THE ACCESS BIBLE

New Revised
Standard Version
Updated Edition

THE ACCESS
BIBLE

NEW REVISED STANDARD VERSION

WITH THE APOCRYPHAL / DEUTEROCANONICAL BOOKS

UPDATED EDITION

GAIL R. O'DAY   DAVID PETERSEN

General Editors

NEW YORK   OXFORD

OXFORD UNIVERSITY PRESS

Oxford University Press, Inc., publishes works that further Oxford University's objective of excellence in research, scholarship, and education.

Oxford   New York
Auckland   Cape Town   Dar es Salaam   Hong Kong   Karachi
Kuala Lumpur   Madrid   Melbourne   Mexico City   Nairobi
New Delhi   Shanghai   Taipei   Toronto

With offices in
Argentina   Austria   Brazil   Chile   Czech Republic   France   Greece
Guatemala   Hungary   Italy   Japan   Poland   Portugal   Singapore
South Korea   Switzerland   Thailand   Turkey   Ukraine   Vietnam

Published by Oxford University Press, Inc.
198 Madison Avenue, New York, New York 10016
http://www.oup.com

Pritchard, James B., The Ancient Near East: Volume One, An Anthology of Texts and Pictures, copyright © 1958 by Princeton University Press. "From the Assyrian Account of the Siege and Surrender of Jerusalem" and "The Decree of Cyrus" reprinted with permission of Princeton University Press.

The hero chart in Sirach originally appeared in Eisenbaum, Pamela, The Jewish Heroes of Christian History: Hebrews 11 in Literary Context. Copyright 1997 by Scholars Press, Atlanta, GA. Reprinted with permission of Scholars.

ISBN 978-0-19-977753-2

Printing number: 10 9 8 7 6

Printed in Korea

CONTRIBUTORS

David L. Barr   Revelation

John Barton   "The Nature and Formation of the Canon"

Ronald E. Clements   Isaiah

Richard J. Clifford   Job, Proverbs

John J. Collins   1, 2, 3, and 4 Maccabees

Pamela M. Eisenbaum   The Wisdom of Solomon, Sirach (Ecclesiasticus)

Theodore Hiebert   Hosea, Joel, Amos, Obadiah, Jonah, Micah, Nahum, Habakkuk, Zephaniah, Haggai, Zechariah, Malachi

Karina Martin Hogan   2 Esdras

Kenneth G. Hoglund   1 and 2 Chronicles, Ezra, Nehemiah

Carl R. Holladay   Romans, 1 and 2 Corinthians, Galatians

Ralph W. Klein   1 Esdras

Amy-Jill Levine   Matthew, Mark

J. Clinton McCann Jr.   Psalms, Psalm 151, Prayer of Manasseh

Steven L. McKenzie   1 and 2 Samuel, 1 and 2 Kings

Richard D. Nelson   Deuteronomy, Joshua, Judges

Jerome H. Neyrey, S.J.   Hebrews, James, 1 and 2 Peter, Jude

Julia M. O'Brien   Ruth, Esther (Hebrew), Ecclesiastes, Song of Solomon, Lamentations, Esther (Greek)

Kathleen M. O'Connor   Jeremiah

Gail R. O'Day   "A Reader's Guide to the Books of the Bible," "The Apocryphal/Deuterocanonical Books," "New Testament Narratives: The Gospels and Acts," "Letters or Epistles," and "Apocalyptic Literature"

Dennis T. Olson   Genesis, Exodus, Leviticus, Numbers

John Painter   John, 1, 2, and 3 John

David Petersen   "What Is Bible Study?" "Torah/Pentateuch," "Historical Literature," "Short Stories," "Hebrew Poetry and Wisdom Literature," and "Prophetic Literature"

TO THE READER

following the publication of the Revised Standard Version and revisions of the Bible were produced by committees and by individual scholars—not to mention even five other translations and revisions of the New Testament alone. One of the

This preface is addressed to you by the Committee of translators, who wish to explain, as briefly as possible, the origin and character of our work. The publication of our revision is yet another step in the long, continual process of making the Bible available in the form of the English language that is most widely current in our day. To summarize in a single sentence: the New Revised Standard Version of the Bible is an authorized revision of the Revised Standard Version, published in 1952, which was a revision of the American Standard Version, published in 1901, which, in turn, embodied earlier revisions of the King James Version, published in 1611.

In the course of time, the King James Version came to be regarded as "the Authorized Version." With good reason it has been termed "the noblest monument of English prose," and it has entered, as no other book has, into the making of the personal character and the public institutions of the English-speaking peoples. We owe to it an incalculable debt.

Yet the King James Version has serious defects. By the middle of the nineteenth century, the development of biblical studies and the discovery of many biblical manuscripts more ancient than those on which the King James Version was based made it apparent that these defects were so many as to call for revision. The task was begun, by authority of the Church of England, in 1870. The (British) Revised Version of the Bible was published in 1881–1885; and the American Standard Version, its variant embodying the preferences of the American scholars associated with the work, was published, as was mentioned above, in 1901. In 1928 the copyright of the latter was acquired by the International Council of Religious Education and thus passed into the ownership of the churches of the United States and Canada that were associated in this Council through their boards of education and publication.

The Council appointed a committee of scholars to have charge of the text of the American Standard Version and to undertake inquiry concerning the need for further revision. After studying the questions whether or not revision should be undertaken, and if so, what its nature and extent should be, in 1937 the Council authorized a revision. The scholars who served as members of the Committee worked in two sections, one dealing with the Old Testament and one with the New Testament. In 1946 the Revised Standard Version of the New Testament was published. The publication of the Revised Standard Version of the Bible, containing the Old and New Testaments, took place on September 30, 1952. A translation of the Apocryphal/Deuterocanonical Books of the Old Testament followed in 1957. In 1977 this collection was issued in an expanded edition, containing three additional texts received by Eastern Orthodox communions (3 and 4 Maccabees and Psalm 151). Thereafter the Revised Standard Version gained the distinction of being officially authorized for use by all major Christian churches: Protestant, Anglican, Roman Catholic, and Eastern Orthodox.

The Revised Standard Version Bible Committee is a continuing body, comprising about thirty members, both men and women. Ecumenical in representation, it includes scholars affiliated with various Protestant denominations, as well as several Roman Catholic members, an Eastern Orthodox member, and a Jewish member who serves in the Old Testament section. For a period of time the Committee included several members from Canada and from England.

Because no translation of the Bible is perfect or is acceptable to all groups of readers, and because discoveries of older manuscripts and further investigation of linguistic features of the text continue to become available, renderings of the Bible have proliferated. During the years following the publication of the Revised Standard Version, twenty-six other English translations and revisions of the Bible were produced by committees and by individual scholars—not to mention twenty-five other translations and revisions of the New Testament alone. One of the latter was the second edition of the RSV New Testament, issued in 1971, twenty-five years after its initial publication.

Following the publication of the RSV Old Testament in 1952, significant advances were made in the discovery and interpretation of documents in Semitic languages related to Hebrew. In addition to the information that had become available in the late 1940s from the Dead Sea texts of Isaiah and Habakkuk, subsequent acquisitions from the same area brought to light many other early copies of all the books of the Hebrew Scriptures (except Esther), though most of these copies are fragmentary. During the same period early Greek manuscript copies of books of the New Testament also became available.

In order to take these discoveries into account, along with recent studies of documents in Semitic languages related to Hebrew, in 1974 the Policies Committee of the Revised Standard Version, which is a standing committee of the National Council of the Churches of Christ in the U.S.A., authorized the preparation of a revision of the entire RSV Bible.

For the Old Testament the Committee has made use of the *Biblia Hebraica Stuttgartensia* (1977; ed. sec. emendata, 1983). This is an edition of the Hebrew and Aramaic text as current early in the Christian era and fixed by Jewish scholars (the "Masoretes") of the sixth to the ninth centuries. The vowel signs, which were added by the Masoretes, are accepted in the main, but where a more probable and convincing reading can be obtained by assuming different vowels, this has been done. No notes are given in such cases, because the vowel points are less ancient and reliable than the consonants. When an alternative reading given by the Masoretes is translated in a footnote, this is identified by the words "Another reading is."

Departures from the consonantal text of the best manuscripts have been made only where it seems clear that errors in copying had been made before the text was standardized. Most of the corrections adopted are based on the ancient versions (translations into Greek, Aramaic, Syriac, and Latin), which were made prior to the time of the work of the Masoretes and which therefore may reflect earlier forms of the Hebrew text. In such instances a footnote specifies the version or versions from which the correction has been derived and also gives a translation of the Masoretic Text. Where it was deemed appropriate to do so, information is supplied in footnotes from subsidiary Jewish traditions concerning other textual readings (the *Tiqqune Sopherim*, "emendations of the scribes"). These are identified in the footnotes as "Ancient Heb tradition."

Occasionally it is evident that the text has suffered in transmission and that none of the versions provides a satisfactory restoration. Here we can only follow the best judgment of competent scholars as to the most probable reconstruction of the original text. Such reconstructions are indicated in footnotes by the abbreviation Cn ("Correction"), and a translation of the Masoretic Text is added.

For the Apocryphal/Deuterocanonical Books of the Old Testament the Committee has made use of a number of texts. For most of these books the basic Greek text from which the present translation was made is the edition of the Septuagint prepared by Alfred Rahlfs and published by the Württemberg Bible Society (Stuttgart, 1935). For several of the books the more recently published individual volumes of the Göttingen Septuagint project were utilized. For the book of Tobit it was decided to follow the form of the Greek text found in codex Sinaiticus (supported as it is by evidence from Qumran); where this text is defective, it was supplemented and corrected by other Greek manuscripts. For the three Additions to Daniel (namely, Susanna, the Prayer of Azariah and the Song of the Three Jews, and Bel and the Dragon) the Committee continued to use the Greek version attributed to Theodotion (the so-called "Theodotion-Daniel"). In translating Ecclesiasticus (Sirach), while constant reference was made to the Hebrew fragments of a large portion of this book (those discovered at Qumran and Masada as well as those recovered from the Cairo Geniza), the Committee generally followed the Greek text (including verse numbers) published by Joseph Ziegler in the Göttingen Septuagint (1965). But in many places the Committee has translated the Hebrew text when this provides a reading that is clearly superior to the Greek; the Syriac and Latin versions were also consulted throughout and occasionally adopted. The basic text adopted in rendering 2 Esdras is the Latin version given in *Biblia Sacra*, edited by Robert Weber (Stuttgart, 1971). This was supplemented by consulting the Latin text as edited by R. L. Bensly (1895) and by Bruno Violet (1910), as well as by taking into account the several Oriental versions of 2 Esdras, namely, the Syriac, Ethiopic, Arabic (two forms, referred to as Arabic 1 and Arabic 2), Armenian, and Georgian versions. Finally, since the Additions to the Book of Esther are disjointed and quite unintelligible as they stand in most editions of the Apocrypha, we have provided them with their original context by translating the whole of the Greek version of Esther from Robert Hanhart's Göttingen edition (1983).

For the New Testament the Committee has based its work on the most recent edition of *The Greek New Testament*, prepared by an interconfessional and international committee and published by the United Bible Societies (1966; 3rd ed. corrected, 1983; information concerning changes to be introduced into the critical apparatus of the forthcoming 4th edition was available to the Committee). As in that edition, double brackets are used to enclose a few passages that are generally regarded to be later additions to the text, but which we have retained because of their evident antiquity and their importance in the textual tradition. Only in very rare instances have we replaced the text or the punctuation of the Bible Societies' edition by an alternative that seemed to us to be superior. Here and there in the footnotes the phrase, "Other ancient authorities read," identifies alternative readings preserved by Greek manuscripts and early versions. In both Testaments, alternative renderings of the text are indicated by the word "Or."

As for the style of English adopted for the present revision, among the mandates given to the Committee in 1980 by the Division of Education and Ministry of the National Council of Churches of Christ (which now holds the copyright of the RSV Bible) was the directive to continue in the tradition of the King James Bible, but to introduce such changes as are warranted on the basis of accuracy, clarity, euphony, and current English usage. Within the constraints set by the original texts and by the mandates of the Division, the Committee has followed the maxim, "As literal as possible, as free as necessary." As a consequence, the New Revised Standard Version (NRSV) remains essentially a literal translation. Paraphrastic renderings have been adopted only sparingly, and then chiefly to compensate for a deficiency in the English language—the lack of a common gender third person singular pronoun.

During the almost half a century since the publication of the RSV, many in the churches have become sensitive to the danger of linguistic sexism arising from the inherent bias of the English language towards the masculine gender, a bias that in the case of the Bible has often restricted or obscured the meaning of the original text. The mandates from the Division specified that, in references to men and women, masculine-oriented language should be eliminated as far as this can be done without altering passages that reflect the historical situation of ancient patriarchal culture. As can be appreciated, more than once the Committee found that the several mandates stood in tension and even in conflict. The various concerns had to be balanced case by case in order to provide a faithful and acceptable rendering without using contrived English. Only very occasionally has the pronoun "he" or "him" been retained in passages where the reference may have been to a woman as well as to a man; for example, in several legal texts in Leviticus and Deuteronomy. In such instances of formal, legal language, the options of either putting the passage in the plural or of introducing additional nouns to avoid masculine pronouns in English seemed to the Committee to obscure the historic structure and literary character of the original. In the vast majority of cases, however, inclusiveness has been attained by simple rephrasing or by introducing plural forms when this does not distort the meaning of the passage. Of course, in narrative and in parable no attempt was made to generalize the sex of individual persons.

Another aspect of style will be detected by readers who compare the more stately English rendering of the Old Testament with the less formal rendering adopted for the New Testament. For example, the traditional distinction between *shall* and *will* in English has been retained in the Old Testament as appropriate in rendering a document that embodies what may be termed the classic form of Hebrew, while in the New Testament the abandonment of such distinctions in the usage of the future tense in English reflects the more colloquial nature of the koine Greek used by most New Testament authors except when they are quoting the Old Testament.

Careful readers will notice that here and there in the Old Testament the word LORD (or in certain cases GOD) is printed in capital letters. This represents the traditional manner in English versions of rendering the Divine Name, the "Tetragrammaton" (see the notes on Exodus 3.14, 15), following the precedent of the ancient Greek and Latin translators and the long established practice in the reading of the Hebrew Scriptures in the synagogue. While it is almost if not quite certain that the Name was originally pronounced "Yahweh," this pronunciation was not indicated when the Masoretes added vowel sounds to the consonantal Hebrew text. To the four consonants YHWH of the Name, which had come to be regarded as too sacred to be pronounced, they attached vowel signs indicating that in its place should be read the Hebrew word *Adonai* meaning "Lord" (or *Elohim* meaning "God"). Ancient Greek translators employed the word *Kyrios* ("Lord") for the Name. The Vulgate likewise used the Latin word *Dominus* ("Lord"). The form "Jehovah" is of late medieval origin; it is a combination of the consonants of the Divine Name and the vowels attached to it by the Masoretes but belonging to an entirely different word. Although the American Standard Version (1901) had used "Jehovah" to render the Tetragrammaton (the sound of Y being represented by J and the sound of W by V, as in Latin), for two reasons the Committees that produced the RSV and the NRSV returned to the more familiar usage of the King James Version. (1) The word "Jehovah" does not accurately represent any form of the Name ever used in Hebrew. (2) The use of any proper name for the one and only God, as though there were other gods from whom the true God had to be distinguished, began to be discontinued in Judaism before the Christian era and is inappropriate for the universal faith of the Christian Church.

It will be seen that in the Psalms and in other prayers addressed to God the archaic second person singular pronouns (*thee, thou, thine*) and verb forms (*art, hast, hadst*) are no longer used. Although some readers may regret this change, it should be pointed out that in the original languages neither the Old Testament nor the New makes any linguistic distinction between addressing a human being and addressing the Deity. Furthermore, in the tradition of the King James Version one will not expect to find the use of capital letters for pronouns that refer to the Deity—such capitalization is an unnecessary innovation that has only recently been introduced into a few English translations of the Bible. Finally, we have left to the discretion of the licensed

CONTENTS

CONTENTS

NAMES AND ORDER OF THE BOOKS
of the Old and New Testaments
with the Apocryphal/Deuterocanonical Books

THE HEBREW SCRIPTURES

Genesis   47

Exodus   115

Leviticus   169

Numbers   208

Deuteronomy   265

Joshua   315

Judges   346

Ruth   378

1 Samuel   384
   (1 Kingdoms in Greek)

2 Samuel   428
   (2 Kingdoms in Greek)

1 Kings   464
   (3 Kingdoms in Greek)

2 Kings   504
   (4 Kingdoms in Greek)

1 Chronicles   545
   (1 Paralipomenon in Greek)

2 Chronicles   584
   (2 Paralipomenon in Greek)

Ezra   630
   (2 Esdras in Greek)

Nehemiah   650
   (2 Esdras in Greek)

Esther   675

Job   685

Psalms   733

Proverbs   861

Ecclesiastes   901

Song of Solomon   913

Isaiah   927

Jeremiah   1023

Lamentations   1106

Ezekiel   1118

Daniel   1189

Hosea   1211

Joel   1228

Amos   1235

Obadiah   1249

Jonah   1252

Micah   1256

Nahum   1267

Habakkuk   1271

Zephaniah   1276

Haggai   1281

Zechariah   1285

Malachi   1300

THE APOCRYPHAL/DEUTEROCANONICAL BOOKS

The Apocryphal/Deuterocanonical Books are listed here in four groupings, as follows:

(a) Books and Additions to Esther and Daniel that are in the Roman Catholic, Greek, and Slavonic Bibles.

Tobit   1309

Judith   1327

The Additions to the Book of Esther
   (with a translation of the entire Greek text of Esther)   1346

Wisdom of Solomon   1360
Ecclesiasticus, or the Wisdom of Jesus Son of Sirach   1388
Baruch   1465
The Letter of Jeremiah (Baruch ch. 6)   1472
The Additions to the Book of Daniel
　　　The Prayer of Azariah and the Song of the Three Jews   1477
　　　Susanna   1481
　　　Bel and the Dragon   1484
1 Maccabees   1487
2 Maccabees   1525

(b) Books in the Greek and Slavonic Bibles; not in the Roman Catholic Canon

1 Esdras (2 Esdras in Slavonic; 3 Esdras in Appendix to Vulgate)   1555
Prayer of Manasseh (in Appendix to Vulgate)   1576
Psalm 151, following Psalm 150 in the Greek Bible   1578
3 Maccabees   1579

(c) In the Slavonic Bible and in the Latin Vulgate Appendix

2 Esdras (3 Esdras in Slavonic; 4 Esdras in Vulgate Appendix)   1594
　(Note: In the Latin Vulgate, Ezra–Nehemiah = 1 and 2 Esdras.)

(d) In an Appendix to the Greek Bible

4 Maccabees   1637

THE NEW TESTAMENT

Matthew   1666
Mark   1713
Luke   1745
John   1794
Acts of the
Apostles   1835
Romans   1890
1 Corinthians   1912
2 Corinthians   1934
Galatians   1948
Ephesians   1957
Philippians   1965
Colossians   1972
1 Thessalonians   1978

2 Thessalonians   1983
1 Timothy   1987
2 Timothy   1994
Titus   1999
Philemon   2003
Hebrews   2006
James   2023
1 Peter   2030
2 Peter   2037
1 John   2043
2 John   2050
3 John   2052
Jude   2054
Revelation   2060

SIDEBAR ESSAYS, MAPS, CHARTS

ALPHABETICAL LISTING
OF THE BOOKS OF THE BIBLE
including the Apocryphal/Deuterocanonical Books

Acts	1835	Jeremiah	1023	Obadiah	1249
The Additions to		Jeremiah,		1 Peter	2030
Esther (Gk)	1346	Letter of	1472	2 Peter	2037
Amos	1235	Job	685	Philemon	2003
Azariah, Prayer of	1477	Joel	1228	Philippians	1965
Baruch	1465	John	1794	Prayer of Azariah	1477
Bel and the		1 John	2043	Prayer of	
Dragon	1484	2 John	2050	Manasseh	1576
1 Chronicles	545	3 John	2052	Proverbs	861
2 Chronicles	584	Jonah	1252	Psalm 151	1578
Colossians	1972	Joshua	315	Psalms	733
1 Corinthians	1912	Jude	2054	Revelation	2060
2 Corinthians	1934	Judges	346	Romans	1890
Daniel	1189	Judith	1327	Ruth	378
Deuteronomy	265	1 Kings	464	1 Samuel	384
Ecclesiastes	901	2 Kings	504	2 Samuel	428
Ecclesiasticus	1388	Lamentations	1106	Sirach, Wisdom	
Ephesians	1957	Letter of		of Jesus Son of	1388
1 Esdras	1555	Jeremiah	1472	Song of Solomon	913
2 Esdras	1594	Leviticus	169	Song of the	
Esther	675	Luke	1745	Three Jews	1477
Esther, (Gk)		1 Maccabees	1487	Susanna	1481
Additions to	1346	2 Maccabees	1525	1 Thessalonians	1978
Exodus	115	3 Maccabees	1579	2 Thessalonians	1983
Ezekiel	1118	4 Maccabees	1637	1 Timothy	1987
Ezra	630	Malachi	1300	2 Timothy	1994
Galatians	1948	Manasseh,		Titus	1999
Genesis	47	Prayer of	1576	Tobit	1309
Habakkuk	1271	Mark	1713	Wisdom of Solomon	1360
Haggai	1281	Matthew	1666	Zechariah	1285
Hebrews	2006	Micah	1256	Zephaniah	1276
Hosea	1211	Nahum	1267		
Isaiah	927	Nehemiah	650		
James	2023	Numbers	208		

ABBREVIATIONS

The following abbreviations are used for the books of the Bible:

Gen	Genesis	2 Chr	2 Chronicles	Dan	Daniel
Ex	Exodus	Ezra	Ezra	Hos	Hosea
Lev	Leviticus	Neh	Nehemiah	Joel	Joel
Num	Numbers	Esth	Esther	Am	Amos
Deut	Deuteronomy	Job	Job	Ob	Obadiah
Josh	Joshua	Ps	Psalms	Jon	Jonah
Judg	Judges	Prov	Proverbs	Mic	Micah
Ruth	Ruth	Eccl	Ecclesiastes	Nah	Nahum
1 Sam	1 Samuel	Song	Song of Solomon	Hab	Habakkuk
2 Sam	2 Samuel	Isa	Isaiah	Zeph	Zephaniah
1 Kings	1 Kings	Jer	Jeremiah	Hag	Haggai
2 Kings	2 Kings	Lam	Lamentations	Zech	Zechariah
1 Chr	1 Chronicles	Ezek	Ezekiel	Mal	Malachi

APOCRYPHAL/DEUTEROCANONICAL BOOKS

Tob	Tobit	Song of Thr	Prayer of Azariah and the
Jdt	Judith		Song of the Three Jews
Add Esth	Additions to Esther	Sus	Susanna
Wis	Wisdom	Bel	Bel and the Dragon
Sir	Sirach (Ecclesiasticus)	1 Macc	1 Maccabees
Bar	Baruch	2 Macc	2 Maccabees
1 Esd	1 Esdras	3 Macc	3 Maccabees
2 Esd	2 Esdras	4 Macc	4 Maccabees
Let Jer	Letter of Jeremiah	Pr Man	Prayer of Manasseh

NEW TESTAMENT

Mt	Matthew	Eph	Ephesians	Heb	Hebrews
Mk	Mark	Phil	Philippians	Jas	James
Lk	Luke	Col	Colossians	1 Pet	1 Peter
Jn	John	1 Thess	1 Thessalonians	2 Pet	2 Peter
Acts	Acts of the Apostles	2 Thess	2 Thessalonians	1 Jn	1 John
Rom	Romans	1 Tim	1 Timothy	2 Jn	2 John
1 Cor	1 Corinthians	2 Tim	2 Timothy	3 Jn	3 John
2 Cor	2 Corinthians	Titus	Titus	Jude	Jude
Gal	Galatians	Philem	Philemon	Rev	Revelation

In the notes to the books of the Old Testament the following abbreviations are used:

Ant.	Josephus, *Antiquities of the Jews*
Aram	Aramaic
Ch, chs	Chapter, chapters
Cn	Correction; made where the text has suffered in transmission and the versions provide no satisfactory restoration but where the Standard Bible Committee agrees with the judgment of competent scholars as to the most probable reconstruction of the original text.
Gk	Septuagint, Greek version of the Old Testament
Heb	Hebrew of the consonantal Masoretic Text of the Old Testament
Josephus	Flavius Josephus (Jewish historian, about A.D. 37 to about 95)
Macc	The book(s) of the Maccabees
Ms(s)	Manuscript(s)
MT	The Hebrew of the pointed Masoretic Text of the Old Testament
OL	Old Latin
Q Ms(s)	Manuscript(s) found at Qumran by the Dead Sea
Sam	Samaritan Hebrew text of the Old Testament
Syr	Syriac Version of the Old Testament
Syr H	Syriac Version of Origen's Hexapla
Tg	Targum
Vg	Vulgate, Latin Version of the Old Testament

THE ACCESS BIBLE

New Revised
Standard Version
Updated Edition

A GUIDE TO THE FEATURES AND USES OF THE ACCESS BIBLE

THE TRANSLATION

This Bible contains the full text of the New Revised Standard Version (NRSV) Bible translation. The NRSV is the most complete translation of the biblical text into English: it contains the Hebrew Scriptures, the Apocryphal/Deuterocanonical Books, and the New Testament. Some editions of the Access Bible are published without the Apocryphal/ Deuterocanonical Books. In editions that do contain these books, the individual introductions contain information about the status of these works in the various Christian churches.

The NRSV Preface, "To the Reader," explains the nature of the NRSV translation, its history, and the scholarly research that lies behind it. The translation also includes footnotes, prepared by the scholars on the translation committee. These footnotes, an important tool for Bible study, explain places where the original language text is unclear, where there is a difference among the various manuscripts that the scholars have consulted (usually indicated in the notes by the phrase, "other ancient authorities read"), or where the original language allows for an alternate translation of the word or phrase (indicated by the word "or"). Some notes provide information about other ancient translations of the Bible that scholars consulted in their translation work. The glossary at the back of this Bible provides information about these different translations (see the entry **ancient translations**). See also "Language and Text" in the essay "What Is Bible Study?" on p. 4.

THE STUDY MATERIALS

The Access Bible is designed to provide study helps that enable the reader to engage the biblical text directly and not simply read about the Bible. That is, the study helps are designed to lead readers into their own careful and reflective reading of the biblical text. The study materials range from full length essays on topics of general interest to the Bible reader to short, dictionary-like entries on particular words or topics. All of the helps are intended to assist the reader in discovering the richness and diversity of the biblical texts.

The Introductory Essays Three introductory essays provide an overview of the Bible as a whole and discuss the nature of Bible study today. "What Is Bible Study?" explains the various ways in which the Bible may be studied. "A Reader's Guide to the Books of the Bible" explains the different books within the Bible and the types of literature they represent. "The Nature and Formation of the Biblical Canon" describes how these many different books came to be gathered together as the Bible and why Jewish, as well as Protestant, Catholic, and Orthodox Christian communities, each hold to a slightly different definition of "canon."

Section Essays At nine places in the text there are essays giving an overview of the different types of biblical literature. These essays, from "Torah/Pentateuch" to "Apocalyptic Literature," provide readers with information about larger units of the biblical text than individual books of the Bible. As such, they can help guide readers to those kinds of writing in which they are most interested, or inform them about the nature and uses of the various kinds of writing in the Bible.

The Book Introductions   In this study Bible, each biblical book is preceded by a brief introduction. The first part enables the modern reader to imagine how the book's content may have been understood by its ancient readers. Information about historical setting, type of literature (e.g., letter, poetry, story), social issues or theological themes all assist in bridging the gap between the ancient world and today's world.

Each introduction also contains a section labeled "Reading Guide," that is primarily directed toward the reading concerns of the modern reader, rather than the questions and needs that probably guided the book's original readers. The included outline helps the reader see a picture of the general sweep of the book before attending to its details.

The Sectional Comments   This Study Bible includes section by section comments on the biblical text. In most cases, the comments follow a segment of Scripture and explain unusual words, ancient religious and social customs, literary features, or the historical setting of that text. They orient the modern reader to the places, people, and events of the biblical world. They also identify key themes or ideas that may be relevant to the reader's own situation.

Within these comments, words in *italics* are those quoted directly from the NRSV text; words in **boldface** describe divisions or individual passages; numbers in boldface are chapter and verse numbers which the comments address. To refer to a translators' footnote, the words "see note on..." are used. "See comment" refers to the running comment on the biblical text, and "see map, chart, or sidebar" refers to the respective study help at the location given.

Other Features within the Text   In addition to section by section comments on the biblical text, this edition contains other helps—maps, charts, and sidebar essays. Each of these helps expands on information mentioned in the comments. The sidebar essays often point beyond the particular biblical text under consideration to broader biblical themes.

Helps at the Back of the Study Bible   At the end of the Bible are three sets of materials that supplement the helps located at each individual book of the Bible. First is a glossary. This lists and defines specialized terms that are used in the running comments; these terms have been marked with a star symbol (✫) to indicate that their definitions can be found in the glossary. The glossary also contains a discussion of other terms not explicitly mentioned in the running comments, but that are helpful for interpreting the biblical text and understanding the biblical world. In addition, many of the glossary entries refer to passages in the Bible that illustrate the entry. The glossary therefore moves in two directions: from the study materials to an explanation in the glossary, or from an explanation in the glossary to an illustration in the biblical text.

Second, the helps contain a brief concordance to the NRSV text. A concordance is a tool for Bible study that enables the reader to compare the use of a word in one biblical verse to its usage elsewhere—either in the same biblical book or another one. By using a concordance, the reader begins to achieve a sense of what individual words meant to the biblical writers and their original readers.

Finally, a full-color set of Oxford Bible Maps is included, along with an index to all of the place names found on the maps. These maps are an important tool for locating the places mentioned in the biblical text and becoming familiar with the geography of the ancient world. The maps also provide a glimpse of the history of the ancient Mediterranean world, since the different maps cover a period of 1,000 years.

Calendar Designation   This Study Bible employs the designations BCE ("before the common era") and CE ("common era") to refer to the time periods often marked by the designations BC ("before Christ") and AD ("in the year of the Lord," *anno domini* in Latin). The designations BCE and CE reflect the way that years are counted in the Western calendar without using terms that derive from the Christian faith tradition, since not all people who follow the Western calendar are members of a Christian community.

USING THIS STUDY BIBLE

The Access Bible is designed to be used in group Bible study settings, classrooms, and for individual Bible reading and study. The helps outlined above can be used in a variety of ways—to assist in verse by verse, chapter by chapter reading of the Bible or to provide information and insight about a particular text or topic.

The editors of the study Bible have designed it in such a way as to put the best resources of biblical scholarship in the hands of the general reader. We have tried to anticipate readers' questions about the ancient world and the complexities of many biblical texts, but in a way that respects both the reader and the Bible. That is, no matter how much Bible study one does, there are some texts in the Bible that are always going to be difficult to understand and that will seem challenging rather than comforting. Nonetheless, the editors hope that the Access Bible will make Bible study a rewarding experience and will make the Bible accessible to the reader— accessible in its contradictions and complexities as well as in its comfort and inspiration.

WHAT IS BIBLE STUDY?

People read the Bible in many settings, such as religious services, personal homes, libraries, hospitals and hotel rooms. Not all Bible reading constitutes Bible study, however. When you read the Bible in a hospital room, you may be seeking to understand your condition from the perspective of your particular religious tradition. You may thus reflect upon illness using the kind of metaphorical language in, for example, Psalm 22:

> I am poured out like water,
>> and all my bones are out of joint;
> my heart is like wax;
>> it is melted within my breast;
> my mouth is dried up like a potsherd,
> and my tongue sticks to my jaws;
>> you lay me in the dust of death. (Ps 22.14–15)

Moreover, you may gain some comfort from the confidence in God expressed in psalms of lament, for example, Ps 55.17. In such a reading, the Bible will have played an important role in your life, but it would be inappropriate to designate that sort of activity as Bible study.

"Bible study" means different things to different people. To some it means sitting at home, reading, and underlining passages in red pencil. To some it means gathering with members of one's church to read and share perceptions about a biblical text or theme. To some it means taking a course devoted to an aspect of the Bible in a college or university classroom. The only real common denominator for these various approaches is attention to the biblical text.

For the purposes of these introductory essays, Bible study means "the disciplined and active reading of the Bible in order to gain new understandings about the biblical text or the reader's own situation." This way of thinking about Bible study includes learning about ancient Israel or early Christianity as well as coming to a new understanding of one's own condition.

We would add one other initial comment about Bible study. Since the Bible derives from ancient cultures, it is, in many ways, a foreign document that requires study in order to be understood properly. Put another way, for the person who takes the Bible seriously, Bible study is not an option but a requirement. The appropriateness of such Bible study is attested in biblical times. Acts 8.26–40 recounts an episode in which an Ethiopian eunuch is reading from the book of Isaiah. Philip approaches him and asks, "Do you understand what you are reading?" The Ethiopian responds, "How can I, unless someone guides me?" The need for guides, whether in the form of a teacher, a book, study materials or an internet site, is even more powerful today than it was in Philip's time.

PRIMARY FEATURES OF BIBLE STUDY

Language and Text　The ancient biblical manuscripts were written in three languages: Hebrew, Aramaic, and Greek. (Aramaic is, like Hebrew, a Semitic language, one that became particularly prominent during the Persian period.) As a result, all English Bibles are translations, scholarly attempts to convey the meaning of these texts into English.

Such a task is no easy enterprise since different theories of translation abound. Some focus on the meaning of individual words, whereas others think the sentence is of primary importance. The former perspective may be called "literal" or "word for word," whereas the latter has often been characterized as a "dynamic-equivalence" approach. Though no translation of the Bible belongs to one or the other approach all the time, the NRSV tends toward the "word for word" style. Such a translation can be useful for Bible study since it will usually translate a Greek or Hebrew word with the same English word, thereby allowing the reader of the English to study individual terms like *mishpat* (a Hebrew word for justice) or *agape* (a Greek word for love) in translation. Still, there are instances in which the original language offers no easy "word for word" option. John 8.15 provides a good example. The NRSV reads: "You judge by human standards" whereas a more literal rendition of the Greek is cited in the translators' note, "You judge according to the flesh."

Despite the best efforts of hundreds of scholars, certain biblical texts remain difficult to translate. As a result, those who created the NRSV have noted many instances in which they have encountered problems in moving from a Hebrew or Greek text to an English version. They also place notes where they have had to interpret the evidence attested in manuscripts written in other languages, such as Latin, Syriac or Coptic. For example, in Habakkuk 3.14, the translators' note on the word "warriors" reads "Vg Compare Gk Syr: Meaning of Heb uncertain." This shorthand statement conveys considerable information. Since the Hebrew term and the phrase in which it is embedded do not follow the normal rules of Hebrew grammar, the translators indicate that they have solved this problem by following the understanding conveyed in the Vulgate (Vg), an early Latin translation. In addition, ancient translations in two other languages—the Gk (Greek or Septuagint) and Syr (Syriac or Peshitta)—provide important information that has helped corroborate their judgments.

Most readers of this study Bible will not be able to consult the Hebrew or Greek texts, much less the Latin and Syriac versions. However, attention to notes of this sort, which are more common than one might suspect, helps the reader to be alert to places of uncertainty. In such a place, one needs to be careful about placing too much interpretive emphasis. In addition, these notes help us appreciate the remarkable complexity of the biblical manuscript traditions along with the various religious communities that produced and used them.

The work of translators is absolutely essential. Without their efforts, there would be no Bibles in modern languages. At the same time, we should recognize subjectivity at work in the creation of a translation, as well as the influence of newly available information for interpreting the ancient texts. Perhaps the best way to appreciate this issue is to compare the NRSV with its earlier counterpart, the Revised Standard Version (RSV).

We offer two such points of comparison. First, compare these two versions of the initial lines of Deut 33.27:

The eternal God is your dwelling place, and underneath are the everlasting arms. (RSV)

He subdues the ancient gods, shatters the forces of old; (NRSV)

"The everlasting arms" have become, as it were, "the forces of old." These two readings represent differing assessments of the rich idioms in ancient Hebrew poetry. The NRSV reflects knowledge about ancient Semitic languages that was unavailable to the translators of the RSV.

Those readers of the biblical text who do not know Hebrew or Greek may well feel at a disadvantage when confronted with such disparities. But there is a way to deal with this issue: It is always appropriate to compare several translations in order to see if there are major differences. At such points of difference, the reader should be careful of placing too much emphasis on a disputed element in the translation. So, in the just mentioned case, the reader of the RSV would do well to avoid offering broad statements concerning the arms of God until after having consulted other good translations, for example, the Revised English Bible, Tanakh or the New American Bible.

As another example, it is useful to compare the RSV and NRSV renditions of Ezek 7. In the RSV, the chapter is printed as prose whereas in the NRSV, most of the chapter is printed as poetry. The scholars responsible for the NRSV had benefitted from recent studies of Hebrew poetry, which enabled them to discern more texts as poetry than had earlier been the case. As we shall see later in this essay, approaching poetry requires different interpretive strategies than reading prose does. And the decision about whether or not a text is poetry can rest in the hands of the translator.

The issues we have just been addressing involve, primarily, questions of language (philology) and translation. However, there is another range of issues related to the texts preserving these ancient readings. None of the original compositions, called "autographs," has been preserved. Moreover, though there is remarkable fixity in the ancient manuscript traditions, they do, on occasion, diverge. The study of the significance of these differences among ancient biblical manuscripts is called textual criticism. Indeed, there are several kinds of text critical issues.

One type of text critical issue is that some manuscripts clearly have a faulty text, one in which a copyist's error or some other accident has occurred. The Cain and Abel story (Gen 4) offers a compelling example. In this well-known tale, God accepts the offering of Abel but not the offering of Cain, whereupon Cain is challenged to "do well." Then, according to the NRSV, "Cain said to his brother Abel, 'Let us go out to the field' " (Gen 4.8). As the translators' note makes clear, the words "Let us go out to the field" are not present in the Hebrew manuscripts, though they are present in the Samaritan Pentateuch, the Septuagint and the Peshitta (the Syriac Old Testament). The phrase has almost certainly fallen out of the Hebrew tradition by mistake, since the text certainly seems to suggest that Cain had engaged in premeditated murder. Scholars who are able to assess the various ancient manuscript evidence have in this case supplied what they deemed to be the more original reading, which has been preserved in manuscripts written in languages other than Hebrew.

Another text critical issue is that ancient texts may offer contrary readings, alternate forms of a story or saying. One of the most interesting examples occurs at the end of Mark's Gospel. Here the question is not one of a mistake but of varying texts. In the ancient manuscripts, the Gospel of Mark can end in three ways: with Mk 16.8, with Mk 16.8 plus what is referred to as "The Shorter Ending of Mark," and with Mk

16.9–20, "The Longer Ending of Mark." The layout of the NRSV, along with the translators' note at the first ending, makes these options very clear.

Option 1 concludes the Gospel on a note of fear. Three women, Mary Magdalene, Mary the mother of James, and Salome, had come to tend to the body of Jesus in the tomb. When they arrived, they were informed by "a young man" that Jesus "has been raised." Whereupon they fled; "and they said nothing to anyone, for they were afraid" (16.8). The note of fear is accompanied by an ironic tone, because they must have told someone, or the scene could not have been recounted in Mark's Gospel. Option 2 removes that ironic tone by reporting explicitly that the women did indeed recount what they had seen and heard "to those around Peter," moving the story beyond the empty tomb into the realm of the disciples. The final portion of the verse introduces the motif of a commission, similar to that found in Mt 28.19. Option 3 removes the note of incompleteness with which Mk 16.8 ends by adding a series of post-resurrection appearances of Jesus. With these verses, the ending of Mark more closely resembles the endings of the other Gospels, which all contain stories of post-resurrection appearances.

The NRSV prints all three options because it is impossible to know how the Gospel of Mark originally ended. The ending at Mk 16.8, while well attested by some very ancient manuscripts, nonetheless seems an abrupt way to end, and the alternatives proposed in many manuscript traditions show how the earliest Christians tried to work with and around this unexpected abruptness. Holy writ there is, but it is on occasion written in more than one way.

Careful study of the Bible, then, particularly for those who do not have access to the ancient languages, will involve comparison of several translations as well as attention to the notes provided by the translators. This form of active reading will alert readers to problem areas in the text as well as to differences among the early biblical witnesses.

Literary Form and Style   If a story begins with "Once upon a time," the reader expects that it will be a traditional tale. The focus will almost certainly be on people and places, not on economic or social history. Similarly, when hearing the phrase "This is the last will and testament of . . . ," the listener knows that the text is a legal document that will outline the disposition of someone's estate. Our initial perception of these texts depends in considerable measure on the sort of literature we think we are hearing.

Just as there are identifiable forms of literature in our own time, so too, both in the ancient Near East and in the Greco-Roman era, readers and listeners (there were far more listeners than readers) were accustomed to encountering discrete forms of literature, many of which are preserved in the Bible. Contemporary readers of the Bible, however, are not always attuned to those ancient forms of literature. Hence, part of Bible study involves becoming aware of and understanding some of these ancient styles of writing.

We have already referred to a primary distinction that occurs in Old Testament literature—prose versus poetry—and we have noted that translators of the Bible differ in their judgments about whether a text is prose or poetry. Some cases are ambiguous. Others are less so, particularly as we learn more about the nature of the Hebrew language and literature. In any case, the reader should discern which style is being used and whether it has significance to the message of the text.

The first two chapters of Genesis in the NRSV present a particularly interesting illustration. The reader can note immediately that Gen 1.27 and Gen 2.23 are written as poetry, surrounded by prose. Is this an accident, or is it important for the interpretation of this literature? Surely, the latter. Both chapters concern God's acts of creation. In the first chapter the entire universe is in view, whereas in the second only the earth and life on it are of concern to the writer. In both cases, these brief poetic pieces occur near the end of the text. In Gen 1 the poem relates to what is happening on the sixth day (vv. 24–31), and in Gen 2 the poem occurs in the final scene (vv. 18–23) of creative activity. These final elements of creation appear as the high point of the texts—creation of humanity in Gen 1 and of woman in Gen 2—and the poetic elements in the text underscore these important moments.

Poetry requires the reader to slow down and focus on the taut relationship between the lines. In Gen 1.27, one confronts the pregnant phrase "the image of God." Though the primary connotation offered by the phrase is something visual—an image, the poem itself offers another angle of vision, by comparing "the image of God" in the second line with "male and female" in the third line. Those relationships make the reader wonder what indeed is conveyed by the notion of God's image. Perhaps it has more to do with community as represented by the relation of the genders and less to do with something visible.

As for Gen 2.23, the writer for the first time gives explicit voice to a human being, and what that individual speaks is a poem. The man testifies to the inextricable connection between male and female, as attested by a wordplay in the Hebrew words for Man (*ish*) and Woman (*ishshah*). (See translators' notes.)

Gaining a better understanding of the categories of prose and poetry is important for readers of biblical literature. Within each of these two basic categories, one may discern a number of sub-types. For example, the following sorts of literature are composed in prose: list (Lev 11.29–30), genealogy (Gen 10), letter (Jer 29.24–28), report (Gen 6.1–2), and story (the book of Ruth). Similarly, another set of literature is written in poetry: e.g., song (Ex 15), prophetic oracle (Mic 1.2–7), and wisdom speech (Prov 6.20–35). To understand a prose text as a story or a poetic text as a song offers the reader special insight into the workings of such literature. Some basic questions can be asked of any story or poem to gain a deeper understanding of the type of literature in question.

Much of the Bible is written in prose. And much, though not all, of the prose conveys stories. Though not all readers are literary critics, everyone knows how to read a story—whether in the historical books of the Old Testament or the parables of the New Testament. We suggest that those engaged in Bible study ask at least three questions of each story that they read. First, what is the basic movement in the plot? Second, what sort of important characters act in the story? Third, what is the main idea or theme of the story?

Let us comment briefly on each of these categories. First, the plot of the story will often begin with a basic situation, from which a complication arises; for example, a husband and wife are unable to bear children. By the end of the story, some change has occurred so that the tension created by the complication has been resolved. Attention to this movement helps readers identify the plot of a story. Second, most stories in the Bible have only a few important characters, and it is always interesting to see if the characters change or develop. Daniel does not seem to change, Paul does. Moreover, some characters are complex: We observe people who struggle, who make mistakes and yet also sometimes do the right thing; they are round, full of depth. Other characters are depicted as totally perfect or sinful; they are flat, without depth. Finally, the reader should try to identify the primary idea with which an author is wrestling in a story. To create that statement of theme requires an active engagement with the art of the author. Individual readers will often write quite different statements of theme, in part because the story may be read in several ways, and in part because the readers understand the story differently. Discussing our statements of theme with others helps us understand the various ways readers respond to prose in biblical literature.

Another type of prose, as mentioned earlier, is the letter. Although there are some letters preserved in the Old Testament, twenty-one of the New Testament books are themselves letters. Hence, it helps to know something about letters in antiquity before encountering this remarkable corpus in the New Testament. Letters in the Greco-Roman world characteristically began by identifying the sender and the receiver or addressee, followed by a thanksgiving to the gods. They concluded with an exchange of greetings. When reading NT letters, it is interesting to look for these opening and closing sections, addressees, and thanksgivings; see, for example, the opening in 1 Cor 1.1–9 and the conclusion in Rom 16.

What special characteristics does poetry have? As we have had occasion to see, poetry challenges readers in a way that prose often does not. Readers of the New Testament will face those challenges less frequently than will readers of the Old Testament because poetry simply does not appear as often in the New Testament. Moreover, much of the poetry that does appear in the New Testament is a quotation of Old Testament texts (for example, Mt 13.14–15). Hence, in most cases, attending to poetry in the Bible involves the reading of Hebrew poetry.

We possess no guidebook in which the rules of ancient Hebrew poetry have been preserved. Rather, the workings of that poetry have been inferred, based on an assessment of poetic texts. For many years, it has been clear that the dominant element in Hebrew poetry is parallelism, typically the juxtaposition of two lines of comparable length. The relationship between the meaning of each line can vary significantly. Often, the lines bear similar meaning, though rarely are they absolutely identical. For example,

> For the bed is too short to stretch oneself on it,
> and the covering too narrow to wrap oneself in it. (Isa 28.20)

These lines offer two related examples of something that is too small, but the absence of a good fit is expressed in different ways: a cramped bed and a skimpy blanket.

So-called antithetic proverbs operate in a different way:

> A soft answer turns away wrath,
> but a harsh word stirs up anger. (Prov 15.1)

The two lines comment on differing forms of behavior, one positive, one negative. Together they work to admonish the reader or hearer toward one form of behavior, the positive one.

Finally, some lines that stand in parallel fashion operate more as a narrative: the thought simply flows from one line to the next.

> My beloved had a vineyard
>   on a very fertile hill.
> He dug it and cleared it of stones,
>   and planted it with choice vines; (Isa 5.1–2)

The person who reads Hebrew poetry will need to be alert to the various ways in which such parallel lines work.

If parallelism is a hallmark of Hebrew poetry, there are other elements that make it similar to that written in other languages: It is filled with rich images, similes (comparisons using "like" or "as") and metaphors (direct comparisons). For example, many psalms give voice to an individual who is suffering (these psalms are often called "individual laments"). These psalms, such as the one that follows, include remarkable descriptions of an individual's plight.

> . . . my bones burn like a furnace.
> My heart is stricken and withered like grass;
>   I am too wasted to eat my bread.
> Because of my loud groaning
>   my bones cling to my skin.
> I am like an owl of the wilderness,
>   like a little owl of the waste places. (Ps 102.3–6)

Four similes depict this person's distress, and because this figure of speech is so prominent, it would be unwise to try to guess precisely what the physical or psychological plight is. Rather than giving a clinical description, the psalm presents images, which could be applied by this person, another Israelite, or even a reader today to reflect on a current situation. To read this psalm as poetry helps us gain access to it as a resource and prevents it from remaining simply a historical artifact of an ancient Israelite's experience.

Formation of Biblical Literature Many books of the Bible grew or developed over time. To be sure, some, like Ruth and 1 Corinthians, were written by a single author. However, many books possess a core of prose or poetry that has been arranged, rearranged and supplemented over time by an editor or reviser (known as a "redactor"). Scholars who study this process engage in "redaction criticism." There are numerous examples of this growth process in the Bible.

In the New Testament, the Synoptic Gospels include many of the same sayings of Jesus. However, their order and configuration is not uniform. For example, the parable of the sower occurs much earlier in Mark's Gospel (4.1–9) than it does in the Gospel of Matthew (13.1–9). Each of the Gospels narrates the account of Jesus and the money-changers in the Jerusalem temple ("the cleansing of the temple"), but whereas in

Matthew, Mark, and Luke that story is positioned in the last week of Jesus' life, in John it is one of the first acts of Jesus' ministry. What we see in such comparisons is the freedom with which ancient collectors and authors could assemble and cast their material.

The Old Testament is full of comparable examples. The book of Psalms is a collection of various songs. The process whereby that collection was made is far from clear. However, even the casual reader soon learns that one element in that organization involves the notion of "books." Just before Psalms 1, 42, 73, 90 and 107, the NRSV includes rubrics, "Book I, II, III, IV and V." Moreover, Ps 41.13; 72.18–19; 89.52; 106.48 and all of Psalm 150 comprise doxologies that conclude each of these "books." In each case, these doxologies stand outside the poetic flow of the psalms to which they have been attached. As a result, one has good reason to think that the psalms have been configured to make them appear in five books. Such a pattern of organization would, of course, make them appear similar to the five book collection—the Pentateuch or Torah—with which the Hebrew Bible begins.

These two examples, taken from the Gospels and Psalms, involve primarily the organization of existing traditions or texts. However, the formation of biblical literature can result from far more aggressive activity than simply the ordering of poems or sayings. The book of Isaiah offers a classic example. Isaiah ben Amoz was active as a prophet in the mid-late eighth and early seventh centuries BCE. During this period, he addressed the people of Judah as they lived through several crises. The sayings of this Isaiah are concentrated in early portions of the book, especially chs. 2–10 and 28–33. Elsewhere in the book, particularly chs. 40–66, the style of the literature changes and the historical context is different. For example, Isa 45.1–8 refers to Cyrus, emperor of the Persian empire (he ruled in the mid sixth century). Moreover, the poetry is more rhetorical and occurs in longer units than does that in the earlier chapters. As a result of such observations, scholars have argued that chs. 40–66 along with many others, for example, chs. 1, 34–35, reflect authors other than Isaiah ben Amoz. Hence, one may surmise that the book of Isaiah reflects a long process of growth, from c. 700 BCE to at least 500 BCE, during which the words of Isaiah were collected and supplemented. Later poets/prophets, particularly in the Persian period, contributed new sayings, which grew out of the theological and literary resources provided by the seminal figure, Isaiah ben Amoz. Understood in this way, the book of Isaiah is very much the product of organic growth. To understand this prophetic book is to understand the generative power of the core sayings along with the literatures that were stimulated by them.

The book of Jeremiah includes a story about how an early form of that book was created. God commands Jeremiah to "Take a scroll and write on it all the words that I have spoken to you. . . " (Jer 36.2). Soon after the scroll is written, it is destroyed, whereupon a new one is created. At the end of Jer 36, which describes this process, the narrator writes, "Then Jeremiah took another scroll and gave it to the secretary Baruch son of Neriah, who wrote on it at Jeremiah's dictation all the words of the scroll that King Jehoiakim of Judah had burned in the fire; and many similar words were added to them" (Jer 36.32). There can be no more graphic statement about one way in which a biblical book developed. Such formative processes hint at the appropriateness, even need, for biblical literature to readdress each new age of readers.

Historical and Cultural Context   One question that readers regularly pose to a biblical text is: When was it written? Knowing something about the people, places or political forces at the time the book was written will help readers gain a deeper understanding of that text. For example, the book of Hosea stems from the early part of the second half of the eighth century BCE (roughly 750–720 BCE). However, as one reads that book, few specific historical references to that period appear. Instead, Hosea uses many ornate figures of speech to depict the fate that awaits Israel: e.g., "they shall reap the whirlwind" (8.7) or "they shall be like the morning mist or like the dew that goes away early" (13.3). In addition, God speaks as if the deity would be an enemy arrayed against Israel: "I will destroy you, O Israel" (13.9) or "I will become like a lion to them" (13.7). This way of speaking does not enable the reader to speak about what, concretely, will happen to Israel.

When one places such language of destruction within the context of what we know about the ancient Near Eastern history of that period, we discover what it is that the prophet is probably anticipating. Other biblical texts are also helpful, in this regard, since the time that Hosea was active is also treated by the biblical historian whose work is preserved in the book of Kings. In addition, archaeologists have discovered texts from the royal archives of the Neo-Assyrian empire, the dominant political force of this era. These varied sources help us understand that the Neo-Assyrian empire was exerting considerable influence on Syria-Palestine during the last half of the eighth century. Their armies were campaigning in the Levant. Hence, when Hosea speaks about sounding an alarm (5.8) or "the tumult of war shall rise against your people" (10.14), we know that there is a very specific reference in Hosea's mind. He perceives that the Neo-Assyrians will destroy Israel. Moreover, he understands military activity from a theological perspective, namely, that such destruction is consistent with Israel's God's intent for Israel—that it be punished.

This is only one of many instances in which understanding the historical context helps the reader. Hence it is always appropriate to raise questions involving a text's historical background when one is studying the Bible. Still, there is a remarkable number of chapters, narratives, and poems about which we can say very little concerning a precise historical context. Such is the case for many psalms. For example, it would be interesting to know when Ps 113 was written or in what specific context it was used in ancient Israel. However, no word or idea in this psalm is specific to a particular moment in ancient Israelite history. The God who dwells above the heavens is a prominent motif in many periods, as is the deity's concern for the poor and the barren woman. Hence, the reader will be wise to avoid struggling to identify a historical setting for this psalm. Instead, a different range of questions—perhaps literary or theological analysis—would be more likely to yield results.

To attend to the context of biblical literature can involve more than simply asking about the historical point of origin. Both the Old and New Testaments are literatures that emerged within cultural contexts that influenced them in important ways. Jewish and Greco-Roman religious impulses fed into early Christian discourse at the very outset of its existence. Likewise, ancient Israelite society and culture was informed by the cultural heritage of the ancient Near East.

Let us take the example of two types of legal material in the Old Testament to demonstrate the importance of paying attention to cultural context. Many of the laws in the Israelite collections follow a standard form: If something happens, then such and such will be the penalty, often termed "case law." Exodus 21.33–34 offers a biblical example, and similar case laws were also prominent in collections from ancient Mesopotamian cultures. These laws surely grew out of actual cases adjudicated by Israelite or Meso-potamian courts. However, elsewhere in the Israelite collections, we find laws of a different sort: "you shall not do something." Exodus 22.18 is characteristic of this form, as are several of the ten commandments. When consulting the ancient Near Eastern collections, one learns that this form of law is much less frequent than it is in the Israelite material. This comparison suggests that these laws of prohibition directed to an individual, a "you," do not seem to derive from the ancient court system and may reflect some other tradition, which was particularly prominent in ancient Israel.

When undertaking Bible study, it is often useful to consult a commentary or the notes in a study Bible to discover if there is an important issue of cultural context that might be pursued. Many of the ancient texts with which biblical literature may be compared are now available in translations and are more readily available than they have been in the past: for example, texts from ancient Egypt or those written by Flavius Josephus. Attention to such literatures can help us understand the ways in which ancient Isra-elites, Jews, and early Christians shared important beliefs and values with those with whom they interacted. Moreover, such study can make clear instances in which those who wrote the Bible stood apart from others in their culture.

Finally, we should note the important resource that the work of archaeologists pro-vides for biblical study. Though few would now speak of something called "biblical archaeology," the work of archaeologists has informed significantly the way in which we understand ancient Israel and early Christianity, not so much by attesting or veri-fying events or places mentioned in the Bible as by helping us understand how these ancient societies worked. Of course, the discovery of texts has a special significance, whether ancient flood stories from Babylon or the Dead Sea Scrolls from the Wadi Qumran, but even when excavations or surveys do not yield texts, we learn a great deal about the context out of which biblical literature emerged.

For example, there are numerous references to city gates in the Old Testament. North American readers of the Bible are probably more familiar with city gates in a European context than those of the ancient Near East. The typical city gate in ancient Israel was like a major corridor into which a number of open rooms were built. When one entered the city, one passed through several chambers, often lined with benches. The ancient city gate had several functions. It afforded the opportunity for assembly as well as entry and, of course, defense. Such knowledge about city gates helps us understand a text such as Ruth 4.1–2, which in this case refers to the city gate as a place of legal assembly. As did Boaz, one could go to the gate and collect a group of individuals—here they were elders of the city—who were those enfranchised to constitute the legal assembly. Were we to have only the European picture, we might imagine this group of elders clogging a small door to the village of Bethlehem.

Recently, archaeologists have been doing more than excavating monuments (for ex-ample, city walls) and finding texts—they have attempted to reconstruct the ways in which people lived. Hence, the nature of family life, for example, has become part of their scope. How many people lived in a household? What sort of food did they produce and eat? What relation did a family outside of a city have to the city? Such studies are having a major impact on the ways we understand the forms of social life depicted in biblical literature.

Social World Issues   Attention to the world of family life is also consistent with another way of studying the Bible: namely, asking broader questions about social structure, economics, culture, and political order. These four labels are related directly to what some would call the social sciences. Earlier in this chapter, we were addressing literary, historical, and philological questions, topics that would normally be addressed in humanities courses. Now we move to another range of discourse, that represented especially by sociology, economics, anthropology, and political science.

Since ancient Israel was a society that existed in a particular period, it is amenable to all these forms of analysis, just as are early Christian communities. In both settings, it is useful to know something about the economies in which people lived. Such knowledge helps us either when we have questions about the economic "sins" that the prophets attack or when we want to ask what early Christians thought about the relation of their faith to possession of property. Similarly, Israel existed in quite different political modes over time—clans, monarchy, religious communities. Other nations and communities have existed in these forms as well. And it is useful to compare the various communities that have been ruled by priests (hierocracies) in order to understand the internal dynamics that were at work in those societies. In this regard, it is no accident that the role of the "high priest" apparently did not exist until after Israel and Judah ceased to exist as nations.

When addressing social world issues, it is very important to distinguish, at least initially, the social world in the text versus the social world behind the text. We may use the book of Genesis as a case in point. In order to study the social world that produced the text, one would need to determine the time it was produced. If, for example, one thought that Genesis had been written during the time of Solomon (tenth century BCE), one would attempt to discern the ways in which issues important to that time are addressed by the Genesis narratives. Similarly, if one thought that Genesis had been written during the time of Ezra (fifth century BCE), then one would seek ways in which Israel's existence as a district in the Persian empire is reflected in it. One would read the book of Genesis in quite different ways, based upon differing judgments about its point of origin.

Scholars currently disagree about when Genesis was written. Hence it would be risky indeed to postulate a social world that produced this important biblical book. It would be very difficult to speak about the social structure or economic system in which its author or authors were embedded. So, unlike the situation with Amos or Romans, it would be unwise to attempt to speak with precision about the social world behind or outside this particular text.

On the other hand, there is a social world conveyed in the book of Genesis. We read about the people planting crops, engaging in animal husbandry, buying and selling land. Hence, we can attempt to determine whether these reports make up an intelligible economic system. The same may be said of family life. People are born, undergo puberty rites, marry, have children, grow old and die. Some of the patterns of family behavior may seem strange to us—for example, Abraham marrying Sarah and then having a child with Sarah's servant Hagar, or Jacob's marrying two sisters, Rachel and Leah. However, scholars familiar with family life in many cultures recognize these practices as part of a well-attested family structure in which property is passed through a particular type of kinship structure. Similar things can be said about patterns of religious behavior. People build altars, engage in blood rituals, whether circumcision or animal sacrifice. Here too, these patterns of religious activity can be understood, based on cross-cultural analysis—without appeal to a specific historical context. This world in the text—whether that of social structure or religious behavior—can be studied and found to be intelligible, even though we may not know when the text was written.

Many readers of the Bible will be familiar with their own social worlds, but not with those of other cultures, including those that might be more similar to those in the Bible. In such situations, it will be important, at a minimum, to allow the biblical text to speak for itself. In the previous paragraph, we mentioned marriage patterns in Genesis that are quite different from those practiced in North America today. Whether or not readers know about other cultures in which such marriages are practiced, they should attempt to discern what cultural values are being addressed by such practices and whether or not these marriage patterns elicit censure by the biblical authors. We need to be careful not to impose our own culture's practices and values on texts that derive from a radically different context. Attention to the social world in the text will help us understand how different that world might be from that of our own.

The Worlds of Readers   All texts are the products of human authors, and readers have often assumed that their task is to figure out what the authors intended them to find in the text. The act of reading itself, however, is very important for the "creation of meaning." Reading involves far more than discovering "the meaning" of a text. Readers come from varied social, economic, and geographical contexts. Some are women, some are men. And, most important, each reader brings his or her own unique history to the text. All these factors regularly manifest themselves in diverse questions or sensitivities that readers bring to texts.

We offer two examples of the ways in which Bible study can be affected by different readers' worlds. First, women will often bring a different set of experiences and questions to biblical texts than will men. Such modes of interpretation, as exemplified by *The Women's Bible Commentary*, have significantly enriched our ability to study the Bible. One scholar has written an interpretation of the book of Judges based on a study of the female characters in it. Seen from this vantage point, Judges, particularly after the time of Deborah, is truly a violent world, one in which "all the people did what was right in their own eyes" (Judg 21.25). And not much was right. In the New Testament, scholars have noted the remarkable prominence of women among Jesus' early followers. Even more, the first resurrection reports are attributed to women: "Now it was Mary Magdalene, Joanna, Mary the mother of James, and the other women with them . . . " (Lk 24.10).

Second, people's own individual experiences affect their interpretations of biblical materials. Genesis 22 offers a useful example. This narrative, often called "the sacrifice of Isaac," has both perplexed and stimulated readers for centuries. It perplexed the Danish theologian Søren Kierkegaard, and it stimulated the Dutch artist Rembrandt. Reading and seeing the results of their work enriches our perception of this text. However, the reader who has suffered as a child at the hands of an abusive parent reads this text from a very different perspective. And that reader's perception, too, can enrich our study of this problematic tale.

There is, of course, a danger in emphasizing the role of the reader. Readers can import their own meanings into the text (often called "eisegesis" or "reading into") as opposed to drawing meaning out of the text (often called "exegesis" or "reading out of"). Each reader should be aware of critical elements in his or her identity. They are obviously important and will, inevitably, affect the way that an individual constructs meaning during the reading process. Such awareness will enable that individual to learn from other readers who might share certain elements of that identity, but that same awareness will make it possible for the individual to seek out others whose experience is different, creating the possibility for true dialogue in Bible study.

The text should, in principle, be able to challenge any reader's preconceptions about what it is saying. Hence, it is always appropriate for readers to be conscious of the questions and the perspectives with which they are approaching a text. Readers might well ask whether their question is literary, sociological, theological or historical.

SUMMARY

There are many ways to study the Bible. Obviously the materials provided in this study Bible do not offer an exhaustive guide. They hint at possible points of engagement and provide some of the basic information needed in order to begin to understand the text. Still, an important element of study are the questions that each reader brings to the text. Readers will serve themselves well if they routinely address a broad range of questions, ranging from literary, historical, and philological subjects to social world issues. In so doing, they will make fruitful biblical study possible for themselves and for others.

A READER'S GUIDE TO THE
BOOKS OF THE BIBLE

The signs in a bookstore or the category headings in the card catalogue at the library inform us whether a book is history or science, fiction or non-fiction, poetry or drama, and so we are able to prepare ourselves for our reading in advance. We would read a biography with a different set of expectations, for example, from those with which we would read an autobiography; a collection of essays on contemporary social problems calls for a different approach to reading than does a novel that focuses on one of those problems. The more readily we as readers are able to recognize the type of literature that we are reading, the more deeply we will be able to engage what that literature has to offer.

For example, the knowledge that *Anne Frank: The Diary of a Young Girl* is the actual journal of a young Jewish girl who lived in hiding during the Nazi occupation of the Second World War raises a different set of reading expectations and responses than would a novel built around the same set of circumstances. Reading the journal of a real person's experiences is different from reading a fictional representation of what those experiences might have been like. Moreover, our reading can be diminished if we mis-understand what type of literature we are reading. If, for example, we read a book on military tactics and strategy with the expectation that it will focus on the emotional costs of battle and so enable us to experience the human face of war, we will inevitably be disappointed or confused. Likewise, if we read a war novel expecting to learn how the high command developed its specific strategies and deployed the troops, we most likely will be disappointed again.

Although it is common to refer to the Bible as a faith community's book (singular), in reality the Bible is a collection of many different books (plural). The very word "bible" signifies a collection of books, because the word's origins can be traced back (through the Latin *biblia*) to the Greek phrase *ta biblia*, which means "the little scrolls." In the Jewish community as well, the diversity of books is reflected in the word used to refer to its Scriptures; "Tanakh" is an acronym formed from the first letters of the Jewish threefold division of Scripture: Law ("torah"), Prophets ("nevi'im") and Writings ("kethubim").

Bound within one cover, then, are many different books, each of which demands something different from the reader. In the New Testament, for example, one can read Paul's own accounts of his ministry in his letters and someone else's account of Paul's ministry in the stories of the Acts of the Apostles. As with *The Diary of A Young Girl*, reading Paul's own words and reading what someone else presents as Paul's words are two very different reading experiences. And unlike the signs and classifications that guide the modern reader through the bookstore or the library, the markers that identify the various types of literature found in the Bible are not as obvious at a casual glance. The titles of the different books of the Bible, for example, do not automatically indicate what we will find there. A man's personal name is the title of many books of the Bible, but reading Amos and reading Philemon are completely different experiences. The rest of this essay suggests the categories in the card catalogue at the library under which the books of the Bible might be filed, if they were filed as individual books, and so equips all readers for a deeper and fuller engagement with the Bible.

NARRATIVE AND NON-NARRATIVE BOOKS

One of the first classifications would involve the broad distinction between narrative and non-narrative books. Narrative books are those that tell a story and that, by and large, follow the traditional forms of storytelling—plot, character, setting, dialogue, etc. The narrative books of the Bible are often the best-known and the most beloved because they tell stories that people remember and retell—Genesis, 1 and 2 Samuel, Ruth, Esther, the four Gospels—but in reality, narrative and non-narrative books are fairly evenly balanced in the full sweep of biblical literature. Non-narrative books are those that, in contrast, do not tell stories. Non-narrative books in the Bible range from the poetry of the Psalms to the community instructions in Paul's letters.

Again, a comparison between Paul's letters and the book of Acts may be the most helpful way to illustrate the difference between narrative and non-narrative books. In the Acts of the Apostles, one of the goals of the author, Luke, is to tell the story of the rise of the Christian church, as the good news of Christ spread to the Gentile world. The reader is positioned to see the story of early Christianity the way Luke sees it and to understand that this story forms the foundation of the future life of the Christian church in the world, right up to the present day. As such, the stories about the mission to individuals or communities stand as illustrations of this basic story line. Paul's letters, by contrast, are not stories about the spread of the gospel in the Gentile world, nor does Paul write them so that the reader can see how the church grew and developed. Rather, Paul's letters are the urgent writings of someone on the front lines, so to speak, written to communities who have only a beginning sense of what it means to embrace the gospel that Paul preaches. A story could be constructed about each of the communities to which Paul writes (which to some extent Luke does in Acts), but that is not Paul's goal in writing. Paul writes to help these newly formed communities resolve particular theological and pastoral issues or crises with which they struggle. He addresses his readers directly through the letter: He talks to them about their own situation, not about another situation, as is the case with the audience of the stories in Acts.

Acts and the letters of Paul, then, give the Bible reader very different exposures to the life of the early Christian church by virtue of the differences in their literary type. Acts, a narrative book, offers a story of the church that has a beginning, middle, and end (however open-ended that ending may be; see the commentary on Acts). It has a cast of characters and a clearly defined plot. Paul's letters, non-narrative books, have none of that. With the exception of Paul and a few of his co-workers, there is no clear cast of characters, only the largely anonymous members of the church to whom each letter is sent. There is no defined story line, because Paul's letters are written out of and to ongoing struggles and situations, so we as modern readers find ourselves in the middle of a situation to which we are outsiders.

Paul cannot provide what Acts does—an ordered story—and Acts cannot provide what Paul's letters do—the sense of urgency and intensity that comes from addressing a crisis. Reading a story and reading a letter are two very different things. Each of these two types of literature, one narrative, the other non-narrative, has something valuable to contribute to our engagement with the biblical writings, but in order to grasp this experience we must read, assess, and appreciate each one on its own terms.

DIFFERENT TYPES OF NARRATIVE BOOKS

The broad distinction between narrative and non-narrative books is a start in orienting us to the spectrum of books gathered together in the Bible. It needs further specification, however, because there are many variations among the books that constitute these two large categories. The category "narrative" is a good way to begin to look at the storytelling of the Bible, but narrative books of the Bible tell different types of stories and tell them in different ways. Some narrative books of the Bible tell one continuous story from beginning to end. The most notable examples of this *novelistic* type of narrative would be the books of Ruth and Esther in the Hebrew Scriptures, and Judith, Tobit, Susanna, and Bel and the Dragon in the Apocrypha. Jonah also fits into this category, because even though it is one of the books of the prophets, it is a narrative of the adventures of one prophet who is trying to avoid his call.

Some narrative books are formed from the combination of many smaller stories and are more like *epics* than novels. Genesis, for example, combines many different stories—the story of the genesis of human beings and their foibles and failings (Gen. 1–11), and the stories of Abraham and his descendants (Gen. 12–50) that tell the distinctive story of the ancestors of the Israelite people. The remaining books of the Pentateuch—Exodus, Leviticus, Numbers, and Deuteronomy—work together to tell the sweeping story of Israel's exodus from slavery in Egypt, journey in the wilderness, and arrival at the promised land, while at the same time telling the life story of one man, Moses.

Shorter story units are also brought together to construct the *historical narratives* that play such a major role in biblical literature. Historical narratives appear in the Hebrew Scriptures, the Apocrypha, and the New Testament. These narratives tell the stories of a particular period in biblical history, but do so not by providing a simple record or chronicle of the events, but by looking at the events through the authors' understanding of the role and place of God in those events. Joshua and Judges tell the story of the conquest and occupation of the promised land, and the books of Samuel, Kings, and Chronicles tell the rich and contentious story of the rise and fall of the Davidic monarchy and dynasty. The last chapters of 2 Chronicles take the story through the fall of Jerusalem at the hands of the Babylonians and the Babylonian exile to the rise of King Cyrus and the Persian Empire. The books of Ezra and Nehemiah pick up the historical narrative at that point, and tell the story of the restoration of Jerusalem under Persian rule.

A comparison of the books of Samuel and Kings with those of Chronicles clearly illustrates that biblical histories are not simply objective recordings of events. The same events are recounted with very different narrative and theological emphases, because the Samuel–Kings tradition and the Chronicles tradition interpreted the events through different lenses (see the commentaries on the respective books). Interestingly, despite their different perspectives, both traditions end their storytelling of the Babylonian exile on a note of hope rather than desolation, another indication that biblical historical narratives are about more than simply recording the "facts."

In the Apocrypha, historical narratives are represented by the books of 1 Esdras and 1 and 2 Maccabees. First Esdras, like the books of Chronicles before it, draws heavily on other biblical histories (2 Chron 35–36, Ezra, and parts of Nehemiah) to tell its story of the Persian period. First and Second Maccabees tell the story of Israel after the death of Alexander the Great, when the Jews, under Hasmonean leadership, rebelled against foreign domination. First Maccabees in particular is highly reminiscent in style and tone of the biblical histories of Samuel and Kings. Again, the fact that 1 Esdras retells so much of a history already available in other books provides an important clue about the nature of biblical histories. Their function is not simply to record the facts—if that were the case, one version of any event would suffice—but to use the telling and retelling of history to think through what it means to be a people who have these stories as part of its heritage.

The Acts of the Apostles is the New Testament's example of a biblical history. The focus and function of the history change dramatically from the historical narratives cited above to Acts. Acts is no longer concerned with telling Israel's national story, but the author of Acts uses the models of the biblical histories that were at his disposal to shape his telling of the story of the rise of the Christian church.

Two other types of biblical narrative need to be discussed—*gospel* and *apocalypse*. The predominant form of narrative literature in the New Testament is the *gospel*, which has many similarities to the narrative forms discussed above, but is also distinct from them. Like Genesis and the biblical historical narratives, each of the four New Testament Gospels, Matthew, Mark, Luke, and John, also combine many smaller stories into one narrative unity, but they do so not to tell the sweeping story of many generations of a family or to cover several centuries in Israel's history. Rather, like the more novelistic narratives of Ruth or Jonah, the Gospels tell one continuous story from beginning to end—the story of the life and death of one man, Jesus. Yet because the focus of this story is primarily on the words and works of Jesus' public ministry and not on the full scope of his life, it is not accurate to label the Gospels as biography either, because their shaping concern is not a portrait of the life of a great man. The Gospels tell the story of Jesus as a way of telling the story of God at work in the world, and are written by people who believe God to be at work in the story they tell. In this way, the Gospel writers are like the authors of the historical narratives of the Hebrew Scriptures, recounting not "facts" alone, but what those facts tell about God and the people who attempt to live in accordance with their faith in that God. The Gospels represent a unique narrative form in the Bible, but one that is closely linked to the various narrative types of the Jewish Scriptures.

The *apocalypse* is represented in the Bible by the books of Daniel and Revelation, and in the Apocrypha by 2 Esdras. To be more specific, Daniel contains two distinct narrative types: Daniel 1–6 belongs to the novelistic type of narrative and so is closely linked in form to the Additions to Daniel found in the Apocrypha (Susanna and Bel and the Dragon), while Daniel 7–12 is an apocalyptic narrative. Daniel 7–12, Revelation, and 2 Esdras do tell a story, but it is not a story that adheres to the conventional expectations of storytelling. Indeed, the "story" of these books is the most sweeping in scope of any narrative in the Bible, for it tells God's cosmic story of the present and future of the created order. Much of Daniel 7–12, Revelation, and 2 Esdras are presented as visions revealed to the author, so that these books, like other biblical narratives, combine shorter narrative units to form the whole. An apocalypse can be among the most difficult books of the Bible to read, because we are tempted to ignore the narrative world that it creates and force it to adhere to our storytelling expectations. More than any other narratives in the Bible, the apocalypses ask the reader to step completely into the imagistic world created by the storyteller and view the whole creation through that perspective. The challenge is to allow these cosmic stories to shape our reading, rather than the other way around.

NON-NARRATIVE BOOKS

As different as the types of narrative books are, they all share the common trait that they tell stories. There is no comparable common characteristic among the non-narrative books of the Bible, and one finds a vast array of such literature—from poetical books to prophetic books to wisdom books to letters. The non-narrative books of the Bible present the reader with a completely different reading challenge and experience than do the narrative books.

Prophetic Books The prophetic books of the Old Testament may be the furthest removed from the biblical narratives. Stories draw the reader into someone else's life or history, but these books directly address a particular audience and focus on the diagnosis and resolution of a particular community problem. The prophetic books are not telling stories about foreign domination and economic injustice for anyone to read; they are engaging in political, economic, and theological analysis for a very specific community situation in what is for them the present moment.

The prophetic books give the reader access to many prophets whose words and actions have been preserved in writing: Isaiah, Jeremiah, Ezekiel, Hosea, Joel, Amos, Obadiah, Micah, Nahum, Habakkuk, Zephaniah, Haggai, Zechariah, Malachi. (Although Jonah appears in the group of the twelve minor prophets, between Obadiah and Micah, it is closer in form to the narrative books than the other prophets; see discussion of Jonah above.) But the narratives of the Hebrew Scriptures also describe many other prophets, most notably Elijah and Elisha in 1 and 2 Kings. We must therefore be careful not to view the nature and place of prophecy in Israel solely through the prophetic books. The prophetic books of the Bible contain a particular form of religious literature which forms part, but not all, of an important religious activity in the life of Israel.

The dominant literary characteristic of the prophetic books is the presence of preaching and prophetic oracles in poetic form. The prophetic oracle, usually a poem, is the prophet's announcement of the word and will of God, often prefaced by the phrase, "Thus says the LORD. . . ." The prophets used the poetry of their preaching and the prophetic oracle to analyze their current political and economic situations, often highlighting the failure of Israel's political and religious leadership, as well as the ordinary people, to live out the righteousness and justice of God.

It may seem odd to the modern reader, used to thinking of poetry primarily as fanciful and artistic language, that the prophets should use poetry to deliver their often harsh messages of social and economic injustice and impending judgment, instead of speaking in the nuts and bolts language common to newspaper editorials and other contemporary forms of social criticism. Perhaps it would help to think instead of the eloquent sermons of Martin Luther King, Jr., whose preaching combined poetry, social urgency, and theological conviction just as the prophets do.

The prophetic books also contain autobiographical and biographical material about the prophets' lives and work. This material may locate a prophet's ministry in a particular historical setting (for instance, Am 1.1) or show how the prophet's own life embodies the will of God that he speaks about in the oracles and sermons (for instance, Am 1.10–17; Jer 13.1–11). Just as biblical narratives are formed from a combination of shorter stories, the prophetic books are formed from a combination of different traditions. And interestingly, as is the case with the biblical histories of Samuel and Chronicles (and Acts in the New Testament), in most instances, the traditions have been gathered together in such a way as to end on a note of hope (for example, Am 9.9–15, Hab 3). The oracles of hope do not diminish the urgency of the judgment, but point toward the ongoing possibility of this faith community's future with God.

Wisdom Literature   At the other end of the spectrum from the prophets are the wisdom books. In the Hebrew Scriptures, Proverbs, Ecclesiastes and Job are classified as wisdom books, with Sirach and Wisdom of Solomon representing wisdom in the Apocrypha. Where the prophets are radically devoted to Yahweh, the God of Israel, constantly appeal to the possibilities for righteousness and faithfulness in Israel's history with this God, and call for reform of specific religious and political institutions, the wisdom books are almost completely silent on these topics (Sir 44–50 and Wis 10.1–21, 11–19 are exceptions). Where the prophetic books are a distinctly biblical literary form, without real parallels in the literature of the ancient Near East, the wisdom books are a universal literary form, one also found in Egypt, Mesopotamia, and other parts of the ancient Mediterranean world. The wisdom books are concerned with everyday experience and what it means to be human, and their subject matter runs from mundane instructions on proper behavior (Proverbs) to a skeptical consideration of the meaning of life (Ecclesiastes).

Wisdom books are poetic in form, with one of their central literary traits being the use of aphorisms or proverbs. The aphorisms usually have an instructional purpose—either to educate the younger generation about what it means to be a productive and moral member of society, or to inculcate traditional wisdom literature values more generally (teachings of wealth and poverty, appropriate speech, how to select one's friends). Proverbs 10–31 and Sirach both represent this traditional didactic wisdom book. Some wisdom teachings are less concerned with practical wisdom and more with an almost philosophical wisdom, reflecting on the nature of wisdom itself (for instance, Prov 1–9, Wis 6–9) and on the goodness and reliability of God's created order (for instance, Prov 8, Sir 16–18, Wis 19.18–21).

Yet biblical wisdom literature also contains two books, Job and Ecclesiastes, that present other important strands of the wisdom tradition, that which engages in skeptical wisdom and questions traditional religious assumptions about God and creation. Job is a complex poetic dialogue on the nature of divine justice and the problem of suffering, and the famous opening lines of Ecclesiastes, ". . . vanity of vanities, all is vanity," set the tone for this skeptical reflection on the meaning of human existence. It is as essential for all readers to struggle with the often jarring and disturbing reflections of Job and Ecclesiastes as it is to read the more traditionally affirmative aphorisms of Proverbs, because it is only when all the perspectives voiced in wisdom literature are taken together that one begins to get a sense of the complexity of biblical faith.

The New Testament book of James, even though its opening address gives it the external form of a letter (see below), is actually much closer to the wisdom teachings of Proverbs or Sirach. Like these books, its focus is instructional and it explicitly hails wisdom as a virtue and equates wisdom with righteousness (Jas 3.13–18).

Poetical Books The discussions of prophetic and wisdom books noted their use of poetic forms, but there are some books of the Bible that consist entirely of poems. The poetical books of the Bible include songs, hymns, and prayers. The best-known of these poetical books is Psalms, a collection of Israel's hymns and prayers. Psalms is often referred to as Israel's hymnbook, and that term gives an accurate sense of the place of poetical books in the Bible. Lamentations also contains hymns for the faith community's worship, in this case laments over the destruction of Jerusalem. The poetical books in the Apocrypha (the Prayer of Manasseh, the Prayer of Azariah and Song of the Three Jews, and Psalm 151) are also in this hymnic and prayer tradition. One poetical book stands slightly apart from the hymns and prayers of the other poetical books: the Song of Solomon (Song of Songs). This book contains joyous love songs between a man and a woman, perhaps to be used at a wedding.

Although the techniques used in Hebrew poetry may seem complicated to modern readers (see discussions of Hebrew poetry in comments and glossary), the power of the poetical books to communicate deeply and immediately to almost everyone remains undiminished. This poetry is able to span chronological and cultural distance and speak as directly to us as it did to its first readers. Not only that, the biblical hymns and prayers have provided Jews and Christians across the centuries with the words needed to pray and sing their own laments and fears, hopes and thanksgivings.

Epistles Like wisdom literature, epistles are a literary form common to the literature of the ancient Mediterranean world. Letter writing was the only way to communicate across long distances, and it therefore should not be surprising, given the missionary nature of the early Christian church, that epistles (letters) are the predominant literary form in the New Testament. Ancient letter writing followed certain conventions and these conventions are adhered to in the New Testament epistles. For example, ancient letters always began with a greeting, in which the letter's sender and recipient are both named. This opening greeting was followed by an expression of thanksgiving, often for a safe journey or rescue from danger, or a prayer on behalf of the recipient. Ancient letters also closed with greetings, in which the writers often passed along greetings from those with them to those at the letter's destination point. The letter of Paul to Philemon, the shortest of Paul's letters, gives the modern reader a good sense of what ancient letters were like.

Although New Testament readers tend to identify the letter form with Paul's writings, twenty-one of the New Testament's twenty-seven books have characteristics of the letter form. Some of these books, most notably James and Revelation, share important characteristics with other literary types (see the discussions of apocalyptic and wisdom books above), but nonetheless contain some stylistic conventions that link them with the letter form. There are no epistles as separate books in the Hebrew Scriptures, but the Apocrypha contains one, the Letter of Jeremiah.

Perhaps the most important thing to remember when reading the New Testament letters is that they are real letters, real communication between two parties, preserved through time, and when we read them we are quite literally eavesdropping on someone else's conversation. This puts modern readers at a certain disadvantage to the original recipients, who knew more about the circumstances that evoked and shaped those letters than we ever can. It is our task to find meaning for ourselves in these letters through the prior experience and struggles of the original readers, and we must be attentive to what those prior situations may have been before leaping to our own situation. Yet these letters also give modern readers a vivid portrait of ancient faith communities struggling with the meaning of their emerging Christianity for their own lives and their conduct in the world, and so provide an invaluable conversation partner for contemporary communities of faith. The reader of the New Testament epistles is never a solitary reader, but is always in the company of the letter's sender and original recipients.

CONCLUSION

This essay began by broadly categorizing the various books of the Bible under the headings "narrative" and "non-narrative." Those basic divisions hold true, but they also need some final clarification, because many of the books of the Bible combine these two categories to some degree. Many of the Bible's narratives contain non-narrative material, and many non-narrative books have strong narrative elements. Exodus and Numbers, for example, narrative books of the Pentateuch, contain important non-narrative sections, most notably the sections of legal codes (for instance, Ex 20–23). The Gospels, likewise, incorporate much non-narrative material into their stories (for instance, the Sermon on the Mount in Mt 5–7). As noted above, the prophetic books include biographical and autobiographical stories about the prophets. Job, a wisdom book, is set within a narrative frame. A letter is part of the narrative in Ezra (4.11–22).

As we have also seen, one biblical book can fit into more than one category. Revelation is the Bible's fullest example of an apocalypse, a narrative form, but it also can be categorized as one of the New Testament epistles. Jonah is a novelistic narrative, but it also is categorized canonically as one of the prophetic books. Daniel is both novelistic and apocalyptic narrative. Some Psalms, for instance Ps 37, can also be considered as wisdom literature, or at least as having been influenced by wisdom traditions. Also, many of the broad categories can be further refined. Hebrews and 1 Peter, for example, New Testament epistles, can also be categorized as sermons in letter form.

The categories suggested in this essay, then, are only a starting point. They provide the basic tools necessary to recognize the varieties of literary types that make up the books of the Bible, but each reader will discover ways to refine, expand, and deepen these categories through continued Bible reading and study. And while each of us will have our favorite biblical book or favorite literary type, it is only when the Bible is allowed to speak in all its variety that we can perceive the span and depth of biblical faith.

THE NATURE AND FORMATION OF THE BIBLICAL CANON

DEFINITION

By the *biblical canon* is meant the official list of the books which make up the Scriptures of the Old and New Testaments. Books which appear on this list are called *canonical* and all other books *non-canonical*. There are also books accepted as Scripture by some Christians but not others, and these are called *deuterocanonical*, meaning "belonging to a second level of canonicity" (Greek *deuteros* means "second"). These categories do not express value judgments about the books in question: to call a book non-canonical is not to say that it is necessarily unimportant or worthless. It is simply to say that it does not belong to the Christian Bible.

CONTENTS

The New Testament contains twenty-seven books, and all Christians agree on which these are. They fall into three categories. First, there are the four Gospels and the Acts of the Apostles, which contain the story of Jesus and of the earliest days of the Christian Church. Secondly, there are a number of letters or "epistles," some written to churches and others to individuals. The bulk of the letters are, or claim to be, by Paul. One of these is to the church in Rome, two to Corinth, one to Galatia, one to Ephesus, one to Colossae, and two to Thessalonica, together with personal letters to Timothy (two), Titus, and Philemon. Other letters claim to be by James, Peter (two), and Jude. Tradition ascribes three letters to John, though the name does not appear in the text itself. In addition there is the Letter to the Hebrews, which does not tell us who wrote it, though some people since ancient times have thought it was by Paul. Thirdly, we have the book of Revelation, sometimes called the Apocalypse. This begins with letters to churches, but consists mostly of a series of visions of the end of the world and the creation of a "new heaven and new earth." All these books were written in Greek.

Things are more complicated where the Old Testament is concerned, because here Christians do not agree. We will begin by discussing the books about which there is no disagreement, which are also regarded as Holy Scripture by Jews. If we follow the order presented in the NRSV (and there are others), we can say that, as in the New Testament, there are basically three kinds of books.

First, there are books of *narrative* or history. Together these amount to about half of the Old Testament. Genesis, Exodus, Leviticus, Numbers, Deuteronomy, Joshua, Judges, Ruth, 1 & 2 Samuel, and 1 & 2 Kings tell the story of God and his people from the creation of the world down to the exile of the people of Israel from their own land to Babylon, after the Babylonians conquered Jerusalem. This story is then repeated, but with enormous differences, in the two books of Chronicles. Following Chronicles, Ezra and Nehemiah relate the return of some Israelites to their land and the establishment of the Jewish state once again during the time of the Persian empire. The Old Testament does not take the story any further than this. The book of Esther tells us of some events at the Persian court which affected the safety of the Jews.

Secondly, the Old Testament contains books of *poetry* and *wisdom*. Job presents the problem of innocent suffering through a story about a righteous man whom God allows to suffer severe trials. Psalms contains many of the hymns that may have been used in Israel's worship. Proverbs includes collections of wise sayings. Ecclesiastes (also known by its Hebrew name, Qoheleth) provides a sceptical reflection on the teachings of other wise men. The Song of Solomon (or Song of Songs) is a collection of love poetry. None of these books is connected to any particular event in the history of Israel, and it is difficult to date them precisely.

The third part of the Old Testament consists of the books of the *prophets*. Three of these (Isaiah, Jeremiah together with Lamentations, and Ezekiel) are very long, and along with a fourth, shorter book—Daniel—are known as the *major prophets*. Last come the twelve *minor prophets*, Hosea, Joel, Amos, Obadiah, Jonah, Micah, Nahum, Habakkuk, Zephaniah, Haggai, Zechariah, and Malachi. ("Major" and "minor" here refer to length, not to importance.) The prophetic books consist of the prophets' *oracles*, which offer comments on contemporary society and predictions of the future, together with some stories about the prophets' lives.

Thus there is a certain parallel between the shape of the Old and New Testaments as they have come down to us—though as we shall see it is partly accidental. Both start with history (Genesis–2 Kings, Gospels and Acts), continue with books of teaching (poetic and wisdom books, letters) and conclude with prophecy (prophetic books, Revelation):

OLD TESTAMENT	NEW TESTAMENT
1. Histories	1. Gospels and Acts
2. Poetry and Wisdom	2. Letters
3. Prophecy	3. Revelation

Remembering this (rough) parallel can be useful as an aid to remembering how the Old and New Testaments are arranged in our Bibles.

All the books of the Old Testament were written in Hebrew, with the exception of a few chapters in Ezra and Daniel which are in Aramaic, a related language spoken across wide areas of the ancient world.

The Old Testament canon thus contains a wide variety of books. In fact the variety is even greater than indicated so far. Among the narrative or "historical" books there are wide variations in content. For example, whereas Genesis consists almost entirely of stories about the beginnings of the world and the early Hebrew ancestors, Exodus contains both history and law. It starts with the story of the exodus from Egypt under the leadership of Moses, but once the escaping Israelites reach Mount Sinai, the narrative pauses while we hear of the laws that Moses received from God. These begin with the Ten Commandments (Ex 20) but go on to include detailed rules for social life and the right ordering of worship. The laws continue all the way through Leviticus and the first half of Numbers, and it is only at Num 20 that continuous narrative resumes. Deuteronomy also consists mostly of laws.

In the same way the books of the prophets are far more varied than people often expect. Alongside oracles about the future (both optimistic and pessimistic) there are also stories, poems, passages that read like sermons, and denunciations of the state of society. It is often difficult or impossible to understand how the prophetic books are organized, with the result that they present a muddled appearance to the reader.

As well as the Old and New Testaments, many Bibles contain a section headed *The Apocrypha* (NRSV: *The Apocryphal/Deuterocanonical Books*). This consists of books whose authority as Scripture is accepted by some Christians but not others. Some Christians regard them as authoritative, but on a lower level from the books of the Old Testament; no Jews regard them as scriptural. The ancient texts of these books are available only in Greek (or certain other languages) rather than Hebrew. Although we know that some of them were originally written in Hebrew, for the most part the original Hebrew text is lost. (A partial exception is the book called Ecclesiasticus. Large portions of this book in Hebrew were found in Egypt at the beginning of the twentieth century.)

There is a traditional way of listing these additional books, but the NRSV prefers to collect them in sections according to which Christian communities accept their authority.

1. There are some books found in all Greek, Latin, and Slavonic Bibles, and are consequently accepted by Catholics, and by Greek and Russian Orthodox Christians. Tobit and Judith, two stories about the adventures of pious Jews, are in some ways rather reminiscent of Esther. Esther itself exists in a short form in the Hebrew Bible, but in Greek, Latin, and Slavonic Bibles it appears in a longer form with additional incidents, speeches, and prayers. Protestant Apocryphas usually print simply the parts that are additional under the heading "Additions to Esther." But these make no sense on their own, so the NRSV has translated The Greek Esther in full. Then there are two wisdom books that stand in the tradition of Proverbs: the Wisdom of Solomon and Ecclesiasticus, also known as the Wisdom of Jesus Son of Sirach (sometimes Sirach or Ben Sira). The book of Baruch combines further wisdom with prophetic teaching about the future glory of Jerusalem. Its sixth and final chapter, known as the Letter of Jeremiah, is sometimes printed separately, as it is in the NRSV. Additions to the book of Daniel follow: the Prayer of Azariah and the Song of the Three Jews, which belongs in the story of the burning fiery furnace (Dan 3), and the stories called Susanna and Bel and the Dragon. Then there are two history books, 1 and 2 Maccabees, which tell the story of Israel in the second century BCE.

2. Christians in the Greek and Russian Orthodox churches recognize four other works beyond even those in the Latin Bible. One is 1 Esdras, a narrative book—the Slavonic Bible calls it 2 Esdras, and Latin Bibles sometimes print it as an appendix under the name 3 Esdras. The Prayer of Manasseh, a penitential text, is also found in an appendix in some Latin Bibles. Psalm 151 and 3 Maccabees are peculiar to the Greek and Slavonic Bibles and not found in Latin Bibles.

3. The Slavonic Bible alone recognizes a work which it calls 3 Esdras, but which in the Latin Bible appendix is called 4 Esdras. This was originally written in Latin, and may be dated to the early Christian era. It is basically a Jewish work, but contains some Christian insertions. So it is later than many books in the New Testament. In Protestant Apocryphas it is usually called 2 Esdras. The titles and numbers of the books said to be composed by Ezra (Esdras in Greek) seem designed to baffle the memories of most readers!

4. Finally, the Greek Bible too has an appendix, which contains a further narrative book called 4 Maccabees. This is found in no other Bibles.

Whereas in Protestant Bibles, and in the NRSV, the apocryphal/deuterocanonical books are thus kept in a special section, in Greek, Slavonic, and Latin Bibles they are mingled in among the other books of the Old Testament, usually placed next to those they are most like. Thus Tobit and Judith stand next to Esther, and Wisdom and Ecclesiasticus next to Proverbs.

This overview demonstrates that the Old Testament and Apocrypha is a much more complex body of material than the New Testament. All Christians agree on the contents of the New Testament, but the Old Testament—though it obviously has a fixed core, the books that exist in Hebrew and are regarded as Scripture in Judaism—is much fuzzier at the edges. If one asks a well-informed Christian in a Protestant, Catholic, Greek Orthodox, or Russian Orthodox church what the books of the Old Testament are, one will get four different answers, though they will all agree in including the books which Jews recognize as their Bible.

ARRANGEMENT

The arrangement of the New Testament, like its contents, is now standardized among Christians. But it is interesting to note that the current arrangement was not the usual one in the first few Christian centuries. Modern Bibles group together all the narratives—the four Gospels and Acts. But Christians in the early centuries linked Acts with the so-called catholic epistles. "Catholic" here means "addressed to all Christians," and in practice the catholic epistles are the letters which are neither by Paul nor attributed to him. His letters each had a specific Christian church in mind, whereas the letters of the other apostles (James, Peter, John, and Jude) seem to envisage a wider group, rather like later papal encyclicals. Early Christian Bibles put Acts, the story of what the apostles did, at the beginning of the section containing the letters they wrote. The Gospels form a section on their own, and so do the letters of Paul (usually taken to include Hebrews). Revelation is the only member of a fourth category. So an early Christian Bible does not have quite the pattern we traced above, and the parallel drawn above with the Old Testament breaks down.

The Old Testament once again offers a more complicated case. Christian Bibles of all sorts usually have the shape described above, with histories followed by poetic books followed by prophets. As we have seen, what is included in each section varies. Catholic Bibles include Wisdom and Ecclesiasticus along with Proverbs and Ecclesiastes, Protestant Bibles exclude them. But the big difference in the arrangement of the Old Testament lies between Christian and Jewish Bibles.

The Hebrew Bible, as we saw, contains only the books that Protestants now accept as Holy Scripture. This does not mean that Jews follow Protestants! It results from the fact that, at the Reformation, Protestants decided to follow the Jewish canon for the books of the Old Testament. But the internal arrangement of the Hebrew books is strikingly different from that of Christian Bibles. There are still three sections, but their logic is a completely different one. The arrangement can be seen by looking at modern Jewish translations of the Bible into English, such as that of the Jewish Publication Society.

The first section of the Hebrew Bible is called the Torah, sometimes translated into English as "the Law." However, Torah has a wider meaning than the English word "law." Though Torah includes the sense of law, it also means teaching, instruction, and guidance. By calling the first section of the Bible "Torah," Jews are signalling that for them it forms the heart of Scripture, the books which are the supreme authority in matters of faith and life. The Torah consists of the *Pentateuch* or five "books of Moses"— Genesis, Exodus, Leviticus, Numbers, and Deuteronomy. Christians often think of these simply as five "historical books," running on without a break into Joshua. But in Judaism they are see not primarily as history but as instruction. They do of course contain historical narratives, but the purpose of these is to guide the life of their Jewish readers, not simply to record information about the past.

The second section of the Hebrew Bible is called the Prophets. This contains all the books called prophets in Christian Bibles (except Daniel), but it also includes the books of Joshua, Judges, Samuel, and Kings. Since the Middle Ages these historical books have come to be known as the "Former Prophets," with the books that are prophetic in the ordinary sense (for example Isaiah, Jeremiah, Amos) described as the "Latter Prophets," but this is not seen as a very important distinction. Why the histories were included under the same heading as the prophecies no-one knows: perhaps they were thought to have prophets as their authors. (Jewish sources tend, for example, to regard Samuel as the author of the books of Samuel, and Jeremiah of the books of Kings.) The Prophets section is important in Jewish worship. After the weekly reading from the Torah, there is a second reading, and it always comes from the Prophets, whether Former or Latter. There is a tendency to think of the Prophets as a kind of second tier in Scripture, of slightly lower status than the Torah though still, of course, highly authoritative.

For the third section the rather bland name Writings is the official term—sometimes modern writers use the Greek form Hagiographa, meaning "sacred writings." This is the section to which everything in Scripture that is not Torah or Prophets is assigned. Such an organization of the texts causes some surprises to those used to the Christian Bible. Chronicles, Ezra, and Nehemiah, which Christian Bibles treat as histories and place after Kings, appear in Hebrew Bibles in the Writings section. What is more, they are usually arranged out of chronological order: Ezra, Nehemiah, Chronicles. Daniel is also reckoned among the Writings, not with the Prophets. Here appear also the five books that were read at Jewish festivals: Lamentations, Ruth, Esther, Song of Solomon, and Ecclesiastes. The order of books in the Writings is not regarded as very significant: ancient and medieval manuscripts sometimes have different orders. The Writings are sometimes thought of as somewhat lower in status than the Prophets, though for practical purposes it is the distinction between the Torah and the rest that is really important. Early rabbis sometimes lumped Prophets and Writings together as "Qabbalah," or tradition.

There has never been a Christian Bible that followed the Jewish arrangement, and this perhaps is puzzling. When Protestants decided to remove the deuterocanonical books from their canon, leaving only the same Hebrew books that were also accepted by Jews, they did not rearrange what remained to make it follow the Hebrew order. They simply extracted the deuterocanonical books, and left everything else as it was.

Consequently we could say that the Protestant "Old Testament" is the Hebrew Bible arranged in the Christian order—something of a hybrid Scripture.

FORMATION OF THE OLD TESTAMENT

The canon of the Old Testament was not fixed by a decision of some authoritative body. In the New Testament period, we do hear dimly from a few Jewish sources that some books were of doubtful status. The Song of Solomon, Ezekiel, Esther, Ecclesiastes, and Proverbs were all regarded by some as anomalous or of doubtful status, though it is far from clear that there was ever any suggestion that that they were not yet canonical, or that they should be removed from the canon. Only in the case of Ecclesiasticus is there record of a decision by rabbis to exclude it from the canon. This decision was taken on the grounds that, though edifying, the book was known to have been written (in 180 BCE) long after the time at which, according to Jewish belief, scriptural books ceased to be written (roughly sometime in the fifth or fourth century BCE). (Daniel, though also written in the second century BCE, did become part of the canon, probably because its attribution to a figure of the sixth century was believed to be correct.) The books that form the Hebrew Bible were never controversial. The canon simply grew, as books were gradually accepted as Holy Scripture and revered by successive generations.

The threefold division of the Hebrew Bible reflects, to some extent, the order in which the books came to be recognized as Scripture. The Pentateuch—the Torah—must have been completed at some time during the Persian period, which lasted from 540 BCE or so until 333 BCE, when Alexander the Great conquered the Persian empire. A date sometime in the fifth century BCE is likely. If so, then we have an explanation for the high prestige of this part of the canon: it is the oldest part of the Bible. There may be books, or parts of books, in the Prophets and Writings that are older, taken individually. For example, the books of Amos, Hosea, Isaiah, and Micah probably include genuine words of those prophets who lived in the eighth century BCE. But as a *collection* the Torah is older than the Prophets and the Writings.

Possibly the Prophets formed next, with the Writings put together last of all, some time not long before the period when the New Testament was written. This would help to explain why the last books to be written appear, on the whole, in the Writings: Daniel, for example, and probably also Ruth and Esther. By the time these books were written, the Torah already existed as a finished whole. Daniel, in fact, even refers to the book of Jeremiah (see Dan 9.1), which indicates that the book of Jeremiah already existed, and possibly that the collection of the Prophets did as well.

Still, there is one piece of evidence that makes it less certain that Prophets and Writings represent successive stages in the formation of the canon. We have already observed that some rabbinic sayings link the two collections together under the single term "Qabbalah." Moreover, the New Testament also tends to treat them as a single whole, when it speaks of "the law and the prophets," meaning by this not Torah and Prophets in the technical sense, but Torah and other scriptural books. In other words, for the New Testament writers the distinction between Prophets and Writings seems not to exist. At most there could be an allusion to it in Lk 24.44, which refers to Scripture as "the law of Moses, the prophets, and the psalms"—the psalms might stand for the Writings. There may also be a reference to the threefold division in the Prologue to Ecclesiasticus, which speaks of "the law and the prophets and the other writings"—though the third category here may mean "other writings in general," not necessarily "the Writings." It seems likely that many people, even as late as the New Testament writers (first century CE), were not yet familiar with the threefold division of the canon, and that it was not generally established until some time in the Common Era.

The situation of all the books other than the Torah forming a single, shapeless category as late as the first century CE might help to explain why the Jewish and Christian Bibles diverge in the way they are arranged, and also in which books they contain. Most of the early Christians whose writings are represented in the New Testament were Greek speakers; and many Jews by this time also spoke Greek as their first, or even their only language. For their benefit the Hebrew Bible had been translated into Greek, mostly in Egypt at Alexandria, during the last three centuries BCE. Moreover, most of the deuterocanonical books, as we have seen, were written in Greek or else existed in Greek translations. For a Greek-speaking Jew living in Egypt it would have been far from clear that (for example) Proverbs, which he or she would know in its Greek version, was Holy Scripture, whereas the (rather similar) Wisdom of Solomon, which was originally composed in Greek, was not. The Jews of Alexandria probably had, alongside the Torah, a rather larger category of second-order books than their fellow Jews in Palestine who knew only the Hebrew books. This "Alexandrian canon" was what the Christians inherited, for most of them lived outside Palestine and did not understand Hebrew: they naturally adopted the Greek version of the Jewish Bible as their own. In arranging the books other than the Torah in a different way from what would become the Hebrew canon, they may not, therefore, have been deliberately changing anything. No one had yet had the idea that there was a "correct" way of arranging them.

An important witness to the state of the canon in the first century CE is the Jewish writer Josephus. He lived in Palestine, but was familiar with the Bible in Greek (he wrote in Greek himself). In one of his writings he claims that the Jews recognize only twenty-two books as Scripture. Most scholars think he is referring to the books of the Hebrew Bible as Jews now have it, though this is usually said to contain twenty-*four* books—the exact number depends on whether, for example, 1 and 2 Samuel are counted as one book or two, whether Lamentations is thought of as part of Jeremiah, and so on. But what is interesting is that Josephus' description of what these twenty-two books contain actually sounds as though he knew them in an order different from any known to us, but having similarities to the Greek Bible—which was to become the Christian Bible. Thus he says that

> five are the books of Moses, comprising the laws and the traditional history down to the death of the lawgiver. . . . From the death of Moses until Artaxerxes, who succeeded Xerxes as king of Persia, the prophets subsequent to Moses wrote the history of the events of their own times in thirteen books. The remaining four books contain hymns to God and precepts for the conduct of human life (*Against Apion* 1.42).

Like the Hebrew Bible, this appears to lump together the Former and the Latter Prophets, treating their writers primarily as historians. But it also recognizes a category of poetic and wisdom books, which is more like the central, poetic section of the Greek Bible than it is like the Writings of the Hebrew one. Perhaps what Josephus shows us is that Jews had not yet agreed on any particular way of arranging the books outside the Torah, so that he was free to classify them in whatever way would be most helpful to his readers.

At some point all Jews came to the conclusion that only the books that are now in the Hebrew Bible were to be treated as Holy Scripture. Christians, on the other hand, tended to follow the longer selection which we find in the Greek Bible and its descendants, the Latin and Slavonic Bibles. We do not know why Jews opted for the shorter canon, nor why they divided it into the three sections described above. But the threefold division was definitely established by the end of the second century CE.

We also do not know why the Church decided to accept the longer Greek canon. But it is clear that many early Christian writers thought that many of the works only to be found there had great authority. Manuscripts of the Christian Old Testament also contain the additional Greek books. There were occasional disagreements. For example, toward the end of the second century CE Melito, bishop of Sardis (in what is now Turkey), went on a fact-finding tour to the Holy Land and discovered that the Jews there accepted only the Hebrew books. (This is one reason why we know that for Jews the Hebrew canon must have been in force by then.) He decided on the strength of this that Christian Old Testaments ought not to contain the extra books; but no one paid him much attention.

Two later Christian leaders also tried to limit the canon to the Hebrew books. Athanasius (c. 296–373 CE), bishop of Alexandria, maintained that the deuterocanonical books ought not to be part of the canon. He would have reduced the Old Testament to the Hebrew books and treated the other books as non-canonical. Strikingly, however, he himself continued to make just as much use of these books after he had pronounced on the subject as he had before—especially the Wisdom of Solomon, which for him as for many early Christian writers was a favorite text.

In the following century Jerome (c. 345–420) set himself the task of translating the whole Bible into Latin, producing the work known as the Vulgate, which is the official version still used by the Catholic Church. (Latin translations already existed, but they were less accurate than Jerome's.) In the process Jerome learned Hebrew from Jewish friends, and inevitably became aware that the Jews recognized only the Hebrew books. He proposed that the Church, too, should abandon the deuterocanonical works. He engaged in a fierce debate with Augustine (345–430), bishop of Hippo in North Africa. Augustine believed that the universal consensus among Christians that the deuterocanonical books were part of the Bible should overrule the fact that the Jews did not accept them. The matter was resolved in Augustine's favor, because the Church continued to use these additional books, and Jerome, indeed, translated them despite his misgivings about their status.

It is important to see that the point at issue was whether the deuterocanonical books should be thought of as Scripture. No one suggested that they were bad or worthless. There is no contradiction in thinking a book to be good but not regarding it as part of the Bible! The problem was that the Church always had regarded these books as Scripture. Although they are quoted little in the New Testament, Christian writers throughout the second century CE used them freely, and treated them exactly as if they were on a par with the "canonical" books. Hence writers like Augustine could argue that, whatever Jews thought about the canon, for Christians the matter was settled by a long tradition in the Church.

Augustine may have had the best of the argument. If we thought of the deuterocanonical books as books added to the Bible by Christians, it would be natural to say that the "original" Old Testament did not contain them. Then we might, with Jerome, think they should be removed. But as we have seen, this way of thinking is not likely to be the explanation of the longer canon in the Christian Bible. There are two more likely explanations. One is the "Alexandrian canon" theory, which says that some Jews already had a longer canon in the New Testament period. The shorter canon is the Bible of Palestinian Jews, the longer is that of the Jews of Alexandria. Everyone agrees that the majority of the Greek books in the longer canon, after all, are Jewish in origin—no one is suggesting that Christians *wrote* them, only that they accepted them. The other plausible explanation is that in New Testament times neither Jews nor Christians had yet decided on the exact selection of books they would regard as canonical. When they did eventually decide, Jews opted for the shorter, Hebrew canon, Christians for the longer, Greek one. In other words, Jerome's argument rested on what Jews *in his own day* thought about the limits of Scripture, but this is not necessarily what Jews had believed several centuries earlier.

After Augustine the matter was regarded as closed in the Christian Church, and throughout subsequent centuries Christian Bibles always included the deuterocanonical books, incorporated into the main body of the Old Testament in the way we have described. It was not until the Reformation in the sixteenth century that the matter was discussed fully again. The major Reformers, Luther and Calvin, both went back to Jerome and Athanasius, and argued strongly that only the Hebrew books should be accepted as Holy Scripture. However, even within Protestantism there were differences of opinion. Calvin and those who followed him in the Reformed tradition regarded the deuterocanonical books as no different in principle from any other ordinary books, and wanted them to have no special position in the Church at all. Sometimes they even argued—which was not strictly necessary to this point of view, as we have seen—that the deuterocanonical books were badly flawed. Luther, on the other hand, regarded these books as good and edifying, and wanted to see Christians continue to read them. But he placed them in an appendix to the Old Testament. In practice Lutherans do not make much use of these additional books, and most Lutheran Bibles do not contain them. Of the other churches of the Reformation, the Anglican (Episcopalian) churches have adopted a position like the Lutheran one, but have tended to use these books in worship and private reading to a greater extent. According to the Church of England's thirty-nine Articles of Religion (1571) "the other books [that is, the deuterocanonical books] the Church doth read for example of life and instruction of manners; but yet doth it not apply them to establish any doctrine." Even so, few Anglicans know these books at all well, and they are read in Church rather seldom, though the *Book of Common Prayer* includes the Song of the Three Jews in its service of Morning Prayer, and Anglican lectionaries have always drawn on the Apocrypha to provide readings for saints' days. Sirach 44.1ff. is familiar to many as a reading for All Saints' Day, is commonly used in Britain at memorial services, and will be familiar to many from the opening of the film "Chariots of Fire."

The Catholic church had to react to the Reformers' decisions about the deuterocanonical books, and did so at the Council of Trent in 1546. The traditional teaching that all the books of the Latin Bible were to be regarded as canonical was reaffirmed, and the special place of the Vulgate translation was emphasized. The Council expressed doubts only about the books usually called 1 and 2 Esdras (see above), which it placed in an appendix following the New Testament. The First Vatican Council in 1870 reaffirmed the position set out at Trent.

Because of the special status allowed for the deuterocanonical books in the thirty-nine Articles of Religion, the translators of the King James Version translated these books, which therefore form a third section to this Bible, between Old and New Testaments, called "The Apocrypha." Consequently their influence on English literature has been greater than might be expected on the basis of official pronouncements about their status.

In the twentieth century nothing has changed regarding the status of the deuterocanonical books. Catholics still regard them as part of the Bible, on an equal footing with the universally accepted books. In the Orthodox churches there have been no debates about them like those at the Reformation in the West, so they remain firmly in place within that religious tradition. The Protestant churches have continued to reject them or to be ambivalent about them. Consequently it is possible to buy Bibles either with or without the Apocrypha. The NRSV is the first western Bible to include the books which are not recognized even in the Catholic church, but only by the Orthodox churches. In this it recognizes an important fact about this vexed issue, namely, whatever status the churches officially claim for the deuterocanonical books, they are certainly important, and deserve to be read and studied. In practice all students of the Bible, whether they are Jewish, Catholic, Protestant, Orthodox, or of no religion need to know about these books. Discussion of the status of the Apocrypha does not seem to be on the agenda in any of the churches; in practice old feuds about them have become rather less important in the modern period.

FORMATION OF THE NEW TESTAMENT

Compared with the Old Testament, the books of the New Testament were all written in a very short space of time—probably not much more than fifty or sixty years, from the 40s CE till the beginning of the second century. As we saw above, by the time there were manuscripts of the whole New Testament the books clearly fell into groups, and presumably this is how they were first collected. One obvious group is the collection of Paul's letters, sometimes called the *Pauline corpus*. Paul's letters were all written to a very specific situation, dealing with problems and difficulties that had arisen in this or that Christian community. But he himself probably expected his letters to be read outside the church to which they were originally written—though the only explicit statement of such an intention is found in Col 4.16 ("when this letter has been read among you, have it read also in the church of the Laodiceans; and see that you read also the letter from Laodicea"), in a letter regarded by many modern scholars as not genuinely Pauline. The custom seems to have grown up of passing Paul's letters around, and it was a short step from this to making a collection of them.

The Pauline corpus seems to go back to the second or third generation after Paul himself. In almost all manuscripts, the letters are arranged in order of length, within two categories. The first category consists of letters to churches: Romans, 1 and 2 Corinthians, Galatians, Ephesians, Philippians, Colossians, 1 and 2 Thessalonians (Ephesians is in fact slightly longer than Galatians, but this is always the order). The second category comprises letters to individuals: 1 and 2 Timothy, Titus, and Philemon. Some people have speculated that Philemon holds the clue to the collection. Perhaps Onesimus, the runaway slave who is the subject of this letter, became a leader in one of the churches founded by Paul, and decided to collect all his letters together. This theory might explain why a letter so completely personal is included in a collection intended for the Church at large. However, such speculation is really the stuff of a biblical novel rather than a matter of hard evidence! Whatever the cause, copies of Paul's letter collection were circulating by the beginning of the second century CE.

The collection of the Four Gospels seems to be equally old. It had a greater effect on the way the Gospels came to be understood than the collection of Paul's letters had on the individual letters. Each Gospel seems originally to be intended to tell the definitive version of the life, death, and resurrection of Jesus. Luke, in fact, tells us explicitly that he wanted to correct existing accounts and to tell the story in its true form (see Lk 1.1). If everything in any one of the Gospels is true exactly as stated, then none of the other Gospels can be completely true, for they present divergent accounts of the same events. But once it came to be accepted that there were four Gospels, all with equal authority, people inevitably had to read them as complementing and completing, rather than contradicting each other. This perspective was fully established by the late second century, when Irenaeus of Lyons (c. 130–c. 200 CE) defended the existence of four Gospels, rather than a single authoritative one, as a positive blessing to the Church. His argument was that four witnesses to such crucial events provided a guarantee greater than would be given by only one, and that the discrepancies do not affect the overall reliability of all four accounts.

Before Irenaeus there had been two attempts to establish just one version of the Gospel as definitive. Marcion (died 160 CE), a native of Asia Minor who taught for a time in Rome, believed that there was only one correct Gospel, the Gospel according to Luke. But he thought that even that Gospel had been contaminated by wrong teaching, so he "corrected" it, and combined it with a selection of Paul's letters to form a kind of rudimentary New Testament. Marcion's attachment to Luke resulted from the fact that it is the least "Jewish" of the Gospels, in the sense that it stresses more than the others the central importance of non-Jews in God's plan, and does not quote the Old Testament as much as does (for instance) Matthew. Even so, Marcion had to delete a number of passages to remove references to the Old Testament. He wanted to do this because he believed that the God of Jesus was quite distinct from the Jewish God, and that Christianity had no kind of connection or continuity with Judaism. For this the Church condemned him as a heretic, because Christians believed that the God revealed in Jesus was, on the contrary, the God who had been known to the Jews for so long through the pages of the Old Testament. But in condemning Marcion, the Church also ruled out the possibility of allowing anyone to claim that only one of the Gospels was a true record, and endorsed the four-Gospel canon.

The second attempt to produce a single Gospel account was made by Tatian (who wrote about 160 CE), who came from Assyria but also studied in Rome. He worked differently from Marcion. Instead of taking one Gospel and expurgating it, he accepted all four Gospels but made a "harmony" of them. He followed different Gospels for different incidents and sayings in Jesus' life, blending the four accounts together to make a single, consistent one. His work, the Diatessaron, became widely popular in the Church, especially in Syria and the East, and was still in use there instead of the four Gospels two or more centuries later. Indeed, it was translated into many languages, and was still used by some people in Western Europe in the Middle Ages. It represents in many ways a common sense reaction to the problem of four inconsistent Gospels. That the Church eventually rejected it shows that the prestige of the four-Gospel canon was high in most areas of Christendom from an early period.

We do not know when the "catholic" letters (James, 1 and 2 Peter, 1, 2, and 3 John, and Jude) were collected together, but we do know that they usually circulated with the Acts of the Apostles. It is almost as if these works together were felt to add up to a kind of apostolic equivalent of the Gospels: just as in the Gospels we learn of Jesus' actions and his teaching, so in this collection we learn of the deeds of the apostles (in Acts) and their teachings (in the letters). From early times, this section of the New Testament was used conspicuously less by Christian writers than the Gospels and Paul. Quotations from Acts are far less common than those from its "first volume," Luke, and the catholic letters are rarely mentioned. Nevertheless, there is no record of any opposition to these books. They were accepted by all as authoritative, even if they were not much used.

Finally, there are the book of Revelation and the Letter to the Hebrews. Revelation had a checkered history. When Christian writers such as Eusebius of Caesarea (c. 260–c. 340 CE), the first Church historian, discuss which books are part of the New Testament, they often express doubts about the status of Revelation. It seems to have been especially unpopular in the Eastern Mediterranean world, and to have been more widely accepted in the West. Revelation's acceptance there may be connected with its predictions of the end of the world in the context of fierce denunciations of the Roman empire. By the fourth century, however, Revelation was firmly ensconced in the canon, perhaps partly because, like the Fourth Gospel and the three Letters of John, it was assumed to have been written by the Apostle John.

As the case of Revelation demonstrates, authorship was often an important factor in deciding which books would be accepted into the canon. We see this also in the case of Hebrews. This letter (if it really is a letter) had the opposite fate from Revelation, since doubts about it tended to be expressed chiefly in the West—possibly because of its very harsh attitude to sins committed after baptism (10.26–31). But doubts about its authority may have been related to doubts about who wrote it. Many Christians assumed it was by Paul, even though it nowhere says so. (Paul's authorship is stated in the *title* in the King James Version, "The Epistle of Paul the Apostle to the Hebrews," but there is nothing about it in the *text* of the letter.) When they did, they tended also to think it must be a valid part of the New Testament, and to quote it more often than those who thought it was by someone else. The question of authorship also affects where it appears in the Pauline corpus. For people who thought Hebrews was written by Paul, it was natural to include it between Romans and 1 Corinthians, because it is next to Romans in length. Where it was not thought to be Pauline, it tended to appear where we now have it, after all the Pauline letters.

The formation of the New Testament differs from that of the Old in two particularly important ways. First, the Old Testament began life as a series of scrolls. Each major book had its own scroll, which had the effect of determining how long a book could be. Although the Pentateuch is a continuous whole, it was divided up into five separate scrolls. Similarly, the "Former Prophets" tell a continuous story from the exodus to the exile, but they are divided up—not always in the most natural places—to make a set of scrolls of roughly equal length. On the other hand, several short books might be grouped together on a single scroll. This is the case with the twelve minor prophets, which in Judaism in ancient times tended to be regarded as a single book—the "Book of the Twelve"—and not seen as having much individual character, because they all appeared on the same scroll. But the New Testament did not start as a set of scrolls. For some reason which no-one has yet discovered, Christian texts from the very beginnings were written in what are technically known as "codices" (singular: "codex"), which are what we call "books"—many pages sewn together with covers, and opening flat. In the ancient world codices were normally used only for informal purposes, as notebooks, and it was a startling innovation for Christians to write their most treasured possessions, the Gospels, in this form.

The use of a codex form had a major effect on the emergence of the New Testament. For one thing, a codex can hold considerably more than a scroll without becoming unwieldy, and so it was possible to have a codex of all four Gospels, of all the Pauline letters, and in due course of the whole New Testament. Secondly, books arranged in a codex come in a certain order. Mark follows Matthew in the straightforward sense that you finish reading Matthew, turn the page, and there is Mark. Scrolls can never be in an "order" in quite this sense, and Jewish discussions of the order of biblical books in ancient times were always rather more theoretical than Christian ones, because scrolls can be moved around relative to each other whereas the order of books in a codex, once they have been written out, is fixed. Christians soon began transferring their methods of writing their own books in codices on to the Old Testament too, so that the Greek Old Testament has a definite order in a stronger sense than the Hebrew Bible ever had—at least until the time when Jews, too, began to use the codex.

Secondly, and possibly linked with their use of the codex form, Christians seem to have had a rather different attitude to their own books, or at least to the Gospels, than they had towards the Old Testament Scriptures. Whereas the Old Testament was seen as a fixed and sacred text, the Gospels were often perceived more as rather informal records of the life and teaching of Jesus, on the basis of which early Christian preachers could to some extent improvise. Although there was enormous reverence for what Jesus had said and done, this referent was not necessarily seen as identical with exactly the words of this or that Gospel, but more as a matter of tradition passed on by word of mouth, which the Gospels were an aid to remembering and recalling. People knew that Jesus had spoken in Aramaic, and that the Gospels contained only translations of his words, not the very words themselves. This is probably one reason why four partly inconsistent Gospels were not seen as a problem. Nothing hung on the *precise* details of this or that incident or saying.

There is something of a paradox here. Only the Old Testament was "Scripture" for the very earliest Christians: their own books were still seen as something less formal than a "Bible." Yet on the other hand those books were their own special possession in a way that the Old Testament was not; and the traditions about Jesus that they knew, whether they were recorded in books or not, were of literally earth-shaking significance in their minds. So they saw the New Testament as less "scriptural" than the Old Testament, yet in many ways as more important. This is a vital point to grasp if we are to understand the significance of what would become the New Testament in the minds of early Christians. Sometimes people say that only the Old Testament was Holy Scripture for the first Christians, and that the New Testament only gradually came to be accepted as of equal status. This is true in one sense; but at another level it fails to take account of how committed Christians were to their not-yet-scriptural writings, which contained the record of something which they thought had changed the world.

Whereas with the Old Testament we cannot point to a definite date when the collection was complete (either for the Hebrew or the Greek version), with the New Testament it is possible to identify a series of official decisions about what was to count as "Scripture." The matter was discussed and ruled on at the council of Laodicea 363 CE, and soon after this we can point to a final moment of "canonization" in the writings of Athanasius, bishop of Alexandria (296–373). Every year before Easter Athanasius wrote to the churches under his care a so-called "Festal Letter." In 367 CE he chose to include an account of the books of the New Testament, and there for the first time we find exactly the list which is now accepted in all the churches. The arrangement is still the old one, with Acts at the head of the catholic letters rather than between the Gospels and Paul, but the specific books are precisely those that are now in our New Testament. In the western Church, councils at Hippo (393) and Carthage (397 and 419) confirmed Athanasius' list as definitive.

THE EXCLUSIVE CANON

There is one further element that needs to be present before we can speak strictly of the biblical canon as fixed and complete. This is that the books in the list are seen as *exclusive*, in the sense that these *and only these* books form the Bible. It is theoretically possible to have an official list of all the books that have *so far* been recognized as authoritative. Perhaps this is what Josephus, for example, is doing in the passage quoted above from *Against Apion*: listing the books that Jews do in fact recognize, and saying that they could only recognize others if they were equally ancient. But when Athanasius lays down the limits of the New Testament canon, he is saying these books are *for all time* the Bible that Christians must accept.

The idea that some books are to be excluded from the Bible is much older than the fourth century CE. As we saw, Jewish authorities had already decided that the Wisdom of Jesus ben Sirach (Ecclesiasticus) did not qualify for the status of Holy Scripture. Tertullian (c. 160–c. 225) tells us that the Church of his day had a list of books that Christians were not supposed to read, the remote ancestor of the Vatican's *Index of*

Prohibited Books, which persisted down into our own time. But it seems to have been in roughly the fourth century that Christians started to abandon a rough-and-ready system in which some books were definitely in and others definitely out, but in which there was a grey area of books whose status was rather unclear. Instead they tried to formulate a definitive and exclusive list of canonical works. The creation of such a list does not mean the works on it were of doubtful authority until then. The great majority of books in the New Testament, like the great majority in the Old, did not become "scriptural" because some authority decided they should be, but established themselves over time in people's minds. All that someone like Athanasius did was to endorse the books that everyone accepted already, and to give a ruling on a few doubtful cases. No-one created the biblical canon: it grew.

THE HEBREW SCRIPTURES COMMONLY CALLED THE OLD TESTAMENT

New Revised Standard Version

TORAH / PENTATEUCH

The first five books of the Bible—Genesis, Exodus, Leviticus, Numbers, and Deuteronomy—have often been looked at as one long work. Some readers know it as the Torah,* others as the Pentateuch.* The decision about whether to characterize the first five books of the Bible as Torah or as the Pentateuch holds great significance. To call them "Torah" is to emphasize the unity of instruction or guidance provided in these books. To label them "the Pentateuch" underscores the variety present in the five books, each of which bears a distinct title.

The word "Pentateuch" means five books. The Hebrew word "Torah" is more difficult to translate easily into English. In the Hebrew Bible, it can mean "instruction," "direction," and "law." The word appears in phrases like "as it is written in the book of the Torah of Moses," (Josh 8.32) or "as it is written in the Torah of Moses" (1 Kings 2.3), or "the book of the Torah of Moses" (Neh 8.1), which reflects the conviction that there is a definitive Torah, one associated with Moses. (The phrase "this Torah," [Deut 1.5] reinforces the singularity of Mosaic Torah.) The phrase was probably first used to refer to an early form of the book of Deuteronomy (Deut 28.61 refers to "the book of this law," namely, the laws that have just been promulgated in Deut; 2 Kings 22.8 refers to "the book of the Torah," probably an early form of that biblical book).

Moses figured prominently in Exodus–Numbers, the books that immediately precede Deuteronomy. Hence, Torah came to be used for the entirety of the Bible up to and including Deuteronomy, even though Moses does not appear in Genesis. Still, Genesis sets the stage for the Mosaic period by placing the people of Israel in Egypt, despite the fact that it does not share many of the literary features of the next four biblical books.

That these five books have been understood as one entity is, in some measure, surprising. Israel's story about itself, which, at the beginning of Genesis, reaches back to the creation of the universe, is markedly incomplete at the end of Deuteronomy. The Torah concludes with a tribute to the now-dead Moses and with Israel on the east side of the Jordan River. Although there had been an ill-fated attempt to conquer the land (Num 14.39–45), the people as a whole had yet to enter the territory promised to them in Genesis. Some interpreters therefore propose that the first six books of the Bible make up an Hexateuch (Genesis through Joshua), a literary entity that concludes with Israel in possession of the land. As it stands, however, the Pentateuch leaves Israel in a figurative exile, "in the plains of Moab by the Jordan" (Num 36.13).

The Torah contains diverse kinds of literature: narratives,* poems, reports, genealogies,* sermons, dialogues, and laws among them. For many readers, the narratives, such as those about the flood or about Israel's escape from Egypt, are the most memorable part of the Pentateuch. The Pentateuch moves through a series of basic narrative moments: creation and the primeval period (Gen 1.1–11.26), the primal family (Gen 11.27–50.26), slavery in Egypt (Ex 1.1–13.16), Israel in the wilderness (Ex 13.17–18.27), Israel at Sinai (Ex 19.1–Num 10.10), Israel in the wilderness (Num 10.11–22.1), and Israel in the plains of Moab (Num 22.1–Deut 34.12). Of these moments, the longest by far is Israel at Sinai, which occupies fifty-four biblical chapters. (Of these, only five [Ex 19–20, 32–34] include substantial narrative material.) Sinai is prominent because of what God announces there and because of the powerful figure with whom God speaks on the mountain, the character who towers over the final four books of Torah: Moses.

Many different kinds of stories appear within these narrative moments. Some are very short, almost sketchlike in nature. One story about Abraham passing off his wife as his sister (Gen 12.10–20) extends over only eleven verses. By comparison, the story concerning Joseph covers fourteen chapters. Some narratives focus on a person, others on a place. Some recount flat characters, others present fully fleshed-out figures. Some make sense immediately, like Moses and the burning bush (Ex 3.1–6); others remain baffling, like the brief account in which the LORD met and tried to kill Moses (Ex 4.24–26). Some seem devoid of religious significance (Gen 34), others are full of theological reflection (Gen 18.22–33).

Genesis contains little legal material, but roughly 50 percent of Exodus through Deuteronomy is made up of what are called prescriptive texts, directions for what to do or what not to do, and penalties for doing wrong. These prescriptions occur in several basic forms: "if someone is caught kidnapping another Israelite...then the kidnapper shall die" (Deut 24.7); "you shall not revile God" (Ex 22.28); "whoever strikes father or mother shall be put to death" (Ex 21.15). All such formulations are known to exist in legal texts from the ancient Near East, for instance, Hammurabi's law code. Some prescriptions are designed to be enacted only once, as with the instructions for building the tabernacle* or tent of worship (Ex 25.1–31.18). Others are designed to sustain Israel's life over time ("Three times in the year you shall hold a festival for me," Ex 23.14).

The legal formulations appear in differing settings within the Torah. Some occur in the midst of biblical narratives (for instance, Gen 9.4, 17.11). Some appear interspersed between narratives, for instance, the prescriptions in Numbers 15 are surrounded by narrative material. Still others appear in legal collections: the book of the covenant* (Ex 20.22–23.33), the holiness code (Lev 17–26), and the Deuteronomic* law code (Deut 12–26). The Ten Commandments (Ex 20.2–17; Deut 5.6–21) function more as a summary of Israel's prescriptive tradition than a series of laws reflecting very specific cases, for instance, Exodus 21.35–36. The Ten Commandments do however reflect both religious concerns (for instance, keeping the Sabbath) and nonritual ones (for instance, perjury) as do the Old Testament's legal collections.

When poetry appears in the Torah, it often emphasizes or intensifies a prose text. (On Hebrew poetry, see "Hebrew Poetry and Wisdom Literature," 730–732) For example, the pivotal moment of God's defeat of Pharaoh's forces is recounted in a poem (Ex 15). Moreover, the climactic statements about the creation of humans (Gen 1.27, 2.23) are expressed in brief poems. The book of Numbers appears to cite poetic collections when recounting Israel's military deeds (for instance, Num 21.14, 17–18).

Genealogies* are prominent and important throughout the Torah, and they can appear in outline form or in stories. Genealogies lie behind many of the stories in Genesis. For example, the story Israel told about Lot and his daughters (Gen 19) reflects the genealogy reported in Genesis 11.27–32. Lot is of interest because he was Abraham's nephew. However, in the story, Israel was also commenting on the disreputable origins of the Moabites, a nation that had its origins in the family to which Israel belonged.

Genealogies in outline form are of two basic sorts, vertical and horizontal. Within Israel, horizontal or branching genealogies become prominent when the twelve sons/tribes of Israel/Jacob are described, for instance in Numbers 26. Horizontal genealogies regularly address relationships between individuals in the same generation. In contrast, vertical genealogies typically trace an individual back to a primal ancestor in order to give the most recent member of the family a certain level of status or authority. Genesis 5, the so-called Sethite genealogy, allows the survivor of the flood to trace his ancestry back to the first human. In lineal genealogies, there is little interest in more than one individual during a single generation.

Although the five books of the Torah are distinct books, one can identify elements that appear prominently throughout all five. God is the protagonist—creating, commanding, responding, redeeming. Whether named "God" (Gen 1.1), "the LORD God" (Gen 2.4), "the LORD" (Gen 4.1),

"God Most High" (Gen 14.19), "the God of my father" (Gen 31.5), "the God of your ancestors, the God of Abraham, the God of Isaac, and the God of Jacob" (Ex 3.15), "the Fear of Isaac" (Gen 31.42), "the Mighty One of Jacob," (Gen 49.24), the deity appears more frequently than any human character (cf. Ex 6.2–3 for Israel's reflection about the relationship of these names). God appears in various ways—sometimes as an almost human character (Gen 2–3), other times working behind the scenes (Gen 50.20).

Humanity is the other major actor. God initially interacts with humanity in its totality, but focuses, beginning in Genesis 12, on one family, Terah and his descendants. What is described as a family in Genesis becomes a "people" (Ex 1.9) in Exodus–Deuteronomy. Much of the Torah is devoted to addressing the issue of how the deity will interact with humanity, the family, and the people of Israel. In all three cases, the biblical writers demonstrate that the parties exist in a covenantal relationship. After the flood, God made a covenant with humanity (Gen 9.8–17), the primary purpose of which was the deity's promise never again to destroy "all flesh" with a flood. Then, in Genesis 15 and 17, the deity makes a covenant with Abraham and his family, promising him both progeny and a land in which to settle. This covenant involves the requirement that Abraham and his male offspring must be circumcised.* Finally, God makes a covenant with the people of Israel (Ex 24.1–8). According to this covenant, the people are required to live up to certain prescribed expectations. Blessings of various forms would ensue if Israel obeyed the covenant; curses would befall them if they did not live up to those expectations. The covenant made between God and the people at Sinai is reaffirmed in the covenant made on the plains of Moab (Deut 29). God relates to humanity, the family, and the people through differing covenants.

The Torah emerged over a long period of time and resulted from the work of many authors and editors. Scholars have offered a number of theories to explain this formation of the Torah. Throughout much of the twentieth century, the source critical hypothesis held sway. Source criticism held that the Pentateuch was comprised of three sources, deriving from different times and locales, and extending from Genesis through Numbers. For example, the priestly source (generally referred to as P) offered one account of creation, focusing on the creation of the universe (Gen 1.1–2.4a) whereas another one, the Yahwistic source (known as J, from the German "Jahveh"), provided another account, focusing on the creation of humanity (Gen 2.4b–25). Another source, the Elohistic tradition (E) that uses the name "Elohim" for God, rather than "Yahweh" in most places, is more fragmentary, and many scholars doubt that it was a separate, fully realized narrative. Deuteronomy (termed D) was its own source. Such a theory enabled scholars to explain the presence of multiple versions of the same basic event and of distinctive vocabulary that was related to differing theological perspectives. Those responsible for this hypothesis held that these sources were combined early in the Second Temple* period (the Second Temple was dedicated in 515 BCE). A second theory, the supplemental hypothesis, imagined an early version of Israel's story, which evolved over a period of time. Some versions of this theory postulate an original poetic version (for instance, as preserved in Ex 15), which was rewritten as prose. Like the source critical hypothesis, the supplementary hypothesis presumes that Israel's early story began in Genesis and continued up to the time just before Israel entered the land. Finally, the so-called fragmentary hypothesis differs from the other two, since it does not assume the presence of an original narrative that extends throughout the first four books of the Bible. Rather, those who advocate this view think that a number of smaller and discrete traditions, for instance, those about Abraham or those about Sinai, circulated independently and were integrated into a longer narrative only after the Exile.* Consistent with this view is the idea that several of the books in the Pentateuch, for instance Genesis and Deuteronomy, may be read as quite distinct books. Although these three theories (source, supplemental, fragmentary) offer very different models for the formation of the Pentateuch, they share one essential tenet: that those five books developed over a long period. Such a process helps explain the presence of diverse theological perspectives as well as different literary styles in the Pentateuch.

GENESIS

Introduction

Genesis is made up of two large sections. The first part (chs. 1–11) begins with stories of God's creation of the heavens and the earth and the first generations of human beings on the earth. Other ancient cultures in biblical times also had their own stories of the beginnings of the world, worldwide floods, and interaction between multiple gods and humans. Some parallels exist between these other ancient accounts and chs. 1–11. However, the biblical writers reshaped these ancient traditions in distinctive ways that were true to their Israelite understanding of the one God who created all things. The second part (chs. 12–50) involves stories about one particular family line whom God selected from among all the families of the earth. This family eventually became the people of Israel, whose story continues throughout the rest of the Old Testament. Israel's family line begins with Abraham and Sarah and their son Isaac (chs. 12–25). These family stories continue with tales about Isaac's son Jacob (chs. 25–36). Genesis concludes with stories about Jacob's children, especially Joseph and Judah (chs. 37–50).

In the first part of Genesis (chs. 1–11), God works with all humanity to restore the broken relationships caused by human rebellion and disobedience. God's repeated attempts to respond to these rebellions through punishment and continued blessing do not succeed in restoring harmony between God and humans. Thus, in the second part (chs. 12–50), God embarks upon a new strategy. God concentrates on working with and through one particular family, the ancestors of the people of Israel. This one family is chosen so that through them "all the families of the earth shall be blessed" (12.3). In this way, the two major parts of Genesis depend upon one another. Most scholars believe that the present form of the book of Genesis is the result of various stages of oral storytelling, writing, and editing over hundreds of years. Certain texts in Genesis may have arisen quite early in ancient Israel's history. Other texts may have been written much later. They have, however, been combined into an artful and extended story about the beginning of the world and Israel's earliest ancestors.

The date and setting for the final form of Genesis is probably the time when the people of Judah were in exile in Babylon (sixth century BCE) or when the Babylonian exiles returned home to Judah under the Persian empire (fifth century BCE). The time of exile and the return home forced Israel to think hard about its identity as a people and its mission as the people of God among the nations of the world. Remembering the Genesis stories about the beginnings of the world and Israel's earliest ancestors was a way to return to their roots and think about who they were as an exiled people who were returning home to Judah. They could identify with the Genesis ancestors of Israel, who were also a family on the move. Just as the family of Abraham and Sarah migrated back and forth from Mesopotamia to Canaan, so the exiles would migrate from Babylon back to Judah. The key promise in the midst of this wandering and yearning to return home was the promise God made to Jacob: "Know that I am with you and will keep you wherever you go, and will bring you back to this land" (28.15).

READING GUIDE

Chapters 1–11, which describe the beginnings of the world and the human race, contain elements that are clearly not part of our everyday experience. These include a talking serpent (3.1), individuals who live to be nearly a thousand years old (5.5), divine beings called "sons of God" who came down to earth (6.1–4), a worldwide flood (7.17–24), and all people of the world talking one language (11.1). The world of these stories may seem strange to us and very distant. Nevertheless, the narratives★ seek to teach profound truths about the nature of reality, the meaning of life, and the purpose of human existence. Two major themes weave in and out among these initial stories of all humankind. The first theme is the emergence of broken relationships among humans, God, and nature. Examples include the human disobedience in the Garden of Eden (ch. 3), the flood story of Noah and the ark (chs. 6–9), and the building of the tower of Babel (ch. 11). The second theme is God's good creation and his continued blessing of humans and creation in spite of human disobedience.

A similar two-part theme also moves in and out of the family stories of Israel's ancestors in chs. 12–50. God makes a major promise of blessing, land, and many descendants to the family of Abraham and Sarah (12.1–3). One theme repeated throughout these stories is the regular endangerment and threat to God's promise coming true. Sarah is unable to have children (11.30). God tells Abraham to kill his only son (22.1–2). Jacob's life is threatened by his brother Esau (27.41). Joseph's own brothers threaten to kill him and then sell him into slavery in Egypt (37.17–28). The second major theme in these ancestor stories is God's continuing commitment to the promise he first made to Abraham and Sarah. The family line continues in spite of all the struggles and obstacles. This sustained blessing of God is marked most clearly throughout Genesis by the birth of children, the gift of prosperity, and the recurring family trees or genealogical lists that form the literary backbone of the narrative.

1–11   The creation of the world and the beginning of humankind
12–25   The family stories of Abraham and Sarah and their son Isaac
25–36   The family stories of Isaac's son, Jacob
37–50   The family stories of Jacob's sons, especially Joseph and Judah

1 In the beginning when God created*a* the heavens and the earth, ²the earth was a formless void and darkness covered the face of the deep, while a wind from God*b* swept over the face of the waters. ³Then God said, "Let there be light"; and there was light. ⁴And God saw that the light was good; and God separated the light from the darkness. ⁵God called the light Day, and the darkness he called Night. And there was evening and there was morning, the first day.

6 And God said, "Let there be a dome in the midst of the waters, and let it separate the waters from the waters." ⁷So God made the dome and separated the waters that were under the dome from the waters that were above the dome. And it was so. ⁸God called the dome Sky. And there was evening and there was morning, the second day.

9 And God said, "Let the waters under the sky be gathered together into one place, and let the dry land appear." And it was so. ¹⁰God called the dry land Earth, and the waters that were gathered together he called Seas. And God saw that it was good. ¹¹Then God said, "Let the earth put forth vegetation: plants yielding seed, and fruit trees of every kind on earth that bear fruit with the seed in it." And it was so. ¹²The earth brought forth vegetation: plants yielding seed of every kind, and trees of every kind bearing fruit with the seed in it. And God saw that it was good. ¹³And there was evening and there was morning, the third day.

14 And God said, "Let there be lights in the dome of the sky to separate the day from

a Or when God began to create or In the beginning God created   b Or while the spirit of God or while a mighty wind the night; and let them be for signs and for seasons and for days and years, [15]and let them be lights in the dome of the sky to give light upon the earth." And it was so. [16]God made the two great lights—the greater light to rule the day and the lesser light to rule the night—and the stars. [17]God set them in the dome of the sky to give light upon the earth, [18]to rule over the day and over the night, and to separate the light from the darkness. And God saw that it was good. [19]And there was evening and there was morning, the fourth day.

20 And God said, "Let the waters bring forth swarms of living creatures, and let birds fly above the earth across the dome of the sky." [21]So God created the great sea monsters and every living creature that moves, of every kind, with which the waters swarm, and every winged bird of every kind. And God saw that it was good. [22]God blessed them, saying, "Be fruitful and multiply and fill the waters in the seas, and let birds multiply on the earth." [23]And there was evening and there was morning, the fifth day.

24 And God said, "Let the earth bring forth living creatures of every kind: cattle and creeping things and wild animals of the earth of every kind." And it was so. [25]God made the wild animals of the earth of every kind, and the cattle of every kind, and everything that creeps upon the ground of every kind. And God saw that it was good.

1.1–2.3: The creation of the heavens and the earth. 1.2: *The face of the deep* and *the face of the waters* are descriptions of a watery and disordered chaos. God's creation involves separating, setting boundaries, and ordering this watery chaos in order to create a space for life to flourish. **3:** God creates by simply speaking a verbal command. **6:** God's creation of *a dome in the midst of the waters* assumes a flat earth and a clear dome that pushes back the lower waters and the blue upper waters to form the space for the sky. **11:** *Let the earth put forth vegetation:* Parts of creation are invited to join with God in the process of creating and ruling (1.17, 24, 28). **14:** The first three days of creation form three regions: Day 1—the region of light and darkness (1.3–5); Day 2—the region of the sky (1.6–8); and Day 3—the region of the earth with its vegetation (1.9–13). Beginning in v. 14, the

next three days of creation provide the inhabitants for each of these regions: Day 4—the sun, moon, and stars occupy the region of light and darkness (1.14–19); Day 5—the birds fill the sky and the fish fill the lower waters (1.20–23); and Day 6—the animals and humans occupy the earth. **21:** *So God created the great sea monsters:* In other ancient stories of creation, the sea monsters are portrayed as independent gods of evil and chaos. Here the sea monsters are made by God and subject to God's control (Ps 148.7).

~~~~~~~~~~~~~~~~~~~~~~~~~~~~

26 Then God said, "Let us make humankind[a] in our image, according to our likeness; and let them have dominion over the fish of the sea, and over the birds of the air, and over the cattle, and over all the wild animals of the earth,[b] and over every creeping thing that creeps upon the earth."
[27] So God created humankind[a] in his
        image,
    in the image of God he created them;[c]
    male and female he created them.
[28]God blessed them, and God said to them, "Be fruitful and multiply, and fill the earth and subdue it; and have dominion over the fish of the sea and over the birds of the air and over every living thing that moves upon the earth." [29]God said, "See, I have given you every plant yielding seed that is upon the face of all the earth, and every tree with seed in its fruit; you shall have them for food. [30]And to every beast of the earth, and to every bird of the air, and to everything that creeps on the earth, everything that has the breath of life, I have given every green plant for food." And it was so. [31]God saw everything that he had made, and indeed, it was very good. And there was evening and there was morning, the sixth day.

1.26–31. 26: The plural *us* and *our image* is probably a reference to an ancient motif* of an assembly of divine beings, here God and God's divine advisers (compare 1 Kings 22; Job 1). They resolve to create humankind in their *image* or *likeness*. The divine image characterizes the human vocation of *dominion* or caring for the fish, birds, and animals. Human dominion

a Heb *adam*   *b* Syr: Heb *and over all the earth*
c Heb *him*

Two Different Creation Stories

The Bible begins with two different versions of the story of the beginning of the world. The two versions arose at different periods in Israel's history. Most scholars would date the creation story in Gen 2.4–25 earlier than 1.1–2.3. The former was probably written during the time Israel had kings reigning in Jerusalem and before the exile to Babylon in 587 BCE. The usual scholarly designation for this earlier tradition, which extends intermittently throughout the Pentateuch* (Genesis—Deuteronomy), is the Yahwist or J tradition. Most scholars would date the later creation story in Gen 1.1–2.3 to a time after 587 BCE and the exile to Babylon. It may have been written even later, after the return to Judah in 539 BCE during the Persian period. Scholars call this later tradition the Priestly or P tradition. The Priestly tradition also extends into other parts of Genesis as well as the Pentateuch, especially the books of Leviticus and Numbers. There are a number of differences between the Priestly (P) creation story and the Yahwist's (J) creation story: the divine names (P—"God"; J—"LORD God"); the condition of the world before creation (P—watery chaos–1.2; J—dry desert–2.5–6); the sequence of creation (P—six days with both man and woman created at the same time; J—man created first, then animals, then woman); the manner of creation (P—the word of God–1.3, 6, 9; J—God "formed," "planted," "made"); the depiction of the deity (P—more majestic and transcendent; J—more intimate and hands-on); and the recurring literary structure and refrains in P versus the absence of such repetitions in J. Allowing two different versions of the creation story to stand side by side suggests that the ancient writers were not interested in defining precisely how the world began in a scientific sense. Rather, they were interested in exploring larger questions of meaning and purpose through multiple perspectives on the same event of creation.

or rule is to be similar to the way God rules over and cares for all creation. **27:** The human *image of God* includes both *male and female*. **31:** God's final evaluation that the creation *was very good* concludes a series of refrains throughout Gen 1 about the goodness of creation (1.4, 12, 18, 21).

2 Thus the heavens and the earth were finished, and all their multitude. ²And on the seventh day God finished the work that he had done, and he rested on the seventh day from all the work that he had done. ³So God blessed the seventh day and hallowed it, because on it God rested from all the work that he had done in creation.

2.1–3: God's resting *on the seventh day* of creation became an explanation for one of the Ten Commandments, that the seventh day of every week be set apart as a sabbath, a day of rest and no work (Ex 20.8–11).

The word "sabbath" comes from the Hebrew word "shabat" meaning "to rest."

4 These are the generations of the heavens and the earth when they were created.

In the day that the LORD God made the earth and the heavens, ⁵when no plant of the field was yet in the earth and no herb of the field had yet sprung up—for the LORD God had not caused it to rain upon the earth, and there was no one to till the ground; ⁶but a stream would rise from the earth, and water the whole face of the ground— ⁷then the LORD God formed man from the dust of the ground,ᵃ and breathed into his nostrils the breath of life; and the man became a living being. ⁸And the LORD God planted a gar-

a Or *formed a man* (Heb *adam*) *of dust from the ground* (Heb *adamah*) den in Eden, in the east; and there he put the man whom he had formed. 9Out of the ground the LORD God made to grow every tree that is pleasant to the sight and good for food, the tree of life also in the midst of the garden, and the tree of the knowledge of good and evil.

10 A river flows out of Eden to water the garden, and from there it divides and becomes four branches. 11The name of the first is Pishon; it is the one that flows around the whole land of Havilah, where there is gold; 12and the gold of that land is good; bdellium and onyx stone are there. 13The name of the second river is Gihon; it is the one that flows around the whole land of Cush. 14The name of the third river is Tigris, which flows east of Assyria. And the fourth river is the Euphrates.

2.4–14: A second creation story—the garden of Eden. 4: The opening formula, *These are the generations of* (sometime alternately translated as "these are the descendants of" or "this is the story of"), marks the beginning of new sections throughout Genesis (6.9; 10.1; 11.27; 25.19; 37.2). *In the day that the LORD God made the earth and the heavens:* a heading for this second and different creation story. The creation story in Gen 2 uses a different divine name, *LORD God*, instead of simply "God" in Gen 1. Genesis 2 begins not with chaotic waters of the deep as in 1.1–2 but with a dry desert. Like the watery deep, the dry wilderness is a biblical image of evil and chaos (Isa 21.1–3; 43.15–21). **7:** The Hebrew word for *man* ("adam") is closely related to the word for *ground* ("adamah"). This Hebrew wordplay underscores the close relationship of humans and the soil (3.19). *The LORD God formed man from the dust* like a potter forming clay. This earth creature becomes a living human only when the LORD God breathes into it *the breath of life.* **8:** The *garden of Eden* means literally "garden of delight." **9:** Two trees, *the tree of life* and *the tree of the knowledge of good and evil,* stand in the middle of the garden. They will become important later in the story (2.17; 3.1–7, 22–24). Eating from the tree of life would give immortality, and eating from the tree of knowledge would provide wisdom, moral discernment, and the experience of pleasure and pain. **10–14:** The image is that of a lush garden at the center of the known world from which four major rivers flow to water the earth. We know the location of only two

of the rivers, the *Tigris* and the *Euphrates.* They are in Mesopotamia. *Havilah* (v. 11) may be in Arabia, and *Cush* (v. 13) may be associated with Africa.

15 The LORD God took the man and put him in the garden of Eden to till it and keep it. 16And the LORD God commanded the man, "You may freely eat of every tree of the garden; 17but of the tree of the knowledge of good and evil you shall not eat, for in the day that you eat of it you shall die."

18 Then the LORD God said, "It is not good that the man should be alone; I will make him a helper as his partner." 19So out of the ground the LORD God formed every animal of the field and every bird of the air, and brought them to the man to see what he would call them; and whatever the man called every living creature, that was its name. 20The man gave names to all cattle, and to the birds of the air, and to every animal of the field; but for the man*a* there was not found a helper as his partner. 21So the LORD God caused a deep sleep to fall upon the man, and he slept; then he took one of his ribs and closed up its place with flesh. 22And the rib that the LORD God had taken from the man he made into a woman and brought her to the man. 23Then the man said,

"This at last is bone of my bones
    and flesh of my flesh;
this one shall be called Woman,*b*
    for out of Man*c* this one was taken."

24Therefore a man leaves his father and his mother and clings to his wife, and they become one flesh. 25And the man and his wife were both naked, and were not ashamed.

2.15–25. 15: The garden of Eden is not a paradise of luxury but a place for human work. Humans will *till* the garden *and keep it.* **16–17:** The command not to eat from the tree of the knowledge of good and evil carries a grave consequence, which in Hebrew reads literally: "you shall *surely* die." **18:** The term *helper* does not imply an inferior assistant but a genuine partner who comes to the aid of another. God is often

a Or *for Adam*   *b* Heb *ishshah*   *c* Heb *ish*

called a "helper" for those in need (Ps 10.14; 54.4). **19–20:** God's first attempt to satisfy the human's loneliness (animals) fails. God invites the human to participate in shaping the character of the animals by giving them names. **21–22:** God tries a second strategy to satisfy the human's loneliness. God fashions a woman from the rib of the sleeping man. **23:** Unlike the animals, the woman instantly evokes a joyous response from the man. The man's brief poetic response plays on the Hebrew words "ish" (*Man*) and "ishshah" (*Woman*). **24:** *They become one flesh* suggests not only sexual union but also a unity through a common household and the raising of children.

3 Now the serpent was more crafty than any other wild animal that the LORD God had made. He said to the woman, "Did God say, 'You shall not eat from any tree in the garden'?" 2The woman said to the serpent, "We may eat of the fruit of the trees in the garden; 3but God said, 'You shall not eat of the fruit of the tree that is in the middle of the garden, nor shall you touch it, or you shall die.'" 4But the serpent said to the woman, "You will not die; 5for God knows that when you eat of it your eyes will be opened, and you will be like God,*a* knowing good and evil." 6So when the woman saw that the tree was good for food, and that it was a delight to the eyes, and that the tree was to be desired to make one wise, she took of its fruit and ate; and she also gave some to her husband, who was with her, and he ate. 7Then the eyes of both were opened, and they knew that they were naked; and they sewed fig leaves together and made loincloths for themselves.

8 They heard the sound of the LORD God walking in the garden at the time of the evening breeze, and the man and his wife hid themselves from the presence of the LORD God among the trees of the garden. 9But the LORD God called to the man, and said to him, "Where are you?" 10He said, "I heard the sound of you in the garden, and I was afraid, because I was naked; and I hid myself." 11He said, "Who told you that you were naked? Have you eaten from the tree of which I commanded you not to eat?" 12The man said, "The woman whom you gave to be with me, she gave me fruit from the tree, and

I ate." 13Then the LORD God said to the woman, "What is this that you have done?" The woman said, "The serpent tricked me, and I ate." 14The LORD God said to the serpent,

"Because you have done this,
    cursed are you among all animals
    and among all wild creatures;
upon your belly you shall go,
    and dust you shall eat
    all the days of your life.
15 I will put enmity between you and the
        woman,
    and between your offspring and hers;
he will strike your head,
    and you will strike his heel."
16To the woman he said,
"I will greatly increase your pangs in
        childbearing;
    in pain you shall bring forth children,
yet your desire shall be for your
        husband,
    and he shall rule over you."
17And to the man*b* he said,
"Because you have listened to the voice
        of your wife,
    and have eaten of the tree
    about which I commanded you,
    'You shall not eat of it,'
cursed is the ground because of you;
    in toil you shall eat of it all the days
        of your life;
18 thorns and thistles it shall bring forth
        for you;
    and you shall eat the plants of the
        field.
19 By the sweat of your face
    you shall eat bread
until you return to the ground,
    for out of it you were taken;
you are dust,
    and to dust you shall return."

20 The man named his wife Eve,*c* because she was the mother of all living. 21And the LORD God made garments of skins for the man*d* and for his wife, and clothed them.

22 Then the LORD God said, "See, the man has become like one of us, knowing

a Or *gods* *b* Or *to Adam* *c* In Heb *Eve* resembles the word for *living* *d* Or *for Adam* good and evil; and now, he might reach out his hand and take also from the tree of life, and eat, and live forever"— 23therefore the LORD God sent him forth from the garden of Eden, to till the ground from which he was taken. 24He drove out the man; and at the east of the garden of Eden he placed the cherubim, and a sword flaming and turning to guard the way to the tree of life.

3.1–24: A serpent's temptation and human disobedience. 1: The *serpent* is not an alien being but simply one of the garden's more intelligent and *crafty* animals *that the LORD God had made.* **3:** The woman repeats the command given by God in 2.17 but then attaches her own additional prohibition, *nor shall you touch it.* Once she disobeys her own prohibition (touching the fruit), it will be easier to take the next step and disobey God's prohibition (eating the fruit). **4–6:** The serpent assures the woman that *you will not die.* In an odd way, the serpent will be correct. God will not cause the humans to die "in the day that you eat of it." However, the humans will come to *know good and evil* by experiencing new intensities of pain as a consequence of their rebellion. The man's quick willingness to eat the forbidden fruit along with the woman suggests equal responsibility for the disobedient act. **7:** The humans now know *that they were naked.* They experience shame and the pain of an intimate human bond that has been broken. The innocence, trust, and openness of their former relationship must now be hidden behind clothes made of *fig leaves.* The prickly fig leaves would make for uncomfortable clothing. **8:** The portrait of *the LORD God walking in the garden* in the cool of the evening implies God's close relationship and involvement with the creation. God's closeness contrasts with the humans' sudden desire for distance as they *hid themselves from the presence of the LORD God.* **14–15:** The serpent is directly cursed by God. The curse provides an ancient explanation for why the snake has no legs and why humans often have a negative reaction to snakes. **16–17:** Neither the woman nor the man are directly cursed as was the serpent. But negative consequences flow from the disobedient act. For the woman, the pain of childbirth will increase, and the man *shall rule over you.* This inequality contrasts with God's original will for mutuality and interdependence between the man and woman in 2.18–22. **17–19:** Like the woman and unlike the serpent, the man is not directly cursed. However, God declares, *cursed is the ground because*

of you. The man will struggle in hard *toil* and *sweat* to produce food from the ground. The earlier story of human creation in 2.7 had already recounted the man's origin from the dust of the ground. Now, for the first time, human death is explicitly mentioned: *to dust you shall return* (3.19). However, the original prohibition in 2.17 had decreed death on the very day that the forbidden fruit would be eaten. God does not enforce this death sentence immediately. God mercifully allows the humans to continue to live for some time and produce children for future generations. **21:** God graciously replaces the prickly fig leaf clothing (2.7) with softer *garments of skins.* **22–24:** God seals the entrance to the garden to make sure the humans do not *take also from the tree of life, and eat, and live forever.* The *cherubim** are winged creatures who are half human and half beast. They guard holy areas. For example, cherubim guard the holiest sections of the Temple* in Jerusalem (1 Kings 8.6–7).

4 Now the man knew his wife Eve, and she conceived and bore Cain, saying, "I have produced*a* a man with the help of the LORD." 2Next she bore his brother Abel. Now Abel was a keeper of sheep, and Cain a tiller of the ground. 3In the course of time Cain brought to the LORD an offering of the fruit of the ground, 4and Abel for his part brought of the firstlings of his flock, their fat portions. And the LORD had regard for Abel and his offering, 5but for Cain and his offering he had no regard. So Cain was very angry, and his countenance fell. 6The LORD said to Cain, "Why are you angry, and why has your countenance fallen? 7If you do well, will you not be accepted? And if you do not do well, sin is lurking at the door; its desire is for you, but you must master it."

8 Cain said to his brother Abel, "Let us go out to the field."*b* And when they were in the field, Cain rose up against his brother Abel, and killed him. 9Then the LORD said to Cain, "Where is your brother Abel?" He said, "I do not know; am I my brother's keeper?" 10And the LORD said, "What have you done? Listen; your brother's blood is crying out to me from the ground! 11And now you are cursed from the ground, which has

a The verb in Heb resembles the word for *Cain*
b Sam Gk Syr Compare Vg: MT lacks *Let us go out to the field*

opened its mouth to receive your brother's blood from your hand. ¹²When you till the ground, it will no longer yield to you its strength; you will be a fugitive and a wanderer on the earth." ¹³Cain said to the LORD, "My punishment is greater than I can bear! ¹⁴Today you have driven me away from the soil, and I shall be hidden from your face; I shall be a fugitive and a wanderer on the earth, and anyone who meets me may kill me." ¹⁵Then the LORD said to him, "Not so!ᵃ Whoever kills Cain will suffer a sevenfold vengeance." And the LORD put a mark on Cain, so that no one who came upon him would kill him. ¹⁶Then Cain went away from the presence of the LORD, and settled in the land of Nod,ᵇ east of Eden.

17 Cain knew his wife, and she conceived and bore Enoch; and he built a city, and named it Enoch after his son Enoch. ¹⁸To Enoch was born Irad; and Irad was the father of Mehujael, and Mehujael the father of Methushael, and Methushael the father of Lamech. ¹⁹Lamech took two wives; the name of the one was Adah, and the name of the other Zillah. ²⁰Adah bore Jabal; he was the ancestor of those who live in tents and have livestock. ²¹His brother's name was Jubal; he was the ancestor of all those who play the lyre and pipe. ²²Zillah bore Tubal-cain, who made all kinds of bronze and iron tools. The sister of Tubal-cain was Naamah.

23 Lamech said to his wives:

"Adah and Zillah, hear my voice;
    you wives of Lamech, listen to what I
        say:
I have killed a man for wounding me,
    a young man for striking me.
24 If Cain is avenged sevenfold,
    truly Lamech seventy-sevenfold."

25 Adam knew his wife again, and she bore a son and named him Seth, for she said, "God has appointedᶜ for me another child instead of Abel, because Cain killed him." ²⁶To Seth also a son was born, and he named him Enosh. At that time people began to invoke the name of the LORD.

Eve (3.20). Now Eve in turn names a man, her son *Cain*. In a wordplay on the name *Cain* ("qayin"), the woman creates or "produces" ("qnh") *a man with the help of the LORD.* **4–5:** The text gives no reason why God accepts Abel's animal offering but rejects Cain's grain offering. God reserves the divine right to accept or be merciful to whomever he wills (Ex 33.19). **7:** If Cain acts properly in response to his brother's acceptance and his own rejection, then Cain himself will be accepted. But if Cain does not *do well, sin is lurking at the door* like an animal eager to consume his life. This is the first occurrence of the word *sin* in the Bible. **9:** Cain's cynical question, *Am I my brother's keeper?*, may imply that God should be the one responsible for "keeping" or "guarding" his brother (Ps 121.5; Isa 27.3). **10–11:** The blood of any human or animal is considered sacred because it is believed to contain the essence of life. Thus, any spilling of blood is a matter for God's attention (Deut 12.23–24; Lev 17.10–14). **14:** As a *fugitive and wanderer* in foreign lands, Cain will have no rights or protection. He will be vulnerable to blood revenge for the murder of his brother. 2 Sam 24.1–24 provides an example of such a case. **17–22:** Cain is a fugitive from the settled rural life of farming. His descendants become the founders of cities (v. 17), wandering shepherds (v. 20), developers of culture (v. 21), and makers of tools (v. 22). **23–24:** Lamech takes revenge into his own hands in an increasing spiral of violence. He kills someone in revenge for a simple injury against himself. Earlier, the LORD had tried to limit revenge and violence (4.15). **25–26:** Adam and Eve have a third son, Seth. The family line of Adam and Eve, through their son Seth, will be traced over ten generations in Gen 5.

5 This is the list of the descendants of Adam. When God created humankind,ᵈ he made themᵉ in the likeness of God. ²Male and female he created them, and he blessed them and named them "Humankind"ᵈ when they were created.

3 When Adam had lived one hundred thirty years, he became the father of a son in his likeness, according to his image, and named him Seth. ⁴The days of Adam after he became the father of Seth were eight hundred years; and he had other sons and

4.1–26: Cain and Abel—the first murder. 1: *The man knew his wife* implies intimate knowledge, in this case sexual intercourse. The man had earlier named his wife

a Gk Syr Vg: Heb *Therefore*   b That is *Wandering*
c The verb in Heb resembles the word for *Seth*
d Heb *adam*   e Heb *him*

[54] HEBREW BIBLE

daughters. 5Thus all the days that Adam lived were nine hundred thirty years; and he died.

6 When Seth had lived one hundred five years, he became the father of Enosh. 7Seth lived after the birth of Enosh eight hundred seven years, and had other sons and daughters. 8Thus all the days of Seth were nine hundred twelve years; and he died.

9 When Enosh had lived ninety years, he became the father of Kenan. 10Enosh lived after the birth of Kenan eight hundred fifteen years, and had other sons and daughters. 11Thus all the days of Enosh were nine hundred five years; and he died.

12 When Kenan had lived seventy years, he became the father of Mahalalel. 13Kenan lived after the birth of Mahalalel eight hundred and forty years, and had other sons and daughters. 14Thus all the days of Kenan were nine hundred and ten years; and he died.

15 When Mahalalel had lived sixty-five years, he became the father of Jared. 16Mahalalel lived after the birth of Jared eight hundred thirty years, and had other sons and daughters. 17Thus all the days of Mahalalel were eight hundred ninety-five years; and he died.

18 When Jared had lived one hundred sixty-two years he became the father of Enoch. 19Jared lived after the birth of Enoch eight hundred years, and had other sons and daughters. 20Thus all the days of Jared were nine hundred sixty-two years; and he died.

21 When Enoch had lived sixty-five years, he became the father of Methuselah. 22Enoch walked with God after the birth of Methuselah three hundred years, and had other sons and daughters. 23Thus all the days of Enoch were three hundred sixty-five years. 24Enoch walked with God; then he was no more, because God took him.

25 When Methuselah had lived one hundred eighty-seven years, he became the father of Lamech. 26Methuselah lived after the birth of Lamech seven hundred eighty-two years, and had other sons and daughters. 27Thus all the days of Methuselah were nine hundred sixty-nine years; and he died.

28 When Lamech had lived one hundred eighty-two years, he became the father of a son; 29he named him Noah, saying, "Out of the ground that the LORD has cursed this one shall bring us relief from our work and from the toil of our hands." 30Lamech lived after the birth of Noah five hundred ninety-five years, and had other sons and daughters. 31Thus all the days of Lamech were seven hundred seventy-seven years; and he died.

32 After Noah was five hundred years old, Noah became the father of Shem, Ham, and Japheth.

5.1–32: Ten generations from Adam and Eve to Noah. This list of ten generations links the story of Adam and Eve (Gen 2–4) with the next major character and story, Noah and the flood (Gen 6–9). Such genealogies, or family trees, occur at important transition points throughout Genesis (from Adam and Eve to Noah—5.1–32; from Noah's son Shem to Abraham—11.10–26; the descendants of Abraham's grandson Jacob—46.8–27). **3:** Adam has a son Seth who is *in his likeness, according to his image.* These same words are used for the first humans before the disobedient act in the garden of Eden (1.26–27; 5.1). The humans' sin did not erase God's image from them as it passes on to the next generation (9.6). **24:** *Because God took him* suggests that Enoch* did not die a normal death. An analogy may be the way in which the prophet* Elijah was taken up into heaven by God (2 Kings 2.11–12). Enoch comes to have a place of honor in later Jewish tradition as one who *walked with God.* **27:** Methuselah's age of 969 years makes him the oldest human being. **29:** *The ground that the LORD has cursed* refers to Adam's punishment in 3.17 and Cain's punishment in 4.11. The verb "to bring relief" (Hebrew "nḥm") is seen as a wordplay on the name Noah (Hebrew "nḥ").

6 When people began to multiply on the face of the ground, and daughters were born to them, 2the sons of God saw that they were fair; and they took wives for themselves of all that they chose. 3Then the LORD said, "My spirit shall not abide*a* in mortals forever, for they are flesh; their days shall be one hundred twenty years." 4The Nephilim were on the earth in those days—and also

a Meaning of Heb uncertain

afterward—when the sons of God went in to the daughters of humans, who bore children to them. These were the heroes that were of old, warriors of renown.

***

6.1–4: The origins of a legendary* line of giant warriors. 1–2: This brief story portrays the breaking of the created boundary between heaven and earth. Divine beings called *the sons of God* cross the boundary and have sexual intercourse with human daughters. **3:** God decides to place tighter limits on the length of human life. Before this, individuals had lived for over 900 years (5.5, 8). In this next stage, humans will live no more than 120 years. Later biblical tradition will declare the typical limit of human life to be 70–80 years which is closer to our normal experience (Ps 90.10). The advancing power of death accompanies the appearance of human sin. **4:** *The Nephilim* were remembered as a superhuman race of legendary warriors born of mixed human and divine parents. Later in Israel's history, Israelite spies will report seeing the giant Nephilim warriors in the land of Canaan (Num 13.32–33).

***

STARTING OVER—NOAH AND THE FLOOD

6.5–8.22: Many scholars believe that two parallel versions of this flood story were woven together into the present combined single story. For example, two separate introductions to the flood story stand side by side (compare one version in 6.5–8, 7.1–5 with the second version in 6.9–22). Scholars have also noted some striking parallels and differences between the biblical flood story and ancient flood stories from Babylon and Mesopotamia.

***

5 The LORD saw that the wickedness of humankind was great in the earth, and that every inclination of the thoughts of their hearts was only evil continually. 6And the LORD was sorry that he had made humankind on the earth, and it grieved him to his heart. 7So the LORD said, "I will blot out from the earth the human beings I have created—people together with animals and creeping things and birds of the air, for I am sorry that I have made them." 8But Noah found favor in the sight of the LORD.

9 These are the descendants of Noah. Noah was a righteous man, blameless in his generation; Noah walked with God. 10And

Noah had three sons, Shem, Ham, and Japheth.

11 Now the earth was corrupt in God's sight, and the earth was filled with violence. 12And God saw that the earth was corrupt; for all flesh had corrupted its ways upon the earth. 13And God said to Noah, "I have determined to make an end of all flesh, for the earth is filled with violence because of them; now I am going to destroy them along with the earth. 14Make yourself an ark of cypress*a* wood; make rooms in the ark, and cover it inside and out with pitch. 15This is how you are to make it: the length of the ark three hundred cubits, its width fifty cubits, and its height thirty cubits. 16Make a roof*b* for the ark, and finish it to a cubit above; and put the door of the ark in its side; make it with lower, second, and third decks. 17For my part, I am going to bring a flood of waters on the earth, to destroy from under heaven all flesh in which is the breath of life; everything that is on the earth shall die. 18But I will establish my covenant with you; and you shall come into the ark, you, your sons, your wife, and your sons' wives with you. 19And of every living thing, of all flesh, you shall bring two of every kind into the ark, to keep them alive with you; they shall be male and female. 20Of the birds according to their kinds, and of the animals according to their kinds, of every creeping thing of the ground according to its kind, two of every kind shall come in to you, to keep them alive. 21Also take with you every kind of food that is eaten, and store it up; and it shall serve as food for you and for them." 22Noah did this; he did all that God commanded him.

***

6.5–22. 5: The human *heart* is the point where the intellect (knowing what is right or wrong) and the will (wanting to do right or wrong) come together. **9:** To be *righteous* means to be in a trusting and loyal relationship with God. To *walk with God* means to obey and follow God's will (Judg 2.22; 2 Kings 21.22). **14:** An *ark* is a "chest," "box," or "basket." The baby Moses floated in the Nile River in a "basket" (same Hebrew word as *ark*). Like Noah's ark, the basket was sealed with pitch, and it saved Moses from death (Ex

***

a Meaning of Heb uncertain   *b* Or *window*

Clean and Unclean Animals

The difference between *clean animals* (7.2) and *animals that are not clean* (7.8) involves a whole system of dividing animals and other parts of life into two categories: clean and unclean. Thus, any animals that have two or more characteristics that usually go together are considered clean. For example, animals that live in the sea typically have fins and scales. Therefore, all fish are clean since they have the fins and scales that sea creatures usually have. However, other sea creatures such as clams or oysters are unclean, because they live in the sea but they do not have fins or scales. They cross created boundaries or mix characteristics that do not normally belong together. See Lev 11.1–47 and Deut 14.3–21. This system of dividing between clean and unclean underlies the Jewish dietary laws of kosher* eating.

2.1–10). **15:** A *cubit* is the length of a forearm, about 20 inches long. Thus, the size of the ark or large boat is about 450 feet long, 75 feet wide, and 45 feet high. **18:** A *covenant** is a formal agreement or promise made between two parties. One or both of the covenant partners commit themselves to fulfill certain promises or obligations. Here God makes a covenant with Noah and his family. The content of the covenant will be spelled out more fully later (9.8–17). God makes several important covenants with his people throughout the Old Testament.

7 Then the LORD said to Noah, "Go into the ark, you and all your household, for I have seen that you alone are righteous before me in this generation. ²Take with you seven pairs of all clean animals, the male and its mate; and a pair of the animals that are not clean, the male and its mate; ³and seven pairs of the birds of the air also, male and female, to keep their kind alive on the face of all the earth. ⁴For in seven days I will send rain on the earth for forty days and forty nights; and every living thing that I have made I will blot out from the face of the ground." ⁵And Noah did all that the LORD had commanded him.

6 Noah was six hundred years old when the flood of waters came on the earth. ⁷And Noah with his sons and his wife and his sons' wives went into the ark to escape the waters of the flood. ⁸Of clean animals, and of animals that are not clean, and of birds, and of everything that creeps on the ground, ⁹two and two, male and female, went into the ark

with Noah, as God had commanded Noah. ¹⁰And after seven days the waters of the flood came on the earth.

11 In the six hundredth year of Noah's life, in the second month, on the seventeenth day of the month, on that day all the fountains of the great deep burst forth, and the windows of the heavens were opened. ¹²The rain fell on the earth forty days and forty nights. ¹³On the very same day Noah with his sons, Shem and Ham and Japheth, and Noah's wife and the three wives of his sons entered the ark, ¹⁴they and every wild animal of every kind, and all domestic animals of every kind, and every creeping thing that creeps on the earth, and every bird of every kind—every bird, every winged creature. ¹⁵They went into the ark with Noah, two and two of all flesh in which there was the breath of life. ¹⁶And those that entered, male and female of all flesh, went in as God had commanded him; and the LORD shut him in.

17 The flood continued forty days on the earth; and the waters increased, and bore up the ark, and it rose high above the earth. ¹⁸The waters swelled and increased greatly on the earth; and the ark floated on the face of the waters. ¹⁹The waters swelled so mightily on the earth that all the high mountains under the whole heaven were covered; ²⁰the waters swelled above the mountains, covering them fifteen cubits deep. ²¹And all flesh died that moved on the earth, birds, domestic animals, wild animals, all swarm-

ing creatures that swarm on the earth, and all human beings; 22everything on dry land in whose nostrils was the breath of life died. 23He blotted out every living thing that was on the face of the ground, human beings and animals and creeping things and birds of the air; they were blotted out from the earth. Only Noah was left, and those that were with him in the ark. 24And the waters swelled on the earth for one hundred fifty days.

7.11–24. 11: In this version, the flood results from the upper and lower waters of chaos pouring back into the earth. In essence, God reverses the creation of Gen 1. *All the fountains of the great deep burst forth* from below the earth. Above the earth, God opens *the windows of the heavens* in the dome of the sky (1.6–8) and allows the watery chaos to pour onto the earth. 17–24: The gradual flooding and disappearance of the dry land and the death of humans, animals, creeping things, and birds returns the world to its pre-creation state, undoing what God did in Gen 1.9–27.

8 But God remembered Noah and all the wild animals and all the domestic animals that were with him in the ark. And God made a wind blow over the earth, and the waters subsided; 2the fountains of the deep and the windows of the heavens were closed, the rain from the heavens was restrained, 3and the waters gradually receded from the earth. At the end of one hundred fifty days the waters had abated; 4and in the seventh month, on the seventeenth day of the month, the ark came to rest on the mountains of Ararat. 5The waters continued to abate until the tenth month; in the tenth month, on the first day of the month, the tops of the mountains appeared.

6 At the end of forty days Noah opened the window of the ark that he had made 7and sent out the raven; and it went to and fro until the waters were dried up from the earth. 8Then he sent out the dove from him, to see if the waters had subsided from the face of the ground; 9but the dove found no place to set its foot, and it returned to him to the ark, for the waters were still on the face of the whole earth. So he put out his hand and took it and brought it into the ark with him. 10He waited another seven days,

and again he sent out the dove from the ark; 11and the dove came back to him in the evening, and there in its beak was a freshly plucked olive leaf; so Noah knew that the waters had subsided from the earth. 12Then he waited another seven days, and sent out the dove; and it did not return to him any more.

13 In the six hundred first year, in the first month, on the first day of the month, the waters were dried up from the earth; and Noah removed the covering of the ark, and looked, and saw that the face of the ground was drying. 14In the second month, on the twenty-seventh day of the month, the earth was dry. 15Then God said to Noah, 16"Go out of the ark, you and your wife, and your sons and your sons' wives with you. 17Bring out with you every living thing that is with you of all flesh—birds and animals and every creeping thing that creeps on the earth—so that they may abound on the earth, and be fruitful and multiply on the earth." 18So Noah went out with his sons and his wife and his sons' wives. 19And every animal, every creeping thing, and every bird, everything that moves on the earth, went out of the ark by families.

20 Then Noah built an altar to the LORD, and took of every clean animal and of every clean bird, and offered burnt offerings on the altar. 21And when the LORD smelled the pleasing odor, the LORD said in his heart, "I will never again curse the ground because of humankind, for the inclination of the human heart is evil from youth; nor will I ever again destroy every living creature as I have done. 22 As long as the earth endures,

seedtime and harvest, cold and heat,
summer and winter, day and night,
shall not cease."

8.1–22. 1: The great turning point in the story is the phrase, *God remembered Noah* and all the animals that were with him in the ark. God remembered the covenant* promises made to Noah in 6.18 and shifted from destruction to reconstruction. God's remembering previous covenant promises is often the signal of a major positive change in the fortunes of his people (Ex 2.24). God begins a whole new creation. He makes *a wind blow* over the watery chaos, just as God's wind

Two Biblical Versions of the Flood Story

Two different versions of the flood story have been woven together to form the present unified story in Gen 6–9. The two versions correspond to two originally separate traditions in ancient Israel, the earlier Yahwist (J) tradition and the later Priestly (P) tradition (see sidebar, "Two Different Creation Stories," p. 50). The existence of two originally separate versions is evident from a number of consistent variations, doublets, and other tensions in the story. These include the following:

- Focus only on human corruption and the destruction of only living things in 6.5–7 (J) versus a broader focus on the corruption of "all flesh" (both humans and animals) and the destruction of "the earth" in 6.11–13 (P)
- The reason God chose Noah is that he "found favor" in God's eyes in 6.8 (J) versus "Noah was a righteous man" in 6.9 (P)
- The portrayal of the flood as a simple rainstorm in 7.4 (J) versus the flood as the return to the watery chaos before creation in Gen 1.2 in 6.17 (P)
- The number of animals as seven pairs of all clean animals and one pair of unclean animals in 7.2 (J) versus one pair of all animals of every kind in 6.19 (P)
- The duration of the flood as 40 days and nights in 7.12, 17; 8.6 (J) versus 150 days with the water standing for over a year in 7.11, 24; 8.3b–5, 13a, 15 (P)
- The divine name of "the LORD" in J versus "God" in P

The two biblical versions of the flood story may be divided in the following way:

	Yahwist version (J)	Priestly version (P)
The condition of the world and God's decision	6.5–8	6.9–13
Instructions concerning the ark and the animals	7.1–5	6.14–22
Boarding the ark as the flood begins	7.7–8, 10, 12, 16b	7.6, 9, 11, 13–16a
The flood	7.17, 22–23	7.18–21, 24
The end of the flood	8.2b–3a, 6–12, 13b	8.1–2a, 3b–5, 13a, 14–19
God's promise	8.20–22	9.1–7
The covenant* of the rainbow		9.8–17
The sons of Noah	9.18–27	
The age of Noah and his death		9.28–29

over the deep had begun the first creation (1.2). **2–12:** The destroying flood of 7.11–24 is gradually reversed. *The mountains of Ararat* are located in a region in modern-day southeast Turkey and northwest Iran. The *raven* and the *dove* are sent out to test whether they find dry land. The dove is sent out three times. The first time the dove returns with nothing, then returns with an *olive leaf* or branch (v. 11), and finally does not return at all (v. 12). The dove with an olive branch has become a symbol of peace, hope, and new life. In the story, the dove with the olive branch is a sign of hope that the waters have partially receded below the level of olive trees. **17:** The phrase *be fruitful and multiply* calls to mind the same words used in the first creation story in 1.28. **20–22:** Noah's first building project after leaving the ark is an altar. Noah offers ritually clean animals (7.2–3) upon the altar as burnt offerings to give thanks to God. God smells *the pleasing odor* of the burnt offerings as the smoke rises to the heavens (Lev 1.9). God resolves never again to *curse the ground* as he had done before (3.17; 4.11) and never again to *destroy every living creature* (v. 21). The flood is not successful in changing the basic problem: *the inclination of the human heart is evil from youth* (v. 21). From here on, God will have to live with that fact and work within its reality. In the meantime, God promises not to disrupt the basic created order of the seasons and the agricultural rhythms of life (v. 22).

9 God blessed Noah and his sons, and said to them, "Be fruitful and multiply, and fill the earth. ²The fear and dread of you shall rest on every animal of the earth, and on every bird of the air, on everything that creeps on the ground, and on all the fish of the sea; into your hand they are delivered. ³Every moving thing that lives shall be food for you; and just as I gave you the green plants, I give you everything. ⁴Only, you shall not eat flesh with its life, that is, its blood. ⁵For your own lifeblood I will surely require a reckoning: from every animal I will require it and from human beings, each one for the blood of another, I will require a reckoning for human life.

6 Whoever sheds the blood of a human,
     by a human shall that person's blood
          be shed;
  for in his own image
     God made humankind.

⁷And you, be fruitful and multiply, abound on the earth and multiply in it."

8 Then God said to Noah and to his sons with him, ⁹"As for me, I am establishing my covenant with you and your descendants after you, ¹⁰and with every living creature that is with you, the birds, the domestic animals, and every animal of the earth with you, as many as came out of the ark.ᵃ ¹¹I establish my covenant with you, that never again shall all flesh be cut off by the waters of a flood, and never again shall there be a flood to de-

stroy the earth." ¹²God said, "This is the sign of the covenant that I make between me and you and every living creature that is with you, for all future generations: ¹³I have set my bow in the clouds, and it shall be a sign of the covenant between me and the earth. ¹⁴When I bring clouds over the earth and the bow is seen in the clouds, ¹⁵I will remember my covenant that is between me and you and every living creature of all flesh; and the waters shall never again become a flood to destroy all flesh. ¹⁶When the bow is in the clouds, I will see it and remember the everlasting covenant between God and every living creature of all flesh that is on the earth." ¹⁷God said to Noah, "This is the sign of the covenant that I have established between me and all flesh that is on the earth."

18 The sons of Noah who went out of the ark were Shem, Ham, and Japheth. Ham was the father of Canaan. ¹⁹These three were the sons of Noah; and from these the whole earth was peopled.

20 Noah, a man of the soil, was the first to plant a vineyard. ²¹He drank some of the wine and became drunk, and he lay uncovered in his tent. ²²And Ham, the father of Canaan, saw the nakedness of his father, and told his two brothers outside. ²³Then Shem and Japheth took a garment, laid it on both their shoulders, and walked backward and covered the nakedness of their father; their faces were turned away, and they did not see their father's nakedness. ²⁴When Noah awoke from his wine and knew what his youngest son had done to him, ²⁵he said,

  "Cursed be Canaan;
     lowest of slaves shall he be to his
          brothers."
²⁶He also said,

  "Blessed by the LORD my God be Shem;
     and let Canaan be his slave.
27 May God make space forᵇ Japheth,
     and let him live in the tents of Shem;
     and let Canaan be his slave."

28 After the flood Noah lived three hundred fifty years. ²⁹All the days of Noah were nine hundred fifty years; and he died.

a Gk: Heb adds *every animal of the earth*   *b* Heb *yapht*, a play on *Japheth*

9.1–29: God's covenant* with creation and Noah's curse of Canaan. 3–4: God expands the original vegetarian diet for humans (1.29) to include the meat of animals, which *shall be food for you.* However, the blood of any animal is to be drained from it before its flesh is eaten (Deut 12.23–25). The blood represents life, and returning it to the ground acknowledges that life belongs to God. **5–6:** Every killing of a human being is a serious threat to the social and moral order of society since it crosses the created boundary between life and death. In addition, God requires *a reckoning* or severe consequence (a life for a life) because humans are created in God's *own image* (1.26–27). God requires a reckoning even from an animal that kills a human (v. 5; Ex 21.28–32). **8–17:** God establishes a covenant relationship with Noah and with all living creatures. God promises never again *shall there be a flood to destroy the earth* (v. 11). This promise fills out the contents of the earlier covenant mentioned in 6.18. The *sign of the covenant* is the rainbow in the sky. The bow will be a sign to jog the divine memory so that God will *remember the everlasting covenant between God and every living creature* (v. 16). In the ancient world, the rainbow was associated with the bow used by God to shoot arrows of lightning (Ps 7.12–13). To hang up the bow in the sky symbolized peace. Worldwide destruction would no longer be a strategy used by God. **18–19:** The three sons of Noah become the ancestors of all living human beings because all other humans had died in the flood (7.21–23). **20:** Noah becomes the world's first winemaker. The intoxicating effect of wine fulfills the words Noah's father spoke at his birth concerning Noah's role in producing something that would bring relief from work (5.29). **21–23:** Noah overindulges in the intoxicating fruits of his own labors and lies *uncovered in his tent.* Noah's son Ham, the father of Canaan, sees *the nakedness of his father.* This may suggest some form of incest or other improper sexual activity (Lev 18.6–8, 24–30). **24–27:** Although Ham is the one who acted improperly, it is Ham's son Canaan who is cursed to be a slave and Shem who is blessed. As the following genealogy, or family tree, in Gen 10 shows, these sons of Noah represent geographical nations and peoples in the known world of the ancient Near East. Ham represents the Hamitic peoples associated with Egypt and areas under Egyptian control, including at some time the land of Canaan. Shem represents the Semitic people, which will eventually include Israel and other related nations. Japheth included a number of groups from Asia Minor. The cursing of Canaan and the blessing of Shem provide a backdrop and justification for the eventual conquest of the Canaanites and the settlement of the Israelites into the land of Canaan in the book of Joshua.

10 These are the descendants of Noah's sons, Shem, Ham, and Japheth; children were born to them after the flood.

2 The descendants of Japheth: Gomer, Magog, Madai, Javan, Tubal, Meshech, and Tiras. 3The descendants of Gomer: Ashkenaz, Riphath, and Togarmah. 4The descendants of Javan: Elishah, Tarshish, Kittim, and Rodanim.ᵃ 5From these the coastland peoples spread. These are the descendants of Japhethᵇ in their lands, with their own language, by their families, in their nations.

6 The descendants of Ham: Cush, Egypt, Put, and Canaan. 7The descendants of Cush: Seba, Havilah, Sabtah, Raamah, and Sabteca. The descendants of Raamah: Sheba and Dedan. 8Cush became the father of Nimrod; he was the first on earth to become a mighty warrior. 9He was a mighty hunter before the LORD; therefore it is said, "Like Nimrod a mighty hunter before the LORD." 10The beginning of his kingdom was Babel, Erech, and Accad, all of them in the land of Shinar. 11From that land he went into Assyria, and built Nineveh, Rehoboth-ir, Calah, and 12Resen between Nineveh and Calah; that is the great city. 13Egypt became the father of Ludim, Anamim, Lehabim, Naphtuhim, 14Pathrusim, Casluhim, and Caphtorim, from which the Philistines come.ᶜ

15 Canaan became the father of Sidon his firstborn, and Heth, 16and the Jebusites, the Amorites, the Girgashites, 17the Hivites, the Arkites, the Sinites, 18the Arvadites, the Zemarites, and the Hamathites. Afterward the families of the Canaanites spread abroad. 19And the territory of the Canaanites extended from Sidon, in the direction of

---

a Heb Mss Sam Gk See 1 Chr 1.7: MT *Dodanim*
b Compare verses 20, 31. Heb lacks *These are the descendants of Japheth*　　*c* Cn: Heb *Casluhim, from which the Philistines come, and Caphtorim*

The Gilgamesh Epic

Other cultures in the ancient Near East had their own versions of a story about a worldwide flood. A Mesopotamian version, the story of Atrahasis, tells of a flood, a boat sealed with bitumen (pitch or tar), and other details that parallel the Genesis story. The Babylonian version involves a scene from the "Epic of Gilgamesh"* and dates roughly to 3000 BCE. A comparison of the biblical flood story and its Babylonian counterpart displays a number of striking parallels. The hero's name in the Babylonian flood story is Utnapishtim. The god Ea tells Utnapishtim in a dream to build an ark or large boat shaped as an exact cube. Ea warns him that other gods are planning to send a flood to destroy the earth. Utnapishtim builds the wooden ark and seals it with pitch. He loads the ark with his family, possessions, animals, and skilled workers. A fierce storm blows in, and even the gods cower in terror before the storm. The rain covers the whole earth by the seventh day. The ark eventually comes to rest on a mountain. After six days, Utnapishtim sends out a dove and then later a swallow. Both birds return because they cannot find a resting place. Then he sends out a raven which does not return, indicating that the waters have receded and dry land has appeared.

Utnapishtim then leaves the ark and offers up a burnt animal sacrifice to delight the gods. The gods "smelled the sweet odor" and "hovered like flies" over the sacrifice. They are apparently hungry because no sacrifices have been offered to them during the flood. The gods vow that there will never be a flood like this again. The gods take Utnapishtim away from his human and earthly existence to live in the heavens as an immortal divine being.

Gerar, as far as Gaza, and in the direction of Sodom, Gomorrah, Admah, and Zeboiim, as far as Lasha. ²⁰These are the descendants of Ham, by their families, their languages, their lands, and their nations.

21 To Shem also, the father of all the children of Eber, the elder brother of Japheth, children were born. ²²The descendants of Shem: Elam, Asshur, Arpachshad, Lud, and Aram. ²³The descendants of Aram: Uz, Hul, Gether, and Mash. ²⁴Arpachshad became the father of Shelah; and Shelah became the father of Eber. ²⁵To Eber were born two sons: the name of the one was Peleg,ᵃ for in his days the earth was divided, and his brother's name was Joktan. ²⁶Joktan became the father of Almodad, Sheleph, Hazarmaveth, Jerah, ²⁷Hadoram, Uzal, Diklah, ²⁸Obal, Abimael, Sheba, ²⁹Ophir, Havilah, and Jobab; all these were the descendants of Joktan. ³⁰The territory in which they lived extended from Mesha in the direction of Sephar, the hill country of the east. ³¹These are

the descendants of Shem, by their families, their languages, their lands, and their nations.

32 These are the families of Noah's sons, according to their genealogies, in their nations; and from these the nations spread abroad on the earth after the flood.

10.1–32: A list of nations descended from Noah's three sons. This genealogy* traces the family line of all the known peoples of the earth back to the three sons of Noah: Japheth, Ham, and Shem. Each of the peoples or groups listed have their own *families, their languages, their lands, and their nations:* This refrain is repeated three times (10.5, 20, 31). **2–5:** *The descendants of Japheth* include peoples to the north and west of Canaan in Greece and Asia Minor and the *coastland peoples* of the Mediterranean Sea such as the Philistines. **6–20:** *The descendants of Ham* represent the nations under Egypt's influence at the time in Africa and Mesopotamia, including the land in and

a That is Division

around Canaan itself (vv. 15–20). The list of nations contains an old legend* about a great warrior named Nimrod. Nimrod conquered *the land of Shinar* or Babylon (see *Babel* in v. 10) and the land of Assyria with its *great city* of Nineveh (vv. 11–12; see Mic 5.5–6). The story of the tower of Babel will be set in the land of Shinar (11.2). **21–31:** *Shem* is the ancestor of the Semitic peoples who lived in and around Assyria and the Arabian Peninsula. Shem is *the father of all the children of Eber* (v. 21). *Eber* may be related to the word "Hebrew," which describes a number of wandering peoples on the margins of society. One of these groups formed the core of the Hebrew or Israelite people (14.13; Ex 9.13).

11 Now the whole earth had one language and the same words. [2]And as they migrated from the east,[a] they came upon a plain in the land of Shinar and settled there. [3]And they said to one another, "Come, let us make bricks, and burn them thoroughly." And they had brick for stone, and bitumen for mortar. [4]Then they said, "Come, let us build ourselves a city, and a tower with its top in the heavens, and let us make a name for ourselves; otherwise we shall be scattered abroad upon the face of the whole earth." [5]The LORD came down to see the city and the tower, which mortals had built. [6]And the LORD said, "Look, they are one people, and they have all one language; and this is only the beginning of what they will do; nothing that they propose to do will now be impossible for them. [7]Come, let us go down, and confuse their language there, so that they will not understand one another's speech." [8]So the LORD scattered them abroad from there over the face of all the earth, and they left off building the city. [9]Therefore it was called Babel, because there the LORD confused[b] the language of all the earth; and from there the LORD scattered them abroad over the face of all the earth.

11.1–9: The tower of Babel and the confusion of human language. This story of the tower of Babel explains the geographical scattering of humans and the division of human speech into many different languages (Gen 10). Like that of the garden of Eden, the story continues the theme of God's limits on excessive human pride and presumption. **2:** *The land of Shinar* is Babylon (10.10). **4:** *A tower with its top in the heavens* probably alludes to a very high pyramid-like structure called a ziggurat. The tall structure functioned as a temple in which to worship the gods in ancient Babylon. In the story, however, the humans' root desire is not to worship the gods but to *make a name* for themselves. **7:** God says, *Let us go down.* He is speaking to a divine council of advisers as in 1.26. **9:** The name *Babel* in the language of Babylon means "Gate of God," which would be appropriate for a temple. However, the Hebrew storyteller links the name instead with the Hebrew word "balal" ("to confuse").

10 These are the descendants of Shem. When Shem was one hundred years old, he became the father of Arpachshad two years after the flood; [11]and Shem lived after the birth of Arpachshad five hundred years, and had other sons and daughters.

12 When Arpachshad had lived thirty-five years, he became the father of Shelah; [13]and Arpachshad lived after the birth of Shelah four hundred three years, and had other sons and daughters.

14 When Shelah had lived thirty years, he became the father of Eber; [15]and Shelah lived after the birth of Eber four hundred three years, and had other sons and daughters.

16 When Eber had lived thirty-four years, he became the father of Peleg; [17]and Eber lived after the birth of Peleg four hundred thirty years, and had other sons and daughters.

18 When Peleg had lived thirty years, he became the father of Reu; [19]and Peleg lived after the birth of Reu two hundred nine years, and had other sons and daughters.

20 When Reu had lived thirty-two years, he became the father of Serug; [21]and Reu lived after the birth of Serug two hundred seven years, and had other sons and daughters.

22 When Serug had lived thirty years, he became the father of Nahor; [23]and Serug lived after the birth of Nahor two hundred years, and had other sons and daughters.

a Or *migrated eastward*   *b* Heb *balal,* meaning *to confuse*

24 When Nahor had lived twenty-nine years, he became the father of Terah; 25 and Nahor lived after the birth of Terah one hundred nineteen years, and had other sons and daughters.

26 When Terah had lived seventy years, he became the father of Abram, Nahor, and Haran.

27 Now these are the descendants of Terah. Terah was the father of Abram, Nahor, and Haran; and Haran was the father of Lot. 28 Haran died before his father Terah in the land of his birth, in Ur of the Chaldeans. 29 Abram and Nahor took wives; the name of Abram's wife was Sarai, and the name of Nahor's wife was Milcah. She was the daughter of Haran the father of Milcah and Iscah. 30 Now Sarai was barren; she had no child.

31 Terah took his son Abram and his grandson Lot son of Haran, and his daughter-in-law Sarai, his son Abram's wife, and they went out together from Ur of the Chaldeans to go into the land of Canaan; but when they came to Haran, they settled there. 32 The days of Terah were two hundred five years; and Terah died in Haran.

11.10–32: The family line from Shem to Abraham. The genealogy in Gen 10, before the tower of Babel story, had named all the siblings of a given generation. These siblings had represented the spread of God's blessing over all peoples of the earth. A major transition occurs with the genealogy in Gen 11. The family line of promises becomes more narrowly focused on one person in each generation. The family line begins with Noah's son Shem (v. 10) and extends for ten generations until we come to Abram (later called Abraham; 17.5) and Sarai (later called Sarah; 17.15). This genealogy builds the literary bridge from stories about all humanity in Gen 1–11 to the more narrowly focused stories on the one family of Abraham and Sarah, the ancestors of Israel, in Gen 12–50. **28:** The memory of this family includes the tragedy of a son (Haran) who died at a young age, while his father was still living. The theme of a son's premature death will continue to haunt this family line. The young sons of Abraham (22.2), Isaac (27.41), and Jacob (37.29–36) will all be endangered or presumed to be dead. **30:** Abram's wife, Sarai, was barren and unable to have children. This condition will become a major obstacle and cause for suspense when God promises Abram and Sarai that

they will have many descendants and become a great nation (12.2; 17.16). The theme of the barren mother unable to have children will also be repeated in succeeding generations with Rebekah (25.21) and Rachel (29.31). **31:** *Haran,* a city in northern Mesopotamia, is the place where Abraham grew up. Abraham will later see to it that his son Isaac obtains a wife from his hometown of Haran, also known as the city of Nahor (24.10). Abraham's grandson, Jacob, will likewise return to Haran to work for his uncle Laban and marry Laban's two daughters (29.4).

12 Now the LORD said to Abram, "Go from your country and your kindred and your father's house to the land that I will show you. 2 I will make of you a great nation, and I will bless you, and make your name great, so that you will be a blessing. 3 I will bless those who bless you, and the one who curses you I will curse; and in you all the families of the earth shall be blessed."[a]

4 So Abram went, as the LORD had told him; and Lot went with him. Abram was seventy-five years old when he departed from Haran. 5 Abram took his wife Sarai and his brother's son Lot, and all the possessions that they had gathered, and the persons whom they had acquired in Haran; and they set forth to go to the land of Canaan. When they had come to the land of Canaan, 6 Abram passed through the land to the place at Shechem, to the oak[b] of Moreh. At that time the Canaanites were in the land. 7 Then the LORD appeared to Abram, and said, "To your offspring[c] I will give this land." So he built there an altar to the LORD, who had appeared to him. 8 From there he moved on to the hill country on the east of Bethel, and pitched his tent, with Bethel on the west and Ai on the east; and there he built an altar to the LORD and invoked the name of the LORD. 9 And Abram journeyed on by stages toward the Negeb.

12.1–9: God calls Abram and promises great blessing. 1–3: This first promise to Abram of *land,* many descendants in the form of *a great nation,* and bless-

---

a Or by you all the families of the earth shall bless themselves   b Or terebinth   c Heb seed ings that will extend to *all the families of the earth* is a foundation for all of God's future promises to Israel. The promise of land and descendants will run like a thread throughout Genesis (13.15–17; 15.5–7, 18–21; 17.1–8; 22.15–18; 26.2–4; 28.1–4, 13–15) and beyond (Ex 6.4, 8; Deut 34.4). God promises Abram to *make your name great* as one who will be a blessing to other nations (v. 2). This element stands in contrast to the tower builders of Babel, who sought to make a name for themselves by their own selfish efforts (11.4). **4:** Abram immediately obeys God's command to leave his homeland and go to a place where he will receive great blessing. Later God will call Abraham a second time to go and sacrifice his son and apparently give up his blessing (22.1–3).

10 Now there was a famine in the land. So Abram went down to Egypt to reside there as an alien, for the famine was severe in the land. ¹¹When he was about to enter Egypt, he said to his wife Sarai, "I know well that you are a woman beautiful in appearance; ¹²and when the Egyptians see you, they will say, 'This is his wife'; then they will kill me, but they will let you live. ¹³Say you are my sister, so that it may go well with me because of you, and that my life may be spared on your account." ¹⁴When Abram entered Egypt the Egyptians saw that the woman was very beautiful. ¹⁵When the officials of Pharaoh saw her, they praised her to Pharaoh. And the woman was taken into Pharaoh's house. ¹⁶And for her sake he dealt well with Abram; and he had sheep, oxen, male donkeys, male and female slaves, female donkeys, and camels.

17 But the LORD afflicted Pharaoh and his house with great plagues because of Sarai, Abram's wife. ¹⁸So Pharaoh called Abram, and said, "What is this you have done to me? Why did you not tell me that she was your wife? ¹⁹Why did you say, 'She is my sister,' so that I took her for my wife? Now then, here is your wife, take her, and be gone." ²⁰And Pharaoh gave his men orders concerning him; and they set him on the way, with his wife and all that he had.

12.10–20: Abram pretends Sarai is his sister and not his wife. 10: *A famine in the land* of Canaan forces Abram and Sarai to travel to Egypt. The same situation

will occur later with Abraham's descendants when Jacob's sons come to Egypt looking for food (41.53–42.3). *An alien* is a traveler who lives for a time in a foreign land. Such a person has no rights as a citizen and thus is vulnerable to abuse. **11–16:** Sarai is so *beautiful in appearance* that Abram is convinced that the Egyptians will take Sarai and kill Abram if they find out they are husband and wife. Therefore, Abram instructs Sarai to lie and say that she is Abram's sister. Abram endangers Sarai's life in order to save his own. **17–20:** The LORD afflicts the Egyptian Pharaoh with plagues to force him to let go of Sarai. During the Israelite exodus out of Egypt, the LORD will again send plagues on Egypt and Pharaoh, which will cause him to set free the Israelite slaves (Ex 11.1). This wife-sister story will reappear with Abraham and Sarah in 20.1–17 and with Isaac and Rebekah in 26.6–11.

13 So Abram went up from Egypt, he and his wife, and all that he had, and Lot with him, into the Negeb.

2 Now Abram was very rich in livestock, in silver, and in gold. ³He journeyed on by stages from the Negeb as far as Bethel, to the place where his tent had been at the beginning, between Bethel and Ai, ⁴to the place where he had made an altar at the first; and there Abram called on the name of the LORD. ⁵Now Lot, who went with Abram, also had flocks and herds and tents, ⁶so that the land could not support both of them living together; for their possessions were so great that they could not live together, ⁷and there was strife between the herders of Abram's livestock and the herders of Lot's livestock. At that time the Canaanites and the Perizzites lived in the land.

8 Then Abram said to Lot, "Let there be no strife between you and me, and between your herders and my herders; for we are kindred. ⁹Is not the whole land before you? Separate yourself from me. If you take the left hand, then I will go to the right; or if you take the right hand, then I will go to the left." ¹⁰Lot looked about him, and saw that the plain of the Jordan was well watered everywhere like the garden of the LORD, like the land of Egypt, in the direction of Zoar; this was before the LORD had destroyed Sodom and Gomorrah. ¹¹So Lot chose for himself all the plain of the Jordan, and Lot journeyed

eastward; thus they separated from each other. ¹²Abram settled in the land of Canaan, while Lot settled among the cities of the Plain and moved his tent as far as Sodom. ¹³Now the people of Sodom were wicked, great sinners against the LORD.

14 The LORD said to Abram, after Lot had separated from him, "Raise your eyes now, and look from the place where you are, northward and southward and eastward and westward; ¹⁵for all the land that you see I will give to you and to your offspring[a] forever. ¹⁶I will make your offspring like the dust of the earth; so that if one can count the dust of the earth, your offspring also can be counted. ¹⁷Rise up, walk through the length and the breadth of the land, for I will give it to you." ¹⁸So Abram moved his

tent, and came and settled by the oaks[b] of Mamre, which are at Hebron; and there he built an altar to the LORD.

13.1–18: Abram and his nephew Lot separate into different territories. 3: After the famine is over, Abram and Sarai return to Canaan *where his tent had been at the beginning* (12.8). **8–9:** As the elder uncle, Abram could have chosen whatever land he wished. Instead, Abram graciously allows his young nephew Lot to select land first. **10:** The green and lush *plain of the Jordan* looked *like the garden of the LORD,* an allusion to the garden of Eden in Gen 2. *Like the land of Egypt* points forward to Israel's experience in Egypt where the Nile River provides fertile crops. But the lush

a Heb *seed*   *b* Or *terebinths*

Map   **The journeys of Abram and Sarai**

appearance of the area is deceptive: The people of the area are *wicked, great sinners* (v. 13). Genesis 19 will tell the story of the destruction of *Sodom and Gomorrah.* This destruction will dramatically change the lush land into a dry desert (19.24–25). **11:** Lot will become the ancestor of two nations that will border Canaan or Israel on its eastern boundary, Moab and Ammon (19.30–38). **14–18:** The first promise to Abram had not specified the exact land God would give him (12.2). But now God invites Abram to lay claim to a specific piece of real estate by making a full survey of it. God also reaffirms that Abram will have descendants as numerous as *the dust of the earth* (v. 16). God's promises of land and children become more visible and real to Abram.

14 In the days of King Amraphel of Shinar, King Arioch of Ellasar, King Chedorlaomer of Elam, and King Tidal of Goiim, 2these kings made war with King Bera of Sodom, King Birsha of Gomorrah, King Shinab of Admah, King Shemeber of Zeboiim, and the king of Bela (that is, Zoar). 3All these joined forces in the Valley of Siddim (that is, the Dead Sea).*a* 4Twelve years they had served Chedorlaomer, but in the thirteenth year they rebelled. 5In the fourteenth year Chedorlaomer and the kings who were with him came and subdued the Rephaim in Ashteroth-karnaim, the Zuzim in Ham, the Emim in Shaveh-kiriathaim, 6and the Horites in the hill country of Seir as far as El-paran on the edge of the wilderness; 7then they turned back and came to En-mishpat (that is, Kadesh), and subdued all the country of the Amalekites, and also the Amorites who lived in Hazazon-tamar. 8Then the king of Sodom, the king of Gomorrah, the king of Admah, the king of Zeboiim, and the king of Bela (that is, Zoar) went out, and they joined battle in the Valley of Siddim 9with King Chedorlaomer of Elam, King Tidal of Goiim, King Amraphel of Shinar, and King Arioch of Ellasar, four kings against five. 10Now the Valley of Siddim was full of bitumen pits; and as the kings of Sodom and Gomorrah fled, some fell into them, and the rest fled to the hill country. 11So the enemy took all the goods of Sodom and Gomorrah, and all their provisions, and went their way; 12they also took Lot, the son of Abram's brother, who lived in Sodom, and his goods, and departed.

13 Then one who had escaped came and told Abram the Hebrew, who was living by the oaks*b* of Mamre the Amorite, brother of Eshcol and of Aner; these were allies of Abram. 14When Abram heard that his nephew had been taken captive, he led forth his trained men, born in his house, three hundred eighteen of them, and went in pursuit as far as Dan. 15He divided his forces against them by night, he and his servants, and routed them and pursued them to Hobah, north of Damascus. 16Then he brought back all the goods, and also brought back his nephew Lot with his goods, and the women and the people.

17 After his return from the defeat of Chedorlaomer and the kings who were with him, the king of Sodom went out to meet him at the Valley of Shaveh (that is, the King's Valley). 18And King Melchizedek of Salem brought out bread and wine; he was priest of God Most High.*c* 19He blessed him and said,

"Blessed be Abram by God Most High,*c*
    maker of heaven and earth;
20 and blessed be God Most High,*c*
    who has delivered your enemies into
        your hand!"
And Abram gave him one-tenth of everything. 21Then the king of Sodom said to Abram, "Give me the persons, but take the goods for yourself." 22But Abram said to the king of Sodom, "I have sworn to the LORD, God Most High,*c* maker of heaven and earth, 23that I would not take a thread or a sandal-thong or anything that is yours, so that you might not say, 'I have made Abram rich.' 24I will take nothing but what the young men have eaten, and the share of the men who went with me—Aner, Eshcol, and Mamre. Let them take their share."

14.1–24: The rescue of Lot and the blessing of Abram. 1–11: A coalition of kings from the east attacks the area around Sodom and Gomorrah. *Shinar* (v. 1) is probably Babylon (10.10; 11.2). Most of these

a Heb *Salt Sea*   *b* Or *terebinths*   *c* Heb *El Elyon* names of kings are not known historically from other ancient sources. **12:** The mention of *Lot, the son of Abram's brother,* gives the reason the story is included. The story suggests that Lot's choice of this initially attractive land may not have been so wise (13.10–11). **13–16:** Abram's small band of 318 fighters is able to defeat the coalition of forces from the east. Abram rescues Lot and his family. Abram's concern for Lot is an example of Abram as a blessing to other families of the earth (12.3). **17–18:** Two kings of Sodom and Salem come out to thank Abram for defeating the eastern kings who had attacked them. Salem is another name for the city of Jerusalem (Ps 76.2). The Canaanite king, *Melchizedek of Salem,* was also a Canaanite priest of a god named *God Most High* (v. 18). The title "Most High" or "God Most High" is an ancient divine title used also for the LORD in the Old Testament (Num 24.16; Deut 32.8) and especially in the Psalms (Ps 57.2). Abram himself links Melchizedek's *God Most High* with *the LORD* in 14.22. The king-priest Melchizedek is not known from other historical sources. He is mentioned only once elsewhere in the Old Testament, in a psalm or blessing addressed to one of Israel's later kings (Ps 110.4). **19–24:** Abram again shows great generosity to people of other nations. He is a blessing to other families of the earth (12.3).

15 After these things the word of the LORD came to Abram in a vision, "Do not be afraid, Abram, I am your shield; your reward shall be very great." ²But Abram said, "O Lord GOD, what will you give me, for I continue childless, and the heir of my house is Eliezer of Damascus?"*ᵃ* ³And Abram said, "You have given me no offspring, and so a slave born in my house is to be my heir." ⁴But the word of the LORD came to him, "This man shall not be your heir; no one but your very own issue shall be your heir." ⁵He brought him outside and said, "Look toward heaven and count the stars, if you are able to count them." Then he said to him, "So shall your descendants be." ⁶And he believed the LORD; and the LORD *ᵇ* reckoned it to him as righteousness.

7 Then he said to him, "I am the LORD who brought you from Ur of the Chaldeans, to give you this land to possess." ⁸But he said, "O Lord GOD, how am I to know that I shall possess it?" ⁹He said to him, "Bring me a heifer three years old, a female goat three years old, a ram three years old, a turtledove, and a young pigeon." ¹⁰He brought him all these and cut them in two, laying each half over against the other; but he did not cut the birds in two. ¹¹And when birds of prey came down on the carcasses, Abram drove them away.

12 As the sun was going down, a deep sleep fell upon Abram, and a deep and terrifying darkness descended upon him. ¹³Then the LORD *ᵇ* said to Abram, "Know this for certain, that your offspring shall be aliens in a land that is not theirs, and shall be slaves there, and they shall be oppressed for four hundred years; ¹⁴but I will bring judgment on the nation that they serve, and afterward they shall come out with great possessions. ¹⁵As for yourself, you shall go to your ancestors in peace; you shall be buried in a good old age. ¹⁶And they shall come back here in the fourth generation; for the iniquity of the Amorites is not yet complete."

17 When the sun had gone down and it was dark, a smoking fire pot and a flaming torch passed between these pieces. ¹⁸On that day the LORD made a covenant with Abram, saying, "To your descendants I give this land, from the river of Egypt to the great river, the river Euphrates, ¹⁹the land of the Kenites, the Kenizzites, the Kadmonites, ²⁰the Hittites, the Perizzites, the Rephaim, ²¹the Amorites, the Canaanites, the Girgashites, and the Jebusites."

15.1–21: God's covenant* with Abram. This story probably developed over a long period of time. It contains a very ancient covenant ceremony (vv. 7–10, 17) and later additions that point to future events in the exodus out of Egypt and the conquest of Canaan (vv. 12–16). **2–3:** Abram complains to God that the promise of many children and descendants shows no signs of being fulfilled. Abram's only apparent heir is his household slave, Eliezer, which reflects a custom that a chief servant could inherit the possessions of a couple who died without children. **6:** This key verse is the basis for Abram's reputation as a man of great trust in God (Gal 3.6–9). *He believed the LORD* means Abram trusted God to make good on the promise. *The LORD* in turn *reckoned* or evaluated Abram's trust in God as

a Meaning of Heb uncertain   *b* Heb *he*

righteousness. *Righteousness* denotes a relationship that is in good order. **7–8:** The topic turns from the promise of children to the promise of land. Again, Abram pleads for a sign of reassurance. **9–10:** God responds to Abram's request for a sign by setting up an ancient covenant ceremony. The bodies of animals are cut in two and laid out on two sides with a path between them. By walking down the path, the one making the covenant promise apparently pledges that he will be cut in two like the animals if he does not fulfill the promise made. Jeremiah 34.18 mentions a similar covenant ceremony. **11:** The hovering *birds of prey* symbolize future obstacles that will threaten the fulfillment of the promise. **12–16:** The general future threat symbolized in v. 11 is specified in Abram's dream. Abram's *offspring shall be aliens* and *slaves* in a *land that is not theirs* (v. 13), a reference to Israel's future slavery in Egypt (Ex 1–15). The LORD promises that Abram's family will eventually return and settle in the land of Canaan (v. 16). *Amorites* (v. 16) is an alternate name for Canaanites. **17–21:** The *smoking fire pot* and the *flaming torch* represent the LORD walking down the path between the animal carcasses. In effect, the LORD's action means, "I will be split in two like these animals if I do not fulfill the promise." Abram does not walk through the animals. This is a one-sided and unconditional promise from God to Abram.

16 Now Sarai, Abram's wife, bore him no children. She had an Egyptian slave-girl whose name was Hagar, ²and Sarai said to Abram, "You see that the LORD has prevented me from bearing children; go in to my slave-girl; it may be that I shall obtain children by her." And Abram listened to the voice of Sarai. ³So, after Abram had lived ten years in the land of Canaan, Sarai, Abram's wife, took Hagar the Egyptian, her slave-girl, and gave her to her husband Abram as a wife. ⁴He went in to Hagar, and she conceived; and when she saw that she had conceived, she looked with contempt on her mistress. ⁵Then Sarai said to Abram, "May the wrong done to me be on you! I gave my slave-girl to your embrace, and when she saw that she had conceived, she looked on me with contempt. May the LORD judge between you and me!" ⁶But Abram said to Sarai, "Your slave-girl is in your power; do to her as you please." Then Sarai dealt harshly with her, and she ran away from her.

7 The angel of the LORD found her by a spring of water in the wilderness, the spring on the way to Shur. ⁸And he said, "Hagar, slave-girl of Sarai, where have you come from and where are you going?" She said, "I am running away from my mistress Sarai." ⁹The angel of the LORD said to her, "Return to your mistress, and submit to her." ¹⁰The angel of the LORD also said to her, "I will so greatly multiply your offspring that they cannot be counted for multitude." ¹¹And the angel of the LORD said to her,

"Now you have conceived and shall bear
        a son;
    you shall call him Ishmael,ᵃ
    for the LORD has given heed to your
        affliction.
12 He shall be a wild ass of a man,
    with his hand against everyone,
        and everyone's hand against him;
    and he shall live at odds with all his
        kin."

¹³So she named the LORD who spoke to her, "You are El-roi";ᵇ for she said, "Have I really seen God and remained alive after seeing him?"ᶜ ¹⁴Therefore the well was called Beer-lahai-roi;ᵈ it lies between Kadesh and Bered.

15 Hagar bore Abram a son; and Abram named his son, whom Hagar bore, Ishmael. ¹⁶Abram was eighty-six years old when Hagar bore himᵉ Ishmael.

16.1–16: Hagar, Sarai, and the birth of Ishmael. 2: Because Sarai could have no children on her own, ancient custom allowed her to have a child through one of her women servants (30.3, 9). **6:** Sarai *dealt harshly* with the Egyptian slave-girl, Hagar. The same Hebrew verb meaning "to deal harshly, oppress" is used to describe the Egyptians' treatment of the Israelite slaves in Ex 1.11. Israel was capable of the same oppression it would experience at the hands of the Egyptians. **10:** *The angel of the LORD* gives a promise to Hagar that is virtually identical to the promise the LORD made to Abram (15.5). **11:** The name of Hagar's son will be *Ishmael,* which means "God hears." The LORD *has given heed to* or heard Hagar's cry for help. God responds to the cry of the oppressed, including non-

ᵃ That is *God hears*   ᵇ Perhaps *God of seeing* or *God who sees*   ᶜ Meaning of Heb uncertain   ᵈ That is *the Well of the Living One who sees me*   ᵉ Heb *Abram*

Israelites like Hagar. **12:** Ishmael will be the ancestor of a people known for their defiance and conflict. **13:** Hagar *named the LORD: "You are El-roi,"* which means "You are a God who sees." This is the only example in the Old Testament of a human being giving a name to God. In all other cases, God is the one who reveals the divine name to humans. **14:** Place names in Genesis often recall important stories or events. Here *Beer-lahai-roi* means "the well of the living one who sees me."

17 When Abram was ninety-nine years old, the LORD appeared to Abram, and said to him, "I am God Almighty;[a] walk before me, and be blameless. [2]And I will make my covenant between me and you, and will make you exceedingly numerous." [3]Then Abram fell on his face; and God said to him, [4]"As for me, this is my covenant with you: You shall be the ancestor of a multitude of nations. [5]No longer shall your name be Abram,[b] but your name shall be Abraham;[c] for I have made you the ancestor of a multitude of nations. [6]I will make you exceedingly fruitful; and I will make nations of you, and kings shall come from you. [7]I will establish my covenant between me and you, and your offspring after you throughout their generations, for an everlasting covenant, to be God to you and to your offspring[d] after you. [8]And I will give to you, and to your offspring after you, the land where you are now an alien, all the land of Canaan, for a perpetual holding; and I will be their God."

[9] God said to Abraham, "As for you, you shall keep my covenant, you and your offspring after you throughout their generations. [10]This is my covenant, which you shall keep, between me and you and your offspring after you: Every male among you shall be circumcised. [11]You shall circumcise the flesh of your foreskins, and it shall be a sign of the covenant between me and you. [12]Throughout your generations every male among you shall be circumcised when he is eight days old, including the slave born in your house and the one bought with your money from any foreigner who is not of your offspring. [13]Both the slave born in your house and the one bought with your money must be circumcised. So shall my covenant be in your flesh an everlasting covenant. [14]Any uncircumcised male who is not circumcised in the flesh of his foreskin shall be cut off from his people; he has broken my covenant."

[15] God said to Abraham, "As for Sarai your wife, you shall not call her Sarai, but Sarah shall be her name. [16]I will bless her, and moreover I will give you a son by her. I will bless her, and she shall give rise to nations; kings of peoples shall come from her." [17]Then Abraham fell on his face and laughed, and said to himself, "Can a child be born to a man who is a hundred years old? Can Sarah, who is ninety years old, bear a child?" [18]And Abraham said to God, "O that Ishmael might live in your sight!" [19]God said, "No, but your wife Sarah shall bear you a son, and you shall name him Isaac.[e] I will establish my covenant with him as an everlasting covenant for his offspring after him. [20]As for Ishmael, I have heard you; I will bless him and make him fruitful and exceedingly numerous; he shall be the father of twelve princes, and I will make him a great nation. [21]But my covenant I will establish with Isaac, whom Sarah shall bear to you at this season next year." [22]And when he had finished talking with him, God went up from Abraham.

[23] Then Abraham took his son Ishmael and all the slaves born in his house or bought with his money, every male among the men of Abraham's house, and he circumcised the flesh of their foreskins that very day, as God had said to him. [24]Abraham was ninety-nine years old when he was circumcised in the flesh of his foreskin. [25]And his son Ishmael was thirteen years old when he was circumcised in the flesh of his foreskin. [26]That very day Abraham and his son Ishmael were circumcised; [27]and all the men of his house, slaves born in the house and those bought with money from a foreigner, were circumcised with him.

17.1–27: Another covenant* promise to Abraham and Sarah. God provides another version of the cov-

a Traditional rendering of Heb *El Shaddai*   b That is *exalted ancestor*   c Here taken to mean *ancestor of a multitude*   d Heb *seed*   e That is *he laughs* enant promise, similar to the one made in Gen 15. For the first time, however, God clearly names both Abraham *and Sarah* as the parents of the promised child. The names of Abram and Sarai are changed to mark the importance of this new promise. God also introduces the ritual of circumcision★ as a physical sign of belonging to the covenant people of God. **1:** Abram is 99 years old, which makes his son Ishmael 13 years old (16.16). **5:** God changes the name *Abram* (meaning "exalted ancestor") to *Abraham* (meaning "ancestor of a multitude") as a further guarantee that God will keep the promise of many descendants. **7–8:** God introduces a new element of assurance involving time. The covenant is *everlasting,* and Abraham's family will possess the land of Canaan as a *perpetual holding.* God also promises a continuing relationship: *I will be their God.* **9–14:** The ritual of circumcision involves cutting off the foreskin of the male penis. The ritual was practiced by neighboring cultures around Israel as well as by Israel itself. It continues to be practiced by Jews and Muslims today. Circumcision is a physical sign for males that they are members of the covenant people of God. The story in Ex 4.24–26 apparently alludes to the rite of circumcision, although the story is somewhat unclear. **15–16:** God changes *Sarai's* name to *Sarah* to indicate that she is now clearly part of the promise. She will be the mother of the long expected child and of future kings. **17–22:** Abraham laughs at the thought that he and Sarah will have a child at their ages of 100 and 90 years old. Abraham pleads with God to keep Ishmael, who is now 13 years old, as the promised son rather than wait for yet another son (v. 18). But God insists that Sarah will have another son whose name will be *Isaac,* which means "he laughs." The theme of laughter and Isaac will come up again (18.12–15; 21.5–6). God also responds to Abraham's concern for Ishmael. God promises to *bless him,* make him *exceedingly numerous,* and *a great nation.* These are the same promises that Abraham originally received (12.1–3) and that now extend to Isaac as the child of promise.

18 The LORD appeared to Abraham[a] by the oaks[b] of Mamre, as he sat at the entrance of his tent in the heat of the day. [2]He looked up and saw three men standing near him. When he saw them, he ran from the tent entrance to meet them, and bowed down to the ground. [3]He said, "My lord, if I find favor with you, do not pass by your servant. [4]Let a little water be brought, and wash

your feet, and rest yourselves under the tree. [5]Let me bring a little bread, that you may refresh yourselves, and after that you may pass on—since you have come to your servant." So they said, "Do as you have said." [6]And Abraham hastened into the tent to Sarah, and said, "Make ready quickly three measures[c] of choice flour, knead it, and make cakes." [7]Abraham ran to the herd, and took a calf, tender and good, and gave it to the servant, who hastened to prepare it. [8]Then he took curds and milk and the calf that he had prepared, and set it before them; and he stood by them under the tree while they ate.

[9] They said to him, "Where is your wife Sarah?" And he said, "There, in the tent." [10]Then one said, "I will surely return to you in due season, and your wife Sarah shall have a son." And Sarah was listening at the tent entrance behind him. [11]Now Abraham and Sarah were old, advanced in age; it had ceased to be with Sarah after the manner of women. [12]So Sarah laughed to herself, saying, "After I have grown old, and my husband is old, shall I have pleasure?" [13]The LORD said to Abraham, "Why did Sarah laugh, and say, 'Shall I indeed bear a child, now that I am old?' [14]Is anything too wonderful for the LORD? At the set time I will return to you, in due season, and Sarah shall have a son." [15]But Sarah denied, saying, "I did not laugh"; for she was afraid. He said, "Oh yes, you did laugh."

18.1–15: The LORD visits Abraham and Sarah. This epiphany★ occurs at *the oaks of Mamre,* namely, "a tree shrine at Mamre," a holy place. The depiction of the deity is ambiguous. Is the LORD one among the *three men?* Or is the LORD symbolized by all three individuals? **4–5:** Abraham's description, *little water* and *little bread,* understates the lavish feast that Abraham and Sarah actually prepare for the guests (vv. 7–8). **9–15:** Sarah's laughter at the apparently impossible promise of a child appears to provoke the deity. *Laugh* ("tshq") puns on the name Isaac ("yitshaq").

[16] Then the men set out from there, and they looked toward Sodom; and Abraham

a Heb *him*   *b* Or *terebinths*   *c* Heb *seahs*

went with them to set them on their way.
¹⁷The LORD said, "Shall I hide from Abraham what I am about to do, ¹⁸seeing that Abraham shall become a great and mighty nation, and all the nations of the earth shall be blessed in him?ᵃ ¹⁹No, for I have chosenᵇ him, that he may charge his children and his household after him to keep the way of the LORD by doing righteousness and justice; so that the LORD may bring about for Abraham what he has promised him." ²⁰Then the LORD said, "How great is the outcry against Sodom and Gomorrah and how very grave their sin! ²¹I must go down and see whether they have done altogether according to the outcry that has come to me; and if not, I will know."

22 So the men turned from there, and went toward Sodom, while Abraham remained standing before the LORD.ᶜ ²³Then Abraham came near and said, "Will you indeed sweep away the righteous with the wicked? ²⁴Suppose there are fifty righteous within the city; will you then sweep away the place and not forgive it for the fifty righteous who are in it? ²⁵Far be it from you to do such a thing, to slay the righteous with the wicked, so that the righteous fare as the wicked! Far be that from you! Shall not the Judge of all the earth do what is just?" ²⁶And the LORD said, "If I find at Sodom fifty righteous in the city, I will forgive the whole place for their sake." ²⁷Abraham answered, "Let me take it upon myself to speak to the Lord, I who am but dust and ashes. ²⁸Suppose five of the fifty righteous are lacking? Will you destroy the whole city for lack of five?" And he said, "I will not destroy it if I find forty-five there." ²⁹Again he spoke to him, "Suppose forty are found there." He answered, "For the sake of forty I will not do it." ³⁰Then he said, "Oh do not let the Lord be angry if I speak. Suppose thirty are found there." He answered, "I will not do it, if I find thirty there." ³¹He said, "Let me take it upon myself to speak to the Lord. Suppose twenty are found there." He answered, "For the sake of twenty I will not destroy it." ³²Then he said, "Oh do not let the Lord be angry if I speak just once more. Suppose ten are found there." He answered, "For the sake of ten I will not destroy

it." ³³And the LORD went his way, when he had finished speaking to Abraham; and Abraham returned to his place.

18.16–33: Dialogue about Sodom. 16–21: After reflecting on the promises already made to Abraham, the LORD tells Abraham why he is concerned about Sodom. **22–33:** Abraham addresses the LORD six times, pleading for the fate of the *righteous* people in a sinful city. God clarifies the status of Sodom, should some righteous people be found in it. There is talk of forgiveness (v. 26) but, more frequently, simply the absence of destruction is indicated. Abraham may be negotiating on behalf of his nephew, Lot, who lives in Sodom.

19 The two angels came to Sodom in the evening, and Lot was sitting in the gateway of Sodom. When Lot saw them, he rose to meet them, and bowed down with his face to the ground. ²He said, "Please, my lords, turn aside to your servant's house and spend the night, and wash your feet; then you can rise early and go on your way." They said, "No; we will spend the night in the square." ³But he urged them strongly; so they turned aside to him and entered his house; and he made them a feast, and baked unleavened bread, and they ate. ⁴But before they lay down, the men of the city, the men of Sodom, both young and old, all the people to the last man, surrounded the house; ⁵and they called to Lot, "Where are the men who came to you tonight? Bring them out to us, so that we may know them." ⁶Lot went out of the door to the men, shut the door after him, ⁷and said, "I beg you, my brothers, do not act so wickedly. ⁸Look, I have two daughters who have not known a man; let me bring them out to you, and do to them as you please; only do nothing to these men, for they have come under the shelter of my roof." ⁹But they replied, "Stand back!" And they said, "This fellow came here as an alien, and he would play the judge! Now we will deal worse with you than with them." Then they pressed hard against the man Lot, and came near the door to break it down. ¹⁰But

a Or and all the nations of the earth shall bless themselves by him   b Heb known   c Another ancient tradition reads while the LORD remained standing before Abraham the men inside reached out their hands and brought Lot into the house with them, and shut the door. ¹¹And they struck with blindness the men who were at the door of the house, both small and great, so that they were unable to find the door.

19.1–11: The wickedness of Sodom. The generous hospitality that the visitors received from Abraham and Sarah in 18.1–15 contrasts sharply with the incredible lack of hospitality shown by the inhabitants of Sodom. **1:** *Two angels* come to Sodom. The angels are divine messengers who look like ordinary human beings. They are apparently two of the same "men" who visited Abraham and Sarah (18.22). **5:** The men of Sodom desire to *know* the visitors sexually. They threaten homosexual rape.

12 Then the men said to Lot, "Have you anyone else here? Sons-in-law, sons, daughters, or anyone you have in the city—bring them out of the place. ¹³For we are about to destroy this place, because the outcry against its people has become great before the LORD, and the LORD has sent us to destroy it." ¹⁴So Lot went out and said to his sons-in-law, who were to marry his daughters, "Up, get out of this place; for the LORD is about to destroy the city." But he seemed to his sons-in-law to be jesting.

15 When morning dawned, the angels urged Lot, saying, "Get up, take your wife and your two daughters who are here, or else you will be consumed in the punishment of the city." ¹⁶But he lingered; so the men seized him and his wife and his two daughters by the hand, the LORD being merciful to him, and they brought him out and left him outside the city. ¹⁷When they had brought them outside, theyᵃ said, "Flee for your life; do not look back or stop anywhere in the Plain; flee to the hills, or else you will be consumed." ¹⁸And Lot said to them, "Oh, no, my lords; ¹⁹your servant has found favor with you, and you have shown me great kindness in saving my life; but I cannot flee to the hills, for fear the disaster will overtake me and I die. ²⁰Look, that city is near enough to flee to, and it is a little one. Let me escape there—is it not a little one?—and my life will be saved!" ²¹He said to him,

"Very well, I grant you this favor too, and will not overthrow the city of which you have spoken. ²²Hurry, escape there, for I can do nothing until you arrive there." Therefore the city was called Zoar.ᵇ ²³The sun had risen on the earth when Lot came to Zoar.

24 Then the LORD rained on Sodom and Gomorrah sulfur and fire from the LORD out of heaven; ²⁵and he overthrew those cities, and all the Plain, and all the inhabitants of the cities, and what grew on the ground. ²⁶But Lot's wife, behind him, looked back, and she became a pillar of salt.

27 Abraham went early in the morning to the place where he had stood before the LORD; ²⁸and he looked down toward Sodom and Gomorrah and toward all the land of the Plain and saw the smoke of the land going up like the smoke of a furnace.

29 So it was that, when God destroyed the cities of the Plain, God remembered Abraham, and sent Lot out of the midst of the overthrow, when he overthrew the cities in which Lot had settled.

19.12–29: The LORD destroys Sodom and Gomorrah. 24: This area southeast of the Dead Sea is an arid desert region with extensive sulfur and other mineral deposits. This story explains why the area is no longer the green "garden of the LORD" that Lot first saw (13.10). **26:** This comment probably explained a certain salt formation in the area. **29:** Abraham again plays a role in saving his nephew Lot and Lot's two daughters. Abraham continues to be a blessing to other families of the earth (12.3).

30 Now Lot went up out of Zoar and settled in the hills with his two daughters, for he was afraid to stay in Zoar; so he lived in a cave with his two daughters. ³¹And the firstborn said to the younger, "Our father is old, and there is not a man on earth to come in to us after the manner of all the world. ³²Come, let us make our father drink wine, and we will lie with him, so that we may preserve offspring through our father." ³³So they made their father drink wine that night; and the firstborn went in, and lay with her father; he did not know when she lay down

a Gk Syr Vg: Heb *he*   *b* That is *Little*

or when she rose. 34On the next day, the firstborn said to the younger, "Look, I lay last night with my father; let us make him drink wine tonight also; then you go in and lie with him, so that we may preserve offspring through our father." 35So they made their father drink wine that night also; and the younger rose, and lay with him; and he did not know when she lay down or when she rose. 36Thus both the daughters of Lot became pregnant by their father. 37The firstborn bore a son, and named him Moab; he is the ancestor of the Moabites to this day. 38The younger also bore a son and named him Ben-ammi; he is the ancestor of the Ammonites to this day.

19.30–38: Lot becomes the ancestor of Moab and Ammon. The unflattering story of drunkenness and incest explains the origins of two nations that border Canaan on the east, Moab and Ammon. **31–32:** *Come in to us* and *lie with him* describe sexual intercourse.

20 From there Abraham journeyed toward the region of the Negeb, and settled between Kadesh and Shur. While residing in Gerar as an alien, 2Abraham said of his wife Sarah, "She is my sister." And King Abimelech of Gerar sent and took Sarah. 3But God came to Abimelech in a dream by night, and said to him, "You are about to die because of the woman whom you have taken; for she is a married woman." 4Now Abimelech had not approached her; so he said, "Lord, will you destroy an innocent people? 5Did he not himself say to me, 'She is my sister'? And she herself said, 'He is my brother.' I did this in the integrity of my heart and the innocence of my hands." 6Then God said to him in the dream, "Yes, I know that you did this in the integrity of your heart; furthermore it was I who kept you from sinning against me. Therefore I did not let you touch her. 7Now then, return the man's wife; for he is a prophet, and he will pray for you and you shall live. But if you do not restore her, know that you shall surely die, you and all that are yours."

8 So Abimelech rose early in the morning, and called all his servants and told them all these things; and the men were very much afraid. 9Then Abimelech called Abraham, and said to him, "What have you done to us? How have I sinned against you, that you have brought such great guilt on me and my kingdom? You have done things to me that ought not to be done." 10And Abimelech said to Abraham, "What were you thinking of, that you did this thing?" 11Abraham said, "I did it because I thought, There is no fear of God at all in this place, and they will kill me because of my wife. 12Besides, she is indeed my sister, the daughter of my father but not the daughter of my mother; and she became my wife. 13And when God caused me to wander from my father's house, I said to her, 'This is the kindness you must do me: at every place to which we come, say of me, He is my brother.' " 14Then Abimelech took sheep and oxen, and male and female slaves, and gave them to Abraham, and restored his wife Sarah to him. 15Abimelech said, "My land is before you; settle where it pleases you." 16To Sarah he said, "Look, I have given your brother a thousand pieces of silver; it is your exoneration before all who are with you; you are completely vindicated." 17Then Abraham prayed to God; and God healed Abimelech, and also healed his wife and female slaves so that they bore children. 18For the LORD had closed fast all the wombs of the house of Abimelech because of Sarah, Abraham's wife.

20.1–18: Abraham again pretends Sarah is his sister and not his wife. Abraham had earlier lied about Sarah's being his wife in 12.10–20. It was not at that point clear that Sarah was supposed to be the mother of the child promised to Abraham. However, now Sarah will be the mother of the child (18.10). Thus, Abraham's willingness to endanger his wife Sarah and the promise of God in this case is a much more serious matter. In this story, Abraham appears much less righteous than his hosts. **3–7:** The narrator wants to make clear that there is absolutely no possibility that the child born to Sarah in the next chapter (ch. 21) is King Abimelech's child rather than Abraham's child. *He is a prophet:** the only time Abraham is called a prophet (v. 7). **11:** Abraham's concern that Abimelech and the people of Gerar would have *no fear of God* is directly contradicted by 20.8. **12:** Abraham tries, weakly, to justify his lie by indicating that technically Sarah is his half-sister. Later biblical laws prohibited such marriages (Lev 18.9–11). **16:** The payment of money is an *exoneration* designed to compensate Sarah's family for any injury to her family's honor.

21 The LORD dealt with Sarah as he had said, and the LORD did for Sarah as he had promised. [2] Sarah conceived and bore Abraham a son in his old age, at the time of which God had spoken to him. [3] Abraham gave the name Isaac to his son whom Sarah bore him. [4] And Abraham circumcised his son Isaac when he was eight days old, as God had commanded him. [5] Abraham was a hundred years old when his son Isaac was born to him. [6] Now Sarah said, "God has brought laughter for me; everyone who hears will laugh with me." [7] And she said, "Who would ever have said to Abraham that Sarah would nurse children? Yet I have borne him a son in his old age."

21.1–7: The birth of Isaac. At long last, the LORD begins to fulfill the promises of a great nation and many descendants (12.2; 15.5) through the birth of Isaac. **4:** Circumcision* is the ritual cutting off of the foreskin of the male penis. It is a physical sign of a male's belonging to God's covenant* people (17.9–14). **6:** The words *laughter* and *laugh* ("tshq'") are puns on the child's name Isaac ("yitshaq'") in v. 4.

8 The child grew, and was weaned; and Abraham made a great feast on the day that Isaac was weaned. [9] But Sarah saw the son of Hagar the Egyptian, whom she had borne to Abraham, playing with her son Isaac.[a] [10] So she said to Abraham, "Cast out this slave woman with her son; for the son of this slave woman shall not inherit along with my son Isaac." [11] The matter was very distressing to Abraham on account of his son. [12] But God said to Abraham, "Do not be distressed because of the boy and because of your slave woman; whatever Sarah says to you, do as she tells you, for it is through Isaac that offspring shall be named for you. [13] As for the son of the slave woman, I will make a nation of him also, because he is your offspring." [14] So Abraham rose early in the morning, and took bread and a skin of water, and gave it to Hagar, putting it on her shoulder, along with the child, and sent her away. And she departed, and wandered about in the wilderness of Beer-sheba.

[15] When the water in the skin was gone, she cast the child under one of the bushes. [16] Then she went and sat down opposite him a good way off, about the distance of a bowshot; for she said, "Do not let me look on the death of the child." And as she sat opposite him, she lifted up her voice and wept. [17] And God heard the voice of the boy; and the angel of God called to Hagar from heaven, and said to her, "What troubles you, Hagar? Do not be afraid; for God has heard the voice of the boy where he is. [18] Come, lift up the boy and hold him fast with your hand, for I will make a great nation of him." [19] Then God opened her eyes and she saw a well of water. She went, and filled the skin with water, and gave the boy a drink.

20 God was with the boy, and he grew up; he lived in the wilderness, and became an expert with the bow. [21] He lived in the wilderness of Paran; and his mother got a wife for him from the land of Egypt.

21.8–21: Abraham and Sarah send Hagar and Ishmael away. This episode contains elements similar to the earlier story of Hagar and Ishmael in 16.1–16: conflict between Sarah and Hagar, journey into the desert, encounter with a divine angel, a well of water, promises concerning Ishmael, and a play on the word "hear" related to the name Ishmael. A key difference this time is that Hagar is forcibly expelled by Sarah, whereas before Hagar had left voluntarily. **10–13:** Sarah's demand to send Hagar and Ishmael away is *very distressing* to Abraham because it will mean giving up his son Ishmael. But God commands Abraham to send Ishmael away, and Abraham obeys. In 22.2, God will similarly command Abraham to give up his only remaining son Isaac. **16:** Hagar's words *Do not let me look* reflect the theme of seeing and not seeing in the story (21.9, 16, 19). **17:** That God *heard* and *has heard* ("shm'") is a pun on the child's name, Ishmael, which means "God hears."

22 At that time Abimelech, with Phicol the commander of his army, said to Abraham, "God is with you in all that you do;

a Gk Vg: Heb lacks *with her son Isaac*

23now therefore swear to me here by God that you will not deal falsely with me or with my offspring or with my posterity, but as I have dealt loyally with you, you will deal with me and with the land where you have resided as an alien." 24And Abraham said, "I swear it."

25 When Abraham complained to Abimelech about a well of water that Abimelech's servants had seized, 26Abimelech said, "I do not know who has done this; you did not tell me, and I have not heard of it until today." 27So Abraham took sheep and oxen and gave them to Abimelech, and the two men made a covenant. 28Abraham set apart seven ewe lambs of the flock. 29And Abimelech said to Abraham, "What is the meaning of these seven ewe lambs that you have set apart?" 30He said, "These seven ewe lambs you shall accept from my hand, in order that you may be a witness for me that I dug this well." 31Therefore that place was called Beer-sheba;a because there both of them swore an oath. 32When they had made a covenant at Beer-sheba, Abimelech, with Phicol the commander of his army, left and returned to the land of the Philistines. 33Abrahamb planted a tamarisk tree in Beer-sheba, and called there on the name of the LORD, the Everlasting God.c 34And Abraham resided as an alien many days in the land of the Philistines.

21.22–34: Abraham reconciles with Abimelech. The Canaanite king *Abimelech,* who Abraham had earlier thought had no "fear of God" (20.11), shows a remarkable reverence toward Abraham's God and a willingness to reconcile a human conflict with Abraham. **31:** *Beer-sheba* can mean either "well of the oath" (referring to the loyalty oath between Abraham and Abimelech in vv. 22–24) or "well of seven" (referring to the *seven ewe lambs* Abraham gave to Abimelech in return for acknowledging that the well belonged to Abraham in vv. 28–30). **33:** The planting of the *tamarisk tree* establishes the site as a holy place of worship. *Everlasting God* ("El Olam") may have been the name of an earlier deity worshipped at the site that the story now appropriates as an additional title for the LORD.

~~~~~~

22 After these things God tested Abraham. He said to him, "Abraham!"

And he said, "Here I am." 2He said, "Take your son, your only son Isaac, whom you love, and go to the land of Moriah, and offer him there as a burnt offering on one of the mountains that I shall show you." 3So Abraham rose early in the morning, saddled his donkey, and took two of his young men with him, and his son Isaac; he cut the wood for the burnt offering, and set out and went to the place in the distance that God had shown him. 4On the third day Abraham looked up and saw the place far away. 5Then Abraham said to his young men, "Stay here with the donkey; the boy and I will go over there; we will worship, and then we will come back to you." 6Abraham took the wood of the burnt offering and laid it on his son Isaac, and he himself carried the fire and the knife. So the two of them walked on together. 7Isaac said to his father Abraham, "Father!" And he said, "Here I am, my son." He said, "The fire and the wood are here, but where is the lamb for a burnt offering?" 8Abraham said, "God himself will provide the lamb for a burnt offering, my son." So the two of them walked on together.

9 When they came to the place that God had shown him, Abraham built an altar there and laid the wood in order. He bound his son Isaac, and laid him on the altar, on top of the wood. 10Then Abraham reached out his hand and took the knife to killd his son. 11But the angel of the LORD called to him from heaven, and said, "Abraham, Abraham!" And he said, "Here I am." 12He said, "Do not lay your hand on the boy or do anything to him; for now I know that you fear God, since you have not withheld your son, your only son, from me." 13And Abraham looked up and saw a ram, caught in a thicket by its horns. Abraham went and took the ram and offered it up as a burnt offering instead of his son. 14So Abraham called that place "The LORD will provide";e as it is said to this day, "On the mount of the LORD it shall be provided."f

a That is *Well of seven* or *Well of the oath*   b Heb *He*
c Or *the LORD, El Olam*   d Or *to slaughter*
e Or *will see*; Heb traditionally transliterated *Jehovah Jireh*   f Or *he shall be seen*

15 The angel of the LORD called to Abraham a second time from heaven, 16and said, "By myself I have sworn, says the LORD: Because you have done this, and have not withheld your son, your only son, 17I will indeed bless you, and I will make your offspring as numerous as the stars of heaven and as the sand that is on the seashore. And your offspring shall possess the gate of their enemies, 18and by your offspring shall all the nations of the earth gain blessing for themselves, because you have obeyed my voice." 19So Abraham returned to his young men, and they arose and went together to Beer-sheba; and Abraham lived at Beer-sheba.

20 Now after these things it was told Abraham, "Milcah also has borne children, to your brother Nahor: 21Uz the firstborn, Buz his brother, Kemuel the father of Aram, 22Chesed, Hazo, Pildash, Jidlaph, and Bethuel." 23Bethuel became the father of Rebekah. These eight Milcah bore to Nahor, Abraham's brother. 24Moreover, his concubine, whose name was Reumah, bore Tebah, Gaham, Tahash, and Maacah.

22.1–24: God commands Abraham to sacrifice Isaac. God puts Abraham through a remarkable test of his obedience and trust in God. God commands Abraham to sacrifice his only remaining son, an act that seems to deny everything God had promised concerning a great nation and many descendants (12.2; 15.5). **2:** The location of Mount Moriah is not known. A later tradition identified Moriah with the mountain on which the Temple* in the city of Jerusalem stood (2 Chr 3.1). **14:** The phrase the LORD will provide plays on the verb "to see" and may be translated "the LORD will see to it" or "the LORD will be seen." **15–18:** God reaffirms the earlier promises of many descendants because of Abraham's extraordinary obedience and trust in God. **20–24:** The list of children born to Abraham's extended family includes Rebekah (v. 23), who will eventually become the wife of his son Isaac (24.1–67).

23 Sarah lived one hundred twenty-seven years; this was the length of Sarah's life. 2And Sarah died at Kiriath-arba (that is, Hebron) in the land of Canaan; and Abraham went in to mourn for Sarah and to weep for her. 3Abraham rose up from beside his dead, and said to the Hittites, 4"I am a stranger and an alien residing among you; give me property among you for a burying place, so that I may bury my dead out of my sight." 5The Hittites answered Abraham, 6"Hear us, my lord; you are a mighty prince among us. Bury your dead in the choicest of our burial places; none of us will withhold from you any burial ground for burying your dead." 7Abraham rose and bowed to the Hittites, the people of the land. 8He said to them, "If you are willing that I should bury my dead out of my sight, hear me, and entreat for me Ephron son of Zohar, 9so that he may give me the cave of Machpelah, which he owns; it is at the end of his field. For the full price let him give it to me in your presence as a possession for a burying place." 10Now Ephron was sitting among the Hittites; and Ephron the Hittite answered Abraham in the hearing of the Hittites, of all who went in at the gate of his city, 11"No, my lord, hear me; I give you the field, and I give you the cave that is in it; in the presence of my people I give it to you; bury your dead." 12Then Abraham bowed down before the people of the land. 13He said to Ephron in the hearing of the people of the land, "If you only will listen to me! I will give the price of the field; accept it from me, so that I may bury my dead there." 14Ephron answered Abraham, 15"My lord, listen to me; a piece of land worth four hundred shekels of silver—what is that between you and me? Bury your dead." 16Abraham agreed with Ephron; and Abraham weighed out for Ephron the silver that he had named in the hearing of the Hittites, four hundred shekels of silver, according to the weights current among the merchants.

17 So the field of Ephron in Machpelah, which was to the east of Mamre, the field with the cave that was in it and all the trees that were in the field, throughout its whole area, passed 18to Abraham as a possession in the presence of the Hittites, in the presence of all who went in at the gate of his city. 19After this, Abraham buried Sarah his wife in the cave of the field of Machpelah facing Mamre (that is, Hebron) in the land of Canaan. 20The field and the cave that is in it

passed from the Hittites into Abraham's possession as a burying place.

23.1–20: Abraham buys a piece of the promised land. Sarah dies and Abraham buys a cave and field in Canaan as a burial place for her. In the indirect style of Near Eastern bargaining, the Hittites' extravagant offers of generosity (vv. 6, 11, 15) mean that the price Abraham will have to pay for the land will be very high. But, in the end, Abraham does hold title to at least a small piece of the land God had promised (15.18–21). **15:** *Four hundred shekels** of silver is a very high price for the field. The prophet* Jeremiah bought a field for only seventeen shekels (Jer 32.9). **19:** The land becomes the burial place for Sarah. It will also be the burial place for Abraham (25.8–10), Isaac, Rebekah, Jacob, and Leah (49.29–31).

24 Now Abraham was old, well advanced in years; and the LORD had blessed Abraham in all things. 2Abraham said to his servant, the oldest of his house, who had charge of all that he had, "Put your hand under my thigh 3and I will make you swear by the LORD, the God of heaven and earth, that you will not get a wife for my son from the daughters of the Canaanites, among whom I live, 4but will go to my country and to my kindred and get a wife for my son Isaac." 5The servant said to him, "Perhaps the woman may not be willing to follow me to this land; must I then take your son back to the land from which you came?" 6Abraham said to him, "See to it that you do not take my son back there. 7The LORD, the God of heaven, who took me from my father's house and from the land of my birth, and who spoke to me and swore to me, 'To your offspring I will give this land,' he will send his angel before you, and you shall take a wife for my son from there. 8But if the woman is not willing to follow you, then you will be free from this oath of mine; only you must not take my son back there." 9So the servant put his hand under the thigh of Abraham his master and swore to him concerning this matter.

10 Then the servant took ten of his master's camels and departed, taking all kinds of choice gifts from his master; and he set out and went to Aram-naharaim, to the city of Nahor. 11He made the camels kneel down outside the city by the well of water; it was toward evening, the time when women go out to draw water. 12And he said, "O LORD, God of my master Abraham, please grant me success today and show steadfast love to my master Abraham. 13I am standing here by the spring of water, and the daughters of the townspeople are coming out to draw water. 14Let the girl to whom I shall say, 'Please offer your jar that I may drink,' and who shall say, 'Drink, and I will water your camels'— let her be the one whom you have appointed for your servant Isaac. By this I shall know that you have shown steadfast love to my master."

15 Before he had finished speaking, there was Rebekah, who was born to Bethuel son of Milcah, the wife of Nahor, Abraham's brother, coming out with her water jar on her shoulder. 16The girl was very fair to look upon, a virgin, whom no man had known. She went down to the spring, filled her jar, and came up. 17Then the servant ran to meet her and said, "Please let me sip a little water from your jar." 18"Drink, my lord," she said, and quickly lowered her jar upon her hand and gave him a drink. 19When she had finished giving him a drink, she said, "I will draw for your camels also, until they have finished drinking." 20So she quickly emptied her jar into the trough and ran again to the well to draw, and she drew for all his camels. 21The man gazed at her in silence to learn whether or not the LORD had made his journey successful.

22 When the camels had finished drinking, the man took a gold nose-ring weighing a half shekel, and two bracelets for her arms weighing ten gold shekels, 23and said, "Tell me whose daughter you are. Is there room in your father's house for us to spend the night?" 24She said to him, "I am the daughter of Bethuel son of Milcah, whom she bore to Nahor." 25She added, "We have plenty of straw and fodder and a place to spend the night." 26The man bowed his head and worshiped the LORD 27and said, "Blessed be the LORD, the God of my master Abraham, who has not forsaken his steadfast love and his faithfulness toward my master. As for me,

the LORD has led me on the way to the house of my master's kin.'"

28 Then the girl ran and told her mother's household about these things. [29]Rebekah had a brother whose name was Laban; and Laban ran out to the man, to the spring. [30]As soon as he had seen the nose-ring, and the bracelets on his sister's arms, and when he heard the words of his sister Rebekah, "Thus the man spoke to me," he went to the man; and there he was, standing by the camels at the spring. [31]He said, "Come in, O blessed of the LORD. Why do you stand outside when I have prepared the house and a place for the camels?" [32]So the man came into the house; and Laban unloaded the camels, and gave him straw and fodder for the camels, and water to wash his feet and the feet of the men who were with him. [33]Then food was set before him to eat; but he said, "I will not eat until I have told my errand." He said, "Speak on."

34 So he said, "I am Abraham's servant. [35]The LORD has greatly blessed my master, and he has become wealthy; he has given him flocks and herds, silver and gold, male and female slaves, camels and donkeys. [36]And Sarah my master's wife bore a son to my master when she was old; and he has given him all that he has. [37]My master made me swear, saying, 'You shall not take a wife for my son from the daughters of the Canaanites, in whose land I live; [38]but you shall go to my father's house, to my kindred, and get a wife for my son.' [39]I said to my master, 'Perhaps the woman will not follow me.' [40]But he said to me, 'The LORD, before whom I walk, will send his angel with you and make your way successful. You shall get a wife for my son from my kindred, from my father's house. [41]Then you will be free from my oath, when you come to my kindred; even if they will not give her to you, you will be free from my oath.'

42 "I came today to the spring, and said, 'O LORD, the God of my master Abraham, if now you will only make successful the way I am going! [43]I am standing here by the spring of water; let the young woman who comes out to draw, to whom I shall say, "Please give me a little water from your jar to drink," [44]and who will say to me, "Drink, and I will draw for your camels also"—let her be the woman whom the LORD has appointed for my master's son.'

45 "Before I had finished speaking in my heart, there was Rebekah coming out with her water jar on her shoulder; and she went down to the spring, and drew. I said to her, 'Please let me drink.' [46]She quickly let down her jar from her shoulder, and said, 'Drink, and I will also water your camels.' So I drank, and she also watered the camels. [47]Then I asked her, 'Whose daughter are you?' She said, 'The daughter of Bethuel, Nahor's son, whom Milcah bore to him.' So I put the ring on her nose, and the bracelets on her arms. [48]Then I bowed my head and worshiped the LORD, and blessed the LORD, the God of my master Abraham, who had led me by the right way to obtain the daughter of my master's kinsman for his son. [49]Now then, if you will deal loyally and truly with my master, tell me; and if not, tell me, so that I may turn either to the right hand or to the left."

50 Then Laban and Bethuel answered, "The thing comes from the LORD; we cannot speak to you anything bad or good. [51]Look, Rebekah is before you, take her and go, and let her be the wife of your master's son, as the LORD has spoken."

52 When Abraham's servant heard their words, he bowed himself to the ground before the LORD. [53]And the servant brought out jewelry of silver and of gold, and garments, and gave them to Rebekah; he also gave to her brother and to her mother costly ornaments. [54]Then he and the men who were with him ate and drank, and they spent the night there. When they rose in the morning, he said, "Send me back to my master." [55]Her brother and her mother said, "Let the girl remain with us a while, at least ten days; after that she may go." [56]But he said to them, "Do not delay me, since the LORD has made my journey successful; let me go that I may go to my master." [57]They said, "We will call the girl, and ask her." [58]And they called Rebekah, and said to her, "Will you go with this man?" She said, "I will." [59]So they sent away their sister Rebekah and her nurse

along with Abraham's servant and his men. 60And they blessed Rebekah and said to her,

"May you, our sister, become
thousands of myriads;
may your offspring gain possession
of the gates of their foes."

61Then Rebekah and her maids rose up, mounted the camels, and followed the man; thus the servant took Rebekah, and went his way.

62 Now Isaac had come from*a* Beer-lahai-roi, and was settled in the Negeb. 63Isaac went out in the evening to walk*b* in the field; and looking up, he saw camels coming. 64And Rebekah looked up, and when she saw Isaac, she slipped quickly from the camel, 65and said to the servant, "Who is the man over there, walking in the field to meet us?" The servant said, "It is my master." So she took her veil and covered herself. 66And the servant told Isaac all the things that he had done. 67Then Isaac brought her into his mother Sarah's tent. He took Rebekah, and she became his wife; and he loved her. So Isaac was comforted after his mother's death.

24.1–67: Isaac secures a wife, Rebekah. 2: Abraham's command to the servant to *put your hand under my thigh,* near his reproductive organs, was a customary way of taking an intimate and solemn oath. **10:** *Aram-naharaim* and *Nahor* are part of Abraham's original home territory in Mesopotamia where he and his family lived before migrating to Canaan (11.31). Most of his extended family apparently remained there. **12–14:** The servant asks the LORD to guide the selection process for Isaac's wife. Rebekah fulfills the conditions perfectly (vv. 15–21). **62:** Isaac comes from *Beer-lahai-roi,* the place where the LORD had guided and comforted Hagar (16.14).

25 Abraham took another wife, whose name was Keturah. 2She bore him Zimran, Jokshan, Medan, Midian, Ishbak, and Shuah. 3Jokshan was the father of Sheba and Dedan. The sons of Dedan were Asshurim, Letushim, and Leummim. 4The sons of Midian were Ephah, Epher, Hanoch, Abida, and Eldaah. All these were the children of Keturah. 5Abraham gave all he had to Isaac. 6But to the sons of his concubines Abraham gave gifts, while he was still living, and he sent them away from his son Isaac, eastward to the east country.

7 This is the length of Abraham's life, one hundred seventy-five years. 8Abraham breathed his last and died in a good old age, an old man and full of years, and was gathered to his people. 9His sons Isaac and Ishmael buried him in the cave of Machpelah, in the field of Ephron son of Zohar the Hittite, east of Mamre, 10the field that Abraham purchased from the Hittites. There Abraham was buried, with his wife Sarah. 11After the death of Abraham God blessed his son Isaac. And Isaac settled at Beer-lahai-roi.

12 These are the descendants of Ishmael, Abraham's son, whom Hagar the Egyptian, Sarah's slave-girl, bore to Abraham. 13These are the names of the sons of Ishmael, named in the order of their birth: Nebaioth, the firstborn of Ishmael; and Kedar, Adbeel, Mibsam, 14Mishma, Dumah, Massa, 15Hadad, Tema, Jetur, Naphish, and Kedemah. 16These are the sons of Ishmael and these are their names, by their villages and by their encampments, twelve princes according to their tribes. 17(This is the length of the life of Ishmael, one hundred thirty-seven years; he breathed his last and died, and was gathered to his people.) 18They settled from Havilah to Shur, which is opposite Egypt in the direction of Assyria; he settled down*c* alongside of*d* all his people.

25.1–18: Abraham's death and the family he leaves behind. 1–6: Abraham takes another wife, Keturah. She is a *concubine** (v. 6), a woman servant with whom he has additional children. However, Isaac remains the favored son (v. 5). The *sons of Midian* are associated with nomadic tribes called Midianites who live *eastward* from Canaan (vv. 4, 6). **10:** The story of the field *purchased from the Hittites* is told in 23.1–20. **16:** Ishmael's descendants form twelve tribes, a grouping similar to the twelve tribes of Israel. They dwell in Arabia (v. 18).

19 These are the descendants of Isaac, Abraham's son: Abraham was the father of

a Syr Tg: Heb *from coming to*   *b* Meaning of Heb word is uncertain   *c* Heb *he fell*   *d* Or *down in opposition to*

Isaac, ²⁰and Isaac was forty years old when he married Rebekah, daughter of Bethuel the Aramean of Paddan-aram, sister of Laban the Aramean. ²¹Isaac prayed to the LORD for his wife, because she was barren; and the LORD granted his prayer, and his wife Rebekah conceived. ²²The children struggled together within her; and she said, "If it is to be this way, why do I live?"ᵃ So she went to inquire of the LORD. ²³And the LORD said to her,

"Two nations are in your womb,
    and two peoples born of you shall be
        divided;
    the one shall be stronger than the other,
        the elder shall serve the younger."

²⁴When her time to give birth was at hand, there were twins in her womb. ²⁵The first came out red, all his body like a hairy mantle; so they named him Esau. ²⁶Afterward his brother came out, with his hand gripping Esau's heel; so he was named Jacob.ᵇ Isaac was sixty years old when she bore them.

27 When the boys grew up, Esau was a skillful hunter, a man of the field, while Jacob was a quiet man, living in tents. ²⁸Isaac loved Esau, because he was fond of game; but Rebekah loved Jacob.

29 Once when Jacob was cooking a stew, Esau came in from the field, and he was famished. ³⁰Esau said to Jacob, "Let me eat some of that red stuff, for I am famished!" (Therefore he was called Edom.ᶜ) ³¹Jacob said, "First sell me your birthright." ³²Esau said, "I am about to die; of what use is a birthright to me?" ³³Jacob said, "Swear to me first."ᵈ So he swore to him, and sold his birthright to Jacob. ³⁴Then Jacob gave Esau bread and lentil stew, and he ate and drank, and rose and went his way. Thus Esau despised his birthright.

25.19–34: The birth and rivalry of Jacob and Esau. 23: The twin boys in Rebekah's womb represent the *two nations* of Israel (Jacob; 32.28) and Edom (Esau; 36.1). Esau is the elder son. Thus, according to the LORD's prediction, the nation of Edom will be less powerful and serve Israel. 25: The first baby born is *Esau*, whose body is *red* (Hebrew "admoni"). This is a wordplay on the name "Edom" (v. 30). 26: The name *Jacob* may have two meanings, both of which describe Ja-

cob's character throughout his life. The name may mean "he takes by the heel" in line with Jacob's tendency to take advantage of others for his own self-interest. The other meaning is "he supplants"; Jacob the younger brother will supplant or take over the privileged position of his elder brother Esau by stealing his birthright and blessing. 30: A famished Esau asks for Jacob's stew, *that red stuff* ("adom"), a pun on Esau's other name, *Edom*.

26 Now there was a famine in the land, besides the former famine that had occurred in the days of Abraham. And Isaac went to Gerar, to King Abimelech of the Philistines. ²The LORD appeared to Isaacᵉ and said, "Do not go down to Egypt; settle in the land that I shall show you. ³Reside in this land as an alien, and I will be with you, and will bless you; for to you and to your descendants I will give all these lands, and I will fulfill the oath that I swore to your father Abraham. ⁴I will make your offspring as numerous as the stars of heaven, and will give to your offspring all these lands; and all the nations of the earth shall gain blessing for themselves through your offspring, ⁵because Abraham obeyed my voice and kept my charge, my commandments, my statutes, and my laws."

6 So Isaac settled in Gerar. ⁷When the men of the place asked him about his wife, he said, "She is my sister"; for he was afraid to say, "My wife," thinking, "or else the men of the place might kill me for the sake of Rebekah, because she is attractive in appearance." ⁸When Isaac had been there a long time, King Abimelech of the Philistines looked out of a window and saw him fondling his wife Rebekah. ⁹So Abimelech called for Isaac, and said, "So she is your wife! Why then did you say, 'She is my sister'?" Isaac said to him, "Because I thought I might die because of her." ¹⁰Abimelech said, "What is this you have done to us? One of the people might easily have lain with your wife, and you would have brought guilt upon us." ¹¹So Abimelech warned all the people, saying,

a Syr: Meaning of Heb uncertain   b That is *He takes by the heel* or *He supplants*   c That is *Red*
d Heb *today*   e Heb *him*

"Whoever touches this man or his wife shall be put to death."

12 Isaac sowed seed in that land, and in the same year reaped a hundredfold. The LORD blessed him, 13and the man became rich; he prospered more and more until he became very wealthy. 14He had possessions of flocks and herds, and a great household, so that the Philistines envied him. 15(Now the Philistines had stopped up and filled with earth all the wells that his father's servants had dug in the days of his father Abraham.) 16And Abimelech said to Isaac, "Go away from us; you have become too powerful for us."

17 So Isaac departed from there and camped in the valley of Gerar and settled there. 18Isaac dug again the wells of water that had been dug in the days of his father Abraham; for the Philistines had stopped them up after the death of Abraham; and he gave them the names that his father had given them. 19But when Isaac's servants dug in the valley and found there a well of spring water, 20the herders of Gerar quarreled with Isaac's herders, saying, "The water is ours." So he called the well Esek,ᵃ because they contended with him. 21Then they dug another well, and they quarreled over that one also; so he called it Sitnah.ᵇ 22He moved from there and dug another well, and they did not quarrel over it; so he called it Rehoboth,ᶜ saying, "Now the LORD has made room for us, and we shall be fruitful in the land."

23 From there he went up to Beer-sheba. 24And that very night the LORD appeared to him and said, "I am the God of your father Abraham; do not be afraid, for I am with you and will bless you and make your offspring numerous for my servant Abraham's sake." 25So he built an altar there, called on the name of the LORD, and pitched his tent there. And there Isaac's servants dug a well.

26 Then Abimelech went to him from Gerar, with Ahuzzath his adviser and Phicol the commander of his army. 27Isaac said to them, "Why have you come to me, seeing that you hate me and have sent me away from you?" 28They said, "We see plainly that the LORD has been with you; so we say, let there be an oath between you and us, and let us make a covenant with you 29so that you will do us no harm, just as we have not touched you and have done to you nothing but good and have sent you away in peace. You are now the blessed of the LORD." 30So he made them a feast, and they ate and drank. 31In the morning they rose early and exchanged oaths; and Isaac set them on their way, and they departed from him in peace. 32That same day Isaac's servants came and told him about the well that they had dug, and said to him, "We have found water!" 33He called it Shibah;ᵈ therefore the name of the city is Beer-shebaᵉ to this day.

26.1–33: Stories about Isaac and Abimelech. Several incidents in Isaac's life repeat similar events in the life of his father Abraham. Examples include divine promises of land and descendants (12.1–3; 26.1–5, 24), the building of altars (12.7–8; 13.18; 26.25), a wife-sister incident with Abimelech (20.1–18; 26.6–11), conflicts over the ownership of wells (21.25–34; 26.17–25), and a covenant* of peace with Abimelech (21.22–24; 26.26–31). **8:** The writer again puns on the name Isaac: The king saw *Isaac* ("yitshaq") *fondling* ("met-saheq") his wife. **33:** *Shibah* is a wordplay on the Hebrew verb "to exchange an oath" ("shb," v. 31). Shibah is an alternate place name for *Beer-sheba* ("Well of the oath," 21.31).

~~~~~~~~~~

34 When Esau was forty years old, he married Judith daughter of Beeri the Hittite, and Basemath daughter of Elon the Hittite; 35and they made life bitter for Isaac and Rebekah.

27 When Isaac was old and his eyes were dim so that he could not see, he called his elder son Esau and said to him, "My son"; and he answered, "Here I am." 2He said, "See, I am old; I do not know the day of my death. 3Now then, take your weapons, your quiver and your bow, and go out to the field, and hunt game for me. 4Then prepare for me savory food, such as I like, and bring it to me to eat, so that I may bless you before I die."

---

a That is *Contention*   *b* That is *Enmity*   *c* That is *Broad places* or *Room*   *d* A word resembling the word for *oath*   *e* That is *Well of the oath* or *Well of seven*

5 Now Rebekah was listening when Isaac spoke to his son Esau. So when Esau went to the field to hunt for game and bring it, 6Rebekah said to her son Jacob, "I heard your father say to your brother Esau, 7'Bring me game, and prepare for me savory food to eat, that I may bless you before the LORD before I die.' 8Now therefore, my son, obey my word as I command you. 9Go to the flock, and get me two choice kids, so that I may prepare from them savory food for your father, such as he likes; 10and you shall take it to your father to eat, so that he may bless you before he dies." 11But Jacob said to his mother Rebekah, "Look, my brother Esau is a hairy man, and I am a man of smooth skin. 12Perhaps my father will feel me, and I shall seem to be mocking him, and bring a curse on myself and not a blessing." 13His mother said to him, "Let your curse be on me, my son; only obey my word, and go, get them for me." 14So he went and got them and brought them to his mother; and his mother prepared savory food, such as his father loved. 15Then Rebekah took the best garments of her elder son Esau, which were with her in the house, and put them on her younger son Jacob; 16and she put the skins of the kids on his hands and on the smooth part of his neck. 17Then she handed the savory food, and the bread that she had prepared, to her son Jacob.

18 So he went in to his father, and said, "My father"; and he said, "Here I am; who are you, my son?" 19Jacob said to his father, "I am Esau your firstborn. I have done as you told me; now sit up and eat of my game, so that you may bless me." 20But Isaac said to his son, "How is it that you have found it so quickly, my son?" He answered, "Because the LORD your God granted me success." 21Then Isaac said to Jacob, "Come near, that I may feel you, my son, to know whether you are really my son Esau or not." 22So Jacob went up to his father Isaac, who felt him and said, "The voice is Jacob's voice, but the hands are the hands of Esau." 23He did not recognize him, because his hands were hairy like his brother Esau's hands; so he blessed him. 24He said, "Are you really my son Esau?" He answered, "I am." 25Then he said,

"Bring it to me, that I may eat of my son's game and bless you." So he brought it to him, and he ate; and he brought him wine, and he drank. 26Then his father Isaac said to him, "Come near and kiss me, my son." 27So he came near and kissed him; and he smelled the smell of his garments, and blessed him, and said,

"Ah, the smell of my son
    is like the smell of a field that the
        LORD has blessed.
28 May God give you of the dew of heaven,
    and of the fatness of the earth,
    and plenty of grain and wine.
29 Let peoples serve you,
    and nations bow down to you.
Be lord over your brothers,
    and may your mother's sons bow
        down to you.
Cursed be everyone who curses you,
    and blessed be everyone who blesses
        you!"

30 As soon as Isaac had finished blessing Jacob, when Jacob had scarcely gone out from the presence of his father Isaac, his brother Esau came in from his hunting. 31He also prepared savory food, and brought it to his father. And he said to his father, "Let my father sit up and eat of his son's game, so that you may bless me." 32His father Isaac said to him, "Who are you?" He answered, "I am your firstborn son, Esau." 33Then Isaac trembled violently, and said, "Who was it then that hunted game and brought it to me, and I ate it all[a] before you came, and I have blessed him?—yes, and blessed he shall be!" 34When Esau heard his father's words, he cried out with an exceedingly great and bitter cry, and said to his father, "Bless me, me also, father!" 35But he said, "Your brother came deceitfully, and he has taken away your blessing." 36Esau said, "Is he not rightly named Jacob?[b] For he has supplanted me these two times. He took away my birthright; and look, now he has taken away my blessing." Then he said, "Have you not reserved a blessing for me?" 37Isaac answered Esau, "I have already made him your

a Cn: Heb of all   b That is He supplants or He takes by the heel lord, and I have given him all his brothers as servants, and with grain and wine I have sustained him. What then can I do for you, my son?" 38 Esau said to his father, "Have you only one blessing, father? Bless me, me also, father!" And Esau lifted up his voice and wept.

39 Then his father Isaac answered him:
"See, away from*a* the fatness of the
earth shall your home be,
and away from*b* the dew of heaven on
high.
40 By your sword you shall live,
and you shall serve your brother;
but when you break loose,*c*
you shall break his yoke from your
neck."

41 Now Esau hated Jacob because of the blessing with which his father had blessed him, and Esau said to himself, "The days of mourning for my father are approaching; then I will kill my brother Jacob." 42 But the words of her elder son Esau were told to Rebekah; so she sent and called her younger son Jacob and said to him, "Your brother Esau is consoling himself by planning to kill you. 43 Now therefore, my son, obey my voice; flee at once to my brother Laban in Haran, 44 and stay with him a while, until your brother's fury turns away— 45 until your brother's anger against you turns away, and he forgets what you have done to him; then I will send, and bring you back from there. Why should I lose both of you in one day?"

46 Then Rebekah said to Isaac, "I am weary of my life because of the Hittite women. If Jacob marries one of the Hittite women such as these, one of the women of the land, what good will my life be to me?"

28 Then Isaac called Jacob and blessed him, and charged him, "You shall not marry one of the Canaanite women. 2 Go at once to Paddan-aram to the house of Bethuel, your mother's father; and take as wife from there one of the daughters of Laban, your mother's brother. 3 May God Almighty*d* bless you and make you fruitful and numerous, that you may become a company of peoples. 4 May he give to you the blessing of Abraham, to you and to your offspring with you, so that you may take possession of the land where you now live as an alien—land that God gave to Abraham." 5 Thus Isaac sent Jacob away; and he went to Paddan-aram, to Laban son of Bethuel the Aramean, the brother of Rebekah, Jacob's and Esau's mother.

6 Now Esau saw that Isaac had blessed Jacob and sent him away to Paddan-aram to take a wife from there, and that as he blessed him he charged him, "You shall not marry one of the Canaanite women," 7 and that Jacob had obeyed his father and his mother and gone to Paddan-aram. 8 So when Esau saw that the Canaanite women did not please his father Isaac, 9 Esau went to Ishmael and took Mahalath daughter of Abraham's son Ishmael, and sister of Nebaioth, to be his wife in addition to the wives he had.

26.34–28.9: Jacob steals Esau's blessing. Jacob deceives his old and blind father Isaac. Jacob pretends to be his older brother Esau so that he can receive the blessing and inheritance that belong to the firstborn son. **26.34–35:** Esau marries two Hittite or native Canaanite women who bring trouble to the family. This comment places Esau in a negative light. **27.34–38:** The grief and anger of Isaac and Esau presuppose that the words and power of a blessing cannot be taken back once they have been spoken. **39:** Esau can only receive the opposite of what Jacob already received. Jacob will receive *of* (the Hebrew preposition "min") *the fatness of the earth* (v. 28) while Esau will live *away from* (the same preposition "min") *the fatness of the earth.* The land of Edom was not an agriculturally rich area. **41:** *I will kill my brother Jacob:* These are the last words we hear from Esau concerning Jacob until they meet many years later in ch. 33. **46:** Rebekah's excuse to Isaac for sending Jacob away is to avoid Jacob's marrying one of the Hittite or Canaanite *women of the land* as Esau had done (26.34–35). Her real reason is to stop Esau from murdering his brother Jacob (vv. 42–45). **28.1–5:** Isaac instructs Jacob to return to the original homeland of Abraham and of his mother Rebekah in Mesopotamia to obtain a wife as Isaac had done (ch. 24; 25.20).

10 Jacob left Beer-sheba and went toward Haran. 11 He came to a certain place and

a Or *See, of* *b* Or *and of* *c* Meaning of Heb uncertain *d* Traditional rendering of Heb *El Shaddai* stayed there for the night, because the sun had set. Taking one of the stones of the place, he put it under his head and lay down in that place. 12And he dreamed that there was a ladder[a] set up on the earth, the top of it reaching to heaven; and the angels of God were ascending and descending on it. 13And the LORD stood beside him[b] and said, "I am the LORD, the God of Abraham your father and the God of Isaac; the land on which you lie I will give to you and to your offspring; 14and your offspring shall be like the dust of the earth, and you shall spread abroad to the west and to the east and to the north and to the south; and all the families of the earth shall be blessed[c] in you and in your offspring. 15Know that I am with you and will keep you wherever you go, and will bring you back to this land; for I will not leave you until I have done what I have promised you." 16Then Jacob woke from his sleep and said, "Surely the LORD is in this place—and I did not know it!" 17And he was afraid, and said, "How awesome is this place! This is none other than the house of God, and this is the gate of heaven."

18 So Jacob rose early in the morning, and he took the stone that he had put under his head and set it up for a pillar and poured oil on the top of it. 19He called that place Bethel;[d] but the name of the city was Luz at the first. 20Then Jacob made a vow, saying, "If God will be with me, and will keep me in this way that I go, and will give me bread to eat and clothing to wear, 21so that I come again to my father's house in peace, then the LORD shall be my God, 22and this stone, which I have set up for a pillar, shall be God's house; and of all that you give me I will surely give one-tenth to you."

28.10–22: This story of Jacob's encounter with God and God's blessing as he leaves Canaan is the first of two such encounters. When Jacob returns to Canaan twenty years later, he will encounter angels or divine messengers a second time (32.1–2). He will also wrestle with God and receive a blessing (32.22–32). 13–15: God reaffirms the promises made to Abraham and Isaac as belonging also to Jacob (12.1–3; 26.2–5). 17: The house of God ("beth'el") becomes the basis for the name of the place, Bethel (v. 19). 18: Jacob's act

of *pouring oil on top of* the stone *pillar* marked the location as a holy place. 20–21: Jacob is always a tough negotiator for his own self-interest (25.29–34). True to his nature, Jacob vows to let God *be my God* on the condition that God cares for all his needs.

29 Then Jacob went on his journey, and came to the land of the people of the east. 2As he looked, he saw a well in the field and three flocks of sheep lying there beside it; for out of that well the flocks were watered. The stone on the well's mouth was large, 3and when all the flocks were gathered there, the shepherds would roll the stone from the mouth of the well, and water the sheep, and put the stone back in its place on the mouth of the well.

4 Jacob said to them, "My brothers, where do you come from?" They said, "We are from Haran." 5He said to them, "Do you know Laban son of Nahor?" They said, "We do." 6He said to them, "Is it well with him?" "Yes," they replied, "and here is his daughter Rachel, coming with the sheep." 7He said, "Look, it is still broad daylight; it is not time for the animals to be gathered together. Water the sheep, and go, pasture them." 8But they said, "We cannot until all the flocks are gathered together, and the stone is rolled from the mouth of the well; then we water the sheep."

9 While he was still speaking with them, Rachel came with her father's sheep; for she kept them. 10Now when Jacob saw Rachel, the daughter of his mother's brother Laban, and the sheep of his mother's brother Laban, Jacob went up and rolled the stone from the well's mouth, and watered the flock of his mother's brother Laban. 11Then Jacob kissed Rachel, and wept aloud. 12And Jacob told Rachel that he was her father's kinsman, and that he was Rebekah's son; and she ran and told her father.

13 When Laban heard the news about his sister's son Jacob, he ran to meet him; he embraced him and kissed him, and brought him to his house. Jacob[e] told Laban all these

a Or *stairway* or *ramp*   b Or *stood above it*
c Or *shall bless themselves*   d That is *House of God*
e Heb *He*

things, ¹⁴and Laban said to him, "Surely you are my bone and my flesh!" And he stayed with him a month.

15 Then Laban said to Jacob, "Because you are my kinsman, should you therefore serve me for nothing? Tell me, what shall your wages be?" ¹⁶Now Laban had two daughters; the name of the elder was Leah, and the name of the younger was Rachel. ¹⁷Leah's eyes were lovely,ᵃ and Rachel was graceful and beautiful. ¹⁸Jacob loved Rachel; so he said, "I will serve you seven years for your younger daughter Rachel." ¹⁹Laban said, "It is better that I give her to you than that I should give her to any other man; stay with me." ²⁰So Jacob served seven years for Rachel, and they seemed to him but a few days because of the love he had for her.

21 Then Jacob said to Laban, "Give me my wife that I may go in to her, for my time is completed." ²²So Laban gathered together all the people of the place, and made a feast. ²³But in the evening he took his daughter Leah and brought her to Jacob; and he went in to her. ²⁴(Laban gave his maid Zilpah to his daughter Leah to be her maid.) ²⁵When morning came, it was Leah! And Jacob said to Laban, "What is this you have done to me? Did I not serve with you for Rachel? Why then have you deceived me?" ²⁶Laban said, "This is not done in our country—giving the younger before the firstborn. ²⁷Complete the week of this one, and we will give you the other also in return for serving me another seven years." ²⁸Jacob did so, and completed her week; then Laban gave him his daughter Rachel as a wife. ²⁹(Laban gave his maid Bilhah to his daughter Rachel to be her maid.) ³⁰So Jacob went in to Rachel also, and he loved Rachel more than Leah. He served Labanᵇ for another seven years.

29.1–30: Jacob marries Leah and Rachel. Jacob the deceiver (ch. 27) meets his match in his uncle Laban, who deceives Jacob (v. 25). Jacob agrees to work seven years in order to marry Rachel. Laban tricks Jacob into working for him for twice as many years (14 years). Jacob also ends up marrying both of Laban's daughters instead of only Rachel, the wife he truly wanted. **17:** The Hebrew word for *lovely* is unclear and may also mean weak or unattractive. This may

partly explain why Jacob preferred Rachel over Leah (v. 30).

31 When the LORD saw that Leah was unloved, he opened her womb; but Rachel was barren. ³²Leah conceived and bore a son, and she named him Reuben;ᶜ for she said, "Because the LORD has looked on my affliction; surely now my husband will love me." ³³She conceived again and bore a son, and said, "Because the LORD has heardᵈ that I am hated, he has given me this son also"; and she named him Simeon. ³⁴Again she conceived and bore a son, and said, "Now this time my husband will be joinedᵉ to me, because I have borne him three sons"; therefore he was named Levi. ³⁵She conceived again and bore a son, and said, "This time I will praiseᶠ the LORD"; therefore she named him Judah; then she ceased bearing.

30 When Rachel saw that she bore Jacob no children, she envied her sister; and she said to Jacob, "Give me children, or I shall die!" ²Jacob became very angry with Rachel and said, "Am I in the place of God, who has withheld from you the fruit of the womb?" ³Then she said, "Here is my maid Bilhah; go in to her, that she may bear upon my knees and that I too may have children through her." ⁴So she gave him her maid Bilhah as a wife; and Jacob went in to her. ⁵And Bilhah conceived and bore Jacob a son. ⁶Then Rachel said, "God has judged me, and has also heard my voice and given me a son"; therefore she named him Dan.ᵍ ⁷Rachel's maid Bilhah conceived again and bore Jacob a second son. ⁸Then Rachel said, "With mighty wrestlings I have wrestledʰ with my sister, and have prevailed"; so she named him Naphtali.

9 When Leah saw that she had ceased bearing children, she took her maid Zilpah and gave her to Jacob as a wife. ¹⁰Then Leah's maid Zilpah bore Jacob a son. ¹¹And Leah said, "Good fortune!" so she named him Gad.ⁱ ¹²Leah's maid Zilpah bore Jacob a second son. ¹³And Leah said, "Happy am

---

ᵃ Meaning of Heb uncertain   ᵇ Heb *him*   ᶜ That is *See, a son*   ᵈ Heb *shama*   ᵉ Heb *lawah*   ᶠ Heb *hodah*   ᵍ That is *He judged*   ʰ Heb *niphtal*   ⁱ That is *Fortune*

I! For the women will call me happy"; so she named him Asher.[a]

14 In the days of wheat harvest Reuben went and found mandrakes in the field, and brought them to his mother Leah. Then Rachel said to Leah, "Please give me some of your son's mandrakes." [15]But she said to her, "Is it a small matter that you have taken away my husband? Would you take away my son's mandrakes also?" Rachel said, "Then he may lie with you tonight for your son's mandrakes." [16]When Jacob came from the field in the evening, Leah went out to meet him, and said, "You must come in to me; for I have hired you with my son's mandrakes." So he lay with her that night. [17]And God heeded Leah, and she conceived and bore Jacob a fifth son. [18]Leah said, "God has given me my hire[b] because I gave my maid to my husband"; so she named him Issachar. [19]And Leah conceived again, and she bore Jacob a sixth son. [20]Then Leah said, "God has endowed me with a good dowry; now my husband will honor[c] me, because I have borne him six sons"; so she named him Zebulun. [21]Afterwards she bore a daughter, and named her Dinah.

22 Then God remembered Rachel, and God heeded her and opened her womb. [23]She conceived and bore a son, and said, "God has taken away my reproach"; [24]and she named him Joseph,[d] saying, "May the LORD add to me another son!"

29.31–30.24: The birth of Jacob's eleven sons and one daughter. The sons born to Jacob will become the ancestors of the twelve tribes of Israel. The birth of the twelfth and last son, Benjamin, is described in ch. 35. The relative status of the mother of each of the sons reflected the relative status of the corresponding tribe at some point in Israel's history. For example, the Joseph tribe was once one of the most powerful tribes, a status reflected by his mother, the most favored wife (vv. 22–24; 29.30). Leah's children and the children of the maid would have been less favored or influential. Each child's name has some meaning attached to it. 30.14–16: As the favored wife, Rachel has the first rights of sleeping with Jacob. However, she barters that right away to Leah for a night in exchange for some *mandrakes*. Mandrakes are herbs thought to aid in fertility. The childless Rachel is apparently anxious to do what she can to have children with Jacob. Rachel eventually succeeds with God's help (30.22–24).

25 When Rachel had borne Joseph, Jacob said to Laban, "Send me away, that I may go to my own home and country. [26]Give me my wives and my children for whom I have served you, and let me go; for you know very well the service I have given you." [27]But Laban said to him, "If you will allow me to say so, I have learned by divination that the LORD has blessed me because of you; [28]name your wages, and I will give it." [29]Jacob said to him, "You yourself know how I have served you, and how your cattle have fared with me. [30]For you had little before I came, and it has increased abundantly; and the LORD has blessed you wherever I turned. But now when shall I provide for my own household also?" [31]He said, "What shall I give you?" Jacob said, "You shall not give me anything; if you will do this for me, I will again feed your flock and keep it: [32]let me pass through all your flock today, removing from it every speckled and spotted sheep and every black lamb, and the spotted and speckled among the goats; and such shall be my wages. [33]So my honesty will answer for me later, when you come to look into my wages with you. Every one that is not speckled and spotted among the goats and black among the lambs, if found with me, shall be counted stolen." [34]Laban said, "Good! Let it be as you have said." [35]But that day Laban removed the male goats that were striped and spotted, and all the female goats that were speckled and spotted, every one that had white on it, and every lamb that was black, and put them in charge of his sons; [36]and he set a distance of three days' journey between himself and Jacob, while Jacob was pasturing the rest of Laban's flock.

37 Then Jacob took fresh rods of poplar and almond and plane, and peeled white streaks in them, exposing the white of the rods. [38]He set the rods that he had peeled in front of the flocks in the troughs, that is, the watering places, where the flocks came to

a That is *Happy*   b Heb *sakar*   c Heb *zabal*
d That is *He adds*

drink. And since they bred when they came to drink, ³⁹the flocks bred in front of the rods, and so the flocks produced young that were striped, speckled, and spotted. ⁴⁰Jacob separated the lambs, and set the faces of the flocks toward the striped and the completely black animals in the flock of Laban; and he put his own droves apart, and did not put them with Laban's flock. ⁴¹Whenever the stronger of the flock were breeding, Jacob laid the rods in the troughs before the eyes of the flock, that they might breed among the rods, ⁴²but for the feebler of the flock he did not lay them there; so the feebler were Laban's, and the stronger Jacob's. ⁴³Thus the man grew exceedingly rich, and had large flocks, and male and female slaves, and camels and donkeys.

30.25–43: Jacob prospers and Laban loses. Laban promises to give Jacob all the sheep and goats that are spotted or black (vv. 32–34). But then Laban secretly removes all the spotted and black animals from the herd and sends them away so nothing is left for Jacob (vv. 35–36). Jacob places striped or spotted almond or poplar branches in front of the strong sheep and goats as they mate. The assumption was that whatever the animals saw while they mated would determine whether their offspring would be a solid or a spotted color. An underlying biological fact is that even though the parent animals were both all white, they could carry the recessive gene for black or a spotted color. As a result of his genetic engineering, Jacob *grew exceedingly rich* (v. 43).

31 Now Jacob heard that the sons of Laban were saying, "Jacob has taken all that was our father's; he has gained all this wealth from what belonged to our father." ²And Jacob saw that Laban did not regard him as favorably as he did before. ³Then the LORD said to Jacob, "Return to the land of your ancestors and to your kindred, and I will be with you." ⁴So Jacob sent and called Rachel and Leah into the field where his flock was, ⁵and said to them, "I see that your father does not regard me as favorably as he did before. But the God of my father has been with me. ⁶You know that I have served your father with all my strength; ⁷yet your father has cheated me and changed my

wages ten times, but God did not permit him to harm me. ⁸If he said, 'The speckled shall be your wages,' then all the flock bore speckled; and if he said, 'The striped shall be your wages,' then all the flock bore striped. ⁹Thus God has taken away the livestock of your father, and given them to me.

10 During the mating of the flock I once had a dream in which I looked up and saw that the male goats that leaped upon the flock were striped, speckled, and mottled. ¹¹Then the angel of God said to me in the dream, 'Jacob,' and I said, 'Here I am!' ¹²And he said, 'Look up and see that all the goats that leap on the flock are striped, speckled, and mottled; for I have seen all that Laban is doing to you. ¹³I am the God of Bethel,*ᵃ* where you anointed a pillar and made a vow to me. Now leave this land at once and return to the land of your birth.' " ¹⁴Then Rachel and Leah answered him, "Is there any portion or inheritance left to us in our father's house? ¹⁵Are we not regarded by him as foreigners? For he has sold us, and he has been using up the money given for us. ¹⁶All the property that God has taken away from our father belongs to us and to our children; now then, do whatever God has said to you."

17 So Jacob arose, and set his children and his wives on camels; ¹⁸and he drove away all his livestock, all the property that he had gained, the livestock in his possession that he had acquired in Paddan-aram, to go to his father Isaac in the land of Canaan.

19 Now Laban had gone to shear his sheep, and Rachel stole her father's household gods. ²⁰And Jacob deceived Laban the Aramean, in that he did not tell him that he intended to flee. ²¹So he fled with all that he had; starting out he crossed the Euphrates,*ᵇ* and set his face toward the hill country of Gilead.

22 On the third day Laban was told that Jacob had fled. ²³So he took his kinsfolk with him and pursued him for seven days until he caught up with him in the hill country of Gilead. ²⁴But God came to Laban the Aramean in a dream by night, and said to him,

a Cn: Meaning of Heb uncertain   *b* Heb *the river*

"Take heed that you say not a word to Jacob, either good or bad."

25 Laban overtook Jacob. Now Jacob had pitched his tent in the hill country, and Laban with his kinsfolk camped in the hill country of Gilead. 26 Laban said to Jacob, "What have you done? You have deceived me, and carried away my daughters like captives of the sword. 27 Why did you flee secretly and deceive me and not tell me? I would have sent you away with mirth and songs, with tambourine and lyre. 28 And why did you not permit me to kiss my sons and my daughters farewell? What you have done is foolish. 29 It is in my power to do you harm; but the God of your father spoke to me last night, saying, 'Take heed that you speak to Jacob neither good nor bad.' 30 Even though you had to go because you longed greatly for your father's house, why did you steal my gods?" 31 Jacob answered Laban, "Because I was afraid, for I thought that you would take your daughters from me by force. 32 But anyone with whom you find your gods shall not live. In the presence of our kinsfolk, point out what I have that is yours, and take it." Now Jacob did not know that Rachel had stolen the gods.[a]

33 So Laban went into Jacob's tent, and into Leah's tent, and into the tent of the two maids, but he did not find them. And he went out of Leah's tent, and entered Rachel's. 34 Now Rachel had taken the household gods and put them in the camel's saddle, and sat on them. Laban felt all about in the tent, but did not find them. 35 And she said to her father, "Let not my lord be angry that I cannot rise before you, for the way of women is upon me." So he searched, but did not find the household gods.

36 Then Jacob became angry, and upbraided Laban. Jacob said to Laban, "What is my offense? What is my sin, that you have hotly pursued me? 37 Although you have felt about through all my goods, what have you found of all your household goods? Set it here before my kinsfolk and your kinsfolk, so that they may decide between us two. 38 These twenty years I have been with you; your ewes and your female goats have not miscarried, and I have not eaten the rams of your flocks. 39 That which was torn by wild beasts I did not bring to you; I bore the loss of it myself; of my hand you required it, whether stolen by day or stolen by night. 40 It was like this with me: by day the heat consumed me, and the cold by night, and my sleep fled from my eyes. 41 These twenty years I have been in your house; I served you fourteen years for your two daughters, and six years for your flock, and you have changed my wages ten times. 42 If the God of my father, the God of Abraham and the Fear[b] of Isaac, had not been on my side, surely now you would have sent me away empty-handed. God saw my affliction and the labor of my hands, and rebuked you last night."

43 Then Laban answered and said to Jacob, "The daughters are my daughters, the children are my children, the flocks are my flocks, and all that you see is mine. But what can I do today about these daughters of mine, or about their children whom they have borne? 44 Come now, let us make a covenant, you and I; and let it be a witness between you and me." 45 So Jacob took a stone, and set it up as a pillar. 46 And Jacob said to his kinsfolk, "Gather stones," and they took stones, and made a heap; and they ate there by the heap. 47 Laban called it Jegar-sahadutha:[c] but Jacob called it Galeed.[d] 48 Laban said, "This heap is a witness between you and me today." Therefore he called it Galeed, 49 and the pillar[e] Mizpah,[f] for he said, "The LORD watch between you and me, when we are absent one from the other. 50 If you ill-treat my daughters, or if you take wives in addition to my daughters, though no one else is with us, remember that God is witness between you and me."

51 Then Laban said to Jacob, "See this heap and see the pillar, which I have set between you and me. 52 This heap is a witness, and the pillar is a witness, that I will not pass beyond this heap to you, and you will not pass beyond this heap and this pillar to me, for harm. 53 May the God of Abraham and

---

a Heb *them*   b Meaning of Heb uncertain
c In Aramaic *The heap of witness*   d In Hebrew *The heap of witness*   e Compare Sam: MT lacks *the pillar*
f That is *Watchpost*

the God of Nahor"—the God of their father—"judge between us." So Jacob swore by the Fear[a] of his father Isaac, ⁵⁴and Jacob offered a sacrifice on the height and called his kinsfolk to eat bread; and they ate bread and tarried all night in the hill country.

⁵⁵[b] Early in the morning Laban rose up, and kissed his grandchildren and his daughters and blessed them; then he departed and returned home.

31.1–55: Jacob flees from Laban with his family and flocks. 1–2: Envy and conflict within the extended families of Jacob and Laban increase as Jacob's wealth and flocks increase. **14–16:** After having experienced conflict between themselves (30.1, 15), Leah and Rachel are now united in their negative feelings toward their father Laban. **19:** The *household gods* were idols that were believed to carry with them power, prosperity, and the legal claim to the family's property. **32:** Jacob unknowingly predicts what will happen to Rachel. She will soon die prematurely in childbirth (35.16–20). **35:** *The way of women* refers to her menstrual period. **47–48:** The site for the boundary covenant* or agreement between Jacob and Laban has two names. One name, *Jegar-sahadutha*, means "the heap of witness" in the Aramaic* language spoken by Laban the Aramean (25.20). The other name for the same site, *Galeed*, also means "the heap of witness," but in the Hebrew language spoken by Jacob. The names refer to the heap of stones that mark the boundary between Laban's Arameans and Jacob's Israelites. **49:** Laban names the pillar *Mizpah*, meaning "watchpost."

---

32 Jacob went on his way and the angels of God met him; ²and when Jacob saw them he said, "This is God's camp!" So he called that place Mahanaim.[c]

3 Jacob sent messengers before him to his brother Esau in the land of Seir, the country of Edom, ⁴instructing them, "Thus you shall say to my lord Esau: Thus says your servant Jacob, 'I have lived with Laban as an alien, and stayed until now; ⁵and I have oxen, donkeys, flocks, male and female slaves; and I have sent to tell my lord, in order that I may find favor in your sight.' "

6 The messengers returned to Jacob, saying, "We came to your brother Esau, and he is coming to meet you, and four hundred men are with him." ⁷Then Jacob was greatly afraid and distressed; and he divided the people that were with him, and the flocks and herds and camels, into two companies, ⁸thinking, "If Esau comes to the one company and destroys it, then the company that is left will escape."

9 And Jacob said, "O God of my father Abraham and God of my father Isaac, O LORD who said to me, 'Return to your country and to your kindred, and I will do you good,' ¹⁰I am not worthy of the least of all the steadfast love and all the faithfulness that you have shown to your servant, for with only my staff I crossed this Jordan; and now I have become two companies. ¹¹Deliver me, please, from the hand of my brother, from the hand of Esau, for I am afraid of him; he may come and kill us all, the mothers with the children. ¹²Yet you have said, 'I will surely do you good, and make your offspring as the sand of the sea, which cannot be counted because of their number.' "

13 So he spent that night there, and from what he had with him he took a present for his brother Esau, ¹⁴two hundred female goats and twenty male goats, two hundred ewes and twenty rams, ¹⁵thirty milch camels and their colts, forty cows and ten bulls, twenty female donkeys and ten male donkeys. ¹⁶These he delivered into the hand of his servants, every drove by itself, and said to his servants, "Pass on ahead of me, and put a space between drove and drove." ¹⁷He instructed the foremost, "When Esau my brother meets you, and asks you, 'To whom do you belong? Where are you going? And whose are these ahead of you?' ¹⁸then you shall say, 'They belong to your servant Jacob; they are a present sent to my lord Esau; and moreover he is behind us.' " ¹⁹He likewise instructed the second and the third and all who followed the droves, "You shall say the same thing to Esau when you meet him, ²⁰and you shall say, 'Moreover your servant Jacob is behind us.' " For he thought, "I may appease him with the present that goes

---

a Meaning of Heb uncertain *b* Ch 32.1 in Heb
c Here taken to mean *Two camps*

ahead of me, and afterwards I shall see his face; perhaps he will accept me." ²¹So the present passed on ahead of him; and he himself spent that night in the camp.

32.1–21: Jacob prepares to meet his brother Esau. After twenty years of separation, the reader recalls that the last words we heard from Esau were, "I will kill my brother Jacob" (27.41). Jacob's preparations to meet Esau exhibit great anxiety about whether Esau still carries this threat with him (v. 11). **1–2:** *Angels of God* again meet Jacob as he enters Canaan, just as the angels visited him when he left Canaan (28.12). Jacob names the place *Mahanaim*, "two camps," because it is *God's camp*. Bethel, "house of God," was the place name of the previous encounter with angels (28.19). **3–8:** Jacob sends gifts to appease his brother Esau. Jacob hears the ominous news that Esau is coming to meet him with an army of *four hundred men* (v. 6). Jacob has good reason to be *greatly afraid and distressed* (v. 7).

22 The same night he got up and took his two wives, his two maids, and his eleven children, and crossed the ford of the Jabbok. ²³He took them and sent them across the stream, and likewise everything that he had. ²⁴Jacob was left alone; and a man wrestled with him until daybreak. ²⁵When the man saw that he did not prevail against Jacob, he struck him on the hip socket; and Jacob's hip was put out of joint as he wrestled with him. ²⁶Then he said, "Let me go, for the day is breaking." But Jacob said, "I will not let you go, unless you bless me." ²⁷So he said to him, "What is your name?" And he said, "Jacob." ²⁸Then the man*ᵃ* said, "You shall no longer be called Jacob, but Israel,*ᵇ* for you have striven with God and with humans,*ᶜ* and have prevailed." ²⁹Then Jacob asked him, "Please tell me your name." But he said, "Why is it that you ask my name?" And there he blessed him. ³⁰So Jacob called the place Peniel,*ᵈ* saying, "For I have seen God face to face, and yet my life is preserved." ³¹The sun rose upon him as he passed Penuel, limping because of his hip. ³²Therefore to this day the Israelites do not eat the thigh muscle that is on the hip socket, because he struck Jacob on the hip socket at the thigh muscle.

32.22–32: Jacob wrestles with God. This is an ancient story that has played several roles in its long history. The story explained the reason for the place name, *Peniel* ("Face of God," v. 30). It also explained the reason for the dietary law that Israelites do not eat the thigh muscle of any animal (v. 32) and the reason for the change of Jacob's name to Israel (v. 28). Jacob's life as an individual becomes a portrait of Israel's life as a nation. Israel as a people will struggle with God and limp away with a blessing. **24:** The sudden and unexplained appearance of *a man* in the night suggests a mysterious or supernatural figure. **25:** Jacob was winning the wrestling match until he was crippled by a wrestler's trick that dislocated his hip. **28:** The identity of the "man" is now revealed: Jacob has *striven with God*. **30:** Jacob's experience is remarkable in light of a prevailing Old Testament tradition that no human can see *God face to face* and live (Ex 33.11–23; Judg 6.22–23).

33 Now Jacob looked up and saw Esau coming, and four hundred men with him. So he divided the children among Leah and Rachel and the two maids. ²He put the maids with their children in front, then Leah with her children, and Rachel and Joseph last of all. ³He himself went on ahead of them, bowing himself to the ground seven times, until he came near his brother.

4 But Esau ran to meet him, and embraced him, and fell on his neck and kissed him, and they wept. ⁵When Esau looked up and saw the women and children, he said, "Who are these with you?" Jacob said, "The children whom God has graciously given your servant." ⁶Then the maids drew near, they and their children, and bowed down; ⁷Leah likewise and her children drew near and bowed down; and finally Joseph and Rachel drew near, and they bowed down. ⁸Esau said, "What do you mean by all this company that I met?" Jacob answered, "To find favor with my lord." ⁹But Esau said, "I have enough, my brother; keep what you have for yourself." ¹⁰Jacob said, "No, please; if I find favor with you, then accept my present from

a Heb *he*   *b* That is *The one who strives with God* or *God strives*   *c* Or *with divine and human beings*
d That is *The face of God*

my hand; for truly to see your face is like seeing the face of God—since you have received me with such favor. ¹¹Please accept my gift that is brought to you, because God has dealt graciously with me, and because I have everything I want." So he urged him, and he took it.

12 Then Esau said, "Let us journey on our way, and I will go alongside you." ¹³But Jacob said to him, "My lord knows that the children are frail and that the flocks and herds, which are nursing, are a care to me; and if they are overdriven for one day, all the flocks will die. ¹⁴Let my lord pass on ahead of his servant, and I will lead on slowly, according to the pace of the cattle that are before me and according to the pace of the children, until I come to my lord in Seir."

15 So Esau said, "Let me leave with you some of the people who are with me." But he said, "Why should my lord be so kind to me?" ¹⁶So Esau returned that day on his way to Seir. ¹⁷But Jacob journeyed to Succoth,ᵃ and built himself a house, and made booths for his cattle; therefore the place is called Succoth.

33.1–17: Jacob reconciles with Esau. 10: Jacob's words link his encounter with God in ch. 32 with his encounter with Esau: *To see your face is like seeing the face of God* (see 32.30). **11:** Jacob's offer of a *gift* ("berakah") to Esau in effect returns the "blessing" ("berakah") Jacob had stolen from Esau twenty years earlier (27.36). **12–16:** Although Jacob and Esau reconcile with one another, Jacob is still wary of his brother. Jacob tries diplomatically to keep a distance between himself and Esau, although Esau wants them to stay together. **17:** *Succoth* means "booths" and is a name of a town just across the Jordan River and east of Canaan (Josh 13.27).

---

18 Jacob came safely to the city of Shechem, which is in the land of Canaan, on his way from Paddan-aram; and he camped before the city. ¹⁹And from the sons of Hamor, Shechem's father, he bought for one hundred pieces of moneyᵇ the plot of land on which he had pitched his tent. ²⁰There he erected an altar and called it El-Elohe-Israel.ᶜ

34 Now Dinah the daughter of Leah, whom she had borne to Jacob, went out to visit the women of the region. ²When Shechem son of Hamor the Hivite, prince of the region, saw her, he seized her and lay with her by force. ³And his soul was drawn to Dinah daughter of Jacob; he loved the girl, and spoke tenderly to her. ⁴So Shechem spoke to his father Hamor, saying, "Get me this girl to be my wife."

5 Now Jacob heard that Shechemᵈ had defiled his daughter Dinah; but his sons were with his cattle in the field, so Jacob held his peace until they came. ⁶And Hamor the father of Shechem went out to Jacob to speak with him, ⁷just as the sons of Jacob came in from the field. When they heard of it, the men were indignant and very angry, because he had committed an outrage in Israel by lying with Jacob's daughter, for such a thing ought not to be done.

8 But Hamor spoke with them, saying, "The heart of my son Shechem longs for your daughter; please give her to him in marriage. ⁹Make marriages with us; give your daughters to us, and take our daughters for yourselves. ¹⁰You shall live with us; and the land shall be open to you; live and trade in it, and get property in it." ¹¹Shechem also said to her father and to her brothers, "Let me find favor with you, and whatever you say to me I will give. ¹²Put the marriage present and gift as high as you like, and I will give whatever you ask me; only give me the girl to be my wife."

13 The sons of Jacob answered Shechem and his father Hamor deceitfully, because he had defiled their sister Dinah. ¹⁴They said to them, "We cannot do this thing, to give our sister to one who is uncircumcised, for that would be a disgrace to us. ¹⁵Only on this condition will we consent to you: that you will become as we are and every male among you be circumcised. ¹⁶Then we will give our daughters to you, and we will take your daughters for ourselves, and we will live among you and become one people. ¹⁷But if

---

a That is *Booths*   b Heb *one hundred qesitah*
c That is *God, the God of Israel*   d Heb *he*

you will not listen to us and be circumcised, then we will take our daughter and be gone." 18 Their words pleased Hamor and Hamor's son Shechem. 19And the young man did not delay to do the thing, because he was delighted with Jacob's daughter. Now he was the most honored of all his family. 20So Hamor and his son Shechem came to the gate of their city and spoke to the men of their city, saying, 21"These people are friendly with us; let them live in the land and trade in it, for the land is large enough for them; let us take their daughters in marriage, and let us give them our daughters. 22Only on this condition will they agree to live among us, to become one people: that every male among us be circumcised as they are circumcised. 23Will not their livestock, their property, and all their animals be ours? Only let us agree with them, and they will live among us." 24And all who went out of the city gate heeded Hamor and his son Shechem; and every male was circumcised, all who went out of the gate of his city.

25 On the third day, when they were still in pain, two of the sons of Jacob, Simeon and Levi, Dinah's brothers, took their swords and came against the city unawares, and killed all the males. 26They killed Hamor and his son Shechem with the sword, and took Dinah out of Shechem's house, and went away. 27And the other sons of Jacob came upon the slain, and plundered the city, because their sister had been defiled. 28They took their flocks and their herds, their donkeys, and whatever was in the city and in the field. 29All their wealth, all their little ones and their wives, all that was in the houses, they captured and made their prey. 30Then Jacob said to Simeon and Levi, "You have brought trouble on me by making me odious to the inhabitants of the land, the Canaanites and the Perizzites; my numbers are few, and if they gather themselves against me and attack me, I shall be destroyed, both I and my household." 31But they said, "Should our sister be treated like a whore?"

33.18–34.31: The rape of Jacob's daughter, Dinah. This story of rape and revenge is the first example of violence in the interaction of Israelites and Canaanites.

Their relationships up to this point in Genesis have been cordial and peaceful. **33.18–19:** *Shechem* is both the name of the city and the name of the son of Hamor, the "prince of the region" (34.2). **20:** *El-Elohe-Israel* means "God, the God of Israel." The ancient divine name "El" appears elsewhere in Genesis, usually combined with another word: El Elyon (14.19), El Shaddai (17.1), El Olam (21.33), and El-bethel (35.7). **34.2–3:** The story reports that Shechem raped Dinah and then *loved* and *spoke tenderly to her.* Dinah's response or feelings are not given. **15:** To be *circumcised* involves cutting off the foreskin of the male penis. Circumcision* was a physical sign of a male's belonging to the covenant* people of Israel (17.9–14). **25–29:** The violence of the revenge (killing all males, taking all their possessions, and capturing their wives and children) seems excessive. That is especially true if the self-interests of the brothers rather than the interests of Dinah are being served. The story seems intentionally ambiguous at key points in order to draw the reader into wrestling with the moral dilemmas and issues raised by the narrative.* **26:** The reader is suddenly aware that Dinah has been staying in *Shechem's house.* Was she there because she wanted to be? Or was she held there by force? Again, we do not know Dinah's feelings. **30–31:** The ethical debate between Jacob (concerned with pragmatic realities) and his sons (concerned with moral principle) ends without resolution.

35 God said to Jacob, "Arise, go up to Bethel, and settle there. Make an altar there to the God who appeared to you when you fled from your brother Esau." 2So Jacob said to his household and to all who were with him, "Put away the foreign gods that are among you, and purify yourselves, and change your clothes; 3then come, let us go up to Bethel, that I may make an altar there to the God who answered me in the day of my distress and has been with me wherever I have gone." 4So they gave to Jacob all the foreign gods that they had, and the rings that were in their ears; and Jacob hid them under the oak that was near Shechem.

5 As they journeyed, a terror from God fell upon the cities all around them, so that no one pursued them. 6Jacob came to Luz (that is, Bethel), which is in the land of Canaan, he and all the people who were with

him, [7]and there he built an altar and called the place El-bethel,[a] because it was there that God had revealed himself to him when he fled from his brother. [8]And Deborah, Rebekah's nurse, died, and she was buried under an oak below Bethel. So it was called Allon-bacuth.[b]

[9] God appeared to Jacob again when he came from Paddan-aram, and he blessed him. [10]God said to him, "Your name is Jacob; no longer shall you be called Jacob, but Israel shall be your name." So he was called Israel. [11]God said to him, "I am God Almighty:[c] be fruitful and multiply; a nation and a company of nations shall come from you, and kings shall spring from you. [12]The land that I gave to Abraham and Isaac I will give to you, and I will give the land to your offspring after you." [13]Then God went up from him at the place where he had spoken with him. [14]Jacob set up a pillar in the place where he had spoken with him, a pillar of stone; and he poured out a drink offering on it, and poured oil on it. [15]So Jacob called the place where God had spoken with him Bethel.

35.1–15: Jacob returns to Bethel. After many years, Jacob returns to Bethel where God had first encountered and blessed Jacob when he was fleeing from his brother Esau (28.10–22). **2:** *The foreign gods that are among you* probably included the household gods or idols that Rachel had stolen from her father Laban when they fled from him (31.19). **7:** *El-bethel* means "God of Bethel" or "God of the house of God." *God had revealed himself* to Jacob there at Bethel in 28.10–22. **14:** As elsewhere in Genesis (28.18), setting up *a pillar of stone* and *pouring oil on it* marks the location as a holy site at which the deity was worshipped. **15:** *Bethel* means "house of God."

---

[16] Then they journeyed from Bethel; and when they were still some distance from Ephrath, Rachel was in childbirth, and she had hard labor. [17]When she was in her hard labor, the midwife said to her, "Do not be afraid; for now you will have another son." [18]As her soul was departing (for she died), she named him Ben-oni;[d] but his father called him Benjamin.[e] [19]So Rachel died, and she was buried on the way to Ephrath

(that is, Bethlehem), [20]and Jacob set up a pillar at her grave; it is the pillar of Rachel's tomb, which is there to this day. [21]Israel journeyed on, and pitched his tent beyond the tower of Eder.

[22] While Israel lived in that land, Reuben went and lay with Bilhah his father's concubine; and Israel heard of it.

Now the sons of Jacob were twelve. [23]The sons of Leah: Reuben (Jacob's firstborn), Simeon, Levi, Judah, Issachar, and Zebulun. [24]The sons of Rachel: Joseph and Benjamin. [25]The sons of Bilhah, Rachel's maid: Dan and Naphtali. [26]The sons of Zilpah, Leah's maid: Gad and Asher. These were the sons of Jacob who were born to him in Paddan-aram.

[27] Jacob came to his father Isaac at Mamre, or Kiriath-arba (that is, Hebron), where Abraham and Isaac had resided as aliens. [28]Now the days of Isaac were one hundred eighty years. [29]And Isaac breathed his last; he died and was gathered to his people, old and full of days; and his sons Esau and Jacob buried him.

35.16–29: Benjamin is born and Rachel dies. 18: *Ben-oni* means "son of my sorrow," reflecting Rachel's suffering in childbirth. Jacob changes the name slightly to *Benjamin*, "son of the right hand." Sitting at the right hand of a ruler or elder is a position of honor. Benjamin is the son of Jacob's favored wife (29.30) and thus Jacob's favored son (see 42.36–38). **22:** Jacob's firstborn son Reuben had sexual relations *with Bilhah his father's concubine,** a grievous offense. This incident is the reason Reuben's status as firstborn son will be diminished in Jacob's blessing of his twelve sons (49.3–4). **27–29:** The last days of Isaac provide an occasion for reconciliation between Jacob and his father (v. 27; see 27.35). The two sons, Esau and Jacob, join together in burying their father, Isaac (v. 29), just as earlier the brothers Isaac and Ishmael had joined together to bury their father, Abraham (25.9).

36

These are the descendants of Esau (that is, Edom). [2]Esau took his wives from the Canaanites: Adah daughter of Elon

---

a That is *God of Bethel*   b That is *Oak of weeping*
c Traditional rendering of Heb *El Shaddai*   d That is *Son of my sorrow*   e That is *Son of the right hand* or *Son of the South*

the Hittite, Oholibamah daughter of Anah son[a] of Zibeon the Hivite, 3and Basemath, Ishmael's daughter, sister of Nebaioth. 4Adah bore Eliphaz to Esau; Basemath bore Reuel; 5and Oholibamah bore Jeush, Jalam, and Korah. These are the sons of Esau who were born to him in the land of Canaan.

6 Then Esau took his wives, his sons, his daughters, and all the members of his household, his cattle, all his livestock, and all the property he had acquired in the land of Canaan; and he moved to a land some distance from his brother Jacob. 7For their possessions were too great for them to live together; the land where they were staying could not support them because of their livestock. 8So Esau settled in the hill country of Seir; Esau is Edom.

9 These are the descendants of Esau, ancestor of the Edomites, in the hill country of Seir. 10These are the names of Esau's sons: Eliphaz son of Adah the wife of Esau; Reuel, the son of Esau's wife Basemath. 11The sons of Eliphaz were Teman, Omar, Zepho, Gatam, and Kenaz. 12(Timna was a concubine of Eliphaz, Esau's son; she bore Amalek to Eliphaz.) These were the sons of Adah, Esau's wife. 13These were the sons of Reuel: Nahath, Zerah, Shammah, and Mizzah. These were the sons of Esau's wife, Basemath. 14These were the sons of Esau's wife Oholibamah, daughter of Anah son[b] of Zibeon: she bore to Esau Jeush, Jalam, and Korah.

15 These are the clans[c] of the sons of Esau. The sons of Eliphaz the firstborn of Esau: the clans[c] Teman, Omar, Zepho, Kenaz, 16Korah, Gatam, and Amalek; these are the clans[c] of Eliphaz in the land of Edom; they are the sons of Adah. 17These are the sons of Esau's son Reuel: the clans[c] Nahath, Zerah, Shammah, and Mizzah; these are the clans[c] of Reuel in the land of Edom; they are the sons of Esau's wife Basemath. 18These are the sons of Esau's wife Oholibamah: the clans[c] Jeush, Jalam, and Korah; these are the clans[c] born of Esau's wife Oholibamah, the daughter of Anah. 19These are the sons of Esau (that is, Edom), and these are their clans.[c]

20 These are the sons of Seir the Horite, the inhabitants of the land: Lotan, Shobal, Zibeon, Anah, 21Dishon, Ezer, and Dishan; these are the clans[c] of the Horites, the sons of Seir in the land of Edom. 22The sons of Lotan were Hori and Heman; and Lotan's sister was Timna. 23These are the sons of Shobal: Alvan, Manahath, Ebal, Shepho, and Onam. 24These are the sons of Zibeon: Aiah and Anah; he is the Anah who found the springs[d] in the wilderness, as he pastured the donkeys of his father Zibeon. 25These are the children of Anah: Dishon and Oholibamah daughter of Anah. 26These are the sons of Dishon: Hemdan, Eshban, Ithran, and Cheran. 27These are the sons of Ezer: Bilhan, Zaavan, and Akan. 28These are the sons of Dishan: Uz and Aran. 29These are the clans[c] of the Horites: the clans[c] Lotan, Shobal, Zibeon, Anah, 30Dishon, Ezer, and Dishan; these are the clans[c] of the Horites, clan by clan[e] in the land of Seir.

31 These are the kings who reigned in the land of Edom, before any king reigned over the Israelites. 32Bela son of Beor reigned in Edom, the name of his city being Dinhabah. 33Bela died, and Jobab son of Zerah of Bozrah succeeded him as king. 34Jobab died, and Husham of the land of the Temanites succeeded him as king. 35Husham died, and Hadad son of Bedad, who defeated Midian in the country of Moab, succeeded him as king, the name of his city being Avith. 36Hadad died, and Samlah of Masrekah succeeded him as king. 37Samlah died, and Shaul of Rehoboth on the Euphrates succeeded him as king. 38Shaul died, and Baal-hanan son of Achbor succeeded him as king. 39Baal-hanan son of Achbor died, and Hadar succeeded him as king, the name of his city being Pau; his wife's name was Mehetabel, the daughter of Matred, daughter of Me-zahab.

40 These are the names of the clans[c] of Esau, according to their families and their localities by their names: the clans[c] Timna, Alvah, Jetheth, 41Oholibamah, Elah, Pinon, 42Kenaz, Teman, Mibzar, 43Magdiel, and Iram; these are the clans[c] of Edom (that is,

a Sam Gk Syr: Heb *daughter*   b Gk Syr: Heb *daughter*
c Or *chiefs*   d Meaning of Heb uncertain
e Or *chief by chief*

Esau, the father of Edom), according to their settlements in the land that they held.

36.1–43: Esau's descendants. The list here of Esau's descendants and the list of Jacob's twelve sons in 35.22–26 represent a partial fulfillment of the promises of many descendants made to Abraham (15.5), Isaac (26.4), and Jacob (28.14). **1:** Jacob's brother *Esau* is the ancestor of the nation of *Edom*. Edom lies just south and east of Canaan. The land of Canaan will later become the nation of Israel, whose ancestor is Jacob (25.23, 30). **31:** This list of *kings who reigned in the land of Edom* precedes the time of Israel's King David, who conquered and ruled over Edom (2 Sam 8.13–14).

THE STORY OF JOSEPH

Chs. 37–50: The story about Jacob's son, Joseph, is the longest continuous narrative* in Genesis. The story runs from ch. 37 to ch. 50. It is interrupted by an inserted story about Judah and Tamar in ch. 38, although even this story has thematic connections to the Joseph narrative. The Joseph story provides a fitting conclusion to the Genesis ancestor stories as the family grows larger to become the people or nation of Israel. The story also functions as a literary bridge to the events in Egypt in the book of Exodus. Joseph will be the first of the Israelites to be enslaved in Egypt and then rescued, a fate all Israel will eventually share.

---

37 Jacob settled in the land where his father had lived as an alien, the land of Canaan. ²This is the story of the family of Jacob.

Joseph, being seventeen years old, was shepherding the flock with his brothers; he was a helper to the sons of Bilhah and Zilpah, his father's wives; and Joseph brought a bad report of them to their father. ³Now Israel loved Joseph more than any other of his children, because he was the son of his old age; and he had made him a long robe with sleeves.ª ⁴But when his brothers saw that their father loved him more than all his brothers, they hated him, and could not speak peaceably to him.

5 Once Joseph had a dream, and when he told it to his brothers, they hated him even more. ⁶He said to them, "Listen to this dream that I dreamed. ⁷There we were, binding sheaves in the field. Suddenly my sheaf rose and stood upright; then your sheaves gathered around it, and bowed down to my sheaf." ⁸His brothers said to him, "Are you indeed to reign over us? Are you indeed to have dominion over us?" So they hated him even more because of his dreams and his words.

9 He had another dream, and told it to his brothers, saying, "Look, I have had another dream: the sun, the moon, and eleven stars were bowing down to me." ¹⁰But when he told it to his father and to his brothers, his father rebuked him, and said to him, "What kind of dream is this that you have had? Shall we indeed come, I and your mother and your brothers, and bow to the ground before you?" ¹¹So his brothers were jealous of him, but his father kept the matter in mind.

12 Now his brothers went to pasture their father's flock near Shechem. ¹³And Israel said to Joseph, "Are not your brothers pasturing the flock at Shechem? Come, I will send you to them." He answered, "Here I am." ¹⁴So he said to him, "Go now, see if it is well with your brothers and with the flock; and bring word back to me." So he sent him from the valley of Hebron.

He came to Shechem, ¹⁵and a man found him wandering in the fields; the man asked him, "What are you seeking?" ¹⁶"I am seeking my brothers," he said; "tell me, please, where they are pasturing the flock." ¹⁷The man said, "They have gone away, for I heard them say, 'Let us go to Dothan.'" So Joseph went after his brothers, and found them at Dothan. ¹⁸They saw him from a distance, and before he came near to them, they conspired to kill him. ¹⁹They said to one another, "Here comes this dreamer. ²⁰Come now, let us kill him and throw him into one of the pits; then we shall say that a wild animal has devoured him, and we shall see what will become of his dreams." ²¹But when Reuben heard it, he delivered him out of their hands, saying, "Let us not take his life." ²²Reuben said to them, "Shed no blood; throw him into this pit here in the

a Traditional rendering (compare Gk): *a coat of many colors;* Meaning of Heb uncertain wilderness, but lay no hand on him"—that he might rescue him out of their hand and restore him to his father. 23So when Joseph came to his brothers, they stripped him of his robe, the long robe with sleeves*a* that he wore; 24and they took him and threw him into a pit. The pit was empty; there was no water in it.

25 Then they sat down to eat; and looking up they saw a caravan of Ishmaelites coming from Gilead, with their camels carrying gum, balm, and resin, on their way to carry it down to Egypt. 26Then Judah said to his brothers, "What profit is it if we kill our brother and conceal his blood? 27Come, let us sell him to the Ishmaelites, and not lay our hands on him, for he is our brother, our own flesh." And his brothers agreed. 28When some Midianite traders passed by, they drew Joseph up, lifting him out of the pit, and sold him to the Ishmaelites for twenty pieces of silver. And they took Joseph to Egypt.

29 When Reuben returned to the pit and saw that Joseph was not in the pit, he tore his clothes. 30He returned to his brothers, and said, "The boy is gone; and I, where can I turn?" 31Then they took Joseph's robe, slaughtered a goat, and dipped the robe in the blood. 32They had the long robe with sleeves*a* taken to their father, and they said, "This we have found; see now whether it is your son's robe or not." 33He recognized it, and said, "It is my son's robe! A wild animal has devoured him; Joseph is without doubt torn to pieces." 34Then Jacob tore his garments, and put sackcloth on his loins, and mourned for his son many days. 35All his sons and all his daughters sought to comfort him; but he refused to be comforted, and said, "No, I shall go down to Sheol to my son, mourning." Thus his father bewailed him. 36Meanwhile the Midianites had sold him in Egypt to Potiphar, one of Pharaoh's officials, the captain of the guard.

voring of one child over another and the conflict that results is an important theme in Genesis (4.4–5; 21.10; 25.28). *A long robe with sleeves,* since it is impossible to do manual labor while wearing it, suggests a life of leisure for Joseph, who seems prone to sleep and dreams (vv. 5, 9). **5–11:** Dreams will play a role throughout the Joseph story. Each of the three dream sequences (37.5–11; 40.5–23; 41.1–36) contains two paired dreams. The story assumes that these dreams allow one to know the future, which is part of a divine plan. Jacob had some experience with dreams and divine plans in the episode at Bethel (28.10–22), so he *kept the matter in mind* (v. 11). *Binding sheaves* refers to tying newly cut stalks of grain into bundles; these stand in the field for a time to dry (v. 7). **15–28:** The changing of Joseph's clothes, here the stripping of his robe, will mark major transitions in his life throughout the story. Joseph moves from being a favored son to a hired slave. Joseph's brothers first plot to kill him, but *Reuben* (v. 21) and *Judah* (vv. 26–27) intervene to restrain them. Instead, they sell Joseph as a slave to some passing *Midianite traders* and *Ishmaelites.* Both of these groups were descended from Abraham and one of two women slaves, Hagar (16.15) and Keturah (25.1–4). Those whom Israel had formerly enslaved turn around and enslave an Israelite, Joseph. **33:** The brothers show the bloodied robe to their father Jacob without explanation. Jacob himself draws the conclusion that *a wild animal has devoured* Joseph. **34:** Jacob *tore his garments* and wore coarse *sackcloth,*★ both traditional acts of anguish and mourning the dead (v. 29). **35:** *Sheol*★ is a dry, dusty pit under the earth where the dead go at the end of their earthly existence.

〰〰〰〰〰〰〰〰〰〰〰〰〰〰〰〰〰〰〰

38 It happened at that time that Judah went down from his brothers and settled near a certain Adullamite whose name was Hirah. 2There Judah saw the daughter of a certain Canaanite whose name was Shua; he married her and went in to her. 3She conceived and bore a son; and he named him Er. 4Again she conceived and bore a son whom she named Onan. 5Yet again she bore a son, and she named him Shelah. She*b* was in Chezib when she bore him. 6Judah took a wife for Er his firstborn; her name was Tamar. 7But Er, Judah's firstborn, was wicked in the sight of the LORD,

37.1–36: Joseph's dreams and his brothers' schemes. 2: *This is the story of the family of* is a formula that literally in Hebrew reads, "These are the generations of." This formula occurs throughout Genesis as a heading for major new sections; examples include Gen 2.4; 6.9; 10.1; 11.27; 25.19. **3–4:** The fa-

a See note on 37.3   *b* Gk: Heb *He*

and the LORD put him to death. 8Then Judah said to Onan, "Go in to your brother's wife and perform the duty of a brother-in-law to her; raise up offspring for your brother." 9But since Onan knew that the offspring would not be his, he spilled his semen on the ground whenever he went in to his brother's wife, so that he would not give offspring to his brother. 10What he did was displeasing in the sight of the LORD, and he put him to death also. 11Then Judah said to his daughter-in-law Tamar, "Remain a widow in your father's house until my son Shelah grows up"—for he feared that he too would die, like his brothers. So Tamar went to live in her father's house.

12 In course of time the wife of Judah, Shua's daughter, died; when Judah's time of mourning was over,ᵃ he went up to Timnah to his sheepshearers, he and his friend Hirah the Adullamite. 13When Tamar was told, "Your father-in-law is going up to Timnah to shear his sheep," 14she put off her widow's garments, put on a veil, wrapped herself up, and sat down at the entrance to Enaim, which is on the road to Timnah. She saw that Shelah was grown up, yet she had not been given to him in marriage. 15When Judah saw her, he thought her to be a prostitute, for she had covered her face. 16He went over to her at the roadside, and said, "Come, let me come in to you," for he did not know that she was his daughter-in-law. She said, "What will you give me, that you may come in to me?" 17He answered, "I will send you a kid from the flock." And she said, "Only if you give me a pledge, until you send it." 18He said, "What pledge shall I give you?" She replied, "Your signet and your cord, and the staff that is in your hand." So he gave them to her, and went in to her, and she conceived by him. 19Then she got up and went away, and taking off her veil she put on the garments of her widowhood.

20 When Judah sent the kid by his friend the Adullamite, to recover the pledge from the woman, he could not find her. 21He asked the townspeople, "Where is the temple prostitute who was at Enaim by the wayside?" But they said, "No prostitute has been here." 22So he returned to Judah, and said,

"I have not found her; moreover the townspeople said, 'No prostitute has been here.'" 23Judah replied, "Let her keep the things as her own, otherwise we will be laughed at; you see, I sent this kid, and you could not find her."

24 About three months later Judah was told, "Your daughter-in-law Tamar has played the whore; moreover she is pregnant as a result of whoredom." And Judah said, "Bring her out, and let her be burned." 25As she was being brought out, she sent word to her father-in-law, "It was the owner of these who made me pregnant." And she said, "Take note, please, whose these are, the signet and the cord and the staff." 26Then Judah acknowledged them and said, "She is more in the right than I, since I did not give her to my son Shelah." And he did not lie with her again.

27 When the time of her delivery came, there were twins in her womb. 28While she was in labor, one put out a hand; and the midwife took and bound on his hand a crimson thread, saying, "This one came out first." 29But just then he drew back his hand, and out came his brother; and she said, "What a breach you have made for yourself!" Therefore he was named Perez.ᵇ 30Afterward his brother came out with the crimson thread on his hand; and he was named Zerah.ᶜ

38.1–30: Tamar and Judah. This story interrupts the Joseph narrative* which runs from ch. 37 to ch. 50. However, some of its themes and images are related to images and themes in the larger Joseph narrative. Examples include the function of the goat (37.31 and 38.17, 20), recognizing and deceiving with clothes (37.31–33 and 38.13–17, 26), and irregular sexual activity (38.14–18 and 39.7–18). The climax* of the Tamar-Judah story is the birth of Perez and Zerah. Perez becomes an ancestor of Israel's great King David (Ruth 4.18–22). The long road of the divine promise to David included this irregular detour through Tamar and Judah. This irregularity ties in with the larger theme of the Joseph story as a whole: God manages to bless Joseph and his brothers in spite of and through the many detours of sibling rivalry, deception, slavery, im-

a Heb *when Judah was comforted*   b That is *A breach*
c That is *Brightness;* perhaps alluding to the crimson thread

prisonment, and famine. **7:** The story does not explain the way in which Er was *wicked* nor precisely how *the LORD put him to death.* The details are not necessary to the plot. **8:** *The duty of a brother-in-law* involves the custom of a levirate marriage.* The levirate obligation requires the brother of a married man who has died childless to have sexual intercourse with the dead man's wife. The brother must do so until she becomes pregnant and has a child who will carry on the dead man's name (Deut 25.5–10). **9–10:** *Onan spilled his semen on the ground. . . . What he did was displeasing.* This is not meant as a generalized judgment against masturbation or birth control. It involves only a specialized case of failure to fulfill the levirate obligation. **11:** Judah has no intention of allowing Shelah to perform the levirate duty of a brother-in-law with Tamar. He apparently assumes association with Tamar somehow caused the death of his other sons. He does not want the same to happen to his only remaining son, Shelah (v. 14). **14:** In light of Tamar's deception and Judah's blindness to what is actually going on, the meanings of the place names are significant. *Entrance to Enaim* means "opening of the eyes." *Timnah* means "conceal." **16:** *Let me come in to you* is a request to have sexual intercourse. **18:** *The signet* was a ring with a distinctive design or stamp which could be used as a personal signature on official or commercial documents. It was often tied to a *cord* and worn around the neck. The *staff* was a walking stick, often with a distinctive family emblem carved on it. The modern-day equivalent of your signet, cord, and staff would be your driver's license and all your credit cards. **21–22:** Judah's messenger asks for the *temple prostitute* ("kedeshah," literally "holy woman," v. 21). The story assumes the presence of prostitutes associated with fertility rituals at Canaanite temples. The term "temple prostitute" is more dignified than the term for an ordinary *prostitute* ("zonah," v. 22). **28–30:** The twin boys repeat the experience of the twins Jacob and Esau. The second-born son comes out ahead of the first-born son (25.22–24). The name *Perez* means "breach" or "breaking forth" out of the womb ahead of his older brother. *Zerah* means "brightness," perhaps in reference to the bright red or crimson thread. Perez is an ancestor of the great King David (Ruth 4.18–22). Like Perez, David was also the youngest among his brothers (1 Sam 16.1–13).

39 Now Joseph was taken down to Egypt, and Potiphar, an officer of Pharaoh, the captain of the guard, an Egyp-

tian, bought him from the Ishmaelites who had brought him down there. [2]The LORD was with Joseph, and he became a successful man; he was in the house of his Egyptian master. [3]His master saw that the LORD was with him, and that the LORD caused all that he did to prosper in his hands. [4]So Joseph found favor in his sight and attended him; he made him overseer of his house and put him in charge of all that he had. [5]From the time that he made him overseer in his house and over all that he had, the LORD blessed the Egyptian's house for Joseph's sake; the blessing of the LORD was on all that he had, in house and field. [6]So he left all that he had in Joseph's charge; and, with him there, he had no concern for anything but the food that he ate.

Now Joseph was handsome and good-looking. [7]And after a time his master's wife cast her eyes on Joseph and said, "Lie with me." [8]But he refused and said to his master's wife, "Look, with me here, my master has no concern about anything in the house, and he has put everything that he has in my hand. [9]He is not greater in this house than I am, nor has he kept back anything from me except yourself, because you are his wife. How then could I do this great wickedness, and sin against God?" [10]And although she spoke to Joseph day after day, he would not consent to lie beside her or to be with her. [11]One day, however, when he went into the house to do his work, and while no one else was in the house, [12]she caught hold of his garment, saying, "Lie with me!" But he left his garment in her hand, and fled and ran outside. [13]When she saw that he had left his garment in her hand and had fled outside, [14]she called out to the members of her household and said to them, "See, my husband[a] has brought among us a Hebrew to insult us! He came in to me to lie with me, and I cried out with a loud voice; [15]and when he heard me raise my voice and cry out, he left his garment beside me, and fled outside." [16]Then she kept his garment by her until his master came home, [17]and she told him the same story, saying, "The Hebrew servant, whom

a Heb *he*

you have brought among us, came in to me to insult me; 18but as soon as I raised my voice and cried out, he left his garment beside me, and fled outside."

19 When his master heard the words that his wife spoke to him, saying, "This is the way your servant treated me," he became enraged. 20And Joseph's master took him and put him into the prison, the place where the king's prisoners were confined; he remained there in prison. 21But the LORD was with Joseph and showed him steadfast love; he gave him favor in the sight of the chief jailer. 22The chief jailer committed to Joseph's care all the prisoners who were in the prison, and whatever was done there, he was the one who did it. 23The chief jailer paid no heed to anything that was in Joseph's care, because the LORD was with him; and whatever he did, the LORD made it prosper.

39.1–23: Joseph and Potiphar's wife. The story of Joseph resumes after the interlude with Tamar and Judah. **1:** *Pharaoh* is the title for the king of Egypt. **2:** The refrain *the LORD was with Joseph* begins and concludes this episode (vv. 21, 23). **7–20:** Some parallels exist between this scene and an ancient Egyptian story entitled "A Tale of Two Brothers." A man resists the sexual invitations of his brother's wife but then is falsely accused.

---

40 Some time after this, the cupbearer of the king of Egypt and his baker offended their lord the king of Egypt. 2Pharaoh was angry with his two officers, the chief cupbearer and the chief baker, 3and he put them in custody in the house of the captain of the guard, in the prison where Joseph was confined. 4The captain of the guard charged Joseph with them, and he waited on them; and they continued for some time in custody. 5One night they both dreamed—the cupbearer and the baker of the king of Egypt, who were confined in the prison—each his own dream, and each dream with its own meaning. 6When Joseph came to them in the morning, he saw that they were troubled. 7So he asked Pharaoh's officers, who were with him in custody in his master's house, "Why are your faces downcast today?" 8They said to him, "We have had dreams, and there

is no one to interpret them." And Joseph said to them, "Do not interpretations belong to God? Please tell them to me."

9 So the chief cupbearer told his dream to Joseph, and said to him, "In my dream there was a vine before me, 10and on the vine there were three branches. As soon as it budded, its blossoms came out and the clusters ripened into grapes. 11Pharaoh's cup was in my hand; and I took the grapes and pressed them into Pharaoh's cup, and placed the cup in Pharaoh's hand." 12Then Joseph said to him, "This is its interpretation: the three branches are three days; 13within three days Pharaoh will lift up your head and restore you to your office; and you shall place Pharaoh's cup in his hand, just as you used to do when you were his cupbearer. 14But remember me when it is well with you; please do me the kindness to make mention of me to Pharaoh, and so get me out of this place. 15For in fact I was stolen out of the land of the Hebrews; and here also I have done nothing that they should have put me into the dungeon."

16 When the chief baker saw that the interpretation was favorable, he said to Joseph, "I also had a dream: there were three cake baskets on my head, 17and in the uppermost basket there were all sorts of baked food for Pharaoh, but the birds were eating it out of the basket on my head." 18And Joseph answered, "This is its interpretation: the three baskets are three days; 19within three days Pharaoh will lift up your head—from you!—and hang you on a pole; and the birds will eat the flesh from you."

20 On the third day, which was Pharaoh's birthday, he made a feast for all his servants, and lifted up the head of the chief cupbearer and the head of the chief baker among his servants. 21He restored the chief cupbearer to his cupbearing, and he placed the cup in Pharaoh's hand; 22but the chief baker he hanged, just as Joseph had interpreted to them. 23Yet the chief cupbearer did not remember Joseph, but forgot him.

40.1–23: Joseph interprets the dreams of two prisoners. 5: This is the second of three dream sequences in the Joseph narrative* (37.5–11; 40.5–23; 41.1–36).

The dreams always occur in pairs, here with quite different futures predicted. Joseph shifts his role from the dreamer of dreams to an interpreter of others' dreams. **13:** The phrase *Pharaoh will lift up your head* has a positive meaning of exaltation for the cupbearer. The same phrase in v. 19 has a very negative meaning of execution by hanging for the baker (vv. 20–22).

41 After two whole years, Pharaoh dreamed that he was standing by the Nile, 2and there came up out of the Nile seven sleek and fat cows, and they grazed in the reed grass. 3Then seven other cows, ugly and thin, came up out of the Nile after them, and stood by the other cows on the bank of the Nile. 4The ugly and thin cows ate up the seven sleek and fat cows. And Pharaoh awoke. 5Then he fell asleep and dreamed a second time; seven ears of grain, plump and good, were growing on one stalk. 6Then seven ears, thin and blighted by the east wind, sprouted after them. 7The thin ears swallowed up the seven plump and full ears. Pharaoh awoke, and it was a dream. 8In the morning his spirit was troubled; so he sent and called for all the magicians of Egypt and all its wise men. Pharaoh told them his dreams, but there was no one who could interpret them to Pharaoh.

9 Then the chief cupbearer said to Pharaoh, "I remember my faults today. 10Once Pharaoh was angry with his servants, and put me and the chief baker in custody in the house of the captain of the guard. 11We dreamed on the same night, he and I, each having a dream with its own meaning. 12A young Hebrew was there with us, a servant of the captain of the guard. When we told him, he interpreted our dreams to us, giving an interpretation to each according to his dream. 13As he interpreted to us, so it turned out; I was restored to my office, and the baker was hanged."

14 Then Pharaoh sent for Joseph, and he was hurriedly brought out of the dungeon. When he had shaved himself and changed his clothes, he came in before Pharaoh. 15And Pharaoh said to Joseph, "I have had a dream, and there is no one who can interpret it. I have heard it said of you that when you hear a dream you can interpret it." 16Joseph answered Pharaoh, "It is not I; God will give Pharaoh a favorable answer." 17Then Pharaoh said to Joseph, "In my dream I was standing on the banks of the Nile; 18and seven cows, fat and sleek, came up out of the Nile and fed in the reed grass. 19Then seven other cows came up after them, poor, very ugly, and thin. Never had I seen such ugly ones in all the land of Egypt. 20The thin and ugly cows ate up the first seven fat cows, 21but when they had eaten them no one would have known that they had done so, for they were still as ugly as before. Then I awoke. 22I fell asleep a second time*a* and I saw in my dream seven ears of grain, full and good, growing on one stalk, 23and seven ears, withered, thin, and blighted by the east wind, sprouting after them; 24and the thin ears swallowed up the seven good ears. But when I told it to the magicians, there was no one who could explain it to me."

25 Then Joseph said to Pharaoh, "Pharaoh's dreams are one and the same; God has revealed to Pharaoh what he is about to do. 26The seven good cows are seven years, and the seven good ears are seven years; the dreams are one. 27The seven lean and ugly cows that came up after them are seven years, as are the seven empty ears blighted by the east wind. They are seven years of famine. 28It is as I told Pharaoh; God has shown to Pharaoh what he is about to do. 29There will come seven years of great plenty throughout all the land of Egypt. 30After them there will arise seven years of famine, and all the plenty will be forgotten in the land of Egypt; the famine will consume the land. 31The plenty will no longer be known in the land because of the famine that will follow, for it will be very grievous. 32And the doubling of Pharaoh's dream means that the thing is fixed by God, and God will shortly bring it about. 33Now therefore let Pharaoh select a man who is discerning and wise, and set him over the land of Egypt. 34Let Pharaoh proceed to appoint overseers over the land, and take one-fifth of the produce of the land of Egypt during the seven plenteous years. 35Let them gather all the food of these

a Gk Syr Vg: Heb lacks *I fell asleep a second time*

good years that are coming, and lay up grain under the authority of Pharaoh for food in the cities, and let them keep it. ³⁶That food shall be a reserve for the land against the seven years of famine that are to befall the land of Egypt, so that the land may not perish through the famine."

37 The proposal pleased Pharaoh and all his servants. ³⁸Pharaoh said to his servants, "Can we find anyone else like this—one in whom is the spirit of God?" ³⁹So Pharaoh said to Joseph, "Since God has shown you all this, there is no one so discerning and wise as you. ⁴⁰You shall be over my house, and all my people shall order themselves as you command; only with regard to the throne will I be greater than you." ⁴¹And Pharaoh said to Joseph, "See, I have set you over all the land of Egypt." ⁴²Removing his signet ring from his hand, Pharaoh put it on Joseph's hand; he arrayed him in garments of fine linen, and put a gold chain around his neck. ⁴³He had him ride in the chariot of his second-in-command; and they cried out in front of him, "Bow the knee!"ᵃ Thus he set him over all the land of Egypt. ⁴⁴Moreover Pharaoh said to Joseph, "I am Pharaoh, and without your consent no one shall lift up hand or foot in all the land of Egypt." ⁴⁵Pharaoh gave Joseph the name Zaphenath-paneah; and he gave him Asenath daughter of Potiphera, priest of On, as his wife. Thus Joseph gained authority over the land of Egypt.

46 Joseph was thirty years old when he entered the service of Pharaoh king of Egypt. And Joseph went out from the presence of Pharaoh, and went through all the land of Egypt. ⁴⁷During the seven plenteous years the earth produced abundantly. ⁴⁸He gathered up all the food of the seven years when there was plentyᵇ in the land of Egypt, and stored up food in the cities; he stored up in every city the food from the fields around it. ⁴⁹So Joseph stored up grain in such abundance—like the sand of the sea—that he stopped measuring it; it was beyond measure.

50 Before the years of famine came, Joseph had two sons, whom Asenath daughter of Potiphera, priest of On, bore to him. ⁵¹Joseph named the firstborn Manasseh,ᶜ "For,"

he said, "God has made me forget all my hardship and all my father's house." ⁵²The second he named Ephraim,ᵈ "For God has made me fruitful in the land of my misfortunes."

53 The seven years of plenty that prevailed in the land of Egypt came to an end; ⁵⁴and the seven years of famine began to come, just as Joseph had said. There was famine in every country, but throughout the land of Egypt there was bread. ⁵⁵When all the land of Egypt was famished, the people cried to Pharaoh for bread. Pharaoh said to all the Egyptians, "Go to Joseph; what he says to you, do." ⁵⁶And since the famine had spread over all the land, Joseph opened all the storehouses,ᵉ and sold to the Egyptians, for the famine was severe in the land of Egypt. ⁵⁷Moreover, all the world came to Joseph in Egypt to buy grain, because the famine became severe throughout the world.

41.1–57: Joseph interprets the dreams of Pharaoh. This story marks the key turning point in Joseph's fortunes: His ability as a dream interpreter elevates him to second in command of all Egypt. **1–7:** This is the third of the three dream sequences in the Joseph story. The dreams again appear as a pair, one about *cows* (vv. 2–4) and one about *grain* (vv. 5–7). The *Nile* River that runs through the otherwise dry landscape is Egypt's primary source of water, fertility, and life (vv. 1–4). **14:** Joseph's change of clothes marks major transitions in his life throughout the story (37.23; 39.12; 41.42). **32:** Joseph explains why all of the dreams have been doubled throughout the story (37.5–11; 40.5–23; 41.1–36). The doubling demonstrates that God has predetermined the events that are soon to happen. **42:** Pharaoh's *signet ring* has the Pharaoh's official stamp or "signature." He gives it to Joseph as a sign of his elevation to power as Pharaoh's representative. Joseph's new *garments of fine linen* mark yet another transition in his life (see v. 14). **51–52:** The two names of Joseph's sons, *Manasseh* ("making to forget") and *Ephraim* ("to be fruitful"), celebrate Jo-

---

ᵃ **Abrek,** apparently an Egyptian word similar in sound to the Hebrew word meaning *to kneel*　　ᵇ Sam Gk: MT *the seven years that were*　　ᶜ That is *Making to forget*　ᵈ From a Hebrew word meaning *to be fruitful*　ᵉ Gk Vg Compare Syr: Heb *opened all that was in* (or, *among*) *them* seph's elevation out of slavery and prison. **57:** The material benefit of providing food in the midst of famine *throughout the world* is another example of the fulfillment of the promise to Abraham that his family would be a blessing "to all the families of the earth" (12.3). The verse also provides a transition to the famine in Canaan and explains why Joseph's brothers will come to Egypt seeking food.

42 When Jacob learned that there was grain in Egypt, he said to his sons, "Why do you keep looking at one another? ²I have heard," he said, "that there is grain in Egypt; go down and buy grain for us there, that we may live and not die." ³So ten of Joseph's brothers went down to buy grain in Egypt. ⁴But Jacob did not send Joseph's brother Benjamin with his brothers, for he feared that harm might come to him. ⁵Thus the sons of Israel were among the other people who came to buy grain, for the famine had reached the land of Canaan.

6 Now Joseph was governor over the land; it was he who sold to all the people of the land. And Joseph's brothers came and bowed themselves before him with their faces to the ground. ⁷When Joseph saw his brothers, he recognized them, but he treated them like strangers and spoke harshly to them. "Where do you come from?" he said. They said, "From the land of Canaan, to buy food." ⁸Although Joseph had recognized his brothers, they did not recognize him. ⁹Joseph also remembered the dreams that he had dreamed about them. He said to them, "You are spies; you have come to see the nakedness of the land!" ¹⁰They said to him, "No, my lord; your servants have come to buy food. ¹¹We are all sons of one man; we are honest men; your servants have never been spies." ¹²But he said to them, "No, you have come to see the nakedness of the land!" ¹³They said, "We, your servants, are twelve brothers, the sons of a certain man in the land of Canaan; the youngest, however, is now with our father, and one is no more." ¹⁴But Joseph said to them, "It is just as I have said to you; you are spies! ¹⁵Here is how you shall be tested: as Pharaoh lives, you shall not leave this place unless your youngest brother comes here! ¹⁶Let one of you go and bring your brother, while the rest of you remain in prison, in order that your words may be tested, whether there is truth in you; or else, as Pharaoh lives, surely you are spies." ¹⁷And he put them all together in prison for three days.

18 On the third day Joseph said to them, "Do this and you will live, for I fear God: ¹⁹if you are honest men, let one of your brothers stay here where you are imprisoned. The rest of you shall go and carry grain for the famine of your households, ²⁰and bring your youngest brother to me. Thus your words will be verified, and you shall not die." And they agreed to do so. ²¹They said to one another, "Alas, we are paying the penalty for what we did to our brother; we saw his anguish when he pleaded with us, but we would not listen. That is why this anguish has come upon us." ²²Then Reuben answered them, "Did I not tell you not to wrong the boy? But you would not listen. So now there comes a reckoning for his blood." ²³They did not know that Joseph understood them, since he spoke with them through an interpreter. ²⁴He turned away from them and wept; then he returned and spoke to them. And he picked out Simeon and had him bound before their eyes. ²⁵Joseph then gave orders to fill their bags with grain, to return every man's money to his sack, and to give them provisions for their journey. This was done for them.

42.1–25: Joseph's brothers seek food in Egypt. 4: *Benjamin* is the youngest of Jacob's sons. He is the one full brother that Joseph has since Benjamin and Joseph are the only children of Jacob's favored wife, Rachel. **6:** Joseph's brothers unknowingly fulfill the prediction in Joseph's earlier two dreams in 37.5–11: They *bowed themselves before him.* **22:** *A reckoning for his blood* assumes a moral order in which murder or other wrongful actions will bring inevitable punishment (4.10; 9.5).

26 They loaded their donkeys with their grain, and departed. ²⁷When one of them opened his sack to give his donkey fodder at the lodging place, he saw his money at the top of the sack. ²⁸He said to his brothers, "My money has been put back; here it is in my sack!" At this they lost heart and turned

trembling to one another, saying, "What is this that God has done to us?"

29 When they came to their father Jacob in the land of Canaan, they told him all that had happened to them, saying, ³⁰"The man, the lord of the land, spoke harshly to us, and charged us with spying on the land. ³¹But we said to him, 'We are honest men, we are not spies. ³²We are twelve brothers, sons of our father; one is no more, and the youngest is now with our father in the land of Canaan.' ³³Then the man, the lord of the land, said to us, 'By this I shall know that you are honest men: leave one of your brothers with me, take grain for the famine of your households, and go your way. ³⁴Bring your youngest brother to me, and I shall know that you are not spies but honest men. Then I will release your brother to you, and you may trade in the land.' "

35 As they were emptying their sacks, there in each one's sack was his bag of money. When they and their father saw their bundles of money, they were dismayed. ³⁶And their father Jacob said to them, "I am the one you have bereaved of children: Joseph is no more, and Simeon is no more, and now you would take Benjamin. All this has happened to me!" ³⁷Then Reuben said to his father, "You may kill my two sons if I do not bring him back to you. Put him in my hands, and I will bring him back to you." ³⁸But he said, "My son shall not go down with you, for his brother is dead, and he alone is left. If harm should come to him on the journey that you are to make, you would bring down my gray hairs with sorrow to Sheol."

42.38: *Sheol** is a dusty pit under the earth where all the dead go. Jacob does not want to die an old man (*my gray hairs*) consumed by sorrow.

43 Now the famine was severe in the land. ²And when they had eaten up the grain that they had brought from Egypt, their father said to them, "Go again, buy us a little more food." ³But Judah said to him, "The man solemnly warned us, saying, 'You shall not see my face unless your brother is with you.' ⁴If you will send our brother with us, we will go down and buy you food; ⁵but

if you will not send him, we will not go down, for the man said to us, 'You shall not see my face, unless your brother is with you.' " ⁶Israel said, "Why did you treat me so badly as to tell the man that you had another brother?" ⁷They replied, "The man questioned us carefully about ourselves and our kindred, saying, 'Is your father still alive? Have you another brother?' What we told him was in answer to these questions. Could we in any way know that he would say, 'Bring your brother down'?" ⁸Then Judah said to his father Israel, "Send the boy with me, and let us be on our way, so that we may live and not die—you and we and also our little ones. ⁹I myself will be surety for him; you can hold me accountable for him. If I do not bring him back to you and set him before you, then let me bear the blame forever. ¹⁰If we had not delayed, we would now have returned twice."

11 Then their father Israel said to them, "If it must be so, then do this: take some of the choice fruits of the land in your bags, and carry them down as a present to the man— a little balm and a little honey, gum, resin, pistachio nuts, and almonds. ¹²Take double the money with you. Carry back with you the money that was returned in the top of your sacks; perhaps it was an oversight. ¹³Take your brother also, and be on your way again to the man; ¹⁴may God Almighty*ᵃ* grant you mercy before the man, so that he may send back your other brother and Benjamin. As for me, if I am bereaved of my children, I am bereaved." ¹⁵So the men took the present, and they took double the money with them, as well as Benjamin. Then they went on their way down to Egypt, and stood before Joseph.

16 When Joseph saw Benjamin with them, he said to the steward of his house, "Bring the men into the house, and slaughter an animal and make ready, for the men are to dine with me at noon." ¹⁷The man did as Joseph said, and brought the men to Joseph's house. ¹⁸Now the men were afraid because they were brought to Joseph's house, and they said, "It is because of the money, replaced in our sacks the first time, that we

a Traditional rendering of Heb *El Shaddai*

have been brought in, so that he may have an opportunity to fall upon us, to make slaves of us and take our donkeys." ¹⁹So they went up to the steward of Joseph's house and spoke with him at the entrance to the house. ²⁰They said, "Oh, my lord, we came down the first time to buy food; ²¹and when we came to the lodging place we opened our sacks, and there was each one's money in the top of his sack, our money in full weight. So we have brought it back with us. ²²Moreover we have brought down with us additional money to buy food. We do not know who put our money in our sacks." ²³He replied, "Rest assured, do not be afraid; your God and the God of your father must have put treasure in your sacks for you; I received your money." Then he brought Simeon out to them. ²⁴When the steward*a* had brought the men into Joseph's house, and given them water, and they had washed their feet, and when he had given their donkeys fodder, ²⁵they made the present ready for Joseph's coming at noon, for they had heard that they would dine there.

26 When Joseph came home, they brought him the present that they had carried into the house, and bowed to the ground before him. ²⁷He inquired about their welfare, and said, "Is your father well, the old man of whom you spoke? Is he still alive?" ²⁸They said, "Your servant our father is well; he is still alive." And they bowed their heads and did obeisance. ²⁹Then he looked up and saw his brother Benjamin, his mother's son, and said, "Is this your youngest brother, of whom you spoke to me? God be gracious to you, my son!" ³⁰With that, Joseph hurried out, because he was overcome with affection for his brother, and he was about to weep. So he went into a private room and wept there. ³¹Then he washed his face and came out; and controlling himself he said, "Serve the meal." ³²They served him by himself, and them by themselves, and the Egyptians who ate with him by themselves, because the Egyptians could not eat with the Hebrews, for that is an abomination to the Egyptians. ³³When they were seated before him, the firstborn according to his birthright and the youngest according to his youth, the men

looked at one another in amazement. ³⁴Portions were taken to them from Joseph's table, but Benjamin's portion was five times as much as any of theirs. So they drank and were merry with him.

43.1–34: Joseph's brothers return to Egypt with Benjamin. 8–9: Judah puts himself on the line and reassures his father Jacob concerning Benjamin's safe return. Judah's words prepare the reader for his later actions in 44.18–34. **23:** Their brother *Simeon* had been detained in their first journey to Egypt (42.19, 24). He is now freed to return to his brothers. **26:** The prediction of Joseph's earlier dreams is fulfilled a second time when Joseph's brothers *bowed to the ground before him* (37.5–11; 42.6). **29:** Joseph and Benjamin were the only sons of their mother, Rachel. Thus, they are full brothers. **33–34:** The order of honor is typically the firstborn as most honored and the youngest as least honored. But Benjamin as the youngest of the twelve brothers receives preferential treatment. This continues the important theme throughout Genesis of the favored younger son (20.10; 25.23; 37.3, 8).

44 Then he commanded the steward of his house, "Fill the men's sacks with food, as much as they can carry, and put each man's money in the top of his sack. ²Put my cup, the silver cup, in the top of the sack of the youngest, with his money for the grain." And he did as Joseph told him. ³As soon as the morning was light, the men were sent away with their donkeys. ⁴When they had gone only a short distance from the city, Joseph said to his steward, "Go, follow after the men; and when you overtake them, say to them, 'Why have you returned evil for good? Why have you stolen my silver cup?*b* ⁵Is it not from this that my lord drinks? Does he not indeed use it for divination? You have done wrong in doing this.'"

6 When he overtook them, he repeated these words to them. ⁷They said to him, "Why does my lord speak such words as these? Far be it from your servants that they should do such a thing! ⁸Look, the money that we found at the top of our sacks, we brought back to you from the land of Ca-

a Heb *the man*   *b* Gk Compare Vg: Heb lacks *Why have you stolen my silver cup?*

naan; why then would we steal silver or gold from your lord's house? 9Should it be found with any one of your servants, let him die; moreover the rest of us will become my lord's slaves." 10He said, "Even so; in accordance with your words, let it be: he with whom it is found shall become my slave, but the rest of you shall go free." 11Then each one quickly lowered his sack to the ground, and each opened his sack. 12He searched, beginning with the eldest and ending with the youngest; and the cup was found in Benjamin's sack. 13At this they tore their clothes. Then each one loaded his donkey, and they returned to the city.

14 Judah and his brothers came to Joseph's house while he was still there; and they fell to the ground before him. 15Joseph said to them, "What deed is this that you have done? Do you not know that one such as I can practice divination?" 16And Judah said, "What can we say to my lord? What can we speak? How can we clear ourselves? God has found out the guilt of your servants; here we are then, my lord's slaves, both we and also the one in whose possession the cup has been found." 17But he said, "Far be it from me that I should do so! Only the one in whose possession the cup was found shall be my slave; but as for you, go up in peace to your father."

18 Then Judah stepped up to him and said, "O my lord, let your servant please speak a word in my lord's ears, and do not be angry with your servant; for you are like Pharaoh himself. 19My lord asked his servants, saying, 'Have you a father or a brother?' 20And we said to my lord, 'We have a father, an old man, and a young brother, the child of his old age. His brother is dead; he alone is left of his mother's children, and his father loves him.' 21Then you said to your servants, 'Bring him down to me, so that I may set my eyes on him.' 22We said to my lord, 'The boy cannot leave his father, for if he should leave his father, his father would die.' 23Then you said to your servants, 'Unless your youngest brother comes down with you, you shall see my face no more.' 24When we went back to your servant my father we told him the words of my lord. 25And when

our father said, 'Go again, buy us a little food,' 26we said, 'We cannot go down. Only if our youngest brother goes with us, will we go down; for we cannot see the man's face unless our youngest brother is with us.' 27Then your servant my father said to us, 'You know that my wife bore me two sons; 28one left me, and I said, Surely he has been torn to pieces; and I have never seen him since. 29If you take this one also from me, and harm comes to him, you will bring down my gray hairs in sorrow to Sheol.' 30Now therefore, when I come to your servant my father and the boy is not with us, then, as his life is bound up in the boy's life, 31when he sees that the boy is not with us, he will die; and your servants will bring down the gray hairs of your servant our father with sorrow to Sheol. 32For your servant became surety for the boy to my father, saying, 'If I do not bring him back to you, then I will bear the blame in the sight of my father all my life.' 33Now therefore, please let your servant remain as a slave to my lord in place of the boy; and let the boy go back with his brothers. 34For how can I go back to my father if the boy is not with me? I fear to see the suffering that would come upon my father."

44.1–34: Joseph puts his brothers to the test. 4: *Why have you returned evil for good?* This question sounds a theme central to the Joseph story as a whole. Joseph's words to his brothers in 50.20 summarize the theme of the interplay of good and evil. **5:** *Divination* is the skill of determining the divine will or plan for the future. This was apparently done by observing the effects created by certain objects placed in the water contained in the sacred *silver cup* (v. 4). **9:** The brothers' words unknowingly put Benjamin under the threat of death since the silver cup was planted in his sack (vv. 2, 12). **13:** *They tore their clothes,* a sign of intense anguish and grief. **14:** The story places *Judah* in the foreground as the leader of his brothers. He is about to play a key role as the hero in this scene. Joseph's earlier dreams in 37.5–11 are again fulfilled as the brothers *fell to the ground before him.* **16:** *Here we are then, my lord's slaves:* Those who once sold Joseph as a slave (37.28) offer themselves as slaves to Joseph. **17:** Joseph offers the other brothers the temptation to save themselves by sacrificing Benjamin. The test is a replay of the brothers' earlier decision to sacrifice their brother Joseph for their own benefit (37.28). **29, 31:** *Sheol** is the place of the dead. **33–34:** Judah offers himself *in place of the boy,* Benjamin. Judah's willingness to sacrifice himself to save Benjamin redeems his earlier involvement in the plot to sell Joseph as a slave (37.26).

45

Then Joseph could no longer control himself before all those who stood by him, and he cried out, "Send everyone away from me." So no one stayed with him when Joseph made himself known to his brothers. [2]And he wept so loudly that the Egyptians heard it, and the household of Pharaoh heard it. [3]Joseph said to his brothers, "I am Joseph. Is my father still alive?" But his brothers could not answer him, so dismayed were they at his presence.

4 Then Joseph said to his brothers, "Come closer to me." And they came closer. He said, "I am your brother, Joseph, whom you sold into Egypt. [5]And now do not be distressed, or angry with yourselves, because you sold me here; for God sent me before you to preserve life. [6]For the famine has been in the land these two years; and there are five more years in which there will be neither plowing nor harvest. [7]God sent me before you to preserve for you a remnant on earth, and to keep alive for you many survivors. [8]So it was not you who sent me here, but God; he has made me a father to Pharaoh, and lord of all his house and ruler over all the land of Egypt. [9]Hurry and go up to my father and say to him, 'Thus says your son Joseph, God has made me lord of all Egypt; come down to me, do not delay. [10]You shall settle in the land of Goshen, and you shall be near me, you and your children and your children's children, as well as your flocks, your herds, and all that you have. [11]I will provide for you there—since there are five more years of famine to come—so that you and your household, and all that you have, will not come to poverty.' [12]And now your eyes and the eyes of my brother Benjamin see that it is my own mouth that speaks to you. [13]You must tell my father how greatly I am honored in Egypt, and all that you have seen. Hurry and bring my father down here."

[14]Then he fell upon his brother Benjamin's neck and wept, while Benjamin wept upon his neck. [15]And he kissed all his brothers and wept upon them; and after that his brothers talked with him.

16 When the report was heard in Pharaoh's house, "Joseph's brothers have come," Pharaoh and his servants were pleased. [17]Pharaoh said to Joseph, "Say to your brothers, 'Do this: load your animals and go back to the land of Canaan. [18]Take your father and your households and come to me, so that I may give you the best of the land of Egypt, and you may enjoy the fat of the land.' [19]You are further charged to say, 'Do this: take wagons from the land of Egypt for your little ones and for your wives, and bring your father, and come. [20]Give no thought to your possessions, for the best of all the land of Egypt is yours.'"

21 The sons of Israel did so. Joseph gave them wagons according to the instruction of Pharaoh, and he gave them provisions for the journey. [22]To each one of them he gave a set of garments; but to Benjamin he gave three hundred pieces of silver and five sets of garments. [23]To his father he sent the following: ten donkeys loaded with the good things of Egypt, and ten female donkeys loaded with grain, bread, and provision for his father on the journey. [24]Then he sent his brothers on their way, and as they were leaving he said to them, "Do not quarrel[a] along the way."

25 So they went up out of Egypt and came to their father Jacob in the land of Canaan. [26]And they told him, "Joseph is still alive! He is even ruler over all the land of Egypt." He was stunned; he could not believe them. [27]But when they told him all the words of Joseph that he had said to them, and when he saw the wagons that Joseph had sent to carry him, the spirit of their father Jacob revived. [28]Israel said, "Enough! My son Joseph is still alive. I must go and see him before I die."

45.1–28: Joseph reveals his true identity to his brothers. 5: Joseph recognizes that his slavery and

a Or *be agitated*

coming to Egypt were part of a larger divine plan *to preserve life* for both his own family and "all the families of the earth" (12.3). **10:** *Goshen* is a fertile pasture land in the delta region of the Nile River in northeast Egypt (47.1–6).

46 When Israel set out on his journey with all that he had and came to Beer-sheba, he offered sacrifices to the God of his father Isaac. ²God spoke to Israel in visions of the night, and said, "Jacob, Jacob." And he said, "Here I am." ³Then he said, "I am God,ᵃ the God of your father; do not be afraid to go down to Egypt, for I will make of you a great nation there. ⁴I myself will go down with you to Egypt, and I will also bring you up again; and Joseph's own hand shall close your eyes."

5 Then Jacob set out from Beer-sheba; and the sons of Israel carried their father Jacob, their little ones, and their wives, in the wagons that Pharaoh had sent to carry him. ⁶They also took their livestock and the goods that they had acquired in the land of Canaan, and they came into Egypt, Jacob and all his offspring with him, ⁷his sons, and his sons' sons with him, his daughters, and his sons' daughters; all his offspring he brought with him into Egypt.

8 Now these are the names of the Israelites, Jacob and his offspring, who came to Egypt. Reuben, Jacob's firstborn, ⁹and the children of Reuben: Hanoch, Pallu, Hezron, and Carmi. ¹⁰The children of Simeon: Jemuel, Jamin, Ohad, Jachin, Zohar, and Shaul,ᵇ the son of a Canaanite woman. ¹¹The children of Levi: Gershon, Kohath, and Merari. ¹²The children of Judah: Er, Onan, Shelah, Perez, and Zerah (but Er and Onan died in the land of Canaan); and the children of Perez were Hezron and Hamul. ¹³The children of Issachar: Tola, Puvah, Jashub,ᶜ and Shimron. ¹⁴The children of Zebulun: Sered, Elon, and Jahleel ¹⁵(these are the sons of Leah, whom she bore to Jacob in Paddan-aram, together with his daughter Dinah; in all his sons and his daughters numbered thirty-three). ¹⁶The children of Gad: Ziphion, Haggi, Shuni, Ezbon, Eri, Arodi, and Areli. ¹⁷The children of Asher: Imnah, Ishvah, Ishvi, Beriah, and their sister Serah.

The children of Beriah: Heber and Malchiel ¹⁸(these are the children of Zilpah, whom Laban gave to his daughter Leah; and these she bore to Jacob—sixteen persons). ¹⁹The children of Jacob's wife Rachel: Joseph and Benjamin. ²⁰To Joseph in the land of Egypt were born Manasseh and Ephraim, whom Asenath daughter of Potiphera, priest of On, bore to him. ²¹The children of Benjamin: Bela, Becher, Ashbel, Gera, Naaman, Ehi, Rosh, Muppim, Huppim, and Ard ²²(these are the children of Rachel, who were born to Jacob—fourteen persons in all). ²³The children of Dan: Hashum.ᵈ ²⁴The children of Naphtali: Jahzeel, Guni, Jezer, and Shillem ²⁵(these are the children of Bilhah, whom Laban gave to his daughter Rachel, and these she bore to Jacob—seven persons in all). ²⁶All the persons belonging to Jacob who came into Egypt, who were his own offspring, not including the wives of his sons, were sixty-six persons in all. ²⁷The children of Joseph, who were born to him in Egypt, were two; all the persons of the house of Jacob who came into Egypt were seventy.

28 Israelᵉ sent Judah ahead to Joseph to lead the way before him into Goshen. When they came to the land of Goshen, ²⁹Joseph made ready his chariot and went up to meet his father Israel in Goshen. He presented himself to him, fell on his neck, and wept on his neck a good while. ³⁰Israel said to Joseph, "I can die now, having seen for myself that you are still alive." ³¹Joseph said to his brothers and to his father's household, "I will go up and tell Pharaoh, and will say to him, 'My brothers and my father's household, who were in the land of Canaan, have come to me. ³²The men are shepherds, for they have been keepers of livestock; and they have brought their flocks, and their herds, and all that they have.' ³³When Pharaoh calls you, and says, 'What is your occupation?' ³⁴you shall say, 'Your servants have been keepers of livestock from our youth even until now, both we and our ancestors'—in order that you may settle in the land of Goshen, be-

ᵃ Heb *the God*   ᵇ Or *Saul*   ᶜ Compare Sam Gk Num 26.24; 1 Chr 7.1: MT *Iob*   ᵈ Gk: Heb *Hushim* ᵉ Heb *He* cause all shepherds are abhorrent to the Egyptians."

46.1–47.31: Jacob moves his family to live with Joseph in Egypt. 46.1–4: Jacob had once before received a vision at night in which God spoke words of assurance and blessing when he had left Canaan (28.10–22). Then as now, God promised Jacob, *"I myself will go down with you* and *bring you up again"* (v. 4; 28.15). **27:** The *seventy* members of *the house of Jacob* are a partial fulfillment of the promise of many descendants repeated throughout Genesis (15.5; 28.14). **34:** *Goshen* is a pasture land in the Nile River delta isolated from the rest of Egypt. *Shepherds are abhorrent to the Egyptians:* Egyptian agriculture was based more on crops and field agriculture that would be endangered by wandering herds of grazing animals.

47 So Joseph went and told Pharaoh, "My father and my brothers, with their flocks and herds and all that they possess, have come from the land of Canaan; they are now in the land of Goshen." [2]From among his brothers he took five men and presented them to Pharaoh. [3]Pharaoh said to his brothers, "What is your occupation?" And they said to Pharaoh, "Your servants are shepherds, as our ancestors were." [4]They said to Pharaoh, "We have come to reside as aliens in the land; for there is no pasture for your servants' flocks because the famine is severe in the land of Canaan. Now, we ask you, let your servants settle in the land of Goshen." [5]Then Pharaoh said to Joseph, "Your father and your brothers have come to you. [6]The land of Egypt is before you; settle your father and your brothers in the best part of the land; let them live in the land of Goshen; and if you know that there are capable men among them, put them in charge of my livestock."

[7] Then Joseph brought in his father Jacob, and presented him before Pharaoh, and Jacob blessed Pharaoh. [8]Pharaoh said to Jacob, "How many are the years of your life?" [9]Jacob said to Pharaoh, "The years of my earthly sojourn are one hundred thirty; few and hard have been the years of my life. They do not compare with the years of the life of my ancestors during their long sojourn." [10]Then Jacob blessed Pharaoh, and went out

from the presence of Pharaoh. [11]Joseph settled his father and his brothers, and granted them a holding in the land of Egypt, in the best part of the land, in the land of Rameses, as Pharaoh had instructed. [12]And Joseph provided his father, his brothers, and all his father's household with food, according to the number of their dependents.

[13] Now there was no food in all the land, for the famine was very severe. The land of Egypt and the land of Canaan languished because of the famine. [14]Joseph collected all the money to be found in the land of Egypt and in the land of Canaan, in exchange for the grain that they bought; and Joseph brought the money into Pharaoh's house. [15]When the money from the land of Egypt and from the land of Canaan was spent, all the Egyptians came to Joseph, and said, "Give us food! Why should we die before your eyes? For our money is gone." [16]And Joseph answered, "Give me your livestock, and I will give you food in exchange for your livestock, if your money is gone." [17]So they brought their livestock to Joseph; and Joseph gave them food in exchange for the horses, the flocks, the herds, and the donkeys. That year he supplied them with food in exchange for all their livestock. [18]When that year was ended, they came to him the following year, and said to him, "We can not hide from my lord that our money is all spent; and the herds of cattle are my lord's. There is nothing left in the sight of my lord but our bodies and our lands. [19]Shall we die before your eyes, both we and our land? Buy us and our land in exchange for food. We with our land will become slaves to Pharaoh; just give us seed, so that we may live and not die, and that the land may not become desolate."

[20] So Joseph bought all the land of Egypt for Pharaoh. All the Egyptians sold their fields, because the famine was severe upon them; and the land became Pharaoh's. [21]As for the people, he made slaves of them[a] from one end of Egypt to the other. [22]Only the land of the priests he did not buy; for the

---

a Sam Gk Compare Vg: MT *He removed them to the cities*

priests had a fixed allowance from Pharaoh, and lived on the allowance that Pharaoh gave them; therefore they did not sell their land. 23 Then Joseph said to the people, "Now that I have this day bought you and your land for Pharaoh, here is seed for you; sow the land. 24 And at the harvests you shall give one-fifth to Pharaoh, and four-fifths shall be your own, as seed for the field and as food for yourselves and your households, and as food for your little ones." 25 They said, "You have saved our lives; may it please my lord, we will be slaves to Pharaoh." 26 So Joseph made it a statute concerning the land of Egypt, and it stands to this day, that Pharaoh should have the fifth. The land of the priests alone did not become Pharaoh's.

27 Thus Israel settled in the land of Egypt, in the region of Goshen; and they gained possessions in it, and were fruitful and multiplied exceedingly. 28 Jacob lived in the land of Egypt seventeen years; so the days of Jacob, the years of his life, were one hundred forty-seven years.

29 When the time of Israel's death drew near, he called his son Joseph and said to him, "If I have found favor with you, put your hand under my thigh and promise to deal loyally and truly with me. Do not bury me in Egypt. 30 When I lie down with my ancestors, carry me out of Egypt and bury me in their burial place." He answered, "I will do as you have said." 31 And he said, "Swear to me"; and he swore to him. Then Israel bowed himself on the head of his bed.

48 After this Joseph was told, "Your father is ill." So he took with him his two sons, Manasseh and Ephraim. 2 When Jacob was told, "Your son Joseph has come to you," he[a] summoned his strength and sat up in bed. 3 And Jacob said to Joseph, "God Almighty[b] appeared to me at Luz in the land of Canaan, and he blessed me, 4 and said to me, 'I am going to make you fruitful and increase your numbers; I will make of you a company of peoples, and will give this land to your offspring after you for a perpetual holding.' 5 Therefore your two sons, who were born to you in the land of Egypt before I came to you in Egypt, are now mine; Ephraim and Manasseh shall be mine, just as Reuben and Simeon are. 6 As for the offspring born to you after them, they shall be yours. They shall be recorded under the names of their brothers with regard to their inheritance. 7 For when I came from Paddan, Rachel, alas, died in the land of Canaan on the way, while there was still some distance to go to Ephrath; and I buried her there on the way to Ephrath" (that is, Bethlehem).

8 When Israel saw Joseph's sons, he said, "Who are these?" 9 Joseph said to his father, "They are my sons, whom God has given me here." And he said, "Bring them to me, please, that I may bless them." 10 Now the eyes of Israel were dim with age, and he could not see well. So Joseph brought them near him; and he kissed them and embraced them. 11 Israel said to Joseph, "I did not expect to see your face; and here God has let me see your children also." 12 Then Joseph removed them from his father's knees,[c] and he bowed himself with his face to the earth. 13 Joseph took them both, Ephraim in his right hand toward Israel's left, and Manasseh in his left hand toward Israel's right, and brought them near him. 14 But Israel stretched out his right hand and laid it on the head of Ephraim, who was the younger, and his left hand on the head of Manasseh, crossing his hands, for Manasseh was the firstborn. 15 He blessed Joseph, and said,

47.1–31. 11: *The land of Rameses* is another name for Goshen. Rameses was the name of a pharaoh in Egypt (Ex 1.11). 13–26: The severity of the famine in Egypt forces the population gradually to give up their money, livestock, land, and freedom to the authority of Pharaoh. The program is managed by Joseph. Joseph's role in making slaves of the Egyptians (v. 25) will be reversed in Ex 1.8–14 when a new pharaoh will enslave the Israelites. 29: Jacob's instruction to Joseph to *put your hand under my thigh,* near the male reproductive organs, is a ritual of making an intimate and solemn oath or promise (see 24.2). 30: *Their burial place* is the cave at Machpelah, which Abraham had purchased from the Hittites (23.1–20).

a Heb *Israel*   b Traditional rendering of Heb *El Shaddai*   c Heb *from his knees*

"The God before whom my ancestors
        Abraham and Isaac walked,
    the God who has been my shepherd all
        my life to this day,
16 the angel who has redeemed me from
        all harm, bless the boys;
    and in them let my name be
        perpetuated, and the name of my
        ancestors Abraham and Isaac;
    and let them grow into a multitude on
        the earth."

17 When Joseph saw that his father laid his right hand on the head of Ephraim, it displeased him; so he took his father's hand, to remove it from Ephraim's head to Manasseh's head. 18Joseph said to his father, "Not so, my father! Since this one is the firstborn, put your right hand on his head." 19But his father refused, and said, "I know, my son, I know; he also shall become a people, and he also shall be great. Nevertheless his younger brother shall be greater than he, and his offspring shall become a multitude of nations." 20So he blessed them that day, saying,

    "By you[a] Israel will invoke blessings,
        saying,
    'God make you[a] like Ephraim and like
        Manasseh.'"

So he put Ephraim ahead of Manasseh. 21Then Israel said to Joseph, "I am about to die, but God will be with you and will bring you again to the land of your ancestors. 22I now give to you one portion[b] more than to your brothers, the portion[b] that I took from the hand of the Amorites with my sword and with my bow."

48.1–22: Jacob blesses Joseph's two sons. 3: Jacob refers to God's first blessing given to him at Bethel (also known as Luz) in 28.10–22. **5–6:** Jacob adopts his two grandsons, *Ephraim and Manasseh,* as his own sons on a par with the oldest sons, Reuben and Simeon. This action explains why Manasseh and Ephraim will be listed in place of Joseph in later lists of the twelve tribes of Israel (Num 1.32–35; Josh 17.17). These tribes were dominant in certain periods of Israel's history. **13–14:** The blessing by Jacob (also known as Israel) with the *right hand* would imply a more favored status than a blessing with the left hand. The firstborn son would normally receive the right-hand blessing, but Jacob lays his right hand on

Ephraim, who was the younger (v. 14). **19:** Old blind Jacob (v. 10) refuses Joseph's request to give the favored right-hand blessing to the elder Manasseh. The scene is a replay of the elderly and blind Isaac blessing the younger Jacob in place of Esau (27.1–40). **22:** Jacob gives to Joseph *the portion that I took from the hand of the Amorites* in battle. The word for *portion* ("shekem") is a wordplay on the Canaanite or Amorite town of Shechem, which Jacob and his sons captured in a violent raid (34.25–29). Shechem was located on the border between Ephraim and Manasseh, the two Joseph tribes.

49 Then Jacob called his sons, and said: "Gather around, that I may tell you what will happen to you in days to come.
2 Assemble and hear, O sons of Jacob;
        listen to Israel your father.

3 Reuben, you are my firstborn,
        my might and the first fruits of my
            vigor,
        excelling in rank and excelling in
            power.
4 Unstable as water, you shall no longer
        excel
    because you went up onto your
        father's bed;
    then you defiled it—you[c] went up
        onto my couch!

5 Simeon and Levi are brothers;
        weapons of violence are their swords.
6 May I never come into their council;
        may I not be joined to their
            company—
    for in their anger they killed men,
        and at their whim they hamstrung
            oxen.
7 Cursed be their anger, for it is fierce,
        and their wrath, for it is cruel!
    I will divide them in Jacob,
        and scatter them in Israel.

8 Judah, your brothers shall praise you;
        your hand shall be on the neck of
            your enemies;

a you here is singular in Heb   *b* Or *mountain slope* (Heb *shekem,* a play on the name of the town and district of Shechem)   *c* Gk Syr Tg: Heb *he*

your father's sons shall bow down
　　before you.

9 Judah is a lion's whelp;
　　from the prey, my son, you have gone
　　　up.
He crouches down, he stretches out like
　　a lion,
　　like a lioness—who dares rouse him
　　　up?

10 The scepter shall not depart from
　　Judah,
　　nor the ruler's staff from between his
　　　feet,
until tribute comes to him;[a]
　　and the obedience of the peoples is
　　　his.

11 Binding his foal to the vine
　　and his donkey's colt to the choice
　　　vine,
he washes his garments in wine
　　and his robe in the blood of grapes;

12 his eyes are darker than wine,
　　and his teeth whiter than milk.

13 Zebulun shall settle at the shore of the
　　sea;
　　he shall be a haven for ships,
　　and his border shall be at Sidon.

14 Issachar is a strong donkey,
　　lying down between the sheepfolds;

15 he saw that a resting place was good,
　　and that the land was pleasant;
so he bowed his shoulder to the
　　burden,
　　and became a slave at forced labor.

16 Dan shall judge his people
　　as one of the tribes of Israel.

17 Dan shall be a snake by the roadside,
　　a viper along the path,
that bites the horse's heels
　　so that its rider falls backward.

18 I wait for your salvation, O LORD.

19 Gad shall be raided by raiders,
　　but he shall raid at their heels.

20 Asher's[b] food shall be rich,
　　and he shall provide royal delicacies.

21 Naphtali is a doe let loose
　　that bears lovely fawns.[c]

22 Joseph is a fruitful bough,
　　a fruitful bough by a spring;
　　his branches run over the wall.[d]

23 The archers fiercely attacked him;
　　they shot at him and pressed him
　　　hard.

24 Yet his bow remained taut,
　　and his arms[e] were made agile
by the hands of the Mighty One of
　　Jacob,
　　by the name of the Shepherd, the
　　　Rock of Israel,

25 by the God of your father, who will help
　　you,
　　by the Almighty[f] who will bless you
with blessings of heaven above,
blessings of the deep that lies beneath,
blessings of the breasts and of the
　　womb.

26 The blessings of your father
　　are stronger than the blessings of the
　　　eternal mountains,
　　the bounties[g] of the everlasting hills;
may they be on the head of Joseph,
　　on the brow of him who was set apart
　　　from his brothers.

27 Benjamin is a ravenous wolf,
　　in the morning devouring the prey,
　　and at evening dividing the spoil."

28 All these are the twelve tribes of Israel,
and this is what their father said to them
when he blessed them, blessing each one of
them with a suitable blessing.

29 Then he charged them, saying to
them, "I am about to be gathered to my people. Bury me with my ancestors—in the cave
in the field of Ephron the Hittite, 30in the
cave in the field at Machpelah, near Mamre,
in the land of Canaan, in the field that Abra-

a Or until Shiloh comes or until he comes to Shiloh or
(with Syr) until he comes to whom it belongs
b Gk Vg Syr: Heb From Asher　　c Or that gives
beautiful words　　d Meaning of Heb uncertain
e Heb the arms of his hands　　f Traditional rendering of
Heb Shaddai　　g Cn Compare Gk: Heb of my progenitors
to the boundaries

ham bought from Ephron the Hittite as a burial site. 31There Abraham and his wife Sarah were buried; there Isaac and his wife Rebekah were buried; and there I buried Leah— 32the field and the cave that is in it were purchased from the Hittites." 33When Jacob ended his charge to his sons, he drew up his feet into the bed, breathed his last, and was gathered to his people.

49.1–33: Jacob's last words to his sons. Jacob's deathbed blessing of his sons is ancient Hebrew poetry, although the varied blessings and condemnations may reflect later historical fortunes (v. 28). **3–4:** *Reuben* should be exalted as Jacob's *firstborn* son, but he will be demoted in status because he *defiled* his *father's bed.* Reuben had sexual relations with one of Jacob's concubines* (35.22). **5–7:** Jacob's condemnation of Simeon and Levi stems from their leadership in the violent killing of the men of Shechem (34.25–26, 30). Jacob's pledge to *divide* and *scatter* them points to Simeon's absorption into the tribe of Judah (Josh 19.9) and Levi's becoming a landless priestly tribe (Num 18.6–7, 20). **8–12:** The name *Judah* puns on the phrase *shall praise you* ("yoduka"). These verses anticipate the preeminence and prosperity of the royal line of King David, who arose out of the tribe of Judah. **16:** The name *Dan* plays on the verb *judge* ("yadin"). **19:** The name *Gad* plays on the words *raided, raiders,* and *raid* ("god"). **22–26:** This large section celebrates the future fertility and strength of the tribe of Joseph. **29–30:** Abraham's purchase of the burial cave is recounted in 23.1–20.

50

Then Joseph threw himself on his father's face and wept over him and kissed him. 2Joseph commanded the physicians in his service to embalm his father. So the physicians embalmed Israel; 3they spent forty days in doing this, for that is the time required for embalming. And the Egyptians wept for him seventy days.

4 When the days of weeping for him were past, Joseph addressed the household of Pharaoh, "If now I have found favor with you, please speak to Pharaoh as follows: 5My father made me swear an oath; he said, 'I am about to die. In the tomb that I hewed out for myself in the land of Canaan, there you shall bury me.' Now therefore let me go up, so that I may bury my father; then I will re-

turn." 6Pharaoh answered, "Go up, and bury your father, as he made you swear to do."

7 So Joseph went up to bury his father. With him went up all the servants of Pharaoh, the elders of his household, and all the elders of the land of Egypt, 8as well as all the household of Joseph, his brothers, and his father's household. Only their children, their flocks, and their herds were left in the land of Goshen. 9Both chariots and charioteers went up with him. It was a very great company. 10When they came to the threshing floor of Atad, which is beyond the Jordan, they held there a very great and sorrowful lamentation; and he observed a time of mourning for his father seven days. 11When the Canaanite inhabitants of the land saw the mourning on the threshing floor of Atad, they said, "This is a grievous mourning on the part of the Egyptians." Therefore the place was named Abel-mizraim;*a* it is beyond the Jordan. 12Thus his sons did for him as he had instructed them. 13They carried him to the land of Canaan and buried him in the cave of the field at Machpelah, the field near Mamre, which Abraham bought as a burial site from Ephron the Hittite. 14After he had buried his father, Joseph returned to Egypt with his brothers and all who had gone up with him to bury his father.

50.1–14: Jacob is embalmed and buried. 2: *To embalm* the dead body of Jacob was an Egyptian custom of treating the corpse so that it would be preserved. The preservation would allow Joseph to return the body to Canaan and bury it there as Jacob had requested.

15 Realizing that their father was dead, Joseph's brothers said, "What if Joseph still bears a grudge against us and pays us back in full for all the wrong that we did to him?" 16So they approached*b* Joseph, saying, "Your father gave this instruction before he died, 17'Say to Joseph: I beg you, forgive the crime of your brothers and the wrong they did in harming you.' Now therefore please forgive the crime of the servants of the God

a That is *mourning* (or *meadow*) of Egypt   b Gk Syr:
Heb *they commanded*

of your father." Joseph wept when they spoke to him. [18]Then his brothers also wept,[a] fell down before him, and said, "We are here as your slaves." [19]But Joseph said to them, "Do not be afraid! Am I in the place of God? [20]Even though you intended to do harm to me, God intended it for good, in order to preserve a numerous people, as he is doing today. [21]So have no fear; I myself will provide for you and your little ones." In this way he reassured them, speaking kindly to them.

22 So Joseph remained in Egypt, he and his father's household; and Joseph lived one hundred ten years. [23]Joseph saw Ephraim's children of the third generation; the children of Machir son of Manasseh were also born on Joseph's knees.

24 Then Joseph said to his brothers, "I am about to die; but God will surely come to you, and bring you up out of this land to the land that he swore to Abraham, to Isaac, and to Jacob." [25]So Joseph made the Israelites swear, saying, "When God comes to you, you shall carry up my bones from here." [26]And Joseph died, being one hundred ten years old; he was embalmed and placed in a coffin in Egypt.

50.15–26: Joseph once again forgives his brothers. 18: The brothers' words, *we are here as your slaves,* unintentionally anticipate the slavery of the Israelites in Egypt in Ex 1.8–14. **19–21:** Joseph's words sound the overriding theme of the Joseph story: the divine ability to guide events and to turn evil into good. **25:** The book of Genesis ends with the promise to Joseph that his body would be buried in the land of Canaan. The Israelites fulfill the promise in Ex 13.19 and Josh 24.32.

a Cn: Heb *also came*

EXODUS

Introduction

The book of Exodus is a book about freedom and obligation, telling one of the Old Testament's central stories. It is the story of the liberation of Israel out of slavery in Egypt (chs. 1–15). But the book of Exodus is not only about Israel's freedom. It is also about the people of Israel's entering into a formal covenant* relationship of laws and obligations with God on their way to the promised land of Canaan (chs. 16–40). Exodus contains diverse forms of literature: narratives,* poetry, commandments, and laws. Among these diverse literatures, the poetic Song of the Sea in ch. 15 is probably one of the oldest texts within the entire Bible. The book of Exodus began its long history of development with early traditions like ch. 15, the Ten Commandments in ch. 20, and the earliest collection of laws in the Bible, the "Covenant Code" in chs. 21–23. Later writers and editors added many narratives, laws, and traditions over hundreds of years as the book of Exodus reached its final form, sometime in the sixth or fifth century BCE. The many traditions and laws of Exodus are joined together into a coherent story with a central human character, Moses, who led Israel out of slavery and into its covenant relationship with God.

The story of Israel's exodus out of Egypt forms one of the most important, influential narratives of the Bible. The Passover* festival celebrates the event as an annual ritual (ch. 12). Israel's experience of slavery in Egypt shaped many Old Testament laws designed to protect the disadvantaged (23.9; Lev 19.33–34). The Old Testament prophets* used the exodus from Egypt as a continuing model of God's saving power when Israel was in crisis (Isa 51.10). The Ten Commandments in ch. 20 and the other laws in Exodus formed the basis for ongoing ethical and legal reflection in Israel's life as a nation and people. The story of Israel's worship of the golden calf and the breaking of the formal relationship of exclusive loyalty to God resonated with the Israelites in exile in Babylon in the sixth century BCE. Most important, God's resolve to remain present in the midst of this sinful people in spite of their sin provided a word of hope to exiles who wondered if the Exile* marked an end or a new beginning in their relationship with God.

READING GUIDE

Three critical moments punctuate the book of Exodus. Each moment is marked by a buildup of tension, suspense, and preparation. The first critical moment is Israel's crossing the Red Sea into the safety and freedom of the other side. God sends ten plagues against Egypt, each time demanding that the Egyptian leader, Pharaoh, set Israel free. Only after the tenth and final plague, including the death of the firstborn sons of Egypt, does Pharaoh finally set Israel free (chs. 12–15). The second key moment in Exodus is the establishment of the formal relationship or covenant between God and Israel at Mount Sinai. After witnessing the dramatic display of God's power and presence on Mount Sinai, the Israelites pledge to enter a special relationship with God and to obey God's laws and commandments (chs. 19–24). The third critical moment in Exodus comes when Israel worships the golden calf and jeopardizes the exclusive relationship with God. God nevertheless continues to lead the Israelites in their wilderness journey to Canaan, even though they are a rebellious and sinful people (chs. 32–34). These three moments—freedom, obligation, and the renewal of a relationship—define the primary turning points in the story of Israel in Exodus.

1 These are the names of the sons of Israel who came to Egypt with Jacob, each with his household: ²Reuben, Simeon, Levi, and Judah, ³Issachar, Zebulun, and Benjamin, ⁴Dan and Naphtali, Gad and Asher. ⁵The total number of people born to Jacob was seventy. Joseph was already in Egypt. ⁶Then Joseph died, and all his brothers, and that whole generation. ⁷But the Israelites were fruitful and prolific; they multiplied and grew exceedingly strong, so that the land was filled with them.

8 Now a new king arose over Egypt, who did not know Joseph. ⁹He said to his people, "Look, the Israelite people are more numerous and more powerful than we. ¹⁰Come, let us deal shrewdly with them, or they will increase and, in the event of war, join our enemies and fight against us and escape from the land." ¹¹Therefore they set taskmasters over them to oppress them with forced labor. They built supply cities, Pithom and Rameses, for Pharaoh. ¹²But the more they were oppressed, the more they multiplied and spread, so that the Egyptians came to dread the Israelites. ¹³The Egyptians became ruthless in imposing tasks on the Israelites, ¹⁴and made their lives bitter with hard service in mortar and brick and in every kind of field labor. They were ruthless in all the tasks that they imposed on them.

15 The king of Egypt said to the Hebrew midwives, one of whom was named Shiphrah and the other Puah, ¹⁶"When you act as midwives to the Hebrew women, and see them on the birthstool, if it is a boy, kill him; but if it is a girl, she shall live." ¹⁷But the midwives feared God; they did not do as the king of Egypt commanded them, but they let the boys live. ¹⁸So the king of Egypt summoned the midwives and said to them, "Why have you done this, and allowed the boys to live?" ¹⁹The midwives said to Pharaoh, "Because the Hebrew women are not like the Egyptian women; for they are vigorous and give birth before the midwife comes to them." ²⁰So God dealt well with the midwives; and the people multiplied and became very strong. ²¹And because the midwives feared God, he gave them families. ²²Then Pharaoh commanded all his people, "Every boy that is born to the Hebrews*a* you shall throw into the Nile, but you shall let every girl live."

1.1–22: A new king arises in Egypt and forces the Israelites to become slaves. Exodus continues the story of the family of Jacob in Egypt which concluded the book of Genesis. Israel's turn in fortunes from a people of honor to a people of slavery fulfills God's words to Abraham in Gen 15.12–16: Israel will go to a land not theirs and become slaves for four hundred years. **7:** The growing number and strength of the Israelites fulfills the promises of many descendants made to the ancestors in Genesis (Gen 13.16; 32.12). **8:** The *new king* of Egypt is not named, but some identify him as Rameses II (13th century BCE) in light of 1.11 and the building of a city called Rameses. The new ruler did not have the same high regard for Joseph and his family as had the previous ruler (Gen 47.1–12). **9:** The claim that the Israelites are *more numerous and more powerful* than the Egyptians may well be an exaggeration that shows the paranoia of the Egyptian ruler. **15:** It is not clear whether these two midwives are *Hebrew midwives* or Egyptians who act as midwives for the Hebrew women. The names of these heroic women, Shiphrah and Puah, suggest they may be Hebrew in origin. On the other hand, the information in vv. 17 and 21 that they *feared God* can refer to non-Israelites who acknowledge or obey Israel's God (Gen 20.1–11). **16:** Killing all the baby boys would cut off all the male lines of descent and thus eventually kill off

a Sam Gk Tg: Heb lacks *to the Hebrews*

the whole people. **19:** The midwives' deceptive claim that Hebrew women give birth more quickly is a way to cover up their refusal to obey the ruler's command to kill the Israelite babies. **22:** The Egyptian ruler or Pharaoh expands the command to kill Israelite boys to *all his people,* not just the midwives. All Egyptians are now guilty and will be subject to God's judgment.

2 Now a man from the house of Levi went and married a Levite woman. ²The woman conceived and bore a son; and when she saw that he was a fine baby, she hid him three months. ³When she could hide him no longer she got a papyrus basket for him, and plastered it with bitumen and pitch; she put the child in it and placed it among the reeds on the bank of the river. ⁴His sister stood at a distance, to see what would happen to him.

5 The daughter of Pharaoh came down to bathe at the river, while her attendants walked beside the river. She saw the basket among the reeds and sent her maid to bring it. ⁶When she opened it, she saw the child. He was crying, and she took pity on him. "This must be one of the Hebrews' children," she said. ⁷Then his sister said to Pharaoh's daughter, "Shall I go and get you a nurse from the Hebrew women to nurse the child for you?" ⁸Pharaoh's daughter said to her, "Yes." So the girl went and called the child's mother. ⁹Pharaoh's daughter said to her, "Take this child and nurse it for me, and I will give you your wages." So the woman took the child and nursed it. ¹⁰When the child grew up, she brought him to Pharaoh's daughter, and she took him as her son. She named him Moses,ᵃ "because," she said, "I drew him outᵇ of the water."

2.1–10: Moses is born and saved from the Nile River. This story of Moses' birth and rescue from the river includes parallels to other birth stories of heroes, especially the Legend* of King Sargon of Akkad (8th century BCE). **1:** Moses is born of parents from the Israelite tribe of *Levi.* The Levite tribe became a tribe of priests or servants dedicated to the worship of God (32.25–29). The family tree for the tribe of Levi in 6.14–27 names Moses' parents as Amram and Jochebed (6.20). Moses' brother is Aaron. **3:** The Bible uses this rare word for *basket* only one other time. It is the same word used for Noah's "ark" in Gen 6.14, another

story of dramatic rescue from water. **4:** Moses' *sister* is not named here. Later we will discover that she is Miriam, a sister to Aaron (15.20) and to Moses (Num 26.59). Micah 6.4 lists these three siblings—Moses, Aaron, and Miriam—as the leaders of Israel in their wilderness trek from Egypt to the promised land of Canaan. **9:** Pharaoh's own daughter conspires with Hebrew women to resist her father's vicious program against Israelite children. In a satisfying twist of fate, Pharaoh's daughter will pay *wages* to Moses' mother for nursing the mother's own child. **10:** The name *Moses* ("Mosheh") plays on the verb "to draw out" ("mashah").

11 One day, after Moses had grown up, he went out to his people and saw their forced labor. He saw an Egyptian beating a Hebrew, one of his kinsfolk. ¹²He looked this way and that, and seeing no one he killed the Egyptian and hid him in the sand. ¹³When he went out the next day, he saw two Hebrews fighting; and he said to the one who was in the wrong, "Why do you strike your fellow Hebrew?" ¹⁴He answered, "Who made you a ruler and judge over us? Do you mean to kill me as you killed the Egyptian?" Then Moses was afraid and thought, "Surely the thing is known." ¹⁵When Pharaoh heard of it, he sought to kill Moses.

But Moses fled from Pharaoh. He settled in the land of Midian, and sat down by a well. ¹⁶The priest of Midian had seven daughters. They came to draw water, and filled the troughs to water their father's flock. ¹⁷But some shepherds came and drove them away. Moses got up and came to their defense and watered their flock. ¹⁸When they returned to their father Reuel, he said, "How is it that you have come back so soon today?" ¹⁹They said, "An Egyptian helped us against the shepherds; he even drew water for us and watered the flock." ²⁰He said to his daughters, "Where is he? Why did you leave the man? Invite him to break bread." ²¹Moses agreed to stay with the man, and he gave Moses his daughter Zipporah in marriage. ²²She bore a son, and he named him Gershom; for he said, "I have been an alienᶜ residing in a foreign land."

a Heb *Mosheh*   *b* Heb *mashah*   *c* Heb *ger*

Moses and the Legend of Sargon

The story of the infant Moses in a basket floating in the river resembles other ancient Near Eastern stories about the birth and infancy of a hero. For example, there are some striking parallels between the Legend★ of Sargon and the biblical account. Sargon was the king of the nation of Akkad in Mesopotamia and reigned around 2600 BCE. The legend recounts how Sargon's mother gave birth to a child in secrecy. She placed the baby "in a basket of rushes; with bitumen she sealed the lid." She placed the basket in a river. A person named Akki saw the baby in the river, rescued him, and raised him as his own son. Eventually the baby became a leader and king of the people of Akkad. The story about Moses in ch. 2 seems to draw from a tradition similar to this legend.

23 After a long time the king of Egypt died. The Israelites groaned under their slavery, and cried out. Out of the slavery their cry for help rose up to God. 24God heard their groaning, and God remembered his covenant with Abraham, Isaac, and Jacob. 25God looked upon the Israelites, and God took notice of them.

2.11–25: Moses kills an Egyptian and flees to Midian. 11: The story moves immediately from Moses as a baby (2.1–10) to Moses as an adult. **13:** The Hebrew verb for *strike* ("nakah") is the same verb used in v. 12 when Moses *killed* the Egyptian, in v. 11 when the Egyptian was *beating* the Hebrew, and the word used as God "strikes" Egypt with the plagues later in the story (3.20; 12.12–13). **15:** Genesis 25.2 portrays the people of *Midian* as descended from Abraham and Keturah. They are a wandering people associated with the Sinai Peninsula south of Canaan and with northern Arabia, which lies east and north of Canaan. **18:** The name of Moses' father-in-law is *Reuel* here, but the name varies in other biblical traditions. His name is sometimes Jethro (3.1; 18.1) or Hobab (Num 10.29; Judg 4.11). **22:** Moses gives his son the name *Gershom* as a wordplay on the word for *alien* ("ger"). In a sense, Moses is an alien or stranger in every land. The Midianites consider him an "Egyptian" (2.19). The Egyptians seek to kill him as a Hebrew sympathizer (2.15). The Hebrews reject him as not one of their own (2.14). **23–24:** God *heard* Israel's cry of distress and God *remembered his covenant★* or promise made to Israel's ancestors in Genesis (*Abraham*—Gen 15.12–16; *Isaac*—26.24; *Jacob*—35.11–12).

**God calls Moses to lead Israel out of Egypt
3.1–4.31:** Moses encounters God veiled in a burning bush at Mount Horeb, otherwise known as Mount Sinai. God calls Moses to leave Midian and return to Egypt to lead Israel out of slavery to freedom. Moses responds with five objections or reasons why he should not lead Israel (3.11, 13; 4. 1, 10, 13). However, God patiently responds to each objection and insists that Moses go. Finally, Moses obeys (4.18–20).

3 Moses was keeping the flock of his father-in-law Jethro, the priest of Midian; he led his flock beyond the wilderness, and came to Horeb, the mountain of God. 2There the angel of the LORD appeared to him in a flame of fire out of a bush; he looked, and the bush was blazing, yet it was not consumed. 3Then Moses said, "I must turn aside and look at this great sight, and see why the bush is not burned up." 4When the LORD saw that he had turned aside to see, God called to him out of the bush, "Moses, Moses!" And he said, "Here I am." 5Then he said, "Come no closer! Remove the sandals from your feet, for the place on which you are standing is holy ground." 6He said further, "I am the God of your father, the God of Abraham, the God of Isaac, and the God of Jacob." And Moses hid his face, for he was afraid to look at God.

7 Then the LORD said, "I have observed the misery of my people who are in Egypt; I

have heard their cry on account of their task-masters. Indeed, I know their sufferings, 8and I have come down to deliver them from the Egyptians, and to bring them up out of that land to a good and broad land, a land flowing with milk and honey, to the country of the Canaanites, the Hittites, the Amorites, the Perizzites, the Hivites, and the Jebusites. 9The cry of the Israelites has now come to me; I have also seen how the Egyptians oppress them. 10So come, I will send you to Pharaoh to bring my people, the Israelites, out of Egypt." 11But Moses said to God, "Who am I that I should go to Pharaoh, and bring the Israelites out of Egypt?" 12He said, "I will be with you; and this shall be the sign for you that it is I who sent you: when you have brought the people out of Egypt, you shall worship God on this mountain."

13 But Moses said to God, "If I come to the Israelites and say to them, 'The God of your ancestors has sent me to you,' and they ask me, 'What is his name?' what shall I say to them?" 14God said to Moses, "I AM WHO I AM."[a] He said further, "Thus you shall say to the Israelites, 'I AM has sent me to you.' " 15God also said to Moses, "Thus you shall say to the Israelites, 'The LORD,[b] the God of your ancestors, the God of Abraham, the God of Isaac, and the God of Jacob, has sent me to you':

This is my name forever,
   and this my title for all generations.

16Go and assemble the elders of Israel, and say to them, 'The LORD, the God of your ancestors, the God of Abraham, of Isaac, and of Jacob, has appeared to me, saying: I have given heed to you and to what has been done to you in Egypt. 17I declare that I will bring you up out of the misery of Egypt, to the land of the Canaanites, the Hittites, the Amorites, the Perizzites, the Hivites, and the Jebusites, a land flowing with milk and honey.' 18They will listen to your voice; and you and the elders of Israel shall go to the king of Egypt and say to him, 'The LORD, the God of the Hebrews, has met with us; let us now go a three days' journey into the wilderness, so that we may sacrifice to the LORD our God.' 19I know, however, that the king of Egypt will not let you go unless compelled by a mighty hand.[c] 20So I will stretch out my hand and strike Egypt with all my wonders that I will perform in it; after that he will let you go. 21I will bring this people into such favor with the Egyptians that, when you go, you will not go empty-handed; 22each woman shall ask her neighbor and any woman living in the neighbor's house for jewelry of silver and of gold, and clothing, and you shall put them on your sons and on your daughters; and so you shall plunder the Egyptians."

3.1–22. 1: *Jethro* is an alternate name for Moses' *father-in-law,* who is otherwise known as Reuel (2.18) or Hobab (Num 10.29). Mount *Horeb* is an alternate name for Mount Sinai (19.11). *The mountain of God* reflects a common notion in the ancient Near East that mountain tops were the special dwelling places of the divine. **2:** *Fire* is a frequent biblical image for the deity's presence (Gen 15.17). **4:** *The LORD* is considered interchangeable with *the angel of the LORD* in v. 2. **6:** *To look at God* was a fearful thing because it could mean instant death (33.20; Isa 6.5). **8:** This is the first of many biblical examples in which the phrase *a land flowing with milk and honey* describes the goodness and fertility of the promised land of Canaan (13.5; Num 13.27). This list of peoples—*the Canaanites, the Hittites, the Amorites, the Perizzites, the Hivites, and the Jebusites*—is the traditional listing of the native inhabitants of the land of Canaan (Gen 15.19–21; Deut 7.1). **11–12:** This is the first of a series of five objections which Moses raises to God's call to lead Israel out of Egypt. Moses feels inadequate for the mission, but God assures him that God will be with him. As a sign, God promises that Moses and the Israelites will return to worship *on this mountain* of Horeb or Sinai (19.11). **13–15:** Moses' second objection is a request for God's name. God reveals the new divine name as *I AM WHO I AM* ("ehyeh asher ehyeh") or *I WILL BE WHO I WILL BE.* This name is a wordplay on the divine name "yhwh," usually pronounced "Yahweh." The name "Yahweh" derives from the verb "to be" ("hayah") and may be translated "he causes to be" or "he creates." Ancient Jewish practice considered the divine name "Yahweh" so holy and special that it should never be pro-

a Or *I AM WHAT I AM* or *I WILL BE WHAT I WILL BE*
b The word "LORD" when spelled with capital letters stands for the divine name, *YHWH,* which is here connected with the verb *hayah,* "to be" c Gk Vg: Heb *no, not by a mighty hand*

nounced. Wherever the name occurred, the reader used instead the Hebrew word for "the Lord" ("adonai"). This NRSV translation follows this ancient practice, substituting "the Lord" for every occurrence of "Yahweh" in the Hebrew text. The divine name, *I AM WHO I AM*, reveals God's intention to be present with Israel. At the same time, the name hides some of God's character until a later time of disclosure (33.19; 34.6–7). Moreover, the text underscores the identification of *the God of Abraham, the God of Isaac, and the God of Jacob* from the book of Genesis with the same God whose new name is revealed as *the Lord* ("Yahweh"). **18:** *Sacrifice* involves the killing of an animal and offering part of it to the deity as an act of worship and devotion. **22:** God's pressure on the Egyptians to release the Israelites will eventually become so strong that the Egyptians will be anxious to send them away with gold, silver, and fine clothing. In this way, Israel will *plunder the Egyptians* and take their war booty as a sign that God has won the victory in the battle with Pharaoh and the Egyptians. The promise is fulfilled in 12.33–36.

4 Then Moses answered, "But suppose they do not believe me or listen to me, but say, 'The Lord did not appear to you.' " ²The Lord said to him, "What is that in your hand?" He said, "A staff." ³And he said, "Throw it on the ground." So he threw the staff on the ground, and it became a snake; and Moses drew back from it. ⁴Then the Lord said to Moses, "Reach out your hand, and seize it by the tail"—so he reached out his hand and grasped it, and it became a staff in his hand— ⁵"so that they may believe that the Lord, the God of their ancestors, the God of Abraham, the God of Isaac, and the God of Jacob, has appeared to you."

6 Again, the Lord said to him, "Put your hand inside your cloak." He put his hand into his cloak; and when he took it out, his hand was leprous,ᵃ as white as snow. ⁷Then God said, "Put your hand back into your cloak"—so he put his hand back into his cloak, and when he took it out, it was restored like the rest of his body— ⁸"If they will not believe you or heed the first sign, they may believe the second sign. ⁹If they will not believe even these two signs or heed you, you shall take some water from the Nile and pour it on the dry ground; and the water

that you shall take from the Nile will become blood on the dry ground."

10 But Moses said to the Lord, "O my Lord, I have never been eloquent, neither in the past nor even now that you have spoken to your servant; but I am slow of speech and slow of tongue." ¹¹Then the Lord said to him, "Who gives speech to mortals? Who makes them mute or deaf, seeing or blind? Is it not I, the Lord? ¹²Now go, and I will be with your mouth and teach you what you are to speak." ¹³But he said, "O my Lord, please send someone else." ¹⁴Then the anger of the Lord was kindled against Moses and he said, "What of your brother Aaron the Levite? I know that he can speak fluently; even now he is coming out to meet you, and when he sees you his heart will be glad. ¹⁵You shall speak to him and put the words in his mouth; and I will be with your mouth and with his mouth, and will teach you what you shall do. ¹⁶He indeed shall speak for you to the people; he shall serve as a mouth for you, and you shall serve as God for him. ¹⁷Take in your hand this staff, with which you shall perform the signs."

18 Moses went back to his father-in-law Jethro and said to him, "Please let me go back to my kindred in Egypt and see whether they are still living." And Jethro said to Moses, "Go in peace." ¹⁹The Lord said to Moses in Midian, "Go back to Egypt; for all those who were seeking your life are dead." ²⁰So Moses took his wife and his sons, put them on a donkey, and went back to the land of Egypt; and Moses carried the staff of God in his hand.

21 And the Lord said to Moses, "When you go back to Egypt, see that you perform before Pharaoh all the wonders that I have put in your power; but I will harden his heart, so that he will not let the people go. ²²Then you shall say to Pharaoh, 'Thus says the Lord: Israel is my firstborn son. ²³I said to you, "Let my son go that he may worship me." But you refused to let him go; now I will kill your firstborn son.' "

24 On the way, at a place where they

_____

ᵃ A term for several skin diseases; precise meaning uncertain spent the night, the LORD met him and tried to kill him. 25But Zipporah took a flint and cut off her son's foreskin, and touched Moses'ᵃ feet with it, and said, "Truly you are a bridegroom of blood to me!" 26So he let him alone. It was then she said, "A bridegroom of blood by circumcision."

27 The LORD said to Aaron, "Go into the wilderness to meet Moses." So he went; and he met him at the mountain of God and kissed him. 28Moses told Aaron all the words of the LORD with which he had sent him, and all the signs with which he had charged him. 29Then Moses and Aaron went and assembled all the elders of the Israelites. 30Aaron spoke all the words that the LORD had spoken to Moses, and performed the signs in the sight of the people. 31The people believed; and when they heard that the LORD had given heed to the Israelites and that he had seen their misery, they bowed down and worshiped.

4.1–31. 1: Moses raises a third objection. God responds by offering three signs to be performed to bolster the people's confidence in Moses (vv. 2–9). Moses and his brother Aaron perform the signs in 4.30. Moses' brother Aaron will use the sign of the staff's turning into a serpent (vv. 2–5) as a means to try to convince Pharaoh (7.8–13). The third sign, the Nile River's turning into blood (v. 9), will become the first plague against Egypt (7.14–25). **10:** Moses' fourth objection is his inability as a speaker: *slow of speech and slow of tongue.* **13:** In a final desperate objection, Moses asks that God *send someone else.* **14:** For the first time, *the anger of the LORD* appears after much patience with Moses. God promises to send Moses' brother Aaron as his mouthpiece (vv. 14–17). **21:** The theme of God's *hardening the heart* of Pharaoh plays an important role throughout the story of Israel's exodus out of Egypt. Ancient Israel understood the *heart* as the intersecting point of human intellect and the human will. God repeatedly stiffens or hardens the heart or will of Pharaoh against letting Israel go (9.12; 14.8). This emphasis on God's control of Pharaoh ensures that Egypt will finally come to acknowledge God's power. On the other hand, the texts also repeatedly declare that Pharaoh hardens his own heart or will (7.13–14; 9.7, 34–35). Thus, Pharaoh can also be held morally responsible for his own willful actions. Pharaoh even confesses his own sin and responsibility for wrongdoing (9.27–28). The story holds together affir-

mations of divine guidance and control along with human freedom and responsibility. **23:** The threat to Pharaoh to *kill your firstborn son* will be accomplished in the tenth and final plague (12.29–32). In this way, God will reclaim Israel as God's *firstborn son* (v. 22). **24–26:** This story of the deity's attack and circumcision's⋆ role as a defense against the deity is difficult to understand. We have lost some of the historical context that underlies the original story. However, the mention of Pharaoh's "firstborn son" in the preceding verse (v. 23) suggests a connection to the final plague when the deity killed all the Egyptian firstborn. The protective power of the blood on the doorposts of the Israelites' houses caused the LORD to pass over their houses and not kill the Israelites' firstborn (12.12, 22–23). In the same way, the protective blood of circumcision here protects either Moses or his son (the pronoun "him" in vv. 24–26 is ambiguous). Circumcision is a ritual involving cutting off the foreskin of the male penis. A *flint* is a sharpened stone used in the ritual. *Moses' feet* is probably an alternate way of saying his genitals. *A bridegroom of blood* may reflect the practice of some cultures that called the circumcised male "a bridegroom." The theme of the deity's attack against those whom the deity has chosen for a special mission occurs elsewhere in the Bible (Gen 32.22–32; Num 22.22–35; Josh 5.13–15; Judg 2.1–5). **27:** *The mountain of God* is Mount Horeb, also known as Mount Sinai (3.1).

5 Afterward Moses and Aaron went to Pharaoh and said, "Thus says the LORD, the God of Israel, 'Let my people go, so that they may celebrate a festival to me in the wilderness.'" 2But Pharaoh said, "Who is the LORD, that I should heed him and let Israel go? I do not know the LORD, and I will not let Israel go." 3Then they said, "The God of the Hebrews has revealed himself to us; let us go a three days' journey into the wilderness to sacrifice to the LORD our God, or he will fall upon us with pestilence or sword." 4But the king of Egypt said to them, "Moses and Aaron, why are you taking the people away from their work? Get to your labors!" 5Pharaoh continued, "Now they are more numerous than the people of the landᵇ and yet you want them to stop working!"

a Heb *his*   *b* Sam: Heb *The people of the land are now many*

6That same day Pharaoh commanded the taskmasters of the people, as well as their supervisors, 7"You shall no longer give the people straw to make bricks, as before; let them go and gather straw for themselves. 8But you shall require of them the same quantity of bricks as they have made previously; do not diminish it, for they are lazy; that is why they cry, 'Let us go and offer sacrifice to our God.' 9Let heavier work be laid on them; then they will labor at it and pay no attention to deceptive words."

10 So the taskmasters and the supervisors of the people went out and said to the people, "Thus says Pharaoh, 'I will not give you straw. 11Go and get straw yourselves, wherever you can find it; but your work will not be lessened in the least.' " 12So the people scattered throughout the land of Egypt, to gather stubble for straw. 13The taskmasters were urgent, saying, "Complete your work, the same daily assignment as when you were given straw." 14And the supervisors of the Israelites, whom Pharaoh's taskmasters had set over them, were beaten, and were asked, "Why did you not finish the required quantity of bricks yesterday and today, as you did before?"

15 Then the Israelite supervisors came to Pharaoh and cried, "Why do you treat your servants like this? 16No straw is given to your servants, yet they say to us, 'Make bricks!' Look how your servants are beaten! You are unjust to your own people."a 17He said, "You are lazy, lazy; that is why you say, 'Let us go and sacrifice to the LORD.' 18Go now, and work; for no straw shall be given you, but you shall still deliver the same number of bricks." 19The Israelite supervisors saw that they were in trouble when they were told, "You shall not lessen your daily number of bricks." 20As they left Pharaoh, they came upon Moses and Aaron who were waiting to meet them. 21They said to them, "The LORD look upon you and judge! You have brought us into bad odor with Pharaoh and his officials, and have put a sword in their hand to kill us."

22 Then Moses turned again to the LORD and said, "O LORD, why have you mistreated this people? Why did you ever send me?

23Since I first came to Pharaoh to speak in your name, he has mistreated this people, and you have done nothing at all to deliver your people."

5.1–23: Moses and Aaron confront Pharaoh for the first time. 2: Pharaoh's words, *I do not know the LORD*, introduce a major theme of knowing the LORD, which plays a role throughout this section of Exodus (7.5, 17; 8.10; 9.14; 14.18). **3:** The threat of *pestilence or sword* points indirectly to the plagues that will begin soon. **5:** The claim that the number of Israelites exceeds that of the Egyptians is probably an exaggeration of a paranoid Pharaoh (1.9). The need *to stop working* in order to worship the LORD will become a defining practice of the Israelite community with the commandment concerning the sabbath (20.8–11; Deut 5.12–15). **21:** *Bad odor with Pharaoh* foreshadows the bad odor that will accompany the first two plagues (7.21; 8.13–14). **22–23:** This is another example of Moses' boldness to speak words of resistance, correction, or complaint to God (chs. 3–4; 32.11–14; 33.12–23).

6 Then the LORD said to Moses, "Now you shall see what I will do to Pharaoh: Indeed, by a mighty hand he will let them go; by a mighty hand he will drive them out of his land."

2 God also spoke to Moses and said to him: "I am the LORD. 3I appeared to Abraham, Isaac, and Jacob as God Almighty,b but by my name 'The LORD'c I did not make myself known to them. 4I also established my covenant with them, to give them the land of Canaan, the land in which they resided as aliens. 5I have also heard the groaning of the Israelites whom the Egyptians are holding as slaves, and I have remembered my covenant. 6Say therefore to the Israelites, 'I am the LORD, and I will free you from the burdens of the Egyptians and deliver you from slavery to them. I will redeem you with an outstretched arm and with mighty acts of judgment. 7I will take you as my people, and I will be your God. You shall know that I am the LORD your God, who has freed you from the burdens of the Egyptians. 8I will bring you into the land that I swore to give to Abra-

---

a Gk Compare Syr Vg: Heb *beaten, and the sin of your people*   b Traditional rendering of Heb *El Shaddai*   c Heb *YHWH;* see note at 3.15

ham, Isaac, and Jacob; I will give it to you for a possession. I am the LORD.' " 9Moses told this to the Israelites; but they would not listen to Moses, because of their broken spirit and their cruel slavery.

10 Then the LORD spoke to Moses, 11"Go and tell Pharaoh king of Egypt to let the Israelites go out of his land." 12But Moses spoke to the LORD, "The Israelites have not listened to me; how then shall Pharaoh listen to me, poor speaker that I am?"*a* 13Thus the LORD spoke to Moses and Aaron, and gave them orders regarding the Israelites and Pharaoh king of Egypt, charging them to free the Israelites from the land of Egypt.

The LORD reaffirms the mission of Moses and Aaron

6.1–7.7: The LORD responds to the complaints of Israel (5.21) and of Moses (5.22–23). God reaffirms the role of Moses and Aaron as leaders of Israel and the divine intention to rescue Israel as God's chosen people from slavery. This section provides an alternate version to chs. 3–4 and is often attributed to the later Priestly tradition (see sidebar, "Two Different Creation Stories, p. 50). **6.1:** *By a mighty hand* refers to Pharaoh's power and authority. **2–3:** On the significance of the divine name *the LORD*, see the comment on 3.13–15. The name *God Almighty* (*El Shaddai*) literally means "God of the Mountain" which is an appropriate name for this deity who appears on Mount Horeb/Sinai. The claim here that the ancestors in Genesis did not know the name *the LORD* ("Yahweh") contradicts an alternate tradition that Abraham, Isaac, and Jacob did know and use the name *the LORD* (Gen 12.8; 26.22; 32.9). **6:** To *redeem* means to pay a ransom in order to set free and regain possession of a family member or plot of land that has been taken over by another person or owner (Lev 25.25–28, 47–49). *With an outstretched arm* refers to the extension of God's power against the Egyptians. The promise is literally fulfilled when Moses "stretched out his hand" and God parted the Red Sea (14.21) and then allowed the water to rush back upon the Egyptians (14.26–28). **7:** *You shall know* continues the important theme concerning the purpose of the exodus out of Egypt: the knowledge of God by both Egyptians and Israelites (see comment on 5.2). **8:** God *swore* or made a promise to each of the ancestors in Genesis: Abraham (Gen 13.14–15), Isaac (Gen 26.3), and Jacob (Gen 28.13).

14 The following are the heads of their ancestral houses: the sons of Reuben, the firstborn of Israel: Hanoch, Pallu, Hezron, and Carmi; these are the families of Reuben. 15The sons of Simeon: Jemuel, Jamin, Ohad, Jachin, Zohar, and Shaul,*b* the son of a Canaanite woman; these are the families of Simeon. 16The following are the names of the sons of Levi according to their genealogies: Gershon,*c* Kohath, and Merari, and the length of Levi's life was one hundred thirty-seven years. 17The sons of Gershon:*c* Libni and Shimei, by their families. 18The sons of Kohath: Amram, Izhar, Hebron, and Uzziel, and the length of Kohath's life was one hundred thirty-three years. 19The sons of Merari: Mahli and Mushi. These are the families of the Levites according to their genealogies. 20Amram married Jochebed his father's sister and she bore him Aaron and Moses, and the length of Amram's life was one hundred thirty-seven years. 21The sons of Izhar: Korah, Nepheg, and Zichri. 22The sons of Uzziel: Mishael, Elzaphan, and Sithri. 23Aaron married Elisheba, daughter of Amminadab and sister of Nahshon, and she bore him Nadab, Abihu, Eleazar, and Ithamar. 24The sons of Korah: Assir, Elkanah, and Abiasaph; these are the families of the Korahites. 25Aaron's son Eleazar married one of the daughters of Putiel, and she bore him Phinehas. These are the heads of the ancestral houses of the Levites by their families.

6.14–25: This genealogy★ or family tree traces the family line of Jacob's three oldest sons: Reuben (v. 14), Simeon (v. 15), and Levi (vv. 16–25). The focus is clearly on the descendants of Levi, a family of priests. The family tree of Levi has two functions: to identify Moses and Aaron as Levites and brothers, and to trace the priestly line through Aaron to his son Eleazar (vv. 23–24) and his grandson Phinehas (v. 25). Eleazar takes over Aaron's role as high priest in Num 20.22–29. God commissions Phinehas and his descendants as priests in Num 25.6–13.

26 It was this same Aaron and Moses to whom the LORD said, "Bring the Israelites

a Heb *me? I am uncircumcised of lips*   *b* Or *Saul*
c Also spelled *Gershom;* see 2.22

out of the land of Egypt, company by company." 27 It was they who spoke to Pharaoh king of Egypt to bring the Israelites out of Egypt, the same Moses and Aaron.

28 On the day when the LORD spoke to Moses in the land of Egypt, 29 he said to him, "I am the LORD; tell Pharaoh king of Egypt all that I am speaking to you." 30 But Moses said in the LORD's presence, "Since I am a poor speaker," why would Pharaoh listen to me?"

7 The LORD said to Moses, "See, I have made you like God to Pharaoh, and your brother Aaron shall be your prophet. 2 You shall speak all that I command you, and your brother Aaron shall tell Pharaoh to let the Israelites go out of his land. 3 But I will harden Pharaoh's heart, and I will multiply my signs and wonders in the land of Egypt. 4 When Pharaoh does not listen to you, I will lay my hand upon Egypt and bring my people the Israelites, company by company, out of the land of Egypt by great acts of judgment. 5 The Egyptians shall know that I am the LORD, when I stretch out my hand against Egypt and bring the Israelites out from among them." 6 Moses and Aaron did so; they did just as the LORD commanded them. 7 Moses was eighty years old and Aaron eighty-three when they spoke to Pharaoh.

6.26–7.7. 1: The relationship between Moses and Aaron as his mouthpiece will be similar to the relationship between God and Moses. Just as Moses is God's *prophet** or messenger, so Aaron will be Moses' prophet or spokesperson. 3: *Harden Pharaoh's heart:* See comment on 4.21. 5: *Stretch out my hand:* See comment on 6.6. 7: Contrary to expectations, the younger brother Moses is superior to the older brother Aaron. This is a frequent motif* in biblical narratives* (Gen 25.23; 37.5–11).

8 The LORD said to Moses and Aaron, 9 "When Pharaoh says to you, 'Perform a wonder,' then you shall say to Aaron, 'Take your staff and throw it down before Pharaoh, and it will become a snake.'" 10 So Moses and Aaron went to Pharaoh and did as the LORD had commanded; Aaron threw down his staff before Pharaoh and his officials, and it became a snake. 11 Then Pharaoh summoned the wise men and the sorcerers; and they also, the magicians of Egypt, did the same by their secret arts. 12 Each one threw down his staff, and they became snakes; but Aaron's staff swallowed up theirs. 13 Still Pharaoh's heart was hardened, and he would not listen to them, as the LORD had said.

7.8–13: Aaron's staff turns into a snake before Pharaoh. Aaron uses the same miraculous sign to try to convince Pharaoh of God's power that he had earlier used to convince the Israelites (4.1–5; 30). 12: The word *snake* is the same word translated as "dragon" in Ezek 29.3, where it describes the Egyptian Pharaoh: "Thus says the Lord GOD: I am against you, Pharaoh king of Egypt, the great dragon." Aaron's snake swallowing the Egyptians' snakes foreshadows the future victory of Israel's God over Pharaoh. 13: *Pharaoh's heart was hardened:* See comment on 4.21.

14 Then the LORD said to Moses, "Pharaoh's heart is hardened; he refuses to let the people go. 15 Go to Pharaoh in the morning, as he is going out to the water; stand by at the river bank to meet him, and take in your hand the staff that was turned into a snake. 16 Say to him, 'The LORD, the God of the Hebrews, sent me to you to say, "Let my people go, so that they may worship me in the wilderness." But until now you have not listened. 17 Thus says the LORD, "By this you shall know that I am the LORD." See, with the staff that is in my hand I will strike the water that is in the Nile, and it shall be turned to blood. 18 The fish in the river shall die, the river itself shall stink, and the Egyptians shall be unable to drink water from the Nile.'" 19 The LORD said to Moses, "Say to Aaron, 'Take your staff and stretch out your hand over the waters of Egypt—over its rivers, its canals, and its ponds, and all its pools of water—so that they may become blood; and there shall be blood throughout the whole land of Egypt, even in vessels of wood and in vessels of stone.'"

20 Moses and Aaron did just as the LORD commanded. In the sight of Pharaoh and of his officials he lifted up the staff and struck

a Heb *am uncircumcised of lips;* see 6.12

the water in the river, and all the water in the river was turned into blood, 21and the fish in the river died. The river stank so that the Egyptians could not drink its water, and there was blood throughout the whole land of Egypt. 22But the magicians of Egypt did the same by their secret arts; so Pharaoh's heart remained hardened, and he would not listen to them, as the LORD had said. 23Pharaoh turned and went into his house, and he did not take even this to heart. 24And all the Egyptians had to dig along the Nile for water to drink, for they could not drink the water of the river.

25 Seven days passed after the LORD had struck the Nile.

7.14–25: The first plague: The Nile turns to blood. The Nile River was the primary source of water and life for Egypt. However, the Egyptians had earlier used the Nile as an instrument of death when Pharaoh ordered every Hebrew baby boy to be thrown into the river (1.22). This first plague, the river's turning to blood, recalls that previous atrocity. The plague also recalls one of the first miraculous signs God gave to Moses to convince the Israelites of God's power (4.9). **14:** *Pharaoh's heart is hardened:* See comment on 4.21. See also 7.22. **19:** The same phrase, *pools of water,* appears in the creation story in Gen 1.10 translated, "waters that were gathered together." Pharaoh's unjust enslavement of Israel prompts this series of ecological disasters. In effect, the plagues undo the life-giving order and structure of creation in Gen 1. **22:** A progression is evident in the experience of *the magicians of Egypt* throughout the ten plagues. They are able to duplicate the first and second plagues (7.14; 8.7). However, they cannot duplicate the third plague (8.18–19). In the fifth plague, not only do the magicians fail to duplicate the plague of boils, they themselves suffer its effects (9.11). The Egyptian magicians disappear entirely during the last five plagues.

8 *a*Then the LORD said to Moses, "Go to Pharaoh and say to him, 'Thus says the LORD: Let my people go, so that they may worship me. 2If you refuse to let them go, I will plague your whole country with frogs. 3The river shall swarm with frogs; they shall come up into your palace, into your bedchamber and your bed, and into the houses of your officials and of your people,*b* and

into your ovens and your kneading bowls. 4The frogs shall come up on you and on your people and on all your officials.' " 5*c* And the LORD said to Moses, "Say to Aaron, 'Stretch out your hand with your staff over the rivers, the canals, and the pools, and make frogs come up on the land of Egypt.' " 6So Aaron stretched out his hand over the waters of Egypt; and the frogs came up and covered the land of Egypt. 7But the magicians did the same by their secret arts, and brought frogs up on the land of Egypt.

8 Then Pharaoh called Moses and Aaron, and said, "Pray to the LORD to take away the frogs from me and my people, and I will let the people go to sacrifice to the LORD." 9Moses said to Pharaoh, "Kindly tell me when I am to pray for you and for your officials and for your people, that the frogs may be removed from you and your houses and be left only in the Nile." 10And he said, "Tomorrow." Moses said, "As you say! So that you may know that there is no one like the LORD our God, 11the frogs shall leave you and your houses and your officials and your people; they shall be left only in the Nile." 12Then Moses and Aaron went out from Pharaoh; and Moses cried out to the LORD concerning the frogs that he had brought upon Pharaoh.*d* 13And the LORD did as Moses requested: the frogs died in the houses, the courtyards, and the fields. 14And they gathered them together in heaps, and the land stank. 15But when Pharaoh saw that there was a respite, he hardened his heart, and would not listen to them, just as the LORD had said.

8.1–15: The second plague: Swarms of frogs invade the land. The second plague involves the rupture of the created boundary that separates creatures of the water (frogs) and the dry land of Egypt. **3:** The same word, *swarm,* occurs in the creation story in Gen 1.20 to describe the creatures of the waters. **7:** On *the magicians,* see comment on 7.22. **8:** This is the first of several times when Pharaoh will seem to surrender but then quickly harden his heart and refuse to let the Israelites go (v. 15; see 8.28, 32; 9.27–28, 34–35;

a Ch 7.26 in Heb   b Gk: Heb *upon your people*
c Ch 8.1 in Heb   d Or *frogs, as he had agreed with Pharaoh*

10.16–17, 20, 24, 27). **15:** On Pharaoh's *hardened heart,* see comment on 4.21.

16 Then the LORD said to Moses, "Say to Aaron, 'Stretch out your staff and strike the dust of the earth, so that it may become gnats throughout the whole land of Egypt.'" ¹⁷And they did so; Aaron stretched out his hand with his staff and struck the dust of the earth, and gnats came on humans and animals alike; all the dust of the earth turned into gnats throughout the whole land of Egypt. ¹⁸The magicians tried to produce gnats by their secret arts, but they could not. There were gnats on both humans and animals. ¹⁹And the magicians said to Pharaoh, "This is the finger of God!" But Pharaoh's heart was hardened, and he would not listen to them, just as the LORD had said.

8.16–19: The third plague: Dust turns into gnats. 18: For the first time, the Egyptian *magicians* are unable to duplicate the plague. See comment on 7.22. **19:** On Pharaoh's *hardened heart,* see comment on 4.21.

20 Then the LORD said to Moses, "Rise early in the morning and present yourself before Pharaoh, as he goes out to the water, and say to him, 'Thus says the LORD: Let my people go, so that they may worship me. ²¹For if you will not let my people go, I will send swarms of flies on you, your officials, and your people, and into your houses; and the houses of the Egyptians shall be filled with swarms of flies; so also the land where they live. ²²But on that day I will set apart the land of Goshen, where my people live, so that no swarms of flies shall be there, that you may know that I the LORD am in this land. ²³Thus I will make a distinction*ᵃ* between my people and your people. This sign shall appear tomorrow.'" ²⁴The LORD did so, and great swarms of flies came into the house of Pharaoh and into his officials' houses; in all of Egypt the land was ruined because of the flies.

25 Then Pharaoh summoned Moses and Aaron, and said, "Go, sacrifice to your God within the land." ²⁶But Moses said, "It would not be right to do so; for the sacrifices

that we offer to the LORD our God are offensive to the Egyptians. If we offer in the sight of the Egyptians sacrifices that are offensive to them, will they not stone us? ²⁷We must go a three days' journey into the wilderness and sacrifice to the LORD our God as he commands us." ²⁸So Pharaoh said, "I will let you go to sacrifice to the LORD your God in the wilderness, provided you do not go very far away. Pray for me." ²⁹Then Moses said, "As soon as I leave you, I will pray to the LORD that the swarms of flies may depart tomorrow from Pharaoh, from his officials, and from his people; only do not let Pharaoh again deal falsely by not letting the people go to sacrifice to the LORD."

30 So Moses went out from Pharaoh and prayed to the LORD. ³¹And the LORD did as Moses asked: he removed the swarms of flies from Pharaoh, from his officials, and from his people; not one remained. ³²But Pharaoh hardened his heart this time also, and would not let the people go.

8.20–32: The fourth plague: Swarms of flies invade Egyptian but not Israelite houses. 22: Israel had lived apart from the Egyptians in *the land of Goshen,* a fertile area in the delta region of the Nile River, since the days of Joseph (Gen 45.10). Israelite shepherds offended the Egyptians (Gen 43.32; 46.34). This offense and subsequent separation from other Egyptians proves to be advantageous, since the people of Israel are untouched by the plagues that terrorize Egypt (9.4, 26; 10.23). The tenth plague, with its blood on the doorpost of each individual Israelite house, seems to reflect another tradition in which the Israelites lived not apart from but among the other Egyptian homes (11.7; 12.23). **26:** The *sacrifices* probably involved sheep (12.1–10), and Egyptians found shepherds and sheep *offensive* (Gen 46.34). **28:** See v. 32 and the comment on 8.8. **32:** See comment on 4.21.

9 Then the LORD said to Moses, "Go to Pharaoh, and say to him, 'Thus says the LORD, the God of the Hebrews: Let my people go, so that they may worship me. ²For if you refuse to let them go and still hold them, ³the hand of the LORD will strike with a deadly pestilence your livestock in the field:

a Gk Vg: Heb *will set redemption*

the horses, the donkeys, the camels, the herds, and the flocks. 4But the LORD will make a distinction between the livestock of Israel and the livestock of Egypt, so that nothing shall die of all that belongs to the Israelites.' " 5The LORD set a time, saying, "Tomorrow the LORD will do this thing in the land." 6And on the next day the LORD did so; all the livestock of the Egyptians died, but of the livestock of the Israelites not one died. 7Pharaoh inquired and found that not one of the livestock of the Israelites was dead. But the heart of Pharaoh was hardened, and he would not let the people go.

9.1–7: The fifth plague: Disease kills Egyptian but not Israelite animals. 6: The claim that *all the livestock of the Egyptians died* is in some tension with the later plagues, when more Egyptian livestock are repeatedly involved (9.10, 19–21; 11.5; 12.29). 7: On Pharaoh's *hardened heart,* see comment on 4.21.

8 Then the LORD said to Moses and Aaron, "Take handfuls of soot from the kiln, and let Moses throw it in the air in the sight of Pharaoh. 9It shall become fine dust all over the land of Egypt, and shall cause festering boils on humans and animals throughout the whole land of Egypt." 10So they took soot from the kiln, and stood before Pharaoh, and Moses threw it in the air, and it caused festering boils on humans and animals. 11The magicians could not stand before Moses because of the boils, for the boils afflicted the magicians as well as all the Egyptians. 12But the LORD hardened the heart of Pharaoh, and he would not listen to them, just as the LORD had spoken to Moses.

9.8–12: The sixth plague: Soot and ashes cause boils on humans and animals. 10: This is the first plague in which *humans* are directly affected along with the *animals.* 11: On the *magicians,* see comment on 7.22. 12: On Pharaoh's *hardened heart,* see comment on 4.21. This is the first time *the LORD* explicitly *hardened his heart.*

13 Then the LORD said to Moses, "Rise up early in the morning and present yourself before Pharaoh, and say to him, 'Thus says the LORD, the God of the Hebrews: Let my people go, so that they may worship me. 14For this time I will send all my plagues upon you yourself, and upon your officials, and upon your people, so that you may know that there is no one like me in all the earth. 15For by now I could have stretched out my hand and struck you and your people with pestilence, and you would have been cut off from the earth. 16But this is why I have let you live: to show you my power, and to make my name resound through all the earth. 17You are still exalting yourself against my people, and will not let them go. 18Tomorrow at this time I will cause the heaviest hail to fall that has ever fallen in Egypt from the day it was founded until now. 19Send, therefore, and have your livestock and everything that you have in the open field brought to a secure place; every human or animal that is in the open field and is not brought under shelter will die when the hail comes down upon them.' " 20Those officials of Pharaoh who feared the word of the LORD hurried their slaves and livestock off to a secure place. 21Those who did not regard the word of the LORD left their slaves and livestock in the open field.

22 The LORD said to Moses, "Stretch out your hand toward heaven so that hail may fall on the whole land of Egypt, on humans and animals and all the plants of the field in the land of Egypt." 23Then Moses stretched out his staff toward heaven, and the LORD sent thunder and hail, and fire came down on the earth. And the LORD rained hail on the land of Egypt; 24there was hail with fire flashing continually in the midst of it, such heavy hail as had never fallen in all the land of Egypt since it became a nation. 25The hail struck down everything that was in the open field throughout all the land of Egypt, both human and animal; the hail also struck down all the plants of the field, and shattered every tree in the field. 26Only in the land of Goshen, where the Israelites were, there was no hail.

27 Then Pharaoh summoned Moses and Aaron, and said to them, "This time I have sinned; the LORD is in the right, and I and my people are in the wrong. 28Pray to the LORD! Enough of God's thunder and hail! I

will let you go; you need stay no longer." 29 Moses said to him, "As soon as I have gone out of the city, I will stretch out my hands to the LORD; the thunder will cease, and there will be no more hail, so that you may know that the earth is the LORD's. 30 But as for you and your officials, I know that you do not yet fear the LORD God." 31 (Now the flax and the barley were ruined, for the barley was in the ear and the flax was in bud. 32 But the wheat and the spelt were not ruined, for they are late in coming up.) 33 So Moses left Pharaoh, went out of the city, and stretched out his hands to the LORD; then the thunder and the hail ceased, and the rain no longer poured down on the earth. 34 But when Pharaoh saw that the rain and the hail and the thunder had ceased, he sinned once more and hardened his heart, he and his officials. 35 So the heart of Pharaoh was hardened, and he would not let the Israelites go, just as the LORD had spoken through Moses.

9.13–35: The seventh plague: Thunder, hail, and fire pour out of the skies. 20–21: The story acknowledges for the first time a distinction between some Egyptians *who feared the word of the LORD* and *those who did not regard the word of the LORD*. **22:** The plagues' disruption of the order established by God at creation now extends to the *plants* as well as animals and humans (Gen 1.11–12, 2.5). **26:** On the separation of Israelites *in the land of Goshen,* see comment on 8.22. **27:** This is the first time Pharaoh confesses, *"I have sinned."* He will do so one more time in 10.16. **32:** Some plants survive, only to be devoured in the next plague (10.12, 15). **34–35:** On Pharaoh's *hardened heart,* see comment on 4.21.

10 Then the LORD said to Moses, "Go to Pharaoh; for I have hardened his heart and the heart of his officials, in order that I may show these signs of mine among them, 2 and that you may tell your children and grandchildren how I have made fools of the Egyptians and what signs I have done among them—so that you may know that I am the LORD."

3 So Moses and Aaron went to Pharaoh, and said to him, "Thus says the LORD, the God of the Hebrews, 'How long will you refuse to humble yourself before me? Let my

people go, so that they may worship me. 4 For if you refuse to let my people go, tomorrow I will bring locusts into your country. 5 They shall cover the surface of the land, so that no one will be able to see the land. They shall devour the last remnant left you after the hail, and they shall devour every tree of yours that grows in the field. 6 They shall fill your houses, and the houses of all your officials and of all the Egyptians—something that neither your parents nor your grandparents have seen, from the day they came on earth to this day.' " Then he turned and went out from Pharaoh.

7 Pharaoh's officials said to him, "How long shall this fellow be a snare to us? Let the people go, so that they may worship the LORD their God; do you not yet understand that Egypt is ruined?" 8 So Moses and Aaron were brought back to Pharaoh, and he said to them, "Go, worship the LORD your God! But which ones are to go?" 9 Moses said, "We will go with our young and our old; we will go with our sons and daughters and with our flocks and herds, because we have the LORD's festival to celebrate." 10 He said to them, "The LORD indeed will be with you, if ever I let your little ones go with you! Plainly, you have some evil purpose in mind. 11 No, never! Your men may go and worship the LORD, for that is what you are asking." And they were driven out from Pharaoh's presence.

12 Then the LORD said to Moses, "Stretch out your hand over the land of Egypt, so that the locusts may come upon it and eat every plant in the land, all that the hail has left." 13 So Moses stretched out his staff over the land of Egypt, and the LORD brought an east wind upon the land all that day and all that night; when morning came, the east wind had brought the locusts. 14 The locusts came upon all the land of Egypt and settled on the whole country of Egypt, such a dense swarm of locusts as had never been before, nor ever shall be again. 15 They covered the surface of the whole land, so that the land was black; and they ate all the plants in the land and all the fruit of the trees that the hail had left; nothing green was left, no tree, no plant in the field, in all

the land of Egypt. 16Pharaoh hurriedly summoned Moses and Aaron and said, "I have sinned against the LORD your God, and against you. 17Do forgive my sin just this once, and pray to the LORD your God that at the least he remove this deadly thing from me." 18So he went out from Pharaoh and prayed to the LORD. 19The LORD changed the wind into a very strong west wind, which lifted the locusts and drove them into the Red Sea;*a* not a single locust was left in all the country of Egypt. 20But the LORD hardened Pharaoh's heart, and he would not let the Israelites go.

10.1–20: The eighth plague: An east wind brings swarms of locusts. 7: This is the first time Pharaoh's own *officials* seek to persuade him to *let the people go*. **13:** The blowing of *the east wind* and the duration *all that night* anticipates the parallel events when "a strong east wind" blows back the waters of the Red Sea "all night" (14.21) to expose dry land so that the Israelites can cross safely. **15:** The land *black* with locusts anticipates the next plague of darkness (vv. 21–22). **16:** This is the second and last time Pharaoh confesses his guilt, *"I have sinned"* (see 9.27). **19:** The mention of the *wind* and the *Red Sea* foreshadows the Red Sea crossing (14.21, 28). **20:** On Pharaoh's *hardened heart*, see comment on 4.21.

21 Then the LORD said to Moses, "Stretch out your hand toward heaven so that there may be darkness over the land of Egypt, a darkness that can be felt." 22So Moses stretched out his hand toward heaven, and there was dense darkness in all the land of Egypt for three days. 23People could not see one another, and for three days they could not move from where they were; but all the Israelites had light where they lived. 24Then Pharaoh summoned Moses, and said, "Go, worship the LORD. Only your flocks and your herds shall remain behind. Even your children may go with you." 25But Moses said, "You must also let us have sacrifices and burnt offerings to sacrifice to the LORD our God. 26Our livestock also must go with us; not a hoof shall be left behind, for we must choose some of them for the worship of the LORD our God, and we will not know what to use to worship the LORD until

we arrive there." 27But the LORD hardened Pharaoh's heart, and he was unwilling to let them go. 28Then Pharaoh said to him, "Get away from me! Take care that you do not see my face again, for on the day you see my face you shall die." 29Moses said, "Just as you say! I will never see your face again."

10.21–29: The ninth plague: A dense darkness sweeps over all Egypt. 23: The Israelites again are separated and thus do not suffer the effects of the plagues on the Egyptians. See comment on 8.22. **27:** On Pharaoh's *hardened heart*, see comment on 4.21. **28–29:** Moses pledges not to seek an audience with Pharaoh again, but Pharaoh will in fact summon Moses one more time during the tenth and final plague (12.31). Moses' words may also hint at the death of Pharaoh and his army at the Red Sea crossing (14.13, 26–29).

11 The LORD said to Moses, "I will bring one more plague upon Pharaoh and upon Egypt; afterwards he will let you go from here; indeed, when he lets you go, he will drive you away. 2Tell the people that every man is to ask his neighbor and every woman is to ask her neighbor for objects of silver and gold." 3The LORD gave the people favor in the sight of the Egyptians. Moreover, Moses himself was a man of great importance in the land of Egypt, in the sight of Pharaoh's officials and in the sight of the people.

4 Moses said, "Thus says the LORD: About midnight I will go out through Egypt. 5Every firstborn in the land of Egypt shall die, from the firstborn of Pharaoh who sits on his throne to the firstborn of the female slave who is behind the handmill, and all the firstborn of the livestock. 6Then there will be a loud cry throughout the whole land of Egypt, such as has never been or will ever be again. 7But not a dog shall growl at any of the Israelites—not at people, not at animals—so that you may know that the LORD makes a distinction between Egypt and Israel. 8Then all these officials of yours shall come down to me, and bow low to me, saying, 'Leave us, you and all the people who

a Or *Sea of Reeds*

follow you.' After that I will leave." And in hot anger he left Pharaoh.

9 The LORD said to Moses, "Pharaoh will not listen to you, in order that my wonders may be multiplied in the land of Egypt." 10Moses and Aaron performed all these wonders before Pharaoh; but the LORD hardened Pharaoh's heart, and he did not let the people of Israel go out of his land.

11.1–10: Moses warns Pharaoh about the tenth and final plague. 1–2: The horror of the final plague will cause Pharaoh and the other Egyptians to plead with Israel to leave their land. The Egyptians will voluntarily surrender *objects of silver and gold* (v. 2) as predicted in 3.22 and fulfilled in 12.35–36. This plundering of the Egyptians signifies Egypt's defeat in the battle with Israel's God. Israel will carry away the spoils of war. **5:** The coming death of *every firstborn in the land of Egypt* expands the earlier judgment of 4.22–23, which predicted the death only of Pharaoh's firstborn son. Part of the background to this judgment is the deity's claim to all firstborn among humans and animals as God's rightful possession (13.1–2). **10:** On Pharaoh's *hardened heart,* see comment on 4.21.

12 The LORD said to Moses and Aaron in the land of Egypt: 2This month shall mark for you the beginning of months; it shall be the first month of the year for you. 3Tell the whole congregation of Israel that on the tenth of this month they are to take a lamb for each family, a lamb for each household. 4If a household is too small for a whole lamb, it shall join its closest neighbor in obtaining one; the lamb shall be divided in proportion to the number of people who eat of it. 5Your lamb shall be without blemish, a year-old male; you may take it from the sheep or from the goats. 6You shall keep it until the fourteenth day of this month; then the whole assembled congregation of Israel shall slaughter it at twilight. 7They shall take some of the blood and put it on the two doorposts and the lintel of the houses in which they eat it. 8They shall eat the lamb that same night; they shall eat it roasted over the fire with unleavened bread and bitter herbs. 9Do not eat any of it raw or boiled in water, but roasted over the fire, with its head, legs, and inner organs. 10You shall let none of it

remain until the morning; anything that remains until the morning you shall burn. 11This is how you shall eat it: your loins girded, your sandals on your feet, and your staff in your hand; and you shall eat it hurriedly. It is the passover of the LORD. 12For I will pass through the land of Egypt that night, and I will strike down every firstborn in the land of Egypt, both human beings and animals; on all the gods of Egypt I will execute judgments: I am the LORD. 13The blood shall be a sign for you on the houses where you live: when I see the blood, I will pass over you, and no plague shall destroy you when I strike the land of Egypt.

14 This day shall be a day of remembrance for you. You shall celebrate it as a festival to the LORD; throughout your generations you shall observe it as a perpetual ordinance. 15Seven days you shall eat unleavened bread; on the first day you shall remove leaven from your houses, for whoever eats leavened bread from the first day until the seventh day shall be cut off from Israel. 16On the first day you shall hold a solemn assembly, and on the seventh day a solemn assembly; no work shall be done on those days; only what everyone must eat, that alone may be prepared by you. 17You shall observe the festival of unleavened bread, for on this very day I brought your companies out of the land of Egypt: you shall observe this day throughout your generations as a perpetual ordinance. 18In the first month, from the evening of the fourteenth day until the evening of the twenty-first day, you shall eat unleavened bread. 19For seven days no leaven shall be found in your houses; for whoever eats what is leavened shall be cut off from the congregation of Israel, whether an alien or a native of the land. 20You shall eat nothing leavened; in all your settlements you shall eat unleavened bread.

21 Then Moses called all the elders of Israel and said to them, "Go, select lambs for your families, and slaughter the passover lamb. 22Take a bunch of hyssop, dip it in the blood that is in the basin, and touch the lintel and the two doorposts with the blood in the basin. None of you shall go outside the door of your house until morning. 23For the

LORD will pass through to strike down the Egyptians; when he sees the blood on the lintel and on the two doorposts, the LORD will pass over that door and will not allow the destroyer to enter your houses to strike you down. 24You shall observe this rite as a perpetual ordinance for you and your children. 25When you come to the land that the LORD will give you, as he has promised, you shall keep this observance. 26And when your children ask you, 'What do you mean by this observance?' 27you shall say, 'It is the passover sacrifice to the LORD, for he passed over the houses of the Israelites in Egypt, when he struck down the Egyptians but spared our houses.'" And the people bowed down and worshiped.

28 The Israelites went and did just as the LORD had commanded Moses and Aaron.

12.1–28: The LORD provides instructions for the annual festivals of Passover* and Unleavened Bread. The flow of the exodus story is interrupted by instructions for celebrating the two festivals of Passover and Unleavened Bread. The immediate purpose of the Passover is to mark every Israelite home with blood so that it will be protected from the effects of the tenth plague, the death of all Egyptian firstborn. After Israel leaves Egypt, the annual festivals of Passover and Unleavened Bread will enable future generations to remember and identify the story of the Exodus as their own (vv. 14–17). 2: This month begins the new year. It occurs in the springtime (March—April) and is called either Abib (13.4; Deut 16.1) or Nisan (Esth 3.7) in later biblical traditions. Older biblical traditions begin the new year in the fall (23.16; 34.22). 7: The smearing of the lamb's blood on the doorposts and lintel or upper door frame will mark the house as Israelite and thus protect it from the plague, which will kill all the Egyptian firstborn (vv. 12–13, 21–23). 8: Unleavened bread, or biscuits without yeast, is quickly baked bread. Verses 33–34 provide the connection with the Exodus: The Israelites had to hurry out of Egypt and so could not wait for their bread dough to rise. The bitter herbs recall the bitterness of Israel's slavery. 9: The lamb is to be roasted rather than eaten raw or boiled to ensure all of its blood is drained. The blood is the essence of life and must be returned to the deity and not eaten in recognition that life belongs to God (Gen 9.4; Lev 17.10–14). 13: The verb pass over ("pasah," also in vv. 23, 27) is the basis for the festival's

name, Passover ("pesah," v. 11). 22: Hyssop* is an aromatic plant or bush that is used for ritual purification (Lev 14.4; Num 19.6). 23: The destroyer is an agent that brings death and is here distinguished from the LORD.

~~~~~~~~~~~~~~~~~~~~~~~~~~~~~~

29 At midnight the LORD struck down all the firstborn in the land of Egypt, from the firstborn of Pharaoh who sat on his throne to the firstborn of the prisoner who was in the dungeon, and all the firstborn of the livestock. 30Pharaoh arose in the night, he and all his officials and all the Egyptians; and there was a loud cry in Egypt, for there was not a house without someone dead. 31Then he summoned Moses and Aaron in the night, and said, "Rise up, go away from my people, both you and the Israelites! Go, worship the LORD, as you said. 32Take your flocks and your herds, as you said, and be gone. And bring a blessing on me too!"

33 The Egyptians urged the people to hasten their departure from the land, for they said, "We shall all be dead." 34So the people took their dough before it was leavened, with their kneading bowls wrapped up in their cloaks on their shoulders. 35The Israelites had done as Moses told them; they had asked the Egyptians for jewelry of silver and gold, and for clothing, 36and the LORD had given the people favor in the sight of the Egyptians, so that they let them have what they asked. And so they plundered the Egyptians.

37 The Israelites journeyed from Rameses to Succoth, about six hundred thousand men on foot, besides children. 38A mixed crowd also went up with them, and livestock in great numbers, both flocks and herds. 39They baked unleavened cakes of the dough that they had brought out of Egypt; it was not leavened, because they were driven out of Egypt and could not wait, nor had they prepared any provisions for themselves.

40 The time that the Israelites had lived in Egypt was four hundred thirty years. 41At the end of four hundred thirty years, on that very day, all the companies of the LORD went out from the land of Egypt. 42That was for the LORD a night of vigil, to bring them out of the land of Egypt. That same night is a

vigil to be kept for the LORD by all the Israelites throughout their generations.

43 The LORD said to Moses and Aaron: This is the ordinance for the passover: no foreigner shall eat of it, 44but any slave who has been purchased may eat of it after he has been circumcised; 45no bound or hired servant may eat of it. 46It shall be eaten in one house; you shall not take any of the animal outside the house, and you shall not break any of its bones. 47The whole congregation of Israel shall celebrate it. 48If an alien who resides with you wants to celebrate the passover to the LORD, all his males shall be circumcised; then he may draw near to celebrate it; he shall be regarded as a native of the land. But no uncircumcised person shall eat of it; 49there shall be one law for the native and for the alien who resides among you.

50 All the Israelites did just as the LORD had commanded Moses and Aaron. 51That very day the LORD brought the Israelites out of the land of Egypt, company by company.

12.29–51: Egypt's firstborn die and Israel departs from Egypt. 34: The haste to leave Egypt provides a rationale for the haste in eating the Passover* meal (vv. 8, 11) and for celebrating the festival of Unleavened Bread (v. 39; 13.3–10). 35–36: The people of Israel *plundered* Egypt as they received *silver and gold* from their former oppressors. The plundered jewelry is Israel's war booty and implies the victory of Israel's God over Pharaoh. 37: *Six hundred thousand men* apart from women, children, and elderly would mean an amazing total population of about two million Israelites. This large number appears again in the census list in Num 1.46 (603,550 Israelite warriors). A typical large army in this ancient period would be 15,000–20,000 warriors. 38: *A mixed crowd* suggests an ethnically mixed group that joins the Israelites in fleeing Egypt (see Num 11.4). 41: Gen 15.13 predicted 400 years of slavery in Egypt. Gen 15.16 predicted four generations or about 160 years (assuming 40 years per generation). 43–49: The LORD provides further instructions about the Passover as it applies to *an alien who resides with you.* The instructions follow appropriately the earlier mention of the "mixed crowd" that joined Israel's exodus (v. 38).

13 The LORD said to Moses: 2Consecrate to me all the firstborn; whatever is the first to open the womb among the Israelites, of human beings and animals, is mine.

3 Moses said to the people, "Remember this day on which you came out of Egypt, out of the house of slavery, because the LORD brought you out from there by strength of hand; no leavened bread shall be eaten. 4Today, in the month of Abib, you are going out. 5When the LORD brings you into the land of the Canaanites, the Hittites, the Amorites, the Hivites, and the Jebusites, which he swore to your ancestors to give you, a land flowing with milk and honey, you shall keep this observance in this month. 6Seven days you shall eat unleavened bread, and on the seventh day there shall be a festival to the LORD. 7Unleavened bread shall be eaten for seven days; no leavened bread shall be seen in your possession, and no leaven shall be seen among you in all your territory. 8You shall tell your child on that day, 'It is because of what the LORD did for me when I came out of Egypt.' 9It shall serve for you as a sign on your hand and as a reminder on your forehead, so that the teaching of the LORD may be on your lips; for with a strong hand the LORD brought you out of Egypt. 10You shall keep this ordinance at its proper time from year to year.

11 "When the LORD has brought you into the land of the Canaanites, as he swore to you and your ancestors, and has given it to you, 12you shall set apart to the LORD all that first opens the womb. All the firstborn of your livestock that are males shall be the LORD's. 13But every firstborn donkey you shall redeem with a sheep; if you do not redeem it, you must break its neck. Every firstborn male among your children you shall redeem. 14When in the future your child asks you, 'What does this mean?' you shall answer, 'By strength of hand the LORD brought us out of Egypt, from the house of slavery. 15When Pharaoh stubbornly refused to let us go, the LORD killed all the firstborn in the land of Egypt, from human firstborn to the firstborn of animals. Therefore I sacrifice to the LORD every male that first opens the womb, but every firstborn of my sons I redeem.' 16It shall serve as a sign on your hand

and as an emblem^a on your forehead that by strength of hand the LORD brought us out of Egypt."

13.1–16: Unleavened Bread and the firstborn: God provides instructions for life in Canaan. The death of Egypt's firstborn (12.29) prompts the LORD to instruct Israel concerning the dedication or consecration of Israel's firstborn to God (vv. 1–2, 11–16). The instructions for Passover* (12.1–28, 43–51) also prompt God to provide laws for celebrating a closely related festival, the festival of Unleavened Bread (vv. 3–10). Both obligations will begin later, *when the LORD* brings you into the land of the Canaanites (vv. 5, 11). As such, the laws function as a promise for the future. **4:** On *the month of Abib*, see comment on 12.2. **5:** This listing of peoples—*the Canaanites, the Hittites, the Amorites, the Hivites, and the Jebusites*—is a traditional list of the native inhabitants of the promised land of Canaan (Gen 15.19–21; Deut 7.1). **9:** *Sign on your hand* and *reminder on your forehead* indicate ornaments that came to be worn in worship in remembrance of the Exodus. In Jewish practice, they are called phylacteries. See v. 16 and Deut 6.8. **13:** The *donkey* is ritually unclean (Lev 11.3). Therefore, a ritually clean animal (a sheep) must be offered to *redeem* or purchase back the firstborn donkey from God. If the owner does not redeem the donkey with a sheep, the owner *must break its neck* and kill it since it cannot be ritually slaughtered as a clean animal. The firstborn donkey belongs to God and cannot be used by humans without redeeming it. *Every firstborn male* child must be redeemed or purchased back from God, either with money (Num 18.16; five shekels*) or the substitution of a member of the priestly tribe of Levi (Num 3.11–13). On the meaning of *redeem*, see comment on 6.6. **16:** See comment on v. 9.

17 When Pharaoh let the people go, God did not lead them by way of the land of the Philistines, although that was nearer; for God thought, "If the people face war, they may change their minds and return to Egypt." ¹⁸So God led the people by the roundabout way of the wilderness toward the Red Sea.^b The Israelites went up out of the land of Egypt prepared for battle. ¹⁹And Moses took with him the bones of Joseph who had required a solemn oath of the Israelites, saying, "God will surely take notice of you, and then you must carry my bones with you

from here." ²⁰They set out from Succoth, and camped at Etham, on the edge of the wilderness. ²¹The LORD went in front of them in a pillar of cloud by day, to lead them along the way, and in a pillar of fire by night, to give them light, so that they might travel by day and by night. ²²Neither the pillar of cloud by day nor the pillar of fire by night left its place in front of the people.

13.17–22: Led by the pillars of cloud and fire, Israel begins to leave Egypt. 17: *The Philistines* were a people who lived on the western border of Canaan near the shores of the Mediterranean Sea. Their territory would have been the most direct route from Goshen (the Nile Delta region of Egypt) to Canaan. However, the reference to *the Philistines* here may represent a later tradition since the Philistines settled this region sometime later than the traditional date for Israel's exodus (after 1200 BCE). **18:** Some scholars argue that the *Red Sea* ("yam suf") is too far south and too large a body of water to have been the sea Israel would eventually cross (14.21–28). Thus, some prefer to call it the "Sea of Reeds" and assume it was a shallow body of water farther north in Egypt near the Mediterranean Sea. However, later readers in ancient Israel may have known only about the larger Red Sea. **19:** See Gen 50.24–26. **20:** The place name *Succoth* in Hebrew means "Booths" or temporary shelters. The locations of Succoth and Ethan are uncertain, except that they are on the eastern border of Egypt. **21:** The two pillars or columns of cloud and fire are apparently one and the same (14.24–25). The cloud by itself is visible by day. At night, only the fire within the cloud is visible. The cloud and fire are visible signs of God's presence among the Israelites.

14 Then the LORD said to Moses: ²Tell the Israelites to turn back and camp in front of Pi-hahiroth, between Migdol and the sea, in front of Baal-zephon; you shall camp opposite it, by the sea. ³Pharaoh will say of the Israelites, "They are wandering aimlessly in the land; the wilderness has closed in on them." ⁴I will harden Pharaoh's heart, and he will pursue them, so that I will gain glory for myself over Pharaoh and all his

a Or *as a frontlet*; Meaning of Heb uncertain
b Or *Sea of Reeds*

army; and the Egyptians shall know that I am the LORD. And they did so.

5 When the king of Egypt was told that the people had fled, the minds of Pharaoh and his officials were changed toward the people, and they said, "What have we done, letting Israel leave our service?" 6So he had his chariot made ready, and took his army with him; 7he took six hundred picked chariots and all the other chariots of Egypt with officers over all of them. 8The LORD hardened the heart of Pharaoh king of Egypt and he pursued the Israelites, who were going out boldly. 9The Egyptians pursued them, all Pharaoh's horses and chariots, his chariot drivers and his army; they overtook them camped by the sea, by Pi-hahiroth, in front of Baal-zephon.

10 As Pharaoh drew near, the Israelites looked back, and there were the Egyptians advancing on them. In great fear the Israelites cried out to the LORD. 11They said to Moses, "Was it because there were no graves in Egypt that you have taken us away to die in the wilderness? What have you done to us, bringing us out of Egypt? 12Is this not the very thing we told you in Egypt, 'Let us alone and let us serve the Egyptians'? For it would have been better for us to serve the Egyptians than to die in the wilderness." 13But Moses said to the people, "Do not be afraid, stand firm, and see the deliverance that the LORD will accomplish for you today; for the Egyptians whom you see today you shall never see again. 14The LORD will fight for you, and you have only to keep still."

15 Then the LORD said to Moses, "Why do you cry out to me? Tell the Israelites to go forward. 16But you lift up your staff, and stretch out your hand over the sea and divide it, that the Israelites may go into the sea on dry ground. 17Then I will harden the hearts of the Egyptians so that they will go in after them; and so I will gain glory for myself over Pharaoh and all his army, his chariots, and his chariot drivers. 18And the Egyptians shall know that I am the LORD, when I have gained glory for myself over Pharaoh, his chariots, and his chariot drivers."

19 The angel of God who was going before the Israelite army moved and went behind them; and the pillar of cloud moved from in front of them and took its place behind them. 20It came between the army of Egypt and the army of Israel. And so the cloud was there with the darkness, and it lit up the night; one did not come near the other all night.

21 Then Moses stretched out his hand over the sea. The LORD drove the sea back by a strong east wind all night, and turned the sea into dry land; and the waters were divided. 22The Israelites went into the sea on dry ground, the waters forming a wall for them on their right and on their left. 23The Egyptians pursued, and went into the sea after them, all of Pharaoh's horses, chariots, and chariot drivers. 24At the morning watch the LORD in the pillar of fire and cloud looked down upon the Egyptian army, and threw the Egyptian army into panic. 25He clogged[a] their chariot wheels so that they turned with difficulty. The Egyptians said, "Let us flee from the Israelites, for the LORD is fighting for them against Egypt."

26 Then the LORD said to Moses, "Stretch out your hand over the sea, so that the water may come back upon the Egyptians, upon their chariots and chariot drivers." 27So Moses stretched out his hand over the sea, and at dawn the sea returned to its normal depth. As the Egyptians fled before it, the LORD tossed the Egyptians into the sea. 28The waters returned and covered the chariots and the chariot drivers, the entire army of Pharaoh that had followed them into the sea; not one of them remained. 29But the Israelites walked on dry ground through the sea, the waters forming a wall for them on their right and on their left.

30 Thus the LORD saved Israel that day from the Egyptians; and Israel saw the Egyptians dead on the seashore. 31Israel saw the great work that the LORD did against the Egyptians. So the people feared the LORD and believed in the LORD and in his servant Moses.

14.1–31: **Israel crosses the Red Sea, and God defeats the Egyptians.** As Pharaoh had tried to drown

a Sam Gk Syr: MT *removed*

The Red Sea Crossing and Creation Stories

The *dividing* of *the sea* and the drying up of the sea to clear *dry ground* (14.16, 21–22; 15.8) contain echoes of some accounts of the world's creation in the ancient world, including Israel. Creation occurs as the LORD splits or cuts into pieces the primeval sea monster or dragon named Rahab or Leviathan.* Alternatively, the LORD defeats the watery primeval chaos by drying up the sea. In this regard, Isa 51.9–10 addresses the LORD: "Was it not you who cut Rahab in pieces, who pierced the dragon? Was it not you who dried up the sea, the waters of the great deep?" Psalm 74.12–15 speaks in a similar vein: "You divided the sea by your might; you broke the heads of the dragons in the waters. You crushed the heads of Leviathan . . . You dried up ever-flowing streams." These creation themes help to interpret the larger significance of Israel's exodus out of Egypt as the deity's defeat of the primal forces of evil and chaos in the world.

Israel's children in the Nile River (1.22), so Pharaoh and his army will drown in the Red Sea. The sea crossing is one of the central events in ancient Israel's collective memory. **2:** *Pi-hahiroth, Migdol,* and *Baal-zephon* appear here as sites on the eastern boundary of Egypt, just before Israel crosses into the wilderness of the Sinai Peninsula. **4:** On Pharaoh's *hardened heart,* see comment on 4.21. **8:** On Pharaoh's *hardened heart,* see v. 4 and comment on 4.21. **13:** *The Egyptians . . . you shall never see again* recalls Moses' words to Pharaoh in 10.28–29. **14:** The image of *the* LORD as a divine warrior* who *will fight for you* is a frequent biblical theme (15.3; Ps 24.8; Isa 42.13). **17:** On the *hardening of the heart,* see comment on 4.21. **19:** The *angel* is an alternate way of describing the presence of the LORD (v. 24).

Moses and Miriam sing songs of victory
15.1–21: These songs of Moses and Miriam represent some of the earliest traditions of the Bible. The elevated language of Hebrew poetry in the songs contains many examples of parallelism,* or doubling of thoughts and images in consecutive lines. A recurring image in the poem is the stone. Israel's enemy sinks or freezes in fear like a lead stone (vv. 5, 10, 16) in contrast to the eternal security of God's stone mountain sanctuary (vv. 17–18). The Song of Moses (vv. 1–18) retells the story of ch. 14 with some differences in details. For example, Israel's crossing the sea on dry land (14.22) is not described in the song.

15 Then Moses and the Israelites sang this song to the LORD:

"I will sing to the LORD, for he has
    triumphed gloriously;
horse and rider he has thrown into
    the sea.
2 The LORD is my strength and my might,[a]
    and he has become my salvation;
this is my God, and I will praise him,
    my father's God, and I will exalt him.
3 The LORD is a warrior;
    the LORD is his name.

4 "Pharaoh's chariots and his army he
    cast into the sea;
his picked officers were sunk in the
    Red Sea.[b]
5 The floods covered them;
    they went down into the depths like a
    stone.
6 Your right hand, O LORD, glorious in
    power—
    your right hand, O LORD, shattered
    the enemy.
7 In the greatness of your majesty you
    overthrew your adversaries;
you sent out your fury, it consumed
    them like stubble.
8 At the blast of your nostrils the waters
    piled up,
    the floods stood up in a heap;
    the deeps congealed in the heart of
    the sea.

a Or *song*   *b* Or *Sea of Reeds*

9 The enemy said, 'I will pursue, I will
      overtake,
    I will divide the spoil, my desire shall
      have its fill of them.
    I will draw my sword, my hand shall
      destroy them.'
10 You blew with your wind, the sea
      covered them;
    they sank like lead in the mighty
      waters.

11 "Who is like you, O LORD, among the
      gods?
    Who is like you, majestic in holiness,
      awesome in splendor, doing wonders?
12 You stretched out your right hand,
    the earth swallowed them.

13 "In your steadfast love you led the
      people whom you redeemed;
    you guided them by your strength to
      your holy abode.
14 The peoples heard, they trembled;
    pangs seized the inhabitants of
      Philistia.
15 Then the chiefs of Edom were
      dismayed;
    trembling seized the leaders of Moab;
    all the inhabitants of Canaan melted
      away.
16 Terror and dread fell upon them;
    by the might of your arm, they
      became still as a stone
    until your people, O LORD, passed by,
    until the people whom you acquired
      passed by.
17 You brought them in and planted them
      on the mountain of your own
      possession,
    the place, O LORD, that you made
      your abode,
    the sanctuary, O LORD, that your
      hands have established.
18 The LORD will reign forever and ever."

19 When the horses of Pharaoh with his
chariots and his chariot drivers went into the
sea, the LORD brought back the waters of the
sea upon them; but the Israelites walked
through the sea on dry ground.

20 Then the prophet Miriam, Aaron's sister, took a tambourine in her hand; and all
the women went out after her with tambourines and with dancing. 21And Miriam sang
to them:

  "Sing to the LORD, for he has
    triumphed gloriously;
  horse and rider he has thrown into the
    sea."

15.1–21. 3: *The* LORD *is a warrior:* see comment on
14.14. **4:** On *the Red Sea,* see comment on 13.18. **11:**
Who is like you, O LORD *, among the gods?* This question assumes that the LORD is the one superior god
above a number of other lesser gods gathered in a
heavenly council. This theme occurs in other ancient
biblical poems (Ps 86.8; 89.6–8). **13:** The poem turns
from the victory against the Egyptians and describes
God leading Israel to the land of Canaan. **14–16:** *Philistia* (v. 14), *Edom, Moab,* and *Canaan* (v. 15) are
nations in and around the promised land of Canaan
whom Israel will encounter on the way there. **17:** *The
mountain* may be a reference to the much later establishment of the LORD's Temple* on Mount Zion* in
the city of Jerusalem (Ps 48.1–3) or to the hill country
of Canaan in general (Ps 78.54). **20–21:** *The prophet**
Miriam may have been the original bard or singer in
an earlier version of the tradition. It was women who
typically sang victory songs after military victories in
ancient Israel (Judg 11.34; 1 Sam 18.6–7).

Israel complains and God responds
15.22–17.7: God provides water and food in response
to the legitimate complaints of Israel as they enter into
the dry desert of the Sinai Peninsula. Similar complaints about food and water later (see Num 11.1–9,
31–35; 20.1–13) provoke God's anger and punishment.

22 Then Moses ordered Israel to set out
from the Red Sea,[a] and they went into the
wilderness of Shur. They went three days in
the wilderness and found no water. 23When
they came to Marah, they could not drink
the water of Marah because it was bitter.
That is why it was called Marah.[b] 24And the
people complained against Moses, saying,
"What shall we drink?" 25He cried out to the
LORD; and the LORD showed him a piece of
wood;[c] he threw it into the water, and the
water became sweet.

a Or *Sea of Reeds*   *b* That is *Bitterness*   *c* Or *a tree*

There the LORD[a] made for them a statute and an ordinance and there he put them to the test. 26He said, "If you will listen carefully to the voice of the LORD your God, and do what is right in his sight, and give heed to his commandments and keep all his statutes, I will not bring upon you any of the diseases that I brought upon the Egyptians; for I am the LORD who heals you."

27 Then they came to Elim, where there were twelve springs of water and seventy palm trees; and they camped there by the water.

16 The whole congregation of the Israelites set out from Elim; and Israel came to the wilderness of Sin, which is between Elim and Sinai, on the fifteenth day of the second month after they had departed from the land of Egypt. 2The whole congregation of the Israelites complained against Moses and Aaron in the wilderness. 3The Israelites said to them, "If only we had died by the hand of the LORD in the land of Egypt, when we sat by the fleshpots and ate our fill of bread; for you have brought us out into this wilderness to kill this whole assembly with hunger."

4 Then the LORD said to Moses, "I am going to rain bread from heaven for you, and each day the people shall go out and gather enough for that day. In that way I will test them, whether they will follow my instruction or not. 5On the sixth day, when they prepare what they bring in, it will be twice as much as they gather on other days." 6So Moses and Aaron said to all the Israelites, "In the evening you shall know that it was the LORD who brought you out of the land of Egypt, 7and in the morning you shall see the glory of the LORD, because he has heard your complaining against the LORD. For what are we, that you complain against us?" 8And Moses said, "When the LORD gives you meat to eat in the evening and your fill of bread in the morning, because the LORD has heard the complaining that you utter against him—what are we? Your complaining is not against us but against the LORD."

15.22–16.8. 23: The place name *Marah* means "Bitterness," a wordplay on the *bitter* water there.

25: Traditional cultures believed that certain kinds of *wood* or trees had the ability to "heal" poisonous water and make it *sweet* or drinkable. **16.1:** *The wilderness of Sin* is in the Sinai Peninsula just east of Egypt. **5:** They will gather *twice as much* on the *sixth day* in order that they may rest on the seventh day. The seventh day is the day of sabbath rest when no work is to be done (vv. 22–30; see the commandment in 20.8–11).

9 Then Moses said to Aaron, "Say to the whole congregation of the Israelites, 'Draw near to the LORD, for he has heard your complaining.' " 10And as Aaron spoke to the whole congregation of the Israelites, they looked toward the wilderness, and the glory of the LORD appeared in the cloud. 11The LORD spoke to Moses and said, 12"I have heard the complaining of the Israelites; say to them, 'At twilight you shall eat meat, and in the morning you shall have your fill of bread; then you shall know that I am the LORD your God.' "

13 In the evening quails came up and covered the camp; and in the morning there was a layer of dew around the camp. 14When the layer of dew lifted, there on the surface of the wilderness was a fine flaky substance, as fine as frost on the ground. 15When the Israelites saw it, they said to one another, "What is it?"[b] For they did not know what it was. Moses said to them, "It is the bread that the LORD has given you to eat. 16This is what the LORD has commanded: 'Gather as much of it as each of you needs, an omer to a person according to the number of persons, all providing for those in their own tents.' " 17The Israelites did so, some gathering more, some less. 18But when they measured it with an omer, those who gathered much had nothing over, and those who gathered little had no shortage; they gathered as much as each of them needed. 19And Moses said to them, "Let no one leave any of it over until morning." 20But they did not listen to Moses; some left part of it until morning, and it bred worms and became foul. And Moses was angry with them. 21Morning by morning

a Heb *he* b Or "*It is manna*" (Heb *man hu*, see verse 31) they gathered it, as much as each needed; but when the sun grew hot, it melted.

22 On the sixth day they gathered twice as much food, two omers apiece. When all the leaders of the congregation came and told Moses, 23he said to them, "This is what the LORD has commanded: 'Tomorrow is a day of solemn rest, a holy sabbath to the LORD; bake what you want to bake and boil what you want to boil, and all that is left over put aside to be kept until morning.'" 24So they put it aside until morning, as Moses commanded them; and it did not become foul, and there were no worms in it. 25Moses said, "Eat it today, for today is a sabbath to the LORD; today you will not find it in the field. 26Six days you shall gather it; but on the seventh day, which is a sabbath, there will be none."

27 On the seventh day some of the people went out to gather, and they found none. 28The LORD said to Moses, "How long will you refuse to keep my commandments and instructions? 29See! The LORD has given you the sabbath, therefore on the sixth day he gives you food for two days; each of you stay where you are; do not leave your place on the seventh day." 30So the people rested on the seventh day.

31 The house of Israel called it manna; it was like coriander seed, white, and the taste of it was like wafers made with honey. 32Moses said, "This is what the LORD has commanded: 'Let an omer of it be kept throughout your generations, in order that they may see the food with which I fed you in the wilderness, when I brought you out of the land of Egypt.'" 33And Moses said to Aaron, "Take a jar, and put an omer of manna in it, and place it before the LORD, to be kept throughout your generations." 34As the LORD commanded Moses, so Aaron placed it before the covenant,ᵃ for safekeeping. 35The Israelites ate manna forty years, until they came to a habitable land; they ate manna, until they came to the border of the land of Canaan. 36An omer is a tenth of an ephah.

17 From the wilderness of Sin the whole congregation of the Israelites journeyed by stages, as the LORD com-manded. They camped at Rephidim, but there was no water for the people to drink. 2The people quarreled with Moses, and said, "Give us water to drink." Moses said to them, "Why do you quarrel with me? Why do you test the LORD?" 3But the people thirsted there for water; and the people complained against Moses and said, "Why did you bring us out of Egypt, to kill us and our children and livestock with thirst?" 4So Moses cried out to the LORD, "What shall I do with this people? They are almost ready to stone me." 5The LORD said to Moses, "Go on ahead of the people, and take some of the elders of Israel with you; take in your hand the staff with which you struck the Nile, and go. 6I will be standing there in front of you on the rock at Horeb. Strike the rock, and water will come out of it, so that the people may drink." Moses did so, in the sight of the elders of Israel. 7He called the place Massahᵇ and Meribah,ᶜ because the Israelites quarreled and tested the LORD, saying, "Is the LORD among us or not?"

16.9–17.7. 15: The phrase *What is it?* ("man hu") is a pun on the name of the food "manna" (v. 31). 16: *An omer* is a unit of dry measure, less than a gallon. See v. 36 where the *omer* is defined as one-tenth of an "ephah." An "ephah" is about 20 liters. 34: *The covenant** refers to the two stone tablets on which the Ten Commandments were written. The tablets were carried in an ornate container called the "ark" or "ark of the covenant" (25.16). Aaron placed the jar of manna into the same ark. 35: The transition from *manna* to the produce of *Canaan* occurs in Josh 5.12. 17.7: *Massah* means "Test," and *Meribah* means "Quarrel."

---

8 Then Amalek came and fought with Israel at Rephidim. 9Moses said to Joshua, "Choose some men for us and go out, fight with Amalek. Tomorrow I will stand on the top of the hill with the staff of God in my hand." 10So Joshua did as Moses told him, and fought with Amalek, while Moses, Aaron, and Hur went up to the top of the hill. 11Whenever Moses held up his hand,

a Or *treaty* or *testimony*; Heb *eduth*   *b* That is *Test*
c That is *Quarrel*

Israel prevailed; and whenever he lowered his hand, Amalek prevailed. 12But Moses' hands grew weary; so they took a stone and put it under him, and he sat on it. Aaron and Hur held up his hands, one on one side, and the other on the other side; so his hands were steady until the sun set. 13And Joshua defeated Amalek and his people with the sword.

14 Then the LORD said to Moses, "Write this as a reminder in a book and recite it in the hearing of Joshua: I will utterly blot out the remembrance of Amalek from under heaven." 15And Moses built an altar and called it, The LORD is my banner. 16He said, "A hand upon the banner of the LORD!a The LORD will have war with Amalek from generation to generation."

17.8–16: Amalek attacks Israel, but Israel defeats them. 8: *Amalek* is a desert tribe from the nation of Edom (Gen 36.12) that lives in the wilderness around Kadesh (Num 13.29). **9:** This is the first mention of *Joshua.* Joshua is Moses' young assistant (24.13; 33.11) and Israel's military commander. Joshua becomes leader of all Israel after Moses' death (Num 27.12–23; Josh 1.1–11). **10:** *Hur* is a leader in the Israelite tribe of Judah (24.14; 31.2). **11–12:** Moses' raised hands are a sign of divine power that aids the Israelites in their battle against Amalek. **14:** *Write . . . in a book:* This is the first reference to Moses' writing in a book or scroll. 1 Chronicles 4.41–43 recounts the final defeat of Amalek during the reign of Hezekiah, king of Judah. **15:** The word *banner* ("nas") puns on the verb "test" ("nasah," v. 7). **16:** *War with Amalek* continues for many generations (1 Sam 15.1–9; 30.1–20).

Jethro gives administrative advice
18.1–27: Alternate versions of this story in which Jethro is not involved occur in Num 11.10–30 and Deut 1.9–18.

18 Jethro, the priest of Midian, Moses' father-in-law, heard of all that God had done for Moses and for his people Israel, how the LORD had brought Israel out of Egypt. 2After Moses had sent away his wife Zipporah, his father-in-law Jethro took her back, 3along with her two sons. The name of the one was Gershom (for he said, "I have

been an alienb in a foreign land"), 4and the name of the other, Eliezerc (for he said, "The God of my father was my help, and delivered me from the sword of Pharaoh"). 5Jethro, Moses' father-in-law, came into the wilderness where Moses was encamped at the mountain of God, bringing Moses' sons and wife to him. 6He sent word to Moses, "I, your father-in-law Jethro, am coming to you, with your wife and her two sons." 7Moses went out to meet his father-in-law; he bowed down and kissed him; each asked after the other's welfare, and they went into the tent. 8Then Moses told his father-in-law all that the LORD had done to Pharaoh and to the Egyptians for Israel's sake, all the hardship that had beset them on the way, and how the LORD had delivered them. 9Jethro rejoiced for all the good that the LORD had done to Israel, in delivering them from the Egyptians.

10 Jethro said, "Blessed be the LORD, who has delivered you from the Egyptians and from Pharaoh. 11Now I know that the LORD is greater than all gods, because he delivered the people from the Egyptians,d when they dealt arrogantly with them." 12And Jethro, Moses' father-in-law, brought a burnt offering and sacrifices to God; and Aaron came with all the elders of Israel to eat bread with Moses' father-in-law in the presence of God.

13 The next day Moses sat as judge for the people, while the people stood around him from morning until evening. 14When Moses' father-in-law saw all that he was doing for the people, he said, "What is this that you are doing for the people? Why do you sit alone, while all the people stand around you from morning until evening?" 15Moses said to his father-in-law, "Because the people come to me to inquire of God. 16When they have a dispute, they come to me and I decide between one person and another, and I make known to them the statutes and instructions of God." 17Moses' father-in-law said to him, "What you are doing is not good. 18You will surely wear yourself out, both you and these

a Cn: Meaning of Heb uncertain   *b* Heb *ger*
c Heb *Eli,* my God; *ezer,* help   *d* The clause
because . . . Egyptians has been transposed from verse 10

people with you. For the task is too heavy for you; you cannot do it alone. ¹⁹Now listen to me. I will give you counsel, and God be with you! You should represent the people before God, and you should bring their cases before God; ²⁰teach them the statutes and instructions and make known to them the way they are to go and the things they are to do. ²¹You should also look for able men among all the people, men who fear God, are trustworthy, and hate dishonest gain; set such men over them as officers over thousands, hundreds, fifties and tens. ²²Let them sit as judges for the people at all times; let them bring every important case to you, but decide every minor case themselves. So it will be easier for you, and they will bear the burden with you. ²³If you do this, and God so commands you, then you will be able to endure, and all these people will go to their home in peace."

24 So Moses listened to his father-in-law and did all that he had said. ²⁵Moses chose able men from all Israel and appointed them as heads over the people, as officers over thousands, hundreds, fifties, and tens. ²⁶And they judged the people at all times;

Map Israel's exodus out of Egypt and wilderness journey

hard cases they brought to Moses, but any minor case they decided themselves. 27 Then Moses let his father-in-law depart, and he went off to his own country.

18.1–27. 1: The name of Moses' father-in-law is *Jethro* here, but the name varies in other biblical traditions. His name is sometimes Reuel (2.18) or Hobab (Num 10.29; Judg 4.11). **2:** Moses' Midianite wife Zipporah (2.21–22) went with Moses from Midian to Egypt (4.20). At some point, *Moses had sent away his wife.* Now Jethro brings her and the two sons back to join Moses (vv. 5–6). **3:** On *Gershom*, see comment on 2.22. **4:** The name *Eliezer* means "my God [is] help." **5:** *The mountain of God* is Mount Horeb, otherwise known as Mount Sinai (3.1). **21:** These numbered divisions of the population most often appear in military contexts (2 Sam 18.1).

Israel prepares for the covenant with the LORD
19.1–25: This chapter begins a major new section within the book of Exodus, 19.1–24.18. God initiates a formal relationship or covenant agreement with Israel. This covenant includes lists of obligations for Israel in the form of the Ten Commandments (20.1–17) and the laws in the Book of the Covenant (20.22–23.19). Israel will remain encamped in this area at Sinai until Num 10.11–12.

19 On the third new moon after the Israelites had gone out of the land of Egypt, on that very day, they came into the wilderness of Sinai. 2 They had journeyed from Rephidim, entered the wilderness of Sinai, and camped in the wilderness; Israel camped there in front of the mountain. 3 Then Moses went up to God; the LORD called to him from the mountain, saying, "Thus you shall say to the house of Jacob, and tell the Israelites: 4 You have seen what I did to the Egyptians, and how I bore you on eagles' wings and brought you to myself. 5 Now therefore, if you obey my voice and keep my covenant, you shall be my treasured possession out of all the peoples. Indeed, the whole earth is mine, 6 but you shall be for me a priestly kingdom and a holy nation. These are the words that you shall speak to the Israelites."

7 So Moses came, summoned the elders of the people, and set before them all these

words that the LORD had commanded him. 8 The people all answered as one: "Everything that the LORD has spoken we will do." Moses reported the words of the people to the LORD. 9 Then the LORD said to Moses, "I am going to come to you in a dense cloud, in order that the people may hear when I speak with you and so trust you ever after."

When Moses had told the words of the people to the LORD, 10 the LORD said to Moses: "Go to the people and consecrate them today and tomorrow. Have them wash their clothes 11 and prepare for the third day, because on the third day the LORD will come down upon Mount Sinai in the sight of all the people. 12 You shall set limits for the people all around, saying, 'Be careful not to go up the mountain or to touch the edge of it. Any who touch the mountain shall be put to death. 13 No hand shall touch them, but they shall be stoned or shot with arrows;*a* whether animal or human being, they shall not live.' When the trumpet sounds a long blast, they may go up on the mountain." 14 So Moses went down from the mountain to the people. He consecrated the people, and they washed their clothes. 15 And he said to the people, "Prepare for the third day; do not go near a woman."

16 On the morning of the third day there was thunder and lightning, as well as a thick cloud on the mountain, and a blast of a trumpet so loud that all the people who were in the camp trembled. 17 Moses brought the people out of the camp to meet God. They took their stand at the foot of the mountain. 18 Now Mount Sinai was wrapped in smoke, because the LORD had descended upon it in fire; the smoke went up like the smoke of a kiln, while the whole mountain shook violently. 19 As the blast of the trumpet grew louder and louder, Moses would speak and God would answer him in thunder. 20 When the LORD descended upon Mount Sinai, to the top of the mountain, the LORD summoned Moses to the top of the mountain, and Moses went up. 21 Then the LORD said to Moses, "Go down and warn the people not to break through to the LORD to look; oth-

a Heb lacks *with arrows*

erwise many of them will perish. ²²Even the priests who approach the LORD must consecrate themselves or the LORD will break out against them." ²³Moses said to the LORD, "The people are not permitted to come up to Mount Sinai; for you yourself warned us, saying, 'Set limits around the mountain and keep it holy.' " ²⁴The LORD said to him, "Go down, and come up bringing Aaron with you; but do not let either the priests or the people break through to come up to the LORD; otherwise he will break out against them." ²⁵So Moses went down to the people and told them.

19.1–25. 1: *The wilderness of Sinai* in the Sinai Peninsula east of Egypt contains many mountains. The exact location of Mount Sinai is not known. The mountain is traditionally located in the south-central area of the Sinai Peninsula. 4: The image of God leading Israel out of Egypt like an eagle is expanded in Deut 32.11. 6: Israel as *a priestly kingdom and a holy nation* implies that God has set Israel apart from other nations. Israel has a higher standard of holiness and a mission to mediate between God and other nations. 12–13: The mountain is holy because of God's presence. Holiness and ritual impurity cannot mix. Unless a person is properly prepared, any human contact with the realm of God's holiness leads to death (vv. 21–24). 15: Sexual relations rendered a person ritually unclean for a day (1 Sam 21.4). 16: Ancient Israel and its neighboring cultures often portrayed the appearance of the deity with an accompanying storm of *thunder, lightning,* and a *thick cloud* (Ps 29; 68). 21–24: On the danger of crossing the boundary of holiness, see comment on vv. 12–13.

The Ten Commandments
20.1–21: These ten rules form the core of Israel's obligation in its relationship with God. Moses repeats these Ten Commandments in slightly altered form to a new generation in Deut 5.6–21. God is the one who writes the Ten Commandments on two stone tablets (31.18). The commandments are a central element of the faith of Judaism and Christianity.

20 Then God spoke all these words: ²I am the LORD your God, who brought you out of the land of Egypt, out of the house of slavery; ³you shall have no other gods before*ᵃ* me.

4 You shall not make for yourself an idol, whether in the form of anything that is in heaven above, or that is on the earth beneath, or that is in the water under the earth. ⁵You shall not bow down to them or worship them; for I the LORD your God am a jealous God, punishing children for the iniquity of parents, to the third and the fourth generation of those who reject me, ⁶but showing steadfast love to the thousandth generation*ᵇ* of those who love me and keep my commandments.

7 You shall not make wrongful use of the name of the LORD your God, for the LORD will not acquit anyone who misuses his name.

8 Remember the sabbath day, and keep it holy. ⁹Six days you shall labor and do all your work. ¹⁰But the seventh day is a sabbath to the LORD your God; you shall not do any work—you, your son or your daughter, your male or female slave, your livestock, or the alien resident in your towns. ¹¹For in six days the LORD made heaven and earth, the sea, and all that is in them, but rested the seventh day; therefore the LORD blessed the sabbath day and consecrated it.

12 Honor your father and your mother, so that your days may be long in the land that the LORD your God is giving you.

13 You shall not murder.*ᶜ*

14 You shall not commit adultery.

15 You shall not steal.

16 You shall not bear false witness against your neighbor.

17 You shall not covet your neighbor's house; you shall not covet your neighbor's wife, or male or female slave, or ox, or donkey, or anything that belongs to your neighbor.

18 When all the people witnessed the thunder and lightning, the sound of the trumpet, and the mountain smoking, they were afraid*ᵈ* and trembled and stood at a distance, ¹⁹and said to Moses, "You speak to us, and we will listen; but do not let God speak to us, or we will die." ²⁰Moses said to

a Or besides *b* Or to thousands *c* Or kill
d Sam Gk Syr Vg: MT *they saw*

the people, "Do not be afraid; for God has come only to test you and to put the fear of him upon you so that you do not sin." ²¹Then the people stood at a distance, while Moses drew near to the thick darkness where God was.

20.1–21. 4: The description assumes a three-level universe: *heaven above, earth beneath,* and *water under the earth.* See Gen 1.6–10. **7:** The prohibition against the *wrongful use of the name of the* LORD is aimed particularly at violating oaths made in the deity's name (Lev 19.12). **8:** The root meaning of the *sabbath* is "to stop, to rest." To *keep it holy* signifies setting the seventh day apart as different from all other days of the week. **11:** In the creation story in Gen 1, God created the world in six days and rested on the seventh (Gen 2.1–3). **12:** The commandment concerning parents may have originally been aimed especially at the care of elderly parents. **13:** *Murder* refers to any killing not sanctioned by the community, including personal acts of revenge. **16:** The prohibition of *false witness* involves false testimony in judicial cases and disputes. **17:** To *covet* refers to the inner yearning and strong desire to take something that rightfully belongs to others, especially the poor and less powerful.

Additional laws in the Book of the Covenant
20.22–23.19: Most scholars consider this group of laws to be the oldest of all the legal collections of the Bible. These biblical laws have several parallels in subject matter and form to ancient Babylonian law codes. The laws alternate between religious concerns and criminal, social, and economic matters.

---

22 The LORD said to Moses: Thus you shall say to the Israelites: "You have seen for yourselves that I spoke with you from heaven. ²³You shall not make gods of silver alongside me, nor shall you make for yourselves gods of gold. ²⁴You need make for me only an altar of earth and sacrifice on it your burnt offerings and your offerings of well-being, your sheep and your oxen; in every place where I cause my name to be remembered I will come to you and bless you. ²⁵But if you make for me an altar of stone, do not build it of hewn stones; for if you use a chisel upon it you profane it. ²⁶You shall not go up by steps to my altar, so that your nakedness may not be exposed on it."

$2\,1$ These are the ordinances that you shall set before them:

2 When you buy a male Hebrew slave, he shall serve six years, but in the seventh he shall go out a free person, without debt. ³If he comes in single, he shall go out single; if he comes in married, then his wife shall go out with him. ⁴If his master gives him a wife and she bears him sons or daughters, the wife and her children shall be her master's and he shall go out alone. ⁵But if the slave declares, "I love my master, my wife, and my children; I will not go out a free person," ⁶then his master shall bring him before God.^a He shall be brought to the door or the doorpost; and his master shall pierce his ear with an awl; and he shall serve him for life.

7 When a man sells his daughter as a slave, she shall not go out as the male slaves do. ⁸If she does not please her master, who designated her for himself, then he shall let her be redeemed; he shall have no right to sell her to a foreign people, since he has dealt unfairly with her. ⁹If he designates her for his son, he shall deal with her as with a daughter. ¹⁰If he takes another wife to himself, he shall not diminish the food, clothing, or marital rights of the first wife.^b ¹¹And if he does not do these three things for her, she shall go out without debt, without payment of money.

12 Whoever strikes a person mortally shall be put to death. ¹³If it was not premeditated, but came about by an act of God, then I will appoint for you a place to which the killer may flee. ¹⁴But if someone willfully attacks and kills another by treachery, you shall take the killer from my altar for execution.

20.22–21.14. 20.26: The concern for stairs and the exposure of *nakedness* implies that those doing the sacrificing at the altar wore robes that were open at the bottom. **21.6:** The blood on the doorpost from the *pierced ear* was a sign of the permanent attachment of the slave to the household. **8:** The case deals with a husband's taking a slave as a wife or concubine* through whom he might have children (Gen 21.10–13). **13–14:** Accidental killers could flee to designated

a Or *to the judges*　　*b* Heb *of her*

"cities of refuge" where they could live protected from family members of the victim who would seek revenge (Num 35.9–28).

15 Whoever strikes father or mother shall be put to death.

16 Whoever kidnaps a person, whether that person has been sold or is still held in possession, shall be put to death.

17 Whoever curses father or mother shall be put to death.

18 When individuals quarrel and one strikes the other with a stone or fist so that the injured party, though not dead, is confined to bed, 19but recovers and walks around outside with the help of a staff, then the assailant shall be free of liability, except to pay for the loss of time, and to arrange for full recovery.

20 When a slaveowner strikes a male or female slave with a rod and the slave dies immediately, the owner shall be punished. 21But if the slave survives a day or two, there is no punishment; for the slave is the owner's property.

22 When people who are fighting injure a pregnant woman so that there is a miscarriage, and yet no further harm follows, the one responsible shall be fined what the woman's husband demands, paying as much as the judges determine. 23If any harm follows, then you shall give life for life, 24eye for eye, tooth for tooth, hand for hand, foot for foot, 25burn for burn, wound for wound, stripe for stripe.

26 When a slaveowner strikes the eye of a male or female slave, destroying it, the owner shall let the slave go, a free person, to compensate for the eye. 27If the owner knocks out a tooth of a male or female slave, the slave shall be let go, a free person, to compensate for the tooth.

28 When an ox gores a man or a woman to death, the ox shall be stoned, and its flesh shall not be eaten; but the owner of the ox shall not be liable. 29If the ox has been accustomed to gore in the past, and its owner has been warned but has not restrained it, and it kills a man or a woman, the ox shall be stoned, and its owner also shall be put to death. 30If a ransom is imposed on the owner, then the owner shall pay whatever is imposed for the redemption of the victim's life. 31If it gores a boy or a girl, the owner shall be dealt with according to this same rule. 32If the ox gores a male or female slave, the owner shall pay to the slaveowner thirty shekels of silver, and the ox shall be stoned.

33 If someone leaves a pit open, or digs a pit and does not cover it, and an ox or a donkey falls into it, 34the owner of the pit shall make restitution, giving money to its owner, but keeping the dead animal.

35 If someone's ox hurts the ox of another, so that it dies, then they shall sell the live ox and divide the price of it; and the dead animal they shall also divide. 36But if it was known that the ox was accustomed to gore in the past, and its owner has not restrained it, the owner shall restore ox for ox, but keep the dead animal.

21.15–36. 23–24: The principle of *life for life* seeks to limit the extent of any revenge. The principle also means that simply paying money to a victim or victim's family cannot compensate for the loss of a priceless life or limb. 28: The *ox shall be stoned* and *not eaten* because it has become ritually impure by causing the death of a human.

22 aWhen someone steals an ox or a sheep, and slaughters it or sells it, the thief shall pay five oxen for an ox, and four sheep for a sheep.b The thief shall make restitution, but if unable to do so, shall be sold for the theft. 4When the animal, whether ox or donkey or sheep, is found alive in the thief's possession, the thief shall pay double.

2c If a thief is found breaking in, and is beaten to death, no bloodguilt is incurred; 3but if it happens after sunrise, bloodguilt is incurred.

5 When someone causes a field or vineyard to be grazed over, or lets livestock loose to graze in someone else's field, restitution shall be made from the best in the owner's field or vineyard.

6 When fire breaks out and catches in

a Ch 21.37 in Heb   b Verses 2, 3, and 4 rearranged thus: 3b, 4, 2, 3a   c Ch 22.1 in Heb thorns so that the stacked grain or the standing grain or the field is consumed, the one who started the fire shall make full restitution.

7 When someone delivers to a neighbor money or goods for safekeeping, and they are stolen from the neighbor's house, then the thief, if caught, shall pay double. 8 If the thief is not caught, the owner of the house shall be brought before God,[a] to determine whether or not the owner had laid hands on the neighbor's goods.

9 In any case of disputed ownership involving ox, donkey, sheep, clothing, or any other loss, of which one party says, "This is mine," the case of both parties shall come before God;[a] the one whom God condemns[b] shall pay double to the other.

10 When someone delivers to another a donkey, ox, sheep, or any other animal for safekeeping, and it dies or is injured or is carried off, without anyone seeing it, 11 an oath before the LORD shall decide between the two of them that the one has not laid hands on the property of the other; the owner shall accept the oath, and no restitution shall be made. 12 But if it was stolen, restitution shall be made to its owner. 13 If it was mangled by beasts, let it be brought as evidence; restitution shall not be made for the mangled remains.

14 When someone borrows an animal from another and it is injured or dies, the owner not being present, full restitution shall be made. 15 If the owner was present, there shall be no restitution; if it was hired, only the hiring fee is due.

16 When a man seduces a virgin who is not engaged to be married, and lies with her, he shall give the bride-price for her and make her his wife. 17 But if her father refuses to give her to him, he shall pay an amount equal to the bride-price for virgins.

18 You shall not permit a female sorcerer to live.

19 Whoever lies with an animal shall be put to death.

20 Whoever sacrifices to any god, other than the LORD alone, shall be devoted to destruction.

21 You shall not wrong or oppress a resident alien, for you were aliens in the land of Egypt. 22 You shall not abuse any widow or orphan. 23 If you do abuse them, when they cry out to me, I will surely heed their cry; 24 my wrath will burn, and I will kill you with the sword, and your wives shall become widows and your children orphans.

25 If you lend money to my people, to the poor among you, you shall not deal with them as a creditor; you shall not exact interest from them. 26 If you take your neighbor's cloak in pawn, you shall restore it before the sun goes down; 27 for it may be your neighbor's only clothing to use as cover; in what else shall that person sleep? And if your neighbor cries out to me, I will listen, for I am compassionate.

28 You shall not revile God, or curse a leader of your people.

29 You shall not delay to make offerings from the fullness of your harvest and from the outflow of your presses.[c]

The firstborn of your sons you shall give to me. 30 You shall do the same with your oxen and with your sheep: seven days it shall remain with its mother; on the eighth day you shall give it to me.

22.21–30. 21–24: Israel's experience of being *aliens in the land of Egypt* motivated these laws against oppressing *a resident alien** or other marginal people in the community (see 23.9). Israel also knew firsthand the power of the oppressed who *cry out* to arouse God's saving action (see 2.23–25). **30:** The *seven days* of waiting is the time required for the mother and the baby to become ritually clean after the birth (Lev 12.2–3).

---

31 You shall be people consecrated to me; therefore you shall not eat any meat that is mangled by beasts in the field; you shall throw it to the dogs.

23 You shall not spread a false report. You shall not join hands with the wicked to act as a malicious witness. 2 You shall not follow a majority in wrongdoing; when you bear witness in a lawsuit, you shall not side with the majority so as to pervert

---

a Or *before the judges*　　b Or *the judges condemn*
c Meaning of Heb uncertain

justice; ³nor shall you be partial to the poor in a lawsuit.

4 When you come upon your enemy's ox or donkey going astray, you shall bring it back.

5 When you see the donkey of one who hates you lying under its burden and you would hold back from setting it free, you must help to set it free.*ᵃ*

6 You shall not pervert the justice due to your poor in their lawsuits. ⁷Keep far from a false charge, and do not kill the innocent and those in the right, for I will not acquit the guilty. ⁸You shall take no bribe, for a bribe blinds the officials, and subverts the cause of those who are in the right.

9 You shall not oppress a resident alien; you know the heart of an alien, for you were aliens in the land of Egypt.

10 For six years you shall sow your land and gather in its yield; ¹¹but the seventh year you shall let it rest and lie fallow, so that the poor of your people may eat; and what they leave the wild animals may eat. You shall do the same with your vineyard, and with your olive orchard.

12 Six days you shall do your work, but on the seventh day you shall rest, so that your ox and your donkey may have relief, and your homeborn slave and the resident alien may be refreshed. ¹³Be attentive to all that I have said to you. Do not invoke the names of other gods; do not let them be heard on your lips.

14 Three times in the year you shall hold a festival for me. ¹⁵You shall observe the festival of unleavened bread; as I commanded you, you shall eat unleavened bread for seven days at the appointed time in the month of Abib, for in it you came out of Egypt.

No one shall appear before me empty-handed.

16 You shall observe the festival of harvest, of the first fruits of your labor, of what you sow in the field. You shall observe the festival of ingathering at the end of the year, when you gather in from the field the fruit of your labor. ¹⁷Three times in the year all your males shall appear before the Lord GOD.

18 You shall not offer the blood of my sacrifice with anything leavened, or let the fat of my festival remain until the morning.

19 The choicest of the first fruits of your ground you shall bring into the house of the LORD your God.

You shall not boil a kid in its mother's milk.

23.15–19. 15: On *the festival of unleavened bread,* see 13.3–10. **19:** The prohibition against boiling a young goat or *kid in its mother's milk* involves the ritual impurity of crossing the boundary between life and death. The mother's milk gives life, but using it to boil meat mixes it with death.

~~~~~~~~~~

20 I am going to send an angel in front of you, to guard you on the way and to bring you to the place that I have prepared. ²¹Be attentive to him and listen to his voice; do not rebel against him, for he will not pardon your transgression; for my name is in him.

22 But if you listen attentively to his voice and do all that I say, then I will be an enemy to your enemies and a foe to your foes.

23 When my angel goes in front of you, and brings you to the Amorites, the Hittites, the Perizzites, the Canaanites, the Hivites, and the Jebusites, and I blot them out, ²⁴you shall not bow down to their gods, or worship them, or follow their practices, but you shall utterly demolish them and break their pillars in pieces. ²⁵You shall worship the LORD your God, and I*ᵇ* will bless your bread and your water; and I will take sickness away from among you. ²⁶No one shall miscarry or be barren in your land; I will fulfill the number of your days. ²⁷I will send my terror in front of you, and will throw into confusion all the people against whom you shall come, and I will make all your enemies turn their backs to you. ²⁸And I will send the pestilence*ᶜ* in front of you, which shall drive out the Hivites, the Canaanites, and the Hittites from before you. ²⁹I will not drive them out from before you in one year, or the land would become desolate and the wild animals would multiply against you. ³⁰Little by little I will

ᵃ Meaning of Heb uncertain   *ᵇ* Gk Vg: Heb *he*
ᶜ Or *hornets*: Meaning of Heb uncertain

drive them out from before you, until you have increased and possess the land. 31I will set your borders from the Red Sea*a* to the sea of the Philistines, and from the wilderness to the Euphrates; for I will hand over to you the inhabitants of the land, and you shall drive them out before you. 32You shall make no covenant with them and their gods. 33They shall not live in your land, or they will make you sin against me; for if you worship their gods, it will surely be a snare to you.

23.20–33: God gives promises and instructions regarding Israel's future entry into Canaan. 20: The LORD promises to send *an angel* as a divine representative to protect and fight for the Israelites (see v. 23 and 14.19). Discussion about the angel continues in 32.34 and 33.2. The angel will reappear in Josh 5.13–15 and Judg 2.1–5. **31:** *The sea of the Philistines* is the Mediterranean Sea to the west of Canaan. *The wilderness* is probably the Negev region south of Canaan. The boundaries correspond roughly to the size of Israel under King Solomon (1 Kings 4.21).

24 Then he said to Moses, "Come up to the LORD, you and Aaron, Nadab, and Abihu, and seventy of the elders of Israel, and worship at a distance. 2Moses alone shall come near the LORD; but the others shall not come near, and the people shall not come up with him."

3 Moses came and told the people all the words of the LORD and all the ordinances; and all the people answered with one voice, and said, "All the words that the LORD has spoken we will do." 4And Moses wrote down all the words of the LORD. He rose early in the morning, and built an altar at the foot of the mountain, and set up twelve pillars, corresponding to the twelve tribes of Israel. 5He sent young men of the people of Israel, who offered burnt offerings and sacrificed oxen as offerings of well-being to the LORD. 6Moses took half of the blood and put it in basins, and half of the blood he dashed against the altar. 7Then he took the book of the covenant, and read it in the hearing of the people; and they said, "All that the LORD has spoken we will do, and we will be obedient." 8Moses took the blood and dashed it on the people, and said, "See the blood of the covenant that

the LORD has made with you in accordance with all these words."

9 Then Moses and Aaron, Nadab, and Abihu, and seventy of the elders of Israel went up, 10and they saw the God of Israel. Under his feet there was something like a pavement of sapphire stone, like the very heaven for clearness. 11God*b* did not lay his hand on the chief men of the people of Israel; also they beheld God, and they ate and drank.

12 The LORD said to Moses, "Come up to me on the mountain, and wait there; and I will give you the tablets of stone, with the law and the commandment, which I have written for their instruction." 13So Moses set out with his assistant Joshua, and Moses went up into the mountain of God. 14To the elders he had said, "Wait here for us, until we come to you again; for Aaron and Hur are with you; whoever has a dispute may go to them."

15 Then Moses went up on the mountain, and the cloud covered the mountain. 16The glory of the LORD settled on Mount Sinai, and the cloud covered it for six days; on the seventh day he called to Moses out of the cloud. 17Now the appearance of the glory of the LORD was like a devouring fire on the top of the mountain in the sight of the people of Israel. 18Moses entered the cloud, and went up on the mountain. Moses was on the mountain for forty days and forty nights.

24.1–18: The LORD, Moses, and the people formally enter into a covenant* relationship. 1: Nadab and Abihu are two sons of Aaron who serve as priests (see 6.23). **6–8:** *The altar* represents God's presence (v. 6). Sprinkling blood on the altar and then the people signifies their binding together in relationship. *The book of the covenant* is presumably some form of the laws and commandments in chs. 20–23. **9:** On *Nadab and Abihu*, see comment on v. 1. **14:** *Hur* is a leader from the Israelite tribe of Judah (17.10; 31.2).

Furnishings for the tabernacle
25.1–40: This unit begins an extended section of instructions for building and furnishing the portable sanctuary or shrine called the tabernacle* (25.1–

a Or *Sea of Reeds*   *b* Heb *He*

31.18). The tabernacle is to be the vehicle of God's presence as they leave God's dwelling place of Mount Sinai and set off on the journey through the wilderness to the promised land. The tabernacle will not be built until after the golden calf rebellion (ch. 32) and the renewal of the covenant* (chs. 33–34).

25

The LORD said to Moses: ²Tell the Israelites to take for me an offering; from all whose hearts prompt them to give you shall receive the offering for me. ³This is the offering that you shall receive from them: gold, silver, and bronze, ⁴blue, purple, and crimson yarns and fine linen, goats' hair, ⁵tanned rams' skins, fine leather,ᵃ acacia wood, ⁶oil for the lamps, spices for the anointing oil and for the fragrant incense, ⁷onyx stones and gems to be set in the ephod and for the breastpiece. ⁸And have them make me a sanctuary, so that I may dwell among them. ⁹In accordance with all that I show you concerning the pattern of the tabernacle and of all its furniture, so you shall make it.

10 They shall make an ark of acacia wood; it shall be two and a half cubits long, a cubit and a half wide, and a cubit and a half high. ¹¹You shall overlay it with pure gold, inside and outside you shall overlay it, and you shall make a molding of gold upon it all around. ¹²You shall cast four rings of gold for it and put them on its four feet, two rings on the one side of it, and two rings on the other side. ¹³You shall make poles of acacia wood, and overlay them with gold. ¹⁴And you shall put the poles into the rings on the sides of the ark, by which to carry the ark. ¹⁵The poles shall remain in the rings of the ark; they shall not be taken from it. ¹⁶You shall put into the ark the covenantᵇ that I shall give you.

17 Then you shall make a mercy seatᶜ of pure gold; two cubits and a half shall be its length, and a cubit and a half its width. ¹⁸You shall make two cherubim of gold; you shall make them of hammered work, at the two ends of the mercy seat.ᵈ ¹⁹Make one cherub at the one end, and one cherub at the other; of one piece with the mercy seatᵈ you shall make the cherubim at its two ends. ²⁰The cherubim shall spread out their wings above, overshadowing the mercy seatᵈ with their wings. They shall face one to another; the faces of the cherubim shall be turned toward the mercy seat.ᵈ ²¹You shall put the mercy seatᵈ on the top of the ark; and in the ark you shall put the covenantᵇ that I shall give you. ²²There I will meet with you, and from above the mercy seat,ᵈ from between the two cherubim that are on the ark of the covenant,ᵇ I will deliver to you all my commands for the Israelites.

23 You shall make a table of acacia wood, two cubits long, one cubit wide, and a cubit and a half high. ²⁴You shall overlay it with pure gold, and make a molding of gold around it. ²⁵You shall make around it a rim a handbreadth wide, and a molding of gold around the rim. ²⁶You shall make for it four rings of gold, and fasten the rings to the four corners at its four legs. ²⁷The rings that hold the poles used for carrying the table shall be close to the rim. ²⁸You shall make the poles of acacia wood, and overlay them with gold, and the table shall be carried with these. ²⁹You shall make its plates and dishes for incense, and its flagons and bowls with which to pour drink offerings; you shall make them of pure gold. ³⁰And you shall set the bread of the Presence on the table before me always.

25.1–30. 3: The *gold* and *silver* and other finery derive presumably from what the Egyptians gave to the Israelites as they fled Egypt (12.35–36). 7: On the *ephod,** see comment on 28.6. 10: The wooden *ark* is a container that functions as a throne or footstool for the divine presence. 16: The two tablets of stone that contain the Ten Commandments are *the covenant* that will be carried in the ark. 17–22: *Cherubim** are half-human and half-animal creatures with wings. The head is human, and the body is usually a lion or bull. They guard holy areas as well as kings. The *mercy seat* is the throne for the deity's presence. 21: On *the covenant*, see comment on v. 16. 30: *The bread of the Presence* is set out *on the table* as a sign of hospitality to the deity, but the priests actually eat the bread (Lev 24.5–9).

ᵃ Meaning of Heb uncertain   ᵇ Or *treaty*, or *testimony*; Heb *eduth*   ᶜ Or *a cover*   ᵈ Or *the cover*

31 You shall make a lampstand of pure gold. The base and the shaft of the lampstand shall be made of hammered work; its cups, its calyxes, and its petals shall be of one piece with it; 32and there shall be six branches going out of its sides, three branches of the lampstand out of one side of it and three branches of the lampstand out of the other side of it; 33three cups shaped like almond blossoms, each with calyx and petals, on one branch, and three cups shaped like almond blossoms, each with calyx and petals, on the other branch—so for the six branches going out of the lampstand. 34On the lampstand itself there shall be four cups shaped like almond blossoms, each with its calyxes and petals. 35There shall be a calyx of one piece with it under the first pair of branches, a calyx of one piece with it under the next pair of branches, and a calyx of one piece with it under the last pair of branches—so for the six branches that go out of the lampstand. 36Their calyxes and their branches shall be of one piece with it, the whole of it one hammered piece of pure gold. 37You shall make the seven lamps for it; and the lamps shall be set up so as to give light on the space in front of it. 38Its snuffers and trays shall be of pure gold. 39It, and all these utensils, shall be made from a talent of pure gold. 40And see that you make them according to the pattern for them, which is being shown you on the mountain.

Instructions concerning the tabernacle's frame and curtains
26.1–37: The description of the tabernacle includes some parallels to the description of Solomon's Temple* in Jerusalem (1 Kings 6) and the vision of the new Temple in Ezek 40–43.

26 Moreover you shall make the tabernacle with ten curtains of fine twisted linen, and blue, purple, and crimson yarns; you shall make them with cherubim skillfully worked into them. 2The length of each curtain shall be twenty-eight cubits, and the width of each curtain four cubits; all the curtains shall be of the same size. 3Five curtains shall be joined to one another; and the other five curtains shall be joined to one another. 4You shall make loops of blue on the edge of the outermost curtain in the first set; and likewise you shall make loops on the edge of the outermost curtain in the second set. 5You shall make fifty loops on the one curtain, and you shall make fifty loops on the edge of the curtain that is in the second set; the loops shall be opposite one another. 6You shall make fifty clasps of gold, and join the curtains to one another with the clasps, so that the tabernacle may be one whole.

7 You shall also make curtains of goats' hair for a tent over the tabernacle; you shall make eleven curtains. 8The length of each curtain shall be thirty cubits, and the width of each curtain four cubits; the eleven curtains shall be of the same size. 9You shall join five curtains by themselves, and six curtains by themselves, and the sixth curtain you shall double over at the front of the tent. 10You shall make fifty loops on the edge of the curtain that is outermost in one set, and fifty loops on the edge of the curtain that is outermost in the second set.

11 You shall make fifty clasps of bronze, and put the clasps into the loops, and join the tent together, so that it may be one whole. 12The part that remains of the curtains of the tent, the half curtain that remains, shall hang over the back of the tabernacle. 13The cubit on the one side, and the cubit on the other side, of what remains in the length of the curtains of the tent, shall hang over the sides of the tabernacle, on this side and that side, to cover it. 14You shall make for the tent a covering of tanned rams' skins and an outer covering of fine leather.ᵃ

15 You shall make upright frames of acacia wood for the tabernacle. 16Ten cubits shall be the length of a frame, and a cubit and a half the width of each frame. 17There shall be two pegs in each frame to fit the frames together; you shall make these for all the frames of the tabernacle. 18You shall make the frames for the tabernacle: twenty frames for the south side; 19and you shall make forty bases of silver under the twenty frames, two bases under the first frame for its two pegs, and two bases under the next

a Meaning of Heb uncertain

frame for its two pegs; 20and for the second side of the tabernacle, on the north side twenty frames, 21and their forty bases of silver, two bases under the first frame, and two bases under the next frame; 22and for the rear of the tabernacle westward you shall make six frames. 23You shall make two frames for corners of the tabernacle in the rear; 24they shall be separate beneath, but joined at the top, at the first ring; it shall be the same with both of them; they shall form the two corners. 25And so there shall be eight frames, with their bases of silver, sixteen bases; two bases under the first frame, and two bases under the next frame.

26 You shall make bars of acacia wood, five for the frames of the one side of the tabernacle, 27and five bars for the frames of the other side of the tabernacle, and five bars for the frames of the side of the tabernacle at the rear westward. 28The middle bar, halfway up the frames, shall pass through from end to end. 29You shall overlay the frames with gold, and shall make their rings of gold to hold the bars; and you shall overlay the bars with gold. 30Then you shall erect the tabernacle according to the plan for it that you were shown on the mountain.

31 You shall make a curtain of blue, purple, and crimson yarns, and of fine twisted linen; it shall be made with cherubim skillfully worked into it. 32You shall hang it on four pillars of acacia overlaid with gold, which have hooks of gold and rest on four bases of silver. 33You shall hang the curtain under the clasps, and bring the ark of the covenant*a* in there, within the curtain; and the curtain shall separate for you the holy place from the most holy. 34You shall put the mercy seat*b* on the ark of the covenant*a* in the most holy place. 35You shall set the table outside the curtain, and the lampstand on the south side of the tabernacle opposite the table; and you shall put the table on the north side.

36 You shall make a screen for the entrance of the tent, of blue, purple, and crimson yarns, and of fine twisted linen, embroidered with needlework. 37You shall make for the screen five pillars of acacia, and overlay them with gold; their hooks shall be of gold,

and you shall cast five bases of bronze for them.

Constructing the altar, the court, and the lamps
27.1–21: These instructions pertain to items and areas outside and surrounding the tabernacle* itself.

27 You shall make the altar of acacia wood, five cubits long and five cubits wide; the altar shall be square, and it shall be three cubits high. 2You shall make horns for it on its four corners; its horns shall be of one piece with it, and you shall overlay it with bronze. 3You shall make pots for it to receive its ashes, and shovels and basins and forks and firepans; you shall make all its utensils of bronze. 4You shall also make for it a grating, a network of bronze; and on the net you shall make four bronze rings at its four corners. 5You shall set it under the ledge of the altar so that the net shall extend halfway down the altar. 6You shall make poles for the altar, poles of acacia wood, and overlay them with bronze; 7the poles shall be put through the rings, so that the poles shall be on the two sides of the altar when it is carried. 8You shall make it hollow, with boards. They shall be made just as you were shown on the mountain.

9 You shall make the court of the tabernacle. On the south side the court shall have hangings of fine twisted linen one hundred cubits long for that side; 10its twenty pillars and their twenty bases shall be of bronze, but the hooks of the pillars and their bands shall be of silver. 11Likewise for its length on the north side there shall be hangings one hundred cubits long, their pillars twenty and their bases twenty, of bronze, but the hooks of the pillars and their bands shall be of silver. 12For the width of the court on the west side there shall be fifty cubits of hangings, with ten pillars and ten bases. 13The width of the court on the front to the east shall be fifty cubits. 14There shall be fifteen cubits of hangings on the one side, with three pillars and three bases. 15There shall be fifteen cubits of hangings on the other side, with three pillars and three bases. 16For the gate of the

a Or *treaty*, or *testimony*; Heb *eduth*   *b* Or *the cover* court there shall be a screen twenty cubits long, of blue, purple, and crimson yarns, and of fine twisted linen, embroidered with needlework; it shall have four pillars and with them four bases. 17All the pillars around the court shall be banded with silver; their hooks shall be of silver, and their bases of bronze. 18The length of the court shall be one hundred cubits, the width fifty, and the height five cubits, with hangings of fine twisted linen and bases of bronze. 19All the utensils of the tabernacle for every use, and all its pegs and all the pegs of the court, shall be of bronze.

20 You shall further command the Israelites to bring you pure oil of beaten olives for the light, so that a lamp may be set up to burn regularly. 21In the tent of meeting, outside the curtain that is before the covenant,ᵃ Aaron and his sons shall tend it from evening to morning before the LORD. It shall be a perpetual ordinance to be observed throughout their generations by the Israelites.

28 Then bring near to you your brother Aaron, and his sons with him, from among the Israelites, to serve me as priests—Aaron and Aaron's sons, Nadab and Abihu, Eleazar and Ithamar. 2You shall make sacred vestments for the glorious adornment of your brother Aaron. 3And you shall speak to all who have ability, whom I have endowed with skill, that they make Aaron's vestments to consecrate him for my priesthood. 4These are the vestments that they shall make: a breastpiece, an ephod, a robe, a checkered tunic, a turban, and a sash. When they make these sacred vestments for your brother Aaron and his sons to serve me as priests, 5they shall use gold, blue, purple, and crimson yarns, and fine linen.

6 They shall make the ephod of gold, of blue, purple, and crimson yarns, and of fine twisted linen, skillfully worked. 7It shall have two shoulder-pieces attached to its two edges, so that it may be joined together. 8The decorated band on it shall be of the same workmanship and materials, of gold, of blue, purple, and crimson yarns, and of fine twisted linen. 9You shall take two onyx stones, and engrave on them the names of the sons of Israel, 10six of their names on the one stone, and the names of the remaining six on the other stone, in the order of their birth. 11As a gem-cutter engraves signets, so you shall engrave the two stones with the names of the sons of Israel; you shall mount them in settings of gold filigree. 12You shall set the two stones on the shoulder-pieces of the ephod, as stones of remembrance for the sons of Israel; and Aaron shall bear their names before the LORD on his two shoulders for remembrance. 13You shall make settings of gold filigree, 14and two chains of pure gold, twisted like cords; and you shall attach the corded chains to the settings.

15 You shall make a breastpiece of judgment, in skilled work; you shall make it in the style of the ephod; of gold, of blue and purple and crimson yarns, and of fine twisted linen you shall make it. 16It shall be square and doubled, a span in length and a span in width. 17You shall set in it four rows of stones. A row of carnelian,ᵇ chrysolite, and emerald shall be the first row; 18and the second row a turquoise, a sapphireᶜ and a moonstone; 19and the third row a jacinth, an agate, and an amethyst; 20and the fourth row a beryl, an onyx, and a jasper; they shall be set in gold filigree. 21There shall be twelve stones with names corresponding to the names of the sons of Israel; they shall be like signets, each engraved with its name, for the twelve tribes. 22You shall make for the breastpiece chains of pure gold, twisted like cords; 23and you shall make for the breastpiece two rings of gold, and put the two rings on the two edges of the breastpiece. 24You shall put the two cords of gold in the two rings at the edges of the breastpiece; 25the two ends of the two cords you shall attach to the two settings, and so attach it in front to the shoulder-pieces of the ephod. 26You shall make two rings of gold, and put them at the two ends of the breastpiece, on its inside edge next to the ephod. 27You shall make two rings of gold, and attach them in front to the lower part of the two shoulder-pieces of the ephod, at its joining above the

a Or treaty, or testimony; Heb eduth   b The identity of several of these stones is uncertain   c Or lapis lazuli decorated band of the ephod. 28 The breastpiece shall be bound by its rings to the rings of the ephod with a blue cord, so that it may lie on the decorated band of the ephod, and so that the breastpiece shall not come loose from the ephod. 29 So Aaron shall bear the names of the sons of Israel in the breastpiece of judgment on his heart when he goes into the holy place, for a continual remembrance before the LORD. 30 In the breastpiece of judgment you shall put the Urim and the Thummim, and they shall be on Aaron's heart when he goes in before the LORD; thus Aaron shall bear the judgment of the Israelites on his heart before the LORD continually.

31 You shall make the robe of the ephod all of blue. 32 It shall have an opening for the head in the middle of it, with a woven binding around the opening, like the opening in a coat of mail,ᵃ so that it may not be torn. 33 On its lower hem you shall make pomegranates of blue, purple, and crimson yarns, all around the lower hem, with bells of gold between them all around— 34 a golden bell and a pomegranate alternating all around the lower hem of the robe. 35 Aaron shall wear it when he ministers, and its sound shall be heard when he goes into the holy place before the LORD, and when he comes out, so that he may not die.

36 You shall make a rosette of pure gold, and engrave on it, like the engraving of a signet, "Holy to the LORD." 37 You shall fasten it on the turban with a blue cord; it shall be on the front of the turban. 38 It shall be on Aaron's forehead, and Aaron shall take on himself any guilt incurred in the holy offering that the Israelites consecrate as their sacred donations; it shall always be on his forehead, in order that they may find favor before the LORD.

39 You shall make the checkered tunic of fine linen, and you shall make a turban of fine linen, and you shall make a sash embroidered with needlework.

40 For Aaron's sons you shall make tunics and sashes and headdresses; you shall make them for their glorious adornment. 41 You shall put them on your brother Aaron, and on his sons with him, and shall anoint them and ordain them and consecrate them, so that they may serve me as priests. 42 You shall make for them linen undergarments to cover their naked flesh; they shall reach from the hips to the thighs; 43 Aaron and his sons shall wear them when they go into the tent of meeting, or when they come near the altar to minister in the holy place; or they will bring guilt on themselves and die. This shall be a perpetual ordinance for him and for his descendants after him.

28.1–43: The LORD gives guidelines for making the priestly garments. 6: *The ephod*⋆ is a long priestly robe; it was sometimes used to obtain an oracle⋆ or message from the deity (1 Sam 23.9–12). **15–30:** The *breastpiece of judgment* functioned as a means to obtain divine messages and guidance. It was a pouch containing the *Urim and Thummim,* light and dark stones used to determine the deity's will in a given situation (v. 30).

Instructions for the ordination of the priests
29.1–46: These instructions for ordination⋆ are carried out when Aaron and his sons are formally set apart as priests in Lev 8–9. Blood is considered a sacred substance with power to purify and make holy (Lev 17.11). Thus, blood plays an important role in purifying the priests and the altar throughout this section.

29 Now this is what you shall do to them to consecrate them, so that they may serve me as priests. Take one young bull and two rams without blemish, 2 and unleavened bread, unleavened cakes mixed with oil, and unleavened wafers spread with oil. You shall make them of choice wheat flour. 3 You shall put them in one basket and bring them in the basket, and bring the bull and the two rams. 4 You shall bring Aaron and his sons to the entrance of the tent of meeting, and wash them with water. 5 Then you shall take the vestments, and put on Aaron the tunic and the robe of the ephod, and the ephod, and the breastpiece, and gird him with the decorated band of the ephod; 6 and you shall set the turban on his head, and put the holy diadem on the turban. 7 You shall take the anointing oil, and pour it on his head and

ᵃ Meaning of Heb uncertain

anoint him. 8Then you shall bring his sons, and put tunics on them, 9and you shall gird them with sashes[a] and tie headdresses on them; and the priesthood shall be theirs by a perpetual ordinance. You shall then ordain Aaron and his sons.

10 You shall bring the bull in front of the tent of meeting. Aaron and his sons shall lay their hands on the head of the bull, 11and you shall slaughter the bull before the LORD, at the entrance of the tent of meeting, 12and shall take some of the blood of the bull and put it on the horns of the altar with your finger, and all the rest of the blood you shall pour out at the base of the altar. 13You shall take all the fat that covers the entrails, and the appendage of the liver, and the two kidneys with the fat that is on them, and turn them into smoke on the altar. 14But the flesh of the bull, and its skin, and its dung, you shall burn with fire outside the camp; it is a sin offering.

15 Then you shall take one of the rams, and Aaron and his sons shall lay their hands on the head of the ram, 16and you shall slaughter the ram, and shall take its blood and dash it against all sides of the altar. 17Then you shall cut the ram into its parts, and wash its entrails and its legs, and put them with its parts and its head, 18and turn the whole ram into smoke on the altar; it is a burnt offering to the LORD; it is a pleasing odor, an offering by fire to the LORD.

19 You shall take the other ram; and Aaron and his sons shall lay their hands on the head of the ram, 20and you shall slaughter the ram, and take some of its blood and put it on the lobe of Aaron's right ear and on the lobes of the right ears of his sons, and on the thumbs of their right hands, and on the big toes of their right feet, and dash the rest of the blood against all sides of the altar. 21Then you shall take some of the blood that is on the altar, and some of the anointing oil, and sprinkle it on Aaron and his vestments and on his sons and his sons' vestments with him; then he and his vestments shall be holy, as well as his sons and his sons' vestments.

22 You shall also take the fat of the ram, the fat tail, the fat that covers the entrails, the appendage of the liver, the two kidneys with the fat that is on them, and the right thigh (for it is a ram of ordination), 23and one loaf of bread, one cake of bread made with oil, and one wafer, out of the basket of unleavened bread that is before the LORD; 24and you shall place all these on the palms of Aaron and on the palms of his sons, and raise them as an elevation offering before the LORD. 25Then you shall take them from their hands, and turn them into smoke on the altar on top of the burnt offering of pleasing odor before the LORD; it is an offering by fire to the LORD.

26 You shall take the breast of the ram of Aaron's ordination and raise it as an elevation offering before the LORD; and it shall be your portion. 27You shall consecrate the breast that was raised as an elevation offering and the thigh that was raised as an elevation offering from the ram of ordination, from that which belonged to Aaron and his sons. 28These things shall be a perpetual ordinance for Aaron and his sons from the Israelites, for this is an offering; and it shall be an offering by the Israelites from their sacrifice of offerings of well-being, their offering to the LORD.

29 The sacred vestments of Aaron shall be passed on to his sons after him; they shall be anointed in them and ordained in them. 30The son who is priest in his place shall wear them seven days, when he comes into the tent of meeting to minister in the holy place.

31 You shall take the ram of ordination, and boil its flesh in a holy place; 32and Aaron and his sons shall eat the flesh of the ram and the bread that is in the basket, at the entrance of the tent of meeting. 33They themselves shall eat the food by which atonement is made, to ordain and consecrate them, but no one else shall eat of them, because they are holy. 34If any of the flesh for the ordination, or of the bread, remains until the morning, then you shall burn the remainder with fire; it shall not be eaten, because it is holy.

35 Thus you shall do to Aaron and to his sons, just as I have commanded you; through

a Gk: Heb sashes, Aaron and his sons

seven days you shall ordain them. ³⁶Also every day you shall offer a bull as a sin offering for atonement. Also you shall offer a sin offering for the altar, when you make atonement for it, and shall anoint it, to consecrate it. ³⁷Seven days you shall make atonement for the altar, and consecrate it, and the altar shall be most holy; whatever touches the altar shall become holy.

38 Now this is what you shall offer on the altar: two lambs a year old regularly each day. ³⁹One lamb you shall offer in the morning, and the other lamb you shall offer in the evening; ⁴⁰and with the first lamb one-tenth of a measure of choice flour mixed with one-fourth of a hin of beaten oil, and one-fourth of a hin of wine for a drink offering. ⁴¹And the other lamb you shall offer in the evening, and shall offer with it a grain offering and its drink offering, as in the morning, for a pleasing odor, an offering by fire to the LORD. ⁴²It shall be a regular burnt offering throughout your generations at the entrance of the tent of meeting before the LORD, where I will meet with you, to speak to you there. ⁴³I will meet with the Israelites there, and it shall be sanctified by my glory; ⁴⁴I will consecrate the tent of meeting and the altar; Aaron also and his sons I will consecrate, to serve me as priests. ⁴⁵I will dwell among the Israelites, and I will be their God. ⁴⁶And they shall know that I am the LORD their God, who brought them out of the land of Egypt that I might dwell among them; I am the LORD their God.

29.33–40. 33–37: *To consecrate* the priests means to set them apart in a formal ceremony for special service. **40:** *A measure* is an ephah, which is equivalent to about 20 liters. A *hin* is one-sixth of an ephah, about 3 liters.

30

You shall make an altar on which to offer incense; you shall make it of acacia wood. ²It shall be one cubit long, and one cubit wide; it shall be square, and shall be two cubits high; its horns shall be of one piece with it. ³You shall overlay it with pure gold, its top, and its sides all around and its horns; and you shall make for it a molding of gold all around. ⁴And you shall make two golden rings for it; under its molding on two opposite sides of it you shall make them, and they shall hold the poles with which to carry it. ⁵You shall make the poles of acacia wood, and overlay them with gold. ⁶You shall place it in front of the curtain that is above the ark of the covenant,^a in front of the mercy seat^b that is over the covenant,^a where I will meet with you. ⁷Aaron shall offer fragrant incense on it; every morning when he dresses the lamps he shall offer it, ⁸and when Aaron sets up the lamps in the evening, he shall offer it, a regular incense offering before the LORD throughout your generations. ⁹You shall not offer unholy incense on it, or a burnt offering, or a grain offering; and you shall not pour a drink offering on it. ¹⁰Once a year Aaron shall perform the rite of atonement on its horns. Throughout your generations he shall perform the atonement for it once a year with the blood of the atoning sin offering. It is most holy to the LORD.

11 The LORD spoke to Moses: ¹²When you take a census of the Israelites to register them, at registration all of them shall give a ransom for their lives to the LORD, so that no plague may come upon them for being registered. ¹³This is what each one who is registered shall give: half a shekel according to the shekel of the sanctuary (the shekel is twenty gerahs), half a shekel as an offering to the LORD. ¹⁴Each one who is registered, from twenty years old and upward, shall give the LORD's offering. ¹⁵The rich shall not give more, and the poor shall not give less, than the half shekel, when you bring this offering to the LORD to make atonement for your lives. ¹⁶You shall take the atonement money from the Israelites and shall designate it for the service of the tent of meeting; before the LORD it will be a reminder to the Israelites of the ransom given for your lives.

17 The LORD spoke to Moses: ¹⁸You shall make a bronze basin with a bronze stand for washing. You shall put it between the tent of meeting and the altar, and you shall put water in it; ¹⁹with the water^c Aaron and his sons shall wash their hands and their feet.

a Or *treaty*, or *testimony*; Heb *eduth*   b Or *the cover*
c Heb *it*

20When they go into the tent of meeting, or when they come near the altar to minister, to make an offering by fire to the LORD, they shall wash with water, so that they may not die. 21They shall wash their hands and their feet, so that they may not die: it shall be a perpetual ordinance for them, for him and for his descendants throughout their generations.

22 The LORD spoke to Moses: 23Take the finest spices: of liquid myrrh five hundred shekels, and of sweet-smelling cinnamon half as much, that is, two hundred fifty, and two hundred fifty of aromatic cane, 24and five hundred of cassia—measured by the sanctuary shekel—and a hin of olive oil; 25and you shall make of these a sacred anointing oil blended as by the perfumer; it shall be a holy anointing oil. 26With it you shall anoint the tent of meeting and the ark of the covenant,ᵃ 27and the table and all its utensils, and the lampstand and its utensils, and the altar of incense, 28and the altar of burnt offering with all its utensils, and the basin with its stand; 29you shall consecrate them, so that they may be most holy; whatever touches them will become holy. 30You shall anoint Aaron and his sons, and consecrate them, in order that they may serve me as priests. 31You shall say to the Israelites, "This shall be my holy anointing oil throughout your generations. 32It shall not be used in any ordinary anointing of the body, and you shall make no other like it in composition; it is holy, and it shall be holy to you. 33Whoever compounds any like it or whoever puts any of it on an unqualified person shall be cut off from the people."

34 The LORD said to Moses: Take sweet spices, stacte, and onycha, and galbanum, sweet spices with pure frankincense (an equal part of each), 35and make an incense blended as by the perfumer, seasoned with salt, pure and holy; 36and you shall beat some of it into powder, and put part of it before the covenantᵃ in the tent of meeting where I shall meet with you; it shall be for you most holy. 37When you make incense according to this composition, you shall not make it for yourselves; it shall be regarded by you as holy to the LORD. 38Whoever

makes any like it to use as perfume shall be cut off from the people.

31 The LORD spoke to Moses: 2See, I have called by name Bezalel son of Uri son of Hur, of the tribe of Judah: 3and I have filled him with divine spirit,ᵇ with ability, intelligence, and knowledge in every kind of craft, 4to devise artistic designs, to work in gold, silver, and bronze, 5in cutting stones for setting, and in carving wood, in every kind of craft. 6Moreover, I have appointed with him Oholiab son of Ahisamach, of the tribe of Dan; and I have given skill to all the skillful, so that they may make all that I have commanded you: 7the tent of meeting, and the ark of the covenant,ᵃ and the mercy seatᶜ that is on it, and all the furnishings of the tent, 8the table and its utensils, and the pure lampstand with all its utensils, and the altar of incense, 9and the altar of burnt offering with all its utensils, and the basin with its stand, 10and the finely worked vestments, the holy vestments for the priest Aaron and the vestments of his sons, for their service as priests, 11and the anointing oil and the fragrant incense for the holy place. They shall do just as I have commanded you.

30.1–31.11: The LORD gives instructions for other matters related to the priests and the worship sanctuary. 30.10: *Once a year* would be the Day of Atonement★ as specified in greater detail in Lev 16. **11–13:** The act of taking *a census* or counting the people for military or administrative purposes was believed to arouse the deity's anger, thereby bringing on *a plague* (2 Sam 24.10). Thus, each person had to pay a *ransom* or fee of *half a shekel★* in order to ward off the plague. Numbers 1.17–47 records the first census taken of the Israelites in the wilderness. **31.2–6:** The *divine spirit* (v. 3) fills the two skilled workers, *Bezalel* (v. 2) and *Oholiab* (v. 6), with *ability, intelligence, and knowledge* in their particular skills of artistry and construction.

12 The LORD said to Moses: 13You yourself are to speak to the Israelites: "You shall keep my sabbaths, for this is a sign between me and you throughout your generations,

a Or *treaty,* or *testimony;* Heb *eduth*   *b* Or *with the spirit of God*   *c* Or *the cover* given in order that you may know that I, the LORD, sanctify you. 14You shall keep the sabbath, because it is holy for you; everyone who profanes it shall be put to death; whoever does any work on it shall be cut off from among the people. 15Six days shall work be done, but the seventh day is a sabbath of solemn rest, holy to the LORD; whoever does any work on the sabbath day shall be put to death. 16Therefore the Israelites shall keep the sabbath, observing the sabbath throughout their generations, as a perpetual covenant. 17It is a sign forever between me and the people of Israel that in six days the LORD made heaven and earth, and on the seventh day he rested, and was refreshed."

18 When God*a* finished speaking with Moses on Mount Sinai, he gave him the two tablets of the covenant,*b* tablets of stone, written with the finger of God.

31.12–18: God gives a concluding reminder of the sabbath commandment. Reference to work on the tabernacle* in the preceding section (31.1–11) occasions the reminder about the regular need to rest from work on the sabbath day (20.8–11). Like the tabernacle that sets apart a sacred space in the community, the sabbath sets apart sacred time in the ongoing life of the community. **18:** This action fulfills the promise God made to Moses in 24.12. The two *tablets of stone* will figure prominently in the next story of the golden calf. They will become signs of the breaking of the old covenant* (32.15–16, 19) and the making of a new covenant (34.1, 4).

Israel worships a golden calf
32.1–35: Israel makes an idol in the form of a golden calf and worships it. This deed violates the important prohibition in the Ten Commandments against worshipping other gods and making idols (20.3–4). The story has a parallel in a later account about King Jeroboam, who sets up golden calves at two worship sites in northern Israel (1 Kings 12.25–33).

32 When the people saw that Moses delayed to come down from the mountain, the people gathered around Aaron, and said to him, "Come, make gods for us, who shall go before us; as for this Moses, the man who brought us up out of the land of Egypt, we do not know what has become of him."

2Aaron said to them, "Take off the gold rings that are on the ears of your wives, your sons, and your daughters, and bring them to me." 3So all the people took off the gold rings from their ears, and brought them to Aaron. 4He took the gold from them, formed it in a mold,*c* and cast an image of a calf; and they said, "These are your gods, O Israel, who brought you up out of the land of Egypt!" 5When Aaron saw this, he built an altar before it; and Aaron made proclamation and said, "Tomorrow shall be a festival to the LORD." 6They rose early the next day, and offered burnt offerings and brought sacrifices of well-being; and the people sat down to eat and drink, and rose up to revel.

7 The LORD said to Moses, "Go down at once! Your people, whom you brought up out of the land of Egypt, have acted perversely; 8they have been quick to turn aside from the way that I commanded them; they have cast for themselves an image of a calf, and have worshiped it and sacrificed to it, and said, 'These are your gods, O Israel, who brought you up out of the land of Egypt!' " 9The LORD said to Moses, "I have seen this people, how stiff-necked they are. 10Now let me alone, so that my wrath may burn hot against them and I may consume them; and of you I will make a great nation."

11 But Moses implored the LORD his God, and said, "O LORD, why does your wrath burn hot against your people, whom you brought out of the land of Egypt with great power and with a mighty hand? 12Why should the Egyptians say, 'It was with evil intent that he brought them out to kill them in the mountains, and to consume them from the face of the earth'? Turn from your fierce wrath; change your mind and do not bring disaster on your people. 13Remember Abraham, Isaac, and Israel, your servants, how you swore to them by your own self, saying to them, 'I will multiply your descendants like the stars of heaven, and all this land that I have promised I will give to your descendants, and they shall inherit it forever.' " 14And the LORD changed his mind about the

b Heb *he*   *a* Or *treaty,* or *testimony;* Heb *eduth*
c Or *fashioned it with a graving tool;* Meaning of Heb uncertain

disaster that he planned to bring on his people.

32.1–14. 2–3: The *gold rings* presumably come from the gold jewelry given to the Israelites by the Egyptians when they fled Egypt (12.35–36). **4:** The *calf* or young bull was a common image for certain Canaanite gods. **7:** The LORD tells Moses that now the Israelites are *your people*. They are no longer God's people. **10:** The LORD plans to *consume* or completely destroy the Israelites for their disobedience. The LORD will then take Moses alone and make of him *a great nation*. That is the same promise God first made to Abraham (Gen 12.2). **11–14:** Moses pleads to God on behalf of the Israelites. Moses reminds God that they are *your people* (vv. 11, 12; see 33.13). To destroy Israel would do harm to the LORD's international reputation (v. 12). It would also violate God's promise to Abraham, Isaac, and Jacob (v. 13; see 6.2–8). God *swore* or made a promise to each of the ancestors in Genesis: Abraham (Gen 13.14–15), Isaac (Gen 26.3), and Jacob/Israel (Gen 28.13). Remarkably, Moses succeeds. *The LORD* changed his *mind* about destroying Israel.

15 Then Moses turned and went down from the mountain, carrying the two tablets of the covenant*a* in his hands, tablets that were written on both sides, written on the front and on the back. 16 The tablets were the work of God, and the writing was the writing of God, engraved upon the tablets. 17 When Joshua heard the noise of the people as they shouted, he said to Moses, "There is a noise of war in the camp." 18 But he said,

"It is not the sound made by victors,
    or the sound made by losers;
    it is the sound of revelers that I hear."

19 As soon as he came near the camp and saw the calf and the dancing, Moses' anger burned hot, and he threw the tablets from his hands and broke them at the foot of the mountain. 20 He took the calf that they had made, burned it with fire, ground it to powder, scattered it on the water, and made the Israelites drink it.

21 Moses said to Aaron, "What did this people do to you that you have brought so great a sin upon them?" 22 And Aaron said, "Do not let the anger of my lord burn hot; you know the people, that they are bent on evil. 23 They said to me, 'Make us gods, who

shall go before us; as for this Moses, the man who brought us up out of the land of Egypt, we do not know what has become of him.' 24 So I said to them, 'Whoever has gold, take it off'; so they gave it to me, and I threw it into the fire, and out came this calf!"

25 When Moses saw that the people were running wild (for Aaron had let them run wild, to the derision of their enemies), 26 then Moses stood in the gate of the camp, and said, "Who is on the LORD's side? Come to me!" And all the sons of Levi gathered around him. 27 He said to them, "Thus says the LORD, the God of Israel, 'Put your sword on your side, each of you! Go back and forth from gate to gate throughout the camp, and each of you kill your brother, your friend, and your neighbor.' " 28 The sons of Levi did as Moses commanded, and about three thousand of the people fell on that day. 29 Moses said, "Today you have ordained yourselves*b* for the service of the LORD, each one at the cost of a son or a brother, and so have brought a blessing on yourselves this day."

30 On the next day Moses said to the people, "You have sinned a great sin. But now I will go up to the LORD; perhaps I can make atonement for your sin." 31 So Moses returned to the LORD and said, "Alas, this people has sinned a great sin; they have made for themselves gods of gold. 32 But now, if you will only forgive their sin—but if not, blot me out of the book that you have written." 33 But the LORD said to Moses, "Whoever has sinned against me I will blot out of my book. 34 But now go, lead the people to the place about which I have spoken to you; see, my angel shall go in front of you. Nevertheless, when the day comes for punishment, I will punish them for their sin."

35 Then the LORD sent a plague on the people, because they made the calf—the one that Aaron made.

32.15–35. 15: On *the two tablets of the covenant,* see comment on 31.18. **17:** *Joshua* is Moses' young assistant (24.13). **19:** Moses *broke* the stone *tablets* on

a Or *treaty*, or *testimony*; Heb *eduth*   *b* Gk Vg Compare Tg: Heb *Today ordain yourselves* which God had written the Ten Commandments (vv. 15–16). The act dramatized Israel's severe disobedience, which broke the formal relationship between God and the people. **21–23**: In contrast to Moses, who takes responsibility and pleads to God on behalf of the people, Aaron blames the people in order to escape his own responsibility for the rebellion. **24**: Aaron's version of the story suggests that the golden calf emerged by itself miraculously out of the fire. The earlier account clearly tells the real story: Aaron himself was the one responsible for making the golden calf (v. 4; see vv. 25, 35). **26–29**: The members of the tribe of *Levi* obey Moses. Thus, Moses *ordained* or set them apart *for the service of the LORD* as priests. The ordination* of the Levites occurs in Num 8. Numbers 16–18 suggests that the Levites will be subordinate to Aaron and the priests in his line. **34**: The LORD promises to send *my angel*, a subordinate divine messenger and commander, to lead Israel into Canaan (23.20, 23). The question will become whether, in addition to the angel, God's own divine presence will go in the midst of Israel to lead them (33.2–3).

33 The LORD said to Moses, "Go, leave this place, you and the people whom you have brought up out of the land of Egypt, and go to the land of which I swore to Abraham, Isaac, and Jacob, saying, 'To your descendants I will give it.' ²I will send an angel before you, and I will drive out the Canaanites, the Amorites, the Hittites, the Perizzites, the Hivites, and the Jebusites. ³Go up to a land flowing with milk and honey; but I will not go up among you, or I would consume you on the way, for you are a stiff-necked people."

4 When the people heard these harsh words, they mourned, and no one put on ornaments. ⁵For the LORD had said to Moses, "Say to the Israelites, 'You are a stiff-necked people; if for a single moment I should go up among you, I would consume you. So now take off your ornaments, and I will decide what to do to you.' " ⁶Therefore the Israelites stripped themselves of their ornaments, from Mount Horeb onward.

7 Now Moses used to take the tent and pitch it outside the camp, far off from the camp; he called it the tent of meeting. And everyone who sought the LORD would go out to the tent of meeting, which was outside the camp. ⁸Whenever Moses went out to the tent, all the people would rise and stand, each of them, at the entrance of their tents and watch Moses until he had gone into the tent. ⁹When Moses entered the tent, the pillar of cloud would descend and stand at the entrance of the tent, and the LORD would speak with Moses. ¹⁰When all the people saw the pillar of cloud standing at the entrance of the tent, all the people would rise and bow down, all of them, at the entrance of their tent. ¹¹Thus the LORD used to speak to Moses face to face, as one speaks to a friend. Then he would return to the camp; but his young assistant, Joshua son of Nun, would not leave the tent.

12 Moses said to the LORD, "See, you have said to me, 'Bring up this people'; but you have not let me know whom you will send with me. Yet you have said, 'I know you by name, and you have also found favor in my sight.' ¹³Now if I have found favor in your sight, show me your ways, so that I may know you and find favor in your sight. Consider too that this nation is your people." ¹⁴He said, "My presence will go with you, and I will give you rest." ¹⁵And he said to him, "If your presence will not go, do not carry us up from here. ¹⁶For how shall it be known that I have found favor in your sight, I and your people, unless you go with us? In this way, we shall be distinct, I and your people, from every people on the face of the earth."

17 The LORD said to Moses, "I will do the very thing that you have asked; for you have found favor in my sight, and I know you by name." ¹⁸Moses said, "Show me your glory, I pray." ¹⁹And he said, "I will make all my goodness pass before you, and will proclaim before you the name, 'The LORD';ᵃ and I will be gracious to whom I will be gracious, and will show mercy on whom I will show mercy. ²⁰But," he said, "you cannot see my face; for no one shall see me and live." ²¹And the LORD continued, "See, there is a place by me where you shall stand on the rock; ²²and while my glory passes by I will put you in a cleft of the rock, and I will cover you with my hand until I have passed by; ²³then I will

a Heb *YHWH*; see note at 3.15

take away my hand, and you shall see my back; but my face shall not be seen."

33.1–23: Moses seeks assurance of God's presence with Israel. 2–3: The LORD promises to *send an angel,* a subordinate divine messenger. However, God's own presence cannot go with Israel lest God's own holiness come in contact with and *consume* the *stiff-necked* people of Israel. **5–6:** The *stripping* of Israel's *ornaments* involves letting go of the jewelry Israel had stripped from the Egyptians (12.35–36). **7:** *The tent of meeting* reflects an older tradition of a tent or shrine in which the deity delivers oracles.* Although the tent of meeting probably preceded the tabernacle* tradition, the two came to be associated with one another (27.19–21). Moses pitches the tent of meeting *far off from the camp* rather than at its center in this interim time while God decides what to do with Israel (v. 5). The tent will eventually be located in the middle of the Israelite camp (Num 2.2). **14:** God's words in Hebrew are literally *"My presence will go"* (not *"with you"*). God will go to Canaan but not "with" or "in the midst of" Israel because of its sin. **16:** Moses asks that God not only *go* to Canaan (v. 14), but Moses insists that God go *with us* or "in our midst." In v. 17, God relents and agrees to Moses' request. **19:** On the divine name *LORD,* see comment on 3.13–15. This verse and God's character revealed to Moses in 34.6–7 add new dimensions by accenting God's compassion and mercy. In 3.13–15, the LORD's name is "I will be who I will be." Here the name is *I will be gracious to whom I will be gracious.* **20–23:** A human could not look directly into the deity's face, for it would cause death (v. 20; see 3.6; Isa 6.5). However, Moses will see more of God than before; he will see God's *back* (v. 23).

God reveals the divine character and makes a new covenant

34.1–35: This chapter represents a significant turning point in Exodus. Worship of the golden calf threatened Israel's relationship with God. However, Moses urges God to provide a deeper revelation of God's character. This deeper revelation (vv. 6–7) enabled a new covenant to be restored (vv. 10–11, 27–28). The new covenant repeats a number of laws given earlier in Exodus with an emphasis on not worshipping other gods and laws relating to the exodus and the sabbath (vv. 12–26).

34 The LORD said to Moses, "Cut two tablets of stone like the former ones,

and I will write on the tablets the words that were on the former tablets, which you broke. ²Be ready in the morning, and come up in the morning to Mount Sinai and present yourself there to me, on the top of the mountain. ³No one shall come up with you, and do not let anyone be seen throughout all the mountain; and do not let flocks or herds graze in front of that mountain." ⁴So Moses cut two tablets of stone like the former ones; and he rose early in the morning and went up on Mount Sinai, as the LORD had commanded him, and took in his hand the two tablets of stone. ⁵The LORD descended in the cloud and stood with him there, and proclaimed the name, "The LORD."*a* ⁶The LORD passed before him, and proclaimed,

"The LORD, the LORD,
a God merciful and gracious,
slow to anger,
and abounding in steadfast love and
faithfulness,
⁷ keeping steadfast love for the
thousandth generation,*b*
forgiving iniquity and transgression and
sin,
yet by no means clearing the guilty,
but visiting the iniquity of the parents
upon the children
and the children's children,
to the third and the fourth generation."

⁸And Moses quickly bowed his head toward the earth, and worshiped. ⁹He said, "If now I have found favor in your sight, O Lord, I pray, let the Lord go with us. Although this is a stiff-necked people, pardon our iniquity and our sin, and take us for your inheritance."

10 He said: I hereby make a covenant. Before all your people I will perform marvels, such as have not been performed in all the earth or in any nation; and all the people among whom you live shall see the work of the LORD; for it is an awesome thing that I will do with you.

11 Observe what I command you today. See, I will drive out before you the Amorites, the Canaanites, the Hittites, the Perizzites, the Hivites, and the Jebusites. ¹²Take care

a Heb *YHWH;* see note at 3.15   *b* Or *for thousands*

Accenting God's Mercy over God's Judgment

Israel's worship of the golden calf caused its covenant* relationship with God to be broken. The restoration of a new covenant between God and Israel was made possible through a deeper revealing of God's character that accented God's mercy and compassion. This deeper revelation is evident when the reader compares the first description of God's character in 20.5–6 and the second description in 34.6–7.

Exodus 20.5–6
I the LORD your God am a jealous God, punishing children for the iniquity of parents, to the third and the fourth generation of those who reject me, but showing steadfast love to the thousandth generation of those who love me and keep my commandments.

Exodus 34.6–7
The LORD, the LORD, a God merciful and gracious, slow to anger, and abounding in steadfast love and faithfulness, keeping steadfast love for the thousandth generation, forgiving iniquity and transgression and sin, yet by no means clearing the guilty, but visiting the iniquity of parents upon the children and the children's children, to the third and the fourth generation.

A number of differences are evident between the two similar texts. Exodus 20.5–6 places God's punishment as the first element of God's character that is emphasized, whereas 34.6–7 places this punishment as a secondary part of God's nature. The steadfast love, in secondary position in 20.5–6, moves to the front in 34.6–7. Exodus 34.6–7 also expands considerably the description of God's compassionate nature: slowness to anger, abundance of mercy, grace, and faithfulness. The condition that God shows steadfast love to "those who love me and keep my commandments" in 20.5–6 is removed in 34.6–7. Instead, 34.6–7 speaks of God as "forgiving iniquity."

Variations of this important description of God's nature occur in several other texts in the Old Testament: Num 14.18; Neh 9.17; Ps 103.8; Joel 2.13; Jon 4.2. Because of its repeated use, the description appears to have functioned as a creed or confession of faith in ancient Israel.

not to make a covenant with the inhabitants of the land to which you are going, or it will become a snare among you. [13]You shall tear down their altars, break their pillars, and cut down their sacred poles[a] [14](for you shall worship no other god, because the LORD, whose name is Jealous, is a jealous God). [15]You shall not make a covenant with the inhabitants of the land, for when they prostitute themselves to their gods and sacrifice to their gods, someone among them will invite you, and you will eat of the sacrifice. [16]And you will take wives from among their daughters for your sons, and their daughters who prostitute themselves to their gods will make your sons also prostitute themselves to their gods.

34.1–16. 4: Moses had broken the *former tablets of stone* when Israel worshipped the idol of the golden calf. Their idolatry* threatened to destroy their relationship with God (32.19). **6–7:** These verses reflect important differences in the description of God's character when compared to a similar description in

a Heb *Asherim*

20.5–6. The changes place more emphasis on God's mercy, grace, and forgiveness while still retaining the element of God's punishment for disobedience. **13:** *Pillars* of stone and *sacred poles* ("asherim") of wood were used in native Canaanite fertility religion in worshipping the gods Baal★ and Asherah★ (Judg 6.25).

～～～～～～～～～～～～～～

17 You shall not make cast idols.

18 You shall keep the festival of unleavened bread. Seven days you shall eat unleavened bread, as I commanded you, at the time appointed in the month of Abib; for in the month of Abib you came out from Egypt.

19 All that first opens the womb is mine, all your male[a] livestock, the firstborn of cow and sheep. 20The firstborn of a donkey you shall redeem with a lamb, or if you will not redeem it you shall break its neck. All the firstborn of your sons you shall redeem.

No one shall appear before me empty-handed.

21 Six days you shall work, but on the seventh day you shall rest; even in plowing time and in harvest time you shall rest. 22You shall observe the festival of weeks, the first fruits of wheat harvest, and the festival of ingathering at the turn of the year. 23Three times in the year all your males shall appear before the LORD God, the God of Israel. 24For I will cast out nations before you, and enlarge your borders; no one shall covet your land when you go up to appear before the LORD your God three times in the year.

25 You shall not offer the blood of my sacrifice with leaven, and the sacrifice of the festival of the passover shall not be left until the morning.

26 The best of the first fruits of your ground you shall bring to the house of the LORD your God.

You shall not boil a kid in its mother's milk.

27 The LORD said to Moses: Write these words; in accordance with these words I have made a covenant with you and with Israel. 28He was there with the LORD forty days and forty nights; he neither ate bread nor drank water. And he wrote on the tablets the words of the covenant, the ten commandments.[b]

29 Moses came down from Mount Sinai. As he came down from the mountain with the two tablets of the covenant[c] in his hand, Moses did not know that the skin of his face shone because he had been talking with God. 30When Aaron and all the Israelites saw Moses, the skin of his face was shining, and they were afraid to come near him. 31But Moses called to them; and Aaron and all the leaders of the congregation returned to him, and Moses spoke with them. 32Afterward all the Israelites came near, and he gave them in commandment all that the LORD had spoken with him on Mount Sinai. 33When Moses had finished speaking with them, he put a veil on his face; 34but whenever Moses went in before the LORD to speak with him, he would take the veil off, until he came out; and when he came out, and told the Israelites what he had been commanded, 35the Israelites would see the face of Moses, that the skin of his face was shining; and Moses would put the veil on his face again, until he went in to speak with him.

───────────────

34.17–35. 19–20: On *redeeming the firstborn*, see comment on 13.13. **24:** To *covet* refers to the inner yearning and strong desire to take something that rightfully belongs to others, especially the poor and less powerful. **29:** Moses' unique and close relationship with God caused some of God's divine radiance or light to pass onto Moses. Thus, *the skin of his face shone*. **33:** Just as the cloud veiled the deity's fiery radiance or glory (24.15–18), so Moses *put a veil on his face* to shield the people from his own shining radiance.

───────────────

Moses prepares to construct the tabernacle
35.1–36.7: This section begins an extensive unit dealing with the actual construction of the tabernacle★ (chs. 35–40). The tabernacle is the tangible and mobile sign of God's presence in the midst of the Israelites as they leave Mount Sinai and travel through the wilderness to Canaan. The instructions for building the tabernacle were first given in chs. 25–31. The golden calf crisis (ch. 32) had endangered the tabernacle project. However, the resolution and new covenant★ in chs. 33–34 enabled the tabernacle construction to move forward. The construction obediently follows the instructions that were previously given. The detailed nature of the instructions and process for building the tabernacle resembles the detailed account of

a Gk Theodotion Vg Tg: Meaning of Heb uncertain
b Heb *words*   c Or *treaty*, or *testimony*; Heb *eduth*

the building of Solomon's Temple* (1 Kings 6–8) and the detailed character of Ezekiel's promise of a new Temple in Jerusalem (Ezek 40–43).

---

35 Moses assembled all the congregation of the Israelites and said to them: These are the things that the LORD has commanded you to do:

2 Six days shall work be done, but on the seventh day you shall have a holy sabbath of solemn rest to the LORD; whoever does any work on it shall be put to death. ³You shall kindle no fire in all your dwellings on the sabbath day.

4 Moses said to all the congregation of the Israelites: This is the thing that the LORD has commanded: ⁵Take from among you an offering to the LORD; let whoever is of a generous heart bring the LORD's offering: gold, silver, and bronze; ⁶blue, purple, and crimson yarns, and fine linen; goats' hair, ⁷tanned rams' skins, and fine leather;*ᵃ acacia wood, ⁸oil for the light, spices for the anointing oil and for the fragrant incense, ⁹and onyx stones and gems to be set in the ephod and the breastpiece.

10 All who are skillful among you shall come and make all that the LORD has commanded: the tabernacle, ¹¹its tent and its covering, its clasps and its frames, its bars, its pillars, and its bases; ¹²the ark with its poles, the mercy seat,ᵇ and the curtain for the screen; ¹³the table with its poles and all its utensils, and the bread of the Presence; ¹⁴the lampstand also for the light, with its utensils and its lamps, and the oil for the light; ¹⁵and the altar of incense, with its poles, and the anointing oil and the fragrant incense, and the screen for the entrance, the entrance of the tabernacle; ¹⁶the altar of burnt offering, with its grating of bronze, its poles, and all its utensils, the basin with its stand; ¹⁷the hangings of the court, its pillars and its bases, and the screen for the gate of the court; ¹⁸the pegs of the tabernacle and the pegs of the court, and their cords; ¹⁹the finely worked vestments for ministering in the holy place, the holy vestments for the priest Aaron, and the vestments of his sons, for their service as priests.

20 Then all the congregation of the Isra-elites withdrew from the presence of Moses. ²¹And they came, everyone whose heart was stirred, and everyone whose spirit was willing, and brought the LORD's offering to be used for the tent of meeting, and for all its service, and for the sacred vestments. ²²So they came, both men and women; all who were of a willing heart brought brooches and earrings and signet rings and pendants, all sorts of gold objects, everyone bringing an offering of gold to the LORD. ²³And everyone who possessed blue or purple or crimson yarn or fine linen or goats' hair or tanned rams' skins or fine leather,ᵃ brought them. ²⁴Everyone who could make an offering of silver or bronze brought it as the LORD's offering; and everyone who possessed acacia wood of any use in the work, brought it. ²⁵All the skillful women spun with their hands, and brought what they had spun in blue and purple and crimson yarns and fine linen; ²⁶all the women whose hearts moved them to use their skill spun the goats' hair. ²⁷And the leaders brought onyx stones and gems to be set in the ephod and the breastpiece, ²⁸and spices and oil for the light, and for the anointing oil, and for the fragrant incense. ²⁹All the Israelite men and women whose hearts made them willing to bring anything for the work that the LORD had commanded by Moses to be done, brought it as a freewill offering to the LORD.

30 Then Moses said to the Israelites: See, the LORD has called by name Bezalel son of Uri son of Hur, of the tribe of Judah; ³¹he has filled him with divine spirit,ᶜ with skill, intelligence, and knowledge in every kind of craft, ³²to devise artistic designs, to work in gold, silver, and bronze, ³³in cutting stones for setting, and in carving wood, in every kind of craft. ³⁴And he has inspired him to teach, both him and Oholiab son of Ahisamach, of the tribe of Dan. ³⁵He has filled them with skill to do every kind of work done by an artisan or by a designer or by an embroiderer in blue, purple, and crimson yarns, and in fine linen, or by a weaver—by any sort of artisan or skilled designer.

---

a Meaning of Heb uncertain   *b* Or *the cover*
c Or *the spirit of God*

35.1–35. 2–3: Just as the sabbath law had concluded the instructions for building the tabernacle (31.12–17), the sabbath law now introduces the actual work of construction. **22–29:** The people offer willingly what they have for the tabernacle. Presumably some of it included the gold, silver, jewelry, and clothing that the Egyptians gave to them when they fled Egypt (12.35–36). **30–35:** The passage about *Bezalel* and *Oholiab* elaborates 31.1–5. The *divine spirit* gives them *knowledge in every kind of craft* (v. 31) as in 31.3. Additionally, the spirit of God *inspired* them *to teach* others their skills (v. 34).

36 Bezalel and Oholiab and every skillful one to whom the LORD has given skill and understanding to know how to do any work in the construction of the sanctuary shall work in accordance with all that the LORD has commanded.

2 Moses then called Bezalel and Oholiab and every skillful one to whom the LORD had given skill, everyone whose heart was stirred to come to do the work; ³and they received from Moses all the freewill offerings that the Israelites had brought for doing the work on the sanctuary. They still kept bringing him freewill offerings every morning, ⁴so that all the artisans who were doing every sort of task on the sanctuary came, each from the task being performed, ⁵and said to Moses, "The people are bringing much more than enough for doing the work that the LORD has commanded us to do." ⁶So Moses gave command, and word was proclaimed throughout the camp: "No man or woman is to make anything else as an offering for the sanctuary." So the people were restrained from bringing; ⁷for what they had already brought was more than enough to do all the work.

36.5–7: Pharaoh's oppressive complaint about the laziness of Israelite slave workers at the beginning of the book (5.4–9) contrasts sharply with Israel's eagerness and enthusiasm in working on the tabernacle here at the end of the book.

The ark of the covenant, the tabernacle, and its furnishings
36.8–39.43: The construction of the tabernacle and its contents follows closely and methodically the instruc-

tions first given in chs. 25–31 with some minor omissions. The sequence proceeds from first constructing the outside frames and curtains and then moving inward to make the holiest furnishings and objects inside the tabernacle. This pattern reverses the sequence of the instructions in chs. 25–31, which move from the innermost, holiest furnishings to the outer objects and surroundings.

8 All those with skill among the workers made the tabernacle with ten curtains; they were made of fine twisted linen, and blue, purple, and crimson yarns, with cherubim skillfully worked into them. ⁹The length of each curtain was twenty-eight cubits, and the width of each curtain four cubits; all the curtains were of the same size.

10 He joined five curtains to one another, and the other five curtains he joined to one another. ¹¹He made loops of blue on the edge of the outermost curtain of the first set; likewise he made them on the edge of the outermost curtain of the second set; ¹²he made fifty loops on the one curtain, and he made fifty loops on the edge of the curtain that was in the second set; the loops were opposite one another. ¹³And he made fifty clasps of gold, and joined the curtains one to the other with clasps; so the tabernacle was one whole.

14 He also made curtains of goats' hair for a tent over the tabernacle; he made eleven curtains. ¹⁵The length of each curtain was thirty cubits, and the width of each curtain four cubits; the eleven curtains were of the same size. ¹⁶He joined five curtains by themselves, and six curtains by themselves. ¹⁷He made fifty loops on the edge of the outermost curtain of the one set, and fifty loops on the edge of the other connecting curtain. ¹⁸He made fifty clasps of bronze to join the tent together so that it might be one whole. ¹⁹And he made for the tent a covering of tanned rams' skins and an outer covering of fine leather.ª

20 Then he made the upright frames for the tabernacle of acacia wood. ²¹Ten cubits was the length of a frame, and a cubit and a half the width of each frame. ²²Each frame

a Meaning of Heb uncertain

had two pegs for fitting together; he did this for all the frames of the tabernacle. 23The frames for the tabernacle he made in this way: twenty frames for the south side; 24and he made forty bases of silver under the twenty frames, two bases under the first frame for its two pegs, and two bases under the next frame for its two pegs. 25For the second side of the tabernacle, on the north side, he made twenty frames 26and their forty bases of silver, two bases under the first frame and two bases under the next frame. 27For the rear of the tabernacle westward he made six frames. 28He made two frames for corners of the tabernacle in the rear. 29They were separate beneath, but joined at the top, at the first ring; he made two of them in this way, for the two corners. 30There were eight frames with their bases of silver: sixteen bases, under every frame two bases.

31 He made bars of acacia wood, five for the frames of the one side of the tabernacle, 32and five bars for the frames of the other side of the tabernacle, and five bars for the frames of the tabernacle at the rear westward. 33He made the middle bar to pass through from end to end halfway up the frames. 34And he overlaid the frames with gold, and made rings of gold for them to hold the bars, and overlaid the bars with gold.

35 He made the curtain of blue, purple, and crimson yarns, and fine twisted linen, with cherubim skillfully worked into it. 36For it he made four pillars of acacia, and overlaid them with gold; their hooks were of gold, and he cast for them four bases of silver. 37He also made a screen for the entrance to the tent, of blue, purple, and crimson yarns, and fine twisted linen, embroidered with needlework; 38and its five pillars with their hooks. He overlaid their capitals and their bases with gold, but their five bases were of bronze.

37 Bezalel made the ark of acacia wood; it was two and a half cubits long, a cubit and a half wide, and a cubit and a half high. 2He overlaid it with pure gold inside and outside, and made a molding of gold around it. 3He cast for it four rings of gold for its four feet, two rings on its one side and two rings on its other side. 4He made poles of acacia wood, and overlaid them with gold,

5and put the poles into the rings on the sides of the ark, to carry the ark. 6He made a mercy seat*a* of pure gold; two cubits and a half was its length, and a cubit and a half its width. 7He made two cherubim of hammered gold; at the two ends of the mercy seat*b* he made them, 8one cherub at the one end, and one cherub at the other end; of one piece with the mercy seat*b* he made the cherubim at its two ends. 9The cherubim spread out their wings above, overshadowing the mercy seat*b* with their wings. They faced one another; the faces of the cherubim were turned toward the mercy seat.*b*

10 He also made the table of acacia wood, two cubits long, one cubit wide, and a cubit and a half high. 11He overlaid it with pure gold, and made a molding of gold around it. 12He made around it a rim a handbreadth wide, and made a molding of gold around the rim. 13He cast for it four rings of gold, and fastened the rings to the four corners at its four legs. 14The rings that held the poles used for carrying the table were close to the rim. 15He made the poles of acacia wood to carry the table, and overlaid them with gold. 16And he made the vessels of pure gold that were to be on the table, its plates and dishes for incense, and its bowls and flagons with which to pour drink offerings.

17 He also made the lampstand of pure gold. The base and the shaft of the lampstand were made of hammered work; its cups, its calyxes, and its petals were of one piece with it. 18There were six branches going out of its sides, three branches of the lampstand out of one side of it and three branches of the lampstand out of the other side of it; 19three cups shaped like almond blossoms, each with calyx and petals, on one branch, and three cups shaped like almond blossoms, each with calyx and petals, on the other branch—so for the six branches going out of the lampstand. 20On the lampstand itself there were four cups shaped like almond blossoms, each with its calyxes and petals. 21There was a calyx of one piece with it under the first pair of branches, a calyx of one piece with it under the next pair of

a Or *a cover*   *b* Or *the cover*

branches, and a calyx of one piece with it under the last pair of branches. 22 Their calyxes and their branches were of one piece with it, the whole of it one hammered piece of pure gold. 23 He made its seven lamps and its snuffers and its trays of pure gold. 24 He made it and all its utensils of a talent of pure gold.

25　He made the altar of incense of acacia wood, one cubit long, and one cubit wide; it was square, and was two cubits high; its horns were of one piece with it. 26 He overlaid it with pure gold, its top, and its sides all around, and its horns; and he made for it a molding of gold all around, 27 and made two golden rings for it under its molding, on two opposite sides of it, to hold the poles with which to carry it. 28 And he made the poles of acacia wood, and overlaid them with gold.

29　He made the holy anointing oil also, and the pure fragrant incense, blended as by the perfumer.

38 He made the altar of burnt offering also of acacia wood; it was five cubits long, and five cubits wide; it was square, and three cubits high. 2 He made horns for it on its four corners; its horns were of one piece with it, and he overlaid it with bronze. 3 He made all the utensils of the altar, the pots, the shovels, the basins, the forks, and the firepans: all its utensils he made of bronze. 4 He made for the altar a grating, a network of bronze, under its ledge, extending halfway down. 5 He cast four rings on the four corners of the bronze grating to hold the poles; 6 he made the poles of acacia wood, and overlaid them with bronze. 7 And he put the poles through the rings on the sides of the altar, to carry it with them; he made it hollow, with boards.

8　He made the basin of bronze with its stand of bronze, from the mirrors of the women who served at the entrance to the tent of meeting.

9　He made the court; for the south side the hangings of the court were of fine twisted linen, one hundred cubits long; 10 its twenty pillars and their twenty bases were of bronze, but the hooks of the pillars and their bands were of silver. 11 For the north side there were hangings one hundred cubits long; its twenty pillars and their twenty bases were of bronze, but the hooks of the pillars and their bands were of silver. 12 For the west side there were hangings fifty cubits long, with ten pillars and ten bases; the hooks of the pillars and their bands were of silver. 13 And for the front to the east, fifty cubits. 14 The hangings for one side of the gate were fifteen cubits, with three pillars and three bases. 15 And so for the other side; on each side of the gate of the court were hangings of fifteen cubits, with three pillars and three bases. 16 All the hangings around the court were of fine twisted linen. 17 The bases for the pillars were of bronze, but the hooks of the pillars and their bands were of silver; the overlaying of their capitals was also of silver, and all the pillars of the court were banded with silver. 18 The screen for the entrance to the court was embroidered with needlework in blue, purple, and crimson yarns and fine twisted linen. It was twenty cubits long and, along the width of it, five cubits high, corresponding to the hangings of the court. 19 There were four pillars; their four bases were of bronze, their hooks of silver, and the overlaying of their capitals and their bands of silver. 20 All the pegs for the tabernacle and for the court all around were of bronze.

21　These are the records of the tabernacle, the tabernacle of the covenant,ᵃ which were drawn up at the commandment of Moses, the work of the Levites being under the direction of Ithamar son of the priest Aaron. 22 Bezalel son of Uri son of Hur, of the tribe of Judah, made all that the LORD commanded Moses; 23 and with him was Oholiab son of Ahisamach, of the tribe of Dan, engraver, designer, and embroiderer in blue, purple, and crimson yarns, and in fine linen.

24　All the gold that was used for the work, in all the construction of the sanctuary, the gold from the offering, was twenty-nine talents and seven hundred thirty shekels, measured by the sanctuary shekel. 25 The silver from those of the congregation who were counted was one hundred talents and one thousand seven hundred seventy-five shek-

a　Or *treaty*, or *testimony*; Heb *eduth*

els, measured by the sanctuary shekel; 26a beka a head (that is, half a shekel, measured by the sanctuary shekel), for everyone who was counted in the census, from twenty years old and upward, for six hundred three thousand, five hundred fifty men. 27The hundred talents of silver were for casting the bases of the sanctuary, and the bases of the curtain; one hundred bases for the hundred talents, a talent for a base. 28Of the thousand seven hundred seventy-five shekels he made hooks for the pillars, and overlaid their capitals and made bands for them. 29The bronze that was contributed was seventy talents, and two thousand four hundred shekels; 30with it he made the bases for the entrance of the tent of meeting, the bronze altar and the bronze grating for it and all the utensils of the altar, 31the bases all around the court, and the bases of the gate of the court, all the pegs of the tabernacle, and all the pegs around the court.

38.26: The *census* and its total count of 603,550 men reflects the results of the census in Num 1.45–46. The law concerning payment during a census occurs in 30.12–14.

39 Of the blue, purple, and crimson yarns they made finely worked vestments, for ministering in the holy place; they made the sacred vestments for Aaron; as the LORD had commanded Moses.

2 He made the ephod of gold, of blue, purple, and crimson yarns, and of fine twisted linen. 3Gold leaf was hammered out and cut into threads to work into the blue, purple, and crimson yarns and into the fine twisted linen, in skilled design. 4They made for the ephod shoulder-pieces, joined to it at its two edges. 5The decorated band on it was of the same materials and workmanship, of gold, of blue, purple, and crimson yarns, and of fine twisted linen; as the LORD had commanded Moses.

6 The onyx stones were prepared, enclosed in settings of gold filigree and engraved like the engravings of a signet, according to the names of the sons of Israel. 7He set them on the shoulder-pieces of the ephod, to be stones of remembrance for the sons of Israel; as the LORD had commanded Moses.

8 He made the breastpiece, in skilled work, like the work of the ephod, of gold, of blue, purple, and crimson yarns, and of fine twisted linen. 9It was square; the breastpiece was made double, a span in length and a span in width when doubled. 10They set in it four rows of stones. A row of carnelian,*a* chrysolite, and emerald was the first row; 11and the second row, a turquoise, a sapphire,*b* and a moonstone; 12and the third row, a jacinth, an agate, and an amethyst; 13and the fourth row, a beryl, an onyx, and a jasper; they were enclosed in settings of gold filigree. 14There were twelve stones with names corresponding to the names of the sons of Israel; they were like signets, each engraved with its name, for the twelve tribes. 15They made on the breastpiece chains of pure gold, twisted like cords; 16and they made two settings of gold filigree and two gold rings, and put the two rings on the two edges of the breastpiece; 17and they put the two cords of gold in the two rings at the edges of the breastpiece. 18Two ends of the two cords they had attached to the two settings of filigree; in this way they attached it in front to the shoulder-pieces of the ephod. 19Then they made two rings of gold, and put them at the two ends of the breastpiece, on its inside edge next to the ephod. 20They made two rings of gold, and attached them in front to the lower part of the two shoulder-pieces of the ephod, at its joining above the decorated band of the ephod. 21They bound the breastpiece by its rings to the rings of the ephod with a blue cord, so that it should lie on the decorated band of the ephod, and that the breastpiece should not come loose from the ephod; as the LORD had commanded Moses.

22 He also made the robe of the ephod woven all of blue yarn; 23and the opening of the robe in the middle of it was like the opening in a coat of mail,*c* with a binding around the opening, so that it might not be torn.

a The identification of several of these stones is uncertain   *b* Or *lapis lazuli*   *c* Meaning of Heb uncertain

24On the lower hem of the robe they made pomegranates of blue, purple, and crimson yarns, and of fine twisted linen. 25They also made bells of pure gold, and put the bells between the pomegranates on the lower hem of the robe all around, between the pomegranates; 26a bell and a pomegranate, a bell and a pomegranate all around on the lower hem of the robe for ministering; as the LORD had commanded Moses.

27 They also made the tunics, woven of fine linen, for Aaron and his sons, 28and the turban of fine linen, and the headdresses of fine linen, and the linen undergarments of fine twisted linen, 29and the sash of fine twisted linen, and of blue, purple, and crimson yarns, embroidered with needlework; as the LORD had commanded Moses.

30 They made the rosette of the holy diadem of pure gold, and wrote on it an inscription, like the engraving of a signet, "Holy to the LORD." 31They tied to it a blue cord, to fasten it on the turban above; as the LORD had commanded Moses.

39.1–31: This section recounts the making of Aaron's priestly vestments or clothing. The refrain *as the LORD had commanded Moses* recurs seven times throughout the chapter (vv. 1, 5, 7, 21, 26, 29, 31). This sevenfold refrain mirrors the sevenfold refrain and structure of the seven days of creation in Gen 1.1–2.4.

32 In this way all the work of the tabernacle of the tent of meeting was finished; the Israelites had done everything just as the LORD had commanded Moses. 33Then they brought the tabernacle to Moses, the tent and all its utensils, its hooks, its frames, its bars, its pillars, and its bases; 34the covering of tanned rams' skins and the covering of fine leather,*a* and the curtain for the screen; 35the ark of the covenant*b* with its poles and the mercy seat;*c* 36the table with all its utensils, and the bread of the Presence; 37the pure lampstand with its lamps set on it and all its utensils, and the oil for the light; 38the golden altar, the anointing oil and the fragrant incense, and the screen for the entrance of the tent; 39the bronze altar, and its grating of bronze, its poles, and all its utensils; the basin with its stand; 40the hangings

of the court, its pillars, and its bases, and the screen for the gate of the court, its cords, and its pegs; and all the utensils for the service of the tabernacle, for the tent of meeting; 41the finely worked vestments for ministering in the holy place, the sacred vestments for the priest Aaron, and the vestments of his sons to serve as priests. 42The Israelites had done all of the work just as the LORD had commanded Moses. 43When Moses saw that they had done all the work just as the LORD had commanded, he blessed them.

40 The LORD spoke to Moses: 2On the first day of the first month you shall set up the tabernacle of the tent of meeting. 3You shall put in it the ark of the covenant,*b* and you shall screen the ark with the curtain. 4You shall bring in the table, and arrange its setting; and you shall bring in the lampstand, and set up its lamps. 5You shall put the golden altar for incense before the ark of the covenant,*b* and set up the screen for the entrance of the tabernacle. 6You shall set the altar of burnt offering before the entrance of the tabernacle of the tent of meeting, 7and place the basin between the tent of meeting and the altar, and put water in it. 8You shall set up the court all around, and hang up the screen for the gate of the court. 9Then you shall take the anointing oil, and anoint the tabernacle and all that is in it, and consecrate it and all its furniture, so that it shall become holy. 10You shall also anoint the altar of burnt offering and all its utensils, and consecrate the altar, so that the altar shall be most holy. 11You shall also anoint the basin with its stand, and consecrate it. 12Then you shall bring Aaron and his sons to the entrance of the tent of meeting, and shall wash them with water, 13and put on Aaron the sacred vestments, and you shall anoint him and consecrate him, so that he may serve me as priest. 14You shall bring his sons also and put tunics on them, 15and anoint them, as you anointed their father, that they may serve me as priests: and their anointing shall admit them to a perpetual priesthood throughout all generations to come.

a Meaning of Heb uncertain   *b* Or *treaty,* or *testimony;* Heb *eduth*   *c* Or *the cover*

16 Moses did everything just as the LORD had commanded him. [17] In the first month in the second year, on the first day of the month, the tabernacle was set up. [18] Moses set up the tabernacle; he laid its bases, and set up its frames, and put in its poles, and raised up its pillars; [19] and he spread the tent over the tabernacle, and put the covering of the tent over it; as the LORD had commanded Moses. [20] He took the covenant[a] and put it into the ark, and put the poles on the ark, and set the mercy seat[b] above the ark; [21] and he brought the ark into the tabernacle, and set up the curtain for screening, and screened the ark of the covenant;[a] as the LORD had commanded Moses. [22] He put the table in the tent of meeting, on the north side of the tabernacle, outside the curtain, [23] and set the bread in order on it before the LORD; as the LORD had commanded Moses. [24] He put the lampstand in the tent of meeting, opposite the table on the south side of the tabernacle, [25] and set up the lamps before the LORD; as the LORD had commanded Moses. [26] He put the golden altar in the tent of meeting before the curtain, [27] and offered fragrant incense on it; as the LORD had commanded Moses. [28] He also put in place the screen for the entrance of the tabernacle. [29] He set the altar of burnt offering at the entrance of the tabernacle of the tent of meeting, and offered on it the burnt offering and the grain offering as the LORD had commanded Moses. [30] He set the basin between the tent of meeting and the altar, and put water in it for washing, [31] with which Moses and Aaron and his sons washed their hands and their feet. [32] When they went into the tent of meeting, and when they approached the altar, they washed; as the LORD had commanded Moses. [33] He set up the court around the tabernacle and the altar, and put up the screen at the gate of the court. So Moses finished the work.

40.1–33: Moses completes the work by erecting the tabernacle and arranging its furnishings. 2: The es- tablishment of the tabernacle *on the first day of the first month* marks the beginning of the rhythms, seasons, and festivals of the new cultic year. The construction of the universe (Gen 1.1–2.4) had provided order and structure out of chaos that enabled the beginning of time and of life. In a similar way, Israel's construction of the tabernacle out of the chaos of the golden calf (ch. 32) provides order and structure for the beginning of Israel's worship and cultic life as it journeys through the wilderness. The text again brings together the *tabernacle* tradition and the older tradition of the *tent of meeting* (39.32, 40; 40.6, 22, 24, 29, 35; see comment on 33.7). **17:** Israel had arrived at Mount Sinai in the third month of the first year after going out of Egypt (19.1). Moses sets up the tabernacle nine months later *in the first month in the second year.*

34 Then the cloud covered the tent of meeting, and the glory of the LORD filled the tabernacle. [35] Moses was not able to enter the tent of meeting because the cloud settled upon it, and the glory of the LORD filled the tabernacle. [36] Whenever the cloud was taken up from the tabernacle, the Israelites would set out on each stage of their journey; [37] but if the cloud was not taken up, then they did not set out until the day that it was taken up. [38] For the cloud of the LORD was on the tabernacle by day, and fire was in the cloud[c] by night, before the eyes of all the house of Israel at each stage of their journey.

40.34–38: The glory and cloud of God's presence fill the tabernacle. 34–35: The presence of God in the form of the LORD's "glory" and the "cloud" had "covered" and "settled on" Mount Sinai in 24.15–18. The same divine *glory* and *cloud covered* and *settled upon* the *tent of meeting* and the *tabernacle.* **36:** *Each stage of their journey* looks forward to Israel's continuing trek through the wilderness toward the land of Canaan. The departure from Mount Sinai will actually begin in Num 10.11–36. **38:** On the *cloud by day* and the *fire by night,* see comment on 13.21.

a Or *treaty,* or *testimony;* Heb *eduth*   b Or *the cover* c Heb *it*

LEVITICUS

Introduction

Leviticus is a collection of laws related to worship, priests, sacrifices, and holiness. The title, "Leviticus," derives from the Greek and Latin titles for the book meaning "the book of the Levites." The Levites themselves, a tribe of priests within ancient Israel, are mentioned only once in Leviticus (25.32–34). However, some biblical traditions trace the ancestry of the high priest Aaron to the tribe of Levi (Ex 6.16–20), and Aaron is the focus of many laws in Leviticus. The book underscores the holiness of Israel's God and the need for the priests and people of Israel to reflect that holiness in all aspects of their lives. The LORD repeatedly commands the people of Israel, "Be holy, for I am holy" (11.44–45; 19.2; 20.26).

Leviticus consists almost entirely of laws and commands with only two brief narrative★ sections, 10.1–7 and 24.10–16. The book presents its many laws and instructions as divine commands mediated through Moses and Aaron at Mount Sinai during Israel's wilderness journey from Egypt to the promised land of Canaan (27.34). However, many scholars agree that these laws actually arose later in Israel's history, from the late pre-exilic period (perhaps seventh century BCE) to the Persian period (fifth century BCE). The laws in Leviticus were probably collected over time in at least two major stages, with the earlier material gathered in chs. 1–16 and the later material concentrated in chs. 17–27. These two editorial stages display two different perspectives on matters of holiness. The earlier material in chs. 1–16 restricted its concern for holiness to the tabernacle★ or worship sanctuary, which was the seat of the divine presence in the midst of Israel in the wilderness. This earlier stage of the laws of Leviticus also viewed holiness as a concern primarily of the priests and not the whole people of Israel. In contrast, the later material in Leviticus (especially chs. 17–27) expands its concern for holiness to the land of Israel and to all the people, not just the priests (18.26; 22.32).

Leviticus contains many earlier traditions, but its final form probably emerged in the post-exilic period. In the midst of this crisis and transition in its national life, Leviticus helped Israel recover its distinctive identity and mission. Israel was to be a holy community centered in the worship of the LORD who dwelled in its midst. The Exile involved the end of monarchy, the destruction of the Temple, and the need to rebuild the structure of the community. The priestly manual of Leviticus provided one important resource in the reconstitution of Israel's life and identity as a nation and as the people of God.

The place of Leviticus within the Pentateuch★ (the first five books of the Bible) provides an important clue to understanding its laws. The book of Exodus precedes Leviticus and includes an elaborate set of instructions for building the mobile tent of worship or the sanctuary called the tabernacle (chs. 25–31). The tabernacle contains the ark of the covenant,★ an elaborate box, over which God appears in the midst of Israel. In spite of Israel's grave sin of idolatry★ in worshipping the golden calf (Ex 32.1–35), God mercifully allows the Israelites to build the tabernacle (Ex 34.10–40.38). The laws of Leviticus provide guidelines for the conduct of worship and sacrifices connected with this newly constructed tabernacle. The laws also establish boundaries of holiness, order, and purity to preserve the life and well-being of Israel. The observance of these boundaries of holiness and purity ensures that God's holy presence among this sinful people will be not a threat but a blessing as Israel continues its wilderness journey toward the land of Canaan (Numbers—Deuteronomy).

READING GUIDE

Leviticus is a difficult book for modern readers since it contains few narratives and many laws dealing with unfamiliar matters (the sacrifice of animals and grain, the need to maintain ritual purity and cleanness). A first-time reader might begin by reading three shorter sections of Leviticus to sample its concerns. First, the account of the ordination⋆ of the priests and the beginning of the tabernacle worship service in chs. 8–10 provides insights about the priesthood as well as the power and danger of God's holy presence in the midst of Israel. Second, ch. 19 addresses matters related to holiness: from worship to food to the treatment of neighbors, including the famous injunction, "you shall love your neighbor as yourself" (19.18; see Mk 12.28–31). Third, ch. 25 sets forth a set of laws related to the use of land, the treatment of the poor, and the periodic cancellation of debts from which interpreters have drawn implications for environmental and economic policies.

1–7	Laws concerning sacrifices and offerings
8–10	The consecration of priests and inauguration of tabernacle worship
11–15	Laws distinguishing between clean and unclean
16	Ceremony for the Day of Atonement⋆
17–26	Laws concerning Israel's life as a holy people
27	Laws related to vows and gifts dedicated to God

Burnt offerings

1.1–17: The LORD gives laws to Moses concerning the sacrifice of whole animals as burnt offerings. These laws begin a section of instructions for voluntary offerings to God (Lev 1–3). Such offerings stand in contrast to other sacrifices of animals and produce that are required at certain fixed times and festivals during the year (chs. 16, 23).

---

1 The LORD summoned Moses and spoke to him from the tent of meeting, saying: 2Speak to the people of Israel and say to them: When any of you bring an offering of livestock to the LORD, you shall bring your offering from the herd or from the flock.

3 If the offering is a burnt offering from the herd, you shall offer a male without blemish; you shall bring it to the entrance of the tent of meeting, for acceptance in your behalf before the LORD. 4You shall lay your hand on the head of the burnt offering, and it shall be acceptable in your behalf as atonement for you. 5The bull shall be slaughtered before the LORD; and Aaron's sons the

priests shall offer the blood, dashing the blood against all sides of the altar that is at the entrance of the tent of meeting. 6The burnt offering shall be flayed and cut up into its parts. 7The sons of the priest Aaron shall put fire on the altar and arrange wood on the fire. 8Aaron's sons the priests shall arrange the parts, with the head and the suet, on the wood that is on the fire on the altar; 9but its entrails and its legs shall be washed with water. Then the priest shall turn the whole into smoke on the altar as a burnt offering, an offering by fire of pleasing odor to the LORD.

10 If your gift for a burnt offering is from the flock, from the sheep or goats, your offering shall be a male without blemish. 11It shall be slaughtered on the north side of the altar before the LORD, and Aaron's sons the priests shall dash its blood against all sides of the altar. 12It shall be cut up into its parts, with its head and its suet, and the priest shall arrange them on the wood that is on the fire on the altar; 13but the entrails and the legs shall be washed with water. Then the priest

shall offer the whole and turn it into smoke on the altar; it is a burnt offering, an offering by fire of pleasing odor to the LORD.

14 If your offering to the LORD is a burnt offering of birds, you shall choose your offering from turtledoves or pigeons. 15 The priest shall bring it to the altar and wring off its head, and turn it into smoke on the altar; and its blood shall be drained out against the side of the altar. 16 He shall remove its crop with its contents*a* and throw it at the east side of the altar, in the place for ashes. 17 He shall tear it open by its wings without severing it. Then the priest shall turn it into smoke on the altar, on the wood that is on the fire; it is a burnt offering, an offering by fire of pleasing odor to the LORD.

1.1–17. 1: *The tent of meeting* came to be identified with the tabernacle,* the mobile tent of worship in the wilderness. In earlier traditions, it was probably different from the tabernacle. Exodus 33.7–11 mentions the tent of meeting as existing before the tabernacle was constructed (Ex 35.1–40.38). 3: The *burnt offering* is unique among the many sacrifices in that it was entirely consumed in the fire on the altar. All other types of sacrifices involved only a portion to be burned on the altar; the remainder was given back as food to be eaten by the priests, the poor, other dependent members of the community, or the donor. The requirement that the male animal be *without blemish* means that the animal is not blind, lame, or sick. The prophet* in Mal 1.8 asks, "When you offer blind animals in sacrifice, is that not wrong? And when you offer those that are lame or sick, is that not wrong?" 4: To *lay your hand on the head* of the sacrificed animal signifies the donor's ownership of the animal that is being offered to God and the donor's receipt of the benefits of the sacrifice. In this case, the benefits include *atonement** for sin, that is, the forgiveness or "covering over" of offenses against God. Burnt offerings especially involved cases of sins of omission or sinful thoughts. Job 1.5 portrays the righteous man named Job who "would rise early in the morning and offer burnt offerings . . . For Job said, 'It may be that my children have sinned, and cursed God in their hearts.'" 5: Ancient Israelites considered *blood* to carry the sacred essence of life; it had the power to cleanse ritual impurity and sin (17.11; Gen 9.4). The act of *dashing the blood against the altar* signifies God's involvement in the ritual and the reconciliation

with the one who offered the animal (see Ex 24.6–8). The priests who presided at the sacrifices were *Aaron's sons* since the Israelite priesthood was a hereditary office and Aaron was the first high priest (Ex 28.1–5; Num 18.1–7). 9: The fire of sacrifice transforms the animal into smoke that rises to the heavenly dwelling place of God. The sacrificed animal thus becomes a *pleasing odor to the LORD,* a phrase indicating God's acceptance of the offering; see Gen 8.20–22. 14–17: The poor who are not able to afford the sacrifice of cattle or sheep have the option of presenting an *offering of birds;* compare 12.2–8.

Grain offerings

2.1–16: The LORD gives instructions for grain offerings. Three different kinds of grain offerings are discussed in these laws: choice flour with olive oil and the spice frankincense (vv. 1–3), unleavened or yeastless cakes mixed with oil (vv. 4–7), and parched or baked grain with oil and frankincense (vv. 14–16).

2 When anyone presents a grain offering to the LORD, the offering shall be of choice flour; the worshiper shall pour oil on it, and put frankincense on it, 2 and bring it to Aaron's sons the priests. After taking from it a handful of the choice flour and oil, with all its frankincense, the priest shall turn this token portion into smoke on the altar, an offering by fire of pleasing odor to the LORD. 3 And what is left of the grain offering shall be for Aaron and his sons, a most holy part of the offerings by fire to the LORD.

4 When you present a grain offering baked in the oven, it shall be of choice flour: unleavened cakes mixed with oil, or unleavened wafers spread with oil. 5 If your offering is grain prepared on a griddle, it shall be of choice flour mixed with oil, unleavened; 6 break it in pieces, and pour oil on it; it is a grain offering. 7 If your offering is grain prepared in a pan, it shall be made of choice flour in oil. 8 You shall bring to the LORD the grain offering that is prepared in any of these ways; and when it is presented to the priest, he shall take it to the altar. 9 The priest shall remove from the grain offering its token portion and turn this into smoke on the altar, an offering by fire of pleasing odor to the

a Meaning of Heb uncertain

LORD. [10]And what is left of the grain offering shall be for Aaron and his sons; it is a most holy part of the offerings by fire to the LORD.

[11] No grain offering that you bring to the LORD shall be made with leaven, for you must not turn any leaven or honey into smoke as an offering by fire to the LORD. [12]You may bring them to the LORD as an offering of choice products, but they shall not be offered on the altar for a pleasing odor. [13]You shall not omit from your grain offerings the salt of the covenant with your God; with all your offerings you shall offer salt.

[14] If you bring a grain offering of first fruits to the LORD, you shall bring as the grain offering of your first fruits coarse new grain from fresh ears, parched with fire. [15]You shall add oil to it and lay frankincense on it; it is a grain offering. [16]And the priest shall turn a token portion of it into smoke—some of the coarse grain and oil with all its frankincense; it is an offering by fire to the LORD.

2.11: Any fermented flour or grain product was considered ritually unclean and thus not acceptable as a sacrifice to God. Like leaven or yeast, honey caused flour to ferment and thus could not be part of any grain offering. **13:** In contrast to leaven and honey that ferment and change grain products and thus render them ritually impure, salt is a preservative of food products. Thus, salt was considered a purifying agent. The *salt of the covenant** may suggest a traditional association of salt with the enduring preservation of a covenant relationship in a ritual meal of covenant making.

Offerings of well-being

3.1–17: The LORD offers guidelines for offerings of well-being. These laws concern the burnt offering of the fat and kidneys of animals on the altar in order to allow the consumption of the animal's meat by the donor. The procedure is similar to the whole burnt offerings in 1.1–17, except that the meat is not burned on the altar but consumed by worshippers in a covenant* meal of well-being or peace. The meal binds together the worshippers and the LORD.

---

3 If the offering is a sacrifice of well-being, if you offer an animal of the herd, whether male or female, you shall offer one without blemish before the LORD. [2]You shall lay your hand on the head of the offering and slaughter it at the entrance of the tent of meeting; and Aaron's sons the priests shall dash the blood against all sides of the altar. [3]You shall offer from the sacrifice of well-being, as an offering by fire to the LORD, the fat that covers the entrails and all the fat that is around the entrails; [4]the two kidneys with the fat that is on them at the loins, and the appendage of the liver, which he shall remove with the kidneys. [5]Then Aaron's sons shall turn these into smoke on the altar, with the burnt offering that is on the wood on the fire, as an offering by fire of pleasing odor to the LORD.

[6] If your offering for a sacrifice of well-being to the LORD is from the flock, male or female, you shall offer one without blemish. [7]If you present a sheep as your offering, you shall bring it before the LORD [8]and lay your hand on the head of the offering. It shall be slaughtered before the tent of meeting, and Aaron's sons shall dash its blood against all sides of the altar. [9]You shall present its fat from the sacrifice of well-being, as an offering by fire to the LORD: the whole broad tail, which shall be removed close to the backbone, the fat that covers the entrails, and all the fat that is around the entrails; [10]the two kidneys with the fat that is on them at the loins, and the appendage of the liver, which you shall remove with the kidneys. [11]Then the priest shall turn these into smoke on the altar as a food offering by fire to the LORD.

[12] If your offering is a goat, you shall bring it before the LORD [13]and lay your hand on its head; it shall be slaughtered before the tent of meeting; and the sons of Aaron shall dash its blood against all sides of the altar. [14]You shall present as your offering from it, as an offering by fire to the LORD, the fat that covers the entrails, and all the fat that is around the entrails; [15]the two kidneys with the fat that is on them at the loins, and the appendage of the liver, which you shall remove with the kidneys. [16]Then the priest shall turn these into smoke on the altar as a food offering by fire for a pleasing odor.

All fat is the LORD's. [17]It shall be a perpetual statute throughout your generations, in all your settlements: you must not eat any fat or any blood.

Purification offerings

4.1–5.13: The LORD gives directives for purification offerings to be given when an individual or group unintentionally sins or becomes ritually unclean. The first group of laws in this section (4.1–35) is organized by the status of the person who sins inadvertently: a priest (4.1–12), the whole congregation of Israel (4.13–21), a ruler (4.22–26), or an ordinary individual (4.27–35). The second group of laws in 5.1–13 also concerns unintentional sins and is organized by the relative financial resources of the offender: a person of some means (5.1–6), a person of lesser means (5.7–10), and a person of minimal means (5.11–13).

4 The LORD spoke to Moses, saying, 2Speak to the people of Israel, saying: When anyone sins unintentionally in any of the LORD's commandments about things not to be done, and does any one of them: 3 If it is the anointed priest who sins, thus bringing guilt on the people, he shall offer for the sin that he has committed a bull of the herd without blemish as a sin offering to the LORD. 4He shall bring the bull to the entrance of the tent of meeting before the LORD and lay his hand on the head of the bull; the bull shall be slaughtered before the LORD. 5The anointed priest shall take some of the blood of the bull and bring it into the tent of meeting. 6The priest shall dip his finger in the blood and sprinkle some of the blood seven times before the LORD in front of the curtain of the sanctuary. 7The priest shall put some of the blood on the horns of the altar of fragrant incense that is in the tent of meeting before the LORD; and the rest of the blood of the bull he shall pour out at the base of the altar of burnt offering, which is at the entrance of the tent of meeting. 8He shall remove all the fat from the bull of sin offering: the fat that covers the entrails and all the fat that is around the entrails; 9the two kidneys with the fat that is on them at the loins; and the appendage of the liver, which he shall remove with the kidneys, 10just as these are removed from the ox of the sacrifice of well-being. The priest

shall turn them into smoke upon the altar of burnt offering. 11But the skin of the bull and all its flesh, as well as its head, its legs, its entrails, and its dung— 12all the rest of the bull—he shall carry out to a clean place outside the camp, to the ash heap, and shall burn it on a wood fire; at the ash heap it shall be burned.

13 If the whole congregation of Israel errs unintentionally and the matter escapes the notice of the assembly, and they do any one of the things that by the LORD's commandments ought not to be done and incur guilt; 14when the sin that they have committed becomes known, the assembly shall offer a bull of the herd for a sin offering and bring it before the tent of meeting. 15The elders of the congregation shall lay their hands on the head of the bull before the LORD, and the bull shall be slaughtered before the LORD. 16The anointed priest shall bring some of the blood of the bull into the tent of meeting, 17and the priest shall dip his finger in the blood and sprinkle it seven times before the LORD, in front of the curtain. 18He shall put some of the blood on the horns of the altar that is before the LORD in the tent of meeting; and the rest of the blood he shall pour out at the base of the altar of burnt offering that is at the entrance of the tent of meeting. 19He shall remove all its fat and turn it into smoke on the altar. 20He shall do with the bull just as is done with the bull of sin offering; he shall do the same with this. The priest shall make atonement for them, and they shall be forgiven. 21He shall carry the bull outside the camp, and burn it as he burned the first bull; it is the sin offering for the assembly.

4.1–21. 6: Sprinkling blood or oil *seven times* reflects the quality of completeness and wholeness associated with the number seven in the Bible. For example, a whole weekly cycle ends on the sabbath or seventh day of the week (Ex 20.8–11). The seven sprinklings of blood purify the whole sanctuary or place of worship. **8–12:** The holiest portions of the animal, the fat and kidneys, are burned as a sacrifice on the altar. The remainder of the animal, which has symbolically absorbed the unintentional guilt of the offending priest, is carried to a ritually clean *ash heap* outside the camp or city where it is burned. Jeremiah 31.40 refers to such an ash heap of dead animal carcasses outside the city of Jerusalem. This ash heap was probably associated with the purification offerings connected with the Temple* in Jerusalem and performed in accordance with these laws in Leviticus. **15:** *The elders* represent the whole congregation as they *lay their hands on the head of the bull.* This ritual act signifies the transfer of guilt from the community to the animal. The removal of the animal to an area outside the camp symbolizes the removal of the community's guilt and impurity (v. 21).

22 When a ruler sins, doing unintentionally any one of all the things that by commandments of the LORD his God ought not to be done and incurs guilt, 23once the sin that he has committed is made known to him, he shall bring as his offering a male goat without blemish. 24He shall lay his hand on the head of the goat; it shall be slaughtered at the spot where the burnt offering is slaughtered before the LORD; it is a sin offering. 25The priest shall take some of the blood of the sin offering with his finger and put it on the horns of the altar of burnt offering, and pour out the rest of its blood at the base of the altar of burnt offering. 26All its fat he shall turn into smoke on the altar, like the fat of the sacrifice of well-being. Thus the priest shall make atonement on his behalf for his sin, and he shall be forgiven.

27 If anyone of the ordinary people among you sins unintentionally in doing any one of the things that by the LORD's commandments ought not to be done and incurs guilt, 28when the sin that you have committed is made known to you, you shall bring a female goat without blemish as your offering, for the sin that you have committed. 29You shall lay your hand on the head of the sin offering; and the sin offering shall be slaughtered at the place of the burnt offering. 30The priest shall take some of its blood with his finger and put it on the horns of the altar of burnt offering, and he shall pour out the rest of its blood at the base of the altar. 31He shall remove all its fat, as the fat is removed from the offering of well-being, and the priest shall turn it into smoke on the altar for a pleasing odor to the LORD. Thus the

priest shall make atonement on your behalf, and you shall be forgiven.

32 If the offering you bring as a sin offering is a sheep, you shall bring a female without blemish. 33You shall lay your hand on the head of the sin offering; and it shall be slaughtered as a sin offering at the spot where the burnt offering is slaughtered. 34The priest shall take some of the blood of the sin offering with his finger and put it on the horns of the altar of burnt offering, and pour out the rest of its blood at the base of the altar. 35You shall remove all its fat, as the fat of the sheep is removed from the sacrifice of well-being, and the priest shall turn it into smoke on the altar, with the offerings by fire to the LORD. Thus the priest shall make atonement on your behalf for the sin that you have committed, and you shall be forgiven.

5 When any of you sin in that you have heard a public adjuration to testify and—though able to testify as one who has seen or learned of the matter—do not speak up, you are subject to punishment. 2Or when any of you touch any unclean thing—whether the carcass of an unclean beast or the carcass of unclean livestock or the carcass of an unclean swarming thing—and are unaware of it, you have become unclean, and are guilty. 3Or when you touch human uncleanness—any uncleanness by which one can become unclean—and are unaware of it, when you come to know it, you shall be guilty. 4Or when any of you utter aloud a rash oath for a bad or a good purpose, whatever people utter in an oath, and are unaware of it, when you come to know it, you shall in any of these be guilty. 5When you realize your guilt in any of these, you shall confess the sin that you have committed. 6And you shall bring to the LORD, as your penalty for the sin that you have committed, a female from the flock, a sheep or a goat, as a sin offering; and the priest shall make atonement on your behalf for your sin.

7 But if you cannot afford a sheep, you shall bring to the LORD, as your penalty for the sin that you have committed, two turtledoves or two pigeons, one for a sin offering and the other for a burnt offering. 8You shall

bring them to the priest, who shall offer first the one for the sin offering, wringing its head at the nape without severing it. [9]He shall sprinkle some of the blood of the sin offering on the side of the altar, while the rest of the blood shall be drained out at the base of the altar; it is a sin offering. [10]And the second he shall offer for a burnt offering according to the regulation. Thus the priest shall make atonement on your behalf for the sin that you have committed, and you shall be forgiven.

[11] But if you cannot afford two turtledoves or two pigeons, you shall bring as your offering for the sin that you have committed one-tenth of an ephah of choice flour for a sin offering; you shall not put oil on it or lay frankincense on it, for it is a sin offering. [12]You shall bring it to the priest, and the priest shall scoop up a handful of it as its memorial portion, and turn this into smoke on the altar, with the offerings by fire to the LORD; it is a sin offering. [13]Thus the priest shall make atonement on your behalf for whichever of these sins you have committed, and you shall be forgiven. Like the grain offering, the rest shall be for the priest.

4.22–5.13. 2–3: For more extensive discussion of ritual cleanness and uncleanness, see 11.1–15.33. **5–6:** To *confess the sin* involves a verbal acknowledgment to the priest of inadvertent guilt. Such confession is a necessary complement to the offering of the animal sacrifice in this ritual of atonement* or forgiveness. **7–13:** Poor persons who *cannot afford a sheep* (v. 7) may offer two birds. Those who cannot even afford two birds may substitute a grain offering for the animal sacrifice in the ritual of forgiveness (vv. 11–13).

Restitution offerings
5.14–6.7: The LORD requires restitution offerings for the misuse of holy sanctuary objects or the LORD's holy name. These laws stipulate certain repayments and purification offerings to those who desecrate holy objects of the sanctuary, fail to fulfill vows to God, or deceive a neighbor by swearing a false oath in the name of God.

---

[14] The LORD spoke to Moses, saying: [15]When any of you commit a trespass and sin unintentionally in any of the holy things of the LORD, you shall bring, as your guilt offering to the LORD, a ram without blemish

from the flock, convertible into silver by the sanctuary shekel; it is a guilt offering. [16]And you shall make restitution for the holy thing in which you were remiss, and shall add one-fifth to it and give it to the priest. The priest shall make atonement on your behalf with the ram of the guilt offering, and you shall be forgiven.

[17] If any of you sin without knowing it, doing any of the things that by the LORD's commandments ought not to be done, you have incurred guilt, and are subject to punishment. [18]You shall bring to the priest a ram without blemish from the flock, or the equivalent, as a guilt offering; and the priest shall make atonement on your behalf for the error that you committed unintentionally, and you shall be forgiven. [19]It is a guilt offering; you have incurred guilt before the LORD.

6 [a]The LORD spoke to Moses, saying: [2]When any of you sin and commit a trespass against the LORD by deceiving a neighbor in a matter of a deposit or a pledge, or by robbery, or if you have defrauded a neighbor, [3]or have found something lost and lied about it—if you swear falsely regarding any of the various things that one may do and sin thereby— [4]when you have sinned and realize your guilt, and would restore what you took by robbery or by fraud or the deposit that was committed to you, or the lost thing that you found, [5]or anything else about which you have sworn falsely, you shall repay the principal amount and shall add one-fifth to it. You shall pay it to its owner when you realize your guilt. [6]And you shall bring to the priest, as your guilt offering to the LORD, a ram without blemish from the flock, or its equivalent, for a guilt offering. [7]The priest shall make atonement on your behalf before the LORD, and you shall be forgiven for any of the things that one may do and incur guilt thereby.

6.1–7: The previous laws in Leviticus have dealt largely with obligations and sacrifices to God. These laws concern injury to a neighbor. The principle is that restitution must be made to the neighbor before the of-

a Ch 5.20 in Heb

fender can be reconciled to God through a guilt or purification offering (see Mt 5.23–24).

Supplementary instructions

6.8–7.38: The LORD provides supplementary instructions to the priests concerning a number of different sacrifices.

8[a] The LORD spoke to Moses, saying: 9Command Aaron and his sons, saying: This is the ritual of the burnt offering. The burnt offering itself shall remain on the hearth upon the altar all night until the morning, while the fire on the altar shall be kept burning. 10The priest shall put on his linen vestments after putting on his linen undergarments next to his body; and he shall take up the ashes to which the fire has reduced the burnt offering on the altar, and place them beside the altar. 11Then he shall take off his vestments and put on other garments, and carry the ashes out to a clean place outside the camp. 12The fire on the altar shall be kept burning; it shall not go out. Every morning the priest shall add wood to it, lay out the burnt offering on it, and turn into smoke the fat pieces of the offerings of well-being. 13A perpetual fire shall be kept burning on the altar; it shall not go out.

14 This is the ritual of the grain offering: The sons of Aaron shall offer it before the LORD, in front of the altar. 15They shall take from it a handful of the choice flour and oil of the grain offering, with all the frankincense that is on the offering, and they shall turn its memorial portion into smoke on the altar as a pleasing odor to the LORD. 16Aaron and his sons shall eat what is left of it; it shall be eaten as unleavened cakes in a holy place; in the court of the tent of meeting they shall eat it. 17It shall not be baked with leaven. I have given it as their portion of my offerings by fire; it is most holy, like the sin offering and the guilt offering. 18Every male among the descendants of Aaron shall eat of it, as their perpetual due throughout your generations, from the LORD's offerings by fire; anything that touches them shall become holy.

19 The LORD spoke to Moses, saying: 20This is the offering that Aaron and his sons shall offer to the LORD on the day when he is anointed: one-tenth of an ephah of choice flour as a regular offering, half of it in the morning and half in the evening. 21It shall be made with oil on a griddle; you shall bring it well soaked, as a grain offering of baked[b] pieces, and you shall present it as a pleasing odor to the LORD. 22And so the priest, anointed from among Aaron's descendants as a successor, shall prepare it; it is the LORD's—a perpetual due—to be turned entirely into smoke. 23Every grain offering of a priest shall be wholly burned; it shall not be eaten.

24 The LORD spoke to Moses, saying: 25Speak to Aaron and his sons, saying: This is the ritual of the sin offering. The sin offering shall be slaughtered before the LORD at the spot where the burnt offering is slaughtered; it is most holy. 26The priest who offers it as a sin offering shall eat of it; it shall be eaten in a holy place, in the court of the tent of meeting. 27Whatever touches its flesh shall become holy; and when any of its blood is spattered on a garment, you shall wash the bespattered part in a holy place. 28An earthen vessel in which it was boiled shall be broken; but if it is boiled in a bronze vessel, that shall be scoured and rinsed in water. 29Every male among the priests shall eat of it; it is most holy. 30But no sin offering shall be eaten from which any blood is brought into the tent of meeting for atonement in the holy place; it shall be burned with fire.

6.8–30. 10–11: The special priestly garments are considered holy and worn only when the priests are in the sanctuary or altar area (Ex 28.40–43). Therefore, the priest must change into other clothes whenever he carries the ashes from the altar to a designated area outside the camp. **12–13:** The perpetual *fire on the altar* that cannot go out is probably based on the events recounted in 9.24, the official inauguration of the worship and sacrifices of the tabernacle* in the wilderness. The requirement to maintain a perpetual fire may reflect a tradition to keep this divine fire going so that all sacrifices would be made sacred by its miraculous flame. **24–29:** These laws assume that the

a Ch 6.1 in Heb   *b* Meaning of Heb uncertain

qualities of ritual cleanness and uncleanness can be passed from one object or person to another through contagious touch.

7 This is the ritual of the guilt offering. It is most holy; ²at the spot where the burnt offering is slaughtered, they shall slaughter the guilt offering, and its blood shall be dashed against all sides of the altar. ³All its fat shall be offered: the broad tail, the fat that covers the entrails, ⁴the two kidneys with the fat that is on them at the loins, and the appendage of the liver, which shall be removed with the kidneys. ⁵The priest shall turn them into smoke on the altar as an offering by fire to the LORD; it is a guilt offering. ⁶Every male among the priests shall eat of it; it shall be eaten in a holy place; it is most holy.

7 The guilt offering is like the sin offering, there is the same ritual for them; the priest who makes atonement with it shall have it. ⁸So, too, the priest who offers anyone's burnt offering shall keep the skin of the burnt offering that he has offered. ⁹And every grain offering baked in the oven, and all that is prepared in a pan or on a griddle, shall belong to the priest who offers it. ¹⁰But every other grain offering, mixed with oil or dry, shall belong to all the sons of Aaron equally.

11 This is the ritual of the sacrifice of the offering of well-being that one may offer to the LORD. ¹²If you offer it for thanksgiving, you shall offer with the thank offering unleavened cakes mixed with oil, unleavened wafers spread with oil, and cakes of choice flour well soaked in oil. ¹³With your thanksgiving sacrifice of well-being you shall bring your offering with cakes of leavened bread. ¹⁴From this you shall offer one cake from each offering, as a gift to the LORD; it shall belong to the priest who dashes the blood of the offering of well-being. ¹⁵And the flesh of your thanksgiving sacrifice of well-being shall be eaten on the day it is offered; you shall not leave any of it until morning. ¹⁶But if the sacrifice you offer is a votive offering or a freewill offering, it shall be eaten on the day that you offer your sacrifice, and what is left of it shall be eaten the next day; ¹⁷but

what is left of the flesh of the sacrifice shall be burned up on the third day. ¹⁸If any of the flesh of your sacrifice of well-being is eaten on the third day, it shall not be acceptable, nor shall it be credited to the one who offers it; it shall be an abomination, and the one who eats of it shall incur guilt.

19 Flesh that touches any unclean thing shall not be eaten; it shall be burned up. As for other flesh, all who are clean may eat such flesh. ²⁰But those who eat flesh from the LORD's sacrifice of well-being while in a state of uncleanness shall be cut off from their kin. ²¹When any one of you touches any unclean thing—human uncleanness or an unclean animal or any unclean creature—and then eats flesh from the LORD's sacrifice of well-being, you shall be cut off from your kin.

22 The LORD spoke to Moses, saying: ²³Speak to the people of Israel, saying: You shall eat no fat of ox or sheep or goat. ²⁴The fat of an animal that died or was torn by wild animals may be put to any other use, but you must not eat it. ²⁵If any one of you eats the fat from an animal of which an offering by fire may be made to the LORD, you who eat it shall be cut off from your kin. ²⁶You must not eat any blood whatever, either of bird or of animal, in any of your settlements. ²⁷Any one of you who eats any blood shall be cut off from your kin.

28 The LORD spoke to Moses, saying: ²⁹Speak to the people of Israel, saying: Any one of you who would offer to the LORD your sacrifice of well-being must yourself bring to the LORD your offering from your sacrifice of well-being. ³⁰Your own hands shall bring the LORD's offering by fire; you shall bring the fat with the breast, so that the breast may be raised as an elevation offering before the LORD. ³¹The priest shall turn the fat into smoke on the altar, but the breast shall belong to Aaron and his sons. ³²And the right thigh from your sacrifices of well-being you shall give to the priest as an offering; ³³the one among the sons of Aaron who offers the blood and fat of the offering of well-being shall have the right thigh for a portion. ³⁴For I have taken the breast of the elevation offering, and the thigh that is offered, from the

people of Israel, from their sacrifices of well-being, and have given them to Aaron the priest and to his sons, as a perpetual due from the people of Israel. 35This is the portion allotted to Aaron and to his sons from the offerings made by fire to the LORD, once they have been brought forward to serve the LORD as priests; 36these the LORD commanded to be given them, when he anointed them, as a perpetual due from the people of Israel throughout their generations.

37 This is the ritual of the burnt offering, the grain offering, the sin offering, the guilt offering, the offering of ordination, and the sacrifice of well-being, 38which the LORD commanded Moses on Mount Sinai, when he commanded the people of Israel to bring their offerings to the LORD, in the wilderness of Sinai.

7.1–38. 13: The instructions here seem to combine the thanksgiving offering and the offering of well-being into one *thanksgiving sacrifice of well-being*. Elsewhere in Leviticus the two offerings are distinct (22.21, 29). 16: A *votive offering* is a sacrifice offered to God by a person who has successfully fulfilled a vow made to God. An example is Hannah, who vowed to dedicate her son Samuel to the service of God. She and her husband brought the child and left him with the priest Eli and then "they slaughtered the bull" (1 Sam 1.11, 24–25; see Lev 27.1–33). A *freewill offering* is a sacrifice donated to God as a voluntary and spontaneous expression of happiness and gratitude. 19–21: For more detailed laws about which things, conditions, and animals are considered ritually unclean, see 11.1–15.33. 30: The *elevation offering* involves the worshipper's lifting up the sacrifice that is offered and transferring it to the elevated hands of the priest (see Ex 29.24). The transfer signifies the lifting up of the sacrifice to God through the mediation of the priest.

Aaron and his sons ordained

8.1–36: The LORD directs Moses to consecrate or induct Aaron and his sons into the priesthood. The chapter's frequent phrase *as the LORD commanded Moses* (vv. 9, 13, 17, 21, 29, 36) affirms Moses' strict adherence to the procedures for priestly ordination* first outlined in the laws in Ex 29.

---

8 The LORD spoke to Moses, saying: 2Take Aaron and his sons with him, the vest-

ments, the anointing oil, the bull of sin offering, the two rams, and the basket of unleavened bread; 3and assemble the whole congregation at the entrance of the tent of meeting. 4And Moses did as the LORD commanded him. When the congregation was assembled at the entrance of the tent of meeting, 5Moses said to the congregation, "This is what the LORD has commanded to be done."

6 Then Moses brought Aaron and his sons forward, and washed them with water. 7He put the tunic on him, fastened the sash around him, clothed him with the robe, and put the ephod on him. He then put the decorated band of the ephod around him, tying the ephod to him with it. 8He placed the breastpiece on him, and in the breastpiece he put the Urim and the Thummim. 9And he set the turban on his head, and on the turban, in front, he set the golden ornament, the holy crown, as the LORD commanded Moses.

10 Then Moses took the anointing oil and anointed the tabernacle and all that was in it, and consecrated them. 11He sprinkled some of it on the altar seven times, and anointed the altar and all its utensils, and the basin and its base, to consecrate them. 12He poured some of the anointing oil on Aaron's head and anointed him, to consecrate him. 13And Moses brought forward Aaron's sons, and clothed them with tunics, and fastened sashes around them, and tied headdresses on them, as the LORD commanded Moses.

14 He led forward the bull of sin offering; and Aaron and his sons laid their hands upon the head of the bull of sin offering, 15and it was slaughtered. Moses took the blood and with his finger put some on each of the horns of the altar, purifying the altar; then he poured out the blood at the base of the altar. Thus he consecrated it, to make atonement for it. 16Moses took all the fat that was around the entrails, and the appendage of the liver, and the two kidneys with their fat, and turned them into smoke on the altar. 17But the bull itself, its skin and flesh and its dung, he burned with fire outside the camp, as the LORD commanded Moses. 18 Then he brought forward the ram of

burnt offering. Aaron and his sons laid their hands on the head of the ram, [19]and it was slaughtered. Moses dashed the blood against all sides of the altar. [20]The ram was cut into its parts, and Moses turned into smoke the head and the parts and the suet. [21]And after the entrails and the legs were washed with water, Moses turned into smoke the whole ram on the altar; it was a burnt offering for a pleasing odor, an offering by fire to the LORD, as the LORD commanded Moses.

[22] Then he brought forward the second ram, the ram of ordination. Aaron and his sons laid their hands on the head of the ram, [23]and it was slaughtered. Moses took some of its blood and put it on the lobe of Aaron's right ear and on the thumb of his right hand and on the big toe of his right foot. [24]After Aaron's sons were brought forward, Moses put some of the blood on the lobes of their right ears and on the thumbs of their right hands and on the big toes of their right feet; and Moses dashed the rest of the blood against all sides of the altar. [25]He took the fat—the broad tail, all the fat that was around the entrails, the appendage of the liver, and the two kidneys with their fat—and the right thigh. [26]From the basket of unleavened bread that was before the LORD, he took one cake of unleavened bread, one cake of bread with oil, and one wafer, and placed them on the fat and on the right thigh. [27]He placed all these on the palms of Aaron and on the palms of his sons, and raised them as an elevation offering before the LORD. [28]Then Moses took them from their hands and turned them into smoke on the altar with the burnt offering. This was an ordination offering for a pleasing odor, an offering by fire to the LORD. [29]Moses took the breast and raised it as an elevation offering before the LORD; it was Moses' portion of the ram of ordination, as the LORD commanded Moses.

[30] Then Moses took some of the anointing oil and some of the blood that was on the altar and sprinkled them on Aaron and his vestments, and also on his sons and their vestments. Thus he consecrated Aaron and his vestments, and also his sons and their vestments.

[31] And Moses said to Aaron and his sons, "Boil the flesh at the entrance of the tent of meeting, and eat it there with the bread that is in the basket of ordination offerings, as I was commanded, 'Aaron and his sons shall eat it'; [32]and what remains of the flesh and the bread you shall burn with fire. [33]You shall not go outside the entrance of the tent of meeting for seven days, until the day when your period of ordination is completed. For it will take seven days to ordain you; [34]as has been done today, the LORD has commanded to be done to make atonement for you. [35]You shall remain at the entrance of the tent of meeting day and night for seven days, keeping the LORD's charge so that you do not die; for so I am commanded." [36]Aaron and his sons did all the things that the LORD commanded through Moses.

8.1–36. 7: *The ephod* ★ is a long and ornate robe or apron hanging as two shoulder pieces on the shoulders of the priest. Stones engraved with the names of the twelve tribes of Israel were attached to the ephod as a remembrance of Israel before the deity (Ex 28.6– 14). 8: *The Urim and the Thummim* were stones used to determine the deity's will or guidance when a decision needed to be made. They were kept in a pouch in the breastpiece worn on the chest of the priest. 10–13: Pouring *the anointing* ★ *oil* on the head of a person was a means of designating him or her to a special office in the community such as a prophet, ★ king, or priest (1 Kings 19.6; Ex 29.7). Objects such as the *tabernacle* ★ (v. 10) and the *altar* (v. 11) were also anointed to set them apart as holy within the community (Ex 40.9–10). On the *tabernacle* (v. 10), see comment on 1.1. On the sprinkling of oil *seven times* (v. 11), see comment on 4.6. 23: The blood smeared on the body's extremities (*ear, thumb,* and *big toe*) purifies Aaron's whole body and protects him from impurities. 33–35: The seven-day period completes the cycle of transition for Aaron and his sons from service in the common sphere to service in the sacred sphere of worship and the sanctuary.

Aaron as high priest

9.1–24: Aaron commences his work as priest by offering a number of the sacrifices for which instructions have been given in the preceding chapters. Those sacrifices include the *sin offering* (v. 8; see 4.1–35), the *burnt offering* (v. 12; see 1.1–17), the *grain offering*

(v. 17; 2.1–16), the *sacrifice of well-being* (v. 18; see 3.1–17), and the *elevation offering* (v. 21; see 7.30).

9 On the eighth day Moses summoned Aaron and his sons and the elders of Israel. [2] He said to Aaron, "Take a bull calf for a sin offering and a ram for a burnt offering, without blemish, and offer them before the LORD. [3] And say to the people of Israel, 'Take a male goat for a sin offering; a calf and a lamb, yearlings without blemish, for a burnt offering; [4] and an ox and a ram for an offering of well-being to sacrifice before the LORD; and a grain offering mixed with oil. For today the LORD will appear to you.' " [5] They brought what Moses commanded to the front of the tent of meeting; and the whole congregation drew near and stood before the LORD. [6] And Moses said, "This is the thing that the LORD commanded you to do, so that the glory of the LORD may appear to you." [7] Then Moses said to Aaron, "Draw near to the altar and sacrifice your sin offering and your burnt offering, and make atonement for yourself and for the people; and sacrifice the offering of the people, and make atonement for them; as the LORD has commanded."

8 Aaron drew near to the altar, and slaughtered the calf of the sin offering, which was for himself. [9] The sons of Aaron presented the blood to him, and he dipped his finger in the blood and put it on the horns of the altar; and the rest of the blood he poured out at the base of the altar. [10] But the fat, the kidneys, and the appendage of the liver from the sin offering he turned into smoke on the altar, as the LORD commanded Moses; [11] and the flesh and the skin he burned with fire outside the camp.

12 Then he slaughtered the burnt offering. Aaron's sons brought him the blood, and he dashed it against all sides of the altar. [13] And they brought him the burnt offering piece by piece, and the head, which he turned into smoke on the altar. [14] He washed the entrails and the legs and, with the burnt offering, turned them into smoke on the altar.

15 Next he presented the people's offering. He took the goat of the sin offering that was for the people, and slaughtered it, and

presented it as a sin offering like the first one. [16] He presented the burnt offering, and sacrificed it according to regulation. [17] He presented the grain offering, and, taking a handful of it, he turned it into smoke on the altar, in addition to the burnt offering of the morning.

18 He slaughtered the ox and the ram as a sacrifice of well-being for the people. Aaron's sons brought him the blood, which he dashed against all sides of the altar, [19] and the fat of the ox and of the ram—the broad tail, the fat that covers the entrails, the two kidneys and the fat on them,[a] and the appendage of the liver. [20] They first laid the fat on the breasts, and the fat was turned into smoke on the altar; [21] and the breasts and the right thigh Aaron raised as an elevation offering before the LORD, as Moses had commanded.

22 Aaron lifted his hands toward the people and blessed them; and he came down after sacrificing the sin offering, the burnt offering, and the offering of well-being. [23] Moses and Aaron entered the tent of meeting, and then came out and blessed the people; and the glory of the LORD appeared to all the people. [24] Fire came out from the LORD and consumed the burnt offering and the fat on the altar; and when all the people saw it, they shouted and fell on their faces.

9.1–24. 1: *The eighth day* comes at the end of the seven-day consecration period in 8.33–35. **6:** The purpose of the sacrifices and worship of the people is *that the glory of the LORD may appear to you*. Israel was often reminded that God's presence among them was not an automatic result of their rituals. **22:** Priests lifted up their hands and *blessed* the people. The traditional priestly blessing of Aaron is recorded in Num 6.24–26: "The LORD bless you and keep you; the LORD make his face to shine upon you, and be gracious to you; the LORD lift up his countenance upon you, and give you peace." **23–24:** *The glory of the LORD* appeared to Israel in the wilderness as a pillar of fire shrouded in a cloud (Ex 24.17; 40.38). When *fire came out from the LORD* to light this first fire for the burning of the sacrifices, the fire presumably came from the fiery cloud of the divine presence.

a Gk: Heb *the broad tail, and that which covers, and the kidneys*

Nadab and Abihu

10.1–20: Aaron's sons, Nadab and Abihu, die as a consequence of their improper sacrifice. The chapter explores the dangers associated with priestly duties because of the nearness of the divine presence and the need for strict observance of proper procedures.

10 Now Aaron's sons, Nadab and Abihu, each took his censer, put fire in it, and laid incense on it; and they offered unholy fire before the LORD, such as he had not commanded them. ²And fire came out from the presence of the LORD and consumed them, and they died before the LORD. ³Then Moses said to Aaron, "This is what the LORD meant when he said,

'Through those who are near me
　I will show myself holy,
　and before all the people
　I will be glorified.'"

And Aaron was silent.

4 Moses summoned Mishael and Elzaphan, sons of Uzziel the uncle of Aaron, and said to them, "Come forward, and carry your kinsmen away from the front of the sanctuary to a place outside the camp." ⁵They came forward and carried them by their tunics out of the camp, as Moses had ordered. ⁶And Moses said to Aaron and to his sons Eleazar and Ithamar, "Do not dishevel your hair, and do not tear your vestments, or you will die and wrath will strike all the congregation; but your kindred, the whole house of Israel, may mourn the burning that the LORD has sent. ⁷You shall not go outside the entrance of the tent of meeting, or you will die; for the anointing oil of the LORD is on you." And they did as Moses had ordered.

8 And the LORD spoke to Aaron: ⁹Drink no wine or strong drink, neither you nor your sons, when you enter the tent of meeting, that you may not die; it is a statute forever throughout your generations. ¹⁰You are to distinguish between the holy and the common, and between the unclean and the clean; ¹¹and you are to teach the people of Israel all the statutes that the LORD has spoken to them through Moses.

12 Moses spoke to Aaron and to his remaining sons, Eleazar and Ithamar: Take the grain offering that is left from the LORD's offerings by fire, and eat it unleavened beside the altar, for it is most holy; ¹³you shall eat it in a holy place, because it is your due and your sons' due, from the offerings by fire to the LORD; for so I am commanded. ¹⁴But the breast that is elevated and the thigh that is raised, you and your sons and daughters as well may eat in any clean place; for they have been assigned to you and your children from the sacrifices of the offerings of well-being of the people of Israel. ¹⁵The thigh that is raised and the breast that is elevated they shall bring, together with the offerings by fire of the fat, to raise for an elevation offering before the LORD; they are to be your due and that of your children forever, as the LORD has commanded.

10.1–15. 1: A *censer* is a container for burning incense. Nadab and Abihu somehow defied the rules when they offered *unholy fire before the LORD*. The coals may not have been properly prepared or were taken from the altar of another god. See Num 16.36–40. **3:** *Aaron was silent.* In other words, Aaron refrained from the normal cries and lament* of mourning because this was prohibited for the high priest and priests sprinkled with anointing* oil (21.10–12). **6–7:** Moses' prohibition to Aaron and his remaining sons not to *dishevel your hair* or *tear your vestments* is a command not to carry out the normal customs of mourning the death of a family member. Coming near or in contact with a corpse rendered a person ritually unclean or impure for seven days (Num 19.11). Such ritual uncleanness would defile any sacrifices that the priests would perform during the period of seven days. Thus, priests were not allowed to attend a funeral or come near a corpse except that of a close family member (21.1–3). However, the high priest (Aaron) or priests sprinkled with oil (Aaron's other sons, Eleazar and Ithamar) were not even permitted to mourn close family members such as a son or brother as here (21.10–12). **10:** Teaching the distinctions between the *holy and the common* and the *unclean and the clean* involves teaching the subject matter of chs. 11–15.

16 Then Moses made inquiry about the goat of the sin offering, and—it had already been burned! He was angry with Eleazar and Ithamar, Aaron's remaining sons, and said, ¹⁷"Why did you not eat the sin offering in

Ritual Purity and Cleanness

The concern for ritual purity or cleanness was an important aspect of ancient Israelite society that may be unfamiliar to many in our own culture. Purity in ancient Israel meant being free from any physical, moral, or ritual contamination. Impurity or uncleanness came about through such things as contact with a corpse, the involuntary flow of bodily fluids (for example, blood or semen), certain skin diseases (often translated incorrectly in some English versions as "leprosy"), or the eating of prohibited foods. Becoming impure or unclean from various causes was a common occurrence for most people (attending a funeral, unintentionally eating unclean food, menstruation). Thus, rituals of purification were readily available to make oneself clean again. Impurity was not sin and could always be removed through various ritual washings, the passage of time, or specified offerings.

The purity laws functioned as part of a social symbol system that identified certain natural boundaries in order to protect the society from destructive or dangerous powers. When something or someone crossed over or confused these boundaries, the result was uncleanness. For example, unclean animals were those that in some way mixed or crossed over perceived boundaries. Certain sea creatures were unclean because they lacked the fins and scales usually associated with fish who lived in the sea. These unclean sea creatures (for example, clams) did not fit within the boundaries of typical sea animals. The most powerful or dangerous purity boundary was the one between life and death. Purity regulations touched on such matters as food, sex and marriage, family relationships, business practices, physical anomalies, and abhorrent worship practices of other gods by other nations. No single principle or concept can explain all the aspects of the purity laws. However, these laws preserve certain boundaries of holiness and separation within the community of God's people, which is holy or sacred by virtue of God's presence in its midst (26.11–13).

the sacred area? For it is most holy, and God[a] has given it to you that you may remove the guilt of the congregation, to make atonement on their behalf before the LORD. [18]Its blood was not brought into the inner part of the sanctuary. You should certainly have eaten it in the sanctuary, as I commanded." [19]And Aaron spoke to Moses, "See, today they offered their sin offering and their burnt offering before the LORD; and yet such things as these have befallen me! If I had eaten the sin offering today, would it have been agreeable to the LORD?" [20]And when Moses heard that, he agreed.

10.16–20: Moses *was angry* with Aaron's two sons, Eleazar and Ithamar, because they *did not eat the sin offering in the sacred area* (vv. 16–17). Normally, the priests were required to eat the meat of the sin offering

rather than burn it on the altar (6.24–26). In this case, however, Aaron's sons burned the flesh of the goat (the sin offering) rather than eat it. The reason may be that earlier the sacrifice had been defiled by the sin and death of their brothers (vv. 1–2). This reasoning seems implied in Aaron's response to Moses (v. 19), which Moses then accepts (v. 20). The case provides a model for negotiation among conflicting laws and requirements in special circumstances.

Laws regarding purity
11.1–15.33 This section of laws deals with matters of purity and the distinction between clean and unclean. The laws specify four primary sources of uncleanness: animal carcasses (ch. 11), childbirth (ch. 12), skin diseases (chs. 13–14), and genital discharges such as semen or menstrual blood (ch. 15). The fifth and most

a Heb *he*

powerful source of impurity is the human corpse, which is discussed in the laws in Num 19. Ancient Israelites understood many of these sources of impurity to derive from crossing the dangerous and powerful boundary between life and death. (See sidebar, p. 182.)

11 The LORD spoke to Moses and Aaron, saying to them: 2 Speak to the people of Israel, saying:

From among all the land animals, these are the creatures that you may eat. 3 Any animal that has divided hoofs and is cleft-footed and chews the cud—such you may eat. 4 But among those that chew the cud or have divided hoofs, you shall not eat the following: the camel, for even though it chews the cud, it does not have divided hoofs; it is unclean for you. 5 The rock badger, for even though it chews the cud, it does not have divided hoofs; it is unclean for you. 6 The hare, for even though it chews the cud, it does not have divided hoofs; it is unclean for you. 7 The pig, for even though it has divided hoofs and is cleft-footed, it does not chew the cud; it is unclean for you. 8 Of their flesh you shall not eat, and their carcasses you shall not touch; they are unclean for you.

9 These you may eat, of all that are in the waters. Everything in the waters that has fins and scales, whether in the seas or in the streams—such you may eat. 10 But anything in the seas or the streams that does not have fins and scales, of the swarming creatures in the waters and among all the other living creatures that are in the waters—they are detestable to you 11 and detestable they shall remain. Of their flesh you shall not eat, and their carcasses you shall regard as detestable. 12 Everything in the waters that does not have fins and scales is detestable to you.

13 These you shall regard as detestable among the birds. They shall not be eaten; they are an abomination: the eagle, the vulture, the osprey, 14 the buzzard, the kite of any kind; 15 every raven of any kind; 16 the ostrich, the nighthawk, the sea gull, the hawk of any kind; 17 the little owl, the cormorant, the great owl, 18 the water hen, the desert owl,*a* the carrion vulture, 19 the stork, the heron of any kind, the hoopoe, and the bat.*b*

20 All winged insects that walk upon all fours are detestable to you. 21 But among the winged insects that walk on all fours you may eat those that have jointed legs above their feet, with which to leap on the ground. 22 Of them you may eat: the locust according to its kind, the bald locust according to its kind, the cricket according to its kind, and the grasshopper according to its kind. 23 But all other winged insects that have four feet are detestable to you.

24 By these you shall become unclean; whoever touches the carcass of any of them shall be unclean until the evening, 25 and whoever carries any part of the carcass of any of them shall wash his clothes and be unclean until the evening. 26 Every animal that has divided hoofs but is not cleft-footed or does not chew the cud is unclean for you; everyone who touches one of them shall be unclean. 27 All that walk on their paws, among the animals that walk on all fours, are unclean for you; whoever touches the carcass of any of them shall be unclean until the evening, 28 and the one who carries the carcass shall wash his clothes and be unclean until the evening; they are unclean for you.

29 These are unclean for you among the creatures that swarm upon the earth: the weasel, the mouse, the great lizard according to its kind, 30 the gecko, the land crocodile, the lizard, the sand lizard, and the chameleon. 31 These are unclean for you among all that swarm; whoever touches one of them when they are dead shall be unclean until the evening. 32 And anything upon which any of them falls when they are dead shall be unclean, whether an article of wood or cloth or skin or sacking, any article that is used for any purpose; it shall be dipped into water, and it shall be unclean until the evening, and then it shall be clean. 33 And if any of them falls into any earthen vessel, all that is in it shall be unclean, and you shall break the vessel. 34 Any food that could be eaten shall be unclean if water from any such vessel comes upon it; and any liquid that could be drunk

a Or *pelican*   *b* Identification of several of the birds in verses 13–19 is uncertain shall be unclean if it was in any such vessel. [35]Everything on which any part of the carcass falls shall be unclean; whether an oven or stove, it shall be broken in pieces; they are unclean, and shall remain unclean for you. [36]But a spring or a cistern holding water shall be clean, while whatever touches the carcass in it shall be unclean. [37]If any part of their carcass falls upon any seed set aside for sowing, it is clean; [38]but if water is put on the seed and any part of their carcass falls on it, it is unclean for you.

39 If an animal of which you may eat dies, anyone who touches its carcass shall be unclean until the evening. [40]Those who eat of its carcass shall wash their clothes and be unclean until the evening; and those who carry the carcass shall wash their clothes and be unclean until the evening.

41 All creatures that swarm upon the earth are detestable; they shall not be eaten. [42]Whatever moves on its belly, and whatever moves on all fours, or whatever has many feet, all the creatures that swarm upon the earth, you shall not eat; for they are detestable. [43]You shall not make yourselves detestable with any creature that swarms; you shall not defile yourselves with them, and so become unclean. [44]For I am the LORD your God; sanctify yourselves therefore, and be holy, for I am holy. You shall not defile yourselves with any swarming creature that moves on the earth. [45]For I am the LORD who brought you up from the land of Egypt, to be your God; you shall be holy, for I am holy.

46 This is the law pertaining to land animal and bird and every living creature that moves through the waters and every creature that swarms upon the earth, [47]to make a distinction between the unclean and the clean, and between the living creature that may be eaten and the living creature that may not be eaten.

11.1–47: The LORD gives instructions to Moses and Aaron regarding clean and unclean foods. 7: The biblical tradition came to consider the pig as a particularly unclean animal, associated with rituals of other gods (Isa 65.4; 66.17). 24–25: Ritual uncleanness in matters of food could be removed by bathing the body, washing the clothes, and waiting the required amount of time (*until the evening*). 32–38: Objects as well as animals and people can be rendered unclean by touching what is unclean. Thus, an earthenware pot (v. 33) or earthenware stove (v. 35) must be broken into pieces and never used again if it becomes ritually contaminated. Unlike metal, impurity cannot be removed from clay or earthenware objects.

---

12 The LORD spoke to Moses, saying: [2]Speak to the people of Israel, saying:

If a woman conceives and bears a male child, she shall be ceremonially unclean seven days; as at the time of her menstruation, she shall be unclean. [3]On the eighth day the flesh of his foreskin shall be circumcised. [4]Her time of blood purification shall be thirty-three days; she shall not touch any holy thing, or come into the sanctuary, until the days of her purification are completed. [5]If she bears a female child, she shall be unclean two weeks, as in her menstruation; her time of blood purification shall be sixty-six days.

6 When the days of her purification are completed, whether for a son or for a daughter, she shall bring to the priest at the entrance of the tent of meeting a lamb in its first year for a burnt offering, and a pigeon or a turtledove for a sin offering. [7]He shall offer it before the LORD, and make atonement on her behalf; then she shall be clean from her flow of blood. This is the law for her who bears a child, male or female. [8]If she cannot afford a sheep, she shall take two turtledoves or two pigeons, one for a burnt offering and the other for a sin offering; and the priest shall make atonement on her behalf, and she shall be clean.

12.1–8: The LORD issues laws concerning the purification of women after childbirth. 2: That the woman is *ceremonially unclean* after childbirth does not imply any moral evil or sin. It is the flow of blood associated with childbirth and the dangerous mixture of life (the birth of a child) and death (the flow of blood) that renders the mother ritually unclean for the specified time period. 6: The *sin offering* is more properly a purification offering since the woman has committed no sin. The birth of a child is a blessing in ancient Israel, but it involves crossing boundaries of life and death and thus creates a condition of ceremonial uncleanness.

Skin diseases

13.1–59: The LORD mandates procedures for dealing with the ritual impurity associated with various skin diseases. The withering and discoloration of human skin often accompanies the process of death. Thus, any skin disease on a living person whose symptoms resemble what happens to a person's skin in death mixes or confuses the boundaries of life and death. Such mixtures or confusions render that person ritually impure. The priest's role in such cases is to determine whether a given skin condition is sufficiently severe to render a person unclean for a shorter or longer time.

13.2–4. 2: The phrase *leprous disease* should be understood not as the particular disease of leprosy but as a variety of skin diseases that are severe enough to render a person ritually impure. This is true of the phrase as it is used throughout the chapter. **4:** Confining the diseased person involves a concern that the person not contaminate another person with ritual impurity. The priest is not a medical doctor, so the process of isolation is for ritual reasons, not medical.

13 The LORD spoke to Moses and Aaron, saying:

2 When a person has on the skin of his body a swelling or an eruption or a spot, and it turns into a leprous[a] disease on the skin of his body, he shall be brought to Aaron the priest or to one of his sons the priests. ³The priest shall examine the disease on the skin of his body, and if the hair in the diseased area has turned white and the disease appears to be deeper than the skin of his body, it is a leprous[a] disease; after the priest has examined him he shall pronounce him ceremonially unclean. ⁴But if the spot is white in the skin of his body, and appears no deeper than the skin, and the hair in it has not turned white, the priest shall confine the diseased person for seven days. ⁵The priest shall examine him on the seventh day, and if he sees that the disease is checked and the disease has not spread in the skin, then the priest shall confine him seven days more. ⁶The priest shall examine him again on the seventh day, and if the disease has abated and the disease has not spread in the skin, the priest shall pronounce him clean; it is only an eruption; and he shall wash his clothes, and be clean. ⁷But if the eruption spreads in the skin after he has shown himself to the priest for his cleansing, he shall appear again before the priest. ⁸The priest shall make an examination, and if the eruption has spread in the skin, the priest shall pronounce him unclean; it is a leprous[a] disease.

9 When a person contracts a leprous[a] disease, he shall be brought to the priest. ¹⁰The priest shall make an examination, and if there is a white swelling in the skin that has turned the hair white, and there is quick raw flesh in the swelling, ¹¹it is a chronic leprous[a] disease in the skin of his body. The priest shall pronounce him unclean; he shall not confine him, for he is unclean. ¹²But if the disease breaks out in the skin, so that it covers all the skin of the diseased person from head to foot, so far as the priest can see, ¹³then the priest shall make an examination, and if the disease has covered all his body, he shall pronounce him clean of the disease; since it has all turned white, he is clean. ¹⁴But if raw flesh ever appears on him, he shall be unclean; ¹⁵the priest shall examine the raw flesh and pronounce him unclean. Raw flesh is unclean, for it is a leprous[a] disease. ¹⁶But if the raw flesh again turns white, he shall come to the priest; ¹⁷the priest shall examine him, and if the disease has turned white, the priest shall pronounce the diseased person clean. He is clean.

18 When there is on the skin of one's body a boil that has healed, ¹⁹and in the place of the boil there appears a white swelling or a reddish-white spot, it shall be shown to the priest. ²⁰The priest shall make an examination, and if it appears deeper than the skin and its hair has turned white, the priest shall pronounce him unclean; this is a leprous[a] disease, broken out in the boil. ²¹But if the priest examines it and the hair on it is not white, nor is it deeper than the skin but has abated, the priest shall confine him

a A term for several skin diseases; precise meaning uncertain

seven days. 22 If it spreads in the skin, the priest shall pronounce him unclean; it is diseased. 23 But if the spot remains in one place and does not spread, it is the scar of the boil; the priest shall pronounce him clean.

24 Or, when the body has a burn on the skin and the raw flesh of the burn becomes a spot, reddish-white or white, 25 the priest shall examine it. If the hair in the spot has turned white and it appears deeper than the skin, it is a leprous*a* disease; it has broken out in the burn, and the priest shall pronounce him unclean. This is a leprous*a* disease. 26 But if the priest examines it and the hair in the spot is not white, and it is no deeper than the skin but has abated, the priest shall confine him seven days. 27 The priest shall examine him the seventh day; if it is spreading in the skin, the priest shall pronounce him unclean. This is a leprous*a* disease. 28 But if the spot remains in one place and does not spread in the skin but has abated, it is a swelling from the burn, and the priest shall pronounce him clean; for it is the scar of the burn.

29 When a man or woman has a disease on the head or in the beard, 30 the priest shall examine the disease. If it appears deeper than the skin and the hair in it is yellow and thin, the priest shall pronounce him unclean; it is an itch, a leprous*a* disease of the head or the beard. 31 If the priest examines the itching disease, and it appears no deeper than the skin and there is no black hair in it, the priest shall confine the person with the itching disease for seven days. 32 On the seventh day the priest shall examine the itch; if the itch has not spread, and there is no yellow hair in it, and the itch appears to be no deeper than the skin, 33 he shall shave, but the itch he shall not shave. The priest shall confine the person with the itch for seven days more. 34 On the seventh day the priest shall examine the itch; if the itch has not spread in the skin and it appears to be no deeper than the skin, the priest shall pronounce him clean. He shall wash his clothes and be clean. 35 But if the itch spreads in the skin after he was pronounced clean, 36 the priest shall examine him. If the itch has spread in the skin, the priest need not seek

for the yellow hair; he is unclean. 37 But if in his eyes the itch is checked, and black hair has grown in it, the itch is healed, he is clean; and the priest shall pronounce him clean.

38 When a man or a woman has spots on the skin of the body, white spots, 39 the priest shall make an examination, and if the spots on the skin of the body are of a dull white, it is a rash that has broken out on the skin; he is clean.

40 If anyone loses the hair from his head, he is bald but he is clean. 41 If he loses the hair from his forehead and temples, he has baldness of the forehead but he is clean. 42 But if there is on the bald head or the bald forehead a reddish-white diseased spot, it is a leprous*a* disease breaking out on his bald head or his bald forehead. 43 The priest shall examine him; if the diseased swelling is reddish-white on his bald head or on his bald forehead, which resembles a leprous*a* disease in the skin of the body, 44 he is leprous,*a* he is unclean. The priest shall pronounce him unclean; the disease is on his head.

45 The person who has the leprous*a* disease shall wear torn clothes and let the hair of his head be disheveled; and he shall cover his upper lip and cry out, "Unclean, unclean." 46 He shall remain unclean as long as he has the disease; he is unclean. He shall live alone; his dwelling shall be outside the camp.

47 Concerning clothing: when a leprous*a* disease appears in it, in woolen or linen cloth, 48 in warp or woof of linen or wool, or in a skin or in anything made of skin, 49 if the disease shows greenish or reddish in the garment, whether in warp or woof or in skin or in anything made of skin, it is a leprous*a* disease and shall be shown to the priest. 50 The priest shall examine the disease, and put the diseased article aside for seven days. 51 He shall examine the disease on the seventh day. If the disease has spread in the cloth, in warp or woof, or in the skin, whatever be the use of the skin, this is a spreading leprous*a* disease; it is unclean. 52 He shall burn the cloth-

a A term for several skin diseases; precise meaning uncertain

ing, whether diseased in warp or woof, woolen or linen, or anything of skin, for it is a spreading leprous*a* disease; it shall be burned in fire.

53 If the priest makes an examination, and the disease has not spread in the clothing, in warp or woof or in anything of skin, 54the priest shall command them to wash the article in which the disease appears, and he shall put it aside seven days more. 55The priest shall examine the diseased article after it has been washed. If the diseased spot has not changed color, though the disease has not spread, it is unclean; you shall burn it in fire, whether the leprous*a* spot is on the inside or on the outside.

56 If the priest makes an examination, and the disease has abated after it is washed, he shall tear the spot out of the cloth, in warp or woof, or out of skin. 57If it appears again in the garment, in warp or woof, or in anything of skin, it is spreading; you shall burn with fire that in which the disease appears. 58But the cloth, warp or woof, or anything of skin from which the disease disappears when you have washed it, shall then be washed a second time, and it shall be clean. 59 This is the ritual for a leprous*a* disease in a cloth of wool or linen, either in warp or woof, or in anything of skin, to decide whether it is clean or unclean.

Three purification rituals
14.1–57: The LORD specifies three purification rituals that allow a person healed of skin disease to resume life within the community. The process of progressive reintegration into the society involves one purification ritual on the first day (vv. 2–8), a second ritual on the seventh day (v. 9), and a third ritual on the eighth day (vv. 10–32).

14 The LORD spoke to Moses, saying: 2This shall be the ritual for the leprous*a* person at the time of his cleansing:

He shall be brought to the priest; 3the priest shall go out of the camp, and the priest shall make an examination. If the disease is healed in the leprous*a* person, 4the priest shall command that two living clean birds and cedarwood and crimson yarn and hyssop be brought for the one who is to be cleansed.

5The priest shall command that one of the birds be slaughtered over fresh water in an earthen vessel. 6He shall take the living bird with the cedarwood and the crimson yarn and the hyssop, and dip them and the living bird in the blood of the bird that was slaughtered over the fresh water. 7He shall sprinkle it seven times upon the one who is to be cleansed of the leprous*a* disease; then he shall pronounce him clean, and he shall let the living bird go into the open field. 8The one who is to be cleansed shall wash his clothes, and shave off all his hair, and bathe himself in water, and he shall be clean. After that he shall come into the camp, but shall live outside his tent seven days. 9On the seventh day he shall shave all his hair: of head, beard, eyebrows; he shall shave all his hair. Then he shall wash his clothes, and bathe his body in water, and he shall be clean.

14.1–9. 4: The function of the *cedarwood and crimson yarn* is not clear. Their reddish color may be associated with the color of blood, which is considered a purifying agent. *Hyssop*★ is an aromatic plant associated with rituals of purification. In Ex 12.22, hyssop was the plant used to apply blood on the doorposts during the Passover★ in order to protect the Israelites from death (see also Num 19.6). **6–8:** The *living bird* that is dipped in the blood of another bird and then set free carries away enough of the healed person's uncleanness to allow him or her to *come into the camp* but not yet into *his tent*. **9:** The second round of shaving and bathing on the seventh day allows the person to rejoin his or her family in the tent.

10 On the eighth day he shall take two male lambs without blemish, and one ewe lamb in its first year without blemish, and a grain offering of three-tenths of an ephah of choice flour mixed with oil, and one log*b* of oil. 11The priest who cleanses shall set the person to be cleansed, along with these things, before the LORD, at the entrance of the tent of meeting. 12The priest shall take one of the lambs, and offer it as a guilt offering, along with the log*b* of oil, and raise them as an elevation offering before the

a A term for several skin diseases; precise meaning uncertain *b* A liquid measure

LORD. [13]He shall slaughter the lamb in the place where the sin offering and the burnt offering are slaughtered in the holy place; for the guilt offering, like the sin offering, belongs to the priest: it is most holy. [14]The priest shall take some of the blood of the guilt offering and put it on the lobe of the right ear of the one to be cleansed, and on the thumb of the right hand, and on the big toe of the right foot. [15]The priest shall take some of the log[a] of oil and pour it into the palm of his own left hand, [16]and dip his right finger in the oil that is in his left hand and sprinkle some oil with his finger seven times before the LORD. [17]Some of the oil that remains in his hand the priest shall put on the lobe of the right ear of the one to be cleansed, and on the thumb of the right hand, and on the big toe of the right foot, on top of the blood of the guilt offering. [18]The rest of the oil that is in the priest's hand he shall put on the head of the one to be cleansed. Then the priest shall make atonement on his behalf before the LORD: [19]the priest shall offer the sin offering, to make atonement for the one to be cleansed from his uncleanness. Afterward he shall slaughter the burnt offering; [20]and the priest shall offer the burnt offering and the grain offering on the altar. Thus the priest shall make atonement on his behalf and he shall be clean.

[21] But if he is poor and cannot afford so much, he shall take one male lamb for a guilt offering to be elevated, to make atonement on his behalf, and one-tenth of an ephah of choice flour mixed with oil for a grain offering and a log[a] of oil; [22]also two turtledoves or two pigeons, such as he can afford, one for a sin offering and the other for a burnt offering. [23]On the eighth day he shall bring them for his cleansing to the priest, to the entrance of the tent of meeting, before the LORD; [24]and the priest shall take the lamb of the guilt offering and the log[a] of oil, and the priest shall raise them as an elevation offering before the LORD. [25]The priest shall slaughter the lamb of the guilt offering and shall take some of the blood of the guilt offering, and put it on the lobe of the right ear of the one to be cleansed, and on the thumb

of the right hand, and on the big toe of the right foot. [26]The priest shall pour some of the oil into the palm of his own left hand, [27]and shall sprinkle with his right finger some of the oil that is in his left hand seven times before the LORD. [28]The priest shall put some of the oil that is in his hand on the lobe of the right ear of the one to be cleansed, and on the thumb of the right hand, and the big toe of the right foot, where the blood of the guilt offering was placed. [29]The rest of the oil that is in the priest's hand he shall put on the head of the one to be cleansed, to make atonement on his behalf before the LORD. [30]And he shall offer, of the turtledoves or pigeons such as he can afford, [31]one[b] for a sin offering and the other for a burnt offering, along with a grain offering; and the priest shall make atonement before the LORD on behalf of the one being cleansed. [32]This is the ritual for the one who has a leprous[c] disease, who cannot afford the offerings for his cleansing.

[33] The LORD spoke to Moses and Aaron, saying: [34] When you come into the land of Canaan, which I give you for a possession, and I put a leprous[c] disease in a house in the land of your possession, [35]the owner of the house shall come and tell the priest, saying, "There seems to me to be some sort of disease in my house." [36]The priest shall command that they empty the house before the priest goes to examine the disease, or all that is in the house will become unclean; and afterward the priest shall go in to inspect the house. [37]He shall examine the disease; if the disease is in the walls of the house with greenish or reddish spots, and if it appears to be deeper than the surface, [38]the priest shall go outside to the door of the house and shut up the house seven days. [39]The priest shall come again on the seventh day and make an inspection; if the disease has spread in the walls of the house, [40]the priest shall command that the stones in which the disease appears be taken out and thrown into an unclean place outside the city. [41]He shall have

a A liquid measure   b Gk Syr: Heb afford, [31]such as he can afford, one   c A term for several skin diseases; precise meaning uncertain the inside of the house scraped thoroughly, and the plaster that is scraped off shall be dumped in an unclean place outside the city. 42They shall take other stones and put them in the place of those stones, and take other plaster and plaster the house.

43 If the disease breaks out again in the house, after he has taken out the stones and scraped the house and plastered it, 44the priest shall go and make inspection; if the disease has spread in the house, it is a spreading leprous^a disease in the house; it is unclean. 45He shall have the house torn down, its stones and timber and all the plaster of the house, and taken outside the city to an unclean place. 46All who enter the house while it is shut up shall be unclean until the evening; 47and all who sleep in the house shall wash their clothes; and all who eat in the house shall wash their clothes.

48 If the priest comes and makes an inspection, and the disease has not spread in the house after the house was plastered, the priest shall pronounce the house clean; the disease is healed. 49For the cleansing of the house he shall take two birds, with cedarwood and crimson yarn and hyssop, 50and shall slaughter one of the birds over fresh water in an earthen vessel, 51and shall take the cedarwood and the hyssop and the crimson yarn, along with the living bird, and dip them in the blood of the slaughtered bird and the fresh water, and sprinkle the house seven times. 52Thus he shall cleanse the house with the blood of the bird, and with the fresh water, and with the living bird, and with the cedarwood and hyssop and crimson yarn; 53and he shall let the living bird go out of the city into the open field; so he shall make atonement for the house, and it shall be clean.

54 This is the ritual for any leprous^a disease: for an itch, 55for leprous^a diseases in clothing and houses, 56and for a swelling or an eruption or a spot, 57to determine when it is unclean and when it is clean. This is the ritual for leprous^a diseases.

holy object or worship space to become unclean and other unintentional offenses (see 5.1–19). The dabbing of blood (v. 14) and oil (vv. 17–18) on the extremities of the healed person (ear, thumb, big toe) cleanses the entire person (see the cleansing of the priest in 8.30). **33–53:** These instructions involve cleansing or restoring a house that has been infected by an unclean fungus or rot (v. 37). The contagion of an unclean house affects all persons who come under its roof (v. 46). The ritual for reinstating a *healed* house (vv. 48–53) is similar to the first step in reinstating a healed person to the community (vv. 2–8).

Eliminating the uncleanness of bodily discharges
15.1–33: The purity laws concerning bodily emissions treat two different situations: more serious genital emissions of fluid that are irregular or a sign of disease and thus require sacrifices for purification (vv. 2–15, 25–30), and less serious genital emissions that are natural and thus require only bathing for purification (vv. 19–24). Such genital emissions enter into the realm of purity concerns because the flow of blood and semen from the body represents the loss of life. On the other hand, the genitalia are associated with the procreation of life. This mixture of the powerful forces and boundaries of life and death creates impure or unclean conditions that require purification.

15 The LORD spoke to Moses and Aaron, saying: 2Speak to the people of Israel and say to them:

When any man has a discharge from his member,^b his discharge makes him ceremonially unclean. 3The uncleanness of his discharge is this: whether his member^b flows with his discharge, or his member^b is stopped from discharging, it is uncleanness for him. 4Every bed on which the one with the discharge lies shall be unclean; and everything on which he sits shall be unclean. 5Anyone who touches his bed shall wash his clothes, and bathe in water, and be unclean until the evening. 6All who sit on anything on which the one with the discharge has sat shall wash their clothes, and bathe in water, and be unclean until the evening. 7All who touch the body of the one with the discharge shall wash their clothes, and bathe in water,

---

14.10–57. 10–20: These offerings by the healed person on the eighth day are related to the offerings of restitution or repayment for inadvertently causing a

a A term for several skin diseases; precise meaning uncertain　*b* Heb *flesh* and be unclean until the evening. 8If the one with the discharge spits on persons who are clean, then they shall wash their clothes, and bathe in water, and be unclean until the evening. 9Any saddle on which the one with the discharge rides shall be unclean. 10All who touch anything that was under him shall be unclean until the evening, and all who carry such a thing shall wash their clothes, and bathe in water, and be unclean until the evening. 11All those whom the one with the discharge touches without his having rinsed his hands in water shall wash their clothes, and bathe in water, and be unclean until the evening. 12Any earthen vessel that the one with the discharge touches shall be broken; and every vessel of wood shall be rinsed in water.

13 When the one with a discharge is cleansed of his discharge, he shall count seven days for his cleansing; he shall wash his clothes and bathe his body in fresh water, and he shall be clean. 14On the eighth day he shall take two turtledoves or two pigeons and come before the LORD to the entrance of the tent of meeting and give them to the priest. 15The priest shall offer them, one for a sin offering and the other for a burnt offering; and the priest shall make atonement on his behalf before the LORD for his discharge.

16 If a man has an emission of semen, he shall bathe his whole body in water, and be unclean until the evening. 17Everything made of cloth or of skin on which the semen falls shall be washed with water, and be unclean until the evening. 18If a man lies with a woman and has an emission of semen, both of them shall bathe in water, and be unclean until the evening.

19 When a woman has a discharge of blood that is her regular discharge from her body, she shall be in her impurity for seven days, and whoever touches her shall be unclean until the evening. 20Everything upon which she lies during her impurity shall be unclean; everything also upon which she sits shall be unclean. 21Whoever touches her bed shall wash his clothes, and bathe in water, and be unclean until the evening. 22Whoever touches anything upon which she sits shall wash his clothes, and bathe in water, and be unclean until the evening; 23whether it is the bed or anything upon which she sits, when he touches it he shall be unclean until the evening. 24If any man lies with her, and her impurity falls on him, he shall be unclean seven days; and every bed on which he lies shall be unclean.

25 If a woman has a discharge of blood for many days, not at the time of her impurity, or if she has a discharge beyond the time of her impurity, all the days of the discharge she shall continue in uncleanness; as in the days of her impurity, she shall be unclean. 26Every bed on which she lies during all the days of her discharge shall be treated as the bed of her impurity; and everything on which she sits shall be unclean, as in the uncleanness of her impurity. 27Whoever touches these things shall be unclean, and shall wash his clothes, and bathe in water, and be unclean until the evening. 28If she is cleansed of her discharge, she shall count seven days, and after that she shall be clean. 29On the eighth day she shall take two turtledoves or two pigeons and bring them to the priest at the entrance of the tent of meeting. 30The priest shall offer one for a sin offering and the other for a burnt offering; and the priest shall make atonement on her behalf before the LORD for her unclean discharge.

31 Thus you shall keep the people of Israel separate from their uncleanness, so that they do not die in their uncleanness by defiling my tabernacle that is in their midst.

32 This is the ritual for those who have a discharge: for him who has an emission of semen, becoming unclean thereby, 33for her who is in the infirmity of her period, for anyone, male or female, who has a discharge, and for the man who lies with a woman who is unclean.

15.1–33. 16–18: The normal act of sexual intercourse and the emission of semen render both the man and the woman unclean with the minor purification of bathing and one day's time required. The Bible does not view sex as evil but as a gift from God (see Song of Solomon). However, sexual union involves powerful forces of life and thus is protected by rituals of purification. **31:** Concern for the holiness of the *tabernacle* is at the heart of these purity laws as well as other laws in Leviticus. The tabernacle is the ornate tent of worship that contains the seat of God's presence in the midst of Israel's wilderness camp (see 1.1). The issue is not so much to protect God but to protect the people from coming in contact with the holiness of God *so that they do not die in their uncleanness.*

Rituals for the Day of Atonement*
16.1–34: The function of this annual ritual is two-fold: First, the purification offerings purge the tabernacle* or place of worship from uncleanness (vv. 16–19); second, the priestly confession of sin, the setting free of the scapegoat, and the people's refraining from work and food purge the people from their sin (vv. 21–31). Atonement refers to the forgiveness or "covering over" of human sin and ritual impurity.

16 The LORD spoke to Moses after the death of the two sons of Aaron, when they drew near before the LORD and died. ²The LORD said to Moses:

Tell your brother Aaron not to come just at any time into the sanctuary inside the curtain before the mercy seat*" that is upon the ark, or he will die; for I appear in the cloud upon the mercy seat.*" ³Thus shall Aaron come into the holy place: with a young bull for a sin offering and a ram for a burnt offering. ⁴He shall put on the holy linen tunic, and shall have the linen undergarments next to his body, fasten the linen sash, and wear the linen turban; these are the holy vestments. He shall bathe his body in water, and then put them on. ⁵He shall take from the congregation of the people of Israel two male goats for a sin offering, and one ram for a burnt offering.

6 Aaron shall offer the bull as a sin offering for himself, and shall make atonement for himself and for his house. ⁷He shall take the two goats and set them before the LORD at the entrance of the tent of meeting; ⁸and Aaron shall cast lots on the two goats, one lot for the LORD and the other lot for Azazel.*ᵇ ⁹Aaron shall present the goat on which the lot fell for the LORD, and offer it as a sin offering; ¹⁰but the goat on which the lot fell for Azazel*ᵇ shall be presented alive before the LORD to make atonement over it, that it

may be sent away into the wilderness to Azazel.*ᵇ

11 Aaron shall present the bull as a sin offering for himself, and shall make atonement for himself and for his house; he shall slaughter the bull as a sin offering for himself. ¹²He shall take a censer full of coals of fire from the altar before the LORD, and two handfuls of crushed sweet incense, and he shall bring it inside the curtain ¹³and put the incense on the fire before the LORD, that the cloud of the incense may cover the mercy seat*" that is upon the covenant,*ᶜ or he will die. ¹⁴He shall take some of the blood of the bull, and sprinkle it with his finger on the front of the mercy seat,*" and before the mercy seat*" he shall sprinkle the blood with his finger seven times.

16.1–14. 1: The remembrance of the earlier story of the death of *the two sons of Aaron* in 10.1–7 emphasizes the danger of the priestly function of drawing near to God's presence on behalf of the people. The laws concerning purification that have intervened between the story in ch. 10 and the atonement ritual in ch. 16 define the varied conditions of uncleanness that the Day of Atonement may eliminate. **2:** The high priest is allowed to enter the inner sanctuary only at certain times, not *any* time. The instruction appended to the end of the chapter specifies "once in the year" (v. 34). On the *curtain, the mercy seat,* and *the ark,* see Ex 25.17–22; 26.31–35. **7–9:** The *two goats* bear the sins of the people. One goat is killed and sacrificed *as a sin offering* (v. 9). The second goat is kept alive and symbolically carries the sin of the people out of the camp and into the wilderness (v. 10; see vv. 21–22). *Azazel* was the name of a goat-demon who was thought to inhabit desolate places (17.7; Isa 34.14). Here the name simply designates a remote wilderness place to which the goat carries the sins and impurity of the community. **13:** This verse reflects biblical traditions that stipulate that any human who sees God will die (Ex 33.20). The cloud of smoke from the incense veils the deity and also placates the deity with the sweet aroma (1.9).

15 He shall slaughter the goat of the sin offering that is for the people and bring its blood inside the curtain, and do with its

a Or *the cover*   *b* Traditionally rendered *a scapegoat*
c Or *treaty,* or *testament;* Heb *eduth*

blood as he did with the blood of the bull, sprinkling it upon the mercy seat[a] and before the mercy seat.[a] 16Thus he shall make atonement for the sanctuary, because of the uncleannesses of the people of Israel, and because of their transgressions, all their sins; and so he shall do for the tent of meeting, which remains with them in the midst of their uncleannesses. 17No one shall be in the tent of meeting from the time he enters to make atonement in the sanctuary until he comes out and has made atonement for himself and for his house and for all the assembly of Israel. 18Then he shall go out to the altar that is before the LORD and make atonement on its behalf, and shall take some of the blood of the bull and of the blood of the goat, and put it on each of the horns of the altar. 19He shall sprinkle some of the blood on it with his finger seven times, and cleanse it and hallow it from the uncleannesses of the people of Israel.

20 When he has finished atoning for the holy place and the tent of meeting and the altar, he shall present the live goat. 21Then Aaron shall lay both his hands on the head of the live goat, and confess over it all the iniquities of the people of Israel, and all their transgressions, all their sins, putting them on the head of the goat, and sending it away into the wilderness by means of someone designated for the task.[b] 22The goat shall bear on itself all their iniquities to a barren region; and the goat shall be set free in the wilderness.

23 Then Aaron shall enter the tent of meeting, and shall take off the linen vestments that he put on when he went into the holy place, and shall leave them there. 24He shall bathe his body in water in a holy place, and put on his vestments; then he shall come out and offer his burnt offering and the burnt offering of the people, making atonement for himself and for the people. 25The fat of the sin offering he shall turn into smoke on the altar. 26The one who sets the goat free for Azazel[c] shall wash his clothes and bathe his body in water, and afterward may come into the camp. 27The bull of the sin offering and the goat of the sin offering, whose blood was brought in to make atone-

ment in the holy place, shall be taken outside the camp; their skin and their flesh and their dung shall be consumed in fire. 28The one who burns them shall wash his clothes and bathe his body in water, and afterward may come into the camp.

29 This shall be a statute to you forever: In the seventh month, on the tenth day of the month, you shall deny yourselves,[d] and shall do no work, neither the citizen nor the alien who resides among you. 30For on this day atonement shall be made for you, to cleanse you; from all your sins you shall be clean before the LORD. 31It is a sabbath of complete rest to you, and you shall deny yourselves;[d] it is a statute forever. 32The priest who is anointed and consecrated as priest in his father's place shall make atonement, wearing the linen vestments, the holy vestments. 33He shall make atonement for the sanctuary, and he shall make atonement for the tent of meeting and for the altar, and he shall make atonement for the priests and for all the people of the assembly. 34This shall be an everlasting statute for you, to make atonement for the people of Israel once in the year for all their sins. And Moses did as the LORD had commanded him.

16.15–34. 22: All the sin of the people is transferred to *the goat,* which carries their sins outside the camp and into *the wilderness.* 26: On *Azazel,* see comment on vv. 7–9. 30–31: The *day of atonement* is to be a *sabbath,* a day of rest when the people refrain from work (see Ex 20.8–11).

Laws regarding holiness
17.1–26.46: The section of laws in chs. 17–26 once formed an independent collection. These laws (especially chs. 19–23) focus on maintaining the holiness of the whole Israelite community and the holiness of the land of Canaan where they will live. The laws are often called the "Holiness Code." See sidebar, p. 195.

17 The LORD spoke to Moses: 2 Speak to Aaron and his sons and to all the people of Israel and say to them:

a Or *the cover*　　b Meaning of Heb uncertain
c Traditionally rendered *a scapegoat*　　d Or *shall fast*

This is what the LORD has commanded. ³If anyone of the house of Israel slaughters an ox or a lamb or a goat in the camp, or slaughters it outside the camp, ⁴and does not bring it to the entrance of the tent of meeting, to present it as an offering to the LORD before the tabernacle of the LORD, he shall be held guilty of bloodshed; he has shed blood, and he shall be cut off from the people. ⁵This is in order that the people of Israel may bring their sacrifices that they offer in the open field, that they may bring them to the LORD, to the priest at the entrance of the tent of meeting, and offer them as sacrifices of well-being to the LORD. ⁶The priest shall dash the blood against the altar of the LORD at the entrance of the tent of meeting, and turn the fat into smoke as a pleasing odor to the LORD, ⁷so that they may no longer offer their sacrifices for goat-demons, to whom they prostitute themselves. This shall be a statute forever to them throughout their generations.

8 And say to them further: Anyone of the house of Israel or of the aliens who reside among them who offers a burnt offering or sacrifice, ⁹and does not bring it to the entrance of the tent of meeting, to sacrifice it to the LORD, shall be cut off from the people.

10 If anyone of the house of Israel or of the aliens who reside among them eats any blood, I will set my face against that person who eats blood, and will cut that person off from the people. ¹¹For the life of the flesh is in the blood; and I have given it to you for making atonement for your lives on the altar; for, as life, it is the blood that makes atonement. ¹²Therefore I have said to the people of Israel: No person among you shall eat blood, nor shall any alien who resides among you eat blood. ¹³And anyone of the people of Israel, or of the aliens who reside among them, who hunts down an animal or bird that may be eaten shall pour out its blood and cover it with earth.

14 For the life of every creature—its blood is its life; therefore I have said to the people of Israel: You shall not eat the blood of any creature, for the life of every creature is its blood; whoever eats it shall be cut off. ¹⁵All persons, citizens or aliens, who eat what dies of itself or what has been torn by wild animals, shall wash their clothes, and bathe themselves in water, and be unclean until the evening; then they shall be clean. ¹⁶But if they do not wash themselves or bathe their body, they shall bear their guilt.

17.1–16: The LORD issues instructions for slaughtering animals. 5: The implication is that all animal meat used for food must be first offered to the LORD as a sacrifice and then eaten. **7:** The reason for regulating animal slaughter is to prevent sacrifices from being offered to *goat-demons.* The word for *goat-demon* is the same as the word "Azazel" used elsewhere (16.26; Isa 34.14). To *prostitute themselves* is a metaphor* for the worship of other gods or idols (20.5). **11:** On *the blood* and *atonement,** see comments on 1.4 and 1.5.

18 The LORD spoke to Moses, saying: 2 Speak to the people of Israel and say to them: I am the LORD your God. ³You shall not do as they do in the land of Egypt, where you lived, and you shall not do as they do in the land of Canaan, to which I am bringing you. You shall not follow their statutes. ⁴My ordinances you shall observe and my statutes you shall keep, following them: I am the LORD your God. ⁵You shall keep my statutes and my ordinances; by doing so one shall live: I am the LORD.

6 None of you shall approach anyone near of kin to uncover nakedness: I am the LORD. ⁷You shall not uncover the nakedness of your father, which is the nakedness of your mother; she is your mother, you shall not uncover her nakedness. ⁸You shall not uncover the nakedness of your father's wife; it is the nakedness of your father. ⁹You shall not uncover the nakedness of your sister, your father's daughter or your mother's daughter, whether born at home or born abroad. ¹⁰You shall not uncover the nakedness of your son's daughter or of your daughter's daughter, for their nakedness is your own nakedness. ¹¹You shall not uncover the nakedness of your father's wife's daughter, begotten by your father, since she is your sister. ¹²You shall not uncover the nakedness of your father's sister; she is your father's flesh. ¹³You shall not uncover the nakedness of your mother's sister, for she is your

mother's flesh. ¹⁴You shall not uncover the nakedness of your father's brother, that is, you shall not approach his wife; she is your aunt. ¹⁵You shall not uncover the nakedness of your daughter-in-law: she is your son's wife; you shall not uncover her nakedness. ¹⁶You shall not uncover the nakedness of your brother's wife; it is your brother's nakedness. ¹⁷You shall not uncover the nakedness of a woman and her daughter, and you shall not take*ᵃ* her son's daughter or her daughter's daughter to uncover her nakedness; they are your*ᵇ* flesh; it is depravity. ¹⁸And you shall not take*ᵃ* a woman as a rival to her sister, uncovering her nakedness while her sister is still alive.

19 You shall not approach a woman to uncover her nakedness while she is in her menstrual uncleanness. ²⁰You shall not have sexual relations with your kinsman's wife, and defile yourself with her. ²¹You shall not give any of your offspring to sacrifice them*ᶜ* to Molech, and so profane the name of your God: I am the LORD. ²²You shall not lie with a male as with a woman; it is an abomination. ²³You shall not have sexual relations with any animal and defile yourself with it, nor shall any woman give herself to an animal to have sexual relations with it: it is perversion.

24 Do not defile yourselves in any of these ways, for by all these practices the nations I am casting out before you have defiled themselves. ²⁵Thus the land became defiled; and I punished it for its iniquity, and the land vomited out its inhabitants. ²⁶But you shall keep my statutes and my ordinances and commit none of these abominations, either the citizen or the alien who resides among you ²⁷(for the inhabitants of the land, who were before you, committed all of these abominations, and the land became defiled); ²⁸otherwise the land will vomit you out for defiling it, as it vomited out the nation that was before you. ²⁹For whoever commits any of these abominations shall be cut off from their people. ³⁰So keep my charge not to commit any of these abominations that were done before you, and not to defile yourselves by them: I am the LORD your God.

18.1–30: The LORD lays out prohibitions concerning sexual relations. 6: To *approach* and to *uncover nakedness* are euphemisms* for sexual intercourse. **9–18:** A number of earlier biblical characters violated some of these laws. Abraham married his half-sister (v. 11; Gen 20.12). Amram (the father of Moses) married Jochebed, who was the sister of Amram's father (v. 12; Ex 6.20). Judah married Tamar, his daughter-in-law (v. 15; Gen 38). Jacob married the two sisters, Rachel and Leah (v. 18; Gen 29.15–30). These violations, however, occurred before the laws of Leviticus came into force. Moreover, the custom of levirate marriage* in which the brother of a dead husband has an obligation to marry the dead man's widow in order to father children seems to be an exception to v. 16 (see Deut 25.5–10). **21:** *Molech* was the pagan deity of the nation of Ammon, which was located just east of Canaan. The Bible associates the rite of child sacrifice with the god Molech (2 Kings 23.10; Jer 32.35).

19 The LORD spoke to Moses, saying: 2 Speak to all the congregation of the people of Israel and say to them: You shall be holy, for I the LORD your God am holy. ³You shall each revere your mother and father, and you shall keep my sabbaths: I am the LORD your God. ⁴Do not turn to idols or make cast images for yourselves: I am the LORD your God.

5 When you offer a sacrifice of well-being to the LORD, offer it in such a way that it is acceptable in your behalf. ⁶It shall be eaten on the same day you offer it, or on the next day; and anything left over until the third day shall be consumed in fire. ⁷If it is eaten at all on the third day, it is an abomination; it will not be acceptable. ⁸All who eat it shall be subject to punishment, because they have profaned what is holy to the LORD; and any such person shall be cut off from the people.

9 When you reap the harvest of your land, you shall not reap to the very edges of your field, or gather the gleanings of your harvest. ¹⁰You shall not strip your vineyard bare, or gather the fallen grapes of your vineyard; you shall leave them for the poor and the alien: I am the LORD your God.

11 You shall not steal; you shall not deal

a Or *marry*   *b* Gk: Heb lacks *your*   *c* Heb *to pass them over*

■▬▬■

The Concept of Holiness

Holiness in Leviticus involves two dimensions. The first dimension is holiness as separation. The sacred is separate from the ordinary or common. The holiness of God as a divine being is separate and distinct from humanity. Circles of graduated holiness extend out from the center of Israel's community. The sanctuary in the middle is the holiest part of the Israelite camp because of its association with the presence of God. The priests are separate from the other members of the community because of their service to God and the worship life of the people. Moreover, Israel as God's holy people is distinct from other nations. These boundaries of separation between what is holy and not holy are related to the boundaries of purity and impurity in some of the other laws in Leviticus (ch. 11; see sidebar, "Ritual Purity and Cleanness," p. 182).

A second dimension of holiness in Leviticus is the more positive concept of holiness as a goal toward which Israel should strive. Leviticus is clearly aware of the threat presented by sinfulness and impurity (chs. 16, 26). However, it also holds up the holiness of God as a model to be imitated. "You shall be holy, for I the LORD your God am holy" (19.2). Such holiness is made concrete in specific moral and ethical commands and behaviors outlined in Lev 19. The most comprehensive of these commands is the injunction to love your neighbor (19.18) and to love the alien (19.34). Holiness is not so much an abstract quality or concept but more a set of actions and behaviors that arise out of Israel's unique relationship with a holy God.

■▬▬■

falsely; and you shall not lie to one another. ¹²And you shall not swear falsely by my name, profaning the name of your God: I am the LORD.

13 You shall not defraud your neighbor; you shall not steal; and you shall not keep for yourself the wages of a laborer until morning. ¹⁴You shall not revile the deaf or put a stumbling block before the blind; you shall fear your God: I am the LORD.

15 You shall not render an unjust judgment; you shall not be partial to the poor or defer to the great: with justice you shall judge your neighbor. ¹⁶You shall not go around as a slanderer[a] among your people, and you shall not profit by the blood[b] of your neighbor: I am the LORD.

17 You shall not hate in your heart anyone of your kin; you shall reprove your neighbor, or you will incur guilt yourself. ¹⁸You shall not take vengeance or bear a grudge against any of your people, but you shall love your neighbor as yourself: I am the LORD.

19 You shall keep my statutes. You shall not let your animals breed with a different kind; you shall not sow your field with two kinds of seed; nor shall you put on a garment made of two different materials.

20 If a man has sexual relations with a woman who is a slave, designated for another man but not ransomed or given her freedom, an inquiry shall be held. They shall not be put to death, since she has not been freed; ²¹but he shall bring a guilt offering for himself to the LORD, at the entrance of the tent of meeting, a ram as guilt offering. ²²And the priest shall make atonement for him with the ram of guilt offering before the LORD for his sin that he committed; and the sin he committed shall be forgiven him.

23 When you come into the land and plant all kinds of trees for food, then you shall regard their fruit as forbidden;[c] three years it shall be forbidden[d] to you, it must not be eaten. ²⁴In the fourth year all their fruit shall be set apart for rejoicing in the LORD. ²⁵But in the fifth year you may eat of

a Meaning of Heb uncertain   b Heb stand against the blood   c Heb as their uncircumcision
d Heb uncircumcision

their fruit, that their yield may be increased for you: I am the LORD your God.

26 You shall not eat anything with its blood. You shall not practice augury or witchcraft. ²⁷You shall not round off the hair on your temples or mar the edges of your beard. ²⁸You shall not make any gashes in your flesh for the dead or tattoo any marks upon you: I am the LORD.

29 Do not profane your daughter by making her a prostitute, that the land not become prostituted and full of depravity. ³⁰You shall keep my sabbaths and reverence my sanctuary: I am the LORD.

31 Do not turn to mediums or wizards; do not seek them out, to be defiled by them: I am the LORD your God.

32 You shall rise before the aged, and defer to the old; and you shall fear your God: I am the LORD.

33 When an alien resides with you in your land, you shall not oppress the alien. ³⁴The alien who resides with you shall be to you as the citizen among you; you shall love the alien as yourself, for you were aliens in the land of Egypt: I am the LORD your God.

35 You shall not cheat in measuring length, weight, or quantity. ³⁶You shall have honest balances, honest weights, an honest ephah, and an honest hin: I am the LORD your God, who brought you out of the land of Egypt. ³⁷You shall keep all my statutes and all my ordinances, and observe them: I am the LORD.

19.1–37: The LORD commands holiness in ethical and ritual spheres of life. 2: This verse supplies the central principle, *you shall be holy*, and its primary justification, *for I the LORD your God am holy*, which underlie all the laws that follow. On the concept of holiness, see sidebar on p. 195. **3:** The *sabbath* is the seventh day of every week. On the sabbath day, rest was commanded and work prohibited (Ex 20.8–11). **5:** On *the sacrifice of well-being*, see comment on 3.1–17. **18:** To *love your neighbor as yourself* is cited in Mk 12.31 as one of two laws that summarize all the commandments. The *neighbor* refers to a fellow Israelite. Verses 33–34 extend the same obligation of love to the resident alien.* *Love* in this context is less an emotion and more an action of kindness and fairness. **19:** The prohibition of mixing animal species, plant seeds,

or other materials is grounded in God's creation, which set up boundaries of separation between each species (Gen 1). Crossing such boundaries created dangerous situations of impurity, not unlike mixing forces of life and death. Holiness is closely connected to notions of separation and distinctiveness. See sidebar, " Ritual Purity and Cleanness," p. 182. **26:** *Augury or witchcraft* involve pagan rites used in consulting the dead spirits. An example is King Saul, who went to the witch of Endor in order to rouse the dead spirit of the prophet* Samuel (1 Sam 28.3–25). **27–28:** These are customs associated with mourning the dead in the pagan worship of other gods. **30:** On the *sabbath*, see comment on v. 3. **36:** The *ephah* and the *hin* were units of measure used in business transactions.

---

20 The LORD spoke to Moses, saying: ²Say further to the people of Israel:

Any of the people of Israel, or of the aliens who reside in Israel, who give any of their offspring to Molech shall be put to death; the people of the land shall stone them to death. ³I myself will set my face against them, and will cut them off from the people, because they have given of their offspring to Molech, defiling my sanctuary and profaning my holy name. ⁴And if the people of the land should ever close their eyes to them, when they give of their offspring to Molech, and do not put them to death, ⁵I myself will set my face against them and against their family, and will cut them off from among their people, them and all who follow them in prostituting themselves to Molech.

6 If any turn to mediums and wizards, prostituting themselves to them, I will set my face against them, and will cut them off from the people. ⁷Consecrate yourselves therefore, and be holy; for I am the LORD your God. ⁸Keep my statutes, and observe them; I am the LORD; I sanctify you. ⁹All who curse father or mother shall be put to death; having cursed father or mother, their blood is upon them.

10 If a man commits adultery with the wife of[a] his neighbor, both the adulterer and the adulteress shall be put to death. ¹¹The man who lies with his father's wife has uncovered his father's nakedness; both of them

---

a Heb repeats *if a man commits adultery with the wife of* shall be put to death; their blood is upon them. 12If a man lies with his daughter-in-law, both of them shall be put to death; they have committed perversion, their blood is upon them. 13If a man lies with a male as with a woman, both of them have committed an abomination; they shall be put to death; their blood is upon them. 14If a man takes a wife and her mother also, it is depravity; they shall be burned to death, both he and they, that there may be no depravity among you. 15If a man has sexual relations with an animal, he shall be put to death; and you shall kill the animal. 16If a woman approaches any animal and has sexual relations with it, you shall kill the woman and the animal; they shall be put to death, their blood is upon them.

17 If a man takes his sister, a daughter of his father or a daughter of his mother, and sees her nakedness, and she sees his nakedness, it is a disgrace, and they shall be cut off in the sight of their people; he has uncovered his sister's nakedness, he shall be subject to punishment. 18If a man lies with a woman having her sickness and uncovers her nakedness, he has laid bare her flow and she has laid bare her flow of blood; both of them shall be cut off from their people. 19You shall not uncover the nakedness of your mother's sister or of your father's sister, for that is to lay bare one's own flesh; they shall be subject to punishment. 20If a man lies with his uncle's wife, he has uncovered his uncle's nakedness; they shall be subject to punishment; they shall die childless. 21If a man takes his brother's wife, it is impurity; he has uncovered his brother's nakedness; they shall be childless.

22 You shall keep all my statutes and all my ordinances, and observe them, so that the land to which I bring you to settle in may not vomit you out. 23You shall not follow the practices of the nation that I am driving out before you. Because they did all these things, I abhorred them. 24But I have said to you: You shall inherit their land, and I will give it to you to possess, a land flowing with milk and honey. I am the LORD your God; I have separated you from the peoples. 25You shall therefore make a distinction between the clean animal and the unclean, and between the unclean bird and the clean; you shall not bring abomination on yourselves by animal or by bird or by anything with which the ground teems, which I have set apart for you to hold unclean. 26You shall be holy to me; for I the LORD am holy, and I have separated you from the other peoples to be mine.

27 A man or a woman who is a medium or a wizard shall be put to death; they shall be stoned to death, their blood is upon them.

20.1–27: The chapter largely repeats several laws from chs. 18–19 but adds specific penalties for violations of the laws. **2–5:** *Molech:* See comment on 18.21. **10–21:** The sexual transgressions listed here exhibit varying severity as indicated by the punishments specified: vv. 10–16, death; vv. 17–19, banishment from the community; and vv. 20–21, childlessness. **25:** Descriptions of which animals are clean or unclean appear in ch. 11. On the notions of *clean* and *unclean,* see sidebar," Ritual Purity and Cleanness," p. 182. **26:** The verse is another statement of the foundational principle of these holiness laws: *You shall be holy . . . for I the LORD am holy* (see 19.2).

The holiness of priests

21.1–22.33: The LORD offers guidelines to protect the holiness of priests and the holiness of the sacrifices they administer. The requirements of holiness are more stringent for priests than for lay persons.

---

21 The LORD said to Moses: Speak to the priests, the sons of Aaron, and say to them:

No one shall defile himself for a dead person among his relatives, 2except for his nearest kin: his mother, his father, his son, his daughter, his brother; 3likewise, for a virgin sister, close to him because she has had no husband, he may defile himself for her. 4But he shall not defile himself as a husband among his people and so profane himself. 5They shall not make bald spots upon their heads, or shave off the edges of their beards, or make any gashes in their flesh. 6They shall be holy to their God, and not profane the name of their God; for they offer the LORD's offerings by fire, the food of their God; therefore they shall be holy. 7They shall not marry a prostitute or a woman who has been defiled; neither shall they marry a woman divorced from her husband. For they are holy to their God, 8and you shall treat them as holy, since they offer the food of your God; they shall be holy to you, for I the LORD, I who sanctify you, am holy. 9When the daughter of a priest profanes herself through prostitution, she profanes her father; she shall be burned to death.

10 The priest who is exalted above his fellows, on whose head the anointing oil has been poured and who has been consecrated to wear the vestments, shall not dishevel his hair, nor tear his vestments. 11He shall not go where there is a dead body; he shall not defile himself even for his father or mother. 12He shall not go outside the sanctuary and thus profane the sanctuary of his God; for the consecration of the anointing oil of his God is upon him: I am the LORD. 13He shall marry only a woman who is a virgin. 14A widow, or a divorced woman, or a woman who has been defiled, a prostitute, these he shall not marry. He shall marry a virgin of his own kin, 15that he may not profane his offspring among his kin; for I am the LORD; I sanctify him.

21.1–11. 1–3: Contact with or proximity to a human corpse was considered the most severe source of impurity (Num 19). Thus, priests were prohibited from attending funerals for the dead except for close family members. 5: These disfigurements were associated with mourning rites in neighboring pagan religions (19.27–28). 7: *A woman who has been defiled* is one who has been involved in sexual activity outside the bonds of marriage (for example, a woman who has been raped). 10–11: See vv. 1–3.

16 The LORD spoke to Moses, saying: 17Speak to Aaron and say: No one of your offspring throughout their generations who has a blemish may approach to offer the food of his God. 18For no one who has a blemish shall draw near, one who is blind or lame, or one who has a mutilated face or a limb too long, 19or one who has a broken foot or a broken hand, 20or a hunchback, or a dwarf, or a man with a blemish in his eyes or an itching disease or scabs or crushed testicles.

21No descendant of Aaron the priest who has a blemish shall come near to offer the LORD's offerings by fire; since he has a blemish, he shall not come near to offer the food of his God. 22He may eat the food of his God, of the most holy as well as of the holy. 23But he shall not come near the curtain or approach the altar, because he has a blemish, that he may not profane my sanctuaries; for I am the LORD; I sanctify them. 24Thus Moses spoke to Aaron and to his sons and to all the people of Israel.

22 The LORD spoke to Moses, saying: 2Direct Aaron and his sons to deal carefully with the sacred donations of the people of Israel, which they dedicate to me, so that they may not profane my holy name; I am the LORD. 3Say to them: If anyone among all your offspring throughout your generations comes near the sacred donations, which the people of Israel dedicate to the LORD, while he is in a state of uncleanness, that person shall be cut off from my presence: I am the LORD. 4No one of Aaron's offspring who has a leprous[a] disease or suffers a discharge may eat of the sacred donations until he is clean. Whoever touches anything made unclean by a corpse or a man who has had an emission of semen, 5and whoever touches any swarming thing by which he may be made unclean or any human being by whom he may be made unclean—whatever his uncleanness may be— 6the person who touches any such shall be unclean until evening and shall not eat of the sacred donations unless he has washed his body in water. 7When the sun sets he shall be clean; and afterward he may eat of the sacred donations, for they are his food. 8That which died or was torn by wild animals he shall not eat, becoming unclean by it: I am the LORD. 9They shall keep my charge, so that they may not incur guilt and die in the sanctuary[b] for having profaned it: I am the LORD; I sanctify them.

10 No lay person shall eat of the sacred donations. No bound or hired servant of the priest shall eat of the sacred donations; 11but

a A term for several skin diseases; precise meaning uncertain b Vg: Heb *incur guilt for it and die in it* if a priest acquires anyone by purchase, the person may eat of them; and those that are born in his house may eat of his food. 12If a priest's daughter marries a layman, she shall not eat of the offering of the sacred donations; 13but if a priest's daughter is widowed or divorced, without offspring, and returns to her father's house, as in her youth, she may eat of her father's food. No lay person shall eat of it. 14If a man eats of the sacred donation unintentionally, he shall add one-fifth of its value to it, and give the sacred donation to the priest. 15No one shall profane the sacred donations of the people of Israel, which they offer to the LORD, 16causing them to bear guilt requiring a guilt offering, by eating their sacred donations: for I am the LORD; I sanctify them.

22.2–16: The *sacred donations* are the portions of the animal and grain sacrifices that the priest reserves for his own consumption. This is in accord with the laws in 2.3, 6.25–26, and 7.31–32.

17 The LORD spoke to Moses, saying: 18Speak to Aaron and his sons and all the people of Israel and say to them: When anyone of the house of Israel or of the aliens residing in Israel presents an offering, whether in payment of a vow or as a freewill offering that is offered to the LORD as a burnt offering, 19to be acceptable in your behalf it shall be a male without blemish, of the cattle or the sheep or the goats. 20You shall not offer anything that has a blemish, for it will not be acceptable in your behalf. 21 When anyone offers a sacrifice of well-being to the LORD, in fulfillment of a vow or as a freewill offering, from the herd or from the flock, to be acceptable it must be perfect; there shall be no blemish in it. 22Anything blind, or injured, or maimed, or having a discharge or an itch or scabs—these you shall not offer to the LORD or put any of them on the altar as offerings by fire to the LORD. 23An ox or a lamb that has a limb too long or too short you may present for a freewill offering; but it will not be accepted for a vow. 24Any animal that has its testicles bruised or crushed or torn or cut, you shall not offer to the LORD; such you shall not do

within your land, 25nor shall you accept any such animals from a foreigner to offer as food to your God; since they are mutilated, with a blemish in them, they shall not be accepted in your behalf.

26 The LORD spoke to Moses, saying: 27When an ox or a sheep or a goat is born, it shall remain seven days with its mother, and from the eighth day on it shall be acceptable as the LORD's offering by fire. 28But you shall not slaughter, from the herd or the flock, an animal with its young on the same day. 29When you sacrifice a thanksgiving offering to the LORD, you shall sacrifice it so that it may be acceptable in your behalf. 30It shall be eaten on the same day; you shall not leave any of it until morning: I am the LORD. 31 Thus you shall keep my commandments and observe them: I am the LORD. 32You shall not profane my holy name, that I may be sanctified among the people of Israel: I am the LORD; I sanctify you, 33I who brought you out of the land of Egypt to be your God: I am the LORD.

The yearly festivals

23.1–44: These laws apply to all Israelites, especially farmers, since they deal mainly with agricultural matters. Other biblical laws for festivals appear in Ex 23.14–17, 34.21–23, and Deut 16.

23 The LORD spoke to Moses, saying: 2Speak to the people of Israel and say to them: These are the appointed festivals of the LORD that you shall proclaim as holy convocations, my appointed festivals. 3 Six days shall work be done; but the seventh day is a sabbath of complete rest, a holy convocation; you shall do no work: it is a sabbath to the LORD throughout your settlements. 4 These are the appointed festivals of the LORD, the holy convocations, which you shall celebrate at the time appointed for them. 5In the first month, on the fourteenth day of the month, at twilight,*a* there shall be a passover offering to the LORD, 6and on the fifteenth day of the same month is the festival of unleavened bread to the LORD; seven

a Heb *between the two evenings*

days you shall eat unleavened bread. [7]On the first day you shall have a holy convocation; you shall not work at your occupations. [8]For seven days you shall present the LORD's offerings by fire; on the seventh day there shall be a holy convocation: you shall not work at your occupations.

23.1–8. 3: On the *sabbath* as a day of *rest,* see Ex 20.8–11. **5–8:** The festivals of Passover* and Unleavened Bread are commemorations of Israel's exodus out of Egypt (Ex 12–13). They were originally two different festivals, but they came to be connected and celebrated together (Deut 16.1–8).

---

9 The LORD spoke to Moses: [10]Speak to the people of Israel and say to them: When you enter the land that I am giving you and you reap its harvest, you shall bring the sheaf of the first fruits of your harvest to the priest. [11]He shall raise the sheaf before the LORD, that you may find acceptance; on the day after the sabbath the priest shall raise it. [12]On the day when you raise the sheaf, you shall offer a lamb a year old, without blemish, as a burnt offering to the LORD. [13]And the grain offering with it shall be two-tenths of an ephah of choice flour mixed with oil, an offering by fire of pleasing odor to the LORD; and the drink offering with it shall be of wine, one-fourth of a hin. [14]You shall eat no bread or parched grain or fresh ears until that very day, until you have brought the offering of your God: it is a statute forever throughout your generations in all your settlements.

15 And from the day after the sabbath, from the day on which you bring the sheaf of the elevation offering, you shall count off seven weeks; they shall be complete. [16]You shall count until the day after the seventh sabbath, fifty days; then you shall present an offering of new grain to the LORD. [17]You shall bring from your settlements two loaves of bread as an elevation offering, each made of two-tenths of an ephah; they shall be of choice flour, baked with leaven, as first fruits to the LORD. [18]You shall present with the bread seven lambs a year old without blemish, one young bull, and two rams; they shall be a burnt offering to the LORD, along with

their grain offering and their drink offerings, an offering by fire of pleasing odor to the LORD. [19]You shall also offer one male goat for a sin offering, and two male lambs a year old as a sacrifice of well-being. [20]The priest shall raise them with the bread of the first fruits as an elevation offering before the LORD, together with the two lambs; they shall be holy to the LORD for the priest. [21]On that same day you shall make proclamation; you shall hold a holy convocation; you shall not work at your occupations. This is a statute forever in all your settlements throughout your generations.

22 When you reap the harvest of your land, you shall not reap to the very edges of your field, or gather the gleanings of your harvest; you shall leave them for the poor and for the alien: I am the LORD your God.

23 The LORD spoke to Moses, saying: [24]Speak to the people of Israel, saying: In the seventh month, on the first day of the month, you shall observe a day of complete rest, a holy convocation commemorated with trumpet blasts. [25]You shall not work at your occupations; and you shall present the LORD's offering by fire.

26 The LORD spoke to Moses, saying: [27]Now, the tenth day of this seventh month is the day of atonement; it shall be a holy convocation for you: you shall deny yourselves[a] and present the LORD's offering by fire; [28]and you shall do no work during that entire day; for it is a day of atonement, to make atonement on your behalf before the LORD your God. [29]For anyone who does not practice self-denial[b] during that entire day shall be cut off from the people. [30]And anyone who does any work during that entire day, such a one I will destroy from the midst of the people. [31]You shall do no work: it is a statute forever throughout your generations in all your settlements. [32]It shall be to you a sabbath of complete rest, and you shall deny yourselves;[a] on the ninth day of the month at evening, from evening to evening you shall keep your sabbath.

33 The LORD spoke to Moses, saying: [34]Speak to the people of Israel, saying: On

a Or shall fast   b Or does not fast

the fifteenth day of this seventh month, and lasting seven days, there shall be the festival of booths *a* to the LORD. 35The first day shall be a holy convocation; you shall not work at your occupations. 36Seven days you shall present the LORD's offerings by fire; on the eighth day you shall observe a holy convocation and present the LORD's offerings by fire; it is a solemn assembly; you shall not work at your occupations.

37 These are the appointed festivals of the LORD, which you shall celebrate as times of holy convocation, for presenting to the LORD offerings by fire—burnt offerings and grain offerings, sacrifices and drink offerings, each on its proper day— 38apart from the sabbaths of the LORD, and apart from your gifts, and apart from all your votive offerings, and apart from all your freewill offerings, which you give to the LORD.

39 Now, the fifteenth day of the seventh month, when you have gathered in the produce of the land, you shall keep the festival of the LORD, lasting seven days; a complete rest on the first day, and a complete rest on the eighth day. 40On the first day you shall take the fruit of majestic *b* trees, branches of palm trees, boughs of leafy trees, and willows of the brook; and you shall rejoice before the LORD your God for seven days. 41You shall keep it as a festival to the LORD seven days in the year; you shall keep it in the seventh month as a statute forever throughout your generations. 42You shall live in booths for seven days; all that are citizens in Israel shall live in booths, 43so that your generations may know that I made the people of Israel live in booths when I brought them out of the land of Egypt: I am the LORD your God.

44 Thus Moses declared to the people of Israel the appointed festivals of the LORD.

23.9–44. 9–14: The offering of *first fruits* occurred at the beginning of the barley harvest in the spring of the year. **15–22:** The festival of *weeks* is celebrated *seven weeks* (v. 15) or *fifty days* (v. 16) after the festival of Unleavened Bread. The festival is also called "Pentecost"* (from a Greek word meaning "fifty"). The festival marks the harvest of *new grain* (v. 16), namely, wheat. **23–24:** The festival of trumpets observes the beginning of the new year in the old agricultural calendar.* *The seventh month* (v. 24) is in the autumn (September—October). **26–32:** Details for *the day of atonement** occur in ch. 16. **33–36:** *The festival of booths* or tabernacles* was a feast of thanksgiving during the autumn harvest. Additional provisions for this festival are given in vv. 39–43. The festival came to be associated with God's care of Israel in the wilderness journey from Egypt to the promised land (v. 43). **38:** On the *sabbath* as a day of rest, see Ex 20.8–11. Numbers 28–29 enumerates further details about the various *offerings by fire* (v. 37) to be given at each festival.

24 The LORD spoke to Moses, saying: 2Command the people of Israel to bring you pure oil of beaten olives for the lamp, that a light may be kept burning regularly. 3Aaron shall set it up in the tent of meeting, outside the curtain of the covenant,*c* to burn from evening to morning before the LORD regularly; it shall be a statute forever throughout your generations. 4He shall set up the lamps on the lampstand of pure gold *d* before the LORD regularly.

5 You shall take choice flour, and bake twelve loaves of it; two-tenths of an ephah shall be in each loaf. 6You shall place them in two rows, six in a row, on the table of pure gold.*e* 7You shall put pure frankincense with each row, to be a token offering for the bread, as an offering by fire to the LORD. 8Every sabbath day Aaron shall set them in order before the LORD regularly as a commitment of the people of Israel, as a covenant forever. 9They shall be for Aaron and his descendants, who shall eat them in a holy place, for they are most holy portions for him from the offerings by fire to the LORD, a perpetual due.

10 A man whose mother was an Israelite and whose father was an Egyptian came out among the people of Israel; and the Israelite woman's son and a certain Israelite began fighting in the camp. 11The Israelite woman's son blasphemed the Name in a curse. And they brought him to Moses— now his mother's name was Shelomith,

a Or *tabernacles:* Heb *succoth*   *b* Meaning of Heb uncertain   *c* Or *treaty,* or *testament;* Heb *eduth*   *d* Heb *pure lampstand*   *e* Heb *pure table* daughter of Dibri, of the tribe of Dan— [12]and they put him in custody, until the decision of the LORD should be made clear to them.

13 The LORD said to Moses, saying: [14]Take the blasphemer outside the camp; and let all who were within hearing lay their hands on his head, and let the whole congregation stone him. [15]And speak to the people of Israel, saying: Anyone who curses God shall bear the sin. [16]One who blasphemes the name of the LORD shall be put to death; the whole congregation shall stone the blasphemer. Aliens as well as citizens, when they blaspheme the Name, shall be put to death. [17]Anyone who kills a human being shall be put to death. [18]Anyone who kills an animal shall make restitution for it, life for life. [19]Anyone who maims another shall suffer the same injury in return: [20]fracture for fracture, eye for eye, tooth for tooth; the injury inflicted is the injury to be suffered. [21]One who kills an animal shall make restitution for it; but one who kills a human being shall be put to death. [22]You shall have one law for the alien and for the citizen: for I am the LORD your God. [23]Moses spoke thus to the people of Israel; and they took the blasphemer outside the camp, and stoned him to death. The people of Israel did as the LORD had commanded Moses.

24.1–23: The LORD issues laws related to the lamp and bread in the sanctuary and the punishment of blasphemy in the camp. 1–4: On the pure oil for the *lamp* in *the tent of meeting*, see Ex 27.20–21. 5–9: On the *bread* for the sanctuary (v. 7), see Ex 25.23–30. *An ephah* is a unit of measure (v. 5). *Frankincense* is an aromatic spice (v. 7). The *sabbath* (v. 8) is the seventh day of the week and is kept holy by refraining from work (Ex 20.8–11). 11: To *blaspheme* is to show contempt or lack of reverence for God. *The Name* is the sacred name for God (YHWH) given to Moses and the Israelites in Ex 3.13–15. The offense involves both blaspheming the divine name (see Ex 20.7) and cursing God (Ex 22.28) as indicated in vv. 15–16. 14: The spoken curse using the powerful divine name contaminates with guilt both the speaker and those who hear it. When the people *lay their hands* on the speaker's head, they transfer their guilt back to the blasphemer (16.21–22). To *stone him* is a communal act of public

execution. Pelting the guilty person with stones until he dies cleanses the community from the evil (Deut 17.2–7). 20: This principle is the so-called "lex talionis" or "law of retribution," *eye for eye, tooth for tooth.* It is designed to limit the amount of punishment. 22: Any distinction in the treatment of Israelites versus non-Israelites is prohibited. This principle is occasioned by the previous case of the blasphemer, who was half-Israelite and half-Egyptian (v. 10).

Laws regarding the sabbatical year and the jubilee year
25.1–55: The basic principle behind these laws is that the land is ultimately owned by God (v. 23). Humans have only temporary possession of it. Thus, humans should avoid excessive economic exploitation of the land or other people. Similar laws about the periodic release of land, slaves, and debts occur in Ex 21.2–6, Ex 23.10–11, and Deut 15.1–18.

25 The LORD spoke to Moses on Mount Sinai, saying: [2]Speak to the people of Israel and say to them: When you enter the land that I am giving you, the land shall observe a sabbath for the LORD. [3]Six years you shall sow your field, and six years you shall prune your vineyard, and gather in their yield; [4]but in the seventh year there shall be a sabbath of complete rest for the land, a sabbath for the LORD: you shall not sow your field or prune your vineyard. [5]You shall not reap the aftergrowth of your harvest or gather the grapes of your unpruned vine: it shall be a year of complete rest for the land. [6]You may eat what the land yields during its sabbath—you, your male and female slaves, your hired and your bound laborers who live with you; [7]for your livestock also, and for the wild animals in your land all its yield shall be for food.

8 You shall count off seven weeks[a] of years, seven times seven years, so that the period of seven weeks of years gives forty-nine years. [9]Then you shall have the trumpet sounded loud; on the tenth day of the seventh month—on the day of atonement—you shall have the trumpet sounded throughout all your land. [10]And you shall hallow the fiftieth year and you shall proclaim liberty

a Or *sabbaths*

throughout the land to all its inhabitants. It shall be a jubilee for you: you shall return, every one of you, to your property and every one of you to your family. ¹¹That fiftieth year shall be a jubilee for you: you shall not sow, or reap the aftergrowth, or harvest the unpruned vines. ¹²For it is a jubilee; it shall be holy to you: you shall eat only what the field itself produces.

13 In this year of jubilee you shall return, every one of you, to your property. ¹⁴When you make a sale to your neighbor or buy from your neighbor, you shall not cheat one another. ¹⁵When you buy from your neighbor, you shall pay only for the number of years since the jubilee; the seller shall charge you only for the remaining crop years. ¹⁶If the years are more, you shall increase the price, and if the years are fewer, you shall diminish the price; for it is a certain number of harvests that are being sold to you. ¹⁷You shall not cheat one another, but you shall fear your God; for I am the LORD your God.

18 You shall observe my statutes and faithfully keep my ordinances, so that you may live on the land securely. ¹⁹The land will yield its fruit, and you will eat your fill and live on it securely. ²⁰Should you ask, "What shall we eat in the seventh year, if we may not sow or gather in our crop?" ²¹I will order my blessing for you in the sixth year, so that it will yield a crop for three years. ²²When you sow in the eighth year, you will be eating from the old crop; until the ninth year, when its produce comes in, you shall eat the old. ²³The land shall not be sold in perpetuity, for the land is mine; with me you are but aliens and tenants. ²⁴Throughout the land that you hold, you shall provide for the redemption of the land.

occurs after the conquest of Canaan in Josh 13–22. The function of the law is both periodic economic equalization and support of the clan and family social structure. **13–17:** Land may be bought and sold as a temporary lease between each jubilee year. However, the buyer knows that the land will revert to the original owner in the fiftieth year of the jubilee. **23:** The ultimate divine ownership of the land is the theological presupposition behind the sabbatical and jubilee laws of release. *In perpetuity* means forever. In other words, every sale of land must be only temporary so that its ownership may periodically revert to the original owners. **24:** *Redemption* involves a relative or family member's taking back land or persons that originally belonged to the family (see v. 25).

25 If anyone of your kin falls into difficulty and sells a piece of property, then the next of kin shall come and redeem what the relative has sold. ²⁶If the person has no one to redeem it, but then prospers and finds sufficient means to do so, ²⁷the years since its sale shall be computed and the difference shall be refunded to the person to whom it was sold, and the property shall be returned. ²⁸But if there are not sufficient means to recover it, what was sold shall remain with the purchaser until the year of jubilee; in the jubilee it shall be released, and the property shall be returned.

29 If anyone sells a dwelling house in a walled city, it may be redeemed until a year has elapsed since its sale; the right of redemption shall be one year. ³⁰If it is not redeemed before a full year has elapsed, a house that is in a walled city shall pass in perpetuity to the purchaser, throughout the generations; it shall not be released in the jubilee. ³¹But houses in villages that have no walls around them shall be classed as open country; they may be redeemed, and they shall be released in the jubilee. ³²As for the cities of the Levites, the Levites shall forever have the right of redemption of the houses in the cities belonging to them. ³³Such property as may be redeemed from the Levites—houses sold in a city belonging to them—shall be released in the jubilee; because the houses in the cities of the Levites are their possession among the people of Israel. ³⁴But the open land around their

25.1–24. 2–7: The *sabbath* (v. 2) typically refers to the seventh day of the week, a day of rest from work (Ex 20.8–11). Here the term applies to every *seventh year* (v. 4). The land rests by having no crops planted on it. **8–12:** The *jubilee* year (vv. 11–12) occurs after every seven times seven years (v. 8) or, in other words, every fiftieth year (v. 10). The *return to your property* and *to your family* presupposes a return to the original allocation of the plots of land in Canaan assigned to each Israelite tribe, clan,* and family. This allocation of land cities may not be sold; for that is their possession for all time.

35 If any of your kin fall into difficulty and become dependent on you,[a] you shall support them; they shall live with you as though resident aliens. 36Do not take interest in advance or otherwise make a profit from them, but fear your God; let them live with you. 37You shall not lend them your money at interest taken in advance, or provide them food at a profit. 38I am the LORD your God, who brought you out of the land of Egypt, to give you the land of Canaan, to be your God.

39 If any who are dependent on you become so impoverished that they sell themselves to you, you shall not make them serve as slaves. 40They shall remain with you as hired or bound laborers. They shall serve with you until the year of the jubilee. 41Then they and their children with them shall be free from your authority; they shall go back to their own family and return to their ancestral property. 42For they are my servants, whom I brought out of the land of Egypt; they shall not be sold as slaves are sold. 43You shall not rule over them with harshness, but shall fear your God. 44As for the male and female slaves whom you may have, it is from the nations around you that you may acquire male and female slaves. 45You may also acquire them from among the aliens residing with you, and from their families that are with you, who have been born in your land; and they may be your property. 46You may keep them as a possession for your children after you, for them to inherit as property. These you may treat as slaves, but as for your fellow Israelites, no one shall rule over the other with harshness.

47 If resident aliens among you prosper, and if any of your kin fall into difficulty with one of them and sell themselves to an alien, or to a branch of the alien's family, 48after they have sold themselves they shall have the right of redemption; one of their brothers may redeem them, 49or their uncle or their uncle's son may redeem them, or anyone of their family who is of their own flesh may redeem them; or if they prosper they may redeem themselves. 50They shall compute with the purchaser the total from the year when they sold themselves to the alien until the jubilee year; the price of the sale shall be applied to the number of years: the time they were with the owner shall be rated as the time of a hired laborer. 51If many years remain, they shall pay for their redemption in proportion to the purchase price; 52and if few years remain until the jubilee year, they shall compute thus: according to the years involved they shall make payment for their redemption. 53As a laborer hired by the year they shall be under the alien's authority, who shall not, however, rule with harshness over them in your sight. 54And if they have not been redeemed in any of these ways, they and their children with them shall go free in the jubilee year. 55For to me the people of Israel are servants; they are my servants whom I brought out from the land of Egypt: I am the LORD your God.

25.25–55: These laws deal with four progressively more serious economic situations of need: (1) the need to sell off a part of the family land holdings (vv. 25–34); (2) the need to become dependent on a fellow Israelite (vv. 35–38); (3) the need to sell oneself as a hired laborer to a fellow Israelite (vv. 39–46); and (4) the need to sell oneself as a hired laborer to a resident alien* or non-Israelite (vv. 47–55). On the *right of redemption* (vv. 29, 32), see comment on v. 24. Since the Levites (a priestly tribe within Israel) did not receive an allotment of land as did the other tribes, they received instead a number of cities throughout Israel (Num 18.20–24; 35.1–8). The basic theological conviction behind the laws in vv. 25–55 is that the Israelites should be slaves or servants to no one other than the LORD (vv. 42, 55).

Blessings for obedience and curses for disobedience

26.1–46: The laws of Leviticus conclude with a list of blessings and curses, a typical part of other ancient Near Eastern law codes and treaties. Similar blessings and curses conclude a collection of laws in Ex 23.20–33 and Deut 28.1–68.

26 You shall make for yourselves no idols and erect no carved images or

a Meaning of Heb uncertain

pillars, and you shall not place figured stones in your land, to worship at them; for I am the LORD your God. 2You shall keep my sabbaths and reverence my sanctuary: I am the LORD.

26.1–2. 1: The prohibited *idols, images,* and *pillars* may refer both to images of Israel's God and to images of foreign gods. 2: The *sabbaths* include the seventh day of every week as a day of rest (19.3; Ex 20.8–11) and the sabbath years (ch. 25).

3 If you follow my statutes and keep my commandments and observe them faithfully, 4I will give you your rains in their season, and the land shall yield its produce, and the trees of the field shall yield their fruit. 5Your threshing shall overtake the vintage, and the vintage shall overtake the sowing; you shall eat your bread to the full, and live securely in your land. 6And I will grant peace in the land, and you shall lie down, and no one shall make you afraid; I will remove dangerous animals from the land, and no sword shall go through your land. 7You shall give chase to your enemies, and they shall fall before you by the sword. 8Five of you shall give chase to a hundred, and a hundred of you shall give chase to ten thousand; your enemies shall fall before you by the sword. 9I will look with favor upon you and make you fruitful and multiply you; and I will maintain my covenant with you. 10You shall eat old grain long stored, and you shall have to clear out the old to make way for the new. 11I will place my dwelling in your midst, and I shall not abhor you. 12And I will walk among you, and will be your God, and you shall be my people. 13I am the LORD your God who brought you out of the land of Egypt, to be their slaves no more; I have broken the bars of your yoke and made you walk erect.

14 But if you will not obey me, and do not observe all these commandments, 15if you spurn my statutes, and abhor my ordinances, so that you will not observe all my commandments, and you break my covenant, 16I in turn will do this to you: I will bring terror on you; consumption and fever that waste the eyes and cause life to pine away. You shall sow your seed in vain, for your enemies shall eat it. 17I will set my face against you, and you shall be struck down by your enemies; your foes shall rule over you, and you shall flee though no one pursues you. 18And if in spite of this you will not obey me, I will continue to punish you sevenfold for your sins. 19I will break your proud glory, and I will make your sky like iron and your earth like copper. 20Your strength shall be spent to no purpose: your land shall not yield its produce, and the trees of the land shall not yield their fruit.

21 If you continue hostile to me, and will not obey me, I will continue to plague you sevenfold for your sins. 22I will let loose wild animals against you, and they shall bereave you of your children and destroy your livestock; they shall make you few in number, and your roads shall be deserted.

23 If in spite of these punishments you have not turned back to me, but continue hostile to me, 24then I too will continue hostile to you: I myself will strike you sevenfold for your sins. 25I will bring the sword against you, executing vengeance for the covenant; and if you withdraw within your cities, I will send pestilence among you, and you shall be delivered into enemy hands. 26When I break your staff of bread, ten women shall bake your bread in a single oven, and they shall dole out your bread by weight; and though you eat, you shall not be satisfied.

27 But if, despite this, you disobey me, and continue hostile to me, 28I will continue hostile to you in fury; I in turn will punish you myself sevenfold for your sins. 29You shall eat the flesh of your sons, and you shall eat the flesh of your daughters. 30I will destroy your high places and cut down your incense altars; I will heap your carcasses on the carcasses of your idols. I will abhor you. 31I will lay your cities waste, will make your sanctuaries desolate, and I will not smell your pleasing odors. 32I will devastate the land, so that your enemies who come to settle in it shall be appalled at it. 33And you I will scatter among the nations, and I will unsheathe the sword against you; your land shall be a desolation, and your cities a waste.

34 Then the land shall enjoy*a* its sabbath years as long as it lies desolate, while you are in the land of your enemies; then the land shall rest, and enjoy*a* its sabbath years. 35As long as it lies desolate, it shall have the rest it did not have on your sabbaths when you were living on it. 36And as for those of you who survive, I will send faintness into their hearts in the lands of their enemies; the sound of a driven leaf shall put them to flight, and they shall flee as one flees from the sword, and they shall fall though no one pursues. 37They shall stumble over one another, as if to escape a sword, though no one pursues; and you shall have no power to stand against your enemies. 38You shall perish among the nations, and the land of your enemies shall devour you. 39And those of you who survive shall languish in the land of your enemies because of their iniquities; also they shall languish because of the iniquities of their ancestors.

40 But if they confess their iniquity and the iniquity of their ancestors, in that they committed treachery against me and, moreover, that they continued hostile to me— 41so that I, in turn, continued hostile to them and brought them into the land of their enemies; if then their uncircumcised heart is humbled and they make amends for their iniquity, 42then will I remember my covenant with Jacob; I will remember also my covenant with Isaac and also my covenant with Abraham, and I will remember the land. 43For the land shall be deserted by them, and enjoy*a* its sabbath years by lying desolate without them, while they shall make amends for their iniquity, because they dared to spurn my ordinances, and they abhorred my statutes. 44Yet for all that, when they are in the land of their enemies, I will not spurn them, or abhor them so as to destroy them utterly and break my covenant with them; for I am the LORD their God; 45but I will remember in their favor the covenant with their ancestors whom I brought out of the land of Egypt in the sight of the nations, to be their God: I am the LORD.

26.32–45: These descriptions of deportation from the land of Canaan and life in exile in a foreign country recall northern Israel's experience under the Assyrian empire in 722 BCE (2 Kings 17) and southern Judah's later exile to Babylon in 587 BCE (2 Kings 24–25). On the *land* and its *sabbath years,* see 25.1–7. The *uncircumcised* heart* (v. 41) is a metaphor* for Israel's stubborn and rebellious will (Deut 10.16). Circumcision* is a ritual involving cutting off the foreskin of the penis as a sign of belonging to the covenant* community.

46 These are the statutes and ordinances and laws that the LORD established between himself and the people of Israel on Mount Sinai through Moses.

27 The LORD spoke to Moses, saying: 2Speak to the people of Israel and say to them: When a person makes an explicit vow to the LORD concerning the equivalent for a human being, 3the equivalent for a male shall be: from twenty to sixty years of age the equivalent shall be fifty shekels of silver by the sanctuary shekel. 4If the person is a female, the equivalent is thirty shekels. 5If the age is from five to twenty years of age, the equivalent is twenty shekels for a male and ten shekels for a female. 6If the age is from one month to five years, the equivalent for a male is five shekels of silver, and for a female the equivalent is three shekels of silver. 7And if the person is sixty years old or over, then the equivalent for a male is fifteen shekels, and for a female ten shekels. 8If any cannot afford the equivalent, they shall be brought before the priest and the priest shall assess them; the priest shall assess them according to what each one making a vow can afford.

9 If it concerns an animal that may be brought as an offering to the LORD, any such that may be given to the LORD shall be holy. 10Another shall not be exchanged or substituted for it, either good for bad or bad for good; and if one animal is substituted for another, both that one and its substitute shall be holy. 11If it concerns any unclean animal that may not be brought as an offering to the LORD, the animal shall be presented before the priest. 12The priest shall assess it: whether good or bad, according to the as-

---

a Or *make up for*

sessment of the priest, so it shall be. ¹³But if it is to be redeemed, one-fifth must be added to the assessment.

14 If a person consecrates a house to the LORD, the priest shall assess it: whether good or bad, as the priest assesses it, so it shall stand. ¹⁵And if the one who consecrates the house wishes to redeem it, one-fifth shall be added to its assessed value, and it shall revert to the original owner.

16 If a person consecrates to the LORD any inherited landholding, its assessment shall be in accordance with its seed requirements: fifty shekels of silver to a homer of barley seed. ¹⁷If the person consecrates the field as of the year of jubilee, that assessment shall stand; ¹⁸but if the field is consecrated after the jubilee, the priest shall compute the price for it according to the years that remain until the year of jubilee, and the assessment shall be reduced. ¹⁹And if the one who consecrates the field wishes to redeem it, then one-fifth shall be added to its assessed value, and it shall revert to the original owner; ²⁰but if the field is not redeemed, or if it has been sold to someone else, it shall no longer be redeemable. ²¹But when the field is released in the jubilee, it shall be holy to the LORD as a devoted field; it becomes the priest's holding. ²²If someone consecrates to the LORD a field that has been purchased, which is not a part of the inherited landholding, ²³the priest shall compute for it the proportionate assessment up to the year of jubilee, and the assessment shall be paid as of that day, a sacred donation to the LORD. ²⁴In the year of jubilee the field shall return to the one from whom it was bought, whose holding the land is. ²⁵All assessments shall be by the sanctuary shekel: twenty gerahs shall make a shekel.

26 A firstling of animals, however, which as a firstling belongs to the LORD, cannot be consecrated by anyone; whether ox or sheep, it is the LORD's. ²⁷If it is an unclean animal, it shall be ransomed at its assessment, with one-fifth added; if it is not redeemed, it shall be sold at its assessment.

28 Nothing that a person owns that has been devoted to destruction for the LORD, be it human or animal, or inherited landholding, may be sold or redeemed; every devoted thing is most holy to the LORD. ²⁹No human beings who have been devoted to destruction can be ransomed; they shall be put to death.

30 All tithes from the land, whether the seed from the ground or the fruit from the tree, are the LORD's; they are holy to the LORD. ³¹If persons wish to redeem any of their tithes, they must add one-fifth to them. ³²All tithes of herd and flock, every tenth one that passes under the shepherd's staff, shall be holy to the LORD. ³³Let no one inquire whether it is good or bad, or make substitution for it; if one makes substitution for it, then both it and the substitute shall be holy and cannot be redeemed.

34 These are the commandments that the LORD gave to Moses for the people of Israel on Mount Sinai.

27.1–34: The LORD issues rules for those who wish to redeem or buy back special sacrifices or donations previously dedicated to God. Persons often dedicated a gift to the sanctuary in the context of a vow to God made after experiencing a special blessing or deliverance from evil (1 Sam 1.11; Ps 66.13–15). 3: A *shekel*★ is a standard unit of weight. 11, 27: On *unclean animals*, see ch. 11. 16: A *homer* is a standard unit of volume. 18: On the *year of jubilee*, see 25.8–24. 25: Both the *shekel* and the *gerah* are standard units of weight. 28–29: *Devoted to destruction* refers to property or humans taken as booty in holy war.★ The booty is dedicated to God and thus could not be kept and used by lay people. Property and animals were given to the priests in the sanctuary, and humans were put to death. 30–33: A *tithe* is a one-tenth portion of a crop or flock that is given as an offering to God for use by the priests serving in the sanctuary. In Numbers, the tithe offering belongs to the Levites (Num 18.21). In Deuteronomy, the tithe offering reverts to the donor and is shared with the Levites, aliens, orphans, and widows (Deut 12.5–12; 26.10–13).

NUMBERS

Introduction

The book of Numbers, the fourth book of the Old Testament, derives its name from the two census lists that number the people in each of the twelve tribes of Israel (chs. 1, 26). The Hebrew title for the book, "In the Wilderness," comes from the first verse of the book and accurately describes its setting. Numbers is the story of the people of Israel in the wilderness as they travel from Egypt and the wilderness mountain of Sinai toward the promised land of Canaan. The most important transition in the story is the death of the old and rebellious generation of Israelites and the birth of a new generation of Israelites in the wilderness. This new generation of hope stands poised to enter the land of Canaan at the end of the book of Numbers.

An important feature of Numbers is its great variety of literary forms and topics. The reader will encounter a mixture of stories and laws, travel itineraries and census lists, lists of personal names and lists of instructions for worship, reports of military battles and accounts of legal disputes. Some of the material is earlier and some later in origin. However, this diverse collection of literature has been woven together into a coherent story of Israel's holy camp on the move through the wilderness.

The final form of the story of Numbers probably emerged in light of Israel's experience of exile* in Babylon (587 BCE) and shortly after its return to the homeland of Judah (539 BCE). The passage from an old and rebellious generation that had died in the wilderness and the birth of a generation of hope provided an enduring paradigm for new generations of Israelites who returned home from exile to the promised land of Judah. The struggles, conflicts, and rebellions of Israel in the wilderness provided a mirror for Israel's struggles in exile and in its return to rebuild the Jewish community in Judah.

READING GUIDE

The transition from the old generation of the wilderness to the new generation of hope and promise on the edge of the promised land forms the primary theme and structure for the book of Numbers. This structure is marked by the two census lists of the twelve tribes of Israel in chs. 1 and 26. The first census list in Num 1 introduces the first half of the book, chs. 1–25. Israel's obedient preparations for the march through the wilderness in chs. 1–10 abruptly turn into Israel's disobedient rebellions against God and Moses in chs. 11–25. The climactic rebellion story is the spy story of chs. 13–14, the key narrative* in Numbers. As a result of this growing rebellion against God, the old generation of Israelites is condemned to die in the wilderness and not allowed to enter the promised land of Canaan (14.20–38). However, the LORD promises to bring a new generation of young Israelites born during the wilderness journey into the land of Canaan (14.31).

The second census list in Num 26 marks the rise of this new generation of hope (26.63–65). This census list introduces the second half of the book, chs. 26–36, which displays a significantly different mood and tone. Whereas the first half of Numbers was dominated by themes of rebellion and death, this second half resonates with new life, hope, obedience, and the resolution of potential conflict through negotiation and dialogue.

The book of Numbers contains many well-known biblical passages and images. Some of them include the priestly benediction or blessing (ch. 6), manna as food for Israel in the wilderness (ch. 11), Miriam's leprosy (ch. 12), water from the rock (ch. 20), the bronze serpent (ch. 21), Balaam's talking donkey (ch. 22), and the bold daughters of Zelophehad (chs. 27, 36).

1–10	Preparations for Israel's march through the wilderness
11–20	The old generation's slide into rebellion and death
21–25	Signs of hope in the midst of the death of the old generation
26–36	The rise of a new generation on the edge of the promised land

A census of the twelve tribes of Israel
1.1–46: The purpose of this numbering of Israelite males over twenty years of age is to determine the number of soldiers who will be *able to go to war* (v. 3) in the upcoming battles for the conquest of Canaan. However, the later rebellions of this generation of Israelites will disqualify them from taking part in the battles for Canaan (chs. 13–14). A similar census in ch. 26 will number an entirely new generation of Israelites whom the LORD will allow to enter the promised land of Canaan (26.63–65).

1 The LORD spoke to Moses in the wilderness of Sinai, in the tent of meeting, on the first day of the second month, in the second year after they had come out of the land of Egypt, saying: ²Take a census of the whole congregation of Israelites, in their clans, by ancestral houses, according to the number of names, every male individually; ³from twenty years old and upward, everyone in Israel able to go to war. You and Aaron shall enroll them, company by company. ⁴A man from each tribe shall be with you, each man the head of his ancestral house. ⁵These are the names of the men who shall assist you:
    From Reuben, Elizur son of Shedeur.
   ⁶ From Simeon, Shelumiel son of
       Zurishaddai.
   ⁷ From Judah, Nahshon son of
       Amminadab.
   ⁸ From Issachar, Nethanel son of Zuar.
   ⁹ From Zebulun, Eliab son of Helon.
 ¹⁰ From the sons of Joseph:
   from Ephraim, Elishama son of
      Ammihud;
   from Manasseh, Gamaliel son of
      Pedahzur.

¹¹ From Benjamin, Abidan son of Gideoni.
¹² From Dan, Ahiezer son of
    Ammishaddai.
¹³ From Asher, Pagiel son of Ochran.
¹⁴ From Gad, Eliasaph son of Deuel.
¹⁵ From Naphtali, Ahira son of Enan.
¹⁶These were the ones chosen from the congregation, the leaders of their ancestral tribes, the heads of the divisions of Israel.

1.1–16. 1: Israel's camp has been situated in *the wilderness of Sinai* since Ex 19.1–2. The *tent of meeting* covers the tabernacle*, a portable sanctuary or shrine. The tent is the place where Moses, the leader of Israel, receives oracles* and instructions from the LORD. Formerly, the tent of meeting stood outside Israel's camp, but now it will be situated in the middle of the camp (see Ex 33.7–11; Num 2.2). *The first day of the second month* means one month has elapsed since Israel finished constructing the portable tabernacle or shrine (Ex 40.17). **2:** Israel was divided into twelve tribes. Each tribe contained a number of smaller groups called *clans*. Each clan in turn contained a number of smaller family groups called *ancestral houses*. **5–15:** This list of the twelve tribes of Israel largely reflects the sequence of the births of the twelve sons of Jacob in Gen 29.31–30.24 and Gen 35.16–18, grouped according to the status of their mothers. The children of Leah and Rachel (Jacob's favored wives) are listed first. The children born of the servant women (Bilhah and Zilpah) are listed last.

17 Moses and Aaron took these men who had been designated by name, ¹⁸and on the first day of the second month they assembled the whole congregation together. They registered themselves in their clans, by their ancestral houses, according to the number of names from twenty years old and upward,

individually, [19] as the LORD commanded Moses. So he enrolled them in the wilderness of Sinai.

20 The descendants of Reuben, Israel's firstborn, their lineage, in their clans, by their ancestral houses, according to the number of names, individually, every male from twenty years old and upward, everyone able to go to war: [21] those enrolled of the tribe of Reuben were forty-six thousand five hundred.

22 The descendants of Simeon, their lineage, in their clans, by their ancestral houses, those of them that were numbered, according to the number of names, individually, every male from twenty years old and upward, everyone able to go to war: [23] those enrolled of the tribe of Simeon were fifty-nine thousand three hundred.

24 The descendants of Gad, their lineage, in their clans, by their ancestral houses, according to the number of the names, from twenty years old and upward, everyone able to go to war: [25] those enrolled of the tribe of Gad were forty-five thousand six hundred fifty.

26 The descendants of Judah, their lineage, in their clans, by their ancestral houses, according to the number of names, from twenty years old and upward, everyone able to go to war: [27] those enrolled of the tribe of Judah were seventy-four thousand six hundred.

28 The descendants of Issachar, their lineage, in their clans, by their ancestral houses, according to the number of names, from twenty years old and upward, everyone able to go to war: [29] those enrolled of the tribe of Issachar were fifty-four thousand four hundred.

30 The descendants of Zebulun, their lineage, in their clans, by their ancestral houses, according to the number of names, from twenty years old and upward, everyone able to go to war: [31] those enrolled of the tribe of Zebulun were fifty-seven thousand four hundred.

32 The descendants of Joseph, namely, the descendants of Ephraim, their lineage, in their clans, by their ancestral houses, according to the number of names, from twenty years old and upward, everyone able to go to war: [33] those enrolled of the tribe of Ephraim were forty thousand five hundred.

34 The descendants of Manasseh, their lineage, in their clans, by their ancestral houses, according to the number of names, from twenty years old and upward, everyone able to go to war: [35] those enrolled of the tribe of Manasseh were thirty-two thousand two hundred.

36 The descendants of Benjamin, their lineage, in their clans, by their ancestral houses, according to the number of names, from twenty years old and upward, everyone able to go to war: [37] those enrolled of the tribe of Benjamin were thirty-five thousand four hundred.

38 The descendants of Dan, their lineage, in their clans, by their ancestral houses, according to the number of names, from twenty years old and upward, everyone able to go to war: [39] those enrolled of the tribe of Dan were sixty-two thousand seven hundred.

40 The descendants of Asher, their lineage, in their clans, by their ancestral houses, according to the number of names, from twenty years old and upward, everyone able to go to war: [41] those enrolled of the tribe of Asher were forty-one thousand five hundred.

42 The descendants of Naphtali, their lineage, in their clans, by their ancestral houses, according to the number of names, from twenty years old and upward, everyone able to go to war: [43] those enrolled of the tribe of Naphtali were fifty-three thousand four hundred.

44 These are those who were enrolled, whom Moses and Aaron enrolled with the help of the leaders of Israel, twelve men, each representing his ancestral house. [45] So the whole number of the Israelites, by their ancestral houses, from twenty years old and upward, everyone able to go to war in Israel— [46] their whole number was six hundred three thousand five hundred fifty. [47] The Levites, however, were not numbered by their ancestral tribe along with them.

48 The LORD had said to Moses: [49] Only the tribe of Levi you shall not enroll, and you

shall not take a census of them with the other Israelites. [50]Rather you shall appoint the Levites over the tabernacle of the covenant,[a] and over all its equipment, and over all that belongs to it; they are to carry the tabernacle and all its equipment, and they shall tend it, and shall camp around the tabernacle. [51]When the tabernacle is to set out, the Levites shall take it down; and when the tabernacle is to be pitched, the Levites shall set it up. And any outsider who comes near shall be put to death. [52]The other Israelites shall camp in their respective regimental camps, by companies; [53]but the Levites shall camp around the tabernacle of the covenant,[a] that there may be no wrath on the congregation of the Israelites; and the Levites shall perform the guard duty of the tabernacle of the covenant.[a] [54]The Israelites did so; they did just as the LORD commanded Moses.

1.17–54. 17–46: The numbers for each individual tribe as well as the total number of male warriors for all twelve tribes (603,550; vv. 44–46) have seemed impossibly high to many commentators. The number of soldiers assumes a total population of men, women, and children of around two million Israelites. Several solutions have been offered to bring down the number to a more plausible figure. However, the present form of the text assumes the full number of 603,550 Israelite soldiers. As such, the census numbers demonstrate the LORD's partial fulfillment of the promises of innumerable descendants made earlier to Israel's ancestors (Gen 15.5; 22.17). 47–54: The tribe of Levi (v. 49) stands apart as a priestly tribe exempted from military service and dedicated to the care and administration of the tabernacle of the covenant* (v. 50). Therefore, the Levites have their own separate census. The tabernacle is the portable sanctuary or shrine at which the powerful and holy presence of God could be present in the midst of the Israelites. The Levites camp around the tabernacle as a protective buffer between God's presence and the rest of the Israelite camp so that there may be no wrath on the congregation of the Israelites (v. 53). An outsider in this case is anyone who is not from the priestly tribe of Levi (v. 51).

---

2 The LORD spoke to Moses and Aaron, saying: [2]The Israelites shall camp each in their respective regiments, under ensigns by their ancestral houses; they shall camp facing the tent of meeting on every side. [3]Those to camp on the east side toward the sunrise shall be of the regimental encampment of Judah by companies. The leader of the people of Judah shall be Nahshon son of Amminadab, [4]with a company as enrolled of seventy-four thousand six hundred. [5]Those to camp next to him shall be the tribe of Issachar. The leader of the Issacharites shall be Nethanel son of Zuar, [6]with a company as enrolled of fifty-four thousand four hundred. [7]Then the tribe of Zebulun: The leader of the Zebulunites shall be Eliab son of Helon, [8]with a company as enrolled of fifty-seven thousand four hundred. [9]The total enrollment of the camp of Judah, by companies, is one hundred eighty-six thousand four hundred. They shall set out first on the march.

10 On the south side shall be the regimental encampment of Reuben by companies. The leader of the Reubenites shall be Elizur son of Shedeur, [11]with a company as enrolled of forty-six thousand five hundred. [12]And those to camp next to him shall be the tribe of Simeon. The leader of the Simeonites shall be Shelumiel son of Zurishaddai, [13]with a company as enrolled of fifty-nine thousand three hundred. [14]Then the tribe of Gad: The leader of the Gadites shall be Eliasaph son of Reuel, [15]with a company as enrolled of forty-five thousand six hundred fifty. [16]The total enrollment of the camp of Reuben, by companies, is one hundred fifty-one thousand four hundred fifty. They shall set out second.

17 The tent of meeting, with the camp of the Levites, shall set out in the center of the camps; they shall set out just as they camp, each in position, by their regiments.

18 On the west side shall be the regimental encampment of Ephraim by companies. The leader of the people of Ephraim shall be Elishama son of Ammihud, [19]with a company as enrolled of forty thousand five hundred. [20]Next to him shall be the tribe of Manasseh. The leader of the people of Manasseh shall be Gamaliel son of Pedah-

a Or treaty, or testimony; Heb eduth

zur, 21with a company as enrolled of thirty-two thousand two hundred. 22Then the tribe of Benjamin: The leader of the Benjaminites shall be Abidan son of Gideoni, 23with a company as enrolled of thirty-five thousand four hundred. 24The total enrollment of the camp of Ephraim, by companies, is one hundred eight thousand one hundred. They shall set out third on the march.

25 On the north side shall be the regimental encampment of Dan by companies. The leader of the Danites shall be Ahiezer son of Ammishaddai, 26with a company as enrolled of sixty-two thousand seven hundred. 27Those to camp next to him shall be the tribe of Asher. The leader of the Asherites shall be Pagiel son of Ochran, 28with a company as enrolled of forty-one thousand five hundred. 29Then the tribe of Naphtali: The leader of the Naphtalites shall be Ahira son of Enan, 30with a company as enrolled of fifty-three thousand four hundred. 31The total enrollment of the camp of Dan is one hundred fifty-seven thousand six hundred. They shall set out last, by companies.*a*

32 This was the enrollment of the Israelites by their ancestral houses; the total enrollment in the camps by their companies was six hundred three thousand five hundred fifty. 33Just as the LORD had commanded Moses, the Levites were not enrolled among the other Israelites.

34 The Israelites did just as the LORD had commanded Moses: They camped by regiments, and they set out the same way, everyone by clans, according to ancestral houses.

2.1–34: The arrangement of Israel's camp and the order of marching. The tent of meeting, which contains the tabernacle* or portable sanctuary, stands in the middle of the Israelite camp (vv. 2, 17). The Levites form a protective inner circle around the tent of meeting (1.53). In the outer circle of the camp, the twelve tribes divide into four groups of three tribes each. Each group of three tribes camps at one of the four cardinal points (east, south, west, north) relative to the tent of meeting. **2:** *Ensigns* are symbols or flags with unique designs that represent the individual *ancestral houses* or family groups. **3:** The order of march begins with the eastern tribes led by *Judah*, the preeminent tribe

among the twelve. Then the tribes of the south (vv. 10–16), the tent of meeting and Levites (v. 17), the tribes of the west (vv. 18–24), and the tribes of the north (vv. 25–31) follow in order during the march. **32:** On the incredibly large number of Israelites who were counted in the census, see comment on 1.17–46.

3 This is the lineage of Aaron and Moses at the time when the LORD spoke with Moses on Mount Sinai. 2These are the names of the sons of Aaron: Nadab the firstborn, and Abihu, Eleazar, and Ithamar; 3these are the names of the sons of Aaron, the anointed priests, whom he ordained to minister as priests. 4Nadab and Abihu died before the LORD when they offered unholy fire before the LORD in the wilderness of Sinai, and they had no children. Eleazar and Ithamar served as priests in the lifetime of their father Aaron.

5 Then the LORD spoke to Moses, saying: 6Bring the tribe of Levi near, and set them before Aaron the priest, so that they may assist him. 7They shall perform duties for him and for the whole congregation in front of the tent of meeting, doing service at the tabernacle; 8they shall be in charge of all the furnishings of the tent of meeting, and attend to the duties for the Israelites as they do service at the tabernacle. 9You shall give the Levites to Aaron and his descendants; they are unreservedly given to him from among the Israelites. 10But you shall make a register of Aaron and his descendants; it is they who shall attend to the priesthood, and any outsider who comes near shall be put to death.

11 Then the LORD spoke to Moses, saying: 12I hereby accept the Levites from among the Israelites as substitutes for all the firstborn that open the womb among the Israelites. The Levites shall be mine, 13for all the firstborn are mine; when I killed all the firstborn in the land of Egypt, I consecrated for my own all the firstborn in Israel, both human and animal; they shall be mine. I am the LORD.

14 Then the LORD spoke to Moses in the

a Compare verses 9, 16, 24: Heb *by their regiments*

wilderness of Sinai, saying: 15 Enroll the Levites by ancestral houses and by clans. You shall enroll every male from a month old and upward. 16 So Moses enrolled them according to the word of the LORD, as he was commanded. 17 The following were the sons of Levi, by their names: Gershon, Kohath, and Merari. 18 These are the names of the sons of Gershon by their clans: Libni and Shimei. 19 The sons of Kohath by their clans: Amram, Izhar, Hebron, and Uzziel. 20 The sons of Merari by their clans: Mahli and Mushi. These are the clans of the Levites, by their ancestral houses.

21 To Gershon belonged the clan of the Libnites and the clan of the Shimeites; these were the clans of the Gershonites. 22 Their enrollment, counting all the males from a month old and upward, was seven thousand five hundred. 23 The clans of the Gershonites were to camp behind the tabernacle on the west, 24 with Eliasaph son of Lael as head of the ancestral house of the Gershonites. 25 The responsibility of the sons of Gershon in the tent of meeting was to be the tabernacle, the tent with its covering, the screen for the entrance of the tent of meeting, 26 the hangings of the court, the screen for the entrance of the court that is around the tabernacle and the altar, and its cords—all the service pertaining to these.

27 To Kohath belonged the clan of the Amramites, the clan of the Izharites, the clan of the Hebronites, and the clan of the Uzzielites; these are the clans of the Kohathites. 28 Counting all the males, from a month old and upward, there were eight thousand six hundred, attending to the duties of the sanctuary. 29 The clans of the Kohathites were to camp on the south side of the tabernacle, 30 with Elizaphan son of Uzziel as head of the ancestral house of the clans of the Kohathites. 31 Their responsibility was to be the ark, the table, the lampstand, the altars, the vessels of the sanctuary with which the priests minister, and the screen—all the service pertaining to these. 32 Eleazar son of Aaron the priest was to be chief over the leaders of the Levites, and to have oversight of those who had charge of the sanctuary.

33 To Merari belonged the clan of the Mahlites and the clan of the Mushites: these are the clans of Merari. 34 Their enrollment, counting all the males from a month old and upward, was six thousand two hundred. 35 The head of the ancestral house of the clans of Merari was Zuriel son of Abihail; they were to camp on the north side of the tabernacle. 36 The responsibility assigned to the sons of Merari was to be the frames of the tabernacle, the bars, the pillars, the bases, and all their accessories—all the service pertaining to these; 37 also the pillars of the court all around, with their bases and pegs and cords.

38 Those who were to camp in front of the tabernacle on the east—in front of the tent of meeting toward the east—were Moses and Aaron and Aaron's sons, having charge of the rites within the sanctuary, whatever had to be done for the Israelites; and any outsider who came near was to be put to death. 39 The total enrollment of the Levites whom Moses and Aaron enrolled at the commandment of the LORD, by their clans, all the males from a month old and upward, was twenty-two thousand.

3.1–51: The duties, census, and function of the Levites. 1: The two leaders, Aaron and Moses, are listed here because they are brothers and both belong to the tribe of Levi (see Ex 6.23). **3:** *The sons of Aaron* are special *anointed* priests* whom the other Levites assist (v. 6). **4:** The story of the death of Nadab and Abihu occurs in Lev 10.1–7. **8:** On *the tent of meeting* and the *tabernacle,** see comment on 1.1. **10:** An *outsider* is anyone who is not from the priestly tribe of Levi (see also v. 38). **11–13:** Earlier laws (Ex 13.2; 22.29–30) commanded that all human firstborn male children should be given to the LORD. This entailed either a lifetime of religious service or being redeemed or bought back through animal sacrifices or monetary offerings. However, this law allows the whole tribe of Levi to function as substitutes for the other Israelite firstborn children. **15:** The earlier census of the twelve tribes had counted all the males twenty years and older (1.3). The census of the Levites counts all the males who are one month and older, since they will be substitutes for all Israelite firstborn males who are one month or older (vv. 40–43). **17–39:** The three clans* of the Levites surround the tabernacle or portable shrine on three sides: the *Gershonites* on the *west* (v. 23), the *Kohath-*

ites on the *south* (v. 29), and the *clans of Merari* on the *north* (v. 35). The prestigious eastern side of the tabernacle is occupied by the families of *Moses and Aaron and Aaron's sons* (v. 38). An *outsider* is any person not from the tribe of Levi (v. 38). On details on the *ark* (v. 31), the furnishings of the *tabernacle* (v. 23), and the *tent of meeting* (v. 25), see Ex 25–27; 30.

~~~~~~~~~~~~~~~~~~~~~~~~~~~~~~~~~~

40 Then the LORD said to Moses: Enroll all the firstborn males of the Israelites, from a month old and upward, and count their names. 41But you shall accept the Levites for me—I am the LORD—as substitutes for all the firstborn among the Israelites, and the livestock of the Levites as substitutes for all the firstborn among the livestock of the Israelites. 42So Moses enrolled all the firstborn among the Israelites, as the LORD commanded him. 43The total enrollment, all the firstborn males from a month old and upward, counting the number of names, was twenty-two thousand two hundred seventy-three.

44 Then the LORD spoke to Moses, saying: 45Accept the Levites as substitutes for all the firstborn among the Israelites, and the livestock of the Levites as substitutes for their livestock; and the Levites shall be mine. I am the LORD. 46As the price of redemption of the two hundred seventy-three of the firstborn of the Israelites, over and above the number of the Levites, 47you shall accept five shekels apiece, reckoning by the shekel of the sanctuary, a shekel of twenty gerahs. 48Give to Aaron and his sons the money by which the excess number of them is redeemed. 49So Moses took the redemption money from those who were over and above those redeemed by the Levites; 50from the firstborn of the Israelites he took the money, one thousand three hundred sixty-five shekels, reckoned by the shekel of the sanctuary; 51and Moses gave the redemption money to Aaron and his sons, according to the word of the LORD, as the LORD had commanded Moses.

3.40–51: The total number of Levites who could be substitutes for the other Israelite firstborn children was 22,000 (v. 39). The total number of Israelite firstborn was 22,273 (v. 43). The remaining 273 Israelite first-

born could be redeemed or purchased back for *five shekels** each (vv. 46–47). The *shekel* and the *gerah* were standard units of weight used in calculating the monetary value of silver and gold. The *shekel of the sanctuary* was the governing standard for the weight of the shekel (v. 47).

A second census of Levites eligible for priestly duties

4.1–49: The earlier census of the Levites (3.14–39) had determined the number of Levites available to substitute for other Israelite firstborn males. This second levitical census numbers those who are 30–50 years old and thus eligible for priestly service.

----

4 The LORD spoke to Moses and Aaron, saying: 2Take a census of the Kohathites separate from the other Levites, by their clans and their ancestral houses, 3from thirty years old up to fifty years old, all who qualify to do work relating to the tent of meeting. 4The service of the Kohathites relating to the tent of meeting concerns the most holy things.

5 When the camp is to set out, Aaron and his sons shall go in and take down the screening curtain, and cover the ark of the covenant*a* with it; 6then they shall put on it a covering of fine leather,*b* and spread over that a cloth all of blue, and shall put its poles in place. 7Over the table of the bread of the Presence they shall spread a blue cloth, and put on it the plates, the dishes for incense, the bowls, and the flagons for the drink offering; the regular bread also shall be on it; 8then they shall spread over them a crimson cloth, and cover it with a covering of fine leather,*b* and shall put its poles in place. 9They shall take a blue cloth, and cover the lampstand for the light, with its lamps, its snuffers, its trays, and all the vessels for oil with which it is supplied; 10and they shall put it with all its utensils in a covering of fine leather,*b* and put it on the carrying frame. 11Over the golden altar they shall spread a blue cloth, and cover it with a covering of fine leather,*b* and shall put its poles in place; 12and they shall take all the utensils of the

a Or *treaty*, or *testimony*; Heb *eduth*   *b* Meaning of Heb uncertain service that are used in the sanctuary, and put them in a blue cloth, and cover them with a covering of fine leather,*a* and put them on the carrying frame. 13They shall take away the ashes from the altar, and spread a purple cloth over it; 14and they shall put on it all the utensils of the altar, which are used for the service there, the firepans, the forks, the shovels, and the basins, all the utensils of the altar; and they shall spread on it a covering of fine leather,*a* and shall put its poles in place. 15When Aaron and his sons have finished covering the sanctuary and all the furnishings of the sanctuary, as the camp sets out, after that the Kohathites shall come to carry these, but they must not touch the holy things, or they will die. These are the things of the tent of meeting that the Kohathites are to carry.

16 Eleazar son of Aaron the priest shall have charge of the oil for the light, the fragrant incense, the regular grain offering, and the anointing oil, the oversight of all the tabernacle and all that is in it, in the sanctuary and in its utensils.

17 Then the LORD spoke to Moses and Aaron, saying: 18You must not let the tribe of the clans of the Kohathites be destroyed from among the Levites. 19This is how you must deal with them in order that they may live and not die when they come near to the most holy things: Aaron and his sons shall go in and assign each to a particular task or burden. 20But the Kohathites*b* must not go in to look on the holy things even for a moment; otherwise they will die.

21 Then the LORD spoke to Moses, saying: 22Take a census of the Gershonites also, by their ancestral houses and by their clans; 23from thirty years old up to fifty years old you shall enroll them, all who qualify to do work in the tent of meeting. 24This is the service of the clans of the Gershonites, in serving and bearing burdens: 25They shall carry the curtains of the tabernacle, and the tent of meeting with its covering, and the outer covering of fine leather*a* that is on top of it, and the screen for the entrance of the tent of meeting, 26and the hangings of the court, and the screen for the entrance of the gate of the court that is around the tab-

ernacle and the altar, and their cords, and all the equipment for their service; and they shall do all that needs to be done with regard to them. 27All the service of the Gershonites shall be at the command of Aaron and his sons, in all that they are to carry, and in all that they have to do; and you shall assign to their charge all that they are to carry. 28This is the service of the clans of the Gershonites relating to the tent of meeting, and their responsibilities are to be under the oversight of Ithamar son of Aaron the priest.

29 As for the Merarites, you shall enroll them by their clans and their ancestral houses; 30from thirty years old up to fifty years old you shall enroll them, everyone who qualifies to do the work of the tent of meeting. 31This is what they are charged to carry, as the whole of their service in the tent of meeting: the frames of the tabernacle, with its bars, pillars, and bases, 32and the pillars of the court all around with their bases, pegs, and cords, with all their equipment and all their related service; and you shall assign by name the objects that they are required to carry. 33This is the service of the clans of the Merarites, the whole of their service relating to the tent of meeting, under the hand of Ithamar son of Aaron the priest.

4.4–33: *The ark of the covenant★* (v. 5) is a wooden container that contains the stone tablets of the Ten Commandments and also functions as a throne or footstool for the divine presence (Ex 25.10–22). The ark is housed in the inner room of the tabernacle within the tent of meeting. On details of the ark, the tabernacle furnishings, and the tent of meeting, see Ex 25–27; 30. The warning concerning the special danger to the Kohathites (vv. 17–20) stems from their responsibility to handle *the most holy things* (v. 4).

34 So Moses and Aaron and the leaders of the congregation enrolled the Kohathites, by their clans and their ancestral houses, 35from thirty years old up to fifty years old, everyone who qualified for work relating to the tent of meeting; 36and their enrollment by clans was two thousand seven hundred fifty. 37This was the enrollment of the clans

a Meaning of Heb uncertain   *b* Heb *they*

of the Kohathites, all who served at the tent of meeting, whom Moses and Aaron enrolled according to the commandment of the LORD by Moses.

38 The enrollment of the Gershonites, by their clans and their ancestral houses, 39from thirty years old up to fifty years old, everyone who qualified for work relating to the tent of meeting— 40their enrollment by their clans and their ancestral houses was two thousand six hundred thirty. 41This was the enrollment of the clans of the Gershonites, all who served at the tent of meeting, whom Moses and Aaron enrolled according to the commandment of the LORD.

42 The enrollment of the clans of the Merarites, by their clans and their ancestral houses, 43from thirty years old up to fifty years old, everyone who qualified for work relating to the tent of meeting— 44their enrollment by their clans was three thousand two hundred. 45This is the enrollment of the clans of the Merarites, whom Moses and Aaron enrolled according to the commandment of the LORD by Moses.

46 All those who were enrolled of the Levites, whom Moses and Aaron and the leaders of Israel enrolled, by their clans and their ancestral houses, 47from thirty years old up to fifty years old, everyone who qualified to do the work of service and the work of bearing burdens relating to the tent of meeting, 48their enrollment was eight thousand five hundred eighty. 49According to the commandment of the LORD through Moses they were appointed to their several tasks of serving or carrying; thus they were enrolled by him, as the LORD commanded Moses.

5 The LORD spoke to Moses, saying: 2Command the Israelites to put out of the camp everyone who is leprous,ᵃ or has a discharge, and everyone who is unclean through contact with a corpse; 3you shall put out both male and female, putting them outside the camp; they must not defile their camp, where I dwell among them. 4The Israelites did so, putting them outside the camp; as the LORD had spoken to Moses, so the Israelites did.

5 The LORD spoke to Moses, saying: 6Speak to the Israelites: When a man or a woman wrongs another, breaking faith with the LORD, that person incurs guilt 7and shall confess the sin that has been committed. The person shall make full restitution for the wrong, adding one-fifth to it, and giving it to the one who was wronged. 8If the injured party has no next of kin to whom restitution may be made for the wrong, the restitution for wrong shall go to the LORD for the priest, in addition to the ram of atonement with which atonement is made for the guilty party. 9Among all the sacred donations of the Israelites, every gift that they bring to the priest shall be his. 10The sacred donations of all are their own; whatever anyone gives to the priest shall be his.

5.1–10: Impurity and sins against the neighbor. This section begins a series of laws in chs. 5–6 designed to preserve the holiness and purity of the Israelite camp. **1–4:** Since the Israelite camp contains the tabernacle where, the LORD says, *I dwell among them*, the ritual purity of the camp and its inhabitants must be preserved. On the concept of ritual purity and defilement, see sidebar, "Ritual Purity and Cleanness," p. 182. Three causes of impurity are named here: *leprous* or diseased skin (see Lev 13), a genital *discharge* (see Lev 15), or *contact with a corpse* (see Num 19.11–13). **5–9:** This legal case is an addition to the law of restitution to injured parties and their families in Lev 6.1–7. The case stipulates procedures when *the injured party has no next of kin to whom restitution may be made* (v. 8). On *the ram of atonement★* (v. 8), see Lev 6.6–7.

11 The LORD spoke to Moses, saying: 12Speak to the Israelites and say to them: If any man's wife goes astray and is unfaithful to him, 13if a man has had intercourse with her but it is hidden from her husband, so that she is undetected though she has defiled herself, and there is no witness against her since she was not caught in the act; 14if a spirit of jealousy comes on him, and he is jealous of his wife who has defiled herself; or if a spirit of jealousy comes on him, and he is jealous of his wife, though she has not defiled herself; 15then the man shall bring

a A term for several skin diseases; precise meaning uncertain his wife to the priest. And he shall bring the offering required for her, one-tenth of an ephah of barley flour. He shall pour no oil on it and put no frankincense on it, for it is a grain offering of jealousy, a grain offering of remembrance, bringing iniquity to remembrance.

16 Then the priest shall bring her near, and set her before the LORD; 17the priest shall take holy water in an earthen vessel, and take some of the dust that is on the floor of the tabernacle and put it into the water. 18The priest shall set the woman before the LORD, dishevel the woman's hair, and place in her hands the grain offering of remembrance, which is the grain offering of jealousy. In his own hand the priest shall have the water of bitterness that brings the curse. 19Then the priest shall make her take an oath, saying, "If no man has lain with you, if you have not turned aside to uncleanness while under your husband's authority, be immune to this water of bitterness that brings the curse. 20But if you have gone astray while under your husband's authority, if you have defiled yourself and some man other than your husband has had intercourse with you," 21—let the priest make the woman take the oath of the curse and say to the woman—"the LORD make you an execration and an oath among your people, when the LORD makes your uterus drop, your womb discharge; 22now may this water that brings the curse enter your bowels and make your womb discharge, your uterus drop!" And the woman shall say, "Amen. Amen."

23 Then the priest shall put these curses in writing, and wash them off into the water of bitterness. 24He shall make the woman drink the water of bitterness that brings the curse, and the water that brings the curse shall enter her and cause bitter pain. 25The priest shall take the grain offering of jealousy out of the woman's hand, and shall elevate the grain offering before the LORD and bring it to the altar; 26and the priest shall take a handful of the grain offering, as its memorial portion, and turn it into smoke on the altar, and afterward shall make the woman drink the water. 27When he has made her drink the water, then, if she has defiled herself and has been unfaithful to her husband, the water that brings the curse shall enter into her and cause bitter pain, and her womb shall discharge, her uterus drop, and the woman shall become an execration among her people. 28But if the woman has not defiled herself and is clean, then she shall be immune and be able to conceive children.

29 This is the law in cases of jealousy, when a wife, while under her husband's authority, goes astray and defiles herself, 30or when a spirit of jealousy comes on a man and he is jealous of his wife; then he shall set the woman before the LORD, and the priest shall apply this entire law to her. 31The man shall be free from iniquity, but the woman shall bear her iniquity.

5.11–31: The case of a woman suspected of adultery. Those convicted of adultery by the evidence of witnesses were subject to the death penalty (Lev 20.10). This supplemental case involves instances in which a husband has a suspicion of adultery or *a spirit of jealousy* (v. 14) but *there is no witness against her* (v. 13). **15:** An *ephah* is a unit of dry measure, roughly half a bushel. Grain offerings were typically accompanied by olive *oil* and *frankincense,* an aromatic spice (Lev 2.1), but this is a special *grain offering of jealousy* and *remembrance.* **17:** The *holy water* is the water used by the priests for ritual washing and purification (Ex 30.17–21, 28–29). **18:** To *dishevel the hair* is a custom associated with mourning (Lev 10.6) or a sign of uncleanness (Lev 13.45). **19–28:** The oath forms the basis for the trial by ordeal, a practice known elsewhere in the ancient world. The woman expresses her acceptance of the trial and the oath by saying, "*Amen, amen*" (v. 22). When the woman drinks the holy *water of bitterness* (v. 19), two results are possible. If she is indeed guilty of adultery as the husband suspected, she will suffer a collapsed uterus and become an *execration* (v. 27), that is, a person under a curse. If she is not guilty, she will be *immune* from the effects of the bitter water and *able to conceive children* (v. 28). **31:** The husband will be *free from iniquity* and not suffer punishment if his wife proves to be innocent through the ordeal. He has the right to request that his wife go through the trial by ordeal.

6 The LORD spoke to Moses, saying: 2Speak to the Israelites and say to them: When either men or women make a special

vow, the vow of a nazirite,[a] to separate themselves to the LORD, [3]they shall separate themselves from wine and strong drink; they shall drink no wine vinegar or other vinegar, and shall not drink any grape juice or eat grapes, fresh or dried. [4]All their days as nazirites[b] they shall eat nothing that is produced by the grapevine, not even the seeds or the skins.

[5] All the days of their nazirite vow no razor shall come upon the head; until the time is completed for which they separate themselves to the LORD, they shall be holy; they shall let the locks of the head grow long.

[6] All the days that they separate themselves to the LORD they shall not go near a corpse. [7]Even if their father or mother, brother or sister, should die, they may not defile themselves; because their consecration to God is upon the head. [8]All their days as nazirites[b] they are holy to the LORD.

[9] If someone dies very suddenly nearby, defiling the consecrated head, then they shall shave the head on the day of their cleansing; on the seventh day they shall shave it. [10]On the eighth day they shall bring two turtledoves or two young pigeons to the priest at the entrance of the tent of meeting, [11]and the priest shall offer one as a sin offering and the other as a burnt offering, and make atonement for them, because they incurred guilt by reason of the corpse. They shall sanctify the head that same day, [12]and separate themselves to the LORD for their days as nazirites,[b] and bring a male lamb a year old as a guilt offering. The former time shall be void, because the consecrated head was defiled.

[13] This is the law for the nazirites[b] when the time of their consecration has been completed: they shall be brought to the entrance of the tent of meeting, [14]and they shall offer their gift to the LORD, one male lamb a year old without blemish as a burnt offering, one ewe lamb a year old without blemish as a sin offering, one ram without blemish as an offering of well-being, [15]and a basket of unleavened bread, cakes of choice flour mixed with oil and unleavened wafers spread with oil, with their grain offering and their drink offerings. [16]The priest shall present them

before the LORD and offer their sin offering and burnt offering, [17]and shall offer the ram as a sacrifice of well-being to the LORD, with the basket of unleavened bread; the priest also shall make the accompanying grain offering and drink offering. [18]Then the nazirites[b] shall shave the consecrated head at the entrance of the tent of meeting, and shall take the hair from the consecrated head and put it on the fire under the sacrifice of well-being. [19]The priest shall take the shoulder of the ram, when it is boiled, and one unleavened cake out of the basket, and one unleavened wafer, and shall put them in the palms of the nazirites,[b] after they have shaved the consecrated head. [20]Then the priest shall elevate them as an elevation offering before the LORD; they are a holy portion for the priest, together with the breast that is elevated and the thigh that is offered. After that the nazirites[b] may drink wine.

[21] This is the law for the nazirites[b] who take a vow. Their offering to the LORD must be in accordance with the nazirite[a] vow, apart from what else they can afford. In accordance with whatever vow they take, so they shall do, following the law for their consecration.

6.1–21: **The vow of the nazirites.** Nazirites were men and women who took vows to offer themselves for special service to the LORD for a specified time. Biblical examples of lifelong nazirites include Samson (Judg 13.2–14) and Samuel (1 Sam 1.11). The nazirite law here assumes a limited duration of special service, not a lifetime. **7:** *Consecration* means dedication to special service to God. **9–12:** *Suddenly* and unexpectedly coming in contact with a corpse causes the nazirite to become ritually unclean (*defiling the consecrated head*, v. 9). Such defilement requires the nazirite to be ritually cleansed and rededicated. **13–20:** On the background of the various offerings to mark the end of the nazirite's vow, see Lev 1–4. On the *elevation offering*, see Lev 7.32–34.

[22] The LORD spoke to Moses, saying: [23]Speak to Aaron and his sons, saying, Thus

---

a That is *one separated* or *one consecrated*   b That is *those separated* or *those consecrated* you shall bless the Israelites: You shall say to them,

24 The LORD bless you and keep you;
25 the LORD make his face to shine upon
        you, and be gracious to you;
26 the LORD lift up his countenance upon
        you, and give you peace.

27 So they shall put my name on the Israelites, and I will bless them.

6.22–27: The priestly blessing. Priests concluded communal worship with these words of blessing and peace. Two silver cylinders discovered by archaeologists and dated to 600 BCE contain portions of this ancient priestly blessing written in Hebrew. To *shine* the *face* and *lift up* the *countenance* or "face of the LORD" are images of protection, favor, and graciousness (vv. 25–26; see Ps 67.1–2; Job 34.29). *Peace* ("shalom") connotes well-being and wholeness in all aspects of one's life (v. 26). Putting the divine *name on the Israelites* implies that they belong exclusively to the LORD and that the LORD will care for them.

The offerings of the leaders of the twelve tribes
7.1–89: Chapter 7 begins a larger section (chs. 7–10) that is set in a flashback to one month earlier than the time specified at the beginning of Numbers. *The day when Moses had finished setting up the tabernacle** (v. 1) was the first day of the first month (Ex 40.17). In contrast, Num 1.1 begins on the first day of the second month. The time frame will return to the second month in Num 10.11. The long list of offerings in ch. 7 was part of the ceremony consecrating or dedicating the tabernacle and altar. The sequence of the twelve tribes in vv. 12–83 follows the same sequence as in 2.3–31, and the names of the tribal leaders are the same as in 1.5–15. Each tribal leader presents exactly the same offering.

---

7 On the day when Moses had finished setting up the tabernacle, and had anointed and consecrated it with all its furnishings, and had anointed and consecrated the altar with all its utensils, 2the leaders of Israel, heads of their ancestral houses, the leaders of the tribes, who were over those who were enrolled, made offerings. 3They brought their offerings before the LORD, six covered wagons and twelve oxen, a wagon for every two of the leaders, and for each one an ox; they presented them before the taber-

nacle. 4Then the LORD said to Moses: 5Accept these from them, that they may be used in doing the service of the tent of meeting, and give them to the Levites, to each according to his service. 6So Moses took the wagons and the oxen, and gave them to the Levites. 7Two wagons and four oxen he gave to the Gershonites, according to their service; 8and four wagons and eight oxen he gave to the Merarites, according to their service, under the direction of Ithamar son of Aaron the priest. 9But to the Kohathites he gave none, because they were charged with the care of the holy things that had to be carried on the shoulders.

10 The leaders also presented offerings for the dedication of the altar at the time when it was anointed; the leaders presented their offering before the altar. 11The LORD said to Moses: They shall present their offerings, one leader each day, for the dedication of the altar.

12 The one who presented his offering the first day was Nahshon son of Amminadab, of the tribe of Judah; 13his offering was one silver plate weighing one hundred thirty shekels, one silver basin weighing seventy shekels, according to the shekel of the sanctuary, both of them full of choice flour mixed with oil for a grain offering; 14one golden dish weighing ten shekels, full of incense; 15one young bull, one ram, one male lamb a year old, for a burnt offering; 16one male goat for a sin offering; 17and for the sacrifice of well-being, two oxen, five rams, five male goats, and five male lambs a year old. This was the offering of Nahshon son of Amminadab.

7.13: On *the shekel of the sanctuary*, see comment on 3.40–51.

---

18 On the second day Nethanel son of Zuar, the leader of Issachar, presented an offering; 19he presented for his offering one silver plate weighing one hundred thirty shekels, one silver basin weighing seventy shekels, according to the shekel of the sanctuary, both of them full of choice flour mixed with oil for a grain offering; 20one golden dish weighing ten shekels, full of incense;

21 one young bull, one ram, one male lamb a year old, as a burnt offering; 22 one male goat as a sin offering; 23 and for the sacrifice of well-being, two oxen, five rams, five male goats, and five male lambs a year old. This was the offering of Nethanel son of Zuar.

24 On the third day Eliab son of Helon, the leader of the Zebulunites: 25 his offering was one silver plate weighing one hundred thirty shekels, one silver basin weighing seventy shekels, according to the shekel of the sanctuary, both of them full of choice flour mixed with oil for a grain offering; 26 one golden dish weighing ten shekels, full of incense; 27 one young bull, one ram, one male lamb a year old, for a burnt offering; 28 one male goat for a sin offering; 29 and for the sacrifice of well-being, two oxen, five rams, five male goats, and five male lambs a year old. This was the offering of Eliab son of Helon.

30 On the fourth day Elizur son of Shedeur, the leader of the Reubenites: 31 his offering was one silver plate weighing one hundred thirty shekels, one silver basin weighing seventy shekels, according to the shekel of the sanctuary, both of them full of choice flour mixed with oil for a grain offering; 32 one golden dish weighing ten shekels, full of incense; 33 one young bull, one ram, one male lamb a year old, for a burnt offering; 34 one male goat for a sin offering; 35 and for the sacrifice of well-being, two oxen, five rams, five male goats, and five male lambs a year old. This was the offering of Elizur son of Shedeur.

36 On the fifth day Shelumiel son of Zurishaddai, the leader of the Simeonites: 37 his offering was one silver plate weighing one hundred thirty shekels, one silver basin weighing seventy shekels, according to the shekel of the sanctuary, both of them full of choice flour mixed with oil for a grain offering; 38 one golden dish weighing ten shekels, full of incense; 39 one young bull, one ram, one male lamb a year old, for a burnt offering; 40 one male goat for a sin offering; 41 and for the sacrifice of well-being, two oxen, five rams, five male goats, and five male lambs a year old. This was the offering of Shelumiel son of Zurishaddai.

42 On the sixth day Eliasaph son of Deuel, the leader of the Gadites: 43 his offering was one silver plate weighing one hundred thirty shekels, one silver basin weighing seventy shekels, according to the shekel of the sanctuary, both of them full of choice flour mixed with oil for a grain offering; 44 one golden dish weighing ten shekels, full of incense; 45 one young bull, one ram, one male lamb a year old, for a burnt offering; 46 one male goat for a sin offering; 47 and for the sacrifice of well-being, two oxen, five rams, five male goats, and five male lambs a year old. This was the offering of Eliasaph son of Deuel.

48 On the seventh day Elishama son of Ammihud, the leader of the Ephraimites: 49 his offering was one silver plate weighing one hundred thirty shekels, one silver basin weighing seventy shekels, according to the shekel of the sanctuary, both of them full of choice flour mixed with oil for a grain offering; 50 one golden dish weighing ten shekels, full of incense; 51 one young bull, one ram, one male lamb a year old, for a burnt offering; 52 one male goat for a sin offering; 53 and for the sacrifice of well-being, two oxen, five rams, five male goats, and five male lambs a year old. This was the offering of Elishama son of Ammihud.

54 On the eighth day Gamaliel son of Pedahzur, the leader of the Manassites: 55 his offering was one silver plate weighing one hundred thirty shekels, one silver basin weighing seventy shekels, according to the shekel of the sanctuary, both of them full of choice flour mixed with oil for a grain offering; 56 one golden dish weighing ten shekels, full of incense; 57 one young bull, one ram, one male lamb a year old, for a burnt offering; 58 one male goat for a sin offering; 59 and for the sacrifice of well-being, two oxen, five rams, five male goats, and five male lambs a year old. This was the offering of Gamaliel son of Pedahzur.

60 On the ninth day Abidan son of Gideoni, the leader of the Benjaminites: 61 his offering was one silver plate weighing one hundred thirty shekels, one silver basin weighing seventy shekels, according to the shekel of the sanctuary, both of them full of

choice flour mixed with oil for a grain offering; 62one golden dish weighing ten shekels, full of incense; 63one young bull, one ram, one male lamb a year old, for a burnt offering; 64one male goat for a sin offering; 65and for the sacrifice of well-being, two oxen, five rams, five male goats, and five male lambs a year old. This was the offering of Abidan son of Gideoni.

66 On the tenth day Ahiezer son of Ammishaddai, the leader of the Danites: 67his offering was one silver plate weighing one hundred thirty shekels, one silver basin weighing seventy shekels, according to the shekel of the sanctuary, both of them full of choice flour mixed with oil for a grain offering; 68one golden dish weighing ten shekels, full of incense; 69one young bull, one ram, one male lamb a year old, for a burnt offering; 70one male goat for a sin offering; 71and for the sacrifice of well-being, two oxen, five rams, five male goats, and five male lambs a year old. This was the offering of Ahiezer son of Ammishaddai.

72 On the eleventh day Pagiel son of Ochran, the leader of the Asherites: 73his offering was one silver plate weighing one hundred thirty shekels, one silver basin weighing seventy shekels, according to the shekel of the sanctuary, both of them full of choice flour mixed with oil for a grain offering; 74one golden dish weighing ten shekels, full of incense; 75one young bull, one ram, one male lamb a year old, for a burnt offering; 76one male goat for a sin offering; 77and for the sacrifice of well-being, two oxen, five rams, five male goats, and five male lambs a year old. This was the offering of Pagiel son of Ochran.

78 On the twelfth day Ahira son of Enan, the leader of the Naphtalites: 79his offering was one silver plate weighing one hundred thirty shekels, one silver basin weighing seventy shekels, according to the shekel of the sanctuary, both of them full of choice flour mixed with oil for a grain offering; 80one golden dish weighing ten shekels, full of incense; 81one young bull, one ram, one male lamb a year old, for a burnt offering; 82one male goat for a sin offering; 83and for the sacrifice of well-being, two oxen, five rams,

five male goats, and five male lambs a year old. This was the offering of Ahira son of Enan.

84 This was the dedication offering for the altar, at the time when it was anointed, from the leaders of Israel: twelve silver plates, twelve silver basins, twelve golden dishes, 85each silver plate weighing one hundred thirty shekels and each basin seventy, all the silver of the vessels two thousand four hundred shekels according to the shekel of the sanctuary, 86the twelve golden dishes, full of incense, weighing ten shekels apiece according to the shekel of the sanctuary, all the gold of the dishes being one hundred twenty shekels; 87all the livestock for the burnt offering twelve bulls, twelve rams, twelve male lambs a year old, with their grain offering; and twelve male goats for a sin offering; 88and all the livestock for the sacrifice of well-being twenty-four bulls, the rams sixty, the male goats sixty, the male lambs a year old sixty. This was the dedication offering for the altar, after it was anointed.

89 When Moses went into the tent of meeting to speak with the LORD,*a* he would hear the voice speaking to him from above the mercy seat*b* that was on the ark of the covenant*c* from between the two cherubim; thus it spoke to him.

8 The LORD spoke to Moses, saying: 2Speak to Aaron and say to him: When you set up the lamps, the seven lamps shall give light in front of the lampstand. 3Aaron did so; he set up its lamps to give light in front of the lampstand, as the LORD had commanded Moses. 4Now this was how the lampstand was made, out of hammered work of gold. From its base to its flowers, it was hammered work; according to the pattern that the LORD had shown Moses, so he made the lampstand.

8.1–26: The seven lamps and the dedication of the Levites. 1–4: The instructions for the seven lamps in the tabernacle were given in Ex 25.31–40.

5 The LORD spoke to Moses, saying: 6Take the Levites from among the Israelites

a Heb *him*   *b* Or *the cover*   *c* Or *treaty,* or *testimony*; Heb *eduth* and cleanse them. 7Thus you shall do to them, to cleanse them: sprinkle the water of purification on them, have them shave their whole body with a razor and wash their clothes, and so cleanse themselves. 8Then let them take a young bull and its grain offering of choice flour mixed with oil, and you shall take another young bull for a sin offering. 9You shall bring the Levites before the tent of meeting, and assemble the whole congregation of the Israelites. 10When you bring the Levites before the LORD, the Israelites shall lay their hands on the Levites, 11and Aaron shall present the Levites before the LORD as an elevation offering from the Israelites, that they may do the service of the LORD. 12The Levites shall lay their hands on the heads of the bulls, and he shall offer the one for a sin offering and the other for a burnt offering to the LORD, to make atonement for the Levites. 13Then you shall have the Levites stand before Aaron and his sons, and you shall present them as an elevation offering to the LORD.

14 Thus you shall separate the Levites from among the other Israelites, and the Levites shall be mine. 15Thereafter the Levites may go in to do service at the tent of meeting, once you have cleansed them and presented them as an elevation offering. 16For they are unreservedly given to me from among the Israelites; I have taken them for myself, in place of all that open the womb, the firstborn of all the Israelites. 17For all the firstborn among the Israelites are mine, both human and animal. On the day that I struck down all the firstborn in the land of Egypt I consecrated them for myself, 18but I have taken the Levites in place of all the firstborn among the Israelites. 19Moreover, I have given the Levites as a gift to Aaron and his sons from among the Israelites, to do the service for the Israelites at the tent of meeting, and to make atonement for the Israelites, in order that there may be no plague among the Israelites for coming too close to the sanctuary.

20 Moses and Aaron and the whole congregation of the Israelites did with the Levites accordingly; the Israelites did with the Levites just as the LORD had commanded Moses concerning them. 21The Levites purified themselves from sin and washed their clothes; then Aaron presented them as an elevation offering before the LORD, and Aaron made atonement for them to cleanse them. 22Thereafter the Levites went in to do their service in the tent of meeting in attendance on Aaron and his sons. As the LORD had commanded Moses concerning the Levites, so they did with them.

23 The LORD spoke to Moses, saying: 24This applies to the Levites: from twenty-five years old and upward they shall begin to do duty in the service of the tent of meeting; 25and from the age of fifty years they shall retire from the duty of the service and serve no more. 26They may assist their brothers in the tent of meeting in carrying out their duties, but they shall perform no service. Thus you shall do with the Levites in assigning their duties.

8.5–26. 6: The Levites must be ritually *cleansed* so that they can handle the holy objects with which they are entrusted. On the concept of ritual purity and cleansing, see the sidebar on p. 182. 10: The Israelites *lay their hands on the Levites* as an act of identification and substitution. The Levites represent all Israel and substitute for Israel's obligation to sacrifice its firstborn to the LORD through the Levites' service in the sanctuary or place of worship (see 3.11–13; 8.16–18). 11: The *elevation offering* signifies the transference of the Levites from the status of a common tribe to a holy tribe dedicated to *the service of the LORD* (see Lev 7.30). 12: Any unintentional guilt or impurity among the Levites is transferred to the bulls when they *lay their hands on the heads of the bulls*. The *sin offering* and the *burnt offering* serve to *make atonement** or remove the impurity or guilt of wrongful actions. See Lev 1.3–9; 4.20–21.

9 The LORD spoke to Moses in the wilderness of Sinai, in the first month of the second year after they had come out of the land of Egypt, saying: 2Let the Israelites keep the passover at its appointed time. 3On the fourteenth day of this month, at twilight,*a* you shall keep it at its appointed time; according to all its statutes and all its regu-

a Heb *between the two evenings*

lations you shall keep it. ⁴So Moses told the Israelites that they should keep the passover. ⁵They kept the passover in the first month, on the fourteenth day of the month, at twilight,ᵃ in the wilderness of Sinai. Just as the LORD had commanded Moses, so the Israelites did. ⁶Now there were certain people who were unclean through touching a corpse, so that they could not keep the passover on that day. They came before Moses and Aaron on that day, ⁷and said to him, "Although we are unclean through touching a corpse, why must we be kept from presenting the LORD's offering at its appointed time among the Israelites?" ⁸Moses spoke to them, "Wait, so that I may hear what the LORD will command concerning you."

9 The LORD spoke to Moses, saying: ¹⁰Speak to the Israelites, saying: Anyone of you or your descendants who is unclean through touching a corpse, or is away on a journey, shall still keep the passover to the LORD. ¹¹In the second month on the fourteenth day, at twilight,ᵃ they shall keep it; they shall eat it with unleavened bread and bitter herbs. ¹²They shall leave none of it until morning, nor break a bone of it; according to all the statute for the passover they shall keep it. ¹³But anyone who is clean and is not on a journey, and yet refrains from keeping the passover, shall be cut off from the people for not presenting the LORD's offering at its appointed time; such a one shall bear the consequences for the sin. ¹⁴Any alien residing among you who wishes to keep the passover to the LORD shall do so according to the statute of the passover and according to its regulation; you shall have one statute for both the resident alien and the native.

9.1–14: Celebrating Passover*: uncleanness and resident aliens. 1: On the date of *the first month of the second year,* see comment on 7.1–89. **2–5:** The festival of Passover celebrates the freedom and exodus out of slavery in Egypt (Ex 12.1–28). **6–13:** Becoming *unclean through touching a corpse* (v. 6) represented a severe ritual impurity (see sidebar, "Ritual Purity and Cleanness," p. 182) that would prevent an Israelite from fulfilling the obligation to observe the Passover on the designated date of *the fourteenth day* of *the first month.* Being *away on a journey* (v. 10) would

also prevent observance. Moses consults the LORD in this unprecedented legal case. The decision is made to allow an alternate date one month later for celebrating Passover (*in the second month on the fourteenth day,* v. 11). **14:** An *alien residing among you* is a foreigner who has taken up permanent residence among the Israelites (Ex 12.43–49).

15 On the day the tabernacle was set up, the cloud covered the tabernacle, the tent of the covenant;ᵇ and from evening until morning it was over the tabernacle, having the appearance of fire. ¹⁶It was always so: the cloud covered it by dayᶜ and the appearance of fire by night. ¹⁷Whenever the cloud lifted from over the tent, then the Israelites would set out; and in the place where the cloud settled down, there the Israelites would camp. ¹⁸At the command of the LORD the Israelites would set out, and at the command of the LORD they would camp. As long as the cloud rested over the tabernacle, they would remain in camp. ¹⁹Even when the cloud continued over the tabernacle many days, the Israelites would keep the charge of the LORD, and would not set out. ²⁰Sometimes the cloud would remain a few days over the tabernacle, and according to the command of the LORD they would remain in camp; then according to the command of the LORD they would set out. ²¹Sometimes the cloud would remain from evening until morning; and when the cloud lifted in the morning, they would set out, or if it continued for a day and a night, when the cloud lifted they would set out. ²²Whether it was two days, or a month, or a longer time, that the cloud continued over the tabernacle, resting upon it, the Israelites would remain in camp and would not set out; but when it lifted they would set out. ²³At the command of the LORD they would camp, and at the command of the LORD they would set out. They kept the charge of the LORD, at the command of the LORD by Moses.

9.15–23: The fiery cloud veiling the divine presence. 15: *The day the tabernacle* was set up* was the same date as in v. 1, 7.1, and Ex 40.17. *The cloud* that

a Heb *between the two evenings*   b Or *treaty,* or *testimony;* Heb *eduth*   c Gk Syr Vg: Heb lacks *by day* had *the appearance of fire* veiled the divine presence while also providing visible assurance that the LORD was present and guiding the Israelites in their wilderness journey (Ex 13.21–22; 40.34–35). On the *tabernacle*, the *tent of the covenant** (also known as the tent of meeting), see comments on 1.1 and 1.47–54.

10 The LORD spoke to Moses, saying: 2Make two silver trumpets; you shall make them of hammered work; and you shall use them for summoning the congregation, and for breaking camp. 3When both are blown, the whole congregation shall assemble before you at the entrance of the tent of meeting. 4But if only one is blown, then the leaders, the heads of the tribes of Israel, shall assemble before you. 5When you blow an alarm, the camps on the east side shall set out; 6when you blow a second alarm, the camps on the south side shall set out. An alarm is to be blown whenever they are to set out. 7But when the assembly is to be gathered, you shall blow, but you shall not sound an alarm. 8The sons of Aaron, the priests, shall blow the trumpets; this shall be a perpetual institution for you throughout your generations. 9When you go to war in your land against the adversary who oppresses you, you shall sound an alarm with the trumpets, so that you may be remembered before the LORD your God and be saved from your enemies. 10Also on your days of rejoicing, at your appointed festivals, and at the beginnings of your months, you shall blow the trumpets over your burnt offerings and over your sacrifices of well-being; they shall serve as a reminder on your behalf before the LORD your God: I am the LORD your God.

10.1–10: The two silver trumpets. The two silver trumpets are sacred instruments blown by priests for four purposes: to call together the whole *congregation* or the *leaders* for an assembly (vv. 3–4), to provide a signal to *set out* from camp on the wilderness sojourn (vv. 5–6), to *sound an alarm* at the time of war (v. 9), and to call a celebration *on your days of rejoicing* (v. 10). According to the ancient Jewish historian Josephus* and as depicted on ancient Jewish coins, the silver trumpets are about twelve inches long with a slender body and wide mouth.

11 In the second year, in the second month, on the twentieth day of the month, the cloud lifted from over the tabernacle of the covenant.*a* 12Then the Israelites set out by stages from the wilderness of Sinai, and the cloud settled down in the wilderness of Paran. 13They set out for the first time at the command of the LORD by Moses. 14The standard of the camp of Judah set out first, company by company, and over the whole company was Nahshon son of Amminadab. 15Over the company of the tribe of Issachar was Nethanel son of Zuar; 16and over the company of the tribe of Zebulun was Eliab son of Helon.

17 Then the tabernacle was taken down, and the Gershonites and the Merarites, who carried the tabernacle, set out. 18Next the standard of the camp of Reuben set out, company by company; and over the whole company was Elizur son of Shedeur. 19Over the company of the tribe of Simeon was Shelumiel son of Zurishaddai, 20and over the company of the tribe of Gad was Eliasaph son of Deuel.

21 Then the Kohathites, who carried the holy things, set out; and the tabernacle was set up before their arrival. 22Next the standard of the Ephraimite camp set out, company by company, and over the whole company was Elishama son of Ammihud. 23Over the company of the tribe of Manasseh was Gamaliel son of Pedahzur, 24and over the company of the tribe of Benjamin was Abidan son of Gideoni.

25 Then the standard of the camp of Dan, acting as the rear guard of all the camps, set out, company by company, and over the whole company was Ahiezer son of Ammishaddai. 26Over the company of the tribe of Asher was Pagiel son of Ochran, 27and over the company of the tribe of Naphtali was Ahira son of Enan. 28This was the order of march of the Israelites, company by company, when they set out.

29 Moses said to Hobab son of Reuel the Midianite, Moses' father-in-law, "We are setting out for the place of which the LORD said, 'I will give it to you'; come with us, and

a Or *treaty*, or *testimony*; Heb *eduth*

we will treat you well; for the LORD has promised good to Israel." 30But he said to him, "I will not go, but I will go back to my own land and to my kindred." 31He said, "Do not leave us, for you know where we should camp in the wilderness, and you will serve as eyes for us. 32Moreover, if you go with us, whatever good the LORD does for us, the same we will do for you."

33 So they set out from the mount of the LORD three days' journey with the ark of the covenant of the LORD going before them three days' journey, to seek out a resting place for them, 34the cloud of the LORD being over them by day when they set out from the camp.

35 Whenever the ark set out, Moses would say,

"Arise, O LORD, let your enemies be
　　scattered,
　　and your foes flee before you."
36And whenever it came to rest, he would say,

"Return, O LORD of the ten thousand
　　thousands of Israel."[a]

10.11–36: The actual beginning of the march of the holy camp of Israel. 11: The date now moves ahead to *the second month, on the twentieth day* which is nineteen days after the census was taken in 1.1 (see comment on 7.1). On *the cloud* and *the tabernacle of the covenant,* see comment on 9.15. **12:** The Israelites move from *the wilderness of Sinai* in the southern part of the Sinai peninsula to *the wilderness of Paran* in the northern part of the Sinai peninsula on their way north to the land of Canaan. **14–28:** On the sequence of the twelve tribes and the Levites as they set out on the march, see chs. 2–3. The list of tribal leaders corresponds to the list in 1.5–15. According to ch. 2, the twelve Israelite tribes are divided into four groups of three tribes each. The four groups of tribes each had their own *standard* (a flag or other symbol, vv. 14, 18, 22, 25). **29:** *Moses' father-in-law* is known here as *Hobab,* but in other biblical traditions he is sometimes known as Jethro (Ex 3.1) or Reuel (Ex 2.18). Hobab is a member of the *Midianite* people, but in Judg 4.11 he is called a Kenite, a group probably related to the Midianites. Israel's relationships with Midianites or Kenites are often positive (Ex 2.11–22), but at times there is conflict (Num 25; 31). **33:** On *the ark of the covenant,* see comment on 1.1. **34:** On *the cloud of*

the LORD, see comment on 9.15. **35–36:** These two ancient battle cries associate the portable *ark* with the presence of the *LORD* as the Divine Warrior* who fights on Israel's behalf in holy war* against Israel's *enemies.*

〜〜〜〜〜〜〜〜〜〜〜〜〜〜〜

11 Now when the people complained in the hearing of the LORD about their misfortunes, the LORD heard it and his anger was kindled. Then the fire of the LORD burned against them, and consumed some outlying parts of the camp. 2But the people cried out to Moses; and Moses prayed to the LORD, and the fire abated. 3So that place was called Taberah,[b] because the fire of the LORD burned against them.

4 The rabble among them had a strong craving; and the Israelites also wept again, and said, "If only we had meat to eat! 5We remember the fish we used to eat in Egypt for nothing, the cucumbers, the melons, the leeks, the onions, and the garlic; 6but now our strength is dried up, and there is nothing at all but this manna to look at."

7 Now the manna was like coriander seed, and its color was like the color of gum resin. 8The people went around and gathered it, ground it in mills or beat it in mortars, then boiled it in pots and made cakes of it; and the taste of it was like the taste of cakes baked with oil. 9When the dew fell on the camp in the night, the manna would fall with it.

11.1–35: Israel's abrupt turn to rebellion in the wilderness. Chapters 1–10 portrayed Israel as very obedient to the LORD's every command. Suddenly and unexpectedly, Israel begins to complain about the hardships of the wilderness and to rebel against the LORD and Moses. **1:** *The fire of the LORD* presumably originated from the fiery cloud of the divine presence in the midst of the camp (see 9.15–16; Lev 10.1–2). **4:** *The rabble* is a disorderly mob of non-Israelites who traveled with Israel out of Egypt. In Ex 12.38, they are called a "mixed crowd" (see Lev 24.10). **6–9:** *Manna* was a special food from the LORD provided daily in the desert for the Israelites (Ex 16).

〜〜〜〜〜〜〜〜〜〜〜〜〜〜〜

10 Moses heard the people weeping throughout their families, all at the en-

---

a Meaning of Heb uncertain　　*b* That is *Burning*

trances of their tents. Then the LORD became very angry, and Moses was displeased. [11]So Moses said to the LORD, "Why have you treated your servant so badly? Why have I not found favor in your sight, that you lay the burden of all this people on me? [12]Did I conceive all this people? Did I give birth to them, that you should say to me, 'Carry them in your bosom, as a nurse carries a sucking child,' to the land that you promised on oath to their ancestors? [13]Where am I to get meat to give to all this people? For they come weeping to me and say, 'Give us meat to eat!' [14]I am not able to carry all this people alone, for they are too heavy for me. [15]If this is the way you are going to treat me, put me to death at once—if I have found favor in your sight—and do not let me see my misery."

16 So the LORD said to Moses, "Gather for me seventy of the elders of Israel, whom you know to be the elders of the people and officers over them; bring them to the tent of meeting, and have them take their place there with you. [17]I will come down and talk with you there; and I will take some of the spirit that is on you and put it on them; and they shall bear the burden of the people along with you so that you will not bear it all by yourself. [18]And say to the people: Consecrate yourselves for tomorrow, and you shall eat meat; for you have wailed in the hearing of the LORD, saying, 'If only we had meat to eat! Surely it was better for us in Egypt.' Therefore the LORD will give you meat, and you shall eat. [19]You shall eat not only one day, or two days, or five days, or ten days, or twenty days, [20]but for a whole month—until it comes out of your nostrils and becomes loathsome to you—because you have rejected the LORD who is among you, and have wailed before him, saying, 'Why did we ever leave Egypt?' " [21]But Moses said, "The people I am with number six hundred thousand on foot; and you say, 'I will give them meat, that they may eat for a whole month'! [22]Are there enough flocks and herds to slaughter for them? Are there enough fish in the sea to catch for them?" [23]The LORD said to Moses, "Is the LORD's power limited?[a] Now you shall see whether my word will come true for you or not."

24 So Moses went out and told the people the words of the LORD; and he gathered seventy elders of the people, and placed them all around the tent. [25]Then the LORD came down in the cloud and spoke to him, and took some of the spirit that was on him and put it on the seventy elders; and when the spirit rested upon them, they prophesied. But they did not do so again.

26 Two men remained in the camp, one named Eldad, and the other named Medad, and the spirit rested on them; they were among those registered, but they had not gone out to the tent, and so they prophesied in the camp. [27]And a young man ran and told Moses, "Eldad and Medad are prophesying in the camp." [28]And Joshua son of Nun, the assistant of Moses, one of his chosen men,[b] said, "My lord Moses, stop them!" [29]But Moses said to him, "Are you jealous for my sake? Would that all the LORD's people were prophets, and that the LORD would put his spirit on them!" [30]And Moses and the elders of Israel returned to the camp.

31 Then a wind went out from the LORD, and it brought quails from the sea and let them fall beside the camp, about a day's journey on this side and a day's journey on the other side, all around the camp, about two cubits deep on the ground. [32]So the people worked all that day and night and all the next day, gathering the quails; the least anyone gathered was ten homers; and they spread them out for themselves all around the camp. [33]But while the meat was still between their teeth, before it was consumed, the anger of the LORD was kindled against the people, and the LORD struck the people with a very great plague. [34]So that place was called Kibroth-hattaavah,[c] because there they buried the people who had the craving. [35]From Kibroth-hattaavah the people journeyed to Hazeroth.

11.10–35. 12: Moses' rhetorical* questions imply that the LORD and not Moses is the one who *conceived* and *gave birth* to Israel. Thus, Moses argues, the LORD and

a Heb LORD's *hand too short?*   b Or *of Moses from his youth*   c That is *Graves of craving* not Moses should be responsible for nursing Israel as *a sucking child*. These female images of mother and wet nurse for the Lord are rare but not unique (Deut 32.18; Isa 66.12–13). **15:** Like Moses, several biblical leaders plead with God to put them to death when caught in desperate circumstances. Examples include the prophets* Elijah (1 Kings 19.4), Jeremiah (Jer 20.17), and Jonah (Jon 4.3), and the judge Samson (Judg 16.30). **16–17:** In an alternate version of the story, Jethro (the father-in-law of Moses) offers a similar solution of Moses' sharing leadership with seventy elders (Ex 18.13–26). The divine *spirit* (v. 17) is often associated with leaders and prophets in the Bible (Judg 3.10) and can be transferred from one person to another (vv. 24–25; 2 Kings 2.9–10). **18:** The command to the people to *consecrate yourselves* involves ritual purification and preparation before encountering the holy presence of the Lord. **25:** The elders temporarily *prophesied* or mediated messages from the Lord but then ceased. This suggests that Moses remains the one authoritative prophet or mediator of the Lord's words to the people. **26–30:** The scene appears to assume *the tent* of meeting which contains the tabernacle* and the ark (see 1.1) is located outside *the camp* of Israelite tribes (see Ex 33.7–11). Another tradition in Numbers places the tent and its contents in the middle of the Israelite camp (2.2). **31:** The two scenes of the *spirit* distributed upon the seventy elders (vv. 16–30) and the *wind* bearing the quails share the same key word in Hebrew, "ruah," which can mean either "wind" or "spirit." A similar quails story occurs in Ex 16.13, although in Numbers the quails become a means of judgment and not favor because of the people's rejection of the manna (vv. 4–6). **32:** A *homer* is a unit of dry measure equal to several bushels.

12 While they were at Hazeroth, Miriam and Aaron spoke against Moses because of the Cushite woman whom he had married (for he had indeed married a Cushite woman); ²and they said, "Has the Lord spoken only through Moses? Has he not spoken through us also?" And the Lord heard it. ³Now the man Moses was very humble,ᵃ more so than anyone else on the face of the earth. ⁴Suddenly the Lord said to Moses, Aaron, and Miriam, "Come out, you three, to the tent of meeting." So the three of them came out. ⁵Then the Lord came down in a pillar of cloud, and stood at the entrance of the tent, and called Aaron and Miriam; and

they both came forward. ⁶And he said, "Hear my words:

When there are prophets among you,
    I the Lord make myself known to
        them in visions;
    I speak to them in dreams.
⁷Not so with my servant Moses;
    he is entrusted with all my house.
⁸ With him I speak face to face—clearly,
        not in riddles;
    and he beholds the form of the
        Lord.

Why then were you not afraid to speak against my servant Moses?" ⁹And the anger of the Lord was kindled against them, and he departed.

10 When the cloud went away from over the tent, Miriam had become leprous,ᵇ as white as snow. And Aaron turned towards Miriam and saw that she was leprous. ¹¹Then Aaron said to Moses, "Oh, my lord, do not punish usᶜ for a sin that we have so foolishly committed. ¹²Do not let her be like one stillborn, whose flesh is half consumed when it comes out of its mother's womb." ¹³And Moses cried to the Lord, "O God, please heal her." ¹⁴But the Lord said to Moses, "If her father had but spit in her face, would she not bear her shame for seven days? Let her be shut out of the camp for seven days, and after that she may be brought in again." ¹⁵So Miriam was shut out of the camp for seven days; and the people did not set out on the march until Miriam had been brought in again. ¹⁶After that the people set out from Hazeroth, and camped in the wilderness of Paran.

12.1–16: The jealous rebellion of Miriam and Aaron. Israel's rebellion spreads from the "outlying parts of the camp" among "the rabble" (11.1, 4) to the inner circle of leaders. Miriam and Aaron are the sister and brother of Moses (26.59) and co-leaders with him (Mic 6.4). **1:** The region of *Cush* in the Bible usually refers to Ethiopia but at times refers to the Arabian region of Midian. Habakkuk 3.7 names "Cushan" as parallel to Midian. Since Moses' wife Zipporah was from Midian

a Or *devout*   *b* A term for several skin diseases; precise meaning uncertain   *c* Heb *do not lay sin upon us*

(Ex 2.15–21), the charge that she is a *Cushite* probably refers to her Midianite origins. **4–5:** On *the tent of meeting* and *the cloud* that veiled the divine presence, see comments on 1.1 and 9.15. **6–8:** *Prophets* may legitimately receive mediated messages from God through *visions* and *dreams* (Joel 2.28). However, such prophets are secondary in authority to Moses who speaks with God *face to face* and directly without the intermediation of visions or dreams (Ex 33.12–34.9). According to Ex 33.23, Moses sees the "back" of God, which may provide the background for the claim that *he beholds the form of the LORD* (v. 8). **10–11:** It is not clear why only Miriam is punished with skin disease. It may be that Aaron could not be allowed to have a leprous skin disease since the resultant ritual impurity would have disqualified him in his priestly duties for a time (Lev 13; 21.16–24). Aaron's reference to Moses as *my lord* and his plea for Moses' help is an ironic* confirmation of what Aaron and Miriam had earlier denied—Moses' unique relationship to God. **14:** A parent spitting in a child's face is a sign of shame (Deut 25.9; Isa 50.6). God orders Miriam to bear her shame by being shut out of the camp for seven days.

13 The LORD said to Moses, 2"Send men to spy out the land of Canaan, which I am giving to the Israelites; from each of their ancestral tribes you shall send a man, every one a leader among them." 3So Moses sent them from the wilderness of Paran, according to the command of the LORD, all of them leading men among the Israelites. 4These were their names: From the tribe of Reuben, Shammua son of Zaccur; 5from the tribe of Simeon, Shaphat son of Hori; 6from the tribe of Judah, Caleb son of Jephunneh; 7from the tribe of Issachar, Igal son of Joseph; 8from the tribe of Ephraim, Hoshea son of Nun; 9from the tribe of Benjamin, Palti son of Raphu; 10from the tribe of Zebulun, Gaddiel son of Sodi; 11from the tribe of Joseph (that is, from the tribe of Manasseh), Gaddi son of Susi; 12from the tribe of Dan, Ammiel son of Gemalli; 13from the tribe of Asher, Sethur son of Michael; 14from the tribe of Naphtali, Nahbi son of Vophsi; 15from the tribe of Gad, Geuel son of Machi. 16These were the names of the men whom Moses sent to spy out the land. And Moses changed the name of Hoshea son of Nun to Joshua.

17 Moses sent them to spy out the land of Canaan, and said to them, "Go up there into the Negeb, and go up into the hill country, 18and see what the land is like, and whether the people who live in it are strong or weak, whether they are few or many, 19and whether the land they live in is good or bad, and whether the towns that they live in are unwalled or fortified, 20and whether the land is rich or poor, and whether there are trees in it or not. Be bold, and bring some of the fruit of the land." Now it was the season of the first ripe grapes.

21 So they went up and spied out the land from the wilderness of Zin to Rehob, near Lebo-hamath. 22They went up into the Negeb, and came to Hebron; and Ahiman, Sheshai, and Talmai, the Anakites, were there. (Hebron was built seven years before Zoan in Egypt.) 23And they came to the Wadi Eshcol, and cut down from there a branch with a single cluster of grapes, and they carried it on a pole between two of them. They also brought some pomegranates and figs. 24That place was called the Wadi Eshcol,*a* because of the cluster that the Israelites cut down from there.

13.1–33: The spy mission into Canaan. 4–16: The sequence of the twelve tribes is the same as the sequence in 1.5–15, but the names of the tribal leaders who are spies are different. *Caleb* is designated as the representative of the tribe of Judah (v. 6). However, other traditions suggest that Caleb was originally not an Israelite but a Kenizzite (32.12; Josh 14.6, 14). The narrative* assumes, however, that he was adopted into the tribe of Judah. **17:** *The Negeb* is the region north of the wilderness of Paran and just south of the land of Canaan. **21:** This later addition to an earlier version of the spy story expands the area surveyed by the spies to include the whole land of Canaan from the far south (*wilderness of Zin*) to the far north in what will become the tribal territory of Dan (*Rehob, near Lebo-hamath*). The older version of the spy story (vv. 22–24) focuses only on the area of the *Negeb* and southern Canaan near *Hebron* (v. 22). **22:** *The Anakites* are one of the native groups living within Canaan. They were a people known for their great physical stature (Deut 9.2). According to later biblical accounts,

a That is *Cluster*

remnants of these giants remained west of Canaan in the Philistine regions of Gaza, Gath, and Ashdod (Josh 11.21–22). Four of these giants were killed by David's men (2 Sam 21.18–22), and the giant Goliath of Gath was slain by the young warrior David with a slingshot (1 Sam 17).

25 At the end of forty days they returned from spying out the land. 26And they came to Moses and Aaron and to all the congregation of the Israelites in the wilderness of Paran, at Kadesh; they brought back word to them and to all the congregation, and showed them the fruit of the land. 27And they told him, "We came to the land to which you sent us; it flows with milk and honey, and this is its fruit. 28Yet the people who live in the land are strong, and the towns are fortified and very large; and besides, we saw the descendants of Anak there. 29The Amalekites live in the land of the Negeb; the Hittites, the Jebusites, and the Amorites live in the hill country; and the Canaanites live by the sea, and along the Jordan."

30 But Caleb quieted the people before Moses, and said, "Let us go up at once and occupy it, for we are well able to overcome it." 31Then the men who had gone up with him said, "We are not able to go up against this people, for they are stronger than we." 32So they brought to the Israelites an unfavorable report of the land that they had spied out, saying, "The land that we have gone through as spies is a land that devours its inhabitants; and all the people that we saw in it are of great size. 33There we saw the Nephilim (the Anakites come from the Nephilim); and to ourselves we seemed like grasshoppers, and so we seemed to them."

13.25–33. 26: The desert oasis of *Kadesh* or Kadesh-barnea (32.8) will be the location of the Israelite camp for much of their remaining years in the wilderness (Num 13–20; see 20.1, 22). **27:** *The land flowing with milk and honey* is a frequent biblical phrase that describes the lush fertility of the promised land of Canaan (Ex 3.17; Josh 5.6). **28:** *The descendants of Anak* are the same Anakites mentioned in v. 22. **29:** *The Amalekites* were often involved in hostilities with Israel throughout the biblical story (Ex 17.8–16; 1 Sam 15.1–9). *The Hittites, the Jebusites, the Amorites, and*

the Canaanites constitute the traditional list of Canaan's native inhabitants (Gen 15.19–21; Deut 7.1). **30–31:** In the earlier version of the spy story, Caleb is the only faithful one among the twelve spies; he encourages the people to go ahead with the plan to conquer the land of Canaan. In verses that reflect a later version of the story, Joshua is added as a faithful spy along with Caleb (note the name change in vv. 8, 16 and the inclusion of Joshua with Caleb in 14.6, 38). **32:** Earlier the spies had reported that the land was fertile and good (v. 27), but now the spies change their story. They demonize the land as a monster that *devours its inhabitants.* **33:** The spies continue to exaggerate the dangers of Canaan by invoking the threat of *the Nephilim,* a semi-divine and mythological race of giants. The Nephilim (literally "fallen ones") were purported to be the semi-divine offspring of divine beings who had fallen from the heavens and mated with humans (Gen 6.4).

14 Then all the congregation raised a loud cry, and the people wept that night. 2And all the Israelites complained against Moses and Aaron; the whole congregation said to them, "Would that we had died in the land of Egypt! Or would that we had died in this wilderness! 3Why is the LORD bringing us into this land to fall by the sword? Our wives and our little ones will become booty; would it not be better for us to go back to Egypt?" 4So they said to one another, "Let us choose a captain, and go back to Egypt."

14.1–45: The decisive rebellion: the old generation's refusal to enter the promised land. This key narrative* forms the basis for the overall structure of the book of Numbers, which divides into the death of the old generation of the wilderness (chs. 1–25) and the birth of a new generation of hope on the edge of the promised land (chs. 26–36). The old rebellious generation is condemned to wander for forty years and die in the wilderness (vv. 22–23, 29–30). Only the new generation of *little ones* (along with the two faithful spies Caleb and Joshua) will be allowed to enter the land of Canaan (vv. 24, 30–31; see 26.63–65). **3:** The Israelites' concern that their wives and children *will become booty* means that they believe they will be defeated by the inhabitants of Canaan and their families will be carried off as the spoils of war. They are unwilling to trust the LORD's promise and power to conquer the Canaanites and their gods. **4:** The Israelites had often yearned to go back to Egypt in earlier episodes (Ex 16.3; Num 11.5). However, the Israelites now actually seek a new leader and adopt a plan by which to return to Egypt. The plan to return to Egyptian slavery is an outright rejection of the LORD "who brought you out of the land of Egypt, out of the house of slavery" (Ex 20.2).

5 Then Moses and Aaron fell on their faces before all the assembly of the congregation of the Israelites. 6And Joshua son of Nun and Caleb son of Jephunneh, who were among those who had spied out the land,

tore their clothes 7and said to all the congregation of the Israelites, "The land that we went through as spies is an exceedingly good land. 8If the LORD is pleased with us, he will bring us into this land and give it to us, a land that flows with milk and honey. 9Only, do not rebel against the LORD; and do not fear the people of the land, for they are no more than bread for us; their protection is removed from them, and the LORD is with us; do not fear them." 10But the whole congregation threatened to stone them.

Then the glory of the LORD appeared at the tent of meeting to all the Israelites.

Map   Canaan at the time of the Conquest

11And the LORD said to Moses, "How long will this people despise me? And how long will they refuse to believe in me, in spite of all the signs that I have done among them? 12I will strike them with pestilence and disinherit them, and I will make of you a nation greater and mightier than they."

13 But Moses said to the LORD, "Then the Egyptians will hear of it, for in your might you brought up this people from among them, 14and they will tell the inhabitants of this land. They have heard that you, O LORD, are in the midst of this people; for you, O LORD, are seen face to face, and your cloud stands over them and you go in front of them, in a pillar of cloud by day and in a pillar of fire by night. 15Now if you kill this people all at one time, then the nations who have heard about you will say, 16'It is because the LORD was not able to bring this people into the land he swore to give them that he has slaughtered them in the wilderness.' 17And now, therefore, let the power of the LORD be great in the way that you promised when you spoke, saying,

18 'The LORD is slow to anger,
    and abounding in steadfast love,
    forgiving iniquity and transgression,
    but by no means clearing the guilty,
    visiting the iniquity of the parents
    upon the children
    to the third and the fourth generation.'
19Forgive the iniquity of this people according to the greatness of your steadfast love, just as you have pardoned this people, from Egypt even until now."

20 Then the LORD said, "I do forgive, just as you have asked; 21nevertheless—as I live, and as all the earth shall be filled with the glory of the LORD— 22none of the people who have seen my glory and the signs that I did in Egypt and in the wilderness, and yet have tested me these ten times and have not obeyed my voice, 23shall see the land that I swore to give to their ancestors; none of those who despised me shall see it. 24But my servant Caleb, because he has a different spirit and has followed me wholeheartedly, I will bring into the land into which he went, and his descendants shall possess it. 25Now, since the Amalekites and the Canaanites live in the valleys, turn tomorrow and set out for the wilderness by the way to the Red Sea."*a*

14.5–25. 5: *Fell on their faces:* This gesture of Moses and Aaron is an act of humility and request before God to lessen the severity of the divine judgment they know will come. **10:** To *stone them* is to kill them by throwing heavy stones at them. *The glory of the LORD* is associated with the appearance of the fiery cloud of the divine presence (Ex 16.10). On *the tent of meeting,* see comment on 1.1. **12:** The LORD threatens to annihilate all Israel and to start over to form a new nation with Moses alone. A similar threat against Israel and a similar offer to Moses was made when Israel worshipped the golden calf (Ex 32.10). **17–18:** Moses appeals to the promise of the LORD's gracious and forgiving character that was made to him on Mount Sinai after the golden calf incident (Ex 34.1–9). **19–23:** The LORD's response is true to both dimensions of the divine character that Moses cited in v. 18: "abounding in steadfast love" and "by no means clearing the guilty." Thus, the LORD will *forgive the iniquity* and not annihilate all the Israelites (v. 20). *Nevertheless,* none of the old generation *shall see the land* of Canaan (vv. 21–23). Only the children of this old generation, their "little ones" (v. 31), will enter the land of Canaan. **24:** *Caleb* is listed alone as the one faithful member of the old generation who will be allowed to enter the promised land. Joshua will also be included with Caleb (vv. 30, 38). See comment on 13.30–31.

26 And the LORD spoke to Moses and to Aaron, saying: 27How long shall this wicked congregation complain against me? I have heard the complaints of the Israelites, which they complain against me. 28Say to them, "As I live," says the LORD, "I will do to you the very things I heard you say: 29your dead bodies shall fall in this very wilderness; and of all your number, included in the census, from twenty years old and upward, who have complained against me, 30not one of you shall come into the land in which I swore to settle you, except Caleb son of Jephunneh and Joshua son of Nun. 31But your little ones, who you said would become booty, I will bring in, and they shall know the land that you have despised. 32But as for you,

a Or *Sea of Reeds*

your dead bodies shall fall in this wilderness. ³³And your children shall be shepherds in the wilderness for forty years, and shall suffer for your faithlessness, until the last of your dead bodies lies in the wilderness. ³⁴According to the number of the days in which you spied out the land, forty days, for every day a year, you shall bear your iniquity, forty years, and you shall know my displeasure." ³⁵I the LORD have spoken; surely I will do thus to all this wicked congregation gathered together against me: in this wilderness they shall come to a full end, and there they shall die.

36 And the men whom Moses sent to spy out the land, who returned and made all the congregation complain against him by bringing a bad report about the land— ³⁷the men who brought an unfavorable report about the land died by a plague before the LORD. ³⁸But Joshua son of Nun and Caleb son of Jephunneh alone remained alive, of those men who went to spy out the land.

39 When Moses told these words to all the Israelites, the people mourned greatly. ⁴⁰They rose early in the morning and went up to the heights of the hill country, saying, "Here we are. We will go up to the place that the LORD has promised, for we have sinned." ⁴¹But Moses said, "Why do you continue to transgress the command of the LORD? That will not succeed. ⁴²Do not go up, for the LORD is not with you; do not let yourselves be struck down before your enemies. ⁴³For the Amalekites and the Canaanites will confront you there, and you shall fall by the sword; because you have turned back from following the LORD, the LORD will not be with you." ⁴⁴But they presumed to go up to the heights of the hill country, even though the ark of the covenant of the LORD, and Moses, had not left the camp. ⁴⁵Then the Amalekites and the Canaanites who lived in that hill country came down and defeated them, pursuing them as far as Hormah.

14.26–45. 28: *As I live* is a typical oath formula for making a binding promise or threat; see v. 20. **29:** *The census* of the Israelites is the count taken in ch. 1. **30:** See comment on 13.30–31. **31:** See v. 3. **34:** See 13.25. **43–45:** *The Amalekites* and *the*

Canaanites are native inhabitants of the land of Canaan. On *the ark of the covenant,*＊ see comment on 4.5–33. The absence of the ark from among the Israelites in their attack was a visible sign that the LORD was not with them, guaranteeing their defeat. *Hormah* is located south and east of Canaan in the area of Edom.

15 The LORD spoke to Moses, saying: ²Speak to the Israelites and say to them: When you come into the land you are to inhabit, which I am giving you, ³and you make an offering by fire to the LORD from the herd or from the flock—whether a burnt offering or a sacrifice, to fulfill a vow or as a freewill offering or at your appointed festivals—to make a pleasing odor for the LORD, ⁴then whoever presents such an offering to the LORD shall present also a grain offering, one-tenth of an ephah of choice flour, mixed with one-fourth of a hin of oil. ⁵Moreover, you shall offer one-fourth of a hin of wine as a drink offering with the burnt offering or the sacrifice, for each lamb. ⁶For a ram, you shall offer a grain offering, two-tenths of an ephah of choice flour mixed with one-third of a hin of oil; ⁷and as a drink offering you shall offer one-third of a hin of wine, a pleasing odor to the LORD. ⁸When you offer a bull as a burnt offering or a sacrifice, to fulfill a vow or as an offering of well-being to the LORD, ⁹then you shall present with the bull a grain offering, three-tenths of an ephah of choice flour, mixed with half a hin of oil, ¹⁰and you shall present as a drink offering half a hin of wine, as an offering by fire, a pleasing odor to the LORD.

11 Thus it shall be done for each ox or ram, or for each of the male lambs or the kids. ¹²According to the number that you offer, so you shall do with each and every one. ¹³Every native Israelite shall do these things in this way, in presenting an offering by fire, a pleasing odor to the LORD. ¹⁴An alien who lives with you, or who takes up permanent residence among you, and wishes to offer an offering by fire, a pleasing odor to the LORD, shall do as you do. ¹⁵As for the assembly, there shall be for both you and the resident alien a single statute, a perpetual statute throughout your generations; you and the

alien shall be alike before the LORD. 16You and the alien who resides with you shall have the same law and the same ordinance.

17 The LORD spoke to Moses, saying: 18Speak to the Israelites and say to them: After you come into the land to which I am bringing you, 19whenever you eat of the bread of the land, you shall present a donation to the LORD. 20From your first batch of dough you shall present a loaf as a donation; you shall present it just as you present a donation from the threshing floor. 21Throughout your generations you shall give to the LORD a donation from the first of your batch of dough.

22 But if you unintentionally fail to observe all these commandments that the LORD has spoken to Moses— 23everything that the LORD has commanded you by Moses, from the day the LORD gave commandment and thereafter, throughout your generations— 24then if it was done unintentionally without the knowledge of the congregation, the whole congregation shall offer one young bull for a burnt offering, a pleasing odor to the LORD, together with its grain offering and its drink offering, according to the ordinance, and one male goat for a sin offering. 25The priest shall make atonement for all the congregation of the Israelites, and they shall be forgiven; it was unintentional, and they have brought their offering, an offering by fire to the LORD, and their sin offering before the LORD, for their error. 26All the congregation of the Israelites shall be forgiven, as well as the aliens residing among them, because the whole people was involved in the error.

27 An individual who sins unintentionally shall present a female goat a year old for a sin offering. 28And the priest shall make atonement before the LORD for the one who commits an error, when it is unintentional, to make atonement for the person, who then shall be forgiven. 29For both the native among the Israelites and the alien residing among them—you shall have the same law for anyone who acts in error. 30But whoever acts high-handedly, whether a native or an alien, affronts the LORD, and shall be cut off from among the people. 31Because of having

despised the word of the LORD and broken his commandment, such a person shall be utterly cut off and bear the guilt.

32 When the Israelites were in the wilderness, they found a man gathering sticks on the sabbath day. 33Those who found him gathering sticks brought him to Moses, Aaron, and to the whole congregation. 34They put him in custody, because it was not clear what should be done to him. 35Then the LORD said to Moses, "The man shall be put to death; all the congregation shall stone him outside the camp." 36The whole congregation brought him outside the camp and stoned him to death, just as the LORD had commanded Moses.

37 The LORD said to Moses: 38Speak to the Israelites, and tell them to make fringes on the corners of their garments throughout their generations and to put a blue cord on the fringe at each corner. 39You have the fringe so that, when you see it, you will remember all the commandments of the LORD and do them, and not follow the lust of your own heart and your own eyes. 40So you shall remember and do all my commandments, and you shall be holy to your God. 41I am the LORD your God, who brought you out of the land of Egypt, to be your God: I am the LORD your God.

15.1–41: Regulations that reassure a future life in the promised land. These laws interrupt the old generation's downward slide into rebellion with laws which assume that future generations of Israelites will eventually carry on life in the promised land of Canaan: *when you come into the land you are to inhabit* (v. 2). **1–16:** These laws prescribe additional grain and drink offerings to accompany burnt offerings (Lev 1) and offerings of well-being (Lev 3). *A pleasing odor for the LORD* (v. 3) is a phrase indicating the LORD's acceptance of the offering as the aroma arises from the burning of the sacrifice (see Gen 8.20–22). An *ephah* is a unit of dry measure of roughly half a bushel, and a *hin* is a unit of liquid measure somewhere between a quart and a gallon (vv. 4–10). **17–21:** This law about offering the *first batch of dough* supplements the law of offering first fruits in Lev 23.9–14. **22–31:** These laws summarize and supplement the laws for unintentional acts of disobedience in Lev 4–5. To *make atonement** (vv. 25, 28) means to make clean, forgive, or cover over guilt or impurity. To *act high-handedly* (v. 30) is to sin deliberately and boldly as opposed to *unintentional* errors (v. 28). The punishment for high-handed or intentional sin is to *be utterly cut off*, probably meaning the death penalty or expulsion from the community (vv. 30–31). The Israelites' refusal to enter the land of Canaan (chs. 13–14) was probably understood as a "high-handed" and intentional act of disobedience for which the old generation suffered death. **32–36:** The earlier law in the background of this case is one prohibiting lighting a fire on the sabbath in Ex 35.2–3. A man demonstrates the intention to light a fire on the sabbath by *gathering sticks* (v. 32). The case demonstrates that the intention to disobey carries the same penalty and guilt as the actual act of disobedience itself. **37–41:** The royal *blue cord* (v. 38) stands out in color among the white fringes of the garment, just as the commandments of God should stand out in the mind of the worshipper (vv. 38–39). Such fringes, called "tallit," are still worn on traditional Jewish prayer shawls.

16 Now Korah son of Izhar son of Kohath son of Levi, along with Dathan and Abiram sons of Eliab, and On son of Peleth—descendants of Reuben—took [2]two hundred fifty Israelite men, leaders of the congregation, chosen from the assembly, well-known men,[a] and they confronted Moses. [3]They assembled against Moses and against Aaron, and said to them, "You have gone too far! All the congregation are holy, every one of them, and the LORD is among them. So why then do you exalt yourselves above the assembly of the LORD?" [4]When Moses heard it, he fell on his face. [5]Then he said to Korah and all his company, "In the morning the LORD will make known who is his, and who is holy, and who will be allowed to approach him; the one whom he will choose he will allow to approach him. [6]Do this: take censers, Korah and all your[b] company, [7]and tomorrow put fire in them, and lay incense on them before the LORD; and the man whom the LORD chooses shall be the holy one. You Levites have gone too far!" [8]Then Moses said to Korah, "Hear now, you Levites! [9]Is it too little for you that the God of Israel has separated you from the congregation of Israel, to allow you to approach him in order to perform the duties of the LORD's

tabernacle, and to stand before the congregation and serve them? [10]He has allowed you to approach him, and all your brother Levites with you; yet you seek the priesthood as well! [11]Therefore you and all your company have gathered together against the LORD. What is Aaron that you rail against him?"

12 Moses sent for Dathan and Abiram sons of Eliab; but they said, "We will not come! [13]Is it too little that you have brought us up out of a land flowing with milk and honey to kill us in the wilderness, that you must also lord it over us? [14]It is clear you have not brought us into a land flowing with milk and honey, or given us an inheritance of fields and vineyards. Would you put out the eyes of these men? We will not come!"

15 Moses was very angry and said to the LORD, "Pay no attention to their offering. I have not taken one donkey from them, and I have not harmed any one of them." [16]And Moses said to Korah, "As for you and all your company, be present tomorrow before the LORD, you and they and Aaron; [17]and let each one of you take his censer, and put incense on it, and each one of you present his censer before the LORD, two hundred fifty censers; you also, and Aaron, each his censer." [18]So each man took his censer, and they put fire in the censers and laid incense on them, and they stood at the entrance of the tent of meeting with Moses and Aaron. [19]Then Korah assembled the whole congregation against them at the entrance of the tent of meeting. And the glory of the LORD appeared to the whole congregation.

20 Then the LORD spoke to Moses and to Aaron, saying: [21]Separate yourselves from this congregation, so that I may consume them in a moment. [22]They fell on their faces, and said, "O God, the God of the spirits of all flesh, shall one person sin and you become angry with the whole congregation?"

23 And the LORD spoke to Moses, saying: [24]Say to the congregation: Get away from the dwellings of Korah, Dathan, and Abiram. [25]So Moses got up and went to Dathan and Abiram; the elders of Israel followed him.

a Cn: Heb *and they confronted Moses, and two hundred fifty men . . . well-known men*   *b* Heb *his*

26 He said to the congregation, "Turn away from the tents of these wicked men, and touch nothing of theirs, or you will be swept away for all their sins." 27 So they got away from the dwellings of Korah, Dathan, and Abiram; and Dathan and Abiram came out and stood at the entrance of their tents, together with their wives, their children, and their little ones. 28 And Moses said, "This is how you shall know that the LORD has sent me to do all these works; it has not been of my own accord: 29 If these people die a natural death, or if a natural fate comes on them, then the LORD has not sent me. 30 But if the LORD creates something new, and the ground opens its mouth and swallows them up, with all that belongs to them, and they go down alive into Sheol, then you shall know that these men have despised the LORD."

31 As soon as he finished speaking all these words, the ground under them was split apart. 32 The earth opened its mouth and swallowed them up, along with their households—everyone who belonged to Korah and all their goods. 33 So they with all that belonged to them went down alive into Sheol; the earth closed over them, and they perished from the midst of the assembly. 34 All Israel around them fled at their outcry, for they said, "The earth will swallow us too!" 35 And fire came out from the LORD and consumed the two hundred fifty men offering the incense.

36ᵃ Then the LORD spoke to Moses, saying: 37 Tell Eleazar son of Aaron the priest to take the censers out of the blaze; then scatter the fire far and wide. 38 For the censers of these sinners have become holy at the cost of their lives. Make them into hammered plates as a covering for the altar, for they presented them before the LORD and they became holy. Thus they shall be a sign to the Israelites. 39 So Eleazar the priest took the bronze censers that had been presented by those who were burned; and they were hammered out as a covering for the altar— 40 a reminder to the Israelites that no outsider, who is not of the descendants of Aaron, shall approach to offer incense before the LORD, so as not to become like Korah and his company—just as the LORD had said to him through Moses.

41 On the next day, however, the whole congregation of the Israelites rebelled against Moses and against Aaron, saying, "You have killed the people of the LORD." 42 And when the congregation had assembled against them, Moses and Aaron turned toward the tent of meeting; the cloud had covered it and the glory of the LORD appeared. 43 Then Moses and Aaron came to the front of the tent of meeting, 44 and the LORD spoke to Moses, saying, 45 "Get away from this congregation, so that I may consume them in a moment." And they fell on their faces. 46 Moses said to Aaron, "Take your censer, put fire on it from the altar and lay incense on it, and carry it quickly to the congregation and make atonement for them. For wrath has gone out from the LORD; the plague has begun." 47 So Aaron took it as Moses had ordered, and ran into the middle of the assembly, where the plague had already begun among the people. He put on the incense, and made atonement for the people. 48 He stood between the dead and the living; and the plague was stopped. 49 Those who died by the plague were fourteen thousand seven hundred, besides those who died in the affair of Korah. 50 When the plague was stopped, Aaron returned to Moses at the entrance of the tent of meeting.

16.1–50: The rebellions continue: Levites, leaders, and all the people. Many scholars suggest that this story probably developed out of several stages of editing. The earliest form of the narrative* may have focused only on a revolt against Moses by the leaders Dathan and Abiram from the tribe of Reuben (vv. 12–15). The story was then enlarged to include 250 lay leaders who claimed the right to act as priests and received punishment (vv. 2, 4–7, 18, 35). One of the last stages in the story's formation was the introduction of a rebel leader from the tribe of Levi named Korah (vv. 1, 8–11, 16–17). **1:** The figure of *On son of Peleth* is mentioned only here as one of the Reubenite leaders. *Dathan and Abiram* are the rebel leaders from the tribe of Reuben who will reappear throughout the story. **5:** The question of *who will be allowed to ap-*

ᵃ Ch 17.1 in Heb

proach the LORD involves the issue of who can legitimately perform the duties of the priest in offering incense and sacrifices at the central altar. **6:** *Censers* are bowls containing hot coals in which incense could be burned. **7–11:** According to previous sections in Numbers, the *Levites* are a tribe of priests. However, most of the Levites serve and assist the one family among the Levites who may legitimately serve as high priests and preside at all sacrifices—the line of Aaron and his sons (3.1–10). The Levites take care of the objects and structure of the *tabernacle** (v. 9), the portable tent of worship that houses the altar and is the visible sign of the divine presence in the midst of Israel's camp. **12:** Dathan and Abiram are from the tribe of Reuben, not the priestly tribe of Levi. Like Korah and the Levites, they too demand the right to act as high priests like Aaron and his sons. **13:** Dathan and Abiram use the phrase *a land flowing with milk and honey* to refer to the land of Israel's slavery, Egypt, rather than its usual referent, the promised land of Canaan (13.27). **21:** The LORD threatens to *consume* the whole congregation of Israel for the rebellions of its leaders. This generation has already been condemned to die in the wilderness (14.29–30), but the LORD threatens to annihilate them immediately. **22:** *Fell on their faces:* See comment on 14.5. **24:** The LORD responds to Moses and Aaron's gesture of humility and request for forgiveness (falling on their faces, v. 22) by restricting the threat of death to the rebel leaders and their families—Korah, Dathan, and Abiram. **30, 33:** *Sheol** is a dry and dusty place under the surface of the earth where all humans who die were believed to go. Sheol is sometimes personified as a monster who opens its mouth to swallow people (13.32; Isa 5.14). **35:** When *fire came out from the LORD,* the fire presumably came out from the fiery cloud of the divine presence (9.15–16). **37–39:** On *censers,* see comment on v. 6. **42:** On *the glory of the LORD,* see comment on 14.10. On *the tent of meeting,* see comment on 1.1. **45:** The LORD threatens to annihilate all Israel a second time (see v. 21). Again, the action of Moses and Aaron restricts the scope of the LORD's punishment (vv. 46–49). **46–47:** To *make atonement** means to make clean, forgive, or cover over guilt or impurity.

17 *a*The LORD spoke to Moses, saying: ²Speak to the Israelites, and get twelve staffs from them, one for each ancestral house, from all the leaders of their ancestral houses. Write each man's name on his staff, ³and write Aaron's name on the

staff of Levi. For there shall be one staff for the head of each ancestral house. ⁴Place them in the tent of meeting before the covenant,*b* where I meet with you. ⁵And the staff of the man whom I choose shall sprout; thus I will put a stop to the complaints of the Israelites that they continually make against you. ⁶Moses spoke to the Israelites; and all their leaders gave him staffs, one for each leader, according to their ancestral houses, twelve staffs; and the staff of Aaron was among theirs. ⁷So Moses placed the staffs before the LORD in the tent of the covenant.*b*

8 When Moses went into the tent of the covenant*b* on the next day, the staff of Aaron for the house of Levi had sprouted. It put forth buds, produced blossoms, and bore ripe almonds. ⁹Then Moses brought out all the staffs from before the LORD to all the Israelites; and they looked, and each man took his staff. ¹⁰And the LORD said to Moses, "Put back the staff of Aaron before the covenant,*b* to be kept as a warning to rebels, so that you may make an end of their complaints against me, or else they will die." ¹¹Moses did so; just as the LORD commanded him, so he did.

12 The Israelites said to Moses, "We are perishing; we are lost, all of us are lost! ¹³Everyone who approaches the tabernacle of the LORD will die. Are we all to perish?"

17.1–12: Aaron's flowering staff. 2: The *twelve staffs* are specially decorated rods representing each of the twelve Israelite tribes or *ancestral houses*. **3:** The high priest Aaron is a member of the tribe of Levi (Ex 6.16–20). **7–8:** The *tent of the covenant** is also known as the tent of meeting. See comments on 1.1 and 1.47–54. **10:** *Before the covenant* is shorthand for "before the ark of the covenant." See comment on 4.5–33. **13:** On *the tabernacle,* see comment on 1.47–54.

18 The LORD said to Aaron: You and your sons and your ancestral house with you shall bear responsibility for offenses connected with the sanctuary, while you and your sons alone shall bear responsibility for

a Ch 17.16 in Heb   *b* Or *treaty,* or *testimony;* Heb *eduth* offenses connected with the priesthood. ²So bring with you also your brothers of the tribe of Levi, your ancestral tribe, in order that they may be joined to you, and serve you while you and your sons with you are in front of the tent of the covenant.ᵃ ³They shall perform duties for you and for the whole tent. But they must not approach either the utensils of the sanctuary or the altar, otherwise both they and you will die. ⁴They are attached to you in order to perform the duties of the tent of meeting, for all the service of the tent; no outsider shall approach you. ⁵You yourselves shall perform the duties of the sanctuary and the duties of the altar, so that wrath may never again come upon the Israelites. ⁶It is I who now take your brother Levites from among the Israelites; they are now yours as a gift, dedicated to the LORD, to perform the service of the tent of meeting. ⁷But you and your sons with you shall diligently perform your priestly duties in all that concerns the altar and the area behind the curtain. I give your priesthood as a gift; ᵇ any outsider who approaches shall be put to death.

8 The LORD spoke to Aaron: I have given you charge of the offerings made to me, all the holy gifts of the Israelites; I have given them to you and your sons as a priestly portion due you in perpetuity. ⁹This shall be yours from the most holy things, reserved from the fire: every offering of theirs that they render to me as a most holy thing, whether grain offering, sin offering, or guilt offering, shall belong to you and your sons. ¹⁰As a most holy thing you shall eat it; every male may eat it; it shall be holy to you. ¹¹This also is yours: I have given to you, together with your sons and daughters, as a perpetual due, whatever is set aside from the gifts of all the elevation offerings of the Israelites; everyone who is clean in your house may eat them. ¹²All the best of the oil and all the best of the wine and of the grain, the choice produce that they give to the LORD, I have given to you. ¹³The first fruits of all that is in their land, which they bring to the LORD, shall be yours; everyone who is clean in your house may eat of it. ¹⁴Every devoted thing in Israel shall be yours. ¹⁵The first issue of the womb

of all creatures, human and animal, which is offered to the LORD, shall be yours; but the firstborn of human beings you shall redeem, and the firstborn of unclean animals you shall redeem. ¹⁶Their redemption price, reckoned from one month of age, you shall fix at five shekels of silver, according to the shekel of the sanctuary (that is, twenty gerahs). ¹⁷But the firstborn of a cow, or the firstborn of a sheep, or the firstborn of a goat, you shall not redeem; they are holy. You shall dash their blood on the altar, and shall turn their fat into smoke as an offering by fire for a pleasing odor to the LORD; ¹⁸but their flesh shall be yours, just as the breast that is elevated and as the right thigh are yours. ¹⁹All the holy offerings that the Israelites present to the LORD I have given to you, together with your sons and daughters, as a perpetual due; it is a covenant of salt forever before the LORD for you and your descendants as well. ²⁰Then the LORD said to Aaron: You shall have no allotment in their land, nor shall you have any share among them; I am your share and your possession among the Israelites.

18.1–32: The duties and support of the priests and Levites. This chapter makes a crucial distinction between Aaron and his sons as the Levites who serve as high priests and the other members of the tribe of Levi, who serve as assistants to Aaron and his sons (3.5–10). **2, 4:** On *the tent of the covenant*⋆ (v. 2) and its alternate designation as *the tent of meeting* (v. 4), see comments on 1.1 and 1.47–54. An *outsider* is any member of the Israelite community who is not from the priestly tribe of Levi or the family of Aaron. **7:** On the *outsider*, see comment on 18.2, 4. *The area behind the curtain* is the so-called "most holy place," the innermost room of the tabernacle,⋆ which contains the ark of the covenant, the seat of the divine presence (see comment on 4.4–33). **9, 11:** On the *grain offering*, the *sin offering*, the *guilt offering*, and the *elevation offering*, see Lev 2; 4–7. **13:** On offering *the first fruits* of the harvest, see Lev 23.9–14. **14:** A *devoted thing* is something that a worshipper has dedicated to God (Lev 23.21, 28). **15–16:** On the offering of the *firstborn* and their *redemption* or monetary substitu-

---

a Or *treaty,* or *testimony;* Heb *eduth*   *b* Heb *as a service of gift* tion, see 3.11–13, 40–51. The *shekel* and the *gerah* were standard measures of weight used to calculate the monetary value of gold and silver. The *shekel of the sanctuary* was the governing standard of weight. **17:** See Lev 27.26. *A pleasing odor to the L*ORD signifies the L ORD's acceptance of the burnt offering. **19:** A *covenant of salt* derives its significance from the use of salt as a long-term preservative; salt was used in meals that celebrated the making of covenants or agreements in the ancient Near East. A *covenant of salt* was an unbreakable and enduring agreement. According to Lev 2.13, salt accompanied all offerings and sacrifices. **20:** Aaron and his priestly descendants will not be allowed to own any land in Canaan. They will rely only on donations and offerings to the L ORD presented by worshippers.

21 To the Levites I have given every tithe in Israel for a possession in return for the service that they perform, the service in the tent of meeting. 22From now on the Israelites shall no longer approach the tent of meeting, or else they will incur guilt and die. 23But the Levites shall perform the service of the tent of meeting, and they shall bear responsibility for their own offenses; it shall be a perpetual statute throughout your generations. But among the Israelites they shall have no allotment, 24because I have given to the Levites as their portion the tithe of the Israelites, which they set apart as an offering to the LORD. Therefore I have said of them that they shall have no allotment among the Israelites.

25 Then the LORD spoke to Moses, saying: 26You shall speak to the Levites, saying: When you receive from the Israelites the tithe that I have given you from them for your portion, you shall set apart an offering from it to the LORD, a tithe of the tithe. 27It shall be reckoned to you as your gift, the same as the grain of the threshing floor and the fullness of the wine press. 28Thus you also shall set apart an offering to the LORD from all the tithes that you receive from the Israelites; and from them you shall give the LORD's offering to the priest Aaron. 29Out of all the gifts to you, you shall set apart every offering due to the LORD; the best of all of them is the part to be consecrated. 30Say also to them: When you have set apart the

best of it, then the rest shall be reckoned to the Levites as produce of the threshing floor, and as produce of the wine press. 31You may eat it in any place, you and your households; for it is your payment for your service in the tent of meeting. 32You shall incur no guilt by reason of it, when you have offered the best of it. But you shall not profane the holy gifts of the Israelites, on pain of death.

18.21–32: Apart from Aaron and his sons, the other members of the tribe of Levi will be given cities and surrounding pasture land (35.1–8) as well as a portion of the offerings given by the Israelites (vv. 21–32). The *tithe* (vv. 21, 24, 26, 28) is a one-tenth portion of grain or produce that is required as an offering to the L ORD (Lev 27.30–32). On *the tent of meeting* (vv. 22, 23, 31), see comment on 1.1. On the duties of the Levites in connection with the tent of meeting, see 3.5–10; 4.1–33.

19 The LORD spoke to Moses and Aaron, saying: 2This is a statute of the law that the LORD has commanded: Tell the Israelites to bring you a red heifer without defect, in which there is no blemish and on which no yoke has been laid. 3You shall give it to the priest Eleazar, and it shall be taken outside the camp and slaughtered in his presence. 4The priest Eleazar shall take some of its blood with his finger and sprinkle it seven times towards the front of the tent of meeting. 5Then the heifer shall be burned in his sight; its skin, its flesh, and its blood, with its dung, shall be burned. 6The priest shall take cedarwood, hyssop, and crimson material, and throw them into the fire in which the heifer is burning. 7Then the priest shall wash his clothes and bathe his body in water, and afterwards he may come into the camp; but the priest shall remain unclean until evening. 8The one who burns the heifer*a* shall wash his clothes in water and bathe his body in water; he shall remain unclean until evening. 9Then someone who is clean shall gather up the ashes of the heifer, and deposit them outside the camp in a clean place; and they shall be kept for the congregation of the Israelites for the water for

a Heb *it*

cleansing. It is a purification offering. ¹⁰The one who gathers the ashes of the heifer shall wash his clothes and be unclean until evening.

This shall be a perpetual statute for the Israelites and for the alien residing among them. ¹¹Those who touch the dead body of any human being shall be unclean seven days. ¹²They shall purify themselves with the water on the third day and on the seventh day, and so be clean; but if they do not purify themselves on the third day and on the seventh day, they will not become clean. ¹³All who touch a corpse, the body of a human being who has died, and do not purify themselves, defile the tabernacle of the LORD; such persons shall be cut off from Israel. Since water for cleansing was not dashed on them, they remain unclean; their uncleanness is still on them.

14 This is the law when someone dies in a tent: everyone who comes into the tent, and everyone who is in the tent, shall be unclean seven days. ¹⁵And every open vessel with no cover fastened on it is unclean. ¹⁶Whoever in the open field touches one who has been killed by a sword, or who has died naturally,ᵃ or a human bone, or a grave, shall be unclean seven days. ¹⁷For the unclean they shall take some ashes of the burnt purification offering, and running water shall be added in a vessel; ¹⁸then a clean person shall take hyssop, dip it in the water, and sprinkle it on the tent, on all the furnishings, on the persons who were there, and on whoever touched the bone, the slain, the corpse, or the grave. ¹⁹The clean person shall sprinkle the unclean ones on the third day and on the seventh day, thus purifying them on the seventh day. Then they shall wash their clothes and bathe themselves in water, and at evening they shall be clean. ²⁰Any who are unclean but do not purify themselves, those persons shall be cut off from the assembly, for they have defiled the sanctuary of the LORD. Since the water for cleansing has not been dashed on them, they are unclean.

21 It shall be a perpetual statute for them. The one who sprinkles the water for cleansing shall wash his clothes, and whoever touches the water for cleansing shall be

unclean until evening. ²²Whatever the unclean person touches shall be unclean, and anyone who touches it shall be unclean until evening.

19.1–22: The ashes of the red cow and the purification of the unclean. 2: The ritual associated with the ashes of the *red heifer* (better translated as "red cow") treats the severe impurity caused by contact with a human corpse (v. 11). On ritual purity and cleanness, see the sidebar on p. 182. The redness of the cow probably symbolizes the redness of blood, a powerful purifying agent according to biblical tradition. **3:** *Eleazar* is the son of Aaron. The red cow is slaughtered *outside the camp,* unlike other sacrifices that occur at the altar in the middle of the camp. This is likely due to the severity of the impurity of corpse contamination with which the red cow is associated. **6:** The reddish *crimson material* has a color association with blood similar to that of the red cow (see comment on v. 1). This association is also suggested by the unusual burning of the blood (v. 5). *Hyssop** is an aromatic plant often associated with purification rituals. **12:** Although a priest (in this case, Eleazar; v. 3) is required when ashes of the red cow are created, the ritual of purification using the ashes mixed with water may be performed by any person in the community. **13:** On the *tabernacle,** see comment on 1.47–54. **14–16:** The uncleanness or impurity of corpse contamination is perceived as a contagious condition. This corpse contagion can be transferred to persons and *open vessels* through touch or simply through being under the same roof of a *tent* or dwelling as a corpse. **18:** On *hyssop,* see comment on v. 6.

20 The Israelites, the whole congregation, came into the wilderness of Zin in the first month, and the people stayed in Kadesh. Miriam died there, and was buried there.

2 Now there was no water for the congregation; so they gathered together against Moses and against Aaron. ³The people quarreled with Moses and said, "Would that we had died when our kindred died before the LORD! ⁴Why have you brought the assembly of the LORD into this wilderness for us and our livestock to die here? ⁵Why have you brought us up out of Egypt, to bring us to

ᵃ Heb lacks *naturally*

this wretched place? It is no place for grain, or figs, or vines, or pomegranates; and there is no water to drink." 6Then Moses and Aaron went away from the assembly to the entrance of the tent of meeting; they fell on their faces, and the glory of the LORD appeared to them. 7The LORD spoke to Moses, saying: 8Take the staff, and assemble the congregation, you and your brother Aaron, and command the rock before their eyes to yield its water. Thus you shall bring water out of the rock for them; thus you shall provide drink for the congregation and their livestock.

20.1–29: The waters of Meribah and the deaths of Miriam and Aaron. 1: *Miriam* is the sister of Aaron and Moses (26.59) and a leader with them (Mic 6.4). **2:** A similar story about the people's complaint about the lack of water occurred at Meribah in Ex 17.1–7. **6:** When Moses and Aaron *fell on their faces,* they were humbly seeking the LORD's forgiveness for the people's complaint about the lack of water. On the *tent of meeting,* see comment on 1.1. *The glory of the* LORD is the divine presence veiled in a fiery cloud that traveled with Israel throughout the wilderness (see Ex 16.10; 40.34–38). **8:** *The staff* is presumably the same staff or rod used by Moses during the exodus out of Egypt (Ex 7.20–21) and in the Exodus version of the water at Meribah story (Ex 17.5–6). It may be significant that the LORD's explicit command for Moses to "strike the rock" in Ex 17.6 is absent in the parallel story here.

---

9 So Moses took the staff from before the LORD, as he had commanded him. 10Moses and Aaron gathered the assembly together before the rock, and he said to them, "Listen, you rebels, shall we bring water for you out of this rock?" 11Then Moses lifted up his hand and struck the rock twice with his staff; water came out abundantly, and the congregation and their livestock drank. 12But the LORD said to Moses and Aaron, "Because you did not trust in me, to show my holiness before the eyes of the Israelites, therefore you shall not bring this assembly into the land that I have given them." 13These are the waters of Meribah,*a* where the people of Israel quarreled with the LORD, and by which he showed his holiness.

14 Moses sent messengers from Kadesh to the king of Edom, "Thus says your brother Israel: You know all the adversity that has befallen us: 15how our ancestors went down to Egypt, and we lived in Egypt a long time; and the Egyptians oppressed us and our ancestors; 16and when we cried to the LORD, he heard our voice, and sent an angel and brought us out of Egypt; and here we are in Kadesh, a town on the edge of your territory. 17Now let us pass through your land. We will not pass through field or vineyard, or drink water from any well; we will go along the King's Highway, not turning aside to the right hand or to the left until we have passed through your territory."

18 But Edom said to him, "You shall not pass through, or we will come out with the sword against you." 19The Israelites said to him, "We will stay on the highway; and if we drink of your water, we and our livestock, then we will pay for it. It is only a small matter; just let us pass through on foot." 20But he said, "You shall not pass through." And Edom came out against them with a large force, heavily armed. 21Thus Edom refused to give Israel passage through their territory; so Israel turned away from them.

22 They set out from Kadesh, and the Israelites, the whole congregation, came to Mount Hor. 23Then the LORD said to Moses and Aaron at Mount Hor, on the border of the land of Edom, 24"Let Aaron be gathered to his people. For he shall not enter the land that I have given to the Israelites, because you rebelled against my command at the waters of Meribah. 25Take Aaron and his son Eleazar, and bring them up Mount Hor; 26strip Aaron of his vestments, and put them on his son Eleazar. But Aaron shall be gathered to his people,*b* and shall die there." 27Moses did as the LORD had commanded; they went up Mount Hor in the sight of the whole congregation. 28Moses stripped Aaron of his vestments, and put them on his son Eleazar; and Aaron died there on the top of the mountain. Moses and Eleazar came down from the mountain. 29When all the congregation saw that Aaron had died, all

a That is *Quarrel*   *b* Heb lacks *to his people*

the house of Israel mourned for Aaron thirty days.

20.9–29. 9: The staff may also be Aaron's staff, which flowered in Num 17. Aaron's staff was placed before the ark of the covenant★ (17.10), an alternative description of the phrase *before the LORD.* **12:** The LORD's angry response and punishment of Moses and Aaron is surprising and difficult to explain. Commentators have offered many possible solutions, but no clear explanation emerges out of the narrative★ itself. Did Moses' act of striking the rock disobey the LORD's instruction only to "command the rock" (v. 8)? Did Moses and Aaron in some way take credit themselves and away from the LORD (v. 10)? Did Moses and Aaron in some way imply that the LORD was unable or unwilling to give water to the people (v. 10)? Both Moses and Aaron are condemned to join the old generation in death outside the promised land of Canaan. Aaron's death is recorded in 20.22–29, and Moses' death is recorded in Deut 34.1–8. **13:** The place name *Meribah* is a play on the Hebrew verb meaning *quarrel* ("rib"). **14:** *Edom* is a nation that lies south and east of the land of Canaan. Israel recalled times of both friendly (2 Kings 3.4–27) and hostile (1 Kings 11.14–17) relationships with Edom. The story of Jacob and Esau (Gen 25.22–28; 33.1–17) represents in part the conflict and reconciliation of two brother nations, Israel (Gen 32.28) and Edom (Gen 25.30). This story lies in the background as Moses speaks to the king of Edom of *your brother Israel.* **16:** On the *angel* as an agent of divine guidance, see Ex 14.19 and Num 22.22–35. *Kadesh* is the desert oasis where Israel spent much of its time in the wilderness (13.26; 20.1). **17:** *The King's Highway* was a main route from the Gulf of Aqaba in the south through the nations of Edom, Moab, and Ammon, ending in Syria to the north. The highway ran roughly parallel to the eastern boundary of Canaan. **24:** To *be gathered to his people* means that Aaron will join his ancestors in death. On the events at *the waters of Meribah,* see vv. 2–13. **26:** Aaron's *vestments* are the vestments of the office of high priest (Ex 28; Lev 8.7–9).

21 When the Canaanite, the king of Arad, who lived in the Negeb, heard that Israel was coming by the way of Atharim, he fought against Israel and took some of them captive. ²Then Israel made a vow to the LORD and said, "If you will indeed give this people into our hands, then we will utterly destroy their towns." ³The LORD listened to the voice of Israel, and handed over the Canaanites; and they utterly destroyed them and their towns; so the place was called Hormah.ᵃ

4 From Mount Hor they set out by the way to the Red Sea,ᵇ to go around the land of Edom; but the people became impatient on the way. ⁵The people spoke against God and against Moses, "Why have you brought us up out of Egypt to die in the wilderness? For there is no food and no water, and we detest this miserable food." ⁶Then the LORD sent poisonousᶜ serpents among the people, and they bit the people, so that many Israelites died. ⁷The people came to Moses and said, "We have sinned by speaking against the LORD and against you; pray to the LORD to take away the serpents from us." So Moses prayed for the people. ⁸And the LORD said to Moses, "Make a poisonousᵈ serpent, and set it on a pole; and everyone who is bitten shall look at it and live." ⁹So Moses made a serpent of bronze, and put it upon a pole; and whenever a serpent bit someone, that person would look at the serpent of bronze and live.

21.1–35: Victories and plagues along the journey. 1–3: This account of Israel's obedience and military victory against a southern Canaanite enemy at *Hormah* ("Destruction") forms a counterpoint to Israel's earlier disobedience and military defeat in southern Canaan at the end of the spy story in 14.39–45 ("pursuing them as far as Hormah," 14.45). **5:** The Israelites typically complained against Moses or Aaron in previous murmuring stories (11.2; 14.2; 16.3). However, this time their rebellion is more serious in that they aim their complaint *against God and against Moses.* **6:** The Hebrew word for "poisonous" literally means "fiery," a reference to the burning pain of a snake bite (see also v. 8). **9:** *A serpent of bronze* is a wordplay in Hebrew, "nehash" ("serpent") and "nehoshet" ("bronze"). Later in Israel's history, King Hezekiah tore down and destroyed what was alleged to be Moses' bronze serpent called "Nehushtan." The sacred object had become an idolatrous object of worship and was thus destroyed (2 Kings 18.4). In the ancient world,

a Heb *Destruction*   *b* Or *Sea of Reeds*   *c* Or *fiery;* Heb *seraphim*   *d* Or *fiery;* Heb *seraph* the snake was a complex and powerful symbol of evil, conveying death as well as fertility, life, and healing.

~~~~~~

10 The Israelites set out, and camped in Oboth. [11]They set out from Oboth, and camped at Iye-abarim, in the wilderness bordering Moab toward the sunrise. [12]From there they set out, and camped in the Wadi Zered. [13]From there they set out, and camped on the other side of the Arnon, in[a] the wilderness that extends from the boundary of the Amorites; for the Arnon is the boundary of Moab, between Moab and the Amorites. [14]Wherefore it is said in the Book of the Wars of the LORD,

"Waheb in Suphah and the wadis.
The Arnon [15]and the slopes of the
    wadis
that extend to the seat of Ar,
and lie along the border of Moab."[b]

16 From there they continued to Beer;[c] that is the well of which the LORD said to Moses, "Gather the people together, and I will give them water." [17]Then Israel sang this song:

"Spring up, O well!—Sing to it!—
[18] the well that the leaders sank,
    that the nobles of the people dug,
    with the scepter, with the staff."

From the wilderness to Mattanah, [19]from Mattanah to Nahaliel, from Nahaliel to Bamoth, [20]and from Bamoth to the valley lying in the region of Moab by the top of Pisgah that overlooks the wasteland.[d]

21 Then Israel sent messengers to King Sihon of the Amorites, saying, [22]"Let me pass through your land; we will not turn aside into field or vineyard; we will not drink the water of any well; we will go by the King's Highway until we have passed through your territory." [23]But Sihon would not allow Israel to pass through his territory. Sihon gathered all his people together, and went out against Israel to the wilderness; he came to Jahaz, and fought against Israel. [24]Israel put him to the sword, and took possession of his land from the Arnon to the Jabbok, as far as to the Ammonites; for the boundary of the Ammonites was strong. [25]Israel took all these towns, and Israel settled in all the towns of the Amorites, in Heshbon, and in all its villages. [26]For Heshbon was the city of King Sihon of the Amorites, who had fought against the former king of Moab and captured all his land as far as the Arnon. [27]Therefore the ballad singers say,

"Come to Heshbon, let it be built;
    let the city of Sihon be established.
28 For fire came out from Heshbon,
    flame from the city of Sihon.
It devoured Ar of Moab,
    and swallowed up[e] the heights of the
        Arnon.
29 Woe to you, O Moab!
    You are undone, O people of
        Chemosh!
He has made his sons fugitives,
    and his daughters captives,
    to an Amorite king, Sihon.
30 So their posterity perished
    from Heshbon[f] to Dibon,
    and we laid waste until fire spread to
        Medeba."[g]

31 Thus Israel settled in the land of the Amorites. [32]Moses sent to spy out Jazer; and they captured its villages, and dispossessed the Amorites who were there.

33 Then they turned and went up the road to Bashan; and King Og of Bashan came out against them, he and all his people, to battle at Edrei. [34]But the LORD said to Moses, "Do not be afraid of him; for I have given him into your hand, with all his people, and all his land. You shall do to him as you did to King Sihon of the Amorites, who ruled in Heshbon." [35]So they killed him, his sons, and all his people, until there was no survivor left; and they took possession of his land.

21.10–33. 10–13: The locations mentioned center around the land of Moab on the eastern boundary of Canaan. 14: This one biblical reference to *the Book of the Wars of the LORD* suggests it is an ancient poetic collection describing Israel's early military conquests. Another such collection is mentioned in Josh 10.13 and 2 Sam 1.18 ("Book of Jashar"). The content of these works is otherwise unknown. 15: *Ar* is apparently

a Gk: Heb *which is in*   b Meaning of Heb uncertain   c That is *Well*   d Or *Jeshimon*   e Gk: Heb *and the lords of*   f Gk: Heb *we have shot at them; Heshbon has perished*   g Compare Sam Gk: Meaning of MT uncertain an important city in Moab (see v. 28). **16:** The place name *Beer* is the Hebrew word for a *well* of water. **19–20:** Several of these place names are otherwise unknown. Moab is a nation that lies on the eastern boundary of Canaan. *Pisgah* is a high plateau that looks out to the west over a *wasteland*, the Jordan River valley, and on to the land of Canaan (Deut 34.1–4). **21:** *The Amorites* occupy a small nation just north of Moab. **22:** On *the King's Highway*, see comment on 20.17. **24:** Israel captured the land between two rivers or wadis,* the *Arnon* to the south and the *Jabbok* to the north. **27–30:** This ancient poem is a taunt song that celebrates an earlier Amorite conquest of a part of Moab's territory. *Chemosh* (v. 29) is the god of the Moabites. **33:** *Bashan* is another small Amorite nation just north of the Jabbok river.

22 The Israelites set out, and camped in the plains of Moab across the Jordan from Jericho. ²Now Balak son of Zippor saw all that Israel had done to the Amorites. ³Moab was in great dread of the people, because they were so numerous; Moab was overcome with fear of the people of Israel. ⁴And Moab said to the elders of Midian, "This horde will now lick up all that is around us, as an ox licks up the grass of the field." Now Balak son of Zippor was king of Moab at that time. ⁵He sent messengers to Balaam son of Beor at Pethor, which is on the Euphrates, in the land of Amaw,ᵃ to summon him, saying, "A people has come out of Egypt; they have spread over the face of the earth, and they have settled next to me. ⁶Come now, curse this people for me, since they are stronger than I; perhaps I shall be able to defeat them and drive them from the land; for I know that whomever you bless is blessed, and whomever you curse is cursed."

7 So the elders of Moab and the elders of Midian departed with the fees for divination in their hand; and they came to Balaam, and gave him Balak's message. ⁸He said to them, "Stay here tonight, and I will bring back word to you, just as the LORD speaks to me"; so the officials of Moab stayed with Balaam. ⁹God came to Balaam and said, "Who are these men with you?" ¹⁰Balaam said to God, "King Balak son of Zippor of Moab, has sent me this message: ¹¹'A people has come out

of Egypt and has spread over the face of the earth; now come, curse them for me; perhaps I shall be able to fight against them and drive them out.'" ¹²God said to Balaam, "You shall not go with them; you shall not curse the people, for they are blessed." ¹³So Balaam rose in the morning, and said to the officials of Balak, "Go to your own land, for the LORD has refused to let me go with you." ¹⁴So the officials of Moab rose and went to Balak, and said, "Balaam refuses to come with us."

22.1–40: The prophet★ Balaam, King Balak, and three encounters with the angel of the LORD. Balak, king of Moab, hears of the Israelite victories against the Amorites and becomes afraid. He hires a prophet or seer from Mesopotamia named Balaam to come and place a curse on Israel. Balaam, however, ends up becoming an instrument of the LORD, blessing Israel rather than cursing it. **2:** On *all that Israel had done to the Amorites*, see 21.21–35. **4:** On the connections between Moab, Midian, and Balaam the prophet, see chs. 25 and 31. **5:** *The Euphrates* is a major river in Mesopotamia. **6:** A prophet's spoken words of *curse* or *blessing* were believed to unleash either negative or positive powers that would shape the outcome of future events. **7:** Balaam is a hired prophet★ who charged *fees for divination*. *Divination* was an ancient means of finding information about future events by interpreting some object such as the configuration of spots on the liver of a sacrificed animal. **8:** Surprisingly, although Balaam is a non-Israelite prophet, he says he will obey Israel's God, the LORD (see vv. 18, 20).

15 Once again Balak sent officials, more numerous and more distinguished than these. ¹⁶They came to Balaam and said to him, "Thus says Balak son of Zippor: 'Do not let anything hinder you from coming to me; ¹⁷for I will surely do you great honor, and whatever you say to me I will do; come, curse this people for me.'" ¹⁸But Balaam replied to the servants of Balak, "Although Balak were to give me his house full of silver and gold, I could not go beyond the command of the LORD my God, to do less or more. ¹⁹You remain here, as the others did, so that I may learn what more the LORD may say to me."

a Or land of his kinsfolk

The Prophet Balaam

In the history of biblical interpretation,⋆ the prophet⋆ or seer named Balaam has received mixed reviews. Some commentators have viewed Balaam as a true and obedient prophet of God. Others have labeled him an evil and false prophet. The variation in evaluating Balaam's character is due in part to the complexity of the biblical record itself. The figure of Balaam emerges from Num 22–24 in a largely positive light. Although Balaam is lampooned in the donkey episode in 22.22–35, he ends up obediently speaking God's word of blessing rather than curse. The prophet Micah affirms the way Balaam turned back the evil scheme of King Balak (Mic 6.5). On the other hand, Deut 23.3–6 portrays Balaam negatively and uses his association with Moab as a reason for prohibiting Moabites and Ammonites from entering the assembly of God's people. Later Balaam is killed for having counseled the Midianite women to lead Israel astray in the worship of a false god named Baal⋆ of Peor (see Num 25; 31.8, 16).

This ambivalence toward the character of Balaam reflects a long history. Stories about a legendary prophet named Balaam circulated not only in Israel but also among its Near Eastern neighbors. Archaeologists have discovered plaster panels in a non-Israelite temple at Deir 'Allah in modern-day Jordan that include the name of a famed prophet named Balaam. The inscription, which is dated to the eighth century BCE, recounts Balaam's vision from the gods at night. The vision includes a message from a council of gods called the "shaddai" gods. Interestingly, the Hebrew word "Shaddai" (translated as "the Almighty") is used as a title for Israel's God in the biblical oracles⋆ of Balaam. Balaam is described as the one "who sees the vision of the Almighty ('Shaddai')" in Num 24.4, 16. In the inscription at Deir 'Allah, the gods inform Balaam that a drought is about to come on the land and the order of nature is about to be overturned. Balaam prays to the gods to reverse their decision and avoid such a calamity. The character of Balaam portrayed in Num 22–24 is probably built upon a legendary prophet who was known in the area near Moab and the Jordan River where the biblical story of Balaam is set.

20That night God came to Balaam and said to him, "If the men have come to summon you, get up and go with them; but do only what I tell you to do." 21So Balaam got up in the morning, saddled his donkey, and went with the officials of Moab.

22 God's anger was kindled because he was going, and the angel of the LORD took his stand in the road as his adversary. Now he was riding on the donkey, and his two servants were with him. 23The donkey saw the angel of the LORD standing in the road, with a drawn sword in his hand; so the donkey turned off the road, and went into the field; and Balaam struck the donkey, to turn it back onto the road. 24Then the angel of the LORD stood in a narrow path between the vineyards, with a wall on either side. 25When the donkey saw the angel of the LORD, it scraped against the wall, and scraped Balaam's foot against the wall; so he struck it again. 26Then the angel of the LORD went ahead, and stood in a narrow place, where there was no way to turn either to the right or to the left. 27When the donkey saw the angel of the LORD, it lay down under Balaam; and Balaam's anger was kindled, and he struck the donkey with his staff. 28Then the LORD opened the mouth of the donkey, and it said to Balaam, "What have I done to

you, that you have struck me these three times?" 29 Balaam said to the donkey, "Because you have made a fool of me! I wish I had a sword in my hand! I would kill you right now!" 30 But the donkey said to Balaam, "Am I not your donkey, which you have ridden all your life to this day? Have I been in the habit of treating you this way?" And he said, "No."

31 Then the LORD opened the eyes of Balaam, and he saw the angel of the LORD standing in the road, with his drawn sword in his hand; and he bowed down, falling on his face. 32 The angel of the LORD said to him, "Why have you struck your donkey these three times? I have come out as an adversary, because your way is perverse*a* before me. 33 The donkey saw me, and turned away from me these three times. If it had not turned away from me, surely just now I would have killed you and let it live." 34 Then Balaam said to the angel of the LORD, "I have sinned, for I did not know that you were standing in the road to oppose me. Now therefore, if it is displeasing to you, I will return home." 35 The angel of the LORD said to Balaam, "Go with the men; but speak only what I tell you to speak." So Balaam went on with the officials of Balak.

36 When Balak heard that Balaam had come, he went out to meet him at Ir-moab, on the boundary formed by the Arnon, at the farthest point of the boundary. 37 Balak said to Balaam, "Did I not send to summon you? Why did you not come to me? Am I not able to honor you?" 38 Balaam said to Balak, "I have come to you now, but do I have power to say just anything? The word God puts in my mouth, that is what I must say." 39 Then Balaam went with Balak, and they came to Kiriath-huzoth. 40 Balak sacrificed oxen and sheep, and sent them to Balaam and to the officials who were with him.

22.15–40. 22: Although the LORD had just commanded Balaam to go to King Balak (v. 20), the LORD becomes angry at Balaam *because he was going.* As a result, *the angel of the LORD* blocks Balaam's way. The threat of an angel contending against a person whom God has just commanded to go on a mission is a motif★ that occurs elsewhere in the Bible. Moses is

threatened by the LORD when he begins his mission to lead Israel out of Egypt (Ex 4.24–26). Joshua encounters an angelic commander of the LORD's army with a drawn sword as he begins his mission to conquer Canaan (Josh 5.13–15). Jacob wrestles with God as he returns home to Canaan (Gen 22–32). These stories emphasize that even those sent by God remain subject to God's will and are not immune from correction or judgment. **23:** Balaam is supposed to be a professional diviner and prophet. However, his own *donkey* is able to see what he does not see, *the angel of the LORD* standing in front of him. **28:** The talking donkey gives this scene the character of a fable,★ which makes fun of Balaam. Just as *the LORD opened the mouth of the donkey,* so the LORD will need to open the eyes of Balaam (v. 31). Verbs of "seeing" and "looking" are key words throughout the Balaam story of chs. 22–24. **32, 35:** The LORD's commands to go (v. 20), to stop (v. 32), and to go again (v. 35) demonstrate to Balaam that the LORD is in sole command of him. The LORD will be ready to attack Balaam if he does not do God's will and bless Israel. **36:** The *Arnon* river is the northern boundary of the nation of Moab. **40:** The sacrifices of oxen and sheep were likely part of the ritual of divination (see comment on v. 7).

Balaam's four oracles of blessing
22.41–24.25: The contents of Balaam's first two oracles★ or pronouncements of blessing (23.7–10 and 23.18–24) are intricately related to and dependent on the surrounding narrative★ about Balaam and Balak. In contrast, the contents of Balaam's third and fourth oracles of blessing (24.3–9 and 24.15–24) are less tied to the narrative. Thus, they may have had an independent life prior to being incorporated into the present story.

---

41 On the next day Balak took Balaam and brought him up to Bamoth-baal; and from there he could see part of the people of 23 Israel.*b* 1 Then Balaam said to Balak, "Build me seven altars here, and prepare seven bulls and seven rams for me." 2 Balak did as Balaam had said; and Balak and Balaam offered a bull and a ram on each altar. 3 Then Balaam said to Balak, "Stay here beside your burnt offerings while I go aside. Perhaps the LORD will come to meet

a Meaning of Heb uncertain   *b* Heb lacks *of Israel*

me. Whatever he shows me I will tell you." And he went to a bare height.

4 Then God met Balaam; and Balaam said to him, "I have arranged the seven altars, and have offered a bull and a ram on each altar." 5The LORD put a word in Balaam's mouth, and said, "Return to Balak, and this is what you must say." 6So he returned to Balak,*a* who was standing beside his burnt offerings with all the officials of Moab. 7Then Balaam*b* uttered his oracle, saying:

"Balak has brought me from Aram,
   the king of Moab from the eastern
      mountains:
'Come, curse Jacob for me;
   Come, denounce Israel!'
8 How can I curse whom God has not
      cursed?
   How can I denounce those whom the
      LORD has not denounced?
9 For from the top of the crags I see him,
   from the hills I behold him;
Here is a people living alone,
   and not reckoning itself among the
      nations!
10 Who can count the dust of Jacob,
   or number the dust-cloud*c* of Israel?
Let me die the death of the upright,
   and let my end be like his!"

11 Then Balak said to Balaam, "What have you done to me? I brought you to curse my enemies, but now you have done nothing but bless them." 12He answered, "Must I not take care to say what the LORD puts into my mouth?"

13 So Balak said to him, "Come with me to another place from which you may see them; you shall see only part of them, and shall not see them all; then curse them for me from there." 14So he took him to the field of Zophim, to the top of Pisgah. He built seven altars, and offered a bull and a ram on each altar. 15Balaam said to Balak, "Stand here beside your burnt offerings, while I meet the LORD over there." 16The LORD met Balaam, put a word into his mouth, and said, "Return to Balak, and this is what you shall say." 17When he came to him, he was standing beside his burnt offerings with the officials of Moab. Balak said to him, "What has

the LORD said?" 18Then Balaam uttered his oracle, saying:

"Rise, Balak, and hear;
   listen to me, O son of Zippor:
19 God is not a human being, that he
      should lie,
   or a mortal, that he should change his
      mind.
Has he promised, and will he not do it?
Has he spoken, and will he not
      fulfill it?
20 See, I received a command to bless;
   he has blessed, and I cannot revoke it.
21 He has not beheld misfortune in Jacob;
   nor has he seen trouble in Israel.
The LORD their God is with them,
   acclaimed as a king among them.
22 God, who brings them out of Egypt,
   is like the horns of a wild ox for them.
23 Surely there is no enchantment against
      Jacob,
   no divination against Israel;
now it shall be said of Jacob and Israel,
   'See what God has done!'
24 Look, a people rising up like a lioness,
   and rousing itself like a lion!
It does not lie down until it has eaten
      the prey
   and drunk the blood of the slain."

25 Then Balak said to Balaam, "Do not curse them at all, and do not bless them at all." 26But Balaam answered Balak, "Did I not tell you, 'Whatever the LORD says, that is what I must do'?"

27 So Balak said to Balaam, "Come now, I will take you to another place; perhaps it will please God that you may curse them for me from there." 28So Balak took Balaam to the top of Peor, which overlooks the wasteland.*d* 29Balaam said to Balak, "Build me seven altars here, and prepare seven bulls and seven rams for me." 30So Balak did as Balaam had said, and offered a bull and a ram on each altar.

22.41–23.30. 7: *Aram* is the biblical name for the nation of Syria, which lies north and east of Moab. **10:** *The dust of Jacob* is a reference to God's promises in

a Heb *him*   *b* Heb *he*   *c* Or *fourth part*
d Or *overlooks Jeshimon*

Genesis that the descendants of Abraham and Jacob would be as numerous as the dust of the earth (Gen 13.16; 28.14). **14:** On *Pisgah,* see comment on 21.19–20. **19:** God does not *change his mind* about promises of blessing and good fortune. On the other hand, God can sometimes be swayed to alter divine decisions about threatened judgments and punishments (Gen 18.16–33; Ex 32.1–14). **24:** On the images of the *rising lion* and *lioness,* see comment on 24.17. **28:** *Peor* is located east of the Jordan river near Pisgah (21.20).

24 Now Balaam saw that it pleased the LORD to bless Israel, so he did not go, as at other times, to look for omens, but set his face toward the wilderness. 2Balaam looked up and saw Israel camping tribe by tribe. Then the spirit of God came upon him, 3and he uttered his oracle, saying:
"The oracle of Balaam son of Beor,
    the oracle of the man whose eye is
        clear,*a*
4   the oracle of one who hears the words
        of God,
    who sees the vision of the Almighty,*b*
    who falls down, but with eyes
        uncovered:
5   how fair are your tents, O Jacob,
        your encampments, O Israel!
6   Like palm groves that stretch far away,
        like gardens beside a river,
    like aloes that the LORD has planted,
        like cedar trees beside the waters.
7   Water shall flow from his buckets,
        and his seed shall have abundant
        water,
    his king shall be higher than Agag,
        and his kingdom shall be exalted.
8   God who brings him out of Egypt,
        is like the horns of a wild ox
            for him;
    he shall devour the nations that are his
        foes
        and break their bones.
    He shall strike with his arrows.*c*
9   He crouched, he lay down like a lion,
        and like a lioness; who will rouse
            him up?
    Blessed is everyone who blesses you,
        and cursed is everyone who curses
        you."

10 Then Balak's anger was kindled against Balaam, and he struck his hands together. Balak said to Balaam, "I summoned you to curse my enemies, but instead you have blessed them these three times. 11Now be off with you! Go home! I said, 'I will reward you richly,' but the LORD has denied you any reward." 12And Balaam said to Balak, "Did I not tell your messengers whom you sent to me, 13'If Balak should give me his house full of silver and gold, I would not be able to go beyond the word of the LORD, to do either good or bad of my own will; what the LORD says, that is what I will say'? 14So now, I am going to my people; let me advise you what this people will do to your people in days to come."
15 So he uttered his oracle, saying:
"The oracle of Balaam son of Beor,
    the oracle of the man whose eye is
        clear,*a*
16 the oracle of one who hears the words
        of God,
    and knows the knowledge of the Most
        High,*d*
    who sees the vision of the Almighty,*b*
    who falls down, but with his eyes
        uncovered:
17 I see him, but not now;
        I behold him, but not near—
    a star shall come out of Jacob,
        and a scepter shall rise out of Israel;
    it shall crush the borderlands*e* of Moab,
        and the territory*f* of all the Shethites.
18 Edom will become a possession,
        Seir a possession of its enemies,*g*
            while Israel does valiantly.
19 One out of Jacob shall rule,
        and destroy the survivors of Ir."
20 Then he looked on Amalek, and uttered his oracle, saying:
"First among the nations was Amalek,
    but its end is to perish forever."
21 Then he looked on the Kenite, and uttered his oracle, saying:
"Enduring is your dwelling place,
    and your nest is set in the rock;

a Or *closed* or *open*   *b* Traditional rendering of Heb *Shaddai*   *c* Meaning of Heb uncertain   *d* Or *of Elyon*   *e* Or *forehead*   *f* Some Mss read *skull*   *g* Heb *Seir, its enemies, a possession*

22 yet Kain is destined for burning.
     How long shall Asshur take you away
          captive?"
   23 Again he uttered his oracle, saying:
     "Alas, who shall live when God does this?
24   But ships shall come from Kittim
     and shall afflict Asshur and Eber;
          and he also shall perish forever."
   25 Then Balaam got up and went back to
his place, and Balak also went his way.

25 While Israel was staying at Shittim, the people began to have sexual relations with the women of Moab. ²These invited the people to the sacrifices of their gods, and the people ate and bowed down to their gods. ³Thus Israel yoked itself to the Baal of Peor, and the LORD's anger was kindled against Israel. ⁴The LORD said to Moses, "Take all the chiefs of the people, and impale them in the sun before the LORD, in order that the fierce anger of the LORD may turn away from Israel." ⁵And Moses said to the judges of Israel, "Each of you shall kill any of your people who have yoked themselves to the Baal of Peor."

6 Just then one of the Israelites came and brought a Midianite woman into his family, in the sight of Moses and in the sight of the whole congregation of the Israelites, while they were weeping at the entrance of the tent of meeting. ⁷When Phinehas son of Eleazar, son of Aaron the priest, saw it, he got up and left the congregation. Taking a spear in his hand, ⁸he went after the Israelite man into the tent, and pierced the two of them, the Israelite and the woman, through the belly. So the plague was stopped among the people of Israel. ⁹Nevertheless those that died by the plague were twenty-four thousand.

10 The LORD spoke to Moses, saying: ¹¹"Phinehas son of Eleazar, son of Aaron the priest, has turned back my wrath from the Israelites by manifesting such zeal among them on my behalf that in my jealousy I did not consume the Israelites. ¹²Therefore say, 'I hereby grant him my covenant of peace. ¹³It shall be for him and for his descendants after him a covenant of perpetual priesthood, because he was zealous for his God, and made atonement for the Israelites.' "

14 The name of the slain Israelite man, who was killed with the Midianite woman, was Zimri son of Salu, head of an ancestral house belonging to the Simeonites. ¹⁵The name of the Midianite woman who was killed was Cozbi daughter of Zur, who was the head of a clan, an ancestral house in Midian.

16 The LORD said to Moses, ¹⁷"Harass the Midianites, and defeat them; ¹⁸for they have harassed you by the trickery with which

24.1–25. 1: An *omen* is information derived from divination (see comment on 22.7). 2: That *the spirit of God came upon* Balaam suggests a more direct mode of divine inspiration and guidance than reliance on omens (v. 1). 4: *The Almighty* (Heb., "Shaddai") is an ancient divine name applied to the LORD (Gen 17.1; Ex 6.3). The Balaam inscription found by archaeologists at Deir 'Allah includes mention of "Shaddai" gods (see the sidebar on p. 244). 7: Some commentators link this *Agag* to King Agag of the Amalekites whom the Israelite king Saul defeated in 1 Sam 15. 9: On the images of the roused *lion* and *lioness,* see comment on 24.17. 13: See 22.18. 16: *The Most High* (Heb., "Elyon") is an ancient divine name used for the LORD in other biblical contexts (Gen 14.18–24; Deut 32.8). On *the Almighty* as a divine name, see comment on 24.4. 17: The image of *a star* could be used as a metaphor* for a king (Isa 14.12). The *scepter* or royal staff symbolized royal authority, much like the staffs of Moses and Aaron represented their authority as leader and priest of Israel (17.10; 20.8). Many commentators understand these images of a future royal figure as pointing to King David and his victories over Moab and Edom (2 Sam 8.2, 11–14). The blessing of Jacob in Gen 49.9–10 uses the image of the crouching lion and lioness waiting to be roused for the tribe of Judah (the tribe of King David). These same images appear in Balaam's oracles* (23.24; 24.9). The *Shethites* may be an ethnic group within the nation of Moab. 18: The nation of *Edom* is also known as *Seir* (Gen 32.3). 19: *Ir* is apparently a town in Moab (see 22.36). 20: On *Amalek* and the Amalekites, see comment on 13.29. 21–22: On *the Kenites*, see comment on 10.29. The mention of *Kain* with the Kenites suggests a link to the Genesis ancestors, Cain and Tubalcain (Gen 4.1–22). 22, 24: These final verses of the oracle are somewhat obscure. *Asshur* (v. 22, 24) is the biblical name for the empire of Assyria. *Kittim* (v. 24) is usually another name for Cyprus. *Eber* is uncertain.

they deceived you in the affair of Peor, and in the affair of Cozbi, the daughter of a leader of Midian, their sister; she was killed on the day of the plague that resulted from Peor."

25.1–18: The final rebellion: Israel's worship of a foreign god and entanglements with foreign women. The chapter combines two incidents in which the old wilderness generation of Israelites rebel against God's commands. One incident involves Israelite men having sexual relations with women from Moab, which leads them to worship the Moabite god Baal* of Peor (vv. 1–5). A second incident involves an Israelite from the tribe of Simeon who has sexual relations with a woman from Midian (vv. 6–15). Intermarriage with foreign peoples was feared since it was believed to lead to the worship of foreign gods (Deut 7.1–5). Yet other biblical traditions do not condemn intermarriage. Moses himself was married to a Midianite woman (Ex 2.15–22), and the book of Ruth portrays an Israelite man's marriage to a Moabite woman named Ruth in a very favorable light. The LORD sends a plague as punishment that kills 24,000 Israelites (v. 9). Those who are killed are presumably the last remnants of the old generation, which had been condemned to die in the wilderness in the spy story of Num 13–14 (see 14.28–30). This old generation had been counted in the first census list in Num 1. The new census list in Num 26 will mark the emergence of an entirely new generation of Israelites, who will be allowed to enter the promised land of Canaan (see 26.63–65). **1:** *Shittim* may be the same as Abel-shittim, which is located on the plains of Moab (33.49). The Hebrew verb "znh," translated here as *to have sexual relations with,* may also mean "to prostitute themselves with." The same verb can also be used for the forbidden worship of foreign gods (Ex 34.12–16: "your sons also prostitute themselves to their gods," v. 16). **3:** *Baal* means "lord," but the title is used here for the name of a non-Israelite god, *Baal of Peor.* **6:** On *the tent of meeting,* see comment on 1.1. **7:** *Phinehas* is the grandson of the high priest Aaron (see Ex 6.23–25). **12–13:** A *covenant** of peace is a promise of well-being (Ezek 37.26). The *perpetual priesthood* offered to Phinehas is an extension of the perpetual priesthood first given to Aaron and his sons (Ex 40.12–15). **16–18:** The military defeat of *the Midianites* commanded here will be carried out by the new generation of Israelites in Num 31. The earlier incident involving the Moabite women and the god Baal of

Peor (vv. 1–5) is joined together with the Midianite incident (vv. 6–15) as essentially one episode.

A second census of a new generation of Israelites 26.1–65: The first census list in Num 1 had counted the twelve tribes of Israel who had been born in Egypt and experienced the exodus out of Egypt. This old generation rebelled against the LORD; hence the LORD condemned them to die in the wilderness without entering the promised land of Canaan (14.28–35). However, the LORD promised to bring the new generation of Israelites into the land of Canaan. This second census list in Num 26 marks the beginning of the story of this new generation of Israelites who will enter the land of Canaan (26.63–65).

26 After the plague the LORD said to Moses and to Eleazar son of Aaron the priest, 2"Take a census of the whole congregation of the Israelites, from twenty years old and upward, by their ancestral houses, everyone in Israel able to go to war." 3Moses and Eleazar the priest spoke with them in the plains of Moab by the Jordan opposite Jericho, saying, 4"Take a census of the people,*a* from twenty years old and upward," as the LORD commanded Moses.

The Israelites, who came out of the land of Egypt, were:

5 Reuben, the firstborn of Israel. The descendants of Reuben: of Hanoch, the clan of the Hanochites; of Pallu, the clan of the Palluites; 6of Hezron, the clan of the Hezronites; of Carmi, the clan of the Carmites. 7These are the clans of the Reubenites; the number of those enrolled was forty-three thousand seven hundred thirty. 8And the descendants of Pallu: Eliab. 9The descendants of Eliab: Nemuel, Dathan, and Abiram. These are the same Dathan and Abiram, chosen from the congregation, who rebelled against Moses and Aaron in the company of Korah, when they rebelled against the LORD, 10and the earth opened its mouth and swallowed them up along with Korah, when that company died, when the fire devoured two hundred fifty men; and they became a warning. 11Notwithstanding, the sons of Korah did not die.

a Heb lacks *take a census of the people*: Compare verse 2

12 The descendants of Simeon by their clans: of Nemuel, the clan of the Nemuelites; of Jamin, the clan of the Jaminites; of Jachin, the clan of the Jachinites; 13 of Zerah, the clan of the Zerahites; of Shaul, the clan of the Shaulites.[a] 14 These are the clans of the Simeonites, twenty-two thousand two hundred.

15 The children of Gad by their clans: of Zephon, the clan of the Zephonites; of Haggi, the clan of the Haggites; of Shuni, the clan of the Shunites; 16 of Ozni, the clan of the Oznites; of Eri, the clan of the Erites; 17 of Arod, the clan of the Arodites; of Areli, the clan of the Arelites. 18 These are the clans of the Gadites: the number of those enrolled was forty thousand five hundred.

19 The sons of Judah: Er and Onan; Er and Onan died in the land of Canaan. 20 The descendants of Judah by their clans were: of Shelah, the clan of the Shelanites; of Perez, the clan of the Perezites; of Zerah, the clan of the Zerahites. 21 The descendants of Perez were: of Hezron, the clan of the Hezronites; of Hamul, the clan of the Hamulites. 22 These are the clans of Judah: the number of those enrolled was seventy-six thousand five hundred.

23 The descendants of Issachar by their clans: of Tola, the clan of the Tolaites; of Puvah, the clan of the Punites; 24 of Jashub, the clan of the Jashubites; of Shimron, the clan of the Shimronites. 25 These are the clans of Issachar: sixty-four thousand three hundred enrolled.

26 The descendants of Zebulun by their clans: of Sered, the clan of the Seredites; of Elon, the clan of the Elonites; of Jahleel, the clan of the Jahleelites. 27 These are the clans of the Zebulunites; the number of those enrolled was sixty thousand five hundred.

28 The sons of Joseph by their clans: Manasseh and Ephraim. 29 The descendants of Manasseh: of Machir, the clan of the Machirites; and Machir was the father of Gilead; of Gilead, the clan of the Gileadites. 30 These are the descendants of Gilead: of Iezer, the clan of the Iezerites; of Helek, the clan of the Helekites; 31 and of Asriel, the clan of the Asrielites; and of Shechem, the clan of the Shechemites; 32 and of She-mida, the clan of the Shemidaites; and of Hepher, the clan of the Hepherites. 33 Now Zelophehad son of Hepher had no sons, but daughters: and the names of the daughters of Zelophehad were Mahlah, Noah, Hoglah, Milcah, and Tirzah. 34 These are the clans of Manasseh; the number of those enrolled was fifty-two thousand seven hundred.

35 These are the descendants of Ephraim according to their clans: of Shuthelah, the clan of the Shuthelahites; of Becher, the clan of the Becherites; of Tahan, the clan of the Tahanites. 36 And these are the descendants of Shuthelah: of Eran, the clan of the Eranites. 37 These are the clans of the Ephraimites: the number of those enrolled was thirty-two thousand five hundred. These are the descendants of Joseph by their clans.

38 The descendants of Benjamin by their clans: of Bela, the clan of the Belaites; of Ashbel, the clan of the Ashbelites; of Ahiram, the clan of the Ahiramites; 39 of Shephupham, the clan of the Shuphamites; of Hupham, the clan of the Huphamites. 40 And the sons of Bela were Ard and Naaman: of Ard, the clan of the Ardites; of Naaman, the clan of the Naamites. 41 These are the descendants of Benjamin by their clans; the number of those enrolled was forty-five thousand six hundred.

42 These are the descendants of Dan by their clans: of Shuham, the clan of the Shuhamites. These are the clans of Dan by their clans. 43 All the clans of the Shuhamites: sixty-four thousand four hundred enrolled.

44 The descendants of Asher by their families: of Imnah, the clan of the Imnites; of Ishvi, the clan of the Ishvites; of Beriah, the clan of the Beriites. 45 Of the descendants of Beriah: of Heber, the clan of the Heberites; of Malchiel, the clan of the Malchielites. 46 And the name of the daughter of Asher was Serah. 47 These are the clans of the Asherites: the number of those enrolled was fifty-three thousand four hundred.

48 The descendants of Naphtali by their clans: of Jahzeel, the clan of the Jahzeelites; of Guni, the clan of the Gunites; 49 of Jezer,

a Or Saul . . . Saulites

the clan of the Jezerites; of Shillem, the clan of the Shillemites. ⁵⁰These are the Naphtalites*a* by their clans: the number of those enrolled was forty-five thousand four hundred.

⁵¹ This was the number of the Israelites enrolled: six hundred and one thousand seven hundred thirty.

⁵² The LORD spoke to Moses, saying: ⁵³To these the land shall be apportioned for inheritance according to the number of names. ⁵⁴To a large tribe you shall give a large inheritance, and to a small tribe you shall give a small inheritance; every tribe shall be given its inheritance according to its enrollment. ⁵⁵But the land shall be apportioned by lot; according to the names of their ancestral tribes they shall inherit. ⁵⁶Their inheritance shall be apportioned according to lot between the larger and the smaller.

⁵⁷ This is the enrollment of the Levites by their clans: of Gershon, the clan of the Gershonites; of Kohath, the clan of the Kohathites; of Merari, the clan of the Merarites. ⁵⁸These are the clans of Levi: the clan of the Libnites, the clan of the Hebronites, the clan of the Mahlites, the clan of the Mushites, the clan of the Korahites. Now Kohath was the father of Amram. ⁵⁹The name of Amram's wife was Jochebed daughter of Levi, who was born to Levi in Egypt; and she bore to Amram: Aaron, Moses, and their sister Miriam. ⁶⁰To Aaron were born Nadab, Abihu, Eleazar, and Ithamar. ⁶¹But Nadab and Abihu died when they offered unholy fire before the LORD. ⁶²The number of those enrolled was twenty-three thousand, every male one month old and upward; for they were not enrolled among the Israelites because there was no allotment given to them among the Israelites.

⁶³ These were those enrolled by Moses and Eleazar the priest, who enrolled the Israelites in the plains of Moab by the Jordan opposite Jericho. ⁶⁴Among these there was not one of those enrolled by Moses and Aaron the priest, who had enrolled the Israelites in the wilderness of Sinai. ⁶⁵For the LORD had said of them, "They shall die in the wilderness." Not one of them was left, except Caleb son of Jephunneh and Joshua son of Nun.

a Heb *clans of Naphtali*

26.1–65. 1: *After the plague* is a reference to the plague in 25.8–9. *Eleazar* is the son of Aaron who became the high priest at Aaron's death (20.22–29). **5–50:** This second census list is similar in form to the census list in Num 1, but there are some notable differences. The total numbers for each of the twelve tribes are different. The tribe of Simeon sustained the greatest loss of numbers, perhaps as a result of the Simeonite's sin in 25.14 (compare 26.12–14 and 1.23). The sequence of the twelve tribes is slightly different from Num 1 and closer to the order of the tribes in Num 2. Another difference between Num 1 and 26 is that various sub-clans* are added in Num 26 under each tribe as a sign of the birth of a new generation. These clan names are similar to those listed in Gen 46.8–27. **51:** The total here of 601,730 Israelites is slightly less than the first census total of 603,550 in 1.46. **52–56:** In addition to the need to determine the number of warriors who are able to go to war (v. 2), this new census has a second purpose. The numbers will determine the relative sizes of the allotments of land necessary for each tribe when Israel conquers the land of Canaan (see Josh 13–19). **57–62:** As in the first census (3.14–39), the Levites have a separate census. The death of *Nadab and Abihu* (v. 61) is recounted in Lev 10.1–2. **64–65:** The enrollment in *the wilderness of Sinai* was the census in Num 1. Everyone of the old generation counted in Num 1 was condemned to *die in the wilderness* because of their refusal to go and conquer Canaan (14.20–25, 28–35). Because of their faithfulness, only *Caleb* and *Joshua* would live to enter the promised land (14.30, 38).

27 Then the daughters of Zelophehad came forward. Zelophehad was son of Hepher son of Gilead son of Machir son of Manasseh son of Joseph, a member of the Manasseh clans. The names of his daughters were: Mahlah, Noah, Hoglah, Milcah, and Tirzah. ²They stood before Moses, Eleazar the priest, the leaders, and all the congregation, at the entrance of the tent of meeting, and they said, ³"Our father died in the wilderness; he was not among the company of those who gathered themselves together against the LORD in the company of Korah, but died for his own sin; and he had no sons. ⁴Why should the name of our father be taken away from his clan because he had no

son? Give to us a possession among our father's brothers."

5 Moses brought their case before the LORD. 6And the LORD spoke to Moses, saying: 7The daughters of Zelophehad are right in what they are saying; you shall indeed let them possess an inheritance among their father's brothers and pass the inheritance of their father on to them. 8You shall also say to the Israelites, "If a man dies, and has no son, then you shall pass his inheritance on to his daughter. 9If he has no daughter, then you shall give his inheritance to his brothers. 10If he has no brothers, then you shall give his inheritance to his father's brothers. 11And if his father has no brothers, then you shall give his inheritance to the nearest kinsman of his clan, and he shall possess it. It shall be for the Israelites a statute and ordinance, as the LORD commanded Moses."

27.1–11: The daughters of Zelophehad and the inheritance of land. This legal case involves the conflict between two principles. On one hand, Israelite land normally passed from father to son and not to daughters. On the other hand, a high priority was given to maintaining a given land allotment within a particular family or clan* in order to maintain a fair distribution of the land among family groups. On the basis of the priority of this latter principle, the five daughters of a man named Zelophehad argue that they ought to receive their father's allotment of land as an inheritance. In the end, the LORD and Moses agree. In Num 36, the case is taken up again with some restrictions on whom the daughters of Zelophehad can marry in order to preserve the land in the family group. **1:** Zelophehad's death and a report about his children is cited in the census in 26.33. **2:** On *the tent of meeting,* see 1.1. **3:** The daughters deny their father's involvement in the rebellion of Korah in Num 16. **4:** *The name of our father* is a reference to the family name and the inheritance of land to which it is attached.

12 The LORD said to Moses, "Go up this mountain of the Abarim range, and see the land that I have given to the Israelites. 13When you have seen it, you also shall be gathered to your people, as your brother Aaron was, 14because you rebelled against my word in the wilderness of Zin when the congregation quarreled with me.a You did

not show my holiness before their eyes at the waters." (These are the waters of Meribathkadesh in the wilderness of Zin.) 15Moses spoke to the LORD, saying, 16"Let the LORD, the God of the spirits of all flesh, appoint someone over the congregation 17who shall go out before them and come in before them, who shall lead them out and bring them in, so that the congregation of the LORD may not be like sheep without a shepherd." 18So the LORD said to Moses, "Take Joshua son of Nun, a man in whom is the spirit, and lay your hand upon him; 19have him stand before Eleazar the priest and all the congregation, and commission him in their sight. 20You shall give him some of your authority, so that all the congregation of the Israelites may obey. 21But he shall stand before Eleazar the priest, who shall inquire for him by the decision of the Urim before the LORD; at his word they shall go out, and at his word they shall come in, both he and all the Israelites with him, the whole congregation." 22So Moses did as the LORD commanded him. He took Joshua and had him stand before Eleazar the priest and the whole congregation; 23he laid his hands on him and commissioned him—as the LORD had directed through Moses.

27.12–23: The succession of leadership from Moses to Joshua. 13: Aaron's death is recorded in 20.22–29. **14:** Moses sinned in the incident in Num 20.2–13. **18:** The divine *spirit* is often associated with leaders and prophets* in the Bible (Judg 3.10) and can be transferred from one person to another (Num 11.24–25; 2 Kings 2.9–10). See the distribution of the spirit among the leaders of Israel in 11.16–17. To *lay your hand* on another involves the transfer of a power or status from one person to another. In this case, Moses' authority transfers in part to Joshua. **20:** Moses' leadership remains unique and unrepeatable so that Joshua receives only a part or *some* of Moses' *authority* (see Deut 34.9–10). **21:** Joshua's leadership will be supplemented by the priest Eleazar, who will seek guidance from the LORD through *the Urim. The Urim* are objects (perhaps light and dark stones) used by Israelite priests in determining the deity's will in a given situation (Ex 28.30; 1 Sam 14.41).

a Heb lacks *with me*

Appointed offerings for various festivals and times

28.1–29.40: Other biblical lists of offerings at festivals include Lev 23 and Deut 16.1–17. The *ephah* and *hin* are frequently mentioned in these laws as measurements of grain and oil. An *ephah* is a unit of dry measure of roughly half a bushel, and a *hin* is a unit of liquid measure somewhere between a quart and a gallon. Another frequent phrase among these laws, *a pleasing odor to the LORD*, indicates a divinely accepted offering as the aroma arises from the burning of the sacrifice (see Gen 8.20–22).

28 The LORD spoke to Moses, saying: ²Command the Israelites, and say to them: My offering, the food for my offerings by fire, my pleasing odor, you shall take care to offer to me at its appointed time. ³And you shall say to them, This is the offering by fire that you shall offer to the LORD: two male lambs a year old without blemish, daily, as a regular offering. ⁴One lamb you shall offer in the morning, and the other lamb you shall offer at twilight;ᵃ ⁵also one-tenth of an ephah of choice flour for a grain offering, mixed with one-fourth of a hin of beaten oil. ⁶It is a regular burnt offering, ordained at Mount Sinai for a pleasing odor, an offering by fire to the LORD. ⁷Its drink offering shall be one-fourth of a hin for each lamb; in the sanctuary you shall pour out a drink offering of strong drink to the LORD. ⁸The other lamb you shall offer at twilightᵃ with a grain offering and a drink offering like the one in the morning; you shall offer it as an offering by fire, a pleasing odor to the LORD.

9 On the sabbath day: two male lambs a year old without blemish, and two-tenths of an ephah of choice flour for a grain offering, mixed with oil, and its drink offering— ¹⁰this is the burnt offering for every sabbath, in addition to the regular burnt offering and its drink offering.

11 At the beginnings of your months you shall offer a burnt offering to the LORD: two young bulls, one ram, seven male lambs a year old without blemish; ¹²also three-tenths of an ephah of choice flour for a grain offering, mixed with oil, for each bull; and two-tenths of choice flour for a grain offering, mixed with oil, for the one ram; ¹³and one-tenth of choice flour mixed with oil as a grain offering for every lamb—a burnt offering of pleasing odor, an offering by fire to the LORD. ¹⁴Their drink offerings shall be half a hin of wine for a bull, one-third of a hin for a ram, and one-fourth of a hin for a lamb. This is the burnt offering of every month throughout the months of the year. ¹⁵And there shall be one male goat for a sin offering to the LORD; it shall be offered in addition to the regular burnt offering and its drink offering.

16 On the fourteenth day of the first month there shall be a passover offering to the LORD. ¹⁷And on the fifteenth day of this month is a festival; seven days shall unleavened bread be eaten. ¹⁸On the first day there shall be a holy convocation. You shall not work at your occupations. ¹⁹You shall offer an offering by fire, a burnt offering to the LORD: two young bulls, one ram, and seven male lambs a year old; see that they are without blemish. ²⁰Their grain offering shall be of choice flour mixed with oil: three-tenths of an ephah shall you offer for a bull, and two-tenths for a ram; ²¹one-tenth shall you offer for each of the seven lambs; ²²also one male goat for a sin offering, to make atonement for you. ²³You shall offer these in addition to the burnt offering of the morning, which belongs to the regular burnt offering. ²⁴In the same way you shall offer daily, for seven days, the food of an offering by fire, a pleasing odor to the LORD; it shall be offered in addition to the regular burnt offering and its drink offering. ²⁵And on the seventh day you shall have a holy convocation; you shall not work at your occupations.

26 On the day of the first fruits, when you offer a grain offering of new grain to the LORD at your festival of weeks, you shall have a holy convocation; you shall not work at your occupations. ²⁷You shall offer a burnt offering, a pleasing odor to the LORD: two young bulls, one ram, seven male lambs a year old. ²⁸Their grain offering shall be of choice flour mixed with oil, three-tenths of

a Heb *between the two evenings*

an ephah for each bull, two-tenths for one ram, 29one-tenth for each of the seven lambs; 30with one male goat, to make atonement for you. 31In addition to the regular burnt offering with its grain offering, you shall offer them and their drink offering. They shall be without blemish.

28.1–31. 9: *The sabbath day* is every seventh day. The sabbath, a day of rest and no work, is holy to the LORD (see Ex 20.8–11). **16:** *Passover** is a springtime festival that celebrates Israel's exodus out of Egypt (Ex 12.1–13.10). **17:** *Unleavened bread* is a yeastless bread that does not rise during baking. It is associated with Passover since the Israelites hurriedly left Egypt and could not wait for their bread to rise when baking it (Ex 12.33–34). **26:** The *festival of weeks* or Pentecost* marks the beginning of the wheat harvest (Lev 23.15–21).

---

29 On the first day of the seventh month you shall have a holy convocation; you shall not work at your occupations. It is a day for you to blow the trumpets, 2and you shall offer a burnt offering, a pleasing odor to the LORD: one young bull, one ram, seven male lambs a year old without blemish. 3Their grain offering shall be of choice flour mixed with oil, three-tenths of one ephah for the bull, two-tenths for the ram, 4and one-tenth for each of the seven lambs; 5with one male goat for a sin offering, to make atonement for you. 6These are in addition to the burnt offering of the new moon and its grain offering, and the regular burnt offering and its grain offering, and their drink offerings, according to the ordinance for them, a pleasing odor, an offering by fire to the LORD.

7 On the tenth day of this seventh month you shall have a holy convocation, and deny yourselves;[a] you shall do no work. 8You shall offer a burnt offering to the LORD, a pleasing odor: one young bull, one ram, seven male lambs a year old. They shall be without blemish. 9Their grain offering shall be of choice flour mixed with oil, three-tenths of an ephah for the bull, two-tenths for the one ram, 10one-tenth for each of the seven lambs; 11with one male goat for a sin offering, in addition to the sin offering of atone-

ment, and the regular burnt offering and its grain offering, and their drink offerings.

12 On the fifteenth day of the seventh month you shall have a holy convocation; you shall not work at your occupations. You shall celebrate a festival to the LORD seven days. 13You shall offer a burnt offering, an offering by fire, a pleasing odor to the LORD: thirteen young bulls, two rams, fourteen male lambs a year old. They shall be without blemish. 14Their grain offering shall be of choice flour mixed with oil, three-tenths of an ephah for each of the thirteen bulls, two-tenths for each of the two rams, 15and one-tenth for each of the fourteen lambs; 16also one male goat for a sin offering, in addition to the regular burnt offering, its grain offering and its drink offering.

17 On the second day: twelve young bulls, two rams, fourteen male lambs a year old without blemish, 18with the grain offering and the drink offerings for the bulls, for the rams, and for the lambs, as prescribed in accordance with their number; 19also one male goat for a sin offering, in addition to the regular burnt offering and its grain offering, and their drink offerings.

20 On the third day: eleven bulls, two rams, fourteen male lambs a year old without blemish, 21with the grain offering and the drink offerings for the bulls, for the rams, and for the lambs, as prescribed in accordance with their number; 22also one male goat for a sin offering, in addition to the regular burnt offering and its grain offering and its drink offering.

23 On the fourth day: ten bulls, two rams, fourteen male lambs a year old without blemish, 24with the grain offering and the drink offerings for the bulls, for the rams, and for the lambs, as prescribed in accordance with their number; 25also one male goat for a sin offering, in addition to the regular burnt offering, its grain offering and its drink offering.

26 On the fifth day: nine bulls, two rams, fourteen male lambs a year old without blemish, 27with the grain offering and the drink offerings for the bulls, for the rams,

a Or *and fast*

and for the lambs, as prescribed in accordance with their number; 28also one male goat for a sin offering, in addition to the regular burnt offering and its grain offering and its drink offering.

29 On the sixth day: eight bulls, two rams, fourteen male lambs a year old without blemish, 30with the grain offering and the drink offerings for the bulls, for the rams, and for the lambs, as prescribed in accordance with their number; 31also one male goat for a sin offering, in addition to the regular burnt offering, its grain offering, and its drink offerings.

32 On the seventh day: seven bulls, two rams, fourteen male lambs a year old without blemish, 33with the grain offering and the drink offerings for the bulls, for the rams, and for the lambs, as prescribed in accordance with their number; 34also one male goat for a sin offering, besides the regular burnt offering, its grain offering, and its drink offering.

35 On the eighth day you shall have a solemn assembly; you shall not work at your occupations. 36You shall offer a burnt offering, an offering by fire, a pleasing odor to the LORD: one bull, one ram, seven male lambs a year old without blemish, 37and the grain offering and the drink offerings for the bull, for the ram, and for the lambs, as prescribed in accordance with their number; 38also one male goat for a sin offering, in addition to the regular burnt offering and its grain offering and its drink offering.

39 These you shall offer to the LORD at your appointed festivals, in addition to your votive offerings and your freewill offerings, as your burnt offerings, your grain offerings, your drink offerings, and your offerings of well-being.

40ᵃ So Moses told the Israelites everything just as the LORD had commanded Moses.

seventh month is the festival of booths or Sukkot (Lev 23.33–36). It was a feast of thanksgiving during the autumn harvest and a remembrance of God's care over Israel during its wilderness journey from Egypt to Canaan.

30 Then Moses said to the heads of the tribes of the Israelites: This is what the LORD has commanded. 2When a man makes a vow to the LORD, or swears an oath to bind himself by a pledge, he shall not break his word; he shall do according to all that proceeds out of his mouth.

3 When a woman makes a vow to the LORD, or binds herself by a pledge, while within her father's house, in her youth, 4and her father hears of her vow or her pledge by which she has bound herself, and says nothing to her; then all her vows shall stand, and any pledge by which she has bound herself shall stand. 5But if her father expresses disapproval to her at the time that he hears of it, no vow of hers, and no pledge by which she has bound herself, shall stand; and the LORD will forgive her, because her father had expressed to her his disapproval.

6 If she marries, while obligated by her vows or any thoughtless utterance of her lips by which she has bound herself, 7and her husband hears of it and says nothing to her at the time that he hears, then her vows shall stand, and her pledges by which she has bound herself shall stand. 8But if, at the time that her husband hears of it, he expresses disapproval to her, then he shall nullify the vow by which she was obligated, or the thoughtless utterance of her lips, by which she bound herself; and the LORD will forgive her. 9(But every vow of a widow or of a divorced woman, by which she has bound herself, shall be binding upon her.) 10And if she made a vow in her husband's house, or bound herself by a pledge with an oath, 11and her husband heard it and said nothing to her, and did not express disapproval to her, then all her vows shall stand, and any pledge by which she bound herself shall stand. 12But if her husband nullifies them at the time that he hears them, then whatever

29.1–40. 1: *The first day of the seventh month* is New Year's Day (Rosh Hashanah, "head of the year,") and occurs in the autumn of the year. 7: *The tenth day of the seventh month* is the Day of Atonement* or Yom Kippur (Lev 23.26–32). **12:** *The fifteenth day of the*

a Ch 30.1 in Heb

proceeds out of her lips concerning her vows, or concerning her pledge of herself, shall not stand. Her husband has nullified them, and the LORD will forgive her. ¹³Any vow or any binding oath to deny herself,ᵃ her husband may allow to stand, or her husband may nullify. ¹⁴But if her husband says nothing to her from day to day,ᵇ then he validates all her vows, or all her pledges, by which she is obligated; he has validated them, because he said nothing to her at the time that he heard of them. ¹⁵But if he nullifies them some time after he has heard of them, then he shall bear her guilt.

16 These are the statutes that the LORD commanded Moses concerning a husband and his wife, and a father and his daughter while she is still young and in her father's house.

30.1–16: Men, women, and the fulfillment of vows. These laws concerning vows by men and women reflect an ancient society in which young women or married women were normally under the responsibility and supervision of men, whether fathers or husbands. **9:** *A widow* or *a divorced woman* is not under the supervision or care of a man and thus has full responsibility for her own vow. **15:** Under certain circumstances, the husband *shall bear* the wife's *guilt*, meaning that he is responsible for fulfilling the vow she made.

---

31 The LORD spoke to Moses, saying, ²"Avenge the Israelites on the Midianites; afterward you shall be gathered to your people." ³So Moses said to the people, "Arm some of your number for the war, so that they may go against Midian, to execute the LORD's vengeance on Midian. ⁴You shall send a thousand from each of the tribes of Israel to the war." ⁵So out of the thousands of Israel, a thousand from each tribe were conscripted, twelve thousand armed for battle. ⁶Moses sent them to the war, a thousand from each tribe, along with Phinehas son of Eleazar the priest,ᶜ with the vessels of the sanctuary and the trumpets for sounding the alarm in his hand. ⁷They did battle against Midian, as the LORD had commanded Moses, and killed every male. ⁸They killed the kings of Midian: Evi, Rekem, Zur, Hur, and

Reba, the five kings of Midian, in addition to others who were slain by them; and they also killed Balaam son of Beor with the sword. ⁹The Israelites took the women of Midian and their little ones captive; and they took all their cattle, their flocks, and all their goods as booty. ¹⁰All their towns where they had settled, and all their encampments, they burned, ¹¹but they took all the spoil and all the booty, both people and animals. ¹²Then they brought the captives and the booty and the spoil to Moses, to Eleazar the priest, and to the congregation of the Israelites, at the camp on the plains of Moab by the Jordan at Jericho.

13 Moses, Eleazar the priest, and all the leaders of the congregation went to meet them outside the camp. ¹⁴Moses became angry with the officers of the army, the commanders of thousands and the commanders of hundreds, who had come from service in the war. ¹⁵Moses said to them, "Have you allowed all the women to live? ¹⁶These women here, on Balaam's advice, made the Israelites act treacherously against the LORD in the affair of Peor, so that the plague came among the congregation of the LORD. ¹⁷Now therefore, kill every male among the little ones, and kill every woman who has known a man by sleeping with him. ¹⁸But all the young girls who have not known a man by sleeping with him, keep alive for yourselves. ¹⁹Camp outside the camp seven days; whoever of you has killed any person or touched a corpse, purify yourselves and your captives on the third and on the seventh day. ²⁰You shall purify every garment, every article of skin, everything made of goats' hair, and every article of wood."

21 Eleazar the priest said to the troops who had gone to battle: "This is the statute of the law that the LORD has commanded Moses: ²²gold, silver, bronze, iron, tin, and lead— ²³everything that can withstand fire, shall be passed through fire, and it shall be clean. Nevertheless it shall also be purified with the water for purification; and whatever cannot withstand fire, shall be passed

---

a Or *to fast*   *b* Or *from that day to the next*
c Gk: Heb adds *to the war*

through the water. ²⁴You must wash your clothes on the seventh day, and you shall be clean; afterward you may come into the camp."

25 The Lord spoke to Moses, saying, ²⁶"You and Eleazar the priest and the heads of the ancestral houses of the congregation make an inventory of the booty captured, both human and animal. ²⁷Divide the booty into two parts, between the warriors who went out to battle and all the congregation. ²⁸From the share of the warriors who went out to battle, set aside as tribute for the Lord, one item out of every five hundred, whether persons, oxen, donkeys, sheep, or goats. ²⁹Take it from their half and give it to Eleazar the priest as an offering to the Lord. ³⁰But from the Israelites' half you shall take one out of every fifty, whether persons, oxen, donkeys, sheep, or goats—all the animals—and give them to the Levites who have charge of the tabernacle of the Lord."

31 Then Moses and Eleazar the priest did as the Lord had commanded Moses:

32 The booty remaining from the spoil that the troops had taken totaled six hundred seventy-five thousand sheep, ³³seventy-two thousand oxen, ³⁴sixty-one thousand donkeys, ³⁵and thirty-two thousand persons in all, women who had not known a man by sleeping with him.

36 The half-share, the portion of those who had gone out to war, was in number three hundred thirty-seven thousand five hundred sheep and goats, ³⁷and the Lord's tribute of sheep and goats was six hundred seventy-five. ³⁸The oxen were thirty-six thousand, of which the Lord's tribute was seventy-two. ³⁹The donkeys were thirty thousand five hundred, of which the Lord's tribute was sixty-one. ⁴⁰The persons were sixteen thousand, of which the Lord's tribute was thirty-two persons. ⁴¹Moses gave the tribute, the offering for the Lord, to Eleazar the priest, as the Lord had commanded Moses.

42 As for the Israelites' half, which Moses separated from that of the troops, ⁴³the congregation's half was three hundred thirty-seven thousand five hundred sheep and goats, ⁴⁴thirty-six thousand oxen, ⁴⁵thirty

thousand five hundred donkeys, ⁴⁶and sixteen thousand persons. ⁴⁷From the Israelites' half Moses took one of every fifty, both of persons and of animals, and gave them to the Levites who had charge of the tabernacle of the Lord; as the Lord had commanded Moses.

48 Then the officers who were over the thousands of the army, the commanders of thousands and the commanders of hundreds, approached Moses, ⁴⁹and said to Moses, "Your servants have counted the warriors who are under our command, and not one of us is missing. ⁵⁰And we have brought the Lord's offering, what each of us found, articles of gold, armlets and bracelets, signet rings, earrings, and pendants, to make atonement for ourselves before the Lord." ⁵¹Moses and Eleazar the priest received the gold from them, all in the form of crafted articles. ⁵²And all the gold of the offering that they offered to the Lord, from the commanders of thousands and the commanders of hundreds, was sixteen thousand seven hundred fifty shekels. ⁵³(The troops had all taken plunder for themselves.) ⁵⁴So Moses and Eleazar the priest received the gold from the commanders of thousands and of hundreds, and brought it into the tent of meeting as a memorial for the Israelites before the Lord.

31.1–54: Holy war* against Midian. 2: The Lord's command to *avenge the Israelites on the Midianites* stems from the Midianites' role in drawing Israel into the worship of a god other than the Lord in the incident at Peor (25.1–18). Moses will soon die and *be gathered to* and join his *people*, namely, his dead ancestors (Deut 34). **6:** The trumpets for sounding the alarm were first introduced in 10.9. The involvement of the priest and objects from the tabernacle* or mobile worship *sanctuary* indicate that this is a holy war. In a holy war, the Lord fights with Israel; every adult male is to be killed; women and children may be taken as captives; and a percentage of all items of value are to be offered to the Lord and given to the priests (Deut 20.1–18). **8:** The Israelites kill the prophet* Balaam. Balaam had spoken words of blessing on Israel (chs. 22–24). However, Balaam had also urged the Midianite women to entice the Israelites to worship a foreign god and thus abandon the Lord (v. 16). **16:** Although *Balaam* is never mentioned in the story of

Israel's sin at Peor in ch. 25, this verse condemns *Ba-laam's* secret involvement *in the affair of Peor.* **17:** Young Midianite males are killed in order to ensure that they will not become part of that country's army. However, Midianites will reappear as Israel's enemy in Judg 6–8. **18:** Any Midianite women who may have had illicit sexual relations with Israelite men are killed. All Midianite virgins are allowed to live. **19–24:** On the concept of ritual purification and cleanness, see sidebar on p. 182. On the ritual contamination of those who *killed a person or touched a corpse* (v. 19), see the purification ritual with water and the ashes of the red cow in ch. 19. **52:** A *shekel* is a standard unit of weight used to calculate the monetary value of gold and silver. **54:** On *the tent of meeting,* see 1.1.

Reuben and Gad's request
32.1–42: Two of the Israelite tribes, Reuben and Gad, request permission from Moses to settle outside Canaan in the area just east of the Jordan River in the plains of Moab. Israel had captured this land from King Sihon and King Og in 21.21–35. Moses eventually grants the request, and the land is actually distributed to these two tribes along with a portion to the half-tribe of Manasseh (v. 33) in Josh 13.8–32; 22.

32 Now the Reubenites and the Gadites owned a very great number of cattle. When they saw that the land of Jazer and the land of Gilead was a good place for cattle, 2the Gadites and the Reubenites came and spoke to Moses, to Eleazar the priest, and to the leaders of the congregation, saying, 3"Ataroth, Dibon, Jazer, Nimrah, Heshbon, Elealeh, Sebam, Nebo, and Beon— 4the land that the LORD subdued before the congregation of Israel—is a land for cattle; and your servants have cattle." 5They continued, "If we have found favor in your sight, let this land be given to your servants for a possession; do not make us cross the Jordan."

6 But Moses said to the Gadites and to the Reubenites, "Shall your brothers go to war while you sit here? 7Why will you discourage the hearts of the Israelites from going over into the land that the LORD has given them? 8Your fathers did this, when I sent them from Kadesh-barnea to see the land. 9When they went up to the Wadi Eshcol and saw the land, they discouraged the hearts of the Israelites from going into the land that the LORD had given them. 10The LORD's anger was kindled on that day and he swore, saying, 11'Surely none of the people who came up out of Egypt, from twenty years old and upward, shall see the land that I swore to give to Abraham, to Isaac, and to Jacob, because they have not unreservedly followed me— 12none except Caleb son of Jephunneh the Kenizzite and Joshua son of Nun, for they have unreservedly followed the LORD.' 13And the LORD's anger was kindled against Israel, and he made them wander in the wilderness for forty years, until all the generation that had done evil in the sight of the LORD had disappeared. 14And now you, a brood of sinners, have risen in place of your fathers, to increase the LORD's fierce anger against Israel! 15If you turn away from following him, he will again abandon them in the wilderness; and you will destroy all this people."

16 Then they came up to him and said, "We will build sheepfolds here for our flocks, and towns for our little ones, 17but we will take up arms as a vanguard*a* before the Israelites, until we have brought them to their place. Meanwhile our little ones will stay in the fortified towns because of the inhabitants of the land. 18We will not return to our homes until all the Israelites have obtained their inheritance. 19We will not inherit with them on the other side of the Jordan and beyond, because our inheritance has come to us on this side of the Jordan to the east."

20 So Moses said to them, "If you do this—if you take up arms to go before the LORD for the war, 21and all those of you who bear arms cross the Jordan before the LORD, until he has driven out his enemies from before him 22and the land is subdued before the LORD—then after that you may return and be free of obligation to the LORD and to Israel, and this land shall be your possession before the LORD. 23But if you do not do this, you have sinned against the LORD; and be sure your sin will find you out. 24Build towns for your little ones, and folds for your flocks; but do what you have promised."

a Cn: Heb *hurrying*

25 Then the Gadites and the Reubenites said to Moses, "Your servants will do as my lord commands. 26Our little ones, our wives, our flocks, and all our livestock shall remain there in the towns of Gilead; 27but your servants will cross over, everyone armed for war, to do battle for the LORD, just as my lord orders."

28 So Moses gave command concerning them to Eleazar the priest, to Joshua son of Nun, and to the heads of the ancestral houses of the Israelite tribes. 29And Moses said to them, "If the Gadites and the Reubenites, everyone armed for battle before the LORD, will cross over the Jordan with you and the land shall be subdued before you, then you shall give them the land of Gilead for a possession; 30but if they will not cross over with you armed, they shall have possessions among you in the land of Canaan." 31The Gadites and the Reubenites answered, "As the LORD has spoken to your servants, so we will do. 32We will cross over armed before the LORD into the land of Canaan, but the possession of our inheritance shall remain with us on this side of*a* the Jordan."

33 Moses gave to them—to the Gadites and to the Reubenites and to the half-tribe of Manasseh son of Joseph—the kingdom of King Sihon of the Amorites and the kingdom of King Og of Bashan, the land and its towns, with the territories of the surrounding towns. 34And the Gadites rebuilt Dibon, Ataroth, Aroer, 35Atroth-shophan, Jazer, Jogbehah, 36Beth-nimrah, and Beth-haran, fortified cities, and folds for sheep. 37And the Reubenites rebuilt Heshbon, Elealeh, Kiriathaim, 38Nebo, and Baal-meon (some names being changed), and Sibmah; and they gave names to the towns that they rebuilt. 39The descendants of Machir son of Manasseh went to Gilead, captured it, and dispossessed the Amorites who were there; 40so Moses gave Gilead to Machir son of Manasseh, and he settled there. 41Jair son of Manasseh went and captured their villages, and renamed them Havvoth-jair.*b* 42And Nobah went and captured Kenath and its villages, and renamed it Nobah after himself.

32.1–42. 1: *Jazer* is part of the territory captured from King Sihon of the Amorites (21.32). *Gilead* is the lush hill country east of the Jordan River (Gen 31.21). **2:** *Eleazar* has taken over his father Aaron's role as high priest (20.22–29). **8–15:** Moses recalls the disastrous events of the spy story in chs. 13–14. Moses is afraid that the Israelites may again be discouraged from entering the land of Canaan if the two tribes of Reuben and Gad do not join Israel's army in crossing the Jordan River and conquering Canaan. **16–32:** Reuben and Gad offer a compromise in response to Moses' objections. They will be allowed to settle in the territory east of the Jordan River, but they will first join with the other Israelites in fighting the Canaanites and capturing the land west of the Jordan River in Canaan. Moses accepts their compromise solution. **33:** *The half-tribe of Manasseh* unexpectedly appears as it joins Reuben and Gad in settling in the territory east of the Jordan River outside Canaan. The other half of the tribe of Manasseh eventually settled west of the Jordan River in Canaan near Shechem (Josh 13.29–31; 17.1–13). On Israel's conquest of the territory of King Sihon and Og, see 21.21–35. **34–42:** The actual settlement of these territories occurs in Josh 13.8–32.

33 These are the stages by which the Israelites went out of the land of Egypt in military formation under the leadership of Moses and Aaron. 2Moses wrote down their starting points, stage by stage, by command of the LORD; and these are their stages according to their starting places. 3They set out from Rameses in the first month, on the fifteenth day of the first month; on the day after the passover the Israelites went out boldly in the sight of all the Egyptians, 4while the Egyptians were burying all their firstborn, whom the LORD had struck down among them. The LORD executed judgments even against their gods.

5 So the Israelites set out from Rameses, and camped at Succoth. 6They set out from Succoth, and camped at Etham, which is on the edge of the wilderness. 7They set out from Etham, and turned back to Pi-hahiroth, which faces Baal-zephon; and they camped before Migdol. 8They set out from Pi-hahiroth, passed through the sea into the wilder-

a Heb *beyond*   *b* That is *the villages of Jair*

ness, went a three days' journey in the wilderness of Etham, and camped at Marah. ⁹They set out from Marah and came to Elim; at Elim there were twelve springs of water and seventy palm trees, and they camped there. ¹⁰They set out from Elim and camped by the Red Sea.ᵃ ¹¹They set out from the Red Seaᵃ and camped in the wilderness of Sin. ¹²They set out from the wilderness of Sin and camped at Dophkah. ¹³They set out from Dophkah and camped at Alush. ¹⁴They set out from Alush and camped at Rephidim, where there was no water for the people to drink. ¹⁵They set out from Rephidim and camped in the wilderness of Sinai. ¹⁶They set out from the wilderness of Sinai and camped at Kibroth-hattaavah. ¹⁷They set out from Kibroth-hattaavah and camped at Hazeroth. ¹⁸They set out from Hazeroth and camped at Rithmah. ¹⁹They set out from Rithmah and camped at Rimmon-perez. ²⁰They set out from Rimmon-perez and camped at Libnah. ²¹They set out from Libnah and camped at Rissah. ²²They set out from Rissah and camped at Kehelathah. ²³They set out from Kehelathah and camped at Mount Shepher. ²⁴They set out from Mount Shepher and camped at Haradah. ²⁵They set out from Haradah and camped at Makheloth. ²⁶They set out from Makheloth and camped at Tahath. ²⁷They set out from Tahath and camped at Terah. ²⁸They set out from Terah and camped at Mithkah. ²⁹They set out from Mithkah and camped at Hashmonah. ³⁰They set out from Hashmonah and camped at Moseroth. ³¹They set out from Moseroth and camped at Bene-jaakan. ³²They set out from Bene-jaakan and camped at Hor-haggidgad. ³³They set out from Hor-haggidgad and camped at Jotbathah. ³⁴They set out from Jotbathah and camped at Abronah. ³⁵They set out from Abronah and camped at Ezion-geber. ³⁶They set out from Ezion-geber and camped in the wilderness of Zin (that is, Kadesh). ³⁷They set out from Kadesh and camped at Mount Hor, on the edge of the land of Edom.

38 Aaron the priest went up Mount Hor at the command of the LORD and died there in the fortieth year after the Israelites had come out of the land of Egypt, on the first day of the fifth month. ³⁹Aaron was one hundred twenty-three years old when he died on Mount Hor.

40 The Canaanite, the king of Arad, who lived in the Negeb in the land of Canaan, heard of the coming of the Israelites.

41 They set out from Mount Hor and camped at Zalmonah. ⁴²They set out from Zalmonah and camped at Punon. ⁴³They set out from Punon and camped at Oboth. ⁴⁴They set out from Oboth and camped at Iye-abarim, in the territory of Moab. ⁴⁵They set out from Iyim and camped at Dibon-gad. ⁴⁶They set out from Dibon-gad and camped at Almon-diblathaim. ⁴⁷They set out from Almon-diblathaim and camped in the mountains of Abarim, before Nebo. ⁴⁸They set out from the mountains of Abarim and camped in the plains of Moab by the Jordan at Jericho; ⁴⁹they camped by the Jordan from Beth-jeshimoth as far as Abel-shittim in the plains of Moab.

50 In the plains of Moab by the Jordan at Jericho, the LORD spoke to Moses, saying: ⁵¹Speak to the Israelites, and say to them: When you cross over the Jordan into the land of Canaan, ⁵²you shall drive out all the inhabitants of the land from before you, destroy all their figured stones, destroy all their cast images, and demolish all their high places. ⁵³You shall take possession of the land and settle in it, for I have given you the land to possess. ⁵⁴You shall apportion the land by lot according to your clans; to a large one you shall give a large inheritance, and to a small one you shall give a small inheritance; the inheritance shall belong to the person on whom the lot falls; according to your ancestral tribes you shall inherit. ⁵⁵But if you do not drive out the inhabitants of the land from before you, then those whom you let remain shall be as barbs in your eyes and thorns in your sides; they shall trouble you in the land where you are settling. ⁵⁶And I will do to you as I thought to do to them.

33.1–56: The stages of Israel's wilderness journey from Egypt to Canaan. 3–5: On the death of Egypt's

ᵃ Or *Sea of Reeds*

firstborn and Israel's travel from *Rameses* to *Succoth*, see *Ex 12.29–37.* **6–15:** Israel's travel *from Succoth* (v. 6) to *the wilderness of Sinai* (v. 15) is recounted in Ex 13.17–19.1. **16–49:** Israel's journey *from the wilderness of Sinai* (v. 16) to *the plains of Moab* (vv. 49–50) is narrated in 10.11–22.1. The death of *Aaron the priest* (vv. 38–39) is recounted in 20.22–29. **50–56:** The LORD commands Moses to *speak to the Israelites* (v. 51) and warn them about the need to *drive out all the inhabitants of the land* of Canaan and all their gods (v. 52). Otherwise, the LORD says to Israel, *I will do to you as I thought to do to them* [the Canaanites] (v. 56). Moses fulfills this divine command to speak to Israel in the book of Deuteronomy with a series of instructional speeches. In the end, however, Israel will not drive out the Canaanites from the land. As a result, Israel will suffer difficulty and oppression during the period of the judges (Judg 1.1–3.6).

34 The LORD spoke to Moses, saying: [2]Command the Israelites, and say to them: When you enter the land of Canaan (this is the land that shall fall to you for an inheritance, the land of Canaan, defined by its boundaries), [3]your south sector shall extend from the wilderness of Zin along the side of Edom. Your southern boundary shall begin from the end of the Dead Sea[a] on the east; [4]your boundary shall turn south of the ascent of Akrabbim, and cross to Zin, and its outer limit shall be south of Kadesh-barnea; then it shall go on to Hazar-addar, and cross to Azmon; [5]the boundary shall turn from Azmon to the Wadi of Egypt, and its termination shall be at the Sea.

[6] For the western boundary, you shall have the Great Sea and its[b] coast; this shall be your western boundary.

[7] This shall be your northern boundary: from the Great Sea you shall mark out your line to Mount Hor; [8]from Mount Hor you shall mark it out to Lebo-hamath, and the outer limit of the boundary shall be at Zedad; [9]then the boundary shall extend to Ziphron, and its end shall be at Hazar-enan; this shall be your northern boundary.

[10] You shall mark out your eastern boundary from Hazar-enan to Shepham; [11]and the boundary shall continue down from Shepham to Riblah on the east side of Ain; and the boundary shall go down, and

reach the eastern slope of the sea of Chinnereth; [12]and the boundary shall go down to the Jordan, and its end shall be at the Dead Sea.[a] This shall be your land with its boundaries all around.

[13] Moses commanded the Israelites, saying: This is the land that you shall inherit by lot, which the LORD has commanded to give to the nine tribes and to the half-tribe; [14]for the tribe of the Reubenites by their ancestral houses and the tribe of the Gadites by their ancestral houses have taken their inheritance, and also the half-tribe of Manasseh; [15]the two tribes and the half-tribe have taken their inheritance beyond the Jordan at Jericho eastward, toward the sunrise.

[16] The LORD spoke to Moses, saying: [17]These are the names of the men who shall apportion the land to you for inheritance: the priest Eleazar and Joshua son of Nun. [18]You shall take one leader of every tribe to apportion the land for inheritance. [19]These are the names of the men: Of the tribe of Judah, Caleb son of Jephunneh. [20]Of the tribe of the Simeonites, Shemuel son of Ammihud. [21]Of the tribe of Benjamin, Elidad son of Chislon. [22]Of the tribe of the Danites a leader, Bukki son of Jogli. [23]Of the Josephites: of the tribe of the Manassites a leader, Hanniel son of Ephod, [24]and of the tribe of the Ephraimites a leader, Kemuel son of Shiphtan. [25]Of the tribe of the Zebulunites a leader, Eli-zaphan son of Parnach. [26]Of the tribe of the Issacharites a leader, Paltiel son of Azzan. [27]And of the tribe of the Asherites a leader, Ahihud son of Shelomi. [28]Of the tribe of the Naphtalites a leader, Pedahel son of Ammihud. [29]These were the ones whom the LORD commanded to apportion the inheritance for the Israelites in the land of Canaan.

34.1–29: The boundaries of Canaan and tribal supervisors for dividing the land. 1–12: This delineation of the boundaries of the promised land follows closely the description of the area covered by the spies in chs. 13–14. The southern boundary is the wilderness of Zin (13.21; see v. 3), and the northern boundary

a Heb *Salt Sea*   *b* Syr: Heb lacks *its*

reaches to Lebo-hamath (13.21; see v. 8). The Jordan River forms the eastern boundary of Canaan, and "the Sea" or "Great Sea" (the Mediterranean) forms the western border (13.29; see vv. 6, 12). These are ideal boundaries since Israel's historical boundaries never actually extended as far west as the Mediterranean Sea in the biblical period. Israel reached its greatest territorial size under King David and King Solomon (2 Sam 8.1–14; 1 Kings 8.65). Israel's settlement of the land is recounted in Josh 13–19. **13–15:** The story of *the Reubenites, the Gadites,* and *the half-tribe of Manasseh* settling east of the Jordan River outside Canaan is narrated in ch. 32. **17:** *Eleazar* has already taken over the role of high priest from his father Aaron (20.22–29). *Joshua* will replace Moses as leader of the people when the Israelites cross the Jordan River into Canaan (27.12–23). Moses' sin at Meribah prevented him from entering Canaan (20.2–13). **18–29:** These names of tribal leaders appear here for the first time with the exception of *Caleb,* the leader of *the tribe of Judah* (v. 19; see 13.6, 30; 14.30).

35 In the plains of Moab by the Jordan at Jericho, the LORD spoke to Moses, saying: 2Command the Israelites to give, from the inheritance that they possess, towns for the Levites to live in; you shall also give to the Levites pasture lands surrounding the towns. 3The towns shall be theirs to live in, and their pasture lands shall be for their cattle, for their livestock, and for all their animals. 4The pasture lands of the towns, which you shall give to the Levites, shall reach from the wall of the town outward a thousand cubits all around. 5You shall measure, outside the town, for the east side two thousand cubits, for the south side two thousand cubits, for the west side two thousand cubits, and for the north side two thousand cubits, with the town in the middle; this shall belong to them as pasture land for their towns.

6 The towns that you give to the Levites shall include the six cities of refuge, where you shall permit a slayer to flee, and in addition to them you shall give forty-two towns. 7The towns that you give to the Levites shall total forty-eight, with their pasture lands. 8And as for the towns that you shall give from the possession of the Israelites, from the larger tribes you shall take many, and from the smaller tribes you shall take few; each, in proportion to the inheritance that it obtains, shall give of its towns to the Levites.

9 The LORD spoke to Moses, saying: 10Speak to the Israelites, and say to them: When you cross the Jordan into the land of Canaan, 11then you shall select cities to be cities of refuge for you, so that a slayer who kills a person without intent may flee there. 12The cities shall be for you a refuge from the avenger, so that the slayer may not die until there is a trial before the congregation.

13 The cities that you designate shall be six cities of refuge for you: 14you shall designate three cities beyond the Jordan, and three cities in the land of Canaan, to be cities of refuge. 15These six cities shall serve as refuge for the Israelites, for the resident or transient alien among them, so that anyone who kills a person without intent may flee there.

16 But anyone who strikes another with an iron object, and death ensues, is a murderer; the murderer shall be put to death. 17Or anyone who strikes another with a stone in hand that could cause death, and death ensues, is a murderer; the murderer shall be put to death. 18Or anyone who strikes another with a weapon of wood in hand that could cause death, and death ensues, is a murderer; the murderer shall be put to death. 19The avenger of blood is the one who shall put the murderer to death; when they meet, the avenger of blood shall execute the sentence. 20Likewise, if someone pushes another from hatred, or hurls something at another, lying in wait, and death ensues, 21or in enmity strikes another with the hand, and death ensues, then the one who struck the blow shall be put to death; that person is a murderer; the avenger of blood shall put the murderer to death, when they meet.

22 But if someone pushes another suddenly without enmity, or hurls any object without lying in wait, 23or, while handling any stone that could cause death, unintentionally*a* drops it on another and death en-

a Heb *without seeing*

sues, though they were not enemies, and no harm was intended, ²⁴then the congregation shall judge between the slayer and the avenger of blood, in accordance with these ordinances; ²⁵and the congregation shall rescue the slayer from the avenger of blood. Then the congregation shall send the slayer back to the original city of refuge. The slayer shall live in it until the death of the high priest who was anointed with the holy oil. ²⁶But if the slayer shall at any time go outside the bounds of the original city of refuge, ²⁷and is found by the avenger of blood outside the bounds of the city of refuge, and is killed by the avenger, no bloodguilt shall be incurred. ²⁸For the slayer must remain in the city of refuge until the death of the high priest; but after the death of the high priest the slayer may return home.

29　These things shall be a statute and ordinance for you throughout your generations wherever you live.

30　If anyone kills another, the murderer shall be put to death on the evidence of witnesses; but no one shall be put to death on the testimony of a single witness. ³¹Moreover you shall accept no ransom for the life of a murderer who is subject to the death penalty; a murderer must be put to death. ³²Nor shall you accept ransom for one who has fled to a city of refuge, enabling the fugitive to return to live in the land before the death of the high priest. ³³You shall not pollute the land in which you live; for blood pollutes the land, and no expiation can be made for the land, for the blood that is shed in it, except by the blood of the one who shed it. ³⁴You shall not defile the land in which you live, in which I also dwell; for I the LORD dwell among the Israelites.

35.1–34: Cities for the Levites, cities of refuge, and borderline cases involving murder and blood revenge. 1–8: *The plains of Moab* lie just east of the *Jordan* River. *Jericho* is the town that lies just west of the Jordan River inside the land of Canaan (v. 1). The priestly tribe of *Levites* is unique among the tribes of Israel. They will receive *towns to live in* rather than an allotment of tribal land when Israel conquers Canaan (v. 2; see 18.20–24; Josh 21). A *cubit* is a unit of length, approximately one and a half feet. Thus, a *thousand*

cubits is about 1,500 feet. On *the cities of refuge*, see 35.9–15. **9–15:** The *cities of refuge* (v. 11) provide a safe place for those who have accidentally or unintentionally killed someone. The *avenger* (v. 12), a member of the dead victim's family, would exact revenge for the person's death by killing the murderer. *Beyond the Jordan* (v. 14) is the area east of the Jordan River just outside Canaan where Reuben, Gad, and the half-tribe of Manasseh settled (Num 32). **16–34:** The laws distinguish between intentional or negligent murder versus accidental killing. In intentional murders but not accidental killings, the community allows the *avenger of blood* (vv. 19, 21) to kill the murderer in revenge for the death of a family member (see comment on vv. 9–15). The spilling of human blood *pollutes the land* (v. 33), even if it is an unintentional killing. The killer is made clean from the impurity or pollution through the atoning *death of the high priest* in the city of refuge (vv. 25–28). A *ransom* (vv. 31–32) is a payment of money or other items of value that repay and wipe out the impurity caused by an unclean act or condition. In this case, the loss of a human's life cannot be repaid or atoned through money or property but only through the death of the murderer or (in the case of accidental killings) through *the death of the high priest* (v. 32).

~~~~~~

36 The heads of the ancestral houses of the clans of the descendants of Gilead son of Machir son of Manasseh, of the Josephite clans, came forward and spoke in the presence of Moses and the leaders, the heads of the ancestral houses of the Israelites; ²they said, "The LORD commanded my lord to give the land for inheritance by lot to the Israelites; and my lord was commanded by the LORD to give the inheritance of our brother Zelophehad to his daughters. ³But if they are married into another Israelite tribe, then their inheritance will be taken from the inheritance of our ancestors and added to the inheritance of the tribe into which they marry; so it will be taken away from the allotted portion of our inheritance. ⁴And when the jubilee of the Israelites comes, then their inheritance will be added to the inheritance of the tribe into which they have married; and their inheritance will be taken from the inheritance of our ancestral tribe."

5　Then Moses commanded the Israelites according to the word of the LORD, saying,

"The descendants of the tribe of Joseph are right in what they are saying. 6This is what the LORD commands concerning the daughters of Zelophehad, 'Let them marry whom they think best; only it must be into a clan of their father's tribe that they are married, 7so that no inheritance of the Israelites shall be transferred from one tribe to another; for all Israelites shall retain the inheritance of their ancestral tribes. 8Every daughter who possesses an inheritance in any tribe of the Israelites shall marry one from the clan of her father's tribe, so that all Israelites may continue to possess their ancestral inheritance. 9No inheritance shall be transferred from one tribe to another; for each of the tribes of the Israelites shall retain its own inheritance.'"

10 The daughters of Zelophehad did as the LORD had commanded Moses. 11Mahlah, Tirzah, Hoglah, Milcah, and Noah, the daughters of Zelophehad, married sons of their father's brothers. 12They were married into the clans of the descendants of Manasseh son of Joseph, and their inheritance remained in the tribe of their father's clan.

13 These are the commandments and the ordinances that the LORD commanded through Moses to the Israelites in the plains of Moab by the Jordan at Jericho.

36.1–13: The daughters of Zelophehad revisited: maintaining the fair distribution of tribal lands. This legal judgment provides a supplement to the earlier case involving the daughters of Zelophehad in 27.1–11. The daughters are required to marry within their own tribe so that the land they have inherited will not pass into the hands of another tribe and thus upset the balanced distribution of Canaan's land among the Israelite tribes. **2:** On the prior decision about the daughters' being allowed to inherit the land of their father Zelophehad, see 27.4–8. **3–4:** This complaint about the possibility of the daughters' land being transferred from one tribe to another tribe assumes that any land the new bride owns passes into the possession of her husband at marriage. *The jubilee* occurs every fifty years. It involves the free return of all tribal lands that have been bought or sold during the previous fifty-year period back to the original tribal owners of the land (Lev 25.8–55). However, in this case the potential transfer of the land did not occur through buying or selling but through marriage. Therefore, the land would not be returned to the first tribe who originally owned it, since the jubilee involves only land that has been bought and sold. This practice would adversely affect the original balance and distribution of land among the tribes. Thus, any Israelite daughters who receive an inheritance of land can marry only within their own tribe. **13:** On *the plains of Moab, the Jordan* River, and *Jericho*, see comments on 35.1–8.

DEUTERONOMY

Introduction

Deuteronomy presents itself as an address by Moses to Israel just before the invasion of the promised land. Moses proclaims the law by which Israel is to shape its life in the land as God's faithful people. This law (Deut 12–26) calls on Israel to reform itself. It urges exclusive loyalty to the LORD by demanding that all sacrificial worship be centralized in a single location. It also seeks to make Israel a just and humane society by advocating concern for the poor and disadvantaged. Moses prefaces this law by reviewing the history of the last generation (chs. 1–4) and motivating Israel to careful obedience (chs. 5–11). After teaching the law, Moses refers to the future implications of the covenant* that God has established (chs. 27–30) and recites two poems (chs. 32–33). Narratives* about the transition of leadership and the death of Moses (chs. 31, 34) lead into the upcoming narratives about Israel's conquest (Joshua) and life in the land (Judges, 1–2 Samuel, 1–2 Kings).

The law of reform in Deuteronomy was originally produced in a time of religious, political, and social crisis. Religious loyalty was being undermined by the worship of other gods and an unfaithful monarchy. Some classes of society had fallen into poverty. There are indications that Deuteronomy was originally directed to the northern kingdom of Israel rather than to Judah. Deuteronomy was later expanded to serve as the introduction to the Deuteronomistic* History (see the introduction to Joshua). The distinctive theology, style, and language of Deuteronomy strongly influenced that later work.

READING GUIDE

Deuteronomy contains both narrative and law. Readers may follow the story of Israel under the leadership of Moses by concentrating on Deut 1–3, 9–10, 31, and 34. Those interested in Deuteronomy's distinctive guidelines for Israel's religious and social life will want to begin with chs. 12–18 and 20. Deuteronomy offers updates or revisions of older laws found in Ex 21–23. Readers can discover Deuteronomy's special outlook by comparing these chapters in Exodus and the laws in Deuteronomy.

1–4	Moses reviews Israel's history
5–11	Moses preaches about the law
12–26	Moses proclaims the law
27–30	Moses makes a covenant in Moab
31–34	Moses concludes with warnings and blessings

1 These are the words that Moses spoke to all Israel beyond the Jordan—in the wilderness, on the plain opposite Suph, between Paran and Tophel, Laban, Hazeroth, and Di-zahab. ²(By the way of Mount Seir it takes eleven days to reach Kadesh-barnea from Horeb.) ³In the fortieth year, on the first day of the eleventh month, Moses spoke to the Israelites just as the LORD had commanded him to speak to them. ⁴This was after he had defeated King Sihon of the Amorites, who reigned in Heshbon, and King Og of Bashan, who reigned in Ashtaroth and*a* in Edrei. ⁵Beyond the Jordan in the

a Gk Syr Vg Compare Josh 12.4: Heb lacks *and*

land of Moab, Moses undertook to expound this law as follows:

6 The LORD our God spoke to us at Horeb, saying, "You have stayed long enough at this mountain. 7 Resume your journey, and go into the hill country of the Amorites as well as into the neighboring regions—the Arabah, the hill country, the Shephelah, the Negeb, and the seacoast—the land of the Canaanites and the Lebanon, as far as the great river, the river Euphrates. 8 See, I have set the land before you; go in and take possession of the land that I[a] swore to your ancestors, to Abraham, to Isaac, and to Jacob, to give to them and to their descendants after them."

1.1–8: Setting the scene. 1–3: Moses addresses Israel just before they invade the promised land. He speaks to a new generation born in the wilderness. **5:** Israel will soon cross the *Jordan* westward into Canaan from *Moab.* **6:** *Horeb* is Deuteronomy's name for Mount Sinai. **7:** The promised land is envisioned as extending north to *the river Euphrates,* although Israel actually occupied a much smaller area.

9 At that time I said to you, "I am unable by myself to bear you. 10 The LORD your God has multiplied you, so that today you are as numerous as the stars of heaven. 11 May the LORD, the God of your ancestors, increase you a thousand times more and bless you, as he has promised you! 12 But how can I bear the heavy burden of your disputes all by myself? 13 Choose for each of your tribes individuals who are wise, discerning, and reputable to be your leaders." 14 You answered me, "The plan you have proposed is a good one." 15 So I took the leaders of your tribes, wise and reputable individuals, and installed them as leaders over you, commanders of thousands, commanders of hundreds, commanders of fifties, commanders of tens, and officials, throughout your tribes. 16 I charged your judges at that time: "Give the members of your community a fair hearing, and judge rightly between one person and another, whether citizen or resident alien. 17 You must not be partial in judging: hear out the small and the great alike; you shall not be intimidated by anyone, for the judgment is God's.

Any case that is too hard for you, bring to me, and I will hear it." 18 So I charged you at that time with all the things that you should do.

1.9–18: Judicial leaders. 10–11: Moses' overwork has been caused by Israel's population growth, a fulfillment of the LORD's promise to Abraham (Gen 15.5). **15–16:** This justice system is comprehensive, reaching down to the level of *commanders of tens.* It is to be fair, even when a disdained *resident alien** is involved. **17:** Fair decisions are ensured by impartiality and appeals to Moses' special expertise.

19 Then, just as the LORD our God had ordered us, we set out from Horeb and went through all that great and terrible wilderness that you saw, on the way to the hill country of the Amorites, until we reached Kadesh-barnea. 20 I said to you, "You have reached the hill country of the Amorites, which the LORD our God is giving us. 21 See, the LORD your God has given the land to you; go up, take possession, as the LORD, the God of your ancestors, has promised you; do not fear or be dismayed."

22 All of you came to me and said, "Let us send men ahead of us to explore the land for us and bring back a report to us regarding the route by which we should go up and the cities we will come to." 23 The plan seemed good to me, and I selected twelve of you, one from each tribe. 24 They set out and went up into the hill country, and when they reached the Valley of Eshcol they spied it out 25 and gathered some of the land's produce, which they brought down to us. They brought back a report to us, and said, "It is a good land that the LORD our God is giving us."

26 But you were unwilling to go up. You rebelled against the command of the LORD your God; 27 you grumbled in your tents and said, "It is because the LORD hates us that he has brought us out of the land of Egypt, to hand us over to the Amorites to destroy us. 28 Where are we headed? Our kindred have made our hearts melt by reporting, 'The people are stronger and taller than we; the cities are large and fortified up to heaven!

a Sam Gk: MT *the* LORD

Related Nations

Israel thought of *Edom, Moab, and Ammon* as kindred peoples and expressed this in terms of lineage. The ancestor of Edom was Esau the brother to Jacob. Moab and Ammon were understood to be sons of Abraham's nephew Lot. Like Israel, these nations had dispossessed the previous inhabitants of their territory (2.20–23).

We actually saw there the offspring of the Anakim!' " ²⁹I said to you, "Have no dread or fear of them. ³⁰The LORD your God, who goes before you, is the one who will fight for you, just as he did for you in Egypt before your very eyes, ³¹and in the wilderness, where you saw how the LORD your God carried you, just as one carries a child, all the way that you traveled until you reached this place. ³²But in spite of this, you have no trust in the LORD your God, ³³who goes before you on the way to seek out a place for you to camp, in fire by night, and in the cloud by day, to show you the route you should take."

34 When the LORD heard your words, he was wrathful and swore: ³⁵"Not one of these—not one of this evil generation—shall see the good land that I swore to give to your ancestors, ³⁶except Caleb son of Jephunneh. He shall see it, and to him and to his descendants I will give the land on which he set foot, because of his complete fidelity to the LORD." ³⁷Even with me the LORD was angry on your account, saying, "You also shall not enter there. ³⁸Joshua son of Nun, your assistant, shall enter there; encourage him, for he is the one who will secure Israel's possession of it. ³⁹And as for your little ones, who you thought would become booty, your children, who today do not yet know right from wrong, they shall enter there; to them I will give it, and they shall take possession of it. ⁴⁰But as for you, journey back into the wilderness, in the direction of the Red Sea."ᵃ

41 You answered me, "We have sinned against the LORD! We are ready to go up and fight, just as the LORD our God commanded us." So all of you strapped on your battle gear, and thought it easy to go up into the hill country. ⁴²The LORD said to me, "Say to them, 'Do not go up and do not fight, for I am not in the midst of you; otherwise you will be defeated by your enemies.' " ⁴³Although I told you, you would not listen. You rebelled against the command of the LORD and presumptuously went up into the hill country. ⁴⁴The Amorites who lived in that hill country then came out against you and chased you as bees do. They beat you down in Seir as far as Hormah. ⁴⁵When you returned and wept before the LORD, the LORD would neither heed your voice nor pay you any attention.

1.19–45: A failed attempt at conquest. 19: *Amorites* is a general term for the inhabitants of the land, but especially for those in the hills. *Kadesh-barnea* is a southern oasis in the Negeb. **22:** Sending out advance scouts was standard practice (Josh 2; Judg 18.1–10). **24–25:** *Eshcol* means "cluster of grapes," underscoring the land's fruitfulness. At first, only the positive aspects of the scouts' report are mentioned (contrast v. 28), which adds to the surprise when Israel proves unwilling to attack. **28:** The fabled* *Anakim* were reputed to be of gigantic size. **29–33:** Moses gives three reasons why they should *have no dread or fear* (v. 29): The LORD has already fought for them (v. 30), carried them like a child (v. 31), and guided them on their journey (v. 33). **34–38:** All the adults of that generation were to die outside the land except for *Caleb* (v. 36) and *Joshua* (v. 38). According to Num 13–14, these two were the only spies who urged Israel to attack. The exclusion of Moses from the land is seen here as the people's fault (contrast 32.51). **39:** These *little ones* are the new generation to whom Moses is now speaking the words of Deuteronomy. **41–45:** When-

a Or *Sea of Reeds*

ever it fought as the LORD's army, Israel prevailed, but in this case it defiantly fought on its own.

~~~~~~

2 46 After you had stayed at Kadesh as many days as you did, ¹we journeyed back into the wilderness, in the direction of the Red Sea,ᵃ as the LORD had told me and skirted Mount Seir for many days. ²Then the LORD said to me: ³"You have been skirting this hill country long enough. Head north, ⁴and charge the people as follows: You are about to pass through the territory of your kindred, the descendants of Esau, who live in Seir. They will be afraid of you, so, be very careful ⁵not to engage in battle with them, for I will not give you even so much as a foot's length of their land, since I have given Mount Seir to Esau as a possession. ⁶You shall purchase food from them for money, so that you may eat; and you shall also buy water from them for money, so that you may drink. ⁷Surely the LORD your God has blessed you in all your undertakings; he knows your going through this great wilderness. These forty years the LORD your God has been with you; you have lacked nothing." ⁸So we passed by our kin, the descendants of Esau who live in Seir, leaving behind the route of the Arabah, and leaving behind Elath and Ezion-geber.

When we had headed out along the route of the wilderness of Moab, ⁹the LORD said to me: "Do not harass Moab or engage them in battle, for I will not give you any of its land as a possession, since I have given Ar as a possession to the descendants of Lot." ¹⁰(The Emim—a large and numerous people, as tall as the Anakim—had formerly inhabited it. ¹¹Like the Anakim, they are usually reckoned as Rephaim, though the Moabites call them Emim. ¹²Moreover, the Horim had formerly inhabited Seir, but the descendants of Esau dispossessed them, destroying them and settling in their place, as Israel has done in the land that the LORD gave them as a possession.) ¹³"Now then, proceed to cross over the Wadi Zered."

So we crossed over the Wadi Zered. ¹⁴And the length of time we had traveled from Kadesh-barnea until we crossed the Wadi

Zered was thirty-eight years, until the entire generation of warriors had perished from the camp, as the LORD had sworn concerning them. ¹⁵Indeed, the LORD's own hand was against them, to root them out from the camp, until all had perished.

16 Just as soon as all the warriors had died off from among the people, ¹⁷the LORD spoke to me, saying, ¹⁸"Today you are going to cross the boundary of Moab at Ar. ¹⁹When you approach the frontier of the Ammonites, do not harass them or engage them in battle, for I will not give the land of the Ammonites to you as a possession, because I have given it to the descendants of Lot." ²⁰(It also is usually reckoned as a land of Rephaim. Rephaim formerly inhabited it, though the Ammonites call them Zamzummim, ²¹a strong and numerous people, as tall as the Anakim. But the LORD destroyed them from before the Ammonites so that they could dispossess them and settle in their place. ²²He did the same for the descendants of Esau, who live in Seir, by destroying the Horim before them so that they could dispossess them and settle in their place even to this day. ²³As for the Avvim, who had lived in settlements in the vicinity of Gaza, the Caphtorim, who came from Caphtor, destroyed them and settled in their place.) ²⁴"Proceed on your journey and cross the Wadi Arnon. See, I have handed over to you King Sihon the Amorite of Heshbon, and his land. Begin to take possession by engaging him in battle. ²⁵This day I will begin to put the dread and fear of you upon the peoples everywhere under heaven; when they hear report of you, they will tremble and be in anguish because of you."

1.46–2.25: Through Edom and Moab. 1.46: Numbers 20.14–21 and 21.10–20 report another version of this story. *Many days* covers thirty-eight years and the death of the first generation (2.14). **2.1:** *Mount Seir* refers to Edom's territory. **8:** *Elath and Ezion-geber* were located on the shore of the Red Sea, south of Edom. **9:** Here *Ar* indicates the territory of Moab in general, while in v. 18 it refers to a specific city. **10–12:** Details about fabled* and extinct peoples (compare

ᵃ *Or Sea of Reeds*

vv. 20–23) were of interest to ancient readers. **13:** The *Wadi* Zered* marked the boundary between Edom and Moab. **14–16:** The death of the last of the previous generation means that conquest can begin. **18:** To move north out of Moab means that war with King Sihon is inevitable. **19:** Ammonite territory lay just to the east of Israel's line of advance. **24–25:** *Wadi Arnon* was the border between Moab and the territory of King Sihon. The language of divine warrior* theology indicates certain victory: *I have handed over.* The LORD as divine warrior uses the weapons of *dread and fear.*

26 So I sent messengers from the wilderness of Kedemoth to King Sihon of Heshbon with the following terms of peace: ²⁷ "If you let me pass through your land, I will travel only along the road; I will turn aside neither to the right nor to the left. ²⁸You shall sell me food for money, so that I may eat, and supply me water for money, so that I may drink. Only allow me to pass through on foot— ²⁹just as the descendants of Esau who live in Seir have done for me and likewise the Moabites who live in Ar—until I cross the Jordan into the land that the LORD our God is giving us." ³⁰But King Sihon of Heshbon was not willing to let us pass through, for the LORD your God had hardened his spirit and made his heart defiant in order to hand him over to you, as he has now done.

31 The LORD said to me, "See, I have begun to give Sihon and his land over to you. Begin now to take possession of his land." ³²So when Sihon came out against us, he and all his people for battle at Jahaz, ³³the LORD our God gave him over to us; and we struck him down, along with his offspring and all his people. ³⁴At that time we captured all his towns, and in each town we utterly destroyed men, women, and children. We left not a single survivor. ³⁵Only the livestock we kept as spoil for ourselves, as well as the plunder of the towns that we had captured. ³⁶From Aroer on the edge of the Wadi Arnon (including the town that is in the wadi itself) as far as Gilead, there was no citadel too high for us. The LORD our God gave everything to us. ³⁷You did not encroach, however, on the land of the Ammonites, avoiding

the whole upper region of the Wadi Jabbok as well as the towns of the hill country, just as^a the LORD our God had charged.

2.26–37: Defeating King Sihon. 27–29: Moses asks for safe passage as a way of luring Sihon into battle. Sihon's rejection of this apparently reasonable request justifies Israel's attack. **30:** *Hardened his spirit* indicates that the LORD was behind Sihon's resistance. God's ultimate control of the events that follow is shown by the expression *hand over* (v. 30) and the repetition of "give" (vv. 31, 33, 36). **34–35:** *Utterly destroyed* indicates that the entire population of each captured town fell under the ban* (see 20.16–18; Josh 6.21). The *livestock* and other *plunder* were not destroyed, but kept for Israel's use. **36:** The line *from Aroer* northward *as far as Gilead* encompasses all of Sihon's territory.

3 When we headed up the road to Bashan, King Og of Bashan came out against us, he and all his people, for battle at Edrei. ²The LORD said to me, "Do not fear him, for I have handed him over to you, along with his people and his land. Do to him as you did to King Sihon of the Amorites, who reigned in Heshbon." ³So the LORD our God also handed over to us King Og of Bashan and all his people. We struck him down until not a single survivor was left. ⁴At that time we captured all his towns; there was no citadel that we did not take from them—sixty towns, the whole region of Argob, the kingdom of Og in Bashan. ⁵All these were fortress towns with high walls, double gates, and bars, besides a great many villages. ⁶And we utterly destroyed them, as we had done to King Sihon of Heshbon, in each city utterly destroying men, women, and children. ⁷But all the livestock and the plunder of the towns we kept as spoil for ourselves.

3.1–7: Defeating King Og. 1: *Bashan* designates the territory north of Gilead. **4–5:** This emphasizes the extent and marvel of Israel's victory. **6–7:** The practice of *utterly destroying* (banning*) the population testifies that it is the LORD as divine warrior* who is responsible for Israel's triumph (compare 2.34–35).

a Gk Tg: Heb *and all*

8 So at that time we took from the two kings of the Amorites the land beyond the Jordan, from the Wadi Arnon to Mount Hermon 9(the Sidonians call Hermon Sirion, while the Amorites call it Senir), 10all the towns of the tableland, the whole of Gilead, and all of Bashan, as far as Salecah and Edrei, towns of Og's kingdom in Bashan. 11(Now only King Og of Bashan was left of the remnant of the Rephaim. In fact his bed, an iron bed, can still be seen in Rabbah of the Ammonites. By the common cubit it is nine cubits long and four cubits wide.) 12As for the land that we took possession of at that time, I gave to the Reubenites and Gadites the territory north of Aroer,*a* that is on the edge of the Wadi Arnon, as well as half the hill country of Gilead with its towns, 13and I gave to the half-tribe of Manasseh the rest of Gilead and all of Bashan, Og's kingdom. (The whole region of Argob: all that portion of Bashan used to be called a land of Rephaim; 14Jair the Manassite acquired the whole region of Argob as far as the border of the Geshurites and the Maacathites, and he named them—that is, Bashan—after himself, Havvoth-jair,*b* as it is to this day.) 15To Machir I gave Gilead. 16And to the Reubenites and the Gadites I gave the territory from Gilead as far as the Wadi Arnon, with the middle of the wadi as a boundary, and up to the Jabbok, the wadi being boundary of the Ammonites; 17the Arabah also, with the Jordan and its banks, from Chinnereth down to the sea of the Arabah, the Dead Sea,*c* with the lower slopes of Pisgah on the east.

18 At that time, I charged you as follows: "Although the LORD your God has given you this land to occupy, all your troops shall cross over armed as the vanguard of your Israelite kin. 19Only your wives, your children, and your livestock—I know that you have much livestock—shall stay behind in the towns that I have given to you. 20When the LORD gives rest to your kindred, as to you, and they too have occupied the land that the LORD your God is giving them beyond the Jordan, then each of you may return to the property that I have given to you." 21And I charged Joshua as well at that time, saying: "Your own eyes have seen everything that the

LORD your God has done to these two kings; so the LORD will do to all the kingdoms into which you are about to cross. 22Do not fear them, for it is the LORD your God who fights for you."

3.8–22: Moses assigns land east of the Jordan. **8–11:** *At that time* (vv. 8, 12, 18, 21, 23) marks off a series of topics. Geographic description emphasizes the size of the territory captured. Og's fabled* size as one of the *Rephaim* (mythic giants; v. 11) increases the wonder of the victory. His *bed* was probably a rock formation linked to him by local tradition. **12–17:** Reuben and Gad receive the southern part of the territory and Manasseh the northern part. Because Manasseh settled on both sides of the Jordan, it is called *the half-tribe of Manasseh* (v. 13). The territories of two important clans* of Manasseh are described as land grants to their founding ancestors: *Jair* (v. 14) and *Machir* (v. 15). **18–20:** Moses' speech reflects Deuteronomy's characteristic emphasis on community solidarity. *Rest* (v. 20) means the complete achievement of God's plans and a peaceful life enjoyed in the land. **21–22:** Moses urges Joshua to have confidence in the upcoming conquest, based on the past victories of the divine warrior* *who fights for you.*

---

23 At that time, too, I entreated the LORD, saying: 24"O Lord GOD, you have only begun to show your servant your greatness and your might; what god in heaven or on earth can perform deeds and mighty acts like yours! 25Let me cross over to see the good land beyond the Jordan, that good hill country and the Lebanon." 26But the LORD was angry with me on your account and would not heed me. The LORD said to me, "Enough from you! Never speak to me of this matter again! 27Go up to the top of Pisgah and look around you to the west, to the north, to the south, and to the east. Look well, for you shall not cross over this Jordan. 28But charge Joshua, and encourage and strengthen him, because it is he who shall cross over at the head of this people and who shall secure their possession of the land that you will see." 29So we remained in the valley opposite Beth-peor.

a Heb *territory from Aroer*   *b* That is *Settlement of Jair*
c Heb *Salt Sea*

3.23–29: Moses is forbidden to enter Canaan. 26: The LORD's anger at Moses refers to what is said in 1.37, but the reason for this anger is never entirely explained. **27:** Moses will climb Mount *Pisgah* just before his death (ch. 34). **29:** Moses' review of history stops at this point. The narrative* action will not resume until ch. 31. *Beth-peor* is a more precise designation for the place where Moses is delivering his speech (1.5; 4.46).

4 So now, Israel, give heed to the statutes and ordinances that I am teaching you to observe, so that you may live to enter and occupy the land that the LORD, the God of your ancestors, is giving you. 2You must neither add anything to what I command you nor take away anything from it, but keep the commandments of the LORD your God with which I am charging you. 3You have seen for yourselves what the LORD did with regard to the Baal of Peor—how the LORD your God destroyed from among you everyone who followed the Baal of Peor, 4while those of you who held fast to the LORD your God are all alive today.

5 See, just as the LORD my God has charged me, I now teach you statutes and ordinances for you to observe in the land that you are about to enter and occupy. 6You must observe them diligently, for this will show your wisdom and discernment to the peoples, who, when they hear all these statutes, will say, "Surely this great nation is a wise and discerning people!" 7For what other great nation has a god so near to it as the LORD our God is whenever we call to him? 8And what other great nation has statutes and ordinances as just as this entire law that I am setting before you today?

9 But take care and watch yourselves closely, so as neither to forget the things that your eyes have seen nor to let them slip from your mind all the days of your life; make them known to your children and your children's children— 10how you once stood before the LORD your God at Horeb, when the LORD said to me, "Assemble the people for me, and I will let them hear my words, so that they may learn to fear me as long as they live on the earth, and may teach their chil-

dren so"; 11you approached and stood at the foot of the mountain while the mountain was blazing up to the very heavens, shrouded in dark clouds. 12Then the LORD spoke to you out of the fire. You heard the sound of words but saw no form; there was only a voice. 13He declared to you his covenant, which he charged you to observe, that is, the ten commandments;*a* and he wrote them on two stone tablets. 14And the LORD charged me at that time to teach you statutes and ordinances for you to observe in the land that you are about to cross into and occupy.

15 Since you saw no form when the LORD spoke to you at Horeb out of the fire, take care and watch yourselves closely, 16so that you do not act corruptly by making an idol for yourselves, in the form of any figure— the likeness of male or female, 17the likeness of any animal that is on the earth, the likeness of any winged bird that flies in the air, 18the likeness of anything that creeps on the ground, the likeness of any fish that is in the water under the earth. 19And when you look up to the heavens and see the sun, the moon, and the stars, all the host of heaven, do not be led astray and bow down to them and serve them, things that the LORD your God has allotted to all the peoples everywhere under heaven. 20But the LORD has taken you and brought you out of the iron-smelter, out of Egypt, to become a people of his very own possession, as you are now.

21 The LORD was angry with me because of you, and he vowed that I should not cross the Jordan and that I should not enter the good land that the LORD your God is giving for your possession. 22For I am going to die in this land without crossing over the Jordan, but you are going to cross over to take possession of that good land. 23So be careful not to forget the covenant that the LORD your God made with you, and not to make for yourselves an idol in the form of anything that the LORD your God has forbidden you. 24For the LORD your God is a devouring fire, a jealous God.

a Heb *the ten words*

4.1–24: A summons to obedience. 1–2: Moses shifts from reviewing history to encouraging obedience to the law he is about to proclaim (vv. 5, 14). **3–4:** The *Baal* of Peor* incident is recounted in Num 25.1–13. It reflects a basic tenet of Deuteronomy: If you disobey you will be destroyed (v. 24); if you obey you will live (v. 1). **6–8:** An appeal to ethnic pride motivates obedience, along with a reminder of the saving acts of the LORD (v. 7; also v. 20). **9:** Teaching the next generation is a central concern of Deuteronomy (6.20–25). **15–19:** According to Deuteronomy, idolatry* and the worship of other gods were the most serious sins Israel could commit. **20:** The image of an *iron-smelter* emphasizes the brutality of slavery in Egypt. **23–24:** *A jealous God* means a God who is zealously committed to *the covenant** made with Israel.

25 When you have had children and children's children, and become complacent in the land, if you act corruptly by making an idol in the form of anything, thus doing what is evil in the sight of the LORD your God, and provoking him to anger, 26 I call heaven and earth to witness against you today that you will soon utterly perish from the land that you are crossing the Jordan to occupy; you will not live long on it, but will be utterly destroyed. 27 The LORD will scatter you among the peoples; only a few of you will be left among the nations where the LORD will lead you. 28 There you will serve other gods made by human hands, objects of wood and stone that neither see, nor hear, nor eat, nor smell. 29 From there you will seek the LORD your God, and you will find him if you search after him with all your heart and soul. 30 In your distress, when all these things have happened to you in time to come, you will return to the LORD your God and heed him. 31 Because the LORD your God is a merciful God, he will neither abandon you nor destroy you; he will not forget the covenant with your ancestors that he swore to them.

32 For ask now about former ages, long before your own, ever since the day that God created human beings on the earth; ask from one end of heaven to the other: has anything so great as this ever happened or has its like ever been heard of? 33 Has any people ever heard the voice of a god speaking out of a fire, as you have heard, and lived? 34 Or has any god ever attempted to go and take a nation for himself from the midst of another nation, by trials, by signs and wonders, by war, by a mighty hand and an outstretched arm, and by terrifying displays of power, as the LORD your God did for you in Egypt before your very eyes? 35 To you it was shown so that you would acknowledge that the LORD is God; there is no other besides him. 36 From heaven he made you hear his voice to discipline you. On earth he showed you his great fire, while you heard his words coming out of the fire. 37 And because he loved your ancestors, he chose their descendants after them. He brought you out of Egypt with his own presence, by his great power, 38 driving out before you nations greater and mightier than yourselves, to bring you in, giving you their land for a possession, as it is still today. 39 So acknowledge today and take to heart that the LORD is God in heaven above and on the earth beneath; there is no other. 40 Keep his statutes and his commandments, which I am commanding you today for your own well-being and that of your descendants after you, so that you may long remain in the land that the LORD your God is giving you for all time.

4.25–40. 25–31: A look to the future. 27–28: What Moses foresees as Israel's possible future (idolatry,* national destruction, exile into pagan lands) would already have been contemporary reality for some of Deuteronomy's early readers. **29–30:** Readers enduring exile are challenged to repent and *return to the LORD.* **31:** Exiles are to rely on the LORD's character as *a merciful God* who would *not forget the covenant.** **32–40: Israel's unique experience of God. 32:** Moses motivates obedience and loyalty by highlighting Israel's unique experience with the LORD. **33:** The sound and fire of the Mount Horeb revelation taught discipline (v. 36). **34:** The exodus from Egypt and its aftermath revealed God's love (vv. 37–38).

41 Then Moses set apart on the east side of the Jordan three cities 42 to which a homicide could flee, someone who unintentionally kills another person, the two not having been at enmity before; the homicide could flee to one of these cities and live:

43Bezer in the wilderness on the tableland belonging to the Reubenites, Ramoth in Gilead belonging to the Gadites, and Golan in Bashan belonging to the Manassites.

44 This is the law that Moses set before the Israelites. 45These are the decrees and the statutes and ordinances that Moses spoke to the Israelites when they had come out of Egypt, 46beyond the Jordan in the valley opposite Beth-peor, in the land of King Sihon of the Amorites, who reigned at Heshbon, whom Moses and the Israelites defeated when they came out of Egypt. 47They occupied his land and the land of King Og of Bashan, the two kings of the Amorites on the eastern side of the Jordan: 48from Aroer, which is on the edge of the Wadi Arnon, as far as Mount Sirion*a* (that is, Hermon), 49together with all the Arabah on the east side of the Jordan as far as the Sea of the Arabah, under the slopes of Pisgah.

4.41–49. 41–43: **Cities of refuge**. To shelter the unintentional killer from vengeful relatives (19.1–13). Joshua will set up three other cities west of the Jordan (Josh 20). **44–49: Introduction to the law. 45–46:** This sets the scene for Moses' proclamation of the law (compare 1.1–5). **49:** *The Arabah on the east side of the Jordan* describes the Jordan valley running south to the Dead Sea (*Sea of the Arabah*).

5 Moses convened all Israel, and said to them:

Hear, O Israel, the statutes and ordinances that I am addressing to you today; you shall learn them and observe them diligently. 2The LORD our God made a covenant with us at Horeb. 3Not with our ancestors did the LORD make this covenant, but with us, who are all of us here alive today. 4The LORD spoke with you face to face at the mountain, out of the fire. 5(At that time I was standing between the LORD and you to declare to you the words *b* of the LORD; for you were afraid because of the fire and did not go up the mountain.) And he said:

6 I am the LORD your God, who brought you out of the land of Egypt, out of the house of slavery; 7you shall have no other gods before*c* me.

8 You shall not make for yourself an idol, whether in the form of anything that is in heaven above, or that is on the earth beneath, or that is in the water under the earth. 9You shall not bow down to them or worship them; for I the LORD your God am a jealous God, punishing children for the iniquity of parents, to the third and fourth generation of those who reject me, 10but showing steadfast love to the thousandth generation*d* of those who love me and keep my commandments.

11 You shall not make wrongful use of the name of the LORD your God, for the LORD will not acquit anyone who misuses his name.

12 Observe the sabbath day and keep it holy, as the LORD your God commanded you. 13Six days you shall labor and do all your work. 14But the seventh day is a sabbath to the LORD your God; you shall not do any work—you, or your son or your daughter, or your male or female slave, or your ox or your donkey, or any of your livestock, or the resident alien in your towns, so that your male and female slave may rest as well as you. 15Remember that you were a slave in the land of Egypt, and the LORD your God brought you out from there with a mighty hand and an outstretched arm; therefore the LORD your God commanded you to keep the sabbath day.

16 Honor your father and your mother, as the LORD your God commanded you, so that your days may be long and that it may go well with you in the land that the LORD your God is giving you.

17 You shall not murder.*e*

18 Neither shall you commit adultery.

19 Neither shall you steal.

20 Neither shall you bear false witness against your neighbor.

21 Neither shall you covet your neighbor's wife.

Neither shall you desire your neighbor's house, or field, or male or female slave, or ox, or donkey, or anything that belongs to your neighbor.

a Syr: Heb *Sion*　*b* Q Mss Sam Gk Syr Vg Tg: MT *word*　*c* Or *besides*　*d* Or *to thousands*　*e* Or *kill*

5.1–21: The ten commandments. 3: The ten words (the Hebrew expression, see note *a* at 4.13) epitomize the *covenant** God has made with every new generation of readers (*with us*). **4–5:** There is tension between the tradition that the LORD spoke directly to the people (*face to face*) and the notion that Moses served as go-between or mediator. **6–7:** The LORD's self-identification as the one who delivered Israel *out of the land of Egypt* justifies a claim on Israel's obedience and encourages Israel's exclusive loyalty. The translation *before me* implies that no other god should take priority over the LORD or appear in the LORD's presence. The translation *besides me* (note c) emphasizes exclusive allegiance. **8–10:** The prohibition of idols is based on the LORD's jealous intolerance that demands absolute fidelity. The threat to three or four generations of those who repudiate the LORD is numerically overwhelmed by God's covenant* loyalty (*steadfast love;* v. 10) shown to thousands of generations (or perhaps individuals, note d). **11:** God's personal name "Yahweh" is not to be used to swear false oaths or do harmful magic. **15:** In contrast to Ex 20.11, Deuteronomy motivates sabbath rest by reference to slavery in Egypt. **16:** This addresses the situation of adult children living in extended family units under the authority of aged parents. **17:** Outright murder, death by careless accident, and unauthorized blood vengeance are forbidden. The translation *murder* is too narrow, but *kill* (note e) is too broad. **21:** Moral concern extends beyond outward action to internal attitude.

22 These words the LORD spoke with a loud voice to your whole assembly at the mountain, out of the fire, the cloud, and the thick darkness, and he added no more. He wrote them on two stone tablets, and gave them to me. 23When you heard the voice out of the darkness, while the mountain was burning with fire, you approached me, all the heads of your tribes and your elders; 24and you said, "Look, the LORD our God has shown us his glory and greatness, and we have heard his voice out of the fire. Today we have seen that God may speak to someone and the person may still live. 25So now why should we die? For this great fire will consume us; if we hear the voice of the LORD our God any longer, we shall die. 26For who is there of all flesh that has heard the voice of the living God speaking out of fire, as we

have, and remained alive? 27Go near, you yourself, and hear all that the LORD our God will say. Then tell us everything that the LORD our God tells you, and we will listen and do it."

28 The LORD heard your words when you spoke to me, and the LORD said to me: "I have heard the words of this people, which they have spoken to you; they are right in all that they have spoken. 29If only they had such a mind as this, to fear me and to keep all my commandments always, so that it might go well with them and with their children forever! 30Go say to them, 'Return to your tents.' 31But you, stand here by me, and I will tell you all the commandments, the statutes and the ordinances, that you shall teach them, so that they may do them in the land that I am giving them to possess." 32You must therefore be careful to do as the LORD your God has commanded you; you shall not turn to the right or to the left. 33You must follow exactly the path that the LORD your God has commanded you, so that you may live, and that it may go well with you, and that you may live long in the land that you are to possess.

5.22–33: Moses as intermediary. 23–26: It was commonly assumed that to be near the deity was to risk mortal danger. **27:** In other words, Deuteronomy is nothing less than the authentic voice of God as mediated by Moses (compare v. 31). **32–33:** Emphasizing the rewards of obedience motivates readers *to follow exactly the path* commanded in Deuteronomy.

6 Now this is the commandment—the statutes and the ordinances—that the LORD your God charged me to teach you to observe in the land that you are about to cross into and occupy, 2so that you and your children and your children's children may fear the LORD your God all the days of your life, and keep all his decrees and his commandments that I am commanding you, so that your days may be long. 3Hear therefore, O Israel, and observe them diligently, so that it may go well with you, and so that you may multiply greatly in a land flowing with milk and honey, as the LORD, the God of your ancestors, has promised you.

4 Hear, O Israel: The LORD is our God, the LORD alone.[a] 5You shall love the LORD your God with all your heart, and with all your soul, and with all your might. 6Keep these words that I am commanding you to-day in your heart. 7Recite them to your children and talk about them when you are at home and when you are away, when you lie down and when you rise. 8Bind them as a sign on your hand, fix them as an emblem[b] on your forehead, 9and write them on the doorposts of your house and on your gates.

6.1–9: The essence of the law. 1–3: Obedience to the law *in the land* (v. 1) is rewarded by long life, prosperity, and population growth in that same land (v. 3). *Flowing with milk and honey* (v. 3) is a conventional description of material abundance. **4–5:** The LORD is unique in power and unity and thus has an exclusive claim on Israel's love and loyalty. The translation *alone* accents the LORD's incomparability. The translations offered in note *a* emphasize the LORD's unity in contrast to belief in a multiplicity of gods. **6–9:** Striking metaphors* call on Israel to internalize the law (*in your heart,* v. 6) and take it personally (*bind them,* v. 8), so that it pervades every aspect of life (*talk about them,* v. 7; *write them,* v. 9). *Recite* (v. 7) literally means to "sharpen up" for instruction.

~~~~~

10 When the LORD your God has brought you into the land that he swore to your ancestors, to Abraham, to Isaac, and to Jacob, to give you—a land with fine, large cities that you did not build, 11houses filled with all sorts of goods that you did not fill, hewn cisterns that you did not hew, vineyards and olive groves that you did not plant—and when you have eaten your fill, 12take care that you do not forget the LORD, who brought you out of the land of Egypt, out of the house of slavery. 13The LORD your God you shall fear; him you shall serve, and by his name alone you shall swear. 14Do not follow other gods, any of the gods of the peoples who are all around you, 15because the LORD your God, who is present with you, is a jealous God. The anger of the LORD your God would be kindled against you and he would destroy you from the face of the earth.

16 Do not put the LORD your God to the test, as you tested him at Massah. 17You must diligently keep the commandments of the LORD your God, and his decrees, and his statutes that he has commanded you. 18Do what is right and good in the sight of the LORD, so that it may go well with you, and so that you may go in and occupy the good land that the LORD swore to your ancestors to give you, 19thrusting out all your enemies from before you, as the LORD has promised.

20 When your children ask you in time to come, "What is the meaning of the decrees and the statutes and the ordinances that the LORD our God has commanded you?" 21then you shall say to your children, "We were Pharaoh's slaves in Egypt, but the LORD brought us out of Egypt with a mighty hand. 22The LORD displayed before our eyes great and awesome signs and wonders against Egypt, against Pharaoh and all his household. 23He brought us out from there in order to bring us in, to give us the land that he promised on oath to our ancestors. 24Then the LORD commanded us to observe all these statutes, to fear the LORD our God, for our lasting good, so as to keep us alive, as is now the case. 25If we diligently observe this entire commandment before the LORD our God, as he has commanded us, we will be in the right."

6.10–25: Keep this law in the new land. 10–12: That the LORD is the source of these good things undercuts any pride Israel might feel in its prosperity. **15:** Israel's loyalty is motivated by the LORD's basic nature as *a jealous God,* one who is so passionately concerned with Israel's exclusive allegiance that national destruction is a real possibility. **16:** See Ex 17.1–7. **20–25:** Deuteronomy is regularly concerned with the instruction of the next generation (vv. 3, 7). This retelling of the story of salvation includes each succeeding generation by repeatedly using *we* and *us.*

~~~~~

7 When the LORD your God brings you into the land that you are about to enter and occupy, and he clears away many nations before you—the Hittites, the Girgashites, the Amorites, the Canaanites, the

---

a Or *The* LORD *our God is one* LORD, or *The* LORD *our God, the* LORD *is one,* or *The* LORD *is our God, the* LORD *is one* *b* Or *as a frontlet*

Perizzites, the Hivites, and the Jebusites, seven nations mightier and more numerous than you— 2and when the LORD your God gives them over to you and you defeat them, then you must utterly destroy them. Make no covenant with them and show them no mercy. 3Do not intermarry with them, giving your daughters to their sons or taking their daughters for your sons, 4for that would turn away your children from following me, to serve other gods. Then the anger of the LORD would be kindled against you, and he would destroy you quickly. 5But this is how you must deal with them: break down their altars, smash their pillars, hew down their sacred poles,*a* and burn their idols with fire. 6For you are a people holy to the LORD your God; the LORD your God has chosen you out of all the peoples on earth to be his people, his treasured possession.

7 It was not because you were more numerous than any other people that the LORD set his heart on you and chose you—for you were the fewest of all peoples. 8It was because the LORD loved you and kept the oath that he swore to your ancestors, that the LORD has brought you out with a mighty hand, and redeemed you from the house of slavery, from the hand of Pharaoh king of Egypt. 9Know therefore that the LORD your God is God, the faithful God who maintains covenant loyalty with those who love him and keep his commandments, to a thousand generations, 10and who repays in their own person those who reject him. He does not delay but repays in their own person those who reject him. 11Therefore, observe diligently the commandment—the statutes and the ordinances—that I am commanding you today.

12 If you heed these ordinances, by diligently observing them, the LORD your God will maintain with you the covenant loyalty that he swore to your ancestors; 13he will love you, bless you, and multiply you; he will bless the fruit of your womb and the fruit of your ground, your grain and your wine and your oil, the increase of your cattle and the issue of your flock, in the land that he swore to your ancestors to give you. 14You shall be the most blessed of peoples, with neither ste-rility nor barrenness among you or your livestock. 15The LORD will turn away from you every illness; all the dread diseases of Egypt that you experienced, he will not inflict on you, but he will lay them on all who hate you. 16You shall devour all the peoples that the LORD your God is giving over to you, showing them no pity; you shall not serve their gods, for that would be a snare to you.

7.1–16: Keep yourself separate. 2: Israel must *utterly destroy* the foreign population by enforcing the ban★ of 20.16–18 (see 2.34; Josh 6.21). **3–4:** Marriage forms social and religious affiliations between families and would lead the Israelite partner to worship or *serve other gods.* Isolation is not motivated by ethnic pride, but is needed to keep Israel loyal. **5:** The temptation of idolatry★ is suppressed by destroying shrines and equipment. **13–14:** The LORD's promise of fruitfulness in family, field, and flock discredits the claims of Canaanite fertility religion.

17 If you say to yourself, "These nations are more numerous than I; how can I dispossess them?" 18do not be afraid of them. Just remember what the LORD your God did to Pharaoh and to all Egypt, 19the great trials that your eyes saw, the signs and wonders, the mighty hand and the outstretched arm by which the LORD your God brought you out. The LORD your God will do the same to all the peoples of whom you are afraid. 20Moreover, the LORD your God will send the pestilence*b* against them, until even the survivors and the fugitives are destroyed. 21Have no dread of them, for the LORD your God, who is present with you, is a great and awesome God. 22The LORD your God will clear away these nations before you little by little; you will not be able to make a quick end of them, otherwise the wild animals would become too numerous for you. 23But the LORD your God will give them over to you, and throw them into great panic, until they are destroyed. 24He will hand their kings over to you and you shall blot out their name from under heaven; no one will be able to stand against you, until you have de-

a Heb *Asherim*   *b* Or *hornets:* Meaning of Heb uncertain stroyed them. 25 The images of their gods you shall burn with fire. Do not covet the silver or the gold that is on them and take it for yourself, because you could be ensnared by it; for it is abhorrent to the LORD your God. 26 Do not bring an abhorrent thing into your house, or you will be set apart for destruction like it. You must utterly detest and abhor it, for it is set apart for destruction.

7.17–26: Do not fear, remember the Exodus. 20: *Pestilence* echoes the plagues against Egypt. The translation *hornets* (note *b*) may be a metaphor* for panic or a swarming invader. **23:** *Great panic* is the classic weapon of the divine warrior* (Judg 7.19–22). **25–26:** The total eradication called for by the holy war* ban* must be rigorously applied, lest Israel itself fall into the category of what is banned or *set apart for destruction* (see Josh 6.18; 7.12).

8 This entire commandment that I command you today you must diligently observe, so that you may live and increase, and go in and occupy the land that the LORD promised on oath to your ancestors. 2 Remember the long way that the LORD your God has led you these forty years in the wilderness, in order to humble you, testing you to know what was in your heart, whether or not you would keep his commandments. 3 He humbled you by letting you hunger, then by feeding you with manna, with which neither you nor your ancestors were acquainted, in order to make you understand that one does not live by bread alone, but by every word that comes from the mouth of the LORD.ᵃ 4 The clothes on your back did not wear out and your feet did not swell these forty years. 5 Know then in your heart that as a parent disciplines a child so the LORD your God disciplines you. 6 Therefore keep the commandments of the LORD your God, by walking in his ways and by fearing him. 7 For the LORD your God is bringing you into a good land, a land with flowing streams, with springs and underground waters welling up in valleys and hills, 8 a land of wheat and barley, of vines and fig trees and pomegranates, a land of olive trees and honey, 9 a land where you may eat bread without scarcity, where you will lack nothing, a land whose stones are

iron and from whose hills you may mine copper. 10 You shall eat your fill and bless the LORD your God for the good land that he has given you.

11 Take care that you do not forget the LORD your God, by failing to keep his commandments, his ordinances, and his statutes, which I am commanding you today. 12 When you have eaten your fill and have built fine houses and live in them, 13 and when your herds and flocks have multiplied, and your silver and gold is multiplied, and all that you have is multiplied, 14 then do not exalt yourself, forgetting the LORD your God, who brought you out of the land of Egypt, out of the house of slavery, 15 who led you through the great and terrible wilderness, an arid wasteland with poisonousᵇ snakes and scorpions. He made water flow for you from flint rock, 16 and fed you in the wilderness with manna that your ancestors did not know, to humble you and to test you, and in the end to do you good. 17 Do not say to yourself, "My power and the might of my own hand have gotten me this wealth." 18 But remember the LORD your God, for it is he who gives you power to get wealth, so that he may confirm his covenant that he swore to your ancestors, as he is doing today. 19 If you do forget the LORD your God and follow other gods to serve and worship them, I solemnly warn you today that you shall surely perish. 20 Like the nations that the LORD is destroying before you, so shall you perish, because you would not obey the voice of the LORD your God.

8.1–20: Remember the LORD's saving acts. 2–6: The story of *manna* (v. 3) is reported in Ex 16. The wilderness experience (vv. 2–4) educated and disciplined Israel to keep the law in the new land (vv. 5–6). **7–20:** Israel's good life in the land (vv. 7–10) would be jeopardized by forgetfulness and pride (vv. 11–14, 17, 19–20). The remedy is to remember the LORD's saving deeds and wilderness lessons (vv. 14–16, 18).

9 Hear, O Israel! You are about to cross the Jordan today, to go in and dispossess

a Or *by anything that the LORD decrees*　　*b* Or *fiery*; Heb *seraph* nations larger and mightier than you, great cities, fortified to the heavens, 2a strong and tall people, the offspring of the Anakim, whom you know. You have heard it said of them, "Who can stand up to the Anakim?" 3Know then today that the LORD your God is the one who crosses over before you as a devouring fire; he will defeat them and subdue them before you, so that you may dispossess and destroy them quickly, as the LORD has promised you.

4 When the LORD your God thrusts them out before you, do not say to yourself, "It is because of my righteousness that the LORD has brought me in to occupy this land"; it is rather because of the wickedness of these nations that the LORD is dispossessing them before you. 5It is not because of your righteousness or the uprightness of your heart that you are going in to occupy their land; but because of the wickedness of these nations the LORD your God is dispossessing them before you, in order to fulfill the promise that the LORD made on oath to your ancestors, to Abraham, to Isaac, and to Jacob.

9.1–5: **Do not be smug or self-righteous. 1–3:** The reader is reminded of the circumstances behind Moses' speech (1.1–5). Moses is imitating the address typically given to encourage warriors before a battle (see 20.2–4). **4–5:** Do not be self-satisfied. The conquest is not a confirmation of your *righteousness,* but of Canaanite *wickedness.*

---

6 Know, then, that the LORD your God is not giving you this good land to occupy because of your righteousness; for you are a stubborn people. 7Remember and do not forget how you provoked the LORD your God to wrath in the wilderness; you have been rebellious against the LORD from the day you came out of the land of Egypt until you came to this place.

8 Even at Horeb you provoked the LORD to wrath, and the LORD was so angry with you that he was ready to destroy you. 9When I went up the mountain to receive the stone tablets, the tablets of the covenant that the LORD made with you, I remained on the mountain forty days and forty nights; I neither ate bread nor drank water. 10And the

LORD gave me the two stone tablets written with the finger of God; on them were all the words that the LORD had spoken to you at the mountain out of the fire on the day of the assembly. 11At the end of forty days and forty nights the LORD gave me the two stone tablets, the tablets of the covenant. 12Then the LORD said to me, "Get up, go down quickly from here, for your people whom you have brought from Egypt have acted corruptly. They have been quick to turn from the way that I commanded them; they have cast an image for themselves." 13Furthermore the LORD said to me, "I have seen that this people is indeed a stubborn people. 14Let me alone that I may destroy them and blot out their name from under heaven; and I will make of you a nation mightier and more numerous than they."

15 So I turned and went down from the mountain, while the mountain was ablaze; the two tablets of the covenant were in my two hands. 16Then I saw that you had indeed sinned against the LORD your God, by casting for yourselves an image of a calf; you had been quick to turn from the way that the LORD had commanded you. 17So I took hold of the two tablets and flung them from my two hands, smashing them before your eyes. 18Then I lay prostrate before the LORD as before, forty days and forty nights; I neither ate bread nor drank water, because of all the sin you had committed, provoking the LORD by doing what was evil in his sight. 19For I was afraid that the anger that the LORD bore against you was so fierce that he would destroy you. But the LORD listened to me that time also. 20The LORD was so angry with Aaron that he was ready to destroy him, but I interceded also on behalf of Aaron at that same time. 21Then I took the sinful thing you had made, the calf, and burned it with fire and crushed it, grinding it thoroughly, until it was reduced to dust; and I threw the dust of it into the stream that runs down the mountain.

22 At Taberah also, and at Massah, and at Kibroth-hattaavah, you provoked the LORD to wrath. 23And when the LORD sent you from Kadesh-barnea, saying, "Go up and occupy the land that I have given you," you

rebelled against the command of the LORD your God, neither trusting him nor obeying him. 24You have been rebellious against the LORD as long as he has[a] known you.

9.6–24: Remember your rebellion and God's pardon. 7: A repetition of *you have been rebellious against the LORD* encloses this section (see v. 24). **12:** The LORD's words carry a message of rejection: They are *your people*, Moses, not mine. **14:** *Let me alone* indicates that Moses should not intercede for Israel. The LORD proposes restarting the process of forming a chosen people from the beginning. **17:** *Smashing* the tablets symbolizes that the covenant* has itself been shattered. **22–24:** Moses cites history to prove that Israel has always *been rebellious* (v. 24). The incident at *Taberah* is reported in Num 11.1–3, *Massah* in Ex 17.1–7, and *Kibroth-hattaavah* in Num 11.31–34. The rebellion at *Kadesh-barnea* is recounted in Deut 1.19–33.

---

25 Throughout the forty days and forty nights that I lay prostrate before the LORD when the LORD intended to destroy you, 26I prayed to the LORD and said, "Lord GOD, do not destroy the people who are your very own possession, whom you redeemed in your greatness, whom you brought out of Egypt with a mighty hand. 27Remember your servants, Abraham, Isaac, and Jacob; pay no attention to the stubbornness of this people, their wickedness and their sin, 28otherwise the land from which you have brought us might say, 'Because the LORD was not able to bring them into the land that he promised them, and because he hated them, he has brought them out to let them die in the wilderness.' 29For they are the people of your very own possession, whom you brought out by your great power and by your outstretched arm."

10 At that time the LORD said to me, "Carve out two tablets of stone like the former ones, and come up to me on the mountain, and make an ark of wood. 2I will write on the tablets the words that were on the former tablets, which you smashed, and you shall put them in the ark." 3So I made an ark of acacia wood, cut two tablets of stone like the former ones, and went up the mountain with the two tablets in my hand.

4Then he wrote on the tablets the same words as before, the ten commandments[b] that the LORD had spoken to you on the mountain out of the fire on the day of the assembly; and the LORD gave them to me. 5So I turned and came down from the mountain, and put the tablets in the ark that I had made; and there they are, as the LORD commanded me.

6 (The Israelites journeyed from Beeroth-bene-jaakan[c] to Moserah. There Aaron died, and there he was buried; his son Eleazar succeeded him as priest. 7From there they journeyed to Gudgodah, and from Gudgodah to Jotbathah, a land with flowing streams. 8At that time the LORD set apart the tribe of Levi to carry the ark of the covenant of the LORD, to stand before the LORD to minister to him, and to bless in his name, to this day. 9Therefore Levi has no allotment or inheritance with his kindred; the LORD is his inheritance, as the LORD your God promised him.)

10 I stayed on the mountain forty days and forty nights, as I had done the first time. And once again the LORD listened to me. The LORD was unwilling to destroy you. 11The LORD said to me, "Get up, go on your journey at the head of the people, that they may go in and occupy the land that I swore to their ancestors to give them."

9.25–10.11: Intercession and forgiveness. 9.25: Moses returns to the incident described in 9.18–19. The flashback is enclosed by the phrase *forty days and forty nights* (see 10.10). **10.1–4:** Israel is back to where it started in 9.10. **10.10:** *The first time* refers to 9.11.

---

12 So now, O Israel, what does the LORD your God require of you? Only to fear the LORD your God, to walk in all his ways, to love him, to serve the LORD your God with all your heart and with all your soul, 13and to keep the commandments of the LORD your God[d] and his decrees that I am commanding you today, for your own well-being. 14Although heaven and the heaven of heav-

---

a Sam Gk: MT *I have*   b Heb *the ten words*
c Or *the wells of the Bene-jaakan*   d Q Ms Gk Syr: MT lacks *your God*

ens belong to the LORD your God, the earth with all that is in it, 15yet the LORD set his heart in love on your ancestors alone and chose you, their descendants after them, out of all the peoples, as it is today. 16Circumcise, then, the foreskin of your heart, and do not be stubborn any longer. 17For the LORD your God is God of gods and Lord of lords, the great God, mighty and awesome, who is not partial and takes no bribe, 18who executes justice for the orphan and the widow, and who loves the strangers, providing them food and clothing. 19You shall also love the stranger, for you were strangers in the land of Egypt. 20You shall fear the LORD your God; him alone you shall worship; to him you shall hold fast, and by his name you shall swear. 21He is your praise; he is your God, who has done for you these great and awesome things that your own eyes have seen. 22Your ancestors went down to Egypt seventy persons; and now the LORD your God has made you as numerous as the stars in heaven.

10.12–22: What the LORD requires of you. 12: *To fear* is to be reverent and obedient (also v. 20). *To love* God is part of a mutual circle that begins with the LORD's elective love for Israel's ancestors (v. 15) and culminates in the love that both God and Israel have for the needy stranger (vv. 18–19). *To serve* is to worship. **16:** *Circumcise . . . the foreskin of your heart* means to remove any obstacle to willing obedience. **21:** *He is your praise* means either that God is the true object of Israel's praise or the reason they are praised by others.

11 You shall love the LORD your God, therefore, and keep his charge, his decrees, his ordinances, and his commandments always. 2Remember today that it was not your children (who have not known or seen the discipline of the LORD your God), but it is you who must acknowledge his greatness, his mighty hand and his outstretched arm, 3his signs and his deeds that he did in Egypt to Pharaoh, the king of Egypt, and to all his land; 4what he did to the Egyptian army, to their horses and chariots, how he made the water of the Red Sea*a* flow over them as they pursued you, so that the LORD has destroyed them to this day;

5what he did to you in the wilderness, until you came to this place; 6and what he did to Dathan and Abiram, sons of Eliab son of Reuben, how in the midst of all Israel the earth opened its mouth and swallowed them up, along with their households, their tents, and every living being in their company; 7for it is your own eyes that have seen every great deed that the LORD did.

8 Keep, then, this entire commandment that I am commanding you today, so that you may have strength to go in and occupy the land that you are crossing over to occupy, 9and so that you may live long in the land that the LORD swore to your ancestors to give them and to their descendants, a land flowing with milk and honey. 10For the land that you are about to enter to occupy is not like the land of Egypt, from which you have come, where you sow your seed and irrigate by foot like a vegetable garden. 11But the land that you are crossing over to occupy is a land of hills and valleys, watered by rain from the sky, 12a land that the LORD your God looks after. The eyes of the LORD your God are always on it, from the beginning of the year to the end of the year.

13 If you will only heed his every commandment*b* that I am commanding you today—loving the LORD your God, and serving him with all your heart and with all your soul— 14then he*c* will give the rain for your land in its season, the early rain and the later rain, and you will gather in your grain, your wine, and your oil; 15and he*c* will give grass in your fields for your livestock, and you will eat your fill. 16Take care, or you will be seduced into turning away, serving other gods and worshiping them, 17for then the anger of the LORD will be kindled against you and he will shut up the heavens, so that there will be no rain and the land will yield no fruit; then you will perish quickly off the good land that the LORD is giving you.

18 You shall put these words of mine in your heart and soul, and you shall bind them as a sign on your hand, and fix them as an emblem*d* on your forehead. 19Teach them

a Or *Sea of Reeds*   *b* Compare Gk: Heb *my commandments*   *c* Sam Gk Vg: MT *I*   *d* Or *as a frontlet* to your children, talking about them when you are at home and when you are away, when you lie down and when you rise. [20]Write them on the doorposts of your house and on your gates, [21]so that your days and the days of your children may be multiplied in the land that the LORD swore to your ancestors to give them, as long as the heavens are above the earth.

22 If you will diligently observe this entire commandment that I am commanding you, loving the LORD your God, walking in all his ways, and holding fast to him, [23]then the LORD will drive out all these nations before you, and you will dispossess nations larger and mightier than yourselves. [24]Every place on which you set foot shall be yours; your territory shall extend from the wilderness to the Lebanon and from the River, the river Euphrates, to the Western Sea. [25]No one will be able to stand against you; the LORD your God will put the fear and dread of you on all the land on which you set foot, as he promised you.

11.1–25: Three reasons to obey. 2–7: The first is God's past discipline. For *Dathan and Abiram* (v. 6), see Num 16. **9–12:** Israel's second motive is the richness of the land. Rainless Egypt demanded that farmers *irrigate by foot* (v. 10), a tedious procedure using a foot-powered device. In contrast, Canaan is watered by God's trustworthy providence (vv. 11–12). **14:** *Early rain and later rain* are showers that fall in October and then in April. **18–21:** Concentration on the law is to be intense and personal (compare 6.4–9). **22–25:** Israel's third reason to obey is God's promise of an extensive and easy conquest. The optimistic territorial claim of v. 24 (see 1.7) corresponds to the jurisdiction of David and Solomon (1 Kings 4.21, 24).

26 See, I am setting before you today a blessing and a curse: [27]the blessing, if you obey the commandments of the LORD your God that I am commanding you today; [28]and the curse, if you do not obey the commandments of the LORD your God, but turn from the way that I am commanding you today, to follow other gods that you have not known.

29 When the LORD your God has brought you into the land that you are entering to occupy, you shall set the blessing on Mount Gerizim and the curse on Mount Ebal. [30]As you know, they are beyond the Jordan, some distance to the west, in the land of the Canaanites who live in the Arabah, opposite Gilgal, beside the oak[a] of Moreh.

31 When you cross the Jordan to go in to occupy the land that the LORD your God is giving you, and when you occupy it and live in it, [32]you must diligently observe all the statutes and ordinances that I am setting before you today.

11.26–32: Choose either blessing or curse. 26–28: A section of blessings and curses concludes Deuteronomy (ch. 28). **29:** Chapter 27 gives detailed instructions for this ceremony, which Joshua will eventually perform (Josh 8.30–35). **30:** The geography is confusing. *Gilgal* is nowhere near these two mountains. **32:** Moses concludes his introduction with a final appeal for obedience.

12 These are the statutes and ordinances that you must diligently observe in the land that the LORD, the God of your ancestors, has given you to occupy all the days that you live on the earth.

2 You must demolish completely all the places where the nations whom you are about to dispossess served their gods, on the mountain heights, on the hills, and under every leafy tree. [3]Break down their altars, smash their pillars, burn their sacred poles[b] with fire, and hew down the idols of their gods, and thus blot out their name from their places. [4]You shall not worship the LORD your God in such ways. [5]But you shall seek the place that the LORD your God will choose out of all your tribes as his habitation to put his name there. You shall go there, [6]bringing there your burnt offerings and your sacrifices, your tithes and your donations, your votive gifts, your freewill offerings, and the firstlings of your herds and flocks. [7]And you shall eat there in the presence of the LORD your God, you and your households together, rejoicing in all the undertakings in which the LORD your God has blessed you.

a Gk Syr: Compare Gen 12.6; Heb *oaks* or *terebinths*
b Heb *Asherim*

Worship at a Central Sanctuary

The centralization of sacrifice is Deuteronomy's most distinctive demand. Sacrificial worship was to take place only at a single, central sanctuary at a location to be chosen by the LORD (12.5, 11, 14, 18, 26). Earlier practice had permitted sacrifice at many local altars scattered around the country (Ex 20.24). Deuteronomy never identifies the site of this central sanctuary. This radical reform was imposed on Judah by King Josiah, who considered Jerusalem to be the LORD's chosen place (2 Kings 23.4–20).

8 You shall not act as we are acting here today, all of us according to our own desires, 9for you have not yet come into the rest and the possession that the LORD your God is giving you. 10When you cross over the Jordan and live in the land that the LORD your God is allotting to you, and when he gives you rest from your enemies all around so that you live in safety, 11then you shall bring everything that I command you to the place that the LORD your God will choose as a dwelling for his name: your burnt offerings and your sacrifices, your tithes and your donations, and all your choice votive gifts that you vow to the LORD. 12And you shall rejoice before the LORD your God, you together with your sons and your daughters, your male and female slaves, and the Levites who reside in your towns (since they have no allotment or inheritance with you).

13 Take care that you do not offer your burnt offerings at any place you happen to see. 14But only at the place that the LORD will choose in one of your tribes—there you shall offer your burnt offerings and there you shall do everything I command you.

15 Yet whenever you desire you may slaughter and eat meat within any of your towns, according to the blessing that the LORD your God has given you; the unclean and the clean may eat of it, as they would of gazelle or deer. 16The blood, however, you must not eat; you shall pour it out on the ground like water. 17Nor may you eat within your towns the tithe of your grain, your wine, and your oil, the firstlings of your herds and your flocks, any of your votive gifts that you vow, your freewill offerings, or your dona-

tions; 18these shall eat in the presence of the LORD your God at the place that the LORD your God will choose, you together with your son and your daughter, your male and female slaves, and the Levites resident in your towns, rejoicing in the presence of the LORD your God in all your undertakings. 19Take care that you do not neglect the Levite as long as you live in your land.

20 When the LORD your God enlarges your territory, as he has promised you, and you say, "I am going to eat some meat," because you wish to eat meat, you may eat meat whenever you have the desire. 21If the place where the LORD your God will choose to put his name is too far from you, and you slaughter as I have commanded you any of your herd or flock that the LORD has given you, then you may eat within your towns whenever you desire. 22Indeed, just as gazelle or deer is eaten, so you may eat it; the unclean and the clean alike may eat it. 23Only be sure that you do not eat the blood; for the blood is the life, and you shall not eat the life with the meat. 24Do not eat it; you shall pour it out on the ground like water. 25Do not eat it, so that all may go well with you and your children after you, because you do what is right in the sight of the LORD. 26But the sacred donations that are due from you, and your votive gifts, you shall bring to the place that the LORD will choose. 27You shall present your burnt offerings, both the meat and the blood, on the altar of the LORD your God; the blood of your other sacrifices shall be poured out beside*a* the al-

a Or *on*

tar of the LORD your God, but the meat you may eat.

28 Be careful to obey all these words that I command you today,[a] so that it may go well with you and with your children after you forever, because you will be doing what is good and right in the sight of the LORD your God.

12.1–28: Centralize all sacrifice. 2–3: Israel's local worship sites were often also used for Canaanite worship. *Sacred poles* (*Asherim*, note *b*) were wooden symbols of the goddess Asherah.* **5:** The LORD is not present there directly, but in the form of *his name*. The central sanctuary is to be a focus of pilgrimage (*go there*). **6:** Every sacrifice and offering must be taken there (vv. 11, 13–14, 17, 26–27). **7:** Most sacrifices culminated in a joyous meal. **12:** The worship assembly is to be inclusive, including women and marginalized groups (also vv. 18–19). **15:** All animal slaughter was potentially a religious act. Centralizing sacrifice meant that killing animals locally would now be a purely secular affair. Those who ate such non-sacrificial meat could be in a state of ritual uncleanness (also vv. 21–22). **16:** *Blood* was dangerous and powerful and could never be eaten. It must be disposed of in a completely non-sacrificial manner, poured on the ground *like water* (also vv. 23–25).

29 When the LORD your God has cut off before you the nations whom you are about to enter to dispossess them, when you have dispossessed them and live in their land, [30]take care that you are not snared into imitating them, after they have been destroyed before you: do not inquire concerning their gods, saying, "How did these nations worship their gods? I also want to do the same." [31]You must not do the same for the LORD your God, because every abhorrent thing that the LORD hates they have done for their gods. They would even burn their sons and their daughters in the fire to their gods. [32][b]You must diligently observe everything that I command you; do not add to it or take anything from it.

13 [c]If prophets or those who divine by dreams appear among you and promise you omens or portents, [2]and the omens or the portents declared by them take place, and they say, "Let us follow other gods"

(whom you have not known) "and let us serve them," [3]you must not heed the words of those prophets or those who divine by dreams; for the LORD your God is testing you, to know whether you indeed love the LORD your God with all your heart and soul. [4]The LORD your God you shall follow, him alone you shall fear, his commandments you shall keep, his voice you shall obey, him you shall serve, and to him you shall hold fast. [5]But those prophets or those who divine by dreams shall be put to death for having spoken treason against the LORD your God— who brought you out of the land of Egypt and redeemed you from the house of slavery—to turn you from the way in which the LORD your God commanded you to walk. So you shall purge the evil from your midst.

6 If anyone secretly entices you—even if it is your brother, your father's son or[d] your mother's son, or your own son or daughter, or the wife you embrace, or your most intimate friend—saying, "Let us go worship other gods," whom neither you nor your ancestors have known, [7]any of the gods of the peoples that are around you, whether near you or far away from you, from one end of the earth to the other, [8]you must not yield to or heed any such persons. Show them no pity or compassion and do not shield them. [9]But you shall surely kill them; your own hand shall be first against them to execute them, and afterwards the hand of all the people. [10]Stone them to death for trying to turn you away from the LORD your God, who brought you out of the land of Egypt, out of the house of slavery. [11]Then all Israel shall hear and be afraid, and never again do any such wickedness.

12 If you hear it said about one of the towns that the LORD your God is giving you to live in, [13]that scoundrels from among you have gone out and led the inhabitants of the town astray, saying, "Let us go and worship other gods," whom you have not known, [14]then you shall inquire and make a thorough investigation. If the charge is estab-

a Gk Sam Syr: MT lacks *today*   *b* Ch 13.1 in Heb
c Ch 13.2 in Heb   *d* Sam Gk Compare Tg: MT lacks *your father's son or*

lished that such an abhorrent thing has been done among you, 15you shall put the inhabitants of that town to the sword, utterly destroying it and everything in it—even putting its livestock to the sword. 16All of its spoil you shall gather into its public square; then burn the town and all its spoil with fire, as a whole burnt offering to the LORD your God. It shall remain a perpetual ruin, never to be rebuilt. 17Do not let anything devoted to destruction stick to your hand, so that the LORD may turn from his fierce anger and show you compassion, and in his compassion multiply you, as he swore to your ancestors, 18if you obey the voice of the LORD your God by keeping all his commandments that I am commanding you today, doing what is right in the sight of the LORD your God.

12.29–13.18: Do not be enticed by other gods. 12.30: One source of temptation is curiosity and a desire to imitate. **13.1–5:** False prophets* are another lure. Their message would be especially tempting if they could authenticate it with *omens* and *portents* (v. 2; contrast 18.22). **6–11:** Temptation could also come *secretly* (v. 6) from someone very close. In contrast to its long history with the LORD during the Exodus (vv. 5, 10), Israel has had no experience with these *other gods* (vv. 6, 13). **12–18:** An apostate town is to be treated as the object of holy war* (20.16–18). In this case, not only are humans *utterly destroyed* (v. 15), but cattle, all moveable property, and the town itself are to be *devoted to destruction* (vv. 16–17; compare Josh 6.21, 24).

14 You are children of the LORD your God. You must not lacerate yourselves or shave your forelocks for the dead. 2For you are a people holy to the LORD your God; it is you the LORD has chosen out of all the peoples on earth to be his people, his treasured possession.

3 You shall not eat any abhorrent thing. 4These are the animals you may eat: the ox, the sheep, the goat, 5the deer, the gazelle, the roebuck, the wild goat, the ibex, the antelope, and the mountain-sheep. 6Any animal that divides the hoof and has the hoof cleft in two, and chews the cud, among the animals, you may eat. 7Yet of those that chew the cud or have the hoof cleft you shall

not eat these: the camel, the hare, and the rock badger, because they chew the cud but do not divide the hoof; they are unclean for you. 8And the pig, because it divides the hoof but does not chew the cud, is unclean for you. You shall not eat their meat, and you shall not touch their carcasses.

9 Of all that live in water you may eat these: whatever has fins and scales you may eat. 10And whatever does not have fins and scales you shall not eat; it is unclean for you.

11 You may eat any clean birds. 12But these are the ones that you shall not eat: the eagle, the vulture, the osprey, 13the buzzard, the kite of any kind; 14every raven of any kind; 15the ostrich, the nighthawk, the sea gull, the hawk of any kind; 16the little owl and the great owl, the water hen 17and the desert owl,*a* the carrion vulture and the cormorant, 18the stork, the heron of any kind; the hoopoe and the bat.*b* 19And all winged insects are unclean for you; they shall not be eaten. 20You may eat any clean winged creature.

21 You shall not eat anything that dies of itself; you may give it to aliens residing in your towns for them to eat, or you may sell it to a foreigner. For you are a people holy to the LORD your God.

You shall not boil a kid in its mother's milk.

14.1–21: Clean and unclean foods. 1: These mourning rituals may have been part of Canaanite worship. **3:** Any *abhorrent thing* would damage one's relationship with God (see 7.26; 12.31). **6–7:** Domestic animals provide the standard for what may be eaten. **8:** The *pig* may have been used in Canaanite rituals. **9–10:** Ordinary fish are the standard for what is clean. **21:** Whatever died a natural death would contain forbidden blood. These dietary rules do not apply to non-Israelites. Boiling a baby goat in its own *mother's milk* may have been a Canaanite ritual.

22 Set apart a tithe of all the yield of your seed that is brought in yearly from the field. 23In the presence of the LORD your God, in the place that he will choose as a dwelling

a Or *pelican*   *b* Identification of several of the birds in verses 12–18 is uncertain

Ritual Purity

Israel's purity system categorized persons, objects, and foods. It had nothing to do with modern notions of hygiene. Those who ate unclean food became ritually unclean. They were excluded from social contact and the worship assembly until their impurity was removed. A similar list of clean and unclean animals is given in Lev 11.

for his name, you shall eat the tithe of your grain, your wine, and your oil, as well as the firstlings of your herd and flock, so that you may learn to fear the LORD your God always. 24But if, when the LORD your God has blessed you, the distance is so great that you are unable to transport it, because the place where the LORD your God will choose to set his name is too far away from you, 25then you may turn it into money. With the money secure in hand, go to the place that the LORD your God will choose; 26spend the money for whatever you wish—oxen, sheep, wine, strong drink, or whatever you desire. And you shall eat there in the presence of the LORD your God, you and your household rejoicing together. 27As for the Levites resident in your towns, do not neglect them, because they have no allotment or inheritance with you.

28 Every third year you shall bring out the full tithe of your produce for that year, and store it within your towns; 29the Levites, because they have no allotment or inheritance with you, as well as the resident aliens, the orphans, and the widows in your towns, may come and eat their fill so that the LORD your God may bless you in all the work that you undertake.

14.22–29: Set apart tithes. 22–23: Ten percent of one's crop, along with firstborn animals, are taken to the central sanctuary and eaten as a sacrificial meal (12.17–18). **24–26:** If transportation is a problem, the tithe may be converted to cash to buy a joyful banquet at the central sanctuary. **27–29:** Every three years, a second tenth is stored up to provide for the needy. Apparently this practice took place on the third and sixth year of every seven-year cycle (15.1).

15 Every seventh year you shall grant a remission of debts. 2And this is the manner of the remission: every creditor shall remit the claim that is held against a neighbor, not exacting it of a neighbor who is a member of the community, because the LORD's remission has been proclaimed. 3Of a foreigner you may exact it, but you must remit your claim on whatever any member of your community owes you. 4There will, however, be no one in need among you, because the LORD is sure to bless you in the land that the LORD your God is giving you as a possession to occupy, 5if only you will obey the LORD your God by diligently observing this entire commandment that I command you today. 6When the LORD your God has blessed you, as he promised you, you will lend to many nations, but you will not borrow; you will rule over many nations, but they will not rule over you.

7 If there is among you anyone in need, a member of your community in any of your towns within the land that the LORD your God is giving you, do not be hard-hearted or tight-fisted toward your needy neighbor. 8You should rather open your hand, willingly lending enough to meet the need, whatever it may be. 9Be careful that you do not entertain a mean thought, thinking, "The seventh year, the year of remission, is near," and therefore view your needy neighbor with hostility and give nothing; your neighbor might cry to the LORD against you, and you would incur guilt. 10Give liberally and be ungrudging when you do so, for on this account the LORD your God will bless you in all your work and in all that you undertake. 11Since there will never cease to be some in need on the earth, I therefore command you, "Open

your hand to the poor and needy neighbor in your land."

15.1–11: Remit debts every seventh year. 1: This is a revision of Ex 23.10–11. *A remission of debts* prevents the creation of a permanent debtor class. **4–5:** The ideal result of perfect obedience (*no one in need*) stands in tension with v. 11. **8–9:** Generous lending is understood as a form of social service. **11:** The permanent reality of poverty provides an opportunity for generosity.

~~~~~~~~~~~~~~~~~~~~~~~~~~~

12 If a member of your community, whether a Hebrew man or a Hebrew woman, is sold*a* to you and works for you six years, in the seventh year you shall set that person free. 13And when you send a male slave*b* out from you a free person, you shall not send him out empty-handed. 14Provide liberally out of your flock, your threshing floor, and your wine press, thus giving to him some of the bounty with which the LORD your God has blessed you. 15Remember that you were a slave in the land of Egypt, and the LORD your God redeemed you; for this reason I lay this command upon you today. 16But if he says to you, "I will not go out from you," because he loves you and your household, since he is well off with you, 17then you shall take an awl and thrust it through his earlobe into the door, and he shall be your slave*c* forever.

You shall do the same with regard to your female slave.*d*

18 Do not consider it a hardship when you send them out from you free persons, because for six years they have given you services worth the wages of hired laborers; and the LORD your God will bless you in all that you do.

19 Every firstling male born of your herd and flock you shall consecrate to the LORD your God; you shall not do work with your firstling ox nor shear the firstling of your flock. 20You shall eat it, you together with your household, in the presence of the LORD your God year by year at the place that the LORD will choose. 21But if it has any defect—any serious defect, such as lameness or blindness—you shall not sacrifice it to the LORD your God; 22within your towns you

may eat it, the unclean and the clean alike, as you would a gazelle or deer. 23Its blood, however, you must not eat; you shall pour it out on the ground like water.

15.12–23. 12–18: Hebrew slaves. 12: This fellow *Hebrew* would have been *sold* (but see note *a*) to meet unpaid debts. Release comes on the *seventh year* of service (not the seven-year cycle of vv. 1–11). **14–15:** This law is a revision of Ex 21.2–6. Its socially compassionate provisions are typical of Deuteronomy, as is the motivating reference to the Exodus (compare 5.15). **17:** Explicit concern for a *female slave* is typical of Deuteronomy (21.10–17). **19–23: Consecrate firstborn male animals. 19–20:** This is a revision of Ex 22.30. Because the animal belongs to the LORD, no economic benefit may be derived from it. It is to be eaten as a sacrifice at the central sanctuary. **21–23:** If too defective to sacrifice, it becomes a secular meal at home (compare 12.15–16, 20–25).

~~~~~~~~~~~~~~~~~~~~~~~~~~~

16 Observe the month*e* of Abib by keeping the passover to the LORD your God, for in the month of Abib the LORD your God brought you out of Egypt by night. 2You shall offer the passover sacrifice to the LORD your God, from the flock and the herd, at the place that the LORD will choose as a dwelling for his name. 3You must not eat with it anything leavened. For seven days you shall eat unleavened bread with it—the bread of affliction—because you came out of the land of Egypt in great haste, so that all the days of your life you may remember the day of your departure from the land of Egypt. 4No leaven shall be seen with you in all your territory for seven days; and none of the meat of what you slaughter on the evening of the first day shall remain until morning. 5You are not permitted to offer the passover sacrifice within any of your towns that the LORD your God is giving you. 6But at the place that the LORD your God will choose as a dwelling for his name, only there shall you offer the passover sacrifice, in the evening at sunset, the time of day when you departed from Egypt. 7You shall cook it and eat it at the place that the LORD your God will

---

a Or *sells himself or herself*   *b* Heb *him*
c Or *bondman*   *d* Or *bondwoman*   *e* Or *new moon*

choose; the next morning you may go back to your tents. ⁸For six days you shall continue to eat unleavened bread, and on the seventh day there shall be a solemn assembly for the LORD your God, when you shall do no work.

9 You shall count seven weeks; begin to count the seven weeks from the time the sickle is first put to the standing grain. ¹⁰Then you shall keep the festival of weeks to the LORD your God, contributing a freewill offering in proportion to the blessing that you have received from the LORD your God. ¹¹Rejoice before the LORD your God—you and your sons and your daughters, your male and female slaves, the Levites resident in your towns, as well as the strangers, the orphans, and the widows who are among you—at the place that the LORD your God will choose as a dwelling for his name. ¹²Remember that you were a slave in Egypt, and diligently observe these statutes.

13 You shall keep the festival of booths*a* for seven days, when you have gathered in the produce from your threshing floor and your wine press. ¹⁴Rejoice during your festival, you and your sons and your daughters, your male and female slaves, as well as the Levites, the strangers, the orphans, and the widows resident in your towns. ¹⁵Seven days you shall keep the festival to the LORD your God at the place that the LORD will choose; for the LORD your God will bless you in all your produce and in all your undertakings, and you shall surely celebrate.

16 Three times a year all your males shall appear before the LORD your God at the place that he will choose: at the festival of unleavened bread, at the festival of weeks, and at the festival of booths.*a* They shall not appear before the LORD empty-handed; ¹⁷all shall give as they are able, according to the blessing of the LORD your God that he has given you.

16.1–17: Celebrate three pilgrimage festivals. 1: *Passover*★ takes place in *Abib,* when the first grain is harvested. 2: Deuteronomy's revision of Ex 23.14–17 turns previously local observances into festivals at the central sanctuary (also vv. 11, 15). 5–6: The former practice of offering the Passover sacrifice *within any of*

your towns is replaced by a centralized festival. This centralization was instituted in Judah by King Josiah (2 Kings 23.21–23). Passover reverted to a domestic celebration when the destruction of the Temple★ by Rome made sacrifice impossible. 9–10: Seven weeks later in early summer is the *festival of weeks.* 11: Including society's marginalized groups is typical of Deuteronomy (v. 14). 13–14: The autumn grape harvest marks the end of the agricultural year and the *festival of booths.* Deuteronomy fails to mention this festival's most distinctive feature, residence in temporary shelters or *booths,* but emphasizes all-inclusive merrymaking.

18 You shall appoint judges and officials throughout your tribes, in all your towns that the LORD your God is giving you, and they shall render just decisions for the people. ¹⁹You must not distort justice; you must not show partiality; and you must not accept bribes, for a bribe blinds the eyes of the wise and subverts the cause of those who are in the right. ²⁰Justice, and only justice, you shall pursue, so that you may live and occupy the land that the LORD your God is giving you.

21 You shall not plant any tree as a sacred pole*b* beside the altar that you make for the LORD your God; ²²nor shall you set up a stone pillar—things that the LORD your God hates.

17 You must not sacrifice to the LORD your God an ox or a sheep that has a defect, anything seriously wrong; for that is abhorrent to the LORD your God.

2 If there is found among you, in one of your towns that the LORD your God is giving you, a man or woman who does what is evil in the sight of the LORD your God, and transgresses his covenant ³by going to serve other gods and worshiping them—whether the sun or the moon or any of the host of heaven, which I have forbidden— ⁴and if it is reported to you or you hear of it, and you make a thorough inquiry, and the charge is proved true that such an abhorrent thing has occurred in Israel, ⁵then you shall bring out to your gates that man or that woman who has committed this crime and you shall stone the

a Or *tabernacles*; Heb *succoth*   *b* Heb *Asherah*

man or woman to death. 6On the evidence of two or three witnesses the death sentence shall be executed; a person must not be put to death on the evidence of only one witness. 7The hands of the witnesses shall be the first raised against the person to execute the death penalty, and afterward the hands of all the people. So you shall purge the evil from your midst.

8 If a judicial decision is too difficult for you to make between one kind of bloodshed and another, one kind of legal right and another, or one kind of assault and another— any such matters of dispute in your towns—then you shall immediately go up to the place that the LORD your God will choose, 9where you shall consult with the levitical priests and the judge who is in office in those days; they shall announce to you the decision in the case. 10Carry out exactly the decision that they announce to you from the place that the LORD will choose, diligently observing everything they instruct you. 11You must carry out fully the law that they interpret for you or the ruling that they announce to you; do not turn aside from the decision that they announce to you, either to the right or to the left. 12As for anyone who presumes to disobey the priest appointed to minister there to the LORD your God, or the judge, that person shall die. So you shall purge the evil from Israel. 13All the people will hear and be afraid, and will not act presumptuously again.

14 When you have come into the land that the LORD your God is giving you, and have taken possession of it and settled in it, and you say, "I will set a king over me, like all the nations that are around me," 15you may indeed set over you a king whom the LORD your God will choose. One of your own community you may set as king over you; you are not permitted to put a foreigner over you, who is not of your own community. 16Even so, he must not acquire many horses for himself, or return the people to Egypt in order to acquire more horses, since the LORD has said to you, "You must never return that way again." 17And he must not acquire many wives for himself, or else his heart will turn away; also silver and gold he must not acquire in great quantity for himself. 18When he has taken the throne of his kingdom, he shall have a copy of this law written for him in the presence of the levitical priests. 19It shall remain with him and he shall read in it all the days of his life, so that he may learn to fear the LORD his God, diligently observing all the words of this law and these statutes, 20neither exalting himself above other members of the community nor turning aside from the commandment, either to the right or to the left, so that he and his descendants may reign long over his kingdom in Israel.

17.14–20: The king. 16–17: Deuteronomy has a low opinion of kingship and restricts its usual perquisites. The grandeur of King Solomon serves as a negative example (compare 1 Kings 10–11). 18–19: Monarchy is brought under the control of the law. 20: The king is to be an obedient "constitutional monarch" on the same level with ordinary citizens.

16.18–17.13: Maintain a fair justice system. 16.19: The phrase beginning a bribe blinds the eyes quotes a proverb (Ex 23.8). 16.21–17.1: Three short laws forbid improper ritual practices. A sacred pole (16.21) was a symbol of the goddess Asherah* (note b). 2–6: The sample case of someone who worships other gods (v. 3) illustrates a fair and rigorous judicial procedure. Fairness requires a thorough inquiry (v. 4) and more than one eyewitness to the crime (v. 6). 7: Witnesses cast the first stones in order to affirm the truth of their testimony (Jn 8.7; Acts 7.58). 8–13: Before sanctuary centralization, priests of the local shrines advised on legal fine points. Deuteronomy instead establishes a centralized court of appeal, staffed by both civil and priestly judges (vv. 9, 12).

18 The levitical priests, the whole tribe of Levi, shall have no allotment or inheritance within Israel. They may eat the sacrifices that are the LORD's portion[a] 2but they shall have no inheritance among the other members of the community; the LORD is their inheritance, as he promised them.

3 This shall be the priests' due from the people, from those offering a sacrifice,

a Meaning of Heb uncertain

whether an ox or a sheep: they shall give to the priest the shoulder, the two jowls, and the stomach. ⁴The first fruits of your grain, your wine, and your oil, as well as the first of the fleece of your sheep, you shall give him. ⁵For the LORD your God has chosen Levi*ᵃ* out of all your tribes, to stand and minister in the name of the LORD, him and his sons for all time.

6 If a Levite leaves any of your towns, from wherever he has been residing in Israel, and comes to the place that the LORD will choose (and he may come whenever he wishes), ⁷then he may minister in the name of the LORD his God, like all his fellow-Levites who stand to minister there before the LORD. ⁸They shall have equal portions to eat, even though they have income from the sale of family possessions.*ᵇ*

9 When you come into the land that the LORD your God is giving you, you must not learn to imitate the abhorrent practices of those nations. ¹⁰No one shall be found among you who makes a son or daughter pass through fire, or who practices divination, or is a soothsayer, or an augur, or a sorcerer, ¹¹or one who casts spells, or who consults ghosts or spirits, or who seeks oracles from the dead. ¹²For whoever does these things is abhorrent to the LORD; it is because of such abhorrent practices that the LORD your God is driving them out before you. ¹³You must remain completely loyal to the LORD your God. ¹⁴Although these nations that you are about to dispossess do give heed to soothsayers and diviners, as for you, the LORD your God does not permit you to do so.

15 The LORD your God will raise up for you a prophet*ᶜ* like me from among your own people; you shall heed such a prophet.*ᵈ* ¹⁶This is what you requested of the LORD your God at Horeb on the day of the assembly when you said: "If I hear the voice of the LORD my God any more, or ever again see this great fire, I will die." ¹⁷Then the LORD replied to me: "They are right in what they have said. ¹⁸I will raise up for them a prophet*ᶜ* like you from among their own people; I will put my words in the mouth of the prophet,*ᵉ* who shall speak to them everything that I command. ¹⁹Anyone who does

not heed the words that the prophet*ᶠ* shall speak in my name, I myself will hold accountable. ²⁰But any prophet who speaks in the name of other gods, or who presumes to speak in my name a word that I have not commanded the prophet to speak—that prophet shall die." ²¹You may say to yourself, "How can we recognize a word that the LORD has not spoken?" ²²If a prophet speaks in the name of the LORD but the thing does not take place or prove true, it is a word that the LORD has not spoken. The prophet has spoken it presumptuously; do not be frightened by it.

18.1–22. 1–8: The levitical priests. 1: Deuteronomy does not make any sharp distinction between *levitical priests* and other members of the *tribe of Levi*. **3–4:** Although priests may have income from other sources (v. 8), they are supported by designated portions of the sacrifices. **6–8:** This provision blunts the devastating economic impact that sanctuary centralization would have on local priests. Any Levite who relocates to the central sanctuary is to receive a priestly appointment. **9–22: True and false prophets.** ★ **10–11:** Various methods of divination and practitioners of secret arts are listed and labeled as abominations. Seeking *oracles★ from the dead* is illustrated by 1 Sam 28.6–19. **15:** A series of *prophets* like Moses is intended, rather than only a single one (notes *c, d, e*). **20–22:** Prophecy in the name of another god is easily rejected, but false prophecy in the name of the LORD poses a more difficult problem. The suggested practical standard (*the thing does not take place,* v. 22) could be applied to a prophet's overall message, but not to individual oracles.

19 When the LORD your God has cut off the nations whose land the LORD your God is giving you, and you have dispossessed them and settled in their towns and in their houses, ²you shall set apart three cities in the land that the LORD your God is giving you to possess. ³You shall calculate the distances*ᵍ* and divide into three regions the land that the LORD your God gives you as a possession, so that any homicide can flee to one of them.

a Heb *him*   *b* Meaning of Heb uncertain
c Or *prophets*   *d* Or *such prophets*   *e* Or *mouths of the prophets*   *f* Heb *he*   *g* Or *prepare roads to them*

4 Now this is the case of a homicide who might flee there and live, that is, someone who has killed another person unintentionally when the two had not been at enmity before: 5Suppose someone goes into the forest with another to cut wood, and when one of them swings the ax to cut down a tree, the head slips from the handle and strikes the other person who then dies; the killer may flee to one of these cities and live. 6But if the distance is too great, the avenger of blood in hot anger might pursue and overtake and put the killer to death, although a death sentence was not deserved, since the two had not been at enmity before. 7Therefore I command you: You shall set apart three cities.

8 If the LORD your God enlarges your territory, as he swore to your ancestors—and he will give you all the land that he promised your ancestors to give you, 9provided you diligently observe this entire commandment that I command you today, by loving the LORD your God and walking always in his ways—then you shall add three more cities to these three, 10so that the blood of an innocent person may not be shed in the land that the LORD your God is giving you as an inheritance, thereby bringing bloodguilt upon you.

11 But if someone at enmity with another lies in wait and attacks and takes the life of that person, and flees into one of these cities, 12then the elders of the killer's city shall send to have the culprit taken from there and handed over to the avenger of blood to be put to death. 13Show no pity; you shall purge the guilt of innocent blood from Israel, so that it may go well with you.

14 You must not move your neighbor's boundary marker, set up by former generations, on the property that will be allotted to you in the land that the LORD your God is giving you to possess.

15 A single witness shall not suffice to convict a person of any crime or wrongdoing in connection with any offense that may be committed. Only on the evidence of two or three witnesses shall a charge be sustained. 16If a malicious witness comes forward to accuse someone of wrongdoing, 17then both parties to the dispute shall appear before the

LORD, before the priests and the judges who are in office in those days, 18and the judges shall make a thorough inquiry. If the witness is a false witness, having testified falsely against another, 19then you shall do to the false witness just as the false witness had meant to do to the other. So you shall purge the evil from your midst. 20The rest shall hear and be afraid, and a crime such as this shall never again be committed among you. 21Show no pity: life for life, eye for eye, tooth for tooth, hand for hand, foot for foot.

19.1–21. 1–13: **Cities of asylum. 3:** Intentional murder was punished by retaliation from the victim's family. Before sanctuary centralization, someone who had killed accidentally (vv. 4–5) could find asylum at a local altar (Ex 21.12–14). Fairness requires easy approach to the three places of asylum, either in regard to *the distances* or the quality of access roads (note g). **6:** The *avenger of blood,* a close relative designated by custom to hunt down the killer, would not weigh the claims of the accused fairly. **8–9:** Moses set up three cities east of the Jordan (4.41–43), and Joshua three on the west (Josh 20). **11–12:** This case contrasts with that of vv. 4–6, so the right of asylum does not apply. **14–21: Boundary markers and witnesses. 14:** This could be done openly through economic pressure against poor landowners as well as in secret (27.17). Ancestral land is a gift from the LORD and not to be alienated from the family that owns it. **16–19:** This law restates Ex 23.1 in light of the central court of 17.8–13. **21:** Justice in Israel depended almost entirely on eyewitness testimony, so stern punishment is in order.

---

20 When you go out to war against your enemies, and see horses and chariots, an army larger than your own, you shall not be afraid of them; for the LORD your God is with you, who brought you up from the land of Egypt. 2Before you engage in battle, the priest shall come forward and speak to the troops, 3and shall say to them: "Hear, O Israel! Today you are drawing near to do battle against your enemies. Do not lose heart, or be afraid, or panic, or be in dread of them; 4for it is the LORD your God who goes with you, to fight for you against your enemies, to give you victory." 5Then the officials shall address the troops, saying, "Has anyone built a new house but not dedicated

it? He should go back to his house, or he might die in the battle and another dedicate it. 6Has anyone planted a vineyard but not yet enjoyed its fruit? He should go back to his house, or he might die in the battle and another be first to enjoy its fruit. 7Has anyone become engaged to a woman but not yet married her? He should go back to his house, or he might die in the battle and another marry her." 8The officials shall continue to address the troops, saying, "Is anyone afraid or disheartened? He should go back to his house, or he might cause the heart of his comrades to melt like his own." 9When the officials have finished addressing the troops, then the commanders shall take charge of them.

10 When you draw near to a town to fight against it, offer it terms of peace. 11If it accepts your terms of peace and surrenders to you, then all the people in it shall serve you at forced labor. 12If it does not submit to you peacefully, but makes war against you, then you shall besiege it; 13and when the LORD your God gives it into your hand, you shall put all its males to the sword. 14You may, however, take as your booty the women, the children, livestock, and everything else in the town, all its spoil. You may enjoy the spoil of your enemies, which the LORD your God has given you. 15Thus you shall treat all the towns that are very far from you, which are not towns of the nations here. 16But as for the towns of these peoples that the LORD your God is giving you as an inheritance, you must not let anything that breathes remain alive. 17You shall annihilate them—the Hittites and the Amorites, the Canaanites and the Perizzites, the Hivites and the Jebusites—just as the LORD your God has commanded, 18so that they may not teach you to do all the abhorrent things that they do for their gods, and you thus sin against the LORD your God.

19 If you besiege a town for a long time, making war against it in order to take it, you must not destroy its trees by wielding an ax against them. Although you may take food from them, you must not cut them down. Are trees in the field human beings that they should come under siege from you? 20You

may destroy only the trees that you know do not produce food; you may cut them down for use in building siegeworks against the town that makes war with you, until it falls.

20.1–20: Holy war. **1:** In holy war confident faith is a prerequisite for victory. **2–4:** First comes a priestly war sermon. **5–8:** Exemptions are provided for any who deserve to enjoy some new venture and those whose fear might undercut the army's courage. **10–15:** Besieged cities outside the promised land (*far from you*, v. 15) are to be offered terms. If they resist, all potential warriors are to be killed, but women and children may be enslaved and everything else plundered. **16–18:** By contrast, the entire population of an enemy city inside the promised land is to be put to the ban* and devoted to destruction (*you shall annihilate them*, v. 17). **19–20:** This limits the devastation of siege warfare.

21 If, in the land that the LORD your God is giving you to possess, a body is found lying in open country, and it is not known who struck the person down, 2then your elders and your judges shall come out to measure the distances to the towns that are near the body. 3The elders of the town nearest the body shall take a heifer that has never been worked, one that has not pulled in the yoke; 4the elders of that town shall bring the heifer down to a wadi with running water, which is neither plowed nor sown, and shall break the heifer's neck there in the wadi. 5Then the priests, the sons of Levi, shall come forward, for the LORD your God has chosen them to minister to him and to pronounce blessings in the name of the LORD, and by their decision all cases of dispute and assault shall be settled. 6All the elders of that town nearest the body shall wash their hands over the heifer whose neck was broken in the wadi, 7and they shall declare: "Our hands did not shed this blood, nor were we witnesses to it. 8Absolve, O LORD, your people Israel, whom you redeemed; do not let the guilt of innocent blood remain in the midst of your people Israel." Then they will be absolved of bloodguilt. 9So you shall purge the guilt of innocent blood from your midst, because you must do what is right in the sight of the LORD.

21.1–9: Unsolved murder. 1–2: The objective reality of bloodguilt endangers the nearest community. **3–4:** Guilt is eliminated by the death of a heifer and a symbolic ritual of hand washing. That the heifer *has never been worked* and the land *neither plowed nor sown* indicates that no human benefit has been derived from them. **6:** Washing hands *over the heifer* dramatically declares innocence and perhaps conveys the guilt to the carcass.

10 When you go out to war against your enemies, and the LORD your God hands them over to you and you take them captive, 11 suppose you see among the captives a beautiful woman whom you desire and want to marry, 12 and so you bring her home to your house: she shall shave her head, pare her nails, 13 discard her captive's garb, and shall remain in your house a full month, mourning for her father and mother; after that you may go in to her and be her husband, and she shall be your wife. 14 But if you are not satisfied with her, you shall let her go free and not sell her for money. You must not treat her as a slave, since you have dishonored her.

15 If a man has two wives, one of them loved and the other disliked, and if both the loved and the disliked have borne him sons, the firstborn being the son of the one who is disliked, 16 then on the day when he wills his possessions to his sons, he is not permitted to treat the son of the loved as the firstborn in preference to the son of the disliked, who is the firstborn. 17 He must acknowledge as firstborn the son of the one who is disliked, giving him a double portion*a* of all that he has; since he is the first issue of his virility, the right of the firstborn is his.

18 If someone has a stubborn and rebellious son who will not obey his father and mother, who does not heed them when they discipline him, 19 then his father and his mother shall take hold of him and bring him out to the elders of his town at the gate of that place. 20 They shall say to the elders of his town, "This son of ours is stubborn and rebellious. He will not obey us. He is a glutton and a drunkard." 21 Then all the men of the town shall stone him to death. So you

shall purge the evil from your midst; and all Israel will hear, and be afraid.

21.10–21: Laws for family life. 10–14: A female captive desired as a wife would have no male relatives to safeguard her rights. She is protected from a later reduction to slave status. Their sexual relationship (*you have dishonored her,* v. 14) establishes the husband's obligation. **15–17:** The law giving the oldest son a larger inheritance cannot be set aside because of favoritism. *Double portion* (v. 17) points to the custom of dividing an inheritance into shares equal to the number of sons plus one and giving the eldest two shares (but compare note a). **18–21:** Disrespect for both *father and mother* is the issue, and both parents must agree to take action. The seriousness of this offense is revealed by the extreme punishment, intended to be a public deterrent.

22 When someone is convicted of a crime punishable by death and is executed, and you hang him on a tree, 23 his corpse must not remain all night upon the tree; you shall bury him that same day, for anyone hung on a tree is under God's curse. You must not defile the land that the LORD your God is giving you for possession.

22 You shall not watch your neighbor's ox or sheep straying away and ignore them; you shall take them back to their owner. 2 If the owner does not reside near you or you do not know who the owner is, you shall bring it to your own house, and it shall remain with you until the owner claims it; then you shall return it. 3 You shall do the same with a neighbor's donkey; you shall do the same with a neighbor's garment; and you shall do the same with anything else that your neighbor loses and you find. You may not withhold your help.

4 You shall not see your neighbor's donkey or ox fallen on the road and ignore it; you shall help to lift it up.

5 A woman shall not wear a man's apparel, nor shall a man put on a woman's garment; for whoever does such things is abhorrent to the LORD your God.

6 If you come on a bird's nest, in any tree or on the ground, with fledglings or eggs,

a Heb *two-thirds*

with the mother sitting on the fledglings or on the eggs, you shall not take the mother with the young. 7 Let the mother go, taking only the young for yourself, in order that it may go well with you and you may live long.

8 When you build a new house, you shall make a parapet for your roof; otherwise you might have bloodguilt on your house, if anyone should fall from it.

9 You shall not sow your vineyard with a second kind of seed, or the whole yield will have to be forfeited, both the crop that you have sown and the yield of the vineyard itself.

10 You shall not plow with an ox and a donkey yoked together.

11 You shall not wear clothes made of wool and linen woven together.

12 You shall make tassels on the four corners of the cloak with which you cover yourself.

21.22–22.12: Laws of purity and community life. 21.22–23: Extended exposure of a hanged body would *defile the land,* putting it into a state of ritual impurity. **22.1–4:** This law revises Ex 23.4–5, widening the circle of neighborly responsibility. **5:** Impurity results from a blurring of culturally defined gender boundaries. **6–7:** This hints at good conservation practices and a respect for parental relationships even among animals (compare 14.21b). **8:** Houses had flat roofs used as living and working space. **9–11:** Forbidden mixtures cause impurity by violating distinctions made in creation. **12:** According to Num 15.38–40, *tassels* serve as reminders to obey the law.

13 Suppose a man marries a woman, but after going in to her, he dislikes her 14 and makes up charges against her, slandering her by saying, "I married this woman; but when I lay with her, I did not find evidence of her virginity." 15 The father of the young woman and her mother shall then submit the evidence of the young woman's virginity to the elders of the city at the gate. 16 The father of the young woman shall say to the elders: "I gave my daughter in marriage to this man but he dislikes her; 17 now he has made up charges against her, saying, 'I did not find evidence of your daughter's virginity.' But here is the evidence of my daughter's virgin-

ity." Then they shall spread out the cloth before the elders of the town. 18 The elders of that town shall take the man and punish him; 19 they shall fine him one hundred shekels of silver (which they shall give to the young woman's father) because he has slandered a virgin of Israel. She shall remain his wife; he shall not be permitted to divorce her as long as he lives.

20 If, however, this charge is true, that evidence of the young woman's virginity was not found, 21 then they shall bring the young woman out to the entrance of her father's house and the men of her town shall stone her to death, because she committed a disgraceful act in Israel by prostituting herself in her father's house. So you shall purge the evil from your midst.

22 If a man is caught lying with the wife of another man, both of them shall die, the man who lay with the woman as well as the woman. So you shall purge the evil from Israel.

23 If there is a young woman, a virgin already engaged to be married, and a man meets her in the town and lies with her, 24 you shall bring both of them to the gate of that town and stone them to death, the young woman because she did not cry for help in the town and the man because he violated his neighbor's wife. So you shall purge the evil from your midst.

25 But if the man meets the engaged woman in the open country, and the man seizes her and lies with her, then only the man who lay with her shall die. 26 You shall do nothing to the young woman; the young woman has not committed an offense punishable by death, because this case is like that of someone who attacks and murders a neighbor. 27 Since he found her in the open country, the engaged woman may have cried for help, but there was no one to rescue her.

28 If a man meets a virgin who is not engaged, and seizes her and lies with her, and they are caught in the act, 29 the man who lay with her shall give fifty shekels of silver to the young woman's father, and she shall become his wife. Because he violated her he shall not be permitted to divorce her as long as he lives.

30[a] A man shall not marry his father's wife, thereby violating his father's rights.[b]

22.13–30: Laws about sex and marriage. 13–19: Rather than simply exercising his right of divorce, the husband viciously slanders his unwanted wife. The *evidence of her virginity* (v. 14) is the bloodstain on the *cloth* (v. 17) on which the couple consummated their marriage. Both parents defend their daughter, but the father alone addresses the elders. The space around *the gate* (v. 15) was the standard location for legal business. **20–21:** *Disgraceful act* refers to outrageous behavior that violates community standards. **22:** Because she is the *wife of another man,* the adultery is seen as a violation of his rights. **23–27:** Engagement is the equivalent of marriage. Again it is only the husband's rights that are at issue (v. 24). The second case is rape: *The man seizes her* (v. 25). Fairness requires that she be given the benefit of the doubt. **28–29:** If the raped woman is not married or engaged, it is a crime against her father, who has suffered the loss of her bride price. The victim's respectable status as wife is permanently protected. **30:** Forbidding marriage to one's father's former wife protects the integrity of the extended family.

23 No one whose testicles are crushed or whose penis is cut off shall be admitted to the assembly of the LORD.

2 Those born of an illicit union shall not be admitted to the assembly of the LORD. Even to the tenth generation, none of their descendants shall be admitted to the assembly of the LORD.

3 No Ammonite or Moabite shall be admitted to the assembly of the LORD. Even to the tenth generation, none of their descendants shall be admitted to the assembly of the LORD, 4because they did not meet you with food and water on your journey out of Egypt, and because they hired against you Balaam son of Beor, from Pethor of Mesopotamia, to curse you. 5(Yet the LORD your God refused to heed Balaam; the LORD your God turned the curse into a blessing for you, because the LORD your God loved you.) 6You shall never promote their welfare or their prosperity as long as you live.

7 You shall not abhor any of the Edomites, for they are your kin. You shall not abhor any of the Egyptians, because you were an alien residing in their land. 8The children of the third generation that are born to them may be admitted to the assembly of the LORD.

9 When you are encamped against your enemies you shall guard against any impropriety.

10 If one of you becomes unclean because of a nocturnal emission, then he shall go outside the camp; he must not come within the camp. 11When evening comes, he shall wash himself with water, and when the sun has set, he may come back into the camp.

12 You shall have a designated area outside the camp to which you shall go. 13With your utensils you shall have a trowel; when you relieve yourself outside, you shall dig a hole with it and then cover up your excrement. 14Because the LORD your God travels along with your camp, to save you and to hand over your enemies to you, therefore your camp must be holy, so that he may not see anything indecent among you and turn away from you.

23.1–14: Laws guarding community purity. 1–6: As a sacral gathering, the *assembly of the LORD* must exclude anyone who would be ritually impure on a permanent basis. Any lack of bodily wholeness or being the offspring of an *illicit union* (v. 2) would cause this. Ammonites and Moabites had a history of intractable hostility to Israel (vv. 3–4). Moreover, Israel viewed both nations as deriving from incestuous relationships (Gen 19.30–38). **9–14:** The LORD as divine warrior* is present in the war camp (v. 14), so ritual impurity must be prevented.

15 Slaves who have escaped to you from their owners shall not be given back to them. 16They shall reside with you, in your midst, in any place they choose in any one of your towns, wherever they please; you shall not oppress them.

17 None of the daughters of Israel shall be a temple prostitute; none of the sons of Israel shall be a temple prostitute. 18You shall not bring the fee of a prostitute or the

a Ch 23.1 in Heb   *b* Heb *uncovering his father's skirt* wages of a male prostitute^a into the house of the LORD your God in payment for any vow, for both of these are abhorrent to the LORD your God.

19 You shall not charge interest on loans to another Israelite, interest on money, interest on provisions, interest on anything that is lent. 20On loans to a foreigner you may charge interest, but on loans to another Israelite you may not charge interest, so that the LORD your God may bless you in all your undertakings in the land that you are about to enter and possess.

21 If you make a vow to the LORD your God, do not postpone fulfilling it; for the LORD your God will surely require it of you, and you would incur guilt. 22But if you refrain from vowing, you will not incur guilt. 23Whatever your lips utter you must diligently perform, just as you have freely vowed to the LORD your God with your own mouth.

24 If you go into your neighbor's vineyard, you may eat your fill of grapes, as many as you wish, but you shall not put any in a container.

25 If you go into your neighbor's standing grain, you may pluck the ears with your hand, but you shall not put a sickle to your neighbor's standing grain.

23.15–25: Laws about harmony in relationships. 15–16: Asylum is granted to slaves who have fled from a foreign master. **17:** The words translated *temple prostitute* refer to prohibited female and male religious personnel of some kind, but not necessarily to any involvement with sex. **18:** Temple obligations must not be paid with money derived from ordinary prostitution or the earnings of "a dog" (note *a*), usually assumed to be a homosexual *male prostitute*. **19–20:** This law restates Ex 22.25. The wealthy are to assist poor Israelites with interest-free loans. **21–23:** A *vow* was a sacrifice promised in expectation of divine assistance. **24–25:** The landowner is protected from unfair exploitation by the poor, who were permitted to gather food in this way (24.19–22).

24 Suppose a man enters into marriage with a woman, but she does not please him because he finds something objectionable about her, and so he writes her a certificate of divorce, puts it in her hand, and

sends her out of his house; she then leaves his house 2and goes off to become another man's wife. 3Then suppose the second man dislikes her, writes her a bill of divorce, puts it in her hand, and sends her out of his house (or the second man who married her dies); 4her first husband, who sent her away, is not permitted to take her again to be his wife after she has been defiled; for that would be abhorrent to the LORD, and you shall not bring guilt on the land that the LORD your God is giving you as a possession.

5 When a man is newly married, he shall not go out with the army or be charged with any related duty. He shall be free at home one year, to be happy with the wife whom he has married.

6 No one shall take a mill or an upper millstone in pledge, for that would be taking a life in pledge.

7 If someone is caught kidnaping another Israelite, enslaving or selling the Israelite, then that kidnaper shall die. So you shall purge the evil from your midst.

8 Guard against an outbreak of a leprous^b skin disease by being very careful; you shall carefully observe whatever the levitical priests instruct you, just as I have commanded them. 9Remember what the LORD your God did to Miriam on your journey out of Egypt.

10 When you make your neighbor a loan of any kind, you shall not go into the house to take the pledge. 11You shall wait outside, while the person to whom you are making the loan brings the pledge out to you. 12If the person is poor, you shall not sleep in the garment given you as^c the pledge. 13You shall give the pledge back by sunset, so that your neighbor may sleep in the cloak and bless you; and it will be to your credit before the LORD your God.

14 You shall not withhold the wages of poor and needy laborers, whether other Israelites or aliens who reside in your land in one of your towns. 15You shall pay them their wages daily before sunset, because they

a Heb *a dog*   *b* A term for several skin diseases; precise meaning uncertain   *c* Heb lacks *the garment given you as* are poor and their livelihood depends on them; otherwise they might cry to the LORD against you, and you would incur guilt.

16 Parents shall not be put to death for their children, nor shall children be put to death for their parents; only for their own crimes may persons be put to death.

17 You shall not deprive a resident alien or an orphan of justice; you shall not take a widow's garment in pledge. [18]Remember that you were a slave in Egypt and the LORD your God redeemed you from there; therefore I command you to do this.

19 When you reap your harvest in your field and forget a sheaf in the field, you shall not go back to get it; it shall be left for the alien, the orphan, and the widow, so that the LORD your God may bless you in all your undertakings. [20]When you beat your olive trees, do not strip what is left; it shall be for the alien, the orphan, and the widow.

21 When you gather the grapes of your vineyard, do not glean what is left; it shall be for the alien, the orphan, and the widow. [22]Remember that you were a slave in the land of Egypt; therefore I am commanding you to do this.

24.1–22: Laws protecting social harmony. 1–4: Divorce was the sole prerogative of the husband, who could initiate it for even trivial reasons (vv. 1, 3). The woman receives a *certificate* or *bill of divorce* (the Hebrew phrase in vv. 1 and 3 is identical), clarifying her freedom to remarry. 6: The household *mill* ground daily bread needed for *life*. 7: This law restates Ex 21.16. 8–9: *Leprous skin disease* covers a wide range of ailments (note *b*). The Miriam incident is reported in Num 12.10–15. 10–13: These rules, restating Ex 22.26–27, defend the dignity of poor people who have defaulted on a loan and forfeited their collateral. 14–15: Workers who live from hand to mouth are protected from oppression, while employers are protected from guilt. 17–22: Israel's own experience of slavery motivates compassion for impoverished groups.

25 Suppose two persons have a dispute and enter into litigation, and the judges decide between them, declaring one to be in the right and the other to be in the wrong. [2]If the one in the wrong deserves to be flogged, the judge shall make that person

lie down and be beaten in his presence with the number of lashes proportionate to the offense. [3]Forty lashes may be given but not more; if more lashes than these are given, your neighbor will be degraded in your sight.

4 You shall not muzzle an ox while it is treading out the grain.

5 When brothers reside together, and one of them dies and has no son, the wife of the deceased shall not be married outside the family to a stranger. Her husband's brother shall go in to her, taking her in marriage, and performing the duty of a husband's brother to her, [6]and the firstborn whom she bears shall succeed to the name of the deceased brother, so that his name may not be blotted out of Israel. [7]But if the man has no desire to marry his brother's widow, then his brother's widow shall go up to the elders at the gate and say, "My husband's brother refuses to perpetuate his brother's name in Israel; he will not perform the duty of a husband's brother to me." [8]Then the elders of his town shall summon him and speak to him. If he persists, saying, "I have no desire to marry her," [9]then his brother's wife shall go up to him in the presence of the elders, pull his sandal off his foot, spit in his face, and declare, "This is what is done to the man who does not build up his brother's house." [10]Throughout Israel his family shall be known as "the house of him whose sandal was pulled off."

11 If men get into a fight with one another, and the wife of one intervenes to rescue her husband from the grip of his opponent by reaching out and seizing his genitals, [12]you shall cut off her hand; show no pity.

13 You shall not have in your bag two kinds of weights, large and small. [14]You shall not have in your house two kinds of measures, large and small. [15]You shall have only a full and honest weight; you shall have only a full and honest measure, so that your days may be long in the land that the LORD your God is giving you. [16]For all who do such things, all who act dishonestly, are abhorrent to the LORD your God.

17 Remember what Amalek did to you on your journey out of Egypt, [18]how he attacked you on the way, when you were faint and

weary, and struck down all who lagged behind you; he did not fear God. ¹⁹Therefore when the LORD your God has given you rest from all your enemies on every hand, in the land that the LORD your God is giving you as an inheritance to possess, you shall blot out the remembrance of Amalek from under heaven; do not forget.

25.1–19: Laws protecting members of society. 1–3: The dignity of the offender is preserved by proper supervision of punishment and limits to its severity. **4:** Even domestic animals have rights (compare 22.10). **5–10:** This custom (levirate marriage*) protects the deceased by ensuring him a son to inherit his property and carry on his name. It also protects the widow from the calamities of poverty and childlessness. It presupposes that these brothers *reside together* (v. 5) in an extended family. The living brother may refuse to perform his duty, but must then endure public shame. **11–12:** Her punishment is severe, perhaps because she has compromised the man's fertility. **13–16:** Commercial dishonesty undermines Israel's relationship with the LORD. **17–19:** This is reported in Ex 17.8–16.

26 When you have come into the land that the LORD your God is giving you as an inheritance to possess, and you possess it, and settle in it, ²you shall take some of the first of all the fruit of the ground, which you harvest from the land that the LORD your God is giving you, and you shall put it in a basket and go to the place that the LORD your God will choose as a dwelling for his name. ³You shall go to the priest who is in office at that time, and say to him, "Today I declare to the LORD your God that I have come into the land that the LORD swore to our ancestors to give us." ⁴When the priest takes the basket from your hand and sets it down before the altar of the LORD your God, ⁵you shall make this response before the LORD your God: "A wandering Aramean was my ancestor; he went down into Egypt and lived there as an alien, few in number, and there he became a great nation, mighty and populous. ⁶When the Egyptians treated us harshly and afflicted us, by imposing hard labor on us, ⁷we cried to the LORD, the God of our ancestors; the LORD heard our voice and saw our affliction, our toil, and our op-

pression. ⁸The LORD brought us out of Egypt with a mighty hand and an outstretched arm, with a terrifying display of power, and with signs and wonders; ⁹and he brought us into this place and gave us this land, a land flowing with milk and honey. ¹⁰So now I bring the first of the fruit of the ground that you, O LORD, have given me." You shall set it down before the LORD your God and bow down before the LORD your God. ¹¹Then you, together with the Levites and the aliens who reside among you, shall celebrate with all the bounty that the LORD your God has given to you and to your house.

12 When you have finished paying all the tithe of your produce in the third year (which is the year of the tithe), giving it to the Levites, the aliens, the orphans, and the widows, so that they may eat their fill within your towns, ¹³then you shall say before the LORD your God: "I have removed the sacred portion from the house, and I have given it to the Levites, the resident aliens, the orphans, and the widows, in accordance with your entire commandment that you commanded me; I have neither transgressed nor forgotten any of your commandments: ¹⁴I have not eaten of it while in mourning; I have not removed any of it while I was unclean; and I have not offered any of it to the dead. I have obeyed the LORD my God, doing just as you commanded me. ¹⁵Look down from your holy habitation, from heaven, and bless your people Israel and the ground that you have given us, as you swore to our ancestors—a land flowing with milk and honey."

26.1–15: First fruits and tithes. 4: The first symbolic presentation is made by the priest, who has access to the *altar of the LORD.* **5–9:** This creedal prayer reviews the history of salvation. *A wandering Aramean* refers to Jacob, linked in tradition with Syria ("Aram"; Gen 29–31). **10:** The farmer makes a second presentation of the basket. **11:** It is characteristic of Deuteronomy that impoverished social groups share in the feast. **12:** The tithe of the *third year* is distributed to the poor, not taken to the central sanctuary (14.28–29). **13–14:** As a *sacred portion,* the tithe must be kept from contact with *unclean* persons or forbidden activities.

16 This very day the LORD your God is commanding you to observe these statutes and ordinances; so observe them diligently with all your heart and with all your soul. 17Today you have obtained the LORD's agreement: to be your God; and for you to walk in his ways, to keep his statutes, his commandments, and his ordinances, and to obey him. 18Today the LORD has obtained your agreement: to be his treasured people, as he promised you, and to keep his commandments; 19for him to set you high above all nations that he has made, in praise and in fame and in honor; and for you to be a people holy to the LORD your God, as he promised.

26.16–19: Conclusion to the law. 17–18: *Today* refers to the day on which Deuteronomy was spoken (compare 15.5; 19.9). The LORD and Israel have agreed to abide by the principles of a covenant* relationship.

---

27 Then Moses and the elders of Israel charged all the people as follows: Keep the entire commandment that I am commanding you today. 2On the day that you cross over the Jordan into the land that the LORD your God is giving you, you shall set up large stones and cover them with plaster. 3You shall write on them all the words of this law when you have crossed over, to enter the land that the LORD your God is giving you, a land flowing with milk and honey, as the LORD, the God of your ancestors, promised you. 4So when you have crossed over the Jordan, you shall set up these stones, about which I am commanding you today, on Mount Ebal, and you shall cover them with plaster. 5And you shall build an altar there to the LORD your God, an altar of stones on which you have not used an iron tool. 6You must build the altar of the LORD your God of unhewn*a* stones. Then offer up burnt offerings on it to the LORD your God, 7make sacrifices of well-being, and eat them there, rejoicing before the LORD your God. 8You shall write on the stones all the words of this law very clearly.

9 Then Moses and the levitical priests spoke to all Israel, saying: Keep silence and hear, O Israel! This very day you have be-come the people of the LORD your God. 10Therefore obey the LORD your God, observing his commandments and his statutes that I am commanding you today.

11 The same day Moses charged the people as follows: 12When you have crossed over the Jordan, these shall stand on Mount Gerizim for the blessing of the people: Simeon, Levi, Judah, Issachar, Joseph, and Benjamin. 13And these shall stand on Mount Ebal for the curse: Reuben, Gad, Asher, Zebulun, Dan, and Naphtali. 14Then the Levites shall declare in a loud voice to all the Israelites:

27.1–13: The covenant* ceremony at Shechem. 4: *Mount Ebal* stands just north of Shechem, and Mount Gerizim (v. 12) rises to the south. **8:** These *stones* are the ones referred to in vv. 2–4, not the altar stones. **12–13:** The two groups are either receiving a blessing and curse spoken by the Levites (compare v. 14) or are proclaiming the blessing and curse themselves.

---

15 "Cursed be anyone who makes an idol or casts an image, anything abhorrent to the LORD, the work of an artisan, and sets it up in secret." All the people shall respond, saying, "Amen!"

16 "Cursed be anyone who dishonors father or mother." All the people shall say, "Amen!"

17 "Cursed be anyone who moves a neighbor's boundary marker." All the people shall say, "Amen!"

18 "Cursed be anyone who misleads a blind person on the road." All the people shall say, "Amen!"

19 "Cursed be anyone who deprives the alien, the orphan, and the widow of justice." All the people shall say, "Amen!"

20 "Cursed be anyone who lies with his father's wife, because he has violated his father's rights."*b* All the people shall say, "Amen!"

21 "Cursed be anyone who lies with any animal." All the people shall say, "Amen!"

22 "Cursed be anyone who lies with his sister, whether the daughter of his father or the daughter of his mother." All the people shall say, "Amen!"

a Heb *whole*   *b* Heb *uncovered his father's skirt*

23 "Cursed be anyone who lies with his mother-in-law." All the people shall say, "Amen!"

24 "Cursed be anyone who strikes down a neighbor in secret." All the people shall say, "Amen!"

25 "Cursed be anyone who takes a bribe to shed innocent blood." All the people shall say, "Amen!"

26 "Cursed be anyone who does not uphold the words of this law by observing them." All the people shall say, "Amen!"

27.14–26: Twelve curses. 15: Curses are powerful words that bring on unavoidable misfortune. The people's *amen* turns the destructive potential of each curse upon themselves. Most of these curses deal with actions committed *in secret* (also v. 24) that could not be controlled by public sanctions. **26:** This last summary curse motivates obedience to the entire law of Deuteronomy.

28 If you will only obey the LORD your God, by diligently observing all his commandments that I am commanding you today, the LORD your God will set you high above all the nations of the earth; 2all these blessings shall come upon you and overtake you, if you obey the LORD your God:

3 Blessed shall you be in the city, and blessed shall you be in the field.

4 Blessed shall be the fruit of your womb, the fruit of your ground, and the fruit of your livestock, both the increase of your cattle and the issue of your flock.

5 Blessed shall be your basket and your kneading bowl.

6 Blessed shall you be when you come in, and blessed shall you be when you go out.

7 The LORD will cause your enemies who rise against you to be defeated before you; they shall come out against you one way, and flee before you seven ways. 8The LORD will command the blessing upon you in your barns, and in all that you undertake; he will bless you in the land that the LORD your God is giving you. 9The LORD will establish you as his holy people, as he has sworn to you, if you keep the commandments of the LORD your God and walk in his ways. 10All the peoples of the earth shall see that you are called by the name of the LORD, and they shall be afraid of you. 11The LORD will make you abound in prosperity, in the fruit of your womb, in the fruit of your livestock, and in the fruit of your ground in the land that the LORD swore to your ancestors to give you. 12The LORD will open for you his rich storehouse, the heavens, to give the rain of your land in its season and to bless all your undertakings. You will lend to many nations, but you will not borrow. 13The LORD will make you the head, and not the tail; you shall be only at the top, and not at the bottom— if you obey the commandments of the LORD your God, which I am commanding you today, by diligently observing them, 14and if you do not turn aside from any of the words that I am commanding you today, either to the right or to the left, following other gods to serve them.

28.1–14: Blessings for obedience. 1: Israel's high status among the nations is a repeated theme (vv. 9–10, 13). **2:** A blessing is an effective power-laden word that brings about well-being and prosperity. These are conditional blessings, dependent on Israel's obedience (vv. 13–14). **4–5:** Israel often associated fertility (vv. 8, 11) and rain (v. 12) with the gods of Canaan, but here they are affirmed as blessings from the LORD.

15 But if you will not obey the LORD your God by diligently observing all his commandments and decrees, which I am commanding you today, then all these curses shall come upon you and overtake you:

16 Cursed shall you be in the city, and cursed shall you be in the field.

17 Cursed shall be your basket and your kneading bowl.

18 Cursed shall be the fruit of your womb, the fruit of your ground, the increase of your cattle and the issue of your flock.

19 Cursed shall you be when you come in, and cursed shall you be when you go out.

20 The LORD will send upon you disaster, panic, and frustration in everything you attempt to do, until you are destroyed and perish quickly, on account of the evil of your deeds, because you have forsaken me. 21The LORD will make the pestilence cling to you until it has consumed you off the land that

you are entering to possess. 22The LORD will afflict you with consumption, fever, inflammation, with fiery heat and drought, and with blight and mildew; they shall pursue you until you perish. 23The sky over your head shall be bronze, and the earth under you iron. 24The LORD will change the rain of your land into powder, and only dust shall come down upon you from the sky until you are destroyed.

25 The LORD will cause you to be defeated before your enemies; you shall go out against them one way and flee before them seven ways. You shall become an object of horror to all the kingdoms of the earth. 26Your corpses shall be food for every bird of the air and animal of the earth, and there shall be no one to frighten them away. 27The LORD will afflict you with the boils of Egypt, with ulcers, scurvy, and itch, of which you cannot be healed. 28The LORD will afflict you with madness, blindness, and confusion of mind; 29you shall grope about at noon as blind people grope in darkness, but you shall be unable to find your way; and you shall be continually abused and robbed, without anyone to help. 30You shall become engaged to a woman, but another man shall lie with her. You shall build a house, but not live in it. You shall plant a vineyard, but not enjoy its fruit. 31Your ox shall be butchered before your eyes, but you shall not eat of it. Your donkey shall be stolen in front of you, and shall not be restored to you. Your sheep shall be given to your enemies, without anyone to help you. 32Your sons and daughters shall be given to another people, while you look on; you will strain your eyes looking for them all day but be powerless to do anything. 33A people whom you do not know shall eat up the fruit of your ground and of all your labors; you shall be continually abused and crushed, 34and driven mad by the sight that your eyes shall see. 35The LORD will strike you on the knees and on the legs with grievous boils of which you cannot be healed, from the sole of your foot to the crown of your head. 36The LORD will bring you, and the king whom you set over you, to a nation that neither you nor your ancestors have known, where you shall serve other gods, of wood and stone. 37You shall become an object of horror, a proverb, and a byword among all the peoples where the LORD will lead you.

38 You shall carry much seed into the field but shall gather little in, for the locust shall consume it. 39You shall plant vineyards and dress them, but you shall neither drink the wine nor gather the grapes, for the worm shall eat them. 40You shall have olive trees throughout all your territory, but you shall not anoint yourself with the oil, for your olives shall drop off. 41You shall have sons and daughters, but they shall not remain yours, for they shall go into captivity. 42All your trees and the fruit of your ground the cicada shall take over. 43Aliens residing among you shall ascend above you higher and higher, while you shall descend lower and lower. 44They shall lend to you but you shall not lend to them; they shall be the head and you shall be the tail.

45 All these curses shall come upon you, pursuing and overtaking you until you are destroyed, because you did not obey the LORD your God, by observing the commandments and the decrees that he commanded you. 46They shall be among you and your descendants as a sign and a portent forever.

47 Because you did not serve the LORD your God joyfully and with gladness of heart for the abundance of everything, 48therefore you shall serve your enemies whom the LORD will send against you, in hunger and thirst, in nakedness and lack of everything. He will put an iron yoke on your neck until he has destroyed you. 49The LORD will bring a nation from far away, from the end of the earth, to swoop down on you like an eagle, a nation whose language you do not understand, 50a grim-faced nation showing no respect to the old or favor to the young. 51It shall consume the fruit of your livestock and the fruit of your ground until you are destroyed, leaving you neither grain, wine, and oil, nor the increase of your cattle and the issue of your flock, until it has made you perish. 52It shall besiege you in all your towns until your high and fortified walls, in which you trusted, come down throughout your land; it shall besiege you in all your towns

throughout the land that the LORD your God has given you. 53 In the desperate straits to which the enemy siege reduces you, you will eat the fruit of your womb, the flesh of your own sons and daughters whom the LORD your God has given you. 54 Even the most refined and gentle of men among you will begrudge food to his own brother, to the wife whom he embraces, and to the last of his remaining children, 55 giving to none of them any of the flesh of his children whom he is eating, because nothing else remains to him, in the desperate straits to which the enemy siege will reduce you in all your towns. 56 She who is the most refined and gentle among you, so gentle and refined that she does not venture to set the sole of her foot on the ground, will begrudge food to the husband whom she embraces, to her own son, and to her own daughter, 57 begrudging even the afterbirth that comes out from between her thighs, and the children that she bears, because she is eating them in secret for lack of anything else, in the desperate straits to which the enemy siege will reduce you in your towns.

58 If you do not diligently observe all the words of this law that are written in this book, fearing this glorious and awesome name, the LORD your God, 59 then the LORD will overwhelm both you and your offspring with severe and lasting afflictions and grievous and lasting maladies. 60 He will bring back upon you all the diseases of Egypt, of which you were in dread, and they shall cling to you. 61 Every other malady and affliction, even though not recorded in the book of this law, the LORD will inflict on you until you are destroyed. 62 Although once you were as numerous as the stars in heaven, you shall be left few in number, because you did not obey the LORD your God. 63 And just as the LORD took delight in making you prosperous and numerous, so the LORD will take delight in bringing you to ruin and destruction; you shall be plucked off the land that you are entering to possess. 64 The LORD will scatter you among all peoples, from one end of the earth to the other; and there you shall serve other gods, of wood and stone, which neither you nor your ancestors have known.

65 Among those nations you shall find no ease, no resting place for the sole of your foot. There the LORD will give you a trembling heart, failing eyes, and a languishing spirit. 66 Your life shall hang in doubt before you; night and day you shall be in dread, with no assurance of your life. 67 In the morning you shall say, "If only it were evening!" and at evening you shall say, "If only it were morning!"—because of the dread that your heart shall feel and the sights that your eyes shall see. 68 The LORD will bring you back in ships to Egypt, by a route that I promised you would never see again; and there you shall offer yourselves for sale to your enemies as male and female slaves, but there will be no buyer.

28.15–68: Curses for disobedience. 15: The preponderance of curses over blessings emphasizes the urgent need to reform. **16–19:** These curses correspond to the blessings of vv. 3–6. **23–24:** These curses oppose the blessing of v. 12. **25:** This malediction corresponds to v. 7. **43–44:** These curses counter vv. 12–13. **45–46:** A temporary conclusion is reached, but even more curses follow. **47–57:** In this second section, Israel's disobedience seems to be an inescapable certainty. The curses focus on the horrors of invasion and siege. **58–68:** This third section describes a systematic reversal of the LORD's saving acts.

29 [a] These are the words of the covenant that the LORD commanded Moses to make with the Israelites in the land of Moab, in addition to the covenant that he had made with them at Horeb.

2 [b] Moses summoned all Israel and said to them: You have seen all that the LORD did before your eyes in the land of Egypt, to Pharaoh and to all his servants and to all his land, 3 the great trials that your eyes saw, the signs, and those great wonders. 4 But to this day the LORD has not given you a mind to understand, or eyes to see, or ears to hear. 5 I have led you forty years in the wilderness. The clothes on your back have not worn out, and the sandals on your feet have not worn out; 6 you have not eaten bread, and you have not drunk wine or strong drink—so that you

a Ch 28.69 in Heb   b Ch 29.1 in Heb

may know that I am the LORD your God. 7When you came to this place, King Sihon of Heshbon and King Og of Bashan came out against us for battle, but we defeated them. 8We took their land and gave it as an inheritance to the Reubenites, the Gadites, and the half-tribe of Manasseh. 9Therefore diligently observe the words of this covenant, in order that you may succeed[a] in everything that you do.

10 You stand assembled today, all of you, before the LORD your God—the leaders of your tribes,[b] your elders, and your officials, all the men of Israel, 11your children, your women, and the aliens who are in your camp, both those who cut your wood and those who draw your water— 12to enter into the covenant of the LORD your God, sworn by an oath, which the LORD your God is making with you today; 13in order that he may establish you today as his people, and that he may be your God, as he promised you and as he swore to your ancestors, to Abraham, to Isaac, and to Jacob. 14I am making this covenant, sworn by an oath, not only with you who stand here with us today before the LORD our God, 15but also with those who are not here with us today. 16You know how we lived in the land of Egypt, and how we came through the midst of the nations through which you passed. 17You have seen their detestable things, the filthy idols of wood and stone, of silver and gold, that were among them. 18It may be that there is among you a man or woman, or a family or tribe, whose heart is already turning away from the LORD our God to serve the gods of those nations. It may be that there is among you a root sprouting poisonous and bitter growth. 19All who hear the words of this oath and bless themselves, thinking in their hearts, "We are safe even though we go our own stubborn ways" (thus bringing disaster on moist and dry alike)[c]— 20the LORD will be unwilling to pardon them, for the LORD's anger and passion will smoke against them. All the curses written in this book will descend on them, and the LORD will blot out their names from under heaven. 21The LORD will single them out from all the tribes of Israel for calamity, in accordance with all the

curses of the covenant written in this book of the law. 22The next generation, your children who rise up after you, as well as the foreigner who comes from a distant country, will see the devastation of that land and the afflictions with which the LORD has afflicted it— 23all its soil burned out by sulfur and salt, nothing planted, nothing sprouting, unable to support any vegetation, like the destruction of Sodom and Gomorrah, Admah and Zeboiim, which the LORD destroyed in his fierce anger— 24they and indeed all the nations will wonder, "Why has the LORD done thus to this land? What caused this great display of anger?" 25They will conclude, "It is because they abandoned the covenant of the LORD, the God of their ancestors, which he made with them when he brought them out of the land of Egypt. 26They turned and served other gods, worshiping them, gods whom they had not known and whom he had not allotted to them; 27so the anger of the LORD was kindled against that land, bringing on it every curse written in this book. 28The LORD uprooted them from their land in anger, fury, and great wrath, and cast them into another land, as is now the case." 29The secret things belong to the LORD our God, but the revealed things belong to us and to our children forever, to observe all the words of this law.

29.1–29: The covenant* made in Moab. 1: The covenant once made *at Horeb* (compare 5.2) is renewed *in the land of Moab,* just before Israel crosses into its new land (compare 1.5). **2–8:** The LORD's providence has been revealed through past events, but it is only now that these lessons can be understood (v. 4). **10–11:** The covenant community is all-inclusive, incorporating even resident *aliens** and menial servants. **14–15:** Deuteronomy's readers are also part of this covenant community. **19:** The obscure *moist and dry alike* (note *c*) means that all will suffer, innocent or guilty. **24–28:** An imagined dialogue warns of destruction and exile if the covenant is violated (compare 1 Kings 9.8–9). **29:** The LORD's ways will always remain a mystery* best left to God, but Israel's task is to obey *revealed things,* that is *the words of this law.*

---

a Or *deal wisely*   *b* Gk Syr: Heb *your leaders, your tribes*   *c* Meaning of Heb uncertain

30 When all these things have happened to you, the blessings and the curses that I have set before you, if you call them to mind among all the nations where the LORD your God has driven you, 2and return to the LORD your God, and you and your children obey him with all your heart and with all your soul, just as I am commanding you today, 3then the LORD your God will restore your fortunes and have compassion on you, gathering you again from all the peoples among whom the LORD your God has scattered you. 4Even if you are exiled to the ends of the world,ᵃ from there the LORD your God will gather you, and from there he will bring you back. 5The LORD your God will bring you into the land that your ancestors possessed, and you will possess it; he will make you more prosperous and numerous than your ancestors.

6 Moreover, the LORD your God will circumcise your heart and the heart of your descendants, so that you will love the LORD your God with all your heart and with all your soul, in order that you may live. 7The LORD your God will put all these curses on your enemies and on the adversaries who took advantage of you. 8Then you shall again obey the LORD, observing all his commandments that I am commanding you today, 9and the LORD your God will make you abundantly prosperous in all your undertakings, in the fruit of your body, in the fruit of your livestock, and in the fruit of your soil. For the LORD will again take delight in prospering you, just as he delighted in prospering your ancestors, 10when you obey the LORD your God by observing his commandments and decrees that are written in this book of the law, because you turn to the LORD your God with all your heart and with all your soul.

11 Surely, this commandment that I am commanding you today is not too hard for you, nor is it too far away. 12It is not in heaven, that you should say, "Who will go up to heaven for us, and get it for us so that we may hear it and observe it?" 13Neither is it beyond the sea, that you should say, "Who will cross to the other side of the sea for us, and get it for us so that we may hear it and observe it?" 14No, the word is very near to you; it is in your mouth and in your heart for you to observe.

15 See, I have set before you today life and prosperity, death and adversity. 16If you obey the commandments of the LORD your Godᵇ that I am commanding you today, by loving the LORD your God, walking in his ways, and observing his commandments, decrees, and ordinances, then you shall live and become numerous, and the LORD your God will bless you in the land that you are entering to possess. 17But if your heart turns away and you do not hear, but are led astray to bow down to other gods and serve them, 18I declare to you today that you shall perish; you shall not live long in the land that you are crossing the Jordan to enter and possess. 19I call heaven and earth to witness against you today that I have set before you life and death, blessings and curses. Choose life so that you and your descendants may live, 20loving the LORD your God, obeying him, and holding fast to him; for that means life to you and length of days, so that you may live in the land that the LORD swore to give to your ancestors, to Abraham, to Isaac, and to Jacob.

30.1–20. 1–10: Repentance leads to restoration. 1–5: Even exile will not mean the end of Israel's peoplehood if they repent (compare 4.29–31). **6:** In contrast to the demand of 10.16 that Israel do this, here it is the LORD who will remove all obstacles to wholehearted devotion (*circumcise your heart*). Love for the LORD will become second nature. **7–9:** Then the *curses* will fall on the *enemies* (v. 7), while Israel will enjoy the blessings (v. 9). **11–20: Choose life. 11–14:** This law is "user-friendly," easy to grasp and easy to accomplish. The impossibility of climbing up to *heaven* (v. 12) and the difficulty of crossing *the sea* (v. 13) were both proverbial. **15:** Israel's choice is simplicity itself: Obey and live, or disobey by worshipping other gods and perish. **19:** Ancient covenants* were witnessed by the gods of the parties involved. Here the witnesses are *heaven and earth*.

---

a Heb *of heaven*　　*b* Gk: Heb lacks *If you obey the commandments of the* LORD *your God*

31 When Moses had finished speaking all[a] these words to all Israel, 2he said to them: "I am now one hundred twenty years old. I am no longer able to get about, and the LORD has told me, 'You shall not cross over this Jordan.' 3The LORD your God himself will cross over before you. He will destroy these nations before you, and you shall dispossess them. Joshua also will cross over before you, as the LORD promised. 4The LORD will do to them as he did to Sihon and Og, the kings of the Amorites, and to their land, when he destroyed them. 5The LORD will give them over to you and you shall deal with them in full accord with the command that I have given to you. 6Be strong and bold; have no fear or dread of them, because it is the LORD your God who goes with you; he will not fail you or forsake you."

7 Then Moses summoned Joshua and said to him in the sight of all Israel: "Be strong and bold, for you are the one who will go with this people into the land that the LORD has sworn to their ancestors to give them; and you will put them in possession of it. 8It is the LORD who goes before you. He will be with you; he will not fail you or forsake you. Do not fear or be dismayed."

9 Then Moses wrote down this law, and gave it to the priests, the sons of Levi, who carried the ark of the covenant of the LORD, and to all the elders of Israel. 10Moses commanded them: "Every seventh year, in the scheduled year of remission, during the festival of booths,[b] 11when all Israel comes to appear before the LORD your God at the place that he will choose, you shall read this law before all Israel in their hearing. 12Assemble the people—men, women, and children, as well as the aliens residing in your towns—so that they may hear and learn to fear the LORD your God and to observe diligently all the words of this law, 13and so that their children, who have not known it, may hear and learn to fear the LORD your God, as long as you live in the land that you are crossing over the Jordan to possess."

14 The LORD said to Moses, "Your time to die is near; call Joshua and present yourselves in the tent of meeting, so that I may commission him." So Moses and Joshua went and presented themselves in the tent of meeting, 15and the LORD appeared at the tent in a pillar of cloud; the pillar of cloud stood at the entrance to the tent.

31.1–15: Preparing for the future. 1: The narrative* action picks up from where it stopped in 3.23–29. **3–8:** Attention shifts to Israel's future under Joshua (also vv. 14–15) and in the land (also vv. 9–13). **10:** The *year of remission* is described in 15.1–11 and the *festival of booths* in 16.13–15. **12–13:** No distinction is made between men and women; both need to *hear and learn* the law. Concern for the education of *children* is typical of Deuteronomy (6.2, 7). **14–15:** The LORD came to communicate with Israel from time to time at *the tent of meeting* (Ex 33.7–11).

16 The LORD said to Moses, "Soon you will lie down with your ancestors. Then this people will begin to prostitute themselves to the foreign gods in their midst, the gods of the land into which they are going; they will forsake me, breaking my covenant that I have made with them. 17My anger will be kindled against them in that day. I will forsake them and hide my face from them; they will become easy prey, and many terrible troubles will come upon them. In that day they will say, 'Have not these troubles come upon us because our God is not in our midst?' 18On that day I will surely hide my face on account of all the evil they have done by turning to other gods. 19Now therefore write this song, and teach it to the Israelites; put it in their mouths, in order that this song may be a witness for me against the Israelites. 20For when I have brought them into the land flowing with milk and honey, which I promised on oath to their ancestors, and they have eaten their fill and grown fat, they will turn to other gods and serve them, despising me and breaking my covenant. 21And when many terrible troubles come upon them, this song will confront them as a witness, because it will not be lost from the mouths of their descendants. For I know what they are inclined to do even now, before I have brought them into the land that

a Q Ms Gk: MT *Moses went and spoke*
b Or *tabernacles;* Heb *succoth*

I promised them on oath." 22That very day Moses wrote this song and taught it to the Israelites.

23 Then the LORD commissioned Joshua son of Nun and said, "Be strong and bold, for you shall bring the Israelites into the land that I promised them; I will be with you."

24 When Moses had finished writing down in a book the words of this law to the very end, 25Moses commanded the Levites who carried the ark of the covenant of the LORD, saying, 26"Take this book of the law and put it beside the ark of the covenant of the LORD your God; let it remain there as a witness against you. 27For I know well how rebellious and stubborn you are. If you already have been so rebellious toward the LORD while I am still alive among you, how much more after my death! 28Assemble to me all the elders of your tribes and your officials, so that I may recite these words in their hearing and call heaven and earth to witness against them. 29For I know that after my death you will surely act corruptly, turning aside from the way that I have commanded you. In time to come trouble will befall you, because you will do what is evil in the sight of the LORD, provoking him to anger through the work of your hands."

31.16–30: The song and the law as witnesses. 16: Moses predicts a disobedient future during which the song of Moses (vv. 19, 21) and the written law (v. 26) will serve as witnesses against Israel. Prostitution is a powerful metaphor* for Israel's disloyalty. **17–18:** *Hide my face* describes the removal of God's presence (compare 32.20). **19:** *Put it in their mouths* means to make them memorize it. **26:** The *book of the law* (Deuteronomy) is to be a concrete *witness* that Israel agreed to the terms of the covenant* they have broken (vv. 16, 20).

30 Then Moses recited the words of this song, to the very end, in the hearing of the whole assembly of Israel:

32

Give ear, O heavens, and I will speak;
　　let the earth hear the words of my mouth.
2 May my teaching drop like the rain,
　　my speech condense like the dew;

like gentle rain on grass,
　　like showers on new growth.
3 For I will proclaim the name of the LORD;
　　ascribe greatness to our God!

4 The Rock, his work is perfect,
　　and all his ways are just.
A faithful God, without deceit,
　　just and upright is he;
5 yet his degenerate children have dealt falsely with him,*a*
　　a perverse and crooked generation.
6 Do you thus repay the LORD,
　　O foolish and senseless people?
Is not he your father, who created you,
　　who made you and established you?
7 Remember the days of old,
　　consider the years long past;
ask your father, and he will inform you;
　　your elders, and they will tell you.
8 When the Most High*b* apportioned the nations,
　　when he divided humankind,
he fixed the boundaries of the peoples
　　according to the number of the gods;*c*
9 the LORD's own portion was his people,
　　Jacob his allotted share.

10 He sustained*d* him in a desert land,
　　in a howling wilderness waste;
he shielded him, cared for him,
　　guarded him as the apple of his eye.
11 As an eagle stirs up its nest,
　　and hovers over its young;
as it spreads its wings, takes them up,
　　and bears them aloft on its pinions,
12 the LORD alone guided him;
　　no foreign god was with him.
13 He set him atop the heights of the land,
　　and fed him with*e* produce of the field;
he nursed him with honey from the crags,
　　with oil from flinty rock;

a Meaning of Heb uncertain　　*b* Traditional rendering of Heb *Elyon*　　*c* Q Ms Compare Gk Tg: MT *the Israelites*　　*d* Sam Gk Compare Tg: MT *found*　　*e* Sam Gk Syr Tg: MT *he ate*

14 curds from the herd, and milk from the
        flock,
    with fat of lambs and rams;
    Bashan bulls and goats,
        together with the choicest wheat—
    you drank fine wine from the blood of
        grapes.
15 Jacob ate his fill;[a]
    Jeshurun grew fat, and kicked.
    You grew fat, bloated, and gorged!
    He abandoned God who made him,
        and scoffed at the Rock of his
        salvation.
16 They made him jealous with strange
        gods,
    with abhorrent things they provoked
        him.
17 They sacrificed to demons, not God,
        to deities they had never known,
    to new ones recently arrived,
        whom your ancestors had not feared.
18 You were unmindful of the Rock that
        bore you;[b]
    you forgot the God who gave you
        birth.

19 The LORD saw it, and was jealous;[c]
    he spurned[d] his sons and daughters.
20 He said: I will hide my face from them,
        I will see what their end will be;
    for they are a perverse generation,
        children in whom there is no
        faithfulness.
21 They made me jealous with what is no
        god,
        provoked me with their idols.
    So I will make them jealous with what
        is no people,
        provoke them with a foolish nation.
22 For a fire is kindled by my anger,
        and burns to the depths of Sheol;
    it devours the earth and its increase,
        and sets on fire the foundations of
        the mountains.
23 I will heap disasters upon them,
        spend my arrows against them:
24 wasting hunger,
        burning consumption,
        bitter pestilence.
    The teeth of beasts I will send against
        them,

with venom of things crawling in the
        dust.
25 In the street the sword shall bereave,
        and in the chambers terror,
    for young man and woman alike,
        nursing child and old gray head.
26 I thought to scatter them[e]
        and blot out the memory of them
        from humankind;
27 but I feared provocation by the enemy,
        for their adversaries might
        misunderstand
    and say, "Our hand is triumphant;
        it was not the LORD who did all this."

28 They are a nation void of sense;
        there is no understanding in them.
29 If they were wise, they would
        understand this;
    they would discern what the end
        would be.
30 How could one have routed a thousand,
        and two put a myriad to flight,
    unless their Rock had sold them,
        the LORD had given them up?
31 Indeed their rock is not like our Rock;
        our enemies are fools.[e]
32 Their vine comes from the vinestock of
        Sodom,
        from the vineyards of Gomorrah;
    their grapes are grapes of poison,
        their clusters are bitter;
33 their wine is the poison of serpents,
        the cruel venom of asps.

34 Is not this laid up in store with me,
        sealed up in my treasuries?
35 Vengeance is mine, and recompense,
        for the time when their foot shall slip;
    because the day of their calamity is at
        hand,
        their doom comes swiftly.
36 Indeed the LORD will vindicate his
        people,
        have compassion on his servants,

a Q Mss Sam Gk: MT lacks *Jacob ate his fill*
b Or *that begot you*   c Q Mss Gk: MT lacks *was jealous*
d Cn: Heb *he spurned because of provocation*
e Gk: Meaning of Heb uncertain

when he sees that their power is gone,
　　neither bond nor free remaining.
37 Then he will say: Where are their gods,
　　the rock in which they took refuge,
38 who ate the fat of their sacrifices,
　　and drank the wine of their libations?
Let them rise up and help you,
　　let them be your protection!

39 See now that I, even I, am he;
　　there is no god besides me.
I kill and I make alive;
　　I wound and I heal;
　　and no one can deliver from my
　　　　hand.
40 For I lift up my hand to heaven,
　　and swear: As I live forever,
41 when I whet my flashing sword,
　　and my hand takes hold on judgment;
I will take vengeance on my adversaries,
　　and will repay those who hate me.
42 I will make my arrows drunk with blood,
　　and my sword shall devour flesh—
with the blood of the slain and the
　　　　captives,
　　from the long-haired enemy.
43 Praise, O heavens,[a] his people,[b]
　　worship him, all you gods![b]
For he will avenge the blood of his
　　　　children,[c]
　　and take vengeance on his
　　　　adversaries;
he will repay those who hate him,[b]
　　and cleanse the land for his people.[d]

cannot understand that their earlier victories were the result of the LORD's abandonment of Israel. **35:** *Vengeance* (see vv. 41, 43) implies vindication of the LORD's rights as Israel's God and the restoration of Israel's status. **37–39:** In contrast to false gods, the LORD is the only one worthy of the designation "God." **40–42:** The LORD takes a war oath to be vindicated against all enemies. **43:** The poet calls upon the gods to praise the LORD as the victorious divine warrior* (restored text; notes a–d).

44 Moses came and recited all the words of this song in the hearing of the people, he and Joshua[e] son of Nun. 45When Moses had finished reciting all these words to all Israel, 46he said to them: "Take to heart all the words that I am giving in witness against you today; give them as a command to your children, so that they may diligently observe all the words of this law. 47This is no trifling matter for you, but rather your very life; through it you may live long in the land that you are crossing over the Jordan to possess."

48 On that very day the LORD addressed Moses as follows: 49"Ascend this mountain of the Abarim, Mount Nebo, which is in the land of Moab, across from Jericho, and view the land of Canaan, which I am giving to the Israelites for a possession; 50you shall die there on the mountain that you ascend and shall be gathered to your kin, as your brother Aaron died on Mount Hor and was gathered to his kin; 51because both of you broke faith with me among the Israelites at the waters of Meribath-kadesh in the wilderness of Zin, by failing to maintain my holiness among the Israelites. 52Although you may view the land from a distance, you shall not enter it—the land that I am giving to the Israelites."

32.1–43: The song of Moses. 1: God employs the format of a lawsuit to charge Israel with infidelity. The *heavens* and *earth* are called as witnesses to the lawsuit. **4:** The dominant poetic image is God as *Rock*, symbolizing strength and security (vv. 15, 18, 30, 31). **7–14:** Israel's story begins with their election as God's people. While dividing up the nations among the lesser gods (v. 8; note c), the LORD chose Israel as a personal inheritance (v. 9). **15–18:** The next stage is disobedience. *Jeshurun* (v. 15) is a poetic name for Israel, meaning "the upright one." God is portrayed as a mother *Rock* who gave birth to Israel (v. 18). **19–27:** Israel's treachery leads to punishment. The LORD moderates this punishment out of self-concern, not because Israel deserves it (vv. 26–27). **28–30:** The song concludes with God's vindication. The foolish enemy

32.44–52: Transition to the death of Moses. 46: *All the words* refers to the song and *this law.* Both will serve as future *witnesses* against Israel (31.19, 21, 26). **51:** According to Num 20.10–13, 24 and 27.12–14, Moses and Aaron sinned while securing water from the rock at *Meribath-kadesh* (Meribah).

a Q Ms Gk: MT *nations*　　b Q Ms Gk: MT lacks this line　　c Q Ms Gk: MT *his servants*　　d Q Ms Sam Gk Vg: MT *his land his people*　　e Sam Gk Syr Vg: MT *Hoshea*

33

This is the blessing with which Moses, the man of God, blessed the Israelites before his death. ²He said:

The LORD came from Sinai,
    and dawned from Seir upon us;*ᵃ*
    he shone forth from Mount Paran.
With him were myriads of holy ones;*ᵇ*
    at his right, a host of his own.*ᶜ*
³ Indeed, O favorite among*ᵈ* peoples,
    all his holy ones were in your charge;
they marched at your heels,
    accepted direction from you.
⁴ Moses charged us with the law,
    as a possession for the assembly of
        Jacob.
⁵ There arose a king in Jeshurun,
    when the leaders of the people
        assembled—
    the united tribes of Israel.

⁶ May Reuben live, and not die out,
    even though his numbers are few.

⁷And this he said of Judah:
    O LORD, give heed to Judah,
    and bring him to his people;
    strengthen his hands for him,*ᵉ*
    and be a help against his adversaries.

⁸And of Levi he said:
    Give to Levi*ᶠ* your Thummim,
    and your Urim to your loyal one,
    whom you tested at Massah,
    with whom you contended at the
        waters of Meribah;
⁹ who said of his father and mother,
    "I regard them not";
he ignored his kin,
    and did not acknowledge his children.
For they observed your word,
    and kept your covenant.
¹⁰ They teach Jacob your ordinances,
    and Israel your law;
they place incense before you,
    and whole burnt offerings on your
        altar.
¹¹ Bless, O LORD, his substance,
    and accept the work of his hands;
crush the loins of his adversaries,
    of those that hate him, so that they
        do not rise again.

¹²Of Benjamin he said:
    The beloved of the LORD rests in
        safety—
    the High God*ᵍ* surrounds him all day
        long—
    the beloved*ʰ* rests between his
        shoulders.

¹³And of Joseph he said:
Blessed by the LORD be his land,
    with the choice gifts of heaven
        above,
    and of the deep that lies beneath;
¹⁴ with the choice fruits of the sun,
    and the rich yield of the months;
¹⁵ with the finest produce of the ancient
        mountains,
    and the abundance of the everlasting
        hills;
¹⁶ with the choice gifts of the earth and its
        fullness,
    and the favor of the one who dwells
        on Sinai.*ⁱ*
Let these come on the head of Joseph,
    on the brow of the prince among his
        brothers.
¹⁷ A firstborn*ʲ* bull—majesty is his!
    His horns are the horns of a wild ox;
with them he gores the peoples,
    driving them to*ᵏ* the ends of the
        earth;
such are the myriads of Ephraim,
    such the thousands of Manasseh.

¹⁸And of Zebulun he said:
    Rejoice, Zebulun, in your going out;
    and Issachar, in your tents.
¹⁹ They call peoples to the mountain;
    there they offer the right sacrifices;
for they suck the affluence of the seas
    and the hidden treasures of the
        sand.

a Gk Syr Vg Compare Tg: Heb *upon them*
b Cn Compare Gk Sam Syr Vg: MT *He came from*
Ribeboth-kodesh, *c* Cn Compare Gk: meaning of Heb
uncertain *d* Or *O lover of the* *e* Cn: Heb *with his*
hands he contended *f* Q Ms Gk: MT lacks *Give to Levi*
g Heb *above him* *h* Heb *he* *i* Cn: Heb *in the bush*
j Q Ms Gk Syr Vg: MT *His firstborn* *k* Cn: Heb *the*
peoples, together

²⁰And of Gad he said:
Blessed be the enlargement of Gad!
    Gad lives like a lion;
    he tears at arm and scalp.
²¹ He chose the best for himself,
    for there a commander's allotment
      was reserved;
    he came at the head of the people,
    he executed the justice of the LORD,
    and his ordinances for Israel.

²²And of Dan he said:
    Dan is a lion's whelp
    that leaps forth from Bashan.

²³And of Naphtali he said:
    O Naphtali, sated with favor,
    full of the blessing of the LORD,
    possess the west and the south.

²⁴And of Asher he said:
    Most blessed of sons be Asher;
    may he be the favorite of his brothers,
    and may he dip his foot in oil.
²⁵ Your bars are iron and bronze;
    and as your days, so is your strength.

²⁶ There is none like God, O Jeshurun,
    who rides through the heavens to
      your help,
    majestic through the skies.
²⁷ He subdues the ancient gods,ᵃ
    shattersᵇ the forces of old;ᶜ
    he drove out the enemy before you,
    and said, "Destroy!"
²⁸ So Israel lives in safety,
    untroubled is Jacob's abodeᵈ
    in a land of grain and wine,
    where the heavens drop down dew.
²⁹ Happy are you, O Israel! Who is like
      you,
    a people saved by the LORD,
    the shield of your help,
    and the sword of your triumph!
    Your enemies shall come fawning to
      you,
    and you shall tread on their backs.

33.1–29: The blessing of Moses. 2–3: The LORD as divine warrior* advances into battle from the mountains of the southern wilderness, leading an army of heavenly beings (*holy ones;* but see note b). There are similar descriptions in Judg 5.4–5 and Hab 3.3–15. **5:** This *king* is Israel's triumphant God. *Jeshurun* (v. 26; 32.15) is a poetic name for Israel. **6:** Verses 6–25 form a collection of traditional sayings and wishes about the tribes similar to Gen 49. *Reuben* has dwindled and is struggling. **7:** A northern perspective is indicated by the absence of Simeon and a reference to the separation of Judah (*bring him to his people*). **8–11:** Several traditions describe the proverbial loyalty of *Levi* (Ex 17.1–7; 32.26–29; Num 25.1–13). *Thummim* and *Urim* (v. 8) were the sacred lots through which the LORD's will could be learned. Teaching God's *law* and offering sacrifice were basic priestly prerogatives (v. 10). **12:** *Benjamin* is protected by *shoulders,* either those of God or the slopes of their hills. **13–17:** *Ephraim* and *Manasseh* (v. 17; descended from Joseph,* Gen 48) are extolled for their military prowess, using the image of an aggressive bull. The tradition of the LORD as *one who dwells on Sinai* or "in the bush" (note *i*) is reflected in Ex 3.1–3. **18–19:** *Zebulun* and *Issachar* are known for their tribal sanctuary (probably on Mount Tabor) and the riches they enjoy from access to the Mediterranean Sea. **20–21:** *Gad* requested the rich territory east of the Jordan (Num 32.1–5, 16–19), thus choosing *the best for himself.* **22:** *Dan* is aggressive, like a lion *from Bashan.* **23–25:** *Naphtali* and *Asher* are acclaimed for their territory's fertility. To dip one's *foot in oil* (v. 24) is a metaphor* for enjoying abundance. **26–29:** The poem returns to the theme of the divine warrior (compare vv. 1–5), whose victory benefits Israel with a secure life in a rich land. Verse 27 is perplexing and suggested translations vary widely (notes *a–c*).

~~~~~~~~~~~~~~~~~~~~

34 Then Moses went up from the plains of Moab to Mount Nebo, to the top of Pisgah, which is opposite Jericho, and the LORD showed him the whole land: Gilead as far as Dan, ²all Naphtali, the land of Ephraim and Manasseh, all the land of Judah as far as the Western Sea, ³the Negeb, and the Plain—that is, the valley of Jericho, the city of palm trees—as far as Zoar. ⁴The LORD said to him, "This is the land of which I swore to Abraham, to Isaac, and to Jacob, saying, 'I will give it to your descendants'; I

---

a Or *The eternal God is a dwelling place*   *b* Cn: Heb *from underneath*   *c* Or *the everlasting arms*
d Or *fountain*

have let you see it with your eyes, but you shall not cross over there." 5 Then Moses, the servant of the LORD, died there in the land of Moab, at the LORD's command. 6 He was buried in a valley in the land of Moab, opposite Beth-peor, but no one knows his burial place to this day. 7 Moses was one hundred twenty years old when he died; his sight was unimpaired and his vigor had not abated. 8 The Israelites wept for Moses in the plains of Moab thirty days; then the period of mourning for Moses was ended.

9 Joshua son of Nun was full of the spirit of wisdom, because Moses had laid his hands on him; and the Israelites obeyed him, doing as the LORD had commanded Moses.

10 Never since has there arisen a prophet in Israel like Moses, whom the LORD knew face to face. 11 He was unequaled for all the signs and wonders that the LORD sent him to perform in the land of Egypt, against Pharaoh and all his servants and his entire land, 12 and for all the mighty deeds and all the terrifying displays of power that Moses performed in the sight of all Israel.

34.1–12: The death of Moses. 1–3: The narrative* continues directly from 32.52. From *Mount Nebo,* east of the north shore of the Dead Sea, Moses is shown a westward panorama from north (*Dan*) to south (*the Negeb* and *Zoar*). **4:** The reason that Moses had to die outside the land is never clearly stated (1.37; 4.21–22; 32.50–51). **7:** *One hundred twenty years* is the maximum life span according to Gen 6.3. A long and vigorous life was the expected reward for righteousness. **10:** Moses was a *prophet,* speaking to the people for God (5.27) and interceding for them (9.18–20, 25–29; 10.10–11). *Face to face* implies direct and unmediated communication.

HISTORICAL LITERATURE

Just as is the case with the Torah*/Pentateuch* (see 43–46), the literature that follows Deuteronomy in the Hebrew Bible is known in various ways. The Hebrew Scriptures* understands Joshua, Judges, Samuel, Kings, and all the individually titled prophetic books as the Nevi'im* or "prophets."* Joshua–Kings appear as the Former Prophets with Isaiah–Malachi as the Latter Prophets. There is no dominant Christian title for Joshua through 2 Kings, although one often finds the phrase "historical literature" in indices to Christian Bibles. The books included under this name differ from those that fall under the Jewish category of the prophets. Historical literature in this sense regularly includes not only Joshua through 2 Kings but also 1 and 2 Chronicles, Ezra, and Nehemiah in the Protestant Bible and also 1 and 2 Maccabees in the Roman Catholic canon* (and 3 Maccabees in the Orthodox canon). The book of Ruth appears between Judges and 1 Samuel in Christian Bibles, but it is not normally thought to be part of the historical literature. (See "Short Stories," 674)

The Jewish canonical title, "prophets," makes overt sense when applied to Isaiah–Malachi (in the Jewish canon, Daniel is not part of the "prophets"). Each of the books in the Latter Prophets is named for an individual who was remembered as a prophet. Less clear is the rationale for construing Joshua–Kings as "prophets." Moses, the hero of the Pentateuch, was thought to be similar to a prophet (Deut 18.15–18, 34.10). This is not true of his successor, Joshua, who was commanded to obey the book of the Torah as he led Israel into the land (Josh 1). Moving on to Judges, one finds charismatic heroes, individuals who were empowered by "the spirit of the LORD," (Judg 3.10). Such empowerment by "the spirit" is attributed to some (e.g., Ezek 37.1), though certainly not all of Israel's prophets. Further, Judges knows about both a prophet (Judg 6.8) and a prophetess (Judg 4.4). Still, in Joshua and Judges, prophetic matters occupy minimal space. This situation changes with the books of Samuel and Kings. In Samuel, one finds individuals known by various prophetic titles: Samuel was known as a "seer" (1 Sam 9.11) as was Gad (2 Sam 24.11). And early in the narratives* about David, Nathan, a "prophet" associated with David's court (2 Sam 7.2), appears. Then, in 1 and 2 Kings, prophets appear with considerable frequency. Elijah and Elisha are the most prominent, though other named (e.g., Micaiah son of Imlah [1 Kings 22], Huldah [2 Kings 22]) and unnamed prophets (1Kings 13) appear. Oddly, only two prophets who are associated with books in the Latter Prophets appear in Kings: Isaiah (2 Kings 19–20) and Jonah (2 Kings 14.25). So, as one moves through the presentation of Israel's history in the "former prophets," individual prophets become increasingly prominent. In addition, the books of Kings attest to a conviction about the power of prophetic words. Things happened so that a prophetic word would be fulfilled. For example, Ahijah the Shilonite announced that God would remove ten tribes from Solomon's control and grant them to Jeroboam (1 Kings 11.31–32). When this happened, the writer concluded, "it was a turn of affairs brought about by the LORD that he might fulfill his word, which the LORD had spoken by Ahijah the Shilonite to Jeroboam son of Nebat" (1 Kings 12.15). This same "prophecy-fulfillment" scheme could cover even longer periods of time. When narrating Nebuchadnezzar's attack on Judah, the writer claimed that this event was done "according to the word of the LORD that he spoke by his servants the prophets" (2 Kings 24.2). This biblical historian deemed prophetic words to shape history. These are at least some of the reasons why Joshua–Kings have been known as "prophets."

The category of historical literature as a description of Joshua–Kings is of a different sort. On the one hand, prophets refers, in the final analysis, to people—an Isaiah or a Hosea. One could contrast prophets with priests or scribes. On the other hand, historical literature refers to a kind of literature; other comparable categories include myth, saga, and legend.* The typical reader might have an easier time characterizing Joshua or 2 Kings as historical literature rather than as prophetic. Both of these biblical books portray events from the past. Topics typically found in political history, for instance, military conflict between nations, are prominent in both books. Both books highlight the exploits of certain individuals, for instance, Joshua and Josiah. Concern for a precise presentation of data, whether nations conquered (Josh 12) or chronology (2 Kings 8.25–26), appears in both books. These are the sorts of things one normally associates with historical literature.

This initial impulse to characterize books such as Joshua or 2 Kings as "historical" requires refinement. Scholars who study history regularly distinguish between *historiographic* literature and *historical* literature. Historiographic literature is the larger category; it includes historical literature but other types of literature as well. This broader category refers to the various forms of literature in which people refer to the past. In the ancient Near East, the past was recounted in various ways. There were, for example, king lists. As the title suggests, they were little more than names, sometimes accompanied by the dates of a king's reign. The Turin Canon, which recounts the names of pharaohs and the dates for their reigns, is a classic example. There are royal inscriptions in which a king might report that he had built a palace or temple. Annals also belong to the genre* of royal inscriptions; they are texts that report what happened on one or more military campaigns. And there are chronicles,* texts that report events relevant to a nation in chronological order and that can cover the reigns of multiple kings. For example, the Babylonian Chronicles extend from the eighth to the sixth centuries BCE. In sum, in the ancient cultural context out of which Israel emerged, there were many different ways in which the past could be presented.

Many scholars distinguish between the forms just identified and historical literature. The hallmarks of historical literature include a purpose for the writing, stated or clearly assumed, attention to a community about which the history is being written, and an attempt to identify reasons why things happened. In addition, history writing does not always concern itself with an accurate accounting of the past. More important is creating a statement about the meaning of that past.

The Hebrew Bible contains two major extended examples of historical literature: the primary history (Josh, Judg, 1 and 2 Sam, 1 and 2 Kings) and the secondary history (1 and 2 Chr, Ezra, Neh). The primary history is "introduced" by the Pentateuch. In fact, one standard view about the primary history is that Deuteronomy belongs with it. The so-called Deuteronomistic History* begins with Deuteronomy and concludes with 2 Kings. Both biblical histories are made up of diverse source material. The Deuteronomistic History includes everything from military annals to stories about prophets. The Chronicler's history is heavy with genealogies* and has added the major postscript of Ezra–Nehemiah. Both are written from distinctive theological perspectives.

The Deuteronomistic History has a number of distinctive features:

- **First,** it is divided into a series of periods: Mosaic leadership, Joshua and entry into the land, the judges, and that of the kings. The author of this historical work does not hesitate to offer judgments, either about individuals or on entire epochs. As for individuals, the narrator reports about King David, immediately after he had Bathsheba's husband killed, "but the thing that David had done displeased the LORD" (2 Sam 11.27). Moreover, the historian surveyed the end of the period of the judges and wrote, "In those days, there was no king in Israel; all the people did what was right in their own eyes." (Judg 17.6, 21.25; cf. 18.1, 19.1). This historian was interested in assessing both individuals and periods of time.

- **Second**, with the exception of the period of the judges, signal figures offer prominent speeches: Moses's discourses throughout Deuteronomy (for instance, 4.1–40); Joshua's two speeches at the end of that book (Josh 23, 24.2–15); Samuel's address introducing kingship (2 Sam 12); David's prayer (2 Sam 7.18–28); Solomon's prayer (1 Kings 8.22–53). These speeches give voice to what the biblical historian thought was important.
- **Third**, the ethos of the Sinai covenant,* as expressed in Exodus 20–24 and refracted in the covenant made on the plains of Moab (Deut 29), provides the primary theological underpinning for this historical work. Israel had entered into a covenantal relationship with Yahweh. The requirements of that relationship had been spelled out in comprehensive fashion: for instance, the deuteronomic law code (Deut 12–26) and summary, for instance, the Ten Commandments (Deut 5.6–21). If Israel obeyed the stipulations of the covenant, they could enjoy a blessed life (Deut 28.1–14). If, however, Israel did not conform to the norms of the covenant, they would be cursed (Deut 28.15–68). The deuteronomistic historian could explain military defeats as the arrival of these covenant curses.
- **Fourth**, although the law codes that are included in the Deuteronomistic History are comprehensive, addressing economic and political as well as religious issues, the standards that the historian uses to evaluate kings focus on religious issues. The first positive requirement present in the deuteronomic law code is that of worshiping Yahweh at the one place where the deity has chosen to place his name, namely, Jerusalem. This mandate allowed the deuteronomistic historian to offer a devastating critique of all the kings of the Northern Kingdom, since they followed Jeroboam's lead by worshiping at Israelite temples, most notably Bethel. The standard critique was: "He did what was evil in the sight of the LORD; he did not turn away from the sins of Jeroboam" (2 Kings 15.24). In addition, the historian indicts Judah's kings for worshiping "other gods." This happened as early as Solomon (1 Kings 11.4) and continued down to the reign of Josiah (2 Kings 23).
- **Fifth,** the history includes summaries that explain why and how things happen. The historian offers a mini-essay to explain why the Northern Kingdom was defeated, "This occurred because..." (2 Kings 17.7–23).
- **Sixth**, the Deuteronomistic History may well have been written in stages. One version may derive from the time of Hezekiah (2 Kings 18.5), another from that of Josiah (2 Kings 23.25a), and a final one from the early postexilic period (2 Kings 25.27–30).

In sum, the Deuteronomistic History is far more than a neutral annal of events that happened during the lives of Israel's history after the time of Moses. It is rather an expansive history that extends from the era of Moses to the time just after Judah and Jerusalem were destroyed. The history is written from a specific theological perspective, one associated with the covenant theology of the book of Deuteronomy.

The Chronicler's work also deserves to be known as historical literature—and also of a highly theological sort. However, it differs from the Deuteronomistic History in many ways due to the interests and goals of its author:

- It begins with the primeval age and Adam and continues down to members of the David lineage who would have been alive around 400 BCE (1 Chr 3). As such it is a history, written by the Judean community after many have returned from Exile,* after the Temple* has been rebuilt, and for a community that is focused on the Temple as the central point of its religious life.

- The Chronicler, like the deuteronomistic historian, appeals to sources, but they are of a different sort from those in the books of Kings. When concluding the report about Rehoboam's reign, the Chronicler refers to "records of the prophet Shemaiah and of the seer Iddo" (2 Chr 12.15). In the Deuteronomistic History, at this same point, the historian refers to "the Book of the Annals of the Kings." (1 Kings 14.29). According to Chronicles, the prophets had become historians; not so in the Deuteronomistic History.

- The Chronicler emphasizes a theology in which individuals receive their due in their lifetime. Here one may compare the two histories in their portrayal of Manasseh. According to 2 Kings 21, Manasseh reintroduced the veneration of gods other than Yahweh. As a result, the deity would destroy Jerusalem and Judah, but only many years after Manasseh's death. The Chronicler holds a different view, namely that Manasseh, whom the deuteronomistic historian recorded as having had a peaceful death, repented from his sins and therefore, deservedly, did not suffer for his sins (2 Chr 33). In similar fashion, the Chronicler indicts Josiah for not obeying God's word to him in order to offer a reason for his death on the battlefield (2 Chr 35.22). By way of contrast, Josiah's death remains unwarranted in the eyes of the deuteronomistic historian.

- David has a far more significant role in the Chronicler's history than he does in the Deuteronomistic History. He sets the stage not only for the building of the Temple but also for the service of worship that will be held there, even after the monarchy has fallen. In addition, the Chronicler does not include episodes that might put David in an unfavorable light, for instance, the episode with Bathsheba present in 2 Samuel 11. For the Chronicler, David was less important as a king than as a leader who instituted forms of worship that existed when Chronicles was written.

The historical works present in the Old Testament offer some of the most vivid and memorable narratives in the Bible (for instance, Samson and Delilah; David and Abigail, Elijah at Mount Carmel). These works are significant not only as history writing but also as literature of the highest order.

JOSHUA

Introduction

Joshua consists of three types of material. Narratives* of conquest under the leadership of the LORD, who fought for Israel as a warrior, make up Josh 2–11. Chapters 12–21 consist of geography in the form of lists and descriptions. Theological addresses constitute the book's introduction (ch. 1) and conclusions (chs. 23–24). Narrative, geography, and address all claim the land of promise for Israel. The individual stories in Joshua, which began as folktales about local victories, were written down and gathered into a connected narrative as the triumphs of a unified Israel (chs. 2–11). Later this story was re-edited (growing to chs. 1–12, 23) to form part of a history of Israel in the land told from the perspective of Deuteronomy's theology. Scholars call this larger work (Deuteronomy through 2 Kings except for Ruth) the Deuteronomistic* History. It was written just before or just after the end of the monarchy in Judah (late seventh or early sixth century BCE). Finally, the geographical material of chs. 13–21, the story of ch. 22, and a second conclusion in ch. 24 were added.

Israel's possession of the land was almost always endangered by outside attack or foreign rule. The threat came first from their local neighbors, but later from the major world empires of Assyria, Babylon, and Persia. The book of Joshua served generation after generation as a call to obedient loyalty to God and as a claim on the land God had promised them.

READING GUIDE

The narrative portions of Joshua, chs. 1–11, 22–24, are the most interesting. They may be read straight through as a connected story beginning with the death of Moses and ending with the death of Joshua. The reader should look for the interconnections among the individual stories: Rahab (ch. 2) leads to Jericho (ch. 6), which leads to Achan (ch. 7), which leads in turn to the capture of Ai (ch. 8), and so forth. It is a good idea to keep a map or Bible atlas open in order to follow the action. The geography of conquest falls into three campaigns: central (chs. 6–8), south (ch. 10), and north (ch. 11). In addition, it is helpful to read the battle reports from the perspective of holy war,* as presented in Deut 20.

1–12	Joshua conquers the land
13–21	Joshua divides the land
22–24	Warnings about the future

1 After the death of Moses the servant of the LORD, the LORD spoke to Joshua son of Nun, Moses' assistant, saying, 2"My servant Moses is dead. Now proceed to cross the Jordan, you and all this people, into the land that I am giving to them, to the Israelites. 3Every place that the sole of your foot will tread upon I have given to you, as I promised to Moses. 4From the wilderness and the Lebanon as far as the great river, the river Euphrates, all the land of the Hittites, to the Great Sea in the west shall be your territory. 5No one shall be able to stand against you all the days of your life. As I was with Moses, so I will be with you; I will not fail you or forsake you. 6Be strong and courageous; for you shall put this people in possession of the land that I swore to their ancestors to give them. 7Only be strong and very courageous, being careful to act in ac-

cordance with all the law that my servant Moses commanded you; do not turn from it to the right hand or to the left, so that you may be successful wherever you go. 8This book of the law shall not depart out of your mouth; you shall meditate on it day and night, so that you may be careful to act in accordance with all that is written in it. For then you shall make your way prosperous, and then you shall be successful. 9I hereby command you: Be strong and courageous; do not be frightened or dismayed, for the LORD your God is with you wherever you go."

1.1–9: The LORD commissions Joshua. 2: Joshua is to move westward across the river in order to give Israel possession of the land (v. 6). **3:** To walk over land was a way of legally claiming it. **4:** The idea that the land of promise extends to *the river Euphrates* reflects Deut 11.24 and royal ideology (Ps 72.8). **5:** The LORD as divine warrior* promises Joshua military success (see v. 3) and a supportive presence (v. 9). **7–8:** The theology reflects Deuteronomy: Undeviating obedience to the *book of the law* produces prosperity and success. Joshua is to be like the ideal king of Deut 17.18–20.

10 Then Joshua commanded the officers of the people, 11"Pass through the camp, and command the people: 'Prepare your provisions; for in three days you are to cross over the Jordan, to go in to take possession of the land that the LORD your God gives you to possess.'"

12 To the Reubenites, the Gadites, and the half-tribe of Manasseh Joshua said, 13"Remember the word that Moses the servant of the LORD commanded you, saying, 'The LORD your God is providing you a place of rest, and will give you this land.' 14Your wives, your little ones, and your livestock shall remain in the land that Moses gave you beyond the Jordan. But all the warriors among you shall cross over armed before your kindred and shall help them, 15until the LORD gives rest to your kindred as well as to you, and they too take possession of the land that the LORD your God is giving them. Then you shall return to your own land and take possession of it, the land that Moses the servant of the LORD gave you beyond the Jordan to the east."

16 They answered Joshua: "All that you have commanded us we will do, and wherever you send us we will go. 17Just as we obeyed Moses in all things, so we will obey you. Only may the LORD your God be with you, as he was with Moses! 18Whoever rebels against your orders and disobeys your words, whatever you command, shall be put to death. Only be strong and courageous."

1.10–18: Joshua commands the people. 11: These *three days* are concluded by 3.2. **12–15:** These tribes have already occupied land east of the Jordan. The command of Moses is reported in Deut 3.18–20. *Rest* (vv. 13, 15) is security in the land established by defeat of the enemy (21.44; 23.1). **17–18:** The eastern tribes agree with enthusiasm, but their double use of *only* introduces some tension into the plot. Will the LORD *be with* Joshua? Will Joshua *be strong and courageous?*

2 Then Joshua son of Nun sent two men secretly from Shittim as spies, saying, "Go, view the land, especially Jericho." So they went, and entered the house of a prostitute whose name was Rahab, and spent the night there. 2The king of Jericho was told, "Some Israelites have come here tonight to search out the land." 3Then the king of Jericho sent orders to Rahab, "Bring out the men who have come to you, who entered your house, for they have come only to search out the whole land." 4But the woman took the two men and hid them. Then she said, "True, the men came to me, but I did not know where they came from. 5And when it was time to close the gate at dark, the men went out. Where the men went I do not know. Pursue them quickly, for you can overtake them." 6She had, however, brought them up to the roof and hidden them with the stalks of flax that she had laid out on the roof. 7So the men pursued them on the way to the Jordan as far as the fords. As soon as the pursuers had gone out, the gate was shut.

8 Before they went to sleep, she came up to them on the roof 9and said to the men: "I know that the LORD has given you the land, and that dread of you has fallen on us, and that all the inhabitants of the land melt in fear before you. 10For we have heard how

the LORD dried up the water of the Red Sea*a* before you when you came out of Egypt, and what you did to the two kings of the Amorites that were beyond the Jordan, to Sihon and Og, whom you utterly destroyed. 11As soon as we heard it, our hearts melted, and there was no courage left in any of us because of you. The LORD your God is indeed God in heaven above and on earth below. 12Now then, since I have dealt kindly with you, swear to me by the LORD that you in turn will deal kindly with my family. Give me a sign of good faith 13that you will spare my father and mother, my brothers and sisters, and all who belong to them, and deliver our lives from death." 14The men said to her, "Our life for yours! If you do not tell this business of ours, then we will deal kindly and faithfully with you when the LORD gives us the land."

2.1–14: Rahab outsmarts the spies. 1: Rahab is a legally independent woman with her own *house,* where the presence of strangers would not be questioned. The spies apparently think this is a good place to gather information. **3:** *Come to you* (also v. 4) has a double meaning. Understood as "come into you" it can imply sexual intercourse. **6–7:** Although she saves them from the king, they find themselves trapped on her roof with the city gate shut. Their situation gives her leverage to negotiate an agreement. *The pursuers* block their route back, deepening their predicament. **8:** Rahab takes the initiative in the negotiations. **9–11:** She provides the content of the spies' eventual report (v. 24) and confesses that the LORD is the universal God (echoing Deut 4.39). Sihon and Og were *utterly destroyed* (v. 10), that is, devoted to destruction in holy war.* This is the fate Rahab seeks to avoid. **12–14:** She suggests a pact of reciprocal protection, and the spies agree. She has *dealt kindly* (v. 12) by showing faithfulness to the relationship between host and guest. In return they are to *deal kindly* by honoring an agreement to protect her extended family.

15 Then she let them down by a rope through the window, for her house was on the outer side of the city wall and she resided within the wall itself. 16She said to them, "Go toward the hill country, so that the pursuers may not come upon you. Hide yourselves there three days, until the pursuers

have returned; then afterward you may go your way." 17The men said to her, "We will be released from this oath that you have made us swear to you 18if we invade the land and you do not tie this crimson cord in the window through which you let us down, and you do not gather into your house your father and mother, your brothers, and all your family. 19If any of you go out of the doors of your house into the street, they shall be responsible for their own death, and we shall be innocent; but if a hand is laid upon any who are with you in the house, we shall bear the responsibility for their death. 20But if you tell this business of ours, then we shall be released from this oath that you made us swear to you." 21She said, "According to your words, so be it." She sent them away and they departed. Then she tied the crimson cord in the window.

22 They departed and went into the hill country and stayed there three days, until the pursuers returned. The pursuers had searched all along the way and found nothing. 23Then the two men came down again from the hill country. They crossed over, came to Joshua son of Nun, and told him all that had happened to them. 24They said to Joshua, "Truly the LORD has given all the land into our hands; moreover all the inhabitants of the land melt in fear before us."

2.15–24: The spies renegotiate. 15: It is difficult to reconcile the location of Rahab's house with the collapse of Jericho's wall in Josh 6. **16:** She is still in charge. These *three days* are difficult to correlate with the three days of 1.11 and 3.2. **17–20:** Once they are safely out of Rahab's trap, the spies seek to clarify their obligations in order to avoid violating them unintentionally. They insist on a conspicuous means of identification, strict concentration of Rahab's family in one place, and that their secret be kept. **24:** The spies report only what Rahab has told them (vv. 9, 11).

3 Early in the morning Joshua rose and set out from Shittim with all the Israelites, and they came to the Jordan. They camped there before crossing over. 2At the end of three days the officers went through the

a Or *Sea of Reeds*

camp ³and commanded the people, "When you see the ark of the covenant of the LORD your God being carried by the levitical priests, then you shall set out from your place. Follow it, ⁴so that you may know the way you should go, for you have not passed this way before. Yet there shall be a space between you and it, a distance of about two thousand cubits; do not come any nearer to it." ⁵Then Joshua said to the people, "Sanctify yourselves; for tomorrow the LORD will do wonders among you." ⁶To the priests Joshua said, "Take up the ark of the covenant, and pass on in front of the people." So they took up the ark of the covenant and went in front of the people.

7 The LORD said to Joshua, "This day I will begin to exalt you in the sight of all Israel, so that they may know that I will be with you as I was with Moses. ⁸You are the one who shall command the priests who bear the ark of the covenant, 'When you come to the edge of the waters of the Jordan, you shall stand still in the Jordan.' " ⁹Joshua then said to the Israelites, "Draw near and hear the words of the LORD your God." ¹⁰Joshua said, "By this you shall know that among you is the living God who without fail will drive out from before you the Canaanites, Hittites, Hivites, Perizzites, Girgashites, Amorites, and Jebusites: ¹¹the ark of the covenant of the Lord of all the earth is going to pass before you into the Jordan. ¹²So now select twelve men from the tribes of Israel, one from each tribe. ¹³When the soles of the feet of the priests who bear the ark of the LORD, the Lord of all the earth, rest in the waters of the Jordan, the waters of the Jordan flowing from above shall be cut off; they shall stand in a single heap."

14 When the people set out from their tents to cross over the Jordan, the priests bearing the ark of the covenant were in front of the people. ¹⁵Now the Jordan overflows all its banks throughout the time of harvest. So when those who bore the ark had come to the Jordan, and the feet of the priests bearing the ark were dipped in the edge of the water, ¹⁶the waters flowing from above stood still, rising up in a single heap far off at Adam, the city that is beside Zarethan,

while those flowing toward the sea of the Arabah, the Dead Sea,^a were wholly cut off. Then the people crossed over opposite Jericho. ¹⁷While all Israel were crossing over on dry ground, the priests who bore the ark of the covenant of the LORD stood on dry ground in the middle of the Jordan, until the entire nation finished crossing over the Jordan.

3.1–17: Crossing the Jordan. 3: The crossing is described as a religious procession led by the ark. **4:** Because the ark is dangerously holy (compare 2 Sam 6.6– 7), the people must keep their distance. **5:** To be ready for a miraculous event, the people are to perform a ceremony to make themselves holy. **7:** The concern raised by 1.17 is resolved here and in 6.27: The LORD is indeed *with* Joshua. **10:** As *the living God,* the LORD will be alive and active in the upcoming conquest. **12:** The selection of twelve men anticipates 4.2. **15:** That the Jordan *overflows all its banks* increases the wonder of the miracle and makes it possible for the priests' feet to touch *the edge of the water.* **16:** Because the flow *stood still* sixteen miles (twenty-five kilometers) upstream at *Adam,* the water that would have flowed downstream was *cut off.*

4 When the entire nation had finished crossing over the Jordan, the LORD said to Joshua: ²"Select twelve men from the people, one from each tribe, ³and command them, 'Take twelve stones from here out of the middle of the Jordan, from the place where the priests' feet stood, carry them over with you, and lay them down in the place where you camp tonight.' " ⁴Then Joshua summoned the twelve men from the Israelites, whom he had appointed, one from each tribe. ⁵Joshua said to them, "Pass on before the ark of the LORD your God into the middle of the Jordan, and each of you take up a stone on his shoulder, one for each of the tribes of the Israelites, ⁶so that this may be a sign among you. When your children ask in time to come, 'What do those stones mean to you?' ⁷then you shall tell them that the waters of the Jordan were cut off in front of the ark of the covenant of the LORD. When it crossed over the Jordan, the waters of the

a Heb *Salt Sea*

Jordan were cut off. So these stones shall be to the Israelites a memorial forever."

8 The Israelites did as Joshua commanded. They took up twelve stones out of the middle of the Jordan, according to the number of the tribes of the Israelites, as the LORD told Joshua, carried them over with them to the place where they camped, and laid them down there. 9 (Joshua set up twelve stones in the middle of the Jordan, in the place where the feet of the priests bearing the ark of the covenant had stood; and they are there to this day.)

4.1–9: Commemorative stones. 1: Verse 11 repeats words from this verse and 3.17 to indicate that vv. 2–10 happened while the crossing was still going on. **3:** The stones are temporarily deposited in the camp, but will be set up permanently at Gilgal (v. 20). **6–7:** The stones memorialize the crossing for future generations (compare Deut 6.20–25). This answer highlights the role of the *ark* and that the water was *cut off* (in contrast to vv. 22–24). **9:** What is apparently a second group of stones is installed in the river itself.

10 The priests who bore the ark remained standing in the middle of the Jordan, until everything was finished that the LORD commanded Joshua to tell the people, according to all that Moses had commanded Joshua. The people crossed over in haste. 11As soon as all the people had finished crossing over, the ark of the LORD, and the priests, crossed over in front of the people. 12The Reubenites, the Gadites, and the half-tribe of Manasseh crossed over armed before the Israelites, as Moses had ordered them. 13About forty thousand armed for war crossed over before the LORD to the plains of Jericho for battle.

14 On that day the LORD exalted Joshua in the sight of all Israel; and they stood in awe of him, as they had stood in awe of Moses, all the days of his life.

15 The LORD said to Joshua, 16"Command the priests who bear the ark of the covenant,ᵃ to come up out of the Jordan." 17Joshua therefore commanded the priests, "Come up out of the Jordan." 18When the priests bearing the ark of the covenant of the LORD came up from the middle of the Jor-

dan, and the soles of the priests' feet touched dry ground, the waters of the Jordan returned to their place and overflowed all its banks, as before.

19 The people came up out of the Jordan on the tenth day of the first month, and they camped in Gilgal on the east border of Jericho. 20Those twelve stones, which they had taken out of the Jordan, Joshua set up in Gilgal, 21 saying to the Israelites, "When your children ask their parents in time to come, 'What do these stones mean?' 22then you shall let your children know, 'Israel crossed over the Jordan here on dry ground.' 23For the LORD your God dried up the waters of the Jordan for you until you crossed over, as the LORD your God did to the Red Sea,ᵇ which he dried up for us until we crossed over, 24so that all the peoples of the earth may know that the hand of the LORD is mighty, and so that you may fear the LORD your God forever."

4.10–24: The crossing completed. 11: The action of crossing is picked up again from v. 1. **12–13:** Particular mention of the eastern tribes emphasizes that all Israel engaged in the conquest together, a motif* also present in Deut 3.18–20. **14:** This exaltation fulfills the pledge of 3.7. **18:** The events of 3.15–16 are reversed item by item. **19:** The date points forward to Passover* in 5.10. **22–24:** This answer (in contrast to vv. 6–7) focuses on similarities to crossing the Red Sea on *dry ground* (Ex 14.22).

5 When all the kings of the Amorites beyond the Jordan to the west, and all the kings of the Canaanites by the sea, heard that the LORD had dried up the waters of the Jordan for the Israelites until they had crossed over, their hearts melted, and there was no longer any spirit in them, because of the Israelites.

2 At that time the LORD said to Joshua, "Make flint knives and circumcise the Israelites a second time." 3So Joshua made flint knives, and circumcised the Israelites at Gibeath-haaraloth.ᶜ 4This is the reason why Joshua circumcised them: all the males of

a Or *treaty*, or *testimony*; Heb *eduth*   *b* Or *Sea of Reeds*   *c* That is *the Hill of the Foreskins* the people who came out of Egypt, all the warriors, had died during the journey through the wilderness after they had come out of Egypt. ⁵Although all the people who came out had been circumcised, yet all the people born on the journey through the wilderness after they had come out of Egypt had not been circumcised. ⁶For the Israelites traveled forty years in the wilderness, until all the nation, the warriors who came out of Egypt, perished, not having listened to the voice of the Lord. To them the Lord swore that he would not let them see the land that he had sworn to their ancestors to give us, a land flowing with milk and honey. ⁷So it was their children, whom he raised up in their place, that Joshua circumcised; for they were uncircumcised, because they had not been circumcised on the way.

8 When the circumcising of all the nation was done, they remained in their places in the camp until they were healed. ⁹The Lord said to Joshua, "Today I have rolled away from you the disgrace of Egypt." And so that place is called Gilgal*a* to this day.

10 While the Israelites were camped in Gilgal they kept the passover in the evening on the fourteenth day of the month in the plains of Jericho. ¹¹On the day after the passover, on that very day, they ate the produce of the land, unleavened cakes and parched grain. ¹²The manna ceased on the day they ate the produce of the land, and the Israelites no longer had manna; they ate the crops of the land of Canaan that year.

5.1–12: A new start in a new land. 1: Enemy fear repeats Rahab's observations (2.9–11) and will motivate enemy strategy (9.1–2; 10.1–5; 11.1–5). 2: The use of *flint knives* demonstrates the conservatism of ritual. Israel's circumcised generation had died in the wilderness. Circumcision★ *a second time* applies to the men of the post-exodus generation. 3: Apparently this explains the name of a hill near Gilgal (note c). 9: *The disgrace of Egypt* may refer to Israel's former status as slaves or insults suffered from the Egyptians. Probably *Gilgal* originally referred to a circle of stones, but here it is explained by reference to Joshua's circumcision (note a). 11–12: The end of manna coordinates with the first Passover★ in the land. It signifies that Israel has moved from the wilderness into an agriculturally pro-

ductive land. *Unleavened cakes* and *parched grain* could be prepared quickly and would be appropriate foods for the first day of this new situation.

13 Once when Joshua was by Jericho, he looked up and saw a man standing before him with a drawn sword in his hand. Joshua went to him and said to him, "Are you one of us, or one of our adversaries?" ¹⁴He replied, "Neither; but as commander of the army of the Lord I have now come." And Joshua fell on his face to the earth and worshiped, and he said to him, "What do you command your servant, my lord?" ¹⁵The commander of the army of the Lord said to Joshua, "Remove the sandals from your feet, for the place where you stand is holy." And Joshua did so.

5.13–15: The commander of the Lord's army. 13: *By Jericho* must be understood as "in the general vicinity of Jericho." The *drawn sword* indicates that war is imminent. Apparently assuming that the *man* is a human soldier, Joshua challenges him. 14: The commander is not part of either human army, but a visible sign that the Lord's supernatural forces will be fighting for Israel. 15: A quotation from Ex 3.5 draws a parallel between Joshua and Moses.

6 Now Jericho was shut up inside and out because of the Israelites; no one came out and no one went in. ²The Lord said to Joshua, "See, I have handed Jericho over to you, along with its king and soldiers. ³You shall march around the city, all the warriors circling the city once. Thus you shall do for six days, ⁴with seven priests bearing seven trumpets of rams' horns before the ark. On the seventh day you shall march around the city seven times, the priests blowing the trumpets. ⁵When they make a long blast with the ram's horn, as soon as you hear the sound of the trumpet, then all the people shall shout with a great shout; and the wall of the city will fall down flat, and all the people shall charge straight ahead." ⁶So Joshua son of Nun summoned the priests and said to them, "Take up the ark of the covenant, and have seven priests carry seven trumpets

a Related to Heb *galal* to roll

of rams' horns in front of the ark of the LORD." 7To the people he said, "Go forward and march around the city; have the armed men pass on before the ark of the LORD."

8 As Joshua had commanded the people, the seven priests carrying the seven trumpets of rams' horns before the LORD went forward, blowing the trumpets, with the ark of the covenant of the LORD following them. 9And the armed men went before the priests who blew the trumpets; the rear guard came after the ark, while the trumpets blew continually. 10To the people Joshua gave this command: "You shall not shout or let your voice be heard, nor shall you utter a word, until the day I tell you to shout. Then you shall shout." 11So the ark of the LORD went around the city, circling it once; and they came into the camp, and spent the night in the camp.

12 Then Joshua rose early in the morning, and the priests took up the ark of the LORD. 13The seven priests carrying the seven trumpets of rams' horns before the ark of the LORD passed on, blowing the trumpets continually. The armed men went before them, and the rear guard came after the ark of the LORD, while the trumpets blew continually. 14On the second day they marched around the city once and then returned to the camp. They did this for six days.

15 On the seventh day they rose early, at dawn, and marched around the city in the same manner seven times. It was only on that day that they marched around the city seven times. 16And at the seventh time, when the priests had blown the trumpets, Joshua said to the people, "Shout! For the LORD has given you the city. 17The city and all that is in it shall be devoted to the LORD for destruction. Only Rahab the prostitute and all who are with her in her house shall live because she hid the messengers we sent. 18As for you, keep away from the things devoted to destruction, so as not to covet[a] and take any of the devoted things and make the camp of Israel an object for destruction, bringing trouble upon it. 19But all silver and gold, and vessels of bronze and iron, are sacred to the LORD; they shall go into the treasury of the LORD." 20So the people shouted,

and the trumpets were blown. As soon as the people heard the sound of the trumpets, they raised a great shout, and the wall fell down flat; so the people charged straight ahead into the city and captured it. 21Then they devoted to destruction by the edge of the sword all in the city, both men and women, young and old, oxen, sheep, and donkeys.

6.1–21: The capture of Jericho. 1: The problem facing Israel is Jericho's impregnable defensive wall. 2: An assurance of victory was part of holy war* tradition (8.1; 10.8). 3: Israel is to engage in a ceremonial siege. 5: A *long blast* on a trumpet will signal the attack, and *a great shout* will initiate it (vv. 16, 20). Both are part of holy war tradition. 8–9: The order of march is: *armed men* followed by *seven priests* with trumpets, then *the ark,* and finally *the rear guard.* 18: To *take any of the devoted things* would put Israel itself under the ban* (*an object for destruction*) by the principle of contagion. This will be Achan's crime (7.21). 20: Israel makes an assault from all sides at once.

~~~~~~

22 Joshua said to the two men who had spied out the land, "Go into the prostitute's house, and bring the woman out of it and all who belong to her, as you swore to her." 23So the young men who had been spies went in and brought Rahab out, along with her father, her mother, her brothers, and all who belonged to her—they brought all her kindred out—and set them outside the camp of Israel. 24They burned down the city, and everything in it; only the silver and gold, and the vessels of bronze and iron, they put into the treasury of the house of the LORD. 25But Rahab the prostitute, with her family and all who belonged to her, Joshua spared. Her family[b] has lived in Israel ever since. For she hid the messengers whom Joshua sent to spy out Jericho.

26 Joshua then pronounced this oath, saying,

"Cursed before the LORD be anyone
    who tries
  to build this city—this Jericho!

a Gk: Heb *devote to destruction* Compare 7.21
b Heb *She*

The Spoils of Holy War

Because it was the divine warrior* who achieved Israel's victories, booty won in holy war* belonged partly or entirely to the LORD. Such booty fell under the ban* (Heb., "herem"; NRSV "devote to destruction," "utterly destroy," "annihilate"). It belonged irrevocably to the LORD and had to be kept from human use. As potential slaves, the entire enemy population routinely fell under the ban and was to be killed (Deut 20.16–17). Normally, non-living booty and cattle did not come under the ban (8.2; 11.14), but Jericho is a special case. Its domestic animals are killed along with its people (v. 21), and valuable metals are deposited in the sanctuary (vv. 19, 24).

At the cost of his firstborn he shall lay
    its foundation,
and at the cost of his youngest he
    shall set up its gates!"

27 So the LORD was with Joshua; and his fame was in all the land.

6.22–27: The aftermath of Jericho's fall. 23: Rahab's family stays *outside the camp* because the holy war* encampment must remain ritually clean (Deut 23.9–14). **25:** The Rahab story explains and justifies the existence of a foreign group still living *in Israel*. **26:** Joshua caps Jericho's state of being banned* (devoted to destruction; v. 21) with a curse blocking its reconstruction (compare Deut 13.16). 1 Kings 16.34 reports the consequences of this curse.

7 But the Israelites broke faith in regard to the devoted things: Achan son of Carmi son of Zabdi son of Zerah, of the tribe of Judah, took some of the devoted things; and the anger of the LORD burned against the Israelites. 2 Joshua sent men from Jericho to Ai, which is near Beth-aven, east of Bethel, and said to them, "Go up and spy out the land." And the men went up and spied out Ai. 3 Then they returned to Joshua and said to him, "Not all the people need go up; about two or three thousand men should go up and attack Ai. Since they are so few, do not make the whole people toil up there." 4 So about three thousand of the people went up there; and they fled before the men of Ai. 5 The men of Ai killed about thirty-six of them, chasing them from outside the gate as far as Sheb-

arim and killing them on the slope. The hearts of the people melted and turned to water.

6 Then Joshua tore his clothes, and fell to the ground on his face before the ark of the LORD until the evening, he and the elders of Israel; and they put dust on their heads. 7 Joshua said, "Ah, Lord GOD! Why have you brought this people across the Jordan at all, to hand us over to the Amorites so as to destroy us? Would that we had been content to settle beyond the Jordan! 8 O Lord, what can I say, now that Israel has turned their backs to their enemies! 9 The Canaanites and all the inhabitants of the land will hear of it, and surround us, and cut off our name from the earth. Then what will you do for your great name?"

10 The LORD said to Joshua, "Stand up! Why have you fallen upon your face? 11 Israel has sinned; they have transgressed my covenant that I imposed on them. They have taken some of the devoted things; they have stolen, they have acted deceitfully, and they have put them among their own belongings. 12 Therefore the Israelites are unable to stand before their enemies; they turn their backs to their enemies, because they have become a thing devoted for destruction themselves. I will be with you no more, unless you destroy the devoted things from among you. 13 Proceed to sanctify the people, and say, 'Sanctify yourselves for tomorrow; for thus says the LORD, the God of Israel, "There are devoted things among you, O Israel; you will be unable to stand before

your enemies until you take away the devoted things from among you." [14]In the morning therefore you shall come forward tribe by tribe. The tribe that the LORD takes shall come near by clans, the clan that the LORD takes shall come near by households, and the household that the LORD takes shall come near one by one. [15]And the one who is taken as having the devoted things shall be burned with fire, together with all that he has, for having transgressed the covenant of the LORD, and for having done an outrageous thing in Israel.' "

7.1–15: The consequences of Achan's sin. 1: Achan, a man of impeccable ancestry, has ignored Joshua's explicit warning concerning the ban* (6.18). He acted alone, but the principle of corporate responsibility means that all *the Israelites broke faith* (also v. 11). Thus *the anger of the LORD* is directed against the entire nation. **2:** Sending spies was a typical first step in a campaign (2.1; Judg 1.23). **5:** Such a great panic associated with only *thirty-six* deaths indicates something is seriously amiss. Israel experiences the fear their enemies have felt: *The hearts of the people melted* (contrast 2.11; 5.1). **7–9:** Joshua follows the pattern of typical lament* prayers such as Ps 44 or 74. He questions the LORD's motives and seeks to provoke a response by highlighting the potential damage to the LORD's reputation (*great name*). **11:** As a violation of the *covenant** (also v. 15), Achan's crime endangers Israel's relationship with the LORD in a fundamental way. **12:** The contagious effect of items *devoted for destruction* (compare 6.18) means that the entire nation has fallen under the ban. **13:** The people must engage in a ceremony to make themselves holy in order to prepare for contact with God's action (compare 3.5). **14:** The procedure for discovering the culprit involves the use of the sacred lot (1 Sam 14.40–42). **15:** An *outrageous thing in Israel* means a heinous crime against society that endangers the whole nation.

[16] So Joshua rose early in the morning, and brought Israel near tribe by tribe, and the tribe of Judah was taken. [17]He brought near the clans of Judah, and the clan of the Zerahites was taken; and he brought near the clan of the Zerahites, family by family,[a] and Zabdi was taken. [18]And he brought near his household one by one, and Achan son of Carmi son of Zabdi son of Zerah, of the tribe

of Judah, was taken. [19]Then Joshua said to Achan, "My son, give glory to the LORD God of Israel and make confession to him. Tell me now what you have done; do not hide it from me." [20]And Achan answered Joshua, "It is true; I am the one who sinned against the LORD God of Israel. This is what I did: [21]when I saw among the spoil a beautiful mantle from Shinar, and two hundred shekels of silver, and a bar of gold weighing fifty shekels, then I coveted them and took them. They now lie hidden in the ground inside my tent, with the silver underneath."

[22] So Joshua sent messengers, and they ran to the tent; and there it was, hidden in his tent with the silver underneath. [23]They took them out of the tent and brought them to Joshua and all the Israelites; and they spread them out before the LORD. [24]Then Joshua and all Israel with him took Achan son of Zerah, with the silver, the mantle, and the bar of gold, with his sons and daughters, with his oxen, donkeys, and sheep, and his tent and all that he had; and they brought them up to the Valley of Achor. [25]Joshua said, "Why did you bring trouble on us? The LORD is bringing trouble on you today." And all Israel stoned him to death; they burned them with fire, cast stones on them, [26]and raised over him a great heap of stones that remains to this day. Then the LORD turned from his burning anger. Therefore that place to this day is called the Valley of Achor.[b]

7.16–26: Discovery and punishment. 16–18: That *Joshua rose early in the morning* signals obedient zeal (3.1; 6.12). The sacred lot gave only a yes or no answer, so the discovery process moves down through smaller and smaller social units: *tribe, clan,** family (household). **19:** Because confession acknowledges God's justice, it is the equivalent of giving *glory to the LORD.* **21:** Cloth, silver, and gold are typical items of plunder (2 Kings 7.8). The *mantle from Shinar* would be a costly outer robe imported from Babylon. **22:** Discovery of *the silver underneath* (v. 21) communicates the complete accuracy of Achan's confession. **25–26:** The *trouble* (better: "state of ritual isolation"; 6.18) brought on by Achan connects to the *Valley of Achor*

a Mss Syr: MT *man by man*   *b* That is *Trouble*

(note b), where later generations could view the stone pile that marked his grave.

8 Then the LORD said to Joshua, "Do not fear or be dismayed; take all the fighting men with you, and go up now to Ai. See, I have handed over to you the king of Ai with his people, his city, and his land. 2You shall do to Ai and its king as you did to Jericho and its king; only its spoil and its livestock you may take as booty for yourselves. Set an ambush against the city, behind it."

3 So Joshua and all the fighting men set out to go up against Ai. Joshua chose thirty thousand warriors and sent them out by night 4with the command, "You shall lie in ambush against the city, behind it; do not go very far from the city, but all of you stay alert. 5I and all the people who are with me will approach the city. When they come out against us, as before, we shall flee from them. 6They will come out after us until we have drawn them away from the city; for they will say, 'They are fleeing from us, as before.' While we flee from them, 7you shall rise up from the ambush and seize the city; for the LORD your God will give it into your hand. 8And when you have taken the city, you shall set the city on fire, doing as the LORD has ordered; see, I have commanded you." 9So Joshua sent them out; and they went to the place of ambush, and lay between Bethel and Ai, to the west of Ai; but Joshua spent that night in the camp.*a*

10 In the morning Joshua rose early and mustered the people, and went up, with the elders of Israel, before the people to Ai. 11All the fighting men who were with him went up, and drew near before the city, and camped on the north side of Ai, with a ravine between them and Ai. 12Taking about five thousand men, he set them in ambush between Bethel and Ai, to the west of the city. 13So they stationed the forces, the main encampment that was north of the city and its rear guard west of the city. But Joshua spent that night in the valley. 14When the king of Ai saw this, he and all his people, the inhabitants of the city, hurried out early in the morning to the meeting place facing the Arabah to meet Israel in battle; but he did not know that there was an ambush against him behind the city. 15And Joshua and all Israel made a pretense of being beaten before them, and fled in the direction of the wilderness. 16So all the people who were in the city were called together to pursue them, and as they pursued Joshua they were drawn away from the city. 17There was not a man left in Ai or Bethel who did not go out after Israel; they left the city open, and pursued Israel.

8.1–13: Setting the trap at Ai. 2: From now on, Israel is to follow the more usual pattern of killing all potential slaves, but keeping the other spoils of war. Even though ultimate victory is given by the LORD (vv. 1, 7, 18), human strategy (*an ambush*) is still required. **3:** Here the ambush is *thirty thousand* strong; in v. 12 it will number only five thousand. Such irregularities resulted when different narrative* versions were blended together. **8:** The tactical purpose of setting *the city on fire* is not revealed until v. 20. Unanswered questions boost reader interest.

18 Then the LORD said to Joshua, "Stretch out the sword that is in your hand toward Ai; for I will give it into your hand." And Joshua stretched out the sword that was in his hand toward the city. 19As soon as he stretched out his hand, the troops in ambush rose quickly out of their place and rushed forward. They entered the city, took it, and at once set the city on fire. 20So when the men of Ai looked back, the smoke of the city was rising to the sky. They had no power to flee this way or that, for the people who fled to the wilderness turned back against the pursuers. 21When Joshua and all Israel saw that the ambush had taken the city and that the smoke of the city was rising, then they turned back and struck down the men of Ai. 22And the others came out from the city against them; so they were surrounded by Israelites, some on one side, and some on the other; and Israel struck them down until no one was left who survived or escaped. 23But the king of Ai was taken alive and brought to Joshua.

24 When Israel had finished slaughtering

a Heb *among the people*

all the inhabitants of Ai in the open wilderness where they pursued them, and when all of them to the very last had fallen by the edge of the sword, all Israel returned to Ai, and attacked it with the edge of the sword. 25 The total of those who fell that day, both men and women, was twelve thousand—all the people of Ai. 26 For Joshua did not draw back his hand, with which he stretched out the sword, until he had utterly destroyed all the inhabitants of Ai. 27 Only the livestock and the spoil of that city Israel took as their booty, according to the word of the LORD that he had issued to Joshua. 28 So Joshua burned Ai, and made it forever a heap of ruins, as it is to this day. 29 And he hanged the king of Ai on a tree until evening; and at sunset Joshua commanded, and they took his body down from the tree, threw it down at the entrance of the gate of the city, and raised over it a great heap of stones, which stands there to this day.

8.14–29: Victory at Ai. 14–15: The sight of Israel's main army draws the forces of Ai out to the north. Israel's withdrawal pulls them farther away from the city *in the direction of the wilderness,* that is, eastward away from the ambush on the west (vv. 12–13). **19:** Joshua's extended sword signals the ambush to overrun the undefended (v. 17) city. **20–21:** *The smoke of the city* both disheartens the defenders and signals the Israelite main body to turn and attack. Biblical narratives* are not always in strict chronological order: v. 21 overlaps with the last part of v. 20. **22:** The Israelite ambush comes out of Ai to attack the enemy's rear, *so they were surrounded by Israelites.* **25–27:** Devoting the enemy population to destruction (*utterly destroyed;* v. 26) but sparing the booty follows the pattern set by v. 2. **28:** Joshua's action explains the name of *Ai,* which means "the ruin." **29:** Exposing an enemy's body was a great insult (1 Sam 31.10). Joshua is careful not to violate Deut 21.22–23. This *great heap of stones* was presumably a well-known landmark (compare 7.26; 10.27).

~~~

30 Then Joshua built on Mount Ebal an altar to the LORD, the God of Israel, 31 just as Moses the servant of the LORD had commanded the Israelites, as it is written in the book of the law of Moses, "an altar of unhewn[a] stones, on which no iron tool has

been used"; and they offered on it burnt offerings to the LORD, and sacrificed offerings of well-being. 32 And there, in the presence of the Israelites, Joshua[b] wrote on the stones a copy of the law of Moses, which he had written. 33 All Israel, alien as well as citizen, with their elders and officers and their judges, stood on opposite sides of the ark in front of the levitical priests who carried the ark of the covenant of the LORD, half of them in front of Mount Gerizim and half of them in front of Mount Ebal, as Moses the servant of the LORD had commanded at the first, that they should bless the people of Israel. 34 And afterward he read all the words of the law, blessings and curses, according to all that is written in the book of the law. 35 There was not a word of all that Moses commanded that Joshua did not read before all the assembly of Israel, and the women, and the little ones, and the aliens who resided among them.

8.30–35: Building an altar, reading the law. 30–31: Joshua obeys Mosaic ordinance (Deut 11.29–30; 27.2–13) by building an altar for sacrifice, writing on stones (v. 32), and arranging the people for blessing and cursing (v. 33). Deuteronomy 27.5 is quoted directly. **32:** These are not the altar stones, but others set up in accordance with Deut 27.4. **34–35:** In obedience to Deut 31.10–12, Joshua reads *the book of the law* (Deuteronomy), including the *blessings and curses* of Deut 28. There is an emphasis on totality: *All the words* and *all that is written* are read to *all the assembly.*

~~~

9 Now when all the kings who were beyond the Jordan in the hill country and in the lowland all along the coast of the Great Sea toward Lebanon—the Hittites, the Amorites, the Canaanites, the Perizzites, the Hivites, and the Jebusites—heard of this, 2 they gathered together with one accord to fight Joshua and Israel.

3 But when the inhabitants of Gibeon heard what Joshua had done to Jericho and to Ai, 4 they on their part acted with cunning: they went and prepared provisions,[c] and took worn-out sacks for their donkeys, and

a Heb *whole*   *b* Heb *he*   *c* Cn: Meaning of Heb uncertain wineskins, worn-out and torn and mended, [5]with worn-out, patched sandals on their feet, and worn-out clothes; and all their provisions were dry and moldy. [6]They went to Joshua in the camp at Gilgal, and said to him and to the Israelites, "We have come from a far country; so now make a treaty with us." [7]But the Israelites said to the Hivites, "Perhaps you live among us; then how can we make a treaty with you?" [8]They said to Joshua, "We are your servants." And Joshua said to them, "Who are you? And where do you come from?" [9]They said to him, "Your servants have come from a very far country, because of the name of the LORD your God; for we have heard a report of him, of all that he did in Egypt, [10]and of all that he did to the two kings of the Amorites who were beyond the Jordan, King Sihon of Heshbon, and King Og of Bashan who lived in Ashtaroth. [11]So our elders and all the inhabitants of our country said to us, 'Take provisions in your hand for the journey; go to meet them, and say to them, "We are your servants; come now, make a treaty with us." ' [12]Here is our bread; it was still warm when we took it from our houses as our food for the journey, on the day we set out to come to you, but now, see, it is dry and moldy; [13]these wineskins were new when we filled them, and see, they are burst; and these garments and sandals of ours are worn out from the very long journey." [14]So the leaders[a] partook of their provisions, and did not ask direction from the LORD. [15]And Joshua made peace with them, guaranteeing their lives by a treaty; and the leaders of the congregation swore an oath to them.

9.1–15: The Gibeonite deception. 1–4: There are two contrasting reactions to the news about Israel's victories. The kings of the various peoples *gathered . . . to fight* (v. 2). But the citizens of Gibeon *acted with cunning* (v. 4). **6:** Their argument rests on being from *a far country* (also v. 9), exempting them from the extermination required by Deut 20.16–18. **7:** In reality they are *Hivites*, one of the nations to be destroyed (9.1; Deut. 20.17). A *treaty* with any who *live among* Israel was forbidden (Deut 7.2). **8:** Their language about being *servants* is respectful, but it is also ironic* in light of vv. 21, 23, 27. **9–10:** Their speech is similar

to Rahab's confession (2.10–11), but is hypocritical. **15:** All three Israelite parties fall for the ruse. The ordinary Israelites of vv. 6 and 7 ("men" is the better reading, note *a*) taste the evidence. Joshua makes *peace*. The *leaders of the congregation* swear *an oath*. Gibeonites retained their special status as a foreign enclave down to the reign of David (2 Sam 21.1–6).

[16] But when three days had passed after they had made a treaty with them, they heard that they were their neighbors and were living among them. [17]So the Israelites set out and reached their cities on the third day. Now their cities were Gibeon, Chephirah, Beeroth, and Kiriath-jearim. [18]But the Israelites did not attack them, because the leaders of the congregation had sworn to them by the LORD, the God of Israel. Then all the congregation murmured against the leaders. [19]But all the leaders said to all the congregation, "We have sworn to them by the LORD, the God of Israel, and now we must not touch them. [20]This is what we will do to them: We will let them live, so that wrath may not come upon us, because of the oath that we swore to them." [21]The leaders said to them, "Let them live." So they became hewers of wood and drawers of water for all the congregation, as the leaders had decided concerning them.

[22] Joshua summoned them, and said to them, "Why did you deceive us, saying, 'We are very far from you,' while in fact you are living among us? [23]Now therefore you are cursed, and some of you shall always be slaves, hewers of wood and drawers of water for the house of my God." [24]They answered Joshua, "Because it was told to your servants for a certainty that the LORD your God had commanded his servant Moses to give you all the land, and to destroy all the inhabitants of the land before you; so we were in great fear for our lives because of you, and did this thing. [25]And now we are in your hand: do as it seems good and right in your sight to do to us." [26]This is what he did for them: he saved them from the Israelites; and they did not kill them. [27]But on that day Joshua made them hewers of wood and drawers of water for the

a Gk: Heb *men*

congregation and for the altar of the LORD, to continue to this day, in the place that he should choose.

9.16–27: Discovery and punishment. 16: The fears of v. 7 are realized; the Gibeonites indeed are *living among them.* **20–21:** The sanctity of the oath must be preserved, but this deception has endangered the community and must be punished. The expression *hewers of wood and drawers of water* indicates a sub-servient servant class (Deut 29.11). **22:** Joshua summarizes their deceit by contrasting *very far* (see vv. 6, 9) with *living among us* (see vv. 7, 16). **23:** Some Gibeonites are to be servants of the *house of my God,* that is, the Temple.*

10

When King Adoni-zedek of Jerusalem heard how Joshua had taken Ai, and had utterly destroyed it, doing to Ai and its king as he had done to Jericho and its king, and how the inhabitants of Gibeon had made peace with Israel and were among them, ²he^a became greatly frightened, because Gibeon was a large city, like one of the royal cities, and was larger than Ai, and all its men were warriors. ³So King Adoni-zedek of Jerusalem sent a message to King Hoham of Hebron, to King Piram of Jarmuth, to King Japhia of Lachish, and to King Debir of Eglon, saying, ⁴"Come up and help me, and let us attack Gibeon; for it has made peace with Joshua and with the Israelites." ⁵Then the five kings of the Amorites—the king of Jerusalem, the king of Hebron, the king of Jarmuth, the king of Lachish, and the king of Eglon—gathered their forces, and went up with all their armies and camped against Gibeon, and made war against it.

6 And the Gibeonites sent to Joshua at the camp in Gilgal, saying, "Do not abandon your servants; come up to us quickly, and save us, and help us; for all the kings of the Amorites who live in the hill country are gathered against us." ⁷So Joshua went up from Gilgal, he and all the fighting force with him, all the mighty warriors. ⁸The LORD said to Joshua, "Do not fear them, for I have handed them over to you; not one of them shall stand before you." ⁹So Joshua came upon them suddenly, having marched up all night from Gilgal. ¹⁰And the LORD threw

them into a panic before Israel, who inflicted a great slaughter on them at Gibeon, chased them by the way of the ascent of Beth-horon, and struck them down as far as Azekah and Makkedah. ¹¹As they fled before Israel, while they were going down the slope of Beth-horon, the LORD threw down huge stones from heaven on them as far as Azekah, and they died; there were more who died because of the hailstones than the Israelites killed with the sword.

10.1–11: Victory at Gibeon. 1: News of Israel's success motivates enemy action (compare 5.1; 9.1–2; 11.1–3). **2:** Israel's treaty with *Gibeon* threatened Jerusalem's northern approaches. **3:** These four cities are south and west of Jerusalem. **6:** *All the kings of the Amorites* is an exaggeration to motivate Israel's response. **10:** *Panic* is a standard weapon of the divine warrior* (Ex 14.24; Judg 7.21–22). The pursuit extends westward from Gibeon, down through the pass at *the ascent of Beth-horon,* then far southward. **11:** Weather phenomena are also weapons of the divine warrior (Isa 30.30).

12 On the day when the LORD gave the Amorites over to the Israelites, Joshua spoke to the LORD; and he said in the sight of Israel,

"Sun, stand still at Gibeon,
    and Moon, in the valley of Aijalon."
13 And the sun stood still, and the moon
    stopped,
    until the nation took vengeance on
        their enemies.
Is this not written in the Book of Jashar? The sun stopped in midheaven, and did not hurry to set for about a whole day. ¹⁴There has been no day like it before or since, when the LORD heeded a human voice; for the LORD fought for Israel.

15 Then Joshua returned, and all Israel with him, to the camp at Gilgal.

10.12–15: The sun stands still. 12–13: A prose framework encloses and reinterprets an older poetic text from *the Book of Jashar* (see 2 Sam 1.18). According to the framework, Joshua's request *to the LORD* (v. 12) for extended daylight causes the sun to stop in its noon

^a Heb *they*

position (*in midheaven*, v. 13) and delay its setting. The poem itself actually addresses the moon and sun, not God. The poet calls upon them to freeze in stunned amazement at the scope of Israel's victory (compare Ex 15.16; Hab 3.11). **14:** That *the LORD fought for Israel* perfectly summarizes the divine warrior* tradition.

16 Meanwhile, these five kings fled and hid themselves in the cave at Makkedah. [17]And it was told Joshua, "The five kings have been found, hidden in the cave at Makkedah." [18]Joshua said, "Roll large stones against the mouth of the cave, and set men by it to guard them; [19]but do not stay there yourselves; pursue your enemies, and attack them from the rear. Do not let them enter their towns, for the LORD your God has given them into your hand." [20]When Joshua and the Israelites had finished inflicting a very great slaughter on them, until they were wiped out, and when the survivors had entered into the fortified towns, [21]all the people returned safe to Joshua in the camp at Makkedah; no one dared to speak*a* against any of the Israelites.

22 Then Joshua said, "Open the mouth of the cave, and bring those five kings out to me from the cave." [23]They did so, and brought the five kings out to him from the cave, the king of Jerusalem, the king of Hebron, the king of Jarmuth, the king of Lachish, and the king of Eglon. [24]When they brought the kings out to Joshua, Joshua summoned all the Israelites, and said to the chiefs of the warriors who had gone with him, "Come near, put your feet on the necks of these kings." Then they came near and put their feet on their necks. [25]And Joshua said to them, "Do not be afraid or dismayed; be strong and courageous; for thus the LORD will do to all the enemies against whom you fight." [26]Afterward Joshua struck them down and put them to death, and he hung them on five trees. And they hung on the trees until evening. [27]At sunset Joshua commanded, and they took them down from the trees and threw them into the cave where they had hidden themselves; they set large stones against the mouth of the cave, which remain to this very day.

10.16–27: Executing the five kings. 16: *Makkedah* was the southernmost limit of the enemy's flight (v. 10) and the starting point for the final phase of the campaign (v. 28). **20:** In spite of Joshua's energetic pursuit (v. 19), *survivors* do escape to *the fortified towns,* thus setting up the need for attacks on Lachish, Eglon, and Hebron (vv. 31, 34, 36). **24:** *Feet on the necks* of enemy kings symbolizes total victory (Ps 110.1). **26–27:** Exposing enemy bodies was a humiliating insult (1 Sam 31.10; 2 Sam 4.12). Joshua obeys Deut 21.22–23. These *large stones* were presumably a well-known landmark (compare 7.26; 8.29).

28 Joshua took Makkedah on that day, and struck it and its king with the edge of the sword; he utterly destroyed every person in it; he left no one remaining. And he did to the king of Makkedah as he had done to the king of Jericho.

29 Then Joshua passed on from Makkedah, and all Israel with him, to Libnah, and fought against Libnah. [30]The LORD gave it also and its king into the hand of Israel; and he struck it with the edge of the sword, and every person in it; he left no one remaining in it; and he did to its king as he had done to the king of Jericho.

31 Next Joshua passed on from Libnah, and all Israel with him, to Lachish, and laid siege to it, and assaulted it. [32]The LORD gave Lachish into the hand of Israel, and he took it on the second day, and struck it with the edge of the sword, and every person in it, as he had done to Libnah.

33 Then King Horam of Gezer came up to help Lachish; and Joshua struck him and his people, leaving him no survivors.

34 From Lachish Joshua passed on with all Israel to Eglon; and they laid siege to it, and assaulted it; [35]and they took it that day, and struck it with the edge of the sword; and every person in it he utterly destroyed that day, as he had done to Lachish.

36 Then Joshua went up with all Israel from Eglon to Hebron; they assaulted it, [37]and took it, and struck it with the edge of the sword, and its king and its towns, and every person in it; he left no one remaining,

a Heb *moved his tongue*

just as he had done to Eglon, and utterly destroyed it with every person in it.

38 Then Joshua, with all Israel, turned back to Debir and assaulted it, 39 and he took it with its king and all its towns; they struck them with the edge of the sword, and utterly destroyed every person in it; he left no one remaining; just as he had done to Hebron, and, as he had done to Libnah and its king, so he did to Debir and its king.

40 So Joshua defeated the whole land, the hill country and the Negeb and the lowland and the slopes, and all their kings; he left no one remaining, but utterly destroyed all that breathed, as the LORD God of Israel commanded. 41 And Joshua defeated them from Kadesh-barnea to Gaza, and all the country of Goshen, as far as Gibeon. 42 Joshua took all these kings and their land at one time, because the LORD God of Israel fought for Israel. 43 Then Joshua returned, and all Israel with him, to the camp at Gilgal.

10.28–43: Capturing five cities. 31: Three cites (*Lachish,* Eglon, and Hebron) were part of the earlier coalition, but Jerusalem and Jarmuth (v. 3) are not attacked. No mention is made of the kings of Lachish or Eglon; they have already been killed (vv. 23, 26). **33:** *Gezer* is not captured. It did not become part of Israel until the reign of Solomon (1 Kings 9.16–17). **37:** Mention of a king of Hebron seems to contradict vv. 23, 26. **41:** This describes the land conquered so far: The south boundary runs east to west from *Kadesh-barnea to Gaza.* Northward it extends *as far as Gibeon.* The extent of *the country of Goshen* (11.16; perhaps 15.51) is unknown.

11 When King Jabin of Hazor heard of this, he sent to King Jobab of Madon, to the king of Shimron, to the king of Achshaph, 2 and to the kings who were in the northern hill country, and in the Arabah south of Chinneroth, and in the lowland, and in Naphoth-dor on the west, 3 to the Canaanites in the east and the west, the Amorites, the Hittites, the Perizzites, and the Jebusites in the hill country, and the Hivites under Hermon in the land of Mizpah. 4 They came out, with all their troops, a great army, in number like the sand on the seashore, with very many horses and chariots. 5 All these kings joined their forces, and came and camped together at the waters of Merom, to fight with Israel.

6 And the LORD said to Joshua, "Do not be afraid of them, for tomorrow at this time I will hand over all of them, slain, to Israel; you shall hamstring their horses, and burn their chariots with fire." 7 So Joshua came suddenly upon them with all his fighting force, by the waters of Merom, and fell upon them. 8 And the LORD handed them over to Israel, who attacked them and chased them as far as Great Sidon and Misrephoth-maim, and eastward as far as the valley of Mizpeh. They struck them down, until they had left no one remaining. 9 And Joshua did to them as the LORD commanded him; he hamstrung their horses, and burned their chariots with fire.

10 Joshua turned back at that time, and took Hazor, and struck its king down with the sword. Before that time Hazor was the head of all those kingdoms. 11 And they put to the sword all who were in it, utterly destroying them; there was no one left who breathed, and he burned Hazor with fire. 12 And all the towns of those kings, and all their kings, Joshua took, and struck them with the edge of the sword, utterly destroying them, as Moses the servant of the LORD had commanded. 13 But Israel burned none of the towns that stood on mounds except Hazor, which Joshua did burn. 14 All the spoil of these towns, and the livestock, the Israelites took for their booty; but all the people they struck down with the edge of the sword, until they had destroyed them, and they did not leave any who breathed. 15 As the LORD had commanded his servant Moses, so Moses commanded Joshua, and so Joshua did; he left nothing undone of all that the LORD had commanded Moses.

11.1–15: Conquests in the north. 1–3: Deborah and Barak also confront a *King Jabin of Hazor* in Judg 4–5. *Jabin* may have been a dynastic name for Hazor's kings. Separate folk traditions about Hazor simply used this well-known name. Jabin's response parallels the pattern of 10.1–5. **4:** Israel's enemies had the advantage of *horses and chariots,* a sophisticated and expensive weapons system. **6:** To *hamstring* a horse means to cut its rear leg tendons so that it could no longer be used in war (2 Sam 8.4). Israel was unable to support and use chariots until the reign of Solomon. **8:** The LORD is always the real victor in holy war* tradition. **11:** The language for the holy war ban,* *no one left who breathed* (also v. 14), is taken from Deut 20.16. **13:** Israel did not destroy most captured cities, but took them over in accordance with the principle of Deut 6.10–11.

16 So Joshua took all that land: the hill country and all the Negeb and all the land of Goshen and the lowland and the Arabah and the hill country of Israel and its lowland, ¹⁷from Mount Halak, which rises toward Seir, as far as Baal-gad in the valley of Lebanon below Mount Hermon. He took all their kings, struck them down, and put them to death. ¹⁸Joshua made war a long time with all those kings. ¹⁹There was not a town that made peace with the Israelites, except the Hivites, the inhabitants of Gibeon; all were taken in battle. ²⁰For it was the LORD's doing to harden their hearts so that they would come against Israel in battle, in order that they might be utterly destroyed, and might receive no mercy, but be exterminated, just as the LORD had commanded Moses.

21 At that time Joshua came and wiped out the Anakim from the hill country, from Hebron, from Debir, from Anab, and from all the hill country of Judah, and from all the hill country of Israel; Joshua utterly destroyed them with their towns. ²²None of the Anakim was left in the land of the Israelites; some remained only in Gaza, in Gath, and in Ashdod. ²³So Joshua took the whole land, according to all that the LORD had spoken to Moses; and Joshua gave it for an inheritance to Israel according to their tribal allotments. And the land had rest from war.

11.16–23: Culmination of the conquest. 16: The description parallels 10.40. **17:** A line of territorial extent reaches from *Mount Halak* in the south on the border with Edom to *Baal-gad* somewhere near *Mount Hermon* on Israel's north (12.7; 13.5–6). **20:** The stubborn hostility and incessant attacks of the enemy were *the LORD's doing,* part of a divine plan to wipe them out. **21–22:** In Israelite folklore, *the Anakim* were an ancient

indigenous race of unusual stature. **23:** The LORD has kept the promise made in 1.3–5, and Joshua has completed the task assigned in 1.6. With the words *the land had rest from war,* the conquest draws to a close.

12 Now these are the kings of the land, whom the Israelites defeated, whose land they occupied beyond the Jordan toward the east, from the Wadi Arnon to Mount Hermon, with all the Arabah eastward: ²King Sihon of the Amorites who lived at Heshbon, and ruled from Aroer, which is on the edge of the Wadi Arnon, and from the middle of the valley as far as the river Jabbok, the boundary of the Ammonites, that is, half of Gilead, ³and the Arabah to the Sea of Chinneroth eastward, and in the direction of Beth-jeshimoth, to the sea of the Arabah, the Dead Sea,ᵃ southward to the foot of the slopes of Pisgah; ⁴and King Ogᵇ of Bashan, one of the last of the Rephaim, who lived at Ashtaroth and at Edrei ⁵and ruled over Mount Hermon and Salecah and all Bashan to the boundary of the Geshurites and the Maacathites, and over half of Gilead to the boundary of King Sihon of Heshbon. ⁶Moses, the servant of the LORD, and the Israelites defeated them; and Moses the servant of the LORD gave their land for a possession to the Reubenites and the Gadites and the half-tribe of Manasseh.

7 The following are the kings of the land whom Joshua and the Israelites defeated on the west side of the Jordan, from Baal-gad in the valley of Lebanon to Mount Halak, that rises toward Seir (and Joshua gave their land to the tribes of Israel as a possession according to their allotments, ⁸in the hill country, in the lowland, in the Arabah, in the slopes, in the wilderness, and in the Negeb, the land of the Hittites, Amorites, Canaanites, Perizzites, Hivites, and Jebusites):

⁹ the king of Jericho   one
  the king of Ai, which is next to
      Bethel   one
¹⁰ the king of Jerusalem   one
  the king of Hebron   one
¹¹ the king of Jarmuth   one
  the king of Lachish   one

a Heb *Salt Sea*   *b* Gk: Heb *the boundary of King Og*

12 the king of Eglon　　　　　　　　　　　one
　　the king of Gezer　　　　　　　　　　　one
13 the king of Debir　　　　　　　　　　　one
　　the king of Geder　　　　　　　　　　　one
14 the king of Hormah　　　　　　　　　　one
　　the king of Arad　　　　　　　　　　　one
15 the king of Libnah　　　　　　　　　　one
　　the king of Adullam　　　　　　　　　one
16 the king of Makkedah　　　　　　　　one
　　the king of Bethel　　　　　　　　　　one
17 the king of Tappuah　　　　　　　　　one
　　the king of Hepher　　　　　　　　　　one
18 the king of Aphek　　　　　　　　　　one
　　the king of Lasharon　　　　　　　　one
19 the king of Madon　　　　　　　　　　one
　　the king of Hazor　　　　　　　　　　one
20 the king of Shimron-meron　　　　　one
　　the king of Achshaph　　　　　　　　one
21 the king of Taanach　　　　　　　　　one
　　the king of Megiddo　　　　　　　　　one
22 the king of Kedesh　　　　　　　　　　one
　　the king of Jokneam in Carmel　　　one
23 the king of Dor in Naphath-dor　　one
　　the king of Goiim in Galilee,*a*　　one
24 the king of Tirzah　　　　　　　　　　one
thirty-one kings in all.

12.1–24: A list of defeated kings. 1–6: Moses defeated two kings east of the Jordan. The territories seized from *Sihon* are delineated in vv. 2–3 and those taken from *Og* in vv. 4–5. **7–8:** Joshua seized territory from thirty-one kings (v. 24). This description mirrors 11.16–17. **9–24:** *Jericho* and *Ai* naturally come first (v. 9). The five cities of 10.3 are listed in vv. 10–12a. The four cities of 11.1 are listed in vv. 19–20.

13 Now Joshua was old and advanced in years; and the LORD said to him, "You are old and advanced in years, and very much of the land still remains to be possessed. ²This is the land that still remains: all the regions of the Philistines, and all those of the Geshurites ³(from the Shihor, which is east of Egypt, northward to the boundary of Ekron, it is reckoned as Canaanite; there are five rulers of the Philistines, those of Gaza, Ashdod, Ashkelon, Gath, and Ekron), and those of the Avvim ⁴in the south; all the land of the Canaanites, and Mearah that belongs to the Sidonians, to Aphek, to the boundary of the Amorites,

⁵and the land of the Gebalites, and all Lebanon, toward the east, from Baal-gad below Mount Hermon to Lebo-hamath, ⁶all the inhabitants of the hill country from Lebanon to Misrephoth-maim, even all the Sidonians. I will myself drive them out from before the Israelites; only allot the land to Israel for an inheritance, as I have commanded you. ⁷Now therefore divide this land for an inheritance to the nine tribes and the half-tribe of Manasseh."

13.1–7: The land that remains. 1: Joshua's advanced age prompts the distribution of territory west of the Jordan (v. 7). **2–6:** A parenthetical digression describes Philistine territory and areas to the north in Phoenicia and Lebanon as land yet to be conquered. The LORD will eventually drive these peoples out, but for now Joshua is to allot the land already conquered (v. 6).

8 With the other half-tribe of Manasseh*b* the Reubenites and the Gadites received their inheritance, which Moses gave them, beyond the Jordan eastward, as Moses the servant of the LORD gave them: ⁹from Aroer, which is on the edge of the Wadi Arnon, and the town that is in the middle of the valley, and all the tableland from*c* Medeba as far as Dibon; ¹⁰and all the cities of King Sihon of the Amorites, who reigned in Heshbon, as far as the boundary of the Ammonites; ¹¹and Gilead, and the region of the Geshurites and Maacathites, and all Mount Hermon, and all Bashan to Salecah; ¹²all the kingdom of Og in Bashan, who reigned in Ashtaroth and in Edrei (he alone was left of the survivors of the Rephaim); these Moses had defeated and driven out. ¹³Yet the Israelites did not drive out the Geshurites or the Maacathites; but Geshur and Maacath live within Israel to this day.

14 To the tribe of Levi alone Moses gave no inheritance; the offerings by fire to the LORD God of Israel are their inheritance, as he said to them.

15 Moses gave an inheritance to the tribe of the Reubenites according to their clans. ¹⁶Their territory was from Aroer, which is on

a Gk: Heb *Gilgal*　　*b* Cn: Heb *With it*　　*c* Compare Gk: Heb lacks *from*

■▲▲▲■

Dividing Up the Promised Land

The geographical information in Josh 13–19 comes in two forms: tribal boundary descriptions and town lists. The town lists are mostly derived from administrative sources from a period later than the events described in Joshua. The difference between tribal and town lists is particularly clear for 15.20–62 and 18.21–28.

■▲▲▲■

the edge of the Wadi Arnon, and the town that is in the middle of the valley, and all the tableland by Medeba; 17with Heshbon, and all its towns that are in the tableland; Dibon, and Bamoth-baal, and Beth-baal-meon, 18and Jahaz, and Kedemoth, and Mephaath, 19and Kiriathaim, and Sibmah, and Zereth-shahar on the hill of the valley, 20and Beth-peor, and the slopes of Pisgah, and Beth-jeshimoth, 21that is, all the towns of the tableland, and all the kingdom of King Sihon of the Amorites, who reigned in Heshbon, whom Moses defeated with the leaders of Midian, Evi and Rekem and Zur and Hur and Reba, as princes of Sihon, who lived in the land. 22Along with the rest of those they put to death, the Israelites also put to the sword Balaam son of Beor, who practiced divination. 23And the border of the Reubenites was the Jordan and its banks. This was the inheritance of the Reubenites according to their families, with their towns and villages.

24 Moses gave an inheritance also to the tribe of the Gadites, according to their families. 25Their territory was Jazer, and all the towns of Gilead, and half the land of the Ammonites, to Aroer, which is east of Rabbah, 26and from Heshbon to Ramath-mizpeh and Betonim, and from Mahanaim to the territory of Debir,ᵃ 27and in the valley Beth-haram, Beth-nimrah, Succoth, and Zaphon, the rest of the kingdom of King Sihon of Heshbon, the Jordan and its banks, as far as the lower end of the Sea of Chinnereth, eastward beyond the Jordan. 28This is the inheritance of the Gadites according to their clans, with their towns and villages.

29 Moses gave an inheritance to the half-tribe of Manasseh; it was allotted to the half-

tribe of the Manassites according to their families. 30Their territory extended from Mahanaim, through all Bashan, the whole kingdom of King Og of Bashan, and all the settlements of Jair, which are in Bashan, sixty towns, 31and half of Gilead, and Ash-taroth, and Edrei, the towns of the kingdom of Og in Bashan; these were allotted to the people of Machir son of Manasseh according to their clans—for half the Machirites.

32 These are the inheritances that Moses distributed in the plains of Moab, beyond the Jordan east of Jericho. 33But to the tribe of Levi Moses gave no inheritance; the LORD God of Israel is their inheritance, as he said to them.

13.8–33: East of the Jordan. 8–14: A general outline moves from south to north. *Aroer* on the edge of the *Wadi★ Arnon* (v. 9) forms the boundary with Moab on the south. *Mount Hermon* and the former *kingdom of Og in Bashan* mark off the north (vv. 11–12). There are two exceptions: *Geshur and Maacath* remain as alien enclaves (v. 13) and *the tribe of Levi* receives no allotment (vv. 14, 33). **15–23:** Reuben's territory is described by a line of extent drawn north *from Aroer* (v. 16) and a list of towns (vv. 17–20). **24–28:** Gad lies to the north of Reuben. Two boundary lines run northward *from Heshbon* and *from Mahanaim* (v. 26). There is a short list of four towns in the first part of v. 27. **29–31:** The clans★ of Manasseh east of the Jordan occupy territory north and east of Gad.

〜〜〜〜〜〜〜〜〜〜〜〜〜〜〜〜〜〜〜〜〜〜〜〜

14 These are the inheritances that the Israelites received in the land of Canaan, which the priest Eleazar, and Joshua son of Nun, and the heads of the families of the tribes of the Israelites distributed to

ᵃ Gk Syr Vg: Heb *Lidebir*

them. ²Their inheritance was by lot, as the LORD had commanded Moses for the nine and one-half tribes. ³For Moses had given an inheritance to the two and one-half tribes beyond the Jordan; but to the Levites he gave no inheritance among them. ⁴For the people of Joseph were two tribes, Manasseh and Ephraim; and no portion was given to the Levites in the land, but only towns to live in, with their pasture lands for their flocks and herds. ⁵The Israelites did as the LORD commanded Moses; they allotted the land.

6 Then the people of Judah came to Joshua at Gilgal; and Caleb son of Jephunneh the Kenizzite said to him, "You know what the LORD said to Moses the man of God in Kadesh-barnea concerning you and me. ⁷I was forty years old when Moses the servant of the LORD sent me from Kadesh-barnea to spy out the land; and I brought him an honest report. ⁸But my companions who went up with me made the heart of the people melt; yet I wholeheartedly followed the LORD my God. ⁹And Moses swore on that day, saying, 'Surely the land on which your foot has trodden shall be an inheritance for you and your children forever, because you have wholeheartedly followed the LORD my God.' ¹⁰And now, as you see, the LORD has kept me alive, as he said, these forty-five years since the time that the LORD spoke this word to Moses, while Israel was journeying through the wilderness; and here I am today, eighty-five years old. ¹¹I am still as strong today as I was on the day that Moses sent me; my strength now is as my strength was then, for war, and for going and coming. ¹²So now give me this hill country of which the LORD spoke on that day; for you heard on that day how the Anakim were there, with great fortified cities; it may be that the LORD will be with me, and I shall drive them out, as the LORD said."

13 Then Joshua blessed him, and gave Hebron to Caleb son of Jephunneh for an inheritance. ¹⁴So Hebron became the inheritance of Caleb son of Jephunneh the Kenizzite to this day, because he wholeheartedly followed the LORD, the God of Israel. ¹⁵Now the name of Hebron formerly was Kiriath-arba;ᵃ this Arba wasᵇ the greatest man

among the Anakim. And the land had rest from war.

14.1–15: Prelude to land distribution. 1: Joshua is joined by *the priest Eleazar* because casting the sacred lot was a priestly monopoly (Deut 33.8). **2:** Distribution *by lot* confirms that the results are in accordance with divine will. **4:** The total number of allotments comes out to twelve because Joseph gave rise to two tribes and Levi received no territory. **6–12:** *Caleb* claims a special grant of territory based on his honest and loyal behavior as a spy (vv. 7–8; Num 13) and the promise of Moses (v. 9). He supports his case by reference to his great age and warlike vigor (vv. 10–11). It was Israel's fear of the *Anakim* (vv. 12, 15) that had caused the original problem (Num 13.28).

15 The lot for the tribe of the people of Judah according to their families reached southward to the boundary of Edom, to the wilderness of Zin at the farthest south. ²And their south boundary ran from the end of the Dead Sea,ᶜ from the bay that faces southward; ³it goes out southward of the ascent of Akrabbim, passes along to Zin, and goes up south of Kadesh-barnea, along by Hezron, up to Addar, makes a turn to Karka, ⁴passes along to Azmon, goes out by the Wadi of Egypt, and comes to its end at the sea. This shall be your south boundary. ⁵And the east boundary is the Dead Sea,ᶜ to the mouth of the Jordan. And the boundary on the north side runs from the bay of the sea at the mouth of the Jordan; ⁶and the boundary goes up to Beth-hoglah, and passes along north of Beth-arabah; and the boundary goes up to the Stone of Bohan, Reuben's son; ⁷and the boundary goes up to Debir from the Valley of Achor, and so northward, turning toward Gilgal, which is opposite the ascent of Adummim, which is on the south side of the valley; and the boundary passes along to the waters of En-shemesh, and ends at En-rogel; ⁸then the boundary goes up by the valley of the son of Hinnom at the southern slope of the Jebusites (that is, Jerusalem); and the boundary goes up to the top of

a That is *the city of Arba*　b Heb lacks *this Arba was*　c Heb *Salt Sea* the mountain that lies over against the valley of Hinnom, on the west, at the northern end of the valley of Rephaim; [9]then the boundary extends from the top of the mountain to the spring of the Waters of Nephtoah, and from there to the towns of Mount Ephron; then the boundary bends around to Baalah (that is, Kiriath-jearim); [10]and the boundary circles west of Baalah to Mount Seir, passes along to the northern slope of Mount Jearim (that is, Chesalon), and goes down to Beth-shemesh, and passes along by Timnah; [11]the boundary goes out to the slope of the hill north of Ekron, then the boundary bends around to Shikkeron, and passes along to Mount Baalah, and goes out to Jabneel; then the boundary comes to an end at the sea. [12]And the west boundary was the Mediterranean with its coast. This is the boundary surrounding the people of Judah according to their families.

15.1–12: The boundaries of Judah. 1–4: Judah's south border (running east to west) is similar to Num 34.3–6. 5–11: The north border with Benjamin is reported in great detail from east to west and coincides with 18.15–19.

13 According to the commandment of the LORD to Joshua, he gave to Caleb son of Jephunneh a portion among the people of Judah, Kiriath-arba,[a] that is, Hebron (Arba was the father of Anak). [14]And Caleb drove out from there the three sons of Anak: Sheshai, Ahiman, and Talmai, the descendants of Anak. [15]From there he went up against the inhabitants of Debir; now the name of Debir formerly was Kiriath-sepher. [16]And Caleb said, "Whoever attacks Kiriath-sepher and takes it, to him I will give my daughter Achsah as wife." [17]Othniel son of Kenaz, the brother of Caleb, took it; and he gave him his daughter Achsah as wife. [18]When she came to him, she urged him to ask her father for a field. As she dismounted from her donkey, Caleb said to her, "What do you wish?" [19]She said to him, "Give me a present; since you have set me in the land of the Negeb, give me springs of water as well." So Caleb gave her the upper springs and the lower springs.

15.13–19: A land grant for Achsah. 13–15: This parallels the account given in 14.6–15. 17–18: Although Achsah prods her husband to ask for a field, nothing of this sort apparently happens. 19: Instead she herself goes on to request springs of water from her father. Because her land is arid she calls it land of the Negeb (the Negeb is arid territory). Achsah's story (paralleled in Judg 1.10–15) explains why the Othniel clan* controlled both Debir and two springs associated with Hebron.

20 This is the inheritance of the tribe of the people of Judah according to their families. [21]The towns belonging to the tribe of the people of Judah in the extreme south, toward the boundary of Edom, were Kabzeel, Eder, Jagur, [22]Kinah, Dimonah, Adadah, [23]Kedesh, Hazor, Ithnan, [24]Ziph, Telem, Bealoth, [25]Hazor-hadattah, Kerioth-hezron (that is, Hazor), [26]Amam, Shema, Moladah, [27]Hazar-gaddah, Heshmon, Beth-pelet, [28]Hazar-shual, Beer-sheba, Biziothiah, [29]Baalah, Iim, Ezem, [30]Eltolad, Chesil, Hormah, [31]Ziklag, Madmannah, Sansannah, [32]Lebaoth, Shilhim, Ain, and Rimmon: in all, twenty-nine towns, with their villages.

33 And in the lowland, Eshtaol, Zorah, Ashnah, [34]Zanoah, En-gannim, Tappuah, Enam, [35]Jarmuth, Adullam, Socoh, Azekah, [36]Shaaraim, Adithaim, Gederah, Gederothaim: fourteen towns with their villages.

37 Zenan, Hadashah, Migdal-gad, [38]Dilan, Mizpeh, Jokthe-el, [39]Lachish, Bozkath, Eglon, [40]Cabbon, Lahmam, Chitlish, [41]Gederoth, Beth-dagon, Naamah, and Makkedah: sixteen towns with their villages.

42 Libnah, Ether, Ashan, [43]Iphtah, Ashnah, Nezib, [44]Keilah, Achzib, and Mareshah: nine towns with their villages.

45 Ekron, with its dependencies and its villages; [46]from Ekron to the sea, all that were near Ashdod, with their villages.

47 Ashdod, its towns and its villages; Gaza, its towns and its villages; to the Wadi of Egypt, and the Great Sea with its coast.

48 And in the hill country, Shamir, Jattir, Socoh, [49]Dannah, Kiriath-sannah (that is, Debir), [50]Anab, Eshtemoh, Anim, [51]Go-

a That is the city of Arba

shen, Holon, and Giloh: eleven towns with their villages.

52 Arab, Dumah, Eshan, 53Janim, Beth-tappuah, Aphekah, 54Humtah, Kiriath-arba (that is, Hebron), and Zior: nine towns with their villages.

55 Maon, Carmel, Ziph, Juttah, 56Jezreel, Jokdeam, Zanoah, 57Kain, Gibeah, and Timnah: ten towns with their villages.

58 Halhul, Beth-zur, Gedor, 59Maarath, Beth-anoth, and Eltekon: six towns with their villages.

60 Kiriath-baal (that is, Kiriath-jearim) and Rabbah: two towns with their villages.

61 In the wilderness, Beth-arabah, Middin, Secacah, 62Nibshan, the City of Salt, and En-gedi: six towns with their villages.

63 But the people of Judah could not drive out the Jebusites, the inhabitants of Jerusalem; so the Jebusites live with the people of Judah in Jerusalem to this day.

15.20–63: The towns of Judah. 20: This description was taken from an authentic source cataloging the administrative districts of the kingdom of Judah. The remainder of this list was used to portray Benjamin (18.21–28). 21–32: Districts are grouped and labeled geographically. This first district is in the *south* (v. 21; Heb., "the Negeb"). Each district concludes with an enumeration of *towns, with their villages* (v. 32). 33–44: Three districts are in the *lowland* (Heb., "Shephelah"). 45–47: This district of Philistine towns does not follow the pattern and was not part of the original source document. 48–60: Other districts are in the *hill country.* 61–62: One district is in the *wilderness.* 63: Jerusalem became part of Israel only under David (2 Sam 5.6–9).

16 The allotment of the Josephites went from the Jordan by Jericho, east of the waters of Jericho, into the wilderness, going up from Jericho into the hill country to Bethel; 2then going from Bethel to Luz, it passes along to Ataroth, the territory of the Archites; 3then it goes down westward to the territory of the Japhletites, as far as the territory of Lower Beth-horon, then to Gezer, and it ends at the sea.

4 The Josephites—Manasseh and Ephraim—received their inheritance.

5 The territory of the Ephraimites by their families was as follows: the boundary of their inheritance on the east was Ataroth-addar as far as Upper Beth-horon, 6and the boundary goes from there to the sea; on the north is Michmethath; then on the east the boundary makes a turn toward Taanath-shiloh, and passes along beyond it on the east to Janoah, 7then it goes down from Janoah to Ataroth and to Naarah, and touches Jericho, ending at the Jordan. 8From Tappuah the boundary goes westward to the Wadi Kanah, and ends at the sea. Such is the inheritance of the tribe of the Ephraimites by their families, 9together with the towns that were set apart for the Ephraimites within the inheritance of the Manassites, all those towns with their villages. 10They did not, however, drive out the Canaanites who lived in Gezer: so the Canaanites have lived within Ephraim to this day but have been made to do forced labor.

16.1–10: Ephraim. 1–3: As sons of Joseph, Ephraim and Manasseh together make up the *Josephites.* Their south boundary is also the north boundary of Benjamin (18.12–13). 5–9: Ephraim's north boundary is traced from its center point, first eastward and southward from *Michmethath* (vv. 6–7), then westward from nearby *Tappuah* (v. 8). 10: *Gezer* remained Canaanite until the reign of Solomon (1 Kings 9.16–17).

17 Then allotment was made to the tribe of Manasseh, for he was the firstborn of Joseph. To Machir the firstborn of Manasseh, the father of Gilead, were allotted Gilead and Bashan, because he was a warrior. 2And allotments were made to the rest of the tribe of Manasseh, by their families, Abiezer, Helek, Asriel, Shechem, Hepher, and Shemida; these were the male descendants of Manasseh son of Joseph, by their families.

3 Now Zelophehad son of Hepher son of Gilead son of Machir son of Manasseh had no sons, but only daughters; and these are the names of his daughters: Mahlah, Noah, Hoglah, Milcah, and Tirzah. 4They came before the priest Eleazar and Joshua son of Nun and the leaders, and said, "The LORD commanded Moses to give us an inheritance

along with our male kin." So according to the commandment of the Lord he gave them an inheritance among the kinsmen of their father. [5]Thus there fell to Manasseh ten portions, besides the land of Gilead and Bashan, which is on the other side of the Jordan, [6]because the daughters of Manasseh received an inheritance along with his sons. The land of Gilead was allotted to the rest of the Manassites.

[7] The territory of Manasseh reached from Asher to Michmethath, which is east of Shechem; then the boundary goes along southward to the inhabitants of En-tappuah. [8]The land of Tappuah belonged to Manasseh, but the town of Tappuah on the boundary of Manasseh belonged to the Ephraimites. [9]Then the boundary went down to the Wadi Kanah. The towns here, to the south of the wadi, among the towns of Manasseh, belong to Ephraim. Then the boundary of Manasseh goes along the north side of the wadi and ends at the sea. [10]The land to the south is Ephraim's and that to the north is Manasseh's, with the sea forming its boundary; on the north Asher is reached, and on the east Issachar. [11]Within Issachar and Asher, Manasseh had Beth-shean and its villages, Ibleam and its villages, the inhabitants of Dor and its villages, the inhabitants of En-dor and its villages, the inhabitants of Taanach and its villages, and the inhabitants of Megiddo and its villages (the third is Naphath).[a] [12]Yet the Manassites could not take possession of those towns; but the Canaanites continued to live in that land. [13]But when the Israelites grew strong, they put the Canaanites to forced labor, but did not utterly drive them out.

17.1–13: Manasseh. 1: Elements of Manasseh tracing descent from *Machir* occupied territory east of the Jordan. **2:** Six clans* traced descent through Manasseh's male heirs. **3–6:** Five other clans descended from the female heirs of Manasseh, the daughters of *Zelophehad.* Joshua fulfills the command of Moses reported in Num 27.1–11. **7–9:** The south boundary parallels Ephraim's north boundary (16.6, 8). **11–12:** Idealized boundaries did not always match the reality of tribal affiliation (compare 16.9).

[14] The tribe of Joseph spoke to Joshua, saying, "Why have you given me but one lot and one portion as an inheritance, since we are a numerous people, whom all along the Lord has blessed?" [15]And Joshua said to them, "If you are a numerous people, go up to the forest, and clear ground there for yourselves in the land of the Perizzites and the Rephaim, since the hill country of Ephraim is too narrow for you." [16]The tribe of Joseph said, "The hill country is not enough for us; yet all the Canaanites who live in the plain have chariots of iron, both those in Beth-shean and its villages and those in the Valley of Jezreel." [17]Then Joshua said to the house of Joseph, to Ephraim and Manasseh, "You are indeed a numerous people, and have great power; you shall not have one lot only, [18]but the hill country shall be yours, for though it is a forest, you shall clear it and possess it to its farthest borders; for you shall drive out the Canaanites, though they have chariots of iron, and though they are strong."

17.14–18: More territory for Joseph. 14–15: Ephraim and Manasseh together as *the tribe of Joseph* complain that they have too little land. Joshua points out that their size gives them the resources to clear the highland forests. **16:** Unsatisfied, they go on to lament* that the military strength of the Canaanites keeps them from settling the plains. **17–18:** The large population of Ephraim and Manasseh is actually not a problem, but an opportunity for an expansive future. In addition to clearing the forests, they will eventually *drive out the Canaanites.*

---

18 Then the whole congregation of the Israelites assembled at Shiloh, and set up the tent of meeting there. The land lay subdued before them.

[2] There remained among the Israelites seven tribes whose inheritance had not yet been apportioned. [3]So Joshua said to the Israelites, "How long will you be slack about going in and taking possession of the land that the Lord, the God of your ancestors, has given you? [4]Provide three men from each tribe, and I will send them out that they

---

a Meaning of Heb uncertain

may begin to go throughout the land, writing a description of it with a view to their inheritances. Then come back to me. 5They shall divide it into seven portions, Judah continuing in its territory on the south, and the house of Joseph in their territory on the north. 6You shall describe the land in seven divisions and bring the description here to me; and I will cast lots for you here before the Lord our God. 7The Levites have no portion among you, for the priesthood of the Lord is their heritage; and Gad and Reuben and the half-tribe of Manasseh have received their inheritance beyond the Jordan eastward, which Moses the servant of the Lord gave them."

8 So the men started on their way; and Joshua charged those who went to write the description of the land, saying, "Go throughout the land and write a description of it, and come back to me; and I will cast lots for you here before the Lord in Shiloh." 9So the men went and traversed the land and set down in a book a description of it by towns in seven divisions; then they came back to Joshua in the camp at Shiloh, 10and Joshua cast lots for them in Shiloh before the Lord; and there Joshua apportioned the land to the Israelites, to each a portion.

18.1–10: Dividing the land into seven portions. 1: So far the process of dividing the land has taken place at Gilgal (14.6). Now it abruptly moves to the sanctuary of *Shiloh*, where the Lord is present in the *tent of meeting*. 4–5: The remaining seven tribes will engage in a lottery for territory. In preparation, the land is divided into equitable allotments by a representative commission. 6: The division is conducted fairly by sacred lot under the Lord's supervision (compare v. 10). 9: The result of the commission's work is a document (NRSV: *book*) delineating the divisions *by towns*. This seems to describe the source used to create chs. 18–19, in which town lists play an important part.

11 The lot of the tribe of Benjamin according to its families came up, and the territory allotted to it fell between the tribe of Judah and the tribe of Joseph. 12On the north side their boundary began at the Jordan; then the boundary goes up to the slope of Jericho on the north, then up through the hill country westward; and it ends at the wilderness of Beth-aven. 13From there the boundary passes along southward in the direction of Luz, to the slope of Luz (that is, Bethel), then the boundary goes down to Ataroth-addar, on the mountain that lies south of Lower Beth-horon. 14Then the boundary goes in another direction, turning on the western side southward from the mountain that lies to the south, opposite Beth-horon, and it ends at Kiriath-baal (that is, Kiriath-jearim), a town belonging to the tribe of Judah. This forms the western side. 15The southern side begins at the outskirts of Kiriath-jearim; and the boundary goes from there to Ephron,ᵃ to the spring of the Waters of Nephtoah; 16then the boundary goes down to the border of the mountain that overlooks the valley of the son of Hinnom, which is at the north end of the valley of Rephaim; and it then goes down the valley of Hinnom, south of the slope of the Jebusites, and downward to En-rogel; 17then it bends in a northerly direction going on to En-shemesh, and from there goes to Geliloth, which is opposite the ascent of Adummim; then it goes down to the Stone of Bohan, Reuben's son; 18and passing on to the north of the slope of Beth-arabahᵇ it goes down to the Arabah; 19then the boundary passes on to the north of the slope of Beth-hoglah; and the boundary ends at the northern bay of the Dead Sea,ᶜ at the south end of the Jordan: this is the southern border. 20The Jordan forms its boundary on the eastern side. This is the inheritance of the tribe of Benjamin, according to its families, boundary by boundary all around.

21 Now the towns of the tribe of Benjamin according to their families were Jericho, Beth-hoglah, Emek-keziz, 22Beth-arabah, Zemaraim, Bethel, 23Avvim, Parah, Ophrah, 24Chephar-ammoni, Ophni, and Geba— twelve towns with their villages: 25Gibeon, Ramah, Beeroth, 26Mizpeh, Chephirah, Mozah, 27Rekem, Irpeel, Taralah, 28Zela, Haeleph, Jebusᵈ (that is, Jerusalem), Gib-

ᵃ Cn See 15.9. Heb *westward*   ᵇ Gk: Heb *to the slope over against the Arabah*   ᶜ Heb *Salt Sea*   ᵈ Gk Syr Vg: Heb *the Jebusite* eah*a* and Kiriath-jearim*b*—fourteen towns with their villages. This is the inheritance of the tribe of Benjamin according to its families.

18.11–28: The lot for Benjamin. 12–13: Its boundaries are described in a counter-clockwise direction (vv. 11–20). The north border parallels that of Ephraim (16.1–3). **15–19:** The south border parallels 15.5–9 (Judah's north border) but is given in the reverse direction (west to east). **21–24:** Benjamin's two districts come from the same source as those of Judah (15.21–62). Benjamin was split by the breakup of Israel after Solomon's death (1 Kings 12). This district describes towns located in the northern kingdom. **25–28:** This district consists of towns located in the kingdom of Judah.

---

19 The second lot came out for Simeon, for the tribe of Simeon, according to its families; its inheritance lay within the inheritance of the tribe of Judah. 2It had for its inheritance Beer-sheba, Sheba, Moladah, 3Hazar-shual, Balah, Ezem, 4Eltolad, Bethul, Hormah, 5Ziklag, Beth-marcaboth, Hazar-susah, 6Beth-lebaoth, and Sharuhen—thirteen towns with their villages; 7Ain, Rimmon, Ether, and Ashan—four towns with their villages; 8together with all the villages all around these towns as far as Baalath-beer, Ramah of the Negeb. This was the inheritance of the tribe of Simeon according to its families. 9The inheritance of the tribe of Simeon formed part of the territory of Judah; because the portion of the tribe of Judah was too large for them, the tribe of Simeon obtained an inheritance within their inheritance.

10 The third lot came up for the tribe of Zebulun, according to its families. The boundary of its inheritance reached as far as Sarid; 11then its boundary goes up westward, and on to Maralah, and touches Dabbesheth, then the wadi that is east of Jokneam; 12from Sarid it goes in the other direction eastward toward the sunrise to the boundary of Chisloth-tabor; from there it goes to Daberath, then up to Japhia; 13from there it passes along on the east toward the sunrise to Gath-hepher, to Eth-kazin, and going on to Rimmon it bends toward Neah; 14then on the north the boundary makes a turn to Hannathon, and it ends at the valley of Iphtah-el; 15and Kattath, Nahalal, Shimron, Idalah, and Bethlehem—twelve towns with their villages. 16This is the inheritance of the tribe of Zebulun, according to its families—these towns with their villages.

17 The fourth lot came out for Issachar, for the tribe of Issachar, according to its families. 18Its territory included Jezreel, Chesulloth, Shunem, 19Hapharaim, Shion, Anaharath, 20Rabbith, Kishion, Ebez, 21Remeth, En-gannim, En-haddah, Beth-pazzez; 22the boundary also touches Tabor, Shahazumah, and Beth-shemesh, and its boundary ends at the Jordan—sixteen towns with their villages. 23This is the inheritance of the tribe of Issachar, according to its families—the towns with their villages.

24 The fifth lot came out for the tribe of Asher according to its families. 25Its boundary included Helkath, Hali, Beten, Achshaph, 26Allammelech, Amad, and Mishal; on the west it touches Carmel and Shihor-libnath, 27then it turns eastward, goes to Beth-dagon, and touches Zebulun and the valley of Iphtah-el northward to Beth-emek and Neiel; then it continues in the north to Cabul, 28Ebron, Rehob, Hammon, Kanah, as far as Great Sidon; 29then the boundary turns to Ramah, reaching to the fortified city of Tyre; then the boundary turns to Hosah, and it ends at the sea; Mahalab,*c* Achzib, 30Ummah, Aphek, and Rehob—twenty-two towns with their villages. 31This is the inheritance of the tribe of Asher according to its families—these towns with their villages.

32 The sixth lot came out for the tribe of Naphtali, for the tribe of Naphtali, according to its families. 33And its boundary ran from Heleph, from the oak in Zaanannim, and Adami-nekeb, and Jabneel, as far as Lakkum; and it ended at the Jordan; 34then the boundary turns westward to Aznoth-tabor, and goes from there to Hukkok, touching Zebulun at the south, and Asher on the west, and Judah on the east at the Jordan. 35The fortified towns are Ziddim, Zer, Hammath,

---

a Heb *Gibeath*　　*b* Gk: Heb *Kiriath*　　*c* Cn Compare Gk: Heb *Mehebel*

Rakkath, Chinnereth, 36Adamah, Ramah, Hazor, 37Kedesh, Edrei, En-hazor, 38Iron, Migdal-el, Horem, Beth-anath, and Beth-shemesh—nineteen towns with their villages. 39This is the inheritance of the tribe of Naphtali according to its families—the towns with their villages.

40 The seventh lot came out for the tribe of Dan, according to its families. 41The territory of its inheritance included Zorah, Eshtaol, Ir-shemesh, 42Shaalabbin, Aijalon, Ithlah, 43Elon, Timnah, Ekron, 44Eltekeh, Gibbethon, Baalath, 45Jehud, Bene-berak, Gath-rimmon, 46Me-jarkon, and Rakkon at the border opposite Joppa. 47When the territory of the Danites was lost to them, the Danites went up and fought against Leshem, and after capturing it and putting it to the sword, they took possession of it and settled in it, calling Leshem, Dan, after their ancestor Dan. 48This is the inheritance of the tribe of Dan, according to their families—these towns with their villages.

49 When they had finished distributing the several territories of the land as inheritances, the Israelites gave an inheritance among them to Joshua son of Nun. 50By command of the LORD they gave him the town that he asked for, Timnath-serah in the hill country of Ephraim; he rebuilt the town, and settled in it.

51 These are the inheritances that the priest Eleazar and Joshua son of Nun and the heads of the families of the tribes of the Israelites distributed by lot at Shiloh before the LORD, at the entrance of the tent of meeting. So they finished dividing the land.

20 Then the LORD spoke to Joshua, saying, 2"Say to the Israelites, 'Appoint the cities of refuge, of which I spoke to you through Moses, 3so that anyone who kills a person without intent or by mistake may flee there; they shall be for you a refuge from the avenger of blood. 4The slayer shall flee to one of these cities and shall stand at the entrance of the gate of the city, and explain the case to the elders of that city; then the fugitive shall be taken into the city, and given a place, and shall remain with them. 5And if the avenger of blood is in pursuit, they shall not give up the slayer, because the neighbor was killed by mistake, there having been no enmity between them before. 6The slayer shall remain in that city until there is a trial before the congregation, until the death of the one who is high priest at the time: then the slayer may return home, to the town in which the deed was done.'"

7 So they set apart Kedesh in Galilee in the hill country of Naphtali, and Shechem in the hill country of Ephraim, and Kiriath-arba (that is, Hebron) in the hill country of Judah. 8And beyond the Jordan east of Jericho, they appointed Bezer in the wilderness on the tableland, from the tribe of Reuben, and Ramoth in Gilead, from the tribe of Gad, and Golan in Bashan, from the tribe of Manasseh. 9These were the cities designated for all the Israelites, and for the aliens residing among them, that anyone who killed a person without intent could flee there, so as not to die by the hand of the avenger of blood, until there was a trial before the congregation.

19.1–51: The other six lots. 1–9: Because its territory lies inside that of Judah (vv. 1, 9), Simeon has no boundary description. Its towns are listed in two districts (vv. 2–6 and 7). 10–16: For Zebulun, a detailed boundary description (vv. 10–14) is followed by a town list (v. 15). The south border is traced westward from Sarid (vv. 10–11), then eastward from the same town (v. 12). The east border is given in v. 13 and the north border in v. 14. 17–23: Issachar is described by a town list (vv. 18–21) followed by a small portion of north boundary (v. 22). 24–31: The boundary description for Asher is confusingly mingled with items from a town list. 32–39: The boundary description for Naphtali (vv. 33–34) is followed by a town list (vv. 35–38). 40–48: Dan is described on the basis of a town list (vv. 41–46). Dan's move north to a new home is reported in Judges 18. 51: The priest Eleazar cast the lot at the tent of meeting, which emphasizes that all was done in accordance with God's will.

20.1–9: Cities of refuge. 2–3: Murders were avenged by a near relative of the victim, the avenger of blood (see v. 5). Easily accessible cities of refuge prevented any miscarriage of justice in cases of unintentional manslaughter (Num 35.13–28; Deut 19.1–13). 7–8:

Cities are designated for six regions, three on each side of the Jordan.

〰〰〰〰〰〰〰〰〰〰〰〰〰〰〰

21 Then the heads of the families of the Levites came to the priest Eleazar and to Joshua son of Nun and to the heads of the families of the tribes of the Israelites; ²they said to them at Shiloh in the land of Canaan, "The LORD commanded through Moses that we be given towns to live in, along with their pasture lands for our livestock." ³So by command of the LORD the Israelites gave to the Levites the following towns and pasture lands out of their inheritance.

4 The lot came out for the families of the Kohathites. So those Levites who were descendants of Aaron the priest received by lot thirteen towns from the tribes of Judah, Simeon, and Benjamin.

5 The rest of the Kohathites received by lot ten towns from the families of the tribe of Ephraim, from the tribe of Dan, and the half-tribe of Manasseh.

6 The Gershonites received by lot thirteen towns from the families of the tribe of Issachar, from the tribe of Asher, from the tribe of Naphtali, and from the half-tribe of Manasseh in Bashan.

7 The Merarites according to their families received twelve towns from the tribe of Reuben, the tribe of Gad, and the tribe of Zebulun.

8 These towns and their pasture lands the Israelites gave by lot to the Levites, as the LORD had commanded through Moses.

9 Out of the tribe of Judah and the tribe of Simeon they gave the following towns mentioned by name, ¹⁰which went to the descendants of Aaron, one of the families of the Kohathites who belonged to the Levites, since the lot fell to them first. ¹¹They gave them Kiriath-arba (Arba being the father of Anak), that is Hebron, in the hill country of Judah, along with the pasture lands around it. ¹²But the fields of the town and its villages had been given to Caleb son of Jephunneh as his holding.

13 To the descendants of Aaron the priest they gave Hebron, the city of refuge for the slayer, with its pasture lands, Libnah with its pasture lands, ¹⁴Jattir with its pasture lands, Eshtemoa with its pasture lands, ¹⁵Holon with its pasture lands, Debir with its pasture lands, ¹⁶Ain with its pasture lands, Juttah with its pasture lands, and Beth-shemesh with its pasture lands—nine towns out of these two tribes. ¹⁷Out of the tribe of Benjamin: Gibeon with its pasture lands, Geba with its pasture lands, ¹⁸Anathoth with its pasture lands, and Almon with its pasture lands—four towns. ¹⁹The towns of the descendants of Aaron—the priests—were thirteen in all, with their pasture lands.

20 As to the rest of the Kohathites belonging to the Kohathite families of the Levites, the towns allotted to them were out of the tribe of Ephraim. ²¹To them were given Shechem, the city of refuge for the slayer, with its pasture lands in the hill country of Ephraim, Gezer with its pasture lands, ²²Kibzaim with its pasture lands, and Beth-horon with its pasture lands—four towns. ²³Out of the tribe of Dan: Elteke with its pasture lands, Gibbethon with its pasture lands, ²⁴Aijalon with its pasture lands, Gath-rimmon with its pasture lands—four towns. ²⁵Out of the half-tribe of Manasseh: Taanach with its pasture lands, and Gath-rimmon with its pasture lands—two towns. ²⁶The towns of the families of the rest of the Kohathites were ten in all, with their pasture lands.

27 To the Gershonites, one of the families of the Levites, were given out of the half-tribe of Manasseh, Golan in Bashan with its pasture lands, the city of refuge for the slayer, and Beeshterah with its pasture lands—two towns. ²⁸Out of the tribe of Issachar: Kishion with its pasture lands, Daberath with its pasture lands, ²⁹Jarmuth with its pasture lands, En-gannim with its pasture lands—four towns. ³⁰Out of the tribe of Asher: Mishal with its pasture lands, Abdon with its pasture lands, ³¹Helkath with its pasture lands, and Rehob with its pasture lands—four towns. ³²Out of the tribe of Naphtali: Kedesh in Galilee with its pasture lands, the city of refuge for the slayer, Hammoth-dor with its pasture lands, and Kartan with its pasture lands—three towns. ³³The towns of the several families of the Gershonites were in all thirteen, with their pasture lands.

34 To the rest of the Levites—the Merarite families—were given out of the tribe of Zebulun: Jokneam with its pasture lands, Kartah with its pasture lands, 35Dimnah with its pasture lands, Nahalal with its pasture lands—four towns. 36Out of the tribe of Reuben: Bezer with its pasture lands, Jahzah with its pasture lands, 37Kedemoth with its pasture lands, and Mephaath with its pasture lands—four towns. 38Out of the tribe of Gad: Ramoth in Gilead with its pasture lands, the city of refuge for the slayer, Mahanaim with its pasture lands, 39Heshbon with its pasture lands, Jazer with its pasture lands—four towns in all. 40As for the towns of the several Merarite families, that is, the remainder of the families of the Levites, those allotted to them were twelve in all.

41 The towns of the Levites within the holdings of the Israelites were in all forty-eight towns with their pasture lands. 42Each of these towns had its pasture lands around it; so it was with all these towns.

43 Thus the LORD gave to Israel all the land that he swore to their ancestors that he would give them; and having taken possession of it, they settled there. 44And the LORD gave them rest on every side just as he had sworn to their ancestors; not one of all their enemies had withstood them, for the LORD had given all their enemies into their hands. 45Not one of all the good promises that the LORD had made to the house of Israel had failed; all came to pass.

21.1–45. 1–42: **Cities for the Levites. 2:** Although Levi receives no allotment for agriculture, the tribe is assigned residence towns and grazing land. For this command, see Num 35.2–8. **4–7:** The levitical cities appear in four divisions. Levi was divided into three clans,* and the *Kohathites* were further subdivided into the *descendants of Aaron* (v. 4; the priests) and those not of priestly descent. **13–19:** The thirteen towns for *the descendants of Aaron* reflect an older source list. The other three lists were created by collecting names from Joshua 13, 16–17, 19, and 20. **32:** Because the source list (vv. 13–19) contained thirteen towns, *Naphtali* contributes only *three towns* instead of the usual four in order to achieve the ideal total of forty-eight (v. 41). **43–45:** All has been achieved (v. 43) and all promises fulfilled (v. 45). *Rest on every*

side (v. 44) means war has been replaced by peace (1.13, 15; 22.4).

22 Then Joshua summoned the Reubenites, the Gadites, and the half-tribe of Manasseh, 2and said to them, "You have observed all that Moses the servant of the LORD commanded you, and have obeyed me in all that I have commanded you; 3you have not forsaken your kindred these many days, down to this day, but have been careful to keep the charge of the LORD your God. 4And now the LORD your God has given rest to your kindred, as he promised them; therefore turn and go to your tents in the land where your possession lies, which Moses the servant of the LORD gave you on the other side of the Jordan. 5Take good care to observe the commandment and instruction that Moses the servant of the LORD commanded you, to love the LORD your God, to walk in all his ways, to keep his commandments, and to hold fast to him, and to serve him with all your heart and with all your soul." 6So Joshua blessed them and sent them away, and they went to their tents.

7 Now to the one half of the tribe of Manasseh Moses had given a possession in Bashan; but to the other half Joshua had given a possession beside their fellow Israelites in the land west of the Jordan. And when Joshua sent them away to their tents and blessed them, 8he said to them, "Go back to your tents with much wealth, and with very much livestock, with silver, gold, bronze, and iron, and with a great quantity of clothing; divide the spoil of your enemies with your kindred." 9So the Reubenites and the Gadites and the half-tribe of Manasseh returned home, parting from the Israelites at Shiloh, which is in the land of Canaan, to go to the land of Gilead, their own land of which they had taken possession by command of the LORD through Moses.

22.1–9: **The eastern tribes return home. 4:** Because *rest* has been achieved (21.44), the commitments made in 1.13, 15 can now be fulfilled. *Go to your tents* reflects traditional language for the dispersal of the national assembly (1 Kings 12.16) or tribal militia. **7:** Manasseh's situation is unique, with territory both east and west of the Jordan. **8:** Sharing out the *spoil* of conquest corresponds to Israel's traditional custom (1 Sam 30.21–25).

〰〰〰〰〰〰〰〰〰〰〰〰

10 When they came to the region*ᵃ* near the Jordan that lies in the land of Canaan, the Reubenites and the Gadites and the half-tribe of Manasseh built there an altar by the Jordan, an altar of great size. ¹¹The Israelites heard that the Reubenites and the Gadites and the half-tribe of Manasseh had built an altar at the frontier of the land of Canaan, in the region*ᵇ* near the Jordan, on the side that belongs to the Israelites. ¹²And when the people of Israel heard of it, the whole assembly of the Israelites gathered at Shiloh, to make war against them.

13 Then the Israelites sent the priest Phinehas son of Eleazar to the Reubenites and the Gadites and the half-tribe of Manasseh, in the land of Gilead, ¹⁴and with him ten chiefs, one from each of the tribal families of Israel, every one of them the head of a family among the clans of Israel. ¹⁵They came to the Reubenites, the Gadites, and the half-tribe of Manasseh, in the land of Gilead, and they said to them, ¹⁶"Thus says the whole congregation of the LORD, 'What is this treachery that you have committed against the God of Israel in turning away today from following the LORD, by building yourselves an altar today in rebellion against the LORD? ¹⁷Have we not had enough of the sin at Peor from which even yet we have not cleansed ourselves, and for which a plague came upon the congregation of the LORD, ¹⁸that you must turn away today from following the LORD! If you rebel against the LORD today, he will be angry with the whole congregation of Israel tomorrow. ¹⁹But now, if your land is unclean, cross over into the LORD's land where the LORD's tabernacle now stands, and take for yourselves a possession among us; only do not rebel against the LORD, or rebel against us*ᶜ* by building yourselves an altar other than the altar of the LORD our God. ²⁰Did not Achan son of Zerah break faith in the matter of the devoted things, and wrath fell upon all the congregation of Israel? And he did not perish alone for his iniquity!'"

21 Then the Reubenites, the Gadites, and the half-tribe of Manasseh said in answer to the heads of the families of Israel, ²²"The LORD, God of gods! The LORD, God of gods! He knows; and let Israel itself know! If it was in rebellion or in breach of faith toward the LORD, do not spare us today ²³for building an altar to turn away from following the LORD; or if we did so to offer burnt offerings or grain offerings or offerings of well-being on it, may the LORD himself take vengeance. ²⁴No! We did it from fear that in time to come your children might say to our children, 'What have you to do with the LORD, the God of Israel? ²⁵For the LORD has made the Jordan a boundary between us and you, you Reubenites and Gadites; you have no portion in the LORD.' So your children might make our children cease to worship the LORD. ²⁶Therefore we said, 'Let us now build an altar, not for burnt offering, nor for sacrifice, ²⁷but to be a witness between us and you, and between the generations after us, that we do perform the service of the LORD in his presence with our burnt offerings and sacrifices and offerings of well-being; so that your children may never say to our children in time to come, "You have no portion in the LORD."' ²⁸And we thought, If this should be said to us or to our descendants in time to come, we could say, 'Look at this copy of the altar of the LORD, which our ancestors made, not for burnt offerings, nor for sacrifice, but to be a witness between us and you.' ²⁹Far be it from us that we should rebel against the LORD, and turn away this day from following the LORD by building an altar for burnt offering, grain offering, or sacrifice, other than the altar of the LORD our God that stands before his tabernacle!"

30 When the priest Phinehas and the chiefs of the congregation, the heads of the families of Israel who were with him, heard the words that the Reubenites and the Gadites and the Manassites spoke, they were satisfied. ³¹The priest Phinehas son of Eleazar said to the Reubenites and the Gadites and

a Or *to Geliloth*   *b* Or *at Geliloth*   *c* Or *make rebels of us* the Manassites, "Today we know that the LORD is among us, because you have not committed this treachery against the LORD; now you have saved the Israelites from the hand of the LORD."

32 Then the priest Phinehas son of Eleazar and the chiefs returned from the Reubenites and the Gadites in the land of Gilead to the land of Canaan, to the Israelites, and brought back word to them. ³³The report pleased the Israelites; and the Israelites blessed God and spoke no more of making war against them, to destroy the land where the Reubenites and the Gadites were settled. ³⁴The Reubenites and the Gadites called the altar Witness;ᵃ "For," said they, "it is a witness between us that the LORD is God."

22.10–34: The altar of witness. 10: The story presupposes that only one altar for sacrifice is permissible. Dissension focuses on whether this *altar by the Jordan* is evidence of apostasy (vv. 16–20) or actually a token of loyalty (vv. 22–29). Its *great size* relates to its intended function as a visible witness (vv. 27–28, 34). **12:** The story is told from the perspective of the western tribes, describing them as *the Israelites* to the exclusion of the eastern tribes (also vv. 32, 33). **17:** The incident at *Peor* is reported in Num 25. **18:** The principle of collective responsibility means the whole nation is endangered by the rebellion of some (compare v. 20). **19:** Territory outside of Canaan might be ritually *unclean,* a place where loyalty to the LORD would be impossible. **22:** The eastern tribes begin with a confessional exclamation (compare 1 Kings 18.39) and a hypothetical self-condemnation that asserts their fidelity in the strongest terms. **27:** The eastern tribes repeatedly cite lists of sacrifices (vv. 23, 26, 29) to deny that they intend to offer them at the newly built altar. Here they use a similar catalog to affirm their loyalty. **28:** The altar's purpose is finally revealed. It is only a *copy,* a replica pointing to loyal service at the legitimate altar at Shiloh. **34:** The altar's name does not appear in the Hebrew text (note *a*). What is important is its function as a *witness between us,* that is, between the eastern and western tribes.

23 A long time afterward, when the LORD had given rest to Israel from all their enemies all around, and Joshua was old and well advanced in years, ²Joshua summoned all Israel, their elders and heads, their judges and officers, and said to them, "I am now old and well advanced in years; ³and you have seen all that the LORD your God has done to all these nations for your sake, for it is the LORD your God who has fought for you. ⁴I have allotted to you as an inheritance for your tribes those nations that remain, along with all the nations that I have already cut off, from the Jordan to the Great Sea in the west. ⁵The LORD your God will push them back before you, and drive them out of your sight; and you shall possess their land, as the LORD your God promised you. ⁶Therefore be very steadfast to observe and do all that is written in the book of the law of Moses, turning aside from it neither to the right nor to the left, ⁷so that you may not be mixed with these nations left here among you, or make mention of the names of their gods, or swear by them, or serve them, or bow yourselves down to them, ⁸but hold fast to the LORD your God, as you have done to this day. ⁹For the LORD has driven out before you great and strong nations; and as for you, no one has been able to withstand you to this day. ¹⁰One of you puts to flight a thousand, since it is the LORD your God who fights for you, as he promised you. ¹¹Be very careful, therefore, to love the LORD your God. ¹²For if you turn back, and join the survivors of these nations left here among you, and intermarry with them, so that you marry their women and they yours, ¹³know assuredly that the LORD your God will not continue to drive out these nations before you; but they shall be a snare and a trap for you, a scourge on your sides, and thorns in your eyes, until you perish from this good land that the LORD your God has given you.

14 "And now I am about to go the way of all the earth, and you know in your hearts and souls, all of you, that not one thing has failed of all the good things that the LORD your God promised concerning you; all have come to pass for you, not one of them has failed. ¹⁵But just as all the good things that the LORD your God promised concerning you have been fulfilled for you, so the LORD

a Cn Compare Syr: Heb lacks *Witness*

will bring upon you all the bad things, until he has destroyed you from this good land that the LORD your God has given you. 16If you transgress the covenant of the LORD your God, which he enjoined on you, and go and serve other gods and bow down to them, then the anger of the LORD will be kindled against you, and you shall perish quickly from the good land that he has given to you."

23.1–16: Joshua's farewell. 1: Joshua's great age (13.1) motivates an exhortation* to faithfulness and a warning about the future. *Rest* signals the end of the conquest (21.44; 22.4). **4:** In spite of many victories, some enemy nations still *remain.* They represent both opportunities for further success (v. 5) and dangerous enticements to infidelity (vv. 7, 12–13). **6:** Future success requires that the whole nation show the same undeviating obedience to *the book of the law* (Deuteronomy) that was enjoined on Joshua in 1.7–8. **12:** Intermarriage would establish complex relationships between families resulting in religious disloyalty (Deut 7.3–4). **13:** The metaphors* of *a snare and a trap* signify loss of freedom, and *a scourge* communicates political oppression (1 Kings 12.11). Exile *from this good land* is threatened three times (vv. 13, 15, 16). **14–15:** The LORD has been trustworthy in keeping past promises (see 21.45), but this means that the LORD's threatened punishments are equally certain to take place.

24 Then Joshua gathered all the tribes of Israel to Shechem, and summoned the elders, the heads, the judges, and the officers of Israel; and they presented themselves before God. 2And Joshua said to all the people, "Thus says the LORD, the God of Israel: Long ago your ancestors—Terah and his sons Abraham and Nahor—lived beyond the Euphrates and served other gods. 3Then I took your father Abraham from beyond the River and led him through all the land of Canaan and made his offspring many. I gave him Isaac; 4and to Isaac I gave Jacob and Esau. I gave Esau the hill country of Seir to possess, but Jacob and his children went down to Egypt. 5Then I sent Moses and Aaron, and I plagued Egypt with what I did in its midst; and afterwards I brought you out. 6When I brought your ancestors out of Egypt, you came to the sea; and the Egyptians pursued your ancestors with chariots

and horsemen to the Red Sea.*a* 7When they cried out to the LORD, he put darkness between you and the Egyptians, and made the sea come upon them and cover them; and your eyes saw what I did to Egypt. Afterwards you lived in the wilderness a long time. 8Then I brought you to the land of the Amorites, who lived on the other side of the Jordan; they fought with you, and I handed them over to you, and you took possession of their land, and I destroyed them before you. 9Then King Balak son of Zippor of Moab, set out to fight against Israel. He sent and invited Balaam son of Beor to curse you, 10but I would not listen to Balaam; therefore he blessed you; so I rescued you out of his hand. 11When you went over the Jordan and came to Jericho, the citizens of Jericho fought against you, and also the Amorites, the Perizzites, the Canaanites, the Hittites, the Girgashites, the Hivites, and the Jebusites; and I handed them over to you. 12I sent the hornet*b* ahead of you, which drove out before you the two kings of the Amorites; it was not by your sword or by your bow. 13I gave you a land on which you had not labored, and towns that you had not built, and you live in them; you eat the fruit of vineyards and oliveyards that you did not plant.

24.1–13: The saving acts of God. 1: A long list of participants emphasizes that *all the tribes of Israel* appeared *before God,* that is, at the sanctuary of *Shechem.* **2:** *Thus says the LORD* indicates that Joshua is speaking as a prophet.* **3:** The *River* is the Euphrates. **7:** This protective *darkness* is mentioned in Ex 14.20. **9–10:** The story of Balaam is reported in Num 22–24. **11:** The detail that *the citizens of Jericho fought* relies on a tradition different from that of Joshua 6. **12:** *Hornet* (note *b*; Deut 7.20) may be a metaphor* for panic (compare 10.10). **13:** This description of the land reflects Deut 6.10–11.

14 "Now therefore revere the LORD, and serve him in sincerity and in faithfulness; put away the gods that your ancestors served beyond the River and in Egypt, and serve the LORD. 15Now if you are unwilling to serve the LORD, choose this day whom you will

a Or *Sea of Reeds* *b* Meaning of Heb uncertain

serve, whether the gods your ancestors served in the region beyond the River or the gods of the Amorites in whose land you are living; but as for me and my household, we will serve the LORD."

16 Then the people answered, "Far be it from us that we should forsake the LORD to serve other gods; [17]for it is the LORD our God who brought us and our ancestors up from the land of Egypt, out of the house of slavery, and who did those great signs in our sight. He protected us along all the way that we went, and among all the peoples through whom we passed; [18]and the LORD drove out before us all the peoples, the Amorites who lived in the land. Therefore we also will serve the LORD, for he is our God."

19 But Joshua said to the people, "You cannot serve the LORD, for he is a holy God. He is a jealous God; he will not forgive your transgressions or your sins. [20]If you forsake the LORD and serve foreign gods, then he will turn and do you harm, and consume you, after having done you good." [21]And the people said to Joshua, "No, we will serve the LORD!" [22]Then Joshua said to the people, "You are witnesses against yourselves that you have chosen the LORD, to serve him." And they said, "We are witnesses." [23]He said, "Then put away the foreign gods that are among you, and incline your hearts to the LORD, the God of Israel." [24]The people said to Joshua, "The LORD our God we will serve, and him we will obey." [25]So Joshua made a covenant with the people that day, and made statutes and ordinances for them at Shechem. [26]Joshua wrote these words in the book of the law of God; and he took a large stone, and set it up there under the oak in the sanctuary of the LORD. [27]Joshua said to all the people, "See, this stone shall be a witness against us; for it has heard all the words of the LORD that he spoke to us; therefore it shall be a witness against you, if you deal falsely with your God." [28]So Joshua sent the people away to their inheritances.

24.14–28: Joshua insists on religious fidelity. 14–15: Three types of gods had proven to be ineffective. Abraham was taken away from the territory of the *gods beyond the River* (v. 3), and the gods of *Egypt* and of

the *Amorites* could not protect their worshippers (vv. 5–7 and 8–13). **19–20:** With a rhetorical* jolt, Joshua warns Israel of the difficulties and dangers implicit in their commitment: *You cannot serve the LORD.* The obstacle is God's basic nature as a *jealous God,* one who is passionately determined to be Israel's only God. **23:** *Incline your heart* calls for personal conviction, not just outward conformity (1 Kings 8.58). The demand to *put away the foreign gods* may reflect a ceremony of burying idols at Shechem (compare Gen 35.2–4). **25–26:** Joshua performed three actions to give structure and effectiveness to Israel's commitment: He *made a covenant,** wrote down its rules in *the book of the law,* and set up a witness stone *under the oak* (see Judg 9.6). **27:** The stone is a witness in the sense of being a visible public reminder (compare 22.27, 34), but also because it was present when *all the words of the LORD* (that is, vv. 2–13) were proclaimed.

29 After these things Joshua son of Nun, the servant of the LORD, died, being one hundred ten years old. [30]They buried him in his own inheritance at Timnath-serah, which is in the hill country of Ephraim, north of Mount Gaash.

31 Israel served the LORD all the days of Joshua, and all the days of the elders who outlived Joshua and had known all the work that the LORD did for Israel.

32 The bones of Joseph, which the Israelites had brought up from Egypt, were buried at Shechem, in the portion of ground that Jacob had bought from the children of Hamor, the father of Shechem, for one hundred pieces of money;[a] it became an inheritance of the descendants of Joseph.

33 Eleazar son of Aaron died; and they buried him at Gibeah, the town of his son Phinehas, which had been given him in the hill country of Ephraim.

24.29–33: Burial traditions. 29–30: Great age is a sign of exceptional faithfulness (Gen 50.26; Deut 34.7). *Timnath-serah* was granted to Joshua in 19.49–50. **31:** This looks forward to the book of Judges (compare Judg 2.9). **32:** These traditions are reported in Gen 33.18–20; 50.24–25; Ex 13.19. **33:** *Eleazar* has played an important role in Joshua (14.1; 17.4; 19.51; 21.1).

a Heb one hundred *qesitah*

JUDGES

Introduction

Judges continues the story of the Deuteronomistic* History (see the introduction to Joshua) from the death of Joshua (Judg 2.8) to just before the birth of Samuel (1 Sam 1). After an incomplete conquest that leaves much in the hands of Israel's foes (ch. 1), Israel's life in the land follows a recurring pattern of disloyalty to God followed by oppression by enemies. When Israel cries out in repentance, the LORD sends deliverers (judges). Most of these judges are military leaders (chs. 2–12). In contrast, the judge Samson is a solitary champion (chs. 13–16). Finally Israel is described as descending into idolatry,* violence, and civil war, as a result of not yet having a king (chs. 17–21). The stories of the six judges were originally individual tales of local heroes, but were gathered together and converted into a succession of leaders of national importance. Judges illustrates the principle that disloyalty to God leads to national catastrophe, while repentance and obedience can lead to deliverance.

Israel's hold on the land of promise was often insecure. The two kingdoms that made up Israel eventually collapsed (2 Kings 17, 24, 25), and many inhabitants were taken into exile. Judges is one answer to what went wrong. Israel had not always been loyal to God, and this tendency for disobedience began early. Yet the cyclical pattern of Judges also offered hope in times of national distress. To cry to the LORD might once again lead to deliverance.

READING GUIDE

Judges may be read theologically as a cautionary tale about disloyalty to God and its consequences. It can also be enjoyed as great literature about improbable heroes. The reader might choose to compare the characters' contrasting personality traits as revealed by their words and actions. Readers may also wish to explore issues of oppression and patriarchal power by comparing the dreadful stories about Jephthah's daughter (11.29–40), the Levite's concubine* (ch. 19), and the efforts made to get replacement wives for the decimated tribe of Benjamin (ch. 21).

1 After the death of Joshua, the Israelites inquired of the LORD, "Who shall go up first for us against the Canaanites, to fight against them?" 2The LORD said, "Judah shall go up. I hereby give the land into his hand." 3Judah said to his brother Simeon, "Come up with me into the territory allotted to me, that we may fight against the Canaanites; then I too will go with you into the territory allotted to you." So Simeon went with him. 4Then Judah went up and the LORD gave the Canaanites and the Perizzites into their hand; and they defeated ten thousand of them at Bezek. 5They came upon Adoni-bezek at Bezek, and fought against him, and defeated the Canaanites and the Perizzites. 6Adoni-bezek fled; but they pursued him, and caught him, and cut off his thumbs and big toes. 7Adoni-bezek said, "Seventy kings with their thumbs and big toes cut off used to pick up scraps under my table; as I have done, so God has paid me

back." They brought him to Jerusalem, and he died there.

8 Then the people of Judah fought against Jerusalem and took it. They put it to the sword and set the city on fire. 9Afterward the people of Judah went down to fight against the Canaanites who lived in the hill country, in the Negeb, and in the lowland. 10Judah went against the Canaanites who lived in Hebron (the name of Hebron was formerly Kiriath-arba); and they defeated Sheshai and Ahiman and Talmai.

11 From there they went against the inhabitants of Debir (the name of Debir was formerly Kiriath-sepher). 12Then Caleb said, "Whoever attacks Kiriath-sepher and takes it, I will give him my daughter Achsah as wife." 13And Othniel son of Kenaz, Caleb's younger brother, took it; and he gave him his daughter Achsah as wife. 14When she came to him, she urged him to ask her father for a field. As she dismounted from her donkey, Caleb said to her, "What do you wish?" 15She said to him, "Give me a present; since you have set me in the land of the Negeb, give me also Gulloth-mayim."*a* So Caleb gave her Upper Gulloth and Lower Gulloth.

16 The descendants of Hobab*b* the Kenite, Moses' father-in-law, went up with the people of Judah from the city of palms into the wilderness of Judah, which lies in the Negeb near Arad. Then they went and settled with the Amalekites.*c* 17Judah went with his brother Simeon, and they defeated the Canaanites who inhabited Zephath, and devoted it to destruction. So the city was called Hormah. 18Judah took Gaza with its territory, Ashkelon with its territory, and Ekron with its territory. 19The LORD was with Judah, and he took possession of the hill country, but could not drive out the inhabitants of the plain, because they had chariots of iron. 20Hebron was given to Caleb, as Moses had said; and he drove out from it the three sons of Anak. 21But the Benjaminites did not drive out the Jebusites who lived in Jerusalem; so the Jebusites have lived in Jerusalem among the Benjaminites to this day.

**1.1–21: Successful conquests by Judah and Simeon.
1:** In contrast to the complete conquest described in

Joshua (Josh 11.23; 21.43–45), Judg 1 portrays an ongoing conquest that continued *after the death of Joshua.* **2:** Judah's successes contrast with the comparative failures of the northern tribes (vv. 22–36). Divine guidance in tactics and an assurance of victory were elements of holy war* tradition. **3:** The tribes *Judah* and *Simeon* are personified as individuals. **8:** This assertion is in tension with v. 21. Jerusalem first became Israelite under David (2 Sam 5.6–9). **10:** These accomplishments are credited to Caleb in v. 20 (and Josh 15.14). **11–15:** The story of Achsah is duplicated in Josh 15.13–19. She argues that she needs pools (note *a*) because she has received arid land (metaphorically,* *land of the Negeb*). **16:** The Kenites were a foreign group associated with Israel (5.24; 1 Sam 15.6). They *settled* with the "people" Israel (the better reading, note *c*). **17:** *Hormah* is a wordplay on the Hebrew word "herem," the holy war ban* inflicted on it when Judah and Simeon *devoted it to destruction.* **19:** *Chariots* with *iron* fittings gave battlefield superiority outside the broken terrain of *the hill country.* **21:** Native *Jebusites* remained a distinct group in *Jerusalem* even after David's capture of the city (2 Sam 24.18).

22 The house of Joseph also went up against Bethel; and the LORD was with them. 23The house of Joseph sent out spies to Bethel (the name of the city was formerly Luz). 24When the spies saw a man coming out of the city, they said to him, "Show us the way into the city, and we will deal kindly with you." 25So he showed them the way into the city; and they put the city to the sword, but they let the man and all his family go. 26So the man went to the land of the Hittites and built a city, and named it Luz; that is its name to this day.

27 Manasseh did not drive out the inhabitants of Beth-shean and its villages, or Taanach and its villages, or the inhabitants of Dor and its villages, or the inhabitants of Ibleam and its villages, or the inhabitants of Megiddo and its villages; but the Canaanites continued to live in that land. 28When Israel grew strong, they put the Canaanites to forced labor, but did not in fact drive them out.

29 And Ephraim did not drive out the

a That is *Basins of Water*   *b* Gk: Heb lacks *Hobab*
c See 1 Sam 15.6: Heb *people*

Canaanites who lived in Gezer; but the Canaanites lived among them in Gezer.

30 Zebulun did not drive out the inhabitants of Kitron, or the inhabitants of Nahalol; but the Canaanites lived among them, and became subject to forced labor.

31 Asher did not drive out the inhabitants of Acco, or the inhabitants of Sidon, or of Ahlab, or of Achzib, or of Helbah, or of Aphik, or of Rehob; 32 but the Asherites lived among the Canaanites, the inhabitants of the land; for they did not drive them out.

33 Naphtali did not drive out the inhabitants of Beth-shemesh, or the inhabitants of Beth-anath, but lived among the Canaanites, the inhabitants of the land; nevertheless the inhabitants of Beth-shemesh and of Beth-anath became subject to forced labor for them.

34 The Amorites pressed the Danites back into the hill country; they did not allow them to come down to the plain. 35 The Amorites continued to live in Har-heres, in Aijalon, and in Shaalbim, but the hand of the house of Joseph rested heavily on them, and they became subject to forced labor. 36 The border of the Amorites ran from the ascent of Akrabbim, from Sela and upward.

1.22–36: Failures of the northern tribes. 22–26: The capture of Bethel is the only success reported. 27–29: This information is duplicated in Josh 16.10; 17.11–13. These cities did not become part of Israel until the reigns of David and Solomon. 34: For the saga of the Danites, see Judg 18.

2 Now the angel of the LORD went up from Gilgal to Bochim, and said, "I brought you up from Egypt, and brought you into the land that I had promised to your ancestors. I said, 'I will never break my covenant with you. 2 For your part, do not make a covenant with the inhabitants of this land; tear down their altars.' But you have not obeyed my command. See what you have done! 3 So now I say, I will not drive them out before you; but they shall become adversaries[a] to you, and their gods shall be a snare to you." 4 When the angel of the LORD spoke these words to all the Israelites, the people lifted up their voices and wept. 5 So they named that place Bochim,[b] and there they sacrificed to the LORD.

2.1–5: The angel of the LORD appears. 1: *The angel of the LORD* is a manifestation by which the LORD appears directly to humans (6.11; 13.3). The Hebrew word "mal'ak" can also be translated "messenger." *Gilgal,* Joshua's former headquarters, abruptly reappears without explanation. 2–3: Because Israel has failed to keep aloof from the native population (Ex 34.12–13; Deut 7.2, 5), the LORD has implemented the punishment anticipated in Josh 23.13. 5: This tradition originally explained the name of a sanctuary (note b).

6 When Joshua dismissed the people, the Israelites all went to their own inheritances to take possession of the land. 7 The people worshiped the LORD all the days of Joshua, and all the days of the elders who outlived Joshua, who had seen all the great work that the LORD had done for Israel. 8 Joshua son of Nun, the servant of the LORD, died at the age of one hundred ten years. 9 So they buried him within the bounds of his inheritance in Timnath-heres, in the hill country of Ephraim, north of Mount Gaash. 10 Moreover, that whole generation was gathered to their ancestors, and another generation grew up after them, who did not know the LORD or the work that he had done for Israel.

11 Then the Israelites did what was evil in the sight of the LORD and worshiped the Baals; 12 and they abandoned the LORD, the God of their ancestors, who had brought them out of the land of Egypt; they followed other gods, from among the gods of the peoples who were all around them, and bowed down to them; and they provoked the LORD to anger. 13 They abandoned the LORD, and worshiped Baal and the Astartes. 14 So the anger of the LORD was kindled against Israel, and he gave them over to plunderers who plundered them, and he sold them into the power of their enemies all around, so that they could no longer withstand their enemies. 15 Whenever they marched out, the hand of the LORD was against them to bring misfortune, as the LORD had warned them

a OL Vg Compare Gk: Heb *sides* b That is *Weepers*

and sworn to them; and they were in great distress. 16 Then the LORD raised up judges, who delivered them out of the power of those who plundered them. 17Yet they did not listen even to their judges; for they lusted after other gods and bowed down to them. They soon turned aside from the way in which their ancestors had walked, who had obeyed the commandments of the LORD; they did not follow their example. 18Whenever the LORD raised up judges for them, the LORD was with the judge, and he delivered them from the hand of their enemies all the days of the judge; for the LORD would be moved to pity by their groaning because of those who persecuted and oppressed them. 19But whenever the judge died, they would relapse and behave worse than their ancestors, following other gods, worshiping them and bowing down to them. They would not drop any of their practices or their stubborn ways. 20So the anger of the LORD was kindled against Israel; and he said, "Because this people have transgressed my covenant that I commanded their ancestors, and have not obeyed my voice, 21I will no longer drive out before them any of the nations that Joshua left when he died." 22In order to test Israel, whether or not they would take care to walk in the way of the LORD as their ancestors did, 23the LORD had left those nations, not driving them out at once, and had not handed them over to Joshua.

3 Now these are the nations that the LORD left to test all those in Israel who had no experience of any war in Canaan 2(it was only that successive generations of Israelites might know war, to teach those who had no experience of it before): 3the five lords of the Philistines, and all the Canaanites, and the Sidonians, and the Hivites who lived on Mount Lebanon, from Mount Baal-hermon as far as Lebo-hamath. 4They were for the testing of Israel, to know whether Israel would obey the commandments of the LORD, which he commanded their ancestors by Moses. 5So the Israelites lived among the Canaanites, the Hittites, the Amorites, the Perizzites, the Hivites, and the Jebusites; 6and they took their daughters as wives for

themselves, and their own daughters they gave to their sons; and they worshiped their gods.

2.6–3.6. 2.6–19: The cyclical pattern. 6–9: This statement is duplicated in Josh 24.28–31. The dismissal seems to close the assembly described in Josh 24.1–27, thereby skipping back over Judg 1.1–2.5. **10:** In contrast to the elders of v. 7, the ignorance of *another generation* sets in motion a repeated pattern of events. **11–13:** First Israel would abandon the LORD for other gods. *Baals*★ (vv. 11, 13) and *the Astartes*★ (v. 13) represent Canaanite religion as a whole (10.6). **14–15:** This would in turn lead to the LORD's anger and oppression by enemies. **16–18:** The LORD would then send *judges* (military leaders) to deliver Israel. **19:** But each time, the people would revert to the worship of other gods and begin the cycle again. **2.20–3.6: The nations left in the land. 2.20–23:** Israel's failure to complete the conquest was both a punishment (vv. 20–21) and a test of obedience (vv. 22–23; 3.1, 4). **3.2:** Another explanation is offered: They remained to train Israel for war. **3.6:** Intermarriage unavoidably entangled Israel in idolatry★ (Deut 7.3–4).

~~~~~~

7 The Israelites did what was evil in the sight of the LORD, forgetting the LORD their God, and worshiping the Baals and the Asherahs. 8Therefore the anger of the LORD was kindled against Israel, and he sold them into the hand of King Cushan-rishathaim of Aram-naharaim; and the Israelites served Cushan-rishathaim eight years. 9But when the Israelites cried out to the LORD, the LORD raised up a deliverer for the Israelites, who delivered them, Othniel son of Kenaz, Caleb's younger brother. 10The spirit of the LORD came upon him, and he judged Israel; he went out to war, and the LORD gave King Cushan-rishathaim of Aram into his hand; and his hand prevailed over Cushan-rishathaim. 11So the land had rest forty years. Then Othniel son of Kenaz died.

3.7–11: Othniel. 7: Apostasy begins the cyclical pattern set forth in 2.11–19. The plural *Baals*★ *and Asherahs*★ denotes the worship of these divinities at multiple local shrines. Asherah was worshipped as the consort of Baal★ or Yahweh and represented by a wooden pole (6.25). **8:** Subjugation follows. *Cushan-rishathaim* is otherwise unknown and sounds like a feature of folklore rather than history ("Cushan of Double Wickedness"). *Aram-naharaim* refers to northwestern Mesopotamia. **9:** The pattern is completed by Israel's cry to the LORD and deliverance. **10:** *The spirit of the LORD* is a force that empowers chosen heroes to perform extraordinary deeds of strength and leadership. **11:** The individual judges are unified by a chronological structure (see also v. 8) that reaches to 1 Kings 6.1.

12 The Israelites again did what was evil in the sight of the LORD; and the LORD strengthened King Eglon of Moab against Israel, because they had done what was evil in the sight of the LORD. ¹³In alliance with the Ammonites and the Amalekites, he went and defeated Israel; and they took possession of the city of palms. ¹⁴So the Israelites served King Eglon of Moab eighteen years.

15 But when the Israelites cried out to the LORD, the LORD raised up for them a deliverer, Ehud son of Gera, the Benjaminite, a left-handed man. The Israelites sent tribute by him to King Eglon of Moab. ¹⁶Ehud made for himself a sword with two edges, a cubit in length; and he fastened it on his right thigh under his clothes. ¹⁷Then he presented the tribute to King Eglon of Moab. Now Eglon was a very fat man. ¹⁸When Ehud had finished presenting the tribute, he sent the people who carried the tribute on their way. ¹⁹But he himself turned back at the sculptured stones near Gilgal, and said, "I have a secret message for you, O king." So the king said,ᵃ "Silence!" and all his attendants went out from his presence. ²⁰Ehud came to him, while he was sitting alone in his cool roof chamber, and said, "I have a message from God for you." So he rose from his seat. ²¹Then Ehud reached with his left hand, took the sword from his right thigh, and thrust it into Eglon'sᵇ belly; ²²the hilt also went in after the blade, and the fat closed over the blade, for he did not draw the sword out of his belly; and the dirt came out.ᶜ ²³Then Ehud went out into the vestibule,ᵈ and closed the doors of the roof chamber on him, and locked them.

24 After he had gone, the servants came. When they saw that the doors of the roof chamber were locked, they thought, "He must be relieving himselfᵉ in the cool chamber." ²⁵So they waited until they were embarrassed. When he still did not open the doors of the roof chamber, they took the key and opened them. There was their lord lying dead on the floor.

26 Ehud escaped while they delayed, and passed beyond the sculptured stones, and escaped to Seirah. ²⁷When he arrived, he sounded the trumpet in the hill country of Ephraim; and the Israelites went down with him from the hill country, having him at their head. ²⁸He said to them, "Follow after me; for the LORD has given your enemies the Moabites into your hand." So they went down after him, and seized the fords of the Jordan against the Moabites, and allowed no one to cross over. ²⁹At that time they killed about ten thousand of the Moabites, all strong, able-bodied men; no one escaped. ³⁰So Moab was subdued that day under the hand of Israel. And the land had rest eighty years.

31 After him came Shamgar son of Anath, who killed six hundred of the Philistines with an oxgoad. He too delivered Israel.

3.12–31. 12–30: Ehud. 13: *The city of palms* is Jericho. **15–16:** That Ehud was *left-handed* lets him hide his short sword (*with two edges* for stabbing) in an unexpected place on his *right thigh*. **20:** Eglon *rose from his seat,* expecting to hear a divine oracle.* **24:** Readers would enjoy rough humor at the expense of their enemies. The delay gives Ehud time to escape and raise a rebellion. **28:** Holding *the fords of the Jordan* prevented the enemy from escaping back across to Moab. **31: Shamgar.** Since 4.1 refers to Ehud, this mysterious figure (compare 5.6) is not part of the book's system of judges. Since *son of* indicates membership in a group or class and *Anath* was a war goddess, Shamgar may have been a mercenary.

4 The Israelites again did what was evil in the sight of the LORD, after Ehud died. ²So the LORD sold them into the hand of King Jabin of Canaan, who reigned in Hazor; the commander of his army was Sisera, who

a Heb *he said*   *b* Heb *his*   *c* With Tg Vg: Meaning of Heb uncertain   *d* Meaning of Heb uncertain   *e* Heb *covering his feet* lived in Harosheth-ha-goiim. ³Then the Israelites cried out to the LORD for help; for he had nine hundred chariots of iron, and had oppressed the Israelites cruelly twenty years.

4 At that time Deborah, a prophetess, wife of Lappidoth, was judging Israel. ⁵She used to sit under the palm of Deborah between Ramah and Bethel in the hill country of Ephraim; and the Israelites came up to her for judgment. ⁶She sent and summoned Barak son of Abinoam from Kedesh in Naphtali, and said to him, "The LORD, the God of Israel, commands you, 'Go, take position at Mount Tabor, bringing ten thousand from the tribe of Naphtali and the tribe of Zebulun. ⁷I will draw out Sisera, the general of Jabin's army, to meet you by the Wadi Kishon with his chariots and his troops; and I will give him into your hand.'" ⁸Barak said to her, "If you will go with me, I will go; but if you will not go with me, I will not go." ⁹And she said, "I will surely go with you; nevertheless, the road on which you are going will not lead to your glory, for the LORD will sell Sisera into the hand of a woman." Then Deborah got up and went with Barak to Kedesh. ¹⁰Barak summoned Zebulun and Naphtali to Kedesh; and ten thousand warriors went up behind him; and Deborah went up with him.

11 Now Heber the Kenite had separated from the other Kenites,ᵃ that is, the descendants of Hobab the father-in-law of Moses, and had encamped as far away as Elon-bezaanannim, which is near Kedesh.

4.1–11: Deborah and Barak prepare for battle. 2: *Jabin* is also named as king of *Hazor* in Josh 11.1–11. **3:** *Chariots* with *iron* fittings gave a decisive tactical advantage. **4:** Here *judging* refers to settling disputes, but the verb also means to serve as military leader (3.10). As a *prophetess** Deborah delivers messages from the LORD (vv. 6–7, 14). **6–7:** In accord with holy war* tradition, the LORD dictates tactics and gives an assurance of victory. The territories of *Naphtali* and *Zebulun* touched at *Mount Tabor*. **9:** Barak is penalized for his fainthearted response. The reader who assumes that *the hand of a woman* refers to Deborah is in for a surprise.

12 When Sisera was told that Barak son of Abinoam had gone up to Mount Tabor, ¹³Sisera called out all his chariots, nine hundred chariots of iron, and all the troops who were with him, from Harosheth-ha-goiim to the Wadi Kishon. ¹⁴Then Deborah said to Barak, "Up! For this is the day on which the LORD has given Sisera into your hand. The LORD is indeed going out before you." So Barak went down from Mount Tabor with ten thousand warriors following him. ¹⁵And the LORD threw Sisera and all his chariots and all his army into a panicᵇ before Barak; Sisera got down from his chariot and fled away on foot, ¹⁶while Barak pursued the chariots and the army to Harosheth-ha-goiim. All the army of Sisera fell by the sword; no one was left.

17 Now Sisera had fled away on foot to the tent of Jael wife of Heber the Kenite; for there was peace between King Jabin of Hazor and the clan of Heber the Kenite. ¹⁸Jael came out to meet Sisera, and said to him, "Turn aside, my lord, turn aside to me; have no fear." So he turned aside to her into the tent, and she covered him with a rug. ¹⁹Then he said to her, "Please give me a little water to drink; for I am thirsty." So she opened a skin of milk and gave him a drink and covered him. ²⁰He said to her, "Stand at the entrance of the tent, and if anybody comes and asks you, 'Is anyone here?' say, 'No.'" ²¹But Jael wife of Heber took a tent peg, and took a hammer in her hand, and went softly to him and drove the peg into his temple, until it went down into the ground—he was lying fast asleep from weariness—and he died. ²²Then, as Barak came in pursuit of Sisera, Jael went out to meet him, and said to him, "Come, and I will show you the man whom you are seeking." So he went into her tent; and there was Sisera lying dead, with the tent peg in his temple.

23 So on that day God subdued King Jabin of Canaan before the Israelites. ²⁴Then the hand of the Israelites bore harder and harder on King Jabin of Canaan, until they destroyed King Jabin of Canaan.

ᵃ Heb *from the Kain*   ᵇ Heb adds *to the sword;* compare verse 16

JUDGES

defeat and Jael's exploit. **13:** The
... ace in the plain of the *Wadi** Kishon*,
... unt Tabor. **15:** *Panic* is a standard weapon
... vine warrior* (Josh 10.10). The circumstances
... and this panic are not described (but see 5.20–21).
... **6:** *Barak pursued the chariots*, but Sisera has abandoned his and run off (vv. 15, 17). **17:** This *peace* explains why Sisera feels comfortable seeking refuge with
Jael. **18–19:** *Jael* takes the initiative, going out to invite
him in. The *rug* and *milk* sound like courteous hospitality, but by encouraging sleep, Jael is setting him up
for the kill. **20:** Sisera's request reveals both his unmanly fear and his misplaced confidence in Jael. **21:**
Hammering tent pegs would have been a routine task
for a woman in this culture.

5 Then Deborah and Barak son of Abinoam sang on that day, saying:
2 "When locks are long in Israel,
    when the people offer themselves
        willingly—
    bless *a* the LORD!

3 "Hear, O kings; give ear, O princes;
    to the LORD I will sing,
    I will make melody to the LORD, the
        God of Israel.

4 "LORD, when you went out from Seir,
    when you marched from the region of
        Edom,
    the earth trembled,
    and the heavens poured,
    the clouds indeed poured water.
5 The mountains quaked before the
        LORD, the One of Sinai,
    before the LORD, the God of
        Israel.

6 "In the days of Shamgar son of Anath,
    in the days of Jael, caravans ceased
    and travelers kept to the byways.
7 The peasantry prospered in Israel,
    they grew fat on plunder,
    because you arose, Deborah,
    arose as a mother in Israel.
8 When new gods were chosen,
    then war was in the gates.
    Was shield or spear to be seen
    among forty thousand in Israel?

9 My heart goes out to the commanders
        of Israel
    who offered themselves willingly
        among the people.
    Bless the LORD.

5.1–31: The song of Deborah. **2:** Archaic language
makes this poem difficult to interpret (notes *a, b, d*).
Locks are long may refer to vows of military dedication,
similar to Samson's long hair. **4–5:** The poetic format
of a "theophany"* describes the awe-inspiring approach of the divine warrior* (compare Deut 33.2–3).
6–8: Israel's precarious situation before the victory (vv.
6, 8), is contrasted with the good fortune that followed
(v. 7). *Mother in Israel* (v. 7) is an honorific title signifying authority and leadership.

10 "Tell of it, you who ride on white
        donkeys,
    you who sit on rich carpets *b*
    and you who walk by the way.
11 To the sound of musicians *b* at the
        watering places,
    there they repeat the triumphs of the
        LORD,
    the triumphs of his peasantry in
        Israel.

    "Then down to the gates marched the
        people of the LORD.

12 "Awake, awake, Deborah!
    Awake, awake, utter a song!
    Arise, Barak, lead away your captives,
        O son of Abinoam.
13 Then down marched the remnant of the
        noble;
    the people of the LORD marched
        down for him *c* against the
        mighty.
14 From Ephraim they set out *d* into the
        valley, *e*
    following you, Benjamin, with your
        kin;
    from Machir marched down the
        commanders,

a Or *You who offer yourselves willingly among the people,
bless*   *b* Meaning of Heb uncertain   *c* Gk: Heb *me*
d Cn: Heb *From Ephraim their root*   *e* Gk: Heb in
Amalek

and from Zebulun those who bear the
  marshal's staff;
15 the chiefs of Issachar came with
  Deborah,
  and Issachar faithful to Barak;
  into the valley they rushed out at his
  heels.
  Among the clans of Reuben
  there were great searchings of heart.
16 Why did you tarry among the sheepfolds,
  to hear the piping for the flocks?
  Among the clans of Reuben
  there were great searchings of heart.
17 Gilead stayed beyond the Jordan;
  and Dan, why did he abide with the
  ships?
  Asher sat still at the coast of the sea,
  settling down by his landings.
18 Zebulun is a people that scorned death;
  Naphtali too, on the heights of the
  field.

5.10–18: Everyone is to celebrate, both aristocrats who
ride and *sit on rich carpets* and ordinary folk who *walk.*
Watering places were customary spots for social interaction. 14–18: Reflecting a stage of tribal affinity earlier
than the conventional twelve-tribe system, the poem
alludes to ten groups and censures four of them for
not participating. *Machir* (v. 14) and *Gilead* (v. 17)
appear in place of Manasseh and Gad. Judah, Simeon,
and Levi are not mentioned at all.

19 "The kings came, they fought;
  then fought the kings of Canaan,
  at Taanach, by the waters of Megiddo;
  they got no spoils of silver.
20 The stars fought from heaven,
  from their courses they fought against
  Sisera.
21 The torrent Kishon swept them away,
  the onrushing torrent, the torrent
  Kishon.
  March on, my soul, with might!
22 "Then loud beat the horses' hoofs
  with the galloping, galloping of his
  steeds.
23 "Curse Meroz, says the angel of the
  LORD,
  curse bitterly its inhabitants,

because they did not come to the help
  of the LORD,
  to the help of the LORD against the
  mighty.
24 "Most blessed of women be Jael,
  the wife of Heber the Kenite,
  of tent-dwelling women most blessed.
25 He asked water and she gave him milk,
  she brought him curds in a lordly bowl.
26 She put her hand to the tent peg
  and her right hand to the workmen's
  mallet;
  she struck Sisera a blow,
  she crushed his head,
  she shattered and pierced his temple.
27 He sank, he fell,
  he lay still at her feet;
  at her feet he sank, he fell;
  where he sank, there he fell dead.

5.19–27. 20–21: The heavenly forces of the divine
warrior* fight, and the Kishon River overwhelms the
enemy. 22: The escaping chariot horses are vividly described. 23: Both the town *Meroz* and the incident
cited are otherwise unknown. 26–27: In this version
Sisera seems to be standing when attacked (contrast
4.21). The penetrating tent peg and his fall "between
her feet" (NRSV: *at her feet*) probably have sexual implications. This scene may be a reversal of the customary rape alluded to in v. 30.

28 "Out of the window she peered,
  the mother of Sisera gazed*a* through
  the lattice:
  'Why is his chariot so long in coming?
  Why tarry the hoofbeats of his
  chariots?'
29 Her wisest ladies make answer,
  indeed, she answers the question
  herself:
30 'Are they not finding and dividing the
  spoil?—
  A girl or two for every man;
  spoil of dyed stuffs for Sisera,
  spoil of dyed stuffs embroidered,
  two pieces of dyed work embroidered
  for my neck as spoil?'

a Gk Compare Tg: Heb *exclaimed*

5.28–30: With delicious sarcasm, the poet describes Sisera's mother waiting in vain. Her reference to *hoofbeats* (v. 28) is ironic* in light of v. 22. Her son is not ravishing captive women (v. 30), but has been ravished himself.

31 "So perish all your enemies, O LORD!
    But may your friends be like the sun
        as it rises in its might."

And the land had rest forty years.

6 The Israelites did what was evil in the sight of the LORD, and the LORD gave them into the hand of Midian seven years. ²The hand of Midian prevailed over Israel; and because of Midian the Israelites provided for themselves hiding places in the mountains, caves and strongholds. ³For whenever the Israelites put in seed, the Midianites and the Amalekites and the people of the east would come up against them. ⁴They would encamp against them and destroy the produce of the land, as far as the neighborhood of Gaza, and leave no sustenance in Israel, and no sheep or ox or donkey. ⁵For they and their livestock would come up, and they would even bring their tents, as thick as locusts; neither they nor their camels could be counted; so they wasted the land as they came in. ⁶Thus Israel was greatly impoverished because of Midian; and the Israelites cried out to the LORD for help.

7 When the Israelites cried to the LORD on account of the Midianites, ⁸the LORD sent a prophet to the Israelites; and he said to them, "Thus says the LORD, the God of Israel: I led you up from Egypt, and brought you out of the house of slavery; ⁹and I delivered you from the hand of the Egyptians, and from the hand of all who oppressed you, and drove them out before you, and gave you their land; ¹⁰and I said to you, 'I am the LORD your God; you shall not pay reverence to the gods of the Amorites, in whose land you live.' But you have not given heed to my voice."

6.1–10: Oppression by Midian. 3–4: Nomadic raiders are devastating the local food supply. **7–10:** These accusations reflect the indictment delivered at Bochim

(2.1–5). To *give heed* to the LORD's *voice* (v. 10) means to obey.

11 Now the angel of the LORD came and sat under the oak at Ophrah, which belonged to Joash the Abiezrite, as his son Gideon was beating out wheat in the wine press, to hide it from the Midianites. ¹²The angel of the LORD appeared to him and said to him, "The LORD is with you, you mighty warrior." ¹³Gideon answered him, "But sir, if the LORD is with us, why then has all this happened to us? And where are all his wonderful deeds that our ancestors recounted to us, saying, 'Did not the LORD bring us up from Egypt?' But now the LORD has cast us off, and given us into the hand of Midian." ¹⁴Then the LORD turned to him and said, "Go in this might of yours and deliver Israel from the hand of Midian; I hereby commission you." ¹⁵He responded, "But sir, how can I deliver Israel? My clan is the weakest in Manasseh, and I am the least in my family." ¹⁶The LORD said to him, "But I will be with you, and you shall strike down the Midianites, every one of them." ¹⁷Then he said to him, "If now I have found favor with you, then show me a sign that it is you who speak with me. ¹⁸Do not depart from here until I come to you, and bring out my present, and set it before you." And he said, "I will stay until you return."

19 So Gideon went into his house and prepared a kid, and unleavened cakes from an ephah of flour; the meat he put in a basket, and the broth he put in a pot, and brought them to him under the oak and presented them. ²⁰The angel of God said to him, "Take the meat and the unleavened cakes, and put them on this rock, and pour out the broth." And he did so. ²¹Then the angel of the LORD reached out the tip of the staff that was in his hand, and touched the meat and the unleavened cakes; and fire sprang up from the rock and consumed the meat and the unleavened cakes; and the angel of the LORD vanished from his sight. ²²Then Gideon perceived that it was the angel of the LORD; and Gideon said, "Help me, Lord GOD! For I have seen the angel of the LORD face to face." ²³But the LORD

said to him, "Peace be to you; do not fear, you shall not die." 24Then Gideon built an altar there to the LORD, and called it, The LORD is peace. To this day it still stands at Ophrah, which belongs to the Abiezrites.

6.11–24: The call of Gideon. 11: *The angel of the* LORD is a visible manifestation of the LORD's presence (compare v. 14). *Wheat* would normally be beaten or threshed* on a windy hilltop, not in the confined space of a *wine press.* **15:** Objections are a standard element of call stories (Ex 3.10–12). **24:** One purpose of this traditional story was to authenticate a local altar of sacrifice.

---

25 That night the LORD said to him, "Take your father's bull, the second bull seven years old, and pull down the altar of Baal that belongs to your father, and cut down the sacred pole*a* that is beside it; 26and build an altar to the LORD your God on the top of the stronghold here, in proper order; then take the second bull, and offer it as a burnt offering with the wood of the sacred pole*a* that you shall cut down." 27So Gideon took ten of his servants, and did as the LORD had told him; but because he was too afraid of his family and the townspeople to do it by day, he did it by night. 28 When the townspeople rose early in the morning, the altar of Baal was broken down, and the sacred pole*a* beside it was cut down, and the second bull was offered on the altar that had been built. 29So they said to one another, "Who has done this?" After searching and inquiring, they were told, "Gideon son of Joash did it." 30Then the townspeople said to Joash, "Bring out your son, so that he may die, for he has pulled down the altar of Baal and cut down the sacred pole*a* beside it." 31But Joash said to all who were arrayed against him, "Will you contend for Baal? Or will you defend his cause? Whoever contends for him shall be put to death by morning. If he is a god, let him contend for himself, because his altar has been pulled down." 32Therefore on that day Gideon*b* was called Jerubbaal, that is to say, "Let Baal contend against him," because he pulled down his altar.

6.25–32: Gideon pulls down Baal's* altar. 25–26: The *sacred pole* was a symbol of the goddess Asherah* (note *a*). Using it as firewood would be a calculated desecration. **27:** Gideon is an ambivalent hero (v. 15, 17); he prefers to act *by night.* **31:** *If he is a god:* A god unable to defend its own interests is not really a god at all. **32:** Gideon's other name, *Jerubbaal* ("let Baal contend"), would have been offensive to later believers. Here it receives an orthodox interpretation* as a reminder of Baal's humiliation.

---

33 Then all the Midianites and the Amalekites and the people of the east came together, and crossing the Jordan they encamped in the Valley of Jezreel. 34But the spirit of the LORD took possession of Gideon; and he sounded the trumpet, and the Abiezrites were called out to follow him. 35He sent messengers throughout all Manasseh, and they too were called out to follow him. He also sent messengers to Asher, Zebulun, and Naphtali, and they went up to meet them.

36 Then Gideon said to God, "In order to see whether you will deliver Israel by my hand, as you have said, 37I am going to lay a fleece of wool on the threshing floor; if there is dew on the fleece alone, and it is dry on all the ground, then I shall know that you will deliver Israel by my hand, as you have said." 38And it was so. When he rose early next morning and squeezed the fleece, he wrung enough dew from the fleece to fill a bowl with water. 39Then Gideon said to God, "Do not let your anger burn against me, let me speak one more time; let me, please, make trial with the fleece just once more; let it be dry only on the fleece, and on all the ground let there be dew." 40And God did so that night. It was dry on the fleece only, and on all the ground there was dew.

6.33–40: Assembling troops and seeking a sign. 34–35: The dynamic power of *the spirit of the* LORD inspires an unexpected act of leadership. Beginning with his own clan,* *the Abiezrites,* Gideon attracts his own tribe and three neighboring ones. **36–40:** Gideon's repeated quest for certainty corresponds to his ambivalent character (6.15, 17, 27), but is not actually

a Heb *Asherah*   *b* Heb *he*

condemned in the narrative.* Assurance of victory was an important element in holy war* tradition.

7 Then Jerubbaal (that is, Gideon) and all the troops that were with him rose early and encamped beside the spring of Harod; and the camp of Midian was north of them, below[a] the hill of Moreh, in the valley.

2 The LORD said to Gideon, "The troops with you are too many for me to give the Midianites into their hand. Israel would only take the credit away from me, saying, 'My own hand has delivered me.' 3 Now therefore proclaim this in the hearing of the troops, 'Whoever is fearful and trembling, let him return home.'" Thus Gideon sifted them out;[b] twenty-two thousand returned, and ten thousand remained.

4 Then the LORD said to Gideon, "The troops are still too many; take them down to the water and I will sift them out for you there. When I say, 'This one shall go with you,' he shall go with you; and when I say, 'This one shall not go with you,' he shall not go." 5 So he brought the troops down to the water; and the LORD said to Gideon, "All those who lap the water with their tongues, as a dog laps, you shall put to one side; all those who kneel down to drink, putting their hands to their mouths,[c] you shall put to the other side." 6 The number of those that lapped was three hundred; but all the rest of the troops knelt down to drink water. 7 Then the LORD said to Gideon, "With the three hundred that lapped I will deliver you, and give the Midianites into your hand. Let all the others go to their homes." 8 So he took the jars of the troops from their hands,[d] and their trumpets; and he sent all the rest of Israel back to their own tents, but retained the three hundred. The camp of Midian was below him in the valley.

9 That same night the LORD said to him, "Get up, attack the camp; for I have given it into your hand. 10 But if you fear to attack, go down to the camp with your servant Purah; 11 and you shall hear what they say, and afterward your hands shall be strengthened to attack the camp." Then he went down with his servant Purah to the outposts of the armed men that were in the camp.

12 The Midianites and the Amalekites and all the people of the east lay along the valley as thick as locusts; and their camels were without number, countless as the sand on the seashore. 13 When Gideon arrived, there was a man telling a dream to his comrade; and he said, "I had a dream, and in it a cake of barley bread tumbled into the camp of Midian, and came to the tent, and struck it so that it fell; it turned upside down, and the tent collapsed." 14 And his comrade answered, "This is no other than the sword of Gideon son of Joash, a man of Israel; into his hand God has given Midian and all the army."

7.1–14: Preparing for battle. 2: In holy war,* the LORD alone wins the victory. **3:** Sending home the *fearful* accords with Deut 20.8. **4–6:** The Hebrew text of the second test is perplexing (note *c*), and the point of preferring *those who lap* over *those who kneel* (v. 5) is baffling. Few Israelites lap water, so that only a tiny fraction of the original ten thousand remain. **8:** Those who stay take the provisions of those who are leaving (retaining the Hebrew text, note *d*). **10:** That Gideon would still *fear to attack* after the LORD's word of assurance in v. 9 typifies his character. **13–14:** Dreams were regarded as premonitions of the future. The symbols are appropriate: a *tent* for Midianite nomads and *barley bread* for Israelite farmers.

15 When Gideon heard the telling of the dream and its interpretation, he worshiped; and he returned to the camp of Israel, and said, "Get up; for the LORD has given the army of Midian into your hand." 16 After he divided the three hundred men into three companies, and put trumpets into the hands of all of them, and empty jars, with torches inside the jars, 17 he said to them, "Look at me, and do the same; when I come to the outskirts of the camp, do as I do. 18 When I blow the trumpet, I and all who are with me, then you also blow the trumpets around the whole camp, and shout, 'For the LORD and for Gideon!'"

19 So Gideon and the hundred who were

a Heb *from*   *b* Cn: Heb *home, and depart from Mount Gilead'*   *c* Heb places the words *putting their hands to their mouths* after the word *lapped* in verse 6
d Cn: Heb *So the people took provisions in their hands*

with him came to the outskirts of the camp at the beginning of the middle watch, when they had just set the watch; and they blew the trumpets and smashed the jars that were in their hands. 20So the three companies blew the trumpets and broke the jars, holding in their left hands the torches, and in their right hands the trumpets to blow; and they cried, "A sword for the LORD and for Gideon!" 21Every man stood in his place all around the camp, and all the men in camp ran; they cried out and fled. 22When they blew the three hundred trumpets, the LORD set every man's sword against his fellow and against all the army; and the army fled as far as Beth-shittah toward Zererah,a as far as the border of Abel-meholah, by Tabbath. 23And the men of Israel were called out from Naphtali and from Asher and from all Manasseh, and they pursued after the Midianites.

24 Then Gideon sent messengers throughout all the hill country of Ephraim, saying, "Come down against the Midianites and seize the waters against them, as far as Beth-barah, and also the Jordan." So all the men of Ephraim were called out, and they seized the waters as far as Beth-barah, and also the Jordan. 25They captured the two captains of Midian, Oreb and Zeeb; they killed Oreb at the rock of Oreb, and Zeeb they killed at the wine press of Zeeb, as they pursued the Midianites. They brought the heads of Oreb and Zeeb to Gideon beyond the Jordan.

8 Then the Ephraimites said to him, "What have you done to us, not to call us when you went to fight against the Midianites?" And they upbraided him violently. 2So he said to them, "What have I done now in comparison with you? Is not the gleaning of the grapes of Ephraim better than the vintage of Abiezer? 3God has given into your hands the captains of Midian, Oreb and Zeeb; what have I been able to do in comparison with you?" When he said this, their anger against him subsided.

7.15–8.3: Victory over Midian. 7.16: The torches remain inside the jars to preserve the element of surprise. 19: The beginning of the middle watch is a psycho-

logically appropriate moment to attack. 21–22: The result is panic, the classic weapon of the divine warrior* (4.15). This victory became a proverbial example (Ps 83.9–11; Isa 9.4). 8.1–2: The Ephraimites resent being left out of the original summons (6.35; 7.23), but Gideon responds wisely with a soothing compliment: The dregs of Ephraim are better than the very best my clan* has to offer.

4 Then Gideon came to the Jordan and crossed over, he and the three hundred who were with him, exhausted and famished.b 5So he said to the people of Succoth, "Please give some loaves of bread to my followers, for they are exhausted, and I am pursuing Zebah and Zalmunna, the kings of Midian." 6But the officials of Succoth said, "Do you already have in your possession the hands of Zebah and Zalmunna, that we should give bread to your army?" 7Gideon replied, "Well then, when the LORD has given Zebah and Zalmunna into my hand, I will trample your flesh on the thorns of the wilderness and on briers." 8From there he went up to Penuel, and made the same request of them; and the people of Penuel answered him as the people of Succoth had answered. 9So he said to the people of Penuel, "When I come back victorious, I will break down this tower."

10 Now Zebah and Zalmunna were in Karkor with their army, about fifteen thousand men, all who were left of all the army of the people of the east; for one hundred twenty thousand men bearing arms had fallen. 11So Gideon went up by the caravan route east of Nobah and Jogbehah, and attacked the army; for the army was off its guard. 12Zebah and Zalmunna fled; and he pursued them and took the two kings of Midian, Zebah and Zalmunna, and threw all the army into a panic.

13 When Gideon son of Joash returned from the battle by the ascent of Heres, 14he caught a young man, one of the people of Succoth, and questioned him; and he listed for him the officials and elders of Succoth, seventy-seven people. 15Then he came to the people of Succoth, and said, "Here are Zebah and Zalmunna, about whom you taunted

a Another reading is Zeredah   b Gk: Heb pursuing

me, saying, 'Do you already have in your possession the hands of Zebah and Zalmunna, that we should give bread to your troops who are exhausted?'" 16So he took the elders of the city and he took thorns of the wilderness and briers and with them he trampled*a* the people of Succoth. 17He also broke down the tower of Penuel, and killed the men of the city.

18 Then he said to Zebah and Zalmunna, "What about the men whom you killed at Tabor?" They answered, "As you are, so were they, every one of them; they resembled the sons of a king." 19And he replied, "They were my brothers, the sons of my mother; as the LORD lives, if you had saved them alive, I would not kill you." 20So he said to Jether his firstborn, "Go kill them!" But the boy did not draw his sword, for he was afraid, because he was still a boy. 21Then Zebah and Zalmunna said, "You come and kill us; for as the man is, so is his strength." So Gideon proceeded to kill Zebah and Zalmunna; and he took the crescents that were on the necks of their camels.

8.4–21: Pursuit and vengeance. 5: *Zebah and Zalmunna* represent a different story-telling tradition from that featuring Oreb and Zeeb (7.25). **6:** The *hands* of the enemy could be cut off to serve as evidence of their capture or death. **19:** Gideon demands personal blood vengeance. *Sons of my mother* indicates these were his full brothers, an important consideration in a polygamous society. **20–21:** To have a mere *boy* kill them would be a grave insult.

22 Then the Israelites said to Gideon, "Rule over us, you and your son and your grandson also; for you have delivered us out of the hand of Midian." 23Gideon said to them, "I will not rule over you, and my son will not rule over you; the LORD will rule over you." 24Then Gideon said to them, "Let me make a request of you; each of you give me an earring he has taken as booty." (For the enemy*b* had golden earrings, because they were Ishmaelites.) 25"We will willingly give them," they answered. So they spread a garment, and each threw into it an earring he had taken as booty. 26The weight of the golden earrings that he requested was one

thousand seven hundred shekels of gold (apart from the crescents and the pendants and the purple garments worn by the kings of Midian, and the collars that were on the necks of their camels). 27Gideon made an ephod of it and put it in his town, in Ophrah; and all Israel prostituted themselves to it there, and it became a snare to Gideon and to his family. 28So Midian was subdued before the Israelites, and they lifted up their heads no more. So the land had rest forty years in the days of Gideon.

29 Jerubbaal son of Joash went to live in his own house. 30Now Gideon had seventy sons, his own offspring, for he had many wives. 31His concubine who was in Shechem also bore him a son, and he named him Abimelech. 32Then Gideon son of Joash died at a good old age, and was buried in the tomb of his father Joash at Ophrah of the Abiezrites.

33 As soon as Gideon died, the Israelites relapsed and prostituted themselves with the Baals, making Baal-berith their god. 34The Israelites did not remember the LORD their God, who had rescued them from the hand of all their enemies on every side; 35and they did not exhibit loyalty to the house of Jerubbaal (that is, Gideon) in return for all the good that he had done to Israel.

8.22–35: Israel offers Gideon hereditary rule. 23: *The* LORD *will rule over you* expresses the traditional notion that choosing human kings violates the LORD's kingship (1 Sam 8.7). **24:** *Ishmaelites* were similar in culture to the Midianites, but these were distinct nationalities (Gen 16; 25.1–4). **27:** *Ephod*★ usually describes a priestly vestment, which could be used for divination. Perhaps this gold ephod was used to robe an idol. **31:** A *concubine*★ was a subordinate wife with lower legal status. **33:** *Baal-berith* (Baal★ of the Covenant; 9.4) was a god worshipped in Shechem, probably the same as El-berith (9.46).

9 Now Abimelech son of Jerubbaal went to Shechem to his mother's kinsfolk and said to them and to the whole clan of his mother's family, 2"Say in the hearing of all

a With verse 7, Compare Gk: Heb *he taught*
b Heb *they*

the lords of Shechem, 'Which is better for you, that all seventy of the sons of Jerubbaal rule over you, or that one rule over you?' Remember also that I am your bone and your flesh." [3] So his mother's kinsfolk spoke all these words on his behalf in the hearing of all the lords of Shechem; and their hearts inclined to follow Abimelech, for they said, "He is our brother." [4] They gave him seventy pieces of silver out of the temple of Baal-berith with which Abimelech hired worthless and reckless fellows, who followed him. [5] He went to his father's house at Ophrah, and killed his brothers the sons of Jerubbaal, seventy men, on one stone; but Jotham, the youngest son of Jerubbaal, survived, for he hid himself. [6] Then all the lords of Shechem and all Beth-millo came together, and they went and made Abimelech king, by the oak of the pillar[a] at Shechem.

9.1–6: Abimelech seizes royal power. 1–3: Abimelech's mother belonged to a clan* of Shechem (8.31). **5:** *On one stone* may indicate a parody of sacrifice (1 Sam 14.33–34), but clearly communicates that the killing was deliberate and cold-blooded. **6:** *Beth-millo* indicates a building (literally "House on Filled-Up Ground"), but here must refer to a group in Shechem's system of government (v. 20; compare "White House").

---

[7] When it was told to Jotham, he went and stood on the top of Mount Gerizim, and cried aloud and said to them, "Listen to me, you lords of Shechem, so that God may listen to you.

[8] The trees once went out
         to anoint a king over themselves.
     So they said to the olive tree,
         'Reign over us.'
[9] The olive tree answered them,
         'Shall I stop producing my rich oil
             by which gods and mortals are
                 honored,
             and go to sway over the trees?'
[10] Then the trees said to the fig tree,
         'You come and reign over us.'
[11] But the fig tree answered them,
         'Shall I stop producing my sweetness
             and my delicious fruit,
             and go to sway over the trees?'

[12] Then the trees said to the vine,
         'You come and reign over us.'
[13] But the vine said to them,
         'Shall I stop producing my wine
             that cheers gods and mortals,
             and go to sway over the trees?'
[14] So all the trees said to the bramble,
         'You come and reign over us.'
[15] And the bramble said to the trees,
         'If in good faith you are anointing me
             king over you,
             then come and take refuge in my
                 shade;
             but if not, let fire come out of the
                 bramble
             and devour the cedars of
                 Lebanon.'

[16] "Now therefore, if you acted in good faith and honor when you made Abimelech king, and if you have dealt well with Jerubbaal and his house, and have done to him as his actions deserved— [17] for my father fought for you, and risked his life, and rescued you from the hand of Midian; [18] but you have risen up against my father's house this day, and have killed his sons, seventy men on one stone, and have made Abimelech, the son of his slave woman, king over the lords of Shechem, because he is your kinsman— [19] if, I say, you have acted in good faith and honor with Jerubbaal and with his house this day, then rejoice in Abimelech, and let him also rejoice in you; [20] but if not, let fire come out from Abimelech, and devour the lords of Shechem, and Beth-millo; and let fire come out from the lords of Shechem, and from Beth-millo, and devour Abimelech." [21] Then Jotham ran away and fled, going to Beer, where he remained for fear of his brother Abimelech.

9.7–21: Jotham's fable.* 8–13: This fable displays a cynicism about kingship similar to 1 Samuel 8. The useful plants (representing Gideon; 8.22–23) refuse kingship as a waste of their valuable aptitudes. **14–15:** The worthless *bramble* (Abimelech) accepts. But beware! The bramble's *shade* is prickly and meager, and its potential for *fire* threatens danger. **16:** The rest of

a Cn: Meaning of Heb uncertain

Jotham's speech is an extended curse that culminates in vv. 19–20. **17–18:** The curse is interrupted to demonstrate that the leaders of Shechem have not acted fairly. **20:** *Fire* represents the dissension that is soon to unfold. Jotham's curse reaches fulfillment in vv. 56–57.

22 Abimelech ruled over Israel three years. ²³But God sent an evil spirit between Abimelech and the lords of Shechem; and the lords of Shechem dealt treacherously with Abimelech. ²⁴This happened so that the violence done to the seventy sons of Jerubbaal might be avenged*ᵃ* and their blood be laid on their brother Abimelech, who killed them, and on the lords of Shechem, who strengthened his hands to kill his brothers. ²⁵So, out of hostility to him, the lords of Shechem set ambushes on the mountain tops. They robbed all who passed by them along that way; and it was reported to Abimelech.

26 When Gaal son of Ebed moved into Shechem with his kinsfolk, the lords of Shechem put confidence in him. ²⁷They went out into the field and gathered the grapes from their vineyards, trod them, and celebrated. Then they went into the temple of their god, ate and drank, and ridiculed Abimelech. ²⁸Gaal son of Ebed said, "Who is Abimelech, and who are we of Shechem, that we should serve him? Did not the son of Jerubbaal and Zebul his officer serve the men of Hamor father of Shechem? Why then should we serve him? ²⁹If only this people were under my command! Then I would remove Abimelech; I would say*ᵇ* to him, 'Increase your army, and come out.'"

30 When Zebul the ruler of the city heard the words of Gaal son of Ebed, his anger was kindled. ³¹He sent messengers to Abimelech at Arumah,*ᶜ* saying, "Look, Gaal son of Ebed and his kinsfolk have come to Shechem, and they are stirring up*ᵈ* the city against you. ³²Now therefore, go by night, you and the troops that are with you, and lie in wait in the fields. ³³Then early in the morning, as soon as the sun rises, get up and rush on the city; and when he and the troops that are with him come out against you, you may deal with them as best you can."

9.22–33: The plot against Abimelech. 23: *An evil spirit* creates a relationship of mutual distrust (1 Sam 16.14). **24:** Israel believed that evil deeds spontaneously brought on their own appropriate penalty. *Violence* and *blood* (bloodshed) would naturally rebound on the culprits. **25:** A breakdown in civil order (compare 5.6) undermines Abimelech's authority and diminishes the collection of royal tolls. **26:** *Gaal* and his relatives relocate to Shechem, but his nationalistic rhetoric★ (vv. 28–29) indicates that he has ethnic ties there. **27:** Talk would be loose and emotions would run high at this celebration of the wine harvest. **28:** Gaal's argument appeals to ethnic pride: Abimelech is an upstart outsider. Both Jerubbaal and *Zebul* (Abimelech's deputy, v. 30) once served the authentic native leadership of Shechem, *the men of Hamor*. Hamor was a renowned character from Shechem's past (Gen 33.19). **33:** Zebul intends to make sure that Gaal and his troops *come out against* Abimelech (v. 38).

34 So Abimelech and all the troops with him got up by night and lay in wait against Shechem in four companies. ³⁵When Gaal son of Ebed went out and stood in the entrance of the gate of the city, Abimelech and the troops with him rose from the ambush. ³⁶And when Gaal saw them, he said to Zebul, "Look, people are coming down from the mountain tops!" And Zebul said to him, "The shadows on the mountains look like people to you." ³⁷Gaal spoke again and said, "Look, people are coming down from Tabbur-erez, and one company is coming from the direction of Elon-meonenim."*ᵉ* ³⁸Then Zebul said to him, "Where is your boast*ᶠ* now, you who said, 'Who is Abimelech, that we should serve him?' Are not these the troops you made light of? Go out now and fight with them." ³⁹So Gaal went out at the head of the lords of Shechem, and fought with Abimelech. ⁴⁰Abimelech chased him, and he fled before him. Many fell wounded, up to the entrance of the gate. ⁴¹So Abimelech resided at Arumah; and Zebul drove out Gaal and his kinsfolk, so that they could not live on at Shechem.

---

a Heb *might come*   *b* Gk: Heb *and he said*
c Cn See 9.41. Heb *Tormah*   *d* Cn: Heb *are besieging*
e That is *Diviners' Oak*   *f* Heb *mouth*

42 On the following day the people went out into the fields. When Abimelech was told, [43]he took his troops and divided them into three companies, and lay in wait in the fields. When he looked and saw the people coming out of the city, he rose against them and killed them. [44]Abimelech and the company that was[a] with him rushed forward and stood at the entrance of the gate of the city, while the two companies rushed on all who were in the fields and killed them. [45]Abimelech fought against the city all that day; he took the city, and killed the people that were in it; and he razed the city and sowed it with salt.

46 When all the lords of the Tower of Shechem heard of it, they entered the stronghold of the temple of El-berith. [47]Abimelech was told that all the lords of the Tower of Shechem were gathered together. [48]So Abimelech went up to Mount Zalmon, he and all the troops that were with him. Abimelech took an ax in his hand, cut down a bundle of brushwood, and took it up and laid it on his shoulder. Then he said to the troops with him, "What you have seen me do, do quickly, as I have done." [49]So every one of the troops cut down a bundle and following Abimelech put it against the stronghold, and they set the stronghold on fire over them, so that all the people of the Tower of Shechem also died, about a thousand men and women.

9.34–49: Abimelech defeats Shechem. 34: By dividing his troops into *four companies*, Abimelech improves their chance of approaching unobserved. **39:** Gaal leads out Shechem's aristocrats (*the lords of Shechem*), who are driven back into the city with heavy losses. **41:** Although Abimelech does not storm the city at this point, Zebul is able to expel Gaal and his supporters. **42:** The ordinary farmers go out to work in the fields, perhaps to harvest (v. 27). **44:** The detachment under Abimelech's direct command blocks escape back into Shechem, while the other two contingents trap and slaughter the common folk. **45:** This is total war. Abimelech pulls down buildings and blocks resettlement by sowing Shechem with salt as a symbolic curse. **46:** Although the identity of *the lords of the Tower of Shechem* is unclear, they are an aristocratic group who seek safety in the city's last

citadel. Ancient temples were often constructed as strongholds.

50 Then Abimelech went to Thebez, and encamped against Thebez, and took it. [51]But there was a strong tower within the city, and all the men and women and all the lords of the city fled to it and shut themselves in; and they went to the roof of the tower. [52]Abimelech came to the tower, and fought against it, and came near to the entrance of the tower to burn it with fire. [53]But a certain woman threw an upper millstone on Abimelech's head, and crushed his skull. [54]Immediately he called to the young man who carried his armor and said to him, "Draw your sword and kill me, so people will not say about me, 'A woman killed him.'" So the young man thrust him through, and he died. [55]When the Israelites saw that Abimelech was dead, they all went home. [56]Thus God repaid Abimelech for the crime he committed against his father in killing his seventy brothers; [57]and God also made all the wickedness of the people of Shechem fall back on their heads, and on them came the curse of Jotham son of Jerubbaal.

9.50–57: The death of Abimelech. 51–52: This narrative* begins as a replay of his assault on Shechem. **53:** *An upper millstone* was commonly used by women. It was of a size to be picked up in two hands and thrown. **54:** Although Abimelech seeks to avoid the notoriety of being killed by a woman (compare 4.9), he became a proverbial example of such a death (2 Sam 11.21). **56–57:** God's retributive justice (v. 24) and Jotham's curse (v. 20) have worked together to achieve a satisfying conclusion.

10 After Abimelech, Tola son of Puah son of Dodo, a man of Issachar, who lived at Shamir in the hill country of Ephraim, rose to deliver Israel. [2]He judged Israel twenty-three years. Then he died, and was buried at Shamir.

3 After him came Jair the Gileadite, who judged Israel twenty-two years. [4]He had thirty sons who rode on thirty donkeys; and they had thirty towns, which are in the land

a Vg and some Gk Mss: Heb *companies that were*

The Judges of Israel

In addition to the six so-called major judges, tradition preserved a concise list of others who "judged Israel" (10.1–5; 12.7–15). Family details (10.4; 12.9, 14) glorify their wealth and eminence. These minor judges seem to have been civil officials rather than military leaders.

of Gilead, and are called Havvoth-jair to this day. ⁵Jair died, and was buried in Kamon.

6 The Israelites again did what was evil in the sight of the LORD, worshiping the Baals and the Astartes, the gods of Aram, the gods of Sidon, the gods of Moab, the gods of the Ammonites, and the gods of the Philistines. Thus they abandoned the LORD, and did not worship him. ⁷So the anger of the LORD was kindled against Israel, and he sold them into the hand of the Philistines and into the hand of the Ammonites, ⁸and they crushed and oppressed the Israelites that year. For eighteen years they oppressed all the Israelites that were beyond the Jordan in the land of the Amorites, which is in Gilead. ⁹The Ammonites also crossed the Jordan to fight against Judah and against Benjamin and against the house of Ephraim; so that Israel was greatly distressed.

10 So the Israelites cried to the LORD, saying, "We have sinned against you, because we have abandoned our God and have worshiped the Baals." ¹¹And the LORD said to the Israelites, "Did I not deliver you*a* from the Egyptians and from the Amorites, from the Ammonites and from the Philistines? ¹²The Sidonians also, and the Amalekites, and the Maonites, oppressed you; and you cried to me, and I delivered you out of their hand. ¹³Yet you have abandoned me and worshiped other gods; therefore I will deliver you no more. ¹⁴Go and cry to the gods whom you have chosen; let them deliver you in the time of your distress." ¹⁵And the Israelites said to the LORD, "We have sinned; do to us whatever seems good to you; but deliver us this day!" ¹⁶So they put away the foreign gods from among them and worshiped the LORD; and he could no longer bear to see Israel suffer.

17 Then the Ammonites were called to arms, and they encamped in Gilead; and the Israelites came together, and they encamped at Mizpah. ¹⁸The commanders of the people of Gilead said to one another, "Who will begin the fight against the Ammonites? He shall be head over all the inhabitants of Gilead."

10.1–18. 1–5: Minor judges: Tola and Jair. 1–2: *Tola* is the only minor judge credited with a military role (*rose to deliver Israel*). Tradition preserves the names *Tola* and *Puah* (as *Puvah*) as clans* of *Issachar* (Gen 46.13). 3–5: *Jair* was remembered as a pioneer in the settlement of Gilead (Josh 13.30; 1 Kings 4.13). *Havvoth-jair* means "tent villages of Jair." 6–18: Oppression by Ammon. 6: A long catalog of gods emphasizes the magnitude of Israel's infidelity. 7–8: *The Ammonites* lived to the east and south of Israel's territory in *Gilead*. 12: Traditions of deliverance from *the Sidonians* or the otherwise unknown *Maonites* are not preserved elsewhere. 13: The LORD has fulfilled the threat made in 2.3. 16: To *put away the foreign gods* may reflect an established ceremony (Gen 35.2–4; Josh 24.23). The LORD's relationship to Israel is described as an emotional attachment.

11 Now Jephthah the Gileadite, the son of a prostitute, was a mighty warrior. Gilead was the father of Jephthah. ²Gilead's wife also bore him sons; and when his wife's sons grew up, they drove Jephthah away, saying to him, "You shall not inherit anything in our father's house; for you are the son of another woman." ³Then Jephthah fled from his brothers and lived in the land of Tob. Outlaws collected around Jephthah and went raiding with him.

a Heb lacks *Did I not deliver you*

4 After a time the Ammonites made war against Israel. 5And when the Ammonites made war against Israel, the elders of Gilead went to bring Jephthah from the land of Tob. 6They said to Jephthah, "Come and be our commander, so that we may fight with the Ammonites." 7But Jephthah said to the elders of Gilead, "Are you not the very ones who rejected me and drove me out of my father's house? So why do you come to me now when you are in trouble?" 8The elders of Gilead said to Jephthah, "Nevertheless, we have now turned back to you, so that you may go with us and fight with the Ammonites, and become head over us, over all the inhabitants of Gilead." 9Jephthah said to the elders of Gilead, "If you bring me home again to fight with the Ammonites, and the LORD gives them over to me, I will be your head." 10And the elders of Gilead said to Jephthah, "The LORD will be witness between us; we will surely do as you say." 11So Jephthah went with the elders of Gilead, and the people made him head and commander over them; and Jephthah spoke all his words before the LORD at Mizpah.

11.1–11: Jephthah becomes leader of Gilead. 3: Jephthah's career as a brigand parallels David's early history (1 Sam 22.2). 6: The elders first offer the apparently temporary position of military *commander*. 8: Jephthah holds out for a better offer: permanent *head* or ruler *over all the inhabitants of Gilead* (10.18). 11: He validates the agreement by reciting it in the witnessing presence of the LORD at the shrine *at Mizpah*.

12 Then Jephthah sent messengers to the king of the Ammonites and said, "What is there between you and me, that you have come to me to fight against my land?" 13The king of the Ammonites answered the messengers of Jephthah, "Because Israel, on coming from Egypt, took away my land from the Arnon to the Jabbok and to the Jordan; now therefore restore it peaceably." 14Once again Jephthah sent messengers to the king of the Ammonites 15and said to him: "Thus says Jephthah: Israel did not take away the land of Moab or the land of the Ammonites, 16but when they came up from Egypt, Israel

went through the wilderness to the Red Sea[a] and came to Kadesh. 17Israel then sent messengers to the king of Edom, saying, 'Let us pass through your land'; but the king of Edom would not listen. They also sent to the king of Moab, but he would not consent. So Israel remained at Kadesh. 18Then they journeyed through the wilderness, went around the land of Edom and the land of Moab, arrived on the east side of the land of Moab, and camped on the other side of the Arnon. They did not enter the territory of Moab, for the Arnon was the boundary of Moab. 19Israel then sent messengers to King Sihon of the Amorites, king of Heshbon; and Israel said to him, 'Let us pass through your land to our country.' 20But Sihon did not trust Israel to pass through his territory; so Sihon gathered all his people together, and encamped at Jahaz, and fought with Israel. 21Then the LORD, the God of Israel, gave Sihon and all his people into the hand of Israel, and they defeated them; so Israel occupied all the land of the Amorites, who inhabited that country. 22They occupied all the territory of the Amorites from the Arnon to the Jabbok and from the wilderness to the Jordan. 23So now the LORD, the God of Israel, has conquered the Amorites for the benefit of his people Israel. Do you intend to take their place? 24Should you not possess what your god Chemosh gives you to possess? And should we not be the ones to possess everything that the LORD our God has conquered for our benefit? 25Now are you any better than King Balak son of Zippor of Moab? Did he ever enter into conflict with Israel, or did he ever go to war with them? 26While Israel lived in Heshbon and its villages, and in Aroer and its villages, and in all the towns that are along the Arnon, three hundred years, why did you not recover them within that time? 27It is not I who have sinned against you, but you are the one who does me wrong by making war on me. Let the LORD, who is judge, decide today for the Israelites or for the Ammonites." 28But the king of the Ammonites did not heed the message that Jephthah sent him.

a Or Sea of Reeds

11.12–28: Jephthah's diplomacy fails. 13: The king asserts that Israel has unlawfully occupied land north of *the Arnon* River and south of the *Jabbok,* directly west of the Ammonite homeland. Later statements indicate that Ammon is claiming this territory on the basis that it once belonged to Moab. **15:** Jephthah's position is that Israel did not take this territory from either *Moab* or *the Ammonites,* but rather obtained it 300 years ago (v. 26) by conquering the Amorite king Sihon (vv. 21–22). **18:** He emphasizes that Israel did not go into Moab. Even at that time *the Arnon was the boundary of Moab.* **24:** Early Israel believed that the gods of other nations existed and legitimately guarded the interests of their own people. *Chemosh,* the god of Moab, was associated with the territory under dispute.

29 Then the spirit of the LORD came upon Jephthah, and he passed through Gilead and Manasseh. He passed on to Mizpah of Gilead, and from Mizpah of Gilead he passed on to the Ammonites. ³⁰And Jephthah made a vow to the LORD, and said, "If you will give the Ammonites into my hand, ³¹then whoever comes out of the doors of my house to meet me, when I return victorious from the Ammonites, shall be the LORD's, to be offered up by me as a burnt offering." ³²So Jephthah crossed over to the Ammonites to fight against them; and the LORD gave them into his hand. ³³He inflicted a massive defeat on them from Aroer to the neighborhood of Minnith, twenty towns, and as far as Abel-keramim. So the Ammonites were subdued before the people of Israel.

34 Then Jephthah came to his home at Mizpah; and there was his daughter coming out to meet him with timbrels and with dancing. She was his only child; he had no son or daughter except her. ³⁵When he saw her, he tore his clothes, and said, "Alas, my daughter! You have brought me very low; you have become the cause of great trouble to me. For I have opened my mouth to the LORD, and I cannot take back my vow." ³⁶She said to him, "My father, if you have opened your mouth to the LORD, do to me according to what has gone out of your mouth, now that the LORD has given you vengeance against your enemies, the Ammonites." ³⁷And she

said to her father, "Let this thing be done for me: Grant me two months, so that I may go and wander*ᵃ* on the mountains, and bewail my virginity, my companions and I." ³⁸"Go," he said and sent her away for two months. So she departed, she and her companions, and bewailed her virginity on the mountains. ³⁹At the end of two months, she returned to her father, who did with her according to the vow he had made. She had never slept with a man. So there arose an Israelite custom that ⁴⁰for four days every year the daughters of Israel would go out to lament the daughter of Jephthah the Gileadite.

11.29–40: Jephthah's vow. 29: Only now *the spirit of the LORD* empowers Jephthah, perhaps reflecting the LORD's earlier reluctance to deliver Israel (10.13–16). **30:** Another example of a war vow can be found in Num 21.2. **31:** His vow is rash, careless, and egocentric. The language does not necessarily specify that this will be a human sacrifice (NRSV *whoever* could also be "whatever"). Israelites shared their houses with farm animals. *Burnt offering* suggests an animal, although human sacrifice was not unknown in Israel. **34:** She is doing an expected and predictable thing. Israelite women customarily celebrated victories *with timbrels and with dancing* (Ex 15.20–21; 1 Sam 18.6–7). **35:** He is distraught (*tore his clothes*), but also sounds as though he is blaming her. Every ancient reader would agree that his vow was irrevocable. **36–37:** She is courageous and suitably devout, but also seizes control of how she will spend the last months of her life. *Bewail my virginity:* To die without the possibility of motherhood was a dreadful tragedy in Israelite culture (reemphasized in v. 39). Jephthah too is now childless (v. 34). **40:** This annual commemoration may have preserved her story for later generations.

12 The men of Ephraim were called to arms, and they crossed to Zaphon and said to Jephthah, "Why did you cross over to fight against the Ammonites, and did not call us to go with you? We will burn your house down over you!" ²Jephthah said to them, "My people and I were engaged in conflict with the Ammonites who oppressed us*ᵇ* severely. But when I called you, you did

a Cn: Heb *go down*   *b* Gk OL, Syr H: Heb lacks *who oppressed us* not deliver me from their hand. [3]When I saw that you would not deliver me, I took my life in my hand, and crossed over against the Ammonites, and the LORD gave them into my hand. Why then have you come up to me this day, to fight against me?" [4]Then Jephthah gathered all the men of Gilead and fought with Ephraim; and the men of Gilead defeated Ephraim, because they said, "You are fugitives from Ephraim, you Gileadites—in the heart of Ephraim and Manasseh."[a] [5]Then the Gileadites took the fords of the Jordan against the Ephraimites. Whenever one of the fugitives of Ephraim said, "Let me go over," the men of Gilead would say to him, "Are you an Ephraimite?" When he said, "No," [6]they said to him, "Then say Shibboleth," and he said, "Sibboleth," for he could not pronounce it right. Then they seized him and killed him at the fords of the Jordan. Forty-two thousand of the Ephraimites fell at that time.

[7] Jephthah judged Israel six years. Then Jephthah the Gileadite died, and was buried in his town in Gilead.[b]

[8] After him Ibzan of Bethlehem judged Israel. [9]He had thirty sons. He gave his thirty daughters in marriage outside his clan and brought in thirty young women from outside for his sons. He judged Israel seven years. [10]Then Ibzan died, and was buried at Bethlehem.

[11] After him Elon the Zebulunite judged Israel; and he judged Israel ten years. [12]Then Elon the Zebulunite died, and was buried at Aijalon in the land of Zebulun.

[13] After him Abdon son of Hillel the Pirathonite judged Israel. [14]He had forty sons and thirty grandsons, who rode on seventy donkeys; he judged Israel eight years. [15]Then Abdon son of Hillel the Pirathonite died, and was buried at Pirathon in the land of Ephraim, in the hill country of the Amalekites.

12.1–15. 1–7: War between Ephraim and Gilead. **1–3:** The reader does not know which side to believe. No such appeal to Ephraim by Jephthah has been reported. **4:** Ephraim insults Gilead as being nothing but *fugitives* or refugees from Ephraim, insisting that Gilead is really only a part *of Ephraim and Manasseh* (but

see note *a*). **5:** Gilead blocks the way back across the Jordan and uses a difference in local dialect as a password. The phrase *fugitives of Ephraim* grimly echoes their earlier taunt (v. 4). **7:** This information seems to derive from the list of minor judges (10.1–5; 12.8–15). **8–15: Minor judges: Ibzan, Elon, and Abdon. 12:** *Elon* is remembered as a clan* ancestor in Zebulun (Gen 46.14).

13

The Israelites again did what was evil in the sight of the LORD, and the LORD gave them into the hand of the Philistines forty years.

[2] There was a certain man of Zorah, of the tribe of the Danites, whose name was Manoah. His wife was barren, having borne no children. [3]And the angel of the LORD appeared to the woman and said to her, "Although you are barren, having borne no children, you shall conceive and bear a son. [4]Now be careful not to drink wine or strong drink, or to eat anything unclean, [5]for you shall conceive and bear a son. No razor is to come on his head, for the boy shall be a nazirite[c] to God from birth. It is he who shall begin to deliver Israel from the hand of the Philistines." [6]Then the woman came and told her husband, "A man of God came to me, and his appearance was like that of an angel[d] of God, most awe-inspiring; I did not ask him where he came from, and he did not tell me his name; [7]but he said to me, 'You shall conceive and bear a son. So then drink no wine or strong drink, and eat nothing unclean, for the boy shall be a nazirite[c] to God from birth to the day of his death.' "

13.1–7: Samson's birth foretold. 3: *The angel of the LORD* represents the LORD's visible presence. **4:** *Wine or strong drink* (Num 6.3) were forbidden to a nazirite. She is to keep away from these because her unborn son must be untouched by them. **5:** A *nazirite* lived a special lifestyle dedicated to God's purposes (see note *c*; Num 6.1–21; 1 Sam 1.11). Normally nazirites took a temporary vow of dedication; Samson was to be a permanent nazirite *from birth*. **6:** She supposes she has encountered *a man of God*, that is, a prophet,* but

a Meaning of Heb uncertain: Gk omits *because . . . Manasseh*   *b* Gk: Heb *in the towns of Gilead*
c That is *one separated* or *one consecrated*   *d* Or *the angel*

from his striking appearance she comes close to sensing the actual truth—that he was a divine messenger.

8 Then Manoah entreated the LORD, and said, "O LORD, I pray, let the man of God whom you sent come to us again and teach us what we are to do concerning the boy who will be born." 9God listened to Manoah, and the angel of God came again to the woman as she sat in the field; but her husband Manoah was not with her. 10So the woman ran quickly and told her husband, "The man who came to me the other day has appeared to me." 11Manoah got up and followed his wife, and came to the man and said to him, "Are you the man who spoke to this woman?" And he said, "I am." 12Then Manoah said, "Now when your words come true, what is to be the boy's rule of life; what is he to do?" 13The angel of the LORD said to Manoah, "Let the woman give heed to all that I said to her. 14She may not eat of anything that comes from the vine. She is not to drink wine or strong drink, or eat any unclean thing. She is to observe everything that I commanded her."

15 Manoah said to the angel of the LORD, "Allow us to detain you, and prepare a kid for you." 16The angel of the LORD said to Manoah, "If you detain me, I will not eat your food; but if you want to prepare a burnt offering, then offer it to the LORD." (For Manoah did not know that he was the angel of the LORD.) 17Then Manoah said to the angel of the LORD, "What is your name, so that we may honor you when your words come true?" 18But the angel of the LORD said to him, "Why do you ask my name? It is too wonderful."

19 So Manoah took the kid with the grain offering, and offered it on the rock to the LORD, to him who works^a wonders.^b 20When the flame went up toward heaven from the altar, the angel of the LORD ascended in the flame of the altar while Manoah and his wife looked on; and they fell on their faces to the ground. 21The angel of the LORD did not appear again to Manoah and his wife. Then Manoah realized that it was the angel of the LORD. 22And Manoah said to his wife, "We shall surely die, for we have seen God." 23But his wife said to him, "If the LORD had meant to kill us, he would not have accepted a burnt offering and a grain offering at our hands, or shown us all these things, or now announced to us such things as these."

24 The woman bore a son, and named him Samson. The boy grew, and the LORD blessed him. 25The spirit of the LORD began to stir him in Mahaneh-dan, between Zorah and Eshtaol.

13.8–25: The angel reappears. 13–14: Manoah discovers nothing new from the second appearance for which he has prayed. 15–16: Manoah offers the customary hospitality for important visitors (6.19; Gen 18.3–5). He still has no idea who this is. 18: *Wonderful* implies that the name is beyond human understanding. 19–20: Gideon's experience was similar (6.20–21). 22: This is the standard reaction after experiencing a visible manifestation of God (6.22). 23: Throughout the narrative,* she is more perceptive than her husband. 25: At this point, *the spirit of the LORD* is only a latent stirring or agitation (contrast 14.6).

14 Once Samson went down to Timnah, and at Timnah he saw a Philistine woman. 2Then he came up, and told his father and mother, "I saw a Philistine woman at Timnah; now get her for me as my wife." 3But his father and mother said to him, "Is there not a woman among your kin, or among all our^c people, that you must go to take a wife from the uncircumcised Philistines?" But Samson said to his father, "Get her for me, because she pleases me." 4His father and mother did not know that this was from the LORD; for he was seeking a pretext to act against the Philistines. At that time the Philistines had dominion over Israel.

5 Then Samson went down with his father and mother to Timnah. When he came to the vineyards of Timnah, suddenly a young lion roared at him. 6The spirit of the LORD rushed on him, and he tore the lion apart barehanded as one might tear apart a kid. But he did not tell his father or his mother what he had done. 7Then he went

a Gk Vg: Heb *and working*   b Heb *wonders, while Manoah and his wife looked on*   c Cn: Heb *my* down and talked with the woman, and she pleased Samson. 8After a while he returned to marry her, and he turned aside to see the carcass of the lion, and there was a swarm of bees in the body of the lion, and honey. 9He scraped it out into his hands, and went on, eating as he went. When he came to his father and mother, he gave some to them, and they ate it. But he did not tell them that he had taken the honey from the carcass of the lion.

10 His father went down to the woman, and Samson made a feast there as the young men were accustomed to do. 11When the people saw him, they brought thirty companions to be with him. 12Samson said to them, "Let me now put a riddle to you. If you can explain it to me within the seven days of the feast, and find it out, then I will give you thirty linen garments and thirty festal garments. 13But if you cannot explain it to me, then you shall give me thirty linen garments and thirty festal garments." So they said to him, "Ask your riddle; let us hear it." 14He said to them,

"Out of the eater came something to
     eat.
Out of the strong came something
     sweet."

But for three days they could not explain the riddle.

15 On the fourth*a* day they said to Samson's wife, "Coax your husband to explain the riddle to us, or we will burn you and your father's house with fire. Have you invited us here to impoverish us?" 16So Samson's wife wept before him, saying, "You hate me; you do not really love me. You have asked a riddle of my people, but you have not explained it to me." He said to her, "Look, I have not told my father or my mother. Why should I tell you?" 17She wept before him the seven days that their feast lasted; and because she nagged him, on the seventh day he told her. Then she explained the riddle to her people. 18The men of the town said to him on the seventh day before the sun went down,

"What is sweeter than honey?
 What is stronger than a lion?"

And he said to them,

"If you had not plowed with my heifer, you would not have found out my riddle." 19Then the spirit of the LORD rushed on him, and he went down to Ashkelon. He killed thirty men of the town, took their spoil, and gave the festal garments to those who had explained the riddle. In hot anger he went back to his father's house. 20And Samson's wife was given to his companion, who had been his best man.

14.1–20: Samson's riddle. 3: Their hesitation is fitting, for intermarriage often leads to apostasy (Deut 7.3–4). **4:** God works behind ordinary human events (compare 9.24). **5:** The first trip to *Timnah* is for parental negotiations and a meeting of the couple (v. 7). **6:** *The spirit of the LORD* gave other judges the ability to serve as military leaders (3.10; 6.34; 11.29), but infuses Samson with physical strength (v. 19). **8–9:** Samson's second trip was *to marry her*. Does he discover the honey on his way back from Timnah? **10:** Now *his father* arrives in Timnah, and Samson gives *a feast*. **11:** *Companions* were a standard feature of marriage celebrations (Ps 45.14). **14:** Proposing and solving *riddles* was a favorite intellectual exercise in the ancient world. **16–17:** Her persistence is akin to Delilah's (16.6–17; compare *you do not really love me* with 16.15). **18:** Their solution sounds like a riddle itself. Is "love" a more profound answer to their question? Samson's response also occurs in riddle form. By exploiting his wife, they have *plowed with* his *heifer*. **19:** The people of *Ashkelon* were also Philistines. Samson can pay off his wager and still not really lose.

15 After a while, at the time of the wheat harvest, Samson went to visit his wife, bringing along a kid. He said, "I want to go into my wife's room." But her father would not allow him to go in. 2Her father said, "I was sure that you had rejected her; so I gave her to your companion. Is not her younger sister prettier than she? Why not take her instead?" 3Samson said to them, "This time, when I do mischief to the Philistines, I will be without blame." 4So Samson went and caught three hundred foxes, and took some torches; and he turned the foxes*b* tail to tail, and put a torch between

a Gk Syr: Heb *seventh*   *b* Heb *them*

each pair of tails. 5When he had set fire to the torches, he let the foxes go into the standing grain of the Philistines, and burned up the shocks and the standing grain, as well as the vineyards and*a* olive groves. 6Then the Philistines asked, "Who has done this?" And they said, "Samson, the son-in-law of the Timnite, because he has taken Samson's wife and given her to his companion." So the Philistines came up, and burned her and her father. 7Samson said to them, "If this is what you do, I swear I will not stop until I have taken revenge on you." 8He struck them down hip and thigh with great slaughter; and he went down and stayed in the cleft of the rock of Etam.

15.1–8: Samson's revenge. 1: This may have been a form of marriage in which the woman continued to live with her parents. **2:** That he had *rejected her* (divorced her) was a reasonable conclusion in light of 14.19. Ancient readers would have seen the offer of *her younger sister* as a sensible compromise. **4:** The *foxes* are a way of spreading the fire widely and quickly. **6:** This was precisely the fate Samson's wife had hoped to avoid (14.15). **8:** The meaning of *hip and thigh* is uncertain, but implies ferocious physical combat.

9 Then the Philistines came up and encamped in Judah, and made a raid on Lehi. 10The men of Judah said, "Why have you come up against us?" They said, "We have come up to bind Samson, to do to him as he did to us." 11Then three thousand men of Judah went down to the cleft of the rock of Etam, and they said to Samson, "Do you not know that the Philistines are rulers over us? What then have you done to us?" He replied, "As they did to me, so I have done to them." 12They said to him, "We have come down to bind you, so that we may give you into the hands of the Philistines." Samson answered them, "Swear to me that you yourselves will not attack me." 13They said to him, "No, we will only bind you and give you into their hands; we will not kill you." So they bound him with two new ropes, and brought him up from the rock.

14 When he came to Lehi, the Philistines came shouting to meet him; and the spirit of the LORD rushed on him, and the ropes that were on his arms became like flax that has caught fire, and his bonds melted off his hands. 15Then he found a fresh jawbone of a donkey, reached down and took it, and with it he killed a thousand men. 16And Samson said,

"With the jawbone of a donkey,
    heaps upon heaps,
  with the jawbone of a donkey
    I have slain a thousand men."

17When he had finished speaking, he threw away the jawbone; and that place was called Ramath-lehi.*b*

18 By then he was very thirsty, and he called on the LORD, saying, "You have granted this great victory by the hand of your servant. Am I now to die of thirst, and fall into the hands of the uncircumcised?" 19So God split open the hollow place that is at Lehi, and water came from it. When he drank, his spirit returned, and he revived. Therefore it was named En-hakkore,*c* which is at Lehi to this day. 20And he judged Israel in the days of the Philistines twenty years.

15.9–20: Samson retaliates at Lehi. 11: The dispatch of *three thousand men* to capture a single individual is humorous. **13:** That these are *two new ropes* adds to the wonder of his escape. **14:** *Shouting* (Heb., "yelling a war cry") conveys their triumph and jubilation. Two vivid images communicate the strength infused by the *spirit of the LORD.* **16:** The words for *donkey* and *heap* are the same in Hebrew. **17:** The story of Samson's exploit was preserved by its attachment to two landmarks (notes *b, c*). **19:** His *spirit returned,* that is, his vigor and positive attitude.

16 Once Samson went to Gaza, where he saw a prostitute and went in to her. 2The Gazites were told,*d* "Samson has come here." So they circled around and lay in wait for him all night at the city gate. They kept quiet all night, thinking, "Let us wait until the light of the morning; then we will kill him." 3But Samson lay only until midnight. Then at midnight he rose up, took

a Gk Tg Vg: Heb lacks *and*   *b* That is *The Hill of the Jawbone*   *c* That is *The Spring of the One who Called*   *d* Gk: Heb lacks *were told* hold of the doors of the city gate and the two posts, pulled them up, bar and all, put them on his shoulders, and carried them to the top of the hill that is in front of Hebron.

4 After this he fell in love with a woman in the valley of Sorek, whose name was Delilah. 5 The lords of the Philistines came to her and said to her, "Coax him, and find out what makes his strength so great, and how we may overpower him, so that we may bind him in order to subdue him; and we will each give you eleven hundred pieces of silver." 6 So Delilah said to Samson, "Please tell me what makes your strength so great, and how you could be bound, so that one could subdue you." 7 Samson said to her, "If they bind me with seven fresh bowstrings that are not dried out, then I shall become weak, and be like anyone else." 8 Then the lords of the Philistines brought her seven fresh bowstrings that had not dried out, and she bound him with them. 9 While men were lying in wait in an inner chamber, she said to him, "The Philistines are upon you, Samson!" But he snapped the bowstrings, as a strand of fiber snaps when it touches the fire. So the secret of his strength was not known.

10 Then Delilah said to Samson, "You have mocked me and told me lies; please tell me how you could be bound." 11 He said to her, "If they bind me with new ropes that have not been used, then I shall become weak, and be like anyone else." 12 So Delilah took new ropes and bound him with them, and said to him, "The Philistines are upon you, Samson!" (The men lying in wait were in an inner chamber.) But he snapped the ropes off his arms like a thread.

13 Then Delilah said to Samson, "Until now you have mocked me and told me lies; tell me how you could be bound." He said to her, "If you weave the seven locks of my head with the web and make it tight with the pin, then I shall become weak, and be like anyone else." 14 So while he slept, Delilah took the seven locks of his head and wove them into the web,[a] and made them tight with the pin. Then she said to him, "The Philistines are upon you, Samson!" But he awoke from his sleep, and pulled away the pin, the loom, and the web.

15 Then she said to him, "How can you say, 'I love you,' when your heart is not with me? You have mocked me three times now and have not told me what makes your strength so great." 16 Finally, after she had nagged him with her words day after day, and pestered him, he was tired to death. 17 So he told her his whole secret, and said to her, "A razor has never come upon my head; for I have been a nazirite[b] to God from my mother's womb. If my head were shaved, then my strength would leave me; I would become weak, and be like anyone else."

18 When Delilah realized that he had told her his whole secret, she sent and called the lords of the Philistines, saying, "This time come up, for he has told his whole secret to me." Then the lords of the Philistines came up to her, and brought the money in their hands. 19 She let him fall asleep on her lap; and she called a man, and had him shave off the seven locks of his head. He began to weaken,[c] and his strength left him. 20 Then she said, "The Philistines are upon you, Samson!" When he awoke from his sleep, he thought, "I will go out as at other times, and shake myself free." But he did not know that the LORD had left him. 21 So the Philistines seized him and gouged out his eyes. They brought him down to Gaza and bound him with bronze shackles; and he ground at the mill in the prison. 22 But the hair of his head began to grow again after it had been shaved.

16.1–22: Delilah betrays Samson. 1–3: *Gaza* was one of the five Philistine cities. *Hebron* is about forty miles (sixty kilometers) uphill from Gaza. 4: Because she lives in *the valley of Sorek,* she is probably a Philistine. 7: *Bowstrings* were made of animal tendons. They are to be *fresh* because new things were thought to have magical powers. 11: Specifying *new ropes* again points to magical notions. 13: *The web* and *the pin* were parts of a loom (v. 14). Perhaps to entangle Samson in something so domestic as weaving would magically drain his warrior powers. By involving his hair, Samson has revealed part of his secret. 20: The loss of his nazirite status (13.5) means *the LORD had left him,* so that the spirit would no longer empower his mighty

a Compare Gk: in verses 13–14, Heb lacks *and make it tight . . . into the web*   b That is *one separated* or *one consecrated*   c Gk: Heb *She began to torment him* feats (14.6, 19; 15.14). **21:** Samson grinds grain with a hand mill, a menial task performed by women and slaves (compare Lam 5.13).

23 Now the lords of the Philistines gathered to offer a great sacrifice to their god Dagon, and to rejoice; for they said, "Our god has given Samson our enemy into our hand." 24When the people saw him, they praised their god; for they said, "Our god has given our enemy into our hand, the ravager of our country, who has killed many of us." 25And when their hearts were merry, they said, "Call Samson, and let him entertain us." So they called Samson out of the prison, and he performed for them. They made him stand between the pillars; 26and Samson said to the attendant who held him by the hand, "Let me feel the pillars on which the house rests, so that I may lean against them." 27Now the house was full of men and women; all the lords of the Philistines were there, and on the roof there were about three thousand men and women, who looked on while Samson performed.

28 Then Samson called to the LORD and said, "Lord GOD, remember me and strengthen me only this once, O God, so that with this one act of revenge I may pay back the Philistines for my two eyes."*a* 29And Samson grasped the two middle pillars on which the house rested, and he leaned his weight against them, his right hand on the one and his left hand on the other. 30Then Samson said, "Let me die with the Philistines." He strained with all his might; and the house fell on the lords and all the people who were in it. So those he killed at his death were more than those he had killed during his life. 31Then his brothers and all his family came down and took him and brought him up and buried him between Zorah and Eshtaol in the tomb of his father Manoah. He had judged Israel twenty years.

16.23–31: Samson's retaliation. 23: *Dagon* was a Canaanite grain god adopted by the Philistines (1 Sam 5.1–5). **26:** *The house* is either Dagon's temple or a large hall. **28:** This *one act* will avenge two wrongs (but see note *a*).

17 There was a man in the hill country of Ephraim whose name was Micah. 2He said to his mother, "The eleven hundred pieces of silver that were taken from you, about which you uttered a curse, and even spoke it in my hearing,—that silver is in my possession; I took it; but now I will return it to you."*b* And his mother said, "May my son be blessed by the LORD!" 3Then he returned the eleven hundred pieces of silver to his mother; and his mother said, "I consecrate the silver to the LORD from my hand for my son, to make an idol of cast metal." 4So when he returned the money to his mother, his mother took two hundred pieces of silver, and gave it to the silversmith, who made it into an idol of cast metal; and it was in the house of Micah. 5This man Micah had a shrine, and he made an ephod and teraphim, and installed one of his sons, who became his priest. 6In those days there was no king in Israel; all the people did what was right in their own eyes.

7 Now there was a young man of Bethlehem in Judah, of the clan of Judah. He was a Levite residing there. 8This man left the town of Bethlehem in Judah, to live wherever he could find a place. He came to the house of Micah in the hill country of Ephraim to carry on his work.*c* 9Micah said to him, "From where do you come?" He replied, "I am a Levite of Bethlehem in Judah, and I am going to live wherever I can find a place." 10Then Micah said to him, "Stay with me, and be to me a father and a priest, and I will give you ten pieces of silver a year, a set of clothes, and your living."*d* 11The Levite agreed to stay with the man; and the young man became to him like one of his sons. 12So Micah installed the Levite, and the young man became his priest, and was in the house of Micah. 13Then Micah said, "Now I know that the LORD will prosper me, because the Levite has become my priest."

a Or *so that I may be avenged upon the Philistines for one of my two eyes*   *b* The words *but now I will return it to you* are transposed from the end of verse 3 in Heb   *c* Or *Ephraim, continuing his journey*   *d* Heb *living, and the Levite went*

17.1–13: Micah builds a shrine and hires a priest. 2: Micah confesses to a theft that has put him under a *curse*. His mother seeks to counteract the curse with a blessing. NRSV considers the text scrambled and re-arranges it (note *b*). **3–4:** She takes further action to nullify the curse, using part of the consecrated silver for an *idol of cast metal*. **5:** This is a private, family sanctuary (Heb., "house of God"). The *ephod** (a priestly garment) and *teraphim* (figurines) were uti-lized to discover God's will. **6:** This editorial refrain (18.1; 19.1; 21.25) approves of kingship and com-municates displeasure with Micah's actions. **7:** He was *of the clan** *of Judah* in the sense of living with them as a resident alien.* **10:** *Father* is an honorific title (compare 5.7). **13:** By virtue of his lineage, *the Levite* is preferable as priest to Micah's son (v. 5).

18 In those days there was no king in Israel. And in those days the tribe of the Danites was seeking for itself a territory to live in; for until then no territory among the tribes of Israel had been allotted to them. 2So the Danites sent five valiant men from the whole number of their clan, from Zorah and from Eshtaol, to spy out the land and to explore it; and they said to them, "Go, ex-plore the land." When they came to the hill country of Ephraim, to the house of Micah, they stayed there. 3While they were at Mi-cah's house, they recognized the voice of the young Levite; so they went over and asked him, "Who brought you here? What are you doing in this place? What is your business here?" 4He said to them, "Micah did such and such for me, and he hired me, and I have become his priest." 5Then they said to him, "Inquire of God that we may know whether the mission we are undertaking will suc-ceed." 6The priest replied, "Go in peace. The mission you are on is under the eye of the LORD."

7 The five men went on, and when they came to Laish, they observed the people who were there living securely, after the manner of the Sidonians, quiet and unsuspecting, lacking*a* nothing on earth, and possessing wealth.*b* Furthermore, they were far from the Sidonians and had no dealings with Aram.*c* 8When they came to their kinsfolk at Zorah and Eshtaol, they said to them,

"What do you report?" 9They said, "Come, let us go up against them; for we have seen the land, and it is very good. Will you do nothing? Do not be slow to go, but enter in and possess the land. 10When you go, you will come to an unsuspecting people. The land is broad—God has indeed given it into your hands—a place where there is no lack of anything on earth."

18.1–10: Dan searches for a new home. 2: Conquest stories typically begin with the dispatch of spies (1.24; Josh 2). **3:** Apparently they recognized his regional ac-cent. **5:** Part of a priest's job was to discover God's will.

11 Six hundred men of the Danite clan, armed with weapons of war, set out from Zo-rah and Eshtaol, 12and went up and en-camped at Kiriath-jearim in Judah. On this account that place is called Mahaneh-dan*d* to this day; it is west of Kiriath-jearim. 13From there they passed on to the hill country of Ephraim, and came to the house of Micah.

14 Then the five men who had gone to spy out the land (that is, Laish) said to their comrades, "Do you know that in these build-ings there are an ephod, teraphim, and an idol of cast metal? Now therefore consider what you will do." 15So they turned in that direction and came to the house of the young Levite, at the home of Micah, and greeted him. 16While the six hundred men of the Danites, armed with their weapons of war, stood by the entrance of the gate, 17the five men who had gone to spy out the land pro-ceeded to enter and take the idol of cast metal, the ephod, and the teraphim.*e* The priest was standing by the entrance of the gate with the six hundred men armed with weapons of war. 18When the men went into Micah's house and took the idol of cast metal, the ephod, and the teraphim, the priest said to them, "What are you doing?" 19They said to him, "Keep quiet! Put your hand over your mouth, and come with us,

a Cn Compare 18.10: Meaning of Heb uncertain
b Meaning of Heb uncertain　　*c* Symmachus: Heb *with anyone*　　*d* That is *Camp of Dan*　　*e* Compare 17.4, 5; 18.14: Heb *teraphim and the cast metal*

and be to us a father and a priest. Is it better for you to be priest to the house of one person, or to be priest to a tribe and clan in Israel?" 20Then the priest accepted the offer. He took the ephod, the teraphim, and the idol, and went along with the people.

21 So they resumed their journey, putting the little ones, the livestock, and the goods in front of them. 22When they were some distance from the home of Micah, the men who were in the houses near Micah's house were called out, and they overtook the Danites. 23They shouted to the Danites, who turned around and said to Micah, "What is the matter that you come with such a company?" 24He replied, "You take my gods that I made, and the priest, and go away, and what have I left? How then can you ask me, 'What is the matter?'" 25And the Danites said to him, "You had better not let your voice be heard among us or else hot-tempered fellows will attack you, and you will lose your life and the lives of your household." 26Then the Danites went their way. When Micah saw that they were too strong for him, he turned and went back to his home.

27 The Danites, having taken what Micah had made, and the priest who belonged to him, came to Laish, to a people quiet and unsuspecting, put them to the sword, and burned down the city. 28There was no deliverer, because it was far from Sidon and they had no dealings with Aram.a It was in the valley that belongs to Beth-rehob. They rebuilt the city, and lived in it. 29They named the city Dan, after their ancestor Dan, who was born to Israel; but the name of the city was formerly Laish. 30Then the Danites set up the idol for themselves. Jonathan son of Gershom, son of Moses,b and his sons were priests to the tribe of the Danites until the time the land went into captivity. 31So they maintained as their own Micah's idol that he had made, as long as the house of God was at Shiloh.

became a national shrine of the northern kingdom (1 Kings 12.29–30). *Jonathan* is presumably the previously unnamed Levite. The priestly family in charge of Dan descended from *Moses* (but see note b). *Captivity* refers to the results of the Assyrian conquests (2 Kings 15.29; 17.5–6). **31:** The true *house of God* was at Shiloh (1 Sam 1–2). The illegitimate background of the sanctuary of Dan has been emphasized at every turn: pilfered silver (17.2–3), stolen illicit image (17.5–6; 18.16–18, 24), opportunistic priest (17.9; 18.19–20).

19 In those days, when there was no king in Israel, a certain Levite, residing in the remote parts of the hill country of Ephraim, took to himself a concubine from Bethlehem in Judah. 2But his concubine became angry withc him, and she went away from him to her father's house at Bethlehem in Judah, and was there some four months. 3Then her husband set out after her, to speak tenderly to her and bring her back. He had with him his servant and a couple of donkeys. When he reachedd her father's house, the girl's father saw him and came with joy to meet him. 4His father-in-law, the girl's father, made him stay, and he remained with him three days; so they ate and drank, and hee stayed there. 5On the fourth day they got up early in the morning, and he prepared to go; but the girl's father said to his son-in-law, "Fortify yourself with a bit of food, and after that you may go." 6So the two men sat and ate and drank together; and the girl's father said to the man, "Why not spend the night and enjoy yourself?" 7When the man got up to go, his father-in-law kept urging him until he spent the night there again. 8On the fifth day he got up early in the morning to leave; and the girl's father said, "Fortify yourself." So they lingeredf until the day declined, and the two of them ate and drank.g 9When the man with his concubine and his servant got up to leave, his father-in-law, the girl's father, said to him, "Look, the day has worn on until it is almost evening.

18.11–31: Dan establishes a sanctuary. 21: The most vulnerable members of the party are protected from pursuit. **25:** *Hot-tempered fellows:* Dan had a reputation for belligerence (Gen 49.17; Deut 33.22). **30:** Dan

a Cn Compare verse 7: Heb *with anyone*   b Another reading is *son of Manasseh*   c Gk OL: Heb *prostituted herself against*   d Gk: Heb *she brought him*   e Compare verse 7 and Gk: Heb *they*   f Cn: Heb *Linger*   g Gk: Heb lacks *and drank*

Spend the night. See, the day has drawn to a close. Spend the night here and enjoy yourself. Tomorrow you can get up early in the morning for your journey, and go home."

10 But the man would not spend the night; he got up and departed, and arrived opposite Jebus (that is, Jerusalem). He had with him a couple of saddled donkeys, and his concubine was with him. ¹¹When they were near Jebus, the day was far spent, and the servant said to his master, "Come now, let us turn aside to this city of the Jebusites, and spend the night in it." ¹²But his master said to him, "We will not turn aside into a city of foreigners, who do not belong to the people of Israel; but we will continue on to Gibeah." ¹³Then he said to his servant, "Come, let us try to reach one of these places, and spend the night at Gibeah or at Ramah." ¹⁴So they passed on and went their way; and the sun went down on them near Gibeah, which belongs to Benjamin. ¹⁵They turned aside there, to go in and spend the night at Gibeah. He went in and sat down in the open square of the city, but no one took them in to spend the night.

16 Then at evening there was an old man coming from his work in the field. The man was from the hill country of Ephraim, and he was residing in Gibeah. (The people of the place were Benjaminites.) ¹⁷When the old man looked up and saw the wayfarer in the open square of the city, he said, "Where are you going and where do you come from?" ¹⁸He answered him, "We are passing from Bethlehem in Judah to the remote parts of the hill country of Ephraim, from which I come. I went to Bethlehem in Judah; and I am going to my home.ᵃ Nobody has offered to take me in. ¹⁹We your servants have straw and fodder for our donkeys, with bread and wine for me and the woman and the young man along with us. We need nothing more." ²⁰The old man said, "Peace be to you. I will care for all your wants; only do not spend the night in the square." ²¹So he brought him into his house, and fed the donkeys; they washed their feet, and ate and drank.

19.1–21: Spending the night in Gibeah. 1: *In those days . . . Israel:* This refrain (17.6; 18.1; 21.25) suggests

that a king would make such horrifying lawlessness unlikely. As *a concubine** she is a recognized wife with inferior legal status. **2:** She returns to her family of origin (*father's house*), but the circumstances are unclear (note *c*). **4–9:** The point of this prolonged account is that they left much later in the afternoon than was wise. **12:** The irony* is sharp. Jerusalem as *a city of foreigners* is rejected as inhospitable in favor of shelter with *the people of Israel*. **15:** That *no one took them in* would be considered outrageous; hospitality was an important civic virtue. **16:** The *old man* is a fellow countryman (*hill country of Ephraim*; v. 1) living as a resident alien* *in Gibeah*.

22 While they were enjoying themselves, the men of the city, a perverse lot, surrounded the house, and started pounding on the door. They said to the old man, the master of the house, "Bring out the man who came into your house, so that we may have intercourse with him." ²³And the man, the master of the house, went out to them and said to them, "No, my brothers, do not act so wickedly. Since this man is my guest, do not do this vile thing. ²⁴Here are my virgin daughter and his concubine; let me bring them out now. Ravish them and do whatever you want to them; but against this man do not do such a vile thing." ²⁵But the men would not listen to him. So the man seized his concubine, and put her out to them. They wantonly raped her, and abused her all through the night until the morning. And as the dawn began to break, they let her go. ²⁶As morning appeared, the woman came and fell down at the door of the man's house where her master was, until it was light.

27 In the morning her master got up, opened the doors of the house, and when he went out to go on his way, there was his concubine lying at the door of the house, with her hands on the threshold. ²⁸"Get up," he said to her, "we are going." But there was no answer. Then he put her on the donkey; and the man set out for his home. ²⁹When he had entered his house, he took a knife, and grasping his concubine he cut her into twelve pieces, limb by limb, and sent her throughout all the territory of Israel. ³⁰Then

---

a Gk Compare 19.29. Heb *to the house of the* LORD

he commanded the men whom he sent, saying, "Thus shall you say to all the Israelites, 'Has such a thing ever happened*a* since the day that the Israelites came up from the land of Egypt until this day? Consider it, take counsel, and speak out.' "

19.22–30: The rape of the Levite's concubine.* 22: Their threat of homosexual rape is the polar opposite of suitable hospitality. It parallels the behavior of the men of Sodom (Gen 19.5). **23–24:** For *the master of the house,* the obligations of hospitality take precedence over family loyalties. However, he does not extend the protection of hospitality to the concubine. *Vile thing* denotes a loathsome and foolish act, especially a sexual crime. **25–26:** The cowardly Levite acts to save himself. The powerful description of rape and the poignant final scene at the door fuel the reader's outrage against Gibeah. Her husband (v. 3) is now called *her master;* he has treated her as a disposable object. **27–28:** The affecting image of *her hands on the threshold* provides a sharp contrast to his brusque unconcern. **29:** Her body is treated as an object, a signal to rally the nation (compare 1 Sam 11.7).

20 Then all the Israelites came out, from Dan to Beer-sheba, including the land of Gilead, and the congregation assembled in one body before the LORD at Mizpah. ²The chiefs of all the people, of all the tribes of Israel, presented themselves in the assembly of the people of God, four hundred thousand foot-soldiers bearing arms. ³(Now the Benjaminites heard that the people of Israel had gone up to Mizpah.) And the Israelites said, "Tell us, how did this criminal act come about?" ⁴The Levite, the husband of the woman who was murdered, answered, "I came to Gibeah that belongs to Benjamin, I and my concubine, to spend the night. ⁵The lords of Gibeah rose up against me, and surrounded the house at night. They intended to kill me, and they raped my concubine until she died. ⁶Then I took my concubine and cut her into pieces, and sent her throughout the whole extent of Israel's territory; for they have committed a vile outrage in Israel. ⁷So now, you Israelites, all of you, give your advice and counsel here."

8 All the people got up as one, saying, "We will not any of us go to our tents, nor will any of us return to our houses. ⁹But now this is what we will do to Gibeah: we will go up*b* against it by lot. ¹⁰We will take ten men of a hundred throughout all the tribes of Israel, and a hundred of a thousand, and a thousand of ten thousand, to bring provisions for the troops, who are going to repay*c* Gibeah of Benjamin for all the disgrace that they have done in Israel." ¹¹So all the men of Israel gathered against the city, united as one.

12 The tribes of Israel sent men through all the tribe of Benjamin, saying, "What crime is this that has been committed among you? ¹³Now then, hand over those scoundrels in Gibeah, so that we may put them to death, and purge the evil from Israel." But the Benjaminites would not listen to their kinsfolk, the Israelites. ¹⁴The Benjaminites came together out of the towns to Gibeah, to go out to battle against the Israelites. ¹⁵On that day the Benjaminites mustered twenty-six thousand armed men from their towns, besides the inhabitants of Gibeah. ¹⁶Of all this force, there were seven hundred picked men who were left-handed; every one could sling a stone at a hair, and not miss. ¹⁷And the Israelites, apart from Benjamin, mustered four hundred thousand armed men, all of them warriors.

20.1–17: Israel assembles to attack Benjamin. 1: *From Dan to Beer-sheba* designates the north and south limits of Israel. **3:** Because Gibeah is Benjaminite (19.16), the Ephraimite Levite's personal quarrel escalates into intertribal conflict. **5:** The Levite's version omits important details in order to magnify the threat to himself and conceal his own culpability. **6:** *Vile outrage* signifies an intentional affront to Israel's core values. **9:** *By lot* refers to the way the ten percent of the next verse are to be chosen. **15–17:** Although Israel has an overwhelming numerical advantage, Benjamin's contingent of crack marksmen (v. 16) suggests that things will not be so simple.

18 The Israelites proceeded to go up to Bethel, where they inquired of God, "Which

a Compare Gk: Heb ³⁰*And all who saw it said, "Such a thing has not happened or been seen* *b* Gk: Heb lacks *we will go up* *c* Compare Gk: Meaning of Heb uncertain of us shall go up first to battle against the Benjaminites?" And the LORD answered, "Judah shall go up first."

19 Then the Israelites got up in the morning, and encamped against Gibeah. 20The Israelites went out to battle against Benjamin; and the Israelites drew up the battle line against them at Gibeah. 21The Benjaminites came out of Gibeah, and struck down on that day twenty-two thousand of the Israelites. 23ᵃThe Israelites went up and wept before the LORD until the evening; and they inquired of the LORD, "Shall we again draw near to battle against our kinsfolk the Benjaminites?" And the LORD said, "Go up against them." 22The Israelites took courage, and again formed the battle line in the same place where they had formed it on the first day.

24 So the Israelites advanced against the Benjaminites the second day. 25Benjamin moved out against them from Gibeah the second day, and struck down eighteen thousand of the Israelites, all of them armed men. 26Then all the Israelites, the whole army, went back to Bethel and wept, sitting there before the LORD; they fasted that day until evening. Then they offered burnt offerings and sacrifices of well-being before the LORD. 27And the Israelites inquired of the LORD (for the ark of the covenant of God was there in those days, 28and Phinehas son of Eleazar, son of Aaron, ministered before it in those days), saying, "Shall we go out once more to battle against our kinsfolk the Benjaminites, or shall we desist?" The LORD answered, "Go up, for tomorrow I will give them into your hand."

20.18–28: Benjamin's initial victories. 18: Nearby *Bethel* was the chief sanctuary of central Israel. The answer comes either by the sacred lots or through an oracle* delivered by a priest. 23–24: *Before the LORD* indicates that they returned to the sanctuary of Bethel to weep (v. 26). 28: Only this third answer includes a promise of victory (contrast vv. 18, 23).

29 So Israel stationed men in ambush around Gibeah. 30Then the Israelites went up against the Benjaminites on the third day, and set themselves in array against Gibeah,

as before. 31When the Benjaminites went out against the army, they were drawn away from the city. As before they began to inflict casualties on the troops, along the main roads, one of which goes up to Bethel and the other to Gibeah, as well as in the open country, killing about thirty men of Israel. 32The Benjaminites thought, "They are being routed before us, as previously." But the Israelites said, "Let us retreat and draw them away from the city toward the roads." 33The main body of the Israelites drew back its battle line to Baal-tamar, while those Israelites who were in ambush rushed out of their place westᵇ of Geba. 34There came against Gibeah ten thousand picked men out of all Israel, and the battle was fierce. But the Benjaminites did not realize that disaster was close upon them.

35 The LORD defeated Benjamin before Israel; and the Israelites destroyed twenty-five thousand one hundred men of Benjamin that day, all of them armed.

36 Then the Benjaminites saw that they were defeated.ᶜ

The Israelites gave ground to Benjamin, because they trusted to the troops in ambush that they had stationed against Gibeah. 37The troops in ambush rushed quickly upon Gibeah. Then they put the whole city to the sword. 38Now the agreement between the main body of Israel and the men in ambush was that when they sent up a cloud of smoke out of the city 39the main body of Israel should turn in battle. But Benjamin had begun to inflict casualties on the Israelites, killing about thirty of them; so they thought, "Surely they are defeated before us, as in the first battle." 40But when the cloud, a column of smoke, began to rise out of the city, the Benjaminites looked behind them—and there was the whole city going up in smoke toward the sky! 41Then the main body of Israel turned, and the Benjaminites were dismayed, for they saw that disaster was close upon them. 42Therefore they turned away from the Israelites in the direction of the wilderness; but the battle overtook them, and

---

a Verses 22 and 23 are transposed   *b* Gk Vg: Heb *in the plain*   *c* This sentence is continued by verse 45.

those who came out of the city*a* were slaughtering them in between.*b* 43Cutting down*c* the Benjaminites, they pursued them from Nohah*d* and trod them down as far as a place east of Gibeah. 44Eighteen thousand Benjaminites fell, all of them courageous fighters. 45When they turned and fled toward the wilderness to the rock of Rimmon, five thousand of them were cut down on the main roads, and they were pursued as far as Gidom, and two thousand of them were slain. 46So all who fell that day of Benjamin were twenty-five thousand arms-bearing men, all of them courageous fighters. 47But six hundred turned and fled toward the wilderness to the rock of Rimmon, and remained at the rock of Rimmon for four months. 48Meanwhile, the Israelites turned back against the Benjaminites, and put them to the sword— the city, the people, the animals, and all that remained. Also the remaining towns they set on fire.

20.29–48: Israel crushes Benjamin. 33: The tactics of *ambush* and simulated retreat parallel Josh 8.3–23. **35:** The magnitude of the disaster is clear when the number killed (v. 46) is compared with Benjamin's starting total (v. 15). **36:** The course of the battle is recounted twice in overlapping parallel stories: vv. 29–36 (as far as note *c*) and vv. 36–43. **40–41:** The role of the *smoke* is the same as in Josh 8.20–21. **42:** Benjamin is trapped and butchered between the main army (*the Israelites*) and the ambush (*those who came out of the city*). **47– 48:** These *six hundred* are the only survivors. Near total annihilation of the Benjaminites sets up the situation for the next chapter.

21 Now the Israelites had sworn at Mizpah, "No one of us shall give his daughter in marriage to Benjamin." 2And the people came to Bethel, and sat there until evening before God, and they lifted up their voices and wept bitterly. 3They said, "O LORD, the God of Israel, why has it come to pass that today there should be one tribe lacking in Israel?" 4On the next day, the people got up early, and built an altar there, and offered burnt offerings and sacrifices of well-being. 5Then the Israelites said, "Which of all the tribes of Israel did not come up in the assembly to the LORD?" For a solemn oath

had been taken concerning whoever did not come up to the LORD to Mizpah, saying, "That one shall be put to death." 6But the Israelites had compassion for Benjamin their kin, and said, "One tribe is cut off from Israel this day. 7What shall we do for wives for those who are left, since we have sworn by the LORD that we will not give them any of our daughters as wives?"

8 Then they said, "Is there anyone from the tribes of Israel who did not come up to the LORD to Mizpah?" It turned out that no one from Jabesh-gilead had come to the camp, to the assembly. 9For when the roll was called among the people, not one of the inhabitants of Jabesh-gilead was there. 10So the congregation sent twelve thousand soldiers there and commanded them, "Go, put the inhabitants of Jabesh-gilead to the sword, including the women and the little ones. 11This is what you shall do; every male and every woman that has lain with a male you shall devote to destruction." 12And they found among the inhabitants of Jabesh-gilead four hundred young virgins who had never slept with a man and brought them to the camp at Shiloh, which is in the land of Canaan.

13 Then the whole congregation sent word to the Benjaminites who were at the rock of Rimmon, and proclaimed peace to them. 14Benjamin returned at that time; and they gave them the women whom they had saved alive of the women of Jabesh-gilead; but they did not suffice for them.

21.1–14: Wives for Benjamin from Jabesh-gilead. 1: This oath is considered unbreakable (v. 5). **8:** Although others from Gilead had participated (20.1), *Jabesh-gilead* did not. **10–11:** As a result of their vow, they treat this as a holy war* and *devote to destruction* everyone not useful for their plan. **14:** This tradition may explain why Jabesh-gilead and King Saul (a Benjaminite from Gibeah) had friendly relations (1 Sam 11.1–11; 31.11–13). Four hundred women are not enough for the six hundred surviving men.

a Compare Vg and some Gk Mss: Heb *cities*
b Compare Syr: Meaning of Heb uncertain
c Gk: Heb *Surrounding*   *d* Gk: Heb *pursued them at their resting place*

15 The people had compassion on Benjamin because the LORD had made a breach in the tribes of Israel. 16 So the elders of the congregation said, "What shall we do for wives for those who are left, since there are no women left in Benjamin?" 17 And they said, "There must be heirs for the survivors of Benjamin, in order that a tribe may not be blotted out from Israel. 18 Yet we cannot give any of our daughters to them as wives." For the Israelites had sworn, "Cursed be anyone who gives a wife to Benjamin." 19 So they said, "Look, the yearly festival of the LORD is taking place at Shiloh, which is north of Bethel, on the east of the highway that goes up from Bethel to Shechem, and south of Lebonah." 20 And they instructed the Benjaminites, saying, "Go and lie in wait in the vineyards, 21 and watch; when the young women of Shiloh come out to dance in the dances, then come out of the vineyards and each of you carry off a wife for himself from the young women of Shiloh, and go to the land of Benjamin. 22 Then if their fathers or their brothers come to complain to us, we will say to them, 'Be generous and allow us to have them; because we did not capture in battle a wife for each man. But neither did you incur guilt by giving your daughters to them.' " 23 The Benjaminites did so; they took wives for each of them from the dancers whom they abducted. Then they went and returned to their territory, and rebuilt the towns, and lived in them. 24 So the Israelites departed from there at that time by tribes and families, and they went out from there to their own territories.

25 In those days there was no king in Israel; all the people did what was right in their own eyes.

21.15–25: Capturing wives at Shiloh. 17: Although not *blotted out*, Benjamin remained one of the smaller tribes. 21: This may reflect an on-going custom of obtaining wives by ritualized capture at the annual festival at Shiloh. 22: *Brothers* are the natural protectors of their unmarried sisters (Song 8.8–9), and *fathers* would lose financially if marriage bypassed the usual negotiations. 25: Rape, civil war, genocide—all resulted because Israel had *no king*.

RUTH

Introduction

The book of Ruth opens with a crisis: While living in Moab, an Israelite woman named Naomi loses her husband and sons. In a society in which property is passed down through males, she thus is left destitute in a foreign land. The book works toward this problem's solution, as her Moabite daughter-in-law Ruth secures for both women land and offspring, with the help of a wealthy Judean landowner named Boaz. The genealogy★ that closes the book reveals that the child born to Ruth and Boaz is the ancestor of none other than King David.

Scholars who focus on the narrative★ quality of the book (calling it an "idyll" or a "novella" or a "short story") believe the genealogy was added to the book to encourage the book's acceptance into the canon.★ Other interpreters see the genealogy as a key to the purpose of its composition: to celebrate David or to give Davidic authority to marriage between Judeans and non-Judeans. If the genealogy is original, then the book was likely written close to the time of the Davidic monarchy. If the primary concern is to authorize intermarriage, then the book may have been part of the larger discussion of intermarriage in the time of Ezra and Nehemiah (Ezra 8).

In the Jewish canon, the book is found in The Writings,★ at the close of the Bible. There, Ruth is clustered with Esther, Ecclesiastes, Song of Solomon, and Lamentations, and together they are called the megillot (singular, "megillah"★)—the scrolls read in annual Jewish festivals. Because of its agricultural setting and concerns, Ruth is linked with the festival of Shavuot★ (also called The Feast of Weeks,★ or Pentecost★), a harvest celebration. At least by the eighth century CE, Shavuot was also identified as the time during which Moses received the Torah★ at Mt. Sinai. The compilers of the Christian canon grouped Ruth with the historical books, putting it there because of its chronological setting "when the judges ruled" (Ruth 1.1).

Both explicit allusions and similarities in theme link Ruth with other narratives of the Hebrew Bible. Like Tamar (Gen 38), Ruth goes to extraordinary measures to procure a son; like Abraham (Gen 12), she leaves her family to go to a foreign land; like Sarah and Rachel (Gen 12–30), she and Naomi struggle with the absence of sons in a society in which land and authority are male prerogatives.

READING GUIDE

Because of its brevity, the book of Ruth is easily read in its entirety, allowing readers the luxury of reading it multiple times. After understanding the story's basic plot, the reader can subsequently ask: Are the characters portrayed as models of perfect behavior or are they complex personalities? What are their motives? How does the strong focus on women fit with the book's "happy ending" of the birth of a male? How often is God mentioned in this book and in what contexts?

1 The problem: famine, death and childlessness
2 Ruth temporarily provides for Naomi and herself
3 Ruth, Naomi, and Boaz work toward more permanent arrangements
4 Resolution: Ruth and Boaz marry and a child is born

1 In the days when the judges ruled, there was a famine in the land, and a certain man of Bethlehem in Judah went to live in the country of Moab, he and his wife and two sons. 2 The name of the man was Elimelech and the name of his wife Naomi, and the names of his two sons were Mahlon and Chilion; they were Ephrathites from Bethlehem in Judah. They went into the country of Moab and remained there. 3 But Elimelech, the husband of Naomi, died, and she was left with her two sons. 4 These took Moabite wives; the name of the one was Orpah and the name of the other Ruth. When they had lived there about ten years, 5 both Mahlon and Chilion also died, so that the woman was left without her two sons and her husband.

1.1–5: Famine and death. 1: *When the judges ruled* sets the story of Ruth before the rise of kingship, when charismatic leaders led Israel against its foes. The book of Judges portrays this period as one of instability, when faithfulness to God led to success, but idolatry* led to failure (see Judg 3.10). When, ironically,* *Bethlehem* (literally "house of bread") becomes a place of *famine*, a *man, his wife,* and his *two sons* move to *Moab,* a suspect place in biblical tradition (Gen 19.37; Deut 23.3). **2:** *Elimelech:* "My god is king." The rhyming names *Mahlon* and *Chilion* mean "weakness" and "consumption." *Ephrathites:* Elsewhere, Ephratha is linked with *Bethlehem* (Mic 5.2; 1 Sam 17.12) and may refer to the large clan* in which Bethlehem was located. **3:** In a sudden reversal, Naomi takes center stage. *Elimelech* (now called Naomi's husband) dies and, after ten years, so do Mahlon and Chilion, leaving Naomi without *her husband* and *her two sons.*

6 Then she started to return with her daughters-in-law from the country of Moab, for she had heard in the country of Moab that the LORD had considered his people and given them food. 7 So she set out from the place where she had been living, she and her two daughters-in-law, and they went on their way to go back to the land of Judah. 8 But Naomi said to her two daughters-in-law, "Go back each of you to your mother's house. May the LORD deal kindly with you, as you have dealt with the dead and with me. 9 The LORD grant that you may find security, each

of you in the house of your husband." Then she kissed them, and they wept aloud. 10 They said to her, "No, we will return with you to your people." 11 But Naomi said, "Turn back, my daughters, why will you go with me? Do I still have sons in my womb that they may become your husbands? 12 Turn back, my daughters, go your way, for I am too old to have a husband. Even if I thought there was hope for me, even if I should have a husband tonight and bear sons, 13 would you then wait until they were grown? Would you then refrain from marrying? No, my daughters, it has been far more bitter for me than for you, because the hand of the LORD has turned against me." 14 Then they wept aloud again. Orpah kissed her mother-in-law, but Ruth clung to her.

15 So she said, "See, your sister-in-law has gone back to her people and to her gods; return after your sister-in-law." 16 But Ruth said,

"Do not press me to leave you
  or to turn back from following you!
Where you go, I will go;
  where you lodge, I will lodge;
your people shall be my people,
  and your God my God.
17 Where you die, I will die—
  there will I be buried.
May the LORD do thus and so to me,
  and more as well,
if even death parts me from you!"
18 When Naomi saw that she was determined to go with her, she said no more to her.

19 So the two of them went on until they came to Bethlehem. When they came to Bethlehem, the whole town was stirred because of them; and the women said, "Is this Naomi?" 20 She said to them,

"Call me no longer Naomi,*a*
  call me Mara,*b*
  for the Almighty*c* has dealt bitterly
    with me.
21 I went away full,
  but the LORD has brought me back
    empty;

a That is *Pleasant*   *b* That is *Bitter*   *c* Traditional rendering of Heb *Shaddai*

why call me Naomi
  when the LORD has dealt harshly with[a]
    me,
  and the Almighty[b] has brought
    calamity upon me?"

22 So Naomi returned together with Ruth the Moabite, her daughter-in-law, who came back with her from the country of Moab. They came to Bethlehem at the beginning of the barley harvest.

1.6–22: Two return to Bethlehem. Naomi decides to return to Bethlehem (reversing Elimelech's decision to go to Moab). Her impassioned speech assumes that if she cannot offer Orpah and Ruth husbands then they have no future with her. **8–14:** Told to return to the house of their mothers ("house of the father" is more common), Orpah obeys Naomi, but Ruth *clings* to her (in Gen 1.24, this verb describes marital union). **16–17:** Ruth's beautiful poem of loyalty states her willingness to exchange her gods, family, and land in order to be with Naomi. *May the LORD do thus and so* is a typical oath formula. **19–22:** Naomi's silence, her insistence on being called *Mara* ("bitter") upon her entry into Bethlehem, and her reference to returning *empty* indicate that Naomi is not initially comforted by the presence of her Moabite daughter-in-law.

2 Now Naomi had a kinsman on her husband's side, a prominent rich man, of the family of Elimelech, whose name was Boaz. [2]And Ruth the Moabite said to Naomi, "Let me go to the field and glean among the ears of grain, behind someone in whose sight I may find favor." She said to her, "Go, my daughter." [3]So she went. She came and gleaned in the field behind the reapers. As it happened, she came to the part of the field belonging to Boaz, who was of the family of Elimelech. [4]Just then Boaz came from Bethlehem. He said to the reapers, "The LORD be with you." They answered, "The LORD bless you." [5]Then Boaz said to his servant who was in charge of the reapers, "To whom does this young woman belong?" [6]The servant who was in charge of the reapers answered, "She is the Moabite who came back with Naomi from the country of Moab. [7]She said, 'Please, let me glean and gather among the sheaves behind the reapers.' So she came, and she has been on her feet from early this

morning until now, without resting even for a moment."[c]

8 Then Boaz said to Ruth, "Now listen, my daughter, do not go to glean in another field or leave this one, but keep close to my young women. [9]Keep your eyes on the field that is being reaped, and follow behind them. I have ordered the young men not to bother you. If you get thirsty, go to the vessels and drink from what the young men have drawn." [10]Then she fell prostrate, with her face to the ground, and said to him, "Why have I found favor in your sight, that you should take notice of me, when I am a foreigner?" [11]But Boaz answered her, "All that you have done for your mother-in-law since the death of your husband has been fully told me, and how you left your father and mother and your native land and came to a people that you did not know before. [12]May the LORD reward you for your deeds, and may you have a full reward from the LORD, the God of Israel, under whose wings you have come for refuge!" [13]Then she said, "May I continue to find favor in your sight, my lord, for you have comforted me and spoken kindly to your servant, even though I am not one of your servants."

14 At mealtime Boaz said to her, "Come here, and eat some of this bread, and dip your morsel in the sour wine." So she sat beside the reapers, and he heaped up for her some parched grain. She ate until she was satisfied, and she had some left over. [15]When she got up to glean, Boaz instructed his young men, "Let her glean even among the standing sheaves, and do not reproach her. [16]You must also pull out some handfuls for her from the bundles, and leave them for her to glean, and do not rebuke her."

17 So she gleaned in the field until evening. Then she beat out what she had gleaned, and it was about an ephah of barley. [18]She picked it up and came into the town, and her mother-in-law saw how much she had gleaned. Then she took out and gave her what was left over after she herself had been

a Or *has testified against*   *b* Traditional rendering of Heb *Shaddai*   *c* Compare Gk Vg: Meaning of Heb uncertain satisfied. [19]Her mother-in-law said to her, "Where did you glean today? And where have you worked? Blessed be the man who took notice of you." So she told her mother-in-law with whom she had worked, and said, "The name of the man with whom I worked today is Boaz." [20]Then Naomi said to her daughter-in-law, "Blessed be he by the LORD, whose kindness has not forsaken the living or the dead!" Naomi also said to her, "The man is a relative of ours, one of our nearest kin."[a] [21]Then Ruth the Moabite said, "He even said to me, 'Stay close by my servants, until they have finished all my harvest.'" [22]Naomi said to Ruth, her daughter-in-law, "It is better, my daughter, that you go out with his young women, otherwise you might be bothered in another field." [23]So she stayed close to the young women of Boaz, gleaning until the end of the barley and wheat harvests; and she lived with her mother-in-law.

2.1–23: Ruth in Boaz's field. Although the reader is told about the relationship between Boaz and Naomi, Ruth seems unaware of this information (it was *as it happened* that she arrived in Boaz's field, v. 3). **4:** As she arrived, *just then Boaz came*. These felicitous "coincidences" hold a key to the theology of Ruth, demonstrating a God who works behind the scenes and through human action. **7:** Ruth's request to *glean* among the sheaves is beyond the scope of common gleaning privileges (Lev 19.9; 23.22; Deut 24.19), and thereby requires the consent of the landowner. Boaz not only approves Ruth's request, but grants her more favors in the field. He offers her protection and the familial privileges of sharing water and the common meal. **15–18:** Boaz extends Ruth's gleaning privileges even further. She gathers an *ephah* of grain, variously calculated at 29–50 pounds. Ruth shares the grain, as well as her lunch leftovers, with Naomi. **19–22:** Naomi reveals to Ruth what the reader already knows: Boaz is a *relative*, one obligated to keep land within the family (Lev 25.25). Ruth alters Boaz's words in her report to Naomi (*stay close by my servants*, v. 21; *keep close to my young women*, v. 8). **23:** As both the barley and wheat harvests draw to a close, the women face difficult months ahead.

3 Naomi her mother-in-law said to her, "My daughter, I need to seek some security for you, so that it may be well with you. [2]Now here is our kinsman Boaz, with whose young women you have been working. See, he is winnowing barley tonight at the threshing floor. [3]Now wash and anoint yourself, and put on your best clothes and go down to the threshing floor; but do not make yourself known to the man until he has finished eating and drinking. [4]When he lies down, observe the place where he lies; then, go and uncover his feet and lie down; and he will tell you what to do." [5]She said to her, "All that you tell me I will do."

[6] So she went down to the threshing floor and did just as her mother-in-law had instructed her. [7]When Boaz had eaten and drunk, and he was in a contented mood, he went to lie down at the end of the heap of grain. Then she came stealthily and uncovered his feet, and lay down. [8]At midnight the man was startled, and turned over, and there, lying at his feet, was a woman! [9]He said, "Who are you?" And she answered, "I am Ruth, your servant; spread your cloak over your servant, for you are next-of-kin."[a] [10]He said, "May you be blessed by the LORD, my daughter; this last instance of your loyalty is better than the first; you have not gone after young men, whether poor or rich. [11]And now, my daughter, do not be afraid, I will do for you all that you ask, for all the assembly of my people know that you are a worthy woman. [12]But now, though it is true that I am a near kinsman, there is another kinsman more closely related than I. [13]Remain this night, and in the morning, if he will act as next-of-kin[a] for you, good; let him do it. If he is not willing to act as next-of-kin[a] for you, then, as the LORD lives, I will act as next-of-kin[a] for you. Lie down until the morning."

[14] So she lay at his feet until morning, but got up before one person could recognize another; for he said, "It must not be known that the woman came to the threshing floor." [15]Then he said, "Bring the cloak you are wearing and hold it out." So she held it, and he measured out six measures of barley, and put it on her back; then he went into the city.

a Or *one with the right to redeem*

16She came to her mother-in-law, who said, "How did things go with you,ᵃ my daughter?" Then she told her all that the man had done for her, 17saying, "He gave me these six measures of barley, for he said, 'Do not go back to your mother-in-law empty-handed.' " 18She replied, "Wait, my daughter, until you learn how the matter turns out, for the man will not rest, but will settle the matter today."

3.1–18: At the threshing* floor. 2–3: At Naomi's initiative, Ruth *washes and anoints** herself and goes to the *threshing floor*, where grain is winnowed* in the early evening breeze. An important man like Boaz might not personally winnow or protect the grain; some believe that he was performing religious responsibilities. **4:** *Uncover his feet and lie down:* The instructions of Naomi are provocative. The word for *feet* ("margelot") is related to the more common word "regel," which often in the Bible refers to sexual organs. **6–11:** Ruth requests not only that Boaz act as *next-of-kin* but also that he *spread* his *cloak* over her, suggesting marriage. **12–13:** *Another kinsman more related than I:* The complication of a closer relative is often seen as referring to the practice of levirate marriage,* in which the brother of a deceased man is expected to have sexual relations with his widow in order to sire an heir for the dead man (Deut 25.5–10). The situation in Ruth does not fit the levirate marriage, since Boaz was not brother to Mahlon or Chilion. Hence, Boaz's speech may indicate that two issues are at stake in Ruth's proposition: marriage and the redemption of Elimelech's land. **14–18:** Ruth's visit must be kept secret until the encounter with the other relative, so she leaves in the darkness. Boaz gives her an unidentified *six measures of barley.* Ruth's report, unlike Boaz's speech, mentions Naomi.

4 No sooner had Boaz gone up to the gate and sat down there than the next-of-kin,ᵇ of whom Boaz had spoken, came passing by. So Boaz said, "Come over, friend; sit down here." And he went over and sat down. 2Then Boaz took ten men of the elders of the city, and said, "Sit down here"; so they sat down. 3He then said to the next-of-kin,ᵇ "Naomi, who has come back from the country of Moab, is selling the parcel of land that belonged to our kinsman Elimelech. 4So I thought I would tell you of it, and say: Buy it in the presence of those sitting here, and in the presence of the elders of my people. If you will redeem it, redeem it; but if you will not, tell me, so that I may know; for there is no one prior to you to redeem it, and I come after you." So he said, "I will redeem it." 5Then Boaz said, "The day you acquire the field from the hand of Naomi, you are also acquiring Ruthᶜ the Moabite, the widow of the dead man, to maintain the dead man's name on his inheritance." 6At this, the next-of-kinᵇ said, "I cannot redeem it for myself without damaging my own inheritance. Take my right of redemption yourself, for I cannot redeem it."

7 Now this was the custom in former times in Israel concerning redeeming and exchanging: to confirm a transaction, the one took off a sandal and gave it to the other; this was the manner of attesting in Israel. 8So when the next-of-kinᵇ said to Boaz, "Acquire it for yourself," he took off his sandal. 9Then Boaz said to the elders and all the people, "Today you are witnesses that I have acquired from the hand of Naomi all that belonged to Elimelech and all that belonged to Chilion and Mahlon. 10I have also acquired Ruth the Moabite, the wife of Mahlon, to be my wife, to maintain the dead man's name on his inheritance, in order that the name of the dead may not be cut off from his kindred and from the gate of his native place; today you are witnesses." 11Then all the people who were at the gate, along with the elders, said, "We are witnesses. May the LORD make the woman who is coming into your house like Rachel and Leah, who together built up the house of Israel. May you produce children in Ephrathah and bestow a name in Bethlehem; 12and, through the children that the LORD will give you by this young woman, may your house be like the house of Perez, whom Tamar bore to Judah."

13 So Boaz took Ruth and she became his wife. When they came together, the LORD made her conceive, and she bore a son. 14Then the women said to Naomi, "Blessed be the LORD, who has not left you this day without next-of-kin;ᵇ and may his name be

a Or *"Who are you,*   *b* Or *one with the right to redeem*
c OL Vg: Heb *from the hand of Naomi and from Ruth*

renowned in Israel! 15He shall be to you a restorer of life and a nourisher of your old age; for your daughter-in-law who loves you, who is more to you than seven sons, has borne him." 16Then Naomi took the child and laid him in her bosom, and became his nurse. 17The women of the neighborhood gave him a name, saying, "A son has been born to Naomi." They named him Obed; he became the father of Jesse, the father of David.

18 Now these are the descendants of Perez: Perez became the father of Hezron, 19Hezron of Ram, Ram of Amminadab, 20Amminadab of Nahshon, Nahshon of Salmon, 21Salmon of Boaz, Boaz of Obed, 22Obed of Jesse, and Jesse of David.

4.1–22: At the city gate. 1–2: In ancient Israel, business was transacted at the city *gate* and was witnessed by *elders*. **3–6:** Boaz offers to buy Naomi's land (implying that she owned the property) if the other man does not wish to do so. The next-of-kin retracts his offer when Boaz links land redemption to the marriage of Ruth. If the man begets a child with Ruth, the land will revert to Naomi. **7:** The removing of a *sandal* to seal a business deal differs from the practice in Deut 25.9, in which a man who refuses to perform levirate marriage* is shamed by the dead man's widow. **9–10:** Boaz announces his intention both to redeem the land and to marry Ruth. **11–12:** The crowds link Ruth with other biblical characters: with *Rachel and Leah,* two sisters who struggled for love and children (Gen 30); and with *Perez,* born after *Tamar* tricked *Judah* into fulfilling the duties of the levirate marriage (Gen 38). **13–17:** Naomi's security is sealed by the birth of a male child, whom Boaz designates as the redeemer of her land. In a story that assumes the inheritance rights of men, the praise that Ruth is more to Naomi *than seven sons* is striking. **18–22:** Boaz, like many other important biblical figures, appears in seventh place in the genealogy* traced from Perez (4.12). While the book began with a man's decision and ends with a list of male names, the women Ruth and Naomi remain solidly in the heart of the story.

1 SAMUEL

Introduction

The books of 1 and 2 Samuel were originally a single book recounting the beginning of the monarchy and the reigns of its first two kings, Saul and David. The book was named after Samuel because he plays a prominent role in its beginning section, which was even attributed to his authorship. The name is not entirely appropriate, however, since Samuel dies well before 1 Samuel ends (25.1). This book was also part of a larger unit known as the Deuteronomistic* History, which incorporates the present books of Deuteronomy, Joshua, Judges, 1–2 Samuel, and 1–2 Kings. The Deuteronomistic History is the central history of Israel in the Hebrew Bible, or Old Testament. It relates Israel's history from their conquest of the land under Joshua (related in Josh 1–12) to the end of the kingdoms of Israel (2 Kings 17) and Judah (2 Kings 24–25). It evaluates that history according to the laws and theology of the book of Deuteronomy, with which it begins. The Deuteronomistic History as a whole stresses such matters as obedience to the law, God's choice of Jerusalem as a central place of worship for Israel, and the kingship of David. This history was composed by one or more authors whose names have not come down to us, and who are therefore referred to as "deuteronomists." It was probably written during the Exile* (after 586 BCE) as a way of collecting Israel's traditions and editing them into a single, running historical account. The collectors or editors occasionally inserted commentary, sometimes in the form of speeches and always in their own distinctive deuteronomistic style. First Samuel 8, with its reference to the Exodus (v. 8) and the people crying out (v. 18), and 1 Sam 12, with its review of Israel's history and its command to "heed the voice of the LORD" (vv. 14–15), give examples of deuteronomistic style.

While the book of Samuel may contain older source material, its final composition as part of the Deuteronomistic History took place in the Exile (after 586 BCE). This was hundreds of years after the events described in Samuel (David reigned around 1000 BCE). The author/editor was attempting to offer a theological explanation for the great crisis of the Exile and perhaps some hope and even a model for restoration in David. Hence, David is the central character not only in 1–2 Samuel but in the entire Deuteronomistic History.

READING GUIDE

As the outline below shows, 1 Samuel falls into three main sections, each organized around one of its principal characters, Samuel, Saul, and David. Samuel and Saul both prepare the way for David. Samuel is a transitional figure—the last of the judges and the prophet* who anoints* Saul and then announces his rejection by the LORD and anoints David in his place. Saul is a tragic figure—plucked from obscurity and thrust into a position of power for which he is unfit. Everything he does is a mistake. His rapid decline is balanced by David's meteoric rise. David can do no wrong. Like Saul, he is presented as humble and without personal ambition for kingship. But unlike Saul, "the LORD was with David"—a major theme in the book. David, for his part, consistently trusts in the LORD to guide his movements and actions. While Samuel is a literary masterpiece, the reader may draw closer to actual history by asking whether Saul was really so bad and David so innocent as their portraits in 1 Samuel indicate.

1 There was a certain man of Ramathaim, a Zuphite*a* from the hill country of Ephraim, whose name was Elkanah son of Jeroham son of Elihu son of Tohu son of Zuph, an Ephraimite. 2He had two wives; the name of the one was Hannah, and the name of the other Peninnah. Peninnah had children, but Hannah had no children.

3 Now this man used to go up year by year from his town to worship and to sacrifice to the LORD of hosts at Shiloh, where the two sons of Eli, Hophni and Phinehas, were priests of the LORD. 4On the day when Elkanah sacrificed, he would give portions to his wife Peninnah and to all her sons and daughters; 5but to Hannah he gave a double portion,*b* because he loved her, though the LORD had closed her womb. 6Her rival used to provoke her severely, to irritate her, because the LORD had closed her womb. 7So it went on year by year; as often as she went up to the house of the LORD, she used to provoke her. Therefore Hannah wept and would not eat. 8Her husband Elkanah said to her, "Hannah, why do you weep? Why do you not eat? Why is your heart sad? Am I not more to you than ten sons?"

9 After they had eaten and drunk at Shiloh, Hannah rose and presented herself before the LORD.*c* Now Eli the priest was sitting on the seat beside the doorpost of the temple of the LORD. 10She was deeply distressed and prayed to the LORD, and wept bitterly. 11She made this vow: "O LORD of hosts, if only you will look on the misery of your servant, and remember me, and not forget your servant, but will give to your servant a male child, then I will set him before you as a nazirite*d* until the day of his death. He shall drink neither wine nor intoxicants,*e* and no razor shall touch his head."

12 As she continued praying before the LORD, Eli observed her mouth. 13Hannah was praying silently; only her lips moved, but her voice was not heard; therefore Eli thought she was drunk. 14So Eli said to her, "How long will you make a drunken spectacle of yourself? Put away your wine." 15But Hannah answered, "No, my lord, I am a woman deeply troubled; I have drunk neither wine nor strong drink, but I have been pouring out my soul before the LORD. 16Do not regard your servant as a worthless woman, for I have been speaking out of my great anxiety and vexation all this time." 17Then Eli answered, "Go in peace; the God of Israel grant the petition you have made to him." 18And she said, "Let your servant find favor in your sight." Then the woman went to her quarters,*f* ate and drank with her husband,*g* and her countenance was sad no longer.*h*

1.1–18: Hannah's request. 3: Elkanah's annual pilgrimage to the temple of Yahweh or *house of the LORD* (v. 7) in Shiloh shows him to be a righteous man. *LORD of hosts* or "armies" (Hebrew "sebaoth") describes the LORD's leadership in wars both divine and on behalf of Israel. **5–8:** The value of a woman's ability to bear children in ancient Israel lies behind Hannah's depression. Her barrenness is comparable to that of Sarah, Rebekah, and Rachel in Genesis and of Samson's mother in Judg 13. **11:** *Nazirites* were "devoted" to the LORD for some special purpose and were prohibited from drinking alcohol or eating grapes, cutting their hair or beards, and approaching a dead body (Num 6.1–21). *Intoxicants* refers to a form of beer. **13:** *Eli thought she was drunk* either because his eyesight was poor (3.2) or because he had lost the capacity to discern the sacred from the secular, and therefore could not tell that Hannah was praying.

19 They rose early in the morning and worshiped before the LORD; then they went

a Compare Gk and 1 Chr 6.35–36: Heb *Ramathaim-zophim*   *b* Syr: Meaning of Heb uncertain
c Gk: Heb lacks *and presented herself before the LORD*
d That is *one separated* or *one consecrated*
e Cn Compare Gk Q Ms 1.22: MT *then I will give him to the LORD all the days of his life*   *f* Gk: Heb *went her way*   *g* Gk: Heb lacks *and drank with her husband*
h Gk: Meaning of Heb uncertain

back to their house at Ramah. Elkanah knew his wife Hannah, and the LORD remembered her. 20In due time Hannah conceived and bore a son. She named him Samuel, for she said, "I have asked him of the LORD."

21 The man Elkanah and all his household went up to offer to the LORD the yearly sacrifice, and to pay his vow. 22But Hannah did not go up, for she said to her husband, "As soon as the child is weaned, I will bring him, that he may appear in the presence of the LORD, and remain there forever; I will offer him as a nazirite*a* for all time."*b* 23Her husband Elkanah said to her, "Do what seems best to you, wait until you have weaned him; only—may the LORD establish his word."*c* So the woman remained and nursed her son, until she weaned him. 24When she had weaned him, she took him up with her, along with a three-year-old bull,*d* an ephah of flour, and a skin of wine. She brought him to the house of the LORD at Shiloh; and the child was young. 25Then they slaughtered the bull, and they brought the child to Eli. 26And she said, "Oh, my lord! As you live, my lord, I am the woman who was standing here in your presence, praying to the LORD. 27For this child I prayed; and the LORD has granted me the petition that I made to him. 28Therefore I have lent him to the LORD; as long as he lives, he is given to the LORD."

She left him there for*e* the LORD.

1.19–28: Samuel's birth. The gift of a son to Hannah shows God's favor toward the disadvantaged and indicates that Samuel is chosen for a special purpose. **19:** *Elkanah knew his wife:* An idiom for sexual relations. **20:** *Samuel's* name ostensibly means "God has heard," so the reader expects Hannah to say that she named her son Samuel because "God heard" her prayer. Her statement that she *asked him of the LORD* is a pun on the name of Saul instead. **28:** *Given* is another pun on Saul's name. This is exactly the same as Saul's name in Hebrew ("sha'ul"). It might even be translated, "He is Saul to the LORD." These puns may indicate that this story was originally about Saul's birth rather than Samuel's, or they may simply be the author's way of alluding to Saul as Israel's first king.

2 Hannah prayed and said,
  "My heart exults in the LORD;
    my strength is exalted in my God.*f*
  My mouth derides my enemies,
    because I rejoice in my*g* victory.

2 "There is no Holy One like the LORD,
    no one besides you;
    there is no Rock like our God.
3 Talk no more so very proudly,
    let not arrogance come from your
      mouth;
  for the LORD is a God of knowledge,
    and by him actions are weighed.
4 The bows of the mighty are broken,
    but the feeble gird on strength.
5 Those who were full have hired
      themselves out for bread,
  but those who were hungry are fat
    with spoil.
  The barren has borne seven,
  but she who has many children is
    forlorn.
6 The LORD kills and brings to life;
    he brings down to Sheol and raises
      up.
7 The LORD makes poor and makes rich;
    he brings low, he also exalts.
8 He raises up the poor from the dust;
    he lifts the needy from the ash
      heap,
  to make them sit with princes
    and inherit a seat of honor.*h*
  For the pillars of the earth are the
    LORD's,
    and on them he has set the world.

9 "He will guard the feet of his faithful
      ones,
  but the wicked shall be cut off in
    darkness;
  for not by might does one prevail.

---

a That is *one separated* or *one consecrated*
b Cn Compare Q Ms: MT lacks *I will offer him as a nazirite for all time*   *c* MT: Q Ms Gk Compare Syr *that which goes out of your mouth*   *d* Q Ms Gk Syr: MT *three bulls*   *e* Gk (Compare Q Ms) and Gk at 2.11: MT *And he* (that is, Elkanah) *worshiped there before*
f Gk: Heb *the LORD*   *g* Q Ms: MT *your*
h Gk (Compare Q Ms) adds *He grants the vow of the one who vows, and blesses the years of the just*

10 The LORD! His adversaries shall be
   shattered;
   the Most High[a] will thunder in
   heaven.
The LORD will judge the ends of the
   earth;
   he will give strength to his king,
   and exalt the power of his anointed."

***

2.1–10: The song of Hannah. This is a psalm of thanksgiving for a national victory that has been placed in Hannah's mouth. **1:** *Strength,* literally, "horn," seems to make use of the image of a proud animal. **5:** *The barren has borne seven:* This line probably led to the psalm's insertion. Hannah had only six children (2.21). **6:** *Sheol*★ was the place of the dead, the underworld. **10:** The reference to *his king* shows that the psalm was written later than Hannah since there was no king of Israel yet in her time. *Anointed,*★ (Heb., "mashiah") was a title for the king and the source of the term "messiah."★

11 Then Elkanah went home to Ramah, while the boy remained to minister to the LORD, in the presence of the priest Eli.

12 Now the sons of Eli were scoundrels; they had no regard for the LORD [13] or for the duties of the priests to the people. When anyone offered sacrifice, the priest's servant would come, while the meat was boiling, with a three-pronged fork in his hand, [14] and he would thrust it into the pan, or kettle, or caldron, or pot; all that the fork brought up the priest would take for himself.[b] This is what they did at Shiloh to all the Israelites who came there. [15] Moreover, before the fat was burned, the priest's servant would come and say to the one who was sacrificing, "Give meat for the priest to roast; for he will not accept boiled meat from you, but only raw." [16] And if the man said to him, "Let them burn the fat first, and then take whatever you wish," he would say, "No, you must give it now; if not, I will take it by force." [17] Thus the sin of the young men was very great in the sight of the LORD; for they treated the offerings of the LORD with contempt.

18 Samuel was ministering before the LORD, a boy wearing a linen ephod. [19] His mother used to make for him a little robe and take it to him each year, when she went up with her husband to offer the yearly sacrifice. [20] Then Eli would bless Elkanah and his wife, and say, "May the LORD repay[c] you with children by this woman for the gift that she made to[d] the LORD"; and then they would return to their home.

21 And[e] the LORD took note of Hannah; she conceived and bore three sons and two daughters. And the boy Samuel grew up in the presence of the LORD.

22 Now Eli was very old. He heard all that his sons were doing to all Israel, and how they lay with the women who served at the entrance to the tent of meeting. [23] He said to them, "Why do you do such things? For I hear of your evil dealings from all these people. [24] No, my sons; it is not a good report that I hear the people of the LORD spreading abroad. [25] If one person sins against another, someone can intercede for the sinner with the LORD;[f] but if someone sins against the LORD, who can make intercession?" But they would not listen to the voice of their father; for it was the will of the LORD to kill them.

26 Now the boy Samuel continued to grow both in stature and in favor with the LORD and with the people.

***

2.11–26: The wicked sons of Eli. Samuel's faithful service contrasts with the evil deeds of Eli's sons and hints that he will replace Eli. **12–17:** Priests made their living by receiving a portion of the sacrifices. The custom in Shiloh (vv. 13–14), which is different from that prescribed elsewhere (Lev 7.28–36; Deut 18.3), was for the priest to get whatever the fork brought up while the meat was boiling. By demanding the fat portion, which properly belonged to God, and taking it first, before the sacrifice was made, Eli's sons were sinning directly against the LORD (v. 25) by treating him with contempt (vv. 12, 17). Moreover, they threatened violence against worshippers who tried to do right (v. 16). **18:** The *linen ephod*★ was a kind of apron worn by priests. **22:** The *tent of meeting* is another name for the tabernacle,★ a moveable shrine. Apparently the temple of the LORD at Shiloh (1.3) was actually a tent shrine. **25:** *It was the will of the LORD to kill them:* This

a Cn Heb *against him he*   *b* Gk Syr Vg: Heb *with it*
c Q Ms Gk: MT *give*   *d* Q Ms Gk: MT *for the petition that she asked of*   *e* Q Ms Gk: MT *When*
f Gk Compare Q Ms: MT *another, God will mediate for him*

explanation of the obstinacy of Eli's sons is like God's hardening of Pharaoh's heart in Ex 4–12.

~~~~~~~~~~~~~~~~~~~~~~

27 A man of God came to Eli and said to him, "Thus the LORD has said, 'I revealed[a] myself to the family of your ancestor in Egypt when they were slaves[b] to the house of Pharaoh. [28]I chose him out of all the tribes of Israel to be my priest, to go up to my altar, to offer incense, to wear an ephod before me; and I gave to the family of your ancestor all my offerings by fire from the people of Israel. [29]Why then look with greedy eye[c] at my sacrifices and my offerings that I commanded, and honor your sons more than me by fattening yourselves on the choicest parts of every offering of my people Israel?' [30]Therefore the LORD the God of Israel declares: 'I promised that your family and the family of your ancestor should go in and out before me forever'; but now the LORD declares: 'Far be it from me; for those who honor me I will honor, and those who despise me shall be treated with contempt. [31]See, a time is coming when I will cut off your strength and the strength of your ancestor's family, so that no one in your family will live to old age. [32]Then in distress you will look with greedy eye[d] on all the prosperity that shall be bestowed upon Israel; and no one in your family shall ever live to old age. [33]The only one of you whom I shall not cut off from my altar shall be spared to weep out his[e] eyes and grieve his[f] heart; all the members of your household shall die by the sword.[g] [34]The fate of your two sons, Hophni and Phinehas, shall be the sign to you—both of them shall die on the same day. [35]I will raise up for myself a faithful priest, who shall do according to what is in my heart and in my mind. I will build him a sure house, and he shall go in and out before my anointed one forever. [36]Everyone who is left in your family shall come to implore him for a piece of silver or a loaf of bread, and shall say, Please put me in one of the priest's places, that I may eat a morsel of bread.' "

2.27–36: The oracle* against Eli. This was probably written by the deuteronomistic* editor. **27:** *Your ancestor* may allude to Moses, to whom Eli's family

traced their ancestry, rather than the tribe of Levi. The names of Eli's sons, Hophni and Phinehas (1.3; 2.34), are actually Egyptian, which is consistent with the phrase *in Egypt*. **28:** *To go up to my altar, to offer incense, to wear an ephod** refer to three principal duties of priests. Going up to the altar refers to making animal sacrifices. **31–33:** The cutting off of Eli's household refers not to the death of Eli and his sons in 1 Sam 4 but to Saul's annihilation of the priests of Nob in 1 Sam 22. Abiathar is the one spared. **35–36:** The *faithful priest* is Zadok, who came to prominence when Abiathar was banished by Solomon (1 Kings 1–2). The Zadokites were Aaron's descendants, and this passage may reflect a rivalry between the descendants of Moses and Aaron for the priesthood.

~~~~~~~~~~~~~~~~~~~~~~

3 Now the boy Samuel was ministering to the LORD under Eli. The word of the LORD was rare in those days; visions were not widespread.

2 At that time Eli, whose eyesight had begun to grow dim so that he could not see, was lying down in his room; [3]the lamp of God had not yet gone out, and Samuel was lying down in the temple of the LORD, where the ark of God was. [4]Then the LORD called, "Samuel! Samuel!"[h] and he said, "Here I am!" [5]and ran to Eli, and said, "Here I am, for you called me." But he said, "I did not call; lie down again." So he went and lay down. [6]The LORD called again, "Samuel!" Samuel got up and went to Eli, and said, "Here I am, for you called me." But he said, "I did not call, my son; lie down again." [7]Now Samuel did not yet know the LORD, and the word of the LORD had not yet been revealed to him. [8]The LORD called Samuel again, a third time. And he got up and went to Eli, and said, "Here I am, for you called me." Then Eli perceived that the LORD was calling the boy. [9]Therefore Eli said to Samuel, "Go, lie down; and if he calls you, you shall say, 'Speak, LORD, for your servant is listening.' " So Samuel went and lay down in his place.

10 Now the LORD came and stood there,

---

a Gk Tg Syr: Heb *Did I reveal*   *b* Q Ms Gk: MT lacks *slaves*   *c* Q Ms Gk: MT *then kick*   *d* Q Ms Gk: MT *will kick*   *e* Q Ms Gk: MT *your*   *f* Q Ms Gk: Heb *your*   *g* Q Ms See Gk: MT *die like mortals*   *h* Q Ms Gk See 3.10: MT *the LORD called Samuel* calling as before, "Samuel! Samuel!" And Samuel said, "Speak, for your servant is listening." 11Then the LORD said to Samuel, "See, I am about to do something in Israel that will make both ears of anyone who hears of it tingle. 12On that day I will fulfill against Eli all that I have spoken concerning his house, from beginning to end. 13For I have told him that I am about to punish his house forever, for the iniquity that he knew, because his sons were blaspheming God,ᵃ and he did not restrain them. 14Therefore I swear to the house of Eli that the iniquity of Eli's house shall not be expiated by sacrifice or offering forever."

15 Samuel lay there until morning; then he opened the doors of the house of the LORD. Samuel was afraid to tell the vision to Eli. 16But Eli called Samuel and said, "Samuel, my son." He said, "Here I am." 17Eli said, "What was it that he told you? Do not hide it from me. May God do so to you and more also, if you hide anything from me of all that he told you." 18So Samuel told him everything and hid nothing from him. Then he said, "It is the LORD; let him do what seems good to him."

19 As Samuel grew up, the LORD was with him and let none of his words fall to the ground. 20And all Israel from Dan to Beersheba knew that Samuel was a trustworthy prophet of the LORD. 21The LORD continued to appear at Shiloh, for the LORD revealed himself to Samuel at Shiloh by the word of the LORD. 1And the word of Samuel came to all Israel.

4

3.1–4.1a: Samuel's call. 1: *Word of the LORD . . . visions* are means of prophetic* revelation. 3: The lamp in the temple was to burn at night (Ex 27.21). Since *the lamp of God had not yet gone out,* it must have been just before dawn. Samuel's bed was in the temple near the inner sanctuary where the *ark of God* was kept. 7: *Samuel did not yet know the LORD:* Samuel's role as a prophet had not yet been established since *the word of the LORD had not yet been revealed to him.* That he would "know" the LORD provides a further contrast to Eli's sons, who did not regard or "know" the LORD (2.12). 14: Eli's sons are guilty of profaning the sacrifices that might otherwise have atoned for their sins. 17: *May God do so to you and more also* is a typical oath formula. Eli adjures Samuel, forcing him to reveal his conversation with the LORD. 19–21: All of Samuel's prophecies come true (none *fall to the ground*), and this is known *from Dan to Beer-sheba,* the traditional northern and southern boundaries of Israel. All Israel recognizes Samuel as a reliable prophet of the LORD.

~~~~~~~~~~~~~~~~~~~~~~~~~~~~~~~~~~~~~

In those days the Philistines mustered for war against Israel,ᵇ and Israel went out to battle against them;ᶜ they encamped at Ebenezer, and the Philistines encamped at Aphek. 2The Philistines drew up in line against Israel, and when the battle was joined,ᵈ Israel was defeated by the Philistines, who killed about four thousand men on the field of battle. 3When the troops came to the camp, the elders of Israel said, "Why has the LORD put us to rout today before the Philistines? Let us bring the ark of the covenant of the LORD here from Shiloh, so that he may come among us and save us from the power of our enemies." 4So the people sent to Shiloh, and brought from there the ark of the covenant of the LORD of hosts, who is enthroned on the cherubim. The two sons of Eli, Hophni and Phinehas, were there with the ark of the covenant of God.

5 When the ark of the covenant of the LORD came into the camp, all Israel gave a mighty shout, so that the earth resounded. 6When the Philistines heard the noise of the shouting, they said, "What does this great shouting in the camp of the Hebrews mean?" When they learned that the ark of the LORD had come to the camp, 7the Philistines were afraid; for they said, "Gods haveᵉ come into the camp." They also said, "Woe to us! For nothing like this has happened before. 8Woe to us! Who can deliver us from the power of these mighty gods? These are the gods who struck the Egyptians with every sort of plague in the wilderness. 9Take courage, and be men, O Philistines, in order not to become slaves to the Hebrews as they have been to you; be men and fight."

a Another reading is *for themselves*   b Gk: Heb lacks
In those days the Philistines mustered for war against Israel
c Gk: Heb *against the Philistines*   d Meaning of Heb
uncertain   e Or A god has

10 So the Philistines fought; Israel was defeated, and they fled, everyone to his home. There was a very great slaughter, for there fell of Israel thirty thousand foot soldiers. 11The ark of God was captured; and the two sons of Eli, Hophni and Phinehas, died.

12 A man of Benjamin ran from the battle line, and came to Shiloh the same day, with his clothes torn and with earth upon his head. 13When he arrived, Eli was sitting upon his seat by the road watching, for his heart trembled for the ark of God. When the man came into the city and told the news, all the city cried out. 14When Eli heard the sound of the outcry, he said, "What is this uproar?" Then the man came quickly and told Eli. 15Now Eli was ninety-eight years old and his eyes were set, so that he could not see. 16The man said to Eli, "I have just come from the battle; I fled from the battle today." He said, "How did it go, my son?" 17The messenger replied, "Israel has fled before the Philistines, and there has also been a great slaughter among the troops; your two sons also, Hophni and Phinehas, are dead, and the ark of God has been captured." 18When he mentioned the ark of God, Eli*a* fell over backward from his seat by the side of the gate; and his neck was broken and he died, for he was an old man, and heavy. He had judged Israel forty years.

19 Now his daughter-in-law, the wife of Phinehas, was pregnant, about to give birth. When she heard the news that the ark of God was captured, and that her father-in-law and her husband were dead, she bowed and gave birth; for her labor pains overwhelmed her. 20As she was about to die, the women attending her said to her, "Do not be afraid, for you have borne a son." But she did not answer or give heed. 21She named the child Ichabod, meaning, "The glory has departed from Israel," because the ark of God had been captured and because of her father-in-law and her husband. 22She said, "The glory has departed from Israel, for the ark of God has been captured."

an old "ark narrative"* which described the capture and return of the ark. **1b:** The *Philistines* came from the northwestern Mediterranean area (especially the island of Crete) and entered Palestine (which is derived from "Philistine") in approximately 1200 BCE, about the same time the Israelites were emerging in the central highlands. In this period they were Israel's traditional enemy. **4:** *Cherubim** were mythical griffin-like creatures with body parts from different creatures, often including wings and human heads. They were commonly depicted in palaces and temples. The ark is described as the throne of "the LORD of hosts who sits *enthroned on the cherubim,*" and the Israelites believe that the LORD is therefore present with them in battle. **6:** *Hebrews* is a term commonly used in the Bible by foreigners speaking of the Israelites. It may designate a socioeconomic group rather than an ethnic or family unit. **7–8:** *Gods:* The Philistines assume that the Israelites, like themselves, are polytheists. **18:** *Forty years* in the Bible is a round number for a single generation. **21–22:** *Ichabod* probably means "Where is the glory?" Phinehas's wife gives her son this name in lamentation* for the capture of the ark, which represents the LORD's presence or glory.

5 When the Philistines captured the ark of God, they brought it from Ebenezer to Ashdod; 2then the Philistines took the ark of God and brought it into the house of Dagon and placed it beside Dagon. 3When the people of Ashdod rose early the next day, there was Dagon, fallen on his face to the ground before the ark of the LORD. So they took Dagon and put him back in his place. 4But when they rose early on the next morning, Dagon had fallen on his face to the ground before the ark of the LORD, and the head of Dagon and both his hands were lying cut off upon the threshold; only the trunk of*b* Dagon was left to him. 5This is why the priests of Dagon and all who enter the house of Dagon do not step on the threshold of Dagon in Ashdod to this day.

6 The hand of the LORD was heavy upon the people of Ashdod, and he terrified and struck them with tumors, both in Ashdod and in its territory. 7And when the inhabitants of Ashdod saw how things were, they said, "The ark of the God of Israel must not

---

4.1b–22: The capture of the ark. Many scholars believe that 4.1–7.1 and possibly 2 Sam 6 are based on

a Heb *he*   *b* Heb lacks *the trunk of*

remain with us; for his hand is heavy on us and on our god Dagon." [8]So they sent and gathered together all the lords of the Philistines, and said, "What shall we do with the ark of the God of Israel?" The inhabitants of Gath replied, "Let the ark of God be moved on to us."[a] So they moved the ark of the God of Israel to Gath.[b] [9]But after they had brought it to Gath,[c] the hand of the LORD was against the city, causing a very great panic; he struck the inhabitants of the city, both young and old, so that tumors broke out on them. [10]So they sent the ark of the God of Israel[d] to Ekron. But when the ark of God came to Ekron, the people of Ekron cried out, "Why[e] have they brought around to us[f] the ark of the God of Israel to kill us[f] and our[g] people?" [11]They sent therefore and gathered together all the lords of the Philistines, and said, "Send away the ark of the God of Israel, and let it return to its own place, that it may not kill us and our people." For there was a deathly panic[h] throughout the whole city. The hand of God was very heavy there; [12]those who did not die were stricken with tumors, and the cry of the city went up to heaven.

5.1–12: The LORD's triumph. In the ancient Near East, wars between nations were interpreted as contests between their respective gods. This story explains that even though the Philistines defeated Israel, the LORD was superior to Dagon, a Philistine god. 1: *Ashdod* was one of five principal Philistine cities. The other four were Ashkelon, Ekron, Gath, and Gaza. 2: *Beside Dagon* means beside the idol or statue of Dagon in his temple or *house*. Dagon was a Canaanite fertility god adopted by the Philistines. 3: After the first night the Philistines find the idol of Dagon bowing prostrate before the ark. 4–5: This is an etiology* for the practice of jumping over thresholds in order to avoid offending the spirits of a particular building or space (compare Zeph 1.9). 6–12: The tumors and mice (in the next chapter) have led to the identification of this outbreak as bubonic plague, which was common in coastal areas. According to this story, however, the plague is the LORD's doing. 8: The *lords of the Philistines* are the rulers of the five Philistine cities. The word for *lord* here ("seren") is Philistine and cognate with the Greek word "tyrannos," or tyrant.

6 The ark of the LORD was in the country of the Philistines seven months. [2]Then the Philistines called for the priests and the diviners and said, "What shall we do with the ark of the LORD? Tell us what we should send with it to its place." [3]They said, "If you send away the ark of the God of Israel, do not send it empty, but by all means return him a guilt offering. Then you will be healed and will be ransomed;[i] will not his hand then turn from you?" [4]And they said, "What is the guilt offering that we shall return to him?" They answered, "Five gold tumors and five gold mice, according to the number of the lords of the Philistines; for the same plague was upon all of you and upon your lords. [5]So you must make images of your tumors and images of your mice that ravage the land, and give glory to the God of Israel; perhaps he will lighten his hand on you and your gods and your land. [6]Why should you harden your hearts as the Egyptians and Pharaoh hardened their hearts? After he had made fools of them, did they not let the people go, and they departed? [7]Now then, get ready a new cart and two milch cows that have never borne a yoke, and yoke the cows to the cart, but take their calves home, away from them. [8]Take the ark of the LORD and place it on the cart, and put in a box at its side the figures of gold, which you are returning to him as a guilt offering. Then send it off, and let it go its way. [9]And watch; if it goes up on the way to its own land, to Beth-shemesh, then it is he who has done us this great harm; but if not, then we shall know that it is not his hand that struck us; it happened to us by chance."

[10] The men did so; they took two milch cows and yoked them to the cart, and shut up their calves at home. [11]They put the ark of the LORD on the cart, and the box with the gold mice and the images of their tu-

a Gk Compare Q Ms: MT *They answered, "Let the ark of the God of Israel be brought around to Gath."*
b Gk: Heb lacks *to Gath*   c Q Ms: MT lacks *to Gath*
d Q Ms Gk: MT lacks *of Israel*   e Q Ms Gk: MT lacks *Why*   f Heb *me*   g Heb *my*   h Q Ms reads *a panic from the LORD*   i Q Ms Gk: MT *and it will be known to you*

mors. 12The cows went straight in the direction of Beth-shemesh along one highway, lowing as they went; they turned neither to the right nor to the left, and the lords of the Philistines went after them as far as the border of Beth-shemesh.

13 Now the people of Beth-shemesh were reaping their wheat harvest in the valley. When they looked up and saw the ark, they went with rejoicing to meet it.*ᵃ 14The cart came into the field of Joshua of Beth-shemesh, and stopped there. A large stone was there; so they split up the wood of the cart and offered the cows as a burnt offering to the LORD. 15The Levites took down the ark of the LORD and the box that was beside it, in which were the gold objects, and set them upon the large stone. Then the people of Beth-shemesh offered burnt offerings and presented sacrifices on that day to the LORD. 16When the five lords of the Philistines saw it, they returned that day to Ekron.

17 These are the gold tumors, which the Philistines returned as a guilt offering to the LORD: one for Ashdod, one for Gaza, one for Ashkelon, one for Gath, one for Ekron; 18also the gold mice, according to the number of all the cities of the Philistines belonging to the five lords, both fortified cities and unwalled villages. The great stone, beside which they set down the ark of the LORD, is a witness to this day in the field of Joshua of Beth-shemesh.

19 The descendants of Jeconiah did not rejoice with the people of Beth-shemesh when they greetedᵇ the ark of the LORD; and he killed seventy men of them.ᶜ The people mourned because the LORD had made a great slaughter among the people. 20Then the people of Beth-shemesh said, "Who is able to stand before the LORD, this holy God? To whom shall he go so that we may be rid of him?" 21So they sent messengers to the inhabitants of Kiriath-jearim, saying, "The Philistines have returned the ark of the LORD. Come down and take it up to you."

7 ¹And the people of Kiriath-jearim came and took up the ark of the LORD, and brought it to the house of Abinadab on the hill. They consecrated his son, Eleazar, to have charge of the ark of the LORD.

6.1–7.1: The return of the ark. Suspecting that the ark is the source of their problems, the Philistines decide to send it back to Israel. They include with it a *guilt offering* (v. 3), which should probably be understood as compensation for having taken the ark and in hopes of appeasing the LORD and avoiding further punishment from him. There is one gold tumor and one gold mouse for each of the five Philistine cities (vv. 4, 17–18). **7:** The cart is new and therefore ritually pure. The two cows have never been yoked and are therefore fit to be sacrificed (compare Num 19.2; Deut 21.3). They are also *milch cows,* meaning that they have young calves. This is part of the test described in v. 9. **9:** Unaccustomed to pulling a cart, these two cows would be expected to wander aimlessly in search of their calves. If, contrary to this expectation, the cows headed straight for Israelite territory, the Philistines would know that their sufferings had indeed been sent by the LORD. **12:** The cows take the most direct route into Israelite territory. **15:** This verse is likely a later addition by a scribe* concerned to have the Levites, the priestly tribe, handle the ark. **20:** *Who is able to stand before the LORD* is apparently a technical expression for priestly service. The people are asking whether there is a priest who can handle the ark.

2 From the day that the ark was lodged at Kiriath-jearim, a long time passed, some twenty years, and all the house of Israel lamentedᵈ after the LORD.

3 Then Samuel said to all the house of Israel, "If you are returning to the LORD with all your heart, then put away the foreign gods and the Astartes from among you. Direct your heart to the LORD, and serve him only, and he will deliver you out of the hand of the Philistines." 4So Israel put away the Baals and the Astartes, and they served the LORD only.

5 Then Samuel said, "Gather all Israel at Mizpah, and I will pray to the LORD for you." 6So they gathered at Mizpah, and drew water and poured it out before the LORD. They fasted that day, and said, "We have sinned against the LORD." And Samuel judged the people of Israel at Mizpah.

a Gk: Heb *rejoiced to see it*   *b* Gk: Heb *And he killed some of the people of Beth-shemesh, because they looked into*   *c* Heb *killed seventy men, fifty thousand men*   *d* Meaning of Heb uncertain

7 When the Philistines heard that the people of Israel had gathered at Mizpah, the lords of the Philistines went up against Israel. And when the people of Israel heard of it they were afraid of the Philistines. 8 The people of Israel said to Samuel, "Do not cease to cry out to the LORD our God for us, and pray that he may save us from the hand of the Philistines." 9 So Samuel took a sucking lamb and offered it as a whole burnt offering to the LORD; Samuel cried out to the LORD for Israel, and the LORD answered him. 10 As Samuel was offering up the burnt offering, the Philistines drew near to attack Israel; but the LORD thundered with a mighty voice that day against the Philistines and threw them into confusion; and they were routed before Israel. 11 And the men of Israel went out of Mizpah and pursued the Philistines, and struck them down as far as beyond Beth-car.

12 Then Samuel took a stone and set it up between Mizpah and Jeshanah,*a* and named it Ebenezer;*b* for he said, "Thus far the LORD has helped us." 13 So the Philistines were subdued and did not again enter the territory of Israel; the hand of the LORD was against the Philistines all the days of Samuel. 14 The towns that the Philistines had taken from Israel were restored to Israel, from Ekron to Gath; and Israel recovered their territory from the hand of the Philistines. There was peace also between Israel and the Amorites.

15 Samuel judged Israel all the days of his life. 16 He went on a circuit year by year to Bethel, Gilgal, and Mizpah; and he judged Israel in all these places. 17 Then he would come back to Ramah, for his home was there; he administered justice there to Israel, and built there an altar to the LORD.

7.2–17: Samuel judges Israel. Samuel is described as a transitional figure between the era of the judges and the monarchy. He embodies the roles of priest, prophet,* and now judge. **2:** *Twenty years* is a way of designating half a generation. The phrase fits Samuel into the structure of the book of Judges in which a period of foreign oppression precedes Israel's repentance. **3–4:** The call for *returning to the LORD with all your heart* from the sin of idolatry* marks these verses

as an addition by the deuteronomistic* editor. *Baal** and *Astarte** were the leading male and female fertility gods of Canaan. **5:** *Mizpah* became the administrative and religious capital after Jerusalem's destruction in 586 BCE. The setting of this story in Mizpah may indicate a late date of composition. **6:** The libations and fasting described here are part of a community purification ritual, perhaps in preparation for war. **8–9:** Samuel is depicted as an intercessor for the people in the tradition of Moses and Jeremiah. **10:** The first part of this verse is parenthetical; Yahweh's answer is the thunder. **12:** An etiology* for the name *Ebenezer,* whose original meaning was religious and military: "stone of the helper/warrior." **13–14:** The typical deuteronomistic formulas for the judges are here applied to Samuel (compare Judg 3.30; 8.28; 11.33). **15–17:** The book of Judges describes two types of judges: military leaders and legal figures. This chapter ascribes both roles to Samuel. The towns of *Bethel, Gilgal, Mizpah,* and *Ramah* were all within the territories of the tribes of Ephraim and Benjamin.

CHOOSING A KING

Chs. 8–12: Chapters 9–11 contain three accounts of Saul's being chosen king that have been bound together editorially and surrounded by Samuel's convocations of the people in chs. 8 and 12.

---

8 When Samuel became old, he made his sons judges over Israel. 2 The name of his firstborn son was Joel, and the name of his second, Abijah; they were judges in Beersheba. 3 Yet his sons did not follow in his ways, but turned aside after gain; they took bribes and perverted justice.

4 Then all the elders of Israel gathered together and came to Samuel at Ramah, 5 and said to him, "You are old and your sons do not follow in your ways; appoint for us, then, a king to govern us, like other nations." 6 But the thing displeased Samuel when they said, "Give us a king to govern us." Samuel prayed to the LORD, 7 and the LORD said to Samuel, "Listen to the voice of the people in all that they say to you; for they have not rejected you, but they have rejected me from being king over them. 8 Just as they have

a Gk Syr: Heb *Shen*   *b* That is *Stone of Help*

done to me,[a] from the day I brought them up out of Egypt to this day, forsaking me and serving other gods, so also they are doing to you. 9Now then, listen to their voice; only—you shall solemnly warn them, and show them the ways of the king who shall reign over them."

10 So Samuel reported all the words of the LORD to the people who were asking him for a king. 11He said, "These will be the ways of the king who will reign over you: he will take your sons and appoint them to his chariots and to be his horsemen, and to run before his chariots; 12and he will appoint for himself commanders of thousands and commanders of fifties, and some to plow his ground and to reap his harvest, and to make his implements of war and the equipment of his chariots. 13He will take your daughters to be perfumers and cooks and bakers. 14He will take the best of your fields and vineyards and olive orchards and give them to his courtiers. 15He will take one-tenth of your grain and of your vineyards and give it to his officers and his courtiers. 16He will take your male and female slaves, and the best of your cattle[b] and donkeys, and put them to his work. 17He will take one-tenth of your flocks, and you shall be his slaves. 18And in that day you will cry out because of your king, whom you have chosen for yourselves; but the LORD will not answer you in that day."

19 But the people refused to listen to the voice of Samuel; they said, "No! but we are determined to have a king over us, 20so that we also may be like other nations, and that our king may govern us and go out before us and fight our battles." 21When Samuel had heard all the words of the people, he repeated them in the ears of the LORD. 22The LORD said to Samuel, "Listen to their voice and set a king over them." Samuel then said to the people of Israel, "Each of you return home."

against the practice of hereditary leadership. Like Eli's sons, Samuel's sons are evil. **4–9:** Both Samuel and the LORD are displeased by the people's request for a king. This does not necessarily mean that monarchy itself is bad but only that the people's request demonstrates a lack of faith in the LORD. **8:** The review of Israel's history as one of forsaking the LORD is indicative of the deuteronomistic* narrator's view. **10:** *Asking* is a play on the name "Saul." **11–17:** These verses preview the social consequences of monarchy by detailing *the ways of the king.* The Hebrew word translated *ways* means "custom" or "judgment." Ironically,* the king to whom the people look for justice will follow the typical ancient Near Eastern practices of taxation and conscription of workers for his service. The items in this list appear to be based on Solomon's reign. **18:** The language of this verse is characteristic of the deuteronomistic narrator and resembles that of the framework of the book of Judges. **20:** *Govern,* or "judge." **22:** The LORD permits the people to have a king even though he does not approve of their demand.

9 There was a man of Benjamin whose name was Kish son of Abiel son of Zeror son of Becorath son of Aphiah, a Benjaminite, a man of wealth. 2He had a son whose name was Saul, a handsome young man. There was not a man among the people of Israel more handsome than he; he stood head and shoulders above everyone else.

3 Now the donkeys of Kish, Saul's father, had strayed. So Kish said to his son Saul, "Take one of the boys with you; go and look for the donkeys." 4He passed through the hill country of Ephraim and passed through the land of Shalishah, but they did not find them. And they passed through the land of Shaalim, but they were not there. Then he passed through the land of Benjamin, but they did not find them.

5 When they came to the land of Zuph, Saul said to the boy who was with him, "Let us turn back, or my father will stop worrying about the donkeys and worry about us." 6But he said to him, "There is a man of God in this town; he is a man held in honor. Whatever he says always comes true. Let us go

8.1–22: Israel demands a king. 1–3: *Beer-sheba* was the southernmost city in Judah and far outside of Samuel's jurisdiction in 7.15–17. It became an administrative center during the period of the monarchy of Judah. These facts suggest 8.1–3 may have been written

a Gk: Heb lacks *to me*   *b* Gk: Heb *young men*

there now; perhaps he will tell us about the journey on which we have set out." [7]Then Saul replied to the boy, "But if we go, what can we bring the man? For the bread in our sacks is gone, and there is no present to bring to the man of God. What have we?" [8]The boy answered Saul again, "Here, I have with me a quarter shekel of silver; I will give it to the man of God, to tell us our way." [9](Formerly in Israel, anyone who went to inquire of God would say, "Come, let us go to the seer"; for the one who is now called a prophet was formerly called a seer.) [10]Saul said to the boy, "Good; come, let us go." So they went to the town where the man of God was.

9.1–10.16: Saul's anointing. * **9.2:** Saul's height and handsomeness are qualities typically attributed to a king. **3:** *Donkeys* were ridden by kings (Zech 9.9; Mt 21.1–9), so that the story already hints at Saul's kingship. *One of the boys* refers to a servant who may or may not have been young. **6:** *Man of God* is a title for a prophet.* This prophet turns out to be Samuel (v. 14). But the identification is secondary, since Saul and his servant do not initially seem to know who Samuel is. In the original tale, Saul's encounter was with an anonymous seer. The *town* would have been understood as Ramah, Samuel's home. **7:** The *present* was necessary as a sort of payment to the man of God for divining the whereabouts of the donkeys. **8:** A *shekel* * was not a coin but a measure of weight of less than half an ounce. **9:** This is an obvious editorial comment identifying a *seer* as a *prophet*.

[11] As they went up the hill to the town, they met some girls coming out to draw water, and said to them, "Is the seer here?" [12]They answered, "Yes, there he is just ahead of you. Hurry; he has come just now to the town, because the people have a sacrifice today at the shrine. [13]As soon as you enter the town, you will find him, before he goes up to the shrine to eat. For the people will not eat until he comes, since he must bless the sacrifice; afterward those eat who are invited. Now go up, for you will meet him immediately." [14]So they went up to the town. As they were entering the town, they saw Samuel coming out toward them on his way up to the shrine.

9.11–14. 11: Cities were built on hills for protection. Drawing water was typically done by women, usually in the morning or evening when it was cooler. This suggests that it was around sundown. **12:** The *shrine* or "high place" was a hill or raised platform where worship, especially sacrifices, took place. Since deuteronomistic* literature generally condemns the high places,* this reference is probably part of the original tale. **13:** Some sacrifices provided occasions for feasting after the portion of the animal designated for God was burned.

[15] Now the day before Saul came, the LORD had revealed to Samuel: [16]"Tomorrow about this time I will send to you a man from the land of Benjamin, and you shall anoint him to be ruler over my people Israel. He shall save my people from the hand of the Philistines; for I have seen the suffering of[a] my people, because their outcry has come to me." [17]When Samuel saw Saul, the LORD told him, "Here is the man of whom I spoke to you. He it is who shall rule over my people." [18]Then Saul approached Samuel inside the gate, and said, "Tell me, please, where is the house of the seer?" [19]Samuel answered Saul, "I am the seer; go up before me to the shrine, for today you shall eat with me, and in the morning I will let you go and will tell you all that is on your mind. [20]As for your donkeys that were lost three days ago, give no further thought to them, for they have been found. And on whom is all Israel's desire fixed, if not on you and on all your ancestral house?" [21]Saul answered, "I am only a Benjaminite, from the least of the tribes of Israel, and my family is the humblest of all the families of the tribe of Benjamin. Why then have you spoken to me in this way?"

9.15–21. 16: Anointing* involved smearing a person's head with scented olive oil as a way of designating the person for a particular office. *Ruler* in Hebrew is "nagid," which means "king designate" in this verse. **18:** The *gate* of a city was a well-fortified entrance to a walled city. It was the site of commerce and the place where trials were held. **19–20:** In the original tale, the seer consulted God overnight in order to address

a Gk: Heb lacks *the suffering of*

Saul's need. But the old tale has been transformed editorially so that Samuel has been told to expect Saul (vv. 15–17) and now goes ahead and tells him *all that is on* his *mind* by assuring him that the donkeys have been found (v. 20). The next morning is reserved for Saul's anointing. **21:** Saul's objection is typical of people who receive a divine call in the Bible, such as Moses (Ex 4.10–17) and Jeremiah (Jer 1.6). It also shows Saul's humility and God's preference for the small and weak.

22 Then Samuel took Saul and his servant-boy and brought them into the hall, and gave them a place at the head of those who had been invited, of whom there were about thirty. 23And Samuel said to the cook, "Bring the portion I gave you, the one I asked you to put aside." 24The cook took up the thigh and what went with it*a* and set them before Saul. Samuel said, "See, what was kept is set before you. Eat; for it is set*b* before you at the appointed time, so that you might eat with the guests."*c*

So Saul ate with Samuel that day. 25When they came down from the shrine into the town, a bed was spread for Saul*d* on the roof, and he lay down to sleep.*e* 26Then at the break of dawn*f* Samuel called to Saul upon the roof, "Get up, so that I may send you on your way." Saul got up, and both he and Samuel went out into the street.

9.22–26. 22–24: Saul is treated as a highly honored guest. He is given *the thigh,* which is usually reserved for the deity or the priests. **25:** Saul sleeps *on the roof,* which was flat and where there was a cool breeze, indicating that the story is set in the summer.

27 As they were going down to the outskirts of the town, Samuel said to Saul, "Tell the boy to go on before us, and when he has passed on, stop here yourself for a while, that I may make known to you the word of God."

10 1Samuel took a vial of oil and poured it on his head, and kissed him; he said, "The LORD has anointed you ruler over his people Israel. You shall reign over the people of the LORD and you will save them from the hand of their enemies all around. Now this shall be the sign to you that the LORD has anointed you ruler*g* over his her-

itage: 2When you depart from me today you will meet two men by Rachel's tomb in the territory of Benjamin at Zelzah; they will say to you, 'The donkeys that you went to seek are found, and now your father has stopped worrying about them and is worrying about you, saying: What shall I do about my son?' 3Then you shall go on from there further and come to the oak of Tabor; three men going up to God at Bethel will meet you there, one carrying three kids, another carrying three loaves of bread, and another carrying a skin of wine. 4They will greet you and give you two loaves of bread, which you shall accept from them. 5After that you shall come to Gibeath-elohim,*h* at the place where the Philistine garrison is; there, as you come to the town, you will meet a band of prophets coming down from the shrine with harp, tambourine, flute, and lyre playing in front of them; they will be in a prophetic frenzy. 6Then the spirit of the LORD will possess you, and you will be in a prophetic frenzy along with them and be turned into a different person. 7Now when these signs meet you, do whatever you see fit to do, for God is with you. 8And you shall go down to Gilgal ahead of me; then I will come down to you to present burnt offerings and offer sacrifices of well-being. Seven days you shall wait, until I come to you and show you what you shall do."

9 As he turned away to leave Samuel, God gave him another heart; and all these signs were fulfilled that day. 10When they were going from there*i* to Gibeah,*j* a band of prophets met him; and the spirit of God possessed him, and he fell into a prophetic frenzy along with them. 11When all who knew him before saw how he prophesied with the prophets, the people said to one another, "What has come over the son of Kish? Is Saul also among the prophets?" 12A man of the place answered, "And who is their fa-

a Meaning of Heb uncertain   *b* Q Ms Gk: MT *it was kept*   *c* Cn: Heb *it was kept for you, saying, I have invited the people*   *d* Gk: Heb *and he spoke with Saul*   *e* Gk: Heb lacks *and he lay down to sleep*   *f* Gk: Heb *and they arose early and at break of dawn*   *g* Gk: Heb lacks *over his people Israel. You shall . . . anointed you ruler*   *h* Or *the Hill of God*   *i* Gk: Heb *they came there*   *j* Or *the hill* ther?" Therefore it became a proverb, "Is Saul also among the prophets?" [13]When his prophetic frenzy had ended, he went home.[a]

14 Saul's uncle said to him and to the boy, "Where did you go?" And he replied, "To seek the donkeys; and when we saw they were not to be found, we went to Samuel." [15]Saul's uncle said, "Tell me what Samuel said to you." [16]Saul said to his uncle, "He told us that the donkeys had been found." But about the matter of the kingship, of which Samuel had spoken, he did not tell him anything.

9.27–10.16. 1: The LORD's *heritage* is the land of Israel. The original idea behind this expression is that every nation is the inheritance of the god it worships. **3–4:** The *three men going up to God at Bethel* are carrying items for sacrifice. They give *two loaves of bread* to Saul, one for him and one for his servant. A better reading, found in the Greek translation known as the Septuagint,* is "two offerings of bread." Thus, Saul again receives the portion of a priest. **5–7:** Music was often used to induce an ecstasy in which prophets* uttered their oracles* (2 Kings 3.15–16). The judges were also moved to action by the spirit of the LORD. Saul's instruction to *do whatever you see fit to do* is a military commission. **8:** This verse connects this story to 13.7b–15. **10–13:** These verses describe the fulfillment of the third sign. The description is also an etiology* for the proverb, *Is Saul also among the prophets?* (v. 11). A different explanation occurs in 19.19–24. Whatever its origin, the proverb seems to have a positive meaning in this context. The LORD's spirit empowers Saul both to prophesy and to rule. The *father* of a group of prophets (v. 12) is their leader. **14–16:** It is surprising that Saul's uncle rather than his father questions him, since the uncle has not been mentioned before in the story. These verses are editorial and set the stage for the following story (10.17–27a). Since Saul's anointing* was private, there is a need for a public proclamation that he is king.

17 Samuel summoned the people to the LORD at Mizpah [18]and said to them,[b] "Thus says the LORD, the God of Israel, 'I brought up Israel out of Egypt, and I rescued you from the hand of the Egyptians and from the hand of all the kingdoms that were oppressing you.' [19]But today you have rejected your God, who saves you from all your calamities

and your distresses; and you have said, 'No! but set a king over us.' Now therefore present yourselves before the LORD by your tribes and by your clans."

20 Then Samuel brought all the tribes of Israel near, and the tribe of Benjamin was taken by lot. [21]He brought the tribe of Benjamin near by its families, and the family of the Matrites was taken by lot. Finally he brought the family of the Matrites near man by man,[c] and Saul the son of Kish was taken by lot. But when they sought him, he could not be found. [22]So they inquired again of the LORD, "Did the man come here?"[d] and the LORD said, "See, he has hidden himself among the baggage." [23]Then they ran and brought him from there. When he took his stand among the people, he was head and shoulders taller than any of them. [24]Samuel said to all the people, "Do you see the one whom the LORD has chosen? There is no one like him among all the people." And all the people shouted, "Long live the king!"

25 Samuel told the people the rights and duties of the kingship; and he wrote them in a book and laid it up before the LORD. Then Samuel sent all the people back to their homes. [26]Saul also went to his home at Gibeah, and with him went warriors whose hearts God had touched. [27]But some worthless fellows said, "How can this man save us?" They despised him and brought him no present. But he held his peace.

10.17–27a: Saul is chosen by lot. 18–19: These verses offer another example of deuteronomistic* language. **20–21:** Israelite society was structured according to a hierarchy: tribe, clan,* family ("house of the father"), and individual. Elsewhere in the Bible (Josh 7.14; 1 Sam 14.41) the lot is used to find a person guilty of breaking a law or vow. Some scholars believe that two stories are combined at this point, one in which Saul was present and chosen by lot and another in which he was chosen by oracle* or because of his height. **22:** *Inquired* is another pun on Saul's name. **25:** *The rights and duties of the kingship* probably set out the responsibilities of king and people to each other. The

a Cn: Heb *he came to the shrine*   *b* Heb *to the people of Israel*   *c* Gk: Heb lacks *Finally . . . man by man* *d* Gk: Heb *Is there yet a man to come here?*

expression here is nearly identical to "the ways of the king" in 8.9, 11, although the two passages seem to refer to two different lists or documents. **26–27a:** Saul's return to Gibeah and the doubts of the *worthless fellows* prepare the way for the subsequent story in which Saul will prove his ability to save Israel.

Now Nahash, king of the Ammonites, had been grievously oppressing the Gadites and the Reubenites. He would gouge out the right eye of each of them and would not grant Israel a deliverer. No one was left of the Israelites across the Jordan whose right eye Nahash, king of the Ammonites, had not gouged out. But there were seven thousand men who had escaped from the Ammonites and had entered Jabesh-gilead.*a*

11 About a month later,*b* Nahash the Ammonite went up and besieged Jabesh-gilead; and all the men of Jabesh said to Nahash, "Make a treaty with us, and we will serve you." 2But Nahash the Ammonite said to them, "On this condition I will make a treaty with you, namely that I gouge out everyone's right eye, and thus put disgrace upon all Israel." 3The elders of Jabesh said to him, "Give us seven days' respite that we may send messengers through all the territory of Israel. Then, if there is no one to save us, we will give ourselves up to you." 4When the messengers came to Gibeah of Saul, they reported the matter in the hearing of the people; and all the people wept aloud.

5 Now Saul was coming from the field behind the oxen; and Saul said, "What is the matter with the people, that they are weeping?" So they told him the message from the inhabitants of Jabesh. 6And the spirit of God came upon Saul in power when he heard these words, and his anger was greatly kindled. 7He took a yoke of oxen, and cut them in pieces and sent them throughout all the territory of Israel by messengers, saying, "Whoever does not come out after Saul and Samuel, so shall it be done to his oxen!" Then the dread of the LORD fell upon the people, and they came out as one. 8When he mustered them at Bezek, those from Israel were three hundred thousand, and those from Judah seventy*c* thousand. 9They said

to the messengers who had come, "Thus shall you say to the inhabitants of Jabesh-gilead: 'Tomorrow, by the time the sun is hot, you shall have deliverance.' " When the messengers came and told the inhabitants of Jabesh, they rejoiced. 10So the inhabitants of Jabesh said, "Tomorrow we will give ourselves up to you, and you may do to us whatever seems good to you." 11The next day Saul put the people in three companies. At the morning watch they came into the camp and cut down the Ammonites until the heat of the day; and those who survived were scattered, so that no two of them were left together.

12 The people said to Samuel, "Who is it that said, 'Shall Saul reign over us?' Give them to us so that we may put them to death." 13But Saul said, "No one shall be put to death this day, for today the LORD has brought deliverance to Israel."

14 Samuel said to the people, "Come, let us go to Gilgal and there renew the kingship." 15So all the people went to Gilgal, and there they made Saul king before the LORD in Gilgal. There they sacrificed offerings of well-being before the LORD, and there Saul and all the Israelites rejoiced greatly.

10.27b–11.15: Saul defeats the Ammonites. 10.27b: This paragraph was lost from the Hebrew text but can now be restored from a Dead Sea Scroll fragment of Samuel, as the translator's note indicates. The missing material explains the reason for the conflict in ch. 11. *The Gadites and the Reubenites* were Israelites living east of the Jordan River in territory which the Ammonite king, Nahash, considered his, but which Israel also claimed. The city of Jabesh in Gilead was farther north and outside of the disputed area, but Nahash threatened it because some of the Israelites from Gad and Reuben had fled there. **11.3:** The messengers are not sent directly to Saul but *through all the territory of Israel.* **4–5:** Even in Gibeah the messengers do not seek out Saul, but he learns of their mission because of the weeping of the people as he returns from the field.

a Q Ms Compare Josephus, *Antiquities* VI.v.1 (68–71): MT lacks *Now Nahash . . . entered Jabesh-gilead.*
b Q Ms Gk: MT lacks *About a month later*   *c* Q Ms Gk: MT *thirty*

Thus, the story does not seem to assume that Saul is king. **6:** The *spirit of God* spurs Saul to military action as it had some of the deliverers in the book of Judges. **7:** Saul's action symbolizes a threat against the animals and perhaps the people themselves who do not join in the war. References to dismemberment occur in ancient treaties, so that Saul's actions assume a covenant* relationship among the tribes. **8:** The division between Israel and Judah is reflected here though it did not occur until after Solomon's reign. **10:** *We will give ourselves up to you* means literally, "we will come out to you." What sounds to Nahash like a surrender cleverly masks a threat. The people of Jabesh will come out to fight! **11:** *The next day* actually began at sunset according to Israelite reckoning, and *the morning watch* was in the early hours before sunrise. This was a surprise attack before dawn. **12–14:** These verses are editorial and bind 10.17–27a with 10.27b–11.15. It was the "worthless fellows" in 10.27a who asked, *Shall Saul reign over us?* The editor adds Samuel to the story at this point even though he plays no role in the battle account. The editor also speaks of *renew(ing) the kingship.* **15:** The original story did not assume that Saul was already king but explained that the people *made Saul king* as a result of his victory on this occasion.

12 Samuel said to all Israel, "I have listened to you in all that you have said to me, and have set a king over you. ²See, it is the king who leads you now; I am old and gray, but my sons are with you. I have led you from my youth until this day. ³Here I am; testify against me before the LORD and before his anointed. Whose ox have I taken? Or whose donkey have I taken? Or whom have I defrauded? Whom have I oppressed? Or from whose hand have I taken a bribe to blind my eyes with it? Testify against me*a* and I will restore it to you." ⁴They said, "You have not defrauded us or oppressed us or taken anything from the hand of anyone." ⁵He said to them, "The LORD is witness against you, and his anointed is witness this day, that you have not found anything in my hand." And they said, "He is witness."

6 Samuel said to the people, "The LORD is witness, who*b* appointed Moses and Aaron and brought your ancestors up out of the land of Egypt. ⁷Now therefore take your stand, so that I may enter into judgment with

you before the LORD, and I will declare to you*c* all the saving deeds of the LORD that he performed for you and for your ancestors. ⁸When Jacob went into Egypt and the Egyptians oppressed them,*d* then your ancestors cried to the LORD and the LORD sent Moses and Aaron, who brought forth your ancestors out of Egypt, and settled them in this place. ⁹But they forgot the LORD their God; and he sold them into the hand of Sisera, commander of the army of King Jabin of*e* Hazor, and into the hand of the Philistines, and into the hand of the king of Moab; and they fought against them. ¹⁰Then they cried to the LORD, and said, 'We have sinned, because we have forsaken the LORD, and have served the Baals and the Astartes; but now rescue us out of the hand of our enemies, and we will serve you.' ¹¹And the LORD sent Jerubbaal and Barak,*f* and Jephthah, and Samson,*g* and rescued you out of the hand of your enemies on every side; and you lived in safety. ¹²But when you saw that King Nahash of the Ammonites came against you, you said to me, 'No, but a king shall reign over us,' though the LORD your God was your king. ¹³See, here is the king whom you have chosen, for whom you have asked; see, the LORD has set a king over you. ¹⁴If you will fear the LORD and serve him and heed his voice and not rebel against the commandment of the LORD, and if both you and the king who reigns over you will follow the LORD your God, it will be well; ¹⁵but if you will not heed the voice of the LORD, but rebel against the commandment of the LORD, then the hand of the LORD will be against you and your king.*h* ¹⁶Now therefore take your stand and see this great thing that the LORD will do before your eyes. ¹⁷Is it not the wheat harvest today? I will call upon the LORD, that he may send thunder and rain; and you shall know and see that the wick-

a Gk: Heb lacks *Testify against me*
b Gk: Heb lacks *is witness, who*
c Gk: Heb lacks *and I will declare to you*
d Gk: Heb lacks *and the Egyptians oppressed them*
e Gk: Heb lacks *King Jabin of*   *f* Gk Syr: Heb *Bedan*   *g* Gk: Heb *Samuel*   *h* Gk: Heb *and your ancestors*

edness that you have done in the sight of the LORD is great in demanding a king for yourselves." 18So Samuel called upon the LORD, and the LORD sent thunder and rain that day; and all the people greatly feared the LORD and Samuel.

12.1–25: Samuel's farewell. 3: Samuel's words are reminiscent of Moses' in Num 16.15 and contrast with the "ways of the king" that he listed in 1 Sam 8. **6–12:** This long retrospective on Israel's history expresses the opinions and concerns of the deuteronomistic* editor. **13–15:** Even though the people's request for a king evinced a lack of faith, they and their king can still prosper as long as they will serve the LORD. **16–18:** The *wheat harvest* was in early summer. The lack of rain was a threat to the crops. Thus, this miracle shows the LORD's response to Samuel and hints at his displeasure with the people.

19 All the people said to Samuel, "Pray to the LORD your God for your servants, so that we may not die; for we have added to all our sins the evil of demanding a king for ourselves." 20And Samuel said to the people, "Do not be afraid; you have done all this evil, yet do not turn aside from following the LORD, but serve the LORD with all your heart; 21and do not turn aside after useless things that cannot profit or save, for they are useless. 22For the LORD will not cast away his people, for his great name's sake, because it has pleased the LORD to make you a people for himself. 23Moreover as for me, far be it from me that I should sin against the LORD by ceasing to pray for you; and I will instruct you in the good and the right way. 24Only fear the LORD, and serve him faithfully with all your heart; for consider what great things he has done for you. 25But if you still do wickedly, you shall be swept away, both you and your king."

12.19–25: Samuel is again described as an intercessor on behalf of the people. The language of these verses, especially vv. 24–25, underlines the main themes of the Deuteronomistic* History. *For his great name's sake* in v. 22 means that Yahweh's own reputation might be damaged if he were not patient with his people but destroyed them too readily.

13 Saul was . . .[a] years old when he began to reign; and he reigned . . . and two[b] years over Israel.

2 Saul chose three thousand out of Israel; two thousand were with Saul in Michmash and the hill country of Bethel, and a thousand were with Jonathan in Gibeah of Benjamin; the rest of the people he sent home to their tents. 3Jonathan defeated the garrison of the Philistines that was at Geba; and the Philistines heard of it. And Saul blew the trumpet throughout all the land, saying, "Let the Hebrews hear!" 4When all Israel heard that Saul had defeated the garrison of the Philistines, and also that Israel had become odious to the Philistines, the people were called out to join Saul at Gilgal.

5 The Philistines mustered to fight with Israel, thirty thousand chariots, and six thousand horsemen, and troops like the sand on the seashore in multitude; they came up and encamped at Michmash, to the east of Bethaven. 6When the Israelites saw that they were in distress (for the troops were hard pressed), the people hid themselves in caves and in holes and in rocks and in tombs and in cisterns. 7Some Hebrews crossed the Jordan to the land of Gad and Gilead. Saul was still at Gilgal, and all the people followed him trembling.

8 He waited seven days, the time appointed by Samuel; but Samuel did not come to Gilgal, and the people began to slip away from Saul.[c] 9So Saul said, "Bring the burnt offering here to me, and the offerings of well-being." And he offered the burnt offering. 10As soon as he had finished offering the burnt offering, Samuel arrived; and Saul went out to meet him and salute him. 11Samuel said, "What have you done?" Saul replied, "When I saw that the people were slipping away from me, and that you did not come within the days appointed, and that the Philistines were mustering at Michmash, 12I said, 'Now the Philistines will come down upon me at Gilgal, and I have not entreated the favor of the LORD'; so I forced myself,

a The number is lacking in the Heb text (the verse is lacking in the Septuagint). *b Two* is not the entire number; something has dropped out. *c* Heb *him* and offered the burnt offering." [13]Samuel said to Saul, "You have done foolishly; you have not kept the commandment of the LORD your God, which he commanded you. The LORD would have established your kingdom over Israel forever, [14]but now your kingdom will not continue; the LORD has sought out a man after his own heart; and the LORD has appointed him to be ruler over his people, because you have not kept what the LORD commanded you." [15]And Samuel left and went on his way from Gilgal.[a] The rest of the people followed Saul to join the army; they went up from Gilgal toward Gibeah of Benjamin.[b]

13.1–14.52: Saul's wars with the Philistines. 13.1: Saul's age at his accession* is unknown. The Hebrew text actually says he was one year old, which is, of course, impossible. It also says that he reigned two years, but the events recounted for his reign indicate a much longer period. **3–4:** *Jonathan*, Saul's son, is mentioned here for the first time. Since he is a grown man, this story is substantially later than 9.1–10.16, where Saul appears as a young man. Both Jonathan and Saul are credited with defeating the Philistine garrison. This may indicate the composite nature of this account, or Saul, as king, may have received the credit for his son's victory. *Geba* and Gibeah are very similar in Hebrew and appear to be confused here. **7b–15a:** This story of Saul's rejection alludes to Samuel's order in 10.8. Both passages refer to an interval of *seven days* between them, but the intervening events in chs. 10–12 would require a much longer time. The nature of Saul's sin is not altogether clear. Perhaps he is condemned for trying to usurp Samuel's role of religious leadership. The *man after [Yahweh's] own heart* is an allusion to David. It does not imply any special quality of David but is simply a way of saying that he is chosen by the LORD.

Saul counted the people who were present with him, about six hundred men. [16]Saul, his son Jonathan, and the people who were present with them stayed in Geba of Benjamin; but the Philistines encamped at Michmash. [17]And raiders came out of the camp of the Philistines in three companies; one company turned toward Ophrah, to the land of Shual, [18]another company turned toward Bethhoron, and another company turned toward

the mountain[c] that looks down upon the valley of Zeboim toward the wilderness.

19 Now there was no smith to be found throughout all the land of Israel; for the Philistines said, "The Hebrews must not make swords or spears for themselves"; [20]so all the Israelites went down to the Philistines to sharpen their plowshares, mattocks, axes, or sickles;[d] [21]The charge was two-thirds of a shekel[e] for the plowshares and for the mattocks, and one-third of a shekel for sharpening the axes and for setting the goads.[f] [22]So on the day of the battle neither sword nor spear was to be found in the possession of any of the people with Saul and Jonathan; but Saul and his son Jonathan had them.

13.15b–22: These verses set the stage for the battle account in the next chapter. *Geba* and *Michmash* (v. 16) were across from each other on opposite sides of a valley. The Philistine *raiders* (vv. 17–18) customarily went north, west, and east from Michmash to attack Israelite settlements and keep them subdued. The Philistines also controlled the Israelites by maintaining a monopoly on iron working (vv. 19–22).

---

23 Now a garrison of the Philistines had gone out to the pass of Michmash. **14** [1]One day Jonathan son of Saul said to the young man who carried his armor, "Come, let us go over to the Philistine garrison on the other side." But he did not tell his father. [2]Saul was staying in the outskirts of Gibeah under the pomegranate tree that is at Migron; the troops that were with him were about six hundred men, [3]along with Ahijah son of Ahitub, Ichabod's brother, son of Phinehas son of Eli, the priest of the LORD in Shiloh, carrying an ephod. Now the people did not know that Jonathan had gone. [4]In the pass,[g] by which Jonathan tried to go over to the Philistine garrison, there was a rocky crag on one side and a rocky crag on the other; the name of the one was Bozez, and the name of the other

---

a Gk: Heb *went up from Gilgal to Gibeah of Benjamin*
b Gk: Heb lacks *The rest . . . of Benjamin*
c Cn Compare Gk: Heb *toward the border*   d Gk: Heb *plowshare*   e Heb *was a pim*   f Cn: Meaning of Heb uncertain   g Heb *Between the passes*

Seneh. ⁵One crag rose on the north in front of Michmash, and the other on the south in front of Geba.

6 Jonathan said to the young man who carried his armor, "Come, let us go over to the garrison of these uncircumcised; it may be that the LORD will act for us; for nothing can hinder the LORD from saving by many or by few." ⁷His armor-bearer said to him, "Do all that your mind inclines to.ᵃ I am with you; as your mind is, so is mine."ᵇ ⁸Then Jonathan said, "Now we will cross over to those men and will show ourselves to them. ⁹If they say to us, 'Wait until we come to you,' then we will stand still in our place, and we will not go up to them. ¹⁰But if they say, 'Come up to us,' then we will go up; for the LORD has given them into our hand. That will be the sign for us." ¹¹So both of them showed themselves to the garrison of the Philistines; and the Philistines said, "Look, Hebrews are coming out of the holes where they have hidden themselves." ¹²The men of the garrison hailed Jonathan and his armor-bearer, saying, "Come up to us, and we will show you something." Jonathan said to his armor-bearer, "Come up after me; for the LORD has given them into the hand of Israel." ¹³Then Jonathan climbed up on his hands and feet, with his armor-bearer following after him. The Philistinesᶜ fell before Jonathan, and his armor-bearer, coming after him, killed them. ¹⁴In that first slaughter Jonathan and his armor-bearer killed about twenty men within an area about half a furrow long in an acreᵈ of land. ¹⁵There was a panic in the camp, in the field, and among all the people; the garrison and even the raiders trembled; the earth quaked; and it became a very great panic.

16 Saul's lookouts in Gibeah of Benjamin were watching as the multitude was surging back and forth.ᵉ ¹⁷Then Saul said to the troops that were with him, "Call the roll and see who has gone from us." When they had called the roll, Jonathan and his armor-bearer were not there. ¹⁸Saul said to Ahijah, "Bring the arkᶠ of God here." For at that time the arkᶠ of God went with the Israelites. ¹⁹While Saul was talking to the priest, the tumult in the camp of the Philistines in-

creased more and more; and Saul said to the priest, "Withdraw your hand." ²⁰Then Saul and all the people who were with him rallied and went into the battle; and every sword was against the other, so that there was very great confusion. ²¹Now the Hebrews who previously had been with the Philistines and had gone up with them into the camp turned and joined the Israelites who were with Saul and Jonathan. ²²Likewise, when all the Israelites who had gone into hiding in the hill country of Ephraim heard that the Philistines were fleeing, they too followed closely after them in the battle. ²³So the LORD gave Israel the victory that day.

13.23–14.23a. 13.23: The battle begins with the Philistines' movement to the pass on their side of the valley. **14.1:** The *young man who carried his armor:* The armor-bearer was a formidable soldier as the involvement of this man in the battle shows. **3:** This *ephod★* was an object that was carried by priests and used to divine the will of God. It was carried in priestly garments, which may explain why the same word was used for both (1 Sam 2.18). *The people* is often used to mean the army. **6:** *These uncircumcised★* is a derogatory term for the Philistines. **13:** Jonathan wounded the Philistines, and his armor-bearer finished them off. **19:** *Withdraw your hand:* Saul had called Ahijah the priest with the intention of consulting the LORD through him (the Greek text reads "ephod" instead of "ark"). Before receiving an answer to his inquiry, Saul decided to attack. **21:** The *Hebrews* here are distinguished from the *Israelites.* They are first allied with the Philistines and then turn against them. They may have been mercenaries of some kind.

~~~~~~~~~~~~~~~~~~~~~~~~~~~~~~~~~~~~~

The battle passed beyond Beth-aven, and the troops with Saul numbered altogether about ten thousand men. The battle spread out over the hill country of Ephraim.

24 Now Saul committed a very rash act on that day.ᵍ He had laid an oath on the troops, saying, "Cursed be anyone who eats food before it is evening and I have been avenged on my enemies." So none of the

---

a Gk: Heb *Do all that is in your mind. Turn*
b Gk: Heb *lacks so is mine*　　c Heb *They*　　d Heb *yoke*
e Gk: Heb *they went and there*　　f Gk *the ephod*
g Gk: Heb *The Israelites were distressed that day*

troops tasted food. 25All the troops*a* came upon a honeycomb; and there was honey on the ground. 26When the troops came upon the honeycomb, the honey was dripping out; but they did not put their hands to their mouths, for they feared the oath. 27But Jonathan had not heard his father charge the troops with the oath; so he extended the staff that was in his hand, and dipped the tip of it in the honeycomb, and put his hand to his mouth; and his eyes brightened. 28Then one of the soldiers said, "Your father strictly charged the troops with an oath, saying, 'Cursed be anyone who eats food this day.' And so the troops are faint." 29Then Jonathan said, "My father has troubled the land; see how my eyes have brightened because I tasted a little of this honey. 30How much better if today the troops had eaten freely of the spoil taken from their enemies; for now the slaughter among the Philistines has not been great."

31 After they had struck down the Philistines that day from Michmash to Aijalon, the troops were very faint; 32so the troops flew upon the spoil, and took sheep and oxen and calves, and slaughtered them on the ground; and the troops ate them with the blood. 33Then it was reported to Saul, "Look, the troops are sinning against the LORD by eating with the blood." And he said, "You have dealt treacherously; roll a large stone before me here."*b* 34Saul said, "Disperse yourselves among the troops, and say to them, 'Let all bring their oxen or their sheep, and slaughter them here, and eat; and do not sin against the LORD by eating with the blood.'" So all of the troops brought their oxen with them that night, and slaughtered them there. 35And Saul built an altar to the LORD; it was the first altar that he built to the LORD.

be slaughtered upon the stone, thereby allowing the blood to be drained before the meat was cooked and eaten.

36 Then Saul said, "Let us go down after the Philistines by night and despoil them until the morning light; let us not leave one of them." They said, "Do whatever seems good to you." But the priest said, "Let us draw near to God here." 37So Saul inquired of God, "Shall I go down after the Philistines? Will you give them into the hand of Israel?" But he did not answer him that day. 38Saul said, "Come here, all you leaders of the people; and let us find out how this sin has arisen today. 39For as the LORD lives who saves Israel, even if it is in my son Jonathan, he shall surely die!" But there was no one among all the people who answered him. 40He said to all Israel, "You shall be on one side, and I and my son Jonathan will be on the other side." The people said to Saul, "Do what seems good to you." 41Then Saul said, "O LORD God of Israel, why have you not answered your servant today? If this guilt is in me or in my son Jonathan, O LORD God of Israel, give Urim; but if this guilt is in your people Israel,*c* give Thummim." And Jonathan and Saul were indicated by the lot, but the people were cleared. 42Then Saul said, "Cast the lot between me and my son Jonathan." And Jonathan was taken.

43 Then Saul said to Jonathan, "Tell me what you have done." Jonathan told him, "I tasted a little honey with the tip of the staff that was in my hand; here I am, I will die." 44Saul said, "God do so to me and more also; you shall surely die, Jonathan!" 45Then the people said to Saul, "Shall Jonathan die, who has accomplished this great victory in Israel? Far from it! As the LORD lives, not one hair of his head shall fall to the ground; for he has worked with God today." So the people ransomed Jonathan, and he did not die. 46Then Saul withdrew from pursuing the Philistines; and the Philistines went to their own place.

14.23b–35. 24–30: Saul's foolish oath caused his troops to be faint and prevented them from gaining a complete victory. 31–35: A further result of Saul's oath was that it led his hungry soldiers to commit a ritual offense by slaughtering animals *on the ground* so that the blood did not drain out. Hence, they ate meat cooked *with the blood*. Saul then commanded them to *roll a large stone* to the site so that animals could

a Heb *land*   *b* Gk: Heb *me this day*   *c* Vg Compare Gk: Heb *41Saul said to the LORD, the God of Israel*

14.36–46: Finally, Saul's oath nearly cost the life of Jonathan. The inquiry through the priest (v. 37) involves yes/no questions, with the additional possibility that no answer will be forthcoming. Verses 40–42 illustrate at least one method of divination or lot casting. Neither the mechanism nor the meaning of the Urim and Thummim are known, but they functioned to answer yes/no questions or to choose between two alternatives. **45:** It is not clear exactly how *the people ransomed Jonathan*. Perhaps this situation foreshadows Jonathan's death before he can succeed Saul.

47 When Saul had taken the kingship over Israel, he fought against all his enemies on every side—against Moab, against the Ammonites, against Edom, against the kings of Zobah, and against the Philistines; wherever he turned he routed them. ⁴⁸He did valiantly, and struck down the Amalekites, and rescued Israel out of the hands of those who plundered them.

49 Now the sons of Saul were Jonathan, Ishvi, and Malchishua; and the names of his two daughters were these: the name of the firstborn was Merab, and the name of the younger, Michal. ⁵⁰The name of Saul's wife was Ahinoam daughter of Ahimaaz. And the name of the commander of his army was Abner son of Ner, Saul's uncle; ⁵¹Kish was the father of Saul, and Ner the father of Abner was the son of Abiel.

52 There was hard fighting against the Philistines all the days of Saul; and when Saul saw any strong or valiant warrior, he took him into his service.

14.47–52. 47–48: These verses indicate Saul's military success as king. *Moab, the Ammonites,* and *Edom* were the three countries on the other side of the Jordan from Israel. *Zobah* was an important Aramean (Syrian) city-state. The *Amalekites* were a nomadic tribe south of Judah. This reference to Saul's defeat of them is contradicted by the story in ch. 15. **49:** *Ishvi* may be the same as Ishbaal, Saul's successor, who is otherwise not named in this list. **52:** The reference to Saul's draft of *any strong or valiant warrior* is an appropriate introduction to the story of David beginning in 16.14.

15 Samuel said to Saul, "The LORD sent me to anoint you king over his people Israel; now therefore listen to the words of the LORD. ²Thus says the LORD of hosts, 'I will punish the Amalekites for what they did in opposing the Israelites when they came up out of Egypt. ³Now go and attack Amalek, and utterly destroy all that they have; do not spare them, but kill both man and woman, child and infant, ox and sheep, camel and donkey.' "

4 So Saul summoned the people, and numbered them in Telaim, two hundred thousand foot soldiers, and ten thousand soldiers of Judah. ⁵Saul came to the city of the Amalekites and lay in wait in the valley. ⁶Saul said to the Kenites, "Go! Leave! Withdraw from among the Amalekites, or I will destroy you with them; for you showed kindness to all the people of Israel when they came up out of Egypt." So the Kenites withdrew from the Amalekites. ⁷Saul defeated the Amalekites, from Havilah as far as Shur, which is east of Egypt. ⁸He took King Agag of the Amalekites alive, but utterly destroyed all the people with the edge of the sword. ⁹Saul and the people spared Agag, and the best of the sheep and of the cattle and of the fatlings, and the lambs, and all that was valuable, and would not utterly destroy them; all that was despised and worthless they utterly destroyed.

15.1–35: Another rejection of Saul. 2: An allusion to the story in Ex 17.8–16, which is also recalled in Deut 25.17–19. **3:** The order to *utterly destroy* the Amalekites reflects the practice of the "ban"* or "devotion to destruction" (Heb., "herem"), used by Israel and other peoples in the ancient Middle East. When it was implemented, the enemy and all their property were annihilated as a kind of sacrifice to the deity. **4:** Saul's army is unbelievably large. Either the figures have been exaggerated or the Hebrew word translated "thousand" actually refers to a military unit much smaller than a thousand men. **6:** The precise event in which the Kenites *showed kindness* is unknown.

10 The word of the LORD came to Samuel: ¹¹"I regret that I made Saul king, for he has turned back from following me, and has not carried out my commands." Samuel was

angry; and he cried out to the LORD all night. [12]Samuel rose early in the morning to meet Saul, and Samuel was told, "Saul went to Carmel, where he set up a monument for himself, and on returning he passed on down to Gilgal." [13]When Samuel came to Saul, Saul said to him, "May you be blessed by the LORD; I have carried out the command of the LORD." [14]But Samuel said, "What then is this bleating of sheep in my ears, and the lowing of cattle that I hear?" [15]Saul said, "They have brought them from the Amalekites; for the people spared the best of the sheep and the cattle, to sacrifice to the LORD your God; but the rest we have utterly destroyed." [16]Then Samuel said to Saul, "Stop! I will tell you what the LORD said to me last night." He replied, "Speak."

17 Samuel said, "Though you are little in your own eyes, are you not the head of the tribes of Israel? The LORD anointed you king over Israel. [18]And the LORD sent you on a mission, and said, 'Go, utterly destroy the sinners, the Amalekites, and fight against them until they are consumed.' [19]Why then did you not obey the voice of the LORD? Why did you swoop down on the spoil, and do what was evil in the sight of the LORD?" [20]Saul said to Samuel, "I have obeyed the voice of the LORD, I have gone on the mission on which the LORD sent me, I have brought Agag the king of Amalek, and I have utterly destroyed the Amalekites. [21]But from the spoil the people took sheep and cattle, the best of the things devoted to destruction, to sacrifice to the LORD your God in Gilgal." [22]And Samuel said,

"Has the LORD as great delight in burnt
    offerings and sacrifices,
  as in obedience to the voice of the
    LORD?
  Surely, to obey is better than sacrifice,
    and to heed than the fat of rams.
23 For rebellion is no less a sin than
    divination,
  and stubbornness is like iniquity and
    idolatry.
Because you have rejected the word of
    the LORD,
  he has also rejected you from being
    king."

15.10–23. 15: Saul defends himself by blaming his troops (*the people*) for sparing the best of the sheep and cattle, though he is implicated in v. 9. He also says that the animals were spared for sacrifice, and this is the ground for Samuel's subsequent rebuke. **22:** *The fat of rams* was the part of the animal burned in sacrifice to the LORD. **23:** The kind of *divination* prohibited here is related to foreign idolatry* and does not include divination through a legitimate priest of the LORD. *Rebellion* and *stubbornness* are like *divination* and *idolatry* because they involve turning away from the LORD.

24 Saul said to Samuel, "I have sinned; for I have transgressed the commandment of the LORD and your words, because I feared the people and obeyed their voice. [25]Now therefore, I pray, pardon my sin, and return with me, so that I may worship the LORD." [26]Samuel said to Saul, "I will not return with you; for you have rejected the word of the LORD, and the LORD has rejected you from being king over Israel." [27]As Samuel turned to go away, Saul caught hold of the hem of his robe, and it tore. [28]And Samuel said to him, "The LORD has torn the kingdom of Israel from you this very day, and has given it to a neighbor of yours, who is better than you. [29]Moreover the Glory of Israel will not recant[a] or change his mind; for he is not a mortal, that he should change his mind." [30]Then Saul[b] said, "I have sinned; yet honor me now before the elders of my people and before Israel, and return with me, so that I may worship the LORD your God." [31]So Samuel turned back after Saul; and Saul worshiped the LORD.

32 Then Samuel said, "Bring Agag king of the Amalekites here to me." And Agag came to him haltingly.[c] Agag said, "Surely this is the bitterness of death."[d] [33]But Samuel said,

"As your sword has made women
      childless,
    so your mother shall be childless
      among women."

And Samuel hewed Agag in pieces before the LORD in Gilgal.

a Q Ms Gk: MT *deceive*   b Heb *he*   c Cn Compare Gk: Meaning of Heb uncertain   d Q Ms Gk: MT *Surely the bitterness of death is past*

34 Then Samuel went to Ramah; and Saul went up to his house in Gibeah of Saul. [35]Samuel did not see Saul again until the day of his death, but Samuel grieved over Saul. And the LORD was sorry that he had made Saul king over Israel.

15.24–35. 27: Grasping the *hem* of a person's garment was a way of submitting or pleading. **28:** Samuel uses the torn hem as an object lesson. The LORD *has torn the kingdom* from Saul and given it to his *neighbor,* an allusion to David. **29:** The point of this verse is that the LORD will not *change his mind,* so Saul's further pleading is futile. *The Glory of Israel* is an epithet* for the LORD not used elsewhere in the Hebrew Bible. The general message of the verse seems to contradict the larger context in which the LORD has changed his mind about allowing Saul to be king. Some scholars address this contradiction by positing v. 29 as a later addition. **33:** Agag's dismemberment *before the LORD* at the hands of Samuel was a ritual execution as punishment either for war crimes or for violation of an unknown treaty. **35:** The statement that *Samuel did not see Saul again until the day of his death* anticipates the story in 1 Sam 28 but stands in tension with 1 Sam 19.18–24.

16 The LORD said to Samuel, "How long will you grieve over Saul? I have rejected him from being king over Israel. Fill your horn with oil and set out; I will send you to Jesse the Bethlehemite, for I have provided for myself a king among his sons." [2]Samuel said, "How can I go? If Saul hears of it, he will kill me." And the LORD said, "Take a heifer with you, and say, 'I have come to sacrifice to the LORD.' [3]Invite Jesse to the sacrifice, and I will show you what you shall do; and you shall anoint for me the one whom I name to you." [4]Samuel did what the LORD commanded, and came to Bethlehem. The elders of the city came to meet him trembling, and said, "Do you come peaceably?" [5]He said, "Peaceably; I have come to sacrifice to the LORD; sanctify yourselves and come with me to the sacrifice." And he sanctified Jesse and his sons and invited them to the sacrifice.

6 When they came, he looked on Eliab and thought, "Surely the LORD's anointed is now before the LORD."[a] [7]But the LORD said

to Samuel, "Do not look on his appearance or on the height of his stature, because I have rejected him; for the LORD does not see as mortals see; they look on the outward appearance, but the LORD looks on the heart." [8]Then Jesse called Abinadab, and made him pass before Samuel. He said, "Neither has the LORD chosen this one." [9]Then Jesse made Shammah pass by. And he said, "Neither has the LORD chosen this one." [10]Jesse made seven of his sons pass before Samuel, and Samuel said to Jesse, "The LORD has not chosen any of these." [11]Samuel said to Jesse, "Are all your sons here?" And he said, "There remains yet the youngest, but he is keeping the sheep." And Samuel said to Jesse, "Send and bring him; for we will not sit down until he comes here." [12]He sent and brought him in. Now he was ruddy, and had beautiful eyes, and was handsome. The LORD said, "Rise and anoint him; for this is the one." [13]Then Samuel took the horn of oil, and anointed him in the presence of his brothers; and the spirit of the LORD came mightily upon David from that day forward. Samuel then set out and went to Ramah.

16.1–13: David's anointing.* 4–5: The *elders of the city* were nobles who functioned as a council of civic leaders. Jesse seems to be among the elders of Bethlehem. **6–7:** Like Saul, Eliab is tall and handsome. Samuel is impressed but is warned that the LORD regards the inner qualities or *heart* as more important than outer appearance. The writer is building a contrast between Saul and David. **8–9:** David's brothers are rejected one by one. Samuel is probably using some device like the Urim and Thummim to determine whether each of the sons is the one chosen by the LORD. **10:** This verse agrees with 17.12 in crediting Jesse with eight sons, but 1 Chr 2.13–15 mentions only seven with David as the youngest. Since the number seven had special meaning as a symbol for completeness or for largeness, the seventh son may have been seen as specially blessed. Perhaps David was originally the seventh son and the tradition became altered over time. Or perhaps he is described as the eighth son as a way of highlighting his humble origins. **11:** The word translated *the youngest* may also mean "the smallest" and again contrasts David with Saul. David is also

a Heb *him*

keeping the sheep. The image of a shepherd was a common metaphor* for kings (2 Sam 5.2). **12**: *Ruddy* means "reddish" of hair and complexion (Gen 25.25).

~~~~~~~~~~~~~~~~

14 Now the spirit of the LORD departed from Saul, and an evil spirit from the LORD tormented him. 15And Saul's servants said to him, "See now, an evil spirit from God is tormenting you. 16Let our lord now command the servants who attend you to look for someone who is skillful in playing the lyre; and when the evil spirit from God is upon you, he will play it, and you will feel better." 17So Saul said to his servants, "Provide for me someone who can play well, and bring him to me." 18One of the young men answered, "I have seen a son of Jesse the Bethlehemite who is skillful in playing, a man of valor, a warrior, prudent in speech, and a man of good presence; and the LORD is with him." 19So Saul sent messengers to Jesse, and said, "Send me your son David who is with the sheep." 20Jesse took a donkey loaded with bread, a skin of wine, and a kid, and sent them by his son David to Saul. 21And David came to Saul, and entered his service. Saul loved him greatly, and he became his armor-bearer. 22Saul sent to Jesse, saying, "Let David remain in my service, for he has found favor in my sight." 23And whenever the evil spirit from God came upon Saul, David took the lyre and played it with his hand, and Saul would be relieved and feel better, and the evil spirit would depart from him.

16.14–23: David comes to Saul's court. **14**: The contrast between David and Saul continues. The *spirit of the LORD* came upon David (v. 13) but left Saul. In its place Saul is tormented by an *evil spirit from the LORD*. This may be an ancient way of describing mental illness. The theological point is that the LORD has abandoned Saul. **16**: The *lyre* was a hand-held stringed instrument. Musicians were used in the ancient world to ward off evil spirits. **18**: *A man of valor* is a "nobleman." In 9.1 the same expression is translated "a man of wealth." *Prudent in speech* or "skilled of speech" implies both eloquence and cleverness. *The LORD is with him* expresses a central theme of the David story, which has its beginning in this text. **19**: David's role as a shepherd again hints at his future as king. **21**: The

word "love" expressed not only affection but also loyalty. Because *Saul loved [David] greatly* he established a relationship with him and made a commitment to him, appointing him as his *armor-bearer*, which indicates David's skill as a warrior.

~~~~~~~~~~~~~~~~

17 Now the Philistines gathered their armies for battle; they were gathered at Socoh, which belongs to Judah, and encamped between Socoh and Azekah, in Ephes-dammim. 2Saul and the Israelites gathered and encamped in the valley of Elah, and formed ranks against the Philistines. 3The Philistines stood on the mountain on the one side, and Israel stood on the mountain on the other side, with a valley between them. 4And there came out from the camp of the Philistines a champion named Goliath, of Gath, whose height was six*a* cubits and a span. 5He had a helmet of bronze on his head, and he was armed with a coat of mail; the weight of the coat was five thousand shekels of bronze. 6He had greaves of bronze on his legs and a javelin of bronze slung between his shoulders. 7The shaft of his spear was like a weaver's beam, and his spear's head weighed six hundred shekels of iron; and his shield-bearer went before him. 8He stood and shouted to the ranks of Israel, "Why have you come out to draw up for battle? Am I not a Philistine, and are you not servants of Saul? Choose a man for yourselves, and let him come down to me. 9If he is able to fight with me and kill me, then we will be your servants; but if I prevail against him and kill him, then you shall be our servants and serve us." 10And the Philistine said, "Today I defy the ranks of Israel! Give me a man, that we may fight together." 11When Saul and all Israel heard these words of the Philistine, they were dismayed and greatly afraid.

17.1–58: David defeats the Philistine champion. An initial version of this story in vv. 1–11, 32–49, 51–54 has been extensively supplemented in the Hebrew text by vv. 12–31, 50, 55–58; 18.1–5. The supplementary material does not occur in the old Greek translation (known as the Septuagint* and abbreviated as LXX*).

a MT: Q Ms Gk *four*

Its addition has caused a series of tensions within the story relating to David's presence in Saul's army, the way in which the Philistine died, and Saul's acquaintance with David (see below). **4**: *Goliath* is a genuine Philistine name. But it occurs only here and in v. 23, which is supplemental. Otherwise, David's opponent is simply called "the Philistine." The name has come into the story under the influence of 2 Sam 21.19, which says that a man named Elhanan killed Goliath. *Six cubits and a span* was about nine and one-half feet. The Greek reading, "four cubits and a span," about six and one-half feet, is more realistic and probably original. **5–7**: The armor described here is not genuinely Philistine but reflects items from different armies at different times. It is designed to paint a very imposing picture of the Philistine. *Five thousand shekels** was almost 126 pounds. **6**: The *javelin* was more likely a curved sword or scimitar. **7**: The spear's description is borrowed from 2 Sam 21.19. The comparison of the shaft with *a weaver's beam* is obscure. It may refer to size or to a leather thong attached to some spears to facilitate hurling. *Six hundred shekels of iron* was more than 15 pounds.

12 Now David was the son of an Ephrathite of Bethlehem in Judah, named Jesse, who had eight sons. In the days of Saul the man was already old and advanced in years.ᵃ ¹³The three eldest sons of Jesse had followed Saul to the battle; the names of his three sons who went to the battle were Eliab the firstborn, and next to him Abinadab, and the third Shammah. ¹⁴David was the youngest; the three eldest followed Saul, ¹⁵but David went back and forth from Saul to feed his father's sheep at Bethlehem. ¹⁶For forty days the Philistine came forward and took his stand, morning and evening.

17 Jesse said to his son David, "Take for your brothers an ephah of this parched grain and these ten loaves, and carry them quickly to the camp to your brothers; ¹⁸also take these ten cheeses to the commander of their thousand. See how your brothers fare, and bring some token from them."

19 Now Saul, and they, and all the men of Israel, were in the valley of Elah, fighting with the Philistines. ²⁰David rose early in the morning, left the sheep with a keeper, took the provisions, and went as Jesse had commanded him. He came to the encampment as the army was going forth to the battle line, shouting the war cry. ²¹Israel and the Philistines drew up for battle, army against army. ²²David left the things in charge of the keeper of the baggage, ran to the ranks, and went and greeted his brothers. ²³As he talked with them, the champion, the Philistine of Gath, Goliath by name, came up out of the ranks of the Philistines, and spoke the same words as before. And David heard him.

24 All the Israelites, when they saw the man, fled from him and were very much afraid. ²⁵The Israelites said, "Have you seen this man who has come up? Surely he has come up to defy Israel. The king will greatly enrich the man who kills him, and will give him his daughter and make his family free in Israel." ²⁶David said to the men who stood by him, "What shall be done for the man who kills this Philistine, and takes away the reproach from Israel? For who is this uncircumcised Philistine that he should defy the armies of the living God?" ²⁷The people answered him in the same way, "So shall it be done for the man who kills him."

17.12–27. 12: The *Ephrathites* were a subgroup within the Calebite clan,* which was part of Judah. **14–15**: Here, David is a shepherd boy running errands for his father rather than a warrior already in the army as in 16.14–23. **16**: In this supplementary version of the story, the Philistine had been challenging the Israelites *for forty days*, while in the initial version David fights him the first time he comes out. **17**: *An ephah* was about half a bushel. **18**: *Some token* refers to a personal effect that would indicate that the brothers had received the gift from their father and that they were well. **25**: *Free* meant exempt from slavery and from taxes and conscription. **26**: David's courage comes from his recognition that the LORD will help him because the Philistine has reproached the *living God*.

28 His eldest brother Eliab heard him talking to the men; and Eliab's anger was kindled against David. He said, "Why have you come down? With whom have you left those few sheep in the wilderness? I know your presumption and the evil of your heart;

ᵃ Gk Syr: Heb *among men*

for you have come down just to see the battle." 29 David said, "What have I done now? It was only a question." 30 He turned away from him toward another and spoke in the same way; and the people answered him again as before.

31 When the words that David spoke were heard, they repeated them before Saul; and he sent for him. 32 David said to Saul, "Let no one's heart fail because of him; your servant will go and fight with this Philistine." 33 Saul said to David, "You are not able to go against this Philistine to fight with him; for you are just a boy, and he has been a warrior from his youth." 34 But David said to Saul, "Your servant used to keep sheep for his father; and whenever a lion or a bear came, and took a lamb from the flock, 35 I went after it and struck it down, rescuing the lamb from its mouth; and if it turned against me, I would catch it by the jaw, strike it down, and kill it. 36 Your servant has killed both lions and bears; and this uncircumcised Philistine shall be like one of them, since he has defied the armies of the living God." 37 David said, "The LORD, who saved me from the paw of the lion and from the paw of the bear, will save me from the hand of this Philistine." So Saul said to David, "Go, and may the LORD be with you!"

38 Saul clothed David with his armor; he put a bronze helmet on his head and clothed him with a coat of mail. 39 David strapped Saul's sword over the armor, and he tried in vain to walk, for he was not used to them. Then David said to Saul, "I cannot walk with these; for I am not used to them." So David removed them. 40 Then he took his staff in his hand, and chose five smooth stones from the wadi, and put them in his shepherd's bag, in the pouch; his sling was in his hand, and he drew near to the Philistine.

staff, little more than a stick. The *sling* was not a shepherd's toy but a deadly weapon of war wielded by entire divisions of armies. It consisted of two cords attached to a pouch from which a stone was hurled, potentially with great accuracy (Judg 20.16).

41 The Philistine came on and drew near to David, with his shield-bearer in front of him. 42 When the Philistine looked and saw David, he disdained him, for he was only a youth, ruddy and handsome in appearance. 43 The Philistine said to David, "Am I a dog, that you come to me with sticks?" And the Philistine cursed David by his gods. 44 The Philistine said to David, "Come to me, and I will give your flesh to the birds of the air and to the wild animals of the field." 45 But David said to the Philistine, "You come to me with sword and spear and javelin; but I come to you in the name of the LORD of hosts, the God of the armies of Israel, whom you have defied. 46 This very day the LORD will deliver you into my hand, and I will strike you down and cut off your head; and I will give the dead bodies of the Philistine army this very day to the birds of the air and to the wild animals of the earth, so that all the earth may know that there is a God in Israel, 47 and that all this assembly may know that the LORD does not save by sword and spear; for the battle is the LORD's and he will give you into our hand."

17.41–47: An element of ancient warfare involved taunting the opponent and boasting of one's own superiority. The Philistine is distracted by David's staff (v. 43) and overlooks his real weapon, the sling. David's reply (vv. 45–47) is religious in nature and promises retribution for the Philistine's defiance of the LORD. David does not need the Philistine's arms because the LORD fights for him.

48 When the Philistine drew nearer to meet David, David ran quickly toward the battle line to meet the Philistine. 49 David put his hand in his bag, took out a stone, slung it, and struck the Philistine on his forehead; the stone sank into his forehead, and he fell face down on the ground. 50 So David prevailed over the Philistine with a sling and a stone, striking down the

17.28–40. 33–37: While David has experience fighting wild animals as a shepherd, he is still not the warrior described in 16.18. This tension results from the addition to the originally independent story in ch. 17. **38–39:** David's inability to move in Saul's armor emphasizes his lack of experience as a soldier. But it also shows Saul's failure to understand that David's advantage lay in his mobility. **40:** *His staff* was a shepherd's

Philistine and killing him; there was no
sword in David's hand. 51Then David ran
and stood over the Philistine; he grasped his
sword, drew it out of its sheath, and killed
him; then he cut off his head with it.

When the Philistines saw that their champion was dead, they fled. 52The troops of Israel and Judah rose up with a shout and pursued the Philistines as far as Gath*a* and the
gates of Ekron, so that the wounded Philistines fell on the way from Shaaraim as far as
Gath and Ekron. 53The Israelites came back
from chasing the Philistines, and they plundered their camp. 54David took the head of
the Philistine and brought it to Jerusalem;
but he put his armor in his tent.

55 When Saul saw David go out against
the Philistine, he said to Abner, the commander of the army, "Abner, whose son is
this young man?" Abner said, "As your soul
lives, O king, I do not know." 56The king
said, "Inquire whose son the stripling is."
57On David's return from killing the Philistine, Abner took him and brought him before
Saul, with the head of the Philistine in his
hand. 58Saul said to him, "Whose son are
you, young man?" And David answered, "I
am the son of your servant Jesse the
Bethlehemite."

17.48–58. 49: It is not by chance that David's stone
strikes the Philistine in a spot where he is vulnerable.
David's speech shows that this is understood as God's
doing. 50: This supplemental verse is a summary of
the action. It causes some tension with v. 51, which
says that David killed the Philistine with his own sword
after felling him with the sling and then beheaded
him. 54: This verse contains an anachronism,* since
Jerusalem was not conquered until David became king
of Israel (2 Sam 5). *His tent:* Goliath's sword later surfaces among the priests at Nob (21.9), suggesting that
this phrase should be read as "the tent (shrine) of Yahweh." 55: *Whose son is this young man?* is idiomatic.
Saul is not asking who David's father is. Again, this
question indicates the story's originally independent
nature, since according to 16.14–23 Saul and David
already had a close relationship.

~~~~~~

18 When David*b* had finished speaking
to Saul, the soul of Jonathan was
bound to the soul of David, and Jonathan

loved him as his own soul. 2Saul took him
that day and would not let him return to his
father's house. 3Then Jonathan made a covenant with David, because he loved him as
his own soul. 4Jonathan stripped himself of
the robe that he was wearing, and gave it to
David, and his armor, and even his sword
and his bow and his belt. 5David went out
and was successful wherever Saul sent him;
as a result, Saul set him over the army. And
all the people, even the servants of Saul,
approved.

18.1–30: Saul's jealousy of David. 1–5: These verses
interrupt the initial narrative,* which continues in v. 6
with the return home after David's victory. They continue the supplemental material from ch. 17. **2–3:** Jonathan's love for David implies political loyalty in addition to personal affection. **4:** Jonathan's act is highly
symbolic. By giving his royal robe and armor to David,
Jonathan, in effect, hands over the succession to the
throne. **5:** This verse is also supplemental. In the initial
narrative David is promoted for quite a different reason
(vv. 12–13).

~~~~~~

6 As they were coming home, when David
returned from killing the Philistine, the
women came out of all the towns of Israel,
singing and dancing, to meet King Saul, with
tambourines, with songs of joy, and with musical instruments.*c* 7And the women sang to
one another as they made merry,

"Saul has killed his thousands,
    and David his ten thousands."

8Saul was very angry, for this saying displeased him. He said, "They have ascribed to
David ten thousands, and to me they have
ascribed thousands; what more can he have
but the kingdom?" 9So Saul eyed David from
that day on.

10 The next day an evil spirit from God
rushed upon Saul, and he raved within his
house, while David was playing the lyre, as
he did day by day. Saul had his spear in his
hand; 11and Saul threw the spear, for he
thought, "I will pin David to the wall." But
David eluded him twice.

12 Saul was afraid of David, because the

---

a Gk Syr: Heb *Gai*   *b* Heb *he*   *c* Or *triangles,* or
three-stringed instruments

LORD was with him but had departed from Saul. 13 So Saul removed him from his presence, and made him a commander of a thousand; and David marched out and came in, leading the army. 14 David had success in all his undertakings; for the LORD was with him. 15 When Saul saw that he had great success, he stood in awe of him. 16 But all Israel and Judah loved David; for it was he who marched out and came in leading them.

17 Then Saul said to David, "Here is my elder daughter Merab; I will give her to you as a wife; only be valiant for me and fight the LORD's battles." For Saul thought, "I will not raise a hand against him; let the Philistines deal with him." 18 David said to Saul, "Who am I and who are my kinsfolk, my father's family in Israel, that I should be son-in-law to the king?" 19 But at the time when Saul's daughter Merab should have been given to David, she was given to Adriel the Meholathite as a wife.

18.6–19. 9: *Saul eyed David* means that Saul kept a wary eye on him. **10–11:** These verses are also supplemental. In the initial story, Saul's attempt to kill David with his spear (19.8–10) provides the climax* to a series of subtle moves against David. *He raved* is the same word translated "prophesy" elsewhere. It refers to ecstatic (irrational) behavior. **13–14:** Saul promotes David because he is afraid to have David near him. He also hopes that David will be killed in battle. *Marched out and came in* is an idiom for "went to war." **16:** *All Israel and Judah loved David* again expresses political loyalty, thus giving Saul all the more reason to fear. **17–19:** These verses are supplemental as they are not included in the original Greek or Septuagint* version (LXX*). If these verses are related to 17.25, Saul has changed the conditions of his promise. David's response in v. 18 shows his humility and lack of ambition to be king. The *son-in-law to the king* was an important political position, since he was potentially an heir to the throne. In the end (v. 19), Saul goes back on his promise despite David's heroic deeds.

20 Now Saul's daughter Michal loved David. Saul was told, and the thing pleased him. 21 Saul thought, "Let me give her to him that she may be a snare for him and that the hand of the Philistines may be against him."

Therefore Saul said to David a second time,ª "You shall now be my son-in-law." 22 Saul commanded his servants, "Speak to David in private and say, 'See, the king is delighted with you, and all his servants love you; now then, become the king's son-in-law.'" 23 So Saul's servants reported these words to David in private. And David said, "Does it seem to you a little thing to become the king's son-in-law, seeing that I am a poor man and of no repute?" 24 The servants of Saul told him, "This is what David said." 25 Then Saul said, "Thus shall you say to David, 'The king desires no marriage present except a hundred foreskins of the Philistines, that he may be avenged on the king's enemies.'" Now Saul planned to make David fall by the hand of the Philistines. 26 When his servants told David these words, David was well pleased to be the king's son-in-law. Before the time had expired, 27 David rose and went, along with his men, and killed one hundredᵇ of the Philistines; and David brought their foreskins, which were given in full number to the king, that he might become the king's son-in-law. Saul gave him his daughter Michal as a wife. 28 But when Saul realized that the LORD was with David, and that Saul's daughter Michal loved him, 29 Saul was still more afraid of David. So Saul was David's enemy from that time forward.

30 Then the commanders of the Philistines came out to battle; and as often as they came out, David had more success than all the servants of Saul, so that his fame became very great.

18.20–30. **20:** *Michal* was Saul's younger daughter. **21:** This plan of Saul's is slightly more direct than his hope that David's promotion over the army would lead to his death. **23–25:** The *marriage present* or "bride price" was set by the bride's father and paid to him by the groom. **26:** *David was well pleased to be the king's son-in-law*, despite his claim to lack of ambition. **28:** *Michal loved him:* Even Saul's own daughter was loyal to David, as she would shortly demonstrate.

---

a Heb *by two*　　*b* Gk Compare 2 Sam 3.14: Heb *two hundred*

Saul spoke with his son Jonathan and with all his servants about killing David. But Saul's son Jonathan took great delight in David. ²Jonathan told David, "My father Saul is trying to kill you; therefore be on guard tomorrow morning; stay in a secret place and hide yourself. ³I will go out and stand beside my father in the field where you are, and I will speak to my father about you; if I learn anything I will tell you." ⁴Jonathan spoke well of David to his father Saul, saying to him, "The king should not sin against his servant David, because he has not sinned against you, and because his deeds have been of good service to you; ⁵for he took his life in his hand when he attacked the Philistine, and the LORD brought about a great victory for all Israel. You saw it, and rejoiced; why then will you sin against an innocent person by killing David without cause?" ⁶Saul heeded the voice of Jonathan; Saul swore, "As the LORD lives, he shall not be put to death." ⁷So Jonathan called David and related all these things to him. Jonathan then brought David to Saul, and he was in his presence as before.

8 Again there was war, and David went out to fight the Philistines. He launched a heavy attack on them, so that they fled before him. ⁹Then an evil spirit from the LORD came upon Saul, as he sat in his house with his spear in his hand, while David was playing music. ¹⁰Saul sought to pin David to the wall with the spear; but he eluded Saul, so that he struck the spear into the wall. David fled and escaped that night.

11 Saul sent messengers to David's house to keep watch over him, planning to kill him in the morning. David's wife Michal told him, "If you do not save your life tonight, tomorrow you will be killed." ¹²So Michal let David down through the window; he fled away and escaped. ¹³Michal took an idol*a* and laid it on the bed; she put a net*b* of goats' hair on its head, and covered it with the clothes. ¹⁴When Saul sent messengers to take David, she said, "He is sick." ¹⁵Then Saul sent the messengers to see David for themselves. He said, "Bring him up to me in the bed, that I may kill him." ¹⁶When the messengers came in, the idol*c* was in the bed, with the covering*b* of goats' hair on its head. ¹⁷Saul said to Michal, "Why have you deceived me like this, and let my enemy go, so that he has escaped?" Michal answered Saul, "He said to me, 'Let me go; why should I kill you?'"

18 Now David fled and escaped; he came to Samuel at Ramah, and told him all that Saul had done to him. He and Samuel went and settled at Naioth. ¹⁹Saul was told, "David is at Naioth in Ramah." ²⁰Then Saul sent messengers to take David. When they saw the company of the prophets in a frenzy, with Samuel standing in charge of*b* them, the spirit of God came upon the messengers of Saul, and they also fell into a prophetic frenzy. ²¹When Saul was told, he sent other messengers, and they also fell into a frenzy. Saul sent messengers again the third time, and they also fell into a frenzy. ²²Then he himself went to Ramah. He came to the great well that is in Secu;*d* he asked, "Where are Samuel and David?" And someone said, "They are at Naioth in Ramah." ²³He went there, toward Naioth in Ramah; and the spirit of God came upon him. As he was going, he fell into a prophetic frenzy, until he came to Naioth in Ramah. ²⁴He too stripped off his clothes, and he too fell into a frenzy before Samuel. He lay naked all that day and all that night. Therefore it is said, "Is Saul also among the prophets?"

19.1–24: More attempts on David's life. 5: Killing an innocent person was a serious crime that could taint an entire nation and bring the wrath of God. **11–17:** This was originally the continuation of the story of David's marriage in 18.20–29 and took place on the couple's wedding night. **12:** The house was evidently built into the city wall, so that David went *through the window* and escaped the city. **13:** *An idol:* The Hebrew word, "teraphim," refers to household gods like those that Rachel took from her father (Gen 31.33–35). The one used by Michal must have been close to life-size. **17:** Michal lies to protect herself. A threat from David could not explain her ruse with the bed after his de-

a Heb *took the teraphim*   *b* Meaning of Heb uncertain
c Heb *the teraphim*   *d* Gk reads *to the well of the threshing floor on the bare height*

parture. **18:** *Ramah*, Samuel's hometown, was about two miles north of Gibeah, while David's home, Bethlehem and Judah, lay to the south. David would hardly have fled north. The story is included here for literary and theological reasons. *Naioth* may be not a proper name but a word meaning "camps" or "huts" where the prophets* lived near their leader Samuel. **23–24:** The saying *Is Saul also among the prophets?* has a different explanation here from the one offered in 10.10–12. The perspective on Saul in this latter case is negative. The depiction of him lying *naked* is degrading. The fact that the LORD's spirit comes upon him to prevent him from arresting David clearly shows that God is on David's side against Saul.

20 David fled from Naioth in Ramah. He came before Jonathan and said, "What have I done? What is my guilt? And what is my sin against your father that he is trying to take my life?" ²He said to him, "Far from it! You shall not die. My father does nothing either great or small without disclosing it to me; and why should my father hide this from me? Never!" ³But David also swore, "Your father knows well that you like me; and he thinks, 'Do not let Jonathan know this, or he will be grieved.' But truly, as the LORD lives and as you yourself live, there is but a step between me and death." ⁴Then Jonathan said to David, "Whatever you say, I will do for you." ⁵David said to Jonathan, "Tomorrow is the new moon, and I should not fail to sit with the king at the meal; but let me go, so that I may hide in the field until the third evening. ⁶If your father misses me at all, then say, 'David earnestly asked leave of me to run to Bethlehem his city; for there is a yearly sacrifice there for all the family.' ⁷If he says, 'Good!' it will be well with your servant; but if he is angry, then know that evil has been determined by him. ⁸Therefore deal kindly with your servant, for you have brought your servant into a sacred covenant*ᵃ* with you. But if there is guilt in me, kill me yourself; why should you bring me to your father?" ⁹Jonathan said, "Far be it from you! If I knew that it was decided by my father that evil should come upon you, would I not tell you?" ¹⁰Then David said to Jonathan, "Who will tell me if your father answers you harshly?" ¹¹Jona-

than replied to David, "Come, let us go out into the field." So they both went out into the field.

12 Jonathan said to David, "By the LORD, the God of Israel! When I have sounded out my father, about this time tomorrow, or on the third day, if he is well disposed toward David, shall I not then send and disclose it to you? ¹³But if my father intends to do you harm, the LORD do so to Jonathan, and more also, if I do not disclose it to you, and send you away, so that you may go in safety. May the LORD be with you, as he has been with my father. ¹⁴If I am still alive, show me the faithful love of the LORD; but if I die,*ᵇ* ¹⁵never cut off your faithful love from my house, even if the LORD were to cut off every one of the enemies of David from the face of the earth." ¹⁶Thus Jonathan made a covenant with the house of David, saying, "May the LORD seek out the enemies of David." ¹⁷Jonathan made David swear again by his love for him; for he loved him as he loved his own life.

20.1–42: The covenant* of David and Jonathan. 2: Jonathan is unaware that Saul has tried to kill David and still believes that his father would not act without first consulting him. **5:** The *new moon** in ancient Israel was a day of sacrificing and feasting. **8:** Jonathan asks David to *deal kindly* or "loyally" with him. The term implies faithfulness to a treaty, and Jonathan goes on to mention the covenant between them. **13:** *The LORD do so to Jonathan, and more also:* Jonathan swears that he will warn David. Jonathan's wish that the LORD be with David as he was with Saul suggests that David will be king. **14–15:** *Faithful love* also means "loyalty." *My house* means Jonathan's descendants. David's oath of loyalty to Jonathan's house anticipates the account of his treatment of Jonathan's son in 2 Sam 9. **16:** *The enemies of David* include Saul. **17:** *Love* again expresses political loyalty.

18 Jonathan said to him, "Tomorrow is the new moon; you will be missed, because your place will be empty. ¹⁹On the day after tomorrow, you shall go a long way down; go

a Heb *a covenant of the LORD*   *b* Meaning of Heb uncertain to the place where you hid yourself earlier, and remain beside the stone there.*a* 20 I will shoot three arrows to the side of it, as though I shot at a mark. 21 Then I will send the boy, saying, 'Go, find the arrows.' If I say to the boy, 'Look, the arrows are on this side of you, collect them,' then you are to come, for, as the LORD lives, it is safe for you and there is no danger. 22 But if I say to the young man, 'Look, the arrows are beyond you,' then go; for the LORD has sent you away. 23 As for the matter about which you and I have spoken, the LORD is witness*b* between you and me forever."

24 So David hid himself in the field. When the new moon came, the king sat at the feast to eat. 25 The king sat upon his seat, as at other times, upon the seat by the wall. Jonathan stood, while Abner sat by Saul's side; but David's place was empty.

26 Saul did not say anything that day; for he thought, "Something has befallen him; he is not clean, surely he is not clean." 27 But on the second day, the day after the new moon, David's place was empty. And Saul said to his son Jonathan, "Why has the son of Jesse not come to the feast, either yesterday or today?" 28 Jonathan answered Saul, "David earnestly asked leave of me to go to Bethlehem; 29 he said, 'Let me go; for our family is holding a sacrifice in the city, and my brother has commanded me to be there. So now, if I have found favor in your sight, let me get away, and see my brothers.' For this reason he has not come to the king's table."

30 Then Saul's anger was kindled against Jonathan. He said to him, "You son of a perverse, rebellious woman! Do I not know that you have chosen the son of Jesse to your own shame, and to the shame of your mother's nakedness? 31 For as long as the son of Jesse lives upon the earth, neither you nor your kingdom shall be established. Now send and bring him to me, for he shall surely die." 32 Then Jonathan answered his father Saul, "Why should he be put to death? What has he done?" 33 But Saul threw his spear at him to strike him; so Jonathan knew that it was the decision of his father to put David to death. 34 Jonathan rose from the table in fierce anger and ate no food on the second day of the month, for he was grieved for David, and because his father had disgraced him.

35 In the morning Jonathan went out into the field to the appointment with David, and with him was a little boy. 36 He said to the boy, "Run and find the arrows that I shoot." As the boy ran, he shot an arrow beyond him. 37 When the boy came to the place where Jonathan's arrow had fallen, Jonathan called after the boy and said, "Is the arrow not beyond you?" 38 Jonathan called after the boy, "Hurry, be quick, do not linger." So Jonathan's boy gathered up the arrows and came to his master. 39 But the boy knew nothing; only Jonathan and David knew the arrangement. 40 Jonathan gave his weapons to the boy and said to him, "Go and carry them to the city." 41 As soon as the boy had gone, David rose from beside the stone heap*c* and prostrated himself with his face to the ground. He bowed three times, and they kissed each other, and wept with each other; David wept the more.*d* 42 Then Jonathan said to David, "Go in peace, since both of us have sworn in the name of the LORD, saying, 'The LORD shall be between me and you, and between my descendants and your descendants, forever.' " He got up and left; and Jonathan went into the city.*e*

20.18–42. 30: *Nakedness* is a euphemism* for the genitals. Saul's remark is coarse and insulting. He accuses Jonathan of treason and says that he is a shame to his mother's genitals. 31: Saul perceives that David will be king if he is not killed. 33: Saul tries to kill Jonathan with his spear just as he tried to kill David. 41–42a: This is an addition emphasizing the affection and loyalty between David and Jonathan. If the two had been able to meet openly like this, the sign in the previous verses would be unnecessary.

21 *f* David came to Nob to the priest Ahimelech. Ahimelech came trembling to meet David, and said to him, "Why are you alone, and no one with you?" 2 David

a Meaning of Heb uncertain   *b* Gk: Heb lacks *witness*
c Gk: Heb *from beside the south*   *d* Vg: Meaning of Heb uncertain   *e* This sentence is 21.1 in Heb
f Ch 21.2 in Heb

said to the priest Ahimelech, "The king has charged me with a matter, and said to me, 'No one must know anything of the matter about which I send you, and with which I have charged you.' I have made an appointment[a] with the young men for such and such a place. 3Now then, what have you at hand? Give me five loaves of bread, or whatever is here." 4The priest answered David, "I have no ordinary bread at hand, only holy bread—provided that the young men have kept themselves from women." 5David answered the priest, "Indeed women have been kept from us as always when I go on an expedition; the vessels of the young men are holy even when it is a common journey; how much more today will their vessels be holy?" 6So the priest gave him the holy bread; for there was no bread there except the bread of the Presence, which is removed from before the LORD, to be replaced by hot bread on the day it is taken away.

7 Now a certain man of the servants of Saul was there that day, detained before the LORD; his name was Doeg the Edomite, the chief of Saul's shepherds.

8 David said to Ahimelech, "Is there no spear or sword here with you? I did not bring my sword or my weapons with me, because the king's business required haste." 9The priest said, "The sword of Goliath the Philistine, whom you killed in the valley of Elah, is here wrapped in a cloth behind the ephod; if you will take that, take it, for there is none here except that one." David said, "There is none like it; give it to me."

10 David rose and fled that day from Saul; he went to King Achish of Gath. 11The servants of Achish said to him, "Is this not David the king of the land? Did they not sing to one another of him in dances,

'Saul has killed his thousands,
　and David his ten thousands'?"

12David took these words to heart and was very much afraid of King Achish of Gath. 13So he changed his behavior before them; he pretended to be mad when in their presence.[b] He scratched marks on the doors of the gate, and let his spittle run down his beard. 14Achish said to his servants, "Look, you see the man is mad; why then have you

brought him to me? 15Do I lack madmen, that you have brought this fellow to play the madman in my presence? Shall this fellow come into my house?"

21.1–15: David visits Nob. 1: *Ahimelech* was the brother of *Ahijah, Saul's* chaplain, and the great-grandson of Eli. He *came trembling to meet David* perhaps because David was alone, and Ahimelech suspected something was wrong. **4–5:** Sexual abstinence, as expressed in the phrase *have kept themselves from women*, was practiced by soldiers preparing for war and by worshippers. David affirms that he and his men are on a holy mission and so have been abstinent. Although *vessels* can refer to tools, weapons, or other implements, here it is a euphemism★ for the sexual organs. **7:** The fact that *Doeg* was *detained before the LORD* probably means that he had a vow to fulfill. *Shepherds* may be a mistake for "runners"; the words are very similar in Hebrew. Kings were often escorted by runners. **9:** David had placed *the sword of Goliath* in his own tent according to 17.54, but see the comment on that verse. The *ephod*★ mentioned here seems to be an idol (Judg 8.27) rather than a priestly garment. **10:** *Achish,* like Goliath, is a genuine Philistine name. **11:** If it is not a simple anachronism,★ the Philistines recognize David already as *the king of the land.* **13– 15:** *To be mad* was seen in the ancient world as being divinely "touched." Hence, the Philistines, fearing divine wrath, leave David alone. The story also jabs fun at the Philistines who cannot tell madness from sanity and who, by their own admission, have plenty of *madmen.*

22 David left there and escaped to the cave of Adullam; when his brothers and all his father's house heard of it, they went down there to him. 2Everyone who was in distress, and everyone who was in debt, and everyone who was discontented gathered to him; and he became captain over them. Those who were with him numbered about four hundred.

3 David went from there to Mizpeh of Moab. He said to the king of Moab, "Please let my father and mother come[c] to you, until I know what God will do for me." 4He left them with the king of Moab, and they stayed

---

a Q Ms Vg Compare Gk: Meaning of MT uncertain
b Heb *in their hands*　　*c* Syr Vg: Heb *come out*

with him all the time that David was in the stronghold. ⁵Then the prophet Gad said to David, "Do not remain in the stronghold; leave, and go into the land of Judah." So David left, and went into the forest of Hereth.

22.1–23: David gains a following. 1–5: The account of David's travels related here delays the continuation of the story of the priests of Nob, but it also shows David building an army. *Adullam* was in Judah and served as David's headquarters. The *cave* may be an error for *stronghold;* the two words are similar in Hebrew. This suggests that the otherwise unknown stronghold in v. 4 is also Adullam. **2:** David's army consists of those who are unhappy with Saul. Many of these people may have fled earlier to the wilderness of Judah to escape Saul's reach. **3–4:** The connection of David's family with Moab is attested by Ruth 4.17–22. **5:** The image of a king sitting in council under a sacred tree was a common one in the ancient Near East.

6 Saul heard that David and those who were with him had been located. Saul was sitting at Gibeah, under the tamarisk tree on the height, with his spear in his hand, and all his servants were standing around him. ⁷Saul said to his servants who stood around him, "Hear now, you Benjaminites; will the son of Jesse give every one of you fields and vineyards, will he make you all commanders of thousands and commanders of hundreds? ⁸Is that why all of you have conspired against me? No one discloses to me when my son makes a league with the son of Jesse, none of you is sorry for me or discloses to me that my son has stirred up my servant against me, to lie in wait, as he is doing today." ⁹Doeg the Edomite, who was in charge of Saul's servants, answered, "I saw the son of Jesse coming to Nob, to Ahimelech son of Ahitub; ¹⁰he inquired of the LORD for him, gave him provisions, and gave him the sword of Goliath the Philistine."

22.6–10. 7: *The son of Jesse* is a disparaging reference to David. It was common for the king to reward his loyal servants. David may have been making promises of rewards to his followers. But Saul is saying that because they are not from Judah, David's tribe, the Benjaminites can expect no such rewards if David becomes king. **10:** Chapter 21 does not mention that

Ahimelech *inquired of the LORD for [David]*, but this plays an important role in the confrontation to follow.

11 The king sent for the priest Ahimelech son of Ahitub and for all his father's house, the priests who were at Nob; and all of them came to the king. ¹²Saul said, "Listen now, son of Ahitub." He answered, "Here I am, my lord." ¹³Saul said to him, "Why have you conspired against me, you and the son of Jesse, by giving him bread and a sword, and by inquiring of God for him, so that he has risen against me, to lie in wait, as he is doing today?"

14 Then Ahimelech answered the king, "Who among all your servants is so faithful as David? He is the king's son-in-law, and is quick*ᵃ* to do your bidding, and is honored in your house. ¹⁵Is today the first time that I have inquired of God for him? By no means! Do not let the king impute anything to his servant or to any member of my father's house; for your servant has known nothing of all this, much or little." ¹⁶The king said, "You shall surely die, Ahimelech, you and all your father's house." ¹⁷The king said to the guard who stood around him, "Turn and kill the priests of the LORD, because their hand also is with David; they knew that he fled, and did not disclose it to me." But the servants of the king would not raise their hand to attack the priests of the LORD. ¹⁸Then the king said to Doeg, "You, Doeg, turn and attack the priests." Doeg the Edomite turned and attacked the priests; on that day he killed eighty-five who wore the linen ephod. ¹⁹Nob, the city of the priests, he put to the sword; men and women, children and infants, oxen, donkeys, and sheep, he put to the sword.

20 But one of the sons of Ahimelech son of Ahitub, named Abiathar, escaped and fled after David. ²¹Abiathar told David that Saul had killed the priests of the LORD. ²²David said to Abiathar, "I knew on that day, when Doeg the Edomite was there, that he would surely tell Saul. I am responsible*ᵇ* for the

---

a Heb *and turns aside*   *b* Gk Vg: Meaning of Heb uncertain lives of all your father's house. 23 Stay with me, and do not be afraid; for the one who seeks my life seeks your life; you will be safe with me."

22.11–23. 13: Saul accuses Ahimelech of treason. 14–15: Ahimelech's eloquent defense makes the point that David is Saul's most loyal servant and son-in-law and that he (Ahimelech) was unaware of any change in their relationship. 16–17: These reminders only infuriate Saul more, and he orders the death of the priests. 18: Only Doeg, who is an Edomite, dares to attack the LORD's priests. 19: Saul devotes Nob to destruction. Ironically,* this is what he failed to do against the Amalekites in ch. 15. 20–23: The one escapee is Abiathar in fulfillment of the oracle* against the house of Eli in 2.27–36. He will prove a useful asset to David.

23 Now they told David, "The Philistines are fighting against Keilah, and are robbing the threshing floors." 2 David inquired of the LORD, "Shall I go and attack these Philistines?" The LORD said to David, "Go and attack the Philistines and save Keilah." 3 But David's men said to him, "Look, we are afraid here in Judah; how much more then if we go to Keilah against the armies of the Philistines?" 4 Then David inquired of the LORD again. The LORD answered him, "Yes, go down to Keilah; for I will give the Philistines into your hand." 5 So David and his men went to Keilah, fought with the Philistines, brought away their livestock, and dealt them a heavy defeat. Thus David rescued the inhabitants of Keilah.

6 When Abiathar son of Ahimelech fled to David at Keilah, he came down with an ephod in his hand. 7 Now it was told Saul that David had come to Keilah. And Saul said, "God has given[a] him into my hand; for he has shut himself in by entering a town that has gates and bars." 8 Saul summoned all the people to war, to go down to Keilah, to besiege David and his men. 9 When David learned that Saul was plotting evil against him, he said to the priest Abiathar, "Bring the ephod here." 10 David said, "O LORD, the God of Israel, your servant has heard that Saul seeks to come to Keilah, to destroy the city on my account. 11 And now, will[b] Saul

come down as your servant has heard? O LORD, the God of Israel, I beseech you, tell your servant." The LORD said, "He will come down." 12 Then David said, "Will the men of Keilah surrender me and my men into the hand of Saul?" The LORD said, "They will surrender you." 13 Then David and his men, who were about six hundred, set out and left Keilah; they wandered wherever they could go. When Saul was told that David had escaped from Keilah, he gave up the expedition. 14 David remained in the strongholds in the wilderness, in the hill country of the Wilderness of Ziph. Saul sought him every day, but the LORD[c] did not give him into his hand.

23.1–29: Narrow escapes. 1–6: This episode illustrates the importance of Abiathar's ability to divine through the ephod* as explained in v. 6. *Keilah* was an independent city within Philistine territory. Both times when *David inquired* his questions required an answer of yes or no, which could be determined through casting lots. Abiathar's *ephod* (v. 6) was just such an instrument. 7–14: Although David was hoping to cultivate the loyalty of the people of Keilah, they were willing to betray him to Saul. The ephod forewarned him and allowed him to escape Saul.

15 David was in the Wilderness of Ziph at Horesh when he learned that[d] Saul had come out to seek his life. 16 Saul's son Jonathan set out and came to David at Horesh; there he strengthened his hand through the LORD.[e] 17 He said to him, "Do not be afraid; for the hand of my father Saul shall not find you; you shall be king over Israel, and I shall be second to you; my father Saul also knows that this is so." 18 Then the two of them made a covenant before the LORD; David remained at Horesh, and Jonathan went home. 19 Then some Ziphites went up to Saul at Gibeah and said, "David is hiding among us in the strongholds of Horesh, on the hill of Hachilah, which is south of Jeshimon. 20 Now, O king, whenever you wish to come

---

a Gk Tg: Heb *made a stranger of*　　b Q Ms Compare Gk: MT *Will the men of Keilah surrender me into his hand? Will*　　c Q Ms Gk: MT *God*　　d Or *saw that*　　e Compare Q Ms Gk: MT *God* down, do so; and our part will be to surrender him into the king's hand." 21 Saul said, "May you be blessed by the LORD for showing me compassion! 22 Go and make sure once more; find out exactly where he is, and who has seen him there; for I am told that he is very cunning. 23 Look around and learn all the hiding places where he lurks, and come back to me with sure information. Then I will go with you; and if he is in the land, I will search him out among all the thousands of Judah." 24 So they set out and went to Ziph ahead of Saul.

David and his men were in the wilderness of Maon, in the Arabah to the south of Jeshimon. 25 Saul and his men went to search for him. When David was told, he went down to the rock and stayed in the wilderness of Maon. When Saul heard that, he pursued David into the wilderness of Maon. 26 Saul went on one side of the mountain, and David and his men on the other side of the mountain. David was hurrying to get away from Saul, while Saul and his men were closing in on David and his men to capture them. 27 Then a messenger came to Saul, saying, "Hurry and come; for the Philistines have made a raid on the land." 28 So Saul stopped pursuing David, and went against the Philistines; therefore that place was called the Rock of Escape.[a] 29[b] David then went up from there, and lived in the strongholds of En-gedi.

23.15–29. 17: The recognition that David will be king and Jonathan the second in command is extraordinary in the mouth of Jonathan himself, the crown prince. 19–29: Saul is frustrated that David stays one jump ahead of him, which he is able to do because of the ephod (v. 22). This time (v. 26) David is trapped on one side of a hill which Saul's force is circling from both directions. The last-minute notice about the Philistines (v. 27) shows Yahweh's protection of David. Either meaning for the etiology* in v. 28 ("rock of escape" or "rock of division") is appropriate in the context of this story.

24 When Saul returned from following the Philistines, he was told, "David is in the wilderness of En-gedi." 2 Then Saul took three thousand chosen men out of all Israel, and went to look for David and his men in the direction of the Rocks of the Wild Goats. 3 He came to the sheepfolds beside the road, where there was a cave; and Saul went in to relieve himself.[c] Now David and his men were sitting in the innermost parts of the cave. 4 The men of David said to him, "Here is the day of which the LORD said to you, 'I will give your enemy into your hand, and you shall do to him as it seems good to you.'" Then David went and stealthily cut off a corner of Saul's cloak. 5 Afterward David was stricken to the heart because he had cut off a corner of Saul's cloak. 6 He said to his men, "The LORD forbid that I should do this thing to my lord, the LORD's anointed, to raise my hand against him; for he is the LORD's anointed." 7 So David scolded his men severely and did not permit them to attack Saul. Then Saul got up and left the cave, and went on his way.

24.1–22: David spares Saul. 3: To relieve himself (literally, "to cover his feet") is a euphemism* for defecation. The portrait of Saul at this point is particularly degrading. 4a: The prophecy to which David's men refer here is not recorded. 4b–5: These verses probably originally were located after v. 7a. David's cutting off Saul's hem may be seen as symbolic emasculation or a symbol of his taking Saul's kingdom. This may be why David's conscience bothered him. 6: To attack Saul, the LORD's anointed,* was to attack the LORD. 7a: David scolds his men for their suggestion in v. 4a that he kill Saul.

8 Afterwards David also rose up and went out of the cave and called after Saul, "My lord the king!" When Saul looked behind him, David bowed with his face to the ground, and did obeisance. 9 David said to Saul, "Why do you listen to the words of those who say, 'David seeks to do you harm'? 10 This very day your eyes have seen how the LORD gave you into my hand in the cave; and some urged me to kill you, but I spared[d] you. I said, 'I will not raise my hand against my lord; for he is the LORD's anointed.' 11 See,

a Or Rock of Division; Meaning of Heb uncertain
b Ch 24.1 in Heb   c Heb to cover his feet   d Gk Syr
Tg Vg: Heb it (my eye) spared

my father, see the corner of your cloak in my hand; for by the fact that I cut off the corner of your cloak, and did not kill you, you may know for certain that there is no wrong or treason in my hands. I have not sinned against you, though you are hunting me to take my life. 12May the LORD judge between me and you! May the LORD avenge me on you; but my hand shall not be against you. 13As the ancient proverb says, 'Out of the wicked comes forth wickedness'; but my hand shall not be against you. 14Against whom has the king of Israel come out? Whom do you pursue? A dead dog? A single flea? 15May the LORD therefore be judge, and give sentence between me and you. May he see to it, and plead my cause, and vindicate me against you."

16 When David had finished speaking these words to Saul, Saul said, "Is this your voice, my son David?" Saul lifted up his voice and wept. 17He said to David, "You are more righteous than I; for you have repaid me good, whereas I have repaid you evil. 18Today you have explained how you have dealt well with me, in that you did not kill me when the LORD put me into your hands. 19For who has ever found an enemy, and sent the enemy safely away? So may the LORD reward you with good for what you have done to me this day. 20Now I know that you shall surely be king, and that the kingdom of Israel shall be established in your hand. 21Swear to me therefore by the LORD that you will not cut off my descendants after me, and that you will not wipe out my name from my father's house." 22So David swore this to Saul. Then Saul went home; but David and his men went up to the stronghold.

24.8–22. 11: *My father* is a respectful address from the younger David to the older Saul; it may also imply David's right to inherit Saul's kingdom. 14: *A dead dog? A single flea?* These terms of self-disparagement may be read in two ways. David could be saying he is insignificant or that Saul is mistaken if he thinks David is insignificant. 20: Even Saul recognizes that David will succeed him. 21–22: David's oath not to wipe out Saul's descendants anticipates his treatment of Jonathan's son, Mephibosheth, in 2 Sam 9.

25 Now Samuel died; and all Israel assembled and mourned for him. They buried him at his home in Ramah.

Then David got up and went down to the wilderness of Paran.

2 There was a man in Maon, whose property was in Carmel. The man was very rich; he had three thousand sheep and a thousand goats. He was shearing his sheep in Carmel. 3Now the name of the man was Nabal, and the name of his wife Abigail. The woman was clever and beautiful, but the man was surly and mean; he was a Calebite. 4David heard in the wilderness that Nabal was shearing his sheep. 5So David sent ten young men; and David said to the young men, "Go up to Carmel, and go to Nabal, and greet him in my name. 6Thus you shall salute him: 'Peace be to you, and peace be to your house, and peace be to all that you have. 7I hear that you have shearers; now your shepherds have been with us, and we did them no harm, and they missed nothing, all the time they were in Carmel. 8Ask your young men, and they will tell you. Therefore let my young men find favor in your sight; for we have come on a feast day. Please give whatever you have at hand to your servants and to your son David.'"

9 When David's young men came, they said all this to Nabal in the name of David; and then they waited. 10But Nabal answered David's servants, "Who is David? Who is the son of Jesse? There are many servants today who are breaking away from their masters. 11Shall I take my bread and my water and the meat that I have butchered for my shearers, and give it to men who come from I do not know where?" 12So David's young men turned away, and came back and told him all this. 13David said to his men, "Every man strap on his sword!" And every one of them strapped on his sword; David also strapped on his sword; and about four hundred men went up after David, while two hundred remained with the baggage.

14 But one of the young men told Abigail, Nabal's wife, "David sent messengers out of the wilderness to salute our master; and he shouted insults at them. 15Yet the men were very good to us, and we suffered no harm,

and we never missed anything when we were in the fields, as long as we were with them; [16]they were a wall to us both by night and by day, all the while we were with them keeping the sheep. [17]Now therefore know this and consider what you should do; for evil has been decided against our master and against all his house; he is so ill-natured that no one can speak to him."

18 Then Abigail hurried and took two hundred loaves, two skins of wine, five sheep ready dressed, five measures of parched grain, one hundred clusters of raisins, and two hundred cakes of figs. She loaded them on donkeys [19]and said to her young men, "Go on ahead of me; I am coming after you." But she did not tell her husband Nabal. [20]As she rode on the donkey and came down under cover of the mountain, David and his men came down toward her; and she met them. [21]Now David had said, "Surely it was in vain that I protected all that this fellow has in the wilderness, so that nothing was missed of all that belonged to him; but he has returned me evil for good. [22]God do so to David[a] and more also, if by morning I leave so much as one male of all who belong to him."

25.1–43: Nabal and Abigail. The placement of this story between the two accounts of David's chances to kill Saul (chs. 24 and 26) is significant. While David avoids shedding Saul's blood, he is almost guilty of killing many innocent people in Nabal's household. 2–3: Nabal is like Saul in many ways. He is "rich as a king" and was probably an important figure, perhaps the chieftain, among the Calebites, one of the leading clans* of Judah. The name Nabal means "fool" or "brute." It was probably not the man's real name but represents his character. His wife, Abigail, on the other hand, is his complete opposite. The only other Abigail in the Bible is David's sister (1 Chr 2.16). 4–8: Shearing sheep was a festival time in Israel. David requests a gift, hoping that Nabal, in the spirit of the festival, will be generous. The gift David expects is more or less obligatory as payment for not harming or "protecting" Nabal's shepherds. The ten young men whom David sends should give Nabal an idea of the size of gift David is expecting, namely, as much as ten men can carry. 10–11: Nabal's reply is insulting. His questions, Who is David? Who is the son of Jesse?, are a way of

saying that David is insignificant and do not mean that Nabal does not know who David is. Nabal calls David, in effect, a runaway slave and a vagabond. 14–17: Nabal's own servants recognize that he is ill-natured and untrustworthy. In this emergency they go to Abigail. 18: Five measures: The Hebrew word is "se'ah." Five se'ahs was about a bushel. Cakes of figs were clumps rather than a bakery product. 22: David vows to annihilate every male in Nabal's household. This sets the stage for the arrival of Abigail, who, as a female, is the only person who can prevent a tragedy.

23 When Abigail saw David, she hurried and alighted from the donkey, and fell before David on her face, bowing to the ground. [24]She fell at his feet and said, "Upon me alone, my lord, be the guilt; please let your servant speak in your ears, and hear the words of your servant. [25]My lord, do not take seriously this ill-natured fellow, Nabal; for as his name is, so is he; Nabal[b] is his name, and folly is with him; but I, your servant, did not see the young men of my lord, whom you sent.

26 "Now then, my lord, as the LORD lives, and as you yourself live, since the LORD has restrained you from bloodguilt and from taking vengeance with your own hand, now let your enemies and those who seek to do evil to my lord be like Nabal. [27]And now let this present that your servant has brought to my lord be given to the young men who follow my lord. [28]Please forgive the trespass of your servant; for the LORD will certainly make my lord a sure house, because my lord is fighting the battles of the LORD; and evil shall not be found in you so long as you live. [29]If anyone should rise up to pursue you and to seek your life, the life of my lord shall be bound in the bundle of the living under the care of the LORD your God; but the lives of your enemies he shall sling out as from the hollow of a sling. [30]When the LORD has done to my lord according to all the good that he has spoken concerning you, and has appointed you prince over Israel, [31]my lord shall have no cause of grief, or pangs of conscience, for having shed blood without cause or for hav-

a Gk Compare Syr: Heb the enemies of David
b That is Fool

ing saved himself. And when the LORD has dealt well with my lord, then remember your servant."

32 David said to Abigail, "Blessed be the LORD, the God of Israel, who sent you to meet me today! 33 Blessed be your good sense, and blessed be you, who have kept me today from bloodguilt and from avenging myself by my own hand! 34 For as surely as the LORD the God of Israel lives, who has restrained me from hurting you, unless you had hurried and come to meet me, truly by morning there would not have been left to Nabal so much as one male." 35 Then David received from her hand what she had brought him; he said to her, "Go up to your house in peace; see, I have heeded your voice, and I have granted your petition."

36 Abigail came to Nabal; he was holding a feast in his house, like the feast of a king. Nabal's heart was merry within him, for he was very drunk; so she told him nothing at all until the morning light. 37 In the morning, when the wine had gone out of Nabal, his wife told him these things, and his heart died within him; he became like a stone. 38 About ten days later the LORD struck Nabal, and he died.

39 When David heard that Nabal was dead, he said, "Blessed be the LORD who has judged the case of Nabal's insult to me, and has kept back his servant from evil; the LORD has returned the evildoing of Nabal upon his own head." Then David sent and wooed Abigail, to make her his wife. 40 When David's servants came to Abigail at Carmel, they said to her, "David has sent us to you to take you to him as his wife." 41 She rose and bowed down, with her face to the ground, and said, "Your servant is a slave to wash the feet of the servants of my lord." 42 Abigail got up hurriedly and rode away on a donkey; her five maids attended her. She went after the messengers of David and became his wife.

43 David also married Ahinoam of Jezreel; both of them became his wives. 44 Saul had given his daughter Michal, David's wife, to Palti son of Laish, who was from Gallim.

25.23–43. 23: Unlike Nabal, Abigail is very respectful toward David, treating him as a king. **24–31:** Abigail's

speech is the model of eloquence and tact. She refers to herself as David's *servant* (v. 24) and begs him to ignore the *ill-natured fellow, Nabal.* Verse 26 seems to anticipate the conclusion of the story, according to which Nabal died, but not by David's hand. Abigail diplomatically refers to the supplies she brings to David as a *present* for his men (v. 27). Her reference to the LORD's giving David a *sure house* means she knows he will be king. The mention of anyone who *should rise up to pursue [David] and to seek [his] life* (v. 29) alludes to Saul. The *bundle of the living* is the list of those who live. Abigail's wish that God *sling out* David's enemies is reminiscent of David's victory in ch. 17 and anticipates Nabal's death in v. 37. Abigail closes her speech by gently suggesting that shedding innocent blood would be an obstacle to his kingship (vv. 30–31). *When the LORD has dealt well with my lord* could refer to David's becoming king or, in an ironic* way, to Nabal's death. *Remember your servant* is a marriage proposal. **34–35:** David perceives that it is the LORD, through Abigail, who has prevented him from committing a great offense. **37:** Nabal's *heart became like a stone* may refer to a coma. **43:** Saul's wife was also named *Ahinoam* (14.50).

---

26 Then the Ziphites came to Saul at Gibeah, saying, "David is in hiding on the hill of Hachilah, which is opposite Jeshimon."*a* 2 So Saul rose and went down to the Wilderness of Ziph, with three thousand chosen men of Israel, to seek David in the Wilderness of Ziph. 3 Saul encamped on the hill of Hachilah, which is opposite Jeshimon*a* beside the road. But David remained in the wilderness. When he learned that Saul had come after him into the wilderness, 4 David sent out spies, and learned that Saul had indeed arrived. 5 Then David set out and came to the place where Saul had encamped; and David saw the place where Saul lay, with Abner son of Ner, the commander of his army. Saul was lying within the encampment, while the army was encamped around him.

6 Then David said to Ahimelech the Hittite, and to Joab's brother Abishai son of Zeruiah, "Who will go down with me into the camp to Saul?" Abishai said, "I will go down with you." 7 So David and Abishai went to the

---

a Or *opposite the wasteland*

army by night; there Saul lay sleeping within the encampment, with his spear stuck in the ground at his head; and Abner and the army lay around him. 8Abishai said to David, "God has given your enemy into your hand today; now therefore let me pin him to the ground with one stroke of the spear; I will not strike him twice." 9But David said to Abishai, "Do not destroy him; for who can raise his hand against the LORD's anointed, and be guiltless?" 10David said, "As the LORD lives, the LORD will strike him down; or his day will come to die; or he will go down into battle and perish. 11The LORD forbid that I should raise my hand against the LORD's anointed; but now take the spear that is at his head, and the water jar, and let us go." 12So David took the spear that was at Saul's head and the water jar, and they went away. No one saw it, or knew it, nor did anyone awake; for they were all asleep, because a deep sleep from the LORD had fallen upon them.

26.1–25: A second opportunity to kill Saul. This story is very similar to the one in ch. 24, and the two may be variants of a single original. 6: *Joab* was David's nephew (1 Chr 2.16) and would become the commander of his army. 8: David can kill Saul with the same *spear* Saul once used against David. 12: The LORD is again protecting David.

13 Then David went over to the other side, and stood on top of a hill far away, with a great distance between them. 14David called to the army and to Abner son of Ner, saying, "Abner! Will you not answer?" Then Abner replied, "Who are you that calls to the king?" 15David said to Abner, "Are you not a man? Who is like you in Israel? Why then have you not kept watch over your lord the king? For one of the people came in to destroy your lord the king. 16This thing that you have done is not good. As the LORD lives, you deserve to die, because you have not kept watch over your lord, the LORD's anointed. See now, where is the king's spear, or the water jar that was at his head?"

17 Saul recognized David's voice, and said, "Is this your voice, my son David?" David said, "It is my voice, my lord, O king." 18And he added, "Why does my lord pursue

his servant? For what have I done? What guilt is on my hands? 19Now therefore let my lord the king hear the words of his servant. If it is the LORD who has stirred you up against me, may he accept an offering; but if it is mortals, may they be cursed before the LORD, for they have driven me out today from my share in the heritage of the LORD, saying, 'Go, serve other gods.' 20Now therefore, do not let my blood fall to the ground, away from the presence of the LORD; for the king of Israel has come out to seek a single flea, like one who hunts a partridge in the mountains."

21 Then Saul said, "I have done wrong; come back, my son David, for I will never harm you again, because my life was precious in your sight today; I have been a fool, and have made a great mistake." 22David replied, "Here is the spear, O king! Let one of the young men come over and get it. 23The LORD rewards everyone for his righteousness and his faithfulness; for the LORD gave you into my hand today, but I would not raise my hand against the LORD's anointed. 24As your life was precious today in my sight, so may my life be precious in the sight of the LORD, and may he rescue me from all tribulation." 25Then Saul said to David, "Blessed be you, my son David! You will do many things and will succeed in them." So David went his way, and Saul returned to his place.

26.13–25. 13: *David went over to the other side* so that if Saul pursues him he can lead the army away from his unsuspecting men. 16: *You deserve to die* hints at Abner's assassination (2 Sam 3). 19: David curses any persons who have caused Saul to pursue him because this has driven him from the land of Israel, which is the LORD's *heritage*. The *other gods* are the gods of countries outside of Israel where David says he has been driven. 20: *A partridge* is literally "the caller" or "calling bird." The comparison is apt since David is calling to Saul from a mountain. 25: Saul's blessing subtly indicates that David will be king.

27 David said in his heart, "I shall now perish one day by the hand of Saul; there is nothing better for me than to escape to the land of the Philistines; then Saul will despair of seeking me any longer within the

borders of Israel, and I shall escape out of his hand." ²So David set out and went over, he and the six hundred men who were with him, to King Achish son of Maoch of Gath. ³David stayed with Achish at Gath, he and his troops, every man with his household, and David with his two wives, Ahinoam of Jezreel, and Abigail of Carmel, Nabal's widow. ⁴When Saul was told that David had fled to Gath, he no longer sought for him.

5 Then David said to Achish, "If I have found favor in your sight, let a place be given me in one of the country towns, so that I may live there; for why should your servant live in the royal city with you?" ⁶So that day Achish gave him Ziklag; therefore Ziklag has belonged to the kings of Judah to this day. ⁷The length of time that David lived in the country of the Philistines was one year and four months.

8 Now David and his men went up and made raids on the Geshurites, the Girzites, and the Amalekites; for these were the landed settlements from Telam* on the way to Shur and on to the land of Egypt. ⁹David struck the land, leaving neither man nor woman alive, but took away the sheep, the oxen, the donkeys, the camels, and the clothing, and came back to Achish. ¹⁰When Achish asked, "Against whom*b* have you made a raid today?" David would say, "Against the Negeb of Judah," or "Against the Negeb of the Jerahmeelites," or, "Against the Negeb of the Kenites." ¹¹David left neither man nor woman alive to be brought back to Gath, thinking, "They might tell about us, and say, 'David has done so and so.' " Such was his practice all the time he lived in the country of the Philistines. ¹²Achish trusted David, thinking, "He has made himself utterly abhorrent to his people Israel; therefore he shall always be my servant."

28 In those days the Philistines gathered their forces for war, to fight against Israel. Achish said to David, "You know, of course, that you and your men are to go out with me in the army." ²David said to Achish, "Very well, then you shall know what your servant can do." Achish said to David, "Very well, I will make you my bodyguard for life."

27.1–28.2: David with the Philistines. 1–4: David is driven by Saul's pursuits to flee to the Philistines. *Achish* is the same character as in 21.10. But the two passages are in tension, since David would not have gone to Achish after pretending to be mad in 21.10–15. **6:** It was common for kings to give grants of land to faithful servants. In this case Achish also benefited because *Ziklag* guarded the southern frontier of Philistine territory. **8:** The mention of the *Amalekites* stands in tension with ch. 15 where they are all killed. **10:** *The Negeb* is the southern wilderness area of Palestine. *Kenites* should be read as "Kenizzites." They and *the Jerahmeelites* were clans* within Judah. David was attacking other peoples and then fooling Achish by telling him that he had attacked parts of Judah. **12:** Achish felt confident of David's loyalty because he thought David had alienated himself from his own people. **28.2:** *Then you shall know what your servant can do* has a double meaning. Achish thinks David is saying that he will show his potential against Israel. David is actually saying that in the heat of battle Achish will find out how David remains loyal to Israel.

3 Now Samuel had died, and all Israel had mourned for him and buried him in Ramah, his own city. Saul had expelled the mediums and the wizards from the land. ⁴The Philistines assembled, and came and encamped at Shunem. Saul gathered all Israel, and they encamped at Gilboa. ⁵When Saul saw the army of the Philistines, he was afraid, and his heart trembled greatly. ⁶When Saul inquired of the LORD, the LORD did not answer him, not by dreams, or by Urim, or by prophets. ⁷Then Saul said to his servants, "Seek out for me a woman who is a medium, so that I may go to her and inquire of her." His servants said to him, "There is a medium at Endor."

28.3–25: Saul consults a ghost. 3: *Mediums and wizards* are often used in conjunction and refer to devices used to communicate with the dead. Such practices are condemned by the law in Deut 18.10. **4:** *Shunem* and *Gilboa* locate the site of the battle near the Jezreel Valley, far north of the Negeb where the previous stories were set. **6:** Three means of divining were *dreams,*

---

a Compare Gk 15.4: Heb *from of old*   *b* Q Ms Gk Vg: MT lacks *whom* or incubation, in which one expected the answer to an inquiry to be given at night, in a dream, often when one slept at a holy place; *Urim,* or lots, which have been used earlier in 1 Samuel; and *prophets,** like the man of God in 9.1–10.16. **7:** *A woman who is a medium* literally means "a woman of (who deals with) spirits," using the word translated "medium" in v. 3.

~~~~~~~~~~~~~~~

8 So Saul disguised himself and put on other clothes and went there, he and two men with him. They came to the woman by night. And he said, "Consult a spirit for me, and bring up for me the one whom I name to you." ⁹The woman said to him, "Surely you know what Saul has done, how he has cut off the mediums and the wizards from the land. Why then are you laying a snare for my life to bring about my death?" ¹⁰But Saul swore to her by the LORD, "As the LORD lives, no punishment shall come upon you for this thing." ¹¹Then the woman said, "Whom shall I bring up for you?" He answered, "Bring up Samuel for me." ¹²When the woman saw Samuel, she cried out with a loud voice; and the woman said to Saul, "Why have you deceived me? You are Saul!" ¹³The king said to her, "Have no fear; what do you see?" The woman said to Saul, "I see a divine being*a* coming up out of the ground." ¹⁴He said to her, "What is his appearance?" She said, "An old man is coming up; he is wrapped in a robe." So Saul knew that it was Samuel, and he bowed with his face to the ground, and did obeisance.

15 Then Samuel said to Saul, "Why have you disturbed me by bringing me up?" Saul answered, "I am in great distress, for the Philistines are warring against me, and God has turned away from me and answers me no more, either by prophets or by dreams; so I have summoned you to tell me what I should do." ¹⁶Samuel said, "Why then do you ask me, since the LORD has turned from you and become your enemy? ¹⁷The LORD has done to you just as he spoke by me; for the LORD has torn the kingdom out of your hand, and given it to your neighbor, David. ¹⁸Because you did not obey the voice of the LORD, and did not carry out his fierce wrath against Amalek, therefore the LORD has done this thing to you today. ¹⁹Moreover the LORD will give Israel along with you into the hands of the Philistines; and tomorrow you and your sons shall be with me; the LORD will also give the army of Israel into the hands of the Philistines."

20 Immediately Saul fell full length on the ground, filled with fear because of the words of Samuel; and there was no strength in him, for he had eaten nothing all day and all night. ²¹The woman came to Saul, and when she saw that he was terrified, she said to him, "Your servant has listened to you; I have taken my life in my hand, and have listened to what you have said to me. ²²Now therefore, you also listen to your servant; let me set a morsel of bread before you. Eat, that you may have strength when you go on your way." ²³He refused, and said, "I will not eat." But his servants, together with the woman, urged him; and he listened to their words. So he got up from the ground and sat on the bed. ²⁴Now the woman had a fatted calf in the house. She quickly slaughtered it, and she took flour, kneaded it, and baked unleavened cakes. ²⁵She put them before Saul and his servants, and they ate. Then they rose and went away that night.

28.8–25. 8: *Saul disguised himself* because he was breaking his own law (v. 3) by visiting the woman. **11–12a:** These verses are an insertion identifying Samuel as the ghost. Originally, the woman recognized Saul because of his oath in v. 10 not to punish her. **13:** *The ground* can also mean "the underworld." *Divine being* can refer to a god or to a ghost or spirit. **14:** The *robe* was Samuel's characteristic garment and the apparent means by which Saul recognized him. **17–18:** These verses refer to the story in ch. 15. **19:** *Tomorrow you and your sons shall be with me:* They will be dead. **24:** *A fatted calf in the house:* Livestock were typically kept on the ground floor of Israelite houses with sleeping quarters above them on a second floor.

~~~~~~~~~~~~~~~

29 Now the Philistines gathered all their forces at Aphek, while the Israelites were encamped by the fountain that is in Jezreel. ²As the lords of the Philistines

a Or *a god;* or *gods*

were passing on by hundreds and by thousands, and David and his men were passing on in the rear with Achish, ³the commanders of the Philistines said, "What are these Hebrews doing here?" Achish said to the commanders of the Philistines, "Is this not David, the servant of King Saul of Israel, who has been with me now for days and years? Since he deserted to me I have found no fault in him to this day." ⁴But the commanders of the Philistines were angry with him; and the commanders of the Philistines said to him, "Send the man back, so that he may return to the place that you have assigned to him; he shall not go down with us to battle, or else he may become an adversary to us in the battle. For how could this fellow reconcile himself to his lord? Would it not be with the heads of the men here? ⁵Is this not David, of whom they sing to one another in dances,

'Saul has killed his thousands,
    and David his ten thousands'?"

6 Then Achish called David and said to him, "As the LORD lives, you have been honest, and to me it seems right that you should march out and in with me in the campaign; for I have found nothing wrong in you from the day of your coming to me until today. Nevertheless the lords do not approve of you. ⁷So go back now; and go peaceably; do nothing to displease the lords of the Philistines." ⁸David said to Achish, "But what have I done? What have you found in your servant from the day I entered your service until now, that I should not go and fight against the enemies of my lord the king?" ⁹Achish replied to David, "I know that you are as blameless in my sight as an angel of God; nevertheless, the commanders of the Philistines have said, 'He shall not go up with us to the battle.' ¹⁰Now then rise early in the morning, you and the servants of your lord who came with you, and go to the place that I appointed for you. As for the evil report, do not take it to heart, for you have done well before me.ᵃ Start early in the morning, and leave as soon as you have light." ¹¹So David set out with his men early in the morning, to return to the land of the Philistines. But the Philistines went up to Jezreel.

29.1–11: The Philistines reject David. 2: *The lords of the Philistines* are the rulers of the five main Philistine cities. **3:** The *commanders* of the Philistine army who will actually be in battle object to the presence of David and his men, whom they refer to as *Hebrews*, possibly a term for mercenaries. **6:** It is surprising that *Achish,* the Philistine, swears here by the LORD, that is, Yahweh, the God of Israel. **8:** David's wish to *fight against the enemies of my lord the king* is ambiguous. David's "lord" is Saul, but Achish takes it as a reference to himself. **10:** *The place that I appointed for you* is Ziklag.

30 Now when David and his men came to Ziklag on the third day, the Amalekites had made a raid on the Negeb and on Ziklag. They had attacked Ziklag, burned it down, ²and taken captive the women and allᵇ who were in it, both small and great; they killed none of them, but carried them off, and went their way. ³When David and his men came to the city, they found it burned down, and their wives and sons and daughters taken captive. ⁴Then David and the people who were with him raised their voices and wept, until they had no more strength to weep. ⁵David's two wives also had been taken captive, Ahinoam of Jezreel, and Abigail the widow of Nabal of Carmel. ⁶David was in great danger; for the people spoke of stoning him, because all the people were bitter in spirit for their sons and daughters. But David strengthened himself in the LORD his God.

30.1–31: David defeats the Amalekites. 1: *On the third day:* Ziklag is over 50 miles from Aphek. The journey took three days. The writer emphasizes David's distance from the battle where Saul is killed. The Amalekite *raid* on Ziklag may have been in retaliation for David's raids against the Amalekites (27.8). This story stands in tension with ch. 15 where the Amalekites were supposedly all destroyed. **2:** *The women and all:* The men were all with David. *Both small and great* is a figure of speech referring to two extremes and everything in the middle. Here, the terms describe poverty or wealth and obscurity or social prominence. **6:**

a Gk: Heb lacks *and go to the place . . . done well before me*   *b* Gk: Heb lacks *and all*

Stoning as a type of execution implies that David had been accused of failing as a leader to provide adequate protection. Strengthened himself may mean summoning courage as well as gathering support within the army. David is here depicted as an ideal ruler.

～～～～～～～～～

7 David said to the priest Abiathar son of Ahimelech, "Bring me the ephod." So Abiathar brought the ephod to David. 8David inquired of the LORD, "Shall I pursue this band? Shall I overtake them?" He answered him, "Pursue; for you shall surely overtake and shall surely rescue." 9So David set out, he and the six hundred men who were with him. They came to the Wadi Besor, where those stayed who were left behind. 10But David went on with the pursuit, he and four hundred men; two hundred stayed behind, too exhausted to cross the Wadi Besor.

11 In the open country they found an Egyptian, and brought him to David. They gave him bread and he ate; they gave him water to drink; 12they also gave him a piece of fig cake and two clusters of raisins. When he had eaten, his spirit revived; for he had not eaten bread or drunk water for three days and three nights. 13Then David said to him, "To whom do you belong? Where are you from?" He said, "I am a young man of Egypt, servant to an Amalekite. My master left me behind because I fell sick three days ago. 14We had made a raid on the Negeb of the Cherethites and on that which belongs to Judah and on the Negeb of Caleb; and we burned Ziklag down." 15David said to him, "Will you take me down to this raiding party?" He said, "Swear to me by God that you will not kill me, or hand me over to my master, and I will take you down to them."

16 When he had taken him down, they were spread out all over the ground, eating and drinking and dancing, because of the great amount of spoil they had taken from the land of the Philistines and from the land of Judah. 17David attacked them from twilight until the evening of the next day. Not one of them escaped, except four hundred young men, who mounted camels and fled. 18David recovered all that the Amalekites had taken; and David rescued his two wives. 19Nothing was missing, whether small or great, sons or daughters, spoil or anything that had been taken; David brought back everything. 20David also captured all the flocks and herds, which were driven ahead of the other cattle; people said, "This is David's spoil."

21 Then David came to the two hundred men who had been too exhausted to follow David, and who had been left at the Wadi Besor. They went out to meet David and to meet the people who were with him. When David drew near to the people he saluted them. 22Then all the corrupt and worthless fellows among the men who had gone with David said, "Because they did not go with us, we will not give them any of the spoil that we have recovered, except that each man may take his wife and children, and leave." 23But David said, "You shall not do so, my brothers, with what the LORD has given us; he has preserved us and handed over to us the raiding party that attacked us. 24Who would listen to you in this matter? For the share of the one who goes down into the battle shall be the same as the share of the one who stays by the baggage; they shall share alike." 25From that day forward he made it a statute and an ordinance for Israel; it continues to the present day.

26 When David came to Ziklag, he sent part of the spoil to his friends, the elders of Judah, saying, "Here is a present for you from the spoil of the enemies of the LORD"; 27it was for those in Bethel, in Ramoth of the Negeb, in Jattir, 28in Aroer, in Siphmoth, in Eshtemoa, 29in Racal, in the towns of the Jerahmeelites, in the towns of the Kenites, 30in Hormah, in Bor-ashan, in Athach, 31in Hebron, all the places where David and his men had roamed.

30.7–31. 7–8: The ephod* was used by priests to divine the answers to yes/no questions such as those in v. 8. 12: Fig cake was a clump of figs. 14: The Cherethites were mercenaries from the island of Crete who were closely associated with the Philistines. 23–25: This is an etiology* for a custom in the writer's day. David's decree of a statute and an ordinance for Israel shows his kingly decisiveness and authority. 26–31: The cities listed here were all in southern Judah. David's gifts to the elders of these cities would cause them to look favorably upon him when the time came to choose a king over Judah.

31

Now the Philistines fought against Israel; and the men of Israel fled before the Philistines, and many fell[a] on Mount Gilboa. [2]The Philistines overtook Saul and his sons; and the Philistines killed Jonathan and Abinadab and Malchishua, the sons of Saul. [3]The battle pressed hard upon Saul; the archers found him, and he was badly wounded by them. [4]Then Saul said to his armor-bearer, "Draw your sword and thrust me through with it, so that these uncircumcised may not come and thrust me through, and make sport of me." But his armor-bearer was unwilling; for he was terrified. So Saul took his own sword and fell upon it. [5]When his armor-bearer saw that Saul was dead, he also fell upon his sword and died with him. [6]So Saul and his three sons and his armor-bearer and all his men died together on the same day. [7]When the men of Israel who were on the other side of the valley and those beyond the Jordan saw that the men of Israel had fled and that Saul and his sons were dead, they forsook their towns and fled; and the Philistines came and occupied them.

8 The next day, when the Philistines came to strip the dead, they found Saul and his three sons fallen on Mount Gilboa. [9]They cut off his head, stripped off his armor, and sent messengers throughout the land of the Philistines to carry the good news to the houses of their idols and to the people. [10]They put his armor in the temple of Astarte;[b] and they fastened his body to the wall of Beth-shan. [11]But when the inhabitants of Jabesh-gilead heard what the Philistines had done to Saul, [12]all the valiant men set out, traveled all night long, and took the body of Saul and the bodies of his sons from the wall of Beth-shan. They came to Jabesh and burned them there. [13]Then they took their bones and buried them under the tamarisk tree in Jabesh, and fasted seven days.

31.1–13: Saul's death. 1 Chronicles 10 contains a parallel account. **4:** *These uncircumcised** are the Philistines. Saul does not want to suffer humiliation and torture at their hands, so he asks his armor-bearer to finish him off. The armor-bearer refuses, perhaps out of respect for the Lord's anointed.* **11–13:** The men of Jabesh rescue Saul's body. They are moved to do this because of Saul's rescue of their city at the beginning of his reign (10.27b–11.15). It is unusual that they burned the bodies of Saul and his sons (v. 12), since cremation was not practiced by the Israelites.

a Heb *and they fell slain*   *b* Heb plural

2 SAMUEL

Introduction

The book of 2 Samuel is the continuation of 1 Samuel in the Deuteronomistic History* (see the introduction to 1 Samuel). The first half of the book relates how David, after Saul's death (2 Sam 1), became king of Judah (ch. 2) and then Israel (ch. 5). It tells how he built a small empire through military conquest and how he established a capital and a dynasty* in Jerusalem. The LORD's promise to David of an eternal dynasty (ch. 7) is a key passage in the Deuteronomistic History. It brings together the themes of Jerusalem as the divinely chosen center for worship and the Davidic line as the chosen family of kings in Judah. The second half of the book describes David's problems, which are all political problems within Israel and arise from within David's extended family. These include his adultery with Bathsheba (chs. 11–12), the rape of Tamar and murder of Amnon (ch. 13), and the revolts of Absalom and Sheba (chs. 13–20). This last section at least has been judged by scholars to have been an independent unit known as the "Succession Narrative" or "Court History." It lacks signs of deuteronomistic style and seems therefore to have been separate in some way from the Deuteronomistic History. There is no consensus about where it begins, however (some say ch. 9, others 2.8–4.12), and the once widely held view that the "Succession Narrative" represented realistic history can no longer be sustained.

The date and setting of 2 Samuel are, of course, the same as for 1 Samuel. Scholars are of two minds, however, about how the message of the book addresses its context. Some believe that the book, especially its second half, continues the defense of David evident in 1 Samuel as a way of promoting at least the hope in the restoration of the monarchy. Others, however, see it as strongly anti-Davidic, in opposition to any attempt to reinstitute kingship in Israel. A great deal hinges on how the story in 2 Sam 11–12 is understood.

READING GUIDE

The ambiguity of 2 Samuel is a mark of its literary sophistication. The mixture of praise for David with hints of cynical political calculation renders interpretation of the book open-ended. 2 Samuel recounts many deaths as David attains and retains power: Abner, Ishbosheth, Amnon, Absalom, Amasa. Is the writer attempting to defend David against charges of murder and usurpation? Does the book continue the contrast between Saul and David, showing how the annihilation of Saul's house and the rise of David took place according to the will of the LORD? Or is the author more cynical and subtle, contending that abuse of power is inherent with monarchs? Close attention to the interaction of the characters in 2 Samuel will help readers to answer these questions for themselves. The reader may also benefit from an awareness of the literary depth of the material. The story of Absalom's revolt, for example, may originally have been independent, with its own set of social and political causes. As it now stands, however, it is explained theologically as a consequence of David's sin with Bathsheba.

1–10	David's reign over Judah, then over Israel
11–12	David's sin with Bathsheba
13–20	Absalom's revolt
21–24	Miscellaneous materials about David's reign

1 After the death of Saul, when David had returned from defeating the Amalekites, David remained two days in Ziklag. 2On the third day, a man came from Saul's camp, with his clothes torn and dirt on his head. When he came to David, he fell to the ground and did obeisance. 3David said to him, "Where have you come from?" He said to him, "I have escaped from the camp of Israel." 4David said to him, "How did things go? Tell me!" He answered, "The army fled from the battle, but also many of the army fell and died; and Saul and his son Jonathan also died." 5Then David asked the young man who was reporting to him, "How do you know that Saul and his son Jonathan died?" 6The young man reporting to him said, "I happened to be on Mount Gilboa; and there was Saul leaning on his spear, while the chariots and the horsemen drew close to him. 7When he looked behind him, he saw me, and called to me. I answered, 'Here sir.' 8And he said to me, 'Who are you?' I answered him, 'I am an Amalekite.' 9He said to me, 'Come, stand over me and kill me; for convulsions have seized me, and yet my life still lingers.' 10So I stood over him, and killed him, for I knew that he could not live after he had fallen. I took the crown that was on his head and the armlet that was on his arm, and I have brought them here to my lord."

11 Then David took hold of his clothes and tore them; and all the men who were with him did the same. 12They mourned and wept, and fasted until evening for Saul and for his son Jonathan, and for the army of the LORD and for the house of Israel, because they had fallen by the sword. 13David said to the young man who had reported to him, "Where do you come from?" He answered, "I am the son of a resident alien, an Amalekite." 14David said to him, "Were you not afraid to lift your hand to destroy the LORD's anointed?" 15Then David called one of the young men and said, "Come here and strike him down." So he struck him down and he died. 16David said to him, "Your blood be on your head; for your own mouth has testified against you, saying, 'I have killed the LORD's anointed.' "

1.1–16: David learns of Saul's death. 2: *With his clothes torn and dirt on his head:* Conventional signs of grief. **5–10:** The Amalekite who brings the news to David tells a different version of Saul's death from the one in 1 Sam 31. His casual attitude (*I happened to be on Mount Gilboa*, v. 6) in the heat of battle suggests that he is lying in hopes of gaining David's favor. The fact that he is an *Amalekite* (v. 8) does not endear him to David and his men, who have just come from fighting the Amalekites. The account of this battle is difficult to reconcile with 1 Sam 15, where Saul's army killed all the Amalekites except their king. But it also provides an ironic* view of Saul's sin: Saul is condemned for failing to annihilate the Amalekites completely, and now one of those Amalekites claims to have killed him. David's predicament is clear: Although he presumably wanted Saul to be dead, he cannot even seem to have anything to do with killing Saul, since that would leave him open to charges of usurping the throne. The *crown* and *armlet* (v. 10) were Saul's royal insignia. David's possession of them would have to be explained. **13–16:** A *resident alien** is a non-Israelite who lives in Israel, which may also explain how this Amalekite escaped being slaughtered by Saul's army in 1 Sam 15. It also gives David the opening he needs: Since the Amalekite would have been responsible for following Israelite laws and customs, David judges him guilty of the capital offense of having killed the LORD's anointed.*

17 David intoned this lamentation over Saul and his son Jonathan. 18(He ordered that The Song of the Bow*a* be taught to the people of Judah; it is written in the Book of Jashar.) He said:
19 Your glory, O Israel, lies slain upon your
    high places!
      How the mighty have fallen!
20 Tell it not in Gath,
      proclaim it not in the streets of
        Ashkelon;
    or the daughters of the Philistines will
      rejoice,
        the daughters of the uncircumcised
          will exult.

21 You mountains of Gilboa,
      let there be no dew or rain upon you,
        nor bounteous fields!*b*

a Heb *that The Bow*   *b* Meaning of Heb uncertain

For there the shield of the mighty was
   defiled,
    the shield of Saul, anointed with oil
     no more.

22 From the blood of the slain,
   from the fat of the mighty,
    the bow of Jonathan did not turn back,
     nor the sword of Saul return empty.

23 Saul and Jonathan, beloved and lovely!
   In life and in death they were not
    divided;
   they were swifter than eagles,
    they were stronger than lions.

24 O daughters of Israel, weep over Saul,
   who clothed you with crimson, in
    luxury,
   who put ornaments of gold on your
    apparel.

25 How the mighty have fallen
   in the midst of the battle!

Jonathan lies slain upon your high
   places.
26 I am distressed for you, my brother
   Jonathan;
   greatly beloved were you to me;
    your love to me was wonderful,
    passing the love of women.

27 How the mighty have fallen,
   and the weapons of war perished!

**1.17–27: David's lament* over Saul and Jonathan.
18:** The title, *The Song of the Bow,* may reflect a textual error. If original, it refers to the tune to which the
lament was sung. *The Book of Jashar* was a collection
of poems that no longer exists. **20:** *Gath* and *Ashkelon*
were Philistine cities. The poem pleads that the news
of Saul's and Jonathan's deaths not be proclaimed in
Philistine cities, where there would be rejoicing over it.
21: *Gilboa* was the mountain where Saul and Jonathan
died in battle. It is being cursed along with the surrounding hills because of this tragedy. Shields were
made of leather and *anointed* with oil* in preparation
for battle. Saul's shield now lies *defiled* from bloody
battle and unused because its owner is dead. **24:** The

poem calls upon the Israelites to mourn because they
prospered under Saul's rule.

2 After this David inquired of the LORD,
"Shall I go up into any of the cities of
Judah?" The LORD said to him, "Go up." David said, "To which shall I go up?" He said,
"To Hebron." 2 So David went up there,
along with his two wives, Ahinoam of Jezreel,
and Abigail the widow of Nabal of Carmel.
3 David brought up the men who were with
him, every one with his household; and they
settled in the towns of Hebron. 4 Then the
people of Judah came, and there they
anointed David king over the house of Judah.

When they told David, "It was the people
of Jabesh-gilead who buried Saul," 5 David
sent messengers to the people of Jabesh-
gilead, and said to them, "May you be
blessed by the LORD, because you showed
this loyalty to Saul your lord, and buried him!
6 Now may the LORD show steadfast love and
faithfulness to you! And I too will reward you
because you have done this thing. 7 Therefore let your hands be strong, and be valiant;
for Saul your lord is dead, and the house of
Judah has anointed me king over them."

2.1–32: Civil war. 1: David *inquired of the LORD* by
means of some device, like lots, which could provide
answers to yes/no questions. Hence, his question
about going to *any of the cities of Judah* received a yes
answer. By process of elimination he then determined
that *Hebron* was the chosen city. Hebron was the capital of Judah. **2:** David's two wives, *Ahinoam* and *Abigail,* were both from the area around Hebron and were
therefore important political assets for his assumption
of the throne of Judah. Through his marriage to Abigail, David had assumed the wealth and position of a
prominent Calebite leader, perhaps their chieftain
(1 Sam 25). The Calebites were a prominent clan* in
Judah. **4a:** *The people of Judah* may be the same as
the elders of Judah to whom David distributed the
spoil from his defeat of the Amalekites (1 Sam
30.26–31). They *anointed** David by smearing oil on
his head. This was a symbol of election. "Messiah" is
a transliteration of the Hebrew word for anointed.
4b–7: The people of *Jabesh* in the region of *Gilead*
were among Saul's most loyal supporters. He had rescued them at the beginning of his reign (1 Sam
10.27b–11.15), and they had returned the favor by

rescuing his corpse from the Philistines (1 Sam 31.11–13). David congratulates them for their loyalty (v. 5) and then invites them to join with him as Saul's replacement (vv. 6–7). By making overtures to the enclaves of Saul's strongest support he forces the hand of Saul's successor, Ishbaal, whereupon civil war between Israel and Judah ensues.

8 But Abner son of Ner, commander of Saul's army, had taken Ishbaal[a] son of Saul, and brought him over to Mahanaim. 9He made him king over Gilead, the Ashurites, Jezreel, Ephraim, Benjamin, and over all Israel. 10Ishbaal,[a] Saul's son, was forty years old when he began to reign over Israel, and he reigned two years. But the house of Judah followed David. 11The time that David was king in Hebron over the house of Judah was seven years and six months.

2.8–11: *Abner* was Saul's cousin or uncle (1 Sam 14.50). He is obviously the power behind *Ishbaal's* throne. The Hebrew text reads "Ish-bosheth" instead of "Ishbaal." Later scribes* substituted the word "bosheth," meaning "abomination," for the name of the Canaanite god Baal.* The word "baal" means "lord;" rather than indicating that Saul worshipped Baal, it may have been used as a title for the LORD (Yahweh). *Mahanaim* was east of the Jordan. Abner took Ishbaal there for protection because the Philistines had captured most of the Israelite territory. Thus, the description of Ishbaal's domain in v. 9 was more ideal than real at this point. *Ashurites* or "Assyrians" is impossible. A better reading is "Geshurites," who lived east of the Sea of Galilee. *Forty years* (v. 10) is a round number for a generation. If Ishbaal reigned *two years* over Israel during David's *seven years and six months* over Judah, five and a half years remain unaccounted for. Either there was an interregnum* in Israel after Saul's death before Ishbaal came to power, or David became king of Judah while Saul was still alive.

~~~~~~~~

12 Abner son of Ner, and the servants of Ishbaal[a] son of Saul, went out from Mahanaim to Gibeon. 13Joab son of Zeruiah, and the servants of David, went out and met them at the pool of Gibeon. One group sat on one side of the pool, while the other sat on the other side of the pool. 14Abner said to Joab, "Let the young men come forward and have a contest before us." Joab said, "Let them come forward." 15So they came forward and were counted as they passed by, twelve for Benjamin and Ishbaal[a] son of Saul, and twelve of the servants of David. 16Each grasped his opponent by the head, and thrust his sword in his opponent's side; so they fell down together. Therefore that place was called Helkath-hazzurim,[b] which is at Gibeon. 17The battle was very fierce that day; and Abner and the men of Israel were beaten by the servants of David.

18 The three sons of Zeruiah were there, Joab, Abishai, and Asahel. Now Asahel was as swift of foot as a wild gazelle. 19Asahel pursued Abner, turning neither to the right nor to the left as he followed him. 20Then Abner looked back and said, "Is it you, Asahel?" He answered, "Yes, it is." 21Abner said to him, "Turn to your right or to your left, and seize one of the young men, and take his spoil." But Asahel would not turn away from following him. 22Abner said again to Asahel, "Turn away from following me; why should I strike you to the ground? How then could I show my face to your brother Joab?" 23But he refused to turn away. So Abner struck him in the stomach with the butt of his spear, so that the spear came out at his back. He fell there, and died where he lay. And all those who came to the place where Asahel had fallen and died, stood still.

24 But Joab and Abishai pursued Abner. As the sun was going down they came to the hill of Ammah, which lies before Giah on the way to the wilderness of Gibeon. 25The Benjaminites rallied around Abner and formed a single band; they took their stand on the top of a hill. 26Then Abner called to Joab, "Is the sword to keep devouring forever? Do you not know that the end will be bitter? How long will it be before you order your people to turn from the pursuit of their kinsmen?" 27Joab said, "As God lives, if you had not spoken, the people would have continued to pursue their kinsmen, not stopping until morning." 28Joab sounded the trumpet and all the people stopped; they no longer pursued Israel or engaged in battle any further.

a Gk Compare 1 Chr 8.33; 9.39: Heb *Ish-bosheth,* "man of shame"   *b* That is *Field of Sword-edges*

29 Abner and his men traveled all that night through the Arabah; they crossed the Jordan, and, marching the whole forenoon,*a* they came to Mahanaim. 30 Joab returned from the pursuit of Abner; and when he had gathered all the people together, there were missing of David's servants nineteen men besides Asahel. 31 But the servants of David had killed of Benjamin three hundred sixty of Abner's men. 32 They took up Asahel and buried him in the tomb of his father, which was at Bethlehem. Joab and his men marched all night, and the day broke upon them at Hebron.

2.12–32: 12: According to 2 Sam 21.1–9, the people of *Gibeon* held a grudge against Saul and may have helped David. 13: *Zeruiah* was David's sister and *Joab* his cousin, according to 1 Chr 2.16. Joab was also the commander of David's army. The *pool of Gibeon* may refer to an enormous pit that has been discovered at the site of the ancient city. The pit descended to the city's water supply. 14–16: The *contest* here is a representative combat: a tournament between a small group from each side, rather than a full battle involving everyone. It provides an etiology* for the name in v. 16—*Helkath-hazzurim* means "field of the flint swords," or field of sword-edges. Since the contest is indecisive, a full battle breaks out (v. 17). 18–23: The death of *Asahel* gives his brother, Joab, a personal incentive for killing Abner (3.26–30). 26: *People* often means the army. 29: The *Arabah* is the geological depression from the Sea of Galilee to the Gulf of Aqabah. Here it refers to the Jordan Valley north of the Dead Sea.

3 There was a long war between the house of Saul and the house of David; David grew stronger and stronger, while the house of Saul became weaker and weaker.

2 Sons were born to David at Hebron: his firstborn was Amnon, of Ahinoam of Jezreel; 3 his second, Chileab, of Abigail the widow of Nabal of Carmel; the third, Absalom son of Maacah, daughter of King Talmai of Geshur; 4 the fourth, Adonijah son of Haggith; the fifth, Shephatiah son of Abital; 5 and the sixth, Ithream, of David's wife Eglah. These were born to David in Hebron.

6 While there was war between the house of Saul and the house of David, Abner was making himself strong in the house of Saul. 7 Now Saul had a concubine whose name was Rizpah daughter of Aiah. And Ishbaal*b* said to Abner, "Why have you gone in to my father's concubine?" 8 The words of Ishbaal*c* made Abner very angry; he said, "Am I a dog's head for Judah? Today I keep showing loyalty to the house of your father Saul, to his brothers, and to his friends, and have not given you into the hand of David; and yet you charge me now with a crime concerning this woman. 9 So may God do to Abner and so may he add to it! For just what the LORD has sworn to David, that will I accomplish for him, 10 to transfer the kingdom from the house of Saul, and set up the throne of David over Israel and over Judah, from Dan to Beer-sheba." 11 And Ishbaal*b* could not answer Abner another word, because he feared him.

12 Abner sent messengers to David at Hebron,*d* saying, "To whom does the land belong? Make your covenant with me, and I will give you my support to bring all Israel over to you." 13 He said, "Good; I will make a covenant with you. But one thing I require of you: you shall never appear in my presence unless you bring Saul's daughter Michal when you come to see me." 14 Then David sent messengers to Saul's son Ishbaal,*e* saying, "Give me my wife Michal, to whom I became engaged at the price of one hundred foreskins of the Philistines." 15 Ishbaal*e* sent and took her from her husband Paltiel the son of Laish. 16 But her husband went with her, weeping as he walked behind her all the way to Bahurim. Then Abner said to him, "Go back home!" So he went back.

17 Abner sent word to the elders of Israel, saying, "For some time past you have been seeking David as king over you. 18 Now then bring it about; for the LORD has promised David: Through my servant David I will save my people Israel from the hand of the Philistines, and from all their enemies." 19 Abner also spoke directly to the Benjaminites; then Abner went to tell David at Hebron all that

a Meaning of Heb uncertain *b* Heb *And he*
c Gk Compare 1 Chr 8.33; 9.39: Heb *Ish-bosheth*,
"man of shame" *d* Gk: Heb *where he was*
e Heb *Ish-bosheth*

Israel and the whole house of Benjamin were ready to do.

3.1–39: The assassination of Abner. 2–5: A similar list of David's sons born in Hebron occurs in 1 Chr 3.1–4. *Chileab* is there called Daniel. His name is uncertain and, like *Shephatiah* and *Ithream*, is not mentioned again. He may have died as a child. David's marriage to *Maacah* probably sealed a treaty with her father, the king of Geshur. **7:** A *concubine** was a female slave used for sexual purposes. To sleep with a member of the harem was to stake a claim to the throne. Thus, Ishbaal's question accuses Abner of treason. **8:** Abner responds angrily because the power is in his hands and he has been loyal to Saul and Ishbaal. He says Ishbaal is treating him as a *dog's head*. This expression is unique but obviously reproachful. **9–10:** *So may God do . . . and so may he add* is an oath formula. Abner swears that he will join David, and since he holds the true power, he will thereby *transfer the kingdom* of Israel to David. *From Dan to Beer-sheba* marks the traditional boundaries, north and south, of the united kingdom of Israel. **13–16:** David requires the return of his wife Michal since, as Saul's daughter, she is the basis for his claim to Saul's throne (1 Sam 20–29). *Ishbaal* may have been legally obligated to return Michal to her first husband. *Paltiel* or "Palti" was Michal's second husband after she was taken from David (1 Sam 25.44). **17:** The *elders of Israel* were the leaders of the tribes. **19:** *Benjamin* was the native tribe of both Saul and Abner.

20 When Abner came with twenty men to David at Hebron, David made a feast for Abner and the men who were with him. 21 Abner said to David, "Let me go and rally all Israel to my lord the king, in order that they may make a covenant with you, and that you may reign over all that your heart desires." So David dismissed Abner, and he went away in peace.

22 Just then the servants of David arrived with Joab from a raid, bringing much spoil with them. But Abner was not with David at Hebron, for David[a] had dismissed him, and he had gone away in peace. 23 When Joab and all the army that was with him came, it was told Joab, "Abner son of Ner came to the king, and he has dismissed him, and he has gone away in peace." 24 Then Joab went to the king and said, "What have you done? Abner came to you; why did you dismiss him, so that he got away? 25 You know that Abner son of Ner came to deceive you, and to learn your comings and goings and to learn all that you are doing."

26 When Joab came out from David's presence, he sent messengers after Abner, and they brought him back from the cistern of Sirah; but David did not know about it. 27 When Abner returned to Hebron, Joab took him aside in the gateway to speak with him privately, and there he stabbed him in the stomach. So he died for shedding[b] the blood of Asahel, Joab's[c] brother. 28 Afterward, when David heard of it, he said, "I and my kingdom are forever guiltless before the LORD for the blood of Abner son of Ner. 29 May the guilt[d] fall on the head of Joab, and on all his father's house; and may the house of Joab never be without one who has a discharge, or who is leprous,[e] or who holds a spindle, or who falls by the sword, or who lacks food!" 30 So Joab and his brother Abishai murdered Abner because he had killed their brother Asahel in the battle at Gibeon.

31 Then David said to Joab and to all the people who were with him, "Tear your clothes, and put on sackcloth, and mourn over Abner." And King David followed the bier. 32 They buried Abner at Hebron. The king lifted up his voice and wept at the grave of Abner, and all the people wept. 33 The king lamented for Abner, saying,

"Should Abner die as a fool dies?
34 Your hands were not bound,
    your feet were not fettered;
 as one falls before the wicked
    you have fallen."

And all the people wept over him again. 35 Then all the people came to persuade David to eat something while it was still day; but David swore, saying, "So may God do to me, and more, if I taste bread or anything else before the sun goes down!" 36 All the people took notice of it, and it pleased them; just as everything the king did pleased all the people. 37 So all the people and all Israel un-

a Heb *he*   b Heb lacks *shedding*   c Heb *his*
d Heb *May it*   e A term for several skin diseases; precise meaning uncertain

derstood that day that the king had no part in the killing of Abner son of Ner. 38And the king said to his servants, "Do you not know that a prince and a great man has fallen this day in Israel? 39Today I am powerless, even though anointed king; these men, the sons of Zeruiah, are too violent for me. The LORD pay back the one who does wickedly in accordance with his wickedness!"

3.20–39. 21–23: The story repeats that Abner left David *in peace* as a way of emphasizing David's innocence in Abner's death. Joab's return after Abner had left (v. 22) suggests that David had sent Joab away in order to avoid a confrontation. 25: *Comings and goings* are military maneuvers. Joab is accusing Abner of spying. 27: Joab kills Abner in revenge for Abner's killing Asahel (2.18–23). The story hints that Joab may also have acted to preserve his place as army commander. 29: David curses Joab's descendants with illness because of his act. A *spindle* may also mean a crutch. 30: *Abishai* is not mentioned in the story but may have been involved with Joab in planning Abner's murder. 31: *Sackcloth* was an unknown kind of material worn by mourners. 33: *Fool* is a translation of the Hebrew "nabal" and is reminiscent of the story in 1 Sam 25.

4 When Saul's son Ishbaal*a* heard that Abner had died at Hebron, his courage failed, and all Israel was dismayed. 2Saul's son had two captains of raiding bands; the name of the one was Baanah, and the name of the other Rechab. They were sons of Rimmon a Benjaminite from Beeroth—for Beeroth is considered to belong to Benjamin. 3(Now the people of Beeroth had fled to Gittaim and are there as resident aliens to this day).

4 Saul's son Jonathan had a son who was crippled in his feet. He was five years old when the news about Saul and Jonathan came from Jezreel. His nurse picked him up and fled; and, in her haste to flee, it happened that he fell and became lame. His name was Mephibosheth.*b*

5 Now the sons of Rimmon the Beerothite, Rechab and Baanah, set out, and about the heat of the day they came to the house of Ishbaal,*c* while he was taking his noonday rest. 6They came inside the house as though

to take wheat, and they struck him in the stomach; then Rechab and his brother Baanah escaped.*d* 7Now they had come into the house while he was lying on his couch in his bedchamber; they attacked him, killed him, and beheaded him. Then they took his head and traveled by way of the Arabah all night long. 8They brought the head of Ishbaal*c* to David at Hebron and said to the king, "Here is the head of Ishbaal,*c* son of Saul, your enemy, who sought your life; the LORD has avenged my lord the king this day on Saul and on his offspring."

9 David answered Rechab and his brother Baanah, the sons of Rimmon the Beerothite, "As the LORD lives, who has redeemed my life out of every adversity, 10when the one who told me, 'See, Saul is dead,' thought he was bringing good news, I seized him and killed him at Ziklag—this was the reward I gave him for his news. 11How much more then, when wicked men have killed a righteous man on his bed in his own house! And now shall I not require his blood at your hand, and destroy you from the earth?" 12So David commanded the young men, and they killed them; they cut off their hands and feet, and hung their bodies beside the pool at Hebron. But the head of Ishbaal*c* they took and buried in the tomb of Abner at Hebron.

4.1–12: The assassination of Ishbaal. 2–3: *Beeroth* was one of the Gibeonite cities that joined Israel (Josh 9.17). Its residents fled and were presumably replaced by Israelites from Benjamin. 4: *Mephibosheth:* The original form of the name was Meribbaal as in 1 Chr 8.34; 9.40. The notice in this verse interrupts the narrative* but makes the point that there is no other suitable candidate for king in Saul's line after Ishbaal, a situation that prepares the way for the events narrated in 5.1. 7: *The Arabah* here refers to the Jordan Valley. 11: David refers to Ishbaal as a *righteous man* rather than as Yahweh's anointed,* suggesting that he does not recognize Ishbaal's kingship. 12: The kind of ritual execution described in this verse was reserved for traitors.

a Heb lacks *Ishbaal*   *b* In 1 Chr 8.34 and 9.40, *Merib-baal*   *c* Heb *Ish-bosheth*   *d* Meaning of Heb of verse 6 uncertain

5 Then all the tribes of Israel came to David at Hebron, and said, "Look, we are your bone and flesh. ²For some time, while Saul was king over us, it was you who led out Israel and brought it in. The Lord said to you: It is you who shall be shepherd of my people Israel, you who shall be ruler over Israel." ³So all the elders of Israel came to the king at Hebron; and King David made a covenant with them at Hebron before the Lord, and they anointed David king over Israel. ⁴David was thirty years old when he began to reign, and he reigned forty years. ⁵At Hebron he reigned over Judah seven years and six months; and at Jerusalem he reigned over all Israel and Judah thirty-three years.

6 The king and his men marched to Jerusalem against the Jebusites, the inhabitants of the land, who said to David, "You will not come in here, even the blind and the lame will turn you back"—thinking, "David cannot come in here." ⁷Nevertheless David took the stronghold of Zion, which is now the city of David. ⁸David had said on that day, "Whoever would strike down the Jebusites, let him get up the water shaft to attack the lame and the blind, those whom David hates."ᵃ Therefore it is said, "The blind and the lame shall not come into the house." ⁹David occupied the stronghold, and named it the city of David. David built the city all around from the Millo inward. ¹⁰And David became greater and greater, for the Lord, the God of hosts, was with him.

11 King Hiram of Tyre sent messengers to David, along with cedar trees, and carpenters and masons who built David a house. ¹²David then perceived that the Lord had established him king over Israel, and that he had exalted his kingdom for the sake of his people Israel.

13 In Jerusalem, after he came from Hebron, David took more concubines and wives; and more sons and daughters were born to David. ¹⁴These are the names of those who were born to him in Jerusalem: Shammua, Shobab, Nathan, Solomon, ¹⁵Ibhar, Elishua, Nepheg, Japhia, ¹⁶Elishama, Eliada, and Eliphelet.

5.1–16: David becomes king of Israel. 1–2: These verses are probably an editorial addition as they anticipate the action of the elders in v. 3. *Bone and flesh* means blood kinship. The people of Israel claim David as one of their own even though he was from Judah. *Led out* and *brought in* are idioms for military leadership. *Shepherd* is a common metaphor* for *ruler* or king. **3:** The *elders* were the senior leaders of the tribes. **4:** *Forty years* is a round number for a generation. **6–8:** The exact meaning of these verses is not clear. 1 Chr 11.5–6 differs, indicating that even the Chronicler found these verses confusing. The important point is that David conquered Jerusalem, which provided him a neutral capital in his effort to unite Israel and Judah. **9:** *Millo* means "fill" and apparently refers to a landfill or artificial platform created near the *stronghold*. **10:** The *hosts* are the armies, heavenly and earthly. **11:** *Tyre* was the capital of Phoenicia, the country north of Israel. Its *cedar* was a luxury item in the ancient Near East.

17 When the Philistines heard that David had been anointed king over Israel, all the Philistines went up in search of David; but David heard about it and went down to the stronghold. ¹⁸Now the Philistines had come and spread out in the valley of Rephaim. ¹⁹David inquired of the Lord, "Shall I go up against the Philistines? Will you give them into my hand?" The Lord said to David, "Go up; for I will certainly give the Philistines into your hand." ²⁰So David came to Baal-perazim, and David defeated them there. He said, "The Lord has burst forth against ᵇ my enemies before me, like a bursting flood." Therefore that place is called Baal-perazim.ᶜ ²¹The Philistines abandoned their idols there, and David and his men carried them away.

22 Once again the Philistines came up, and were spread out in the valley of Rephaim. ²³When David inquired of the Lord, he said, "You shall not go up; go around to their rear, and come upon them opposite the balsam trees. ²⁴When you hear the sound of marching in the tops of the balsam trees, then be on the alert; for then the Lord has gone out before you to strike down the army

a Another reading is *those who hate David*
b Heb *paraz*   c That is *Lord of Bursting Forth*

of the Philistines." 25David did just as the LORD had commanded him; and he struck down the Philistines from Geba all the way to Gezer.

5.17–25: David defeats the Philistines. 17: David's defeat of the Philistines probably preceded his conquest of Jerusalem, since they stood between Hebron and Jerusalem and would have resisted the unification of Israel and Judah. David's *stronghold* here is probably Adullam, not Jerusalem. **19:** *David inquired of the LORD* by means of some device that provided answers to yes/no questions. **20:** This verse is an etiology* for the name *Baal-perazim*, which means "Lord of bursting forth." **21:** A victorious army typically captured the idols that its opponent brought to the battlefield to show the superiority of its own gods. **22–25:** David's victory on this occasion is divinely directed.

---

6 David again gathered all the chosen men of Israel, thirty thousand. 2David and all the people with him set out and went from Baale-judah, to bring up from there the ark of God, which is called by the name of the LORD of hosts who is enthroned on the cherubim. 3They carried the ark of God on a new cart, and brought it out of the house of Abinadab, which was on the hill. Uzzah and Ahio,*a* the sons of Abinadab, were driving the new cart 4with the ark of God;*b* and Ahio*a* went in front of the ark. 5David and all the house of Israel were dancing before the LORD with all their might, with songs*c* and lyres and harps and tambourines and castanets and cymbals.

6 When they came to the threshing floor of Nacon, Uzzah reached out his hand to the ark of God and took hold of it, for the oxen shook it. 7The anger of the LORD was kindled against Uzzah; and God struck him there because he reached out his hand to the ark;*d* and he died there beside the ark of God. 8David was angry because the LORD had burst forth with an outburst upon Uzzah; so that place is called Perez-uzzah,*e* to this day. 9David was afraid of the LORD that day; he said, "How can the ark of the LORD come into my care?" 10So David was unwilling to take the ark of the LORD into his care in the city of David; instead David took it to the house of Obed-edom the Gittite. 11The

ark of the LORD remained in the house of Obed-edom the Gittite three months; and the LORD blessed Obed-edom and all his household.

12 It was told King David, "The LORD has blessed the household of Obed-edom and all that belongs to him, because of the ark of God." So David went and brought up the ark of God from the house of Obed-edom to the city of David with rejoicing; 13and when those who bore the ark of the LORD had gone six paces, he sacrificed an ox and a fatling. 14David danced before the LORD with all his might; David was girded with a linen ephod. 15So David and all the house of Israel brought up the ark of the LORD with shouting, and with the sound of the trumpet.

16 As the ark of the LORD came into the city of David, Michal daughter of Saul looked out of the window, and saw King David leaping and dancing before the LORD; and she despised him in her heart.

17 They brought in the ark of the LORD, and set it in its place, inside the tent that David had pitched for it; and David offered burnt offerings and offerings of well-being before the LORD. 18When David had finished offering the burnt offerings and the offerings of well-being, he blessed the people in the name of the LORD of hosts, 19and distributed food among all the people, the whole multitude of Israel, both men and women, to each a cake of bread, a portion of meat,*f* and a cake of raisins. Then all the people went back to their homes.

20 David returned to bless his household. But Michal the daughter of Saul came out to meet David, and said, "How the king of Israel honored himself today, uncovering himself today before the eyes of his servants' maids, as any vulgar fellow might shamelessly uncover himself!" 21David said to Michal, "It was before the LORD, who chose me in place of your father and all his household, to appoint me as prince over Israel, the

---

a Or *and his brother*   *b* Compare Gk: Heb *and brought it out of the house of Abinadab, which was on the hill with the ark of God*   *c* Q Ms Gk 1 Chr 13.8: Heb *fir trees*
d 1 Chr 13.10 Compare Q Ms: Meaning of Heb uncertain   *e* That is *Bursting Out Against Uzzah*
f Vg: Meaning of Heb uncertain

people of the LORD, that I have danced before the LORD. 22I will make myself yet more contemptible than this, and I will be abased in my own eyes; but by the maids of whom you have spoken, by them I shall be held in honor." 23And Michal the daughter of Saul had no child to the day of her death.

6.1–23: David brings the ark to Jerusalem. 1: The word translated "thousand" designates a military unit of much smaller size. Then, *thirty thousand* would be thirty units. **2:** *Baale-judah* is another name for Kiriath-jearim, according to Josh 15.9. This is where the ark was left in 1 Sam 7.1. The *ark* was viewed as the throne of the LORD. *Cherubim* were mythical griffins that often guarded temples and palaces. **6–8:** *Uzzah's* death shows the awesome holiness of the ark. The story also provides an etiological* explanation for the name Perez-uzzah (see note *e*). **10:** *Obed-edom* was from Gath (*the Gittite*) and was apparently among the Philistines who followed David from his days with the Philistines. **14:** A *linen ephod** was an apron typically worn by priests (1 Sam 2.18). **20:** Michal accuses David of fraternizing with the lowest element of society, thus implying that he is not dignified enough to be king. **21–22:** David replies that the LORD made him king in place of her father, Saul. **23:** Michal had no children either because the LORD prevented it or because David had no relations with her. Her children would have been Saul's heirs and therefore a threat to David's rule.

---

7 Now when the king was settled in his house, and the LORD had given him rest from all his enemies around him, 2the king said to the prophet Nathan, "See now, I am living in a house of cedar, but the ark of God stays in a tent." 3Nathan said to the king, "Go, do all that you have in mind; for the LORD is with you."

4 But that same night the word of the LORD came to Nathan: 5Go and tell my servant David: Thus says the LORD: Are you the one to build me a house to live in? 6I have not lived in a house since the day I brought up the people of Israel from Egypt to this day, but I have been moving about in a tent and a tabernacle. 7Wherever I have moved about among all the people of Israel, did I ever speak a word with any of the tribal leaders*a* of Israel, whom I commanded to shep-

herd my people Israel, saying, "Why have you not built me a house of cedar?" 8Now therefore thus you shall say to my servant David: Thus says the LORD of hosts: I took you from the pasture, from following the sheep to be prince over my people Israel; 9and I have been with you wherever you went, and have cut off all your enemies from before you; and I will make for you a great name, like the name of the great ones of the earth. 10And I will appoint a place for my people Israel and will plant them, so that they may live in their own place, and be disturbed no more; and evildoers shall afflict them no more, as formerly, 11from the time that I appointed judges over my people Israel; and I will give you rest from all your enemies. Moreover the LORD declares to you that the LORD will make you a house. 12When your days are fulfilled and you lie down with your ancestors, I will raise up your offspring after you, who shall come forth from your body, and I will establish his kingdom. 13He shall build a house for my name, and I will establish the throne of his kingdom forever. 14I will be a father to him, and he shall be a son to me. When he commits iniquity, I will punish him with a rod such as mortals use, with blows inflicted by human beings. 15But I will not take*b* my steadfast love from him, as I took it from Saul, whom I put away from before you. 16Your house and your kingdom shall be made sure forever before me;*c* your throne shall be established forever. 17In accordance with all these words and with all this vision, Nathan spoke to David.

18 Then King David went in and sat before the LORD, and said, "Who am I, O Lord GOD, and what is my house, that you have brought me thus far? 19And yet this was a small thing in your eyes, O Lord GOD; you have spoken also of your servant's house for a great while to come. May this be instruction for the people,*d* O Lord GOD! 20And what more can David say to you? For you know your servant, O Lord GOD! 21Because of your promise, and according to your own

a Or *any of the tribes*   *b* Gk Syr Vg 1 Chr 17.13: Heb *shall not depart*   *c* Gk Heb Mss: MT *before you;* Compare 2 Sam 7.26, 29   *d* Meaning of Heb uncertain heart, you have wrought all this greatness, so that your servant may know it. 22Therefore you are great, O LORD God; for there is no one like you, and there is no God besides you, according to all that we have heard with our ears. 23Who is like your people, like Israel? Is there another*a* nation on earth whose God went to redeem it as a people, and to make a name for himself, doing great and awesome things for them,*b* by driving out*c* before his people nations and their gods?*d* 24And you established your people Israel for yourself to be your people forever; and you, O LORD, became their God. 25And now, O LORD God, as for the word that you have spoken concerning your servant and concerning his house, confirm it forever; do as you have promised. 26Thus your name will be magnified forever in the saying, 'The LORD of hosts is God over Israel'; and the house of your servant David will be established before you. 27For you, O LORD of hosts, the God of Israel, have made this revelation to your servant, saying, 'I will build you a house'; therefore your servant has found courage to pray this prayer to you. 28And now, O Lord GOD, you are God, and your words are true, and you have promised this good thing to your servant; 29now therefore may it please you to bless the house of your servant, so that it may continue forever before you; for you, O Lord GOD, have spoken, and with your blessing shall the house of your servant be blessed forever."

7.1–29: A dynasty* for David. 1: The second half of this verse, about the LORD giving David rest, is not in the parallel version in 1 Chr 17.1. It is also contradicted by the subsequent accounts of David's wars and by the statement in 1 Kings 5.3–4 that rest came only to Solomon. **5–7:** There is a play throughout the chapter on the word "house." The *house* David proposes to build is a temple. But the LORD declines David's offer and says instead that he will build David a house, that is, a dynasty. The claim in vv. 6–7 that the LORD has never had a *house* (temple) seems to overlook the temple in Shiloh (1 Sam 1–3). **10:** The *place* mentioned here is probably a place of worship, namely the Jerusalem Temple. **11–12:** The *house* that the LORD promises David is a dynasty. **13:** It is David's son who will build the Temple. **16:** David's dynasty will be per-

---

manent and *established forever*. **23:** David here refers to the exodus from Egypt and the conquest of Canaan.

~~~~~~~~~~~~~~~~~~~~~~~~~~~~~~~~~~~~~

8 Some time afterward, David attacked the Philistines and subdued them; David took Metheg-ammah out of the hand of the Philistines.

2 He also defeated the Moabites and, making them lie down on the ground, measured them off with a cord; he measured two lengths of cord for those who were to be put to death, and one length*e* for those who were to be spared. And the Moabites became servants to David and brought tribute.

3 David also struck down King Hadadezer son of Rehob of Zobah, as he went to restore his monument*f* at the river Euphrates. 4David took from him one thousand seven hundred horsemen, and twenty thousand foot soldiers. David hamstrung all the chariot horses, but left enough for a hundred chariots. 5When the Arameans of Damascus came to help King Hadadezer of Zobah, David killed twenty-two thousand men of the Arameans. 6Then David put garrisons among the Arameans of Damascus; and the Arameans became servants to David and brought tribute. The LORD gave victory to David wherever he went. 7David took the gold shields that were carried by the servants of Hadadezer, and brought them to Jerusalem. 8From Betah and from Berothai, towns of Hadadezer, King David took a great amount of bronze.

9 When King Toi of Hamath heard that David had defeated the whole army of Hadadezer, 10Toi sent his son Joram to King David, to greet him and to congratulate him because he had fought against Hadadezer and defeated him. Now Hadadezer had often been at war with Toi. Joram brought with him articles of silver, gold, and bronze; 11these also King David dedicated to the LORD, together with the silver and gold that he dedicated from all the nations he subdued, 12from Edom, Moab, the Ammonites,

---

a Gk: Heb *one*   *b* Heb *you*   *c* Gk 1 Chr 17.21: Heb *for your land*   *d* Cn: Heb *before your people, whom you redeemed for yourself from Egypt, nations and its gods*   *e* Heb *one full length*   *f* Compare 1 Sam 15.12 and 2 Sam 18.18

the Philistines, Amalek, and from the spoil of King Hadadezer son of Rehob of Zobah.

13 David won a name for himself. When he returned, he killed eighteen thousand Edomites[a] in the Valley of Salt. 14He put garrisons in Edom; throughout all Edom he put garrisons, and all the Edomites became David's servants. And the LORD gave victory to David wherever he went.

15 So David reigned over all Israel; and David administered justice and equity to all his people. 16Joab son of Zeruiah was over the army; Jehoshaphat son of Ahilud was recorder; 17Zadok son of Ahitub and Ahimelech son of Abiathar were priests; Seraiah was secretary; 18Benaiah son of Jehoiada was over[b] the Cherethites and the Pelethites; and David's sons were priests.

8.1–18: David's wars. 1: The meaning of *Methegammah* is uncertain. **2:** The *Moabites* lived on the other side of the Dead Sea from Israel. **3:** *Zobah* was an Aramean (Syrian) city-state. The word *restore* may also be read as "leave." Thus, David, rather than *Hadadezer,* may have been traveling to the Euphrates to erect a monument. **4:** David *hamstrung* the horses he could not use to keep someone else from using them against him. Joshua was commanded to do the same thing with the chariot horses he captured (Josh 11.6). This suggests that the Israelites did not yet use chariots extensively in battle. **5:** *Twenty-two thousand* may be twenty-two military units, which numbered much less than a thousand. **9:** *Hamath* was an important city-state north of Syria. **10:** *Joram,* the son of *King Toi,* has an Israelite name! **13–14:** *Edom* was the southernmost country east of the Jordan. **15–17:** The exact functions of the *recorder* and the *secretary* in David's administration are unknown. **18:** The *Cherethites and Pelethites* were the royal bodyguard (23.23) and were related to if not identical with the Philistines. Apparently, in David's day the king and his sons could serve as priests.

9 David asked, "Is there still anyone left of the house of Saul to whom I may show kindness for Jonathan's sake?" 2Now there was a servant of the house of Saul whose name was Ziba, and he was summoned to David. The king said to him, "Are you Ziba?" And he said, "At your service!" 3The king said, "Is there anyone remaining of the house of Saul to whom I may show the kindness of God?" Ziba said to the king, "There remains a son of Jonathan; he is crippled in his feet." 4The king said to him, "Where is he?" Ziba said to the king, "He is in the house of Machir son of Ammiel, at Lo-debar." 5Then King David sent and brought him from the house of Machir son of Ammiel, at Lo-debar. 6Mephibosheth[c] son of Jonathan son of Saul came to David, and fell on his face and did obeisance. David said, "Mephibosheth!"[c] He answered, "I am your servant." 7David said to him, "Do not be afraid, for I will show you kindness for the sake of your father Jonathan; I will restore to you all the land of your grandfather Saul, and you yourself shall eat at my table always." 8He did obeisance and said, "What is your servant, that you should look upon a dead dog such as I?"

9 Then the king summoned Saul's servant Ziba, and said to him, "All that belonged to Saul and to all his house I have given to your master's grandson. 10You and your sons and your servants shall till the land for him, and shall bring in the produce, so that your master's grandson may have food to eat; but your master's grandson Mephibosheth[c] shall always eat at my table." Now Ziba had fifteen sons and twenty servants. 11Then Ziba said to the king, "According to all that my lord the king commands his servant, so your servant will do." Mephibosheth[c] ate at David's[d] table, like one of the king's sons. 12Mephibosheth[c] had a young son whose name was Mica. And all who lived in Ziba's house became Mephibosheth's[e] servants. 13Mephibosheth[c] lived in Jerusalem, for he always ate at the king's table. Now he was lame in both his feet.

9.1–13: Jonathan's son. 1: The story in 21.1–14 originally preceded this one. It tells of the execution of a group of Saul's sons and grandsons, which provides background to David's question, *Is there still anyone left of the house of Saul?* David's *kindness for Jonathan's sake* fulfills the promise of loyalty that he made

a Gk: Heb *returned from striking down eighteen thousand Arameans*   b Syr Tg Vg 20.23; 1 Chr 18.17: Heb lacks *was over*   c Or *Merib-baal:* See 4.4 note
d Gk: Heb *my*   e Or *Merib-baal's:* See 4.4 note

to Jonathan in several places in 1 Sam. **3:** *Crippled in his feet:* See comment on 4.4. This handicap made him unable to go to war and therefore unsuitable to be king. **4:** *Machir* became a loyal supporter of David (17.27). *Lo-debar* was a northern Israelite city east of the Jordan. **6:** *Mephibosheth's* name was originally Merib-baal. **7:** Eating at the king's table was a sign of favor. It also gave David the chance to keep a close watch on Merib-baal, who was still heir to Saul's kingdom. **8:** *Dead dog* was a term of self-reproach. **9–13:** While he lived in Jerusalem with David, Merib-baal would receive the income from Saul's lands, which Ziba and his family would work.

10 Some time afterward, the king of the Ammonites died, and his son Hanun succeeded him. ²David said, "I will deal loyally with Hanun son of Nahash, just as his father dealt loyally with me." So David sent envoys to console him concerning his father. When David's envoys came into the land of the Ammonites, ³the princes of the Ammonites said to their lord Hanun, "Do you really think that David is honoring your father just because he has sent messengers with condolences to you? Has not David sent his envoys to you to search the city, to spy it out, and to overthrow it?" ⁴So Hanun seized David's envoys, shaved off half the beard of each, cut off their garments in the middle at their hips, and sent them away. ⁵When David was told, he sent to meet them, for the men were greatly ashamed. The king said, "Remain at Jericho until your beards have grown, and then return."

6 When the Ammonites saw that they had become odious to David, the Ammonites sent and hired the Arameans of Beth-rehob and the Arameans of Zobah, twenty thousand foot soldiers, as well as the king of Maacah, one thousand men, and the men of Tob, twelve thousand men. ⁷When David heard of it, he sent Joab and all the army with the warriors. ⁸The Ammonites came out and drew up in battle array at the entrance of the gate; but the Arameans of Zobah and of Rehob, and the men of Tob and Maacah, were by themselves in the open country.

9 When Joab saw that the battle was set against him both in front and in the rear, he chose some of the picked men of Israel, and

arrayed them against the Arameans; ¹⁰the rest of his men he put in the charge of his brother Abishai, and he arrayed them against the Ammonites. ¹¹He said, "If the Arameans are too strong for me, then you shall help me; but if the Ammonites are too strong for you, then I will come and help you. ¹²Be strong, and let us be courageous for the sake of our people, and for the cities of our God; and may the LORD do what seems good to him." ¹³So Joab and the people who were with him moved forward into battle against the Arameans; and they fled before him. ¹⁴When the Ammonites saw that the Arameans fled, they likewise fled before Abishai, and entered the city. Then Joab returned from fighting against the Ammonites, and came to Jerusalem.

15 But when the Arameans saw that they had been defeated by Israel, they gathered themselves together. ¹⁶Hadadezer sent and brought out the Arameans who were beyond the Euphrates; and they came to Helam, with Shobach the commander of the army of Hadadezer at their head. ¹⁷When it was told David, he gathered all Israel together, and crossed the Jordan, and came to Helam. The Arameans arrayed themselves against David and fought with him. ¹⁸The Arameans fled before Israel; and David killed of the Arameans seven hundred chariot teams, and forty thousand horsemen,ᵃ and wounded Shobach the commander of their army, so that he died there. ¹⁹When all the kings who were servants of Hadadezer saw that they had been defeated by Israel, they made peace with Israel, and became subject to them. So the Arameans were afraid to help the Ammonites any more.

10.1–19: The Ammonite war. 2: *Nahash* was Saul's enemy in 1 Sam 10.27b–11.15. He and David had a treaty. *Hanun's* actions here indicate that Israel was the superior partner in the treaty or that David was trying to make Israel the superior partner. **4:** *Hanun's* treatment of the *envoys* is symbolic emasculation. The *beard* was a symbol of masculinity. Cutting off *their garments* below the waist was a symbolic castration. **5:** *Jericho* was the closest Israelite city west of the Jor-

a 1 Chr 19.18 and some Gk Mss read *foot soldiers*

dan opposite Ammon. **6:** *Beth-rehob* and *Zobah* were Aramean (Syrian) city-states. The word for *thousand* may refer to a much smaller military unit. *Maacah* and *Tob* were states in northern Palestine east of the Jordan. **9:** *Joab* made a tactical mistake that led to having enemies on two opposing sides. **12:** Joab encouraged his men to fight for the *cities* that Israel claimed east of the Jordan.

11 In the spring of the year, the time when kings go out to battle, David sent Joab with his officers and all Israel with him; they ravaged the Ammonites, and besieged Rabbah. But David remained at Jerusalem.

2 It happened, late one afternoon, when David rose from his couch and was walking about on the roof of the king's house, that he saw from the roof a woman bathing; the woman was very beautiful. 3 David sent someone to inquire about the woman. It was reported, "This is Bathsheba daughter of Eliam, the wife of Uriah the Hittite." 4 So David sent messengers to get her, and she came to him, and he lay with her. (Now she was purifying herself after her period.) Then she returned to her house. 5 The woman conceived; and she sent and told David, "I am pregnant."

6 So David sent word to Joab, "Send me Uriah the Hittite." And Joab sent Uriah to David. 7 When Uriah came to him, David asked how Joab and the people fared, and how the war was going. 8 Then David said to Uriah, "Go down to your house, and wash your feet." Uriah went out of the king's house, and there followed him a present from the king. 9 But Uriah slept at the entrance of the king's house with all the servants of his lord, and did not go down to his house. 10 When they told David, "Uriah did not go down to his house," David said to Uriah, "You have just come from a journey. Why did you not go down to your house?" 11 Uriah said to David, "The ark and Israel and Judah remain in booths;[a] and my lord Joab and the servants of my lord are camping in the open field; shall I then go to my house, to eat and to drink, and to lie with my wife? As you live, and as your soul lives, I will not do such a thing." 12 Then David said to

Uriah, "Remain here today also, and tomorrow I will send you back." So Uriah remained in Jerusalem that day. On the next day, 13 David invited him to eat and drink in his presence and made him drunk; and in the evening he went out to lie on his couch with the servants of his lord, but he did not go down to his house.

14 In the morning David wrote a letter to Joab, and sent it by the hand of Uriah. 15 In the letter he wrote, "Set Uriah in the forefront of the hardest fighting, and then draw back from him, so that he may be struck down and die." 16 As Joab was besieging the city, he assigned Uriah to the place where he knew there were valiant warriors. 17 The men of the city came out and fought with Joab; and some of the servants of David among the people fell. Uriah the Hittite was killed as well. 18 Then Joab sent and told David all the news about the fighting; 19 and he instructed the messenger, "When you have finished telling the king all the news about the fighting, 20 then, if the king's anger rises, and if he says to you, 'Why did you go so near the city to fight? Did you not know that they would shoot from the wall? 21 Who killed Abimelech son of Jerubbaal?[b] Did not a woman throw an upper millstone on him from the wall, so that he died at Thebez? Why did you go so near the wall?' then you shall say, 'Your servant Uriah the Hittite is dead too.' "

22 So the messenger went, and came and told David all that Joab had sent him to tell. 23 The messenger said to David, "The men gained an advantage over us, and came out against us in the field; but we drove them back to the entrance of the gate. 24 Then the archers shot at your servants from the wall; some of the king's servants are dead; and your servant Uriah the Hittite is dead also." 25 David said to the messenger, "Thus you shall say to Joab, 'Do not let this matter trouble you, for the sword devours now one and now another; press your attack on the city, and overthrow it.' And encourage him."

26 When the wife of Uriah heard that her husband was dead, she made lamentation for

a Or *at Succoth*   *b* Gk Syr Judg 7.1: Heb *Jerubbesheth* him. 27When the mourning was over, David sent and brought her to his house, and she became his wife, and bore him a son.

11.1–27: David and Bathsheba. 1: This story is set a year after the events in the previous chapter. It is not clear why *David remained at Jerusalem,* but the story in 21.15–17 may lie in the background. **2:** David had been taking an afternoon nap on *the roof of the king's house* where it was cool. From there he was able to look down into the courtyard of surrounding houses where he saw the *woman bathing. Uriah* was one of David's best soldiers, according to 23.39. **4:** Bathsheba *was purifying herself after her period* by bathing according to Lev 15.19–28. She was at the most fertile time of her cycle when she slept with David. This also makes it clear that her child must be David's, not Uriah's. **7:** It must have seemed strange to Uriah to be called back from battle for a personal audience with the king only to be asked the most general questions. Perhaps this raised his suspicions and caused him to be on his best behavior. The *people* are the army. **8:** *Wash your feet* is a euphemism* for sexual intercourse. In Hebrew idiom, the *feet* often refer to the genitals. **9:** As a pious soldier who is consecrated for war (see 1 Sam 21.5), Uriah refuses to sleep with his wife. **14:** David has confidence enough in Uriah's loyalty to send his death warrant by his own hand knowing that Uriah, even if he could read, would not read it. **16–21:** Joab also uses Uriah's death to cover up his mistake in drawing too close to the city wall. The story of *Abimelech* (v. 21) is in Judg 9. **27:** This verse provides a transition to the continuation of the story in the next chapter.

---

12 But the thing that David had done displeased the LORD, 1and the LORD sent Nathan to David. He came to him, and said to him, "There were two men in a certain city, the one rich and the other poor. 2The rich man had very many flocks and herds; 3but the poor man had nothing but one little ewe lamb, which he had bought. He brought it up, and it grew up with him and with his children; it used to eat of his meager fare, and drink from his cup, and lie in his bosom, and it was like a daughter to him. 4Now there came a traveler to the rich man, and he was loath to take one of his own flock or herd to prepare for the wayfarer who had come to him, but he took the poor

man's lamb, and prepared that for the guest who had come to him." 5Then David's anger was greatly kindled against the man. He said to Nathan, "As the LORD lives, the man who has done this deserves to die; 6he shall restore the lamb fourfold, because he did this thing, and because he had no pity."

7 Nathan said to David, "You are the man! Thus says the LORD, the God of Israel: I anointed you king over Israel, and I rescued you from the hand of Saul; 8I gave you your master's house, and your master's wives into your bosom, and gave you the house of Israel and of Judah; and if that had been too little, I would have added as much more. 9Why have you despised the word of the LORD, to do what is evil in his sight? You have struck down Uriah the Hittite with the sword, and have taken his wife to be your wife, and have killed him with the sword of the Ammonites. 10Now therefore the sword shall never depart from your house, for you have despised me, and have taken the wife of Uriah the Hittite to be your wife. 11Thus says the LORD: I will raise up trouble against you from within your own house; and I will take your wives before your eyes, and give them to your neighbor, and he shall lie with your wives in the sight of this very sun. 12For you did it secretly; but I will do this thing before all Israel, and before the sun." 13David said to Nathan, "I have sinned against the LORD." Nathan said to David, "Now the LORD has put away your sin; you shall not die. 14Nevertheless, because by this deed you have utterly scorned the LORD,ᵃ the child that is born to you shall die." 15Then Nathan went to his house.

The LORD struck the child that Uriah's wife bore to David, and it became very ill. 16David therefore pleaded with God for the child; David fasted, and went in and lay all night on the ground. 17The elders of his house stood beside him, urging him to rise from the ground; but he would not, nor did he eat food with them. 18On the seventh day the child died. And the servants of David were afraid to tell him that the child was

---

a Ancient scribal tradition: Compare 1 Sam 25.22 note: Heb *scorned the enemies of the* LORD dead; for they said, "While the child was still alive, we spoke to him, and he did not listen to us; how then can we tell him the child is dead? He may do himself some harm." [19] But when David saw that his servants were whispering together, he perceived that the child was dead; and David said to his servants, "Is the child dead?" They said, "He is dead."

20 Then David rose from the ground, washed, anointed himself, and changed his clothes. He went into the house of the LORD, and worshiped; he then went to his own house; and when he asked, they set food before him and he ate. [21] Then his servants said to him, "What is this thing that you have done? You fasted and wept for the child while it was alive; but when the child died, you rose and ate food." [22] He said, "While the child was still alive, I fasted and wept; for I said, 'Who knows? The LORD may be gracious to me, and the child may live.' [23] But now he is dead; why should I fast? Can I bring him back again? I shall go to him, but he will not return to me."

24 Then David consoled his wife Bathsheba, and went to her, and lay with her; and she bore a son, and he named him Solomon. The LORD loved him, [25] and sent a message by the prophet Nathan; so he named him Jedidiah,[a] because of the LORD.

26 Now Joab fought against Rabbah of the Ammonites, and took the royal city. [27] Joab sent messengers to David, and said, "I have fought against Rabbah; moreover, I have taken the water city. [28] Now, then, gather the rest of the people together, and encamp against the city, and take it; or I myself will take the city, and it will be called by my name." [29] So David gathered all the people together and went to Rabbah, and fought against it and took it. [30] He took the crown of Milcom[b] from his head; the weight of it was a talent of gold, and in it was a precious stone; and it was placed on David's head. He also brought forth the spoil of the city, a very great amount. [31] He brought out the people who were in it, and set them to work with saws and iron picks and iron axes, or sent them to the brickworks. Thus did he to all the cities of the Ammonites. Then David and all the people returned to Jerusalem.

12.1–31: David's punishment. 1–6: Nathan brings a legal case before David. As king he was responsible for ensuring the rights of the poor. The fourfold restoration mentioned in v. 6 is prescribed in Ex 22.1. Other textual witnesses have "sevenfold." **8:** There is some textual support for reading "daughter(s)" instead of *house* in this verse. The point in any case is that David had many women as wives and concubines.* But like the rich man in Nathan's parable,* he stole what belonged to his poor neighbor. The mention of *your master's wives* assumes that David took over Saul's harem. **11–12:** These verses allude to Absalom's revolt, specifically his deed in 16.20–23. **13–18:** David's sin is transferred to his newborn son, who then dies because of it. **20:** The *house of the LORD* is the Temple* in Jerusalem, which had not yet been built. This appears, therefore, to be an anachronism.* **24–25:** *Solomon* means "his replacement." He was a replacement for the dead child. But his name *Jedidiah* ("beloved of Yahweh"), which does not occur for Solomon anywhere else, hints that he will replace David (whose name means "beloved") as king. **26–29:** Joab captured the citadel and the water supply of Rabbah, the Ammonite capital, so that David's conquest of the rest of the city was fairly simple. **30:** *Milcom* was the national god of the Ammonites. *A talent* was about 75 pounds.

13 Some time passed. David's son Absalom had a beautiful sister whose name was Tamar; and David's son Amnon fell in love with her. [2] Amnon was so tormented that he made himself ill because of his sister Tamar, for she was a virgin and it seemed impossible to Amnon to do anything to her. [3] But Amnon had a friend whose name was Jonadab, the son of David's brother Shimeah; and Jonadab was a very crafty man. [4] He said to him, "O son of the king, why are you so haggard morning after morning? Will you not tell me?" Amnon said to him, "I love Tamar, my brother Absalom's sister." [5] Jonadab said to him, "Lie down on your bed, and pretend to be ill; and when your father comes to see you, say to him, 'Let my sister Tamar come and give me something to eat, and prepare the food in my sight, so that I may see it and eat it from her

a That is *Beloved of the* LORD　　*b* Gk See 1 Kings 11.5, 33: Heb *their kings* hand.' " 6So Amnon lay down, and pretended to be ill; and when the king came to see him, Amnon said to the king, "Please let my sister Tamar come and make a couple of cakes in my sight, so that I may eat from her hand."

7 Then David sent home to Tamar, saying, "Go to your brother Amnon's house, and prepare food for him." 8So Tamar went to her brother Amnon's house, where he was lying down. She took dough, kneaded it, made cakes in his sight, and baked the cakes. 9Then she took the pan and set them*a* out before him, but he refused to eat. Amnon said, "Send out everyone from me." So everyone went out from him. 10Then Amnon said to Tamar, "Bring the food into the chamber, so that I may eat from your hand." So Tamar took the cakes she had made, and brought them into the chamber to Amnon her brother. 11But when she brought them near him to eat, he took hold of her, and said to her, "Come, lie with me, my sister." 12She answered him, "No, my brother, do not force me; for such a thing is not done in Israel; do not do anything so vile! 13As for me, where could I carry my shame? And as for you, you would be as one of the scoundrels in Israel. Now therefore, I beg you, speak to the king; for he will not withhold me from you." 14But he would not listen to her; and being stronger than she, he forced her and lay with her.

15 Then Amnon was seized with a very great loathing for her; indeed, his loathing was even greater than the lust he had felt for her. Amnon said to her, "Get out!" 16But she said to him, "No, my brother;*b* for this wrong in sending me away is greater than the other that you did to me." But he would not listen to her. 17He called the young man who served him and said, "Put this woman out of my presence, and bolt the door after her." 18(Now she was wearing a long robe with sleeves; for this is how the virgin daughters of the king were clothed in earlier times.*c*) So his servant put her out, and bolted the door after her. 19But Tamar put ashes on her head, and tore the long robe that she was wearing; she put her hand on her head, and went away, crying aloud as she went.

20 Her brother Absalom said to her, "Has Amnon your brother been with you? Be quiet for now, my sister; he is your brother; do not take this to heart." So Tamar remained, a desolate woman, in her brother Absalom's house. 21When King David heard of all these things, he became very angry, but he would not punish his son Amnon, because he loved him, for he was his firstborn.*d* 22But Absalom spoke to Amnon neither good nor bad; for Absalom hated Amnon, because he had raped his sister Tamar.

13.1–22: The rape of Tamar. 1: Tamar was Absalom's full *sister* but Amnon's half-sister. David was the father of all three, but Tamar's and Absalom's mother was different from Amnon's. **2:** As a virgin daughter of the king, Tamar was probably guarded and therefore it *seemed impossible to Amnon to do anything to her.* **6:** The word for *cakes* is similar to the Hebrew word for "heart." This may describe their shape. It also suggests Amnon's love. **11:** The term *my sister* reflects the kinship of Amnon to Tamar. It is also common in ancient love poetry and expresses his sexual desire (compare Song 4.9–10; 5.1). **12:** *Such a thing* may refer to incest or rape or both. **13:** Tamar suggests that David would allow their marriage despite its incestuous nature. In part, at least, she is trying to buy time. **16:** Exodus 22.16 and Deut 22.28–29 required marriage in similar cases. Tamar may have such laws in mind when she says that in sending her away Amnon is committing a *greater* wrong than the rape itself. **17:** Having robbed Tamar of her virginity, Amnon takes her identity as well, contemptuously calling her *this woman.* **18:** The exact nature of the *long robe with sleeves* is unknown. The same expression is used for Joseph's garment in Gen 37.3. **19:** Putting ashes on the head and tearing the clothes were signs of grief, though Tamar may also have torn *the long robe* worn by the king's virgin daughters because it was no longer appropriate. **20:** By *desolate* is meant unmarried. **22:** *Neither good nor bad* means not at all. It indicates Absalom's silence and his self-restraint.

23 After two full years Absalom had sheepshearers at Baal-hazor, which is near Ephraim, and Absalom invited all the king's

a Heb *and poured*   *b* Cn Compare Gk Vg: Meaning of Heb uncertain   *c* Cn: Heb *were clothed in robes* *d* Q Ms Gk: MT lacks *but he would not punish . . . firstborn* sons. 24Absalom came to the king, and said, "Your servant has sheepshearers; will the king and his servants please go with your servant?" 25But the king said to Absalom, "No, my son, let us not all go, or else we will be burdensome to you." He pressed him, but he would not go but gave him his blessing. 26Then Absalom said, "If not, please let my brother Amnon go with us." The king said to him, "Why should he go with you?" 27But Absalom pressed him until he let Amnon and all the king's sons go with him. Absalom made a feast like a king's feast.*a* 28Then Absalom commanded his servants, "Watch when Amnon's heart is merry with wine, and when I say to you, 'Strike Amnon,' then kill him. Do not be afraid; have I not myself commanded you? Be courageous and valiant." 29So the servants of Absalom did to Amnon as Absalom had commanded. Then all the king's sons rose, and each mounted his mule and fled.

30 While they were on the way, the report came to David that Absalom had killed all the king's sons, and not one of them was left. 31The king rose, tore his garments, and lay on the ground; and all his servants who were standing by tore their garments. 32But Jonadab, the son of David's brother Shimeah, said, "Let not my lord suppose that they have killed all the young men the king's sons; Amnon alone is dead. This has been determined by Absalom from the day Amnon*b* raped his sister Tamar. 33Now therefore, do not let my lord the king take it to heart, as if all the king's sons were dead; for Amnon alone is dead."

34 But Absalom fled. When the young man who kept watch looked up, he saw many people coming from the Horonaim road*c* by the side of the mountain. 35Jonadab said to the king, "See, the king's sons have come; as your servant said, so it has come about." 36As soon as he had finished speaking, the king's sons arrived, and raised their voices and wept; and the king and all his servants also wept very bitterly.

37 But Absalom fled, and went to Talmai son of Ammihud, king of Geshur. David mourned for his son day after day. 38Absalom, having fled to Geshur, stayed there three years. 39And the heart of*d* the king went out, yearning for Absalom; for he was now consoled over the death of Amnon.

13.23–39: Amnon's murder. 23: Sheepshearing was a time of celebration. **27:** The *feast* was a drinking bout. **29:** David and his sons rode on *mules* (18.9; 1 Kings 1.33). **30–33:** David initially thought that Absalom had killed all the king's sons, which would make sense if he were attempting a coup. But his intention at this point is purely revenge against Amnon. The clever *Jonadab* appears as a false friend to Amnon. **37:** *Talmai*, the *king of Geshur*, was Absalom's maternal grandfather (3.3). **39:** The first part of this verse may mean that David was tired of marching out in pursuit of Absalom rather than that he yearned for him. This would explain David's reluctance in the next chapter to allow Absalom back into his presence.

14 Now Joab son of Zeruiah perceived that the king's mind was on Absalom. 2Joab sent to Tekoa and brought from there a wise woman. He said to her, "Pretend to be a mourner; put on mourning garments, do not anoint yourself with oil, but behave like a woman who has been mourning many days for the dead. 3Go to the king and speak to him as follows." And Joab put the words into her mouth.

4 When the woman of Tekoa came to the king, she fell on her face to the ground and did obeisance, and said, "Help, O king!" 5The king asked her, "What is your trouble?" She answered, "Alas, I am a widow; my husband is dead. 6Your servant had two sons, and they fought with one another in the field; there was no one to part them, and one struck the other and killed him. 7Now the whole family has risen against your servant. They say, 'Give up the man who struck his brother, so that we may kill him for the life of his brother whom he murdered, even if we destroy the heir as well.' Thus they would quench my one remaining ember, and leave to my husband neither name nor remnant on the face of the earth."

8 Then the king said to the woman, "Go to your house, and I will give orders con-

a Gk Compare Q Ms: MT lacks *Absalom made a feast like a king's feast*   b Heb *he*   c Cn Compare Gk: Heb *the road behind him*   d Q Ms Gk: MT *And David* cerning you." ⁹The woman of Tekoa said to the king, "On me be the guilt, my lord the king, and on my father's house; let the king and his throne be guiltless." ¹⁰The king said, "If anyone says anything to you, bring him to me, and he shall never touch you again." ¹¹Then she said, "Please, may the king keep the LORD your God in mind, so that the avenger of blood may kill no more, and my son not be destroyed." He said, "As the LORD lives, not one hair of your son shall fall to the ground."

14.1–33: Absalom's return. 1: The fact that *the king's mind was on Absalom* does not mean that he was now favorably inclined toward Absalom, as this story makes clear. **2:** *Tekoa* was a village south of Bethlehem. Perhaps David took an interest in this case because the woman was from his home territory. *Wise* also means skilled. This woman was a skilled actress. **8–11:** David grants the woman's request and swears by the LORD that her one remaining son will not be harmed. The woman will urge David to apply this oath to his situation with Absalom. Since David's ruling is contrary to the customary punishment, the woman accepts any guilt that David may incur (v. 9).

---

12 Then the woman said, "Please let your servant speak a word to my lord the king." He said, "Speak." ¹³The woman said, "Why then have you planned such a thing against the people of God? For in giving this decision the king convicts himself, inasmuch as the king does not bring his banished one home again. ¹⁴We must all die; we are like water spilled on the ground, which cannot be gathered up. But God will not take away a life; he will devise plans so as not to keep an outcast banished forever from his presence.ᵃ ¹⁵Now I have come to say this to my lord the king because the people have made me afraid; your servant thought, 'I will speak to the king; it may be that the king will perform the request of his servant. ¹⁶For the king will hear, and deliver his servant from the hand of the man who would cut both me and my son off from the heritage of God.' ¹⁷Your servant thought, 'The word of my lord the king will set me at rest'; for my lord the king is like the angel of God, discerning good and evil. The LORD your God be with you!"

18 Then the king answered the woman, "Do not withhold from me anything I ask you." The woman said, "Let my lord the king speak." ¹⁹The king said, "Is the hand of Joab with you in all this?" The woman answered and said, "As surely as you live, my lord the king, one cannot turn right or left from anything that my lord the king has said. For it was your servant Joab who commanded me; it was he who put all these words into the mouth of your servant. ²⁰In order to change the course of affairs your servant Joab did this. But my lord has wisdom like the wisdom of the angel of God to know all things that are on the earth."

21 Then the king said to Joab, "Very well, I grant this; go, bring back the young man Absalom." ²²Joab prostrated himself with his face to the ground and did obeisance, and blessed the king; and Joab said, "Today your servant knows that I have found favor in your sight, my lord the king, in that the king has granted the request of his servant." ²³So Joab set off, went to Geshur, and brought Absalom to Jerusalem. ²⁴The king said, "Let him go to his own house; he is not to come into my presence." So Absalom went to his own house, and did not come into the king's presence.

25 Now in all Israel there was no one to be praised so much for his beauty as Absalom; from the sole of his foot to the crown of his head there was no blemish in him. ²⁶When he cut the hair of his head (for at the end of every year he used to cut it; when it was heavy on him, he cut it), he weighed the hair of his head, two hundred shekels by the king's weight. ²⁷There were born to Absalom three sons, and one daughter whose name was Tamar; she was a beautiful woman.

28 So Absalom lived two full years in Jerusalem, without coming into the king's presence. ²⁹Then Absalom sent for Joab to send him to the king; but Joab would not come to him. He sent a second time, but Joab would not come. ³⁰Then he said to his servants, "Look, Joab's field is next to mine,

ᵃ Meaning of Heb uncertain

and he has barley there; go and set it on fire." So Absalom's servants set the field on fire. 31Then Joab rose and went to Absalom at his house, and said to him, "Why have your servants set my field on fire?" 32Absalom answered Joab, "Look, I sent word to you: Come here, that I may send you to the king with the question, 'Why have I come from Geshur? It would be better for me to be there still.' Now let me go into the king's presence; if there is guilt in me, let him kill me!" 33Then Joab went to the king and told him; and he summoned Absalom. So he came to the king and prostrated himself with his face to the ground before the king; and the king kissed Absalom.

14.12–33. 14: Amnon is dead and cannot be brought to life again, but David can accept Absalom, who is still alive. 15–17: These verses are out of place; the woman continues to plead for her son, but David has already rendered his decision. They probably originally went after v. 7. *The man who would cut both me and my son off* is the blood avenger, a member of the clan* appointed to avenge the death of the murdered son. *The heritage of God* refers not only to the land of Israel but to its people. 21–24: David allows Absalom to return but refuses to see him personally. 26: *Two hundred shekels** would be over five pounds, an extraordinary amount of hair. 27: Absalom named his daughter after his sister, *Tamar* (ch. 13). 28–33: This episode shows Absalom's rash nature and suggests that Joab may have held a grudge against him.

15 After this Absalom got himself a chariot and horses, and fifty men to run ahead of him. 2Absalom used to rise early and stand beside the road into the gate; and when anyone brought a suit before the king for judgment, Absalom would call out and say, "From what city are you?" When the person said, "Your servant is of such and such a tribe in Israel," 3Absalom would say, "See, your claims are good and right; but there is no one deputed by the king to hear you." 4Absalom said moreover, "If only I were judge in the land! Then all who had a suit or cause might come to me, and I would give them justice." 5Whenever people came near to do obeisance to him, he would put out his hand and take hold of them, and kiss

them. 6Thus Absalom did to every Israelite who came to the king for judgment; so Absalom stole the hearts of the people of Israel.

7 At the end of four*a* years Absalom said to the king, "Please let me go to Hebron and pay the vow that I have made to the LORD. 8For your servant made a vow while I lived at Geshur in Aram: If the LORD will indeed bring me back to Jerusalem, then I will worship the LORD in Hebron."*b* 9The king said to him, "Go in peace." So he got up, and went to Hebron. 10But Absalom sent secret messengers throughout all the tribes of Israel, saying, "As soon as you hear the sound of the trumpet, then shout: Absalom has become king at Hebron!" 11Two hundred men from Jerusalem went with Absalom; they were invited guests, and they went in their innocence, knowing nothing of the matter. 12While Absalom was offering the sacrifices, he sent for*c* Ahithophel the Gilonite, David's counselor, from his city Giloh. The conspiracy grew in strength, and the people with Absalom kept increasing.

15.1–12: The revolt begins. 1: The *chariot and horses* and *fifty men to run ahead* were trappings of kingship (1 Kings 1.5). The fifty men were probably a royal bodyguard. 5: Absalom would not allow anyone to bow or *do obeisance to him* but fashioned himself as a "man of the people." 6: *Stole the hearts* is translated "deceived" in Gen 31.20 and is appropriate here also. 7–10: *Hebron* was the capital of Judah, where David had been made king of both Judah and Israel and had ruled Judah for seven years. Absalom was mirroring his father's rise by declaring himself king in Hebron. His revolt, however, was not limited to Judah but spread *throughout all the tribes of Israel* (v. 10). 8: *Geshur* was the Aramean city-state where Absalom fled after killing Amnon (13.37–39). 12: On the great wisdom of *David's counselor, Ahithophel*, see 16.15–23.

13 A messenger came to David, saying, "The hearts of the Israelites have gone after Absalom." 14Then David said to all his officials who were with him at Jerusalem, "Get up! Let us flee, or there will be no escape for us from Absalom. Hurry, or he will soon

a Gk Syr: Heb *forty*   *b* Gk Mss: Heb lacks *in Hebron*
c Or *he sent*

overtake us, and bring disaster down upon us, and attack the city with the edge of the sword." 15The king's officials said to the king, "Your servants are ready to do whatever our lord the king decides." 16So the king left, followed by all his household, except ten concubines whom he left behind to look after the house. 17The king left, followed by all the people; and they stopped at the last house. 18All his officials passed by him; and all the Cherethites, and all the Pelethites, and all the six hundred Gittites who had followed him from Gath, passed on before the king.

19 Then the king said to Ittai the Gittite, "Why are you also coming with us? Go back, and stay with the king; for you are a foreigner, and also an exile from your home. 20You came only yesterday, and shall I today make you wander about with us, while I go wherever I can? Go back, and take your kinsfolk with you; and may the LORD show*a* steadfast love and faithfulness to you." 21But Ittai answered the king, "As the LORD lives, and as my lord the king lives, wherever my lord the king may be, whether for death or for life, there also your servant will be." 22David said to Ittai, "Go then, march on." So Ittai the Gittite marched on, with all his men and all the little ones who were with him. 23The whole country wept aloud as all the people passed by; the king crossed the Wadi Kidron, and all the people moved on toward the wilderness.

24 Abiathar came up, and Zadok also, with all the Levites, carrying the ark of the covenant of God. They set down the ark of God, until the people had all passed out of the city. 25Then the king said to Zadok, "Carry the ark of God back into the city. If I find favor in the eyes of the LORD, he will bring me back and let me see both it and the place where it stays. 26But if he says, 'I take no pleasure in you,' here I am, let him do to me what seems good to him." 27The king also said to the priest Zadok, "Look,*b* go back to the city in peace, you and Abiathar,*c* with your two sons, Ahimaaz your son, and Jonathan son of Abiathar. 28See, I will wait at the fords of the wilderness until word comes from you to inform me." 29So Zadok and Abi-

athar carried the ark of God back to Jerusalem, and they remained there.

30 But David went up the ascent of the Mount of Olives, weeping as he went, with his head covered and walking barefoot; and all the people who were with him covered their heads and went up, weeping as they went. 31David was told that Ahithophel was among the conspirators with Absalom. And David said, "O LORD, I pray you, turn the counsel of Ahithophel into foolishness."

32 When David came to the summit, where God was worshiped, Hushai the Archite came to meet him with his coat torn and earth on his head. 33David said to him, "If you go on with me, you will be a burden to me. 34But if you return to the city and say to Absalom, 'I will be your servant, O king; as I have been your father's servant in time past, so now I will be your servant,' then you will defeat for me the counsel of Ahithophel. 35The priests Zadok and Abiathar will be with you there. So whatever you hear from the king's house, tell it to the priests Zadok and Abiathar. 36Their two sons are with them there, Zadok's son Ahimaaz and Abiathar's son Jonathan; and by them you shall report to me everything you hear." 37So Hushai, David's friend, came into the city, just as Absalom was entering Jerusalem.

15.13–16.14: David flees Jerusalem. 15.16: *Concubines* were female slaves used for sexual purposes. **17:** *The last house* refers to the last house on the outskirts of Jerusalem. **18:** *The Cherethites* and *Pelethites* were related to or identical with Philistines who served as the royal bodyguard. *Gittites* were Philistines from Gath. All of these groups had followed David from his days with the Philistines. **23:** The *Wadi Kidron* is the valley between Jerusalem and the Mount of Olives. David is heading east toward the Jordan. **24:** *Abiathar* and *Zadok* were David's two priests. **31–34:** David was disheartened to learn that his wise adviser, Ahithophel (see 16.15–23) had joined Absalom. As he walked up the *Mount of Olives* (v. 30), he prayed for help against Ahithophel. His prayer was answered at the *summit* when he met *Hushai,* who would help him defeat

a Gk Compare 2.6: Heb lacks *may the LORD show*
b Gk: Heb *Are you a seer* or *Do you see?*   *c* Cn: Heb lacks *and Abiathar*

Ahithophel's advice. **37:** *David's friend* may have been a title for an intimate adviser or "best man."

16

When David had passed a little beyond the summit, Ziba the servant of Mephibosheth[a] met him, with a couple of donkeys saddled, carrying two hundred loaves of bread, one hundred bunches of raisins, one hundred of summer fruits, and one skin of wine. 2The king said to Ziba, "Why have you brought these?" Ziba answered, "The donkeys are for the king's household to ride, the bread and summer fruit for the young men to eat, and the wine is for those to drink who faint in the wilderness." 3The king said, "And where is your master's son?" Ziba said to the king, "He remains in Jerusalem; for he said, 'Today the house of Israel will give me back my grandfather's kingdom.'" 4Then the king said to Ziba, "All that belonged to Mephibosheth[a] is now yours." Ziba said, "I do obeisance; let me find favor in your sight, my lord the king."

5 When King David came to Bahurim, a man of the family of the house of Saul came out whose name was Shimei son of Gera; he came out cursing. 6He threw stones at David and at all the servants of King David; now all the people and all the warriors were on his right and on his left. 7Shimei shouted while he cursed, "Out! Out! Murderer! Scoundrel! 8The LORD has avenged on all of you the blood of the house of Saul, in whose place you have reigned; and the LORD has given the kingdom into the hand of your son Absalom. See, disaster has overtaken you; for you are a man of blood."

9 Then Abishai son of Zeruiah said to the king, "Why should this dead dog curse my lord the king? Let me go over and take off his head." 10But the king said, "What have I to do with you, you sons of Zeruiah? If he is cursing because the LORD has said to him, 'Curse David,' who then shall say, 'Why have you done so?'" 11David said to Abishai and to all his servants, "My own son seeks my life; how much more now may this Benjaminite! Let him alone, and let him curse; for the LORD has bidden him. 12It may be that the LORD will look on my distress,[b] and the LORD will repay me with good for this curs-

ing of me today." 13So David and his men went on the road, while Shimei went along on the hillside opposite him and cursed as he went, throwing stones and flinging dust at him. 14The king and all the people who were with him arrived weary at the Jordan;[c] and there he refreshed himself.

16.1–14. 3–4: *Your master's son* is Merib-baal. His grandfather was Saul, and Ziba claims that he is hoping to take over his grandfather's place as king. But Ziba may be lying (19.24–30). David rewards Ziba by giving him Saul's property. There is some question about whether David has the legal right to do this. **5:** *Shimei* belonged not only to Saul's tribe (Benjamin) but also to his *family* or clan.* **6–8:** Shimei accused David of murdering members of Saul's family and usurping the throne. He may have in mind the deaths of Abner and Ishbaal or those of Saul's sons and grandsons in 21.1–14. **9:** *Abishai* was Joab's brother. Both are recognized in 2 Samuel as violent men. He calls Shimei a *dead dog,* a term of reproach.

15 Now Absalom and all the Israelites[d] came to Jerusalem; Ahithophel was with him. 16When Hushai the Archite, David's friend, came to Absalom, Hushai said to Absalom, "Long live the king! Long live the king!" 17Absalom said to Hushai, "Is this your loyalty to your friend? Why did you not go with your friend?" 18Hushai said to Absalom, "No; but the one whom the LORD and this people and all the Israelites have chosen, his I will be, and with him I will remain. 19Moreover, whom should I serve? Should it not be his son? Just as I have served your father, so I will serve you."

20 Then Absalom said to Ahithophel, "Give us your counsel; what shall we do?" 21Ahithophel said to Absalom, "Go in to your father's concubines, the ones he has left to look after the house; and all Israel will hear that you have made yourself odious to your father, and the hands of all who are with you will be strengthened." 22So they pitched a tent for Absalom upon the roof; and Absalom went in to his father's concubines in the sight of all Israel. 23Now in those days the

a Or *Merib-baal:* See 4.4 note   b Gk Vg: Heb *iniquity*
c Gk: Heb lacks *at the Jordan*   d Gk: Heb *all the people, the men of Israel*

counsel that Ahithophel gave was as if one consulted the oracle*a* of God; so all the counsel of Ahithophel was esteemed, both by David and by Absalom.

17 Moreover Ahithophel said to Absalom, "Let me choose twelve thousand men, and I will set out and pursue David tonight. ²I will come upon him while he is weary and discouraged, and throw him into a panic; and all the people who are with him will flee. I will strike down only the king, ³and I will bring all the people back to you as a bride comes home to her husband. You seek the life of only one man,*b* and all the people will be at peace." ⁴The advice pleased Absalom and all the elders of Israel.

16.15–17.29: Overcoming Ahithophel. 16.16–19: Hushai's words are duplicitous. When he says, *Long live the king* (v. 16), he means David. Similarly, when he affirms his loyalty to *the one whom the Lord and this people* have chosen, he also means David. In both cases, Absalom takes these statements as a reference to himself. **20–22:** By sleeping with David's concubines,✶ Absalom makes his claim to the throne emphatic. His deed fulfills Nathan's oracle✶ (12.12). **23:** The *counsel that Ahithophel gave* was very highly prized. His motive for joining Absalom is not certain, but it is possible that he was Bathsheba's grandfather (compare 11.3 and 23.34) and may have held a grudge against David for his treatment of Bathsheba and Uriah. **17.1–4:** *Ahithophel's* advice is to attack while David's forces are weak from fleeing.

---

5 Then Absalom said, "Call Hushai the Archite also, and let us hear too what he has to say." ⁶When Hushai came to Absalom, Absalom said to him, "This is what Ahithophel has said; shall we do as he advises? If not, you tell us." ⁷Then Hushai said to Absalom, "This time the counsel that Ahithophel has given is not good." ⁸Hushai continued, "You know that your father and his men are warriors, and that they are enraged, like a bear robbed of her cubs in the field. Besides, your father is expert in war; he will not spend the night with the troops. ⁹Even now he has hidden himself in one of the pits, or in some other place. And when some of our troops*c* fall at the first attack, whoever hears it will say, 'There has been a slaughter among the troops who follow Absalom.' ¹⁰Then even the valiant warrior, whose heart is like the heart of a lion, will utterly melt with fear; for all Israel knows that your father is a warrior, and that those who are with him are valiant warriors. ¹¹But my counsel is that all Israel be gathered to you, from Dan to Beer-sheba, like the sand by the sea for multitude, and that you go to battle in person. ¹²So we shall come upon him in whatever place he may be found, and we shall light on him as the dew falls on the ground; and he will not survive, nor will any of those with him. ¹³If he withdraws into a city, then all Israel will bring ropes to that city, and we shall drag it into the valley, until not even a pebble is to be found there." ¹⁴Absalom and all the men of Israel said, "The counsel of Hushai the Archite is better than the counsel of Ahithophel." For the Lord had ordained to defeat the good counsel of Ahithophel, so that the Lord might bring ruin on Absalom.

15 Then Hushai said to the priests Zadok and Abiathar, "Thus and so did Ahithophel counsel Absalom and the elders of Israel; and thus and so I have counseled. ¹⁶Therefore send quickly and tell David, 'Do not lodge tonight at the fords of the wilderness, but by all means cross over; otherwise the king and all the people who are with him will be swallowed up.' " ¹⁷Jonathan and Ahimaaz were waiting at En-rogel; a servant-girl used to go and tell them, and they would go and tell King David; for they could not risk being seen entering the city. ¹⁸But a boy saw them, and told Absalom; so both of them went away quickly, and came to the house of a man at Bahurim, who had a well in his courtyard; and they went down into it. ¹⁹The man's wife took a covering, stretched it over the well's mouth, and spread out grain on it; and nothing was known of it. ²⁰When Absalom's servants came to the woman at the house, they said, "Where are Ahimaaz and Jonathan?" The woman said to them, "They have crossed over the brook*d* of water." And when they had searched and could not find them, they returned to Jerusalem.

a Heb *word*   *b* Gk: Heb *like the return of the whole (is) the man whom you seek*   *c* Gk Mss: Heb *some of them*
d Meaning of Heb uncertain

21 After they had gone, the men came up out of the well, and went and told King David. They said to David, "Go and cross the water quickly; for thus and so has Ahithophel counseled against you." 22So David and all the people who were with him set out and crossed the Jordan; by daybreak not one was left who had not crossed the Jordan.

23 When Ahithophel saw that his counsel was not followed, he saddled his donkey and went off home to his own city. He set his house in order, and hanged himself; he died and was buried in the tomb of his father.

24 Then David came to Mahanaim, while Absalom crossed the Jordan with all the men of Israel. 25Now Absalom had set Amasa over the army in the place of Joab. Amasa was the son of a man named Ithra the Ishmaelite,ᵃ who had married Abigal daughter of Nahash, sister of Zeruiah, Joab's mother. 26The Israelites and Absalom encamped in the land of Gilead.

27 When David came to Mahanaim, Shobi son of Nahash from Rabbah of the Ammonites, and Machir son of Ammiel from Lo-debar, and Barzillai the Gileadite from Rogelim, 28brought beds, basins, and earthen vessels, wheat, barley, meal, parched grain, beans and lentils,ᵇ 29honey and curds, sheep, and cheese from the herd, for David and the people with him to eat; for they said, "The troops are hungry and weary and thirsty in the wilderness."

17.5–29. 5–14: *Hushai* advises that Absalom wait and then attack David with the full force of *all Israel* (v. 11). Of course, Hushai is trying to give David time to recuperate and reorganize. He also plays on Absalom's ego, saying that all the people will follow him, and he can lead them into battle (v. 12). Even though Ahithophel's advice is obviously better than Hushai's, *the* LORD *had ordained* that Absalom would be persuaded to follow Hushai. **15–16:** *Hushai* sends word to David through the priests and their sons. He has bought David some time but urges him to cross the Jordan quickly and escape. **18–19:** The *well* was a simple pit; its opening could be covered with a blanket and *grain* spread over it for perfect camouflage. **23:** *Ahithophel* committed suicide perhaps because he knew that the end of Absalom's reign was imminent. **24:** *Mahanaim* was a site east of the Jordan that was easily defensible.

25: *Amasa* was David's nephew, the son of his sister *Zeruiah*. She is called the daughter of *Nahash* here rather than the daughter of Jesse. This may be a scribal error (Nahash occurs in v. 27), or Abigail may have been David's half-sister. **27:** This *Nahash* is the Ammonite king with whom David had a treaty (10.1–2). His son, *Shobi*, loyal to the treaty, now helps David in exile.

18 Then David mustered the men who were with him, and set over them commanders of thousands and commanders of hundreds. 2And David divided the army into three groups:ᶜ one third under the command of Joab, one third under the command of Abishai son of Zeruiah, Joab's brother, and one third under the command of Ittai the Gittite. The king said to the men, "I myself will also go out with you." 3But the men said, "You shall not go out. For if we flee, they will not care about us. If half of us die, they will not care about us. But you are worth ten thousand of us;ᵈ therefore it is better that you send us help from the city." 4The king said to them, "Whatever seems best to you I will do." So the king stood at the side of the gate, while all the army marched out by hundreds and by thousands. 5The king ordered Joab and Abishai and Ittai, saying, "Deal gently for my sake with the young man Absalom." And all the people heard when the king gave orders to all the commanders concerning Absalom.

6 So the army went out into the field against Israel; and the battle was fought in the forest of Ephraim. 7The men of Israel were defeated there by the servants of David, and the slaughter there was great on that day, twenty thousand men. 8The battle spread over the face of all the country; and the forest claimed more victims that day than the sword.

9 Absalom happened to meet the servants of David. Absalom was riding on his mule, and the mule went under the thick branches of a great oak. His head caught fast in the oak, and he was left hangingᵉ between

a 1 Chr 2.17: Heb *Israelite*　　*b* Heb *and lentils and parched grain*　　*c* Gk: Heb *sent forth the army* *d* Gk Vg Symmachus: Heb *for now there are ten thousand such as we*　　*e* Gk Syr Tg: Heb *was put* heaven and earth, while the mule that was under him went on. [10]A man saw it, and told Joab, "I saw Absalom hanging in an oak." [11]Joab said to the man who told him, "What, you saw him! Why then did you not strike him there to the ground? I would have been glad to give you ten pieces of silver and a belt." [12]But the man said to Joab, "Even if I felt in my hand the weight of a thousand pieces of silver, I would not raise my hand against the king's son; for in our hearing the king commanded you and Abishai and Ittai, saying: For my sake protect the young man Absalom! [13]On the other hand, if I had dealt treacherously against his life[a] (and there is nothing hidden from the king), then you yourself would have stood aloof." [14]Joab said, "I will not waste time like this with you." He took three spears in his hand, and thrust them into the heart of Absalom, while he was still alive in the oak. [15]And ten young men, Joab's armor-bearers, surrounded Absalom and struck him, and killed him.

[16] Then Joab sounded the trumpet, and the troops came back from pursuing Israel, for Joab restrained the troops. [17]They took Absalom, threw him into a great pit in the forest, and raised over him a very great heap of stones. Meanwhile all the Israelites fled to their homes. [18]Now Absalom in his lifetime had taken and set up for himself a pillar that is in the King's Valley, for he said, "I have no son to keep my name in remembrance"; he called the pillar by his own name. It is called Absalom's Monument to this day.

18.1–19.10: The defeat and death of Absalom.
18.1–8: By following Hushai's advice to delay in Jerusalem, Absalom gave David the opportunity to regroup his forces and to choose the battle site. David and his men used the rugged *forest of Ephraim* to counter the larger numbers of Absalom's army. **9:** The *mule* was the royal mount for King David and his sons. Thus, Absalom's unseating from the mule symbolizes his loss of the kingdom. His predicament, being caught by the head, reminds one of his glorious hair (14.26) and suggests that his pride was his downfall. **14:** *Spears* may also be translated "sticks." Apparently, Joab stabbed or struck Absalom with them in order to dislodge him from the tree and finish him off (v. 15).

17: Burial under a *heap of stones* was a sign of a cursed person (Josh 7.26).

[19] Then Ahimaaz son of Zadok said, "Let me run, and carry tidings to the king that the LORD has delivered him from the power of his enemies." [20]Joab said to him, "You are not to carry tidings today; you may carry tidings another day, but today you shall not do so, because the king's son is dead." [21]Then Joab said to a Cushite, "Go, tell the king what you have seen." The Cushite bowed before Joab, and ran. [22]Then Ahimaaz son of Zadok said again to Joab, "Come what may, let me also run after the Cushite." And Joab said, "Why will you run, my son, seeing that you have no reward[b] for the tidings?" [23]"Come what may," he said, "I will run." So he said to him, "Run." Then Ahimaaz ran by the way of the Plain, and outran the Cushite.

[24] Now David was sitting between the two gates. The sentinel went up to the roof of the gate by the wall, and when he looked up, he saw a man running alone. [25]The sentinel shouted and told the king. The king said, "If he is alone, there are tidings in his mouth." He kept coming, and drew near. [26]Then the sentinel saw another man running; and the sentinel called to the gatekeeper and said, "See, another man running alone!" The king said, "He also is bringing tidings." [27]The sentinel said, "I think the running of the first one is like the running of Ahimaaz son of Zadok." The king said, "He is a good man, and comes with good tidings."

[28] Then Ahimaaz cried out to the king, "All is well!" He prostrated himself before the king with his face to the ground, and said, "Blessed be the LORD your God, who has delivered up the men who raised their hand against my lord the king." [29]The king said, "Is it well with the young man Absalom?" Ahimaaz answered, "When Joab sent your servant,[c] I saw a great tumult, but I do not know what it was." [30]The king said, "Turn aside, and stand here." So he turned aside, and stood still.

a Another reading is *at the risk of my life*   *b* Meaning of Heb uncertain   *c* Heb *the king's servant, your servant*

31 Then the Cushite came; and the Cushite said, "Good tidings for my lord the king! For the LORD has vindicated you this day, delivering you from the power of all who rose up against you." 32The king said to the Cushite, "Is it well with the young man Absalom?" The Cushite answered, "May the enemies of my lord the king, and all who rise up to do you harm, be like that young man."

18.19–32: 19: *Ahimaaz* wants to deliver the good news of the victory to David. **20:** *Because the king's son [was] dead* may be the narrator's words rather than Joab's. **21:** A *Cushite* was an Ethiopian. **29:** *Ahimaaz* apparently does not know that Absalom is dead. **32:** The *Cushite* thinks that Absalom's death is also good news.

33[a] The king was deeply moved, and went up to the chamber over the gate, and wept; and as he went, he said, "O my son Absalom, my son, my son Absalom! Would I had died instead of you, O Absalom, my son, my son!"

19 It was told Joab, "The king is weeping and mourning for Absalom." 2So the victory that day was turned into mourning for all the troops; for the troops heard that day, "The king is grieving for his son." 3The troops stole into the city that day as soldiers steal in who are ashamed when they flee in battle. 4The king covered his face, and the king cried with a loud voice, "O my son Absalom, O Absalom, my son, my son!" 5Then Joab came into the house to the king, and said, "Today you have covered with shame the faces of all your officers who have saved your life today, and the lives of your sons and your daughters, and the lives of your wives and your concubines, 6for love of those who hate you and for hatred of those who love you. You have made it clear today that commanders and officers are nothing to you; for I perceive that if Absalom were alive and all of us were dead today, then you would be pleased. 7So go out at once and speak kindly to your servants; for I swear by the LORD, if you do not go, not a man will stay with you this night; and this will be worse for you than any disaster that has come upon you from your youth until now."

8Then the king got up and took his seat in the gate. The troops were all told, "See, the king is sitting in the gate"; and all the troops came before the king.

19.6: *Love* and *hate* can be political terms for loyalty and disloyalty. Joab's point is that David shows love to those who are disloyal to him (Absalom) while failing to show love or appreciation toward his loyal subjects.

Meanwhile, all the Israelites had fled to their homes. 9All the people were disputing throughout all the tribes of Israel, saying, "The king delivered us from the hand of our enemies, and saved us from the hand of the Philistines; and now he has fled out of the land because of Absalom. 10But Absalom, whom we anointed over us, is dead in battle. Now therefore why do you say nothing about bringing the king back?"

11 King David sent this message to the priests Zadok and Abiathar, "Say to the elders of Judah, 'Why should you be the last to bring the king back to his house? The talk of all Israel has come to the king.[b] 12You are my kin, you are my bone and my flesh; why then should you be the last to bring back the king?' 13And say to Amasa, 'Are you not my bone and my flesh? So may God do to me, and more, if you are not the commander of my army from now on, in place of Joab.' " 14Amasa[c] swayed the hearts of all the people of Judah as one, and they sent word to the king, "Return, both you and all your servants." 15So the king came back to the Jordan; and Judah came to Gilgal to meet the king and to bring him over the Jordan.

19.11–43: David returns to Jerusalem. 11: David contacts the leaders or *elders* of Judah to encourage them to welcome him back as king. **13:** David appoints Amasa as his army commander in place of Joab. Amasa was David's nephew (17.25) and had been Absalom's commander. This provides a motive for Joab's murder of Amasa (20.10). **14:** Amasa, in turn, persuades the *people* (army) of Judah to return to David.

a Ch 19.1 in Heb   *b* Gk: Heb *to the king, to his house*
c Heb *He*

16 Shimei son of Gera, the Benjaminite, from Bahurim, hurried to come down with the people of Judah to meet King David; 17with him were a thousand people from Benjamin. And Ziba, the servant of the house of Saul, with his fifteen sons and his twenty servants, rushed down to the Jordan ahead of the king, 18while the crossing was taking place,^a to bring over the king's household, and to do his pleasure.

Shimei son of Gera fell down before the king, as he was about to cross the Jordan, 19and said to the king, "May my lord not hold me guilty or remember how your servant did wrong on the day my lord the king left Jerusalem; may the king not bear it in mind. 20For your servant knows that I have sinned; therefore, see, I have come this day, the first of all the house of Joseph to come down to meet my lord the king." 21Abishai son of Zeruiah answered, "Shall not Shimei be put to death for this, because he cursed the LORD's anointed?" 22But David said, "What have I to do with you, you sons of Zeruiah, that you should today become an adversary to me? Shall anyone be put to death in Israel this day? For do I not know that I am this day king over Israel?" 23The king said to Shimei, "You shall not die." And the king gave him his oath.

19.16–23: *Shimei* and those with him were from the tribe of *Benjamin*, Saul's tribe. Shimei had ridiculed David when he fled from Jerusalem (16.5–13). Now that David is victorious, he asks forgiveness. He and the Benjaminites are the first of the Israelites or the *house of Joseph* (v. 20) to welcome David back. *Abishai* still wants to kill Shimei (16.9), but David refuses. It may have been customary for a new king to pardon criminals on the day of his coronation (see 1 Sam 11.13).

24 Mephibosheth^b grandson of Saul came down to meet the king; he had not taken care of his feet, or trimmed his beard, or washed his clothes, from the day the king left until the day he came back in safety. 25When he came from Jerusalem to meet the king, the king said to him, "Why did you not go with me, Mephibosheth?"^b 26He answered, "My lord, O king, my servant deceived me; for your servant said to him, 'Saddle a donkey for me,^c so that I may ride on it and go with the king.' For your servant is lame. 27He has slandered your servant to my lord the king. But my lord the king is like the angel of God; do therefore what seems good to you. 28For all my father's house were doomed to death before my lord the king; but you set your servant among those who eat at your table. What further right have I, then, to appeal to the king?" 29The king said to him, "Why speak any more of your affairs? I have decided: you and Ziba shall divide the land." 30Mephibosheth^b said to the king, "Let him take it all, since my lord the king has arrived home safely."

19.24–30. 24: *Taken care of his feet* may mean trimmed his toenails, since the writer cites it as evidence that Merib-baal (*Mephibosheth*) had been mourning David's exile. 26–30: *Ziba* had accused Merib-baal of plotting to take the throne (16.1–4). Merib-baal here defends himself, saying that Ziba refused to help him to flee with David, and he could not leave on his own accord because he is crippled. David's decision (v. 29) indicates that he does not know which of them is telling the truth.

31 Now Barzillai the Gileadite had come down from Rogelim; he went on with the king to the Jordan, to escort him over the Jordan. 32Barzillai was a very aged man, eighty years old. He had provided the king with food while he stayed at Mahanaim, for he was a very wealthy man. 33The king said to Barzillai, "Come over with me, and I will provide for you in Jerusalem at my side." 34But Barzillai said to the king, "How many years have I still to live, that I should go up with the king to Jerusalem? 35Today I am eighty years old; can I discern what is pleasant and what is not? Can your servant taste what he eats or what he drinks? Can I still listen to the voice of singing men and singing women? Why then should your servant be an added burden to my lord the king? 36Your servant will go a little way over the Jordan with the king. Why should the king recom-

a Cn: Heb *the ford crossed*   b Or *Merib-baal*: See 4.4 note   c Gk Syr Vg: Heb *said, 'I will saddle a donkey for myself* pense me with such a reward? 37Please let your servant return, so that I may die in my own town, near the graves of my father and my mother. But here is your servant Chimham; let him go over with my lord the king; and do for him whatever seems good to you." 38The king answered, "Chimham shall go over with me, and I will do for him whatever seems good to you; and all that you desire of me I will do for you." 39Then all the people crossed over the Jordan, and the king crossed over; the king kissed Barzillai and blessed him, and he returned to his own home. 40The king went on to Gilgal, and Chimham went on with him; all the people of Judah, and also half the people of Israel, brought the king on his way.

19.31–40: *Barzillai* had helped to provide for David in exile (17.27). David now invites him to come live in his palace in Jerusalem. Barzillai replies that he is too old to enjoy it but arranges for the king to take his son *Chimham* instead.

41 Then all the people of Israel came to the king, and said to him, "Why have our kindred the people of Judah stolen you away, and brought the king and his household over the Jordan, and all David's men with him?" 42All the people of Judah answered the people of Israel, "Because the king is near of kin to us. Why then are you angry over this matter? Have we eaten at all at the king's expense? Or has he given us any gift?" 43But the people of Israel answered the people of Judah, "We have ten shares in the king, and in David also we have more than you. Why then did you despise us? Were we not the first to speak of bringing back our king?" But the words of the people of Judah were fiercer than the words of the people of Israel.

19.41–43. 41: Because of David's invitation (vv. 11–12) the army (*people*) of Judah welcomes David back before the army of Israel. **42:** The army of Judah denies that it has received any special favors or bribes from David. **43:** The *ten shares* are the ten northern tribes of Israel.

20 Now a scoundrel named Sheba son of Bichri, a Benjaminite, happened

to be there. He sounded the trumpet and cried out,

"We have no portion in David,
    no share in the son of Jesse!
    Everyone to your tents, O Israel!"

2So all the people of Israel withdrew from David and followed Sheba son of Bichri; but the people of Judah followed their king steadfastly from the Jordan to Jerusalem. 3 David came to his house at Jerusalem; and the king took the ten concubines whom he had left to look after the house, and put them in a house under guard, and provided for them, but did not go in to them. So they were shut up until the day of their death, living as if in widowhood.

20.1–26: Sheba's revolt. 1: *Everyone to your tents* is an idiom for military demobilization. Sheba is calling for the army of Israel to withdraw from David. **2:** *All the people of Israel* refers only to the northern tribes, as the rest of the verse shows. The phrase probably exaggerates the extent of the northern disaffection with David (see v. 21). **3:** David no longer had sexual relations with the *ten concubines*⋆ he had left behind because Absalom had slept with them (16.20–22).

4 Then the king said to Amasa, "Call the men of Judah together to me within three days, and be here yourself." 5So Amasa went to summon Judah; but he delayed beyond the set time that had been appointed him. 6David said to Abishai, "Now Sheba son of Bichri will do us more harm than Absalom; take your lord's servants and pursue him, or he will find fortified cities for himself, and escape from us." 7Joab's men went out after him, along with the Cherethites, the Pelethites, and all the warriors; they went out from Jerusalem to pursue Sheba son of Bichri. 8When they were at the large stone that is in Gibeon, Amasa came to meet them. Now Joab was wearing a soldier's garment and over it was a belt with a sword in its sheath fastened at his waist; as he went forward it fell out. 9Joab said to Amasa, "Is it well with you, my brother?" And Joab took Amasa by the beard with his right hand to kiss him. 10But Amasa did not notice the sword in Joab's hand; Joab struck him in the belly so that his entrails poured out on the

ground, and he died. He did not strike a second blow.

Then Joab and his brother Abishai pursued Sheba son of Bichri. ¹¹And one of Joab's men took his stand by Amasa, and said, "Whoever favors Joab, and whoever is for David, let him follow Joab." ¹²Amasa lay wallowing in his blood on the highway, and the man saw that all the people were stopping. Since he saw that all who came by him were stopping, he carried Amasa from the highway into a field, and threw a garment over him. ¹³Once he was removed from the highway, all the people went on after Joab to pursue Sheba son of Bichri.

20.4–13. 7: *The Cherethites* and *Pelethites* were the royal bodyguard. They were closely related to if not identical with the Philistines. 8–10: *Joab's* assassination of *Amasa* is similar to his murder of Abner (3.26–39). His motive is not explained but presumably had to do with the fact that Amasa had taken Joab's place as army commander.

---

14 Sheba*ᵃ* passed through all the tribes of Israel to Abel of Beth-maacah;*ᵇ* and all the Bichrites*ᶜ* assembled, and followed him inside. ¹⁵Joab's forces*ᵈ* came and besieged him in Abel of Beth-maacah; they threw up a siege ramp against the city, and it stood against the rampart. Joab's forces were battering the wall to break it down. ¹⁶Then a wise woman called from the city, "Listen! Listen! Tell Joab, 'Come here, I want to speak to you.' " ¹⁷He came near her; and the woman said, "Are you Joab?" He answered, "I am." Then she said to him, "Listen to the words of your servant." He answered, "I am listening." ¹⁸Then she said, "They used to say in the old days, 'Let them inquire at Abel'; and so they would settle a matter. ¹⁹I am one of those who are peaceable and faithful in Israel; you seek to destroy a city that is a mother in Israel; why will you swallow up the heritage of the LORD?" ²⁰Joab answered, "Far be it from me, far be it, that I should swallow up or destroy! ²¹That is not the case! But a man of the hill country of Ephraim, called Sheba son of Bichri, has lifted up his hand against King David; give him up alone, and I will withdraw from the

city." The woman said to Joab, "His head shall be thrown over the wall to you." ²²Then the woman went to all the people with her wise plan. And they cut off the head of Sheba son of Bichri, and threw it out to Joab. So he blew the trumpet, and they dispersed from the city, and all went to their homes, while Joab returned to Jerusalem to the king.

23 Now Joab was in command of all the army of Israel;*ᵉ* Benaiah son of Jehoiada was in command of the Cherethites and the Pelethites; ²⁴Adoram was in charge of the forced labor; Jehoshaphat son of Ahilud was the recorder; ²⁵Sheva was secretary; Zadok and Abiathar were priests; ²⁶and Ira the Jairite was also David's priest.

20.14–26. 14: *Abel* is at the northern extreme of Israel. 15: Ancient Israelite cities were surrounded by thick walls that had to be broken through with battering rams. 16: This *wise woman* is both intelligent and eloquent. She may have been a city official. 18–19: The woman says that *Abel* is one of Israel's original cities and should not be destroyed. 21: The woman does not know about Sheba, indicating that his revolt did not reach to all Israel but included only part of Benjamin and *the hill country of Ephraim*. 23–26: This cabinet list is very similar to the one in 8.16–18. It probably came to this location by attachment to 21.1–14. The *forced labor* was conscripted from the northern tribes by David and Solomon. Its leader, *Adoram* or Adoniram, was later stoned when the Israelites rebelled against the Davidic dynasty* (1 Kings 12.18).

---

21 Now there was a famine in the days of David for three years, year after year; and David inquired of the LORD. The LORD said, "There is bloodguilt on Saul and on his house, because he put the Gibeonites to death." ²So the king called the Gibeonites and spoke to them. (Now the Gibeonites were not of the people of Israel, but of the remnant of the Amorites; although the people of Israel had sworn to spare them, Saul had tried to wipe them out in his zeal for the people of Israel and Judah.) ³David said to the Gibeonites, "What shall I do for you?

a Heb *He*   *b* Compare 20.15: Heb *and Beth-maacah*
c Compare Gk Vg: Heb *Berites*   *d* Heb *They*
e Cn: Heb *Joab to all the army, Israel*

How shall I make expiation, that you may bless the heritage of the LORD?" ⁴The Gibeonites said to him, "It is not a matter of silver or gold between us and Saul or his house; neither is it for us to put anyone to death in Israel." He said, "What do you say that I should do for you?" ⁵They said to the king, "The man who consumed us and planned to destroy us, so that we should have no place in all the territory of Israel— ⁶let seven of his sons be handed over to us, and we will impale them before the LORD at Gibeon on the mountain of the LORD."ᵃ The king said, "I will hand them over."

7 But the king spared Mephibosheth,ᵇ the son of Saul's son Jonathan, because of the oath of the LORD that was between them, between David and Jonathan son of Saul. ⁸The king took the two sons of Rizpah daughter of Aiah, whom she bore to Saul, Armoni and Mephibosheth;ᵇ and the five sons of Merabᶜ daughter of Saul, whom she bore to Adriel son of Barzillai the Meholathite; ⁹he gave them into the hands of the Gibeonites, and they impaled them on the mountain before the LORD. The seven of them perished together. They were put to death in the first days of harvest, at the beginning of barley harvest.

10 Then Rizpah the daughter of Aiah took sackcloth, and spread it on a rock for herself, from the beginning of harvest until rain fell on them from the heavens; she did not allow the birds of the air to come on the bodiesᵈ by day, or the wild animals by night. ¹¹When David was told what Rizpah daughter of Aiah, the concubine of Saul, had done, ¹²David went and took the bones of Saul and the bones of his son Jonathan from the people of Jabesh-gilead, who had stolen them from the public square of Beth-shan, where the Philistines had hung them up, on the day the Philistines killed Saul on Gilboa. ¹³He brought up from there the bones of Saul and the bones of his son Jonathan; and they gathered the bones of those who had been impaled. ¹⁴They buried the bones of Saul and of his son Jonathan in the land of Benjamin in Zela, in the tomb of his father Kish; they did all that the king commanded. After that, God heeded supplications for the land.

21.1–14: The execution of Saul's heirs. 1–2: The *Gibeonites* had a special treaty with Israel (Josh 9). This story assumes that the violation of that treaty brought divine wrath. The Bible nowhere recounts Saul's attempted extermination of the Gibeonites. **3:** The LORD's *heritage* is both the land and the people of Israel. **4:** This is a matter for blood vengeance, but as resident aliens* in Israel the Gibeonites do not have that right. **5–9:** It was typical for the founder of a new dynasty* to annihilate the potential claimants from the previous dynasty. David does this here. Saul's alleged offense provides a religious legitimation for this political act. Only Merib-baal is spared (v. 7), probably because he was crippled and could not therefore be king, though this may also reflect David's affection for Jonathan. This story originally came before 9.1, in which David asks if anyone is left in Saul's house. The event took place early in David's reign over Israel. *Sons* (v. 6) may also include grandsons. *Mephibosheth* or Mephibaal in v. 8 is the proper reading. This was not Jonathan's son, Merib-baal, who was spared. The *barley harvest* was in April—May. **10:** *Rizpah* was Saul's concubine.* **11–14:** As a result of Rizpah's action, David tries to honor the memory of Saul and Jonathan. According to 1 Sam 31.12, their *bones* were burned. This is either a contradiction, or David gathered only their ashes.

15 The Philistines went to war again with Israel, and David went down together with his servants. They fought against the Philistines, and David grew weary. ¹⁶Ishbi-benob, one of the descendants of the giants, whose spear weighed three hundred shekels of bronze, and who was fitted out with new weapons,ᵉ said he would kill David. ¹⁷But Abishai son of Zeruiah came to his aid, and attacked the Philistine and killed him. Then David's men swore to him, "You shall not go out with us to battle any longer, so that you do not quench the lamp of Israel."

18 After this a battle took place with the Philistines, at Gob; then Sibbecai the Hushathite killed Saph, who was one of the descendants of the giants. ¹⁹Then there was another battle with the Philistines at Gob;

ᵃ Cn Compare Gk and 21.9: Heb *at Gibeah of Saul, the chosen of the LORD*   ᵇ Or *Merib-baal:* See 4.4 note
ᶜ Two Heb Mss Syr Compare Gk: MT *Michal*
ᵈ Heb *them*   ᵉ Heb *was belted anew*

and Elhanan son of Jaare-oregim, the Bethlehemite, killed Goliath the Gittite, the shaft of whose spear was like a weaver's beam. 20There was again war at Gath, where there was a man of great size, who had six fingers on each hand, and six toes on each foot, twenty-four in number; he too was descended from the giants. 21When he taunted Israel, Jonathan son of David's brother Shimei, killed him. 22These four were descended from the giants in Gath; they fell by the hands of David and his servants.

21.16–19. 16: *Three hundred shekels* was almost eight pounds. **19:** Some of the information in this verse has been secondarily added to the story in 1 Sam 17.

22 David spoke to the LORD the words of this song on the day when the LORD delivered him from the hand of all his enemies, and from the hand of Saul. 2He said:

The LORD is my rock, my fortress, and my deliverer,
3   my God, my rock, in whom I take refuge,
my shield and the horn of my salvation,
my stronghold and my refuge,
my savior; you save me from violence.
4 I call upon the LORD, who is worthy to be praised,
and I am saved from my enemies.

5 For the waves of death encompassed me,
the torrents of perdition assailed me;
6 the cords of Sheol entangled me,
the snares of death confronted me.

7 In my distress I called upon the LORD;
to my God I called.
From his temple he heard my voice,
and my cry came to his ears.

22.1–51: A psalm of praise. This psalm, which is the same as Psalm 18, was written long after David's time but is inserted here as appropriate to David's sentiments. **2–3:** The image of the LORD as a protective *rock* is common in the Bible. **5–6:** *Perdition* is a reference to the underworld, the abode of the dead, known in the Bible as *Sheol*. **7:** The mention of the *temple* is an

indication that this psalm was written after David, since the Temple was built by Solomon.

8 Then the earth reeled and rocked;
the foundations of the heavens trembled
and quaked, because he was angry.
9 Smoke went up from his nostrils,
and devouring fire from his mouth;
glowing coals flamed forth from him.
10 He bowed the heavens, and came down;
thick darkness was under his feet.
11 He rode on a cherub, and flew;
he was seen upon the wings of the wind.
12 He made darkness around him a canopy,
thick clouds, a gathering of water.
13 Out of the brightness before him coals of fire flamed forth.
14 The LORD thundered from heaven;
the Most High uttered his voice.
15 He sent out arrows, and scattered them
—lightning, and routed them.
16 Then the channels of the sea were seen,
the foundations of the world were laid bare
at the rebuke of the LORD,
at the blast of the breath of his nostrils.

22.8–16. 8: The LORD's appearance is accompanied by an earthquake. **9:** The LORD is pictured here as a fire-breathing dragon. **11–16:** The LORD is depicted here as the storm God. A *cherub* (v. 11) was a mythical, griffin-like creature. God's *voice* (v. 14) is thunder, and he throws lightning bolts at his enemies (v. 15). The psalmist envisions the world as flat and is trapped in the underworld beneath *the foundations of the world,* which the LORD's roar uncovers (v. 16).

17 He reached from on high, he took me,
he drew me out of mighty waters.
18 He delivered me from my strong enemy,
from those who hated me;
for they were too mighty for me.
19 They came upon me in the day of my calamity,
but the LORD was my stay.

20 He brought me out into a broad place;
    he delivered me, because he delighted
       in me.
21 The LORD rewarded me according to my
    righteousness;
    according to the cleanness of my
       hands he recompensed me.
22 For I have kept the ways of the LORD,
    and have not wickedly departed from
       my God.
23 For all his ordinances were before me,
    and from his statutes I did not turn
       aside.
24 I was blameless before him,
    and I kept myself from guilt.
25 Therefore the LORD has recompensed
    me according to my
       righteousness,
    according to my cleanness in his
       sight.

26 With the loyal you show yourself loyal;
    with the blameless you show yourself
       blameless;
27 with the pure you show yourself pure,
    and with the crooked you show
       yourself perverse.
28 You deliver a humble people,
    but your eyes are upon the haughty to
       bring them down.
29 Indeed, you are my lamp, O LORD,
    the LORD lightens my darkness.
30 By you I can crush a troop,
    and by my God I can leap over a
       wall.
31 This God—his way is perfect;
    the promise of the LORD proves true;
    he is a shield for all who take refuge
       in him.

32 For who is God, but the LORD?
    And who is a rock, except our God?
33 The God who has girded me with
    strength*a*
    has opened wide my path.*b*
34 He made my*c* feet like the feet of deer,
    and set me secure on the heights.
35 He trains my hands for war,
    so that my arms can bend a bow of
       bronze.

36 You have given me the shield of your
       salvation,
    and your help*d* has made me great.
37 You have made me stride freely,
    and my feet do not slip;
38 I pursued my enemies and destroyed
       them,
    and did not turn back until they were
       consumed.
39 I consumed them; I struck them down,
    so that they did not rise;
    they fell under my feet.
40 For you girded me with strength for the
       battle;
    you made my assailants sink under
       me.
41 You made my enemies turn their backs
       to me,
    those who hated me, and I destroyed
       them.
42 They looked, but there was no one to
       save them;
    they cried to the LORD, but he did
       not answer them.
43 I beat them fine like the dust of the
       earth,
    I crushed them and stamped them
       down like the mire of the streets.

22.32–37. 32: This is a monotheistic claim; the LORD
(Yahweh) alone is God. **33–37:** The LORD equips the
psalmist for battle.

44 You delivered me from strife with the
       peoples;*e*
    you kept me as the head of the
       nations;
    people whom I had not known served
       me.
45 Foreigners came cringing to me;
    as soon as they heard of me, they
       obeyed me.
46 Foreigners lost heart,
    and came trembling out of their
       strongholds.

a Q Ms Gk Syr Vg Compare Ps 18.32: MT *God is my
strong refuge*   *b* Meaning of Heb uncertain
c Another reading is *his*   *d* Q Ms: MT *your answering*
e Gk: Heb *from strife with my people*

47 The LORD lives! Blessed be my rock,
   and exalted be my God, the rock of
      my salvation,
48 the God who gave me vengeance
   and brought down peoples under
      me,
49 who brought me out from my enemies;
   you exalted me above my adversaries,
   you delivered me from the violent.

50 For this I will extol you, O LORD,
      among the nations,
   and sing praises to your name.
51 He is a tower of salvation for his king,
   and shows steadfast love to his
      anointed,
      to David and his descendants
         forever.

22.51: *Steadfast love* can also mean loyalty. *Anointed**
was a title for the king; it is the word "messiah."* The
reference to *David and his descendants,* if original to
the psalm, would indicate that it comes from royal circles in Judah.

23 Now these are the last words of
   David:
The oracle of David, son of Jesse,
   the oracle of the man whom God
      exalted,ᵃ
   the anointed of the God of Jacob,
      the favorite of the Strong One of
         Israel:

2 The spirit of the LORD speaks through
      me,
   his word is upon my tongue.
3 The God of Israel has spoken,
   the Rock of Israel has said to me:
One who rules over people justly,
   ruling in the fear of God,
4 is like the light of morning,
   like the sun rising on a cloudless
      morning,
   gleaming from the rain on the grassy
      land.

5 Is not my house like this with God?
   For he has made with me an
      everlasting covenant,

ordered in all things and secure.
   Will he not cause to prosper
      all my help and my desire?
6 But the godless areᵇ all like thorns that
      are thrown away;
   for they cannot be picked up with the
      hand;
7 to touch them one uses an iron bar
   or the shaft of a spear.
      And they are entirely consumed in
         fire on the spot.ᶜ

23.1–7: The last words of David. This is another
poem attributed to David. Its date is uncertain. **3–4:**
The image of the king as the sun was common in the
ancient Near East, especially in Egypt, though it was
less common in Israel. **5:** The *house* of the king is his
dynasty.* The *everlasting covenant** refers to the
LORD's promise of an eternal dynasty for David in
2 Sam 7. **6–7:** These verses continue the image of vv.
3–4. The *godless* are like *thorns* consumed by the sun's
heat.

8 These are the names of the warriors
whom David had: Josheb-basshebeth a Tah-
chemonite; he was chief of the Three;ᵈ he
wielded his spearᵉ against eight hundred
whom he killed at one time.
   9 Next to him among the three warriors
was Eleazar son of Dodo son of Ahohi. He
was with David when they defied the Philistines who were gathered there for battle.
The Israelites withdrew, ¹⁰but he stood his
ground. He struck down the Philistines until
his arm grew weary, though his hand clung
to the sword. The LORD brought about a
great victory that day. Then the people came
back to him—but only to strip the dead.
   11 Next to him was Shammah son of
Agee, the Hararite. The Philistines gathered
together at Lehi, where there was a plot of
ground full of lentils; and the army fled from
the Philistines. ¹²But he took his stand in
the middle of the plot, defended it, and killed
the Philistines; and the LORD brought about
a great victory.

a Q Ms: MT *who was raised on high*   b Heb *But
worthlessness*   c Heb *in sitting*   d Gk Vg Compare
1 Chr 11.11: Meaning of Heb uncertain   e 1 Chr
11.11: Meaning of Heb uncertain

13 Towards the beginning of harvest three of the thirty[a] chiefs went down to join David at the cave of Adullam, while a band of Philistines was encamped in the valley of Rephaim. 14David was then in the stronghold; and the garrison of the Philistines was then at Bethlehem. 15David said longingly, "O that someone would give me water to drink from the well of Bethlehem that is by the gate!" 16Then the three warriors broke through the camp of the Philistines, drew water from the well of Bethlehem that was by the gate, and brought it to David. But he would not drink of it; he poured it out to the LORD, 17for he said, "The LORD forbid that I should do this. Can I drink the blood of the men who went at the risk of their lives?" Therefore he would not drink it. The three warriors did these things.

18 Now Abishai son of Zeruiah, the brother of Joab, was chief of the Thirty.[b] With his spear he fought against three hundred men and killed them, and won a name beside the Three. 19He was the most renowned of the Thirty,[c] and became their commander; but he did not attain to the Three.

20 Benaiah son of Jehoiada was a valiant warrior[d] from Kabzeel, a doer of great deeds; he struck down two sons of Ariel[e] of Moab. He also went down and killed a lion in a pit on a day when snow had fallen. 21And he killed an Egyptian, a handsome man. The Egyptian had a spear in his hand; but Benaiah went against him with a staff, snatched the spear out of the Egyptian's hand, and killed him with his own spear. 22Such were the things Benaiah son of Jehoiada did, and won a name beside the three warriors. 23He was renowned among the Thirty, but he did not attain to the Three. And David put him in charge of his bodyguard.

24 Among the Thirty were Asahel brother of Joab; Elhanan son of Dodo of Bethlehem; 25Shammah of Harod; Elika of Harod; 26Helez the Paltite; Ira son of Ikkesh of Tekoa; 27Abiezer of Anathoth; Mebunnai the Hushathite; 28Zalmon the Ahohite; Maharai of Netophah; 29Heleb son of Baanah of Netophah; Ittai son of Ribai of Gibeah of the Ben-jaminites; 30Benaiah of Pirathon; Hiddai of the torrents of Gaash; 31Abi-albon the Arbathite; Azmaveth of Bahurim; 32Eliahba of Shaalbon; the sons of Jashen: Jonathan 33son of[f] Shammah the Hararite; Ahiam son of Sharar the Hararite; 34Eliphelet son of Ahasbai of Maacah; Eliam son of Ahithophel the Gilonite; 35Hezro[g] of Carmel; Paarai the Arbite; 36Igal son of Nathan of Zobah; Bani the Gadite; 37Zelek the Ammonite; Naharai of Beeroth, the armorbearer of Joab son of Zeruiah; 38Ira the Ithrite; Gareb the Ithrite; 39Uriah the Hittite—thirty-seven in all.

23.8–39: David's heroes. 8–12: Nothing more is known about *the three* greatest warriors in David's army besides what is reported here. **13–17:** The story in these verses is not about the three warriors just listed but about three anonymous members of the honor guard of *the thirty*. At *the beginning of the harvest* (v. 13) the weather was hot and dry, which is why David became thirsty. The *stronghold* (v. 14) was the fortress at Adullam. Since a *garrison of the Philistines was then at Bethlehem,* this must have been early in David's reign. Bethlehem was David's hometown, which accounts for his fond remembrance of the water there. **16–17:** Pouring out the water was a way of honoring the three men. Water was often poured out as a libation or sacrifice to God. **20:** *Benaiah* was the commander of David's bodyguard and later of the army under Solomon. **24:** It is strange to find *Asahel* in this list since he seems to be a young warrior aspiring to greatness at the time of his death (2.18–23). *Elhanan* killed Goliath (21.19). **30:** This is a different *Benaiah* from the one in vv. 20–23. **39:** *Uriah* was Bathsheba's husband (ch. 11). It is uncertain how the count of *thirty-seven* is achieved. The addition of the "Three" plus Abishai and Benaiah brings the number to thirty-five. Joab may have been counted as a member of this elite group, though his name is not specifically mentioned. The list in vv. 24–39 has thirty names in it. But there are textual variations where an additional name may have been read.

a Heb adds *head*   b Two Heb Mss Syr: MT *Three*
c Syr Compare 1 Chr 11.25: Heb *Was he the most renowned of the Three?*   d Another reading is *the son of Ish-hai*   e Gk: Heb lacks *sons of*   f Gk: Heb lacks *son of*   g Another reading is *Hezrai*

24 Again the anger of the LORD was kindled against Israel, and he incited David against them, saying, "Go, count the people of Israel and Judah." 2So the king said to Joab and the commanders of the army,*a* who were with him, "Go through all the tribes of Israel, from Dan to Beer-sheba, and take a census of the people, so that I may know how many there are." 3But Joab said to the king, "May the LORD your God increase the number of the people a hundredfold, while the eyes of my lord the king can still see it! But why does my lord the king want to do this?" 4But the king's word prevailed against Joab and the commanders of the army. So Joab and the commanders of the army went out from the presence of the king to take a census of the people of Israel. 5They crossed the Jordan, and began from*b* Aroer and from the city that is in the middle of the valley, toward Gad and on to Jazer. 6Then they came to Gilead, and to Kadesh in the land of the Hittites;*c* and they came to Dan, and from Dan*d* they went around to Sidon, 7and came to the fortress of Tyre and to all the cities of the Hivites and Canaanites; and they went out to the Negeb of Judah at Beer-sheba. 8So when they had gone through all the land, they came back to Jerusalem at the end of nine months and twenty days. 9Joab reported to the king the number of those who had been recorded: in Israel there were eight hundred thousand soldiers able to draw the sword, and those of Judah were five hundred thousand.

24.1–25: David's census. 1: *Again* implies that this story is the sequel to an earlier one, perhaps 21.1–14. This same story is found in 1 Chr 21, where v.1 says that Satan rather than the LORD *incited* David. A census provided the basis for conscription and taxation. The fact that a plague ensued suggests that some ritual taboo was broken. **2:** *From Dan to Beer-sheba* were the traditional northern and southern boundaries of Israel. **9:** The count is limited to men of military age. The Hebrew word translated *thousand* may refer to a much smaller military unit. Israel and Judah are numbered separately because Judah was exempted from taxation.

---

10 But afterward, David was stricken to the heart because he had numbered the peo-

ple. David said to the LORD, "I have sinned greatly in what I have done. But now, O LORD, I pray you, take away the guilt of your servant; for I have done very foolishly." 11When David rose in the morning, the word of the LORD came to the prophet Gad, David's seer, saying, 12"Go and say to David: Thus says the LORD: Three things I offer*e* you; choose one of them, and I will do it to you." 13So Gad came to David and told him; he asked him, "Shall three*f* years of famine come to you on your land? Or will you flee three months before your foes while they pursue you? Or shall there be three days' pestilence in your land? Now consider, and decide what answer I shall return to the one who sent me." 14Then David said to Gad, "I am in great distress; let us fall into the hand of the LORD, for his mercy is great; but let me not fall into human hands."

15 So the LORD sent a pestilence on Israel from that morning until the appointed time; and seventy thousand of the people died, from Dan to Beer-sheba. 16But when the angel stretched out his hand toward Jerusalem to destroy it, the LORD relented concerning the evil, and said to the angel who was bringing destruction among the people, "It is enough; now stay your hand." The angel of the LORD was then by the threshing floor of Araunah the Jebusite. 17When David saw the angel who was destroying the people, he said to the LORD, "I alone have sinned, and I alone have done wickedly; but these sheep, what have they done? Let your hand, I pray, be against me and against my father's house."

18 That day Gad came to David and said to him, "Go up and erect an altar to the LORD on the threshing floor of Araunah the Jebusite." 19Following Gad's instructions, David went up, as the LORD had commanded. 20When Araunah looked down, he saw the king and his servants coming toward him; and Araunah went out and prostrated

---

a 1 Chr 21.2 Gk: Heb *to Joab the commander of the army* *b* Gk Mss: Heb *encamped in Aroer south of* *c* Gk: Heb *to the land of Tahtim-hodshi* *d* Cn Compare Gk: Heb *they came to Dan-jaan and* *e* Or *hold over* *f* 1 Chr 21.12 Gk: Heb *seven* himself before the king with his face to the ground. 21Araunah said, "Why has my lord the king come to his servant?" David said, "To buy the threshing floor from you in order to build an altar to the LORD, so that the plague may be averted from the people." 22Then Araunah said to David, "Let my lord the king take and offer up what seems good to him; here are the oxen for the burnt offering, and the threshing sledges and the yokes of the oxen for the wood. 23All this, O king, Araunah gives to the king." And Araunah said to the king, "May the LORD your God respond favorably to you."

24 But the king said to Araunah, "No, but I will buy them from you for a price; I will not offer burnt offerings to the LORD my God that cost me nothing." So David bought the threshing floor and the oxen for fifty shekels of silver. 25David built there an altar to the LORD, and offered burnt offerings and offerings of well-being. So the LORD an-

swered his supplication for the land, and the plague was averted from Israel.

24.10–25. 10–14: David is given a choice of three punishments. He chooses *the hand of the LORD*, an idiom for plague, trusting in the LORD's mercy. **15–16:** David's strategy works. The plague is stopped after only one day. *The appointed time* (v. 15) may be the time of the evening meal. *Evil* (v. 16) is not moral evil but destruction. *Araunah* is called Ornan in 1 Chr 21. A *threshing* floor* was a flat, high area where grain was separated from the chaff.* In the Bible, God often appears to people at threshing floors (Judg 6.11–12). **17:** The *sheep* are the people of Jerusalem. The image is of David, the king, as their shepherd. **18–25:** These verses indicate that the plague was stopped after David built his altar and made his offerings rather than by the LORD's free will as in v. 16. The site of David's altar is the location of the later altar of burnt offering of Solomon's Temple. *Fifty shekels** (v. 24) was about one and a quarter pounds.

1 KINGS

Introduction

The book of 1 Kings continues the narrative★ of 1–2 Samuel. It begins with the account of David's death and the (unexpected) succession of his son Solomon (chs. 1–11). The deuteronomistic★ author/editor gives a theological explanation (Solomon's sin) for the subsequent division of the kingdom. The account then alternates between kings of Israel and Judah. The Israelite kings are all wicked and continue in the "sin of Jeroboam," which the writer believes is the idolatry★ at Bethel and other places of worship outside Jerusalem. Hence, one dynasty★ after another falls. The kings of Judah fare slightly better, but this is mainly because of David's faithfulness and the LORD's promise to him of an enduring "house." The central part of the book (chs. 12–16), therefore, is a little like a list of kings that has been expanded by anecdotes. The final chapters, however, are filled with the fantastic exploits of prophets,★ especially of the legendary★ Elijah as he confronts his archenemy, Jezebel, the wife of King Ahab.

As with 1–2 Samuel, the final version of 1 Kings was produced in the Exile,★ the writer trying to account theologically for the events of Israel's history. The division of the kingdom is the result of Solomon's sin (11.32–37). The kingdom of Judah lasted longer and was more stable than the kingdom of Israel because of David's loyalty and the LORD's promise. The standard practice whereby the founder of a new dynasty would annihilate the male rivals of the old is also given a theological framework by the author of 1 Kings in a series of prophecies and fulfillments. The stories of the prophets, including most of the ones about Elijah, do not reflect deuteronomistic editing and may have been added later. More than preachers or even oracle★ givers, these prophets are miracle-working "men of God" whose stories are comparable to the legends surrounding early Christian saints.

READING GUIDE

The reader should be aware that the criteria by which the deuteronomistic historian evaluates the kings of Israel and Judah arose at a much later date. For instance, the idea that Jerusalem was the only legitimate place of worship (centralization) comes from the period of the final kings of Judah, at the earliest. 1 Kings, therefore, is primarily a work of theology, not of history. The history it conveys is interpreted through the eyes of a theologian. Nowhere is this clearer than with the presentation of the reign of Omri (16.21–28). Although he was likely the most important king of Israel, his reign is treated in very cursory fashion. The reign of his son Ahab, in contrast, receives a great deal of attention—but only because it is the setting of the great religious conflict between Elijah and Jezebel.

1–11   The reign of Solomon

12–16   The Israelite dynasties of Jeroboam and Baasha and their individual counterparts in Judah

17–22   The reign of Ahab and Jezebel and stories of Elijah and other prophets

1 King David was old and advanced in years; and although they covered him with clothes, he could not get warm. 2So his servants said to him, "Let a young virgin be sought for my lord the king, and let her wait on the king, and be his attendant; let her lie in your bosom, so that my lord the king may be warm." 3So they searched for a beautiful girl throughout all the territory of Israel, and found Abishag the Shunammite, and brought her to the king. 4The girl was very beautiful. She became the king's attendant and served him, but the king did not know her sexually.

5 Now Adonijah son of Haggith exalted himself, saying, "I will be king"; he prepared for himself chariots and horsemen, and fifty men to run before him. 6His father had never at any time displeased him by asking, "Why have you done thus and so?" He was also a very handsome man, and he was born next after Absalom. 7He conferred with Joab son of Zeruiah and with the priest Abiathar, and they supported Adonijah. 8But the priest Zadok, and Benaiah son of Jehoiada, and the prophet Nathan, and Shimei, and Rei, and David's own warriors did not side with Adonijah.

9 Adonijah sacrificed sheep, oxen, and fatted cattle by the stone Zoheleth, which is beside En-rogel, and he invited all his brothers, the king's sons, and all the royal officials of Judah, 10but he did not invite the prophet Nathan or Benaiah or the warriors or his brother Solomon.

1.1–53: Solomon succeeds David. 1–4: The choice of *Abishag* (v. 3) to *serve* David (v. 4) is a test of his virility. The fact that *he did not know her sexually* (v. 4) indicates that he is impotent and therefore no longer fit to be king. 5: The knowledge of David's impotence spurs *Adonijah* to declare himself king. The *chariots and horsemen, and fifty men to run before him* were trappings of kingship (2 Sam 15.1). 6: As the *next after Absalom*, Adonijah was David's oldest living son (see 2 Sam 3.2–5; nothing is known about Chileab, and many scholars assume he died in infancy). Therefore, he was by all rights the heir to the throne. 7–8: The court is divided between those who support Adonijah for king (Joab and Abiathar, v. 7) and those who support Solomon (Zadok, Benaiah, and Nathan, among

others, v. 8). Since Adonijah was the rightful heir, it must be explained how Solomon came to succeed David. That is the topic of the rest of the chapter. 9–10: Adonijah holds a sacrifice to celebrate his coronation. Such sacrifices were like banquets because the meat from the sacrificed animals was eaten. Adonijah recognized Solomon as his rival and did not invite him or those who supported him to the sacrifice.

11 Then Nathan said to Bathsheba, Solomon's mother, "Have you not heard that Adonijah son of Haggith has become king and our lord David does not know it? 12Now therefore come, let me give you advice, so that you may save your own life and the life of your son Solomon. 13Go in at once to King David, and say to him, 'Did you not, my lord the king, swear to your servant, saying: Your son Solomon shall succeed me as king, and he shall sit on my throne? Why then is Adonijah king?' 14Then while you are still there speaking with the king, I will come in after you and confirm your words."

15 So Bathsheba went to the king in his room. The king was very old; Abishag the Shunammite was attending the king. 16Bathsheba bowed and did obeisance to the king, and the king said, "What do you wish?" 17She said to him, "My lord, you swore to your servant by the LORD your God, saying: Your son Solomon shall succeed me as king, and he shall sit on my throne. 18But now suddenly Adonijah has become king, though you, my lord the king, do not know it. 19He has sacrificed oxen, fatted cattle, and sheep in abundance, and has invited all the children of the king, the priest Abiathar, and Joab the commander of the army; but your servant Solomon he has not invited. 20But you, my lord the king—the eyes of all Israel are on you to tell them who shall sit on the throne of my lord the king after him. 21Otherwise it will come to pass, when my lord the king sleeps with his ancestors, that my son Solomon and I will be counted offenders."

1.11–21. 11: It is surprising to find Nathan and Bathsheba in cahoots; when they were mentioned together previously (2 Sam 11–12), Nathan was condemning David for his adultery with Bathsheba and murder of her husband. 12: Nathan advises Bathsheba on how to *save your own life and the life of your son Solomon*. The lives of Bathsheba and Solomon were in danger if Adonijah became king, since new kings customarily killed off all their potential rivals (compare v. 21). **17:** The promise Bathsheba cites here is not recorded elsewhere and may be fictional. She may be taking advantage of David's senility in order to have Solomon declared king.

22 While she was still speaking with the king, the prophet Nathan came in. 23 The king was told, "Here is the prophet Nathan." When he came in before the king, he did obeisance to the king, with his face to the ground. 24 Nathan said, "My lord the king, have you said, 'Adonijah shall succeed me as king, and he shall sit on my throne'? 25 For today he has gone down and has sacrificed oxen, fatted cattle, and sheep in abundance, and has invited all the king's children, Joab the commander*a* of the army, and the priest Abiathar, who are now eating and drinking before him, and saying, 'Long live King Adonijah!' 26 But he did not invite me, your servant, and the priest Zadok, and Benaiah son of Jehoiada, and your servant Solomon. 27 Has this thing been brought about by my lord the king and you have not let your servants know who should sit on the throne of my lord the king after him?"

28 King David answered, "Summon Bathsheba to me." So she came into the king's presence, and stood before the king. 29 The king swore, saying, "As the LORD lives, who has saved my life from every adversity, 30 as I swore to you by the LORD, the God of Israel, 'Your son Solomon shall succeed me as king, and he shall sit on my throne in my place,' so will I do this day." 31 Then Bathsheba bowed with her face to the ground, and did obeisance to the king, and said, "May my lord King David live forever!"

32 King David said, "Summon to me the priest Zadok, the prophet Nathan, and Benaiah son of Jehoiada." When they came before the king, 33 the king said to them, "Take with you the servants of your lord, and have my son Solomon ride on my own mule, and bring him down to Gihon. 34 There let the priest Zadok and the prophet Nathan anoint him king over Israel; then blow the trumpet,

and say, 'Long live King Solomon!' 35 You shall go up following him. Let him enter and sit on my throne; he shall be king in my place; for I have appointed him to be ruler over Israel and over Judah." 36 Benaiah son of Jehoiada answered the king, "Amen! May the LORD, the God of my lord the king, so ordain. 37 As the LORD has been with my lord the king, so may he be with Solomon, and make his throne greater than the throne of my lord King David."

1.22–37. 28–32: The movements of Bathsheba and Nathan are confusing and may indicate editorial work of some sort. As it stands, the reader must assume that each of them leaves the king's presence when he interviews the other. **33:** The *mule* was the royal mount (2 Sam 18.9). The *Gihon* spring was the water source for the city of Jerusalem.

38 So the priest Zadok, the prophet Nathan, and Benaiah son of Jehoiada, and the Cherethites and the Pelethites, went down and had Solomon ride on King David's mule, and led him to Gihon. 39 There the priest Zadok took the horn of oil from the tent and anointed Solomon. Then they blew the trumpet, and all the people said, "Long live King Solomon!" 40 And all the people went up following him, playing on pipes and rejoicing with great joy, so that the earth quaked at their noise.

41 Adonijah and all the guests who were with him heard it as they finished feasting. When Joab heard the sound of the trumpet, he said, "Why is the city in an uproar?" 42 While he was still speaking, Jonathan son of the priest Abiathar arrived. Adonijah said, "Come in, for you are a worthy man and surely you bring good news." 43 Jonathan answered Adonijah, "No, for our lord King David has made Solomon king; 44 the king has sent with him the priest Zadok, the prophet Nathan, and Benaiah son of Jehoiada, and the Cherethites and the Pelethites; and they had him ride on the king's mule; 45 the priest Zadok and the prophet Nathan have anointed him king at Gihon; and they have gone up from there rejoicing, so that the city

a Gk: Heb *the commanders*

is in an uproar. This is the noise that you heard. [46]Solomon now sits on the royal throne. [47]Moreover the king's servants came to congratulate our lord King David, saying, 'May God make the name of Solomon more famous than yours, and make his throne greater than your throne.' The king bowed in worship on the bed [48]and went on to pray thus, 'Blessed be the LORD, the God of Israel, who today has granted one of my offspring[a] to sit on my throne and permitted me to witness it.' "

[49] Then all the guests of Adonijah got up trembling and went their own ways. [50]Adonijah, fearing Solomon, got up and went to grasp the horns of the altar. [51]Solomon was informed, "Adonijah is afraid of King Solomon; see, he has laid hold of the horns of the altar, saying, 'Let King Solomon swear to me first that he will not kill his servant with the sword.' " [52]So Solomon responded, "If he proves to be a worthy man, not one of his hairs shall fall to the ground; but if wickedness is found in him, he shall die." [53]Then King Solomon sent to have him brought down from the altar. He came to do obeisance to King Solomon; and Solomon said to him, "Go home."

1.38–53. 38: *The Cherethites and Pelethites* were the royal bodyguard; they were Philistines or associated with the Philistines. **39:** Anointing* was a way of designating a person for some special office. It involved dripping or smearing fine olive oil on the person's head. **50:** The *horns of the altar* were projections from each corner of a sacrificial altar. Since the altar was holy, grasping the horns was a way of seeking sanctuary from execution.

2 When David's time to die drew near, he charged his son Solomon, saying: [2]"I am about to go the way of all the earth. Be strong, be courageous, [3]and keep the charge of the LORD your God, walking in his ways and keeping his statutes, his commandments, his ordinances, and his testimonies, as it is written in the law of Moses, so that you may prosper in all that you do and wherever you turn. [4]Then the LORD will establish his word that he spoke concerning me: 'If your heirs take heed to their way, to walk

before me in faithfulness with all their heaı and with all their soul, there shall not faiı you a successor on the throne of Israel.'

[5] "Moreover you know also what Joab son of Zeruiah did to me, how he dealt with the two commanders of the armies of Israel, Abner son of Ner, and Amasa son of Jether, whom he murdered, retaliating in time of peace for blood that had been shed in war, and putting the blood of war on the belt around his waist, and on the sandals on his feet. [6]Act therefore according to your wisdom, but do not let his gray head go down to Sheol in peace. [7]Deal loyally, however, with the sons of Barzillai the Gileadite, and let them be among those who eat at your table; for with such loyalty they met me when I fled from your brother Absalom. [8]There is also with you Shimei son of Gera, the Benjaminite from Bahurim, who cursed me with a terrible curse on the day when I went to Mahanaim; but when he came down to meet me at the Jordan, I swore to him by the LORD, 'I will not put you to death with the sword.' [9]Therefore do not hold him guiltless, for you are a wise man; you will know what you ought to do to him, and you must bring his gray head down with blood to Sheol."

2.1–46: Solomon deals with his rivals. 1–4: David's charge to Solomon is in deuteronomistic* style and is typical of the charges that one leader gives to another in the Deuteronomistic History, especially Moses' charge to Joshua and the people (Deut 4.40; 32.23). **5–9:** David's orders justify Solomon's actions in the rest of the chapter. He is told to execute Joab because of Joab's murders of Abner (2 Sam 3.26–30) and Amasa (2 Sam 20.4–10). However, these murders were committed years earlier, so that punishing Joab at this point makes little sense. Solomon's true motive for Joab's execution was political—Joab had supported Adonijah. *Sheol* (v. 6) was the abode of the dead. *Barzillai* had helped David when he fled from Absalom (2 Sam 17.27), and David had promised to take care of Barzillai's son as a reward (2 Sam 19.31–40). *Shimei* had cursed David when he fled from Absalom (2 Sam 16.5–8) and then apologized when David returned victorious (2 Sam 19.16–23).

a Gk: Heb *one*

10 Then David slept with his ancestors, and was buried in the city of David. 11The time that David reigned over Israel was forty years; he reigned seven years in Hebron, and thirty-three years in Jerusalem. 12So Solomon sat on the throne of his father David; and his kingdom was firmly established.

13 Then Adonijah son of Haggith came to Bathsheba, Solomon's mother. She asked, "Do you come peaceably?" He said, "Peaceably." 14Then he said, "May I have a word with you?" She said, "Go on." 15He said, "You know that the kingdom was mine, and that all Israel expected me to reign; however, the kingdom has turned about and become my brother's, for it was his from the LORD. 16And now I have one request to make of you; do not refuse me." She said to him, "Go on." 17He said, "Please ask King Solomon—he will not refuse you—to give me Abishag the Shunammite as my wife." 18Bathsheba said, "Very well; I will speak to the king on your behalf."

19 So Bathsheba went to King Solomon, to speak to him on behalf of Adonijah. The king rose to meet her, and bowed down to her; then he sat on his throne, and had a throne brought for the king's mother, and she sat on his right. 20Then she said, "I have one small request to make of you; do not refuse me." And the king said to her, "Make your request, my mother; for I will not refuse you." 21She said, "Let Abishag the Shunammite be given to your brother Adonijah as his wife." 22King Solomon answered his mother, "And why do you ask Abishag the Shunammite for Adonijah? Ask for him the kingdom as well! For he is my elder brother; ask not only for him but also for the priest Abiathar and for Joab son of Zeruiah!" 23Then King Solomon swore by the LORD, "So may God do to me, and more also, for Adonijah has devised this scheme at the risk of his life! 24Now therefore as the LORD lives, who has established me and placed me on the throne of my father David, and who has made me a house as he promised, today Adonijah shall be put to death." 25So King Solomon sent Benaiah son of Jehoiada; he struck him down, and he died.

David's death and burial. *Forty years* (v. 11) is often a round number for a generation in the Bible. **12–25:** The story of Adonijah's request is not very believable. To take a member of the harem, such as Abishag, would be a blatant play for the throne. Adonijah would hardly have been foolish enough to make such a request with Solomon in power. Besides, he could not have chosen a worse advocate than the king's own mother. Solomon's true motive for having Adonijah killed was again political; he was removing his rival for kingship.

26 The king said to the priest Abiathar, "Go to Anathoth, to your estate; for you deserve death. But I will not at this time put you to death, because you carried the ark of the Lord GOD before my father David, and because you shared in all the hardships my father endured." 27So Solomon banished Abiathar from being priest to the LORD, thus fulfilling the word of the LORD that he had spoken concerning the house of Eli in Shiloh.

2.26–27: Abiathar was the only supporter Adonijah had not killed, apparently because he was a priest. He was banished instead. The prophecy *concerning the house of Eli in Shiloh* is in 1 Sam 2.27–36. This story also explains the dominance of the Zadokite priests in Jerusalem at the expense of their rivals in the line of Eli.

28 When the news came to Joab—for Joab had supported Adonijah though he had not supported Absalom—Joab fled to the tent of the LORD and grasped the horns of the altar. 29When it was told King Solomon, "Joab has fled to the tent of the LORD and now is beside the altar," Solomon sent Benaiah son of Jehoiada, saying, "Go, strike him down." 30So Benaiah came to the tent of the LORD and said to him, "The king commands, 'Come out.'" But he said, "No, I will die here." Then Benaiah brought the king word again, saying, "Thus said Joab, and thus he answered me." 31The king replied to him, "Do as he has said, strike him down and bury him; and thus take away from me and from my father's house the guilt for the blood that Joab shed without cause. 32The LORD will bring back his bloody deeds on his own

head, because, without the knowledge of my father David, he attacked and killed with the sword two men more righteous and better than himself, Abner son of Ner, commander of the army of Israel, and Amasa son of Jether, commander of the army of Judah. 33 So shall their blood come back on the head of Joab and on the head of his descendants forever; but to David, and to his descendants, and to his house, and to his throne, there shall be peace from the LORD forevermore." 34 Then Benaiah son of Jehoiada went up and struck him down and killed him; and he was buried at his own house near the wilderness. 35 The king put Benaiah son of Jehoiada over the army in his place, and the king put the priest Zadok in the place of Abiathar.

36 Then the king sent and summoned Shimei, and said to him, "Build yourself a house in Jerusalem, and live there, and do not go out from there to any place whatever. 37 For on the day you go out, and cross the Wadi Kidron, know for certain that you shall die; your blood shall be on your own head." 38 And Shimei said to the king, "The sentence is fair; as my lord the king has said, so will your servant do." So Shimei lived in Jerusalem many days.

39 But it happened at the end of three years that two of Shimei's slaves ran away to King Achish son of Maacah of Gath. When it was told Shimei, "Your slaves are in Gath," 40 Shimei arose and saddled a donkey, and went to Achish in Gath, to search for his slaves; Shimei went and brought his slaves from Gath. 41 When Solomon was told that Shimei had gone from Jerusalem to Gath and returned, 42 the king sent and summoned Shimei, and said to him, "Did I not make you swear by the LORD, and solemnly adjure you, saying, 'Know for certain that on the day you go out and go to any place whatever, you shall die'? And you said to me, 'The sentence is fair; I accept.' 43 Why then have you not kept your oath to the LORD and the commandment with which I charged you?" 44 The king also said to Shimei, "You know in your own heart all the evil that you did to my father David; so the LORD will bring back your evil on your own head. 45 But King Sol-

omon shall be blessed, and the throne of David shall be established before the LORD forever." 46 Then the king commanded Benaiah son of Jehoiada; and he went out and struck him down, and he died.

So the kingdom was established in the hand of Solomon.

2.28–46. 28–35: Joab is executed, ostensibly at David's command, despite his plea for sanctuary at the *horns of the altar* (v. 28; see 1.50). **36–46a:** Solomon confined Shimei to Jerusalem, perhaps to prevent him from causing any trouble in his home tribe of Benjamin (also Saul's tribe). When he violated his confinement, Solomon had him executed. **46b:** *The kingdom was established in the hand of Solomon* because all his rivals were removed.

3 Solomon made a marriage alliance with Pharaoh king of Egypt; he took Pharaoh's daughter and brought her into the city of David, until he had finished building his own house and the house of the LORD and the wall around Jerusalem. 2 The people were sacrificing at the high places, however, because no house had yet been built for the name of the LORD.

3 Solomon loved the LORD, walking in the statutes of his father David; only, he sacrificed and offered incense at the high places. 4 The king went to Gibeon to sacrifice there, for that was the principal high place; Solomon used to offer a thousand burnt offerings on that altar. 5 At Gibeon the LORD appeared to Solomon in a dream by night; and God said, "Ask what I should give you." 6 And Solomon said, "You have shown great and steadfast love to your servant my father David, because he walked before you in faithfulness, in righteousness, and in uprightness of heart toward you; and you have kept for him this great and steadfast love, and have given him a son to sit on his throne today. 7 And now, O LORD my God, you have made your servant king in place of my father David, although I am only a little child; I do not know how to go out or come in. 8 And your servant is in the midst of the people whom you have chosen, a great people, so numerous they cannot be numbered or counted. 9 Give your servant therefore an un-

derstanding mind to govern your people, able to discern between good and evil; for who can govern this your great people?"

10 It pleased the Lord that Solomon had asked this. ¹¹God said to him, "Because you have asked this, and have not asked for yourself long life or riches, or for the life of your enemies, but have asked for yourself understanding to discern what is right, ¹²I now do according to your word. Indeed I give you a wise and discerning mind; no one like you has been before you and no one like you shall arise after you. ¹³I give you also what you have not asked, both riches and honor all your life; no other king shall compare with you. ¹⁴If you will walk in my ways, keeping my statutes and my commandments, as your father David walked, then I will lengthen your life."

15 Then Solomon awoke; it had been a dream. He came to Jerusalem where he stood before the ark of the covenant of the LORD. He offered up burnt offerings and offerings of well-being, and provided a feast for all his servants.

3.1–15: Solomon's gift of wisdom. 1: A *marriage alliance* was a treaty sealed with a marriage, a common practice in the ancient Near East. This verse anticipates 11.1, where foreign women prove to be Solomon's undoing. **2–4:** *High places* were raised platforms where worship took place. They are usually condemned in the Bible. But these verses explain that the use of them during Solomon's early reign, especially his use of the one at Gibeon, was permissible since the Temple* had not yet been built. Solomon's actions here may be a dream incubation—a way of seeking divine revelation through a dream by petitioning a deity and then sleeping at that god's shrine. **5–9:** Solomon's reference to himself as *a little child* (v. 7) expresses his feelings of being overwhelmed by his responsibility as king and is not to be taken literally. He requests *an understanding mind* in order to *govern* (lit., "judge") the numerous people of Israel. **10–14:** The LORD grants Solomon's request and promises him wealth as well. Thus, Solomon's traditional wisdom and magnificence are explained as gifts from God.

16 Later, two women who were prostitutes came to the king and stood before him.

¹⁷The one woman said, "Please, my lord, this woman and I live in the same house; and I gave birth while she was in the house. ¹⁸Then on the third day after I gave birth, this woman also gave birth. We were together; there was no one else with us in the house, only the two of us were in the house. ¹⁹Then this woman's son died in the night, because she lay on him. ²⁰She got up in the middle of the night and took my son from beside me while your servant slept. She laid him at her breast, and laid her dead son at my breast. ²¹When I rose in the morning to nurse my son, I saw that he was dead; but when I looked at him closely in the morning, clearly it was not the son I had borne." ²²But the other woman said, "No, the living son is mine, and the dead son is yours." The first said, "No, the dead son is yours, and the living son is mine." So they argued before the king.

23 Then the king said, "The one says, 'This is my son that is alive, and your son is dead'; while the other says, 'Not so! Your son is dead, and my son is the living one.' " ²⁴So the king said, "Bring me a sword," and they brought a sword before the king. ²⁵The king said, "Divide the living boy in two; then give half to the one, and half to the other." ²⁶But the woman whose son was alive said to the king—because compassion for her son burned within her—"Please, my lord, give her the living boy; certainly do not kill him!" The other said, "It shall be neither mine nor yours; divide it." ²⁷Then the king responded: "Give the first woman the living boy; do not kill him. She is his mother." ²⁸All Israel heard of the judgment that the king had rendered; and they stood in awe of the king, because they perceived that the wisdom of God was in him, to execute justice.

3.16–28: An illustration of Solomon's wisdom. The king served as a kind of "supreme court," and it was his responsibility to see that justice was equitably disbursed in the land. This seemingly impossible case shows Solomon's great wisdom in judgment.

4 King Solomon was king over all Israel, ²and these were his high officials: Azariah son of Zadok was the priest; ³Elihoreph

and Ahijah sons of Shisha were secretaries; Jehoshaphat son of Ahilud was recorder; [4]Benaiah son of Jehoiada was in command of the army; Zadok and Abiathar were priests; [5]Azariah son of Nathan was over the officials; Zabud son of Nathan was priest and king's friend; [6]Ahishar was in charge of the palace; and Adoniram son of Abda was in charge of the forced labor.

[7] Solomon had twelve officials over all Israel, who provided food for the king and his household; each one had to make provision for one month in the year. [8]These were their names: Ben-hur, in the hill country of Ephraim; [9]Ben-deker, in Makaz, Shaalbim, Beth-shemesh, and Elon-beth-hanan; [10]Ben-hesed, in Arubboth (to him belonged Socoh and all the land of Hepher); [11]Ben-abinadab, in all Naphath-dor (he had Taphath, Solomon's daughter, as his wife); [12]Baana son of Ahilud, in Taanach, Megiddo, and all Beth-shean, which is beside Zarethan below Jezreel, and from Beth-shean to Abel-meholah, as far as the other side of Jokmeam; [13]Ben-geber, in Ramoth-gilead (he had the villages of Jair son of Manasseh, which are in Gilead, and he had the region of Argob, which is in Bashan, sixty great cities with walls and bronze bars); [14]Ahinadab son of Iddo, in Mahanaim; [15]Ahimaaz, in Naphtali (he had taken Basemath, Solomon's daughter, as his wife); [16]Baana son of Hushai, in Asher and Bealoth; [17]Jehoshaphat son of Paruah, in Issachar; [18]Shimei son of Ela, in Benjamin; [19]Geber son of Uri, in the land of Gilead, the country of King Sihon of the Amorites and of King Og of Bashan. And there was one official in the land of Judah.

[20] Judah and Israel were as numerous as the sand by the sea; they ate and drank and were happy. [21][a]Solomon was sovereign over all the kingdoms from the Euphrates to the land of the Philistines, even to the border of Egypt; they brought tribute and served Solomon all the days of his life.

ince had to provide for the king one month in the year (v. 7). Judah is listed separately (v. 19) because it was exempted from taxation as David's and Solomon's home tribe. **20–21:** This is an idealized statement, as the revolt immediately after Solomon's death indicates. The extent of his actual rule may also be exaggerated here.

[22] Solomon's provision for one day was thirty cors of choice flour, and sixty cors of meal, [23]ten fat oxen, and twenty pasture-fed cattle, one hundred sheep, besides deer, gazelles, roebucks, and fatted fowl. [24]For he had dominion over all the region west of the Euphrates from Tiphsah to Gaza, over all the kings west of the Euphrates; and he had peace on all sides. [25]During Solomon's lifetime Judah and Israel lived in safety, from Dan even to Beer-sheba, all of them under their vines and fig trees. [26]Solomon also had forty thousand stalls of horses for his chariots, and twelve thousand horsemen. [27]Those officials supplied provisions for King Solomon and for all who came to King Solomon's table, each one in his month; they let nothing be lacking. [28]They also brought to the required place barley and straw for the horses and swift steeds, each according to his charge.

[29] God gave Solomon very great wisdom, discernment, and breadth of understanding as vast as the sand on the seashore, [30]so that Solomon's wisdom surpassed the wisdom of all the people of the east, and all the wisdom of Egypt. [31]He was wiser than anyone else, wiser than Ethan the Ezrahite, and Heman, Calcol, and Darda, children of Mahol; his fame spread throughout all the surrounding nations. [32]He composed three thousand proverbs, and his songs numbered a thousand and five. [33]He would speak of trees, from the cedar that is in the Lebanon to the hyssop that grows in the wall; he would speak of animals, and birds, and reptiles, and fish. [34]People came from all the nations to hear the wisdom of Solomon; they came from all the kings of the earth who had heard of his wisdom.

4.1–34: Solomon's administration. 1–6: Similar lists are found for David's cabinet in 2 Sam 8.15–18; 20.23–26. **7–19:** Solomon reorganized Israel into twelve provinces for purposes of taxation. Each prov-

a Ch 5.1 in Heb

4.22–34. 22–28: A *cor* (v. 22) was about eleven bushels. *From Dan to Beer-sheba* (v. 25) marked the traditional boundaries of Israel and Judah. The expression *all of them under their vine and fig trees* was an idiom for tranquillity and agricultural prosperity. **29–34:** Solomon's legendary* wisdom is said to exceed that of *the people of the east*, which is probably a reference to Mesopotamia (roughly modern Iraq), and *of Egypt* (v. 30), the two great civilizations of the ancient Near East. Wisdom in the sense used here involved not only wise judgment but also the composition of wisdom literature,* such as proverbs, and the observation of the natural world (vv. 32–33).

5 *a* Now King Hiram of Tyre sent his servants to Solomon, when he heard that they had anointed him king in place of his father; for Hiram had always been a friend to David. [2]Solomon sent word to Hiram, saying, [3]"You know that my father David could not build a house for the name of the LORD his God because of the warfare with which his enemies surrounded him, until the LORD put them under the soles of his feet.*b* [4]But now the LORD my God has given me rest on every side; there is neither adversary nor misfortune. [5]So I intend to build a house for the name of the LORD my God, as the LORD said to my father David, 'Your son, whom I will set on your throne in your place, shall build the house for my name.' [6]Therefore command that cedars from the Lebanon be cut for me. My servants will join your servants, and I will give you whatever wages you set for your servants; for you know that there is no one among us who knows how to cut timber like the Sidonians."

7 When Hiram heard the words of Solomon, he rejoiced greatly, and said, "Blessed be the LORD today, who has given to David a wise son to be over this great people." [8]Hiram sent word to Solomon, "I have heard the message that you have sent to me; I will fulfill all your needs in the matter of cedar and cypress timber. [9]My servants shall bring it down to the sea from the Lebanon; I will make it into rafts to go by sea to the place you indicate. I will have them broken up there for you to take away. And you shall meet my needs by providing food for my

household." [10]So Hiram supplied Solomon's every need for timber of cedar and cypress. [11]Solomon in turn gave Hiram twenty thousand cors of wheat as food for his household, and twenty cors of fine oil. Solomon gave this to Hiram year by year. [12]So the LORD gave Solomon wisdom, as he promised him. There was peace between Hiram and Solomon; and the two of them made a treaty.

13 King Solomon conscripted forced labor out of all Israel; the levy numbered thirty thousand men. [14]He sent them to the Lebanon, ten thousand a month in shifts; they would be a month in the Lebanon and two months at home; Adoniram was in charge of the forced labor. [15]Solomon also had seventy thousand laborers and eighty thousand stonecutters in the hill country, [16]besides Solomon's three thousand three hundred supervisors who were over the work, having charge of the people who did the work. [17]At the king's command, they quarried out great, costly stones in order to lay the foundation of the house with dressed stones. [18]So Solomon's builders and Hiram's builders and the Gebalites did the stonecutting and prepared the timber and the stone to build the house.

5.1–18: Solomon prepares to build the Temple.* **1:** *Tyre* was a Phoenician city-state on the Mediterranean coast north of Israel, essentially modern Lebanon. The trees from this area were highly valued in antiquity. King Hiram provided building materials to David for his palace in Jerusalem (2 Sam 5.11–12). In the ancient Near East a god's house was his temple. **3:** The *house for the name of the LORD* is the temple of Yahweh. Since the LORD does not actually reside in the Temple, it is built for his "name." **4:** *Rest* is an important theme in the Deuteronomistic* History (see 2 Sam 7.1). The LORD promised the people rest when they had entered the promised land and come to the "place" where he would make his name dwell (Deut 12.10–11). With Solomon the promise of rest is fulfilled so that the Temple can now be built in Jerusalem. This emphasis on rest may be a play on Solomon's name, which sounds like the Hebrew word "shalom," meaning peace (see 1 Chr 22.9). **6:** The *Sidonians* were people from Sidon,

a Ch 5.15 in Heb *b* Gk Tg Vg: Heb *my feet* or *his feet* another Phoenician city-state. Here, however, it seems to refer to Phoenicians in general. **13:** Solomon's labor force was conscripted from *Israel* as distinguished from Judah. It is clear from ch. 12 that the use of this conscripted labor continued after the Temple was completed. **18:** *Gebalites* were people from the Phoenician city-state of Byblos (also known as Gebal).

6 In the four hundred eightieth year after the Israelites came out of the land of Egypt, in the fourth year of Solomon's reign over Israel, in the month of Ziv, which is the second month, he began to build the house of the LORD. ²The house that King Solomon built for the LORD was sixty cubits long, twenty cubits wide, and thirty cubits high. ³The vestibule in front of the nave of the house was twenty cubits wide, across the width of the house. Its depth was ten cubits in front of the house. ⁴For the house he made windows with recessed frames.*ᵃ* ⁵He also built a structure against the wall of the house, running around the walls of the house, both the nave and the inner sanctuary; and he made side chambers all around. ⁶The lowest story*ᵇ* was five cubits wide, the middle one was six cubits wide, and the third was seven cubits wide; for around the outside of the house he made offsets on the wall in order that the supporting beams should not be inserted into the walls of the house.

7 The house was built with stone finished at the quarry, so that neither hammer nor ax nor any tool of iron was heard in the temple while it was being built.

8 The entrance for the middle story was on the south side of the house: one went up by winding stairs to the middle story, and from the middle story to the third. ⁹So he built the house, and finished it; he roofed the house with beams and planks of cedar. ¹⁰He built the structure against the whole house, each story*ᶜ* five cubits high, and it was joined to the house with timbers of cedar.

11 Now the word of the LORD came to Solomon, ¹²"Concerning this house that you are building, if you will walk in my statutes, obey my ordinances, and keep all my commandments by walking in them, then I will establish my promise with you, which I made to your father David. ¹³I will dwell among the children of Israel, and will not forsake my people Israel."

6.1–38: The Temple* building. 1: *The fourth year of Solomon's reign* would be about 960 BCE, placing the date of the Exodus at 1440. But *the four hundred eightieth year* is probably an artificial number, perhaps representing twelve generations using the traditional round number of forty years for a generation. *The month of Ziv* was in the spring (April—May). **2:** A *cubit* was about eighteen inches. **3–5:** The basic design of the building with its three main parts—here translated the *vestibule, nave,* and *inner sanctuary*—was typical of the style of temples in ancient Syria and Phoenicia. **7:** Iron tools were forbidden for the construction of altars (Deut 27.5; Josh 8.31). Something of this same prohibition may have been at work in the Temple building. **11–13:** These verses are in typical deuteronomistic* language. They make the promise to David and Yahweh's presence among the people conditional upon Solomon's obedience.

14 So Solomon built the house, and finished it. ¹⁵He lined the walls of the house on the inside with boards of cedar; from the floor of the house to the rafters of the ceiling, he covered them on the inside with wood; and he covered the floor of the house with boards of cypress. ¹⁶He built twenty cubits of the rear of the house with boards of cedar from the floor to the rafters, and he built this within as an inner sanctuary, as the most holy place. ¹⁷The house, that is, the nave in front of the inner sanctuary, was forty cubits long. ¹⁸The cedar within the house had carvings of gourds and open flowers; all was cedar, no stone was seen. ¹⁹The inner sanctuary he prepared in the innermost part of the house, to set there the ark of the covenant of the LORD. ²⁰The interior of the inner sanctuary was twenty cubits long, twenty cubits wide, and twenty cubits high; he overlaid it with pure gold. He also overlaid the altar with cedar.*ᵈ* ²¹Solomon overlaid the inside of the house with pure gold, then he drew chains of gold across, in front of the inner sanctuary, and overlaid it with gold. ²²Next

a Gk: Meaning of Heb uncertain   *b* Gk: Heb *structure*
c Heb lacks *each story*   *d* Meaning of Heb uncertain

he overlaid the whole house with gold, in order that the whole house might be perfect; even the whole altar that belonged to the inner sanctuary he overlaid with gold.

23 In the inner sanctuary he made two cherubim of olivewood, each ten cubits high. 24Five cubits was the length of one wing of the cherub, and five cubits the length of the other wing of the cherub; it was ten cubits from the tip of one wing to the tip of the other. 25The other cherub also measured ten cubits; both cherubim had the same measure and the same form. 26The height of one cherub was ten cubits, and so was that of the other cherub. 27He put the cherubim in the innermost part of the house; the wings of the cherubim were spread out so that a wing of one was touching the one wall, and a wing of the other cherub was touching the other wall; their other wings toward the center of the house were touching wing to wing. 28He also overlaid the cherubim with gold.

29 He carved the walls of the house all around about with carved engravings of cherubim, palm trees, and open flowers, in the inner and outer rooms. 30The floor of the house he overlaid with gold, in the inner and outer rooms.

31 For the entrance to the inner sanctuary he made doors of olivewood; the lintel and the doorposts were five-sided.*a* 32He covered the two doors of olivewood with carvings of cherubim, palm trees, and open flowers; he overlaid them with gold, and spread gold on the cherubim and on the palm trees.

33 So also he made for the entrance to the nave doorposts of olivewood, four-sided each, 34and two doors of cypress wood; the two leaves of the one door were folding, and the two leaves of the other door were folding. 35He carved cherubim, palm trees, and open flowers, overlaying them with gold evenly applied upon the carved work. 36He built the inner court with three courses of dressed stone to one course of cedar beams.

37 In the fourth year the foundation of the house of the LORD was laid, in the month of Ziv. 38In the eleventh year, in the month of Bul, which is the eighth month, the house was finished in all its parts, and according to

all its specifications. He was seven years in building it.

6.14–38. 14–36: The interior of the Temple* was lavishly decorated. The various designs of plants and fruits were likely symbols of fertility. The *cherubim** (plural of *cherub*, vv. 23–29) were mythical griffin-like creatures whose statues often guarded the entrances to temples and palaces in the ancient Near East. **37:** This verse refers to v. 1. **38:** The month of *Bul* was in the fall (October–November).

7 Solomon was building his own house thirteen years, and he finished his entire house.

2 He built the House of the Forest of the Lebanon one hundred cubits long, fifty cubits wide, and thirty cubits high, built on four rows of cedar pillars, with cedar beams on the pillars. 3It was roofed with cedar on the forty-five rafters, fifteen in each row, which were on the pillars. 4There were window frames in the three rows, facing each other in the three rows. 5All the doorways and doorposts had four-sided frames, opposite, facing each other in the three rows.

6 He made the Hall of Pillars fifty cubits long and thirty cubits wide. There was a porch in front with pillars, and a canopy in front of them.

7 He made the Hall of the Throne where he was to pronounce judgment, the Hall of Justice, covered with cedar from floor to floor.

8 His own house where he would reside, in the other court back of the hall, was of the same construction. Solomon also made a house like this hall for Pharaoh's daughter, whom he had taken in marriage.

9 All these were made of costly stones, cut according to measure, sawed with saws, back and front, from the foundation to the coping, and from outside to the great court. 10The foundation was of costly stones, huge stones, stones of eight and ten cubits. 11There were costly stones above, cut to measure, and cedarwood. 12The great court had three courses of dressed stone to one

a Meaning of Heb uncertain

layer of cedar beams all around; so had the inner court of the house of the LORD, and the vestibule of the house.

7.1–12: Solomon's palace complex. 1: Solomon spent *thirteen* years on his own palace and only seven on the Temple* (7.38). But the writer of 1 Kings stresses the Temple by spending much more time on it. Also, in the Hebrew (Masoretic*) text the material about Solomon's palace is sandwiched between accounts dealing with the Temple (6.1–38 and 7.13–51). The order of the Greek or Septuagint* (LXX*) text is different. Whichever placement is original, both Hebrew and Greek versions show that, for the author of 1 Kings, the Temple was of greater importance. **2–5:** The *House of the Forest of the Lebanon* may have derived its name from its rows of cedar pillars.

---

13 Now King Solomon invited and received Hiram from Tyre. 14He was the son of a widow of the tribe of Naphtali, whose father, a man of Tyre, had been an artisan in bronze; he was full of skill, intelligence, and knowledge in working bronze. He came to King Solomon, and did all his work.

15 He cast two pillars of bronze. Eighteen cubits was the height of the one, and a cord of twelve cubits would encircle it; the second pillar was the same.*a* 16He also made two capitals of molten bronze, to set on the tops of the pillars; the height of the one capital was five cubits, and the height of the other capital was five cubits. 17There were nets of checker work with wreaths of chain work for the capitals on the tops of the pillars; seven*b* for the one capital, and seven*b* for the other capital. 18He made the columns with two rows around each latticework to cover the capitals that were above the pomegranates; he did the same with the other capital. 19Now the capitals that were on the tops of the pillars in the vestibule were of lily-work, four cubits high. 20The capitals were on the two pillars and also above the rounded projection that was beside the latticework; there were two hundred pomegranates in rows all around; and so with the other capital. 21He set up the pillars at the vestibule of the temple; he set up the pillar on the south and called it Jachin; and he set up the pillar on the north and called it Boaz. 22On the tops

of the pillars was lily-work. Thus the work of the pillars was finished.

23 Then he made the molten sea; it was round, ten cubits from brim to brim, and five cubits high. A line of thirty cubits would encircle it completely. 24Under its brim were panels all around it, each of ten cubits, surrounding the sea; there were two rows of panels, cast when it was cast. 25It stood on twelve oxen, three facing north, three facing west, three facing south, and three facing east; the sea was set on them. The hindquarters of each were toward the inside. 26Its thickness was a handbreadth; its brim was made like the brim of a cup, like the flower of a lily; it held two thousand baths.*c*

7.13–51: The bronze furnishings of the Temple.* 13–14: This *Hiram* is not the king but a craftsman. 2 Chronicles 2.12–13 calls him Huram-Abi. *Skill*, literally "wisdom." This word may also mean skill at a particular craft, and that is doubtless its nuance here. **15–22:** The *two pillars* had some symbolic meaning that is no longer clear. Their names, *Jachin* ("he establishes") and *Boaz* ("in him is strength") may represent the LORD's foundation of the earth or sacred trees (v. 21). **23–26:** The *molten sea* probably represented the primeval chaos which the LORD had defeated before making the world, in one version of creation. Another possibility is that the *molten sea* represents the primeval deep out of which the LORD created the universe, according to Gen 1. The *twelve oxen* on which it stood (v. 25) were fertility symbols.

---

27 He also made the ten stands of bronze; each stand was four cubits long, four cubits wide, and three cubits high. 28This was the construction of the stands: they had borders; the borders were within the frames; 29on the borders that were set in the frames were lions, oxen, and cherubim. On the frames, both above and below the lions and oxen, there were wreaths of beveled work. 30Each stand had four bronze wheels and axles of bronze; at the four corners were supports for a basin. The supports were cast with wreaths at the side of each. 31Its opening was within the crown whose height was one cubit; its

a Cn: Heb *and a cord of twelve cubits encircled the second pillar*; Compare Jer 52.21　　*b* Heb: Gk *a net*
c A Heb measure of volume

opening was round, as a pedestal is made; it was a cubit and a half wide. At its opening there were carvings; its borders were four-sided, not round. 32The four wheels were underneath the borders; the axles of the wheels were in the stands; and the height of a wheel was a cubit and a half. 33The wheels were made like a chariot wheel; their axles, their rims, their spokes, and their hubs were all cast. 34There were four supports at the four corners of each stand; the supports were of one piece with the stands. 35On the top of the stand there was a round band half a cubit high; on the top of the stand, its stays and its borders were of one piece with it. 36On the surfaces of its stays and on its borders he carved cherubim, lions, and palm trees, where each had space, with wreaths all around. 37In this way he made the ten stands; all of them were cast alike, with the same size and the same form.

38 He made ten basins of bronze; each basin held forty baths,*a* each basin measured four cubits; there was a basin for each of the ten stands. 39He set five of the stands on the south side of the house, and five on the north side of the house; he set the sea on the southeast corner of the house.

40 Hiram also made the pots, the shovels, and the basins. So Hiram finished all the work that he did for King Solomon on the house of the LORD: 41the two pillars, the two bowls of the capitals that were on the tops of the pillars, the two latticeworks to cover the two bowls of the capitals that were on the tops of the pillars; 42the four hundred pomegranates for the two latticeworks, two rows of pomegranates for each latticework, to cover the two bowls of the capitals that were on the pillars; 43the ten stands, the ten basins on the stands; 44the one sea, and the twelve oxen underneath the sea.

45 The pots, the shovels, and the basins, all these vessels that Hiram made for King Solomon for the house of the LORD were of burnished bronze. 46In the plain of the Jordan the king cast them, in the clay ground between Succoth and Zarethan. 47Solomon left all the vessels unweighed, because there were so many of them; the weight of the bronze was not determined.

48 So Solomon made all the vessels that were in the house of the LORD: the golden altar, the golden table for the bread of the Presence, 49the lampstands of pure gold, five on the south side and five on the north, in front of the inner sanctuary; the flowers, the lamps, and the tongs, of gold; 50the cups, snuffers, basins, dishes for incense, and fire-pans, of pure gold; the sockets for the doors of the innermost part of the house, the most holy place, and for the doors of the nave of the temple, of gold.

51 Thus all the work that King Solomon did on the house of the LORD was finished. Solomon brought in the things that his father David had dedicated, the silver, the gold, and the vessels, and stored them in the treasuries of the house of the LORD.

7.27–51. 27–39: The *ten stands* and *ten lavers* were also richly decorated with symbols of fertility and divine power. 48: The *golden altar* was apparently for burning incense. On the *bread of the Presence,* see Lev 24.5–9. 49: The *lampstands* were made to hold lamps consisting of a container for oil and a wick. They were not candlesticks.

8 Then Solomon assembled the elders of Israel and all the heads of the tribes, the leaders of the ancestral houses of the Israelites, before King Solomon in Jerusalem, to bring up the ark of the covenant of the LORD out of the city of David, which is Zion. 2All the people of Israel assembled to King Solomon at the festival in the month Ethanim, which is the seventh month. 3And all the elders of Israel came, and the priests carried the ark. 4So they brought up the ark of the LORD, the tent of meeting, and all the holy vessels that were in the tent; the priests and the Levites brought them up. 5King Solomon and all the congregation of Israel, who had assembled before him, were with him before the ark, sacrificing so many sheep and oxen that they could not be counted or numbered. 6Then the priests brought the ark of the covenant of the LORD to its place, in the inner sanctuary of the house, in the most holy

a A Heb measure of volume

place, underneath the wings of the cherubim. 7For the cherubim spread out their wings over the place of the ark, so that the cherubim made a covering above the ark and its poles. 8The poles were so long that the ends of the poles were seen from the holy place in front of the inner sanctuary; but they could not be seen from outside; they are there to this day. 9There was nothing in the ark except the two tablets of stone that Moses had placed there at Horeb, where the LORD made a covenant with the Israelites, when they came out of the land of Egypt. 10And when the priests came out of the holy place, a cloud filled the house of the LORD, 11so that the priests could not stand to minister because of the cloud; for the glory of the LORD filled the house of the LORD.

12 Then Solomon said,

"The LORD has said that he would dwell
    in thick darkness.
13 I have built you an exalted house,
    a place for you to dwell in forever."

14 Then the king turned around and blessed all the assembly of Israel, while all the assembly of Israel stood. 15He said, "Blessed be the LORD, the God of Israel, who with his hand has fulfilled what he promised with his mouth to my father David, saying, 16'Since the day that I brought my people Israel out of Egypt, I have not chosen a city from any of the tribes of Israel in which to build a house, that my name might be there; but I chose David to be over my people Israel.' 17My father David had it in mind to build a house for the name of the LORD, the God of Israel. 18But the LORD said to my father David, 'You did well to consider building a house for my name; 19nevertheless you shall not build the house, but your son who shall be born to you shall build the house for my name.' 20Now the LORD has upheld the promise that he made; for I have risen in the place of my father David; I sit on the throne of Israel, as the LORD promised, and have built the house for the name of the LORD, the God of Israel. 21There I have provided a place for the ark, in which is the covenant of the LORD that he made with our ancestors when he brought them out of the land of Egypt."

8.1–66: The dedication of the Temple.* **2:** *The month* of *Ethanim,* also called Tishri, was in the fall (September—October). This means that the dedication of the Temple occurred nearly a year after its completion, perhaps to coincide with the autumn new year celebration. **7–8:** The ark was carried by *poles* inside of rings on either side of the box that was the ark proper. The expression *to this day* may indicate that the writer lived while the Temple was still standing. **11:** The *glory of the LORD* was the thick cloud that symbolized the LORD's presence. **15–21:** Solomon's speech beginning in this verse is a deuteronomistic* composition. It links the promise to David of a dynasty* (2 Sam 7) with that of rest for Israel (Deut 12.11–12). It therefore identifies the "place" described in Deuteronomy with Solomon's Temple.

22 Then Solomon stood before the altar of the LORD in the presence of all the assembly of Israel, and spread out his hands to heaven. 23He said, "O LORD, God of Israel, there is no God like you in heaven above or on earth beneath, keeping covenant and steadfast love for your servants who walk before you with all their heart, 24the covenant that you kept for your servant my father David as you declared to him; you promised with your mouth and have this day fulfilled with your hand. 25Therefore, O LORD, God of Israel, keep for your servant my father David that which you promised him, saying, 'There shall never fail you a successor before me to sit on the throne of Israel, if only your children look to their way, to walk before me as you have walked before me.' 26Therefore, O God of Israel, let your word be confirmed, which you promised to your servant my father David.

27 "But will God indeed dwell on the earth? Even heaven and the highest heaven cannot contain you, much less this house that I have built! 28Regard your servant's prayer and his plea, O LORD my God, heeding the cry and the prayer that your servant prays to you today; 29that your eyes may be open night and day toward this house, the place of which you said, 'My name shall be there,' that you may heed the prayer that your servant prays toward this place. 30Hear the plea of your servant and of your people

Israel when they pray toward this place; O hear in heaven your dwelling place; heed and forgive.

31 "If someone sins against a neighbor and is given an oath to swear, and comes and swears before your altar in this house, 32then hear in heaven, and act, and judge your servants, condemning the guilty by bringing their conduct on their own head, and vindicating the righteous by rewarding them according to their righteousness.

33 "When your people Israel, having sinned against you, are defeated before an enemy but turn again to you, confess your name, pray and plead with you in this house, 34then hear in heaven, forgive the sin of your people Israel, and bring them again to the land that you gave to their ancestors.

35 "When heaven is shut up and there is no rain because they have sinned against you, and then they pray toward this place, confess your name, and turn from their sin, because you punish*a* them, 36then hear in heaven, and forgive the sin of your servants, your people Israel, when you teach them the good way in which they should walk; and grant rain on your land, which you have given to your people as an inheritance.

37 "If there is famine in the land, if there is plague, blight, mildew, locust, or caterpillar; if their enemy besieges them in any*b* of their cities; whatever plague, whatever sickness there is; 38whatever prayer, whatever plea there is from any individual or from all your people Israel, all knowing the afflictions of their own hearts so that they stretch out their hands toward this house; 39then hear in heaven your dwelling place, forgive, act, and render to all whose hearts you know— according to all their ways, for only you know what is in every human heart— 40so that they may fear you all the days that they live in the land that you gave to our ancestors.

41 "Likewise when a foreigner, who is not of your people Israel, comes from a distant land because of your name 42—for they shall hear of your great name, your mighty hand, and your outstretched arm—when a foreigner comes and prays toward this house, 43then hear in heaven your dwelling place, and do according to all that the foreigner calls to you, so that all the peoples of the earth may know your name and fear you, as do your people Israel, and so that they may know that your name has been invoked on this house that I have built.

44 "If your people go out to battle against their enemy, by whatever way you shall send them, and they pray to the LORD toward the city that you have chosen and the house that I have built for your name, 45then hear in heaven their prayer and their plea, and maintain their cause.

46 "If they sin against you—for there is no one who does not sin—and you are angry with them and give them to an enemy, so that they are carried away captive to the land of the enemy, far off or near; 47yet if they come to their senses in the land to which they have been taken captive, and repent, and plead with you in the land of their captors, saying, 'We have sinned, and have done wrong; we have acted wickedly'; 48if they repent with all their heart and soul in the land of their enemies, who took them captive, and pray to you toward their land, which you gave to their ancestors, the city that you have chosen, and the house that I have built for your name; 49then hear in heaven your dwelling place their prayer and their plea, maintain their cause 50and forgive your people who have sinned against you, and all their transgressions that they have committed against you; and grant them compassion in the sight of their captors, so that they may have compassion on them 51(for they are your people and heritage, which you brought out of Egypt, from the midst of the iron-smelter). 52Let your eyes be open to the plea of your servant, and to the plea of your people Israel, listening to them whenever they call to you. 53For you have separated them from among all the peoples of the earth, to be your heritage, just as you promised through Moses, your servant, when you brought our ancestors out of Egypt, O Lord GOD."

8.22–53: Solomon's prayer contains seven petitions, which address various future problems and ask the LORD to heed the prayers made in and toward the

a Or *when you answer*   *b* Gk Syr: Heb *in the land*

Temple.* Scholars debate whether this prayer or part of it comes before the Exile* or after it. Verses 44–53, in particular, are often considered a later expansion of the prayer. The idea behind the word *heritage* in v. 53 is that each nation has its own god and each god his own people; the LORD's heritage is Israel.

54 Now when Solomon finished offering all this prayer and this plea to the LORD, he arose from facing the altar of the LORD, where he had knelt with hands outstretched toward heaven; 55he stood and blessed all the assembly of Israel with a loud voice:

56 "Blessed be the LORD, who has given rest to his people Israel according to all that he promised; not one word has failed of all his good promise, which he spoke through his servant Moses. 57The LORD our God be with us, as he was with our ancestors; may he not leave us or abandon us, 58but incline our hearts to him, to walk in all his ways, and to keep his commandments, his statutes, and his ordinances, which he commanded our ancestors. 59Let these words of mine, with which I pleaded before the LORD, be near to the LORD our God day and night, and may he maintain the cause of his servant and the cause of his people Israel, as each day requires; 60so that all the peoples of the earth may know that the LORD is God; there is no other. 61Therefore devote yourselves completely to the LORD our God, walking in his statutes and keeping his commandments, as at this day."

8.54–61: The benediction mentions *[the LORD's] commandments, his statutes, and his ordinances* (v. 58), which is a way of referring to the law of Moses. The confession that *the LORD is God; there is no other* (v. 60) is very similar to the traditional confession of Judaism known as the "shema" (Deut 6.4).

62 Then the king, and all Israel with him, offered sacrifice before the LORD. 63Solomon offered as sacrifices of well-being to the LORD twenty-two thousand oxen and one hundred twenty thousand sheep. So the king and all the people of Israel dedicated the house of the LORD. 64The same day the king consecrated the middle of the court that was in front of the house of the LORD; for there

he offered the burnt offerings and the grain offerings and the fat pieces of the sacrifices of well-being, because the bronze altar that was before the LORD was too small to receive the burnt offerings and the grain offerings and the fat pieces of the sacrifices of well-being.

65 So Solomon held the festival at that time, and all Israel with him—a great assembly, people from Lebo-hamath to the Wadi of Egypt—before the LORD our God, seven days.*a* 66On the eighth day he sent the people away; and they blessed the king, and went to their tents, joyful and in good spirits because of all the goodness that the LORD had shown to his servant David and to his people Israel.

8.62–66: These verses describe Solomon's great sacrifices and celebration at the Temple* dedication. The *bronze altar* (v. 64) was the altar of burnt offering, which, oddly, was not described among the bronze works of Hiram in ch. 7. *The festival* was the Feast of Tabernacles* or Booths ("sukkot") described in Lev 23.33–43; Num 29.12–38. *From Lebo-hamath to the Wadi* of *Egypt* describes the idealized boundaries of Israel during the reigns of David and Solomon, from northern Syria to the Egyptian border.

9 When Solomon had finished building the house of the LORD and the king's house and all that Solomon desired to build, 2the LORD appeared to Solomon a second time, as he had appeared to him at Gibeon. 3The LORD said to him, "I have heard your prayer and your plea, which you made before me; I have consecrated this house that you have built, and put my name there forever; my eyes and my heart will be there for all time. 4As for you, if you will walk before me, as David your father walked, with integrity of heart and uprightness, doing according to all that I have commanded you, and keeping my statutes and my ordinances, 5then I will establish your royal throne over Israel forever, as I promised your father David, saying, 'There shall not fail you a successor on the throne of Israel.'

a Compare Gk: Heb *seven days and seven days, fourteen days*

6 "If you turn aside from following me, you or your children, and do not keep my commandments and my statutes that I have set before you, but go and serve other gods and worship them, 7then I will cut Israel off from the land that I have given them; and the house that I have consecrated for my name I will cast out of my sight; and Israel will become a proverb and a taunt among all peoples. 8This house will become a heap of ruins;*a* everyone passing by it will be astonished, and will hiss; and they will say, 'Why has the LORD done such a thing to this land and to this house?' 9Then they will say, 'Because they have forsaken the LORD their God, who brought their ancestors out of the land of Egypt, and embraced other gods, worshiping them and serving them; therefore the LORD has brought this disaster upon them.'"

9.1–9: The LORD appears to Solomon again. The promise to David of an eternal dynasty* is extended to Solomon, but only on the condition of his obedience. Verses 6–9 anticipate the disobedience of Solomon and other kings, as well as the Exile.*

10 At the end of twenty years, in which Solomon had built the two houses, the house of the LORD and the king's house, 11King Hiram of Tyre having supplied Solomon with cedar and cypress timber and gold, as much as he desired, King Solomon gave to Hiram twenty cities in the land of Galilee. 12But when Hiram came from Tyre to see the cities that Solomon had given him, they did not please him. 13Therefore he said, "What kind of cities are these that you have given me, my brother?" So they are called the land of Cabul*b* to this day. 14But Hiram had sent to the king one hundred twenty talents of gold.

9.10–28: Other activities of Solomon. 10–14: Solomon seems to be in financial difficulties and is forced to sell land, though his bargaining appears shrewd. *Cabul* (v. 13) is explained as meaning "as nothing." This is a popular etymology or even an etiology* (a story or report that explains something's origin). The real meaning of the name is unknown. The *talent* was a measure of weight. Its amount varied, but it could be as much as 130 pounds.

15 This is the account of the forced labor that King Solomon conscripted to build the house of the LORD and his own house, the Millo and the wall of Jerusalem, Hazor, Megiddo, Gezer 16(Pharaoh king of Egypt had gone up and captured Gezer and burned it down, had killed the Canaanites who lived in the city, and had given it as dowry to his daughter, Solomon's wife; 17so Solomon rebuilt Gezer), Lower Beth-horon, 18Baalath, Tamar in the wilderness, within the land, 19as well as all of Solomon's storage cities, the cities for his chariots, the cities for his cavalry, and whatever Solomon desired to build, in Jerusalem, in Lebanon, and in all the land of his dominion. 20All the people who were left of the Amorites, the Hittites, the Perizzites, the Hivites, and the Jebusites, who were not of the people of Israel— 21their descendants who were still left in the land, whom the Israelites were unable to destroy completely—these Solomon conscripted for slave labor, and so they are to this day. 22But of the Israelites Solomon made no slaves; they were the soldiers, they were his officials, his commanders, his captains, and the commanders of his chariotry and cavalry.

23 These were the chief officers who were over Solomon's work: five hundred fifty, who had charge of the people who carried on the work.

24 But Pharaoh's daughter went up from the city of David to her own house that Solomon had built for her; then he built the Millo.

25 Three times a year Solomon used to offer up burnt offerings and sacrifices of well-being on the altar that he built for the LORD, offering incense*c* before the LORD. So he completed the house.

26 King Solomon built a fleet of ships at Ezion-geber, which is near Eloth on the shore of the Red Sea,*d* in the land of Edom. 27Hiram sent his servants with the fleet, sailors who were familiar with the sea, together with the servants of Solomon. 28They went

a Syr Old Latin: Heb *will become high*   *b* Perhaps meaning *a land good for nothing*   *c* Gk: Heb *offering incense with it that was*   *d* Or *Sea of Reeds* to Ophir, and imported from there four hundred twenty talents of gold, which they delivered to King Solomon.

9.15–28. 15–22: The *Millo*, probably meaning "fill," seems to have been earthwork connecting the Temple* area to the palace complex on the south. *Hazor, Megiddo,* and *Gezer* (v. 15) were all important administrative centers for Solomon. The *Amorites, Hittites, Perizzites, Hivites, and Jebusites* (v. 20) are names the Bible uses for different native Canaanite peoples. They are familiar from the book of Genesis (Gen 15.19–20). The claim (v. 22) that Solomon did not force Israelites to work in his levy of slaves seems contradicted by 5.13; 11.28; and the events in ch. 12. **24:** *Pharaoh's daughter* is a subtheme in chs. 1–11 (see 3.1; 9.16) that leads up to the report of his sin in ch. 11. **26–28:** The location of *Ophir* is unknown; it may have been in southern Arabia. On the weight of a *talent,* see comment on v. 14.

10 When the queen of Sheba heard of the fame of Solomon (fame due to*a* the name of the LORD), she came to test him with hard questions. ²She came to Jerusalem with a very great retinue, with camels bearing spices, and very much gold, and precious stones; and when she came to Solomon, she told him all that was on her mind. ³Solomon answered all her questions; there was nothing hidden from the king that he could not explain to her. ⁴When the queen of Sheba had observed all the wisdom of Solomon, the house that he had built, ⁵the food of his table, the seating of his officials, and the attendance of his servants, their clothing, his valets, and his burnt offerings that he offered at the house of the LORD, there was no more spirit in her.

6 So she said to the king, "The report was true that I heard in my own land of your accomplishments and of your wisdom, ⁷but I did not believe the reports until I came and my own eyes had seen it. Not even half had been told me; your wisdom and prosperity far surpass the report that I had heard. ⁸Happy are your wives!*b* Happy are these your servants, who continually attend you and hear your wisdom! ⁹Blessed be the LORD your God, who has delighted in you and set you on the throne of Israel! Because the LORD

loved Israel forever, he has made you king to execute justice and righteousness." ¹⁰Then she gave the king one hundred twenty talents of gold, a great quantity of spices, and precious stones; never again did spices come in such quantity as that which the queen of Sheba gave to King Solomon.

11 Moreover, the fleet of Hiram, which carried gold from Ophir, brought from Ophir a great quantity of almug wood and precious stones. ¹²From the almug wood the king made supports for the house of the LORD, and for the king's house, lyres also and harps for the singers; no such almug wood has come or been seen to this day.

13 Meanwhile King Solomon gave to the queen of Sheba every desire that she expressed, as well as what he gave her out of Solomon's royal bounty. Then she returned to her own land, with her servants.

10.1–13: The queen of Sheba visits. *Sheba* was in Arabia, perhaps modern Yemen. The *queen* may have come on a trade mission from one of the tribes living in that area. The story has been greatly elaborated as a display of Solomon's wealth and wisdom. **5:** *Spirit* may also mean "breath." **9:** It is rather surprising that a foreigner blesses by the name of Israel's God, Yahweh. This may be what the writer thinks she must have said. **10:** On the weight of a *talent,* see comment on 9.14. **12:** The reference to *almug wood* occurs only here in the Bible; the exact species is unknown.

14 The weight of gold that came to Solomon in one year was six hundred sixty-six talents of gold, ¹⁵besides that which came from the traders and from the business of the merchants, and from all the kings of Arabia and the governors of the land. ¹⁶King Solomon made two hundred large shields of beaten gold; six hundred shekels of gold went into each large shield. ¹⁷He made three hundred shields of beaten gold; three minas of gold went into each shield; and the king put them in the House of the Forest of Lebanon. ¹⁸The king also made a great ivory throne, and overlaid it with the finest gold. ¹⁹The throne had six steps. The top of the throne was rounded in the back, and on each

a Meaning of Heb uncertain   *b* Gk Syr: Heb *men*

side of the seat were arm rests and two lions standing beside the arm rests, 20while twelve lions were standing, one on each end of a step on the six steps. Nothing like it was ever made in any kingdom. 21All King Solomon's drinking vessels were of gold, and all the vessels of the House of the Forest of Lebanon were of pure gold; none were of silver—it was not considered as anything in the days of Solomon. 22For the king had a fleet of ships of Tarshish at sea with the fleet of Hiram. Once every three years the fleet of ships of Tarshish used to come bringing gold, silver, ivory, apes, and peacocks.[a]

23 Thus King Solomon excelled all the kings of the earth in riches and in wisdom. 24The whole earth sought the presence of Solomon to hear his wisdom, which God had put into his mind. 25Every one of them brought a present, objects of silver and gold, garments, weaponry, spices, horses, and mules, so much year by year.

26 Solomon gathered together chariots and horses; he had fourteen hundred chariots and twelve thousand horses, which he stationed in the chariot cities and with the king in Jerusalem. 27The king made silver as common in Jerusalem as stones, and he made cedars as numerous as the sycamores of the Shephelah. 28Solomon's import of horses was from Egypt and Kue, and the king's traders received them from Kue at a price. 29A chariot could be imported from Egypt for six hundred shekels of silver, and a horse for one hundred fifty; so through the king's traders they were exported to all the kings of the Hittites and the kings of Aram.

10.14–29: More on Solomon's wealth and activities. 14: *Six hundred sixty-six talents of gold* would be an enormous sum—between thirty and eighty-five tons! See comment on 9.14. **16–17:** There were 50 *shekels** in a mina and 60 *minas* in a talent, which could weigh between 45 and 130 pounds. Thus the large shields would have weighed between 9 and 26 pounds and the small ones half as much. **22:** *Ships of Tarshish* were probably large ships capable of making a long voyage. Tarshish was a site in southern Spain that represented the western extreme of the world known to the biblical writers. **27:** The *Shephelah* is the lowland area in southern Palestine between the Mediterranean coast-

land and the central highlands. **28:** *Kue* was in southeastern Anatolia (Turkey) near Cilicia. *Egypt* (Heb., "Misrayim") may be a mistake for Musri, also in Anatolia north of Kue.

11 King Solomon loved many foreign women along with the daughter of Pharaoh: Moabite, Ammonite, Edomite, Sidonian, and Hittite women, 2from the nations concerning which the LORD had said to the Israelites, "You shall not enter into marriage with them, neither shall they with you; for they will surely incline your heart to follow their gods"; Solomon clung to these in love. 3Among his wives were seven hundred princesses and three hundred concubines; and his wives turned away his heart. 4For when Solomon was old, his wives turned away his heart after other gods; and his heart was not true to the LORD his God, as was the heart of his father David. 5For Solomon followed Astarte the goddess of the Sidonians, and Milcom the abomination of the Ammonites. 6So Solomon did what was evil in the sight of the LORD, and did not completely follow the LORD, as his father David had done. 7Then Solomon built a high place for Chemosh the abomination of Moab, and for Molech the abomination of the Ammonites, on the mountain east of Jerusalem. 8He did the same for all his foreign wives, who offered incense and sacrificed to their gods.

9 Then the LORD was angry with Solomon, because his heart had turned away from the LORD, the God of Israel, who had appeared to him twice, 10and had commanded him concerning this matter, that he should not follow other gods; but he did not observe what the LORD commanded. 11Therefore the LORD said to Solomon, "Since this has been your mind and you have not kept my covenant and my statutes that I have commanded you, I will surely tear the kingdom from you and give it to your servant. 12Yet for the sake of your father David I will not do it in your lifetime; I will tear it out of the hand of your son. 13I will not, however, tear away the entire kingdom; I will give one

a Or *baboons*

tribe to your son, for the sake of my servant David and for the sake of Jerusalem, which I have chosen."

14 Then the LORD raised up an adversary against Solomon, Hadad the Edomite; he was of the royal house in Edom. 15For when David was in Edom, and Joab the commander of the army went up to bury the dead, he killed every male in Edom 16(for Joab and all Israel remained there six months, until he had eliminated every male in Edom); 17but Hadad fled to Egypt with some Edomites who were servants of his father. He was a young boy at that time. 18They set out from Midian and came to Paran; they took people with them from Paran and came to Egypt, to Pharaoh king of Egypt, who gave him a house, assigned him an allowance of food, and gave him land. 19Hadad found great favor in the sight of Pharaoh, so that he gave him his sister-in-law for a wife, the sister of Queen Tahpenes. 20The sister of Tahpenes gave birth by him to his son Genubath, whom Tahpenes weaned in Pharaoh's house; Genubath was in Pharaoh's house among the children of Pharaoh. 21When Hadad heard in Egypt that David slept with his ancestors and that Joab the commander of the army was dead, Hadad said to Pharaoh, "Let me depart, that I may go to my own country." 22But Pharaoh said to him, "What do you lack with me that you now seek to go to your own country?" And he said, "No, do let me go."

23 God raised up another adversary against Solomon,ᵃ Rezon son of Eliada, who had fled from his master, King Hadadezer of Zobah. 24He gathered followers around him and became leader of a marauding band, after the slaughter by David; they went to Damascus, settled there, and made him king in Damascus. 25He was an adversary of Israel all the days of Solomon, making trouble as Hadad did; he despised Israel and reigned over Aram.

11.1–43: Solomon's troubles. The writer has divided the account of Solomon's reign into two parts for theological reasons. The first part (chs. 1–10) told of his successes, the greatest of which was the building of the Temple.* But the division of the kingdom after

Solomon required an explanation, which the writer furnishes in the account of Solomon's religious failures in ch. 11. **1:** Solomon's many foreign wives were partly the result of treaties with other nations. **2:** See Deut 7.1–4 for the law prohibiting foreign marriages. **3:** A large harem was also a symbol of royal grandeur. The *princesses* were not all of royal birth but had gained royal status through marriage. *Concubines,*★ on the other hand, had no royal status but were female slaves used for sexual purposes. **4:** The statement that Solomon's *heart was not true* is a pun on his name. The word "true" in Hebrew is "shalem," which sounds like "Shelomoh," Solomon in Hebrew. **5:** *Astarte*★ was a prominent Phoenician and Canaanite goddess. The Hebrew text deliberately distorts her name to "Ashtoreth" to rhyme with the word "bosheth," meaning "abomination." *Milcom* was the chief god of the Ammonites, who lived in the area of modern northern Jordan. **7:** *Chemosh* was the chief god of the Moabites in central Jordan. *Molech* is a distortion of the name Milcom. **11–13:** The announcement of Solomon's punishment anticipates the story of the division of the kingdom under Rehoboam in the next chapter. **14–25:** Solomon's first two adversaries are foreign. The word *adversary* is "satan," which does not imply any supernatural force in this case. The fact that both *Hadad the Edomite* and *Rezon* began their careers during David's reign indicates that they caused trouble for Solomon early in his reign. However, the writer has placed their stories here because of the partitioning of the account of Solomon into "positive" and "negative" sections.

26 Jeroboam son of Nebat, an Ephraimite of Zeredah, a servant of Solomon, whose mother's name was Zeruah, a widow, rebelled against the king. 27The following was the reason he rebelled against the king. Solomon built the Millo, and closed up the gap in the wallᵇ of the city of his father David. 28The man Jeroboam was very able, and when Solomon saw that the young man was industrious he gave him charge over all the forced labor of the house of Joseph. 29About that time, when Jeroboam was leaving Jerusalem, the prophet Ahijah the Shilonite found him on the road. Ahijah had clothed himself with a new garment. The two of

a Heb *him*   *b* Heb lacks *in the wall*

them were alone in the open country [30]when Ahijah laid hold of the new garment he was wearing and tore it into twelve pieces. [31]He then said to Jeroboam: Take for yourself ten pieces; for thus says the LORD, the God of Israel, "See, I am about to tear the kingdom from the hand of Solomon, and will give you ten tribes. [32]One tribe will remain his, for the sake of my servant David and for the sake of Jerusalem, the city that I have chosen out of all the tribes of Israel. [33]This is because he has[a] forsaken me, worshiped Astarte the goddess of the Sidonians, Chemosh the god of Moab, and Milcom the god of the Ammonites, and has[a] not walked in my ways, doing what is right in my sight and keeping my statutes and my ordinances, as his father David did. [34]Nevertheless I will not take the whole kingdom away from him but will make him ruler all the days of his life, for the sake of my servant David whom I chose and who did keep my commandments and my statutes; [35]but I will take the kingdom away from his son and give it to you—that is, the ten tribes. [36]Yet to his son I will give one tribe, so that my servant David may always have a lamp before me in Jerusalem, the city where I have chosen to put my name. [37]I will take you, and you shall reign over all that your soul desires; you shall be king over Israel. [38]If you will listen to all that I command you, walk in my ways, and do what is right in my sight by keeping my statutes and my commandments, as David my servant did, I will be with you, and will build you an enduring house, as I built for David, and I will give Israel to you. [39]For this reason I will punish the descendants of David, but not forever." [40]Solomon sought therefore to kill Jeroboam; but Jeroboam promptly fled to Egypt, to King Shishak of Egypt, and remained in Egypt until the death of Solomon.

41 Now the rest of the acts of Solomon, all that he did as well as his wisdom, are they not written in the Book of the Acts of Solomon? [42]The time that Solomon reigned in Jerusalem over all Israel was forty years. [43]Solomon slept with his ancestors and was buried in the city of his father David; and his son Rehoboam succeeded him.

11.26–43. 26: *Jeroboam* was Solomon's third adversary. **27:** The *reason he rebelled* against Solomon was Ahijah's oracle* (vv. 29–39) promising him kingship over the northern tribes. **29–32:** One tribe is either missing or presumed in Ahijah's symbolic division of the kingdom, since Jeroboam receives *ten pieces* and only one of the twelve pieces is kept for David. Different scholars have proposed that the tribes of Benjamin, Simeon, or Levi are assumed to accompany Judah. **36:** The word translated *lamp* can refer to a "fiefdom" or minor domain. **37–38:** Jeroboam receives the same promise of an enduring dynasty* that was given to David if he will be obedient to Yahweh. **40:** It is not clear how Solomon found out about Ahijah's oracle to Jeroboam. **41–43:** This is typical of the concluding notices the deuteronomist* supplies for the reigns of kings. The *Book of the Acts of Solomon* is no longer extant. *Forty years* (v. 42) is a round number for the length of a generation. That *Solomon slept with his ancestors* is an idiomatic way of saying that he died.

12 Rehoboam went to Shechem, for all Israel had come to Shechem to make him king. [2]When Jeroboam son of Nebat heard of it (for he was still in Egypt, where he had fled from King Solomon), then Jeroboam returned from[b] Egypt. [3]And they sent and called him; and Jeroboam and all the assembly of Israel came and said to Rehoboam, [4]"Your father made our yoke heavy. Now therefore lighten the hard service of your father and his heavy yoke that he placed on us, and we will serve you." [5]He said to them, "Go away for three days, then come again to me." So the people went away.

6 Then King Rehoboam took counsel with the older men who had attended his father Solomon while he was still alive, saying, "How do you advise me to answer this people?" [7]They answered him, "If you will be a servant to this people today and serve them, and speak good words to them when you answer them, then they will be your servants forever." [8]But he disregarded the advice that the older men gave him, and consulted with the young men who had grown up with him and now attended him. [9]He said to them, "What do you advise that we answer this peo-

a Gk Syr Vg: Heb *they have*   b Gk Vg Compare 2 Chr 10.2: Heb *lived in* ple who have said to me, 'Lighten the yoke that your father put on us'?" ¹⁰The young men who had grown up with him said to him, "Thus you should say to this people who spoke to you, 'Your father made our yoke heavy, but you must lighten it for us'; thus you should say to them, 'My little finger is thicker than my father's loins. ¹¹Now, whereas my father laid on you a heavy yoke, I will add to your yoke. My father disciplined you with whips, but I will discipline you with scorpions.' "

12 So Jeroboam and all the people came to Rehoboam the third day, as the king had said, "Come to me again the third day." ¹³The king answered the people harshly. He disregarded the advice that the older men had given him ¹⁴and spoke to them according to the advice of the young men, "My father made your yoke heavy, but I will add to your yoke; my father disciplined you with whips, but I will discipline you with scorpions." ¹⁵So the king did not listen to the people, because it was a turn of affairs brought about by the LORD that he might fulfill his word, which the LORD had spoken by Ahijah the Shilonite to Jeroboam son of Nebat.

12.1–24: The division of the kingdom. 2–3a: These verses are contradicted by v. 20, in which Jeroboam does not return until after the secession of the northern tribes. Verses 2–3a are not in the Greek (Septuagint,* LXX*) version of 1 Kings and are probably a secondary scribal gloss. **10:** *My father's loins* is a euphemism.* Rehoboam is saying that he is more of a man than his father so that the people can expect harsher treatment from him than from Solomon. **11:** Rehoboam makes the same point here, where *scorpions* may refer to a particularly vicious kind of whip. **12:** *Jeroboam*'s name is secondary here, having been added under the influence of vv. 2–3a. **15:** The author interprets the events in explicitly theological terms as the LORD's doing to fulfill Ahijah's oracle* in 11.29–39.

16 When all Israel saw that the king would not listen to them, the people answered the king,

"What share do we have in David?
    We have no inheritance in the son of
        Jesse.
To your tents, O Israel!

Look now to your own house,
    O David."
So Israel went away to their tents. ¹⁷But Rehoboam reigned over the Israelites who were living in the towns of Judah. ¹⁸When King Rehoboam sent Adoram, who was taskmaster over the forced labor, all Israel stoned him to death. King Rehoboam then hurriedly mounted his chariot to flee to Jerusalem. ¹⁹So Israel has been in rebellion against the house of David to this day.

20 When all Israel heard that Jeroboam had returned, they sent and called him to the assembly and made him king over all Israel. There was no one who followed the house of David, except the tribe of Judah alone.

21 When Rehoboam came to Jerusalem, he assembled all the house of Judah and the tribe of Benjamin, one hundred eighty thousand chosen troops to fight against the house of Israel, to restore the kingdom to Rehoboam son of Solomon. ²²But the word of God came to Shemaiah the man of God: ²³Say to King Rehoboam of Judah, son of Solomon, and to all the house of Judah and Benjamin, and to the rest of the people, ²⁴"Thus says the LORD, You shall not go up or fight against your kindred the people of Israel. Let everyone go home, for this thing is from me." So they heeded the word of the LORD and went home again, according to the word of the LORD.

12.16–24. 16: *To your tents, O Israel* is a summons to military demobilization. The people, especially the army, of Israel is withdrawing from Rehoboam. A similar cry went up at Sheba's revolt in 2 Sam 20.1. **18:** *Adoram* is mentioned in 2 Sam 20.24 and 1 Kings 4.6 (Adoniram) as the head of the forced labor for David and Solomon. His presence was a particularly bitter and insulting reminder to the Israelite people of the burden of labor they had been forced to endure under Solomon. Hence, they stoned him. **19:** Even though the bulk of Israel left the house of David and sided with Rehoboam, the writer speaks of Israel's being *in rebellion*, indicating that his perspective is that of a citizen of Judah. In addition, the phrase *to this day* shows that the writer lived at a considerably later date. **21–24:** *Shemaiah*'s oracle expresses the view of v. 15 that the division was the LORD's doing. It addresses *Judah and Benjamin* (v. 23), while v. 20 speaks of Judah alone as the southern kingdom. Benjamin was probably divided between the two countries.

~~~~~~~~~~

25 Then Jeroboam built Shechem in the hill country of Ephraim, and resided there; he went out from there and built Penuel. 26Then Jeroboam said to himself, "Now the kingdom may well revert to the house of David. 27If this people continues to go up to offer sacrifices in the house of the LORD at Jerusalem, the heart of this people will turn again to their master, King Rehoboam of Judah; they will kill me and return to King Rehoboam of Judah." 28So the king took counsel, and made two calves of gold. He said to the people,*a* "You have gone up to Jerusalem long enough. Here are your gods, O Israel, who brought you up out of the land of Egypt." 29He set one in Bethel, and the other he put in Dan. 30And this thing became a sin, for the people went to worship before the one at Bethel and before the other as far as Dan.*b* 31He also made houses*c* on high places, and appointed priests from among all the people, who were not Levites. 32Jeroboam appointed a festival on the fifteenth day of the eighth month like the festival that was in Judah, and he offered sacrifices on the altar; so he did in Bethel, sacrificing to the calves that he had made. And he placed in Bethel the priests of the high places that he had made. 33He went up to the altar that he had made in Bethel on the fifteenth day in the eighth month, in the month that he alone had devised; he appointed a festival for the people of Israel, and he went up to the altar to offer incense.

_____

12.25–33: The sin of Jeroboam. 25: *Jeroboam built Shechem* and *Penuel* not in the sense of building them from the ground up but in the sense of fortifying already existing sites. **28:** Images of calves and bulls were commonly used in the ancient Near East to represent deities, especially fertility gods like Baal.★ The *golden calves* and Jeroboam's words to the people about them are reminiscent of the golden calf built by Aaron in Ex 32 and his words in 32.4. **29:** *Dan* was regarded as the northernmost city in Israel. *Bethel* was near the border between Israel and Judah. **31:** The *houses on the high places*★ were temples at various local shrines. Besides the royal sanctuaries at Dan and

Bethel, making it unnecessary to make a pilgrimage to Jerusalem, the writer accuses Jeroboam of setting up temples throughout his land. These were probably shrines to the LORD, but the writer regards Jerusalem as the only legitimate place to worship the LORD. Another aspect of Jeroboam's apostasy, in the writer's view, was his appointment of non-Levites as priests at the local shrines. **32:** Jeroboam is also accused of changing the religious calendar★ by establishing a festival in the eighth month to rival the Feast of Tabernacles★ in the seventh month in Jerusalem when the Temple★ there was dedicated (see 8.65).

~~~~~~~~~~

13 While Jeroboam was standing by the altar to offer incense, a man of God came out of Judah by the word of the LORD to Bethel 2and proclaimed against the altar by the word of the LORD, and said, "O altar, altar, thus says the LORD: 'A son shall be born to the house of David, Josiah by name; and he shall sacrifice on you the priests of the high places who offer incense on you, and human bones shall be burned on you.'" 3He gave a sign the same day, saying, "This is the sign that the LORD has spoken: 'The altar shall be torn down, and the ashes that are on it shall be poured out.'" 4When the king heard what the man of God cried out against the altar at Bethel, Jeroboam stretched out his hand from the altar, saying, "Seize him!" But the hand that he stretched out against him withered so that he could not draw it back to himself. 5The altar also was torn down, and the ashes poured out from the altar, according to the sign that the man of God had given by the word of the LORD. 6The king said to the man of God, "Entreat now the favor of the LORD your God, and pray for me, so that my hand may be restored to me." So the man of God entreated the LORD; and the king's hand was restored to him, and became as it was before. 7Then the king said to the man of God, "Come home with me and dine, and I will give you a gift." 8But the man of God said to the king, "If you give me half your kingdom, I will not go in with you; nor will I eat food or drink water in this place. 9For thus I was

a Gk: Heb *to them*   *b* Compare Gk: Heb *went to the one as far as Dan*   *c* Gk Vg Compare 13.32: Heb *a house* commanded by the word of the LORD: You shall not eat food, or drink water, or return by the way that you came." ¹⁰So he went another way, and did not return by the way that he had come to Bethel.

13.1–10: The oracle* against the altar at Bethel. The prophetic* legend* in this chapter was probably inserted here after the completion of the Deuteronomistic* History. Its setting, however, is Jeroboam's ascent to the altar at Bethel, apparently at its dedication (see 12.33). **2:** This story probably arose after the time of *Josiah* (640–609 BCE), who is credited with destroying the shrine at Bethel (2 Kings 23.15–18), some 300 years after Jeroboam. **3:** *Sign* here implies an unusual or miraculous occurrence. It looks ahead to v. 5, though it is not clear there how the altar was torn down. **4:** Jeroboam's withered *hand* or arm is miraculous, but it is not called a sign. **9:** Eating and drinking at Bethel would have indicated approval of the shrine there.

11 Now there lived an old prophet in Bethel. One of his sons came and told him all that the man of God had done that day in Bethel; the words also that he had spoken to the king, they told to their father. ¹²Their father said to them, "Which way did he go?" And his sons showed him the way that the man of God who came from Judah had gone. ¹³Then he said to his sons, "Saddle a donkey for me." So they saddled a donkey for him, and he mounted it. ¹⁴He went after the man of God, and found him sitting under an oak tree. He said to him, "Are you the man of God who came from Judah?" He answered, "I am." ¹⁵Then he said to him, "Come home with me and eat some food." ¹⁶But he said, "I cannot return with you, or go in with you; nor will I eat food or drink water with you in this place; ¹⁷for it was said to me by the word of the LORD: You shall not eat food or drink water there, or return by the way that you came." ¹⁸Then the other*ᵃ* said to him, "I also am a prophet as you are, and an angel spoke to me by the word of the LORD: Bring him back with you into your house so that he may eat food and drink water." But he was deceiving him. ¹⁹Then the man of God*ᵃ* went back with him, and ate food and drank water in his house.

13.11–34: The young man of God and the old prophet.* This is the main part of the story. It has nothing to do with Jeroboam but concerns obedience to the prophetic word and has affinities with other prophetic legends* such as 1 Kings 20 and the stories about Elijah and Elisha. **18:** The motive of the old prophet in lying to his younger colleague is not explained.

20 As they were sitting at the table, the word of the LORD came to the prophet who had brought him back; ²¹and he proclaimed to the man of God who came from Judah, "Thus says the LORD: Because you have disobeyed the word of the LORD, and have not kept the commandment that the LORD your God commanded you, ²²but have come back and have eaten food and drunk water in the place of which he said to you, 'Eat no food, and drink no water,' your body shall not come to your ancestral tomb." ²³After the man of God*ᵃ* had eaten food and had drunk, they saddled for him a donkey belonging to the prophet who had brought him back. ²⁴Then as he went away, a lion met him on the road and killed him. His body was thrown in the road, and the donkey stood beside it; the lion also stood beside the body. ²⁵People passed by and saw the body thrown in the road, with the lion standing by the body. And they came and told it in the town where the old prophet lived.

26 When the prophet who had brought him back from the way heard of it, he said, "It is the man of God who disobeyed the word of the LORD; therefore the LORD has given him to the lion, which has torn him and killed him according to the word that the LORD spoke to him." ²⁷Then he said to his sons, "Saddle a donkey for me." So they saddled one, ²⁸and he went and found the body thrown in the road, with the donkey and the lion standing beside the body. The lion had not eaten the body or attacked the donkey. ²⁹The prophet took up the body of the man of God, laid it on the donkey, and brought it back to the city,*ᵇ* to mourn and to bury him. ³⁰He laid the body in his own grave; and

a Heb *he*   *b* Gk: Heb *he came to the town of the old prophet* they mourned over him, saying, "Alas, my brother!" [31] After he had buried him, he said to his sons, "When I die, bury me in the grave in which the man of God is buried; lay my bones beside his bones. [32] For the saying that he proclaimed by the word of the LORD against the altar in Bethel, and against all the houses of the high places that are in the cities of Samaria, shall surely come to pass."

33 Even after this event Jeroboam did not turn from his evil way, but made priests for the high places again from among all the people; any who wanted to be priests he consecrated for the high places. [34] This matter became sin to the house of Jeroboam, so as to cut it off and to destroy it from the face of the earth.

13.20–34. 20–25: The harsh judgment is meant to teach a lesson. The young man of God should have obeyed the LORD rather than trusting another prophet. 31–32: The oracle* is fulfilled in the purge of Josiah (2 Kings 23.15–18), who saves the bones of the old prophet. The reference to the *cities of Samaria* can be no earlier than 721 BCE, when Israel was annexed by the Assyrians and turned into an Assyrian province. 33–34: After the prophetic legend, the narrative* returns to the topic of Jeroboam's apostasy.

14 At that time Abijah son of Jeroboam fell sick. [2] Jeroboam said to his wife, "Go, disguise yourself, so that it will not be known that you are the wife of Jeroboam, and go to Shiloh; for the prophet Ahijah is there, who said of me that I should be king over this people. [3] Take with you ten loaves, some cakes, and a jar of honey, and go to him; he will tell you what shall happen to the child."

4 Jeroboam's wife did so; she set out and went to Shiloh, and came to the house of Ahijah. Now Ahijah could not see, for his eyes were dim because of his age. [5] But the LORD said to Ahijah, "The wife of Jeroboam is coming to inquire of you concerning her son; for he is sick. Thus and thus you shall say to her."

When she came, she pretended to be another woman. [6] But when Ahijah heard the sound of her feet, as she came in at the door, he said, "Come in, wife of Jeroboam; why do you pretend to be another? For I am charged with heavy tidings for you. [7] Go, tell Jeroboam, 'Thus says the LORD, the God of Israel: Because I exalted you from among the people, made you leader over my people Israel, [8] and tore the kingdom away from the house of David to give it to you; yet you have not been like my servant David, who kept my commandments and followed me with all his heart, doing only that which was right in my sight, [9] but you have done evil above all those who were before you and have gone and made for yourself other gods, and cast images, provoking me to anger, and have thrust me behind your back; [10] therefore, I will bring evil upon the house of Jeroboam. I will cut off from Jeroboam every male, both bond and free in Israel, and will consume the house of Jeroboam, just as one burns up dung until it is all gone. [11] Anyone belonging to Jeroboam who dies in the city, the dogs shall eat; and anyone who dies in the open country, the birds of the air shall eat; for the LORD has spoken.' [12] Therefore set out, go to your house. When your feet enter the city, the child shall die. [13] All Israel shall mourn for him and bury him; for he alone of Jeroboam's family shall come to the grave, because in him there is found something pleasing to the LORD, the God of Israel, in the house of Jeroboam. [14] Moreover the LORD will raise up for himself a king over Israel, who shall cut off the house of Jeroboam today, even right now!*

15 "The LORD will strike Israel, as a reed is shaken in the water; he will root up Israel out of this good land that he gave to their ancestors, and scatter them beyond the Euphrates, because they have made their sacred poles,*b* provoking the LORD to anger. [16] He will give Israel up because of the sins of Jeroboam, which he sinned and which he caused Israel to commit."

17 Then Jeroboam's wife got up and went away, and she came to Tirzah. As she came to the threshold of the house, the child died. [18] All Israel buried him and mourned for him, according to the word of the LORD,

a Meaning of Heb uncertain   *b* Heb *Asherim*

which he spoke by his servant the prophet Ahijah.

14.1–18: The oracle* against Jeroboam. 3: The *ten loaves, some cakes, and a jar of honey* are payment to a seer for revealing the future. **6:** *Ahijah*, as a true man of God, knows that his visitor is the *wife of Jeroboam* despite his blindness (v. 4) and her disguise (vv. 2, 5). **7–11:** These verses, a deuteronomistic* insertion, focus on the fate of Jeroboam's royal house rather than on that of his ill son. Jeroboam had the opportunity to establish a dynasty* like David's (v. 8), but his sin will prevent that from happening. All of Jeroboam's *male* heirs (v. 10, male is literally "one who urinates on a wall") will be killed by a usurper. The threat in v. 11 is drawn from a curse of non-burial. **12–14:** The original oracle told of the impending death of Jeroboam's son and mentioned the coming of a new royal house, but without elaboration. **15:** *Sacred poles* were fertility symbols used in the worship of the Canaanite goddess, Asherah.* **17–18:** The fulfillment of Ahijah's prophecy.

19 Now the rest of the acts of Jeroboam, how he warred and how he reigned, are written in the Book of the Annals of the Kings of Israel. 20The time that Jeroboam reigned was twenty-two years; then he slept with his ancestors, and his son Nadab succeeded him.

21 Now Rehoboam son of Solomon reigned in Judah. Rehoboam was forty-one years old when he began to reign, and he reigned seventeen years in Jerusalem, the city that the LORD had chosen out of all the tribes of Israel, to put his name there. His mother's name was Naamah the Ammonite. 22Judah did what was evil in the sight of the LORD; they provoked him to jealousy with their sins that they committed, more than all that their ancestors had done. 23For they also built for themselves high places, pillars, and sacred poles*a* on every high hill and under every green tree; 24there were also male temple prostitutes in the land. They committed all the abominations of the nations that the LORD drove out before the people of Israel.

25 In the fifth year of King Rehoboam, King Shishak of Egypt came up against Jerusalem; 26he took away the treasures of the house of the LORD and the treasures of the

king's house; he took everything. He also took away all the shields of gold that Solomon had made; 27so King Rehoboam made shields of bronze instead, and committed them to the hands of the officers of the guard, who kept the door of the king's house. 28As often as the king went into the house of the LORD, the guard carried them and brought them back to the guardroom.

29 Now the rest of the acts of Rehoboam, and all that he did, are they not written in the Book of the Annals of the Kings of Judah? 30There was war between Rehoboam and Jeroboam continually. 31Rehoboam slept with his ancestors and was buried with his ancestors in the city of David. His mother's name was Naamah the Ammonite. His son Abijam succeeded him.

14.19–31: The reigns of Jeroboam and Rehoboam. Most of these verses are the standard deuteronomistic formulas for kings. **19:** The *Book of the Annals of the Kings of Israel* no longer exists, so its exact nature is unknown. **20:** *Slept with his ancestors* is an idiom for death. **21–24:** The typical beginning formula for a king of Judah included the name of the "queen mother," the mother of the king. *High places** were shrines used for worship. *Pillars* were standing stones used in worship. The biblical writers connect them especially with service to other gods. On *sacred poles,* see comment on v. 15. **25–26:** *Shishak* (also called Shoshenq or Sheshonk) invaded Palestine around 922 BCE. His annals mention sites in Israel but not Jerusalem, apparently because Rehoboam paid him off. **29:** The *Book of the Annals of the Kings of Judah* also no longer exists. **31:** *Ancestors* is literally "fathers." Rehoboam is buried with the previous kings of Judah, as are subsequent kings as well, *in the city of David.* The location of these tombs is not known, but it was probably not within the walls of Jerusalem.

15 Now in the eighteenth year of King Jeroboam son of Nebat, Abijam began to reign over Judah. 2He reigned for three years in Jerusalem. His mother's name was Maacah daughter of Abishalom. 3He committed all the sins that his father did before him; his heart was not true to the LORD his God, like the heart of his father David.

a Heb *Asherim*

4Nevertheless for David's sake the LORD his God gave him a lamp in Jerusalem, setting up his son after him, and establishing Jerusalem; 5because David did what was right in the sight of the LORD, and did not turn aside from anything that he commanded him all the days of his life, except in the matter of Uriah the Hittite. 6The war begun between Rehoboam and Jeroboam continued all the days of his life. 7The rest of the acts of Abijam, and all that he did, are they not written in the Book of the Annals of the Kings of Judah? There was war between Abijam and Jeroboam. 8Abijam slept with his ancestors, and they buried him in the city of David. Then his son Asa succeeded him.

15.1–8: Abijam of Judah. 1: *Abijam* is called Abijah in 2 Chr 13.1 and is judged in Chronicles to be good. **2:** *Abishalom* is apparently Absalom, David's rebellious son (2 Sam 13–19). If so, *Maacah* would have been David's granddaughter. **4:** *A lamp* may also mean a fiefdom or minor domain. **6:** This verse is repetitive; see 14.30.

9 In the twentieth year of King Jeroboam of Israel, Asa began to reign over Judah; 10he reigned forty-one years in Jerusalem. His mother's name was Maacah daughter of Abishalom. 11Asa did what was right in the sight of the LORD, as his father David had done. 12He put away the male temple prostitutes out of the land, and removed all the idols that his ancestors had made. 13He also removed his mother Maacah from being queen mother, because she had made an abominable image for Asherah; Asa cut down her image and burned it at the Wadi Kidron. 14But the high places were not taken away. Nevertheless the heart of Asa was true to the LORD all his days. 15He brought into the house of the LORD the votive gifts of his father and his own votive gifts—silver, gold, and utensils.

16 There was war between Asa and King Baasha of Israel all their days. 17King Baasha of Israel went up against Judah, and built Ramah, to prevent anyone from going out or coming in to King Asa of Judah. 18Then Asa took all the silver and the gold that were left in the treasures of the house of the LORD and the treasures of the king's house, and gave them into the hands of his servants. King Asa sent them to King Ben-hadad son of Tabrimmon son of Hezion of Aram, who resided in Damascus, saying, 19"Let there be an alliance between me and you, like that between my father and your father: I am sending you a present of silver and gold; go, break your alliance with King Baasha of Israel, so that he may withdraw from me." 20Ben-hadad listened to King Asa, and sent the commanders of his armies against the cities of Israel. He conquered Ijon, Dan, Abel-beth-maacah, and all Chinneroth, with all the land of Naphtali. 21When Baasha heard of it, he stopped building Ramah and lived in Tirzah. 22Then King Asa made a proclamation to all Judah, none was exempt: they carried away the stones of Ramah and its timber, with which Baasha had been building; with them King Asa built Geba of Benjamin and Mizpah. 23Now the rest of all the acts of Asa, all his power, all that he did, and the cities that he built, are they not written in the Book of the Annals of the Kings of Judah? But in his old age he was diseased in his feet. 24Then Asa slept with his ancestors, and was buried with his ancestors in the city of his father David; his son Jehoshaphat succeeded him.

15.9–24: Asa of Judah. 12: The term for *idols* is a disparaging one and sounds like the word for "dung" in 14.10. **13:** The nature of Maacah's *abominable image* is not known; it may have been related to Asherah's* role as a Canaanite fertility goddess. **14:** The *high places** were shrines. Here, they were apparently used for the worship of the LORD, not of other gods. **17:** *Ramah* was in Benjamin on the main road between north and south. **20:** The places listed in this verse are all in northern Israel. Thus, Asa used Ben-hadad to divert Baasha's attention from his southern border with Judah. **22:** *None was exempt* means that Asa conscripted a labor force of all the men of Judah for this project. *Geba* and *Mizpah* were on opposite sides of a pass along the north-south road a little north of Ramah. Asa was, therefore, extending his northern border. **23:** *Feet* is probably a euphemism for the sexual organs; Asa likely died of a venereal disease. This verse implies that the disease was punishment for some unnamed sin.

25 Nadab son of Jeroboam began to reign over Israel in the second year of King Asa of Judah; he reigned over Israel two years. 26He did what was evil in the sight of the LORD, walking in the way of his ancestor and in the sin that he caused Israel to commit.

27 Baasha son of Ahijah, of the house of Issachar, conspired against him; and Baasha struck him down at Gibbethon, which belonged to the Philistines; for Nadab and all Israel were laying siege to Gibbethon. 28So Baasha killed Nadab*a* in the third year of King Asa of Judah, and succeeded him. 29As soon as he was king, he killed all the house of Jeroboam; he left to the house of Jeroboam not one that breathed, until he had destroyed it, according to the word of the LORD that he spoke by his servant Ahijah the Shilonite— 30because of the sins of Jeroboam that he committed and that he caused Israel to commit, and because of the anger to which he provoked the LORD, the God of Israel.

31 Now the rest of the acts of Nadab, and all that he did, are they not written in the Book of the Annals of the Kings of Israel? 32There was war between Asa and King Baasha of Israel all their days.

15.25–32: Nadab of Israel. 25: *Nadab* marks the end of the royal house of Jeroboam. **26:** *His ancestor* is literally "his father," Jeroboam. **27:** *Baasha* was an army general who led a government takeover. **29–30:** After assassinating Nadab, Baasha killed all of Jeroboam's male heirs because they were potential rivals for the throne. This was a customary practice for the founders of new royal houses. The deuteronomist,* however, sees this as punishment for Jeroboam as prophesied by Ahijah (14.7–11).

33 In the third year of King Asa of Judah, Baasha son of Ahijah began to reign over all Israel at Tirzah; he reigned twenty-four years. 34He did what was evil in the sight of the LORD, walking in the way of Jeroboam and in the sin that he caused Israel to commit.

16 The word of the LORD came to Jehu son of Hanani against Baasha, saying, 2"Since I exalted you out of the dust and made you leader over my people Israel, and

you have walked in the way of Jeroboam, and have caused my people Israel to sin, provoking me to anger with their sins, 3therefore, I will consume Baasha and his house, and I will make your house like the house of Jeroboam son of Nebat. 4Anyone belonging to Baasha who dies in the city the dogs shall eat; and anyone of his who dies in the field the birds of the air shall eat."

5 Now the rest of the acts of Baasha, what he did, and his power, are they not written in the Book of the Annals of the Kings of Israel? 6Baasha slept with his ancestors, and was buried at Tirzah; and his son Elah succeeded him. 7Moreover the word of the LORD came by the prophet Jehu son of Hanani against Baasha and his house, both because of all the evil that he did in the sight of the LORD, provoking him to anger with the work of his hands, in being like the house of Jeroboam, and also because he destroyed it.

15.33–16.7: Baasha of Israel. 15.34: *The sin that [Jeroboam] caused Israel to commit* was the worship at the shrines of Dan and Bethel (12.25–33). **16.1–4:** This oracle* predicts the demise of the house of Baasha in terms very similar to the one against Jeroboam in 14.7–11. Both are likely the work of the deuteronomist. **7:** This verse seems secondary because it is repetitive of vv. 1–4 and because it follows the closing formula for Baasha in vv. 5–6. The last clause, *and also because he destroyed it,* has been understood by some as "even though he destroyed [the house of Jeroboam]."

8 In the twenty-sixth year of King Asa of Judah, Elah son of Baasha began to reign over Israel in Tirzah; he reigned two years. 9But his servant Zimri, commander of half his chariots, conspired against him. When he was at Tirzah, drinking himself drunk in the house of Arza, who was in charge of the palace at Tirzah, 10Zimri came in and struck him down and killed him, in the twenty-seventh year of King Asa of Judah, and succeeded him. 11When he began to reign, as soon as he had seated himself on his throne, he killed all the house of Baasha; he did not leave him

a Heb *him*

a single male of his kindred or his friends. ¹²Thus Zimri destroyed all the house of Baasha, according to the word of the LORD, which he spoke against Baasha by the prophet Jehu— ¹³because of all the sins of Baasha and the sins of his son Elah that they committed, and that they caused Israel to commit, provoking the LORD God of Israel to anger with their idols. ¹⁴Now the rest of the acts of Elah, and all that he did, are they not written in the Book of the Annals of the Kings of Israel?

16.8–14: Elah of Israel. 9: Like Baasha, *Zimri* was a general in the army who led a revolt. 11–13: Zimri follows the standard practice of wiping out all the male heirs of the previous royal house. Again, the deuteronomist explains this theologically as punishment from the LORD as predicted by a prophet.*

---

15 In the twenty-seventh year of King Asa of Judah, Zimri reigned seven days in Tirzah. Now the troops were encamped against Gibbethon, which belonged to the Philistines, ¹⁶and the troops who were encamped heard it said, "Zimri has conspired, and he has killed the king"; therefore all Israel made Omri, the commander of the army, king over Israel that day in the camp. ¹⁷So Omri went up from Gibbethon, and all Israel with him, and they besieged Tirzah. ¹⁸When Zimri saw that the city was taken, he went into the citadel of the king's house; he burned down the king's house over himself with fire, and died— ¹⁹because of the sins that he committed, doing evil in the sight of the LORD, walking in the way of Jeroboam, and for the sin that he committed, causing Israel to sin. ²⁰Now the rest of the acts of Zimri, and the conspiracy that he made, are they not written in the Book of the Annals of the Kings of Israel?

16.15–20: Zimri of Israel. The formulaic nature of the deuteronomistic* evaluation is clear in this case from the fact that Zimri reigned only *seven days* (v. 15), yet he is still condemned for all the sins of his predecessors (v. 19).

---

21 Then the people of Israel were divided into two parts; half of the people followed Tibni son of Ginath, to make him king, and half followed Omri. ²²But the people who followed Omri overcame the people who followed Tibni son of Ginath; so Tibni died, and Omri became king. ²³In the thirty-first year of King Asa of Judah, Omri began to reign over Israel; he reigned for twelve years, six of them in Tirzah.

24 He bought the hill of Samaria from Shemer for two talents of silver; he fortified the hill, and called the city that he built, Samaria, after the name of Shemer, the owner of the hill.

25 Omri did what was evil in the sight of the LORD; he did more evil than all who were before him. ²⁶For he walked in all the way of Jeroboam son of Nebat, and in the sins that he caused Israel to commit, provoking the LORD, the God of Israel, to anger by their idols. ²⁷Now the rest of the acts of Omri that he did, and the power that he showed, are they not written in the Book of the Annals of the Kings of Israel? ²⁸Omri slept with his ancestors, and was buried in Samaria; his son Ahab succeeded him.

16.21–28: Omri of Israel. 21–22: The civil war described here was between two other military commanders, *Omri* and *Tibni*, with Omri eventually being victorious. 24: Omri's acquisition of *Samaria* and his designation of it as his capital was similar to David's acquisition and establishment of Jerusalem as his capital. 25–28: Historically, Omri was one of the most powerful and important kings of Israel. He founded a dynasty* that lasted through five kings. Israel was known by other countries as the "house of Omri" for generations after Omri's death. The fact that the deuteronomist disposes of Omri in just a few verses using the same formulas as for all other kings indicates that his interests are primarily theological rather than historical.

---

29 In the thirty-eighth year of King Asa of Judah, Ahab son of Omri began to reign over Israel; Ahab son of Omri reigned over Israel in Samaria twenty-two years. ³⁰Ahab son of Omri did evil in the sight of the LORD more than all who were before him.

31 And as if it had been a light thing for him to walk in the sins of Jeroboam son of Nebat, he took as his wife Jezebel daughter

of King Ethbaal of the Sidonians, and went and served Baal, and worshiped him. 32 He erected an altar for Baal in the house of Baal, which he built in Samaria. 33 Ahab also made a sacred pole.*a* Ahab did more to provoke the anger of the LORD, the God of Israel, than had all the kings of Israel who were before him. 34 In his days Hiel of Bethel built Jericho; he laid its foundation at the cost of Abiram his firstborn, and set up its gates at the cost of his youngest son Segub, according to the word of the LORD, which he spoke by Joshua son of Nun.

16.29–34: The beginning of Ahab's reign. Like his father, Ahab was also a powerful king. His prominence in the Bible, however, is due to religious reasons. He is regarded as the most wicked king of Israel (v. 33), largely because of his wife, Jezebel (v. 32). His reign also stands out in 1 Kings as the setting of the Elijah stories. **31:** *Jezebel* means "Where is the prince?" and comes from ritual lamentation* in the worship of Baal.* *Ethbaal* means "Baal exists." These names set the stage for the conflict between the LORD (Yahweh) and Baal in the following stories. Ethbaal was king of Tyre, a city-state of the Phoenicians, who are here called *Sidonians.* **34:** This verse alludes to the curse in Josh 6.26. It is unclear whether *at the cost of* implies accidental death of the sons or a deliberate sacrifice. The practice of burying children in the foundation of buildings to bring good fortune is known from elsewhere in the ancient Near East.

17 Now Elijah the Tishbite, of Tishbe*b* in Gilead, said to Ahab, "As the LORD the God of Israel lives, before whom I stand, there shall be neither dew nor rain these years, except by my word." 2 The word of the LORD came to him, saying, 3 "Go from here and turn eastward, and hide yourself by the Wadi Cherith, which is east of the Jordan. 4 You shall drink from the wadi, and I have commanded the ravens to feed you there." 5 So he went and did according to the word of the LORD; he went and lived by the Wadi Cherith, which is east of the Jordan. 6 The ravens brought him bread and meat in the morning, and bread and meat in the evening; and he drank from the wadi. 7 But after a while the wadi dried up, because there was no rain in the land.

8 Then the word of the LORD came to him, saying, 9 "Go now to Zarephath, which belongs to Sidon, and live there; for I have commanded a widow there to feed you." 10 So he set out and went to Zarephath. When he came to the gate of the town, a widow was there gathering sticks; he called to her and said, "Bring me a little water in a vessel, so that I may drink." 11 As she was going to bring it, he called to her and said, "Bring me a morsel of bread in your hand." 12 But she said, "As the LORD your God lives, I have nothing baked, only a handful of meal in a jar, and a little oil in a jug; I am now gathering a couple of sticks, so that I may go home and prepare it for myself and my son, that we may eat it, and die." 13 Elijah said to her, "Do not be afraid; go and do as you have said; but first make me a little cake of it and bring it to me, and afterwards make something for yourself and your son. 14 For thus says the LORD the God of Israel: The jar of meal will not be emptied and the jug of oil will not fail until the day that the LORD sends rain on the earth." 15 She went and did as Elijah said, so that she as well as he and her household ate for many days. 16 The jar of meal was not emptied, neither did the jug of oil fail, according to the word of the LORD that he spoke by Elijah.

17.1–24: Elijah and the drought. 1: *Elijah* means "Yahweh is (my) God," and it sets the theme for the following chapters. The cessation of rain shows that it is the LORD (Yahweh), not Baal,* who controls the elements and therefore fertility. **3:** A *Wadi* was a stream bed with or without water rather than a brook, as it has been translated. **9:** Elijah is sent north into Phoenician territory. The two stories that follow show Elijah's status as a miracle-working man of God.

17 After this the son of the woman, the mistress of the house, became ill; his illness was so severe that there was no breath left in him. 18 She then said to Elijah, "What have you against me, O man of God? You have come to me to bring my sin to remembrance, and to cause the death of my son!"

a Heb *Asherah*   *b* Gk: Heb *of the settlers*

19But he said to her, "Give me your son." He took him from her bosom, carried him up into the upper chamber where he was lodging, and laid him on his own bed. 20He cried out to the LORD, "O LORD my God, have you brought calamity even upon the widow with whom I am staying, by killing her son?" 21Then he stretched himself upon the child three times, and cried out to the LORD, "O LORD my God, let this child's life come into him again." 22The LORD listened to the voice of Elijah; the life of the child came into him again, and he revived. 23Elijah took the child, brought him down from the upper chamber into the house, and gave him to his mother; then Elijah said, "See, your son is alive." 24So the woman said to Elijah, "Now I know that you are a man of God, and that the word of the LORD in your mouth is truth."

17.17–24. 17: The woman who was previously described as destitute is here called *the mistress of the house*. This is one indication that the story in vv. 17–24 has been adapted from or influenced by the story about Elisha in 2 Kings 4.11–37. 18: The woman implies that her son's death is divine punishment for some sin. 19: *The upper chamber* is another element drawn from the story in 2 Kings 4, which explains how the chamber was built for the prophet.* 21–22: Elijah's actions suggest that *life* or "breath" went from Elijah's body into the boy's so that he revived. Examples of this kind of contactual magic are found elsewhere from the ancient Near East. The point of the story, however, is that this was the LORD's doing.

18 After many days the word of the LORD came to Elijah, in the third year of the drought,ᵃ saying, "Go, present yourself to Ahab; I will send rain on the earth." 2So Elijah went to present himself to Ahab. The famine was severe in Samaria. 3Ahab summoned Obadiah, who was in charge of the palace. (Now Obadiah revered the LORD greatly; 4when Jezebel was killing off the prophets of the LORD, Obadiah took a hundred prophets, hid them fifty to a cave, and provided them with bread and water.) 5Then Ahab said to Obadiah, "Go through the land to all the springs of water and to all the wadis; perhaps we may find grass to keep the horses and mules alive, and not lose

some of the animals." 6So they divided the land between them to pass through it; Ahab went in one direction by himself, and Obadiah went in another direction by himself.

7 As Obadiah was on the way, Elijah met him; Obadiah recognized him, fell on his face, and said, "Is it you, my lord Elijah?" 8He answered him, "It is I. Go, tell your lord that Elijah is here." 9And he said, "How have I sinned, that you would hand your servant over to Ahab, to kill me? 10As the LORD your God lives, there is no nation or kingdom to which my lord has not sent to seek you; and when they would say, 'He is not here,' he would require an oath of the kingdom or nation, that they had not found you. 11But now you say, 'Go, tell your lord that Elijah is here.' 12As soon as I have gone from you, the spirit of the LORD will carry you I know not where; so, when I come and tell Ahab and he cannot find you, he will kill me, although I your servant have revered the LORD from my youth. 13Has it not been told my lord what I did when Jezebel killed the prophets of the LORD, how I hid a hundred of the LORD's prophets fifty to a cave, and provided them with bread and water? 14Yet now you say, 'Go, tell your lord that Elijah is here'; he will surely kill me." 15Elijah said, "As the LORD of hosts lives, before whom I stand, I will surely show myself to him today." 16So Obadiah went to meet Ahab, and told him; and Ahab went to meet Elijah.

18.1–46: **Contest on Mount Carmel. 3:** *Obadiah* is loyal to Yahweh; his name means "servant of Yahweh." **4:** There is no story preserved about Jezebel *killing off the prophets** of the LORD. **5:** *Ahab* is more concerned about saving his animals than about his wife's slaughter of the LORD's prophets. **7–8:** Obadiah calls Elijah *my lord*, but Elijah refers to Ahab as *your lord*, thus hinting that he is not pleased about Obadiah being a servant to such a wicked king. **12:** Obadiah's fear about Elijah's disappearance shows the aura of mystery* and power that surrounded the prophet. **15:** *LORD of hosts* is a title for Yahweh indicating his authority over the armies or hosts of both heaven and earth.

ᵃ Heb lacks *of the drought*

17 When Ahab saw Elijah, Ahab said to him, "Is it you, you troubler of Israel?" 18He answered, "I have not troubled Israel; but you have, and your father's house, because you have forsaken the commandments of the LORD and followed the Baals. 19Now therefore have all Israel assemble for me at Mount Carmel, with the four hundred fifty prophets of Baal and the four hundred prophets of Asherah, who eat at Jezebel's table."

20 So Ahab sent to all the Israelites, and assembled the prophets at Mount Carmel. 21Elijah then came near to all the people, and said, "How long will you go limping with two different opinions? If the LORD is God, follow him; but if Baal, then follow him." The people did not answer him a word. 22Then Elijah said to the people, "I, even I only, am left a prophet of the LORD; but Baal's prophets number four hundred fifty. 23Let two bulls be given to us; let them choose one bull for themselves, cut it in pieces, and lay it on the wood, but put no fire to it; I will prepare the other bull and lay it on the wood, but put no fire to it. 24Then you call on the name of your god and I will call on the name of the LORD; the god who answers by fire is indeed God." All the people answered, "Well spoken!" 25Then Elijah said to the prophets of Baal, "Choose for yourselves one bull and prepare it first, for you are many; then call on the name of your god, but put no fire to it." 26So they took the bull that was given them, prepared it, and called on the name of Baal from morning until noon, crying, "O Baal, answer us!" But there was no voice, and no answer. They limped about the altar that they had made. 27At noon Elijah mocked them, saying, "Cry aloud! Surely he is a god; either he is meditating, or he has wandered away, or he is on a journey, or perhaps he is asleep and must be awakened." 28Then they cried aloud and, as was their custom, they cut themselves with swords and lances until the blood gushed out over them. 29As midday passed, they raved on until the time of the offering of the oblation, but there was no voice, no answer, and no response.

18.17–29. 17–18: Ahab blames Elijah for the drought and calls him the *troubler of Israel*, but Elijah points out that it is Ahab's apostasy that has brought trouble to Israel. **19:** *Baal** and *Asherah** were the leading male and female deities, respectively, in the fertility religion of ancient Canaan. *Carmel* means "vineyard of (the god) El" and implies affiliation with Canaanite fertility religion. Mount Carmel is near the Mediterranean coast in northern Israel and held a place for worship near its summit. **21:** *Elijah* accuses the people of *limping with two different opinions* or "straddling the fence" between the worship of Yahweh and that of Baal. The word "limping" is echoed later (v. 26) in referring to the ritual dance of the prophets of Baal. **22:** *Elijah* is overstating the case when he says, *I, even I only, am left a prophet of the LORD* since there are at least the 150 prophets of the LORD saved by Obadiah. **23–24:** Elijah proposes a decisive test to determine whether the LORD (Yahweh) or Baal truly controls the storm. The *fire* for which each of them prays is lightning. **26:** *No voice* or "sound" means that there was no thunder. When the prophets *limped about the altar* they were apparently engaged in a ritual dance. **27:** *He is meditating* may mean that he is relieving himself (see Gen 24.63), which would certainly fit with Elijah's mocking. **28:** This kind of blood-letting was common in ritual as a sign of fervency or perhaps sympathetic magic. **29:** The verb for *raved on* also means "prophesy" and implies trance behavior or some other loss of self-control. The *time of the offering of the oblation,* about 3 p.m. Second Kings 3.20 also mentions a morning oblation. The practice of two daily oblations may have arisen first in the Exile* or later. The reference to the oblation also implies the existence of a central sanctuary and therefore a southern author.

30 Then Elijah said to all the people, "Come closer to me"; and all the people came closer to him. First he repaired the altar of the LORD that had been thrown down; 31Elijah took twelve stones, according to the number of the tribes of the sons of Jacob, to whom the word of the LORD came, saying, "Israel shall be your name"; 32with the stones he built an altar in the name of the LORD. Then he made a trench around the altar, large enough to contain two measures of seed. 33Next he put the wood in order, cut the bull in pieces, and laid it on the wood. He said, "Fill four jars with water and pour it on the

burnt offering and on the wood." ³⁴Then he said, "Do it a second time"; and they did it a second time. Again he said, "Do it a third time"; and they did it a third time, ³⁵so that the water ran all around the altar, and filled the trench also with water.

36 At the time of the offering of the oblation, the prophet Elijah came near and said, "O LORD, God of Abraham, Isaac, and Israel, let it be known this day that you are God in Israel, that I am your servant, and that I have done all these things at your bidding. ³⁷Answer me, O LORD, answer me, so that this people may know that you, O LORD, are God, and that you have turned their hearts back." ³⁸Then the fire of the LORD fell and consumed the burnt offering, the wood, the stones, and the dust, and even licked up the water that was in the trench. ³⁹When all the people saw it, they fell on their faces and said, "The LORD indeed is God; the LORD indeed is God." ⁴⁰Elijah said to them, "Seize the prophets of Baal; do not let one of them escape." Then they seized them; and Elijah brought them down to the Wadi Kishon, and killed them there.

41 Elijah said to Ahab, "Go up, eat and drink; for there is a sound of rushing rain." ⁴²So Ahab went up to eat and to drink. Elijah went up to the top of Carmel; there he bowed himself down upon the earth and put his face between his knees. ⁴³He said to his servant, "Go up now, look toward the sea." He went up and looked, and said, "There is nothing." Then he said, "Go again seven times." ⁴⁴At the seventh time he said, "Look, a little cloud no bigger than a person's hand is rising out of the sea." Then he said, "Go say to Ahab, 'Harness your chariot and go down before the rain stops you.' " ⁴⁵In a little while the heavens grew black with clouds and wind; there was a heavy rain. Ahab rode off and went to Jezreel. ⁴⁶But the hand of the LORD was on Elijah; he girded up his loins and ran in front of Ahab to the entrance of Jezreel.

18.30–46. 30–32: Elijah's repair and use of an altar away from Jerusalem would not have been approved by the deuteronomistic* historian and is one indication that the stories in chs. 17–19 are a later insertion.

32: Two measures (Heb., two "se'ahs") of seed was about three pecks or seven gallons, though this seems too small for the amount indicated in the story. Some have suggested that it refers to the amount of land that could be planted by two measures of seed. But this seems inappropriately large. 33–35: The point of drenching the sacrifice is to make clear that the fire is not accidental and does not originate on the earth. It also makes the test all the more difficult in order to impress the audience with the LORD's power, especially during a drought. 36–39: The LORD answers by sending lightning onto the altar, and the people recognize that Yahweh is the true God, who controls the storm and fertility. 40: The slaughter of the prophets* of Baal* counters Jezebel's slaughter of the LORD's prophets. 41: Elijah tells Ahab to eat and drink. Ahab may have been fasting for ritual purposes before and during the contest. 42–45: Elijah's call for the end of the drought is yet one more sign of the LORD's control over the elements and of Elijah's prowess as a man of God. 46: Jezreel was about 17 miles away! Elijah was able to outrun Ahab's chariot because the hand of the LORD was on [him]; hand often signifies power.

19 Ahab told Jezebel all that Elijah had done, and how he had killed all the prophets with the sword. ²Then Jezebel sent a messenger to Elijah, saying, "So may the gods do to me, and more also, if I do not make your life like the life of one of them by this time tomorrow." ³Then he was afraid; he got up and fled for his life, and came to Beer-sheba, which belongs to Judah; he left his servant there.

4 But he himself went a day's journey into the wilderness, and came and sat down under a solitary broom tree. He asked that he might die: "It is enough; now, O LORD, take away my life, for I am no better than my ancestors." ⁵Then he lay down under the broom tree and fell asleep. Suddenly an angel touched him and said to him, "Get up and eat." ⁶He looked, and there at his head was a cake baked on hot stones, and a jar of water. He ate and drank, and lay down again. ⁷The angel of the LORD came a second time, touched him, and said, "Get up and eat, otherwise the journey will be too much for you." ⁸He got up, and ate and drank; then he went in the strength of that food forty days and forty nights to Horeb the mount of God. ⁹At

that place he came to a cave, and spent the night there.

Then the word of the LORD came to him, saying, "What are you doing here, Elijah?" [10]He answered, "I have been very zealous for the LORD, the God of hosts; for the Israelites have forsaken your covenant, thrown down your altars, and killed your prophets with the sword. I alone am left, and they are seeking my life, to take it away."

11 He said, "Go out and stand on the mountain before the LORD, for the LORD is about to pass by." Now there was a great wind, so strong that it was splitting mountains and breaking rocks in pieces before the LORD, but the LORD was not in the wind; and after the wind an earthquake, but the LORD was not in the earthquake; [12]and after the earthquake a fire, but the LORD was not in the fire; and after the fire a sound of sheer silence. [13]When Elijah heard it, he wrapped his face in his mantle and went out and stood at the entrance of the cave. Then there came a voice to him that said, "What are you doing here, Elijah?" [14]He answered, "I have been very zealous for the LORD, the God of hosts; for the Israelites have forsaken your covenant, thrown down your altars, and killed your prophets with the sword. I alone am left, and they are seeking my life, to take it away." [15]Then the LORD said to him, "Go, return on your way to the wilderness of Damascus; when you arrive, you shall anoint Hazael as king over Aram. [16]Also you shall anoint Jehu son of Nimshi as king over Israel; and you shall anoint Elisha son of Shaphat of Abel-meholah as prophet in your place. [17]Whoever escapes from the sword of Hazael, Jehu shall kill; and whoever escapes from the sword of Jehu, Elisha shall kill. [18]Yet I will leave seven thousand in Israel, all the knees that have not bowed to Baal, and every mouth that has not kissed him."

19 So he set out from there, and found Elisha son of Shaphat, who was plowing. There were twelve yoke of oxen ahead of him, and he was with the twelfth. Elijah passed by him and threw his mantle over him. [20]He left the oxen, ran after Elijah, and said, "Let me kiss my father and my mother, and then I will follow you." Then Elijah[a]

said to him, "Go back again; for what have I done to you?" [21]He returned from following him, took the yoke of oxen, and slaughtered them; using the equipment from the oxen, he boiled their flesh, and gave it to the people, and they ate. Then he set out and followed Elijah, and became his servant.

19.1–21: Elijah on Mount Horeb. 1–3: *Elijah* flees south some 130 miles to *Beer-sheba* out of fear of Jezebel. **8:** Like Moses, Elijah fasts *forty days and forty nights.* Elijah goes to *Horeb the mount of God,* which is called Sinai at other places in the Bible. It is the place where Moses received the law. **9:** The Hebrew text reads "the" *cave,* apparently the same cave where Moses hid when the LORD passed by (Ex 33.17–23). **11–12:** The LORD does not appear in any of these violent forms, which might be associated with the storm god, Baal. Rather, the LORD appears quietly. **13:** Elijah *wrapped his face in his mantle,* apparently because he was afraid. **14:** Again, Elijah is overstating matters when he says *I alone am left.* **15–18:** The LORD evidently accepts Elijah's "resignation." Elijah is assured that he is not alone (v. 18), but he is told to *anoint** or designate Elisha ("my God saves") as his replacement. The other two commissions in these verses are actually carried out by Elisha (2 Kings 8–9). **19:** The introduction of *Elisha* is abrupt. We know nothing of his background except what is narrated here. The *twelve yoke of oxen* (v. 19) suggests that he is from a wealthy family. The *mantle* was a token of the prophetic office. When he *threw his mantle over him,* Elijah was designating Elisha as his replacement. **20:** Elijah's response to Elisha's request in v. 20 is obscure. By asking *What have I done to you?* he may be asking Elisha to keep in mind that he has received an important call. **21:** Elisha's feast is a way of bidding goodbye to his former life.

20 King Ben-hadad of Aram gathered all his army together; thirty-two kings were with him, along with horses and chariots. He marched against Samaria, laid siege to it, and attacked it. [2]Then he sent messengers into the city to King Ahab of Israel, and said to him: "Thus says Ben-hadad: [3]Your silver and gold are mine; your fairest wives and children also are mine." [4]The king of Israel answered, "As you say, my lord,

a Heb *he*

O king, I am yours, and all that I have." [5]The messengers came again and said: "Thus says Ben-hadad: I sent to you, saying, 'Deliver to me your silver and gold, your wives and children'; [6]nevertheless I will send my servants to you tomorrow about this time, and they shall search your house and the houses of your servants, and lay hands on whatever pleases them,ᵃ and take it away."

7 Then the king of Israel called all the elders of the land, and said, "Look now! See how this man is seeking trouble; for he sent to me for my wives, my children, my silver, and my gold; and I did not refuse him." [8]Then all the elders and all the people said to him, "Do not listen or consent." [9]So he said to the messengers of Ben-hadad, "Tell my lord the king: All that you first demanded of your servant I will do; but this thing I cannot do." The messengers left and brought him word again. [10]Ben-hadad sent to him and said, "The gods do so to me, and more also, if the dust of Samaria will provide a handful for each of the people who follow me." [11]The king of Israel answered, "Tell him: One who puts on armor should not brag like one who takes it off." [12]When Ben-hadad heard this message—now he had been drinking with the kings in the booths—he said to his men, "Take your positions!" And they took their positions against the city.

13 Then a certain prophet came up to King Ahab of Israel and said, "Thus says the LORD, Have you seen all this great multitude? Look, I will give it into your hand today; and you shall know that I am the LORD." [14]Ahab said, "By whom?" He said, "Thus says the LORD, By the young men who serve the district governors." Then he said, "Who shall begin the battle?" He answered, "You." [15]Then he mustered the young men who served the district governors, two hundred thirty-two; after them he mustered all the people of Israel, seven thousand.

20.1–43: Tales of other prophets. This chapter probably went originally with ch. 22 as in the Greek (Septuagint*) version of 1 Kings, which has chs. 20 and 21 in reverse order. The stories in chs. 20 and 22 are out of place historically, since they assume a setting in which Israel was dominated by Aram (Syria), which was not the case during Ahab's reign. **1:** The *thirty-two kings* were rulers not of nations but of city-states or chieftains dominated by Damascus. **2:** The king of Israel is here identified as *Ahab,* but this identification is likely secondary. For most of the chapter he is called simply "the king of Israel." **12:** *The booths* probably refer to the army's tents. However, it might also be read as "Sukkoth," a site east of the Jordan. **14:** The *young men who serve the district governors* seems to be a special rank or division within the military, but we no longer know exactly what it means.

~~~~~~~~~~~~~~~~

16 They went out at noon, while Ben-hadad was drinking himself drunk in the booths, he and the thirty-two kings allied with him. [17]The young men who served the district governors went out first. Ben-hadad had sent out scouts,ᵇ and they reported to him, "Men have come out from Samaria." [18]He said, "If they have come out for peace, take them alive; if they have come out for war, take them alive."

19 But these had already come out of the city: the young men who served the district governors, and the army that followed them. [20]Each killed his man; the Arameans fled and Israel pursued them, but King Ben-hadad of Aram escaped on a horse with the cavalry. [21]The king of Israel went out, attacked the horses and chariots, and defeated the Arameans with a great slaughter.

22 Then the prophet approached the king of Israel and said to him, "Come, strengthen yourself, and consider well what you have to do; for in the spring the king of Aram will come up against you."

23 The servants of the king of Aram said to him, "Their gods are gods of the hills, and so they were stronger than we; but let us fight against them in the plain, and surely we shall be stronger than they. [24]Also do this: remove the kings, each from his post, and put commanders in place of them; [25]and muster an army like the army that you have lost, horse for horse, and chariot for chariot; then we will fight against them in the plain, and surely we shall be stronger than they." He heeded their voice, and did so.

ᵃ Gk Syr Vg: Heb *you*   ᵇ Heb lacks *scouts*

26 In the spring Ben-hadad mustered the Arameans and went up to Aphek to fight against Israel. 27After the Israelites had been mustered and provisioned, they went out to engage them; the people of Israel encamped opposite them like two little flocks of goats, while the Arameans filled the country. 28A man of God approached and said to the king of Israel, "Thus says the LORD: Because the Arameans have said, 'The LORD is a god of the hills but he is not a god of the valleys,' therefore I will give all this great multitude into your hand, and you shall know that I am the LORD." 29They encamped opposite one another seven days. Then on the seventh day the battle began; the Israelites killed one hundred thousand Aramean foot soldiers in one day. 30The rest fled into the city of Aphek; and the wall fell on twenty-seven thousand men that were left.

Ben-hadad also fled, and entered the city to hide. 31His servants said to him, "Look, we have heard that the kings of the house of Israel are merciful kings; let us put sackcloth around our waists and ropes on our heads, and go out to the king of Israel; perhaps he will spare your life." 32So they tied sackcloth around their waists, put ropes on their heads, went to the king of Israel, and said, "Your servant Ben-hadad says, 'Please let me live.'" And he said, "Is he still alive? He is my brother." 33Now the men were watching for an omen; they quickly took it up from him and said, "Yes, Ben-hadad is your brother." Then he said, "Go and bring him." So Ben-hadad came out to him; and he had him come up into the chariot. 34Ben-hadad*a* said to him, "I will restore the towns that my father took from your father; and you may establish bazaars for yourself in Damascus, as my father did in Samaria." The king of Israel responded,*b* "I will let you go on those terms." So he made a treaty with him and let him go.

much fewer than a thousand men. **31:** *Sackcloth*★ (Heb., "saq") refers to some type of clothing that was worn to show sorrow. **32–33:** The servants of *Ben-hadad* refer to him as the *servant* of the *king of Israel*. But the king of Israel calls him a *brother*, thus making him an equal. This is also treaty language and indicates that the king of Israel wants to be treaty partners with Ben-hadad. This indication is the sign or *omen* the servants of Ben-hadad were awaiting.

35 At the command of the LORD a certain member of a company of prophets*c* said to another, "Strike me!" But the man refused to strike him. 36Then he said to him, "Because you have not obeyed the voice of the LORD, as soon as you have left me, a lion will kill you." And when he had left him, a lion met him and killed him. 37Then he found another man and said, "Strike me!" So the man hit him, striking and wounding him. 38Then the prophet departed, and waited for the king along the road, disguising himself with a bandage over his eyes. 39As the king passed by, he cried to the king and said, "Your servant went out into the thick of the battle; then a soldier turned and brought a man to me, and said, 'Guard this man; if he is missing, your life shall be given for his life, or else you shall pay a talent of silver.' 40While your servant was busy here and there, he was gone." The king of Israel said to him, "So shall your judgment be; you yourself have decided it." 41Then he quickly took the bandage away from his eyes. The king of Israel recognized him as one of the prophets. 42Then he said to him, "Thus says the LORD, 'Because you have let the man go whom I had devoted to destruction, therefore your life shall be for his life, and your people for his people.'" 43The king of Israel set out toward home, resentful and sullen, and came to Samaria.

20.16–34. 22: *In the spring* is literally "at the turn of the year," which may mean "next year." **23–25:** A *chariot* force would be more useful on flat ground than in hilly or mountainous territory. **30:** *Twenty-seven thousand* may be a simple exaggeration, or the word translated "thousand" may refer to a military unit of

20.35–43. 39: A *talent* was a measure of weight between 45 and 130 pounds. **42:** Devotion to *destruction* was an aspect of holy war★ in which the enemy was killed as a kind of sacrifice. The *king of Israel* is condemned for not carrying out Yahweh's command,

a Heb He *b* Heb lacks The king of Israel responded
c Heb of the sons of the prophets

much the same as Saul is condemned in 1 Sam 15 for the same offense.

21 Later the following events took place: Naboth the Jezreelite had a vineyard in Jezreel, beside the palace of King Ahab of Samaria. 2And Ahab said to Naboth, "Give me your vineyard, so that I may have it for a vegetable garden, because it is near my house; I will give you a better vineyard for it; or, if it seems good to you, I will give you its value in money." 3But Naboth said to Ahab, "The LORD forbid that I should give you my ancestral inheritance." 4Ahab went home resentful and sullen because of what Naboth the Jezreelite had said to him; for he had said, "I will not give you my ancestral inheritance." He lay down on his bed, turned away his face, and would not eat.

5 His wife Jezebel came to him and said, "Why are you so depressed that you will not eat?" 6He said to her, "Because I spoke to Naboth the Jezreelite and said to him, 'Give me your vineyard for money; or else, if you prefer, I will give you another vineyard for it'; but he answered, 'I will not give you my vineyard.' " 7His wife Jezebel said to him, "Do you now govern Israel? Get up, eat some food, and be cheerful; I will give you the vineyard of Naboth the Jezreelite."

8 So she wrote letters in Ahab's name and sealed them with his seal; she sent the letters to the elders and the nobles who lived with Naboth in his city. 9She wrote in the letters, "Proclaim a fast, and seat Naboth at the head of the assembly; 10seat two scoundrels opposite him, and have them bring a charge against him, saying, 'You have cursed God and the king.' Then take him out, and stone him to death." 11The men of his city, the elders and the nobles who lived in his city, did as Jezebel had sent word to them. Just as it was written in the letters that she had sent to them, 12they proclaimed a fast and seated Naboth at the head of the assembly. 13The two scoundrels came in and sat opposite him; and the scoundrels brought a charge against Naboth, in the presence of the people, saying, "Naboth cursed God and the king." So they took him outside the city, and stoned him to death. 14Then they sent to Jez-

ebel, saying, "Naboth has been stoned; he is dead."

21.1–29: Naboth's vineyard. 1: Naboth's vineyard was in *Jezreel,* while the royal palace was in Samaria. The phrase *of Samaria* was probably added later by a scribe* who was influenced by the David and Bathsheba story in 2 Sam 11–12. The story is set in Jezreel where Ahab had another palace. **3:** Israelite law forbade the sale of one's *ancestral inheritance* in perpetuity (Lev 25.23–28). **8–14:** Jezebel's actions show a keen awareness of Israelite law, which required two witnesses in capital cases (Deut 17.6) and condemned blasphemy (Lev 24.10–23) and speaking against the king (Ex 22.28). Her plot against Naboth is not done in ignorance of Israelite tradition but in spite of it.

15 As soon as Jezebel heard that Naboth had been stoned and was dead, Jezebel said to Ahab, "Go, take possession of the vineyard of Naboth the Jezreelite, which he refused to give you for money; for Naboth is not alive, but dead." 16As soon as Ahab heard that Naboth was dead, Ahab set out to go down to the vineyard of Naboth the Jezreelite, to take possession of it.

17 Then the word of the LORD came to Elijah the Tishbite, saying: 18Go down to meet King Ahab of Israel, who rules*a* in Samaria; he is now in the vineyard of Naboth, where he has gone to take possession. 19You shall say to him, "Thus says the LORD: Have you killed, and also taken possession?" You shall say to him, "Thus says the LORD: In the place where dogs licked up the blood of Naboth, dogs will also lick up your blood."

20 Ahab said to Elijah, "Have you found me, O my enemy?" He answered, "I have found you. Because you have sold yourself to do what is evil in the sight of the LORD, 21I will bring disaster on you; I will consume you, and will cut off from Ahab every male, bond or free, in Israel; 22and I will make your house like the house of Jeroboam son of Nebat, and like the house of Baasha son of Ahijah, because you have provoked me to anger and have caused Israel to sin. 23Also concerning Jezebel the LORD said, 'The dogs shall eat Jezebel within the bounds of Jez-

a Heb *who is*

reel.' 24Anyone belonging to Ahab who dies in the city the dogs shall eat; and anyone of his who dies in the open country the birds of the air shall eat."

25 (Indeed, there was no one like Ahab, who sold himself to do what was evil in the sight of the LORD, urged on by his wife Jezebel. 26He acted most abominably in going after idols, as the Amorites had done, whom the LORD drove out before the Israelites.)

27 When Ahab heard those words, he tore his clothes and put sackcloth over his bare flesh; he fasted, lay in the sackcloth, and went about dejectedly. 28Then the word of the LORD came to Elijah the Tishbite: 29"Have you seen how Ahab has humbled himself before me? Because he has humbled himself before me, I will not bring the disaster in his days; but in his son's days I will bring the disaster on his house."

21.15–29. 18: Again, the phrase *in Samaria* is an addition. **20–24:** The oracle* against Ahab has been turned into a prophecy about the fall of the entire dynasty,* similar to those against the houses of Jeroboam (14.7–11) and Baasha (16.1–4). Verse 23, however, is new and is directed specifically against Jezebel. **27–29:** Ahab's repentance delays the fall of the dynasty until after his reign. These verses were likely written by a different author from the one responsible for vv. 25–26, which view Ahab as the worst of all Israelite kings.

22 For three years Aram and Israel continued without war. 2But in the third year King Jehoshaphat of Judah came down to the king of Israel. 3The king of Israel said to his servants, "Do you know that Ramoth-gilead belongs to us, yet we are doing nothing to take it out of the hand of the king of Aram?" 4He said to Jehoshaphat, "Will you go with me to battle at Ramoth-gilead?" Jehoshaphat replied to the king of Israel, "I am as you are; my people are your people, my horses are your horses."

5 But Jehoshaphat also said to the king of Israel, "Inquire first for the word of the LORD." 6Then the king of Israel gathered the prophets together, about four hundred of them, and said to them, "Shall I go to battle against Ramoth-gilead, or shall I refrain?"

They said, "Go up; for the LORD will give it into the hand of the king." 7But Jehoshaphat said, "Is there no other prophet of the LORD here of whom we may inquire?" 8The king of Israel said to Jehoshaphat, "There is still one other by whom we may inquire of the LORD, Micaiah son of Imlah; but I hate him, for he never prophesies anything favorable about me, but only disaster." Jehoshaphat said, "Let the king not say such a thing." 9Then the king of Israel summoned an officer and said, "Bring quickly Micaiah son of Imlah." 10Now the king of Israel and King Jehoshaphat of Judah were sitting on their thrones, arrayed in their robes, at the threshing floor at the entrance of the gate of Samaria; and all the prophets were prophesying before them. 11Zedekiah son of Chenaanah made for himself horns of iron, and he said, "Thus says the LORD: With these you shall gore the Arameans until they are destroyed." 12All the prophets were prophesying the same and saying, "Go up to Ramoth-gilead and triumph; the LORD will give it into the hand of the king."

22.1–53: The prophecy of Micaiah. 2: As in ch. 20, the *king of Israel* in this story was originally not identified. The identification as Ahab is secondary and probably incorrect. **3:** *Ramoth-gilead* was an important site east of the Jordan river. **5:** The fact that *Jehoshaphat* wants to inquire of the LORD reflects the author's positive view of him. The *king of Israel* is depicted as an enemy of the true prophet,* Micaiah. **6:** The *prophets* are probably court prophets who were sustained by the king. It is not clear whether they are even worshippers of the LORD (Yahweh). In fact, the number *four hundred* recalls the prophets of Baal* in 18.19. Their oracle* appears favorable to *the king*, but it could be ambiguous since they do not say which king will be given victory. **7:** *Jehoshaphat* is skeptical of the quick answer and the unanimity of the 400 prophets, so he requests another *prophet of the LORD*, one who is a true prophet of Yahweh but not associated with the 400 court prophets. **8:** The fact that *Micaiah . . . never prophesies anything favorable* about the king *but only disaster* is an indication that Micaiah is a true prophet, since prophets often opposed kings. **10:** A *threshing* floor* was a broad, flat area where grain was separated from the hull. Kings are often pictured in the Bible as sitting enthroned outside in similar settings (1 Sam 14.2; 22.6). **11:** Prophets in the Bible often carried out symbolic acts like the one described here (Jer 13; Ezek 4). Nothing is known outside of this story about this *Zedekiah*. But his name ("the righteousness of Yahweh") indicates that he was a worshipper of the LORD (Yahweh).

13 The messenger who had gone to summon Micaiah said to him, "Look, the words of the prophets with one accord are favorable to the king; let your word be like the word of one of them, and speak favorably." 14But Micaiah said, "As the LORD lives, whatever the LORD says to me, that I will speak."

15 When he had come to the king, the king said to him, "Micaiah, shall we go to Ramoth-gilead to battle, or shall we refrain?" He answered him, "Go up and triumph; the LORD will give it into the hand of the king." 16But the king said to him, "How many times must I make you swear to tell me nothing but the truth in the name of the LORD?" 17Then Micaiah*a* said, "I saw all Israel scattered on the mountains, like sheep that have no shepherd; and the LORD said, 'These have no master; let each one go home in peace.' " 18The king of Israel said to Jehoshaphat, "Did I not tell you that he would not prophesy anything favorable about me, but only disaster?"

19 Then Micaiah*a* said, "Therefore hear the word of the LORD: I saw the LORD sitting on his throne, with all the host of heaven standing beside him to the right and to the left of him. 20And the LORD said, 'Who will entice Ahab, so that he may go up and fall at Ramoth-gilead?' Then one said one thing, and another said another, 21until a spirit came forward and stood before the LORD, saying, 'I will entice him.' 22'How?' the LORD asked him. He replied, 'I will go out and be a lying spirit in the mouth of all his prophets.' Then the LORD*a* said, 'You are to entice him, and you shall succeed; go out and do it.' 23So you see, the LORD has put a lying spirit in the mouth of all these your prophets; the LORD has decreed disaster for you."

caiah's first response agrees completely with that of the court prophets. He may, in fact, be mimicking them. **16:** The *king* of Israel recognizes Micaiah's insincerity and adjures him to speak *the truth in the name of the LORD*. **17:** The image of a king as a *shepherd* was common in the ancient Near East (2 Sam 5.2). The sheep are without a shepherd in *Micaiah*'s vision because the king has died. **19:** The LORD is depicted as a king *sitting on his throne* surrounded by his council of advisers, here called the *host of heaven*. **20:** This is the only time in the story proper that the king of Israel is identified as *Ahab*. The council deliberates how to *entice* him to go to *Ramoth-gilead* where he will *fall*, that is, be killed. **21–23:** A *spirit* or "breath" steps forward and volunteers to deceive Ahab as a *lying spirit in the mouth of his prophets*.

24 Then Zedekiah son of Chenaanah came up to Micaiah, slapped him on the cheek, and said, "Which way did the spirit of the LORD pass from me to speak to you?" 25Micaiah replied, "You will find out on that day when you go in to hide in an inner chamber." 26The king of Israel then ordered, "Take Micaiah, and return him to Amon the governor of the city and to Joash the king's son, 27and say, 'Thus says the king: Put this fellow in prison, and feed him on reduced rations of bread and water until I come in peace.' " 28Micaiah said, "If you return in peace, the LORD has not spoken by me." And he said, "Hear, you peoples, all of you!"

29 So the king of Israel and King Jehoshaphat of Judah went up to Ramoth-gilead. 30The king of Israel said to Jehoshaphat, "I will disguise myself and go into battle, but you wear your robes." So the king of Israel disguised himself and went into battle. 31Now the king of Aram had commanded the thirty-two captains of his chariots, "Fight with no one small or great, but only with the king of Israel." 32When the captains of the chariots saw Jehoshaphat, they said, "It is surely the king of Israel." So they turned to fight against him; and Jehoshaphat cried out. 33When the captains of the chariots saw that it was not the king of Israel, they turned back from pursuing him. 34But a certain man

22.13–23. 13–14: *Micaiah*, unlike the court prophets, cannot speak what he wishes or what the king wants to hear, but only what the LORD says to him. **15:** *Mi-*

a Heb *he*

drew his bow and unknowingly struck the king of Israel between the scale armor and the breastplate; so he said to the driver of his chariot, "Turn around, and carry me out of the battle, for I am wounded." ³⁵The battle grew hot that day, and the king was propped up in his chariot facing the Arameans, until at evening he died; the blood from the wound had flowed into the bottom of the chariot. ³⁶Then about sunset a shout went through the army, "Every man to his city, and every man to his country!"

37 So the king died, and was brought to Samaria; they buried the king in Samaria. ³⁸They washed the chariot by the pool of Samaria; the dogs licked up his blood, and the prostitutes washed themselves in it,ᵃ according to the word of the LORD that he had spoken. ³⁹Now the rest of the acts of Ahab, and all that he did, and the ivory house that he built, and all the cities that he built, are they not written in the Book of the Annals of the Kings of Israel? ⁴⁰So Ahab slept with his ancestors; and his son Ahaziah succeeded him.

41 Jehoshaphat son of Asa began to reign over Judah in the fourth year of King Ahab of Israel. ⁴²Jehoshaphat was thirty-five years old when he began to reign, and he reigned twenty-five years in Jerusalem. His mother's name was Azubah daughter of Shilhi. ⁴³He walked in all the way of his father Asa; he did not turn aside from it, doing what was right in the sight of the LORD; yet the high places were not taken away, and the people still sacrificed and offered incense on the high places. ⁴⁴Jehoshaphat also made peace with the king of Israel.

king of Israel believed Micaiah enough so that he disguised himself in order to avoid being a target of the enemy. This probably means that he did not wear his royal robes as did Jehoshaphat. **32–33:** Something about Jehoshaphat's cry, perhaps his accent, alerted the Arameans that he was not the king of Israel. **36:** Every man to his city, and every man to his country is a cry to military demobilization. See 2 Sam 20.1; 1 Kings 12.16. **38:** The fact that the dogs licked up [Ahab's] blood is evidently meant as a fulfillment of Elijah's word in 21.19. **40:** The idiom slept with his ancestors is not used anywhere else of a king who suffered a violent death. Thus the closing formula for Ahab's reign seems to ignore his death in battle. **43:** The high places* were places for worship outside of Jerusalem.

45 Now the rest of the acts of Jehoshaphat, and his power that he showed, and how he waged war, are they not written in the Book of the Annals of the Kings of Judah? ⁴⁶The remnant of the male temple prostitutes who were still in the land in the days of his father Asa, he exterminated.

47 There was no king in Edom; a deputy was king. ⁴⁸Jehoshaphat made ships of the Tarshish type to go to Ophir for gold; but they did not go, for the ships were wrecked at Ezion-geber. ⁴⁹Then Ahaziah son of Ahab said to Jehoshaphat, "Let my servants go with your servants in the ships," but Jehoshaphat was not willing. ⁵⁰Jehoshaphat slept with his ancestors and was buried with his ancestors in the city of his father David; his son Jehoram succeeded him.

51 Ahaziah son of Ahab began to reign over Israel in Samaria in the seventeenth year of King Jehoshaphat of Judah; he reigned two years over Israel. ⁵²He did what was evil in the sight of the LORD, and walked in the way of his father and mother, and in the way of Jeroboam son of Nebat, who caused Israel to sin. ⁵³He served Baal and worshiped him; he provoked the LORD, the God of Israel, to anger, just as his father had done.

ᵃ Heb lacks in it

22.24–44. 24: Zedekiah claims that the lying spirit is actually in Micaiah. **25:** Micaiah's point is not entirely clear. Apparently, he foresees Zedekiah trying to hide in an inner chamber after Israel's defeat. Another possible interpretation would take Micaiah's meaning to be coarsely sarcastic: You will know the answer to your question (v. 24) the next time you relieve yourself (taking hide in an inner chamber to be a euphemism*). **27–28:** In peace means alive and unharmed. **30:** The

2 KINGS

Introduction

The book of 2 Kings is the continuation of 1 Kings and the final biblical book of the Deuteronomistic★ History (see the introduction to 1 Samuel). In some ways the hand of the deuteronomistic author appears more clearly in 2 Kings than in the previous books of the History, partly because the contents of the book are closer to the author's time than is the case with the previous books. Deuteronomistic editing is especially apparent in the evaluations of the kings. The kings of Israel are all condemned for perpetuating the sin of Jeroboam in the shrines he built at Dan and Bethel. Several of the kings of Judah, on the other hand, are viewed favorably, although most of them are accused of failing to do away with the "high places,"★ shrines other than the Jerusalem Temple,★ which is considered the only legitimate place for worship. The author obviously had access to a king list or perhaps royal annals for information about the kings. In addition, a significant portion of 2 Kings consists of stories about prophets.★ There is reason to believe that many of these stories were inserted by a later writer or editor into the already completed Deuteronomistic History.

The Deuteronomistic History was composed in the Exile.★ 2 Kings recounts the destruction of Jerusalem and the beginning of the Babylonian captivity. The author struggles to explain the cause for the Exile, blaming it on both Manasseh (21.10–15) and Zedekiah and his contemporaries (24.20). Curiously, no attempt is made to explain how the promise of an eternal Davidic dynasty★ is to be understood in the light of the Exile. Indeed, the book ends on an ambiguous note. On the one hand, it offers no explicit hope for restoration. On the other hand, the final four verses mention the release from prison of Jehoiachin, the next-to-last king of Judah, and his elevation in the Babylonian court. They therefore hint at a possible restoration of the Davidic monarchy.

READING GUIDE

The reader may find the names of the kings unfamiliar and the alternation between Israel and Judah difficult to track. What is more important than knowing the details of this history is understanding the author's overall perspective, which entails trying to explain Israel's history theologically. Thus, Judah outlasts Israel because of the LORD's reward of a dynasty for David's faithfulness. Israel's destruction is due to its apostasy, as is Judah's captivity. But in Judah's case there may still be hope for the future. The stories about Elisha and the prophets add another dimension to this narrative.★ While they emphasize the supremacy of the LORD in contrast to other gods, they also display a legendary★ quality in describing the deeds of the prophets, which does not correspond to the deuteronomistic outlook.

1–8	Stories about Elisha and the prophets
9–10	Jehu's revolt
11–16	Various kings; focus on Judah
17	The fall of Israel
18–20	Hezekiah
21	Manasseh and Amon
22–23	Josiah
24–25	The final kings and fall of Judah

1 After the death of Ahab, Moab rebelled against Israel. 2 Ahaziah had fallen through the lattice in his upper chamber in Samaria, and lay injured; so he sent messengers, telling them, "Go, inquire of Baal-zebub, the god of Ekron, whether I shall recover from this injury." 3 But the angel of the LORD said to Elijah the Tishbite, "Get up, go to meet the messengers of the king of Samaria, and say to them, 'Is it because there is no God in Israel that you are going to inquire of Baal-zebub, the god of Ekron?' 4 Now therefore thus says the LORD, 'You shall not leave the bed to which you have gone, but you shall surely die.'" So Elijah went.

5 The messengers returned to the king, who said to them, "Why have you returned?" 6 They answered him, "There came a man to meet us, who said to us, 'Go back to the king who sent you, and say to him: Thus says the LORD: Is it because there is no God in Israel that you are sending to inquire of Baal-zebub, the god of Ekron? Therefore you shall not leave the bed to which you have gone, but shall surely die.'" 7 He said to them, "What sort of man was he who came to meet you and told you these things?" 8 They answered him, "A hairy man, with a leather belt around his waist." He said, "It is Elijah the Tishbite."

9 Then the king sent to him a captain of fifty with his fifty men. He went up to Elijah, who was sitting on the top of a hill, and said to him, "O man of God, the king says, 'Come down.'" 10 But Elijah answered the captain of fifty, "If I am a man of God, let fire come down from heaven and consume you and your fifty." Then fire came down from heaven, and consumed him and his fifty.

11 Again the king sent to him another captain of fifty with his fifty. He went up[a] and said to him, "O man of God, this is the king's order: Come down quickly!" 12 But Elijah answered them, "If I am a man of God, let fire come down from heaven and consume you and your fifty." Then the fire of God came down from heaven and consumed him and his fifty.

13 Again the king sent the captain of a third fifty with his fifty. So the third captain of fifty went up, and came and fell on his knees before Elijah, and entreated him, "O man of God, please let my life, and the life of these fifty servants of yours, be precious in your sight. 14 Look, fire came down from heaven and consumed the two former captains of fifty men with their fifties; but now let my life be precious in your sight." 15 Then the angel of the LORD said to Elijah, "Go down with him; do not be afraid of him." So he set out and went down with him to the king, 16 and said to him, "Thus says the LORD: Because you have sent messengers to inquire of Baal-zebub, the god of Ekron,—is it because there is no God in Israel to inquire of his word?—therefore you shall not leave the bed to which you have gone, but you shall surely die."

17 So he died according to the word of the LORD that Elijah had spoken. His brother,[b] Jehoram succeeded him as king in the second year of King Jehoram son of Jehoshaphat of Judah, because Ahaziah had no son. 18 Now the rest of the acts of Ahaziah that he did, are they not written in the Book of the Annals of the Kings of Israel?

1.1–18: The death of Ahaziah. 1: This verse anticipates the story in 3.4–27 and may be out of place here. **2:** The *lattice* was decorative, but also functional in the sense of admitting light and air while providing some privacy. It was not strong enough to keep a person from falling, as this story shows. Ahaziah sent messengers to *inquire*, a technical term for divination. *Baal-zebub*,★ meaning "lord of the fly," is a deliberate mocking distortion of the name Baal-zebul,★ "Baal★ the prince." **3:** The Hebrew word for *angel* also means messenger. **8:** A *hairy man*, literally "a man of hair," may refer to a coarse garment that was the mantle of prophets★ (Zech 13.4). **10, 12:** The *fire of God from heaven* was probably lightning.

2 Now when the LORD was about to take Elijah up to heaven by a whirlwind, Elijah and Elisha were on their way from Gilgal. 2 Elijah said to Elisha, "Stay here; for the LORD has sent me as far as Bethel." But Elisha said, "As the LORD lives, and as you your-

a Gk Compare verses 9, 13: Heb *He answered*
b Gk Syr: Heb lacks *His brother*

self live, I will not leave you." So they went down to Bethel. ³The company of prophets*ª who were in Bethel came out to Elisha, and said to him, "Do you know that today the LORD will take your master away from you?" And he said, "Yes, I know; keep silent."

4 Elijah said to him, "Elisha, stay here; for the LORD has sent me to Jericho." But he said, "As the LORD lives, and as you yourself live, I will not leave you." So they came to Jericho. ⁵The company of prophets*ª who were at Jericho drew near to Elisha, and said to him, "Do you know that today the LORD will take your master away from you?" And he answered, "Yes, I know; be silent."

6 Then Elijah said to him, "Stay here; for the LORD has sent me to the Jordan." But he said, "As the LORD lives, and as you yourself live, I will not leave you." So the two of them went on. ⁷Fifty men of the company of prophets*ª also went, and stood at some distance from them, as they both were standing by the Jordan. ⁸Then Elijah took his mantle and rolled it up, and struck the water; the water was parted to the one side and to the other, until the two of them crossed on dry ground.

9 When they had crossed, Elijah said to Elisha, "Tell me what I may do for you, before I am taken from you." Elisha said, "Please let me inherit a double share of your spirit." ¹⁰He responded, "You have asked a hard thing; yet, if you see me as I am being taken from you, it will be granted you; if not, it will not." ¹¹As they continued walking and talking, a chariot of fire and horses of fire separated the two of them, and Elijah ascended in a whirlwind into heaven. ¹²Elisha kept watching and crying out, "Father, father! The chariots of Israel and its horsemen!" But when he could no longer see him, he grasped his own clothes and tore them in two pieces.

2.1–12: The translation of Elijah. The stories in this chapter fall outside of the standard wording that marks the beginning and ending of the reigns of the kings, called regnal formulas (1.17–18; 3.1), which may indicate that they, along with other stories about the prophets,* are later additions to the Deuteronomistic* History. **1:** The only other person in the Bible who was taken *up to heaven* without dying was Enoch (Gen 5.24). **3:** The *company of prophets,* literally "the sons of the prophets," were followers of prophets, perhaps even a guild or school of prophets. They were also aware, perhaps through prophetic agency, that *the LORD will take* Elijah away. **8:** Elijah's *mantle* is a symbol of his power as a prophet (see 1.8; Zech 13.4), which Elisha will inherit (2.13). His division of the Jordan here is reminiscent of Moses' division of the Red Sea (Ex 14.21–22) and of Joshua's division of the Jordan (Josh 3.13–17). **9:** *Double share* does not mean twice as much as Elijah but the portion of the first-born son (Deut 21.17), or two-thirds. **12:** Elisha calls Elijah his *father* out of respect for his teacher, not because there is a blood relationship between them. *The chariots of Israel and its horsemen* may allude to the image of the LORD as commander of the heavenly armies ("Yahweh sebaoth," "the LORD of hosts"; see 6.17).

13 He picked up the mantle of Elijah that had fallen from him, and went back and stood on the bank of the Jordan. ¹⁴He took the mantle of Elijah that had fallen from him, and struck the water, saying, "Where is the LORD, the God of Elijah?" When he had struck the water, the water was parted to the one side and to the other, and Elisha went over.

15 When the company of prophets*ª who were at Jericho saw him at a distance, they declared, "The spirit of Elijah rests on Elisha." They came to meet him and bowed to the ground before him. ¹⁶They said to him, "See now, we have fifty strong men among your servants; please let them go and seek your master; it may be that the spirit of the LORD has caught him up and thrown him down on some mountain or into some valley." He responded, "No, do not send them." ¹⁷But when they urged him until he was ashamed, he said, "Send them." So they sent fifty men who searched for three days but did not find him. ¹⁸When they came back to him (he had remained at Jericho), he said to them, "Did I not say to you, Do not go?"

19 Now the people of the city said to Elisha, "The location of this city is good, as my

ª Heb *sons of the prophets*

lord sees; but the water is bad, and the land is unfruitful." 20He said, "Bring me a new bowl, and put salt in it." So they brought it to him. 21Then he went to the spring of water and threw the salt into it, and said, "Thus says the LORD, I have made this water wholesome; from now on neither death nor miscarriage shall come from it." 22So the water has been wholesome to this day, according to the word that Elisha spoke.

23 He went up from there to Bethel; and while he was going up on the way, some small boys came out of the city and jeered at him, saying, "Go away, baldhead! Go away, baldhead!" 24When he turned around and saw them, he cursed them in the name of the LORD. Then two she-bears came out of the woods and mauled forty-two of the boys. 25From there he went on to Mount Carmel, and then returned to Samaria.

2.13–25: Elisha as Elijah's successor. The stories here show that Elisha has inherited Elijah's power as a man of God. 13–14: Elisha *picked up the mantle of Elijah,* which was the symbol of his prophetic* power (1.8; Zech 13.4). He then *struck the water* of the Jordan with it and *parted* it just as Elijah had done (2.8) and much as Joshua did when he succeeded Moses (Ex 14.21–22; Josh 3.13–17). 15: The *company of prophets* (see comment on 2.3) recognize Elisha as Elijah's successor. 16–18: Elisha knows that Elijah has been taken up and will not be found, but he acquiesces to a search at the insistence of the other prophets. 19–22: Elisha's miraculous purification of the spring also shows that he has the power of Elijah. This story offers an etiological* explanation for the renowned spring at Jericho that is still active today. 23–25: This legend* was preserved not for its high ethical quality but to show the power now vested in Elisha and to teach that one should have respect for prophets.

3 In the eighteenth year of King Jehoshaphat of Judah, Jehoram son of Ahab became king over Israel in Samaria; he reigned twelve years. 2He did what was evil in the sight of the LORD, though not like his father and mother, for he removed the pillar of Baal that his father had made. 3Nevertheless he clung to the sin of Jeroboam son of Nebat, which he caused Israel to commit; he did not depart from it.

4 Now King Mesha of Moab was a sheep breeder, who used to deliver to the king of Israel one hundred thousand lambs, and the wool of one hundred thousand rams. 5But when Ahab died, the king of Moab rebelled against the king of Israel. 6So King Jehoram marched out of Samaria at that time and mustered all Israel. 7As he went he sent word to King Jehoshaphat of Judah, "The king of Moab has rebelled against me; will you go with me to battle against Moab?" He answered, "I will; I am with you, my people are your people, my horses are your horses." 8Then he asked, "By which way shall we march?" Jehoram answered, "By the way of the wilderness of Edom."

9 So the king of Israel, the king of Judah, and the king of Edom set out; and when they had made a roundabout march of seven days, there was no water for the army or for the animals that were with them. 10Then the king of Israel said, "Alas! The LORD has summoned us, three kings, only to be handed over to Moab." 11But Jehoshaphat said, "Is there no prophet of the LORD here, through whom we may inquire of the LORD?" Then one of the servants of the king of Israel answered, "Elisha son of Shaphat, who used to pour water on the hands of Elijah, is here." 12Jehoshaphat said, "The word of the LORD is with him." So the king of Israel and Jehoshaphat and the king of Edom went down to him.

3.1–27: The independence of Moab. 1: The information here about the beginning of Jehoram's reign disagrees with that of 1.17. The two verses may be based on two distinct chronologies. 2: A *pillar* was often used, much as an idol would be, as a symbol for a god in worship. 3: *The sin of Jeroboam* was the two shrines at Dan and Bethel (1 Kings 12.25–33). 4: *Moab* was the country across the Dead Sea from Israel. The *lambs* and *wool* that *King Mesha* sent to Israel were the yearly payment of tribute of a subject state to its overlord. 8: *Edom* was east of Judah and south of Moab. It was apparently controlled at this time by Judah. *Jehoram* plans to attack Moab from the south. 11: As in 1 Kings 22.7, it is the righteous King *Jehoshaphat* of Judah who asks for a prophet* of the LORD. To *inquire* is a technical term for divination or seeking an oracle* from God. *Elisha* is here recognized as *Elijah*'s servant *who used to pour water* on his hands.

~~~~~~

13 Elisha said to the king of Israel, "What have I to do with you? Go to your father's prophets or to your mother's." But the king of Israel said to him, "No; it is the LORD who has summoned us, three kings, only to be handed over to Moab." ¹⁴Elisha said, "As the LORD of hosts lives, whom I serve, were it not that I have regard for King Jehoshaphat of Judah, I would give you neither a look nor a glance. ¹⁵But get me a musician." And then, while the musician was playing, the power of the LORD came on him. ¹⁶And he said, "Thus says the LORD, 'I will make this wadi full of pools.' ¹⁷For thus says the LORD, 'You shall see neither wind nor rain, but the wadi shall be filled with water, so that you shall drink, you, your cattle, and your animals.' ¹⁸This is only a trifle in the sight of the LORD, for he will also hand Moab over to you. ¹⁹You shall conquer every fortified city and every choice city; every good tree you shall fell, all springs of water you shall stop up, and every good piece of land you shall ruin with stones." ²⁰The next day, about the time of the morning offering, suddenly water began to flow from the direction of Edom, until the country was filled with water.

─────────────────────────────

3.13–20. 13: *What have I to do with you?* means "We have nothing in common"; Elisha wants nothing to do with the king of Israel. Jehoram's *father* was Ahab and his *mother* Jezebel. Their *prophets* were worshippers of Baal★ and Asherah★ (1 Kings 18.19). **15:** Music was used to induce the prophet's ecstatic experience in which he would give his oracle★ (compare 1 Sam. 10.5, 9–13). **19:** The measures described in this verse would ruin a piece of land for agriculture. **20:** The *morning offering* or oblation was made at dawn. 1 Kings 18.29 refers to a second oblation at about 3 p.m. The practice of two oblations may have begun in the Exile★ or later. This is an indication that this story was written at a later date.

~~~~~~~~~~~~~~~~~~~~~~~~~~~~~~~

21 When all the Moabites heard that the kings had come up to fight against them, all who were able to put on armor, from the youngest to the oldest, were called out and were drawn up at the frontier. ²²When they rose early in the morning, and the sun shone upon the water, the Moabites saw the water opposite them as red as blood. ²³They said, "This is blood; the kings must have fought together, and killed one another. Now then, Moab, to the spoil!" ²⁴But when they came

■~~~~~~■

The Mesha Stele

The Mesha stele (a stele, pronounced "steely," is an inscribed pillar) or Moabite stone was discovered in 1868 in what is now the country of Jordan. It is the only inscription known to exist from the ancient country of Moab and in the language of that country. While it was discovered intact, subsequent feuding over it, especially by Western powers, led the Bedouin Arabs who possessed it to destroy it. Only about half of the original stele remains today in fragmentary form. The rest has been reconstructed. The stele was erected by King Mesha of Moab (2 Kings 3.4) sometime in the second half of the ninth century (850–800) BCE. In it, Mesha claims to have broken free of the domination of Israel under Omri and Ahab. The inscription mentions the LORD (Yahweh) as well as the institution of the ban,★ or devotion to destruction, which is also found in the Bible (for example, 1 Sam 15.3). According to this practice, everything of the enemy's that can breathe—men, women, children, animals—is killed as a sacrifice to the deity. The Mesha stele, therefore, makes it clear that holy war★ was not unique to Israel but was an institution common in the ancient Near East.

■~~~~~~■

to the camp of Israel, the Israelites rose up and attacked the Moabites, who fled before them; as they entered Moab they continued the attack.[a] 25The cities they overturned, and on every good piece of land everyone threw a stone, until it was covered; every spring of water they stopped up, and every good tree they felled. Only at Kir-hareseth did the stone walls remain, until the slingers surrounded and attacked it. 26When the king of Moab saw that the battle was going against him, he took with him seven hundred swordsmen to break through, opposite the king of Edom; but they could not. 27Then he took his firstborn son who was to succeed him, and offered him as a burnt offering on the wall. And great wrath came upon Israel, so they withdrew from him and returned to their own land.

3.21–27. 22: The *red* color of the water is appropriate to Edom, which comes from the word for red and which was known for its red sandstone (see Gen 25.25, 30). 27: Child sacrifice was practiced in the ancient Near East. Here the king of Moab sacrifices his son to Chemosh, Moab's god. It is not clear what is meant by *great wrath came upon Israel*. Perhaps it means that the Israelites became afraid when they witnessed this desperate act, though the most natural interpretation would seem to be that Chemosh's wrath was directed against Israel in some form.

4 Now the wife of a member of the company of prophets[b] cried to Elisha, "Your servant my husband is dead; and you know that your servant feared the LORD, but a creditor has come to take my two children as slaves." 2Elisha said to her, "What shall I do for you? Tell me, what do you have in the house?" She answered, "Your servant has nothing in the house, except a jar of oil." 3He said, "Go outside, borrow vessels from all your neighbors, empty vessels and not just a few. 4Then go in, and shut the door behind you and your children, and start pouring into all these vessels; when each is full, set it aside." 5So she left him and shut the door behind her and her children; they kept bringing vessels to her, and she kept pouring. 6When the vessels were full, she said to her son, "Bring me another vessel." But he said

to her, "There are no more." Then the oil stopped flowing. 7She came and told the man of God, and he said, "Go sell the oil and pay your debts, and you and your children can live on the rest."

4.1–44: Elisha's wonders. 1–7: This story is similar to the one about Elijah in 1 Kings 17.8–16. The sale of oneself or one's family members to pay debts was permitted on a temporary basis by Israelite law (Lev 25.39–42; Deut 15.1–17).

8 One day Elisha was passing through Shunem, where a wealthy woman lived, who urged him to have a meal. So whenever he passed that way, he would stop there for a meal. 9She said to her husband, "Look, I am sure that this man who regularly passes our way is a holy man of God. 10Let us make a small roof chamber with walls, and put there for him a bed, a table, a chair, and a lamp, so that he can stay there whenever he comes to us."

11 One day when he came there, he went up to the chamber and lay down there. 12He said to his servant Gehazi, "Call the Shunammite woman." When he had called her, she stood before him. 13He said to him, "Say to her, Since you have taken all this trouble for us, what may be done for you? Would you have a word spoken on your behalf to the king or to the commander of the army?" She answered, "I live among my own people." 14He said, "What then may be done for her?" Gehazi answered, "Well, she has no son, and her husband is old." 15He said, "Call her." When he had called her, she stood at the door. 16He said, "At this season, in due time, you shall embrace a son." She replied, "No, my lord, O man of God; do not deceive your servant."

17 The woman conceived and bore a son at that season, in due time, as Elisha had declared to her.

18 When the child was older, he went out one day to his father among the reapers. 19He complained to his father, "Oh, my head, my head!" The father said to his ser-

a Compare Gk Syr: Meaning of Heb uncertain
b Heb *the sons of the prophets*

vant, "Carry him to his mother." 20He carried him and brought him to his mother; the child sat on her lap until noon, and he died. 21She went up and laid him on the bed of the man of God, closed the door on him, and left. 22Then she called to her husband, and said, "Send me one of the servants and one of the donkeys, so that I may quickly go to the man of God and come back again." 23He said, "Why go to him today? It is neither new moon nor sabbath." She said, "It will be all right." 24Then she saddled the donkey and said to her servant, "Urge the animal on; do not hold back for me unless I tell you." 25So she set out, and came to the man of God at Mount Carmel.

When the man of God saw her coming, he said to Gehazi his servant, "Look, there is the Shunammite woman; 26run at once to meet her, and say to her, Are you all right? Is your husband all right? Is the child all right?" She answered, "It is all right." 27When she came to the man of God at the mountain, she caught hold of his feet. Gehazi approached to push her away. But the man of God said, "Let her alone, for she is in bitter distress; the LORD has hidden it from me and has not told me." 28Then she said, "Did I ask my lord for a son? Did I not say, Do not mislead me?" 29He said to Gehazi, "Gird up your loins, and take my staff in your hand, and go. If you meet anyone, give no greeting, and if anyone greets you, do not answer; and lay my staff on the face of the child." 30Then the mother of the child said, "As the LORD lives, and as you yourself live, I will not leave without you." So he rose up and followed her. 31Gehazi went on ahead and laid the staff on the face of the child, but there was no sound or sign of life. He came back to meet him and told him, "The child has not awakened."

32 When Elisha came into the house, he saw the child lying dead on his bed. 33So he went in and closed the door on the two of them, and prayed to the LORD. 34Then he got up on the bed[a] and lay upon the child, putting his mouth upon his mouth, his eyes upon his eyes, and his hands upon his hands; and while he lay bent over him, the flesh of the child became warm. 35He got down, walked once to and fro in the room, then got up again and bent over him; the child sneezed seven times, and the child opened his eyes. 36Elisha[b] summoned Gehazi and said, "Call the Shunammite woman." So he called her. When she came to him, he said, "Take your son." 37She came and fell at his feet, bowing to the ground; then she took her son and left.

4.8–37: This story is also similar to one about Elijah in 1 Kings 17.17–24, which it has influenced (see comments on 1 Kings 17). *Mount Carmel* (v. 25) was a holy site and the location of Elijah's victory in 1 Kings 18. It has apparently become Elisha's residence. *Gehazi,* Elisha's servant, is mentioned here (v. 25), without introduction, for the first time. As in 1 Kings 17, Elisha's resuscitation of the boy involves contactual magic (v. 34), though the miracle is clearly seen as the LORD's doing (v. 33). The boy's sneezing (v. 35) is a sign of life.

38 When Elisha returned to Gilgal, there was a famine in the land. As the company of prophets was[c] sitting before him, he said to his servant, "Put the large pot on, and make some stew for the company of prophets."[d] 39One of them went out into the field to gather herbs; he found a wild vine and gathered from it a lapful of wild gourds, and came and cut them up into the pot of stew, not knowing what they were. 40They served some for the men to eat. But while they were eating the stew, they cried out, "O man of God, there is death in the pot!" They could not eat it. 41He said, "Then bring some flour." He threw it into the pot, and said, "Serve the people and let them eat." And there was nothing harmful in the pot.

42 A man came from Baal-shalishah, bringing food from the first fruits to the man of God: twenty loaves of barley and fresh ears of grain in his sack. Elisha said, "Give it to the people and let them eat." 43But his servant said, "How can I set this before a hundred people?" So he repeated, "Give it to the people and let them eat, for thus says the LORD, 'They shall eat and have some left.' "

a Heb lacks *on the bed*   *b* Heb *he*   *c* Heb *sons of the prophets were*   *d* Heb *sons of the prophets*

44He set it before them, they ate, and had some left, according to the word of the LORD.

4.38–44. 38–41: This story is similar to the one in 2.19–22. **42–44:** Compare the New Testament stories of Jesus' multiplication of the loaves (Mt 14.13–21; 15.32–38; and their parallels in the other Gospels).

5 Naaman, commander of the army of the king of Aram, was a great man and in high favor with his master, because by him the LORD had given victory to Aram. The man, though a mighty warrior, suffered from leprosy.a 2Now the Arameans on one of their raids had taken a young girl captive from the land of Israel, and she served Naaman's wife. 3She said to her mistress, "If only my lord were with the prophet who is in Samaria! He would cure him of his leprosy."a 4So Naamanb went in and told his lord just what the girl from the land of Israel had said. 5And the king of Aram said, "Go then, and I will send along a letter to the king of Israel."

He went, taking with him ten talents of silver, six thousand shekels of gold, and ten sets of garments. 6He brought the letter to the king of Israel, which read, "When this letter reaches you, know that I have sent to you my servant Naaman, that you may cure him of his leprosy."a 7When the king of Israel read the letter, he tore his clothes and said, "Am I God, to give death or life, that this man sends word to me to cure a man of his leprosy?a Just look and see how he is trying to pick a quarrel with me."

8 But when Elisha the man of God heard that the king of Israel had torn his clothes, he sent a message to the king, "Why have you torn your clothes? Let him come to me, that he may learn that there is a prophet in Israel." 9So Naaman came with his horses and chariots, and halted at the entrance of Elisha's house. 10Elisha sent a messenger to him, saying, "Go, wash in the Jordan seven times, and your flesh shall be restored and you shall be clean." 11But Naaman became angry and went away, saying, "I thought that for me he would surely come out, and stand and call on the name of the LORD his God,

and would wave his hand over the spot, and cure the leprosy!a 12Are not Abanac and Pharpar, the rivers of Damascus, better than all the waters of Israel? Could I not wash in them, and be clean?" He turned and went away in a rage. 13But his servants approached and said to him, "Father, if the prophet had commanded you to do something difficult, would you not have done it? How much more, when all he said to you was, 'Wash, and be clean'?" 14So he went down and immersed himself seven times in the Jordan, according to the word of the man of God; his flesh was restored like the flesh of a young boy, and he was clean.

15 Then he returned to the man of God, he and all his company; he came and stood before him and said, "Now I know that there is no God in all the earth except in Israel; please accept a present from your servant." 16But he said, "As the LORD lives, whom I serve, I will accept nothing!" He urged him to accept, but he refused. 17Then Naaman said, "If not, please let two mule-loads of earth be given to your servant; for your servant will no longer offer burnt offering or sacrifice to any god except the LORD. 18But may the LORD pardon your servant on one count: when my master goes into the house of Rimmon to worship there, leaning on my arm, and I bow down in the house of Rimmon, when I do bow down in the house of Rimmon, may the LORD pardon your servant on this one count." 19He said to him, "Go in peace."

But when Naaman had gone from him a short distance, 20Gehazi, the servant of Elisha the man of God, thought, "My master has let that Aramean Naaman off too lightly by not accepting from him what he offered. As the LORD lives, I will run after him and get something out of him." 21So Gehazi went after Naaman. When Naaman saw someone running after him, he jumped down from the chariot to meet him and said, "Is everything all right?" 22He replied, "Yes, but my master has sent me to say, 'Two members of a com-

---

a A term for several skin diseases; precise meaning uncertain   b Heb he   c Another reading is Amana pany of prophets[a] have just come to me from the hill country of Ephraim; please give them a talent of silver and two changes of clothing.'" 23Naaman said, "Please accept two talents." He urged him, and tied up two talents of silver in two bags, with two changes of clothing, and gave them to two of his servants, who carried them in front of Gehazi.[b] 24When he came to the citadel, he took the bags[c] from them, and stored them inside; he dismissed the men, and they left.

25 He went in and stood before his master; and Elisha said to him, "Where have you been, Gehazi?" He answered, "Your servant has not gone anywhere at all." 26But he said to him, "Did I not go with you in spirit when someone left his chariot to meet you? Is this a time to accept money and to accept clothing, olive orchards and vineyards, sheep and oxen, and male and female slaves? 27Therefore the leprosy[d] of Naaman shall cling to you, and to your descendants forever." So he left his presence leprous,[d] as white as snow.

5.1–27: The healing of Naaman. 1: The story presupposes a time when *Aram* (Syria) dominates Israel. This was the case during the Jehu dynasty* (see 10.32) but not during the Omri dynasty where this story is set, according to its current placement in 2 Kings. However, neither the *king of Aram* nor the king of Israel (v. 5) is named. *Leprosy* is a broad term for some skin diseases. It was greatly feared because it was regarded as incurable, disfiguring, fatal, and highly contagious. **3:** *The prophet** is later identified as Elisha. The story shows how his fame reached beyond the borders of Israel. **5:** A *talent* could weigh from 45 to 130 pounds. A shekel weighed less than half an ounce. *Six thousand shekels* was probably about 150 pounds. **13:** *Father* is a title of respect here and does not indicate any blood relationship. **15:** Naaman's statement is very similar to Israel's confession of faith (Deut 6.4). **17:** The idea behind *Naaman's* request for *two mule-loads of earth* was that the LORD (Yahweh) could only be worshipped on Israelite soil. **18:** *Rimmon* ("pomegranate") is a mocking distortion of Ramman, a title for the Syrian god Hadad. Naaman continues to worship the deity of his native land only because he is forced to do so; he no longer believes in Hadad. **19b–27:** This episode shows the danger of trying to deceive a prophet.

6 Now the company of prophets[a] said to Elisha, "As you see, the place where we live under your charge is too small for us. 2Let us go to the Jordan, and let us collect logs there, one for each of us, and build a place there for us to live." He answered, "Do so." 3Then one of them said, "Please come with your servants." And he answered, "I will." 4So he went with them. When they came to the Jordan, they cut down trees. 5But as one was felling a log, his ax head fell into the water; he cried out, "Alas, master! It was borrowed." 6Then the man of God said, "Where did it fall?" When he showed him the place, he cut off a stick, and threw it in there, and made the iron float. 7He said, "Pick it up." So he reached out his hand and took it.

8 Once when the king of Aram was at war with Israel, he took counsel with his officers. He said, "At such and such a place shall be my camp." 9But the man of God sent word to the king of Israel, "Take care not to pass this place, because the Arameans are going down there." 10The king of Israel sent word to the place of which the man of God spoke. More than once or twice he warned such a place[e] so that it was on the alert.

6.1–23: More wonders of Elisha. 1–7: This story, in which Elisha makes an *ax head* float, is set near the Jordan River where trees grow because of the abundance of water. **8–10:** Elisha's strategic importance for the Israelites is invaluable, since he is able to warn them of the impeding actions of their enemies, *the Arameans* (Syrians).

11 The mind of the king of Aram was greatly perturbed because of this; he called his officers and said to them, "Now tell me who among us sides with the king of Israel?" 12Then one of his officers said, "No one, my lord king. It is Elisha, the prophet in Israel, who tells the king of Israel the words that you speak in your bedchamber." 13He said, "Go and find where he is; I will send and seize him." He was told, "He is in Dothan." 14So he sent horses and chariots there and

a Heb *sons of the prophets*   b Heb *him*   c Heb lacks *the bags*   d A term for several skin diseases; precise meaning uncertain   e Heb *warned it* a great army; they came by night, and surrounded the city.

15 When an attendant of the man of God rose early in the morning and went out, an army with horses and chariots was all around the city. His servant said, "Alas, master! What shall we do?" 16He replied, "Do not be afraid, for there are more with us than there are with them." 17Then Elisha prayed: "O LORD, please open his eyes that he may see." So the LORD opened the eyes of the servant, and he saw; the mountain was full of horses and chariots of fire all around Elisha. 18When the Arameans[a] came down against him, Elisha prayed to the LORD, and said, "Strike this people, please, with blindness." So he struck them with blindness as Elisha had asked. 19Elisha said to them, "This is not the way, and this is not the city; follow me, and I will bring you to the man whom you seek." And he led them to Samaria.

20 As soon as they entered Samaria, Elisha said, "O LORD, open the eyes of these men so that they may see." The LORD opened their eyes, and they saw that they were inside Samaria. 21When the king of Israel saw them he said to Elisha, "Father, shall I kill them? Shall I kill them?" 22He answered, "No! Did you capture with your sword and your bow those whom you want to kill? Set food and water before them so that they may eat and drink; and let them go to their master." 23So he prepared for them a great feast; after they ate and drank, he sent them on their way, and they went to their master. And the Arameans no longer came raiding into the land of Israel.

6.11–23: 12: The Aramean officer tells his king that Elisha knows even the most intimate words spoken by the king in his *bedchamber*. Though this is certainly an exaggeration, it is quite disconcerting to the king. 13–14: The story stresses Elisha's importance since he is the reason for an invasion by the Arameans. 17: This verse vividly illustrates the title "the LORD of hosts" ("Yahweh sebaoth"), since the LORD controls both earthly and heavenly armies (see 2.11). 21: *Father* is a term of respect for a superior. Thus, in this story the king was subject to the prophet.★

24 Some time later King Ben-hadad of Aram mustered his entire army; he marched against Samaria and laid siege to it. 25As the siege continued, famine in Samaria became so great that a donkey's head was sold for eighty shekels of silver, and one-fourth of a kab of dove's dung for five shekels of silver. 26Now as the king of Israel was walking on the city wall, a woman cried out to him, "Help, my lord king!" 27He said, "No! Let the LORD help you. How can I help you? From the threshing floor or from the wine press?" 28But then the king asked her, "What is your complaint?" She answered, "This woman said to me, 'Give up your son; we will eat him today, and we will eat my son tomorrow.' 29So we cooked my son and ate him. The next day I said to her, 'Give up your son and we will eat him.' But she has hidden her son." 30When the king heard the words of the woman he tore his clothes—now since he was walking on the city wall, the people could see that he had sackcloth on his body underneath— 31and he said, "So may God do to me, and more, if the head of Elisha son of Shaphat stays on his shoulders today." 32So he dispatched a man from his presence.

Now Elisha was sitting in his house, and the elders were sitting with him. Before the messenger arrived, Elisha said to the elders, "Are you aware that this murderer has sent someone to take off my head? When the messenger comes, see that you shut the door and hold it closed against him. Is not the sound of his master's feet behind him?" 33While he was still speaking with them, the king[b] came down to him and said, "This trouble is from the LORD! Why should I hope in the LORD any longer?" 1But Elisha said, "Hear the word of the LORD: thus says the LORD, Tomorrow about this time a measure of choice meal shall be sold for a shekel, and two measures of barley for a shekel, at the gate of Samaria." 2Then the captain on whose hand the king leaned said to the man of God, "Even if the LORD were to make windows in the sky, could such a thing happen?" But he said, "You shall see it

---

a Heb *they*   b See 7.2: Heb *messenger*

with your own eyes, but you shall not eat from it."

6.24–7.20: The siege of Samaria. 6.24–25: In a *siege*, a city was surrounded and its food supply cut off in order to starve out the inhabitants. Thus, food prices within the city soared. A *shekel** was a measure of weight of just less than half an ounce. A *kab* was slightly more than a quart. **27:** The *threshing** *floor* was a flat, raised area where grain was separated from the hull. A *wine press* was where grapes were squeezed for their juice to make wine. The king is replying that he has no more access to food supplies than does the woman who is asking for his help. His wish, *Let the* LORD *help you*, seems sarcastic in this context, as he likely blames the LORD for the predicament of the city. **28–29:** The woman's *complaint* is a legal case, since *the king* is, in effect, the supreme court of the land. The case she brings reflects the desperate straits of the city, where people have resorted to cannibalism. It also recalls, in a distorted way, the case of Solomon's judgment in 1 Kings 3.16–28. **30:** *Sackcloth** is a transliteration of the Hebrew "saq," which refers to some kind of garment worn to symbolize mourning. **31:** It is not clear why the king holds *Elisha* responsible for the siege, but it seems to be a classic case of blaming the messenger for the message. The LORD has sent the trouble (v. 33), and Elisha is the LORD's messenger. **33:** *The king* may be asking why he *should hope in the Lord any longer* or what more (punishment) he can expect from *the* LORD if he kills Elisha. **7.1:** Compare 6.25. Elisha predicts that the availability of food will dramatically increase and hence the prices be drastically reduced within a day. **2:** *On whose hand the king leaned* was a title for a special assistant to the king.

3 Now there were four leprous*a* men outside the city gate, who said to one another, "Why should we sit here until we die? *4*If we say, 'Let us enter the city,' the famine is in the city, and we shall die there; but if we sit here, we shall also die. Therefore, let us desert to the Aramean camp; if they spare our lives, we shall live; and if they kill us, we shall but die." *5*So they arose at twilight to go to the Aramean camp; but when they came to the edge of the Aramean camp, there was no one there at all. *6*For the Lord had caused the Aramean army to hear the sound of chariots, and of horses, the sound of a great army,

so that they said to one another, "The king of Israel has hired the kings of the Hittites and the kings of Egypt to fight against us." *7*So they fled away in the twilight and abandoned their tents, their horses, and their donkeys leaving the camp just as it was, and fled for their lives. *8*When these leprous*a* men had come to the edge of the camp, they went into a tent, ate and drank, carried off silver, gold, and clothing, and went and hid them. Then they came back, entered another tent, carried off things from it, and went and hid them.

9 Then they said to one another, "What we are doing is wrong. This is a day of good news; if we are silent and wait until the morning light, we will be found guilty; therefore let us go and tell the king's household." *10*So they came and called to the gatekeepers of the city, and told them, "We went to the Aramean camp, but there was no one to be seen or heard there, nothing but the horses tied, the donkeys tied, and the tents as they were." *11*Then the gatekeepers called out and proclaimed it to the king's household. *12*The king got up in the night, and said to his servants, "I will tell you what the Arameans have prepared against us. They know that we are starving; so they have left the camp to hide themselves in the open country, thinking, 'When they come out of the city, we shall take them alive and get into the city.'" *13*One of his servants said, "Let some men take five of the remaining horses, since those left here will suffer the fate of the whole multitude of Israel that have perished already;*b* let us send and find out." *14*So they took two mounted men, and the king sent them after the Aramean army, saying, "Go and find out." *15*So they went after them as far as the Jordan; the whole way was littered with garments and equipment that the Arameans had thrown away in their haste. So the messengers returned, and told the king.

16 Then the people went out, and plundered the camp of the Arameans. So a measure of choice meal was sold for a shekel,

---

a A term for several skin diseases; precise meaning uncertain　　*b* Compare Gk Syr Vg: Meaning of Heb uncertain and two measures of barley for a shekel, according to the word of the LORD. [17]Now the king had appointed the captain on whose hand he leaned to have charge of the gate; the people trampled him to death in the gate, just as the man of God had said when the king came down to him. [18]For when the man of God had said to the king, "Two measures of barley shall be sold for a shekel, and a measure of choice meal for a shekel, about this time tomorrow in the gate of Samaria," [19]the captain had answered the man of God, "Even if the LORD were to make windows in the sky, could such a thing happen?" And he had answered, "You shall see it with your own eyes, but you shall not eat from it." [20]It did indeed happen to him; the people trampled him to death in the gate.

7.3–20. 3: On leprosy, see comment on 5.1. People with skin diseases were isolated from society because leprosy was contagious. Hence, these *four leprous men* are *outside the city gate.* **4:** The four men surrender to the Arameans because they have nothing to lose. **6:** *Egypt* (Heb., "Misrayim") may be a mistake for Musri, an area in Anatolia (modern Turkey), which was also the home of the *Hittites.* **17–20:** These verses explain the fulfillment of the oracle* in v. 2.

8 Now Elisha had said to the woman whose son he had restored to life, "Get up and go with your household, and settle wherever you can; for the LORD has called for a famine, and it will come on the land for seven years." [2]So the woman got up and did according to the word of the man of God; she went with her household and settled in the land of the Philistines seven years. [3]At the end of the seven years, when the woman returned from the land of the Philistines, she set out to appeal to the king for her house and her land. [4]Now the king was talking with Gehazi the servant of the man of God, saying, "Tell me all the great things that Elisha has done." [5]While he was telling the king how Elisha had restored a dead person to life, the woman whose son he had restored to life appealed to the king for her house and her land. Gehazi said, "My lord king, here is the woman, and here is her son whom Elisha restored to life." [6]When the king questioned

the woman, she told him. So the king appointed an official for her, saying, "Restore all that was hers, together with all the revenue of the fields from the day that she left the land until now."

8.1–6: Elisha and the Shunammite woman. These verses refer to and may continue the stories in 4.8–37. **1:** *Seven years* is a round number for completeness, indicating that the *famine* was severe and long-lasting. **2:** The *land of the Philistines* was along the southern coast of Palestine near the area known today as the Gaza strip. **3:** It is not clear who is trying to take the woman's land, but they are more than squatters, for they are making a legal claim. **4–5:** The miraculous part of this tale is the timing. The woman appeared just as the fascinated *king* was hearing the story of her involvement with Elisha. *Gehazi* appears here without reference to his leprosy. Either this episode is connected with 4.8–37 or comes from a source completely apart from the story in ch. 5. However, the fact that Gehazi alone is speaking with the king may indicate that this story arose after Elisha's death.

[7] Elisha went to Damascus while King Ben-hadad of Aram was ill. When it was told him, "The man of God has come here," [8]the king said to Hazael, "Take a present with you and go to meet the man of God. Inquire of the LORD through him, whether I shall recover from this illness." [9]So Hazael went to meet him, taking a present with him, all kinds of goods of Damascus, forty camel loads. When he entered and stood before him, he said, "Your son King Ben-hadad of Aram has sent me to you, saying, 'Shall I recover from this illness?'" [10]Elisha said to him, "Go, say to him, 'You shall certainly recover'; but the LORD has shown me that he shall certainly die." [11]He fixed his gaze and stared at him, until he was ashamed. Then the man of God wept. [12]Hazael asked, "Why does my lord weep?" He answered, "Because I know the evil that you will do to the people of Israel; you will set their fortresses on fire, you will kill their young men with the sword, dash in pieces their little ones, and rip up their pregnant women." [13]Hazael said, "What is your servant, who is a mere dog, that he should do this great thing?" Elisha answered, "The LORD has shown me that

you are to be king over Aram." 14Then he left Elisha, and went to his master Ben-hadad,[a] who said to him, "What did Elisha say to you?" And he answered, "He told me that you would certainly recover." 15But the next day he took the bed-cover and dipped it in water and spread it over the king's face, until he died. And Hazael succeeded him.

8.7–15: The designation of Hazael. Elisha here apparently carries out the commission given to Elijah in 1 Kings 19.15. **8:** *Inquire* is a technical term for divination. Stories of inquiry through a prophet* in the case of illness are found also in 1 Kings 14.1–14; 2 Kings 1.2–17. **9:** *Forty camel loads* would be an enormous sum. That this is exaggeration is also clear from the fact that forty is a round number for a large quantity. *Your son* is an expression of humility and self-effacement. *Ben-hadad* is placing Elisha above him. **11:** The subject of these verbs is apparently Elisha. Perhaps Elisha *stared* at Hazael until Hazael *was ashamed*. Another possibility is that Elisha *stared* in a kind of trance until he himself became *ashamed*. **12:** Elisha foresees that Hazael will be the LORD's instrument to punish Israel. **13:** *Hazael* refers to himself as *a mere dog*, not because he sees violent acts described by Elisha as despicable but because he is of low social status and does not have the power to carry out such deeds. Elisha explains, however, that he is to be *king over Aram*. **15:** *Until he died* suggests that *Hazael* is responsible for Ben-hadad's death. The Hebrew is more ambiguous, however. Placing the wet *bed-cover over the king's face* may have been simply a way of cooling him off, and this verse may only explain the time of his death.

16 In the fifth year of King Joram son of Ahab of Israel,[b] Jehoram son of King Jehoshaphat of Judah began to reign. 17He was thirty-two years old when he became king, and he reigned eight years in Jerusalem. 18He walked in the way of the kings of Israel, as the house of Ahab had done, for the daughter of Ahab was his wife. He did what was evil in the sight of the LORD. 19Yet the LORD would not destroy Judah, for the sake of his servant David, since he had promised to give a lamp to him and to his descendants forever.

20 In his days Edom revolted against the rule of Judah, and set up a king of their own. 21Then Joram crossed over to Zair with all his chariots. He set out by night and attacked the Edomites and their chariot commanders who had surrounded him;[c] but his army fled home. 22So Edom has been in revolt against the rule of Judah to this day. Libnah also revolted at the same time. 23Now the rest of the acts of Joram, and all that he did, are they not written in the Book of the Annals of the Kings of Judah? 24So Joram slept with his ancestors, and was buried with them in the city of David; his son Ahaziah succeeded him.

25 In the twelfth year of King Joram son of Ahab of Israel, Ahaziah son of King Jehoram of Judah began to reign. 26Ahaziah was twenty-two years old when he began to reign; he reigned one year in Jerusalem. His mother's name was Athaliah, a granddaughter of King Omri of Israel. 27He also walked in the way of the house of Ahab, doing what was evil in the sight of the LORD, as the house of Ahab had done, for he was son-in-law to the house of Ahab.

28 He went with Joram son of Ahab to wage war against King Hazael of Aram at Ramoth-gilead, where the Arameans wounded Joram. 29King Joram returned to be healed in Jezreel of the wounds that the Arameans had inflicted on him at Ramah, when he fought against King Hazael of Aram. King Ahaziah son of Jehoram of Judah went down to see Joram son of Ahab in Jezreel, because he was wounded.

8.16–29: Regnal formulas for Joram and Ahaziah. **20:** The *king* of *Edom* referred to in 3.9 may have been only a "deputy" under the king of Judah (1 Kings 22.47). **28:** *Ramoth-gilead* was east of the Jordan in territory disputed between Israel and Aram.

9 Then the prophet Elisha called a member of the company of prophets[d] and said to him, "Gird up your loins; take this flask of oil in your hand, and go to Ramoth-gilead. 2When you arrive, look there

a Heb lacks *Ben-hadad*   b Gk Syr: Heb adds *Jehoshaphat being king of Judah,*   c Meaning of Heb uncertain   d Heb *sons of the prophets* for Jehu son of Jehoshaphat, son of Nimshi; go in and get him to leave his companions, and take him into an inner chamber. ³Then take the flask of oil, pour it on his head, and say, 'Thus says the LORD: I anoint you king over Israel.' Then open the door and flee; do not linger."

4 So the young man, the young prophet, went to Ramoth-gilead. ⁵He arrived while the commanders of the army were in council, and he announced, "I have a message for you, commander." "For which one of us?" asked Jehu. "For you, commander." ⁶So Jehu*a* got up and went inside; the young man poured the oil on his head, saying to him, "Thus says the LORD the God of Israel: I anoint you king over the people of the LORD, over Israel. ⁷You shall strike down the house of your master Ahab, so that I may avenge on Jezebel the blood of my servants the prophets, and the blood of all the servants of the LORD. ⁸For the whole house of Ahab shall perish; I will cut off from Ahab every male, bond or free, in Israel. ⁹I will make the house of Ahab like the house of Jeroboam son of Nebat, and like the house of Baasha son of Ahijah. ¹⁰The dogs shall eat Jezebel in the territory of Jezreel, and no one shall bury her." Then he opened the door and fled.

11 When Jehu came back to his master's officers, they said to him, "Is everything all right? Why did that madman come to you?" He answered them, "You know the sort and how they babble." ¹²They said, "Liar! Come on, tell us!" So he said, "This is just what he said to me: 'Thus says the LORD, I anoint you king over Israel.' " ¹³Then hurriedly they all took their cloaks and spread them for him on the bare*b* steps; and they blew the trumpet, and proclaimed, "Jehu is king."

9.1–10.36: Jehu's revolt. 9.1–3: The revolt is begun by Elisha. Again, the anointing* of Jehu is apparently meant as a carrying out of the commission to Elijah (1 Kings 19.16). 7–10a: These verses are an addition by the deuteronomistic* editor. They violate Elisha's order to anoint Jehu and flee (v. 3). They are also comparable to the prophetic oracles* against the houses of Jeroboam (1 Kings 14.7–11), Baasha (1 Kings 16.2–4), and Ahab (1 Kings 21.21–24). As in 1 Kings 21.21–24, the dynasty* here is referred to as the *house of Ahab* (vv. 8–9), even though it is actually the "house of Omri." The reason is the focal role of Ahab's reign in 1–2 Kings and his reputation as the worst king of Israel (1 Kings 21.25). 11: In part because of such ecstatic experiences, a prophet* was sometimes called a *madman* (Jer 29.26; Hos 9.7). 13: By spreading their *cloaks* before him, the other commanders signal their submission to Jehu as their king (Mt 21.8).

14 Thus Jehu son of Jehoshaphat son of Nimshi conspired against Joram. Joram with all Israel had been on guard at Ramoth-gilead against King Hazael of Aram; ¹⁵but King Joram had returned to be healed in Jezreel of the wounds that the Arameans had inflicted on him, when he fought against King Hazael of Aram. So Jehu said, "If this is your wish, then let no one slip out of the city to go and tell the news in Jezreel." ¹⁶Then Jehu mounted his chariot and went to Jezreel, where Joram was lying ill. King Ahaziah of Judah had come down to visit Joram.

17 In Jezreel, the sentinel standing on the tower spied the company of Jehu arriving, and said, "I see a company." Joram said, "Take a horseman; send him to meet them, and let him say, 'Is it peace?' " ¹⁸So the horseman went to meet him; he said, "Thus says the king, 'Is it peace?' " Jehu responded, "What have you to do with peace? Fall in behind me." The sentinel reported, saying, "The messenger reached them, but he is not coming back." ¹⁹Then he sent out a second horseman, who came to them and said, "Thus says the king, 'Is it peace?' " Jehu answered, "What have you to do with peace? Fall in behind me." ²⁰Again the sentinel reported, "He reached them, but he is not coming back. It looks like the driving of Jehu son of Nimshi; for he drives like a maniac." ²¹Joram said, "Get ready." And they got his chariot ready. Then King Joram of Israel and King Ahaziah of Judah set out, each in his chariot, and went to meet Jehu; they met him at the property of Naboth the Jezreelite. ²²When Joram saw Jehu, he said, "Is it

a Heb *he*　　*b* Meaning of Heb uncertain

peace, Jehu?" He answered, "What peace can there be, so long as the many whoredoms and sorceries of your mother Jezebel continue?" 23 Then Joram reined about and fled, saying to Ahaziah, "Treason, Ahaziah!" 24 Jehu drew his bow with all his strength, and shot Joram between the shoulders, so that the arrow pierced his heart; and he sank in his chariot. 25 Jehu said to his aide Bidkar, "Lift him out, and throw him on the plot of ground belonging to Naboth the Jezreelite; for remember, when you and I rode side by side behind his father Ahab how the LORD uttered this oracle against him: 26 'For the blood of Naboth and for the blood of his children that I saw yesterday, says the LORD, I swear I will repay you on this very plot of ground.' Now therefore lift him out and throw him on the plot of ground, in accordance with the word of the LORD."

27 When King Ahaziah of Judah saw this, he fled in the direction of Beth-haggan. Jehu pursued him, saying, "Shoot him also!" And they shot him*a* in the chariot at the ascent to Gur, which is by Ibleam. Then he fled to Megiddo, and died there. 28 His officers carried him in a chariot to Jerusalem, and buried him in his tomb with his ancestors in the city of David.

29 In the eleventh year of Joram son of Ahab, Ahaziah began to reign over Judah.

30 When Jehu came to Jezreel, Jezebel heard of it; she painted her eyes, and adorned her head, and looked out of the window. 31 As Jehu entered the gate, she said, "Is it peace, Zimri, murderer of your master?" 32 He looked up to the window and said, "Who is on my side? Who?" Two or three eunuchs looked out at him. 33 He said, "Throw her down." So they threw her down; some of her blood spattered on the wall and on the horses, which trampled on her. 34 Then he went in and ate and drank; he said, "See to that cursed woman and bury her; for she is a king's daughter." 35 But when they went to bury her, they found no more of her than the skull and the feet and the palms of her hands. 36 When they came back and told him, he said, "This is the word of the LORD, which he spoke by his servant Elijah the Tishbite, 'In the territory of Jezreel the dogs shall eat the flesh of Jezebel; 37 the corpse of Jezebel shall be like dung on the field in the territory of Jezreel, so that no one can say, This is Jezebel.' "

9.14–37. 21, 25–26: Either the story of Jehu's revolt has been tailored as a fulfillment of Elijah's oracle* in 1 Kings 21 in punishment for the murder of Naboth, or these verses reflect the original setting of the oracle against Ahab and Jezebel, which has been changed in order to attribute it to Elijah in 1 Kings 21. **22:** *Whoredoms* probably refers to the worship of other gods, as is frequently the case in the Bible (compare the book of Hosea). *Sorceries* may also refer to other practices (divination and the like) associated with the worship of other gods. **30:** It is not clear why *Jezebel* dresses up. It may be that she is described this way in order to fit the image of a prostitute. **31:** Jezebel calls Jehu *Zimri* because Zimri led a revolt and was the *murderer of [his] master*. Zimri's subsequent reign lasted only seven days, so that Jezebel is also implying that Jehu's kingship will be unsuccessful (1 Kings 16.9–20). **32–33:** *Eunuchs* were used to guard the harem. Jezebel was thrown from the second story of the building. **34–37:** *Jezebel's* death is described as the fulfillment, though elaborated, of *Elijah's* prophecy in 1 Kings 21.23. Her gruesome end fulfills the threat of non-burial in 1 Kings 21.24 (compare 2 Kings 9.10).

10 Now Ahab had seventy sons in Samaria. So Jehu wrote letters and sent them to Samaria, to the rulers of Jezreel,*b* to the elders, and to the guardians of the sons of*c* Ahab, saying, 2 "Since your master's sons are with you and you have at your disposal chariots and horses, a fortified city, and weapons, 3 select the son of your master who is the best qualified, set him on his father's throne, and fight for your master's house." 4 But they were utterly terrified and said, "Look, two kings could not withstand him; how then can we stand?" 5 So the steward of the palace, and the governor of the city, along with the elders and the guardians, sent word to Jehu: "We are your servants; we will do anything you say. We will not make anyone king; do whatever you think right."

a Syr Vg Compare Gk: Heb lacks *and they shot him*
b Or *of the city*; Vg Compare Gk   c Gk: Heb lacks *of the sons of*

6Then he wrote them a second letter, saying, "If you are on my side, and if you are ready to obey me, take the heads of your master's sons and come to me at Jezreel tomorrow at this time." Now the king's sons, seventy persons, were with the leaders of the city, who were charged with their upbringing. 7When the letter reached them, they took the king's sons and killed them, seventy persons; they put their heads in baskets and sent them to him at Jezreel. 8When the messenger came and told him, "They have brought the heads of the king's sons," he said, "Lay them in two heaps at the entrance of the gate until the morning." 9Then in the morning when he went out, he stood and said to all the people, "You are innocent. It was I who conspired against my master and killed him; but who struck down all these? 10Know then that there shall fall to the earth nothing of the word of the LORD, which the LORD spoke concerning the house of Ahab; for the LORD has done what he said through his servant Elijah." 11So Jehu killed all who were left of the house of Ahab in Jezreel, all his leaders, close friends, and priests, until he left him no survivor.

12 Then he set out and went to Samaria. On the way, when he was at Beth-eked of the Shepherds, 13Jehu met relatives of King Ahaziah of Judah and said, "Who are you?" They answered, "We are kin of Ahaziah; we have come down to visit the royal princes and the sons of the queen mother." 14He said, "Take them alive." They took them alive, and slaughtered them at the pit of Beth-eked, forty-two in all; he spared none of them.

15 When he left there, he met Jehonadab son of Rechab coming to meet him; he greeted him, and said to him, "Is your heart as true to mine as mine is to yours?"ᵃ Jehonadab answered, "It is." Jehu said,ᵇ "If it is, give me your hand." So he gave him his hand. Jehu took him up with him into the chariot. 16He said, "Come with me, and see my zeal for the LORD." So heᶜ had him ride in his chariot. 17When he came to Samaria, he killed all who were left to Ahab in Samaria, until he had wiped them out, according to the word of the LORD that he spoke to Elijah.

18 Then Jehu assembled all the people and said to them, "Ahab offered Baal small service; but Jehu will offer much more. 19Now therefore summon to me all the prophets of Baal, all his worshipers, and all his priests; let none be missing, for I have a great sacrifice to offer to Baal; whoever is missing shall not live." But Jehu was acting with cunning in order to destroy the worshipers of Baal. 20Jehu decreed, "Sanctify a solemn assembly for Baal." So they proclaimed it. 21Jehu sent word throughout all Israel; all the worshipers of Baal came, so that there was no one left who did not come. They entered the temple of Baal, until the temple of Baal was filled from wall to wall. 22He said to the keeper of the wardrobe, "Bring out the vestments for all the worshipers of Baal." So he brought out the vestments for them. 23Then Jehu entered the temple of Baal with Jehonadab son of Rechab; he said to the worshipers of Baal, "Search and see that there is no worshiper of the LORD here among you, but only worshipers of Baal." 24Then they proceeded to offer sacrifices and burnt offerings.

Now Jehu had stationed eighty men outside, saying, "Whoever allows any of those to escape whom I deliver into your hands shall forfeit his life." 25As soon as he had finished presenting the burnt offering, Jehu said to the guards and to the officers, "Come in and kill them; let no one escape." So they put them to the sword. The guards and the of-

---

10.1–14. 1: *Sons* probably means descendants, that is, sons and grandsons, although Ahab may have had a large enough harem to produce seventy sons. 9–10: The exact meaning of Jehu's words in v. 9 is unclear. However, he seems to be suggesting that his revolt is more than a rebellion by a single individual and that the LORD is behind it. Hence, the prophecies against Ahab's house will be fulfilled (v. 10). 14: *Forty-two* was also the number of boys killed by bears in 2.24. This may indicate that it was a conventional number for disaster.

---

a Gk: Heb *Is it right with your heart, as my heart is with your heart?* b Gk: Heb lacks *Jehu said* c Gk Syr Tg: Heb *they* ficers threw them out, and then went into the citadel of the temple of Baal. 26They brought out the pillar*a* that was in the temple of Baal, and burned it. 27Then they demolished the pillar of Baal, and destroyed the temple of Baal, and made it a latrine to this day.

28 Thus Jehu wiped out Baal from Israel. 29But Jehu did not turn aside from the sins of Jeroboam son of Nebat, which he caused Israel to commit—the golden calves that were in Bethel and in Dan. 30The LORD said to Jehu, "Because you have done well in carrying out what I consider right, and in accordance with all that was in my heart have dealt with the house of Ahab, your sons of the fourth generation shall sit on the throne of Israel." 31But Jehu was not careful to follow the law of the LORD the God of Israel with all his heart; he did not turn from the sins of Jeroboam, which he caused Israel to commit.

32 In those days the LORD began to trim off parts of Israel. Hazael defeated them throughout the territory of Israel: 33from the Jordan eastward, all the land of Gilead, the Gadites, the Reubenites, and the Manassites, from Aroer, which is by the Wadi Arnon, that is, Gilead and Bashan. 34Now the rest of the acts of Jehu, all that he did, and all his power, are they not written in the Book of the Annals of the Kings of Israel? 35So Jehu slept with his ancestors, and they buried him in Samaria. His son Jehoahaz succeeded him. 36The time that Jehu reigned over Israel in Samaria was twenty-eight years.

11 Now when Athaliah, Ahaziah's mother, saw that her son was dead, she set about to destroy all the royal family. 2But Jehosheba, King Joram's daughter, Ahaziah's sister, took Joash son of Ahaziah, and stole him away from among the king's children who were about to be killed; she put*b* him and his nurse in a bedroom. Thus she*c* hid him from Athaliah, so that he was not killed; 3he remained with her six years, hidden in the house of the LORD, while Athaliah reigned over the land.

4 But in the seventh year Jehoiada summoned the captains of the Carites and of the guards and had them come to him in the house of the LORD. He made a covenant with them and put them under oath in the house of the LORD; then he showed them the king's son. 5He commanded them, "This is what you are to do: one-third of you, those who go off duty on the sabbath and guard the king's house 6(another third being at the gate Sur and a third at the gate behind the guards), shall guard the palace; 7and your two divisions that come on duty in force on the sabbath and guard the house of the LORD*d* 8shall surround the king, each with weapons in hand; and whoever approaches the ranks is to be killed. Be with the king in his comings and goings."

10.15–36. 15: *Son of Rechab* designates *Jehonadab's* clan★ rather than his father. The Rechabites were as-cetics and strict devotees of the LORD (Yahweh). See Jer 35. 24–25: Hosea 1.4 seems to condemn Jehu's bloodshed. 26: The *pillar* was an important element in the worship of Baal;★ it represented him much like an idol. 32: The reigns of Jehu and his descendants were marked by the subjugation of Israel to Aram (Syria). See also 13.3. Many of the stories about prophets★ earlier in 1–2 Kings seem to presuppose this political situation, which was not true under the Omri dynasty.★

11.1–21: The reign of Athaliah and revolt of Je-hoash. 1–3: *Athaliah* was the daughter of Ahab and Jezebel who had married Joram king of Judah in a treaty between Israel and Judah (8.18). After the death of her son, *Ahaziah*, she seized power. No regnal formula is reported for her because the writer of 2 Kings did not consider her a legitimate ruler. 4: *Jehoiada* was a priest. Since the new king, Jehoash (or Joash), was only seven years old, Jehoiada was really in charge of the kingdom. The *Carites* were apparently the royal bodyguard, and this may be an error for Cherethites, the name for the bodyguard under David and Solomon (2 Sam 8.18). 5–7: The parenthetical statement in v. 6 is probably a late gloss or explanatory addition, trying to identify the other two divisions. The *gate Sur* is unknown. Jehoiada chooses the change of the guard

a Gk Vg Syr Tg: Heb *pillars*   *b* With 2 Chr 22.11: Heb lacks *she put*   *c* Gk Syr Vg Compare 2 Chr 22.11: Heb *they*   *d* Heb *the* LORD *to the king* on the *sabbath* as the time for the revolt. This made all the troops available to him in order to protect Jehoash. It was also a time when troop movements would not be suspicious.

9 The captains did according to all that the priest Jehoiada commanded; each brought his men who were to go off duty on the sabbath, with those who were to come on duty on the sabbath, and came to the priest Jehoiada. [10] The priest delivered to the captains the spears and shields that had been King David's, which were in the house of the LORD; [11] the guards stood, every man with his weapons in his hand, from the south side of the house to the north side of the house, around the altar and the house, to guard the king on every side. [12] Then he brought out the king's son, put the crown on him, and gave him the covenant;*a* they proclaimed him king, and anointed him; they clapped their hands and shouted, "Long live the king!"

13 When Athaliah heard the noise of the guard and of the people, she went into the house of the LORD to the people; [14] when she looked, there was the king standing by the pillar, according to custom, with the captains and the trumpeters beside the king, and all the people of the land rejoicing and blowing trumpets. Athaliah tore her clothes and cried, "Treason! Treason!" [15] Then the priest Jehoiada commanded the captains who were set over the army, "Bring her out between the ranks, and kill with the sword anyone who follows her." For the priest said, "Let her not be killed in the house of the LORD." [16] So they laid hands on her; she went through the horses' entrance to the king's house, and there she was put to death.

17 Jehoiada made a covenant between the LORD and the king and people, that they should be the LORD's people; also between the king and the people. [18] Then all the people of the land went to the house of Baal, and tore it down; his altars and his images they broke in pieces, and they killed Mattan, the priest of Baal, before the altars. The priest posted guards over the house of the LORD. [19] He took the captains, the Carites, the guards, and all the people of the land;

then they brought the king down from the house of the LORD, marching through the gate of the guards to the king's house. He took his seat on the throne of the kings. [20] So all the people of the land rejoiced; and the city was quiet after Athaliah had been killed with the sword at the king's house.

[21]*b* Jehoash*c* was seven years old when he began to reign.

11.9–21. 10: The *spears and shields* mentioned here were originally of gold and dedicated by David (2 Sam 8.7). But they had been replaced by Rehoboam with bronze articles after Shishak's invasion (1 Kings 14.26–27). **12:** The *covenant** would have been a written document, perhaps laws or a contract between the people and the king. However, the word may be an error for armlet, associated with the crown in 2 Sam 1.10. See comment on 11.17. **14:** The *pillar* in front of the Temple* is meant here. **17:** Only after Athaliah's removal is the covenant made. It appears to be an agreement between the people and the king to follow the LORD, but its exact nature and its relationship to the laws in the Bible are unknown. **20:** The exact identity of the *people of the land* is disputed. They may have been the landholders or leading citizens of Judah.

12 In the seventh year of Jehu, Jehoash began to reign; he reigned forty years in Jerusalem. His mother's name was Zibiah of Beer-sheba. [2] Jehoash did what was right in the sight of the LORD all his days, because the priest Jehoiada instructed him. [3] Nevertheless the high places were not taken away; the people continued to sacrifice and make offerings on the high places.

4 Jehoash said to the priests, "All the money offered as sacred donations that is brought into the house of the LORD, the money for which each person is assessed—the money from the assessment of persons—and the money from the voluntary offerings brought into the house of the LORD, [5] let the priests receive from each of the donors; and let them repair the house wherever any need of repairs is discovered." [6] But by the twenty-third year of King Jehoash the priests had made no repairs on the house.

a Or *treaty* or *testimony*; Heb *eduth*   *b* Ch 12.1 in Heb
c Another spelling is *Joash*; see verse 19

7Therefore King Jehoash summoned the priest Jehoiada with the other priests and said to them, "Why are you not repairing the house? Now therefore do not accept any more money from your donors but hand it over for the repair of the house." 8So the priests agreed that they would neither accept more money from the people nor repair the house.

9 Then the priest Jehoiada took a chest, made a hole in its lid, and set it beside the altar on the right side as one entered the house of the LORD; the priests who guarded the threshold put in it all the money that was brought into the house of the LORD. 10Whenever they saw that there was a great deal of money in the chest, the king's secretary and the high priest went up, counted the money that was found in the house of the LORD, and tied it up in bags. 11They would give the money that was weighed out into the hands of the workers who had the oversight of the house of the LORD; then they paid it out to the carpenters and the builders who worked on the house of the LORD, 12to the masons and the stonecutters, as well as to buy timber and quarried stone for making repairs on the house of the LORD, as well as for any outlay for repairs of the house. 13But for the house of the LORD no basins of silver, snuffers, bowls, trumpets, or any vessels of gold, or of silver, were made from the money that was brought into the house of the LORD, 14for that was given to the workers who were repairing the house of the LORD with it. 15They did not ask an accounting from those into whose hand they delivered the money to pay out to the workers, for they dealt honestly. 16The money from the guilt offerings and the money from the sin offerings was not brought into the house of the LORD; it belonged to the priests.

17 At that time King Hazael of Aram went up, fought against Gath, and took it. But when Hazael set his face to go up against Jerusalem, 18King Jehoash of Judah took all the votive gifts that Jehoshaphat, Jehoram, and Ahaziah, his ancestors, the kings of Judah, had dedicated, as well as his own votive gifts, all the gold that was found in the trea-suries of the house of the LORD and of the king's house, and sent these to King Hazael of Aram. Then Hazael withdrew from Jerusalem.

19 Now the rest of the acts of Joash, and all that he did, are they not written in the Book of the Annals of the Kings of Judah? 20His servants arose, devised a conspiracy, and killed Joash in the house of Millo, on the way that goes down to Silla. 21It was Jozacar son of Shimeath and Jehozabad son of Shomer, his servants, who struck him down, so that he died. He was buried with his ancestors in the city of David; then his son Amaziah succeeded him.

12.1–21: The reign of Jehoash. 1: *Forty years* is probably a round number for a generation. 3: The *high places** were shrines other than the Temple* of Jerusalem. 4–16: Jehoash repairs the Temple. Jehoash has to admonish the priests (v. 7), who are slow to carry out the repairs. *Money* is literally "silver." Parts of this account, however, seem to assume that the contributions were in the form of coins, which would be an anachronism* since coins began to be used widely in Palestine no earlier than the late sixth century BCE. 18: *Votive gifts* were special items of value that the kings of Judah had dedicated to the Temple. By paying these to Hazael as tribute, Jehoash capitulated to him and in effect bribed him to prevent him from attacking Jerusalem. 19: The *Annals of the Kings of Judah* may have been official records of the monarchy of Judah. They no longer exist. 20: *Millo* means "fill"; it probably refers to the earthwork done by David to fill in the saddle between the Temple area and the palace area south of it (2 Sam 5.9). 21: The motive behind Jehoash's assassination is not explained in 2 Kings. See 2 Chr 24.20–27.

---

13 In the twenty-third year of King Joash son of Ahaziah of Judah, Jehoahaz son of Jehu began to reign over Israel in Samaria; he reigned seventeen years. 2He did what was evil in the sight of the LORD, and followed the sins of Jeroboam son of Nebat, which he caused Israel to sin; he did not depart from them. 3The anger of the LORD was kindled against Israel, so that he gave them repeatedly into the hand of King Hazael of Aram, then into the hand of Benhadad son of Hazael. 4But Jehoahaz en-

treated the LORD, and the LORD heeded him; for he saw the oppression of Israel, how the king of Aram oppressed them. [5]Therefore the LORD gave Israel a savior, so that they escaped from the hand of the Arameans; and the people of Israel lived in their homes as formerly. [6]Nevertheless they did not depart from the sins of the house of Jeroboam, which he caused Israel to sin, but walked[a] in them; the sacred pole[b] also remained in Samaria. [7]So Jehoahaz was left with an army of not more than fifty horsemen, ten chariots and ten thousand footmen; for the king of Aram had destroyed them and made them like the dust at threshing. [8]Now the rest of the acts of Jehoahaz and all that he did, including his might, are they not written in the Book of the Annals of the Kings of Israel? [9]So Jehoahaz slept with his ancestors, and they buried him in Samaria; then his son Joash succeeded him.

10 In the thirty-seventh year of King Joash of Judah, Jehoash son of Jehoahaz began to reign over Israel in Samaria; he reigned sixteen years. [11]He also did what was evil in the sight of the LORD; he did not depart from all the sins of Jeroboam son of Nebat, which he caused Israel to sin, but he walked in them. [12]Now the rest of the acts of Joash, and all that he did, as well as the might with which he fought against King Amaziah of Judah, are they not written in the Book of the Annals of the Kings of Israel? [13]So Joash slept with his ancestors, and Jeroboam sat upon his throne; Joash was buried in Samaria with the kings of Israel.

13.1–13: The reigns of Jehoahaz and Joash. 1: *Joash* and Jehoash are two versions of the same name. **2:** *The sins of Jeroboam* are the shrines at Dan and Bethel (1 Kings 12.25–33). **3:** Like the rest of the regnal formulas, this verse is deuteronomistic* and sounds much like part of the deuteronomistic formula found in the book of Judges (Judg 2.14; 4.1–2; 6.1). **5:** The idea and language are also borrowed from the book of Judges. The identity of this *savior* is not clear, but it may be a reference to Elisha (vv. 14–21). **6:** *The sins of the house of Jeroboam* are the same as the sins of Jeroboam (v. 2). The *sacred pole* was used in the worship of the Canaanite goddess Asherah.* **7:** *Like the*

*dust at threshing** means that the army had scattered. **10:** While they bear the same name, *Joash* king of Judah and *Jehoash* king of Israel are two different people. **13:** This Jeroboam is distinct from the one in 1 Kings 12–14 and is often called Jeroboam II.

~~~~~~~~~~~~~~~~

14 Now when Elisha had fallen sick with the illness of which he was to die, King Joash of Israel went down to him, and wept before him, crying, "My father, my father! The chariots of Israel and its horsemen!" [15]Elisha said to him, "Take a bow and arrows"; so he took a bow and arrows. [16]Then he said to the king of Israel, "Draw the bow"; and he drew it. Elisha laid his hands on the king's hands. [17]Then he said, "Open the window eastward"; and he opened it. Elisha said, "Shoot"; and he shot. Then he said, "The LORD's arrow of victory, the arrow of victory over Aram! For you shall fight the Arameans in Aphek until you have made an end of them." [18]He continued, "Take the arrows"; and he took them. He said to the king of Israel, "Strike the ground with them"; he struck three times, and stopped. [19]Then the man of God was angry with him, and said, "You should have struck five or six times; then you would have struck down Aram until you had made an end of it, but now you will strike down Aram only three times."

20 So Elisha died, and they buried him. Now bands of Moabites used to invade the land in the spring of the year. [21]As a man was being buried, a marauding band was seen and the man was thrown into the grave of Elisha; as soon as the man touched the bones of Elisha, he came to life and stood on his feet.

22 Now King Hazael of Aram oppressed Israel all the days of Jehoahaz. [23]But the LORD was gracious to them and had compassion on them; he turned toward them, because of his covenant with Abraham, Isaac, and Jacob, and would not destroy them; nor has he banished them from his presence until now.

24 When King Hazael of Aram died, his son Ben-hadad succeeded him. [25]Then Jehoash son of Jehoahaz took again from

a Gk Syr Tg Vg: Heb *he walked*   *b* Heb *Asherah*

Ben-hadad son of Hazael the towns that he had taken from his father Jehoahaz in war. Three times Joash defeated him and recovered the towns of Israel.

13.14–25: Elisha's death. This story lies outside of the framework of the regnal formulas. That is, it follows the closing formula for Joash (vv. 12–13) but precedes the beginning formula for Jeroboam II (14.23–24). Since the deuteronomistic* editor regularly uses these formulas as the framework for the history, this story may be either out of place or a later addition. **14:** *My father* is a term of respect showing the king's subordination to the prophet.* The exact sense of *the chariots of Israel and its horsemen* here is uncertain. It recalls previous episodes in the Elisha stories (2.12; 6.17) and may have become a kind of nickname for him because of these episodes. **15–17:** Symbolic acts like this one are frequently carried out by prophets in the Bible, especially by Ezekiel and Jeremiah. In this case, the LORD's *arrow of victory* is shot *eastward* (v. 17), toward *Aram* (Syria), to represent victory over the Arameans. **18–19:** This is an example of bellomancy, the use of weapons of war to foretell the future, which was common in the ancient Near East. **20–21:** Elisha's miraculous powers continue even after his death. **22–23:** While these verses were certainly written after the fall of Israel in 721 BCE, the writer still appeals to the people of the north in stating that the LORD has not ultimately abandoned them. **24–25:** These verses fulfill Elisha's prediction in v. 19.

14 In the second year of King Joash son of Joahaz of Israel, King Amaziah son of Joash of Judah, began to reign. ²He was twenty-five years old when he began to reign, and he reigned twenty-nine years in Jerusalem. His mother's name was Jehoaddin of Jerusalem. ³He did what was right in the sight of the LORD, yet not like his ancestor David; in all things he did as his father Joash had done. ⁴But the high places were not removed; the people still sacrificed and made offerings on the high places. ⁵As soon as the royal power was firmly in his hand he killed his servants who had murdered his father the king. ⁶But he did not put to death the children of the murderers; according to what is written in the book of the law of Moses, where the LORD commanded, "The parents shall not be put to death for the children, or

the children be put to death for the parents; but all shall be put to death for their own sins."

7 He killed ten thousand Edomites in the Valley of Salt and took Sela by storm; he called it Jokthe-el, which is its name to this day.

8 Then Amaziah sent messengers to King Jehoash son of Jehoahaz, son of Jehu, of Israel, saying, "Come, let us look one another in the face." ⁹King Jehoash of Israel sent word to King Amaziah of Judah, "A thornbush on Lebanon sent to a cedar on Lebanon, saying, 'Give your daughter to my son for a wife'; but a wild animal of Lebanon passed by and trampled down the thornbush. ¹⁰You have indeed defeated Edom, and your heart has lifted you up. Be content with your glory, and stay at home; for why should you provoke trouble so that you fall, you and Judah with you?"

14.1–29: The reigns of Amaziah of Judah and Jeroboam II of Israel. 4: The *high places** were shrines other than the Temple* of Jerusalem. **6:** The *law* referred to here is Deut 24.16. **7:** The location of the *Valley of Salt* is uncertain, but most scholars locate it south of the Dead Sea in the same depression in which the Dead Sea or Salt Sea lies. *Sela* means "rock" or "crag." The meaning of *Jokthe-el* is uncertain. One suggestion is that it means "God destroys." **8:** *Let us look one another in the face* is a challenge to battle (v. 11). **9:** The fable* does not imply any marriage treaty or relationship between Amaziah and Joash. Its point, rather, is that Amaziah is trying to make himself more important than he is and that he will be *trampled down* if he continues.

---

11 But Amaziah would not listen. So King Jehoash of Israel went up; he and King Amaziah of Judah faced one another in battle at Beth-shemesh, which belongs to Judah. ¹²Judah was defeated by Israel; everyone fled home. ¹³King Jehoash of Israel captured King Amaziah of Judah son of Jehoash, son of Ahaziah, at Beth-shemesh; he came to Jerusalem, and broke down the wall of Jerusalem from the Ephraim Gate to the Corner Gate, a distance of four hundred cubits. ¹⁴He seized all the gold and silver, and all the vessels that were found in the house of

the LORD and in the treasuries of the king's house, as well as hostages; then he returned to Samaria.

15 Now the rest of the acts that Jehoash did, his might, and how he fought with King Amaziah of Judah, are they not written in the Book of the Annals of the Kings of Israel? ¹⁶Jehoash slept with his ancestors, and was buried in Samaria with the kings of Israel; then his son Jeroboam succeeded him.

17 King Amaziah son of Joash of Judah lived fifteen years after the death of King Jehoash son of Jehoahaz of Israel. ¹⁸Now the rest of the deeds of Amaziah, are they not written in the Book of the Annals of the Kings of Judah? ¹⁹They made a conspiracy against him in Jerusalem, and he fled to Lachish. But they sent after him to Lachish, and killed him there. ²⁰They brought him on horses; he was buried in Jerusalem with his ancestors in the city of David. ²¹All the people of Judah took Azariah, who was sixteen years old, and made him king to succeed his father Amaziah. ²²He rebuilt Elath and restored it to Judah, after King Amaziah*a* slept with his ancestors.

23 In the fifteenth year of King Amaziah son of Joash of Judah, King Jeroboam son of Joash of Israel began to reign in Samaria; he reigned forty-one years. ²⁴He did what was evil in the sight of the LORD; he did not depart from all the sins of Jeroboam son of Nebat, which he caused Israel to sin. ²⁵He restored the border of Israel from Lebohamath as far as the Sea of the Arabah, according to the word of the LORD, the God of Israel, which he spoke by his servant Jonah son of Amittai, the prophet, who was from Gath-hepher. ²⁶For the LORD saw that the distress of Israel was very bitter; there was no one left, bond or free, and no one to help Israel. ²⁷But the LORD had not said that he would blot out the name of Israel from under heaven, so he saved them by the hand of Jeroboam son of Joash.

28 Now the rest of the acts of Jeroboam, and all that he did, and his might, how he fought, and how he recovered for Israel Damascus and Hamath, which had belonged to Judah, are they not written in the Book of the Annals of the Kings of Israel? ²⁹Jero-

boam slept with his ancestors, the kings of Israel; his son Zechariah succeeded him.

14.11–29. 13: A *cubit* was about 18 inches, so 400 cubits is about 200 yards. The *wall* of a city was essential for its protection. **19:** *Lachish* was an important fortress and city about 25 miles southwest of Jerusalem. **22:** *Elath* was an important port city at the tip of the Gulf of Aqaba. Amaziah was able to *rebuild and restore it* to Judah after he had defeated Edom (v. 7). **25:** *Lebo-hamath* represented the idealized northern border of Israel in northern Syria as described for Solomon (1 Kings 8.65). The *Sea of the Arabah* was the Dead Sea. *Jonah* was the prophet* about whom the book of Jonah was written. The oracles* referred to here, however, are not recorded. **28:** *Jeroboam*'s reign was a prosperous one, but he did not restore *Damascus and Hamath* to Israel, nor had they once *belonged to Judah*. The text has been damaged in transmission, and the original reading is uncertain.

15 In the twenty-seventh year of King Jeroboam of Israel King Azariah son of Amaziah of Judah began to reign. ²He was sixteen years old when he began to reign, and he reigned fifty-two years in Jerusalem. His mother's name was Jecoliah of Jerusalem. ³He did what was right in the sight of the LORD, just as his father Amaziah had done. ⁴Nevertheless the high places were not taken away; the people still sacrificed and made offerings on the high places. ⁵The LORD struck the king, so that he was leprous*b* to the day of his death, and lived in a separate house. Jotham the king's son was in charge of the palace, governing the people of the land. ⁶Now the rest of the acts of Azariah, and all that he did, are they not written in the Book of the Annals of the Kings of Judah? ⁷Azariah slept with his ancestors; they buried him with his ancestors in the city of David; his son Jotham succeeded him.

8 In the thirty-eighth year of King Azariah of Judah, Zechariah son of Jeroboam reigned over Israel in Samaria six months. ⁹He did what was evil in the sight of the LORD, as his ancestors had done. He did not depart from the sins of Jeroboam son of Nebat, which he

a Heb *the king*   *b* A term for several skin diseases; precise meaning uncertain caused Israel to sin. ¹⁰Shallum son of Jabesh conspired against him, and struck him down in public and killed him, and reigned in place of him. ¹¹Now the rest of the deeds of Zechariah are written in the Book of the Annals of the Kings of Israel. ¹²This was the promise of the LORD that he gave to Jehu, "Your sons shall sit on the throne of Israel to the fourth generation." And so it happened.

13 Shallum son of Jabesh began to reign in the thirty-ninth year of King Uzziah of Judah; he reigned one month in Samaria. ¹⁴Then Menahem son of Gadi came up from Tirzah and came to Samaria; he struck down Shallum son of Jabesh in Samaria and killed him; he reigned in place of him. ¹⁵Now the rest of the deeds of Shallum, including the conspiracy that he made, are written in the Book of the Annals of the Kings of Israel. ¹⁶At that time Menahem sacked Tiphsah, all who were in it and its territory from Tirzah on; because they did not open it to him, he sacked it. He ripped open all the pregnant women in it.

17 In the thirty-ninth year of King Azariah of Judah, Menahem son of Gadi began to reign over Israel; he reigned ten years in Samaria. ¹⁸He did what was evil in the sight of the LORD; he did not depart all his days from any of the sins of Jeroboam son of Nebat, which he caused Israel to sin. ¹⁹King Pul of Assyria came against the land; Menahem gave Pul a thousand talents of silver, so that he might help him confirm his hold on the royal power. ²⁰Menahem exacted the money from Israel, that is, from all the wealthy, fifty shekels of silver from each one, to give to the king of Assyria. So the king of Assyria turned back, and did not stay there in the land. ²¹Now the rest of the deeds of Menahem, and all that he did, are they not written in the Book of the Annals of the Kings of Israel? ²²Menahem slept with his ancestors, and his son Pekahiah succeeded him.

It was greatly feared because it was regarded as fatal and incurable. Lepers were isolated because the disease was contagious. Hence, Azariah and his son Jotham were co-regents, that is, they ruled together. **12**: The prophecy about the duration of the Jehu dynasty* occurs in 10.30. The rapid succession of contenders to the throne at the end of the Jehu dynasty is reminiscent of the last days of Baasha's house in 1 Kings 16. **15**: *The rest of the deeds* is part of the standard deuteronomistic* formula. Since he reigned only one month (v. 13), *Shallum* did not have time to accomplish many deeds. **16**: *Tiphsah* was a town on the Euphrates, quite out of *Menahem's* reach. A better reading is Tappuah (as in the Septuagint*), which was within Israel. The practice of *rip[ping] open pregnant women* is mentioned elsewhere in the Bible in the context of wars with other countries (2 Kings 8.12; Hos 13.16; Am 1.13). The reason for Menahem's brutality against the town of Tappuah is unknown, but it has been suggested that this was Shallum's hometown. **19**: *Pul* was another name for Tiglath-pileser III, one of the greatest kings of the Assyrian empire (see v. 29). A *talent* was between 45 and 130 pounds. *A thousand talents of silver* was an enormous sum. **20**: A *shekel* was slightly less than half an ounce.

23 In the fiftieth year of King Azariah of Judah, Pekahiah son of Menahem began to reign over Israel in Samaria; he reigned two years. ²⁴He did what was evil in the sight of the LORD; he did not turn away from the sins of Jeroboam son of Nebat, which he caused Israel to sin. ²⁵Pekah son of Remaliah, his captain, conspired against him with fifty of the Gileadites, and attacked him in Samaria, in the citadel of the palace along with Argob and Arieh; he killed him, and reigned in place of him. ²⁶Now the rest of the deeds of Pekahiah, and all that he did, are written in the Book of the Annals of the Kings of Israel.

27 In the fifty-second year of King Azariah of Judah, Pekah son of Remaliah began to reign over Israel in Samaria; he reigned twenty years. ²⁸He did what was evil in the sight of the LORD; he did not depart from the sins of Jeroboam son of Nebat, which he caused Israel to sin.

29 In the days of King Pekah of Israel, King Tiglath-pileser of Assyria came and captured Ijon, Abel-beth-maacah, Janoah, Kedesh, Hazor, Gilead, and Galilee, all the

15.1–38: Azariah and Jotham of Judah; Zechariah, Shallum, Menahem, and Pekahiah of Israel. **1**: *Azariah* is also known as Uzziah (2 Chr 26). **4**: *High places** were shrines other than the Temple* of Jerusalem. **5**: *Leprosy* was a word used for a variety of skin diseases.

land of Naphtali; and he carried the people captive to Assyria. ³⁰Then Hoshea son of Elah made a conspiracy against Pekah son of Remaliah, attacked him, and killed him; he reigned in place of him, in the twentieth year of Jotham son of Uzziah. ³¹Now the rest of the acts of Pekah, and all that he did, are written in the Book of the Annals of the Kings of Israel.

32 In the second year of King Pekah son of Remaliah of Israel, King Jotham son of Uzziah of Judah began to reign. ³³He was twenty-five years old when he began to reign and reigned sixteen years in Jerusalem. His mother's name was Jerusha daughter of Zadok. ³⁴He did what was right in the sight of the LORD, just as his father Uzziah had done. ³⁵Nevertheless the high places were not removed; the people still sacrificed and made offerings on the high places. He built the upper gate of the house of the LORD. ³⁶Now the rest of the acts of Jotham, and all that he did, are they not written in the Book of the Annals of the Kings of Judah? ³⁷In those days the LORD began to send King Rezin of Aram and Pekah son of Remaliah against Judah. ³⁸Jotham slept with his ancestors, and was buried with his ancestors in the city of David, his ancestor; his son Ahaz succeeded him.

15.23–38: 27: *Twenty years* is difficult to fit into a chronology for Israel. If it is not a simple error or exaggeration, it may indicate that Israel was divided and that *Pekah* reigned over a splinter section of it before becoming king over the entire country. 29: The sites listed in this verse are all in northern Israel which, along with Damascus and Syria, was ravaged in 733–732 BCE. 30: Tiglath-pileser helped *Hoshea* to overthrow *Pekah*. The overthrow and Hoshea's pro-Assyrian policy kept Israel from meeting the same fate as Syria in 732. Hoshea's kingdom, however, was only a part of the former state, since the northern part of the country was made into an Assyrian province. 37: *Pekah* and *Rezin* wanted to force Judah to join them in a coalition to resist Tiglath-Pileser of Assyria. The matter came to a head during the reign of Ahaz. See 16.5.

16 In the seventeenth year of Pekah son of Remaliah, King Ahaz son of Jotham of Judah began to reign. ²Ahaz was twenty years old when he began to reign; he reigned sixteen years in Jerusalem. He did not do what was right in the sight of the LORD his God, as his ancestor David had done, ³but he walked in the way of the kings of Israel. He even made his son pass through fire, according to the abominable practices of the nations whom the LORD drove out before the people of Israel. ⁴He sacrificed and made offerings on the high places, on the hills, and under every green tree.

5 Then King Rezin of Aram and King Pekah son of Remaliah of Israel came up to wage war on Jerusalem; they besieged Ahaz but could not conquer him. ⁶At that time the king of Edom*a* recovered Elath for Edom,*b* and drove the Judeans from Elath; and the Edomites came to Elath, where they live to this day. ⁷Ahaz sent messengers to King Tiglath-pileser of Assyria, saying, "I am your servant and your son. Come up, and rescue me from the hand of the king of Aram and from the hand of the king of Israel, who are attacking me." ⁸Ahaz also took the silver and gold found in the house of the LORD and in the treasures of the king's house, and sent a present to the king of Assyria. ⁹The king of Assyria listened to him; the king of Assyria marched up against Damascus, and took it, carrying its people captive to Kir; then he killed Rezin.

10 When King Ahaz went to Damascus to meet King Tiglath-pileser of Assyria, he saw the altar that was at Damascus. King Ahaz sent to the priest Uriah a model of the altar, and its pattern, exact in all its details. ¹¹The priest Uriah built the altar; in accordance with all that King Ahaz had sent from Damascus, just so did the priest Uriah build it, before King Ahaz arrived from Damascus. ¹²When the king came from Damascus, the king viewed the altar. Then the king drew near to the altar, went up on it, ¹³and offered his burnt offering and his grain offering, poured his drink offering, and dashed the blood of his offerings of well-being against the altar. ¹⁴The bronze altar that was before the LORD he removed from the front of the

a Cn: Heb *King Rezin of Aram*   *b* Cn: Heb *Aram*

house, from the place between his altar and the house of the LORD, and put it on the north side of his altar. ¹⁵King Ahaz commanded the priest Uriah, saying, "Upon the great altar offer the morning burnt offering, and the evening grain offering, and the king's burnt offering, and his grain offering, with the burnt offering of all the people of the land, their grain offering, and their drink offering; then dash against it all the blood of the burnt offering, and all the blood of the sacrifice; but the bronze altar shall be for me to inquire by." ¹⁶The priest Uriah did everything that King Ahaz commanded.

17 Then King Ahaz cut off the frames of the stands, and removed the laver from them; he removed the sea from the bronze oxen that were under it, and put it on a pediment of stone. ¹⁸The covered portal for use on the sabbath that had been built inside the palace, and the outer entrance for the king he removed from^a the house of the LORD. He did this because of the king of Assyria. ¹⁹Now the rest of the acts of Ahaz that he did, are they not written in the Book of the Annals of the Kings of Judah? ²⁰Ahaz slept with his ancestors, and was buried with his ancestors in the city of David; his son Hezekiah succeeded him.

16.1–20: The reign of Ahaz. 3: Making *his son pass through fire* is a reference to child sacrifice (see 3.27). 5: This verse refers to the "Syro-Ephraimitic crisis" of 734 BCE. See comment on 15.37. The oracle* of Isaiah in Isa 7 is directed to this situation. 6: Judah's problems with Syria and Israel weakened its hold on *Elath* (see 14.22), and the Edomites took advantage. 7–9: These verses continue with the Syro-Ephraimitic crisis. According to Isa 7, Isaiah counseled Ahaz against seeking the help of the Assyrians. These verses indicate that Ahaz chose to ignore that advice and purchased the aid of *Tiglath-pileser* against Syria and Israel. This placed Judah in a subject relationship to Assyria that would be the source of future problems. *Kir* is the place of the Syrians' origin, according to Am 9.7. It is also mentioned as the place of Syrian exile in Am 1.5. It is obviously in Mesopotamia though its exact location is unknown. 10–16: This story is apparently meant as condemnation of Ahaz to illustrate his importation of foreign elements into the worship of the LORD. It may be, however, that Ahaz intended the new altar to

honor the LORD. *Uriah the priest* is likely the same figure mentioned in Isa 8.2. 17–18: Ahaz was forced to remove some of the *bronze* from the Temple* in order to make his payment of tribute to the Assyrian king. For descriptions of the *bronze oxen under the sea* and the *laver stands*, see 1 Kings 7.23–37. The meaning and nature of *the covered portal for use on the sabbath* (v. 18) is not certain.

17 In the twelfth year of King Ahaz of Judah, Hoshea son of Elah began to reign in Samaria over Israel; he reigned nine years. ²He did what was evil in the sight of the LORD, yet not like the kings of Israel who were before him. ³King Shalmaneser of Assyria came up against him; Hoshea became his vassal, and paid him tribute. ⁴But the king of Assyria found treachery in Hoshea; for he had sent messengers to King So of Egypt, and offered no tribute to the king of Assyria, as he had done year by year; therefore the king of Assyria confined him and imprisoned him.

5 Then the king of Assyria invaded all the land and came to Samaria; for three years he besieged it. ⁶In the ninth year of Hoshea the king of Assyria captured Samaria; he carried the Israelites away to Assyria. He placed them in Halah, on the Habor, the river of Gozan, and in the cities of the Medes.

17.1–41: The fall of Israel. 2: It is not clear why Hoshea is judged to be less evil than his predecessors. 4: Hosea 7.11 may reflect the prophet* Hosea's judgment of the foolishness of *Hoshea's* revolt against Assyria. 5: The fact that Samaria held out for *three years* is a tribute to its defenses. 6: This verse marks the end of the northern kingdom of Israel. The places listed here to which the people of Israel were deported were all close to the Assyrian homeland.

7 This occurred because the people of Israel had sinned against the LORD their God, who had brought them up out of the land of Egypt from under the hand of Pharaoh king of Egypt. They had worshiped other gods ⁸and walked in the customs of the nations whom the LORD drove out before the people

a Cn: Heb lacks *from*

of Israel, and in the customs that the kings of Israel had introduced.[a] 9The people of Israel secretly did things that were not right against the LORD their God. They built for themselves high places at all their towns, from watchtower to fortified city; 10they set up for themselves pillars and sacred poles[b] on every high hill and under every green tree; 11there they made offerings on all the high places, as the nations did whom the LORD carried away before them. They did wicked things, provoking the LORD to anger; 12they served idols, of which the LORD had said to them, "You shall not do this." 13Yet the LORD warned Israel and Judah by every prophet and every seer, saying, "Turn from your evil ways and keep my commandments and my statutes, in accordance with all the law that I commanded your ancestors and that I sent to you by my servants the prophets." 14They would not listen but were stubborn, as their ancestors had been, who did not believe in the LORD their God. 15They despised his statutes, and his covenant that he made with their ancestors, and the warnings that he gave them. They went after false idols and became false; they followed the nations that were around them, concerning whom the LORD had commanded them that they should not do as they did. 16They rejected all the commandments of the LORD their God and made for themselves cast images of two calves; they made a sacred pole,[c] worshiped all the host of heaven, and served Baal. 17They made their sons and their daughters pass through fire; they used divination and augury; and they sold themselves to do evil in the sight of the LORD, provoking him to anger. 18Therefore the LORD was very angry with Israel and removed them out of his sight; none was left but the tribe of Judah alone.

stars). Making *their sons and their daughters pass through fire* is child sacrifice.

19 Judah also did not keep the commandments of the LORD their God but walked in the customs that Israel had introduced. 20The LORD rejected all the descendants of Israel; he punished them and gave them into the hand of plunderers, until he had banished them from his presence.

21 When he had torn Israel from the house of David, they made Jeroboam son of Nebat king. Jeroboam drove Israel from following the LORD and made them commit great sin. 22The people of Israel continued in all the sins that Jeroboam committed; they did not depart from them 23until the LORD removed Israel out of his sight, as he had foretold through all his servants the prophets. So Israel was exiled from their own land to Assyria until this day.

24 The king of Assyria brought people from Babylon, Cuthah, Avva, Hamath, and Sepharvaim, and placed them in the cities of Samaria in place of the people of Israel; they took possession of Samaria, and settled in its cities. 25When they first settled there, they did not worship the LORD; therefore the LORD sent lions among them, which killed some of them. 26So the king of Assyria was told, "The nations that you have carried away and placed in the cities of Samaria do not know the law of the god of the land; therefore he has sent lions among them; they are killing them, because they do not know the law of the god of the land." 27Then the king of Assyria commanded, "Send there one of the priests whom you carried away from there; let him[d] go and live there, and teach them the law of the god of the land." 28So one of the priests whom they had carried away from Samaria came and lived in Bethel; he taught them how they should worship the LORD.

17.7–18: Many scholars regard these verses as a later addition, in deuteronomistic* style, to the initial Deuteronomistic History, since they explain Israel's fall as the result of idolatry,* as opposed to the explanation in vv. 21–23, which culminates the theme of the sin of Jeroboam. *Pillars* and *sacred poles* (vv. 10, 16) were trappings of the worship of Canaanite gods. The *host of heaven* (v. 16) refers to astral deities (sun, moon,

17.19–28. 19–20: These verses are also an addition, perhaps part of the addition in vv. 7–18. They make it clear that Judah was guilty of the same offenses as Is-

a Meaning of Heb uncertain   b Heb *Asherim*
c Heb *Asherah*   d Syr Vg: Heb *them*

rael. They were apparently written in the Exile* (after 586 BCE) as indicated in v. 20, where *all the descendants of Israel* would include both Israel and Judah. **21–23:** These verses conclude the theme of the *sin(s) of Jeroboam,* which refers to the shrines at Dan and Bethel (1 Kings 12.25–33) and which every king of Israel is accused of perpetuating. **24:** In addition to deporting the people of Israel, the Assyrians settled captives from other countries in the former land of Israel. They also renamed the area the Assyrian province of Samaria (Samerina). **25–28:** A widely accepted idea in the ancient Near East was that each country had its own god and each god its own country. It was therefore considered important by the Assyrians that the people whom they had imported into Israel learn the *law of the god of the land* (v. 26), and the attacks by lions were blamed on the failure to do this.

29 But every nation still made gods of its own and put them in the shrines of the high places that the people of Samaria had made, every nation in the cities in which they lived; ³⁰the people of Babylon made Succoth-benoth, the people of Cuth made Nergal, the people of Hamath made Ashima; ³¹the Avvites made Nibhaz and Tartak; the Sepharvites burned their children in the fire to Adrammelech and Anammelech, the gods of Sepharvaim. ³²They also worshiped the LORD and appointed from among themselves all sorts of people as priests of the high places, who sacrificed for them in the shrines of the high places. ³³So they worshiped the LORD but also served their own gods, after the manner of the nations from among whom they had been carried away. ³⁴To this day they continue to practice their former customs.

They do not worship the LORD and they do not follow the statutes or the ordinances or the law or the commandment that the LORD commanded the children of Jacob, whom he named Israel. ³⁵The LORD had made a covenant with them and commanded them, "You shall not worship other gods or bow yourselves to them or serve them or sacrifice to them, ³⁶but you shall worship the LORD, who brought you out of the land of Egypt with great power and with an outstretched arm; you shall bow yourselves to him, and to him you shall sacrifice. ³⁷The

statutes and the ordinances and the law and the commandment that he wrote for you, you shall always be careful to observe. You shall not worship other gods; ³⁸you shall not forget the covenant that I have made with you. You shall not worship other gods, ³⁹but you shall worship the LORD your God; he will deliver you out of the hand of all your enemies." ⁴⁰They would not listen, however, but they continued to practice their former custom.

41 So these nations worshiped the LORD, but also served their carved images; to this day their children and their children's children continue to do as their ancestors did.

17.29–41. 29–34a: The newcomers, however, also retained the gods of their homelands and worshipped them along with the LORD. The names of the gods in vv. 30–31 are distortions or misspellings of the names of gods from different parts of the ancient Near East. However, the errors do not seem to be intentional. Rather, they betray an author (probably the deuteronomist) who is unfamiliar with these different gods and who also writes at a later date, as indicated by the *to this day* statement in v. 34a. **34b–40:** These verses were added by a later writer who viewed the religion of the Samaritans (the residents of the province of Samaria) as illegitimate. Verse 34b, therefore, directly contradicts v. 33. Many faithful Jews hated the Samaritans in part because of their religious practice, which mixed elements from other religions into Jewish observances. Samaritans were also regarded as practicing a form of Judaism, however, particularly at later periods. The animosity between the two groups surfaces in Ezra 4.1–3 and is clearly reflected in stories in the New Testament Gospels (Lk 10.29–37; Jn 4.7–42). **41:** This verse summarizes vv. 29–34a and may have been their original conclusion. It agrees with the viewpoint that the settlers worshiped both the LORD and other gods.

18 In the third year of King Hoshea son of Elah of Israel, Hezekiah son of King Ahaz of Judah began to reign. ²He was twenty-five years old when he began to reign; he reigned twenty-nine years in Jerusalem. His mother's name was Abi daughter of Zechariah. ³He did what was right in the sight of the LORD just as his ancestor David had done. ⁴He removed the high places,

broke down the pillars, and cut down the sacred pole.*a* He broke in pieces the bronze serpent that Moses had made, for until those days the people of Israel had made offerings to it; it was called Nehushtan. 5He trusted in the LORD the God of Israel; so that there was no one like him among all the kings of Judah after him, or among those who were before him. 6For he held fast to the LORD; he did not depart from following him but kept the commandments that the LORD commanded Moses. 7The LORD was with him; wherever he went, he prospered. He rebelled against the king of Assyria and would not serve him. 8He attacked the Philistines as far as Gaza and its territory, from watchtower to fortified city.

18.1–19.37: Hezekiah and the invasion of Sennacherib. The invasion of Sennacherib, king of Assyria, which is recounted in these chapters, took place in 701 BCE and is documented both in the Bible and in Assyrian records. Similar versions of the story are found in 2 Chr 32 and Isa 36. The Assyrian version was recorded in Sennacherib's annals and in a famous relief of the defeat of Lachish on his palace wall in Nineveh. **18.4:** The *high places*★ were shrines other than the Jerusalem Temple.★ They could be used for the worship of the LORD or of other gods. Here it appears to be the latter that is envisioned, since *pillars* and *sacred poles* were used in the worship of Canaanite gods. The *bronze serpent that Moses had made* was to save the people from poisonous snakes (Num 21.6–9). **5:** Statements of incomparability like this one are made also for Moses as a prophet★ (Deut 34.10), for Solomon for wisdom (1 Kings 3.12), and for Josiah for obedience (2 Kings 23.25). **8:** The *Philistines* had remained more or less independent in their land since the time of David. Hezekiah subjugated them to Judah, probably to strengthen the resistance to the Assyrians.

9 In the fourth year of King Hezekiah, which was the seventh year of King Hoshea son of Elah of Israel, King Shalmaneser of Assyria came up against Samaria, besieged it, 10and at the end of three years, took it. In the sixth year of Hezekiah, which was the ninth year of King Hoshea of Israel, Samaria was taken. 11The king of Assyria carried the Israelites away to Assyria, settled them in Halah, on the Habor, the river of Gozan, and in the cities of the Medes, 12because they did not obey the voice of the LORD their God but transgressed his covenant—all that Moses the servant of the LORD had commanded; they neither listened nor obeyed.

13 In the fourteenth year of King Hezekiah, King Sennacherib of Assyria came up against all the fortified cities of Judah and captured them. 14King Hezekiah of Judah sent to the king of Assyria at Lachish, saying, "I have done wrong; withdraw from me; whatever you impose on me I will bear." The king of Assyria demanded of King Hezekiah of Judah three hundred talents of silver and thirty talents of gold. 15Hezekiah gave him all the silver that was found in the house of the LORD and in the treasuries of the king's house. 16At that time Hezekiah stripped the gold from the doors of the temple of the LORD, and from the doorposts that King Hezekiah of Judah had overlaid and gave it to the king of Assyria. 17The king of Assyria sent the Tartan, the Rabsaris, and the Rabshakeh with a great army from Lachish to King Hezekiah at Jerusalem. They went up and came to Jerusalem. When they arrived, they came and stood by the conduit of the upper pool, which is on the highway to the Fuller's Field. 18When they called for the king, there came out to them Eliakim son of Hilkiah, who was in charge of the palace, and Shebnah the secretary, and Joah son of Asaph, the recorder.

19 The Rabshakeh said to them, "Say to Hezekiah: Thus says the great king, the king of Assyria: On what do you base this confidence of yours? 20Do you think that mere words are strategy and power for war? On whom do you now rely, that you have rebelled against me? 21See, you are relying now on Egypt, that broken reed of a staff, which will pierce the hand of anyone who leans on it. Such is Pharaoh king of Egypt to all who rely on him. 22But if you say to me, 'We rely on the LORD our God,' is it not he whose high places and altars Hezekiah has removed, saying to Judah and to Jerusalem, 'You shall worship before this altar in Jerusalem'? 23Come now, make a wager with my

a Heb *Asherah*

master the king of Assyria: I will give you two thousand horses, if you are able on your part to set riders on them. ²⁴How then can you repulse a single captain among the least of my master's servants, when you rely on Egypt for chariots and for horsemen? ²⁵Moreover, is it without the LORD that I have come up against this place to destroy it? The LORD said to me, Go up against this land, and destroy it."

26 Then Eliakim son of Hilkiah, and Shebnah, and Joah said to the Rabshakeh, "Please speak to your servants in the Aramaic language, for we understand it; do not speak to us in the language of Judah within the hearing of the people who are on the wall." ²⁷But the Rabshakeh said to them, "Has my master sent me to speak these words to your master and to you, and not to the people sitting on the wall, who are doomed with you to eat their own dung and to drink their own urine?"

18.9–27. 9–12: These verses reiterate the information about the fall of Israel in ch. 17. 14: A *talent* could weigh between 45 and 130 pounds. 17: *Tartan, Rabsaris,* and *Rabshakeh* are all titles for Assyrian military officers. The exact location of the *conduit of the upper pool* is unknown. 18: The three Assyrians meet with three officials of the court of Judah—*Eliakim, Shebnah,* and *Joah.* The precise functions of their offices as the one *in charge of the palace, secretary,* and *recorder* are uncertain. 19–25: Part of the tactics of ancient warfare involved speeches like this one designed to discourage the enemy. The Rabshakeh makes the point that the Assyrians greatly outnumber the forces of Judah (vv. 23–24) and asks who else the people of Judah are relying on. He observes, quite correctly, that the Egyptians to whom Hezekiah may have looked for help (v. 24), are powerless compared with the Assyrian army. His comparison of Egypt to a *broken reed of a staff* in v. 21 is found also in Ezek 29.6 and may have been a proverb. The other possibility he raises is that they are dependent on the LORD. To counter this, he states that Hezekiah *removed* the LORD's *high places* and altars* (v. 22), which may have been true in a sense. That is, in his effort to centralize the government and religion of Judah, Hezekiah may have outlawed all shrines outside of Jerusalem. The Rabshakeh also claims that the LORD sent the Assyrians against Jerusalem. This claim may also have had a measure of truth

to the extent that Hezekiah or his predecessors likely swore an oath by the LORD to be loyal to their Assyrian overlord. 26: *Aramaic** was the language of diplomacy of that time. *The language of Judah* was Hebrew. 27: The fates described here refer to the conditions of starvation of a city under siege.

28 Then the Rabshakeh stood and called out in a loud voice in the language of Judah, "Hear the word of the great king, the king of Assyria! ²⁹Thus says the king: 'Do not let Hezekiah deceive you, for he will not be able to deliver you out of my hand. ³⁰Do not let Hezekiah make you rely on the LORD by saying, The LORD will surely deliver us, and this city will not be given into the hand of the king of Assyria.' ³¹Do not listen to Hezekiah; for thus says the king of Assyria: 'Make your peace with me and come out to me; then every one of you will eat from your own vine and your own fig tree, and drink water from your own cistern, ³²until I come and take you away to a land like your own land, a land of grain and wine, a land of bread and vineyards, a land of olive oil and honey, that you may live and not die. Do not listen to Hezekiah when he misleads you by saying, The LORD will deliver us. ³³Has any of the gods of the nations ever delivered its land out of the hand of the king of Assyria? ³⁴Where are the gods of Hamath and Arpad? Where are the gods of Sepharvaim, Hena, and Ivvah? Have they delivered Samaria out of my hand? ³⁵Who among all the gods of the countries have delivered their countries out of my hand, that the LORD should deliver Jerusalem out of my hand?'"

18.28–35: The Rabshakeh's second speech is in Hebrew (*the language of Judah,* v. 28), is directed to the common defenders of the city, and is designed to effect a mutiny. He calls on them to surrender, promising prosperity first in their homeland (v. 31) and then in exile (v. 32). The part of the speech regarded as blasphemy by the biblical writers is vv. 33–35, where the Rabshakeh compares the LORD to the gods of other nations, none of whom has been able to save their people from the Assyrian assault.

36 But the people were silent and answered him not a word, for the king's com-

mand was, "Do not answer him." ³⁷Then Eliakim son of Hilkiah, who was in charge of the palace, and Shebna the secretary, and Joah son of Asaph, the recorder, came to Hezekiah with their clothes torn and told him the words of the Rabshakeh.

19 When King Hezekiah heard it, he tore his clothes, covered himself with sackcloth, and went into the house of the LORD. ²And he sent Eliakim, who was in charge of the palace, and Shebna the secretary, and the senior priests, covered with sackcloth, to the prophet Isaiah son of Amoz. ³They said to him, "Thus says Hezekiah, This day is a day of distress, of rebuke, and of disgrace; children have come to the birth, and there is no strength to bring them forth. ⁴It may be that the LORD your God heard all the words of the Rabshakeh, whom his master the king of Assyria has sent to mock the living God, and will rebuke the words that the LORD your God has heard; therefore lift up your prayer for the remnant that is left." ⁵When the servants of King Hezekiah came to Isaiah, ⁶Isaiah said to them, "Say to your master, Thus says the LORD: Do not be afraid because of the words that you have heard, with which the servants of the king of Assyria have reviled me. ⁷I myself will put a spirit in him, so that he shall hear a rumor and return to his own land; I will cause him to fall by the sword in his own land.'"

8 The Rabshakeh returned, and found the king of Assyria fighting against Libnah; for he had heard that the king had left Lachish. ⁹When the king*a* heard concerning King Tirhakah of Ethiopia,*b* "See, he has set out to fight against you," he sent messengers again to Hezekiah, saying, ¹⁰"Thus shall you speak to King Hezekiah of Judah: Do not let your God on whom you rely deceive you by promising that Jerusalem will not be given into the hand of the king of Assyria. ¹¹See, you have heard what the kings of Assyria have done to all lands, destroying them utterly. Shall you be delivered? ¹²Have the gods of the nations delivered them, the nations that my predecessors destroyed, Gozan, Haran, Rezeph, and the people of Eden who were in Telassar? ¹³Where is the king of Hamath, the king of Arpad, the king

of the city of Sepharvaim, the king of Hena, or the king of Ivvah?"

18.36–19.13. 18.37; 19.1–2: Wearing *torn clothes* and *sackcloth*★ (Heb., "saq") were signs of great sorrow or distress. *Isaiah, son of Amoz,* is also the prophet★ behind the book of Isaiah. 3: *Children have come to the birth, and there is no strength to bring them forth* may be a proverb. It alludes to great pain and suffering associated with labor. Here, it expresses frustration because the people of Judah do not have the strength to carry out the rebellion against the Assyrians. 4: It was in his second speech (18.28–35) that the Rabshakeh *mock(ed) the living God.* 8: *Libnah* was southwest of Jerusalem and north of Lachish. 9: *Tirhaka* (Tarhaka) was from Nubia (*Ethiopia*) and did not become king of Egypt until around 690 BCE. His name here is probably an error made by the much later biblical writer. 11–13: The Rabshakeh's letter here is very similar to his speech in 18.33–35.

14 Hezekiah received the letter from the hand of the messengers and read it; then Hezekiah went up to the house of the LORD and spread it before the LORD. ¹⁵And Hezekiah prayed before the LORD, and said: "O LORD the God of Israel, who are enthroned above the cherubim, you are God, you alone, of all the kingdoms of the earth; you have made heaven and earth. ¹⁶Incline your ear, O LORD, and hear; open your eyes, O LORD, and see; hear the words of Sennacherib, which he has sent to mock the living God. ¹⁷Truly, O LORD, the kings of Assyria have laid waste the nations and their lands, ¹⁸and have hurled their gods into the fire, though they were no gods but the work of human hands—wood and stone—and so they were destroyed. ¹⁹So now, O LORD our God, save us, I pray you, from his hand, so that all the kingdoms of the earth may know that you, O LORD, are God alone."

19.14–19. 15: The *cherubim*★ is a reference to the ark, which had two cherubim depicted on its lid. These were mythical, griffin-like creatures whose statues often adorned temples and palaces in the ancient Near East. 16–19: Hezekiah's prayer addresses the Rab-

a Heb *he*   *b* Or *Nubia;* Heb *Cush*

The Siege of Lachish

The city of Lachish, southwest of Jerusalem, was an important and well-fortified outpost of Judah during the reign of King Hezekiah. When the Assyrian emperor Sennacherib came to Palestine in 701 BCE, he besieged and conquered Lachish and then set up his headquarters there, from which he threatened Jerusalem (2 Kings 18.14). In addition to the Bible's accounts of the events of 701 (2 Kings 18–19; 2 Chr 32; Isa 36), we possess Sennacherib's own annals. Unfortunately, these versions of the story do not always agree. For example, Sennacherib claims to have conquered Jerusalem, while the Bible indicates that he never reached Jerusalem. Sennacherib's annals say nothing about the plague which, according to the Bible (2 Kings 19.35), forced him to withdraw from Judah. All accounts agree that Sennacherib left Hezekiah on the throne of Judah, which seems extraordinary considering Hezekiah's rebellion. They also agree that Hezekiah paid tribute to Sennacherib, though they differ about the amount. Sennacherib was so proud of his conquest of Lachish that he had a relief (a raised carving) of the battle included in the decorations of his palace wall in Nineveh. The relief graphically depicts the tactics and weapons used in ancient Near Eastern warfare. The site of ancient Lachish has recently been excavated, and the discoveries there confirm the basic accuracy of the relief.

shakeh's claim that the gods of the nations had not saved them and neither could the LORD save Judah. Through Hezekiah the author makes the point that those gods were not real but only idols. Hence, Hezekiah calls on the LORD for deliverance as a way of showing the world that the LORD (Yahweh) is *God alone.*

20 Then Isaiah son of Amoz sent to Hezekiah, saying, "Thus says the LORD, the God of Israel: I have heard your prayer to me about King Sennacherib of Assyria. 21 This is the word that the LORD has spoken concerning him:

She despises you, she scorns you—
    virgin daughter Zion;
she tosses her head—behind your back,
    daughter Jerusalem.

22 "Whom have you mocked and reviled?
    Against whom have you raised your
        voice
    and haughtily lifted your eyes?
    Against the Holy One of Israel!
23 By your messengers you have mocked
        the Lord,

and you have said, 'With my many
        chariots
I have gone up the heights of the
        mountains,
    to the far recesses of Lebanon;
I felled its tallest cedars,
    its choicest cypresses;
I entered its farthest retreat,
    its densest forest.
24 I dug wells
    and drank foreign waters,
I dried up with the sole of my foot
    all the streams of Egypt.'

25 "Have you not heard
    that I determined it long ago?
I planned from days of old
    what now I bring to pass,
that you should make fortified cities
    crash into heaps of ruins,
26 while their inhabitants, shorn of
        strength,
    are dismayed and confounded;
they have become like plants of the
        field
    and like tender grass,

like grass on the housetops,
  blighted before it is grown.

27 "But I know your rising*a* and your
    sitting,
  your going out and coming in,
    and your raging against me.
28 Because you have raged against me
    and your arrogance has come to my
      ears,
  I will put my hook in your nose
    and my bit in your mouth;
  I will turn you back on the way
    by which you came.

29 "And this shall be the sign for you:
This year you shall eat what grows of itself,
and in the second year what springs from
that; then in the third year sow, reap, plant
vineyards, and eat their fruit. 30The surviving remnant of the house of Judah shall again
take root downward, and bear fruit upward;
31for from Jerusalem a remnant shall go out,
and from Mount Zion a band of survivors.
The zeal of the LORD of hosts will do this.

32 "Therefore thus says the LORD concerning the king of Assyria: He shall not
come into this city, shoot an arrow there,
come before it with a shield, or cast up a
siege ramp against it. 33By the way that he
came, by the same he shall return; he shall
not come into this city, says the LORD. 34For
I will defend this city to save it, for my own
sake and for the sake of my servant David."

35 That very night the angel of the LORD
set out and struck down one hundred eighty-
five thousand in the camp of the Assyrians;
when morning dawned, they were all dead
bodies. 36Then King Sennacherib of Assyria
left, went home, and lived at Nineveh. 37As
he was worshiping in the house of his god
Nisroch, his sons Adrammelech and Sharezer killed him with the sword, and they escaped into the land of Ararat. His son Esar-
haddon succeeded him.

19.20–37. 21: *She* is the *virgin daughter Zion,** a reference to Jerusalem. *Toss(ing) her head* was a way of
showing contempt. The idea is that the city of Jerusalem disdains the Assyrian king Sennacherib. **22–24:**
Sennacherib is caricatured as arrogant and boastful to

the point that he has *reviled* the LORD. The speaker in
vv. 23–24 is Sennacherib. See Isa 10.12–19; 14.24–
27. **25–28:** Now, the LORD speaks. The message in
these verses is that it is the LORD who determined Sennacherib's victories and who will now bring him down
because of his pride. **29–31:** This oracle* is considered
more realistic and thus more original than the surrounding material. The *sign* it describes is a three-year
period before agriculture returns to its normal cycle
and the Assyrian threat is finally removed (v. 29). The
oracle also describes the survival of a *remnant* in the
city of *Jerusalem* from which the countryside will be
repopulated after the Assyrian devastation (vv. 30–31).
32–33: These verses reflect the doctrine of the inviolability of Jerusalem, that is, the belief that the LORD
would never allow the city of Jerusalem to be captured.
The idea may have arisen as a result of the city's survival in 701. It was later countered by the prophet*
Jeremiah (Jer 7). **35:** This verse describes a plague that
devastated Sennacherib's army and forced him to return in shame to Nineveh. The historical veracity of the
event cannot be confirmed or denied. **36–37:** Sennacherib's assassination did not take place until 20
years later in 681 BCE. *Ararat* (v. 37) is modern Armenia
north of Assyria.

20 In those days Hezekiah became sick
and was at the point of death. The
prophet Isaiah son of Amoz came to him, and
said to him, "Thus says the LORD: Set your
house in order, for you shall die; you shall
not recover." 2Then Hezekiah turned his
face to the wall and prayed to the LORD:
3"Remember now, O LORD, I implore you,
how I have walked before you in faithfulness
with a whole heart, and have done what is
good in your sight." Hezekiah wept bitterly.
4Before Isaiah had gone out of the middle
court, the word of the LORD came to him:
5"Turn back, and say to Hezekiah prince of
my people, Thus says the LORD, the God of
your ancestor David: I have heard your
prayer, I have seen your tears; indeed, I will
heal you; on the third day you shall go up to
the house of the LORD. 6I will add fifteen
years to your life. I will deliver you and this
city out of the hand of the king of Assyria; I
will defend this city for my own sake and for
my servant David's sake." 7Then Isaiah said,

---

a Gk Compare Isa 37.27 Q Ms: MT lacks *rising*

"Bring a lump of figs. Let them take it and apply it to the boil, so that he may recover."

8 Hezekiah said to Isaiah, "What shall be the sign that the LORD will heal me, and that I shall go up to the house of the LORD on the third day?" 9Isaiah said, "This is the sign to you from the LORD, that the LORD will do the thing that he has promised: the shadow has now advanced ten intervals; shall it retreat ten intervals?" 10Hezekiah answered, "It is normal for the shadow to lengthen ten intervals; rather let the shadow retreat ten intervals." 11The prophet Isaiah cried to the LORD; and he brought the shadow back the ten intervals, by which the sun*a* had declined on the dial of Ahaz.

12 At that time King Merodach-baladan son of Baladan of Babylon sent envoys with letters and a present to Hezekiah, for he had heard that Hezekiah had been sick. 13Hezekiah welcomed them;*b* he showed them all his treasure house, the silver, the gold, the spices, the precious oil, his armory, all that was found in his storehouses; there was nothing in his house or in all his realm that Hezekiah did not show them. 14Then the prophet Isaiah came to King Hezekiah, and said to him, "What did these men say? From where did they come to you?" Hezekiah answered, "They have come from a far country, from Babylon." 15He said, "What have they seen in your house?" Hezekiah answered, "They have seen all that is in my house; there is nothing in my storehouses that I did not show them."

16 Then Isaiah said to Hezekiah, "Hear the word of the LORD: 17Days are coming when all that is in your house, and that which your ancestors have stored up until this day, shall be carried to Babylon; nothing shall be left, says the LORD. 18Some of your own sons who are born to you shall be taken away; they shall be eunuchs in the palace of the king of Babylon." 19Then Hezekiah said to Isaiah, "The word of the LORD that you have spoken is good." For he thought, "Why not, if there will be peace and security in my days?"

20 The rest of the deeds of Hezekiah, all his power, how he made the pool and the conduit and brought water into the city, are they not written in the Book of the Annals of the Kings of Judah? 21Hezekiah slept with his ancestors; and his son Manasseh succeeded him.

20.1–21: Hezekiah's illness and the Babylonian envoy. The stories in this chapter are probably out of order and originally preceded the invasion of Sennacherib in 701 BCE, since v. 6 promises defense of Jerusalem, and the visit of Merodach-baladan must have preceded Hezekiah's revolt against Assyria. **7:** The *lump of figs* served as a poultice, a medicinal substance applied directly to the skin, to draw out the boil. **8–11:** Comparable to Josh 10.12–13, where the sun stood still, here it retreated 10 hours. **12–19:** *Merodach-baladan* is Marduk-apal-iddina, who ruled in Babylon 720–709 and again in 702 and opposed Assyria. His visit to Jerusalem would have involved plotting for Hezekiah's revolt against Assyria. In this context, however, it has been used to foreshadow the Babylonian Exile. ✻ *Eunuchs* (v. 18) were castrated males who were often employed as guardians and servants in the royal harem. However, the Hebrew word may simply mean a palace servant or official. **20:** The *conduit* by which Hezekiah *brought water into the city* probably refers to the Siloam tunnel in Jerusalem, which contained an inscription describing its construction. **21:** There is no notice about Hezekiah's burial "in the city of David" as there is for his predecessors. The reason is unclear, though it may reflect an actual change in practice. 2 Chr 32.33 says he was buried "on the ascent to the tombs of the descendants of David," which may suggest that the royal tombs of Judah were full.

21 Manasseh was twelve years old when he began to reign; he reigned fifty-five years in Jerusalem. His mother's name was Hephzibah. 2He did what was evil in the sight of the LORD, following the abominable practices of the nations that the LORD drove out before the people of Israel. 3For he rebuilt the high places that his father Hezekiah had destroyed; he erected altars for Baal, made a sacred pole,*c* as King Ahab of Israel had done, worshiped all the host of heaven, and served them. 4He built altars in the house of the LORD, of which the LORD had said, "In Jerusalem I will put my name." 5He

a Syr See Isa 38.8 and Tg: Heb *it*   *b* Gk Vg Syr: Heb *When Hezekiah heard about them*   *c* Heb *Asherah* built altars for all the host of heaven in the two courts of the house of the LORD. 6He made his son pass through fire; he practiced soothsaying and augury, and dealt with mediums and with wizards. He did much evil in the sight of the LORD, provoking him to anger. 7The carved image of Asherah that he had made he set in the house of which the LORD said to David and to his son Solomon, "In this house, and in Jerusalem, which I have chosen out of all the tribes of Israel, I will put my name forever; 8I will not cause the feet of Israel to wander any more out of the land that I gave to their ancestors, if only they will be careful to do according to all that I have commanded them, and according to all the law that my servant Moses commanded them." 9But they did not listen; Manasseh misled them to do more evil than the nations had done that the LORD destroyed before the people of Israel.

10 The LORD said by his servants the prophets, 11"Because King Manasseh of Judah has committed these abominations, has done things more wicked than all that the Amorites did, who were before him, and has caused Judah also to sin with his idols; 12therefore thus says the LORD, the God of Israel, I am bringing upon Jerusalem and Judah such evil that the ears of everyone who hears of it will tingle. 13I will stretch over Jerusalem the measuring line for Samaria, and the plummet for the house of Ahab; I will wipe Jerusalem as one wipes a dish, wiping it and turning it upside down. 14I will cast off the remnant of my heritage, and give them into the hand of their enemies; they shall become a prey and a spoil to all their enemies, 15because they have done what is evil in my sight and have provoked me to anger, since the day their ancestors came out of Egypt, even to this day."

16 Moreover Manasseh shed very much innocent blood, until he had filled Jerusalem from one end to another, besides the sin that he caused Judah to sin so that they did what was evil in the sight of the LORD.

17 Now the rest of the acts of Manasseh, all that he did, and the sin that he committed, are they not written in the Book of the Annals of the Kings of Judah? 18Manasseh slept with his ancestors, and was buried in the garden of his house, in the garden of Uzza. His son Amon succeeded him.

19 Amon was twenty-two years old when he began to reign; he reigned two years in Jerusalem. His mother's name was Meshullemeth daughter of Haruz of Jotbah. 20He did what was evil in the sight of the LORD, as his father Manasseh had done. 21He walked in all the way in which his father walked, served the idols that his father served, and worshiped them; 22he abandoned the LORD, the God of his ancestors, and did not walk in the way of the LORD. 23The servants of Amon conspired against him, and killed the king in his house. 24But the people of the land killed all those who had conspired against King Amon, and the people of the land made his son Josiah king in place of him. 25Now the rest of the acts of Amon that he did, are they not written in the Book of the Annals of the Kings of Judah? 26He was buried in his tomb in the garden of Uzza; then his son Josiah succeeded him.

21.1–26: **Manasseh and Amon. 1:** Manasseh is credited with the longest reign, *fifty-five years*, of any king of Israel or Judah. **3:** A *sacred pole* was an important part of the worship of the Canaanite goddess Asherah.✷ The *host of heaven* refers to the astral gods— sun, moon, and stars. These practices were outlawed by Deuteronomy (12.29–31; 17.3). **6:** *He made his son pass through fire* refers to child sacrifice. *Mediums and wizards* are often used in conjunction and refer to devices used to communicate with the dead. Such practices are condemned by the law in Deuteronomy (18.10). See 1 Sam 28. **7–8:** Here the promise of the central "place" chosen by Yahweh (Deut 12.5) is combined with the promise of a dynasty✷ to *David* (2 Sam 7). **11:** *Amorites* is a general name for the inhabitants of Canaan before the Israelites. **13:** The *measuring line* and *plummet* suggest that Judah will be judged by the same standards by which *Samaria* and its worst kings, *the house of Ahab*, were condemned. Compare Am 7.7–9. To *wipe Jerusalem as one wipes a dish* means to empty it completely. **14:** The LORD's *heritage* is the nation of Israel. Since the northern kingdom is no more, Judah is the *remnant* of that heritage. These verses, therefore, predict the Babylonian Exile✷ and blame it on Manasseh. Quite a different story is told in

2 Chr 33.10–13. **16:** This verse may be an addition, since it does not seem to relate well to the surrounding context. **18:** *Manasseh* also is not *buried* in the city of David but *in the garden of Uzza.* Both the identity of Uzza and the location of this garden are unknown. **24:** The *people of the land* may be the landowning nobility, but their identity is disputed. **26:** *Amon* is also buried in the *garden of Uzza.*

and one of the heroes of the Deuteronomistic* History. He is renowned for his obedience (22.2; 23.25) to the law book found during his reign. **22.3–10:** The Temple* repairs made by Josiah lead to the discovery of a copy of the *book of the law,* which has long been identified as a form of the book of Deuteronomy.

22 Josiah was eight years old when he began to reign; he reigned thirty-one years in Jerusalem. His mother's name was Jedidah daughter of Adaiah of Bozkath. ²He did what was right in the sight of the LORD, and walked in all the way of his father David; he did not turn aside to the right or to the left.

3 In the eighteenth year of King Josiah, the king sent Shaphan son of Azaliah, son of Meshullam, the secretary, to the house of the LORD, saying, ⁴"Go up to the high priest Hilkiah, and have him count the entire sum of the money that has been brought into the house of the LORD, which the keepers of the threshold have collected from the people; ⁵let it be given into the hand of the workers who have the oversight of the house of the LORD; let them give it to the workers who are at the house of the LORD, repairing the house, ⁶that is, to the carpenters, to the builders, to the masons; and let them use it to buy timber and quarried stone to repair the house. ⁷But no accounting shall be asked from them for the money that is delivered into their hand, for they deal honestly."

8 The high priest Hilkiah said to Shaphan the secretary, "I have found the book of the law in the house of the LORD." When Hilkiah gave the book to Shaphan, he read it. ⁹Then Shaphan the secretary came to the king, and reported to the king, "Your servants have emptied out the money that was found in the house, and have delivered it into the hand of the workers who have oversight of the house of the LORD." ¹⁰Shaphan the secretary informed the king, "The priest Hilkiah has given me a book." Shaphan then read it aloud to the king.

11 When the king heard the words of the book of the law, he tore his clothes. ¹²Then the king commanded the priest Hilkiah, Ahikam son of Shaphan, Achbor son of Micaiah, Shaphan the secretary, and the king's servant Asaiah, saying, ¹³"Go, inquire of the LORD for me, for the people, and for all Judah, concerning the words of this book that has been found; for great is the wrath of the LORD that is kindled against us, because our ancestors did not obey the words of this book, to do according to all that is written concerning us."

14 So the priest Hilkiah, Ahikam, Achbor, Shaphan, and Asaiah went to the prophetess Huldah the wife of Shallum son of Tikvah, son of Harhas, keeper of the wardrobe; she resided in Jerusalem in the Second Quarter, where they consulted her. ¹⁵She declared to them, "Thus says the LORD, the God of Israel: Tell the man who sent you to me, ¹⁶Thus says the LORD, I will indeed bring disaster on this place and on its inhabitants—all the words of the book that the king of Judah has read. ¹⁷Because they have abandoned me and have made offerings to other gods, so that they have provoked me to anger with all the work of their hands, therefore my wrath will be kindled against this place, and it will not be quenched. ¹⁸But as to the king of Judah, who sent you to inquire of the LORD, thus shall you say to him, Thus says the LORD, the God of Israel: Regarding the words that you have heard, ¹⁹because your heart was penitent, and you humbled yourself before the LORD, when you heard how I spoke against this place, and against its inhabitants, that they should become a desolation and a curse, and because you have torn your clothes and wept before me, I also have heard you, says the LORD. ²⁰Therefore, I will gather you to your ancestors, and you shall be gathered to your grave in peace; your eyes shall not see all the di-

22.1–23.30: The reign and reform of Josiah. Josiah, along with Hezekiah, is one of the good kings of Judah saster that I will bring on this place." They took the message back to the king.

22.11–20. 11: Tearing *clothes* is a sign of repentance and distress. Josiah is worried because of the punishments threatened in the law for disobedience, since the people of Judah have not kept the law. 13: *Inquire* is a technical term for divining or seeking an oracle★ from God. 14: *The prophetess*★ Huldah is one of the few women in the Bible so designated (Miriam, Ex 15.20; Deborah, Judg 4.4; and Isaiah's wife[?], Isa 8.3). The *Second Quarter* was apparently an expansion of the city of Jerusalem that had taken place, perhaps during Hezekiah's day, in part to accommodate the influx of refugees from Israel. 15–17: *The man who sent you to me* is Josiah. *This place* is Jerusalem. This part of Huldah's oracle anticipates the destruction of Jerusalem and the Babylonian Exile.★ 20: Most scholars believe at least the second half of Huldah's oracle to be genuine because it seems to be contradicted by history. Josiah did not in fact go to his grave peacefully, if this is what *in peace* means. Rather, he was killed in battle (23.29).

23 Then the king directed that all the elders of Judah and Jerusalem should be gathered to him. ²The king went up to the house of the LORD, and with him went all the people of Judah, all the inhabitants of Jerusalem, the priests, the prophets, and all the people, both small and great; he read in their hearing all the words of the book of the covenant that had been found in the house of the LORD. ³The king stood by the pillar and made a covenant before the LORD, to follow the LORD, keeping his commandments, his decrees, and his statutes, with all his heart and all his soul, to perform the words of this covenant that were written in this book. All the people joined in the covenant.

4 The king commanded the high priest Hilkiah, the priests of the second order, and the guardians of the threshold, to bring out of the temple of the LORD all the vessels made for Baal, for Asherah, and for all the host of heaven; he burned them outside Jerusalem in the fields of the Kidron, and carried their ashes to Bethel. ⁵He deposed the idolatrous priests whom the kings of Judah had ordained to make offerings in the high places at the cities of Judah and around Jerusalem; those also who made offerings to Baal, to the sun, the moon, the constellations, and all the host of the heavens. ⁶He brought out the image of*ᵃ* Asherah from the house of the LORD, outside Jerusalem, to the Wadi Kidron, burned it at the Wadi Kidron, beat it to dust and threw the dust of it upon the graves of the common people. ⁷He broke down the houses of the male temple prostitutes that were in the house of the LORD, where the women did weaving for Asherah. ⁸He brought all the priests out of the towns of Judah, and defiled the high places where the priests had made offerings, from Geba to Beer-sheba; he broke down the high places of the gates that were at the entrance of the gate of Joshua the governor of the city, which were on the left at the gate of the city. ⁹The priests of the high places, however, did not come up to the altar of the LORD in Jerusalem, but ate unleavened bread among their kindred. ¹⁰He defiled Topheth, which is in the valley of Ben-hinnom, so that no one would make a son or a daughter pass through fire as an offering to Molech. ¹¹He removed the horses that the kings of Judah had dedicated to the sun, at the entrance to the house of the LORD, by the chamber of the eunuch Nathan-melech, which was in the precincts;*ᵇ* then he burned the chariots of the sun with fire. ¹²The altars on the roof of the upper chamber of Ahaz, which the kings of Judah had made, and the altars that Manasseh had made in the two courts of the house of the LORD, he pulled down from there and broke in pieces, and threw the rubble into the Wadi Kidron. ¹³The king defiled the high places that were east of Jerusalem, to the south of the Mount of Destruction, which King Solomon of Israel had built for Astarte the abomination of the Sidonians, for Chemosh the abomination of Moab, and for Milcom the abomination of the Ammonites. ¹⁴He broke the pillars in pieces, cut down the sacred poles,*ᶜ* and covered the sites with human bones.

a Heb lacks *image of*   *b* Meaning of Heb uncertain
c Heb *Asherim*

23.1–14. 1–3: Huldah's original oracle* may not have been so bleak, or at least it may have been conditional, since it motivated Josiah to try to carry out reforms so as to avoid disaster. On the language of v. 3, compare 23.25 and Deut 6.5. **4–5:** Josiah's reforms included purging the Temple* of the trappings of the worship of other gods. The *Kidron* was the valley between the city of Jerusalem and the Mount of Olives. **6:** Throwing the *dust* from the *image of Asherah** upon the *graves* would defile the image all the more. **7:** The word translated *male temple prostitutes* may actually include both male and female prostitutes who served in the fertility rituals of the worship of Baal* and Asherah. **8:** In bringing the *priests out of the towns of Judah* and destroying the *high places** Josiah was executing the deuteronomic* ideal of centralization, according to which the Temple in Jerusalem was the only legitimate place to worship the LORD. *From Geba to Beer-sheba* was the extent of the kingdom of Judah. **9:** The *priests of the high places,* however, refused to go to Jerusalem. Eating *unleavened bread* accompanied sacrifices (Lev 6.14–18), which apparently continued outside of Jerusalem despite Josiah's efforts. **10:** *Topheth* was a valley that marked Jerusalem's western border. Also known as the valley of (the son of) Hinnom (Heb., "ge' hinnom"), it became Jerusalem's trash dump and was used by Jesus as the image for hell (Gehenna,* see Mt 10.28). It was despised because it had served as a place of child sacrifice to the Ammonite god Molech (a distortion of the name Milcom made by borrowing the vowels from the word "bosheth," meaning "abomination"). **11:** This verse suggests that *horses* were an important part of the worship of the sun, which was imagined as being drawn daily across the sky in a *chariot.* **12:** Offerings from *altars on the roof* are mentioned in Jer 32.29. The *altars that Manasseh had made* are mentioned in 21.5. **13:** *Mount of Destruction* is probably a play on the Hebrew name for the Mount of Olives ("Mount of Anointing") because of the altars to foreign gods erected there. **14:** *Pillars* and *sacred poles* were used in the worship of the Canaanite gods. *Cover(ing) the sites with human bones* would further defile them.

15 Moreover, the altar at Bethel, the high place erected by Jeroboam son of Nebat, who caused Israel to sin—he pulled down that altar along with the high place. He burned the high place, crushing it to dust; he also burned the sacred pole.*a* 16As Josiah turned, he saw the tombs there on the mount; and he sent and took the bones out of the tombs, and burned them on the altar, and defiled it, according to the word of the LORD that the man of God proclaimed,*b* when Jeroboam stood by the altar at the festival; he turned and looked up at the tomb of the man of God who had predicted these things. 17Then he said, "What is that monument that I see?" The people of the city told him, "It is the tomb of the man of God who came from Judah and predicted these things that you have done against the altar at Bethel." 18He said, "Let him rest; let no one move his bones." So they let his bones alone, with the bones of the prophet who came out of Samaria. 19Moreover, Josiah removed all the shrines of the high places that were in the towns of Samaria, which kings of Israel had made, provoking the LORD to anger; he did to them just as he had done at Bethel. 20He slaughtered on the altars all the priests of the high places who were there, and burned human bones on them. Then he returned to Jerusalem.

21 The king commanded all the people, "Keep the passover to the LORD your God as prescribed in this book of the covenant." 22No such passover had been kept since the days of the judges who judged Israel, even during all the days of the kings of Israel and of the kings of Judah; 23but in the eighteenth year of King Josiah this passover was kept to the LORD in Jerusalem.

24 Moreover Josiah put away the mediums, wizards, teraphim,*c* idols, and all the abominations that were seen in the land of Judah and in Jerusalem, so that he established the words of the law that were written in the book that the priest Hilkiah had found in the house of the LORD. 25Before him there was no king like him, who turned to the LORD with all his heart, with all his soul, and with all his might, according to all the law of Moses; nor did any like him arise after him.

26 Still the LORD did not turn from the fierceness of his great wrath, by which his

a Heb *Asherah* *b* Gk: Heb *proclaimed, who had predicted these things* *c* Or *household gods* anger was kindled against Judah, because of all the provocations with which Manasseh had provoked him. ²⁷The LORD said, "I will remove Judah also out of my sight, as I have removed Israel; and I will reject this city that I have chosen, Jerusalem, and the house of which I said, My name shall be there."

28 Now the rest of the acts of Josiah, and all that he did, are they not written in the Book of the Annals of the Kings of Judah? ²⁹In his days Pharaoh Neco king of Egypt went up to the king of Assyria to the river Euphrates. King Josiah went to meet him; but when Pharaoh Neco met him at Megiddo, he killed him. ³⁰His servants carried him dead in a chariot from Megiddo, brought him to Jerusalem, and buried him in his own tomb. The people of the land took Jehoahaz son of Josiah, anointed him, and made him king in place of his father.

23.15–30. 15: On *Jeroboam's altar at Bethel,* see 1 Kings 12.25–33. **16–18:** The story of the *man of God* from Bethel is found in 1 Kings 13. **19–20:** According to these verses, Josiah's reforms reached as far as Samaria. He may have annexed at least part of the territory of the former northern kingdom as his own. **21–23:** On the *passover*⋆ see Ex 12.1–32 and Deut 16.1–8. **24:** On *mediums* and *wizards,* see 21.6. *Teraphim* or "household idols" play a role in stories in Gen 31.33–35 and 1 Sam 19.11–16. **25:** Josiah was incomparably obedient (22.2; Deut 6.5) as Moses was an incomparable prophet⋆ (Deut 34.10), Solomon incomparably wise (1 Kings 3.12), and Hezekiah incomparably faithful (2 Kings 18.5). **26:** This statement is curious because 23.4–14 makes it clear that Josiah corrected *Manasseh's* apostasies. The writer is apparently struggling to find a theological reason for the Exile⋆ and ends up blaming it on Manasseh. **27:** This verse is a reversal of the doctrine in Deuteronomy of a *chosen* place. **29:** *King Josiah's* sudden death came as a shock to those who had placed trust in his reforms.

31 Jehoahaz was twenty-three years old when he began to reign; he reigned three months in Jerusalem. His mother's name was Hamutal daughter of Jeremiah of Libnah. ³²He did what was evil in the sight of the LORD, just as his ancestors had done. ³³Pharaoh Neco confined him at Riblah in the land of Hamath, so that he might not reign in Jerusalem, and imposed tribute on the land of one hundred talents of silver and a talent of gold. ³⁴Pharaoh Neco made Eliakim son of Josiah king in place of his father Josiah, and changed his name to Jehoiakim. But he took Jehoahaz away; he came to Egypt, and died there. ³⁵Jehoiakim gave the silver and the gold to Pharaoh, but he taxed the land in order to meet Pharaoh's demand for money. He exacted the silver and the gold from the people of the land, from all according to their assessment, to give it to Pharaoh Neco.

23.31–35: The reign of Jehoahaz. 32: The judgment that Jehoahaz *did what was evil in the sight of the LORD* is clearly formulaic, since Jehoahaz reigned only three months. **33:** *Pharaoh Neco* apparently deposed Jehoahaz on the way back to Egypt. Jehoahaz, also known as Shallum (Jer 22.11), had evidently been chosen by the people, but Neco did not believe he would be favorable to Egypt and so replaced him. A *talent* varied in weight from 45 to 130 pounds. **34:** *Eliakim* was *Jehoahaz's* older brother. *Neco* found him more suitable. His name, *Jehoiakim,* means "Yahweh establishes" and may have been intended by Neco to remind Jehoiakim that he had sworn an oath of loyalty to Egypt by the LORD (Yahweh).

36 Jehoiakim was twenty-five years old when he began to reign; he reigned eleven years in Jerusalem. His mother's name was Zebidah daughter of Pedaiah of Rumah. ³⁷He did what was evil in the sight of the LORD, just as all his ancestors had done.

24 In his days King Nebuchadnezzar of Babylon came up; Jehoiakim became his servant for three years; then he turned and rebelled against him. ²The LORD sent against him bands of the Chaldeans, bands of the Arameans, bands of the Moabites, and bands of the Ammonites; he sent them against Judah to destroy it, according to the word of the LORD that he spoke by his servants the prophets. ³Surely this came upon Judah at the command of the LORD, to remove them out of his sight, for the sins of Manasseh, for all that he had committed, ⁴and also for the innocent blood that he had shed; for he filled Jerusalem with innocent blood, and the LORD was not willing to par-

don. 5 Now the rest of the deeds of Jehoiakim, and all that he did, are they not written in the Book of the Annals of the Kings of Judah? 6 So Jehoiakim slept with his ancestors; then his son Jehoiachin succeeded him. 7 The king of Egypt did not come again out of his land, for the king of Babylon had taken over all that belonged to the king of Egypt from the Wadi of Egypt to the River Euphrates.

23.36–24.7: The reign of Jehoiakim. 24.1: The new power at the end of the seventh century BCE was *Babylon* (see v. 7). Judah came under Babylonian control around 605 BCE and *rebelled* three years later. **2:** *Chaldeans* is another name for Babylonians. **3–4:** As in 23.26, the Exile* is blamed on *Manasseh*. **7:** Nebuchadnezzar, king of Babylon, had defeated the Egyptians in the battle of Carchemish in 605 BCE, so Egypt no longer controlled Judah.

8 Jehoiachin was eighteen years old when he began to reign; he reigned three months in Jerusalem. His mother's name was Nehushta daughter of Elnathan of Jerusalem. 9 He did what was evil in the sight of the LORD, just as his father had done.

10 At that time the servants of King Nebuchadnezzar of Babylon came up to Jerusalem, and the city was besieged. 11 King Nebuchadnezzar of Babylon came to the city, while his servants were besieging it; 12 King Jehoiachin of Judah gave himself up to the king of Babylon, himself, his mother, his servants, his officers, and his palace officials. The king of Babylon took him prisoner in the eighth year of his reign.

13 He carried off all the treasures of the house of the LORD, and the treasures of the king's house; he cut in pieces all the vessels of gold in the temple of the LORD, which King Solomon of Israel had made, all this as the LORD had foretold. 14 He carried away all Jerusalem, all the officials, all the warriors, ten thousand captives, all the artisans and the smiths; no one remained, except the poorest people of the land. 15 He carried away Jehoiachin to Babylon; the king's mother, the king's wives, his officials, and the elite of the land, he took into captivity

from Jerusalem to Babylon. 16 The king of Babylon brought captive to Babylon all the men of valor, seven thousand, the artisans and the smiths, one thousand, all of them strong and fit for war. 17 The king of Babylon made Mattaniah, Jehoiachin's uncle, king in his place, and changed his name to Zedekiah.

24.8–17: Jehoiachin and the Babylonian incursion. 8–9: Again, since *Jehoiachin* reigned only *three months*, the judgment that he did *evil in the sight of the LORD* is a stereotypical formula. **10–12:** Jehoiakim died after his rebellion but before the Babylonians reached Jerusalem. That, plus the fact that Jehoiachin surrendered himself, may be the reason the Babylonians did not destroy the city in the invasion of 597. Jehoiachin, also called Jeconiah (1 Chr 3.16) and Coniah (Jer 22.24) was the son of Jehoiakim. **14:** The statement that *all Jerusalem* was taken captive is an obvious exaggeration. Evidently, the upper class was exiled. **15:** This wave of captives included King Jehoiachin. The prophet* Ezekiel was also among them (Ezek 1.1). **17:** *Mattaniah* means "gift of Yahweh." Nebuchadnezzar changed it to *Zedekiah*, "the judgment of Yahweh," perhaps as a reminder that the LORD would bring judgment upon him if he broke his oath of loyalty, sworn by the LORD, to Babylon.

18 Zedekiah was twenty-one years old when he began to reign; he reigned eleven years in Jerusalem. His mother's name was Hamutal daughter of Jeremiah of Libnah. 19 He did what was evil in the sight of the LORD, just as Jehoiakim had done. 20 Indeed, Jerusalem and Judah so angered the LORD that he expelled them from his presence.

Zedekiah rebelled against the king of Babylon. 1 And in the ninth year of his reign, in the tenth month, on the tenth day of the month, King Nebuchadnezzar of Babylon came with all his army against Jerusalem, and laid siege to it; they built siegeworks against it all around. 2 So the city was besieged until the eleventh year of King Zedekiah. 3 On the ninth day of the fourth month the famine became so severe in the city that there was no food for the people of the land. 4 Then a breach was made in the city wall;^a the king with all the soldiers fled^b by night by the way of the gate between the two walls, by the king's garden, though the Chaldeans were all around the city. They went in the direction of the Arabah. 5But the army of the Chaldeans pursued the king, and overtook him in the plains of Jericho; all his army was scattered, deserting him. 6Then they captured the king and brought him up to the king of Babylon at Riblah, who passed sentence on him. 7They slaughtered the sons of Zedekiah before his eyes, then put out the eyes of Zedekiah; they bound him in fetters and took him to Babylon.

8 In the fifth month, on the seventh day of the month—which was the nineteenth year of King Nebuchadnezzar, king of Babylon—Nebuzaradan, the captain of the bodyguard, a servant of the king of Babylon, came to Jerusalem. 9He burned the house of the LORD, the king's house, and all the houses of Jerusalem; every great house he burned down. 10All the army of the Chaldeans who were with the captain of the guard broke down the walls around Jerusalem. 11Nebuzaradan the captain of the guard carried into exile the rest of the people who were left in the city and the deserters who had defected to the king of Babylon—all the rest of the population. 12But the captain of the guard left some of the poorest people of the land to be vinedressers and tillers of the soil.

13 The bronze pillars that were in the house of the LORD, as well as the stands and the bronze sea that were in the house of the LORD, the Chaldeans broke in pieces, and carried the bronze to Babylon. 14They took away the pots, the shovels, the snuffers, the dishes for incense, and all the bronze vessels used in the temple service, 15as well as the firepans and the basins. What was made of gold the captain of the guard took away for the gold, and what was made of silver, for the silver. 16As for the two pillars, the one sea, and the stands, which Solomon had made for the house of the LORD, the bronze of all these vessels was beyond weighing. 17The height of the one pillar was eighteen cubits, and on it was a bronze capital; the height of the capital was three cubits; lat-

ticework and pomegranates, all of bronze, were on the capital all around. The second pillar had the same, with the latticework. 18 The captain of the guard took the chief priest Seraiah, the second priest Zephaniah, and the three guardians of the threshold; 19from the city he took an officer who had been in command of the soldiers, and five men of the king's council who were found in the city; the secretary who was the commander of the army who mustered the people of the land; and sixty men of the people of the land who were found in the city. 20Nebuzaradan the captain of the guard took them, and brought them to the king of Babylon at Riblah. 21The king of Babylon struck them down and put them to death at Riblah in the land of Hamath. So Judah went into exile out of its land.

24.18–25.21: The reign of Zedekiah and the fall of Jerusalem. This section is very similar to Jer 52, and the first part of it to Jer 39.1–10. **24.20:** Here the Exile* is blamed mostly on Zedekiah and his generation. **25.2–3:** The city of Jerusalem fell to the Babylonians in 587 or 586 BCE. **4:** *The Arabah* means the Jordan valley north of the Dead Sea. **11:** Jeremiah 52.29 gives the number of captives from this deportation as 832. **13–17:** On the items taken from the Temple,* see 1 Kings 7.15–50; Jer 52.17–23. **18–21:** The other leaders of the city who were considered responsible for fostering the rebellion were executed.

~~~~~~

22 He appointed Gedaliah son of Ahikam son of Shaphan as governor over the people who remained in the land of Judah, whom King Nebuchadnezzar of Babylon had left. 23Now when all the captains of the forces and their men heard that the king of Babylon had appointed Gedaliah as governor, they came with their men to Gedaliah at Mizpah, namely, Ishmael son of Nethaniah, Johanan son of Kareah, Seraiah son of Tanhumeth the Netophathite, and Jaazaniah son of the Maacathite. 24Gedaliah swore to them and their men, saying, "Do not be afraid because of the Chaldean officials; live in the land, serve the king of Babylon, and it shall be well

a Heb lacks *wall*　　*b* Gk Compare Jer 39.4; 52.7: Heb lacks *the king* and lacks *fled* with you." 25But in the seventh month, Ishmael son of Nethaniah son of Elishama, of the royal family, came with ten men; they struck down Gedaliah so that he died, along with the Judeans and Chaldeans who were with him at Mizpah. 26Then all the people, high and low,*a* and the captains of the forces set out and went to Egypt; for they were afraid of the Chaldeans.

25.22–26: The rule and assassination of Gedaliah. 22: The word *governor* does not actually appear in the Hebrew text. Gedaliah is not given any title. **23:** The administrative capital was moved from Jerusalem to *Mizpah.* **25:** Perhaps because he was not a descendant of David, *Gedaliah* was regarded as an illegitimate ruler and was assassinated by members of the *royal family.*

27 In the thirty-seventh year of the exile of King Jehoiachin of Judah, in the twelfth month, on the twenty-seventh day of the month, King Evil-merodach of Babylon, in the year that he began to reign, released King Jehoiachin of Judah from prison; 28he spoke kindly to him, and gave him a seat above the other seats of the kings who were with him in Babylon. 29So Jehoiachin put aside his prison clothes. Every day of his life he dined regularly in the king's presence. 30For his allowance, a regular allowance was given him by the king, a portion every day, as long as he lived.

25.27–30: The elevation of Jehoiachin. The year is around 562, so that there is a gap of about 25 years between the events described in these verses and those in the verses immediately preceding. This may indicate that these verses are a later addition. Their purpose is not clear, but some have suggested that they subtly express the possibility that God may again restore the Davidic monarchy. **27–28:** *Evil-merodach* was Awil-Marduk. His reason for releasing Jehoiachin from prison is not made clear. **29–30:** Even though he remained a captive, probably until he died, Jehoiachin's status was enhanced and his life made more comfortable.

a Or *young and old*

1 CHRONICLES

Introduction to 1, 2 Chronicles

The Chronicler offers his readers a history of what was important from the community's (namely Judah's) past, something quite different from the earlier narratives* of 1 and 2 Samuel and 1 and 2 Kings. While the Deuteronomistic* History (Judges through 2 Kings) tries to justify the destruction of both the northern kingdom of Israel and the southern kingdom of Judah by showing how both communities turned their backs on God by practicing idolatry,* the Chronicler is more concerned to present a positive model from Israel's past. Starting with David as an example, the narratives that stand out in the Chronicler's history are those in which the community or king respond faithfully to God, finding unity and security in response. Good kings are those who "seek the LORD," and in return they experience military and economic success, and their subjects experience great joy in gathering before the Temple* in Jerusalem for worship. These positive models are intended to speak to the Chronicler's readers, to convince them that in "seeking the LORD" at the Temple in their own day, they will find their fullest sense of purpose and community.

The narratives of the Chronicler's history abound with historical problems from the view of a modern reader. David makes provision for the use of marble in building the Temple (1 Chr 29.2); however, marble was not used in Jerusalem until the Hellenistic* age seven hundred years later. David collects "10,000 darics" (1 Chr 29.7) for the Temple, a coin of the Persian empire 500 years after the Davidic period. Impossibly large numbers of military forces are mustered in the field (300,000 from Judah, 280,000 from Benjamin, facing a "million" from Egypt; 2 Chr 14.8–9), and stock numbers are often used (for example, Shishak of Egypt attacks with "1,200 chariots and 60,000 chariots," playing on the number 12 and its multiples; 2 Chr 12.3). The Chronicler never mentions David's transgression in taking Bathsheba as wife (2 Sam 11–12), nor for that matter Solomon's fall into idolatry (1 Kings 11). These tendencies are similar to Hellenistic historians of the same general period, suggesting the Chronicler is simply writing about the past with commonly accepted, perhaps even expected, conventions.

Part of the dilemma over the historical value of 1 and 2 Chronicles involves what potential sources the author had at his disposal. The author cites a number of sources that are otherwise unknown; however, the general stylistic uniformity between narratives where sources are mentioned and where none are indicated raises the suspicion that such sources may not have existed. There is no conclusive evidence to support the Chronicler's use of any sources other than 1 Samuel through 2 Kings.

In its original form, the Hebrew Chronicles would have filled one single scroll. Its division into two parts was accomplished when the codex or book-form of transmitting literature became the standard, probably in the early centuries CE.

While numerous proposals have been offered for the date of the Chronicler's composition, perhaps the most telling points are the interest in military matters and the result of "peace" when the community "seeks the LORD." Following the death of Alexander the Great (around 330 BCE), his successors fought incessantly with each other, often across the landscape of Palestine. Archaeological evidence demonstrates that in the last decades of the fourth century BCE nearly every urban center in Palestine suffered military destruction. It was not until the Ptolemaic★ rulers of Egypt suppressed their Syrian rivals that peace came to Palestine in the early second century BCE. In the midst of such turmoil, a message focusing on the peace that "seeking the LORD" might bring would have been particularly powerful.

The author focuses almost exclusively on the events affecting Jerusalem and the Temple. With regard to the Temple, the author shows particular interest in the activities of the priesthood and individuals given prominence in Temple affairs. Many scholars conclude that the author was a member of the Temple priesthood.

READING GUIDE

When recounting a story of Israel's past, the Chronicler skillfully weaves personal encounters and community responses. A characteristic narrative is the account of the reign of Judah's King Asa (2 Chr 14–16). It opens with the land having "rest," in part because Asa "did what was good and right" in God's view and "commanded Judah to seek the LORD" (2 Chr 14.4). He orders his people to build fortifications around the urban areas since "the land is still ours because we have sought the LORD our God . . . and he has given us peace on every side" (2 Chr 14.7). This sense of security is challenged by Zerah the "Ethiopian," who comes with a million-man army to attack Judah. Asa offers a simple petition for help, and "the LORD defeated the Ethiopians" (2 Chr 14.12). Fresh from this great victory, the Chronicler has an otherwise unattested prophet★ confront the king in a decisive way. This is similar to the style of the Greek historian Herodotus, who uses the figures of various wise counselors to present a ruler with a choice to follow wisdom or pride. In Asa's case, it is "Azariah the son of Oded" who gives voice to the central theological theme of the Chronicler: "The LORD is with you, while you are with him. If you seek him, he will be found by you, but if you abandon him, he will abandon you" (2 Chr 15.2). Taking heart from the prophet's message, Asa convenes all his subjects (Judah and Benjamin) as well as those faithful from the northern kingdom who had joined with Judah (2 Chr 15.9–10). After sacrificing to God, the assembled populace "entered into covenant★ to seek the LORD, the God of their ancestors, with all their heart and with all their soul" (v. 12), an echo of Israel's basic credo of Deut 6.4–5. To emphasize the seriousness of this act, the Chronicler adds that whoever did not join with the covenant "should be put to death" (v. 13). Not wanting to close on a negative note, the Chronicler portrays the community enthusiastically embracing this arrangement: "All Judah rejoiced over the oath; for they had sworn with all their heart, and had sought him with their whole desire, and he was found by them, and the LORD gave them rest all around" (v. 15). This is a paradigm that the Chronicler uses frequently: the king being presented with the need to "seek" God and then the community actively and joyously embracing God.

1 Chronicles
1–9   Genealogical★ prologue
10–20   David's reign
21–29   Transition (centrality of the Temple)
2 Chronicles
1–9   Solomon's rule
10–36   Dissolution of Judah

THE GENEALOGICAL* PROLOGUE

Chs. 1–9: The Chronicler begins his history in a way similar to a number of ancient Greek histories by trying to show the internal connectedness of the nation. After tracing the nation's descent from a common stock of ancestors, the historian focuses on the tribe of Judah and the family line of David, which is of central importance to the destiny of Jerusalem.

1 Adam, Seth, Enosh; 2 Kenan, Mahalalel, Jared; 3 Enoch, Methuselah, Lamech; 4 Noah, Shem, Ham, and Japheth.

5 The descendants of Japheth: Gomer, Magog, Madai, Javan, Tubal, Meshech, and Tiras. 6 The descendants of Gomer: Ashkenaz, Diphath,*a* and Togarmah. 7 The descendants of Javan: Elishah, Tarshish, Kittim, and Rodanim.*b*

8 The descendants of Ham: Cush, Egypt, Put, and Canaan. 9 The descendants of Cush: Seba, Havilah, Sabta, Raama, and Sabteca. The descendants of Raamah: Sheba and Dedan. 10 Cush became the father of Nimrod; he was the first to be a mighty one on the earth.

11 Egypt became the father of Ludim, Anamim, Lehabim, Naphtuhim, 12 Pathrusim, Casluhim, and Caphtorim, from whom the Philistines come.*c*

13 Canaan became the father of Sidon his firstborn, and Heth, 14 and the Jebusites, the Amorites, the Girgashites, 15 the Hivites, the Arkites, the Sinites, 16 the Arvadites, the Zemarites, and the Hamathites.

17 The descendants of Shem: Elam, Asshur, Arpachshad, Lud, Aram, Uz, Hul, Gether, and Meshech.*d* 18 Arpachshad became the father of Shelah; and Shelah became the father of Eber. 19 To Eber were born two sons: the name of the one was Peleg (for in his days the earth was divided), and the name of his brother Joktan. 20 Joktan became the father of Almodad, Sheleph, Hazarmaveth, Jerah, 21 Hadoram, Uzal, Diklah, 22 Ebal, Abimael, Sheba, 23 Ophir, Havilah, and Jobab; all these were the descendants of Joktan.

24 Shem, Arpachshad, Shelah; 25 Eber, Peleg, Reu; 26 Serug, Nahor, Terah; 27 Abram, that is, Abraham.

28 The sons of Abraham: Isaac and Ishmael. 29 These are their genealogies: the firstborn of Ishmael, Nebaioth; and Kedar, Adbeel, Mibsam, 30 Mishma, Dumah, Massa, Hadad, Tema, 31 Jetur, Naphish, and Kedemah. These are the sons of Ishmael. 32 The sons of Keturah, Abraham's concubine: she bore Zimran, Jokshan, Medan, Midian, Ishbak, and Shuah. The sons of Jokshan: Sheba and Dedan. 33 The sons of Midian: Ephah, Epher, Hanoch, Abida, and Eldaah. All these were the descendants of Keturah.

34 Abraham became the father of Isaac. The sons of Isaac: Esau and Israel. 35 The sons of Esau: Eliphaz, Reuel, Jeush, Jalam, and Korah. 36 The sons of Eliphaz: Teman, Omar, Zephi, Gatam, Kenaz, Timna, and Amalek. 37 The sons of Reuel: Nahath, Zerah, Shammah, and Mizzah.

38 The sons of Seir: Lotan, Shobal, Zibeon, Anah, Dishon, Ezer, and Dishan. 39 The sons of Lotan: Hori and Homam; and Lotan's sister was Timna. 40 The sons of Shobal: Alian, Manahath, Ebal, Shephi, and Onam. The sons of Zibeon: Aiah and Anah. 41 The sons of Anah: Dishon. The sons of Dishon: Hamran, Eshban, Ithran, and Cheran. 42 The sons of Ezer: Bilhan, Zaavan, and Jaakan.*e* The sons of Dishan:*f* Uz and Aran.

43 These are the kings who reigned in the land of Edom before any king reigned over the Israelites: Bela son of Beor, whose city was called Dinhabah. 44 When Bela died, Jobab son of Zerah of Bozrah succeeded him. 45 When Jobab died, Husham of the land of the Temanites succeeded him. 46 When Husham died, Hadad son of Bedad, who defeated Midian in the country of Moab, succeeded him; and the name of his city was Avith. 47 When Hadad died, Samlah of Masrekah succeeded him. 48 When Samlah died, Shaul*g* of Rehoboth on the Euphrates succeeded him. 49 When Shaul*g* died, Baal-

a Gen 10.3 Ripath; See Gk Vg   b Gen 10.4 Dodanim; See Syr Vg   c Heb Casluhim, from which the Philistines come, Caphtorim; See Am 9.7, Jer 47.4
d Mash in Gen 10.23   e Or and Akan; See Gen 36.27
f See 1.38: Heb Dishon   g Or Saul

hanan son of Achbor succeeded him. [50]When Baal-hanan died, Hadad succeeded him; the name of his city was Pai, and his wife's name Mehetabel daughter of Matred, daughter of Me-zahab. [51]And Hadad died.

The clans[a] of Edom were: clans[a] Timna, Aliah,[b] Jetheth, [52]Oholibamah, Elah, Pinon, [53]Kenaz, Teman, Mibzar, [54]Magdiel, and Iram; these are the clans[a] of Edom.

1.1–54: Genealogy* of the ancestors. Summarizing much information from Genesis, the Chronicler starts with Adam and takes the sequence down to Jacob (also known as Israel). **43:** *These are the kings who reigned in the land of Edom:* Located to the southeast of the land of Judah and on the other side of the Jordan valley, Edom was always recognized as having a close relationship to Judah. Israel also recognized that Edom had adopted a monarchic form of political organization before Israel had embraced monarchy. **51:** *The clans* of Edom:* In Hebrew the word for "clans" is normally translated as "chiefs." Prior to the emergence of David and the Judean monarchy, Edom was an independent kingdom; however, David was able to assert control over Edom and reduce its leaders to "chiefs."

~~~

2 These are the sons of Israel: Reuben, Simeon, Levi, Judah, Issachar, Zebulun, [2]Dan, Joseph, Benjamin, Naphtali, Gad, and Asher. [3]The sons of Judah: Er, Onan, and Shelah; these three the Canaanite woman Bath-shua bore to him. Now Er, Judah's firstborn, was wicked in the sight of the Lord, and he put him to death. [4]His daughter-in-law Tamar also bore him Perez and Zerah. Judah had five sons in all.

5 The sons of Perez: Hezron and Hamul. [6]The sons of Zerah: Zimri, Ethan, Heman, Calcol, and Dara,[c] five in all. [7]The sons of Carmi: Achar, the troubler of Israel, who transgressed in the matter of the devoted thing; [8]and Ethan's son was Azariah.

2.1–4.23: The tribe of Judah and the line of David. The Chronicler writes from a Judean perspective, emphasizing the events of the southern kingdom as though they were decisive for the larger fate of "all Israel." Accordingly, the lineage of the tribe of Judah and the line of David were of special concern. Their priority for the author is apparent by their placement

first in the lineage of Israel. **2.4:** *His daughter-in-law Tamar also bore him Perez* alludes to the narrative* in Gen 38 where Tamar must seduce Judah by deceit to gain her legitimate rights. David comes from the "Perez" line of the clan.* **7:** *The sons of Carmi: Achar, the troubler of Israel:* Carmi was a descendant of Zerah's line. Achan (for which the Chronicler uses Achar) appears in Josh 7.1–26, where he violates the command to destroy all the possessions of the inhabitants of Jericho. The notice of Zerah's line may have brought to the author's mind the incident with Achar. *Troubler* is a Hebrew pun, a word sounding similar to Achar (see Jn 7.24).

~~~

9 The sons of Hezron, who were born to him: Jerahmeel, Ram, and Chelubai. [10]Ram became the father of Amminadab, and Amminadab became the father of Nahshon, prince of the sons of Judah. [11]Nahshon became the father of Salma, Salma of Boaz, [12]Boaz of Obed, Obed of Jesse. [13]Jesse became the father of Eliab his firstborn, Abinadab the second, Shimea the third, [14]Nethanel the fourth, Raddai the fifth, [15]Ozem the sixth, David the seventh; [16]and their sisters were Zeruiah and Abigail. The sons of Zeruiah: Abishai, Joab, and Asahel, three. [17]Abigail bore Amasa, and the father of Amasa was Jether the Ishmaelite.

18 Caleb son of Hezron had children by his wife Azubah, and by Jerioth; these were her sons: Jesher, Shobab, and Ardon. [19]When Azubah died, Caleb married Ephrath, who bore him Hur. [20]Hur became the father of Uri, and Uri became the father of Bezalel.

21 Afterward Hezron went in to the daughter of Machir father of Gilead, whom he married when he was sixty years old; and she bore him Segub; [22]and Segub became the father of Jair, who had twenty-three towns in the land of Gilead. [23]But Geshur and Aram took from them Havvoth-jair, Kenath and its villages, sixty towns. All these were descendants of Machir, father of Gilead. [24]After the death of Hezron, in Caleb-ephrathah, Abijah wife of Hezron bore him Ashhur, father of Tekoa.

a Or *chiefs*   b Or *Alvah*; See Gen 36.40
c Or *Darda*; Compare Syr Tg some Gk Mss; See
1 Kings 4.31

2.9–24. 10: *Nahshon, prince of the sons of Judah:* The term for "prince" (Heb., "nasi") had a variety of meanings in antiquity. Nahshon may be described in this way to highlight the line of David, since Nahshon's sister married Moses' brother Aaron (Ex 6.23) and thus helped form the primary line of Israel's priesthood. Such a connection would tie the royal and priestly family lines together. **13:** *Jesse became the father of:* The narrative posits ten generations from Judah to Jesse, directly tying the ancestry of David's father to a founder of the nation. **21:** *Machir father of Gilead:* The genealogies* use the term "father" to refer to a person or family lineage that made up a portion of the population of a specific place.

25 The sons of Jerahmeel, the firstborn of Hezron: Ram his firstborn, Bunah, Oren, Ozem, and Ahijah. 26 Jerahmeel also had another wife, whose name was Atarah; she was the mother of Onam. 27 The sons of Ram, the firstborn of Jerahmeel: Maaz, Jamin, and Eker. 28 The sons of Onam: Shammai and Jada. The sons of Shammai: Nadab and Abishur. 29 The name of Abishur's wife was Abihail, and she bore him Ahban and Molid. 30 The sons of Nadab: Seled and Appaim; and Seled died childless. 31 The son*a* of Appaim: Ishi. The son*a* of Ishi: Sheshan. The son*a* of Sheshan: Ahlai. 32 The sons of Jada, Shammai's brother: Jether and Jonathan; and Jether died childless. 33 The sons of Jonathan: Peleth and Zaza. These were the descendants of Jerahmeel. 34 Now Sheshan had no sons, only daughters; but Sheshan had an Egyptian slave, whose name was Jarha. 35 So Sheshan gave his daughter in marriage to his slave Jarha; and she bore him Attai. 36 Attai became the father of Nathan, and Nathan of Zabad. 37 Zabad became the father of Ephlal, and Ephlal of Obed. 38 Obed became the father of Jehu, and Jehu of Azariah. 39 Azariah became the father of Helez, and Helez of Eleasah. 40 Eleasah became the father of Sismai, and Sismai of Shallum. 41 Shallum became the father of Jekamiah, and Jekamiah of Elishama.

42 The sons of Caleb brother of Jerahmeel: Mesha*b* his firstborn, who was father of Ziph. The sons of Mareshah father of Hebron. 43 The sons of Hebron: Korah, Tappuah, Rekem, and Shema. 44 Shema became father of Raham, father of Jorkeam; and Rekem became the father of Shammai. 45 The son of Shammai: Maon; and Maon was the father of Beth-zur. 46 Ephah also, Caleb's concubine, bore Haran, Moza, and Gazez; and Haran became the father of Gazez. 47 The sons of Jahdai: Regem, Jotham, Geshan, Pelet, Ephah, and Shaaph. 48 Maacah, Caleb's concubine, bore Sheber and Tirhanah. 49 She also bore Shaaph father of Madmannah, Sheva father of Machbenah and father of Gibea; and the daughter of Caleb was Achsah. 50 These were the descendants of Caleb.

The sons*c* of Hur the firstborn of Ephrathah: Shobal father of Kiriath-jearim, 51 Salma father of Bethlehem, and Hareph father of Beth-gader. 52 Shobal father of Kiriath-jearim had other sons: Haroeh, half of the Menuhoth. 53 And the families of Kiriath-jearim: the Ithrites, the Puthites, the Shumathites, and the Mishraites; from these came the Zorathites and the Eshtaolites. 54 The sons of Salma: Bethlehem, the Netophathites, Atroth-beth-joab, and half of the Manahathites, the Zorites. 55 The families also of the scribes that lived at Jabez: the Tirathites, the Shimeathites, and the Sucathites. These are the Kenites who came from Hammath, father of the house of Rechab.

3 These are the sons of David who were born to him in Hebron: the firstborn Amnon, by Ahinoam the Jezreelite; the second Daniel, by Abigail the Carmelite; 2 the third Absalom, son of Maacah, daughter of King Talmai of Geshur; the fourth Adonijah, son of Haggith; 3 the fifth Shephatiah, by Abital; the sixth Ithream, by his wife Eglah; 4 six were born to him in Hebron, where he reigned for seven years and six months. And he reigned thirty-three years in Jerusalem. 5 These were born to him in Jerusalem: Shimea, Shobab, Nathan, and Solomon, four by Bath-shua, daughter of Ammiel; 6 then Ibhar, Elishama, Eliphelet, 7 Nogah, Nepheg, Japhia, 8 Elishama, Eliada, and

a Heb *sons*   *b* Gk reads *Mareshah*   *c* Gk Vg: Heb *son*

Eliphelet, nine. [9] All these were David's sons, besides the sons of the concubines; and Tamar was their sister.

10 The descendants of Solomon: Rehoboam, Abijah his son, Asa his son, Jehoshaphat his son, [11] Joram his son, Ahaziah his son, Joash his son, [12] Amaziah his son, Azariah his son, Jotham his son, [13] Ahaz his son, Hezekiah his son, Manasseh his son, [14] Amon his son, Josiah his son. [15] The sons of Josiah: Johanan the firstborn, the second Jehoiakim, the third Zedekiah, the fourth Shallum. [16] The descendants of Jehoiakim: Jeconiah his son, Zedekiah his son; [17] and the sons of Jeconiah, the captive: Shealtiel his son, [18] Malchiram, Pedaiah, Shenazzar, Jekamiah, Hoshama, and Nedabiah; [19] The sons of Pedaiah: Zerubbabel and Shimei; and the sons of Zerubbabel: Meshullam and Hananiah, and Shelomith was their sister; [20] and Hashubah, Ohel, Berechiah, Hasadiah, and Jushab-hesed, five. [21] The sons of Hananiah: Pelatiah and Jeshaiah, his son[a] Rephaiah, his son[a] Arnan, his son[a] Obadiah, his son[a] Shecaniah. [22] The son[b] of Shecaniah: Shemaiah. And the sons of Shemaiah: Hattush, Igal, Bariah, Neariah, and Shaphat, six. [23] The sons of Neariah: Elioenai, Hizkiah, and Azrikam, three. [24] The sons of Elioenai: Hodaviah, Eliashib, Pelaiah, Akkub, Johanan, Delaiah, and Anani, seven.

3.1–24. 1: *These are the sons of David:* This unit begins with the notice of the sons born to David while he reigned as king in Hebron, a time quickly skipped over by the author in the subsequent narratives.* Much of the material is rearranged from several places in 2 Samuel. 10: *The descendants of Solomon* introduces a new listing highlighting the royal succession of the southern kingdom. Of particular interest are the lines extending into the period of the Exile* and beyond, ending sometime in the fourth century BCE. 19: *The sons of Pedaiah: Zerubbabel:* Presumably the author means the same Zerubbabel who acted as governor of the province of Yehud (post-exilic Judah) for the Persians (see Hag 1.1, Ezra 3.2). The Greek Old Testament has a reading of "the sons of Shealtiel" here, which may reflect an effort to harmonize the genealogical* information here with that in other biblical sources such as Ezra. *And Shelomith was their sister:* Shelomith, the only female mentioned in the course of the

royal lineage, is prominently featured in a post-exilic seal impression as the "noble wife" of Elnathan, a Persian period governor who served sometime after Zerubbabel. Elnathan may have been using his marriage to a member of the Davidic lineage to help legitimate his political authority.

4 The sons of Judah: Perez, Hezron, Carmi, Hur, and Shobal. [2] Reaiah son of Shobal became the father of Jahath, and Jahath became the father of Ahumai and Lahad. These were the families of the Zorathites. [3] These were the sons[c] of Etam: Jezreel, Ishma, and Idbash; and the name of their sister was Hazzelelponi, [4] and Penuel was the father of Gedor, and Ezer the father of Hushah. These were the sons of Hur, the firstborn of Ephrathah, the father of Bethlehem. [5] Ashhur father of Tekoa had two wives, Helah and Naarah; [6] Naarah bore him Ahuzzam, Hepher, Temeni, and Haahashtari.[d] These were the sons of Naarah. [7] The sons of Helah: Zereth, Izhar,[e] and Ethnan. [8] Koz became the father of Anub, Zobebah, and the families of Aharhel son of Harum. [9] Jabez was honored more than his brothers; and his mother named him Jabez, saying, "Because I bore him in pain." [10] Jabez called on the God of Israel, saying, "Oh that you would bless me and enlarge my border, and that your hand might be with me, and that you would keep me from hurt and harm!" And God granted what he asked. [11] Chelub the brother of Shuhah became the father of Mehir, who was the father of Eshton. [12] Eshton became the father of Beth-rapha, Paseah, and Tehinnah the father of Ir-nahash. These are the men of Recah. [13] The sons of Kenaz: Othniel and Seraiah; and the sons of Othniel: Hathath and Meonothai.[f] [14] Meonothai became the father of Ophrah; and Seraiah became the father of Joab father of Ge-harashim,[g] so-called because they were artisans. [15] The sons of Caleb son of Jephunneh: Iru, Elah, and Naam; and the son[b] of

a Gk Compare Syr Vg: Heb *sons of*   b Heb *sons*
c Gk Compare Vg: Heb *the father*   d Or *Ahashtari*
e Another reading is *Zohar*   f Gk Vg: Heb lacks *and Meonothai*   g That is *Valley of artisans*

Elah: Kenaz. 16The sons of Jehallelel: Ziph, Ziphah, Tiria, and Asarel. 17The sons of Ezrah: Jether, Mered, Epher, and Jalon. These are the sons of Bithiah, daughter of Pharaoh, whom Mered married;*a* and she conceived and bore*b* Miriam, Shammai, and Ishbah father of Eshtemoa. 18And his Judean wife bore Jered father of Gedor, Heber father of Soco, and Jekuthiel father of Zanoah. 19The sons of the wife of Hodiah, the sister of Naham, were the fathers of Keilah the Garmite and Eshtemoa the Maacathite. 20The sons of Shimon: Amnon, Rinnah, Ben-hanan, and Tilon. The sons of Ishi: Zoheth and Ben-zoheth. 21The sons of Shelah son of Judah: Er father of Lecah, Laadah father of Mareshah, and the families of the guild of linen workers at Beth-ashbea; 22and Jokim, and the men of Cozeba, and Joash, and Saraph, who married into Moab but returned to Lehem*c* (now the records*d* are ancient). 23These were the potters and inhabitants of Netaim and Gederah; they lived there with the king in his service.

4.1–23. 1: *The sons of Judah:* With this phrase the author returns to the point with which the list began (at 2.3), now with the intent of tracing the other branches of this clan.* This material has proven to be very difficult to interpret since the genealogies* are not fully integrated. The author may be compiling material from several different sources. 4: *The father of Bethlehem:* The author again uses family terminology to indicate a portion of the clan that had been responsible for settling well-known locales. 9: *Jabez was honored more than his brothers:* Unattested otherwise in the Old Testament, this notice reflects extraordinary efforts to justify a name. The name "Jabez" means "pain" in Hebrew, even though this individual was honored. Being "honored" more than his brothers may mean that he received a bigger portion of the family inheritance. He also appealed to God for protection that none would cause him pain, ensuring that his name would not lead to harm. 22: *Now the records are ancient:* The term for "records" is more openended, usually translated "matters." The author may simply be indicating he knows nothing beyond the bare facts that these named individuals went to Moab and returned. It is such a scenario that underlies the opening of the book of Ruth.

24 The sons of Simeon: Nemuel, Jamin, Jarib, Zerah, Shaul;*e* 25Shallum was his son, Mibsam his son, Mishma his son. 26The sons of Mishma: Hammuel his son, Zaccur his son, Shimei his son. 27Shimei had sixteen sons and six daughters; but his brothers did not have many children, nor did all their family multiply like the Judeans. 28They lived in Beer-sheba, Moladah, Hazar-shual, 29Bilhah, Ezem, Tolad, 30Bethuel, Hormah, Ziklag, 31Beth-marcaboth, Hazar-susim, Beth-biri, and Shaaraim. These were their towns until David became king. 32And their villages were Etam, Ain, Rimmon, Tochen, and Ashan, five towns, 33along with all their villages that were around these towns as far as Baal. These were their settlements. And they kept a genealogical record.

34 Meshobab, Jamlech, Joshah son of Amaziah, 35Joel, Jehu son of Joshibiah son of Seraiah son of Asiel, 36Elioenai, Jaakobah, Jeshohaiah, Asaiah, Adiel, Jesimiel, Benaiah, 37Ziza son of Shiphi son of Allon son of Jedaiah son of Shimri son of Shemaiah— 38these mentioned by name were leaders in their families, and their clans increased greatly. 39They journeyed to the entrance of Gedor, to the east side of the valley, to seek pasture for their flocks, 40where they found rich, good pasture, and the land was very broad, quiet, and peaceful; for the former inhabitants there belonged to Ham. 41These, registered by name, came in the days of King Hezekiah of Judah, and attacked their tents and the Meunim who were found there, and exterminated them to this day, and settled in their place, because there was pasture there for their flocks. 42And some of them, five hundred men of the Simeonites, went to Mount Seir, having as their leaders Pelatiah, Neariah, Rephaiah, and Uzziel, sons of Ishi; 43they destroyed the remnant of the Amalekites that had escaped, and they have lived there to this day.

4.24–43: **The tribe of Simeon.** Since the author has begun with Judah, it makes some sense to continue the examination of Israel by turning to the family

a The clause: *These are . . . married* is transposed from verse 18   b Heb lacks *and bore*   c Vg Compare Gk: Heb *and Jashubi-lahem*   d Or *matters*   e Or *Saul* group of Simeon, a tribe connected with Judah both by birth (Judah and Simeon were Jacob's sons by the same mother) and by proximity. **28:** *They lived in Beer-sheba:* These places all lie along the extreme southern edge of Judean settlements fringing the Negev desert. **31:** *Until David became king* may mean that these were self-governing cities until they became part of the Davidic kingdom. **39:** *They journeyed to the entrance of Gedor:* The Greek version has "Gerar," which some believe is a more appropriate setting for the story. Gedor is a common place name; either name would place the valley to the west of the Judean heartland. **43:** *They destroyed the remnant of the Amalekites,* one of the peoples inhabiting Canaan prior to Israel's taking of the land. Mt. Seir is normally located on the other side of the Jordan valley in territory controlled by Edom. This territorial claim may indicate some expansion of clan* elements into the southeastern regions outside of Judah.

5 The sons of Reuben the firstborn of Israel. (He was the firstborn, but because he defiled his father's bed his birthright was given to the sons of Joseph son of Israel, so that he is not enrolled in the genealogy according to the birthright; ²though Judah became prominent among his brothers and a ruler came from him, yet the birthright belonged to Joseph.) ³The sons of Reuben, the firstborn of Israel: Hanoch, Pallu, Hezron, and Carmi. ⁴The sons of Joel: Shemaiah his son, Gog his son, Shimei his son, ⁵Micah his son, Reaiah his son, Baal his son, ⁶Beerah his son, whom King Tilgath-pilneser of Assyria carried away into exile; he was a chieftain of the Reubenites. ⁷And his kindred by their families, when the genealogy of their generations was reckoned: the chief, Jeiel, and Zechariah, ⁸and Bela son of Azaz, son of Shema, son of Joel, who lived in Aroer, as far as Nebo and Baal-meon. ⁹He also lived to the east as far as the beginning of the desert this side of the Euphrates, because their cattle had multiplied in the land of Gilead. ¹⁰And in the days of Saul they made war on the Hagrites, who fell by their hand; and they lived in their tents throughout all the region east of Gilead.

5.1–10: The tribe of Reuben. The Chronicler begins a consideration of the tribes of Israel that settled on

the other side of the Jordan. Reference to Simeon's taking territory near Mt. Seir in the preceding chapter may have been intended as the bridge to this block of material. Otherwise, there is no apparent explanation for moving to the traditions of Reuben, the "firstborn" of Jacob. **1:** *Because he defiled his father's bed* is a reference to Reuben's encounter with Bilhah, one of his father's concubines* (Gen 35.22). **6:** *Whom King Tilgath-pilneser of Assyria carried away into exile* is a reference to Tiglath-pilesar III, the Assyrian king most responsible for the westward expansion of Assyria. In 733–732 BCE, he led a campaign into Galilee and the eastern side of the Jordan, which would fit with the author's comment.

11 The sons of Gad lived beside them in the land of Bashan as far as Salecah: ¹²Joel the chief, Shapham the second, Janai, and Shaphat in Bashan. ¹³And their kindred according to their clans: Michael, Meshullam, Sheba, Jorai, Jacan, Zia, and Eber, seven. ¹⁴These were the sons of Abihail son of Huri, son of Jaroah, son of Gilead, son of Michael, son of Jeshishai, son of Jahdo, son of Buz; ¹⁵Ahi son of Abdiel, son of Guni, was chief in their clan; ¹⁶and they lived in Gilead, in Bashan and in its towns, and in all the pasture lands of Sharon to their limits. ¹⁷All of these were enrolled by genealogies in the days of King Jotham of Judah, and in the days of King Jeroboam of Israel.

5.11–17: The tribe of Gad. Following the pattern of reviewing the tribes that settled on the eastern side of the Jordan Valley, the author provides an overview of Gad, usually the eleventh son of Jacob. Structurally, this section is very similar to the previous section on Reuben, and seems unrelated to any other biblical records of the Gadites. **16:** *And in all the pasture lands of Sharon:* This is not the "Sharon" south of the Carmel range along the coastal plain of Israel, but a region north of Moab. All the place names in this narrative* point to a location near the modern Golan.

18 The Reubenites, the Gadites, and the half-tribe of Manasseh had valiant warriors, who carried shield and sword, and drew the bow, expert in war, forty-four thousand seven hundred sixty, ready for service. ¹⁹They made war on the Hagrites, Jetur, Naphish, and Nodab; ²⁰and when they received

help against them, the Hagrites and all who were with them were given into their hands, for they cried to God in the battle, and he granted their entreaty because they trusted in him. 21 They captured their livestock: fifty thousand of their camels, two hundred fifty thousand sheep, two thousand donkeys, and one hundred thousand captives. 22 Many fell slain, because the war was of God. And they lived in their territory until the exile.

5.18–22: The Transjordan war. In the process of reviewing those tribes of Israel who settled in the Transjordan, the Chronicler includes a brief battle narrative* that features all of the tribes to the east of the Jordan cooperating in a major military campaign. The language and theme are characteristic of the Chronicler, suggesting that if a source was used, the Chronicler has thoroughly reworked it. **18:** *Who carried shield and sword, and drew the bow:* This string of descriptive terms indicates a professional, trained military force as opposed to the more common citizen militia. The author is deeply concerned with military matters. **19:** *They made war on the Hagrites, Jetur, Naphish, and Nodab:* These are groups identified in Genesis as descendants of Ishamael. **20:** *For they cried to God in the battle, and he granted their entreaty:* For the Chronicler, military success depends upon seeking divine assistance.

23 The members of the half-tribe of Manasseh lived in the land; they were very numerous from Bashan to Baal-hermon, Senir, and Mount Hermon. 24 These were the heads of their clans: Epher,[a] Ishi, Eliel, Azriel, Jeremiah, Hodaviah, and Jahdiel, mighty warriors, famous men, heads of their clans. 25 But they transgressed against the God of their ancestors, and prostituted themselves to the gods of the peoples of the land, whom God had destroyed before them. 26 So the God of Israel stirred up the spirit of King Pul of Assyria, the spirit of King Tilgath-pilneser of Assyria, and he carried them away, namely, the Reubenites, the Gadites, and the half-tribe of Manasseh, and brought them to Halah, Habor, Hara, and the river Gozan, to this day.

5.23–26: The half-tribe of Manasseh. While a portion of this tribe settled in the central hill country of Sa-

maria, a portion also settled in the Transjordan. The place names indicate an impossibly large area for effective control; the author may mean that members of this tribe were scattered throughout this extensive area. **25:** *But they transgressed against the God of their ancestors:* Following on the Deuteronomistic* History's judgment against the northern kingdom on account of idolatry,* the Chronicler sees idolatry— "prostituting themselves"—as the fundamental reason for their subsequent exile by the Assyrians. There is an ironic* contrast intended here: Just as their common seeking of divine assistance in battle had led to their success, their common departure from God by committing idolatry caused the Transjordanian tribes to be exiled.

6 [b] The sons of Levi: Gershom,[c] Kohath, and Merari. 2 The sons of Kohath: Amram, Izhar, Hebron, and Uzziel. 3 The children of Amram: Aaron, Moses, and Miriam. The sons of Aaron: Nadab, Abihu, Eleazar, and Ithamar. 4 Eleazar became the father of Phinehas, Phinehas of Abishua, 5 Abishua of Bukki, Bukki of Uzzi, 6 Uzzi of Zerahiah, Zerahiah of Meraioth, 7 Meraioth of Amariah, Amariah of Ahitub, 8 Ahitub of Zadok, Zadok of Ahimaaz, 9 Ahimaaz of Azariah, Azariah of Johanan, 10 and Johanan of Azariah (it was he who served as priest in the house that Solomon built in Jerusalem). 11 Azariah became the father of Amariah, Amariah of Ahitub, 12 Ahitub of Zadok, Zadok of Shallum, 13 Shallum of Hilkiah, Hilkiah of Azariah, 14 Azariah of Seraiah, Seraiah of Jehozadak; 15 and Jehozadak went into exile when the LORD sent Judah and Jerusalem into exile by the hand of Nebuchadnezzar.

16 [d] The sons of Levi: Gershom, Kohath, and Merari. 17 These are the names of the sons of Gershom: Libni and Shimei. 18 The sons of Kohath: Amram, Izhar, Hebron, and Uzziel. 19 The sons of Merari: Mahli and Mushi. These are the clans of the Levites according to their ancestry. 20 Of Gershom: Libni his son, Jahath his son, Zimmah his son, 21 Joah his son, Iddo his son, Zerah his son, Jeatherai his son. 22 The sons of Kohath:

a Gk Vg: Heb *and Epher*   *b* Ch 5.27 in Heb
c Heb *Gershon,* variant of *Gershom;* See 6.16
d Ch 6.1 in Heb

Amminadab his son, Korah his son, Assir his son, 23Elkanah his son, Ebiasaph his son, Assir his son, 24Tahath his son, Uriel his son, Uzziah his son, and Shaul his son. 25The sons of Elkanah: Amasai and Ahimoth, 26Elkanah his son, Zophai his son, Nahath his son, 27Eliab his son, Jeroham his son, Elkanah his son. 28The sons of Samuel: Joel*a* his firstborn, the second Abijah.*b* 29The sons of Merari: Mahli, Libni his son, Shimei his son, Uzzah his son, 30Shimea his son, Haggiah his son, and Asaiah his son.

31 These are the men whom David put in charge of the service of song in the house of the LORD, after the ark came to rest there. 32They ministered with song before the tabernacle of the tent of meeting, until Solomon had built the house of the LORD in Jerusalem; and they performed their service in due order. 33These are the men who served; and their sons were: Of the Kohathites: Heman, the singer, son of Joel, son of Samuel, 34son of Elkanah, son of Jeroham, son of Eliel, son of Toah, 35son of Zuph, son of Elkanah, son of Mahath, son of Amasai, 36son of Elkanah, son of Joel, son of Azariah, son of Zephaniah, 37son of Tahath, son of Assir, son of Ebiasaph, son of Korah, 38son of Izhar, son of Kohath, son of Levi, son of Israel; 39and his brother Asaph, who stood on his right, namely, Asaph son of Berechiah, son of Shimea, 40son of Michael, son of Baaseiah, son of Malchijah, 41son of Ethni, son of Zerah, son of Adaiah, 42son of Ethan, son of Zimmah, son of Shimei, 43son of Jahath, son of Gershom, son of Levi. 44On the left were their kindred the sons of Merari: Ethan son of Kishi, son of Abdi, son of Malluch, 45son of Hashabiah, son of Amaziah, son of Hilkiah, 46son of Amzi, son of Bani, son of Shemer, 47son of Mahli, son of Mushi, son of Merari, son of Levi; 48and their kindred the Levites were appointed for all the service of the tabernacle of the house of God.

6.1–66: Priests—Levites and Aaronides. This section, along with that devoted to the tribe of Judah, represents the most elaborate portion of the genealogical* prologue. From the Chronicler's viewpoint, the tribe of Levi and the formal Temple* service responsibilities that only this family can undertake for Israel are of crit-

ical importance for Israel's destiny. By the time of the Chronicler's history, the priesthood of Israel had been segmented into various family lines with differing responsibilities and social standings. Those who belonged to the sons of Aaron were eligible for the high priesthood, the chief administrative office of the Temple.* Those who belonged to the various lines of the Levites other than Aaron's had lesser roles in the Temple. The Chronicler begins consideration of this important family group by tracing the line of Aaron, but with several omissions and rearrangements. **3:** *The children of Amram: Aaron, Moses, and Miriam:* This remarkable family group, which by tradition had offered significant leadership in Israel's early history, is linked to the Levitical tribe. Miriam is the only female in this lineage. **28:** *The sons of Samuel:* With the judgment against Elkanah's line for abuse of their office (1 Sam 2.27–36), Samuel takes on the role of chief priest, thus the Chronicler's interest in his line. **31:** *These are the men whom David put in charge of the service of song:* Although David's son Solomon is the one who built the Temple, the Chronicler asserts that all the main elements of Temple worship were put in place by David. He justifies this perspective by noting that such worship was instigated "after the ark came to rest there," assuming that once the ark had been brought into Jerusalem, regular formal worship would be required. While it is not historically implausible that David would have authorized the formation of dedicated musicians for worship prior to the foundation of the Temple, this elaborate form of the organization suggests the Chronicler is referring to the form of Temple music professionals of his own day.

49 But Aaron and his sons made offerings on the altar of burnt offering and on the altar of incense, doing all the work of the most holy place, to make atonement for Israel, according to all that Moses the servant of God had commanded. 50These are the sons of Aaron: Eleazar his son, Phinehas his son, Abishua his son, 51Bukki his son, Uzzi his son, Zerahiah his son, 52Meraioth his son, Amariah his son, Ahitub his son, 53Zadok his son, Ahimaaz his son.

54 These are their dwelling places according to their settlements within their bor-

a Gk Syr Compare verse 33 and 1 Sam 8.2: Heb lacks *Joel* *b* Heb reads *Vashni, and Abijah* for *the second Abijah,* taking *the second* as a proper name ders: to the sons of Aaron of the families of Kohathites—for the lot fell to them first—⁵⁵to them they gave Hebron in the land of Judah and its surrounding pasture lands, ⁵⁶but the fields of the city and its villages they gave to Caleb son of Jephunneh. ⁵⁷To the sons of Aaron they gave the cities of refuge: Hebron, Libnah with its pasture lands, Jattir, Eshtemoa with its pasture lands, ⁵⁸Hilen*ᵃ* with its pasture lands, Debir with its pasture lands, ⁵⁹Ashan with its pasture lands, and Beth-shemesh with its pasture lands. ⁶⁰From the tribe of Benjamin, Geba with its pasture lands, Alemeth with its pasture lands, and Anathoth with its pasture lands. All their towns throughout their families were thirteen.

61 To the rest of the Kohathites were given by lot out of the family of the tribe, out of the half-tribe, the half of Manasseh, ten towns. ⁶²To the Gershomites according to their families were allotted thirteen towns out of the tribes of Issachar, Asher, Naphtali, and Manasseh in Bashan. ⁶³To the Merarites according to their families were allotted twelve towns out of the tribes of Reuben, Gad, and Zebulun. ⁶⁴So the people of Israel gave the Levites the towns with their pasture lands. ⁶⁵They also gave them by lot out of the tribes of Judah, Simeon, and Benjamin these towns that are mentioned by name.

66 And some of the families of the sons of Kohath had towns of their territory out of the tribe of Ephraim. ⁶⁷They were given the cities of refuge: Shechem with its pasture lands in the hill country of Ephraim, Gezer with its pasture lands, ⁶⁸Jokmeam with its pasture lands, Beth-horon with its pasture lands, ⁶⁹Aijalon with its pasture lands, Gath-rimmon with its pasture lands; ⁷⁰and out of the half-tribe of Manasseh, Aner with its pasture lands, and Bileam with its pasture lands, for the rest of the families of the Kohathites.

cording to all that *Moses the servant of God had commanded:* The Chronicler presents both Moses and David as sources of the customs that govern Temple service. Efforts to reconstruct the form of the Pentateuch* that the Chronicler used by comparing the regulations he attributed to Moses to the present contents of the Pentateuch have yielded conflicting results. Often the Chronicler freely adapts the regulations of the Pentateuch to fit the circumstances of his narrative.* **54:** *These are their dwelling places:* Drawing largely from the list in Josh 21.5–39, the Chronicler may be including this register to show how the Levites were distributed throughout the territory of Israel, emphasizing their importance to the well-being of the nation.

71 To the Gershomites: out of the half-tribe of Manasseh: Golan in Bashan with its pasture lands and Ashtaroth with its pasture lands; ⁷²and out of the tribe of Issachar: Kedesh with its pasture lands, Daberath*ᵇ* with its pasture lands, ⁷³Ramoth with its pasture lands, and Anem with its pasture lands; ⁷⁴out of the tribe of Asher: Mashal with its pasture lands, Abdon with its pasture lands, ⁷⁵Hukok with its pasture lands, and Rehob with its pasture lands; ⁷⁶and out of the tribe of Naphtali: Kedesh in Galilee with its pasture lands, Hammon with its pasture lands, and Kiriathaim with its pasture lands. ⁷⁷To the rest of the Merarites out of the tribe of Zebulun: Rimmono with its pasture lands, Tabor with its pasture lands, ⁷⁸and across the Jordan from Jericho, on the east side of the Jordan, out of the tribe of Reuben: Bezer in the steppe with its pasture lands, Jahzah with its pasture lands, ⁷⁹Kedemoth with its pasture lands, and Mephaath with its pasture lands; ⁸⁰and out of the tribe of Gad: Ramoth in Gilead with its pasture lands, Mahanaim with its pasture lands, ⁸¹Heshbon with its pasture lands, and Jazer with its pasture lands.

7 The sons*ᶜ* of Issachar: Tola, Puah, Jashub, and Shimron, four. ²The sons of Tola: Uzzi, Rephaiah, Jeriel, Jahmai, Ibsam, and Shemuel, heads of their ancestral houses, namely of Tola, mighty warriors of

---

6.49–66. 49: *But Aaron and his sons made offerings on the altar:* One of the prime distinctions between the line of Aaron and the other members of the tribe of Levi is that the sons of Aaron could offer the sacrifices to atone for sin and purify the worshipper. Ac-

a Other readings *Hilez, Holon;* See Josh 21.15
b Or *Dobrath*   *c* Syr Compare Vg: Heb *And to the sons*

their generations, their number in the days of David being twenty-two thousand six hundred. ³The son*ª* of Uzzi: Izrahiah. And the sons of Izrahiah: Michael, Obadiah, Joel, and Isshiah, five, all of them chiefs; ⁴and along with them, by their generations, according to their ancestral houses, were units of the fighting force, thirty-six thousand, for they had many wives and sons. ⁵Their kindred belonging to all the families of Issachar were in all eighty-seven thousand mighty warriors, enrolled by genealogy.

6 The sons of Benjamin: Bela, Becher, and Jediael, three. ⁷The sons of Bela: Ezbon, Uzzi, Uzziel, Jerimoth, and Iri, five, heads of ancestral houses, mighty warriors; and their enrollment by genealogies was twenty-two thousand thirty-four. ⁸The sons of Becher: Zemirah, Joash, Eliezer, Elioenai, Omri, Jeremoth, Abijah, Anathoth, and Alemeth. All these were the sons of Becher; ⁹and their enrollment by genealogies, according to their generations, as heads of their ancestral houses, mighty warriors, was twenty thousand two hundred. ¹⁰The sons of Jediael: Bilhan. And the sons of Bilhan: Jeush, Benjamin, Ehud, Chenaanah, Zethan, Tarshish, and Ahishahar. ¹¹All these were the sons of Jediael according to the heads of their ancestral houses, mighty warriors, seventeen thousand two hundred, ready for service in war. ¹²And Shuppim and Huppim were the sons of Ir, Hushim the son*ª* of Aher.

13 The descendants of Naphtali: Jahziel, Guni, Jezer, and Shallum, the descendants of Bilhah.

7.1–13. 1–5: The tribe of Issachar. The Chronicler had limited knowledge of this northern tribe. His characteristic interest in military factors is evident throughout. 6–12: The tribe of Benjamin. This is the first of two sections dealing with this important tribe. In this section, the Chronicler's military interests predominate. 13: The tribe of Naphtali. The brevity of this section indicates how little the Chronicler knew in his day of this northern tribe.

14 The sons of Manasseh: Asriel, whom his Aramean concubine bore; she bore Machir the father of Gilead. ¹⁵And Machir took a wife for Huppim and for Shuppim. The name of his sister was Maacah. And the name of the second was Zelophehad; and Zelophehad had daughters. ¹⁶Maacah the wife of Machir bore a son, and she named him Peresh; the name of his brother was Sheresh; and his sons were Ulam and Rekem. ¹⁷The son*ª* of Ulam: Bedan. These were the sons of Gilead son of Machir, son of Manasseh. ¹⁸And his sister Hammolecheth bore Ishhod, Abiezer, and Mahlah. ¹⁹The sons of Shemida were Ahian, Shechem, Likhi, and Aniam.

7.14–19: The tribe of Manasseh. This section recounts the lineage of the tribe that settled in the central Samarian hill country, as opposed to the portion that settled in the Transjordan. This section has a number of grammatical and textual difficulties, suggesting that the received form has been corrupted. 15: And Zelophehad had daughters: This is a reference to a significant question concerning the inheritance of property in the absence of a male heir (Num 26.33; 27.1–11; 36.1–12).

20 The sons of Ephraim: Shuthelah, and Bered his son, Tahath his son, Eleadah his son, Tahath his son, ²¹Zabad his son, Shuthelah his son, and Ezer and Elead. Now the people of Gath, who were born in the land, killed them, because they came down to raid their cattle. ²²And their father Ephraim mourned many days, and his brothers came to comfort him. ²³Ephraim*ᵇ* went in to his wife, and she conceived and bore a son; and he named him Beriah, because disaster*ᶜ* had befallen his house. ²⁴His daughter was Sheerah, who built both Lower and Upper Beth-horon, and Uzzen-sheerah. ²⁵Rephah was his son, Resheph his son, Telah his son, Tahan his son, ²⁶Ladan his son, Ammihud his son, Elishama his son, ²⁷Nun*ᵈ* his son, Joshua his son. ²⁸Their possessions and settlements were Bethel and its towns, and eastward Naaran, and westward Gezer and its towns, Shechem and its towns, as far as Ayyah and its towns; ²⁹also along the borders of the Manassites, Beth-shean and its towns, Taanach and its towns, Megiddo and its

a Heb *sons*   *b* Heb *He*   *c* Heb *beraah*
d Here spelled *Non*; see Ex 33.11

towns, Dor and its towns. In these lived the sons of Joseph son of Israel.

7.20–29: The tribe of Ephraim. Manasseh and Ephraim were the two sons of Joseph, which may account for the placement of this section. **21:** *Now the people of Gath, who were born in the land:* Gath was normally associated with the Philistines (1 Sam 7.14) and was said to have been the giant Goliath's home (1 Sam 17.4). Being born in the land would mark them as part of the population of Canaan as opposed to the Philistines who, like the Israelites, had come from another place to settle in the land. **24:** *His daughter was Sheerah:* Although founders of cities or other settlements are often noted, this is the only woman credited with founding cities. Upper and Lower Beth-horon were important centers in ancient Israel; Uzzensheerah is otherwise unmentioned in the Bible.

~~~~~~~~~~~~~~~~

30 The sons of Asher: Imnah, Ishvah, Ishvi, Beriah, and their sister Serah. ³¹The sons of Beriah: Heber and Malchiel, who was the father of Birzaith. ³²Heber became the father of Japhlet, Shomer, Hotham, and their sister Shua. ³³The sons of Japhlet: Pasach, Bimhal, and Ashvath. These are the sons of Japhlet. ³⁴The sons of Shemer: Ahi, Rohgah, Hubbah, and Aram. ³⁵The sons of Helem[a] his brother: Zophah, Imna, Shelesh, and Amal. ³⁶The sons of Zophah: Suah, Harnepher, Shual, Beri, Imrah, ³⁷Bezer, Hod, Shamma, Shilshah, Ithran, and Beera. ³⁸The sons of Jether: Jephunneh, Pispa, and Ara. ³⁹The sons of Ulla: Arah, Hanniel, and Rizia. ⁴⁰All of these were men of Asher, heads of ancestral houses, select mighty warriors, chief of the princes. Their number enrolled by genealogies, for service in war, was twenty-six thousand men.

7.30–40: The tribe of Asher. This concise section raises a number of questions: Many of the names are not Hebrew; the list only follows the lineage of Heber; and the number of warriors is low compared to the other tribes. Some suggest the "Heberites" were a mixed group of Israelites and Canaanites who settled on the western fringes of the Samarian hill country.

~~~~~~~~~~~~~~~~

8 Benjamin became the father of Bela his firstborn, Ashbel the second, Aharah the third, ²Nohah the fourth, and Rapha the

fifth. ³And Bela had sons: Addar, Gera, Abihud,[b] ⁴Abishua, Naaman, Ahoah, ⁵Gera, Shephuphan, and Huram. ⁶These are the sons of Ehud (they were heads of ancestral houses of the inhabitants of Geba, and they were carried into exile to Manahath): ⁷Naaman,[c] Ahijah, and Gera, that is, Heglam,[d] who became the father of Uzza and Ahihud. ⁸And Shaharaim had sons in the country of Moab after he had sent away his wives Hushim and Baara. ⁹He had sons by his wife Hodesh: Jobab, Zibia, Mesha, Malcam, ¹⁰Jeuz, Sachia, and Mirmah. These were his sons, heads of ancestral houses. ¹¹He also had sons by Hushim: Abitub and Elpaal. ¹²The sons of Elpaal: Eber, Misham, and Shemed, who built Ono and Lod with its towns, ¹³and Beriah and Shema (they were heads of ancestral houses of the inhabitants of Aijalon, who put to flight the inhabitants of Gath); ¹⁴and Ahio, Shashak, and Jeremoth. ¹⁵Zebadiah, Arad, Eder, ¹⁶Michael, Ishpah, and Joha were sons of Beriah. ¹⁷Zebadiah, Meshullam, Hizki, Heber, ¹⁸Ishmerai, Izliah, and Jobab were the sons of Elpaal. ¹⁹Jakim, Zichri, Zabdi, ²⁰Elienai, Zillethai, Eliel, ²¹Adaiah, Beraiah, and Shimrath were the sons of Shimei. ²²Ishpan, Eber, Eliel, ²³Abdon, Zichri, Hanan, ²⁴Hananiah, Elam, Anthothijah, ²⁵Iphdeiah, and Penuel were the sons of Shashak. ²⁶Shamsherai, Shehariah, Athaliah, ²⁷Jaareshiah, Elijah, and Zichri were the sons of Jeroham. ²⁸These were the heads of ancestral houses, according to their generations, chiefs. These lived in Jerusalem.

29 Jeiel[e] the father of Gibeon lived in Gibeon, and the name of his wife was Maacah. ³⁰His firstborn son: Abdon, then Zur, Kish, Baal,[f] Nadab, ³¹Gedor, Ahio, Zecher, ³²and Mikloth, who became the father of Shimeah. Now these also lived opposite their kindred in Jerusalem, with their kindred. ³³Ner became the father of Kish, Kish of Saul,[g] Saul[g] of Jonathan, Malchishua, Abinadab, and Esh-baal; ³⁴and the son of Jona-

---

a Or *Hotham;* see 7.32　　b Or *father of Ehud;* see 8.6
c Heb *and Naaman*　　d Or *he carried them into exile*
e Compare 9.35: Heb lacks *Jeiel*　　f Gk Ms adds *Ner;*
Compare 8.33 and 9.36　　g Or *Shaul*

than was Merib-baal; and Merib-baal became the father of Micah. ³⁵The sons of Micah: Pithon, Melech, Tarea, and Ahaz. ³⁶Ahaz became the father of Jehoaddah; and Jehoaddah became the father of Alemeth, Azmaveth, and Zimri; Zimri became the father of Moza. ³⁷Moza became the father of Binea; Raphah was his son, Eleasah his son, Azel his son. ³⁸Azel had six sons, and these are their names: Azrikam, Bocheru, Ishmael, Sheariah, Obadiah, and Hanan; all these were the sons of Azel. ³⁹The sons of his brother Eshek: Ulam his firstborn, Jeush the second, and Eliphelet the third. ⁴⁰The sons of Ulam were mighty warriors, archers, having many children and grandchildren, one hundred fifty. All these were Benjaminites.

8.1–40: The tribe of Benjamin. This is the second listing of the Benjaminite tribe. The Chronicler may have needed this additional material to weave several strands of his narrative* together—the relationship of the Benjaminite and Judean tribes; the lineage of Saul, the first king of Israel; and the centrality of Jerusalem. **33:** *Saul of Jonathan, Malchishua, Abinadab, and Eshbaal:* Of note among the family of Saul are several persons bearing names with the Canaanite god Baal's* name. *Eshbaal* means "man of Baal."

9 So all Israel was enrolled by genealogies; and these are written in the Book of the Kings of Israel. And Judah was taken into exile in Babylon because of their unfaithfulness. ²Now the first to live again in their possessions in their towns were Israelites, priests, Levites, and temple servants.

3 And some of the people of Judah, Benjamin, Ephraim, and Manasseh lived in Jerusalem: ⁴Uthai son of Ammihud, son of Omri, son of Imri, son of Bani, from the sons of Perez son of Judah. ⁵And of the Shilonites: Asaiah the firstborn, and his sons. ⁶Of the sons of Zerah: Jeuel and their kin, six hundred ninety. ⁷Of the Benjaminites: Sallu son of Meshullam, son of Hodaviah, son of Hassenuah, ⁸Ibneiah son of Jeroham, Elah son of Uzzi, son of Michri, and Meshullam son of Shephatiah, son of Reuel, son of Ibnijah; ⁹and their kindred according to their

generations, nine hundred fifty-six. All these were heads of families according to their ancestral houses.

9.1–34: The organization of the post-exilic community. This section opens with a summary of what has gone before (vv. 1–2) and moves on to a detailed listing of those responsible for Jerusalem after the return from exile. The Chronicler places characteristic emphasis on the role of the Levites in maintaining proper worship. **2:** *Now the first . . . were Israelites, priests, Levites, and temple servants:* This is a description in brief of the basic social structure, according to the Chronicler, of post-exilic Yehud. The *Israelites* are all those in the population with no formal Temple* function; the *priests* are the sons of Aaron, those entitled to offer the sacrifices on behalf of the worshippers; the *Levites* are those with non-sacrificial responsibilities in the Temple; and the *temple servants* are a class of persons assigned to assist in the mundane functions of the Temple. The Chronicler spends a large portion of this section on those with a connection to the Temple to underscore its importance. **3:** *And some of the people of Judah, Benjamin, Ephraim, and Manasseh lived in Jerusalem:* Sitting on the boundary of the territories settled by Judah and Benjamin, the presence of these family groups is expected. Ephraim and Manasseh, being northern tribes, would not have been expected to appear in this group. However, the Chronicler includes a theme to be developed in the historical narratives:* The participation of elements of Ephraim and Manasseh confirms the ideal of "all Israel" coming together to seek God.

10 Of the priests: Jedaiah, Jehoiarib, Jachin, ¹¹and Azariah son of Hilkiah, son of Meshullam, son of Zadok, son of Meraioth, son of Ahitub, the chief officer of the house of God; ¹²and Adaiah son of Jeroham, son of Pashhur, son of Malchijah, and Maasai son of Adiel, son of Jahzerah, son of Meshullam, son of Meshillemith, son of Immer; ¹³besides their kindred, heads of their ancestral houses, one thousand seven hundred sixty, qualified for the work of the service of the house of God.

14 Of the Levites: Shemaiah son of Hasshub, son of Azrikam, son of Hashabiah, of the sons of Merari; ¹⁵and Bakbakkar, Heresh, Galal, and Mattaniah son of Mica, son

of Zichri, son of Asaph; 16and Obadiah son of Shemaiah, son of Galal, son of Jeduthun, and Berechiah son of Asa, son of Elkanah, who lived in the villages of the Netophathites.

17 The gatekeepers were: Shallum, Akkub, Talmon, Ahiman; and their kindred Shallum was the chief, 18stationed previously in the king's gate on the east side. These were the gatekeepers of the camp of the Levites. 19Shallum son of Kore, son of Ebiasaph, son of Korah, and his kindred of his ancestral house, the Korahites, were in charge of the work of the service, guardians of the thresholds of the tent, as their ancestors had been in charge of the camp of the LORD, guardians of the entrance. 20And Phinehas son of Eleazar was chief over them in former times; the LORD was with him. 21Zechariah son of Meshelemiah was gatekeeper at the entrance of the tent of meeting. 22All these, who were chosen as gatekeepers at the thresholds, were two hundred twelve. They were enrolled by genealogies in their villages. David and the seer Samuel established them in their office of trust. 23So they and their descendants were in charge of the gates of the house of the LORD, that is, the house of the tent, as guards. 24The gatekeepers were on the four sides, east, west, north, and south; 25and their kindred who were in their villages were obliged to come in every seven days, in turn, to be with them; 26for the four chief gatekeepers, who were Levites, were in charge of the chambers and the treasures of the house of God. 27And they would spend the night near the house of God; for on them lay the duty of watching, and they had charge of opening it every morning.

28 Some of them had charge of the utensils of service, for they were required to count them when they were brought in and taken out. 29Others of them were appointed over the furniture, and over all the holy utensils, also over the choice flour, the wine, the oil, the incense, and the spices. 30Others, of the sons of the priests, prepared the mixing of the spices, 31and Mattithiah, one of the Levites, the firstborn of Shallum the Korahite, was in charge of making the flat cakes. 32Also some of their kindred of the Kohathites had charge of the rows of bread, to prepare them for each sabbath.

33 Now these are the singers, the heads of ancestral houses of the Levites, living in the chambers of the temple free from other service, for they were on duty day and night. 34These were heads of ancestral houses of the Levites, according to their generations; these leaders lived in Jerusalem.

9.10–34. 20: *And Phineas . . . was chief over them in former times:* This notice refers to Num 25.1–13, where Phineas kills an Israelite and his Midianite wife for defiling the tent of meeting. It suggests that the *gatekeepers at the entrance* may have had a role in determining who could enter the Levitical orders and who could not. **22:** *David and the seer Samuel established them in their office of trust* is a curious connection of persons since David had little, in fact, to do with Samuel. The text probably recalls Samuel's condemnation of the priest Eli's line for abuse of office (1 Sam 3.10–18) which, in the Chronicler's view, received royal approval by David's founding of the Temple functionaries.

35 In Gibeon lived the father of Gibeon, Jeiel, and the name of his wife was Maacah. 36His firstborn son was Abdon, then Zur, Kish, Baal, Ner, Nadab, 37Gedor, Ahio, Zechariah, and Mikloth; 38and Mikloth became the father of Shimeam; and these also lived opposite their kindred in Jerusalem, with their kindred. 39Ner became the father of Kish, Kish of Saul, Saul of Jonathan, Malchishua, Abinadab, and Esh-baal; 40and the son of Jonathan was Merib-baal; and Merib-baal became the father of Micah. 41The sons of Micah: Pithon, Melech, Tahrea, and Ahaz;ª 42and Ahaz became the father of Jarah, and Jarah of Alemeth, Azmaveth, and Zimri; and Zimri became the father of Moza. 43Moza became the father of Binea; and Rephaiah was his son, Eleasah his son, Azel his son. 44Azel had six sons, and these are their names: Azrikam, Bocheru, Ishmael, Sheariah, Obadiah, and Hanan; these were the sons of Azel.

---

a Compare 8.35: Heb lacks *and Ahaz*

ACCOUNT OF DAVID'S REIGN

Chs. 10–20: These chapters sometimes repeat, and on occasion summarize, portions of the narratives* of David's reign in 2 Sam 5 through 1 Kings 2. Many of these earlier accounts are completely left out by the Chronicler, and others are rewritten so thoroughly as to bear little resemblance to the earlier account. In these narratives, the Chronicler highlights David's success as king and his role in selecting Jerusalem as the capital, along with preparing for the construction and staffing of the Temple.*

10 Now the Philistines fought against Israel; and the men of Israel fled before the Philistines, and fell slain on Mount Gilboa. ²The Philistines overtook Saul and his sons; and the Philistines killed Jonathan and Abinadab and Malchishua, sons of Saul. ³The battle pressed hard on Saul; and the archers found him, and he was wounded by the archers. ⁴Then Saul said to his armor-bearer, "Draw your sword, and thrust me through with it, so that these uncircumcised may not come and make sport of me." But his armor-bearer was unwilling, for he was terrified. So Saul took his own sword and fell on it. ⁵When his armor-bearer saw that Saul was dead, he also fell on his sword and died. ⁶Thus Saul died; he and his three sons and all his house died together. ⁷When all the men of Israel who were in the valley saw that the army[a] had fled and that Saul and his sons were dead, they abandoned their towns and fled; and the Philistines came and occupied them.

8 The next day when the Philistines came to strip the dead, they found Saul and his sons fallen on Mount Gilboa. ⁹They stripped him and took his head and his armor, and sent messengers throughout the land of the Philistines to carry the good news to their idols and to the people. ¹⁰They put his armor in the temple of their gods, and fastened his head in the temple of Dagon. ¹¹But when all Jabesh-gilead heard everything that the Philistines had done to Saul, ¹²all the valiant warriors got up and took away the body of Saul and the bodies of his sons, and brought them to Jabesh. Then they buried their

bones under the oak in Jabesh, and fasted seven days.

13 So Saul died for his unfaithfulness; he was unfaithful to the Lord in that he did not keep the command of the Lord; moreover, he had consulted a medium, seeking guidance, ¹⁴and did not seek guidance from the Lord. Therefore the Lord[b] put him to death and turned the kingdom over to David son of Jesse.

10.1–14: The death of Saul. As Israel's first king, Saul was of particular interest to the writer of 1 and 2 Samuel. In contrast, the Chronicler gives him little notice. **13:** *So Saul died for his unfaithfulness* is the Chronicler's sad commentary on Saul's moral failure, particularly his seeking instruction from someone other than a prophet* of the Lord.

11 Then all Israel gathered together to David at Hebron and said, "See, we are your bone and flesh. ²For some time now, even while Saul was king, it was you who commanded the army of Israel. The Lord your God said to you: It is you who shall be shepherd of my people Israel, you who shall be ruler over my people Israel." ³So all the elders of Israel came to the king at Hebron, and David made a covenant with them at Hebron before the Lord. And they anointed David king over Israel, according to the word of the Lord by Samuel.

11.1–3: David is chosen king. 1: *All Israel* is a variation on "all the tribes of Israel" in 2 Sam 5. In the Chronicler's time, tribal identity may no longer be certain. **3:** *According to the word of the Lord by Samuel:* The Chronicler betrays his use of 1 and 2 Samuel here since he has not previously mentioned Samuel's anointing* David as king.

4 David and all Israel marched to Jerusalem, that is Jebus, where the Jebusites were, the inhabitants of the land. ⁵The inhabitants of Jebus said to David, "You will not come in here." Nevertheless David took the stronghold of Zion, now the city of David. ⁶David had said, "Whoever attacks the Jebusites first shall be chief and com-

a Heb *they* *b* Heb *he*

mander." And Joab son of Zeruiah went up first, so he became chief. 7David resided in the stronghold; therefore it was called the city of David. 8He built the city all around, from the Millo in complete circuit; and Joab repaired the rest of the city. 9And David became greater and greater, for the LORD of hosts was with him.

11.4–9: David captures Jerusalem. The Chronicler omits his source's mention that David reigned in Hebron for 7 years (2 Sam 5.5) to make it look as though David's first action after becoming king was to conquer Jerusalem. **6:** *Whoever attacks the Jebusites first shall be chief and commander* is a challenge to his men very different from the account in 2 Sam 5.8. **9:** *David became greater and greater, for the* LORD *of Hosts was with him:* For the Chronicler, the measure of success was expressed in terms of the king's closeness to God. This phrase highlights the reason for David's great success as king as recounted in the following narratives.*

10 Now these are the chiefs of David's warriors, who gave him strong support in his kingdom, together with all Israel, to make him king, according to the word of the LORD concerning Israel. 11This is an account of David's mighty warriors: Jashobeam, son of Hachmoni,*a* was chief of the Three;*b* he wielded his spear against three hundred whom he killed at one time.

12 And next to him among the three warriors was Eleazar son of Dodo, the Ahohite. 13He was with David at Pas-dammim when the Philistines were gathered there for battle. There was a plot of ground full of barley. Now the people had fled from the Philistines, 14but he and David took their stand in the middle of the plot, defended it, and killed the Philistines; and the LORD saved them by a great victory.

15 Three of the thirty chiefs went down to the rock to David at the cave of Adullam, while the army of Philistines was encamped in the valley of Rephaim. 16David was then in the stronghold; and the garrison of the Philistines was then at Bethlehem. 17David said longingly, "O that someone would give me water to drink from the well of Bethlehem that is by the gate!" 18Then the Three

broke through the camp of the Philistines, and drew water from the well of Bethlehem that was by the gate, and they brought it to David. But David would not drink of it; he poured it out to the LORD, 19and said, "My God forbid that I should do this. Can I drink the blood of these men? For at the risk of their lives they brought it." Therefore he would not drink it. The three warriors did these things.

20 Now Abishai,*c* the brother of Joab, was chief of the Thirty.*d* With his spear he fought against three hundred and killed them, and won a name beside the Three. 21He was the most renowned*e* of the Thirty,*d* and became their commander; but he did not attain to the Three.

22 Benaiah son of Jehoiada was a valiant man*f* of Kabzeel, a doer of great deeds; he struck down two sons of*g* Ariel of Moab. He also went down and killed a lion in a pit on a day when snow had fallen. 23And he killed an Egyptian, a man of great stature, five cubits tall. The Egyptian had in his hand a spear like a weaver's beam; but Benaiah went against him with a staff, snatched the spear out of the Egyptian's hand, and killed him with his own spear. 24Such were the things Benaiah son of Jehoiada did, and he won a name beside the three warriors. 25He was renowned among the Thirty, but he did not attain to the Three. And David put him in charge of his bodyguard.

11.10–25: David's mighty men. Generally a repetition of 2 Sam 23.8–39 with few minor variations.

26 The warriors of the armies were Asahel brother of Joab, Elhanan son of Dodo of Bethlehem, 27Shammoth of Harod,*h* Helez the Pelonite, 28Ira son of Ikkesh of Tekoa, Abiezer of Anathoth, 29Sibbecai the Hushathite, Ilai the Ahohite, 30Maharai of Netophah, Heled son of Baanah of Netophah,

---

a Or *a Hachmonite*   *b* Compare 2 Sam 23.8: Heb *Thirty* or *captains*   *c* Gk Vg Tg Compare 2 Sam 23.18: Heb *Abshai*   *d* Syr: Heb *Three*   *e* Compare 2 Sam 23.19: Heb *more renowned among the two*   *f* Syr: Heb *the son of a valiant man*   *g* See 2 Sam 23.20: Heb lacks *sons of*   *h* Compare 2 Sam 23.25: Heb *the Harorite*

31Ithai son of Ribai of Gibeah of the Benjaminites, Benaiah of Pirathon, 32Hurai of the wadis of Gaash, Abiel the Arbathite, 33Azmaveth of Baharum, Eliahba of Shaalbon, 34Hashem*a* the Gizonite, Jonathan son of Shagee the Hararite, 35Ahiam son of Sachar the Hararite, Eliphal son of Ur, 36Hepher the Mecherathite, Ahijah the Pelonite, 37Hezro of Carmel, Naarai son of Ezbai, 38Joel the brother of Nathan, Mibhar son of Hagri, 39Zelek the Ammonite, Naharai of Beeroth, the armor-bearer of Joab son of Zeruiah, 40Ira the Ithrite, Gareb the Ithrite, 41Uriah the Hittite, Zabad son of Ahlai, 42Adina son of Shiza the Reubenite, a leader of the Reubenites, and thirty with him, 43Hanan son of Maacah, and Joshaphat the Mithnite, 44Uzzia the Ashterathite, Shama and Jeiel sons of Hotham the Aroerite, 45Jediael son of Shimri, and his brother Joha the Tizite, 46Eliel the Mahavite, and Jeribai and Joshaviah sons of Elnaam, and Ithmah the Moabite, 47Eliel, and Obed, and Jaasiel the Mezobaite.

12 The following are those who came to David at Ziklag, while he could not move about freely because of Saul son of Kish; they were among the mighty warriors who helped him in war. 2They were archers, and could shoot arrows and sling stones with either the right hand or the left; they were Benjaminites, Saul's kindred. 3The chief was Ahiezer, then Joash, both sons of Shemaah of Gibeah; also Jeziel and Pelet sons of Azmaveth; Beracah, Jehu of Anathoth, 4Ishmaiah of Gibeon, a warrior among the Thirty and a leader over the Thirty; Jeremiah,*b* Jahaziel, Johanan, Jozabad of Gederah, 5Eluzai,*c* Jerimoth, Bealiah, Shemariah, Shephatiah the Haruphite; 6Elkanah, Isshiah, Azarel, Joezer, and Jashobeam, the Korahites; 7and Joelah and Zebadiah, sons of Jeroham of Gedor.

8 From the Gadites there went over to David at the stronghold in the wilderness mighty and experienced warriors, expert with shield and spear, whose faces were like the faces of lions, and who were swift as gazelles on the mountains: 9Ezer the chief, Obadiah second, Eliab third, 10Mishmannah fourth, Jeremiah fifth, 11Attai sixth, Eliel seventh,

12Johanan eighth, Elzabad ninth, 13Jeremiah tenth, Machbannai eleventh. 14These Gadites were officers of the army, the least equal to a hundred and the greatest to a thousand. 15These are the men who crossed the Jordan in the first month, when it was overflowing all its banks, and put to flight all those in the valleys, to the east and to the west.

16 Some Benjaminites and Judahites came to the stronghold to David. 17David went out to meet them and said to them, "If you have come to me in friendship, to help me, then my heart will be knit to you; but if you have come to betray me to my adversaries, though my hands have done no wrong, then may the God of our ancestors see and give judgment." 18Then the spirit came upon Amasai, chief of the Thirty, and he said,

"We are yours, O David;
    and with you, O son of Jesse!
  Peace, peace to you,
    and peace to the one who helps you!
    For your God is the one who helps
      you."

Then David received them, and made them officers of his troops.

19 Some of the Manassites deserted to David when he came with the Philistines for the battle against Saul. (Yet he did not help them, for the rulers of the Philistines took counsel and sent him away, saying, "He will desert to his master Saul at the cost of our heads.") 20As he went to Ziklag these Manassites deserted to him: Adnah, Jozabad, Jediael, Michael, Jozabad, Elihu, and Zillethai, chiefs of the thousands in Manasseh. 21They helped David against the band of raiders,*d* for they were all warriors and commanders in the army. 22Indeed from day to day people kept coming to David to help him, until there was a great army, like an army of God.

12.1–22: David's loyal forces. To emphasize the prowess of David's forces, the Chronicler refers to the time when David was trying to keep away from Saul.

a Compare Gk and 2 Sam 23.32: Heb *the sons of Hashem*   *b* Heb verse 5   *c* Heb verse 6
d Or *as officers of his troops*

During this time, experienced and skilled warriors join with David's cause. There is almost no parallel material to these narratives* in 1 Samuel. **18:** *"Peace, peace to you"*: Despite the Chronicler's interest in military matters, one of the marks that the community is on the right path is God's granting of peace. This may also be a wordplay on "Jerusalem," "City of Peace," reminding the audience of Jerusalem's highest goal. **19:** *Some of the Manassites*: The tribe of Manasseh was one of the primary population groups in the central portion of the northern district of Israel. Specific reference to these individuals as well as other northern tribal groups emphasizes the unanimity of support for David as opposed to Saul, the legitimate king of the nation.

23 These are the numbers of the divisions of the armed troops who came to David in Hebron to turn the kingdom of Saul over to him, according to the word of the LORD. ²⁴The people of Judah bearing shield and spear numbered six thousand eight hundred armed troops. ²⁵Of the Simeonites, mighty warriors, seven thousand one hundred. ²⁶Of the Levites four thousand six hundred. ²⁷Jehoiada, leader of the house of Aaron, and with him three thousand seven hundred. ²⁸Zadok, a young warrior, and twenty-two commanders from his own ancestral house. ²⁹Of the Benjaminites, the kindred of Saul, three thousand, of whom the majority had continued to keep their allegiance to the house of Saul. ³⁰Of the Ephraimites, twenty thousand eight hundred, mighty warriors, notables in their ancestral houses. ³¹Of the half-tribe of Manasseh, eighteen thousand, who were expressly named to come and make David king. ³²Of Issachar, those who had understanding of the times, to know what Israel ought to do, two hundred chiefs, and all their kindred under their command. ³³Of Zebulun, fifty thousand seasoned troops, equipped for battle with all the weapons of war, to help David*a* with singleness of purpose. ³⁴Of Naphtali, a thousand commanders, with whom there were thirty-seven thousand armed with shield and spear. ³⁵Of the Danites, twenty-eight thousand six hundred equipped for battle. ³⁶Of Asher, forty thousand seasoned troops ready for battle. ³⁷Of the Reubenites and Gadites and the half-tribe of Manasseh from beyond the Jor-

dan, one hundred twenty thousand armed with all the weapons of war.

12.23: *These are the numbers:* This listing of troop strength seems grossly inflated. Some believe the author has misunderstood terms for "unit" and has understood it as a word for "thousand." Others have argued the numbers are symbolic rather than real.

38 All these, warriors arrayed in battle order, came to Hebron with full intent to make David king over all Israel; likewise all the rest of Israel were of a single mind to make David king. ³⁹They were there with David for three days, eating and drinking, for their kindred had provided for them. ⁴⁰And also their neighbors, from as far away as Issachar and Zebulun and Naphtali, came bringing food on donkeys, camels, mules, and oxen— abundant provisions of meal, cakes of figs, clusters of raisins, wine, oil, oxen, and sheep, for there was joy in Israel.

12.38: *All the rest of Israel were of a single mind to make David king:* The Chronicler emphasizes that the community acts as one throughout the book. Of particular importance to the author is the idea of "all Israel," even though the history focuses almost exclusively on events impacting the region or tribe of Judah only.

13 David consulted with the commanders of the thousands and of the hundreds, with every leader. ²David said to the whole assembly of Israel, "If it seems good to you, and if it is the will of the LORD our God, let us send abroad to our kindred who remain in all the land of Israel, including the priests and Levites in the cities that have pasture lands, that they may come together to us. ³Then let us bring again the ark of our God to us; for we did not turn to it in the days of Saul." ⁴The whole assembly agreed to do so, for the thing pleased all the people.

5 So David assembled all Israel from the Shihor of Egypt to Lebo-hamath, to bring the ark of God from Kiriath-jearim. ⁶And David and all Israel went up to Baalah, that is, to Kiriath-jearim, which belongs to Judah,

a Gk: Heb lacks *David*

to bring up from there the ark of God, the LORD, who is enthroned on the cherubim, which is called by his*a* name. 7They carried the ark of God on a new cart, from the house of Abinadab, and Uzzah and Ahio*b* were driving the cart. 8David and all Israel were dancing before God with all their might, with song and lyres and harps and tambourines and cymbals and trumpets.

9 When they came to the threshing floor of Chidon, Uzzah put out his hand to hold the ark, for the oxen shook it. 10The anger of the LORD was kindled against Uzzah; he struck him down because he put out his hand to the ark; and he died there before God. 11David was angry because the LORD had burst out against Uzzah; so that place is called Perez-uzzah*c* to this day. 12David was afraid of God that day; he said, "How can I bring the ark of God into my care?" 13So David did not take the ark into his care into the city of David; he took it instead to the house of Obed-edom the Gittite. 14The ark of God remained with the household of Obed-edom in his house three months, and the LORD blessed the household of Obed-edom and all that he had.

13.1–14: Moving the ark into Jerusalem. An important prelude to David's effectual rule from Jerusalem was bringing the ark of the covenant* into what will be the "chosen city" of Jerusalem. Rearranging the order of his source (2 Sam 6.1–11), the Chronicler has David acting to bring the divine presence as symbolized by the ark (Num 10.33–36) into the capital city even before beginning his own palace. The Chronicler's deliberate reformatting of the sequence of events highlights the importance the narrative* will give to honoring God's presence in Jerusalem. **2:** *David said to the whole assembly of Israel:* In 2 Samuel, David simply makes the decision to bring the ark into the city; here, the Chronicler has David act on the basis of community consensus and divine will. **3:** *We did not turn to it in the days of Saul:* The ark served as a physical manifestation of God's presence. As such, it could ensure that a prophet* was receiving a message from God himself. This comment also serves to underscore the Chronicler's condemnation of Saul for having failed to consult authorized prophets. **5:** *All Israel from the Shihor of Egypt to Lebo-hamath* is probably the largest amount of territory attributed to Israel in the

Old Testament. Shihor of Egypt was the furthest eastern branch of the Nile in Egypt; Lebo-hamath may have been a divide within the Beqa' Valley of modern Lebanon. **6:** *The ark of God, the LORD, who is enthroned on the cherubim,* which is called by his name: This is an elaborated title for the ark, though of uncertain meaning, possibly emphasizing the uniqueness of this object. **9:** *Threshing* floor of Chidon:* The owner's name was "Nacon" in 2 Sam 6.6. The Chronicler offers no explanation for the change in name.

14 King Hiram of Tyre sent messengers to David, along with cedar logs, and masons and carpenters to build a house for him. 2David then perceived that the LORD had established him as king over Israel, and that his kingdom was highly exalted for the sake of his people Israel.

3 David took more wives in Jerusalem, and David became the father of more sons and daughters. 4These are the names of the children whom he had in Jerusalem: Shammua, Shobab, and Nathan; Solomon, 5Ibhar, Elishua, and Elpelet; 6Nogah, Nepheg, and Japhia; 7Elishama, Beeliada, and Eliphelet.

8 When the Philistines heard that David had been anointed king over all Israel, all the Philistines went up in search of David; and David heard of it and went out against them. 9Now the Philistines had come and made a raid in the valley of Rephaim. 10David inquired of God, "Shall I go up against the Philistines? Will you give them into my hand?" The LORD said to him, "Go up, and I will give them into your hand." 11So he went up to Baal-perazim, and David defeated them there. David said, "God has burst out*d* against my enemies by my hand, like a bursting flood." Therefore that place is called Baal-perazim.*e* 12They abandoned their gods there, and at David's command they were burned.

13 Once again the Philistines made a raid in the valley. 14When David again inquired of God, God said to him, "You shall not go up after them; go around and come on them

a Heb lacks *his*   *b* Or *and his brother*   *c* That is *Bursting Out Against Uzzah*   *d* Heb *paraz*   *e* That is *Lord of Bursting Out* opposite the balsam trees. ¹⁵When you hear the sound of marching in the tops of the balsam trees, then go out to battle; for God has gone out before you to strike down the army of the Philistines." ¹⁶David did as God had commanded him, and they struck down the Philistine army from Gibeon to Gezer. ¹⁷The fame of David went out into all lands, and the LORD brought the fear of him on all nations.

14.1–17: Consolidation of David's rule. As the prelude to the movement of the ark into Jerusalem, David's claim on Jerusalem is solidified. **1:** *King Hiram of Tyre sent messengers to David, along with cedar logs:* The cedars of Lebanon were prized in antiquity as a prime building material. Cedar, which is naturally resistant to rot, symbolized eternity in the ancient Near East. **10:** *David inquired of God* is the technical language for consulting with a prophet* to seek God's will. **12:** *They abandoned their gods there and at David's command they were burned:* In the Chronicler's source (2 Sam 5.21), David and his forces "carry away" the idols. Here, the Chronicler has David following more explicitly the Pentateuchal* regulations for the disposal of idols (Deut 12.3). **16:** *They struck down the Philistine army from Gibeon to Gezer:* Gibeon was slightly north of Jerusalem; Gezer lay at the boundary of the hill country and the coastal plain. Essentially this description would confine the Philistines to the strip of land that constitutes the coastal plain. There is some archaeological evidence that at the time of David's reign, Philistine expansion into the hill country was reversed.

15 David^a built houses for himself in the city of David, and he prepared a place for the ark of God and pitched a tent for it. ²Then David commanded that no one but the Levites were to carry the ark of God, for the LORD had chosen them to carry the ark of the LORD and to minister to him forever. ³David assembled all Israel in Jerusalem to bring up the ark of the LORD to its place, which he had prepared for it. ⁴Then David gathered together the descendants of Aaron and the Levites: ⁵of the sons of Kohath, Uriel the chief, with one hundred twenty of his kindred; ⁶of the sons of Merari, Asaiah the chief, with two hundred twenty of his kindred; ⁷of the sons of Gershom, Joel

the chief, with one hundred thirty of his kindred; ⁸of the sons of Elizaphan, Shemaiah the chief, with two hundred of his kindred; ⁹of the sons of Hebron, Eliel the chief, with eighty of his kindred; ¹⁰of the sons of Uzziel, Amminadab the chief, with one hundred twelve of his kindred.

15.1–16.43: The ark is installed in Jerusalem. Unlike Saul, David had properly consulted with, and obeyed, the messages he received from God. With Jerusalem secured as the capital of the nascent kingdom, David was ready to bring the ark into the city. Much of this chapter is the Chronicler's elaboration on his source, 2 Sam 6.12–16. Characteristic of the Chronicler's revision is the emphasis on the proper order for such ritual actions. **15.2:** *Then David commanded that no one but the Levites:* The Chronicler conceives that David established some of the regulations governing worship. Here, though there were no preexisting requirements as to who could carry the ark, David sets down the rule that only Levites can carry the ark. *Forever* as the length of such responsibility is in keeping with other charges to the priesthood (see Num 25.13).

11 David summoned the priests Zadok and Abiathar, and the Levites Uriel, Asaiah, Joel, Shemaiah, Eliel, and Amminadab. ¹²He said to them, "You are the heads of families of the Levites; sanctify yourselves, you and your kindred, so that you may bring up the ark of the LORD, the God of Israel, to the place that I have prepared for it. ¹³Because you did not carry it the first time,^b the LORD our God burst out against us, because we did not give it proper care." ¹⁴So the priests and the Levites sanctified themselves to bring up the ark of the LORD, the God of Israel. ¹⁵And the Levites carried the ark of God on their shoulders with the poles, as Moses had commanded according to the word of the LORD.

16 David also commanded the chiefs of the Levites to appoint their kindred as the singers to play on musical instruments, on harps and lyres and cymbals, to raise loud sounds of joy. ¹⁷So the Levites appointed Heman son of Joel; and of his kindred Asaph son of Berechiah; and of the sons of Merari,

a Heb *He*   *b* Meaning of Heb uncertain

their kindred, Ethan son of Kushaiah; [18] and with them their kindred of the second order, Zechariah, Jaaziel, Shemiramoth, Jehiel, Unni, Eliab, Benaiah, Maaseiah, Mattithiah, Eliphelehu, and Mikneiah, and the gatekeepers Obed-edom and Jeiel. [19] The singers Heman, Asaph, and Ethan were to sound bronze cymbals; [20] Zechariah, Aziel, Shemiramoth, Jehiel, Unni, Eliab, Maaseiah, and Benaiah were to play harps according to Alamoth; [21] but Mattithiah, Eliphelehu, Mikneiah, Obed-edom, Jeiel, and Azaziah were to lead with lyres according to the Sheminith. [22] Chenaniah, leader of the Levites in music, was to direct the music, for he understood it. [23] Berechiah and Elkanah were to be gatekeepers for the ark. [24] Shebaniah, Joshaphat, Nethanel, Amasai, Zechariah, Benaiah, and Eliezer, the priests, were to blow the trumpets before the ark of God. Obed-edom and Jehiah also were to be gatekeepers for the ark.

25 So David and the elders of Israel, and the commanders of the thousands, went to bring up the ark of the covenant of the LORD from the house of Obed-edom with rejoicing. [26] And because God helped the Levites who were carrying the ark of the covenant of the LORD, they sacrificed seven bulls and seven rams. [27] David was clothed with a robe of fine linen, as also were all the Levites who were carrying the ark, and the singers, and Chenaniah the leader of the music of the singers; and David wore a linen ephod. [28] So all Israel brought up the ark of the covenant of the LORD with shouting, to the sound of the horn, trumpets, and cymbals, and made loud music on harps and lyres.

29 As the ark of the covenant of the LORD came to the city of David, Michal daughter of Saul looked out of the window, and saw King David leaping and dancing; and she despised him in her heart.

15.11–29. 12: *He said to them:* The Chronicler typically interspersed speeches by the main figures of the narratives,* underlining his particular concerns at critical points. This same technique was often employed by ancient Greek historians as a way of enabling the reader to see what the historian believed were the crucial elements behind decisive actions. Here David un-

derscores the lineage of those to whom he is entrusting the ritual of moving the ark. This depiction stands in contrast to the earlier effort to move the ark, which ended in failure because *we did not give it proper care* (v. 13). For the Chronicler, maintenance of the community's relationship to God is directly related to the degree of care taken in approaching or handing holy things. **16:** *To raise loud sounds of joy:* For the Chronicler, events in which the community is united in worship are marked by joy and celebration. **22:** *Chenaniah . . . was to direct the music, for he understood it:* The word translated "music" here is difficult. This translation may well reflect the proper understanding of the passage, or the text may relate to the carrying or transporting of the ark. The emphasis is on having someone direct the process either of singing or carrying the ark because they know how to give it "proper care." **28:** *So all Israel brought up the ark of the covenant* of the LORD: Again the Chronicler's emphasis is on the unity of the community in undertaking a critical effort. **29:** *Michal daughter of Saul . . . saw King David leaping and dancing; and she despised him in her heart:* This is an abridged version of 2 Sam 6.20–23, but without the observation that David's nakedness disturbed Michal. The Chronicler may be trying to draw another contrast between Saul and David by portraying Michal's displeasure at David's joy in bringing the ark to Jerusalem.

16 They brought in the ark of God, and set it inside the tent that David had pitched for it; and they offered burnt offerings and offerings of well-being before God. [2] When David had finished offering the burnt offerings and the offerings of well-being, he blessed the people in the name of the LORD; [3] and he distributed to every person in Israel—man and woman alike—to each a loaf of bread, a portion of meat,[a] and a cake of raisins.

4 He appointed certain of the Levites as ministers before the ark of the LORD, to invoke, to thank, and to praise the LORD, the God of Israel. [5] Asaph was the chief, and second to him Zechariah, Jeiel, Shemiramoth, Jehiel, Mattithiah, Eliab, Benaiah, Obed-edom, and Jeiel, with harps and lyres; Asaph was to sound the cymbals, [6] and the priests

a Compare Gk Syr Vg: Meaning of Heb uncertain

Benaiah and Jahaziel were to blow trumpets regularly, before the ark of the covenant of God.

7 Then on that day David first appointed the singing of praises to the LORD by Asaph and his kindred.

16.1–7. 2: *When David had finished offering:* David is the only royal figure the Chronicler portrays positively when he acts in a priestly manner. He offers sacrifices and blesses the people, both priestly actions. 4: *To invoke, to thank, and to praise the LORD, the God of Israel:* Each action is related to a specific type of Psalm: To invoke God's actions by the psalms of lament,* to thank God by a psalm of thanksgiving, and to praise God by one of the hymns in the Psalter. Through the offering of music before the ark these Levites act on behalf of the community. 7: *The singing of praises to the LORD by Asaph and his kindred:* What follows is a psalm constructed from portions of several of the canonical* Psalms (96, 105, and 106), illustrating the praising, thanking, and invoking of God. It reflects the form of hymn composition common in the Chronicler's own day.

〰〰〰〰〰〰〰〰〰〰〰

8 O give thanks to the LORD, call on his
    name,
  make known his deeds among the
    peoples.
9 Sing to him, sing praises to him,
  tell of all his wonderful works.
10 Glory in his holy name;
  let the hearts of those who seek the
    LORD rejoice.
11 Seek the LORD and his strength,
  seek his presence continually.
12 Remember the wonderful works he has
    done,
  his miracles, and the judgments he
    uttered,
13 O offspring of his servant Israel,ᵃ
  children of Jacob, his chosen ones.

14 He is the LORD our God;
  his judgments are in all the earth.
15 Remember his covenant forever,
  the word that he commanded, for a
    thousand generations,
16 the covenant that he made with
    Abraham,
  his sworn promise to Isaac,

17 which he confirmed to Jacob as a
    statute,
  to Israel as an everlasting covenant,
18 saying, "To you I will give the land of
    Canaan
  as your portion for an inheritance."

19 When they were few in number,
  of little account, and strangers in the
    land,ᵇ
20 wandering from nation to nation,
  from one kingdom to another
    people,
21 he allowed no one to oppress them;
  he rebuked kings on their account,
22 saying, "Do not touch my anointed
    ones;
  do my prophets no harm."

23 Sing to the LORD, all the earth.
  Tell of his salvation from day to day.
24 Declare his glory among the nations,
  his marvelous works among all the
    peoples.
25 For great is the LORD, and greatly to be
    praised;
  he is to be revered above all gods.
26 For all the gods of the peoples are
    idols,
  but the LORD made the heavens.
27 Honor and majesty are before him;
  strength and joy are in his place.

28 Ascribe to the LORD, O families of the
    peoples,
  ascribe to the LORD glory and
    strength.
29 Ascribe to the LORD the glory due his
    name;
  bring an offering, and come before
    him.
  Worship the LORD in holy splendor;
30   tremble before him, all the earth.
  The world is firmly established; it
    shall never be moved.
31 Let the heavens be glad, and let the
    earth rejoice,
  and let them say among the nations,
    "The LORD is king!"

a Another reading is *Abraham* (compare Ps 105.6)
b Heb *in it*

32 Let the sea roar, and all that fills it;
    let the field exult, and everything in
        it.
33 Then shall the trees of the forest sing
        for joy
    before the LORD, for he comes to
        judge the earth.
34 O give thanks to the LORD, for he is
        good;
    for his steadfast love endures forever.

35 Say also:
  "Save us, O God of our salvation,
    and gather and rescue us from among
        the nations,
  that we may give thanks to your holy
        name,
  and glory in your praise.
36 Blessed be the LORD, the God of Israel,
    from everlasting to everlasting."
Then all the people said "Amen!" and praised
the LORD.

37 David left Asaph and his kinsfolk there
before the ark of the covenant of the LORD
to minister regularly before the ark as each
day required, 38and also Obed-edom and
his*a* sixty-eight kinsfolk; while Obed-edom
son of Jeduthun and Hosah were to be gatekeepers. 39And he left the priest Zadok and
his kindred the priests before the tabernacle
of the LORD in the high place that was at
Gibeon, 40to offer burnt offerings to the
LORD on the altar of burnt offering regularly,
morning and evening, according to all that is
written in the law of the LORD that he commanded Israel. 41With them were Heman
and Jeduthun, and the rest of those chosen
and expressly named to render thanks to the
LORD, for his steadfast love endures forever.
42Heman and Jeduthun had with them
trumpets and cymbals for the music, and instruments for sacred song. The sons of Jeduthun were appointed to the gate.

16.39: *He left the priest Zadok . . . before the
tabernacle* of the LORD *in the high place* that was at
Gibeon: Since no permanent structure had been
erected in Jerusalem for the ark, sacrifices continue to
be offered at Gibeon. The author understands this activity to be in accord with God's wishes. This assessment is in contrast to the Deuteronomistic* History,

which sees any place of offering outside of Jerusalem
as problematical (1 Kings 3.3–4).

43 Then all the people departed to their
homes, and David went home to bless his
household.

17 Now when David settled in his
house, David said to the prophet Nathan, "I am living in a house of cedar, but
the ark of the covenant of the LORD is under
a tent." 2Nathan said to David, "Do all that
you have in mind, for God is with you."

17.1–27: The Davidic covenant. Though he follows
his source (2 Sam 7.1–29) fairly closely, the Chronicler
makes a few adjustments to subtly shift the meaning
of several passages. These changes emphasize both
Solomon's coming kingdom as the fulfillment of the
promises to David and God's eternal rule over Israel.
1: *Now when David settled in his house:* The setting
of the promises to David in the Chronicler's history
makes much more sense than in 2 Samuel. Here, David
has just returned to his home, and in this opening David realizes how well-provided his own palace is in contrast to the tent that houses the ark.

---

3 But that same night the word of the
LORD came to Nathan, saying: 4Go and tell
my servant David: Thus says the LORD: You
shall not build me a house to live in. 5For I
have not lived in a house since the day I
brought out Israel to this very day, but I have
lived in a tent and a tabernacle.*b* 6Wherever
I have moved about among all Israel, did I
ever speak a word with any of the judges of
Israel, whom I commanded to shepherd my
people, saying, Why have you not built me a
house of cedar? 7Now therefore thus you
shall say to my servant David: Thus says the
LORD of hosts: I took you from the pasture,
from following the sheep, to be ruler over my
people Israel; 8and I have been with you
wherever you went, and have cut off all your
enemies before you; and I will make for you
a name, like the name of the great ones of
the earth. 9I will appoint a place for my people Israel, and will plant them, so that they
may live in their own place, and be disturbed

a Gk Syr Vg: Heb *their*   *b* Gk 2 Sam 7.6: Heb *but I
have been from tent to tent and from tabernacle*

no more; and evildoers shall wear them down no more, as they did formerly, [10]from the time that I appointed judges over my people Israel; and I will subdue all your enemies.

Moreover I declare to you that the LORD will build you a house. [11]When your days are fulfilled to go to be with your ancestors, I will raise up your offspring after you, one of your own sons, and I will establish his kingdom. [12]He shall build a house for me, and I will establish his throne forever. [13]I will be a father to him, and he shall be a son to me. I will not take my steadfast love from him, as I took it from him who was before you, [14]but I will confirm him in my house and in my kingdom forever, and his throne shall be established forever. [15]In accordance with all these words and all this vision, Nathan spoke to David.

[16] Then King David went in and sat before the LORD, and said, "Who am I, O LORD God, and what is my house, that you have brought me thus far? [17]And even this was a small thing in your sight, O God; you have also spoken of your servant's house for a great while to come. You regard me as someone of high rank,[a] O LORD God! [18]And what more can David say to you for honoring your servant? You know your servant. [19]For your servant's sake, O LORD, and according to your own heart, you have done all these great deeds, making known all these great things. [20]There is no one like you, O LORD, and there is no God besides you, according to all that we have heard with our ears. [21]Who is like your people Israel, one nation on the earth whom God went to redeem to be his people, making for yourself a name for great and terrible things, in driving out nations before your people whom you redeemed from Egypt? [22]And you made your people Israel to be your people forever; and you, O LORD, became their God.

[23] "And now, O LORD, as for the word that you have spoken concerning your servant and concerning his house, let it be established forever, and do as you have promised. [24]Thus your name will be established and magnified forever in the saying, 'The LORD of hosts, the God of Israel, is Israel's God'; and the house of your servant David

will be established in your presence. [25]For you, my God, have revealed to your servant that you will build a house for him; therefore your servant has found it possible to pray before you. [26]And now, O LORD, you are God, and you have promised this good thing to your servant; [27]therefore may it please you to bless the house of your servant, that it may continue forever before you. For you, O LORD, have blessed and are blessed[b] forever."

17.3–27. 10: *And I will subdue all your enemies:* Unlike 2 Samuel where this statement is in the past tense, the Chronicler places it in the future, anticipating the conditions that will make it possible to build the Temple.★ **14:** *I will confirm him in my house and in my kingdom:* In 2 Samuel, the promise is that David's house (dynasty★) and kingdom will be established forever. The Chronicler here affirms a strongly theocratic perspective: The kingdom belongs to God, not some successor from David's line. **16:** *Then King David went in and sat before the LORD:* David's response of overwhelming gratitude to God is taken without major alteration from 2 Samuel.

David's military success
18.1–20.8: A precondition of God's promise to David was that God would subdue all the king's enemies. This motif★ becomes the primary point of these closing chapters on David's reign, recounting his great success against a variety of the surrounding peoples. While many of the individual sections closely follow their sources in 2 Samuel, the Chronicler has lifted them from several different settings to combine them for a more dramatic effect.

18 Some time afterward, David attacked the Philistines and subdued them; he took Gath and its villages from the Philistines.

2 He defeated Moab, and the Moabites became subject to David and brought tribute.

3 David also struck down King Hadadezer of Zobah, toward Hamath,[a] as he went to set up a monument at the river Euphrates. [4]David took from him one thousand chariots, seven thousand cavalry, and twenty

a Meaning of Heb uncertain   b Or *and it is blessed*

thousand foot soldiers. David hamstrung all the chariot horses, but left one hundred of them. 5When the Arameans of Damascus came to help King Hadadezer of Zobah, David killed twenty-two thousand Arameans. 6Then David put garrisons*a* in Aram of Damascus; and the Arameans became subject to David, and brought tribute. The LORD gave victory to David wherever he went. 7David took the gold shields that were carried by the servants of Hadadezer, and brought them to Jerusalem. 8From Tibhath and from Cun, cities of Hadadezer, David took a vast quantity of bronze; with it Solomon made the bronze sea and the pillars and the vessels of bronze.

18.6–8. 6: *The LORD gave victory to David wherever he went:* For the Chronicler, it is God's support, not David's skill as a warrior, that ensures the victory. 8: *David took a vast quantity of bronze:* Not in the Chronicler's source, this aside underlies the author's concern to show that the fabrication of the Temple* was the combined work of both David and Solomon.

9 When King Tou of Hamath heard that David had defeated the whole army of King Hadadezer of Zobah, 10he sent his son Hadoram to King David, to greet him and to congratulate him, because he had fought against Hadadezer and defeated him. Now Hadadezer had often been at war with Tou. He sent all sorts of articles of gold, of silver, and of bronze; 11these also King David dedicated to the LORD, together with the silver and gold that he had carried off from all the nations, from Edom, Moab, the Ammonites, the Philistines, and Amalek.

18.11: *These also King David dedicated to the LORD, together with the silver and gold that he carried off:* Though this information is present in 2 Samuel, here the emphasis is on David's setting aside these items for God to prepare for construction of the Temple.

12 Abishai son of Zeruiah killed eighteen thousand Edomites in the Valley of Salt. 13He put garrisons in Edom; and all the Edomites became subject to David. And the LORD gave victory to David wherever he went.

14 So David reigned over all Israel; and he administered justice and equity to all his people. 15Joab son of Zeruiah was over the army; Jehoshaphat son of Ahilud was recorder; 16Zadok son of Ahitub and Ahimelech son of Abiathar were priests; Shavsha was secretary; 17Benaiah son of Jehoiada was over the Cherethites and the Pelethites; and David's sons were the chief officials in the service of the king.

19 Some time afterward, King Nahash of the Ammonites died, and his son succeeded him. 2David said, "I will deal loyally with Hanun son of Nahash, for his father dealt loyally with me." So David sent messengers to console him concerning his father. When David's servants came to Hanun in the land of the Ammonites, to console him, 3the officials of the Ammonites said to Hanun, "Do you think, because David has sent consolers to you, that he is honoring your father? Have not his servants come to you to search and to overthrow and to spy out the land?" 4So Hanun seized David's servants, shaved them, cut off their garments in the middle at their hips, and sent them away; 5and they departed. When David was told about the men, he sent messengers to them, for they felt greatly humiliated. The king said, "Remain at Jericho until your beards have grown, and then return."

6 When the Ammonites saw that they had made themselves odious to David, Hanun and the Ammonites sent a thousand talents of silver to hire chariots and cavalry from Mesopotamia, from Aram-maacah and from Zobah. 7They hired thirty-two thousand chariots and the king of Maacah with his army, who came and camped before Medeba. And the Ammonites were mustered from their cities and came to battle. 8When David heard of it, he sent Joab and all the army of the warriors. 9The Ammonites came out and drew up in battle array at the entrance of the city, and the kings who had come were by themselves in the open country.

10 When Joab saw that the line of battle was set against him both in front and in the

a Gk Vg 2 Sam 8.6 Compare Syr: Heb lacks *garrisons*

rear, he chose some of the picked men of Israel and arrayed them against the Arameans; [11] the rest of his troops he put in the charge of his brother Abishai, and they were arrayed against the Ammonites. [12] He said, "If the Arameans are too strong for me, then you shall help me; but if the Ammonites are too strong for you, then I will help you. [13] Be strong, and let us be courageous for our people and for the cities of our God; and may the LORD do what seems good to him." [14] So Joab and the troops who were with him advanced toward the Arameans for battle; and they fled before him. [15] When the Ammonites saw that the Arameans fled, they likewise fled before Abishai, Joab's brother, and entered the city. Then Joab came to Jerusalem.

16 But when the Arameans saw that they had been defeated by Israel, they sent messengers and brought out the Arameans who were beyond the Euphrates, with Shophach the commander of the army of Hadadezer at their head. [17] When David was informed, he gathered all Israel together, crossed the Jordan, came to them, and drew up his forces against them. When David set the battle in array against the Arameans, they fought with him. [18] The Arameans fled before Israel; and David killed seven thousand Aramean charioteers and forty thousand foot soldiers, and also killed Shophach the commander of their army. [19] When the servants of Hadadezer saw that they had been defeated by Israel, they made peace with David, and became subject to him. So the Arameans were not willing to help the Ammonites any more.

19.18: *David killed seven thousand Aramean charioteers and forty thousand foot soldiers:* In 2 Sam 10.18, the number of charioteers is given as seven hundred. The Chronicler has a pronounced tendency to prefer larger numbers, which may be the result of misunderstanding the numbers of his source, or a deliberate revision in light of military practices of his own day. David's slaughter of so many during his military campaigns comes back to haunt him as a reason that he cannot build the Temple★ (1 Chr 22.8).

20 In the spring of the year, the time when kings go out to battle, Joab led out the army, ravaged the country of the Ammonites, and came and besieged Rabbah. But David remained at Jerusalem. Joab attacked Rabbah, and overthrew it. [2] David took the crown of Milcom[a] from his head; he found that it weighed a talent of gold, and in it was a precious stone; and it was placed on David's head. He also brought out the booty of the city, a very great amount. [3] He brought out the people who were in it, and set them to work[b] with saws and iron picks and axes.[c] Thus David did to all the cities of the Ammonites. Then David and all the people returned to Jerusalem.

4 After this, war broke out with the Philistines at Gezer; then Sibbecai the Hushathite killed Sippai, who was one of the descendants of the giants; and the Philistines were subdued. [5] Again there was war with the Philistines; and Elhanan son of Jair killed Lahmi the brother of Goliath the Gittite, the shaft of whose spear was like a weaver's beam. [6] Again there was war at Gath, where there was a man of great size, who had six fingers on each hand, and six toes on each foot, twenty-four in number; he also was descended from the giants. [7] When he taunted Israel, Jonathan son of Shimea, David's brother, killed him. [8] These were descended from the giants in Gath; they fell by the hand of David and his servants.

20.5: *Elhanan son of Jair killed Lahmi the brother of Goliath:* It appears the Chronicler is deliberately trying to harmonize two different traditions in 1 and 2 Samuel—that David killed Goliath (1 Sam 17) and that Elhanan the Bethlehemite killed Goliath (2 Sam 21.19).

TRANSITION IN REIGNS

Chs. 21–29: While David is still clearly on the throne, this section provides a number of points of continuity between David's reign, which is ending, and Solomon's, which is beginning. Along the way, David makes all the necessary provisions to ensure the successful completion of the Temple★ and the continuing

a Gk Vg See 1 Kings 11.5, 33: MT *of their king*
b Compare 2 Sam 12.31: Heb *and he sawed*
c Compare 2 Sam 12.31: Heb *saws*

growth of Jerusalem. The Chronicler's version is in marked contrast to the opening chapters of 1 Kings where Solomon apparently gains the throne at the last minute thanks to the resourceful intervention of the prophet* Nathan and Solomon's mother Bathsheba. While palace infighting and splits among the influential court officials are evident in the account of 1 Kings, Chronicles has "all Israel" along with all the royal household and high court officials enthusiastically support Solomon as David's successor. This revision of the process by which Solomon gains the throne underlines the Chronicler's concern about presenting a positive model of community unity as a way of preparing to "seek God." It also shows that the completion of the Temple was accomplished by the legitimate heir of David's throne, who fulfilled David's intention to build the Temple.

21 Satan stood up against Israel, and incited David to count the people of Israel. ²So David said to Joab and the commanders of the army, "Go, number Israel, from Beer-sheba to Dan, and bring me a report, so that I may know their number." ³But Joab said, "May the LORD increase the number of his people a hundredfold! Are they not, my lord the king, all of them my lord's servants? Why then should my lord require this? Why should he bring guilt on Israel?" ⁴But the king's word prevailed against Joab. So Joab departed and went throughout all Israel, and came back to Jerusalem. ⁵Joab gave the total count of the people to David. In all Israel there were one million one hundred thousand men who drew the sword, and in Judah four hundred seventy thousand who drew the sword. ⁶But he did not include Levi and Benjamin in the numbering, for the king's command was abhorrent to Joab.

21.1–27: The plague against Israel. Following on the heels of David's string of military victories, disaster strikes in the form of a plague triggered by David's taking of a census. While the Chronicler has closely followed his source in 2 Sam 24, the author has also made significant alterations to bring into strong relief several critical themes. **1:** *Satan stood up against Israel:* This is the only place in the Hebrew Bible where Satan appears as a proper name. In Job and Zech 3 "the Satan" appears as an agent of God, but here Satan acts as an agent opposed to God. Why a census of the peo-

ple would be considered such a grievous offense is unclear. Possibly the Chronicler thought such a census presumed human ownership of the kingdom that in reality was God's, thus inciting God's anger. **5:** *In all Israel there were one million one hundred thousand men who drew the sword:* 2 Samuel has 800,000, but the Chronicler may have been thinking the numbers in 2 Samuel did not include some of the other tribes, hence his assumption of a larger number.

7 But God was displeased with this thing, and he struck Israel. ⁸David said to God, "I have sinned greatly in that I have done this thing. But now, I pray you, take away the guilt of your servant; for I have done very foolishly." ⁹The LORD spoke to Gad, David's seer, saying, ¹⁰"Go and say to David, 'Thus says the LORD: Three things I offer you; choose one of them, so that I may do it to you.' " ¹¹So Gad came to David and said to him, "Thus says the LORD, 'Take your choice: ¹²either three years of famine; or three months of devastation by your foes, while the sword of your enemies overtakes you; or three days of the sword of the LORD, pestilence on the land, and the angel of the LORD destroying throughout all the territory of Israel.' Now decide what answer I shall return to the one who sent me." ¹³Then David said to Gad, "I am in great distress; let me fall into the hand of the LORD, for his mercy is very great; but let me not fall into human hands."

21.7–13. 7: *God was displeased with this thing, and he struck Israel:* This is an addition by the Chronicler. In 2 Sam 24, following Joab's report David realizes his sin and repents before God. For the Chronicler, the realization of sin most often follows on some direct word or action. The author offers no suggestion as to what is meant by God *struck* Israel. **13:** *David said to Gad, "I am in great distress; let me fall into the hand of the LORD":* The Chronicler's source has "let us," putting the emphasis on the welfare of the community. The Chronicler has instead subtly shifted the focus onto David.

14 So the LORD sent a pestilence on Israel; and seventy thousand persons fell in Israel. ¹⁵And God sent an angel to Jerusalem to destroy it; but when he was about to de-

stroy it, the LORD took note and relented concerning the calamity; he said to the destroying angel, "Enough! Stay your hand." The angel of the LORD was then standing by the threshing floor of Ornan the Jebusite. [16]David looked up and saw the angel of the LORD standing between earth and heaven, and in his hand a drawn sword stretched out over Jerusalem. Then David and the elders, clothed in sackcloth, fell on their faces. [17]And David said to God, "Was it not I who gave the command to count the people? It is I who have sinned and done very wickedly. But these sheep, what have they done? Let your hand, I pray, O LORD my God, be against me and against my father's house; but do not let your people be plagued!"

21.15: *And God sent an angel to Jerusalem to destroy it:* As the center of David's human reign, special judgment was reserved for Jerusalem. God's recognition of the impeding disaster triggered the mercy that David had hoped for. *The angel of the LORD was then standing by the threshing* floor of Ornan the Jebusite:* A threshing floor was usually located on an exposed height where a steady wind would be available to allow the separation of the chaff* from the grain. When David and the elders of Israel see the angel, they repent immediately.

18 Then the angel of the LORD commanded Gad to tell David that he should go up and erect an altar to the LORD on the threshing floor of Ornan the Jebusite. [19]So David went up following Gad's instructions, which he had spoken in the name of the LORD. [20]Ornan turned and saw the angel; and while his four sons who were with him hid themselves, Ornan continued to thresh wheat. [21]As David came to Ornan, Ornan looked and saw David; he went out from the threshing floor, and did obeisance to David with his face to the ground. [22]David said to Ornan, "Give me the site of the threshing floor that I may build on it an altar to the LORD—give it to me at its full price—so that the plague may be averted from the people." [23]Then Ornan said to David, "Take it; and let my lord the king do what seems good to him; see, I present the oxen for burnt offerings, and the threshing sledges for the wood,

and the wheat for a grain offering. I give it all." [24]But King David said to Ornan, "No; I will buy them for the full price. I will not take for the LORD what is yours, nor offer burnt offerings that cost me nothing." [25]So David paid Ornan six hundred shekels of gold by weight for the site. [26]David built there an altar to the LORD and presented burnt offerings and offerings of well-being. He called upon the LORD, and he answered him with fire from heaven on the altar of burnt offering. [27]Then the LORD commanded the angel, and he put his sword back into its sheath.

21.18–27.18: *Then the angel of the LORD commanded Gad to tell David that he should go up and erect an altar to the LORD on the threshing floor:* In 2 Samuel Gad goes directly to David without prompting. The Chronicler wants the reader to understand more clearly that the foundation of the Temple* is the result of divine initiative, so an angel prompts Gad to pass along the command to build an altar. There is a tradition in the Bible of marking places of divine disclosure by building altars. **26:** *He called upon the LORD, and he answered him with fire from heaven on the altar of burnt offering:* In 2 Samuel God hears David's appeal and averts the plague. The Chronicler has reworked this simpler report into a miraculous affirmation of God's choice of the location, with echoes of the inauguration of Aaron's priesthood (Lev 9.24) and Elijah's victory over the prophets* of Baal* (1 Kings 18.38).

28 At that time, when David saw that the LORD had answered him at the threshing floor of Ornan the Jebusite, he made his sacrifices there. [29]For the tabernacle of the LORD, which Moses had made in the wilderness, and the altar of burnt offering were at that time in the high place at Gibeon; [30]but David could not go before it to inquire of God, for he was afraid of the sword of the angel of the LORD. **22** [1]Then David said, "Here shall be the house of the LORD God and here the altar of burnt offering for Israel."

2 David gave orders to gather together the aliens who were residing in the land of Israel, and he set stonecutters to prepare dressed stones for building the house of God. [3]David

also provided great stores of iron for nails for the doors of the gates and for clamps, as well as bronze in quantities beyond weighing, ⁴and cedar logs without number—for the Sidonians and Tyrians brought great quantities of cedar to David. ⁵For David said, "My son Solomon is young and inexperienced, and the house that is to be built for the LORD must be exceedingly magnificent, famous and glorified throughout all lands; I will therefore make preparation for it." So David provided materials in great quantity before his death.

21.28–22.19: Preparations for the Temple.★ While 2 Sam 24 does not explicitly draw the connection between the resolution of the plague and the selection of the site for the Temple, the Chronicler makes certain the connection is clear. The Chronicler also makes the connection with David explicit by having David make extraordinary provision for a building his son will actually build. Using the device of a major speech, this section ends with David giving voice to some of the most characteristic themes of the Chronicler's history. Most of this material does not appear in 2 Samuel. **21.28:** *He made his sacrifices there* refers to David's own personal sacrifices in contrast to the sacrifices made to stay the plague. **29:** *The high place*★ *at Gibeon:* While Gibeon was an important religious center, only the Chronicler attests a tradition that the tabernacle★ and altar were present there (16.39). **30:** *For he was afraid of the sword of the angel:* Though the plague had been stayed, just prior to the vision of the angel over Jerusalem David had offered himself and his lineage in place of the larger community (21.17). To go into the presence of God at a location other than the one where God had stayed his judgment, in the Chronicler's view, would have exposed David to potential harm. **22.1:** *Here shall be the house of the LORD God and here the altar of burnt offering for Israel:* The house of the LORD is the standard title for the Temple. The altar of burnt offering for Israel is the place where the annual sacrifice for the atonement★ of the community's sins could be made. **5:** *The house that is to be built for the LORD must be exceedingly magnificent, famous and glorified throughout all lands:* The Chronicler wants the Temple to be a stunning accomplishment not for the glory of David or Solomon, but to bring the world's attention to Israel's god.

⁶ Then he called for his son Solomon and charged him to build a house for the LORD, the God of Israel. ⁷David said to Solomon, "My son, I had planned to build a house to the name of the LORD my God. ⁸But the word of the LORD came to me, saying, 'You have shed much blood and have waged great wars; you shall not build a house to my name, because you have shed so much blood in my sight on the earth. ⁹See, a son shall be born to you; he shall be a man of peace. I will give him peace from all his enemies on every side; for his name shall be Solomon,^a and I will give peace^b and quiet to Israel in his days. ¹⁰He shall build a house for my name. He shall be a son to me, and I will be a father to him, and I will establish his royal throne in Israel forever.' ¹¹Now, my son, the LORD be with you, so that you may succeed in building the house of the LORD your God, as he has spoken concerning you. ¹²Only, may the LORD grant you discretion and understanding, so that when he gives you charge over Israel you may keep the law of the LORD your God. ¹³Then you will prosper if you are careful to observe the statutes and the ordinances that the LORD commanded Moses for Israel. Be strong and of good courage. Do not be afraid or dismayed. ¹⁴With great pains I have provided for the house of the LORD one hundred thousand talents of gold, one million talents of silver, and bronze and iron beyond weighing, for there is so much of it; timber and stone too I have provided. To these you must add more. ¹⁵You have an abundance of workers: stonecutters, masons, carpenters, and all kinds of artisans without number, skilled in working ¹⁶gold, silver, bronze, and iron. Now begin the work, and the LORD be with you."

17 David also commanded all the leaders of Israel to help his son Solomon, saying, ¹⁸"Is not the LORD your God with you? Has he not given you peace on every side? For he has delivered the inhabitants of the land into my hand; and the land is subdued before the LORD and his people. ¹⁹Now set your mind and heart to seek the LORD your God. Go and build the sanctuary of the LORD God so

a Heb *Shelomoh*   *b* Heb *shalom*

that the ark of the covenant of the LORD and the holy vessels of God may be brought into a house built for the name of the LORD."

22.6–19. 6: He called for his son Solomon and charged him to build a house for the LORD: Given the conditions of the promise made to David and his line in ch. 17, David's charge to Solomon carries the strong implication that Solomon will succeed his father on the throne. **8:** *But the word of the LORD came to me, saying, "You have shed much blood":* The opening wording of this verse suggests a message from a prophet.* The shedding of blood is not, in and of itself, an offense that would make one ritually impure. The Chronicler is seeking a larger purpose here, to connect the Temple* and Jerusalem—City of Peace. Solomon, because his name can be understood as "Man of peace," will be the builder of the Temple; David, man of war, cannot build it. **12:** *Only, may the LORD grant you discretion and understanding, so that . . . you may keep the law of the LORD:* This is a reflection of 1 Kings 3 where God grants Solomon an understanding mind and the ability to discern between good and evil. The Chronicler's version narrows the scope of Solomon's fabled* wisdom by defining its purpose as directing one in the law. **13:** *Be strong and of good courage. Do not be afraid or be dismayed:* The thing feared is not specified. This is the language of "holy war,"* used prominently in Joshua (see Josh 1.9). **19:** *Now set your mind and heart to seek the LORD your God:* David's call for the leaders of Israel to help Solomon is also a tacit call for them to recognize his legitimacy as king. For the Chronicler, part of maintaining a relationship with God involves the willful seeking after God, as David calls on the leadership to do.

23 When David was old and full of days, he made his son Solomon king over Israel.

2 David assembled all the leaders of Israel and the priests and the Levites. 3The Levites, thirty years old and upward, were counted, and the total was thirty-eight thousand. 4"Twenty-four thousand of these," David said, "shall have charge of the work in the house of the LORD, six thousand shall be officers and judges, 5four thousand gatekeepers, and four thousand shall offer praises to the LORD with the instruments that I have made for praise." 6And David organized them in divisions corresponding to

the sons of Levi: Gershon,[a] Kohath, and Merari.

7 The sons of Gershon[b] were Ladan and Shimei. 8The sons of Ladan: Jehiel the chief, Zetham, and Joel, three. 9The sons of Shimei: Shelomoth, Haziel, and Haran, three. These were the heads of families of Ladan. 10And the sons of Shimei: Jahath, Zina, Jeush, and Beriah. These four were the sons of Shimei. 11Jahath was the chief, and Zizah the second; but Jeush and Beriah did not have many sons, so they were enrolled as a single family.

12 The sons of Kohath: Amram, Izhar, Hebron, and Uzziel, four. 13The sons of Amram: Aaron and Moses. Aaron was set apart to consecrate the most holy things, so that he and his sons forever should make offerings before the LORD, and minister to him and pronounce blessings in his name forever; 14but as for Moses the man of God, his sons were to be reckoned among the tribe of Levi. 15The sons of Moses: Gershom and Eliezer. 16The sons of Gershom: Shebuel the chief. 17The sons of Eliezer: Rehabiah the chief; Eliezer had no other sons, but the sons of Rehabiah were very numerous. 18The sons of Izhar: Shelomith the chief. 19The sons of Hebron: Jeriah the chief, Amariah the second, Jahaziel the third, and Jekameam the fourth. 20The sons of Uzziel: Micah the chief and Isshiah the second.

21 The sons of Merari: Mahli and Mushi. The sons of Mahli: Eleazar and Kish. 22Eleazar died having no sons, but only daughters; their kindred, the sons of Kish, married them. 23The sons of Mushi: Mahli, Eder, and Jeremoth, three.

24 These were the sons of Levi by their ancestral houses, the heads of families as they were enrolled according to the number of the names of the individuals from twenty years old and upward who were to do the work for the service of the house of the LORD. 25For David said, "The LORD, the God of Israel, has given rest to his people; and he resides in Jerusalem forever. 26And so the Levites no longer need to carry the

a Or *Gershom*; See 1 Chr 6.1, note, and 23.15
b Vg Compare Gk Syr: Heb *to the Gershonite*

tabernacle or any of the things for its service"— 27for according to the last words of David these were the number of the Levites from twenty years old and upward— 28"but their duty shall be to assist the descendants of Aaron for the service of the house of the LORD, having the care of the courts and the chambers, the cleansing of all that is holy, and any work for the service of the house of God; 29to assist also with the rows of bread, the choice flour for the grain offering, the wafers of unleavened bread, the baked offering, the offering mixed with oil, and all measures of quantity or size. 30And they shall stand every morning, thanking and praising the LORD, and likewise at evening, 31and whenever burnt offerings are offered to the LORD on sabbaths, new moons, and appointed festivals, according to the number required of them, regularly before the LORD. 32Thus they shall keep charge of the tent of meeting and the sanctuary, and shall attend the descendants of Aaron, their kindred, for the service of the house of the LORD."

23.1–32: The appointment of the Levites. By the Chronicler's day, the personnel involved in the administration of formal religious observance were divided broadly into two groups. The priests were those of the tribe of Levi who came from the line of Aaron, the brother of Moses. From the ranks of the priests the High Priest was chosen, and the priests were the only ones who could offer sacrifices in the Temple.* The larger group of Temple personnel consisted of members of the tribe of Levi who had lineages different from Aaron's line. These were apparently organized in a variety of guilds with various forms of service within the Temple and/or the formal religious life of the community. **3:** *The Levites, thirty years old and upward, were counted* following the general date when they could begin official duties (Num 4.3). **6:** *David organized them in divisions corresponding to the sons of Levi:* This wording may mean David simply organized them into three divisions and used the traditional names of Levi's sons as a way to delineate them. **25:** *He resides in Jerusalem forever:* One of the Chronicler's chief purposes is to convince his readers of the importance of Jerusalem despite the disasters it has experienced in the past. The divine presence residing in Jerusalem meant that no other religious center held the same importance for worship that Jerusalem now held,

thus diminishing Gibeon, where the Chronicler places the tabernacle* and the altar of burnt offering.

24

The divisions of the descendants of Aaron were these. The sons of Aaron: Nadab, Abihu, Eleazar, and Ithamar. 2But Nadab and Abihu died before their father, and had no sons; so Eleazar and Ithamar became the priests. 3Along with Zadok of the sons of Eleazar, and Ahimelech of the sons of Ithamar, David organized them according to the appointed duties in their service. 4Since more chief men were found among the sons of Eleazar than among the sons of Ithamar, they organized them under sixteen heads of ancestral houses of the sons of Eleazar, and eight of the sons of Ithamar. 5They organized them by lot, all alike, for there were officers of the sanctuary and officers of God among both the sons of Eleazar and the sons of Ithamar. 6The scribe Shemaiah son of Nethanel, a Levite, recorded them in the presence of the king, and the officers, and Zadok the priest, and Ahimelech son of Abiathar, and the heads of ancestral houses of the priests and of the Levites; one ancestral house being chosen for Eleazar and one chosen for Ithamar.

7 The first lot fell to Jehoiarib, the second to Jedaiah, 8the third to Harim, the fourth to Seorim, 9the fifth to Malchijah, the sixth to Mijamin, 10the seventh to Hakkoz, the eighth to Abijah, 11the ninth to Jeshua, the tenth to Shecaniah, 12the eleventh to Eliashib, the twelfth to Jakim, 13the thirteenth to Huppah, the fourteenth to Jeshebeab, 14the fifteenth to Bilgah, the sixteenth to Immer, 15the seventeenth to Hezir, the eighteenth to Happizzez, 16the nineteenth to Pethahiah, the twentieth to Jehezkel, 17the twenty-first to Jachin, the twenty-second to Gamul, 18the twenty-third to Delaiah, the twenty-fourth to Maaziah. 19These had as their appointed duty in their service to enter the house of the LORD according to the procedure established for them by their ancestor Aaron, as the LORD God of Israel had commanded him.

24.1–19: The appointment of the priests. The priests held the foremost position within the Temple.* Their service in the Temple was divided into a sequence of twenty-four divisions, each of which was on duty for half a month out of the year.

20 And of the rest of the sons of Levi: of the sons of Amram, Shubael; of the sons of Shubael, Jehdeiah. 21 Of Rehabiah: of the sons of Rehabiah, Isshiah the chief. 22 Of the Izharites, Shelomoth; of the sons of Shelomoth, Jahath. 23 The sons of Hebron:*a* Jeriah the chief,*b* Amariah the second, Jahaziel the third, Jekameam the fourth. 24 The sons of Uzziel, Micah; of the sons of Micah, Shamir. 25 The brother of Micah, Isshiah; of the sons of Isshiah, Zechariah. 26 The sons of Merari: Mahli and Mushi. The sons of Jaaziah: Beno.*c* 27 The sons of Merari: of Jaaziah, Beno,*c* Shoham, Zaccur, and Ibri. 28 Of Mahli: Eleazar, who had no sons. 29 Of Kish, the sons of Kish: Jerahmeel. 30 The sons of Mushi: Mahli, Eder, and Jerimoth. These were the sons of the Levites according to their ancestral houses. 31 These also cast lots corresponding to their kindred, the descendants of Aaron, in the presence of King David, Zadok, Ahimelech, and the heads of ancestral houses of the priests and of the Levites, the chief as well as the youngest brother.

24.20–31: Updating the appointments of Levites. This section fits very poorly in its present setting. There is no introduction to the section, and the material largely repeats 1 Chr 23.6–23, but with additions to the various family lines, suggesting that the narrative* has been revised to provide an updating of the listing of the Levites, ending with twenty-four courses of Levites to match the twenty-four courses of the priests.

25 David and the officers of the army also set apart for the service the sons of Asaph, and of Heman, and of Jeduthun, who should prophesy with lyres, harps, and cymbals. The list of those who did the work and of their duties was: 2 Of the sons of Asaph: Zaccur, Joseph, Nethaniah, and Asarelah, sons of Asaph, under the direction of Asaph, who prophesied under the direction of the king. 3 Of Jeduthun, the sons of Jeduthun: Gedaliah, Zeri, Jeshaiah, Shimei,*d* Hashabiah, and Mattithiah, six, under the direction of their father Jeduthun, who prophesied with the lyre in thanksgiving and praise to the LORD. 4 Of Heman, the sons of Heman: Bukkiah, Mattaniah, Uzziel, Shebuel, and Jerimoth, Hananiah, Hanani, Eliathah, Giddalti, and Romamti-ezer, Joshbekashah, Mallothi, Hothir, Mahazioth. 5 All these were the sons of Heman the king's seer, according to the promise of God to exalt him; for God had given Heman fourteen sons and three daughters. 6 They were all under the direction of their father for the music in the house of the LORD with cymbals, harps, and lyres for the service of the house of God. Asaph, Jeduthun, and Heman were under the order of the king. 7 They and their kindred, who were trained in singing to the LORD, all of whom were skillful, numbered two hundred eighty-eight. 8 And they cast lots for their duties, small and great, teacher and pupil alike.

9 The first lot fell for Asaph to Joseph; the second to Gedaliah, to him and his brothers and his sons, twelve; 10 the third to Zaccur, his sons and his brothers, twelve; 11 the fourth to Izri, his sons and his brothers, twelve; 12 the fifth to Nethaniah, his sons and his brothers, twelve; 13 the sixth to Bukkiah, his sons and his brothers, twelve; 14 the seventh to Jesarelah,*e* his sons and his brothers, twelve; 15 the eighth to Jeshaiah, his sons and his brothers, twelve; 16 the ninth to Mattaniah, his sons and his brothers, twelve; 17 the tenth to Shimei, his sons and his brothers, twelve; 18 the eleventh to Azarel, his sons and his brothers, twelve; 19 the twelfth to Hashabiah, his sons and his brothers, twelve; 20 to the thirteenth, Shubael, his sons and his brothers, twelve; 21 to the fourteenth, Mattithiah, his sons and his brothers, twelve; 22 to the fifteenth, to Jeremoth, his sons and his brothers, twelve; 23 to the sixteenth, to Hananiah, his sons and his brothers, twelve; 24 to the seventeenth, to Joshbekashah, his sons and his brothers, twelve; 25 to the eighteenth, to Hanani, his sons and his brothers, twelve; 26 to the nine-

a See 23.19: Heb lacks *Hebron*   *b* See 23.19: Heb lacks *the chief*   *c* Or *his son*: Meaning of Heb uncertain   *d* One Ms: Gk: MT lacks *Shimei*   *e* Or *Asarelah*; see 25.2

teenth, to Mallothi, his sons and his brothers, twelve; 27to the twentieth, to Eliathah, his sons and his brothers, twelve; 28to the twenty-first, to Hothir, his sons and his brothers, twelve; 29to the twenty-second, to Giddalti, his sons and his brothers, twelve; 30to the twenty-third, to Mahazioth, his sons and his brothers, twelve; 31to the twenty-fourth, to Romamti-ezer, his sons and his brothers, twelve.

25.1–31: The appointment of musical service. Music as a part of the formal worship conducted in the Temple* almost certainly predates the Exile.* However, the intricacy of the musical arrangements for Temple service reflected in Chronicles more likely represents the forms known by the Chronicler.

26 As for the divisions of the gatekeepers: of the Korahites, Meshelemiah son of Kore, of the sons of Asaph. 2Meshelemiah had sons: Zechariah the firstborn, Jediael the second, Zebadiah the third, Jathniel the fourth, 3Elam the fifth, Jehohanan the sixth, Eliehoenai the seventh. 4Obed-edom had sons: Shemaiah the firstborn, Jehozabad the second, Joah the third, Sachar the fourth, Nethanel the fifth, 5Ammiel the sixth, Issachar the seventh, Peullethai the eighth; for God blessed him. 6Also to his son Shemaiah sons were born who exercised authority in their ancestral houses, for they were men of great ability. 7The sons of Shemaiah: Othni, Rephael, Obed, and Elzabad, whose brothers were able men, Elihu and Semachiah. 8All these, sons of Obed-edom with their sons and brothers, were able men qualified for the service; sixty-two of Obed-edom. 9Meshelemiah had sons and brothers, able men, eighteen. 10Hosah, of the sons of Merari, had sons: Shimri the chief (for though he was not the firstborn, his father made him chief), 11Hilkiah the second, Tebaliah the third, Zechariah the fourth: all the sons and brothers of Hosah totaled thirteen.

12 These divisions of the gatekeepers, corresponding to their leaders, had duties, just as their kindred did, ministering in the house of the LORD; 13and they cast lots by ancestral houses, small and great alike, for

their gates. 14The lot for the east fell to Shelemiah. They cast lots also for his son Zechariah, a prudent counselor, and his lot came out for the north. 15Obed-edom's came out for the south, and to his sons was allotted the storehouse. 16For Shuppim and Hosah it came out for the west, at the gate of Shallecheth on the ascending road. Guard corresponded to guard. 17On the east there were six Levites each day,*a* on the north four each day, on the south four each day, as well as two and two at the storehouse; 18and for the colonnade*b* on the west there were four at the road and two at the colonnade.*b* 19These were the divisions of the gatekeepers among the Korahites and the sons of Merari.

26.1–19: The appointment of the gatekeepers. The Temple* precincts were entered by means of a series of gateways, with each gate guarded by Levites. In David's day, there would have been no reason to have such officials appointed, but the Chronicler wants to present all major Temple assignments as coming from David to emphasize the importance of the Temple.

20 And of the Levites, Ahijah had charge of the treasuries of the house of God and the treasuries of the dedicated gifts. 21The sons of Ladan, the sons of the Gershonites belonging to Ladan, the heads of families belonging to Ladan the Gershonite: Jehieli.*c* 22 The sons of Jehieli, Zetham and his brother Joel, were in charge of the treasuries of the house of the LORD. 23Of the Amramites, the Izharites, the Hebronites, and the Uzzielites: 24Shebuel son of Gershom, son of Moses, was chief officer in charge of the treasuries. 25His brothers: from Eliezer were his son Rehabiah, his son Jeshaiah, his son Joram, his son Zichri, and his son Shelomoth. 26This Shelomoth and his brothers were in charge of all the treasuries of the dedicated gifts that King David, and the heads of families, and the officers of the thousands and the hundreds, and the commanders of the army, had dedicated. 27From booty won in battles they dedicated gifts for

a Gk: Heb lacks *each day*   *b* Heb *parbar*: meaning uncertain   *c* The Hebrew text of verse 21 is confused the maintenance of the house of the LORD. [28]Also all that Samuel the seer, and Saul son of Kish, and Abner son of Ner, and Joab son of Zeruiah had dedicated—all dedicated gifts were in the care of Shelomoth[a] and his brothers.

26.20–28: The appointment of financial overseers. David and his warriors had already been reported as making substantial donations from their military booty to the Temple.* Keeping watch over these resources as well as future revenues was a responsibility of one of the Levitical orders.

[29] Of the Izharites, Chenaniah and his sons were appointed to outside duties for Israel, as officers and judges. [30]Of the Hebronites, Hashabiah and his brothers, one thousand seven hundred men of ability, had the oversight of Israel west of the Jordan for all the work of the LORD and for the service of the king. [31]Of the Hebronites, Jerijah was chief of the Hebronites. (In the fortieth year of David's reign search was made, of whatever genealogy or family, and men of great ability among them were found at Jazer in Gilead.) [32]King David appointed him and his brothers, two thousand seven hundred men of ability, heads of families, to have the oversight of the Reubenites, the Gadites, and the half-tribe of the Manassites for everything pertaining to God and for the affairs of the king.

26.29–32: The appointment of judicial officials. One of the Chronicler's themes is the responsibility of royal figures for ensuring the proper observance of religious regulations. The appointment of Levitical groups for this responsibility accords with other evidence that the Levites explained the meaning of the law to worshippers (see Neh 8.7–8). **32:** *Everything pertaining to God and for the affairs of the king:* As royal appointees, though their primary duties may relate to religious matters, they could also be called upon to administer royal regulations.

27 This is the list of the people of Israel, the heads of families, the commanders of the thousands and the hundreds, and their officers who served the king in all matters concerning the divisions that came and went, month after month throughout the year, each division numbering twenty-four thousand:

[2] Jashobeam son of Zabdiel was in charge of the first division in the first month; in his division were twenty-four thousand. [3]He was a descendant of Perez, and was chief of all the commanders of the army for the first month. [4]Dodai the Ahohite was in charge of the division of the second month; Mikloth was the chief officer of his division. In his division were twenty-four thousand. [5]The third commander, for the third month, was Benaiah son of the priest Jehoiada, as chief; in his division were twenty-four thousand. [6]This is the Benaiah who was a mighty man of the Thirty and in command of the Thirty; his son Ammizabad was in charge of his division.[b] [7]Asahel brother of Joab was fourth, for the fourth month, and his son Zebadiah after him; in his division were twenty-four thousand. [8]The fifth commander, for the fifth month, was Shamhuth, the Izrahite; in his division were twenty-four thousand. [9]Sixth, for the sixth month, was Ira son of Ikkesh the Tekoite; in his division were twenty-four thousand. [10]Seventh, for the seventh month, was Helez the Pelonite, of the Ephraimites; in his division were twenty-four thousand. [11]Eighth, for the eighth month, was Sibbecai the Hushathite, of the Zerahites; in his division were twenty-four thousand. [12]Ninth, for the ninth month, was Abiezer of Anathoth, a Benjaminite; in his division were twenty-four thousand. [13]Tenth, for the tenth month, was Maharai of Netophah, of the Zerahites; in his division were twenty-four thousand. [14]Eleventh, for the eleventh month, was Benaiah of Pirathon, of the Ephraimites; in his division were twenty-four thousand. [15]Twelfth, for the twelfth month, was Heldai the Netophathite, of Othniel; in his division were twenty-four thousand.

[16] Over the tribes of Israel, for the Reubenites, Eliezer son of Zichri was chief officer; for the Simeonites, Shephatiah son of Maacah; [17]for Levi, Hashabiah son of

a Gk Compare 26.28: Heb *Shelomith*   *b* Gk Vg: Heb *Ammizabad was his division*

Kemuel; for Aaron, Zadok; 18for Judah, Elihu, one of David's brothers; for Issachar, Omri son of Michael; 19for Zebulun, Ishmaiah son of Obadiah; for Naphtali, Jerimoth son of Azriel; 20for the Ephraimites, Hoshea son of Azaziah; for the half-tribe of Manasseh, Joel son of Pedaiah; 21for the half-tribe of Manasseh in Gilead, Iddo son of Zechariah; for Benjamin, Jaasiel son of Abner; 22for Dan, Azarel son of Jeroham. These were the leaders of the tribes of Israel. 23David did not count those below twenty years of age, for the LORD had promised to make Israel as numerous as the stars of heaven. 24Joab son of Zeruiah began to count them, but did not finish; yet wrath came upon Israel for this, and the number was not entered into the account of the Annals of King David.

27.1–24: The military organization of the kingdom. The Chronicler believes national security depends on seeking God in the proper way. Having arrayed the various levels of priests and Levites, and thus having arranged for the proper seeking of God, the Chronicler posits David attending to the ordering of military affairs. The overall description is of a conscripted army that would be called together in the event of national emergency. Each tribe presents 24,000 men (twice 12,000), to be available for service each month of the year, on a parallel with the priestly service. The names of the various commanders seem to be largely drawn from the list of David's heroes found in 1 Chr 11. **23:** *David did not count those below twenty years of age, for the LORD had promised to make Israel as numerous as the stars of heaven:* Twenty years of age was the point at which most men would have already been married and had children (Num 1.3). The reference to God's promise refers to the time of Abraham, when God promised his descendants would be as numerous as the stars (Gen 15.5; 22.17).

25 Over the king's treasuries was Azmaveth son of Adiel. Over the treasuries in the country, in the cities, in the villages and in the towers, was Jonathan son of Uzziah. 26Over those who did the work of the field, tilling the soil, was Ezri son of Chelub. 27Over the vineyards was Shimei the Ramathite. Over the produce of the vineyards for the wine cellars was Zabdi the Shiphmite.

28Over the olive and sycamore trees in the Shephelah was Baal-hanan the Gederite. Over the stores of oil was Joash. 29Over the herds that pastured in Sharon was Shitrai the Sharonite. Over the herds in the valleys was Shaphat son of Adlai. 30Over the camels was Obil the Ishmaelite. Over the donkeys was Jehdeiah the Meronothite. Over the flocks was Jaziz the Hagrite. 31All these were stewards of King David's property.

32 Jonathan, David's uncle, was a counselor, being a man of understanding and a scribe; Jehiel son of Hachmoni attended the king's sons. 33Ahithophel was the king's counselor, and Hushai the Archite was the king's friend. 34After Ahithophel came Jehoiada son of Benaiah, and Abiathar. Joab was commander of the king's army.

27.25–34: Miscellaneous royal officials. Just as the military affairs were placed in proper order by David, the Chronicler notes David's efforts at organizing the affairs of the royal administration. Stewards were needed for the various royal properties that were part of the king's wealth.

28 David assembled at Jerusalem all the officials of Israel, the officials of the tribes, the officers of the divisions that served the king, the commanders of the thousands, the commanders of the hundreds, the stewards of all the property and cattle of the king and his sons, together with the palace officials, the mighty warriors, and all the warriors. 2Then King David rose to his feet and said: "Hear me, my brothers and my people. I had planned to build a house of rest for the ark of the covenant of the LORD, for the footstool of our God; and I made preparations for building. 3But God said to me, 'You shall not build a house for my name, for you are a warrior and have shed blood.' 4Yet the LORD God of Israel chose me from all my ancestral house to be king over Israel forever; for he chose Judah as leader, and in the house of Judah my father's house, and among my father's sons he took delight in making me king over all Israel. 5And of all my sons, for the LORD has given me many, he has chosen my son Solomon to sit upon the throne of the kingdom of the

LORD over Israel. 6He said to me, 'It is your son Solomon who shall build my house and my courts, for I have chosen him to be a son to me, and I will be a father to him. 7I will establish his kingdom forever if he continues resolute in keeping my commandments and my ordinances, as he is today.' 8Now therefore in the sight of all Israel, the assembly of the LORD, and in the hearing of our God, observe and search out all the commandments of the LORD your God; that you may possess this good land, and leave it for an inheritance to your children after you forever.

9 "And you, my son Solomon, know the God of your father, and serve him with single mind and willing heart; for the LORD searches every mind, and understands every plan and thought. If you seek him, he will be found by you; but if you forsake him, he will abandon you forever. 10Take heed now, for the LORD has chosen you to build a house as the sanctuary; be strong, and act."

11 Then David gave his son Solomon the plan of the vestibule of the temple, and of its houses, its treasuries, its upper rooms, and its inner chambers, and of the room for the mercy seat;ᵃ 12and the plan of all that he had in mind: for the courts of the house of the LORD, all the surrounding chambers, the treasuries of the house of God, and the treasuries for dedicated gifts; 13for the divisions of the priests and of the Levites, and all the work of the service in the house of the LORD; for all the vessels for the service in the house of the LORD, 14the weight of gold for all golden vessels for each service, the weight of silver vessels for each service, 15the weight of the golden lampstands and their lamps, the weight of gold for each lampstand and its lamps, the weight of silver for a lampstand and its lamps, according to the use of each in the service, 16the weight of gold for each table for the rows of bread, the silver for the silver tables, 17and pure gold for the forks, the basins, and the cups; for the golden bowls and the weight of each; for the silver bowls and the weight of each; 18for the altar of incense made of refined gold, and its weight; also his plan for the golden chariot of the cherubim that spread their wings and covered the ark of the covenant of the LORD.

19 "All this, in writing at the LORD's direction, he made clear to me—the plan of all the works."

20 David said further to his son Solomon, "Be strong and of good courage, and act. Do not be afraid or dismayed; for the LORD God, my God, is with you. He will not fail you or forsake you, until all the work for the service of the house of the LORD is finished. 21Here are the divisions of the priests and the Levites for all the service of the house of God; and with you in all the work will be every volunteer who has skill for any kind of service; also the officers and all the people will be wholly at your command."

28.1–21: David's charge to Solomon. Employing again the royal speech as a means of giving voice to his own concerns, the Chronicler has David offer this important charge at the conclusion of organizing the community for the future. **2:** *A house of rest for the ark of the covenant* of the LORD, for the footstool of our God:* These are terms found in Ps 132, which praises God for having chosen Jerusalem as his eternal dwelling place. **8:** *In the sight of all Israel, the assembly of the LORD, and in the hearing of our God:* The whole community is proclaimed to be the "assembly" or corporate entity of God. As with other settings, it is "all Israel" that receives the unified resolve of the leadership. **9:** *If you seek him, he will be found by you; but if you forsake him, he will abandon you forever:* In brief, this is the Chronicler's primary theology. **11:** *Then David gave his son Solomon the plan,* as in the design and manner of ordering. **19:** *All this, in writing at the LORD's direction, he made clear to me:* David functions as a prophetic* figure, receiving the ordering of the Temple* just as Moses received the law from God. In effect, the Chronicler places the commands of David and the commands of Moses on equal footing, making the proper order of the Temple rituals as essential as the Mosaic regulations for what one may eat.

29 King David said to the whole assembly, "My son Solomon, whom alone God has chosen, is young and inexperienced, and the work is great; for the templeᵇ will not be for mortals but for the LORD God. 2So

a Or the cover   *b* Heb fortress

I have provided for the house of my God, so far as I was able, the gold for the things of gold, the silver for the things of silver, and the bronze for the things of bronze, the iron for the things of iron, and wood for the things of wood, besides great quantities of onyx and stones for setting, antimony, colored stones, all sorts of precious stones, and marble in abundance. ³Moreover, in addition to all that I have provided for the holy house, I have a treasure of my own of gold and silver, and because of my devotion to the house of my God I give it to the house of my God: ⁴three thousand talents of gold, of the gold of Ophir, and seven thousand talents of refined silver, for overlaying the walls of the house, ⁵and for all the work to be done by artisans, gold for the things of gold and silver for the things of silver. Who then will offer willingly, consecrating themselves today to the LORD?"

6 Then the leaders of ancestral houses made their freewill offerings, as did also the leaders of the tribes, the commanders of the thousands and of the hundreds, and the officers over the king's work. ⁷They gave for the service of the house of God five thousand talents and ten thousand darics of gold, ten thousand talents of silver, eighteen thousand talents of bronze, and one hundred thousand talents of iron. ⁸Whoever had precious stones gave them to the treasury of the house of the LORD, into the care of Jehiel the Gershonite. ⁹Then the people rejoiced because these had given willingly, for with single mind they had offered freely to the LORD; King David also rejoiced greatly.

10 Then David blessed the LORD in the presence of all the assembly; David said: "Blessed are you, O LORD, the God of our ancestor Israel, forever and ever. ¹¹Yours, O LORD, are the greatness, the power, the glory, the victory, and the majesty; for all that is in the heavens and on the earth is yours; yours is the kingdom, O LORD, and you are exalted as head above all. ¹²Riches and honor come from you, and you rule over all. In your hand are power and might; and it is in your hand to make great and to give

strength to all. ¹³And now, our God, we give thanks to you and praise your glorious name.

29.1–22a: Provision of offerings for construction. Having made arrangements for the funding of the building of the Temple,* it now remains for David to make one last gesture of his devotion to God. **3:** *I have a treasure of my own of gold and silver, and because of my devotion to the house of my God I give it to the house of my God:* David gives of his own personal wealth to accomplish the building of the Temple. **9:** *Then the people rejoiced because these had given willingly, for with single mind they had offered freely to the LORD:* The assembled company of people are touched by this demonstration of personal commitment. The Chronicler highlights the unity of purpose. **11:** *Yours is the kingdom, O LORD:* This underscores the concept that the kingdom of Israel is God's, not the line of David's.

---

14 "But who am I, and what is my people, that we should be able to make this freewill offering? For all things come from you, and of your own have we given you. ¹⁵For we are aliens and transients before you, as were all our ancestors; our days on the earth are like a shadow, and there is no hope. ¹⁶O LORD our God, all this abundance that we have provided for building you a house for your holy name comes from your hand and is all your own. ¹⁷I know, my God, that you search the heart, and take pleasure in uprightness; in the uprightness of my heart I have freely offered all these things, and now I have seen your people, who are present here, offering freely and joyously to you. ¹⁸O LORD, the God of Abraham, Isaac, and Israel, our ancestors, keep forever such purposes and thoughts in the hearts of your people, and direct their hearts toward you. ¹⁹Grant to my son Solomon that with single mind he may keep your commandments, your decrees, and your statutes, performing all of them, and that he may build the temple*ᵃ* for which I have made provision."

20 Then David said to the whole assembly, "Bless the LORD your God." And all the assembly blessed the LORD, the God of their

a Heb *fortress*

ancestors, and bowed their heads and prostrated themselves before the LORD and the king. 21On the next day they offered sacrifices and burnt offerings to the LORD, a thousand bulls, a thousand rams, and a thousand lambs, with their libations, and sacrifices in abundance for all Israel; 22and they ate and drank before the LORD on that day with great joy.

29.14–22a. 18: *Keep forever such purposes and thoughts in the hearts of your people:* The Chronicler uses David's prayer to remind his audience of the need for proper piety. 22: *And they ate and drank before the LORD on that day with great joy:* When the community is unified in purpose and commitment, then worship results in great joy for all Israel, a recurring motif* in the Chronicler's history.

They made David's son Solomon king a second time; they anointed him as the LORD's prince, and Zadok as priest. 23Then Solomon sat on the throne of the LORD, succeeding his father David as king; he prospered, and all Israel obeyed him. 24All the leaders and the mighty warriors, and also all the sons of King David, pledged their allegiance to King Solomon. 25The LORD highly exalted Solomon in the sight of all Israel, and bestowed upon him such royal majesty as had not been on any king before him in Israel.

26 Thus David son of Jesse reigned over all Israel. 27The period that he reigned over Israel was forty years; he reigned seven years

in Hebron, and thirty-three years in Jerusalem. 28He died in a good old age, full of days, riches, and honor; and his son Solomon succeeded him. 29Now the acts of King David, from first to last, are written in the records of the seer Samuel, and in the records of the prophet Nathan, and in the records of the seer Gad, 30with accounts of all his rule and his might and of the events that befell him and Israel and all the kingdoms of the earth.

29.22b–30: Summary of the transition. This section accomplishes two main tasks: providing the reader with a preview of Solomon's successful reign, and closing out the narratives* on David. 22b: *They made David's son Solomon king a second time:* "They" refers to the assembled officialdom and people of Israel, who had already affirmed Solomon as king in ch. 22. The appointment of Solomon as *the LORD's prince* underscores the Chronicler's point that the kingdom is God's, and the line of David rules not by divine right but by permission of God. 24: *All the leaders . . . pledged their allegiance to King Solomon:* This revises the account of courtly dissension in 1 Kings 1. Unity of the community is an important theme to the Chronicler's presentation. 28: *His son Solomon succeeded him* is a further affirmation of the legitimacy of Solomon's rule. 29: *Written in the records of the seer Samuel:* It is uncertain if the Chronicler is referring to the canonical* books of 1 and 2 Samuel by this title. The *records of the prophet* Nathan and records of the seer Gad* are unknown outside of Chronicles and may constitute literary devices designed to lend authenticity to the narrative.

2 CHRONICLES

Introduction

The Access Bible treats 1 and 2 Chronicles as a single work; for convenience the introductory material from 1 Chronicles is repeated here.

The Chronicler offers his readers a history of what was important from the community's (namely Judah's) past, something quite different from the earlier narratives★ of 1 and 2 Samuel and 1 and 2 Kings. While the Deuteronomistic★ History (Judges through 2 Kings) tries to justify the destruction of both the northern kingdom of Israel and the southern kingdom of Judah by showing how both communities turned their backs on God by practicing idolatry,★ the Chronicler is more concerned to present a positive model from Israel's past. Starting with David as an example, the narratives that stand out in the Chronicler's history are those in which the community or king respond faithfully to God, finding unity and security in response. Good kings are those who "seek the LORD," and in return they experience military and economic success, and their subjects experience great joy in gathering before the Temple★ in Jerusalem for worship. These positive models are intended to speak to the Chronicler's readers, to convince them that in "seeking the LORD" at the Temple in their own day, they will find their fullest sense of purpose and community.

The narratives of the Chronicler's history abound with historical problems from the view of a modern reader. David makes provision for the use of marble in building the Temple (1 Chr 29.2); however, marble was not used in Jerusalem until the Hellenistic★ age seven hundred years later. David collects "10,000 darics" (1 Chr 29.7) for the Temple, a coin of the Persian empire 500 years after the Davidic period. Impossibly large numbers of military forces are mustered in the field (300,000 from Judah, 280,000 from Benjamin, facing a "million" from Egypt; 2 Chr 14.8–9), and stock numbers are often used (for example, Shishak of Egypt attacks with "1,200 chariots and 60,000 chariots," playing on the number 12 and its multiples; 2 Chr 12.3). The Chronicler never mentions David's transgression in taking Bathsheba as wife (2 Sam 11–12), nor for that matter Solomon's fall into idolatry (1 Kings 11). These tendencies are similar to Hellenistic historians of the same general period, suggesting the Chronicler is simply writing about the past with commonly accepted, perhaps even expected, conventions.

Part of the dilemma over the historical value of 1 and 2 Chronicles involves what potential sources the author had at his disposal. The author cites a number of sources that are otherwise unknown; however, the general stylistic uniformity between narratives where sources are mentioned and where none are indicated raises the suspicion that such sources may not have existed. There is no conclusive evidence to support the Chronicler's use of any sources other than 1 Samuel through 2 Kings.

In its original form, the Hebrew Chronicles would have filled one single scroll. Its division into two parts was accomplished when the codex or book-form of transmitting literature became the standard, probably in the early centuries CE.

While numerous proposals have been offered for the date of the Chronicler's composition, perhaps the most telling points are the interest in military matters and the result of "peace" when the community "seeks the LORD." Following the death of Alexander the Great (around 330 BCE), his successors fought incessantly with each other, often across the landscape of Palestine. Archaeological evidence demonstrates that in the last decades of the fourth century BCE nearly every urban center in Palestine suffered military destruction. It was not until the Ptolemaic★ rulers of Egypt suppressed their Syrian rivals that peace came to Palestine in the early second century BCE. In the midst of such turmoil, a message focusing on the peace that "seeking the LORD" might bring would have been particularly powerful.

The author focuses almost exclusively on the events affecting Jerusalem and the Temple. With regard to the Temple, the author shows particular interest in the activities of the priesthood and individuals given prominence in Temple affairs. Many scholars conclude that the author was a member of the Temple priesthood.

READING GUIDE

When recounting a story of Israel's past, the Chronicler skillfully weaves personal encounters and community responses. A characteristic narrative is the account of the reign of Judah's King Asa (2 Chr 14–16). It opens with the land having "rest," in part because Asa "did what was good and right" in God's view and "commanded Judah to seek the LORD" (2 Chr 14.4). He orders his people to build fortifications around the urban areas since "the land is still ours because we have sought the LORD our God . . . and he has given us peace on every side" (2 Chr 14.7). This sense of security is challenged by Zerah the "Ethiopian," who comes with a million-man army to attack Judah. Asa offers a simple petition for help, and "the LORD defeated the Ethiopians" (2 Chr 14.12). Fresh from this great victory, the Chronicler has an otherwise unattested prophet★ confront the king in a decisive way. This is similar to the style of the Greek historian Herodotus, who uses the figures of various wise counselors to present a ruler with a choice to follow wisdom or pride. In Asa's case, it is "Azariah the son of Oded" who gives voice to the central theological theme of the Chronicler: "The LORD is with you, while you are with him. If you seek him, he will be found by you, but if you abandon him, he will abandon you" (2 Chr 15.2). Taking heart from the prophet's message, Asa convenes all his subjects (Judah and Benjamin) as well as those faithful from the northern kingdom who had joined with Judah (2 Chr 15.9–10). After sacrificing to God, the assembled populace "entered into covenant★ to seek the LORD, the God of their ancestors, with all their heart and with all their soul" (v. 12), an echo of Israel's basic credo of Deut 6.4–5. To emphasize the seriousness of this act, the Chronicler adds that whoever did not join with the covenant "should be put to death" (v. 13). Not wanting to close on a negative note, the Chronicler portrays the community enthusiastically embracing this arrangement: "All Judah rejoiced over the oath; for they had sworn with all their heart, and had sought him with their whole desire, and he was found by them, and the LORD gave them rest all around" (v. 15). This is a paradigm that the Chronicler uses frequently: the king being presented with the need to "seek" God and then the community actively and joyously embracing God.

1 Chronicles

1–9   Genealogical★ prologue
10–20   David's reign
21–29   Transition (centrality of the Temple)

2 Chronicles

1–9   Solomon's rule
10–36   Dissolution of Judah

SOLOMON'S REIGN

Chs. 1–9: These chapters emphasize the success of Solomon as king over Israel. They attribute that success to Solomon's careful fulfillment of all that David had planned, particularly with regard to the Temple* and the conduct of proper worship. One of the basic points made in this section is that the Temple is the result of the combined efforts of David and Solomon. The Chronicler closely follows his source in 1 Kings 1–11, but by selective editing and rearranging, he creates his own distinctive understanding of Solomon's importance.

1 Solomon son of David established himself in his kingdom; the LORD his God was with him and made him exceedingly great. 2 Solomon summoned all Israel, the commanders of the thousands and of the hundreds, the judges, and all the leaders of all Israel, the heads of families. ³Then Solomon, and the whole assembly with him, went to the high place that was at Gibeon; for God's tent of meeting, which Moses the servant of the LORD had made in the wilderness, was there. ⁴(But David had brought the ark of God up from Kiriath-jearim to the place that David had prepared for it; for he had pitched a tent for it in Jerusalem.) ⁵Moreover the bronze altar that Bezalel son of Uri, son of Hur, had made, was there in front of the tabernacle of the LORD. And Solomon and the assembly inquired at it. ⁶Solomon went up there to the bronze altar before the LORD, which was at the tent of meeting, and offered a thousand burnt offerings on it.

7 That night God appeared to Solomon, and said to him, "Ask what I should give you." ⁸Solomon said to God, "You have shown great and steadfast love to my father David, and have made me succeed him as king. ⁹O LORD God, let your promise to my father David now be fulfilled, for you have made me king over a people as numerous as the dust of the earth. ¹⁰Give me now wisdom and knowledge to go out and come in before this people, for who can rule this great people of yours?" ¹¹God answered Solomon,

"Because this was in your heart, and you have not asked for possessions, wealth, honor, or the life of those who hate you, and have not even asked for long life, but have asked for wisdom and knowledge for yourself that you may rule my people over whom I have made you king, ¹²wisdom and knowledge are granted to you. I will also give you riches, possessions, and honor, such as none of the kings had who were before you, and none after you shall have the like." ¹³So Solomon came from*ᵃ* the high place at Gibeon, from the tent of meeting, to Jerusalem. And he reigned over Israel.

14 Solomon gathered together chariots and horses; he had fourteen hundred chariots and twelve thousand horses, which he stationed in the chariot cities and with the king in Jerusalem. ¹⁵The king made silver and gold as common in Jerusalem as stone, and he made cedar as plentiful as the sycamore of the Shephelah. ¹⁶Solomon's horses were imported from Egypt and Kue; the king's traders received them from Kue at the prevailing price. ¹⁷They imported from Egypt, and then exported, a chariot for six hundred shekels of silver, and a horse for one hundred fifty; so through them these were exported to all the kings of the Hittites and the kings of Aram.

1.1–17: Solomon's wisdom. This section sets the stage for the following narratives,* which develop Solomon's concern with building the Temple.* **1:** *Solomon son of David established himself in his kingdom:* It is not clear when the Chronicler understood this to be happening; he may conceive of Solomon's sacrifice occurring just after David's death. **2:** *Solomon summoned all Israel:* The community is unified in worship. **3:** *The high place* that was at Gibeon:* In 1 Kings 3, Solomon's going to Gibeon was viewed negatively since the Deuteronomistic* Historian saw any worship center outside of Jerusalem as heretical. For the Chronicler, Gibeon is the place where the tabernacle* and the altar of burnt offering are situated, and going there to worship is thereby acceptable. **10:** *Give me now wisdom and knowledge to go out and come in before this people* is a rephrasing of the Chronicler's source (1 Kings 3.9), where Solomon requests wisdom to

a Gk Vg: Heb *to*

know good and evil in order to be able to govern. In this rephrasing, Solomon is asking for wisdom to know how to conduct his life as king, a broader goal. **13:** *So Solomon came from the high place at Gibeon:* The Chronicler leaves out the narrative in his source (1 Kings 3.16–28) of Solomon's deciding between two prostitutes claiming the same child. In Kings, the story illustrates how Solomon's wisdom allows him to discern where justice lay and how to execute it. Since the Chronicler sees Solomon's wisdom as leading him to build the Temple, such a powerful story would be distracting. **15:** *The king made silver and gold as common in Jerusalem as stone:* The overview of Solomon's achievements serves to confirm how shrewdly he could conduct himself.

2 ^{a}Solomon decided to build a temple for the name of the LORD, and a royal palace for himself. 2^{b}Solomon conscripted seventy thousand laborers and eighty thousand stonecutters in the hill country, with three thousand six hundred to oversee them.

3 Solomon sent word to King Huram of Tyre: "Once you dealt with my father David and sent him cedar to build himself a house to live in. 4I am now about to build a house for the name of the LORD my God and dedicate it to him for offering fragrant incense before him, and for the regular offering of the rows of bread, and for burnt offerings morning and evening, on the sabbaths and the new moons and the appointed festivals of the LORD our God, as ordained forever for Israel. 5The house that I am about to build will be great, for our God is greater than other gods. 6But who is able to build him a house, since heaven, even highest heaven, cannot contain him? Who am I to build a house for him, except as a place to make offerings before him? 7So now send me an artisan skilled to work in gold, silver, bronze, and iron, and in purple, crimson, and blue fabrics, trained also in engraving, to join the skilled workers who are with me in Judah and Jerusalem, whom my father David provided. 8Send me also cedar, cypress, and algum timber from Lebanon, for I know that your servants are skilled in cutting Lebanon timber. My servants will work with your servants 9to prepare timber for me in abundance, for the house I am about to build will

be great and wonderful. 10I will provide for your servants, those who cut the timber, twenty thousand cors of crushed wheat, twenty thousand cors of barley, twenty thousand baths^c of wine, and twenty thousand baths of oil."

11 Then King Huram of Tyre answered in a letter that he sent to Solomon, "Because the LORD loves his people he has made you king over them." 12Huram also said, "Blessed be the LORD God of Israel, who made heaven and earth, who has given King David a wise son, endowed with discretion and understanding, who will build a temple for the LORD, and a royal palace for himself. 13 "I have dispatched Huram-abi, a skilled artisan, endowed with understanding, 14the son of one of the Danite women, his father a Tyrian. He is trained to work in gold, silver, bronze, iron, stone, and wood, and in purple, blue, and crimson fabrics and fine linen, and to do all sorts of engraving and execute any design that may be assigned him, with your artisans, the artisans of my lord, your father David. 15Now, as for the wheat, barley, oil, and wine, of which my lord has spoken, let him send them to his servants. 16We will cut whatever timber you need from Lebanon, and bring it to you as rafts by sea to Joppa; you will take it up to Jerusalem."

17 Then Solomon took a census of all the aliens who were residing in the land of Israel, after the census that his father David had taken; and there were found to be one hundred fifty-three thousand six hundred. 18Seventy thousand of them he assigned as laborers, eighty thousand as stonecutters in the hill country, and three thousand six hundred as overseers to make the people work.

2.1–18: Preparation for building the Temple.* The Chronicler now turns to Solomon's actively putting into place the pieces for assembling the Temple. Much of this portion has used 1 Kings 5.1–18, but the rearranging and supplementation has created a very different narrative.* **1:** *Solomon decided to build a tem-*

a Ch 1.18 in Heb   *b* Ch 2.1 in Heb   *c* A Hebrew measure of volume ple for the name of the LORD: Taken by itself, this statement seems odd given all the earlier commands David had given Solomon. However, these verses introduce what follows; *decided* means Solomon has resolved on his own to undertake the Temple. **4:** *I am now about to build a house for the name of the LORD my God:* Clarifying the meaning of v. 1, Solomon is ready to put the preparations for the Temple into action. *As ordained forever for Israel:* The Chronicler understands the regular appointed festivals to be an eternal obligation for Israel. The offerings specified prior to this conclusion are drawn from several different places in the Pentateuch.* **11:** *Because the LORD loves his people he has made you king over them:* Solomon, in the author's view, does not rule because of the promise God made to David, but because of God's great love for the community. **12:** *Blessed be the LORD God of Israel, who made heaven and earth:* Spoken by Huram of Tyre, this is the classic expression for those outside Israel about Israel's unique faith (see Jon 1.9). It is the only place where the Chronicler makes such a clear statement concerning creation. **13:** *I have dispatched Huram-abi, a skilled artisan, endowed with understanding:* In the original source (1 Kings 7.14) the artisan is identified as a specialist only in bronze. The Chronicler expands this description to create a parallel between Huram-abi and the figure of Bezalel, who assisted Moses in fabricating the tabernacle* (Ex 31.1–5), thus creating a parallel between the tabernacle in the wilderness and the Temple in Jerusalem. Solomon's census of the aliens was intended to support Temple construction, not to assess military strength, so it was not objectionable to God as David's had been. The term "aliens" relates to residual Canaanite groups still inhabiting the land. For the Chronicler, they cannot be considered part of Israel.

3 Solomon began to build the house of the LORD in Jerusalem on Mount Moriah, where the LORD had appeared to his father David, at the place that David had designated, on the threshing floor of Ornan the Jebusite. ²He began to build on the second day of the second month of the fourth year of his reign. ³These are Solomon's measurements*a* for building the house of God: the length, in cubits of the old standard, was sixty cubits, and the width twenty cubits. ⁴The vestibule in front of the nave of the house was twenty cubits long, across the width of the house;*b* and its height was one hundred twenty cubits. He overlaid it on the inside with pure gold. ⁵The nave he lined with cypress, covered it with fine gold, and made palms and chains on it. ⁶He adorned the house with settings of precious stones. The gold was gold from Parvaim. ⁷So he lined the house with gold—its beams, its thresholds, its walls, and its doors; and he carved cherubim on the walls.

3.1–5.1: Construction of the Temple. In this elaborate section, the Chronicler relies mainly on 1 Kings but adds points and elements of his own. **3.1:** *Solomon began to build the house of the LORD in Jerusalem on Mount Moriah:* Only in Chronicles is the Temple mount identified as the place where Abraham nearly sacrificed his son Isaac before God (Gen 22). **3:** *In cubits of the old standard,* possibly before the cubit was standardized in Judean practice. The cubit was a measure of linear size; the older standard was more than 17 inches. **6:** *The gold was gold from Parvaim,* an unknown place that may have produced highly refined gold.

8 He made the most holy place; its length, corresponding to the width of the house, was twenty cubits, and its width was twenty cubits; he overlaid it with six hundred talents of fine gold. ⁹The weight of the nails was fifty shekels of gold. He overlaid the upper chambers with gold.

10 In the most holy place he made two carved cherubim and overlaid*c* them with gold. ¹¹The wings of the cherubim together extended twenty cubits: one wing of the one, five cubits long, touched the wall of the house, and its other wing, five cubits long, touched the wing of the other cherub; ¹²and of this cherub, one wing, five cubits long, touched the wall of the house, and the other wing, also five cubits long, was joined to the wing of the first cherub. ¹³The wings of these cherubim extended twenty cubits; the cherubim*d* stood on their feet, facing the nave. ¹⁴And Solomon*e* made the curtain of blue and purple and crimson fabrics and fine linen, and worked cherubim into it.

a Syr: Heb *foundations*   *b* Compare 1 Kings 6.3: Meaning of Heb uncertain   *c* Heb *they overlaid* *d* Heb *they*   *e* Heb *he*

3.14: *And Solomon made the curtain of blue and purple and crimson fabrics:* The term for "curtain" has more the sense of "veil." In Solomon's Temple a door separated the inner chamber from the rest of the building. In the rebuilt Temple of the post-exilic period, a veil served the same purpose, but the description the Chronicler offers is more like the veil in the tabernacle* (Ex 26.31–32).

15 In front of the house he made two pillars thirty-five cubits high, with a capital of five cubits on the top of each. [16]He made encircling[a] chains and put them on the tops of the pillars; and he made one hundred pomegranates, and put them on the chains. [17]He set up the pillars in front of the temple, one on the right, the other on the left; the one on the right he called Jachin, and the one on the left, Boaz.

4 He made an altar of bronze, twenty cubits long, twenty cubits wide, and ten cubits high. [2]Then he made the molten sea; it was round, ten cubits from rim to rim, and five cubits high. A line of thirty cubits would encircle it completely. [3]Under it were panels all around, each of ten cubits, surrounding the sea; there were two rows of panels, cast when it was cast. [4]It stood on twelve oxen, three facing north, three facing west, three facing south, and three facing east; the sea was set on them. The hindquarters of each were toward the inside. [5]Its thickness was a handbreadth; its rim was made like the rim of a cup, like the flower of a lily; it held three thousand baths.[b] [6]He also made ten basins in which to wash, and set five on the right side, and five on the left. In these they were to rinse what was used for the burnt offering. The sea was for the priests to wash in.

7 He made ten golden lampstands as prescribed, and set them in the temple, five on the south side and five on the north. [8]He also made ten tables and placed them in the temple, five on the right side and five on the left. And he made one hundred basins of gold. [9]He made the court of the priests, and the great court, and doors for the court; he overlaid their doors with bronze. [10]He set the sea at the southeast corner of the house.

11 And Huram made the pots, the shovels, and the basins. Thus Huram finished the work that he did for King Solomon on the house of God: [12]the two pillars, the bowls, and the two capitals on the top of the pillars; and the two latticeworks to cover the two bowls of the capitals that were on the top of the pillars; [13]the four hundred pomegranates for the two latticeworks, two rows of pomegranates for each latticework, to cover the two bowls of the capitals that were on the pillars. [14]He made the stands, the basins on the stands, [15]the one sea, and the twelve oxen underneath it. [16]The pots, the shovels, the forks, and all the equipment for these Huram-abi made of burnished bronze for King Solomon for the house of the LORD. [17]In the plain of the Jordan the king cast them, in the clay ground between Succoth and Zeredah. [18]Solomon made all these things in great quantities, so that the weight of the bronze was not determined.

19 So Solomon made all the things that were in the house of God: the golden altar, the tables for the bread of the Presence, [20]the lampstands and their lamps of pure gold to burn before the inner sanctuary, as prescribed; [21]the flowers, the lamps, and the tongs, of purest gold; [22]the snuffers, basins, ladles, and firepans, of pure gold. As for the entrance to the temple: the inner doors to the most holy place and the doors of the nave of the temple were of gold.

5 Thus all the work that Solomon did for the house of the LORD was finished. Solomon brought in the things that his father David had dedicated, and stored the silver, the gold, and all the vessels in the treasuries of the house of God.

5.1: *Thus all the work that Solomon did for the house of the LORD was finished:* The Chronicler concludes his descriptions with this formal ending.

2 Then Solomon assembled the elders of Israel and all the heads of the tribes, the leaders of the ancestral houses of the people

a Cn: Heb *in the inner sanctuary*   *b* A Hebrew measure of volume of Israel, in Jerusalem, to bring up the ark of the covenant of the LORD out of the city of David, which is Zion. [3]And all the Israelites assembled before the king at the festival that is in the seventh month. [4]And all the elders of Israel came, and the Levites carried the ark. [5]So they brought up the ark, the tent of meeting, and all the holy vessels that were in the tent; the priests and the Levites brought them up. [6]King Solomon and all the congregation of Israel, who had assembled before him, were before the ark, sacrificing so many sheep and oxen that they could not be numbered or counted. [7]Then the priests brought the ark of the covenant of the LORD to its place, in the inner sanctuary of the house, in the most holy place, underneath the wings of the cherubim. [8]For the cherubim spread out their wings over the place of the ark, so that the cherubim made a covering above the ark and its poles. [9]The poles were so long that the ends of the poles were seen from the holy place in front of the inner sanctuary; but they could not be seen from outside; they are there to this day. [10]There was nothing in the ark except the two tablets that Moses put there at Horeb, where the LORD made a covenant[a] with the people of Israel after they came out of Egypt.

[11] Now when the priests came out of the holy place (for all the priests who were present had sanctified themselves, without regard to their divisions), [12]all the levitical singers, Asaph, Heman, and Jeduthun, their sons and kindred, arrayed in fine linen, with cymbals, harps, and lyres, stood east of the altar with one hundred twenty priests who were trumpeters. [13]It was the duty of the trumpeters and singers to make themselves heard in unison in praise and thanksgiving to the LORD, and when the song was raised, with trumpets and cymbals and other musical instruments, in praise to the LORD,

  "For he is good,
    for his steadfast love endures
       forever,"
the house, the house of the LORD, was filled with a cloud, [14]so that the priests could not stand to minister because of the cloud; for the glory of the LORD filled the house of God.

5.2–14: Installing the ark. Now that the structure of the Temple* has been completed, the Chronicler turns to the final act of centralizing worship at the Temple by narrating the entry of the ark into the structure. Alterations to his source in 1 Kings 8 are relatively minor. **5:** *So they brought up the ark, the tent of meeting, and all the holy vessels that were in the tent* underscores the Chronicler's sense that all the essential elements for formal worship are being brought into the Temple. *The priests and the Levites brought them up:* In 1 Kings 8.4 most translations note only the Levites, though the wording is the same as here. The phrase is normally understood to mean "levitical priests," used most often in the book of Deuteronomy and a very unusual expression for the Chronicler. His understanding of the term may have been different from Deuteronomy, since for the Chronicler it is not certain that Levites could carry the holy vessels. **11:** *(For all the priests who were present had sanctified themselves):* This parenthetical insert is not found in 1 Kings 8 and reflects the Chronicler's concern for proper ritual order. **13:** *It was the duty of the trumpeters and singers to make themselves heard in unison* reflects the Temple worship of the Chronicler's day and his concern with unified expressions of worship. *And when the song was raised . . . the house, the house of the LORD, was filled with a cloud:* Significantly, the Chronicler has God's presence, symbolized by the cloud, inhabit the Temple in response to the unified worship of the priests and Levites, who had taken the proper care to fulfill all the ritual requirements.

6 Then Solomon said, "The LORD has said that he would reside in thick darkness. [2]I have built you an exalted house, a place for you to reside in forever."

[3] Then the king turned around and blessed all the assembly of Israel, while all the assembly of Israel stood. [4]And he said, "Blessed be the LORD, the God of Israel, who with his hand has fulfilled what he promised with his mouth to my father David, saying, [5]'Since the day that I brought my people out of the land of Egypt, I have not chosen a city from any of the tribes of Israel in which to build a house, so that my name might be there, and I chose no one as ruler over my people Israel; [6]but I have chosen Jerusalem

a Heb lacks *a covenant*

in order that my name may be there, and I have chosen David to be over my people Israel.' [7]My father David had it in mind to build a house for the name of the LORD, the God of Israel. [8]But the LORD said to my father David, 'You did well to consider building a house for my name; [9]nevertheless you shall not build the house, but your son who shall be born to you shall build the house for my name.' [10]Now the LORD has fulfilled his promise that he made; for I have succeeded my father David, and sit on the throne of Israel, as the LORD promised, and have built the house for the name of the LORD, the God of Israel. [11]There I have set the ark, in which is the covenant of the LORD that he made with the people of Israel."

12 Then Solomon[a] stood before the altar of the LORD in the presence of the whole assembly of Israel, and spread out his hands. [13]Solomon had made a bronze platform five cubits long, five cubits wide, and three cubits high, and had set it in the court; and he stood on it. Then he knelt on his knees in the presence of the whole assembly of Israel, and spread out his hands toward heaven. [14]He said, "O LORD, God of Israel, there is no God like you, in heaven or on earth, keeping covenant in steadfast love with your servants who walk before you with all their heart— [15]you who have kept for your servant, my father David, what you promised to him. Indeed, you promised with your mouth and this day have fulfilled with your hand. [16]Therefore, O LORD, God of Israel, keep for your servant, my father David, that which you promised him, saying, 'There shall never fail you a successor before me to sit on the throne of Israel, if only your children keep to their way, to walk in my law as you have walked before me.' [17]Therefore, O LORD, God of Israel, let your word be confirmed, which you promised to your servant David.

6.1–7.11: Dedication of the Temple.* Now that God's presence dwells within the Temple, the Chronicler offers two prayers by Solomon, each emphasizing different aspects of the Temple's dedication. This section marks the mid-point of the Chronicler's history. 6.6: *I have chosen Jerusalem in order that my name*

may be there, and I have chosen David to be over my people Israel: This prayer links the building of the Temple with Solomon's legitimacy as a ruler. The Chronicler draws a strong contrast between God's previous actions and the "new order" now that God dwells in the Temple. Just as God's presence in the Temple demonstrates he has chosen Jerusalem, having one of the line of David build the Temple demonstrates God has chosen that line to be the legitimate rulers of Israel. **13:** *Then he knelt on his knees in the presence of the whole assembly of Israel:* In 1 Kings 8 Solomon stands throughout his prayer. While the Chronicler has him begin by standing, he portrays Solomon as humbled by the honor that has been bestowed on him. **16:** *If only your children keep to their way, to walk in my law as you have walked before me:* This phrase adds a conditionality to the succession of the Davidic line promised in 1 Chr 17. A ruler from the line of David is assured only if *they walk in my law,* possibly reflecting the larger role of the Pentateuch* in regulating daily life in the time of the Chronicler.

18 "But will God indeed reside with mortals on earth? Even heaven and the highest heaven cannot contain you, how much less this house that I have built! [19]Regard your servant's prayer and his plea, O LORD my God, heeding the cry and the prayer that your servant prays to you. [20]May your eyes be open day and night toward this house, the place where you promised to set your name, and may you heed the prayer that your servant prays toward this place. [21]And hear the plea of your servant and of your people Israel, when they pray toward this place; may you hear from heaven your dwelling place; hear and forgive.

22 "If someone sins against another and is required to take an oath and comes and swears before your altar in this house, [23]may you hear from heaven, and act, and judge your servants, repaying the guilty by bringing their conduct on their own head, and vindicating those who are in the right by rewarding them in accordance with their righteousness.

24 "When your people Israel, having sinned against you, are defeated before an

a Heb *he*

enemy but turn again to you, confess your name, pray and plead with you in this house, 25may you hear from heaven, and forgive the sin of your people Israel, and bring them again to the land that you gave to them and to their ancestors.

26 "When heaven is shut up and there is no rain because they have sinned against you, and then they pray toward this place, confess your name, and turn from their sin, because you punish them, 27may you hear in heaven, forgive the sin of your servants, your people Israel, when you teach them the good way in which they should walk; and send down rain upon your land, which you have given to your people as an inheritance.

28 "If there is famine in the land, if there is plague, blight, mildew, locust, or caterpillar; if their enemies besiege them in any of the settlements of the lands; whatever suffering, whatever sickness there is; 29whatever prayer, whatever plea from any individual or from all your people Israel, all knowing their own suffering and their own sorrows so that they stretch out their hands toward this house; 30may you hear from heaven, your dwelling place, forgive, and render to all whose heart you know, according to all their ways, for only you know the human heart. 31Thus may they fear you and walk in your ways all the days that they live in the land that you gave to our ancestors.

32 "Likewise when foreigners, who are not of your people Israel, come from a distant land because of your great name, and your mighty hand, and your outstretched arm, when they come and pray toward this house, 33may you hear from heaven your dwelling place, and do whatever the foreigners ask of you, in order that all the peoples of the earth may know your name and fear you, as do your people Israel, and that they may know that your name has been invoked on this house that I have built.

34 "If your people go out to battle against their enemies, by whatever way you shall send them, and they pray to you toward this city that you have chosen and the house that I have built for your name, 35then hear from heaven their prayer and their plea, and maintain their cause.

36 "If they sin against you—for there is no one who does not sin—and you are angry with them and give them to an enemy, so that they are carried away captive to a land far or near; 37then if they come to their senses in the land to which they have been taken captive, and repent, and plead with you in the land of their captivity, saying, 'We have sinned, and have done wrong; we have acted wickedly'; 38if they repent with all their heart and soul in the land of their captivity, to which they were taken captive, and pray toward their land, which you gave to their ancestors, the city that you have chosen, and the house that I have built for your name, 39then hear from heaven your dwelling place their prayer and their pleas, maintain their cause and forgive your people who have sinned against you. 40Now, O my God, let your eyes be open and your ears attentive to prayer from this place.

41 "Now rise up, O LORD God, and go to your resting place,
    you and the ark of your might.
Let your priests, O LORD God, be clothed with salvation,
    and let your faithful rejoice in your goodness.
42 O LORD God, do not reject your anointed one.
    Remember your steadfast love for your servant David."

6.18–42. 39: *Then hear from heaven your dwelling place their prayer and their pleas, maintain their cause and forgive your people:* As the Chronicler prepares to close Solomon's prayer, he departs significantly from the source in 1 Kings 8. Although in Kings Solomon requests that God act to grant Israel compassion in the sight of their captors (Kings was written while many Israelites lived in captivity in Babylon), the Chronicler makes no mention of captivity or captors. Rather, the appeal is more general, that God forgive. **40:** *Let your eyes be open and your ears attentive to prayer from this place:* God's dwelling in the Temple makes it a place of special "connectedness" to heaven, and prayers uttered at the Temple were understood to be particularly effective. **41:** *Now rise up, O LORD God, and go to your resting place:* The Chronicler closes with portions of Psalm 132, which reaffirms God's choice of the line of David and of Jerusalem, both appropriate themes to highlight the potential for Israel that is available under Solomon.

7 When Solomon had ended his prayer, fire came down from heaven and consumed the burnt offering and the sacrifices; and the glory of the LORD filled the temple. 2The priests could not enter the house of the LORD, because the glory of the LORD filled the LORD's house. 3When all the people of Israel saw the fire come down and the glory of the LORD on the temple, they bowed down on the pavement with their faces to the ground, and worshiped and gave thanks to the LORD, saying,

"For he is good,
　　for his steadfast love endures forever."

4 Then the king and all the people offered sacrifice before the LORD. 5King Solomon offered as a sacrifice twenty-two thousand oxen and one hundred twenty thousand sheep. So the king and all the people dedicated the house of God. 6The priests stood at their posts; the Levites also, with the instruments for music to the LORD that King David had made for giving thanks to the LORD—for his steadfast love endures forever—whenever David offered praises by their ministry. Opposite them the priests sounded trumpets; and all Israel stood.

7 Solomon consecrated the middle of the court that was in front of the house of the LORD; for there he offered the burnt offerings and the fat of the offerings of well-being because the bronze altar Solomon had made could not hold the burnt offering and the grain offering and the fat parts.

8 At that time Solomon held the festival for seven days, and all Israel with him, a very great congregation, from Lebo-hamath to the Wadi of Egypt. 9On the eighth day they held a solemn assembly; for they had observed the dedication of the altar seven days and the festival seven days. 10On the twenty-third day of the seventh month he sent the people away to their homes, joyful and in good spirits because of the goodness that the LORD had shown to David and to Solomon and to his people Israel.

11 Thus Solomon finished the house of the LORD and the king's house; all that Solomon had planned to do in the house of the LORD and in his own house he successfully accomplished.

7.1–11. 1: *Fire came down from heaven and consumed the burnt offering and the sacrifices:* Not present in 1 Kings 8, this allusion connects the dedication of the Temple with the altar of burnt offering in the wilderness (Lev 9.24) and with the affirmation of the reality of Israel's God by the prophet* Elijah on Mount Carmel (1 Kings 18.38). 3: *For he is good, for his steadfast love endures forever:* This affirmation by the people echoes the praise offered God by the Levites (5.13). 6: *Opposite them the priests sounded trumpets; and all Israel stood:* This depiction of the service of dedication is not in the Chronicler's source (1 Kings 8.62–63). Characteristic of the Chronicler's depiction of worship is the maintenance of proper order, the offering of praise, and the unified spirit of all the people.

12 Then the LORD appeared to Solomon in the night and said to him: "I have heard your prayer, and have chosen this place for myself as a house of sacrifice. 13When I shut up the heavens so that there is no rain, or command the locust to devour the land, or send pestilence among my people, 14if my people who are called by my name humble themselves, pray, seek my face, and turn from their wicked ways, then I will hear from heaven, and will forgive their sin and heal their land. 15Now my eyes will be open and my ears attentive to the prayer that is made in this place. 16For now I have chosen and consecrated this house so that my name may be there forever; my eyes and my heart will be there for all time. 17As for you, if you walk before me, as your father David walked, doing according to all that I have commanded you and keeping my statutes and my ordinances, 18then I will establish your royal throne, as I made covenant with your father David saying, 'You shall never lack a successor to rule over Israel.'

19 "But if you*a* turn aside and forsake my statutes and my commandments that I have set before you, and go and serve other gods and worship them, 20then I will pluck you*b* up from the land that I have given you;*b* and

a The word *you* in this verse is plural　　*b* Heb *them*

this house, which I have consecrated for my name, I will cast out of my sight, and will make it a proverb and a byword among all peoples. 21And regarding this house, now exalted, everyone passing by will be astonished, and say, 'Why has the LORD done such a thing to this land and to this house?' 22Then they will say, 'Because they abandoned the LORD the God of their ancestors who brought them out of the land of Egypt, and they adopted other gods, and worshiped them and served them; therefore he has brought all this calamity upon them.' "

7.12–22: God's second appearance. God first appeared to Solomon at Gibeon, shortly after the death of David. In this account, God communicates two basic points to Solomon. One is the uniqueness of the Temple,* the second is the conditionality of the rule of the line of David over Israel. While he has supplemented it at points, the Chronicler has generally followed his source (1 Kings 9.1–9). 12: *I have heard your prayer and have chosen this place for myself as a house of sacrifice:* For the Chronicler, the Temple is important because God has consecrated the place by choosing it for himself. This interpretation* by the Chronicler is related to the idea in Deuteronomy of God's choosing a place for his name to dwell (Deut 12.11, 14). The concept of a *house of sacrifice* places emphasis on the ritual aspects of Temple service and its role as a place of mediation between God and the community. 14: *If my people . . . humble themselves, pray, seek my face, and turn from their wicked ways* is a classic expression of the Chronicler's theology. When under divine judgment, the community must initiate its contact with God and seek God's face. 16: *My name may be there forever; my eyes and my heart will be there for all time:* This underscores the finality of God's choice of the Temple.

8 At the end of twenty years, during which Solomon had built the house of the LORD and his own house, 2Solomon rebuilt the cities that Huram had given to him, and settled the people of Israel in them.

3 Solomon went to Hamath-zobah, and captured it. 4He built Tadmor in the wilderness and all the storage towns that he built in Hamath. 5He also built Upper Beth-horon and Lower Beth-horon, fortified cities, with walls, gates, and bars, 6and Baalath, as well as all Solomon's storage towns, and all the towns for his chariots, the towns for his cavalry, and whatever Solomon desired to build, in Jerusalem, in Lebanon, and in all the land of his dominion. 7All the people who were left of the Hittites, the Amorites, the Perizzites, the Hivites, and the Jebusites, who were not of Israel, 8from their descendants who were still left in the land, whom the people of Israel had not destroyed—these Solomon conscripted for forced labor, as is still the case today. 9But of the people of Israel Solomon made no slaves for his work; they were soldiers, and his officers, the commanders of his chariotry and cavalry. 10These were the chief officers of King Solomon, two hundred fifty of them, who exercised authority over the people.

8.1–17: Highlights of Solomon's reign. The Chronicler now offers a series of brief reports, each reflecting Solomon's success and personal piety. Most of these reports touch on some aspect of the Temple.* 6: *Whatever Solomon desired to build, in Jerusalem, in Lebanon, and in all the land of his dominion:* Having built the Temple first, the way was now open for Solomon to engage in great public works projects.

11 Solomon brought Pharaoh's daughter from the city of David to the house that he had built for her, for he said, "My wife shall not live in the house of King David of Israel, for the places to which the ark of the LORD has come are holy."

12 Then Solomon offered up burnt offerings to the LORD on the altar of the LORD that he had built in front of the vestibule, 13as the duty of each day required, offering according to the commandment of Moses for the sabbaths, the new moons, and the three annual festivals—the festival of unleavened bread, the festival of weeks, and the festival of booths. 14According to the ordinance of his father David, he appointed the divisions of the priests for their service, and the Levites for their offices of praise and ministry alongside the priests as the duty of each day required, and the gatekeepers in their divisions for the several gates; for so David the man of God had commanded. 15They did not turn away from what the king had com-

manded the priests and Levites regarding anything at all, or regarding the treasuries.

16 Thus all the work of Solomon was accomplished from[a] the day the foundation of the house of the LORD was laid until the house of the LORD was finished completely.

8.11–16. 11: *My wife shall not live in the house of King David of Israel:* The Chronicler presumes throughout that his readers are familiar with 1 Kings 7.8, which notes Solomon's marriage to an Egyptian princess. The Chronicler's wording is ambiguous in Hebrew, but it seems to refer not to the places but to the people and things surrounding the ark. As a non-Israelite, Solomon's Egyptian wife could not fit the category of holy persons. 13: *Offering according to the commandment of Moses:* The Chronicler is concerned with proper ritual. The regulations for such sacrifices are in Num 28. 14: *According to the ordinance of his father David:* Just as Moses is recognized as a source of authority for the rules of worship, David occupies an esteemed position as source of proper ritual. 16: *Thus all the work of Solomon was accomplished:* With this formal closure, the Chronicler has described as much of Solomon's activity as he felt was necessary.

---

17 Then Solomon went to Ezion-geber and Eloth on the shore of the sea, in the land of Edom. [18]Huram sent him, in the care of his servants, ships and servants familiar with the sea. They went to Ophir, together with the servants of Solomon, and imported from there four hundred fifty talents of gold and brought it to King Solomon.

9 When the queen of Sheba heard of the fame of Solomon, she came to Jerusalem to test him with hard questions, having a very great retinue and camels bearing spices and very much gold and precious stones. When she came to Solomon, she discussed with him all that was on her mind. [2]Solomon answered all her questions; there was nothing hidden from Solomon that he could not explain to her. [3]When the queen of Sheba had observed the wisdom of Solomon, the house that he had built, [4]the food of his table, the seating of his officials, and the attendance of his servants, and their clothing, his valets, and their clothing, and his burnt offerings[b] that he offered at the house of the LORD, there was no more spirit left in her.

5 So she said to the king, "The report was true that I heard in my own land of your accomplishments and of your wisdom, [6]but I did not believe the[c] reports until I came and my own eyes saw it. Not even half of the greatness of your wisdom had been told to me; you far surpass the report that I had heard. [7]Happy are your people! Happy are these your servants, who continually attend you and hear your wisdom! [8]Blessed be the LORD your God, who has delighted in you and set you on his throne as king for the LORD your God. Because your God loved Israel and would establish them forever, he has made you king over them, that you may execute justice and righteousness." [9]Then she gave the king one hundred twenty talents of gold, a very great quantity of spices, and precious stones: there were no spices such as those that the queen of Sheba gave to King Solomon.

10 Moreover the servants of Huram and the servants of Solomon who brought gold from Ophir brought algum wood and precious stones. [11]From the algum wood, the king made steps[d] for the house of the LORD and for the king's house, lyres also and harps for the singers; there never was seen the like of them before in the land of Judah.

12 Meanwhile King Solomon granted the queen of Sheba every desire that she expressed, well beyond what she had brought to the king. Then she returned to her own land, with her servants.

13 The weight of gold that came to Solomon in one year was six hundred sixty-six talents of gold, [14]besides that which the traders and merchants brought; and all the kings of Arabia and the governors of the land brought gold and silver to Solomon. [15]King Solomon made two hundred large shields of beaten gold; six hundred shekels of beaten gold went into each large shield. [16]He made three hundred shields of beaten gold; three hundred shekels of gold went into each shield; and the king put them in the House of the Forest of Lebanon. [17]The king also

---

a Gk Syr Vg: Heb *to*   *b* Gk Syr Vg 1 Kings 10.5: Heb *ascent*   *c* Heb *their*   *d* Gk Vg: Meaning of Heb uncertain made a great ivory throne, and overlaid it with pure gold. 18 The throne had six steps and a footstool of gold, which were attached to the throne, and on each side of the seat were arm rests and two lions standing beside the arm rests, 19 while twelve lions were standing, one on each end of a step on the six steps. The like of it was never made in any kingdom. 20 All King Solomon's drinking vessels were of gold, and all the vessels of the House of the Forest of Lebanon were of pure gold; silver was not considered as anything in the days of Solomon. 21 For the king's ships went to Tarshish with the servants of Huram; once every three years the ships of Tarshish used to come bringing gold, silver, ivory, apes, and peacocks.*

22 Thus King Solomon excelled all the kings of the earth in riches and in wisdom. 23 All the kings of the earth sought the presence of Solomon to hear his wisdom, which God had put into his mind. 24 Every one of them brought a present, objects of silver and gold, garments, weaponry, spices, horses, and mules, so much year by year. 25 Solomon had four thousand stalls for horses and chariots, and twelve thousand horses, which he stationed in the chariot cities and with the king in Jerusalem. 26 He ruled over all the kings from the Euphrates to the land of the Philistines, and to the border of Egypt. 27 The king made silver as common in Jerusalem as stone, and cedar as plentiful as the sycamore of the Shephelah. 28 Horses were imported for Solomon from Egypt and from all lands.

29 Now the rest of the acts of Solomon, from first to last, are they not written in the history of the prophet Nathan, and in the prophecy of Ahijah the Shilonite, and in the visions of the seer Iddo concerning Jeroboam son of Nebat? 30 Solomon reigned in Jerusalem over all Israel forty years. 31 Solomon slept with his ancestors and was buried in the city of his father David; and his son Rehoboam succeeded him.

9.1–31: Evidence of Solomon's greatness. These narratives* are offered by the Chronicler as a way of affirming the extraordinary reign of Solomon. They relate the concepts of Solomon's great wisdom, received

from God, and his immense wealth, built in part by his wisdom. Generally, the Chronicler follows his source in 1 Kings closely. The Chronicler contends that having lavished his own wealth on the Temple,* Solomon (and the kingdom) receives great reward for such devotion. **2:** *Solomon answered all her questions:* Part of the plot of the story of the queen of Sheba's visit is that she came prepared with "hard questions," ready to present a test to Solomon. His success in answering her questions led to her honoring him with extravagant gifts. **16:** *The king put them in the House of the Forest of Lebanon,* part of the royal palace complex. **22:** *King Solomon excelled all the kings of the earth in riches and in wisdom:* Having built the Temple as soon as he was able, Solomon demonstrated his personal commitment to God's plans for Israel. As a result, he has military success, economic prosperity, and the recognition of powerful persons outside Israel. **29:** *Are they not written in the history of the prophet* Nathan, *and in the prophecy of Ahijah the Shilonite, and in the visions of the seer Iddo concerning Jeroboam son of Nebat?* These are figures from the Deuteronomistic* History, but there are no other indications that these individuals wrote accounts of Solomon's reign.

THE DISSOLUTION OF JUDAH

Chs. 10–36: Having described the high point of Israel under David and Solomon, the Chronicler now turns his attention to the flow of Israel's history after the division of the kingdom into two parts. Writing in Jerusalem during the post-exilic period, the Chronicler wants to present positive models for his own readership from Israel's past. These models share with David and Solomon a desire to ensure the proper worship of God in the Temple* and to instill in the community the ideal of seeking God. Focused on the Temple in Jerusalem, the Chronicler recounts the historical ebb and flow of the Davidic line that ruled Judah, only rarely incorporating any of the northern kingdom's history into his narrative.* When handling a positive model, the Chronicler follows a set pattern in which a prophet* brings a message to the king, offering a choice between God's way and a human way. The king chooses to obey God, does something good for the Temple, and all the community joins him in joyful obedience. The king goes on to enjoy military success and a positive rule. The figures from Israel's past particularly attractive to the Chronicler are Asa

a Or *baboons*

(14.1–16.14), Jehoshaphat (17.1–20.37), Joash (22.10–24.27), Hezekiah (29.1–32.33) and Josiah (34.1–35.27). In the case of the last two royal figures, the Chronicler is particularly lavish in praising the positive aspects of their rule. In general, the Chronicler adapts large portions of the narratives of 1 and 2 Kings in constructing his account, but there are extensive blocks of material that seem to have been generated by the Chronicler himself. Whether there were any sources for these materials is a debated issue.

10 Rehoboam went to Shechem, for all Israel had come to Shechem to make him king. ²When Jeroboam son of Nebat heard of it (for he was in Egypt, where he had fled from King Solomon), then Jeroboam returned from Egypt. ³They sent and called him; and Jeroboam and all Israel came and said to Rehoboam, ⁴"Your father made our yoke heavy. Now therefore lighten the hard service of your father and his heavy yoke that he placed on us, and we will serve you." ⁵He said to them, "Come to me again in three days." So the people went away.

6 Then King Rehoboam took counsel with the older men who had attended his father Solomon while he was still alive, saying, "How do you advise me to answer this people?" ⁷They answered him, "If you will be kind to this people and please them, and speak good words to them, then they will be your servants forever." ⁸But he rejected the advice that the older men gave him, and consulted the young men who had grown up with him and now attended him. ⁹He said to them, "What do you advise that we answer this people who have said to me, 'Lighten the yoke that your father put on us'?" ¹⁰The young men who had grown up with him said to him, "Thus should you speak to the people who said to you, 'Your father made our yoke heavy, but you must lighten it for us'; tell them, 'My little finger is thicker than my father's loins. ¹¹Now, whereas my father laid on you a heavy yoke, I will add to your yoke. My father disciplined you with whips, but I will discipline you with scorpions.'"

¹²So Jeroboam and all the people came to Rehoboam the third day, as the king had said, "Come to me again the third day." ¹³The king answered them harshly. King Re-

hoboam rejected the advice of the older men; ¹⁴he spoke to them in accordance with the advice of the young men, "My father made your yoke heavy, but I will add to it; my father disciplined you with whips, but I will discipline you with scorpions." ¹⁵So the king did not listen to the people, because it was a turn of affairs brought about by God so that the LORD might fulfill his word, which he had spoken by Ahijah the Shilonite to Jeroboam son of Nebat.

16 When all Israel saw that the king would not listen to them, the people answered the king,

"What share do we have in David?
    We have no inheritance in the son of
        Jesse.
Each of you to your tents, O Israel!
    Look now to your own house,
        O David."

So all Israel departed to their tents. ¹⁷But Rehoboam reigned over the people of Israel who were living in the cities of Judah. ¹⁸When King Rehoboam sent Hadoram, who was taskmaster over the forced labor, the people of Israel stoned him to death. King Rehoboam hurriedly mounted his chariot to flee to Jerusalem. ¹⁹So Israel has been in rebellion against the house of David to this day.

10.1–19: Revolt of the north. Jumping quickly into the reign of Rehoboam, Solomon's son, the Chronicler presents the root causes of the division between north and south as stemming from Solomon's excesses, in general following his source (1 Kings 12.1–19). However, he does have a basic problem, since he has excised from his narrative* the report of Solomon's failure to maintain sole allegiance to Israel's god (1 Kings 11). As a result, the division of the kingdom appears to result from arbitrary factors of human politics rather than God's rule. This he handles by a quick gesture to the narrative in 1 Kings, assuming his readers are familiar with the account. **4:** *Your father made our yoke heavy* is a reference to the burden of taxation to support public building projects, as well as labor gangs that each region was obligated to supply to the court. **15:** *It was a turn of affairs brought about by God so that the LORD might fulfill his word:* Not content to portray the affairs of Israel as subject only to human political ambition, the Chronicler notes that the revolt of the northern tribes triggered by Rehoboam's insensitivity was God's doing. The word *spoken by Ahijah the Shilonite* condemned Solomon for committing idolatry* (1 Kings 11.26–40) and fulfilled the promise that Jeroboam would rule over the larger part of the nation. **19:** *So Israel has been in rebellion against the house of David to this day,* using "Israel" in the formal sense of the northern kingdom formed from the tribes that objected to Rehoboam's policies. The loss of the greater portion of the nation's population and the more economically productive portion of the land must have been seen as a great disaster by Rehoboam.

11 When Rehoboam came to Jerusalem, he assembled one hundred eighty thousand chosen troops of the house of Judah and Benjamin to fight against Israel, to restore the kingdom to Rehoboam. ²But the word of the LORD came to Shemaiah the man of God: ³Say to King Rehoboam of Judah, son of Solomon, and to all Israel in Judah and Benjamin, ⁴"Thus says the LORD: You shall not go up or fight against your kindred. Let everyone return home, for this thing is from me." So they heeded the word of the LORD and turned back from the expedition against Jeroboam.

5 Rehoboam resided in Jerusalem, and he built cities for defense in Judah. ⁶He built up Bethlehem, Etam, Tekoa, ⁷Beth-zur, Soco, Adullam, ⁸Gath, Mareshah, Ziph, ⁹Adoraim, Lachish, Azekah, ¹⁰Zorah, Aijalon, and Hebron, fortified cities that are in Judah and in Benjamin. ¹¹He made the fortresses strong, and put commanders in them, and stores of food, oil, and wine. ¹²He also put large shields and spears in all the cities, and made them very strong. So he held Judah and Benjamin.

11.1–12.16: The reign of Rehoboam. Given the division of the kingdom, the Chronicler now turns to consider Rehoboam's rule. Rehoboam is seen in both positive and negative terms by the Chronicler. **11.1:** *When Rehoboam came to Jerusalem, he assembled . . . troops of the house of Judah and Benjamin to fight against Israel, to restore the kingdom:* A normal response to revolt against his rule would be to attack before the new kingdom can organize itself. **4:** *Thus says the LORD: You shall not go up or fight against your kindred:* Prophets* function in the Chronicler's

scheme to make the reader and the protagonist aware of an important decision that must be made. Here the dilemma is clear: follow God's word and allow the division of the community and the diminishment of the Davidic kingdom, or attack quickly and try to regain the kingdom. *So they heeded the word of the LORD:* No motivation is offered, but Rehoboam makes the right decision and follows God's desires. **12:** *So he held Judah and Benjamin:* Having followed God's desires, Rehoboam is able to achieve his military goals of fortifying the northern border and creating strongholds to defend his realm.

13 The priests and the Levites who were in all Israel presented themselves to him from all their territories. ¹⁴The Levites had left their common lands and their holdings and had come to Judah and Jerusalem, because Jeroboam and his sons had prevented them from serving as priests of the LORD, ¹⁵and had appointed his own priests for the high places, and for the goat-demons, and for the calves that he had made. ¹⁶Those who had set their hearts to seek the LORD God of Israel came after them from all the tribes of Israel to Jerusalem to sacrifice to the LORD, the God of their ancestors. ¹⁷They strengthened the kingdom of Judah, and for three years they made Rehoboam son of Solomon secure, for they walked for three years in the way of David and Solomon.

11.13–17. 13: *The priests and Levites who were in all Israel presented themselves to him:* Rehoboam's following the word from God brings additional support from those devoted to serving God by worship. **16:** *Those who had set their hearts to seek the LORD God of Israel came after them:* In addition to receiving the support of priests and Levites from "all Israel," all those who truly sought God came and joined Rehoboam's kingdom.

18 Rehoboam took as his wife Mahalath daughter of Jerimoth son of David, and of Abihail daughter of Eliab son of Jesse. ¹⁹She bore him sons: Jeush, Shemariah, and Zaham. ²⁰After her he took Maacah daughter of Absalom, who bore him Abijah, Attai, Ziza, and Shelomith. ²¹Rehoboam loved Maacah daughter of Absalom more than all his other wives and concubines (he took

eighteen wives and sixty concubines, and became the father of twenty-eight sons and sixty daughters). 22Rehoboam appointed Abijah son of Maacah as chief prince among his brothers, for he intended to make him king. 23He dealt wisely, and distributed some of his sons through all the districts of Judah and Benjamin, in all the fortified cities; he gave them abundant provisions, and found many wives for them.

12 When the rule of Rehoboam was established and he grew strong, he abandoned the law of the LORD, he and all Israel with him. 2In the fifth year of King Rehoboam, because they had been unfaithful to the LORD, King Shishak of Egypt came up against Jerusalem 3with twelve hundred chariots and sixty thousand cavalry. A countless army came with him from Egypt—Libyans, Sukkiim, and Ethiopians.*a* 4He took the fortified cities of Judah and came as far as Jerusalem. 5Then the prophet Shemaiah came to Rehoboam and to the officers of Judah, who had gathered at Jerusalem because of Shishak, and said to them, "Thus says the LORD: You abandoned me, so I have abandoned you to the hand of Shishak." 6Then the officers of Israel and the king humbled themselves and said, "The LORD is in the right." 7When the LORD saw that they humbled themselves, the word of the LORD came to Shemaiah, saying: "They have humbled themselves; I will not destroy them, but I will grant them some deliverance, and my wrath shall not be poured out on Jerusalem by the hand of Shishak. 8Nevertheless they shall be his servants, so that they may know the difference between serving me and serving the kingdoms of other lands."

12.1–8. 1: *When the rule of Rehoboam was established and he grew strong, he abandoned the law of the LORD, he and all Israel with him:* Having emphasized the positive elements of Rehoboam's rule, the historian now turns to the downside. The *law* (Torah*) refers to the Pentateuchal* regulations for bringing everyday life into accord with God's ways. 2: *Because they had been unfaithful to the LORD:* Historical experience is shaped by the degree to which the community seeks God. Since the people have abandoned the law, God now abandons the community and allows

an enemy to gain the upper hand. 5: *You abandoned me, so I have abandoned you to the hand of Shishak:* This is a classic expression of the Chronicler's sense of immediate retribution, that God repays the community for good or ill depending on the community's action toward God. While the Chronicler is using some of the materials in 1 Kings 14.21–28, in this source the connection is not explicitly drawn between the community's actions and Shishak's campaign. 7: *They have humbled themselves; I will not destroy them, but I will grant them some deliverance:* The second word from God by the prophet* Shemaiah contains God's immediate response to Israel's leaders who have humbled themselves. Though the community will not be destroyed, they will be "humbled" by having to serve the Egyptian king.

9 So King Shishak of Egypt came up against Jerusalem; he took away the treasures of the house of the LORD and the treasures of the king's house; he took everything. He also took away the shields of gold that Solomon had made; 10but King Rehoboam made in place of them shields of bronze, and committed them to the hands of the officers of the guard, who kept the door of the king's house. 11Whenever the king went into the house of the LORD, the guard would come along bearing them, and would then bring them back to the guardroom. 12Because he humbled himself the wrath of the LORD turned from him, so as not to destroy them completely; moreover, conditions were good in Judah.

13 So King Rehoboam established himself in Jerusalem and reigned. Rehoboam was forty-one years old when he began to reign; he reigned seventeen years in Jerusalem, the city that the LORD had chosen out of all the tribes of Israel to put his name there. His mother's name was Naamah the Ammonite. 14He did evil, for he did not set his heart to seek the LORD.

15 Now the acts of Rehoboam, from first to last, are they not written in the records of the prophet Shemaiah and of the seer Iddo, recorded by genealogy? There were continual wars between Rehoboam and Jeroboam.

a Or *Nubians;* Heb *Cushites*

16Rehoboam slept with his ancestors and was buried in the city of David; and his son Abijah succeeded him.

12.9–16. 9: *So King Shishak of Egypt came up against Jerusalem:* In the Chronicler's view, the historical experience of the community is determined by the community's action toward God. In Egyptian temple wall reliefs at Thebes, there are fragmentary scenes showing Shishak's (Sheshonq I) campaign into Syria-Palestine around the year 930 BCE. Shishak was apparently trying to reassert Egyptian control over the weaker nation-states in the region. 12: *Moreover, conditions were good in Judah:* The Chronicler softens the impact of this humiliation by noting Judah did well despite Egyptian control. 14: *He did evil, for he did not set his heart to seek the LORD:* In the summary of Rehoboam's reign, the Chronicler adds this evaluation, expressing his judgment that "seeking" or "abandoning" God depends on a human's willingness to act in a proper way.

13 In the eighteenth year of King Jeroboam, Abijah began to reign over Judah. 2He reigned for three years in Jerusalem. His mother's name was Micaiah daughter of Uriel of Gibeah.

Now there was war between Abijah and Jeroboam. 3Abijah engaged in battle, having an army of valiant warriors, four hundred thousand picked men; and Jeroboam drew up his line of battle against him with eight hundred thousand picked mighty warriors. 4Then Abijah stood on the slope of Mount Zemaraim that is in the hill country of Ephraim, and said, "Listen to me, Jeroboam and all Israel! 5Do you not know that the LORD God of Israel gave the kingship over Israel forever to David and his sons by a covenant of salt? 6Yet Jeroboam son of Nebat, a servant of Solomon son of David, rose up and rebelled against his lord; 7and certain worthless scoundrels gathered around him and defied Rehoboam son of Solomon, when Rehoboam was young and irresolute and could not withstand them.

13.1–22: **The reign of Abijah.** After Rehoboam's checkered rule, Abijah appears as a defender of Davidic prerogatives. The Chronicler has greatly expanded the brief account in his source (1 Kings 15.1–8), using the

dramatic setting of assembled armies and stirring speeches. While the deuteronomistic* historian saw Abijah as evil, the Chronicler rehabilitates the figure of Abijah into a positive example for his readers. 5: *Do you not know that the LORD God of Israel gave the kingship over Israel forever to David and his sons:* In 1 and 2 Kings, the Davidic privilege of rule over all Israel was removed because of Solomon's idolatrous actions (1 Kings 11.9–13), but the Chronicler has excised this incident from his recounting of Solomon's reign. In the Chronicler's narrative,* God's covenant* with David is still in effect; the northern tribes are in revolt against the Davidic line and God. 7: *Certain worthless scoundrels gathered around him and defied Rehoboam* constitutes a revision of sorts from his earlier account of the split in the kingdom (10.1–19). It is not Rehoboam's disdain for the request of the northern tribes for economic relief that motivated the split, but unsavory types who have backed Jeroboam's revolt.

8 "And now you think that you can withstand the kingdom of the LORD in the hand of the sons of David, because you are a great multitude and have with you the golden calves that Jeroboam made as gods for you. 9Have you not driven out the priests of the LORD, the descendants of Aaron, and the Levites, and made priests for yourselves like the peoples of other lands? Whoever comes to be consecrated with a young bull or seven rams becomes a priest of what are no gods. 10But as for us, the LORD is our God, and we have not abandoned him. We have priests ministering to the LORD who are descendants of Aaron, and Levites for their service. 11They offer to the LORD every morning and every evening burnt offerings and fragrant incense, set out the rows of bread on the table of pure gold, and care for the golden lampstand so that its lamps may burn every evening; for we keep the charge of the LORD our God, but you have abandoned him. 12See, God is with us at our head, and his priests have their battle trumpets to sound the call to battle against you. O Israelites, do not fight against the LORD, the God of your ancestors; for you cannot succeed."

13.8–12. 9: *Have you not driven out the priests of the LORD, the descendants of Aaron, and the Levites:* This is a slight recasting of the Chronicler's earlier account (11.13–15) where the religious personnel had simply been prevented from officiating. The more serious charge, *made priests for yourselves like the peoples of other lands,* indicates that the northern kingdom had abandoned their distinctiveness as a people of God and had reduced themselves to being like any other human political entity. **10:** *As for us, the* LORD *is our God, and we have not abandoned him:* For the Chronicler this is the ultimate statement of community fidelity, expressed most clearly in concern for proper worship and Temple* service. *We have priests ministering to the* LORD *who are descendants of Aaron, and Levites for their service:* By maintaining the proper order for worship and approach to God, the community expresses its desire to seek him. **12:** *Do not fight against the* LORD, *the God of your ancestors; for you cannot succeed:* Military success depends upon the community's relationship to God, whether "seeking" him or "abandoning" him. With God beside them, the Chronicler cannot imagine a military defeat.

13 Jeroboam had sent an ambush around to come on them from behind; thus his troops*a* were in front of Judah, and the ambush was behind them. ¹⁴When Judah turned, the battle was in front of them and behind them. They cried out to the LORD, and the priests blew the trumpets. ¹⁵Then the people of Judah raised the battle shout. And when the people of Judah shouted, God defeated Jeroboam and all Israel before Abijah and Judah. ¹⁶The Israelites fled before Judah, and God gave them into their hands. ¹⁷Abijah and his army defeated them with great slaughter; five hundred thousand picked men of Israel fell slain. ¹⁸Thus the Israelites were subdued at that time, and the people of Judah prevailed, because they relied on the LORD, the God of their ancestors. ¹⁹Abijah pursued Jeroboam, and took cities from him: Bethel with its villages and Jeshanah with its villages and Ephron*b* with its villages. ²⁰Jeroboam did not recover his power in the days of Abijah; the LORD struck him down, and he died. ²¹But Abijah grew strong. He took fourteen wives, and became the father of twenty-two sons and sixteen daughters. ²²The rest of the acts of Abijah, his behavior and his deeds, are written in the story of the prophet Iddo.

13.13–22. 14: *They cried out to the* LORD, *and the priests blew the trumpets:* Sensing the battle was turning in the northern kingdom's favor, the armies of Judah call on God for assistance. **15:** *God defeated Jeroboam and all Israel before Abijah and Judah:* The victory is not won by military strategy but by God's direct intervention. **21:** *Abijah grew strong,* in contrast to Jeroboam and the northern kingdom. Abijah's success is the result of his, and Judah's, reliance on the proper means of worship and the offering of continual service to God. Taking such care to maintain the right relationship to God provided the community with its security and well-being, a model for the Chronicler's reader.

14 ᶜSo Abijah slept with his ancestors, and they buried him in the city of David. His son Asa succeeded him. In his days the land had rest for ten years. ²ᵈAsa did what was good and right in the sight of the LORD his God. ³He took away the foreign altars and the high places, broke down the pillars, hewed down the sacred poles,*e* ⁴and commanded Judah to seek the LORD, the God of their ancestors, and to keep the law and the commandment. ⁵He also removed from all the cities of Judah the high places and the incense altars. And the kingdom had rest under him. ⁶He built fortified cities in Judah while the land had rest. He had no war in those years, for the LORD gave him peace. ⁷He said to Judah, "Let us build these cities, and surround them with walls and towers, gates and bars; the land is still ours because we have sought the LORD our God; we have sought him, and he has given us peace on every side." So they built and prospered. ⁸Asa had an army of three hundred thousand from Judah, armed with large shields and spears, and two hundred eighty thousand troops from Benjamin who carried shields and drew bows; all these were mighty warriors.

14.1–16.14: The reign of Asa. In this classic expansion of his source in 1 Kings, the Chronicler takes a mere

---

a Heb *they*　　*b* Another reading is *Ephrain*
c Ch 13.23 in Heb　　*d* Ch 14.1 in Heb
e Heb *Asherim*

seven verses on the reign of Asa and develops three chapters with complex plots and a rich theological content. The Chronicler portrays Asa as a model ruler who succeeds in bringing the community into peace, security, and joy by his devotion to God. **2**: *Asa did what was good and right in the sight of the LORD:* The first evaluation the reader receives of Asa is that he acted to suppress idolatry.* **4**: *And commanded Judah to seek the LORD, the God of their ancestors, and to keep the law and the commandment:* In his office as king, Asa also served as the chief legal authority in the realm. The Chronicler has him legislate the observance of Pentateuchal* law, presumably enforced by royal agents.

9 Zerah the Ethiopian*a* came out against them with an army of a million men and three hundred chariots, and came as far as Mareshah. [10]Asa went out to meet him, and they drew up their lines of battle in the valley of Zephathah at Mareshah. [11]Asa cried to the LORD his God, "O LORD, there is no difference for you between helping the mighty and the weak. Help us, O LORD our God, for we rely on you, and in your name we have come against this multitude. O LORD, you are our God; let no mortal prevail against you." [12]So the LORD defeated the Ethiopians*b* before Asa and before Judah, and the Ethiopians*b* fled. [13]Asa and the army with him pursued them as far as Gerar, and the Ethiopians*b* fell until no one remained alive; for they were broken before the LORD and his army. The people of Judah*c* carried away a great quantity of booty. [14]They defeated all the cities around Gerar, for the fear of the LORD was on them. They plundered all the cities; for there was much plunder in them. [15]They also attacked the tents of those who had livestock,*d* and carried away sheep and goats in abundance, and camels. Then they returned to Jerusalem.

14.9–15. 9: *Zerah the Ethiopian came out against them with an army of a million men:* Zerah may have been a general of Osorkon I, who ruled Egypt in the opening decades of the ninth century BCE. The figure of a million men may be a of convention for expressing a large massed force rather than a specific number. **13**: *The Ethiopians fell until no one remained alive; for they were broken before the LORD and his army:* Since God

was fighting on behalf of Judah, the Chronicler envisions this as a compelling victory. God's army is the Judean force of Asa.

15 The spirit of God came upon Azariah son of Oded. [2]He went out to meet Asa and said to him, "Hear me, Asa, and all Judah and Benjamin: The LORD is with you, while you are with him. If you seek him, he will be found by you, but if you abandon him, he will abandon you. [3]For a long time Israel was without the true God, and without a teaching priest, and without law; [4]but when in their distress they turned to the LORD, the God of Israel, and sought him, he was found by them. [5]In those times it was not safe for anyone to go or come, for great disturbances afflicted all the inhabitants of the lands. [6]They were broken in pieces, nation against nation and city against city, for God troubled them with every sort of distress. [7]But you, take courage! Do not let your hands be weak, for your work shall be rewarded."

8 When Asa heard these words, the prophecy of Azariah son of Oded,*e* he took courage, and put away the abominable idols from all the land of Judah and Benjamin and from the towns that he had taken in the hill country of Ephraim. He repaired the altar of the LORD that was in front of the vestibule of the house of the LORD.*f* [9]He gathered all Judah and Benjamin, and those from Ephraim, Manasseh, and Simeon who were residing as aliens with them, for great numbers had deserted to him from Israel when they saw that the LORD his God was with him. [10]They were gathered at Jerusalem in the third month of the fifteenth year of the reign of Asa. [11]They sacrificed to the LORD on that day, from the booty that they had brought, seven hundred oxen and seven thousand sheep. [12]They entered into a covenant to seek the LORD, the God of their ancestors, with all their heart and with all their soul. [13]Whoever would not seek the LORD, the God of Israel, should be put to death,

a Or Nubian; Heb Cushite   *b* Or Nubians; Heb Cushites   *c* Heb They   *d* Meaning of Heb uncertain   *e* Compare Syr Vg: Heb the prophecy, the prophet Obed   *f* Heb the vestibule of the LORD whether young or old, man or woman. [14]They took an oath to the LORD with a loud voice, and with shouting, and with trumpets, and with horns. [15]All Judah rejoiced over the oath; for they had sworn with all their heart, and had sought him with their whole desire, and he was found by them, and the LORD gave them rest all around.

15.1–15. 2: *The LORD is with you, while you are with him. If you seek him, he will be found by you, but if you abandon him, he will abandon you:* This is a succinct expression of the Chronicler's understanding of God's relationship to Israel. The entire message brought by Azariah is intended to present Asa with an opportunity to act further on behalf of God. **3:** *Israel was without the true God and without a teaching priest and without law:* This indefinite reference possibly relates to the period before Moses, the period of the judges, or some period of anarchy, though perhaps no specific period is intended. The Chronicler noted these items to help his readers appreciate what was present in their own time: the inheritance of God, teaching priests, and law. **9:** *For great numbers had deserted to him:* Asa's actions in response to Azariah's word receive affirmation from others who come to Judah to join with Asa. **12:** *They entered into a covenant* to seek the LORD, the God of their ancestors, with all their heart and all their soul:* This echoes Deut 6.5, which calls on Israel to love God with complete commitment. **15:** *All Judah rejoiced over the oath; for they had sworn with all their heart, and had sought him with their whole desire, and he was found by them, and the LORD gave them rest all around:* When the community is unified in intent, then God will respond. The "seeking" of God had been committed without reservation, and as the result of finding God, the community enjoyed peace.

---

16 King Asa even removed his mother Maacah from being queen mother because she had made an abominable image for Asherah. Asa cut down her image, crushed it, and burned it at the Wadi Kidron. [17]But the high places were not taken out of Israel. Nevertheless the heart of Asa was true all his days. [18]He brought into the house of God the votive gifts of his father and his own votive gifts—silver, gold, and utensils. [19]And there was no more war until the thirty-fifth year of the reign of Asa.

16 In the thirty-sixth year of the reign of Asa, King Baasha of Israel went up against Judah, and built Ramah, to prevent anyone from going out or coming into the territory of[a] King Asa of Judah. [2]Then Asa took silver and gold from the treasures of the house of the LORD and the king's house, and sent them to King Ben-hadad of Aram, who resided in Damascus, saying, [3]"Let there be an alliance between me and you, like that between my father and your father; I am sending to you silver and gold; go, break your alliance with King Baasha of Israel, so that he may withdraw from me." [4]Ben-hadad listened to King Asa, and sent the commanders of his armies against the cities of Israel. They conquered Ijon, Dan, Abel-maim, and all the store-cities of Naphtali. [5]When Baasha heard of it, he stopped building Ramah, and let his work cease. [6]Then King Asa brought all Judah, and they carried away the stones of Ramah and its timber, with which Baasha had been building, and with them he built up Geba and Mizpah.

7 At that time the seer Hanani came to King Asa of Judah, and said to him, "Because you relied on the king of Aram, and did not rely on the LORD your God, the army of the king of Aram has escaped you. [8]Were not the Ethiopians[b] and the Libyans a huge army with exceedingly many chariots and cavalry? Yet because you relied on the LORD, he gave them into your hand. [9]For the eyes of the LORD range throughout the entire earth, to strengthen those whose heart is true to him. You have done foolishly in this; for from now on you will have wars." [10]Then Asa was angry with the seer, and put him in the stocks, in prison, for he was in a rage with him because of this. And Asa inflicted cruelties on some of the people at the same time.

11 The acts of Asa, from first to last, are written in the Book of the Kings of Judah and Israel. [12]In the thirty-ninth year of his reign Asa was diseased in his feet, and his disease became severe; yet even in his disease he did not seek the LORD, but sought help from physicians. [13]Then Asa slept with his ances-

a Heb lacks *the territory of*   *b* Or *Nubians*; Heb *Cushites* tors, dying in the forty-first year of his reign. [14] They buried him in the tomb that he had hewn out for himself in the city of David. They laid him on a bier that had been filled with various kinds of spices prepared by the perfumer's art; and they made a very great fire in his honor.

15.16–16.14. 16.7: *Because you relied on the king of Aram, and did not rely on the LORD your God:* Asa's use of Temple* treasures to bribe the king of Aram into attacking the northern kingdom was a breech of faith in the ability of God to act on Judah's behalf. The penalty for this breech is continuing military conflict. 14: *They made a very great fire in his honor:* The Chronicler alone records the custom of making a "great fire" in honor of a deceased ruler, a custom found on the island of Cyprus, among other cultures.

17 His son Jehoshaphat succeeded him, and strengthened himself against Israel. [2] He placed forces in all the fortified cities of Judah, and set garrisons in the land of Judah, and in the cities of Ephraim that his father Asa had taken. [3] The LORD was with Jehoshaphat, because he walked in the earlier ways of his father;[a] he did not seek the Baals, [4] but sought the God of his father and walked in his commandments, and not according to the ways of Israel. [5] Therefore the LORD established the kingdom in his hand. All Judah brought tribute to Jehoshaphat, and he had great riches and honor. [6] His heart was courageous in the ways of the LORD; and furthermore he removed the high places and the sacred poles[b] from Judah.

17.1–20.37: **The reign of Jehoshaphat.** This is another of the Chronicler's expansions of limited material in the narratives* of 1 and 2 Kings. The Chronicler takes an initially positive assessment of Jehoshaphat and expands his role into a model of bringing the community into accord with God. 4: *Sought the God of his father and walked in his commandments and not according to the ways of Israel:* Israel was the formal name for the northern kingdom. A prime motif* in this narrative is the danger the idolatrous north presented to the faithful southern kingdom, Judah. The Chronicler begins early in this narrative to underscore the contrast. 6: *His heart was courageous in the ways*

of the LORD: The *heart* was often seen as the intellectual center or seat of the will in ancient Israel. The expression here conveys Jehoshaphat's desire to conform to the will of God despite the opposition he may encounter.

7 In the third year of his reign he sent his officials, Ben-hail, Obadiah, Zechariah, Nethanel, and Micaiah, to teach in the cities of Judah. [8] With them were the Levites, Shemaiah, Nethaniah, Zebadiah, Asahel, Shemiramoth, Jehonathan, Adonijah, Tobijah, and Tob-adonijah; and with these Levites, the priests Elishama and Jehoram. [9] They taught in Judah, having the book of the law of the LORD with them; they went around through all the cities of Judah and taught among the people.

10 The fear of the LORD fell on all the kingdoms of the lands around Judah, and they did not make war against Jehoshaphat. [11] Some of the Philistines brought Jehoshaphat presents, and silver for tribute; and the Arabs also brought him seven thousand seven hundred rams and seven thousand seven hundred male goats. [12] Jehoshaphat grew steadily greater. He built fortresses and storage cities in Judah. [13] He carried out great works in the cities of Judah. He had soldiers, mighty warriors, in Jerusalem. [14] This was the muster of them by ancestral houses: Of Judah, the commanders of the thousands: Adnah the commander, with three hundred thousand mighty warriors, [15] and next to him Jehohanan the commander, with two hundred eighty thousand, [16] and next to him Amasiah son of Zichri, a volunteer for the service of the LORD, with two hundred thousand mighty warriors. [17] Of Benjamin: Eliada, a mighty warrior, with two hundred thousand armed with bow and shield; [18] and next to him Jehozabad with one hundred eighty thousand armed for war. [19] These were in the service of the king, besides those whom the king had placed in the fortified cities throughout all Judah.

17.7–19. 7–9: *They taught in Judah, having the book of the law of the LORD with them:* This extensive teach-

a Another reading is *his father David*   *b* Heb *Asherim* ing mission is undertaken with representatives of the court (*officials*), the central religious authorities (*priests*), and those entrusted with the task of teaching the religious traditions of the community (*Levites*). The *book of the law of the LORD* may refer to the present book of Deuteronomy. **12:** *Jehoshaphat grew steadily greater:* The reward for his faithfulness was peace and prosperity, allowing the king to build stronger fortifications and an ever stronger military force.

18 Now Jehoshaphat had great riches and honor; and he made a marriage alliance with Ahab. 2 After some years he went down to Ahab in Samaria. Ahab slaughtered an abundance of sheep and oxen for him and for the people who were with him, and induced him to go up against Ramoth-gilead. 3 King Ahab of Israel said to King Jehoshaphat of Judah, "Will you go with me to Ramoth-gilead?" He answered him, "I am with you, my people are your people. We will be with you in the war."

4 But Jehoshaphat also said to the king of Israel, "Inquire first for the word of the LORD." 5 Then the king of Israel gathered the prophets together, four hundred of them, and said to them, "Shall we go to battle against Ramoth-gilead, or shall I refrain?" They said, "Go up; for God will give it into the hand of the king." 6 But Jehoshaphat said, "Is there no other prophet of the LORD here of whom we may inquire?" 7 The king of Israel said to Jehoshaphat, "There is still one other by whom we may inquire of the LORD, Micaiah son of Imlah; but I hate him, for he never prophesies anything favorable about me, but only disaster." Jehoshaphat said, "Let the king not say such a thing." 8 Then the king of Israel summoned an officer and said, "Bring quickly Micaiah son of Imlah." 9 Now the king of Israel and King Jehoshaphat of Judah were sitting on their thrones, arrayed in their robes; and they were sitting at the threshing floor at the entrance of the gate of Samaria; and all the prophets were prophesying before them. 10 Zedekiah son of Chenaanah made for himself horns of iron, and he said, "Thus says the LORD: With these you shall gore the Arameans until they are destroyed." 11 All the prophets were prophesying the same and saying, "Go up to Ramoth-gilead and triumph; the LORD will give it into the hand of the king."

12 The messenger who had gone to summon Micaiah said to him, "Look, the words of the prophets with one accord are favorable to the king; let your word be like the word of one of them, and speak favorably." 13 But Micaiah said, "As the LORD lives, whatever my God says, that I will speak."

18.1–13. 1: *He made a marriage alliance with Ahab:* The Chronicler assumes throughout that his readers know the evils Omri and his son Ahab had brought on the north by idolatrous worship. Closely following his source (1 Kings 22.1–28), the Chronicler also uses his source's anti-Ahab stance to make his own points. Ahab had engaged in extensive trade and hence an alliance may have been economically beneficial to Jehoshaphat. **9:** *They were sitting at the threshing* floor at the entrance of the gate of Samaria; and all the prophets* were prophesying before them:* Threshing floors were associated with activities of importance to the community. Being on a height to catch prevailing winds, such clear, open areas would be more suitable for a large gathering than small spaces within the defensive city walls. **13:** *But Micaiah said, "As the LORD lives, whatever my God says, that I will speak":* Despite the pressure to go along with the words of the other prophets, Micaiah offers a classic statement of the prophet's obligation to be obedient to God alone. The expression is very close to that of the pagan prophet Balaam (Num 22.38).

14 When he had come to the king, the king said to him, "Micaiah, shall we go to Ramoth-gilead to battle, or shall I refrain?" He answered, "Go up and triumph; they will be given into your hand." 15 But the king said to him, "How many times must I make you swear to tell me nothing but the truth in the name of the LORD?" 16 Then Micaiah*a* said, "I saw all Israel scattered on the mountains, like sheep without a shepherd; and the LORD said, 'These have no master; let each one go home in peace.' " 17 The king of Israel said to Jehoshaphat, "Did I not tell you that he would not prophesy anything favorable about me, but only disaster?"

18 Then Micaiah*a* said, "Therefore hear

a Heb *he*

the word of the LORD: I saw the LORD sitting on his throne, with all the host of heaven standing to the right and to the left of him. 19And the LORD said, 'Who will entice King Ahab of Israel, so that he may go up and fall at Ramoth-gilead?' Then one said one thing, and another said another, 20until a spirit came forward and stood before the LORD, saying, 'I will entice him.' The LORD asked him, 'How?' 21He replied, 'I will go out and be a lying spirit in the mouth of all his prophets.' Then the LORD*a* said, 'You are to entice him, and you shall succeed; go out and do it.' 22So you see, the LORD has put a lying spirit in the mouth of these your prophets; the LORD has decreed disaster for you."

23 Then Zedekiah son of Chenaanah came up to Micaiah, slapped him on the cheek, and said, "Which way did the spirit of the LORD pass from me to speak to you?" 24Micaiah replied, "You will find out on that day when you go in to hide in an inner chamber." 25The king of Israel then ordered, "Take Micaiah, and return him to Amon the governor of the city and to Joash the king's son; 26and say, 'Thus says the king: Put this fellow in prison, and feed him on reduced rations of bread and water until I return in peace.' " 27Micaiah said, "If you return in peace, the LORD has not spoken by me." And he said, "Hear, you peoples, all of you!"

28 So the king of Israel and King Jehoshaphat of Judah went up to Ramoth-gilead. 29The king of Israel said to Jehoshaphat, "I will disguise myself and go into battle, but you wear your robes." So the king of Israel disguised himself, and they went into battle. 30Now the king of Aram had commanded the captains of his chariots, "Fight with no one small or great, but only with the king of Israel." 31When the captains of the chariots saw Jehoshaphat, they said, "It is the king of Israel." So they turned to fight against him; and Jehoshaphat cried out, and the LORD helped him. God drew them away from him, 32for when the captains of the chariots saw that it was not the king of Israel, they turned back from pursuing him. 33But a certain man drew his bow and unknowingly struck the king of Israel between the scale armor and the breastplate; so he said to the driver

of his chariot, "Turn around, and carry me out of the battle, for I am wounded." 34The battle grew hot that day, and the king of Israel propped himself up in his chariot facing the Arameans until evening; then at sunset he died.

19 King Jehoshaphat of Judah returned in safety to his house in Jerusalem. 2Jehu son of Hanani the seer went out to meet him and said to King Jehoshaphat, "Should you help the wicked and love those who hate the LORD? Because of this, wrath has gone out against you from the LORD. 3Nevertheless, some good is found in you, for you destroyed the sacred poles*b* out of the land, and have set your heart to seek God."

4 Jehoshaphat resided at Jerusalem; then he went out again among the people, from Beer-sheba to the hill country of Ephraim, and brought them back to the LORD, the God of their ancestors. 5He appointed judges in the land in all the fortified cities of Judah, city by city, 6and said to the judges, "Consider what you are doing, for you judge not on behalf of human beings but on the LORD's behalf; he is with you in giving judgment. 7Now, let the fear of the LORD be upon you; take care what you do, for there is no perversion of justice with the LORD our God, or partiality, or taking of bribes."

8 Moreover in Jerusalem Jehoshaphat appointed certain Levites and priests and heads of families of Israel, to give judgment for the LORD and to decide disputed cases. They had their seat at Jerusalem. 9He charged them: "This is how you shall act: in the fear of the LORD, in faithfulness, and with your whole heart; 10whenever a case comes to you from your kindred who live in their cities, concerning bloodshed, law or commandment, statutes or ordinances, then you shall instruct them, so that they may not incur guilt before the LORD and wrath may not come on you and your kindred. Do so, and you will not incur guilt. 11See, Amariah the chief priest is over you in all matters of the LORD; and Zebadiah son of Ishmael, the governor of the house of Judah, in all the

a Heb he   *b* Heb Asheroth

king's matters; and the Levites will serve you as officers. Deal courageously, and may the LORD be with the good!"

18.14–19.11. 19.2: *Should you help the wicked and love those who hate the LORD?* Following on the disastrous outcome of the battle with the Arameans, this word from the prophet* Jehu serves as the incentive for Jehoshaphat's renewed efforts at bringing the community into accord with God's law. **4:** *Then he went out again among the people . . . and brought them back to the LORD:* Whereas earlier he sent his officials and other representatives, now the king himself undertakes an itinerant mission to teach the law to the people. **9:** *This is how you shall act: in the fear of the LORD, in faithfulness, and with your whole heart:* He lists a unique combination of elements from various portions of the Hebrew Bible. *Fear of the LORD* is necessary to ensure wisdom (Prov 1.7), *faithfulness* to adhere to the traditions and commandments of God, and *whole heart* to ensure full commitment of mind and will to administer justice.

20 After this the Moabites and Ammonites, and with them some of the Meunites,*ᵃ* came against Jehoshaphat for battle. ²Messengers*ᵇ* came and told Jehoshaphat, "A great multitude is coming against you from Edom,*ᶜ* from beyond the sea; already they are at Hazazon-tamar" (that is, En-gedi). ³Jehoshaphat was afraid; he set himself to seek the LORD, and proclaimed a fast throughout all Judah. ⁴Judah assembled to seek help from the LORD; from all the towns of Judah they came to seek the LORD.

5 Jehoshaphat stood in the assembly of Judah and Jerusalem, in the house of the LORD, before the new court, ⁶and said, "O LORD, God of our ancestors, are you not God in heaven? Do you not rule over all the kingdoms of the nations? In your hand are power and might, so that no one is able to withstand you. ⁷Did you not, O our God, drive out the inhabitants of this land before your people Israel, and give it forever to the descendants of your friend Abraham? ⁸They have lived in it, and in it have built you a sanctuary for your name, saying, ⁹'If disaster comes upon us, the sword, judgment,*ᵈ* or pestilence, or famine, we will stand before this house, and before you, for your name is

in this house, and cry to you in our distress, and you will hear and save.' ¹⁰See now, the people of Ammon, Moab, and Mount Seir, whom you would not let Israel invade when they came from the land of Egypt, and whom they avoided and did not destroy— ¹¹they reward us by coming to drive us out of your possession that you have given us to inherit. ¹²O our God, will you not execute judgment upon them? For we are powerless against this great multitude that is coming against us. We do not know what to do, but our eyes are on you."

13 Meanwhile all Judah stood before the LORD, with their little ones, their wives, and their children. ¹⁴Then the spirit of the LORD came upon Jahaziel son of Zechariah, son of Benaiah, son of Jeiel, son of Mattaniah, a Levite of the sons of Asaph, in the middle of the assembly. ¹⁵He said, "Listen, all Judah and inhabitants of Jerusalem, and King Jehoshaphat: Thus says the LORD to you: 'Do not fear or be dismayed at this great multitude; for the battle is not yours but God's. ¹⁶Tomorrow go down against them; they will come up by the ascent of Ziz; you will find them at the end of the valley, before the wilderness of Jeruel. ¹⁷This battle is not for you to fight; take your position, stand still, and see the victory of the LORD on your behalf, O Judah and Jerusalem.' Do not fear or be dismayed; tomorrow go out against them, and the LORD will be with you."

20.1–17. 1: *The Moabites and Ammonites, and with them some of the Meunites came against Jehoshaphat:* Presumably these are all peoples across the Jordan River to the east, though it would not be expected for Judah to face a challenge from these peoples. **15:** *Do not fear or be dismayed at this great multitude; for the battle is not yours but God's:* Jehoshaphat's reward for his renewed efforts to bring the nation into compliance with God is God's protection against this invasion. The implication in the Chronicler's narrative* is that no matter what the transgression, renewed seeking of God can renew the right relationship with him.

a Compare 26.7: Heb *Ammonites*   *b* Heb *They*
c One Ms: MT *Aram*   *d* Or *the sword of judgment*

18 Then Jehoshaphat bowed down with his face to the ground, and all Judah and the inhabitants of Jerusalem fell down before the LORD, worshiping the LORD. 19And the Levites, of the Kohathites and the Korahites, stood up to praise the LORD, the God of Israel, with a very loud voice.

20 They rose early in the morning and went out into the wilderness of Tekoa; and as they went out, Jehoshaphat stood and said, "Listen to me, O Judah and inhabitants of Jerusalem! Believe in the LORD your God and you will be established; believe his prophets." 21When he had taken counsel with the people, he appointed those who were to sing to the LORD and praise him in holy splendor, as they went before the army, saying,

"Give thanks to the LORD,
    for his steadfast love endures
        forever."

22As they began to sing and praise, the LORD set an ambush against the Ammonites, Moab, and Mount Seir, who had come against Judah, so that they were routed. 23For the Ammonites and Moab attacked the inhabitants of Mount Seir, destroying them utterly; and when they had made an end of the inhabitants of Seir, they all helped to destroy one another.

24 When Judah came to the watchtower of the wilderness, they looked toward the multitude; they were corpses lying on the ground; no one had escaped. 25When Jehoshaphat and his people came to take the booty from them, they found livestock*a* in great numbers, goods, clothing, and precious things, which they took for themselves until they could carry no more. They spent three days taking the booty, because of its abundance. 26On the fourth day they assembled in the Valley of Beracah, for there they blessed the LORD; therefore that place has been called the Valley of Beracah*b* to this day. 27Then all the people of Judah and Jerusalem, with Jehoshaphat at their head, returned to Jerusalem with joy, for the LORD had enabled them to rejoice over their enemies. 28They came to Jerusalem, with harps and lyres and trumpets, to the house of the LORD. 29The fear of God came on all the kingdoms of the countries when they heard that the LORD had fought against the enemies of Israel. 30And the realm of Jehoshaphat was quiet, for his God gave him rest all around.

31 So Jehoshaphat reigned over Judah. He was thirty-five years old when he began to reign; he reigned twenty-five years in Jerusalem. His mother's name was Azubah daughter of Shilhi. 32He walked in the way of his father Asa and did not turn aside from it, doing what was right in the sight of the LORD. 33Yet the high places were not removed; the people had not yet set their hearts upon the God of their ancestors.

34 Now the rest of the acts of Jehoshaphat, from first to last, are written in the Annals of Jehu son of Hanani, which are recorded in the Book of the Kings of Israel.

35 After this King Jehoshaphat of Judah joined with King Ahaziah of Israel, who did wickedly. 36He joined him in building ships to go to Tarshish; they built the ships in Ezion-geber. 37Then Eliezer son of Dodavahu of Mareshah prophesied against Jehoshaphat, saying, "Because you have joined with Ahaziah, the LORD will destroy what you have made." And the ships were wrecked and were not able to go to Tarshish.

20.18–37. 27: *Then all the people of Judah and Jerusalem, with Jehoshaphat at their head, returned to Jerusalem with joy:* The total destruction and looting of their enemies allowed the people of Judah to experience the joy of being "found" by God. **37:** *Because you have joined with Ahaziah, the LORD will destroy what you have made:* For apparently seeking a commercial alliance again with the idolatrous northern kingdom, Jehoshaphat's punishment was limited simply to the destruction of the means of the alliance, the ships prepared for the venture.

21 Jehoshaphat slept with his ancestors and was buried with his ancestors in the city of David; his son Jehoram succeeded him. 2He had brothers, the sons of Jehoshaphat: Azariah, Jehiel, Zechariah, Azariah, Michael, and Shephatiah; all these were the

a Gk: Heb *among them*   *b* That is *Blessing*

sons of King Jehoshaphat of Judah.ᵃ ³Their father gave them many gifts, of silver, gold, and valuable possessions, together with fortified cities in Judah; but he gave the kingdom to Jehoram, because he was the firstborn. ⁴When Jehoram had ascended the throne of his father and was established, he put all his brothers to the sword, and also some of the officials of Israel. ⁵Jehoram was thirty-two years old when he began to reign; he reigned eight years in Jerusalem. ⁶He walked in the way of the kings of Israel, as the house of Ahab had done; for the daughter of Ahab was his wife. He did what was evil in the sight of the LORD. ⁷Yet the LORD would not destroy the house of David because of the covenant that he had made with David, and since he had promised to give a lamp to him and to his descendants forever.

8 In his days Edom revolted against the rule of Judah and set up a king of their own. ⁹Then Jehoram crossed over with his commanders and all his chariots. He set out by night and attacked the Edomites, who had surrounded him and his chariot commanders. ¹⁰So Edom has been in revolt against the rule of Judah to this day. At that time Libnah also revolted against his rule, because he had forsaken the LORD, the God of his ancestors.

11 Moreover he made high places in the hill country of Judah, and led the inhabitants of Jerusalem into unfaithfulness, and made Judah go astray. ¹²A letter came to him from the prophet Elijah, saying: "Thus says the LORD, the God of your father David: Because you have not walked in the ways of your father Jehoshaphat or in the ways of King Asa of Judah, ¹³but have walked in the way of the kings of Israel, and have led Judah and the inhabitants of Jerusalem into unfaithfulness, as the house of Ahab led Israel into unfaithfulness, and because you also have killed your brothers, members of your father's house, who were better than yourself, ¹⁴see, the LORD will bring a great plague on your people, your children, your wives, and all your possessions, ¹⁵and you yourself will have a severe sickness with a disease of your bowels, until your bowels come out, day after day, because of the disease."

16 The LORD aroused against Jehoram the anger of the Philistines and of the Arabs who are near the Ethiopians.ᵇ ¹⁷They came up against Judah, invaded it, and carried away all the possessions they found that belonged to the king's house, along with his sons and his wives, so that no son was left to him except Jehoahaz, his youngest son.

18 After all this the LORD struck him in his bowels with an incurable disease. ¹⁹In course of time, at the end of two years, his bowels came out because of the disease, and he died in great agony. His people made no fire in his honor, like the fires made for his ancestors. ²⁰He was thirty-two years old when he began to reign; he reigned eight years in Jerusalem. He departed with no one's regret. They buried him in the city of David, but not in the tombs of the kings.

21.1–20: The reign of Jehoram. The Chronicler expands the limited information available in his source (2 Kings 8.16–19). This is the first king of Judah whom the Chronicler evaluates as uniformly evil: The personal disaster unfaithfulness brings is clearly highlighted. **4:** *He put all his brothers to the sword,* removing any potential rivals to the throne and probably taking control of their wealth. This aside quickly establishes Jehoram as an unjust individual. **6:** *He walked in the way of the kings of Israel* by encouraging idolatry* if not directly engaging in it himself. **10:** *So Edom has been in revolt against the rule of Judah to this day:* Edom, located to the east of Judah on the other side of the Jordan, had been subject to Judah since the reign of David. The loss of Edom was one of the consequences of Jehoram's sin. **12:** *A letter came to him from the prophet* Elijah:* In 1 and 2 Kings, Elijah's prophetic ministry, largely located in the northern kingdom, offered a clear condemnation of idolatry. He also attacked the religious policies of Ahab, the king of Israel to whom Jehoram was related by marriage. The letter's contents and language are strongly colored with the Chronicler's style. The letter condemns Jehoram for killing his brothers and promoting idolatry. **20:** *He departed with no one's regret:* The Chronicler makes an ironic* comment on Jehoram's utter failure as king. The decease of the king was not marked by the ceremonial fire, and in the final insult, he was not buried with the other kings of the line of David.

~~~~~~~

22 The inhabitants of Jerusalem made his youngest son Ahaziah king as his successor; for the troops who came with the Arabs to the camp had killed all the older sons. So Ahaziah son of Jehoram reigned as king of Judah. ²Ahaziah was forty-two years old when he began to reign; he reigned one year in Jerusalem. His mother's name was Athaliah, a granddaughter of Omri. ³He also walked in the ways of the house of Ahab, for his mother was his counselor in doing wickedly. ⁴He did what was evil in the sight of the LORD, as the house of Ahab had done; for after the death of his father they were his counselors, to his ruin. ⁵He even followed their advice, and went with Jehoram son of King Ahab of Israel to make war against King Hazael of Aram at Ramoth-gilead. The Arameans wounded Joram, ⁶and he returned to be healed in Jezreel of the wounds that he had received at Ramah, when he fought King Hazael of Aram. And Ahaziah son of King Jehoram of Judah went down to see Joram son of Ahab in Jezreel, because he was sick.

7 But it was ordained by God that the downfall of Ahaziah should come about through his going to visit Joram. For when he came there he went out with Jehoram to meet Jehu son of Nimshi, whom the LORD had anointed to destroy the house of Ahab. ⁸When Jehu was executing judgment on the house of Ahab, he met the officials of Judah and the sons of Ahaziah's brothers, who attended Ahaziah, and he killed them. ⁹He searched for Ahaziah, who was captured while hiding in Samaria and was brought to Jehu, and put to death. They buried him, for they said, "He is the grandson of Jehoshaphat, who sought the LORD with all his heart." And the house of Ahaziah had no one able to rule the kingdom.

22.1–9: The reign of Ahaziah. The Chronicler greatly reduces the narrative* from his source (2 Kings 8.25–29; 9.14–16, 27–29). The historian is not interested in negative examples for their own sake, but only as examples or warnings of the community's relationship to God. This account provides a brief transition to Athaliah's seizing of the throne. **3:** *He also walked in the ways of the house of Ahab,* that is, he promoted idolatry.* **8:** *When Jehu was executing judgment on the house of Ahab:* The Chronicler assumes his readers are familiar with the account in 2 Kings 9–10 where God anoints* Jehu to take the throne of the northern kingdom from the line of Ahab. **9:** *They buried him, for they said, "He is the grandson of Jehoshaphat, who sought the LORD with all his heart":* In his source, the Chronicler simply had the statement that Ahaziah was taken back to Jerusalem and buried. He expanded this simple statement to create a contrast between the faithful example of Jehoshaphat and the disastrous reigns of Jehoram and Ahaziah.

~~~~~~~

10 Now when Athaliah, Ahaziah's mother, saw that her son was dead, she set about to destroy all the royal family of the house of Judah. ¹¹But Jehoshabeath, the king's daughter, took Joash son of Ahaziah, and stole him away from among the king's children who were about to be killed; she put him and his nurse in a bedroom. Thus Jehoshabeath, daughter of King Jehoram and wife of the priest Jehoiada—because she was a sister of Ahaziah—hid him from Athaliah, so that she did not kill him; ¹²he remained with them six years, hidden in the house of God, while Athaliah reigned over the land.

23 But in the seventh year Jehoiada took courage, and entered into a compact with the commanders of the hundreds, Azariah son of Jeroham, Ishmael son of Jehohanan, Azariah son of Obed, Maaseiah son of Adaiah, and Elishaphat son of Zichri. ²They went around through Judah and gathered the Levites from all the towns of Judah, and the heads of families of Israel, and they came to Jerusalem. ³Then the whole assembly made a covenant with the king in the house of God. Jehoiada*ᵃ* said to them, "Here is the king's son! Let him reign, as the LORD promised concerning the sons of David. ⁴This is what you are to do: one-third of you, priests and Levites, who come on duty on the sabbath, shall be gatekeepers, ⁵one-third shall be at the king's house, and one-third at the Gate of the Foundation; and

a Heb *He*

all the people shall be in the courts of the house of the LORD. 6Do not let anyone enter the house of the LORD except the priests and ministering Levites; they may enter, for they are holy, but all the other*a* people shall observe the instructions of the LORD. 7The Levites shall surround the king, each with his weapons in his hand; and whoever enters the house shall be killed. Stay with the king in his comings and goings."

22.10–24.27: The reign of Joash. Although at points following closely his source in 2 Kings 11–12, the Chronicler has expanded selected parts of the account to incorporate his own concerns and has added an entire phase of Joash's later rule, marked by apostasy. The focus of the first part of the narrative* is not so much on Joash as on the figure of the high priest Jehoiada, who functions as the model of faithfulness and the example of seeking God. **22.10:** *She set about to destroy all the royal family of the house of Judah,* possibly in revenge for Jehu's killing of the house of Ahab, to which she belonged. **11:** *Jehoshabeath, daughter of King Jehoram and wife of the priest Jehoiada . . . hid him from Athaliah:* 2 Kings presents Jehoshabeath's royal lineage, but not her marriage to Jehoiada. Her heroic action in sheltering the Davidic heir is motivated in several ways, from familial loyalty to her brother to self-interested preservation of the privileges of the Temple* in Jerusalem. **23.2:** *They went around through Judah and gathered the Levites:* While 2 Kings presents the effort to put Joash on the throne as the combined effort of military commanders and Jehoiada, the Chronicler places the conspiracy squarely among the religious personnel, the priests and Levites. The elaborate preparations were designed to conceal the assembly of such a large company of armed Levites.

8 The Levites and all Judah did according to all that the priest Jehoiada commanded; each brought his men, who were to come on duty on the sabbath, with those who were to go off duty on the sabbath; for the priest Jehoiada did not dismiss the divisions. 9The priest Jehoiada delivered to the captains the spears and the large and small shields that had been King David's, which were in the house of God; 10and he set all the people as a guard for the king, everyone with weapon in hand, from the south side of the house to the north side of the house, around the altar and the house. 11Then he brought out the king's son, put the crown on him, and gave him the covenant;*b* they proclaimed him king, and Jehoiada and his sons anointed him; and they shouted, "Long live the king!"

12 When Athaliah heard the noise of the people running and praising the king, she went into the house of the LORD to the people; 13and when she looked, there was the king standing by his pillar at the entrance, and the captains and the trumpeters beside the king, and all the people of the land rejoicing and blowing trumpets, and the singers with their musical instruments leading in the celebration. Athaliah tore her clothes, and cried, "Treason! Treason!" 14Then the priest Jehoiada brought out the captains who were set over the army, saying to them, "Bring her out between the ranks; anyone who follows her is to be put to the sword." For the priest said, "Do not put her to death in the house of the LORD." 15So they laid hands on her; she went into the entrance of the Horse Gate of the king's house, and there they put her to death.

16 Jehoiada made a covenant between himself and all the people and the king that they should be the LORD's people. 17Then all the people went to the house of Baal, and tore it down; his altars and his images they broke in pieces, and they killed Mattan, the priest of Baal, in front of the altars. 18Jehoiada assigned the care of the house of the LORD to the levitical priests whom David had organized to be in charge of the house of the LORD, to offer burnt offerings to the LORD, as it is written in the law of Moses, with rejoicing and with singing, according to the order of David. 19He stationed the gatekeepers at the gates of the house of the LORD so that no one should enter who was in any way unclean. 20And he took the captains, the nobles, the governors of the people, and all the people of the land, and they brought the king down from the house of the LORD, marching through the upper gate to the king's house. They set the king on the royal throne. 21So

a Heb lacks *other*   *b* Or *treaty,* or *testimony;* Heb *eduth* all the people of the land rejoiced, and the city was quiet after Athaliah had been killed with the sword.

23.8–21. 16: *Jehoiada made a covenant* between himself and all the people and the king that they should be the LORD's people,* thus committing themselves to the exclusive worship of the God of Israel. **18:** *Jehoiada assigned the care of the house of the LORD to the levitical priests whom David had organized to be in charge of the house of the LORD, to offer burnt offerings to the LORD, as it is written in the law of Moses, with rejoicing and with singing, according to the order of David:* This is confusing since only priests, the sons of Aaron, could offer burnt offerings to the LORD. There may be a textual confusion, and the term "levitical priests" may have read "priest and Levites," which would resolve the confusion. The reinstallation of these responsibilities by Jehoiada implies that under Athaliah normal Temple functions were disrupted and now needed to be restored. **19:** *So that no one should enter who was in any way unclean:* This means unclean in a ritual sense, that is, unacceptable to come into God's presence. Such a protection preserves the holiness of the Temple precinct.

---

24 Joash was seven years old when he began to reign; he reigned forty years in Jerusalem; his mother's name was Zibiah of Beer-sheba. ²Joash did what was right in the sight of the LORD all the days of the priest Jehoiada. ³Jehoiada got two wives for him, and he became the father of sons and daughters.

4 Some time afterward Joash decided to restore the house of the LORD. ⁵He assembled the priests and the Levites and said to them, "Go out to the cities of Judah and gather money from all Israel to repair the house of your God, year by year; and see that you act quickly." But the Levites did not act quickly. ⁶So the king summoned Jehoiada the chief, and said to him, "Why have you not required the Levites to bring in from Judah and Jerusalem the tax levied by Moses, the servant of the LORD, on*ᵃ* the congregation of Israel for the tent of the covenant?"*ᵇ* ⁷For the children of Athaliah, that wicked woman, had broken into the house of God, and had even used all the dedicated things of the house of the LORD for the Baals.

8 So the king gave command, and they made a chest, and set it outside the gate of the house of the LORD. ⁹A proclamation was made throughout Judah and Jerusalem to bring in for the LORD the tax that Moses the servant of God laid on Israel in the wilderness. ¹⁰All the leaders and all the people rejoiced and brought their tax and dropped it into the chest until it was full. ¹¹Whenever the chest was brought to the king's officers by the Levites, when they saw that there was a large amount of money in it, the king's secretary and the officer of the chief priest would come and empty the chest and take it and return it to its place. So they did day after day, and collected money in abundance. ¹²The king and Jehoiada gave it to those who had charge of the work of the house of the LORD, and they hired masons and carpenters to restore the house of the LORD, and also workers in iron and bronze to repair the house of the LORD. ¹³So those who were engaged in the work labored, and the repairing went forward at their hands, and they restored the house of God to its proper condition and strengthened it. ¹⁴When they had finished, they brought the rest of the money to the king and Jehoiada, and with it were made utensils for the house of the LORD, utensils for the service and for the burnt offerings, and ladles, and vessels of gold and silver. They offered burnt offerings in the house of the LORD regularly all the days of Jehoiada.

15 But Jehoiada grew old and full of days, and died; he was one hundred thirty years old at his death. ¹⁶And they buried him in the city of David among the kings, because he had done good in Israel, and for God and his house.

17 Now after the death of Jehoiada the officials of Judah came and did obeisance to the king; then the king listened to them. ¹⁸They abandoned the house of the LORD, the God of their ancestors, and served the sacred poles*ᶜ* and the idols. And wrath came upon Judah and Jerusalem for this guilt of theirs. ¹⁹Yet he sent prophets among them

---

a Compare Vg: Heb *and*   *b* Or *treaty*, or *testimony*; Heb *eduth*   *c* Heb *Asherim* to bring them back to the LORD; they testified against them, but they would not listen.

20 Then the spirit of God took possession of[a] Zechariah son of the priest Jehoiada; he stood above the people and said to them, "Thus says God: Why do you transgress the commandments of the LORD, so that you cannot prosper? Because you have forsaken the LORD, he has also forsaken you." 21 But they conspired against him, and by command of the king they stoned him to death in the court of the house of the LORD. 22 King Joash did not remember the kindness that Jehoiada, Zechariah's father, had shown him, but killed his son. As he was dying, he said, "May the LORD see and avenge!"

23 At the end of the year the army of Aram came up against Joash. They came to Judah and Jerusalem, and destroyed all the officials of the people from among them, and sent all the booty they took to the king of Damascus. 24 Although the army of Aram had come with few men, the LORD delivered into their hand a very great army, because they had abandoned the LORD, the God of their ancestors. Thus they executed judgment on Joash.

25 When they had withdrawn, leaving him severely wounded, his servants conspired against him because of the blood of the son[b] of the priest Jehoiada, and they killed him on his bed. So he died; and they buried him in the city of David, but they did not bury him in the tombs of the kings. 26 Those who conspired against him were Zabad son of Shimeath the Ammonite, and Jehozabad son of Shimrith the Moabite. 27 Accounts of his sons, and of the many oracles against him, and of the rebuilding[c] of the house of God are written in the Commentary on the Book of the Kings. And his son Amaziah succeeded him.

24.1–27. 10: *All the leaders and all the people rejoiced and brought their tax and dropped it into the chest:* Having come on the throne with the support of the priests and Levites and "all the people," Joash reaffirms his faithfulness by seeking to repair and restore the Temple.* By having the Levites fail to go out and collect the tax for the Temple, the Chronicler can portray

the people coming in joy to pay their obligation and note that the money came in abundantly. **16:** *They buried him in the city of David among the kings,* a remarkable honor for Jehoiada. The Chronicler underscores Jehoiada's contributions by depicting him as the restorer of the legitimate heir to the throne of David, and as the restorer of proper worship to the Temple. **18:** *They abandoned the house of the LORD:* As in the Chronicler's earlier statements, if Israel abandons God, God abandons the community. This is the message of the prophet* Zechariah, son of Jehoiada, which only succeeds in earning his murder. Joash's reign ends in military disaster and conspiracy against the king.

〰〰〰〰〰〰〰〰〰〰〰〰〰〰〰〰〰〰〰〰

25 Amaziah was twenty-five years old when he began to reign, and he reigned twenty-nine years in Jerusalem. His mother's name was Jehoaddan of Jerusalem. 2 He did what was right in the sight of the LORD, yet not with a true heart. 3 As soon as the royal power was firmly in his hand he killed his servants who had murdered his father the king. 4 But he did not put their children to death, according to what is written in the law, in the book of Moses, where the LORD commanded, "The parents shall not be put to death for the children, or the children be put to death for the parents; but all shall be put to death for their own sins."

5 Amaziah assembled the people of Judah, and set them by ancestral houses under commanders of the thousands and of the hundreds for all Judah and Benjamin. He mustered those twenty years old and upward, and found that they were three hundred thousand picked troops fit for war, able to handle spear and shield. 6 He also hired one hundred thousand mighty warriors from Israel for one hundred talents of silver. 7 But a man of God came to him and said, "O king, do not let the army of Israel go with you, for the LORD is not with Israel—all these Ephraimites. 8 Rather, go by yourself and act; be strong in battle, or God will fling you down before the enemy; for God has power to help or to overthrow." 9 Amaziah said to the man of God, "But what shall we do about

a Heb *clothed itself with*　　*b* Gk Vg: Heb *sons*
c Heb *founding*

the hundred talents that I have given to the army of Israel?" The man of God answered, "The LORD is able to give you much more than this." 10Then Amaziah discharged the army that had come to him from Ephraim, letting them go home again. But they became very angry with Judah, and returned home in fierce anger.

25.1–28: The reign of Amaziah. Expanding considerably on his source in 2 Kings 14.1–22, the Chronicler elaborates several characteristic themes in recounting Amaziah's rule. In several ways it is similar to the reign of Joash, starting off on the right moral ground but declining into idolatry* with the inescapable judgment against the king and the community. **2:** *He did what was right in the sight of the LORD, yet not with a true heart:* Though technically Amaziah was in the right, the commitment of will and intellect the Chronicler sees as essential was not present. **4:** *According to what is written in the law, in the book of Moses:* This indicates how important the written collection of the Pentateuch* was becoming. Deuteronomy 24.16 provides the specific reference. **7:** *O king, do not let the army of Israel go with you, for the LORD is not with Israel:* Having conducted himself correctly, Amaziah is assured of military success. His hiring of mercenaries from the northern kingdom does not meet with God's approval. The unnamed prophet* (*man of God*) offers him a chance to return to God's favor, an opportunity that Amaziah takes. The result is a great victory for Judah.

---

11 Amaziah took courage, and led out his people; he went to the Valley of Salt, and struck down ten thousand men of Seir. 12The people of Judah captured another ten thousand alive, took them to the top of Sela, and threw them down from the top of Sela, so that all of them were dashed to pieces. 13But the men of the army whom Amaziah sent back, not letting them go with him to battle, fell on the cities of Judah from Samaria to Beth-horon; they killed three thousand people in them, and took much booty.

14 Now after Amaziah came from the slaughter of the Edomites, he brought the gods of the people of Seir, set them up as his gods, and worshiped them, making offerings to them. 15The LORD was angry with Amaziah and sent to him a prophet, who said to

him, "Why have you resorted to a people's gods who could not deliver their own people from your hand?" 16But as he was speaking the king*a* said to him, "Have we made you a royal counselor? Stop! Why should you be put to death?" So the prophet stopped, but said, "I know that God has determined to destroy you, because you have done this and have not listened to my advice."

25.11–16. 14: *He brought the gods of the people of Seir, set them up as his gods, and worshiped them:* Having begun his rule correctly, Amaziah now succumbs to idolatry. **16:** *I know that God has determined to destroy you, because you have done this and have not listened to my advice:* The prophet's offer of an opportunity for repentance is abruptly halted by Amaziah, and the prophet gives voice to the Chronicler's view of what such pride leads to. His reign ends in dishonor as conspirators murder him.

---

17 Then King Amaziah of Judah took counsel and sent to King Joash son of Jehoahaz son of Jehu of Israel, saying, "Come, let us look one another in the face." 18King Joash of Israel sent word to King Amaziah of Judah, "A thornbush on Lebanon sent to a cedar on Lebanon, saying, 'Give your daughter to my son for a wife'; but a wild animal of Lebanon passed by and trampled down the thornbush. 19You say, 'See, I have defeated Edom,' and your heart has lifted you up in boastfulness. Now stay at home; why should you provoke trouble so that you fall, you and Judah with you?"

20 But Amaziah would not listen—it was God's doing, in order to hand them over, because they had sought the gods of Edom. 21So King Joash of Israel went up; he and King Amaziah of Judah faced one another in battle at Beth-shemesh, which belongs to Judah. 22Judah was defeated by Israel; everyone fled home. 23King Joash of Israel captured King Amaziah of Judah, son of Joash, son of Ahaziah, at Beth-shemesh; he brought him to Jerusalem, and broke down the wall of Jerusalem from the Ephraim Gate to the Corner Gate, a distance of four hundred cubits. 24He seized all the gold and silver, and

a Heb *he*

all the vessels that were found in the house of God, and Obed-edom with them; he seized also the treasuries of the king's house, also hostages; then he returned to Samaria.

25 King Amaziah son of Joash of Judah, lived fifteen years after the death of King Joash son of Jehoahaz of Israel. 26 Now the rest of the deeds of Amaziah, from first to last, are they not written in the Book of the Kings of Judah and Israel? 27 From the time that Amaziah turned away from the LORD they made a conspiracy against him in Jerusalem, and he fled to Lachish. But they sent after him to Lachish, and killed him there. 28 They brought him back on horses; he was buried with his ancestors in the city of David.

26 Then all the people of Judah took Uzziah, who was sixteen years old, and made him king to succeed his father Amaziah. 2 He rebuilt Eloth and restored it to Judah, after the king slept with his ancestors. 3 Uzziah was sixteen years old when he began to reign, and he reigned fifty-two years in Jerusalem. His mother's name was Jecoliah of Jerusalem. 4 He did what was right in the sight of the LORD, just as his father Amaziah had done. 5 He set himself to seek God in the days of Zechariah, who instructed him in the fear of God; and as long as he sought the LORD, God made him prosper.

6 He went out and made war against the Philistines, and broke down the wall of Gath and the wall of Jabneh and the wall of Ashdod; he built cities in the territory of Ashdod and elsewhere among the Philistines. 7 God helped him against the Philistines, against the Arabs who lived in Gur-baal, and against the Meunites. 8 The Ammonites paid tribute to Uzziah, and his fame spread even to the border of Egypt, for he became very strong. 9 Moreover Uzziah built towers in Jerusalem at the Corner Gate, at the Valley Gate, and at the Angle, and fortified them. 10 He built towers in the wilderness and hewed out many cisterns, for he had large herds, both in the Shephelah and in the plain, and he had farmers and vinedressers in the hills and in the fertile lands, for he loved the soil. 11 Moreover Uzziah had an army of soldiers, fit for war, in divisions according to the num-

bers in the muster made by the secretary Jeiel and the officer Maaseiah, under the direction of Hananiah, one of the king's commanders. 12 The whole number of the heads of ancestral houses of mighty warriors was two thousand six hundred. 13 Under their command was an army of three hundred seven thousand five hundred, who could make war with mighty power, to help the king against the enemy. 14 Uzziah provided for all the army the shields, spears, helmets, coats of mail, bows, and stones for slinging. 15 In Jerusalem he set up machines, invented by skilled workers, on the towers and the corners for shooting arrows and large stones. And his fame spread far, for he was marvelously helped until he became strong.

16 But when he had become strong he grew proud, to his destruction. For he was false to the LORD his God, and entered the temple of the LORD to make offering on the altar of incense. 17 But the priest Azariah went in after him, with eighty priests of the LORD who were men of valor; 18 they withstood King Uzziah, and said to him, "It is not for you, Uzziah, to make offering to the LORD, but for the priests the descendants of Aaron, who are consecrated to make offering. Go out of the sanctuary; for you have done wrong, and it will bring you no honor from the LORD God." 19 Then Uzziah was angry. Now he had a censer in his hand to make offering, and when he became angry with the priests a leprous[b] disease broke out on his forehead, in the presence of the priests in the house of the LORD, by the altar of incense. 20 When the chief priest Azariah, and all the priests, looked at him, he was leprous[a] in his forehead. They hurried him out, and he himself hurried to get out, because the LORD had struck him. 21 King Uzziah was leprous[a] to the day of his death, and being leprous[a] lived in a separate house, for he was excluded from the house of the LORD. His son Jotham was in charge of the palace of the king, governing the people of the land.

22 Now the rest of the acts of Uzziah, from first to last, the prophet Isaiah son of

_a_ A term for several skin diseases; precise meaning uncertain

Amoz wrote. [23]Uzziah slept with his ancestors; they buried him near his ancestors in the burial field that belonged to the kings, for they said, "He is leprous."[a] His son Jotham succeeded him.

26.1–23: The reign of Uzziah. Greatly expanding on his source (2 Kings 14.21–22; 15.1–3), the Chronicler presents another cycle of good beginnings that end in dishonor. Of particular interest is the incident of Uzziah's taking on the prerogatives of the priesthood. **5:** *He set himself to seek God in the days of Zechariah, who instructed him in the fear of God:* The identity of this Zechariah is uncertain; possibly he is a member of the family of the high priest Jehoiada, whose son was named Zechariah. Uzziah's intent to seek God is highlighted. Being on the right path early in his reign, Uzziah has military and economic success. **16:** *But when he had become strong he grew proud, to his destruction:* Despite his good start, Uzziah moved apart from the law of God. **18:** *It is not for you, Uzziah, to make offering to the LORD, but for the priests the descendants of Aaron:* The intercessory role of the priesthood is understood by the Chronicler to be ordained by God (see Num 16). The priests act as the prophets* do in other settings, bringing an offer to the protagonist to make the right moral choice. **19:** *When he became angry with the priests a leprous disease broke out on his forehead:* His anger at the priests was, indirectly, anger at God's chosen means of regulating worship. Being struck with leprosy made Uzziah unclean, unable to approach the Temple* precinct and unable to conduct normal commerce with those who observed the Mosaic rules regulating ritual cleanliness. **23:** *They buried him near his ancestors,* but because of his uncleanness, he could not be buried with the other kings of the line of David.

---

27 Jotham was twenty-five years old when he began to reign; he reigned sixteen years in Jerusalem. His mother's name was Jerushah daughter of Zadok. [2]He did what was right in the sight of the LORD just as his father Uzziah had done—only he did not invade the temple of the LORD. But the people still followed corrupt practices. [3]He built the upper gate of the house of the LORD, and did extensive building on the wall of Ophel. [4]Moreover he built cities in the hill country of Judah, and forts and towers on the wooded hills. [5]He fought with the king of the

Ammonites and prevailed against them. The Ammonites gave him that year one hundred talents of silver, ten thousand cors of wheat and ten thousand of barley. The Ammonites paid him the same amount in the second and the third years. [6]So Jotham became strong because he ordered his ways before the LORD his God. [7]Now the rest of the acts of Jotham, and all his wars and his ways, are written in the Book of the Kings of Israel and Judah. [8]He was twenty-five years old when he began to reign; he reigned sixteen years in Jerusalem. [9]Jotham slept with his ancestors, and they buried him in the city of David; and his son Ahaz succeeded him.

27.1–9: The reign of Jotham. Of not much interest to the Chronicler, Jotham's rule receives very short notice. **2:** His main attribute is that *he did not invade the temple,* the primary failing of his father Uzziah.

---

28 Ahaz was twenty years old when he began to reign; he reigned sixteen years in Jerusalem. He did not do what was right in the sight of the LORD, as his ancestor David had done, [2]but he walked in the ways of the kings of Israel. He even made cast images for the Baals; [3]and he made offerings in the valley of the son of Hinnom, and made his sons pass through fire, according to the abominable practices of the nations whom the LORD drove out before the people of Israel. [4]He sacrificed and made offerings on the high places, on the hills, and under every green tree.

[5] Therefore the LORD his God gave him into the hand of the king of Aram, who defeated him and took captive a great number of his people and brought them to Damascus. He was also given into the hand of the king of Israel, who defeated him with great slaughter. [6]Pekah son of Remaliah killed one hundred twenty thousand in Judah in one day, all of them valiant warriors, because they had abandoned the LORD, the God of their ancestors. [7]And Zichri, a mighty warrior of Ephraim, killed the king's son Maaseiah, Azrikam the commander of the palace,

---

a A term for several skin diseases; precise meaning uncertain

and Elkanah the next in authority to the king.

8 The people of Israel took captive two hundred thousand of their kin, women, sons, and daughters; they also took much booty from them and brought the booty to Samaria. 9But a prophet of the LORD was there, whose name was Oded; he went out to meet the army that came to Samaria, and said to them, "Because the LORD, the God of your ancestors, was angry with Judah, he gave them into your hand, but you have killed them in a rage that has reached up to heaven. 10Now you intend to subjugate the people of Judah and Jerusalem, male and female, as your slaves. But what have you except sins against the LORD your God? 11Now hear me, and send back the captives whom you have taken from your kindred, for the fierce wrath of the LORD is upon you." 12Moreover, certain chiefs of the Ephraimites, Azariah son of Johanan, Berechiah son of Meshillemoth, Jehizkiah son of Shallum, and Amasa son of Hadlai, stood up against those who were coming from the war, 13and said to them, "You shall not bring the captives in here, for you propose to bring on us guilt against the LORD in addition to our present sins and guilt. For our guilt is already great, and there is fierce wrath against Israel." 14So the warriors left the captives and the booty before the officials and all the assembly. 15Then those who were mentioned by name got up and took the captives, and with the booty they clothed all that were naked among them; they clothed them, gave them sandals, provided them with food and drink, and anointed them; and carrying all the feeble among them on donkeys, they brought them to their kindred at Jericho, the city of palm trees. Then they returned to Samaria.

16 At that time King Ahaz sent to the king*a* of Assyria for help. 17For the Edomites had again invaded and defeated Judah, and carried away captives. 18And the Philistines had made raids on the cities in the Shephelah and the Negeb of Judah, and had taken Beth-shemesh, Aijalon, Gederoth, Soco with its villages, Timnah with its villages, and Gimzo with its villages; and they settled there. 19For the LORD brought Judah low because of King Ahaz of Israel, for he had behaved without restraint in Judah and had been faithless to the LORD. 20So King Tilgath-pilneser of Assyria came against him, and oppressed him instead of strengthening him. 21For Ahaz plundered the house of the LORD and the houses of the king and of the officials, and gave tribute to the king of Assyria; but it did not help him.

22 In the time of his distress he became yet more faithless to the LORD—this same King Ahaz. 23For he sacrificed to the gods of Damascus, which had defeated him, and said, "Because the gods of the kings of Aram helped them, I will sacrifice to them so that they may help me." But they were the ruin of him, and of all Israel. 24Ahaz gathered together the utensils of the house of God, and cut in pieces the utensils of the house of God. He shut up the doors of the house of the LORD and made himself altars in every corner of Jerusalem. 25In every city of Judah he made high places to make offerings to other gods, provoking to anger the LORD, the God of his ancestors. 26Now the rest of his acts and all his ways, from first to last, are written in the Book of the Kings of Judah and Israel. 27Ahaz slept with his ancestors, and they buried him in the city, in Jerusalem; but they did not bring him into the tombs of the kings of Israel. His son Hezekiah succeeded him.

28.1–27: The reign of Ahaz. Having portrayed how serious a violation of the Temple* was in the case of Uzziah, the Chronicler has led his readers to one of the turning points in Judean history, the rule of Ahaz. While relying closely on his source (2 Kings 16.1–20), the Chronicler has expanded his materials considerably. **5:** *Therefore the LORD his God gave him into the hand of the king of Aram:* Ahaz's pattern of idolatry* had inescapable consequences in the Chronicler's view. **6:** *Pekah son of Remaliah killed one hundred twenty thousand in Judah in one day . . . because they had abandoned the LORD:* The Chronicler sees Ahaz's apostasy as representative of a more general abandonment of God by the people under his rule. **9:** *But you have killed them in a rage that has reached up to heaven:* With a large body of captives in tow that will

a Gk Syr Vg Compare 2 Kings 16.7: Heb *kings*

be enslaved, the warriors confront the prophet* Oded, who makes clear the choice before them. They choose wisely, and the captives are returned to Jericho. **24:** *He shut up the doors of the house of the* LORD: Ahaz's closure of the doors meant the suspension of the normal daily rituals of the Temple, the very offerings that David and Solomon had taken such care to ensure were performed properly. The Chronicler is stating that Ahaz had undone all the good that David and Solomon had accomplished. **27:** *They did not bring him into the tombs of the kings of Israel:* Like Uzziah, Ahaz was unclean because of his open participation in idolatry and his closure of the Temple. His burial with the other kings would have rendered their tombs unclean.

29 Hezekiah began to reign when he was twenty-five years old; he reigned twenty-nine years in Jerusalem. His mother's name was Abijah daughter of Zechariah. ²He did what was right in the sight of the LORD, just as his ancestor David had done.

29.1–32.33: The reign of Hezekiah. One of the great narratives* of the Chronicler's history is the account of Hezekiah. Incorporating large portions of his source in 2 Kings 18–20, he adds considerable materials concerning Hezekiah's reforms and the great worshipping assemblies, in which the king tries to bring the community back into alignment with God. A number of literary forms are employed, including dramatic speeches, sweeping descriptions, and detailed lists of personnel. **29.2:** *He did what was right in the sight of the* LORD, *just as his ancestor David had done:* This is an unusual opening for the Chronicler, linking Hezekiah's rule to David's.

3 In the first year of his reign, in the first month, he opened the doors of the house of the LORD and repaired them. ⁴He brought in the priests and the Levites and assembled them in the square on the east. ⁵He said to them, "Listen to me, Levites! Sanctify yourselves, and sanctify the house of the LORD, the God of your ancestors, and carry out the filth from the holy place. ⁶For our ancestors have been unfaithful and have done what was evil in the sight of the LORD our God; they have forsaken him, and have turned away their faces from the dwelling of the LORD, and turned their backs. ⁷They also

shut the doors of the vestibule and put out the lamps, and have not offered incense or made burnt offerings in the holy place to the God of Israel. ⁸Therefore the wrath of the LORD came upon Judah and Jerusalem, and he has made them an object of horror, of astonishment, and of hissing, as you see with your own eyes. ⁹Our fathers have fallen by the sword and our sons and our daughters and our wives are in captivity for this. ¹⁰Now it is in my heart to make a covenant with the LORD, the God of Israel, so that his fierce anger may turn away from us. ¹¹My sons, do not now be negligent, for the LORD has chosen you to stand in his presence to minister to him, and to be his ministers and make offerings to him."

29.3–11. 3: *In the first year of his reign, in the first month, he opened the doors of the house of the* LORD, demonstrating by the priority assigned to this task his dedication to God. **5:** *Sanctify yourselves, and sanctify the house of the* LORD *. . . and carry out the filth from the holy place:* The closure of the Temple* had dangerously imperiled its sanctity. There are also suggestions that Ahaz had cultivated idolatrous* worship in the Temple precinct itself (2 Kings 16.11–16). To set the Temple service back on the proper course, all the elements of idolatrous worship needed to be removed, and all the proper worship implements and utensils restored to their places.

12 Then the Levites arose, Mahath son of Amasai, and Joel son of Azariah, of the sons of the Kohathites; and of the sons of Merari, Kish son of Abdi, and Azariah son of Jehallelel; and of the Gershonites, Joah son of Zimmah, and Eden son of Joah; ¹³and of the sons of Elizaphan, Shimri and Jeuel; and of the sons of Asaph, Zechariah and Mattaniah; ¹⁴and of the sons of Heman, Jehuel and Shimei; and of the sons of Jeduthun, Shemaiah and Uzziel. ¹⁵They gathered their brothers, sanctified themselves, and went in as the king had commanded, by the words of the LORD, to cleanse the house of the LORD. ¹⁶The priests went into the inner part of the house of the LORD to cleanse it, and they brought out all the unclean things that they found in the temple of the LORD into the court of the house of the LORD; and the Le-

vites took them and carried them out to the Wadi Kidron. 17They began to sanctify on the first day of the first month, and on the eighth day of the month they came to the vestibule of the LORD; then for eight days they sanctified the house of the LORD, and on the sixteenth day of the first month they finished. 18Then they went inside to King Hezekiah and said, "We have cleansed all the house of the LORD, the altar of burnt offering and all its utensils, and the table for the rows of bread and all its utensils. 19All the utensils that King Ahaz repudiated during his reign when he was faithless, we have made ready and sanctified; see, they are in front of the altar of the LORD."

20 Then King Hezekiah rose early, assembled the officials of the city, and went up to the house of the LORD. 21They brought seven bulls, seven rams, seven lambs, and seven male goats for a sin offering for the kingdom and for the sanctuary and for Judah. He commanded the priests the descendants of Aaron to offer them on the altar of the LORD. 22So they slaughtered the bulls, and the priests received the blood and dashed it against the altar; they slaughtered the rams and their blood was dashed against the altar; they also slaughtered the lambs and their blood was dashed against the altar. 23Then the male goats for the sin offering were brought to the king and the assembly; they laid their hands on them, 24and the priests slaughtered them and made a sin offering with their blood at the altar, to make atonement for all Israel. For the king commanded that the burnt offering and the sin offering should be made for all Israel.

25 He stationed the Levites in the house of the LORD with cymbals, harps, and lyres, according to the commandment of David and of Gad the king's seer and of the prophet Nathan, for the commandment was from the LORD through his prophets. 26The Levites stood with the instruments of David, and the priests with the trumpets. 27Then Hezekiah commanded that the burnt offering be offered on the altar. When the burnt offering began, the song to the LORD began also, and the trumpets, accompanied by the instruments of King David of Israel. 28The whole

assembly worshiped, the singers sang, and the trumpeters sounded; all this continued until the burnt offering was finished. 29When the offering was finished, the king and all who were present with him bowed down and worshiped. 30King Hezekiah and the officials commanded the Levites to sing praises to the LORD with the words of David and of the seer Asaph. They sang praises with gladness, and they bowed down and worshiped.

31 Then Hezekiah said, "You have now consecrated yourselves to the LORD; come near, bring sacrifices and thank offerings to the house of the LORD." The assembly brought sacrifices and thank offerings; and all who were of a willing heart brought burnt offerings. 32The number of the burnt offerings that the assembly brought was seventy bulls, one hundred rams, and two hundred lambs; all these were for a burnt offering to the LORD. 33The consecrated offerings were six hundred bulls and three thousand sheep. 34But the priests were too few and could not skin all the burnt offerings, so, until other priests had sanctified themselves, their kindred, the Levites, helped them until the work was finished—for the Levites were more conscientious[a] than the priests in sanctifying themselves. 35Besides the great number of burnt offerings there was the fat of the offerings of well-being, and there were the drink offerings for the burnt offerings. Thus the service of the house of the LORD was restored. 36And Hezekiah and all the people rejoiced because of what God had done for the people; for the thing had come about suddenly.

29.12–36. 21: For a sin offering for the kingdom and for the sanctuary and for Judah: Once the Temple is cleansed, Hezekiah moves quickly to restore the Temple services. To initiate normal services, the king and the community leaders offer a sequence of offerings to atone for sins by the community. 27: When the burnt offering began, the song to the LORD began also: Restarting the Temple sacrifices was accompanied by the reinstitution of choral praise to God that David had initiated. 36: Hezekiah and all the people rejoiced be-

a Heb upright in heart

cause of what God had done for the people: Having been able to restore the Temple service, the assembly sensed that a reversal of God's judgment against Judah was also beginning.

30 Hezekiah sent word to all Israel and Judah, and wrote letters also to Ephraim and Manasseh, that they should come to the house of the LORD at Jerusalem, to keep the passover to the LORD the God of Israel. ²For the king and his officials and all the assembly in Jerusalem had taken counsel to keep the passover in the second month ³(for they could not keep it at its proper time because the priests had not sanctified themselves in sufficient number, nor had the people assembled in Jerusalem). ⁴The plan seemed right to the king and all the assembly. ⁵So they decreed to make a proclamation throughout all Israel, from Beer-sheba to Dan, that the people should come and keep the passover to the LORD the God of Israel, at Jerusalem; for they had not kept it in great numbers as prescribed. ⁶So couriers went throughout all Israel and Judah with letters from the king and his officials, as the king had commanded, saying, "O people of Israel, return to the LORD, the God of Abraham, Isaac, and Israel, so that he may turn again to the remnant of you who have escaped from the hand of the kings of Assyria. ⁷Do not be like your ancestors and your kindred, who were faithless to the LORD God of their ancestors, so that he made them a desolation, as you see. ⁸Do not now be stiff-necked as your ancestors were, but yield yourselves to the LORD and come to his sanctuary, which he has sanctified forever, and serve the LORD your God, so that his fierce anger may turn away from you. ⁹For as you return to the LORD, your kindred and your children will find compassion with their captors, and return to this land. For the LORD your God is gracious and merciful, and will not turn away his face from you, if you return to him."

10 So the couriers went from city to city through the country of Ephraim and Manasseh, and as far as Zebulun; but they laughed them to scorn, and mocked them. ¹¹Only a few from Asher, Manasseh, and Zebulun humbled themselves and came to Jerusalem. ¹²The hand of God was also on Judah to give them one heart to do what the king and the officials commanded by the word of the LORD.

30.1–12. 5: *So they decreed to make a proclamation throughout all Israel, from Beer-sheba to Dan, that the people should come and keep the passover*:* These boundaries are the traditional southern and northern points of Israel. The inclusion of both northern and southern portions of the country may be a deliberate effort to connect Hezekiah with the first "united" rule over north and south since the time of Solomon. It is doubtful that Judean rule under Hezekiah could have been extended very far to the north. **12:** *The hand of God was also on Judah to give them one heart to do what the king and the officials commanded by the word of the LORD:* The unity of the people is an important theme to the Chronicler's history.

13 Many people came together in Jerusalem to keep the festival of unleavened bread in the second month, a very large assembly. ¹⁴They set to work and removed the altars that were in Jerusalem, and all the altars for offering incense they took away and threw into the Wadi Kidron. ¹⁵They slaughtered the passover lamb on the fourteenth day of the second month. The priests and the Levites were ashamed, and they sanctified themselves and brought burnt offerings into the house of the LORD. ¹⁶They took their accustomed posts according to the law of Moses the man of God; the priests dashed the blood that they received*ᵃ* from the hands of the Levites. ¹⁷For there were many in the assembly who had not sanctified themselves; therefore the Levites had to slaughter the passover lamb for everyone who was not clean, to make it holy to the LORD. ¹⁸For a multitude of the people, many of them from Ephraim, Manasseh, Issachar, and Zebulun, had not cleansed themselves, yet they ate the passover otherwise than as prescribed. But Hezekiah prayed for them, saying, "The good LORD pardon all ¹⁹who set their hearts to seek God, the LORD the God of their ancestors, even though not in accordance with the

a Heb lacks *that they received*

sanctuary's rules of cleanness." 20 The LORD heard Hezekiah, and healed the people. 21 The people of Israel who were present at Jerusalem kept the festival of unleavened bread seven days with great gladness; and the Levites and the priests praised the LORD day by day, accompanied by loud instruments for the LORD. 22 Hezekiah spoke encouragingly to all the Levites who showed good skill in the service of the LORD. So the people ate the food of the festival for seven days, sacrificing offerings of well-being and giving thanks to the LORD the God of their ancestors.

23 Then the whole assembly agreed together to keep the festival for another seven days; so they kept it for another seven days with gladness. 24 For King Hezekiah of Judah gave the assembly a thousand bulls and seven thousand sheep for offerings, and the officials gave the assembly a thousand bulls and ten thousand sheep. The priests sanctified themselves in great numbers. 25 The whole assembly of Judah, the priests and the Levites, and the whole assembly that came out of Israel, and the resident aliens who came out of the land of Israel, and the resident aliens who lived in Judah, rejoiced. 26 There was great joy in Jerusalem, for since the time of Solomon son of King David of Israel there had been nothing like this in Jerusalem. 27 Then the priests and the Levites stood up and blessed the people, and their voice was heard; their prayer came to his holy dwelling in heaven.

30.13–27. 18–19: *The good LORD pardon all who set their hearts to seek God:* Since some had come from the north to worship in Jerusalem, they had not subscribed to the proper forms of purity to approach the Temple* precinct. Hezekiah's successful intercession on their behalf is remarkable. **26:** *There was great joy in Jerusalem, for since the time of Solomon son of King David of Israel there had been nothing like this in Jerusalem:* Hezekiah's actions serve to reverse the policies not only of Ahaz, but also of other kings who had aided the division of Israel into northern and southern states. The Chronicler envisions a unified community in which the old divisions are overwhelmed by consciousness of an even older unity.

31 Now when all this was finished, all Israel who were present went out to the cities of Judah and broke down the pillars, hewed down the sacred poles," and pulled down the high places and the altars throughout all Judah and Benjamin, and in Ephraim and Manasseh, until they had destroyed them all. Then all the people of Israel returned to their cities, all to their individual properties.

2 Hezekiah appointed the divisions of the priests and of the Levites, division by division, everyone according to his service, the priests and the Levites, for burnt offerings and offerings of well-being, to minister in the gates of the camp of the LORD and to give thanks and praise. 3 The contribution of the king from his own possessions was for the burnt offerings: the burnt offerings of morning and evening, and the burnt offerings for the sabbaths, the new moons, and the appointed festivals, as it is written in the law of the LORD. 4 He commanded the people who lived in Jerusalem to give the portion due to the priests and the Levites, so that they might devote themselves to the law of the LORD. 5 As soon as the word spread, the people of Israel gave in abundance the first fruits of grain, wine, oil, honey, and of all the produce of the field; and they brought in abundantly the tithe of everything. 6 The people of Israel and Judah who lived in the cities of Judah also brought in the tithe of cattle and sheep, and the tithe of the dedicated things that had been consecrated to the LORD their God, and laid them in heaps. 7 In the third month they began to pile up the heaps, and finished them in the seventh month. 8 When Hezekiah and the officials came and saw the heaps, they blessed the LORD and his people Israel. 9 Hezekiah questioned the priests and the Levites about the heaps. 10 The chief priest Azariah, who was of the house of Zadok, answered him, "Since they began to bring the contributions into the house of the LORD, we have had enough to eat and have plenty to spare; for the LORD has blessed his people, so that we have this great supply left over."

a Heb *Asherim*

31.4: *He commanded the people who lived in Jerusalem to give the portion due to the priests and the Levites, so that they might devote themselves to the law of the LORD:* As recipients of blessing from God's having chosen Jerusalem, the inhabitants were obligated to make extra provision to ensure the Temple* personnel were free to pursue their study and teaching of the law.

11 Then Hezekiah commanded them to prepare store-chambers in the house of the LORD; and they prepared them. 12 Faithfully they brought in the contributions, the tithes and the dedicated things. The chief officer in charge of them was Conaniah the Levite, with his brother Shimei as second; 13 while Jehiel, Azaziah, Nahath, Asahel, Jerimoth, Jozabad, Eliel, Ismachiah, Mahath, and Benaiah were overseers assisting Conaniah and his brother Shimei, by the appointment of King Hezekiah and of Azariah the chief officer of the house of God. 14 Kore son of Imnah the Levite, keeper of the east gate, was in charge of the freewill offerings to God, to apportion the contribution reserved for the LORD and the most holy offerings. 15 Eden, Miniamin, Jeshua, Shemaiah, Amariah, and Shecaniah were faithfully assisting him in the cities of the priests, to distribute the portions to their kindred, old and young alike, by divisions, 16 except those enrolled by genealogy, males from three years old and upwards, all who entered the house of the LORD as the duty of each day required, for their service according to their offices, by their divisions. 17 The enrollment of the priests was according to their ancestral houses; that of the Levites from twenty years old and upwards was according to their offices, by their divisions. 18 The priests were enrolled with all their little children, their wives, their sons, and their daughters, the whole multitude; for they were faithful in keeping themselves holy. 19 And for the descendants of Aaron, the priests, who were in the fields of common land belonging to their towns, town by town, the people designated by name were to distribute portions to every male among the priests and to everyone among the Levites who was enrolled.

20 Hezekiah did this throughout all Judah; he did what was good and right and faithful before the LORD his God. 21 And every work that he undertook in the service of the house of God, and in accordance with the law and the commandments, to seek his God, he did with all his heart; and he prospered.

32 After these things and these acts of faithfulness, King Sennacherib of Assyria came and invaded Judah and encamped against the fortified cities, thinking to win them for himself. 2 When Hezekiah saw that Sennacherib had come and intended to fight against Jerusalem, 3 he planned with his officers and his warriors to stop the flow of the springs that were outside the city; and they helped him. 4 A great many people were gathered, and they stopped all the springs and the wadi that flowed through the land, saying, "Why should the Assyrian kings come and find water in abundance?" 5 Hezekiah*a* set to work resolutely and built up the entire wall that was broken down, and raised towers on it,*b* and outside it he built another wall; he also strengthened the Millo in the city of David, and made weapons and shields in abundance. 6 He appointed combat commanders over the people, and gathered them together to him in the square at the gate of the city and spoke encouragingly to them, saying, 7 "Be strong and of good courage. Do not be afraid or dismayed before the king of Assyria and all the horde that is with him; for there is one greater with us than with him. 8 With him is an arm of flesh; but with us is the LORD our God, to help us and to fight our battles." The people were encouraged by the words of King Hezekiah of Judah.

9 After this, while King Sennacherib of Assyria was at Lachish with all his forces, he sent his servants to Jerusalem to King Hezekiah of Judah and to all the people of Judah that were in Jerusalem, saying, 10 "Thus says King Sennacherib of Assyria: On what are you relying, that you undergo the siege of Jerusalem? 11 Is not Hezekiah misleading

a Heb He   *b* Vg: Heb *and raised on the towers*

you, handing you over to die by famine and by thirst, when he tells you, 'The LORD our God will save us from the hand of the king of Assyria'? 12Was it not this same Hezekiah who took away his high places and his altars and commanded Judah and Jerusalem, saying, 'Before one altar you shall worship, and upon it you shall make your offerings'? 13Do you not know what I and my ancestors have done to all the peoples of other lands? Were the gods of the nations of those lands at all able to save their lands out of my hand? 14Who among all the gods of those nations that my ancestors utterly destroyed was able to save his people from my hand, that your God should be able to save you from my hand? 15Now therefore do not let Hezekiah deceive you or mislead you in this fashion, and do not believe him, for no god of any nation or kingdom has been able to save his people from my hand or from the hand of my ancestors. How much less will your God save you out of my hand!"

16 His servants said still more against the Lord GOD and against his servant Hezekiah. 17He also wrote letters to throw contempt on the LORD the God of Israel and to speak against him, saying, "Just as the gods of the nations in other lands did not rescue their people from my hands, so the God of Hezekiah will not rescue his people from my hand." 18They shouted it with a loud voice in the language of Judah to the people of Jerusalem who were on the wall, to frighten and terrify them, in order that they might take the city. 19They spoke of the God of Jerusalem as if he were like the gods of the peoples of the earth, which are the work of human hands.

32.19: *They spoke of the God of Jerusalem as if he were like the gods of the peoples of the earth:* Sennacherib came against Judah because Hezekiah had ceased to pay his annual tribute as a vassal of Assyria. The Chronicler understands this invasion as a test of God's ability to defend his people and to avoid being viewed simply as one of hundreds of national deities in the ancient world.

20 Then King Hezekiah and the prophet Isaiah son of Amoz prayed because of this and cried to heaven. 21And the LORD sent an angel who cut off all the mighty warriors and commanders and officers in the camp of the king of Assyria. So he returned in disgrace to his own land. When he came into the house of his god, some of his own sons struck him down there with the sword. 22So the LORD saved Hezekiah and the inhabitants of Jerusalem from the hand of King Sennacherib of Assyria and from the hand of all his enemies; he gave them rest[a] on every side. 23Many brought gifts to the LORD in Jerusalem and precious things to King Hezekiah of Judah, so that he was exalted in the sight of all nations from that time onward.

32.23: *Many brought gifts to the LORD in Jerusalem and precious things to King Hezekiah:* Just as Solomon had received such honors in his time, Hezekiah's rule is affirmed by recognition from outside Israel. The Chronicler concludes his narrative* by drawing a picture of a prosperous and powerful monarch, in much the same way as Solomon was depicted.

24 In those days Hezekiah became sick and was at the point of death. He prayed to the LORD, and he answered him and gave him a sign. 25But Hezekiah did not respond according to the benefit done to him, for his heart was proud. Therefore wrath came upon him and upon Judah and Jerusalem. 26Then Hezekiah humbled himself for the pride of his heart, both he and the inhabitants of Jerusalem, so that the wrath of the LORD did not come upon them in the days of Hezekiah.

27 Hezekiah had very great riches and honor; and he made for himself treasuries for silver, for gold, for precious stones, for spices, for shields, and for all kinds of costly objects; 28storehouses also for the yield of grain, wine, and oil; and stalls for all kinds of cattle, and sheepfolds.[b] 29He likewise provided cities for himself, and flocks and herds in abundance; for God had given him very great possessions. 30This same Hezekiah closed the upper outlet of the waters of

a Gk Vg: Heb *guided them*   b Gk Vg: Heb *flocks for folds*

Gihon and directed them down to the west side of the city of David. Hezekiah prospered in all his works. [31]So also in the matter of the envoys of the officials of Babylon, who had been sent to him to inquire about the sign that had been done in the land, God left him to himself, in order to test him and to know all that was in his heart.

32 Now the rest of the acts of Hezekiah, and his good deeds, are written in the vision of the prophet Isaiah son of Amoz in the Book of the Kings of Judah and Israel. [33]Hezekiah slept with his ancestors, and they buried him on the ascent to the tombs of the descendants of David; and all Judah and the inhabitants of Jerusalem did him honor at his death. His son Manasseh succeeded him.

33 Manasseh was twelve years old when he began to reign; he reigned fifty-five years in Jerusalem. [2]He did what was evil in the sight of the LORD, according to the abominable practices of the nations whom the LORD drove out before the people of Israel. [3]For he rebuilt the high places that his father Hezekiah had pulled down, and erected altars to the Baals, made sacred poles,[a] worshiped all the host of heaven, and served them. [4]He built altars in the house of the LORD, of which the LORD had said, "In Jerusalem shall my name be forever." [5]He built altars for all the host of heaven in the two courts of the house of the LORD. [6]He made his son pass through fire in the valley of the son of Hinnom, practiced soothsaying and augury and sorcery, and dealt with mediums and with wizards. He did much evil in the sight of the LORD, provoking him to anger. [7]The carved image of the idol that he had made he set in the house of God, of which God said to David and to his son Solomon, "In this house, and in Jerusalem, which I have chosen out of all the tribes of Israel, I will put my name forever; [8]I will never again remove the feet of Israel from the land that I appointed for your ancestors, if only they will be careful to do all that I have commanded them, all the law, the statutes, and the ordinances given through Moses." [9]Manasseh misled Judah and the in-

habitants of Jerusalem, so that they did more evil than the nations whom the LORD had destroyed before the people of Israel.

10 The LORD spoke to Manasseh and to his people, but they gave no heed. [11]Therefore the LORD brought against them the commanders of the army of the king of Assyria, who took Manasseh captive in manacles, bound him with fetters, and brought him to Babylon. [12]While he was in distress he entreated the favor of the LORD his God and humbled himself greatly before the God of his ancestors. [13]He prayed to him, and God received his entreaty, heard his plea, and restored him again to Jerusalem and to his kingdom. Then Manasseh knew that the LORD indeed was God.

14 Afterward he built an outer wall for the city of David west of Gihon, in the valley, reaching the entrance at the Fish Gate; he carried it around Ophel, and raised it to a very great height. He also put commanders of the army in all the fortified cities in Judah. [15]He took away the foreign gods and the idol from the house of the LORD, and all the altars that he had built on the mountain of the house of the LORD and in Jerusalem, and he threw them out of the city. [16]He also restored the altar of the LORD and offered on it sacrifices of well-being and of thanksgiving; and he commanded Judah to serve the LORD the God of Israel. [17]The people, however, still sacrificed at the high places, but only to the LORD their God.

18 Now the rest of the acts of Manasseh, his prayer to his God, and the words of the seers who spoke to him in the name of the LORD God of Israel, these are in the Annals of the Kings of Israel. [19]His prayer, and how God received his entreaty, all his sin and his faithlessness, the sites on which he built high places and set up the sacred poles[b] and the images, before he humbled himself, these are written in the records of the seers.[c] [20]So Manasseh slept with his ancestors, and they buried him in his house. His son Amon succeeded him.

a Heb Asheroth   b Heb Asherim   c One Ms Gk: MT of Hozai

33.1–20: The reign of Manasseh. The Chronicler follows his source closely (2 Kings 21), though the account of Manasseh's repentance is unique to the Chronicler. While he is presented as the paradigm of wickedness in 2 Kings, the Chronicler leaves his readers with a portrait of the repentant person whose seeking God brings him back to Jerusalem. Some believe this is pure fiction by the Chronicler, an effort to create a parallel between the repentant Manasseh and the exilic community. **13:** *Then Manasseh knew that the* Lord *indeed was God:* This echoes a recurring expression in the prophet* Ezekiel.

21 Amon was twenty-two years old when he began to reign; he reigned two years in Jerusalem. 22 He did what was evil in the sight of the Lord, as his father Manasseh had done. Amon sacrificed to all the images that his father Manasseh had made, and served them. 23 He did not humble himself before the Lord, as his father Manasseh had humbled himself, but this Amon incurred more and more guilt. 24 His servants conspired against him and killed him in his house. 25 But the people of the land killed all those who had conspired against King Amon; and the people of the land made his son Josiah king to succeed him.

33.21–25: The reign of Amon. Of little interest to the Chronicler, Amon simply serves to show what would have happened if Manasseh had not repented.

34 Josiah was eight years old when he began to reign; he reigned thirty-one years in Jerusalem. 2 He did what was right in the sight of the Lord, and walked in the ways of his ancestor David; he did not turn aside to the right or to the left. 3 For in the eighth year of his reign, while he was still a boy, he began to seek the God of his ancestor David, and in the twelfth year he began to purge Judah and Jerusalem of the high places, the sacred poles,*a* and the carved and the cast images. 4 In his presence they pulled down the altars of the Baals; he demolished the incense altars that stood above them. He broke down the sacred poles*a* and the carved and the cast images; he made dust of them

and scattered it over the graves of those who had sacrificed to them. 5 He also burned the bones of the priests on their altars, and purged Judah and Jerusalem. 6 In the towns of Manasseh, Ephraim, and Simeon, and as far as Naphtali, in their ruins*b* all around, 7 he broke down the altars, beat the sacred poles*a* and the images into powder, and demolished all the incense altars throughout all the land of Israel. Then he returned to Jerusalem.

8 In the eighteenth year of his reign, when he had purged the land and the house, he sent Shaphan son of Azaliah, Maaseiah the governor of the city, and Joah son of Joahaz, the recorder, to repair the house of the Lord his God. 9 They came to the high priest Hilkiah and delivered the money that had been brought into the house of God, which the Levites, the keepers of the threshold, had collected from Manasseh and Ephraim and from all the remnant of Israel and from all Judah and Benjamin and from the inhabitants of Jerusalem. 10 They delivered it to the workers who had the oversight of the house of the Lord, and the workers who were working in the house of the Lord gave it for repairing and restoring the house. 11 They gave it to the carpenters and the builders to buy quarried stone, and timber for binders, and beams for the buildings that the kings of Judah had let go to ruin. 12 The people did the work faithfully. Over them were appointed the Levites Jahath and Obadiah, of the sons of Merari, along with Zechariah and Meshullam, of the sons of the Kohathites, to have oversight. Other Levites, all skillful with instruments of music, 13 were over the burden bearers and directed all who did work in every kind of service; and some of the Levites were scribes, and officials, and gatekeepers.

14 While they were bringing out the money that had been brought into the house of the Lord, the priest Hilkiah found the book of the law of the Lord given through Moses. 15 Hilkiah said to the secretary Shaphan, "I have found the book of the law in

a Heb *Asherim*　*b* Meaning of Heb uncertain

the house of the LORD"; and Hilkiah gave the book to Shaphan. ¹⁶Shaphan brought the book to the king, and further reported to the king, "All that was committed to your servants they are doing. ¹⁷They have emptied out the money that was found in the house of the LORD and have delivered it into the hand of the overseers and the workers." ¹⁸The secretary Shaphan informed the king, "The priest Hilkiah has given me a book." Shaphan then read it aloud to the king.

19 When the king heard the words of the law he tore his clothes. ²⁰Then the king commanded Hilkiah, Ahikam son of Shaphan, Abdon son of Micah, the secretary Shaphan, and the king's servant Asaiah: ²¹"Go, inquire of the LORD for me and for those who are left in Israel and in Judah, concerning the words of the book that has been found; for the wrath of the LORD that is poured out on us is great, because our ancestors did not keep the word of the LORD, to act in accordance with all that is written in this book."

22 So Hilkiah and those whom the king had sent went to the prophet Huldah, the wife of Shallum son of Tokhath son of Hasrah, keeper of the wardrobe (who lived in Jerusalem in the Second Quarter) and spoke to her to that effect. ²³She declared to them, "Thus says the LORD, the God of Israel: Tell the man who sent you to me, ²⁴Thus says the LORD: I will indeed bring disaster upon this place and upon its inhabitants, all the curses that are written in the book that was read before the king of Judah. ²⁵Because they have forsaken me and have made offerings to other gods, so that they have provoked me to anger with all the works of their hands, my wrath will be poured out on this place and will not be quenched. ²⁶But as to the king of Judah, who sent you to inquire of the LORD, thus shall you say to him: Thus says the LORD, the God of Israel: Regarding the words that you have heard, ²⁷because your heart was penitent and you humbled yourself before God when you heard his words against this place and its inhabitants, and you have humbled yourself before me, and have torn your clothes and wept before

me, I also have heard you, says the LORD. ²⁸I will gather you to your ancestors and you shall be gathered to your grave in peace; your eyes shall not see all the disaster that I will bring on this place and its inhabitants." They took the message back to the king.

29 Then the king sent word and gathered together all the elders of Judah and Jerusalem. ³⁰The king went up to the house of the LORD, with all the people of Judah, the inhabitants of Jerusalem, the priests and the Levites, all the people both great and small; he read in their hearing all the words of the book of the covenant that had been found in the house of the LORD. ³¹The king stood in his place and made a covenant before the LORD, to follow the LORD, keeping his commandments, his decrees, and his statutes, with all his heart and all his soul, to perform the words of the covenant that were written in this book. ³²Then he made all who were present in Jerusalem and in Benjamin pledge themselves to it. And the inhabitants of Jerusalem acted according to the covenant of God, the God of their ancestors. ³³Josiah took away all the abominations from all the territory that belonged to the people of Israel, and made all who were in Israel worship the LORD their God. All his days they did not turn away from following the LORD the God of their ancestors.

35 Josiah kept a passover to the LORD in Jerusalem; they slaughtered the passover lamb on the fourteenth day of the first month. ²He appointed the priests to their offices and encouraged them in the service of the house of the LORD. ³He said to the Levites who taught all Israel and who were holy to the LORD, "Put the holy ark in the house that Solomon son of David, king of Israel, built; you need no longer carry it on your shoulders. Now serve the LORD your God and his people Israel. ⁴Make preparations by your ancestral houses by your divisions, following the written directions of King David of Israel and the written directions of his son Solomon. ⁵Take position in the holy place according to the groupings of the ancestral houses of your kindred the people, and let there be Levites for each division

of an ancestral house.ᵃ ⁶Slaughter the passover lamb, sanctify yourselves, and on behalf of your kindred make preparations, acting according to the word of the LORD by Moses."

7 Then Josiah contributed to the people, as passover offerings for all that were present, lambs and kids from the flock to the number of thirty thousand, and three thousand bulls; these were from the king's possessions. ⁸His officials contributed willingly to the people, to the priests, and to the Levites. Hilkiah, Zechariah, and Jehiel, the chief officers of the house of God, gave to the priests for the passover offerings two thousand six hundred lambs and kids and three hundred bulls. ⁹Conaniah also, and his brothers Shemaiah and Nethanel, and Hashabiah and Jeiel and Jozabad, the chiefs of the Levites, gave to the Levites for the passover offerings five thousand lambs and kids and five hundred bulls.

10 When the service had been prepared for, the priests stood in their place, and the Levites in their divisions according to the king's command. ¹¹They slaughtered the passover lamb, and the priests dashed the blood that they receivedᵇ from them, while the Levites did the skinning. ¹²They set aside the burnt offerings so that they might distribute them according to the groupings of the ancestral houses of the people, to offer to the LORD, as it is written in the book of Moses. And they did the same with the bulls. ¹³They roasted the passover lamb with fire according to the ordinance; and they boiled the holy offerings in pots, in caldrons, and in pans, and carried them quickly to all the people. ¹⁴Afterward they made preparations for themselves and for the priests, because the priests the descendants of Aaron were occupied in offering the burnt offerings and the fat parts until night; so the Levites made preparations for themselves and for the priests, the descendants of Aaron. ¹⁵The singers, the descendants of Asaph, were in their place according to the command of David, and Asaph, and Heman, and the king's seer Jeduthun. The gatekeepers were at each gate; they did not need to interrupt their service, for their kindred the Levites made preparations for them.

16 So all the service of the LORD was prepared that day, to keep the passover and to offer burnt offerings on the altar of the LORD, according to the command of King Josiah. ¹⁷The people of Israel who were present kept the passover at that time, and the festival of unleavened bread seven days. ¹⁸No passover like it had been kept in Israel since the days of the prophet Samuel; none of the kings of Israel had kept such a passover as was kept by Josiah, by the priests and the Levites, by all Judah and Israel who were present, and by the inhabitants of Jerusalem. ¹⁹In the eighteenth year of the reign of Josiah this passover was kept.

20 After all this, when Josiah had set the temple in order, King Neco of Egypt went up to fight at Carchemish on the Euphrates, and Josiah went out against him. ²¹But Necoᶜ sent envoys to him, saying, "What have I to do with you, king of Judah? I am not coming against you today, but against the house with which I am at war; and God has commanded me to hurry. Cease opposing God, who is with me, so that he will not destroy you." ²²But Josiah would not turn away from him, but disguised himself in order to fight with him. He did not listen to the words of Neco from the mouth of God, but joined battle in the plain of Megiddo. ²³The archers shot King Josiah; and the king said to his servants, "Take me away, for I am badly wounded." ²⁴So his servants took him out of the chariot and carried him in his second chariotᵈ and brought him to Jerusalem. There he died, and was buried in the tombs of his ancestors. All Judah and Jerusalem mourned for Josiah. ²⁵Jeremiah also uttered a lament for Josiah, and all the singing men and singing women have spoken of Josiah in their laments to this day. They made these a custom in Israel; they are recorded in the Laments. ²⁶Now the rest of the acts of Josiah and his faithful deeds in accordance with what is written in the law of the LORD, ²⁷and

a Meaning of Heb uncertain   b Heb lacks that they received   c Heb he   d Or the chariot of his deputy his acts, first and last, are written in the Book of the Kings of Israel and Judah.

34.1–35.27: The reign of Josiah. Though a king of interest to the Chronicler, Josiah does not have the same prominence in the Chronicler's history that he was accorded in Kings. The Chronicler follows closely his source (2 Kings 22–23) but does not praise him in the same superlatives as Hezekiah. **34.3:** *In the twelfth year he began to purge Judah and Jerusalem of the high places*:* The Chronicler places Josiah's efforts at suppressing idolatry* before the "Book of the Law" is found in the Temple,* the reverse of the narrative* in 2 Kings. For the Chronicler, if a king truly sought God, he would not tolerate rampant idolatry.

36 The people of the land took Jehoahaz son of Josiah and made him king to succeed his father in Jerusalem. ²Jehoahaz was twenty-three years old when he began to reign; he reigned three months in Jerusalem. ³Then the king of Egypt deposed him in Jerusalem and laid on the land a tribute of one hundred talents of silver and one talent of gold. ⁴The king of Egypt made his brother Eliakim king over Judah and Jerusalem, and changed his name to Jehoiakim; but Neco took his brother Jehoahaz and carried him to Egypt.

5 Jehoiakim was twenty-five years old when he began to reign; he reigned eleven years in Jerusalem. He did what was evil in the sight of the LORD his God. ⁶Against him King Nebuchadnezzar of Babylon came up, and bound him with fetters to take him to Babylon. ⁷Nebuchadnezzar also carried some of the vessels of the house of the LORD to Babylon and put them in his palace in Babylon. ⁸Now the rest of the acts of Jehoiakim, and the abominations that he did, and what was found against him, are written in the Book of the Kings of Israel and Judah; and his son Jehoiachin succeeded him.

9 Jehoiachin was eight years old when he began to reign; he reigned three months and ten days in Jerusalem. He did what was evil in the sight of the LORD. ¹⁰In the spring of the year King Nebuchadnezzar sent and brought him to Babylon, along with the precious vessels of the house of the LORD, and

made his brother Zedekiah king over Judah and Jerusalem.

36.1–10. 1–4: The reign of Jehoahaz. The Chronicler says little about the short reign of this minor figure in Judah's history. **5–8: The reign of Jehoiakim.** Apart from his doing evil and suffering disaster because of it, the Chronicler offers no details of Jehoiakim's reign. **9–10: The reign of Jehoiachin.** Another of the minor figures at the close of Judean history, the Chronicler asserts he did evil, though he was only *eight years old.*

11 Zedekiah was twenty-one years old when he began to reign; he reigned eleven years in Jerusalem. ¹²He did what was evil in the sight of the LORD his God. He did not humble himself before the prophet Jeremiah who spoke from the mouth of the LORD. ¹³He also rebelled against King Nebuchadnezzar, who had made him swear by God; he stiffened his neck and hardened his heart against turning to the LORD, the God of Israel. ¹⁴All the leading priests and the people also were exceedingly unfaithful, following all the abominations of the nations; and they polluted the house of the LORD that he had consecrated in Jerusalem.

15 The LORD, the God of their ancestors, sent persistently to them by his messengers, because he had compassion on his people and on his dwelling place; ¹⁶but they kept mocking the messengers of God, despising his words, and scoffing at his prophets, until the wrath of the LORD against his people became so great that there was no remedy.

17 Therefore he brought up against them the king of the Chaldeans, who killed their youths with the sword in the house of their sanctuary, and had no compassion on young man or young woman, the aged or the feeble; he gave them all into his hand. ¹⁸All the vessels of the house of God, large and small, and the treasures of the house of the LORD, and the treasures of the king and of his officials, all these he brought to Babylon. ¹⁹They burned the house of God, broke down the wall of Jerusalem, burned all its palaces with fire, and destroyed all its precious vessels. ²⁰He took into exile in Babylon those who had escaped from the sword, and they be-

came servants to him and to his sons until the establishment of the kingdom of Persia, 21to fulfill the word of the LORD by the mouth of Jeremiah, until the land had made up for its sabbaths. All the days that it lay desolate it kept sabbath, to fulfill seventy years.

22 In the first year of King Cyrus of Persia, in fulfillment of the word of the LORD spoken by Jeremiah, the LORD stirred up the spirit of King Cyrus of Persia so that he sent a herald throughout all his kingdom and also declared in a written edict: 23"Thus says King Cyrus of Persia: The LORD, the God of heaven, has given me all the kingdoms of the earth, and he has charged me to build him a house at Jerusalem, which is in Judah. Whoever is among you of all his people, may the LORD his God be with him! Let him go up."

36.11–23: The fall of Jerusalem. With a string of bad kings following on Josiah's death, the kingdom was doomed. Zedekiah comes to the throne, and the Chronicler regards him as evil because of his opposition to the prophets* and his rebellion against Nebuchadnezzar. 14: Lest the king be held the only one at fault, the Chronicler sees the *leading priests and people* as sharing in the blame, particularly for desecrating the Temple.* 21: The Chronicler ends his history with a word of promise: The land *made up for its sabbaths* by being vacant, and Cyrus, king of Persia, called for a new Temple to be built in Jerusalem. The community can once again enjoy finding and being found by God at the new Temple, if they take to heart the examples of devotion and faithfulness from Israel's past.

1 and 2 Chronicles and Ezra-Nehemiah have extended genealogical lists. While this view may still predominate, the last two decades have seen the emergence of a serious challenge from scholars who argue for the independence of Ezra-Nehemiah and 1 and 2 Chronicles. They have sought to base this conclusion on a number of differences in vocabulary, theology and ideology between the two works. The issue is complex, but here we will look at Ezra-Nehemiah as it is an independent composition on its own terms.

In literary form, Ezra-Nehemiah is difficult to characterize. The author has employed citations of documents, lists of personnel or community members, historical narratives, and first-person narratives that are often termed "memoirs." Some of the more notable portions are Rehum's correspondence with King Artaxerxes (Ezra 4:7–22), Tattenai's correspondence with King Darius (5:6–17; 6:6–12), a list of those who returned from Babylon (Ezra 2:1–67, repeated in Neh 7:6–68), the "Ezra memoir" (Ezra 7–10), and the "Nehemiah memoir" (mainly Neh 1:1–7:5).

The normal approach to the work has been to read it as a historical narrative, but throughout the work elements appear dislocated and far off the mark for history-writing. Given the lack of characterized flow to the work, it would be better to consider it a historical apologetic, or a defense of a particular position or viewpoint, loosely using the events of the community to support a theological perspective.

Squarely set in the midst of the Persian empire, the work focuses on two imperial functionaries, Ezra and Nehemiah, and the reforms they attempted. If Ezra is placed before Nehemiah, as seems the intent of the author, then Ezra came to Jerusalem in 458 BCE, and Nehemiah's first stint as governor was in 445 BCE. When scholars examine the lists of names, they can determine that the latest names on some lists date from a generation or so after the time of the mid-fifth century. They therefore conclude that the work was written around 400 BCE.

Both Ezra and Nehemiah as literary figures are portrayed as disturbed by intermarriage with foreigners in the community, and both condemn this activity using a language loaded with religious connotations. This concern fundamentally seems to fit with Ezra 1–6, where the struggle to rebuild the Temple in Jerusalem almost a century earlier dominates.

EZRA

Introduction to Ezra, Nehemiah

In the form found in most English Bibles, Ezra and Nehemiah are divided into two separate books. This format follows a tradition established in the early centuries of the Christian church, when the Vulgate* (the Bible in Latin) divided these two works. It was only in the fifteenth century CE that Hebrew manuscripts adopted the same custom. In actuality, the most ancient tradition we can trace kept these two works together as one. Most of the ancient lists of books of the Hebrew Bible list them together. Moreover, the two share a number of literary elements, suggesting that they are related.

It has become commonplace in scholarship to see Ezra-Nehemiah as a continuation of the same narrative* as 1 and 2 Chronicles, all these works having been written by the same hand. The reasons are many, but some of the main points are that Ezra-Nehemiah opens with a repetition of 2 Chr 36.22–23, that Ezra-Nehemiah and 1 and 2 Chronicles share vocabulary for Temple* personnel and objects that are not found elsewhere in the Hebrew Bible, and that both 1 and 2 Chronicles and Ezra-Nehemiah have extended genealogical* lists. While this view may still predominate, the last two decades have seen the emergence of a serious challenge from scholars who argue for the independence of Ezra-Nehemiah and 1 and 2 Chronicles. They have sought to base this conclusion on a number of differences in vocabulary, theology, and ideology between the two works. The issue is complex, but here we will look at Ezra-Nehemiah as if it is an independent composition on its own terms.

In literary form, Ezra-Nehemiah is difficult to characterize. The author has employed citations of documents, lists of personnel or community members, historical narratives, and first-person narratives that are often termed "memoirs." Some of the more notable portions are Rehum's correspondence with King Artaxerxes (Ezra 4.7–22), Tattenai's correspondence with King Darius (5.6–17; 6.6–12), a list of those who returned from Babylon (Ezra 2.1–67, repeated in Neh 7.6–68), the "Ezra memoir" (Ezra 7–10), and the "Nehemiah memoir" (mainly Neh 1.1–7.5).

The normal approach to the work has been to read it as a historical narrative, but throughout the work elements appear dislocated and far off the mark for history writing. Given the lack of chronological flow to the work, it would be better to consider it a historical apologetic,* or a defense of a particular position or viewpoint, loosely using the events of the community to support a theological perspective.

Squarely set in the midst of the Persian empire, the work focuses on two imperial functionaries, Ezra and Nehemiah, and the reforms they attempted. If Ezra is placed before Nehemiah, as seems the intent of the author, then Ezra came to Jerusalem in 458 BCE, and Nehemiah's first stint as governor was in 445 BCE. When scholars examine the lists of names, they can determine that the latest names on some lists date from a generation or so after the time of the mid fifth century. They therefore conclude that the work was written around 400 BCE.

Both Ezra and Nehemiah as literary figures are portrayed as disturbed by intermarriage with "foreigners" in the community, and both condemn this activity using a language loaded with religious connotations. This concern hardly seems to fit with Ezra 1–6, where the struggle to rebuild the Temple in Jerusalem almost a century earlier dominates.

Linking the various parts of the work together is the theme of the "house of God." Beginning with the rebuilding of the physical structure of the Temple, the work moves through to the reformation of the community as the "house of God." A subsidiary theme is the rebuilding of the walls of Jerusalem, which would separate the community from the surrounding region, both physically and religiously. These themes are cast in highly religious language, leading the reader to the inevitable assessment of the righteousness of this redefinition of the community.

The Persian empire faced troubled conditions in the mid fifth century as a serious revolt in Egypt, coupled with the assistance of the Greek city-states, openly challenged the empire's control of the Mediterranean. The territory of Yehud, as the region of Jerusalem and the surrounding area was called, suddenly had strategic importance for the empire. One of the techniques the Persian empire used to control subject populations was controlling their access to the land. Since most of the population was engaged in farming or farming-related employment, access to the land was essential for survival, and thus the empire maintained control over the peoples they had conquered. The ability to control land access was threatened when adjacent communities began to intermarry, since this blurred the definition of who had access to what lands. The narratives of Ezra-Nehemiah present two individuals who are charged directly by the Persian king to undertake vaguely described missions, the result of which is the strengthening of the community boundaries by directly attacking the practice of intermarriage. Such a redefinition of the community probably met with strong opposition, and the present literary work of Ezra-Nehemiah sought to provide a theological rationale for accepting what was essentially an imperial dictate.

READING GUIDE

Given the complicated mixture of literary forms in Ezra-Nehemiah, it is difficult to follow all the elements of the narrative. Readers should watch for the "house of God" theme in the various sections; how does the author want us to understand the "house of God"? Also, it is helpful to notice who is allowed to participate in the community, and who is being excluded.

A useful place to begin reading is Ezra 9 where an important transfer takes place, moving from the sanctity of the Temple to the general population of the region. Running throughout the chapter is the consciousness of the Exile★ as a punishment and a lesson from the past to serve as an incentive to follow the ways of God more closely in the future.

Ezra

1–2	Prologue
3–6	Rebuilding the house of God
7–10	Ezra's inquiry

Nehemiah

1.1–7.5	Nehemiah's mission
7.6–13.3	Forming the house of God
13.4–30	Postlogue

PROLOGUE

Chs. 1–2 The beginning of Ezra-Nehemiah seeks to establish the legitimacy of rebuilding the house of God, the Temple.* This is expressed by opening with the imperial order to return to Jerusalem and rebuild the Temple, immediately jumping to a listing of those who did return, and concluding with the tangible signs of devotion among them. The repetition of Cyrus's decree (Ezra 1.1–4 and 2 Chr 36.22–23) introduces the theme of Ezra and is not a direct link to the end of 2 Chronicles.

1 In the first year of King Cyrus of Persia, in order that the word of the LORD by the mouth of Jeremiah might be accomplished, the LORD stirred up the spirit of King Cyrus of Persia so that he sent a herald throughout all his kingdom, and also in a written edict declared:

2 "Thus says King Cyrus of Persia: The LORD, the God of heaven, has given me all the kingdoms of the earth, and he has charged me to build him a house at Jerusalem in Judah. ³Any of those among you who are of his people—may their God be with them!—are now permitted to go up to Jerusalem in Judah, and rebuild the house of the LORD, the God of Israel—he is the God who is in Jerusalem; ⁴and let all survivors, in whatever place they reside, be assisted by the people of their place with silver and gold, with goods and with animals, besides freewill offerings for the house of God in Jerusalem."

5 The heads of the families of Judah and Benjamin, and the priests and the Levites—everyone whose spirit God had stirred—got ready to go up and rebuild the house of the LORD in Jerusalem. ⁶All their neighbors aided them with silver vessels, with gold, with goods, with animals, and with valuable gifts, besides all that was freely offered. ⁷King Cyrus himself brought out the vessels of the house of the LORD that Nebuchadnezzar had carried away from Jerusalem and placed in the house of his gods. ⁸King Cyrus of Persia had them released into the charge of Mithredath the treasurer, who counted them out to Sheshbazzar the prince

of Judah. ⁹And this was the inventory: gold basins, thirty; silver basins, one thousand; knives,ᵃ twenty-nine; ¹⁰gold bowls, thirty; other silver bowls, four hundred ten; other vessels, one thousand; ¹¹the total of the gold and silver vessels was five thousand four hundred. All these Sheshbazzar brought up, when the exiles were brought up from Babylonia to Jerusalem.

1.1–11: The decree of Cyrus and its results. The legitimation pattern is opened by having Cyrus, the dominant founder of the Persian empire as Israel experienced it, decree that all those from Jerusalem should return and *rebuild the house of the LORD.* **1–2:** *In order that the word of the LORD by the mouth of Jeremiah might be accomplished:* Jeremiah had claimed the Exile* in Babylon would last 70 years (Jer 29.10). The *first year* of Cyrus is probably a reference to his first year over the Babylonian empire, which he captured in 539 BCE. The decree that follows is substantially the one that closes 2 Chr 36. *Charged me to build him a house at Jerusalem* is not the confession of Cyrus's belief in Israel's God, but rather a balanced polytheistic way of claiming that all subjugated peoples' gods have empowered Persian rule. Thus the Persian king, by virtue of having rule, should honor the gods who have permitted it. In other ancient sources, Cyrus claims the same divine approval from Marduk, the chief Babylonian god. **3:** *He is the God who is in Jerusalem* reflects the common ancient Near Eastern concept that gods and goddesses are specially present and should be worshipped in particular locations. **4:** *For the house of God in Jerusalem* is an expansion of the decree in 2 Chr 36 that allows for the collection of offerings for the Temple* in Jerusalem by all those living outside the city. **5:** *The heads of the families of Judah and Benjamin, and the priests and the Levites:* The primary tribes populating the southern kingdom of Judah were Judah and Benjamin. The priests and Levites were usually counted separately from the tribes. **7:** *King Cyrus himself brought out the vessels of the house of the LORD that Nebuchadnezzar had carried away from Jerusalem:* When Jerusalem and the Temple were destroyed in 587 BCE, the Babylonians looted the Temple precinct, including the gold and silver vessels used in the Temple service. The return of these vessels links the Temple of Solomon that had

a Vg: Meaning of Heb uncertain

been destroyed by the Babylonians with the Temple that will be built after the Exile. **8:** *Sheshbazzar the prince of Judah:* There is no consensus on what this title may have meant in this time period. In Ezra 5.14 Sheshbazzar is called a "governor" of the province, so it may be that the author is using "prince" to indicate a leading citizen. **9:** *And this was the inventory:* This list possibly has been copied from an authentic inventory of the returned vessels.

2 Now these were the people of the province who came from those captive exiles whom King Nebuchadnezzar of Babylon had carried captive to Babylonia; they returned to Jerusalem and Judah, all to their own towns. ²They came with Zerubbabel, Jeshua, Nehemiah, Seraiah, Reelaiah, Mordecai, Bilshan, Mispar, Bigvai, Rehum, and Baanah.

The number of the Israelite people: ³the descendants of Parosh, two thousand one hundred seventy-two. ⁴Of Shephatiah, three hundred seventy-two. ⁵Of Arah, seven hundred seventy-five. ⁶Of Pahath-moab, namely the descendants of Jeshua and Joab, two thousand eight hundred twelve. ⁷Of Elam, one thousand two hundred fifty-four. ⁸Of Zattu, nine hundred forty-five. ⁹Of Zaccai, seven hundred sixty. ¹⁰Of Bani, six hundred forty-two. ¹¹Of Bebai, six hundred twenty-three. ¹²Of Azgad, one thousand two hundred twenty-two. ¹³Of Adonikam, six hundred sixty-six. ¹⁴Of Bigvai, two thousand fifty-six. ¹⁵Of Adin, four hundred fifty-four. ¹⁶Of Ater, namely of Hezekiah, ninety-eight. ¹⁷Of Bezai, three hundred twenty-three. ¹⁸Of Jorah, one hundred twelve. ¹⁹Of Hashum, two hundred twenty-three. ²⁰Of Gibbar, ninety-five. ²¹Of Bethlehem, one hundred twenty-three. ²²The people of Netophah, fifty-six. ²³Of Anathoth, one hundred twenty-eight. ²⁴The descendants of Azmaveth, forty-two. ²⁵Of Kiriatharim, Chephirah, and Beeroth, seven hundred forty-three. ²⁶Of Ramah and Geba, six hundred twenty-one. ²⁷The people of Michmas, one hundred twenty-two. ²⁸Of Bethel and Ai, two hundred twenty-three. ²⁹The descendants of Nebo, fifty-two. ³⁰Of Magbish, one hundred fifty-six. ³¹Of the other Elam, one thousand two hundred fifty-four. ³²Of Harim, three hundred twenty. ³³Of Lod, Hadid, and Ono, seven hundred twenty-five. ³⁴Of Jericho, three hundred forty-five. ³⁵Of Senaah, three thousand six hundred thirty.

2.1–70: The list of those who returned from Babylon. At first glance, the list would seem to be a well-organized, coherent presentation broken into sections by category of occupations. A closer examination reveals that some persons are identified by their family lineage, others by their place of residence. This and other differences suggest the list is a composite product, possibly listing returnees from several different stages of the formation of the community in Jerusalem. From what meager records have survived, the usual conclusion drawn is that following Cyrus's decree several different groups left Babylon for Jerusalem at different times. The list is repeated with some variations in Neh 7.6–73. From a close comparison of the two lists, the list here in Ezra 2 appears to summarize the information in Neh 7, and consequently may be derived from that list. The use of duplicate lists in Ezra-Nehemiah is a deliberate framing device by the author, directing the reader's attention to the level of the individuals who form the "house of God." **2:** *They came with Zerubbabel, Jeshua, Nehemiah, Seraiah, Reelaiah . . . :* Several of these names are well-known governors of Yehud, the Persian province centered in Jerusalem, who were in office at various times from the sixth century onward. Others, such as *Jeshua,* were among the high priests. Some of the individuals were contemporaries of Nehemiah, bringing the close of the list to the mid fifth century. The incorporation of persons over such a range of time shows the essentially nonhistorical interests of the author. *The number of the Israelite people:* The term for *number* is more appropriately "listing," since a formal census does not follow. The first section (vv. 2b–20) lists names by clan★ group, the second (vv. 21–35) mainly by location, the third (vv. 36–39) lists priestly clans, the fourth (vv. 40–42) Levitical groups, and the fifth (vv. 43–58) various orders of Temple★ servants. These are followed by a miscellaneous group that could not demonstrate a connection to known family lineages (vv. 59–63). A numerical summary of the primary attributes of the community follows (vv. 64–67), then there is a report of the devotion of these groups to the Temple (vv. 68–70). The various numbers given are possible in some cases, though some of the amounts may be artificial, such as 666 (v. 13).

36 The priests: the descendants of Jedaiah, of the house of Jeshua, nine hundred seventy-three. [37]Of Immer, one thousand fifty-two. [38]Of Pashhur, one thousand two hundred forty-seven. [39]Of Harim, one thousand seventeen.

40 The Levites: the descendants of Jeshua and Kadmiel, of the descendants of Hodaviah, seventy-four. [41]The singers: the descendants of Asaph, one hundred twenty-eight. [42]The descendants of the gatekeepers: of Shallum, of Ater, of Talmon, of Akkub, of Hatita, and of Shobai, in all one hundred thirty-nine.

43 The temple servants: the descendants of Ziha, Hasupha, Tabbaoth, [44]Keros, Siaha, Padon, [45]Lebanah, Hagabah, Akkub, [46]Hagab, Shamlai, Hanan, [47]Giddel, Gahar, Reaiah, [48]Rezin, Nekoda, Gazzam, [49]Uzza, Paseah, Besai, [50]Asnah, Meunim, Nephisim, [51]Bakbuk, Hakupha, Harhur, [52]Bazluth, Mehida, Harsha, [53]Barkos, Sisera, Temah, [54]Neziah, and Hatipha.

55 The descendants of Solomon's servants: Sotai, Hassophereth, Peruda, [56]Jaalah, Darkon, Giddel, [57]Shephatiah, Hattil, Pochereth-hazzebaim, and Ami.

58 All the temple servants and the descendants of Solomon's servants were three hundred ninety-two.

59 The following were those who came up from Tel-melah, Tel-harsha, Cherub, Addan, and Immer, though they could not prove their families or their descent, whether they belonged to Israel: [60]the descendants of Delaiah, Tobiah, and Nekoda, six hundred fifty-two. [61]Also, of the descendants of the priests: the descendants of Habaiah, Hakkoz, and Barzillai (who had married one of the daughters of Barzillai the Gileadite, and was called by their name). [62]These looked for their entries in the genealogical records, but they were not found there, and so they were excluded from the priesthood as unclean; [63]the governor told them that they were not to partake of the most holy food, until there should be a priest to consult Urim and Thummim.

64 The whole assembly together was forty-two thousand three hundred sixty, [65]besides their male and female servants, of whom there were seven thousand three hundred thirty-seven; and they had two hundred male and female singers. [66]They had seven hundred thirty-six horses, two hundred forty-five mules, [67]four hundred thirty-five camels, and six thousand seven hundred twenty donkeys.

68 As soon as they came to the house of the LORD in Jerusalem, some of the heads of families made freewill offerings for the house of God, to erect it on its site. [69]According to their resources they gave to the building fund sixty-one thousand darics of gold, five thousand minas of silver, and one hundred priestly robes.

70 The priests, the Levites, and some of the people lived in Jerusalem and its vicinity;[a] and the singers, the gatekeepers, and the temple servants lived in their towns, and all Israel in their towns.

2.36–70. 36: *The priests: the descendants of Jedaiah, of the house of Jeshua: Jedaiah* is named as one of the first priestly figures to return to Jerusalem after the Exile* (1 Chr 9.10), and *Jeshua* was an important chief priest under the administration of Zerubbabel in the late sixth century (Ezra 3.8). Apparently, Jedaiah was regarded as the founder of a renewed line for the chief priesthood. 43: *The temple servants* is a technical name for a group devoted to serving the Levites. 55: *Solomon's servants* appear to have been a similar group. 59: *Tel-melah, Tel-harsha, Cherub, Addan, and Immer* are place names of uncertain identification.

REBUILDING THE HOUSE OF GOD

Chs. 3–6: This section, in the form of historical narrative,* includes citations from various documents designed to authenticate the contents. There are disruptions in the chronological order of the narrative, however, and in ch. 4 there is a sudden shift from Hebrew to the Aramaic* language. Recounting events in chronological order is therefore probably not the intention of this section. Rather, the author is interweaving two actions by the community: the rebuilding of the Temple* and the reconstitution of the community as the "house of God." The first happens within a gen-

a 1 Esdras 5.46: Heb lacks *lived in Jerusalem and its vicinity* eration of the return to Jerusalem from the Exile,* but the second can take place only several generations later, after the Jerusalem community is separated by its walls and its covenant* to refrain from intermarriage.

3 When the seventh month came, and the Israelites were in the towns, the people gathered together in Jerusalem. ²Then Jeshua son of Jozadak, with his fellow priests, and Zerubbabel son of Shealtiel with his kin set out to build the altar of the God of Israel, to offer burnt offerings on it, as prescribed in the law of Moses the man of God. ³They set up the altar on its foundation, because they were in dread of the neighboring peoples, and they offered burnt offerings upon it to the LORD, morning and evening. ⁴And they kept the festival of booths,ᵃ as prescribed, and offered the daily burnt offerings by number according to the ordinance, as required for each day, ⁵and after that the regular burnt offerings, the offerings at the new moon and at all the sacred festivals of the LORD, and the offerings of everyone who made a freewill offering to the LORD. ⁶From the first day of the seventh month they began to offer burnt offerings to the LORD. But the foundation of the temple of the LORD was not yet laid. ⁷So they gave money to the masons and the carpenters, and food, drink, and oil to the Sidonians and the Tyrians to bring cedar trees from Lebanon to the sea, to Joppa, according to the grant that they had from King Cyrus of Persia.

3.1–7: The reinstitution of worship. This section describes the resumption of worship at the site of the ruined Temple* as a prelude to the effort to rebuild the Temple, as decreed by the Persian king Cyrus in the opening of the book. **1:** *When the seventh month came* is an enigmatic reference since the year is not disclosed. It may be the seventh month of the earlier date formula of 1.1, that is, the first year of Cyrus (around 539 BCE), though this presents a problem with what follows. The notices of *Jeshua* and *Zerubbabel* (v 2.) focus on two individuals who are usually dated to the early years of the reign of Darius (522–486 BCE). The *seventh month* may refer to the second year of Darius's rule, when a renewed commitment to rebuild-

ing the Temple was made (Hag 2.1). **2:** *As prescribed in the law of Moses the man of God* relates to rules on the composition of the altar found in Ex 20.25. **4:** *And they kept the festival of booths, as prescribed,* reflecting perhaps a concern to follow the rules found in Lev 23.33–43, where the fifteenth day of the seventh month is reserved for the beginning of this important festival. **6:** *But the foundation of the temple of the LORD was not yet laid* distinguishes the resumption of worship from the beginning of rebuilding the physical Temple.

8 In the second year after their arrival at the house of God at Jerusalem, in the second month, Zerubbabel son of Shealtiel and Jeshua son of Jozadak made a beginning, together with the rest of their people, the priests and the Levites and all who had come to Jerusalem from the captivity. They appointed the Levites, from twenty years old and upward, to have the oversight of the work on the house of the LORD. ⁹And Jeshua with his sons and his kin, and Kadmiel and his sons, Binnui and Hodaviahᵇ along with the sons of Henadad, the Levites, their sons and kin, together took charge of the workers in the house of God.

10 When the builders laid the foundation of the temple of the LORD, the priests in their vestments were stationed to praise the LORD with trumpets, and the Levites, the sons of Asaph, with cymbals, according to the directions of King David of Israel; ¹¹and they sang responsively, praising and giving thanks to the LORD,

"For he is good,
     for his steadfast love endures forever
          toward Israel."

And all the people responded with a great shout when they praised the LORD, because the foundation of the house of the LORD was laid. ¹²But many of the priests and Levites and heads of families, old people who had seen the first house on its foundations, wept with a loud voice when they saw this house, though many shouted aloud for joy, ¹³so that the people could not distinguish the sound of the joyful shout from the sound of the

ᵃ Or *tabernacles*; Heb *succoth*   ᵇ Compare 2.40;
Neh 7.43; 1 Esdras 5.58: Heb *sons of Judah*

people's weeping, for the people shouted so loudly that the sound was heard far away.

3.8–13: Laying the foundation of the Temple.* The author highlights the momentous beginning of rebuilding the Temple, emphasizing the devotion of the community. **8:** *In the second year after their arrival at the house of God at Jerusalem* may relate to the third year of Darius, around 519 BCE if the earlier reference was to a time in the reign of Darius. The community arrived at Jerusalem to find the Temple in ruins, hence the need to begin rebuilding. But the author, wanting to connect the Jerusalem community with the sanctified dwelling place of God, has the exiles arriving *at the house of God. They appointed the Levites:* Most likely, Zerubbabel and Jeshua appointed them. **10:** *The priests in their vestments were stationed to praise the* LORD *with trumpets* recalls the priestly trumpeters in 2 Chr 5.12 at the dedication of the first Temple in the days of Solomon. *According to the directions of King David* emphasizes the continuity between this Second Temple and the worship conducted in the First Temple. Despite the trauma of the destruction of Jerusalem and the Temple, and the Exile* in Babylon, nothing has changed in the way the community worships God. **11:** *They sang responsively:* The leaders sang first, and the assembly responded. Another possible meaning is "antiphonally," with one part of the choir initiating a verse and the other part completing it. The hymn that is sung appears as part of a number of Psalms (for example, Ps 106.1; 107.1; 136.1). **12:** *Old people who had seen the first house:* Sixty-eight years had elapsed since the destruction of the first Temple. *Wept with a loud voice when they saw this house:* Presumably what was planned for the rebuilt Temple was less in size and/or grandeur than that of the Temple of Solomon (as in Hag 2.3). The weeping over what had been lost was drowned out by those who *shouted aloud for joy,* shifting the focus to what could be anticipated for the future.

4 When the adversaries of Judah and Benjamin heard that the returned exiles were building a temple to the LORD, the God of Israel, ²they approached Zerubbabel and the heads of families and said to them, "Let us build with you, for we worship your God as you do, and we have been sacrificing to him ever since the days of King Esar-haddon of Assyria who brought us here." ³But Zerubbabel, Jeshua, and the rest of the heads

of families in Israel said to them, "You shall have no part with us in building a house to our God; but we alone will build to the LORD, the God of Israel, as King Cyrus of Persia has commanded us."

4 Then the people of the land discouraged the people of Judah, and made them afraid to build, ⁵and they bribed officials to frustrate their plan throughout the reign of King Cyrus of Persia and until the reign of King Darius of Persia.

4.1–5: Opposition to rebuilding the Temple.* This section shows the surrounding peoples opposing the rebuilding of the Temple, just as the following section will detail opposition by surrounding peoples to the rebuilding of the walls of Jerusalem over half a century later. Such opposition to sacred actions furthers the prohibition of intermarriage with the surrounding peoples. **1:** *The adversaries of Judah and Benjamin:* By characterizing these persons as *adversaries,* the author makes their subsequent request less than truthful. **2:** *We worship your God as you do:* As deportees who had been settled in the land by the Assyrians, the "adversaries" would not have known the Pentateuch* nor the orders for Temple service attributed to King David. Consequently, they could not approach God in the same way as the returned exiles. **3:** *We alone will build to the* LORD, *. . . as King Cyrus of Persia has commanded us:* The community determines to show its devotion on its own, and claims this is required by Cyrus's orders. There is nothing in the decree that restricts who can participate in the rebuilding. **4:** *The people of the land discouraged the people of Judah:* Here *people of the land* is defined by what preceded it, namely they are the deportees who were brought into the land by the Assyrians. However, the author will use the term simply as a generic label for those who are not of Judah. The Hebrew term translated as *discouraged* is better rendered "undermined."

6 In the reign of Ahasuerus, in his accession year, they wrote an accusation against the inhabitants of Judah and Jerusalem.

4.6–24: Opposition to rebuilding Jerusalem. The author now moves from opposition to the Temple rebuilding to opposition to building a wall around Jerusalem. After a brief effort at a chronological transition, there is an exchange of memoranda between several imperial officials and King Artaxerxes I of Persia. As a result, the king orders the suspension of any rebuilding of the city, which the author then ties to opposition to the Temple. While there is no way to authenticate these memos, they have the form and general structure of known imperial memos from the Persian empire, although some elements may have been introduced to carry forward the larger purposes of the book. **6:** *In the reign of Ahasuerus, in his accession* year:* Ahasuerus is the Hebrew version of the name of the Persian king the Greeks called Xerxes. The main royal figure in the book of Esther, Xerxes came to the Persian throne late in the year 486 BCE. The contents of the *accusation* are not specified, nor the consequences of the report. This notice serves to bring the narrative* through a chronological sequence of Persian kings (Cyrus, Darius, Xerxes) to the communications with Artaxerxes.

7 And in the days of Artaxerxes, Bishlam and Mithredath and Tabeel and the rest of their associates wrote to King Artaxerxes of Persia; the letter was written in Aramaic and translated.*ᵃ* 8Rehum the royal deputy and Shimshai the scribe wrote a letter against Jerusalem to King Artaxerxes as follows 9(then Rehum the royal deputy, Shimshai the scribe, and the rest of their associates, the judges, the envoys, the officials, the Persians, the people of Erech, the Babylonians, the people of Susa, that is, the Elamites, 10and the rest of the nations whom the great and noble Osnappar deported and settled in the cities of Samaria and in the rest of the province Beyond the River wrote—and now 11this is a copy of the letter that they sent):

"To King Artaxerxes: Your servants, the people of the province Beyond the River, send greeting. And now 12may it be known to the king that the Jews who came up from you to us have gone to Jerusalem. They are rebuilding that rebellious and wicked city; they are finishing the walls and repairing the foundations. 13Now may it be known to the king that, if this city is rebuilt and the walls finished, they will not pay tribute, custom, or toll, and the royal revenue will be reduced. 14Now because we share the salt of the palace and it is not fitting for us to witness the king's dishonor, therefore we send and inform the king, 15so that a search may be

made in the annals of your ancestors. You will discover in the annals that this is a rebellious city, hurtful to kings and provinces, and that sedition was stirred up in it from long ago. On that account this city was laid waste. 16We make known to the king that, if this city is rebuilt and its walls finished, you will then have no possession in the province Beyond the River."

4.7–16. 7: *And in the days of Artaxerxes:* He came to the throne in 465 BCE and remained in power until 423 BCE. The names of the officials sending the memo are Aramaic* and Persian. *The letter was written in Aramaic:* The normal language for conducting official business in the Persian empire was Aramaic. By making note of this detail, the author affirms the seriousness of this exchange. It was *translated* so that the Jerusalem community could understand it. The footnote points out that the Hebrew text goes on to read *in Aramaic*, indicating that the author is quoting from the Aramaic original as opposed to the translation. From this point until 6.18, the narrative is in Aramaic. **8:** *Wrote a letter against Jerusalem* identifies the city with the house of God. **10:** *The rest of the nations . . . deported and settled* refers to vv. 1–2, where the deportees settled to the north of Jerusalem were the "adversaries" seeking to join in rebuilding the Temple. Here, they oppose the rebuilding of Jerusalem's walls. *Osnapper* is a variant name for the Assyrian king Asshurbanipal (669–633 BCE). *Beyond the River* was the official name of the administrative unit of Syria-Palestine (in Aramaic, "Abarnahara"). From the perspective of Mesopotamia and Persia, the territories of Syria-Palestine were across or "beyond" the river Jordan, terminating at the coast of the Mediterranean. **12:** *They are rebuilding that rebellious and wicked city:* The neighboring peoples charge that Jerusalem, with its history of rebellion against empires, should not be rebuilt. Persian imperial practice was to decentralize populations. Only where security or economic concerns were of central importance were cities rebuilt. **13:** *If this city is rebuilt and the walls finished, they will not pay tribute:* A renewed and refortified Jerusalem will follow its earlier history and will revolt against the taxes and dues that provided the economic lifeblood of the empire. **14:** *We share the salt of the palace:* An

a Heb adds *in Aramaic,* indicating that 4.8–6.18 is in Aramaic. Another interpretation is *The letter was written in the Aramaic script and set forth in the Aramaic language* expression, exact meaning unclear, perhaps saying that the writers are paid in part directly by the palace in the form of salt, a more valued commodity in antiquity than now. **16:** *You will then have no possession in the province Beyond the River:* With hyperbole (exaggeration to make a point) the opponents imply that Jerusalem's revolt would lead to the loss of the whole province.

17 The king sent an answer: "To Rehum the royal deputy and Shimshai the scribe and the rest of their associates who live in Samaria and in the rest of the province Beyond the River, greeting. And now ¹⁸the letter that you sent to us has been read in translation before me. ¹⁹So I made a decree, and someone searched and discovered that this city has risen against kings from long ago, and that rebellion and sedition have been made in it. ²⁰Jerusalem has had mighty kings who ruled over the whole province Beyond the River, to whom tribute, custom, and toll were paid. ²¹Therefore issue an order that these people be made to cease, and that this city not be rebuilt, until I make a decree. ²²Moreover, take care not to be slack in this matter; why should damage grow to the hurt of the king?"

23 Then when the copy of King Artaxerxes' letter was read before Rehum and the scribe Shimshai and their associates, they hurried to the Jews in Jerusalem and by force and power made them cease. ²⁴At that time the work on the house of God in Jerusalem stopped and was discontinued until the second year of the reign of King Darius of Persia.

4.17–24. 19: *I made a decree, and someone searched:* The command was to investigate the charge that Jerusalem had a history of rebellion. Brief accounts of major events were kept for administrative purposes, such as the Babylonian Chronicles, which record the successive revolts of Jerusalem against the Babylonian empire until the city's destruction. **20:** *Jerusalem has had mighty kings who ruled over the whole province Beyond the River:* This would seem to refer to either David or Solomon, who exercised control over a large territory. This makes little sense, however, either in the context or in the kinds of records available to the Persian monarch. The same wording could be translated,

"Moreover, there have been powerful kings over Jerusalem who also ruled over the whole province . . . ," placing Artaxerxes in a series of imperial rulers who had successfully controlled Jerusalem and Beyond the River. **21:** *This city not be rebuilt, until I make a decree:* By stopping the rebuilding, Artaxerxes was not making a permanent decision. A future royal decree is exactly what the narrative concerning Nehemiah envisions. **23:** *By force and power made them cease:* The prompt response of Rehum and Shimshai is accompanied by terms that may refer to infantry and cavalry units whose presence would underscore the imperial concern over the rebuilding effort. **24:** *At that time the work on the house of God in Jerusalem stopped:* If read as a historical narrative, the phrase *at that time* makes little sense. Artaxerxes I makes the decision to have the work halted sometime after 465 BCE, but later the note *until the second year of the reign of King Darius* would have to be 521 BCE. Either the author is hopelessly confused regarding chronology, or the purpose of the narrative is not historical but thematic. The notation here returns the narrative to the issue of rebuilding the Temple, bringing it back to v. 5.

5 Now the prophets, Haggai*ᵃ* and Zechariah son of Iddo, prophesied to the Jews who were in Judah and Jerusalem, in the name of the God of Israel who was over them. ²Then Zerubbabel son of Shealtiel and Jeshua son of Jozadak set out to rebuild the house of God in Jerusalem; and with them were the prophets of God, helping them.

3 At the same time Tattenai the governor of the province Beyond the River and Shethar-bozenai and their associates came to them and spoke to them thus, "Who gave you a decree to build this house and to finish this structure?" ⁴They*ᵇ* also asked them this, "What are the names of the men who are building this building?" ⁵But the eye of their God was upon the elders of the Jews, and they did not stop them until a report reached Darius and then answer was returned by letter in reply to it.

5.1–6.18: Overcoming opposition and rebuilding the Temple.⋆ This section of the book highlights the continued commitment of the community to rebuild-

a Aram adds *the prophet*　　*b* Gk Syr: Aram *We*

ing the house of God, understood as both the physical Temple and the renewed city of Jerusalem. The section is in Aramaic* and, as in the earlier sections, carries the narrative* forward by extensive quotation from various official documents. **5.1:** *Haggai and Zechariah:* The section opens at the end of the sixth century, where ch. 4 ended, with a mention of two prophets* who, along with Zerubbabel the governor and Joshua the high priest, directed a new effort to rebuild the Temple. These are probably the prophets behind the canonical* books bearing their names. **3:** *Who gave you a decree:* The officials who are inquiring about imperial permission may not be opposing the rebuilding of the Temple as much as showing concern that all is being done in accord with imperial sanction.

6 The copy of the letter that Tattenai the governor of the province Beyond the River and Shethar-bozenai and his associates the envoys who were in the province Beyond the River sent to King Darius; ⁷they sent him a report, in which was written as follows: "To Darius the king, all peace! ⁸May it be known to the king that we went to the province of Judah, to the house of the great God. It is being built of hewn stone, and timber is laid in the walls; this work is being done diligently and prospers in their hands. ⁹Then we spoke to those elders and asked them, 'Who gave you a decree to build this house and to finish this structure?' ¹⁰We also asked them their names, for your information, so that we might write down the names of the men at their head. ¹¹This was their reply to us: 'We are the servants of the God of heaven and earth, and we are rebuilding the house that was built many years ago, which a great king of Israel built and finished. ¹²But because our ancestors had angered the God of heaven, he gave them into the hand of King Nebuchadnezzar of Babylon, the Chaldean, who destroyed this house and carried away the people to Babylonia. ¹³However, King Cyrus of Babylon, in the first year of his reign, made a decree that this house of God should be rebuilt. ¹⁴Moreover, the gold and silver vessels of the house of God, which Nebuchadnezzar had taken out of the temple in Jerusalem and had brought into the temple of Babylon, these King Cyrus took out of the temple of Babylon, and they were deliv-

ered to a man named Sheshbazzar, whom he had made governor. ¹⁵He said to him, "Take these vessels; go and put them in the temple in Jerusalem, and let the house of God be rebuilt on its site." ¹⁶Then this Sheshbazzar came and laid the foundations of the house of God in Jerusalem; and from that time until now it has been under construction, and it is not yet finished.' ¹⁷And now, if it seems good to the king, have a search made in the royal archives there in Babylon, to see whether a decree was issued by King Cyrus for the rebuilding of this house of God in Jerusalem. Let the king send us his pleasure in this matter."

5.6–17. 6: *The copy of the letter:* The author offers extracts from official memoranda to fill out the story line. While there can be no certainty, it appears the author was working from actual documents, which may have been modified slightly to fit the narrative. **12:** *But because our ancestors had angered the God of heaven, he gave them into the hand of King Nebuchadnezzar:* The case for rebuilding the Temple depends in part on the assertion that the Temple was destroyed not because the southern kingdom rebelled against Nebuchadnezzar, an imperial king, but because God was angry. **13:** *King Cyrus . . . made a decree:* See 1.1–4.

6 Then King Darius made a decree, and they searched the archives where the documents were stored in Babylon. ²But it was in Ecbatana, the capital in the province of Media, that a scroll was found on which this was written: "A record. ³In the first year of his reign, King Cyrus issued a decree: Concerning the house of God at Jerusalem, let the house be rebuilt, the place where sacrifices are offered and burnt offerings are brought;ᵃ its height shall be sixty cubits and its width sixty cubits, ⁴with three courses of hewn stones and one course of timber; let the cost be paid from the royal treasury. ⁵Moreover, let the gold and silver vessels of the house of God, which Nebuchadnezzar took out of the temple in Jerusalem and brought to Babylon, be restored and brought back to the temple in Jerusalem, each to its

a Meaning of Aram uncertain

place; you shall put them in the house of God."

6 "Now you, Tattenai, governor of the province Beyond the River, Shethar-bozenai, and you, their associates, the envoys in the province Beyond the River, keep away; ⁷let the work on this house of God alone; let the governor of the Jews and the elders of the Jews rebuild this house of God on its site. ⁸Moreover I make a decree regarding what you shall do for these elders of the Jews for the rebuilding of this house of God: the cost is to be paid to these people, in full and without delay, from the royal revenue, the tribute of the province Beyond the River. ⁹Whatever is needed—young bulls, rams, or sheep for burnt offerings to the God of heaven, wheat, salt, wine, or oil, as the priests in Jerusalem require—let that be given to them day by day without fail, ¹⁰so that they may offer pleasing sacrifices to the God of heaven, and pray for the life of the king and his children. ¹¹Furthermore I decree that if anyone alters this edict, a beam shall be pulled out of the house of the perpetrator, who then shall be impaled on it. The house shall be made a dunghill. ¹²May the God who has established his name there overthrow any king or people that shall put forth a hand to alter this, or to destroy this house of God in Jerusalem. I, Darius, make a decree; let it be done with all diligence."

13 Then, according to the word sent by King Darius, Tattenai, the governor of the province Beyond the River, Shethar-bozenai, and their associates did with all diligence what King Darius had ordered. ¹⁴So the elders of the Jews built and prospered, through the prophesying of the prophet Haggai and Zechariah son of Iddo. They finished their building by command of the God of Israel and by decree of Cyrus, Darius, and King Artaxerxes of Persia; ¹⁵and this house was finished on the third day of the month of Adar, in the sixth year of the reign of King Darius.

16 The people of Israel, the priests and the Levites, and the rest of the returned exiles, celebrated the dedication of this house of God with joy. ¹⁷They offered at the dedication of this house of God one hundred bulls, two hundred rams, four hundred lambs, and as a sin offering for all Israel, twelve male goats, according to the number of the tribes of Israel. ¹⁸Then they set the priests in their divisions and the Levites in their courses for the service of God at Jerusalem, as it is written in the book of Moses.

6.1–12. 2: *Ecbatana, the capital of the province of Media:* The search began in Babylon since important royal decrees would be archived there. Ecbatana, at a higher elevation than the main capital of Persepolis, was the location of the Persian kings' summer palace. 4: *Let the cost be paid from the royal treasury:* Cyrus's detailed specifications of the size and form of construction limit how much the rebuilding would cost, since imperial funds were paying for it. 10: *So they may offer pleasing sacrifices . . . and pray for the life of the king and his children:* Persian imperial support for local religious centers is well attested. It was part of a larger policy of bringing local customs into a framework of loyalty to the empire. Darius probably did not worship Israel's God, but that did not prevent him from seeking to convince those who did that Israel's God was concerned with the king's well-being.

6.13–18. 14: *They finished their building by command of the God of Israel and by decree of Cyrus, Darius, and King Artaxerxes of Persia:* In a literal historical reading this makes no sense, since the physical Temple was completed in the reign of Darius, and Artaxerxes had nothing to do with it. However, the formation of the "house of God" involved not only rebuilding the Temple, but also rebuilding the city and separating the community from the surrounding peoples by prohibiting intermarriage. These later steps, under the reformers Ezra and Nehemiah, occurred in the time of Artaxerxes. 15: *The third day of the month of Adar, in the sixth year of the reign of King Darius:* 515 BCE. Some believe the day was originally the twenty-third day of Adar, which would put the completed rebuilding near the anniversary of Solomon's celebration of the completion of the original Temple (2 Chr 7.10) and approximately 70 years after the destruction of that Temple. 17: *As a sin offering for all Israel, twelve male goats, according to the number of the tribes of Israel:* Without a functioning Temple, it was not possible for the priesthood to maintain the regular purification offering for the nation. The offering may be indebted to the vision of a renewed Temple by the prophet Ezekiel (Ezek 43.22–27) in which the sin offering purifies the Temple from the pollutions of Israel's past. **18:** *As it is written in the book of Moses:* In 1 Chr 23–26 it is David who sets up the courses of the priests and the Levites for the worship in the Temple. There is no prescription for these orders as described in the Pentateuch,* normally what the author means by the *book of Moses.* With the arrangements for the offerings and who would be responsible for them, the Temple is now fully functioning.

19 On the fourteenth day of the first month the returned exiles kept the passover. ²⁰For both the priests and the Levites had purified themselves; all of them were clean. So they killed the passover lamb for all the returned exiles, for their fellow priests, and for themselves. ²¹It was eaten by the people of Israel who had returned from exile, and also by all who had joined them and separated themselves from the pollutions of the nations of the land to worship the LORD, the God of Israel. ²²With joy they celebrated the festival of unleavened bread seven days; for the LORD had made them joyful, and had turned the heart of the king of Assyria to them, so that he aided them in the work on the house of God, the God of Israel.

6.19–22: The first Passover* in the rebuilt Temple.* The shift back to Hebrew from Aramaic* draws attention to this central festival. Just as Israel was not a physical nation until they could worship God following their escape from Egypt, celebrated in the Passover, so the exilic community could not be considered a nation until the house of God was fully functioning. With the Temple in place, the Passover celebration had a renewed importance for the community as a sign of their coming into a new status. The author skillfully connects this with the physical separation of the community from the surrounding peoples, a point that Ezra will hammer on as the centerpiece of his reforms. **20:** *The priests and the Levites had purified themselves:* Following the return from exile, there was a new emphasis on the purity regulations of the Pentateuch* and on extending the areas of life they affected. Before undertaking the Passover, the ritual purity of the priests and Levites had to be assured. **21:** *The people of Israel who had returned from exile, and . . . all who had joined them and separated themselves from the pollutions of the nations:* As a celebration of

God's miraculous deliverance and the formation of the people into a nation, Passover was a powerful symbol of identity. Those who had been exiled and returned clearly would be recognized as part of Israel. The population that remained behind joined the Exile* community by separating from the surrounding peoples. *Pollutions:* a term normally reserved for severe violations of the sacral order. It was because of their pollutions, according to some parts of the Hebrew Bible, that God removed the Canaanites from the land (Lev 20.22–24). **22:** *Had turned the heart of the king of Assyria to them, so that he aided them in the work:* An echo of Ezra 1.1–4. The use of the title *king of Assyria* is unclear, though the Persian king did adopt this title since the former Assyrian territory was under his rule. It may be a deliberate reference to King Esarhaddon of Assyria (Ezra 4.2); some of the peoples he transported to the territory north of Jerusalem had indeed "come over" to the side of the returning exiles in opposition to their fellow countryfolk, who opposed the Temple.

EZRA'S INQUIRY

Chs. 7–10: With little in the way of transition, a first-person narrative* recounts the conditions under which Ezra was authorized to undertake a trip to Jerusalem, and his initial concerns once there. The use of a first-person narrative may be the result of the author's use of an authentic source (an "Ezra memoir") or may be a literary device intended to give immediacy and emotional power to the narrative.

7 After this, in the reign of King Artaxerxes of Persia, Ezra son of Seraiah, son of Azariah, son of Hilkiah, ²son of Shallum, son of Zadok, son of Ahitub, ³son of Amariah, son of Azariah, son of Meraioth, ⁴son of Zerahiah, son of Uzzi, son of Bukki, ⁵son of Abishua, son of Phinehas, son of Eleazar, son of the chief priest Aaron— ⁶this Ezra went up from Babylonia. He was a scribe skilled in the law of Moses that the LORD the God of Israel had given; and the king granted him all that he asked, for the hand of the LORD his God was upon him.

7 Some of the people of Israel, and some of the priests and Levites, the singers and gatekeepers, and the temple servants also went up to Jerusalem, in the seventh year of King Artaxerxes. ⁸They came to Jerusalem in

the fifth month, which was in the seventh year of the king. ⁹On the first day of the first month the journey up from Babylon was begun, and on the first day of the fifth month he came to Jerusalem, for the gracious hand of his God was upon him. ¹⁰For Ezra had set his heart to study the law of the LORD, and to do it, and to teach the statutes and ordinances in Israel.

7.1–10: Introduction to the mission of Ezra. The purpose of this third-person narration is to give the reader a sense of who Ezra was and what was significant about his role in relation to the community. **5:** *Son of Eleazar, son of the chief priest Aaron:* Ezra is given a distinguished lineage, concluding with the most important aspect of his family line, that he was a descendant of the primary line of priests in ancient Israel. **6:** *A scribe* skilled in the law:* The ability to read and write led people to expect that scribes could also explain legal issues. *Law of Moses:* apparently the Pentateuch* in some form. *The king granted him all that he asked, for the hand of the LORD his God was upon him:* There is no explanation of how a person who was a specialist in a religious tradition whose followers were a small minority within the empire could get repeated access to the king. *Hand of the LORD . . . was upon him:* A common expression of the presence of God in some sense guiding the person's career. **7:** *Some of the people of Israel:* Presumably only a small portion of the Jewish community in Babylonia chose to return to Jerusalem. Life in exile was more than likely not too difficult, and the prospect of returning to a land devastated by warfare and economic ruin not very attractive. The *seventh year of King Artaxerxes* would be 458 BCE if this was Artaxerxes I of Persia. Since Ezra's opposition to intermarriage receives no mention in the account of Nehemiah, and Nehemiah addresses the same issues as if they had never been raised before, some have argued Ezra really came under Artaxerxes II (the seventh year being 398 BCE). The confusion over Ezra's chronological relation to Nehemiah comes about from trying to read Ezra-Nehemiah as straight history rather than as an apologetic.* The author intends the reader to believe that Ezra came first. **10:** *Ezra had set his heart to study the law of the LORD, and to do it:* Not only was Ezra a student of the law, but he sought to observe its requirements in his everyday life. Out of this study and experience, Ezra would teach the people.

11 This is a copy of the letter that King Artaxerxes gave to the priest Ezra, the scribe, a scholar of the text of the commandments of the LORD and his statutes for Israel: ¹²"Artaxerxes, king of kings, to the priest Ezra, the scribe of the law of the God of heaven: Peace.ᵃ And now ¹³I decree that any of the people of Israel or their priests or Levites in my kingdom who freely offers to go to Jerusalem may go with you. ¹⁴For you are sent by the king and his seven counselors to make inquiries about Judah and Jerusalem according to the law of your God, which is in your hand, ¹⁵and also to convey the silver and gold that the king and his counselors have freely offered to the God of Israel, whose dwelling is in Jerusalem, ¹⁶with all the silver and gold that you shall find in the whole province of Babylonia, and with the freewill offerings of the people and the priests, given willingly for the house of their God in Jerusalem. ¹⁷With this money, then, you shall with all diligence buy bulls, rams, and lambs, and their grain offerings and their drink offerings, and you shall offer them on the altar of the house of your God in Jerusalem. ¹⁸Whatever seems good to you and your colleagues to do with the rest of the silver and gold, you may do, according to the will of your God. ¹⁹The vessels that have been given you for the service of the house of your God, you shall deliver before the God of Jerusalem. ²⁰And whatever else is required for the house of your God, which you are responsible for providing, you may provide out of the king's treasury.

7.11–28: King Artaxerxes' commission to Ezra. The letter that Artaxerxes purportedly gave to Ezra elevates Ezra from a religious teacher to an imperial official, undertaking an important mission at the request of the king. While portions of the letter may well be genuine, there are serious questions about the authenticity of other sections, and the author seems to have taken some significant liberties in editing the document. **12:** *Artaxerxes, king of kings:* Persian kings did refer to themselves this way, suggesting part of an authentic Persian letter. **14:** *You are sent by the king and his seven counselors:* Persian monarchs had a high council

a Syr Vg 1 Esdras 8.9: Aram *Perfect*

of seven trusted advisers who were called upon to help with significant decisions. Ezra is instructed *to make inquiries about Judah and Jerusalem,* a vague task. *According to the law of your God* may suggest that Ezra is ensuring that the worship in the Temple* is being properly conducted. *Which is in your hand* has been variously interpreted. On its simplest level, it means that Ezra is physically carrying a copy of the Pentateuch* from Babylon to Jerusalem, although in Hebrew there are more direct ways to express this. The phrase *in your hand* is attested in several Persian period documents as meaning "in your power" or "in your sphere of authority." In this understanding, Artaxerxes is directing Ezra to conduct his inquiry in terms of the laws that are relevant to the inquiry, laws that apply to Ezra's task. **19:** *The vessels that have been given you:* Like the vessels Nebuchadnezzar had taken and Cyrus had returned to the Temple (1.7–11), these vessels are a royal gift bestowed on the Temple as a sign of gratitude for God's granting Artaxerxes' rule.

21 "I, King Artaxerxes, decree to all the treasurers in the province Beyond the River: Whatever the priest Ezra, the scribe of the law of the God of heaven, requires of you, let it be done with all diligence, 22 up to one hundred talents of silver, one hundred cors of wheat, one hundred baths*ᵃ* of wine, one hundred baths*ᵃ* of oil, and unlimited salt. 23 Whatever is commanded by the God of heaven, let it be done with zeal for the house of the God of heaven, or wrath will come upon the realm of the king and his heirs. 24 We also notify you that it shall not be lawful to impose tribute, custom, or toll on any of the priests, the Levites, the singers, the doorkeepers, the temple servants, or other servants of this house of God.

25 "And you, Ezra, according to the God-given wisdom you possess, appoint magistrates and judges who may judge all the people in the province Beyond the River who know the laws of your God; and you shall teach those who do not know them. 26 All who will not obey the law of your God and the law of the king, let judgment be strictly executed on them, whether for death or for banishment or for confiscation of their goods or for imprisonment."

27 Blessed be the LORD, the God of our ancestors, who put such a thing as this into the heart of the king to glorify the house of the LORD in Jerusalem, 28 and who extended to me steadfast love before the king and his counselors, and before all the king's mighty officers. I took courage, for the hand of the LORD my God was upon me, and I gathered leaders from Israel to go up with me.

7.21–28. 22: *Up to one hundred talents of silver:* Instructions for the imperial treasurers to support Ezra within limits. The quantities for most of the commodities are not unreasonable, but the amount of silver is almost a third of the total annual taxation of the province Beyond the River. **24:** *It shall not be lawful to impose tribute, custom, or toll:* The exemption of professionals involved in staffing temples from any taxation is attested in other parts of the Persian empire, so it would not be out of character for such an exemption to be extended to the Temple personnel in Jerusalem. **25:** *Appoint magistrates and judges:* Ezra is charged to reform the judiciary. *God-given wisdom:* Though it is unlikely that a Persian king would have credited Ezra's wisdom to God, this connection appears in several places in the book of Deuteronomy (Deut 4.6; 16.19–20). **26:** *All who will not obey the law of your God* refers not to all peoples of any cultural heritage living in the province, but to those who *know the laws* of God, that is, other Jews. **27:** *To glorify the house of the LORD in Jerusalem:* Since Ezra's official mission has little to do with the physical Temple, it is likely that the "house of God" is not the Temple as such, but the community's adherence to the distinctive customs of Israel.

8 These are their family heads, and this is the genealogy of those who went up with me from Babylonia, in the reign of King Artaxerxes: 2 Of the descendants of Phinehas, Gershom. Of Ithamar, Daniel. Of David, Hattush, 3 of the descendants of Shecaniah. Of Parosh, Zechariah, with whom were registered one hundred fifty males. 4 Of the descendants of Pahath-moab, Eliehoenai son of Zerahiah, and with him two hundred males. 5 Of the descendants of Zattu,*ᵇ* Shecaniah son of Jahaziel, and with him three hundred males. 6 Of the descendants of

a A Heb measure of volume   *b* Gk 1 Esdras 8.32: Heb lacks *of Zattu*

Adin, Ebed son of Jonathan, and with him fifty males. 7Of the descendants of Elam, Jeshaiah son of Athaliah, and with him seventy males. 8Of the descendants of Shephatiah, Zebadiah son of Michael, and with him eighty males. 9Of the descendants of Joab, Obadiah son of Jehiel, and with him two hundred eighteen males. 10Of the descendants of Bani,*a* Shelomith son of Josiphiah, and with him one hundred sixty males. 11Of the descendants of Bebai, Zechariah son of Bebai, and with him twenty-eight males. 12Of the descendants of Azgad, Johanan son of Hakkatan, and with him one hundred ten males. 13Of the descendants of Adonikam, those who came later, their names being Eliphelet, Jeuel, and Shemaiah, and with them sixty males. 14Of the descendants of Bigvai, Uthai and Zaccur, and with them seventy males.

8.1–14: Listing of those returning with Ezra. Presented in the form of a list, this section has a very artificial structure, leading many to question its authenticity. **2:** *Of the descendants of Phineas:* The list begins with priests first, followed by the descendants of David. The list of David's descendants in 1 Chr 3 carries the list three or four generations after these individuals. **3:** *Of Parosh, Zechariah:* What follows are twelve distinct family groups of persons with no specified occupations. Given the figures for the number of males in each family group, a total of 1,500 men, and an estimated total of 5,000 men, women, and children would have been part of this group.

15 I gathered them by the river that runs to Ahava, and there we camped three days. As I reviewed the people and the priests, I found there none of the descendants of Levi. 16Then I sent for Eliezer, Ariel, Shemaiah, Elnathan, Jarib, Elnathan, Nathan, Zechariah, and Meshullam, who were leaders, and for Joiarib and Elnathan, who were wise, 17and sent them to Iddo, the leader at the place called Casiphia, telling them what to say to Iddo and his colleagues the temple servants at Casiphia, namely, to send us ministers for the house of our God. 18Since the gracious hand of our God was upon us, they brought us a man of discretion, of the descendants of Mahli son of Levi son of Israel,

namely Sherebiah, with his sons and kin, eighteen; 19also Hashabiah and with him Jeshaiah of the descendants of Merari, with his kin and their sons, twenty; 20besides two hundred twenty of the temple servants, whom David and his officials had set apart to attend the Levites. These were all mentioned by name.

8.15–20: An aside concerning the Levites. In the list above (vv. 1–14), although there are priests, there are no Levites. Yet Levites were necessary for the proper functioning of the Temple* since certain duties were exclusively theirs. This section explains how Ezra was able to solve this problem. **15:** *The river that runs to Ahava:* An unknown place in Babylonia. **17:** *The place called Casiphia:* Another unknown place, though the presence of Temple servants there suggests some form of formal worship may have been conducted in this location.

21 Then I proclaimed a fast there, at the river Ahava, that we might deny ourselves*b* before our God, to seek from him a safe journey for ourselves, our children, and all our possessions. 22For I was ashamed to ask the king for a band of soldiers and cavalry to protect us against the enemy on our way, since we had told the king that the hand of our God is gracious to all who seek him, but his power and his wrath are against all who forsake him. 23So we fasted and petitioned our God for this, and he listened to our entreaty.

24 Then I set apart twelve of the leading priests: Sherebiah, Hashabiah, and ten of their kin with them. 25And I weighed out to them the silver and the gold and the vessels, the offering for the house of our God that the king, his counselors, his lords, and all Israel there present had offered; 26I weighed out into their hand six hundred fifty talents of silver, and one hundred silver vessels worth . . . talents,*c* and one hundred talents of gold, 27twenty gold bowls worth a thousand darics, and two vessels of fine polished bronze as precious as gold. 28And I said to them, "You are holy to the LORD, and the

---

a Gk 1 Esdras 8.36: Heb lacks *Bani*   *b* Or *might fast*
c The number of talents is lacking

vessels are holy; and the silver and the gold are a freewill offering to the LORD, the God of your ancestors. 29Guard them and keep them until you weigh them before the chief priests and the Levites and the heads of families in Israel at Jerusalem, within the chambers of the house of the LORD." 30So the priests and the Levites took over the silver, the gold, and the vessels as they were weighed out, to bring them to Jerusalem, to the house of our God.

8.21–30: Preparations for the journey to Jerusalem. There are two distinct parts to this section: a concern about physical dangers (vv. 21–23) and some details on the precious metals being carried for the Temple* (vv. 24–30). In the author's view, it may be that carrying so much gold and silver made the expedition a target for robbers, leading to the concerns for security. **21:** *Then I proclaimed a fast there:* Following the Exile,* fasting seems to have become a more common practice to affirm to God and the community the seriousness with which appeals to God were being made. In this case, the fast underscores the community's desire for God to protect them. **23:** *And he listened to our entreaty* anticipates what the reader is told later, that the journey was made safely. **24:** *Then I set apart twelve of the leading priests:* In Ezra-Nehemiah various groupings of twelve appear frequently, possibly as a way of retaining some sense of the twelve-tribe organization that traditionally made up the members of Israel, even though most of the persons in these groups are from the tribe of Judah. **28:** *You are holy to the LORD, and the vessels are holy* summarizes several Pentateuchal* rules regarding priests (Ex 29.1; Lev 21.6) and vessels used in worship (Ex 29.44; 30.29). Only Temple personnel decreed as holy could transport holy objects (Lev 3.31; 4.12–15).

31 Then we left the river Ahava on the twelfth day of the first month, to go to Jerusalem; the hand of our God was upon us, and he delivered us from the hand of the enemy and from ambushes along the way. 32We came to Jerusalem and remained there three days. 33On the fourth day, within the house of our God, the silver, the gold, and the vessels were weighed into the hands of the priest Meremoth son of Uriah, and with him was Eleazar son of Phinehas, and with them were the Levites, Jozabad son of Jeshua

and Noadiah son of Binnui. 34The total was counted and weighed, and the weight of everything was recorded.

35 At that time those who had come from captivity, the returned exiles, offered burnt offerings to the God of Israel, twelve bulls for all Israel, ninety-six rams, seventy-seven lambs, and as a sin offering twelve male goats; all this was a burnt offering to the LORD. 36They also delivered the king's commissions to the king's satraps and to the governors of the province Beyond the River; and they supported the people and the house of God.

8.31–36: The return to Jerusalem. This section provides a clean closure to the basic duties of the party returning with Ezra: the delivery of the Temple* treasures being donated by the Persian monarchy and the initiation of newly endowed sacrifices. **31:** *The hand of our God was upon us:* The same concept of divine empowerment is found in 7.28. **33:** *On the fourth day:* Possibly the party needed the time to rest before engaging in their business. The gifts were *weighed* out in order to ensure the quantities entrusted to Ezra and his group were fully delivered. **35:** *Those who had come from captivity, the returned exiles:* This enigmatic reference may mean just the group that has returned with Ezra or the entire Jerusalem community. Most likely, given the end of v. 36, the reference is intended to be the group that has just returned. The sacrifices that are offered bear symbolic numbers representative of all Israel. Verses 35–36 are related in a third-person form, leading several to suggest they are the work of a later editor. **36:** *They supported the people and the house of God,* the ultimate commendation of those who came with Ezra.

9 After these things had been done, the officials approached me and said, "The people of Israel, the priests, and the Levites have not separated themselves from the peoples of the lands with their abominations, from the Canaanites, the Hittites, the Perizzites, the Jebusites, the Ammonites, the Moabites, the Egyptians, and the Amorites. 2For they have taken some of their daughters as wives for themselves and for their sons. Thus the holy seed has mixed itself with the peoples of the lands, and in this faithlessness the officials and leaders have led the way."

3When I heard this, I tore my garment and my mantle, and pulled hair from my head and beard, and sat appalled. 4Then all who trembled at the words of the God of Israel, because of the faithlessness of the returned exiles, gathered around me while I sat appalled until the evening sacrifice.

9.1–15: Acknowledgment of intermarriage and Ezra's response. The narrative* dealing with Ezra comes to a dramatic point in this chapter. Portions of the community reveal that intermarriage has taken place, and Ezra offers a long prayer of confession trusting that God will not destroy the community because of this sin. The entire framework is expressed in graphic terms, in which intermarriage is colored by terms associated with the most severe violations of God's sanctity. The aura of holiness and purity which must surround the Temple* as God's dwelling place is now transferred to the community as a whole. The community becomes the house of God. **1:** *After these things:* Ezra has disposed of some of the formalities of his mission, and then is confronted by the issue of intermarriage. The list of peoples contains the seven stock enemies of Israel that appear in a number of places in the Hebrew Bible. While marriage with foreigners was not prohibited, marriage with any of these enemies was considered unacceptable because of the danger of idolatry* (for example, Deut 7.1–4). There is no evidence that such peoples would still have been identifiable in the time of Ezra. **2:** *The holy seed has mixed itself* extends language from the "holiness code" of Lev 19 to the population. In Lev 19.19, mixing different seeds is prohibited as an affront to God's holiness. Such action is characterized as *faithlessness* in this narrative, or acting without regard for God's holiness. The entire condemnation of intermarriage here is a process of creatively combining ideas and themes into a new teaching. **3:** *I tore my garment and my mantle, and pulled hair from my head and beard:* These are traditional signs of deeply felt grief. **4:** *All who trembled at the words of the God of Israel* is a reference to those who took seriously the commandments of God, reflecting the original awe of the people when God first revealed his law upon the mountain (Ex 19.16–20).

5 At the evening sacrifice I got up from my fasting, with my garments and my mantle torn, and fell on my knees, spread out my hands to the LORD my God, 6and said,

"O my God, I am too ashamed and embarrassed to lift my face to you, my God, for our iniquities have risen higher than our heads, and our guilt has mounted up to the heavens. 7From the days of our ancestors to this day we have been deep in guilt, and for our iniquities we, our kings, and our priests have been handed over to the kings of the lands, to the sword, to captivity, to plundering, and to utter shame, as is now the case. 8But now for a brief moment favor has been shown by the LORD our God, who has left us a remnant, and given us a stake in his holy place, in order that he*a* may brighten our eyes and grant us a little sustenance in our slavery. 9For we are slaves; yet our God has not forsaken us in our slavery, but has extended to us his steadfast love before the kings of Persia, to give us new life to set up the house of our God, to repair its ruins, and to give us a wall in Judea and Jerusalem.

9.5–9. 6: *Our iniquities . . . and our guilt* are references to the practice of intermarriage; both terms are often used for severe transgressions of the law. **7:** *To utter shame, as is now the case:* Though the Persian monarchs have generally been supportive, there is still the sense of a diminished community because of the need to rely on Persian support. **8:** *Who has left us a remnant, and given us a stake in his holy place:* God's recent gracious acts are reviewed, including allowing the community to survive at all and providing a point of security in Jerusalem. **9:** *For we are slaves:* Despite the favor the monarchy has granted, the community is still in servitude to the empire. The expression will be echoed in Neh 9.36. *To set up the house of our God* serves as the general heading, the specific actions being to *repair its ruins* and to provide *a wall in Judea and Jerusalem.* The *wall* is a metaphor,* standing for a boundary or separation from the surrounding region by staying away from intermarriage. To violate this *wall* becomes all the more serious, a rejection of God's gift intended to help establish the house of God.

10 "And now, our God, what shall we say after this? For we have forsaken your commandments, 11which you commanded by your servants the prophets, saying, 'The land that you are entering to possess is a land un-

a Heb *our God*

clean with the pollutions of the peoples of the lands, with their abominations. They have filled it from end to end with their uncleanness. 12Therefore do not give your daughters to their sons, neither take their daughters for your sons, and never seek their peace or prosperity, so that you may be strong and eat the good of the land and leave it for an inheritance to your children forever.' 13After all that has come upon us for our evil deeds and for our great guilt, seeing that you, our God, have punished us less than our iniquities deserved and have given us such a remnant as this, 14shall we break your commandments again and intermarry with the peoples who practice these abominations? Would you not be angry with us until you destroy us without remnant or survivor? 15O LORD, God of Israel, you are just, but we have escaped as a remnant, as is now the case. Here we are before you in our guilt, though no one can face you because of this."

9.10–15. 10–11: *For we have forsaken your commandments, which you commanded by your servants the prophets:** The quotation comes from fragments of various texts pieced together, notably Deut 7.1–4; 11.8; 23.6; Isa 1.19; and Lev 18.24–30. **13:** *After all that has come upon us* relates to the destruction of Jerusalem and the subsequent exile of a number of leading citizens under the Babylonians. **14:** *Shall we break your commandments again and intermarry:* This phrasing equates the idolatry of the late Judean kingdom with the practice of intermarriage in Ezra's day. **15:** *You are just:* Despite God's character as a just god (which would mean the community should have been obliterated), the community has survived, yet *guilt* has again come on the community from its intermarriage with the surrounding peoples. The implication is that the community must remove the guilt (that is, intermarriage) or face certain destruction at the hands of a just and holy God.

---

10 While Ezra prayed and made confession, weeping and throwing himself down before the house of God, a very great assembly of men, women, and children gathered to him out of Israel; the people also wept bitterly. 2Shecaniah son of Jehiel, of the descendants of Elam, addressed Ezra,

saying, "We have broken faith with our God and have married foreign women from the peoples of the land, but even now there is hope for Israel in spite of this. 3So now let us make a covenant with our God to send away all these wives and their children, according to the counsel of my lord and of those who tremble at the commandment of our God; and let it be done according to the law. 4Take action, for it is your duty, and we are with you; be strong, and do it." 5Then Ezra stood up and made the leading priests, the Levites, and all Israel swear that they would do as had been said. So they swore.

10.1–5: The people's response. The narrative* now returns briefly to a third-person form to describe the community's reaction to Ezra's sermon in prayer form. The function of this brief notice is to empower Ezra to act on behalf of the community's own request. **1:** *A very great assembly of men, women, and children gathered to him out of Israel:* One of the keys to this section is the idea of an *assembly*. A large number of persons heard Ezra's prayer and *wept bitterly*, indicating their deep grief. **3:** *Now let us make a covenant:** Recognizing the gravity of their situation, the assembly calls for action to remove the foreign wives from the community's midst as a sacred act, to be done as dictated by Ezra and *those who tremble at the commandment of our God*, the members of the community particularly concerned with obedience to the law. **5:** *The leading priests, the Levites, and all Israel:* Reversing the order of the report from the "officials" in 9.1, the account ensures that the community as a whole observes the new covenant.

---

6 Then Ezra withdrew from before the house of God, and went to the chamber of Jehohanan son of Eliashib, where he spent the night.*a* He did not eat bread or drink water, for he was mourning over the faithlessness of the exiles. 7They made a proclamation throughout Judah and Jerusalem to all the returned exiles that they should assemble at Jerusalem, 8and that if any did not come within three days, by order of the officials and the elders all their property should be forfeited, and they themselves banned from the congregation of the exiles.

a 1 Esdras 9.2: Heb *where he went*

9 Then all the people of Judah and Benjamin assembled at Jerusalem within the three days; it was the ninth month, on the twentieth day of the month. All the people sat in the open square before the house of God, trembling because of this matter and because of the heavy rain. 10 Then Ezra the priest stood up and said to them, "You have trespassed and married foreign women, and so increased the guilt of Israel. 11 Now make confession to the LORD the God of your ancestors, and do his will; separate yourselves from the peoples of the land and from the foreign wives." 12 Then all the assembly answered with a loud voice, "It is so; we must do as you have said. 13 But the people are many, and it is a time of heavy rain; we cannot stand in the open. Nor is this a task for one day or for two, for many of us have transgressed in this matter. 14 Let our officials represent the whole assembly, and let all in our towns who have taken foreign wives come at appointed times, and with them the elders and judges of every town, until the fierce wrath of our God on this account is averted from us." 15 Only Jonathan son of Asahel and Jahzeiah son of Tikvah opposed this, and Meshullam and Shabbethai the Levites supported them.

10.6–15: Ezra's decree against intermarriage. Rather than issue a proclamation in his role as imperial representative, Ezra convenes an assembly of the community to deliver the regulation to separate themselves from the peoples of the lands. The narrative* underscores the willingness of the community to reform itself, with few exceptions. **6:** *Ezra withdrew:* Having interceded on behalf of the community, Ezra could now retire to another less public place to plan how the community would enact its reforms. His fasting is a traditional means of expressing sorrow for sin. **7:** *A proclamation:* The call to convene an assembly goes to the *returned exiles,* perhaps to differentiate the community from non-Israelite populations that may have moved into the region after the fall of the Judean kingdom. **8:** *Property . . . forfeited:* a penalty that presupposes community control over each individual's possessions. There is evidence that the Persian empire organized some districts into economic collectives in which the individual had wealth only as a part of the collective. Being excluded from the collective would

have dire economic consequences. *Congregation:* the same word in Hebrew as "assembly" in 10.1. **9:** *The ninth month:* Kislev, approximately December of the modern calendar,* a time of cold rains in Palestine. In a human touch, the author notes the people were *trembling* from the awesomeness of the matter at hand, and the cold rains. **10:** *Trespassed:* The violation of separateness has not only caused individual alienation from God, but has affected the community's relationship to God. **11:** *Separate yourselves:* It is not clear if the order to separate is a general one, for which sending away *the foreign wives* is the specific action, or if an additional issue is involved. **14:** The *whole assembly* agrees to Ezra's proposal but makes a series of practical suggestions for its implementation. The work of sorting through those marriages that needed to be dissolved would continue until intermarriage was no longer the guilt of the community.

16 Then the returned exiles did so. Ezra the priest selected men,*a* heads of families, according to their families, each of them designated by name. On the first day of the tenth month they sat down to examine the matter. 17 By the first day of the first month they had come to the end of all the men who had married foreign women.

18 There were found of the descendants of the priests who had married foreign women, of the descendants of Jeshua son of Jozadak and his brothers: Maaseiah, Eliezer, Jarib, and Gedaliah. 19 They pledged themselves to send away their wives, and their guilt offering was a ram of the flock for their guilt. 20 Of the descendants of Immer: Hanani and Zebadiah. 21 Of the descendants of Harim: Maaseiah, Elijah, Shemaiah, Jehiel, and Uzziah. 22 Of the descendants of Pashhur: Elioenai, Maaseiah, Ishmael, Nethanel, Jozabad, and Elasah.

23 Of the Levites: Jozabad, Shimei, Kelaiah (that is, Kelita), Pethahiah, Judah, and Eliezer. 24 Of the singers: Eliashib. Of the gatekeepers: Shallum, Telem, and Uri.

25 And of Israel: of the descendants of Parosh: Ramiah, Izziah, Malchijah, Mijamin, Eleazar, Hashabiah,*b* and Benaiah. 26 Of the descendants of Elam: Mattaniah,

a 1 Esdras 9.16: Syr: Heb *And there were selected Ezra,*
b 1 Esdras 9.26 Gk: Heb *Malchijah*

Zechariah, Jehiel, Abdi, Jeremoth, and Elijah. [27] Of the descendants of Zattu: Elioenai, Eliashib, Mattaniah, Jeremoth, Zabad, and Aziza. [28] Of the descendants of Bebai: Jehohanan, Hananiah, Zabbai, and Athlai. [29] Of the descendants of Bani: Meshullam, Malluch, Adaiah, Jashub, Sheal, and Jeremoth. [30] Of the descendants of Pahath-moab: Adna, Chelal, Benaiah, Maaseiah, Mattaniah, Bezalel, Binnui, and Manasseh. [31] Of the descendants of Harim: Eliezer, Isshijah, Malchijah, Shemaiah, Shimeon, [32] Benjamin, Malluch, and Shemariah. [33] Of the descendants of Hashum: Mattenai, Mattattah, Zabad, Eliphelet, Jeremai, Manasseh, and Shimei. [34] Of the descendants of Bani: Maadai, Amram, Uel, [35] Benaiah, Bedeiah, Cheluhi, [36] Vaniah, Meremoth, Eliashib, [37] Mattaniah, Mattenai, and Jaasu. [38] Of the descendants of Binnui:[a] Shimei, [39] Shelemiah, Nathan, Adaiah, [40] Machnadebai, Shashai, Sharai, [41] Azarel, Shelemiah, Shemariah, [42] Shallum, Amariah, and Joseph. [43] Of the descendants of Nebo: Jeiel, Mattithiah, Zabad, Zebina, Jaddai, Joel, and Benaiah. [44] All these had married foreign women, and they sent them away with their children.[b]

10.16–44: The listing of men who had married foreign wives. Moving back to a third-person narrative,* the account now describes the process by which the community was examined, and the results of that examination are listed. The emphasis on the actual persons who willingly sent away their foreign wives underscores the community's willingness to take on this level of separation, forming a distinct, "holy" community. **17:** *By the first day of the first month:* The process took three months. **18:** The list is ordered along three lines—the priests, the Levites, and Israel—considering the small enclave of Jerusalem and its surroundings as the totality of the community. **44:** The Hebrew text here is difficult and the translation follows the Greek of 1 Esdras. The Hebrew suggests the children stayed and only the foreign wives were sent away, the children being counted as legitimate members of the community.

~~~~~~~~~~~~~~~~~~~~

a Gk: Heb *Bani, Binnui* *b* 1 Esdras 9.36; Meaning of Heb uncertain

NEHEMIAH

Introduction

The Access Bible treats Ezra-Nehemiah as a single work; for convenience the introductory material from Ezra is repeated here.

In the form found in most English Bibles, Ezra and Nehemiah are divided into two separate books. This format follows a tradition established in the early centuries of the Christian church, when the Vulgate★ (the Bible in Latin) divided these two works. It was only in the fifteenth century CE that Hebrew manuscripts adopted the same custom. In actuality, the most ancient tradition we can trace kept these two works together as one. Most of the ancient lists of books of the Hebrew Bible list them together. Moreover, the two share a number of literary elements, suggesting that they are related.

It has become commonplace in scholarship to see Ezra-Nehemiah as a continuation of the same narrative★ as 1 and 2 Chronicles, all these works having been written by the same hand. The reasons are many, but some of the main points are that Ezra-Nehemiah opens with a repetition of 2 Chr 36.22–23, that Ezra-Nehemiah and 1 and 2 Chronicles share vocabulary for Temple★ personnel and objects that are not found elsewhere in the Hebrew Bible, and that both 1 and 2 Chronicles and Ezra-Nehemiah have extended genealogical★ lists. While this view may still predominate, the last two decades have seen the emergence of a serious challenge from scholars who argue for the independence of Ezra-Nehemiah and 1 and 2 Chronicles. They have sought to base this conclusion on a number of differences in vocabulary, theology, and ideology between the two works. The issue is complex, but here we will look at Ezra-Nehemiah as if it is an independent composition on its own terms.

In literary form, Ezra-Nehemiah is difficult to characterize. The author has employed citations of documents, lists of personnel or community members, historical narratives, and first-person narratives that are often termed "memoirs." Some of the more notable portions are Rehum's correspondence with King Artaxerxes (Ezra 4.7–22), Tattenai's correspondence with King Darius (5.6–17; 6.6–12), a list of those who returned from Babylon (Ezra 2.1–67, repeated in Neh 7.6–68), the "Ezra memoir" (Ezra 7–10), and the "Nehemiah memoir" (mainly Neh 1.1–7.5).

The normal approach to the work has been to read it as a historical narrative, but throughout the work elements appear dislocated and far off the mark for history writing. Given the lack of chronological flow to the work, it would be better to consider it a historical apologetic,★ or a defense of a particular position or viewpoint, loosely using the events of the community to support a theological perspective.

Squarely set in the midst of the Persian empire, the work focuses on two imperial functionaries, Ezra and Nehemiah, and the reforms they attempted. If Ezra is placed before Nehemiah, as seems the intent of the author, then Ezra came to Jerusalem in 458 BCE, and Nehemiah's first stint as governor was in 445 BCE. When scholars examine the lists of names, they can determine that the latest names on some lists date from a generation or so after the time of the mid fifth century. They therefore conclude that the work was written around 400 BCE.

Both Ezra and Nehemiah as literary figures are portrayed as disturbed by intermarriage with "foreigners" in the community, and both condemn this activity using a language loaded with religious connotations. This concern hardly seems to fit with Ezra 1–6, where the struggle to rebuild the Temple in Jerusalem almost a century earlier dominates.

Linking the various parts of the work together is the theme of the "house of God." Beginning with the rebuilding of the physical structure of the Temple, the work moves through to the reformation of the community as the "house of God." A subsidiary theme is the rebuilding of the walls of Jerusalem, which would separate the community from the surrounding region, both physically and religiously. These themes are cast in highly religious language, leading the reader to the inevitable assessment of the righteousness of this redefinition of the community.

The Persian empire faced troubled conditions in the mid fifth century as a serious revolt in Egypt, coupled with the assistance of the Greek city-states, openly challenged the empire's control of the Mediterranean. The territory of Yehud, as the region of Jerusalem and the surrounding area was called, suddenly had strategic importance for the empire. One of the techniques the Persian empire used to control subject populations was controlling their access to the land. Since most of the population was engaged in farming or farming-related employment, access to the land was essential for survival, and thus the empire maintained control over the peoples they had conquered. The ability to control land access was threatened when adjacent communities began to intermarry, since this blurred the definition of who had access to what lands. The narratives of Ezra-Nehemiah present two individuals who are charged directly by the Persian king to undertake vaguely described missions, the result of which is the strengthening of the community boundaries by directly attacking the practice of intermarriage. Such a redefinition of the community probably met with strong opposition, and the present literary work of Ezra-Nehemiah sought to provide a theological rationale for accepting what was essentially an imperial dictate.

READING GUIDE

Given the complicated mixture of literary forms in Ezra-Nehemiah, it is difficult to follow all the elements of the narrative. Readers should watch for the "house of God" theme in the various sections; how does the author want us to understand the "house of God"? Also, it is helpful to notice who is allowed to participate in the community, and who is being excluded.

Ezra

1–2	Prologue
3–6	Rebuilding the house of God
7–10	Ezra's inquiry

Nehemiah

1.1–7.5	Nehemiah's mission
7.6–13.3	Forming the house of God
13.4–30	Postlogue

NEHEMIAH'S MISSION

1.1–7.5: Nehemiah opens with a first-person narrative* relating his concerns over Jerusalem and the Persian monarch's appointment of himself as governor over the province. The bulk of the account covers the various incidents of Nehemiah's rule as governor as he attempted to rebuild the walls of Jerusalem. The narrative must constantly balance Nehemiah's leadership of the community and the active opposition of leaders in the surrounding areas. There are several points of connection (as noted in the comments) with the first-person narratives of the book of Ezra.

1 The words of Nehemiah son of Hacaliah. In the month of Chislev, in the twentieth year, while I was in Susa the capital, ²one of my brothers, Hanani, came with certain men from Judah; and I asked them about the Jews that survived, those who had escaped the captivity, and about Jerusalem. ³They replied, "The survivors there in the province who escaped captivity are in great trouble and shame; the wall of Jerusalem is broken down, and its gates have been destroyed by fire."

4 When I heard these words I sat down and wept, and mourned for days, fasting and praying before the God of heaven. ⁵I said, "O LORD God of heaven, the great and awesome God who keeps covenant and steadfast love with those who love him and keep his commandments; ⁶let your ear be attentive and your eyes open to hear the prayer of your servant that I now pray before you day and night for your servants, the people of Israel, confessing the sins of the people of Israel, which we have sinned against you. Both I and my family have sinned. ⁷We have offended you deeply, failing to keep the commandments, the statutes, and the ordinances that you commanded your servant Moses. ⁸Remember the word that you commanded your servant Moses, 'If you are unfaithful, I will scatter you among the peoples; ⁹but if you return to me and keep my commandments and do them, though your outcasts are under the farthest skies, I will gather them from there and bring them to the place at which I have chosen to establish

my name.' ¹⁰They are your servants and your people, whom you redeemed by your great power and your strong hand. ¹¹O Lord, let your ear be attentive to the prayer of your servant, and to the prayer of your servants who delight in revering your name. Give success to your servant today, and grant him mercy in the sight of this man!"

At the time, I was cupbearer to the king.

1.1–11: Nehemiah's concern over Jerusalem. The opening explains Nehemiah's appointment as governor and his relentless pursuit of the rebuilding of the city walls. The section ends with a lengthy prayer that gives voice to the author's concept of the proper approach to God. **1:** *The words of Nehemiah:* The Hebrew term for *words* can also be rendered "matters." The opening does not necessarily support the existence of a "Nehemiah memoir." *In the twentieth year:* Apparently the twentieth year of King Artaxerxes (see 2.1). *Susa* was a seasonal palace for the Persian monarchs, though Artaxerxes seemed to have favored it and spent protracted periods there. **2:** *One of my brothers* may indicate a family member (see 7.2) or may simply mean a colleague. *The Jews that survived:* It is unclear what specific group or groups Nehemiah is asking about, but the main point is his concern with the entire community's welfare as well as the city's. **3:** *The wall of Jerusalem is broken down:* This should have been well known, following on the destruction of the city by the Babylonians in 587 BCE. Some believe the report must relate to a more recent event, and suggest that the events of Ezra 4.23 may provide the background, though nothing in that account would suggest a destruction of the work that had been accomplished. Possibly the report is taken as a sign of the royal disapproval of Ezra 4.23: The wall of Jerusalem is still broken down, and thus Nehemiah must try a different means to aid Jerusalem. Given the use of terms such as *great trouble and shame,* another possibility is that the *wall* and *gates* are metaphors* for the separation that Ezra was trying to achieve. **4:** *I sat down and wept, and mourned for days:* This is a sign of grief, and also a sign of the literary character of the account, since it is hard to conceive of a figure as forceful as Nehemiah acting so victimized for several months. **5:** *God of heaven* was a characteristic title for God in the Persian period (see Ezra 7.12, 23). **10:** *They are your servants and your people:* After confessing his own guilt, Nehemiah calls on God to remember his people since Nehemiah's prayer is on their behalf. **11:** *Give* success to your servant today, and grant him mercy in the sight of this man: Nehemiah apparently has formed a plan to address the misfortunes of Jerusalem, but the reader does not yet know what it is. Man is clearly a reference to Artaxerxes. In the Persian court, cupbearer was a formal office, with responsibility for ensuring the safety of the king's wine supply as well as acting as a royal adviser.

2 In the month of Nisan, in the twentieth year of King Artaxerxes, when wine was served him, I carried the wine and gave it to the king. Now, I had never been sad in his presence before. ²So the king said to me, "Why is your face sad, since you are not sick? This can only be sadness of the heart." Then I was very much afraid. ³I said to the king, "May the king live forever! Why should my face not be sad, when the city, the place of my ancestors' graves, lies waste, and its gates have been destroyed by fire?" ⁴Then the king said to me, "What do you request?" So I prayed to the God of heaven. ⁵Then I said to the king, "If it pleases the king, and if your servant has found favor with you, I ask that you send me to Judah, to the city of my ancestors' graves, so that I may rebuild it." ⁶The king said to me (the queen also was sitting beside him), "How long will you be gone, and when will you return?" So it pleased the king to send me, and I set him a date. ⁷Then I said to the king, "If it pleases the king, let letters be given me to the governors of the province Beyond the River, that they may grant me passage until I arrive in Judah; ⁸and a letter to Asaph, the keeper of the king's forest, directing him to give me timber to make beams for the gates of the temple fortress, and for the wall of the city, and for the house that I shall occupy." And the king granted me what I asked, for the gracious hand of my God was upon me.

2.1–8: Artaxerxes' grant to Nehemiah. Just as Ezra's mission was the result of a gracious act by Artaxerxes, so Nehemiah's appointment as governor is by the favor of the same king. This account shows the conditions of Nehemiah's appointment and underscores God's working through both Artaxerxes and Nehemiah. **1:** *In the month of Nisan, in the twentieth year:* Nisan, is in early Spring, roughly March—April in our

calendar, some three months after receiving the report of 1.3. The *twentieth year of Artaxerxes* would place this in 445 BCE, about 13 years after Ezra's mission. **3:** *The city, the place of my ancestors' graves, lies waste* is a somewhat exaggerated description, though it is probable that sections of the city remained uninhabitable from the ruins of the Babylonian conquest. **6:** *How long will you be gone, and when will you return?* Artaxerxes's reply assumes the granting of Nehemiah's request to rebuild Jerusalem, and the value of Nehemiah to the court. **8:** *To give me timber to make beams for the gates of the temple fortress, and for the wall of the city:* Nehemiah's task in rebuilding the city will include refortification, something the Persian empire would not allow without royal dispensation. Since the beams over the gateways need to be of larger and stronger wood than is readily available in the region, Nehemiah asks for timber from the imperially controlled sources, probably the cedar forests of Lebanon. The granting of timber supplies was also the empowering of Nehemiah to refortify the city, an act undertaken because of troubled conditions in the Egyptian holdings of the empire. *The gracious hand of my God was upon me* parallels Ezra's claim of divine support (Ezra 7.6, 28).

9 Then I came to the governors of the province Beyond the River, and gave them the king's letters. Now the king had sent officers of the army and cavalry with me. ¹⁰When Sanballat the Horonite and Tobiah the Ammonite official heard this, it displeased them greatly that someone had come to seek the welfare of the people of Israel.

11 So I came to Jerusalem and was there for three days. ¹²Then I got up during the night, I and a few men with me; I told no one what my God had put into my heart to do for Jerusalem. The only animal I took was the animal I rode. ¹³I went out by night by the Valley Gate past the Dragon's Spring and to the Dung Gate, and I inspected the walls of Jerusalem that had been broken down and its gates that had been destroyed by fire. ¹⁴Then I went on to the Fountain Gate and to the King's Pool; but there was no place for the animal I was riding to continue. ¹⁵So I went up by way of the valley by night and inspected the wall. Then I turned back and entered by the Valley Gate, and so returned. ¹⁶The officials did not know where I had

gone or what I was doing; I had not yet told the Jews, the priests, the nobles, the officials, and the rest that were to do the work.

2.9–16: Nehemiah's coming to Jerusalem. As with the account of Ezra, there are few details of the lengthy journey from Persia to Jerusalem. The focus is on significant opposition to Nehemiah's task and his consequent need to be cautious in his planning. **9:** *Gave them the king's letters:* Since Nehemiah came directly from the imperial court, it would be convenient for him to carry vital dispatches as well as official declarations of his office. *The king had sent officers of the army and cavalry with me* highlights both the military nature of Nehemiah's commission and the importance the imperial court placed on his success. **10:** *Sanballat the Horonite and Tobiah the Ammonite official: Sanballat* is a Babylonian name and is known from Aramaic* documents of the Persian period to have been the name of the governor of the Persian district of Samaria. *Horonite* probably means his family was from Beth-horon, two Israelite cities located some 12 miles north of Jerusalem (2 Chr 8.5) and controlling a strategic pass. *Tobiah* is a Hebrew name; his exact role is less certain. *The Ammonite official* is perhaps a reference to his region of administrative responsibility. Some have linked him to a powerful family of the same name of a later period that had significant interests in the Transjordan. Others have suggested he is the same as the *Tabeel* of Ezra 4.7, apparently a junior official in the regional administration. As an *Ammonite* (if this is a reference to family origin), Tobiah would be excluded from the "assembly" of Israel (Deut 23.3–6). *It displeased them:* Perhaps because of the new preference the imperial court is showing to Jerusalem, which will bring new revenues and prestige to the city. **11:** The account of the rest of the *three days* parallels Ezra's account (Ezra 8.32). **13:** *I went out by night by the Valley Gate:* Nehemiah's inspection of the city's fortifications, had it been observed, might have raised objections that could be communicated to the king and cause a delay in the project. His inspection tour seems to follow the area known as the "City of David," a spur of land that lies along the western edge of the Kidron Valley south of the Temple* area. Nehemiah moves from the northwest corner of this region along the city walls, which stretched southeastward until they turned and went back north above the Kidron.

17 Then I said to them, "You see the trouble we are in, how Jerusalem lies in ruins with its gates burned. Come, let us rebuild the wall of Jerusalem, so that we may no longer suffer disgrace." 18 I told them that the hand of my God had been gracious upon me, and also the words that the king had spoken to me. Then they said, "Let us start building!" So they committed themselves to the common good. 19 But when Sanballat the Horonite and Tobiah the Ammonite official, and Geshem the Arab heard of it, they mocked and ridiculed us, saying, "What is this that you are doing? Are you rebelling against the king?" 20 Then I replied to them, "The God of heaven is the one who will give us success, and we his servants are going to start building; but you have no share or claim or historic right in Jerusalem."

2.17–20: Nehemiah's decree to the people, and opposition to the project. Just as the previous section introduced Nehemiah's determination to fulfill the commission given him, and introduced the main personalities who would oppose him, this section brings the community into the picture by Nehemiah's leadership, yet notes the opposition. **17:** *Then I said to them:* The whole community, as defined in v. 16. *Disgrace* was a term often associated with the Exile* as God's punishment of the community; in other words, the refortification of the city would finally put to an end the negative results of God's punishment of the community. **18:** *They committed themselves to the common good:* Just as Ezra had found a willingness to undertake the difficult task of separation from the surrounding peoples, Nehemiah finds the community ready to undertake rebuilding the walls. **19:** *Geshem the Arab* is a new figure among the opponents, thought to be the governor of a region in the Shephelah with an administrative center at Lachish. *Are you rebelling against the king?* would be the normal assumption about an effort to rebuild a city's fortifications since it would provide the means to defy imperial power. It is a hollow taunt since Nehemiah was directly commissioned by the imperial court. **20:** *You have no share or claim or historic right in Jerusalem* was a stinging rebuke to his opponents that essentially undercut their intrusion into Nehemiah's administrative affairs. The expression strongly parallels the rejection of help from "adversaries" in rebuilding the Temple* (Ezra 4.3), joining the theme of reestablishing the "house of God" to the rebuilding of the walls.

3 Then the high priest Eliashib set to work with his fellow priests and rebuilt the Sheep Gate. They consecrated it and set up its doors; they consecrated it as far as the Tower of the Hundred and as far as the Tower of Hananel. [2]And the men of Jericho built next to him. And next to them[a] Zaccur son of Imri built.

3 The sons of Hassenaah built the Fish Gate; they laid its beams and set up its doors, its bolts, and its bars. [4]Next to them Meremoth son of Uriah son of Hakkoz made repairs. Next to them Meshullam son of Berechiah son of Meshezabel made repairs. Next to them Zadok son of Baana made repairs. [5]Next to them the Tekoites made repairs; but their nobles would not put their shoulders to the work of their Lord.[b]

6 Joiada son of Paseah and Meshullam son of Besodeiah repaired the Old Gate; they laid its beams and set up its doors, its bolts, and its bars. [7]Next to them repairs were made by Melatiah the Gibeonite and Jadon the Meronothite—the men of Gibeon and of Mizpah—who were under the jurisdiction of[c] the governor of the province Beyond the River. [8]Next to them Uzziel son of Harhaiah, one of the goldsmiths, made repairs. Next to him Hananiah, one of the perfumers, made repairs; and they restored Jerusalem as far as the Broad Wall. [9]Next to them Rephaiah son of Hur, ruler of half the district of[d] Jerusalem, made repairs. [10]Next to them Jedaiah son of Harumaph made repairs opposite his house; and next to him Hattush son of Hashabneiah made repairs. [11]Malchijah son of Harim and Hasshub son of Pahath-moab repaired another section and the Tower of the Ovens. [12]Next to him Shallum son of Hallohesh, ruler of half the district of[d] Jerusalem, made repairs, he and his daughters.

13 Hanun and the inhabitants of Zanoah repaired the Valley Gate; they rebuilt it and set up its doors, its bolts, and its bars, and repaired a thousand cubits of the wall, as far as the Dung Gate.

14 Malchijah son of Rechab, ruler of the district of[e] Beth-haccherem, repaired the Dung Gate; he rebuilt it and set up its doors, its bolts, and its bars.

15 And Shallum son of Col-hozeh, ruler of the district of[e] Mizpah, repaired the Fountain Gate; he rebuilt it and covered it and set up its doors, its bolts, and its bars; and he built the wall of the Pool of Shelah of the king's garden, as far as the stairs that go down from the City of David. [16]After him Nehemiah son of Azbuk, ruler of half the district of[d] Beth-zur, repaired from a point opposite the graves of David, as far as the artificial pool and the house of the warriors. [17]After him the Levites made repairs: Rehum son of Bani; next to him Hashabiah, ruler of half the district of[d] Keilah, made repairs for his district. [18]After him their kin made repairs: Binnui,[f] son of Henadad, ruler of half the district of[d] Keilah; [19]next to him Ezer son of Jeshua, ruler[g] of Mizpah, repaired another section opposite the ascent to the armory at the Angle. [20]After him Baruch son of Zabbai repaired another section from the Angle to the door of the house of the high priest Eliashib. [21]After him Meremoth son of Uriah son of Hakkoz repaired another section from the door of the house of Eliashib to the end of the house of Eliashib. [22]After him the priests, the men of the surrounding area, made repairs. [23]After them Benjamin and Hasshub made repairs opposite their house. After them Azariah son of Maaseiah son of Ananiah made repairs beside his own house. [24]After him Binnui son of Henadad repaired another section, from the house of Azariah to the Angle and to the corner. [25]Palal son of Uzai repaired opposite the Angle and the tower projecting from the upper house of the king at the court of the guard. After him Pedaiah son of Parosh [26]and the temple servants living[h] on Ophel made repairs up to a point opposite the Water Gate on the east and the projecting tower. [27]After him the Tekoites repaired another section opposite the great projecting tower as far as the wall of Ophel.

28 Above the Horse Gate the priests made repairs, each one opposite his own house. 29After them Zadok son of Immer made repairs opposite his own house. After him Shemaiah son of Shecaniah, the keeper of the East Gate, made repairs. 30After him Hananiah son of Shelemiah and Hanun sixth son of Zalaph repaired another section. After him Meshullam son of Berechiah made repairs opposite his living quarters. 31After him Malchijah, one of the goldsmiths, made repairs as far as the house of the temple servants and of the merchants, opposite the Muster Gate,*a* and to the upper room of the corner. 32And between the upper room of the corner and the Sheep Gate the goldsmiths and the merchants made repairs.

3.1–32: The community organizes to rebuild the walls. This section marks the centerpoint of the combined work Ezra-Nehemiah and places the emphasis squarely on the community's efforts. While Ezra and Nehemiah are marked by having "the hand of God" on them, the heroes of the narrative* are the community members, elaborated in various lists, who willingly undertake the formation of the "house of God." The historical value of this list has been under discussion, and many believe it reflects an authentic, if only partial, record of the organization of the rebuilding effort. 1: *Then the high priest . . . with his fellow priests . . . rebuilt the Sheep Gate:* This gate was located in the northeast corner of the city adjacent to the Temple* precinct and was the principal entry for animals brought for sacrifice. Perhaps because of this, the section of wall is *consecrated* or "made holy." Another possibility is that this section was most vulnerable to attack, and consecrating the wall in effect called on God to help defend it. 5: *Tekoites:* Tekoa was on the fringe of the Judean desert to the south of Jerusalem. It was the traditional village of the prophet* Amos (Am 1.1). The common people's willingness is contrasted with the *nobles,* whose reasons for opposing Nehemiah are not given. It is possible that Tekoa lay near the boundary between Yehud's administrative area and Gershem's, and the nobles may have feared their involvement would bring difficulties with Gershem. *Their Lord* is a probable reference to Nehemiah. 7: *Gibeon and of Mizpah . . . under the jurisdiction of the governor of the province Beyond the River:* The Hebrew phrasing is difficult, but it may be that Miz-

pah, and the city of Gibeon which lies slightly south of it, were under some special status. Mizpah was not destroyed by the Babylonians, and it became the administrative center for their rule over the devastated Judean kingdom (Jer 40.7–10). It may have retained some special status as a provincial center as Jerusalem reemerged as the regional capital.

4 *b*Now when Sanballat heard that we were building the wall, he was angry and greatly enraged, and he mocked the Jews. 2He said in the presence of his associates and of the army of Samaria, "What are these feeble Jews doing? Will they restore things? Will they sacrifice? Will they finish it in a day? Will they revive the stones out of the heaps of rubbish—and burned ones at that?" 3Tobiah the Ammonite was beside him, and he said, "That stone wall they are building—any fox going up on it would break it down!" 4Hear, O our God, for we are despised; turn their taunt back on their own heads, and give them over as plunder in a land of captivity. 5Do not cover their guilt, and do not let their sin be blotted out from your sight; for they have hurled insults in the face of the builders.

6 So we rebuilt the wall, and all the wall was joined together to half its height; for the people had a mind to work.

7*c* But when Sanballat and Tobiah and the Arabs and the Ammonites and the Ashdodites heard that the repairing of the walls of Jerusalem was going forward and the gaps were beginning to be closed, they were very angry, 8and all plotted together to come and fight against Jerusalem and to cause confusion in it. 9So we prayed to our God, and set a guard as a protection against them day and night.

4.1–23: Opposition and the community's response. Though written as a first-person narrative,* presumably from Nehemiah's view, the focus is on the community. The account alternates between the scorn and plots of the adversaries of the rebuilding, and the community's determination to rebuild the walls of Jerusalem. 2: *Will they restore things? Will they sacrifice? Will*

a Or *Hammiphkad Gate*   *b* Ch 3.33 in Heb
c Ch 4.1 in Heb

they finish it in a day? The taunt relates to restoring Jerusalem to its former glory, a task that would take a great deal of time. The community's enthusiasm may be strong at the moment, but as time passes, Sanballat believes they will give up the task. The issue of *sacrifice* relates to dedicating the walls at the completion of the project (see 12.43). **6:** *All the wall was joined together to half its height:* It is unclear if this was half its original height, or half of its planned height (which may have been considerably less, given the restricted resources). **8:** *All plotted together to come and fight,* maybe not as an "official" military force, but perhaps in a series of raids designed to destabilize the building project.

10 But Judah said, "The strength of the burden bearers is failing, and there is too much rubbish so that we are unable to work on the wall." [11]And our enemies said, "They will not know or see anything before we come upon them and kill them and stop the work." [12]When the Jews who lived near them came, they said to us ten times, "From all the places where they live[a] they will come up against us."[b] [13]So in the lowest parts of the space behind the wall, in open places, I stationed the people according to their families,[c] with their swords, their spears, and their bows. [14]After I looked these things over, I stood up and said to the nobles and the officials and the rest of the people, "Do not be afraid of them. Remember the LORD, who is great and awesome, and fight for your kin, your sons, your daughters, your wives, and your homes."

15 When our enemies heard that their plot was known to us, and that God had frustrated it, we all returned to the wall, each to his work. [16]From that day on, half of my servants worked on construction, and half held the spears, shields, bows, and body-armor; and the leaders posted themselves behind the whole house of Judah, [17]who were building the wall. The burden bearers carried their loads in such a way that each labored on the work with one hand and with the other held a weapon. [18]And each of the builders had his sword strapped at his side while he built. The man who sounded the trumpet was beside me. [19]And I said to the nobles, the officials, and the rest of the people, "The work is great and widely spread

out, and we are separated far from one another on the wall. [20]Rally to us wherever you hear the sound of the trumpet. Our God will fight for us."

21 So we labored at the work, and half of them held the spears from break of dawn until the stars came out. [22]I also said to the people at that time, "Let every man and his servant pass the night inside Jerusalem, so that they may be a guard for us by night and may labor by day." [23]So neither I nor my brothers nor my servants nor the men of the guard who followed me ever took off our clothes; each kept his weapon in his right hand.[d]

4.10–23. 10: *But Judah said, "The strength of the burden bearers is failing":* Facing not only external pressure to cease, Nehemiah now had to contend with wavering resolve among the builders. *Judah* is a metaphor* for the whole community. The *burden bearers* hauled materials up to the points on the wall where they were needed. **12:** *They said to us ten times* is an idiom for "repeatedly." These informants want to be sure the community understands that rebuilding may provoke a general raid. **13:** *So in the lowest parts of the space behind the wall, in open places:* Nehemiah's strategy was to place the people where they would be ready to respond to an attack anywhere along the wall line. The *lowest parts* may have been chosen to conceal the force from any attacker. **14:** *Do not be afraid . . . Remember the LORD:* In the biblical tradition of the holy war* the armed force is promised that God will fight on their behalf. **15:** *We all returned to the wall:* The immediate threat of military challenge having passed, the community could now return to the task of rebuilding the wall. Nehemiah's subsequent orders are designed to maximize the work on the wall while demonstrating a preparedness for defense. **16:** *Half of my servants:* Probably a chosen group of individuals under direct employ of Nehemiah and whose loyalty he could count on. With such careful provisions, the danger of general military action against the community was stymied.

5 Now there was a great outcry of the people and of their wives against their Jew-

a Cn: Heb *you return*   b Compare Gk Syr: Meaning of Heb uncertain   c Meaning of Heb uncertain
d Cn: Heb *each his weapon the water*

ish kin. 2For there were those who said, "With our sons and our daughters, we are many; we must get grain, so that we may eat and stay alive." 3There were also those who said, "We are having to pledge our fields, our vineyards, and our houses in order to get grain during the famine." 4And there were those who said, "We are having to borrow money on our fields and vineyards to pay the king's tax. 5Now our flesh is the same as that of our kindred; our children are the same as their children; and yet we are forcing our sons and daughters to be slaves, and some of our daughters have been ravished; we are powerless, and our fields and vineyards now belong to others."

6 I was very angry when I heard their outcry and these complaints. 7After thinking it over, I brought charges against the nobles and the officials; I said to them, "You are all taking interest from your own people." And I called a great assembly to deal with them, 8and said to them, "As far as we were able, we have bought back our Jewish kindred who had been sold to other nations; but now you are selling your own kin, who must then be bought back by us!" They were silent, and could not find a word to say. 9So I said, "The thing that you are doing is not good. Should you not walk in the fear of our God, to prevent the taunts of the nations our enemies? 10Moreover I and my brothers and my servants are lending them money and grain. Let us stop this taking of interest. 11Restore to them, this very day, their fields, their vineyards, their olive orchards, and their houses, and the interest on money, grain, wine, and oil that you have been exacting from them." 12Then they said, "We will restore everything and demand nothing more from them. We will do as you say." And I called the priests, and made them take an oath to do as they had promised. 13I also shook out the fold of my garment and said, "So may God shake out everyone from house and from property who does not perform this promise. Thus may they be shaken out and emptied." And all the assembly said, "Amen," and praised the LORD. And the people did as they had promised.

5.1–13: Economic crisis and Nehemiah's solutions. Told in a first-person fashion, this section recounts a grave economic crisis made worse by the profiteering of some members of the community. Faced with a possible revolt, Nehemiah forcefully takes dramatic steps to alleviate the crisis. **1:** *Now there was a great outcry:* The implication of the placement of this account is that the work of rebuilding was continuing when the crisis reached its potential breaking point. Three different issues are raised by the crowd, all the result of a periodic famine (v. 3). The first issue is the difficulty in getting grain for food (v. 2); the second, the use of fields as collateral to obtain loans for purchasing grain (v. 4); and most seriously, the use of the labor of children as collateral on borrowing money to pay *the king's tax* (v. 5). Normally, taxes were paid in grains in the Persian empire, but when grain was not available, taxes could be paid in the monetary equivalent (usually in terms of weight, such as "so many mina of silver") of the amount of grain owed. In a famine, as the cost of grain escalated, so would the relative value of the taxes owed to the empire. Also, famine was usually triggered by drought, making it difficult for farmers to raise the necessary crop yield to repay a debt. Brokers could loan grains or silver in return for receiving pledges on the future yields of the land or on the available labor in the family group. If the loan was not repaid in the time frame agreed to, the broker could seize all the yield of a given crop, or take members of the family into indentured servitude, often exacting interest on the remaining balance due until the whole loan plus accrued interest was repaid. Nehemiah attempts to address this situation by first calling a *great assembly* (v. 7), announcing the release of new resources into the markets (v. 10). He also requires that productive lands be returned to the debtors so that they will have some means of raising capital to make the debt good (v. 11). The call to *stop this taking of interest* (v. 10) is most likely a reference to the additional interest on the loan when the original repayment schedule cannot be met. This seems to be what the brokers agree to in pledging they will *demand nothing more from them* (v. 12). **13:** *May God shake out everyone from house and from property:* Having forced the brokers to take a solemn oath before the priests (v. 12), Nehemiah engages in a symbolic action, placing a curse on all who violate the pledge. The brokers, being people of means, would take seriously the possibility of losing their wealth. *The people* *did as they had promised* suggests Nehemiah's solutions worked.

14 Moreover from the time that I was appointed to be their governor in the land of Judah, from the twentieth year to the thirty-second year of King Artaxerxes, twelve years, neither I nor my brothers ate the food allowance of the governor. ¹⁵The former governors who were before me laid heavy burdens on the people, and took food and wine from them, besides forty shekels of silver. Even their servants lorded it over the people. But I did not do so, because of the fear of God. ¹⁶Indeed, I devoted myself to the work on this wall, and acquired no land; and all my servants were gathered there for the work. ¹⁷Moreover there were at my table one hundred fifty people, Jews and officials, besides those who came to us from the nations around us. ¹⁸Now that which was prepared for one day was one ox and six choice sheep; also fowls were prepared for me, and every ten days skins of wine in abundance; yet with all this I did not demand the food allowance of the governor, because of the heavy burden of labor on the people. ¹⁹Remember for my good, O my God, all that I have done for this people.

5.14–19: Nehemiah's refusal to collect the food tax.
Having highlighted his generosity in making his own wealth available to those struggling in the famine crisis, in this section Nehemiah shows his refusal to place additional burdens on the populace, despite his right to collect a "food allowance." **14:** *From the twentieth year to the thirty-second year of King Artaxerxes,* or from 445 to 434 BCE. The *food allowance* was apparently the privilege of the local imperial officials to draw their living support from a taxation surcharge. **15:** *Former governors* suggests that Yehud (as the region around Jerusalem was known) had been politically independent for some time prior to Nehemiah. **16:** *I . . . acquired no land:* Imperial privileges included the ability to amass land holdings. Nehemiah's single-mindedness excluded a concern to build wealth. **17:** *There were at my table one hundred fifty people:* Apparently they were all members of his entourage and lesser officials for whom the governor was expected to provide food rations, thereby showing that Nehemiah had every reason to exact the food allowance. **19:** *Remem-*

ber for my good, O my God, all that I have done for this people: This is the first of five separate appeals for God to bear in mind some particular action by, or against, Nehemiah. These appeals make it difficult to assess the character of the so-called "Nehemiah memoir," since such pietistic asides would not be expected in an official report. They do, however, provide insight into the emotions and faith of Nehemiah.

6 Now when it was reported to Sanballat and Tobiah and to Geshem the Arab and to the rest of our enemies that I had built the wall and that there was no gap left in it (though up to that time I had not set up the doors in the gates), ²Sanballat and Geshem sent to me, saying, "Come and let us meet together in one of the villages in the plain of Ono." But they intended to do me harm. ³So I sent messengers to them, saying, "I am doing a great work and I cannot come down. Why should the work stop while I leave it to come down to you?" ⁴They sent to me four times in this way, and I answered them in the same manner. ⁵In the same way Sanballat for the fifth time sent his servant to me with an open letter in his hand. ⁶In it was written, "It is reported among the nations—and Geshem*ᵃ* also says it—that you and the Jews intend to rebel; that is why you are building the wall; and according to this report you wish to become their king. ⁷You have also set up prophets to proclaim in Jerusalem concerning you, 'There is a king in Judah!' And now it will be reported to the king according to these words. So come, therefore, and let us confer together." ⁸Then I sent to him, saying, "No such things as you say have been done; you are inventing them out of your own mind" ⁹—for they all wanted to frighten us, thinking, "Their hands will drop from the work, and it will not be done." But now, O God, strengthen my hands.

10 One day when I went into the house of Shemaiah son of Delaiah son of Mehetabel, who was confined to his house, he said, "Let us meet together in the house of God, within the temple, and let us close the doors of the temple, for they are coming to kill you;

a Heb *Gashmu*

indeed, tonight they are coming to kill you." ¹¹But I said, "Should a man like me run away? Would a man like me go into the temple to save his life? I will not go in!" ¹²Then I perceived and saw that God had not sent him at all, but he had pronounced the prophecy against me because Tobiah and Sanballat had hired him. ¹³He was hired for this purpose, to intimidate me and make me sin by acting in this way, and so they could give me a bad name, in order to taunt me. ¹⁴Remember Tobiah and Sanballat, O my God, according to these things that they did, and also the prophetess Noadiah and the rest of the prophets who wanted to make me afraid.

6.1–14: Nehemiah's life is threatened. While the account of ch. 4 deals with threats against the community, this section continues a focus on Nehemiah as an individual, revealing a series of plots by the "adversaries" to destroy him. Nehemiah's persistence in directing the rebuilding effort preserved him from being entrapped by their plots. **2:** *The plain of Ono* lay to the northwest of Jerusalem. It may have been in a boundary area between Sanballat's district and Nehemiah's. *They intended to do me harm:* The account provides no reason for this conclusion. **6:** *You and the Jews intend to rebel:* In general, walled cities were not built in the Persian empire. The refortification of Jerusalem would provide an opportunity to defy the empire. Sanballat uses the threat of reporting this to the king (v. 7) to draw Nehemiah out. **10:** *Shemaiah . . . was confined to his house:* Though the account is not clear on the timing, there seems to be some time between Sanballat's efforts to get Nehemiah to meet with him, and this plot. It is not certain why Shemaiah was closed in his house, nor why Nehemiah went to see him. *Tonight they are coming to kill you:* Perhaps Shemaiah had sent word to Nehemiah that he had an important message to convey. His advice to meet in the Temple* and *close the doors* because the adversaries were coming to kill Nehemiah would have made the governor look cowardly. **13:** *He was hired for this purpose:* It takes Nehemiah time to see through the plot, but Shemaiah may have been a reputable prophet,* making the deception difficult to detect. **14:** *Remember . . . O my God:* one of Nehemiah's direct appeals to God to keep something before him. Here Nehemiah wants his opponents be repaid according to their deeds, as well as *the prophetess Noadiah and the rest of the prophets*

who may have engaged in the same kinds of deceit as Shemaiah.

15 So the wall was finished on the twenty-fifth day of the month Elul, in fifty-two days. ¹⁶And when all our enemies heard of it, all the nations around us were afraid*a* and fell greatly in their own esteem; for they perceived that this work had been accomplished with the help of our God. ¹⁷Moreover in those days the nobles of Judah sent many letters to Tobiah, and Tobiah's letters came to them. ¹⁸For many in Judah were bound by oath to him, because he was the son-in-law of Shecaniah son of Arah; and his son Jehohanan had married the daughter of Meshullam son of Berechiah. ¹⁹Also they spoke of his good deeds in my presence, and reported my words to him. And Tobiah sent letters to intimidate me.

6.15–7.5: The walls are completed. This section, which recounts the completion of the physical work of refortifying the city, ends with a note on the relatively few people in the city. The rebuilding of the walls is not the final completion of the formation of the "house of God." **6.17:** *The nobles of Judah* are an indefinite group, but presumably related to a traditional aristocracy. **18:** *For many in Judah were bound by oath to him:* The reasons are not specified. Presumably their support of Tobiah results not from opposition to Nehemiah as much as being bound by their oaths.

7 Now when the wall had been built and I had set up the doors, and the gatekeepers, the singers, and the Levites had been appointed, ²I gave my brother Hanani charge over Jerusalem, along with Hananiah the commander of the citadel—for he was a faithful man and feared God more than many. ³And I said to them, "The gates of Jerusalem are not to be opened until the sun is hot; while the gatekeepers*b* are still standing guard, let them shut and bar the doors. Appoint guards from among the inhabitants of Jerusalem, some at their watch posts, and others before their own houses." ⁴The city was wide and large, but the people within it were few and no houses had been built.

a Another reading is *saw* *b* Heb *while they*

5 Then my God put it into my mind to assemble the nobles and the officials and the people to be enrolled by genealogy. And I found the book of the genealogy of those who were the first to come back, and I found the following written in it:

7.1–5. 1: *The gatekeepers, the singers, and the Levites:* The addition of the singers and Levites is unexpected, though since these groups were well organized they may have served as supplementary help to the gatekeepers, who would have to undertake their duties without prior experience. 3: *The gates of Jerusalem are not to be opened until the sun is hot,* perhaps as an additional security measure. 5: *The book of the genealogy:*★ There is no explanation for where or how the book was found. *Those who were the first to come back:* Perhaps those who first returned from the Exile,★ or those who first returned with one of the subsequent waves of exiled persons who migrated to Jerusalem.

FORMING THE HOUSE OF GOD

7.6–13.3: This section drops the first-person style of the "Nehemiah memoir" and the concern with opponents to the rebuilding efforts. Instead, the focus is on the community's concerns and corporate commitments. These are presented by means of several large gatherings of the "assembly" of the people interspersed with lengthy lists of the people involved. The culmination is an extended description of the dedication of the city walls and the separation of "Israel" from all those of "foreign descent," thus paralleling the physical separation of the city from the surrounding peoples.

6 These are the people of the province who came up out of the captivity of those exiles whom King Nebuchadnezzar of Babylon had carried into exile; they returned to Jerusalem and Judah, each to his town. 7They came with Zerubbabel, Jeshua, Nehemiah, Azariah, Raamiah, Nahamani, Mordecai, Bilshan, Mispereth, Bigvai, Nehum, Baanah.

The number of the Israelite people: 8the descendants of Parosh, two thousand one hundred seventy-two. 9Of Shephatiah, three hundred seventy-two. 10Of Arah, six hundred fifty-two. 11Of Pahath-moab, namely the descendants of Jeshua and Joab, two

thousand eight hundred eighteen. 12Of Elam, one thousand two hundred fifty-four. 13Of Zattu, eight hundred forty-five. 14Of Zaccai, seven hundred sixty. 15Of Binnui, six hundred forty-eight. 16Of Bebai, six hundred twenty-eight. 17Of Azgad, two thousand three hundred twenty-two. 18Of Adonikam, six hundred sixty-seven. 19Of Bigvai, two thousand sixty-seven. 20Of Adin, six hundred fifty-five. 21Of Ater, namely of Hezekiah, ninety-eight. 22Of Hashum, three hundred twenty-eight. 23Of Bezai, three hundred twenty-four. 24Of Hariph, one hundred twelve. 25Of Gibeon, ninety-five. 26The people of Bethlehem and Netophah, one hundred eighty-eight. 27Of Anathoth, one hundred twenty-eight. 28Of Beth-azmaveth, forty-two. 29Of Kiriath-jearim, Chephirah, and Beeroth, seven hundred forty-three. 30Of Ramah and Geba, six hundred twenty-one. 31Of Michmas, one hundred twenty-two. 32Of Bethel and Ai, one hundred twenty-three. 33Of the other Nebo, fifty-two. 34The descendants of the other Elam, one thousand two hundred fifty-four. 35Of Harim, three hundred twenty. 36Of Jericho, three hundred forty-five. 37Of Lod, Hadid, and Ono, seven hundred twenty-one. 38Of Senaah, three thousand nine hundred thirty.

39 The priests: the descendants of Jedaiah, namely the house of Jeshua, nine hundred seventy-three. 40Of Immer, one thousand fifty-two. 41Of Pashhur, one thousand two hundred forty-seven. 42Of Harim, one thousand seventeen.

43 The Levites: the descendants of Jeshua, namely of Kadmiel of the descendants of Hodevah, seventy-four. 44The singers: the descendants of Asaph, one hundred forty-eight. 45The gatekeepers: the descendants of Shallum, of Ater, of Talmon, of Akkub, of Hatita, of Shobai, one hundred thirty-eight.

46 The temple servants: the descendants of Ziha, of Hasupha, of Tabbaoth, 47of Keros, of Sia, of Padon, 48of Lebana, of Hagaba, of Shalmai, 49of Hanan, of Giddel, of Gahar, 50of Reaiah, of Rezin, of Nekoda, 51of Gazzam, of Uzza, of Paseah, 52of Besai, of Meunim, of Nephushesim, 53of Bakbuk,

of Hakupha, of Harhur, 54of Bazlith, of Mehida, of Harsha, 55of Barkos, of Sisera, of Temah, 56of Neziah, of Hatipha.

57 The descendants of Solomon's servants: of Sotai, of Sophereth, of Perida, 58of Jaala, of Darkon, of Giddel, 59of Shephatiah, of Hattil, of Pochereth-hazzebaim, of Amon.

60 All the temple servants and the descendants of Solomon's servants were three hundred ninety-two.

61 The following were those who came up from Tel-melah, Tel-harsha, Cherub, Addon, and Immer, but they could not prove their ancestral houses or their descent, whether they belonged to Israel: 62the descendants of Delaiah, of Tobiah, of Nekoda, six hundred forty-two. 63Also, of the priests: the descendants of Hobaiah, of Hakkoz, of Barzillai (who had married one of the daughters of Barzillai the Gileadite and was called by their name). 64These sought their registration among those enrolled in the genealogies, but it was not found there, so they were excluded from the priesthood as unclean; 65the governor told them that they were not to partake of the most holy food, until a priest with Urim and Thummim should come.

66 The whole assembly together was forty-two thousand three hundred sixty, 67besides their male and female slaves, of whom there were seven thousand three hundred thirty-seven; and they had two hundred forty-five singers, male and female. 68They had seven hundred thirty-six horses, two hundred forty-five mules,[a] 69four hundred thirty-five camels, and six thousand seven hundred twenty donkeys.

70 Now some of the heads of ancestral houses contributed to the work. The governor gave to the treasury one thousand darics of gold, fifty basins, and five hundred thirty priestly robes. 71And some of the heads of ancestral houses gave into the building fund twenty thousand darics of gold and two thousand two hundred minas of silver. 72And what the rest of the people gave was twenty thousand darics of gold, two thousand minas of silver, and sixty-seven priestly robes.

73 So the priests, the Levites, the gatekeepers, the singers, some of the people, the temple servants, and all Israel settled in their towns.

7.6–73a: The list of those who returned from Babylon. 6: *These are the people of the province:* Largely repeats the list found in Ezra 2.1–70. Variations between the two lists are minor, but often this list represents a slightly fuller version of the list in Ezra 2. The focus is clearly on *the people,* and the reduplication of the lists shows the author's concern to focus on the community's efforts. **7:** *Nehemiah:* Notice that this is in the third person, rather than the first-person accounts of the "Nehemiah memoir."

When the seventh month came—the people of Israel being settled in their towns— 8 1all the people gathered together into the square before the Water Gate. They told the scribe Ezra to bring the book of the law of Moses, which the LORD had given to Israel. 2Accordingly, the priest Ezra brought the law before the assembly, both men and women and all who could hear with understanding. This was on the first day of the seventh month. 3He read from it facing the square before the Water Gate from early morning until midday, in the presence of the men and the women and those who could understand; and the ears of all the people were attentive to the book of the law. 4The scribe Ezra stood on a wooden platform that had been made for the purpose; and beside him stood Mattithiah, Shema, Anaiah, Uriah, Hilkiah, and Maaseiah on his right hand; and Pedaiah, Mishael, Malchijah, Hashum, Hash-baddanah, Zechariah, and Meshullam on his left hand. 5And Ezra opened the book in the sight of all the people, for he was standing above all the people; and when he opened it, all the people stood up. 6Then Ezra blessed the LORD, the great God, and all the people answered, "Amen, Amen," lifting up their hands. Then they bowed their heads and worshiped the LORD with their faces to the ground. 7Also Jeshua, Bani, Sherebiah, Jamin, Akkub, Shabbethai, Hodiah, Maaseiah, Kelita, Azariah, Jozabad,

a Ezra 2.66 and the margins of some Hebrew Mss: MT lacks *They had . . . forty-five mules*

Hanan, Pelaiah, the Levites,[a] helped the people to understand the law, while the people remained in their places. 8So they read from the book, from the law of God, with interpretation. They gave the sense, so that the people understood the reading.

9 And Nehemiah, who was the governor, and Ezra the priest and scribe, and the Levites who taught the people said to all the people, "This day is holy to the LORD your God; do not mourn or weep." For all the people wept when they heard the words of the law. 10Then he said to them, "Go your way, eat the fat and drink sweet wine and send portions of them to those for whom nothing is prepared, for this day is holy to our LORD; and do not be grieved, for the joy of the LORD is your strength." 11So the Levites stilled all the people, saying, "Be quiet, for this day is holy; do not be grieved." 12And all the people went their way to eat and drink and to send portions and to make great rejoicing, because they had understood the words that were declared to them.

7.73b–8.12: The community gathers to hear the law. This section brings back into the narrative* the figure of Ezra, of whom nothing has been said since the close of the book of Ezra. This sudden reemergence of Ezra and the focus on the importance of the law has led many scholars to conclude that this narrative was originally part of the account of Ezra and was moved to its present position by the editor who has brought Ezra-Nehemiah into its present form. The focus, however, remains on the community's request for the reading of the law, and the way the section is placed makes it clear that the goal is to reform itself into a more obedient community on the eve of the dedication of the city walls. This ceremony also forms the backdrop to the conclusion of this larger section in 13.1–3. **73b:** When the seventh month came: The walls were completed in the month of Elul (6.15), the sixth month of the year. A rough chronological sequence is maintained by the placement, though there is some question if enough time is allowed for the people to return to be settled in their towns before reassembling in Jerusalem. The seventh month was traditionally the time of the Day of Atonement* (on the tenth day) and the Feast of Tabernacles (for a week starting on the fifteenth day). Several scholars have noted that this was also the month specified in Deut

31.10–13 for an assembly of the people to hear a reading of the law every seven years. This is apparently the model on which the account is structured. **8.1:** They told the scribe* Ezra to bring the book: The way Ezra is portrayed as subservient to the wishes of the "assembly," rather than the forceful leader of the community as in the book of Ezra tends to weigh against the idea that this narrative* was originally part of the book of Ezra. In the account of this gathering, Ezra is variously termed the scribe (vv. 1, 4), the priest (v. 2), and the priest and scribe (v. 9), both being roles attributed to him in the book of Ezra. **7:** The Levites helped the people to understand: One of the traditional roles of the Levites was to teach the meaning of the law to Israel (Deut 33.10), and this may have involved a brief exposition of the passage. The Levites may have moved about the crowd answering queries since the people remained in their places. **9:** Nehemiah . . . and Ezra: This is one of only two places in the Hebrew text of Ezra-Nehemiah where the two reformers appear together. This day is holy: The day of the assembly is a specific sacred occasion. While the specified time of the reading of the law could be considered a holy day, the account may imply that the day is the Feast of Trumpets, set on the first day of the seventh month, which was a sacred day (Lev 23.23–25), although no reading of the law is connected with the Feast of Trumpets. Possibly recognizing how far they had strayed from the law, the people wept. **10:** Then he said to them: The he may be Ezra. The specified foods are typical of a festive meal celebrating a sacred occasion. The phrase the joy of the LORD is your strength uses an unusual term for joy, one that occurs here and in 1 Chr 16.27, where "strength and joy are in his place." **12:** All the people went their way . . . to make great rejoicing: Unlike 1 and 2 Chronicles, where the rejoicing takes place in great corporate scenes, this account portrays the people retiring to their homes to rejoice. Their ability to understand the law provides the opportunity to live in accord with the divine will (Ps 119.34–35).

13 On the second day the heads of ancestral houses of all the people, with the priests and the Levites, came together to the scribe Ezra in order to study the words of the law. 14And they found it written in the law, which the LORD had commanded by Moses, that the people of Israel should live in

---

a 1 Esdras 9.48 Vg: Heb and the Levites

booths*a* during the festival of the seventh month, 15and that they should publish and proclaim in all their towns and in Jerusalem as follows, "Go out to the hills and bring branches of olive, wild olive, myrtle, palm, and other leafy trees to make booths,*a* as it is written." 16So the people went out and brought them, and made booths*a* for themselves, each on the roofs of their houses, and in their courts and in the courts of the house of God, and in the square at the Water Gate and in the square at the Gate of Ephraim. 17And all the assembly of those who had returned from the captivity made booths*a* and lived in them; for from the days of Jeshua son of Nun to that day the people of Israel had not done so. And there was very great rejoicing. 18And day by day, from the first day to the last day, he read from the book of the law of God. They kept the festival seven days; and on the eighth day there was a solemn assembly, according to the ordinance.

8.13–18: The community keeps the Festival of Booths. One of the specified holy times of the seventh month was the Festival of Booths (Lev 23.33–43), slated to be observed for a week beginning on the fifteenth day of the month. Along with the celebration of the deliverance from Egypt that is the prime focus of the festival, this account continues the reading, and presumably explanation, of the law. 13: *On the second day* keeps the chronology of 8.2, even though it technically does not observe the festival specifications of the law. This may be an indication that the precise limits of the festival had not been set in the Persian period. In place of the community as a whole, this gathering consists only of the leadership. 17: *All the assembly . . . made booths:* The whole community is involved. *From the days of Jeshua* is a reference to the period of conquest and Israel's inheritance of the land. The completion of the city walls and the reformation of the community are parallel to Israel's beginnings.

9 Now on the twenty-fourth day of this month the people of Israel were assembled with fasting and in sackcloth, and with earth on their heads.*b* 2Then those of Israelite descent separated themselves from all foreigners, and stood and confessed their sins and the iniquities of their ancestors.

3They stood up in their place and read from the book of the law of the LORD their God for a fourth part of the day, and for another fourth they made confession and worshiped the LORD their God. 4Then Jeshua, Bani, Kadmiel, Shebaniah, Bunni, Sherebiah, Bani, and Chenani stood on the stairs of the Levites and cried out with a loud voice to the LORD their God. 5Then the Levites, Jeshua, Kadmiel, Bani, Hashabneiah, Sherebiah, Hodiah, Shebaniah, and Pethahiah, said, "Stand up and bless the LORD your God from everlasting to everlasting. Blessed be your glorious name, which is exalted above all blessing and praise."

6 And Ezra said:*c* "You are the LORD, you alone; you have made heaven, the heaven of heavens, with all their host, the earth and all that is on it, the seas and all that is in them. To all of them you give life, and the host of heaven worships you. 7You are the LORD, the God who chose Abram and brought him out of Ur of the Chaldeans and gave him the name Abraham; 8and you found his heart faithful before you, and made with him a covenant to give to his descendants the land of the Canaanite, the Hittite, the Amorite, the Perizzite, the Jebusite, and the Girgashite; and you have fulfilled your promise, for you are righteous.

9.1–10.27: A day of community confession. This account explains a solemn covenant* to which the community will bind itself. Most of the section is a lengthy prayer, possibly offered by Ezra, which implores God to see the sufferings of the community in the present. The people hope that seeing how they have suffered, God will spare them any additional hardship in spite of their failure to observe the law. The account closes with the names of those who affirmed the covenant. Many have suggested that all or parts of the account fit best after the materials of Ezra 10. 9.1: *The twenty-fourth day of this month:* Following the author's chronology, the Feast of Weeks,* lasting eight days, would have ended on the tenth day of the month. The community had clearly prepared for the expression of grief by *fasting* and being dressed in *sackcloth.* 2: *Separated themselves:* Possibly a reflec-

a Or *tabernacles;* Heb *succoth*   *b* Heb *on them*
c Gk: Heb lacks *And Ezra said*

tion of the "sending away" of the foreign wives of Ezra 10, though the wording here clearly relates to foreign men as well. Since the confession is rooted in the particular experiences of Israel, the wording may simply mean that only those who have continuity with pre-exilic Israel continued with the confession, while converts to Judaism did not participate. **6:** *Ezra said:* This reading follows the Greek translation of Nehemiah (see note *c*). The Hebrew text implies the prayer is offered by the congregation as a whole. The prayer goes on to recount God's special kindness to Israel and the coming into the land of Israel. The prayer also notes the problem of idolatry* that led to judgment, though characterizing these transgressions by the more general casting of the "law behind their backs" (v. 26). Of particular note is the emphasis on God as a "gracious and merciful God" (v. 31).

9 "And you saw the distress of our ancestors in Egypt and heard their cry at the Red Sea.*ᵃ* ¹⁰You performed signs and wonders against Pharaoh and all his servants and all the people of his land, for you knew that they acted insolently against our ancestors. You made a name for yourself, which remains to this day. ¹¹And you divided the sea before them, so that they passed through the sea on dry land, but you threw their pursuers into the depths, like a stone into mighty waters. ¹²Moreover, you led them by day with a pillar of cloud, and by night with a pillar of fire, to give them light on the way in which they should go. ¹³You came down also upon Mount Sinai, and spoke with them from heaven, and gave them right ordinances and true laws, good statutes and commandments, ¹⁴and you made known your holy sabbath to them and gave them commandments and statutes and a law through your servant Moses. ¹⁵For their hunger you gave them bread from heaven, and for their thirst you brought water for them out of the rock, and you told them to go in to possess the land that you swore to give them.

16 "But they and our ancestors acted presumptuously and stiffened their necks and did not obey your commandments; ¹⁷they refused to obey, and were not mindful of the wonders that you performed among them; but they stiffened their necks and determined to return to their slavery in Egypt. But

you are a God ready to forgive, gracious and merciful, slow to anger and abounding in steadfast love, and you did not forsake them. ¹⁸Even when they had cast an image of a calf for themselves and said, 'This is your God who brought you up out of Egypt,' and had committed great blasphemies, ¹⁹you in your great mercies did not forsake them in the wilderness; the pillar of cloud that led them in the way did not leave them by day, nor the pillar of fire by night that gave them light on the way by which they should go. ²⁰You gave your good spirit to instruct them, and did not withhold your manna from their mouths, and gave them water for their thirst. ²¹Forty years you sustained them in the wilderness so that they lacked nothing; their clothes did not wear out and their feet did not swell. ²²And you gave them kingdoms and peoples, and allotted to them every corner,*ᵇ* so they took possession of the land of King Sihon of Heshbon and the land of King Og of Bashan. ²³You multiplied their descendants like the stars of heaven, and brought them into the land that you had told their ancestors to enter and possess. ²⁴So the descendants went in and possessed the land, and you subdued before them the inhabitants of the land, the Canaanites, and gave them into their hands, with their kings and the peoples of the land, to do with them as they pleased. ²⁵And they captured fortress cities and a rich land, and took possession of houses filled with all sorts of goods, hewn cisterns, vineyards, olive orchards, and fruit trees in abundance; so they ate, and were filled and became fat, and delighted themselves in your great goodness.

26 "Nevertheless they were disobedient and rebelled against you and cast your law behind their backs and killed your prophets, who had warned them in order to turn them back to you, and they committed great blasphemies. ²⁷Therefore you gave them into the hands of their enemies, who made them suffer. Then in the time of their suffering they cried out to you and you heard them from heaven, and according to your great mercies you gave them saviors who saved them from

a Or *Sea of Reeds*   *b* Meaning of Heb uncertain

the hands of their enemies. 28But after they had rest, they again did evil before you, and you abandoned them to the hands of their enemies, so that they had dominion over them; yet when they turned and cried to you, you heard from heaven, and many times you rescued them according to your mercies. 29And you warned them in order to turn them back to your law. Yet they acted presumptuously and did not obey your commandments, but sinned against your ordinances, by the observance of which a person shall live. They turned a stubborn shoulder and stiffened their neck and would not obey. 30Many years you were patient with them, and warned them by your spirit through your prophets; yet they would not listen. Therefore you handed them over to the peoples of the lands. 31Nevertheless, in your great mercies you did not make an end of them or forsake them, for you are a gracious and merciful God.

32 "Now therefore, our God—the great and mighty and awesome God, keeping covenant and steadfast love—do not treat lightly all the hardship that has come upon us, upon our kings, our officials, our priests, our prophets, our ancestors, and all your people, since the time of the kings of Assyria until today. 33You have been just in all that has come upon us, for you have dealt faithfully and we have acted wickedly; 34our kings, our officials, our priests, and our ancestors have not kept your law or heeded the commandments and the warnings that you gave them. 35Even in their own kingdom, and in the great goodness you bestowed on them, and in the large and rich land that you set before them, they did not serve you and did not turn from their wicked works. 36Here we are, slaves to this day—slaves in the land that you gave to our ancestors to enjoy its fruit and its good gifts. 37Its rich yield goes to the kings whom you have set over us because of our sins; they have power also over our bodies and over our livestock at their pleasure, and we are in great distress."

38*a* Because of all this we make a firm agreement in writing, and on that sealed document are inscribed the names of our officials, our Levites, and our priests.

9.9–38. 32: *Keeping covenant* and steadfast love* emphasizes God's enduring relationship with Israel. *Do not treat lightly all the hardship that has come upon us* is an appeal that God not add to the community's burden but accept the deep contrition being expressed. **36:** *Here we are, slaves to this day:* Though overly dramatic, the community most likely did find itself in a bound condition under imperial constraints. **38:** *We make a firm agreement:* The confession has noted the community's present predicament, which now calls for a response that takes the law very seriously, not repeating the sins of the past. To commit to the agreement *in writing* further affirms the serious intent here. The author has made this intent more apparent by listing the names of the community leadership affirming this covenant in 10.1–27. Surprisingly, Ezra is absent from the list.

10 *b*Upon the sealed document are the names of Nehemiah the governor, son of Hacaliah, and Zedekiah; 2Seraiah, Azariah, Jeremiah, 3Pashhur, Amariah, Malchijah, 4Hattush, Shebaniah, Malluch, 5Harim, Meremoth, Obadiah, 6Daniel, Ginnethon, Baruch, 7Meshullam, Abijah, Mijamin, 8Maaziah, Bilgai, Shemaiah; these are the priests. 9And the Levites: Jeshua son of Azaniah, Binnui of the sons of Henadad, Kadmiel; 10and their associates, Shebaniah, Hodiah, Kelita, Pelaiah, Hanan, 11Mica, Rehob, Hashabiah, 12Zaccur, Sherebiah, Shebaniah, 13Hodiah, Bani, Beninu. 14The leaders of the people: Parosh, Pahath-moab, Elam, Zattu, Bani, 15Bunni, Azgad, Bebai, 16Adonijah, Bigvai, Adin, 17Ater, Hezekiah, Azzur, 18Hodiah, Hashum, Bezai, 19Hariph, Anathoth, Nebai, 20Magpiash, Meshullam, Hezir, 21Meshezabel, Zadok, Jaddua, 22Pelatiah, Hanan, Anaiah, 23Hoshea, Hananiah, Hasshub, 24Hallohesh, Pilha, Shobek, 25Rehum, Hashabnah, Maaseiah, 26Ahiah, Hanan, Anan, 27Malluch, Harim, and Baanah.

28 The rest of the people, the priests, the Levites, the gatekeepers, the singers, the temple servants, and all who have separated themselves from the peoples of the lands to adhere to the law of God, their wives, their

a Ch 10.1 in Heb   *b* Ch 10.2 in Heb

sons, their daughters, all who have knowledge and understanding, ²⁹join with their kin, their nobles, and enter into a curse and an oath to walk in God's law, which was given by Moses the servant of God, and to observe and do all the commandments of the LORD our Lord and his ordinances and his statutes. ³⁰We will not give our daughters to the peoples of the land or take their daughters for our sons; ³¹and if the peoples of the land bring in merchandise or any grain on the sabbath day to sell, we will not buy it from them on the sabbath or on a holy day; and we will forego the crops of the seventh year and the exaction of every debt.

32 We also lay on ourselves the obligation to charge ourselves yearly one-third of a shekel for the service of the house of our God: ³³for the rows of bread, the regular grain offering, the regular burnt offering, the sabbaths, the new moons, the appointed festivals, the sacred donations, and the sin offerings to make atonement for Israel, and for all the work of the house of our God. ³⁴We have also cast lots among the priests, the Levites, and the people, for the wood offering, to bring it into the house of our God, by ancestral houses, at appointed times, year by year, to burn on the altar of the LORD our God, as it is written in the law. ³⁵We obligate ourselves to bring the first fruits of our soil and the first fruits of all fruit of every tree, year by year, to the house of the LORD; ³⁶also to bring to the house of our God, to the priests who minister in the house of our God, the firstborn of our sons and of our livestock, as it is written in the law, and the firstlings of our herds and of our flocks; ³⁷and to bring the first of our dough, and our contributions, the fruit of every tree, the wine and the oil, to the priests, to the chambers of the house of our God; and to bring to the Levites the tithes from our soil, for it is the Levites who collect the tithes in all our rural towns. ³⁸And the priest, the descendant of Aaron, shall be with the Levites when the Levites receive the tithes; and the Levites shall bring up a tithe of the tithes to the house of our God, to the chambers of the storehouse. ³⁹For the people of Israel and the sons of Levi shall bring the contribution of grain, wine, and oil to the storerooms where the vessels of the sanctuary are, and where the priests that minister, and the gatekeepers and the singers are. We will not neglect the house of our God.

10.28–39: The terms of the covenant.* Having made an extensive confession before God, the community now offers a solemn covenant that covers a wide range of obligations. All these will reform the community and bring it into accord with the law of God. **28:** *The rest of the people,* that is, other than the named signatories. **30:** *We will not give our daughters . . . take their daughters:* The first major commitment is to oppose intermarriage and cease its practice. The dissolution of existing ethnically mixed marriages is not called for. **31:** *We will not buy . . . on the sabbath or on a holy day:* This involves observing the sabbath with new rigor, since the law does not prohibit buying on the sabbath, though selling on the sabbath may have been customarily forbidden (Am 8.5). *Forego the crops of the seventh year:* Crop land is to receive a sabbath (Lev 25.1–7), combined with rules regarding the release of debts (Deut 15.1–18). These rules had not previously been linked. **32:** *One-third of a shekel:*✶ This was an annual Temple✶ tax that continued into the Roman period (Mt 17.24–27). The Temple tax was instituted after the Exile✶ since there was no source of regular royal underwriting of Temple functions. **34:** The community also commits to supply the *wood offering* to support the Temple service. **35:** *First fruits:* While the first cuttings of grain are specified in the law (Deut 26.1–11), no provision is required for the produce of fruit trees. The remaining obligations commit the community to the support of various aspects of Temple service. **39:** The main thrust of this covenant✶ extends the coverage of the law, placing a larger sphere of life into the realm of the holy as part of service for the *house of our God.*

11 Now the leaders of the people lived in Jerusalem; and the rest of the people cast lots to bring one out of ten to live in the holy city Jerusalem, while nine-tenths remained in the other towns. ²And the people blessed all those who willingly offered to live in Jerusalem.

3 These are the leaders of the province who lived in Jerusalem; but in the towns of Judah all lived on their property in their towns: Israel, the priests, the Levites, the

temple servants, and the descendants of Solomon's servants. [4]And in Jerusalem lived some of the Judahites and of the Benjaminites. Of the Judahites: Athaiah son of Uzziah son of Zechariah son of Amariah son of Shephatiah son of Mahalalel, of the descendants of Perez; [5]and Maaseiah son of Baruch son of Col-hozeh son of Hazaiah son of Adaiah son of Joiarib son of Zechariah son of the Shilonite. [6]All the descendants of Perez who lived in Jerusalem were four hundred sixty-eight valiant warriors.

7 And these are the Benjaminites: Sallu son of Meshullam son of Joed son of Pedaiah son of Kolaiah son of Maaseiah son of Ithiel son of Jeshaiah. [8]And his brothers[a] Gabbai, Sallai: nine hundred twenty-eight. [9]Joel son of Zichri was their overseer; and Judah son of Hassenuah was second in charge of the city.

10 Of the priests: Jedaiah son of Joiarib, Jachin, [11]Seraiah son of Hilkiah son of Meshullam son of Zadok son of Meraioth son of Ahitub, officer of the house of God, [12]and their associates who did the work of the house, eight hundred twenty-two; and Adaiah son of Jeroham son of Pelaliah son of Amzi son of Zechariah son of Pashhur son of Malchijah, [13]and his associates, heads of ancestral houses, two hundred forty-two; and Amashsai son of Azarel son of Ahzai son of Meshillemoth son of Immer, [14]and their associates, valiant warriors, one hundred twenty-eight; their overseer was Zabdiel son of Haggedolim.

15 And of the Levites: Shemaiah son of Hasshub son of Azrikam son of Hashabiah son of Bunni; [16]and Shabbethai and Jozabad, of the leaders of the Levites, who were over the outside work of the house of God; [17]and Mattaniah son of Mica son of Zabdi son of Asaph, who was the leader to begin the thanksgiving in prayer, and Bakbukiah, the second among his associates; and Abda son of Shammua son of Galal son of Jeduthun. [18]All the Levites in the holy city were two hundred eighty-four.

19 The gatekeepers, Akkub, Talmon and their associates, who kept watch at the gates, were one hundred seventy-two. [20]And the rest of Israel, and of the priests and the Levites, were in all the towns of Judah, all of them in their inheritance. [21]But the temple servants lived on Ophel; and Ziha and Gishpa were over the temple servants.

22 The overseer of the Levites in Jerusalem was Uzzi son of Bani son of Hashabiah son of Mattaniah son of Mica, of the descendants of Asaph, the singers, in charge of the work of the house of God. [23]For there was a command from the king concerning them, and a settled provision for the singers, as was required every day. [24]And Pethahiah son of Meshezabel, of the descendants of Zerah son of Judah, was at the king's hand in all matters concerning the people.

11.1–24: **The community repopulates Jerusalem.** Further focusing on the community's dedication to the law, this section depicts the repopulation of Jerusalem, ending with another lengthy list of those who moved into Jerusalem. **1:** *One out of ten:* This applies the tithe (Deut 12.17) to the community's total population. This is the first time Jerusalem is called *the holy city,* an extension of the Temple* precinct's sacredness to the entire city now that it is marked by the completed walls. **2:** *The people blessed . . . live in Jerusalem:* The community's desire to undertake this task is emphasized. The listing that follows offers leaders (divided into those of Judah and Benjamin), priests, Levites, and gatekeepers.

25 And as for the villages, with their fields, some of the people of Judah lived in Kiriath-arba and its villages, and in Dibon and its villages, and in Jekabzeel and its villages, [26]and in Jeshua and in Moladah and Beth-pelet, [27]in Hazar-shual, in Beer-sheba and its villages, [28]in Ziklag, in Meconah and its villages, [29]in En-rimmon, in Zorah, in Jarmuth, [30]Zanoah, Adullam, and their villages, Lachish and its fields, and Azekah and its villages. So they camped from Beer-sheba to the valley of Hinnom. [31]The people of Benjamin also lived from Geba onward, at Michmash, Aija, Bethel and its villages, [32]Anathoth, Nob, Ananiah, [33]Hazor, Ramah, Gittaim, [34]Hadid, Zeboim, Neballat, [35]Lod, and Ono, the valley of artisans. [36]And cer-

a Gk Mss: Heb *And after him*

tain divisions of the Levites in Judah were joined to Benjamin.

11.25–36: A note about villages outside Jerusalem. This brief account touches on some of the settlements outside Jerusalem that constituted the territory of Judah. Several of the places on the list were not settled by Jews until the Hellenistic* period, so this list may be an idealized fiction, approximating the settlements of Judah as described in the tribal allotments of the book of Joshua (Josh 15.1–12). In effect, this makes the same point as the notice of the Festival of Booths earlier (8.17).

12 These are the priests and the Levites who came up with Zerubbabel son of Shealtiel, and Jeshua: Seraiah, Jeremiah, Ezra, 2Amariah, Malluch, Hattush, 3Shecaniah, Rehum, Meremoth, 4Iddo, Ginnethoi, Abijah, 5Mijamin, Maadiah, Bilgah, 6Shemaiah, Joiarib, Jedaiah, 7Sallu, Amok, Hilkiah, Jedaiah. These were the leaders of the priests and of their associates in the days of Jeshua.

8 And the Levites: Jeshua, Binnui, Kadmiel, Sherebiah, Judah, and Mattaniah, who with his associates was in charge of the songs of thanksgiving. 9And Bakbukiah and Unno their associates stood opposite them in the service. 10Jeshua was the father of Joiakim, Joiakim the father of Eliashib, Eliashib the father of Joiada, 11Joiada the father of Jonathan, and Jonathan the father of Jaddua.

12 In the days of Joiakim the priests, heads of ancestral houses, were: of Seraiah, Meraiah; of Jeremiah, Hananiah; 13of Ezra, Meshullam; of Amariah, Jehohanan; 14of Malluchi, Jonathan; of Shebaniah, Joseph; 15of Harim, Adna; of Meraioth, Helkai; 16of Iddo, Zechariah; of Ginnethon, Meshullam; 17of Abijah, Zichri; of Miniamin, of Moadiah, Piltai; 18of Bilgah, Shammua; of Shemaiah, Jehonathan; 19of Joiarib, Mattenai; of Jedaiah, Uzzi; 20of Sallai, Kallai; of Amok, Eber; 21of Hilkiah, Hashabiah; of Jedaiah, Nethanel.

22 As for the Levites, in the days of Eliashib, Joiada, Johanan, and Jaddua, there were recorded the heads of ancestral houses; also the priests until the reign of Darius the Persian. 23The Levites, heads of ancestral houses, were recorded in the Book of the Annals until the days of Johanan son of Eliashib. 24And the leaders of the Levites: Hashabiah, Sherebiah, and Jeshua son of Kadmiel, with their associates over against them, to praise and to give thanks, according to the commandment of David the man of God, section opposite to section. 25Mattaniah, Bakbukiah, Obadiah, Meshullam, Talmon, and Akkub were gatekeepers standing guard at the storehouses of the gates. 26These were in the days of Joiakim son of Jeshua son of Jozadak, and in the days of the governor Nehemiah and of the priest Ezra, the scribe.

12.1–26: List of priests and Levites. Though the list appears fairly well organized (priests and Levites from the time of the return, vv. 1–9; high priests during the period of the sixth to fifth centuries, vv. 10–11; priests and Levites from the generation after the return, vv. 12–25; and a chronological summary, v. 26), there is evidence the lists have been expanded over time. While the question of sources and historicity are highly debated, the list in its present position serves to emphasize the sacred character of the newly populated holy city. **24:** *According to the commandment of David:* See the account in 1 Chr 23.30, where David sets several families of Levites aside for this purpose.

27 Now at the dedication of the wall of Jerusalem they sought out the Levites in all their places, to bring them to Jerusalem to celebrate the dedication with rejoicing, with thanksgivings and with singing, with cymbals, harps, and lyres. 28The companies of the singers gathered together from the circuit around Jerusalem and from the villages of the Netophathites; 29also from Beth-gilgal and from the region of Geba and Azmaveth; for the singers had built for themselves villages around Jerusalem. 30And the priests and the Levites purified themselves; and they purified the people and the gates and the wall.

31 Then I brought the leaders of Judah up onto the wall, and appointed two great companies that gave thanks and went in procession. One went to the right on the wall to the Dung Gate; 32and after them went Hoshaiah and half the officials of Judah, 33and

Azariah, Ezra, Meshullam, 34Judah, Benjamin, Shemaiah, and Jeremiah, 35and some of the young priests with trumpets: Zechariah son of Jonathan son of Shemaiah son of Mattaniah son of Micaiah son of Zaccur son of Asaph; 36and his kindred, Shemaiah, Azarel, Milalai, Gilalai, Maai, Nethanel, Judah, and Hanani, with the musical instruments of David the man of God; and the scribe Ezra went in front of them. 37At the Fountain Gate, in front of them, they went straight up by the stairs of the city of David, at the ascent of the wall, above the house of David, to the Water Gate on the east.

38 The other company of those who gave thanks went to the left,*a* and I followed them with half of the people on the wall, above the Tower of the Ovens, to the Broad Wall, 39and above the Gate of Ephraim, and by the Old Gate, and by the Fish Gate and the Tower of Hananel and the Tower of the Hundred, to the Sheep Gate; and they came to a halt at the Gate of the Guard. 40So both companies of those who gave thanks stood in the house of God, and I and half of the officials with me; 41and the priests Eliakim, Maaseiah, Miniamin, Micaiah, Elioenai, Zechariah, and Hananiah, with trumpets; 42and Maaseiah, Shemaiah, Eleazar, Uzzi, Jehohanan, Malchijah, Elam, and Ezer. And the singers sang with Jezrahiah as their leader. 43They offered great sacrifices that day and rejoiced, for God had made them rejoice with great joy; the women and children also rejoiced. The joy of Jerusalem was heard far away.

12.27–43: The dedication of Jerusalem's walls. This section briefly returns to a first-person style, similar to the other sections of the "Nehemiah memoir." It recounts the elaborate dedication ceremony, with the community divided into two large portions processing along the walls until they meet by the Temple.* The dedication is given a religious dimension with priests and Levites actively participating in the ceremony. **27:** *They sought out the Levites in all their places:* The Levites, who lived in common villages, were needed to ensure the full complement of music and praise. **30:** *Purified themselves:* A necessary preparatory step for a religious ceremony. Also necessary was the purification of *the people,* though purifying the *gates and*

walls represents a new level of concern for correctness. Such an act extends the arena of God's presence from the Temple to the entire walled city. **36:** *And the scribe* Ezra *went in front* in recognition of the importance of his contributions to the community. **40:** *Both companies . . . stood in the house of God:* No formal entry into the Temple itself has preceded this point. This makes more sense if the entire walled city is being considered the "house of God." **43:** *The joy of Jerusalem was heard:* This offers a conclusion to the rejoicing and jubilation the community had experienced.

44 On that day men were appointed over the chambers for the stores, the contributions, the first fruits, and the tithes, to gather into them the portions required by the law for the priests and for the Levites from the fields belonging to the towns; for Judah rejoiced over the priests and the Levites who ministered. 45They performed the service of their God and the service of purification, as did the singers and the gatekeepers, according to the command of David and his son Solomon. 46For in the days of David and Asaph long ago there was a leader of the singers, and there were songs of praise and thanksgiving to God. 47In the days of Zerubbabel and in the days of Nehemiah all Israel gave the daily portions for the singers and the gatekeepers. They set apart that which was for the Levites; and the Levites set apart that which was for the descendants of Aaron.

12.44–47: The community ensures Temple* service. Shifting back to a third-person narrative, this section recounts efforts the community made to ensure that the contributions to the Temple stores were properly accounted for. The focus is exclusively on the community and its support for the Temple personnel. **44:** *Men were appointed:* The appointment was by the consensus of the community, not by an individual. Being *over* the stores included the inventorying and redistribution of offerings. Such care was taken because *Judah rejoiced over the priests and the Levites who ministered.* Taking care over the offerings that support these persons was an act of thanksgiving for the joy worship provided to the community. **47:** *The daily portions:* The offering that provided daily rations to the Temple personnel. Paralleling *Zerubbabel,* who rebuilt

a Cn: Heb *opposite*

the Temple, and *Nehemiah*, who rebuilt the walls of Jerusalem, serves the same function as Ezra 1–6 served in mixing the two efforts together: The rebuilding of the walls and subsequent solemn covenant* reformed the house of God just as the physical rebuilding of the building did. To speak of Nehemiah in this manner makes it sound like his term as governor is over.

13 On that day they read from the book of Moses in the hearing of the people; and in it was found written that no Ammonite or Moabite should ever enter the assembly of God, ²because they did not meet the Israelites with bread and water, but hired Balaam against them to curse them—yet our God turned the curse into a blessing. ³When the people heard the law, they separated from Israel all those of foreign descent.

13.1–3: The separation of foreigners. Slipping back into a first-person form, this brief notice highlights again the now sacred character of the community as a whole. **1:** *On that day* is unclear, but in context it must mean on the day of the dedication of the walls. *No Ammonite or Moabite should ever enter the assembly of God* refers to Deut 23.3–6, where "the assembly of God" is the worshipping community appearing in the Temple.* **3:** *They separated from Israel all those of foreign descent,* presumably including non-Ammonite and non-Moabite persons. The Deuteronomic law is being extended to the community as a whole, not just the worshipping body, and to all foreigners, not just Ammonites and Moabites. This marks a further redefinition of the community as a sacred body. Note that intermarriage is not raised here.

THE POSTLOGUE

13.4–31: Having described the communal confession of sin, the entry into a solemn covenant,* the dedication of the walls, and the redefinition of the community as the "house of God," it remains for the author to clarify what happened to Nehemiah. This postlogue offers a sort of conclusion to Nehemiah's mission, showing the reformer forcefully addressing a number of wrongs in the community. The section as a whole is based on the covenant contents of ch. 10, but in reverse order. For example, where the covenant begins with a vow to end intermarriage (10.30), the present section ends with the same issue (vv. 23–27).

Nemehiah's efforts are aimed at trying to get the community to live up to its own promises.

4 Now before this, the priest Eliashib, who was appointed over the chambers of the house of our God, and who was related to Tobiah, ⁵prepared for Tobiah a large room where they had previously put the grain offering, the frankincense, the vessels, and the tithes of grain, wine, and oil, which were given by commandment to the Levites, singers, and gatekeepers, and the contributions for the priests. ⁶While this was taking place I was not in Jerusalem, for in the thirty-second year of King Artaxerxes of Babylon I went to the king. After some time I asked leave of the king ⁷and returned to Jerusalem. I then discovered the wrong that Eliashib had done on behalf of Tobiah, preparing a room for him in the courts of the house of God. ⁸And I was very angry, and I threw all the household furniture of Tobiah out of the room. ⁹Then I gave orders and they cleansed the chambers, and I brought back the vessels of the house of God, with the grain offering and the frankincense.

10 I also found out that the portions of the Levites had not been given to them; so that the Levites and the singers, who had conducted the service, had gone back to their fields. ¹¹So I remonstrated with the officials and said, "Why is the house of God forsaken?" And I gathered them together and set them in their stations. ¹²Then all Judah brought the tithe of the grain, wine, and oil into the storehouses. ¹³And I appointed as treasurers over the storehouses the priest Shelemiah, the scribe Zadok, and Pedaiah of the Levites, and as their assistant Hanan son of Zaccur son of Mattaniah, for they were considered faithful; and their duty was to distribute to their associates. ¹⁴Remember me, O my God, concerning this, and do not wipe out my good deeds that I have done for the house of my God and for his service.

15 In those days I saw in Judah people treading wine presses on the sabbath, and bringing in heaps of grain and loading them on donkeys; and also wine, grapes, figs, and all kinds of burdens, which they brought into Jerusalem on the sabbath day; and I warned

them at that time against selling food. ¹⁶Tyrians also, who lived in the city, brought in fish and all kinds of merchandise and sold them on the sabbath to the people of Judah, and in Jerusalem. ¹⁷Then I remonstrated with the nobles of Judah and said to them, "What is this evil thing that you are doing, profaning the sabbath day? ¹⁸Did not your ancestors act in this way, and did not our God bring all this disaster on us and on this city? Yet you bring more wrath on Israel by profaning the sabbath."

19 When it began to be dark at the gates of Jerusalem before the sabbath, I commanded that the doors should be shut and gave orders that they should not be opened until after the sabbath. And I set some of my servants over the gates, to prevent any burden from being brought in on the sabbath day. ²⁰Then the merchants and sellers of all kinds of merchandise spent the night outside Jerusalem once or twice. ²¹But I warned them and said to them, "Why do you spend the night in front of the wall? If you do so again, I will lay hands on you." From that time on they did not come on the sabbath. ²²And I commanded the Levites that they should purify themselves and come and guard the gates, to keep the sabbath day holy. Remember this also in my favor, O my God, and spare me according to the greatness of your steadfast love.

23 In those days also I saw Jews who had married women of Ashdod, Ammon, and Moab; ²⁴and half of their children spoke the language of Ashdod, and they could not speak the language of Judah, but spoke the language of various peoples. ²⁵And I contended with them and cursed them and beat some of them and pulled out their hair; and I made them take an oath in the name of God, saying, "You shall not give your daughters to their sons, or take their daughters for your sons or for yourselves. ²⁶Did not King Solomon of Israel sin on account of such women? Among the many nations there was no king like him, and he was beloved by his God, and God made him king over all Israel; nevertheless, foreign women made even him to sin. ²⁷Shall we then listen to you and do all this great evil and act treacherously

against our God by marrying foreign women?"

28 And one of the sons of Jehoiada, son of the high priest Eliashib, was the son-in-law of Sanballat the Horonite; I chased him away from me. ²⁹Remember them, O my God, because they have defiled the priesthood, the covenant of the priests and the Levites.

30 Thus I cleansed them from everything foreign, and I established the duties of the priests and Levites, each in his work; ³¹and I provided for the wood offering, at appointed times, and for the first fruits. Remember me, O my God, for good.

13.4–31. 5: *Prepared for Tobiah a large room* in the Temple* precinct: Tobiah was not only one of Nehemiah's primary adversaries, but was an Ammonite, a group to be excluded from the Temple (13.1–2). *They had previously put the grain offering* suggests that the offerings are not coming in as they had been, allowing for the room to be put to other uses. 6: *I was not in Jerusalem:* Nehemiah apparently was called back to the court for reasons not directly relating to his governance of the district. The *thirty-second year* of Artaxerxes would be 432 BCE. 8: *I was very angry:* By making such a public show, Nehemiah may have been hoping to bring the priest Eliashib, a relative of Tobiah, under control. This entire incident is a follow-up to the actions of the community in 13.1–3. 10: *The portions of the Levites had not been given to them:* This is contrary to the pledge made in 10.35–39 not to "neglect the house of our God." It also specifically violates the pledges made in 12.44–47 to ensure the singers could remain at their posts. 17: *Profaning the sabbath day?* This is contrary to the pledges made in 10.31 to keep the sabbath, even if foreign merchants come with goods to sell. 19: *I set some of my servants over the gates,* apparently to ensure that Nehemiah's orders to shut the city gates at the beginning of the sabbath were fulfilled. Cordoning off the city on the sabbath makes the entire city a holy precinct on that day. 22: This explains why Nehemiah commands the *Levites that they should purify themselves and come and guard the gates.* With the entire community turned into a "house of God," the Levites should guard the entryways just as they had previously guarded the entrances into the Temple precincts. 27: *This great evil:* Just as in Ezra, the intermarriage of the community with the surrounding peoples is portrayed in graphic terms as a most serious violation of divine order. The discovery of intermarriage was contrary to the pledges of the community in 10.30. While in ch. 10 the community voluntarily takes on an oath, here Nehemiah made them take an oath, with a strong public display of anger. **28:** *One of the sons of Jehoiada:* Just as Tobiah's relationship to certain of the priests presented a problem at the beginning of this section, now Sanballat's relationship to a member of the high priestly family presents another challenge. **30:** *I cleansed them from everything foreign:* The community, as a "house of God," has been cleansed of patterns that would pull them away from their strict observance of the law. Just as David and Solomon made specific provisions for the care of the Temple personnel, Nehemiah places himself in the same company for establishing *the duties of the priests and Levites, each in his work.* **31:** *For good,* that is, all the good that Nehemiah has accomplished on behalf of the community.

SHORT STORIES

The Old Testament contains literature about numerous characters. Genesis 25.16–37.1 has sometimes been called the story of Jacob while 1 Samuel 16–2 Kings 2.12 could be titled the story of David. In both cases, these chapters that narrate the life of a major figure are integrally embedded in larger narratives* and would be would be difficult to read in isolation from them. In contrast, there are stories that stand apart, either as separate books (Ruth, Jon, Esth, Tob, Jdt) or as relatively independent from their context (Dan 1–6, Sus, Bel). (Some interpreters* would include the Joseph short story here as well.) Although these books were written at different times and offer no uniform theological perspective, scholars have characterized them as short stories or novellas, primarily because of their relative brevity and their interest in a primary character. They do not have the scope of the narratives about Moses or David, that is, following someone from birth or youth to death; the book of Tobit comes close, however. Rather, they typically focus on a discrete period in a person's life. That moment is often fraught with difficulty. As a result, many of the stories contain an element of suspense: Will Susanna surmount the false accusation made against her? Will Daniel die in the lion's den?

These short stories—or at least many of them—share some surprising features that distinguish them from other narratives in the Old Testament. As the names of Ruth, Esther, Judith, and Susanna demonstrate, women are more prominent in short stories than they are in other biblical prose narratives. In addition, the settings for the short stories are striking. Esther, Daniel, Jonah (at least for the second half of the story), Tobit, Bel and the Dragon, and Susanna are all set in Mesopotamia. And the first part of Ruth takes place in Moab. Several of the stories take place at a royal court. It would seem that the authors were particularly interested in exploring what it meant to be a Jew who must live, move, and have one's being in a foreign land. These stories explore both the challenges and the opportunities presented by life outside Syria-Palestine. That setting may also provide the occasion for rethinking traditional gender roles.

Wisdom literature* in the Old Testament shares many features with wisdom literature in both ancient Egypt and ancient Mesopotamia (see "Hebrew Poetry and Wisdom Literature," 730–732). In contrast, there is very little literature in the ancient Near East like the short story as it occurs in the Old Testament. The Wisdom of Ahikar,* a fifth-century BCE text written in Aramaic* and discovered in Egypt, offers a tale of court intrigue, which is then followed by a major collection of proverbs. The story itself recounts the fate of two courtiers, Nabusumiskum and Ahikar. When Sennacherib, the Assyrian king, wanted to kill Nabusumiskum, Ahikar hid him in his house. Later, Sennacherib's son, Esar-haddon, wanted to kill Ahikar, who then asked Nabusumiskum to reciprocate. This is one of the very few exemplars of literature comparable to the Old Testament short story.

Over time, the Old Testament novella developed in noteworthy ways. The book of Ruth, probably the earliest of the short stories, offers a fairly straightforward account about Ruth and Naomi using narrative and dialogue, whereas the later book of Esther displays greater attention to the development of Esther's character. Similar developments are also readily observable when one compares the narrative about Esther preserved in the Hebrew Bible with those present in Greek versions. The latter focus more on the beauty and deeply emotional qualities of Esther; they become more distinctly theological; and they reflect deep concern for Jewish piety. Just as one may speak of the history of the novel in the nineteenth and twentieth centuries, one may reflect about the development of the Old Testament short stories.

ESTHER

Introduction

Set in the royal court of Persia, the book of Esther recounts how, through a series of dramatic events, a Jewish woman becomes queen and uses her influence to win for her people the right to fight off a threat of genocide. The Jewish holiday of Purim, described at the end of the book, celebrates this victory. The book's festival theme groups it within the five "megilloth"★ (scrolls) of Jewish Scripture (along with Ruth, Lamentations, Song of Solomon, and Ecclesiastes). Esther is found among the historical books of the Christian canon.★

There are three ancient versions of the book of Esther: the Masoretic text★ (MT), a Jewish manuscript tradition from the Middle Ages; the Septuagint,★ a Greek version from an earlier period; and another Greek manuscript tradition called the A (or Alpha) Text. The MT is the shortest of the versions and is printed here. The longer Septuagint version is accepted as canon by Roman Catholic and Orthodox Christians and is found in the Apocryphal★/deuterocanonical★ books.

Because details from the book do not easily fit with historical information about the Persian king Xerxes (called in the MT Ahasuerus and in the Septuagint Artaxerxes), the book is best considered "historical fiction." Its acceptance (mixed with gentle mockery) of foreign rule, along with lack of concern with the land of Israel, suggests that it was written in the Diaspora★ (communities living outside of Israel), perhaps late in the Persian era★ (the fourth or early third century BCE).

READING GUIDE

The reader is well served to notice the exaggerated features of the narrative★—the extended period of banqueting, the wild mood swings of Ahasuerus and Haman, the use of royal edicts to control interpersonal disputes, and Esther's year-long beauty treatment. What image was the author painting of the Persian court? Noting that Esther is one of the few biblical books named for a woman, modern readers often ponder the gender message of the book. Is Esther a passive woman, bowing to her uncle and subordinating her life to that of others? Does she grow into her own power as the book continues? Since the book does not mention the name of God, a key to its theology may be the "coincidences" that work to the benefit of the Jewish people.

1–2	Esther becomes queen instead of Vashti; Mordecai thwarts a plot
3–8	Esther counters Haman's plot to destroy the Jews
9.1–16	The Jews fight their enemies
9.17–10.3	Purim is instituted and decrees are sent

1 This happened in the days of Ahasuerus, the same Ahasuerus who ruled over one hundred twenty-seven provinces from India to Ethiopia.[a] 2In those days when King Ahasuerus sat on his royal throne in the citadel of Susa, 3in the third year of his reign, he gave a banquet for all his officials and ministers. The army of Persia and Media and the nobles and governors of the provinces were present, 4while he displayed the great

a Or Nubia; Heb Cush

wealth of his kingdom and the splendor and pomp of his majesty for many days, one hundred eighty days in all.

5 When these days were completed, the king gave for all the people present in the citadel of Susa, both great and small, a banquet lasting for seven days, in the court of the garden of the king's palace. 6There were white cotton curtains and blue hangings tied with cords of fine linen and purple to silver rings[a] and marble pillars. There were couches of gold and silver on a mosaic pavement of porphyry, marble, mother-of-pearl, and colored stones. 7Drinks were served in golden goblets, goblets of different kinds, and the royal wine was lavished according to the bounty of the king. 8Drinking was by flagons, without restraint; for the king had given orders to all the officials of his palace to do as each one desired. 9Furthermore, Queen Vashti gave a banquet for the women in the palace of King Ahasuerus.

1.1–9: In the royal court. 1: *Ahasuerus* is usually identified with Xerxes I (486–465 BCE). "Satrapies" is the more usual description of Persian administrative units than *provinces. One hundred twenty-seven* does not correspond to any reckoning known outside the Bible. **2:** *Susa,* at the foot of the Zagros mountains, was one of three royal residences. It consisted of a *citadel,* or fortified city (enclosed with gates), and an unfortified lower city. **3:** *Media* was a large province of the Achaemenid *Persian* empire. **4–8:** The extended period of banqueting, as well as the extensive list of furnishings, paints a picture of a lavish, extravagant gentile* (non-Jewish) court. **9:** *Vashti* is not mentioned in Persian literature. Although the Greek historian Herodotus reports that Persian men and women banqueted together, Vashti's separate banquet explains to the reader why she must be summoned, and the heavy drinking of the all-male audience may suggest the danger Vashti faced in appearing before them.

---

10 On the seventh day, when the king was merry with wine, he commanded Mehuman, Biztha, Harbona, Bigtha and Abagtha, Zethar and Carkas, the seven eunuchs who attended him, 11to bring Queen Vashti before the king, wearing the royal crown, in order to show the peoples and the officials her beauty; for she was fair to behold. 12But

Queen Vashti refused to come at the king's command conveyed by the eunuchs. At this the king was enraged, and his anger burned within him.

13 Then the king consulted the sages who knew the laws[b] (for this was the king's procedure toward all who were versed in law and custom, 14and those next to him were Carshena, Shethar, Admatha, Tarshish, Meres, Marsena, and Memucan, the seven officials of Persia and Media, who had access to the king, and sat first in the kingdom): 15"According to the law, what is to be done to Queen Vashti because she has not performed the command of King Ahasuerus conveyed by the eunuchs?" 16Then Memucan said in the presence of the king and the officials, "Not only has Queen Vashti done wrong to the king, but also to all the officials and all the peoples who are in all the provinces of King Ahasuerus. 17For this deed of the queen will be made known to all women, causing them to look with contempt on their husbands, since they will say, 'King Ahasuerus commanded Queen Vashti to be brought before him, and she did not come.' 18This very day the noble ladies of Persia and Media who have heard of the queen's behavior will rebel against[c] the king's officials, and there will be no end of contempt and wrath! 19If it pleases the king, let a royal order go out from him, and let it be written among the laws of the Persians and the Medes so that it may not be altered, that Vashti is never again to come before King Ahasuerus; and let the king give her royal position to another who is better than she. 20So when the decree made by the king is proclaimed throughout all his kingdom, vast as it is, all women will give honor to their husbands, high and low alike."

21 This advice pleased the king and the officials, and the king did as Memucan proposed; 22he sent letters to all the royal provinces, to every province in its own script and to every people in its own language, declaring that every man should be master in his own house.[d]

a Or *rods*　　*b* Cn: Heb *times*　　*c* Cn: Heb *will tell*　　*d* Heb adds *and speak according to the language of his people*

1.10–22: Vashti refuses. 10: Throughout the book, *eunuchs* (royal servants, often castrated) bridge gaps between men and women, royals and commoners, insiders and outsiders. **12:** The author gives neither the reason for Vashti's refusal nor a judgment on her decision. *The king was enraged:* Ahauserus (and later Haman) has a quick temper. **13–19:** The importance and permanence of Persian *laws* are themes of the book. As elsewhere, the king does not make his own decisions but defers to advisers and documents. *Memucan* the eunuch, not the king, makes the Vashti affair into a forum on women's subordination. **19:** While biblical tradition indicates that Persian law could not be altered (Dan 6.8), such a strategy would have been impractical. **22:** *In its own language:* The Persians generally accepted the ethnic diversity of their kingdom.

2 After these things, when the anger of King Ahasuerus had abated, he remembered Vashti and what she had done and what had been decreed against her. 2Then the king's servants who attended him said, "Let beautiful young virgins be sought out for the king. 3And let the king appoint commissioners in all the provinces of his kingdom to gather all the beautiful young virgins to the harem in the citadel of Susa under custody of Hegai, the king's eunuch, who is in charge of the women; let their cosmetic treatments be given them. 4And let the girl who pleases the king be queen instead of Vashti." This pleased the king, and he did so.

5 Now there was a Jew in the citadel of Susa whose name was Mordecai son of Jair son of Shimei son of Kish, a Benjaminite. 6Kish*a* had been carried away from Jerusalem among the captives carried away with King Jeconiah of Judah, whom King Nebuchadnezzar of Babylon had carried away. 7Mordecai*b* had brought up Hadassah, that is Esther, his cousin, for she had neither father nor mother; the girl was fair and beautiful, and when her father and her mother died, Mordecai adopted her as his own daughter. 8So when the king's order and his edict were proclaimed, and when many young women were gathered in the citadel of Susa in custody of Hegai, Esther also was taken into the king's palace and put in custody of Hegai, who had charge of the women.

9The girl pleased him and won his favor, and he quickly provided her with her cosmetic treatments and her portion of food, and with seven chosen maids from the king's palace, and advanced her and her maids to the best place in the harem. 10Esther did not reveal her people or kindred, for Mordecai had charged her not to tell. 11Every day Mordecai would walk around in front of the court of the harem, to learn how Esther was and how she fared.

2.1–11: Esther and Mordecai. 2–4: While according to Herodotus the Persian king could only marry from seven noble families, this account explains how a commoner, a Jewish one at that, could marry into royalty. **5–6:** The name *Mordecai* is similar to that of the Babylonian god Marduk. *Shimei, Kish,* and *Benjaminite* provide verbal links to King Saul (1 Sam 9.1; 2 Sam 16.5–8). The Hebrew reads that Mordecai was carried away by the Babylonians (see note *a*), making him over 100 years old. The NRSV suggests, instead, that *Kish* was carried into exile. **7:** *Hadassah,* the Jewish name, means "myrtle." *Esther* sounds similar to the Babylonian goddess Ishtar. **8–11:** Like Joseph (Gen 39.3) and Daniel (Dan 1.9), Esther wins favor in the royal court and is aided by a royal servant. Apparently Jewish identity was not obvious, and there is no mention of Esther's attempts at religious observances like kosher* food regulations.

12 The turn came for each girl to go in to King Ahasuerus, after being twelve months under the regulations for the women, since this was the regular period of their cosmetic treatment, six months with oil of myrrh and six months with perfumes and cosmetics for women. 13When the girl went in to the king she was given whatever she asked for to take with her from the harem to the king's palace. 14In the evening she went in; then in the morning she came back to the second harem in custody of Shaashgaz, the king's eunuch, who was in charge of the concubines; she did not go in to the king again, unless the king delighted in her and she was summoned by name.

15 When the turn came for Esther daughter of Abihail the uncle of Mordecai,

a Heb *a Benjamite* *6*who　*b* Heb *He*

who had adopted her as his own daughter, to go in to the king, she asked for nothing except what Hegai the king's eunuch, who had charge of the women, advised. Now Esther was admired by all who saw her. 16When Esther was taken to King Ahasuerus in his royal palace in the tenth month, which is the month of Tebeth, in the seventh year of his reign, 17the king loved Esther more than all the other women; of all the virgins she won his favor and devotion, so that he set the royal crown on her head and made her queen instead of Vashti. 18Then the king gave a great banquet to all his officials and ministers—"Esther's banquet." He also granted a holiday*a* to the provinces, and gave gifts with royal liberality.

19 When the virgins were being gathered together,*b* Mordecai was sitting at the king's gate. 20Now Esther had not revealed her kindred or her people, as Mordecai had charged her; for Esther obeyed Mordecai just as when she was brought up by him. 21In those days, while Mordecai was sitting at the king's gate, Bigthan and Teresh, two of the king's eunuchs, who guarded the threshold, became angry and conspired to assassinate*c* King Ahasuerus. 22But the matter came to the knowledge of Mordecai, and he told it to Queen Esther, and Esther told the king in the name of Mordecai. 23When the affair was investigated and found to be so, both the men were hanged on the gallows. It was recorded in the book of the annals in the presence of the king.

2.12–23: Esther's and Mordecai's successes. The elaborate procedures portray Esther's chances as a long shot. 15–18: With savvy Esther follows the instructions of the eunuch who has favored her. Her victory is celebrated by the fourth banquet of the book. 19–23: Mordecai's protection of the king, while not yet rewarded, will serve as his salvation from Haman's plot in ch. 6. 21: Threshold: Of the king's private room. Greek sources relate that Ahasuerus died from this type of conspiracy. Mordecai's access to the eunuchs may indicate that he held some official position.

3 After these things King Ahasuerus promoted Haman son of Hammedatha the Agagite, and advanced him and set his seat above all the officials who were with him. 2And all the king's servants who were at the king's gate bowed down and did obeisance to Haman; for the king had so commanded concerning him. But Mordecai did not bow down or do obeisance. 3Then the king's servants who were at the king's gate said to Mordecai, "Why do you disobey the king's command?" 4When they spoke to him day after day and he would not listen to them, they told Haman, in order to see whether Mordecai's words would avail; for he had told them that he was a Jew. 5When Haman saw that Mordecai did not bow down or do obeisance to him, Haman was infuriated. 6But he thought it beneath him to lay hands on Mordecai alone. So, having been told who Mordecai's people were, Haman plotted to destroy all the Jews, the people of Mordecai, throughout the whole kingdom of Ahasuerus.

7 In the first month, which is the month of Nisan, in the twelfth year of King Ahasuerus, they cast Pur—which means "the lot"—before Haman for the day and for the month, and the lot fell on the thirteenth day*d* of the twelfth month, which is the month of Adar. 8Then Haman said to King Ahasuerus, "There is a certain people scattered and separated among the peoples in all the provinces of your kingdom; their laws are different from those of every other people, and they do not keep the king's laws, so that it is not appropriate for the king to tolerate them. 9If it pleases the king, let a decree be issued for their destruction, and I will pay ten thousand talents of silver into the hands of those who have charge of the king's business, so that they may put it into the king's treasuries." 10So the king took his signet ring from his hand and gave it to Haman son of Hammedatha the Agagite, the enemy of the Jews. 11The king said to Haman, "The money is given to you, and the people as well, to do with them as it seems good to you."

12 Then the king's secretaries were summoned on the thirteenth day of the first

a Or an amnesty   *b* Heb adds a second time
c Heb to lay hands on   *d* Cn Compare Gk and verse 13 below: Heb the twelfth month

month, and an edict, according to all that Haman commanded, was written to the king's satraps and to the governors over all the provinces and to the officials of all the peoples, to every province in its own script and every people in its own language; it was written in the name of King Ahasuerus and sealed with the king's ring. 13Letters were sent by couriers to all the king's provinces, giving orders to destroy, to kill, and to annihilate all Jews, young and old, women and children, in one day, the thirteenth day of the twelfth month, which is the month of Adar, and to plunder their goods. 14A copy of the document was to be issued as a decree in every province by proclamation, calling on all the peoples to be ready for that day. 15The couriers went quickly by order of the king, and the decree was issued in the citadel of Susa. The king and Haman sat down to drink; but the city of Susa was thrown into confusion.

3.1–15: Mordecai angers Haman. 1: Haman's *Agagite* identity puts him in tension with the Benjaminite Mordecai (1 Sam 15.7–9). **2:** As in the case of Vashti's refusal, Mordecai's refusal to bow down is not explained. **4–6:** Mordecai having revealed his identity, Haman hatches a plan against all Jews. **7–11:** *Nisan:* As in other post-exilic books, month names are based on the Babylonian calendar.* *Pur:* Akkadian for "lot" (singular, unlike the English usage of "lots"). The date chosen for the pogrom* is 11 months hence. **8:** Haman does not identify the rebellious people, but argues their danger to the empire. **10:** *Signet ring:* Sign of royal authority. **11:** *As it seems good to you:* As usual, the king lets others decide. **12–15:** The *edict,* which bears all the royal trappings, allows destruction and plunder of the Jewish people. Coldly, the men drink after issuing a decree of death.

4 When Mordecai learned all that had been done, Mordecai tore his clothes and put on sackcloth and ashes, and went through the city, wailing with a loud and bitter cry; 2he went up to the entrance of the king's gate, for no one might enter the king's gate clothed with sackcloth. 3In every province, wherever the king's command and his decree came, there was great mourning among the Jews, with fasting and weeping and lamenting, and most of them lay in sackcloth and ashes.

4 When Esther's maids and her eunuchs came and told her, the queen was deeply distressed; she sent garments to clothe Mordecai, so that he might take off his sackcloth; but he would not accept them. 5Then Esther called for Hathach, one of the king's eunuchs, who had been appointed to attend her, and ordered him to go to Mordecai to learn what was happening and why. 6Hathach went out to Mordecai in the open square of the city in front of the king's gate, 7and Mordecai told him all that had happened to him, and the exact sum of money that Haman had promised to pay into the king's treasuries for the destruction of the Jews. 8Mordecai also gave him a copy of the written decree issued in Susa for their destruction, that he might show it to Esther, explain it to her, and charge her to go to the king to make supplication to him and entreat him for her people.

9 Hathach went and told Esther what Mordecai had said. 10Then Esther spoke to Hathach and gave him a message for Mordecai, saying, 11"All the king's servants and the people of the king's provinces know that if any man or woman goes to the king inside the inner court without being called, there is but one law—all alike are to be put to death. Only if the king holds out the golden scepter to someone, may that person live. I myself have not been called to come in to the king for thirty days." 12When they told Mordecai what Esther had said, 13Mordecai told them to reply to Esther, "Do not think that in the king's palace you will escape any more than all the other Jews. 14For if you keep silence at such a time as this, relief and deliverance will rise for the Jews from another quarter, but you and your father's family will perish. Who knows? Perhaps you have come to royal dignity for just such a time as this." 15Then Esther said in reply to Mordecai, 16"Go, gather all the Jews to be found in Susa, and hold a fast on my behalf, and neither eat nor drink for three days, night or day. I and my maids will also fast as you do. After that I will go to the king, though it is against the law; and if I perish, I perish." 17Mordecai

then went away and did everything as Esther had ordered him.

4.1–17: Mordecai petitions Esther. 1: *Torn clothes, sackcloth,** and *ashes* are typical gestures of mourning and distress. **4–5:** Why Esther was *distressed* is not explained: Did she fear for Mordecai's safety? **11:** Despite her status as queen, Esther remains under the authority of the king and of the ever present Persian law. **12–14:** Mordecai is the face of Esther's Jewishness. His speech reminds her that she shares the fate of her people. *Another quarter* may be a veiled reference to God, who is not named explicitly in the book. *Perhaps . . . for just such a time as this* summarizes the book's theme: Esther rises to power just in time to save the Jewish people. **16–17:** For the first time, Esther commands Mordecai, and he does everything she says (compare 2.20). The *fast* is one of the few religious observances in the book and prepares the people for the danger Esther is to face.

---

5 On the third day Esther put on her royal robes and stood in the inner court of the king's palace, opposite the king's hall. The king was sitting on his royal throne inside the palace opposite the entrance to the palace. 2As soon as the king saw Queen Esther standing in the court, she won his favor and he held out to her the golden scepter that was in his hand. Then Esther approached and touched the top of the scepter. 3The king said to her, "What is it, Queen Esther? What is your request? It shall be given you, even to the half of my kingdom." 4Then Esther said, "If it pleases the king, let the king and Haman come today to a banquet that I have prepared for the king." 5Then the king said, "Bring Haman quickly, so that we may do as Esther desires." So the king and Haman came to the banquet that Esther had prepared. 6While they were drinking wine, the king said to Esther, "What is your petition? It shall be granted you. And what is your request? Even to the half of my kingdom, it shall be fulfilled." 7Then Esther said, "This is my petition and request: 8If I have won the king's favor, and if it pleases the king to grant my petition and fulfill my request, let the king and Haman come tomorrow to the banquet that I will prepare for them, and then I will do as the king has said."

5.1–8: Esther requests two banquets. 1: Esther, while bold, shows respect for the king. **3:** *Half of my kingdom:* Another example of Ahasuerus's impulsive style. **4–5:** A clear strategist, Esther feeds the ego of both the king (throwing him a banquet) and Haman (honoring him with an invitation). **6–8:** Esther requests another banquet, the seventh of the book. By postponing her ultimate request, she leaves the reader in suspense and puffs up Haman, preparing him for a yet more dramatic fall.

---

9 Haman went out that day happy and in good spirits. But when Haman saw Mordecai in the king's gate, and observed that he neither rose nor trembled before him, he was infuriated with Mordecai; 10nevertheless Haman restrained himself and went home. Then he sent and called for his friends and his wife Zeresh, 11and Haman recounted to them the splendor of his riches, the number of his sons, all the promotions with which the king had honored him, and how he had advanced him above the officials and the ministers of the king. 12Haman added, "Even Queen Esther let no one but myself come with the king to the banquet that she prepared. Tomorrow also I am invited by her, together with the king. 13Yet all this does me no good so long as I see the Jew Mordecai sitting at the king's gate." 14Then his wife Zeresh and all his friends said to him, "Let a gallows fifty cubits high be made, and in the morning tell the king to have Mordecai hanged on it; then go with the king to the banquet in good spirits." This advice pleased Haman, and he had the gallows made.

5.9–14: Haman's mood swings. In good spirits after the queen has shown him honor, Haman is infuriated by Mordecai's repeated refusal to bow. **11:** Haman's bragging to people who already know him suggests an ego out of control. **14:** Because the pogrom* is still months from its execution, the plan to kill Mordecai immediately on a *gallows 50 cubits high* (75 ft!) leaves Haman in good spirits once again.

---

6 On that night the king could not sleep, and he gave orders to bring the book of records, the annals, and they were read to the king. 2It was found written how Mor-

decai had told about Bigthana and Teresh, two of the king's eunuchs, who guarded the threshold, and who had conspired to assassinate*a* King Ahasuerus. ³Then the king said, "What honor or distinction has been bestowed on Mordecai for this?" The king's servants who attended him said, "Nothing has been done for him." ⁴The king said, "Who is in the court?" Now Haman had just entered the outer court of the king's palace to speak to the king about having Mordecai hanged on the gallows that he had prepared for him. ⁵So the king's servants told him, "Haman is there, standing in the court." The king said, "Let him come in." ⁶So Haman came in, and the king said to him, "What shall be done for the man whom the king wishes to honor?" Haman said to himself, "Whom would the king wish to honor more than me?" ⁷So Haman said to the king, "For the man whom the king wishes to honor, ⁸let royal robes be brought, which the king has worn, and a horse that the king has ridden, with a royal crown on its head. ⁹Let the robes and the horse be handed over to one of the king's most noble officials; let him*b* robe the man whom the king wishes to honor, and let him*b* conduct the man on horseback through the open square of the city, proclaiming before him: 'Thus shall it be done for the man whom the king wishes to honor.'" ¹⁰Then the king said to Haman, "Quickly, take the robes and the horse, as you have said, and do so to the Jew Mordecai who sits at the king's gate. Leave out nothing that you have mentioned." ¹¹So Haman took the robes and the horse and robed Mordecai and led him riding through the open square of the city, proclaiming, "Thus shall it be done for the man whom the king wishes to honor."

12 Then Mordecai returned to the king's gate, but Haman hurried to his house, mourning and with his head covered. ¹³When Haman told his wife Zeresh and all his friends everything that had happened to him, his advisers and his wife Zeresh said to him, "If Mordecai, before whom your downfall has begun, is of the Jewish people, you will not prevail against him, but will surely fall before him."

6.1–14: Royal insomnia benefits Mordecai. In a comic scene, the king passes a sleepless night listening to royal annals. In keeping with the theology of the book, "it just happened" to be the same night Haman hatched his plan; Haman "happens" to be in the court; and Haman's desire for royal treatment "happens" to be given to the very man he wished to hang. **10:** *The Jew Mordecai:* The king makes no connection between Mordecai's ethnicity and the people he had condemned to death in ch. 3. **13:** *If Mordecai . . . is of the Jewish people:* Since Haman had already revealed this information in 5.13, the statement is likely intended as a preview of what is to come.

14 While they were still talking with him, the king's eunuchs arrived and hurried Haman off to the banquet that Esther had prepared. ¹So the king and Haman went in to feast with Queen Esther. ²On the second day, as they were drinking wine, the king again said to Esther, "What is your petition, Queen Esther? It shall be granted you. And what is your request? Even to the half of my kingdom, it shall be fulfilled." ³Then Queen Esther answered, "If I have won your favor, O king, and if it pleases the king, let my life be given me—that is my petition— and the lives of my people—that is my request. ⁴For we have been sold, I and my people, to be destroyed, to be killed, and to be annihilated. If we had been sold merely as slaves, men and women, I would have held my peace; but no enemy can compensate for this damage to the king."*c* ⁵Then King Ahasuerus said to Queen Esther, "Who is he, and where is he, who has presumed to do this?" ⁶Esther said, "A foe and enemy, this wicked Haman!" Then Haman was terrified before the king and the queen. ⁷The king rose from the feast in wrath and went into the palace garden, but Haman stayed to beg his life from Queen Esther, for he saw that the king had determined to destroy him. ⁸When the king returned from the palace garden to the banquet hall, Haman had thrown himself on the couch where Esther was reclining; and the king said, "Will he even assault the

---

a Heb *to lay hands on*　　*b* Heb *them*　　*c* Meaning of Heb uncertain queen in my presence, in my own house?" As the words left the mouth of the king, they covered Haman's face. 9Then Harbona, one of the eunuchs in attendance on the king, said, "Look, the very gallows that Haman has prepared for Mordecai, whose word saved the king, stands at Haman's house, fifty cubits high." And the king said, "Hang him on that." 10So they hanged Haman on the gallows that he had prepared for Mordecai. Then the anger of the king abated.

7.1–10: Haman's downfall. 3–4: Esther strategically heaps up deferential comments to the king and focuses on his loss (*damage to the king*) in her death. **8:** *Reclining* was a common posture for banqueting. Haman's act of supplication is interpreted by Ahasuerus as a sexual attack on Esther. **9:** A eunuch "happens" to be on hand and suggests a "measure for measure" punishment for Haman.

8 On that day King Ahasuerus gave to Queen Esther the house of Haman, the enemy of the Jews; and Mordecai came before the king, for Esther had told what he was to her. 2Then the king took off his signet ring, which he had taken from Haman, and gave it to Mordecai. So Esther set Mordecai over the house of Haman.

3 Then Esther spoke again to the king; she fell at his feet, weeping and pleading with him to avert the evil design of Haman the Agagite and the plot that he had devised against the Jews. 4The king held out the golden scepter to Esther, 5and Esther rose and stood before the king. She said, "If it pleases the king, and if I have won his favor, and if the thing seems right before the king, and I have his approval, let an order be written to revoke the letters devised by Haman son of Hammedatha the Agagite, which he wrote giving orders to destroy the Jews who are in all the provinces of the king. 6For how can I bear to see the calamity that is coming on my people? Or how can I bear to see the destruction of my kindred?" 7Then King Ahasuerus said to Queen Esther and to the Jew Mordecai, "See, I have given Esther the house of Haman, and they have hanged him on the gallows, because he plotted to lay hands on the Jews. 8You may write as you please with regard to the Jews, in the name of the king, and seal it with the king's ring; for an edict written in the name of the king and sealed with the king's ring cannot be revoked."

9 The king's secretaries were summoned at that time, in the third month, which is the month of Sivan, on the twenty-third day; and an edict was written, according to all that Mordecai commanded, to the Jews and to the satraps and the governors and the officials of the provinces from India to Ethiopia,ᵃ one hundred twenty-seven provinces, to every province in its own script and to every people in its own language, and also to the Jews in their script and their language. 10He wrote letters in the name of King Ahasuerus, sealed them with the king's ring, and sent them by mounted couriers riding on fast steeds bred from the royal herd.ᵇ 11By these letters the king allowed the Jews who were in every city to assemble and defend their lives, to destroy, to kill, and to annihilate any armed force of any people or province that might attack them, with their children and women, and to plunder their goods 12on a single day throughout all the provinces of King Ahasuerus, on the thirteenth day of the twelfth month, which is the month of Adar. 13A copy of the writ was to be issued as a decree in every province and published to all peoples, and the Jews were to be ready on that day to take revenge on their enemies. 14So the couriers, mounted on their swift royal steeds, hurried out, urged by the king's command. The decree was issued in the citadel of Susa.

15 Then Mordecai went out from the presence of the king, wearing royal robes of blue and white, with a great golden crown and a mantle of fine linen and purple, while the city of Susa shouted and rejoiced. 16For the Jews there was light and gladness, joy and honor. 17In every province and in every city, wherever the king's command and his edict came, there was gladness and joy among the Jews, a festival and a holiday. Furthermore, many of the peoples of the country

a Or *Nubia*; Heb *Cush*   b Meaning of Heb uncertain

professed to be Jews, because the fear of the Jews had fallen upon them.

8.1–17: Esther and Mordecai issue edicts. 1–2: Yet more reversals: Esther receives Haman's house, and the *signet ring* that Ahasuerus gave to Haman to issue a decree (3.10) is now given to Mordecai to issue a counter-decree. **3:** The king has saved Esther and Mordecai, but she now asks that he save the whole Jewish people. **8:** The irrevocability of a royal edict is both the cause and now the solution to the Jews' problem. **9–11:** *Sivan* (Babylonian "Simanu") was still 9 months from the execution of the original edict. Given free reign to draft the decree, Mordecai allows Jews not only to defend themselves but also to take plunder (though they do not, see 9.10). **15:** Mordecai's *blue and white* robes (as in 1.6) link him with royalty, as foreshadowed in 6.11. **17:** Persians *professed to be Jews*, suggesting that Jewish identity could be chosen for oneself.

9 Now in the twelfth month, which is the month of Adar, on the thirteenth day, when the king's command and edict were about to be executed, on the very day when the enemies of the Jews hoped to gain power over them, but which had been changed to a day when the Jews would gain power over their foes, ²the Jews gathered in their cities throughout all the provinces of King Ahasuerus to lay hands on those who had sought their ruin; and no one could withstand them, because the fear of them had fallen upon all peoples. ³All the officials of the provinces, the satraps and the governors, and the royal officials were supporting the Jews, because the fear of Mordecai had fallen upon them. ⁴For Mordecai was powerful in the king's house, and his fame spread throughout all the provinces as the man Mordecai grew more and more powerful. ⁵So the Jews struck down all their enemies with the sword, slaughtering, and destroying them, and did as they pleased to those who hated them. ⁶In the citadel of Susa the Jews killed and destroyed five hundred people. ⁷They killed Parshandatha, Dalphon, Aspatha, ⁸Poratha, Adalia, Aridatha, ⁹Parmashta, Arisai, Aridai, Vaizatha, ¹⁰the ten sons of Haman son of Hammedatha, the enemy of the Jews; but they did not touch the plunder.

11 That very day the number of those killed in the citadel of Susa was reported to the king. ¹²The king said to Queen Esther, "In the citadel of Susa the Jews have killed five hundred people and also the ten sons of Haman. What have they done in the rest of the king's provinces? Now what is your petition? It shall be granted you. And what further is your request? It shall be fulfilled." ¹³Esther said, "If it pleases the king, let the Jews who are in Susa be allowed tomorrow also to do according to this day's edict, and let the ten sons of Haman be hanged on the gallows." ¹⁴So the king commanded this to be done; a decree was issued in Susa, and the ten sons of Haman were hanged. ¹⁵The Jews who were in Susa gathered also on the fourteenth day of the month of Adar and they killed three hundred persons in Susa; but they did not touch the plunder.

16 Now the other Jews who were in the king's provinces also gathered to defend their lives, and gained relief from their enemies, and killed seventy-five thousand of those who hated them; but they laid no hands on the plunder. ¹⁷This was on the thirteenth day of the month of Adar, and on the fourteenth day they rested and made that a day of feasting and gladness.

9.1–17: The events of Adar. 1: *On the very day* underlines the reversal of fates that has taken place in the book. **5–16:** Jewish self-defense begins *in the citadel of Susa* (vv. 6–12). Fighting *in Susa* (vv. 13–15) may refer to the same locale or the unfortified city; fighting then spreads to other Persian provinces (v. 16). The violence of these verses is variously assessed: Is the killing justified resistance to a planned pogrom*? Is it a troublesome commentary on the excesses of revenge? *They did not touch the plunder* (vv. 10, 15, 16), though Mordecai's edict allowed it, suggesting a religious motive for the fighting. In 1 Sam 15, Saul loses kingship because he took plunder and spared Agag.

18 But the Jews who were in Susa gathered on the thirteenth day and on the fourteenth, and rested on the fifteenth day, making that a day of feasting and gladness. ¹⁹Therefore the Jews of the villages, who live in the open towns, hold the fourteenth day

of the month of Adar as a day for gladness and feasting, a holiday on which they send gifts of food to one another.

20 Mordecai recorded these things, and sent letters to all the Jews who were in all the provinces of King Ahasuerus, both near and far, 21enjoining them that they should keep the fourteenth day of the month Adar and also the fifteenth day of the same month, year by year, 22as the days on which the Jews gained relief from their enemies, and as the month that had been turned for them from sorrow into gladness and from mourning into a holiday; that they should make them days of feasting and gladness, days for sending gifts of food to one another and presents to the poor. 23So the Jews adopted as a custom what they had begun to do, as Mordecai had written to them.

24 Haman son of Hammedatha the Agagite, the enemy of all the Jews, had plotted against the Jews to destroy them, and had cast Pur—that is "the lot"—to crush and destroy them; 25but when Esther came before the king, he gave orders in writing that the wicked plot that he had devised against the Jews should come upon his own head, and that he and his sons should be hanged on the gallows. 26Therefore these days are called Purim, from the word Pur. Thus because of all that was written in this letter, and of what they had faced in this matter, and of what had happened to them, 27the Jews established and accepted as a custom for themselves and their descendants and all who joined them, that without fail they would continue to observe these two days every year, as it was written and at the time appointed. 28These days should be remembered and kept throughout every generation, in every family, province, and city; and these days of Purim should never fall into disuse among the Jews, nor should the commemoration of these days cease among their descendants.

29 Queen Esther daughter of Abihail, along with the Jew Mordecai, gave full written authority, confirming this second letter about Purim. 30Letters were sent wishing peace and security to all the Jews, to the one hundred twenty-seven provinces of the kingdom of Ahasuerus, 31and giving orders that these days of Purim should be observed at their appointed seasons, as the Jew Mordecai and Queen Esther enjoined on the Jews, just as they had laid down for themselves and for their descendants regulations concerning their fasts and their lamentations. 32The command of Queen Esther fixed these practices of Purim, and it was recorded in writing.

9.18–32: Purim celebrations. 18–21: The different days on which the fighting took place here explains why Purim is celebrated for two days. 22: In keeping with the book's strong emphasis on banqueting, Purim observances includes *gifts of food*. 24–26: Ironically,* the festival is named after Haman's plot, first begun in 3.7 with the casting of a lot. 27–28: Because Purim is not found in the Torah* (Pentateuch*), its acceptance would have needed explanation and support. 29–32: The titles of *the Jew Mordecai* (as in 8.7) and *Queen Esther* suggest their different, though complementary, authority for sending letters.

10 King Ahasuerus laid tribute on the land and on the islands of the sea. 2All the acts of his power and might, and the full account of the high honor of Mordecai, to which the king advanced him, are they not written in the annals of the kings of Media and Persia? 3For Mordecai the Jew was next in rank to King Ahasuerus, and he was powerful among the Jews and popular with his many kindred, for he sought the good of his people and interceded for the welfare of all his descendants.

10.1–3: Mordecai honored. 2: Like other key events of the book of Esther, Mordecai's deeds are recorded in *the annals of the kings of Media and Persia*. 3: The closing tribute to *Mordecai*, as opposed to Esther for whom the book is named, is sometimes considered a later addition to the book, though Purim is called "Mordecai's Day" in 2 Macc 15.35.

J O B

Introduction

The book of Job offers a sustained reflection on a single topic—God's governance of the world of human beings. It asks passionately: Is that governance just? Justice is understood actively as the ability of the gods (or God) to uphold the righteous and put down the wicked. The approach of the book is typically biblical: The question is personalized ("There was once *a man* in the land of Uz whose name was Job") and developed in a narrative.✶ The discursive essay, which reaches a conclusion through rational discussion and which modern theologians would use to explore the topic, did not exist in the literature of the time. Modern readers must therefore immerse themselves in the story and, like the friends (2.13), sit a while with Job.

Job shows the probing and critical side of ancient Near Eastern literature, works that pointed to the miseries and inequities of life and the seeming inability of the gods to manage the world justly and wisely. Of these works, the most relevant to Job is "The Babylonian Theodicy" (written about 1000 BCE), a dialogue between a sufferer and a sage to whom he goes for comfort and wisdom. The sage is scolding and didactic, but at the end he is won over by the sufferer's anguish and arguments, conceding finally that the gods have put evil into the world. The sufferer, having won the sage's sympathy, acknowledges his suppliant state and asks the gods for pity. "The Babylonian Theodicy" helps us to understand Job: The problem of suffering is intensely personal (the speaker is actually suffering); the sufferer seeks not only counsel but acceptance and solace from the sage; the sufferer never gives up his judgment that his lot is miserable and that society is corrupt (it is the sage who changes!). Though similar in genre,✶ Job makes its own vigorous statement. Prior to Job, there is nothing like his explicit and unyielding declaration of innocence. One reason is the biblical confession of one God, supremely wise, powerful, and just; the God of Israel is responsible for *everything* that happens in the world. The problem of evil in Job is thus more pressing and poignant than in other religions. A second distinctive mark of Job is that God is a powerful actor in the drama, initiating the action in chs. 1–2, responding to Job's charges in chs. 39–42, and bringing all to a close in 42.7–17.

The author of Job is not known, but he may have been a palace scribe✶ with exceptional poetic and intellectual gifts and an acquaintance with other skeptical literature. The date of composition is also unknown, for the book contains no historical reference, and its language cannot be fitted into a typology of the Hebrew language. Most estimates of the date are between the seventh and the fifth centuries BCE. A possible hint regarding the date is that Job is an Edomite, which may suggest the book was written before the sixth-century Exile✶ when Edomites were hated for taking advantage of Israel.

READING GUIDE

The best approach to Job is to defer discussion of its grand ideas such as justice and suffering and simply to read the entire book as a story. The book has characters and a plot with a beginning, middle, and end. It begins by introducing Job as a righteous sheik (1.1–5). The drama begins in the heavenly court with a wager between God and Satan on whether Job's piety is genuine (chs. 1–2). God agrees to the testing of Job. The wager and testing remain hidden from Job and his friends, contributing to the pervasive irony★ of the book. Irony is present when the reader knows more than the characters in the story know. Only the reader knows that it is not because of his sins (as the friends think) but because of his righteousness that Job suffers. In the first test, Job loses property and children but accepts it humbly. The second test afflicts his person. Initially accepting even this evil (2.7–13), he ultimately erupts in a curse upon the day of his birth (ch. 3). His friends object and heatedly defend divine justice and wisdom by a variety of traditional arguments: Job must have done some evil, perhaps unthinkingly; we are sinners in any case, fragile creatures of a few short years; a human being cannot know all the rules defining proper behavior; entrust yourself to God in an emotional rather than an intellectual solution. His unsympathetic friends provoke Job to abandon his passivity and desire for obliteration. He demands to see God; using legal language, he summons God into court for the adjudication of his complaint. His dialogue with the friends extends over three cycles (chs. 4–27), ending when communication breaks down completely. Alone, Job begins a sustained address to God with an oath of innocence (27.2), continuing it in his summation and final oath in chs. 29–31. In the meantime, an anonymous poem on the inaccessibility of wisdom (ch. 28) suggests the futility of the previous dialogues and points forward to a divine intervention by insisting that God alone knows the way to wisdom. In chs. 32–37, Elihu appears as an absurd answer to Job's demand for a mediator between himself and God. Dramatically, Elihu's speeches retard the action and heighten the expectation of the LORD's appearance in ch. 38. In a long-awaited intervention, God answers Job out of the whirlwind, demonstrating by examples (rather than by arguments) that the world is indeed governed wisely (chs. 38–39) and justly (40.6–41.34). To each speech Job responds humbly and then withdraws his suit and accepts God's version (40.3–5; 42.1–6). In the epilogue, God declares Job has won the disputation with the friends and restores his family and his place in the community. For details on the dramatic movement, see the commentary.

Some scholars regard the poetic cycles (3.1–42.6) as the original core to which a prose framework (chs. 1–2 and 42.7–17) was later added. Many also suggest that the Elihu speeches are secondary. The evidence, however, for the original unity of Job is compelling: Job is the same stalwart man in the dialogues and in the frame; prose and poetry in the Bible are not radically distinct styles; there are verbal cross-references between the poetic cycle and the prose frame; the Elihu speeches make sense in the literary structure.

In Jewish tradition, Job fascinated the rabbis, as is attested by many discussions about him in the Talmud. Interest centered on his status as a gentile★ (some believed he was a Jewish proselyte) and on the question whether he was ultimately motivated by love or by fear. Christian tradition remembers the endurance (the translation "patience" is misleading) of Job (Jas 5.11). Job became a type or example of the virtuous and faithful person to church Fathers. The many homilies of St. Gregory the Great (died 604) sum up patristic tradition about Job and point to medieval usage: Job is an image of Christ★ and of the church, and an example of spiritual and moral life.

1–2	Prologue
3–14	First cycle of speeches
15–21	Second cycle of speeches
22–27	Third cycle of speeches
28	Poem on wisdom
29–31	Final speech of Job

PROLOGUE

Chs. 1–2: God decides to test Job. The action of chs. 1–2 unfolds in alternating scenes on earth (1.1–5, 13–22, and 2.7b–10) and in heaven (1.6–12 and 2.1–7a). Each earthly scene ends with a righteous statement or act by Job (1.5, 22; 2.10). Each heavenly scene begins with the courtiers presenting themselves before the LORD and ends with one member of the court, Satan, leaving to take action.

There was once a man in the land of Uz whose name was Job. That man was blameless and upright, one who feared God and turned away from evil. ²There were born to him seven sons and three daughters. ³He had seven thousand sheep, three thousand camels, five hundred yoke of oxen, five hundred donkeys, and very many servants; so that this man was the greatest of all the people of the east. ⁴His sons used to go and hold feasts in one another's houses in turn; and they would send and invite their three sisters to eat and drink with them. ⁵And when the feast days had run their course, Job would send and sanctify them, and he would rise early in the morning and offer burnt offerings according to the number of them all; for Job said, "It may be that my children have sinned, and cursed God in their hearts." This is what Job always did.

1.1–5: Earthly scene I: Introduction of Job the just. **1.** *Job* is a venerable hero, well known beyond the confines of Israel (Ezek 14.14, 20). His homeland *Uz* is outside the holy land, located to the east, probably in Edom (Lam 4.21), an area south of the Dead Sea on both sides of the Wadi★ Arabah. Job was *blameless and upright*, designations important thematically in the dialogues; they are more fully explained by the following phrases, *feared God* and *turned away from evil*. **4–5:** The children are mentioned to illustrate Job's piety on their behalf and to prepare for their loss in v. 19.

6 One day the heavenly beings[a] came to present themselves before the LORD, and Satan[b] also came among them. ⁷The LORD said to Satan,[b] "Where have you come from?" Satan[b] answered the LORD, "From going to and fro on the earth, and from walking up and down on it." ⁸The LORD said to Satan,[b] "Have you considered my servant Job? There is no one like him on the earth, a blameless and upright man who fears God and turns away from evil." ⁹Then Satan[b] answered the LORD, "Does Job fear God for nothing? ¹⁰Have you not put a fence around him and his house and all that he has, on every side? You have blessed the work of his hands, and his possessions have increased in the land. ¹¹But stretch out your hand now, and touch all that he has, and he will curse you to your face." ¹²The LORD said to Satan,[b] "Very well, all that he has is in your power; only do not stretch out your hand against him!" So Satan[b] went out from the presence of the LORD.

1.6–12: Heavenly scene I: Conversation of God and Satan. People imagined the heavenly court on the model of an earthly one: Courtiers present themselves before the king and officials report to the LORD. *Satan*, literally, "the Satan" or the adversary, is not the enemy of God as in later biblical books, but a member of the court whose particular task is to watch the actions of human beings and report back to the LORD. **8–10:** God is pleased by the utterly just actions of Job, but Satan cynically intimates that Job is doing it only for the abundant blessings he receives in return. God allows Satan to test Job to see whether he, when "touched," will curse God. The reader now knows two things that the friends of Job do not: Job is genuinely just, and God is testing him.

13 One day when his sons and daughters were eating and drinking wine in the eldest brother's house, ¹⁴a messenger came to Job

a Heb *sons of God*   *b* Or *the Accuser*; Heb *ha-satan* and said, "The oxen were plowing and the donkeys were feeding beside them, 15and the Sabeans fell on them and carried them off, and killed the servants with the edge of the sword; I alone have escaped to tell you." 16While he was still speaking, another came and said, "The fire of God fell from heaven and burned up the sheep and the servants, and consumed them; I alone have escaped to tell you." 17While he was still speaking, another came and said, "The Chaldeans formed three columns, made a raid on the camels and carried them off, and killed the servants with the edge of the sword; I alone have escaped to tell you." 18While he was still speaking, another came and said, "Your sons and daughters were eating and drinking wine in their eldest brother's house, 19and suddenly a great wind came across the desert, struck the four corners of the house, and it fell on the young people, and they are dead; I alone have escaped to tell you."

20 Then Job arose, tore his robe, shaved his head, and fell on the ground and worshiped. 21He said, "Naked I came from my mother's womb, and naked shall I return there; the LORD gave, and the LORD has taken away; blessed be the name of the LORD."

22 In all this Job did not sin or charge God with wrongdoing.

1.13–22: Earthly scene II: All that Job has is taken away but Job does not curse God. With divine permission, Satan instigates four attacks, by two peoples (Sabeans, Chaldeans) and two natural forces (the fire of God, a great wind), to wipe out Job's animals, servants, and children. **15:** *The Sabeans* lived in southwest Arabia, contemporary Yemen. Here they must be members of a caravan. **17:** *The Chaldeans* were the rulers of the sixth-century Neo-Babylonian Empire, named here probably to characterize the eastern raiders as devastating. **21–22:** Dramatic suspense is built by postponing Job's response. Contrary to Satan's prediction (v. 11), Job does not curse God but worships and blesses in the sense of praising and acknowledging God's power as almighty.

2 One day the heavenly beings[a] came to present themselves before the LORD, and Satan[b] also came among them to pre-

sent himself before the LORD. 2The LORD said to Satan,[b] "Where have you come from?" Satan[c] answered the LORD, "From going to and fro on the earth, and from walking up and down on it." 3The LORD said to Satan,[b] "Have you considered my servant Job? There is no one like him on the earth, a blameless and upright man who fears God and turns away from evil. He still persists in his integrity, although you incited me against him, to destroy him for no reason." 4Then Satan[b] answered the LORD, "Skin for skin! All that people have they will give to save their lives.[d] 5But stretch out your hand now and touch his bone and his flesh, and he will curse you to your face." 6The LORD said to Satan,[b] "Very well, he is in your power; only spare his life."

7 So Satan[b] went out from the presence of the LORD, and inflicted loathsome sores on Job from the sole of his foot to the crown of his head. 8Job[e] took a potsherd with which to scrape himself, and sat among the ashes.

2.1–7: Heavenly scene II: Conversation of God with Satan. 3: *You incited me against him, to destroy him for no reason,* a seemingly shocking statement made by God. What is happening to Job is the result of a wager in heaven about which he knows nothing. **4:** *Skin for skin!* A proverbial statement apparently meaning that people will only act out of self-interest. **5–6:** Satan will not concede defeat; he moves to a new level. If I can touch Job's very self, *his bone and his flesh,* as opposed to his property and his children, *he will curse you to your face.* The LORD agrees to extend the test to affect Job's person. The LORD will not speak again until ch. 38. **7:** The scene now shifts from heaven to earth.

9 Then his wife said to him, "Do you still persist in your integrity? Curse[f] God, and die." 10But he said to her, "You speak as any foolish woman would speak. Shall we receive the good at the hand of God, and not receive the bad?" In all this Job did not sin with his lips.

a Heb *sons of God*   b Or *the Accuser*; Heb *ha-satan*
c Or *The Accuser*; Heb *ha-satan*   d Or *All that the man has he will give for his life*   e Heb *He*
f Heb *Bless*

21 Their tent-cord is plucked up within
   them,
   and they die devoid of wisdom.'

5 "Call now; is there anyone who will
   answer you?
   To which of the holy ones will you turn?
2 Surely vexation kills the fool,
   and jealousy slays the simple.
3 I have seen fools taking root,
   but suddenly I cursed their dwelling.
4 Their children are far from safety,
   they are crushed in the gate,
   and there is no one to deliver them.
5 The hungry eat their harvest,
   and they take it even out of the
   thorns;[a]
   and the thirsty[b] pant after their
   wealth.
6 For misery does not come from the
   earth,
   nor does trouble sprout from the
   ground;
7 but human beings are born to trouble
   just as sparks[c] fly upward.

8 "As for me, I would seek God,
   and to God I would commit my
   cause.
9 He does great things and unsearchable,
   marvelous things without number.
10 He gives rain on the earth
   and sends waters on the fields;
11 he sets on high those who are lowly,
   and those who mourn are lifted to
   safety.
12 He frustrates the devices of the crafty,
   so that their hands achieve no
   success.
13 He takes the wise in their own
   craftiness;
   and the schemes of the wily are
   brought to a quick end.
14 They meet with darkness in the
   daytime,
   and grope at noonday as in the night.
15 But he saves the needy from the sword
   of their mouth,
   from the hand of the mighty.
16 So the poor have hope,
   and injustice shuts its mouth.

17 "How happy is the one whom God
   reproves;
   therefore do not despise the discipline
   of the Almighty.[d]
18 For he wounds, but he binds up;
   he strikes, but his hands heal.
19 He will deliver you from six troubles;
   in seven no harm shall touch you.
20 In famine he will redeem you from
   death,
   and in war from the power of the
   sword.
21 You shall be hidden from the scourge of
   the tongue,
   and shall not fear destruction when it
   comes.
22 At destruction and famine you shall
   laugh,
   and shall not fear the wild animals of
   the earth.
23 For you shall be in league with the
   stones of the field,
   and the wild animals shall be at peace
   with you.
24 You shall know that your tent is safe,
   you shall inspect your fold and miss
   nothing.
25 You shall know that your descendants
   will be many,
   and your offspring like the grass of
   the earth.
26 You shall come to your grave in ripe old
   age,
   as a shock of grain comes up to the
   threshing floor in its season.
27 See, we have searched this out; it is
   true.
   Hear, and know it for yourself."

4.1–5.27. 4.12–21: Eliphaz's first statement to Job is
based not on traditional lore, as one might expect, but
on a vision in the night, like Abraham's (Gen 15.12).
The content—human beings are insignificant before
their creator—is nonetheless quite traditional. **5.1:** *To
which of the holy ones will you turn?* That human beings are fragile and transient is so obvious that no one,
not even a heavenly being (*holy ones*), will deny it. **17:**

a Meaning of Heb uncertain   b Aquila Symmachus
Syr Vg: Heb *snare*   c Or *birds*; Heb *sons of Resheph*
d Traditional rendering of Heb *Shaddai*

Discipline ("musar") is the training employed by a wisdom teacher; it may involve chastisement but has as its goal the acquisition of wisdom.

___

Job's first response

Chs. 6–7: Job explains that his passionate complaint arises from intense suffering (6.2–7), reaffirms his desire that God annihilate him (6.8–13), rebukes and entreats his friends (6.14–30), and reflects on the miserable lot of the human race (7.1–21).

___

6 Then Job answered:

2 "O that my vexation were weighed,
    and all my calamity laid in the
        balances!
3 For then it would be heavier than the
        sand of the sea;
    therefore my words have been rash.
4 For the arrows of the Almighty*a* are in
        me;
    my spirit drinks their poison;
    the terrors of God are arrayed against
        me.
5 Does the wild ass bray over its grass,
    or the ox low over its fodder?
6 Can that which is tasteless be eaten
        without salt,
    or is there any flavor in the juice of
        mallows?*b*
7 My appetite refuses to touch them;
    they are like food that is loathsome to
        me.*b*

8 "O that I might have my request,
    and that God would grant my desire;
9 that it would please God to crush me,
    that he would let loose his hand and
        cut me off!
10 This would be my consolation;
    I would even exult*b* in unrelenting
        pain;
    for I have not denied the words of the
        Holy One.
11 What is my strength, that I should
        wait?
    And what is my end, that I should be
        patient?
12 Is my strength the strength of stones,
    or is my flesh bronze?
13 In truth I have no help in me,
    and any resource is driven from me.

14 "Those who withhold*c* kindness from a
        friend
    forsake the fear of the Almighty.*a*
15 My companions are treacherous like a
        torrent-bed,
    like freshets that pass away,
16 that run dark with ice,
    turbid with melting snow.
17 In time of heat they disappear;
    when it is hot, they vanish from their
        place.
18 The caravans turn aside from their
        course;
    they go up into the waste, and perish.
19 The caravans of Tema look,
    the travelers of Sheba hope.
20 They are disappointed because they
        were confident;
    they come there and are confounded.
21 Such you have now become to me;*d*
    you see my calamity, and are afraid.
22 Have I said, 'Make me a gift'?
    Or, 'From your wealth offer a bribe
        for me'?
23 Or, 'Save me from an opponent's hand'?
    Or, 'Ransom me from the hand of
        oppressors'?

24 "Teach me, and I will be silent;
    make me understand how I have gone
        wrong.
25 How forceful are honest words!
    But your reproof, what does it
        reprove?
26 Do you think that you can reprove
        words,
    as if the speech of the desperate were
        wind?
27 You would even cast lots over the orphan,
    and bargain over your friend.

28 "But now, be pleased to look at me;
    for I will not lie to your face.
29 Turn, I pray, let no wrong be done.
    Turn now, my vindication is at stake.
30 Is there any wrong on my tongue?
    Cannot my taste discern calamity?

a Traditional rendering of Heb *Shaddai*   *b* Meaning of Heb uncertain   *c* Syr Vg Compare Tg: Meaning of Heb uncertain   *d* Cn Compare Gk Syr: Meaning of Heb uncertain

7 "Do not human beings have a hard
     service on earth,
        and are not their days like the days of
          a laborer?
2 Like a slave who longs for the shadow,
     and like laborers who look for their
       wages,
3 so I am allotted months of emptiness,
     and nights of misery are apportioned
       to me.
4 When I lie down I say, 'When shall I
     rise?'
        But the night is long,
     and I am full of tossing until dawn.
5 My flesh is clothed with worms and
     dirt;
        my skin hardens, then breaks out
          again.
6 My days are swifter than a weaver's
     shuttle,
        and come to their end without hope. a
7 "Remember that my life is a breath;
     my eye will never again see good.
8 The eye that beholds me will see me no
     more;
        while your eyes are upon me, I shall
          be gone.
9 As the cloud fades and vanishes,
     so those who go down to Sheol do not
       come up;
10 they return no more to their houses,
     nor do their places know them any
       more.

11 "Therefore I will not restrain my mouth;
     I will speak in the anguish of my
       spirit;
        I will complain in the bitterness of my
          soul.
12 Am I the Sea, or the Dragon,
     that you set a guard over me?
13 When I say, 'My bed will comfort me,
     my couch will ease my complaint,'
14 then you scare me with dreams
     and terrify me with visions,
15 so that I would choose strangling
     and death rather than this body.
16 I loathe my life; I would not live forever.
     Let me alone, for my days are a
       breath.

17 What are human beings, that you make
     so much of them,
        that you set your mind on them,
18 visit them every morning,
     test them every moment?
19 Will you not look away from me for a
     while,
        let me alone until I swallow my
          spittle?
20 If I sin, what do I do to you, you
     watcher of humanity?
        Why have you made me your target?
        Why have I become a burden to
          you?
21 Why do you not pardon my
     transgression
        and take away my iniquity?
        For now I shall lie in the earth;
          you will seek me, but I shall not be."

6.1–7.21. 6.2: *Vexation* is the mark of a fool (5.2), but
Job pleads his own terrible suffering as the source of
his vexation. If it could be *weighed*, his friends might
see and understand. **5–7**: Obscure. Possibly, Job expresses a desire for the "food" of sympathy. See Ps
69.20–21. **8–13**: At this point, Job is overwhelmed and
simply wants annihilation. He expressed the same wish
in ch. 3. **14–30**: From his bitter depiction of false
friends (vv. 14–21), disappointment at their lack of
sympathy (vv. 22–27), and touching final plea (vv. 28–
30), Job shows how deeply his friends have wounded
and disappointed him. **7.1–21**: A lament* in three sections (vv. 1–8, 9–16, 17–21). Instead of following the
lament convention of mentioning the brevity and misery of human life as a means of winning God's favor,
Job blames God for humanity's (and his own) suffering
(7.8, 12–16, 30). **12**: *The Sea, or the Dragon:* In
mythological texts of neighboring cultures, the storm
god had to defeat a monstrous personified* sea to
become the chief god. The Bible adapted the myth to
portray the God of Israel as supreme. Job is sarcastic:
Why do you hurt me? I am not important to you.
17–18: Continuing in the sarcastic vein, Job parodies
the words of Ps 8.4: "What are human beings that you
are mindful of them, / mortals that you care for
them?" Instead of caring for human beings, God scru-
tinizes them, becoming a *watcher of humanity* (7.20).

a Or *as the thread runs out*

8 Then Bildad the Shuhite answered:
2 "How long will you say these things,
  and the words of your mouth be a
    great wind?
3 Does God pervert justice?
    Or does the Almighty*a* pervert the
      right?
4 If your children sinned against him,
    he delivered them into the power of
      their transgression.
5 If you will seek God
    and make supplication to the
      Almighty,*a*
6 if you are pure and upright,
    surely then he will rouse himself for
      you
    and restore to you your rightful place.
7 Though your beginning was small,
    your latter days will be very great.

8 "For inquire now of bygone generations,
    and consider what their ancestors
      have found;
9 for we are but of yesterday, and we
    know nothing,
    for our days on earth are but a
      shadow.
10 Will they not teach you and tell you
    and utter words out of their
      understanding?
11 "Can papyrus grow where there is no
    marsh?
    Can reeds flourish where there is no
      water?
12 While yet in flower and not cut down,
    they wither before any other plant.
13 Such are the paths of all who forget
    God;
    the hope of the godless shall perish.
14 Their confidence is gossamer,
    a spider's house their trust.
15 If one leans against its house, it will not
    stand;
    if one lays hold of it, it will not
      endure.
16 The wicked thrive*b* before the sun,
    and their shoots spread over the
      garden.
17 Their roots twine around the stoneheap;
    they live among the rocks.*c*

18 If they are destroyed from their place,
    then it will deny them, saying, 'I have
      never seen you.'
19 See, these are their happy ways,*d*
    and out of the earth still others will
      spring.

20 "See, God will not reject a blameless
    person,
    nor take the hand of evildoers.
21 He will yet fill your mouth with
    laughter,
    and your lips with shouts of joy.
22 Those who hate you will be clothed with
    shame,
    and the tent of the wicked will be no
      more."

8.1–22: The response of Bildad the Shuhite. 3: *Does God pervert justice?* Justice in the biblical sense involves upholding the innocent and punishing the guilty. Bildad is shocked that Job would deny God is just. **4:** *Your children:* Because of his simple understanding of justice (sin deserves punishment, therefore punishment only follows sin), Bildad judges the slaughter of Job's children to be due to their sin. **11–12:** Evidently proverbial: Just as plants need water, so human beings need life. **13–19:** Difficult. Some assume two plants are compared as in Ps 1 and Jer 17.5–8: One plant, symbolizing the wicked, withers quickly (vv. 12–15), whereas the other plant (reading "the other" in place of *the wicked* in v. 16) survives. The example of the two plants is meant to bring Job to repentance.

Job's second response
Chs. 9–10: Job admits the uselessness of entering into litigation with God. He takes the friends' statements about divine justice in a strictly legal sense. For example, Eliphaz asked in 4.17 whether mortals can be righteous before God. Job interprets "righteous" as winning a legal case (9.2). Other instances of legal language are 9.2–3, 14–16, 19–21, 24.

---

9 Then Job answered:
2 "Indeed I know that this is so;
    but how can a mortal be just before
      God?

a Traditional rendering of Heb *Shaddai*   *b* Heb *He thrives*   *c* Gk Vg: Meaning of Heb uncertain   *d* Meaning of Heb uncertain

3 If one wished to contend with him,
  one could not answer him once in a
    thousand.
4 He is wise in heart, and mighty in
    strength
  —who has resisted him, and
    succeeded?—
5 he who removes mountains, and they do
    not know it,
  when he overturns them in his
    anger;
6 who shakes the earth out of its place,
  and its pillars tremble;
7 who commands the sun, and it does not
    rise;
  who seals up the stars;
8 who alone stretched out the heavens
  and trampled the waves of the Sea;*a*
9 who made the Bear and Orion,
  the Pleiades and the chambers of the
    south;
10 who does great things beyond
    understanding,
  and marvelous things without
    number.
11 Look, he passes by me, and I do not see
    him;
  he moves on, but I do not perceive
    him.
12 He snatches away; who can stop him?
  Who will say to him, 'What are you
    doing?'
13 "God will not turn back his anger;
  the helpers of Rahab bowed beneath
    him.
14 How then can I answer him,
  choosing my words with him?
15 Though I am innocent, I cannot answer
    him;
  I must appeal for mercy to my
    accuser.*b*
16 If I summoned him and he answered
    me,
  I do not believe that he would listen
    to my voice.
17 For he crushes me with a tempest,
  and multiplies my wounds without
    cause;
18 he will not let me get my breath,
  but fills me with bitterness.

19 If it is a contest of strength, he is the
    strong one!
  If it is a matter of justice, who can
    summon him?*c*
20 Though I am innocent, my own mouth
    would condemn me;
  though I am blameless, he would
    prove me perverse.
21 I am blameless; I do not know myself;
  I loathe my life.
22 It is all one; therefore I say,
  he destroys both the blameless and
    the wicked.
23 When disaster brings sudden death,
  he mocks at the calamity*d* of the
    innocent.
24 The earth is given into the hand of the
    wicked;
  he covers the eyes of its judges—
  if it is not he, who then is it?

25 "My days are swifter than a runner;
  they flee away, they see no good.
26 They go by like skiffs of reed,
  like an eagle swooping on the prey.
27 If I say, 'I will forget my complaint;
  I will put off my sad countenance and
    be of good cheer,'
28 I become afraid of all my suffering,
  for I know you will not hold me
    innocent.
29 I shall be condemned;
  why then do I labor in vain?
30 If I wash myself with soap
  and cleanse my hands with lye,
31 yet you will plunge me into filth,
  and my own clothes will abhor me.
32 For he is not a mortal, as I am, that I
    might answer him,
  that we should come to trial together.
33 There is no umpire*e* between us,
  who might lay his hand on us both.
34 If he would take his rod away from me,
  and not let dread of him terrify me,
35 then I would speak without fear of him,
  for I know I am not what I am
    thought to be.*f*

a Or *trampled the back of the sea dragon*   *b* Or *for my right*   *c* Compare Gk: Heb *me*   *d* Meaning of Heb uncertain   *e* Another reading is *Would that there were an umpire*   *f* Cn: Heb *for I am not so in myself*

9.1–35. 2–3: *Be just before God . . . contend with him . . . answer him:* Job responds to Bildad's assertion in 8.20 ("God will not reject a blameless person") in a strictly legal sense: God will not be summoned into court so that an accused person can be found guilty (rejected, 8.20) or declared innocent (9.20). **4–13:** God is beyond responding to human requests. **25–35:** Job considers three alternatives to taking God to court, only to reject them as impossible: (1) if he drops charges, God will find him guilty anyway (9.25–29); (2) if he attempts to purge himself as in Ps 51.7, God will make him filthy again (9.30–31); (3) there is no one impartial adjudicator (*umpire;* 9.32–35).

10 "I loathe my life;
I will give free utterance to my
complaint;
I will speak in the bitterness of my
soul.

2 I will say to God, Do not condemn me;
let me know why you contend against
me.

3 Does it seem good to you to oppress,
to despise the work of your hands
and favor the schemes of the wicked?

4 Do you have eyes of flesh?
Do you see as humans see?

5 Are your days like the days of mortals,
or your years like human years,

6 that you seek out my iniquity
and search for my sin,

7 although you know that I am not guilty,
and there is no one to deliver out of
your hand?

8 Your hands fashioned and made me;
and now you turn and destroy me.ᵃ

9 Remember that you fashioned me like
clay;
and will you turn me to dust again?

10 Did you not pour me out like milk
and curdle me like cheese?

11 You clothed me with skin and flesh,
and knit me together with bones and
sinews.

12 You have granted me life and steadfast
love,
and your care has preserved my
spirit.

13 Yet these things you hid in your heart;
I know that this was your purpose.

14 If I sin, you watch me,
and do not acquit me of my iniquity.

15 If I am wicked, woe to me!
If I am righteous, I cannot lift up my
head,
for I am filled with disgrace
and look upon my affliction.

16 Bold as a lion you hunt me;
you repeat your exploits against me.

17 You renew your witnesses against me,
and increase your vexation toward
me;
you bring fresh troops against me.ᵇ

10.8–17: Though Job expects no justice, he nonetheless lists his charges against God: You, the one who brought me into being, nonetheless seek to destroy me!

18 "Why did you bring me forth from the
womb?
Would that I had died before any eye
had seen me,

19 and were as though I had not been,
carried from the womb to the grave.

20 Are not the days of my life few?ᶜ
Let me alone, that I may find a little
comfortᵈ

21 before I go, never to return,
to the land of gloom and deep
darkness,

22 the land of gloomᵉ and chaos,
where light is like darkness."

The response of Zophar the Naamathite

Ch 11: Zophar accuses Job of malice in maintaining his innocence (vv. 2–12) and urges him to turn to God, an act of repentance that will assure him prosperity (vv. 13–20). There is profound irony✶ in Zophar's assertion of a hidden dimension in wisdom (vv. 6–12) and of the untroubled existence of the just (v. 20). The reader knows from chs. 1–2 of God's wager, hidden from the actors, and that it is precisely because Job is just that he suffers.

a Cn Compare Gk Syr: Heb *made me together all around, and you destroy me*   b Cn Compare Gk: Heb *toward me; changes and a troop are with me*
c Cn Compare Gk Syr: Heb *Are not my days few? Let him cease!*   d Heb *that I may brighten up a little*
e Heb *gloom as darkness, deep darkness*

11 Then Zophar the Naamathite answered:

2 "Should a multitude of words go
　　unanswered,
　and should one full of talk be
　　vindicated?

3 Should your babble put others to
　　silence,
　and when you mock, shall no one
　　shame you?

4 For you say, 'My conduct[a] is pure,
　and I am clean in God's[b] sight.'

5 But O that God would speak,
　and open his lips to you,

6 and that he would tell you the secrets of
　　wisdom!
　For wisdom is many-sided.[c]
　Know then that God exacts of you less
　　than your guilt deserves.

7 "Can you find out the deep things of
　　God?
　Can you find out the limit of the
　　Almighty?[d]

8 It is higher than heaven[e]—what can
　　you do?
　Deeper than Sheol—what can you
　　know?

9 Its measure is longer than the earth,
　and broader than the sea.

10 If he passes through, and imprisons,
　and assembles for judgment, who can
　　hinder him?

11 For he knows those who are worthless;
　when he sees iniquity, will he not
　　consider it?

12 But a stupid person will get
　　understanding,
　when a wild ass is born human.[c]

13 "If you direct your heart rightly,
　you will stretch out your hands
　　toward him.

14 If iniquity is in your hand, put it far
　　away,
　and do not let wickedness reside in
　　your tents.

15 Surely then you will lift up your face
　　without blemish;
　you will be secure, and will not fear.

16 You will forget your misery;
　you will remember it as waters that
　　have passed away.

17 And your life will be brighter than the
　　noonday;
　its darkness will be like the morning.

18 And you will have confidence, because
　　there is hope;
　you will be protected[f] and take your
　　rest in safety.

19 You will lie down, and no one will make
　　you afraid;
　many will entreat your favor.

20 But the eyes of the wicked will fail;
　all way of escape will be lost to
　　them,
　and their hope is to breathe their
　　last."

Job's third response

Chs. 12–14: Job's speech is the climax* of the first cycle. In essence, he denounces the friends for presuming to speak for God who, being all wise and powerful (12.13, 16), is responsible for everything that takes place (12.13–13.5). Job wants only to be allowed to bring his case directly before God (13.6–28). The prospect brings home to Job how fragile is humanity's grip on life (14.1–22).

12 Then Job answered:

2 "No doubt you are the people,
　and wisdom will die with you.

3 But I have understanding as well as
　　you;
　I am not inferior to you.
　Who does not know such things as
　　these?

4 I am a laughingstock to my friends;
　I, who called upon God and he
　　answered me,
　a just and blameless man, I am a
　　laughingstock.

5 Those at ease have contempt for
　　misfortune,[e]
　but it is ready for those whose feet
　　are unstable.

_a_ Gk: Heb _teaching_　_b_ Heb _your_　_c_ Meaning of Heb uncertain　_d_ Traditional rendering of Heb _Shaddai_　_e_ Heb _The heights of heaven_　_f_ Or _you will look around_

6 The tents of robbers are at peace,
    and those who provoke God are
        secure,
    who bring their god in their hands.[a]

7 "But ask the animals, and they will
        teach you;
    the birds of the air, and they will tell
        you;
8 ask the plants of the earth,[b] and they
        will teach you;
    and the fish of the sea will declare to
        you.
9 Who among all these does not know
    that the hand of the LORD has done
        this?
10 In his hand is the life of every living
        thing
    and the breath of every human being.
11 Does not the ear test words
    as the palate tastes food?
12 Is wisdom with the aged,
    and understanding in length of days?

12.1–12. 1: *You are the people:* Probably, short for
people with land, the elite who believe they alone are
wise. 7: *Ask the animals:* In ch. 8 Bildad urged inquiring
of "bygone generations" (v. 8), that is, tradition, to
demonstrate a point. Here, Job says that even animals
know that nothing happens without God.

---

13 "With God[c] are wisdom and strength;
    he has counsel and understanding.
14 If he tears down, no one can rebuild;
    if he shuts someone in, no one can
        open up.
15 If he withholds the waters, they dry up;
    if he sends them out, they overwhelm
        the land.
16 With him are strength and wisdom;
    the deceived and the deceiver are his.
17 He leads counselors away stripped,
    and makes fools of judges.
18 He looses the sash of kings,
    and binds a waistcloth on their loins.
19 He leads priests away stripped,
    and overthrows the mighty.
20 He deprives of speech those who are
        trusted,
    and takes away the discernment of
        the elders.

21 He pours contempt on princes,
    and looses the belt of the strong.
22 He uncovers the deeps out of darkness,
    and brings deep darkness to light.
23 He makes nations great, then destroys
        them;
    he enlarges nations, then leads them
        away.
24 He strips understanding from the
        leaders[d] of the earth,
    and makes them wander in a pathless
        waste.
25 They grope in the dark without light;
    he makes them stagger like a
        drunkard.

13 "Look, my eye has seen all this,
    my ear has heard and understood it.
2 What you know, I also know;
    I am not inferior to you.
3 But I would speak to the Almighty,[e]
    and I desire to argue my case with
        God.
4 As for you, you whitewash with lies;
    all of you are worthless physicians.
5 If you would only keep silent,
    that would be your wisdom!
6 Hear now my reasoning,
    and listen to the pleadings of my lips.
7 Will you speak falsely for God,
    and speak deceitfully for him?
8 Will you show partiality toward him,
    will you plead the case for God?
9 Will it be well with you when he
        searches you out?
    Or can you deceive him, as one
        person deceives another?
10 He will surely rebuke you
    if in secret you show partiality.
11 Will not his majesty terrify you,
    and the dread of him fall upon you?
12 Your maxims are proverbs of ashes,
    your defenses are defenses of clay.

13.3: *I would speak to the Almighty:* In his earlier
speeches (3.3–26; 6.8–10), Job wanted to disappear,
but a desire to confront God directly has begun to

---

a Or *whom God brought forth by his hand*; Meaning of
Heb uncertain   b Or *speak to the earth*   c Heb *him*
d Heb adds *of the people*   e Traditional rendering of
Heb *Shaddai*

emerge, probably because of the mockery of the friends (12.4) and their claim that he is unaware of the hidden dimension of wisdom (11.6–12).

13 "Let me have silence, and I will speak,
    and let come on me what may.
14 I will take my flesh in my teeth,
    and put my life in my hand.*a*
15 See, he will kill me; I have no hope;*b*
    but I will defend my ways to his
        face.
16 This will be my salvation,
    that the godless shall not come before
        him.
17 Listen carefully to my words,
    and let my declaration be in your
        ears.
18 I have indeed prepared my case;
    I know that I shall be vindicated.
19 Who is there that will contend with
        me?
    For then I would be silent and die.
20 Only grant two things to me,
    then I will not hide myself from your
        face:
21 withdraw your hand far from me,
    and do not let dread of you terrify me.
22 Then call, and I will answer;
    or let me speak, and you reply to me.
23 How many are my iniquities and my
        sins?
    Make me know my transgression and
        my sin.
24 Why do you hide your face,
    and count me as your enemy?
25 Will you frighten a windblown leaf
    and pursue dry chaff?
26 For you write bitter things against me,
    and make me reap*c* the iniquities of
        my youth.
27 You put my feet in the stocks,
    and watch all my paths;
    you set a bound to the soles of my
        feet.
28 One wastes away like a rotten thing,
    like a garment that is moth-eaten.

14 "A mortal, born of woman, few of
        days and full of trouble,
2   comes up like a flower and withers,
    flees like a shadow and does not last.

3 Do you fix your eyes on such a one?
    Do you bring me into judgment with
        you?
4 Who can bring a clean thing out of an
        unclean?
    No one can.
5 Since their days are determined,
    and the number of their months is
        known to you,
    and you have appointed the bounds
        that they cannot pass,
6 look away from them, and desist,*d*
    that they may enjoy, like laborers,
        their days.

7 "For there is hope for a tree,
    if it is cut down, that it will sprout
        again,
    and that its shoots will not cease.
8 Though its root grows old in the
        earth,
    and its stump dies in the ground,
9 yet at the scent of water it will bud
    and put forth branches like a young
        plant.
10 But mortals die, and are laid low;
    humans expire, and where are they?
11 As waters fail from a lake,
    and a river wastes away and dries up,
12 so mortals lie down and do not rise
        again;
    until the heavens are no more, they
        will not awake
    or be roused out of their sleep.
13 O that you would hide me in Sheol,
    that you would conceal me until your
        wrath is past,
    that you would appoint me a set time,
        and remember me!
14 If mortals die, will they live again?
    All the days of my service I would
        wait
    until my release should come.
15 You would call, and I would answer
        you;
    you would long for the work of your
        hands.

a Gk: Heb *Why should I take . . . in my hand?*
b Or *Though he kill me, yet I will trust in him*
c Heb *inherit*   *d* Cn: Heb *that they may desist*

16 For then you would not*a* number my
  steps,
   you would not keep watch over my
    sin;
17 my transgression would be sealed up in
  a bag,
   and you would cover over my
    iniquity.

18 "But the mountain falls and crumbles
  away,
   and the rock is removed from its
    place;
19 the waters wear away the stones;
   the torrents wash away the soil of the
    earth;
   so you destroy the hope of mortals.
20 You prevail forever against them, and
  they pass away;
   you change their countenance, and
    send them away.
21 Their children come to honor, and they
  do not know it;
   they are brought low, and it goes
    unnoticed.
22 They feel only the pain of their own
  bodies,
   and mourn only for themselves."

14.1–22: In vv. 1–6, Job underlines the brevity of human life, asking how God can possibly bring such a miserable creature into judgment (vv. 3–4). In vv. 7–22, Job draws a comparison between the brief human life span and trees ever renewed by water (vv. 7–9) and mountains worn slowly away by water (vv. 18–19). In between he entertains the impossible hope that he might escape the constraints of mortality and be enabled to speak with God beyond the grave (vv. 10–17).

THE BEGINNING OF THE SECOND CYCLE OF SPEECHES

Ch. 15: The response of Eliphaz. Job's talk, according to Eliphaz, does away with genuine religion (vv. 4–6), presumes he has access to the divine assembly (vv. 8–9), and fails to reckon with the insignificance of human beings before God (vv. 12–16). The sages teach that the wicked are severely punished and endure frustration (vv. 17–35).

15 Then Eliphaz the Temanite answered:
2 "Should the wise answer with windy
  knowledge,
   and fill themselves with the east
    wind?
3 Should they argue in unprofitable
  talk,
   or in words with which they can do
    no good?
4 But you are doing away with the fear of
  God,
   and hindering meditation before God.
5 For your iniquity teaches your mouth,
   and you choose the tongue of the
    crafty.
6 Your own mouth condemns you, and
  not I;
   your own lips testify against you.

7 "Are you the firstborn of the human
  race?
   Were you brought forth before the
    hills?
8 Have you listened in the council of God?
   And do you limit wisdom to yourself?
9 What do you know that we do not
  know?
   What do you understand that is not
    clear to us?
10 The gray-haired and the aged are on our
  side,
   those older than your father.
11 Are the consolations of God too small
  for you,
   or the word that deals gently with
    you?
12 Why does your heart carry you away,
   and why do your eyes flash,*b*
13 so that you turn your spirit against God,
   and let such words go out of your
    mouth?
14 What are mortals, that they can be
  clean?
   Or those born of woman, that they
    can be righteous?
15 God puts no trust even in his holy ones,
   and the heavens are not clean in his
    sight;

a Syr: Heb lacks *not* *b* Meaning of Heb uncertain

16 how much less one who is abominable
    and corrupt,
    one who drinks iniquity like water!

17 "I will show you; listen to me;
    what I have seen I will declare—

18 what sages have told,
    and their ancestors have not hidden,

19 to whom alone the land was given,
    and no stranger passed among them.

20 The wicked writhe in pain all their days,
    through all the years that are laid up
    for the ruthless.

21 Terrifying sounds are in their ears;
    in prosperity the destroyer will come
    upon them.

22 They despair of returning from
    darkness,
    and they are destined for the sword.

23 They wander abroad for bread, saying,
    'Where is it?'
    They know that a day of darkness is
    ready at hand;

24 distress and anguish terrify them;
    they prevail against them, like a king
    prepared for battle.

25 Because they stretched out their hands
    against God,
    and bid defiance to the Almighty,*a*

26 running stubbornly against him
    with a thick-bossed shield;

27 because they have covered their faces
    with their fat,
    and gathered fat upon their loins,

28 they will live in desolate cities,
    in houses that no one should inhabit,
    houses destined to become heaps of
    ruins;

29 they will not be rich, and their wealth
    will not endure,
    nor will they strike root in the earth;*b*

30 they will not escape from darkness;
    the flame will dry up their shoots,
    and their blossom*c* will be swept
    away*d* by the wind.

31 Let them not trust in emptiness,
    deceiving themselves;
    for emptiness will be their
    recompense.

32 It will be paid in full before their time,
    and their branch will not be green.

33 They will shake off their unripe grape,
    like the vine,
    and cast off their blossoms, like the
    olive tree.

34 For the company of the godless is
    barren,
    and fire consumes the tents of
    bribery.

35 They conceive mischief and bring forth
    evil
    and their heart prepares deceit."

15.1–35. 2: *Should the wise answer with windy knowledge?* Eliphaz begins with an attack on Job's motives, without bothering to listen to his words. The deterioration of Job's relationship to his friends increases his interest in exploring his relationship to God. **7–10:** Eliphaz refers to a legend⋆ of a primordial human being who had access to divine wisdom. The language is similar to that describing wisdom in Prov 8.22–31. **18:** *What sages have told:* Eliphaz's portrayal of the fate of the wicked is an indirect rebuke of Job, for he judges Job wrong in continuing to assert his innocence.

Job's first response in the second cycle
Chs 16–17: Job complains against God (16.6–17), following it with an expression of hope (16.18–17.1). He next complains against his friends (17.2–10), following it with an expression of despair (17.11–16).

---

16 Then Job answered:
2 "I have heard many such
    things;
    miserable comforters are you all.

3 Have windy words no limit?
    Or what provokes you that you keep
    on talking?

4 I also could talk as you do,
    if you were in my place;
    I could join words together against
    you,
    and shake my head at you.

5 I could encourage you with my mouth,
    and the solace of my lips would
    assuage your pain.

a Traditional rendering of Heb *Shaddai*
b Vg: Meaning of Heb uncertain
c Gk: Heb *mouth*
d Cn: Heb *will depart*

6 "If I speak, my pain is not assuaged,
and if I forbear, how much of it
leaves me?
7 Surely now God has worn me out;
he has^a made desolate all my
company.
8 And he has^a shriveled me up,
which is a witness against me;
my leanness has risen up against me,
and it testifies to my face.
9 He has torn me in his wrath, and hated
me;
he has gnashed his teeth at me;
my adversary sharpens his eyes
against me.
10 They have gaped at me with their
mouths;
they have struck me insolently on the
cheek;
they mass themselves together against
me.
11 God gives me up to the ungodly,
and casts me into the hands of the
wicked.
12 I was at ease, and he broke me in two;
he seized me by the neck and dashed
me to pieces;
he set me up as his target;
13 his archers surround me.
He slashes open my kidneys, and shows
no mercy;
he pours out my gall on the ground.
14 He bursts upon me again and again;
he rushes at me like a warrior.
15 I have sewed sackcloth upon my skin,
and have laid my strength in the dust.
16 My face is red with weeping,
and deep darkness is on my eyelids,
17 though there is no violence in my hands,
and my prayer is pure.

18 "O earth, do not cover my blood;
let my outcry find no resting place.
19 Even now, in fact, my witness is in
heaven,
and he that vouches for me is on high.
20 My friends scorn me;
my eye pours out tears to God,
21 that he would maintain the right of a
mortal with God,
as^b one does for a neighbor.

22 For when a few years have come,
I shall go the way from which I shall
not return.

17 My spirit is broken, my days are
extinct,
the grave is ready for me.
2 Surely there are mockers around me,
and my eye dwells on their
provocation.

3 "Lay down a pledge for me with
yourself;
who is there that will give surety for
me?
4 Since you have closed their minds to
understanding,
therefore you will not let them
triumph.
5 Those who denounce friends for
reward—
the eyes of their children will fail.

6 "He has made me a byword of the
peoples,
and I am one before whom people
spit.
7 My eye has grown dim from grief,
and all my members are like a
shadow.
8 The upright are appalled at this,
and the innocent stir themselves up
against the godless.
9 Yet the righteous hold to their way,
and they that have clean hands grow
stronger and stronger.
10 But you, come back now, all of you,
and I shall not find a sensible person
among you.
11 My days are past, my plans are broken
off,
the desires of my heart.
12 They make night into day;
'The light,' they say, 'is near to the
darkness.'^c
13 If I look for Sheol as my house,
if I spread my couch in darkness,
14 if I say to the Pit, 'You are my father,'
and to the worm, 'My mother,' or 'My
sister,'

a Heb *you have* *b* Syr Vg Tg: Heb *and* *c* Meaning
of Heb uncertain

15 where then is my hope?
   Who will see my hope?
16 Will it go down to the bars of Sheol?
   Shall we descend together into the
      dust?"

16.8–17.16. 16.8: *It testifies to my face:* Job believes his wretched physical state advertises to others his alienation from God. **18:** *O earth, do not cover my blood:* Job hopes that his blood that God has shed by the cruel attacks of vv. 11–14 will cry out for vindication like the spilled blood of Abel (Gen 4.10), and that it will happen before his death (v. 22). **19:** *My witness is in heaven:* The identity of the witness is disputed. Is it God or some third party? Most likely, the witness is a third party who would arbitrate between God and Job and be a truthful witness. The rich irony* of these verses is apparent to the reader of chs. 1–2, where just such a third party was introduced: Satan, who is Job's enemy! **17.3:** *Lay down a pledge with me for yourself:* Job offers to God a pledge or token of his innocence. The effect is that of an oath of innocence. Another instance of such a pledge is Gen 38.17–18, where Judah gives his signet, cord, and staff in pledge of full payment later.

The response of Bildad

Ch. 18: With far greater harshness than his first response in ch. 8, Bildad states that Job is egotistically making himself the center of the world, whereas he is really among the wicked. The speech upholds a rigid doctrine of punishment for wicked deeds.

---

18 Then Bildad the Shuhite answered:
2 "How long will you hunt for
      words?
   Consider, and then we shall speak.
3 Why are we counted as cattle?
   Why are we stupid in your sight?
4 You who tear yourself in your anger—
   shall the earth be forsaken because of
      you,
   or the rock be removed out of its
      place?

5 "Surely the light of the wicked is put
      out,
   and the flame of their fire does not
      shine.
6 The light is dark in their tent,
   and the lamp above them is put out.

---

7 Their strong steps are shortened,
   and their own schemes throw them
      down.
8 For they are thrust into a net by their
      own feet,
   and they walk into a pitfall.
9 A trap seizes them by the heel;
   a snare lays hold of them.
10 A rope is hid for them in the ground,
   a trap for them in the path.
11 Terrors frighten them on every side,
   and chase them at their heels.
12 Their strength is consumed by hunger,[a]
   and calamity is ready for their
      stumbling.
13 By disease their skin is consumed,[b]
   the firstborn of Death consumes their
      limbs.
14 They are torn from the tent in which
      they trusted,
   and are brought to the king of terrors.
15 In their tents nothing remains;
   sulfur is scattered upon their
      habitations.
16 Their roots dry up beneath,
   and their branches wither above.
17 Their memory perishes from the earth,
   and they have no name in the street.
18 They are thrust from light into
      darkness,
   and driven out of the world.
19 They have no offspring or descendant
      among their people,
   and no survivor where they used to
      live.
20 They of the west are appalled at their
      fate,
   and horror seizes those of the east.
21 Surely such are the dwellings of the
      ungodly,
   such is the place of those who do not
      know God."

18.1–21. 2: *How long will you hunt for words?* Literally, "snare with words." Hunting imagery recurs in vv. 7–11, which depict the wicked being hunted and snared. **4:** *Place:* The word appears in the final verse (v. 21), rounding off the thought in an inclusio*: You

---

a Or *Disaster is hungry for them*   *b* Cn: Heb *It consumes the limbs of his skin* cannot move the center of the world (*the rock be removed from its place*, v. 4); the place of the punishment of the wicked is arranged (*such is the place of those who do not know God*, v. 21).

Job's second response

Ch. 19: Far from making himself the center of the universe and far from hunting with words (Bildad's accusations in ch. 18), Job is being hunted by God's net (v. 6) and besieged by God (vv. 11–12). His family life is gone (vv. 13–20), and he can only plead with his friends not to pursue him pitilessly as God does (vv. 21–29).

19 Then Job answered:
2 "How long will you torment me,
　　and break me in pieces with words?
3 These ten times you have cast reproach
　　upon me;
　　are you not ashamed to wrong me?
4 And even if it is true that I have erred,
　　my error remains with me.
5 If indeed you magnify yourselves against
　　me,
　　and make my humiliation an
　　　argument against me,
6 know then that God has put me in the
　　wrong,
　　and closed his net around me.
7 Even when I cry out, 'Violence!' I am
　　not answered;
　　I call aloud, but there is no justice.
8 He has walled up my way so that I
　　cannot pass,
　　and he has set darkness upon my
　　　paths.
9 He has stripped my glory from me,
　　and taken the crown from my head.
10 He breaks me down on every side, and I
　　am gone,
　　he has uprooted my hope like a tree.
11 He has kindled his wrath against me,
　　and counts me as his adversary.
12 His troops come on together;
　　they have thrown up siegeworks*a*
　　　against me,
　　and encamp around my tent.
13 "He has put my family far from me,
　　and my acquaintances are wholly
　　　estranged from me.

14 My relatives and my close friends have
　　failed me;
15 the guests in my house have forgotten
　　me;
　my serving girls count me as a
　　stranger;
　I have become an alien in their
　　eyes.
16 I call to my servant, but he gives me no
　　answer;
　　I must myself plead with him.
17 My breath is repulsive to my wife;
　　I am loathsome to my own family.
18 Even young children despise me;
　　when I rise, they talk against me.
19 All my intimate friends abhor me,
　　and those whom I loved have turned
　　　against me.
20 My bones cling to my skin and to my
　　flesh,
　　and I have escaped by the skin of my
　　　teeth.
21 Have pity on me, have pity on me,
　　　O you my friends,
　　for the hand of God has touched me!
22 Why do you, like God, pursue me,
　　never satisfied with my flesh?

23 "O that my words were written down!
　　O that they were inscribed in a
　　　book!
24 O that with an iron pen and with lead
　　they were engraved on a rock forever!
25 For I know that my Redeemer*b* lives,
　　and that at the last he*c* will stand
　　　upon the earth;*d*
26 and after my skin has been thus
　　destroyed,
　　then in*e* my flesh I shall see God,*f*
27 whom I shall see on my side,*g*
　　and my eyes shall behold, and not
　　　another.
　My heart faints within me!
28 If you say, 'How we will persecute
　　him!'
　　and, 'The root of the matter is found
　　　in him';

a Cn: Heb *their way*　　*b* Or *Vindicator*　　*c* Or *that he the Last*　　*d* Heb *dust*　　*e* Or *without*　　*f* Meaning of Heb of this verse uncertain　　*g* Or *for myself*

29 be afraid of the sword,
  for wrath brings the punishment of
    the sword,
  so that you may know there is a
    judgment."

19.1–29. 13–20: There is no mention of the death of Job's children. Instead, Job gives a standard portrayal of a once-great sheik whose household has disappeared. **21:** *Have pity on my, have pity on me, O you my friends:* Some take Job's pleading as sarcastic, because his friends have been unremittingly harsh. There is a correlation between the harshness of his friends and the harshness of God. **23–27:** The Hebrew is difficult. Just as Job expressed the hope for an impartial umpire in 10.33, for a postmortem trial in 14.12–17, and for a witness in heaven in 16.19, he now wishes he could engrave on a stone marker his side of the case for all to see. He hopes for a redeemer. Who is this redeemer? Some suggest it is God, but, most likely, it is the same third party as the witness (16.19) and umpire (9.33). It is a figure of the heavenly council who would act as his friend and support. **26:** *And after my skin has been thus destroyed:* Though some suggest that Job hopes for a judgment this side of the grave, it is probable that he hopes for some kind of survival after death. **28:** *The root of the matter is found in him:* Because the friends have judged Job guilty, they feel free to persecute him. Job warns them they are attacking an innocent man and hence will experience the divine wrath.

The response of Zophar

Ch. 20: Making an appeal to ancient tradition as in 8.8–20, Zophar states his topic in v. 5 and illustrates it in vv. 6–28. The wicked may rise high, but they inevitably fall (vv. 6–11); they ingest wickedness like delicious food, but they will experience misery (vv. 12–22); God will bring their wickedness upon them (vv. 23–29).

20 Then Zophar the Naamathite answered:
2 "Pay attention! My thoughts urge me to
    answer,
  because of the agitation within me.
3 I hear censure that insults me,
    and a spirit beyond my understanding
    answers me.
4 Do you not know this from of old,

ever since mortals were placed on
    earth,
5 that the exulting of the wicked is
    short,
  and the joy of the godless is but for a
    moment?
6 Even though they mount up high as the
    heavens,
  and their head reaches to the
    clouds,
7 they will perish forever like their own
    dung;
  those who have seen them will say,
    'Where are they?'
8 They will fly away like a dream, and not
    be found;
  they will be chased away like a vision
    of the night.
9 The eye that saw them will see them no
    more,
  nor will their place behold them any
    longer.
10 Their children will seek the favor of the
    poor,
  and their hands will give back their
    wealth.
11 Their bodies, once full of youth,
  will lie down in the dust with them.

12 "Though wickedness is sweet in their
    mouth,
  though they hide it under their
    tongues,
13 though they are loath to let it go,
  and hold it in their mouths,
14 yet their food is turned in their
    stomachs;
  it is the venom of asps within them.
15 They swallow down riches and vomit
    them up again;
  God casts them out of their bellies.
16 They will suck the poison of asps;
  the tongue of a viper will kill them.
17 They will not look on the rivers,
  the streams flowing with honey and
    curds.
18 They will give back the fruit of their
    toil,
  and will not swallow it down;
  from the profit of their trading
    they will get no enjoyment.

19 For they have crushed and abandoned
the poor,
they have seized a house that they did
not build.
20 "They knew no quiet in their bellies;
in their greed they let nothing escape.
21 There was nothing left after they had
eaten;
therefore their prosperity will not
endure.
22 In full sufficiency they will be in
distress;
all the force of misery will come upon
them.
23 To fill their belly to the full
God*a* will send his fierce anger into
them,
and rain it upon them as their food.*b*
24 They will flee from an iron weapon;
a bronze arrow will strike them
through.
25 It is drawn forth and comes out of their
body,
and the glittering point comes out of
their gall;
terrors come upon them.
26 Utter darkness is laid up for their
treasures;
a fire fanned by no one will devour
them;
what is left in their tent will be
consumed.
27 The heavens will reveal their iniquity,
and the earth will rise up against
them.
28 The possessions of their house will be
carried away,
dragged off in the day of God's*c*
wrath.
29 This is the portion of the wicked from
God,
the heritage decreed for them by God."

〰〰〰〰〰〰〰〰〰〰〰〰

Job's third response
Ch. 21: Job closes the second cycle of speeches (chs.
15–21) by addressing his three friends' arguments.

21 Then Job answered:
2 "Listen carefully to my words,
and let this be your consolation.

3 Bear with me, and I will speak;
then after I have spoken, mock on.
4 As for me, is my complaint addressed to
mortals?
Why should I not be impatient?
5 Look at me, and be appalled,
and lay your hand upon your mouth.
6 When I think of it I am dismayed,
and shuddering seizes my flesh.
7 Why do the wicked live on,
reach old age, and grow mighty in
power?
8 Their children are established in their
presence,
and their offspring before their eyes.
9 Their houses are safe from fear,
and no rod of God is upon them.
10 Their bull breeds without fail;
their cow calves and never miscarries.
11 They send out their little ones like a
flock,
and their children dance around.
12 They sing to the tambourine and the
lyre,
and rejoice to the sound of the pipe.
13 They spend their days in prosperity,
and in peace they go down to Sheol.
14 They say to God, 'Leave us alone!
We do not desire to know your ways.
15 What is the Almighty,*d* that we should
serve him?
And what profit do we get if we pray
to him?'
16 Is not their prosperity indeed their own
achievement?*e*
The plans of the wicked are
repugnant to me.
17 "How often is the lamp of the wicked
put out?
How often does calamity come upon
them?
How often does God*a* distribute pains
in his anger?
18 How often are they like straw before the
wind,
and like chaff that the storm carries
away?

a Heb *he*   *b* Cn: Meaning of Heb uncertain
c Heb *his*   *d* Traditional rendering of Heb *Shaddai*
e Heb *in their hand*

19 You say, 'God stores up their iniquity for
　　　their children.'
　　Let it be paid back to them, so that
　　　they may know it.
20 Let their own eyes see their
　　　destruction,
　　and let them drink of the wrath of the
　　　Almighty.*a*
21 For what do they care for their
　　　household after them,
　　when the number of their months is
　　　cut off?
22 Will any teach God knowledge,
　　seeing that he judges those that are
　　　on high?
23 One dies in full prosperity,
　　being wholly at ease and secure,
24 his loins full of milk
　　and the marrow of his bones moist.
25 Another dies in bitterness of soul,
　　never having tasted of good.
26 They lie down alike in the dust,
　　and the worms cover them.
27 "Oh, I know your thoughts,
　　and your schemes to wrong me.
28 For you say, 'Where is the house of the
　　　prince?
　　Where is the tent in which the
　　　wicked lived?'
29 Have you not asked those who travel the
　　　roads,
　　and do you not accept their
　　　testimony,
30 that the wicked are spared in the day of
　　　calamity,
　　and are rescued in the day of wrath?
31 Who declares their way to their face,
　　and who repays them for what they
　　　have done?
32 When they are carried to the grave,
　　a watch is kept over their tomb.
33 The clods of the valley are sweet to
　　　them;
　　everyone will follow after,
　　and those who went before are
　　　innumerable.
34 How then will you comfort me with
　　　empty nothings?
　　There is nothing left of your answers
　　　but falsehood."

21.1–34. 7–16: Job refutes Zophar's assertion (20.5–11) that the joys of the wicked are only temporary. Their children are not impoverished but flourish. **17–26:** Job refutes Bildad (ch. 19). **27–34:** Against the claim that the houses of tyrants are destroyed, travelers (as opposed to pedants like the friends) report their houses flourish and their tombs are honored. **34:** *How then will you comfort me with empty nothings?* Job began his first speech in this second cycle by calling his friends "miserable comforters" (16.2) and ends the cycle by again denouncing their empty comforting.

THE THIRD CYCLE OF SPEECHES

Chs. 22–27: Textual damage makes it impossible to attribute all the speeches to their proper speaker with certainty. Several passages seem to be out of place or attributed to the wrong person: 24.18–25 is attributed to Job but probably best suits Zophar; 26.1–4, which belongs to Job, is in a speech of Bildad (25.1–6 and 26.5–14); 27.13–24 occurs in a speech of Job but is only appropriate to one of the friends. Job's speech in 26.1–4 prefaces his speech in 27.2–12; 27.13–23 may belong to Zophar.

　Ch. 22: The response of Eliphaz. Eliphaz begins the third and final cycle of speeches. In vv. 2–11 he charges Job with wickedness (v. 5). In vv. 12–20 he charges Job with denying God does justice (the probable meaning of *keep to the old way* in v. 15). Eliphaz concludes by exhorting Job to change his ways (vv. 21–25). If Job does so, he will have joy, the assurance of having his prayers heard, success, and the ability to teach others (vv. 26–29). Throughout, Eliphaz assumes Job has sinned. The ironic* statements of this chapter are especially rich.

22 Then Eliphaz the Temanite answered:
2 "Can a mortal be of use to God?
　　Can even the wisest be of service to
　　　him?
3 Is it any pleasure to the Almighty*a* if you
　　　are righteous,
　　or is it gain to him if you make your
　　　ways blameless?
4 Is it for your piety that he reproves you,
　　and enters into judgment with you?
5 Is not your wickedness great?
　　There is no end to your iniquities.

a Traditional rendering of Heb *Shaddai*

6 For you have exacted pledges from your
family for no reason,
and stripped the naked of their
clothing.
7 You have given no water to the weary to
drink,
and you have withheld bread from the
hungry.
8 The powerful possess the land,
and the favored live in it.
9 You have sent widows away empty-
handed,
and the arms of the orphans you have
crushed.*
10 Therefore snares are around you,
and sudden terror overwhelms you,
11 or darkness so that you cannot see;
a flood of water covers you.

22.4: *Is it for your piety that he reproves you?* This is
meant sarcastically by Eliphaz, but the reader knows
from 1.8 and 2.3 that Job's piety has led to this reproof.

12 "Is not God high in the heavens?
See the highest stars, how lofty they
are!
13 Therefore you say, 'What does God know?
Can he judge through the deep
darkness?
14 Thick clouds enwrap him, so that he
does not see,
and he walks on the dome of heaven.'
15 Will you keep to the old way
that the wicked have trod?
16 They were snatched away before their
time;
their foundation was washed away by
a flood.
17 They said to God, 'Leave us alone,'
and 'What can the Almighty*b* do to
us?'*e*
18 Yet he filled their houses with good
things—
but the plans of the wicked are
repugnant to me.
19 The righteous see it and are glad;
the innocent laugh them to scorn,
20 saying, 'Surely our adversaries are cut
off,
and what they left, the fire has
consumed.'

21 "Agree with God,*d* and be at peace;
in this way good will come to you.
22 Receive instruction from his mouth,
and lay up his words in your heart.
23 If you return to the Almighty,*b* you will
be restored,
if you remove unrighteousness from
your tents,
24 if you treat gold like dust,
and gold of Ophir like the stones of
the torrent-bed,
25 and if the Almighty*b* is your gold
and your precious silver,
26 then you will delight yourself in the
Almighty,*b*
and lift up your face to God.
27 You will pray to him, and he will hear
you,
and you will pay your vows.
28 You will decide on a matter, and it will
be established for you,
and light will shine on your ways.
29 When others are humiliated, you say it
is pride;
for he saves the humble.
30 He will deliver even those who are
guilty;
they will escape because of the
cleanness of your hands.'"

Job's first response in the third cycle
Chs. 23–24: Job characteristically interprets his friends'
persistent exhortations* to seek God (8.5–6; 11.13–
20; 22.21–30) in a legal sense—appearing before God
in a court of law where he could lay out his case (23.2–
7). But Job admits he cannot meet God in a court and
even if he could, he would be struck dumb with terror
(23.8–17). He then asks a rhetorical* question: Why
does God not make public *times* (of judgment, 24.1)?
He describes two types of malicious behavior, neither
of which seems to be punished by God: oppression of
the poor (24.2–12, especially v. 12) and violations of
the prohibitions against murder and adultery (24.13–
17, especially v. 17). The end of ch. 24 (vv. 18–24)
wholly contradicts Job's statements in ch. 21 and
should therefore probably be attributed to one of the
friends, perhaps Zophar.

a Gk Syr Tg Vg: Heb *were crushed*   *b* Traditional
rendering of Heb *Shaddai*   *c* Gk Syr: Heb *them*
d Heb *him*   *e* Meaning of Heb uncertain

23 Then Job answered:
² "Today also my complaint is
bitter;[a]
his[b] hand is heavy despite my
groaning.
³ Oh, that I knew where I might find
him,
that I might come even to his
dwelling!
⁴ I would lay my case before him,
and fill my mouth with arguments.
⁵ I would learn what he would answer
me,
and understand what he would say to
me.
⁶ Would he contend with me in the
greatness of his power?
No; but he would give heed to me.
⁷ There an upright person could reason
with him,
and I should be acquitted forever by
my judge.
⁸ "If I go forward, he is not there;
or backward, I cannot perceive him;
⁹ on the left he hides, and I cannot
behold him;
I turn[c] to the right, but I cannot see
him.
¹⁰ But he knows the way that I take;
when he has tested me, I shall come
out like gold.
¹¹ My foot has held fast to his steps;
I have kept his way and have not
turned aside.
¹² I have not departed from the
commandment of his lips;
I have treasured in[d] my bosom the
words of his mouth.
¹³ But he stands alone and who can
dissuade him?
What he desires, that he does.
¹⁴ For he will complete what he appoints
for me;
and many such things are in his
mind.
¹⁵ Therefore I am terrified at his presence;
when I consider, I am in dread of
him.
¹⁶ God has made my heart faint;
the Almighty[e] has terrified me;

¹⁷ If only I could vanish in darkness,
and thick darkness would cover my
face![f]

23.1–17. 3: *Oh, that I knew where I might find him:*
Job has persistently sought to find God (to seek answers), though his friends urge him to find God to seek
forgiveness. **13:** *But he stands alone:* In the monotheistic perspective of the book there are no other gods
who might persuade or dissuade God from a course
of action. **15:** *Therefore I am terrified at his presence*
(lit., "his face"). Earlier (7.14; 9.34), Job expressed his
fear of being overwhelmed by God's majesty.

~~~~~~~~~~~~~~

24 "Why are times not kept by the
Almighty,[e]
and why do those who know him
never see his days?
² The wicked[g] remove landmarks;
they seize flocks and pasture them.
³ They drive away the donkey of the
orphan;
they take the widow's ox for a pledge.
⁴ They thrust the needy off the road;
the poor of the earth all hide
themselves.
⁵ Like wild asses in the desert
they go out to their toil,
scavenging in the wasteland
food for their young.
⁶ They reap in a field not their own
and they glean in the vineyard of the
wicked.
⁷ They lie all night naked, without
clothing,
and have no covering in the cold.
⁸ They are wet with the rain of the
mountains,
and cling to the rock for want of
shelter.
⁹ "There are those who snatch the orphan
child from the breast,
and take as a pledge the infant of the
poor.

---

a Syr Vg Tg: Heb *rebellious*   *b* Gk Syr: Heb *my*
c Syr Vg: Heb *he turns*   *d* Gk Vg: Heb *from*
e Traditional rendering of Heb *Shaddai*   *f* Or *But I*
am not destroyed by the darkness; he has concealed the
thick darkness from me   *g* Gk: Heb *they*

10 They go about naked, without clothing;
    though hungry, they carry the
        sheaves;
11 between their terraces^a they press out
        oil;
    they tread the wine presses, but suffer
        thirst.
12 From the city the dying groan,
    and the throat of the wounded cries
        for help;
    yet God pays no attention to their
        prayer.

13 "There are those who rebel against the
        light,
    who are not acquainted with its ways,
    and do not stay in its paths.
14 The murderer rises at dusk
    to kill the poor and needy,
    and in the night is like a thief.
15 The eye of the adulterer also waits for
        the twilight,
    saying, 'No eye will see me';
    and he disguises his face.
16 In the dark they dig through houses;
    by day they shut themselves up;
    they do not know the light.
17 For deep darkness is morning to all of
        them;
    for they are friends with the terrors of
        deep darkness.

18 "Swift are they on the face of the waters;
    their portion in the land is cursed;
    no treader turns toward their vineyards.
19 Drought and heat snatch away the snow
        waters;
    so does Sheol those who have sinned.
20 The womb forgets them;
    the worm finds them sweet;
    they are no longer remembered;
    so wickedness is broken like a tree.

21 "They harm^b the childless woman,
    and do no good to the widow.
22 Yet God^c prolongs the life of the mighty
        by his power;
    they rise up when they despair of life.
23 He gives them security, and they are
        supported;
    his eyes are upon their ways.

24 They are exalted a little while, and then
        are gone;
    they wither and fade like the
        mallow;^d
    they are cut off like the heads of
        grain.
25 If it is not so, who will prove me a liar,
    and show that there is nothing in
        what I say?"

24.1–25. 17: *For they are friends with the terrors of deep darkness:* The imagery of light and darkness permeates 24.13–17. The wicked "overcome" the light. **18–25:** A fragment of a friend's (Zophar's?) speech. The verses strongly affirm that divine retribution will fall on the two groups described in vv. 1–12 and 13–17. **22–25:** The verses may be read as a concession: God, it is true, allows the wicked to flourish but ultimately will cut them off.

The response of Bildad

25.1–6 and 26.5–14: The Hebrew text has suffered dislocation. Bildad's speech in ch. 25 is too short and Job's speech in ch. 26 shifts abruptly in v. 5. Probably, Bildad's speech was originally 25.1–6 and 26.5–14, because the verses form a coherent whole. Bildad's speech is largely in hymnic form. Hymns to the creator God are found in the speeches of Job (9.5–12; 12.13–25) and his friends (5.9–11). In Job's hymns God's power is portrayed as arbitrary and irrational, whereas Bildad portrays a God so powerful and splendid that everything else, including human beings, is nothing (25.1–6). Verses 5–14 form a cosmogony (an account of creation), which shows how God, like a master builder and a heroic warrior, easily shaped primordial massive elements into a vast universe. Bildad concedes his cosmogony gives only a hint of God's grandeur (26.14). The implication is that Job has no right to question God.

---

25 Then Bildad the Shuhite answered:
2 "Dominion and fear are with
        God;^e
    he makes peace in his high heaven.
3 Is there any number to his armies?
    Upon whom does his light not
        arise?

---

a Meaning of Heb uncertain   *b* Gk Tg: Heb *feed on* or
associate with   *c* Heb *he*   *d* Gk: Heb *like all others*
e Heb *him*

4 How then can a mortal be righteous
    before God?
  How can one born of woman be pure?
5 If even the moon is not bright
    and the stars are not pure in his sight,
6 how much less a mortal, who is a
    maggot,
  and a human being, who is a worm!"

Job's second response

26.1–4 and 27.1–12: The attributions of the speeches have been confused in the transmission of the text. This commentary assumes Job's brief speech in 26.1–4 is the preface to his speech in 27.2–12. It also assumes 27.13–23 belongs not to Job but to Zophar, for it contradicts Job's previous statements and continues themes from Zophar's speech in ch. 20. Job's speech is extremely important in the book, since it brings back phrases from chs. 1–2, concludes the three cycles of speeches, points forward to Job's climactic words in chs. 29–31, and is explicitly quoted by God later on (40.8 cites 27.5–6).

26 Then Job answered:
  2 "How you have helped one who
      has no power!
    How you have assisted the arm that
      has no strength!
  3 How you have counseled one who has
      no wisdom,
    and given much good advice!
  4 With whose help have you uttered
      words,
    and whose spirit has come forth from
      you?
  5 The shades below tremble,
    the waters and their inhabitants.
  6 Sheol is naked before God,
    and Abaddon has no covering.
  7 He stretches out Zaphon[a] over the
      void,
    and hangs the earth upon nothing.
  8 He binds up the waters in his thick
      clouds,
    and the cloud is not torn open by
      them.
  9 He covers the face of the full moon,
    and spreads over it his cloud.
  10 He has described a circle on the face of
      the waters,
    at the boundary between light and
      darkness.

11 The pillars of heaven tremble,
    and are astounded at his rebuke.
12 By his power he stilled the Sea;
    by his understanding he struck down
      Rahab.
13 By his wind the heavens were made fair;
    his hand pierced the fleeing serpent.
14 These are indeed but the outskirts of his
      ways;
    and how small a whisper do we hear
      of him!
    But the thunder of his power who can
      understand?"

26.1–14. 5: *The shades* are inhabitants of the underworld (Ps 88.10; Prov 9.18) who also appear in the myths of Israel's neighbors. God's power prevails even in the underworld, the outermost part of the universe. *The waters* are those under the earth, such as are referred to in Jonah's psalm (Jon 2.2–6). **7:** *Zaphon:* A general designation for the north. It is also the name of a northern mountain, which could be applied to Mount Zion* (Ps 48.2). Here, apparently, Zaphon is conceived as the center of the earth. Like a skilled builder, God easily fits the massive mountain into its proper place over formless chaos. **12:** *He stilled the Sea:* Like a victorious warrior, God defeated the forces of pre-creation chaos, personified* as the dragon Sea. *Rahab* is another name for Sea, or for one of Sea's allies.

27 Job again took up his discourse and
  said:
  2 "As God lives, who has taken away my
      right,
    and the Almighty,[b] who has made my
      soul bitter,
  3 as long as my breath is in me
    and the spirit of God is in my nostrils,
  4 my lips will not speak falsehood,
    and my tongue will not utter deceit.
  5 Far be it from me to say that you are
      right;
    until I die I will not put away my
      integrity from me.
  6 I hold fast my righteousness, and will
      not let it go;
    my heart does not reproach me for
      any of my days.

a Or *the North* b Traditional rendering of Heb *Shaddai*

7 "May my enemy be like the wicked,
and may my opponent be like the
unrighteous.
8 For what is the hope of the godless
when God cuts them off,
when God takes away their lives?
9 Will God hear their cry
when trouble comes upon them?
10 Will they take delight in the Almighty?[a]
Will they call upon God at all times?
11 I will teach you concerning the hand of
God;
that which is with the Almighty[a] I will
not conceal.
12 All of you have seen it yourselves;
why then have you become altogether
vain?

27.1–12. 2: *As God lives:* Job's great oath, vowing his innocence, marks a turning point in the story. The solemn formula *as God lives* invites God to punish the false swearer as in 1 Sam 14.39, 45; 2 Sam 2.27. Job has created a new legal context and also an unprecedented situation: His oath makes God the guarantor of the oath but he believes the same God is his enemy. Ending the conversation, Job turns irrevocably to God. **7:** *May my enemy be like the wicked:* Job adapts legal language to his unique situation. The enemy (singular) evidently is God, whom Job wishes to be somehow declared to be in the wrong, and be made to suffer the same painful experiences that Job has endured (v. 8). **11:** Job turns to his friends for the last time (*you* is plural), speaking to them as one who has endured at first hand *the hand of God.*

The response of Zophar (?)

27.13–23: Verse 13 states the topic—the trouble the wicked experience—and gives examples of retribution in different spheres, destruction of families, loss of inheritance, devastation of families, unforeseen terrors, and ruin from the east wind. Zophar in ch. 20 spoke about the inevitable disaster awaiting the wicked.

---

13 "This is the portion of the wicked with
God,
and the heritage that oppressors
receive from the Almighty:[a]
14 If their children are multiplied, it is for
the sword;
and their offspring have not enough
to eat.

15 Those who survive them the pestilence
buries,
and their widows make no lamentation.
16 Though they heap up silver like dust,
and pile up clothing like clay—
17 they may pile it up, but the just will
wear it,
and the innocent will divide the silver.
18 They build their houses like nests,
like booths made by sentinels of the
vineyard.
19 They go to bed with wealth, but will do
so no more;
they open their eyes, and it is gone.
20 Terrors overtake them like a flood;
in the night a whirlwind carries them
off.
21 The east wind lifts them up and they
are gone;
it sweeps them out of their place.
22 It[b] hurls at them without pity;
they flee from its[c] power in headlong
flight.
23 It[b] claps its[c] hands at them,
and hisses at them from its[c] place.

POEM ON WISDOM

Ch. 28: The anonymous poem breaks the cycle of speeches of Job and his three friends that began in ch. 3. Some consider it a later insertion, but it is original to the story, because it heightens the drama by retarding the action and by raising important questions in the reader's mind. For example, by declaring wisdom inaccessible to human beings, the poem suggests what the reader already suspects, the dialogue between Job and his friends cannot provide a satisfactory answer to his problem. It suggests the answer must come from a non-human source, pointing toward the divine response of chs. 39–42. Structurally, the poem has three sections, vv. 1–11, 12–19, and 20–28. In each section, key words (*place, search, way/path, to see*) play an important role.

---

28 "Surely there is a mine for silver,
and a place for gold to be refined.
2 Iron is taken out of the earth,
and copper is smelted from ore.

---

a Traditional rendering of Heb *Shaddai*   *b* Or *He* (that is God)   *c* Or *his*

3 Miners put[a] an end to darkness,
    and search out to the farthest bound
    the ore in gloom and deep darkness.
4 They open shafts in a valley away from
        human habitation;
    they are forgotten by travelers,
    they sway suspended, remote from
        people.
5 As for the earth, out of it comes bread;
    but underneath it is turned up as by
        fire.
6 Its stones are the place of sapphires,[b]
    and its dust contains gold.

7 "That path no bird of prey knows,
    and the falcon's eye has not seen it.
8 The proud wild animals have not
        trodden it;
    the lion has not passed over it.

9 "They put their hand to the flinty rock,
    and overturn mountains by the roots.
10 They cut out channels in the rocks,
    and their eyes see every precious
        thing.
11 The sources of the rivers they probe;[c]
    hidden things they bring to light.

12 "But where shall wisdom be found?
    And where is the place of
        understanding?
13 Mortals do not know the way to it,[d]
    and it is not found in the land of the
        living.
14 The deep says, 'It is not in me,'
    and the sea says, 'It is not with me.'
15 It cannot be gotten for gold,
    and silver cannot be weighed out as
        its price.
16 It cannot be valued in the gold of
        Ophir,
    in precious onyx or sapphire.[b]
17 Gold and glass cannot equal it,
    nor can it be exchanged for jewels of
        fine gold.
18 No mention shall be made of coral or of
        crystal;
    the price of wisdom is above pearls.
19 The chrysolite of Ethiopia[e] cannot
        compare with it,
    nor can it be valued in pure gold.

20 "Where then does wisdom come from?
    And where is the place of
        understanding?
21 It is hidden from the eyes of all living,
    and concealed from the birds of the
        air.
22 Abaddon and Death say,
    'We have heard a rumor of it with our
        ears.'
23 "God understands the way to it,
    and he knows its place.
24 For he looks to the ends of the earth,
    and sees everything under the
        heavens.
25 When he gave to the wind its weight,
    and apportioned out the waters by
        measure;
26 when he made a decree for the rain,
    and a way for the thunderbolt;
27 then he saw it and declared it;
    he established it, and searched it out.
28 And he said to humankind,
    'Truly, the fear of the Lord, that is
        wisdom;
    and to depart from evil is
        understanding.' "

28.1–28. 7: *That path no bird of prey knows:* Human beings who excavate precious metals in mines surpass the vision of the keenest-eyed birds, yet wisdom lies beyond the vision of the most intrepid human explorers. **28:** *Truly, the fear of the Lord, that is wisdom:* The phrase was used in Job 1.8 and 2.3.

JOB'S FINAL STATEMENT

Chs. 29–31: Job's final speech, the longest speech in the book until the LORD's twin speeches in chs. 38–42, is a statement continuing the legal argument of the earlier speeches. In ch. 29 Job portrays himself in exalted terms as a heroic and just person, favored by God (29.2–6) and honored by all in the community (29.7–25). But now, Job complains, he is ridiculed by the dregs of society (30.1–8), assaulted and humiliated by others (30.9–15), attacked by God and denied justice (30.16–31). In his great oath he denies any wrongdoing whatsoever and swears he has adhered to heroic

a Heb *He puts*   b Or *lapis lazuli*
c Gk Vg: Heb *bind*   d Gk: Heb *its price*
e Or *Nubia;* Heb *Cush*

standards of justice. He ends with a demand to confront God directly (31.35–40).

29

¹ Job again took up his discourse and said:

² "O that I were as in the months of old,
　　as in the days when God watched
　　　over me;
³ when his lamp shone over my head,
　　and by his light I walked through
　　　darkness;
⁴ when I was in my prime,
　　when the friendship of God was upon
　　　my tent;
⁵ when the Almighty*a* was still with me,
　　when my children were around me;
⁶ when my steps were washed with milk,
　　and the rock poured out for me
　　　streams of oil!
⁷ When I went out to the gate of the city,
　　when I took my seat in the square,
⁸ the young men saw me and withdrew,
　　and the aged rose up and stood;
⁹ the nobles refrained from talking,
　　and laid their hands on their mouths;
¹⁰ the voices of princes were hushed,
　　and their tongues stuck to the roof of
　　　their mouths.
¹¹ When the ear heard, it commended me,
　　and when the eye saw, it approved;
¹² because I delivered the poor who cried,
　　and the orphan who had no helper.
¹³ The blessing of the wretched came
　　　upon me,
　　and I caused the widow's heart to
　　　sing for joy.
¹⁴ I put on righteousness, and it clothed
　　　me;
　　my justice was like a robe and a
　　　turban.
¹⁵ I was eyes to the blind,
　　and feet to the lame.
¹⁶ I was a father to the needy,
　　and I championed the cause of the
　　　stranger.
¹⁷ I broke the fangs of the unrighteous,
　　and made them drop their prey from
　　　their teeth.
¹⁸ Then I thought, 'I shall die in my nest,
　　and I shall multiply my days like the
　　　phoenix;*b*

¹⁹ my roots spread out to the waters,
　　with the dew all night on my
　　　branches;
²⁰ my glory was fresh with me,
　　and my bow ever new in my hand.'
²¹ "They listened to me, and waited,
　　and kept silence for my counsel.
²² After I spoke they did not speak again,
　　and my word dropped upon them like
　　　dew.*c*
²³ They waited for me as for the rain;
　　they opened their mouths as for the
　　　spring rain.
²⁴ I smiled on them when they had no
　　　confidence;
　　and the light of my countenance they
　　　did not extinguish.*d*
²⁵ I chose their way, and sat as chief,
　　and I lived like a king among his
　　　troops,
　　like one who comforts mourners.

29.1–25: Job's blessed and heroic life. Job yearns to return to his past life, to the time when he was blessed and honored. The review of his life functions as a kind of self-praise, citing himself as the example of noble conduct and status. **11–17:** The centerpiece of his remembrance is himself as a peerless administrator of justice. Job's treatment of the oppressed and the needy contrasts dramatically with God's treatment of the oppressed and needy Job. **14:** The middle verse of vv. 11–17 is set off by the mention of paired body parts in the surrounding verses (v. 11, *ear, eye*; v. 13, *heart*; v. 15, *eyes, feet*; v. 17, *fangs, teeth*). **18:** *Like the phoenix:* A legendary* bird, which, after living up to 500 years, burned itself to ashes and rose to live another long period. Verses 19–20 continue the images of vitality. **21–25:** Job applies to himself phrases normally applied to God: *spring rain* (v. 23; see also Deut 11.14; Hos 6.3) and *the light of my countenance* (v. 24, compare Ps 4.6; 44.3).

30

¹ "But now they make sport of me,
　　those who are younger than I,
　　whose fathers I would have disdained
　　　to set with the dogs of my flock.

a Traditional rendering of Heb *Shaddai*　　*b* Or *like sand*　　*c* Heb lacks *like dew*　　*d* Meaning of Heb uncertain

2 What could I gain from the strength of
     their hands?
  All their vigor is gone.
3 Through want and hard hunger
     they gnaw the dry and desolate
     ground,
4 they pick mallow and the leaves of
     bushes,
     and to warm themselves the roots of
     broom.
5 They are driven out from society;
     people shout after them as after a
     thief.
6 In the gullies of wadis they must live,
     in holes in the ground, and in the
     rocks.
7 Among the bushes they bray;
     under the nettles they huddle together.
8 A senseless, disreputable brood,
     they have been whipped out of the
     land.

9 "And now they mock me in song;
  I am a byword to them.
10 They abhor me, they keep aloof from me;
     they do not hesitate to spit at the
     sight of me.
11 Because God has loosed my bowstring
     and humbled me,
     they have cast off restraint in my
     presence.
12 On my right hand the rabble rise up;
     they send me sprawling,
     and build roads for my ruin.
13 They break up my path,
     they promote my calamity;
     no one restrains*a* them.
14 As through a wide breach they come;
     amid the crash they roll on.
15 Terrors are turned upon me;
     my honor is pursued as by the wind,
     and my prosperity has passed away
     like a cloud.

16 "And now my soul is poured out within
     me;
     days of affliction have taken hold of
     me.
17 The night racks my bones,
     and the pain that gnaws me takes no
     rest.

18 With violence he seizes my garment;*b*
     he grasps me by*c* the collar of my
     tunic.
19 He has cast me into the mire,
     and I have become like dust and
     ashes.
20 I cry to you and you do not answer me;
     I stand, and you merely look at me.
21 You have turned cruel to me;
     with the might of your hand you
     persecute me.
22 You lift me up on the wind, you make
     me ride on it,
     and you toss me about in the roar of
     the storm.
23 I know that you will bring me to death,
     and to the house appointed for all
     living.

24 "Surely one does not turn against the
     needy,*d*
     when in disaster they cry for help.*e*
25 Did I not weep for those whose day was
     hard?
     Was not my soul grieved for the
     poor?
26 But when I looked for good, evil came;
     and when I waited for light, darkness
     came.
27 My inward parts are in turmoil, and are
     never still;
     days of affliction come to meet me.
28 I go about in sunless gloom;
     I stand up in the assembly and cry for
     help.
29 I am a brother of jackals,
     and a companion of ostriches.
30 My skin turns black and falls from me,
     and my bones burn with heat.
31 My lyre is turned to mourning,
     and my pipe to the voice of those who
     weep.

30.1–31: Job complains he is attacked by human beings and by God, and his cry is not heard. **11:** *God has loosed my bowstring:* God has disarmed Job. **20:** *I cry to you:* The verb *cry* is repeated in v. 28. Job cries

a Cn: Heb *helps*   *b* Gk: Heb *my garment is disfigured*
c Heb *like*   *d* Heb *ruin*   *e* Cn: Meaning of Heb
uncertain

out in vain for justice, though basic decency would
demand the needy be heard.

31 "I have made a covenant with my
      eyes;
    how then could I look upon a virgin?
2 What would be my portion from God
      above,
    and my heritage from the Almighty[a]
      on high?
3 Does not calamity befall the unrighteous,
    and disaster the workers of iniquity?
4 Does he not see my ways,
    and number all my steps?

5 "If I have walked with falsehood,
    and my foot has hurried to deceit—
6 let me be weighed in a just balance,
    and let God know my integrity!—
7 if my step has turned aside from the way,
    and my heart has followed my eyes,
    and if any spot has clung to my
      hands;
8 then let me sow, and another eat;
    and let what grows for me be rooted
      out.

9 "If my heart has been enticed by a
      woman,
    and I have lain in wait at my
      neighbor's door;
10 then let my wife grind for another,
    and let other men kneel over her.
11 For that would be a heinous crime;
    that would be a criminal offense;
12 for that would be a fire consuming
      down to Abaddon,
    and it would burn to the root all my
      harvest.

13 "If I have rejected the cause of my male
      or female slaves,
    when they brought a complaint
      against me;
14 what then shall I do when God rises up?
    When he makes inquiry, what shall I
      answer him?
15 Did not he who made me in the womb
      make them?
    And did not one fashion us in the
      womb?

16 "If I have withheld anything that the
      poor desired,
    or have caused the eyes of the widow
      to fail,
17 or have eaten my morsel alone,
    and the orphan has not eaten from
      it—
18 for from my youth I reared the orphan[b]
      like a father,
    and from my mother's womb I guided
      the widow[c]—
19 if I have seen anyone perish for lack of
      clothing,
    or a poor person without covering,
20 whose loins have not blessed me,
    and who was not warmed with the
      fleece of my sheep;
21 if I have raised my hand against the
      orphan,
    because I saw I had supporters at the
      gate;
22 then let my shoulder blade fall from my
      shoulder,
    and let my arm be broken from its
      socket.
23 For I was in terror of calamity from
      God,
    and I could not have faced his
      majesty.

24 "If I have made gold my trust,
    or called fine gold my confidence;
25 if I have rejoiced because my wealth
      was great,
    or because my hand had gotten much;
26 if I have looked at the sun[d] when it
      shone,
    or the moon moving in splendor,
27 and my heart has been secretly enticed,
    and my mouth has kissed my hand;
28 this also would be an iniquity to be
      punished by the judges,
    for I should have been false to God
      above.

29 "If I have rejoiced at the ruin of those
      who hated me,
    or exulted when evil overtook them—

_a_ Traditional rendering of Heb _Shaddai_   _b_ Heb _him_
_c_ Heb _her_   _d_ Heb _the light_

30 I have not let my mouth sin
　　by asking for their lives with a curse—
31 if those of my tent ever said,
　　'O that we might be sated with his
　　　flesh!'[a]—
32 the stranger has not lodged in the
　　　street;
　　I have opened my doors to the
　　　traveler—
33 if I have concealed my transgressions as
　　　others do,[b]
　　by hiding my iniquity in my bosom,
34 because I stood in great fear of the
　　　multitude,
　　and the contempt of families terrified
　　　me,
　　so that I kept silence, and did not go
　　　out of doors—
35 O that I had one to hear me!
　　(Here is my signature! Let the
　　　Almighty[c] answer me!)
　　O that I had the indictment written
　　　by my adversary!
36 Surely I would carry it on my shoulder;
　　I would bind it on me like a crown;
37 I would give him an account of all my
　　　steps;
　　like a prince I would approach him.

38 "If my land has cried out against me,
　　and its furrows have wept together;
39 if I have eaten its yield without
　　　payment,
　　and caused the death of its owners;
40 let thorns grow instead of wheat,
　　and foul weeds instead of barley."

The words of Job are ended.

31.1–40: In a negative confession, Job swears an oath to clear himself of all charges. Job swears before God that if he has done any of the deeds he describes, then punishment should afflict him. The chapter is structured in "envelope style": vv. 1–3 and 38–40 (the covenant* and its curse) are the outer envelope, vv. 4–6 and 35–37 (the challenge hurled at God) are the inner envelope, and vv. 7–34 are at the center. The central verses list the potential sins and their penalties. Eleven sins are mentioned in vv. 7–34. After each there is a sanction or some comment (except vv. 24–25 and 32). 1: *How then could I look upon a virgin?* An ex-

ample of hyperbole.* Here and elsewhere in the chapter, Job is swearing to an extraordinary level of righteousness. By the same token, the oaths are an indirect attack on Job's opponent at law. 36–37: *Oh, that I had one to hear me!* Job calls out one last time for a public trial with an arbiter present (see 9.33; 16.19; 19.25) to mediate between him and his opponent. 38–40: Job ends his list of oaths by calling upon earth, a primordial element often invoked in ancient legal ceremonies as a witness. If God remains silent now, he will seem to be the guilty party.

THE SPEECHES OF ELIHU

Chs. 32–37: The four Elihu speeches are often judged to have been added later as an attempt to answer Job more effectively than the three friends. The Elihu speeches are most probably original, however: (1) Elihu is a somewhat comic figure, angrily claiming to be wiser than his elders (the mark of a fool) and would hardly be invented to rebut Job definitively; (2) in the book Elihu makes dramatic sense, for he is the comically exaggerated answer to Job's demand for a mediator between himself and God; (3) the omission of his name in the list of friends in the epilogue (42.7, 9) only shows he is not part of the give-and-take of the dialogues; (4) dramatically, he retards the action and prepares for the appearance of the LORD and the cosmic topics in the divine speeches.

Ch. 32: Elihu introduces himself. Elihu makes an impression opposite to the one he wants to create. Instead of patiently and wisely drawing on the teaching of his elders, he angrily dismisses them, inadvertently giving himself away by comparing himself to a new wineskin ready to burst (v. 19).

32 So these three men ceased to answer Job, because he was righteous in his own eyes. [2] Then Elihu son of Barachel the Buzite, of the family of Ram, became angry. He was angry at Job because he justified himself rather than God; [3] he was angry also at Job's three friends because they had found no answer, though they had declared Job to be in the wrong.[d] [4] Now Elihu had waited to speak to Job, because they were older than he. [5] But when Elihu saw that there was no

a Meaning of Heb uncertain   b Or as *Adam did*
c Traditional rendering of Heb *Shaddai*   d Another ancient tradition reads *answer, and had put God in the wrong*

answer in the mouths of these three men, he became angry.

32.2: *Buzite:* The name Buz occurs in Gen 22.21 as the brother of Uz, which is the name of Job's homeland (1.1); it is presumably a place in the same area.

6 Elihu son of Barachel the Buzite answered:
"I am young in years,
   and you are aged;
therefore I was timid and afraid
   to declare my opinion to you.
7 I said, 'Let days speak,
   and many years teach wisdom.'
8 But truly it is the spirit in a mortal,
   the breath of the Almighty,*a* that
      makes for understanding.
9 It is not the old*b* that are wise,
   nor the aged that understand what is
      right.
10 Therefore I say, 'Listen to me;
   let me also declare my opinion.'

11 "See, I waited for your words,
   I listened for your wise sayings,
      while you searched out what to say.
12 I gave you my attention,
   but there was in fact no one that
      confuted Job,
   no one among you that answered his
      words.
13 Yet do not say, 'We have found wisdom;
   God may vanquish him, not a
      human.'
14 He has not directed his words against
      me,
   and I will not answer him with your
      speeches.

15 "They are dismayed, they answer no
      more;
   they have not a word to say.
16 And am I to wait, because they do not
      speak,
   because they stand there, and answer
      no more?
17 I also will give my answer;
   I also will declare my opinion.
18 For I am full of words;
   the spirit within me constrains me.

19 My heart is indeed like wine that has no
      vent;
   like new wineskins, it is ready to
      burst.
20 I must speak, so that I may find relief;
   I must open my lips and answer.
21 I will not show partiality to any person
   or use flattery toward anyone.
22 For I do not know how to flatter—
   or my Maker would soon put an end
      to me!

Elihu's first speech
Ch. 33: Contrary to Job's assertion that God did not respond to him, Elihu teaches that God indeed responds to people, teaching them through dreams (vv. 15–18), through suffering (vv. 19–22), and through healing (vv. 23–28). *Pit* (Sheol,* the underworld) unifies the three sections, appearing in each (vv. 18, 22, 28). Elihu invites Job to allow God to heal him (especially vv. 29–33).

---

33 "But now, hear my speech, O Job,
   and listen to all my words.
2 See, I open my mouth;
   the tongue in my mouth speaks.
3 My words declare the uprightness of my
      heart,
   and what my lips know they speak
      sincerely.
4 The spirit of God has made me,
   and the breath of the Almighty*a* gives
      me life.
5 Answer me, if you can;
   set your words in order before me;
      take your stand.
6 See, before God I am as you are;
   I too was formed from a piece of clay.
7 No fear of me need terrify you;
   my pressure will not be heavy on you.

8 "Surely, you have spoken in my hearing,
   and I have heard the sound of your
      words.
9 You say, 'I am clean, without
      transgression;
   I am pure, and there is no iniquity in
      me.

---

a Traditional rendering of Heb *Shaddai*   *b* Gk Syr Vg:
Heb *many*

10 Look, he finds occasions against me,
    he counts me as his enemy;
11 he puts my feet in the stocks,
    and watches all my paths.'

33.9: *You say, "I am clean, without transgression":*
Elihu makes Job say more than he actually said. Job did
not claim to be clean in an absolute sense even in ch.
31; he claimed only to be innocent of the kind of
wrongdoing that has caused his present suffering.

〰〰〰〰〰〰〰〰〰〰〰〰〰〰〰〰

12 "But in this you are not right. I will
    answer you:
    God is greater than any mortal.
13 Why do you contend against him,
    saying, 'He will answer none of my[a]
    words'?
14 For God speaks in one way,
    and in two, though people do not
    perceive it.
15 In a dream, in a vision of the night,
    when deep sleep falls on mortals,
    while they slumber on their beds,
16 then he opens their ears,
    and terrifies them with warnings,
17 that he may turn them aside from their
    deeds,
    and keep them from pride,
18 to spare their souls from the Pit,
    their lives from traversing the River.
19 They are also chastened with pain upon
    their beds,
    and with continual strife in their bones,
20 so that their lives loathe bread,
    and their appetites dainty food.
21 Their flesh is so wasted away that it
    cannot be seen;
    and their bones, once invisible, now
    stick out.
22 Their souls draw near the Pit,
    and their lives to those who bring
    death.
23 Then, if there should be for one of them
    an angel,
    a mediator, one of a thousand,
    one who declares a person upright,
24 and he is gracious to that person, and
    says,
    'Deliver him from going down into
    the Pit;
    I have found a ransom;

25 let his flesh become fresh with youth;
    let him return to the days of his
    youthful vigor';
26 then he prays to God, and is accepted
    by him,
    he comes into his presence with joy,
    and God[b] repays him for his
    righteousness.
27 That person sings to others and says,
    'I sinned, and perverted what was right,
    and it was not paid back to me.
28 He has redeemed my soul from going
    down to the Pit,
    and my life shall see the light.'

29 "God indeed does all these things,
    twice, three times, with mortals,
30 to bring back their souls from the Pit,
    so that they may see the light of life.[c]
31 Pay heed, Job, listen to me;
    be silent, and I will speak.
32 If you have anything to say, answer me;
    speak, for I desire to justify you.
33 If not, listen to me;
    be silent, and I will teach you
    wisdom."

〰〰〰〰〰〰〰〰〰〰〰〰〰〰〰〰

Elihu's second speech
Ch. 34: Elihu defends God's justice (vv. 2–4) by attacking Job's character (vv. 5–9) and upholding God's
character (vv. 10–15) and mode of governance (vv.
16–30). Therefore, he calls on Job to repent (vv. 31–
33) and gives his own verdict (vv. 34–37).

---

34 Then Elihu continued and said:
2 "Hear my words, you wise men,
    and give ear to me, you who know;
3 for the ear tests words
    as the palate tastes food.
4 Let us choose what is right;
    let us determine among ourselves
    what is good.
5 For Job has said, 'I am innocent,
    and God has taken away my right;
6 in spite of being right I am counted a
    liar;
    my wound is incurable, though I am
    without transgression.'

a Compare Gk: Heb *his*   *b* Heb *he*   *c* Syr: Heb *to*
be lighted with the light of life

7 Who is there like Job,
     who drinks up scoffing like water,
8 who goes in company with evildoers
     and walks with the wicked?
9 For he has said, 'It profits one nothing
     to take delight in God.'

10 "Therefore, hear me, you who have
          sense,
     far be it from God that he should do
          wickedness,
     and from the Almighty*a* that he
          should do wrong.
11 For according to their deeds he will
          repay them,
     and according to their ways he will
          make it befall them.
12 Of a truth, God will not do wickedly,
     and the Almighty*a* will not pervert
          justice.
13 Who gave him charge over the earth
     and who laid on him*b* the whole
          world?
14 If he should take back his spirit*c* to
          himself,
     and gather to himself his breath,
15 all flesh would perish together,
     and all mortals return to dust.

16 "If you have understanding, hear this;
     listen to what I say.
17 Shall one who hates justice govern?
     Will you condemn one who is
          righteous and mighty,
18 who says to a king, 'You scoundrel!'
     and to princes, 'You wicked men!';
19 who shows no partiality to nobles,
     nor regards the rich more than the
          poor,
     for they are all the work of his hands?
20 In a moment they die;
     at midnight the people are shaken
          and pass away,
     and the mighty are taken away by no
          human hand.

21 "For his eyes are upon the ways of
          mortals,
     and he sees all their steps.
22 There is no gloom or deep darkness
     where evildoers may hide themselves.

23 For he has not appointed a time*d* for
          anyone
     to go before God in judgment.
24 He shatters the mighty without
          investigation,
     and sets others in their place.
25 Thus, knowing their works,
     he overturns them in the night, and
          they are crushed.
26 He strikes them for their wickedness
     while others look on,
27 because they turned aside from
          following him,
     and had no regard for any of his ways,
28 so that they caused the cry of the poor
          to come to him,
     and he heard the cry of the
          afflicted—
29 When he is quiet, who can condemn?
     When he hides his face, who can
          behold him,
     whether it be a nation or an
          individual?—
30 so that the godless should not reign,
     or those who ensnare the people.

31 "For has anyone said to God,
     'I have endured punishment; I will
          not offend any more;
32 teach me what I do not see;
     if I have done iniquity, I will do it no
          more'?
33 Will he then pay back to suit you,
     because you reject it?
For you must choose, and not I;
     therefore declare what you know.*e*
34 Those who have sense will say to me,
     and the wise who hear me will say,
35 'Job speaks without knowledge,
     his words are without insight.'
36 Would that Job were tried to the limit,
     because his answers are those of the
          wicked.
37 For he adds rebellion to his sin;
     he claps his hands among us,
     and multiplies his words against
          God."

a Traditional rendering of Heb *Shaddai*   *b* Heb lacks
on him   *c* Heb *his heart his spirit*   *d* Cn: Heb *yet*
e Meaning of Heb of verses 29–33 uncertain

34.1–37. 5: *God has taken away my right* is a legal phrase, meaning that God has denied me litigation. **23:** *For he has not appointed a time for anyone* has a legal meaning: Human beings cannot force God into court, for God and God's governance are faultless and beyond questioning.

Elihu's third speech

Ch. 35: Elihu assesses Job's claim that one gains no advantage from being just (v. 3). How dare Job expect a divine response to his conduct? God is too far away to be affected by human behavior (vv. 5–8). Moreover, most people's cries for help are insincere in any case (vv. 9–13). Elihu then derides Job (vv. 14–16).

35 Elihu continued and said:
2 "Do you think this to be just? You say, 'I am in the right before God.'
3 If you ask, 'What advantage have I? How am I better off than if I had sinned?'
4 I will answer you and your friends with you.
5 Look at the heavens and see; observe the clouds, which are higher than you.
6 If you have sinned, what do you accomplish against him? And if your transgressions are multiplied, what do you do to him?
7 If you are righteous, what do you give to him; or what does he receive from your hand?
8 Your wickedness affects others like you, and your righteousness, other human beings.
9 "Because of the multitude of oppressions people cry out; they call for help because of the arm of the mighty.
10 But no one says, 'Where is God my Maker, who gives strength in the night,
11 who teaches us more than the animals of the earth,

and makes us wiser than the birds of the air?'
12 There they cry out, but he does not answer, because of the pride of evildoers.
13 Surely God does not hear an empty cry, nor does the Almighty[a] regard it.
14 How much less when you say that you do not see him, that the case is before him, and you are waiting for him!
15 And now, because his anger does not punish, and he does not greatly heed transgression,[b]
16 Job opens his mouth in empty talk, he multiplies words without knowledge."

Elihu's fourth and climactic speech

Chs. 36–37: The speech has three parts. Each begins with an address to Job (36.2–4, 16–21; 37.14–22) and then depicts God as just and wise (36.5–15, 22–25; 37.23–24). The depiction of God in the middle section (36.26–37.13) is accomplished by describing God's masterpiece, the storm, which vividly illustrates divine wisdom and power.

36 Elihu continued and said:
2 "Bear with me a little, and I will show you, for I have yet something to say on God's behalf.
3 I will bring my knowledge from far away, and ascribe righteousness to my Maker.
4 For truly my words are not false; one who is perfect in knowledge is with you.
5 "Surely God is mighty and does not despise any; he is mighty in strength of understanding.
6 He does not keep the wicked alive, but gives the afflicted their right.

a Traditional rendering of Heb *Shaddai*   *b* Theodotion Symmachus Compare Vg: Meaning of Heb uncertain

7 He does not withdraw his eyes from the
   righteous,
      but with kings on the throne
      he sets them forever, and they are
         exalted.
8 And if they are bound in fetters
      and caught in the cords of affliction,
9 then he declares to them their work
      and their transgressions, that they are
         behaving arrogantly.
10 He opens their ears to instruction,
      and commands that they return from
         iniquity.
11 If they listen, and serve him,
      they complete their days in
         prosperity,
      and their years in pleasantness.
12 But if they do not listen, they shall
      perish by the sword,
      and die without knowledge.
13 "The godless in heart cherish anger;
      they do not cry for help when he
         binds them.
14 They die in their youth,
      and their life ends in shame.*a*
15 He delivers the afflicted by their
      affliction,
      and opens their ear by adversity.
16 He also allured you out of distress
      into a broad place where there was no
         constraint,
      and what was set on your table was
         full of fatness.

17 "But you are obsessed with the case of
      the wicked;
      judgment and justice seize you.
18 Beware that wrath does not entice you
      into scoffing,
      and do not let the greatness of the
         ransom turn you aside.
19 Will your cry avail to keep you from
      distress,
      or will all the force of your strength?
20 Do not long for the night,
      when peoples are cut off in their
         place.
21 Beware! Do not turn to iniquity;
      because of that you have been tried
         by affliction.

22 See, God is exalted in his power;
      who is a teacher like him?
23 Who has prescribed for him his way,
      or who can say, 'You have done
         wrong'?
24 "Remember to extol his work,
      of which mortals have sung.
25 All people have looked on it;
      everyone watches it from far away.
26 Surely God is great, and we do not
      know him;
      the number of his years is
         unsearchable.
27 For he draws up the drops of water;
      he distills*b* his mist in rain,
28 which the skies pour down
      and drop upon mortals abundantly.
29 Can anyone understand the spreading
      of the clouds,
      the thunderings of his pavilion?
30 See, he scatters his lightning around
      him
      and covers the roots of the sea.
31 For by these he governs peoples;
      he gives food in abundance.
32 He covers his hands with the lightning,
      and commands it to strike the mark.
33 Its crashing*c* tells about him;
      he is jealous*c* with anger against
         iniquity.

37 "At this also my heart trembles,
      and leaps out of its place.
2 Listen, listen to the thunder of his voice
      and the rumbling that comes from his
         mouth.
3 Under the whole heaven he lets it loose,
      and his lightning to the corners of the
         earth.
4 After it his voice roars;
      he thunders with his majestic voice
      and he does not restrain the
         lightnings*d* when his voice is
         heard.
5 God thunders wondrously with his voice;
      he does great things that we cannot
         comprehend.

a Heb *ends among the temple prostitutes*   *b* Cn: Heb
they distill   *c* Meaning of Heb uncertain
d Heb *them*

6 For to the snow he says, 'Fall on the
     earth';
   and the shower of rain, his heavy
     shower of rain,
7 serves as a sign on everyone's hand,
   so that all whom he has made may
     know it.*
8 Then the animals go into their lairs
   and remain in their dens.
9 From its chamber comes the whirlwind,
   and cold from the scattering winds.
10 By the breath of God ice is given,
   and the broad waters are frozen fast.
11 He loads the thick cloud with moisture;
   the clouds scatter his lightning.
12 They turn round and round by his
     guidance,
   to accomplish all that he commands
     them
   on the face of the habitable world.
13 Whether for correction, or for his land,
   or for love, he causes it to happen.

14 "Hear this, O Job;
   stop and consider the wondrous
     works of God.
15 Do you know how God lays his
     command upon them,
   and causes the lightning of his cloud
     to shine?
16 Do you know the balancings of the
     clouds,
   the wondrous works of the one whose
     knowledge is perfect,
17 you whose garments are hot
   when the earth is still because of the
     south wind?
18 Can you, like him, spread out the skies,
   hard as a molten mirror?
19 Teach us what we shall say to him;
   we cannot draw up our case because
     of darkness.
20 Should he be told that I want to speak?
   Did anyone ever wish to be swallowed
     up?
21 Now, no one can look on the light
   when it is bright in the skies,
   when the wind has passed and
     cleared them.
22 Out of the north comes golden splendor;
   around God is awesome majesty.

23 The Almighty*—we cannot find him;
   he is great in power and justice,
   and abundant righteousness he will
     not violate.
24 Therefore mortals fear him;
   he does not regard any who are wise
     in their own conceit."

37.1–24. 15: *Do you know how God lays his command upon them?* This challenging question to Job about the operating of the universe, as well as the similar ones in vv. 15–18, foreshadow the LORD's questions to him in the divine speeches. **23:** *The Almighty—we cannot find him:* Elihu's final speech is full of ironies. Job will soon find the Almighty; God is in the storm that Elihu so eloquently described in 36.26–37.13, but differently than Elihu imagines.

GOD'S TWO SPEECHES TO JOB

38.1–42.6: The LORD's sudden appearance in the storm never fails to astonish even though the ground has been laid for it in Job's oaths and demands of chs. 27 and 29–31 and, in an ironic* way, by Elihu's "appearance" and final statement. God answers Job out of the whirlwind in two speeches (chs. 38–39 and 40–41), each evoking a brief response by Job (40.1–5 and 42.1–6). The structure and the meaning of the speeches have puzzled scholars. Some believe the speeches are deliberately incoherent, irrational divine blasts showing there is no answer to Job's questions except inscrutable divine will. Others rearrange the text, but no rearrangement has won wide acceptance. Most, however, find some kind of logic, even though the speeches are also an example of the mysterious communication of creator to creature. The first speech shows that the world has a design (God is wise, is able to govern), and the second demonstrates the world is just (God upholds the righteous and puts down the wicked).

38.1–40.5: The LORD's first speech and Job's response. God treats Job like a rival claimant to deity. God's questions, despite their variety, come down to one: Did you bring the world into being? Job was the one who established the legal context. Now, under God's relentless legal questioning, he cannot give a single answer. The topic of the speech is *counsel*, which Job is accused of obscuring (38.2). *Who is this*

---

a Meaning of Heb of verse 7 uncertain   *b* Traditional rendering of Heb *Shaddai* that darkens counsel by words without knowledge? *Counsel* is better rendered "plan, design" (as in Ps 14.6; 20.4; Prov 20.5). An example of Job's charge that the earth was purely random and without design is 9.5–6, where Job accuses God of overturning the primordial mountains and earth, that is, of not knowing how to create. God counters by asking Job if he actually witnessed the foundation of the earth, and then reveals how carefully he built with measuring line, sockets, and cornerstone while a festive chorus sang as at a Temple* dedication (38.4–7). Another example is Job's accusation that God does not distinguish between the wicked and the righteous (9.24). On the contrary, dawn exposes the night deeds of the wicked, which does not, however, necessarily lead to their punishment (38.12–15). Even the proverbial stupid ostrich is stupid by design (39.13–18), a reminder that God creates not for human beings but for his own inscrutable purpose. The world includes the useful, the bizarre, and even the playful, all by God's design. The rhetorical* method of the speech is to list eight items of the inanimate world (38.4–38) and eight items of the animal and bird kingdoms (38.39–39.30). In none of them did Job have any role, a conclusion that is made clear by Job's inability to answer the divine questions. Significantly, the human race is not mentioned in either catalog. The human race—including Job—are not the center of the universe.

38 Then the LORD answered Job out of the whirlwind:

2 "Who is this that darkens counsel by
        words without knowledge?
3 Gird up your loins like a man,
        I will question you, and you shall
            declare to me.

4 "Where were you when I laid the
            foundation of the earth?
        Tell me, if you have understanding.
5 Who determined its measurements—
            surely you know!
        Or who stretched the line upon it?
6 On what were its bases sunk,
        or who laid its cornerstone
7 when the morning stars sang together
        and all the heavenly beings[a] shouted
            for joy?

8 "Or who shut in the sea with doors
        when it burst out from the womb?—

9 when I made the clouds its garment,
        and thick darkness its swaddling
            band,
10 and prescribed bounds for it,
        and set bars and doors,
11 and said, 'Thus far shall you come, and
            no farther,
        and here shall your proud waves be
            stopped'?

38.8: *When it burst out from the womb?* A common myth told of sea personified* as a monster whom the storm god defeated in order to create. Here, the monster is reduced to an infant in order to show God's easy control (see Ps 104.26).

12 "Have you commanded the morning
            since your days began,
        and caused the dawn to know its
            place,
13 so that it might take hold of the skirts of
            the earth,
        and the wicked be shaken out of it?
14 It is changed like clay under the seal,
        and it is dyed[b] like a garment.
15 Light is withheld from the wicked,
        and their uplifted arm is broken.

16 "Have you entered into the springs of
            the sea,
        or walked in the recesses of the deep?
17 Have the gates of death been revealed
            to you,
        or have you seen the gates of deep
            darkness?
18 Have you comprehended the expanse of
            the earth?
        Declare, if you know all this.

19 "Where is the way to the dwelling of
            light,
        and where is the place of darkness,
20 that you may take it to its territory
        and that you may discern the paths to
            its home?
21 Surely you know, for you were born
            then,
        and the number of your days is great!

a Heb *sons of God*   b Cn: Heb *and they stand forth*

22 "Have you entered the storehouses of
    the snow,
    or have you seen the storehouses of
    the hail,
23 which I have reserved for the time of
    trouble,
    for the day of battle and war?
24 What is the way to the place where the
    light is distributed,
    or where the east wind is scattered
    upon the earth?

25 "Who has cut a channel for the torrents
    of rain,
    and a way for the thunderbolt,
26 to bring rain on a land where no one
    lives,
    on the desert, which is empty of
    human life,
27 to satisfy the waste and desolate land,
    and to make the ground put forth
    grass?

28 "Has the rain a father,
    or who has begotten the drops of
    dew?
29 From whose womb did the ice come
    forth,
    and who has given birth to the
    hoarfrost of heaven?
30 The waters become hard like stone,
    and the face of the deep is frozen.

31 "Can you bind the chains of the
    Pleiades,
    or loose the cords of Orion?
32 Can you lead forth the Mazzaroth in
    their season,
    or can you guide the Bear with its
    children?
33 Do you know the ordinances of the
    heavens?
    Can you establish their rule on the
    earth?

stellation, well known to ancient star gazers. *Orion* is
a constellation on the equator east of Taurus imagined
by the Greeks as a hunter with belt and sword. The
identifications of *Mazzaroth* and *the Bear* are
uncertain.

~~~~~~~~~~

34 "Can you lift up your voice to the
    clouds,
    so that a flood of waters may cover
    you?
35 Can you send forth lightnings, so that
    they may go
    and say to you, 'Here we are'?
36 Who has put wisdom in the inward
    parts,[a]
    or given understanding to the
    mind?[a]
37 Who has the wisdom to number the
    clouds?
    Or who can tilt the waterskins of the
    heavens,
38 when the dust runs into a mass
    and the clods cling together?

39 "Can you hunt the prey for the lion,
    or satisfy the appetite of the young
    lions,
40 when they crouch in their dens,
    or lie in wait in their covert?
41 Who provides for the raven its prey,
    when its young ones cry to God,
    and wander about for lack of food?

39 "Do you know when the mountain
    goats give birth?
    Do you observe the calving of the
    deer?
2 Can you number the months that they
    fulfill,
    and do you know the time when they
    give birth,
3 when they crouch to give birth to their
    offspring,
    and are delivered of their young?
4 Their young ones become strong, they
    grow up in the open;
    they go forth, and do not return to
    them.

38.26–31. 26: *To bring rain on a land where no one
lives:* God cares for areas where no human beings live,
a rebuke to an anthropocentric view of creation. Human beings are not the measure. **31:** *The Pleiades . . .
Orion . . . Mazzaroth . . . the Bear: The Pleiades* is the
Greek name for a cluster of six stars in the Taurus con-

a Meaning of Heb uncertain

5 "Who has let the wild ass go free?
  Who has loosed the bonds of the
    swift ass,
6 to which I have given the steppe for its
    home,
  the salt land for its dwelling place?
7 It scorns the tumult of the city;
  it does not hear the shouts of the
    driver.
8 It ranges the mountains as its pasture,
  and it searches after every green
    thing.

9 "Is the wild ox willing to serve you?
  Will it spend the night at your crib?
10 Can you tie it in the furrow with ropes,
  or will it harrow the valleys after you?
11 Will you depend on it because its
    strength is great,
  and will you hand over your labor to it?
12 Do you have faith in it that it will return,
  and bring your grain to your threshing
    floor?[a]

13 "The ostrich's wings flap wildly,
  though its pinions lack plumage.[b]
14 For it leaves its eggs to the earth,
  and lets them be warmed on the
    ground,
15 forgetting that a foot may crush them,
  and that a wild animal may trample
    them.
16 It deals cruelly with its young, as if they
    were not its own;
  though its labor should be in vain, yet
    it has no fear;
17 because God has made it forget wisdom,
  and given it no share in understanding.
18 When it spreads its plumes aloft,[b]
  it laughs at the horse and its rider.

19 "Do you give the horse its might?
  Do you clothe its neck with mane?
20 Do you make it leap like the locust?
  Its majestic snorting is terrible.
21 It paws[c] violently, exults mightily;
  it goes out to meet the weapons.
22 It laughs at fear, and is not dismayed;
  it does not turn back from the sword.
23 Upon it rattle the quiver,
  the flashing spear, and the javelin.

24 With fierceness and rage it swallows the
    ground;
  it cannot stand still at the sound of
    the trumpet.
25 When the trumpet sounds, it says 'Aha!'
  From a distance it smells the battle,
  the thunder of the captains, and the
    shouting.

26 "Is it by your wisdom that the hawk
    soars,
  and spreads its wings toward the
    south?
27 Is it at your command that the eagle
    mounts up
  and makes its nest on high?
28 It lives on the rock and makes its home
  in the fastness of the rocky crag.
29 From there it spies the prey;
  its eyes see it from far away.
30 Its young ones suck up blood;
  and where the slain are, there it is."

40 And the LORD said to Job:
2 "Shall a faultfinder contend with
    the Almighty?[d]
  Anyone who argues with God must
    respond."

3 Then Job answered the LORD:
4 "See, I am of small account; what shall
    I answer you?
  I lay my hand on my mouth.
5 I have spoken once, and I will not
    answer;
  twice, but will proceed no further."

40.2: *Shall a faultfinder contend with the Almighty?*
God's concluding question to Job is a legal one: Can
the one who brought me into court answer my
questions?

God's second speech and Job's response
40.6–42.6: The topic of the second speech is God's
justice, which was criticized by Job. *Will you even put
me in the wrong* (v. 8) is, literally, "Would you impugn
my justice?" Justice here, and in the Bible generally, is

---

a Heb *your grain and your threshing floor*   b Meaning
of Heb uncertain   c Gk Syr Vg: Heb *they dig*
d Traditional rendering of Heb *Shaddai*

not the Western concept, passive and impartial (hearing out both sides), but the ancient Near Eastern concept, active and partial (upholding the righteous and putting down the wicked). Job accuses God of being unjust in this sense, that is, allowing the unjust to prosper and the righteous (like Job) to suffer. God's response, in the form of a question (*Have you an arm like God?* v. 9), silences Job, for Job can never be just in this sense. The rhetorical* method of the second speech is surprising in that God simply describes two great animals: *Behemoth** (40.15–24) and *Leviathan** (41.1–34). Both animals are mythological beasts (though Behemoth may be modeled on the hippopotamus). Behemoth and Leviathan symbolize the two great untamed and chaotic areas, respectively, the immense and lifeless desert and the vast and chaotic sea. The first speech (chs. 38–39) refuted Job's charge that God governs unwisely (without design) by demonstrating God cares for a vast world beyond human knowing. The second speech rebuts the charge that God is unjust by demonstrating God indeed can control ultimate cosmic evil (represented by Behemoth and Leviathan), but does not necessarily exercise control over it for the immediate benefit of human beings. God's mastery over the beasts is shown by 40.24 (Heb., "By [Behemoth's] eyes he is captured, by hooks his nose is pierced") and by 41.12 (Heb., uncertain, "Did I not silence [Leviathan's] boasting, his mighty words and martial deeds?"). The two beasts symbolize fearsome power that is beyond our understanding or control, yet they have a place in God's universe. They fulfill no evident function, cannot be domesticated, and do not serve human beings. God allows them to exist under divine control, despite their potential for evil. The world is God's, not man's (Job's).

6 Then the LORD answered Job out of the whirlwind:

7 "Gird up your loins like a man;
   I will question you, and you declare
      to me.
8 Will you even put me in the wrong?
   Will you condemn me that you may
      be justified?
9 Have you an arm like God,
   and can you thunder with a voice like
      his?

10 "Deck yourself with majesty and dignity;
   clothe yourself with glory and
      splendor.

11 Pour out the overflowings of your anger,
   and look on all who are proud, and
      abase them.
12 Look on all who are proud, and bring
      them low;
   tread down the wicked where they
      stand.
13 Hide them all in the dust together;
   bind their faces in the world below.*a*
14 Then I will also acknowledge to you
   that your own right hand can give you
      victory.

40.10: *Deck yourself with majesty and dignity:* God challenges Job to be just in the sense of putting down the wicked (vv. 10–14).

15 "Look at Behemoth,
   which I made just as I made you;
   it eats grass like an ox.
16 Its strength is in its loins,
   and its power in the muscles of its
      belly.
17 It makes its tail stiff like a cedar;
   the sinews of its thighs are knit
      together.
18 Its bones are tubes of bronze,
   its limbs like bars of iron.

19 "It is the first of the great acts of God—
   only its Maker can approach it with
      the sword.
20 For the mountains yield food for it
   where all the wild animals play.
21 Under the lotus plants it lies,
   in the covert of the reeds and in the
      marsh.
22 The lotus trees cover it for shade;
   the willows of the wadi surround it.
23 Even if the river is turbulent, it is not
      frightened;
   it is confident though Jordan rushes
      against its mouth.
24 Can one take it with hooks*b*
   or pierce its nose with a snare?

41 *c*"Can you draw out Leviathan*d* with
      a fishhook,
   or press down its tongue with a cord?

a Heb *the hidden place*   *b* Cn: Heb *in his eyes*
c Ch 40.25 in Heb   *d* Or *the crocodile*

2 Can you put a rope in its nose,
   or pierce its jaw with a hook?
3 Will it make many supplications to you?
   Will it speak soft words to you?
4 Will it make a covenant with you
   to be taken as your servant forever?
5 Will you play with it as with a bird,
   or will you put it on leash for your
      girls?
6 Will traders bargain over it?
   Will they divide it up among the
      merchants?
7 Can you fill its skin with harpoons,
   or its head with fishing spears?
8 Lay hands on it;
   think of the battle; you will not do it
      again!
9*a* Any hope of capturing it*b* will be
      disappointed;
   were not even the gods*c*
      overwhelmed at the sight of it?
10 No one is so fierce as to dare to stir it
      up.
   Who can stand before it?*d*
11 Who can confront it*d* and be safe?*e*
   —under the whole heaven, who?*f*

12 "I will not keep silence concerning its
      limbs,
   or its mighty strength, or its splendid
      frame.
13 Who can strip off its outer garment?
   Who can penetrate its double coat of
      mail?*g*
14 Who can open the doors of its face?
   There is terror all around its teeth.
15 Its back*h* is made of shields in rows,
   shut up closely as with a seal.
16 One is so near to another
   that no air can come between them.
17 They are joined one to another;
   they clasp each other and cannot be
      separated.
18 Its sneezes flash forth light,
   and its eyes are like the eyelids of the
      dawn.
19 From its mouth go flaming torches;
   sparks of fire leap out.
20 Out of its nostrils comes smoke,
   as from a boiling pot and burning
      rushes.

21 Its breath kindles coals,
   and a flame comes out of its mouth.
22 In its neck abides strength,
   and terror dances before it.
23 The folds of its flesh cling together;
   it is firmly cast and immovable.
24 Its heart is as hard as stone,
   as hard as the lower millstone.
25 When it raises itself up the gods are
      afraid;
   at the crashing they are beside
      themselves.
26 Though the sword reaches it, it does not
      avail,
   nor does the spear, the dart, or the
      javelin.
27 It counts iron as straw,
   and bronze as rotten wood.
28 The arrow cannot make it flee;
   slingstones, for it, are turned to
      chaff.
29 Clubs are counted as chaff;
   it laughs at the rattle of javelins.
30 Its underparts are like sharp
      potsherds;
   it spreads itself like a threshing sledge
      on the mire.
31 It makes the deep boil like a pot;
   it makes the sea like a pot of
      ointment.
32 It leaves a shining wake behind it;
   one would think the deep to be white-
      haired.
33 On earth it has no equal,
   a creature without fear.
34 It surveys everything that is lofty;
   it is king over all that are proud."

42 Then Job answered the LORD:
2 "I know that you can do all
   things,
   and that no purpose of yours can be
      thwarted.
3 'Who is this that hides counsel without
      knowledge?'

---

a Ch 41.1 in Heb   *b* Heb *of it*   *c* Cn Compare
Symmachus Syr: Heb *one is*   *d* Heb *me*   *e* Gk: Heb
that I shall repay   *f* Heb *to me*   *g* Gk: Heb *bridle*
h Cn Compare Gk Vg: Heb *pride*

Therefore I have uttered what I did not
    understand,
  things too wonderful for me, which I
      did not know.
4 'Hear, and I will speak;
  I will question you, and you declare
      to me.'
5 I had heard of you by the hearing of the
      ear,
  but now my eye sees you;
6 therefore I despise myself,
  and repent in dust and ashes.'"

42.1–6. 3: *Who is this that hides counsel without
knowledge?* Job cites God's two questions from the
first speech (38.2, 3) as a preface to his final statement
in this verse and in the next. The reprise of the opening
sentence, called an inclusio,* signals to the reader that
the section is concluding. **5:** *But now my eye sees you:*
Job had demanded to see God (19.26–27) and resented God's hiding his face (13.24). God's thunder-
ous speech was an occasion for Job to "see" God. **6:**
*Therefore I despise myself and repent in dust and
ashes:* The meaning of the verse is uncertain because
no object is specified for the first verb. Is the verb re-
flexive or does it have an external object such as Job's
previous words or dust and ashes as the symbol of a
deprived plaintiff? Given the frequent legal language
of the book, it seems better to render "I retract and
give up my dust and ashes," that is, I give up my lawsuit (without necessarily admitting I was wrong).

EPILOGUE

42.7–17: The reappearance of the name of the LORD
and the resumption of the prose that was used in the
prologue signals the reader that the story is ending.
God declares Job the winner in his lengthy disputation
about divine wisdom and justice. Acting at God's command, Job intercedes for his friends as he interceded
for his children in the prologue (vv. 7–9). God gives
Job twice as much as he had before. His newly enlarged family consoles him (vv. 10–17).

7 After the LORD had spoken these words
to Job, the LORD said to Eliphaz the Temanite: "My wrath is kindled against you and
against your two friends; for you have not
spoken of me what is right, as my servant
Job has. 8 Now therefore take seven bulls

and seven rams, and go to my servant Job,
and offer up for yourselves a burnt offering; and my servant Job shall pray for you,
for I will accept his prayer not to deal with
you according to your folly; for you have not
spoken of me what is right, as my servant Job
has done." 9 So Eliphaz the Temanite and
Bildad the Shuhite and Zophar the Naamathite went and did what the LORD had
told them; and the LORD accepted Job's
prayer.

10 And the LORD restored the fortunes of
Job when he had prayed for his friends; and
the LORD gave Job twice as much as he had
before. 11 Then there came to him all his
brothers and sisters and all who had known
him before, and they ate bread with him in
his house; they showed him sympathy and
comforted him for all the evil that the LORD
had brought upon him; and each of them
gave him a piece of money*a* and a gold ring.
12 The LORD blessed the latter days of Job
more than his beginning; and he had fourteen thousand sheep, six thousand camels, a
thousand yoke of oxen, and a thousand donkeys. 13 He also had seven sons and three
daughters. 14 He named the first Jemimah,
the second Keziah, and the third Keren-
happuch. 15 In all the land there were no
women so beautiful as Job's daughters; and
their father gave them an inheritance along
with their brothers. 16 After this Job lived one
hundred and forty years, and saw his children, and his children's children, four generations. 17 And Job died, old and full of days.

42.7–17. 7: *You have not spoken of me what is right,
as my servant Job has:* Job, who protested and accused
God of attacking an innocent man, is declared to have
told the truth about God, whereas the friends, who
defended God and divine justice and wisdom without
regard for truth, are judged to have acted out of folly
and incur God's anger. Job is once again an effective
intercessor (v. 10; compare 1.5). **11:** *They ate bread
with him in his house:* The meal shows the harmony
of the restored family and Job's reconciliation with his
friends.

---

a Heb *a qesitah*

HEBREW POETRY AND WISDOM LITERATURE*

Hebrew Poetry

Poems are embedded throughout the Pentateuch*/Torah* (for instance, Ex 15) and the historical literature (Judg 5), but it is only with Job—if one follows the order of books in the Christian Bible—that readers first confront a book that is predominantly composed as poetry. If reading the Jewish Bible or Hebrew Scriptures,* the first primarily poetic book is Isaiah. All such poetry makes greater demands on readers than does prose. Although one could make some sense of a Japanese haiku or an Elizabethan sonnet without any background knowledge, readers would understand each one more fully if they knew something about the characteristics of a poem written in that style. The situation is the same for Hebrew poetry. Readers are helped if they know what to look for in the poetry of a particular culture.

Some features of the poetry preserved in the Old Testament are shared by poetry from other times and places. Figurative language is typical of poetry the world over. The following examples show the rich trove of devices used in ancient and modern poetry and found in the Old Testament:

Simile:* "The righteous flourish like the palm tree, and
  grow like a cedar in Lebanon." (Ps 92.12)
Metaphor:* "Ephraim was a trained heifer
  that loved to thresh." (Hos 10.11)
Personification:* "Lift up your heads,
  O Gates! and be lifted up, O ancient doors!" (Ps 24.7) or
"Awake, O harp and lyre!
  I will awake the dawn." (Ps 108.2)
Rhetorical Question: "Can you bind the
  chains of the Pleiades or loose the cords of Orion?" (Job 38.31)
Hyperbole:* "I will utterly sweep away
  everything from the face of the earth, says the LORD." (Zeph 1.2)

One can as well find examples of irony,* allusion (or indirect reference to another text), sentences that run from one line to the next without a pause at the end of a poetic line (technically known as enjambment), ambiguity, and acrostic* within Old Testament poetry. Many of these elements can appear in prose, but they occur with greater density and frequency in poetry.

The true hallmark of Hebrew poetry is parallelism,* a phenomenon in which two or more poetic lines can be related in numerous ways. In order for parallelism to exist, there must be a building block, namely, the poetic line. These basic units are regularly presented in English translations as one line in a double-column printed page. For example, Psalm 29:3 is made up of three lines, each of which is very short. In Hebrew, the first line contains four words, the next two lines, three words each. This brevity characterizes much Hebrew poetry.

These brief poetic lines rarely occur without one or more "parallel" lines. Much of the time, the lines are very similar, both in meaning and in structure. Psalm 19.1 exemplifies this case:

The heavens are telling the glory of God;
  and the firmament proclaims his handiwork.

The subject, verb, and object of the first line are mirrored directly in the second. And the order of the grammar is identical. Further, the meanings of the three elements in the two lines are very similar. The firmament or dome that was created and installed on the first day of creation receives the name "heavens" (NRSV "Sky") in Genesis 1.8. The word translated as "heavens" can also mean air or space immediately above the earth. So, heavens and firmament are not quite synonyms. Similarity and difference are present in the remaining portions of the lines. Though both verbs involve the act of speaking, the verb in the second line, "proclaims," is stronger than simply "telling." In the third element, the sense of difference becomes even stronger, since "the glory of God," which elsewhere refers to the very nature of God (Ezek 1.28), is now characterized as something formed by the hand of the deity, "his handiwork." The poet seems to be suggesting that God's glory is suffused throughout the created order.

In other instances, parallel lines can be very different in structure:

> The LORD is my rock, my fortress, and my deliverer,
> my God, my rock in whom I take refuge,
> my shield, and the horn of my salvation, my stronghold. (Ps 18.2)

In these three lines, the basic sentence, "the Lord is my rock," is never repeated. Instead, all the ensuing phrases elucidate the initial predicate, "my rock." And then, sometimes the first line simply continues in the second line,

> He trains my hands for war,
> so that my arms can bend a bow of bronze. (Ps 18.34)

When we read widely in biblical poetry, therefore, we see that parallel lines can be related in very different ways.

Poets could add many parallel lines together to create powerful assemblages. The famous poem in Ecclesiastes 3 ("a time to be born, and a time to die") features strong grammatical similarity and absolute opposites in meaning. Proverbs 23.29–35 presents a set of parallel lines, offering a narrative* vignette of someone who drinks too much. Amos 2.6–8 comprises an overwhelming list of indictments against Israel and structured by parallel lines.

Wisdom Literature

Old Testament wisdom literature includes Proverbs, Job, and Ecclesiastes, though a comprehensive list might also include texts such as wisdom Psalms (for instance Ps 1). These books include a variety of literary forms. Some are simple.

- The **saying**, formulated in the indicative mood and in the present tense, reports that something is the case, for instance, "Fools think their own way is right, but the wise listen to advice" (Prov 12.15). Other sayings use formulae such as "Better is…than…" (Prov 15:16) or "Happy is…" (Prov 28.14).
- **Admonitions** appear in the imperative mood. They can be formulated in positive (Prov 27.11) or negative fashion (Prov 23.9).
- **Speeches** give voice to a character. Woman wisdom (Prov 1.22–33), adulterous woman (Prov 7.14–20), a mother (Prov 31.1–9), and a father (Prov 4.1–9) all have their say, sometimes including sayings or admonitions as a part of their speeches.
- Other forms of wisdom literature are the **riddle** (Judg 14.14), **dialogue** (Job 3–31), and **song** (Job 28).

Wisdom literature in the Old Testament presents a world different from the one that surrounds it in the canon.* The topics and theology are distinctive as are the forms of literature. Further, there are strong similarities between Israelite wisdom literature and wisdom literature in both Mesopotamia and Egypt. The production of wisdom literature, as exemplified by the proverb, is an almost universal feature of human culture, and it was cultivated in the ancient Near East.

Wisdom literature is grounded in observation and personal human experience. It is oriented to matters of daily life: when to get up, when to go to bed, how hard to work, how to work, how to raise children, and the like. Old Testament wisdom literature does not address or seem rooted in the Sinai covenant,* the ritual world, or the history of Israel.

Much of the wisdom literature is undergirded by a theology of creation. Proverbs presents this view by characterizing wisdom as a female. She can speak, both admonishing and offering people wealth, happiness, knowledge, and long life (for instance, Prov 1.20).

Wisdom reports that she was the first act of creation and present with God during the remainder of creation. As a result, one may infer that the created order is ordered and intelligible. One can learn from the created order. Proverbs 6.6–11 offers an admonition, "Go to the ant, you lazybones; consider its ways and be wise." The remainder of the verses reports that ants are industrious and have enough food. Humans should take note and act accordingly. Wisdom is therefore empirical, not depending upon the deity to reveal knowledge. Creation itself is a revelation. Knowledge is to be found in the world of creation that surrounds humans.

Wisdom literature offers many generalizations about the way life works. Those who work hard will be rewarded. Those who are lazy will become poor. Some scholars have characterized this view as the act-consequence system. What someone does sets certain forces in motion that will more or less automatically work themselves out. And there are predictable patterns. At the same time, the world of wisdom literature implicitly encourages people to use their own experiences to challenge those generalizations. That is what happens in both the book of Job and in Ecclesiastes. Job challenges the view that God rewards those who have behaved well since Job was "blameless and upright" and yet suffered egregiously. The author of Ecclesiastes challenges the notion that one can understand the nature of human existence: "no one can find out what is happening under the sun" (Eccl 8.17).

Wisdom depends upon human experience but not just upon one's own experience. A person should learn from one's parents: "Hear, my child, your father's instruction, and do not reject your mother's teaching" (Prov 1.8). One can learn from what happens at the royal court (Prov 19.12; 20.16). One can learn from those who have lived a long and full life, such as from the author of Ecclesiastes. One can learn from those who have come before, from "bygone generations" (Job 8.8).

Wisdom literature is also realistic. It not only deals with real-world, everyday events, it reflects the diversity of human experience. One proverb reports, "Do not answer fools according to their folly, or you will be a fool yourself" (Prov 26.4). The very next proverb moves in another direction, "Answer fools according to their folly, or they will be wise in their own eyes" (Prov 26.5). Clearly there is no one way to react to someone speaking foolishly. Moreover, the world of wisdom literature, although it advocates the search for wisdom, acknowledges that mysteries will always be with us (Prov 30.18–19).

Much wisdom literature sounds secular, for instance, "let your garments always be white; do not let oil be lacking on your head" (Eccl 9.8). Few proverbs refer overtly to God. And yet there is a persistent theological undercurrent in all three wisdom books. Job strives vigorously to encounter and challenge God; and God responds to that challenge. The writer of Ecclesiastes admits that God is responsible for the times of both adversity and prosperity (Eccl 7.14). And the book of Proverbs affirms that "the fear of the LORD is the beginning of knowledge" (Prov 1.7).

PSALMS

Introduction

The Psalms is a collection of 150 songs of praise, prayers, and spiritual poems. All or parts of the book may have served as the hymnbook or prayerbook of the First Temple* (952–587 BCE) or Second Temple (515 BCE–70 CE), as well as the synagogues* that emerged in the Persian era.* The five-book arrangement of the Psalms (1–41, 42–72, 73–89, 90–106, 107–150) parallels the five books of the Torah.* It is likely that Books I–III received their final form earlier than IV–V, since three psalms dealing with the Davidic monarchy appear in crucial positions in Books I–III (2, 72, 89). The sequence seems to be intentional, and the probable purpose was to highlight the apparent failure of the Davidic covenant* with the destruction of Jerusalem and the Temple in 587 BCE (89.38–51). Book IV provides an immediate and effective response at the beginning of Ps 90 by calling attention to Moses, who led the people of God before the existence of monarchy, Temple, or land. Furthermore, Ps 93–99 then provide what many scholars identify as the central theme of the Psalms: the proclamation of God's cosmic and eternal reign (as opposed to the transient Davidic monarchy).

Book V continues to affirm the universal sovereignty of God (107, 145–150), but its more complex structure suggests different nuances. The appearance of Davidic collections (108–110, 138–145) redirects attention toward the Davidic monarchy, but the whole people of God now appears to fulfill the royal function of serving as God's earthly agents (see 144, 149). At the heart of the book, two collections featuring the Exodus (113–118) and Zion* (120–137) surround Ps 119, which upholds the central significance of the Torah. Because it no longer possessed either a land or a monarchy, the post-exilic community reorganized itself around the Torah. The prominence of the Torah in the final shape of the Psalms suggests that the character of the collection shifted as it grew to final form. What started out primarily as a hymnbook or prayerbook took on the additional character of something like a catechism or book of instruction, which is what the word "Torah" essentially means.

The English word "psalm" is derived from a Greek word, which in turn translates a Hebrew word meaning "musical praise." This etymology suggests that the original context of most of the psalms was in Israel's and Judah's worship of God. This probability is reinforced by frequent references to singing, shouting, dancing, and musical instruments. In addition, the Temple is often in view, along with its gates, courts, and altar. Exactly how, where, and when the psalms were used is not known. Undoubtedly the songs of praise were sung as part of worship when the people gathered at the three annual pilgrimage feasts, and they may have been used in daily Temple services and on special occasions and celebrations. The prayers may also have been used at these times. In later times, the psalms would have been used in the synagogues. The prayers may have been used in smaller group settings, possibly even in homes.

Further specificity is difficult to attain. The superscriptions, or headings, of many psalms associate them with particular individuals, especially David, but not with the implication that he was their author. "Of David," for instance, could mean "inspired by David" or "in memory of David." The thirteen instances in which the superscriptions associate the psalm with a specific episode in David's life should be understood as later attempts to provide an imagined narrative* context for the psalm. In this translation, these superscriptions appear in smaller italic type before the first verse of some of the psalms. Psalm 3 gives an example of a superscription linking that Psalm to an event in David's life.

The Psalms are difficult to date. The safest conclusion is that they originated in various periods and had a long and varied history of use, even within the biblical period. The collection in its present form shows signs of having been shaped in response to the crisis of the Exile✫ and its aftermath. The Psalms as a book of scripture made it especially suited for teaching persons about God, humankind, and the life of faith.

READING GUIDE

There are obvious similarities among psalms, and it is helpful to attend to the traditional means of categorizing them:

Song of praise or hymn. The typical elements are an invitation to praise God, followed by reasons for praise that focus upon God's character (100, 117) or upon God's work as creator (8, 104) or deliverer (103). Usually considered as sub-types are psalms known as the enthronement psalms (29, 47, 93, 95–99—hymns that celebrate God's reign) and the songs of Zion (46, 48, 76, 84, 87, 120—hymns that focus praise on the city of Jerusalem, thus praising God more indirectly).

Prayer for help. The prayers, often known as laments✫ or complaints, address God directly. Typical elements include opening address, description of the distress (the lament or complaint proper), petition for help, affirmation of trust, and vow to praise God. Most of the prayers appear to be those of individuals (13, 22), but there are also several communal laments (44, 74). These prayers are the most frequent type of psalm. The situations out of which they arose are unclear. Their language and imagery suggest sickness, persecution by false accusers, and warfare. Reference to foes or enemies appears regularly in the prayers.

Song of thanksgiving. It is helpful to think of these psalms as the expression of the praise that is promised toward the conclusion of the prayers for help. The usual elements include the offering of thanks to God, a description of the former distress, testimony to God's ability to deliver, and an invitation to others to join in praising God (30, 34).

Royal psalms. This category is based more on content than structure. It includes the psalms that mention the king or appear to have been associated with services or rituals involving the monarchy (2, 18, 20, 21, 45, 72, 89, 101, 110, 132, 144).

Wisdom/Torah psalms. Neither songs of praise nor prayers, they are spiritual poems that offer reflections on or advice concerning the faithful life (37, 49, 73) or the Torah (1, 19, 119).

Scholars frequently disagree on the appropriate categorization of particular psalms. Moreover, other psalms do not fit the major categories. They are sometimes given other designations such as entrance liturgies✫ (15, 24), prophetic✫ exhortations✫ (50, 81, 95), psalms of trust (11, 16, 23, 91), and historical psalms (78, 105, 106, 136).

In addition to noticing the features shared by psalms, readers should attend to what is unique in each psalm. The individuality of each psalm is created by the poet's choice of vocabulary and imagery. Also, typical elements are arranged differently to create a certain effect. Thus, readers should attend carefully to the structure of each psalm. The stylistic device of parallelism✫ (expressing essentially the same thought in different words) will be obvious, but it should be noted that only rarely does the second part of a line merely repeat or paraphrase the first part. In the second part, the poet often heightens or intensifies an image or concept. Perhaps the most important stylistic device in the Psalms is repetition. Since the repetition in Hebrew is often obscured by the translation, the following annotations will point out important instances of this device.

Most psalms have a superscription. In addition to personal names, the superscriptions often contain what appear to be liturgical information or instructions. The precise meaning of most of the terms is uncertain, but they may indicate an ancient melody or appropriate musical accompaniment or setting for use in worship. Just as mysterious is the term "Selah," which also appears to have had some liturgical significance, perhaps indicating where a response was to be sung or a musical interlude was to appear.

Because the Psalms in their final form have an instructional intent, the reader may want to keep in mind some of the following questions about the meaning of the Psalms:

How is happiness portrayed in the Psalms, and how does this differ from the varied definitions of happiness today?

How do you assess the claim that God rules the world, especially in light of the reality that God is constantly opposed in the Psalms?

Of what significance is it that "the righteous" in the Psalms are those who constantly find themselves to be the afflicted, poor, persecuted, and needy?

How may the Psalms serve as models for prayer?

What is the theological function of violence and vengeance in the Psalms?

Of what significance is it that complaint and praise are constantly juxtaposed in the Psalms?

BOOK ONE

PSALM 1

1 Happy are those
    who do not follow the advice of the
        wicked,
    or take the path that sinners tread,
    or sit in the seat of scoffers;
2 but their delight is in the law of the
        LORD,
    and on his law they meditate day and
        night.
3 They are like trees
    planted by streams of water,
    which yield their fruit in its season,
    and their leaves do not wither.
    In all that they do, they prosper.

4 The wicked are not so,
    but are like chaff that the wind drives
        away.
5 Therefore the wicked will not stand in
        the judgment,
    nor sinners in the congregation of the
        righteous;

6 for the LORD watches over the way of
        the righteous,
    but the way of the wicked will perish.

1.1–6: Happy are those. 1–2: By defining happiness (2.12) over against *the wicked, sinners,* and *scoffers,* the poet heightens the contrast between two different ways or lifestyles. *Scoffers* refuse to accept instruction (Prov 1.22). The *happy* are those who are constantly open to God's instruction (Josh 1.8). The Hebrew word translated here as *law* is "torah," which would be better translated "instruction" or "teaching." "Torah"* can designate particular legal stipulations, but it can also refer more broadly to the entire tradition of God's revelation. **3–4:** These central verses each contain a comparison. What characterizes *trees planted by streams of water* is their stable rootedness (Jer 17.8). Prosperity should not be understood as a reward but rather as the result of being connected to God. Such rootedness is exactly what *the wicked* lack; they are easily blown away. **5–6:** It is unclear whether judgment should be understood as "the final judgment." In any case, the wicked have no foundation. Lack of connection to God means death, the ultimate contrast to happiness.

PSALM 2

1 Why do the nations conspire,
   and the peoples plot in vain?
2 The kings of the earth set themselves,
   and the rulers take counsel together,
   against the LORD and his anointed,
      saying,
3 "Let us burst their bonds asunder,
   and cast their cords from us."

4 He who sits in the heavens laughs;
   the LORD has them in derision.
5 Then he will speak to them in his
      wrath,
   and terrify them in his fury, saying,
6 "I have set my king on Zion, my holy
      hill."

7 I will tell of the decree of the LORD:
   He said to me, "You are my son;
   today I have begotten you.
8 Ask of me, and I will make the nations
      your heritage,
   and the ends of the earth your
      possession.
9 You shall break them with a rod of iron,
   and dash them in pieces like a
      potter's vessel."

10 Now therefore, O kings, be wise;
   be warned, O rulers of the earth.
11 Serve the LORD with fear,
   with trembling 12kiss his feet,[a]
   or he will be angry, and you will perish
      in the way;
   for his wrath is quickly kindled.

Happy are all who take refuge in him.

2.1–12: The LORD and the anointed.* A royal psalm, it may have been used originally at the coronation of Judean kings. Now paired with Ps 1, it introduces the entire collection. It proclaims God's universal reign, a major theme of the Psalms (Ps 93–99). 1–3: The LORD's anointed (Hebrew "meshiach," usually written "messiah"*) is the Judean king, the earthly agent of God's reign (Ps 72). 4–6: Because God is cosmic ruler, God can laugh at the presumptuous earthly kings (37.13; 59.9). Verse 6 may have been spoken by a priest or prophet.* Zion* is the mountain that Jerusalem oc-

cupies, God's holy hill (3.4; 15.1). 7–9: The speaker in v. 7 is the king, who was viewed as God's adopted son (2 Sam 7.14). Today apparently indicates the day of enthronement. The promises in vv. 8–9 (see 20.2; 21.4) are standard ancient Near Eastern hyperbole.* The king is to represent God's universal sovereignty (72.8–11). 10–12: The rebellious kings and rulers are now admonished to subject themselves to God's rule. The difficult vv. 11b–12a probably are meant to reinforce serve the LORD (see 100.2, where NRSV translates the same verb as "worship"). The words perish and way recall Ps 1, as does happy. To take refuge is to trust God and to live in fundamental dependence upon God, a theme that pervades the Psalms (5.11; 7.1; 144.2).

PSALM 3

*A Psalm of David, when he fled from
his son Absalom.*

1 O LORD, how many are my foes!
   Many are rising against me;
2 many are saying to me,
   "There is no help for you[b] in God."
                                    Selah

3 But you, O LORD, are a shield around
      me,
   my glory, and the one who lifts up my
      head.
4 I cry aloud to the LORD,
   and he answers me from his holy hill.
                                    Selah

5 I lie down and sleep;
   I wake again, for the LORD sustains
      me.
6 I am not afraid of ten thousands of
      people
   who have set themselves against me
      all around.

7 Rise up, O LORD!
   Deliver me, O my God!
   For you strike all my enemies on the
      cheek;
   you break the teeth of the wicked.

---

a Cn: Meaning of Heb of verses 11b and 12a is uncertain   b Syr: Heb him

8 Deliverance belongs to the LORD;
　may your blessing be on your people!
　　　　　　　　　　　　　　Selah

3.1–8: Help belongs to the LORD. The first prayer for help in the psalter. The superscription invites the reader to hear the prayer in conjunction with David's experience in 2 Sam 15–18. **1–2:** The repetition of *many* emphasizes the threat from the *foes,* who contradict 2.12 by advising self-assertion rather than trust in God. The Hebrew for *help* is a form of *deliver* (v. 7) and *deliverance* (v. 8). **3–4:** Deliverance seems to lie in the future (see v. 7), but it is nonetheless sure (v. 8). **5–6:** Such assurance explains how the daily rhythms of life are still possible amid *ten thousands,* which is from the same root as *many* in v. 1. **7–8:** Petition (vv. 7a, 8b) surrounds profession (vv. 7b–8a). As the foes *are rising* (v. 1), God is asked to *rise* (7.6; 9.19) and to *deliver,* which is precisely what the foes said God cannot do. Thus, it is appropriate that the psalmist trusts that God will deliver by aiming at the *cheek* and *teeth* (58.6), organs of speech. *Deliverance* means the opportunity to live fully, a *blessing* (5.12; 28.9) the psalmist desires for others as well.

PSALM 4

To the leader: with stringed instruments.
A Psalm of David.

1 Answer me when I call, O God of my
　　right!
　You gave me room when I was in
　　distress.
　Be gracious to me, and hear my
　　prayer.

2 How long, you people, shall my honor
　　suffer shame?
　How long will you love vain words,
　　and seek after lies?   *Selah*
3 But know that the LORD has set apart
　　the faithful for himself;
　the LORD hears when I call to
　　him.

4 When you are disturbed,[a] do not sin;
　ponder it on your beds, and be silent.
　　　　　　　　　　　　　　Selah
5 Offer right sacrifices,
　and put your trust in the LORD.

6 There are many who say, "O that we
　　might see some good!
　Let the light of your face shine on us,
　　O LORD!"
7 You have put gladness in my heart
　more than when their grain and wine
　　abound.

8 I will both lie down and sleep in peace;
　for you alone, O LORD, make me lie
　　down in safety.

4.1–8: Trust in the LORD. Usually labeled a lament* because of the prayers in vv. 1, 6–8, it also contains the psalmist's questions to others and subsequent counsel (vv. 2–5), which function as a profession of faith. **1:** Three typical pleas surround a remembrance of past help. *Right* signifies that righteousness is a characteristic of God and God's reign (5.8; 9.8; 96.13). **2–3:** The question is apparently addressed to opponents who have injured the psalmist (3.1–2). In response to opposition, the psalmist affirms that he or she belongs to God. **4–5:** The advice to *be silent* has the sense of "Don't worry" or "Be at peace" (v. 8), and prepares for the admonition to *trust,* which is a pervasive theme in the Psalms (9.10; 21.7). It is synonymous with taking refuge in God (2.12; 62.8; 91.2). When the whole self has been yielded to God, *right sacrifices* (51.19) become possible. **6–8:** Verse 7 suggests that what other people prayed for in v. 6 was wealth and possessions. The psalmist is content with a relationship of trust in God. It affords constant *peace* (3.5) as well as *safety,* even amid the opposition and materialism of others.

PSALM 5

To the leader: for the flutes. A Psalm of David.

1 Give ear to my words, O LORD;
　give heed to my sighing.
2 Listen to the sound of my cry,
　my King and my God,
　for to you I pray.
3 O LORD, in the morning you hear my
　　voice;
　in the morning I plead my case to
　　you, and watch.

a Or are angry

4 For you are not a God who delights in
wickedness;
evil will not sojourn with you.
5 The boastful will not stand before your
eyes;
you hate all evildoers.
6 You destroy those who speak lies;
the LORD abhors the bloodthirsty and
deceitful.

7 But I, through the abundance of your
steadfast love,
will enter your house,
I will bow down toward your holy
temple
in awe of you.
8 Lead me, O LORD, in your
righteousness
because of my enemies;
make your way straight before me.

9 For there is no truth in their mouths;
their hearts are destruction;
their throats are open graves;
they flatter with their tongues.
10 Make them bear their guilt, O God;
let them fall by their own counsels;
because of their many transgressions
cast them out,
for they have rebelled against you.

11 But let all who take refuge in you
rejoice;
let them ever sing for joy.
Spread your protection over them,
so that those who love your name
may exult in you.
12 For you bless the righteous, O LORD;
you cover them with favor as with a
shield.

5.1–12: I will enter your house. In this lament,*
appeal to God (vv. 1–3, 7–8, 11–12) alternates
with complaint about the enemies (vv. 4–6, 9–10).
Verses 7–8 form a structural and theological center. 1–
3: The word King is the first time in the psalter that the
Hebrew root "mlk" is used of God. As usual God's sovereignty is proclaimed amid opposition. The morning
seems to have been an appointed time for prayer
(55.17; 59.16). 4–6: Wickedness is followed by six synonyms. The total of seven suggests God's complete

opposition to unrighteousness (1.6; 2.12). 7–8: The
psalmist attributes entry into the Temple* not to personal merit but to God's steadfast love, the first occurrence of "hesed," which is virtually a one-word
summary of God's character (see Ex 34.6–7; Ps 100.5;
107.1). The request for God to lead me (23.6; 31.7)
anticipates vv. 11–12. Entry into the Temple may have
been to make a judicial appeal for vindication from the
false accusations of the enemies. 9–10: Verse 9 features four anatomical terms, three of which are organs
of speech (3.7). Transgressions in v. 10 connotes willful
rebellion. The wicked refuse to be led. 11–12: It was
the responsibility of a King (v. 2) to protect his people,
and refuge (2.12) is what the psalmist requests.

~~~~~~~~~~~~~~~~~~~~

PSALM 6

To the leader: with stringed instruments;
according to The Sheminith. A Psalm of David.

1 O LORD, do not rebuke me in your
anger,
or discipline me in your wrath.
2 Be gracious to me, O LORD, for I am
languishing;
O LORD, heal me, for my bones are
shaking with terror.
3 My soul also is struck with terror,
while you, O LORD—how long?

4 Turn, O LORD, save my life;
deliver me for the sake of your
steadfast love.
5 For in death there is no remembrance
of you;
in Sheol who can give you praise?

6 I am weary with my moaning;
every night I flood my bed with
tears;
I drench my couch with my weeping.
7 My eyes waste away because of grief;
they grow weak because of all
my foes.

8 Depart from me, all you workers of evil,
for the LORD has heard the sound of
my weeping.
9 The LORD has heard my supplication;
the LORD accepts my prayer.
10 All my enemies shall be ashamed and
struck with terror;

they shall turn back, and in a moment
    be put to shame.

6.1–10: Save my life. This lament* may have been
prayed originally in a context of sickness, but the language can be heard metaphorically.* It became one
of the church's Penitential Psalms* (a grouping of
Psalms that derives from the fourth or fifth century and
that are traditionally used in seasons of penitence, such
as Lent; see Ps 32, 38, 51, 102, 130, 143). **1–3:** Verse
1 reflects the ancient belief that sickness was caused
by sin (41.4; Mk 2.1–12). At the same time, the psalmist appeals to God's grace and healing power. *How
long?* is a typical question in the laments. **4–5:** The
plea for God to *turn*, accompanied by the appeal to
God's *steadfast love* (5.7), is reminiscent of Moses'
plea for the people's life (see Ex 32.12; Ps 90.13–14,
which is attributed to Moses). *Sheol** is the realm of
the dead (30.3; 88.3). **6–7:** The central v. 6a recalls vv.
1–3 and introduces vv. 8–10. **8–10:** Trusting that he
or she has been *heard*, the psalmist is transformed. The
terror formerly experienced (vv. 2–3) will become the
enemies'. It is not at all clear that the psalmist has been
healed, but trust has triumphed over the pervasive
weariness articulated in vv. 1–3, 6–7.

PSALM 7

*A Shiggaion of David, which he sang to the
LORD concerning Cush, a Benjaminite.*

1 O LORD my God, in you I take refuge;
    save me from all my pursuers, and
      deliver me,
2 or like a lion they will tear me apart;
    they will drag me away, with no one
      to rescue.

3 O LORD my God, if I have done this,
    if there is wrong in my hands,
4 if I have repaid my ally with harm
    or plundered my foe without cause,
5 then let the enemy pursue and overtake
      me,
    trample my life to the ground,
    and lay my soul in the dust.   *Selah*

6 Rise up, O LORD, in your anger;
    lift yourself up against the fury of my
      enemies;
    awake, O my God;[a] you have
      appointed a judgment.

7 Let the assembly of the peoples be
    gathered around you,
    and over it take your seat[b] on high.
8 The LORD judges the peoples;
    judge me, O LORD, according to my
      righteousness
    and according to the integrity that is
      in me.
9 O let the evil of the wicked come to an
      end,
    but establish the righteous,
    you who test the minds and hearts,
    O righteous God.
10 God is my shield,
    who saves the upright in heart.
11 God is a righteous judge,
    and a God who has indignation every
      day.

12 If one does not repent, God[c] will whet
      his sword;
    he has bent and strung his bow;
13 he has prepared his deadly weapons,
    making his arrows fiery shafts.
14 See how they conceive evil,
    and are pregnant with mischief,
    and bring forth lies.
15 They make a pit, digging it out,
    and fall into the hole that they have
      made.
16 Their mischief returns upon their own
      heads,
    and on their own heads their violence
      descends.

17 I will give to the LORD the thanks due
    to his righteousness,
    and sing praise to the name of the
      LORD, the Most High.

7.1–17: Establish the righteous. The allusion in the
superscription is unclear, since no Cush appears in the
Davidic narratives.* This lament* may originally have
been prayed by a person falsely accused (Ps 5). **1–2:**
Confidence in God as *refuge* (2.12; 5.11) grounds the
petitions. The enemies are often described as animals
(10.9). **3–5:** With an oath formula, the psalmist de-

---

a Or *awake for me*   *b* Cn: Heb *return*   *c* Heb *he* clares innocence. The claim is for innocence in a particular case (see Job 31). **6–8:** *Judgment* (v. 6), *judges* (v. 8), and *judge* (v. 11) derive from the Hebrew "shpt," "to judge" or "do justice," a key word in the psalm. God's commitment to justice follows from God's sovereignty over all (vv. 6–8). *Integrity* connotes innocence (Job 31.6). **9–11:** The other key word is "tsdq," *righteous* (twice in v. 9; see vv. 8, 11, 17), an attribute of God and God's reign (4.1; 5.8; 96.13). The psalmist trusts that God's commitment to justice in the cosmos will also work itself out for individuals. **12–13:** The subject of the verbs is unclear (see note *c*). The NRSV casts God in the role of just warrior (38.2; 64.7). **14–17:** The subject of the verbs is *the wicked* (v. 9). Birth imagery dominates v. 14 (Job 15.35). The psalmist trusts that wickedness destroys itself (9.16; 57.6). The psalmist interprets this as God's *righteousness* and is grateful (v. 17; see 1.6).

PSALM 8

To the leader: according to The Gittith. A Psalm of David.

1 O LORD, our Sovereign,
　　how majestic is your name in all the
　　　earth!

　You have set your glory above the
　　　heavens.
2 　Out of the mouths of babes and
　　　infants
　you have founded a bulwark because of
　　　your foes,
　　to silence the enemy and the avenger.

3 When I look at your heavens, the work
　　　of your fingers,
　　the moon and the stars that you have
　　　established;
4 what are human beings that you are
　　　mindful of them,
　　mortals*a* that you care for them?

5 Yet you have made them a little lower
　　　than God,*b*
　and crowned them with glory and
　　　honor.
6 You have given them dominion over the
　　　works of your hands;
　　you have put all things under their
　　　feet,

7 all sheep and oxen,
　　and also the beasts of the field,
8 the birds of the air, and the fish of the
　　　sea,
　　whatever passes along the paths of
　　　the seas.

9 O LORD, our Sovereign,
　　how majestic is your name in all the
　　　earth!

8.1–9: How majestic is your name. The first song of praise in the psalter, its direct address of God is unique. **1a:** Framing the psalm, the refrain (vv. 1a, 9) proclaims God's world-wide reign. **1b–2:** The NRSV takes v. 1b as a discrete thought, extending the scope of God's sovereignty to *the heavens*. If the sense of v. 2 is that God can use even vulnerable infants as a defense against God's foes, then v. 2 anticipates vv. 3–8 and the affirmation that God uses insignificant humans to exercise God's rule. **3:** The only human action in the psalm is a passive one—to *look*. **4:** The Hebrew behind *what* is the same as *how* in vv. 1, 9, linking the central verse of the psalm to its framework. **5–8:** What is implied by the relationship between vv. 1, 9 and v. 4 is here made explicit. The sovereign God has *crowned* humans with the symbols of sovereignty—*glory and honor*. God's own works are put under the *dominion* of humanity (see Gen 1.26–28). **9:** The word *all* occurs for the fourth time (vv. 1, 6, 7). It is now clear that God's *all*-ness is inextricably bound up with humankind's response.

PSALM 9

*To the leader: according to Muth-labben.
A Psalm of David.*

1 I will give thanks to the LORD with my
　　　whole heart;
　I will tell of all your wonderful deeds.
2 I will be glad and exult in you;
　I will sing praise to your name,
　　O Most High.

3 When my enemies turned back,
　　they stumbled and perished before
　　　you.

a Heb *ben adam*, lit. *son of man*　　*b* Or *than the divine beings* or *angels*: Heb *elohim*

4 For you have maintained my just cause;
    you have sat on the throne giving
      righteous judgment.

5 You have rebuked the nations, you have
      destroyed the wicked;
    you have blotted out their name
      forever and ever.
6 The enemies have vanished in
      everlasting ruins;
    their cities you have rooted out;
    the very memory of them has
      perished.

7 But the LORD sits enthroned forever,
    he has established his throne for
      judgment.
8 He judges the world with righteousness;
    he judges the peoples with equity.

9 The LORD is a stronghold for the
      oppressed,
    a stronghold in times of trouble.
10 And those who know your name put
      their trust in you,
    for you, O LORD, have not forsaken
      those who seek you.

11 Sing praises to the LORD, who dwells in
      Zion.
    Declare his deeds among the peoples.
12 For he who avenges blood is mindful of
      them;
    he does not forget the cry of the
      afflicted.

13 Be gracious to me, O LORD.
    See what I suffer from those who
      hate me;
    you are the one who lifts me up from
      the gates of death,
14 so that I may recount all your praises,
    and, in the gates of daughter Zion,
    rejoice in your deliverance.

15 The nations have sunk in the pit that
      they made;
    in the net that they hid has their own
      foot been caught.

16 The LORD has made himself known, he
      has executed judgment;
    the wicked are snared in the work of
      their own hands. *Higgaion. Selah*

17 The wicked shall depart to Sheol,
    all the nations that forget God.

18 For the needy shall not always be
      forgotten,
    nor the hope of the poor perish
      forever.

19 Rise up, O LORD! Do not let mortals
      prevail;
    let the nations be judged before
      you.
20 Put them in fear, O LORD;
    let the nations know that they are
      only human.   *Selah*

9.1–10.18: The hope of the poor. Psalms 9 and 10 were probably written as a single acrostic* poem, one in which every other line begins with the succeeding letter of the Hebrew alphabet.* The Septuagint* (the ancient Greek translation of the Hebrew Scriptures*) treats them as one, and Ps 10 has no superscription. Psalm 9 has the characteristics of a song of thanksgiving and focuses on rebellious nations. Psalm 10 is a lament* that focuses on the wicked. **9.1–8:** The *wonderful deeds* for which the psalmist *gives thanks* include personal (vv. 3–4) as well as corporate deliverance (vv. 5–6). Such deliverance testifies to God's justice and righteousness (vv. 4, 7–8; see 7.11). These attributes characterize God's rule, which is articulated by *throne* (vv. 5, 7) and *enthroned* (v. 7). **9–12:** Because of God's justice and righteousness, the *oppressed* (v. 9) and *afflicted* (v. 12) are invited to *trust* (v. 10) and *praise* God (v. 11). The Hebrew root of *afflicted* recurs six times; it is translated *poor* (9.18; 10.2, 9), *oppressed* (10.12) and *meek* (10.17). That God *avenges blood* means that God values and protects human life. **13–14:** The repetition of *gates* expresses trust in God's ability to deliver from death to life. *Zion** is Jerusalem, God's city, and the psalmist will be there. **15–18:** God's "justice" (NRSV *judgment*) will be manifest as the wicked destroy themselves (7.15–16). *Sheol** is the realm of the dead (6.5). **19–20:** Focus on *the nations* continues (see vv. 5, 15, 17).

PSALM 10

1 Why, O LORD, do you stand far off?
    Why do you hide yourself in times of
        trouble?
2 In arrogance the wicked persecute the
        poor—
    let them be caught in the schemes
        they have devised.

3 For the wicked boast of the desires of
        their heart,
    those greedy for gain curse and
        renounce the LORD.
4 In the pride of their countenance the
        wicked say, "God will not seek it
        out";
    all their thoughts are, "There is no
        God."

5 Their ways prosper at all times;
    your judgments are on high, out of
        their sight;
    as for their foes, they scoff at them.
6 They think in their heart, "We shall not
        be moved;
    throughout all generations we shall
        not meet adversity."

7 Their mouths are filled with cursing and
        deceit and oppression;
    under their tongues are mischief and
        iniquity.
8 They sit in ambush in the villages;
    in hiding places they murder the
        innocent.

Their eyes stealthily watch for the
        helpless;
9 they lurk in secret like a lion in its
        covert;
    they lurk that they may seize the poor;
    they seize the poor and drag them off
        in their net.

10 They stoop, they crouch,
    and the helpless fall by their might.
11 They think in their heart, "God has
        forgotten,
    he has hidden his face, he will never
        see it."

12 Rise up, O LORD; O God, lift up your
        hand;
    do not forget the oppressed.
13 Why do the wicked renounce God,
    and say in their hearts, "You will not
        call us to account"?

14 But you do see! Indeed you note trouble
        and grief,
    that you may take it into your hands;
    the helpless commit themselves to you;
    you have been the helper of the
        orphan.

15 Break the arm of the wicked and
        evildoers;
    seek out their wickedness until you
        find none.
16 The LORD is king forever and ever;
    the nations shall perish from his land.

17 O LORD, you will hear the desire of the
        meek;
    you will strengthen their heart, you
        will incline your ear
18 to do justice for the orphan and the
        oppressed,
    so that those from earth may strike
        terror no more.*a*

10.1–18. 1–11: The questions in v. 1 mark a transition. Verses 2–11 are an extended description of the wicked, including quotations of their arrogant self-sufficiency and self-assertion (vv. 4, 6, 11). Mocking God, they also think that they can exploit *the poor* with impunity. **12–14:** But the psalmist thinks otherwise, as indicated first by petition (v. 12) and then exclamation (v. 14). *See* is repeated in vv. 11, 14. **15–18:** The psalmist prays that God do what *the wicked* said that God could not do. Naming God *king*, v. 16 recalls 9.4, 7–8. A king's primary commitment is *to do justice*, especially for *the afflicted* (72.1–4).

PSALM 11

To the leader. Of David.

1 In the LORD I take refuge; how can you
        say to me,
    "Flee like a bird to the mountains;*b*

a Meaning of Heb uncertain   *b* Gk Syr Jerome Tg: Heb *flee to your mountain, O bird*

2 for look, the wicked bend the bow,
    they have fitted their arrow to the
        string,
    to shoot in the dark at the upright in
        heart.
3 If the foundations are destroyed,
    what can the righteous do?"

4 The LORD is in his holy temple;
    the LORD's throne is in heaven.
    His eyes behold, his gaze examines
        humankind.
5 The LORD tests the righteous and the
        wicked,
    and his soul hates the lover of violence.
6 On the wicked he will rain coals of fire
        and sulfur;
    a scorching wind shall be the portion
        of their cup.
7 For the LORD is righteous;
    he loves righteous deeds;
    the upright shall behold his face.

11.1–7: What can the righteous do? This psalm of
trust may have been spoken originally in the Temple★
by a person who had been advised to *flee* from enemies (Ps 5, 7). **1–3:** An initial profession of trust utilizes
the important word *refuge* (2.12; 5.11; 7.1). The
psalmist quotes advisers. The situation seems hopeless
(v. 3). *Foundations* indicates the basic fabric of the social order. **4:** The psalmist responds by asserting God's
rule on earth (*holy temple*) and *in heaven*. Verse 4 is
the center of the psalm. **5–7:** The characters in view in
vv. 2–3 return here. God opposes *the wicked* (v. 5; see
7.16). They will be judged (v. 6; see Gen 19.24; Ps
75.9), because God *is righteous* (7.9; 9.4, 8). Those
who share God's identity, *the righteous* (vv. 3, 5), *shall
behold his face* (17.15). Those who trust God will not
be disappointed.

~~~~~~~~~~~~~~~~~~~~~~~~~~~~~~

PSALM 12

To the leader: according to The Sheminith.
A Psalm of David.

1 Help, O LORD, for there is no longer
        anyone who is godly;
    the faithful have disappeared from
        humankind.
2 They utter lies to each other;
    with flattering lips and a double heart
        they speak.

3 May the LORD cut off all flattering
        lips,
    the tongue that makes great boasts,
4 those who say, "With our tongues we
        will prevail;
    our lips are our own—who is our
        master?"

5 "Because the poor are despoiled,
        because the needy groan,
    I will now rise up," says the LORD;
    "I will place them in the safety for
        which they long."
6 The promises of the LORD are promises
        that are pure,
    silver refined in a furnace on the
        ground,
    purified seven times.

7 You, O LORD, will protect us;
    you will guard us from this generation
        forever.
8 On every side the wicked prowl,
    as vileness is exalted among
        humankind.

12.1–8: The promises of the LORD. Usually categorized as a lament,★ it has elements of petition (vv. 1,
3), complaint (vv. 2, 4, 8), and trust (vv. 6–7). Unique
is the inclusion of God's response (v. 5) to the worshipper, perhaps spoken originally in the Temple★
by a prophet★ or priest. **1–4:** The most basic human
prayer, *help*, is followed by complaint. The situation recalls Ps 11. The quotation in v. 4 indicates the
utter self-centeredness of the wicked (10.4, 6, 11, 13;
14.1). **5:** God's response reveals that the wicked are
deceived. God will *rise up* (3.7; 10.12) on behalf
of the *poor* and *needy* (see Ex 3.7; 22.21–24;
Ps 9.18). **6–8:** Whereas the speech of the wicked is
deceptive (v. 2), God's *promises* are reliable (v. 6).
They are followed appropriately by a profession of
faith (v. 7), which is effective even as *the wicked
prowl* (v. 8).

~~~~~~~~~~~~~~~~~~~~~~~~~~~~~~

PSALM 13

To the leader. A Psalm of David.

1 How long, O LORD? Will you forget me
        forever?
    How long will you hide your face
        from me?

2 How long must I bear pain[a] in my soul,
  and have sorrow in my heart all day
    long?
How long shall my enemy be exalted
    over me?

3 Consider and answer me, O LORD my
    God!
Give light to my eyes, or I will sleep
    the sleep of death,
4 and my enemy will say, "I have
    prevailed";
my foes will rejoice because I am
    shaken.

5 But I trusted in your steadfast love;
  my heart shall rejoice in your
    salvation.
6 I will sing to the LORD,
  because he has dealt bountifully with
    me.

13.1–6: How long, O LORD? This prayer for help may
have originally been spoken by a sick person. Complaint (vv. 1–2) is followed by petition (vv. 3–4) and
an expression of trust (vv. 5–6). **1–2:** The four-fold repetition of *How long* conveys urgency. *Exalted* is supposed to be God's position (18.46; 46.10), but the
enemy now occupies it. **3–4:** Each of the three petitions is appropriate in light of the complaints. *Consider*
calls God to remember and show God's face. *Answer*
is appropriate, given the four questions in vv. 1–2.
Give light recalls the mention of God's *face*, which is
often associated with *light* (Num 6.25; Ps 4.6; 31.16).
5–6: Whereas the *foes* had been about to *rejoice* (v. 4),
now the psalmist *shall rejoice*. Uncertainty has become
trust (4.5; 9.10) in God's *steadfast love* (5.7; 6.4). Perhaps the psalmist looks back in gratitude for deliverance; perhaps she or he looks forward in trusting hope;
or perhaps the simultaneity of complaint and praise
represents what the life of faith always involves.

PSALM 14
To the leader. Of David.

1 Fools say in their hearts, "There is no
    God."
They are corrupt, they do abominable
    deeds;
there is no one who does good.

2 The LORD looks down from heaven on
    humankind
to see if there are any who are wise,
  who seek after God.

3 They have all gone astray, they are all
    alike perverse;
there is no one who does good,
  no, not one.

4 Have they no knowledge, all the
    evildoers
who eat up my people as they eat
    bread,
and do not call upon the LORD?

5 There they shall be in great terror,
  for God is with the company of the
    righteous.
6 You would confound the plans of the
    poor,
but the LORD is their refuge.

7 O that deliverance for Israel would
    come from Zion!
When the LORD restores the fortunes
    of his people,
Jacob will rejoice; Israel will be glad.

14.1–7: Foolishness and wisdom. Often categorized
as a prophetic* exhortation* (a psalm that recalls prophetic speech by delivering an indictment of or promise to the people), it is almost identical to Ps 53. **1:**
Foolishness is not ignorance, but rather the failure to
entrust life to God, resulting in wickedness (compare
10.4). **2:** God's position in *heaven* connotes God's
sovereignty, which is precisely what the foolish fail
to acknowledge. **3:** Recalling v. 1, v. 3 indicts all humanity, setting up an apparent tension with vv. 4–6.
4–6: By distinguishing between *evildoers* and those
called *my people, the righteous* and *the poor*, these
verses seem to contradict v. 3. They may reflect a strat-
ified society dominated by a powerful elite (see
Mic 3.1–4). God sides with the victims (9.17–18;
10.17–18; 12.5–7). *There* may suggest that efforts at
oppression by the wicked will be their own undoing
(7.15–16). The oppressed find *refuge* in God (2.12).
The tension between vv. 1–3 and 4–6 preserves the
insight that corporate evil and its effects leave no one

a Syr: Heb *hold counsels*

uninvolved or untouched. **7:** This verse may be an exilic or post-exilic addition, which makes the psalm relevant to an era when the people were oppressed by other nations.

PSALM 15

A Psalm of David.

1 O LORD, who may abide in your tent?
　Who may dwell on your holy hill?

2 Those who walk blamelessly, and do
　　what is right,
　and speak the truth from their
　　heart;
3 who do not slander with their tongue,
　and do no evil to their friends,
　　nor take up a reproach against their
　　　neighbors;
4 in whose eyes the wicked are despised,
　but who honor those who fear the
　　LORD;
　who stand by their oath even to their
　　hurt;
5 who do not lend money at interest,
　and do not take a bribe against the
　　innocent.

　Those who do these things shall never
　　be moved.

15.1–5: Who may abide in your tent? An entrance liturgy,* it may have originated as a response in a ritual used as worshippers entered the Temple* (see Ps 24). If so, it now portrays the lifestyle of those who have been described previously as "the righteous" (1.5–6; 14.5). **1:** *Tent* (27.5–6; 61.4) refers to the Temple, preserving the memory of the wilderness tabernacle* (Ex 33.7). The *holy hill* is Zion,* the Temple mount (2.6; 3.4). **2:** To *walk blamelessly* is not to be sinless but rather to be devoted fully to God. Elsewhere, it is God who is *right* or "righteous" (7.11), as well as *true* or showing "faithfulness" (Ex 34.6). **3–5a:** Speech and actions that oppress others are to be avoided, in accordance with God's character, values, and activity. **5b:** In the context of the prayers in Book I, the closing promise cannot be understood to affirm that the righteous will be unopposed, but rather that they will have a secure foundation for facing anything.

PSALM 16

A Miktam of David.

1 Protect me, O God, for in you I take
　refuge.
2 I say to the LORD, "You are my Lord;
　I have no good apart from you."[a]

3 As for the holy ones in the land, they
　　are the noble,
　in whom is all my delight.

4 Those who choose another god multiply
　　their sorrows;[b]
　their drink offerings of blood I will
　　not pour out
　or take their names upon my lips.

5 The LORD is my chosen portion and my
　　cup;
　you hold my lot.
6 The boundary lines have fallen for me
　　in pleasant places;
　I have a goodly heritage.

7 I bless the LORD who gives me counsel;
　in the night also my heart instructs
　　me.
8 I keep the LORD always before me;
　because he is at my right hand, I shall
　　not be moved.

9 Therefore my heart is glad, and my soul
　　rejoices;
　my body also rests secure.
10 For you do not give me up to Sheol,
　or let your faithful one see the Pit.

11 You show me the path of life.
　In your presence there is fullness of
　　joy;
　in your right hand are pleasures
　　forevermore.

16.1–11: The path of life. A mixture of prayer (vv. 1–2, 9–11) and profession of faith, it is usually classified as a psalm of trust (Ps 11, 23). **1–2:** Petition is followed by an expression of trust (see *refuge* in 2.12;

a Jerome Tg: Meaning of Heb uncertain
b Cn: Meaning of Heb uncertain

11.8; 14.6). LORD asserts God's sovereignty, and casts the psalmist in the role of servant. **3–4**: Verse 3 probably expresses loyalty to God in the form of honoring God's people, and v. 4 expresses loyalty in the form of rejecting idols and their devotees. **5–6**: The vocabulary derives from the book of Joshua and references to the land, of which everyone was to have a *portion* (19.9), determined by *lot* (18.6), as their *heritage* or "inheritance" (14.3; 17.6). **7–8**: *Bless* indicates submission, which includes openness to God's *counsel*. God's accessibility is unfailing, an effective source of stability (15.5). **9–11**: The assurance of security yields joy from the psalmist's whole being. Entrusting the self to God means avoiding *Sheol** and *the Pit*, names for the realm of death (6.5; 88.3–4), traveling instead *the path of life*. The psalmists had no developed doctrine of resurrection, but they anticipate this belief with their poetic assurances of unbroken communion with God.

PSALM 17

A Prayer of David.

1 Hear a just cause, O LORD; attend to
  my cry;
    give ear to my prayer from lips free of
      deceit.
2 From you let my vindication come;
  let your eyes see the right.

3 If you try my heart, if you visit me by
  night,
    if you test me, you will find no
      wickedness in me;
  my mouth does not transgress.
4 As for what others do, by the word of
  your lips
    I have avoided the ways of the violent.
5 My steps have held fast to your paths;
  my feet have not slipped.

6 I call upon you, for you will answer me,
  O God;
    incline your ear to me, hear my
      words.
7 Wondrously show your steadfast love,
  O savior of those who seek refuge
    from their adversaries at your right
      hand.

8 Guard me as the apple of the eye;
  hide me in the shadow of your wings,

9 from the wicked who despoil me,
  my deadly enemies who surround me.
10 They close their hearts to pity;
  with their mouths they speak
    arrogantly.
11 They track me down;[a] now they
  surround me;
    they set their eyes to cast me to the
      ground.
12 They are like a lion eager to tear,
  like a young lion lurking in ambush.

13 Rise up, O LORD, confront them,
  overthrow them!
    By your sword deliver my life from
      the wicked,
14 from mortals—by your hand, O LORD—
  from mortals whose portion in life is
    in this world.
  May their bellies be filled with what you
    have stored up for them;
  may their children have more than
    enough;
  may they leave something over to
    their little ones.

15 As for me, I shall behold your face in
  righteousness;
    when I awake I shall be satisfied,
      beholding your likeness.

17.1–15: Beholding God's face. This prayer for help may originally have been offered in the Temple* by someone who had been falsely accused (see Ps 5). **1–2:** The psalmist is the victim of those whose speech is not *free of deceit*. *Vindication* is more literally "justice." **3–5:** Often known as a protestation of innocence, these verses do not claim sinlessness but rather innocence in a particular case (7.3–5). **6–9:** The psalmist looks to God for *refuge* (2.12; 16.1). The language recalls the Exodus (see *steadfast love* and *right hand* in v. 7 and Ex 15.12–13). The *shadow of your wings* may allude to the wings of the seraphs who accompanied the ark in the Temple (36.7; 57.1; 63.7). **10–12:** The description of the wicked emphasizes their arrogance and violence (5.9; 10.6–11). **13–15:** God is frequently asked to *rise up* (3.7; 10.12) against enemies. The request is more literally "meet their face," anticipating how the psalmist will *behold* God's face (11.7). The

a One Ms Compare Syr: MT *Our steps*

wicked may be *filled* (v. 14) by their treachery, but the psalmist *shall be satisfied* by God (16.11).

P S A L M 1 8

To the leader. A Psalm of David the servant of the LORD, who addressed the words of this song to the LORD on the day when the LORD delivered him from the hand of all his enemies, and from the hand of Saul. He said:

1 I love you, O LORD, my strength.
2 The LORD is my rock, my fortress, and
 my deliverer,
 my God, my rock in whom I take
 refuge,
 my shield, and the horn of my
 salvation, my stronghold.
3 I call upon the LORD, who is worthy to
 be praised,
 so I shall be saved from my enemies.

4 The cords of death encompassed me;
 the torrents of perdition assailed me;
5 the cords of Sheol entangled me;
 the snares of death confronted me.

6 In my distress I called upon the LORD;
 to my God I cried for help.
From his temple he heard my voice,
 and my cry to him reached his ears.

7 Then the earth reeled and rocked;
 the foundations also of the mountains
 trembled
 and quaked, because he was angry.
8 Smoke went up from his nostrils,
 and devouring fire from his mouth;
 glowing coals flamed forth from him.
9 He bowed the heavens, and came
 down;
 thick darkness was under his feet.
10 He rode on a cherub, and flew;
 he came swiftly upon the wings of the
 wind.
11 He made darkness his covering around
 him,
 his canopy thick clouds dark with
 water.
12 Out of the brightness before him
 there broke through his clouds
 hailstones and coals of fire.

13 The LORD also thundered in the
 heavens,
 and the Most High uttered his
 voice.*ᵃ*
14 And he sent out his arrows, and
 scattered them;
 he flashed forth lightnings, and
 routed them.
15 Then the channels of the sea were
 seen,
 and the foundations of the world
 were laid bare
 at your rebuke, O LORD,
 at the blast of the breath of your
 nostrils.

18.1–50: Exalted be the God of my salvation. A royal psalm of thanksgiving, it is nearly identical to 2 Sam 22. Proposed dates range from David's time to the post-exilic era. After the disappearance of the monarchy, it would have fostered hope by recalling the past (see Ps 144). **1–6:** The king's distress is evident. *Sheol*⋆ is the realm of the dead (6.5; 16.10), and the king already has one foot in *Sheol* (v. 5). The preponderance of metaphors⋆ for God in vv. 1–2 suggests that the psalm is as much about God as about the king. *Help* (v. 6) will come from God. **7–15:** God's response (vv. 16–19) is preceded by the description of a theophany,⋆ literally, "an appearance of God." Theophanies employ poetic imagery to emphasize God's cosmic power and presence (50.2–3; 68.7–8). They assert God's sovereignty (29.3–9; 97.1–5; 99.1) and often accompany accounts of deliverances (Ex 15.6–10; Judg 5.4–5).

16 He reached down from on high, he took
 me;
 he drew me out of mighty waters.
17 He delivered me from my strong
 enemy,
 and from those who hated me;
 for they were too mighty for me.
18 They confronted me in the day of my
 calamity;
 but the LORD was my support.
19 He brought me out into a broad place;
 he delivered me, because he delighted
 in me.

a Gk See 2 Sam 22.14: Heb adds *hailstones and coals of fire*

20 The LORD rewarded me according to my
     righteousness;
   according to the cleanness of my
     hands he recompensed me.
21 For I have kept the ways of the LORD,
   and have not wickedly departed from
     my God.
22 For all his ordinances were before me,
   and his statutes I did not put away
     from me.
23 I was blameless before him,
   and I kept myself from guilt.
24 Therefore the LORD has recompensed
     me according to my
     righteousness,
   according to the cleanness of my
     hands in his sight.

25 With the loyal you show yourself loyal;
   with the blameless you show yourself
     blameless;
26 with the pure you show yourself pure;
   and with the crooked you show
     yourself perverse.
27 For you deliver a humble people,
   but the haughty eyes you bring down.
28 It is you who light my lamp;
   the LORD, my God, lights up my
     darkness.
29 By you I can crush a troop,
   and by my God I can leap over a
     wall.
30 This God—his way is perfect;
   the promise of the LORD proves true;
   he is a shield for all who take refuge
     in him.

18.16–30. 16–19: The mention of *mighty waters*,
symbolizing chaos, suggests the cosmic dimension of
the deliverance. The focus is on God's activity. **20–24:**
Attention shifts to the king and to what sounds like
royal boasting. But the focal point of this section is v.
22, which suggests that God's *ordinances* and *statutes*
are the real source of the king's *righteousness* (vv. 20,
25). To be *blameless* is not to be sinless but rather to
depend completely upon God (15.2; 19.13). **25–30:**
These verses sharpen the emphasis on God's power.
God is the real source of the king's life (v. 28; see 2 Sam
21.17), strength (v. 29; see vv. 1, 32), and protection
(v. 30; see v. 2 and 2.12).

31 For who is God except the LORD?
   And who is a rock besides our
     God?—
32 the God who girded me with strength,
   and made my way safe.
33 He made my feet like the feet of a deer,
   and set me secure on the heights.
34 He trains my hands for war,
   so that my arms can bend a bow of
     bronze.
35 You have given me the shield of your
     salvation,
   and your right hand has supported
     me;
   your help[a] has made me great.
36 You gave me a wide place for my steps
     under me,
   and my feet did not slip.
37 I pursued my enemies and overtook
     them;
   and did not turn back until they were
     consumed.
38 I struck them down, so that they were
     not able to rise;
   they fell under my feet.
39 For you girded me with strength for the
     battle;
   you made my assailants sink under
     me.
40 You made my enemies turn their backs
     to me,
   and those who hated me I destroyed.
41 They cried for help, but there was no
     one to save them;
   they cried to the LORD, but he did
     not answer them.
42 I beat them fine, like dust before the
     wind;
   I cast them out like the mire of the
     streets.
43 You delivered me from strife with the
     peoples;[b]
   you made me head of the nations;
   people whom I had not known served
     me.
44 As soon as they heard of me they
     obeyed me;
   foreigners came cringing to me.

a Or *gentleness*   *b* Gk Tg: Heb *people*

45 Foreigners lost heart,
    and came trembling out of their
        strongholds.
46 The LORD lives! Blessed be my rock,
    and exalted be the God of my
        salvation,
47 the God who gave me vengeance
    and subdued peoples under me;
48 who delivered me from my enemies;
    indeed, you exalted me above my
        adversaries;
    you delivered me from the violent.
49 For this I will extol you, O LORD,
        among the nations,
    and sing praises to your name.
50 Great triumphs he gives to his king,
    and shows steadfast love to his
        anointed,
    to David and his descendants forever.

18.31–50: Perhaps originally a victory hymn, these verses function now to express the king's gratitude to God. Both God and king are cast in the role of warrior. While the king claims some credit (vv. 37–38, 42), the victory really belongs to God (vv. 31–32, 40–41, 43–48, 50) and is evidence of God's sovereignty (vv. 43, 47, 49). The military imagery is problematic; it is important to consider the larger context and its claim that God's cause always represents justice, righteousness, and equity (72.1–7, 12–14; 98.7–9). God's victory is the triumph of *steadfast love* (v. 50).

PSALM 19

To the leader. A Psalm of David.

1 The heavens are telling the glory of
        God;
    and the firmament*a* proclaims his
        handiwork.
2 Day to day pours forth speech,
    and night to night declares
        knowledge.
3 There is no speech, nor are there
        words;
    their voice is not heard;
4 yet their voice*b* goes out through all the
        earth,
    and their words to the end of the
        world.

In the heavens*c* he has set a tent for
        the sun,
5 which comes out like a bridegroom from
        his wedding canopy,
    and like a strong man runs its course
        with joy.
6 Its rising is from the end of the heavens,
    and its circuit to the end of them;
    and nothing is hid from its heat.

7 The law of the LORD is perfect,
        reviving the soul;
    the decrees of the LORD are sure,
        making wise the simple;
8 the precepts of the LORD are right,
        rejoicing the heart;
    the commandment of the LORD is
        clear,
        enlightening the eyes;
9 the fear of the LORD is pure,
        enduring forever;
    the ordinances of the LORD are true
        and righteous altogether.
10 More to be desired are they than gold,
        even much fine gold;
    sweeter also than honey,
        and drippings of the honeycomb.

11 Moreover by them is your servant
        warned;
    in keeping them there is great
        reward.
12 But who can detect their errors?
    Clear me from hidden faults.
13 Keep back your servant also from the
        insolent;*d*
    do not let them have dominion over
        me.
    Then I shall be blameless,
        and innocent of great transgression.

14 Let the words of my mouth and the
        meditation of my heart
    be acceptable to you,
        O LORD, my rock and my redeemer.

19.1–14: My rock and redeemer. Scholars often treat Ps 19 as two psalms: 19A (vv. 1–6), a creation hymn,

a Or *dome*   *b* Gk Jerome Compare Syr: Heb *line*
c Heb *In them*   *d* Or *from proud thoughts*

and 19B (vv. 7–14), a meditation on "torah."* However, this psalm is actually a unity that proclaims the all-encompassing importance of God's "torah" (v. 7, NRSV *law*; see Ps 1, 119). **1–6:** It is possible that the psalmist has adopted and modified an ancient hymn to *the sun* (v. 4). But here *the sun* is a created entity which, along with *the heavens,* proclaims God's *glory* (v. 1) in silent but eloquent *speech* (v. 2). **7–10:** The focus shifts to God's "torah," but the transition is a natural one. It affirms that God's "torah," "instruction," is a basic structure of the cosmos. *Perfect* connotes "pervasive" or "all-encompassing." As the sun makes life possible, which is the sense of *reviving the soul,* so does God's instruction. It is responsible for all good things, including wisdom (v. 7), joy (v. 8), vision (v. 8; *enlightening* recalls the work of *the sun*), piety (v. 9a), and order (v. 9b). There is nothing more valuable (v. 10). **11–13:** NRSV *reward* should be translated "consequence." After the psalmist's confession of sin (v. 12), *blameless* must be understood as "forgiven" and *innocent* as "pardoned." **14:** Forgiven by God, the psalmist's *words* (the same Hebrew word as "speech" in vv. 2–3) can be *acceptable. Redeemer* could be translated "next-of-kin." The cosmic God (v. 1–6), by way of God's "torah" (vv. 7–10), has become the psalmist's gracious next-of-kin.

PSALM 20
To the leader. A Psalm of David.

1 The LORD answer you in the day of
    trouble!
    The name of the God of Jacob protect
      you!
2 May he send you help from the
    sanctuary,
    and give you support from Zion.
3 May he remember all your offerings,
    and regard with favor your burnt
      sacrifices.   *Selah*

4 May he grant you your heart's desire,
    and fulfill all your plans.
5 May we shout for joy over your
      victory,
    and in the name of our God set up
      our banners.
    May the LORD fulfill all your petitions.

6 Now I know that the LORD will help his
    anointed;

he will answer him from his holy
    heaven
    with mighty victories by his right hand.
7 Some take pride in chariots, and some
      in horses,
    but our pride is in the name of the
      LORD our God.
8 They will collapse and fall,
    but we shall rise and stand upright.

9 Give victory to the king, O LORD;
    answer us when we call.*a*

20.1–9: The LORD will help. This royal psalm may have been used in the Temple* when Israel prepared for battle. After the demise of the monarchy, it would have expressed hope in God's ability to help. **1–5:** As the people pray for the king, the real focus is on God's activity. *Answer* in v. 1 recurs twice (vv. 6, 9). NRSV often translates *victory* (v. 5) as "deliverance," "salvation," or "help." The root occurs twice in v. 6 (*help, victories*) and again in v. 9. **6–8:** The *anointed** (v. 6) is the king (v. 9; 2.2; 18.50), the earthly agent of God's rule. The people's *pride* or trust is appropriately directed not to the king, but to God (v. 7). **9:** As note *a* suggests, the closing prayer is ambiguous. NRSV construes it as the people's prayer for themselves and *the king.*

PSALM 21
To the leader. A Psalm of David.

1 In your strength the king rejoices,
      O LORD,
    and in your help how greatly he
      exults!
2 You have given him his heart's desire,
    and have not withheld the request of
      his lips.   *Selah*
3 For you meet him with rich blessings;
    you set a crown of fine gold on his
      head.
4 He asked you for life; you gave it to
      him—
    length of days forever and ever.
5 His glory is great through your help;
    splendor and majesty you bestow on
      him.

a Gk: Heb *give victory, O LORD; let the King answer us
when we call*

6 You bestow on him blessings forever;
  you make him glad with the joy of
    your presence.
7 For the king trusts in the LORD,
  and through the steadfast love of the
    Most High he shall not be
    moved.

8 Your hand will find out all your
    enemies;
  your right hand will find out those
    who hate you.
9 You will make them like a fiery furnace
    when you appear.
  The LORD will swallow them up in his
    wrath,
  and fire will consume them.
10 You will destroy their offspring from the
    earth,
  and their children from among
    humankind.
11 If they plan evil against you,
  if they devise mischief, they will not
    succeed.
12 For you will put them to flight;
  you will aim at their faces with your
    bows.

13 Be exalted, O LORD, in your strength!
  We will sing and praise your power.

21.1–13: The king exults in God's help. Linked to Ps
20 by the continued focus on *the king* (20.9; 21.1), it
may have been used originally upon the king's return
from battle. After the demise of the monarchy, it
would have been used to celebrate God's help for the
people. **1–6:** The psalm is encompassed by references
to God's *strength* (vv. 1, 13). *The king* has received
the divine *help* (vv. 1, 5) requested in Ps 20 (compare
20.4 and 21.2). **7:** The king's power is derived from
God's *strength* (vv. 1, 13), and it is fitting that he *trusts
in the LORD* (2 Kings 18.5). God's *steadfast love* is the
foundation of the Davidic dynasty* (2 Sam 7.15;
1 Kings 3.6). **8–12:** It is not clear whether these words
are addressed to *the king* or to God. Since *the king* is
viewed as God's earthly agent, the ambiguity is appropriate (18.31–50). Verse 10 represents the typical
means of claiming sovereignty or victory (2 Kings 8.12;
Ps 137.8–9). **13:** God is clearly addressed, as the people join the king in praising God.

PSALM 22

*To the leader: according to The Deer
of the Dawn. A Psalm of David.*

1 My God, my God, why have you
    forsaken me?
  Why are you so far from helping me,
    from the words of my groaning?
2 O my God, I cry by day, but you do not
    answer;
  and by night, but find no rest.

3 Yet you are holy,
  enthroned on the praises of Israel.
4 In you our ancestors trusted;
  they trusted, and you delivered them.
5 To you they cried, and were saved;
  in you they trusted, and were not put
    to shame.

6 But I am a worm, and not human;
  scorned by others, and despised by
    the people.
7 All who see me mock at me;
  they make mouths at me, they shake
    their heads;
8 "Commit your cause to the LORD; let
    him deliver—
  let him rescue the one in whom he
    delights!"

9 Yet it was you who took me from the
    womb;
  you kept me safe on my mother's
    breast.
10 On you I was cast from my birth,
  and since my mother bore me you
    have been my God.
11 Do not be far from me,
  for trouble is near
  and there is no one to help.

12 Many bulls encircle me,
  strong bulls of Bashan surround me;
13 they open wide their mouths at me,
  like a ravening and roaring lion.

14 I am poured out like water,
  and all my bones are out of joint;
  my heart is like wax;
  it is melted within my breast;

15 my mouth^a is dried up like a potsherd,
    and my tongue sticks to my jaws;
    you lay me in the dust of death.

16 For dogs are all around me;
    a company of evildoers encircles me.
    My hands and feet have shriveled;^b
17 I can count all my bones.
    They stare and gloat over me;
18 they divide my clothes among
        themselves,
    and for my clothing they cast lots.

22.1–31: God rules the nations. The intensity of this lament* is created by its structure. It consists of two complaints (vv. 1–11, 12–21), each with two parts (vv. 1–5, 6–11 and 12–15, 16–21), followed by two sections of praise (vv. 22–26, 27–31). **1–5:** The threefold appearance of the phrase *My God* suggests intimacy that now seems broken (see Mk 15.34). The psalmist cannot understand *why* God is *so far* away (vv. 11, 19). Praise (v. 3) asserts God's sovereign ability to help, which God has done in past times (vv. 4–5). But memory increases misery. **6–11:** Forsakenness by God is accompanied by human abandonment and ridicule (vv. 6–8). The psalmist is utterly dehumanized—a *worm*. **12–18:** Each complaint features animals, symbolizing enemies, which surround the psalmist (vv. 12–13, 16a–b; see 7.2; 10.9). Death threatens, as the anatomical imagery suggests (vv. 14–15, 16c–18). Because they assume death is imminent, the enemies divide the psalmist's possessions (v. 18; see Mk 15.24).

19 But you, O LORD, do not be far away!
    O my help, come quickly to my aid!
20 Deliver my soul from the sword,
    my life^c from the power of the dog!
21   Save me from the mouth of the lion!

    From the horns of the wild oxen you
        have rescued^d me.
22 I will tell of your name to my brothers
        and sisters;^e
    in the midst of the congregation I will
        praise you:
23 You who fear the LORD, praise him!
    All you offspring of Jacob, glorify him;
    stand in awe of him, all you offspring
        of Israel!
24 For he did not despise or abhor
    the affliction of the afflicted;

he did not hide his face from me,^f
    but heard when I^g cried to him.

25 From you comes my praise in the great
        congregation;
    my vows I will pay before those who
        fear him.
26 The poor^h shall eat and be satisfied;
    those who seek him shall praise the
        LORD.
    May your hearts live forever!

27 All the ends of the earth shall remember
    and turn to the LORD;
    and all the families of the nations
        shall worship before him.ⁱ
28 For dominion belongs to the LORD,
    and he rules over the nations.

29 To him,^j indeed, shall all who sleep in^k
        the earth bow down;
    before him shall bow all who go down
        to the dust,
    and I shall live for him.^l
30 Posterity will serve him;
    future generations will be told about
        the Lord,
31 and^m proclaim his deliverance to a
        people yet unborn,
    saying that he has done it.

22.19–31. 19–21: The petitions draw on vocabulary used earlier in the psalm—*far* (vv. 1, 11), *help* (v. 11), *deliver* (v. 8), *save* (see *helping* in v. 1). Through it all, the psalmist still trusts God. Verse 21b marks a transition. To be "answered" (see note *d*) *from the horns of the wild oxen* suggests that the following *praise* comes in the midst of ongoing suffering. **22–26:** Each verse contains the word *praise* except v. 24, which suggests that God is present among *the afflicted*, a community of which gathers around the psalmist (vv. 25–26). The payment of *vows* was part of a ritual of gratitude (56.12; 61.8), probably involving a sacrificial meal. **27–31:** The psalmist's community achieves

a Cn: Heb *strength*   *b* Meaning of Heb uncertain
c Heb *my only one*   *d* Heb *answered*   *e* Or *kindred*
f Heb *him*   *g* Heb *he*   *h* Or *afflicted*   *i* Gk Syr
Jerome: Heb *you*   *j* Cn: Heb *They have eaten and*
k Cn: Heb *all the fat ones*   *l* Compare Gk Syr Vg: Heb
and he who cannot keep himself alive   *m* Compare Gk:
Heb *it will be told about the Lord to the generation,* ³¹*they
will come and*

world-wide proportions. Even the dead will participate (v. 29), as will people *yet unborn* (v. 31). The God who *rules over the nations* (v. 28) claims a universal following.

〜〜〜〜〜〜〜〜〜〜〜〜〜〜〜〜〜

P S A L M 2 3
A Psalm of David.

1 The LORD is my shepherd, I shall not
        want.
2   He makes me lie down in green
            pastures;
  he leads me beside still waters;*a*
3   he restores my soul.*b*
  He leads me in right paths*c*
      for his name's sake.

4 Even though I walk through the darkest
            valley,*d*
    I fear no evil;
  for you are with me;
      your rod and your staff—
      they comfort me.

5 You prepare a table before me
    in the presence of my enemies;
  you anoint my head with oil;
      my cup overflows.
6 Surely*e* goodness and mercy*f* shall
            follow me
    all the days of my life,
  and I shall dwell in the house of the
            LORD
      my whole life long.*g*

────────────

23.1–6: God's love will pursue me. It is a psalm of trust. **1:** *Shepherd* was a royal title in the ancient Near East, and it was the responsibility of kings to provide for their people (Jer 23.1–4; Ezek 34.1–10). The psalmist proclaims loyal submission to God and affirms that God has made complete provision. **2–3:** Details of God's provision are listed: food (*green pastures*), drink (*still waters*), and protection (*right paths*). The result is life; *restores my soul* means "keeps me alive." *For his name's sake* indicates that God keeps people alive because it is God's character to do so. **4:** God's provision endures in the worst of circumstances. The switch to direct address in this central verse heightens the sense of intimate presence, which means no threat is so great as to *fear*. *Rod* can designate a shepherd's equipment, but it also denotes royal authority. **5–6:**

The image shifts to that of a gracious host, who provides as did the *shepherd*—food (*a table*), drink (*my cup*), and protection (*the house of the LORD*). *Enemies* are no threat. Hospitality abounds, signified by the anointing* oil. Abundant life is attributed to God's *goodness* (100.5; 106.1) and *mercy* (usually translated "steadfast love," as in 5.7; 21.7), which "pursue" (rather than *follow*) the psalmist.

〜〜〜〜〜〜〜〜〜〜〜〜〜〜〜〜〜

P S A L M 2 4
Of David. A Psalm.

1 The earth is the LORD's and all that is
            in it,
    the world, and those who live in it;
2 for he has founded it on the seas,
      and established it on the rivers.

3 Who shall ascend the hill of the LORD?
      And who shall stand in his holy
            place?
4 Those who have clean hands and pure
            hearts,
    who do not lift up their souls to what
            is false,
      and do not swear deceitfully.
5 They will receive blessing from the
            LORD,
    and vindication from the God of their
            salvation.
6 Such is the company of those who seek
            him,
    who seek the face of the God of
            Jacob.*h*   *Selah*

7 Lift up your heads, O gates!
    and be lifted up, O ancient doors!
    that the King of glory may come in.
8 Who is the King of glory?
    The LORD, strong and mighty,
    the LORD, mighty in battle.
9 Lift up your heads, O gates!
    and be lifted up, O ancient doors!
    that the King of glory may come in.
10 Who is this King of glory?
    The LORD of hosts,
    he is the King of glory.   *Selah*

────────────

a Heb *waters of rest*   *b* Or *life*   *c* Or *paths of righteousness*   *d* Or *the valley of the shadow of death*   *e* Or *Only*   *f* Or *kindness*   *g* Heb *for length of days*   *h* Gk Syr: Heb *your face, O Jacob*

24.1–10: The King of glory. An entrance liturgy* (see Ps 15), it was probably used originally in a procession as worshippers accompanied the ark of the covenant* into the Temple.* **1–2:** The profession of faith anticipates the explicit affirmation of God's sovereignty in vv. 7–10. The *seas* and *rivers* represent the chaotic waters that God ordered into a cosmos. **3:** The questions may have been asked by a priest as worshippers approached the Temple gates (15.1). **4–6:** The worshippers' response follows. *Clean hands* (73.13) and *pure hearts* (73.1) may reflect exterior and interior preparation. *False* is sometimes associated with idolatry,* and to *not swear deceitfully* indicates proper relationship to other persons (see Ex 20.16). Proper relatedness to God and neighbor constitutes *blessing* and *vindication,* a word usually translated as "righteousness." Seeking God's *face* (11.7; 17.15) may have meant entering the Temple, but also indicates submission to God. **7–10:** These verses have the character of a responsorial ritual between priests and worshippers at the Temple gates. *Mighty in battle* may allude to v. 2, since creation was often portrayed as a battle with chaos. *LORD of hosts* may also have a military ring, since *hosts* can mean an army. *Hosts* can also indicate the heavenly beings surrounding God (29.1–2; 82.1). Verses 7–10 offer a ritual enactment of the claims made in vv. 1–2 (5.2; 98.6).

PSALM 25

Of David.

1 To you, O LORD, I lift up my soul.
2 O my God, in you I trust;
    do not let me be put to shame;
    do not let my enemies exult
        over me.
3 Do not let those who wait for you be
        put to shame;
    let them be ashamed who are
        wantonly treacherous.

4 Make me to know your ways, O LORD;
    teach me your paths.
5 Lead me in your truth, and teach me,
    for you are the God of my salvation;
    for you I wait all day long.

6 Be mindful of your mercy, O LORD, and
        of your steadfast love,
    for they have been from of old.

7 Do not remember the sins of my youth
        or my transgressions;
    according to your steadfast love
        remember me,
    for your goodness' sake, O LORD!

8 Good and upright is the LORD;
    therefore he instructs sinners in the
        way.
9 He leads the humble in what is right,
    and teaches the humble his way.
10 All the paths of the LORD are steadfast
        love and faithfulness,
    for those who keep his covenant and
        his decrees.

11 For your name's sake, O LORD,
    pardon my guilt, for it is great.
12 Who are they that fear the LORD?
    He will teach them the way that they
        should choose.
13 They will abide in prosperity,
    and their children shall possess the
        land.
14 The friendship of the LORD is for those
        who fear him,
    and he makes his covenant known to
        them.
15 My eyes are ever toward the LORD,
    for he will pluck my feet out of the
        net.

16 Turn to me and be gracious to me,
    for I am lonely and afflicted.
17 Relieve the troubles of my heart,
    and bring me*a* out of my distress.
18 Consider my affliction and my trouble,
    and forgive all my sins.
19 Consider how many are my foes,
    and with what violent hatred they
        hate me.
20 O guard my life, and deliver me;
    do not let me be put to shame, for I
        take refuge in you.
21 May integrity and uprightness preserve
        me,
    for I wait for you.

a Or *The troubles of my heart are enlarged; bring me*

22 Redeem Israel, O God,
  out of all its troubles.

25.1–22: For you I wait. A lament,★ it contains petition (vv. 2b–3, 4–7, 11, 16–18, 19–22), praise (vv. 8–10), and assurance (vv. 12–15). Their unique arrangement may be due to the acrostic★ structure (see Ps 9–10). **1–2a:** In keeping with Ps 24.4, the psalmist promises to *lift up my soul* to the LORD (86.4; 143.8). The phrase means to "offer my life," the essence of *trust* (86.2; 143.8). **2b–3:** *Shame* and *wait* become thematic (vv. 5, 20–21). **4–7:** An interest in teaching is introduced (vv. 8–9, 12), as is a focus on God's *way* or *ways* (vv. 4, 8, 9, 12; the same Hebrew root lies behind *leads* in vv. 5, 9). **8–10:** This characterization of God recalls the historic confession in Ex 34.6–7. **11:** This petition is the central line of the psalm; it gives the prayer the character of a confession of sin (see v. 18; Ps 32, 51). **12–15:** The assurance of *prosperity* must be heard in light of ongoing complaint (vv. 16–21). *Prosperity* involves connectedness to God (1.3), which is what God's *friendship* designates. *Fear* (vv. 12, 14) connotes reverence and trust. **16–21:** The psalmist is one of the *afflicted* (v. 16; 22.24) and is opposed by *foes* (v. 19; 3.1). *Refuge* is found in God (2.12; 5.11). *Integrity* results from complete dependence upon God. **22:** Standing outside the acrostic structure, it may have been appended to give the psalm an explicitly corporate orientation.

PSALM 26
Of David.

1 Vindicate me, O LORD,
  for I have walked in my integrity,
  and I have trusted in the LORD
  without wavering.
2 Prove me, O LORD, and try me;
  test my heart and mind.
3 For your steadfast love is before my eyes,
  and I walk in faithfulness to you.*

4 I do not sit with the worthless,
  nor do I consort with hypocrites;
5 I hate the company of evildoers,
  and will not sit with the wicked.

6 I wash my hands in innocence,
  and go around your altar, O LORD,
7 singing aloud a song of thanksgiving,
  and telling all your wondrous deeds.

8 O LORD, I love the house in which you
  dwell,
  and the place where your glory
  abides.
9 Do not sweep me away with sinners,
  nor my life with the bloodthirsty,
10 those in whose hands are evil devices,
  and whose right hands are full of
  bribes.

11 But as for me, I walk in my integrity;
  redeem me, and be gracious to me.
12 My foot stands on level ground;
  in the great congregation I will bless
  the LORD.

26.1–12: Vindicate me, O LORD. This lament★ may have been prayed originally by a falsely accused person seeking help in the Temple★ (see Ps 5, 7, 17). **1–3:** *Vindicate me* could be translated more literally "establish justice for me" (7.8; 17.1–2). *Integrity* (vv. 1, 11; 25.21) denotes complete dependence on God; it is synonymous with *trusted*. The psalmist knows God's ways—*steadfast love* and *faithfulness* (v. 3)—and has nothing to hide (v. 2; 7.9; 17.3). **4–5:** The psalmist asserts that he or she opposes *evil*, just as God does (5.5). The claim is not of sinlessness but rather of innocence in a particular case (7.3–5). **6–8:** The central section focuses on the psalmist and the Temple. Verse 6 describes what priests would have done to prepare themselves for service in the Temple, but it may be heard figuratively. *Love* of the Temple expresses loyalty and trust. **9–10:** As in vv. 4–5, the focus is on *evil* and *evildoers*. **11–12:** Echoing v. 1, the psalmist states with whom he or she *stands*—with God's people, another indication of loyalty and trust. *Bless* originally connoted "to kneel," an act of submission.

PSALM 27
Of David.

1 The LORD is my light and my salvation;
  whom shall I fear?
  The LORD is the stronghold*b* of my life;
  of whom shall I be afraid?

2 When evildoers assail me
  to devour my flesh—

a Or *in your faithfulness*   *b* Or *refuge*

my adversaries and foes—
    they shall stumble and fall.

3 Though an army encamp against me,
    my heart shall not fear;
though war rise up against me,
    yet I will be confident.

4 One thing I asked of the LORD,
    that will I seek after:
to live in the house of the LORD
    all the days of my life,
to behold the beauty of the LORD,
    and to inquire in his temple.

5 For he will hide me in his shelter
    in the day of trouble;
he will conceal me under the cover of
    his tent;
    he will set me high on a rock.

6 Now my head is lifted up
    above my enemies all around me,
and I will offer in his tent
    sacrifices with shouts of joy;
I will sing and make melody to the
    LORD.

7 Hear, O LORD, when I cry aloud,
    be gracious to me and answer me!
8 "Come," my heart says, "seek his
    face!"
    Your face, LORD, do I seek.
9   Do not hide your face from me.

Do not turn your servant away in
    anger,
    you who have been my help.
Do not cast me off, do not forsake me,
    O God of my salvation!
10 If my father and mother forsake me,
    the LORD will take me up.

11 Teach me your way, O LORD,
    and lead me on a level path
    because of my enemies.
12 Do not give me up to the will of
    my adversaries,
    for false witnesses have risen against
    me,
and they are breathing out violence.

13 I believe that I shall see the goodness of
    the LORD
    in the land of the living.
14 Wait for the LORD;
    be strong, and let your heart take
    courage;
    wait for the LORD!

27.1–14: The LORD is my light. Reversing the usual order of a lament,* it begins with assurance (vv. 1–6) and moves to prayer (vv. 7–12) before returning to assurance (vv. 13–14). **1–3:** *Light* symbolizes *life*, which is also what *salvation* means in a context where *life* is threatened (vv. 2–3). *Light* also anticipates vv. 8–9, since God's *face* is often associated with *light* (Num 6.25; Ps 4.6). The military image can be construed metaphorically.* **4–6:** Persecuted by enemies, the psalmist may have literally sought *shelter* in the *temple*, God's *house* or *tent* (15.1). The imagery may be metaphorical for entrusting the self to God. The *temple* mount was a *rock* (Isa 30.29), but God is also addressed as a *rock* (18.2; 28.1). *Behold the beauty* and *to inquire* may refer to unknown rituals. **7–10:** The psalmists regularly *seek* God's *face* or "presence" (11.7; 24.6). To be forsaken by family was to be threatened with death. **11–12:** False accusations and their destructive effects may be the source of the psalmist's complaint (see Ps 7, 17, 26). **13–14:** The opposite of *fear* (v. 1) is faith, and it engenders hope for the self and others (see "wait" in 25.3, 5, 21; 31.24).

PSALM 28
Of David.

1 To you, O LORD, I call;
    my rock, do not refuse to hear me,
for if you are silent to me,
    I shall be like those who go down to
    the Pit.
2 Hear the voice of my supplication,
    as I cry to you for help,
as I lift up my hands
    toward your most holy sanctuary.*a*

3 Do not drag me away with the wicked,
    with those who are workers of evil,
who speak peace with their neighbors,
    while mischief is in their hearts.

a Heb *your innermost sanctuary*

4 Repay them according to their work,
  and according to the evil of their
    deeds;
  repay them according to the work of
    their hands;
  render them their due reward.
5 Because they do not regard the works of
    the LORD,
  or the work of his hands,
  he will break them down and build
    them up no more.

6 Blessed be the LORD,
  for he has heard the sound of my
    pleadings.
7 The LORD is my strength and my
    shield;
  in him my heart trusts;
  so I am helped, and my heart exults,
  and with my song I give thanks to
    him.

8 The LORD is the strength of his
    people;
  he is the saving refuge of his
    anointed.
9 O save your people, and bless your
    heritage;
  be their shepherd, and carry them
    forever.

28.1–9: With my song I give thanks. Most scholars
assume that vv. 6–7 indicate that the prayer of vv. 1–4
has been answered; hence they classify the psalm as a
song of thanksgiving. Others label it a prayer for help,
or even a royal psalm, due to the phrase *his anointed**
in v. 8 (2.2). 1–2: The *Pit* is the realm of death
(116.10). In an unstable situation, the psalmist appeals
to *my rock* (27.5). Uplifted *hands* represent the posture of prayer (63.4). Perhaps the psalm was originally
prayed as the psalmist faced the holy of holies, the site
of God's earthly throne (1 Kings 6.5). 3–5: The prayer
is not so much for revenge as it is for justice, since *the
wicked* pursue their own *work* as opposed to the *works
of the LORD*. 6–7: The psalmist asked God to *hear* (v. 2),
and God *has heard* (v. 6). God has been a protecting
shield (3.4) and has *helped* (22.19). The appropriate
response is gratitude. 8–9: Using the word *strength*
from v. 7, v. 8 introduces a corporate dimension by
mentioning God's *people* and the *anointed*, the king.
Even after affirming that God is a *saving refuge*, the

psalmist still prays, *save your people*. God's work is
never done. As v. 1 suggested, God's constant provision is necessary for the people to live (23.1).

PSALM 29
A Psalm of David.

1 Ascribe to the LORD, O heavenly beings,*ᵃ*
    ascribe to the LORD glory and
      strength.
2 Ascribe to the LORD the glory of his
      name;
    worship the LORD in holy splendor.

3 The voice of the LORD is over the
      waters;
    the God of glory thunders,
    the LORD, over mighty waters.
4 The voice of the LORD is powerful;
    the voice of the LORD is full of
      majesty.

5 The voice of the LORD breaks the
      cedars;
    the LORD breaks the cedars of
      Lebanon.
6 He makes Lebanon skip like a calf,
    and Sirion like a young wild ox.

7 The voice of the LORD flashes forth
      flames of fire.
8 The voice of the LORD shakes the
      wilderness;
    the LORD shakes the wilderness of
      Kadesh.

9 The voice of the LORD causes the oaks
      to whirl,*ᵇ*
    and strips the forest bare;
    and in his temple all say, "Glory!"

10 The LORD sits enthroned over the
      flood;
    the LORD sits enthroned as king
      forever.
11 May the LORD give strength to his
      people!
    May the LORD bless his people with
      peace!

a Heb *sons of gods*   b Or *causes the deer to calve*

29.1–11: The LORD sits enthroned. An enthronement psalm (see v. 10; Ps 93), it may be among the oldest psalms, perhaps an adaptation of a Canaanite hymn to Baal,* the god of the storm. **1–2:** *Ascribe* means to acknowledge. The *heavenly beings*, probably viewed as deposed Canaanite deities (Ps 82), are to yield to God's sovereignty. *Glory* becomes a key word (vv. 1–3, 9; 24.7–10; 96.3). *Holy splendor* may suggest a reverential posture or perhaps appropriate attire. **3–9:** *Voice* occurs seven times, suggesting the complete power of God. In the context, it suggests thunder, since vv. 3–9 describe the effects of a powerful storm hitting the coast of Palestine, complete with gusty winds (vv. 6–7), sharp lightning (v. 7), and thunder (v. 8). Baal's power has been appropriated by the LORD. God's temple may indicate God's heavenly abode (11.4), but the earthly Temple* may also be in view. **10–11:** The *flood* indicates the cosmic waters, over which God is sovereign. The job of a king was to provide for his people. The ultimate goal was "shalom" ("peace"), for which the psalmist prayed in v. 11 (72.7).

PSALM 30

A Psalm. A Song at the dedication of the temple.
Of David.

1 I will extol you, O LORD, for you have
      drawn me up,
   and did not let my foes rejoice over
      me.
2 O LORD my God, I cried to you for
      help,
   and you have healed me.
3 O LORD, you brought up my soul from
      Sheol,
   restored me to life from among those
      gone down to the Pit.*

4 Sing praises to the LORD, O you his
      faithful ones,
   and give thanks to his holy name.
5 For his anger is but for a moment;
   his favor is for a lifetime.
   Weeping may linger for the night,
   but joy comes with the morning.

6 As for me, I said in my prosperity,
   "I shall never be moved."

7 By your favor, O LORD,
   you had established me as a strong
      mountain;
 you hid your face;
   I was dismayed.

8 To you, O LORD, I cried,
   and to the LORD I made supplication:
9 "What profit is there in my death,
   if I go down to the Pit?
 Will the dust praise you?
   Will it tell of your faithfulness?
10 Hear, O LORD, and be gracious to me!
   O LORD, be my helper!"

11 You have turned my mourning into
      dancing;
   you have taken off my sackcloth
   and clothed me with joy,
12 so that my soul[b] may praise you and not
      be silent.
 O LORD my God, I will give thanks to
      you forever.

30.1–12: I will give thanks to you forever. The superscription associates the psalm with *the dedication of the temple,* and rabbinic sources identity it with the Feast of Dedication (Hanukkah). A song of thanksgiving, it may have been used originally by someone who had been *healed* (v. 2) from illness. **1–3:** *Healed* may be heard metaphorically* (147.3; Hos 6.1). In any case, the threat was deadly, since *Sheol** (6.5) and *the Pit* (28.1) designate the realm of the dead. **4–5:** The psalmist now invites others to join the song of thanksgiving. The two verbs in v. 4 recur in v. 12. *Joy* in v. 5 anticipates v. 11. **6–12:** These verses rehearse the distress (vv. 6–10) and deliverance (vv. 11–12). Verses 9–10 apparently quote a portion of the prayer mentioned in v. 2 (6.5; 88.10–12). A comparison of v. 6 with v. 12 suggests the psalmist's move from misplaced confidence in the self to humble gratitude and *praise* that will endure *forever.*

PSALM 31

To the leader. A Psalm of David.

1 In you, O LORD, I seek refuge;
   do not let me ever be put to shame;
   in your righteousness deliver me.

a Or that I should not go down to the Pit   *b Heb that glory*

2 Incline your ear to me;
    rescue me speedily.
  Be a rock of refuge for me,
    a strong fortress to save me.

3 You are indeed my rock and my fortress;
    for your name's sake lead me and
      guide me,
4 take me out of the net that is hidden for
      me,
    for you are my refuge.
5 Into your hand I commit my spirit;
    you have redeemed me, O LORD,
      faithful God.

6 You hate*a* those who pay regard to
      worthless idols,
    but I trust in the LORD.
7 I will exult and rejoice in your steadfast
      love,
    because you have seen my affliction;
    you have taken heed of my
      adversities,
8 and have not delivered me into the hand
      of the enemy;
    you have set my feet in a broad place.

9 Be gracious to me, O LORD, for I am in
      distress;
    my eye wastes away from grief,
    my soul and body also.
10 For my life is spent with sorrow,
    and my years with sighing;
    my strength fails because of my misery,*b*
    and my bones waste away.

11 I am the scorn of all my adversaries,
    a horror*c* to my neighbors,
    an object of dread to my acquaintances;
    those who see me in the street flee
      from me.
12 I have passed out of mind like one who
      is dead;
    I have become like a broken vessel.
13 For I hear the whispering of many—
      terror all around!—
    as they scheme together against me,
    as they plot to take my life.

14 But I trust in you, O LORD;
    I say, "You are my God."

15 My times are in your hand;
    deliver me from the hand of my
      enemies and persecutors.
16 Let your face shine upon your servant;
    save me in your steadfast love.
17 Do not let me be put to shame,
      O LORD,
    for I call on you;
    let the wicked be put to shame;
    let them go dumbfounded to Sheol.
18 Let the lying lips be stilled
    that speak insolently against the
      righteous
    with pride and contempt.

19 O how abundant is your goodness
    that you have laid up for those who
      fear you,
    and accomplished for those who take
      refuge in you,
    in the sight of everyone!
20 In the shelter of your presence you hide
      them
    from human plots;
    you hold them safe under your shelter
    from contentious tongues.

21 Blessed be the LORD,
    for he has wondrously shown his
      steadfast love to me
    when I was beset as a city under
      siege.
22 I had said in my alarm,
    "I am driven far*d* from your sight."
  But you heard my supplications
    when I cried out to you for help.

23 Love the LORD, all you his saints.
    The LORD preserves the faithful,
    but abundantly repays the one who
      acts haughtily.
24 Be strong, and let your heart take
      courage,
    all you who wait for the LORD.

31.1–24: Into your hand I commit my spirit. A prayer
for help, its uniqueness lies in the frequent expressions
of trust that accompany the petitions (see vv. 1a, 3a,

a One Heb Ms Gk Syr Jerome: MT *I hate*   *b* Gk Syr:
Heb *my iniquity*   *c* Cn: Heb *exceedingly*   *d* Another
reading is *cut off*

4b–8, 14–15a, 19–24). **1–5:** *Refuge* (2.12; 18.2) grounds the subsequent petitions and sets the tone for the entire psalm. Verse 5a means "I turn my life over to you" (see Lk 23.46). **6–8:** Verse 6 should begin "I hate" (see note *a*). To show *trust* in God means to oppose those who oppose God (26.5). It also means to embody God's character, which is essentially *steadfast love* (v. 7; see vv. 16, 21). *Broad place* connotes safety and well-being (18.19). **9–13:** In tension with v. 8 is the petition that implies the psalmist's ongoing *distress*, which connotes "narrowness, tight space," the opposite of *broad place*. The distress leads to social abandonment (22. 6–8). *Terror all around* occurs elsewhere only in Jer 20.3, 10; Jeremiah was also abandoned and ridiculed. **14–18:** Returning to *trust*, v. 14 recalls v. 6, and v. 5 is echoed in v. 15, which means, "I turn my future over to you." The psalmist prays for life, symbolized by the light of God's *face* (4.6), and for *the wicked* to be silenced. *Sheol*⁎ is the realm of the dead (30.3). **19–22:** In view of ongoing complaint and petition, God's *goodness* cannot mean material prosperity nor a carefree existence. Rather it suggests the assurance of turning one's life over fully to God (vv. 5, 15) and of knowing God is not absent (vv. 14, 22). **23–24:** Such assurance leads the people to *love the Lord* and *wait for the Lord* (27.14).

PSALM 32

Of David. A Maskil.

1 Happy are those whose transgression is
      forgiven,
   whose sin is covered.
2 Happy are those to whom the Lord
      imputes no iniquity,
   and in whose spirit there is no deceit.

3 While I kept silence, my body wasted
      away
   through my groaning all day long.
4 For day and night your hand was heavy
      upon me;
   my strength was dried up*ᵃ* as by the
      heat of summer. *Selah*

5 Then I acknowledged my sin to you,
   and I did not hide my iniquity;
   I said, "I will confess my transgressions
      to the Lord,"
   and you forgave the guilt of my sin.
      Selah

6 Therefore let all who are faithful
      offer prayer to you;
   at a time of distress,*ᵇ* the rush of
      mighty waters
   shall not reach them.
7 You are a hiding place for me;
   you preserve me from trouble;
   you surround me with glad cries of
      deliverance. *Selah*

8 I will instruct you and teach you the
      way you should go;
   I will counsel you with my eye upon
      you.
9 Do not be like a horse or a mule,
      without understanding,
   whose temper must be curbed with
      bit and bridle,
   else it will not stay near you.

10 Many are the torments of the wicked,
   but steadfast love surrounds those
      who trust in the Lord.
11 Be glad in the Lord and rejoice,
      O righteous,
   and shout for joy, all you upright in
      heart.

32.1–11: I will confess my transgressions. Usually classified as a song of thanksgiving because of the account of deliverance in vv. 3–5, it is one of the church's Penitential Psalms⁎ (see Ps 6). **1–2:** The beatitudes recall 1.1; 2.12. The *righteous* (v. 11) are portrayed as those who have been forgiven rather than those who deserve God's favor (Rom 4.6–8). **3–5:** *Sin* is the most general term, connoting "to miss the mark." *Transgression(s)* connotes intentional rebellion. *Iniquity* includes the destructive effects of disobedience, which are graphically described and which persist until *sin* is confessed. *Forgiven* and *forgive* frame vv. 1–5. **6–7:** The prayer continues, but as a profession of faith focused on God. **8–9:** It is not clear whether the speaker should be understood as God responding to the psalmist (in words originally delivered by a priest or prophet⁎), or as the psalmist stating the intention to share what he or she has learned (51.13). **10–11:** The psalmist, apparently addressing other worshippers (or readers), invites them into his or her experience. The

a Meaning of Heb uncertain   *b* Cn: Heb *at a time of finding only* psalm associates forgiveness with God's *steadfast love* (see Ex 34.6–7) and suggests that the essence of *trust* and the source of *joy* are found in confession and forgiveness.

〰〰〰〰〰〰〰〰〰〰〰〰〰〰〰

PSALM 33

1 Rejoice in the LORD, O you righteous.
   Praise befits the upright.
2 Praise the LORD with the lyre;
   make melody to him with the harp of
      ten strings.
3 Sing to him a new song;
   play skillfully on the strings, with loud
      shouts.

4 For the word of the LORD is upright,
   and all his work is done in
      faithfulness.
5 He loves righteousness and justice;
   the earth is full of the steadfast love
      of the LORD.

6 By the word of the LORD the heavens
      were made,
   and all their host by the breath of his
      mouth.
7 He gathered the waters of the sea as in
      a bottle;
   he put the deeps in storehouses.

8 Let all the earth fear the LORD;
   let all the inhabitants of the world
      stand in awe of him.
9 For he spoke, and it came to be;
   he commanded, and it stood firm.

10 The LORD brings the counsel of the
      nations to nothing;
    he frustrates the plans of the peoples.
11 The counsel of the LORD stands forever,
    the thoughts of his heart to all
      generations.
12 Happy is the nation whose God is the
      LORD,
    the people whom he has chosen as
      his heritage.

13 The LORD looks down from heaven;
    he sees all humankind.

14 From where he sits enthroned he
      watches
    all the inhabitants of the earth—
15 he who fashions the hearts of them all,
    and observes all their deeds.
16 A king is not saved by his great army;
    a warrior is not delivered by his great
      strength.
17 The war horse is a vain hope for victory,
    and by its great might it cannot save.

18 Truly the eye of the LORD is on those
      who fear him,
    on those who hope in his steadfast
      love,
19 to deliver their soul from death,
    and to keep them alive in famine.

20 Our soul waits for the LORD;
    he is our help and shield.
21 Our heart is glad in him,
    because we trust in his holy name.
22 Let your steadfast love, O LORD, be
      upon us,
    even as we hope in you.

33.1–22: The earth is full of the steadfast love of the LORD. This song of praise responds to Ps 32 (compare 32.11 and 33.1), a conclusion reinforced by the lack of a superscription. **1–3:** The *righteous* and *upright* have been portrayed as those whom God forgives (32.11). They owe their lives to God, so *praise befits* them. *Praise* bespeaks submission to God's sovereignty, a concept associated elsewhere with *a new song* (96.1; 98.1). Verses 2–3 are the first references to musical instruments in the body of a psalm (57.8; 71.22). **4–5:** *Righteousness and justice* are attributes of God's reign (89.14; 96.13). Verses 6–22 expound upon the claim that the world is essentially constituted by God's *word* revealed as *steadfast love* (vv. 18, 22; 5.7; 118.1). **6–9:** Repeating *word* from v. 4, the psalmist attributes the universe to God's creative speech (v. 9). The vocabulary recalls Ex 15 and Gen 1. *Fear* (v. 8) means to acknowledge God's sovereignty. **10–12:** The unfolding of history will not thwart God's *counsel* (Prov 19.21). **13–15:** *Enthroned* further sharpens the focus on God's sovereignty (11.4; 14.2). **16–19:** Highly placed persons and their resources offer only the illusion of power (Prov 21.30–31). Only God, implementing divine love (v. 18), will *deliver* (v. 19; 107.4–9). **20–22:** An affirmation of *trust* precedes a final petition, which also bespeaks *hope* (27.14; 31.24) in God's loving *help* (22.19).

~~~~~~~~~~

PSALM 34

Of David, when he feigned madness before Abimelech, so that he drove him out, and he went away.

1 I will bless the LORD at all times;
 his praise shall continually be in my
  mouth.
2 My soul makes its boast in the LORD;
 let the humble hear and be glad.
3 O magnify the LORD with me,
 and let us exalt his name together.

4 I sought the LORD, and he answered
  me,
 and delivered me from all my fears.
5 Look to him, and be radiant;
 so your*a* faces shall never be
  ashamed.
6 This poor soul cried, and was heard by
  the LORD,
 and was saved from every trouble.
7 The angel of the LORD encamps
 around those who fear him, and
  delivers them.
8 O taste and see that the LORD is good;
 happy are those who take refuge in
  him.
9 O fear the LORD, you his holy ones,
 for those who fear him have no want.
10 The young lions suffer want and
  hunger,
 but those who seek the LORD lack no
  good thing.

11 Come, O children, listen to me;
 I will teach you the fear of the LORD.
12 Which of you desires life,
 and covets many days to enjoy good?
13 Keep your tongue from evil,
 and your lips from speaking deceit.
14 Depart from evil, and do good;
 seek peace, and pursue it.

15 The eyes of the LORD are on the
  righteous,
 and his ears are open to their cry.

16 The face of the LORD is against
  evildoers,
 to cut off the remembrance of them
  from the earth.
17 When the righteous cry for help, the
  LORD hears,
 and rescues them from all their
  troubles.
18 The LORD is near to the brokenhearted,
 and saves the crushed in spirit.

19 Many are the afflictions of the righteous,
 but the LORD rescues them from
  them all.
20 He keeps all their bones;
 not one of them will be broken.
21 Evil brings death to the wicked,
 and those who hate the righteous will
  be condemned.
22 The LORD redeems the life of his
  servants;
 none of those who take refuge in him
  will be condemned.

34.1–22: Which of you desires life? An acrostic* song of thanksgiving (see Ps 9–10), its concern to *teach . . . the fear of the* LORD (v. 11) leads some to label it a wisdom psalm. The superscription seems related to 1 Sam 21.13, but there are discrepancies. **1–3:** *Praise* is to be overheard, encouraging others to join *together* with the psalmist. **4–10:** Intending to be exemplary (v. 2), the psalmist recounts God's deliverance, interspersed with invitations for others to *look to* and experience (which is the sense of *taste*) God as well (vv. 5, 8–9). *Fear* connotes trust in and dependence upon God; v. 9 fills out what it means to *take refuge in* God (v. 8; see v. 22; 2.12). **11–14:** Wisdom vocabulary predominates, including the address to *children* (Prov 1.8; 3.1), the theme of *fear of the* LORD (Prov 1.7; 9.10), the goal of *life* (Prov 3.2; 10.17), the concern with proper speech (Prov 4.24; 6.17), and the contrast of *good* and *evil* (Prov 2.20; 3.7). **15–22:** God helps *the righteous* (vv. 15, 17, 19) and opposes *evildoers* (v. 16) and *the wicked* (v. 21). That a mechanistic retributional scheme is not operative is indicated *by the afflictions of the righteous* (v. 19). God's nearness (v. 18; 73.28) offers the resources that make *life* (v. 22) possible in the midst of suffering.

~~~~~~~~~~

a Gk Syr Jerome: Heb *their*

PSALM 35

Of David.

1 Contend, O LORD, with those who
   contend with me;
   fight against those who fight against
      me!
2 Take hold of shield and buckler,
   and rise up to help me!
3 Draw the spear and javelin
   against my pursuers;
   say to my soul,
   "I am your salvation."

4 Let them be put to shame and dishonor
   who seek after my life.
   Let them be turned back and
      confounded
   who devise evil against me.
5 Let them be like chaff before the wind,
   with the angel of the LORD driving
      them on.
6 Let their way be dark and slippery,
   with the angel of the LORD pursuing
      them.

7 For without cause they hid their net[a]
      for me;
   without cause they dug a pit[b] for my
      life.
8 Let ruin come on them unawares.
   And let the net that they hid ensnare
      them;
   let them fall in it—to their ruin.

9 Then my soul shall rejoice in the LORD,
   exulting in his deliverance.
10 All my bones shall say,
   "O LORD, who is like you?
   You deliver the weak
      from those too strong for them,
   the weak and needy from those who
      despoil them."

11 Malicious witnesses rise up;
   they ask me about things I do not
      know.
12 They repay me evil for good;
   my soul is forlorn.
13 But as for me, when they were sick,
   I wore sackcloth;
   I afflicted myself with fasting.

I prayed with head bowed[c] on my
      bosom,
14 as though I grieved for a friend or a
      brother;
   I went about as one who laments for a
      mother,
   bowed down and in mourning.

35.1–28: My soul is forlorn. All the elements of a prayer for help are here, but in no apparent order: petition for help (vv. 1–3, 17, 22–25); petition against the enemies (vv. 4–6, 8, 19, 26); complaint (vv. 7, 11–12, 15–16, 20–21); vow to praise (vv. 9–10, 18, 28); protestation of innocence (vv. 13–14); and an invitation to praise addressed to allies (v. 27). This psalm may have originated as a prayer of one falsely accused (Ps 17, 26) or of one whose sickness (v. 13) was capitalized upon by enemies. **1–3:** *Contend* suggests a legal proceeding, but the legal language is accompanied by military imagery in vv. 2–3. The language can be construed metaphorically.* **4–8:** The petitions against the enemies are motivated not by vengeance but rather by a longing for justice (v. 24), which involves opposition to oppression. The psalmist trusts that *evil* will destroy itself (1.6; 7.15–16). **9–10:** The self-destruction of *evil* represents the activity of God on behalf of *the weak and needy* (v. 10; 9.18). **11–14:** The complaint in vv. 11–12 ends with *forlorn*, a word that may indicate grief over childlessness and anticipates the psalmist's treatment of others as if they were family (vv. 13–14).

---

15 But at my stumbling they gathered in
      glee,
   they gathered together against me;
   ruffians whom I did not know
      tore at me without ceasing;
16 they impiously mocked more and more,[d]
   gnashing at me with their teeth.

17 How long, O LORD, will you look on?
   Rescue me from their ravages,
      my life from the lions!
18 Then I will thank you in the great
      congregation;
   in the mighty throng I will praise you.

---

a Heb *a pit, their net*   *b* The word *pit* is transposed
from the preceding line   *c* Or *My prayer turned back*
d Cn Compare Gk: Heb *like the profanest of mockers of a
cake*

19 Do not let my treacherous enemies
　　　rejoice over me,
　　or those who hate me without cause
　　　wink the eye.
20 For they do not speak peace,
　　but they conceive deceitful words
　　against those who are quiet in the
　　　land.
21 They open wide their mouths against me;
　　they say, "Aha, Aha,
　　our eyes have seen it."

22 You have seen, O LORD; do not be
　　　silent!
　　O Lord, do not be far from me!
23 Wake up! Bestir yourself for my
　　　defense,
　　for my cause, my God and my Lord!
24 Vindicate me, O LORD, my God,
　　according to your righteousness,
　　and do not let them rejoice over me.
25 Do not let them say to themselves,
　　"Aha, we have our heart's desire."
　　Do not let them say, "We have
　　　swallowed you*a* up."

26 Let all those who rejoice at my calamity
　　be put to shame and confusion;
　　let those who exalt themselves against
　　　me
　　be clothed with shame and dishonor.

27 Let those who desire my vindication
　　shout for joy and be glad,
　　and say evermore,
　　"Great is the LORD,
　　who delights in the welfare of his
　　　servant."
28 Then my tongue shall tell of your
　　　righteousness
　　and of your praise all day long.

35.15–28. 15–18: Unlike the psalmist, the opponents
act like ravenous animals (37.12; 58.6). 19–25: Their
arrogance is revealed in their speech (vv. 21, 25). They
think they have *seen* (v. 21), but the psalmist trusts
that God has *seen* (v. 22). Challenging God to *Wake
up!*, the psalmist summarizes the issue as one of justice. *My defense* is literally "my justice," and *vindicate
me* is literally "establish justice for me" (v. 24; 26.1).
The petition is grounded in God's *righteousness* (v. 28;

7.17; 33.5). 26–28: The contrasting of opponents
(v. 26) and allies (v. 27) summarizes the essence of
God's *righteousness* (v. 28) as "shalom," "peace"
(NRSV *welfare*), a contrast to the opponents who *do
not speak peace* (v. 20) and whose behavior results in
persecution *without cause* (vv. 7, 19).

PSALM 36
To the leader. Of David, the servant of the LORD.

1 Transgression speaks to the wicked
　　deep in their hearts;
　　there is no fear of God
　　before their eyes.
2 For they flatter themselves in their own
　　　eyes
　　that their iniquity cannot be found
　　　out and hated.
3 The words of their mouths are mischief
　　　and deceit;
　　they have ceased to act wisely and do
　　　good.
4 They plot mischief while on their beds;
　　they are set on a way that is not good;
　　they do not reject evil.

5 Your steadfast love, O LORD, extends to
　　　the heavens,
　　your faithfulness to the clouds.
6 Your righteousness is like the mighty
　　　mountains,
　　your judgments are like the great
　　　deep;
　　you save humans and animals alike,
　　　O LORD.

7 How precious is your steadfast love,
　　　O God!
　　All people may take refuge in the
　　　shadow of your wings.
8 They feast on the abundance of your
　　　house,
　　and you give them drink from the
　　　river of your delights.
9 For with you is the fountain of life;
　　in your light we see light.

10 O continue your steadfast love to those
　　　who know you,

a Heb *him*

and your salvation to the upright of
  heart!
11 Do not let the foot of the arrogant tread
    on me,
  or the hand of the wicked drive me
    away.
12 There the evildoers lie prostrate;
  they are thrust down, unable to rise.

36.1–12: The fountain of life. It is usually categorized as a lament,* but petition occurs only in vv. 10–11. The repetition of "hesed" (vv. 5, 7, 10) gives it the character of a celebration of God's *steadfast love*. **1–4:** The word *speaks* in v. 1 is used almost exclusively elsewhere of God's speech, but *the wicked* hear only their own rebellious thoughts. Therefore, loyalty to or *fear of God* is replaced by self-assertion, for which the wicked envision no accountability (vv. 2–3; Mic 2.1). **5–6:** *Steadfast love* and *faithfulness* communicate the character of God (Ex 34.6), while *righteousness* and *judgment* (or "acts of justice") summarize God's will (33.4–5; 89.14). Cosmological features, appearing in descending order, suggest that God's *steadfast love* permeates the cosmos. **7–9:** The promise of *refuge in the shadow of your wings* (17.8; 57.1) and the mention of *your house* may suggest an original Temple* setting. The language is probably metaphorical.* God is the *fountain* (68.26) or source of *life*, which *light* symbolizes (4.6). **10–12:** The focus on *the wicked* (v. 11) and *the evildoers* (v. 12) is a reminder of their constant opposition to God and God's people, but the psalmist trusts that God renders ineffective such opposition.

PSALM 37
Of David.

1 Do not fret because of the wicked;
  do not be envious of wrongdoers,
2 for they will soon fade like the grass,
  and wither like the green herb.

3 Trust in the LORD, and do good;
  so you will live in the land, and enjoy
    security.
4 Take delight in the LORD,
  and he will give you the desires of
    your heart.

5 Commit your way to the LORD;
  trust in him, and he will act.

6 He will make your vindication shine like
    the light,
  and the justice of your cause like the
    noonday.

7 Be still before the LORD, and wait
    patiently for him;
  do not fret over those who prosper in
    their way,
  over those who carry out evil devices.

8 Refrain from anger, and forsake wrath.
  Do not fret—it leads only to evil.
9 For the wicked shall be cut off,
  but those who wait for the LORD shall
    inherit the land.

10 Yet a little while, and the wicked will be
    no more;
  though you look diligently for their
    place, they will not be there.
11 But the meek shall inherit the land,
  and delight themselves in abundant
    prosperity.

12 The wicked plot against the righteous,
  and gnash their teeth at them;
13 but the LORD laughs at the wicked,
  for he sees that their day is coming.

14 The wicked draw the sword and bend
    their bows
  to bring down the poor and needy,
  to kill those who walk uprightly;
15 their sword shall enter their own heart,
  and their bows shall be broken.

16 Better is a little that the righteous
    person has
  than the abundance of many wicked.
17 For the arms of the wicked shall be
    broken,
  but the LORD upholds the righteous.

18 The LORD knows the days of the
    blameless,
  and their heritage will abide forever;
19 they are not put to shame in evil times,
  in the days of famine they have
    abundance.

20 But the wicked perish,
 and the enemies of the LORD are like
  the glory of the pastures;
 they vanish—like smoke they vanish
  away.

37.1–40: The LORD loves justice. This acrostic* poem (see Ps 9–10) is usually categorized as a wisdom psalm. It confronts the issue of theodicy* (literally, "the justice of God"), which is raised by the prosperity of *the wicked* (v. 1, plus fourteen more times) and their apparent success in opposing *the righteous* (v. 12, plus eight more times). **1–11:** The advice to the faithful (vv. 1, 3–5, 7–8), to which promises are attached (vv. 2, 6, 9–11), is *Do not fret* (vv. 1, 7, 8). Positively stated, it is *Trust in the LORD* (v. 3; see v. 5). Verse 6 identifies the issue as *justice* (v. 28), and v. 9 introduces the pervading themes: *the wicked shall be cut off* (vv. 22, 28, 34, 38) and *the righteous will inherit the land* (vv. 11, 22, 29, 34). The promise was probably meant figuratively to communicate the assurance of life and future. **12–20:** After vv. 1–11, advice is infrequent (vv. 27, 34). It is replaced by observations that support the promises of vv. 2, 6, 10–11. The LORD *laughs at the wicked*, because they do not threaten divine sovereignty (v. 13; see 2.4). *The wicked* effect their own undoing (vv. 14–15; Ps 7.15–16).

---

21 The wicked borrow, and do not pay
  back,
 but the righteous are generous and
  keep giving;
22 for those blessed by the LORD shall
  inherit the land,
 but those cursed by him shall be cut
  off.

23 Our steps*a* are made firm by the LORD,
 when he delights in our*b* way;
24 though we stumble,*c* we*d* shall not fall
  headlong,
 for the LORD holds us*e* by the hand.

25 I have been young, and now am old,
 yet I have not seen the righteous
  forsaken
 or their children begging bread.
26 They are ever giving liberally and
  lending,
 and their children become a
  blessing.

27 Depart from evil, and do good;
 so you shall abide forever.
28 For the LORD loves justice;
 he will not forsake his faithful ones.

 The righteous shall be kept safe
  forever,
 but the children of the wicked shall
  be cut off.
29 The righteous shall inherit the land,
 and live in it forever.

30 The mouths of the righteous utter
  wisdom,
 and their tongues speak justice.
31 The law of their God is in their hearts;
 their steps do not slip.

32 The wicked watch for the righteous,
 and seek to kill them.
33 The LORD will not abandon them to
  their power,
 or let them be condemned when they
  are brought to trial.

34 Wait for the LORD, and keep to his way,
 and he will exalt you to inherit the
  land;
 you will look on the destruction of
  the wicked.

35 I have seen the wicked oppressing,
 and towering like a cedar of
  Lebanon.*f*
36 Again I*g* passed by, and they were no
  more;
 though I sought them, they could not
  be found.

37 Mark the blameless, and behold the
  upright,
 for there is posterity for the
  peaceable.
38 But transgressors shall be altogether
  destroyed;
 the posterity of the wicked shall be
  cut off.

---

a Heb *A man's steps*   *b* Heb *his*   *c* Heb *he stumbles*
d Heb *he*   *e* Heb *him*   *f* Gk: Meaning of Heb
uncertain   *g* Gk Syr Jerome: Heb *he*

39 The salvation of the righteous is from
  the LORD;
    he is their refuge in the time of
      trouble.
40 The LORD helps them and rescues
  them;
    he rescues them from the wicked,
      and saves them,
    because they take refuge in him.

37.21–40. 21–26: The concepts of *borrow* and *lending* frame this section. Generosity is its own reward (Prov 14.31; 19.17). **27–29:** Verse 27 recalls v. 3; and v. 28 recalls vv. 5–6, highlighting God's *justice*. **30–31:** *The righteous* are oriented to God, reflecting God's *justice* and appropriating God's "torah," "instruction" (NRSV *law*; 1.1–2). **32–38:** A final exhortation* (v. 34) accompanies further assurance that evil is fleeting and that righteousness will endure. **39–40:** Two different Hebrew words for *refuge* highlight the concept (2.12). That the assurances do not constitute a mechanistic doctrine of retribution is indicated by the recognition that *the righteous* will still experience *the time of trouble.*

PSALM 38

A Psalm of David, for the memorial offering.

1 O LORD, do not rebuke me in your
  anger,
    or discipline me in your wrath.
2 For your arrows have sunk into me,
    and your hand has come down
      on me.

3 There is no soundness in my flesh
    because of your indignation;
  there is no health in my bones
    because of my sin.
4 For my iniquities have gone over my
  head;
    they weigh like a burden too heavy for
      me.

5 My wounds grow foul and fester
    because of my foolishness;
6 I am utterly bowed down and prostrate;
    all day long I go around mourning.
7 For my loins are filled with burning,
    and there is no soundness in my
      flesh.

8 I am utterly spent and crushed;
    I groan because of the tumult of my
      heart.

9 O Lord, all my longing is known
    to you;
    my sighing is not hidden from you.
10 My heart throbs, my strength fails me;
    as for the light of my eyes—it also
      has gone from me.
11 My friends and companions stand aloof
    from my affliction,
    and my neighbors stand far off.

12 Those who seek my life lay their snares;
    those who seek to hurt me speak of
      ruin,
    and meditate treachery all day long.

13 But I am like the deaf, I do not hear;
    like the mute, who cannot speak.
14 Truly, I am like one who does not hear,
    and in whose mouth is no retort.

15 But it is for you, O LORD, that I wait;
    it is you, O Lord my God, who will
      answer.
16 For I pray, "Only do not let them rejoice
    over me,
    those who boast against me when my
      foot slips."

17 For I am ready to fall,
    and my pain is ever with me.
18 I confess my iniquity;
    I am sorry for my sin.
19 Those who are my foes without cause*a*
    are mighty,
    and many are those who hate me
      wrongfully.
20 Those who render me evil for good
    are my adversaries because I follow
      after good.

21 Do not forsake me, O LORD;
    O my God, do not be far from me;
22 make haste to help me,
    O Lord, my salvation.

a Q Ms: MT *my living foes*

38.1–22: My pain is ever with me. A prayer for help, it may have originally been used by sick persons (Ps 6). It is one of the church's Penitential Psalms* (Ps 6). **1–4:** The opening petition (6.1) implies that the distress represents punishment, and vv. 2–4 make this explicit (see v. 18). Verse 3a is repeated in v. 7b. **5–8:** *Grow foul and fester* could suggest that the psalmist suffered from leprosy, but the language can be heard metaphorically.* **9–10:** Apparently near death (v. 10), the psalmist is confident that the dire situation is *known* by God (v. 9). This ray of hope anticipates vv. 15–16, 21–22. **11–12:** Constant opposition from enemies may be bad enough (v. 12), but the psalmist has also been abandoned by those who should have offered support (v. 11; 27.10; 55.12–14; 88.8, 18). **13–14:** It is not clear whether the psalmist pretends not to hear, or whether the situation is so irredeemable that there is nothing left to say. **15–16:** The only hope is God. The psalmist petitions not for healing but for vindication. **17–20:** The psalmist is repentant (vv. 18, 20) but still in constant *pain* (v. 17). **21–22:** Recalling Ps 22.1, 11, 19, these verses undercut the notion of retribution implied by the psalmist's earlier linkage of sin and sickness. The psalmist anticipates that ultimately God will respond compassionately to *pain* (see vv. 9, 15).

PSALM 39
To the leader: to Jeduthun. A Psalm of David.

1 I said, "I will guard my ways
  that I may not sin with my tongue;
I will keep a muzzle on my mouth
  as long as the wicked are in my
    presence."
2 I was silent and still;
  I held my peace to no avail;
my distress grew worse,
3   my heart became hot within me.
While I mused, the fire burned;
  then I spoke with my tongue:

4 "LORD, let me know my end,
  and what is the measure of my days;
let me know how fleeting my life is.
5 You have made my days a few
    handbreadths,
  and my lifetime is as nothing in your
    sight.
Surely everyone stands as a mere
  breath. *Selah*

6 Surely everyone goes about like a
    shadow.
Surely for nothing they are in turmoil;
  they heap up, and do not know who
    will gather.

7 "And now, O Lord, what do I wait for?
  My hope is in you.
8 Deliver me from all my transgressions.
  Do not make me the scorn of the
    fool.
9 I am silent; I do not open my mouth,
  for it is you who have done it.
10 Remove your stroke from me;
  I am worn down by the blows[a] of
    your hand.

11 "You chastise mortals
  in punishment for sin,
consuming like a moth what is dear to
    them;
  surely everyone is a mere breath. *Selah*

12 "Hear my prayer, O LORD,
  and give ear to my cry;
  do not hold your peace at my tears.
For I am your passing guest,
  an alien, like all my forebears.
13 Turn your gaze away from me, that I
    may smile again,
  before I depart and am no more."

39.1–13: I am your passing guest. Like a prayer for help, it contains complaint (vv. 4–6), petition (vv. 8, 10, 12–13), and assurance (v. 7). But the generalized nature of the complaint and the puzzling final petition give the psalm the character of a wisdom meditation on the transience of life (Ps 90). **1–3:** The psalmist vows to remain silent, but is compelled to speak (Jer 20.9). **4–6:** Surprisingly, the actual speech is not offensive. It begins with a polite request (v. 4) to *know* something which the psalmist apparently knew well—the transience of human life (vv. 5–6). *Shadow* connotes *fleeting*, as does *breath*, which occurs often in Ecclesiastes (1.2, 14; 2.1; NRSV "vanity"). **7–11:** Again surprisingly, the apparently hopeless psalmist expresses *hope*, and addresses God with pious petitions (vv. 8, 10) which imply a confession of *sin*, a condition af-

a Heb *hostility*

fecting *everyone* (v. 11). **12–13:** While v. 11 sounds hopeless again, the psalmist has at least enough *hope* to continue to pray (v. 12). To be a *passing guest* and *an alien* elsewhere opens one to God's compassion and serves as a basis for petition (Lev 25.23; 1 Chr 29.15). So, it is surprising again that the psalmist ends by asking God to *turn . . . away.* The surprising juxtapositions portray hope and despair as simultaneous realities in the life of the faithful.

PSALM 40

To the leader. Of David. A Psalm.

1 I waited patiently for the LORD;
　　he inclined to me and heard my cry.
2 He drew me up from the desolate pit,[a]
　　out of the miry bog,
　　and set my feet upon a rock,
　　making my steps secure.
3 He put a new song in my mouth,
　　a song of praise to our God.
　Many will see and fear,
　　and put their trust in the LORD.

4 Happy are those who make
　　the LORD their trust,
　who do not turn to the proud,
　　to those who go astray after false
　　　gods.
5 You have multiplied, O LORD my God,
　　your wondrous deeds and your
　　　thoughts toward us;
　　none can compare with you.
　Were I to proclaim and tell of them,
　　they would be more than can be
　　　counted.

6 Sacrifice and offering you do not desire,
　　but you have given me an open ear.[b]
　Burnt offering and sin offering
　　you have not required.
7 Then I said, "Here I am;
　　in the scroll of the book it is written
　　　of me.[c]
8 I delight to do your will, O my God;
　　your law is within my heart."

9 I have told the glad news of deliverance
　　in the great congregation;
　see, I have not restrained my lips,
　　as you know, O LORD.

10 I have not hidden your saving help
　　within my heart,
　I have spoken of your faithfulness and
　　your salvation;
　I have not concealed your steadfast love
　　and your faithfulness
　　from the great congregation.

11 Do not, O LORD, withhold
　　your mercy from me;
　let your steadfast love and your
　　faithfulness
　　keep me safe forever.
12 For evils have encompassed me
　　without number;
　my iniquities have overtaken me,
　　until I cannot see;
　they are more than the hairs of my
　　　head,
　　and my heart fails me.

13 Be pleased, O LORD, to deliver me;
　　O LORD, make haste to help me.
14 Let all those be put to shame and
　　confusion
　who seek to snatch away my life;
　let those be turned back and brought to
　　dishonor
　who desire my hurt.
15 Let those be appalled because of their
　　shame
　who say to me, "Aha, Aha!"

16 But may all who seek you
　　rejoice and be glad in you;
　may those who love your salvation
　　say continually, "Great is the LORD!"
17 As for me, I am poor and needy,
　　but the Lord takes thought for me.
　You are my help and my deliverer;
　　do not delay, O my God.

40.1–17: Your steadfast love and faithfulness will keep me safe forever. It is often treated as two separate psalms: a song of thanksgiving (vv. 1–10) and a prayer for help (vv. 11–17). Verses 13–17 are nearly identical to Ps 70. **1–3:** The psalmist recalls past faithfulness (v. 1a; 27.14; 31.24) and deliverance. The *new song* suggests grateful recognition of God's sover-

a Cn: Heb *pit of tumult*　　b Heb *ears you have dug for me*　　c Meaning of Heb uncertain eignty (33.3; 96.1). The psalmist's response serves as a witness to others to *trust* God (v. 3; see v. 4; 4.5; 33.21). **4–8:** *Trust* in God causes us to be what the Psalms call *happy* (2.12). *Trust* involves offering the whole self to God (v. 7), which is what God wants instead of sacrifice (v. 6; Hos 6.6; Am 5.21–24). God's "torah," "instruction" (NRSV *law*), should be internalized (v. 8; 1.1–2; 37.31). **9–10:** Externally, "trust" means sharing *glad news*. *Deliverance* (v. 9) and *saving help* (v. 10) represent the same Hebrew root, usually translated "righteousness"; it summarizes what God wills. *Faithfulness* and *steadfast love* summarize God's character (Ex 34.6). **11–12:** Verse 11b can be heard as an indicative: "Your steadfast love and your faithfulness will keep me safe forever." Hope is grounded in God's character. **13–17:** The word *help* frames the section of petition. The *poor and needy* (v. 17) are precisely those whom God wills to *help* (9.18; 12.5).

PSALM 41

To the leader. A Psalm of David.

1 Happy are those who consider the poor;*a*
   the LORD delivers them in the day of
      trouble.
2 The LORD protects them and keeps
         them alive;
   they are called happy in the land.
   You do not give them up to the will of
      their enemies.
3 The LORD sustains them on their
         sickbed;
   in their illness you heal all their
      infirmities.*b*

4 As for me, I said, "O LORD, be gracious
      to me;
   heal me, for I have sinned against
      you."
5 My enemies wonder in malice
   when I will die, and my name perish.
6 And when they come to see me, they
         utter empty words,
   while their hearts gather mischief;
   when they go out, they tell it abroad.
7 All who hate me whisper together about
      me;
   they imagine the worst for me.

8 They think that a deadly thing has
         fastened on me,

that I will not rise again from where I
   lie.
9 Even my bosom friend in whom I
      trusted,
   who ate of my bread, has lifted the
      heel against me.
10 But you, O LORD, be gracious to me,
   and raise me up, that I may repay
      them.

11 By this I know that you are pleased with
      me;
   because my enemy has not triumphed
      over me.
12 But you have upheld me because of my
      integrity,
   and set me in your presence forever.

13 Blessed be the LORD, the God of Israel,
   from everlasting to everlasting.
      Amen and Amen.

41.1–13: In your presence forever. It is either a song of thanksgiving or a prayer for help, depending upon whether one concludes that deliverance has already occurred. In either case, it probably originated in a context of illness (vv. 3–4; Ps 38), although the language can be heard metaphorically.* **1–3:** The beatitude (v. 1) and repetition of *happy* recall 1.1–2. Here, however, happiness is defined as openness to others rather than openness to God. **4–10:** Identical petitions in v. 4a surround a complaint about *enemies* who clearly disregard the beatitude of v. 1a, as do the psalmist's former friends (v. 9; 38.11). **11–12:** Regardless of whether healing has already occurred, the psalmist is *upheld* by trusting God, which is what *integrity* means (26.1, 11). The psalmist remains in God's *presence forever*, because God always considers *the poor* (v. 1a; 9.18; 40.17). **13:** The doxology concludes Book I (compare 72.19; 89.52; 106.48).

BOOK TWO

PSALM 42

To the leader. A Maskil of the Korahites.

1 As a deer longs for flowing streams,
   so my soul longs for you, O God.

a Or *weak*   *b* Heb *you change all his bed*

2 My soul thirsts for God,
    for the living God.
When shall I come and behold
    the face of God?
3 My tears have been my food
    day and night,
while people say to me continually,
    "Where is your God?"

4 These things I remember,
    as I pour out my soul:
how I went with the throng, *
    and led them in procession to the
        house of God,
with glad shouts and songs of
        thanksgiving,
    a multitude keeping festival.
5 Why are you cast down, O my soul,
    and why are you disquieted within
        me?
Hope in God; for I shall again praise
        him,
    my help 6and my God.

My soul is cast down within me;
    therefore I remember you
from the land of Jordan and of Hermon,
    from Mount Mizar.
7 Deep calls to deep
    at the thunder of your cataracts;
all your waves and your billows
    have gone over me.
8 By day the LORD commands his
        steadfast love,
and at night his song is with me,
    a prayer to the God of my life.

9 I say to God, my rock,
    "Why have you forgotten me?
Why must I walk about mournfully
    because the enemy oppresses me?"
10 As with a deadly wound in my body,
    my adversaries taunt me,
while they say to me continually,
    "Where is your God?"

11 Why are you cast down, O my soul,
    and why are you disquieted within
        me?
Hope in God; for I shall again praise
        him,
    my help and my God.

42.1–43.5: My help and my God. The two psalms are a unity. A shared refrain concludes each section (42.5, 11; 43.5). Usually classified as a prayer for help, it initiates a collection attributed to *the Korahites*, Levites prominent in the Second Temple* period (Ps 42–49; see also 84–85, 87–88; 1 Chr 9.19). **42.1–5:** The imagery of thirst suggests that God is a necessity of life (63.1; 143.6). It seems that the psalmist was exiled or otherwise prevented from visiting the Temple to *behold the face of God* (11.7; 24.6). Taunting questions (vv. 3, 10) do not help, but the psalmist's own memory is painful also (v. 4). Discouragement is articulated in the refrain, but the final words are *hope* (33.18, 22) and *help*. **6–11:** The psalmist cannot help but *remember* (v. 6; see v. 4). The geographical terms suggest the psalmist may have been in exile; however, the region in view seems to suggest the area where the Jordan River begins, and the terms may simply introduce the water imagery of v. 7. Hope in v. 8 is short-lived, since vv. 9–10 include the psalmist's own questions about God.

PSALM 43

1 Vindicate me, O God, and defend my
        cause
    against an ungodly people;
from those who are deceitful and unjust
    deliver me!
2 For you are the God in whom I take
        refuge;
    why have you cast me off?
Why must I walk about mournfully
    because of the oppression of the
        enemy?

3 O send out your light and your truth;
    let them lead me;
let them bring me to your holy hill
    and to your dwelling.
4 Then I will go to the altar of God,
    to God my exceeding joy;
and I will praise you with the harp,
    O God, my God.

5 Why are you cast down, O my soul,
    and why are you disquieted within
        me?

a Meaning of Heb uncertain

Hope in God; for I shall again praise
    him,
  my help and my God.

43.1–5: *Vindicate me* is literally "establish justice for
me." More questions occur in v. 2 before the petition
continues in v. 3. *Light* may echo the psalmist's desire
to see God's *face,* which is often associated with *light*
(4.6). Verses 3–4 voice the trust that the psalmist will
indeed revisit the Temple (see *holy hill* in 15.1). The
language may be construed literally or figuratively.
The confidence expressed in vv. 3–4 accentuates *hope*
in the final occurrence of the refrain.

PSALM 44

To the leader. Of the Korahites. A Maskil.

1 We have heard with our ears, O God,
     our ancestors have told us,
   what deeds you performed in their days,
     in the days of old:
2 you with your own hand drove out the
       nations,
     but them you planted;
   you afflicted the peoples,
     but them you set free;
3 for not by their own sword did they win
       the land,
     nor did their own arm give them
       victory;
   but your right hand, and your arm,
     and the light of your countenance,
     for you delighted in them.

4 You are my King and my God;
     you command*a* victories for Jacob.
5 Through you we push down our foes;
     through your name we tread down
       our assailants.
6 For not in my bow do I trust,
     nor can my sword save me.
7 But you have saved us from our foes,
     and have put to confusion those who
       hate us.
8 In God we have boasted continually,
     and we will give thanks to your name
       forever.   *Selah*

9 Yet you have rejected us and abased us,
     and have not gone out with our
       armies.

10 You made us turn back from the foe,
      and our enemies have gotten spoil.
11 You have made us like sheep for
        slaughter,
      and have scattered us among
        the nations.
12 You have sold your people for a trifle,
      demanding no high price for them.

13 You have made us the taunt of our
        neighbors,
      the derision and scorn of those
        around us.
14 You have made us a byword among the
        nations,
      a laughingstock*b* among the peoples.
15 All day long my disgrace is before me,
      and shame has covered my face
16 at the words of the taunters and
        revilers,
      at the sight of the enemy and the
        avenger.

17 All this has come upon us,
      yet we have not forgotten you,
      or been false to your covenant.
18 Our heart has not turned back,
      nor have our steps departed from
        your way,
19 yet you have broken us in the haunt of
        jackals,
      and covered us with deep darkness.

20 If we had forgotten the name of our
        God,
      or spread out our hands to a strange
        god,
21 would not God discover this?
      For he knows the secrets of the heart.
22 Because of you we are being killed all
        day long,
      and accounted as sheep for the
        slaughter.

23 Rouse yourself! Why do you sleep,
        O Lord?
      Awake, do not cast us off forever!

---

a Gk Syr: Heb *You are my King, O God; command*
b Heb *a shaking of the head*

24 Why do you hide your face?
    Why do you forget our affliction and
        oppression?
25 For we sink down to the dust;
    our bodies cling to the ground.
26 Rise up, come to our help.
    Redeem us for the sake of your
        steadfast love.

44.1–26: Why do you sleep, O Lord? It is the first communal lament in the psalter. The historical crisis that precipitated it is unknown. It may have arisen during the monarchy and would have been used as subsequent crises arose, such as the destruction of Jerusalem and the Exile.* **1–8:** The rehearsal of God's *deeds* (78.3–4) leads to an affirmation of God's sovereignty (v. 4a), after which *trust* in God is affirmed (21.7; 22.4–5). **9–16:** The opening profession of faith makes this section of complaint all the more poignant. Not a good shepherd, God is letting the *sheep* face *slaughter* (vv. 11, 22). **17–22:** The poignancy increases with this protestation of innocence (7.3–5). The people claim not to have broken *covenant** (v. 17) nor to have *forgotten* God (vv. 17, 20). **23–26:** Beginning with a wake-up call (7.6; 35.23), the psalm concludes with biting questions (13.1), a summary of the complaint (v. 25), and one more petition (v. 26), which appeals to God's *steadfast love* (Ex 34.6; Ps 5.7; 33.5, 18, 22).

P S A L M   4 5

To the leader: according to Lilies.
Of the Korahites. A Maskil. A love song.

1 My heart overflows with a goodly
        theme;
    I address my verses to the king;
    my tongue is like the pen of a ready
        scribe.

2 You are the most handsome of men;
    grace is poured upon your lips;
    therefore God has blessed you
        forever.
3 Gird your sword on your thigh,
        O mighty one,
    in your glory and majesty.

4 In your majesty ride on victoriously
    for the cause of truth and to defend*a*
        the right;

let your right hand teach you dread
    deeds.
5 Your arrows are sharp
    in the heart of the king's enemies;
    the peoples fall under you.

6 Your throne, O God,*b* endures forever
        and ever.
    Your royal scepter is a scepter of
        equity;
7 you love righteousness and hate
        wickedness.
    Therefore God, your God, has anointed
        you
    with the oil of gladness beyond your
        companions;
8 your robes are all fragrant with myrrh
        and aloes and cassia.
    From ivory palaces stringed instruments
        make you glad;
9 daughters of kings are among your
        ladies of honor;
    at your right hand stands the queen
        in gold of Ophir.

10 Hear, O daughter, consider and incline
        your ear;
    forget your people and your father's
        house,
11 and the king will desire your beauty.
    Since he is your lord, bow to him;
12 the people*c* of Tyre will seek your
        favor with gifts,
    the richest of the people 13with all
        kinds of wealth.

The princess is decked in her chamber
        with gold-woven robes;*d*
14 in many-colored robes she is led to
        the king;
    behind her the virgins, her
        companions, follow.
15 With joy and gladness they are led along
    as they enter the palace of the king.

16 In the place of ancestors you, O king,*e*
        shall have sons;

a Cn: Heb *and the meekness of*   *b* Or *Your throne is a*
throne of God, it   *c* Heb *daughter*   *d* Or *people.*
13All glorious is the princess within, gold embroidery is her
clothing   *e* Heb lacks *O king*

you will make them princes in all the
    earth.

17 I will cause your name to be celebrated
    in all generations;
    therefore the peoples will praise you
    forever and ever.

45.1–17: My verses to the king. The superscription, *A love song,* indicates the uniqueness of this royal psalm, which is addressed not to God but *to the king* (v. 1). It was probably written in honor of and for use at the wedding of a Judean or Israelite king. **1–2:** *Grace* is an attribute of God (Ex 34.6). Verse 2 articulates a special relationship between *king* and God. **3–5:** God directs the king's military pursuits (18.31–45), which are aimed at the fulfillment of God's purposes—*truth* (or "faithfulness") and the defense of the oppressed (v. 4; 72.12–14). **6–7:** Verse 6 appears to attribute divinity to the king; but the word in question elsewhere describes human leaders who have been endowed with strength by God (Ex 4.16; 7.1), as v. 7 suggests. The king's job is to enact God's will for *equity* and *righteousness* (98.9). **8–9:** The elaborate attire, music, and attendants suggest a wedding. **10–15:** The *queen* (v. 9) is addressed with admonitions (vv. 10–11) and promises (v. 12). A description of her attire (v. 13) precedes the portrayal of the wedding procession. **16–17:** It is not clear whether these promises should be understood as the poet's or God's (see v. 2).

PSALM 46

To the leader. Of the Korahites.
According to Alamoth. A Song.

1 God is our refuge and strength,
    a very present*a* help in trouble.
2 Therefore we will not fear, though the
    earth should change,
    though the mountains shake in the
    heart of the sea;
3 though its waters roar and foam,
    though the mountains tremble with
    its tumult. *Selah*

4 There is a river whose streams make
    glad the city of God,
    the holy habitation of the Most High.
5 God is in the midst of the city;*b* it shall
    not be moved;
    God will help it when the morning
    dawns.

6 The nations are in an uproar, the
    kingdoms totter;
    he utters his voice, the earth melts.
7 The LORD of hosts is with us;
    the God of Jacob is our refuge.*c* *Selah*

8 Come, behold the works of the LORD;
    see what desolations he has brought
    on the earth.
9 He makes wars cease to the end of the
    earth;
    he breaks the bow, and shatters the
    spear;
    he burns the shields with fire.
10 "Be still, and know that I am God!
    I am exalted among the nations,
    I am exalted in the earth."
11 The LORD of hosts is with us;
    the God of Jacob is our refuge.*c* *Selah*

46.1–11: The LORD of hosts is with us. A song of Zion,★ its focus on Jerusalem (vv. 4–5) is surrounded by proclamations of God's cosmic sovereignty (vv. 1–3, 8–10), thus anticipating Ps 47. **1–3:** God is a powerful protective presence (v. 1; see vv. 7, 11) and worthy of trust in the worst circumstances (vv. 2–3). For *the mountains* to shake meant the world was threatened. **4–6:** *The city of God* is a stable point which *shall not be moved* (*moved* is the same Hebrew word as *shake* in v. 2 and *totter* in v. 6) amid the surrounding *uproar* (v. 6; the same Hebrew word as *roar* in v. 3). The language is symbolic and hyperbolic★ (for instance, there is no river in Jerusalem; see Ezek 47.1–12). That the *earth melts* articulates not destruction but submission to God. **7:** *Hosts* accentuates the emphasis on God's sovereignty (24.10). **8–11:** Verse 8 is sarcastic. God's *desolations* consist of destroying instruments of war. *Be still* suggests "Stop!" It is an order to acknowledge God's sovereignty.

PSALM 47

To the leader. Of the Korahites. A Psalm.

1 Clap your hands, all you peoples;
    shout to God with loud songs of joy.
2 For the LORD, the Most High, is
    awesome,
    a great king over all the earth.

a Or *well proved*   *b* Heb *of it*   *c* Or *fortress*

3 He subdued peoples under us,
   and nations under our feet.
4 He chose our heritage for us,
   the pride of Jacob whom he loves.
                                    Selah

5 God has gone up with a shout,
   the LORD with the sound of a trumpet.
6 Sing praises to God, sing praises;
   sing praises to our King, sing praises.
7 For God is the king of all the earth;
   sing praises with a psalm.[a]

8 God is king over the nations;
   God sits on his holy throne.
9 The princes of the peoples gather
   as the people of the God of Abraham.
   For the shields of the earth belong to
      God;
   he is highly exalted.

47.1–9: God is highly exalted. An enthronement psalm (see Ps 93), it invites recognition of God's sovereignty and describes God's symbolic enthronement in the Temple* (v. 5). 1–4: In keeping with God's cosmic claim (see Ps 46), *all you peoples* are invited to *clap your hands* (v. 1), a joyful acknowledgment of God's kingship and God's subduing of *peoples* and *nations* (vv. 2–3). *Most High* represents the first occurrence of the psalm's key word, which recurs as *gone up* (v. 5) and *exalted* (v. 9). God shares the benefits of sovereignty with those whom God *loves* (v. 4; 78.68). 5: Linked to v. 1 by *shout* and v. 9 by *gone up/exalted*, this central verse portrays the enactment of God's enthronement, originally in the context of worship in the Temple. 6–9: Verse 6 surrounds *God* and *our King* with the invitation to *sing praises. King* recurs in vv. 7–8. *Shields* (v. 9) probably designates kings (89.18). All earthly rulers *belong to God.*

P S A L M   4 8

A Song. A Psalm of the Korahites.

1 Great is the LORD and greatly to be
      praised
   in the city of our God.
   His holy mountain, 2beautiful in
         elevation,
   is the joy of all the earth,
   Mount Zion, in the far north,
      the city of the great King.

3 Within its citadels God
   has shown himself a sure defense.
4 Then the kings assembled,
   they came on together.
5 As soon as they saw it, they were
         astounded;
   they were in panic, they took to flight;
6 trembling took hold of them there,
   pains as of a woman in labor,
7 as when an east wind shatters
   the ships of Tarshish.
8 As we have heard, so have we seen
   in the city of the LORD of hosts,
   in the city of our God,
   which God establishes forever.   *Selah*

9 We ponder your steadfast love, O God,
   in the midst of your temple.
10 Your name, O God, like your praise,
   reaches to the ends of the earth.
   Your right hand is filled with victory.
11   Let Mount Zion be glad,
   let the towns[b] of Judah rejoice
      because of your judgments.

12 Walk about Zion, go all around it,
      count its towers,
13 consider well its ramparts;
      go through its citadels,
   that you may tell the next generation
14   that this is God,
   our God forever and ever.
   He will be our guide forever.

48.1–14: The city of the great King. A song of Zion,* it affirms that Jerusalem symbolizes God's universal sovereignty (see Ps 47). It may have been used originally by pilgrims as they approached and entered Jerusalem. 1–3: The seven titles for Jerusalem communicate its importance. The word translated *north* is "zaphon," the Canaanite mountain of the gods. The God of *Mount Zion* has displaced the Canaanite deities (see Ps 82). 4–7: These verses draw on the tradition of Zion's indestructibility, as well as the tradition of the holy war* in which God wins without an actual fight. *East wind* recalls the defeat of the Egyptians in Ex 14, which led to the planting of God's people "on the mountain of your own possession" (Ex 15.17). 8–11:

a Heb *Maskil*   *b* Heb *daughters*

Just as the sight of Jerusalem had a powerful effect on opposing kings (v. 5), so it also has on pilgrims who approach and enter the *temple*. *Victory* in v. 10 is literally "righteousness," and *judgments* in v. 11 is literally "justices." Entry into the city puts pilgrims in touch with the essence of God's will (97.2), as well as the essence of God's character, *steadfast love* (33.5; 89.14). **12–14:** The city's revelatory power is the rationale for observing its architectural detail. *Count* (v. 12) and *tell* (v. 14) represent the same Hebrew root. Careful observation of the city leads to proclamation about the city's God.

P S A L M   4 9

To the leader. Of the Korahites. A Psalm.

1 Hear this, all you peoples;
    give ear, all inhabitants of the world,
2 both low and high,
    rich and poor together.
3 My mouth shall speak wisdom;
    the meditation of my heart shall be
        understanding.
4 I will incline my ear to a proverb;
    I will solve my riddle to the music of
        the harp.

5 Why should I fear in times of trouble,
    when the iniquity of my persecutors
        surrounds me,
6 those who trust in their wealth
    and boast of the abundance of their
        riches?
7 Truly, no ransom avails for one's life,*ᵃ*
    there is no price one can give to God
        for it.
8 For the ransom of life is costly,
    and can never suffice,
9 that one should live on forever
    and never see the grave.*ᵇ*

10 When we look at the wise, they die;
    fool and dolt perish together
    and leave their wealth to others.
11 Their graves*ᶜ* are their homes forever,
    their dwelling places to all
        generations,
    though they named lands their own.
12 Mortals cannot abide in their pomp;
    they are like the animals that perish.

13 Such is the fate of the foolhardy,
    the end of those*ᵈ* who are pleased
        with their lot.   Selah
14 Like sheep they are appointed for Sheol;
    Death shall be their shepherd;
    straight to the grave they descend,*ᵉ*
    and their form shall waste away;
    Sheol shall be their home.*ᶠ*
15 But God will ransom my soul from the
        power of Sheol,
    for he will receive me.   Selah

16 Do not be afraid when some become
        rich,
    when the wealth of their houses
        increases.
17 For when they die they will carry
        nothing away;
    their wealth will not go down after
        them.
18 Though in their lifetime they count
        themselves happy
    —for you are praised when you do
        well for yourself—
19 they*ᵍ* will go to the company of their
        ancestors,
    who will never again see the light.
20 Mortals cannot abide in their pomp;
    they are like the animals that perish.

49.1–20: Mortals cannot abide in their pomp. This wisdom psalm addresses a *riddle* (v. 4) that can be inferred from the content of its two sections (vv. 5–12, 13–20): How are humans *like the animals* (vv. 12, 20)? **1–4:** *Harp* suggests a setting in worship, but the psalm is ultimately aimed at a universal audience. **5–12:** Persons *who trust in their wealth* (v. 6) live with the illusion that ultimate security can be purchased (vv. 7–9). But death disproves the illusion by sparing no one (vv. 10–11). Humans fare no better than *the animals*, despite their riches, which is what *pomp* means (v. 12). **13–20:** The universality of death is not the final word. *The foolhardy* (v. 13) will permanently reside in *Sheol*,★ the realm of the dead (v. 14; 6.5); but God will *ransom* the psalmist's life in a way that no human can purchase life (vv. 7–8). What is meant by *God . . .*

a Another reading is *no one can ransom a brother*
b Heb *the pit*   *c* Gk Syr Compare Tg: Heb *their inward* (thought)   *d* Tg: Heb *after them*   *e* Cn: Heb *the upright shall have dominion over them in the morning*
f Meaning of Heb uncertain   *g* Cn: Heb *you*

will receive me is unclear, but it pushes beyond the normal view that all persons go to *Sheol* (see 22.19; 73.24; Gen 5.24; 2 Kings 2.1–12). Verse 20 in Hebrew is not identical to v. 12. It should be translated, "Mortals with riches and no understanding are like the animals that perish." For those who understand (v. 3), God offers a hope that no amount of wealth can purchase. Finally then, only *the foolhardy*, who lack understanding and thus fail to *trust* God (see v. 6), die without hope *like the animals*.

PSALM 50

A Psalm of Asaph.

1 The mighty one, God the LORD,
    speaks and summons the earth
    from the rising of the sun to its
      setting.
2 Out of Zion, the perfection of beauty,
    God shines forth.

3 Our God comes and does not keep
      silence,
    before him is a devouring fire,
    and a mighty tempest all around him.
4 He calls to the heavens above
    and to the earth, that he may judge
      his people:
5 "Gather to me my faithful ones,
    who made a covenant with me by
      sacrifice!"
6 The heavens declare his righteousness,
    for God himself is judge.   *Selah*

7 "Hear, O my people, and I will speak,
    O Israel, I will testify against you.
    I am God, your God.
8 Not for your sacrifices do I rebuke you;
    your burnt offerings are continually
      before me.
9 I will not accept a bull from your house,
    or goats from your folds.
10 For every wild animal of the forest is
      mine,
    the cattle on a thousand hills.
11 I know all the birds of the air,[a]
    and all that moves in the field is
      mine.

12 "If I were hungry, I would not tell you,
    for the world and all that is in it is
      mine.

13 Do I eat the flesh of bulls,
    or drink the blood of goats?
14 Offer to God a sacrifice of thanksgiving,[b]
    and pay your vows to the Most High.
15 Call on me in the day of trouble;
    I will deliver you, and you shall glorify
      me."

16 But to the wicked God says:
    "What right have you to recite my
      statutes,
    or take my covenant on your lips?
17 For you hate discipline,
    and you cast my words behind you.
18 You make friends with a thief when you
      see one,
    and you keep company with
      adulterers.

19 "You give your mouth free rein for evil,
    and your tongue frames deceit.
20 You sit and speak against your kin;
    you slander your own mother's child.
21 These things you have done and I have
      been silent;
    you thought that I was one just like
      yourself.
    But now I rebuke you, and lay the
      charge before you.

22 "Mark this, then, you who forget God,
    or I will tear you apart, and there will
      be no one to deliver.
23 Those who bring thanksgiving as their
      sacrifice honor me;
    to those who go the right way[c]
    I will show the salvation of God."

50.1–23: Thanksgiving as sacrifice. A prophetic★ exhortation★ (see Ps 14), it offers the word of God (vv. 5, 7–23), apparently delivered originally by a prophet or priest during worship. *Asaph* was a Levite appointed by David to be "chief" of several "ministers before the ark of the LORD" (1 Chr 16.4–5; see Ps 73–83). **1–6:** The divine speech is introduced with a theophany,★ an appearance of God (vv. 2–3; 18.7–15; 97.2–5). Verses 1–3 assert God's cosmic reign, the attributes of which are justice (see *judge* in vv. 4, 6) and *righteous-*

---

a Gk Syr Tg: Heb *mountains*   *b* Or *make thanksgiving your sacrifice to God*   *c* Heb *who set a way* ness (98.9). God's people have failed to embody these *covenant** standards (v. 5), and are put on trial (Mic 6.1–2). **7–15:** The first charge involves misunderstanding of *sacrifices*. They are not something God needs (vv. 10–13), but rather are to be a means of expressing gratitude to God (v. 14). God desires the proper understanding (40.6–8; 51.19; Hos 6.6; Am 5.21–24). **16–22:** *The wicked* are what God's people have become, and the second *charge* (v. 21) involves disobedience to *covenant* stipulations. Verses 18–19 allude to the Ten Commandments. God has *been silent* but will be no longer (see v. 3). **23:** The first line summarizes vv. 7–15, and the second summarizes vv. 16–22. *Salvation* or life is the promise for those who participate properly in the *covenant*.

P S A L M   5 1

To the leader. A Psalm of David, when the prophet Nathan came to him, after he had gone in to Bathsheba.

1 Have mercy on me, O God,
 according to your steadfast love;
 according to your abundant mercy
 blot out my transgressions.
2 Wash me thoroughly from my iniquity,
 and cleanse me from my sin.

3 For I know my transgressions,
 and my sin is ever before me.
4 Against you, you alone, have I sinned,
 and done what is evil in your sight,
 so that you are justified in your
 sentence
 and blameless when you pass
 judgment.
5 Indeed, I was born guilty,
 a sinner when my mother conceived
 me.

6 You desire truth in the inward being;[a]
 therefore teach me wisdom in my
 secret heart.
7 Purge me with hyssop, and I shall be
 clean;
 wash me, and I shall be whiter than
 snow.
8 Let me hear joy and gladness;
 let the bones that you have crushed
 rejoice.
9 Hide your face from my sins,
 and blot out all my iniquities.

10 Create in me a clean heart, O God,
 and put a new and right[b] spirit within
 me.
11 Do not cast me away from your
 presence,
 and do not take your holy spirit from
 me.
12 Restore to me the joy of your salvation,
 and sustain in me a willing[c] spirit.

13 Then I will teach transgressors your
 ways,
 and sinners will return to you.
14 Deliver me from bloodshed, O God,
 O God of my salvation,
 and my tongue will sing aloud of your
 deliverance.

15 O Lord, open my lips,
 and my mouth will declare your
 praise.
16 For you have no delight in sacrifice;
 if I were to give a burnt offering, you
 would not be pleased.
17 The sacrifice acceptable to God[d] is a
 broken spirit;
 a broken and contrite heart, O God,
 you will not despise.

18 Do good to Zion in your good pleasure;
 rebuild the walls of Jerusalem,
19 then you will delight in right sacrifices,
 in burnt offerings and whole burnt
 offerings;
 then bulls will be offered on your
 altar.

51.1–19: I know my transgressions. A prayer for help, it became one of the church's Penitential Psalms* (Ps 6). The psalmist's complaint involves personal sinfulness, leading the editors of the psalter to associate it with David (2 Sam 11–12). **1–5:** The focus on God's character recalls Israel's fundamental profession in Ex 34.6–7. *Sin* is a more general term than *transgressions*, which suggests intentional rebellion. *Iniquity* and *guilty* represent the same Hebrew word. Verse 5a is literally, "Indeed, I was born into iniquity." Verse 4 recalls 2 Sam 12.13. **6–12:** *Sin* is not the final reality.

a Meaning of Heb uncertain   b Or *steadfast*
c Or *generous*   d Or *My sacrifice, O God,*

There is a God-given *wisdom* (37.30–31) that yields *truth* or "faithfulness," so the psalmist continues to pray for forgiveness (vv. 7–9) and a new start (vv. 10–12). Specific rituals of cleansing may have been involved (v. 7; Lev 14.49, 52). The repetition of *spirit* reinforces the plea for God to *create* (Gen 1.2). The psalmist anticipates a new creation (Ezek 36.25–27). **13–17:** The forgiven and transformed psalmist will be in a position to *teach* others God's *ways* (32.8–9), although not without opposition (v. 14a). The psalmist promises to make public testimony to God's activity with every organ of speech (vv. 14–15) and by offering God the whole self (vv. 16–17). *Broken* connotes humility and gratitude (50.14, 23). **18–19:** These verses were probably added to ensure that vv. 16–17 not be construed to advocate abolition of *sacrifice*.

PSALM 52

To the leader. A Maskil of David, when Doeg
the Edomite came to Saul and said to him,
"David has come to the house of Ahimelech."

1 Why do you boast, O mighty one,
　　of mischief done against the godly?*a*
　　All day long 2you are plotting
　　　　destruction.
　　Your tongue is like a sharp razor,
　　　you worker of treachery.
3 You love evil more than good,
　　and lying more than speaking the
　　　　truth.　　　　　　　　　*Selah*
4 You love all words that devour,
　　O deceitful tongue.

5 But God will break you down forever;
　　he will snatch and tear you from your
　　　　tent;
　　he will uproot you from the land of
　　　　the living.　　　　　　*Selah*
6 The righteous will see, and fear,
　　and will laugh at the evildoer,*b*
　　　saying,
7 "See the one who would not take
　　　refuge in God,
　　but trusted in abundant riches,
　　　and sought refuge in wealth!"*c*

8 But I am like a green olive tree
　　in the house of God.
　I trust in the steadfast love of God
　　forever and ever.

9 I will thank you forever,
　　because of what you have done.
　In the presence of the faithful
　　I will proclaim*d* your name, for it is
　　　good.

52.1–9: I trust in the steadfast love of God. It is classified as a psalm of trust (vv. 8–9), a prophetic* announcement of judgment (vv. 1–5), and a wisdom psalm to instruct *the righteous* (vv. 6–7). The superscription suggests that the *mighty one* (v. 1) is *Doeg*, who betrayed David and killed the priests of Nob (1 Sam 22.9). **1–4:** The psalm is addressed not to God but to a formidable opponent of God and the psalmist. In view of the occurrence of *steadfast love* in v. 8, it should be retained in v. 1, the second line of which would then read, "the steadfast love of God lasts all the day." The opening verse then lays out the option to *evil* that the *mighty one* has rejected but which the psalmist has embraced. Treacherous speech characterizes wickedness (10.7; 35.20; 38.12). **5–7a:** The destiny of the wicked will be a lesson to *the righteous* concerning the proper source of *refuge*. **7b–9:** Whereas the wicked one *trusted . . . in wealth*, the psalmist places *trust* in God's love (see v. 1) and is solidly rooted there (1.3; 92.12–15). Eternal gratitude contrasts with the greed of the *mighty one* (vv. 2–4, 7).

PSALM 53

To the leader: according to Mahalath. A Maskil
of David.

1 Fools say in their hearts, "There is no
　　　God."
　They are corrupt, they commit
　　　abominable acts;
　　there is no one who does good.

2 God looks down from heaven on
　　　humankind
　to see if there are any who are wise,
　　who seek after God.

3 They have all fallen away, they are all
　　　alike perverse;
　there is no one who does good,
　　no, not one.

---

a Cn Compare Syr: Heb *the kindness of God*
b Heb *him*　　c Syr Tg: Heb *in his destruction*
d Cn: Heb *wait for*

4 Have they no knowledge, those
> evildoers,
> who eat up my people as they eat
> > bread,
> and do not call upon God?

5 There they shall be in great terror,
> in terror such as has not been.
> For God will scatter the bones of the
> > ungodly;[a]
> they will be put to shame,[b] for God
> > has rejected them.

6 O that deliverance for Israel would
> > come from Zion!
> When God restores the fortunes of
> > his people,
> Jacob will rejoice; Israel will be glad.

53.1–6: Terror for the ungodly. It is nearly identical to Ps 14, except for v. 5 (compare 14.5–6). The two versions apparently made their way into the psalter because they existed in separate collections. **5:** While 14.5–6 proclaim God's protective presence with the righteous and the poor, v. 5 elaborates upon the *great terror*, which will involve judgment on those who oppose God. This particular direction is fitting following the judgment described in Ps 52.

PSALM 54

To the leader: with stringed instruments.
A Maskil of David, when the Ziphites went and
told Saul, "David is in hiding among us."

1 Save me, O God, by your name,
> and vindicate me by your might.
2 Hear my prayer, O God;
> give ear to the words of my mouth.

3 For the insolent have risen against me,
> the ruthless seek my life;
> they do not set God before them.
> > *Selah*

4 But surely, God is my helper;
> the Lord is the upholder of[c] my life.
5 He will repay my enemies for their
> > evil.
> In your faithfulness, put an end to
> > them.

6 With a freewill offering I will sacrifice
> to you;
> I will give thanks to your name,
> > O LORD, for it is good.
7 For he has delivered me from every
> > trouble,
> and my eye has looked in triumph on
> > my enemies.

54.1–7: Save me, O God, by your name. Usually considered a prayer for help, it is sometimes classified as a song of thanksgiving, since v. 7 may indicate that deliverance has occurred. Originally it may have been used by falsely accused persons seeking sanctuary in the Temple* (see Ps 5, 7). The superscription alludes to 1 Sam 23.19. **1–2:** The opening petitions are typical (17.1; 26.1). *Name* recurs in v. 6; it focuses the issue on God's character as one who is *good* (v. 6) and shows *faithfulness* (v. 5; Ex 34.6). **3–5:** References to opponents encompass the central profession of faith in v. 4 (see 10.14; 22.19). The issue in v. 5 is not so much personal revenge as the establishment of justice. **6–7:** The motive for the psalmist's *freewill offering* (2 Chr 31.14) is gratitude for the actual or anticipated deliverance, which reveals God's character.

PSALM 55

To the leader: with stringed instruments.
A Maskil of David.

1 Give ear to my prayer, O God;
> do not hide yourself from my
> > supplication.
2 Attend to me, and answer me;
> I am troubled in my complaint.
> I am distraught 3by the noise of the
> > enemy,
> because of the clamor of the wicked.
> For they bring[d] trouble upon me,
> and in anger they cherish enmity
> > against me.

4 My heart is in anguish within me,
> the terrors of death have fallen upon
> > me.

a Cn Compare Gk Syr: Heb *him who encamps against
you*   b Gk: Heb *you have put (them) to shame*
c Gk Syr Jerome: Heb *is of those who uphold* or *is with
those who uphold*   d Cn Compare Gk: Heb *they cause
to totter*

5 Fear and trembling come upon me,
   and horror overwhelms me.
6 And I say, "O that I had wings like a
     dove!
   I would fly away and be at rest;
7 truly, I would flee far away;
   I would lodge in the wilderness; *Selah*
8 I would hurry to find a shelter for
     myself
   from the raging wind and tempest."

9 Confuse, O Lord, confound their
     speech;
   for I see violence and strife in the
     city.
10 Day and night they go around it
     on its walls,
   and iniquity and trouble are within it;
11   ruin is in its midst;
   oppression and fraud
     do not depart from its marketplace.

12 It is not enemies who taunt me—
     I could bear that;
   it is not adversaries who deal insolently
     with me—
     I could hide from them.
13 But it is you, my equal,
   my companion, my familiar friend,
14 with whom I kept pleasant company;
   we walked in the house of God with
     the throng.
15 Let death come upon them;
   let them go down alive to Sheol;
   for evil is in their homes and in their
     hearts.

16 But I call upon God,
   and the LORD will save me.
17 Evening and morning and at noon
   I utter my complaint and moan,
   and he will hear my voice.
18 He will redeem me unharmed
   from the battle that I wage,
   for many are arrayed against me.
19 God, who is enthroned from of old,
                 Selah
   will hear, and will humble them—
   because they do not change,
   and do not fear God.

20 My companion laid hands on a friend
   and violated a covenant with me[a]
21 with speech smoother than butter,
   but with a heart set on war;
   with words that were softer than oil,
   but in fact were drawn swords.

22 Cast your burden[b] on the LORD,
   and he will sustain you;
   he will never permit
     the righteous to be moved.

23 But you, O God, will cast them down
     into the lowest pit;
   the bloodthirsty and treacherous
     shall not live out half their days.
   But I will trust in you.

55.1–23: But I call upon God. The typical elements of a prayer for help are present—petition (vv. 1–2a, 9a, 15), complaint (vv. 2b–8, 9b–11, 12–14, 20–21), expression of trust (vv. 16–19, 22–23). Their irregular arrangement may symbolize the chaotic conditions facing the psalmist. **1–5:** The *complaint* suggests powerful opposition. *Terrors* and *trembling* are ordinarily what the judgment of God produces (see Ex 15.15–16). **6–8:** Thus, the psalmist wants to escape *like a dove* (11.1; Jer 9.2–3). **9–11:** Recalling Gen 11.1–9, v. 9 suggests that the enemies also oppose God with their *violence* (7.16; 11.5). **12–15:** Societal chaos is accompanied by personal betrayal (35.12–15; 38.11). The psalmist longs for the opponents to go to *Sheol,*＊ the realm of the dead (6.5). **16–19:** In the midst of *horror* (v. 5), the psalmist looks to God, *enthroned from of old.* Monarchs were responsible for peace, and the psalmist trusts that God will preserve life *unharmed,* literally, "in peace." **20–23:** The psalmist concludes by inviting others to *trust* (v. 23) their life and future to God's care (v. 22).

~~~~~~~~~~~~~~~~~~~~

PSALM 56

*To the leader: according to The Dove on Far-
off Terebinths. Of David. A Miktam, when the
Philistines seized him in Gath.*

1 Be gracious to me, O God, for people
     trample on me;
   all day long foes oppress me;

a Heb lacks *with me*   *b* Or *Cast what he has given you*

2 my enemies trample on me all day long,
　　for many fight against me.
　O Most High, 3when I am afraid,
　　I put my trust in you.
4 In God, whose word I praise,
　　in God I trust; I am not afraid;
　　what can flesh do to me?

5 All day long they seek to injure my
　　　cause;
　　all their thoughts are against me for
　　　evil.
6 They stir up strife, they lurk,
　　they watch my steps.
　As they hoped to have my life,
7　　so repay*a* them for their crime;
　　in wrath cast down the peoples,
　　　O God!

8 You have kept count of my tossings;
　　put my tears in your bottle.
　　Are they not in your record?
9 Then my enemies will retreat
　　in the day when I call.
　　This I know, that*b* God is for me.
10 In God, whose word I praise,
　　in the LORD, whose word I praise,
11 in God I trust; I am not afraid.
　　What can a mere mortal do to me?

12 My vows to you I must perform, O God;
　　I will render thank offerings to you.
13 For you have delivered my soul from
　　　death,
　　and my feet from falling,
　　so that I may walk before God
　　in the light of life.

56.1–13: I am not afraid. Petition and complaint (vv. 1–2, 5–8) suggest this is a prayer for help, but some consider it a song of thanksgiving, concluding that vv. 12–13 indicate that deliverance has occurred (see Ps 54). The superscription alludes to 1 Sam 21.10–14. **1–2:** *Fight* suggests a military context, but *trample* connotes socioeconomic abuse. The language may be metaphorical.* The threat is enduring: *all day long* (vv. 1–2, 5). **3–4:** The crucial contrast is between being *afraid* and putting *trust* in God (vv. 3, 4, 11). *Praise* for God's *word* (vv. 4, 10) occurs only here in the Old Testament; *word* may refer to the whole tradition of God's saving activity or to an implied promise of de-

liverance. **5–11:** Verses 5–7 describe what others *can . . . do to* the psalmist (vv. 4, 10). Known by God (v. 8; see 40.7) and trusting that God is *for me* (v. 9; see 118.6), the psalmist is *not afraid*. **12–13:** *Vows* and *thank offerings* indicate humble gratitude (50.14; 116.17–18) for *life* in God's presence, an enduring source of *light* (4.6; 27.1).

PSALM 57

To the leader: Do Not Destroy. Of David.
A Miktam, when he fled from Saul, in the cave.

1 Be merciful to me, O God, be merciful
　　to me,
　　for in you my soul takes refuge;
　in the shadow of your wings I will take
　　refuge,
　　until the destroying storms pass by.
2 I cry to God Most High,
　　to God who fulfills his purpose for
　　　me.
3 He will send from heaven and save me,
　　he will put to shame those who
　　　trample on me.　　　　*Selah*
　God will send forth his steadfast love
　　and his faithfulness.

4 I lie down among lions
　　that greedily devour*c* human prey;
　their teeth are spears and arrows,
　　their tongues sharp swords.

5 Be exalted, O God, above the heavens.
　　Let your glory be over all the earth.

6 They set a net for my steps;
　　my soul was bowed down.
　They dug a pit in my path,
　　but they have fallen into it
　　　themselves.　　　　*Selah*
7 My heart is steadfast, O God,
　　my heart is steadfast.
　I will sing and make melody.
8　Awake, my soul!
　Awake, O harp and lyre!
　　I will awake the dawn.

---

a Cn: Heb *rescue*　　*b* Or *because*　　*c* Cn: Heb *are*
aflame for

9 I will give thanks to you, O Lord, among
      the peoples;
   I will sing praises to you among the
      nations.
10 For your steadfast love is as high as the
      heavens;
   your faithfulness extends to the
      clouds.

11 Be exalted, O God, above the heavens.
   Let your glory be over all the earth.

57.1–11: Let your glory be over all the earth. Usually classified as a prayer for help, it could be understood as a song of thanksgiving, depending on the interpretation* of v. 6 (see Ps 54, 56). The superscription alludes to 1 Sam 21.1; 24.3. Verse 4 may indicate the prayer was originally that of a falsely accused person (see Ps 5, 7). **1–3:** An extended expression of trust features *refuge* (2.12; 17.8). The psalmist is confident that God's essential character—*steadfast love* and *faithfulness* (Ex 34.6; Ps 33.5; 89.14)—will enact the divine *purpose*. The repetition of *send* reinforces the point. **4–6:** Complaint in vv. 4, 6 surrounds the first occurrence of the refrain in v. 5 (see v. 11). Typically, the wicked are described as weapon-bearing beasts (7.2; 11.2), who also employ *a net* and *a pit* (9.15). **7–8:** Regardless of whether v. 6 indicates the removal of the threat, the psalmist is confident that security lies with God. The psalmist is eager to greet God's help, originally perhaps at the conclusion of a night vigil in the Temple.* **9–11:** The promise of grateful praise arises from the conviction that God's *steadfast love* and *faithfulness* (see v. 3) pervade the cosmos (36.5). Verses 7–11 recur in nearly identical form as 108.1–5.

PSALM 58
To the leader: Do Not Destroy. Of David.
A Miktam.

1 Do you indeed decree what is right, you
      gods?[a]
   Do you judge people fairly?
2 No, in your hearts you devise wrongs;
   your hands deal out violence on
      earth.

3 The wicked go astray from the womb;
   they err from their birth, speaking
      lies.

4 They have venom like the venom of a
      serpent,
   like the deaf adder that stops its ear,
5 so that it does not hear the voice of
      charmers
   or of the cunning enchanter.

6 O God, break the teeth in their mouths;
   tear out the fangs of the young lions,
      O Lord!
7 Let them vanish like water that runs
      away;
   like grass let them be trodden down[b]
      and wither.
8 Let them be like the snail that dissolves
      into slime;
   like the untimely birth that never sees
      the sun.
9 Sooner than your pots can feel the heat
      of thorns,
   whether green or ablaze, may he
      sweep them away!

10 The righteous will rejoice when they see
      vengeance done;
   they will bathe their feet in the blood
      of the wicked.
11 People will say, "Surely there is a
      reward for the righteous;
   surely there is a God who judges on
      earth."

58.1–11: Violence on earth, justice on earth. A prayer for help, its unusual beginning (vv. 1–4) and conclusion (vv. 10–11) give it a prophetic,* instructional tone. **1–2:** It is unclear whether the opening questions are addressed to the *gods* (Ps 82) or to *wicked* persons (Ps 52). **3–5:** *Wicked* persons are clearly targeted in the complaint. They are deceitful and destructive (5.6; 57.4). **6–11:** Despite v. 10, v. 11 makes it clear that the motivation behind the petition in vv. 6–9 is not personal revenge but the desire for justice to prevail. If the violence is to stop, *the wicked* must be disarmed (see v. 6). *Reward* in v. 11 is literally "fruit." *Judges* could be translated "establishes justice." The psalmist affirms, despite appearances (vv. 1–5), that God's justice *on earth* (v. 11) will ultimately triumph over *violence on earth* (v. 2).

---

a Or *mighty lords*   b Cn: Meaning of Heb uncertain

P S A L M   5 9

To the leader: Do Not Destroy. Of David.
A Miktam, when Saul ordered his house to be
watched in order to kill him.

1 Deliver me from my enemies, O my
       God;
   protect me from those who rise up
       against me.
2 Deliver me from those who work evil;
   from the bloodthirsty save me.

3 Even now they lie in wait for my life;
   the mighty stir up strife against me.
   For no transgression or sin of mine,
       O LORD,
4   for no fault of mine, they run and
       make ready.

   Rouse yourself, come to my help and
       see!
5   You, LORD God of hosts, are God of
       Israel.
   Awake to punish all the nations;
       spare none of those who
       treacherously plot evil.   *Selah*

6 Each evening they come back,
   howling like dogs
   and prowling about the city.
7 There they are, bellowing with their
       mouths,
   with sharp words*a* on their lips—
   for "Who," they think,*b* "will hear
       us?"

8 But you laugh at them, O LORD;
   you hold all the nations in derision.
9 O my strength, I will watch for you;
   for you, O God, are my fortress.
10 My God in his steadfast love will meet
       me;
   my God will let me look in triumph
       on my enemies.

11 Do not kill them, or my people may
       forget;
   make them totter by your power, and
       bring them down,
   O Lord, our shield.

12 For the sin of their mouths, the words
       of their lips,
   let them be trapped in their pride.
   For the cursing and lies that they utter,
13   consume them in wrath;
   consume them until they are no
       more.
   Then it will be known to the ends of the
       earth
   that God rules over Jacob.   *Selah*

14 Each evening they come back,
   howling like dogs
   and prowling about the city.
15 They roam about for food,
   and growl if they do not get their fill.

16 But I will sing of your might;
   I will sing aloud of your steadfast love
       in the morning.
   For you have been a fortress for me
   and a refuge in the day of my distress.
17 O my strength, I will sing praises to you,
   for you, O God, are my fortress,
   the God who shows me steadfast love.

59.1–17: In steadfast love, God will meet me. A
prayer for help, it may have originated as the prayer
of a falsely accused person seeking sanctuary in the
Temple* (Ps 5, 7). The superscription associates it with
Saul's threats on David's life (1 Sam 19.11). **1–5:** Petition anticipates subsequent expressions of assurance,
since *protect* is the same Hebrew root as *fortress* (vv.
9, 16–17). A protestation of innocence (vv. 3c–4a;
7.3–5) is followed by a poetic wake-up call (44.23)
addressed to *God of hosts*, which suggests God is in
for a fight (24.10). **6–7:** To help the psalmist, God
must oppose the enemies who are imaged as ravenous
dogs (22.16, 20) and whose arrogant *words* demonstrate an utter lack of accountability (10.4). **8–10:**
God's laughter indicates divine sovereignty (2.4),
which is the basis of the psalmist's trust that God's
steadfast love (vv. 10, 16, 17) will prevail. **11–13:**
While sounding vindictive, the psalmist's motivation is
God-centered. Defeat of the *enemies* will show *that
God rules.* **14–15:** *Growl* also means "lodge," suggesting the persistence of the enemies (see v. 6). **16–
17:** More persistent is God's *steadfast love*, the endur-

a Heb *with swords*   *b* Heb lacks *they think*

ing source of the psalmist's *strength* (vv. 9, 17) and protection.

~~~

PSALM 60

To the leader: according to the Lily
of the Covenant. A Miktam of David;
for instruction; when he struggled with Aram-
naharaim and with Aram-zobah, and when Joab
on his return killed twelve thousand Edomites
in the Valley of Salt.

1 O God, you have rejected us, broken
        our defenses;
    you have been angry; now restore us!
2 You have caused the land to quake; you
        have torn it open;
    repair the cracks in it, for it is
        tottering.
3 You have made your people suffer hard
        things;
    you have given us wine to drink that
        made us reel.

4 You have set up a banner for those who
        fear you,
    to rally to it out of bowshot.*a*   *Selah*
5 Give victory with your right hand, and
        answer us,*b*
    so that those whom you love may be
        rescued.

6 God has promised in his sanctuary:*c*
    "With exultation I will divide up
        Shechem,
    and portion out the Vale of Succoth.
7 Gilead is mine, and Manasseh is mine;
    Ephraim is my helmet;
    Judah is my scepter.
8 Moab is my washbasin;
    on Edom I hurl my shoe;
    over Philistia I shout in triumph."

9 Who will bring me to the fortified city?
    Who will lead me to Edom?
10 Have you not rejected us, O God?
    You do not go out, O God, with our
        armies.
11 O grant us help against the foe,
    for human help is worthless.
12 With God we shall do valiantly;
    it is he who will tread down our foes.

60.1–12: Grant us help against the foe. This communal prayer for help is associated by the editors of the psalter with events described in 2 Sam 8 (see vv. 13–14), although the details of the psalm are not congruent with that narrative.* **1–3:** The complaint attributes the people's misfortune to God's anger (79.5). *Rejected* recurs in v. 10. **4–5:** Verse 4 perhaps should be understood as petition to make it consistent with v. 5. **6–8:** The divine promise locates hope for reversal with God's ownership of all lands and peoples, including Israelite places (vv. 6–7) and enemy territories (v. 8). The images in v. 8a–b may be construed as insults, but the idea may be that *Moab* and *Edom* are God's personal possessions. **9:** *Edom* is singled out as the primary source of the people's problem (137.7). **10–12:** Even so, these verses return to the perspective of vv. 1–5, suggesting God is both the problem and the solution. Only God's *help* (22.19), as opposed to *human help* (146.3), will enable the people to *do valiantly* (118.15–16.)

~~~

PSALM 61

To the leader: with stringed instruments.
Of David.

1 Hear my cry, O God;
    listen to my prayer.
2 From the end of the earth I call to you,
    when my heart is faint.

Lead me to the rock
    that is higher than I;
3 for you are my refuge,
    a strong tower against the enemy.

4 Let me abide in your tent forever,
    find refuge under the shelter of your
        wings.   *Selah*
5 For you, O God, have heard my vows;
    you have given me the heritage of
        those who fear your name.

6 Prolong the life of the king;
    may his years endure to all
        generations!
7 May he be enthroned forever before God;
    appoint steadfast love and
        faithfulness to watch over him!

a Gk Syr Jerome: Heb *because of the truth*   *b* Another
reading is *me*   *c* Or *by his holiness*

8 So I will always sing praises to your
    name,
        as I pay my vows day after day.

61.1–8: Lead me to the rock. A prayer for help, its
petitions (vv. 1, 2c, 4, 6–7) are juxtaposed with expressions of trust (vv. 3, 5, 8). **1–3:** Verse 2a can be
understood geographically, but it can also be heard
metaphorically* to indicate a serious situation. *Lead
me to the rock* (v. 2; 27.5) may indicate the psalmist
was seeking *refuge* (2.12; 5.11) in the Temple* from
false accusers (see Ps 5, 7). **4–5:** Entrance into the Temple may be indicated by *tent* (15.1), and perhaps too
by *the shelter of your wings* (17.8; 57.1; 63.7). That
the psalmist's *vows* have been heard probably expresses the foundation of the previous petitions rather
than indicating that the distress is over (22.25; 65.1).
6–7: It is not clear whether the psalm was prayed originally by *the king*, but probably not. The petition
would have been heard as a prayer for the nation after
the disappearance of the monarchy . **8:** *Vows* recalls v.
5. *Praises* result from trusting that God will indeed be
the psalmist's *refuge* (vv. 3, 4).

PSALM 62

*To the leader: according to Jeduthun. A Psalm
of David.*

1 For God alone my soul waits in
    silence;
        from him comes my salvation.
2 He alone is my rock and my salvation,
        my fortress; I shall never be shaken.

3 How long will you assail a person,
        will you batter your victim, all
            of you,
    as you would a leaning wall, a
        tottering fence?
4 Their only plan is to bring down a
        person of prominence.
    They take pleasure in falsehood;
    they bless with their mouths,
        but inwardly they curse.   *Selah*

5 For God alone my soul waits in
    silence,
        for my hope is from him.
6 He alone is my rock and my salvation,
        my fortress; I shall not be shaken.

7 On God rests my deliverance and my
        honor;
    my mighty rock, my refuge is in God.

8 Trust in him at all times, O people;
        pour out your heart before him;
    God is a refuge for us.   *Selah*

9 Those of low estate are but a breath,
        those of high estate are a delusion;
    in the balances they go up;
        they are together lighter than a
            breath.
10 Put no confidence in extortion,
        and set no vain hopes on robbery;
    if riches increase, do not set your
        heart on them.

11 Once God has spoken;
        twice have I heard this:
    that power belongs to God,
12   and steadfast love belongs to you,
            O Lord.
    For you repay to all
        according to their work.

62.1–12: God alone is my rock. A psalm of trust, it
recalls Ps 61 (compare 61.2–3 with 62.7). **1–6:** The
similar vv. 1–2, 5–6 surround a description of the enemies. *Alone* (vv. 1–2, 5–6) emphasizes the psalmist's
total dependence upon God. **7:** This central verse is
transitional, summing up the direction of vv. 1–6 (see
rock in vv. 1, 6, 7) and anticipating the instruction in
vv. 8–10. **8–10:** *Trust* (v. 8) and *Put . . . confidence*
(v. 10) represent the same Hebrew verb. The psalmist
invites others to the same *trust* he or she has articulated. **11–12:** Hope rests finally on the foundation of
God's *steadfast love* (59.10, 16–17; 63.3).

PSALM 63

*A Psalm of David, when he was
in the Wilderness of Judah.*

1 O God, you are my God, I seek you,
        my soul thirsts for you;
    my flesh faints for you,
        as in a dry and weary land where
            there is no water.
2 So I have looked upon you in the
        sanctuary,
    beholding your power and glory.

3 Because your steadfast love is better
   than life,
   my lips will praise you.
4 So I will bless you as long as I live;
   I will lift up my hands and call on
   your name.

5 My soul is satisfied as with a rich feast,[a]
   and my mouth praises you with joyful
   lips
6 when I think of you on my bed,
   and meditate on you in the watches
   of the night;
7 for you have been my help,
   and in the shadow of your wings I
   sing for joy.
8 My soul clings to you;
   your right hand upholds me.

9 But those who seek to destroy my life
   shall go down into the depths of the
   earth;
10 they shall be given over to the power of
   the sword,
   they shall be prey for jackals.
11 But the king shall rejoice in God;
   all who swear by him shall exult,
   for the mouths of liars will be
   stopped.

63.1–11: My soul thirsts for you. A song of thanksgiving or psalm of trust, it apparently narrates the experience and results of the psalmist's encounter with
God in the Temple* (Ps 17). The editors of the psalter
associated it with David in the wilderness (compare v.
9 with 1 Sam 23.4; 24.2). **1–2:** Lack of *water* (42.2)
symbolizes the need that the psalmist addresses by entering the Temple where *beholding* God occurs (27.4).
3: To see God is to comprehend God's character,
which is *steadfast love* (Ex 34.6–7; Ps 17.7; 62.12). **4:**
The psalmist responds with praise and prayer, indicated by uplifted *hands*. **5–8:** The metaphor* shifts
from thirst to hunger, which is also *satisfied* (17.15;
65.4), leading again to *praises* (v. 5), prayerful meditation (v. 6), and a profession of faith in God's *help*
and protection (see *shadow of your wings* in 17.8;
57.1). **9–11:** Those who *seek* the psalmist's *life* (38.12;
54.3) will be eaten instead of eating (see v. 5). The
prayer may have been prayed originally by *the king*,
but probably not (61.6–7).

P S A L M 6 4

To the leader. A Psalm of David.

1 Hear my voice, O God, in my
   complaint;
   preserve my life from the dread
   enemy.
2 Hide me from the secret plots of the
   wicked,
   from the scheming of evildoers,
3 who whet their tongues like swords,
   who aim bitter words like arrows,
4 shooting from ambush at the blameless;
   they shoot suddenly and without fear.
5 They hold fast to their evil purpose;
   they talk of laying snares secretly,
   thinking, "Who can see us?[b]
6 Who can search out our crimes?[c]
   We have thought out a cunningly
   conceived plot."
   For the human heart and mind are
   deep.

7 But God will shoot his arrow at them;
   they will be wounded suddenly.
8 Because of their tongue he will bring
   them to ruin;[d]
   all who see them will shake with
   horror.
9 Then everyone will fear;
   they will tell what God has brought
   about,
   and ponder what he has done.

10 Let the righteous rejoice in the LORD
   and take refuge in him.
   Let all the upright in heart glory.

64.1–10: What God has brought about. It is a prayer
for help (note *complaint* in v. 1). **1–6:** The *tongues*
and *words* of the wicked act as weapons (57.4; 140.3);
and they believe that they act with impunity (v. 5) and
without accountability (v. 6; 10.4, 6, 11). **7–9:** Verse 7
picks up the vocabulary of vv. 3–4 to affirm God's response, which will serve as a witness and motivation
to others (v. 9; 52.5–6). **10:** In the midst of opposition,
the righteous always have a *refuge* in God (2.12; 62.8).

---

a Heb *with fat and fatness*　　b Syr: Heb *them*
c Cn: Heb *They search out crimes*　　d Cn: Heb *They
will bring him to ruin, their tongue being against them*

PSALM 65

To the leader. A Psalm of David. A Song.

1 Praise is due to you,
    O God, in Zion;
and to you shall vows be performed,
2   O you who answer prayer!
To you all flesh shall come.
3 When deeds of iniquity overwhelm us,
    you forgive our transgressions.
4 Happy are those whom you choose and
    bring near
    to live in your courts.
We shall be satisfied with the goodness
    of your house,
    your holy temple.

5 By awesome deeds you answer us with
    deliverance,
    O God of our salvation;
you are the hope of all the ends of the
    earth
    and of the farthest seas.
6 By your[a] strength you established the
    mountains;
    you are girded with might.
7 You silence the roaring of the seas,
    the roaring of their waves,
    the tumult of the peoples.
8 Those who live at earth's farthest
    bounds are awed by your signs;
you make the gateways of the morning
    and the evening shout for joy.

9 You visit the earth and water it,
    you greatly enrich it;
the river of God is full of water;
    you provide the people with grain,
    for so you have prepared it.
10 You water its furrows abundantly,
    settling its ridges,
softening it with showers,
    and blessing its growth.
11 You crown the year with your bounty;
    your wagon tracks overflow with
    richness.
12 The pastures of the wilderness
    overflow,
    the hills gird themselves with joy,
13 the meadows clothe themselves with
    flocks,

the valleys deck themselves with
    grain,
    they shout and sing together for joy.

65.1–13: Praise is due to you, O God. A communal song of thanksgiving, it may originally have been used at the autumn harvest festival (Succoth). **1–4:** The three-fold *to you* in vv. 1–2 focuses attention on God, who has *satisfied* the people in the *temple*, perhaps an allusion to the ritual meals that accompanied thanksgiving sacrifices. Forgiveness seems to result from God's initiative rather than the people's. **5–8:** God's *answer* (v. 5; see v. 2) affects not only God's people but all people and all creation. God wills and effects security for the world. **9–13:** An illustration of God-given security is the rain which leads to an abundance of *grain* and *flocks*. Appropriately, the created elements *sing together for joy* (v. 13; see v. 8).

PSALM 66

To the leader. A Song. A Psalm.

1 Make a joyful noise to God, all the
    earth;
2   sing the glory of his name;
    give to him glorious praise.
3 Say to God, "How awesome are your
    deeds!
    Because of your great power, your
    enemies cringe before you.
4 All the earth worships you;
    they sing praises to you,
    sing praises to your name."   *Selah*

5 Come and see what God has done:
    he is awesome in his deeds among
    mortals.
6 He turned the sea into dry land;
    they passed through the river on foot.
There we rejoiced in him,
7   who rules by his might forever,
    whose eyes keep watch on the nations—
    let the rebellious not exalt
    themselves.   *Selah*

8 Bless our God, O peoples,
    let the sound of his praise be heard,
9 who has kept us among the living,
    and has not let our feet slip.

---

a Gk Jerome: Heb *his*

10 For you, O God, have tested us;
   you have tried us as silver is tried.
11 You brought us into the net;
   you laid burdens on our backs;
12 you let people ride over our heads;
   we went through fire and through
      water;
   yet you have brought us out to a
      spacious place.*

13 I will come into your house with burnt
      offerings;
   I will pay you my vows,
14 those that my lips uttered
   and my mouth promised when I was
      in trouble.
15 I will offer to you burnt offerings of
      fatlings,
   with the smoke of the sacrifice of
      rams;
   I will make an offering of bulls and
      goats.   *Selah*

16 Come and hear, all you who fear God,
   and I will tell what he has done for
      me.
17 I cried aloud to him,
   and he was extolled with my tongue.
18 If I had cherished iniquity in my heart,
   the Lord would not have listened.
19 But truly God has listened;
   he has given heed to the words of my
      prayer.

20 Blessed be God,
   because he has not rejected my
      prayer
   or removed his steadfast love from
      me.

66.1–20: Come and see, come and hear. In this communal song of thanksgiving, the shift to first-person singular language in v. 13 implies that an individual has personally appropriated the communal story of deliverance. 1–4: *All the earth* (vv. 1, 4) is invited to acknowledge the sovereignty of the cosmic God (100.1). 5–7: The description of *what God has done* (v. 5; 64.9) recalls the Exodus. 8–12: Verses 9 and 12 suggest that the people have been *tested* and *tried* (v. 10) in order that they may be vindicated (17.3). 13–19: Recalling

vv. 5 and 16 suggests that individual deliverance parallels communal deliverance. A personal exodus has occurred, for which the psalmist is thankful and offers appropriate sacrifices (vv. 13–15; 22.25–26; 56.12–13). 20: The psalmist responds as all peoples have been invited to do in v. 8. What God *has done* (v. 16) reveals God's character—*steadfast love* (Ex 34.6–7; Ps 33.5, 18, 22).

~~~~~~~~~~~~~~~~~~~~~

PSALM 67
To the leader: with stringed instruments.
A Psalm. A Song.

1 May God be gracious to us and bless us
   and make his face to shine upon us,
                                    Selah
2 that your way may be known upon
      earth,
   your saving power among all nations.
3 Let the peoples praise you, O God;
   let all the peoples praise you.

4 Let the nations be glad and sing for joy,
   for you judge the peoples with
      equity
   and guide the nations upon earth.
                                    Selah
5 Let the peoples praise you, O God;
   let all the peoples praise you.

6 The earth has yielded its increase;
   God, our God, has blessed us.
7 May God continue to bless us;
   let all the ends of the earth revere
      him.

67.1–7: Let all peoples praise you. A communal song of thanksgiving, it can also be understood as a prayer for God's blessing (vv. 1, 7). 1–2: Verse 1 recalls Num 6.22–27 where blessing and *face* are associated 4.6; 31.16). The blessing of the people will involve *all nations* (Gen 12.1–3). 3–5: A refrain surrounds the central v. 4. Justice (*judge* could be translated "establish justice") and *equity* are attributes of God's reign (98.9). 6–7: The concept of blessing and the universal perspective recall vv. 1–2.

~~~~~~~~~~~~~~~~~~~~~

a Cn Compare Gk Syr Jerome Tg: Heb *to a saturation*

PSALM 68

To the leader. Of David. A Psalm. A Song.

1 Let God rise up, let his enemies be
     scattered;
   let those who hate him flee before
     him.
2 As smoke is driven away, so drive them
     away;
   as wax melts before the fire,
   let the wicked perish before God.
3 But let the righteous be joyful;
   let them exult before God;
   let them be jubilant with joy.

4 Sing to God, sing praises to his name;
   lift up a song to him who rides upon
     the clouds[a]—
   his name is the Lord—
   be exultant before him.

5 Father of orphans and protector of
     widows
   is God in his holy habitation.
6 God gives the desolate a home to live in;
   he leads out the prisoners to
     prosperity,
   but the rebellious live in a parched
     land.

7 O God, when you went out before your
     people,
   when you marched through the
     wilderness,   *Selah*
8 the earth quaked, the heavens poured
     down rain
   at the presence of God, the God of
     Sinai,
   at the presence of God, the God of
     Israel.
9 Rain in abundance, O God, you
     showered abroad;
   you restored your heritage when it
     languished;
10 your flock found a dwelling in it;
   in your goodness, O God, you
     provided for the needy.

11 The Lord gives the command;
   great is the company of those[b] who
     bore the tidings:

12 "The kings of the armies, they flee,
     they flee!"
   The women at home divide the spoil,
13   though they stay among the
     sheepfolds—
   the wings of a dove covered with silver,
     its pinions with green gold.
14 When the Almighty[c] scattered kings
     there,
   snow fell on Zalmon.

15 O mighty mountain, mountain of
     Bashan;
   O many-peaked mountain, mountain
     of Bashan!
16 Why do you look with envy, O many-
     peaked mountain,
   at the mount that God desired for his
     abode,
   where the Lord will reside forever?

17 With mighty chariotry, twice ten
     thousand,
   thousands upon thousands,
   the Lord came from Sinai into the
     holy place.[d]
18 You ascended the high mount,
   leading captives in your train
   and receiving gifts from people,
   even from those who rebel against the
     Lord God's abiding there.
19 Blessed be the Lord,
   who daily bears us up;
   God is our salvation.   *Selah*
20 Our God is a God of salvation,
   and to God, the Lord, belongs escape
     from death.

21 But God will shatter the heads of his
     enemies,
   the hairy crown of those who walk in
     their guilty ways.
22 The Lord said,
   "I will bring them back from Bashan,
   I will bring them back from the depths
     of the sea,

a Or cast up a highway for him who rides through the
deserts   b Or company of the women   c Traditional
rendering of Heb *Shaddai*   d Cn: Heb *The Lord among
them Sinai in the holy* (place)

23 so that you may bathe^a your feet in
    blood,
    so that the tongues of your dogs may
      have their share from the foe."

68.1–35: The processions of my God. A communal
song of thanksgiving, it depicts a processional celebration of God's reign in the Temple,* perhaps involving
the ark (see Ps 24). **1–3:** Verse 1 recalls Num 10.35,
which suggests that the ark of the covenant* symbolized God's victory over enemies. **4–6:** The Canaanite
god Baal* was known as the one *who rides upon the
clouds.* Israel's God has displaced Baal (see Ps 48, 82).
Verses 5–6 allude to the Exodus, suggesting that what
God wills has occurred. **7–18:** The poem proceeds
with further historical allusions: *wilderness* (v. 7), *Sinai*
(v. 8), and possession of the land (vv. 9–14). God and
the people make their way *from Sinai* (v. 17) to *the
high mount* (v. 18), Zion,* rejecting other locations
(vv. 15–16). **19–23:** Having arrived at Zion, the celebration of God's victory over all *enemies* begins. The
result is life (vv. 19–20).

24 Your solemn processions are seen,^b
    O God,
    the processions of my God, my King,
      into the sanctuary—
25 the singers in front, the musicians last,
    between them girls playing
      tambourines:
26 "Bless God in the great congregation,
    the LORD, O you who are of Israel's
      fountain!"
27 There is Benjamin, the least of them, in
    the lead,
    the princes of Judah in a body,
    the princes of Zebulun, the princes of
      Naphtali.

28 Summon your might, O God;
    show your strength, O God, as you
      have done for us before.
29 Because of your temple at Jerusalem
    kings bear gifts to you.
30 Rebuke the wild animals that live
      among the reeds,
    the herd of bulls with the calves of
      the peoples.
    Trample^c under foot those who lust
      after tribute;
    scatter the peoples who delight in war.^d

31 Let bronze be brought from Egypt;
    let Ethiopia^e hasten to stretch out its
      hands to God.

32 Sing to God, O kingdoms of the earth;
    sing praises to the Lord,   *Selah*
33 O rider in the heavens, the ancient
      heavens;
    listen, he sends out his voice, his
      mighty voice.
34 Ascribe power to God,
    whose majesty is over Israel;
    and whose power is in the skies.
35 Awesome is God in his^f sanctuary,
    the God of Israel;
    he gives power and strength to his
      people.

    Blessed be God!

68.24–35. 24–27: God is greeted as *King* (see Ex
15.18; Ps 24.7–10) in a festive procession. These four
tribes seem to represent the whole people. **28–31:**
God's sovereignty is not universally recognized (see Ps
2). A new manifestation of *might* and *strength* is
needed. **32–35:** Verses 32–33 recall v. 4. The Hebrew
behind *might* and *strength* in v. 28 recurs four more
times—*mighty* (v. 33) and *power* (three times in vv.
34–35). Despite opposition, God will prevail; and the
people will share the benefits (vv. 5–6).

PSALM 69

To the leader: according to Lilies. Of David.

1 Save me, O God,
    for the waters have come up to my
      neck.
2 I sink in deep mire,
    where there is no foothold;
    I have come into deep waters,
    and the flood sweeps over me.
3 I am weary with my crying;
    my throat is parched.
    My eyes grow dim
    with waiting for my God.

a Gk Syr Tg: Heb *shatter*   *b* Or *have been seen*
c Cn: Heb *Trampling*   *d* Meaning of Heb of verse 30
is uncertain   *e* Or *Nubia*; Heb *Cush*   *f* Gk: Heb
from your

4 More in number than the hairs of my
    head
  are those who hate me without
    cause;
many are those who would destroy me,
  my enemies who accuse me falsely.
What I did not steal
  must I now restore?
5 O God, you know my folly;
  the wrongs I have done are not
    hidden from you.

6 Do not let those who hope in you be put
    to shame because of me,
  O Lord GOD of hosts;
do not let those who seek you be
    dishonored because of me,
  O God of Israel.
7 It is for your sake that I have borne
    reproach,
  that shame has covered my face.
8 I have become a stranger to my
    kindred,
  an alien to my mother's children.

9 It is zeal for your house that has
    consumed me;
  the insults of those who insult you
    have fallen on me.
10 When I humbled my soul with fasting,ª
  they insulted me for doing so.
11 When I made sackcloth my clothing,
  I became a byword to them.
12 I am the subject of gossip for those who
    sit in the gate,
  and the drunkards make songs about
    me.

13 But as for me, my prayer is to you,
    O LORD.
  At an acceptable time, O God,
  in the abundance of your steadfast
    love, answer me.
With your faithful help 14rescue me
  from sinking in the mire;
let me be delivered from my enemies
  and from the deep waters.
15 Do not let the flood sweep over me,
  or the deep swallow me up,
  or the Pit close its mouth over me.

16 Answer me, O LORD, for your steadfast
    love is good;
  according to your abundant mercy,
    turn to me.
17 Do not hide your face from your
    servant,
  for I am in distress—make haste to
    answer me.
18 Draw near to me, redeem me,
  set me free because of my enemies.

69.1–36: The LORD hears the needy. In this prayer for help, the psalmist is convinced that he or she suffers for God's sake (v. 7). Alternating petition and complaint characterize the first two sections (vv. 1–13b, 13c–29), which are roughly parallel in vocabulary and imagery. Two sections of praise (vv. 30–33, 34–36) follow. **1–3:** *Neck* is the original sense of "nephesh," usually translated "soul" or "life." **4–5:** The original situation may have involved *enemies who accuse . . . falsely* (Ps 5, 7). Verse 5 implies innocence; the persecution is *without cause* (35.7, 19). **6–13b:** The psalmist's isolation (v. 8; 38.11) is for God's sake (vv. 7, 9). The Hebrew behind *reproach* occurs five more times as *insult(s)* in vv. 9, 10, 19, 20. In the midst of trouble, the psalmist prays (v. 13a–b), an act of entrusting life and future to God. **13c–18:** Paralleling vv. 1–4, these verses indicate the psalmist takes his or her stand on God's *steadfast love* (vv. 13, 16), faithfulness (v. 13), and *mercy* (v. 16). The psalmist trusts that God's goodness will correspond to the way that God has revealed the divine self (Ex 34.6–7).

19 You know the insults I receive,
  and my shame and dishonor;
  my foes are all known to you.
20 Insults have broken my heart,
  so that I am in despair.
I looked for pity, but there was none;
  and for comforters, but I found
    none.
21 They gave me poison for food,
  and for my thirst they gave me
    vinegar to drink.

22 Let their table be a trap for them,
  a snare for their allies.

a Gk Syr: Heb I wept, with fasting my soul, or I made my
soul mourn with fasting

23 Let their eyes be darkened so that they
        cannot see,
    and make their loins tremble
        continually.
24 Pour out your indignation upon them,
    and let your burning anger overtake
        them.
25 May their camp be a desolation;
    let no one live in their tents.
26 For they persecute those whom you
        have struck down,
    and those whom you have wounded,
        they attack still more.*
27 Add guilt to their guilt;
    may they have no acquittal from you.
28 Let them be blotted out of the book of
        the living;
    let them not be enrolled among the
        righteous.
29 But I am lowly and in pain;
    let your salvation, O God, protect me.

30 I will praise the name of God with a
        song;
    I will magnify him with thanksgiving.
31 This will please the LORD more than an
        ox
    or a bull with horns and hoofs.
32 Let the oppressed see it and be glad;
    you who seek God, let your hearts
        revive.
33 For the LORD hears the needy,
    and does not despise his own that are
        in bonds.

34 Let heaven and earth praise him,
    the seas and everything that moves in
        them.
35 For God will save Zion
    and rebuild the cities of Judah;
    and his servants shall live* there and
        possess it;
36   the children of his servants shall
        inherit it,
    and those who love his name shall
        live in it.

venge but by a desire for "righteousness," which is
how the Hebrew behind *acquittal* is usually translated.
The psalmist trusts that God stands with the *lowly*
(12.5; 109.22, 31). **30–33:** Thus, the *oppressed* and
needy will want to join the psalmist's praise. The
psalmist's life proves to be exemplary (see v. 6).
34–36: Perhaps a post-exilic addition, these verses extend praise throughout space and time (22.27–31).

PSALM 70

*To the leader. Of David, for the
memorial offering.*

1 Be pleased, O God, to deliver me.
    O LORD, make haste to help me!
2 Let those be put to shame and
        confusion
    who seek my life.
    Let those be turned back and brought
        to dishonor
    who desire to hurt me.
3 Let those who say, "Aha, Aha!"
    turn back because of their shame.

4 Let all who seek you
    rejoice and be glad in you.
    Let those who love your salvation
    say evermore, "God is great!"
5 But I am poor and needy;
    hasten to me, O God!
    You are my help and my deliverer;
    O LORD, do not delay!

70.1–5: Make haste to help me. A prayer for help, it
is nearly identical to 40.13–17. The only major difference is between 40.17 and 70.5, which includes the
petition for God to *hasten* (see v. 1). The translation
memorial offering in the superscription is uncertain.
1–3: *Help* recurs in v. 5, framing the psalm, along with
the concept of deliverance. The petition against the
enemies recalls 69.22–29. **4–5:** These verses recall
69.29, 33. The psalmists regularly affirm that God
stands with the *poor and needy* (9.18; 10.17–18).

PSALM 71

1 In you, O LORD, I take refuge;
    let me never be put to shame.

69.19–36. 19–21: Paralleling vv. 5–11 (see *you know*
in vv. 5, 19), these verses focus on the *foes*, preparing
for vv. 22–29. **22–29:** Petitions against the enemies
(35.4–8; 58.6–9) are motivated not so much by re-

a Gk Syr: Heb *recount the pain of*   *b* Syr: Heb *and
they shall live*

2 In your righteousness deliver me and
rescue me;
incline your ear to me and save me.
3 Be to me a rock of refuge,
a strong fortress,ᵃ to save me,
for you are my rock and my fortress.

4 Rescue me, O my God, from the hand
of the wicked,
from the grasp of the unjust and
cruel.
5 For you, O Lord, are my hope,
my trust, O LORD, from my youth.
6 Upon you I have leaned from my birth;
it was you who took me from my
mother's womb.
My praise is continually of you.

7 I have been like a portent to many,
but you are my strong refuge.
8 My mouth is filled with your praise,
and with your glory all day long.
9 Do not cast me off in the time of old
age;
do not forsake me when my strength
is spent.
10 For my enemies speak concerning me,
and those who watch for my life
consult together.
11 They say, "Pursue and seize that person
whom God has forsaken,
for there is no one to deliver."

12 O God, do not be far from me;
O my God, make haste to help me!
13 Let my accusers be put to shame and
consumed;
let those who seek to hurt me
be covered with scorn and disgrace.
14 But I will hope continually,
and will praise you yet more and
more.
15 My mouth will tell of your righteous
acts,
of your deeds of salvation all day long,
though their number is past my
knowledge.
16 I will come praising the mighty deeds of
the Lord GOD,
I will praise your righteousness, yours
alone.

17 O God, from my youth you have taught
me,
and I still proclaim your wondrous
deeds.
18 So even to old age and gray hairs,
O God, do not forsake me,
until I proclaim your might
to all the generations to come.ᵇ
Your power ¹⁹and your righteousness,
O God,
reach the high heavens.

You who have done great things,
O God, who is like you?
20 You who have made me see many
troubles and calamities
will revive me again;
from the depths of the earth
you will bring me up again.
21 You will increase my honor,
and comfort me once again.

22 I will also praise you with the harp
for your faithfulness, O my God;
I will sing praises to you with the lyre,
O Holy One of Israel.
23 My lips will shout for joy
when I sing praises to you;
my soul also, which you have rescued.
24 All day long my tongue will talk of your
righteous help,
for those who tried to do me harm
have been put to shame, and
disgraced.

71.1–24: O God, who is like you? A prayer for help,
its similarities with Ps 22 and 31 suggest that it may
be an anthology of quotations from other psalms.
1–4: Verses 1–3 are nearly identical to 31.1–3a. **5–8:**
Reminiscent of 22.9–10, these verses reinforce the
psalmist's affirmation of dependence upon God (see
refuge in vv. 1, 7). The mention of *youth* in v. 5 prepares for *old age* in v. 9. The themes recur in vv. 17–
18. **9–13:** As in 22.1, the psalmist is *forsaken* (v. 11;
see vv. 9, 18). Verse 12 recalls 22.19. **14–17:** *Righteous
acts* and *righteousness* are the same Hebrew word.
The conviction that God wills to set things right un-

a Gk Compare 31.3: Heb *to come continually you have
commanded*   *b* Gk Compare Syr: Heb *to a generation,
to all that come*

derlies the petition against the enemies (v. 13). **18–24:** The question *who is like you?* focuses attention on God's character. The psalmist affirms that God's *faithfulness* is fundamental (Ex 34.6) and that it is manifest as *righteous help* (v. 24; see the same Hebrew word in vv. 15, 16, 19).

~~~~~~~~~~~~~~~~~~~~~~~~~~~~~~

P S A L M 7 2

Of Solomon.

1 Give the king your justice, O God,
   and your righteousness to a king's
      son.
2 May he judge your people with
      righteousness,
   and your poor with justice.
3 May the mountains yield prosperity for
      the people,
   and the hills, in righteousness.
4 May he defend the cause of the poor of
      the people,
   give deliverance to the needy,
   and crush the oppressor.

5 May he live*a* while the sun endures,
   and as long as the moon, throughout
      all generations.
6 May he be like rain that falls on the
      mown grass,
   like showers that water the earth.
7 In his days may righteousness flourish
   and peace abound, until the moon is
      no more.

8 May he have dominion from sea to sea,
   and from the River to the ends of the
      earth.
9 May his foes*b* bow down before him,
   and his enemies lick the dust.
10 May the kings of Tarshish and of the
      isles
   render him tribute,
   may the kings of Sheba and Seba
      bring gifts.
11 May all kings fall down before him,
   all nations give him service.

12 For he delivers the needy when they
      call,
   the poor and those who have no
      helper.

13 He has pity on the weak and the needy,
   and saves the lives of the needy.
14 From oppression and violence he
      redeems their life;
   and precious is their blood in his
      sight.

15 Long may he live!
   May gold of Sheba be given to him.
   May prayer be made for him
      continually,
   and blessings invoked for him all day
      long.
16 May there be abundance of grain in the
      land;
   may it wave on the tops of the
      mountains;
   may its fruit be like Lebanon;
   and may people blossom in the cities
   like the grass of the field.
17 May his name endure forever,
   his fame continue as long as the sun.
   May all nations be blessed in him;*c*
   may they pronounce him happy.

18 Blessed be the LORD, the God of Israel,
   who alone does wondrous things.
19 Blessed be his glorious name forever;
   may his glory fill the whole earth.
      Amen and Amen.

20 The prayers of David son of Jesse are
      ended.

72.1–20: Your justice and righteousness. This royal psalm was probably used originally as a prayer for the Judean king on the day of his coronation (see Ps 2). It may date from the time *of Solomon.* After the disappearance of the monarchy, it would have been heard as a prayer for the enactment of God's will for *justice* and *righteousness.* **1–7:** These two key words appear in v. 1 and are repeated. *The king* was the earthly agent of God's will, which always involves *justice* and *righteousness* (98.9; 99.4). When they are enacted, the result is "shalom" (*prosperity* in v. 3; *peace* in v. 7). The petitions suggest that the cosmos will not operate properly apart from *justice* and *righteousness* (36.5–6; 82.5). **8–11:** God's rule enacted by *the king* is to ex-

a Gk: Heb *may they fear you*   *b* Cn: Heb *those who live in the wilderness*   *c* Or *bless themselves by him* tend in both time (v. 7) and space (vv. 8–11). *The River* is probably the Euphrates. *Tarshish* and *the isles* indicate Spain and Mediterranean regions, while *Sheba and Seba* occupy the Arabian peninsula. These place names symbolize God's universal rule. **12–14:** *Justice* and *righteousness* exist when the *needy, poor,* and *weak* are protected and empowered. **15–17:** There are cosmic consequences of the king's enactment of *justice* and *righteousness* (see vv. 5–7). Verse 17 recalls Gen 12.1–3. **18–19:** An appropriate conclusion to the psalm, these verses also provide the concluding doxology for Book II (compare 41.13). **20:** The Davidic collection may be Ps 51–72 or Ps 3–72.

BOOK THREE

PSALM 73

A Psalm of Asaph.

1 Truly God is good to the upright,[a]
　　to those who are pure in heart.
2 But as for me, my feet had almost
　　　　stumbled;
　　my steps had nearly slipped.
3 For I was envious of the arrogant;
　　I saw the prosperity of the wicked.

4 For they have no pain;
　　their bodies are sound and sleek.
5 They are not in trouble as others are;
　　they are not plagued like other
　　　　people.
6 Therefore pride is their necklace;
　　violence covers them like a garment.
7 Their eyes swell out with fatness;
　　their hearts overflow with follies.
8 They scoff and speak with malice;
　　loftily they threaten oppression.
9 They set their mouths against heaven,
　　and their tongues range over the
　　　　earth.
10 Therefore the people turn and praise
　　　　them,[b]
　　and find no fault in them.[c]
11 And they say, "How can God know?
　　Is there knowledge in the
　　　　Most High?"
12 Such are the wicked;
　　always at ease, they increase in
　　　　riches.

13 All in vain I have kept my heart clean
　　and washed my hands in innocence.
14 For all day long I have been plagued,
　　and am punished every morning.

15 If I had said, "I will talk on in this way,"
　　I would have been untrue to the
　　　　circle of your children.
16 But when I thought how to understand
　　　　this,
　　it seemed to me a wearisome task,
17 until I went into the sanctuary of God;
　　then I perceived their end.
18 Truly you set them in slippery places;
　　you make them fall to ruin.
19 How they are destroyed in a moment,
　　swept away utterly by terrors!
20 They are[d] like a dream when one
　　　　awakes;
　　on awaking you despise their
　　　　phantoms.

21 When my soul was embittered,
　　when I was pricked in heart,
22 I was stupid and ignorant;
　　I was like a brute beast toward you.
23 Nevertheless I am continually with you;
　　you hold my right hand.
24 You guide me with your counsel,
　　and afterward you will receive me
　　　　with honor.[e]
25 Whom have I in heaven but you?
　　And there is nothing on earth that I
　　　　desire other than you.
26 My flesh and my heart may fail,
　　but God is the strength[f] of my heart
　　　　and my portion forever.

27 Indeed, those who are far from you will
　　　　perish;
　　you put an end to those who are false
　　　　to you.
28 But for me it is good to be near God;
　　I have made the Lord GOD my
　　　　refuge,
　　to tell of all your works.

a Or *good to Israel*　　b Cn: Heb *his people return here*
c Cn: Heb *abundant waters are drained by them*
d Cn: Heb *Lord*　　e Or *to glory*　　f Heb *rock*

73.1–28: I am continually with you. Often labeled a psalm of trust, its instructional intent suggests it may be a wisdom psalm. It is best divided into three sections (vv. 1–12, 13–17, 18–28), each of which begins with the same Hebrew word, translated *truly* in vv. 1 and 18. It initiates a collection of eleven *Asaph* psalms (see Ps 50). **1–3:** Because of the focus on God's *children* in v. 15, v. 1 should follow the Hebrew to read "Israel" rather than *upright*. *Pure in heart* characterizes the worshipping community (24.4). The psalmist is pulled toward doubt by the *prosperity of the wicked*. **4–12:** This *prosperity* (vv. 4–5, 7, 12) is accompanied by the denial of accountability to God and others (vv. 6, 8–9, 11). Verse 10 seems to indicate that even arrogance attracts others. **13–17:** Verses 13–14 expand upon the doubt expressed in vv. 2–3. It appears that crime does pay; but the psalmist realizes that such *talk* would lead to alienation from the community of faith. The insight expressed in the pivotal v. 15 is consolidated in vv. 16–17 as the psalmist apparently enters the Temple.* **18–20:** Whereas the psalmist *had nearly slipped* (v. 2), now he or she perceives that the wicked are on *slippery* ground. **21–26:** Looking back on former doubt, the psalmist realizes that he or she was and is constantly with God. The key phrase is *with you* (v. 23). Verse 24 probably does not articulate a doctrine of resurrection, but develops typical thinking about the afterlife (22.29; 49.15). **27–28:** *Good* in v. 28 recalls v. 1. Goodness is not the material prosperity the wicked possess, but rather nearness to God. Having found *refuge* in God (2.12; 71.1), the psalmist's *talk* (v. 15) now takes the form of proclamation.

PSALM 74

A Maskil of Asaph.

1 O God, why do you cast us off
      forever?
   Why does your anger smoke against
      the sheep of your pasture?
2 Remember your congregation, which
      you acquired long ago,
   which you redeemed to be the tribe of
      your heritage.
   Remember Mount Zion, where you
      came to dwell.
3 Direct your steps to the perpetual
      ruins;
   the enemy has destroyed everything
      in the sanctuary.

4 Your foes have roared within your holy
      place;
   they set up their emblems there.
5 At the upper entrance they hacked
      the wooden trellis with axes.*a*
6 And then, with hatchets and hammers,
      they smashed all its carved work.
7 They set your sanctuary on fire;
   they desecrated the dwelling place of
      your name,
   bringing it to the ground.
8 They said to themselves, "We will
      utterly subdue them";
   they burned all the meeting places of
      God in the land.

9 We do not see our emblems;
   there is no longer any prophet,
   and there is no one among us who
      knows how long.
10 How long, O God, is the foe to scoff?
   Is the enemy to revile your name
      forever?
11 Why do you hold back your hand;
   why do you keep your hand in*b* your
      bosom?

12 Yet God my King is from of old,
   working salvation in the earth.
13 You divided the sea by your might;
   you broke the heads of the dragons in
      the waters.
14 You crushed the heads of Leviathan;
   you gave him as food*c* for the
      creatures of the wilderness.
15 You cut openings for springs and torrents;
   you dried up ever-flowing streams.
16 Yours is the day, yours also the night;
   you established the luminaries*d* and
      the sun.
17 You have fixed all the bounds of the
      earth;
   you made summer and winter.

18 Remember this, O LORD, how the
      enemy scoffs,
   and an impious people reviles your
      name.

a Cn Compare Gk Syr: Meaning of Heb uncertain
b Cn: Heb *do you consume your right hand from*
c Heb *food for the people*   d Or *moon*; Heb *light*

19 Do not deliver the soul of your dove to
      the wild animals;
  do not forget the life of your poor
      forever.
20 Have regard for your^a covenant,
      for the dark places of the land are full
      of the haunts of violence.
21 Do not let the downtrodden be put to
      shame;
  let the poor and needy praise your
      name.
22 Rise up, O God, plead your cause;
  remember how the impious scoff at
      you all day long.
23 Do not forget the clamor of your foes,
  the uproar of your adversaries that
      goes up continually.

74.1–23: Remember your congregation. This communal prayer for help is usually associated with the destruction of Jerusalem and the Temple* in 587 BCE. **1–11:** The questions in vv. 1, 10–11 frame the section. Verse 2 alludes to the Exodus and entry into the land. *Remember* recurs in vv. 18, 22. Verses 4–8 describe the destruction of the Temple and other holy places. The absence of any sign or word from God (v. 9) leads to the people's questions. **12–17:** That God is *King* is evident in the Exodus (vv. 13–14), the description of which reaches mythic proportions and leads to the affirmation of God's power over *the dragons* and *Leviathan,** symbols of chaotic forces. **18–23:** The Exodus and subsequent *covenant** (Ex 24.1–8; Ps 44.17) at Sinai were evidence of God's concern for the *poor, downtrodden,* and *needy.* The people pray that the scoffing of the *impious* will cause God to *remember* and act as God acted *long ago* (v. 2).

PSALM 75
To the leader: Do Not Destroy. A Psalm
of Asaph. A Song.

1 We give thanks to you, O God;
  we give thanks; your name is near.
  People tell of your wondrous deeds.

2 At the set time that I appoint
  I will judge with equity.
3 When the earth totters, with all its
      inhabitants,
  it is I who keep its pillars steady.
              Selah

4 I say to the boastful, "Do not boast,"
  and to the wicked, "Do not lift up
      your horn;
5 do not lift up your horn on high,
  or speak with insolent neck."
6 For not from the east or from the west
  and not from the wilderness comes
      lifting up;
7 but it is God who executes judgment,
  putting down one and lifting up
      another.
8 For in the hand of the LORD there is a
      cup
  with foaming wine, well mixed;
  he will pour a draught from it,
  and all the wicked of the earth
  shall drain it down to the dregs.
9 But I will rejoice^b forever;
  I will sing praises to the God of
      Jacob.
10 All the horns of the wicked I will cut off,
  but the horns of the righteous shall
      be exalted.

75.1–10: The righteous shall be exalted. Often classified as a prophetic* judgment oracle* (see especially vv. 2, 7, 10), the first divine speech (vv. 2–5) is preceded by praise (v. 1), and the second (v. 10) by a profession of faith (vv. 6–8) and a promise to praise (v. 9). **1:** Gratitude and proclamation of God's *wondrous deeds* go together (9.1; 26.7). **2–5:** In order to *judge,* or "establish justice" (v. 2), God must oppose *the wicked* and their self-assertion. The key word is *lift up* (vv. 4–5; see also vv. 6–7). **6–9:** Echoing vv. 2–5, the psalmist celebrates God's establishment of justice. Oppressors drink the *cup* of destruction (11.6). **10:** *Horns* (vv. 4–5) symbolize power. The self-assertive are humbled; the *righteous* are *exalted.*

PSALM 76
To the leader: with stringed instruments.
A Psalm of Asaph. A Song.

1 In Judah God is known,
  his name is great in Israel.
2 His abode has been established in
      Salem,
  his dwelling place in Zion.

a Gk Syr: Heb *the*   *b* Gk: Heb *declare*

3 There he broke the flashing arrows,
  the shield, the sword, and the
    weapons of war.   *Selah*

4 Glorious are you, more majestic
  than the everlasting mountains."
5 The stouthearted were stripped of their
    spoil;
  they sank into sleep;
  none of the troops
    was able to lift a hand.
6 At your rebuke, O God of Jacob,
  both rider and horse lay stunned.

7 But you indeed are awesome!
  Who can stand before you
    when once your anger is roused?
8 From the heavens you uttered
    judgment;
  the earth feared and was still
9 when God rose up to establish
    judgment,
  to save all the oppressed of the earth.
    Selah

10 Human wrath serves only to praise you,
  when you bind the last bit of your[b]
    wrath around you.
11 Make vows to the LORD your God, and
    perform them;
  let all who are around him bring gifts
    to the one who is awesome,
12 who cuts off the spirit of princes,
  who inspires fear in the kings of the
    earth.

76.1–12: The one who is awesome. A song of Zion,*
but its real focus is upon God (vv. 4, 7, 11–12). **1–3:**
Zion symbolizes God's claim on the whole world (vv.
8–9) and God's will for its well-being. *Salem,*
"shalem," is similar to "shalom," "peace," anticipating v. 3 (46.9). **4–9:** Reminiscent of the Exodus, vv.
4–6 prepare for the affirmation that God wills *judgment* or "justice" (vv. 8–9; 75.2, 7) for *all the oppressed. Awesome* (vv. 7, 11) represents the same Hebrew root as *feared/fear* (vv. 8, 12). **10–12:** Verse 10
suggests that all opposition to God is futile. God's
claim preempts the claims of the most powerful
earthly rulers (v. 12).

P S A L M 7 7

To the leader: according to Jeduthun. Of Asaph.
A Psalm.

1 I cry aloud to God,
  aloud to God, that he may hear me.
2 In the day of my trouble I seek
    the Lord;
  in the night my hand is stretched out
    without wearying;
  my soul refuses to be comforted.
3 I think of God, and I moan;
  I meditate, and my spirit faints. *Selah*

4 You keep my eyelids from closing;
  I am so troubled that I cannot speak.
5 I consider the days of old,
  and remember the years of long ago.
6 I commune[c] with my heart in the night;
  I meditate and search my spirit:[d]
7 "Will the Lord spurn forever,
  and never again be favorable?
8 Has his steadfast love ceased forever?
  Are his promises at an end for all
    time?
9 Has God forgotten to be gracious?
  Has he in anger shut up his
    compassion?"   *Selah*
10 And I say, "It is my grief
  that the right hand of the Most High
    has changed."

11 I will call to mind the deeds of the
    LORD;
  I will remember your wonders of old.
12 I will meditate on all your work,
  and muse on your mighty deeds.
13 Your way, O God, is holy.
  What god is so great as our God?
14 You are the God who works wonders;
  you have displayed your might among
    the peoples.
15 With your strong arm you redeemed
    your people,
  the descendants of Jacob and Joseph.
    Selah

a Gk: Heb *the mountains of prey*   b Heb lacks *your*
c Gk Syr: Heb *My music*   d Syr Jerome: Heb *my spirit*
searches

16 When the waters saw you, O God,
    when the waters saw you, they were
        afraid;
    the very deep trembled.
17 The clouds poured out water;
    the skies thundered;
    your arrows flashed on every side.
18 The crash of your thunder was in the
        whirlwind;
    your lightnings lit up the world;
    the earth trembled and shook.
19 Your way was through the sea,
    your path, through the mighty
        waters;
    yet your footprints were unseen.
20 You led your people like a flock
    by the hand of Moses and Aaron.

77.1–20: I will remember your wonders of old. Resembling a prayer for help, vv.1–10 report the psalmist's anguished meditations (vv. 1–6), bitter questions (vv. 7–9), and hopeless conclusion (v. 10). While the psalmist continues to *meditate* (v. 12; see vv. 3, 6) in vv. 11–20, the tone and conclusions are remarkably different. **1–6:** The outstretched *hand* indicates prayer, but constant prayer and meditation yield only a faint *spirit* (142.3; 143.4). **7–10:** The psalmist's questions employ words that describe God's fundamental character—*steadfast love*, grace, and *compassion* or mercy (Ex 34.6). But God seems to have *changed*. **11–20:** The switch to direct address in v. 11 creates a more intimate tone. The psalmist's memory (v. 11; see v. 5) of God's *wonders of old* now inspires hope. The language and imagery recall the Exodus. Verse 19 suggests a renewed faith that will be effective even when God's *way* is *unseen*.

PSALM 78

A Maskil of Asaph.

1 Give ear, O my people, to my
        teaching;
    incline your ears to the words of my
        mouth.
2 I will open my mouth in a parable;
    I will utter dark sayings from of old,
3 things that we have heard and known,
    that our ancestors have told us.
4 We will not hide them from their
        children;
    we will tell to the coming generation

the glorious deeds of the LORD, and his
    might,
    and the wonders that he has done.

5 He established a decree in Jacob,
    and appointed a law in Israel,
    which he commanded our ancestors
        to teach to their children;
6 that the next generation might know
        them,
    the children yet unborn,
    and rise up and tell them to their
        children,
7   so that they should set their hope in
        God,
    and not forget the works of God,
        but keep his commandments;
8 and that they should not be like their
        ancestors,
    a stubborn and rebellious generation,
    a generation whose heart was not
        steadfast,
    whose spirit was not faithful to God.

9 The Ephraimites, armed with[a] the bow,
    turned back on the day of battle.
10 They did not keep God's covenant,
    but refused to walk according to his
        law.
11 They forgot what he had done,
    and the miracles that he had shown
        them.
12 In the sight of their ancestors he
        worked marvels
    in the land of Egypt, in the fields of
        Zoan.
13 He divided the sea and let them pass
        through it,
    and made the waters stand like
        a heap.
14 In the daytime he led them with
        a cloud,
    and all night long with a fiery light.
15 He split rocks open in the wilderness,
    and gave them drink abundantly as
        from the deep.
16 He made streams come out of the rock,
    and caused waters to flow down like
        rivers.

a *Heb* armed with shooting

17 Yet they sinned still more against him,
   rebelling against the Most High in
      the desert.
18 They tested God in their heart
   by demanding the food they craved.
19 They spoke against God, saying,
   "Can God spread a table in the
      wilderness?
20 Even though he struck the rock so that
      water gushed out
   and torrents overflowed,
   can he also give bread,
   or provide meat for his people?"

78.1–72: The wonders God has done. Usually classified as a historical psalm (one that rehearses major elements of Israel's story), its aim is to teach (vv. 1, 5) and inspire faithfulness (vv. 6–8). Two parallel sections (vv. 12–39, 40–72) follow the introduction (vv. 1–11). **1–11:** The focus on knowing (vv. 3, 6) and teaching (vv. 1, 5), consistent with the goal of faithfulness to the *covenant** (v. 10) and "torah" (*law*, v. 10), recalls both the wisdom literature* and Deuteronomy (see 6.20–25). **12–16:** The recital begins with God's gracious activity—the Exodus and guidance in the *wilderness* (Ex 13.21–22; 14.21–29; 17.1–6). **17–20:** The recital continues with the people's rebellion (Ex 15.22–25; 16.4–36; 17.1–7).

~~~~~~~~~~~~~~~~

21 Therefore, when the LORD heard, he
      was full of rage;
   a fire was kindled against Jacob,
   his anger mounted against Israel,
22 because they had no faith in God,
   and did not trust his saving power.
23 Yet he commanded the skies above,
   and opened the doors of heaven;
24 he rained down on them manna to eat,
   and gave them the grain of heaven.
25 Mortals ate of the bread of angels;
   he sent them food in abundance.
26 He caused the east wind to blow in the
      heavens,
   and by his power he led out the south
      wind;
27 he rained flesh upon them like dust,
   winged birds like the sand of the seas;
28 he let them fall within their camp,
   all around their dwellings.
29 And they ate and were well filled,
   for he gave them what they craved.

30 But before they had satisfied their
      craving,
   while the food was still in their
      mouths,
31 the anger of God rose against them
   and he killed the strongest of them,
   and laid low the flower of Israel.
32 In spite of all this they still sinned;
   they did not believe in his wonders.
33 So he made their days vanish like a
      breath,
   and their years in terror.
34 When he killed them, they sought for
      him;
   they repented and sought God
      earnestly.
35 They remembered that God was their
      rock,
   the Most High God their redeemer.
36 But they flattered him with their
      mouths;
   they lied to him with their tongues.
37 Their heart was not steadfast toward
      him;
   they were not true to his covenant.
38 Yet he, being compassionate,
   forgave their iniquity,
   and did not destroy them;
   often he restrained his anger,
   and did not stir up all his wrath.
39 He remembered that they were but
      flesh,
   a wind that passes and does not come
      again.
40 How often they rebelled against him in
      the wilderness
   and grieved him in the desert!
41 They tested God again and again,
   and provoked the Holy One of Israel.
42 They did not keep in mind his power,
   or the day when he redeemed them
      from the foe;
43 when he displayed his signs in Egypt,
   and his miracles in the fields of Zoan.
44 He turned their rivers to blood,
   so that they could not drink of their
      streams.
45 He sent among them swarms of flies,
   which devoured them,
   and frogs, which destroyed them.

46 He gave their crops to the caterpillar,
    and the fruit of their labor to the
        locust.
47 He destroyed their vines with hail,
    and their sycamores with frost.
48 He gave over their cattle to the hail,
    and their flocks to thunderbolts.
49 He let loose on them his fierce anger,
    wrath, indignation, and distress,
    a company of destroying angels.
50 He made a path for his anger;
    he did not spare them from death,
    but gave their lives over to the
        plague.
51 He struck all the firstborn in Egypt,
    the first issue of their strength in the
        tents of Ham.
52 Then he led out his people like sheep,
    and guided them in the wilderness
        like a flock.
53 He led them in safety, so that they were
        not afraid;
    but the sea overwhelmed their
        enemies.
54 And he brought them to his holy hill,
    to the mountain that his right hand
        had won.
55 He drove out nations before them;
    he apportioned them for a possession
    and settled the tribes of Israel in their
        tents.

56 Yet they tested the Most High God,
    and rebelled against him.
    They did not observe his decrees,
57 but turned away and were faithless like
        their ancestors;
    they twisted like a treacherous bow.
58 For they provoked him to anger with
        their high places;
    they moved him to jealousy with their
        idols.
59 When God heard, he was full of wrath,
    and he utterly rejected Israel.
60 He abandoned his dwelling at Shiloh,
    the tent where he dwelt among
        mortals,
61 and delivered his power to captivity,
    his glory to the hand of the foe.
62 He gave his people to the sword,
    and vented his wrath on his heritage.

63 Fire devoured their young men,
    and their girls had no marriage song.
64 Their priests fell by the sword,
    and their widows made no
        lamentation.
65 Then the Lord awoke as from sleep,
    like a warrior shouting because of
        wine.
66 He put his adversaries to rout;
    he put them to everlasting disgrace.

67 He rejected the tent of Joseph,
    he did not choose the tribe of Ephraim;
68 but he chose the tribe of Judah,
    Mount Zion, which he loves.
69 He built his sanctuary like the high
        heavens,
    like the earth, which he has founded
        forever.
70 He chose his servant David,
    and took him from the sheepfolds;
71 from tending the nursing ewes he
        brought him
    to be the shepherd of his people
        Jacob,
    of Israel, his inheritance.
72 With upright heart he tended them,
    and guided them with skillful hand.

78.21–72. 21–32: Rebellion evokes God's *rage* (v. 21) and *anger* (vv. 21, 31), but God still graciously provides (vv. 23–29; Ex 16.4–36). **33–39:** There are consequences for disobedience (vv. 33–34), but God ultimately proves to be *compassionate* (v. 38). **40–72:** This section demonstrates the same pattern found in vv. 12–39: God's gracious activity (vv. 40–55; Ex 7.14–12.30) is followed by the people's rebellion (vv. 56–58), which evokes God's *wrath* (vv. 59–64; vv. 62–64 seem to allude to 1 Sam 4.10–11), which in turn is followed by God's grace (vv. 65–72). Verse 67 may reflect the destruction of the northern kingdom in 722 BCE. The concluding verses reflect the promises to the Davidic dynasty* (2 Sam 7.1–17; Ps 89.19–37).

PSALM 79

A Psalm of Asaph.

1 O God, the nations have come into your
        inheritance;
    they have defiled your holy temple;
    they have laid Jerusalem in ruins.

2 They have given the bodies of your
    servants
    to the birds of the air for food,
    the flesh of your faithful to the wild
        animals of the earth.
3 They have poured out their blood like
    water
    all around Jerusalem,
    and there was no one to bury them.
4 We have become a taunt to our
    neighbors,
    mocked and derided by those around
    us.
5 How long, O LORD? Will you be angry
    forever?
    Will your jealous wrath burn like fire?
6 Pour out your anger on the nations
    that do not know you,
    and on the kingdoms
    that do not call on your name.
7 For they have devoured Jacob
    and laid waste his habitation.

8 Do not remember against us the
    iniquities of our ancestors;
    let your compassion come speedily to
    meet us,
    for we are brought very low.
9 Help us, O God of our salvation,
    for the glory of your name;
    deliver us, and forgive our sins,
    for your name's sake.
10 Why should the nations say,
    "Where is their God?"
    Let the avenging of the outpoured blood
        of your servants
    be known among the nations before
        our eyes.
11 Let the groans of the prisoners come
    before you;
    according to your great power
    preserve those doomed to die.
12 Return sevenfold into the bosom of our
    neighbors
    the taunts with which they taunted
        you, O Lord!
13 Then we your people, the flock of your
    pasture,
    will give thanks to you forever;

from generation to generation we will
    recount your praise.

79.1–13: Help us, O God. A communal lament,* it probably originated with the destruction of the *temple* and *Jerusalem* (v. 1) in 587 BCE. **1–5:** Unburied bodies (vv. 2–3) compound the uncleanness represented by the entrance of *the nations* into the *temple* (v. 1). The people's status as a *taunt* (v. 4) anticipates the *taunts* against God (v. 12; 44.13). The questions in v. 5 communicate the people's doubt and fear (80.4). **6–12:** The petitions call for a redirecting of God's *anger* (v. 6) and a display of God's *compassion* (v. 8), despite the people's *sins* (v. 9). The question of *the nations* in v. 10 reflects the people's own doubt (42.10; 115.2). The petitions against the nations are motivated not simply by revenge but by a desire for deliverance from oppression. **13:** The pastoral imagery recalls 78.70–72 and anticipates 80.1.

<hr>

PSALM 80

To the leader: on Lilies, a Covenant. Of Asaph.
A Psalm.

1 Give ear, O Shepherd of Israel,
    you who lead Joseph like a flock!
    You who are enthroned upon the
        cherubim, shine forth
2   before Ephraim and Benjamin and
        Manasseh.
    Stir up your might,
    and come to save us!

3 Restore us, O God;
    let your face shine, that we may be
        saved.

4 O LORD God of hosts,
    how long will you be angry with your
        people's prayers?
5 You have fed them with the bread of
        tears,
    and given them tears to drink in full
        measure.
6 You make us the scorn*a* of our
        neighbors;
    our enemies laugh among
        themselves.

a Syr: Heb *strife*

7 Restore us, O God of hosts;
    let your face shine, that we may be
        saved.

8 You brought a vine out of Egypt;
    you drove out the nations and planted
        it.
9 You cleared the ground for it;
    it took deep root and filled the land.
10 The mountains were covered with its
        shade,
    the mighty cedars with its branches;
11 it sent out its branches to the sea,
    and its shoots to the River.
12 Why then have you broken down its
        walls,
    so that all who pass along the way
        pluck its fruit?
13 The boar from the forest ravages it,
    and all that move in the field feed on
        it.

14 Turn again, O God of hosts;
    look down from heaven, and see;
    have regard for this vine,
15   the stock that your right hand
        planted.[a]
16 They have burned it with fire, they have
        cut it down;[b]
    may they perish at the rebuke of your
        countenance.
17 But let your hand be upon the one at
        your right hand,
    the one whom you made strong for
        yourself.
18 Then we will never turn back from you;
    give us life, and we will call on your
        name.

19 Restore us, O LORD God of hosts;
    let your face shine, that we may be
        saved.

80.1–19: Restore us, O God. A fitting companion to Ps 79, it is also a communal lament.* While *Ephraim* and *Manasseh* in v. 2 suggest a northern origin (they were tribes of the northern kingdom; see 1 Kings 12), the psalm orients these references toward the destruction of Jerusalem. The primary structural feature is the refrain (vv. 3, 7, 19) and a variation thereof (v. 14). **1–3:** Calamity does not prevent the people from af-

firming God's sovereignty. *Shepherd* is a royal title (Ezek 34.1–16), and God is *enthroned. Shine forth* suggests the need for a theophany* (a manifestation of the deity in the natural order), a new appearing of God that will *restore* the people (v. 3; Num 6.24–26; Ps 4.6; 67.1). **4–7:** The question in v. 4 (74.10; 79.5) implies the following complaint. *Shepherd* literally means "feeder," but the food has not been appropriate (v. 5). **8–13:** The vine metaphor* recalls the Exodus, establishment in the land, and subsequent demise. **14–19:** *Turn* represents the same Hebrew as *restore.* God's turning must precede the people's restoration (90.13). The *one at your right hand* (v. 17) may be a future king, but v. 18 suggests that it probably refers to the people as a whole.

PSALM 81

To the leader: according to The Gittith.
Of Asaph.

1 Sing aloud to God our strength;
    shout for joy to the God of Jacob.
2 Raise a song, sound the tambourine,
    the sweet lyre with the harp.
3 Blow the trumpet at the new moon,
    at the full moon, on our festal day.
4 For it is a statute for Israel,
    an ordinance of the God of Jacob.
5 He made it a decree in Joseph,
    when he went out over[c] the land of
        Egypt.

    I hear a voice I had not known:
6 "I relieved your[d] shoulder of the
        burden;
    your[d] hands were freed from the
        basket.
7 In distress you called, and I rescued
        you;
    I answered you in the secret place of
        thunder;
    I tested you at the waters of Meribah.
                                    Selah
8 Hear, O my people, while I admonish
        you;
    O Israel, if you would but listen to
        me!

a Heb adds from verse 17 *and upon the one whom you made strong for yourself*   *b* Cn: Heb *it is cut down*   *c* Or *against*   *d* Heb *his*

9 There shall be no strange god among
you;
you shall not bow down to a foreign
god.
10 I am the LORD your God,
who brought you up out of the land
of Egypt.
Open your mouth wide and I will fill it.
11 "But my people did not listen to my
voice;
Israel would not submit to me.
12 So I gave them over to their stubborn
hearts,
to follow their own counsels.
13 O that my people would listen to me,
that Israel would walk in my ways!
14 Then I would quickly subdue their
enemies,
and turn my hand against their foes.
15 Those who hate the LORD would cringe
before him,
and their doom would last forever.
16 I would feed you[a] with the finest of the
wheat,
and with honey from the rock I would
satisfy you."

in the midst of the gods he holds
judgment:
2 "How long will you judge unjustly
and show partiality to the wicked?
Selah
3 Give justice to the weak and the
orphan;
maintain the right of the lowly and
the destitute.
4 Rescue the weak and the needy;
deliver them from the hand of the
wicked."

5 They have neither knowledge nor
understanding,
they walk around in darkness;
all the foundations of the earth are
shaken.

6 I say, "You are gods,
children of the Most High, all of you;
7 nevertheless, you shall die like mortals,
and fall like any prince."[b]

8 Rise up, O God, judge the earth;
for all the nations belong to you!

81.1–16: Hear, O my people. It is usually categorized
as a prophetic* exhortation* (see Ps 50). A prophet
may have originally spoken vv. 6–16 in a worship service. **1–5b:** The divine speech is introduced by a song
of praise. Mention of *the trumpet* (v. 3) suggests a
possible association with the festal season in the seventh month (Lev 23.23–24; Num 29.1–6). **5c:** The
new *voice* marks the beginning of God's word to the
people. **6–10:** The Exodus, Sinai, and wilderness are
recalled, including *Meribah* where Israel is said to have
tested God (Ex 17.7; Ps 95.8). *Hear* and *listen* are the
same Hebrew word (v. 8), phraseology recalling Deut
6.4, the "Shema," and anticipating vv. 11, 13. **11–16:**
By refusing to *listen* (v. 11), past generations chose
their own punishment (v. 12). God desires that the
current hearers not repeat their mistake (v. 13), so as
to thwart God's will to *feed* and *satisfy* (v. 16).

82.1–8: Give justice to the weak. It is often considered a prophetic* exhortation.* The divine speech
(vv. 2–4, 6–7, and perhaps v. 5), however, is addressed
to *the gods* rather than the people. The poem recounts
a trial in heaven, in which *the gods* are indicted (vv.
2–4), convicted (v. 5), and sentenced to death (vv.
6–7). **1:** Israel's *God* precludes the existence of other
gods (81.9–10). **2–4:** The exhortations serve as indictments. *The gods* have failed to administer *justice*, the
crucial criterion of which is whether the *weak* and
needy are enabled to live. The Hebrew "shpt," "to
judge, do justice," is the key word (vv. 1, 2, 3, 8). **5:**
When *justice* is not present, the whole *earth* is desta-
bilized and threatened (Isa 24.18–19; Ps 46.1–3).
6–7: *The gods* will reap the destruction their policies
have advanced. The *divine council* (v. 1; 1 Kings
22.19–23; Ps 58.1–2) is terminated. **8:** The demise of
the gods opens the way for *God* to *judge*, or better,
"establish justice" on *earth*, the role of a true sovereign
(72.1–7).

PSALM 82

A Psalm of Asaph.

1 God has taken his place in the divine
council;

a Cn Compare verse 16b: Heb *he would feed him*
b Or *fall as one man, O princes*

PSALM 83

A Song. A Psalm of Asaph.

1 O God, do not keep silence;
 do not hold your peace or be still,
  O God!
2 Even now your enemies are in tumult;
 those who hate you have raised their
  heads.
3 They lay crafty plans against your
  people;
 they consult together against those
  you protect.
4 They say, "Come, let us wipe them out
  as a nation;
 let the name of Israel be remembered
  no more."
5 They conspire with one accord;
 against you they make a covenant—
6 the tents of Edom and the Ishmaelites,
 Moab and the Hagrites,
7 Gebal and Ammon and Amalek,
 Philistia with the inhabitants of Tyre;
8 Assyria also has joined them;
 they are the strong arm of the
  children of Lot.   *Selah*

9 Do to them as you did to Midian,
 as to Sisera and Jabin at the Wadi
  Kishon,
10 who were destroyed at En-dor,
 who became dung for the ground.
11 Make their nobles like Oreb and Zeeb,
 all their princes like Zebah and
  Zalmunna,
12 who said, "Let us take the pastures of
  God
 for our own possession."

13 O my God, make them like whirling
  dust,[a]
 like chaff before the wind.
14 As fire consumes the forest,
 as the flame sets the mountains
  ablaze,
15 so pursue them with your tempest
 and terrify them with your
  hurricane.
16 Fill their faces with shame,
 so that they may seek your name,
  O LORD.

17 Let them be put to shame and dismayed
  forever;
 let them perish in disgrace.
18 Let them know that you alone,
 whose name is the LORD,
  are the Most High over all the earth.

83.1–18: That they may seek your name, O LORD. A communal prayer for help, its naming of the *enemies* (vv. 6–8) culminates with *Assyria*, suggesting an origin in the ninth to seventh centuries BCE. But the psalm itself may derive from a later period. **1:** *O God* begins and ends the verse, suggesting that God's presence is more encompassing than that of the many *enemies* (vv. 2, 6–8). **2–5:** Verses 2–3 recall the opposition to God and God's people in 2.1–3. **6–8:** The list of *enemies* may be hyperbolic,* suggesting pervasive opposition, or the names may be arranged geographically to indicate that the people are surrounded. *Assyria* may function symbolically as a reference to Israel's enemies, and was eventually heard this way. **9–12:** Past deliverance (Judg 4–8) grounds the petitions against the *enemies.* **13–18:** The violent-sounding petitions are motivated not so much by a desire for vengeance as a desire for justice, which will involve reconciliation (vv. 16, 18).

PSALM 84

To the leader: according to The Gittith.
Of the Korahites. A Psalm.

1 How lovely is your dwelling place,
  O LORD of hosts!
2 My soul longs, indeed it faints
  for the courts of the LORD;
 my heart and my flesh sing for joy
  to the living God.

3 Even the sparrow finds a home,
  and the swallow a nest for herself,
  where she may lay her young,
 at your altars, O LORD of hosts,
  my King and my God.
4 Happy are those who live in your house,
  ever singing your praise.   *Selah*

5 Happy are those whose strength is in you,
  in whose heart are the highways to
  Zion.[b]

---

a Or a tumbleweed   b Heb lacks to Zion

6 As they go through the valley of Baca
   they make it a place of springs;
   the early rain also covers it with
      pools.
7 They go from strength to strength;
   the God of gods will be seen in Zion.

8 O LORD God of hosts, hear my prayer;
   give ear, O God of Jacob!   Selah
9 Behold our shield, O God;
   look on the face of your anointed.

10 For a day in your courts is better
   than a thousand elsewhere.
   I would rather be a doorkeeper in the
      house of my God
   than live in the tents of wickedness.
11 For the LORD God is a sun and shield;
   he bestows favor and honor.
   No good thing does the LORD withhold
   from those who walk uprightly.
12 O LORD of hosts,
   happy is everyone who trusts in you.

84.1–12: Happy are those who live in your house. A song of Zion,⋆ it was probably used originally by pilgrims as they journeyed toward or visited Jerusalem. The focus finally is upon God (vv. 11–12). **1–4:** *LORD of hosts* (vv. 1, 3; see vv. 8, 12) is a title associated with the ark (24.7–10); it bespeaks God's sovereignty, as does the title, *King.* God's *house* (v. 4), the Temple,⋆ is envisioned by the psalmist as his or her true *home* (v. 3). **5–7:** *Happy* functions as a theme (vv. 4, 5, 12); the source of happiness is thoroughly God-centered (1.1; 2.12). Verses 5b–6a affirm that the pilgrims receive *strength* from God (v. 5) and transmit it to others (v. 6). If *Baca* is an actual place, the location is unknown. The word is similar to one meaning "tears." **8–12:** In v. 9, the psalmist prays for the king, whose palace adjoined the Temple. *Better* and *good things,* from the same Hebrew root, frame vv. 10–11. God is the source of all goodness (73.28), a conviction held by a pilgrim *who trusts in God.*

PSALM 85
To the leader. Of the Korahites. A Psalm.

1 LORD, you were favorable to your land;
   you restored the fortunes of Jacob.
2 You forgave the iniquity of your people;
   you pardoned all their sin.   Selah

3 You withdrew all your wrath;
   you turned from your hot anger.

4 Restore us again, O God of our
      salvation,
   and put away your indignation toward
      us.
5 Will you be angry with us forever?
   Will you prolong your anger to all
      generations?
6 Will you not revive us again,
   so that your people may rejoice
      in you?
7 Show us your steadfast love, O LORD,
   and grant us your salvation.

8 Let me hear what God the LORD will
      speak,
   for he will speak peace to his people,
   to his faithful, to those who turn to
      him in their hearts.[a]
9 Surely his salvation is at hand for those
      who fear him,
   that his glory may dwell in our land.

10 Steadfast love and faithfulness
      will meet;
   righteousness and peace will kiss
      each other.
11 Faithfulness will spring up from the
      ground,
   and righteousness will look down
      from the sky.
12 The LORD will give what is good,
   and our land will yield its increase.
13 Righteousness will go before him,
   and will make a path for his steps.

85.1–13: Steadfast love and faithfulness will meet. A communal prayer for help, it may have originated amid the disappointing circumstances of the early post-exilic era. **1–3:** *Restored the fortunes* probably denotes the return from exile (126.1; Jer 30.3), which the prophets⋆ proclaimed was precipitated by God's forgiveness (Isa 40.1–2). **4–7:** But the return was not as glorious as had been hoped. The need for a fuller restoration motivates the petitions, which are framed by *salvation* (vv. 4, 7; see v. 9). **8–13:** While vv. 8–9 sug-

a Gk: Heb *but let them not turn back to folly*

gest the necessity of a response, the promise depicted in vv. 10–13 exceeds what the people could ever deserve. *Steadfast love* and *faithfulness* lie at the essence of God's character, and were revealed preeminently following God's gracious forgiveness of the people (Ex 34.6). *Righteousness* (vv. 10, 11, 13) describes the essence of God's will. Verse 11 suggests the whole earth, from *ground* to *sky*, will be permeated by God's gracious presence and purposes, yielding *what is good* (v. 12; 84.11).

PSALM 86

A Prayer of David.

1 Incline your ear, O LORD, and answer me,
    for I am poor and needy.
2 Preserve my life, for I am devoted to you;
    save your servant who trusts in you.
  You are my God; ³be gracious to me, O Lord,
    for to you do I cry all day long.
4 Gladden the soul of your servant,
    for to you, O Lord, I lift up my soul.
5 For you, O Lord, are good and forgiving,
    abounding in steadfast love to all who call on you.
6 Give ear, O LORD, to my prayer;
    listen to my cry of supplication.
7 In the day of my trouble I call on you,
    for you will answer me.

8 There is none like you among the gods, O Lord,
    nor are there any works like yours.
9 All the nations you have made shall come
    and bow down before you, O Lord,
    and shall glorify your name.
10 For you are great and do wondrous things;
    you alone are God.
11 Teach me your way, O LORD,
    that I may walk in your truth;
    give me an undivided heart to revere your name.
12 I give thanks to you, O Lord my God,
    with my whole heart,
    and I will glorify your name forever.

13 For great is your steadfast love toward me;
    you have delivered my soul from the depths of Sheol.

14 O God, the insolent rise up against me;
    a band of ruffians seeks my life,
    and they do not set you before them.
15 But you, O Lord, are a God merciful and gracious,
    slow to anger and abounding in steadfast love and faithfulness.
16 Turn to me and be gracious to me;
    give your strength to your servant;
    save the child of your serving girl.
17 Show me a sign of your favor,
    so that those who hate me may see it and be put to shame,
    because you, LORD, have helped me and comforted me.

86.1–17: Great is your steadfast love. A prayer for help, its petitions and complaints (vv. 1–7, 14–17) surround a core of praise and affirmation (vv. 8–13) in a unique arrangement that departs from the usual culmination in praise. **1–7:** The psalmist belongs among those whom God especially attends, the *poor and needy* (v. 1; 9.9, 18; 10.12; 82.2–3) who entrust their lives to God (v. 2). To *lift up my soul* means essentially to trust, to offer life to God's keeping (25.1; 143.8). **8–13:** *Name* (vv. 9, 11, 12) focuses attention on God's character, which is unsurpassable (vv. 8, 10). God's essence is *steadfast love* (v. 13; see vv. 5, 15), which evokes the psalmist's gratitude. **14–17:** The renewed petitions are grounded in the conviction that God will act in a way similar to the time when God revealed the divine character to Moses (v. 15; Ex 34.6). Like Moses, the psalmist is God's *servant* (vv. 4, 16; 116.16).

PSALM 87

Of the Korahites. A Psalm. A Song.

1 On the holy mount stands the city he founded;
2   the LORD loves the gates of Zion
    more than all the dwellings of Jacob.
3 Glorious things are spoken of you,
    O city of God.   *Selah*

4 Among those who know me I mention Rahab and Babylon;

Philistia too, and Tyre, with
  Ethiopia[a]—
"This one was born there," they say.

5 And of Zion it shall be said,
  "This one and that one were born in
    it";
  for the Most High himself will
    establish it.
6 The LORD records, as he registers the
    peoples,
  "This one was born there."   *Selah*

7 Singers and dancers alike say,
  "All my springs are in you."

87.1–7: Born in Zion.* A song of *Zion*, it celebrates
Jerusalem as God's place (vv. 1–2), but it also suggests
that Jerusalem represents God's claim on the whole
world and its peoples (vv. 3–7; Ps 48). **1–2:** Jerusalem
occupies a *holy mount* or hill (2.6; 48.1). **3–7:** Praise
of *Zion* in vv. 3, 7 encompasses the verses that share
the word *born*. The speaker in vv. 4–5 could be viewed
as God or a personified* *Zion*. It is remarkable that
traditional enemies look to Jerusalem as their home,
suggesting God's claim on the whole world and its
peoples (Gen 12.3; Isa 19.23–25).

PSALM 88

A Song. A Psalm of the Korahites. To the leader:
  according to Mahalath Leannoth. A Maskil
  of Heman the Ezrahite.

1 O LORD, God of my salvation,
  when, at night, I cry out in your
    presence,
2 let my prayer come before you;
  incline your ear to my cry.

3 For my soul is full of troubles,
  and my life draws near to Sheol.
4 I am counted among those who go
    down to the Pit;
  I am like those who have no help,
5 like those forsaken among the dead,
  like the slain that lie in the grave,
  like those whom you remember
    no more,
  for they are cut off from your hand.
6 You have put me in the depths of the
    Pit,
  in the regions dark and deep.

7 Your wrath lies heavy upon me,
  and you overwhelm me with all your
    waves.   *Selah*

8 You have caused my companions to
    shun me;
  you have made me a thing of horror
    to them.
  I am shut in so that I cannot escape;
9   my eye grows dim through sorrow.
  Every day I call on you, O LORD;
  I spread out my hands to you.
10 Do you work wonders for the dead?
  Do the shades rise up to praise you?
                                   Selah
11 Is your steadfast love declared in the
    grave,
  or your faithfulness in Abaddon?
12 Are your wonders known in the
    darkness,
  or your saving help in the land of
    forgetfulness?

13 But I, O LORD, cry out to you;
  in the morning my prayer comes
    before you.
14 O LORD, why do you cast me off?
  Why do you hide your face from me?
15 Wretched and close to death from my
    youth up,
  I suffer your terrors; I am desperate.[b]
16 Your wrath has swept over me;
  your dread assaults destroy me.
17 They surround me like a flood all day
    long;
  from all sides they close in on me.
18 You have caused friend and neighbor to
    shun me;
  my companions are in darkness.

88.1–18: In the darkness. Unique among the prayers
for help, it contains no explicit movement toward trust
or praise. Three different Hebrew words for *cry out* or
call mark the beginning of its three sections (vv. 1, 9b,
13); each is accompanied by a chronological reference. **1–9a:** Trust is implied in v. 1 and by the fact that
the psalmist continues to pray. *Sheol** and *the Pit*, the
realm of the dead, indicate the urgency of the situation. Abandonment by God (vv. 3–7; 22.1) is accom-

a Or *Nubia*; Heb *Cush*   *b* Meaning of Heb uncertain panied by human isolation (v. 8; 31.11; 38.11). **9b–12:** All the questions in vv. 10–12 are about death, but they imply the psalmist's conviction that God ultimately wills and works for life. **13–18:** Questions continue (v. 14), functioning as in vv. 10–12 as a complaint. Verse 18 recalls v. 8, and the final word of the psalm captures its pervasive mood—*darkness* (see vv. 6, 12).

PSALM 89

A Maskil of Ethan the Ezrahite.

1 I will sing of your steadfast love,
      O Lord,*a* forever;
   with my mouth I will proclaim your
      faithfulness to all generations.
2 I declare that your steadfast love is
      established forever;
   your faithfulness is as firm as the
      heavens.

3 You said, "I have made a covenant with
      my chosen one,
   I have sworn to my servant David:
4 'I will establish your descendants
      forever,
   and build your throne for all
      generations.' "   *Selah*

5 Let the heavens praise your wonders,
      O Lord,
   your faithfulness in the assembly of
      the holy ones.
6 For who in the skies can be compared
      to the Lord?
   Who among the heavenly beings is
      like the Lord,
7 a God feared in the council of the holy
      ones,
   great and awesome*b* above all that
      are around him?
8 O Lord God of hosts,
      who is as mighty as you, O Lord?
   Your faithfulness surrounds you.
9 You rule the raging of the sea;
      when its waves rise, you still them.
10 You crushed Rahab like a carcass;
      you scattered your enemies with your
      mighty arm.
11 The heavens are yours, the earth also is
      yours;

the world and all that is in it—you
      have founded them.
12 The north and the south*c*—you created
      them;
   Tabor and Hermon joyously praise
      your name.
13 You have a mighty arm;
      strong is your hand, high your right
      hand.
14 Righteousness and justice are the
      foundation of your throne;
   steadfast love and faithfulness go
      before you.
15 Happy are the people who know the
      festal shout,
   who walk, O Lord, in the light of
      your countenance;
16 they exult in your name all day long,
      and extol*d* your righteousness.
17 For you are the glory of their strength;
      by your favor our horn is exalted.
18 For our shield belongs to the Lord,
      our king to the Holy One of Israel.

89.1–52: Where is your steadfast love of old? A royal psalm, it contains praise (vv. 1–2, 5–18) and complaint (vv. 38–51). Verses 3–4, 19–37 are offered as divine speech. It probably originated in response to the destruction of Jerusalem and disappearance of the monarchy in 587 BCE. **1–4:** The two key words appear twice in vv. 1–2: *steadfast love* (see vv. 14, 24, 28, 33, 49) and *faithfulness* (see vv. 5, 8, 14, 24, 33, 49). The focus on God (vv. 1–2) is continued in vv. 5–18, while the focus on the Davidic *covenant** (vv. 3–4) continues in vv. 19–37. **5–18:** Among the *heavenly beings, the Lord* is preeminent (vv. 5–8), for God tamed the chaotic powers (vv. 9–10), claimed the whole world (vv. 11–12), and now rules rightly and lovingly (vv. 13–14; 97.2). The appropriate response is worship (vv. 15–18).

19 Then you spoke in a vision to your
      faithful one, and said:
   "I have set the crown*e* on one who is
      mighty,
   I have exalted one chosen from the
      people.

a Gk: Heb *the steadfast love of the Lord*   *b* Gk Syr:
Heb *greatly awesome*   *c* Or *Zaphon and Yamin*
d Cn: Heb *are exalted in*   *e* Cn: Heb *help*

20 I have found my servant David;
　　with my holy oil I have anointed
　　　him;
21 my hand shall always remain with him;
　　my arm also shall strengthen him.
22 The enemy shall not outwit him,
　　the wicked shall not humble him.
23 I will crush his foes before him
　　and strike down those who hate him.
24 My faithfulness and steadfast love shall
　　　be with him;
　　and in my name his horn shall be
　　　exalted.
25 I will set his hand on the sea
　　and his right hand on the rivers.
26 He shall cry to me, 'You are my Father,
　　my God, and the Rock of my
　　　salvation!'
27 I will make him the firstborn,
　　the highest of the kings of the earth.
28 Forever I will keep my steadfast love for
　　　him,
　　and my covenant with him will stand
　　　firm.
29 I will establish his line forever,
　　and his throne as long as the heavens
　　　endure.
30 If his children forsake my law
　　and do not walk according to my
　　　ordinances,
31 if they violate my statutes
　　and do not keep my commandments,
32 then I will punish their transgression
　　　with the rod
　　and their iniquity with scourges;
33 but I will not remove from him my
　　　steadfast love,
　　or be false to my faithfulness.
34 I will not violate my covenant,
　　or alter the word that went forth from
　　　my lips.
35 Once and for all I have sworn by my
　　　holiness;
　　I will not lie to David.
36 His line shall continue forever,
　　and his throne endure before me like
　　　the sun.
37 It shall be established forever like the
　　　moon,
　　an enduring witness in the skies."
　　　　　　　　　　　　　　　　Selah

38 But now you have spurned and rejected
　　　him;
　　you are full of wrath against your
　　　anointed.
39 You have renounced the covenant with
　　　your servant;
　　you have defiled his crown in
　　　the dust.
40 You have broken through all his walls;
　　you have laid his strongholds in ruins.
41 All who pass by plunder him;
　　he has become the scorn of his
　　　neighbors.
42 You have exalted the right hand of his
　　　foes;
　　you have made all his enemies
　　　rejoice.
43 Moreover, you have turned back the
　　　edge of his sword,
　　and you have not supported him in
　　　battle.
44 You have removed the scepter from his
　　　hand,[a]
　　and hurled his throne to the ground.
45 You have cut short the days of his
　　　youth;
　　you have covered him with shame.
　　　　　　　　　　　　　　　　Selah

46 How long, O LORD? Will you hide
　　　yourself forever?
　　How long will your wrath burn like
　　　fire?
47 Remember how short my time is—[b]
　　for what vanity you have created all
　　　mortals!
48 Who can live and never see death?
　　Who can escape the power of Sheol?
　　　　　　　　　　　　　　　　Selah

49 Lord, where is your steadfast love of
　　　old,
　　which by your faithfulness you swore
　　　to David?
50 Remember, O Lord, how your servant is
　　　taunted;
　　how I bear in my bosom the insults of
　　　the peoples,[c]

---

a Cn: Heb *removed his cleanness*   b Meaning of Heb
uncertain   c Cn: Heb *bosom all of many peoples*

51 with which your enemies taunt,
        O LORD,
    with which they taunted the footsteps
        of your anointed.

52 Blessed be the LORD forever.
        Amen and Amen.

89.19–52. 19–37: Recalling 2 Sam 7, Nathan's oracle*
to David, these verses rehearse the promises of the
covenant (vv. 28, 34) with *David* and *his children*. The
repetition of *forever* (vv. 28, 29, 35, 36) makes for a
jarring transition at v. 38. 38–51: The supposedly eternal *covenant* has been *renounced* (v. 39), and God's
*anointed** has been *rejected* (v. 38), precipitating the
questions and petitions summarized in v. 49. 52: The
doxology closes Book III, leaving the question of v. 49
unanswered and inviting the reader forward into Book
IV (see Introduction).

BOOK FOUR

PSALM 90
A Prayer of Moses, the man of God.

1 Lord, you have been our dwelling place*a*
    in all generations.
2 Before the mountains were brought
        forth,
    or ever you had formed the earth and
        the world,
    from everlasting to everlasting you are
        God.

3 You turn us*b* back to dust,
    and say, "Turn back, you mortals."
4 For a thousand years in your sight
    are like yesterday when it is past,
    or like a watch in the night.

5 You sweep them away; they are like a
        dream,
    like grass that is renewed in the
        morning;
6 in the morning it flourishes and is
        renewed;
    in the evening it fades and withers.

7 For we are consumed by your anger;
    by your wrath we are overwhelmed.

8 You have set our iniquities before you,
    our secret sins in the light of your
        countenance.
9 For all our days pass away under your
        wrath;
    our years come to an end*c* like a sigh.
10 The days of our life are seventy years,
    or perhaps eighty, if we are strong;
    even then their span*d* is only toil and
        trouble;
    they are soon gone, and we fly away.

11 Who considers the power of your anger?
    Your wrath is as great as the fear that
        is due you.
12 So teach us to count our days
    that we may gain a wise heart.

13 Turn, O LORD! How long?
    Have compassion on your servants!
14 Satisfy us in the morning with your
        steadfast love,
    so that we may rejoice and be glad all
        our days.
15 Make us glad as many days as you have
        afflicted us,
    and as many years as we have seen
        evil.
16 Let your work be manifest to your
        servants,
    and your glorious power to their
        children.
17 Let the favor of the Lord our God be
        upon us,
    and prosper for us the work of our
        hands—
    O prosper the work of our hands!

90.1–17: Satisfy us with your steadfast love. Often
categorized as a communal prayer for help or a wisdom psalm, it begins Book IV by offering a realistic but
hopeful response to the despairing questions of
89.46–49. In so doing, this psalm responds to the crisis
of exile. This is the only psalm attributed to *Moses* (see
Introduction). 1–2: In contrast to the transience of human life and the homelessness of exile, God is an eter-

---

a Another reading is *our refuge*   *b* Heb *humankind*
c Syr: Heb *we bring our years to an end*   *d* Cn Compare
Gk Syr Jerome Tg: Heb *pride*

nal *dwelling place*. **3–6:** Both vocabulary (*years, yesterday, night, morning, evening*) and poetic structure (for instance, the movement from night to *morning* to *evening* in vv. 5–6) evoke the passage of time, which reveals human transience. **7–11:** The word *wrath* frames this section. It communicates the way that humans experience finitude. **12:** The psalmist asks, in essence, "Teach us to accept each day as a gift," a request that marks the transition from despair to hope. **13–17:** The plea that God *turn* recalls Moses' intercession in Ex 32.12; v. 13b recalls Deut 32.36; and *steadfast love* (v. 14) recalls Ex 34.6–7. The petitions imply trust in God's forgiveness and God's redemption of human time, words which are now associated with joy and gladness. Human time and transience, when entrusted to God, need not be sources of despair. With God, hope is possible.

PSALM 91

1 You who live in the shelter of the Most
        High,
    who abide in the shadow of the
        Almighty,[a]
2 will say to the LORD, "My refuge and
        my fortress;
    my God, in whom I trust."
3 For he will deliver you from the snare of
        the fowler
    and from the deadly pestilence;
4 he will cover you with his pinions,
    and under his wings you will find
        refuge;
    his faithfulness is a shield and
        buckler.
5 You will not fear the terror of the night,
    or the arrow that flies by day,
6 or the pestilence that stalks in darkness,
    or the destruction that wastes at
        noonday.

7 A thousand may fall at your side,
    ten thousand at your right hand,
    but it will not come near you.
8 You will only look with your eyes
    and see the punishment of the
        wicked.

9 Because you have made the LORD your
        refuge,[b]
    the Most High your dwelling place,

10 no evil shall befall you,
    no scourge come near your tent.
11 For he will command his angels
        concerning you
    to guard you in all your ways.
12 On their hands they will bear you up,
    so that you will not dash your foot
        against a stone.
13 You will tread on the lion and the adder,
    the young lion and the serpent you
        will trample under foot.
14 Those who love me, I will deliver;
    I will protect those who know my
        name.
15 When they call to me, I will answer
        them;
    I will be with them in trouble,
    I will rescue them and honor them.
16 With long life I will satisfy them,
    and show them my salvation.

91.1–16: With long life I will satisfy them. A psalm of trust, it seems to respond to the closing petitions of 90.13–17 (compare 90.14 and 91.16). **1–2:** *Trust* characterizes the whole, and *refuge* becomes thematic (see vv. 4, 9; 2.12; 5.11). **3–13:** An extended profession of faith articulates the reasons to *trust*. In the most threatening of circumstances—persecution (v. 3), disease (vv. 5–6), war (vv. 7–8)—God *will deliver* (v. 3). God's *angels* or "messengers" provide constant protection (Ex 23.20; Lk 4.9–12). **14–16:** Divine speech concludes the psalm in an emphatic manner, reinforcing the reasons to *trust* in vv. 3–13.

PSALM 92

A Psalm. A Song for the Sabbath Day.

1 It is good to give thanks to the LORD,
    to sing praises to your name, O Most
        High;
2 to declare your steadfast love in the
        morning,
    and your faithfulness by night,
3 to the music of the lute and the harp,
    to the melody of the lyre.

a Traditional rendering of Heb *Shaddai*   *b* Cn: Heb
Because you, LORD, are my refuge; you have made

4 For you, O LORD, have made me glad
    by your work;
  at the works of your hands I sing for
    joy.

5 How great are your works, O LORD!
  Your thoughts are very deep!
6 The dullard cannot know,
  the stupid cannot understand this:
7 though the wicked sprout like grass
  and all evildoers flourish,
  they are doomed to destruction forever,
8 but you, O LORD, are on high forever.
9 For your enemies, O LORD,
  for your enemies shall perish;
  all evildoers shall be scattered.

10 But you have exalted my horn like that
  of the wild ox;
  you have poured over me*a* fresh oil.
11 My eyes have seen the downfall of my
  enemies;
  my ears have heard the doom of my
  evil assailants.

12 The righteous flourish like the palm
  tree,
  and grow like a cedar in Lebanon.
13 They are planted in the house of the
  LORD;
  they flourish in the courts of our
  God.
14 In old age they still produce fruit;
  they are always green and full of sap,
15 showing that the LORD is upright;
  he is my rock, and there is no
  unrighteousness in him.

92.1–15: How great are your works, O LORD! A song of thanksgiving, it celebrates the experience of *the righteous* (v. 12) in general more than a particular deliverance. This orientation gives it an instructional tone. It is the only psalm assigned *for the Sabbath Day*, though the reason is unclear. **1–4:** Gratitude to God takes the form of constantly celebrating God's character—*steadfast love* and *faithfulness* (v. 2; Ex 34.6)—and God's *work* (v. 4), perhaps a reference to creation, which was also associated with *the sabbath* (Gen 2.1–3; Ex 20.8–11). **5–9:** Repeating *works* from v. 4, the celebration continues in v. 5. References to *the wicked* and God's *enemies* surround the central v. 8,

which asserts God's sovereignty, anticipating 93.4. **10–15:** *Evildoers* may *flourish* briefly (v. 7), but *the righteous* will *flourish* (vv. 12–13) permanently. Their stable rootedness in God's presence assures a vitality and fruitfulness that witnesses to God's righteousness (v. 15; 1.3; 52.8).

PSALM 93

1 The LORD is king, he is robed in
  majesty;
  the LORD is robed, he is girded with
  strength.
  He has established the world; it shall
  never be moved;
2 your throne is established from
  of old;
  you are from everlasting.

3 The floods have lifted up, O LORD,
  the floods have lifted up their voice;
  the floods lift up their roaring.
4 More majestic than the thunders of
  mighty waters,
  more majestic than the waves*b* of the
  sea,
  majestic on high is the LORD!

5 Your decrees are very sure;
  holiness befits your house,
  O LORD, forevermore.

93.1–5: The LORD is king. It is the first in a collection (Ps 93, 95–99) which explicitly proclaims that God *is king*. In its present setting following Ps 89 and 90, the collection proclaims the LORD's kingship in response to the crisis of the disappearance of the Davidic monarchy. **1–2:** *Girded* usually suggests dress for battle, and creation (v. 1c) is often depicted as divine conquest of chaos. **3–4:** The floods represent the chaotic forces that the LORD has tamed and ordered, thus demonstrating sovereignty. **5:** Kings were responsible for establishing justice and righteousness (72.1–7; 97.2) by their *decrees*. God's *house* is apparently the Temple.* The enthronement collection returns to the theme of *holiness* as it concludes (99.3, 5, 9).

---

a Syr: Meaning of Heb uncertain   *b* Cn: Heb *majestic are the waves*

PSALM 94

1 O LORD, you God of vengeance,
   you God of vengeance, shine forth!
2 Rise up, O judge of the earth;
   give to the proud what they deserve!
3 O LORD, how long shall the wicked,
   how long shall the wicked exult?

4 They pour out their arrogant words;
   all the evildoers boast.
5 They crush your people, O LORD,
   and afflict your heritage.
6 They kill the widow and the stranger,
   they murder the orphan,
7 and they say, "The LORD does not see;
   the God of Jacob does not perceive."

8 Understand, O dullest of the people;
   fools, when will you be wise?
9 He who planted the ear, does he not
   hear?
   He who formed the eye, does he
   not see?
10 He who disciplines the nations,
   he who teaches knowledge to
      humankind,
   does he not chastise?
11 The LORD knows our thoughts,[a]
   that they are but an empty breath.

12 Happy are those whom you discipline,
   O LORD,
   and whom you teach out of your law,
13 giving them respite from days of
      trouble,
   until a pit is dug for the wicked.
14 For the LORD will not forsake his
      people;
   he will not abandon his heritage;
15 for justice will return to the righteous,
   and all the upright in heart will follow
      it.

16 Who rises up for me against the
      wicked?
   Who stands up for me against
      evildoers?
17 If the LORD had not been my help,
   my soul would soon have lived in the
      land of silence.

18 When I thought, "My foot is slipping,"
   your steadfast love, O LORD, held me
   up.
19 When the cares of my heart are many,
   your consolations cheer my soul.
20 Can wicked rulers be allied with you,
   those who contrive mischief by
      statute?
21 They band together against the life of
      the righteous,
   and condemn the innocent to death.
22 But the LORD has become my
      stronghold,
   and my God the rock of my refuge.
23 He will repay them for their iniquity
   and wipe them out for their
      wickedness;
   the LORD our God will wipe
      them out.

94.1–23: Your steadfast love, O LORD, held me up.
Starting like a communal prayer for help, it takes on
an instructional tone as it addresses *fools* (vv. 8–11)
and *the righteous* (vv. 14–15). A final prayer (vv.
18–21) is framed by two professions of faith (vv.
16–17, 22–23). Although it seems to interrupt the enthronement collection, its theme of *justice* (v. 15; see
v. 2) is congruent with Ps 93, 95–99. **1–7:** *Vengeance*
serves the function of establishing *justice*. To create
justice for the *widow*, *stranger*, and *orphan* (v. 6), God
must confront oppressors, who view themselves as un-
accountable (v. 7; 10.4, 11; 73.11). **8–11:** The questions in vv. 8–9 respond to the evildoers' assertion in
v. 7. God does *see* (v. 9; 10.14) and God *knows* (v. 11).
12–15: Verse 12 recalls 1.1–2. Despite current appearances, *justice* will prevail. **16–17:** The psalmist answers her or his own questions. Without God's *help*,
she or he would be dead. **18–21:** God's *steadfast love*
(90.14; 92.2) and *consolations* (vv. 18–19) contrast
with the ruthlessness of the *wicked* (vv. 20–21; see vv.
5–7). **22–23:** While v. 12 recalls Ps 1, *refuge* recalls
2.12. Entrusting life to God yields hope.

PSALM 95

1 O come, let us sing to the LORD;
   let us make a joyful noise to the rock
      of our salvation!

---

a Heb *the thoughts of humankind*

2 Let us come into his presence with
thanksgiving;
let us make a joyful noise to him with
songs of praise!
3 For the LORD is a great God,
and a great King above all gods.
4 In his hand are the depths of the earth;
the heights of the mountains are his
also.
5 The sea is his, for he made it,
and the dry land, which his hands
have formed.

6 O come, let us worship and bow down,
let us kneel before the LORD,
our Maker!
7 For he is our God,
and we are the people of his pasture,
and the sheep of his hand.

O that today you would listen to his
voice!
8 Do not harden your hearts, as at
Meribah,
as on the day at Massah in the
wilderness,
9 when your ancestors tested me,
and put me to the proof, though they
had seen my work.
10 For forty years I loathed that generation
and said, "They are a people whose
hearts go astray,
and they do not regard my ways."
11 Therefore in my anger I swore,
"They shall not enter my rest."

95.1–11: O that you would listen! Part of the enthronement collection (see Ps 93), its unique ending
with divine speech reflects a prophetic* exhortation*
(see Ps 81). 1–5: The invitations to *praise* are appropriate for hailing a sovereign, anticipating the title *King*
in v. 3. *Thanksgiving* could designate the offering of a
sacrifice or verbal gratitude (50.23; 100.4). The repetition of *hands* (vv. 4–5) symbolizes God's encompassing ownership of the cosmos. 6–7b: Further invitations and reasons for praise feature God's ownership
of *the people* (100.3). *Maker* recalls both creation
(104.24) and exodus (see 118.24 where "made"
would be better translated as "acted" and alludes to
the Exodus). 7c: This line culminates vv. 1–7b and introduces the following divine speech. 8–11: Recalling

events *in the wilderness* following the Exodus (Ex
17.1–7), the speech calls current hearers (see *today* in
v. 7c) to trust rather than test God.

PSALM 96

1 O sing to the LORD a new song;
sing to the LORD, all the earth.
2 Sing to the LORD, bless his name;
tell of his salvation from day to day.
3 Declare his glory among the nations,
his marvelous works among all the
peoples.
4 For great is the LORD, and greatly to be
praised;
he is to be revered above all gods.
5 For all the gods of the peoples are idols,
but the LORD made the heavens.
6 Honor and majesty are before him;
strength and beauty are in his
sanctuary.

7 Ascribe to the LORD, O families of the
peoples,
ascribe to the LORD glory and
strength.
8 Ascribe to the LORD the glory due his
name;
bring an offering, and come into his
courts.
9 Worship the LORD in holy splendor;
tremble before him, all the earth.

10 Say among the nations, "The LORD is
king!
The world is firmly established; it
shall never be moved.
He will judge the peoples with
equity."
11 Let the heavens be glad, and let the
earth rejoice;
let the sea roar, and all that fills it;
12 let the field exult, and everything in
it.
Then shall all the trees of the forest
sing for joy
13 before the LORD; for he is coming,
for he is coming to judge the earth.
He will judge the world with
righteousness,
and the peoples with his truth.

96.1–13: A new song. An enthronement psalm (see Ps 93), its use in Temple* worship is attested in 1 Chr 16.22–33. **1–3:** The *new song* (v. 1; 98.1) recalls the former song, which the people sang in response to the Exodus (Ex 15.1–21). Psalm 96 may have arisen or been used to respond to the return from exile (see Isa 42.10), as well as to anticipate future acts of deliverance (v. 13). **4–6:** Among all supposed authorities— *the gods—the LORD* is preeminent (97.9). **7–10a:** Verses 7–9 reproduce 29.1–2, except here they are addressed to *families of the peoples.* Verse 10a invites the explicit proclamation of God's reign. **10b–c:** The creator (93.1) will also *judge,* or better, "establish justice" (see v. 13). **11–12a:** All the cosmic elements are invited to acknowledge God's reign (98.4, 7–8). **12b–13:** The hallmarks of God's royal policy are justice and *righteousness* (97.1; 98.9; 99.4).

PSALM 97

1 The LORD is king! Let the earth rejoice;
    let the many coastlands be glad!
2 Clouds and thick darkness are all
        around him;
    righteousness and justice are the
        foundation of his throne.
3 Fire goes before him,
    and consumes his adversaries on
        every side.
4 His lightnings light up the world;
    the earth sees and trembles.
5 The mountains melt like wax before the
        LORD,
    before the Lord of all the earth.

6 The heavens proclaim his righteousness;
    and all the peoples behold his glory.
7 All worshipers of images are put
        to shame,
    those who make their boast in
        worthless idols;
    all gods bow down before him.
8 Zion hears and is glad,
    and the towns*a* of Judah rejoice,
    because of your judgments, O God.
9 For you, O LORD, are most high over all
        the earth;
    you are exalted far above all gods.

10 The LORD loves those who hate*b* evil;
    he guards the lives of his faithful;

he rescues them from the hand of the
        wicked.
11 Light dawns*c* for the righteous,
    and joy for the upright in heart.
12 Rejoice in the LORD, O you righteous,
    and give thanks to his holy name!

97.1–12: Righteousness and justice are the foundations of God's throne. Similar in many ways to the other enthronement psalms (see Ps 93), it is also distinctive, featuring the themes of *joy*/gladness (vv. 1, 8, 11–12) and *righteousness* (vv. 2, 6; see vv. 11–12). **1–5:** The language of theophany,* a description of God's appearing in the natural order (18.7–15; 50.1–6), communicates God's cosmic claim, which is characterized by *righteousness and justice* (89.14; 96.13). **6–9:** Although not all people acknowledge God's sovereignty (v. 7), *the heavens* do and so do *Zion** and *Judah* (v. 8). No other claim can rival God's (v. 9; 96.4–5). **10–12:** Verse 10a should probably be understood as an admonition to God's people (see note b) to *hate evil.* The admonition is followed by promises to the *faithful* (vv. 10b–11) that are in accordance with God's *justice* (see vv. 2, 8). The appropriate response is joy and gratitude (v. 12).

PSALM 98
A Psalm.

1 O sing to the LORD a new song,
    for he has done marvelous things.
    His right hand and his holy arm
        have gotten him victory.
2 The LORD has made known his victory;
    he has revealed his vindication in the
        sight of the nations.
3 He has remembered his steadfast love
        and faithfulness
    to the house of Israel.
    All the ends of the earth have seen
        the victory of our God.

4 Make a joyful noise to the LORD, all the
        earth;
    break forth into joyous song and sing
        praises.
5 Sing praises to the LORD with the lyre,
    with the lyre and the sound of melody.

a Heb *daughters*   *b* Cn: Heb *You who love the LORD hate*   *c* Gk Syr Jerome: Heb *is sown*

6 With trumpets and the sound of the
        horn
    make a joyful noise before the King,
        the LORD.

7 Let the sea roar, and all that fills it;
    the world and those who live in it.
8 Let the floods clap their hands;
    let the hills sing together for joy
9 at the presence of the LORD, for he is
        coming
    to judge the earth.
    He will judge the world with
        righteousness,
        and the peoples with equity.

98.1–9: Make a joyful noise before the King. Part of the enthronement collection (see Ps 93), it recalls especially Ps 96 (compare 96.1 and 98.1). **1–3:** Each of these verses speaks of *victory*, usually translated "salvation." The word recalls the former song, which the people sang after the Exodus (see *salvation* in Ex 15.2). God's gift of life to the people reveals God's *steadfast love and faithfulness* (Ex 34.6; Ps 89.14; 92.2). **4–6:** *Make a joyful noise* frames the invitation to *all the earth* (100.1) to acknowledge God as *King*. **7–9:** People are to be joined by the created order in acknowledging God's reign (96.11–12), which is characterized by justice, *righteousness*, and *equity* (96.10, 13; 97.2).

PSALM 99

1 The LORD is king; let the peoples
        tremble!
    He sits enthroned upon the
        cherubim; let the earth quake!
2 The LORD is great in Zion;
    he is exalted over all the peoples.
3 Let them praise your great and
        awesome name.
    Holy is he!
4 Mighty King,[a] lover of justice,
    you have established equity;
    you have executed justice
    and righteousness in Jacob.
5 Extol the LORD our God;
    worship at his footstool.
    Holy is he!

6 Moses and Aaron were among his
        priests,

Samuel also was among those who
        called on his name.
    They cried to the LORD, and he
        answered them.
7 He spoke to them in the pillar of cloud;
    they kept his decrees,
    and the statutes that he gave them.

8 O LORD our God, you answered them;
    you were a forgiving God to them,
    but an avenger of their wrongdoings.
9 Extol the LORD our God,
    and worship at his holy mountain;
    for the LORD our God is holy.

99.1–9: Holy is the LORD. Culminating the collection of enthronement psalms (see Ps 93), it highlights one of the themes of the collection—holiness (vv. 3, 5, 9; 93.5; 96.9; 97.12; 98.1). **1–3:** Trembling and quaking are consistent with the fundamental sense of holiness, which connotes an overwhelming presence that evokes awe and necessitates separation between God and humans (Ex 19.23). *The cherubim** were mythical creatures who attended the ark (see v. 5). **4–5:** These verses make it clear that the *holy* God does not simply distance the divine self from humanity. God deserves *worship*, because God wills and works for *justice and righteousness* among the people (96.13; 97.2; 98.9). God's *footstool* was the ark, where the heavenly God sat *enthroned* (v. 1) in an earthly location, the Temple,* on God's *holy mountain* (v. 9). **6–9:** Although v. 7 reports that the people obeyed, *Moses, Aaron*, and *Samuel* frequently interceded when the people disobeyed. God proved to be both *forgiving* and *an avenger of their wrongdoings*, a tension reflected also in God's revelation to *Moses* in Ex 34.6–7.

PSALM 100
A Psalm of thanksgiving.

1 Make a joyful noise to the LORD, all the
        earth.
2   Worship the LORD with gladness;
    come into his presence with singing.

3 Know that the LORD is God.
    It is he that made us, and we are his;[b]
    we are his people, and the sheep of
        his pasture.

a Cn: Heb *And a king's strength*   b Another reading is *and not we ourselves*

4 Enter his gates with thanksgiving,
   and his courts with praise.
   Give thanks to him, bless his name.

5 For the LORD is good;
   his steadfast love endures forever,
   and his faithfulness to all generations.

100.1–5: Worship the LORD with gladness. A song of praise, it forms a fitting epilogue to the enthronement psalms (Ps 93, 95–99), recalling especially Ps 95 (compare vv. 1–2, 4 with 95.1–2; v. 3 with 95.7). **1–2:** Three invitations to praise call for a recognition of God's sovereignty. This is especially so of *worship*, which could also be translated "serve" (see 2.11, the only other such invitation). **3–4:** Three more imperative verbs in v. 4 invite grateful praise, and the pattern highlights the central imperative in v. 3, *know*, which is followed by a profession of faith. The people's role as *sheep* suggests that God is the shepherd, a royal title (80.1). **5:** The reasons for praise focus on God's fundamental character—*steadfast love* and *faithfulness*—thus recalling Ex 34.6–7, as does Ps 99 (see 98.3).

PSALM 101
Of David. A Psalm.

1 I will sing of loyalty and of justice;
   to you, O LORD, I will sing.
2 I will study the way that is blameless.
   When shall I attain it?

   I will walk with integrity of heart
      within my house;
3 I will not set before my eyes
      anything that is base.

   I hate the work of those who fall away;
      it shall not cling to me.
4 Perverseness of heart shall be far from
      me;
   I will know nothing of evil.

5 One who secretly slanders a neighbor
      I will destroy.
   A haughty look and an arrogant heart
      I will not tolerate.

6 I will look with favor on the faithful in
      the land,
   so that they may live with me;

whoever walks in the way that is
      blameless
   shall minister to me.

7 No one who practices deceit
      shall remain in my house;
no one who utters lies
      shall continue in my presence.

8 Morning by morning I will destroy
      all the wicked in the land,
   cutting off all evildoers
      from the city of the LORD.

101.1–8: I will walk with integrity. Often classified as a royal psalm, it perhaps originally functioned as a king's oath of office. After the disappearance of the monarchy (see Ps 89), it may have functioned as an implicit plea for restoration and as a description of the *integrity* which everyone should embody. **1–2a:** *Loyalty* represents the word usually translated "steadfast love." The preceding psalms have suggested that it and *justice* characterize God's reign (98.3, 9). *Blameless* and *integrity* (v. 2b) represent the same Hebrew word (see v. 6). God's ways are *blameless;* and as he was supposed to do, the king vows to embody God's character (18.20–25; 72.1–7). **2b–5:** The word *heart* frames this section. *Integrity* will involve the avoidance of all deceit and arrogance. The list recalls 15.3–5 (see "blamelessly" in 15.2). **6–8:** Repeating several words from vv. 2b–5, the king vows to keep and support good company. The *cutting off* of *evildoers* is usually God's prerogative (54.5; 94.23), but the king was viewed as the embodiment of God's reign (18.40; 72.4, 9).

PSALM 102
A prayer of one afflicted, when faint and
pleading before the LORD.

1 Hear my prayer, O LORD;
   let my cry come to you.
2 Do not hide your face from me
   in the day of my distress.
   Incline your ear to me;
      answer me speedily in the day when I
      call.

3 For my days pass away like smoke,
   and my bones burn like a furnace.

⁴ My heart is stricken and withered like
grass;
I am too wasted to eat my bread.
⁵ Because of my loud groaning
my bones cling to my skin.
⁶ I am like an owl of the wilderness,
like a little owl of the waste places.
⁷ I lie awake;
I am like a lonely bird on the
housetop.
⁸ All day long my enemies taunt me;
those who deride me use my name for
a curse.
⁹ For I eat ashes like bread,
and mingle tears with my drink,
¹⁰ because of your indignation and anger;
for you have lifted me up and thrown
me aside.
¹¹ My days are like an evening shadow;
I wither away like grass.

¹² But you, O LORD, are enthroned
forever;
your name endures to all generations.
¹³ You will rise up and have compassion
on Zion,
for it is time to favor it;
the appointed time has come.
¹⁴ For your servants hold its stones dear,
and have pity on its dust.
¹⁵ The nations will fear the name of the
LORD,
and all the kings of the earth your
glory.
¹⁶ For the LORD will build up Zion;
he will appear in his glory.
¹⁷ He will regard the prayer of the
destitute,
and will not despise their prayer.

¹⁸ Let this be recorded for a generation to
come,
so that a people yet unborn may
praise the LORD:
¹⁹ that he looked down from his holy
height,
from heaven the LORD looked at the
earth,
²⁰ to hear the groans of the prisoners,
to set free those who were doomed to
die;

²¹ so that the name of the LORD may be
declared in Zion,
and his praise in Jerusalem,
²² when peoples gather together,
and kingdoms, to worship the LORD.

²³ He has broken my strength in
midcourse;
he has shortened my days.
²⁴ "O my God," I say, "do not take
me away
at the midpoint of my life,
you whose years endure
throughout all generations."

²⁵ Long ago you laid the foundation of the
earth,
and the heavens are the work of your
hands.
²⁶ They will perish, but you endure;
they will all wear out like a garment.
You change them like clothing, and they
pass away;
²⁷ but you are the same, and your years
have no end.
²⁸ The children of your servants shall live
secure;
their offspring shall be established in
your presence.

102.1–28: **Established in your presence.** As the superscription suggests, it is an individual prayer for help,
at least in part (vv. 1–11, 23–24). Other verses consist
of affirmations of God's sovereignty and divine help
for *Zion*★ and God's people (vv. 12–17, 25–28), as
well as an expression of gratitude (or perhaps hope)
for the return of the exiles (vv. 18–22). It became one
of the church's Penitential Psalms★ (Ps 6). **1–11:** Petitions (vv. 1–2) are followed by complaint, which is
framed by references to *my days* (vv. 3, 11) and *like
grass* (vv. 4, 11). The language and imagery suggest
physical illness, but they can be understood metaphorically.★ **12–22:** The shift of focus to God, *Zion*,
and the return of people to *Zion* suggests that vv.
3–11, 23–24 were indeed heard as a metaphorical description of the distress of exile. **23–28:** Individual
complaint recurs (vv. 23–24a) before another shift of
focus to God (vv. 24b–28). The eternal God will secure
the future of God's people, an assurance applicable to
both individuals and the whole people (90.13–17).

PSALM 103

Of David.

1 Bless the LORD, O my soul,
   and all that is within me,
   bless his holy name.
2 Bless the LORD, O my soul,
   and do not forget all his benefits—
3 who forgives all your iniquity,
   who heals all your diseases,
4 who redeems your life from the Pit,
   who crowns you with steadfast love
   and mercy,
5 who satisfies you with good as long as
   you live[a]
   so that your youth is renewed like the
   eagle's.

6 The LORD works vindication
   and justice for all who are oppressed.
7 He made known his ways to Moses,
   his acts to the people of Israel.
8 The LORD is merciful and gracious,
   slow to anger and abounding in
   steadfast love.
9 He will not always accuse,
   nor will he keep his anger forever.
10 He does not deal with us according to
   our sins,
   nor repay us according to our
   iniquities.
11 For as the heavens are high above the
   earth,
   so great is his steadfast love toward
   those who fear him;
12 as far as the east is from the west,
   so far he removes our transgressions
   from us.
13 As a father has compassion for his
   children,
   so the LORD has compassion for
   those who fear him.
14 For he knows how we were made;
   he remembers that we are dust.

15 As for mortals, their days are like grass;
   they flourish like a flower of the
   field;
16 for the wind passes over it, and it is
   gone,
   and its place knows it no more.

17 But the steadfast love of the LORD is
   from everlasting to everlasting
   on those who fear him,
   and his righteousness to children's
   children,
18 to those who keep his covenant
   and remember to do his
   commandments.

19 The LORD has established his throne in
   the heavens,
   and his kingdom rules over all.
20 Bless the LORD, O you his angels,
   you mighty ones who do his bidding,
   obedient to his spoken word.
21 Bless the LORD, all his hosts,
   his ministers that do his will.
22 Bless the LORD, all his works,
   in all places of his dominion.
   Bless the LORD, O my soul.

103.1–22: Bless the LORD. A song of praise, it celebrates God's *benefits* (v. 2) in a comprehensive way as signaled by the repetition of *all* (vv. 1–3, 6, 19, 21–22). **1–2:** The invitation to praise is addressed to the psalmist's own self (v. 1; v. 22; 104.1, 35). *Bless* originally meant "to kneel," so the invitation calls for the recognition of God's sovereignty. **3–6:** The reasons for praise are also comprehensive. God does whatever is needed to enhance life. *Steadfast love* (v. 4) recurs in vv. 8, 11, 17; and the Hebrew translated *mercy* recurs in vv. 8 (*merciful*) and 13 (*compassion*). *Vindication* usually appears as "righteousness"; it and *justice* summarize God's will for humankind (97.2; 98.9). **7–18:** To illustrate God's *justice*, the psalmist recalls the Exodus (v. 7) and the golden calf episode, which concludes with divine forgiveness and God's self-revelation to Moses (see Ex 34.6, which v. 8 quotes). Verses 13, 17, 18 seem to make God's *mercy* depend on *fear* and obedience, a tension also reflected in Ex 34.6–7. **19–22:** Because God *rules over all*, all cosmic beings and features are invited to yield themselves to God's claim.

PSALM 104

1 Bless the LORD, O my soul.
   O LORD my God, you are very great.
   You are clothed with honor and majesty,

a Meaning of Heb uncertain

2   wrapped in light as with a garment.
   You stretch out the heavens like a tent,
3   you set the beams of your*a* chambers
         on the waters,
   you make the clouds your*a* chariot,
      you ride on the wings of the wind,
4 you make the winds your*a* messengers,
      fire and flame your*a* ministers.

5 You set the earth on its foundations,
      so that it shall never be shaken.
6 You cover it with the deep as with a
         garment;
      the waters stood above the
         mountains.
7 At your rebuke they flee;
      at the sound of your thunder they
         take to flight.
8 They rose up to the mountains, ran
         down to the valleys
      to the place that you appointed for
         them.
9 You set a boundary that they may not
         pass,
      so that they might not again cover the
         earth.

10 You make springs gush forth in the
         valleys;
      they flow between the hills,
11 giving drink to every wild animal;
      the wild asses quench their thirst.
12 By the streams*b* the birds of the air
         have their habitation;
      they sing among the branches.
13 From your lofty abode you water the
         mountains;
      the earth is satisfied with the fruit of
         your work.

104.1–35: O LORD, how manifold are your works! A
song of praise linked to Ps 103 by *Bless the LORD, O
my soul*, it seems to a be poetic elaboration of 103.22,
Bless the LORD, all his works (see *work[s]* in vv. 13, 24,
31 as well as the verbal form *make[s]* or *made* in vv.
4, 9, 24). **1–4:** The attributes of sovereignty belong to
the LORD (vv. 1–2a), who has built the cosmos *on the
waters*, which represent mythic forces of chaos and
disorder (74.12–15). In the Canaanite view, Baal★
rode *the clouds*, a role now taken by *the LORD*. **5–13:**
The focus is on *the earth* (vv. 5, 9, 13), which exists as

a result of God's controlling *the waters* (vv. 6–9; Job
38.8–11). *The waters* now serve to sustain God's creatures (vv. 10–13).

14 You cause the grass to grow for the
         cattle,
      and plants for people to use,*c*
   to bring forth food from the earth,
15   and wine to gladden the human
         heart,
   oil to make the face shine,
      and bread to strengthen the human
         heart.
16 The trees of the LORD are watered
         abundantly,
      the cedars of Lebanon that he
         planted.
17 In them the birds build their nests;
      the stork has its home in the fir trees.
18 The high mountains are for the wild
         goats;
      the rocks are a refuge for the coneys.
19 You have made the moon to mark the
         seasons;
      the sun knows its time for setting.
20 You make darkness, and it is night,
      when all the animals of the forest
         come creeping out.
21 The young lions roar for their prey,
      seeking their food from God.
22 When the sun rises, they withdraw
      and lie down in their dens.
23 People go out to their work
      and to their labor until the evening.

24 O LORD, how manifold are your works!
      In wisdom you have made them all;
      the earth is full of your creatures.
25 Yonder is the sea, great and wide,
      creeping things innumerable are
         there,
      living things both small and great.
26 There go the ships,
      and Leviathan that you formed
         to sport in it.

27 These all look to you
      to give them their food in due season;

a Heb *his*   *b* Heb *By them*   *c* Or *to cultivate*

28 when you give to them, they gather it
        up;
    when you open your hand, they are
        filled with good things.
29 When you hide your face, they are
        dismayed;
    when you take away their breath, they
        die
    and return to their dust.
30 When you send forth your spirit,*a* they
        are created;
    and you renew the face of the
        ground.

31 May the glory of the LORD endure
        forever;
    may the LORD rejoice in his
        works—
32 who looks on the earth and it trembles,
    who touches the mountains and they
        smoke.
33 I will sing to the LORD as long as I live;
    I will sing praise to my God while I
        have being.
34 May my meditation be pleasing to him,
    for I rejoice in the LORD.
35 Let sinners be consumed from the
        earth,
    and let the wicked be no more.
    Bless the LORD, O my soul.
    Praise the LORD!

104.14–35. 14–23: This section is bounded by references to *people* (vv. 14, 23), for whom God also provides, along with *trees*, *birds*, and other *animals*.
24–27: Indeed, all *creatures* and other elements in the
created order belong to God and reveal God's *wisdom*
(Prov 3.19; 8.22–31; Jer 10.12). *Sea* creatures, especially *Leviathan*⋆ (Job 41.1–11; Ps 74.14), were associated with chaos; but they too are subject to God.
28–30: *Breath* (v. 29) and *spirit* (v. 30) represent the
Hebrew word "ruach," recalling Gen 1.2 and suggesting that creation is ongoing. **31–35:** After wishing
for the eternity of God's reign (v. 31) and acknowledging God's power in the language of theophany⋆
(v. 32; 97.2–5), the psalmist pledges his or her loyalty
(v. 33). *My meditation* (v. 34) probably refers to the
preceding verses. Requesting the disappearance of *the
wicked* is another way of acknowledging God's
sovereignty.

PSALM 105

1 O give thanks to the LORD, call on his
        name,
    make known his deeds among the
        peoples.
2 Sing to him, sing praises to him;
    tell of all his wonderful works.
3 Glory in his holy name;
    let the hearts of those who seek the
        LORD rejoice.
4 Seek the LORD and his strength;
    seek his presence continually.
5 Remember the wonderful works he has
        done,
    his miracles, and the judgments he
        has uttered,
6 O offspring of his servant Abraham,*b*
    children of Jacob, his chosen ones.

7 He is the LORD our God;
    his judgments are in all the earth.
8 He is mindful of his covenant forever,
    of the word that he commanded, for a
        thousand generations,
9 the covenant that he made with
        Abraham,
    his sworn promise to Isaac,
10 which he confirmed to Jacob as a
        statute,
    to Israel as an everlasting covenant,
11 saying, "To you I will give the land of
        Canaan
    as your portion for an inheritance."

12 When they were few in number,
    of little account, and strangers in it,
13 wandering from nation to nation,
    from one kingdom to another people,
14 he allowed no one to oppress them;
    he rebuked kings on their account,
15 saying, "Do not touch my anointed
        ones;
    do my prophets no harm."

16 When he summoned famine against the
        land,
    and broke every staff of bread,

---

a Or *your breath*   *b* Another reading is *Israel* (compare
1 Chr 16.13)

17 he had sent a man ahead of them,
   Joseph, who was sold as a slave.
18 His feet were hurt with fetters,
   his neck was put in a collar of iron;
19 until what he had said came to pass,
   the word of the LORD kept testing
      him.
20 The king sent and released him;
   the ruler of the peoples set him free.
21 He made him lord of his house,
   and ruler of all his possessions,
22 to instruct*a* his officials at his pleasure,
   and to teach his elders wisdom.

23 Then Israel came to Egypt;
   Jacob lived as an alien in the land of
      Ham.
24 And the LORD made his people very
      fruitful,
   and made them stronger than their
      foes,
25 whose hearts he then turned to hate his
      people,
   to deal craftily with his servants.

105.1–45: Tell of all God's wonderful works. Often classified as a historical psalm (see Ps 78, 106), its recital of God's saving acts is offered in the form of a song of praise. **1–6:** Invitations to grateful praise and remembrance focus on what God *has done*, which will be recounted in the rest of the psalm. **7–11:** The *covenant,*★ a word that occurs in each of vv. 8–10, is traced back to *Abraham* and his descendants (Gen 12.1–3; 15.1–19; 17.1–14). **12–25:** This section features the *wandering* (v. 13) of the matriarchs and patriarchs, which left the people in *Egypt* (v. 23). That the people are designated *anointed*★ *ones,* a royal term, may suggest a post-exilic origin (see Ps 149).

26 He sent his servant Moses,
   and Aaron whom he had chosen.
27 They performed his signs among
      them,
   and miracles in the land of Ham.
28 He sent darkness, and made the land
      dark;
   they rebelled*b* against his words.
29 He turned their waters into blood,
   and caused their fish to die.
30 Their land swarmed with frogs,
   even in the chambers of their kings.

31 He spoke, and there came swarms of
      flies,
   and gnats throughout their country.
32 He gave them hail for rain,
   and lightning that flashed through
      their land.
33 He struck their vines and fig trees,
   and shattered the trees of their
      country.
34 He spoke, and the locusts came,
   and young locusts without number;
35 they devoured all the vegetation in their
      land,
   and ate up the fruit of their ground.
36 He struck down all the firstborn in their
      land,
   the first issue of all their strength.

37 Then he brought Israel*c* out with silver
      and gold,
   and there was no one among their
      tribes who stumbled.
38 Egypt was glad when they departed,
   for dread of them had fallen upon it.
39 He spread a cloud for a covering,
   and fire to give light by night.
40 They asked, and he brought quails,
   and gave them food from heaven in
      abundance.
41 He opened the rock, and water gushed
      out;
   it flowed through the desert like a
      river.
42 For he remembered his holy promise,
   and Abraham, his servant.

43 So he brought his people out with joy,
   his chosen ones with singing.
44 He gave them the lands of the nations,
   and they took possession of the
      wealth of the peoples,
45 that they might keep his statutes
   and observe his laws.
   Praise the LORD!

105.26–45. 26–38: The rehearsal of the Exodus features the plagues (Ex 7.14–12.32). **39–44:** The story continues with God's provision for the people in the

a Gk Syr Jerome: Heb *to bind*   *b* Cn Compare Gk Syr:
Heb *they did not rebel*   *c* Heb *them*

wilderness and the possession of the land. *Chosen* recurs for the third time (vv. 6, 26, 43). **45:** The final invitation to praise recalls vv. 1–6, and it points forward to Ps 106, which will highlight the people's failure to *observe God's laws.*

PSALM 106

1 Praise the LORD!
  O give thanks to the LORD, for he is
    good;
  for his steadfast love endures forever.
2 Who can utter the mighty doings of the
    LORD,
  or declare all his praise?
3 Happy are those who observe justice,
  who do righteousness at all times.

4 Remember me, O LORD, when you
    show favor to your people;
  help me when you deliver them;
5 that I may see the prosperity of your
    chosen ones,
  that I may rejoice in the gladness of
    your nation,
  that I may glory in your heritage.

6 Both we and our ancestors have sinned;
  we have committed iniquity, have
    done wickedly.
7 Our ancestors, when they were in
    Egypt,
  did not consider your wonderful
    works;
  they did not remember the abundance
    of your steadfast love,
  but rebelled against the Most High*a*
    at the Red Sea.*b*
8 Yet he saved them for his name's sake,
  so that he might make known his
    mighty power.
9 He rebuked the Red Sea,*b* and it
    became dry;
  he led them through the deep as
    through a desert.
10 So he saved them from the hand of the
    foe,
  and delivered them from the hand of
    the enemy.
11 The waters covered their adversaries;
  not one of them was left.

12 Then they believed his words;
  they sang his praise.

13 But they soon forgot his works;
  they did not wait for his counsel.
14 But they had a wanton craving in the
    wilderness,
  and put God to the test in the desert;
15 he gave them what they asked,
  but sent a wasting disease among
    them.

16 They were jealous of Moses in
    the camp,
  and of Aaron, the holy one of
    the LORD.
17 The earth opened and swallowed
    up Dathan,
  and covered the faction of Abiram.
18 Fire also broke out in their company;
  the flame burned up the wicked.

19 They made a calf at Horeb
  and worshiped a cast image.
20 They exchanged the glory of God*c*
  for the image of an ox that eats grass.
21 They forgot God, their Savior,
  who had done great things in Egypt,
22 wondrous works in the land of Ham,
  and awesome deeds by the Red Sea.*b*
23 Therefore he said he would destroy
    them—
  had not Moses, his chosen one,
  stood in the breach before him,
  to turn away his wrath from
    destroying them.

106.1–48: Save us, O LORD. Another historical psalm, it covers the same territory as Ps 105; but it tells the story not from the perspective of God's deeds but rather of the people's misdeeds. **1–5:** *Steadfast love* (v. 1) will be the people's only hope (v. 45), even though they regularly forget it (v. 7). The petition in vv. 4–5 anticipates v. 47. **6–12:** Verse 6 summarizes the content of the psalm, introducing the initial focus on the Exodus (Ex 14–15). **13–15:** As v. 13 suggests, the Song of the Sea (Ex 15.1–21) is followed immediately by

a Cn Compare 78.17, 56: Heb *rebelled at the sea*
b Or *Sea of Reeds*   *c* Compare Gk Mss: Heb *exchanged their glory*

the people's complaining (Ex 15.24), which persisted throughout the wilderness era (Ex 17.1–7; Num 11.4–34). **16–18:** The episode occurs in Num 16.1–35. **19–23:** The golden calf incident is in view (Ex 32.1–14).

24 Then they despised the pleasant land,
    having no faith in his promise.
25 They grumbled in their tents,
    and did not obey the voice of
        the LORD.
26 Therefore he raised his hand and swore
        to them
    that he would make them fall in the
        wilderness,
27 and would disperse*a* their descendants
        among the nations,
    scattering them over the lands.

28 Then they attached themselves to the
        Baal of Peor,
    and ate sacrifices offered to the dead;
29 they provoked the LORD to anger with
        their deeds,
    and a plague broke out among them.
30 Then Phinehas stood up and interceded,
    and the plague was stopped.
31 And that has been reckoned to him as
        righteousness
    from generation to generation forever.

32 They angered the LORD *b* at the waters
        of Meribah,
    and it went ill with Moses on their
        account;
33 for they made his spirit bitter,
    and he spoke words that were rash.

34 They did not destroy the peoples,
    as the LORD commanded them,
35 but they mingled with the nations
    and learned to do as they did.
36 They served their idols,
    which became a snare to them.
37 They sacrificed their sons
    and their daughters to the demons;
38 they poured out innocent blood,
    the blood of their sons and daughters,
    whom they sacrificed to the idols of
        Canaan;
    and the land was polluted with blood.

39 Thus they became unclean by their acts,
    and prostituted themselves in their
        doings.
40 Then the anger of the LORD was
        kindled against his people,
    and he abhorred his heritage;
41 he gave them into the hand of the
        nations,
    so that those who hated them ruled
        over them.
42 Their enemies oppressed them,
    and they were brought into subjection
        under their power.
43 Many times he delivered them,
    but they were rebellious in their
        purposes,
    and were brought low through their
        iniquity.
44 Nevertheless he regarded their distress
    when he heard their cry.
45 For their sake he remembered his
        covenant,
    and showed compassion according to
        the abundance of his steadfast
        love.
46 He caused them to be pitied
    by all who held them captive.

47 Save us, O LORD our God,
    and gather us from among the
        nations,
    that we may give thanks to your holy
        name
    and glory in your praise.

48 Blessed be the LORD, the God of Israel,
    from everlasting to everlasting.
    And let all the people say, "Amen."
    Praise the LORD!

106.24–48. 24–27: The people's failure to trust the spies sent into Canaan is reviewed (Num 14.1–25). **28–31:** See Num 25.1–13. **32–33:** See Ex 17.1–7. **34–39:** Faithlessness and disobedience continued after entry into the land. **40–47:** The pattern described in vv. 40–46 recalls the book of Judges, but might also apply to Israel's whole history, including the Exile* and

a Syr Compare Ezek 20.23: Heb *cause to fall*
b Heb *him*

dispersion, which is in view in v. 47. Verse 47 reinforces the conclusion that Book IV offers a response to the Exile (see Introduction; Ps 90). **48:** This doxology concludes Book IV.

~~~~~~

BOOK FIVE

PSALM 107

1 O give thanks to the LORD, for he is
   good;
   for his steadfast love endures forever.
2 Let the redeemed of the LORD say so,
   those he redeemed from trouble
3 and gathered in from the lands,
   from the east and from the west,
   from the north and from the south.*a*

4 Some wandered in desert wastes,
   finding no way to an inhabited town;
5 hungry and thirsty,
   their soul fainted within them.
6 Then they cried to the LORD in their
   trouble,
   and he delivered them from their
   distress;
7 he led them by a straight way,
   until they reached an inhabited town.
8 Let them thank the LORD for his
   steadfast love,
   for his wonderful works to
   humankind.
9 For he satisfies the thirsty,
   and the hungry he fills with good
   things.

10 Some sat in darkness and in gloom,
   prisoners in misery and in irons,
11 for they had rebelled against the words
   of God,
   and spurned the counsel of the Most
   High.
12 Their hearts were bowed down with
   hard labor;
   they fell down, with no one to help.
13 Then they cried to the LORD in their
   trouble,
   and he saved them from their distress;
14 he brought them out of darkness and
   gloom,
   and broke their bonds asunder.

15 Let them thank the LORD for his
   steadfast love,
   for his wonderful works to
   humankind.
16 For he shatters the doors of bronze,
   and cuts in two the bars of iron.

17 Some were sick*b* through their sinful
   ways,
   and because of their iniquities
   endured affliction;
18 they loathed any kind of food,
   and they drew near to the gates of
   death.
19 Then they cried to the LORD in their
   trouble,
   and he saved them from their
   distress;
20 he sent out his word and healed them,
   and delivered them from destruction.
21 Let them thank the LORD for his
   steadfast love,
   for his wonderful works to
   humankind.
22 And let them offer thanksgiving
   sacrifices,
   and tell of his deeds with songs
   of joy.

107.1–43: God delivered them from their distress. A song of thanksgiving, it begins Book V with what seems to be a direct response to Ps 106 (compare 107.2–3 with 106.47). **1–3:** Recalling 106.1, v. 1 introduces the theme of *steadfast love* (see the refrain in vv. 8, 15, 21, 31; plus v. 43). The contrasting theme, *trouble*, is introduced in v. 2 and recurs in another refrain (vv. 6, 13, 19, 28). **4–9:** The *trouble* is stated generally enough to be widely applicable, but it especially recalls the experiences of wilderness and exile. Deliverance typically occurs after needy persons have *cried to the LORD* (Ex 3.7, 9; Ps 106.44). **10–16:** Again, the *trouble* can be understood generally, but *darkness* recalls the Exile* (Isa 42.7), as does *prisoners* (Isa 49.9). Typically, God helps those *with no one to help* them (v. 12; 9.18). **17–22:** The *trouble* seems to be sickness (although see note *b* in v. 17), from which people are *healed* (v. 20). This imagery may be metaphorical* (Isa 57.18–19).

~~~~~~

a Cn: Heb *sea*   *b* Cn: Heb *fools*

23 Some went down to the sea in ships,
 doing business on the mighty
  waters;
24 they saw the deeds of the LORD,
 his wondrous works in the deep.
25 For he commanded and raised the
  stormy wind,
 which lifted up the waves of
  the sea.
26 They mounted up to heaven, they went
  down to the depths;
 their courage melted away in their
  calamity;
27 they reeled and staggered like
  drunkards,
 and were at their wits' end.
28 Then they cried to the LORD in their
  trouble,
 and he brought them out from their
  distress;
29 he made the storm be still,
 and the waves of the sea were
  hushed.
30 Then they were glad because they had
  quiet,
 and he brought them to their desired
  haven.
31 Let them thank the LORD for his
  steadfast love,
 for his wonderful works to
  humankind.
32 Let them extol him in the congregation
  of the people,
 and praise him in the assembly of the
  elders.

33 He turns rivers into a desert,
 springs of water into thirsty ground,
34 a fruitful land into a salty waste,
 because of the wickedness of its
  inhabitants.
35 He turns a desert into pools of water,
 a parched land into springs of
  water.
36 And there he lets the hungry live,
 and they establish a town to live in;
37 they sow fields, and plant vineyards,
 and get a fruitful yield.
38 By his blessing they multiply greatly,
 and he does not let their cattle
  decrease.

39 When they are diminished and brought
  low
 through oppression, trouble,
  and sorrow,
40 he pours contempt on princes
 and makes them wander in trackless
  wastes;
41 but he raises up the needy out of
  distress,
 and makes their families like flocks.
42 The upright see it and are glad;
 and all wickedness stops its mouth.
43 Let those who are wise give heed to
  these things,
 and consider the steadfast love of the
  LORD.

107.23–43. 23–32: Deliverance from distress at *sea* is unique (see Jon 1–2). *The sea, the mighty waters,* and *the depths* may symbolize cosmic chaotic forces (93.3–4). *Wits'* (v. 27) is literally "wisdom," anticipating v. 43. **33–43:** A summary recalling vv. 4–9, this section may have been added to an original vv. 4–32. **43:** Those who heed the preceding instances of deliverance will be taught dependence upon God's *steadfast love,* and such is the essence of wisdom.

~~~~~~~~~~~~

PSALM 108
A Song. A Psalm of David.

1 My heart is steadfast, O God, my heart
  is steadfast;*a*
 I will sing and make melody.
 Awake, my soul!*b*
2 Awake, O harp and lyre!
 I will awake the dawn.
3 I will give thanks to you, O LORD,
  among the peoples,
 and I will sing praises to you among
  the nations.
4 For your steadfast love is higher than
  the heavens,
 and your faithfulness reaches to the
  clouds.

5 Be exalted, O God, above the heavens,
 and let your glory be over all the
  earth.

a Heb Mss Gk Syr: MT lacks *my heart is steadfast*
b Compare 57.8: Heb *also my soul*

6 Give victory with your right hand, and
        answer me,
    so that those whom you love may be
        rescued.

7 God has promised in his sanctuary:[a]
    "With exultation I will divide up
        Shechem,
    and portion out the Vale of Succoth.
8 Gilead is mine; Manasseh is mine;
    Ephraim is my helmet;
    Judah is my scepter.
9 Moab is my washbasin;
    on Edom I hurl my shoe;
    over Philistia I shout in triumph."

10 Who will bring me to the fortified city?
    Who will lead me to Edom?
11 Have you not rejected us, O God?
    You do not go out, O God, with our
        armies.
12 O grant us help against the foe,
    for human help is worthless.
13 With God we shall do valiantly;
    it is he who will tread down
        our foes.

108.1–13: Human help is worthless. Formed
from combining 57.7–11 (108.1–5) and 60.5–12
(108.6–13), it moves from praise (vv. 1–4) to petition
(vv. 5–6) to divine speech (vv. 7–9) to complaint (vv.
10–11) to petition (v. 12) to expression of trust (v. 13).
The reasons for combining portions of Ps 57 and 60
are unclear. In their present context, vv. 1–4 supply
the grateful praise repeatedly called for in Ps 107 (vv.
1, 8, 15, 21, 31). If this praise is a response to the return
from exile, the movement to petition and complaint
may reflect the reality that the return did not solve all
the people's problems. They still found themselves in
need of *help against the foe* (v. 12).

PSALM 109
To the leader. Of David. A Psalm.

1 Do not be silent, O God of my praise.
2 For wicked and deceitful mouths are
        opened against me,
    speaking against me with lying
        tongues.
3 They beset me with words of hate,
    and attack me without cause.

4 In return for my love they accuse me,
    even while I make prayer for them.[b]
5 So they reward me evil for good,
    and hatred for my love.

6 They say,[c] "Appoint a wicked man
        against him;
    let an accuser stand on his right.
7 When he is tried, let him be found
        guilty;
    let his prayer be counted as sin.
8 May his days be few;
    may another seize his position.
9 May his children be orphans,
    and his wife a widow.
10 May his children wander about and beg;
    may they be driven out of[d] the ruins
        they inhabit.
11 May the creditor seize all that he has;
    may strangers plunder the fruits of
        his toil.
12 May there be no one to do him a
        kindness,
    nor anyone to pity his orphaned
        children.
13 May his posterity be cut off;
    may his name be blotted out in the
        second generation.
14 May the iniquity of his father[e] be
        remembered before the LORD,
    and do not let the sin of his mother
        be blotted out.
15 Let them be before the LORD
        continually,
    and may his[f] memory be cut off from
        the earth.
16 For he did not remember to show
        kindness,
    but pursued the poor and needy
    and the brokenhearted to their death.
17 He loved to curse; let curses come on
        him.
    He did not like blessing; may it be far
        from him.
18 He clothed himself with cursing as his
        coat,
    may it soak into his body like water,
    like oil into his bones.

a Or *by his holiness*   b Syr: Heb I *prayer*
c Heb lacks *They say*   d Gk: Heb *and seek*
e Cn: Heb *fathers*   f Gk: Heb *their*

19 May it be like a garment that he wraps
around himself,
like a belt that he wears every day."

**109.1–31: God stands at the right hand of the
needy.** Because it contains petition (vv. 1a, 20–21, 26–
29), complaint (vv. 1b–5, 22–25), and an expression
of praise and trust (vv. 30–31), this psalm is usually
classified as a prayer for help of a person falsely accused (see Ps 5, 7). The extended request for revenge
in vv. 6–19 is unique. **1–5:** The psalmist is a victim,
despite his or her goodness toward others. **6–19:** The
addition of *they say*, which is not in the Hebrew text
(see note c), attributes the desire for revenge to the
psalmist's enemies. The passage should instead be
seen as expressing the psalmist's wishes. The charges
involve the failure to show *kindness*, thus contributing
to the *death* of *poor and needy* persons (v. 16).

20 May that be the reward of my accusers
from the LORD,
of those who speak evil against my
life.
21 But you, O LORD my Lord,
act on my behalf for your name's
sake;
because your steadfast love is good,
deliver me.
22 For I am poor and needy,
and my heart is pierced within me.
23 I am gone like a shadow at evening;
I am shaken off like a locust.
24 My knees are weak through fasting;
my body has become gaunt.
25 I am an object of scorn to my
accusers;
when they see me, they shake their
heads.
26 Help me, O LORD my God!
Save me according to your steadfast
love.
27 Let them know that this is your hand;
you, O LORD, have done it.
28 Let them curse, but you will bless.
Let my assailants be put to shame;[a]
may your servant be glad.
29 May my accusers be clothed with
dishonor;
may they be wrapped in their own
shame as in a mantle.

30 With my mouth I will give great thanks
to the LORD;
I will praise him in the midst of the
throng.
31 For he stands at the right hand of the
needy,
to save them from those who would
condemn them to death.

109.20–31: Even if vv. 6–19 are the words of the enemies, the psalmist claims them (v. 20). The psalmist
appeals to God's *steadfast love* (vv. 21, 26; the same
Hebrew word was translated *kindness* in vv. 12, 16).
The appeal is grounded in the conviction that God
loves and favors the *needy* (v. 31; 9.18), among whom
is the psalmist (v. 22).

PSALM 110

Of David. A Psalm.

1 The LORD says to my lord,
"Sit at my right hand
until I make your enemies your
footstool."

2 The LORD sends out from Zion
your mighty scepter.
Rule in the midst of your foes.
3 Your people will offer themselves
willingly
on the day you lead your forces
on the holy mountains.[b]
From the womb of the morning,
like dew, your youth[c] will come to
you.
4 The LORD has sworn and will not
change his mind,
"You are a priest forever according to
the order of Melchizedek."[d]

5 The Lord is at your right hand;
he will shatter kings on the day of his
wrath.
6 He will execute judgment among the
nations,
filling them with corpses;

---

a Gk: Heb *They have risen up and have been put to
shame* b Another reading is *in holy splendor*
c Cn: Heb *the dew of your youth* d Or *forever, a
rightful king by my edict*

he will shatter heads
  over the wide earth.
7 He will drink from the stream by the
    path;
  therefore he will lift up his head.

110.1–7: The LORD is at your right hand. A royal psalm, it may have been used originally at the coronation of Judean kings (see Ps 2). After the disappearance of the monarchy (see Ps 89), it would have served as a profession of trust in God's continued involvement with the people, to whom Ps 149 attributes the role formerly reserved for kings. **1–3:** Divine speech promises victory over *enemies* (v. 1; 2.1–5, 8–11). The promise is reinforced in v. 2, and probably in v. 3 as well, although its meaning is unclear. **4:** Divine speech resumes in v. 4. *Melchizedek* shared the titles king and priest (Gen 14.18). **5:** *Right hand* designates the position of help (109.31). **6:** Justice will be achieved by God's defeat of oppressors (v. 6; 149.9). The graphic imagery is typical of ancient battle descriptions (2 Kings 8.12; Ps 137.9). **7:** *He* now refers to the king. An uplifted *head* seems to signify deliverance (3.3; 27.6).

PSALM 111

1 Praise the LORD!
  I will give thanks to the LORD with my
    whole heart,
  in the company of the upright, in the
    congregation.
2 Great are the works of the LORD,
    studied by all who delight in them.
3 Full of honor and majesty is his work,
    and his righteousness endures
      forever.
4 He has gained renown by his wonderful
    deeds;
  the LORD is gracious and merciful.
5 He provides food for those who fear him;
  he is ever mindful of his covenant.
6 He has shown his people the power of
    his works,
  in giving them the heritage of the
    nations.
7 The works of his hands are faithful and
    just;
  all his precepts are trustworthy.
8 They are established forever and ever,
    to be performed with faithfulness and
      uprightness.

9 He sent redemption to his people;
  he has commanded his covenant
    forever.
  Holy and awesome is his name.
10 The fear of the LORD is the beginning
    of wisdom;
  all those who practice it[a] have a good
    understanding.
  His praise endures forever.

111.1–10: The works of the LORD. An acrostic* poem (see Ps 25) to be read in conjunction with Ps 112, it is often categorized as a song of praise. An opening invitation (v. 1a) is followed by the psalmist's own response (v. 1b–c) and reasons for praise that focus on God's *works* (vv. 2, 6–7). **1:** The psalmist's wholehearted response (86.12) is offered publicly. **2–3:** God's *works* include actions (vv. 4–6) and words (vv. 7–9). **4–6:** God's *wonderful deeds*, motivated by God's *gracious and merciful* character (Ex 34.6; Ps 112.4), include the Exodus, provision in the wilderness (v. 5), and gift of the land (v. 6). **7–9:** Established by God's action, the *covenant* (vv. 5, 9) involved *precepts* intended to establish justice among the people. **10:** *Fear of the LORD* involves trust and obedience. It is the essence of *praise* and the evidence of true *wisdom* (Job 28.28; Prov 1.7; 9.10).

PSALM 112

1 Praise the LORD!
  Happy are those who fear the LORD,
  who greatly delight in his
    commandments.
2 Their descendants will be mighty in the
    land;
  the generation of the upright will be
    blessed.
3 Wealth and riches are in their houses,
    and their righteousness endures
      forever.
4 They rise in the darkness as a light for
    the upright;
  they are gracious, merciful, and
    righteous.
5 It is well with those who deal
    generously and lend,
  who conduct their affairs with justice.

---

a Gk Syr: Heb *them*

6 For the righteous will never be moved;
   they will be remembered forever.
7 They are not afraid of evil tidings;
   their hearts are firm, secure in the
      LORD.
8 Their hearts are steady, they will not be
      afraid;
   in the end they will look in triumph
      on their foes.
9 They have distributed freely, they have
      given to the poor;
   their righteousness endures forever;
   their horn is exalted in honor.
10 The wicked see it and are angry;
   they gnash their teeth and melt away;
   the desire of the wicked comes
      to nothing.

112.1–10: Happy are those who fear the LORD. An acrostic* poem (see Ps 25), it belongs with Ps 111. It begins like Ps 111, and it features *those who fear the LORD* (v. 1; 111.10). **1–3:** *Happy* and *delight* in v. 1 recall 1.1–2. *Wealth and riches* need not be understood materialistically. The real reward of *the righteous* is stability (vv. 6, 8) and security grounded *in the LORD* (v. 7; 1.3). Because *the righteous* embody God's will, the same thing is said of them that is said of God in 111.3: *their righteousness endures forever* (vv. 3, 9). **4–6:** Like God also, *the righteous* are a source of *light* for others (27.1); and they are *gracious* and *merciful* (v. 4; 111.4). Their lives reflect *justice*, the essence of God's will (72.1–2; 82.3). **7–10:** Because they trust or *fear the LORD* (v. 1), they do not have to be *afraid of evil tidings* (v. 7). Their generosity also models God's will (v. 9), and it sets them apart from *the wicked*, whose behavior *comes to nothing* (literally "perishes"; 1.6).

~~~~~~~~~~~~~~~~~~~~~~~~~~~~~

PSALM 113

1 Praise the LORD!
   Praise, O servants of the LORD;
   praise the name of the LORD.

2 Blessed be the name of the LORD
   from this time on and forevermore.
3 From the rising of the sun to its setting
   the name of the LORD is to be
      praised.
4 The LORD is high above all nations,
   and his glory above the heavens.

5 Who is like the LORD our God,
   who is seated on high,
6 who looks far down
   on the heavens and the earth?
7 He raises the poor from the dust,
   and lifts the needy from the ash heap,
8 to make them sit with princes,
   with the princes of his people.
9 He gives the barren woman a home,
   making her the joyous mother of
      children.
   Praise the LORD!

113.1–9: The God who looks far down. A song of praise, it introduces the Egyptian "Hallel" ("Praise"; Ps 113–118), a collection which, because of its references to the Exodus from Egypt, was and is used at Passover.* **1–4:** Each of the first three verses contains *name of the LORD*, suggesting the importance of God's identity. Verse 4 affirms God's cosmic sovereignty. **5a:** Each of vv. 1–5a contains the name *LORD*. The question specifically raises the issue of the LORD's identity that will be addressed in vv. 5b–9. **5b–9:** God is known by what God does. The God *on high* is one *who looks far down*, or literally, "causes God's self to be low so as to see." This humbling of the divine self leads to exaltation for *the poor* and *needy* (9.18; 109.31). The same Hebrew root underlies *seated* (v. 5b), *sit* (v. 8), and *gives a . . . home* (v. 9). The repetition makes the point that the will of God is done on earth as in heaven (see *heavens and the earth* in v. 6). This constitutes the ultimate reason to *Praise the LORD!*

~~~~~~~~~~~~~~~~~~~~~~~~~~~~~

PSALM 114

1 When Israel went out from Egypt,
   the house of Jacob from a people of
      strange language,
2 Judah became God's[a] sanctuary,
   Israel his dominion.

3 The sea looked and fled;
   Jordan turned back.
4 The mountains skipped like rams,
   the hills like lambs.

5 Why is it, O sea, that you flee?
   O Jordan, that you turn back?

a Heb *his*

6 O mountains, that you skip like rams?
    O hills, like lambs?

7 Tremble, O earth, at the presence of the
    LORD,
    at the presence of the God of Jacob,
8 who turns the rock into a pool of
    water,
    the flint into a spring of water.

114.1–8: When Israel went out from Egypt. It is a poetic accounting of the Exodus (vv. 1, 3a, 5a), wilderness (v. 8), the crossing of the *Jordan* into the land (vv. 3b, 5b), and the possession of the land (v. 2). It is part of the Egyptian "Hallel" (Ps 113–118). **1–2:** Like the Song of the Sea (Ex 15.1–18), the movement is from Exodus to God's *sanctuary* (v. 2; Ex 15.17). **3–4:** The crossing of the *Jordan* into Canaan was remembered as an event like the Exodus (Josh 4.23–24). The imagery depicts the effects of God's appearing (29.6). **5–8:** The questions in vv. 5–6 prepare for the climactic vv. 7–8, where the name *LORD* appears for the first time. To *tremble* is the appropriate response to *the presence of the LORD* (77.16; 97.4).

PSALM 115

1 Not to us, O LORD, not to us, but to
    your name give glory,
    for the sake of your steadfast love and
        your faithfulness.
2 Why should the nations say,
    "Where is their God?"

3 Our God is in the heavens;
    he does whatever he pleases.
4 Their idols are silver and gold,
    the work of human hands.
5 They have mouths, but do not speak;
    eyes, but do not see.
6 They have ears, but do not hear;
    noses, but do not smell.
7 They have hands, but do not feel;
    feet, but do not walk;
    they make no sound in their throats.
8 Those who make them are like them;
    so are all who trust in them.

9 O Israel, trust in the LORD!
    He is their help and their shield.

10 O house of Aaron, trust in the LORD!
    He is their help and their shield.
11 You who fear the LORD, trust in
        the LORD!
    He is their help and their shield.

12 The LORD has been mindful of us; he
        will bless us;
    he will bless the house of Israel;
    he will bless the house of Aaron;
13 he will bless those who fear the LORD,
    both small and great.

14 May the LORD give you increase,
    both you and your children.
15 May you be blessed by the LORD,
    who made heaven and earth.

16 The heavens are the LORD's heavens,
    but the earth he has given to human
        beings.
17 The dead do not praise the LORD,
    nor do any that go down into
        silence.
18 But we will bless the LORD
    from this time on and forevermore.
    Praise the LORD!

115.1–18: Trust in the LORD! Difficult to classify, it has the character of a song of praise and profession of faith. It is part of the Egyptian "Hallel" (Ps 113–118). **1–2:** The double negation emphasizes God's sovereignty and character, the essence of which are *steadfast love* and *faithfulness* (Ex 34.6; Ps 36.5; 98.3). The question (v. 2; 42.3; 79.10) indicates that not all attribute *glory* to God. **3–8:** Reasserting God's sovereignty, v. 3 suggests not that God is whimsical but rather that he is powerful. This situation contrasts with *idols*, whose devotees are also rendered powerless (v. 8; 97.7; Isa 45.16). **9–11:** The issue is *trust* (vv. 8–11). Those who *trust in the LORD* find *help* and protection (33.20). It is unclear whether different groups are addressed (118.2–4; 135.19–20). **12–15:** God remembers (v. 12; 9.12) and *will bless* (5.12; 107.38). Whereas *idols* are made by their devotees (vv. 4, 8), Israel's God *made heaven and earth* (v. 15; 121.2; 124.8). **16–18:** God has chosen to share dominion of *the earth* (v. 16; 8.5–8). The human vocation is to *bless* and *praise* God (v. 18; see v. 1), which means to acknowledge God's ultimate dominion.

PSALM 116

1 I love the LORD, because he has heard
   my voice and my supplications.
2 Because he inclined his ear to me,
      therefore I will call on him as long as
         I live.
3 The snares of death encompassed me;
      the pangs of Sheol laid hold on me;
      I suffered distress and anguish.
4 Then I called on the name of
         the LORD:
   "O LORD, I pray, save my life!"

5 Gracious is the LORD, and righteous;
      our God is merciful.
6 The LORD protects the simple;
      when I was brought low, he
         saved me.
7 Return, O my soul, to your rest,
      for the LORD has dealt bountifully
         with you.

8 For you have delivered my soul from
         death,
      my eyes from tears,
      my feet from stumbling.
9 I walk before the LORD
      in the land of the living.
10 I kept my faith, even when I said,
   "I am greatly afflicted";
11 I said in my consternation,
   "Everyone is a liar."

12 What shall I return to the LORD
      for all his bounty to me?
13 I will lift up the cup of salvation
      and call on the name of the LORD,
14 I will pay my vows to the LORD
      in the presence of all his people.
15 Precious in the sight of the LORD
      is the death of his faithful ones.
16 O LORD, I am your servant;
      I am your servant, the child of your
         serving girl.
      You have loosed my bonds.
17 I will offer to you a thanksgiving
         sacrifice
      and call on the name of the LORD.
18 I will pay my vows to the LORD
      in the presence of all his people,

19 in the courts of the house of the LORD,
      in your midst, O Jerusalem.
   Praise the LORD!

116.1–19: What shall I return to the LORD? In a song of thanksgiving, the psalmist recalls former distress (vv. 3–4, 6b, 8, 10–11), celebrates deliverance (vv. 1–2, 7, 8–9), and renders thanks (vv. 12–19). It is part of the Egyptian "Hallel" (Ps 113–118). **1–4:** *Sheol* (v. 3), the realm of death, was sometimes viewed less as a place and more as a life-invading power (30.3; 49.15). God has delivered the psalmist from a life-threatening situation. The psalmist responds with *love* (v. 1; 5.11; 31.23) and the promise of life-long commitment (v. 2). **5–7:** The deliverance demonstrates God's character (v. 5; 111.3–4) and characteristic activity on behalf of the lowly (v. 6; 113.7). Verse 7a may state the psalmist's intent to visit the Temple* (see vv. 12–19). **8–11:** Recalling again the deliverance *from death* (v. 8) to *living* (v. 9), the psalmist affirms *faith* in God (v. 10) as opposed to human help (v. 11; 108.12). **12–13:** Recalling v. 7, v. 12 asks the question that is answered in v. 13. The *cup of salvation* may indicate a sacrificial offering of some kind (Ex 29.40). **14–19:** Verses 14 and 18 are identical (22.25). The payment includes verbal gratitude (v. 13) and *a thanksgiving sacrifice* (v. 17; Lev 7.12; Ps 107.22), apparently offered in the Temple (v. 19).

PSALM 117

1 Praise the LORD, all you nations!
      Extol him, all you peoples!
2 For great is his steadfast love toward us,
      and the faithfulness of the LORD
         endures forever.
   Praise the LORD!

117.1–2: Praise the LORD! A song of praise, its invitation is followed by reasons for *praise*. It is part of the Egyptian "Hallel" (Ps 113–118). **1:** The invitation typically extends beyond the bounds of God's people (97.1; 99.1; 100.1). A cosmic sovereign gathers a universal congregation. **2:** The reasons feature God's fundamental attributes—*steadfast love* and *faithfulness* (Ex 34.6; Ps 100.5; 115.1).

PSALM 118

1 O give thanks to the LORD, for he is
         good;
      his steadfast love endures forever!

2 Let Israel say,
   "His steadfast love endures forever."
3 Let the house of Aaron say,
   "His steadfast love endures forever."
4 Let those who fear the LORD say,
   "His steadfast love endures forever."

5 Out of my distress I called on the LORD;
   the LORD answered me and set me in
      a broad place.
6 With the LORD on my side I do not fear.
   What can mortals do to me?
7 The LORD is on my side to help me;
   I shall look in triumph on those who
      hate me.
8 It is better to take refuge in the LORD
   than to put confidence in mortals.
9 It is better to take refuge in the LORD
   than to put confidence in princes.

10 All nations surrounded me;
    in the name of the LORD I cut them
       off!
11 They surrounded me, surrounded me on
       every side;
    in the name of the LORD I cut them
       off!
12 They surrounded me like bees;
    they blazed[a] like a fire of thorns;
    in the name of the LORD I cut them
       off!
13 I was pushed hard,[b] so that I was
       falling,
    but the LORD helped me.
14 The LORD is my strength and my might;
    he has become my salvation.

15 There are glad songs of victory in the
       tents of the righteous:
    "The right hand of the LORD does
       valiantly;
16   the right hand of the LORD is exalted;
       the right hand of the LORD does
       valiantly."
17 I shall not die, but I shall live,
    and recount the deeds of the LORD.
18 The LORD has punished me severely,
    but he did not give me over to death.

19 Open to me the gates of righteousness,
    that I may enter through them
    and give thanks to the LORD.

20 This is the gate of the LORD;
    the righteous shall enter through it.

21 I thank you that you have answered me
    and have become my salvation.
22 The stone that the builders rejected
    has become the chief cornerstone.
23 This is the LORD's doing;
    it is marvelous in our eyes.
24 This is the day that the LORD has made;
    let us rejoice and be glad in it.[c]
25 Save us, we beseech you, O LORD!
    O LORD, we beseech you, give us
       success!

26 Blessed is the one who comes in the
       name of the LORD.[d]
    We bless you from the house of the
       LORD.
27 The LORD is God,
    and he has given us light.
    Bind the festal procession with
       branches,
    up to the horns of the altar.[e]

28 You are my God, and I will give thanks
       to you;
    you are my God, I will extol you.

29 O give thanks to the LORD, for he is
       good,
    for his steadfast love endures forever.

118.1–29: God's steadfast love endures forever. Because of the invitation to and the offering of thanks (vv. 19, 21, 28–29) accompanied by a recounting of deliverance from *distress* (vv. 5–18), it is usually classified as a song of thanksgiving of an individual. But the *distress* seems corporate (vv. 10–12), and the celebration of deliverance recalls the Exodus (v. 14). Furthermore, the speaker shifts to the plural in vv. 23–27, in the midst of which is an unexpected petition (v. 25). Hence the psalm possesses both a past and future orientation that is appropriate for the conclusion of the Egyptian "Hallel" (Ps 113–118), which was and is used at Passover.* **1–4:** Each verse contains *steadfast love*,

---

a Gk: Heb *were extinguished* b Gk Syr Jerome: Heb *You pushed me hard* c Or *in him* d Or *Blessed in the name of the* LORD *is the one who comes* e Meaning of Heb uncertain a word that frames the psalm (vv. 1, 29; 107.1) and a divine trait that deliverance reveals. Verses 2–4 anticipate the plural voice in vv. 23–27. **5–9:** Deliverance reveals that God is *on my side* or "for me" (56.9). The repetition of *refuge* (vv. 8–9; 2.12) emphasizes the effectiveness of divine *help* (v. 7) and the ineffectiveness of human agency (146.3). **10–14:** After recounting again that God has *helped* (v. 13; v. 7), the psalmist explicitly recalls the Exodus (v. 14; Ex 15.2). **15–18:** *Victory* (v. 15) is the same Hebrew word as *salvation* in v. 14 (see also v. 21). God's *deeds* deliver the psalmist from *death* (v. 18) to life. **19–29:** These verses suggest a public celebration of the deliverance recounted in vv. 5–18. The psalmist enters the Temple* (vv. 19–20), recounts again the deliverance (vv. 21–22), and then is joined by other voices (vv. 23–27) before concluding (vv. 28–29). Verse 24a could also be translated, "This is the day on which the LORD has acted," thus alluding to the deliverance described in vv. 5–18. *Branches* (v. 27) may indicate an original connection to the Feast of Booths (Lev 23.40). Like v. 14, v. 28 echoes Ex 15.2.

PSALM 119

1 Happy are those whose way is blameless,
  who walk in the law of the LORD.
2 Happy are those who keep his decrees,
  who seek him with their whole heart,
3 who also do no wrong,
  but walk in his ways.
4 You have commanded your precepts
  to be kept diligently.
5 O that my ways may be steadfast
  in keeping your statutes!
6 Then I shall not be put to shame,
  having my eyes fixed on all your
    commandments.
7 I will praise you with an upright heart,
  when I learn your righteous
    ordinances.
8 I will observe your statutes;
  do not utterly forsake me.

9 How can young people keep their way
    pure?
  By guarding it according to your
    word.
10 With my whole heart I seek you;
  do not let me stray from your
    commandments.

11 I treasure your word in my heart,
  so that I may not sin against you.
12 Blessed are you, O LORD;
  teach me your statutes.
13 With my lips I declare
  all the ordinances of your mouth.
14 I delight in the way of your decrees
  as much as in all riches.
15 I will meditate on your precepts,
  and fix my eyes on your ways.
16 I will delight in your statutes;
  I will not forget your word.

17 Deal bountifully with your servant,
  so that I may live and observe your
    word.
18 Open my eyes, so that I may behold
  wondrous things out of your law.
19 I live as an alien in the land;
  do not hide your commandments
    from me.
20 My soul is consumed with longing
  for your ordinances at all times.
21 You rebuke the insolent, accursed ones,
  who wander from your
    commandments;
22 take away from me their scorn and
    contempt,
  for I have kept your decrees.
23 Even though princes sit plotting against
    me,
  your servant will meditate on your
    statutes.
24 Your decrees are my delight,
  they are my counselors.

25 My soul clings to the dust;
  revive me according to your word.
26 When I told of my ways, you answered
    me;
  teach me your statutes.
27 Make me understand the way of your
    precepts,
  and I will meditate on your wondrous
    works.
28 My soul melts away for sorrow;
  strengthen me according to your
    word.
29 Put false ways far from me;
  and graciously teach me your law.

30 I have chosen the way of faithfulness;
      I set your ordinances before me.
31 I cling to your decrees, O LORD;
      let me not be put to shame.
32 I run the way of your commandments,
      for you enlarge my understanding.

119.1–176: The torah* of the LORD. The poem is an acrostic.* The first word of each of vv. 1–8 begins with an "Aleph"; the first word of each of vv. 9–16 begins with "Beth"; and so on throughout the Hebrew alphabet.* Although this psalm contains all types of material—petition, complaint, praise, trust, instruction, admonition—it is usually classified as a "torah"-psalm (see Ps 1, 19). The word "torah" (NRSV *law*) occurs twenty-five times, including at least once in every section except vv. 9–16. In addition, seven synonyms for "torah" occur repeatedly: *decrees, precepts, statutes, command(ment)s, ordinances, word,* and *promise.* Each verse contains one of the eight, except vv. 3, 37, 90, and 122. The psalm's date and origin are unclear. In its current setting, the psalm attests to the importance of "torah" in the post-exilic era as a central feature of communal life (see Introduction). **1–8:** *Happy* and *law* recall the beginning of the psalter (1.1–2; 2.12). While *law* suggests a written code, as do several of the synonyms, "torah" has a broader meaning: "instruction." *Blameless* cannot mean moral perfection, for the psalmist has sinned (v. 176). It connotes dependence upon God that yields happiness, a condition not incompatible with suffering (vv. 22–23, 84–87). **9–16:** *Word* frames the section (vv. 9, 16). Verse 11 recalls Jer 31.33. The psalmist humbly suggests that there is always more to learn. **17–24:** Petition (vv. 17–18) and complaint (v. 19, 21–23) dominate. Verse 19 anticipates v. 54, and the two would have been particularly meaningful in the post-exilic era. **25–32:** Complaint continues (vv. 25a, 28), in the midst of which the psalmist prays for life (v. 25b).

33 Teach me, O LORD, the way of your
        statutes,
      and I will observe it to the end.
34 Give me understanding, that I may keep
        your law
      and observe it with my whole heart.
35 Lead me in the path of your
        commandments,
      for I delight in it.
36 Turn my heart to your decrees,
      and not to selfish gain.

37 Turn my eyes from looking at vanities;
      give me life in your ways.
38 Confirm to your servant your promise,
      which is for those who fear you.
39 Turn away the disgrace that I dread,
      for your ordinances are good.
40 See, I have longed for your precepts;
      in your righteousness give me life.

41 Let your steadfast love come to me,
        O LORD,
      your salvation according to your
        promise.
42 Then I shall have an answer for those
        who taunt me,
      for I trust in your word.
43 Do not take the word of truth utterly
        out of my mouth,
      for my hope is in your ordinances.
44 I will keep your law continually,
      forever and ever.
45 I shall walk at liberty,
      for I have sought your precepts.
46 I will also speak of your decrees before
        kings,
      and shall not be put to shame;
47 I find my delight in your commandments,
      because I love them.
48 I revere your commandments, which I
        love,
      and I will meditate on your statutes.

49 Remember your word to your servant,
      in which you have made me hope.
50 This is my comfort in my distress,
      that your promise gives me life.
51 The arrogant utterly deride me,
      but I do not turn away from your law.
52 When I think of your ordinances from
        of old,
      I take comfort, O LORD.
53 Hot indignation seizes me because of
        the wicked,
      those who forsake your law.
54 Your statutes have been my songs
      wherever I make my home.
55 I remember your name in the night,
        O LORD,
      and keep your law.
56 This blessing has fallen to me,
      for I have kept your precepts.

57 The LORD is my portion;
    I promise to keep your words.
58 I implore your favor with all my heart;
    be gracious to me according to your
        promise.
59 When I think of your ways,
    I turn my feet to your decrees;
60 I hurry and do not delay
    to keep your commandments.
61 Though the cords of the wicked ensnare
        me,
    I do not forget your law.
62 At midnight I rise to praise you,
    because of your righteous
        ordinances.
63 I am a companion of all who fear you,
    of those who keep your precepts.
64 The earth, O LORD, is full of your
        steadfast love;
    teach me your statutes.

119.33–64. 33–40: Petition begins each of vv. 33–39,
requesting that the psalmist be completely oriented to
God, the giver of *life* (v. 40). **41–48:** Assurance becomes the theme—*trust* (v. 42), *hope* (v. 43), *liberty*
(v. 45), *delight* (v. 47). *Steadfast love* is the first of
seven occurrences (vv. 64, 76, 88, 124, 149, 159).
49–56: Remembering, God's and the psalmist's, is featured (vv. 49, 55; see v. 52). Memory leads to *hope*
(v. 49) and *comfort* (vv. 50, 52). **57–64:** *Portion* refers
to the tribal shares in the land, so the affirmation in v.
57a (16.5; 73.26) would have been especially meaningful to a homeless, landless people.

---

65 You have dealt well with your servant,
    O LORD, according to your word.
66 Teach me good judgment and
        knowledge,
    for I believe in your
        commandments.
67 Before I was humbled I went astray,
    but now I keep your word.
68 You are good and do good;
    teach me your statutes.
69 The arrogant smear me with lies,
    but with my whole heart I keep your
        precepts.
70 Their hearts are fat and gross,
    but I delight in your law.
71 It is good for me that I was humbled,
    so that I might learn your statutes.

72 The law of your mouth is better to me
    than thousands of gold and silver
        pieces.
73 Your hands have made and fashioned
        me;
    give me understanding that I may
        learn your commandments.
74 Those who fear you shall see me and
        rejoice,
    because I have hoped in your word.
75 I know, O LORD, that your judgments
        are right,
    and that in faithfulness you have
        humbled me.
76 Let your steadfast love become my
        comfort
    according to your promise to your
        servant.
77 Let your mercy come to me, that I may
        live;
    for your law is my delight.
78 Let the arrogant be put to shame,
    because they have subverted me with
        guile;
    as for me, I will meditate on your
        precepts.
79 Let those who fear you turn to me,
    so that they may know your decrees.
80 May my heart be blameless in your
        statutes,
    so that I may not be put to shame.
81 My soul languishes for your salvation;
    I hope in your word.
82 My eyes fail with watching for your
        promise;
    I ask, "When will you comfort me?"
83 For I have become like a wineskin in
        the smoke,
    yet I have not forgotten your
        statutes.
84 How long must your servant endure?
    When will you judge those who
        persecute me?
85 The arrogant have dug pitfalls for me;
    they flout your law.
86 All your commandments are
        enduring;
    I am persecuted without cause; help
        me!

87 They have almost made an end of me
　　on earth;
　　but I have not forsaken your precepts.
88 In your steadfast love spare my life,
　　so that I may keep the decrees of your
　　mouth.

89 The LORD exists forever;
　　your word is firmly fixed in heaven.
90 Your faithfulness endures to all
　　generations;
　　you have established the earth, and it
　　stands fast.
91 By your appointment they stand today,
　　for all things are your servants.
92 If your law had not been my delight,
　　I would have perished in my misery.
93 I will never forget your precepts,
　　for by them you have given me life.
94 I am yours; save me,
　　for I have sought your precepts.
95 The wicked lie in wait to destroy me,
　　but I consider your decrees.
96 I have seen a limit to all perfection,
　　but your commandment is
　　exceedingly broad.

119.65–96. 65–72: The key word is *well/good/better*
(vv. 65, 66, 68, 71, 72). The reward for obedience is
not material (v. 72) but rather the *delight* (v. 70) of
conformity to God's will (1.2–3). 73–80: In the context
(v. 75), *blameless* (v. 80) means being forgiven rather
than being sinless. The forgiven sinner instructs others
(32.8–9; 51.13). 81–88: The extended complaints reveal the psalmist's suffering, in the midst of which the
psalmist pleads for *life* (vv. 86, 88). 89–96: While not
entirely leaving behind complaint and petition (vv.
94–95), this section consists primarily of a hymnic profession of faith that asserts God's cosmic sovereignty
(vv. 89–91).

---

97 Oh, how I love your law!
　　It is my meditation all day long.
98 Your commandment makes me wiser
　　than my enemies,
　　for it is always with me.
99 I have more understanding than all my
　　teachers,
　　for your decrees are my meditation.
100 I understand more than the aged,
　　for I keep your precepts.

101 I hold back my feet from every evil way,
　　in order to keep your word.
102 I do not turn away from your ordinances,
　　for you have taught me.
103 How sweet are your words to my taste,
　　sweeter than honey to my mouth!
104 Through your precepts I get
　　understanding;
　　therefore I hate every false way.

105 Your word is a lamp to my feet
　　and a light to my path.
106 I have sworn an oath and confirmed it,
　　to observe your righteous ordinances.
107 I am severely afflicted;
　　give me life, O LORD, according to
　　your word.
108 Accept my offerings of praise, O LORD,
　　and teach me your ordinances.
109 I hold my life in my hand continually,
　　but I do not forget your law.
110 The wicked have laid a snare for me,
　　but I do not stray from your precepts.
111 Your decrees are my heritage forever;
　　they are the joy of my heart.
112 I incline my heart to perform your
　　statutes
　　forever, to the end.

113 I hate the double-minded,
　　but I love your law.
114 You are my hiding place and my shield;
　　I hope in your word.
115 Go away from me, you evildoers,
　　that I may keep the commandments
　　of my God.
116 Uphold me according to your promise,
　　that I may live,
　　and let me not be put to shame in my
　　hope.
117 Hold me up, that I may be safe
　　and have regard for your statutes
　　continually.
118 You spurn all who go astray from your
　　statutes;
　　for their cunning is in vain.
119 All the wicked of the earth you count as
　　dross;
　　therefore I love your decrees.
120 My flesh trembles for fear of you,
　　and I am afraid of your judgments.

119.97–120. 97–104: The sensual language of vv. 97, 103 conveys the depth of the psalmist's *love* for God's instruction, which yields wisdom and *understanding* (vv. 98–100). **105–112:** Like God's own self, God's *word* is a *light* (v. 105; 4.6; 27.1). The psalmist's affliction is again in view (vv. 107, 110). **113–120:** Amid the affliction, there is also divine protection and *hope* (v. 114). *Afraid* (v. 120) probably suggests awe and reverence rather than fright.

121 I have done what is just and right;
    do not leave me to my oppressors.
122 Guarantee your servant's well-being;
    do not let the godless oppress me.
123 My eyes fail from watching for your
        salvation,
    and for the fulfillment of your
        righteous promise.
124 Deal with your servant according to
        your steadfast love,
    and teach me your statutes.
125 I am your servant; give me
        understanding,
    so that I may know your decrees.
126 It is time for the LORD to act,
    for your law has been broken.
127 Truly I love your commandments
    more than gold, more than fine gold.
128 Truly I direct my steps by all your
        precepts;[a]
    I hate every false way.

129 Your decrees are wonderful;
    therefore my soul keeps them.
130 The unfolding of your words gives
        light;
    it imparts understanding to the
        simple.
131 With open mouth I pant,
    because I long for your
        commandments.
132 Turn to me and be gracious to me,
    as is your custom toward those who
        love your name.
133 Keep my steps steady according to your
        promise,
    and never let iniquity have dominion
        over me.
134 Redeem me from human oppression,
    that I may keep your precepts.

135 Make your face shine upon your
        servant,
    and teach me your statutes.
136 My eyes shed streams of tears
    because your law is not kept.

137 You are righteous, O LORD,
    and your judgments are right.
138 You have appointed your decrees in
        righteousness
    and in all faithfulness.
139 My zeal consumes me
    because my foes forget your words.
140 Your promise is well tried,
    and your servant loves it.
141 I am small and despised,
    yet I do not forget your precepts.
142 Your righteousness is an everlasting
        righteousness,
    and your law is the truth.
143 Trouble and anguish have come
        upon me,
    but your commandments are my
        delight.
144 Your decrees are righteous forever;
    give me understanding that I may
        live.

145 With my whole heart I cry; answer me,
        O LORD.
    I will keep your statutes.
146 I cry to you; save me,
    that I may observe your decrees.
147 I rise before dawn and cry for help;
    I put my hope in your words.
148 My eyes are awake before each watch of
        the night,
    that I may meditate on your promise.
149 In your steadfast love hear my voice;
    O LORD, in your justice preserve my
        life.
150 Those who persecute me with evil
        purpose draw near;
    they are far from your law.
151 Yet you are near, O LORD,
    and all your commandments are true.
152 Long ago I learned from your decrees
    that you have established them
        forever.

a Gk Jerome: Meaning of Heb uncertain

119.121–152. 121–128: Verse 122 may be the most noticeable in the psalm since it contains none of the eight synonyms for "torah." It highlights the psalmist's *servant* role (see vv. 122, 124–125). **129–136:** *Custom* in v. 132 is, more literally, "justice." The psalmist asserts that God's "justice" is finally to *be gracious.* **137–144:** The key word here is *righteous(ness)* (vv. 137, 138, 142, 144). **145–152:** The opposites *near* and *far* are featured in vv. 150–151. Ultimately, God is *near* (73.28).

153 Look on my misery and rescue me,
for I do not forget your law.
154 Plead my cause and redeem me;
give me life according to your
promise.
155 Salvation is far from the wicked,
for they do not seek your statutes.
156 Great is your mercy, O LORD;
give me life according to your justice.
157 Many are my persecutors and my
adversaries,
yet I do not swerve from your
decrees.
158 I look at the faithless with disgust,
because they do not keep your
commands.
159 Consider how I love your precepts;
preserve my life according to your
steadfast love.
160 The sum of your word is truth;
and every one of your righteous
ordinances endures forever.

161 Princes persecute me without cause,
but my heart stands in awe of your
words.
162 I rejoice at your word
like one who finds great spoil.
163 I hate and abhor falsehood,
but I love your law.
164 Seven times a day I praise you
for your righteous ordinances.
165 Great peace have those who love your
law;
nothing can make them stumble.
166 I hope for your salvation, O LORD,
and I fulfill your commandments.
167 My soul keeps your decrees;
I love them exceedingly.

168 I keep your precepts and decrees,
for all my ways are before you.

169 Let my cry come before you, O LORD;
give me understanding according to
your word.
170 Let my supplication come before you;
deliver me according to your
promise.
171 My lips will pour forth praise,
because you teach me your statutes.
172 My tongue will sing of your promise,
for all your commandments are
right.
173 Let your hand be ready to help me,
for I have chosen your precepts.
174 I long for your salvation, O LORD,
and your law is my delight.
175 Let me live that I may praise you,
and let your ordinances help me.
176 I have gone astray like a lost sheep; seek
out your servant,
for I do not forget your
commandments.

119.153–176. 153–160: The petition for *life* occurs throughout but is concentrated here (vv. 154, 156, 159). **161–168:** It is not clear whether *seven times* is meant literally or whether, since *seven* is the number of completeness, it connotes continual *praise* (v. 164). **169–176:** The psalm concludes with the striking simile* of *a lost sheep. Lost* is more literally "perishing," a word associated with the wicked (1.6). Thus it emphasizes that God's "torah" communicates God's essentially merciful character (vv. 77, 156).

PSALM 120
A Song of Ascents.

1 In my distress I cry to the LORD,
that he may answer me:
2 "Deliver me, O LORD,
from lying lips,
from a deceitful tongue."

3 What shall be given to you?
And what more shall be done to you,
you deceitful tongue?
4 A warrior's sharp arrows,
with glowing coals of the broom
tree!

5 Woe is me, that I am an alien in
    Meshech,
  that I must live among the tents of
    Kedar.
6 Too long have I had my dwelling
  among those who hate peace.
7 I am for peace;
  but when I speak,
  they are for war.

120.1–7: Peace and war. The first of the Songs of Ascents (Ps 120–134), its opening complaint and petition suggest a prayer for help. But its uniqueness makes it appropriate for beginning the Ascents collection. This psalm locates the speaker outside the land (v. 5), while the next two psalms suggest a journey (Ps 121) that ends in Jerusalem (Ps 122; especially *go up* in v. 4, since Jerusalem is on a hill). The Songs of Ascents probably originated as, or became, a collection used by pilgrims as they traveled to and from Jerusalem. Several of the psalms reflect the daily concerns of ordinary folk (Ps 127, 128, 133), and there are numerous references to Jerusalem (Ps 122, 125, 126, 128, 129, 132–134). Psalm 133 suggests that individual families have gathered as the larger family of God, and the concluding Ps 134 sounds like a benediction. **1–4:** The *distress* is a frequent one—deceitful enemies (31.18; 109.2). The *deceitful tongue* is personified* and addressed in v. 3 with questions that are answered in v. 4. In short, justice will be done (140.9–11). **5–7:** Since they are not close together, *Meshech* (Ezek 32.26) and *Kedar* (Isa 21.16–17) may stand metaphorically* for all those *who hate peace*. The longing for *peace* (vv. 6–7) may anticipate the journey to Jerusalem (122.6–8). The repetition of *peace* in successive lines produces a stair-like pattern appropriate for a *Song of Ascents* (*Ascents* can also mean "stairs" or "steps").

PSALM 121
A Song of Ascents.

1 I lift up my eyes to the hills—
  from where will my help come?
2 My help comes from the LORD,
  who made heaven and earth.

3 He will not let your foot be moved;
  he who keeps you will not slumber.
4 He who keeps Israel
  will neither slumber nor sleep.

5 The LORD is your keeper;
  the LORD is your shade at your right
    hand.
6 The sun shall not strike you by day,
  nor the moon by night.

7 The LORD will keep you from all evil;
  he will keep your life.
8 The LORD will keep
  your going out and your coming in
  from this time on and forevermore.

121.1–8: The LORD is your keeper. A psalm of trust and the second *Song of Ascents* (see Ps 120), its unifying motif* is a journey for which the LORD is the psalmist's *keeper* (v. 5). **1–2:** The cosmic creator (v. 2; 115.15; 124.8; 134.3) is also the psalmist's personal *help*. The stair-like repetition is characteristic of the collection (120.5–7). In the present context, *hills* probably includes Zion* (125.1–2). **3–4:** The stair-like pattern (see 120.5–7) continues with *slumber* and *keeps*, which becomes the key word (vv. 5, 7, 8). **5–6:** For travelers, *the sun* could be hazardous (Isa 49.10); and the ancients believed that *the moon* was dangerous (see Mt 17.15 where "epileptic" is literally "moonstruck"). God provides protection. **7–8:** Three more occurrences of *keep* extend the promise of God's protection from a particular journey to all of *life* and *forevermore* (Deut 28.6).

PSALM 122
A Song of Ascents. Of David.

1 I was glad when they said to me,
  "Let us go to the house of the LORD!"
2 Our feet are standing
  within your gates, O Jerusalem.

3 Jerusalem—built as a city
  that is bound firmly together.
4 To it the tribes go up,
  the tribes of the LORD,
  as was decreed for Israel,
  to give thanks to the name of
    the LORD.
5 For there the thrones for judgment were
    set up,
  the thrones of the house of David.

6 Pray for the peace of Jerusalem:
  "May they prosper who love you.

7 Peace be within your walls,
    and security within your towers."
8 For the sake of my relatives and friends
    I will say, "Peace be within you."
9 For the sake of the house of the LORD
      our God,
    I will seek your good.

122.1–9: Pray for the peace of Jerusalem. The focus on *Jerusalem* (vv. 2, 3, 6), makes it a song of Zion* (see Ps 48, 84). It is the only actual pilgrimage song among the Songs of Ascents, which was probably a pilgrimage collection (see Ps 120). **1–2:** The psalmist joyfully responds to the invitation to visit the Temple* (Jer 31.6), and v. 2 locates the pilgrims in *Jerusalem.* **3–5:** The phrase, *bound firmly together,* may celebrate Jerusalem's architecture (48.12–14), but it may also suggest the city's ability to bring people together. Such is the subject of v. 4, where *go up* represents the same Hebrew root as *Ascents. Tribes* represents more stair-like repetition (see 120.5–7). *Judgment* could be translated "justice," which was to be enacted by *the house of David* in accordance with God's will (72.1–2). **6–8:** The key word is *peace,* the Hebrew word for which ("shalom") is an element of the name *Jerusalem. Peace* is the result of doing justice (72.7). **9:** References to *the house of the LORD* frame the psalm (see v. 1). The visit to the Temple has motivated the psalmist to do the *good* that promotes justice and *peace.*

PSALM 123
A Song of Ascents.

1 To you I lift up my eyes,
    O you who are enthroned in the
      heavens!
2 As the eyes of servants
    look to the hand of their master,
  as the eyes of a maid
    to the hand of her mistress,
  so our eyes look to the LORD our God,
    until he has mercy upon us.

3 Have mercy upon us, O LORD, have
      mercy upon us,
    for we have had more than enough of
      contempt.
4 Our soul has had more than its fill
    of the scorn of those who are at ease,
    of the contempt of the proud.

123.1–4: Have mercy upon us, O LORD. If the Songs of Ascents reflect the experience of pilgrims from hostile environments (see Ps 120), then it makes sense that their prayers for help would express trust in the sovereign God (vv. 1–2; see Ps 121), dependence on God's *mercy* (v. 3a), and the frustration of living amid oppression (vv. 3b–4). **1–2:** The repetition of *eyes* maintains a stair-like pattern (see 120.5–7). The pilgrims appropriately posture themselves as *servants* before a cosmic sovereign. The use of *maid* and *mistress* hints at feminine imagery for God (see Ps 131). **3:** The repeated *have mercy* surrounds the LORD with requests for help. **4:** *Contempt* (see also v. 3) and *scorn* recall the conditions that existed in the post-exilic era (see Neh 2.19 where "mocked" and "ridiculed" represent the same Hebrew words).

PSALM 124
A Song of Ascents. Of David.

1 If it had not been the LORD who was on
      our side
    —let Israel now say—
2 if it had not been the LORD who was on
      our side,
    when our enemies attacked us,
3 then they would have swallowed us up
      alive,
    when their anger was kindled against
      us;
4 then the flood would have swept us
      away,
    the torrent would have gone over us;
5 then over us would have gone
    the raging waters.

6 Blessed be the LORD,
    who has not given us
      as prey to their teeth.
7 We have escaped like a bird
    from the snare of the fowlers;
  the snare is broken,
    and we have escaped.

8 Our help is in the name of the LORD,
    who made heaven and earth.

124.1–8: Our help is in the name of the LORD. A communal song of thanksgiving, it is especially appropriate after the prayer for help in Ps 123. As Ps 123 recalls

120, so Ps 124 recalls 121 (compare 121.2 and 124.8), perhaps suggesting an intentional arranging of the Songs of Ascents (see Ps 120). **1–2:** The two *if*-clauses implicitly affirm the *help* proclaimed explicitly in v. 8. The invitation in v. 1b (see 129.1) implies liturgical* use by the pilgrims assembled in Jerusalem (see Ps 122). **3–5:** Without God's *help* (v. 8), the people would have been overwhelmed by chaotic forces, represented by *flood*, *torrent*, and *waters*. **6–7:** The repetitions of *We have escaped* and *snare* is another instance of stair-like repetition (see 120.5–7). The order is important. The instruments of enslavement are encompassed by references to freedom. **8:** The community now affirms what an individual voice affirmed in 121.2.

PSALM 125

A Song of Ascents.

1 Those who trust in the LORD are like
     Mount Zion,
   which cannot be moved, but abides
     forever.
2 As the mountains surround Jerusalem,
   so the LORD surrounds his people,
   from this time on and forevermore.
3 For the scepter of wickedness shall not
     rest
   on the land allotted to the
     righteous,
   so that the righteous might not stretch
     out
   their hands to do wrong.
4 Do good, O LORD, to those who are
     good,
   and to those who are upright in their
     hearts.
5 But those who turn aside to their own
     crooked ways
   the LORD will lead away with
     evildoers.
     Peace be upon Israel!

125.1–5: Trust in the LORD. Like several of the Songs of Ascents (see Ps 120), it focuses on Jerusalem (see Ps 122). **1–2:** Appropriately for pilgrims, their destination—*Mount Zion*—becomes a metaphor* for the faithful life. The surrounding terrain also reminds them of God's eternal protection. **3:** The *land allotted* may have been controlled by the wicked, which may reflect the post-exilic situation. *Trust* (v. 1) must exist

amid opposition, and v. 3 implies the petition that *the righteous* not yield to the temptation to imitate their oppressors (see 141.3–4). **4–5:** Petition becomes explicit in v. 4; whereas v. 5 professes faith in God's ultimate sovereignty, despite *the scepter of wickedness* (v. 3). The sovereign God wills *peace*, and *peace* is what the psalmist proclaims (120.7; 122.6–8; 128.6).

PSALM 126

A Song of Ascents.

1 When the LORD restored the fortunes of
     Zion,*a*
   we were like those who dream.
2 Then our mouth was filled with
     laughter,
   and our tongue with shouts of joy;
   then it was said among the nations,
   "The LORD has done great things for
     them."
3 The LORD has done great things for us,
   and we rejoiced.

4 Restore our fortunes, O LORD,
   like the watercourses in the Negeb.
5 May those who sow in tears
   reap with shouts of joy.
6 Those who go out weeping,
   bearing the seed for sowing,
   shall come home with shouts of joy,
   carrying their sheaves.

126.1–6: Bringing in the sheaves. The focus on *Zion** is characteristic of the Songs of Ascents (see Ps 120), as are the petition for help (120.1–2; 123.3) and trust in future deliverance (121.7–8; 123.2; 124.8). **1–3:** The return from exile is cited in v. 1 (Deut 30.3; Jer 30.3; Ps 85.1). The image of a *dream* come true was a source of *joy* and celebration, as even *the nations* recognized (compare v. 2b with 115.2). **4–6:** Because the return from exile brought problems of its own, the people needed to continue to pray for restoration (vv. 4–5). The image of *watercourses* communicates hope, since dry streambeds could suddenly become rivers during the rainy season. Striking a thematic note, v. 6 clearly articulates the hope of further *joy*.

a Or brought back those who returned to Zion

PSALM 127

A Song of Ascents. Of Solomon.

1 Unless the LORD builds the house,
    those who build it labor in vain.
Unless the LORD guards the city,
    the guard keeps watch in vain.
2 It is in vain that you rise up early
    and go late to rest,
eating the bread of anxious toil;
    for he gives sleep to his beloved.*

3 Sons are indeed a heritage from
        the LORD,
    the fruit of the womb a reward.
4 Like arrows in the hand of a warrior
    are the sons of one's youth.
5 Happy is the man who has
    his quiver full of them.
He shall not be put to shame
    when he speaks with his enemies in
        the gate.

127.1–5: Unless the LORD builds the house. The focus on daily activities (vv. 1–2) and family (vv. 3–5) may reflect the concerns of ordinary pilgrims who originally used the Songs of Ascents (see Ps 120). The attribution to *Solomon* is in keeping with the collection's interest in Jerusalem and the Davidic dynasty.* **1–2:** The key word is *vain*. It, and the repeated *Unless the LORD*, show the stair-like repetition characteristic of the collection (see 120.5–7). Any and every activity will be purposeless unless oriented to God. **3–5:** Because building a house (v. 1) can refer to the establishment of a family, v. 3 follows vv. 1–2 more logically than it may first appear. Children are to be seen as God's gift. The city *gate* was the site of legal activity, so having many children may have brought power and protection in the public arena.

PSALM 128

A Song of Ascents.

1 Happy is everyone who fears
        the LORD,
    who walks in his ways.
2 You shall eat the fruit of the labor of
        your hands;
    you shall be happy, and it shall go
        well with you.

3 Your wife will be like a fruitful vine
    within your house;
your children will be like olive shoots
    around your table.
4 Thus shall the man be blessed
    who fears the LORD.

5 The LORD bless you from Zion.
    May you see the prosperity of
        Jerusalem
    all the days of your life.
6 May you see your children's children.
    Peace be upon Israel!

128.1–6: Happy is everyone who fears the LORD. Linked to Ps 127 by the word *happy*, it also shares the interest in daily activities and family matters that is characteristic of the Songs of Ascents (see Ps 120). **1–2:** Fear connotes trust and obedience. To be *happy* involves orienting life fully to God (1.1–2; 112.1). **3–4:** The focus shifts from the realm of work to that of family. As in v. 1, the crucial component is fear of God. **5–6:** *Blessed* (v. 4) and *bless* (v. 5; 134.3) demonstrate the stair-like repetition that characterizes the collection (see 120.5–7). The effect is to put the daily concerns of families in the broader context of the *peace* of God's larger family, *Israel* (122.6–8; 125.5; 133.3).

PSALM 129

A Song of Ascents.

1 "Often have they attacked me from my
        youth"
    —let Israel now say—
2 "often have they attacked me from my
        youth,
    yet they have not prevailed against
        me.
3 The plowers plowed on my back;
    they made their furrows long."
4 The LORD is righteous;
    he has cut the cords of the wicked.
5 May all who hate Zion
    be put to shame and turned
        backward.
6 Let them be like the grass on the
        housetops
    that withers before it grows up,

a Or *for he provides for his beloved during sleep*

7 with which reapers do not fill their
    hands
    or binders of sheaves their arms,
8 while those who pass by do not say,
    "The blessing of the LORD be upon
      you!
    We bless you in the name of the
      LORD!"

129.1–8: They have not prevailed against me. This psalm is categorized either as a communal prayer for help or communal thanksgiving, since it is not clear whether deliverance has occurred (vv. 2–4) or is still awaited (vv. 5–8). The combination of individual voice and communal voice is understandable if the Songs of Ascents were used as pilgrim songs (see Ps 120). **1–4:** Verse 1 recalls 124.1. That the people continue to exist (v. 2b) despite frequent opposition (vv. 1–2a, 3) is evidence that God *is righteous* (v. 4); that is, God is responsible for the people's life. **5–8:** The interest in *Zion** characterizes the collection (122.6–8; 125.1–2). Verse 8 apparently articulates what the opponents of *Zion* will *not* hear or experience (compare 134.3).

PSALM 130

A Song of Ascents.

1 Out of the depths I cry to you, O LORD.
2   Lord, hear my voice!
Let your ears be attentive
    to the voice of my supplications!

3 If you, O LORD, should mark iniquities,
    Lord, who could stand?
4 But there is forgiveness with you,
    so that you may be revered.

5 I wait for the LORD, my soul waits,
    and in his word I hope;
6 my soul waits for the Lord
    more than those who watch for the
      morning,
    more than those who watch for the
      morning.

7 O Israel, hope in the LORD!
    For with the LORD there is steadfast
      love,
    and with him is great power to
      redeem.

8 It is he who will redeem Israel
    from all its iniquities.

130.1–8: Out of the depths. The juxtaposition with Ps 129 is auspicious, for it indicates that opposition to God occurs also within the ranks of God's people. This *Song of Ascents* (see Ps 120) became one of the church's Penitential Psalms* (see Ps 6). **1–2:** *The depths* represent a chaotic situation from which the psalmist pleads for deliverance. **3–4:** The question in v. 3 implies that the psalmist's own sinfulness has contributed to the current distress. God's *forgiveness* provides the foundation for the subsequent expressions of *hope* (vv. 5, 7). **5–6:** To *wait* and to *hope* are essentially synonymous (27.14; 31.24). The repetition in v. 6 is stair-like (see 120.5–7) and creates the effect of waiting. **7–8:** *Hope* is also associated with *steadfast love* in 33.18. God's *forgiveness* (v. 4) of *iniquities* (vv. 3, 8) is evidence of God's *steadfast love*. It recalls Israel's past (Ex 34.6–7), and the memory is a source of *hope* (131.3).

PSALM 131

A Song of Ascents. Of David.

1 O LORD, my heart is not lifted up,
    my eyes are not raised too high;
I do not occupy myself with things
    too great and too marvelous for me.
2 But I have calmed and quieted my soul,
    like a weaned child with its mother;
    my soul is like the weaned child that
      is with me.[a]

3 O Israel, hope in the LORD
    from this time on and forevermore.

131.1–3: Like a weaned child with its mother. The use of *mother*/child imagery and the likelihood of female authorship (v. 2) fits the pilgrimage context of the Songs of Ascents since whole families may have made the trip to Jerusalem (see Ps 120). The psalm is an expression of humble trust that follows well upon Ps 130, to which Ps 131 is verbally linked (130.7; 131.3). **1:** The psalmist's humility is evident in her attitudes (*heart*), demeanor (*eyes*), and vocation (*occupy*). **2:** Her humility, perhaps forced upon her as a woman in a patriarchal culture, is accompanied by a

a Or *my soul within me is like a weaned child*

sense of peace. *A weaned child* is most likely to return to its *mother* for security, so the phrase *with me* strongly suggests that the author is a woman. **3:** Israel's *hope* is to be based on the same experience described in v. 2. Thus, *the* LORD is portrayed as a loving, nurturing *mother* (see Deut 1.31; Isa 66.13; Jer 31.20).

PSALM 132

A Song of Ascents.

1 O LORD, remember in David's favor
   all the hardships he endured;
2 how he swore to the LORD
   and vowed to the Mighty One of
      Jacob,
3 "I will not enter my house
   or get into my bed;
4 I will not give sleep to my eyes
   or slumber to my eyelids,
5 until I find a place for the LORD,
   a dwelling place for the Mighty One
      of Jacob."

6 We heard of it in Ephrathah;
   we found it in the fields of Jaar.
7 "Let us go to his dwelling place;
   let us worship at his footstool."

8 Rise up, O LORD, and go to your resting
      place,
   you and the ark of your might.
9 Let your priests be clothed with
      righteousness,
   and let your faithful shout for joy.
10 For your servant David's sake
   do not turn away the face of your
      anointed one.

11 The LORD swore to David a sure oath
   from which he will not turn back:
   "One of the sons of your body
   I will set on your throne.
12 If your sons keep my covenant
   and my decrees that I shall teach
      them,
   their sons also, forevermore,
   shall sit on your throne."

13 For the LORD has chosen Zion;
   he has desired it for his habitation:

14 "This is my resting place forever;
   here I will reside, for I have desired
      it.
15 I will abundantly bless its provisions;
   I will satisfy its poor with bread.
16 Its priests I will clothe with salvation,
   and its faithful will shout for joy.
17 There I will cause a horn to sprout up
      for David;
   I have prepared a lamp for my
      anointed one.
18 His enemies I will clothe with
      disgrace,
   but on him, his crown will gleam."

132.1–18: A lamp for my anointed* one. Noticeably longer than the other Songs of Ascents (see Ps 120), it is usually classified as a royal psalm (see Ps 2, 72) or a song of Zion* (see Ps 48, 122). As such, it articulates the reasons that Jerusalem is the pilgrim's destination (v. 13). The use of 132.8–9 is assigned to Solomon's dedication of the Temple* (2 Chr 6.41), but vv. 17–18 suggest the psalm originated after the traumatic disappearance of the monarchy (see Ps 89). **1–5:** The *hardships* (v. 1) of David may refer not so much to the efforts recounted in vv. 3–5, but rather to the eventual loss of the monarchy (see vv. 17–18). David's oath recalls 2 Sam 7.1–2. **6–7:** The identity of *it* is unclear; it could be David's oath (vv. 3–5) or perhaps the ark. *Ephrathah* may indicate the region around Bethlehem, David's home. *Jaar* may be a shortened form of Kiriath-jearim, the location of the ark in 1 Sam 6.19–7.2. If the psalm was used by pilgrims, v. 7 may indicate their intent to retrace David's route in moving the ark to Jerusalem (2 Sam 6). **8–10:** Verse 8 may again recall David's journey with the ark, or it may initiate a prayer for the Temple (v. 8), its officiants and worshippers (v. 9), and the royal house (probably now destroyed). **11–12:** God's oath responds to David's oath (vv. 3–5). It recalls the promises to David in 2 Sam 7, although *covenant** recalls 89.3–4. **13–16:** Corresponding to vv. 6–9, this section indicates God's choice of *Zion* as *my resting place* (v. 14; see v. 8). Verse 16 indicates God's response to the petition in v. 9. **17–18:** These verses respond to the plea of v. 10. *Horn* and *lamp* represent the promise of a future monarch, an *anointed one* (2.2), although this designation could also be applied to the whole people (105.15; see Ps 149).

PSALM 133

A Song of Ascents.

1 How very good and pleasant it is
    when kindred live together in unity!
2 It is like the precious oil on the head,
    running down upon the beard,
on the beard of Aaron,
    running down over the collar of his
        robes.
3 It is like the dew of Hermon,
    which falls on the mountains of Zion.
For there the LORD ordained his
        blessing,
    life forevermore.

133.1–3: When kindred live together in unity. Like other Songs of Ascents (see Ps 120), it features family imagery (v. 1; Ps 127–128) and focuses finally on Zion* (v. 3; Ps 122). It thus recalls Ps 132. The word *blessing* anticipates Ps 134. Ps 133 may represent a final celebration of the pilgrims' unity before a parting blessing. **1:** Perhaps originally a proverbial saying, the focus here is on an extended biological family. **2:** The simile* probably is intended to communicate joy and abundance. The stair-like repetition (see 120.5–7) of *running down* recreates the effect of dripping oil. **3:** *Hermon* was known for abundant *dew*. The simile shifts attention from local families to the whole family of God gathered at *Zion*. It is *there* that the gathered family experiences God's *blessing* of *life forevermore*.

PSALM 134

A Song of Ascents.

1 Come, bless the LORD, all you servants
    of the LORD,
who stand by night in the house of
        the LORD!
2 Lift up your hands to the holy place,
    and bless the LORD.

3 May the LORD, maker of heaven and
        earth,
    bless you from Zion.

134.1–3: Blessing from Zion.* It provides a fitting conclusion to the Songs of Ascents (see Ps 120) by offering a parting benediction (v. 3) to the pilgrims. **1–2:** It may have originally been used at a closing worship service on the *night* before the pilgrims' depar-

ture. Two names for the Temple*—*house of the LORD* and *holy place*—are surrounded by the invitation to *bless the LORD*. **3:** Recalling 121.2 and 124.8, it sends pilgrims on their way with the hope that God will *bless* them (128.5).

PSALM 135

1 Praise the LORD!
    Praise the name of the LORD;
    give praise, O servants of the LORD,
2 you that stand in the house of
        the LORD,
    in the courts of the house of
        our God.
3 Praise the LORD, for the LORD is good;
    sing to his name, for he is gracious.
4 For the LORD has chosen Jacob for
        himself,
    Israel as his own possession.

5 For I know that the LORD is great;
    our Lord is above all gods.
6 Whatever the LORD pleases he does,
    in heaven and on earth,
    in the seas and all deeps.
7 He it is who makes the clouds rise at
        the end of the earth;
    he makes lightnings for the rain
    and brings out the wind from his
        storehouses.

8 He it was who struck down the firstborn
        of Egypt,
    both human beings and animals;
9 he sent signs and wonders
    into your midst, O Egypt,
    against Pharaoh and all his servants.
10 He struck down many nations
    and killed mighty kings—
11 Sihon, king of the Amorites,
    and Og, king of Bashan,
    and all the kingdoms of Canaan—
12 and gave their land as a heritage,
    a heritage to his people Israel.

13 Your name, O LORD, endures forever,
    your renown, O LORD, throughout all
        ages.
14 For the LORD will vindicate his people,
    and have compassion on his servants.

15 The idols of the nations are silver and
        gold,
   the work of human hands.
16 They have mouths, but they do not
        speak;
   they have eyes, but they do not see;
17 they have ears, but they do not hear,
   and there is no breath in their
        mouths.
18 Those who make them
   and all who trust them
   shall become like them.

19 O house of Israel, bless the LORD!
   O house of Aaron, bless the LORD!
20 O house of Levi, bless the LORD!
   You that fear the LORD, bless
        the LORD!
21 Blessed be the LORD from Zion,
   he who resides in Jerusalem.
   Praise the LORD!

135.1–21: Praise the name of the LORD. A song of
praise, it locates the *servants of the LORD* (v. 1) in the
same place as 134.1. Some scholars suggest that it,
along with Ps 136 and 137, form an appendix to the
Songs of Ascents (Ps 120–134). **1–4:** *Praise* (vv. 1, 3)
and *name* (vv. 1, 3, 13) are thematic. *Name* suggests
character, and the psalm will describe who God is and
how God is *good* (v. 3) by rehearsing what God has
done. Verse 4 anticipates v. 14. **5–14:** The sovereignty
of God *above all gods* (v. 5; see vv. 15–18) is evident
in the created order (vv. 6–7; 115.3) as well as in the
Exodus (vv. 8–9) and entry into *Canaan* (vv. 10–11;
Num 21.21–35). The gift of land to oppressed persons
demonstrates God's *compassion* (v. 14; Deut 32.36).
15–18: In contrast to God's dynamic activity, *idols* do
nothing (115.4–8). **19–21:** The four-fold occurrence
of *bless* again recalls Ps 134, as does the final focus on
Zion.* The different addressees may represent different groups, such as the entire congregation and priests
(115.9–11; 118.2–4).

~~~~~~~~~~

PSALM 136

1 O give thanks to the LORD, for he is
        good,
   for his steadfast love endures forever.
2 O give thanks to the God of gods,
   for his steadfast love endures
        forever.

3 O give thanks to the Lord of lords,
   for his steadfast love endures forever;
4 who alone does great wonders,
   for his steadfast love endures forever;
5 who by understanding made the
        heavens,
   for his steadfast love endures forever;
6 who spread out the earth on the
        waters,
   for his steadfast love endures forever;
7 who made the great lights,
   for his steadfast love endures forever;
8 the sun to rule over the day,
   for his steadfast love endures forever;
9 the moon and stars to rule over
        the night,
   for his steadfast love endures forever;
10 who struck Egypt through their
        firstborn,
   for his steadfast love endures forever;
11 and brought Israel out from among
        them,
   for his steadfast love endures forever;
12 with a strong hand and an outstretched
        arm,
   for his steadfast love endures forever;
13 who divided the Red Sea*a* in two,
   for his steadfast love endures forever;
14 and made Israel pass through the midst
        of it,
   for his steadfast love endures forever;
15 but overthrew Pharaoh and his army in
        the Red Sea,*a*
   for his steadfast love endures forever;
16 who led his people through the
        wilderness,
   for his steadfast love endures forever;
17 who struck down great kings,
   for his steadfast love endures forever;
18 and killed famous kings,
   for his steadfast love endures forever;
19 Sihon, king of the Amorites,
   for his steadfast love endures forever;
20 and Og, king of Bashan,
   for his steadfast love endures forever;
21 and gave their land as a heritage,
   for his steadfast love endures forever;

a Or Sea of Reeds

22 a heritage to his servant Israel,
　　for his steadfast love endures
　　　forever.

23 It is he who remembered us in our low
　　　estate,
　　for his steadfast love endures
　　　forever;
24 and rescued us from our foes,
　　for his steadfast love endures
　　　forever;
25 who gives food to all flesh,
　　for his steadfast love endures
　　　forever.

26 O give thanks to the God of heaven,
　　for his steadfast love endures
　　　forever.

136.1–26: God's steadfast love endures forever. A song of praise, it recalls Ps 135 (see *good* in 135.5 and 136.1; compare 136.2–3 with 135.5, 136.5–9 with 135.6–7, and 136.10–22 with 135.8–12). It is also frequently labeled a historical psalm (see Ps 78, 105–106). Its most obvious feature is the refrain that is repeated in every verse, suggesting that God's *steadfast love* pervades Israel's story. The refrain probably represents a sung congregational response. **1–3:** Verse 1 recalls 106.1; 107.1; 118.1, 29. As in Ps 135, God's sovereignty—*God of gods* and *Lord of lords*—is evident by what God has done (vv. 4–25). **4–9:** The focus on creation recalls Gen 1. The refrain suggests that creation was motivated by God's *steadfast love*. **10–22:** Also motivated by God's *steadfast love* is the Exodus (vv. 10–15) and guidance in the wilderness toward entry into the *land* (vv. 16–22). **23–25:** Verses 23–24 seem to refer to the return from exile. The perspective becomes cosmic again in v. 25 (see vv. 4–9) with the mention of *all flesh* (104.27). **26:** Because creation and providence reveal God's *steadfast love*, the appropriate response is gratitude.

PSALM 137

1 By the rivers of Babylon—
　　there we sat down and there we wept
　　when we remembered Zion.
2 On the willows[a] there
　　we hung up our harps.
3 For there our captors
　　asked us for songs,

and our tormentors asked for mirth,
　　saying,
　　"Sing us one of the songs of Zion!"

4 How could we sing the LORD's song
　　in a foreign land?
5 If I forget you, O Jerusalem,
　　let my right hand wither!
6 Let my tongue cling to the roof of my
　　　mouth,
　　if I do not remember you,
　　if I do not set Jerusalem
　　above my highest joy.

7 Remember, O LORD, against the
　　　Edomites
　　the day of Jerusalem's fall,
　　how they said, "Tear it down! Tear it
　　　down!
　　Down to its foundations!"
8 O daughter Babylon, you devastator![b]
　　Happy shall they be who pay
　　　you back
　　what you have done to us!
9 Happy shall they be who take your little
　　　ones
　　and dash them against the rock!

137.1–9: When we remembered Zion. * The focus on *Zion* (vv. 1, 3) and *Jerusalem* (vv. 5–7) recalls the Songs of Ascents, and it is likely that Ps 135–137 form an appendix to that collection. Psalm 137 almost certainly originated during the exile in *Babylon* or shortly after the return. **1–4:** The *rivers of Babylon* refer to the canals between the Tigris and Euphrates Rivers. *Remember* serves as a theme (vv. 1, 6, 7). The *songs of Zion* probably indicate the joyful songs sung by pilgrims visiting the city (Ps 48, 84, 122). Tied closely to the place itself, they cannot be sung elsewhere. **5–6:** Although remembering *Jerusalem* was painful (v. 1), to *forget* the city would mean permanent silence—that is, death. Memory sustains hope. **7–9:** While grief was evident in vv. 1–4, rage is now expressed. The *Edomites* were complicit in *Jerusalem's* fall (Ezek 35.1–15; Obad 1–14), and *Babylon* was directly responsible. Verse 9 reflects the brutality of all warfare (2 Kings 8.12), but requests simply that the punishment fit the crime (see v. 8).

---

a Or poplars　　*b Or* you who are devastated

P S A L M 1 3 8

Of David.

1 I give you thanks, O LORD, with my
        whole heart;
    before the gods I sing your praise;
2 I bow down toward your holy temple
    and give thanks to your name for your
        steadfast love and your
        faithfulness;
    for you have exalted your name and
        your word
    above everything.*a*
3 On the day I called, you answered me,
    you increased my strength of soul.*b*

4 All the kings of the earth shall praise
        you, O LORD,
    for they have heard the words of your
        mouth.
5 They shall sing of the ways of the LORD,
    for great is the glory of the LORD.
6 For though the LORD is high, he regards
        the lowly;
    but the haughty he perceives from far
        away.

7 Though I walk in the midst of trouble,
    you preserve me against the wrath of
        my enemies;
    you stretch out your hand,
    and your right hand delivers me.
8 The LORD will fulfill his purpose
        for me;
    your steadfast love, O LORD, endures
        forever.
    Do not forsake the work of your
        hands.

138.1–8: **With my whole heart.** A song of thanksgiving, it initiates a final Davidic collection (Ps 138–145), the function of which is to respond to the Exile* (see Ps 137) by suggesting that the whole people now fulfills the function formerly served by the Davidic monarchy (Ps 144; see also Ps 149). **1–3:** With his or her whole being (9.1; 119.2), the psalmist is grateful. Reference to *the gods* recalls 135.5 and 136.2–3. God alone is to be worshipped (v. 2), an act that celebrates God's *steadfast love* and *faithfulness* (Ex 34.6; Ps 5.7; 100.5). Acting in character and according to God's *word* (v. 2), God has delivered the psalmist (v. 3; see

v. 7). **4–6:** The psalmist's deliverance, or at least what it represents, is to be universally acclaimed (2.10). God's *ways* involve exalting *the lowly* (113.7–9) and humbling *the haughty*. **7–8:** While v. 7 rehearses the psalmist's deliverance, v. 8 implies an ongoing need, in the midst of which the psalmist is content to trust God's *steadfast love* (v. 2).

P S A L M 1 3 9

To the leader. Of David. A Psalm.

1 O LORD, you have searched me and
        known me.
2 You know when I sit down and when I
        rise up;
    you discern my thoughts from
        far away.
3 You search out my path and my lying
        down,
    and are acquainted with all my ways.
4 Even before a word is on my tongue,
    O LORD, you know it completely.
5 You hem me in, behind and before,
    and lay your hand upon me.
6 Such knowledge is too wonderful for
        me;
    it is so high that I cannot attain it.

7 Where can I go from your spirit?
    Or where can I flee from your
        presence?
8 If I ascend to heaven, you are there;
    if I make my bed in Sheol, you are
        there.
9 If I take the wings of the morning
    and settle at the farthest limits of the
        sea,
10 even there your hand shall lead me,
    and your right hand shall hold me
        fast.
11 If I say, "Surely the darkness shall cover
        me,
    and the light around me become
        night,"
12 even the darkness is not dark to you;
    the night is as bright as the day,
    for darkness is as light to you.

a Cn: Heb *you have exalted your word above all your name*   *b* Syr Compare Gk Tg: Heb *you made me arrogant in my soul with strength*

13 For it was you who formed my inward
    parts;
    you knit me together in my mother's
    womb.
14 I praise you, for I am fearfully and
    wonderfully made.
    Wonderful are your works;
    that I know very well.
15 My frame was not hidden from you,
    when I was being made in secret,
    intricately woven in the depths of the
    earth.
16 Your eyes beheld my unformed
    substance.
    In your book were written
    all the days that were formed for me,
    when none of them as yet existed.
17 How weighty to me are your thoughts,
    O God!
    How vast is the sum of them!
18 I try to count them—they are more
    than the sand;
    I come to the end^a—I am still with
    you.

19 O that you would kill the wicked,
    O God,
    and that the bloodthirsty would
    depart from me—
20 those who speak of you maliciously,
    and lift themselves up against you for
    evil!^{b}
21 Do I not hate those who hate you,
    O LORD?
    And do I not loathe those who rise up
    against you?
22 I hate them with perfect hatred;
    I count them my enemies.
23 Search me, O God, and know my heart;
    test me and know my thoughts.
24 See if there is any wicked^c way in me,
    and lead me in the way everlasting.^{d}

139.1–24: You have searched me and known me.
The petitions in vv. 19–20, 23–24 suggest that the
psalmist has been falsely accused and appeals to God
for vindication (see Ps 7, 17). Several forms of *know*
represent the key word (vv. 1–2, 4, 6, 14, 23). **1–6:**
The psalmist asserts that he or she is fully *known*—
actions and thoughts (v. 2), as well as lifestyle (v. 3)
and speech (v. 4). V. 5 implies a vulnerability that

could be threatening, but the psalmist seems to welcome God's *knowledge* (v. 6). **7–12:** God's *spirit* represents God's *presence*, which is inescapable. *Sheol**
is the realm of the dead and was ordinarily understood
to be devoid of God's presence (6.5; 30.3), but not
here (see Am 9.2). God's *light* dispels even utter *darkness* (vv. 11–12). The psalmist is secure everywhere
(v. 10; 73.23–24). **13–18:** The conceptual background
of vv. 15–16 is unclear. Along with *knit* in v. 13, *woven*
suggests the metaphor* of God as creative weaver.
While the psalmist cannot understand God's *thoughts*
(v. 17; compare v. 2), he or she is assured of being
with God (v. 18; see vv. 12–17). **19–24:** The petition
in vv. 19–20 seeks not so much personal revenge as it
does justice (140.9–12). Loyalty and openness to God
(vv. 23–24; see v. 1) include opposing those who oppose God (vv. 21–22).

〰〰〰〰〰〰〰〰〰〰〰〰〰

PSALM 140

To the leader. A Psalm of David.

1 Deliver me, O LORD, from evildoers;
    protect me from those who are
        violent,
2 who plan evil things in their minds
    and stir up wars continually.
3 They make their tongue sharp as a
        snake's,
    and under their lips is the venom of
        vipers.   *Selah*

4 Guard me, O LORD, from the hands of
        the wicked;
    protect me from the violent
    who have planned my downfall.
5 The arrogant have hidden a trap for me,
    and with cords they have spread a
        net,^{e}
    along the road they have set snares
        for me.   *Selah*

6 I say to the LORD, "You are my God;
    give ear, O LORD, to the voice of my
        supplications."
7 O LORD, my Lord, my strong deliverer,
    you have covered my head in the day
        of battle.

---

a Or *I awake* b Cn: Meaning of Heb uncertain
c Heb *hurtful* d Or *the ancient way*. Compare Jer 6.16
e Or *they have spread cords as a net*

8 Do not grant, O LORD, the desires of
       the wicked;
    do not further their evil plot.*ᵃ   *Selah*

9 Those who surround me lift up their
       heads;ᵇ
    let the mischief of their lips
       overwhelm them!
10 Let burning coals fall on them!
    Let them be flung into pits, no more
       to rise!
11 Do not let the slanderer be established
       in the land;
    let evil speedily hunt down the
       violent!

12 I know that the LORD maintains the
       cause of the needy,
    and executes justice for the poor.
13 Surely the righteous shall give thanks to
       your name;
    the upright shall live in your
       presence.

140.1–13: Protect me from those who are violent.
In this prayer for help, the complaints and petitions
against *the wicked* (vv. 1–5, 8–11) recall 139.19–22,
while the expressions of trust (vv. 6–7, 12–13) recall
139.1–18. **1–5:** Elsewhere too, *the wicked* (v. 4) are
violent (vv. 1, 3; 7.16; 11.5). Verbal abuse (v. 3; 58.4)
accompanies *planned* persecution (vv. 4–5; 9.15;
10.9). **6–7:** In the midst of complaint and petition, the
psalmist professes faith. God has *covered* the psalmist
(5.11; 91.4). **8–13:** The petitions (vv. 8–11) aim not at
personal revenge, but rather at the elimination of violence and oppression. In short, the issue is *justice*
(v. 12), which God wills for all, especially the *needy*
and *poor* (9.18; 82.3–4). Such advocacy is cause for
gratitude (v. 13).

PSALM 141
A Psalm of David.

1 I call upon you, O LORD; come quickly
       to me;
    give ear to my voice when I call to
       you.
2 Let my prayer be counted as incense
       before you,
    and the lifting up of my hands as an
       evening sacrifice.

3 Set a guard over my mouth, O LORD;
    keep watch over the door of my lips.
4 Do not turn my heart to any evil,
       to busy myself with wicked deeds
    in company with those who work
       iniquity;
    do not let me eat of their delicacies.
5 Let the righteous strike me;
    let the faithful correct me.
    Never let the oil of the wicked anoint
       my head,ᶜ
    for my prayer is continuallyᵈ against
       their wicked deeds.
6 When they are given over to those who
       shall condemn them,
    then they shall learn that my words
       were pleasant.
7 Like a rock that one breaks apart and
       shatters on the land,
    so shall their bones be strewn at the
       mouth of Sheol.ᵉ

8 But my eyes are turned toward you,
       O GOD, my Lord;
    in you I seek refuge; do not leave me
       defenseless.
9 Keep me from the trap that they have
       laid for me,
    and from the snares of evildoers.
10 Let the wicked fall into their own nets,
    while I alone escape.

141.1–10: Do not leave me defenseless. A prayer for
help, it recalls Ps 140 and anticipates Ps 142 (see *trap*
in 140.5; 141.9; 142.3). It requests deliverance not
only from the persecutions of *the wicked* (v. 10), but
also from the temptation to imitate them (vv. 3–5).
1–2: Uplifted *hands* are the posture of *prayer* (28.2;
63.4). The psalmist probably intends the *prayer* to accompany rather than replace an *evening sacrifice* (Ezra
9.5). **3–7:** The focus here is upon the psalmist and *the
wicked* (v. 5). The psalmist prays for support against
the enticement of *evil* (vv. 3–5a). Then he or she apparently anticipates v. 10 by envisioning the destruction of *the wicked,* but vv. 5–7 are very unclear (see

a Heb adds *they are exalted*   *b* Cn Compare Gk: Heb
those who surround me are uplifted in head; Heb divides
verses 8 and 9 differently   *c* Gk: Meaning of Heb
uncertain   *d* Cn: Heb *for continually and my prayer*
e Meaning of Heb of verses 5–7 is uncertain

note *e*). **8–10:** Despite the enticement of *evil* and the power of *the wicked,* the psalmist entrusts life to God alone. Amid the threat of being *defenseless* (literally, "naked"), the psalmist looks to God as *refuge* (2.12; 142.5). Protection for *the righteous* (v. 5) must finally mean the demise of *the wicked* (vv. 9–10; 140.9–13).

〜〜〜〜〜〜〜〜〜〜〜〜〜

P S A L M   1 4 2

A Maskil of David. When he was in the cave. A Prayer.

1 With my voice I cry to the LORD;
　　with my voice I make supplication to
　　　the LORD.
2 I pour out my complaint before him;
　　I tell my trouble before him.
3 When my spirit is faint,
　　you know my way.

　In the path where I walk
　　they have hidden a trap for me.
4 Look on my right hand and see—
　　there is no one who takes notice of
　　　me;
　no refuge remains to me;
　　no one cares for me.

5 I cry to you, O LORD;
　　I say, "You are my refuge,
　　my portion in the land of the living."
6 Give heed to my cry,
　　for I am brought very low.

　Save me from my persecutors,
　　for they are too strong for me.
7 Bring me out of prison,
　　so that I may give thanks to your
　　　name.
　The righteous will surround me,
　　for you will deal bountifully with me.

142.1–7: You are my refuge. *Supplication* (v. 1) and *complaint* (v. 2) indicate a prayer for help. It recalls Ps 141 and anticipates Ps 143 (compare 142.3 and 143.4). The superscription is apparently based upon 1 Sam 22.1; 24.3–4 (see Ps 57). Expressions of trust pervade the psalm (vv. 3a, 5, 7b). **1–3a:** Israel's faith was based on the assurance that God hears the needy when they *cry to the LORD* (v. 1; Ex 2.23; Ps 107.12–13). *Faint* indicates the need (107.5; 143.4), which God will *know*. **3b–5:** The need is indicated fur-

ther in renewed *complaint. Trap* recalls 140.5; 141.9. Although apparently abandoned by all, the psalmist again moves from *complaint* to assurance: God is a *refuge* (2.12; 141.8). A *portion* originally indicated a parcel of land and thus access to life; God is the psalmist's access to life (16.5; 73.26). **6–7:** Supplication and complaint recur before a final expression of trust (13.6; 116.7) that anticipates human as well as divine support (see v. 4).

〜〜〜〜〜〜〜〜〜〜〜〜〜

P S A L M   1 4 3

A Psalm of David.

1 Hear my prayer, O LORD;
　　give ear to my supplications in your
　　　faithfulness;
　　answer me in your righteousness.
2 Do not enter into judgment with your
　　　servant,
　　for no one living is righteous before
　　　you.
3 For the enemy has pursued me,
　　crushing my life to the ground,
　　making me sit in darkness like those
　　　long dead.
4 Therefore my spirit faints within me;
　　my heart within me is appalled.
5 I remember the days of old,
　　I think about all your deeds,
　　I meditate on the works of your hands.
6 I stretch out my hands to you;
　　my soul thirsts for you like a parched
　　　land.   *Selah*

7 Answer me quickly, O LORD;
　　my spirit fails.
　Do not hide your face from me,
　　or I shall be like those who go down
　　　to the Pit.
8 Let me hear of your steadfast love in the
　　　morning,
　　for in you I put my trust.
　Teach me the way I should go,
　　for to you I lift up my soul.

9 Save me, O LORD, from my enemies;
　　I have fled to you for refuge.*a*

---

a One Heb Ms Gk: MT *to you I have hidden*

10 Teach me to do your will,
   for you are my God.
   Let your good spirit lead me
   on a level path.
11 For your name's sake, O LORD, preserve
   my life.
   In your righteousness bring me out of
   trouble.
12 In your steadfast love cut off my
   enemies,
   and destroy all my adversaries,
   for I am your servant.

143.1–12: Answer me in your righteousness. The final in a series of prayers for help (Ps 139–143), it became one of the church's Penitential Psalms* (see Ps 6). **1–2:** The opening petitions focus on God's character, which pervades the psalm. The psalmist's future will depend on God's *faithfulness* (v. 1), *righteousness* (vv. 2, 11), and *steadfast love* (vv. 8, 12). To so depend on God is what it means to be God's *servant* (vv. 2, 12). To offer life to those who are not *righteous* is what it means to be God. **3–6:** The *enemy* (v. 3; see vv. 9, 12) threatens the psalmist's *life* (v. 3; see v. 11). Faintness of *spirit* (77.3; 142.3) leads to recollection of God's past *deeds* and *works* on behalf of the oppressed (v. 5). Memory yields the hope expressed in the psalmist's reach toward God (v. 6; 42.1–2; 63.1). **7–9:** *Answer* echoes the plea of v. 1 and *spirit* the complaint of v. 4. *The Pit* is the realm of the dead (28.1; 30.3). God's *steadfast love* (v. 8; see v. 12) promises life. To *lift up* the *soul* (v. 8; 25.1; 86.4) means to offer one's life to God in *trust* and submission to God's *way*. **9–10:** Thus, the psalmist prays not only for life but for God to *teach me* (vv. 8, 10). **11–12:** God's *name's sake* indicates God's character, at the heart of which are *righteousness* and *steadfast love* (Ex 34.6; Ps 36.5–6).

PSALM 144
Of David.

1 Blessed be the LORD, my rock,
   who trains my hands for war, and my
   fingers for battle;
2 my rock[a] and my fortress,
   my stronghold and my deliverer,
   my shield, in whom I take refuge,
   who subdues the peoples[b]
   under me.

3 O LORD, what are human beings that
   you regard them,
   or mortals that you think of them?
4 They are like a breath;
   their days are like a passing
   shadow.

5 Bow your heavens, O LORD, and come
   down;
   touch the mountains so that they
   smoke.
6 Make the lightning flash and scatter
   them;
   send out your arrows and rout
   them.
7 Stretch out your hand from on high;
   set me free and rescue me from the
   mighty waters,
   from the hand of aliens,
8 whose mouths speak lies,
   and whose right hands are false.

9 I will sing a new song to you, O God;
   upon a ten-stringed harp I will play to
   you,
10 the one who gives victory to kings,
   who rescues his servant David.
11 Rescue me from the cruel sword,
   and deliver me from the hand of
   aliens,
   whose mouths speak lies,
   and whose right hands are false.

12 May our sons in their youth
   be like plants full grown,
   our daughters like corner pillars,
   cut for the building of a palace.
13 May our barns be filled,
   with produce of every kind;
   may our sheep increase by thousands,
   by tens of thousands in our fields,
14   and may our cattle be heavy with
   young.
   May there be no breach in the walls,[c]
   no exile,
   and no cry of distress in our streets.

a With 18.2 and 2 Sam 22.2: Heb *my steadfast love*
b Heb Mss Syr Aquila Jerome: MT *my people*
c Heb lacks *in the walls*

15 Happy are the people to whom such
      blessings fall;
   happy are the people whose God is
      the LORD.

144.1–15: A new song to you, O God. Because of the
reference to *David* (v. 10) and because it recalls Ps 18,
Ps 144 is usually categorized as a royal psalm. The label
is problematic, however, since it reflects the realities of
the post-exilic era when the monarchy had disappeared. By rewriting Ps 18, the psalmist suggests that
the whole people have appropriated the former role
of the monarchy and are heir to the promises formerly
attached to it (see Ps 149; Isa 55.3). **1–2:** Recalling
18.1–2, 34, 46–47, these verses also recall the royal Ps
2 and its reminder that God and his purposes are always opposed. **3–8:** Verse 3 is reminiscent of 8.4. An
acute awareness of human transience accompanied
the loss of the monarchy (see the royal Ps 89, vv. 46–
48). Verses 5–8 have transformed the description of a
theophany* in 18.7–15 into a request, indicating a
problem precipitated by *the hand of aliens* (v. 7; see
v. 11). **9–11:** *A new song* is the appropriate response
to God's sovereignty (33.3; 96.1; 98.1). Verse 11 apparently imagines a deposed Davidic monarch praying
to the sovereign God for restoration. **12–14:** The shift
to the plural *our* indicates the transfer of the Davidic
ideology to the whole people. These verses reflect the
pain of the *exile* that persisted into the post-exilic era.
15: Alluding to 33.12, v. 15 leaves the people anticipating the help of God whose sovereignty has been
affirmed in vv. 9–11.

PSALM 145
Praise. Of David.

1 I will extol you, my God and King,
    and bless your name forever and
      ever.
2 Every day I will bless you,
    and praise your name forever
      and ever.
3 Great is the LORD, and greatly to be
      praised;
    his greatness is unsearchable.

4 One generation shall laud your works to
      another,
    and shall declare your mighty acts.
5 On the glorious splendor of your
      majesty,

and on your wondrous works, I will
    meditate.
6 The might of your awesome deeds shall
      be proclaimed,
    and I will declare your greatness.
7 They shall celebrate the fame of your
      abundant goodness,
    and shall sing aloud of your
      righteousness.

8 The LORD is gracious and merciful,
    slow to anger and abounding in
      steadfast love.
9 The LORD is good to all,
    and his compassion is over all that he
      has made.

10 All your works shall give thanks to you,
      O LORD,
    and all your faithful shall bless you.
11 They shall speak of the glory of your
      kingdom,
    and tell of your power,
12 to make known to all people your[a]
      mighty deeds,
    and the glorious splendor of your[b]
      kingdom.
13 Your kingdom is an everlasting
      kingdom,
    and your dominion endures
      throughout all generations.

   The LORD is faithful in all his words,
    and gracious in all his deeds.[c]
14 The LORD upholds all who are falling,
    and raises up all who are bowed
      down.
15 The eyes of all look to you,
    and you give them their food in due
      season.
16 You open your hand,
    satisfying the desire of every living
      thing.
17 The LORD is just in all his ways,
    and kind in all his doings.
18 The LORD is near to all who call on him,
    to all who call on him in truth.
19 He fulfills the desire of all who fear him;

---

a Gk Jerome Syr: Heb *his*   *b* Heb *his*   *c* These two
lines supplied by Q Ms Gk Syr

he also hears their cry, and saves
　　them.
20 The LORD watches over all who
　　love him,
　but all the wicked he will destroy.

21 My mouth will speak the praise of the
　　LORD,
　and all flesh will bless his holy name
　　forever and ever.

145.1–21: My God and King. An acrostic* poem (see
Ps 9–10), it is the only psalm to include *Praise* in the
superscription. It concludes the final Davidic collection
(Ps 138–145); its celebration of God's sovereignty (see
vv. 1, 11–13) follows well upon Ps 144. Psalm 145
anticipates the final outpouring of *praise* that concludes the psalter (Ps 146–150; compare 145.21 and
150.6). **1–2:** Not only will the psalmist *bless* God's
name (103.1), but so will *all flesh* (v. 21). *Bless* connotes the submission appropriate to one who is *King*.
3–6: The section is encompassed by God's *greatness*
(vv. 3, 6; 48.1; 96.4), which is revealed by what God
does and which provides reason for blessing God. **7–
9:** God's activity also reveals his essential character.
Verse 8 cites Ex 34.6, God's self-revelation to Moses
(see 86.15; 103.8). *Merciful* and *compassion* represent
the same Hebrew root that connotes God's motherly
love (see Ps 131). *All* occurs twice in v. 9, and will recur
numerous times. **10–13:** Four occurrences of *kingdom*
reinforce the opening focus on God's sovereignty. The
addition of a missing Hebrew line (see note *c*) surrounds the assertions of God's sovereignty by a consideration of God's character. **14–20:** Returning the focus to God's activity, these verses describe the results
of God's faithful love. The destruction of *the wicked*
(v. 20b) results not from God's intent but rather from
their failure to respond (1.5–6). **21:** Because of the similarity to 150.6, some scholars suggest this may have
been the original end to the psalter.

PSALM 146

1 Praise the LORD!
　Praise the LORD, O my soul!
2 I will praise the LORD as long as I live;
　I will sing praises to my God all my
　　life long.

3 Do not put your trust in princes,
　in mortals, in whom there is no help.

4 When their breath departs, they return
　　to the earth;
　on that very day their plans perish.

5 Happy are those whose help is the God
　　of Jacob,
　whose hope is in the LORD their God,
6 who made heaven and earth,
　the sea, and all that is in them;
　who keeps faith forever;
7 　who executes justice for the
　　oppressed;
　who gives food to the hungry.

　The LORD sets the prisoners free;
8 　the LORD opens the eyes of the blind.
　The LORD lifts up those who are bowed
　　down;
　the LORD loves the righteous.
9 The LORD watches over the strangers;
　he upholds the orphan and the
　　widow,
　but the way of the wicked he brings
　　to ruin.

10 The LORD will reign forever,
　your God, O Zion, for all generations.
　Praise the LORD!

146.1–10: The LORD will reign forever. A song of
praise, it initiates a concluding series of five psalms, all
of which begin and end with *Praise the LORD!* **1–4:**
Songs of praise typically start with an invitation, but
not usually one addressed to *my soul* (but see 103.1;
104.1). *Praise* indicates entrusting of *life* to God, while
vv. 3–4 depict the opposite—to *put* one's *trust* in humans (118.8–9). To do so is ultimately futile (v. 4).
5–9: The final beatitude in the psalter (v. 5) recalls its
opening (1.1; 2.12). To be *happy* means to entrust life
to the God who is creator (v. 6a) and redeemer (v. 6b).
God's advocacy for all in need is summarized by the
word *justice* (v. 7; 82.3–4; 140.12). While *the righteous* seem not to belong in the list, they are regularly
afflicted in the Psalms (34.19). Nevertheless, *the righteous* find happiness in God, while *the wicked* choose
alienation from God and consequent *ruin* (v. 9;
1.5–6; 145.20; 147.6). **10:** Since *justice* is regularly associated with God's sovereignty (97.2; 99.4), the affirmation of God's *reign* provides an appropriate conclusion (145.1, 10–13; 149.2).

PSALM 147

1 Praise the LORD!
How good it is to sing praises to our
God;
for he is gracious, and a song of
praise is fitting.
2 The LORD builds up Jerusalem;
he gathers the outcasts of Israel.
3 He heals the brokenhearted,
and binds up their wounds.
4 He determines the number of the stars;
he gives to all of them their names.
5 Great is our Lord, and abundant
in power;
his understanding is beyond measure.
6 The LORD lifts up the downtrodden;
he casts the wicked to the ground.

7 Sing to the LORD with thanksgiving;
make melody to our God on the lyre.
8 He covers the heavens with clouds,
prepares rain for the earth,
makes grass grow on the hills.
9 He gives to the animals their food,
and to the young ravens when they
cry.
10 His delight is not in the strength of the
horse,
nor his pleasure in the speed of
a runner;[a]
11 but the LORD takes pleasure in those
who fear him,
in those who hope in his steadfast
love.

12 Praise the LORD, O Jerusalem!
Praise your God, O Zion!
13 For he strengthens the bars of
your gates;
he blesses your children within you.
14 He grants peace[b] within your borders;
he fills you with the finest of wheat.
15 He sends out his command to the earth;
his word runs swiftly.
16 He gives snow like wool;
he scatters frost like ashes.
17 He hurls down hail like crumbs—
who can stand before his cold?
18 He sends out his word, and melts them;
he makes his wind blow, and the
waters flow.

19 He declares his word to Jacob,
his statutes and ordinances to Israel.
20 He has not dealt thus with any other
nation;
they do not know his ordinances.
Praise the LORD!

147.1–20: God's word to Jacob. This song of praise features God's activity in the two realms highlighted in Ps 146.6—creation and redemption. Each of three major sections begins with an imperative invitation to praise (vv. 1–6, 7–11, 12–20). **1–6:** A post-exilic setting is reflected in vv. 2–3 (106.47; 107.2–3). The God who cares for the *brokenhearted* (v. 3; Isa 61.1) and *downtrodden* (v. 6) is the God of all the cosmos (vv. 4–5; Isa 40.26). **7–11:** That vv. 8–9 recall 104.14, 27 and vv. 10–11 recall 33.16–18 suggests the possibility that the psalm has been composed with reference to other psalms. *Fear* indicates a trustful obedience that yields *hope*. **12–20:** *Jerusalem* in v. 12 recalls v. 2. It was the place where people went to seek blessing and *peace* (122.6–8; 134.3). God's *word* (Isa 55.12) is addressed to the created order (vv. 15, 18) as well as to *Jacob* (v. 19), suggesting the conviction that God's *ordinances* (vv. 19–20) were intended to order the life of God's people so as to fulfill God's purposes for the whole creation.

PSALM 148

1 Praise the LORD!
Praise the LORD from the heavens;
praise him in the heights!
2 Praise him, all his angels;
praise him, all his host!

3 Praise him, sun and moon;
praise him, all you shining stars!
4 Praise him, you highest heavens,
and you waters above the heavens!

5 Let them praise the name of the LORD,
for he commanded and they
were created.
6 He established them forever and ever;
he fixed their bounds, which cannot
be passed.[c]

a Heb *legs of a person*   b Or *prosperity*   c Or *he set
a law that cannot pass away*

7 Praise the LORD from the earth,
    you sea monsters and all deeps,
8 fire and hail, snow and frost,
    stormy wind fulfilling his command!
9 Mountains and all hills,
    fruit trees and all cedars!
10 Wild animals and all cattle,
    creeping things and flying birds!
11 Kings of the earth and all peoples,
    princes and all rulers of the earth!
12 Young men and women alike,
    old and young together!

13 Let them praise the name of the LORD,
    for his name alone is exalted;
    his glory is above earth and heaven.
14 He has raised up a horn for his people,
    praise for all his faithful,
    for the people of Israel who are close
        to him.
    Praise the LORD!

148.1–14: Praise from the heavens and the earth.
This psalm is the third in a series of songs of praise that
conclude the psalter. Distinctive are the extended invitations to *praise* (vv. 1–5, 7, 13) and the expansive
inclusivity of those invited. **1–6:** *Praise* is invited first
from the heavens, including heavenly beings (v. 2;
29.1; 103.20–21) and bodies (vv. 3–4). The list of participants recalls Gen 1–2, as does the verb *created* (v.
5). **7–13:** *Praise* is now invited *from the earth,* including chaotic forces (v. 7), meteorological phenomena
(v. 8), inanimate things (v. 9a), plants (v. 9b), *animals*
(v. 10), and finally people of all positions and ages (vv.
11–12). The *all*-inclusive invitation anticipates 150.6.
13–14: As in v. 5, *the name of the LORD* is to be praised
(v. 13; 113.1; 149.3). The final verse narrows the focus
to God's *people,* the *faithful* (149.1, 5, 9). They have
experienced God's help, which the image of the *horn*
suggests (75.10; 92.10).

~~~~~~

PSALM 149

1 Praise the LORD!
    Sing to the LORD a new song,
        his praise in the assembly of the
            faithful.
2 Let Israel be glad in its Maker;
    let the children of Zion rejoice in
        their King.

3 Let them praise his name with dancing,
    making melody to him with
        tambourine and lyre.
4 For the LORD takes pleasure in
        his people;
    he adorns the humble with victory.
5 Let the faithful exult in glory;
    let them sing for joy on their couches.
6 Let the high praises of God be in their
        throats
    and two-edged swords in their hands,
7 to execute vengeance on the nations
    and punishment on the peoples,
8 to bind their kings with fetters
    and their nobles with chains of iron,
9 to execute on them the judgment
        decreed.
    This is glory for all his faithful ones.
    Praise the LORD!

149.1–9: Glory for all God's faithful. In many ways a
typical song of praise, it departs from the usual style
in vv. 6–9, which focus on the mission of *the faithful*
(vv. 1, 5; see v. 9). **1–4:** The mention of *a new song*
(96.1; 98.1) and *King* suggests that *praise* involves the
joyful recognition of God's sovereign claim on the
whole world (see Ps 148). The reason for praise in v. 4
may allude to the Exodus. **5:** Renewing the invitation
to *praise,* it is the central verse of the psalm and anticipates the unique vv. 6–9. What *on their couches* indicates is unclear, but perhaps it suggests that *praise*
should continue through the night. **6–9:** *Vengeance*
ordinarily belongs to God (Deut 32.35; Ps 94.1), but
Ps 2 entrusts to the monarchy the task of calling to
account rebellious *kings.* Verses 6–9 recall Ps 2, but the
task of executing *judgment,* or better, "establishing
justice," is now the mission of *all* the *faithful.* The former *glory* of the king (21.5) now belongs to the whole
people, *all* God's *faithful* (see Ps 105, 144).

~~~~~~

PSALM 150

1 Praise the LORD!
    Praise God in his sanctuary;
        praise him in his mighty firmament!*a*
2 Praise him for his mighty deeds;
    praise him according to his surpassing
        greatness!

---

a Or *dome*

3 Praise him with trumpet sound;
  praise him with lute and harp!
4 Praise him with tambourine and dance;
  praise him with strings and pipe!
5 Praise him with clanging cymbals;
  praise him with loud clashing
    cymbals!
6 Let everything that breathes praise the
    LORD!
  Praise the LORD!

150.1–6: Praise the LORD! The final position in the psalter calls for a unique song of praise. It consists almost entirely of invitations to *praise*, although v. 2 implies a reason. **1–2:** God's *sanctuary* suggests the Temple,* but it is clear that God's claim is not limited to earthly places. God's *surpassing greatness* communicates God's cosmic sovereignty. The Hebrew roots of *mighty* (v. 1) and *mighty deeds* (v. 2) occur together in 24.8, which proclaim God to be "King of glory." **3–5:** The *trumpet* elsewhere announces God's reign (47.5–7; 98.6), but it is here to be joined by full instrumentation (33.2–3; 68.24–25). **6:** The symphonic expression of *praise* is to be completed by the participation of *everything that breathes* . The cosmic God invites the response of every creature (145.21) No less a congregation will suffice, and no less a doxology would be appropriate to conclude Book V and the whole book.

PROVERBS

Introduction

The book of Proverbs is an anthology—a collection of instructions plus speeches of Wisdom (chs. 1–9), two large collections of two-line sayings (chs. 10–22 and 25–29), a booklet of counsels (22.17–24.34), and some poems (chs. 30–31). The two chief literary genres* represented in the book are the instruction or lecture and the "proverb" or pithy saying. They are examples of the instruction attested in Mesopotamia, but especially favored in Egypt, where seventeen examples from every historical period are known to exist. In a typical instruction a king, high official, or father instructs his son (or disciple or successor) how to live so as to enjoy the blessings of life and avoid unnecessary trouble. Despite their practical and common-sense approach, instructions were thoroughly religious, for they were written in the assumption that the world yields its blessings to those who respect the gods and direct their lives in accord with the order and rhythms of the divinely fashioned universe. The second genre, the saying or proverb, was also very common in the ancient Near East; Mesopotamian and West Semitic sayings collections are extant. The two-line "proverbs" of Proverbs are broader than the modern proverb, which, in one definition, is "a concise statement of an apparent truth that has currency among the people." Some verses in Proverbs are proverbs in this sense, but there are also witty sayings, paradoxes, and riddles. The sayings are hard to translate; even the best efforts of translators can seem banal. In their original language, however, the sayings are incisive and witty, provoking readers to take a fresh look at life. In the phrase of the great eighteenth-century aphorist, Samuel Johnson, "New things are made familiar, and familiar things are made new."

No single date can be assigned to Proverbs, for its collections arose in different periods. The one datable reference (25.1) suggests that officials of King Hezekiah (715–687 BCE) added a collection of proverbs (chs. 25–29) to an existing Solomonic collection. It is likely that some sayings go back to Solomon (or even earlier), for ancient kings sponsored literature. Moreover, Solomon is remembered as a sage and author (1 Kings 3; 4.29–34, 10). Collections of sayings were arranged through techniques such as catchword ("king," "the LORD"), topic (discretion in speech), or type of parallelism.* (Antithetic* parallelism, where the second line points up the first by expressing its opposite, predominates in chs. 10–15). Exactly when the collections were edited into the present book is difficult to say. Many scholars believe that the latest sections of Proverbs are chs. 1–9 and the poem on the virtuous wife (31.10–31) and that these sections influenced the final shaping of the book, which was edited in the post-exilic period.

Who wrote Proverbs? That question is vigorously debated. Some believe the sayings and instructions originated with scribes* in the royal court (or a hypothetical scribal school), whereas others believe the material originated with tribal elders instructing the young in ancestral traditions and customs, the material being written down later by scribes. Though much material may be ultimately of folk origin, the uniform and sophisticated style of the sayings and the foreign influence on the instructions suggest the book was essentially the work of palace scribes.

READING GUIDE

The instructions in chs. 1–9 on a literal level address a young man at critical points in his life such as leaving his parents' home to found his own (1.8–19), discerning the best course to take in life (2.1–11; 3.1–12, 13–18; 4.1–9, 10–19, 20–27), and being tempted to betray his family and home by following another woman (5.1–22; 6.20–35; 7.1–27). The new literary setting of the instructions, especially the introduction (1.1–7) and the speeches of Wisdom, creates a metaphorical* horizon that makes the instruction relevant to any person who desires to live optimally in God's world and seek wisdom amid counterclaims and temptations.

The sayings (chs. 10–22 and 25–29) do not so much provide information as help readers to make decisions and see a dimension in the world that is not immediately apparent. They use antithetical types (the wise and foolish, the righteous and wicked, the religious and the impious) to show how human choices and actions bring with them blessing (such as long life, domestic happiness, honor, and wealth) or misfortune (such as premature death, shame, destitution). The sayings are written with a robust confidence in divine justice and in human freedom. That confidence should not be interpreted in a metaphysical way, as a naive belief that things always work out for the best. This book does not ask the questions posed by Job and Qoheleth.

Proverbs influenced Sirach (ca. 180 BCE), who developed the saying into "essays." Later, Hebrew ethical wills, in which parents handed their wisdom to their children, drew from the instructions. Jesus was a wisdom teacher who used paradoxical and witty sayings to teach his disciples about God's reign. The Gospel of John, especially, borrowed from Prov 1–9 to depict Jesus as incarnate wisdom descended from on high to offer human beings life and truth. Like Woman Wisdom (Prov 1.20–33; 8), Jesus speaks in long discourses and, like her (Prov 9.2–5), he invites people to his banquet: "I am the bread of life" (6.35). Two early Christian hymns, John 1.1–18 and Col 1.15–20, drew on Prov 8 to identify Jesus with God's creative word and heavenly wisdom. The Letter of James is an instruction (in letter form) reprising wisdom themes.

The universal truths of Proverbs remain relevant today. Proverbs proclaims that God's world is good, yielding its full blessings only to those who seek wisdom, do justice, and revere God. To those, however, who do not listen to the wisdom God has placed in the world and who are hostile to their neighbor, the world will prove a dangerous place: Evil comes back upon the wicked. The virtues of wisdom, justice, and piety are acquired through discipline, a process requiring sincerity, persistence, and openness to those more experienced. The book declares that right, wise, and reverent conduct is the only way to happiness, which God is invited to grant as a gift.

The book is difficult for some modern readers to enjoy. Some find the instructions without content and the sayings trite. It must be remembered that the instructions of chs. 1–9 are concerned with forming character—developing an openhearted person who is faithful to the basic relationships of life (to God, spouse, household, and neighbors) and who rejects easy compromises. The aphorisms contain traditional insights that help us to grow in wisdom as we decode and ponder them.

1–9	Collection of wisdom speeches and instructions
10.1–22.16	Proverbs of Solomon
22.17–24.22	The words of the wise
24.23–34	Appendix to words of the wise
25–29	Proverbs of Solomon edited by Hezekiah's scribes
30.1–14	The words of Agur
30.15–33	Numerical sayings
31.1–9	The words of Lemuel king of Massa
31.10–31	Praise of the capable wife

1 The proverbs of Solomon son of David,
  king of Israel:

2 For learning about wisdom and
      instruction,
    for understanding words of insight,
3 for gaining instruction in wise dealing,
    righteousness, justice, and equity;
4 to teach shrewdness to the simple,
    knowledge and prudence to the
      young—
5 let the wise also hear and gain in
      learning,
    and the discerning acquire skill,
6 to understand a proverb and a figure,
    the words of the wise and their
      riddles.

7 The fear of the LORD is the beginning
      of knowledge;
    fools despise wisdom and instruction.

1.1–9.18: Speeches and instructions. 1.1–7: Introduction and purpose of the book. 1: Egyptian and biblical wisdom books, contrary to the customary anonymity of ancient literature, give the name of the author, who was normally a king or prominent courtier advising his son or disciple. Solomon, famed for his wisdom, is named as the author, or, as we might say, patron of the entire book. **2–7:** There are fourteen (two times seven) different nouns for wisdom or wise sayings in order to show totality. Verses 2–3 are concerned with learning, v. 4 with teaching, v. 5 with the teacher or sage, v. 6 with understanding wisdom writings, and v. 7 (in climactic position) with fear of the LORD. **4:** *The simple* are naive or uninstructed people, either because of their youth or, sometimes, because of their carelessness. In the latter case the term has a negative connotation. **7:** The verse is the climax★ of the introduction, for the LORD is the source of blessings for the wise. The phrase *wisdom and instruction* reprises the same phrase in v. 2a. *Fear of the LORD* is the traditional (and not fully satisfactory) translation of "yir'at YHWH," literally, "revering the LORD." The phrase means giving to one's God what is due, knowing and accepting one's place in the universe. It primarily designates neither an emotion (fear) nor general reverence, but rather a conviction that one should honor and serve a particular god.

8 Hear, my child, your father's
      instruction,
    and do not reject your mother's
      teaching;
9 for they are a fair garland for your head,
    and pendants for your neck.
10 My child, if sinners entice you,
    do not consent.
11 If they say, "Come with us, let us lie in
      wait for blood;
    let us wantonly ambush the innocent;
12 like Sheol let us swallow them alive
    and whole, like those who go down to
      the Pit.
13 We shall find all kinds of costly things;
    we shall fill our houses with booty.
14 Throw in your lot among us;
    we will all have one purse"—
15 my child, do not walk in their way,
    keep your foot from their paths;
16 for their feet run to evil,
    and they hurry to shed blood.
17 For in vain is the net baited
    while the bird is looking on;
18 yet they lie in wait—to kill themselves!
    and set an ambush—for their own
      lives!
19 Such is the end*a* of all who are greedy
      for gain;
    it takes away the life of its possessors.

1.8–19: Parental advice on leaving home. The opening scene of a youth leaving parents and home to establish his own household sets the scene for the entire book. Every reader must establish a household in the sense of learning to live well as an adult, accepting traditional wisdom and discerning where true life is to be found. **10–14:** A group of sinners invites the youth not simply to commit a violent crime but to share in their violent life (*Come with us. . . . Throw in your lot among us*). **16–17:** Verse 16 is a gloss from Isa 59.7 to explain the enigmatic v. 17, which is a parable★ about sinners not seeing the divine retribution that works invisibly. The evil they plan for others will come upon them instead (vv. 18–19).

20 Wisdom cries out in the street;
    in the squares she raises her voice.

a Gk: Heb *are the ways*

21 At the busiest corner she cries out;
    at the entrance of the city gates she
        speaks:
22 "How long, O simple ones, will you love
        being simple?
    How long will scoffers delight in their
        scoffing
    and fools hate knowledge?
23 Give heed to my reproof;
    I will pour out my thoughts to you;
    I will make my words known to you.
24 Because I have called and you refused,
    have stretched out my hand and no
        one heeded,
25 and because you have ignored all my
        counsel
    and would have none of my reproof,
26 I also will laugh at your calamity;
    I will mock when panic strikes you,
27 when panic strikes you like a storm,
    and your calamity comes like a
        whirlwind,
    when distress and anguish come upon
        you.
28 Then they will call upon me, but I will
        not answer;
    they will seek me diligently, but will
        not find me.
29 Because they hated knowledge
    and did not choose the fear of the
        LORD,
30 would have none of my counsel,
    and despised all my reproof,
31 therefore they shall eat the fruit of their
        way
    and be sated with their own devices.
32 For waywardness kills the simple,
    and the complacency of fools destroys
        them;
33 but those who listen to me will be
        secure
    and will live at ease, without dread of
        disaster."

1.20–33: The consequences of not heeding Wisdom. Woman Wisdom warns the simple (who seem to have previously rejected her teaching) that she will not be there when the inevitable disaster comes upon them (vv. 22–32). She nonetheless gives them a last chance to accept her (v. 33). Verses 24–27 and 28–31 are parallel sections. Each gives a reason (*because,* vv.

25, 29) and announces a disaster; the first section employs the grammatical second person, and the second section employs the grammatical third person. **20–21:** *The entrance of the city gates* is the entrance to the upper city, which was the place of business and government. **22–23a:** The best solution to the textual confusion is to drop v. 22b–c as a later insertion and to translate *How long, O simple ones, will you love being simple?* Its parallel verse is best rendered (differently from NRSV) "Will you turn away from *my reproof?*" The translation "turn away" is preferable to NRSV *give heed to* and is based on the meaning of the same root in v. 32a (*waywardness*) and on Hebrew idiom.

2 My child, if you accept my words
    and treasure up my commandments
        within you,
2 making your ear attentive to wisdom
    and inclining your heart to
        understanding;
3 if you indeed cry out for insight,
    and raise your voice for
        understanding;
4 if you seek it like silver,
    and search for it as for hidden
        treasures—
5 then you will understand the fear of the
        LORD
    and find the knowledge of God.
6 For the LORD gives wisdom;
    from his mouth come knowledge and
        understanding;
7 he stores up sound wisdom for the
        upright;
    he is a shield to those who walk
        blamelessly,
8 guarding the paths of justice
    and preserving the way of his faithful
        ones.
9 Then you will understand righteousness
        and justice
    and equity, every good path;
10 for wisdom will come into your heart,
    and knowledge will be pleasant to
        your soul;
11 prudence will watch over you;
    and understanding will guard you.
12 It will save you from the way of evil,
    from those who speak perversely,
13 who forsake the paths of uprightness
    to walk in the ways of darkness,

14 who rejoice in doing evil
    and delight in the perverseness
       of evil;
15 those whose paths are crooked,
    and who are devious in their ways.

16 You will be saved from the loose*
       woman,
    from the adulteress with her smooth
      words,
17 who forsakes the partner of her youth
    and forgets her sacred covenant;
18 for her way[b] leads down to death,
    and her paths to the shades;
19 those who go to her never come back,
    nor do they regain the paths of life.

20 Therefore walk in the way of the good,
    and keep to the paths of the just.
21 For the upright will abide in the land,
    and the innocent will remain in it;
22 but the wicked will be cut off from the
      land,
    and the treacherous will be rooted
      out of it.

2.1–22: Seek wisdom and the LORD will keep you safe. The form is an acrostic* poem of twenty-two lines (the number of consonants in the Hebrew alphabet*). The first letter of the Hebrew alphabet ("aleph") dominates the first half (vv. 1–11; "aleph" is the initial letter in vv. 1, 3, 4, 5, and 9). The middle letter of the Hebrew alphabet ("lamed") dominates the second half (vv. 12–22; "lamed" is the initial letter of vv. 12, 16, 20). The main point of the poem is that if you seek wisdom with all your strength, the LORD will give it to you, and wisdom will safeguard you from wicked men and seductive women with the result that you can walk on the blessed path. Wisdom will be given to anyone who earnestly seeks it. However, one cannot directly take it; it must be given as a gift. **16–19:** *The loose woman . . . the adulteress. Loose* is literally "foreign." The figure of the dangerous and seductive woman appears again in 5.1–6; 6.20–35; 7.1–27; 9.13–18. Elsewhere in the Bible, a "foreign woman" can be a woman outside the community who is forbidden as a marriage partner, a prostitute or a woman otherwise dangerous to a man. Proverbs' focus is not only on her sexuality but also on her seductive and deceitful speech.

3 My child, do not forget my teaching,
    but let your heart keep my
      commandments;
2 for length of days and years of life
    and abundant welfare they will give
      you.

3 Do not let loyalty and faithfulness
      forsake you;
    bind them around your neck,
    write them on the tablet of your
      heart.
4 So you will find favor and good repute
    in the sight of God and of people.

5 Trust in the LORD with all your heart,
    and do not rely on your own insight.
6 In all your ways acknowledge him,
    and he will make straight your paths.
7 Do not be wise in your own eyes;
    fear the LORD, and turn away from
      evil.
8 It will be a healing for your flesh
    and a refreshment for your body.

9 Honor the LORD with your substance
    and with the first fruits of all your
      produce;
10 then your barns will be filled with
      plenty,
    and your vats will be bursting with
      wine.

11 My child, do not despise the LORD's
      discipline
    or be weary of his reproof,
12 for the LORD reproves the one he loves,
    as a father the son in whom he
      delights.

3.1–12: Trust in God makes one prosperous. The lecture consists of six four-line exhortations* of a father (or teacher) to a son (or disciple), in each of which a reward is promised. The teacher invites the disciple to memorize the teaching (vv. 1–2) and to be loyal (vv. 3–4), which leads to trust in God, the great teacher (v. 5). Such trust means not relying on oneself (v. 7), honoring God with due worship, and allowing God to become one's teacher and father (vv. 11–12). Consid-

a Heb *strange*   *b* Cn: Heb *house*

erable trust is necessary, for God *reproves* when educating disciples; there may be suffering.

13 Happy are those who find wisdom,
　　and those who get understanding,
14 for her income is better than silver,
　　and her revenue better than gold.
15 She is more precious than jewels,
　　and nothing you desire can compare
　　　with her.
16 Long life is in her right hand;
　　in her left hand are riches and honor.
17 Her ways are ways of pleasantness,
　　and all her paths are peace.
18 She is a tree of life to those who lay
　　　hold of her;
　　those who hold her fast are called
　　　happy.

19 The LORD by wisdom founded the
　　　earth;
　　by understanding he established the
　　　heavens;
20 by his knowledge the deeps broke open,
　　and the clouds drop down the dew.
21 My child, do not let these escape from
　　　your sight:
　　keep sound wisdom and prudence,
22 and they will be life for your soul
　　and adornment for your neck.
23 Then you will walk on your way securely
　　and your foot will not stumble.
24 If you sit down,*a* you will not be afraid;
　　when you lie down, your sleep will be
　　　sweet.
25 Do not be afraid of sudden panic,
　　or of the storm that strikes the
　　　wicked;
26 for the LORD will be your confidence
　　and will keep your foot from being
　　　caught.

27 Do not withhold good from those to
　　　whom it is due,*b*
　　when it is in your power to do it.
28 Do not say to your neighbor, "Go, and
　　　come again,
　　tomorrow I will give it"—when you
　　　have it with you.
29 Do not plan harm against your neighbor
　　who lives trustingly beside you.

30 Do not quarrel with anyone without
　　　cause,
　　when no harm has been done to you.
31 Do not envy the violent
　　and do not choose any of their ways;
32 for the perverse are an abomination to
　　　the LORD,
　　but the upright are in his confidence.
33 The LORD's curse is on the house of the
　　　wicked,
　　but he blesses the abode of the
　　　righteous.
34 Toward the scorners he is scornful,
　　but to the humble he shows favor.
35 The wise will inherit honor,
　　but stubborn fools, disgrace.

3.13–35. 13–20: Wisdom's benefits and prestige.
Some scholars believe the poem consists of vv. 13–26 rather than 13–20. The poem praises wisdom by listing her benefits to the human race and explains her power by describing her role in creation. Since the world is made by wisdom, all those who follow wisdom will live well in the world. **18:** *Tree of life:* The tree of life occurs in the Hebrew Scriptures* only in Proverbs and in Gen 2–3. In both books the tree is associated with wisdom. Its fruit gives life and prosperity. It is also found in Rev 2.7 and 22.2, 14, 19, where it has been influenced by the picture of the health-giving tree in Ezek 47.12. **21–35: Kindness to the neighbor brings blessing to oneself.** Treating others well brings life to oneself. The blessings are portrayed as accruing to one's very body—eyes (*sight*), throat (*soul:* The throat is the source of life-breath), *neck,* and *foot.* To put wisdom into practice brings her gifts, *life* (v. 22a), honor (*adornment,* v. 22b), and protection from crime and violence (vv. 23–25).

---

4 Listen, children, to a father's instruction,
　　and be attentive, that you may gain*c*
　　　insight;
2 for I give you good precepts:
　　do not forsake my teaching.
3 When I was a son with my father,
　　tender, and my mother's favorite,
4 he taught me, and said to me,
　　"Let your heart hold fast my words;
　　keep my commandments, and live.

a Gk: Heb *lie down*　　*b* Heb *from its owners*
c Heb *know*

5 Get wisdom; get insight: do not forget,
   nor turn away
   from the words of my mouth.
6 Do not forsake her, and she will keep
   you;
   love her, and she will guard you.
7 The beginning of wisdom is this: Get
   wisdom,
   and whatever else you get, get insight.
8 Prize her highly, and she will exalt you;
   she will honor you if you
   embrace her.
9 She will place on your head a fair
   garland;
   she will bestow on you a beautiful
   crown."

4.1–9: The teacher's life as an example of wisdom.
The teacher draws a parallel between his teaching his
sons now and his father's teaching him as a youth. The
authority of the teacher comes from the obedience he
showed to *his* father. The teacher now is a model of
the blessings that come with reverence and obedience. **4–9:** *Get wisdom:* In vv. 4–6, the disciple is to
take in the teacher's words and get wisdom. In vv. 6,
8–9 wisdom herself becomes active, guarding and
honoring the disciple.

10 Hear, my child, and accept my words,
    that the years of your life may
    be many.
11 I have taught you the way of wisdom;
    I have led you in the paths of
    uprightness.
12 When you walk, your step will not be
    hampered;
    and if you run, you will not stumble.
13 Keep hold of instruction; do not let go;
    guard her, for she is your life.
14 Do not enter the path of the wicked,
    and do not walk in the way of
    evildoers.
15 Avoid it; do not go on it;
    turn away from it and pass on.
16 For they cannot sleep unless they have
    done wrong;
    they are robbed of sleep unless they
    have made someone stumble.
17 For they eat the bread of wickedness
    and drink the wine of violence.

18 But the path of the righteous is like the
    light of dawn,
    which shines brighter and brighter
    until full day.
19 The way of the wicked is like deep
    darkness;
    they do not know what they stumble
    over.
20 My child, be attentive to my words;
    incline your ear to my sayings.
21 Do not let them escape from
    your sight;
    keep them within your heart.
22 For they are life to those who
    find them,
    and healing to all their flesh.
23 Keep your heart with all vigilance,
    for from it flow the springs of life.
24 Put away from you crooked speech,
    and put devious talk far from you.
25 Let your eyes look directly forward,
    and your gaze be straight before you.
26 Keep straight the path of your feet,
    and all your ways will be sure.
27 Do not swerve to the right or to
    the left;
    turn your foot away from evil.

4.10–27. 10–19: The two ways. The process of gaining wisdom is essentially the same in all the instructions: One begins by memorizing the teaching and
putting it into practice, then one receives wisdom as
a gift. The passage develops the doctrine of the two
ways, in which the moral life is dramatized as two competing paths, the way of wisdom and the path of the
wicked. Each has its inherent destiny, represented here
by the symbols of light and darkness (vv. 18–19). The
two ways are not static; one must struggle to stay on
the right path. It is possible to leave one path and walk
on the other. **20–27: Heed my words.** This lecture
emphasizes the vigor and sincerity necessary for the
pursuit of wisdom. The poem offers a psychological
picture of discipleship. One perceives the teacher's examples and words through listening and seeing (vv.
20–22) and stores the perceptions in the heart (by
memorizing them) where they are pondered (v. 23).
One then puts into practice what one "knows," that
which is in one's heart or mind. Practicing wisdom
means always speaking the truth (v. 24) and acting
justly (vv. 25–27).

5 My child, be attentive to my wisdom;
  incline your ear to my understanding,
² so that you may hold on to prudence,
  and your lips may guard
    knowledge.
³ For the lips of a loose*a* woman drip
    honey,
  and her speech is smoother than oil;
⁴ but in the end she is bitter as
    wormwood,
  sharp as a two-edged sword.
⁵ Her feet go down to death;
  her steps follow the path to Sheol.
⁶ She does not keep straight to the path
    of life;
  her ways wander, and she does not
    know it.

⁷ And now, my child,*b* listen to me,
  and do not depart from the words of
    my mouth.
⁸ Keep your way far from her,
  and do not go near the door of her
    house;
⁹ or you will give your honor to others,
  and your years to the merciless,
¹⁰ and strangers will take their fill of your
    wealth,
  and your labors will go to the house
    of an alien;
¹¹ and at the end of your life you will
    groan,
  when your flesh and body are
    consumed,
¹² and you say, "Oh, how I hated
    discipline,
  and my heart despised reproof!
¹³ I did not listen to the voice of my
    teachers
  or incline my ear to my instructors.
¹⁴ Now I am at the point of utter ruin
  in the public assembly."

¹⁵ Drink water from your own cistern,
  flowing water from your own well.
¹⁶ Should your springs be scattered
    abroad,
  streams of water in the streets?
¹⁷ Let them be for yourself alone,
  and not for sharing with strangers.

¹⁸ Let your fountain be blessed,
  and rejoice in the wife of your youth,
¹⁹ a lovely deer, a graceful doe.
  May her breasts satisfy you at all times;
  may you be intoxicated always by her
    love.
²⁰ Why should you be intoxicated, my son,
    by another woman
  and embrace the bosom of an
    adulteress?
²¹ For human ways are under the eyes of
    the LORD,
  and he examines all their paths.
²² The iniquities of the wicked ensnare
    them,
  and they are caught in the toils of
    their sin.
²³ They die for lack of discipline,
  and because of their great folly they
    are lost.

5.1–23: Choose the right woman! The teacher exhorts a youth to avoid adulterous liaisons (the "wrong" woman, vv. 3–14) and to enjoy the company of his wife (the "right" woman, vv. 15–19). The poem has four sections (vv. 1–6, 7–14, 15–19, and 20–23), each of which begins with "my child" (implicit in v. 15). Adulterous consorting with the wrong woman leads to loss of health (v. 9), dissipation of family wealth (v. 10), ruined reputation (vv. 9, 14), and bitter regret (vv. 11–13). The context of Proverbs suggests a metaphorical* level of meaning: Seductive and lying words lead one away from one's primary commitment to the tradition and to wisdom. **16:** *Should your springs be scattered abroad?* A disputed phrase. Most probably, *water* is a metaphor for sexual pleasure, as in Song 4.15. The man should exercise his sexuality exclusively with his wife in the context of the household.

6 My child, if you have given your pledge
    to your neighbor,
  if you have bound yourself to
    another,*c*
² you are snared by the utterance of your
    lips,*d*
  caught by the words of your mouth.

a Heb *strange*   *b* Gk Vg: Heb *children*   *c* Or *a stranger*   *d* Cn Compare Gk Syr: Heb *the words of your mouth*

3 So do this, my child, and save yourself,
    for you have come into your
        neighbor's power:
    go, hurry,*a* and plead with your
        neighbor.
4 Give your eyes no sleep
    and your eyelids no slumber;
5 save yourself like a gazelle from the
        hunter,*b*
    like a bird from the hand of the
        fowler.

6 Go to the ant, you lazybones;
    consider its ways, and be wise.
7 Without having any chief
    or officer or ruler,
8 it prepares its food in summer,
    and gathers its sustenance in harvest.
9 How long will you lie there,
        O lazybones?
    When will you rise from your sleep?
10 A little sleep, a little slumber,
    a little folding of the hands to rest,
11 and poverty will come upon you like a
        robber,
    and want, like an armed warrior.

12 A scoundrel and a villain
    goes around with crooked speech,
13 winking the eyes, shuffling the feet,
    pointing the fingers,
14 with perverted mind devising evil,
    continually sowing discord;
15 on such a one calamity will descend
        suddenly;
    in a moment, damage beyond repair.

16 There are six things that the LORD
        hates,
    seven that are an abomination to him:
17 haughty eyes, a lying tongue,
    and hands that shed innocent blood,
18 a heart that devises wicked plans,
    feet that hurry to run to evil,
19 a lying witness who testifies falsely,
    and one who sows discord in
        a family.

6.1–19: Four short pieces. The section is often judged to be an addition on the grounds that its topics and style are very different from the surrounding instruc-

tions. It is possible, however, that the editors wanted to insert related but miscellaneous material at this point. Thematically, the section is concerned not with external obstacles to acquiring wisdom, such as violent men and seductive women, but with internal obstacles, such as poor judgment (vv. 1–5) and laziness (vv. 6–11). It also sketches an evil character (vv. 12–15), which is wholly unacceptable to the LORD (vv. 16–19). **1–5:** *Pledge:* Proverbs is entirely negative on the legal custom of a third party guaranteeing a loan (11.15; 17.18; 22.26), probably because it endangers the guarantor. **6–11:** *Lazybones:* Proverbs looks with disdain, and often humorously, on the lazy person (for example, 10.4; 12.24; 24.30–34), preferring instead the energetic and responsible person. **12–15:** *A scoundrel and a villain:* A Proverbs type, who is here described as corrupt externally (mouth or *speech, eyes, feet, fingers*) and internally (*perverted mind*). An evil destiny hangs over such a type. **16–19:** Proverbs often declares certain behavior "an abomination to the LORD" (see 11.1). *Six* and *seven* are an instance of ascending parallelism* of numbers, like "three" and "four" in 30.18–19, 21–23. The organ such as the eye stands for the entire activity of seeing, an example of metonymy.*

20 My child, keep your father's
        commandment,
    and do not forsake your mother's
        teaching.
21 Bind them upon your heart always;
    tie them around your neck.
22 When you walk, they*c* will lead you;
    when you lie down, they*c* will watch
        over you;
    and when you awake, they*c* will talk
        with you.
23 For the commandment is a lamp and
        the teaching a light,
    and the reproofs of discipline are the
        way of life,
24 to preserve you from the wife of
        another,*d*
    from the smooth tongue of the
        adulteress.
25 Do not desire her beauty in your heart,
    and do not let her capture you with
        her eyelashes;

a Or *humble yourself*   *b* Cn: Heb *from the hand*
c Heb *it*   *d* Gk: MT *the evil woman*

26 for a prostitute's fee is only a loaf of
  bread,*
  but the wife of another stalks a man's
  very life.
27 Can fire be carried in the bosom
  without burning one's clothes?
28 Or can one walk on hot coals
  without scorching the feet?
29 So is he who sleeps with his neighbor's
  wife;
  no one who touches her will go
  unpunished.
30 Thieves are not despised who steal only
  to satisfy their appetite when they are
  hungry.
31 Yet if they are caught, they will pay
  sevenfold;
  they will forfeit all the goods of their
  house.
32 But he who commits adultery has no
  sense;
  he who does it destroys himself.
33 He will get wounds and dishonor,
  and his disgrace will not be wiped
  away.
34 For jealousy arouses a husband's fury,
  and he shows no restraint when he
  takes revenge.
35 He will accept no compensation,
  and refuses a bribe no matter how
  great.

6.20–35: The dangers of adultery. The teaching of
one's parents, once memorized, becomes a *lamp* that
exposes the danger of an adulteress (v. 23). Unlike a
liaison with a prostitute, whose hire is only a matter of
money, an affair with a married woman can destroy
one's life, bringing upon one shame, physical beatings, and an enraged husband. The instruction focuses
more on the practical consequences of adultery rather
than on its theoretical immorality. **30:** *Thieves are not
despised:* A comparison is drawn between getting
caught for satisfying one's appetite for food (a
euphemism* for the sexual appetite) and getting
caught for adultery. In the first case, a monetary payment makes things right. In the second, money cannot
repair the loss of one's position in the community or
protect one from the vengeance of a deceived
husband.

7 My child, keep my words
  and store up my commandments with
  you;
2 keep my commandments and live,
  keep my teachings as the apple of
  your eye;
3 bind them on your fingers,
  write them on the tablet of your
  heart.
4 Say to wisdom, "You are my sister,"
  and call insight your intimate friend,
5 that they may keep you from the loose*
  woman,
  from the adulteress with her smooth
  words.

6 For at the window of my house
  I looked out through my lattice,
7 and I saw among the simple ones,
  I observed among the youths,
  a young man without sense,
8 passing along the street near her corner,
  taking the road to her house
9 in the twilight, in the evening,
  at the time of night and darkness.

10 Then a woman comes toward him,
  decked out like a prostitute, wily of
  heart.*
11 She is loud and wayward;
  her feet do not stay at home;
12 now in the street, now in the squares,
  and at every corner she lies in wait.
13 She seizes him and kisses him,
  and with impudent face she says to
  him:
14 "I had to offer sacrifices,
  and today I have paid my vows;
15 so now I have come out to meet you,
  to seek you eagerly, and I have found
  you!
16 I have decked my couch with coverings,
  colored spreads of Egyptian linen;
17 I have perfumed my bed with myrrh,
  aloes, and cinnamon.
18 Come, let us take our fill of love until
  morning;
  let us delight ourselves with love.

a Cn Compare Gk Syr Vg Tg: Heb *for because of a harlot
to a piece of bread*   b Heb *strange*   c Meaning of
Heb uncertain

19 For my husband is not at home;
   he has gone on a long journey.
20 He took a bag of money with him;
   he will not come home until full
      moon."
21 With much seductive speech she
      persuades him;
   with her smooth talk she
      compels him.
22 Right away he follows her,
   and goes like an ox to the slaughter,
   or bounds like a stag toward the trap^a
23   until an arrow pierces its entrails.
   He is like a bird rushing into a snare,
      not knowing that it will cost him his
         life.

24 And now, my children, listen to me,
   and be attentive to the words of my
      mouth.
25 Do not let your hearts turn aside to her
      ways;
   do not stray into her paths.
26 for many are those she has laid low,
   and numerous are her victims.
27 Her house is the way to Sheol,
   going down to the chambers of death.

_____

7.1–27: An example of seduction by words. The
tenth and final instruction is also the fourth of the four
warnings against the seductive woman (2.16–19;
5.1–23; 6.20–35). The preface (vv. 1–5) urges the disciple to become a lover of Wisdom rather than a foolish
victim of the lying woman whose typical wiles are narrated. The woman is active and aware, speaking and
acting decisively, whereas the youth is passive and naive, led in silence like a lamb to slaughter. The images
are darkness and night, animals of sacrifice or the hunt,
and death. **4:** _You are my sister:_ A designation for the
beloved used in love poetry (Song 4.9, 10, 12; 5.1, 2).
Other love terms are _let us take our fill of love_ (v. 18;
see Song 5.1) and the theme of finding and seeking
(v. 10–15; see Song 3.1–4). **14:** _Today I have paid my
vows:_ An ambivalent statement, which the youth takes
as an invitation to a feast of meat offered in fulfillment
of a vow, but which the woman intends as the sacrifice
of the youth. Comparison with Jephthah's vow (Judg
11.30–31) is illuminating, for Jephthah also sacrifices
an unsuspecting victim. **20:** _He took a bag of money
with him:_ The wife knows from the amount of money

her husband took that he will be gone long enough
for her to dally with the youth.

~~~~~~~~~~~~~~~~~~~~~~~~~~~~

8 Does not wisdom call,
   and does not understanding raise her
      voice?
2 On the heights, beside the way,
   at the crossroads she takes her
      stand;
3 beside the gates in front of the town,
   at the entrance of the portals she
      cries out:
4 "To you, O people, I call,
   and my cry is to all that live.
5 O simple ones, learn prudence;
   acquire intelligence, you who lack it.
6 Hear, for I will speak noble things,
   and from my lips will come what is
      right;
7 for my mouth will utter truth;
   wickedness is an abomination to my
      lips.
8 All the words of my mouth are
      righteous;
   there is nothing twisted or crooked in
      them.
9 They are all straight to one who
      understands
   and right to those who find
      knowledge.
10 Take my instruction instead of silver,
   and knowledge rather than choice
      gold;
11 for wisdom is better than jewels,
   and all that you may desire cannot
      compare with her.
12 I, wisdom, live with prudence,^b
   and I attain knowledge and
      discretion.
13 The fear of the LORD is hatred of evil.
   Pride and arrogance and the way of evil
   and perverted speech I hate.
14 I have good advice and sound wisdom;
   I have insight, I have strength.
15 By me kings reign,
   and rulers decree what is just;
16 by me rulers rule,
   and nobles, all who govern rightly.

_a_ Cn Compare Gk: Meaning of Heb uncertain
_b_ Meaning of Heb uncertain

The Personification of Wisdom

One of the most striking features of Proverbs is its vivid personification★ of wisdom as a woman. Personification is a way of presenting an idea, a natural force, or an abstract concept as if it were a person. Woman Wisdom gives two lengthy speeches in the town square (1.20–33 and 8.1–36), and she invites passers-by to the banquet dedicating her newly built palace (9.1–6). Personification is found in other biblical passages, such as Ps 43.3 ("O send out your light and your truth; let them lead me"), but none have the scale and vigor of Wisdom in Proverbs.

Scholars have sought for parallels to Woman Wisdom in comparable literature. Some believe that personified Wisdom is an example of hypostasis, according to which some quality of a god, such as his anger or wisdom, is considered an entity in itself. Woman would thus be an embodiment of the wisdom of the LORD. Proverbs insists, however, that Wisdom is *distinct* from the LORD. Another suggestion is that Wisdom is an Israelite version of the Egyptian goddess Maat, who symbolizes order in the world and is sometimes personified. There is, however, no exact biblical equivalent to the Egyptian concept of cosmic order. Further, personified Maat is a pale abstraction in comparison with Woman Wisdom. A third suggestion is that Woman Wisdom is modeled on the "apkallu" or "umannu" of Mesopotamian mythology, sages who brought to the human race heavenly wisdom such as metallurgy, writing, and ritual. According to this conception, Wisdom is given to the race by a grand process that begins with the gods, passes through mythic sages, and ends with authoritative human beings such as kings, parents, and teachers. This last antecedent is the most likely for Proverbs for two reasons: first because Wisdom is called an "umannu" (NRSV "master worker") in 8.30, and second because in chs. 1–9, a king (Solomon), parents, and teachers join Wisdom in her task of instructing the human race; they are part of the chain of wisdom.

The book presents a counter-figure to Woman Wisdom—the "loose woman" (2.16–19; 5.1–23; 6.20–35; 7.1–27) and Woman Folly (9.13–18). Ultimately derived from warnings to young men against the wrong kind of women, the loose woman has a metaphorical★ dimension in the book: She seeks to seduce her hearers with words, promising them life but dealing them death. The book thus presents the moral life in dramatic terms; there are two voices (Wisdom and Folly), and there are two ways (the way of the righteous and the way of the wicked). Each person must choose one or the other.

Woman Wisdom's speeches in Proverbs contain no specific advice. Rather, she invites her hearers to become her disciples—to trust and obey her, and even to wait at her gates like a dear friend (8.32–36). She promises to bestow security (1.33), rule, wealth, and success (8.14–21). Her authority rests on her intimacy and honored position with God; she was created before everything and has an intimate relationship with God. In fact, traditional love language is used to describe her relationship to God and to human beings (8.30–31, 34).

Wisdom in Proverbs, and Woman Wisdom in particular, has been interpreted in a variety of ways. Jewish tradition generally views wisdom as the Torah.★ The Jewish sage Ben Sira in the early second century BCE interpreted personified Wisdom as the covenant★ of the Most High God, the law of Moses (Sir 24.23). Early Christians used the concept of personified Wisdom to explain the pre-existence of Christ (Jn 1.1–2; Col 1.15–20). In early Christian controversies about the divinity of Christ, Prov 8.22 ("The LORD created me at the beginning of his work") was used as a proof text.

The personification of wisdom gives Proverbs a metaphorical dimension. The moral life is not simply a series of right actions but a fundamental option—seeking wisdom before all else.

17 I love those who love me,
  and those who seek me diligently find
    me.
18 Riches and honor are with me,
  enduring wealth and prosperity.
19 My fruit is better than gold, even fine
    gold,
  and my yield than choice silver.
20 I walk in the way of righteousness,
  along the paths of justice,
21 endowing with wealth those who love
    me,
  and filling their treasuries.
22 The LORD created me at the beginning^a
    of his work,^b
  the first of his acts of long ago.
23 Ages ago I was set up,
  at the first, before the beginning of
    the earth.
24 When there were no depths I was
    brought forth,
  when there were no springs
    abounding with water.
25 Before the mountains had been shaped,
  before the hills, I was brought forth—
26 when he had not yet made earth and
    fields,^c
  or the world's first bits of soil.
27 When he established the heavens, I was
    there,
  when he drew a circle on the face of
    the deep,
28 when he made firm the skies above,
  when he established the fountains of
    the deep,
29 when he assigned to the sea its limit,
  so that the waters might not
    transgress his command,
  when he marked out the foundations of
    the earth,
30   then I was beside him, like a master
    worker;^d
  and I was daily his^e delight,
  rejoicing before him always,
31 rejoicing in his inhabited world
  and delighting in the human race.

32 "And now, my children, listen to me:
  happy are those who keep my ways.
33 Hear instruction and be wise,
  and do not neglect it.

34 Happy is the one who listens to me,
  watching daily at my gates,
  waiting beside my doors.
35 For whoever finds me finds life
  and obtains favor from the LORD;
36 but those who miss me injure
    themselves;
  all who hate me love death."

8.1–36: Woman Wisdom and her blessings for her loyal disciples. The speech of personified* Wisdom promising blessings balances her first speech (1.20–33) threatening those who left her. She appears in the busiest part of the city (vv. 1–3), and addresses the entire populace there, but singles out the simple (vv. 4–5). She establishes her credibility (vv. 6–11), promises her hearers skill in governing along with riches and honor (vv. 12–21), explains her high status by her closeness to God at creation (vv. 22–31), and asks her followers to wait at her door as disciples (vv. 32–36). Unlike the seductive woman in ch. 7 who speaks to a single youth in the dark of night, Wisdom addresses everyone in broad daylight, speaks trustworthy words, and grants life rather than death. **22–31:** The verses are a cosmogony or creation account, which was used in ancient literature to explain and validate important aspects of reality. The first half of the cosmogony (vv. 22–26) emphasizes the birth of Woman Wisdom *before* all else, thus underlining her unique priority. The second half (vv. 27–31) stresses her presence with God, *I was there* (v. 27) and *I was beside him* (v. 30). **30–31:** *I was daily his delight . . . delighting in the human race:* The repetition of the words *delight* and *rejoicing* establishes a correspondence between Wisdom's delighting in the LORD and her delighting in the human race. She bestows on the human race the wisdom and goodness that God put into creation.

9 Wisdom has built her house,
  she has hewn her seven pillars.
2 She has slaughtered her animals, she
    has mixed her wine,
  she has also set her table.
3 She has sent out her servant-girls, she
    calls
  from the highest places in the town,

a Or *me as the beginning*   *b* Heb *way*   *c* Meaning of Heb uncertain   *d* Another reading is *little child*   *e* Gk: Heb lacks *his*

4 "You that are simple, turn in here!"
To those without sense she says,
5 "Come, eat of my bread
and drink of the wine I have mixed.
6 Lay aside immaturity,[a] and live,
and walk in the way of insight."

7 Whoever corrects a scoffer wins abuse;
whoever rebukes the wicked
gets hurt.
8 A scoffer who is rebuked will only hate
you;
the wise, when rebuked, will love you.
9 Give instruction[b] to the wise, and they
will become wiser still;
teach the righteous and they will gain
in learning.
10 The fear of the LORD is the beginning
of wisdom,
and the knowledge of the Holy One is
insight.
11 For by me your days will be multiplied,
and years will be added to your life.
12 If you are wise, you are wise for
yourself;
if you scoff, you alone will bear it.

13 The foolish woman is loud;
she is ignorant and knows nothing.
14 She sits at the door of her house,
on a seat at the high places of the
town,
15 calling to those who pass by,
who are going straight on their way,
16 "You who are simple, turn in here!"
And to those without sense she says,
17 "Stolen water is sweet,
and bread eaten in secret is pleasant."
18 But they do not know that the dead[c]
are there,
that her guests are in the depths of
Sheol.

9.1–18: The banquets of the two women, plus some aphorisms. Woman Wisdom completes her palace and issues an invitation to the dedicatory banquet (1–6). In vv. 13–18, Woman Folly issues a counter-invitation. Verses 7–12 are individual sayings, which echo some verses in ch. 1 (compare 1.7, "The fear of the LORD is the beginning of knowledge," and 1.22, "How long, O simple ones, will you love being sim-

ple?") and also point ahead to chs. 10–22, where the same two types, the wise and the righteous, are vividly contrasted. **6:** *Lay aside immaturity, and live:* To partake of the banquet creates a bond between Wisdom and her guests, requiring guests to leave behind *immaturity* and ignorance and to become wise. The imperative verb *live* here implies enjoyment of such gifts from Wisdom as a family, riches, and reputation. **11:** *For by me your days will be multiplied:* Originally, this verse probably immediately followed v. 6, for *by me* has no antecedent in the immediately preceding verses. **16–17:** Folly's invitation begins with the same words as Wisdom's (see v. 16 and v. 4), but in v. 17 diverges radically. **17:** In the phrase *stolen water, water* has the erotic meaning it has in 5.15–16, "Drink water from your own cistern, / flowing water from your own well," that is, sexual relations. *Stolen* implies clandestine and adulterous sex. *In secret* evokes the furtive meeting of ch. 7. **18:** *The dead* inhabit the underworld. As in 2.16–18; 5.3–5; 7.24–27, the woman promises life but kills instead.

THE PROVERBS OF SOLOMON

10.1–22.16: Nearly all of chs. 10–15 are antithetic* proverbs, that is, the second line (B) restates the first line (A) in an opposite way. The section contrasts the wicked and the righteous person (treated as types) and emphasizes the consequences of human acts. Chapters 16–22, on the other hand, contain far fewer antitheses and many more exceptions to the rule. A key metaphor* throughout all these chapters is founding or maintaining a house, which continues the same image as in chs. 1–9. The chapters contain over fifty references to father, mother, son, house, wife or servant.

10

The proverbs of Solomon.

A wise child makes a glad father,
but a foolish child is a mother's grief.
2 Treasures gained by wickedness do not
profit,
but righteousness delivers from death.
3 The LORD does not let the righteous go
hungry,
but he thwarts the craving of the
wicked.

---

a Or *simpleness*   b Heb lacks *instruction*
c Heb *shades*

4 A slack hand causes poverty,
  but the hand of the diligent makes
    rich.
5 A child who gathers in summer is
    prudent,
  but a child who sleeps in harvest
    brings shame.
6 Blessings are on the head of the
    righteous,
  but the mouth of the wicked conceals
    violence.
7 The memory of the righteous is a
    blessing,
  but the name of the wicked will rot.
8 The wise of heart will heed
    commandments,
  but a babbling fool will come to ruin.
9 Whoever walks in integrity walks
    securely,
  but whoever follows perverse ways
    will be found out.
10 Whoever winks the eye causes trouble,
  but the one who rebukes boldly
    makes peace.ᵃ
11 The mouth of the righteous is a
    fountain of life,
  but the mouth of the wicked conceals
    violence.
12 Hatred stirs up strife,
  but love covers all offenses.
13 On the lips of one who has
    understanding wisdom is found,
  but a rod is for the back of one who
    lacks sense.
14 The wise lay up knowledge,
  but the babbling of a fool brings ruin
    near.
15 The wealth of the rich is their fortress;
  the poverty of the poor is their ruin.
16 The wage of the righteous leads to life,
  the gain of the wicked to sin.
17 Whoever heeds instruction is on the
    path to life,
  but one who rejects a rebuke goes
    astray.
18 Lying lips conceal hatred,
  and whoever utters slander is a fool.
19 When words are many, transgression is
    not lacking,
  but the prudent are restrained in
    speech.

20 The tongue of the righteous is choice
    silver;
  the mind of the wicked is of
    little worth.
21 The lips of the righteous feed many,
  but fools die for lack of sense.
22 The blessing of the LORD makes rich,
  and he adds no sorrow with it.ᵇ
23 Doing wrong is like sport to a fool,
  but wise conduct is pleasure to a
    person of understanding.
24 What the wicked dread will come upon
    them,
  but the desire of the righteous will be
    granted.
25 When the tempest passes, the wicked
    are no more,
  but the righteous are established
    forever.
26 Like vinegar to the teeth, and smoke to
    the eyes,
  so are the lazy to their employers.
27 The fear of the LORD prolongs life,
  but the years of the wicked will be
    short.
28 The hope of the righteous ends in
    gladness,
  but the expectation of the wicked
    comes to nothing.
29 The way of the LORD is a stronghold for
    the upright,
  but destruction for evildoers.
30 The righteous will never be removed,
  but the wicked will not remain in the
    land.
31 The mouth of the righteous brings forth
    wisdom,
  but the perverse tongue will be cut
    off.
32 The lips of the righteous know what is
    acceptable,
  but the mouth of the wicked what is
    perverse.

10.1–32. 1–3: The first three sayings represent the
three sides of wisdom, the sapiential (wisdom as right
knowledge, v. 1, *wise*), the ethical (wisdom as right
action, v. 2, *righteousness*), and the religious (wisdom

a Gk: Heb *but a babbling fool will come to ruin*
b Or *and toil adds nothing to it*

as right reverence or worship, v. 3, *the LORD*). **1:** In the opening saying, *child*, *father*, and *mother* refer to the instructions of chs. 1–9 (see 1.8) and show the continuity between the instructions and the sayings. **6:** Proverbs often plays on two senses of the verb "to cover": "cover" in the sense of "conceal" and in the sense of "fill" (see vv. 11 and 12). Line B can also be translated in a sense opposite to NRSV, "violence covers the mouth of the wicked." **9:** Proverbs frequently uses the metaphors* of walking and path for conduct (also current in English). "To walk" is "to conduct oneself, to live"; "way" is "conduct"; "straight" and "crooked" (*perverted*) are "good" and "evil." *Integrity* is literally "straight, whole." **15:** Though Proverbs praises diligence and ridicules laziness, it does not ordinarily praise the wealthy and criticize the poor, but rather makes neutral observations on the situation of rich and poor, as here. **19:** Ordinarily, abundance is good, as in vv. 4, 21, and 27, and scarcity is bad, as in vv. 15 and 21. But where words are concerned the situation is reversed. Words should be few and well chosen (see 17.27). **26:** A lazy person is a common type in Proverbs (mentioned fourteen times in the book) and is often the object of scorn or humor. The lazy are as sure to pain an employer as *vinegar* and *smoke* are sure to pain taste buds and eyes, by an almost chemical necessity.

11 A false balance is an abomination to the LORD,
   but an accurate weight is his delight.
2 When pride comes, then comes disgrace;
   but wisdom is with the humble.
3 The integrity of the upright guides them,
   but the crookedness of the treacherous destroys them.
4 Riches do not profit in the day of wrath,
   but righteousness delivers from death.
5 The righteousness of the blameless keeps their ways straight,
   but the wicked fall by their own wickedness.
6 The righteousness of the upright saves them,
   but the treacherous are taken captive by their schemes.

7 When the wicked die, their hope perishes,
   and the expectation of the godless comes to nothing.
8 The righteous are delivered from trouble,
   and the wicked get into it instead.
9 With their mouths the godless would destroy their neighbors,
   but by knowledge the righteous are delivered.
10 When it goes well with the righteous, the city rejoices;
   and when the wicked perish, there is jubilation.
11 By the blessing of the upright a city is exalted,
   but it is overthrown by the mouth of the wicked.
12 Whoever belittles another lacks sense,
   but an intelligent person remains silent.
13 A gossip goes about telling secrets,
   but one who is trustworthy in spirit keeps a confidence.
14 Where there is no guidance, a nation*a* falls,
   but in an abundance of counselors there is safety.
15 To guarantee loans for a stranger brings trouble,
   but there is safety in refusing to do so.
16 A gracious woman gets honor,
   but she who hates virtue is covered with shame.*b*
   The timid become destitute,*c*
   but the aggressive gain riches.
17 Those who are kind reward themselves,
   but the cruel do themselves harm.
18 The wicked earn no real gain,
   but those who sow righteousness get a true reward.
19 Whoever is steadfast in righteousness will live,
   but whoever pursues evil will die.
20 Crooked minds are an abomination to the LORD,

a Or *an army*   *b* Compare Gk Syr: Heb lacks *but she . . . shame*   *c* Gk: Heb lacks *The timid . . . destitute*

but those of blameless ways are his
   delight.

21 Be assured, the wicked will not go
      unpunished,
   but those who are righteous will
      escape.

22 Like a gold ring in a pig's snout
   is a beautiful woman without good
      sense.

23 The desire of the righteous ends only in
      good;
   the expectation of the wicked in
      wrath.

24 Some give freely, yet grow all the richer;
   others withhold what is due, and only
      suffer want.

25 A generous person will be enriched,
   and one who gives water will
      get water.

26 The people curse those who hold back
      grain,
   but a blessing is on the head of those
      who sell it.

27 Whoever diligently seeks good seeks
      favor,
   but evil comes to the one who
      searches for it.

28 Those who trust in their riches will
      wither,[a]
   but the righteous will flourish like
      green leaves.

29 Those who trouble their households will
      inherit wind,
   and the fool will be servant to the
      wise.

30 The fruit of the righteous is a tree of
      life,
   but violence[b] takes lives away.

31 If the righteous are repaid on earth,
   how much more the wicked and the
      sinner!

11.1–31. 4: *The day of wrath* is any life-threatening
disaster as in Job 21.30 and Ezek 7.19. In such mortal
danger riches are of no use; value attaches only to that
which assures ultimate protection—righteousness. **9:**
The difference between impiety and righteousness is
so great that what is expressed by *the godless* harms
others, whereas what is not expressed (*knowledge*
here is what is stored in the heart) by *the righteous*
benefits them. **22:** A humorous statement that wisdom

is more important than beauty in evaluating a woman.
Ear and nose rings were common adornments of
women. The comparison to a pig seems to have been
made on the basis of sound as well as humorous in-
congruity, for the consonant "z" predominates in the
first line: "nezem zahab be'ap hazir," literally, "a ring
of god in the snout of a pig." **27:** The persistent quest
for what is good is ultimately a quest that ends in gaining divine favor, perhaps human favor as well. In other
words, to seek happiness, seek excellence. To seek evil
("ra'â"), on the other hand, means only that trouble
("ra'â") will seek one out. The same Hebrew word can
mean "evil" and "trouble."

12 Whoever loves discipline loves
      knowledge,
   but those who hate to be rebuked are
      stupid.

2 The good obtain favor from the LORD,
   but those who devise evil he
      condemns.

3 No one finds security by wickedness,
   but the root of the righteous will
      never be moved.

4 A good wife is the crown of her
      husband,
   but she who brings shame is like
      rottenness in his bones.

5 The thoughts of the righteous are just;
   the advice of the wicked is
      treacherous.

6 The words of the wicked are a deadly
      ambush,
   but the speech of the upright delivers
      them.

7 The wicked are overthrown and are no
      more,
   but the house of the righteous will
      stand.

8 One is commended for good sense,
   but a perverse mind is despised.

9 Better to be despised and have a
      servant,
   than to be self-important and lack
      food.

10 The righteous know the needs of their
      animals,
   but the mercy of the wicked is cruel.

a Cn: Heb *fall*   *b* Cn Compare Gk Syr: Heb *a wise
man*

11 Those who till their land will have
     plenty of food,
   but those who follow worthless
     pursuits have no sense.
12 The wicked covet the proceeds of
     wickedness,[a]
   but the root of the righteous bears
     fruit.
13 The evil are ensnared by the
     transgression of their lips,
   but the righteous escape from
     trouble.
14 From the fruit of the mouth one is filled
     with good things,
   and manual labor has its reward.
15 Fools think their own way is right,
   but the wise listen to advice.
16 Fools show their anger at once,
   but the prudent ignore an insult.
17 Whoever speaks the truth gives honest
     evidence,
   but a false witness speaks deceitfully.
18 Rash words are like sword thrusts,
   but the tongue of the wise brings
     healing.
19 Truthful lips endure forever,
   but a lying tongue lasts only a
     moment.
20 Deceit is in the mind of those who plan
     evil,
   but those who counsel peace
     have joy.
21 No harm happens to the righteous,
   but the wicked are filled with
     trouble.
22 Lying lips are an abomination to the
     LORD,
   but those who act faithfully are his
     delight.
23 One who is clever conceals knowledge,
   but the mind of a fool[b] broadcasts
     folly.
24 The hand of the diligent will rule,
   while the lazy will be put to forced
     labor.
25 Anxiety weighs down the human heart,
   but a good word cheers it up.
26 The righteous gives good advice
     to friends,[c]
   but the way of the wicked leads
     astray.

27 The lazy do not roast[d] their game,
   but the diligent obtain precious
     wealth.[d]
28 In the path of righteousness there is
     life,
   in walking its path there is no death.

12.1–28. 1: Genuine wisdom is gained through conversation with the wise (*discipline*) and through being criticized (*rebuked*). To reject this educational process is to settle for an animal level of consciousness; the Hebrew word for *stupid* in the second line connotes brutish. 14: Normally, one's mouth is sated from the fruit of the earth, but in this saying one is sated from the words of one's mouth. Words in Proverbs are the prime instance of human activity. One will enjoy the benefits of one's conduct.

13 A wise child loves discipline,[e]
   but a scoffer does not listen to
     rebuke.
2 From the fruit of their words good
     persons eat good things,
   but the desire of the treacherous is
     for wrongdoing.
3 Those who guard their mouths preserve
     their lives;
   those who open wide their lips come
     to ruin.
4 The appetite of the lazy craves, and gets
     nothing,
   while the appetite of the diligent is
     richly supplied.
5 The righteous hate falsehood,
   but the wicked act shamefully and
     disgracefully.
6 Righteousness guards one whose way is
     upright,
   but sin overthrows the wicked.
7 Some pretend to be rich, yet have
     nothing;
   others pretend to be poor, yet have
     great wealth.
8 Wealth is a ransom for a person's life,
   but the poor get no threats.
9 The light of the righteous rejoices,
   but the lamp of the wicked goes out.

a Or *covet the catch of the wicked*   b Heb *the heart of fools*   c Syr: Meaning of Heb uncertain   d Meaning of Heb uncertain   e Cn: Heb *A wise child the discipline of his father*

10 By insolence the heedless make strife,
   but wisdom is with those who take
      advice.
11 Wealth hastily gotten[a] will dwindle,
   but those who gather little by little
      will increase it.
12 Hope deferred makes the heart sick,
   but a desire fulfilled is a tree of life.
13 Those who despise the word bring
      destruction on themselves,
   but those who respect the
      commandment will be rewarded.
14 The teaching of the wise is a fountain of
      life,
   so that one may avoid the snares of
      death.
15 Good sense wins favor,
   but the way of the faithless is their
      ruin.[b]
16 The clever do all things intelligently,
   but the fool displays folly.
17 A bad messenger brings trouble,
   but a faithful envoy, healing.
18 Poverty and disgrace are for the one
      who ignores instruction,
   but one who heeds reproof is
      honored.
19 A desire realized is sweet to the soul,
   but to turn away from evil is an
      abomination to fools.
20 Whoever walks with the wise becomes
      wise,
   but the companion of fools suffers
      harm.
21 Misfortune pursues sinners,
   but prosperity rewards the righteous.
22 The good leave an inheritance to their
      children's children,
   but the sinner's wealth is laid up for
      the righteous.
23 The field of the poor may yield much
      food,
   but it is swept away through
      injustice.
24 Those who spare the rod hate their
      children,
   but those who love them are diligent
      to discipline them.
25 The righteous have enough to satisfy
      their appetite,
   but the belly of the wicked is empty.

13.1–25. 6: *Righteousness* and *sin* are personified* as forces affecting those who commit themselves to them. Fundamental options determine one's course. **24:** The paradox is that one *hates* one's children by being tender with them and *loves* them by being strict, especially at an early age when children can readily change. What is criticized is indulging one's children. The paradoxical language cannot be invoked to justify harsh treatment of children or corporal punishment. Proverbs often states the need of parental discipline: 19.18; 23.13–14; Sir 7.23; 30.1–13.

14 The wise woman[c] builds her house,
   but the foolish tears it down with
      her own hands.
2 Those who walk uprightly fear the
      LORD,
   but one who is devious in conduct
      despises him.
3 The talk of fools is a rod for their backs,[d]
   but the lips of the wise preserve
      them.
4 Where there are no oxen, there is no
      grain;
   abundant crops come by the strength
      of the ox.
5 A faithful witness does not lie,
   but a false witness breathes out lies.
6 A scoffer seeks wisdom in vain,
   but knowledge is easy for one who
      understands.
7 Leave the presence of a fool,
   for there you do not find words of
      knowledge.
8 It is the wisdom of the clever to
      understand where they go,
   but the folly of fools misleads.
9 Fools mock at the guilt offering,[e]
   but the upright enjoy God's favor.
10 The heart knows its own bitterness,
   and no stranger shares its joy.
11 The house of the wicked is destroyed,
   but the tent of the upright flourishes.
12 There is a way that seems right to a
      person,
   but its end is the way to death.[f]

a Gk Vg: Heb *from vanity*   b Cn Compare Gk Syr Vg
Tg: Heb *is enduring*   c Heb *Wisdom of women*
d Cn: Heb *a rod of pride*   e Meaning of Heb uncertain
f Heb *ways of death*

13 Even in laughter the heart is sad,
  and the end of joy is grief.
14 The perverse get what their ways
    deserve,
  and the good, what their deeds
    deserve.*a*
15 The simple believe everything,
  but the clever consider their steps.
16 The wise are cautious and turn away
    from evil,
  but the fool throws off restraint and is
    careless.
17 One who is quick-tempered acts
    foolishly,
  and the schemer is hated.
18 The simple are adorned with*b* folly,
  but the clever are crowned with
    knowledge.
19 The evil bow down before the good,
  the wicked at the gates of the
    righteous.
20 The poor are disliked even by their
    neighbors,
  but the rich have many friends.
21 Those who despise their neighbors are
    sinners,
  but happy are those who are kind to
    the poor.
22 Do they not err that plan evil?
  Those who plan good find loyalty and
    faithfulness.
23 In all toil there is profit,
  but mere talk leads only to poverty.
24 The crown of the wise is their wisdom,*c*
  but folly is the garland*d* of fools.
25 A truthful witness saves lives,
  but one who utters lies is a betrayer.
26 In the fear of the LORD one has strong
    confidence,
  and one's children will have a refuge.
27 The fear of the LORD is a fountain of
    life,
  so that one may avoid the snares of
    death.
28 The glory of a king is a multitude of
    people;
  without people a prince is ruined.
29 Whoever is slow to anger has great
    understanding,
  but one who has a hasty temper exalts
    folly.

30 A tranquil mind gives life to the flesh,
  but passion makes the bones rot.
31 Those who oppress the poor insult their
    Maker,
  but those who are kind to the needy
    honor him.
32 The wicked are overthrown by their
    evildoing,
  but the righteous find a refuge in
    their integrity.*e*
33 Wisdom is at home in the mind of one
    who has understanding,
  but it is not*f* known in the heart of
    fools.
34 Righteousness exalts a nation,
  but sin is a reproach to any people.
35 A servant who deals wisely has the
    king's favor,
  but his wrath falls on one who acts
    shamefully.

14.1–35. 5: How to assess a *witness* in court is a common concern of the book (6.19; 12.17; 19.28). The best criterion is the character of the witness: How does the person ordinarily act? **13:** As observed in v. 10, external behavior does not always mirror internal thought and feeling. People are too complex to be known completely from their actions. **28:** *The glory of a king* is not absolute but depends, surprisingly, on the people he rules. A witty critique of royal power. **30:** *Passion* can also be rendered "jealousy." Inner calmness has a beneficial effect on health.

15 A soft answer turns away wrath,
    but a harsh word stirs up anger.
2 The tongue of the wise dispenses
    knowledge,*g*
  but the mouths of fools pour
    out folly.
3 The eyes of the LORD are in every
    place,
  keeping watch on the evil and the
    good.
4 A gentle tongue is a tree of life,
  but perverseness in it breaks the
    spirit.

a Cn: Heb *from upon him*   *b* Or *inherit*
c Cn Compare Gk: Heb *riches*   *d* Cn: Heb *is the folly*
e Gk Syr: Heb *in their death*   *f* Gk Syr: Heb *lacks not*
g Cn: Heb *makes knowledge good*

5 A fool despises a parent's instruction,
   but the one who heeds admonition is
      prudent.
6 In the house of the righteous there is
      much treasure,
   but trouble befalls the income of the
      wicked.
7 The lips of the wise spread knowledge;
   not so the minds of fools.
8 The sacrifice of the wicked is an
      abomination to the LORD,
   but the prayer of the upright is his
      delight.
9 The way of the wicked is an
      abomination to the LORD,
   but he loves the one who pursues
      righteousness.
10 There is severe discipline for one who
      forsakes the way,
   but one who hates a rebuke will die.
11 Sheol and Abaddon lie open before the
      LORD,
   how much more human hearts!
12 Scoffers do not like to be rebuked;
   they will not go to the wise.
13 A glad heart makes a cheerful
      countenance,
   but by sorrow of heart the spirit is
      broken.
14 The mind of one who has
      understanding seeks knowledge,
   but the mouths of fools feed on folly.
15 All the days of the poor are hard,
   but a cheerful heart has a continual
      feast.
16 Better is a little with the fear of the
      LORD
   than great treasure and trouble with it.
17 Better is a dinner of vegetables where
      love is
   than a fatted ox and hatred with it.
18 Those who are hot-tempered stir up
      strife,
   but those who are slow to anger calm
      contention.
19 The way of the lazy is overgrown with
      thorns,
   but the path of the upright is a level
      highway.
20 A wise child makes a glad father,
   but the foolish despise their mothers.

21 Folly is a joy to one who has no sense,
   but a person of understanding walks
      straight ahead.
22 Without counsel, plans go wrong,
   but with many advisers they succeed.
23 To make an apt answer is a joy to
      anyone,
   and a word in season, how good it is!
24 For the wise the path of life leads
      upward,
   in order to avoid Sheol below.
25 The LORD tears down the house of the
      proud,
   but maintains the widow's
      boundaries.
26 Evil plans are an abomination to the
      LORD,
   but gracious words are pure.
27 Those who are greedy for unjust gain
      make trouble for their
      households,
   but those who hate bribes will live.
28 The mind of the righteous ponders how
      to answer,
   but the mouth of the wicked pours
      out evil.
29 The LORD is far from the wicked,
   but he hears the prayer of the
      righteous.
30 The light of the eyes rejoices the heart,
   and good news refreshes the body.
31 The ear that heeds wholesome
      admonition
   will lodge among the wise.
32 Those who ignore instruction despise
      themselves,
   but those who heed admonition gain
      understanding.
33 The fear of the LORD is instruction in
      wisdom,
   and humility goes before honor.

15.1–33. 1: In responding to angry people, one might
be tempted to use harsh and violent language. The
verse states the paradox that when one responds to
angry people, *soft* is strong and *harsh* is weak. 14:
Heart (*mind*) and mouth are often contrasted as the
organ of storage-reflection (*mind*) and the organ of
expression (*mouth*). Here, the wise use their minds to
seek even more knowledge, whereas fools use their
mouths only to feed on more folly. 26: *Abomination,*

originally a ritual term for an unacceptable offering, is here used metaphorically.* *Pure* in this usage means acceptable to God. **33:** As one must first be low (*humility*) in order to be raised up (*honor*), so *fear of the* Lord comes before wisdom.

16 The plans of the mind belong to mortals,
  but the answer of the tongue is from the Lord.

2 All one's ways may be pure in one's own eyes,
  but the Lord weighs the spirit.

3 Commit your work to the Lord,
  and your plans will be established.

4 The Lord has made everything for its purpose,
  even the wicked for the day of trouble.

5 All those who are arrogant are an abomination to the Lord;
  be assured, they will not go unpunished.

6 By loyalty and faithfulness iniquity is atoned for,
  and by the fear of the Lord one avoids evil.

7 When the ways of people please the Lord,
  he causes even their enemies to be at peace with them.

8 Better is a little with righteousness than large income with injustice.

9 The human mind plans the way,
  but the Lord directs the steps.

10 Inspired decisions are on the lips of a king;
  his mouth does not sin in judgment.

11 Honest balances and scales are the Lord's;
  all the weights in the bag are his work.

12 It is an abomination to kings to do evil,
  for the throne is established by righteousness.

13 Righteous lips are the delight of a king,
  and he loves those who speak what is right.

14 A king's wrath is a messenger of death,
  and whoever is wise will appease it.

15 In the light of a king's face there is life,
  and his favor is like the clouds that bring the spring rain.

16 How much better to get wisdom than gold!
  To get understanding is to be chosen rather than silver.

17 The highway of the upright avoids evil;
  those who guard their way preserve their lives.

18 Pride goes before destruction,
  and a haughty spirit before a fall.

19 It is better to be of a lowly spirit among the poor
  than to divide the spoil with the proud.

20 Those who are attentive to a matter will prosper,
  and happy are those who trust in the Lord.

21 The wise of heart is called perceptive,
  and pleasant speech increases persuasiveness.

22 Wisdom is a fountain of life to one who has it,
  but folly is the punishment of fools.

23 The mind of the wise makes their speech judicious,
  and adds persuasiveness to their lips.

24 Pleasant words are like a honeycomb,
  sweetness to the soul and health to the body.

25 Sometimes there is a way that seems to be right,
  but in the end it is the way to death.

26 The appetite of workers works for them;
  their hunger urges them on.

27 Scoundrels concoct evil,
  and their speech is like a scorching fire.

28 A perverse person spreads strife,
  and a whisperer separates close friends.

29 The violent entice their neighbors,
  and lead them in a way that is not good.

30 One who winks the eyes plans*a* perverse things;
  one who compresses the lips brings evil to pass.

a Gk Syr Vg Tg: Heb *to plan*

31 Gray hair is a crown of glory;
   it is gained in a righteous life.
32 One who is slow to anger is better than
      the mighty,
   and one whose temper is controlled
      than one who captures a city.
33 The lot is cast into the lap,
   but the decision is the LORD's alone.

16.1–33. 1: The heart (*mind*) is the organ of planning and the *tongue* is the organ of speaking and execution. It is not fully in the power of a human being to put plans into effect or control their course. 16: Tradition declares *wisdom* more precious than *gold* and *silver* (3.14; Job 28). Gold and silver can buy many things, but wisdom invites God to give the priceless gifts of long life, wealth, and honor. 20: The saying declares that success and happiness depend both on God and on our own efforts. It does not explore theological issues arising from such an assertion. 27–30: Sayings on three types of wicked people and their speech and demeanor. The first three verses begin with the Hebrew word "'ish," translated "man" or "individual." The second line of each saying states the particular damage a villain's words inflict on others. The final saying (v. 30) sketches the facial mannerisms common to all the malefactors; compare 6.12–15. 33: A *lot*, similar to dice in giving varying results when thrown, was given a designation "yes" or "no" and cast for its answer. See 1 Sam 10.16–26; Num 26.55; Josh 14.2. The answer was believed to be from God.

17 Better is a dry morsel with quiet
   than a house full of feasting with
      strife.
2 A slave who deals wisely will rule over a
      child who acts shamefully,
   and will share the inheritance as one
      of the family.
3 The crucible is for silver, and the
      furnace is for gold,
   but the LORD tests the heart.
4 An evildoer listens to wicked lips;
   and a liar gives heed to a mischievous
      tongue.
5 Those who mock the poor insult their
      Maker;
   those who are glad at calamity will
      not go unpunished.
6 Grandchildren are the crown of
      the aged,

and the glory of children is their
      parents.
7 Fine speech is not becoming to a fool;
   still less is false speech to a ruler.ᵃ
8 A bribe is like a magic stone in the eyes
      of those who give it;
   wherever they turn they prosper.
9 One who forgives an affront fosters
      friendship,
   but one who dwells on disputes will
      alienate a friend.
10 A rebuke strikes deeper into a
      discerning person
   than a hundred blows into a fool.
11 Evil people seek only rebellion,
   but a cruel messenger will be sent
      against them.
12 Better to meet a she-bear robbed of its
      cubs
   than to confront a fool immersed in
      folly.
13 Evil will not depart from the house
   of one who returns evil for good.
14 The beginning of strife is like letting out
      water;
   so stop before the quarrel breaks out.
15 One who justifies the wicked and one
      who condemns the righteous
   are both alike an abomination to the
      LORD.
16 Why should fools have a price in hand
      to buy wisdom, when they have no
      mind to learn?
17 A friend loves at all times,
   and kinsfolk are born to share
      adversity.
18 It is senseless to give a pledge,
   to become surety for a neighbor.
19 One who loves transgression loves strife;
   one who builds a high threshold
      invites broken bones.
20 The crooked of mind do not prosper,
   and the perverse of tongue fall into
      calamity.
21 The one who begets a fool gets trouble;
   the parent of a fool has no joy.
22 A cheerful heart is a good medicine,
   but a downcast spirit dries up
      the bones.

a Or *a noble person*

23 The wicked accept a concealed bribe
    to pervert the ways of justice.
24 The discerning person looks to wisdom,
    but the eyes of a fool to the ends of
        the earth.
25 Foolish children are a grief to their
        father
    and bitterness to her who bore them.
26 To impose a fine on the innocent is not
        right,
    or to flog the noble for their integrity.
27 One who spares words is
        knowledgeable;
    one who is cool in spirit has
        understanding.
28 Even fools who keep silent are
        considered wise;
    when they close their lips, they are
        deemed intelligent.

17.1–28. 2: Wisdom surmounts natural boundaries and limits. Slaves of the time could enter a great household and their conduct, if prudent and trustworthy, would win everyone's respect. A perversely foolish child could lose out to such wise servants. **8:** A neutral observation on money. A *bribe* can seem like a *magic stone* since it opens doors hitherto closed. **9:** A paradox: One finds *friendship* if one loses or hides (*forgives*) *an affront*, and loses (*alienates*) *a friend* if one finds or makes public (*dwells on*) *disputes*. Friendship has a price—bearing with the faults of the other. **13:** Paradoxically, evil stays in the house of anyone who tries to inflict it on others. **19:** Whoever *loves* an offense in the sense of dwelling on it is equivalently asking for a quarrel in the same way that any one who builds an overly *high threshold* is asking for injury.

18 The one who lives alone is self-
        indulgent,
    showing contempt for all who have
        sound judgment.*ᵃ*
2 A fool takes no pleasure in
        understanding,
    but only in expressing personal
        opinion.
3 When wickedness comes, contempt
        comes also;
    and with dishonor comes disgrace.
4 The words of the mouth are deep
        waters;

    the fountain of wisdom is a gushing
        stream.
5 It is not right to be partial to the guilty,
    or to subvert the innocent in
        judgment.
6 A fool's lips bring strife,
    and a fool's mouth invites a flogging.
7 The mouths of fools are their ruin,
    and their lips a snare to themselves.
8 The words of a whisperer are like
        delicious morsels;
    they go down into the inner parts of
        the body.
9 One who is slack in work
    is close kin to a vandal.
10 The name of the LORD is a strong
        tower;
    the righteous run into it and are safe.
11 The wealth of the rich is their strong
        city;
    in their imagination it is like a high
        wall.
12 Before destruction one's heart is
        haughty,
    but humility goes before honor.
13 If one gives answer before hearing,
    it is folly and shame.
14 The human spirit will endure sickness;
    but a broken spirit—who can bear?
15 An intelligent mind acquires knowledge,
    and the ear of the wise seeks
        knowledge.
16 A gift opens doors;
    it gives access to the great.
17 The one who first states a case seems
        right,
    until the other comes and cross-
        examines.
18 Casting the lot puts an end to disputes
    and decides between powerful
        contenders.
19 An ally offended is stronger than a city;*ᵇ*
    such quarreling is like the bars of a
        castle.
20 From the fruit of the mouth one's
        stomach is satisfied;
    the yield of the lips brings
        satisfaction.

a Meaning of Heb uncertain   *b* Gk Syr Vg Tg:
Meaning of Heb uncertain

21 Death and life are in the power of the
     tongue,
     and those who love it will eat
       its fruits.
22 He who finds a wife finds a good thing,
     and obtains favor from the LORD.
23 The poor use entreaties,
     but the rich answer roughly.
24 Some[a] friends play at friendship[b]
     but a true friend sticks closer than
       one's nearest kin.

18.1–24. 1: The probable meaning is that those who
do not listen to others cannot grow wise, for wisdom
comes through interaction with others—a process of
instruction and correction. 4: The *deep waters* of the
mind are revealed by one's words (20.5). The *waters*
become a *stream* nourishing others. 17: The first
speaker in a lawsuit seems entirely in the right. Then
the opponent *cross-examines*. The law court experience teaches a valuable lesson: There are two sides to
every question. 19: *Ally* is a family member, literally,
"brother" or "member of the family." An offended
family member can be more unyielding than a fortress.
21: *Love* has the sense of "choose" as in Deut 4.37;
10.15; Isa 41.8. One chooses either life or death by the
words one speaks. One must *eat* the *fruits* (consequences) of one's acts. For similar vocabulary, see
30.15–20.

19 Better the poor walking in integrity
     than one perverse of speech who is
       a fool.
2 Desire without knowledge is not good,
     and one who moves too hurriedly
       misses the way.
3 One's own folly leads to ruin,
     yet the heart rages against
       the LORD.
4 Wealth brings many friends,
     but the poor are left friendless.
5 A false witness will not go unpunished,
     and a liar will not escape.
6 Many seek the favor of the generous,
     and everyone is a friend to a giver of
       gifts.
7 If the poor are hated even by their kin,
     how much more are they shunned by
       their friends!
     When they call after them, they are not
       there.[c]

8 To get wisdom is to love oneself;
     to keep understanding is to prosper.
9 A false witness will not go unpunished,
     and the liar will perish.
10 It is not fitting for a fool to live
     in luxury,
     much less for a slave to rule over
       princes.
11 Those with good sense are slow
     to anger,
     and it is their glory to overlook an
       offense.
12 A king's anger is like the growling of a
     lion,
     but his favor is like dew on the grass.
13 A stupid child is ruin to a father,
     and a wife's quarreling is a continual
       dripping of rain.
14 House and wealth are inherited from
     parents,
     but a prudent wife is from the LORD.
15 Laziness brings on deep sleep;
     an idle person will suffer hunger.
16 Those who keep the commandment will
     live;
     those who are heedless of their ways
       will die.
17 Whoever is kind to the poor lends to the
     LORD,
     and will be repaid in full.
18 Discipline your children while there is
     hope;
     do not set your heart on their
       destruction.
19 A violent tempered person will pay the
     penalty;
     if you effect a rescue, you will only
       have to do it again.[c]
20 Listen to advice and accept instruction,
     that you may gain wisdom for the
       future.
21 The human mind may devise
     many plans,
     but it is the purpose of the LORD that
       will be established.
22 What is desirable in a person is loyalty,
     and it is better to be poor than a liar.

a Syr Tg: Heb A *man of*   b Cn Compare Syr Vg Tg:
Meaning of Heb uncertain   c Meaning of Heb
uncertain

23 The fear of the LORD is life indeed;
    filled with it one rests secure
    and suffers no harm.
24 The lazy person buries a hand in the
        dish,
    and will not even bring it back to the
        mouth.
25 Strike a scoffer, and the simple will
        learn prudence;
    reprove the intelligent, and they will
        gain knowledge.
26 Those who do violence to their father
        and chase away their mother
    are children who cause shame and
        bring reproach.
27 Cease straying, my child, from the
        words of knowledge,
    in order that you may hear
        instruction.
28 A worthless witness mocks at justice,
    and the mouth of the wicked devours
        iniquity.
29 Condemnation is ready for scoffers,
    and flogging for the backs of fools.

19.1–29. 2: *Desire* (the internal) and *movement* (the
external) without sufficient reflection go nowhere. **13:**
Another saying on the household (from the male point
of view). The two great causes of domestic unhappiness are foolish children and an angry wife or spouse.
Wisdom can help one avoid such unhappiness. **14:** As
if to balance the preceding verse on the angry wife,
this saying asserts the greatest cause of domestic happiness is a suitable wife.

20 Wine is a mocker, strong drink a
        brawler,
    and whoever is led astray by it is not
        wise.
2 The dread anger of a king is like the
        growling of a lion;
    anyone who provokes him to anger
        forfeits life itself.
3 It is honorable to refrain from strife,
    but every fool is quick to quarrel.
4 The lazy person does not plow in season;
    harvest comes, and there is nothing
        to be found.
5 The purposes in the human mind are
        like deep water,
    but the intelligent will draw them out.

6 Many proclaim themselves loyal,
    but who can find one worthy of trust?
7 The righteous walk in integrity—
    happy are the children who follow
        them!
8 A king who sits on the throne of
        judgment
    winnows all evil with his eyes.
9 Who can say, "I have made my heart
        clean;
    I am pure from my sin"?
10 Diverse weights and diverse measures
    are both alike an abomination to the
        LORD.
11 Even children make themselves known
        by their acts,
    by whether what they do is pure and
        right.
12 The hearing ear and the seeing eye—
    the LORD has made them both.
13 Do not love sleep, or else you will come
        to poverty;
    open your eyes, and you will have
        plenty of bread.
14 "Bad, bad," says the buyer,
    then goes away and boasts.
15 There is gold, and abundance of costly
        stones;
    but the lips informed by knowledge
        are a precious jewel.
16 Take the garment of one who has given
        surety for a stranger;
    seize the pledge given as surety for
        foreigners.
17 Bread gained by deceit is sweet,
    but afterward the mouth will be full
        of gravel.
18 Plans are established by taking advice;
    wage war by following wise guidance.
19 A gossip reveals secrets;
    therefore do not associate with a
        babbler.
20 If you curse father or mother,
    your lamp will go out in utter
        darkness.
21 An estate quickly acquired in the
        beginning
    will not be blessed in the end.
22 Do not say, "I will repay evil";
    wait for the LORD, and he will help
        you.

23 Differing weights are an abomination to
        the LORD,
    and false scales are not good.
24 All our steps are ordered by
        the LORD;
    how then can we understand our own
        ways?
25 It is a snare for one to say rashly, "It is
        holy,"
    and begin to reflect only after making
        a vow.
26 A wise king winnows the wicked,
    and drives the wheel over them.
27 The human spirit is the lamp of the
        LORD,
    searching every inmost part.
28 Loyalty and faithfulness preserve the
        king,
    and his throne is upheld by
        righteousness.*a*
29 The glory of youths is their strength,
    but the beauty of the aged is their
        gray hair.
30 Blows that wound cleanse away evil;
    beatings make clean the innermost
        parts.

20.1–30. 15: *Gold* and *costly stones* must refer to jewelry. The most beautiful adornment of a face is not jewelry but wise *lips*, that is, wise words that show the beauty within.

21 The king's heart is a stream of
        water in the hand of the LORD;
    he turns it wherever he will.
2 All deeds are right in the sight of the
        doer,
    but the LORD weighs the heart.
3 To do righteousness and justice
    is more acceptable to the LORD than
        sacrifice.
4 Haughty eyes and a proud heart—
    the lamp of the wicked—are sin.
5 The plans of the diligent lead surely to
        abundance,
    but everyone who is hasty comes only
        to want.
6 The getting of treasures by a lying
        tongue
    is a fleeting vapor and a snare*b* of
        death.

7 The violence of the wicked will sweep
        them away,
    because they refuse to do what
        is just.
8 The way of the guilty is crooked,
    but the conduct of the pure is right.
9 It is better to live in a corner of the
        housetop
    than in a house shared with a
        contentious wife.
10 The souls of the wicked desire evil;
    their neighbors find no mercy in their
        eyes.
11 When a scoffer is punished, the simple
        become wiser;
    when the wise are instructed, they
        increase in knowledge.
12 The Righteous One observes the house
        of the wicked;
    he casts the wicked down to ruin.
13 If you close your ear to the cry of the
        poor,
    you will cry out and not be heard.
14 A gift in secret averts anger;
    and a concealed bribe in the bosom,
        strong wrath.
15 When justice is done, it is a joy to the
        righteous,
    but dismay to evildoers.
16 Whoever wanders from the way of
        understanding
    will rest in the assembly of the dead.
17 Whoever loves pleasure will suffer
        want;
    whoever loves wine and oil will not be
        rich.
18 The wicked is a ransom for the
        righteous,
    and the faithless for the upright.
19 It is better to live in a desert land
    than with a contentious and fretful
        wife.
20 Precious treasure remains*c* in the house
        of the wise,
    but the fool devours it.
21 Whoever pursues righteousness and
        kindness
    will find life*d* and honor.

a Gk: Heb *loyalty*   *b* Gk: Heb *seekers*   *c* Gk: Heb
and oil   *d* Gk: Heb *life and righteousness*

22 One wise person went up against a city
   of warriors
      and brought down the stronghold in
      which they trusted.
23 To watch over mouth and tongue
      is to keep out of trouble.
24 The proud, haughty person, named
   "Scoffer,"
      acts with arrogant pride.
25 The craving of the lazy person is fatal,
      for lazy hands refuse to labor.
26 All day long the wicked covet,[a]
      but the righteous give and do not
      hold back.
27 The sacrifice of the wicked is an
   abomination;
      how much more when brought with
      evil intent.
28 A false witness will perish,
      but a good listener will testify
      successfully.
29 The wicked put on a bold face,
      but the upright give thought to[b] their
      ways.
30 No wisdom, no understanding, no
   counsel,
      can avail against the LORD.
31 The horse is made ready for the day of
   battle,
      but the victory belongs to the LORD.

21.1–31. 14: The wise know the secret of taming *anger* and *strong wrath*—a gift of money. The strategy implies a certain disdain for anger, for a seemingly strong passion can be assuaged by a little money. 17: Those who desire the trappings of wealth will never get them, for wealth does not come to the idle and those who *love pleasure* (see 6.6–11; 10.4; 12.24, 27). 19: Living alone is preferable to living in a house spoiled by a spouse's anger. 29: *The wicked* are defiant (*put on a bold face*) whereas the *upright*, who give thought to their ways, are willing to conform their actions to the teaching of others. The Hebrew text and the ancient versions transmit another reading in the second line: "the upright person *maintains* a faithful course."

22 A good name is to be chosen rather
   than great riches,
      and favor is better than silver
      or gold.

2 The rich and the poor have this in
   common:
      the LORD is the maker of them all.
3 The clever see danger and hide;
      but the simple go on, and suffer for
      it.
4 The reward for humility and fear of the
   LORD
      is riches and honor and life.
5 Thorns and snares are in the way of the
   perverse;
      the cautious will keep far from them.
6 Train children in the right way,
      and when old, they will not stray.
7 The rich rule over the poor,
      and the borrower is the slave of the
      lender.
8 Whoever sows injustice will reap
   calamity,
      and the rod of anger will fail.
9 Those who are generous are blessed,
      for they share their bread with the
      poor.
10 Drive out a scoffer, and strife
   goes out;
      quarreling and abuse will cease.
11 Those who love a pure heart and are
   gracious in speech
      will have the king as a friend.
12 The eyes of the LORD keep watch over
   knowledge,
      but he overthrows the words of the
      faithless.
13 The lazy person says, "There is a lion
   outside!
      I shall be killed in the streets!"
14 The mouth of a loose[c] woman is a deep
   pit;
      he with whom the LORD is angry falls
      into it.
15 Folly is bound up in the heart of
   a boy,
      but the rod of discipline drives it far
      away.
16 Oppressing the poor in order to enrich
   oneself,
      and giving to the rich, will lead only
      to loss.

a Gk: Heb *all day long one covets covetously*   b Another reading is *establish*   c Heb *strange*

22.1–16. 8: Both metaphors* are agricultural. In line A, bad actions are seed yielding trouble. In line B, *the rod* is a flail which cannot thresh* grain. Evil will be frustrated; it will bear no fruit.

THE WORDS OF THE WISE

22.17–24.22: An instruction partly modeled on the thirteenth-century BCE Egyptian "Instruction of Amenemope." Like its Egyptian model, it has *thirty sayings* (22.20) and is introduced by a preface (22.17–21); its first two admonitions (22.22–25) resemble the first two in "Amenemope." *The words of the wise* offer a kind of professional ethics, warning against behavior that can destroy one's humanity and religion (22.22–23.11) and urging resistance to the temptations of youth (23.12–35). It concludes with counsels of a general nature (24.1–22).

---

17   The words of the wise:

Incline your ear and hear my words,*a*
    and apply your mind to my teaching;
18 for it will be pleasant if you keep them
        within you,
    if all of them are ready on your lips.
19 So that your trust may be in the LORD,
    I have made them known to you
        today—yes, to you.
20 Have I not written for you thirty sayings
    of admonition and knowledge,
21 to show you what is right and true,
    so that you may give a true answer to
        those who sent you?

22 Do not rob the poor because they are
        poor,
    or crush the afflicted at the gate;
23 for the LORD pleads their cause
    and despoils of life those who despoil
        them.
24 Make no friends with those given to
        anger,
    and do not associate with hotheads,
25 or you may learn their ways
    and entangle yourself in a snare.
26 Do not be one of those who give pledges,
    who become surety for debts.
27 If you have nothing with which to pay,
    why should your bed be taken from
        under you?

28 Do not remove the ancient landmark
    that your ancestors set up.
29 Do you see those who are skillful in
        their work?
    They will serve kings;
    they will not serve common people.

22.22–23: *The poor* are dangerous to attack, for God will defend them.

23 When you sit down to eat with
        a ruler,
    observe carefully what*b* is before you,
2   and put a knife to your throat
    if you have a big appetite.
3   Do not desire the ruler's*c* delicacies,
    for they are deceptive food.
4   Do not wear yourself out to get rich;
    be wise enough to desist.
5   When your eyes light upon it, it is gone;
    for suddenly it takes wings to itself,
    flying like an eagle toward heaven.
6   Do not eat the bread of the stingy;
    do not desire their delicacies;
7   for like a hair in the throat, so are they.*d*
    "Eat and drink!" they say to you;
    but they do not mean it.
8   You will vomit up the little you have
        eaten,
    and you will waste your pleasant
        words.
9   Do not speak in the hearing of a fool,
    who will only despise the wisdom of
        your words.
10 Do not remove an ancient landmark
    or encroach on the fields of orphans,
11 for their redeemer is strong;
    he will plead their cause against you.
12 Apply your mind to instruction
    and your ear to words of knowledge.
13 Do not withhold discipline from your
        children;
    if you beat them with a rod, they will
        not die.
14 If you beat them with the rod,
    you will save their lives from Sheol.
15 My child, if your heart is wise,
    my heart too will be glad.

a Cn Compare Gk: Heb *Incline your ear, and hear the words of the wise*   *b* Or *who*   *c* Heb *his*
d Meaning of Heb uncertain

16 My soul will rejoice
  when your lips speak what is right.
17 Do not let your heart envy sinners,
  but always continue in the fear of the
    LORD.
18 Surely there is a future,
  and your hope will not be cut off.

19 Hear, my child, and be wise,
  and direct your mind in the way.
20 Do not be among winebibbers,
  or among gluttonous eaters
    of meat;
21 for the drunkard and the glutton will
    come to poverty,
  and drowsiness will clothe them with
    rags.

22 Listen to your father who begot you,
  and do not despise your mother when
    she is old.
23 Buy truth, and do not sell it;
  buy wisdom, instruction, and
    understanding.
24 The father of the righteous will greatly
    rejoice;
  he who begets a wise son will be glad
    in him.
25 Let your father and mother be glad;
  let her who bore you rejoice.

26 My child, give me your heart,
  and let your eyes observe*ᵃ* my ways.
27 For a prostitute is a deep pit;
  an adulteress*ᵇ* is a narrow well.
28 She lies in wait like a robber
  and increases the number of the
    faithless.

23.1–23. 1–3: Dining etiquette, especially moderation with food and drink, is a common topic in Egyptian instructions. Banquets were an occasion for young servants to advance themselves, and self-indulgence would leave a bad impression. 1: *Observe carefully what is before you* refers both to the food and the host. 2: *Put a knife to your throat:* Put your knife in your jaws rather than in the food, that is, restrain your appetite. 6–7: Don't go to banquets when you are not invited or wanted. Though courtesy forces the host to say *"Eat and drink!"*, the words are insincere. The result will be indigestion and frustration for the unwelcome guest.

13–14: Hyperbole* and sardonic humor are used to give advice on raising children. It is not disciplinary blows that will kill a child but uncorrected behavior that will lead to fatal consequences. The humor and hyperbole show the admonition does not espouse the corporal punishment of children. 17–18: A warning against peer-group pressure, which is especially applicable to the young. Why envy the wicked, for they have no future, no descendants? The warning is repeated in 24.1 and 19–20. 22–23: The two commands in v. 23, *buy truth* and *do not sell it*, continue on a metaphorical* level in the two commands in v. 22, *listen* and *do not despise*.

29 Who has woe? Who has sorrow?
    Who has strife? Who has
      complaining?
  Who has wounds without cause?
    Who has redness of eyes?
30 Those who linger late over wine,
  those who keep trying mixed wines.
31 Do not look at wine when it is red,
    when it sparkles in the cup
  and goes down smoothly.
32 At the last it bites like a serpent,
  and stings like an adder.
33 Your eyes will see strange things,
  and your mind utter perverse things.
34 You will be like one who lies down in
      the midst of the sea,
  like one who lies on the top of
      a mast.*ᶜ*
35 "They struck me," you will say,*ᵈ* "but I
      was not hurt;
  they beat me, but I did not feel it.
  When shall I awake?
  I will seek another drink."

24 Do not envy the wicked,
   nor desire to be with them;
2 for their minds devise violence,
  and their lips talk of mischief.

3 By wisdom a house is built,
  and by understanding it is
    established;
4 by knowledge the rooms are filled
  with all precious and pleasant riches.

---

a Another reading is *delight in*   *b* Heb *an alien woman*
c Meaning of Heb uncertain   *d* Gk Syr Vg Tg: Heb lacks *you will say*

5 Wise warriors are mightier than strong
   ones,[a]
   and those who have knowledge than
      those who have strength;
6 for by wise guidance you can wage your
      war,
   and in abundance of counselors there
      is victory.
7 Wisdom is too high for fools;
   in the gate they do not open
      their mouths.

8 Whoever plans to do evil
   will be called a mischief-maker.
9 The devising of folly is sin,
   and the scoffer is an abomination to
      all.

10 If you faint in the day of adversity,
   your strength being small;
11 if you hold back from rescuing those
      taken away to death,
   those who go staggering to the
      slaughter;
12 if you say, "Look, we did not know this"—
   does not he who weighs the heart
      perceive it?
   Does not he who keeps watch over your
      soul know it?
   And will he not repay all according to
      their deeds?

13 My child, eat honey, for it is good,
   and the drippings of the honeycomb
      are sweet to your taste.
14 Know that wisdom is such to your soul;
   if you find it, you will find a future,
   and your hope will not be cut off.

15 Do not lie in wait like an outlaw against
      the home of the righteous;
   do no violence to the place where the
      righteous live;
16 for though they fall seven times, they
      will rise again;
   but the wicked are overthrown by
      calamity.

17 Do not rejoice when your enemies fall,
   and do not let your heart be glad
      when they stumble,

18 or else the LORD will see it and be
      displeased,
   and turn away his anger from them.

19 Do not fret because of evildoers.
   Do not envy the wicked;
20 for the evil have no future;
   the lamp of the wicked will go out.

21 My child, fear the LORD and the king,
   and do not disobey either of them;[b]
22 for disaster comes from them suddenly,
   and who knows the ruin that both
      can bring?

24.3–22. 10–12: The probable meaning of the obscure admonition is that excuses for not aiding one's
neighbor will be useless before the all-seeing God.
17–18: Divine retribution works mysteriously. Human
beings should stand aside and not anticipate its results.

23   These also are sayings of the wise:

   Partiality in judging is not good.
24 Whoever says to the wicked, "You are
      innocent,"
   will be cursed by peoples, abhorred by
      nations;
25 but those who rebuke the wicked will
      have delight,
   and a good blessing will come upon
      them.
26 One who gives an honest answer
   gives a kiss on the lips.

27 Prepare your work outside,
   get everything ready for you in the
      field;
   and after that build your house.

28 Do not be a witness against your
      neighbor without cause,
   and do not deceive with your lips.
29 Do not say, "I will do to others as they
      have done to me;
   I will pay them back for what they
      have done."

---

a Gk Compare Syr Tg: Heb *A wise man is strength*
b Gk: Heb *do not associate with those who change*

30 I passed by the field of one who was
lazy,
by the vineyard of a stupid person;
31 and see, it was all overgrown with
thorns;
the ground was covered with nettles,
and its stone wall was broken down.
32 Then I saw and considered it;
I looked and received instruction.
33 A little sleep, a little slumber,
a little folding of the hands to rest,
34 and poverty will come upon you like a
robber,
and want, like an armed warrior.

24.23–34. Further words of the wise. A carefully arranged appendix to 22.17–24.22. Two areas of life,
law (vv. 23–25, 28–29) and farming (vv. 27, 30–34),
are used to illustrate the effects of wisdom in word
and action. **30–34:** An illustrative story, like those in
6.9–11, ch. 7, and Ps 37.35–36.

25 These are other proverbs of Solomon
that the officials of King Hezekiah of
Judah copied.

2 It is the glory of God to conceal things,
but the glory of kings is to search
things out.
3 Like the heavens for height, like the
earth for depth,
so the mind of kings is unsearchable.
4 Take away the dross from the silver,
and the smith has material for
a vessel;
5 take away the wicked from the presence
of the king,
and his throne will be established in
righteousness.
6 Do not put yourself forward in the
king's presence
or stand in the place of the great;
7 for it is better to be told, "Come up here,"
than to be put lower in the presence
of a noble.

What your eyes have seen
8   do not hastily bring into court;
for*a* what will you do in the end,
when your neighbor puts you to
shame?

9 Argue your case with your neighbor
directly,
and do not disclose another's secret;
10 or else someone who hears you will
bring shame upon you,
and your ill repute will have no end.
11 A word fitly spoken
is like apples of gold in a setting of
silver.
12 Like a gold ring or an ornament
of gold
is a wise rebuke to a listening ear.
13 Like the cold of snow in the time
of harvest
are faithful messengers to those who
send them;
they refresh the spirit of their
masters.
14 Like clouds and wind without rain
is one who boasts of a gift never
given.
15 With patience a ruler may be
persuaded,
and a soft tongue can break bones.
16 If you have found honey, eat only
enough for you,
or else, having too much, you will
vomit it.
17 Let your foot be seldom in your
neighbor's house,
otherwise the neighbor will become
weary of you and hate you.
18 Like a war club, a sword, or a sharp
arrow
is one who bears false witness against
a neighbor.
19 Like a bad tooth or a lame foot
is trust in a faithless person in time of
trouble.
20 Like vinegar on a wound*b*
is one who sings songs to a heavy
heart.
Like a moth in clothing or a worm in
wood,
sorrow gnaws at the human heart.*c*
21 If your enemies are hungry, give them
bread to eat;

a Cn: Heb *or else*   *b* Gk: Heb *Like one who takes off
a garment on a cold day, like vinegar on lye*   *c* Gk Syr
Tg: Heb lacks *Like a moth . . . human heart*

and if they are thirsty, give them
  water to drink;
22 for you will heap coals of fire on their
  heads,
  and the LORD will reward you.
23 The north wind produces rain,
  and a backbiting tongue, angry
  looks.
24 It is better to live in a corner of the
  housetop
  than in a house shared with a
  contentious wife.
25 Like cold water to a thirsty soul,
  so is good news from a far country.
26 Like a muddied spring or a polluted
  fountain
  are the righteous who give way before
  the wicked.
27 It is not good to eat much honey,
  or to seek honor on top of honor.
28 Like a city breached, without walls,
  is one who lacks self-control.

Chs. 25–29: Proverbs of Solomon. 25.1–28. 1: An
important clue to the composition and date of Proverbs. Hezekiah, who was king of Judah from 715–687
BCE, apparently ordered this collection added to an already existing Solomonic collection (perhaps chs.
10–22). 2–3: The world is full of conundrums and puzzles, but the king is there to unravel them and lead
people to serve the gods. The affinity between divine
and royal wisdom is expressed by the repetition of the
first and last word of each phrase (*glory* and *things*)
and by the rhyme in *God* and *king* ("'elohim" and
"melakim"). 7: See Lk 14.8–10. 21–22: An enemy's
vulnerability should not be made an occasion for settling old scores (so also Ex 23.4). Allow God's justice
its proper scope (compare 20.22 and 24.17–18). *Heap
coals of fire on their heads* alludes to no known practice. It may be hyperbole* for punishment. Romans
12.20 cites the Greek version.

26 Like snow in summer or rain in
  harvest,
  so honor is not fitting for a fool.
2 Like a sparrow in its flitting, like a
  swallow in its flying,
  an undeserved curse goes nowhere.
3 A whip for the horse, a bridle for the
  donkey,
  and a rod for the back of fools.

4 Do not answer fools according to their
  folly,
  or you will be a fool yourself.
5 Answer fools according to their folly,
  or they will be wise in their own eyes.
6 It is like cutting off one's foot and
  drinking down violence,
  to send a message by a fool.
7 The legs of a disabled person hang
  limp;
  so does a proverb in the mouth of a
  fool.
8 It is like binding a stone in a sling
  to give honor to a fool.
9 Like a thornbush brandished by the
  hand of a drunkard
  is a proverb in the mouth of a fool.
10 Like an archer who wounds everybody
  is one who hires a passing fool or
  drunkard.*
11 Like a dog that returns to its vomit
  is a fool who reverts to his folly.
12 Do you see persons wise in their own
  eyes?
  There is more hope for fools than for
  them.
13 The lazy person says, "There is a lion in
  the road!
  There is a lion in the streets!"
14 As a door turns on its hinges,
  so does a lazy person in bed.
15 The lazy person buries a hand in the
  dish,
  and is too tired to bring it back to the
  mouth.
16 The lazy person is wiser in self-esteem
  than seven who can answer
  discreetly.
17 Like somebody who takes a passing dog
  by the ears
  is one who meddles in the quarrel of
  another.
18 Like a maniac who shoots deadly
  firebrands and arrows,
19 so is one who deceives a neighbor
  and says, "I am only joking!"
20 For lack of wood the fire goes out,
  and where there is no whisperer,
  quarreling ceases.

a Meaning of Heb uncertain

21 As charcoal is to hot embers and wood
    to fire,
    so is a quarrelsome person for
    kindling strife.
22 The words of a whisperer are like
    delicious morsels;
    they go down into the inner parts of
    the body.
23 Like the glaze[a] covering an earthen
    vessel
    are smooth[b] lips with an
    evil heart.
24 An enemy dissembles in speaking
    while harboring deceit within;
25 when an enemy speaks graciously, do
    not believe it,
    for there are seven abominations
    concealed within;
26 though hatred is covered with guile,
    the enemy's wickedness will be
    exposed in the assembly.
27 Whoever digs a pit will fall into it,
    and a stone will come back on the
    one who starts it rolling.
28 A lying tongue hates its victims,
    and a flattering mouth works ruin.

26.1–28. 4–5: Each saying makes sense in its own
right. Taken together they show the problem, even the
danger, that *fools* pose to their neighbors. **13–16:** Four
sayings on the *lazy person*, whom Proverbs derides on
the grounds that this type of person never acts.

27

Do not boast about tomorrow,
for you do not know what a day
may bring.
2 Let another praise you, and not your
    own mouth—
    a stranger, and not your own lips.
3 A stone is heavy, and sand is weighty,
    but a fool's provocation is heavier
    than both.
4 Wrath is cruel, anger is overwhelming,
    but who is able to stand before
    jealousy?
5 Better is open rebuke
    than hidden love.
6 Well meant are the wounds a friend
    inflicts,
    but profuse are the kisses of an
    enemy.

7 The sated appetite spurns honey,
    but to a ravenous appetite even the
    bitter is sweet.
8 Like a bird that strays from its nest
    is one who strays from home.
9 Perfume and incense make the heart
    glad,
    but the soul is torn by trouble.[c]
10 Do not forsake your friend or the friend
    of your parent;
    do not go to the house of your
    kindred in the day of your
    calamity.
    Better is a neighbor who is nearby
    than kindred who are far away.
11 Be wise, my child, and make my heart
    glad,
    so that I may answer whoever
    reproaches me.
12 The clever see danger and hide;
    but the simple go on, and suffer for
    it.
13 Take the garment of one who has given
    surety for a stranger;
    seize the pledge given as surety for
    foreigners.[d]
14 Whoever blesses a neighbor with a loud
    voice,
    rising early in the morning,
    will be counted as cursing.
15 A continual dripping on a rainy day
    and a contentious wife are alike;
16 to restrain her is to restrain the wind
    or to grasp oil in the right hand.[e]
17 Iron sharpens iron,
    and one person sharpens the wits[f] of
    another.
18 Anyone who tends a fig tree will eat its
    fruit,
    and anyone who takes care of a
    master will be honored.
19 Just as water reflects the face,
    so one human heart reflects
    another.
20 Sheol and Abaddon are never satisfied,
    and human eyes are never satisfied.

a Cn: Heb *silver of dross*   *b* Gk: Heb *burning*
c Gk: Heb *the sweetness of a friend is better than one's
own counsel*   *d* Vg and 20.16: Heb *for a foreign woman*
e Meaning of Heb uncertain   *f* Heb *face*

21 The crucible is for silver, and the
    furnace is for gold,
    so a person is tested[a] by being
    praised.
22 Crush a fool in a mortar with a pestle
    along with crushed grain,
    but the folly will not be driven out.
23 Know well the condition of your flocks,
    and give attention to your herds;
24 for riches do not last forever,
    nor a crown for all generations.
25 When the grass is gone, and new
    growth appears,
    and the herbage of the mountains is
    gathered,
26 the lambs will provide your clothing,
    and the goats the price of a field;
27 there will be enough goats' milk for your
    food,
    for the food of your household
    and nourishment for your servant-
    girls.

27.1–27. 5: To correct someone is difficult, but it is better than passing over a fault in silence out of affection (*hidden love*). **14:** *Blesses* can mean simply "greets" (1 Sam 13.10; 2 Kings 4.29) but the word *cursing* in line C keeps the sense "bless" to the fore. The saying has been interpreted seriously and humorously. If it is taken humorously, *a loud voice* and *early in the morning* describe boorish behavior that provokes a hostile reaction. If it is taken seriously, *a loud voice* refers to an insincere greeting as in v. 6 and 26.23–25, 28, and *early in the morning* means "insistently" as in Jer 7.13. **23–27:** A traditional poem prizing flocks and fields over hoarded treasure on the grounds that wealth in the form of flocks and fields ever renews itself. Vegetation comes up annually from the earth; sheep and goats are transformed into food and clothing.

28

The wicked flee when no one
    pursues,
    but the righteous are as bold as a lion.
2 When a land rebels
    it has many rulers;
    but with an intelligent ruler
    there is lasting order.[b]
3 A ruler[c] who oppresses the poor
    is a beating rain that leaves no food.

4 Those who forsake the law praise the
    wicked,
    but those who keep the law struggle
    against them.
5 The evil do not understand justice,
    but those who seek the LORD
    understand it completely.
6 Better to be poor and walk in integrity
    than to be crooked in one's ways even
    though rich.
7 Those who keep the law are wise
    children,
    but companions of gluttons shame
    their parents.
8 One who augments wealth by exorbitant
    interest
    gathers it for another who is kind to
    the poor.
9 When one will not listen to the law,
    even one's prayers are an
    abomination.
10 Those who mislead the upright into evil
    ways
    will fall into pits of their own
    making,
    but the blameless will have a goodly
    inheritance.
11 The rich is wise in self-esteem,
    but an intelligent poor person sees
    through the pose.
12 When the righteous triumph, there is
    great glory,
    but when the wicked prevail, people
    go into hiding.
13 No one who conceals transgressions will
    prosper,
    but one who confesses and forsakes
    them will obtain mercy.
14 Happy is the one who is never without
    fear,
    but one who is hard-hearted will fall
    into calamity.
15 Like a roaring lion or a charging bear
    is a wicked ruler over a poor people.
16 A ruler who lacks understanding is a
    cruel oppressor;
    but one who hates unjust gain will
    enjoy a long life.

---

a Heb lacks *is tested*   *b* Meaning of Heb uncertain
c Cn: Heb *A poor person*

17 If someone is burdened with the blood
    of another,
    let that killer be a fugitive
      until death;
    let no one offer assistance.
18 One who walks in integrity will be safe,
    but whoever follows crooked ways will
      fall into the Pit.*a*
19 Anyone who tills the land will have
    plenty of bread,
    but one who follows worthless
      pursuits will have plenty
      of poverty.
20 The faithful will abound with
    blessings,
    but one who is in a hurry to be rich
      will not go unpunished.
21 To show partiality is not good—
    yet for a piece of bread a person may
      do wrong.
22 The miser is in a hurry to get rich
    and does not know that loss is sure to
      come.
23 Whoever rebukes a person will
    afterward find more favor
    than one who flatters with
      the tongue.
24 Anyone who robs father or mother
    and says, "That is no crime,"
    is partner to a thug.
25 The greedy person stirs up strife,
    but whoever trusts in the LORD will
      be enriched.
26 Those who trust in their own wits are
    fools;
    but those who walk in wisdom come
      through safely.
27 Whoever gives to the poor will lack
    nothing,
    but one who turns a blind eye will get
      many a curse.
28 When the wicked prevail, people go into
    hiding;
    but when they perish, the righteous
      increase.

28.1–28. 4: *The law* ("torah"*) is taken by some as
the Mosaic law but it is better to understand it as the
traditional instruction of teachers and parents. To defy
such teaching is to promote the designs of the wicked,
whereas to heed it is to defeat them. **9:** An example

of poetic justice. Whoever does not listen to the law
(or instruction), which comes ultimately from God, will
not be heard by God. **24:** Children lived in their parents' home until they married, and even after marriage
could remain under the parental roof. If the parents
grew feeble, the children might become domineering
and gradually take over the house and its wealth. The
saying declares such usurpation to constitute simple
theft. The children have no more right to their parents'
property while the latter are living than a brigand does
who is from outside the family.

29 One who is often reproved, yet
    remains stubborn,
  will suddenly be broken beyond
    healing.
2 When the righteous are in authority, the
    people rejoice;
    but when the wicked rule, the people
      groan.
3 A child who loves wisdom makes a
    parent glad,
    but to keep company with prostitutes
      is to squander one's substance.
4 By justice a king gives stability to the
    land,
    but one who makes heavy exactions
      ruins it.
5 Whoever flatters a neighbor
    is spreading a net for the neighbor's
      feet.
6 In the transgression of the evil there is a
    snare,
    but the righteous sing and rejoice.
7 The righteous know the rights of the
    poor;
    the wicked have no such
      understanding.
8 Scoffers set a city aflame,
    but the wise turn away wrath.
9 If the wise go to law with fools,
    there is ranting and ridicule without
      relief.
10 The bloodthirsty hate the blameless,
    and they seek the life of the upright.
11 A fool gives full vent to anger,
    but the wise quietly holds it back.
12 If a ruler listens to falsehood,
    all his officials will be wicked.

a Syr: Heb *fall all at once*

13 The poor and the oppressor have this in
　　　common:
　　the LORD gives light to the eyes of
　　　both.

14 If a king judges the poor with equity,
　　his throne will be established
　　　forever.

15 The rod and reproof give wisdom,
　　but a mother is disgraced by a
　　　neglected child.

16 When the wicked are in authority,
　　transgression increases,
　　but the righteous will look upon their
　　　downfall.

17 Discipline your children, and they will
　　　give you rest;
　　they will give delight to your heart.

18 Where there is no prophecy, the people
　　cast off restraint,
　　but happy are those who keep
　　　the law.

19 By mere words servants are not
　　　disciplined,
　　for though they understand, they will
　　　not give heed.

20 Do you see someone who is hasty
　　in speech?
　　There is more hope for a fool than for
　　anyone like that.

21 A slave pampered from childhood
　　will come to a bad end.ᵃ

22 One given to anger stirs up strife,
　　and the hothead causes much
　　　transgression.

23 A person's pride will bring humiliation,
　　but one who is lowly in spirit will
　　　obtain honor.

24 To be a partner of a thief is to hate
　　one's own life;
　　one hears the victim's curse, but
　　discloses nothing.ᵇ

25 The fear of othersᶜ lays a snare,
　　but one who trusts in the LORD
　　　is secure.

26 Many seek the favor of a ruler,
　　but it is from the LORD that one gets
　　justice.

27 The unjust are an abomination to the
　　righteous,
　　but the upright are an abomination to
　　the wicked.

29.1–27. 1: *Remains stubborn* is, literally, "stiffens the neck." There is a possible play on words: Stiffening one's neck risks having it broken. *Suddenly* suggests an extraordinary, perhaps divine, intervention. **4:** The saying uses the metaphor* "high" and "low" for prosperity and decline in order to differentiate between good and bad governance. A just king *gives stability*, literally, "raises up the land." But a king who raises taxes *ruins*, literally, brings down, a country. **15:** As with domestic animals, a staff ("shebet" as in Lev 27.32; Zech 11.7; Ps 23.4) is needed to train and control children. Children (and animals) allowed to run free cannot learn. **18:** *Prophecy* and *law* are paired in Ezek 7.26 and Lam 2.9. In this saying *prophecy* has to do with the community and *law* with the individual. Though a people may be demoralized without credible national guidance, an individual can still find happiness by heeding the instruction of teachers. **24:** An aphorism derived from the legal adjuration summoning witnesses to a crime, which is described in Lev 5.1. By not coming forward to testify one becomes an accomplice of the criminal. Moreover, to get mixed up with a crime is to destroy oneself.

30 The words of Agur son of Jakeh. An
　　oracle.

　　Thus says the man: I am weary, O God,
　　I am weary, O God. How can I
　　　prevail?ᵈ
2 Surely I am too stupid to be human;
　　I do not have human understanding.
3 I have not learned wisdom,
　　nor have I knowledge of the
　　　holy ones.ᵉ
4 Who has ascended to heaven and come
　　down?
　　Who has gathered the wind in the
　　　hollow of the hand?
　　Who has wrapped up the waters in a
　　　garment?
　　Who has established all the ends of
　　　the earth?
　　What is the person's name?
　　　And what is the name of the person's
　　　child?
　　Surely you know!

a Vg: Meaning of Heb uncertain　　*b* Meaning of Heb
uncertain　　*c* Or *human fear*　　*d* Or *I am spent*.
Meaning of Heb uncertain　　*e* Or *Holy One*

5 Every word of God proves true;
    he is a shield to those who take
        refuge in him.
6 Do not add to his words,
    or else he will rebuke you, and you
        will be found a liar.

7 Two things I ask of you;
    do not deny them to me before I die:
8 Remove far from me falsehood and
        lying;
    give me neither poverty nor riches;
    feed me with the food that I need,
9 or I shall be full, and deny you,
    and say, "Who is the LORD?"
    or I shall be poor, and steal,
    and profane the name of my God.

10 Do not slander a servant to a master,
    or the servant will curse you, and you
        will be held guilty.

11 There are those who curse their
        fathers
    and do not bless their mothers.
12 There are those who are pure in their
        own eyes
    yet are not cleansed of their
        filthiness.
13 There are those—how lofty are their
        eyes,
    how high their eyelids lift!—
14 there are those whose teeth are swords,
    whose teeth are knives,
    to devour the poor from off the earth,
    the needy from among mortals.

15 The leech*a* has two daughters;
    "Give, give," they cry.
    Three things are never satisfied;
    four never say, "Enough":
16 Sheol, the barren womb,
    the earth ever thirsty for water,
    and the fire that never says,
        "Enough."*a*

17 The eye that mocks a father
    and scorns to obey a mother
    will be pecked out by the ravens of the
        valley
    and eaten by the vultures.

18 Three things are too wonderful for me;
    four I do not understand:
19 the way of an eagle in the sky,
    the way of a snake on a rock,
    the way of a ship on the high seas,
    and the way of a man with a girl.

20 This is the way of an adulteress:
    she eats, and wipes her mouth,
    and says, "I have done no wrong."

21 Under three things the earth trembles;
    under four it cannot bear up:
22 a slave when he becomes king,
    and a fool when glutted with food;
23 an unloved woman when she gets
        a husband,
    and a maid when she succeeds her
        mistress.

24 Four things on earth are small,
    yet they are exceedingly wise:
25 the ants are a people without strength,
    yet they provide their food in
        the summer;
26 the badgers are a people without power,
    yet they make their homes in
        the rocks;
27 the locusts have no king,
    yet all of them march in rank;
28 the lizard*b* can be grasped in the hand,
    yet it is found in kings' palaces.

29 Three things are stately in their stride;
    four are stately in their gait:
30 the lion, which is mightiest among wild
        animals
    and does not turn back before any;
31 the strutting rooster,*c* the he-goat,
    and a king striding before*a* his people.

32 If you have been foolish, exalting
        yourself,
    or if you have been devising evil,
    put your hand on your mouth.
33 For as pressing milk produces curds,
    and pressing the nose produces blood,
    so pressing anger produces strife.

a Meaning of Heb uncertain   *b* Or *spider*   *c* Gk Syr
Tg Compare Vg: Meaning of Heb uncertain

30.1–33. 1–10: This poem is the most puzzling section in Proverbs. Verses 1–6 were the original unit, but later vv. 1–10 were edited to make a new and larger speech. Verses 1–6 evoke old passages such as Ps 18.30 (Prov 30.5), Ps 73.22 (Prov 30.2a), Deut 4.2 (Prov 30.6), Deut 30.11–14 (Prov 30.4a). Also influential are the divine questions beginning with "Who?" in Job 38–41 and Isa 40–45 (see Prov 30.4b–d). In vv. 1–6 Agur delivers an oracle★ ("ne'um," v. 1) that did not come from his own efforts, for he is worn out, incapable of wisdom, and does not know God (vv. 2–3). Indeed, no human being can have divine wisdom, for who is capable of bringing it down from heaven (v. 4a)? In fact, no act of wisdom and power is possible for human beings (v. 4b–d)! In the process of acknowledging his own impotence and ignorance, Agur finds the assuring word of God, which is reliable and protects him just as it protected the psalmists in Ps 12 and 18 (v. 5). One should not add to the divine word (v. 6). Agur now prays to speak the truth and to have the basic necessities of life (vv. 7–8) lest he offend the God who has rescued him from exhaustion and ignorance (v. 9). Verse 10 concludes vv. 1–9, for *Do not* reprises v. 6. *Curse* in v. 10b links it to what follows. **11–14:** The poem is united by anaphora.★ There seems to be a progression from disdaining parental advice (v. 11), to overestimating one's situation (v. 12), to arrogance (v. 13), resulting finally in cruelty directed toward the lowly (v. 14). **18–20:** Anaphora (the repetition of *way*) unites the piece. Each *way* is wondrous: the effortless flight of the eagle (or vulture), the legless movement of the serpent, the massive progress of a ship. The fourth and climactic★ *way* is the course of a man and a woman toward each other, the attraction of the sexes. **32–33:** The syntax is like 6.1–3: If you have done such and such, then you must now do such and such. It is a mark of wisdom to make peace and avoid strife (15.18). There is wordplay in *pressing the nose* ("mits ap") and *pressing anger* ("mits appayim," literally, nostrils; anger).

〰〰〰〰〰〰〰〰〰〰〰〰〰〰〰〰

31 The words of King Lemuel. An oracle that his mother taught him:

2 No, my son! No, son of my womb!
　　No, son of my vows!
3 Do not give your strength to women,
　　your ways to those who destroy
　　　　kings.

4 It is not for kings, O Lemuel,
　　it is not for kings to drink wine,
　　or for rulers to desire*a* strong drink;
5 or else they will drink and forget what
　　has been decreed,
　　and will pervert the rights of all the
　　　　afflicted.
6 Give strong drink to one who is
　　perishing,
　　and wine to those in bitter distress;
7 let them drink and forget their poverty,
　　and remember their misery no more.
8 Speak out for those who cannot speak,
　　for the rights of all the destitute.*b*
9 Speak out, judge righteously,
　　defend the rights of the poor
　　　　and needy.

31.1–9: A queen mother's advice to her son, given with wit and style. The queen mother had an important role in the palace because of her insider's knowledge of palace politics and undoubted loyalty to her son. Verses 3–5 warn the king that abuse of sex and alcohol can lead him to *forget* the *afflicted.* Verses 6–9 counsel rather that alcohol be used to aid the poor so that those who are afflicted (*perishing*) can *forget* their *poverty.* Verses 8–9 urge the king to open his mouth (*speak out*) not to drink alcohol but to speak for the voiceless *poor.* The underlying subject of the poem is the king's duty to bring about justice for the *poor.* The women referred to in v. 3 are the women of his harem. An example of moral callousness from sexual indulgence is David's adultery with Bathsheba and the murder of Uriah (2 Sam 11–12). For the association of liquor with disdain for the poor, see Isa 28.1–8; Am 6.1–7.

〰〰〰〰〰〰〰〰〰〰〰〰〰〰〰〰

10 A capable wife who can find?
　　She is far more precious than
　　　　jewels.
11 The heart of her husband trusts in her,
　　and he will have no lack of gain.
12 She does him good, and not harm,
　　all the days of her life.
13 She seeks wool and flax,
　　and works with willing hands.
14 She is like the ships of the merchant,
　　she brings her food from far away.

a Cn: Heb *where*　　*b* Heb *all children of passing away*

15 She rises while it is still night
 and provides food for her household
 and tasks for her servant-girls.
16 She considers a field and buys it;
 with the fruit of her hands she plants
 a vineyard.
17 She girds herself with strength,
 and makes her arms strong.
18 She perceives that her merchandise is
 profitable.
 Her lamp does not go out at night.
19 She puts her hands to the distaff,
 and her hands hold the spindle.
20 She opens her hand to the poor,
 and reaches out her hands to
 the needy.
21 She is not afraid for her household
 when it snows,
 for all her household are clothed in
 crimson.
22 She makes herself coverings;
 her clothing is fine linen and purple.
23 Her husband is known in the city gates,
 taking his seat among the elders of
 the land.
24 She makes linen garments and sells
 them;
 she supplies the merchant with
 sashes.
25 Strength and dignity are her clothing,
 and she laughs at the time to come.
26 She opens her mouth with wisdom,
 and the teaching of kindness is on her
 tongue.
27 She looks well to the ways of her
 household,
 and does not eat the bread of
 idleness.
28 Her children rise up and call her
 happy;
 her husband too, and he praises her:

29 "Many women have done excellently,
 but you surpass them all."
30 Charm is deceitful, and beauty is vain,
 but a woman who fears the LORD is
 to be praised.
31 Give her a share in the fruit of her
 hands,
 and let her works praise her in the
 city gates.

31.10–31: Praise of the capable wife. An acrostic*
poem of twenty-two lines, each line beginning with a
successive letter of the alphabet.* It is an encomium*
or hymn praising the capable wife. A hymn does not
dwell on the inner feelings or the physical appearance
of its hero but describes the hero's mighty feats of
valor, in this case the wife's extraordinarily wise management of her great household. The narrator first describes the wife's wonderful deeds (vv. 11–27), a description that is completed by her own children and
husband (vv. 28–31). **19–20:** The chiasmus* at the
center of the poem (*hands* ("yad") . . . *hands* ("kap")
// *hand* ("kap") . . . *hands* ("yad") shifts the action
from the domestic to the public sphere in that the
hands that weave cloth (v. 19) now open wide in lar-
gesse to the poor beyond the household gates (v. 20).
She is a blessing not only to her family but to the whole
community. The hymn to the capable wife includes a
metaphorical* dimension. The heroic woman evokes
Woman Wisdom of chs. 1–9. Her abundantly prosperous household illustrates the result of becoming a disciple of Wisdom (ch. 8; 9.6, 11). The book began with
a young person leaving the parental house to found
and maintain a new one. It ends with a splendid
household provided by the wisdom of the capable
wife. Visible within the house are all the blessings of
wisdom—wealth, justice, generosity to the poor, reputation, children, and, most precious of all (compare
19.14), a good wife (or spouse). The pursuit of wisdom
has brought every blessing.

ECCLESIASTES

Introduction

Along with other wisdom literature★ of the Hebrew Bible (Proverbs and Job), Ecclesiastes offers observations based on human experience; but while Proverbs optimistically suggests that humans can use what they have learned to their advantage (see Prov 10.4), Ecclesiastes' repeated refrain "vanity of vanities" and its harsh rejection of wisdom's practical value lead some to hear it as a voice of despair. The book does, however, offer some moderately hopeful advice: Enjoyment of life and its pleasures is possible and appropriate, as long as it is informed by the inevitability of death.

The call to enjoyment explains the book's connection to the Jewish festival of Sukkot, a time of celebration, and thus its inclusion in the Jewish canon★ within the "megilloth," or festival scrolls.★ The Jewish name for the book, Qoheleth, derives from 1.1; a noun derived from the Hebrew "qahal" ("assembly"), it may refer to the one who speaks to a gathering. The English "Ecclesiastes" comes from the Greek translation "ekklesiastes," the one who speaks in the "ekklesia" (later used to designate the church), accounting for the traditional translation, "Preacher" (see note a). The NRSV offers "Teacher" as its modern equivalent.

Although the book begins with a reference to King Solomon and includes later references to "the king," scholars tend to date the book much later than the monarchy. The style of its language bears out the suggestion of a late date: Words like "pesher" ("interpretation," 8.1) and "'inyan" ("business," 1.13 and elsewhere) are derived from Aramaic,★ the common language of the ancient Near East from the seventh century through much of the Hellenistic★ period. The literary motif★ of Solomonic authorship, which may have helped the book be canonized, is also found in the Song of Solomon and in the Wisdom of Solomon (Apocrypha★).

READING GUIDE

Both in its style and in its theme, the book engages in dialogue with the optimistic wisdom typical of the book of Proverbs. Traditional-sounding proverbs, such as the famous poem in 3.1–8 ("For everything there is a season") are often followed by the author's more sober judgments (3.9: "What gain have the workers from their toil?"). Because of this "yes, but" style, the reader cannot assume that every statement made is the position of the author. Readers should consider how statements are modified, corrected, or even contradicted by subsequent verses. Where is the author's own voice heard?

For many readers over the centuries, Ecclesiastes has served as a check on human pride. Like similar "cynical" tales from Egypt and Mesopotamia, it reminds humans of the limitations in their understanding of the world and of the divine. Ecclesiastes, however, avoids utter despair, choosing to remain in conversation with traditional wisdom and remaining convinced that God is present, even if not always understandable.

Attempts to determine a clear structure for the book have proven frustrating. The following outline is one of many ways of understanding the book's movements.

1.1–3	Title and theses
1.4–11	Poem: nothing new

1 The words of the Teacher,[a] the son of David, king in Jerusalem.

2 Vanity of vanities, says the Teacher,[a]
   vanity of vanities! All is vanity.

3 What do people gain from all the toil
   at which they toil under the sun?

4 A generation goes, and a generation
      comes,
   but the earth remains forever.

5 The sun rises and the sun goes down,
   and hurries to the place where
      it rises.

6 The wind blows to the south,
      and goes around to the north;
round and round goes the wind,
   and on its circuits the wind returns.

7 All streams run to the sea,
      but the sea is not full;
to the place where the streams flow,
   there they continue to flow.

8 All things[b] are wearisome;
      more than one can express;
the eye is not satisfied with seeing,
   or the ear filled with hearing.

9 What has been is what will be,
   and what has been done is what will
      be done;
   there is nothing new under the sun.

10 Is there a thing of which it is said,
   "See, this is new"?
It has already been,
   in the ages before us.

11 The people of long ago are not
      remembered,
   nor will there be any remembrance
of people yet to come
   by those who come after them.

vanities is Hebrew superlative: "the most insubstantial thing." **3: The dominant question.** Is there any benefit from life? The reader is introduced to vocabulary that will be repeated throughout the book: *Under the sun* refers to wearisome earthly existence, and *toil* bears a negative connotation. **4–11: Nothing ever changes.** The Teacher laments the inability of human activity to alter the flow of the existence. The *sun, wind,* and *streams* repeat their predictable, "no sum" circuits, just as humans are never satisfied with what they see or hear. **10–11:** Throughout the book, the Teacher grieves that even righteous ones are not remembered after death.

12 I, the Teacher,[a] when king over Israel in Jerusalem, 13 applied my mind to seek and to search out by wisdom all that is done under heaven; it is an unhappy business that God has given to human beings to be busy with. 14 I saw all the deeds that are done under the sun; and see, all is vanity and a chasing after wind.[c]

15 What is crooked cannot be made
      straight,
   and what is lacking cannot
      be counted.

16 I said to myself, "I have acquired great wisdom, surpassing all who were over Jerusalem before me; and my mind has had great experience of wisdom and knowledge." 17 And I applied my mind to know wisdom and to know madness and folly. I perceived that this also is but a chasing after wind.[c]

18 For in much wisdom is much vexation,
   and those who increase knowledge
      increase sorrow.

1.1–11. 1: Superscription. Like many Psalms, the book begins with an editorial comment; it alludes to Solomon. *Teacher:* Hebrew Qoheleth; a form of "qhl" ("assembly"), its meaning is not clear. **2: The book's theme.** *Vanity:* In Hebrew "hevel," meaning "vapor, wind," things transient and impermanent. *Vanity of*

1.12–18. The Teacher's experiment. Though any king of the southern kingdom would fit this description, Solomon is likely implied. **13:** *Mind:* In Hebrew, "heart," the seat of thinking. *Wisdom* refers to prac-

a Heb *Qoheleth*, traditionally rendered *Preacher*
b Or *words*   c Or *a feeding on wind*. See Hos 12.1

tical, as well as speculative, knowledge. The Teacher begins an empirical investigation into what is useful in life. **14:** *Chasing after wind:* Literally, "shepherding the wind," a futile exertion of energy. This phrase will be repeated eight more times in Ecclesiastes. **15:** Given the proverbial ring of the statement, some suggest that the Teacher is quoting a well-known saying. **17:** *Wisdom, madness, folly:* The list of items from one extreme to the other suggests the complete range of experience. **18:** A second proverbial statement, likely original to the Teacher.

2 I said to myself, "Come now, I will make a test of pleasure; enjoy yourself." But again, this also was vanity. ²I said of laughter, "It is mad," and of pleasure, "What use is it?" ³I searched with my mind how to cheer my body with wine—my mind still guiding me with wisdom—and how to lay hold on folly, until I might see what was good for mortals to do under heaven during the few days of their life. ⁴I made great works; I built houses and planted vineyards for myself; ⁵I made myself gardens and parks, and planted in them all kinds of fruit trees. ⁶I made myself pools from which to water the forest of growing trees. ⁷I bought male and female slaves, and had slaves who were born in my house; I also had great possessions of herds and flocks, more than any who had been before me in Jerusalem. ⁸I also gathered for myself silver and gold and the treasure of kings and of the provinces; I got singers, both men and women, and delights of the flesh, and many concubines.*ᵃ*

9 So I became great and surpassed all who were before me in Jerusalem; also my wisdom remained with me. ¹⁰Whatever my eyes desired I did not keep from them; I kept my heart from no pleasure, for my heart found pleasure in all my toil, and this was my reward for all my toil. ¹¹Then I considered all that my hands had done and the toil I had spent in doing it, and again, all was vanity and a chasing after wind,*ᵇ* and there was nothing to be gained under the sun.

2.1–11: Experiment one: pleasure. The preliminary verdict in vv. 1–2 is followed by the empirical data. **4–10:** The literary fiction of Solomonic authorship would lend credibility to these extravagances. Solo-

mon's building projects (1 Kings 7–10), large number of women (1 Kings 7), and wealth were legendary.* **9:** *My wisdom remained:* An experiment, not sheer indulgence. **11:** Despite the initial pleasure, all the work involved in seeking pleasure was unsatisfying. The three-fold verdict on the experiment is devastating: It is *vanity, chasing after wind,* and yet another wearisome matter *under the sun.*

12 So I turned to consider wisdom and madness and folly; for what can the one do who comes after the king? Only what has already been done. ¹³Then I saw that wisdom excels folly as light excels darkness.
¹⁴ The wise have eyes in their head,
  but fools walk in darkness.
Yet I perceived that the same fate befalls all of them. ¹⁵Then I said to myself, "What happens to the fool will happen to me also; why then have I been so very wise?" And I said to myself that this also is vanity. ¹⁶For there is no enduring remembrance of the wise or of fools, seeing that in the days to come all will have been long forgotten. How can the wise die just like fools? ¹⁷So I hated life, because what is done under the sun was grievous to me; for all is vanity and a chasing after wind.*ᵇ*

2.12–17. Experiment two: being wise. 12: *After the king.* How could the successor of the great King Solomon match his wisdom and wealth? The verse may suggest that others need not repeat the experiment since Solomon has done it all. **13–14:** The Teacher sincerely recognizes the superiority of *wisdom* over *folly,* repeating a traditional saying. **15–16:** And yet, being wise doesn't keep you from dying. As throughout the book, the inevitability of death and its power to erase the memory of a person precipitate the Teacher's despair: *How can the wise die just like fools?* **17:** He repeats his three-fold verdict (2.11).

18 I hated all my toil in which I had toiled under the sun, seeing that I must leave it to those who come after me ¹⁹—and who knows whether they will be wise or foolish? Yet they will be master of all for which I toiled and used my wisdom under the sun. This also is vanity. ²⁰So I turned and gave

a Meaning of Heb uncertain
b Or *a feeding on wind.* See Hos 12.1

my heart up to despair concerning all the toil of my labors under the sun, 21 because sometimes one who has toiled with wisdom and knowledge and skill must leave all to be enjoyed by another who did not toil for it. This also is vanity and a great evil. 22 What do mortals get from all the toil and strain with which they toil under the sun? 23 For all their days are full of pain, and their work is a vexation; even at night their minds do not rest. This also is vanity.

24 There is nothing better for mortals than to eat and drink, and find enjoyment in their toil. This also, I saw, is from the hand of God; 25 for apart from him *a* who can eat or who can have enjoyment? 26 For to the one who pleases him God gives wisdom and knowledge and joy; but to the sinner he gives the work of gathering and heaping, only to give to one who pleases God. This also is vanity and a chasing after wind. *b*

2.18–26. Experiment three: work. If humans are destined to die and have no control over who will enjoy the fruits of their labor, why work? The prospect is not only *vanity*, but indeed a *great evil* (v. 21). 23: A grim account of the exhaustion of daily *work*. 24: The Teacher's resulting advice: Enjoy the work itself, and don't make contentment dependent on the outcome of your labor. This ability to enjoy the task itself is seen by the Teacher as a gift *from the hand of God*. 25–26: Though in previous verses the Teacher has attributed a common fate to all humans, here he distinguishes the work of the *sinner* as futile. *Sinner* is synonymous with the fool; it does not refer to the person's moral standards.

3 For everything there is a season, and a time for every matter under heaven:
2   a time to be born, and a time to die;
    a time to plant, and a time to pluck up
        what is planted;
3   a time to kill, and a time to heal;
    a time to break down, and a time to
        build up;
4   a time to weep, and a time to laugh;
    a time to mourn, and a time to dance;
5   a time to throw away stones, and a time
        to gather stones together;
    a time to embrace, and a time to refrain
        from embracing;

6   a time to seek, and a time to lose;
    a time to keep, and a time to
        throw away;
7   a time to tear, and a time to sew;
    a time to keep silence, and a time to
        speak;
8   a time to love, and a time to hate;
    a time for war, and a time for peace.

3.1–8. Poem on times. Contrasting extremes demonstrate that there is proper time for all dimensions of human endeavor. 5: *Throw away stones . . . gather stones.* Interpreted by some early Jewish commentators as a time for sexual relations and a time for abstinence.

9 What gain have the workers from their toil? 10 I have seen the business that God has given to everyone to be busy with. 11 He has made everything suitable for its time; moreover he has put a sense of past and future into their minds, yet they cannot find out what God has done from the beginning to the end. 12 I know that there is nothing better for them than to be happy and enjoy themselves as long as they live; 13 moreover, it is God's gift that all should eat and drink and take pleasure in all their toil. 14 I know that whatever God does endures forever; nothing can be added to it, nor anything taken from it; God has done this, so that all should stand in awe before him. 15 That which is, already has been; that which is to be, already is; and God seeks out what has gone by. *c*

16 Moreover I saw under the sun that in the place of justice, wickedness was there, and in the place of righteousness, wickedness was there as well. 17 I said in my heart, God will judge the righteous and the wicked, for he has appointed a time for every matter, and for every work. 18 I said in my heart with regard to human beings that God is testing them to show that they are but animals. 19 For the fate of humans and the fate of animals is the same; as one dies, so dies the other. They all have the same breath, and humans have no advantage over the animals; for all is vanity. 20 All go to one place; all are

a Gk Syr: Heb *apart from me*   *b* Or *a feeding on wind.* See Hos 12.1   *c* Heb *what is pursued* from the dust, and all turn to dust again. 21Who knows whether the human spirit goes upward and the spirit of animals goes downward to the earth? 22So I saw that there is nothing better than that all should enjoy their work, for that is their lot; who can bring them to see what will be after them?

3.9–22. 9–15: And yet. The punch line robs the reader of whatever comfort the poem has offered: While indeed all things may have their appointed times, human beings are unable to discern those times, much less use the information to their advantage. **11:** *Sense of past and future:* Other possible translations are "sense of eternity," "sense of the world." While humans have intimations of the cosmic dimensions of existence, their knowledge is limited. **12–15:** While this list of what the Teacher knows does not answer his problem, it counterbalances his sense of life's injustice. **16–22: Injustice.** If God determines the times for all things, then God must set a time for judgment. Clearly, however, the *righteous* and the *wicked* have not yet received what they deserve (v. 17). **19:** *Animals and humans* are equal in that they die; they share the *breath* breathed into the human at creation (Gen 2). **20:** *One place:* Sheol,✶ the realm of the dead (1 Sam 2.6; Jon 2.2). Early Israel had no concept of the afterlife (either immortality or resurrection), though these such ideas grew in popularity during the Persian✶ and Hellenistic✶ periods, so that by the turn of the era the resurrection of the body was an article of belief for the Pharisees.✶ **21:** *Who knows?* The question implies a negative answer: "No one knows." The possibility that the *human spirit* might survive cannot be verified empirically, so the Teacher returns to his conclusion: Enjoy your work while you are alive (v. 22).

4 Again I saw all the oppressions that are practiced under the sun. Look, the tears of the oppressed—with no one to comfort them! On the side of their oppressors there was power—with no one to comfort them. 2And I thought the dead, who have already died, more fortunate than the living, who are still alive; 3but better than both is the one who has not yet been, and has not seen the evil deeds that are done under the sun.

4 Then I saw that all toil and all skill in work come from one person's envy of another. This also is vanity and a chasing after wind.ᵃ

5 Fools fold their hands
    and consume their own flesh.
6 Better is a handful with quiet
    than two handfuls with toil,
    and a chasing after wind.ᵃ

7 Again, I saw vanity under the sun: 8the case of solitary individuals, without sons or brothers; yet there is no end to all their toil, and their eyes are never satisfied with riches. "For whom am I toiling," they ask, "and depriving myself of pleasure?" This also is vanity and an unhappy business.

9 Two are better than one, because they have a good reward for their toil. 10For if they fall, one will lift up the other; but woe to one who is alone and falls and does not have another to help. 11Again, if two lie together, they keep warm; but how can one keep warm alone? 12And though one might prevail against another, two will withstand one. A threefold cord is not quickly broken.

13 Better is a poor but wise youth than an old but foolish king, who will no longer take advice. 14One can indeed come out of prison to reign, even though born poor in the kingdom. 15I saw all the living who, moving about under the sun, follow thatᵇ youth who replaced the king;ᶜ 16there was no end to all those people whom he led. Yet those who come later will not rejoice in him. Surely this also is vanity and a chasing after wind.ᵃ

4.1–16. 1–12: Observations on oppression, work, and riches. Three observations and three conclusions. **1–3:** Based on his observation of *oppression,* the Teacher concludes that those who have never experienced the tragedy of life are best. *Better than:* A common phrase in the book (4.6; 4.9; 4.13; 5.1; 5.5) and in traditional wisdom (Prov 15.16–17). **4–6:** Based on his observation of competitive envy and the fate of the lazy, he concludes that more possessions are not worth more strife. **7–9:** Based on his observation of a single person working hard for riches and no one with whom to share, he concludes that companionship is preferable to wealth. **12:** *Threefold cord:* Since the topic has been two, the mention of three is curious; it perhaps refers generically to "strength in numbers."

a Or *a feeding on wind.* See Hos 12.1   *b* Heb *the second*   *c* Heb *him*

13–16: Reversals. *Better than:* See comment on 4.3. The *king* and *youth* may allude to specific people (Saul and David; Pharaoh and Joseph), or the Teacher may be telling a story to make a point (see 8.10–11; 9.14–15). The tale demonstrates the power of wisdom, even to overcome social expectations; yet the hero of one age is not remembered in the next.

5 "Guard your steps when you go to the house of God; to draw near to listen is better than the sacrifice offered by fools; for they do not know how to keep from doing evil.[b] 2[c]Never be rash with your mouth, nor let your heart be quick to utter a word before God, for God is in heaven, and you upon earth; therefore let your words be few.

3 For dreams come with many cares, and a fool's voice with many words.

4 When you make a vow to God, do not delay fulfilling it; for he has no pleasure in fools. Fulfill what you vow. 5It is better that you should not vow than that you should vow and not fulfill it. 6Do not let your mouth lead you into sin, and do not say before the messenger that it was a mistake; why should God be angry at your words, and destroy the work of your hands?

7 With many dreams come vanities and a multitude of words;[d] but fear God.

8 If you see in a province the oppression of the poor and the violation of justice and right, do not be amazed at the matter; for the high official is watched by a higher, and there are yet higher ones over them. 9But all things considered, this is an advantage for a land: a king for a plowed field.[d]

10 The lover of money will not be satisfied with money; nor the lover of wealth, with gain. This also is vanity.

11 When goods increase, those who eat them increase; and what gain has their owner but to see them with his eyes?

12 Sweet is the sleep of laborers, whether they eat little or much; but the surfeit of the rich will not let them sleep.

13 There is a grievous ill that I have seen under the sun: riches were kept by their owners to their hurt, 14and those riches were lost in a bad venture; though they are parents of children, they have nothing in their hands. 15As they came from their mother's womb, so they shall go again, naked as they came; they shall take nothing for their toil, which they may carry away with their hands. 16This also is a grievous ill: just as they came, so shall they go; and what gain do they have from toiling for the wind? 17Besides, all their days they eat in darkness, in much vexation and sickness and resentment.

18 This is what I have seen to be good: it is fitting to eat and drink and find enjoyment in all the toil with which one toils under the sun the few days of the life God gives us; for this is our lot. 19Likewise all to whom God gives wealth and possessions and whom he enables to enjoy them, and to accept their lot and find enjoyment in their toil—this is the gift of God. 20For they will scarcely brood over the days of their lives, because God keeps them occupied with the joy of their hearts.

5.1–9: Guard yourself. These sayings parallel traditional biblical wisdom: Attentiveness is better than sacrifice (1 Sam 15.22); speech is dangerous and should be minimal (Prov 13.3); and vows require fulfillment (Deut 23.21). While the Teacher advises caution in all things, he does not reject the Temple* (*house of God*). **6:** *Messenger:* Likely a servant of the Temple, collecting the payment of a vow. **7:** *Fear God:* A common motif* in wisdom literature,* affirming God's control over all matters. **8–9:** Injustice should surprise no one, since it is part of the structure of society. *King for a plowed field:* Meaning unclear, perhaps "a king is worth his upkeep" or "the benefits of an ordered society are worth the cost of social oppression," a point

5.10–20: Insatiability of greed. One who seeks wealth for its own sake, rather than for what it can provide, cannot be satisfied. **11:** What can one do with possessions other than admire them? **12:** A romantic view of the honest laborer who *sleeps* after great exertion compared to the *rich* person who lies awake worried about acquisitions. **14:** While the Teacher has decried riches, he now considers the unfairness of los-

a Ch 4.17 in Heb   b Cn: Heb *they do not know how to do evil*   c Ch 5.1 in Heb   d Meaning of Heb uncertain ing wealth, especially as a *parent*. **15:** Humans are born *naked* and take nothing with them when they die (Job 1.21). **17:** *Eat in darkness:* Either one is too miserly to use oil, or (metaphorically*) one eats without enjoyment. **18–20:** In light of the foregoing investigation, the Teacher advises: Accept the realities of life and find joy wherever possible.

6 There is an evil that I have seen under the sun, and it lies heavy upon humankind: ²those to whom God gives wealth, possessions, and honor, so that they lack nothing of all that they desire, yet God does not enable them to enjoy these things, but a stranger enjoys them. This is vanity; it is a grievous ill. ³A man may beget a hundred children, and live many years; but however many are the days of his years, if he does not enjoy life's good things, or has no burial, I say that a stillborn child is better off than he. ⁴For it comes into vanity and goes into darkness, and in darkness its name is covered; ⁵moreover it has not seen the sun or known anything; yet it finds rest rather than he. ⁶Even though he should live a thousand years twice over, yet enjoy no good—do not all go to one place?

7 All human toil is for the mouth, yet the appetite is not satisfied. ⁸For what advantage have the wise over fools? And what do the poor have who know how to conduct themselves before the living? ⁹Better is the sight of the eyes than the wandering of desire; this also is vanity and a chasing after wind.*

10 Whatever has come to be has already been named, and it is known what human beings are, and that they are not able to dispute with those who are stronger. ¹¹The more words, the more vanity, so how is one the better? ¹²For who knows what is good for mortals while they live the few days of their vain life, which they pass like a shadow? For who can tell them what will be after them under the sun?

6.1–12: Frustration. In light of his previous advice, the Teacher considers the greatest evil the inability to enjoy what one has. **3:** In the ancient world, many *children* (Deut 11.21) and long life (Ps 91.16) were greatly valued. *No burial:* While the importance of proper burial is clear in the Old Testament (2 Kings 9.30–37), its

inclusion here is a bit surprising. *Stillborn child:* The one who has never experienced life's pain (*seen the sun*) is the most fortunate (4.1–3; Job 3.16). **6:** If one does not enjoy life, it is futile. **9:** *Better is sight . . . than the wandering of desire:* It is better to be content with what one has than constantly to desire more. **10:** See ch 1. **12:** A summary.

7 A good name is better than precious ointment,
    and the day of death, than the day of birth.
² It is better to go to the house of mourning
    than to go to the house of feasting;
  for this is the end of everyone,
    and the living will lay it to heart.
³ Sorrow is better than laughter,
    for by sadness of countenance the heart is made glad.
⁴ The heart of the wise is in the house of mourning;
    but the heart of fools is in the house of mirth.
⁵ It is better to hear the rebuke of the wise
    than to hear the song of fools.
⁶ For like the crackling of thorns under a pot,
    so is the laughter of fools;
    this also is vanity.
⁷ Surely oppression makes the wise foolish,
    and a bribe corrupts the heart.
⁸ Better is the end of a thing than its beginning;
    the patient in spirit are better than the proud in spirit.
⁹ Do not be quick to anger,
    for anger lodges in the bosom of fools.
¹⁰ Do not say, "Why were the former days better than these?"
    For it is not from wisdom that you ask this.
¹¹ Wisdom is as good as an inheritance,
    an advantage to those who see the sun.

a Or *a feeding on wind.* See Hos 12.1

12 For the protection of wisdom is like the
protection of money,
    and the advantage of knowledge is
       that wisdom gives life to the one
       who possesses it.
13 Consider the work of God;
    who can make straight what he has
       made crooked?

14 In the day of prosperity be joyful, and
in the day of adversity consider; God has
made the one as well as the other, so that
mortals may not find out anything that will
come after them.

**7.1–14: Mixture of the Teacher's ideas and tradi-
tional wisdom.** Forms of Hebrew "tob" (*good*, and in
comparative mode, *better*) occur ten times in this section. **1–4:** *Death* is instructive for the living, revealing
the true end of all things and hence life's proper priorities. **3:** *Made glad:* Literally "made good", "improved." **6:** *Crackling . . . vanity:* The words of a fool
are loud but bring no long-term benefit. **7:** While the
Teacher contrasts wisdom with folly, he also recognizes that they are not permanent conditions; in adversity, wisdom may fail. **11–12:** *Wisdom,* while not
stable, is good. **13:** *Crooked:* See 1.15. Since people
do not receive their just rewards, one should avoid being overly pious or overly wicked.

---

15 In my vain life I have seen everything;
there are righteous people who perish in
their righteousness, and there are wicked
people who prolong their life in their evildoing. 16Do not be too righteous, and do not
act too wise; why should you destroy
yourself? 17Do not be too wicked, and do not
be a fool; why should you die before your
time? 18It is good that you should take hold
of the one, without letting go of the other;
for the one who fears God shall succeed with
both.

19 Wisdom gives strength to the wise
more than ten rulers that are in a city.

20 Surely there is no one on earth so righteous as to do good without ever sinning.

21 Do not give heed to everything that
people say, or you may hear your servant
cursing you; 22your heart knows that many
times you have yourself cursed others.

23 All this I have tested by wisdom; I said,
"I will be wise," but it was far from me.

24That which is, is far off, and deep, very
deep; who can find it out? 25I turned my
mind to know and to search out and to seek
wisdom and the sum of things, and to know
that wickedness is folly and that foolishness
is madness. 26I found more bitter than death
the woman who is a trap, whose heart is
snares and nets, whose hands are fetters; one
who pleases God escapes her, but the sinner
is taken by her. 27See, this is what I found,
says the Teacher,[a] adding one thing to another to find the sum, 28which my mind has
sought repeatedly, but I have not found. One
man among a thousand I found, but a
woman among all these I have not found.
29See, this alone I found, that God made human beings straightforward, but they have
devised many schemes.

7.15–29: Practical advice. 18: *One . . . other:* Not being too wise and not being too foolish (compare vv.
16–17). **20:** *No one . . . sinning:* See 1 Kings 8.46. **26:**
The woman: Decries the gossipy, frivolous woman
(Prov 7). Few men, but even fewer women, are righteous. Does the book reflect an anti-female bias? **29:**
Human beings: In Hebrew the word is singular ("ad-
ham"); the same word is translated *man* in v. 28. *Humans* (or just males?) were created good (Gen 1) but
nonetheless sin.

---

8 Who is like the wise man?
   And who knows the interpretation of
    a thing?
   Wisdom makes one's face shine,
     and the hardness of one's
       countenance is changed.

2 Keep[b] the king's command because of
your sacred oath. 3Do not be terrified; go
from his presence, do not delay when the
matter is unpleasant, for he does whatever
he pleases. 4For the word of the king is powerful, and who can say to him, "What are you
doing?" 5Whoever obeys a command will
meet no harm, and the wise mind will know
the time and way. 6For every matter has its
time and way, although the troubles of mortals lie heavy upon them. 7Indeed, they do
not know what is to be, for who can tell them

a Qoheleth, traditionally rendered *Preacher*   *b* Heb I
keep

how it will be? [8]No one has power over the wind[a] to restrain the wind,[a] or power over the day of death; there is no discharge from the battle, nor does wickedness deliver those who practice it. [9]All this I observed, applying my mind to all that is done under the sun, while one person exercises authority over another to the other's hurt.

8.1–9: Wisdom's value and limits. 2–5: Practical advice on dealing with a king: Recognize his power and do not challenge him openly. *Sacred oath:* a pledge of loyalty to the king, made in God's name. **6–8:** The repetition of *time and way* from v. 5 allows the Teacher to reiterate the inability of humans to understand the future or to control their fates any more than they can control the *wind*.

---

[10] Then I saw the wicked buried; they used to go in and out of the holy place, and were praised in the city where they had done such things.[b] This also is vanity. [11]Because sentence against an evil deed is not executed speedily, the human heart is fully set to do evil. [12]Though sinners do evil a hundred times and prolong their lives, yet I know that it will be well with those who fear God, because they stand in fear before him, [13]but it will not be well with the wicked, neither will they prolong their days like a shadow, because they do not stand in fear before God.

[14] There is a vanity that takes place on earth, that there are righteous people who are treated according to the conduct of the wicked, and there are wicked people who are treated according to the conduct of the righteous. I said that this also is vanity. [15]So I commend enjoyment, for there is nothing better for people under the sun than to eat, and drink, and enjoy themselves, for this will go with them in their toil through the days of life that God gives them under the sun.

[16] When I applied my mind to know wisdom, and to see the business that is done on earth, how one's eyes see sleep neither day nor night, [17]then I saw all the work of God, that no one can find out what is happening under the sun. However much they may toil in seeking, they will not find it out; even though those who are wise claim to know, they cannot find it out.

8.10–17: No justice. The public praise given the wicked at their death and the lack of swift, clear punishment encourages people in their evil. **12:** In light of earlier comments, this confidence in God's justice is surprising. **13–14:** One cannot distinguish between the *righteous* and the *wicked* by their rewards. **15–17:** A summary of the book's theme: No one, not even the wise, can understand what happens in life.

9 All this I laid to heart, examining it all, how the righteous and the wise and their deeds are in the hand of God; whether it is love or hate one does not know. Everything that confronts them [2]is vanity,[c] since the same fate comes to all, to the righteous and the wicked, to the good and the evil,[d] to the clean and the unclean, to those who sacrifice and those who do not sacrifice. As are the good, so are the sinners; those who swear are like those who shun an oath. [3]This is an evil in all that happens under the sun, that the same fate comes to everyone. Moreover, the hearts of all are full of evil; madness is in their hearts while they live, and after that they go to the dead. [4]But whoever is joined with all the living has hope, for a living dog is better than a dead lion. [5]The living know that they will die, but the dead know nothing; they have no more reward, and even the memory of them is lost. [6]Their love and their hate and their envy have already perished; never again will they have any share in all that happens under the sun.

[7] Go, eat your bread with enjoyment, and drink your wine with a merry heart; for God has long ago approved what you do. [8]Let your garments always be white; do not let oil be lacking on your head. [9]Enjoy life with the wife whom you love, all the days of your vain life that are given you under the sun, because that is your portion in life and in your toil at which you toil under the sun. [10]Whatever your hand finds to do, do with your might; for there is no work or thought or knowledge or wisdom in Sheol, to which you are going.

---

a Or *breath*　　b Meaning of Heb uncertain
c Syr Compare Gk: Heb *Everything that confronts them*
[2]*is everything*　　d Gk Syr Vg: Heb lacks *and the evil*

11 Again I saw that under the sun the race is not to the swift, nor the battle to the strong, nor bread to the wise, nor riches to the intelligent, nor favor to the skillful; but time and chance happen to them all. 12 For no one can anticipate the time of disaster. Like fish taken in a cruel net, and like birds caught in a snare, so mortals are snared at a time of calamity, when it suddenly falls upon them.

9.1–12: In God's hands. 2: *Clean and unclean, sacrifice and not sacrifice:* References to ritual practices, verifying that the Teacher is not opposed to traditional religion. *Those who swear* are evil. *Those who shun the oath* are good, avoiding unnecessary words (5.2). 3: Less a concept of complete sinfulness than a cry of despair in face of human frailty and mortality. 4: *Dog:* a despised animal in ancient Israel (Prov 26.11). The valuing of life over death is either a contradiction or a development beyond the contrary statements in 6.3–6. 8: *White:* a color for festivals; contrast 7.3–4. 9: *Wife:* Literally, "woman." 10: *Sheol*:* See comment on 3.20.

13 I have also seen this example of wisdom under the sun, and it seemed great to me. 14 There was a little city with few people in it. A great king came against it and besieged it, building great siegeworks against it. 15 Now there was found in it a poor wise man, and he by his wisdom delivered the city. Yet no one remembered that poor man. 16 So I said, "Wisdom is better than might; yet the poor man's wisdom is despised, and his words are not heeded."

17 The quiet words of the wise are more to
be heeded
than the shouting of a ruler among
fools.
18 Wisdom is better than weapons of war,
but one bungler destroys much
good.

9.13–18: The goodness and limits of wisdom. The parable-like* story, followed by traditional sayings, makes the Teacher's point: While wisdom is better than folly, it does not guarantee fame or respect. 16: While the *poor man* apparently saved the city, people did not listen to his advice.

10 Dead flies make the perfumer's
ointment give off a foul odor;
so a little folly outweighs wisdom and
honor.
2 The heart of the wise inclines to the
right,
but the heart of a fool to the left.
3 Even when fools walk on the road, they
lack sense,
and show to everyone that they are
fools.
4 If the anger of the ruler rises against
you, do not leave your post,
for calmness will undo great
offenses.
5 There is an evil that I have seen under the sun, as great an error as if it proceeded from the ruler: 6 folly is set in many high places, and the rich sit in a low place. 7 I have seen slaves on horseback, and princes walking on foot like slaves.
8 Whoever digs a pit will fall into it;
and whoever breaks through a wall
will be bitten by a snake.
9 Whoever quarries stones will be hurt by
them;
and whoever splits logs will be
endangered by them.
10 If the iron is blunt, and one does not
whet the edge,
then more strength must be
exerted;
but wisdom helps one to succeed.
11 If the snake bites before it is charmed,
there is no advantage in a charmer.

10.1–11.10: Traditional sayings, with the Teacher's own observations. 10.2: Ancient Israel considered the *right* the "proper" side (Ex 15.6) and the *left* inferior. 4: Advice for dealing with a king (Prov 19.12). 5–7: The unexpected fates of the foolish and the rich, the latter equated with the wise. 8–11: Inherent risks. *Digs a pit:* See Prov 26.27; 28.10. *Snake:* See Am 5.19.

12 Words spoken by the wise bring them
favor,
but the lips of fools consume them.
13 The words of their mouths begin in
foolishness,
and their talk ends in wicked
madness;

14 yet fools talk on and on.
    No one knows what is to happen,
        and who can tell anyone what the
            future holds?
15 The toil of fools wears them out,
        for they do not even know the way to
            town.
16 Alas for you, O land, when your king is
        a servant,[a]
    and your princes feast in the
        morning!
17 Happy are you, O land, when your king
        is a nobleman,
    and your princes feast at the proper
        time—
    for strength, and not for drunkenness!
18 Through sloth the roof sinks in,
    and through indolence the house
        leaks.
19 Feasts are made for laughter;
    wine gladdens life,
    and money meets every need.
20 Do not curse the king, even in your
            thoughts,
    or curse the rich, even in your
            bedroom;
    for a bird of the air may carry your voice,
        or some winged creature tell
            the matter.

10.12–20. 12–15: The Teacher's own observation
(v. 14) incorporated with traditional views on the *fool*.
16–18: A country suffers if leaders are foolish and do
not know the proper times for *feasting*. **20:** Practical
advice about not speaking ill of powerful people.

〰〰〰〰〰〰〰〰〰〰〰〰〰〰〰

11 Send out your bread upon the
        waters,
    for after many days you will get it
        back.
2 Divide your means seven ways, or even
        eight,
    for you do not know what disaster
        may happen on earth.
3 When clouds are full,
    they empty rain on the earth;
    whether a tree falls to the south or to
        the north,
    in the place where the tree falls, there
        it will lie.

4 Whoever observes the wind will
        not sow;
    and whoever regards the clouds will
        not reap.
5 Just as you do not know how the breath
comes to the bones in the mother's womb,
so you do not know the work of God, who
makes everything.
6 In the morning sow your seed, and at
evening do not let your hands be idle; for you
do not know which will prosper, this or that,
or whether both alike will be good.
7 Light is sweet, and it is pleasant for the
eyes to see the sun.
8 Even those who live many years should
rejoice in them all; yet let them remember
that the days of darkness will be many. All
that comes is vanity.
9 Rejoice, young man, while you are
young, and let your heart cheer you in the
days of your youth. Follow the inclination of
your heart and the desire of your eyes, but
know that for all these things God will bring
you into judgment.
10 Banish anxiety from your mind, and
put away pain from your body; for youth and
the dawn of life are vanity.

11.1–10. 1–2: Likely refers to a trade venture. See Isa
18.2. **3–6:** Adapt to events that are beyond your control (v. 3) and work while you can (v. 6). **8–10:** Enjoy
life when possible, always remaining aware that death
awaits.

〰〰〰〰〰〰〰〰〰〰〰〰〰〰〰

12 Remember your creator in the days
    of your youth, before the days of
trouble come, and the years draw near when
you will say, "I have no pleasure in them";
2before the sun and the light and the moon
and the stars are darkened and the clouds
return with[b] the rain; 3in the day when the
guards of the house tremble, and the strong
men are bent, and the women who grind
cease working because they are few, and
those who look through the windows see
dimly; 4when the doors on the street are
shut, and the sound of the grinding is low,
and one rises up at the sound of a bird, and
all the daughters of song are brought low;

---

a Or *a child*   *b* Or *after*; Heb *'ahar*

[5]when one is afraid of heights, and terrors are in the road; the almond tree blossoms, the grasshopper drags itself along[a] and desire fails; because all must go to their eternal home, and the mourners will go about the streets; [6]before the silver cord is snapped,[b] and the golden bowl is broken, and the pitcher is broken at the fountain, and the wheel broken at the cistern, [7]and the dust returns to the earth as it was, and the breath[c] returns to God who gave it. [8]Vanity of vanities, says the Teacher;[d] all is vanity.

12.1–8: A vision of aging and death. God as *creator*: Job 38, Prov 20. **2–5:** A description of aging and the approach of death. One option is to read the images allegorically:* *Guards of the house* are arms; *strong men* are legs; *women who grind* are teeth; *daughters of song* are birds; *grasshopper* is the image of one walking on crutches. **6–7:** Human death compared to items at the end of their usefulness; perhaps images of a well (*cord, bowl, cistern*). **7:** *Breath returns:* A contradiction or development beyond 3.21. **8:** The body of the book ends with the same phrase with which it began (1.2).

---

9 Besides being wise, the Teacher[d] also taught the people knowledge, weighing and studying and arranging many proverbs. [10]The Teacher[d] sought to find pleasing words, and he wrote words of truth plainly.

11 The sayings of the wise are like goads, and like nails firmly fixed are the collected sayings that are given by one shepherd.[e] [12]Of anything beyond these, my child, beware. Of making many books there is no end, and much study is a weariness of the flesh.

13 The end of the matter; all has been heard. Fear God, and keep his commandments; for that is the whole duty of everyone. [14]For God will bring every deed into judgment, including[f] every secret thing, whether good or evil.

12.9–14: Epilogue. Likely added by an editor, these verses speak in third person and make the book more pious. **13:** *Fear God, keep commandments:* While not the opposite of previous ideas (5.6), this advice ends the book on a traditional note. **14:** The body of the book has been less clear about the distinct rewards of *good* and *evil* (8.13–14).

---

a Or *is a burden* *b* Syr Vg Compare Gk: Heb *is removed* *c* Or *the spirit* *d* *Qoheleth*, traditionally rendered *Preacher* *e* Meaning of Heb uncertain *f* Or *into the judgment on*

THE SONG OF SOLOMON

Introduction

Song of Solomon (Song of Songs or Canticles) is a collection of love poems exchanged between a woman and a man, with occasional remarks by one or more choruses. Throughout, the lovers delight in the tastes, smells, and feel of each other, which they describe in a cascade of comparisons with the world of nature and of urban life. The identity of these lovers has been explained in various ways. (1) Solomonic: Because of references to this famous king of Israel, the poems have been read as describing a wedding between Solomon and a shepherdess. (2) Allegorical: By the turn of the era, some Jewish interpreters read the Song as an allegory★ of God's love for Israel, despite (or perhaps because of) the book's lack of mention of God. Similarly, the Christian tradition of reading the poems as expressing Christ's★ love for the church, or seeing "the bride" as the Virgin Mary, has a long history. (3) Sacred marriage: One school of Hebrew Bible interpretation★ draws parallels between these images and ancient Near Eastern descriptions of the sacred union between a god and goddess. (4) Love poetry: Contemporary scholars tend to accept the book as secular love poetry. The extended description of the lover's body, called a "wasf," and the use of "bride" as a term of endearment are analogous to Egyptian, Arabic, and Syrian love poems.

The allegorical reading explains the book's placement in the Jewish canon★: It appears with the five "megilloth" (or festival scrolls★) and is read at Passover.★ In the Christian canon, Songs appears in the poetical books. Various linguistic features suggest that it was written much later than the tenth century, perhaps in the Persian period;★ the references to Solomon are best read as allusions to the great lover of ancient Israel (1 Kings 11.1–3) rather than as a key to the book's authorship. The book bears a strong women's perspective: The woman speaks more often than the man; the woman's sexuality is celebrated rather than controlled; and mothers rather than fathers are mentioned throughout. Some scholars cite this perspective as evidence that the book was written by or for women.

READING GUIDE

Song of Solomon is not easy to read: The meanings of many words are unknown; the metaphorical★ nature of the language often leaves the referent unclear; and speakers are not clearly marked. One focus for reading is to consider how the author has evoked the feeling of love. How do images of fruit, wine, and flowers allow the lovers to speak provocatively? While the lovers clearly express their affection for one another, they also seem aware of the societal constraints under which they live. What opposition does their love meet and how do they respond? The only references to marriage are a puzzling poem about the wedding procession of King Solomon in 3.6–11 and the woman's description as "bride." Does this celebration of physical love without focus on marriage or procreation surprise you?

1 The Song of Songs, which is Solomon's.

2 Let him kiss me with the kisses of his
        mouth!
  For your love is better than wine,
3   your anointing oils are fragrant,
  your name is perfume poured out;
     therefore the maidens love you.
4 Draw me after you, let us make haste.
     The king has brought me into his
        chambers.
  We will exult and rejoice in you;
     we will extol your love more
        than wine;
     rightly do they love you.

5 I am black and beautiful,
     O daughters of Jerusalem,
  like the tents of Kedar,
     like the curtains of Solomon.
6 Do not gaze at me because I am dark,
     because the sun has gazed on me.
  My mother's sons were angry with me;
     they made me keeper of the
        vineyards,
     but my own vineyard I have not kept!
7 Tell me, you whom my soul loves,
     where you pasture your flock,
     where you make it lie down at noon;
  for why should I be like one who
        is veiled
     beside the flocks of your companions?

8 If you do not know,
     O fairest among women,
  follow the tracks of the flock,
     and pasture your kids
     beside the shepherds' tents.

likely the editor's attempt to link the book with Solomon rather than proof of its authorship. **2–8: The woman speaks of love.** Ancient Near Eastern cultures used many sweet, strong scents on the body as well as in religious ceremonies. Throughout the book, such aromas are compared to the scent of the lovers' bodies. **4:** *The king:* The lovers call each other royal names, indicating their majesty in one another's eyes. **5–6:** *Black and beautiful:* The woman maintains that her sun-darkened skin is beautiful. The verses imply an expectation that women have fair skin, perhaps reflecting an urban perspective. *Kedar:* A mountain range, the name of which means "black." *Mother's sons:* Mothers rather than fathers are mentioned in the book, suggesting a strong female perspective. *Vineyards* throughout the book are connected with sexuality. The first mention is literal: Her brothers required her to work outside. The second reference is metaphorical:☆ She has not been chaste. **7:** *Veiled:* Veiling practices in ancient Israel are difficult to reconstruct. In Gen 38, a prostitute wears a veil, and Gen 29.21–25 may imply that brides wore face coverings. The reference here may be metaphorical: Why should she have difficulty seeing him? **8:** Another voice, the male or a chorus, tells her to follow the sheep to find her lover.

9 I compare you, my love,
     to a mare among Pharaoh's chariots.
10 Your cheeks are comely with
        ornaments,
     your neck with strings of jewels.
11 We will make you ornaments of gold,
     studded with silver.

12 While the king was on his couch,
     my nard gave forth its fragrance.
13 My beloved is to me a bag of myrrh
     that lies between my breasts.
14 My beloved is to me a cluster of henna
        blossoms
     in the vineyards of En-gedi.

1.1–8. 1: Superscription. Like many Psalms, the book begins with background information. *Song of Songs:* Hebrew for "best song." *Which is Solomon's* is more

15 Ah, you are beautiful, my love;
    ah, you are beautiful;
    your eyes are doves.
16 Ah, you are beautiful, my beloved,
    truly lovely.
    Our couch is green;
17   the beams of our house are cedar,
    our rafters[a] are pine.

2 I am a rose[b] of Sharon,
    a lily of the valleys.
2 As a lily among brambles,
    so is my love among maidens.

3 As an apple tree among the trees of the
    wood,
    so is my beloved among young men.
    With great delight I sat in his shadow,
    and his fruit was sweet to my taste.
4 He brought me to the banqueting
    house,
    and his intention toward me was love.
5 Sustain me with raisins,
    refresh me with apples;
    for I am faint with love.
6 O that his left hand were under my
    head,
    and that his right hand embraced me!
7 I adjure you, O daughters of Jerusalem,
    by the gazelles or the wild does:
    do not stir up or awaken love
    until it is ready!

**1.9–2.7: The man and the woman speak of love.
1.9–11:** He uses a wide array of images to describe the
woman. *Mare:* Egyptian sources report the military
strategy of sending a mare out to excite and disturb
the enemy's stallions. **12–17:** The woman likens her
own bodily smells and the delight of her lover between
her breasts to *nard, myrrh* and *henna:* aromatic, precious scents. *En-gedi:* A lush oasis close to the Dead
Sea. **15:** The male speaks. **16–17:** The woman's speech
portrays their trysting place as outdoors. **2.1–2:** The
woman sees herself as one of many common flowers;
but her lover sees her as outstanding in beauty. **3–5:**
Fruit is used as erotic imagery. She compares their
trysting place to a *banqueting house* or "winehouse,"
where they are to take their fill of delicacies. **7:** This
statement, issued as a lesson for others, either suggests
the danger of love or requests that the lovers' intimacy

not be interrupted. *Daughters of Jerusalem* refers to
the young women of the city. In the book, their participation advances the dialogue.

8 The voice of my beloved!
    Look, he comes,
    leaping upon the mountains,
    bounding over the hills.
9 My beloved is like a gazelle
    or a young stag.
    Look, there he stands
    behind our wall,
    gazing in at the windows,
    looking through the lattice.
10 My beloved speaks and says to me:
    "Arise, my love, my fair one,
    and come away;
11 for now the winter is past,
    the rain is over and gone.
12 The flowers appear on the earth;
    the time of singing has come,
    and the voice of the turtledove
    is heard in our land.
13 The fig tree puts forth its figs,
    and the vines are in blossom;
    they give forth fragrance.
    Arise, my love, my fair one,
    and come away.
14 O my dove, in the clefts of the rock,
    in the covert of the cliff,
    let me see your face,
    let me hear your voice;
    for your voice is sweet,
    and your face is lovely.
15 Catch us the foxes,
    the little foxes,
    that ruin the vineyards—
    for our vineyards are in blossom."

16 My beloved is mine and I am his;
    he pastures his flock among the
    lilies.
17 Until the day breathes
    and the shadows flee,
    turn, my beloved, be like a gazelle
    or a young stag on the cleft
    mountains.[c]

a Meaning of Heb uncertain   *b* Heb *crocus*
c Or *on the mountains of Bether:* meaning of Heb
uncertain

2.8–17: She reports his invitation. The man beckons to the woman to join him in the countryside, where springtime has awakened nature and desire. **14:** Their love is expressive, yet secretive. He invites her to private places: *clefts* and the *covert*. **15:** A difficult verse to translate. Some consider it a reference to an ancient riddle, the meaning of which has been lost. If *vineyards* symbolize the woman's sexuality (as elsewhere) then the *foxes* are dangers to their lovemaking. **16:** *Pastures the flock* may either be literal (he is a shepherd) or metaphorical* of their love, since she is called a *lily* (2.1). **17:** *Until the day breathes . . . shadows flee:* Although some interpret the reference as to dawn, it likely refers to sunset. The woman tells the man to depart until later in the evening.

3 Upon my bed at night
    I sought him whom my soul loves;
  I sought him, but found him not;
    I called him, but he gave no answer.*

2 "I will rise now and go about the city,
    in the streets and in the squares;
  I will seek him whom my soul loves."
    I sought him, but found him not.
3 The sentinels found me,
    as they went about in the city.
  "Have you seen him whom my soul
      loves?"
4 Scarcely had I passed them,
    when I found him whom my soul
      loves.
  I held him, and would not let him go
    until I brought him into my mother's
      house,
  and into the chamber of her that
      conceived me.
5 I adjure you, O daughters of Jerusalem,
    by the gazelles or the wild does:
  do not stir up or awaken love
    until it is ready!

3.1–5: Her nighttime search. Having been sent away, the man does not return, and the woman seeks him. **2–3:** *Streets* and *sentinels* indicate an urban setting. **4:** The book has a strong feminine orientation, speaking of the *mother's house* instead of the more normal house of the father (1.6; 8.1–2; see also Ruth 1.8). Did she really bring her lover into her mother's house or is this a dream? **5:** Another warning (2.7; 5.8).

6 What is that coming up from the
      wilderness,
    like a column of smoke,
  perfumed with myrrh and frankincense,
    with all the fragrant powders of the
      merchant?
7 Look, it is the litter of Solomon!
    Around it are sixty mighty men
      of the mighty men of Israel,
8 all equipped with swords
      and expert in war,
  each with his sword at his thigh
    because of alarms by night.
9 King Solomon made himself a
      palanquin
    from the wood of Lebanon.
10 He made its posts of silver,
    its back of gold, its seat of purple;
  its interior was inlaid with love.^b
    Daughters of Jerusalem,
11   come out.
  Look, O daughters of Zion,
    at King Solomon,
  at the crown with which his mother
      crowned him
    on the day of his wedding,
    on the day of the gladness of
      his heart.

3.6–11: A wedding scene. The book's only description of a wedding and of *Solomon* as present, these verses have been variously assessed (1) as a later insertion, modeled on Ps 45 and intended to strengthen the book's connection with Solomon; or (2) as an extended royal image, in which the woman compares the sight of her lover to that of the extravagant entourage of a king known for his love of women (1 Kings 11.1–3). **7:** *Mighty men of Israel*, translated elsewhere in the NRSV as "warriors" (2 Sam 23.8). **8:** *Sword at his thigh:* For easy access (Judg 3.16). **9:** *Wood of Lebanon:* Famous for its aroma and quality (2 Kings 19.23; 1 Kings 4.33). **11:** Jewish sources indicate that, prior to the Roman destruction of Jerusalem in 70 CE, bride and groom wore a wedding *crown*.

4 How beautiful you are, my love,
    how very beautiful!
  Your eyes are doves
    behind your veil.

a Gk: Heb lacks this line   *b* Meaning of Heb uncertain

Your hair is like a flock of goats,
   moving down the slopes of Gilead.
2 Your teeth are like a flock of shorn ewes
   that have come up from the washing,
all of which bear twins,
   and not one among them is bereaved.
3 Your lips are like a crimson thread,
   and your mouth is lovely.
Your cheeks are like halves of a
      pomegranate
   behind your veil.
4 Your neck is like the tower of David,
   built in courses;
on it hang a thousand bucklers,
   all of them shields of warriors.
5 Your two breasts are like two fawns,
   twins of a gazelle,
   that feed among the lilies.
6 Until the day breathes
   and the shadows flee,
I will hasten to the mountain of myrrh
   and the hill of frankincense.
7 You are altogether beautiful, my love;
   there is no flaw in you.
8 Come with me from Lebanon, my bride;
   come with me from Lebanon.
Depart[a] from the peak of Amana,
   from the peak of Senir and Hermon,
from the dens of lions,
   from the mountains of leopards.

4.1–7: The man praises the beauty of his lover. 1:
Veil: See comment on 1.7. *Goats* in Israel are primarily
black, while sheep are white. **2:** Her *teeth* are perfect:
white, proportional. **3:** *Crimson thread* describes the
color of her lips or the part between them. *Pomegranates,* elsewhere connected with sexuality, have a juicy
red pulp. **4:** *Built in courses:* Ancient Near Eastern art
shows women wearing multiple layers of metal neck-
laces. **5:** *Fawns, twins:* Perfectly matched and soft. **6:**
Sunset (See 2.17). *Mountain of myrrh* and *hill of frankincense* refer to parts of the woman's body.

~~~~~~~~~~~~~~~~~~~~~~~~~~~~~~~~~~~~~~

9 You have ravished my heart, my sister,
      my bride,
   you have ravished my heart with a
      glance of your eyes,
   with one jewel of your necklace.
10 How sweet is your love, my sister, my
      bride!

how much better is your love than
      wine,
   and the fragrance of your oils than
      any spice!
11 Your lips distill nectar, my bride;
   honey and milk are under your
      tongue;
   the scent of your garments is like the
      scent of Lebanon.
12 A garden locked is my sister, my bride,
   a garden locked, a fountain sealed.
13 Your channel[b] is an orchard of
      pomegranates
   with all choicest fruits,
   henna with nard,
14 nard and saffron, calamus and
      cinnamon,
   with all trees of frankincense,
myrrh and aloes,
   with all chief spices—
15 a garden fountain, a well of living water,
   and flowing streams from Lebanon.

16 Awake, O north wind,
   and come, O south wind!
Blow upon my garden
   that its fragrance may be wafted
      abroad.
Let my beloved come to his garden,
   and eat its choicest fruits.

5 I come to my garden, my sister,
      my bride;
   I gather my myrrh with my spice,
   I eat my honeycomb with my honey,
   I drink my wine with my milk.

Eat, friends, drink,
   and be drunk with love.

4.8–5.1: The man beckons her closer. While not all
identifiable, the place names are far away and exotic;
he imagines her removed from him. **4.9:** As in ancient
Egyptian poetry, *sister* and *bride* need not be read literally but as a description of the close intimacy of the
pair. **12–13:** *Garden locked* and *fountain sealed* refer
to the woman's chastity (Prov 5.15), though the man
has much knowledge of her *channel,* a more intimate
part of her body. The Hebrew word means "sword"

a Or *Look*   b Meaning of Heb uncertain

or perhaps "sprout." He compares it to exotic, fragrant, desirable anointments and spices. **16:** The woman accepts the comparison and invites him to partake. **5.1:** The man accepts the invitation and delights in what has been offered to him.

2 I slept, but my heart was awake.
　Listen! my beloved is knocking.
　"Open to me, my sister, my love,
　　my dove, my perfect one;
　for my head is wet with dew,
　　my locks with the drops of the night."
3 I had put off my garment;
　　how could I put it on again?
　I had bathed my feet;
　　how could I soil them?
4 My beloved thrust his hand into the
　　opening,
　and my inmost being yearned for him.
5 I arose to open to my beloved,
　　and my hands dripped with myrrh,
　my fingers with liquid myrrh,
　　upon the handles of the bolt.
6 I opened to my beloved,
　　but my beloved had turned and was
　　　gone.
　My soul failed me when he spoke.
　I sought him, but did not find him;
　　I called him, but he gave no answer.
7 Making their rounds in the city
　　the sentinels found me;
　they beat me, they wounded me,
　　they took away my mantle,
　　those sentinels of the walls.
8 I adjure you, O daughters of Jerusalem,
　　if you find my beloved,
　tell him this:
　　I am faint with love.

5.2–8: A second nighttime search. As in 3.1–4, she may either be on an actual search or dreaming. **3:** Although she has prepared herself for his visit, she is reluctant to go to the door. **4:** While likely referring to the window, *opening* also has a sexual connotation. **5:** Because *myrrh* is expensive, dripping suggests excess and luxury. **7:** The *sentinels* guarding the city at night represent the conventions of society, which frown on a young, unaccompanied woman roaming the streets. She does not elaborate on their beating and stripping her, citing this treatment as an example of the lengths to which she will go to find her lover.

8: It is doubtful that the *daughters of Jerusalem* were present during her search. Here, as elsewhere, the chorus adds dramatic effect.

9 What is your beloved more than another
　　beloved,
　　O fairest among women?
　What is your beloved more than another
　　beloved,
　　that you thus adjure us?
10 My beloved is all radiant and ruddy,
　　distinguished among ten thousand.
11 His head is the finest gold;
　　his locks are wavy,
　　black as a raven.
12 His eyes are like doves
　　beside springs of water,
　bathed in milk,
　　fitly set.[a]
13 His cheeks are like beds of spices,
　　yielding fragrance.
　His lips are lilies,
　　distilling liquid myrrh.
14 His arms are rounded gold,
　　set with jewels.
　His body is ivory work,[a]
　　encrusted with sapphires.[b]
15 His legs are alabaster columns,
　　set upon bases of gold.
　His appearance is like Lebanon,
　　choice as the cedars.
16 His speech is most sweet,
　　and he is altogether desirable.
　This is my beloved and this is
　　my friend,
　　O daughters of Jerusalem.

5.9–16: The woman praises her lover. This description offers the Hebrew Bible's only description of a man's body by a woman. **10:** A *ruddy* complexion was considered attractive for men (1 Sam 16.12; Gen 2.7). **11–15:** The description, given from *head* to *legs*, compares the man to conventional ancient Near Eastern statues: head and arms of gold, encrusted with jewels. The mention of *his body* (v. 14) sounds general in a list of specific body parts: Some interpreters suggest "loins" for this reference.

a Meaning of Heb uncertain   *b* Heb *lapis lazuli*

6 Where has your beloved gone,
　O fairest among women?
　Which way has your beloved turned,
　　that we may seek him with you?

2 My beloved has gone down to his
　　garden,
　to the beds of spices,
　to pasture his flock in the gardens,
　　and to gather lilies.
3 I am my beloved's and my beloved is
　　mine;
　he pastures his flock among the lilies.

4 You are beautiful as Tirzah, my love,
　comely as Jerusalem,
　terrible as an army with banners.
5 Turn away your eyes from me,
　for they overwhelm me!
　Your hair is like a flock of goats,
　　moving down the slopes of Gilead.
6 Your teeth are like a flock of ewes,
　　that have come up from the washing;
　all of them bear twins,
　　and not one among them is bereaved.
7 Your cheeks are like halves of a
　　pomegranate
　behind your veil.
8 There are sixty queens and eighty
　　concubines,
　and maidens without number.
9 My dove, my perfect one, is the only one,
　the darling of her mother,
　flawless to her that bore her.
　The maidens saw her and called her
　　happy;
　the queens and concubines also, and
　　they praised her.
10 "Who is this that looks forth like the
　　dawn,
　fair as the moon, bright as the sun,
　terrible as an army with banners?"

6.1–10. 1–3: The lover's whereabouts. A short fragment of a song, in which the woman reiterates earlier
themes. **4–10: The man praises the woman's body.**
While this poem shares many of the agricultural comparisons of 4.1–3 (*hair* like *goats*, *teeth* like *ewes*), it
also introduces regal imagery. The woman is seen as
awe-inspiring. She is compared to important cities (*Tirzah* was the capital of the northern kingdom after the

division; *Jerusalem* of the south), and she would invite
the praise even of *queens* and *concubines.**

11 I went down to the nut orchard,
　　to look at the blossoms of the valley,
　to see whether the vines had budded,
　　whether the pomegranates were in
　　bloom.
12 Before I was aware, my fancy set me
　　in a chariot beside my prince.*a*

13*b* Return, return, O Shulammite!
　Return, return, that we may look
　　upon you.

Why should you look upon the
　　Shulammite,
　as upon a dance before two armies?*c*

6.11–13. 11–12: The woman speaks. The regal imagery continues, as the woman calls her lover *my
prince.* **13: A call to the woman.** *Shulammite:* The
woman is called "the Shulammite," meaning unclear.
It could be a feminine form of the name Solomon,
indicating nobility. An unidentified group asks to gaze
upon her. The man rebuffs the request. *A dance before
two armies* may refer to a specific kind of dance or
perhaps explains that such a display would be as lewd
as a woman dancing in front of two armies of men.

7 How graceful are your feet in sandals,
　O queenly maiden!
　Your rounded thighs are like jewels,
　　the work of a master hand.
2 Your navel is a rounded bowl
　　that never lacks mixed wine.
　Your belly is a heap of wheat,
　　encircled with lilies.
3 Your two breasts are like two fawns,
　　twins of a gazelle.
4 Your neck is like an ivory tower.
　Your eyes are pools in Heshbon,
　　by the gate of Bath-rabbim.
　Your nose is like a tower of Lebanon,
　　overlooking Damascus.
5 Your head crowns you like Carmel,
　　and your flowing locks are like purple;
　a king is held captive in the tresses.*a*

---

a Cn: Meaning of Heb uncertain　　*b* Ch 7.1 in Heb
c Or *dance of Mahanaim*

7.1–5: The man praises the woman's body. In his third description of the beauty of the woman's body, the man reverses his gaze and describes her from foot to head. Greater intimacy is implied by these images: He speaks of her *navel* and *belly*, normally hidden by clothing. **4–7:** The woman is compared to majestic geography and architecture. *Heshbon:* South of Jerusalem, known for its large reservior. *Bath-rabbim:* Literally, "daughter of great ones." *Carmel* is a mountain range in northwestern Israel.

6 How fair and pleasant you are,
   O loved one, delectable maiden!*a*
7 You are stately*b* as a palm tree,
   and your breasts are like its
      clusters.
8 I say I will climb the palm tree
   and lay hold of its branches.
 O may your breasts be like clusters of
      the vine,
   and the scent of your breath like
      apples,
9 and your kisses*c* like the best wine
   that goes down*d* smoothly,
   gliding over lips and teeth.*e*

10 I am my beloved's,
   and his desire is for me.
11 Come, my beloved,
   let us go forth into the fields,
   and lodge in the villages;
12 let us go out early to the vineyards,
   and see whether the vines have
      budded,
 whether the grape blossoms have
      opened
 and the pomegranates are in bloom.
 There I will give you my love.
13 The mandrakes give forth fragrance,
   and over our doors are all choice
      fruits,
 new as well as old,
   which I have laid up for you, O my
      beloved.

7.6–13: Dialogue between the lovers. The man expresses his desire to touch the woman: She is as delectable as fruit and as delicious as wine. **10–13:** The woman invites the man into the *fields:* There, where blooms are opening, she will give herself to him. In

many cultures *mandrakes* are considered aphrodisiacs (Gen 30.14–16).

8 O that you were like a brother to me,
   who nursed at my mother's breast!
 If I met you outside, I would kiss you,
   and no one would despise me.
2 I would lead you and bring you
   into the house of my mother,
   and into the chamber of the one who
      bore me.*f*
 I would give you spiced wine to drink,
   the juice of my pomegranates.
3 O that his left hand were under my
      head,
   and that his right hand embraced me!
4 I adjure you, O daughters of Jerusalem,
   do not stir up or awaken love
   until it is ready!

5 Who is that coming up from the
      wilderness,
   leaning upon her beloved?

 Under the apple tree I awakened you.
 There your mother was in labor with
      you;
   there she who bore you was in labor.

8.1–5: Expressions of desire. The woman is aware of the societal constraints on their expressions of love. She wishes for the same freedom of affection and shared space that she would have with a brother. **2:** As elsewhere, *pomegranates* is a sexual image. **5:** The words of the chorus reveal that the lovers have been together in the countryside, perhaps having consummated their desire. For the third time, the woman connects their intimate moments with events of their own conceptions (3.4; 8.2).

6 Set me as a seal upon your heart,
   as a seal upon your arm;
 for love is strong as death,
   passion fierce as the grave.
 Its flashes are flashes of fire,
   a raging flame.

a Syr: Heb *in delights*   *b* Heb *This your stature is*
c Heb *palate*   *d* Heb *down for my lover*   *e* Gk Syr
Vg: Heb *lips of sleepers*   *f* Gk Syr: Heb *my mother; she (or you) will teach me*

7 Many waters cannot quench love,
    neither can floods drown it.
  If one offered for love
    all the wealth of one's house,
    it would be utterly scorned.

8 We have a little sister,
    and she has no breasts.
  What shall we do for our sister,
    on the day when she is spoken for?
9 If she is a wall,
    we will build upon her a battlement
      of silver;
  but if she is a door,
    we will enclose her with boards of
      cedar.
10 I was a wall,
    and my breasts were like towers;
  then I was in his eyes
    as one who brings*a* peace.
11 Solomon had a vineyard at Baal-hamon;
    he entrusted the vineyard to keepers;
    each one was to bring for its fruit a
      thousand pieces of silver.
12 My vineyard, my very own, is for myself;
    you, O Solomon, may have the
      thousand,
    and the keepers of the fruit two
      hundred!

13 O you who dwell in the gardens,
    my companions are listening for your
      voice;
    let me hear it.

14 Make haste, my beloved,
    and be like a gazelle
  or a young stag
    upon the mountains of spices!

8.6–14. 6–7: Sayings on love. Documents were secured with wax, which were then stamped with a *seal* bearing the owner's distinctive symbol. The woman marks the man as her own. **8–14: Miscellaneous poems.** The brothers, mentioned in ch. 1, speak. **9:** If on her wedding day she has been chaste (*a wall*), they will give her silver ornaments. If she has not, then they will guard her. **10:** She maintains that she is chaste, and mature with full *breasts* (*towers*). **11–12:** The man maintains that his *vineyard* (that is, the woman) is better than that of Solomon, where a single piece of fruit was worth *a thousand pieces of silver. Baal-hamon* means "possessor of wealth." The location is unknown. **13:** The woman speaks these final verses.

a Or *finds*

7 Many waters cannot quench love,
    neither can floods drown it.
  If one offered for love
    all the wealth of one's house,
    it would be utterly scorned.

8 We have a little sister,
    and she has no breasts.
  What shall we do for our sister,
    on the day when she is spoken for?
9 If she is a wall,
    we will build upon her a battlement
      of silver;
  but if she is a door,
    we will enclose her with boards of
      cedar.
10 I was a wall,
    and my breasts were like towers;
  then I was in his eyes
    as one who brings peace.
11 Solomon had a vineyard at Baal-hamon;
    he entrusted the vineyard to keepers;
  each one was to bring for its fruit a
    thousand pieces of silver.
12 My vineyard, my very own, is for myself;
  you, O Solomon, may have the
      thousand,
  and the keepers of the fruit two
      hundred!

13 O you who dwell in the gardens,
    my companions are listening for your
      voice;
    let me hear it.

14 Make haste, my beloved,
    and be like a gazelle
  or a young stag
    upon the mountains of spices.ˣ

8:6–14, 8:7. Sayings on love. Documents were secured with wax, which were then stamped with a seal bearing the owner's distinctive symbol. The woman marks the man as her own. 8–14: Miscellaneous poems. The brothers, mentioned in ch. 1, speak 9: If on her wedding day she has been chaste (a wall), they will give her silver ornaments. If she has not then they will guard her. 10: She maintains that she is chaste, and mature with full breasts (towers). 11–12: The man maintains that his vineyard (that is, the woman) is better than that of Solomon, whose a single piece of fruit was worth a thousand pieces of silver. Baal-hamon means "possessor of wealth." The location is unknown. 13: The woman speaks these final verses.

ˣ Or flocks

PROPHETIC LITERATURE

The phrase "prophetic literature" often brings to mind books such as Isaiah or Micah, books that contain the words of prophets* active in ancient Israel. And those books surely count as prophetic literature. However, prophetic literature includes far more than a book like Micah. At the outset, it is important to know that prophets were active in the ancient Near East long before Israel came to exist. Archaeologists have found texts that record what ancient Mesopotamian prophets uttered, some from a city named Mari, texts that date to about 1800 BCE, others from Nineveh that derive from the seventh century BCE. The prophets in the latter texts would have been contemporaries of Isaiah and Micah. Both Israelite and Mesopotamian prophets were remembered as having spoken in short, poetic oracles.* So, as was the case with wisdom literature,* prophetic literature is something that appears beyond the covers of the Old Testament.

Most of the prophetic literature present in the Old Testament derives from the period of the monarchy, roughly 1000 BCE to 587 BCE. And some of the prophetic literature that postdates the demise of monarchic Israel in 587 remains concerned about the fate of the Davidic lineage, for instance, Haggai 2.20–23. It is not too much to say that prophets regularly addressed kings and nations, even foreign nations. There are major collections devoted to foreign nations in each of the three Latter Prophets (Isa 13–21; Jer 46–51; Ezek 25–32) (See Hebrew Scriptures*). Nahum is concerned about Nineveh (Nah 1.1) and Obadiah primarily with Edom. It is no wonder that at least one prophet was known as "a prophet to the nations" (Jer 1.5).

Prophetic literature in the Old Testament appears both inside and outside prophetic books. If one means by prophetic literature, those texts that derive from the work of a prophet— whether that individual wrote it or someone else did—then prophetic literature appears in the Pentateuch,* the historical literature, and in the prophetic books. In the Pentateuch, the book of Numbers attests to the words and behavior of Balaam, son of Beor, a non-Israelite seer whom the king of Moab had asked curse Israel. (This same Balaam is attested in an inscription dating to the eighth century BCE and that was discovered in Jordan.) Balaam uttered oracles, as did his other ancient Near Eastern and biblical counterparts. On prophets in the historical literature, see "Historical Literature." And, of course, prophetic books are normally deemed to be prophetic literature, with Jonah functioning almost as an ironic* version of a prophetic book.

Though much prophetic literature is written as poetry, a considerable body of prose prophetic literature also exists. There are a number of basic forms that scholars have identified:

- The **symbolic action report** recounts behavior designed to communicate a message. Hosea's marriage to "a wife of whoredom" (Hos 1.2–9), Isaiah's walking naked for three years (Isa 20.1–6), and Ezekiel's portrayal of a siege (Ezek 4.1–3) offer noteworthy and memorable examples. These symbolic actions reports demonstrate that the ability of a prophet to communicate was not limited to that person's ability to speak in oracles. Their actions could speak in lieu of words. Moreover, their actions could make people ask questions of the prophet ("Will you not tell us what these things mean for us, that you are acting this way?" Ezek 24.19).

- The **commissioning report** appears in several prophetic books and is present elsewhere in the Old Testament. (This same basic form of literature is used to describe the commission of Abraham's servant [Gen 24], Moses' call [Ex 3.1–4:16], and Gideon's call [Judg 6.11–24].) Isaiah 6; Jeremiah 1.4–10, and Ezekiel 1.1–3:15 offer accounts of the way in which a prophet perceived and reported his commission. Basic elements recur in the prophetic accounts. The prophet encounters the deity, whether in a vision or in an audition (for instance, "the word of the LORD came to me" in Jer 1.4). As a part of that encounter, the prophet is given a task (for instance, "I appointed you a prophet to the nations" in Jer 1.5), the prophet raises an objection ("Truly I do not know how to speak, for I am only a boy" in Jer 1.6), and the deity responds to the objection "do not say 'I am only a boy'...I have put my words in your mouth" (Jer 1:7–9).

- The **vision report** is one of the most prominent types of prose prophetic literature, no doubt because some prophets were seers (Amaziah to Amos, "O seer..." Am 7.12) and were associated with visionary behavior ("the vision of Isaiah" in Isa 1.1). Vision reports can be terse: "I saw the LORD standing beside the altar and he said..." (Am 9.1). They can be extensive (Ezek 1.1–28). They can involve mundane (Zech 2.1) and bizarre images (Zech 5.5–11). In most cases, visions are understood to be occasions when the deity shows something to the prophet. That individual is privy to scenes and meanings unavailable to ordinary people. There also appears to be a historical development in vision reports. Those attributed to Amos are probably the earlier prophetic vision reports. When God shows Amos a scene of agricultural disaster, Amos immediately understood what he saw and interceded on behalf of Israel (Am 7.1–3). Almost two centuries later, Ezekiel needs a guide to lead him through the visionary experience (Ezek 8.17–18; 40.3–4). Later still, Zechariah, when presented with a vision of four horses, asks "the angel who talked with me, 'What are these, my lord?'" (Zech 6:4). Clearly, Zechariah does not understand what he sees. Visions now require an interpreter,* as will also be the case in apocalyptic* visions (Dan 7.15–18).

- There is also the **legend**.* The term suffers in contemporary usage. It is often now used to mean something that didn't actually happen. In its original sense, a legend was a report or story about something—whether person or place— that was holy or sacred. The account of Moses and the burning bush is properly understood as a legend. Legends deal with the powerful and the world of the miraculous. Some prophets were known by the title, "man of God," as was Elijah in 1 Kings 17.18. They were understood to share in the power of the deity such that the narratives* told about them qualify as legends. They celebrate the power of the holy person who is a prophet, and therefore such narratives may be called prophetic legends. Some are short and simple, as is the report about Elisha's killing of boys who jeered at him (2 Kings 2.23–24). Others are longer, offering more than simply a view of the powerful prophet. The book of 2 Kings 4.1–7 celebrates the power of Elisha in providing oil to a poor widow of one of his disciples. The legend does more because it reports that the widow was told to procure vessels into which oil might be poured. The implication is that had she found even more, the oil would have been more bountiful. Even longer legends explore the character of the holy man himself. Again, 2 Kings 4.8–37 depicts an Elisha grateful to a wealthy woman who had supported him. He decides that she should have a child, which subsequently happens. At this point, the narrative becomes an exploration of the holy man's power and the proper and improper uses of it. In sum, there are various types of prophetic legends.

- Finally, there are **divinatory chronicles**,* accounts in which someone requests information from a prophet. He functions as a diviner. Samuel was, among other things, viewed as a seer in 1 Samuel 9. In that episode, Saul and his companion want Samuel to tell them the location of their lost livestock. In similar fashion, Ezekiel 20.1 reports that "elders of Israel" went to Ezekiel's house in order "to consult the LORD" only to discover that the LORD will not allow them to consult him. Finally, Zechariah 7.3 reports a question posed to the prophet Zechariah by a delegation from Bethel. He answers their question in the following chapter (Zech 8.19).

This brief overview shows that there are diverse kinds of prose prophetic literature.

Most readers associate prophetic literature with poetry. Virtually all poetry makes greater demands on readers than does prose. When a reader approaches a poem such as Exodus 15 or any one of the psalms, there is a discrete text, a first and a last verse. It is not always easy to find these first and last verses of the speeches in prophetic books. Readers can, however, pay attention to formulae to help them identify the boundaries of these poems. Amos 1 includes five oracles, each of which is introduced by the formula "Thus says the LORD." Moreover, three of the oracles conclude with the formula, "says the LORD." The phrase "thus says the LORD"—and similar ones such as "Hear this word" (Am 3.1; 4.1) or "the word of the LORD came to me" (Jer 2.1) frequently appear at the beginning of a prophetic speech whereas "says the LORD" often appears either at the end of a speech (Jer 2.3) or at the end of a section of a speech (Jer 2.12). Attention to these formulae can help discern the boundaries of individual poems.

Unfortunately, these formulae are not consistently present throughout prophetic poetry. Readers can see the consequences of this by comparing different translations. For example, most contemporary translations of prophetic poetry include spaces between individual oracles, as one can see in the spaces between Isaiah 1.3 and 1.4, 1.4 and 1.5, 1.6 and 1.7, and 1.9 and 1.10 in the NRSV. These spaces represent the judgments about the individual oracles that make up a book by the translators and editors responsible for a particular translation. Not all scholars agree on these divisions. So, the white spaces between oracles in the NRSV of Isaiah 1 differ from those in other translations. There is, however, a consensus that Isaiah 1 is made up of a series of poems and is not one extended lyric poem.

As a result of the lack of clues about where breaks might occur in prophetic poetry, readers must rely on other features of the poetry in order to discern the separate poems. These features include the logical structure of the poetry and thematic coherence. Many prophetic speeches are structured into two basic parts: an indictment and a sentence. The prophet demonstrates that the people or their leaders have done something wrong. Then the prophet reports what the result will be. The reader can use the content of the poem to determine where the individual section begins and ends.

In order to do this, the reader must attend to the kinds of prophetic poetry in the various prophetic books. As with prophetic prose, it is possible to discern some basic forms present in poetic prophetic literature:

- **Judgment oracles** are those consisting of an indictment and a sentence. They sometimes appear clearly with the formulae described above. For example, Amos 4.1 begins with "Hear this word," which is followed by an indictment of those in Samaria. Then v. 2, which commences with an oath formula, "the Lord GOD has sworn by his holiness," offers the sentence. In other cases, no formulae are present. Hosea 4.7–10 is structured as a judgment oracle, with vv. 7–8 as the indictment and vv. 9–10 as the sentence, but without any of the formulae. Consistency of theme or imagery also can help readers of prophetic poetry. For example, the imagery of a hot oven helps unify Hosea 6.11b–7.7 whereas the imagery of a child integrates Hosea 11.1–2 with vv. 3–4.

Other forms that prophets used to convey their messages include:

- The **woe oracle** (Isa 10.1–4).
- The **lawsuit** (Mic 1.2–7), which stemmed from the ancient law court.
- **Hymns** (Hab 3.2–15), which arose in Temple worship.
- **Wisdom sayings** (Am 3.3–8) or proverbs, which originated in schools.
- **Allegories**★ (Ezek 17.2–10).
- **Songs** (Isa 5.1–2).

These forms of speaking, as noted, originated in various sectors of ancient Israelite society. As a result, one may infer that the prophets used forms of speaking (or writing) well known to their audience. Still, they were not slavish in their deployment of these forms. For example, though the lament★ had its roots in funeral lamentation, Amos used a lament in reference to Israel (Am 5.1–2), suggesting that they were as good as dead.

Prophetic literature grew over time. Sayings were collected, for instance, those about the foreign nations in Amos 1–2. More sayings were added to the collections, as in Jeremiah 36.32. Some prophecies were updated. Isaiah 16.13 reads, "This was the word that the LORD spoke concerning Moab in the past," referring to that which appears in Isa 15.1–16.12. Isaiah 16.14 then offers a new saying about Moab, "But now the LORD says…." Clearly the prophet was updating his collection of sayings about Moab. In some cases, new prophetic material from a much later period was added to an earlier collection. Most scholars agree that Isaiah 40–66 was composed over one hundred fifty years later than were the oracles spoken by Isaiah son of Amoz and preserved in Isaiah 1–39. And even after prophetic books were more or less complete, additions were made to them. For example, Hosea 14.9 moves beyond the world of figurative and interrogative rhetoric★ that characterizes much of Hosea to the quieter world of wisdom literature. References to the "wise," the "discerning," and "the way(s) of the LORD" are prominent in the book of Proverbs. It is likely that a scribe★ added Hosea 14.9 to that book in order to integrate it with the wisdom literature and, in so doing, suggesting that the wisdom literature and prophetic literature belong together in ways that might not be obvious to the casual reader.

In sum, although prophets were talented speakers and/or writers, they used a number of standard forms to convey their messages. But within these constraints, one of their most distinctive qualities was the figurative speech in which they couched their message. The deuteronomistic★ historian also indicted Israel for worshiping a god or gods other than Yahweh. However, only a great poet would have described Israel's God as "the fountain of living water" and other gods as "cracked cisterns that can hold no water" (Jer 2.13). The same could be said of ringing phrases such as Isaiah's "every valley shall be lifted up, and every mountain and hill be made low," Hosea's "for they sow the wind, and they shall reap the whirlwind" (Hos 8.7), and Amos's "but let justice roll down like waters, and righteousness like an ever-flowing stream" (Am 5.24).

ISAIAH

Introduction

In the second division of the Hebrew Bible canon,* the Prophets, Isaiah is the first of the four major books, or collections, of prophecies. The other three are Jeremiah, Ezekiel, and the twelve minor prophets (Hosea—Malachi) formed into one book. Isaiah contains prophecies originating with Isaiah son of Amoz in the eighth century BCE, which have been recorded, added to, and edited during the following three centuries. Its sixty-six chapters, which comprise a "collection of collections," can bewilder the reader because of the complex manner in which the individual units have been structured. Three major themes dominate the book. First is the unity and destiny of Israel as the people of the LORD God as they face the threat posed by imperial domination from Mesopotamia (Assyria, Babylonia, and Persia). Second, Jerusalem is the spiritual center and symbol of Israel's role among the nations of the world. Third, the Davidic dynasty* bears a special significance. David, the founder, had first established a united kingdom of Israel, with a capital in Jerusalem. The fate of this royal house plays a dominant role in the prophecies of chs. 6–12, but thereafter the theme appears less prominently. This link with the language and themes associated with the Davidic kingship and its future has made Isaiah the "messianic" prophet of the Old Testament. (Messiah* means "anointed* one," a key royal title.)

READING GUIDE

Because the book of Isaiah took shape over a period of several centuries, it is helpful to consider its major divisions separately. These divisions are marked by separate headings and provide evidence of the book's final editorial shaping. Six major units make up the scroll of Isaiah.

1–4	General introduction: Warning and promise for Judah and Jerusalem
5–12	Warnings to Jerusalem and its royal house
13–27	Warnings and laments addressed to foreign nations and peoples
28–39	Threats to Jerusalem and its great deliverance
40–55	The renewal of hope for Jerusalem
56–66	The coming of the light

The primary historical context for the book is reflected in chs. 6–9, the period between 740–732 BCE. The people of Israel had become divided into two kingdoms, Israel and Judah (the prophet calls them "houses"). Israel (Ephraim) and Syria were attempting to depose the reigning Davidic king of Judah. However, the Judahite king, Ahaz, retained his throne, but in order to do so bought support from Assyria, thereby involving the entire region in the oppressive control of this Mesopotamian power. Further encounters with Assyria led to the destruction of Israel (see Isa 9.8–10.4). When Judah also later rebelled against Assyria, both its ruler, Hezekiah, and the city of Jerusalem were spared the fate that had overtaken Israel (see Isa 36.1–37.38). This reprieve helped emphasize the importance of the religious foundations of Jerusalem's life: the Temple* and the royal dynasty of David.

Soon after Babylon replaced Assyria as the oppressing Mesopotamian power, the Babylonians destroyed Jerusalem and its Temple and removed the surviving Davidic ruler. As a result, Israel itself was broken apart, with many taken into captivity and others forced to flee. Thereafter, the overthrow of Babylon as the enemy of God's people became a central issue (13.1–14.23; 47.1–15). The rebuilding of Jerusalem, the return of the scattered exiles to form once again a united people, and (with considerable caution) the reestablishing of the covenant* with the royal house of David (Isa 55.1–6), are the major subject of the prophecies in the later part (chs. 40–66). The very latest sections (especially chs. 24–27) look to a time when the world will be governed by the direct rule of God, who will come in judgment to punish the wicked and establish peace and justice. This reign will end the oppressive rule of foreign powers and of wrongdoers among God's own people. Only then will peace and justice be established under the Davidic royal house in the city of Jerusalem. Isaiah is therefore uniquely within the Bible the prophet of the Kingdom of God.

The book of Isaiah, which reflects events extending through at least three centuries, was written and edited throughout this extended period. The alternative—that the eighth-century prophet foresaw events of a future time and referred to them as having already occurred—would mean that the prophet was meaninglessly and unrealistically detached from the people he addressed. It was vital to the role of the prophet to influence the minds of his hearers, not only in penitence and faith toward God, but in major political decisions of state leading to war or peace. To understand many of the individual prophecies, it is important to understand their political background.

The book itself develops along thematic, rather than narrowly historical, lines. Central among these are promises of the importance of Jerusalem as the city to which the nations of the world will make pilgrimage (see 2.1–4; 60.1–22), the role of the Davidic monarchy in upholding the just rule of God (11.1–5), and the overthrow of Assyria and Babylon as examples of worldly oppression and violence (14.4–11, 12–21). These prophecies declaring God's purpose for the world express broad themes rather than focusing on specific events. Frequently, earlier prophecies are alluded to in later ones and revised or supplemented (this is called intertextuality*). Even more significant are instances in which words, names, and word pictures are used and then later reinterpreted in subsequent prophecies (see, for example, the reinterpretation of the word picture of *briers and thorns* from 5.6 in 7.23–25; 9.18; 10.17; 27.4). Such intertextuality attests to the intricate process according to which new prophecies were formed out of earlier ones. In recognizing this process, we begin to understand how prophetic sayings and then scrolls were built into books. Once the biblical scrolls had achieved a fixed form, Jewish scribes used similar techniques to construct entire books, which became commentaries on the original canonical ones.

Prophets were originally speakers rather than writers, but once their words were recorded, the writings were brought together and edited so that their lasting message could be kept alive and understood. To interpret a prophetic book, we must attend both to the original situation and to the need to relate one saying to other sayings and to the outcome of events addressed by the prophet. By linking together the separate parts of the prophetic book, we can expect to discern a coherent and enduring message from God. The prophet was God's messenger, declaring a word that possessed divine authority, both in rebuke for wrongdoing and disobedience and in promise for future salvation of an entire people. The process of making spoken prophecies into books was one in which questions of authorship and time of origin cannot always now be answered with certainty. The primary issue was the unity, consistency, and integrity of God's purpose.

Isaiah 1–4

GENERAL INTRODUCTION: WARNING AND PROMISE FOR JUDAH AND JERUSALEM

Chapters 1–4 present two major themes that integrate the book's separate parts. The first theme is the promise of God that Jerusalem (Zion*) will become a center of pilgrimage for the nations of the world (2.1–4) and will be the center from which the knowledge of God will radiate (4.2–6). The second theme, which reappears repeatedly, is that Jerusalem itself must first be purged of wrongdoers and its citizens must repent and turn to seek God's righteousness (1.1–31). Proof of the city's ungodly ways is found in the greed, idolatry,* love of luxury, and indifference to the plight of the poor that characterize its citizens (2.6–22; 3.13–4.1). It is because of such deeds that the land lies in ruin and desolation (1.7–9; 3.1–12).

The historical situation of chs. 1–4 is that of the fifth century BCE when Jerusalem lay at the center of a community of Jews settled in Judah, but served also as the spiritual center and focus for a far wider number living in various parts of the Persian empire. Many were settled still further away, in Egypt and North Africa. Given Judah's political weakness, the need for a firm and consistent focus for the religious life and loyalty of all Jews was paramount. The written legacy of the eighth-century prophet Isaiah of Jerusalem presented Jerusalem as a central source of authority and leadership and as the place to which all these scattered communities would return to make Israel once again their national homeland. Authentic prophecies from Isaiah were preserved and edited to provide this message of new hope. The message of chs. 1–4 reflects directly that of 56–66, indicating a planned structure to the finished book.

READING GUIDE

The main theme of these introductory chapters is the call to penitence and a renewal of commitment to the LORD (ch. 1). Hope for the future is given in 2.1–4 and 4.2–6 in visions of the new glory and authority of Jerusalem, the city that provides assurance of God's blessing. Between these promises the prophet points to the ills and wrongs of the community which hinder the fulfillment of God's purpose.

1.1–20	The ruin and desolation of the land of Judah
2.1–22	Jerusalem: its destiny and wrongdoing
3.1–4.1	Confusion in Judah and Jerusalem
3.13–4.1	The LORD's case against the people
4.2–6	The glory of the new Jerusalem

1 The vision of Isaiah son of Amoz, which he saw concerning Judah and Jerusalem in the days of Uzziah, Jotham, Ahaz, and Hezekiah, kings of Judah.

2 Hear, O heavens, and listen, O earth;
    for the LORD has spoken:
I reared children and brought
        them up,
    but they have rebelled against me.

3 The ox knows its owner,
    and the donkey its master's crib;
but Israel does not know,
    my people do not understand.

4 Ah, sinful nation,
    people laden with iniquity,
offspring who do evil,
    children who deal corruptly,

who have forsaken the LORD,
  who have despised the Holy One of
    Israel,
  who are utterly estranged!

5 Why do you seek further beatings?
  Why do you continue to rebel?
The whole head is sick,
  and the whole heart faint.
6 From the sole of the foot even to the
    head,
  there is no soundness in it,
but bruises and sores
  and bleeding wounds;
they have not been drained, or bound up,
  or softened with oil.

7 Your country lies desolate,
  your cities are burned with fire;
in your very presence
  aliens devour your land;
  it is desolate, as overthrown by
    foreigners.
8 And daughter Zion is left
  like a booth in a vineyard,
like a shelter in a cucumber field,
  like a besieged city.
9 If the LORD of hosts
  had not left us a few survivors,
we would have been like Sodom,
  and become like Gomorrah.

**1.1–20: The ruin and desolation of Jerusalem and
the land of Judah. 1–9:** The portrayal of the desolation
of the land and the isolated situation of Jerusalem
probably refers to the events of 701 BCE in which the
Assyrian king, Sennacherib, laid siege to the city (see
36.1–37.38). Such attacks were repeated in later times
and hence provide a context for the whole book. The
prophet's rebuke shows how the people's own wrongdoing had brought about their misfortunes. **8:** The
booth and *shelter* in *vineyard* and *field* were watchmen's huts set up to protect the vines and crops.

---

10 Hear the word of the LORD,
  you rulers of Sodom!
Listen to the teaching of our God,
  you people of Gomorrah!
11 What to me is the multitude of your
    sacrifices?
  says the LORD;

I have had enough of burnt offerings of
    rams
  and the fat of fed beasts;
I do not delight in the blood of bulls,
  or of lambs, or of goats.

12 When you come to appear before me,[a]
  who asked this from your hand?
Trample my courts no more;
13 bringing offerings is futile;
  incense is an abomination to me.
New moon and sabbath and calling of
    convocation—
  I cannot endure solemn assemblies
    with iniquity.
14 Your new moons and your appointed
    festivals
  my soul hates;
they have become a burden to me,
  I am weary of bearing them.
15 When you stretch out your hands,
  I will hide my eyes from you;
even though you make many prayers,
  I will not listen;
your hands are full of blood.
16 Wash yourselves; make yourselves
    clean;
  remove the evil of your doings
    from before my eyes;
cease to do evil,
17   learn to do good;
seek justice,
  rescue the oppressed,
defend the orphan,
  plead for the widow.

18 Come now, let us argue it out,
  says the LORD:
though your sins are like scarlet,
  they shall be like snow;
though they are red like crimson,
  they shall become like wool.
19 If you are willing and obedient,
  you shall eat the good of the land;
20 but if you refuse and rebel,
  you shall be devoured by the sword;
for the mouth of the LORD has
    spoken.

a Or *see my face*

1.10–20: Criticisms of the Temple* rituals and prayers show that without justice and compassion they are meaningless to God, who ignores them.

21 How the faithful city
     has become a whore!
   She that was full of justice,
   righteousness lodged in her—
     but now murderers!
22 Your silver has become dross,
     your wine is mixed with water.
23 Your princes are rebels
     and companions of thieves.
   Everyone loves a bribe
     and runs after gifts.
   They do not defend the orphan,
     and the widow's cause does not come
       before them.

24 Therefore says the Sovereign, the LORD
       of hosts, the Mighty One of
       Israel:
   Ah, I will pour out my wrath on my
       enemies,
     and avenge myself on my foes!
25 I will turn my hand against you;
     I will smelt away your dross as with
       lye
     and remove all your alloy.
26 And I will restore your judges as at the
       first,
     and your counselors as at the
       beginning.
   Afterward you shall be called the city of
       righteousness,
     the faithful city.
27 Zion shall be redeemed by justice,
     and those in her who repent, by
       righteousness.
28 But rebels and sinners shall be
       destroyed together,
     and those who forsake the LORD shall
       be consumed.
29 For you shall be ashamed of the oaks
     in which you delighted;
   and you shall blush for the gardens
     that you have chosen.
30 For you shall be like an oak
     whose leaf withers,
     and like a garden without water.

31 The strong shall become like tinder,
     and their work*a* like a spark;
   they and their work shall burn together,
     with no one to quench them.

1.21–31: As a royal city, Jerusalem was a center for the administration of justice over which the king presided. The failure to uphold such justice allowed the most serious crimes to go unpunished. God would therefore have to take action, not only against the criminal wrongdoers, but also against those whose indifference encouraged evil deeds. **29:** The *oaks* were simple rustic shrines, devoted to fertility and the gods and goddesses who were believed to guarantee life-giving power.

2 The word that Isaiah son of Amoz saw
   concerning Judah and Jerusalem.

2 In days to come
     the mountain of the LORD's house
   shall be established as the highest of the
       mountains,
     and shall be raised above the hills;
   all the nations shall stream to it.
3   Many peoples shall come and say,
   "Come, let us go up to the mountain of
       the LORD,
     to the house of the God of Jacob;
   that he may teach us his ways
     and that we may walk in his paths."
   For out of Zion shall go forth
       instruction,
     and the word of the LORD from
       Jerusalem.
4 He shall judge between the nations,
     and shall arbitrate for many peoples;
   they shall beat their swords into
       plowshares,
     and their spears into pruning hooks;
   nation shall not lift up sword against
       nation,
     neither shall they learn war any more.

2.1–22: Jerusalem: its destiny and wrongdoing. 1–4: From the time of David's adoption of the city as his capital, Jerusalem had been celebrated as the place to which many nations paid homage and brought tribute (see Ps 2.2–11). This memorable prophecy re-

a Or *its makers*

interprets this theme, giving divine assurance that the city will become a center from which God's law will be administered among the nations (the city's name is related to the Hebrew word for peace, "shalom." Peace, God's purpose for all nations (v. 4), can only come when there is justice.

5 O house of Jacob,
    come, let us walk
    in the light of the LORD!
6 For you have forsaken the ways of*a* your
        people,
    O house of Jacob.
    Indeed they are full of diviners*b* from
        the east
    and of soothsayers like the
        Philistines,
    and they clasp hands with foreigners.
7 Their land is filled with silver and gold,
    and there is no end to their treasures;
    their land is filled with horses,
    and there is no end to their chariots.
8 Their land is filled with idols;
    they bow down to the work of their
        hands,
    to what their own fingers have made.
9 And so people are humbled,
    and everyone is brought low—
    do not forgive them!
10 Enter into the rock,
    and hide in the dust
    from the terror of the LORD,
    and from the glory of his majesty.
11 The haughty eyes of people shall be
        brought low,
    and the pride of everyone shall be
        humbled;
    and the LORD alone will be exalted on
        that day.
12 For the LORD of hosts has a day
    against all that is proud and lofty,
    against all that is lifted up and high;*c*
13 against all the cedars of Lebanon,
        lofty and lifted up;
    and against all the oaks of Bashan;
14 against all the high mountains,
    and against all the lofty hills;
15 against every high tower,
    and against every fortified wall;
16 against all the ships of Tarshish,
    and against all the beautiful craft.*d*

17 The haughtiness of people shall be
        humbled,
    and the pride of everyone shall be
        brought low;
    and the LORD alone will be exalted on
        that day.
18 The idols shall utterly pass away.
19 Enter the caves of the rocks
    and the holes of the ground,
    from the terror of the LORD,
    and from the glory of his majesty,
    when he rises to terrify the earth.
20 On that day people will throw away
    to the moles and to the bats
    their idols of silver and their idols of
        gold,
    which they made for themselves to
        worship,
21 to enter the caverns of the rocks
    and the clefts in the crags,
    from the terror of the LORD,
    and from the glory of his majesty,
    when he rises to terrify the earth.
22 Turn away from mortals,
    who have only breath in their
        nostrils,
    for of what account are they?

2.5–22. 5–11: Jerusalem, seeking commercial prosperity and success, neglected its spiritual foundations. *On that day* (v. 11) points to an indefinite time of God's judgment and comes to refer to the great judgment and renewal for Judah and all nations (see Isa 25.9). 12–22: The prophet depicts God's punishment of human pride through the image of bringing down natural features such as tall trees and *high mountains* (vv. 12–15). Arrogance is the root of idolatry★ (vv. 19–20), the belief that human beings can control the divine realm. The Day of the LORD (v. 11) now points to God's judgment against human violence and disregard of the divine laws. The *ships of Tarshish* (v. 16) were the famed trading ships of the maritime nations of the Mediterranean. In Gen 10.4 Tarshish is a great-grandson of Noah, but the several biblical references to it as a place point to its fame as a source of trade, especially trade in precious metals. It is often located in southwestern Spain, but probably more

a Heb lacks *the ways of*　*b* Cn: Heb lacks *of diviners*
c Cn Compare Gk: Heb *low*　*d* Compare Gk: Meaning of Heb uncertain

than one site where mining and metal-refining took place bore such a name.

3 For now the Sovereign, the LORD of hosts,
is taking away from Jerusalem and from Judah
support and staff—
all support of bread,
and all support of water—
2 warrior and soldier,
judge and prophet,
diviner and elder,
3 captain of fifty
and dignitary,
counselor and skillful magician
and expert enchanter.
4 And I will make boys their princes,
and babes shall rule over them.
5 The people will be oppressed,
everyone by another
and everyone by a neighbor;
the youth will be insolent to the elder,
and the base to the honorable.

6 Someone will even seize a relative,
a member of the clan, saying,
"You have a cloak;
you shall be our leader,
and this heap of ruins
shall be under your rule."
7 But the other will cry out on that day,
saying,
"I will not be a healer;
in my house there is neither bread
nor cloak;
you shall not make me
leader of the people."
8 For Jerusalem has stumbled
and Judah has fallen,
because their speech and their deeds
are against the LORD,
defying his glorious presence.

9 The look on their faces bears witness
against them;
they proclaim their sin like Sodom,
they do not hide it.
Woe to them!
For they have brought evil on
themselves.

10 Tell the innocent how fortunate they
are,
for they shall eat the fruit of their
labors.
11 Woe to the guilty! How unfortunate
they are,
for what their hands have done shall
be done to them.
12 My people—children are their
oppressors,
and women rule over them.
O my people, your leaders mislead you,
and confuse the course of your paths.

3.1–4.1: Confusion in Judah and Jerusalem. 1–8: The city and land will suffer famine and the loss of their natural resources, bringing confusion and panic. There will be no capable judges and elders (vv. 1–5), bringing economic ruin and social chaos (v. 6) with the breakdown of law and order. The broader context indicates that this is the consequence of oppressive foreign invasions and interference (see chs. 5–12). 9–12: The readers of that time would know, only too well, the ruined state of Judah and its chief city. Disobedience and indifference to the LORD God had brought such misfortune upon them.

13 The LORD rises to argue his case;
he stands to judge the peoples.
14 The LORD enters into judgment
with the elders and princes of his
people:
It is you who have devoured the
vineyard;
the spoil of the poor is in your houses.
15 What do you mean by crushing my
people,
by grinding the face of the poor? says
the Lord GOD of hosts.

16 The LORD said:
Because the daughters of Zion are
haughty
and walk with outstretched necks,
glancing wantonly with their eyes,
mincing along as they go,
tinkling with their feet;
17 the Lord will afflict with scabs
the heads of the daughters of Zion,
and the LORD will lay bare their
secret parts.

18 In that day the Lord will take away the finery of the anklets, the headbands, and the crescents; 19the pendants, the bracelets, and the scarfs; 20the headdresses, the armlets, the sashes, the perfume boxes, and the amulets; 21the signet rings and nose rings; 22the festal robes, the mantles, the cloaks, and the handbags; 23the garments of gauze, the linen garments, the turbans, and the veils.

24 Instead of perfume there will be a
      stench;
   and instead of a sash, a rope;
 and instead of well-set hair, baldness;
   and instead of a rich robe, a binding
      of sackcloth;
   instead of beauty, shame.ᵃ
25 Your men shall fall by the sword
   and your warriors in battle.
26 And her gates shall lament and mourn;
   ravaged, she shall sit upon the
      ground.

4 Seven women shall take hold of one man in that day, saying,
   "We will eat our own bread and wear
      our own clothes;
   just let us be called by your name;
      take away our disgrace."

3.13–4.1: The Lord's case against the people. The reasons for Judah's misfortunes are detailed in a lawsuit which God is bringing against the people. 15–16: Oppression of the poor and women who indulge in absurd luxury are outward signs of a spiritual sickness. Accordingly, God's punishment will fit the offense (v. 24): The horrors of warfare will reduce many of the women who had so pampered themselves to a state of destitution (3.25–4.1).

2 On that day the branch of the LORD shall be beautiful and glorious, and the fruit of the land shall be the pride and glory of the survivors of Israel. 3Whoever is left in Zion and remains in Jerusalem will be called holy, everyone who has been recorded for life in Jerusalem, 4once the Lord has washed away the filth of the daughters of Zion and cleansed the bloodstains of Jerusalem from its midst by a spirit of judgment and by a spirit of burning. 5Then the LORD will create over the whole site of Mount Zion and over its places of assembly a cloud by day and smoke and the shining of a flaming fire by night. Indeed over all the glory there will be a canopy. 6It will serve as a pavilion, a shade by day from the heat, and a refuge and a shelter from the storm and rain.

4.2–6: The glory of the new Jerusalem. 5–6: Judgment is the necessary path to the renewal of hope and to the dawning of a time of justice and world peace. Hence, the opening chapters conclude with the vision of a chastened and glorified Jerusalem in which the presence of God will be evident everywhere (vv. 5–6). The visionary presentation is filled with symbolic word pictures in which the title the branch of the LORD (v. 2) refers to the new Davidic king (compare 11.1). As God had led the ancestors of the nation through the desert (see Ex 13.21–22), so now the same presence would indicate the protection and blessing of the favored city. The pictures of shade and shelter (v. 6) counter the warnings of the sufferings and trials in 3.1–4.1.

---

a Q Ms: MT lacks shame

Isaiah 5–12

WARNINGS TO JERUSALEM AND ITS ROYAL HOUSE

These chapters, the oldest part of the book, contain prophecies from 740–732 BCE. There may be an Isaiah "memoir" in 6.1–8.18, part of which is written in the first person, and in which the prophet recounts his call and the three children's sign-names that contain divine messages. Chapter 5 prepares for this memoir with a general warning that God's "vineyard" (Israel) will soon be destroyed (5.1–7) by a far-away nation (5.26–30), Assyria. Further threats of danger and destruction follow (8.19–22). Fresh hope beyond these warnings comes with the promise of the birth to the house of David of a new king, who will bring deliverance (9.2–7). Judah's sister kingdom in the north, Ephraim, will not share this deliverance (9.8–21).

The perspective changes with the assurance in 10.5–15 that Assyria also, having been God's instrument of punishment, will itself be punished. A series of warnings in word pictures (10.16–34) reaffirms Assyria's overthrow. Israel's fortunes after the collapse of Assyrian domination with the rise of Babylon are briefly outlined (11.1–16). The glowing hope of 9.2–7, that deliverance will come through the new ruler from the Davidic dynasty,* is developed further in 11.1–5, followed by assurance that the entire world order will be transformed in the new age of salvation (11.6–9). At this time survivors of the kingdoms of Judah and Israel who had become scattered among many nations will return to their homeland (11.10–16). A psalm-like hymn of praise and thanksgiving to God for this great final hope brings the collection to a close in ch. 12.

The memoir of 6.1–8.18 probably belongs to the period of the war between Judah and Ephraim (in alliance with Syria) in the years 735–732 BCE. The death of King Uzziah (6.1) initiated a major political crisis, which threatened the survival of the Davidic dynasty. It brought Assyria onto the scene in a way that proved destructive for the entire region. This memoir has, however, been supplemented by many additions that take account of subsequent events. The impact that Assyria was to have upon Judah and Israel for more than a century colors the prophecies of 10.5–34. Chapter 11 takes into account the subsequent dominance of Babylon when Jerusalem was destroyed (587 BCE).

READING GUIDE

5.1–30   The song of the vineyard
6.1–13   The prophet's call and commission
7.1–8.4   The message of the names of three children
8.5–22   The rejection of the prophet's message
9.1–7   Light in the darkness
9.8–10.4 No respite for the land of Ephraim
10.5–34   Assyria will not escape the judgment of God
11.1–16   The renewal of God's promise
12.1–6   A psalm of thanksgiving

5 Let me sing for my beloved
  my love-song concerning his
      vineyard:
My beloved had a vineyard
  on a very fertile hill.
2 He dug it and cleared it of stones,
  and planted it with choice vines;
he built a watchtower in the midst of it,
  and hewed out a wine vat in it;
he expected it to yield grapes,
  but it yielded wild grapes.

3 And now, inhabitants of Jerusalem
  and people of Judah,

judge between me
  and my vineyard.
4 What more was there to do for my
      vineyard
  that I have not done in it?
When I expected it to yield grapes,
  why did it yield wild grapes?

5 And now I will tell you
  what I will do to my vineyard.
I will remove its hedge,
  and it shall be devoured;
I will break down its wall,
  and it shall be trampled down.

6 I will make it a waste;
   it shall not be pruned or hoed,
   and it shall be overgrown with briers
      and thorns;
I will also command the clouds
   that they rain no rain upon it.

7 For the vineyard of the LORD of hosts
   is the house of Israel,
and the people of Judah
   are his pleasant planting;
he expected justice,
   but saw bloodshed;
righteousness,
   but heard a cry!

8 Ah, you who join house to house,
   who add field to field,
until there is room for no one but you,
   and you are left to live alone
   in the midst of the land!

9 The LORD of hosts has sworn in my
      hearing:
Surely many houses shall be desolate,
   large and beautiful houses, without
      inhabitant.

10 For ten acres of vineyard shall yield but
      one bath,
   and a homer of seed shall yield a
      mere ephah.ᵃ

11 Ah, you who rise early in the morning
   in pursuit of strong drink,
who linger in the evening
   to be inflamed by wine,

12 whose feasts consist of lyre and harp,
   tambourine and flute and wine,
but who do not regard the deeds of the
      LORD,
   or see the work of his hands!

13 Therefore my people go into exile
      without knowledge;
their nobles are dying of hunger,
   and their multitude is parched with
      thirst.

14 Therefore Sheol has enlarged its
      appetite
   and opened its mouth beyond
      measure;
the nobility of Jerusalemᵇ and her
      multitude go down,
   her throng and all who exult in her.

15 People are bowed down, everyone is
      brought low,
   and the eyes of the haughty are
      humbled.

16 But the LORD of hosts is exalted
      by justice,
   and the Holy God shows himself holy
      by righteousness.

17 Then the lambs shall graze as in their
      pasture,
   fatlings and kidsᶜ shall feed among
      the ruins.

18 Ah, you who drag iniquity along with
      cords of falsehood,
   who drag sin along as with cart ropes,

19 who say, "Let him make haste,
   let him speed his work
   that we may see it;
let the plan of the Holy One of Israel
      hasten to fulfillment,
   that we may know it!"

20 Ah, you who call evil good
   and good evil,
who put darkness for light
   and light for darkness,
who put bitter for sweet
   and sweet for bitter!

21 Ah, you who are wise in your own eyes,
   and shrewd in your own sight!

22 Ah, you who are heroes in drinking wine
   and valiant at mixing drink,

23 who acquit the guilty for a bribe,
   and deprive the innocent of their
      rights!

24 Therefore, as the tongue of fire devours
      the stubble,
   and as dry grass sinks down in the
      flame,
so their root will become rotten,
   and their blossom go up like dust;
for they have rejected the instruction of
      the LORD of hosts,
   and have despised the word of the
      Holy One of Israel.

25 Therefore the anger of the LORD was
      kindled against his people,

a The Heb *bath*, *homer*, and *ephah* are measures of
quantity   b Heb *her nobility*   c Cn Compare Gk:
Heb *aliens*

and he stretched out his hand against
  them and struck them;
the mountains quaked,
and their corpses were like refuse
  in the streets.
For all this his anger has not turned
  away,
  and his hand is stretched out still.

5.1–30: The song of the vineyard. 1–7: The parable*
of an unfruitful vineyard is an apparently unremarkable
story whose full meaning only becomes clear when the
storyteller reveals that he is describing Israel and Judah.
The verdict of v. 6 is valid also for this larger meaning:
The land must soon suffer utter devastation and ruin.
This is the theme-message which underlies all the
prophecies of chs. 5–12 (see especially 6.11–13). The
parable is made more complex by the opening address
in which the speaker declares: *Let me sing for my beloved my love-song.* As a "friend" of the injured vineyard owner, the speaker is an interested onlooker or
perhaps the owner's supporter at a feast. In this case,
the claim to present a *love-song* suggests that the story
will be about a disappointed lover (see the use of vineyard imagery for courtship in Song 8.11–12). In v. 7
the vineyard represents both *Israel* and *Judah.* **8–24:**
The conduct of the ruling classes in Jerusalem involved
greed, manipulation of justice, violence, and dishonesty. Divine judgment is therefore necessary. The concluding part of this indictment may occur in 10.1–3,
with 5.25 correspondingly misplaced from 9.8–21.

26 He will raise a signal for a nation far
      away,
    and whistle for a people at the ends
      of the earth;
    Here they come, swiftly, speedily!
27 None of them is weary, none
      stumbles,
    none slumbers or sleeps,
    not a loincloth is loose,
    not a sandal-thong broken;
28 their arrows are sharp,
    all their bows bent,
    their horses' hoofs seem like flint,
    and their wheels like the whirlwind.
29 Their roaring is like a lion,
    like young lions they roar;
    they growl and seize their prey,
    they carry it off, and no one
      can rescue.

30 They will roar over it on that day,
    like the roaring of the sea.
    And if one look to the land—
      only darkness and distress;
    and the light grows dark with clouds.

5.26–30: This key prophetic declaration shows clearly
how the judgment will fall upon the land of Israel and
Judah and that, although a foreign nation will bring
about the devastation, the voice of God has summoned it. The image of God acting against Israel by
raising *a signal for a nation far away* becomes a repeated theme showing how God acts to control human destiny (see 11.10–12; 49.22). Although in this
pronouncement the identity of the distant nation is
not revealed, one quickly discovers that it is Assyria
(see 7.17; 8.4).

6 In the year that King Uzziah died, I saw
  the Lord sitting on a throne, high and
lofty; and the hem of his robe filled the temple. ²Seraphs were in attendance above him;
each had six wings: with two they covered
their faces, and with two they covered their
feet, and with two they flew. ³And one called
to another and said:
  "Holy, holy, holy is the LORD of hosts;
    the whole earth is full of his glory."
⁴The pivots*a* on the thresholds shook at the
voices of those who called, and the house
filled with smoke. ⁵And I said: "Woe is me!
I am lost, for I am a man of unclean lips, and
I live among a people of unclean lips; yet my
eyes have seen the King, the LORD of hosts!"
  ⁶ Then one of the seraphs flew to me,
holding a live coal that had been taken from
the altar with a pair of tongs. ⁷The seraph*b*
touched my mouth with it and said: "Now
that this has touched your lips, your guilt has
departed and your sin is blotted out." ⁸Then
I heard the voice of the Lord saying, "Whom
shall I send, and who will go for us?" And I
said, "Here am I; send me!" ⁹And he said,
"Go and say to this people:
  'Keep listening, but do not comprehend;
  keep looking, but do not understand.'
10 Make the mind of this people dull,
      and stop their ears,
      and shut their eyes,

a Meaning of Heb uncertain   *b* Heb *He*

so that they may not look with their
    eyes,
and listen with their ears,
and comprehend with their minds,
    and turn and be healed."
11 Then I said, "How long, O Lord?" And
    he said:
"Until cities lie waste
    without inhabitant,
and houses without people,
    and the land is utterly desolate;
12 until the LORD sends everyone
        far away,
    and vast is the emptiness in the midst
        of the land.
13 Even if a tenth part remain in it,
        it will be burned again,
    like a terebinth or an oak
        whose stump remains standing
        when it is felled."[a]
    The holy seed is its stump.

6.1–13: The prophet's call and commission. 1–8:
The year in which *King Uzziah died* is not precisely
known, but his death occurred sometime between
742 and 736 BCE. The king (also called Azariah, 2 Kings
15.1–7) had been stricken with severe illness (2 Kings
15.5), which meant that his son Jotham served for a
time as co-regent with him before succeeding to the
throne (2 Kings 15.7). This co-regency period must be
included in the sixteen years ascribed Jotham's reign
(2 Kings 15.33). It was in this time that a major conflict
arose between an alliance of Syria-Israel (Ephraim) and
Judah (2 Kings 15. 37). The central issue was resistance
against Assyrian expansion in the region (see 2 Kings
15.17–20). Judah's neighbors intended to remove
Ahaz from his throne and to replace him with an otherwise unknown figure called Tabeel (7.6). Isaiah's call
therefore came at a time when Assyrian interference
was beginning to cause severe political upheaval in the
region. **9–10:** The sharp irony* of the commission
given to Isaiah implies awareness of the popular hostility to his message and the people's refusal to accept
it (see 8.11–15). **11:** One of Isaiah's central warnings
is that the entire land of Israel will be ruined because
of the rejection of God's message. The continuing relevance of these prophecies led to their preservation in
this book. **12–13:** The cruel Assyrian policy of exiling
whole populations (see 36.17) is reflected in this warning. The further threat that, even after severe devastation, the land will be *burned again* reflects later

awareness of depredations by both Assyrian and Babylonian armies.

7 In the days of Ahaz son of Jotham son
of Uzziah, king of Judah, King Rezin of
Aram and King Pekah son of Remaliah of
Israel went up to attack Jerusalem, but could
not mount an attack against it. 2When the
house of David heard that Aram had allied
itself with Ephraim, the heart of Ahaz[b] and
the heart of his people shook as the trees of
the forest shake before the wind. 3 Then the LORD said to Isaiah, Go out
to meet Ahaz, you and your son Shear-ja-
shub,[c] at the end of the conduit of the upper
pool on the highway to the Fuller's Field,
4and say to him, Take heed, be quiet, do not
fear, and do not let your heart be faint because of these two smoldering stumps of
firebrands, because of the fierce anger of Rezin and Aram and the son of Remaliah. 5Be-
cause Aram—with Ephraim and the son of
Remaliah—has plotted evil against you,
saying, 6Let us go up against Judah and cut
off Jerusalem[d] and conquer it for ourselves
and make the son of Tabeel king in it; 7there-
fore thus says the Lord GOD:
    It shall not stand,
        and it shall not come to pass.
8 For the head of Aram is Damascus,
    and the head of Damascus is Rezin.
    (Within sixty-five years Ephraim will be
shattered, no longer a people.)
9 The head of Ephraim is Samaria,
    and the head of Samaria is the son of
        Remaliah.
    If you do not stand firm in faith,
    you shall not stand at all.

**7.1–8.4: The message of the names of three chil-
dren. 7.1–3:** For the political context, see 2 Kings
16.5–9. The threat to depose Ahaz was an attempt to
force Judah into joining the anti-Assyrian coalition. The
king countered by seeking assistance from Assyria
(2 Kings 16.7–9), trying to secure his throne and gain
an advantage over Ephraim in a territorial quarrel (see
2 Kings 14.25). Ahaz's overture to Assyria was disas-

---

a Meaning of Heb uncertain *b* Heb *his heart*
c That is *A remnant shall return*
d Heb *cut it off*

trous. Isaiah conveys a message through children's names: Shear-jashub, Immanuel, and Maher-Shalal-hashbaz. The first is already the prophet's infant son, whereas the third had not even been conceived when his name was given and inscribed on a tablet (8.1–2). At the child's birth, witnesses would unveil the pre-scribed name (8.2). The name of the second child, Im-manuel (7.14), may indicate a royal figure, an heir to the throne who would assure the future of the dynasty* to the troubled Ahaz. It is more probable, however, that, like the other two, the child is the prophet's and the unnamed young woman of 7.14 is the prophet's wife. **3:** *Shear-jashub,* "a remnant re-turns," implies the defeat of the armies threatening Jerusalem and their return home in greatly reduced numbers. It could later be interpreted in other ways (see 10.20–23). **6:** *The son of Tabeel* is not otherwise identified, and it is not even clear that he was from a Judahite family. The prophet's emphatic form of ad-dress to the king (v. 13) implies that the future of the royal dynasty was threatened. **8:** The note on the dis-solution of *Ephraim* (Israel) reflects an editor's aware-ness that the veiled threat was fulfilled.

10 Again the LORD spoke to Ahaz, saying, ¹¹Ask a sign of the LORD your God; let it be deep as Sheol or high as heaven. ¹²But Ahaz said, I will not ask, and I will not put the LORD to the test. ¹³Then Isaiah*a* said: "Hear then, O house of David! Is it too little for you to weary mortals, that you weary my God also? ¹⁴Therefore the Lord himself will give you a sign. Look, the young woman*b* is with child and shall bear a son, and shall name him Immanuel.*c* ¹⁵He shall eat curds and honey by the time he knows how to refuse the evil and choose the good. ¹⁶For before the child knows how to refuse the evil and choose the good, the land before whose two kings you are in dread will be deserted. ¹⁷The LORD will bring on you and on your people and on your ancestral house such days as have not come since the day that Ephraim departed from Judah—the king of Assyria."

7.10–17. The king rejects a sign, showing that he had not abandoned his plan to seek help from Assyria. **11:** The *sign* indicated that the prophetic word would, in due course, be fulfilled. *Sheol** was the place to which the spirits of the dead descended and is here used for

poetic emphasis. **14:** In spite of the traditional trans-lation of *the young woman* as "virgin," the Hebrew noun implies no more than a woman of marriageable age. The prophet's right to confer the child's name indicates that she was probably his wife. In the context of concern about the future of the Davidic line, how-ever, the child may be a royal heir, possibly Hezekiah, who succeeded Ahaz on the throne of Judah. The later "messianic*" interpretation of prophecies relating to the Davidic kingship belongs to the period after this royal dynasty ceased to rule in Jerusalem (9.2–7; 11.1–5; 55.3–5). *Immanuel,* "God with us," is an ex-clamation used in worship to affirm God's presence and protection (see Ps 46.11). Ahaz had no need to seek help from Assyria when God was his true helper. **15–17:** Eating *curds and honey* and refusing *the evil* and choosing *the good* came at the time (1–2 years of age) when the child would begin to take solid food and respond to parental discipline. Within less than two years Judah's present enemies would have been forced to flee home. *The day that Ephraim departed* refers to the time when the united kingdom of Israel, over which David and Solomon had reigned, split over allegiance to the Davidic dynasty* (see 1 Kings 12.1–19).

18 On that day the LORD will whistle for the fly that is at the sources of the streams of Egypt, and for the bee that is in the land of Assyria. ¹⁹And they will all come and set-tle in the steep ravines, and in the clefts of the rocks, and on all the thornbushes, and on all the pastures.

20 On that day the Lord will shave with a razor hired beyond the River—with the king of Assyria—the head and the hair of the feet, and it will take off the beard as well.

21 On that day one will keep alive a young cow and two sheep, ²²and will eat curds be-cause of the abundance of milk that they give; for everyone that is left in the land shall eat curds and honey.

23 On that day every place where there used to be a thousand vines, worth a thou-sand shekels of silver, will become briers and thorns. ²⁴With bow and arrows one will go there, for all the land will be briers and

a Heb *he*   *b* Gk *the virgin*
c That is *God is with us*

thorns; [25]and as for all the hills that used to be hoed with a hoe, you will not go there for fear of briers and thorns; but they will become a place where cattle are let loose and where sheep tread.

7.18–25: Further interpretations* of the prophet's words. A series of short statements spells out the message of the prophet. **18–19:** The *fly* and the *bee* symbolize the threat from Egypt and Assyria: Israel and Judah were sandwiched between two major world powers. **20:** The hired *razor* is Assyria, which would ravage and destroy Israel's entire land. **21–22:** A further interpretation is given of the sign in v. 15. **23–25:** Three fresh interpretations are provided of the *briers and thorns* from the parable* of the vineyard in 5.1–7. **24:** The *briers and thorns* are soldiers with *bows and arrows.*

8 Then the LORD said to me, Take a large tablet and write on it in common characters, "Belonging to Maher-shalal-hash-baz,"[a] [2]and have it attested[b] for me by reliable witnesses, the priest Uriah and Zechariah son of Jeberechiah. [3]And I went to the prophetess, and she conceived and bore a son. Then the LORD said to me, Name him Maher-shalal-hash-baz; [4]for before the child knows how to call "My father" or "My mother," the wealth of Damascus and the spoil of Samaria will be carried away by the king of Assyria.

8.1–4: The sign-name of Maher-shalal-hash-baz. This is the third message attached to the name of a child, which had not yet been conceived when the name was given. The name, "The spoil speeds, the prey hastens," points to the defeat of the forces threatening Judah. The witnesses would confirm that the name was given before the child had been conceived.

5 The LORD spoke to me again: [6]Because this people has refused the waters of Shiloah that flow gently, and melt in fear before[c] Rezin and the son of Remaliah; [7]therefore, the Lord is bringing up against it the mighty flood waters of the River, the king of Assyria and all his glory; it will rise above all its channels and overflow all its banks; [8]it will sweep on into Judah as a flood, and, pouring over, it will reach up to the neck; and its outspread

wings will fill the breadth of your land, O Immanuel.

[9] Band together, you peoples, and be dismayed;
    listen, all you far countries;
    gird yourselves and be dismayed;
    gird yourselves and be dismayed!
[10] Take counsel together, but it shall be brought to naught;
    speak a word, but it will not stand,
    for God is with us.[d]

11 For the LORD spoke thus to me while his hand was strong upon me, and warned me not to walk in the way of this people, saying: [12]Do not call conspiracy all that this people calls conspiracy, and do not fear what it fears, or be in dread. [13]But the LORD of hosts, him you shall regard as holy; let him be your fear, and let him be your dread. [14]He will become a sanctuary, a stone one strikes against; for both houses of Israel he will become a rock one stumbles over—a trap and a snare for the inhabitants of Jerusalem. [15]And many among them shall stumble; they shall fall and be broken; they shall be snared and taken.

16 Bind up the testimony, seal the teaching among my disciples. [17]I will wait for the LORD, who is hiding his face from the house of Jacob, and I will hope in him. [18]See, I and the children whom the LORD has given me are signs and portents in Israel from the LORD of hosts, who dwells on Mount Zion. [19]Now if people say to you, "Consult the ghosts and the familiar spirits that chirp and mutter; should not a people consult their gods, the dead on behalf of the living, [20]for teaching and for instruction?" surely, those who speak like this will have no dawn! [21]They will pass through the land,[e] greatly distressed and hungry; when they are hungry, they will be enraged and will curse[f] their king and their gods. They will turn their faces upward, [22]or they will look to the earth, but will see only distress and darkness,

a That is *The spoil speeds, the prey hastens*   *b* Q Ms Gk Syr: MT *and I caused to be attested*   *c* Cn: Meaning of Heb uncertain   *d* Heb *immanu el*   *e* Heb *it*   *f* Or *curse by* the gloom of anguish; and they will be thrust into thick darkness.*

8.5–22: The rejection of the prophet's message. 5–8: The message of the names is refused. Isaiah becomes the bearer of a new message: Ahaz will indeed seek military help from Assyria (see 2 Kings 16.7–9), but it would open the floodgates to a torrent that would overwhelm the entire land, immersing Judah as well as the sister kingdom in the north. **9–10:** The prophet proclaims: God will establish justice upon earth (the book's overall message; compare 14.24–27; 17.12–14; and see Introduction to chs. 13–27). **11–22:** The prophet retires from public activity until the truth of his warning is established. Verse 16 refers to the *testimony* of the name inscribed on the tablet in 8.1, so the *disciples* are the witnesses of 8.2. The prophet's written "memoir" would originally have ended at v. 18, reemphasizing the message of his children's names, the message the king had rejected. **12–15:** Isaiah, isolated and spurned, is accused of *conspiracy*, although it was the king who had committed conspiracy against God. **19–22:** Short prophecies warn of the folly of rejecting the true word of God. When, in despair, the people turn to seek assurance and knowledge of the future from the forbidden practice of consulting sorcerers and the spirits of the dead, they will simply plunge themselves into deeper darkness.

9 *b*But there will be no gloom for those who were in anguish. In the former time he brought into contempt the land of Zebulun and the land of Naphtali, but in the latter time he will make glorious the way of the sea, the land beyond the Jordan, Galilee of the nations.
² *c*The people who walked in darkness
    have seen a great light;
  those who lived in a land of deep
       darkness—
  on them light has shined.
³ You have multiplied the nation,
  you have increased its joy;
  they rejoice before you
    as with joy at the harvest,
    as people exult when dividing
       plunder.
⁴ For the yoke of their burden,
  and the bar across their shoulders,
  the rod of their oppressor,

you have broken as on the day of
      Midian.
⁵ For all the boots of the tramping
    warriors
  and all the garments rolled in blood
  shall be burned as fuel for the fire.
⁶ For a child has been born for us,
  a son given to us;
  authority rests upon his shoulders;
  and he is named
  Wonderful Counselor, Mighty God,
  Everlasting Father, Prince of
      Peace.
⁷ His authority shall grow continually,
  and there shall be endless peace
  for the throne of David and his
      kingdom.
  He will establish and uphold it
  with justice and with righteousness
  from this time onward and
      forevermore.
The zeal of the LORD of hosts will do
  this.

9.1–7: Light in the darkness. A brief editorial note looks ahead to the time when the darkness of Assyrian destruction will end and a new era of peace and hope will dawn. The difficult text anticipates the celebrated prophecy of the new king that follows. **2–7: The coming of a new king.** A coronation hymn celebrates the coming of a new king who would restore the honor, fame, and authority of David's royal house (see Ps 2 for a similar royal coronation hymn). The new ruler would reverse the harm wrought by Ahaz. The new king is probably Hezekiah, Ahaz's successor (2 Kings 16.20). His accession* year is uncertain (perhaps 725 or 715 BCE). His ascent to the throne marked the beginning of new royal policy, which was expected to bring a change in the nation's fortunes. Since Hezekiah was not successful in ending Assyria's rule (Isa 36–39), it may be Josiah (639–609 BCE) whose reforming reign is foretold. Under Josiah, Assyrian control over Judah finally ended. The arrival of the new king is described as a royal birth, which involves divine assurance for the royal dynasty. The "birth" probably refers to the king's coronation, a moment of spiritual rebirth (Ps 2.7).

---

a Meaning of Heb uncertain   *b* Ch 8.23 in Heb
c Ch 9.1 in Heb

8 The Lord sent a word against Jacob,
  and it fell on Israel;
9 and all the people knew it—
  Ephraim and the inhabitants of
    Samaria—
  but in pride and arrogance of heart
    they said:
10 "The bricks have fallen,
  but we will build with dressed stones;
  the sycamores have been cut down,
  but we will put cedars in their place."
11 So the LORD raised adversaries[a] against
    them,
  and stirred up their enemies,
12 the Arameans on the east and the
    Philistines on the west,
  and they devoured Israel with open
    mouth.
  For all this his anger has not turned
    away;
  his hand is stretched out still.

13 The people did not turn to him who
    struck them,
  or seek the LORD of hosts.
14 So the LORD cut off from Israel head
    and tail,
  palm branch and reed in one day—
15 elders and dignitaries are the head,
  and prophets who teach lies are the
    tail;
16 for those who led this people led them
    astray,
  and those who were led by them were
    left in confusion.
17 That is why the Lord did not have pity
    on[b] their young people,
  or compassion on their orphans and
    widows;
  for everyone was godless and an
    evildoer,
  and every mouth spoke folly.
  For all this his anger has not turned
    away;
  his hand is stretched out still.

18 For wickedness burned like a fire,
  consuming briers and thorns;
  it kindled the thickets of the forest,
  and they swirled upward in a column
    of smoke.

19 Through the wrath of the LORD of hosts
    the land was burned,
  and the people became like fuel for the
    fire;
  no one spared another.
20 They gorged on the right, but still were
    hungry,
  and they devoured on the left, but
    were not satisfied;
  they devoured the flesh of their own
    kindred;[c]
21 Manasseh devoured Ephraim, and
    Ephraim Manasseh,
  and together they were against Judah.
  For all this his anger has not turned
    away;
  his hand is stretched out still.

10 Ah, you who make iniquitous
      decrees,
  who write oppressive statutes,
2 to turn aside the needy from justice
  and to rob the poor of my people of
    their right,
  that widows may be your spoil,
  and that you may make the orphans
    your prey!
3 What will you do on the day of
    punishment,
  in the calamity that will come from
    far away?
  To whom will you flee for help,
  and where will you leave your
    wealth,
4 so as not to crouch among the
    prisoners
  or fall among the slain?
  For all this his anger has not turned
    away;
  his hand is stretched out still.

**9.8–10.4: No respite for the land of Ephraim.
9.8–21:** The Assyrian intervention proved ruinous.
Judah fared less badly than Ephraim; 2 Kings 17.5–23
tells how Ephraim was destroyed (see also Isa 7.8).
The prophet warns against pride and complacency
(vv. 9–10) in trusting that ruin would be overcome.
During the following half-century, persistent external

a Cn: Heb *the adversaries of Rezin*   b Q Ms: MT
rejoice over   c Or *arm*

interference and internal conflicts ruined the region of Ephraim-Samaria. Not till the reign of Josiah more than a century later were serious attempts made to reunite parts of this land with Judah. **10.1–4:** Verses 1–3 belong to the condemnation of the leaders of Jerusalem in 5.8–24 (note also the use of the refrain from 9.8–21 in 5.25), while 10.4 clearly belongs to the warning against Ephraim (9.8–21).

5 Ah, Assyria, the rod of my anger—
  the club in their hands is my fury!
6 Against a godless nation I send him,
  and against the people of my wrath I
    command him,
  to take spoil and seize plunder,
  and to tread them down like the mire
    of the streets.
7 But this is not what he intends,
  nor does he have this in mind;
  but it is in his heart to destroy,
  and to cut off nations not a few.
8 For he says:
  "Are not my commanders all kings?
9 Is not Calno like Carchemish?
  Is not Hamath like Arpad?
  Is not Samaria like Damascus?
10 As my hand has reached to the
    kingdoms of the idols
  whose images were greater than those
    of Jerusalem and Samaria,
11 shall I not do to Jerusalem and
    her idols
  what I have done to Samaria and her
    images?"

12 When the Lord has finished all his work on Mount Zion and on Jerusalem, he[a] will punish the arrogant boasting of the king of Assyria and his haughty pride. 13For he says:
  "By the strength of my hand I have
    done it,
  and by my wisdom, for I have
    understanding;
  I have removed the boundaries of
    peoples,
  and have plundered their treasures;
  like a bull I have brought down those
    who sat on thrones.
14 My hand has found, like a nest,
  the wealth of the peoples;

  and as one gathers eggs that have been
    forsaken,
  so I have gathered all the earth;
  and there was none that moved a wing,
  or opened its mouth, or chirped."

15 Shall the ax vaunt itself over the one
    who wields it,
  or the saw magnify itself against the
    one who handles it?
  As if a rod should raise the one who lifts
    it up,
  or as if a staff should lift the one who
    is not wood!
16 Therefore the Sovereign, the LORD of
    hosts,
  will send wasting sickness among his
    stout warriors,
  and under his glory a burning will be
    kindled,
  like the burning of fire.
17 The light of Israel will become a fire,
  and his Holy One a flame;
  and it will burn and devour
  his thorns and briers in one day.
18 The glory of his forest and his fruitful
    land
  the LORD will destroy, both soul and
    body,
  and it will be as when an invalid
    wastes away.
19 The remnant of the trees of his forest
    will be so few
  that a child can write them down.

10.5–34: Assyria will not escape the judgment of God. 5–19: Assyria was the agent of God, but its ministers were arrogant and blasphemous (see 36.13–20). When God judged that the time was ripe (v. 2) Assyria would suffer a severe punishment from God (vv. 15–19), set out in a series of word-pictures related to other sayings. **17–19:** The tree imagery is related to the language of "briers and thorns" in 5.6 (see 7.23–25; 9.18; possibly also relates to the wooden rod of 9.4 and 10.5).

20 On that day the remnant of Israel and the survivors of the house of Jacob will no more lean on the one who struck them, but

a Heb *I*

will lean on the LORD, the Holy One of Israel, in truth. 21A remnant will return, the remnant of Jacob, to the mighty God. 22For though your people Israel were like the sand of the sea, only a remnant of them will return. Destruction is decreed, overflowing with righteousness. 23For the Lord GOD of hosts will make a full end, as decreed, in all the earth.*

24 Therefore thus says the Lord GOD of hosts: O my people, who live in Zion, do not be afraid of the Assyrians when they beat you with a rod and lift up their staff against you as the Egyptians did. 25For in a very little while my indignation will come to an end, and my anger will be directed to their destruction. 26The LORD of hosts will wield a whip against them, as when he struck Midian at the rock of Oreb; his staff will be over the sea, and he will lift it as he did in Egypt. 27On that day his burden will be removed from your shoulder, and his yoke will be destroyed from your neck.

He has gone up from Rimmon,*b*
28   he has come to Aiath;
he has passed through Migron,
   at Michmash he stores his baggage;
29 they have crossed over the pass,
   at Geba they lodge for the night;
Ramah trembles,
   Gibeah of Saul has fled.
30 Cry aloud, O daughter Gallim!
   Listen, O Laishah!
   Answer her, O Anathoth!
31 Madmenah is in flight,
   the inhabitants of Gebim flee
      for safety.
32 This very day he will halt at Nob,
   he will shake his fist
   at the mount of daughter Zion,
   the hill of Jerusalem.

33 Look, the Sovereign, the LORD of
      hosts,
   will lop the boughs with terrifying
      power;
   the tallest trees will be cut down,
   and the lofty will be brought low.
34 He will hack down the thickets of the
      forest with an ax,

and Lebanon with its majestic trees*c*
   will fall.

10.20–34. 20–27a: "Shear-jashub" of 7.3, "a remnant returns," could be understood in more than one way, as the three interpretations of vv. 21–23 show. There would be a future nation, but shaped by suffering and loss. Only some of the nation would survive. Similarly, the interpretations in vv. 24–27a of "the rod of their oppressor" (9.4) show that God would free Judah from foreign domination. 27b–32: This short passage probably refers to the march on Jerusalem by Sennacherib in 701 BCE, the background for Isaiah's later prophecies (see chs. 28–30 and 36–37). It is out of chronological sequence with the events in chs. 7–9 (the reign of King Ahaz). However, its abrupt ending with the oppressor threatening, but not attacking, Jerusalem (v. 32) fits the Assyrian punitive campaign into Judah during the reign of Hezekiah, whose accession* is foretold in 9.2–7. 33–34: The outcome of Sennacherib's campaign is presented as the cutting down of the *forest* foretold in vv. 18–19. The failure to complete the punitive attack upon Jerusalem in 701 was a judgment of God upon Assyria's blasphemous boasts. The events in chs. 36–37 are understood to fulfill the punishment on Assyria declared in 10.15–19.

11 A shoot shall come out from the
      stump of Jesse,
   and a branch shall grow out of his
      roots.
2 The spirit of the LORD shall rest
      on him,
   the spirit of wisdom and
      understanding,
   the spirit of counsel and might,
   the spirit of knowledge and the fear
      of the LORD.
3 His delight shall be in the fear of the
      LORD.

He shall not judge by what his eyes see,
   or decide by what his ears hear;
4 but with righteousness he shall judge
      the poor,
   and decide with equity for the meek
      of the earth;

a Or *land*   *b* Cn: Heb *and his yoke from your neck, and a yoke will be destroyed because of fatness*
c Cn Compare Gk Vg: Heb *with a majestic one*

he shall strike the earth with the rod of
his mouth,
and with the breath of his lips he
shall kill the wicked.
5 Righteousness shall be the belt around
his waist,
and faithfulness the belt around his
loins.

6 The wolf shall live with the lamb,
the leopard shall lie down with the
kid,
the calf and the lion and the fatling
together,
and a little child shall lead them.
7 The cow and the bear shall graze,
their young shall lie down together;
and the lion shall eat straw like
the ox.
8 The nursing child shall play over the
hole of the asp,
and the weaned child shall put its
hand on the adder's den.
9 They will not hurt or destroy
on all my holy mountain;
for the earth will be full of the
knowledge of the LORD
as the waters cover the sea.

10 On that day the root of Jesse shall
stand as a signal to the peoples; the nations
shall inquire of him, and his dwelling shall
be glorious.
11 On that day the Lord will extend his
hand yet a second time to recover the remnant that is left of his people, from Assyria,
from Egypt, from Pathros, from Ethiopia,*
from Elam, from Shinar, from Hamath, and
from the coastlands of the sea.
12 He will raise a signal for the nations,
and will assemble the outcasts of
Israel,
and gather the dispersed of Judah
from the four corners of the earth.
13 The jealousy of Ephraim shall depart,
the hostility of Judah shall be cut off;
Ephraim shall not be jealous of Judah,
and Judah shall not be hostile
towards Ephraim.
14 But they shall swoop down on the backs
of the Philistines in the west,

together they shall plunder the people
of the east.
They shall put forth their hand against
Edom and Moab,
and the Ammonites shall obey them.
15 And the LORD will utterly destroy
the tongue of the sea of Egypt;
and will wave his hand over the River
with his scorching wind;
and will split it into seven channels,
and make a way to cross on foot;
16 so there shall be a highway from
Assyria
for the remnant that is left of
his people,
as there was for Israel
when they came up from the land of
Egypt.

11.1–16: The renewal of God's promise. 1–5: The
shoot from *the stump of Jesse* refers to the situation
after the Babylonians had removed the last of the Davidic rulers, Zedekiah (2 Kings 25.1–7). His predecessor and nephew, Jehoiachin, had been taken and held
prisoner in Babylon (2 Kings 24.10–12), and this
prophecy reflects the hope that either he, or one of his
descendants, would return to rule (see 55.1–5; 1 Chr
3.16–24). This hope was not fulfilled, and the promises
of Davidic kingship became a messianic* hope. 6–9:
An addition that conveys a wider message than one of
government and justice: a time of world peace extending throughout the natural order, witnessing the
end of violence, not simply between nations (see Isa
2.4) but between wild and domestic animals. The violence and disorder that had confounded God's purpose since the beginning would be transformed by the
fashioning of a new heaven and a new earth (66.2–3).
As a prominent, and unique, hope in Isaiah, the message is repeated in 65.25. 10–16: Chapters 5–12 form
a connected series of prophecies, from the devastation
foretold in 6.11–13 until the return of survivors to re-
populate it and to rebuild Jerusalem. This promise of
return forms a significant feature of the book's overall
message. Detailed promises of this return begin in chs.
40–55. Prophecies fulfilling that hope are included in
chs. 56–66. As God's judgment had been heralded by
a signal to a "nation far away" (5.26), so the ending
of the period of judgment and the dawning of the age

a Or Nubia; Heb Cush

of peace would begin with a further *signal* to all *nations* (11.10–12).

〜〜〜〜〜〜〜〜〜〜〜〜〜〜〜〜〜〜〜〜〜〜

12 You will say in that day:
I will give thanks to you, O LORD,
for though you were angry with me,
your anger turned away,
and you comforted me.

2 Surely God is my salvation;
I will trust, and will not be afraid,
for the LORD GOD *a* is my strength and
my might;
he has become my salvation.

3 With joy you will draw water from the wells of salvation. ⁴And you will say in that day:

Give thanks to the LORD,
call on his name;
make known his deeds among the
nations;
proclaim that his name is exalted.

⁵ Sing praises to the LORD, for he has
done gloriously;
let this be known *b* in all the
earth.
⁶ Shout aloud and sing for joy, O royal *c*
Zion,
for great in your midst is the Holy
One of Israel.

───────────────

12.1–6: A psalm of thanksgiving. Isaiah has been constructed to form a series of "books within books." A psalm of thanksgiving for the salvation of God which will surely come to Jerusalem concludes the section that began in 5.1. These shorter collections display a broad editorial structure where hope and promise follow threats and warnings. Even the punitive fires of judgment are placed within this larger context of the saving purpose of God.

〜〜〜〜〜〜〜〜〜〜〜〜〜〜〜〜〜〜〜〜〜〜

a Heb *for Yah, the* LORD   *b* Or *this is made known*
c Or *O inhabitant of*

Isaiah 13–27

WARNINGS AND LAMENTS ADDRESSED TO FOREIGN NATIONS AND PEOPLES

This collection contains pronouncements that are predominantly threats to the nations caught up in the world events that had affected Israel and Judah. In chs. 24–27 there is a radical and reassuring promise that these times of trial will end with a new era of God's justice. The prophecies against the nations begin in 13.1–14.23 with oracles* against Babylon. After returning to the renewed announcement of Assyria's inevitable downfall in 14.24–27, they deal in turn with Philistia, Moab, Syria, Egypt, and Arabia. Prophecies relating to Jerusalem (the "valley of vision") in ch. 22 are followed by a lament* for Tyre (Phoenicia) in ch. 23. Chapters 24–27 conclude in 27.12–13 with a promise like that in 11.10–16: The survivors will return to their homeland.

The historical background begins with the first instances of Isaiah's prophesying (see comment on 6.1), when the threat from Assyria marked the first step toward the breakup and dismemberment of Israel and Judah. It extends until sometime after the fall of Babylon to a combined Medo-Persian army in 538 BCE. The prophecies of chs. 24–27 probably derive from this late period, when the further overthrow of this Medo-Persian power was awaited, with the expectation that it would begin the direct rule of God on earth. There is little agreement about the origins of the oracles in chs. 13–23. Some of them are dated (see 14.28; 20.1), but the present shape of this part of the book presents an overview of God's purpose for all nations from the perspective of the years of Assyrian and Babylonian rule over Judah. The context thus extends over more than two centuries.

READING GUIDE

The prophecies concerning foreign cities and nations present a variety of feelings and attitudes. In the case of Babylon there is an understandable sense of exultation that a terrifying oppressor has at last received just punishment. In the case of Moab, one confronts the grievous pain and suffering that the people will endure, while in the case of Tyre there is the theme that God humbles human pride and achievement. The prophecies relating to Egypt are of special interest, partly because Egyptian promises of military aid to Judah had repeatedly failed to materialize and had, thereby, proved disastrous for God's people. Yet there is also a profound spiritual message of hope in the belief that Egypt, too, would eventually share in the universal knowledge and blessing of the one LORD (19.18–25).

13 The oracle concerning Babylon that Isaiah son of Amoz saw.

2 On a bare hill raise a signal,
cry aloud to them;
wave the hand for them to enter
the gates of the nobles.
3 I myself have commanded my
consecrated ones,
have summoned my warriors, my
proudly exulting ones,
to execute my anger.

4 Listen, a tumult on the mountains
as of a great multitude!
Listen, an uproar of kingdoms,
of nations gathering together!
The LORD of hosts is mustering
an army for battle.

5 They come from a distant land,
from the end of the heavens,
the LORD and the weapons of his
indignation,
to destroy the whole earth.

6 Wail, for the day of the LORD is near;
it will come like destruction from the
Almighty!a
7 Therefore all hands will be feeble,
and every human heart will melt,
8 and they will be dismayed.
Pangs and agony will seize them;
they will be in anguish like a woman
in labor.
They will look aghast at one another;
their faces will be aflame.

a Traditional rendering of Heb *Shaddai*

9 See, the day of the LORD comes,
  cruel, with wrath and fierce anger,
  to make the earth a desolation,
    and to destroy its sinners from it.
10 For the stars of the heavens and their
      constellations
    will not give their light;
  the sun will be dark at its rising,
    and the moon will not shed its light.
11 I will punish the world for its evil,
    and the wicked for their iniquity;
  I will put an end to the pride of
      the arrogant,
    and lay low the insolence of
      tyrants.
12 I will make mortals more rare than fine
      gold,
    and humans than the gold of Ophir.
13 Therefore I will make the heavens
      tremble,
  and the earth will be shaken out of its
      place,
    at the wrath of the LORD of hosts
    in the day of his fierce anger.
14 Like a hunted gazelle,
    or like sheep with no one to gather
      them,
  all will turn to their own people,
    and all will flee to their own lands.
15 Whoever is found will be thrust
      through,
  and whoever is caught will fall by the
      sword.
16 Their infants will be dashed to pieces
      before their eyes;
  their houses will be plundered,
    and their wives ravished.
17 See, I am stirring up the Medes against
      them,
  who have no regard for silver
    and do not delight in gold.
18 Their bows will slaughter the young
      men;
  they will have no mercy on the fruit
      of the womb;
    their eyes will not pity children.
19 And Babylon, the glory of kingdoms,
    the splendor and pride of the
      Chaldeans,
  will be like Sodom and Gomorrah
    when God overthrew them.

20 It will never be inhabited
    or lived in for all generations;
  Arabs will not pitch their tents there,
    shepherds will not make their flocks
      lie down there.
21 But wild animals will lie down there,
    and its houses will be full of howling
      creatures;
  there ostriches will live,
    and there goat-demons will dance.
22 Hyenas will cry in its towers,
    and jackals in the pleasant palaces;
  its time is close at hand,
    and its days will not be prolonged.

13.1–22: The overthrow of Babylon. 1–22: It is a surprise that *Babylon,* rather than Assyria, is the great oppressing power to be punished for its excesses and cruelties. The reason lies in the importance of Babylon for
the structure of the book: Chs. 40–55 reflect the period of Babylonian imperial control over the nations
dealt with in chs. 13–23. Reference to the attacking
Medes (v. 17) points to this fierce prophecy as a forewarning of the defeat of Babylon in 538 BCE, later
anticipated so eagerly in chs. 46–47. Judah's bitter
sufferings at the hands of Babylon explain the vengeful spirit in vv. 14–16 and the longing that such a
great kingdom should become a perpetual ruin (vv.
20–22).

14 But the LORD will have compassion
on Jacob and will again choose Israel, and will set them in their own land; and
aliens will join them and attach themselves
to the house of Jacob. 2And the nations will
take them and bring them to their place, and
the house of Israel will possess the nations*a*
as male and female slaves in the LORD's land;
they will take captive those who were their
captors, and rule over those who oppressed
them.

3 When the LORD has given you rest from
your pain and turmoil and the hard service
with which you were made to serve, 4you will
take up this taunt against the king of
Babylon:

  How the oppressor has ceased!
    How his insolence*b* has ceased!

a Heb *them*   *b* Q Ms Compare Gk Syr Vg: Meaning of
MT uncertain

5 The LORD has broken the staff of the
wicked,
the scepter of rulers,
6 that struck down the peoples in wrath
with unceasing blows,
that ruled the nations in anger
with unrelenting persecution.
7 The whole earth is at rest and quiet;
they break forth into singing.
8 The cypresses exult over you,
the cedars of Lebanon, saying,
"Since you were laid low,
no one comes to cut us down."
9 Sheol beneath is stirred up
to meet you when you come;
it rouses the shades to greet you,
all who were leaders of the earth;
it raises from their thrones
all who were kings of the nations.
10 All of them will speak
and say to you:
"You too have become as weak as we!
You have become like us!"
11 Your pomp is brought down to Sheol,
and the sound of your harps;
maggots are the bed beneath you,
and worms are your covering.

12 How you are fallen from heaven,
O Day Star, son of Dawn!
How you are cut down to the ground,
you who laid the nations low!
13 You said in your heart,
"I will ascend to heaven;
I will raise my throne
above the stars of God;
I will sit on the mount of assembly
on the heights of Zaphon;^{a}
14 I will ascend to the tops of the clouds,
I will make myself like the Most High."
15 But you are brought down to Sheol,
to the depths of the Pit.
16 Those who see you will stare at you,
and ponder over you:
"Is this the man who made the earth
tremble,
who shook kingdoms,
17 who made the world like a desert
and overthrew its cities,
who would not let his prisoners go
home?"

18 All the kings of the nations lie in glory,
each in his own tomb;
19 but you are cast out, away from your
grave,
like loathsome carrion,^{b}
clothed with the dead, those pierced by
the sword,
who go down to the stones of the Pit,
like a corpse trampled underfoot.
20 You will not be joined with them
in burial,
because you have destroyed your land,
you have killed your people.

May the descendants of evildoers
nevermore be named!
21 Prepare slaughter for his sons
because of the guilt of their father.^{c}
Let them never rise to possess the earth
or cover the face of the world with
cities.

14.1–23: A mocking lament★ **for the death of the
king of Babylon. 1–2:** The Babylonian threat occupies
most of chs. 40–55, so this great world power takes
on a symbolic role as the supreme example of oppression. This editorial note provides a summary of the
message of hope (chs. 56–66; see also 11.12–16).
3–11: A brilliant, mocking lament for the death of the
king of Babylon ironically contrasts the king's power in
life and powerlessness in death and celebrates the
passing of Babylon as a world power. No ruler is
named, and, apart from the introductory heading in
v. 4, direct identification with Babylon is lacking. The
original subject may be some earlier ruler's death, possibly the Assyrian Shalmaneser V (whose death in 705
occurred during Isaiah's ministry and had major re-
percussions for Judah's political stance). But this passage celebrates the downfall of tyranny rather than the
death of a specific individual. *Sheol*★ (vv. 11, 15) is the
mysterious underworld to which spirits descended after death. The spirits of other dead persons rise up in
amazement that a figure once so proud and supreme
could be brought so low (vv. 16–20). **12–15:** The *Day
Star, son of Dawn* is the Morning Star (Venus). **16–21:**
In extensive royal households other sons were usually
a threat to a crown prince (see 37.38).

---

a Or *assembly in the far north*   *b* Cn Compare Gk:
Heb *like a loathed branch*   *c* Syr Compare Gk: Heb
fathers

22 I will rise up against them, says the LORD of hosts, and will cut off from Babylon name and remnant, offspring and posterity, says the LORD. 23And I will make it a possession of the hedgehog, and pools of water, and I will sweep it with the broom of destruction, says the LORD of hosts.

24 The LORD of hosts has sworn:
   As I have designed,
      so shall it be;
   and as I have planned,
      so shall it come to pass:
25 I will break the Assyrian in my land,
      and on my mountains trample him
         under foot;
   his yoke shall be removed from them,
      and his burden from their shoulders.
26 This is the plan that is planned
      concerning the whole earth;
   and this is the hand that is stretched
         out
      over all the nations.
27 For the LORD of hosts has planned,
      and who will annul it?
   His hand is stretched out,
      and who will turn it back?

14.24–27: Assyria will suffer divine judgment (see 10.5–34), and, although out of chronological sequence, this is a warning to all nations who threaten God's people (vv. 26–27; see 8.9–10; 17.12–14). In the literary and historical structure of Isa 13–27, the historical rise and fall of the great imperial powers was a preparation for God's rule.

28In the year that King Ahaz died this oracle came:

29 Do not rejoice, all you Philistines,
      that the rod that struck you
         is broken,
   for from the root of the snake will come
         forth an adder,
      and its fruit will be a flying
         fiery serpent.
30 The firstborn of the poor will graze,
      and the needy lie down in safety;
   but I will make your root die of
         famine,
      and your remnant I[a] will kill.

31 Wail, O gate; cry, O city;
      melt in fear, O Philistia, all of you!
   For smoke comes out of the north,
      and there is no straggler in its ranks.

32 What will one answer the messengers of
         the nation?
   "The LORD has founded Zion,
      and the needy among his people
      will find refuge in her."

15

An oracle concerning Moab.

Because Ar is laid waste in a night,
      Moab is undone;
because Kir is laid waste in a night,
      Moab is undone.
2 Dibon[b] has gone up to the temple,
      to the high places to weep;
   over Nebo and over Medeba
      Moab wails.
   On every head is baldness,
      every beard is shorn;
3 in the streets they bind on sackcloth;
      on the housetops and in the squares
      everyone wails and melts in tears.
4 Heshbon and Elealeh cry out,
      their voices are heard as far as
         Jahaz;
   therefore the loins of Moab quiver;[c]
      his soul trembles.
5 My heart cries out for Moab;
      his fugitives flee to Zoar,
      to Eglath-shelishiyah.
   For at the ascent of Luhith
      they go up weeping;
   on the road to Horonaim
      they raise a cry of destruction;
6 the waters of Nimrim
      are a desolation;
   the grass is withered, the new growth
         fails,
      the verdure is no more.
7 Therefore the abundance they
         have gained
      and what they have laid up

a Q Ms Vg: MT he   b Cn: Heb the house and Dibon
c Cn Compare Gk Syr: Heb the armed men of Moab cry
aloud

they carry away
   over the Wadi of the Willows.
8 For a cry has gone
   around the land of Moab;
the wailing reaches to Eglaim,
   the wailing reaches to Beer-elim.
9 For the waters of Dibon[a] are full
   of blood;
yet I will bring upon Dibon[a] even
   more—
a lion for those of Moab who escape,
   for the remnant of the land.

15.1–16.13: Prophecies concerning the downfall of Moab. 15.1–9: *Moab* was one of the smaller kingdoms neighboring Judah in the south and to the east of the River Jordan. It covered much of the territory now occupied by Jordan. Moab, though once a part of David's kingdom (2 Sam 8.2), had broken away and suffered Assyrian and Babylonian exploitation. In the course of one or another campaign, this fearful killing took place.

16 Send lambs
   to the ruler of the land,
from Sela, by way of the desert,
   to the mount of daughter Zion.
2 Like fluttering birds,
   like scattered nestlings,
so are the daughters of Moab
   at the fords of the Arnon.
3 "Give counsel,
   grant justice;
make your shade like night
   at the height of noon;
hide the outcasts,
   do not betray the fugitive;
4 let the outcasts of Moab
   settle among you;
be a refuge to them
   from the destroyer."

When the oppressor is no more,
   and destruction has ceased,
and marauders have vanished from the
   land,
5 then a throne shall be established in
   steadfast love
in the tent of David,
   and on it shall sit in faithfulness
a ruler who seeks justice
   and is swift to do what is right.

6 We have heard of the pride of Moab
   —how proud he is!—
of his arrogance, his pride, and his
   insolence;
   his boasts are false.
7 Therefore let Moab wail,
   let everyone wail for Moab.
Mourn, utterly stricken,
   for the raisin cakes of Kir-hareseth.

8 For the fields of Heshbon languish,
   and the vines of Sibmah,
whose clusters once made drunk
   the lords of the nations,
reached to Jazer
   and strayed to the desert;
their shoots once spread abroad
   and crossed over the sea.
9 Therefore I weep with the weeping of
   Jazer
   for the vines of Sibmah;
I drench you with my tears,
   O Heshbon and Elealeh;
for the shout over your fruit harvest
   and your grain harvest has ceased.
10 Joy and gladness are taken away
   from the fruitful field;
and in the vineyards no songs are sung,
   no shouts are raised;
no treader treads out wine in the presses;
   the vintage-shout is hushed.[b]
11 Therefore my heart throbs like a harp
   for Moab,
   and my very soul for Kir-heres.

12 When Moab presents himself, when he wearies himself upon the high place, when he comes to his sanctuary to pray, he will not prevail.

13 This was the word that the LORD spoke concerning Moab in the past. 14 But now the LORD says, In three years, like the years of a hired worker, the glory of Moab will be brought into contempt, in spite of all its great multitude; and those who survive will be very few and feeble.

16.1–13. 1–11: The appeal to Jerusalem to offer refuge to fugitives from this disaster is a sign of hope that

a Q Ms Vg Compare Syr: MT *Dimon*   *b* Gk: Heb I have hushed

Moab would renew allegiance to a Davidic king. This prophecy may allude to the reign of Josiah, a link with the promise of 32.1–8. Verses 6–11 rebuke *the pride of Moab*. **12–13:** Subsequent to the disaster of 586 BCE, the relations between Judah and Moab worsened.

17

An oracle concerning Damascus.

See, Damascus will cease to be a city,
    and will become a heap of ruins.
2 Her towns will be deserted forever;[a]
    they will be places for flocks,
    which will lie down, and no one will
        make them afraid.
3 The fortress will disappear from
        Ephraim,
    and the kingdom from Damascus;
    and the remnant of Aram will be
    like the glory of the children of Israel,
            says the LORD of hosts.

4 On that day
    the glory of Jacob will be brought low,
    and the fat of his flesh will
        grow lean.
5 And it shall be as when reapers gather
        standing grain
    and their arms harvest the ears,
    and as when one gleans the ears
        of grain
    in the Valley of Rephaim.
6 Gleanings will be left in it,
    as when an olive tree is beaten—
    two or three berries
    in the top of the highest bough,
    four or five
    on the branches of a fruit tree,
            says the LORD God of Israel.

7 On that day people will regard their Maker, and their eyes will look to the Holy One of Israel; 8they will not have regard for the altars, the work of their hands, and they will not look to what their own fingers have made, either the sacred poles[b] or the altars of incense.

9 On that day their strong cities will be like the deserted places of the Hivites and the Amorites,[c] which they deserted because of the children of Israel, and there will be desolation.

10 For you have forgotten the God of your
        salvation,
    and have not remembered the Rock
        of your refuge;
    therefore, though you plant pleasant
        plants
    and set out slips of an alien god,
11 though you make them grow on the day
        that you plant them,
    and make them blossom in the
        morning that you sow;
    yet the harvest will flee away
    in a day of grief and incurable pain.

17. 1–11: Prophecies concerning Israel and Damascus. 1–6: The background is that of the alliance of Syria (Damascus) and Ephraim (Israel) against Judah, which is also present in chs. 7–8. The message is that expressed in the name of Isaiah's son Shear-jashub ("a remnant returns," Isa 7.3). Instead of the defeated remnant of an army, this time the image is that of gleanings* after a harvest. **7–9:** The original threat gives only a general reason for the coming disaster (vv. 10–11); this added warning against trust in the power of idols intensifies the threat (see 2.8). **10–11:** Reference to the hyperbolic* growth of plants reflects a form of fertility ritual with religious (and probably also sexual) significance.

12 Ah, the thunder of many peoples,
    they thunder like the thundering of
        the sea!
    Ah, the roar of nations,
    they roar like the roaring of mighty
        waters!
13 The nations roar like the roaring of
        many waters,
    but he will rebuke them, and they will
        flee far away,
    chased like chaff on the mountains
        before the wind
    and whirling dust before the storm.
14 At evening time, lo, terror!
    Before morning, they are no more.
    This is the fate of those who
        despoil us,
    and the lot of those who plunder us.

a Cn Compare Gk: Heb *the cities of Aroer are deserted*
b Heb *Asherim*   c Cn Compare Gk: Heb *places of the wood and the highest bough*

17.12–14: The defeat of a host of nations when they threaten God's people conforms to the warnings in 8.9–10 and 14.24–27.

18 ¹Ah, land of whirring wings
  beyond the rivers of Ethiopia,ᵃ
² sending ambassadors by the Nile
    in vessels of papyrus on the waters!
  Go, you swift messengers,
    to a nation tall and smooth,
  to a people feared near and far,
    a nation mighty and conquering,
    whose land the rivers divide.

³ All you inhabitants of the world,
    you who live on the earth,
  when a signal is raised on the
      mountains, look!
  When a trumpet is blown, listen!
⁴ For thus the LORD said to me:
  I will quietly look from my dwelling
    like clear heat in sunshine,
    like a cloud of dew in the heat
      of harvest.
⁵ For before the harvest, when the
      blossom is over
    and the flower becomes a ripening
      grape,
  he will cut off the shoots with pruning
      hooks,
    and the spreading branches he will
      hew away.
⁶ They shall all be left
    to the birds of prey of the mountains
    and to the animals of the earth.
  And the birds of prey will summer on
      them,
    and all the animals of the earth will
      winter on them.

⁷ At that time gifts will be brought to the LORD of hosts fromᵇ a people tall and smooth, from a people feared near and far, a nation mighty and conquering, whose land the rivers divide, to Mount Zion, the place of the name of the LORD of hosts.

18.1–7: A prophecy concerning Ethiopia. 1–6: This oracle* probably refers to the situation described in 2 Kings 17.4: Judah sent ambassadors to Ethiopia

(Cush) to negotiate an alliance against Assyria in 724 BCE. Isaiah warns that the LORD does not support such an alliance; it will fail. 7: This anticipation of the hope in 45.14 shows how an observant editor has unified the message of the book.

19 ¹An oracle concerning Egypt.

  See, the LORD is riding on a swift cloud
    and comes to Egypt;
  the idols of Egypt will tremble at his
      presence,
    and the heart of the Egyptians will
      melt within them.
² I will stir up Egyptians against
      Egyptians,
    and they will fight, one against the
      other,
  neighbor against neighbor,
    city against city, kingdom against
      kingdom;
³ the spirit of the Egyptians within them
      will be emptied out,
    and I will confound their plans;
  they will consult the idols and the
      spirits of the dead
    and the ghosts and the familiar spirits;
⁴ I will deliver the Egyptians
    into the hand of a hard master;
  a fierce king will rule over them,
    says the Sovereign, the LORD of hosts.

⁵ The waters of the Nile will be dried up,
    and the river will be parched and dry;
⁶ its canals will become foul,
    and the branches of Egypt's Nile will
      diminish and dry up,
    reeds and rushes will rot away.
⁷ There will be bare places by the Nile,
    on the brink of the Nile;
  and all that is sown by the Nile will
      dry up,
    be driven away, and be no more.
⁸ Those who fish will mourn;
    all who cast hooks in the Nile will
      lament,
  and those who spread nets on the
      water will languish.

ᵃ Or Nubia; Heb Cush   ᵇ Q Ms Gk Vg: MT of

9 The workers in flax will be in despair,
    and the carders and those at the loom
        will grow pale.
10 Its weavers will be dismayed,
    and all who work for wages will be
        grieved.

11 The princes of Zoan are utterly foolish;
    the wise counselors of Pharaoh give
        stupid counsel.
    How can you say to Pharaoh,
    "I am one of the sages,
        a descendant of ancient kings"?
12 Where now are your sages?
    Let them tell you and make known
    what the LORD of hosts has planned
        against Egypt.
13 The princes of Zoan have become
        fools,
    and the princes of Memphis
        are deluded;
those who are the cornerstones of its
        tribes
    have led Egypt astray.
14 The LORD has poured into them[a]
    a spirit of confusion;
and they have made Egypt stagger in all
        its doings
    as a drunkard staggers around
        in vomit.
15 Neither head nor tail, palm branch or
        reed,
    will be able to do anything for
        Egypt.

16 On that day the Egyptians will be like women, and tremble with fear before the hand that the LORD of hosts raises against them. 17 And the land of Judah will become a terror to the Egyptians; everyone to whom it is mentioned will fear because of the plan that the LORD of hosts is planning against them.

18 On that day there will be five cities in the land of Egypt that speak the language of Canaan and swear allegiance to the LORD of hosts. One of these will be called the City of the Sun.

19 On that day there will be an altar to the LORD in the center of the land of Egypt, and a pillar to the LORD at its border. 20 It will be a sign and a witness to the LORD of hosts in the land of Egypt; when they cry to the LORD because of oppressors, he will send them a savior, and will defend and deliver them. 21 The LORD will make himself known to the Egyptians; and the Egyptians will know the LORD on that day, and will worship with sacrifice and burnt offering, and they will make vows to the LORD and perform them. 22 The LORD will strike Egypt, striking and healing; they will return to the LORD, and he will listen to their supplications and heal them.

23 On that day there will be a highway from Egypt to Assyria, and the Assyrian will come into Egypt, and the Egyptian into Assyria, and the Egyptians will worship with the Assyrians.

24 On that day Israel will be the third with Egypt and Assyria, a blessing in the midst of the earth, 25 whom the LORD of hosts has blessed, saying, "Blessed be Egypt my people, and Assyria the work of my hands, and Israel my heritage."

19.1–25: Threats concerning Egypt. 1–15: Throughout the period when Assyria and Babylon were assaulting Israel and Judah, Egypt repeatedly promised protection, yet consistently failed to carry through. "For Egypt's help is worthless and empty" (Isa 30.7). The people famed throughout antiquity for learning and literary skill could offer no defense against a ruthless invader (vv. 11–15). **16–25:** In spite of these failures, Judah's relations with Egypt were prolonged and often close. The prophet looks beyond the turmoil of Mesopotamian rule to the time when a community would dwell there who *spoke the language of Canaan* (v. 18) and swore *allegiance to the LORD of hosts.* Even Assyria would one day become with Egypt and Israel *a blessing in the midst of the earth* (v. 24). This series of remarkable short prophecies builds on the aftermath of the disasters that befell Jerusalem at the hands of the Assyrians and Babylonians. Many citizens fled to Egypt and, from the sixth century BCE onwards, substantial settlements of exiled Judeans took refuge there. In this bold look across the spiritual boundaries of the ancient world, a genuine religious universalism begins to ap-

a Gk Compare Tg: Heb *it*

pear (vv. 23–24). The knowledge of God revealed to Israel would be shared among other peoples, replacing the failed learning of the Egyptian sages (v. 11).

20 In the year that the commander-in-chief, who was sent by King Sargon of Assyria, came to Ashdod and fought against it and took it— ²at that time the LORD had spoken to Isaiah son of Amoz, saying, "Go, and loose the sackcloth from your loins and take your sandals off your feet," and he had done so, walking naked and barefoot. ³Then the LORD said, "Just as my servant Isaiah has walked naked and barefoot for three years as a sign and a portent against Egypt and Ethiopia,ᵃ ⁴so shall the king of Assyria lead away the Egyptians as captives and the Ethiopiansᵇ as exiles, both the young and the old, naked and barefoot, with buttocks uncovered, to the shame of Egypt. ⁵And they shall be dismayed and confounded because of Ethiopiaᵃ their hope and of Egypt their boast. ⁶In that day the inhabitants of this coastland will say, 'See, this is what has happened to those in whom we hoped and to whom we fled for help and deliverance from the king of Assyria! And we, how shall we escape?'"

20.1–6: A lesson from the past. A brief narrative* reports an event of 715 BCE: A Philistine rebellion against Assyria led to a campaign against Ashdod, one of the five major cities of the Philistines. The Egyptians promised help for the rebellion and Judah was tempted to join. Isaiah's strange action of appearing *naked and barefoot*, like a prisoner of war being sold into slavery (v. 2), warned against such complicity. Egypt's help would prove to be unreliable and worthless (v. 6). This warning was reaffirmed when Hezekiah trusted Egyptian promises in rebelling against Assyria in 703 BCE.

21 The oracle concerning the wilderness of the sea.

As whirlwinds in the Negeb sweep on,
    it comes from the desert,
    from a terrible land.
² A stern vision is told to me;
    the betrayer betrays,
    and the destroyer destroys.

Go up, O Elam,
    lay siege, O Media;
all the sighing she has caused
    I bring to an end.
³ Therefore my loins are filled
        with anguish;
    pangs have seized me,
    like the pangs of a woman in labor;
I am bowed down so that I cannot hear,
I am dismayed so that I cannot see.
⁴ My mind reels, horror has appalled me;
    the twilight I longed for
    has been turned for me into
        trembling.
⁵ They prepare the table,
    they spread the rugs,
    they eat, they drink.
Rise up, commanders,
    oil the shield!
⁶ For thus the Lord said to me:
"Go, post a lookout,
    let him announce what he sees.
⁷ When he sees riders, horsemen in pairs,
    riders on donkeys, riders on camels,
let him listen diligently,
    very diligently."
⁸ Then the watcherᶜ called out:
"Upon a watchtower I stand, O Lord,
    continually by day,
and at my post I am stationed
    throughout the night.
⁹ Look, there they come, riders,
    horsemen in pairs!"
Then he responded,
    "Fallen, fallen is Babylon;
and all the images of her gods
    lie shattered on the ground."
¹⁰ O my threshed and winnowed one,
    what I have heard from the LORD of
        hosts,
    the God of Israel, I announce to you.

21.1–17: Prophecies concerning Babylon, Edom, and the southern desert lands. 1–10: This anguished warning concerns the fall of *Babylon* (v. 9). The heading (v. 1) addresses the southern desert of the Negeb, but the content points to Babylon. The oracle* may date from the time of the attack on the city by Elam

---

a Or *Nubia*; Heb *Cush*   *b* Or *Nubians*; Heb *Cushites*
c Q Ms: MT *a lion*

and Media (538 BCE), when the Medo-Persian over-throw of Babyon marked its end as a world power. This prophecy would provide a framework for the series of prophecies against the nations that began in ch. 13 with the threat to Babylon. It may also date, however, from 703 BCE when the Assyrian king Sennacherib captured the city of Babylon after it had rebelled against Assyria's rule. At this time, the Babylonian ruler Merodach-baladan sent emissaries to Hezekiah of Judah to coordinate rebellion against Assyria (compare Isa 39.1–8).

~~~~~~~~~~

11 The oracle concerning Dumah.

One is calling to me from Seir,
  "Sentinel, what of the night?
  Sentinel, what of the night?"
12 The sentinel says:
  "Morning comes, and also the night.
  If you will inquire, inquire;
  come back again."

13 The oracle concerning the desert
    plain.

In the scrub of the desert plain you will
    lodge,
  O caravans of Dedanites.
14 Bring water to the thirsty,
  meet the fugitive with bread,
  O inhabitants of the land of Tema.
15 For they have fled from the swords,
  from the drawn sword,
  from the bent bow,
  and from the stress of battle.

16 For thus the Lord said to me: Within a year, according to the years of a hired worker, all the glory of Kedar will come to an end; 17and the remaining bows of Kedar's warriors will be few; for the LORD, the God of Israel, has spoken.

───────────

21.11–17. 11–12: In 691–689 the Assyrian king, Sennacherib, extended his campaigns further to the south and west, penetrating to *Dumah* (Edom) and the northwest tip of Arabia where the famed caravan cities of Kedar and Dedan were located. This brief, inconclusive prophecy may be reporting the ineffectual nature of this particular foray. 13–17: The campaign of Sennacherib to plunder the desert cities of *Dedan* and *Tema* is reflected in vv. 14–15, with vv. 16–17 adding

an additional note reflecting later attempts to exploit the region, probably by Babylonian forces.

~~~~~~~~~~

22 The oracle concerning the valley of vision.

What do you mean that you have
    gone up,
  all of you, to the housetops,
2 you that are full of shoutings,
  tumultuous city, exultant town?
Your slain are not slain by the sword,
  nor are they dead in battle.
3 Your rulers have all fled together;
  they were captured without the use of
    a bow.*
All of you who were found were
    captured,
  though they had fled far away.*
4 Therefore I said:
  Look away from me,
  let me weep bitter tears;
  do not try to comfort me
  for the destruction of my
    beloved people.

5 For the Lord GOD of hosts has a day
  of tumult and trampling and
    confusion
  in the valley of vision,
  a battering down of walls
  and a cry for help to the mountains.
6 Elam bore the quiver
  with chariots and cavalry,*
  and Kir uncovered the shield.
7 Your choicest valleys were full of
    chariots,
  and the cavalry took their stand at the
    gates.
8 He has taken away the covering
    of Judah.

On that day you looked to the weapons of the House of the Forest, 9and you saw that there were many breaches in the city of David, and you collected the waters of the lower pool. 10You counted the houses of Jerusalem, and you broke down the houses to for-

a Or *without their bows*   *b* Gk Syr Vg: Heb *fled from far away*   *c* Meaning of Heb uncertain tify the wall. 11You made a reservoir between the two walls for the water of the old pool. But you did not look to him who did it, or have regard for him who planned it long ago.

12 In that day the Lord GOD of hosts
    called to weeping and mourning,
        to baldness and putting on sackcloth;
13 but instead there was joy and festivity,
        killing oxen and slaughtering sheep,
    eating meat and drinking wine.
    "Let us eat and drink,
        for tomorrow we die."
14 The LORD of hosts has revealed himself
        in my ears:
    Surely this iniquity will not be forgiven
        you until you die,
    says the Lord GOD of hosts.

15 Thus says the Lord GOD of hosts: Come, go to this steward, to Shebna, who is master of the household, and say to him: 16What right do you have here? Who are your relatives here, that you have cut out a tomb here for yourself, cutting a tomb on the height, and carving a habitation for yourself in the rock? 17The LORD is about to hurl you away violently, my fellow. He will seize firm hold on you, 18whirl you round and round, and throw you like a ball into a wide land; there you shall die, and there your splendid chariots shall lie, O you disgrace to your master's house! 19I will thrust you from your office, and you will be pulled down from your post.

20 On that day I will call my servant Eliakim son of Hilkiah, 21and will clothe him with your robe and bind your sash on him. I will commit your authority to his hand, and he shall be a father to the inhabitants of Jerusalem and to the house of Judah. 22I will place on his shoulder the key of the house of David; he shall open, and no one shall shut; he shall shut, and no one shall open. 23I will fasten him like a peg in a secure place, and he will become a throne of honor to his ancestral house. 24And they will hang on him the whole weight of his ancestral house, the offspring and issue, every small vessel, from the cups to all the flagons. 25On that day, says the LORD of hosts, the peg that

was fastened in a secure place will give way; it will be cut down and fall, and the load that was on it will perish, for the LORD has spoken.

22.1–25: Warnings to Jerusalem and its leaders. 1–4: The *valley of vision* is Jerusalem, apparently because Isaiah's call-vision took place there (ch. 6). The prophecies refer to the events described in 2 Kings 18.9–12: The northern Israelite city of Samaria was besieged, captured, and destroyed by the king of Assyria. Jerusalem's escape from a similar fate by the timely, but humiliating, surrender of King Hezekiah (2 Kings 18.13–16) may also be referred to. In celebrating their own escape, the citizens of Jerusalem ignored the suffering of their sister nation. Isaiah strongly believed that both Judah and Israel (Ephraim) were two houses of one people before God (see 8.14; 9.21). **5–8a:** The fate that had so recently overtaken their compatriots would also befall the citizens of Jerusalem. A century later Babylonian forces captured Jerusalem in 598, destroying it in 587 BCE. **8b–11:** Instead of trusting the LORD, the beleaguered citizens trusted their own human defense system. It would fail them, just as surely as the defenses of Samaria had failed. **15–25:** Three short, but related, condemnations (vv. 15–19, 20–23, 24–25) concern *Shebna,* the master of the royal household (v. 15), and *Eliakim son of Hilkiah* (v. 20) who had briefly succeeded him (v. 21). These officials are mentioned in 36.3, 11, 22 and played a prominent role in the negotiations for King Hezekiah's surrender to Assyria (see 2 Kings 18.18). Their personal ambitions and folly, which affected their roles in forming national policy, are condemned. Isaiah also condemned the king for relying upon Egyptian promises of support (see Isa 30).

23 The oracle concerning Tyre.

    Wail, O ships of Tarshish,
        for your fortress is destroyed.[a]
    When they came in from Cyprus
        they learned of it.
2   Be still, O inhabitants of the coast,
        O merchants of Sidon,
    your messengers crossed over the sea[b]
3   and were on the mighty waters;

a Cn Compare verse 14: Heb *for it is destroyed, without houses* b Q Ms: MT *crossing over the sea, they replenished you*

your revenue was the grain of Shihor,
  the harvest of the Nile;
  you were the merchant of the nations.
4 Be ashamed, O Sidon, for the sea has
    spoken,
  the fortress of the sea, saying:
"I have neither labored nor given birth,
  I have neither reared young men
  nor brought up young women."
5 When the report comes to Egypt,
  they will be in anguish over the report
    about Tyre.
6 Cross over to Tarshish—
  wail, O inhabitants of the coast!
7 Is this your exultant city
  whose origin is from days of old,
  whose feet carried her
  to settle far away?
8 Who has planned this
  against Tyre, the bestower of crowns,
  whose merchants were princes,
  whose traders were the honored of
    the earth?
9 The LORD of hosts has planned it—
  to defile the pride of all glory,
  to shame all the honored of the
    earth.
10 Cross over to your own land,
  O ships of[a] Tarshish;
  this is a harbor[b] no more.
11 He has stretched out his hand over the
    sea,
  he has shaken the kingdoms;
  the LORD has given command
    concerning Canaan
  to destroy its fortresses.
12 He said:
You will exult no longer,
  O oppressed virgin daughter Sidon;
  rise, cross over to Cyprus—
  even there you will have no rest.

13 Look at the land of the Chaldeans!
This is the people; it was not Assyria. They
destined Tyre for wild animals. They erected
their siege towers, they tore down her palaces, they made her a ruin.[c]
14 Wail, O ships of Tarshish,
  for your fortress is destroyed.
15 From that day Tyre will be forgotten for
seventy years, the lifetime of one king. At the

end of seventy years, it will happen to Tyre
as in the song about the prostitute:
16 Take a harp,
  go about the city,
  you forgotten prostitute!
Make sweet melody,
  sing many songs,
  that you may be remembered.
17 At the end of seventy years, the LORD will
visit Tyre, and she will return to her trade,
and will prostitute herself with all the
kingdoms of the world on the face of the
earth. 18 Her merchandise and her wages will
be dedicated to the LORD; her profits[d] will
not be stored or hoarded, but her merchandise will supply abundant food and fine
clothing for those who live in the presence
of the LORD.

23.1–18: A prophecy concerning Tyre. 1–12: The
Phoenician cities of *Tyre* and *Sidon* were famous in
antiquity as the seafaring and mercantile trading centers of the Mediterranean world. The pride of Tyre was
its fine buildings, wealth, and honor. In 701 BCE, the
Assyrian ruler Sennacherib laid siege to the Phoenician
cities, forcing Luli, king of Sidon, to flee to the island
of *Cyprus* (v. 12). **13–18:** A brief editorial note (v. 13)
points out that Babylon (from 604 BCE) had replaced
the threat from Assyria (compare the book of Nahum,
which celebrates the fall of Nineveh in 612 BCE). This
succession of Mesopotamian oppressors led the later
compilers to supplement earlier prophecies to provide
a fuller picture of God's purpose. Tyre, like an aging
prostitute (v. 16), will shamelessly pursue wealth (a
reference to the rich merchants for which Tyre was
known). In contrast, the final note (v. 18) recognizes
that wealth, rightly earned, can be used in the service
of God.

**The terror of the day of the LORD and the ensuing
reign of blessedness**
24.1–27.13: Chapters 24–27 contain no clear indications of their time of origin and therefore are difficult
to relate to known events. They contrast a time of fearful judgment upon *the city of chaos* (24.10) with a
new era of blessedness, a spectacular feast on the
mountain of God (25.6–10). These chapters may have

---

a Cn Compare Gk: Heb *like the Nile, daughter*
b Cn: Heb *restraint*   c Meaning of Heb uncertain
d Heb *it*

been a separate prophetic book, but clear references to earlier themes and pronouncements, most notably the "New Song of the Vineyard" (27.2–6; compare 5.1–7), make it more likely that they are a sequel to the prophecies against foreign cities and nations in chs. 13–23. The great empires will be overtaken by a fearful day of God's judgment, followed by a time of peace and justice. The evocative word pictures of doom and disaster, intermixed with hymns of praise and promises of a new age of great peace and blessedness, lift human history into the realm of a great spiritual "super-history" in which evil is overthrown and the faithful are vindicated.

24 Now the LORD is about to lay
waste the earth and make it
desolate,
and he will twist its surface and
scatter its inhabitants.
2 And it shall be, as with the people, so
with the priest;
as with the slave, so with his master;
as with the maid, so with her
mistress;
as with the buyer, so with the seller;
as with the lender, so with the
borrower;
as with the creditor, so with
the debtor.
3 The earth shall be utterly laid waste and
utterly despoiled;
for the LORD has spoken this word.

4 The earth dries up and withers,
the world languishes and withers;
the heavens languish together with
the earth.
5 The earth lies polluted
under its inhabitants;
for they have transgressed laws,
violated the statutes,
broken the everlasting covenant.
6 Therefore a curse devours the earth,
and its inhabitants suffer for their
guilt;
therefore the inhabitants of the earth
dwindled,
and few people are left.
7 The wine dries up,
the vine languishes,
all the merry-hearted sigh.

8 The mirth of the timbrels is stilled,
the noise of the jubilant has ceased,
the mirth of the lyre is stilled.
9 No longer do they drink wine with
singing;
strong drink is bitter to those who
drink it.
10 The city of chaos is broken down,
every house is shut up so that no one
can enter.
11 There is an outcry in the streets for lack
of wine;
all joy has reached its eventide;
the gladness of the earth is banished.
12 Desolation is left in the city,
the gates are battered into ruins.
13 For thus it shall be on the earth
and among the nations,
as when an olive tree is beaten,
as at the gleaning when the grape
harvest is ended.

14 They lift up their voices, they sing for
joy;
they shout from the west over the
majesty of the LORD.
15 Therefore in the east give glory to the
LORD;
in the coastlands of the sea glorify the
name of the LORD, the God of
Israel.
16 From the ends of the earth we hear
songs of praise,
of glory to the Righteous One.
But I say, I pine away,
I pine away. Woe is me!
For the treacherous deal treacherously,
the treacherous deal very
treacherously.

17 Terror, and the pit, and the snare
are upon you, O inhabitant of the
earth!
18 Whoever flees at the sound of the
terror
shall fall into the pit;
and whoever climbs out of the pit
shall be caught in the snare.
For the windows of heaven are opened,
and the foundations of the earth
tremble.

19 The earth is utterly broken,
   the earth is torn asunder,
   the earth is violently shaken.
20 The earth staggers like a drunkard,
   it sways like a hut;
   its transgression lies heavy upon it,
   and it falls, and will not rise again.

21 On that day the LORD will punish
   the host of heaven in heaven,
   and on earth the kings of the earth.
22 They will be gathered together
   like prisoners in a pit;
   they will be shut up in a prison,
   and after many days they will be
   punished.
23 Then the moon will be abashed,
   and the sun ashamed;
   for the LORD of hosts will reign
   on Mount Zion and in Jerusalem,
   and before his elders he will manifest
   his glory.

24.1–23: The day of terror for the city of chaos. This remarkable picture of a tortured and pain-wracked earth views the sufferings of its inhabitants (vv. 17–20) as a consequence of the curse-ridden state of the earth itself (v. 6). The very order of the world, disturbed and in turmoil, can only be put right by divine punishment of evil in a new era of divine rule (vv. 22–23). Despair for the earth combines with trust that ultimately God will prevail, which explains the praise to God in vv. 14–16. Judgment, as proof of divine justice, is itself a necessary part of God's created order. The *city of chaos* (v. 10) is a symbolic city, like Bunyan's Vanity Fair in *Pilgrim's Progress*. Even though the *host of heaven* rebels against God (v. 21), this prophet believes that God will prevail.

25 O LORD, you are my God;
   I will exalt you, I will praise your
   name;
   for you have done wonderful things,
   plans formed of old, faithful and sure.
2 For you have made the city a heap,
   the fortified city a ruin;
   the palace of aliens is a city no more,
   it will never be rebuilt.
3 Therefore strong peoples will glorify
   you;
   cities of ruthless nations will fear you.

4 For you have been a refuge to the poor,
   a refuge to the needy in their distress,
   a shelter from the rainstorm and a
   shade from the heat.
   When the blast of the ruthless was like
   a winter rainstorm,
5 the noise of aliens like heat in a dry
   place,
   you subdued the heat with the shade of
   clouds;
   the song of the ruthless was stilled.

6 On this mountain the LORD of hosts
   will make for all peoples
   a feast of rich food, a feast of well-
   aged wines,
   of rich food filled with marrow, of
   well-aged wines strained clear.
7 And he will destroy on this mountain
   the shroud that is cast over all
   peoples,
   the sheet that is spread over all
   nations;
8 he will swallow up death forever.
   Then the Lord GOD will wipe away the
   tears from all faces,
   and the disgrace of his people he will
   take away from all the earth,
   for the LORD has spoken.
9 It will be said on that day,
   Lo, this is our God; we have waited
   for him, so that he might save us.
   This is the LORD for whom we have
   waited;
   let us be glad and rejoice in his
   salvation.
10 For the hand of the LORD will rest on
   this mountain.

   The Moabites shall be trodden down in
   their place
   as straw is trodden down in a
   dung-pit.
11 Though they spread out their hands in
   the midst of it,
   as swimmers spread out their hands
   to swim,
   their pride will be laid low despite the
   struggle*a* of their hands.

a Meaning of Heb uncertain

12 The high fortifications of his walls will
    be brought down,
laid low, cast to the ground, even to
    the dust.

25.1–12: The banquet of the LORD of hosts. The great festival to be celebrated in Jerusalem on the holy mountain gives pictorial expression to the praise of God (vv. 1–5). Even in the most violent trouble, God is *a refuge to the needy in their distress* (v. 4). The prophetic vision, however, recognizes that there are wrongs and sufferings on earth that cannot be put right by stilling *the blast of the ruthless.* The ultimate resolution of injustice can come only when God overcomes the power of death itself (v. 7; compare 26.19). **10–12. The humiliation of Moab.** This appears to belong with the other warnings in chs. 15–16.

26 On that day this song will be sung in the land of Judah:
We have a strong city;
    he sets up victory
    like walls and bulwarks.
2 Open the gates,
    so that the righteous nation that
    keeps faith
may enter in.
3 Those of steadfast mind you keep
    in peace—
in peace because they trust in you.
4 Trust in the LORD forever,
    for in the LORD GOD *a*
you have an everlasting rock.
5 For he has brought low
    the inhabitants of the height;
    the lofty city he lays low.
He lays it low to the ground,
    casts it to the dust.
6 The foot tramples it,
    the feet of the poor,
    the steps of the needy.

7 The way of the righteous is level;
    O Just One, you make smooth the
    path of the righteous.
8 In the path of your judgments,
    O LORD, we wait for you;
your name and your renown
    are the soul's desire.
9 My soul yearns for you in
    the night,

my spirit within me earnestly seeks
    you.
For when your judgments are in the
    earth,
    the inhabitants of the world learn
    righteousness.
10 If favor is shown to the wicked,
    they do not learn righteousness;
in the land of uprightness they deal
    perversely
    and do not see the majesty of
    the LORD.
11 O LORD, your hand is lifted up,
    but they do not see it.
Let them see your zeal for your people,
    and be ashamed.
Let the fire for your adversaries
    consume them.
12 O LORD, you will ordain peace for us,
    for indeed, all that we have done, you
    have done for us.
13 O LORD our God,
    other lords besides you have ruled
    over us,
    but we acknowledge your name alone.
14 The dead do not live;
    shades do not rise—
because you have punished and
    destroyed them,
    and wiped out all memory of them.
15 But you have increased the nation,
    O LORD,
you have increased the nation; you
    are glorified;
    you have enlarged all the borders of
    the land.

16 O LORD, in distress they sought you,
    they poured out a prayer *b*
    when your chastening was on them.
17 Like a woman with child,
    who writhes and cries out in her pangs
    when she is near her time,
so were we because of you, O LORD;
18 we were with child, we writhed,
    but we gave birth only to wind.
We have won no victories on earth,
    and no one is born to inhabit
    the world.

a Heb *in Yah, the* LORD *b* Meaning of Heb uncertain

19 Your dead shall live, their corpses*a* shall
    rise.
O dwellers in the dust, awake and
    sing for joy!
For your dew is a radiant dew,
    and the earth will give birth to those
    long dead.*b*

20 Come, my people, enter your chambers,
    and shut your doors behind you;
hide yourselves for a little while
    until the wrath is past.
21 For the LORD comes out from his place
    to punish the inhabitants of the earth
    for their iniquity;
the earth will disclose the blood shed
    on it,
    and will no longer cover its slain.

26.1–21: Praise to the God of justice. The hymn of praise to God for the justice of the divine judgments upon earth in vv. 1–15 indicates that chs. 24–27, and probably the entire scroll of Isaiah, were designed to be read, and prayerfully responded to, in acts of worship. The message of God was a call to penitence and faith, so that unresolved questions and doubts could be answered by trust, as in v. 3: *Those of steadfast mind you keep in peace—in peace because they trust in you.* It is necessary to accept the purpose of God and to await salvation without fully understanding the violent wrongs of human history. This trust is expressed in the remarkable outburst of vv. 16–19: When the promises of God appear so far from fulfillment, a new vision breaks in, a vision of life beyond the grave and of life renewed for those long dead. The only other passage in the Hebrew Scriptures that compares with this visionary insight into the world beyond the grave is Dan 12.2. The prophet is attempting to reconcile the righteousness of God with the problems of suffering and conflict.

27 On that day the LORD with his cruel and great and strong sword will punish Leviathan the fleeing serpent, Leviathan the twisting serpent, and he will kill the dragon that is in the sea.

2 On that day:
A pleasant vineyard, sing about it!
3 I, the LORD, am its keeper;
    every moment I water it.

I guard it night and day
    so that no one can harm it;
4 I have no wrath.
If it gives me thorns and briers,
    I will march to battle against it.
    I will burn it up.
5 Or else let it cling to me for protection,
    let it make peace with me,
    let it make peace with me.

6 In days to come*c* Jacob shall take root,
    Israel shall blossom and put
    forth shoots,
    and fill the whole world with fruit.

7 Has he struck them down as he struck
    down those who struck them?
Or have they been killed as their
    killers were killed?
8 By expulsion,*d* by exile you struggled
    against them;
with his fierce blast he removed them
    in the day of the east wind.
9 Therefore by this the guilt of Jacob will
    be expiated,
and this will be the full fruit of the
    removal of his sin:
when he makes all the stones of the
    altars
    like chalkstones crushed to pieces,
    no sacred poles*e* or incense altars will
    remain standing.
10 For the fortified city is solitary,
    a habitation deserted and forsaken,
    like the wilderness;
the calves graze there,
    there they lie down, and strip its
    branches.
11 When its boughs are dry, they
    are broken;
women come and make a fire
    of them.
For this is a people without
    understanding;
therefore he that made them will not
    have compassion on them,
he that formed them will show them
    no favor.

a Cn Compare Syr Tg: Heb *my corpse*   *b* Heb *to the shades*   *c* Heb *Those to come*   *d* Meaning of Heb uncertain   *e* Heb *Asherim*

12 On that day the LORD will thresh from the channel of the Euphrates to the Wadi of Egypt, and you will be gathered one by one, O people of Israel. ¹³And on that day a great trumpet will be blown, and those who were lost in the land of Assyria and those who were driven out to the land of Egypt will come and worship the LORD on the holy mountain at Jerusalem.

27.1–13: The new song of the vineyard. 1: The assurance that the LORD *will punish Leviathan** reflects the ancient belief that the earth was created after a great battle between the creator God and a monster symbolizing chaos. In the Babylonian creation epic, this monster is called Tiamat, but other versions use the name Rahab (compare Isa 51.9). The power of God to impose order is needed not simply in the primary act of creation but in every natural disaster or historical catastrophe, when God's rule needs to be reestablished. **2:** *A pleasant vineyard, sing about it!* Reference to the vineyard parable* of Isa 5.1–7 shows that this new song marks the end of the period in which the former vineyard (Israel) was reduced to a wasteland. **4:** The *thorns and briers* will at last be removed (see 7.23–25; 9.18; 10.17). **7–11:** The restoration has not yet taken place, and the fields of Jacob still lie desolate and *forsaken* (v. 10). The *people without understanding* (v. 11) are those who hold back God's saving work. **12–13.** The promise of return to their homeland for the scattered survivors remains central to the hope for the future in Isaiah. Here and in 11.12–16 (compare 19.23–24), this return is the prelude to the restoration of Israel to its former glory, the completion of God's saving purpose.

Isaiah 28–39

THREATS TO JERUSALEM AND ITS GREAT DELIVERANCE

Chapters 28–31 present sharp prophetic accusations, first against the leaders of Ephraim (28.1–11) and then against those of Jerusalem (28.14–31.9). They charge that these people are pursuing a national policy contrary to God's will, by looking to Egypt rather than to God to provide deliverance from threatening foreign powers. Chapter 32 presents a new hope, beginning in vv. 1–8, with promises of the coming of a just king and responsible and righteous leaders for the nation. Fresh warnings follow, first to Jerusalem and Judah (32.9–33.16), but then to the wider world of other nations (34.1–17). The hope for Jerusalem's future is not abandoned, but rather intensified, with ch. 35 summarizing the later message of chs. 40–66.

Chapters 36–39, largely identical to 2 Kings 18.13–20.19, concern the threatened siege of Jerusalem by the Assyrian king, Sennacherib, in 701 BCE, followed by the reprieve for the beleaguered King Hezekiah and the city (36.1–37.38). A report of Hezekiah's illness and recovery (38.1–9), for which the king offers a psalm of thanksgiving (38.10–20), is followed in 39.1–8 by a visit of emissaries from the Babylonian ruler Merodach-baladan, along with the prophet's ominous warning of danger from that nation.

The background to the prophecies of chs. 28–31 is the situation of 705–701 BCE, when King Hezekiah of Judah joined a rebellion of eastern Mediterranean states against Assyria, following the death of the Assyrian king, Shalmaneser, in 705 BCE. Egypt was the chief instigator and promised military protection for those foolhardy nations that joined in the revolt. These unreliable assurances provide the background to Isaiah's warnings against Egyptian help (chs. 30–31). The revolt was crushed mercilessly in 701. Research into the events behind the accounts of Hezekiah's surrender to Sennacherib, and the extensive reports of the blasphemous speeches of the Assyrian negotiator (called the Rabshakeh) and their rebuff by Isaiah, include the recovery of clay tablets and palace wall illustrations attesting the capture of Lachish and the humiliations inflicted on Hezekiah. These give a very different picture from that in Isa 36–37. Yet, in contrast to the fate of Samaria and its king, reported in 2 Kings 18.9–12, Hezekiah retained his throne and his city survived intact. The Assyrian royal records presumably exaggerate the victory to flatter their king.

READING GUIDE

In the rebuff to the blasphemous claims of the Assyrian negotiator (37.22–29) and in several other memorable utterances, Isaiah calls for a complete faith in God (28.16) and insists that only such faith can bring true peace and strength (30.15). Similarly, his call for integrity before God (29.13) and his insistence that God cannot be deceived by human secrecy and subterfuge (29.15–16) are the basis for Jewish and Christian teaching about the limitations of human learning and the necessity for submission to the superior wisdom of God (29.14).

The LORD is a refuge and protection
28.1–29: The four units of this chapter (1–6; 7–13; 14–22; 23–29) condemn the foolishness of the leaders of both Ephraim (Israel) and Judah, who show by their drunken and mocking behavior that they neither understand their problems nor are able to remedy them. In contrast, Isaiah sets out the simple and direct message: *"One who trusts will not panic"* (v. 16).

28 Ah, the proud garland of the
        drunkards of Ephraim,
    and the fading flower of its glorious
        beauty,
    which is on the head of those bloated
        with rich food, of those overcome
        with wine!
2 See, the Lord has one who is mighty
        and strong;
    like a storm of hail, a destroying
        tempest,
    like a storm of mighty, overflowing
        waters;

with his hand he will hurl them down
        to the earth.
3 Trampled under foot will be
    the proud garland of the drunkards of
        Ephraim.
4 And the fading flower of its glorious
        beauty,
    which is on the head of those bloated
        with rich food,
    will be like a first-ripe fig before the
        summer;
    whoever sees it, eats it up
    as soon as it comes to hand.

5 In that day the LORD of hosts will be a
        garland of glory,
    and a diadem of beauty, to the
        remnant of his people;
6 and a spirit of justice to the one who
        sits in judgment,
    and strength to those who turn back
        the battle at the gate.

28.1–6: The folly of Ephraim's leaders. It is surprising that the opening prophecy focuses on Ephraim, rather than Judah, which Isaiah usually addressed. Yet Ephraim suffered first, and more severely, from the depredations of Assyria. Judah should learn the necessary lesson: As a sudden rainstorm (v. 2) ruins the festival of those leaders who had already eaten and drunk too much, so would God's judgment wreck the complacent peace of the kingdom (compare 9.8–10.4). A brief word of hope and relief (vv. 5–6) shows that God's judgment always has a way of escape for a penitent remnant.

7 These also reel with wine
    and stagger with strong drink;
  the priest and the prophet reel with
      strong drink,
    they are confused with wine,
    they stagger with strong drink;
    they err in vision,
    they stumble in giving judgment.
8 All tables are covered with filthy vomit;
    no place is clean.

9 "Whom will he teach knowledge,
    and to whom will he explain
      the message?
  Those who are weaned from milk,
    those taken from the breast?
10 For it is precept upon precept, precept
      upon precept,
    line upon line, line upon line,
    here a little, there a little."*a*

11 Truly, with stammering lip
    and with alien tongue
  he will speak to this people,
12 to whom he has said,
  "This is rest;
    give rest to the weary;
  and this is repose";
    yet they would not hear.
13 Therefore the word of the LORD will be
    to them,
  "Precept upon precept, precept upon
      precept,
  line upon line, line upon line,
  here a little, there a little;"*a*
  in order that they may go, and fall
    backward,

  and be broken, and snared,
    and taken.

28.7–13: God cannot be mocked with impunity. It is unclear whether this oracle* is addressed to the revelers in vv. 1–4, or whether it is a rebuke to a group of Jerusalem's leaders (compare v. 14). The signs of excess are evident (v. 8) when they turn to mock the prophet and, by implication, God (vv. 9–10). These leaders accuse the prophet of treating them like little children (v. 10). Instead God will teach them a lesson in the language of foreign invaders (v. 11). By rejecting and mocking the prophet's warnings (v. 12), and choosing rebellion against Assyria, they were playing with their own lives and those of the people and would pay the price (v. 13).

14 Therefore hear the word of the LORD,
    you scoffers
  who rule this people in Jerusalem.
15 Because you have said, "We have made
    a covenant with death,
    and with Sheol we have an
      agreement;
  when the overwhelming scourge passes
      through
    it will not come to us;
  for we have made lies our refuge,
    and in falsehood we have taken
      shelter";
16 therefore thus says the Lord GOD,
  See, I am laying in Zion a foundation
      stone,
    a tested stone,
  a precious cornerstone, a sure
      foundation:
  "One who trusts will not panic."
17 And I will make justice the line,
    and righteousness the plummet;
  hail will sweep away the refuge of lies,
    and waters will overwhelm the
      shelter.
18 Then your covenant with death will be
      annulled,
    and your agreement* with Sheol will
      not stand;
  when the overwhelming scourge passes
      through

a Meaning of Heb of this verse uncertain

Assyrian Account of the Siege of Jerusalem

As to Hezekiah, the Jew, he did not submit to my yoke, I laid siege to 46 of his strong cities, walled forts, and to the countless small villages in their vicinity, and conquered (them) by means of well-stamped (earth-) ramps, and battering-rams brought (thus) near (to the walls) (combined with) the attack by foot soldiers, (using) mines, breeches as well as sapper work. I drove out (of them) 200,150 people, young and old, male and female, horses, mules, donkeys, camels, big and small cattle beyond counting, and considered (them) booty. Himself I made a prisoner in Jerusalem, his royal residence, like a bird in a cage. I surrounded him with earthwork in order to molest those who were leaving his city's gate. His towns which I had plundered, I took away from his country and gave them (over) to Mitinti, king of Ashdod, Padi, king of Ekron, and Sillibel, king of Gaza. Thus I reduced his country, but I still increased the tribute and the *katrû* -presents (due) to me (as his) overlord which I imposed (later) upon him beyond the former tribute, to be delivered annually. Hezekiah himself, whom the terror-inspiring splendor of my lordship had overwhelmed and whose irregular and elite troops which he had brought into Jerusalem, his royal residence, in order to strengthen (it), had deserted him, did send me, later, to Nineveh, my lordly city, together with 30 talents of gold, 800 talents of silver, precious stones, antimony, large cuts of red stone, couches (inlaid) with ivory, *nîmedu* -chairs (inlaid) with ivory, elephant-hides, ebony-wood, box-wood (and) all kinds of valuable treasures, his (own) daughters, concubines,⋆ male and female musicians. In order to deliver the tribute and to do obeisance as a slave he sent his (personal) messenger. (From *The Ancient Near East: Volume One, An Anthology of Texts and Pictures,* edited by James B. Pritchard, Princeton University Press, 1958, p. 200.)

you will be beaten down by it.

19 As often as it passes through, it will
take you;
for morning by morning it will pass
through,
by day and by night;
and it will be sheer terror to understand
the message.

20 For the bed is too short to stretch
oneself on it,
and the covering too narrow to wrap
oneself in it.

21 For the LORD will rise up as on Mount
Perazim,
he will rage as in the valley of
Gibeon
to do his deed—strange is his deed!—
and to work his work—alien is his
work!

22 Now therefore do not scoff,
or your bonds will be made stronger;

for I have heard a decree of destruction
from the Lord GOD of hosts upon the
whole land.

28.14–22: God's strange work. This powerful prophecy expresses the fundamentals of Isaiah's conviction: God alone is the defense and protector of the people of Jerusalem. Instead of trusting in God, however, these leaders had chosen *a covenant⋆ with death* and an *agreement with Sheol⋆* (v. 18). These titles may refer to a strange ritual with the god of death to make sure that no harm could come to them. Or more likely, they may be a sharply ironic description of the treaty with Egypt that Judah hoped would protect it against any Assyrian reprisal for rebellion. Egypt is caricatured as the kingdom of death because of its obsession with overcoming death (by constructing great pyramids and embalming national figures). In contrast, Isaiah insists that Judah's actions will simply hasten death's arrival.

23 Listen, and hear my voice;
  Pay attention, and hear my speech.
24 Do those who plow for sowing plow
    continually?
  Do they continually open and harrow
    their ground?
25 When they have leveled its surface,
    do they not scatter dill, sow cummin,
  and plant wheat in rows
  and barley in its proper place,
  and spelt as the border?
26 For they are well instructed;
    their God teaches them.

27 Dill is not threshed with a threshing
    sledge,
  nor is a cart wheel rolled over
    cummin;
  but dill is beaten out with a stick,
  and cummin with a rod.
28 Grain is crushed for bread,
  but one does not thresh it forever;
  one drives the cart wheel and horses
    over it,
  but does not pulverize it.
29 This also comes from the LORD
    of hosts;
  he is wonderful in counsel,
  and excellent in wisdom.

28.23–29: The lesson of the farmer's year. This is one of the most instructive prophetic parables* of the Hebrew Scriptures. The variety of activities that make up the farmer's year illustrate the force of vv. 21–22. To the question, "Would not destroying the city where the Temple* stands be a strange work for God the protector?" the prophet's answer is that, like the farmer, God has many varied tasks to perform—and judging a rebellious people is one of them.

29 Ah, Ariel, Ariel,
    the city where David encamped!
  Add year to year;
    let the festivals run their round.
2 Yet I will distress Ariel,
  and there shall be moaning and
    lamentation,
  and Jerusalem[a] shall be to me like an
    Ariel.[b]
3 And like David[c] I will encamp against
    you;

I will besiege you with towers
    and raise siegeworks against you.
4 Then deep from the earth you
    shall speak,
  from low in the dust your words shall
    come;
  your voice shall come from the ground
    like the voice of a ghost,
  and your speech shall whisper out of
    the dust.

29.1–24: The siege and deliverance of Jerusalem. This chapter centers on the threat to Jerusalem by Sennacherib's campaign in 701 BCE (see chs. 36–37). These oracles* attest to both the danger the city faced and its remarkable escape. Warnings explaining the near catastrophe occur in vv. 9–10, 13–14, and 15–16. Jerusalem's survival demanded further reflection on Isaiah's warnings, and Jerusalem's later destruction (587 BCE) posed further questions. These reflections are in vv. 5–8, with further messages of hope in vv. 17–21 and 22–24. **1–4:** *Ah, Ariel, Ariel, the city where David encamped! Ariel,* "altar hearth," refers to the sacred altar in the city, and the reference to King David recalls the taking of the city in 2 Sam 5.6–10, evoking its unique importance both to God and to Israel.

5 But the multitude of your foes[d] shall be
    like small dust,
  and the multitude of tyrants like
    flying chaff.
  And in an instant, suddenly,
6   you will be visited by the LORD
    of hosts
  with thunder and earthquake and great
    noise,
  with whirlwind and tempest, and the
    flame of a devouring fire.
7 And the multitude of all the nations
    that fight against Ariel,
  all that fight against her and her
    stronghold, and who distress her,
  shall be like a dream, a vision
    of the night.
8 Just as when a hungry person dreams of
    eating
  and wakes up still hungry,

a Heb *she* b Probable meaning, *altar hearth;* compare Ezek 43.15 c Gk: Meaning of Heb uncertain
d Cn: Heb *strangers*

or a thirsty person dreams of drinking
   and wakes up faint, still thirsty,
so shall the multitude of all the nations be
   that fight against Mount Zion.

9 Stupefy yourselves and be in a stupor,
   blind yourselves and be blind!
Be drunk, but not from wine;
   stagger, but not from strong drink!
10 For the LORD has poured out upon you
   a spirit of deep sleep;
he has closed your eyes, you prophets,
   and covered your heads, you seers.

11 The vision of all this has become for
you like the words of a sealed document. If
it is given to those who can read, with the
command, "Read this," they say, "We cannot, for it is sealed." 12And if it is given to
those who cannot read, saying, "Read this,"
they say, "We cannot read."

13 The Lord said:
Because these people draw near with
   their mouths
   and honor me with their lips,
   while their hearts are far from me,
and their worship of me is a human
   commandment learned by rote;
14 so I will again do
   amazing things with this people,
   shocking and amazing.
The wisdom of their wise shall perish,
   and the discernment of the discerning
   shall be hidden.

15 Ha! You who hide a plan too deep for
   the LORD,
   whose deeds are in the dark,
   and who say, "Who sees us? Who
   knows us?"
16 You turn things upside down!
   Shall the potter be regarded as the clay?
Shall the thing made say of its maker,
   "He did not make me";
or the thing formed say of the one who
   formed it,
   "He has no understanding"?

29.5–16. 5–8: The visitation of the LORD of hosts.
God would intervene to protect Jerusalem, but it is not
clear what actually occurred in 701 to explain this report (see comment on 37.36). This assurance may go

back to Isaiah, or it may result from subsequent reflection on the deliverance of the city and King Hezekiah's
continuing reign. The survival of the Davidic dynasty★
in Jerusalem was of great significance when the destruction of Samaria and its royal house was recalled
(see 2 Kings 18.10–12). 9–12: The people's inability
to discern God's purpose is like drunken staggering.
The warning in vv. 11–12 witnesses to the way in
which the spoken word of the prophet was preserved
to become a part of scripture. The reader of the book
takes the place of the hearer of the word. 13–14: *The
wisdom of their wise shall perish.* The foolhardy policies of the royal counselors and advisers would prove
ruinous. 15–16: The prophet mocks the secrecy and
subterfuge by which the royal counselors seek to hide
their policy, with its high risk of military disaster, from
the people.

17 Shall not Lebanon in a very little while
   become a fruitful field,
   and the fruitful field be regarded as a
   forest?
18 On that day the deaf shall hear
   the words of a scroll,
and out of their gloom and darkness
   the eyes of the blind shall see.
19 The meek shall obtain fresh joy in the
   LORD,
   and the neediest people shall exult in
   the Holy One of Israel.
20 For the tyrant shall be no more,
   and the scoffer shall cease to be;
   all those alert to do evil shall be cut
   off—
21 those who cause a person to lose a
   lawsuit,
   who set a trap for the arbiter in the
   gate,
   and without grounds deny justice to
   the one in the right.

22 Therefore thus says the LORD, who redeemed Abraham, concerning the house of
Jacob:
No longer shall Jacob be ashamed,
   no longer shall his face grow pale.
23 For when he sees his children,
   the work of my hands, in his midst,
   they will sanctify my name;
they will sanctify the Holy One of
   Jacob,

and will stand in awe of the God of
Israel.
24 And those who err in spirit will come to
understanding,
and those who grumble will accept
instruction.

29.17–24. 17–21: The renewal of hope. It is not clear
why this message of hope, and the following one, have
been added at this point. Verse 18 affirms that Israel's
period of blindness (see 6.9–10) will pass, suggesting
a link with the renewed warning of this in 29.9. **22–24:**
And those who err in spirit: Israel's foolishness and lack
of discernment (v. 14) requires a look toward God's
deliverance. All who have forsaken God and the path
of righteousness will come to understand the truth.

30 Oh, rebellious children, says the
LORD,
who carry out a plan, but not mine;
who make an alliance, but against my
will,
adding sin to sin;
2 who set out to go down to Egypt
without asking for my counsel,
to take refuge in the protection of
Pharaoh,
and to seek shelter in the shadow of
Egypt;
3 Therefore the protection of Pharaoh
shall become your shame,
and the shelter in the shadow of
Egypt your humiliation.
4 For though his officials are at Zoan
and his envoys reach Hanes,
5 everyone comes to shame
through a people that cannot profit
them,
that brings neither help nor profit,
but shame and disgrace.

**30.1–33: In quietness and in trust shall be your
strength.** These memorable phrases present a central
teaching: Salvation and peace come through trusting
in God, not through human plans and alliances (v. 15).
The chapter is built up from a number of short prophetic sayings (vv. 1–5; 6–7; 12–14; 15–17) deriving
from the time of King Hezekiah's rebellion against Assyria (703–701 BCE) and the negotiations with Egypt
for protection. Subsequently, admonitions (vv. 8–11)
and assurances (vv. 18–26; 29–33) were added. The

assurance includes a warning: God will judge wrongdoers (vv. 27–28). **1–5:** Isaiah rejects Hezekiah's plan
to rebel against Assyria and to trust Egypt's promises
of help. The sending of royal emissaries from Judah to
Egypt (v. 4) must have prompted the original prophecy. This, along with Isaiah's awareness of secret consultations and plans made in Jerusalem (see 29.15),
suggests that he held a privileged position at court.

6 An oracle concerning the animals of the
Negeb.
Through a land of trouble and distress,
of lioness and roaring*a* lion,
of viper and flying serpent,
they carry their riches on the backs of
donkeys,
and their treasures on the humps of
camels,
to a people that cannot profit them.
7 For Egypt's help is worthless and empty,
therefore I have called her,
"Rahab who sits still."*b*
8 Go now, write it before them on
a tablet,
and inscribe it in a book,
so that it may be for the time to come
as a witness forever.
9 For they are a rebellious people,
faithless children,
children who will not hear
the instruction of the LORD;
10 who say to the seers, "Do not see";
and to the prophets, "Do not
prophesy to us what is right;
speak to us smooth things,
prophesy illusions,
11 leave the way, turn aside from the path,
let us hear no more about the Holy
One of Israel."
12 Therefore thus says the Holy One of
Israel:
Because you reject this word,
and put your trust in oppression and
deceit,
and rely on them;
13 therefore this iniquity shall become
for you

a Cn: Heb *from them* *b* Meaning of Heb uncertain

like a break in a high wall, bulging
      out, and about to collapse,
    whose crash comes suddenly, in an
      instant;
14 its breaking is like that of a potter's
      vessel
    that is smashed so ruthlessly
  that among its fragments not a sherd is
      found
      for taking fire from the hearth,
      or dipping water out of the cistern.

15 For thus said the Lord GOD, the Holy
      One of Israel:
  In returning and rest you shall be saved;
    in quietness and in trust shall be your
      strength.
  But you refused 16and said,
    "No! We will flee upon horses"—
    therefore you shall flee!
    and, "We will ride upon swift steeds"—
    therefore your pursuers shall be swift!
17 A thousand shall flee at the threat
      of one,
    at the threat of five you shall flee,
  until you are left
    like a flagstaff on the top of
      a mountain,
    like a signal on a hill.

30.6–17. 6–7: Egypt was famous for palaces and monuments, and as the gateway to Africa for the caravans
that brought wealth and luxuries (see 1 Kings 10). The
prophet contrasts such exotic wealth with the worthlessness of the promises of Egyptian help. *Rahab* (v. 7)
was a dragon monster of ancient story comparable to
the Leviathan* creature (27.1). Since Egyptian religion
was well known for its many deities portrayed in mixed
animal/human form, the ironic title *"Rahab who sits
still"* (v. 7) may allude to the sphinx-like images of
Egypt. **8–11:** The command to *inscribe it in a book* is
a remarkably rare recognition that prophecy was written down and read long after the time when it had
originally been given. The writing is to become *a witness forever* to the truth that Israel was *a rebellious
people* (v. 9). The readers would be no more willing
to heed the message than the original hearers (see
29.11–12). **12–14:** *Its breaking is like that of a potter's
vessel* (v. 14) emphasizes the suddenness and completeness of the disaster that was to come. Hezekiah's
attempt to build security through an alliance with

Egypt would prove disastrously misjudged. **15–17:**
The poetry of *returning, rest, quietness, and trust* attests that God alone is the defense of Jerusalem.

~~~~~~

18 Therefore the LORD waits to be gracious
      to you;
    therefore he will rise up to show
      mercy to you.
    For the LORD is a God of justice;
      blessed are all those who wait for
        him.
  19 Truly, O people in Zion, inhabitants of
Jerusalem, you shall weep no more. He will
surely be gracious to you at the sound of your
cry; when he hears it, he will answer you.
20Though the Lord may give you the bread
of adversity and the water of affliction, yet
your Teacher will not hide himself any more,
but your eyes shall see your Teacher. 21And
when you turn to the right or when you turn
to the left, your ears shall hear a word behind
you, saying, "This is the way; walk in it."
22Then you will defile your silver-covered
idols and your gold-plated images. You will
scatter them like filthy rags; you will say to
them, "Away with you!"
  23 He will give rain for the seed with
which you sow the ground, and grain, the
produce of the ground, which will be rich
and plenteous. On that day your cattle will
graze in broad pastures; 24and the oxen and
donkeys that till the ground will eat silage,
which has been winnowed with shovel and
fork. 25On every lofty mountain and every
high hill there will be brooks running with
water—on a day of the great slaughter, when
the towers fall. 26Moreover the light of the
moon will be like the light of the sun, and
the light of the sun will be sevenfold, like the
light of seven days, on the day when the
LORD binds up the injuries of his people, and
heals the wounds inflicted by his blow.

30.18–26: This poetic reminder of future hope counters any criticism that the message of rest and quietness (v. 15) was too submissive and politically inactive
to end foreign oppression. Human acceptance of the
divine plan for the nations may require patience and
fortitude in enduring the present order. A later scribe
has described more fully (vv. 19–26) what this longed-
for future would bring. Only when God's judgment

puts an end to human violence and oppression—
when the towers fall (v. 25)—will such peace and prosperity come.

27 See, the name of the LORD comes from
    far away,
  burning with his anger, and in thick
    rising smoke;*a*
his lips are full of indignation,
  and his tongue is like a devouring
    fire;
28 his breath is like an overflowing stream
  that reaches up to the neck—
to sift the nations with the sieve of
    destruction,
  and to place on the jaws of the
    peoples a bridle that leads them
    astray.

29 You shall have a song as in the night
when a holy festival is kept; and gladness of
heart, as when one sets out to the sound of
the flute to go to the mountain of the LORD,
to the Rock of Israel. 30And the LORD will
cause his majestic voice to be heard and the
descending blow of his arm to be seen, in
furious anger and a flame of devouring fire,
with a cloudburst and tempest and hailstones. 31The Assyrian will be terror-stricken
at the voice of the LORD, when he strikes
with his rod. 32And every stroke of the staff
of punishment that the LORD lays upon him
will be to the sound of timbrels and lyres;
battling with brandished arm he will fight
with him. 33For his burning place*b* has long
been prepared; truly it is made ready for the
king,*c* its pyre made deep and wide, with fire
and wood in abundance; the breath of the
LORD, like a stream of sulfur, kindles it.

30.27–33: A song in the night. The concluding comments, a later development of the original message,
elaborate on the theme of God's judgment, which will
bring an end to the present unsatisfactory world order
and establish in its place the righteous order of God.
The Assyrian (v. 31) has become symbolic for every
oppressor of God's people.

31 Alas for those who go down to
    Egypt for help
  and who rely on horses,

who trust in chariots because they are
    many
  and in horsemen because they are
    very strong,
but do not look to the Holy One
    of Israel
  or consult the LORD!
2 Yet he too is wise and brings disaster;
  he does not call back his words,
but will rise against the house of the
    evildoers,
  and against the helpers of those who
    work iniquity.
3 The Egyptians are human, and not God;
  their horses are flesh, and not spirit.
When the LORD stretches out his hand,
  the helper will stumble, and the one
    helped will fall,
  and they will all perish together.

4 For thus the LORD said to me,
  As a lion or a young lion growls over its
    prey,
  and—when a band of shepherds is
    called out against it—
is not terrified by their shouting
  or daunted at their noise,
so the LORD of hosts will come down
  to fight upon Mount Zion and upon
    its hill.
5 Like birds hovering overhead, so the
    LORD of hosts
  will protect Jerusalem;
he will protect and deliver it,
  he will spare and rescue it.

6 Turn back to him whom you*d* have
deeply betrayed, O people of Israel. 7For on
that day all of you shall throw away your idols
of silver and idols of gold, which your hands
have sinfully made for you.
8 "Then the Assyrian shall fall by a sword,
    not of mortals;
  and a sword, not of humans, shall
    devour him;
he shall flee from the sword,
  and his young men shall be put to
    forced labor.

a Meaning of Heb uncertain   *b* Or *Topheth*
c Or *Molech*   *d* Heb *they*

⁹ His rock shall pass away in terror,
    and his officers desert the standard in
        panic,"
says the LORD, whose fire is in
        Zion,
    and whose furnace is in Jerusalem.

31.1–9: The lordship of the God of Mount Zion.*
Isaiah continues to warn against complicity with Egypt
in rebellion against Assyria. The LORD *fighting upon
Mount Zion* and *upon its hill* (v. 4) was perhaps originally a threat that God would fight against, not with,
Jerusalem (compare 29.4). Once again, a rebuke
(vv. 1–3) shifts suddenly to assurance (vv. 4–9), raising
the question at what point this new spiritual direction
arose. Was Isaiah compelled to change his warning
into one of promise, or has the situation that occurred
with King Hezekiah's surrender to the Assyrian forces
(2 Kings 18.13–16) necessitated a revised perspective?
The warning and promise introduce (v. 6) the rebuke
that Israel, a rebellious people, must first reject
idolatry* before God's deliverance can come. Threat
and assurance are two aspects of the one consistent,
loving purpose of God, to protect and preserve the
people. The reference to *a sword, not of mortals* (v. 8)
alludes to the angelic slaughter described in 37.36.

32 See, a king will reign in
    righteousness,
    and princes will rule with justice.
² Each will be like a hiding place from
        the wind,
    a covert from the tempest,
like streams of water in a dry place,
    like the shade of a great rock in a
        weary land.
³ Then the eyes of those who have sight
        will not be closed,
    and the ears of those who have
        hearing will listen.
⁴ The minds of the rash will have good
        judgment,
    and the tongues of stammerers will
        speak readily and distinctly.
⁵ A fool will no longer be called noble,
    nor a villain said to be honorable.
⁶ For fools speak folly,
    and their minds plot iniquity:
to practice ungodliness,
    to utter error concerning
        the LORD,

to leave the craving of the hungry
        unsatisfied,
    and to deprive the thirsty of drink.
⁷ The villainies of villains are evil;
    they devise wicked devices
to ruin the poor with lying words,
    even when the plea of the needy is
        right.
⁸ But those who are noble plan noble
        things,
    and by noble things they stand.

⁹ Rise up, you women who are at ease,
        hear my voice;
    you complacent daughters, listen to
        my speech.
¹⁰ In little more than a year
    you will shudder, you complacent
        ones;
for the vintage will fail,
    the fruit harvest will not come.
¹¹ Tremble, you women who are at ease,
    shudder, you complacent ones;
strip, and make yourselves bare,
    and put sackcloth on your loins.
¹² Beat your breasts for the pleasant
        fields,
    for the fruitful vine,
¹³ for the soil of my people
    growing up in thorns and briers;
yes, for all the joyous houses
    in the jubilant city.
¹⁴ For the palace will be forsaken,
    the populous city deserted;
the hill and the watchtower
    will become dens forever,
the joy of wild asses,
    a pasture for flocks;
¹⁵ until a spirit from on high is poured out
        on us,
    and the wilderness becomes a fruitful
        field,
    and the fruitful field is deemed
        a forest.
¹⁶ Then justice will dwell in the
        wilderness,
    and righteousness abide in the
        fruitful field.
¹⁷ The effect of righteousness will be
        peace,
    and the result of righteousness,
        quietness and trust forever.

18 My people will abide in a peaceful
       habitation,
   in secure dwellings, and in quiet
       resting places.
19 The forest will disappear completely,[a]
   and the city will be utterly laid low.
20 Happy will you be who sow beside every
       stream,
   who let the ox and the donkey range
       freely.

32.1–20: A king will reign in righteousness. 1–8: The
deliverance of the city in 701 BCE was a dangerous
precedent: It implied that God's protection could be
relied upon unconditionally. The warning to Hezekiah
in ch. 39 on the occasion of the visit of Babylonian
emissaries was aimed at countering such false expectations. The Davidic kingship could not survive unless
it was founded on just government and compassionate administration. This oracle* may be a portrait of
the great reforming king, Josiah, during whose long
reign (639–609 BCE) Assyrian rule over Judah ended
and the royal administration was reformed (see 2 Kings
22.1–23.25). During this period a substantial part of
Isaiah's prophecies was probably compiled. **9–14:** The
brief respite of hope and renewal during Josiah's reign
ended suddenly and disastrously. Babylonian rule
swiftly replaced Assyrian oppression. Israel would suffer devastation once again, as Isaiah had declared (see
6.11–12) and the rampant growth of *thorns and briers*
(see 5.6) would return. **15–20:** The outpouring of God's
spirit (v. 15) and the transformation of the ruined land
into farmland once again anticipate the hope of the
later chapters, especially 60–62. The *forest* (v. 19) indicates oppressing foreign powers (Assyria and Babylon; see 10.18–19), which will *disappear completely.*

33 Ah, you destroyer,
   who yourself have not been
       destroyed;
   you treacherous one,
   with whom no one has dealt
       treacherously!
   When you have ceased to destroy,
       you will be destroyed;
   and when you have stopped dealing
       treacherously,
   you will be dealt with treacherously.

2 O LORD, be gracious to us; we wait for
   you.

Be our arm every morning,
   our salvation in the time of trouble.
3 At the sound of tumult, peoples fled;
   before your majesty, nations
       scattered.
4 Spoil was gathered as the caterpillar
       gathers;
   as locusts leap, they leaped[b] upon it.
5 The LORD is exalted, he dwells on high;
   he filled Zion with justice and
       righteousness;
6 he will be the stability of your times,
   abundance of salvation, wisdom, and
       knowledge;
   the fear of the LORD is Zion's
       treasure.[c]
7 Listen! the valiant[b] cry in the streets;
   the envoys of peace weep bitterly.
8 The highways are deserted,
   travelers have quit the road.
   The treaty is broken,
   its oaths[d] are despised,
   its obligation[e] is disregarded.
9 The land mourns and languishes;
   Lebanon is confounded and withers
       away;
   Sharon is like a desert;
   and Bashan and Carmel shake off
       their leaves.
10 "Now I will arise," says the LORD,
   "now I will lift myself up;
   now I will be exalted.
11 You conceive chaff, you bring
       forth stubble;
   your breath is a fire that will consume
       you.
12 And the peoples will be as if burned to
       lime,
   like thorns cut down, that are burned
       in the fire."

33.1–24. A miscellany of prophetic themes. This
chapter, and the following two, are difficult to place
in context, but they probably reflect the period after
the fall of Babylon when the fulfillment of the glowing

a Cn: Heb *And it will hail when the forest comes down*
b Meaning of Heb uncertain   c Heb *his treasure;*
meaning of Heb uncertain   d Q Ms: MT *cities*
e Or *everyone*

promises of chs. 40–55 was still awaited. **1–6:** The *destroyer* is not identified, but the general context points to Babylon. Deliverance from oppression is still eagerly awaited, but requires patience and trust in God's purpose (v. 6). **7–12:** The lamentation* of vv. 7–9, revealing the devastated condition of the land, is followed by warnings in vv. 10–16 that the wrongdoing of leaders in Jerusalem now hinders the fulfillment of God's promises.

13 Hear, you who are far away, what I have
      done;
   and you who are near, acknowledge
      my might.
14 The sinners in Zion are afraid;
   trembling has seized the godless:
   "Who among us can live with the
      devouring fire?
   Who among us can live with
      everlasting flames?"
15 Those who walk righteously and speak
      uprightly,
   who despise the gain of oppression,
   who wave away a bribe instead of
      accepting it,
   who stop their ears from hearing of
      bloodshed
   and shut their eyes from looking on
      evil,
16 they will live on the heights;
   their refuge will be the fortresses of
      rocks;
   their food will be supplied, their
      water assured.
17 Your eyes will see the king in his
      beauty;
   they will behold a land that stretches
      far away.
18 Your mind will muse on the terror:
   "Where is the one who counted?
   Where is the one who weighed the
      tribute?
   Where is the one who counted the
      towers?"
19 No longer will you see the insolent
      people,
   the people of an obscure speech that
      you cannot comprehend,
   stammering in a language that you
      cannot understand.

20 Look on Zion, the city of our appointed
      festivals!
   Your eyes will see Jerusalem,
   a quiet habitation, an immovable tent,
   whose stakes will never be pulled up,
      and none of whose ropes will
      be broken.
21 But there the LORD in majesty will be
      for us
   a place of broad rivers and streams,
   where no galley with oars can go,
      nor stately ship can pass.
22 For the LORD is our judge, the LORD is
      our ruler,
   the LORD is our king; he will save us.
23 Your rigging hangs loose;
   it cannot hold the mast firm in its
      place,
   or keep the sail spread out.
   Then prey and spoil in abundance will
      be divided;
   even the lame will fall to plundering.
24 And no inhabitant will say, "I am sick";
   the people who live there will be
      forgiven their iniquity.

33.13–24. 13–16: The reference to those *who are far away* and those *who are near* reflects the divided condition of Israel in the wake of the removal of people into exile. The former nation was in danger of becoming two peoples with some still in the territory of Judah and others scattered among many nations. Isaiah emphasizes the unified purpose of God for both groups and the central significance of Jerusalem as the spiritual capital of all. **17–24:** Babylonian control over Judah and the catastrophes that had befallen Jerusalem had cast doubt on the future of the Davidic kingship. The message of 11.1–5 reveals how eagerly the people awaited a descendant of Judah's royal dynasty, and this hope is further repeated here. Instead of the hated representatives of foreign domination—zealous only for plunder and gain (v. 18)—there would be a king upholding justice and building prosperity (v. 17). Jerusalem would once again become a *quiet habitation* and an *immovable tent* (v. 20). The *broad rivers and streams*, strangely out of place in a city with no major waterways, establish a contrast to the many waterways of Babylon, with their oppressive associations.

34

Draw near, O nations, to hear;
  O peoples, give heed!
Let the earth hear, and all that fills it;
  the world, and all that comes from it.
2 For the LORD is enraged against all the
    nations,
  and furious against all their hordes;
  he has doomed them, has given them
    over for slaughter.
3 Their slain shall be cast out,
  and the stench of their corpses shall
    rise;
  the mountains shall flow with their
    blood.
4 All the host of heaven shall rot away,
  and the skies roll up like a scroll.
All their host shall wither
  like a leaf withering on a vine,
  or fruit withering on a fig tree.

5 When my sword has drunk its fill in the
    heavens,
  lo, it will descend upon Edom,
  upon the people I have doomed to
    judgment.
6 The LORD has a sword; it is sated with
    blood,
  it is gorged with fat,
  with the blood of lambs and goats,
  with the fat of the kidneys of rams.
For the LORD has a sacrifice in Bozrah,
  a great slaughter in the land of Edom.
7 Wild oxen shall fall with them,
  and young steers with the
    mighty bulls.
Their land shall be soaked with blood,
  and their soil made rich with fat.

8 For the LORD has a day of vengeance,
  a year of vindication by Zion's
    cause.[a]
9 And the streams of Edom[b] shall be
    turned into pitch,
  and her soil into sulfur;
  her land shall become burning pitch.
10 Night and day it shall not be quenched;
  its smoke shall go up forever.
From generation to generation it shall
    lie waste;
  no one shall pass through it forever
    and ever.

11 But the hawk[c] and the hedgehog[c] shall
    possess it;
  the owl[c] and the raven shall live in it.
He shall stretch the line of confusion
    over it,
  and the plummet of chaos over[d] its
    nobles.
12 They shall name it No Kingdom There,
  and all its princes shall be nothing.
13 Thorns shall grow over its strongholds,
  nettles and thistles in its fortresses.
It shall be the haunt of jackals,
  an abode for ostriches.
14 Wildcats shall meet with hyenas,
  goat-demons shall call to each other;
there too Lilith shall repose,
  and find a place to rest.
15 There shall the owl nest
  and lay and hatch and brood in its
    shadow;
there too the buzzards shall gather,
  each one with its mate.
16 Seek and read from the book of
    the LORD:
Not one of these shall be missing;
  none shall be without its mate.
For the mouth of the LORD has
    commanded,
  and his spirit has gathered them.
17 He has cast the lot for them,
  his hand has portioned it out to them
    with the line;
they shall possess it forever,
  from generation to generation they
    shall live in it.

34.1–17: The LORD's day of vengeance. Taken together, chs. 34–35 provide a sequel to the prophecies of chs. 24–27, with which they are closely related both in theme and character. The major exception is the warning of the divine punishment that is to befall the people of Edom (34.5–17), a nation that is unexpectedly absent from the foreign peoples included in chs. 13–23. Their inclusion separately at this point may reflect a sharp condemnation of their treacherous role after the destruction of Jerusalem by Babylonian forces in 587 BCE. **1–4:** The opening addresses all nations and peoples with a fearsome warning of judgment to come

a Or of recompense by Zion's defender   b Heb her
streams   c Identification uncertain   d Heb lacks over

upon them all, similar to the warning of 24.1–23. **5–17:** The especially fierce and bloodthirsty warning of the judgment that is to befall Edom foretells that this land will be reduced to a total ruin, with all its population annihilated (vv. 9–13). It will become a home for wild animals, instead of a place of human habitation (vv. 14–17).

〰〰〰〰〰〰〰〰〰〰〰〰〰〰〰〰

35 The wilderness and the dry land
      shall be glad,
   the desert shall rejoice and blossom;
like the crocus ²it shall blossom
      abundantly,
   and rejoice with joy and singing.
The glory of Lebanon shall be given
      to it,
   the majesty of Carmel and Sharon.
They shall see the glory of the LORD,
   the majesty of our God.

³ Strengthen the weak hands,
   and make firm the feeble knees.
⁴ Say to those who are of a fearful
      heart,
   "Be strong, do not fear!
Here is your God.
   He will come with vengeance,
with terrible recompense.
   He will come and save you."

⁵ Then the eyes of the blind shall
      be opened,
   and the ears of the deaf unstopped;
⁶ then the lame shall leap like a deer,
   and the tongue of the speechless sing
      for joy.
For waters shall break forth in the
      wilderness,
   and streams in the desert;
⁷ the burning sand shall become a pool,
   and the thirsty ground springs
      of water;
the haunt of jackals shall become
      a swamp,ᵃ
   the grass shall become reeds and
      rushes.

⁸ A highway shall be there,
   and it shall be called the Holy Way;
the unclean shall not travel on it,ᵇ
   but it shall be for God's people;ᶜ

no traveler, not even fools, shall go
      astray.
⁹ No lion shall be there,
   nor shall any ravenous beast come up
      on it;
they shall not be found there,
   but the redeemed shall walk there.
¹⁰ And the ransomed of the LORD shall
      return,
   and come to Zion with singing;
everlasting joy shall be upon their
      heads;
   they shall obtain joy and gladness,
   and sorrow and sighing shall
      flee away.

35.1–10: The triumph of Zion.* **1–4:** In contrast to the grim and forbidding warnings of ch. 34, ch. 35 presents a picture of the hope that awaits the people of God when they rebuild the land of Judah and reestablish Jerusalem as their capital. It will be a fitting place to which all the scattered survivors of Israel can return. This chapter, without a clear historical context, may have been added to link chs. 40–55 with chs. 5–34. **5–10:** The hope for the special eminence that will come to Jerusalem (*Zion*) is consistent with chs. 60–62. The theme of the *highway* by which the scattered survivors of the nation will be enabled to return to their homeland (40.1) is anticipated in v. 8 (see also 19.23). The opening up of pools in the wilderness alludes to the promise of 41.17–18, while the opening of *eyes* and *ears* (v. 5) marks the end of the time of Israel's blindness and deafness (compare 6.9–10). Chapter 35 summarizes and concludes chs. 5–34, with their many threats and warnings, and opens the path to the more consistently hopeful message of chs. 40–66. Chapters 36–39 bridge these two major collections by reporting a triumphant sign of hope for Judah at the close of the eighth century.

The wonderful deliverance of Jerusalem
36.1–37.38: Jerusalem was saved from destruction when threatened by the forces of the Assyrian king, Sennacherib, in 701 BCE. The account is repeated from 2 Kings 18.17–19.37 because it provides the main background to chs. 28–31 and because of the major part that Isaiah played. The account itself is straight-

---

a Cn: Heb *in the haunt of jackals is her resting place*
b Or *pass it by*   *c* Cn: Heb *for them*

forward: After the Assyrian forces had captured most of the towns and fortified cities of Judah (36.1), the Assyrian king sent his representative, called the Rabshakeh, to King Hezekiah in Jerusalem, urging him to surrender. This ultimatum is exceedingly dismissive of the LORD as protector of Jerusalem, regarding any god save that of the king of Assyria as worthless (36.13–20). A letter effectively repeats the same charges. The Assyrian ultimatum leaves Hezekiah gravely troubled until Isaiah encourages him to refuse (37.22–35). Isaiah insists that the Assyrian king, who has blasphemed God, will be punished accordingly, and that God will defend Jerusalem. Soon afterwards, the angel of the LORD strikes down 185,000 of the besieging force, compelling Sennacherib to return home (37.36–37).

Any effort to reconstruct the actual event needs to take three issues into account. First, 2 Kings 18.13–16 shows that Hezekiah surrendered to Sennacherib after the capture of Lachish and was forced to pay a heavy indemnity. Second, an Assyrian royal chronicle* of the campaign shows that the Assyrian commander regarded Hezekiah's surrender as a victory. Third, some untoward event (37.36) influenced the Assyrian king's return home in haste without destroying Jerusalem and removing its royal head, perhaps severe plague among the soldiers (see Isa 10.16), or news of an Egyptian counterattack (see Isa 37.7, 9). It is unlikely that Sennacherib campaigned against Jerusalem twice, so that the account of the humiliating withdrawal of the Assyrian forces refers to the second occasion, when no formal surrender from Hezekiah took place. It is more likely that Hezekiah did surrender to Sennacherib in 701 BCE, but the terms were remarkably lenient for unknown reasons. The Assyrian royal chronicle presumably omits all details that are less than flattering to the royal commander. To understand the prophetic significance of the narrative, it is important to recognize the contrast between the deliverance of Jerusalem in 701 BCE, and the grievous collapse and surrender of the city to the Babylonian forces in 598 and again in 587 BCE. This contrast is implied in the response of Isaiah to Hezekiah (39.5–8), when Babylonian emissaries visited Jerusalem.

36 In the fourteenth year of King Hezekiah, King Sennacherib of Assyria came up against all the fortified cities of Judah and captured them. 2The king of Assyria sent the Rabshakeh from Lachish to King Hezekiah at Jerusalem, with a great army. He stood by the conduit of the upper pool on the highway to the Fuller's Field. 3And there came out to him Eliakim son of Hilkiah, who was in charge of the palace, and Shebna the secretary, and Joah son of Asaph, the recorder.

4 The Rabshakeh said to them, "Say to Hezekiah: Thus says the great king, the king of Assyria: On what do you base this confidence of yours? 5Do you think that mere words are strategy and power for war? On whom do you now rely, that you have rebelled against me? 6See, you are relying on Egypt, that broken reed of a staff, which will pierce the hand of anyone who leans on it. Such is Pharaoh king of Egypt to all who rely on him. 7But if you say to me, 'We rely on the LORD our God,' is it not he whose high places and altars Hezekiah has removed, saying to Judah and to Jerusalem, 'You shall worship before this altar'? 8Come now, make a wager with my master the king of Assyria: I will give you two thousand horses, if you are able on your part to set riders on them. 9How then can you repulse a single captain among the least of my master's servants, when you rely on Egypt for chariots and for horsemen? 10Moreover, is it without the LORD that I have come up against this land to destroy it? The LORD said to me, Go up against this land, and destroy it."

11 Then Eliakim, Shebna, and Joah said to the Rabshakeh, "Please speak to your servants in Aramaic, for we understand it; do not speak to us in the language of Judah within the hearing of the people who are on the wall." 12But the Rabshakeh said, "Has my master sent me to speak these words to your master and to you, and not to the people sitting on the wall, who are doomed with you to eat their own dung and drink their own urine?"

13 Then the Rabshakeh stood and called out in a loud voice in the language of Judah, "Hear the words of the great king, the king of Assyria! 14Thus says the king: 'Do not let Hezekiah deceive you, for he will not be able to deliver you. 15Do not let Hezekiah make you rely on the LORD by saying, The LORD will surely deliver us; this city will not be given into the hand of the king of Assyria.'

16Do not listen to Hezekiah; for thus says the king of Assyria: 'Make your peace with me and come out to me; then everyone of you will eat from your own vine and your own fig tree and drink water from your own cistern, 17until I come and take you away to a land like your own land, a land of grain and wine, a land of bread and vineyards. 18Do not let Hezekiah mislead you by saying, The LORD will save us. Has any of the gods of the nations saved their land out of the hand of the king of Assyria? 19Where are the gods of Hamath and Arpad? Where are the gods of Sepharvaim? Have they delivered Samaria out of my hand? 20Who among all the gods of these countries have saved their countries out of my hand, that the LORD should save Jerusalem out of my hand?'"

21 But they were silent and answered him not a word, for the king's command was, "Do not answer him." 22Then Eliakim son of Hilkiah, who was in charge of the palace, and Shebna the secretary, and Joah son of Asaph, the recorder, came to Hezekiah with their clothes torn, and told him the words of the Rabshakeh.

37 When King Hezekiah heard it, he tore his clothes, covered himself with sackcloth, and went into the house of the LORD. 2And he sent Eliakim, who was in charge of the palace, and Shebna the secretary, and the senior priests, covered with sackcloth, to the prophet Isaiah son of Amoz. 3They said to him, "Thus says Hezekiah, This day is a day of distress, of rebuke, and of disgrace; children have come to the birth, and there is no strength to bring them forth. 4It may be that the LORD your God heard the words of the Rabshakeh, whom his master the king of Assyria has sent to mock the living God, and will rebuke the words that the LORD your God has heard; therefore lift up your prayer for the remnant that is left."

5 When the servants of King Hezekiah came to Isaiah, 6Isaiah said to them, "Say to your master, 'Thus says the LORD: Do not be afraid because of the words that you have heard, with which the servants of the king of Assyria have reviled me. 7I myself will put a spirit in him, so that he shall hear a rumor,

and return to his own land; I will cause him to fall by the sword in his own land.'"

36.1–37.7: The report of the speech of the Assyrian Rabshakeh and Isaiah's response. Two closely parallel accounts tell the story of the Assyrian address mocking Hezekiah's God along with Isaiah's reply. In the first account (36.1–37.7), the Rabshakeh speaks in the hearing of all Jerusalem, whereas in the second (37.8–38) the ultimatum is conveyed by letter and a much longer reply is given by Isaiah (37.6–7 compared with 37.22–35). **36.2:** *The king of Assyria sent the Rabshakeh from Lachish.* The siege and capture of Lachish formed the major battle of the Assyrian campaign in Judah and was afterwards extensively illustrated in carved wallpanels that decorated Sennacherib's palace. These have been recovered and are now displayed in the British Museum in London.

8 The Rabshakeh returned, and found the king of Assyria fighting against Libnah; for he had heard that the king had left Lachish. 9Now the king*a* heard concerning King Tirhakah of Ethiopia,*b* "He has set out to fight against you." When he heard it, he sent messengers to Hezekiah, saying, 10"Thus shall you speak to King Hezekiah of Judah: Do not let your God on whom you rely deceive you by promising that Jerusalem will not be given into the hand of the king of Assyria. 11See, you have heard what the kings of Assyria have done to all lands, destroying them utterly. Shall you be delivered? 12Have the gods of the nations delivered them, the nations that my predecessors destroyed, Gozan, Haran, Rezeph, and the people of Eden who were in Telassar? 13Where is the king of Hamath, the king of Arpad, the king of the city of Sepharvaim, the king of Hena, or the king of Ivvah?"

14 Hezekiah received the letter from the hand of the messengers and read it; then Hezekiah went up to the house of the LORD and spread it before the LORD. 15And Hezekiah prayed to the LORD, saying: 16"O LORD of hosts, God of Israel, who are enthroned above the cherubim, you are God, you alone, of all the kingdoms of the earth;

a Heb he   *b* Or Nubia; Heb Cush

you have made heaven and earth. 17Incline your ear, O LORD, and hear; open your eyes, O LORD, and see; hear all the words of Sennacherib, which he has sent to mock the living God. 18Truly, O LORD, the kings of Assyria have laid waste all the nations and their lands, 19and have hurled their gods into the fire, though they were no gods, but the work of human hands—wood and stone—and so they were destroyed. 20So now, O LORD our God, save us from his hand, so that all the kingdoms of the earth may know that you alone are the LORD."

21 Then Isaiah son of Amoz sent to Hezekiah, saying: "Thus says the LORD, the God of Israel: Because you have prayed to me concerning King Sennacherib of Assyria, 22this is the word that the LORD has spoken concerning him:

She despises you, she scorns you—
virgin daughter Zion;
she tosses her head—behind
your back,
daughter Jerusalem.

23 "Whom have you mocked and
reviled?
Against whom have you raised your
voice
and haughtily lifted your eyes?
Against the Holy One of Israel!
24 By your servants you have mocked
the Lord,
and you have said, 'With my many
chariots
I have gone up the heights of the
mountains,
to the far recesses of Lebanon;
I felled its tallest cedars,
its choicest cypresses;
I came to its remotest height,
its densest forest.
25 I dug wells
and drank waters,
I dried up with the sole of my foot
all the streams of Egypt.'

26 "Have you not heard
that I determined it long ago?
I planned from days of old
what now I bring to pass,

that you should make fortified cities
crash into heaps of ruins,
27 while their inhabitants, shorn of
strength,
are dismayed and confounded;
they have become like plants of
the field
and like tender grass,
like grass on the housetops,
blighted[a] before it is grown.

28 "I know your rising up[b] and your sitting
down,
your going out and coming in,
and your raging against me.
29 Because you have raged against me
and your arrogance has come to my
ears,
I will put my hook in your nose
and my bit in your mouth;
I will turn you back on the way
by which you came.

30 "And this shall be the sign for you: This year eat what grows of itself, and in the second year what springs from that; then in the third year sow, reap, plant vineyards, and eat their fruit. 31The surviving remnant of the house of Judah shall again take root downward, and bear fruit upward; 32for from Jerusalem a remnant shall go out, and from Mount Zion a band of survivors. The zeal of the LORD of hosts will do this.

33 "Therefore thus says the LORD concerning the king of Assyria: He shall not come into this city, shoot an arrow there, come before it with a shield, or cast up a siege ramp against it. 34By the way that he came, by the same he shall return; he shall not come into this city, says the LORD. 35For I will defend this city to save it, for my own sake and for the sake of my servant David."

36 Then the angel of the LORD set out and struck down one hundred eighty-five

a With 2 Kings 19.26: Heb field   b Q Ms Gk: MT lacks your rising up thousand in the camp of the Assyrians; when morning dawned, they were all dead bodies. [37]Then King Sennacherib of Assyria left, went home, and lived at Nineveh. [38]As he was worshiping in the house of his god Nisroch, his sons Adrammelech and Sharezer killed him with the sword, and they escaped into the land of Ararat. His son Esar-haddon succeeded him.

37.8–38. 9: *When he heard it, he sent messengers to Hezekiah:* A repetition of the Assyrian ultimatum. 15–21: The prayer of Hezekiah demonstrates the trust and piety of the king (see especially v. 21). 21–35: Isaiah replies to the Assyrian letter with a series of prophetic declarations. Jerusalem survived intact and the king retained his throne. These facts were more central to Isaiah's message than the punishment eventually inflicted on Sennacherib, who is accused of blasphemy (37.38). 36: The work of *the angel of the Lord* may have been an outbreak of disease among forces camped in unhygienic conditions (as foretold in 10.16). Verse 37.7 declares: "I myself will put a spirit in him, so that he shall hear a rumor and return to his own land." Other possibilities cannot be ruled out, and no precise information is available. 37–38: Sennacherib's assassination by members of his own family is not reported in Assyrian royal chronicles. The king's death occurred some time after the events of 701, but his insult to the God of Jerusalem was seen to demand personal punishment.

38 In those days Hezekiah became sick and was at the point of death. The prophet Isaiah son of Amoz came to him, and said to him, "Thus says the Lord: Set your house in order, for you shall die; you shall not recover." [2]Then Hezekiah turned his face to the wall, and prayed to the Lord: [3]"Remember now, O Lord, I implore you, how I have walked before you in faithfulness with a whole heart, and have done what is good in your sight." And Hezekiah wept bitterly.

4 Then the word of the Lord came to Isaiah: [5]"Go and say to Hezekiah, Thus says the Lord, the God of your ancestor David: I have heard your prayer, I have seen your tears; I will add fifteen years to your life. [6]I will deliver you and this city out of the hand of the king of Assyria, and defend this city.

7 "This is the sign to you from the Lord, that the Lord will do this thing that he has promised: [8]See, I will make the shadow cast by the declining sun on the dial of Ahaz turn back ten steps." So the sun turned back on the dial the ten steps by which it had declined.[a]

9 A writing of King Hezekiah of Judah, after he had been sick and had recovered from his sickness:

[10] I said: In the noontide of my days
  I must depart;
  I am consigned to the gates of Sheol
    for the rest of my years.
[11] I said, I shall not see the Lord
    in the land of the living;
  I shall look upon mortals no more
    among the inhabitants of the world.
[12] My dwelling is plucked up and removed
        from me
    like a shepherd's tent;
  like a weaver I have rolled up my life;
    he cuts me off from the loom;
  from day to night you bring me to an
        end;[a]
[13]   I cry for help[b] until morning;
  like a lion he breaks all my bones;
    from day to night you bring me to an
        end.[a]

[14] Like a swallow or a crane[a] I clamor,
    I moan like a dove.
  My eyes are weary with looking
        upward.
    O Lord, I am oppressed; be my
        security!
[15] But what can I say? For he has spoken
        to me,
    and he himself has done it.
  All my sleep has fled[c]
    because of the bitterness of my soul.

[16] O Lord, by these things people live,
    and in all these is the life of
        my spirit.[a]
  Oh, restore me to health and make
        me live!

a Meaning of Heb uncertain   b Cn: Meaning of Heb uncertain   c Cn Compare Syr: Heb *I will walk slowly all my years*

17 Surely it was for my welfare
     that I had great bitterness;
 but you have held back*a* my life
     from the pit of destruction,
 for you have cast all my sins
     behind your back.
18 For Sheol cannot thank you,
     death cannot praise you;
 those who go down to the Pit cannot
     hope
     for your faithfulness.
19 The living, the living, they thank you,
     as I do this day;
 fathers make known to children
     your faithfulness.

20 The LORD will save me,
     and we will sing to stringed
         instruments*b*
 all the days of our lives,
     at the house of the LORD.

21 Now Isaiah had said, "Let them take a lump of figs, and apply it to the boil, so that he may recover." 22 Hezekiah also had said, "What is the sign that I shall go up to the house of the LORD?"

38.1–22: Hezekiah's sickness and recovery. The story of Hezekiah's illness (v. 21) is a further illustration of piety (v. 3): His total submissiveness to the will of the LORD God and his subsequent recovery from the sickness are inseparably related to the wonderful deliverance of Jerusalem from the forces of Assyria (v. 6). Signs were evidence of the validity of a prophetic pronouncement (see Isa 7.10–17). The exact nature of the sign is not clear. **10–20:** This psalm of thanksgiving is not included in 2 Kings 20.1–11, but is added as further evidence of the king's piety. It is a personal psalm of thanksgiving for recovery from serious illness. It includes a lamentation during the time of distress (vv. 10–15) and thanksgiving for recovery (vv. 16–20).

39 At that time King Merodach-baladan
     son of Baladan of Babylon sent envoys with letters and a present to Hezekiah, for he heard that he had been sick and had recovered. 2 Hezekiah welcomed them; he showed them his treasure house, the silver, the gold, the spices, the precious oil, his whole armory, all that was found in his store-

houses. There was nothing in his house or in all his realm that Hezekiah did not show them. 3 Then the prophet Isaiah came to King Hezekiah and said to him, "What did these men say? From where did they come to you?" Hezekiah answered, "They have come to me from a far country, from Babylon." 4 He said, "What have they seen in your house?" Hezekiah answered, "They have seen all that is in my house; there is nothing in my storehouses that I did not show them."

5 Then Isaiah said to Hezekiah, "Hear the word of the LORD of hosts: 6 Days are coming when all that is in your house, and that which your ancestors have stored up until this day, shall be carried to Babylon; nothing shall be left, says the LORD. 7 Some of your own sons who are born to you shall be taken away; they shall be eunuchs in the palace of the king of Babylon." 8 Then Hezekiah said to Isaiah, "The word of the LORD that you have spoken is good." For he thought, "There will be peace and security in my days."

39.1–8: The visit of the Babylonian emissaries. The book of Isaiah is built around belief in God's concern with the Davidic dynasty* of kings and the city of Jerusalem where God's Temple* stood. The contrast between the fate of the dynasty and the city in 701 BCE, when Isaiah was active as a prophet, and events a century later when the Babylonian forces confronted Jerusalem (in 598 and again in 587 BCE), effectively divides the book between two main periods—the Assyrian and the Babylonian epochs. The visit of Babylonian emissaries to Hezekiah when Sennacherib threatened the king and his city forms a bridge between these two main sections. The events in vv. 6–7 occurred in 598 BCE when Jehoiachin was removed from the throne and taken prisoner to Babylon, with most of his immediate household (2 Kings 24.10–17). God's protection of Jerusalem and its Davidic dynasty was not unconditional, but depended upon the obedience and submission of each ruler. The comment of Hezekiah, *There will be peace and security in my days* (v.8), is not selfish complacency but a submissive acceptance of the conditions under which God's promise was conferred. More than this could not be given.

a Cn Compare Gk Vg: Heb *loved*   b Heb *my stringed instruments*

Isaiah 40-55

THE RENEWAL OF HOPE FOR JERUSALEM

In 538 BCE, a combined force of Medes and Persians entered the city of Babylon, having previously defeated the Babylonian military might. During the decade before the collapse of Babylonian rule, the prophecies that make up chs. 40–55 were written. They show a remarkable similarity of mood and character and are, with only minor exceptions, attributed to a single prophet. They express in richly poetic language a message of comfort, addressed primarily to Jerusalem, but also to the scattered remnants of the former Israel. They assure the readers that God is Creator and Lord of history. Israel's past experience proves this; the fulfillment of earlier prophecies bears witness to it; and current events confirm it. The prophet points to the rise of Cyrus, the Persian ruler whose victories put an end to Babylon's domination. Unbelief, despair, and idolatry* are all condemned as neglect of the one true God. This emphatic focus on the sole deity of the LORD God of Israel makes these chapters the most forthright declaration of monotheism in the Hebrew Scriptures.

Combined with this message of comfort and reassurance for Israel is a clear promise that those exiled among the nations will return home. A way will open up in the wilderness for this processional return to Jerusalem, and God will providentially support the weak and distressed who make the journey. The city of Babylon will fall (47.1–15) and Jerusalem will be rebuilt (44.28; 54.11–17). Its future will be even more splendid than its past, and a new age of peace and tranquillity will dawn.

Overall, the message balances the warnings and threats that have colored most of chs. 1–39. Even more, however, these chapters allude to earlier prophecies and carry their message further. Clearly the prophet of chs. 40–55, sometimes referred to as Second Isaiah, was close to the scribes who preserved the sayings of the first part, even being described as a "disciple" of the earlier prophet (50.4–6; compare 8.16). Chapters 40–55 carry forward the message about Jerusalem and its future as the symbolic center of Israel as the people of God. The tragedies of the past will become the triumphs of the future in God's plan.

Explicit references to the Persian ruler Cyrus (44.28; 45.1; compare 41.25) point to the events of 545–538 BCE, a time just before the downfall of Babylon. The prophet addresses Israelite captives held in Babylon (42.7, 8) and recognizes the dispersion of many survivors of Israel and Judah among the nations (49.22–23). The fall of Babylon is foretold as imminent, with an expectation of the subsequent release of the captives from Judah and their return home (55.12). Because the prophet alternately addresses Jerusalem and the scattered remnants, it is not clear where he was located. He was clearly sensitive to the sufferings of captives held in Babylon, so he may have been among them. His frequent explicit addresses to Zion and Jerusalem (40.1, 9; 49.14; 52.1), however, may indicate that he cannot have been far from this city, the undoubted spiritual focus of his thinking. Even with this focus, the prophet looks beyond known national boundaries to the undefined coastlands (41.1, 5; 49.1) and the ends of the earth (41.9).

READING GUIDE

Recent study of these sixteen chapters recognizes their psalm-like quality. The prophet's thought and language were evidently deeply colored by the Hebrew psalms. Jerusalem with its Temple* was his spiritual and intellectual home, even though the Temple itself had been in ruins for half a century. Moreover, the prophecies concentrate intensely on hope and encouragement, giving them great power. The original audience was presumably either indifferent to God's message or near despair about its relevance. Consequently, the emphasis upon the most basic religious themes—the creation of the world, the idea of purpose and meaning in human history, the oneness of God and of all nations and peoples in the divine plan—has made these chapters unequaled anywhere else in prophecy.

40 Comfort, O comfort my people,
  says your God.
2 Speak tenderly to Jerusalem,
    and cry to her
  that she has served her term,
    that her penalty is paid,
  that she has received from the LORD's
    hand
  double for all her sins.

3 A voice cries out:
  "In the wilderness prepare the way of
    the LORD,
    make straight in the desert a highway
      for our God.
4 Every valley shall be lifted up,
    and every mountain and hill be made
      low;
  the uneven ground shall become level,
    and the rough places a plain.
5 Then the glory of the LORD shall
      be revealed,
    and all people shall see it together,

for the mouth of the LORD has
    spoken."

6 A voice says, "Cry out!"
    And I said, "What shall I cry?"
  All people are grass,
    their constancy is like the flower of
      the field.
7 The grass withers, the flower fades,
    when the breath of the LORD blows
      upon it;
  surely the people are grass.
8 The grass withers, the flower fades;
    but the word of our God will stand
      forever.
9 Get you up to a high mountain,
    O Zion, herald of good tidings;[a]
  lift up your voice with strength,
    O Jerusalem, herald of good tidings,[b]
  lift it up, do not fear;

a Or O herald of good tidings to Zion   b Or O herald of
good tidings to Jerusalem

say to the cities of Judah,
  "Here is your God!"
10 See, the Lord GOD comes with might,
    and his arm rules for him;
  his reward is with him,
    and his recompense before him.
11 He will feed his flock like a shepherd;
    he will gather the lambs in his arms,
  and carry them in his bosom,
    and gently lead the mother sheep.

40.1–31: A highway for our God. 1–11: The prophet begins by calling on the reader to bring a message of *comfort* to Jerusalem. Her period of servitude is now complete and freedom is at hand (v. 2). This message of hope pictures a great *highway* stretching across the desert and leading to Jerusalem (vv. 3–5), providing a way home for those scattered remnants of the former Israel who have been captive among the nations, particularly in Babylon. God will strengthen the weakened survivors who feel that they cannot make the journey (vv. 10–11; 29–31).

~~~~~~

12 Who has measured the waters in the
      hollow of his hand
    and marked off the heavens with a
      span,
  enclosed the dust of the earth in
    a measure,
    and weighed the mountains in scales
  and the hills in a balance?
13 Who has directed the spirit of the LORD,
    or as his counselor has instructed
      him?
14 Whom did he consult for his
      enlightenment,
    and who taught him the path of
      justice?
  Who taught him knowledge,
    and showed him the way of
      understanding?
15 Even the nations are like a drop from a
      bucket,
    and are accounted as dust on
      the scales;
  see, he takes up the isles like fine
    dust.
16 Lebanon would not provide fuel
      enough,
    nor are its animals enough for a burnt
      offering.

17 All the nations are as nothing before
      him;
    they are accounted by him as less
      than nothing and emptiness.
18 To whom then will you liken God,
    or what likeness compare with him?
19 An idol? —A workman casts it,
    and a goldsmith overlays it with gold,
    and casts for it silver chains.
20 As a gift one chooses mulberry wood[a]
    —wood that will not rot—
  then seeks out a skilled artisan
    to set up an image that will
      not topple.

21 Have you not known? Have you
      not heard?
  Has it not been told you from the
      beginning?
  Have you not understood from the
      foundations of the earth?
22 It is he who sits above the circle of the
      earth,
    and its inhabitants are like
      grasshoppers;
  who stretches out the heavens like a
      curtain,
    and spreads them like a tent to
      live in;
23 who brings princes to naught,
    and makes the rulers of the earth as
      nothing.

24 Scarcely are they planted, scarcely
      sown,
    scarcely has their stem taken root in
      the earth,
  when he blows upon them, and they
      wither,
    and the tempest carries them off like
      stubble.

25 To whom then will you compare me,
    or who is my equal? says the Holy
      One.
26 Lift up your eyes on high and see:
    Who created these?

---

a Meaning of Heb uncertain

He who brings out their host and
numbers them,
calling them all by name;
because he is great in strength,
mighty in power,
not one is missing.

27 Why do you say, O Jacob,
and speak, O Israel,
"My way is hidden from the LORD,
and my right is disregarded by my
God"?
28 Have you not known? Have you
not heard?
The LORD is the everlasting God,
the Creator of the ends of the earth.
He does not faint or grow weary;
his understanding is unsearchable.
29 He gives power to the faint,
and strengthens the powerless.
30 Even youths will faint and be weary,
and the young will fall exhausted;
31 but those who wait for the LORD shall
renew their strength,
they shall mount up with wings like
eagles,
they shall run and not be weary,
they shall walk and not faint.

40.12–31. 12–20: Such a message would be unbelievable if God were other than the sovereign creator of
the entire universe (vv. 12–14). Even the multitude of
the nations of the world *are as nothing* before such
immense power (v. 17). **21–28:** The very stars adhere
to the divine places set for them at creation (v. 26).
Already vv. 19–20 answer the question posed in v. 18:
False ideas of God lead to false expectations about the
divine purpose. Only by abandoning the absurdities
of idolatry* can the people grasp the power of God
(v. 23).

41 Listen to me in silence,
O coastlands;
let the peoples renew their strength;
let them approach, then let
them speak;
let us together draw near for
judgment.

2 Who has roused a victor from the east,
summoned him to his service?

He delivers up nations to him,
and tramples kings under foot;
he makes them like dust with his sword,
like driven stubble with his bow.
3 He pursues them and passes on safely,
scarcely touching the path with his
feet.
4 Who has performed and done this,
calling the generations from the
beginning?
I, the LORD, am first,
and will be with the last.
5 The coastlands have seen and
are afraid,
the ends of the earth tremble;
they have drawn near and come.
6 Each one helps the other,
saying to one another, "Take
courage!"
7 The artisan encourages the goldsmith,
and the one who smooths with the
hammer encourages the one who
strikes the anvil,
saying of the soldering, "It is good";
and they fasten it with nails so that it
cannot be moved.
8 But you, Israel, my servant,
Jacob, whom I have chosen,
the offspring of Abraham, my friend;
9 you whom I took from the ends of the
earth,
and called from its farthest corners,
saying to you, "You are my servant,
I have chosen you and not cast you
off";
10 do not fear, for I am with you,
do not be afraid, for I am your God;
I will strengthen you, I will help you,
I will uphold you with my victorious
right hand.

41.1–29: I am your God. 1–5: The speech of the Assyrian Rabshakeh in 36.20 had asked in complacent
irony:* "Who among all the gods of the countries
have saved their countries out of my hand, that the
LORD should save Jerusalem out of my hand?" The
prophecies of ch. 41 provide a magnificent rejoinder
to this question, showing how and why the God of
Jerusalem is different. The Holy One of Israel is creator
and director of human history. Proof of this is first seen
in the victories that Cyrus, king of the Medes and Per-

sians, has already won (vv. 2–5, 25). This ruler is mentioned by name more fully in 44.28; 45.1–4, 13. The *coastlands* (vv. 1, 5) are the most distant parts of the earth, so that all nations may recognize that a divine plan is at work. **6–10:** Again the prophet ridicules the foolish work of the idol maker (see also 23–24, 29). God had already called Israel to be the servant-people who would fulfill God's special purpose on earth (compare 49.6).

11 Yes, all who are incensed against you
        shall be ashamed and disgraced;
    those who strive against you
        shall be as nothing and
            shall perish.
12 You shall seek those who contend
        with you,
    but you shall not find them;
    those who war against you
        shall be as nothing at all.
13 For I, the LORD your God,
        hold your right hand;
    it is I who say to you, "Do not fear,
    I will help you."

14 Do not fear, you worm Jacob,
        you insect[a] Israel!
    I will help you, says the LORD;
        your Redeemer is the Holy One of
            Israel.
15 Now, I will make of you a threshing
        sledge,
        sharp, new, and having teeth;
    you shall thresh the mountains and
            crush them,
    and you shall make the hills
            like chaff.
16 You shall winnow them and the wind
        shall carry them away,
    and the tempest shall scatter them.
    Then you shall rejoice in the LORD;
        in the Holy One of Israel you shall
            glory.

17 When the poor and needy seek water,
        and there is none,
    and their tongue is parched
            with thirst,
    I the LORD will answer them,
    I the God of Israel will not forsake
            them.

18 I will open rivers on the bare heights,[b]
        and fountains in the midst of
            the valleys;
    I will make the wilderness a pool
            of water,
    and the dry land springs of water.
19 I will put in the wilderness the cedar,
        the acacia, the myrtle, and the olive;
    I will set in the desert the cypress,
        the plane and the pine together,
20 so that all may see and know,
        all may consider and understand,
    that the hand of the LORD has done this,
        the Holy One of Israel has created it.

21 Set forth your case, says the LORD;
        bring your proofs, says the King of
            Jacob.
22 Let them bring them, and tell us
        what is to happen.
    Tell us the former things, what they are,
        so that we may consider them,
    and that we may know their outcome;
        or declare to us the things to come.
23 Tell us what is to come hereafter,
        that we may know that you are gods;
    do good, or do harm,
        that we may be afraid and terrified.
24 You, indeed, are nothing
        and your work is nothing at all;
    whoever chooses you is an
            abomination.

25 I stirred up one from the north, and he
            has come,
        from the rising of the sun he was
            summoned by name.[c]
    He shall trample[d] on rulers as on
            mortar,
        as the potter treads clay.
26 Who declared it from the beginning, so
            that we might know,
        and beforehand, so that we might say,
            "He is right"?
    There was no one who declared it, none
            who proclaimed,
        none who heard your words.

a Syr: Heb *men of*   b Or *trails*   c Cn Compare
Q Ms Gk: MT *and he shall call on my name*
d Cn: Heb *come*

27 I first have declared it to Zion,^a
   and I give to Jerusalem a herald of
      good tidings.
28 But when I look there is no one;
   among these there is no counselor
   who, when I ask, gives an answer.
29 No, they are all a delusion;
   their works are nothing;
   their images are empty wind.

41.11–29. 11–16: The present weakness of Israel (v. 14) is contrasted with the strength that God will confer upon them (vv. 15–16). **17–24:** Israel's tradition taught that, at the beginning of the nation's history, God had provided sustenance for the journey through the wilderness (see Deut 8.1–4), and now that same care would be repeated.

42

Here is my servant, whom
   I uphold,
my chosen, in whom my soul
   delights;
I have put my spirit upon him;
   he will bring forth justice to the
      nations.
2 He will not cry or lift up his voice,
   or make it heard in the street;
3 a bruised reed he will not break,
   and a dimly burning wick he will not
      quench;
   he will faithfully bring forth justice.
4 He will not grow faint or be crushed
   until he has established justice in the
      earth;
   and the coastlands wait for his
      teaching.

5 Thus says God, the LORD,
   who created the heavens and
      stretched them out,
   who spread out the earth and what
      comes from it,
   who gives breath to the people upon it
   and spirit to those who walk in it:
6 I am the LORD, I have called you in
      righteousness,
   I have taken you by the hand and
      kept you;
   I have given you as a covenant to the
      people,^b
   a light to the nations,

7 to open the eyes that are blind,
   to bring out the prisoners from the
      dungeon,
   from the prison those who sit in
      darkness.
8 I am the LORD, that is my name;
   my glory I give to no other,
   nor my praise to idols.
9 See, the former things have come
      to pass,
   and new things I now declare;
   before they spring forth,
   I tell you of them.

10 Sing to the LORD a new song,
   his praise from the end of the earth!
Let the sea roar^c and all that fills it,
   the coastlands and their inhabitants.
11 Let the desert and its towns lift up their
      voice,
   the villages that Kedar inhabits;
let the inhabitants of Sela sing for joy,
   let them shout from the tops of the
      mountains.
12 Let them give glory to the LORD,
   and declare his praise in the
      coastlands.
13 The LORD goes forth like a soldier,
   like a warrior he stirs up his fury;
he cries out, he shouts aloud,
   he shows himself mighty against his
      foes.

42.1–25: The mission of the servant. 1–4: The introduction of the servant (see sidebar, p. 988) follows the pattern of a royal emissary being introduced at court. The authority of the sender is conferred on the deputy who is sent. **5–9:** The servant of God is to bring *a light to the nations* (v. 6). This is the coming of salvation and the ending of Israel's spiritual blindness (v. 7), but is this promise only for the scattered survivors of Israel who dwell among the nations, or is it also for those nations themselves? Verse 49.6 answers this question: It is for everyone, although 45.22 comes very close to anticipating this message. The inescapable force of the argument that the LORD God of Israel is the creator and lord of all nations leads to this larger hope for the

---

a Cn: Heb *First to Zion—Behold, behold them*
b Meaning of Heb uncertain   *c* Cn Compare Ps 96.11;
98.7: Heb *Those who go down to the sea*

The Servant of God

The theme of the "Servant of God" is developed in a distinctive way in 42.1–4, one of four passages that scholars have come to identify as the four "Servant Songs" (the others are 49.1–6; 50.4–9; 52.13–53.12). Their distinctive nature is shown by the role that they ascribe to the servant as having a mission *to raise up the tribes of Jacob* (49.6), and even more remarkably in the intense range of personal suffering endured by the servant (50.6; 53.3–10). These two features have suggested to many scholars that the servant cannot be identical with the Servant-Israel of 41.8 and that the author of the distinctive "Servant Songs" may be different from the author of the rest of chs. 40–55. Yet this conclusion is unnecessary. Although the idea of God's servant is used in more than one way throughout 40–55 (as indeed throughout the book as a whole), the portrayal is consistently that of Israel, suffering, sometimes rebellious, often scattered and disunited. It is this many-sided nature of Israel's servanthood that is presented by the prophet, who recognizes that the servant's task is one that only some within the nation can fulfill.

nations of the world. **10–13:** The revelation of the new task assigned to Israel, God's servant, calls forth a response of praise in the most distant places.

14 For a long time I have held my peace,
    I have kept still and restrained myself;
now I will cry out like a woman in labor,
    I will gasp and pant.
15 I will lay waste mountains and hills,
    and dry up all their herbage;
I will turn the rivers into islands,
    and dry up the pools.
16 I will lead the blind
    by a road they do not know,
by paths they have not known
    I will guide them.
I will turn the darkness before them
    into light,
    the rough places into level ground.
These are the things I will do,
    and I will not forsake them.
17 They shall be turned back and utterly
        put to shame—
    those who trust in carved images,
who say to cast images,
    "You are our gods."

18 Listen, you that are deaf;
    and you that are blind, look up and
        see!

19 Who is blind but my servant,
    or deaf like my messenger whom I
        send?
Who is blind like my dedicated one,
    or blind like the servant of the LORD?
20 He sees many things, but does*a* not
        observe them;
    his ears are open, but he does not hear.
21 The LORD was pleased, for the sake of
        his righteousness,
    to magnify his teaching and make it
        glorious.
22 But this is a people robbed and
        plundered,
    all of them are trapped in holes
    and hidden in prisons;
they have become a prey with no one to
        rescue,
    a spoil with no one to say, "Restore!"
23 Who among you will give heed to this,
    who will attend and listen for the
        time to come?
24 Who gave up Jacob to the spoiler,
    and Israel to the robbers?
Was it not the LORD, against whom we
        have sinned,
    in whose ways they would not walk,
    and whose law they would not obey?

a Heb *You see many things but do*

25 So he poured upon him the heat of his
    anger
    and the fury of war;
    it set him on fire all around, but he did
    not understand;
    it burned him, but he did not take it
    to heart.

42.14–25: The references to the blind and deaf in vv.
16, 18–19 reverse the threatening aspect of the warnings given in 6.9–10 by the eighth-century Isaiah of
Jerusalem (see further 43.8). The descriptions of the
weak and distressed state of the prophet's own people
in v. 22 (see 41.7) may indicate that he himself was
suffering in Babylon. It seems probable, however, that
the descriptions are typical of the misfortunes that had
befallen the former inhabitants of Judah in many
places. The mission of God's servant requires a recollection (v. 24) that Israel's present situation was a consequence of its own wrongdoing.

43 But now thus says the LORD,
    he who created you, O Jacob,
    he who formed you, O Israel:
    Do not fear, for I have redeemed you;
    I have called you by name, you are
    mine.
2 When you pass through the waters, I
    will be with you;
    and through the rivers, they shall not
    overwhelm you;
    when you walk through fire you shall
    not be burned,
    and the flame shall not consume you.
3 For I am the LORD your God,
    the Holy One of Israel, your Savior.
    I give Egypt as your ransom,
    Ethiopia*a* and Seba in exchange
    for you.
4 Because you are precious in my sight,
    and honored, and I love you,
    I give people in return for you,
    nations in exchange for your life.
5 Do not fear, for I am with you;
    I will bring your offspring from the
    east,
    and from the west I will gather you;
6 I will say to the north, "Give them up,"
    and to the south, "Do not
    withhold;
    bring my sons from far away

and my daughters from the end of the
    earth—
7 everyone who is called by my name,
    whom I created for my glory,
    whom I formed and made."

8 Bring forth the people who are blind,
    yet have eyes,
    who are deaf, yet have ears!
9 Let all the nations gather together,
    and let the peoples assemble.
    Who among them declared this,
    and foretold to us the former things?
    Let them bring their witnesses to justify
    them,
    and let them hear and say, "It
    is true."
10 You are my witnesses, says the LORD,
    and my servant whom I have chosen,
    so that you may know and believe me
    and understand that I am he.
    Before me no god was formed,
    nor shall there be any after me.
11 I, I am the LORD,
    and besides me there is no savior.
12 I declared and saved and proclaimed,
    when there was no strange god
    among you;
    and you are my witnesses, says the
    LORD.
13 I am God, and also henceforth I am He;
    there is no one who can deliver from
    my hand;
    I work and who can hinder it?

43.1–28: I will be with you. 1–7: The presence of God
with Israel is assured, in spite of the apparently hopeless situation in which many survivors of the nation
found themselves. Their widely scattered locations
reach far beyond the borders of Judah, or even Babylon. A slave's freedom could be negotiated. God
would ensure that the host nations to which Judah's
citizens had fled for refuge would grant them freedom
to return to their homeland. 8–13: The foretelling of
the *former things* (vv. 9, 18) refers to the fulfillment of
earlier prophecies, probably those now preserved in
the book of Isaiah, as the allusion (v. 8) to the warning
given in 6.9–10 makes clear. The LORD God of Israel
providentially controls all world history and is the only

a Or *Nubia;* Heb *Cush*

true God. Verse 10 shows how the title *my servant* could be used to describe a whole community.

~~~~~~

14 Thus says the LORD,
    your Redeemer, the Holy One
       of Israel:
  For your sake I will send to Babylon
    and break down all the bars,
    and the shouting of the Chaldeans
      will be turned to lamentation.*a*

15 I am the LORD, your Holy One,
    the Creator of Israel, your King.

16 Thus says the LORD,
    who makes a way in the sea,
    a path in the mighty waters,

17 who brings out chariot and horse,
    army and warrior;
  they lie down, they cannot rise,
    they are extinguished, quenched like
      a wick:

18 Do not remember the former things,
    or consider the things of old.

19 I am about to do a new thing;
    now it springs forth, do you not
      perceive it?
  I will make a way in the wilderness
    and rivers in the desert.

20 The wild animals will honor me,
    the jackals and the ostriches;
  for I give water in the wilderness,
    rivers in the desert,
  to give drink to my chosen people,

21   the people whom I formed for myself
  so that they might declare my praise.

22 Yet you did not call upon me, O Jacob;
    but you have been weary of me,
      O Israel!

23 You have not brought me your sheep for
      burnt offerings,
    or honored me with your sacrifices.
  I have not burdened you with offerings,
    or wearied you with frankincense.

24 You have not bought me sweet cane
    with money,
    or satisfied me with the fat of your
      sacrifices.
  But you have burdened me with your
      sins;
  you have wearied me with your
      iniquities.

25 I, I am He
  who blots out your transgressions for
    my own sake,
  and I will not remember your sins.

26 Accuse me, let us go to trial;
  set forth your case, so that you may
    be proved right.

27 Your first ancestor sinned,
  and your interpreters transgressed
    against me.

28 Therefore I profaned the princes of the
    sanctuary,
  I delivered Jacob to utter destruction,
    and Israel to reviling.

43.14–28. 14–21: Verses 16–17 refer to crossing the sea and the destruction of the pursuing Egyptians (Ex 14.15–30). The return of Israel from among the nations will constitute a new exodus. **22–28**: Israel is presented on one hand as God's servant and witness to the nations and on the other as a weak and sinful people who have burdened God with their sins. Both portraits are valid. The sufferings were necessary and inevitable (v. 28). Yet the consequences of Israel's wrongdoing had now been fully atoned for (see 40.2).

~~~~~~

44 But now hear, O Jacob my servant,
  Israel whom I have chosen!

2 Thus says the LORD who made you,
  who formed you in the womb and will
    help you:
  Do not fear, O Jacob my servant,
  Jeshurun whom I have chosen.

3 For I will pour water on the thirsty
    land,
  and streams on the dry ground;
  I will pour my spirit upon your
    descendants,
  and my blessing on your offspring.

4 They shall spring up like a green
    tamarisk,
  like willows by flowing streams.

5 This one will say, "I am the LORD's,"
  another will be called by the name of
    Jacob,
  yet another will write on the hand, "The
    LORD's,"
  and adopt the name of Israel.

a Meaning of Heb uncertain

6 Thus says the LORD, the King of Israel,
  and his Redeemer, the LORD of
    hosts:
I am the first and I am the last;
  besides me there is no god.
7 Who is like me? Let them proclaim it,
  let them declare and set it forth
    before me.
Who has announced from of old the
    things to come?[a]
Let them tell us[b] what is yet to be.
8 Do not fear, or be afraid;
  have I not told you from of old and
    declared it?
You are my witnesses!
Is there any god besides me?
  There is no other rock; I know not
    one.

9 All who make idols are nothing, and the
things they delight in do not profit; their witnesses neither see nor know. And so they will
be put to shame. 10 Who would fashion a god
or cast an image that can do no good?
11 Look, all its devotees shall be put to
shame; the artisans too are merely human.
Let them all assemble, let them stand up;
they shall be terrified, they shall all be put to
shame. 12 The ironsmith fashions it[c] and works
it over the coals, shaping it with hammers,
and forging it with his strong arm; he becomes hungry and his strength fails, he
drinks no water and is faint. 13 The carpenter
stretches a line, marks it out with a stylus,
fashions it with planes, and marks it with a
compass; he makes it in human form, with
human beauty, to be set up in a shrine. 14 He
cuts down cedars or chooses a holm tree or
an oak and lets it grow strong among the
trees of the forest. He plants a cedar and the
rain nourishes it. 15 Then it can be used as
fuel. Part of it he takes and warms himself;
he kindles a fire and bakes bread. Then he
makes a god and worships it, makes it a
carved image and bows down before it.
16 Half of it he burns in the fire; over this half
he roasts meat, eats it and is satisfied. He
also warms himself and says, "Ah, I am
warm, I can feel the fire!" 17 The rest of it he
makes into a god, his idol, bows down to it

and worships it; he prays to it and says, "Save
me, for you are my god!"

18 They do not know, nor do they comprehend; for their eyes are shut, so that they
cannot see, and their minds as well, so that
they cannot understand. 19 No one considers, nor is there knowledge or discernment
to say, "Half of it I burned in the fire; I also
baked bread on its coals, I roasted meat and
have eaten. Now shall I make the rest of it
an abomination? Shall I fall down before a
block of wood?" 20 He feeds on ashes; a deluded mind has led him astray, and he cannot save himself or say, "Is not this thing in
my right hand a fraud?"

44.1–28: Do not fear, or be afraid. 1–8: Just as God's
rainstorm transforms desert into fertile land (v. 3) , so
will God transform scattered and weakened Israel. No
other god can prevent this happening, and the gods
themselves are nothing (v. 6). They have no witnesses
among the nations who can foretell future events
(v. 7). 9–20: A sharp reproof of idolatry: The very fact
that human beings make such images demonstrates
that they are false, since human beings cannot make
gods (v. 20).

21 Remember these things, O Jacob,
  and Israel, for you are my servant;
  I formed you, you are my servant;
  O Israel, you will not be forgotten
    by me.
22 I have swept away your transgressions
    like a cloud,
  and your sins like mist;
  return to me, for I have redeemed you.
23 Sing, O heavens, for the LORD has
    done it;
  shout, O depths of the earth;
  break forth into singing, O mountains,
    O forest, and every tree in it!
  For the LORD has redeemed Jacob,
    and will be glorified in Israel.

24 Thus says the LORD, your Redeemer,
  who formed you in the womb:

a Cn: Heb from my placing an eternal people and things
to come   b Tg: Heb them   c Cn: Heb an ax

I am the LORD, who made all things,
    who alone stretched out the heavens,
    who by myself spread out the earth;
25 who frustrates the omens of liars,
    and makes fools of diviners;
who turns back the wise,
    and makes their knowledge foolish;
26 who confirms the word of his servant,
    and fulfills the prediction of his
      messengers;
who says of Jerusalem, "It shall be
      inhabited,"
    and of the cities of Judah, "They shall
      be rebuilt,
    and I will raise up their ruins";
27 who says to the deep, "Be dry—
    I will dry up your rivers";
28 who says of Cyrus, "He is my shepherd,
    and he shall carry out all my purpose";
and who says of Jerusalem, "It shall be
      rebuilt,"
    and of the temple, "Your foundation
      shall be laid."

44.21–28: Jerusalem will be rebuilt, the restored city will be inhabited once again and a new Temple will be constructed (vv. 26–28). The designation of the Persian ruler Cyrus as God's *shepherd* (v. 28) and "anointed" (45.1) includes titles used of Israelite kings (for "shepherd" as a title of kings and rulers, see Jer 23.1–5; Ezek 34.1–24). Even a foreign and pagan ruler who attained world power did so as the agent of the God of Israel who directed the course of history. Jews living outside the land used this language to show due recognition to the rulers of nations among whom they lived. Such an understanding did not, however, entirely rule out a special role for the surviving dynasty of David (see 55.3–5).

45 Thus says the LORD to his
    anointed, to Cyrus,
    whose right hand I have grasped
to subdue nations before him
    and strip kings of their robes,
to open doors before him—
    and the gates shall not be closed:
2 I will go before you
    and level the mountains,ᵃ
I will break in pieces the doors
    of bronze
    and cut through the bars of iron,

3 I will give you the treasures of darkness
    and riches hidden in secret places,
so that you may know that it is I, the
    LORD,
    the God of Israel, who call you by
      your name.
4 For the sake of my servant Jacob,
    and Israel my chosen,
I call you by your name,
    I surname you, though you do not
      know me.
5 I am the LORD, and there is no other;
    besides me there is no god.
I arm you, though you do not know
      me,
6 so that they may know, from the rising
      of the sun
    and from the west, that there is no
      one besides me;
I am the LORD, and there is no other.
7 I form light and create darkness,
    I make weal and create woe;
    I the LORD do all these things.

45.1–25: **Turn to me and be saved.** *1–7: Cyrus* is the world conqueror whom God had chosen to overthrow the power of Babylon and enable the survivors of Israel to return to their homeland, a reaffirmation of the sovereign power of the LORD God (v. 7). This verse expresses fully the claim that God, as God of all nations, is all-powerful.

8 Shower, O heavens, from above,
    and let the skies rain down
      righteousness;
let the earth open, that salvation may
      spring up,ᵇ
and let it cause righteousness to
      sprout up also;
    I the LORD have created it.

9 Woe to you who strive with your Maker,
    earthen vessels with the potter!ᶜ
Does the clay say to the one who
      fashions it, "What are you
      making"?
    or "Your work has no handles"?

a Q Ms Gk: MT *the swellings*   *b* Q Ms: MT *that they may bring forth salvation*   *c* Cn: Heb *with the potsherds,* or *with the potters*

10 Woe to anyone who says to a father,
  "What are you begetting?"
  or to a woman, "With what are you in
    labor?"
11 Thus says the LORD,
  the Holy One of Israel, and its Maker:
  Will you question me*a* about my
    children,
  or command me concerning the work
    of my hands?
12 I made the earth,
  and created humankind upon it;
  it was my hands that stretched out the
    heavens,
  and I commanded all their host.
13 I have aroused Cyrus*b* in righteousness,
  and I will make all his paths straight;
  he shall build my city
  and set my exiles free,
  not for price or reward,
    says the LORD of hosts.
14 Thus says the LORD:
  The wealth of Egypt and the
    merchandise of Ethiopia,*c*
  and the Sabeans, tall of stature,
  shall come over to you and be yours,
    they shall follow you;
  they shall come over in chains and
    bow down to you.
  They will make supplication to you,
    saying,
  "God is with you alone, and there is
    no other;
  there is no god besides him."
15 Truly, you are a God who hides himself,
  O God of Israel, the Savior.
16 All of them are put to shame and
    confounded,
  the makers of idols go in confusion
    together.
17 But Israel is saved by the LORD
  with everlasting salvation;
  you shall not be put to shame or
    confounded
  to all eternity.

45.8–17: Human beings cannot challenge God's declared purpose any more than *clay* can question a
potter (v. 9). Nor can people question parents as to
the kind of offspring they will bring into the world (vv.
10–11). Even the distant tribes of North Africa will rec-

ognize Israel's God (v. 14). To exchange knowledge of
this true God for the spurious aid of an *idol* would be
utter folly (v. 16).

18 For thus says the LORD,
  who created the heavens
    (he is God!),
  who formed the earth and made it
    (he established it;
  he did not create it a chaos,
    he formed it to be inhabited!):
  I am the LORD, and there is no other.
19 I did not speak in secret,
    in a land of darkness;
  I did not say to the offspring of Jacob,
    "Seek me in chaos."
  I the LORD speak the truth,
    I declare what is right.
20 Assemble yourselves and come together,
    draw near, you survivors of the
      nations!
  They have no knowledge—
    those who carry about their wooden
      idols,
  and keep on praying to a god
    that cannot save.
21 Declare and present your case;
    let them take counsel together!
  Who told this long ago?
    Who declared it of old?
  Was it not I, the LORD?
    There is no other god besides me,
  a righteous God and a Savior;
    there is no one besides me.
22 Turn to me and be saved,
    all the ends of the earth!
  For I am God, and there is no other.
23 By myself I have sworn,
    from my mouth has gone forth in
      righteousness
    a word that shall not return:
  "To me every knee shall bow,
    every tongue shall swear."
24 Only in the LORD, it shall be said of me,
  are righteousness and strength;

a Cn: Heb *Ask me of things to come*   *b* Heb *him*
c Or *Nubia*; Heb *Cush*

all who were incensed against him
    shall come to him and be ashamed.
25 In the LORD all the offspring of Israel
    shall triumph and glory.

45.18–25: The prophet turns to address the many nations of the world. If God can shape the destiny of Israel, God's purpose is that every nation should know that there is no God but one and worship this one God alone. Those who had once made light of it (see 36.18–20) will be ashamed of their foolishness (v. 24) and confess that Israel was the first of many nations to acknowledge the LORD as God.

46 Bel bows down, Nebo stoops,
    their idols are on beasts and cattle;
these things you carry are loaded
    as burdens on weary animals.
2 They stoop, they bow down together;
    they cannot save the burden,
    but themselves go into captivity.

3 Listen to me, O house of Jacob,
    all the remnant of the house of Israel,
who have been borne by me from your
        birth,
    carried from the womb;
4 even to your old age I am he,
    even when you turn gray I will carry
        you.
I have made, and I will bear;
    I will carry and will save.

5 To whom will you liken me and make
        me equal,
    and compare me, as though we were
        alike?
6 Those who lavish gold from the purse,
    and weigh out silver in the scales—
they hire a goldsmith, who makes it into
        a god;
    then they fall down and worship!
7 They lift it to their shoulders, they
        carry it,
    they set it in its place, and it stands
        there;
    it cannot move from its place.
If one cries out to it, it does not answer
    or save anyone from trouble.

8 Remember this and consider,^a
    recall it to mind, you transgressors,

9 remember the former things of old;
    for I am God, and there is no other;
    I am God, and there is no one like
        me,
10 declaring the end from the beginning
    and from ancient times things not yet
        done,
saying, "My purpose shall stand,
    and I will fulfill my intention,"
11 calling a bird of prey from the east,
    the man for my purpose from a far
        country.
I have spoken, and I will bring it
    to pass;
    I have planned, and I will do it.

12 Listen to me, you stubborn of heart,
    you who are far from deliverance:
13 I bring near my deliverance, it is not far
        off,
    and my salvation will not tarry;
I will put salvation in Zion,
    for Israel my glory.

46.1–13: The uselessness of false gods. 1–7: The theme of idolatry* highlights the helpless situation of the priests and worshippers of Babylon. With Babylon facing imminent capture, those who cared for the images of the gods would soon be forced to flee with them to a place of safety (v. 1). Yet they would not find it. There would be no place to hide, and the absurdity of human beings trying to save their gods shows that they are in reality no gods at all. The true deity is the one who carries, not who is carried (vv. 6–7). **8–11:** The true God shapes the destiny of nations (vv. 10–11). The *bird of prey* is *the man for my purpose from a far country,* none other than Cyrus, who will bring release to Israel. **12–13:** Rebuilding and restoring the ruined Jerusalem is God's *salvation.* God's *deliverance* has a very practical aspect to it.

47 Come down and sit in the dust,
    virgin daughter Babylon!
Sit on the ground without a throne,
    daughter Chaldea!
For you shall no more be called
    tender and delicate.
2 Take the millstones and grind meal,
    remove your veil,

---

a Meaning of Heb uncertain

strip off your robe, uncover your legs,
   pass through the rivers.
3 Your nakedness shall be uncovered,
   and your shame shall be seen.
I will take vengeance,
   and I will spare no one.
4 Our Redeemer—the LORD of hosts is
   his name—
is the Holy One of Israel.

5 Sit in silence, and go into darkness,
   daughter Chaldea!
For you shall no more be called
   the mistress of kingdoms.
6 I was angry with my people,
   I profaned my heritage;
I gave them into your hand,
   you showed them no mercy;
on the aged you made your yoke
   exceedingly heavy.
7 You said, "I shall be mistress forever,"
   so that you did not lay these things to
     heart
   or remember their end.

8 Now therefore hear this, you lover of
     pleasures,
who sit securely,
who say in your heart,
  "I am, and there is no one besides me;
I shall not sit as a widow
  or know the loss of children"—
9 both these things shall come upon you
   in a moment, in one day:
the loss of children and widowhood
   shall come upon you in full
     measure,
in spite of your many sorceries
   and the great power of your
     enchantments.

10 You felt secure in your wickedness;
   you said, "No one sees me."
Your wisdom and your knowledge
   led you astray,
and you said in your heart,
  "I am, and there is no one besides
     me."
11 But evil shall come upon you,
   which you cannot charm away;
disaster shall fall upon you,

which you will not be able to ward
     off;
and ruin shall come on you suddenly,
   of which you know nothing.

12 Stand fast in your enchantments
   and your many sorceries,
with which you have labored from
     your youth;
perhaps you may be able to
     succeed,
   perhaps you may inspire terror.
13 You are wearied with your many
     consultations;
   let those who study[a] the heavens
stand up and save you,
   those who gaze at the stars,
and at each new moon predict
   what[b] shall befall you.

14 See, they are like stubble,
   the fire consumes them;
they cannot deliver themselves
   from the power of the flame.
No coal for warming oneself is this,
   no fire to sit before!
15 Such to you are those with whom you
     have labored,
   who have trafficked with you from
     your youth;
they all wander about in their
     own paths;
   there is no one to save you.

47.1–15: The fall of Babylon. 1–9: Babylon is depicted as a mature young lady, accustomed to pampered luxury, but now suddenly seized, stripped, and humiliated. The empire had absorbed many nations and had plundered their lands and treasures, showing no pity even to the weakest (v. 6). The proud assumption that her power would remain unchecked forever (v. 8) had encouraged the city to revel in its excesses, without pity or compassion. Now the pain she had inflicted on others would be brought home to her. **10–15:** It is by divine authority that such terrible retribution comes. Babylon's elaborate rituals and techniques for uncovering the mysteries of the future could not fend off the disaster. The all-consuming fire rav-

a Meaning of Heb uncertain   *b* Gk Syr Compare Vg:
Heb *from what*

aging the countryside concludes this forewarning of Babylon's imminent downfall. This is not gloating over an enemy so much as the conviction that a divine will for justice ultimately shapes the course of human history.

~~~~~~~~~~~~

48 Hear this, O house of Jacob,
who are called by the name of
Israel,
and who came forth from the loins[a]
of Judah;
who swear by the name of the LORD,
and invoke the God of Israel,
but not in truth or right.
2 For they call themselves after the holy
city,
and lean on the God of Israel;
the LORD of hosts is his name.

3 The former things I declared
long ago,
they went out from my mouth and I
made them known;
then suddenly I did them and they
came to pass.
4 Because I know that you are obstinate,
and your neck is an iron sinew
and your forehead brass,
5 I declared them to you from long ago,
before they came to pass I announced
them to you,
so that you would not say, "My idol did
them,
my carved image and my cast image
commanded them."

6 You have heard; now see all this;
and will you not declare it?
From this time forward I make you hear
new things,
hidden things that you have not
known.
7 They are created now, not long ago;
before today you have never heard of
them,
so that you could not say, "I already
knew them."
8 You have never heard, you have never
known,
from of old your ear has not been
opened.

For I knew that you would deal very
treacherously,
and that from birth you were called a
rebel.

48.1–22: Reassurance for God's people. 1–8: A significant change of mood occurs with less attention to the rise of Cyrus, although his imminent defeat of Babylon is still taken for granted (v. 14). Instead the prophet addresses Israel, preparing its survivors to make a positive response to the new message of hope. The high mission of Israel contrasts with the persistent unbelief and self-pity of Israel's response. This ambiguity is clear in the rebuke that is added to the privileged title of Israel: who *invoke the God of Israel, but not in truth or right* (v. 1). Offering fine prayers to God was not in itself proof that they were sincerely meant. The evidence that God is guiding Israel is found in the fulfillment of prophecies (v. 3). Yet if the people had been reluctant to believe and act upon prophecies that had been fulfilled, how would they believe new ones? The failures and rebelliousness of the past are the reason for making sure that such mistakes were not repeated in the present (v. 8).

~~~~~~~~~~~~

9 For my name's sake I defer my anger,
for the sake of my praise I restrain it
for you,
so that I may not cut you off.
10 See, I have refined you, but not like[b]
silver;
I have tested you in the furnace of
adversity.
11 For my own sake, for my own sake,
I do it,
for why should my name[c] be
profaned?
My glory I will not give to another.

12 Listen to me, O Jacob,
and Israel, whom I called:
I am He; I am the first,
and I am the last.
13 My hand laid the foundation of the earth,
and my right hand spread out
the heavens;
when I summon them,
they stand at attention.

a Cn: Heb *waters*   *b* Cn: Heb *with*   *c* Gk Old Latin:
Heb *for why should it*

14 Assemble, all of you, and hear!
   Who among them has declared these
      things?
   The LORD loves him;
      he shall perform his purpose on
         Babylon,
      and his arm shall be against the
         Chaldeans.
15 I, even I, have spoken and called him,
   I have brought him, and he will
      prosper in his way.
16 Draw near to me, hear this!
   From the beginning I have not spoken
      in secret,
   from the time it came to be I have
      been there.
   And now the Lord GOD has sent me
      and his spirit.

17 Thus says the LORD,
   your Redeemer, the Holy One
      of Israel:
   I am the LORD your God,
      who teaches you for your own good,
      who leads you in the way you
         should go.
18 O that you had paid attention to my
      commandments!
   Then your prosperity would have
      been like a river,
   and your success like the waves of
      the sea;
19 your offspring would have been like the
      sand,
   and your descendants like its grains;
   their name would never be cut off
   or destroyed from before me.

20 Go out from Babylon, flee from
      Chaldea,
   declare this with a shout of joy,
      proclaim it,
   send it forth to the end of the earth;
   say, "The LORD has redeemed his
      servant Jacob!"
21 They did not thirst when he led them
      through the deserts;
   he made water flow for them from
      the rock;
   he split open the rock and the water
      gushed out.

22 "There is no peace," says the LORD, "for
      the wicked."

48.9–22. 9–16: Because the LORD is forgiving and gracious, even imperfect Israel may, with God's help, fulfill a great purpose (vv. 9–11). What would be impossible for a people left to their own resources was possible with God (vv. 12–16). **17–22:** The concluding command: *Go out from Babylon, flee from Chaldea.* Fleeing from Babylon would be like the flight from Egypt by which Israel had first achieved its freedom (v. 21). So it was appropriate to recall the providential care which had made that beginning possible. Once again God would, if necessary, bring *water from the rock* to sustain the returning exiles (see Ex 17.1–7). A final word of warning (v. 22) is a necessary addition to the message concerning Israel's rebellious nature that echoes through the chapter (vv. 1, 4, 5, 18). From the very beginning Israel had received great promises but had failed to respond (especially v. 18). That could happen again and those who, in the pursuit of peace, shunned the risks and dangers of the journey home would find that they enjoyed a worthless tranquillity.

49 Listen to me, O coastlands,
   pay attention, you peoples from far
      away!
   The LORD called me before I was born,
      while I was in my mother's womb he
         named me.
2 He made my mouth like a sharp sword,
      in the shadow of his hand he hid me;
   he made me a polished arrow,
      in his quiver he hid me away.
3 And he said to me, "You are my servant,
   Israel, in whom I will be glorified."
4 But I said, "I have labored in vain,
   I have spent my strength for nothing
      and vanity;
   yet surely my cause is with the LORD,
   and my reward with my God."

5 And now the LORD says,
   who formed me in the womb to be his
      servant,
   to bring Jacob back to him,
   and that Israel might be gathered to
      him,
   for I am honored in the sight of the LORD,
   and my God has become my
      strength—

6 he says,
"It is too light a thing that you should
    be my servant
  to raise up the tribes of Jacob
  and to restore the survivors of Israel;
I will give you as a light to the nations,
  that my salvation may reach to the
    end of the earth."

7 Thus says the LORD,
  the Redeemer of Israel and his
    Holy One,
to one deeply despised, abhorred by the
    nations,
  the slave of rulers,
"Kings shall see and stand up,
  princes, and they shall prostrate
    themselves,
because of the LORD, who is faithful,
  the Holy One of Israel, who has
    chosen you."

8 Thus says the LORD:
In a time of favor I have answered you,
  on a day of salvation I have helped
    you;
I have kept you and given you
  as a covenant to the people,^a
to establish the land,
  to apportion the desolate heritages;
9 saying to the prisoners, "Come out,"
  to those who are in darkness, "Show
    yourselves."
They shall feed along the ways,
  on all the bare heights^b shall be their
    pasture;
10 they shall not hunger or thirst,
  neither scorching wind nor sun shall
    strike them down,
for he who has pity on them will lead
    them,
  and by springs of water will guide
    them.
11 And I will turn all my mountains into a
    road,
  and my highways shall be raised up.
12 Lo, these shall come from far away,
  and lo, these from the north and from
    the west,
  and these from the land of Syene.^c

13 Sing for joy, O heavens, and exult,
    O earth;
  break forth, O mountains, into
    singing!
For the LORD has comforted his people,
  and will have compassion on his
    suffering ones.

49.1–26: The servant's mission to the world. 1–6:
The second of the four Servant Songs (see sidebar, p.
988). Israel's servant mission will reach beyond the survivors of the former Israel, and will bring *light* (salvation) *to the nations* (v. 6). Servant-Israel (v. 3) also has
a mission to Israel, suggesting that *Israel* may have
been added later. More probably, one part of the nation has a mission to the other part. **8–13:** The task of
restoring the *tribes of Jacob* (v. 6) consists of establishing the land, apportioning the desolate heritages, and
releasing the prisoners. Exiles will be able to return.
Syene (perhaps southern Egypt) is an example of the
distant locations to which the people had fled.

---

14 But Zion said, "The LORD has
    forsaken me,
  my Lord has forgotten me."
15 Can a woman forget her nursing child,
  or show no compassion for the child
    of her womb?
Even these may forget,
  yet I will not forget you.
16 See, I have inscribed you on the palms
    of my hands;
  your walls are continually before me.
17 Your builders outdo your destroyers,^d
  and those who laid you waste go away
    from you.
18 Lift up your eyes all around and see;
  they all gather, they come to you.
As I live, says the LORD,
  you shall put all of them on like an
    ornament,
  and like a bride you shall bind
    them on.
19 Surely your waste and your desolate
    places
  and your devastated land—

---

a Meaning of Heb uncertain   b Or *the trails*
c Q Ms: MT *Sinim*   d Or *Your children come swiftly;*
your destroyers

surely now you will be too crowded for
    your inhabitants,
and those who swallowed you up will
    be far away.

20 The children born in the time of your
    bereavement
will yet say in your hearing:
"The place is too crowded for me;
    make room for me to settle."

21 Then you will say in your heart,
"Who has borne me these?
I was bereaved and barren,
    exiled and put away—
so who has reared these?
I was left all alone—
    where then have these come from?"

22 Thus says the Lord GOD:
I will soon lift up my hand to the
    nations,
    and raise my signal to the peoples;
and they shall bring your sons in their
    bosom,
    and your daughters shall be carried
      on their shoulders.

23 Kings shall be your foster fathers,
    and their queens your nursing
      mothers.
With their faces to the ground they
      shall bow down to you,
    and lick the dust of your feet.
Then you will know that I am the LORD;
    those who wait for me shall not be
      put to shame.

24 Can the prey be taken from the mighty,
    or the captives of a tyrant[a] be
      rescued?
25 But thus says the LORD:
Even the captives of the mighty shall be
    taken,
    and the prey of the tyrant be rescued;
for I will contend with those who
      contend with you,
    and I will save your children.
26 I will make your oppressors eat their
      own flesh,
    and they shall be drunk with their
      own blood as with wine.
Then all flesh shall know
    that I am the LORD your Savior,

and your Redeemer, the Mighty One
    of Jacob.

49.14–26. 14–21: The apparent impossibility of the
promised restoration of the ruined city is now possible
due to the compassion and love that God has for it
(vv. 14–16). **22–26:** What might sometimes rarely be
possible in human terms—that a human *tyrant* may
set free his *captives* (v. 25)—is possible with God.

---

50 Thus says the LORD:
Where is your mother's bill of
    divorce
with which I put her away?
Or which of my creditors is it
    to whom I have sold you?
No, because of your sins you
      were sold,
    and for your transgressions your
      mother was put away.
2 Why was no one there when I came?
Why did no one answer when I
      called?
Is my hand shortened, that it cannot
      redeem?
    Or have I no power to deliver?
By my rebuke I dry up the sea,
    I make the rivers a desert;
their fish stink for lack of water,
    and die of thirst.[b]
3 I clothe the heavens with blackness,
    and make sackcloth their covering.

4 The Lord GOD has given me
    the tongue of a teacher,[c]
that I may know how to sustain
    the weary with a word.
Morning by morning he wakens—
    wakens my ear
    to listen as those who are taught.
5 The Lord GOD has opened my ear,
    and I was not rebellious,
    I did not turn backward.
6 I gave my back to those who struck me,
    and my cheeks to those who pulled
      out the beard;
I did not hide my face
    from insult and spitting.

---

a Q Ms Syr Vg: MT *of a righteous person*   *b* Or *die on
the thirsty ground*   *c* Cn: Heb *of those who are taught*

7 The Lord GOD helps me;
    therefore I have not been disgraced;
  therefore I have set my face like flint,
    and I know that I shall not be put to
      shame;
8   he who vindicates me is near.
  Who will contend with me?
    Let us stand up together.
  Who are my adversaries?
    Let them confront me.
9   It is the Lord GOD who helps me;
    who will declare me guilty?
  All of them will wear out like a garment;
    the moth will eat them up.

10 Who among you fears the LORD
    and obeys the voice of his servant,
  who walks in darkness
    and has no light,
  yet trusts in the name of the LORD
    and relies upon his God?
11 But all of you are kindlers of fire,
    lighters of firebrands.ᵃ
  Walk in the flame of your fire,
    and among the brands that you have
      kindled!
  This is what you shall have from my
    hand:
    you shall lie down in torment.

50.1–11: Israel: servant and rebel. 1–3: The opening
questions highlight the need for choice between a
positive believing response and an unbelieving rejection. These differing responses show the contrast between the submissive and obedient servant and the
mocking and insolent rebels. **4–9:** The third of the four
Servant Songs (see sidebar, p. 988) shows that the servant undergoes humiliation and rejection in the course
of fulfilling his mission. The autobiographical form
shows how wholeheartedly the prophet identifies himself with the mission of servant-Israel. **10–11:** The
prophet contrasts those who seek *light* (salvation) in
order to walk by it, and those who use torches (*firebrands*) to kindle destruction (see 10.17 for a similar
use of the picture of light becoming fire).

51 Listen to me, you that pursue
    righteousness,
  you that seek the LORD.
  Look to the rock from which you were
    hewn,

and to the quarry from which
    you were dug.
2 Look to Abraham your father
    and to Sarah who bore you;
  for he was but one when I called him,
    but I blessed him and made
      him many.
3 For the LORD will comfort Zion;
    he will comfort all her waste places,
  and will make her wilderness like Eden,
    her desert like the garden of
      the LORD;
  joy and gladness will be found in her,
    thanksgiving and the voice of song.

4 Listen to me, my people,
    and give heed to me, my nation;
  for a teaching will go out from me,
    and my justice for a light to
      the peoples.
5 I will bring near my deliverance swiftly,
    my salvation has gone out
    and my arms will rule the peoples;
  the coastlands wait for me,
    and for my arm they hope.
6 Lift up your eyes to the heavens,
    and look at the earth beneath;
  for the heavens will vanish like smoke,
    the earth will wear out like a
      garment,
  and those who live on it will die like
      gnats;ᵇ
  but my salvation will be forever,
    and my deliverance will never
      be ended.

7 Listen to me, you who know
    righteousness,
  you people who have my teaching in
    your hearts;
  do not fear the reproach of others,
    and do not be dismayed when they
      revile you.
8 For the moth will eat them up like a
    garment,
    and the worm will eat them like wool;
  but my deliverance will be forever,
    and my salvation to all generations.

a Syr: Heb *you gird yourselves with firebrands*   *b* Or *in
like manner*

51.1–23: Stand up, O Jerusalem. 1–8: A fresh argument strengthens the appeal. *Abraham* was *but one* when God *called him* (v. 2). Yet from this one man a whole nation came into being. How much more certainly is God capable of restoring the scattered remnants of Israel. God's salvation is even more certain and secure than is the sky above.

9 Awake, awake, put on strength,
  O arm of the LORD!
Awake, as in days of old,
  the generations of long ago!
Was it not you who cut Rahab in
    pieces,
  who pierced the dragon?
10 Was it not you who dried up the sea,
  the waters of the great deep;
who made the depths of the sea a way
  for the redeemed to cross over?
11 So the ransomed of the LORD shall
    return,
  and come to Zion with singing;
everlasting joy shall be upon their
    heads;
  they shall obtain joy and gladness,
and sorrow and sighing shall
    flee away.

12 I, I am he who comforts you;
  why then are you afraid of a mere
    mortal who must die,
  a human being who fades like grass?
13 You have forgotten the LORD, your
    Maker,
  who stretched out the heavens
  and laid the foundations of the earth.
You fear continually all day long
  because of the fury of the oppressor,
who is bent on destruction.
  But where is the fury of the
    oppressor?
14 The oppressed shall speedily be
    released;
  they shall not die and go down to
    the Pit,
  nor shall they lack bread.
15 For I am the LORD your God,
  who stirs up the sea so that its waves
    roar—
  the LORD of hosts is his name.

16 I have put my words in your mouth,
  and hidden you in the shadow of my
    hand,
stretching out*a* the heavens
  and laying the foundations of
    the earth,
  and saying to Zion, "You are my
    people."

17 Rouse yourself, rouse yourself!
  Stand up, O Jerusalem,
you who have drunk at the hand of
    the LORD
  the cup of his wrath,
who have drunk to the dregs
  the bowl of staggering.
18 There is no one to guide her
  among all the children she
    has borne;
there is no one to take her by the hand
  among all the children she has
    brought up.
19 These two things have befallen you
  —who will grieve with you?—
devastation and destruction, famine and
    sword—
  who will comfort you?*b*
20 Your children have fainted,
  they lie at the head of every street
  like an antelope in a net;
they are full of the wrath of the LORD,
  the rebuke of your God.

21 Therefore hear this, you who are
    wounded,*c*
  who are drunk, but not with wine:
22 Thus says your Sovereign, the LORD,
  your God who pleads the cause of his
    people:
See, I have taken from your hand the
    cup of staggering;
you shall drink no more
  from the bowl of my wrath.
23 And I will put it into the hand of your
    tormentors,
  who have said to you,
  "Bow down, that we may walk
    on you";

a Syr: Heb *planting*   *b* Q Ms Gk Syr Vg: MT *how may I comfort you?*   *c* Or *humbled*

and you have made your back like the
      ground
   and like the street for them to walk
      on.

51.9–23. 9–16: *Cut Rahab in pieces* refers to the ancient pictorial account of creation in which the earth
was formed by cutting in pieces a great dragon monster, here called Rahab (see Leviathan in 27.1). *Dried
up the sea* (v. 10) combines themes from the creation,
when dry land appeared amid the ocean (see Gen 1.9–
10), and the drying up of the sea in the miraculous
crossing, when the ancestors of the nation fled from
Egypt (see Ex 14.21–22). **17–23:** *Jerusalem* is directly
addressed and its ruined state vividly described (v. 23).

$\sim\sim\sim\sim\sim\sim\sim\sim\sim\sim\sim\sim\sim\sim$

52 Awake, awake,
      put on your strength, O Zion!
   Put on your beautiful garments,
      O Jerusalem, the holy city;
   for the uncircumcised and the unclean
      shall enter you no more.
2 Shake yourself from the dust, rise up,
      O captive*a* Jerusalem;
   loose the bonds from your neck,
      O captive daughter Zion!

3 For thus says the LORD: You were sold
for nothing, and you shall be redeemed without money. 4For thus says the Lord GOD:
Long ago, my people went down into Egypt
to reside there as aliens; the Assyrian, too,
has oppressed them without cause. 5Now
therefore what am I doing here, says the
LORD, seeing that my people are taken away
without cause? Their rulers howl, says the
LORD, and continually, all day long, my
name is despised. 6Therefore my people
shall know my name; therefore in that day
they shall know that it is I who speak; here
am I.

7 How beautiful upon the mountains
      are the feet of the messenger who
         announces peace,
   who brings good news,
      who announces salvation,
      who says to Zion, "Your God reigns."
8 Listen! Your sentinels lift up
         their voices,
      together they sing for joy;

   for in plain sight they see
      the return of the LORD to Zion.
9 Break forth together into singing,
      you ruins of Jerusalem;
   for the LORD has comforted his people,
      he has redeemed Jerusalem.
10 The LORD has bared his holy arm
      before the eyes of all the nations;
   and all the ends of the earth shall see
      the salvation of our God.

11 Depart, depart, go out from there!
      Touch no unclean thing;
   go out from the midst of it, purify
         yourselves,
   you who carry the vessels of
         the LORD.
12 For you shall not go out in haste,
      and you shall not go in flight;
   for the LORD will go before you,
      and the God of Israel will be your
         rear guard.

52.1–12: Put on your beautiful garments. 1–2: The
uncircumcised and unclean are the foreigners who
ruled over Jerusalem. Once God's people had returned
to take control of their beloved city, then this hated
foreign rule would be at an end. **3–6:** This short prose
digression summarizes Israel's sufferings at the hands
of foreigners. It looks ahead to the time when the
promises and assurances of chs. 40–55 will have been
fulfilled. **7–10:** In this prophetic image watchmen on
the city walls see a *messenger bringing news* of Israel's
deliverance (from the power of Babylon). When God's
people return to *Zion,*★ then God will return to be with
them (v. 8). **11–12:** The command to *depart* is a reference to the many places of exile to which Jerusalem's
citizens had been driven. In contrast to the departure
of Israel's forbears from Egypt—the event that marked
the beginning of the nation's history—this departure
would not be *in haste* (see Ex 12.39); nor would it
include the plundering of their captors (v. 11; see Ex
12.35–36).

$\sim\sim\sim\sim\sim\sim\sim\sim\sim\sim\sim\sim\sim\sim$

13 See, my servant shall prosper;
      he shall be exalted and lifted up,
      and shall be very high.
14 Just as there were many who were
         astonished at him*b*

---

a Cn: Heb *rise up, sit*   *b* Syr Tg: Heb *you*

—so marred was his appearance,
  beyond human semblance,
and his form beyond that of
  mortals—
15 so he shall startle[a] many nations;
  kings shall shut their mouths because
    of him;
for that which had not been told them
  they shall see,
and that which they had not heard
  they shall contemplate.

53 Who has believed what we have
  heard?
And to whom has the arm of the
  LORD been revealed?
2 For he grew up before him like a young
    plant,
  and like a root out of dry ground;
he had no form or majesty that we
    should look at him,
  nothing in his appearance that we
    should desire him.
3 He was despised and rejected by others;
  a man of suffering[b] and acquainted
    with infirmity;
and as one from whom others hide their
    faces[c]
  he was despised, and we held him of
    no account.

4 Surely he has borne our infirmities
  and carried our diseases;
yet we accounted him stricken,
  struck down by God, and afflicted.
5 But he was wounded for our
    transgressions,
  crushed for our iniquities;
upon him was the punishment that
    made us whole,
  and by his bruises we are healed.
6 All we like sheep have gone astray;
  we have all turned to our own way,
and the LORD has laid on him
  the iniquity of us all.

7 He was oppressed, and he was afflicted,
  yet he did not open his mouth;
like a lamb that is led to the slaughter,
  and like a sheep that before its
    shearers is silent,
  so he did not open his mouth.

8 By a perversion of justice he was taken
    away.
  Who could have imagined his future?
For he was cut off from the land of the
    living,
  stricken for the transgression of my
    people.
9 They made his grave with the wicked
  and his tomb[d] with the rich,[e]
although he had done no violence,
  and there was no deceit in
    his mouth.

10 Yet it was the will of the LORD to crush
  him with pain.[f]
When you make his life an offering for
    sin,[a]
  he shall see his offspring, and shall
    prolong his days;
through him the will of the LORD shall
    prosper.
11 Out of his anguish he shall see light;[g]
  he shall find satisfaction through his
    knowledge.
The righteous one,[h] my servant, shall
    make many righteous,
  and he shall bear their iniquities.
12 Therefore I will allot him a portion with
    the great,
  and he shall divide the spoil with the
    strong;
because he poured out himself to death,
  and was numbered with the
    transgressors;
yet he bore the sin of many,
  and made intercession for the
    transgressors.

52.13–53.12: The suffering servant. One of the most
remarkable passages in all prophetic literature, this is
the fourth of the distinctive Servant passages, or
Songs, which describe the fate of Israel as the servant
of God (see sidebar, p. 988). The servant will suffer as
a result of his commitment to the task (50.4–9). Now
what that suffering entails is spelled out in all its hor-

---

a Meaning of Heb uncertain   b Or *a man of sorrows*
c Or *as one who hides his face from us*   d Q Ms: MT
and in his death   e Cn: Heb *with a rich person*
f Or *by disease*; meaning of Heb uncertain   g Q Mss:
MT lacks *light*   h Or *and he shall find satisfaction.
Through his knowledge, the righteous one*

rifying detail. This enigmatic passage seems to combine many experiences. Even if the references in 53.8–9 are not to actual death but to an extreme of suffering, the prophet himself cannot have written it. It is not the death and torture of one person alone that is being reported here. The servant mission is divisive in its challenge. Not all the prophet's hearers respond to his demands, and many have already shown themselves to be rebellious and unresponsive. It is those who have identified themselves with this servant task, who have borne the rebukes, reproaches, and wounds of their fellows, whose fate is described here. So the prophet has woven into one tapestry of suffering the terrifying experiences that many had undergone. It is a mission portrait of servanthood. There is a positive and reassuring outlook that sees beyond the immediate pain to the rich reward of such endurance (53.12). It is not a resurrection of an individual that is described in *he shall see his offspring, and shall prolong his days* (53.10–11). Rather it is the fruit that will be borne by those who assume the servant's task and find that, for all its pain, it gains *a portion with the great* (v. 12). Moreover, a remarkable sensitivity to the way in which the righteous often suffer at the hands of wrongdoers leads to a new perception of the meaning of suffering. The righteous individual may bear the sin of the many who are guilty.

54 Sing, O barren one who did
    not bear;
  burst into song and shout,
  you who have not been in labor!
  For the children of the desolate woman
      will be more
    than the children of her that is
      married, says the LORD.
2 Enlarge the site of your tent,
    and let the curtains of your
      habitations be stretched out;
  do not hold back; lengthen your cords
    and strengthen your stakes.
3 For you will spread out to the right and
      to the left,
    and your descendants will possess the
      nations
    and will settle the desolate towns.

4 Do not fear, for you will not be
      ashamed;
  do not be discouraged, for you will
      not suffer disgrace;

for you will forget the shame of your
      youth,
  and the disgrace of your widowhood
    you will remember no more.
5 For your Maker is your husband,
    the LORD of hosts is his name;
  the Holy One of Israel is your
      Redeemer,
    the God of the whole earth he
      is called.
6 For the LORD has called you
    like a wife forsaken and grieved in
      spirit,
  like the wife of a man's youth when she
      is cast off,
    says your God.
7 For a brief moment I abandoned you,
    but with great compassion I will
      gather you.
8 In overflowing wrath for a moment
    I hid my face from you,
  but with everlasting love I will have
      compassion on you,
    says the LORD, your Redeemer.

9 This is like the days of Noah to me:
    Just as I swore that the waters
      of Noah
    would never again go over the
      earth,
  so I have sworn that I will not be angry
      with you
    and will not rebuke you.
10 For the mountains may depart
      and the hills be removed,
  but my steadfast love shall not depart
      from you,
    and my covenant of peace shall not
      be removed,
  says the LORD, who has compassion
      on you.

11 O afflicted one, storm-tossed, and not
      comforted,
  I am about to set your stones in
      antimony,
    and lay your foundations with
      sapphires.ᵃ

a Or *lapis lazuli*

12 I will make your pinnacles of rubies,
 your gates of jewels,
 and all your wall of precious
  stones.

13 All your children shall be taught by the
 LORD,
 and great shall be the prosperity of
  your children.

14 In righteousness you shall be
 established;
 you shall be far from oppression, for
  you shall not fear;
 and from terror, for it shall not come
  near you.

15 If anyone stirs up strife,
 it is not from me;
 whoever stirs up strife with you
  shall fall because of you.

16 See it is I who have created the
  smith
 who blows the fire of coals,
 and produces a weapon fit for
  its purpose;
 I have also created the ravager
  to destroy.

17 No weapon that is fashioned against
 you shall prosper,
 and you shall confute every tongue
  that rises against you in
  judgment.
 This is the heritage of the servants of
  the LORD
 and their vindication from me, says
  the LORD.

54.1–17: Consolation for the new Jerusalem. 1–8: The city must put behind it the memory of its past, forgetting its shame and disappointments. It must instead make plans for *enlargement* and growth (vv. 2–3). Using the peaceful imagery of *widowhood*, the prophet looks ahead to the prosperous and bustling future that awaits it (vv. 6–7). **9–17:** Another lesson from the traditions of the past is the lesson of Noah, who after the ending of the Great Deluge was the recipient of a divine promise that never again would such a catastrophe overtake humankind (see Gen 9.8–17). So God would ensure that Jerusalem's citizens were taught the divine way (v. 13), and those who brought strife (v. 15), or made war against the city, would fail in their purpose (v. 17).

---

55 Ho, everyone who thirsts,
 come to the waters;
 and you that have no money,
  come, buy and eat!
 Come, buy wine and milk
  without money and without price.

2 Why do you spend your money for that
  which is not bread,
 and your labor for that which does
  not satisfy?
 Listen carefully to me, and eat what is
  good,
 and delight yourselves in rich food.

3 Incline your ear, and come to me;
 listen, so that you may live.
 I will make with you an everlasting
  covenant,
 my steadfast, sure love for David.

4 See, I made him a witness to
  the peoples,
 a leader and commander for
  the peoples.

5 See, you shall call nations that you do
  not know,
 and nations that do not know you
  shall run to you,
 because of the LORD your God, the
  Holy One of Israel,
 for he has glorified you.

55.1–13: Seek the LORD while he may be found. Although this chapter concludes the work of the prophet of the return, chs. 54 and 55 form a bridge to 56–66. Two separate units are in the present chapter. **1–5:** The first unit concerns God's promise to the royal dynasty★ of David (2 Sam 7.1–17), an *everlasting covenant*★ (v. 3). This covenant is an act of God's love, an unmerited gift. Along with the promises set out in 11.1–5 and 32.1–8, it affirms that God will hold fast to the unqualified promise that, through the authority entrusted to this royal dynasty of kings, Israel will exercise leadership over the nations (v. 5). This can mean either that, although the royal family itself would not return to the throne, leadership among the nations would be shared throughout the servant-nation, or that the restoration of the Davidic monarchy is promised here. The course of events in the following half-century reveals that such an expectation remained alive and exercised a strong political influence, even though it failed to reach fruition. In later years, a larger "messianic" interpretation★ concerning the coming of a divinely sent savior figure was built on this, and the other royal prophecies, of the book of Isaiah and the Psalms.

6 Seek the LORD while he may be found,
    call upon him while he is near;
7 let the wicked forsake their way,
    and the unrighteous their thoughts;
    let them return to the LORD, that he
        may have mercy on them,
    and to our God, for he will
        abundantly pardon.
8 For my thoughts are not your thoughts,
    nor are your ways my ways, says the
        LORD.
9 For as the heavens are higher than the
        earth,
    so are my ways higher than your ways
    and my thoughts than your thoughts.

10 For as the rain and the snow come
        down from heaven,
    and do not return there until they
        have watered the earth,
    making it bring forth and sprout,
    giving seed to the sower and bread to
        the eater,
11 so shall my word be that goes out from
        my mouth;
    it shall not return to me empty,
    but it shall accomplish that which I
        purpose,

and succeed in the thing for which I
    sent it.

12 For you shall go out in joy,
    and be led back in peace;
    the mountains and the hills before you
        shall burst into song,
    and all the trees of the field shall clap
        their hands.
13 Instead of the thorn shall come up the
        cypress;
    instead of the brier shall come up the
        myrtle;
    and it shall be to the LORD for a
        memorial,
    for an everlasting sign that shall not
        be cut off.

55.6–13: The concluding unit (vv. 6–13) makes a rich and memorable appeal concerning the power of the divine word given through the prophet and the certainty that it will accomplish its purpose. What appeared impossible to the human mind was possible with God (vv. 8–9). As *rain and snow* made the earth fertile and productive, so would God's word prove equally effective in achieving its intended purpose (v. 10). The promise of v. 13 summarizes in pictorial language the message of hope for the future by insisting that the ruination of the vineyard of God (Israel) by *briers* and *thorns* would be a feature of the past (see 5.6).

Isaiah 56–66

THE COMING OF THE LIGHT

These chapters fluctuate sharply between stern rebuke and lyrical reassurance. Disloyalty, a return to idol-worship, and conflicts within the community are the central themes of chs. 56–59. Even the keeping of festivals and holding of fasts is fraudulent and insincere, because those who do so do not practice right-dealing with their fellow citizens. This falsity prevents the fulfillment of God's promises. Yet the coming glory of the new Jerusalem is assured (chs. 60–62), although the time of fulfillment is uncertain. Fresh rebukes challenge the insincerity of worship (ch. 65), and fresh lamentations* denounce injustice within the community (63.16–19). Only a new heaven and a new earth can bring the fullness of peace and rejoicing which God has promised (66.22–23).

These chapters were most likely compiled later than chs. 40–55, belonging to the period after the first stages of the return and restoration in Judah around 520–500 BCE, or even during the following half-century. The admonitions in 66.1 appear to refer to the rebuilding of the Jerusalem Temple in 520–516 BCE, but whether they came before or after this event is not clear. There is no mention of attempts to restore a descendant of David to the throne, to which other prophecies of the period certainly testify (see Hag 2.20–23; Zech 4.1–14). Nor are these chapters a unified work. Different prophets addressed the pressing issues that frustrated a community struggling to reestablish its identity. It is unclear whether these prophecies were collected and shaped to provide a conclusion to a "Book of Isaiah" that already existed and that was largely similar to our Isa 1–55. Although chs. 56–59 seem to be integrated, chs. 60–66 appear as individual developments of earlier themes and texts. There does seem, however, to be some deliberate connection between chs. 1–4 and 63–66, which attests to the editorial shaping of the final form of the book.

READING GUIDE

Although appearing to qualify the hope promised in chs. 40–55, these later chapters introduce significant themes such as the nature of community and nationhood, the need for self-critical reflection on worship and self-denial, and the importance of faith in breaking down barriers between hostile groups. Faith is not simply about taking hold of promises, but about compassion, heart-searching, and tolerance, all of which are essential for true religious renewal.

56.1–12   Soon my salvation will come
57.1–21   No peace for the wicked
58.1–14   The fast acceptable to God
59.1–21   Why God's face is hidden
60.1–22   Arise, shine, for your light has come
61.1–11   The year of the LORD's favor
62.1–12   A city not forsaken
63.1–19   The day of vengeance
64.1–12   The silence of God
65.1–25   The promise of new heavens and a new earth
66.1–24   Final warnings and consolations for Jerusalem

56 Thus says the LORD:
Maintain justice, and do what is right,
for soon my salvation will come,
and my deliverance be revealed.

2 Happy is the mortal who does this,
the one who holds it fast,
who keeps the sabbath, not profaning it,
and refrains from doing any evil.

3 Do not let the foreigner joined to the LORD say,
"The LORD will surely separate me from his people";
and do not let the eunuch say,
"I am just a dry tree."

4 For thus says the LORD:
To the eunuchs who keep my sabbaths,
who choose the things that please me
and hold fast my covenant,
5 I will give, in my house and within my walls,
a monument and a name
better than sons and daughters;
I will give them an everlasting name
that shall not be cut off.

6 And the foreigners who join themselves to the LORD,
to minister to him, to love the name of the LORD,
and to be his servants,

all who keep the sabbath, and do not
    profane it,
and hold fast my covenant—
7 these I will bring to my holy mountain,
    and make them joyful in my house of
      prayer;
their burnt offerings and their sacrifices
    will be accepted on my altar;
for my house shall be called a house of
      prayer
    for all peoples.
8 Thus says the Lord GOD,
    who gathers the outcasts of Israel,
I will gather others to them
    besides those already gathered.*a*

9 All you wild animals,
    all you wild animals in the forest,
      come to devour!
10 Israel's*b* sentinels are blind,
    they are all without knowledge;
they are all silent dogs
    that cannot bark;
dreaming, lying down,
    loving to slumber.
11 The dogs have a mighty appetite;
    they never have enough.
The shepherds also have no
      understanding;
they have all turned to their own way,
    to their own gain, one and all.
12 "Come," they say, "let us*c* get wine;
    let us fill ourselves with strong drink.
And tomorrow will be like today,
    great beyond measure."

56.1–12: Soon my salvation will come. 1–8: The call to rebuild Jerusalem had been an open invitation (especially 55.6–7). This openness, however, did not take into account strong traditional rules concerning who belonged in God's family (see Deut 23.1–8). Now these rules were being used to exclude those, such as *foreigners* and *eunuchs,* who were treated as outcasts (v. 3), even though this mocked the Temple* as a *house of prayer* (v. 7). **9–12:** This sharp rebuke addressed to the *blind* and *silent dogs* reflects the bitter divisions that had emerged within the community. Most likely the presence of returned exiles contributed to this bitterness with those already holding positions of power in Jerusalem reluctant to give it up.

57 The righteous perish,
    and no one takes it to heart;
the devout are taken away,
    while no one understands.
For the righteous are taken away from
      calamity,
2 and they enter into peace;
those who walk uprightly
    will rest on their couches.
3 But as for you, come here,
    you children of a sorceress,
    you offspring of an adulterer and a
      whore.*d*
4 Whom are you mocking?
    Against whom do you open your
      mouth wide
    and stick out your tongue?
Are you not children of transgression,
    the offspring of deceit—
5 you that burn with lust among the oaks,
    under every green tree;
you that slaughter your children in the
      valleys,
    under the clefts of the rocks?
6 Among the smooth stones of the valley
    is your portion;
    they, they, are your lot;
to them you have poured out a drink
      offering,
    you have brought a grain offering.
Shall I be appeased for these
      things?
7 Upon a high and lofty mountain
    you have set your bed,
    and there you went up to offer
      sacrifice.
8 Behind the door and the doorpost
    you have set up your symbol;
for, in deserting me,*e* you have
      uncovered your bed,
    you have gone up to it,
    you have made it wide;
and you have made a bargain for
      yourself with them,
    you have loved their bed,
    you have gazed on their nakedness.*f*

a Heb *besides his gathered ones*   *b* Heb *His*
c Q Ms Syr Vg Tg: MT *me*   *d* Heb *an adulterer and
she plays the whore*   *e* Meaning of Heb uncertain
f Or *their phallus;* Heb *the hand*

9 You journeyed to Molech[a] with oil,
  and multiplied your perfumes;
you sent your envoys far away,
  and sent down even to Sheol.
10 You grew weary from your many
    wanderings,
  but you did not say, "It is useless."
You found your desire rekindled,
  and so you did not weaken.

11 Whom did you dread and fear
  so that you lied,
and did not remember me
  or give me a thought?
Have I not kept silent and closed my
    eyes,[b]
  and so you do not fear me?
12 I will concede your righteousness and
    your works,
  but they will not help you.
13 When you cry out, let your collection of
    idols deliver you!
The wind will carry them off,
  a breath will take them away.
But whoever takes refuge in me shall
    possess the land
  and inherit my holy mountain.

14 It shall be said,
  "Build up, build up, prepare the way,
  remove every obstruction from my
    people's way."
15 For thus says the high and lofty one
  who inhabits eternity, whose name is
    Holy:
I dwell in the high and holy place,
  and also with those who are contrite
  and humble in spirit,
to revive the spirit of the humble,
  and to revive the heart of the
    contrite.
16 For I will not continually accuse,
  nor will I always be angry;
for then the spirits would grow faint
  before me,
  even the souls that I have made.
17 Because of their wicked covetousness I
    was angry;
I struck them, I hid and was angry;
  but they kept turning back to their
    own ways.

18 I have seen their ways, but I will heal
    them;
  I will lead them and repay them with
    comfort,
  creating for their mourners the fruit
    of the lips.[c]
19 Peace, peace, to the far and the near,
    says the LORD;
  and I will heal them.
20 But the wicked are like the tossing sea
    that cannot keep still;
  its waters toss up mire and mud.
21 There is no peace, says my God, for the
    wicked.

57.1–21: No peace for the wicked. 1–10: The sense of disunity within Jerusalem reveals that the end of the captivity had not brought an end to its troubles. It had simply given rise to new ones. There was injustice and false and immoral worship, tolerated under foreign rule (vv. 5–7). Old customs of gods worshipped for centuries throughout the region (v. 9) had been revived while the Temple* of the LORD lay in ruins. *Molech* is probably one of the titles of Baal,* a god especially linked with child sacrifice. **11–21:** The sharp prophetic critique of wrongdoing within the community that characterizes earlier prophecies reappears here with added vigor (see 5.11–25). The warning of 48.22 that there would be no peace for the wicked receives a dismal confirmation in the vain efforts of those who try to secure it (vv. 19–21). There is a note of both lamentation and despair in the repetition of God's call to build and be patient (vv. 14–19) and the response of vv. 20–21, affirming that the wicked are incapable of creating peace.

58 Shout out, do not hold back!
  Lift up your voice like a trumpet!
Announce to my people their
    rebellion,
  to the house of Jacob their sins.
2 Yet day after day they seek me
  and delight to know my ways,
  as if they were a nation that practiced
    righteousness
  and did not forsake the ordinance of
    their God;

---

a Or *the king* b Gk Vg: Heb *silent even for a long time*
c Meaning of Heb uncertain

they ask of me righteous judgments,
    they delight to draw near to God.
3 "Why do we fast, but you do not see?
    Why humble ourselves, but you do
        not notice?"
Look, you serve your own interest on
        your fast day,
    and oppress all your workers.
4 Look, you fast only to quarrel and to
        fight
    and to strike with a wicked fist.
Such fasting as you do today
    will not make your voice heard on
        high.
5 Is such the fast that I choose,
    a day to humble oneself?
Is it to bow down the head like a
        bulrush,
    and to lie in sackcloth and ashes?
Will you call this a fast,
    a day acceptable to the LORD?
6 Is not this the fast that I choose:
    to loose the bonds of injustice,
    to undo the thongs of the yoke,
    to let the oppressed go free,
    and to break every yoke?
7 Is it not to share your bread with the
        hungry,
    and bring the homeless poor into your
        house;
    when you see the naked, to cover them,
    and not to hide yourself from your
        own kin?
8 Then your light shall break forth like
        the dawn,
    and your healing shall spring
        up quickly;
your vindicator[a] shall go before you,
    the glory of the LORD shall be your
        rear guard.
9 Then you shall call, and the LORD will
        answer;
    you shall cry for help, and he will say,
        Here I am.

If you remove the yoke from among you,
    the pointing of the finger, the
        speaking of evil,
10 if you offer your food to the hungry
    and satisfy the needs of the afflicted,

then your light shall rise in the darkness
    and your gloom be like the noonday.
11 The LORD will guide you continually,
    and satisfy your needs in parched
        places,
    and make your bones strong;
and you shall be like a watered garden,
    like a spring of water,
    whose waters never fail.
12 Your ancient ruins shall be rebuilt;
    you shall raise up the foundations of
        many generations;
you shall be called the repairer of the
        breach,
    the restorer of streets to live in.

13 If you refrain from trampling the
        sabbath,
    from pursuing your own interests on
        my holy day;
if you call the sabbath a delight
    and the holy day of the LORD
        honorable;
if you honor it, not going your
        own ways,
    serving your own interests, or
        pursuing your own affairs;[b]
14 then you shall take delight in the LORD,
    and I will make you ride upon the
        heights of the earth;
I will feed you with the heritage of your
        ancestor Jacob,
    for the mouth of the LORD has
        spoken.

58.1–14: The fast acceptable to God. 1–10: A fresh problem concerns those who maintain a bold public display of piety, but whose actions and way of life flout the basic requirements of justice and goodness. The central issue is fasting, self-denial aimed at concentrating mind and body on prayer, which was publicly declared by wearing *sackcloth* * (a rough garment) and smearing the face and hands with *ashes* (symbol of mortality) (v. 5). Yet such deeds unaccompanied by compassion and concern for those less fortunate were meaningless to God (vv. 6–9). **11–14:** The efforts to restore Jerusalem had focused on externals—restoring ancient buildings and replanting neglected fields—instead of the inner recovery of spiritual health and

a Or *vindication*   b Heb *or speaking words*

wholeness. Only a renewal of this inner direction of life could bring about the true rebuilding of the city.

59

See, the LORD's hand is not too
short to save,
nor his ear too dull to hear.

2 Rather, your iniquities have been
barriers
between you and your God,
and your sins have hidden his face
from you,
so that he does not hear.

3 For your hands are defiled with blood,
and your fingers with iniquity;
your lips have spoken lies,
your tongue mutters wickedness.

4 No one brings suit justly,
no one goes to law honestly;
they rely on empty pleas, they speak
lies,
conceiving mischief and begetting
iniquity.

5 They hatch adders' eggs,
and weave the spider's web;
whoever eats their eggs dies,
and the crushed egg hatches out a
viper.

6 Their webs cannot serve as clothing;
they cannot cover themselves with
what they make.
Their works are works of iniquity,
and deeds of violence are in their
hands.

7 Their feet run to evil,
and they rush to shed innocent
blood;
their thoughts are thoughts of iniquity,
desolation and destruction are in
their highways.

8 The way of peace they do not know,
and there is no justice in their paths.
Their roads they have made crooked;
no one who walks in them knows
peace.

nized authority to implement justice, or whether because those who wield power in Jerusalem are themselves the chief culprits.

9 Therefore justice is far from us,
and righteousness does not reach us;
we wait for light, and lo! there is
darkness;
and for brightness, but we walk in
gloom.

10 We grope like the blind along a wall,
groping like those who have no eyes;
we stumble at noon as in the twilight,
among the vigorous[a] as though we
were dead.

11 We all growl like bears;
like doves we moan mournfully.
We wait for justice, but there is none;
for salvation, but it is far from us.

12 For our transgressions before you are
many,
and our sins testify against us.
Our transgressions indeed are with us,
and we know our iniquities:

13 transgressing, and denying the LORD,
and turning away from following our
God,
talking oppression and revolt,
conceiving lying words and uttering
them from the heart.

14 Justice is turned back,
and righteousness stands at a
distance;
for truth stumbles in the public square,
and uprightness cannot enter.

15 Truth is lacking,
and whoever turns from evil is
despoiled.

The LORD saw it, and it displeased him
that there was no justice.

16 He saw that there was no one,
and was appalled that there was no
one to intervene;
so his own arm brought him victory,
and his righteousness upheld him.

17 He put on righteousness like a
breastplate,
and a helmet of salvation on his head;

59.1–21: Why God's face is hidden. 1–8. God's salvation has not come, not because God is weak and powerless, but because the people's wrongdoing creates a barrier between themselves and God (vv. 1–2). The rebukes (vv. 3–8) condemn violence, injustice and brigandage, whether arising from lack of any recog-

a Meaning of Heb uncertain

he put on garments of vengeance for
   clothing,
   and wrapped himself in fury as in a
      mantle.
18 According to their deeds, so will he repay;
   wrath to his adversaries, requital to
      his enemies;
   to the coastlands he will render
      requital.
19 So those in the west shall fear the
      name of the LORD,
   and those in the east, his glory;
   for he will come like a pent-up stream
   that the wind of the LORD drives on.

20 And he will come to Zion as Redeemer,
   to those in Jacob who turn from
      transgression, says the LORD.
21And as for me, this is my covenant with
them, says the LORD: my spirit that is upon
you, and my words that I have put in your
mouth, shall not depart out of your mouth,
or out of the mouths of your children, or out
of the mouths of your children's children,
says the LORD, from now on and forever.

59.9–21. 9–15a: The lack of an effective administration of justice allowed violence and corruption to flourish. Those who had won power under foreign masters
were now unwilling to relinquish control and to empower a new order of religious leaders. It was not until
the work of Ezra and Nehemiah, in the middle of the
fifth century BCE, that the situation began to be put
right. **15b–21:** Without the protection that God alone
can bring, the helplessness described so vividly in vv.
10–11 must continue. The assurance in v. 21 that
God's word will prove effective indicates that chs.
56–59, at one time, formed a separate collection to
which this section was a conclusion.

Visions of the new Jerusalem
Chs. 60–62: After the setbacks and dissensions in chs.
56–59, chs. 60–62 recover the vision of the future central to chs. 40–55. Jerusalem will be rebuilt, a city of
peace and righteousness. These chapters reflect the
spiritual reawakening that came with the rebuilding
and restoration of the Temple* in Jerusalem in 520–
516 BCE. More broadly, these chapters express a positive, if ideal, portrayal of human beings living in
peace, prosperity, and harmony. They reveal a goal to
strive for, not a simplistic expectation of a condition of

human happiness that will drop down as a gift from
heaven.

60 Arise, shine; for your light has come,
   and the glory of the LORD has risen
      upon you.
2 For darkness shall cover the earth,
   and thick darkness the peoples;
   but the LORD will arise upon you,
   and his glory will appear over you.
3 Nations shall come to your light,
   and kings to the brightness of your
      dawn.

4 Lift up your eyes and look around;
   they all gather together, they come
      to you;
   your sons shall come from far away,
   and your daughters shall be carried
      on their nurses' arms.
5 Then you shall see and be radiant;
   your heart shall thrill and rejoice,^a
   because the abundance of the sea shall
      be brought to you,
   the wealth of the nations shall come
      to you.
6 A multitude of camels shall cover you,
   the young camels of Midian and
      Ephah;
   all those from Sheba shall come.
   They shall bring gold and frankincense,
   and shall proclaim the praise of the
      LORD.
7 All the flocks of Kedar shall be gathered
      to you,
   the rams of Nebaioth shall minister to
      you;
   they shall be acceptable on my altar,
   and I will glorify my glorious house.
8 Who are these that fly like a cloud,
   and like doves to their windows?
9 For the coastlands shall wait for me,
   the ships of Tarshish first,
   to bring your children from far away,
   their silver and gold with them,
   for the name of the LORD your God,
   and for the Holy One of Israel,
   because he has glorified you.

a Heb *be enlarged*

10 Foreigners shall build up your walls,
    and their kings shall minister to you;
for in my wrath I struck you down,
    but in my favor I have had mercy
        on you.
11 Your gates shall always be open;
    day and night they shall not be shut,
so that nations shall bring you their
        wealth,
    with their kings led in procession.
12 For the nation and kingdom
    that will not serve you shall perish;
    those nations shall be utterly
        laid waste.
13 The glory of Lebanon shall come
        to you,
    the cypress, the plane, and the pine,
to beautify the place of my sanctuary;
    and I will glorify where my feet
        rest.
14 The descendants of those who
        oppressed you
    shall come bending low to you,
and all who despised you
    shall bow down at your feet;
they shall call you the City of the
        LORD,
    the Zion of the Holy One of Israel.
15 Whereas you have been forsaken and
        hated,
    with no one passing through,
I will make you majestic forever,
    a joy from age to age.
16 You shall suck the milk of nations,
    you shall suck the breasts of kings;
and you shall know that I, the LORD,
        am your Savior
    and your Redeemer, the Mighty One
        of Jacob.
17 Instead of bronze I will bring gold,
    instead of iron I will bring silver;
instead of wood, bronze,
    instead of stones, iron.
I will appoint Peace as your overseer
    and Righteousness as your
        taskmaster.
18 Violence shall no more be heard in your
        land,
    devastation or destruction within your
        borders;

you shall call your walls Salvation,
    and your gates Praise.
19 The sun shall no longer be
    your light by day,
nor for brightness shall the moon
    give light to you by night;[a]
but the LORD will be your everlasting
        light,
    and your God will be your glory.
20 Your sun shall no more go down,
    or your moon withdraw itself;
for the LORD will be your everlasting
        light,
    and your days of mourning shall be
        ended.
21 Your people shall all be righteous;
    they shall possess the land forever.
They are the shoot that I planted, the
        work of my hands,
    so that I might be glorified.
22 The least of them shall become a clan,
    and the smallest one a mighty nation;
I am the LORD;
    in its time I will accomplish
        it quickly.

60.1–22: Arise, shine, for your light has come. 1–7: The expected return had not occurred. At best, only token numbers of the former population had come back. The vision of a great return was still a distant dream. A new pattern of Jewish life emerged that established rules of conduct for living as peaceably as possible in alien lands. **8–14:** The high point of the great vision of 45.22–23, that foreigners too would share in the coming salvation and prosperity, is here sharply reduced to granting them the role of being servants and suppliers to the restored Israel. **15–22:** Hope for the future Jerusalem as a city of wealth, learning, and authority contrasts with the revelations of conflict and violence that 59.1–8 has revealed. The need to restore a vision of God's intentions for Jerusalem became urgent as a counterweight to the current difficulties. The Temple* was restored and a new focus provided for those who worshipped the LORD in every land.

61 The spirit of the Lord GOD is
        upon me,
    because the LORD has anointed me;

---

a Q Ms Gk Old Latin Tg: MT lacks *by night*

he has sent me to bring good news to
　　the oppressed,
to bind up the brokenhearted,
to proclaim liberty to the captives,
　　and release to the prisoners;
2 to proclaim the year of the LORD's
　　favor,
　　and the day of vengeance of our God;
　　to comfort all who mourn;
3 to provide for those who mourn in
　　Zion—
　　to give them a garland instead
　　　of ashes,
the oil of gladness instead of mourning,
　　the mantle of praise instead of a faint
　　　spirit.
They will be called oaks of
　　righteousness,
　　the planting of the LORD, to display
　　　his glory.
4 They shall build up the ancient ruins,
　　they shall raise up the former
　　　devastations;
they shall repair the ruined cities,
　　the devastations of many generations.

5 Strangers shall stand and feed
　　　your flocks,
　　foreigners shall till your land and
　　　dress your vines;
6 but you shall be called priests of the
　　LORD,
　　you shall be named ministers of our
　　　God;
you shall enjoy the wealth of
　　the nations,
　　and in their riches you shall glory.
7 Because their*a* shame was double,
　　and dishonor was proclaimed as their
　　　lot,
therefore they shall possess a double
　　portion;
　　everlasting joy shall be theirs.

8 For I the LORD love justice,
　　I hate robbery and wrongdoing;*b*
I will faithfully give them their
　　recompense,
　　and I will make an everlasting
　　covenant with them.

9 Their descendants shall be known
　　among the nations,
　　and their offspring among the
　　　peoples;
all who see them shall acknowledge
　　that they are a people whom the
　　LORD has blessed.
10 I will greatly rejoice in the LORD,
　　my whole being shall exult in my God;
for he has clothed me with the
　　garments of salvation,
he has covered me with the robe of
　　righteousness,
as a bridegroom decks himself with a
　　garland,
　　and as a bride adorns herself with her
　　jewels.
11 For as the earth brings forth its shoots,
　　and as a garden causes what is sown
　　　in it to spring up,
so the Lord GOD will cause
　　righteousness and praise
　　to spring up before all the nations.

61.1–11: The year of the LORD's favor. 1–4: All that
God had promised regarding the rebuilding and restoration of Jerusalem would shortly be fulfilled. **5–9:**
Expectation of God's direct action to overthrow the
present world order becomes a marked feature of the
hope expressed throughout chs. 56–66. Where chs.
40–55 had recognized the hand of God at work in the
rise of Cyrus, king of Persia, to direct the destiny of
Judah, now Israel awaits a more direct divine intervention. **8–11:** Assurance that this transformation will take
place derives from the very nature of God. Love of justice and hatred of all forms of wrongdoing are aspects
of God's rule.

62 For Zion's sake I will not keep
　　　silent,
　　and for Jerusalem's sake I will not
　　　rest,
until her vindication shines out like the
　　dawn,
　　and her salvation like a burning torch.
2 The nations shall see your vindication,
　　and all the kings your glory;
and you shall be called by a new name
　　that the mouth of the LORD will give.

a Heb *your*　　*b* Or *robbery with a burnt offering*

3 You shall be a crown of beauty in the
hand of the LORD,
and a royal diadem in the hand of
your God.
4 You shall no more be termed
Forsaken,[a]
and your land shall no more be
termed Desolate;[b]
but you shall be called My Delight Is in
Her,[c]
and your land Married;[d]
for the LORD delights in you,
and your land shall be married.
5 For as a young man marries a young
woman,
so shall your builder[e] marry you,
and as the bridegroom rejoices over the
bride,
so shall your God rejoice over you.
6 Upon your walls, O Jerusalem,
I have posted sentinels;
all day and all night
they shall never be silent.
You who remind the LORD,
take no rest,
7 and give him no rest
until he establishes Jerusalem
and makes it renowned throughout
the earth.
8 The LORD has sworn by his right hand
and by his mighty arm:
I will not again give your grain
to be food for your enemies,
and foreigners shall not drink the wine
for which you have labored;
9 but those who garner it shall eat it
and praise the LORD,
and those who gather it shall drink it
in my holy courts.

10 Go through, go through the gates,
prepare the way for the people;
build up, build up the highway,
clear it of stones,
lift up an ensign over the peoples.
11 The LORD has proclaimed
to the end of the earth:
Say to daughter Zion,
"See, your salvation comes;
his reward is with him,
and his recompense before him."

12 They shall be called, "The Holy People,
The Redeemed of the LORD";
and you shall be called, "Sought Out,
A City Not Forsaken."

62.1–12: A city not forsaken. 1–5: As the situation in Jerusalem failed to change after the downfall of Babylon, the prophet reassured the people of God's intense love for the city. These are presented here in terms of the intensity of the divine love for the city (vv. 4–5). **6–9:** The wealth and food that foreigners took were prime examples of the frustrations and disappointments of the past. The people must pray that such injustice never again occurs (vv. 8–9). **10–12:** A note of urgency colors the prophet's insistence that God's promise will not fail.

63 "Who is this that comes from
Edom,
from Bozrah in garments stained
crimson?
Who is this so splendidly robed,
marching in his great might?"

"It is I, announcing vindication,
mighty to save."

2 "Why are your robes red,
and your garments like theirs who
tread the wine press?"

3 "I have trodden the wine press alone,
and from the peoples no one was
with me;
I trod them in my anger
and trampled them in my wrath;
their juice spattered on my garments,
and stained all my robes.
4 For the day of vengeance was in my
heart,
and the year for my redeeming work
had come.
5 I looked, but there was no helper;
I stared, but there was no one to
sustain me;
so my own arm brought me victory,
and my wrath sustained me.

a Heb Azubah   b Heb Shemamah   c Heb Hephzibah
d Heb Beulah   e Cn: Heb your sons

6 I trampled down peoples in my anger,
  I crushed them in my wrath,
  and I poured out their lifeblood on
    the earth."

7 I will recount the gracious deeds of the
    LORD,
  the praiseworthy acts of the LORD,
because of all that the LORD has done
    for us,
  and the great favor to the house of
    Israel
that he has shown them according to
    his mercy,
  according to the abundance of his
    steadfast love.
8 For he said, "Surely they are my people,
  children who will not deal falsely";
and he became their savior
9   in all their distress.
It was no messenger[a] or angel
  but his presence that saved them;[b]
in his love and in his pity he redeemed
    them;
  he lifted them up and carried them
    all the days of old.

10 But they rebelled
  and grieved his holy spirit;
therefore he became their enemy;
  he himself fought against them.
11 Then they[c] remembered the days of
    old,
  of Moses his servant.[d]
Where is the one who brought them
    up out of the sea
  with the shepherds of his flock?
Where is the one who put within them
  his holy spirit,
12 who caused his glorious arm
    to march at the right hand of Moses,
who divided the waters before them
    to make for himself an everlasting
      name,
13   who led them through the depths?
Like a horse in the desert,
  they did not stumble.
14 Like cattle that go down into the valley,
  the spirit of the LORD gave them rest.
Thus you led your people,
  to make for yourself a glorious name.

15 Look down from heaven and see,
  from your holy and glorious
    habitation.
Where are your zeal and your might?
  The yearning of your heart and your
    compassion?
They are withheld from me.
16 For you are our father,
  though Abraham does not know us
  and Israel does not acknowledge us;
you, O LORD, are our father;
  our Redeemer from of old is
    your name.
17 Why, O LORD, do you make us stray
    from your ways
  and harden our heart, so that we do
    not fear you?
Turn back for the sake of your servants,
  for the sake of the tribes that are your
    heritage.
18 Your holy people took possession for a
    little while;
  but now our adversaries have
    trampled down your sanctuary.
19 We have long been like those whom you
    do not rule,
  like those not called by your name.

63.1–19: The day of vengeance. 1–6: In vivid and frightening imagery, human frustration and longing for the end of violence calls forth this powerful picture of God acting alone to pass judgment on the warring nations. Where no human ruler could impose justice and peace (v. 5), God had to act directly and decisively (vv. 5–6). **7–14:** In the past, God's presence had accompanied the people and given them victory over their enemies (v. 9). In the present, the rebelliousness of the people grieved the spirit of God, aroused the divine anger, and led to failure and defeat (v. 10). The people of Israel had learned this lesson in the past when failure humbled them (see Josh 7.1–26), and now they had to relearn it (vv. 11–14). **15–19:** Even after temporary success had brought about a partial change in Judah's fortunes (v. 18), new threats and new oppressions had robbed the people of the justice and prosperity they sought (v. 19).

---

a Gk: Heb anguish   b Or savior. 9In all their distress he
was distressed; the angel of his presence saved them;
c Heb he   d Cn: Heb his people

A Summary of the Message of Isaiah

The protection of Jerusalem and its Temple* from the arrogant threats of the Assyrian king, Sennacherib, (chs. 36–37) form a background to the collection of prophecies in Isa 1–39. The hope of rebuilding the Temple after its destruction by the armies of Babylon in 587 BCE are central to the promises of chs. 40–55. The renewed conflicts that surrounded its rebuilding in the years 520–516 BCE color the mixture of threats and warnings of Isa 56–66. What inner meaning and purpose hold together these changing fortunes of the building which aroused such passionate emotions and expectations? Verses 1–2 of chapter 66 offer a fundamental and comprehensive answer by showing how the Temple could be either a means of understanding the reality of God, or a foolish illusion by which God's real claims were evaded. When rightly understood, the Temple was an aid to the humility, obedience, and contrite spirit that God demands.

64 O that you would tear open the
      heavens and come down,
   so that the mountains would quake at
      your presence—
2 *a* as when fire kindles brushwood
      and the fire causes water to boil—
   to make your name known to your
      adversaries,
   so that the nations might tremble at
      your presence!
3 When you did awesome deeds that we
      did not expect,
   you came down, the mountains
      quaked at your presence.
4 From ages past no one has heard,
      no ear has perceived,
   no eye has seen any God besides you,
   who works for those who wait
      for him.
5 You meet those who gladly do right,
      those who remember you in
         your ways.
   But you were angry, and we sinned;
   because you hid yourself we
      transgressed. *b*
6 We have all become like one who is
      unclean,
   and all our righteous deeds are like a
      filthy cloth.
   We all fade like a leaf,
      and our iniquities, like the wind, take
         us away.

7 There is no one who calls on
      your name,
   or attempts to take hold of you;
   for you have hidden your face from us,
      and have delivered *c* us into the hand
         of our iniquity.
8 Yet, O LORD, you are our Father;
   we are the clay, and you are
      our potter;
   we are all the work of your hand.
9 Do not be exceedingly angry, O LORD,
      and do not remember iniquity forever.
   Now consider, we are all your people.
10 Your holy cities have become a
      wilderness,
   Zion has become a wilderness,
      Jerusalem a desolation.
11 Our holy and beautiful house,
      where our ancestors praised you,
   has been burned by fire,
      and all our pleasant places have
         become ruins.
12 After all this, will you restrain yourself,
         O LORD?
      Will you keep silent, and punish us so
         severely?

64.1–12: The silence of God. 1–7: The present situation appeared as a contradiction to God's power

a Ch 64.1 in Heb   *b* Meaning of Heb uncertain
c Gk Syr Old Latin Tg: Heb *melted*

(v. 4). The reason for this lay with the sins of the present generation, which now came in penitent lamentation to confess their rebelliousness to God (vv. 6–7). **8–12:** Even in its failures, Israel remained God's people and could confess its wrongdoing and return to God. The renewed conflict and destruction (v. 11) had arisen in the wake of the rebuilding of the Temple.

65 I was ready to be sought out by
   those who did not ask,
to be found by those who did not seek
   me.
I said, "Here I am, here I am,"
   to a nation that did not call on my
   name.
2 I held out my hands all day long
   to a rebellious people,
who walk in a way that is not good,
   following their own devices;
3 a people who provoke me
   to my face continually,
sacrificing in gardens
   and offering incense on bricks;
4 who sit inside tombs,
   and spend the night in secret places;
who eat swine's flesh,
   with broth of abominable things in
   their vessels;
5 who say, "Keep to yourself,
   do not come near me, for I am too
   holy for you."
These are a smoke in my nostrils,
   a fire that burns all day long.
6 See, it is written before me:
   I will not keep silent, but I will
   repay;
I will indeed repay into their laps
7   their*a* iniquities and their*a* ancestors'
   iniquities together,
                 says the LORD;
because they offered incense on the
   mountains
   and reviled me on the hills,
I will measure into their laps
   full payment for their actions.
8 Thus says the LORD:
As the wine is found in the cluster,
   and they say, "Do not destroy it,
   for there is a blessing in it,"
so I will do for my servants' sake,
   and not destroy them all.

9 I will bring forth descendants*b* from
   Jacob,
   and from Judah inheritors*c* of my
   mountains;
my chosen shall inherit it,
   and my servants shall settle there.
10 Sharon shall become a pasture
   for flocks,
   and the Valley of Achor a place for
   herds to lie down,
for my people who have sought me.
11 But you who forsake the LORD,
   who forget my holy mountain,
who set a table for Fortune
   and fill cups of mixed wine for
   Destiny;
12 I will destine you to the sword,
   and all of you shall bow down to the
   slaughter;
because, when I called, you did
   not answer,
   when I spoke, you did not listen,
but you did what was evil in my sight,
   and chose what I did not delight in.
13 Therefore thus says the Lord GOD:
My servants shall eat,
   but you shall be hungry;
my servants shall drink,
   but you shall be thirsty;
my servants shall rejoice,
   but you shall be put to shame;
14 my servants shall sing for gladness of
   heart,
   but you shall cry out for pain
   of heart,
   and shall wail for anguish of spirit.
15 You shall leave your name to my chosen
   to use as a curse,
   and the Lord GOD will put you
   to death;
but to his servants he will give a
   different name.
16 Then whoever invokes a blessing in the
   land
   shall bless by the God of faithfulness,
and whoever takes an oath in the land
   shall swear by the God of
   faithfulness;

a Gk Syr: Heb *your*   *b* Or *a descendant*   *c* Or *an
inheritor*

because the former troubles are
forgotten
and are hidden from my sight.

17 For I am about to create new heavens
and a new earth;
the former things shall not be
remembered
or come to mind.

18 But be glad and rejoice forever
in what I am creating;
for I am about to create Jerusalem as a
joy,
and its people as a delight.

19 I will rejoice in Jerusalem,
and delight in my people;
no more shall the sound of weeping be
heard in it,
or the cry of distress.

20 No more shall there be in it
an infant that lives but a few days,
or an old person who does not live
out a lifetime;
for one who dies at a hundred years will
be considered a youth,
and one who falls short of a hundred
will be considered accursed.

21 They shall build houses and inhabit
them;
they shall plant vineyards and eat
their fruit.

22 They shall not build and another
inhabit;
they shall not plant and another eat;
for like the days of a tree shall the days
of my people be,
and my chosen shall long enjoy the
work of their hands.

23 They shall not labor in vain,
or bear children for calamity;[a]
for they shall be offspring blessed by the
LORD—
and their descendants as well.

24 Before they call I will answer,
while they are yet speaking I
will hear.

25 The wolf and the lamb shall feed
together,
the lion shall eat straw like the ox;
but the serpent—its food shall
be dust!

They shall not hurt or destroy
on all my holy mountain,
says the LORD.

65.1–25: The promise of new heavens and a new earth. 1–7: Chapters 63–66 carry forward the essential message of Isaiah's prophecies into the new age that came with the return from exile. Idolatry* marked a relapse into indifference to God. The strange and crude rites described in vv. 3–4 were designed to conjure up and manipulate magical power. The belief that human beings could perform symbolic rituals and eat strange foods (magic potions) to make themselves holy (v. 5), and thereby gain power to harm or heal others, represented a very ancient (v. 7) and superstitious tradition. **8–16:** How could God punish the wrongdoers without destroying the whole community of Judah? The prophetic answer is that, for the present, both groups must coexist, but that God has reserved a future judgment to bless those who are faithful, but to punish those who are guilty (vv. 8–13). Then the very different fates allotted to the two groups will become plain (vv. 13–16). **17–25:** God is still in control of human history. The prophet was aware of the promises earlier in Isaiah; v. 25 recalls the promise in 11.6–9.

66 Thus says the LORD:
Heaven is my throne
and the earth is my footstool;
what is the house that you would build
for me,
and what is my resting place?

2 All these things my hand has made,
and so all these things are mine,[b]
says the LORD.
But this is the one to whom I will
look,
to the humble and contrite in spirit,
who trembles at my word.

3 Whoever slaughters an ox is like one
who kills a human being;
whoever sacrifices a lamb, like one
who breaks a dog's neck;
whoever presents a grain offering, like
one who offers swine's blood;[c]

---

a Or *sudden terror*   b Gk Syr: Heb *these things came to be*   c Meaning of Heb uncertain

whoever makes a memorial offering of
 frankincense, like one who
 blesses an idol.
These have chosen their own ways,
 and in their abominations they take
 delight;
4 I also will choose to mock[a] them,
 and bring upon them what they fear;
because, when I called, no one
 answered,
 when I spoke, they did not listen;
but they did what was evil in my sight,
 and chose what did not please me.
5 Hear the word of the LORD,
 you who tremble at his word:
Your own people who hate you
 and reject you for my name's sake
have said, "Let the LORD be glorified,
 so that we may see your joy";
 but it is they who shall be put
 to shame.

6 Listen, an uproar from the city!
 A voice from the temple!
The voice of the LORD,
 dealing retribution to his enemies!

7 Before she was in labor
 she gave birth;
before her pain came upon her
 she delivered a son.
8 Who has heard of such a thing?
 Who has seen such things?
Shall a land be born in one day?
 Shall a nation be delivered in one
 moment?
Yet as soon as Zion was in labor
 she delivered her children.
9 Shall I open the womb and not
 deliver?
 says the LORD;
shall I, the one who delivers, shut the
 womb?
 says your God.

10 Rejoice with Jerusalem, and be glad for
 her,
 all you who love her;
rejoice with her in joy,
 all you who mourn over her—

11 that you may nurse and be satisfied
 from her consoling breast;
that you may drink deeply with
 delight
 from her glorious bosom.

12 For thus says the LORD:
I will extend prosperity to her like a
 river,
 and the wealth of the nations like an
 overflowing stream;
and you shall nurse and be carried on
 her arm,
 and dandled on her knees.
13 As a mother comforts her child,
 so I will comfort you;
you shall be comforted in
 Jerusalem.
14 You shall see, and your heart shall
 rejoice;
 your bodies[b] shall flourish like the
 grass;
and it shall be known that the hand
 of the LORD is with his
 servants,
 and his indignation is against
 his enemies.
15 For the LORD will come in fire,
 and his chariots like the whirlwind,
to pay back his anger in fury,
 and his rebuke in flames of fire.
16 For by fire will the LORD execute
 judgment,
 and by his sword, on all flesh;
 and those slain by the LORD shall be
 many.

17 Those who sanctify and purify themselves to go into the gardens, following the
one in the center, eating the flesh of pigs,
vermin, and rodents, shall come to an end
together, says the LORD.

18 For I know[c] their works and their
thoughts, and I am[d] coming to gather all
nations and tongues; and they shall come
and shall see my glory, 19 and I will set a sign
among them. From them I will send survi-

a Or to punish   b Heb bones   c Gk Syr: Heb lacks
know   d Gk Syr Vg Tg: Heb it is

vors to the nations, to Tarshish, Put,ᵃ and Lud—which draw the bow—to Tubal and Javan, to the coastlands far away that have not heard of my fame or seen my glory; and they shall declare my glory among the nations. 20They shall bring all your kindred from all the nations as an offering to the LORD, on horses, and in chariots, and in litters, and on mules, and on dromedaries, to my holy mountain Jerusalem, says the LORD, just as the Israelites bring a grain offering in a clean vessel to the house of the LORD. 21And I will also take some of them as priests and as Levites, says the LORD.

22 For as the new heavens and the new
        earth,
    which I will make,
shall remain before me, says the LORD;
    so shall your descendants and your
        name remain.
23 From new moon to new moon,
    and from sabbath to sabbath,
all flesh shall come to worship before me,
says the LORD.

24 And they shall go out and look at the dead bodies of the people who have rebelled against me; for their worm shall not die, their fire shall not be quenched, and they shall be an abhorrence to all flesh.

66.1–24: Final warnings and consolations for Jerusalem. 1–5: The final chapter of the book of Isaiah sets out afresh several of the basic themes that have appeared and reappeared throughout the book. Of primary importance is the demand for truth and sincerity in worship. The public performance of ritual and piety shows loyalty to God, but such outward actions must be matched by an inner spirit (see 1.12–17; 29.13). Verse 1 is not a rejection of the Temple, but rather defines its true purpose (see sidebar, p. 1017). **6–11:** In spite of the many conflicts and setbacks that had marred Jerusalem's history, the promises of God for the blessing of Israel as a people remained valid. **12–16:** The message of reassurance and hope for the future of Jerusalem did not mean, however, that wrongdoing would pass without judgment. God's promises required obedience and trust. **17:** Reference to the forbidden foods recalls the warning of 65.4. **18–21:** The return of all those who had been exiled from Judah and Israel would mark the fulfillment of God's promise for the people. **22–23:** The prophecies of Isaiah set a goal for all nations. All humankind (*all flesh*) were bound together in one world and would, therefore, ultimately share a single destiny. **24:** Divine judgment cannot be evaded. God's call is an imperious command, and the disobedient cannot participate in the final glory of God's kingdom.

a Gk: Heb *Pul*

JEREMIAH

Introduction

The book of Jeremiah was written for people in the throes of suffering. A historical tragedy underlies the book. In the sixth century BCE, Babylon invaded the nation of Judah and its capital city Jerusalem. The political structure of the country collapsed and, after resistance broke out, the Babylonians destroyed Jerusalem. Accusation, anguish, and grief run through Jeremiah, but hope and promises of a new future appear as well. The book is an honest, artistic, and sometimes chaotic response to the collapse of the nation during and after the invasion. It seeks to help the community survive that tragedy by retelling it, interpreting it, and imagining a world beyond it.

The book of Jeremiah gathers together a complex collection of poems, stories, and sermons associated with the prophet★ Jeremiah as speaker and actor. A quick review of the book reveals a mixture of prose narrative★ and poetry. The first chapter alone, for example, contains a brief prose introduction (1.1–3), a poem in which God and Jeremiah speak to one another (1.4–10), followed by a further prose narrative that describes Jeremiah's visions (1.11–19). The poetry is largely made up of prophetic oracles. Oracles are poems of judgment and accusation, and sometimes of healing, spoken by a prophet on behalf of God. There are liturgical poems, laments★ by Jeremiah, by God, and by the people. The prose passages include stories about Jeremiah and sermons attributed to Jeremiah. These various literary types are scattered about in the book, except for a few obvious groupings of similar material such as the Oracles against the Nations (chs. 46–51). Both the variety of literary types and their apparent lack of order make reading and interpreting the book difficult.

In the past, scholars have explained this literary disarray as the result of a long process of writing. For most of the twentieth century, interpreters thought that the book contained several levels of material deriving from different historical periods. First was the poetry, thought to be Jeremiah's own words, delivered orally to Judahites in the time before the Exile★ in 587 BCE. To this were added stories about Jeremiah recorded by his companion Baruch. Next came sermons that are assigned to Jeremiah but were thought to have come from a later writer, perhaps from a group influenced by the theology and language of the book of Deuteronomy. The value of this theory about the writing of the book is that it explained some difficulties of reading. The book does not move in order because poems, stories, and sermons from different times and places were added to each other without narrative intention. Interpreters who held this view were interested in the history behind each story or poem rather than how the literature fit together.

In a modification of this theory, one commentator proposed that the book was composed through a process that resembles a snowball rolling down a hill. To a core collection of Jeremiah's poems were added more poems, stories, and sermons by later followers of the prophet. From this perspective, little coherence can be found in the book. But more recently, scholars have begun to find order that is more poetic than chronological or thematic. This coherence or unity appears in images, metaphors,★ and the interplay of voices.

The book is like a conversation among many people as they struggle to survive the invasion and interpret their situation. Besides the voice of Jeremiah, there are other literary characters or voices in the book. Speeches are assigned to the people, to figures like Baruch, Jeremiah's companion, to the nations, and to the city of Jerusalem, which is portrayed as a woman called "daughter Zion." The most frequent speaker—indeed, the most important and dominant voice—is God.

The book divides into two major sections or "books": chs. 1–25 and 26–52. Within these two larger parts are smaller literary divisions.

Book One: Chs. 1–25: How the nation fell
- **1–10** Cosmic destruction
- **11–20** Covenant* destroyed
- **21–25** Aftermath of invasion

Book Two: Chs. 26–52: How the nation will survive
- **26–36** Blame and hope
- **37–45** Baruch's account
- **46–51** Oracles against the nations
- **52** The end

As may be obvious from the brief outline of the book, the material contained in it cannot be reduced to a few isolated themes. Instead, there are a number of interwoven themes that appear, fade, and reappear. These include dramatic accusations of the nation for its sins, poetic portrayal of the military battle that will destroy them, accusation of breaking the covenant relation with God, instructions about how to survive the disaster, and promises that God will ultimately reverse their circumstances and turn their suffering to joy.

The book's primary theological concern, however, is to defend God from accusations of injustice. People in the ancient world believed that if disaster occurred, it must be because God or the gods caused it. The book of Jeremiah tries to show that God was not unjust in punishing Israel for its sins. The historical collapse of the nation and the destruction of Jerusalem happened not because God was careless, unfaithful, or cruel, but because the people of Israel turned away and sought other gods. But the story does not end there: There will be a future.

Themes of hope appear throughout the book in surprising positions—for example, juxtaposed with poems of judgment and accusation. These hopeful themes come to a climax* in a section called the "Little Book of Consolation" (chs. 30–33). There restoration and joy replace accusation and judgment; there the future is imagined as a festive garden filled with feasting. It is curious that the book of Jeremiah does not place hope at the end, as modern western writers might do, but just after the middle. This central placement of hope means that hope is still surrounded by themes of tragedy, sorrow, and judgment. Some scholars have suggested that this literary arrangement reflects the psychological and spiritual reality of the book's audience in Exile. In captivity, they are caught between tragedy and a new vision of the future.

"Oracles Against the Nations," prophecies of doom against Israel's enemies, come toward the end the book (chs. 46–51). These poems may provide hope for the exiles, for in these chapters the vanquished nation changes places with its enemies. The book's conclusion offers a low-key description of the invasion of Jerusalem by Babylon (ch. 52). The account of the invasion almost exactly duplicates the depiction in 2 Kings 25. It provides the book of Jeremiah with a sobering last word. Since the chapter, and thus the book, ends with the release of the Judean king from

Babylonian prison, the chapter may also suggest hope for the exiles. In the king's survival, exiles may anticipate their own survival.

Jeremiah's ministry is described as beginning in the thirteenth year of King Josiah (627 BCE) and extending to the "captivity of Jerusalem" in 587 BCE (Jer 1.1–3). These were troubled times. The weakening of control by the Assyrian empire over Israel in the late seventh century BCE led to competition between Egypt and the emerging neo-Babylonian (also called "Chaldean") empire for dominance in the Mediterranean region. Within Judah, leading groups split between support of Egypt or Babylon. Many in the royal governing party were pro-Egyptian, whereas Jeremiah and his followers were pro-Babylonian. In 605, Babylon won a military victory over Egypt and control of Judah, but internal strife among Israel's factions continued.

In 597, Judah revolted against Babylon. In response, Babylon invaded Jerusalem, the capital city, and deported the king and other leaders. The Babylonians installed Zedekiah as a puppet king, but in 587 Judah revolted again. When the Babylonians invaded a second time in 587, they destroyed mercilessly. The Temple,* palace, and parts of the city were razed; more of the leading citizens were deported to Babylon. Gedaliah was made governor of the occupied land, but he was assassinated, and a third invasion and further suffering and deportations occurred in 582.

Some survivors remained in the devastated land; some escaped to Egypt; some settled into exile in Babylon. The Babylonian exiles were not released from captivity until 50 years later (537). It was probably during the aftermath of invasion, destruction, and deportation that the book of Jeremiah was compiled in an effort to help the survivors deal with the tragedy. The book reflects conflicts among various surviving groups. It portrays Jeremiah on the side of Babylon and opposed to Egypt and those who escape there.

The relationship of the book to the prophet Jeremiah is greatly disputed. Until recently most interpreters traced the book's poetry to Jeremiah and saw in ch. 36 an account of the book's dictation to Baruch, who wrote it on a scroll. A few interpreters thought that Jeremiah even wrote prose portions of the book, but that view has not gained much acceptance. More recently, commentators have found it difficult to decide what role Jeremiah and Baruch had in the book's writing, since evidence is limited largely to the book itself. Some of the stories may be symbolic, and the poems attributed to Jeremiah may have been written by others in order to convey theological and political messages to the community at different times during its struggles for survival. Rather than trying to pin all the poems, stories, and sermons directly to events in Jeremiah's own life, current interpreters try to make sense of the book as it stands. Jeremiah's life plays a major symbolic role in the book. The sufferings that happen to him happen to the people. His survival in captivity provides hope to the exiles—that they too will survive if they listen to the voice of God expressed in Jeremiah's book.

Chart   **Kings of Judah mentioned in Jeremiah**

King Josiah	640–609 BCE	Jehoiachin (Coniah)	598–97
Jehoahaz II (Shallum)	609	Zedekiah	597–587
Jehoiakim	609–598	Gedaliah (governor)	587–582

READING GUIDE

To understand the book of Jeremiah, it is probably best first to skim the whole book. Locate the large divisions listed above and get a sense of the book's many voices and kinds of literature. Then it will be helpful to return to the first chapter, Jeremiah's call, and think of it as an introduction to the book's major themes. It is important to recall that the book is not chronologically arranged. Time does not move in a straight line. Events in the past, promises about the future, and appeals to the reader in the present are braided together. Memories about the past shape the present and remain alive in it, just as future hope changes perceptions of the present. This overlapping of time is particularly true for survivors of trauma and loss. The present and the past weave together, and hopeful anticipation for the future can burst in without preparation upon the present.

1 The words of Jeremiah son of Hilkiah, of the priests who were in Anathoth in the land of Benjamin, ²to whom the word of the LORD came in the days of King Josiah son of Amon of Judah, in the thirteenth year of his reign. ³It came also in the days of King Jehoiakim son of Josiah of Judah, and until the end of the eleventh year of King Zedekiah son of Josiah of Judah, until the captivity of Jerusalem in the fifth month.

4 Now the word of the LORD came to me saying,

5 "Before I formed you in the womb I knew you,
and before you were born I consecrated you;
I appointed you a prophet to the nations."

⁶Then I said, "Ah, Lord GOD! Truly I do not know how to speak, for I am only a boy."

⁷But the LORD said to me,

"Do not say, 'I am only a boy';
for you shall go to all to whom I send you,
and you shall speak whatever I command you.

8 Do not be afraid of them,
for I am with you to deliver you,
                    says the LORD."

⁹Then the LORD put out his hand and touched my mouth; and the LORD said to me,

"Now I have put my words in your mouth.

10 See, today I appoint you over nations and over kingdoms,

to pluck up and to pull down,
to destroy and to overthrow,
to build and to plant."

Chs. 1–10: Cosmic destruction. Ch. 1: Jeremiah's call. 1–3: The introductory verse tells who Jeremiah was and when he prophesied. He was from a family of priests from a town outside Jerusalem, *Anathoth*. His call came during the time of *King Josiah* and extended until the fall of Jerusalem to Babylon in 587 BCE, a 40-year period that symbolically links him with Moses' 40 years of leadership in the wilderness. Jeremiah is presented as a prophet* like Moses, as promised in Deut 18.18. **4–10:** In a poetic conversation between God and Jeremiah, Jeremiah receives his mission. His call before birth indicates that his prophecy was not his own invention but given to him by God. His resistance on the grounds that he is *only a boy* and so cannot speak properly also indicates that God has sent him; he has not chosen this task for himself. God tells him not to be afraid, promises to be with him, and touches his mouth. This gesture symbolizes the divine origin of the words Jeremiah speaks and the words recorded in this book. The book claims that Jeremiah's words are from God. **10:** Jeremiah is a prophet to the *nations* and will tear down and build up. This short poem gives Jeremiah and his book authority in the face of opposition.

11 The word of the LORD came to me, saying, "Jeremiah, what do you see?" And I said, "I see a branch of an almond tree."ᵃ ¹²Then the LORD said to me, "You have seen well, for I am watchingᵇ over my word to

---

a Heb *shaqed* *b* Heb *shoqed*

perform it." 13The word of the LORD came to me a second time, saying, "What do you see?" And I said, "I see a boiling pot, tilted away from the north."

14 Then the LORD said to me: Out of the north disaster shall break out on all the inhabitants of the land. 15For now I am calling all the tribes of the kingdoms of the north, says the LORD; and they shall come and all of them shall set their thrones at the entrance of the gates of Jerusalem, against all its surrounding walls and against all the cities of Judah. 16And I will utter my judgments against them, for all their wickedness in forsaking me; they have made offerings to other gods, and worshiped the works of their own hands. 17But you, gird up your loins; stand up and tell them everything that I command you. Do not break down before them, or I will break you before them. 18And I for my part have made you today a fortified city, an iron pillar, and a bronze wall, against the whole land—against the kings of Judah, its princes, its priests, and the people of the land. 19They will fight against you; but they shall not prevail against you, for I am with you, says the LORD, to deliver you.

1.11–19: Jeremiah's mission gains substance from two visions written in prose. **11–13:** Jeremiah sees a branch of an almond tree, a "shaqed" in Hebrew. In a play on words, God replies, *I am watching* ("shoqed") *over my word to perform it.* What God says through Jeremiah will happen. Next Jeremiah sees *a boiling pot, tilted away from the north.* The boiling pot is a symbol of destruction, overflowing and burning. The north may refer to a historical enemy, but more likely the threat from the north refers to a mythic enemy, coming like a superhuman monster. Only in 20.4 will the foe from the *north* be identified as Babylon. **14–18:** The tilting pot will spill out an army of invaders who will stream upon the land. God is *calling the kingdoms of the north* to invade Jerusalem. Jeremiah himself should have courage throughout the terror, for God will be with him.

The broken family

Chs. 2–3: A story of a broken family underlies and unifies the poetry and prose of this section. The account of this family functions as a summary of the whole book in symbolic form. God appears as husband and father, betrayed, brokenhearted and in search of reconciliation with his unfaithful wife and children.

---

2 The word of the LORD came to me, saying: 2Go and proclaim in the hearing of Jerusalem, Thus says the LORD:
I remember the devotion of your
    youth,
  your love as a bride,
how you followed me in the
    wilderness,
  in a land not sown.
3 Israel was holy to the LORD,
  the first fruits of his harvest.
All who ate of it were held guilty;
  disaster came upon them,
        says the LORD.

2.1–3: God speaks and addresses his wife, remembering how good it was during their honeymoon. Then God addresses male Israel in similar terms. Israel was *holy to the LORD.* Both female and male were set apart and protected.

~~~~~~~~~~~~~~~~~~~~~~~~~~~~~~~~~~~~~~

4 Hear the word of the LORD, O house of Jacob, and all the families of the house of Israel. 5Thus says the LORD:
  What wrong did your ancestors find
        in me
    that they went far from me,
  and went after worthless things, and
        became worthless themselves?
6 They did not say, "Where is the LORD
    who brought us up from the land of
        Egypt,
  who led us in the wilderness,
    in a land of deserts and pits,
  in a land of drought and deep
        darkness,
    in a land that no one passes through,
    where no one lives?"
7 I brought you into a plentiful land
    to eat its fruits and its good things.
  But when you entered you defiled my
        land,
  and made my heritage an
        abomination.
8 The priests did not say, "Where is the
        LORD?"
  Those who handle the law did not
        know me;

the rulers*a* transgressed against me;
 the prophets prophesied by Baal,
 and went after things that do
  not profit.

9 Therefore once more I accuse you,
  says the LORD,
 and I accuse your children's children.
10 Cross to the coasts of Cyprus and look,
 send to Kedar and examine with care;
 see if there has ever been such
  a thing.
11 Has a nation changed its gods,
 even though they are no gods?
 But my people have changed their glory
 for something that does not profit.
12 Be appalled, O heavens, at this,
 be shocked, be utterly desolate,
  says the LORD,
13 for my people have committed two evils:
 they have forsaken me,
 the fountain of living water,
 and dug out cisterns for themselves,
 cracked cisterns
 that can hold no water.
14 Is Israel a slave? Is he a homeborn
  servant?
 Why then has he become plunder?
15 The lions have roared against him,
 they have roared loudly.
 They have made his land a waste;
 his cities are in ruins, without
  inhabitant.
16 Moreover, the people of Memphis and
  Tahpanhes
 have broken the crown of your head.
17 Have you not brought this upon yourself
 by forsaking the LORD your God,
 while he led you in the way?
18 What then do you gain by going to Egypt,
 to drink the waters of the Nile?
 Or what do you gain by going to Assyria,
 to drink the waters of the Euphrates?
19 Your wickedness will punish you,
 and your apostasies will convict you.
 Know and see that it is evil and bitter
 for you to forsake the LORD
  your God;
 the fear of me is not in you,
  says the Lord GOD of hosts.

20 For long ago you broke your yoke
 and burst your bonds,
 and you said, "I will not serve!"
 On every high hill
 and under every green tree
 you sprawled and played the whore.
21 Yet I planted you as a choice vine,
 from the purest stock.
 How then did you turn degenerate
 and become a wild vine?
22 Though you wash yourself with lye
 and use much soap,
 the stain of your guilt is still before me,
  says the Lord GOD.
23 How can you say, "I am not defiled,
 I have not gone after the Baals"?
 Look at your way in the valley;
 know what you have done—
 a restive young camel interlacing her
  tracks,
24 a wild ass at home in the wilderness,
 in her heat sniffing the wind!
 Who can restrain her lust?
 None who seek her need weary
  themselves;
 in her month they will find her.
25 Keep your feet from going unshod
 and your throat from thirst.
 But you said, "It is hopeless,
 for I have loved strangers,
 and after them I will go."
26 As a thief is shamed when caught,
 so the house of Israel shall be
  shamed—
 they, their kings, their officials,
 their priests, and their prophets,
27 who say to a tree, "You are my father,"
 and to a stone, "You gave me birth."
 For they have turned their backs to me,
 and not their faces.
 But in the time of their trouble they say,
 "Come and save us!"
28 But where are your gods
 that you made for yourself?
 Let them come, if they can save you,
 in your time of trouble;
 for you have as many gods
 as you have towns, O Judah.

a Heb *shepherds*

29 Why do you complain against me?
    You have all rebelled against me,
          says the LORD.
30 In vain I have struck down
          your children;
    they accepted no correction.
    Your own sword devoured your
          prophets
    like a ravening lion.
31 And you, O generation, behold the word
          of the LORD!*a*
    Have I been a wilderness to Israel,
    or a land of thick darkness?
    Why then do my people say, "We are
          free,
    we will come to you no more"?
32 Can a girl forget her ornaments,
    or a bride her attire?
    Yet my people have forgotten me,
    days without number.

33 How well you direct your course
    to seek lovers!
    So that even to wicked women
    you have taught your ways.
34 Also on your skirts is found
    the lifeblood of the innocent poor,
    though you did not catch them
          breaking in.
    Yet in spite of all these things*a*
35 you say, "I am innocent;
    surely his anger has turned from me."
    Now I am bringing you to judgment
    for saying, "I have not sinned."
36 How lightly you gad about,
    changing your ways!
    You shall be put to shame by Egypt
    as you were put to shame by Assyria.
37 From there also you will come away
    with your hands on your head;
    for the LORD has rejected those in
          whom you trust,
    and you will not prosper through
          them.

3 If*b* a man divorces his wife
    and she goes from him
    and becomes another man's wife,
    will he return to her?
    Would not such a land be greatly
          polluted?

You have played the whore with many
          lovers;
    and would you return to me?
          says the LORD.
2 Look up to the bare heights,*c* and see!
    Where have you not been lain with?
    By the waysides you have sat waiting for
          lovers,
    like a nomad in the wilderness.
    You have polluted the land
    with your whoring and wickedness.
3 Therefore the showers have been
          withheld,
    and the spring rain has not come;
    yet you have the forehead of a whore,
    you refuse to be ashamed.
4 Have you not just now called to me,
    "My Father, you are the friend of my
          youth—
5 will he be angry forever,
    will he be indignant to the end?"
    This is how you have spoken,
    but you have done all the evil that
          you could.

2.4–3.5: In these poems, the divine speaker alternates in addressing male Israel (2.4–16; 2.26–32) and female Judah, portrayed as God's wife (2.17–25; 2.33–3.5). The effect of this switch from male to female is to accuse both figures of infidelity and of going after other gods or lovers. Male Israel changes its gods (2.11), forsakes God, *the fountain of living water* (2.13), digs its own sources of water (2.13) and worships idols (2.27–28). Wife Judah also betrays God, but in more intimate ways. Though she is GOD's wife, she *played the whore* (2.20), went after other lovers (2.23–25, 33; 3.1), and would not *return* to her husband (3.1). The Hebrew word for return also means "to repent." The divine husband, therefore, divorces her (3.1–5). The relationship between God and his wife, symbolizing all the people of Israel and Judah, is over. The family is broken and there appears to be no future.

6 The LORD said to me in the days of King Josiah: Have you seen what she did, that faithless one, Israel, how she went up on

a Meaning of Heb uncertain   *b* Q Ms Gk Syr: MT *Saying, If*   *c* Or *the trails* every high hill and under every green tree, and played the whore there? 7And I thought, "After she has done all this she will return to me"; but she did not return, and her false sister Judah saw it. 8She*a* saw that for all the adulteries of that faithless one, Israel, I had sent her away with a decree of divorce; yet her false sister Judah did not fear, but she too went and played the whore. 9Because she took her whoredom so lightly, she polluted the land, committing adultery with stone and tree. 10Yet for all this her false sister Judah did not return to me with her whole heart, but only in pretense, says the LORD.

11 Then the LORD said to me: Faithless Israel has shown herself less guilty than false Judah. 12Go, and proclaim these words toward the north, and say:

Return, faithless Israel,
              says the LORD.
I will not look on you in anger,
  for I am merciful,
              says the LORD;
I will not be angry forever.
13 Only acknowledge your guilt,
  that you have rebelled against the
    LORD your God,
and scattered your favors among
  strangers under every green tree,
  and have not obeyed my voice,
              says the LORD.
14 Return, O faithless children,
             says the LORD,
  for I am your master;
I will take you, one from a city and two
  from a family,
  and I will bring you to Zion.

15 I will give you shepherds after my own heart, who will feed you with knowledge and understanding. 16And when you have multiplied and increased in the land, in those days, says the LORD, they shall no longer say, "The ark of the covenant of the LORD." It shall not come to mind, or be remembered, or missed; nor shall another one be made. 17At that time Jerusalem shall be called the throne of the LORD, and all nations shall gather to it, to the presence of the LORD in Jerusalem, and they shall no longer stubbornly follow their own evil will. 18In those days the house of Judah shall join the house of Israel, and together they shall come from the land of the north to the land that I gave your ancestors for a heritage.

3.6–18. 6–10: Jeremiah replaces the husband as speaker and reports that the husband had previously had another wife, Israel, who also betrayed him and whom he had also divorced. In this story of the family, both the northern and southern kingdoms have betrayed God and been cast off. Since the northern kingdom of Israel fell to Assyria in 721 BCE, this story explains that historical tragedy in the symbolic terms of betrayal in marriage. **11–18:** The divine husband sends Jeremiah to speak to the first wife and invite her to return. The text reports no response from her. Then the invitation to return is addressed to the children (v. 14). Their father promises them restoration and reunification of the whole people in Jerusalem (vv. 15–18).

19 I thought
  how I would set you among
    my children,
and give you a pleasant land,
  the most beautiful heritage of all the
    nations.
And I thought you would call me, My
    Father,
  and would not turn from following
    me.
20 Instead, as a faithless wife leaves her
    husband,
  so you have been faithless to me,
    O house of Israel,
             says the LORD.

21 A voice on the bare heights*b* is heard,
  the plaintive weeping of Israel's
    children,
because they have perverted their way,
  they have forgotten the LORD their
    God:
22 Return, O faithless children,
  I will heal your faithlessness.

"Here we come to you;
  for you are the LORD our God.

a Q Ms Gk Mss Syr: MT I   *b* Or *the trails*

23 Truly the hills are[a] a delusion,
  the orgies on the mountains.
 Truly in the LORD our God
  is the salvation of Israel.
24 "But from our youth the shameful
thing has devoured all for which our ancestors had labored, their flocks and their herds,
their sons and their daughters. 25 Let us lie
down in our shame, and let our dishonor
cover us; for we have sinned against the
LORD our God, we and our ancestors, from
our youth even to this day; and we have not
obeyed the voice of the LORD our God."

3.19–24: Though still nostalgic for his wife (2.19–20), the husband/father again invites the children to "return" and promises to heal them. **22–24:** The children then begin to speak, addressing the father directly and repenting of their infidelity and idolatry.* The family is partially restored. The account of the broken family symbolically retells the entire course of Judah's history up to the Exile.* It is likely that the children symbolize the exiles who were invited to return and promised a renewed future in allegiance to their father. The story of this broken family explains the Exile symbolically. The historical destruction of Judah and Jerusalem was not God's fault but was punishment for idolatry and betrayal. That betrayal by all the people appears the more intimate and wrong because it is like betrayal by a spouse.

THE COSMIC BATTLE

Chs. 4–10: Chapter 4 turns away from the story of the broken family to give prominence to announce-ments of imminent invasion by the "foe from the north." The material in this section is largely poetic, but there are some prose passages as well (7.1–8.3). Although individual passages probably come from many different times, they are collected here around the theme of cosmic destruction at the hands of the mythic "foe from the north."

4 If you return, O Israel,
              says the LORD,
 if you return to me,
 if you remove your abominations from
  my presence,
  and do not waver,
2 and if you swear, "As the LORD lives!"
  in truth, in justice, and in uprightness,

then nations shall be blessed[b] by him,
  and by him they shall boast.
3 For thus says the LORD to the people
of Judah and to the inhabitants of Jerusalem:
 Break up your fallow ground,
  and do not sow among thorns.
4 Circumcise yourselves to the LORD,
  remove the foreskin of your hearts,
  O people of Judah and inhabitants of
   Jerusalem,
 or else my wrath will go forth like fire,
  and burn with no one to quench it,
  because of the evil of your doings.

4.1–4: Repent. This poem reaches back to the broken marriage by repeating the invitation to "return," and it extends forward in the book by promising God's wrathful judgment against those who do not repent.

The approaching enemy

Chs. 4–6: No narrative* unifies these poems, but the approaching foe looms over the chapters and gives them menacing drama. The voices of God, Jeremiah, a narrator, the people, daughter Zion, and the foe from the north—all speak and argue about God's role in the coming invasion. The battle poems use great art in portraying war. Scenes of approaching armies ap-peal to the senses and give the superhuman enemy from the north shape in the imagination. With a few details of sight and sound, the poems place readers in the thick of battle.

---

5 Declare in Judah, and proclaim in Jerusalem, and say:
 Blow the trumpet through the land;
  shout aloud[c] and say,
 "Gather together, and let us go
  into the fortified cities!"
6 Raise a standard toward Zion,
  flee for safety, do not delay,
 for I am bringing evil from the north,
  and a great destruction.
7 A lion has gone up from its thicket,
  a destroyer of nations has set out;
  he has gone out from his place

---

a Gk Syr Vg: Heb *Truly from the hills is*
b Or *shall bless themselves*
c Or *shout, take your weapons*: Heb *shout, fill*
(your hand)

to make your land a waste;
    your cities will be ruins
    without inhabitant.
8 Because of this put on sackcloth,
    lament and wail:
"The fierce anger of the LORD
    has not turned away from us."

⁹On that day, says the LORD, courage shall fail the king and the officials; the priests shall be appalled and the prophets astounded. ¹⁰Then I said, "Ah, Lord GOD, how utterly you have deceived this people and Jerusalem, saying, 'It shall be well with you,' even while the sword is at the throat!"

11 At that time it will be said to this people and to Jerusalem: A hot wind comes from me out of the bare heights*a* in the desert toward my poor people, not to winnow or cleanse— ¹²a wind too strong for that. Now it is I who speak in judgment against them.
13 Look! He comes up like clouds,
    his chariots like the whirlwind;
his horses are swifter than eagles—
    woe to us, for we are ruined!
14 O Jerusalem, wash your heart clean of
    wickedness
    so that you may be saved.
How long shall your evil schemes
    lodge within you?
15 For a voice declares from Dan
    and proclaims disaster from Mount
      Ephraim.
16 Tell the nations, "Here they are!"
    Proclaim against Jerusalem,
"Besiegers come from a distant land;
    they shout against the cities of
      Judah.
17 They have closed in around her like
    watchers of a field,
    because she has rebelled against me,
        says the LORD.
18 Your ways and your doings
    have brought this upon you.
This is your doom; how bitter it is!
    It has reached your very heart."

19 My anguish, my anguish! I writhe in
    pain!
    Oh, the walls of my heart!

My heart is beating wildly;
    I cannot keep silent;
for I*b* hear the sound of the trumpet,
    the alarm of war.
20 Disaster overtakes disaster,
    the whole land is laid waste.
Suddenly my tents are destroyed,
    my curtains in a moment.
21 How long must I see the standard,
    and hear the sound of the trumpet?
22 "For my people are foolish,
    they do not know me;
they are stupid children,
    they have no understanding.
They are skilled in doing evil,
    but do not know how to do good."

4.5–31: The sound of the trumpet and the sight of the standard or flag of the army evoke the battle. 6–7: References to the mythic foe add to the unearthly terror coming upon the nation. The enemy is a *lion,* magnified into *a destroyer of nations.* Since God is the one bringing the foe, supernatural forces are arrayed against the nation. 19–22: Although God brings the enemy, God also witnesses the battle with uncontrollable anguish.

23 I looked on the earth, and lo, it was
    waste and void;
    and to the heavens, and they had no
      light.
24 I looked on the mountains, and lo, they
    were quaking,
    and all the hills moved to and fro.
25 I looked, and lo, there was no one at all,
    and all the birds of the air had fled.
26 I looked, and lo, the fruitful land was a
    desert,
    and all its cities were laid in ruins
    before the LORD, before his fierce
      anger.

27 For thus says the LORD: The whole land shall be a desolation; yet I will not make a full end.
28 Because of this the earth shall mourn,
    and the heavens above grow black;
for I have spoken, I have purposed;
    I have not relented nor will I turn
      back.

a Or *the trails*   *b* Another reading is *for you, O my soul,*

29 At the noise of horseman and archer
 every town takes to flight;
they enter thickets; they climb among
  rocks;
 all the towns are forsaken,
 and no one lives in them.
30 And you, O desolate one,
 what do you mean that you dress in
  crimson,
 that you deck yourself with
  ornaments of gold,
 that you enlarge your eyes with paint?
In vain you beautify yourself.
 Your lovers despise you;
 they seek your life.
31 For I heard a cry as of a woman
  in labor,
 anguish as of one bringing forth her
  first child,
 the cry of daughter Zion gasping for
  breath,
stretching out her hands,
"Woe is me! I am fainting before
  killers!"

4.23–31. 23–28: Creation destroyed. The speaker describes a terrifying vision of destruction that reverses the world's creation in the first chapter of Genesis. This picture of the earth as a devastated landscape, *waste and void,* implies that the cosmic battle somehow overturns the world. The impact of the historical invasion of Judah by Babylon meant the end of their national world, the collapse of daily life in their land. The poem describes the symbolic effects of that invasion. Judah's world has come to an end. **29–31:** The battle draws near as suggested by the noise of the attack and the flight of the inhabitants. The poem portrays the city of Jerusalem as a woman called *daughter Zion.* She is probably God's first wife in 2.1–3.25. Portraying the city as a woman indicates how impossible defense against the advancing army is for her and creates pity in the reader.

5 Run to and fro through the streets of
  Jerusalem,
 look around and take note!
Search its squares and see
 if you can find one person
who acts justly
 and seeks truth—
so that I may pardon Jerusalem.^a

2 Although they say, "As the LORD lives,"
 yet they swear falsely.
3 O LORD, do your eyes not look
  for truth?
You have struck them,
 but they felt no anguish;
you have consumed them,
 but they refused to take correction.
They have made their faces harder than
  rock;
 they have refused to turn back.

4 Then I said, "These are only the poor,
 they have no sense;
for they do not know the way of
  the LORD,
 the law of their God.
5 Let me go to the rich^b
 and speak to them;
surely they know the way of the LORD,
 the law of their God."
But they all alike had broken the yoke,
 they had burst the bonds.

6 Therefore a lion from the forest shall
  kill them,
 a wolf from the desert shall destroy
  them.
A leopard is watching against
  their cities;
 everyone who goes out of them shall
  be torn in pieces—
because their transgressions are many,
 their apostasies are great.

5.1–31: God's reluctance to send the attackers. These loosely connected poems show that God does not wish to destroy the nation. Instead, the people are at fault because they will not act justly or repent. God is neither arbitrary nor whimsical in orchestrating the attack on the nation. **1–6:** God will not destroy the nation if Jeremiah can find one righteous person. Though he runs up and down the streets of Jerusalem to the rich and the poor, Jeremiah's search is unsuccessful. God promises invasion by wild animals, which symbolize the invading enemy.

7 How can I pardon you?
 Your children have forsaken me,

a Heb *it*   *b* Or *the great*

and have sworn by those who are no
gods.
When I fed them to the full,
they committed adultery
and trooped to the houses of
prostitutes.
8 They were well-fed lusty stallions,
each neighing for his neighbor's wife.
9 Shall I not punish them for these
things?
says the LORD;
and shall I not bring retribution
on a nation such as this?

10 Go up through her vine-rows
and destroy,
but do not make a full end;
strip away her branches,
for they are not the LORD's.
11 For the house of Israel and the house of
Judah
have been utterly faithless to me,
says the LORD.
12 They have spoken falsely of the LORD,
and have said, "He will do nothing.
No evil will come upon us,
and we shall not see sword or
famine."
13 The prophets are nothing but wind,
for the word is not in them.
Thus shall it be done to them!

14 Therefore thus says the LORD, the God
of hosts:
Because they[a] have spoken this word,
I am now making my words in your
mouth a fire,
and this people wood, and the fire
shall devour them.
15 I am going to bring upon you
a nation from far away, O house of
Israel,
says the LORD.
It is an enduring nation,
it is an ancient nation,
a nation whose language you do
not know,
nor can you understand what they
say.
16 Their quiver is like an open tomb;
all of them are mighty warriors.

17 They shall eat up your harvest and your
food;
they shall eat up your sons and your
daughters;
they shall eat up your flocks and your
herds;
they shall eat up your vines and your
fig trees;
they shall destroy with the sword
your fortified cities in which
you trust.

18 But even in those days, says the LORD,
I will not make a full end of you. 19And when
your people say, "Why has the LORD our God
done all these things to us?" you shall say to
them, "As you have forsaken me and served
foreign gods in your land, so you shall serve
strangers in a land that is not yours."

5.7–19. 7–11: A question that will be repeated (5.29)
addresses an unnamed female. She is probably daughter Zion and God's unfaithful wife (2.1–3.5). God asks
if there is a way to pardon her, but she and her children
have been adulterous. There is no way to avoid punishment. **12–18:** Further accusations of infidelity introduce another announcement of the approaching invader, a mighty nation, superhuman in its capabilities.
However, a prose comment promises not to completely destroy the nation. If the book's audience is the
people in exile, v. 18 speaks to them directly. They are
the remnant who remain after the invasion.

---

20 Declare this in the house of Jacob,
proclaim it in Judah:
21 Hear this, O foolish and senseless
people,
who have eyes, but do not see,
who have ears, but do not hear.
22 Do you not fear me? says the LORD;
Do you not tremble before me?
I placed the sand as a boundary for the
sea,
a perpetual barrier that it cannot
pass;
though the waves toss, they cannot
prevail,
though they roar, they cannot pass
over it.

a Heb you

23 But this people has a stubborn and
    rebellious heart;
  they have turned aside and
    gone away.
24 They do not say in their hearts,
  "Let us fear the LORD our God,
who gives the rain in its season,
  the autumn rain and the spring rain,
and keeps for us
  the weeks appointed for the harvest."
25 Your iniquities have turned these away,
  and your sins have deprived you of
    good.
26 For scoundrels are found among
    my people;
  they take over the goods of others.
Like fowlers they set a trap;[a]
  they catch human beings.
27 Like a cage full of birds,
  their houses are full of treachery;
therefore they have become great and
    rich,
28   they have grown fat and sleek.
They know no limits in deeds of
    wickedness;
  they do not judge with justice
the cause of the orphan, to make
    it prosper,
  and they do not defend the rights of
    the needy.
29 Shall I not punish them for these things?
              says the LORD,
  and shall I not bring retribution
on a nation such as this?

5.20–29: God's reluctance to punish is overcome because neither Jacob, the northern kingdom that fell to Assyria in 721 BCE, nor Judah, the southern kingdom that falls to Babylon in 587, sees, hears, or fears the Creator. Unlike the sea and the rains that stay in place and come at the proper times, the people know no boundaries in their wickedness.

30 An appalling and horrible thing
  has happened in the land:
31 the prophets prophesy falsely,
  and the priests rule as the prophets
    direct;[b]
my people love to have it so,
  but what will you do when the end
    comes?

6 Flee for safety, O children of
    Benjamin,
  from the midst of Jerusalem!
Blow the trumpet in Tekoa,
  and raise a signal on Beth-
    haccherem;
for evil looms out of the north,
  and great destruction.
2 I have likened daughter Zion
  to the loveliest pasture.[c]
3 Shepherds with their flocks shall come
    against her.
  They shall pitch their tents around
    her;
  they shall pasture, all in their places.
4 "Prepare war against her;
  up, and let us attack at noon!"
"Woe to us, for the day declines,
  the shadows of evening lengthen!"
5 "Up, and let us attack by night,
  and destroy her palaces!"
6 For thus says the LORD of hosts:
Cut down her trees;
  cast up a siege ramp against
    Jerusalem.
This is the city that must be
    punished;[d]
  there is nothing but oppression within
    her.
7 As a well keeps its water fresh,
  so she keeps fresh her wickedness;
violence and destruction are heard
  within her;
  sickness and wounds are ever
    before me.
8 Take warning, O Jerusalem,
  or I shall turn from you in disgust,
and make you a desolation,
  an uninhabited land.

9 Thus says the LORD of hosts:
Glean[e] thoroughly as a vine
  the remnant of Israel;
like a grape-gatherer, pass your hand
    again
  over its branches.

a Meaning of Heb uncertain   *b* Or *rule by their own*
authority   *c* Or *I will destroy daughter Zion, the loveliest*
pasture   *d* Or *the city of license*   *e* Cn: Heb *They*
shall glean

10 To whom shall I speak and give warning,
   that they may hear?
See, their ears are closed,*ᵃ*
   they cannot listen.
The word of the LORD is to them an
   object of scorn;
   they take no pleasure in it.
11 But I am full of the wrath of the LORD;
   I am weary of holding it in.

Pour it out on the children in the street,
   and on the gatherings of young men
      as well;
both husband and wife shall be taken,
   the old folk and the very aged.
12 Their houses shall be turned over to
      others,
   their fields and wives together;
for I will stretch out my hand
   against the inhabitants of the land,
            says the LORD.

6.1–30: Daughter Zion is attacked. This chapter gathers images of the cosmic battle into a collection of poems from a chorus of speakers. The mythic nature of the battle increases when the text identifies daughter Zion as the object of attack. A ferocious military nation wages war against Jerusalem, portrayed as a weak, wanton woman, defenseless in the face of her foe. **1:** A voice urges the *children of Benjamin,* one of the tribes in Judah, to flee the city *for evil looms out of the north.* **4–7:** The poem quotes the enemies' shouts as they prepare for attack. They believe they are acting under divine orders against a wicked city. **10–12:** Jeremiah laments the people's stubbornness. They are not even capable of hearing the prophet's* warning.

13 For from the least to the greatest
      of them,
   everyone is greedy for unjust gain;
and from prophet to priest,
   everyone deals falsely.
14 They have treated the wound of my
      people carelessly,
   saying, "Peace, peace,"
   when there is no peace.
15 They acted shamefully, they committed
      abomination;
   yet they were not ashamed,
   they did not know how to blush.

Therefore they shall fall among those
   who fall;
at the time that I punish them, they
   shall be overthrown,
            says the LORD.
16 Thus says the LORD:
Stand at the crossroads, and look,
   and ask for the ancient paths,
where the good way lies; and walk in it,
   and find rest for your souls.
But they said, "We will not walk in it."
17 Also I raised up sentinels for you:
   "Give heed to the sound of the
      trumpet!"
But they said, "We will not give heed."
18 Therefore hear, O nations,
   and know, O congregation, what will
      happen to them.
19 Hear, O earth; I am going to bring
      disaster on this people,
   the fruit of their schemes,
because they have not given heed to my
      words;
   and as for my teaching, they have
      rejected it.
20 Of what use to me is frankincense that
      comes from Sheba,
   or sweet cane from a distant land?
Your burnt offerings are not acceptable,
   nor are your sacrifices pleasing to me.
21 Therefore thus says the LORD:
See, I am laying before this people
   stumbling blocks against which they
      shall stumble;
parents and children together,
   neighbor and friend shall perish.

6.13–21. 13–15: A refrain that will reappear in 8.10–13 charges the entire community with guilt—from the people to the leaders. Everyone is greedy and leaders lie; therefore, God is justified in punishing them. **16–21:** God assembles the nations and the earth itself as witnesses against them in a covenant* lawsuit.

22 Thus says the LORD:
See, a people is coming from the land of
      the north,
   a great nation is stirring from the
      farthest parts of the earth.

a Heb *are uncircumcised*

23 They grasp the bow and the javelin,
　　they are cruel and have no mercy,
　　their sound is like the roaring sea;
　they ride on horses,
　　equipped like a warrior for battle,
　　against you, O daughter Zion!

24 "We have heard news of them,
　　our hands fall helpless;
　anguish has taken hold of us,
　　pain as of a woman in labor.
25 Do not go out into the field,
　　or walk on the road;
　for the enemy has a sword,
　　terror is on every side."

26 O my poor people, put on sackcloth,
　　and roll in ashes;
　make mourning as for an only child,
　　most bitter lamentation:
　for suddenly the destroyer
　　will come upon us.

27 I have made you a tester and a refiner[a]
　　among my people
　so that you may know and test their
　　ways.
28 They are all stubbornly rebellious,
　　going about with slanders;
　they are bronze and iron,
　　all of them act corruptly.
29 The bellows blow fiercely,
　　the lead is consumed by the fire;
　in vain the refining goes on,
　　for the wicked are not removed.
30 They are called "rejected silver,"
　　for the LORD has rejected them.

6.22–30: The attacking army continues to advance *against you, O daughter Zion* (v. 23). **26:** As the symbol of the city there is nothing for her to do but to lament her fate. **27:** God speaks to Jeremiah to tell him his role is like one who tests the authenticity of silver. **30:** Judah is *rejected silver.*

The Temple sermon

Chs. 7–8: This long prose sermon presented by Jeremiah at the Temple* in Jerusalem appears to interrupt the poetry of chs. 1–10. The poetry contains multiple images and voices that intrude upon each other

and, in chs. 4–6, focus on the cosmic battle. The prose sermon, by contrast, contains only the voice of Jeremiah as the divine spokesperson. The sermon's subject is the hypocrisy and arrogance of the people's worship. Rather than completely changing the subject from the poetry, the Temple sermon focuses attention on one more aspect of the people's sinfulness. The people themselves, not God, should be blamed for the destruction of the nation. Judah and its capital city, Jerusalem, fell to Babylon in the sixth century BCE because their worship was false. The sermon must have been immensely shocking for its original audience. Since the time of David, the king and the Temple had been closely bound together in the people's thinking. When David came to the throne, God promised that David's son would build the Temple and that David and his throne would be established forever (1 Sam 7.1–7). A century earlier than Jeremiah, the prophet Isaiah had interpreted the promises to David as unconditional assurance of Jerusalem's safety (Isa 36–37). By the time of Jeremiah, the people of Judah seemed to think they were safe no matter what they did.

7 The word that came to Jeremiah from the LORD: ²Stand in the gate of the LORD's house, and proclaim there this word, and say, Hear the word of the LORD, all you people of Judah, you that enter these gates to worship the LORD. ³Thus says the LORD of hosts, the God of Israel: Amend your ways and your doings, and let me dwell with you[b] in this place. ⁴Do not trust in these deceptive words: "This is[c] the temple of the LORD, the temple of the LORD, the temple of the LORD."

5 For if you truly amend your ways and your doings, if you truly act justly one with another, ⁶if you do not oppress the alien, the orphan, and the widow, or shed innocent blood in this place, and if you do not go after other gods to your own hurt, ⁷then I will dwell with you in this place, in the land that I gave of old to your ancestors forever and ever.

7.1–7: Standing at the gates of the Temple,* Jeremiah tells the people that they must change their ways to dwell *in this place* (7.3, 7, 10, 11). The "place" prob-

a Or *a fortress*　　*b* Or *and I will let you dwell*
c Heb *They are*

ably refers to the Temple, the land, and the city. To live there, they must stop their false reliance on the place itself. Instead, they must act justly toward one another. They claim God's protection in the Temple even though, by oppressing weak members of their society, they act as if they are not God's people. The threat to the nation stems not only from the invading foe but also from their own behavior.

8 Here you are, trusting in deceptive words to no avail. 9Will you steal, murder, commit adultery, swear falsely, make offerings to Baal, and go after other gods that you have not known, 10and then come and stand before me in this house, which is called by my name, and say, "We are safe!"—only to go on doing all these abominations? 11Has this house, which is called by my name, become a den of robbers in your sight? You know, I too am watching, says the LORD. 12Go now to my place that was in Shiloh, where I made my name dwell at first, and see what I did to it for the wickedness of my people Israel. 13And now, because you have done all these things, says the LORD, and when I spoke to you persistently, you did not listen, and when I called you, you did not answer, 14therefore I will do to the house that is called by my name, in which you trust, and to the place that I gave to you and to your ancestors, just what I did to Shiloh. 15And I will cast you out of my sight, just as I cast out all your kinsfolk, all the offspring of Ephraim.

16 As for you, do not pray for this people, do not raise a cry or prayer on their behalf, and do not intercede with me, for I will not hear you. 17Do you not see what they are doing in the towns of Judah and in the streets of Jerusalem? 18The children gather wood, the fathers kindle fire, and the women knead dough, to make cakes for the queen of heaven; and they pour out drink offerings to other gods, to provoke me to anger. 19Is it I whom they provoke? says the LORD. Is it not themselves, to their own hurt? 20Therefore thus says the Lord GOD: My anger and my wrath shall be poured out on this place, on human beings and animals, on the trees of the field and the fruit of the ground; it will burn and not be quenched.

7.8–8.3: The sermon moves in a downward spiral of offenses. **7.9:** The people commit crimes and worship *Baal,* a storm deity, not the God of Israel. **12–15:** For these offenses, Jerusalem will become like *Shiloh,* a shrine in the northern kingdom that was destroyed by the Philistines. The Jerusalem Temple* will meet the same fate if the people of Judah do not repent. **16–17:** Yet the sins of Judah are so great that God prohibits Jeremiah from interceding on behalf of the people. **18–19:** Entire families worship the astral deity called *the queen of heaven.*

21 Thus says the LORD of hosts, the God of Israel: Add your burnt offerings to your sacrifices, and eat the flesh. 22For in the day that I brought your ancestors out of the land of Egypt, I did not speak to them or command them concerning burnt offerings and sacrifices. 23But this command I gave them, "Obey my voice, and I will be your God, and you shall be my people; and walk only in the way that I command you, so that it may be well with you." 24Yet they did not obey or incline their ear, but, in the stubbornness of their evil will, they walked in their own counsels, and looked backward rather than forward. 25From the day that your ancestors came out of the land of Egypt until this day, I have persistently sent all my servants the prophets to them, day after day; 26yet they did not listen to me, or pay attention, but they stiffened their necks. They did worse than their ancestors did.

27 So you shall speak all these words to them, but they will not listen to you. You shall call to them, but they will not answer you. 28You shall say to them: This is the nation that did not obey the voice of the LORD their God, and did not accept discipline; truth has perished; it is cut off from their lips.

29 Cut off your hair and throw it away;
　　raise a lamentation on the bare
　　　　heights,*a*
　for the LORD has rejected and forsaken
　　the generation that provoked
　　　　his wrath.

30 For the people of Judah have done evil in my sight, says the LORD; they have set

a Or *the trails*

their abominations in the house that is called by my name, defiling it. 31And they go on building the high place*a* of Topheth, which is in the valley of the son of Hinnom, to burn their sons and their daughters in the fire— which I did not command, nor did it come into my mind. 32Therefore, the days are surely coming, says the LORD, when it will no more be called Topheth, or the valley of the son of Hinnom, but the valley of Slaughter: for they will bury in Topheth until there is no more room. 33The corpses of this people will be food for the birds of the air, and for the animals of the earth; and no one will frighten them away. 34And I will bring to an end the sound of mirth and gladness, the voice of the bride and bridegroom in the cities of Judah and in the streets of Jerusalem; for the land shall become a waste.

7.21–34. 29: A poetic verse urges the people to lament,* for God has rejected their worship. 30–32: People offer their children in sacrifice on *Topheth in the valley of Hinnom.* 33–34: For these crimes the nation will be destroyed. Their corpses will be littered about, normal life in the land will cease, and *the land shall become a waste.*

8 At that time, says the LORD, the bones of the kings of Judah, the bones of its officials, the bones of the priests, the bones of the prophets, and the bones of the inhabitants of Jerusalem shall be brought out of their tombs; 2and they shall be spread before the sun and the moon and all the host of heaven, which they have loved and served, which they have followed, and which they have inquired of and worshiped; and they shall not be gathered or buried; they shall be like dung on the surface of the ground. 3Death shall be preferred to life by all the remnant that remains of this evil family in all the places where I have driven them, says the LORD of hosts.

8.1–3: In the horrifying conclusion to the sermon, the kings, who are not only the leaders but also symbolize the nation itself, will die and their corpses will be dishonored. The sermon seeks to bring about obedience and true worship. The people must listen to the voice of God through the prophet.* If the book's audience lives in exile, then the sermon makes clear that only true worship will bring about renewed life in the land.

Weeping and lamentation
8.4–10.25: Poetry resumes in this section that continues to announce the impending cosmic battle and also emphasizes themes of weeping and lamentation.* The only response left in the face of the community's stubbornness and infidelity is to weep at the tragedy that is certain to come. The poems gathered here fall into four groupings: 8.4–17 continues to explain why the cosmic battle must come; 8.18–9.26 begins the weeping as if at a funeral for the nation; 10.1–16 contains a communal prayer of loyalty to God; 10.17–25 announces the Exile* as the enemy from the north comes closer. As in earlier chapters in the book, many voices announce, comment upon, or respond to the approaching disaster. Voices of lamentation and weeping that appeared in 3.21; 4.19; 6.26; and 7.29 burst out here with abundant tears that flow from God, Jeremiah, and the people.

4 You shall say to them, Thus says the
    LORD:
When people fall, do they not get up
    again?
    If they go astray, do they not turn
      back?
5 Why then has this people*b* turned away
    in perpetual backsliding?
They have held fast to deceit,
    they have refused to return.
6 I have given heed and listened,
    but they do not speak honestly;
no one repents of wickedness,
    saying, "What have I done!"
All of them turn to their own course,
    like a horse plunging headlong into
      battle.
7 Even the stork in the heavens
    knows its times;
and the turtledove, swallow, and crane*c*
    observe the time of their coming;
but my people do not know
    the ordinance of the LORD.

8 How can you say, "We are wise,
    and the law of the LORD is with us,"

a Gk Tg: Heb *high places*   *b* One Ms Gk: MT *this people, Jerusalem,*   *c* Meaning of Heb uncertain

when, in fact, the false pen of the scribes
has made it into a lie?

9 The wise shall be put to shame,
they shall be dismayed and taken;
since they have rejected the word
of the LORD,
what wisdom is in them?

10 Therefore I will give their wives
to others
and their fields to conquerors,
because from the least to the greatest
everyone is greedy for unjust gain;
from prophet to priest
everyone deals falsely.

11 They have treated the wound of my
people carelessly,
saying, "Peace, peace,"
when there is no peace.

12 They acted shamefully, they committed
abomination;
yet they were not at all ashamed,
they did not know how to blush.
Therefore they shall fall among those
who fall;
at the time when I punish them, they
shall be overthrown,
says the LORD.

13 When I wanted to gather them, says the
LORD,
there are*a* no grapes on the vine,
nor figs on the fig tree;
even the leaves are withered,
and what I gave them has passed
away from them.*b*

14 Why do we sit still?
Gather together, let us go into the
fortified cities
and perish there;
for the LORD our God has doomed us to
perish,
and has given us poisoned water to
drink,
because we have sinned against
the LORD.

15 We look for peace, but find no good,
for a time of healing, but there is
terror instead.

16 The snorting of their horses is heard
from Dan;

at the sound of the neighing of their
stallions
the whole land quakes.
They come and devour the land and all
that fills it,
the city and those who live in it.

17 See, I am letting snakes loose among you,
adders that cannot be charmed,
and they shall bite you,
says the LORD.

8.4–17: Why the attack will come. God speaks to Jeremiah in continued perplexity about the people's failure to repent. **6–7:** They behave like wild animals. **8–9:** Their punishment will be captivity. The aftermath of military attack shows wives and fields captured by others. **10–12:** The refrain of accusation from 6.13–15 is repeated here to explain why the invasion must occur. Everyone is deluded and everyone sins. **14–15:** The people speak in confusion and blame God for failing them. Their voice may reflect the feelings of the book's audience in exile, even though their speech is here set before the recounting of the tragedy. **16–17:** God replies by calling attention to the sound of the approaching battle.

18 My joy is gone, grief is upon me,
my heart is sick.

19 Hark, the cry of my poor people
from far and wide in the land:
"Is the LORD not in Zion?
Is her King not in her?"
("Why have they provoked me to anger
with their images,
with their foreign idols?")

20 "The harvest is past, the summer
is ended,
and we are not saved."

21 For the hurt of my poor people I am
hurt,
I mourn, and dismay has taken hold
of me.

22 Is there no balm in Gilead?
Is there no physician there?
Why then has the health of my poor
people
not been restored?

a Or *I will make an end of them, says the* LORD. *There are*
b Meaning of Heb uncertain

9 [a] O that my head were a spring of
water,
    and my eyes a fountain of tears,
so that I might weep day and night
    for the slain of my poor people!
2 [b] O that I had in the desert
    a traveler's lodging place,
that I might leave my people
    and go away from them!
For they are all adulterers,
    a band of traitors.
3 They bend their tongues like bows;
    they have grown strong in the land for
        falsehood, and not for truth;
for they proceed from evil to evil,
    and they do not know me, says the
        LORD.

8.18–9.26: Weeping. God, the earth, and official mourning women weep to signify the certainty of the nation's destruction. The poetry of weeping also suggests that God joins with the people and the earth in expressing vulnerability, pain, and grief over the invasion that will destroy life in the land. **8.18–9.3:** There is disagreement among scholars about the identity of the principal speaker in this poem, but it is probably God. **21:** The God who suffered in the story of the broken family (2.1–3.25) is in pain and *dismay* again over the *hurt of my poor people.* The Hebrew text reads "daughter of my people," to suggest that God is still lamenting over the broken family relationship. **9.1:** The divine speaker then expresses a wish: *O that my head were a spring of water, and my eyes a fountain of tears, so that I might weep day and night for the slain of my poor people!* Divine tears, unlike divine anger, create a brief solidarity and empathy with the people. If the audience is Israel during the Exile,* divine tears suggest that God has not rejected them forever but suffers with them. **2:** The speaker's mood changes quickly. God desires to escape from the midst of the sinners, an unfaithful people.

4 Beware of your neighbors,
    and put no trust in any of your kin; [c]
for all your kin [d] are supplanters,
    and every neighbor goes around like a
        slanderer.
5 They all deceive their neighbors,
    and no one speaks the truth;
they have taught their tongues to speak
    lies;

they commit iniquity and are too
    weary to repent. [e]
6 Oppression upon oppression, deceit [f]
    upon deceit!
They refuse to know me, says
    the LORD.

7 Therefore thus says the LORD of hosts:
I will now refine and test them,
    for what else can I do with my sinful
        people? [g]
8 Their tongue is a deadly arrow;
    it speaks deceit through the mouth.
They all speak friendly words to their
    neighbors,
    but inwardly are planning to lay an
        ambush.
9 Shall I not punish them for these
    things? says the LORD;
    and shall I not bring retribution
        on a nation such as this?

10 Take up [h] weeping and wailing for the
    mountains,
    and a lamentation for the pastures of
        the wilderness,
because they are laid waste so that no
    one passes through,
    and the lowing of cattle is not heard;
both the birds of the air and the animals
    have fled and are gone.
11 I will make Jerusalem a heap of ruins,
    a lair of jackals;
and I will make the towns of Judah a
    desolation,
    without inhabitant.

12 Who is wise enough to understand this? To whom has the mouth of the LORD spoken, so that they may declare it? Why is the land ruined and laid waste like a wilderness, so that no one passes through? 13 And the LORD says: Because they have forsaken my law that I set before them, and have not obeyed my voice, or walked in accordance

a Ch 8.23 in Heb   *b* Ch 9.1 in Heb   *c* Heb *in a brother*   *d* Heb *for every brother*   *e* Cn Compare Gk: Heb *they weary themselves with iniquity.* 6*Your dwelling*   *f* Cn: Heb *Your dwelling in the midst of deceit*   *g* Or *my poor people*   *h* Gk Syr: Heb *I will take up* with it, 14but have stubbornly followed their own hearts and have gone after the Baals, as their ancestors taught them. 15Therefore thus says the LORD of hosts, the God of Israel: I am feeding this people with wormwood, and giving them poisonous water to drink. 16I will scatter them among nations that neither they nor their ancestors have known; and I will send the sword after them, until I have consumed them.

9.4–16. 4–8: Accusations against the people include their unfaithfulness to each other as they lie, slander, and deceive. In punishment God will refine them like silver. **9:** But God expresses hesitancy with a question also asked earlier (5.9, 29): How can punishment be avoided? **10–11:** The command to weep indicates that the destruction of the earth and of the city of Jerusalem cannot be turned away. The poem implies the end of the world for the inhabitants of Judah. Invasion by the foe from the north will end normal life. **12–16:** These prose verses interpret further the tragedy about to happen, but which for the audience of the book has already occurred. **13–14:** The people did not keep God's law nor listen to God's voice. Instead, they worshipped the *Baals.**

17 Thus says the LORD of hosts:
　Consider, and call for the mourning
　　　women to come;
　send for the skilled women to come;
18 let them quickly raise a dirge over us,
　　so that our eyes may run down with
　　　tears,
　and our eyelids flow with water.
19 For a sound of wailing is heard from
　　　Zion:
　"How we are ruined!
　We are utterly shamed,
　because we have left the land,
　　because they have cast down our
　　　dwellings."

20 Hear, O women, the word of the LORD,
　and let your ears receive the word of
　　　his mouth;
　teach to your daughters a dirge,
　　and each to her neighbor a lament.
21 "Death has come up into our windows,
　　it has entered our palaces,
　to cut off the children from the streets

and the young men from
　　　the squares."
22 Speak! Thus says the LORD:
　"Human corpses shall fall
　　like dung upon the open field,
　like sheaves behind the reaper,
　　and no one shall gather them."

23 Thus says the LORD: Do not let the wise boast in their wisdom, do not let the mighty boast in their might, do not let the wealthy boast in their wealth; 24but let those who boast boast in this, that they understand and know me, that I am the LORD; I act with steadfast love, justice, and righteousness in the earth, for in these things I delight, says the LORD.

25 The days are surely coming, says the LORD, when I will attend to all those who are circumcised only in the foreskin: 26Egypt, Judah, Edom, the Ammonites, Moab, and all those with shaven temples who live in the desert. For all these nations are uncircumcised, and all the house of Israel is uncircumcised in heart.

9.17–25. 17: *Mourning women:* In ancient Israel, official mourning women were called to funerals to lead the community in weeping. **21:** Here they are summoned to weep over the destruction of the nation, for *death has come up into our windows.* The funeral to which the people are invited is their own. **23–26:** A prose comment, which seems to continue from 9.12–16 rather than from the weeping poem, announces that God acts in justice for those who *know me.*

10 Hear the word that the LORD speaks to you, O house of Israel. 2Thus says the LORD:
　Do not learn the way of the nations,
　　or be dismayed at the signs of the
　　　heavens;
　for the nations are dismayed at them.
3 For the customs of the peoples are false:
　a tree from the forest is cut down,
　　and worked with an ax by the hands
　　　of an artisan;
4 people deck it with silver and gold;
　　they fasten it with hammer and nails
　　so that it cannot move.

5 Their idols[a] are like scarecrows in a
    cucumber field,
  and they cannot speak;
  they have to be carried,
    for they cannot walk.
  Do not be afraid of them,
    for they cannot do evil,
    nor is it in them to do good.

6 There is none like you, O LORD;
    you are great, and your name is great
    in might.
7 Who would not fear you, O King of the
    nations?
  For that is your due;
  among all the wise ones of the nations
    and in all their kingdoms
  there is no one like you.
8 They are both stupid and foolish;
    the instruction given by idols
    is no better than wood![b]
9 Beaten silver is brought from Tarshish,
    and gold from Uphaz.
  They are the work of the artisan and of
    the hands of the goldsmith;
  their clothing is blue and purple;
  they are all the product of skilled
    workers.
10 But the LORD is the true God;
    he is the living God and the
    everlasting King.
  At his wrath the earth quakes,
    and the nations cannot endure his
    indignation.

11 Thus shall you say to them: The gods
who did not make the heavens and the earth
shall perish from the earth and from under
the heavens.[c]

12 It is he who made the earth by
    his power,
  who established the world by
    his wisdom,
  and by his understanding stretched
    out the heavens.
13 When he utters his voice, there is a
    tumult of waters in the heavens,
  and he makes the mist rise from the
    ends of the earth.
  He makes lightnings for the rain,

  and he brings out the wind from his
    storehouses.
14 Everyone is stupid and without
    knowledge;
  goldsmiths are all put to shame by
    their idols;
  for their images are false,
    and there is no breath in them.
15 They are worthless, a work of delusion;
    at the time of their punishment they
    shall perish.
16 Not like these is the LORD,[d] the portion
    of Jacob,
  for he is the one who formed
    all things,
  and Israel is the tribe of his inheritance;
    the LORD of hosts is his name.

10.1–16: Hymn of praise. These verses contain a hymn that expresses loyalty to the one true God and makes fun of other gods as worthless idols. The hymn, which seems to follow 9.22, serves as a model of repentance and reconciliation for the exiles surviving the nation's collapse. The poem is similar in subject and worship style to the repentance of the children from the broken family (3.22–25). **2–5:** The people should neither become like the nations around them nor adopt their idolatrous* customs. **6:** Israel's God is the true king of the nations. **8–11:** By contrast, the gods of the nations are stupid, human creations. **12–16:** Only the God of Israel is the Creator whose wisdom made the world. Israel is God's special inheritance. In this hymn, creation's harmony is reestablished.

17 Gather up your bundle from the
    ground,
    O you who live under siege!
18 For thus says the LORD:
  I am going to sling out the inhabitants
    of the land
  at this time,
  and I will bring distress on them,
    so that they shall feel it.

19 Woe is me because of my hurt!
    My wound is severe.
  But I said, "Truly this is my
    punishment,

---

a Heb *They*   b Meaning of Heb uncertain
c This verse is in Aramaic   d Heb lacks *the* LORD

and I must bear it."

20 My tent is destroyed,
    and all my cords are broken;
my children have gone from me,
    and they are no more;
there is no one to spread my tent again,
    and to set up my curtains.
21 For the shepherds are stupid,
    and do not inquire of the LORD;
therefore they have not prospered,
    and all their flock is scattered.

22 Hear, a noise! Listen, it is coming—
    a great commotion from the land of
        the north
to make the cities of Judah a desolation,
    a lair of jackals.

23 I know, O LORD, that the way of human
        beings is not in their control,
    that mortals as they walk cannot
        direct their steps.
24 Correct me, O LORD, but in
        just measure;
not in your anger, or you will bring
    me to nothing.

25 Pour out your wrath on the nations that
        do not know you,
    and on the peoples that do not call on
        your name;
for they have devoured Jacob;
    they have devoured him and
        consumed him,
and have laid waste his habitation.

10.17–25: Exile. These verses shift back to the time before the Exile,* and God announces that the attack, expected throughout chs. 4–10, is about to come (vv. 17–18, 22). **19–20:** A second voice, probably that of Jerusalem personified* as daughter Zion, laments her fate. She is abandoned and her children are gone. **23–25:** She admits her sins and asks for divine justice in punishment of both herself and the nations who *devour Jacob,* another name for Israel.

COVENANT DESTROYED

Chs. 11–20: Like the previous chapters, this section of the book seeks to explain the tragedy that has befallen Judah and to defend God from charges of cruelty. It claims that the people brought the catastrophe upon themselves. These chapters continue the poetic accusations of chs. 2–10, but in addition, Jeremiah himself moves into the foreground as a major character in the book. Stories show Jeremiah engaged in symbolic actions (chs. 13, 18, 19, 20). Symbolic actions are prophetic activities that express the prophetic message in dramatic behavior. In addition, this section also includes poems called the "confessions" or "laments*" of Jeremiah (see sidebar on p. 1047). The confessions portray Jeremiah's sufferings as he tries to be faithful to his prophetic mission. The covenant* sermon begins the next ten chapters with a curse whose fulfillment becomes inevitable by ch. 20. No blessings, which usually accompany curses, appear here. Their absence suggests that the curse—defeat of Judah— has already occurred and that the audience in exile is asking why it happened and if it is reversible. The sermon interprets their loss of land as the result of their infidelity. Only obedience to God's voice through this prophetic book can set things right.

---

11 The word that came to Jeremiah from the LORD: 2Hear the words of this covenant, and speak to the people of Judah and the inhabitants of Jerusalem. 3You shall say to them, Thus says the LORD, the God of Israel: Cursed be anyone who does not heed the words of this covenant, 4which I commanded your ancestors when I brought them out of the land of Egypt, from the iron-smelter, saying, Listen to my voice, and do all that I command you. So shall you be my people, and I will be your God, 5that I may perform the oath that I swore to your ancestors, to give them a land flowing with milk and honey, as at this day. Then I answered, "So be it, LORD."

6 And the LORD said to me: Proclaim all these words in the cities of Judah, and in the streets of Jerusalem: Hear the words of this covenant and do them. 7For I solemnly warned your ancestors when I brought them up out of the land of Egypt, warning them persistently, even to this day, saying, Obey my voice. 8Yet they did not obey or incline their ear, but everyone walked in the stubbornness of an evil will. So I brought upon them all the words of this covenant, which I commanded them to do, but they did not.

9 And the LORD said to me: Conspiracy exists among the people of Judah and the inhabitants of Jerusalem. 10They have turned back to the iniquities of their ancestors of old, who refused to heed my words; they have gone after other gods to serve them; the house of Israel and the house of Judah have broken the covenant that I made with their ancestors. 11Therefore, thus says the LORD, assuredly I am going to bring disaster upon them that they cannot escape; though they cry out to me, I will not listen to them. 12Then the cities of Judah and the inhabitants of Jerusalem will go and cry out to the gods to whom they make offerings, but they will never save them in the time of their trouble. 13For your gods have become as many as your towns, O Judah; and as many as the streets of Jerusalem are the altars to shame you have set up, altars to make offerings to Baal.

14 As for you, do not pray for this people, or lift up a cry or prayer on their behalf, for I will not listen when they call to me in the time of their trouble. 15What right has my beloved in my house, when she has done vile deeds? Can vows*a* and sacrificial flesh avert your doom? Can you then exult? 16The LORD once called you, "A green olive tree, fair with goodly fruit"; but with the roar of a great tempest he will set fire to it, and its branches will be consumed. 17The LORD of hosts, who planted you, has pronounced evil against you, because of the evil that the house of Israel and the house of Judah have done, provoking me to anger by making offerings to Baal.

them. **14–17:** Once again God tells Jeremiah not to intercede for the people because they are so sinful.

18 It was the LORD who made it known to
        me, and I knew;
    then you showed me their evil deeds.
19 But I was like a gentle lamb
        led to the slaughter.
    And I did not know it was against me
        that they devised schemes, saying,
    "Let us destroy the tree with its fruit,
        let us cut him off from the land of the
            living,
        so that his name will no longer be
            remembered!"
20 But you, O LORD of hosts, who judge
        righteously,
    who try the heart and the mind,
    let me see your retribution upon them,
        for to you I have committed my cause.

21 Therefore thus says the LORD concerning the people of Anathoth, who seek your life, and say, "You shall not prophesy in the name of the LORD, or you will die by our hand"— 22therefore thus says the LORD of hosts: I am going to punish them; the young men shall die by the sword; their sons and their daughters shall die by famine; 23and not even a remnant shall be left of them. For I will bring disaster upon the people of Anathoth, the year of their punishment.

12 You will be in the right, O LORD,
        when I lay charges against you;
    but let me put my case to you.
    Why does the way of the guilty prosper?
    Why do all who are treacherous
        thrive?
2 You plant them, and they take root;
        they grow and bring forth fruit;
    you are near in their mouths
        yet far from their hearts.
3 But you, O LORD, know me;
        You see me and test me—my heart is
            with you.
    Pull them out like sheep for the
        slaughter,
    and set them apart for the day
        of slaughter.

11.1–17: The covenant* curse. In this prose sermon, similar in style to the Temple* sermon (7.1–8.3), Jeremiah announces a curse upon anyone *who does not heed the words* of the covenant (v. 3). The covenant refers to the relationship of loyalty and love that God made with them at Mount Sinai (Ex 19). This sermon has one point that is presented with great simplicity: To possess the land, the people must obey the covenant. **4:** They must *listen to my voice*. The covenant is a two-way relationship. If they obey, then *so shall you be my people, and I will be your God.* **5:** That obedience is the condition of living in the land *flowing with milk and honey.* **6–13:** Otherwise disaster will fall upon

a Gk: Heb *Can many*

4 How long will the land mourn,
 and the grass of every field wither?
For the wickedness of those who live
 in it
 the animals and the birds are swept
 away,
 and because people said, "He is blind
 to our ways."[a]

5 If you have raced with foot-runners and
 they have wearied you,
 how will you compete with horses?
And if in a safe land you fall down,
 how will you fare in the thickets of
 the Jordan?
6 For even your kinsfolk and your own
 family,
 even they have dealt treacherously
 with you;
 they are in full cry after you;
 do not believe them,
 though they speak friendly words
 to you.

11.18–12.6: Jeremiah's first confession. See sidebar on p. 1047. **18–19:** Jeremiah complains that he is under attack from unidentified enemies. He quotes their plots to get rid of him. **20:** He appeals to God, the just judge, to take vengeance against them. **21–23:** In a prose comment, God promises to punish the enemies, who are identified as people from Jeremiah's own town of Anathoth. But Jeremiah then accuses the just judge of planting and nourishing wickedness. **12.5–6:** The judge replies that things will get worse; even Jeremiah's family will turn against him.

---

7 I have forsaken my house,
 I have abandoned my heritage;
I have given the beloved of my heart
 into the hands of her enemies.
8 My heritage has become to me
 like a lion in the forest;
 she has lifted up her voice against me—
 therefore I hate her.
9 Is the hyena greedy[b] for my heritage at
 my command?
 Are the birds of prey all around her?
Go, assemble all the wild animals;
 bring them to devour her.
10 Many shepherds have destroyed
 my vineyard,

they have trampled down my portion,
 they have made my pleasant portion
 a desolate wilderness.
11 They have made it a desolation;
 desolate, it mourns to me.
The whole land is made desolate,
 but no one lays it to heart.
12 Upon all the bare heights[c] in the desert
 spoilers have come;
 for the sword of the LORD devours
 from one end of the land to the other;
 no one shall be safe.
13 They have sown wheat and have reaped
 thorns,
 they have tired themselves out but
 profit nothing.
They shall be ashamed of their[d] harvests
 because of the fierce anger of
 the LORD.

14 Thus says the LORD concerning all my evil neighbors who touch the heritage that I have given my people Israel to inherit: I am about to pluck them up from their land, and I will pluck up the house of Judah from among them. 15And after I have plucked them up, I will again have compassion on them, and I will bring them again to their heritage and to their land, everyone of them. 16And then, if they will diligently learn the ways of my people, to swear by my name, "As the LORD lives," as they taught my people to swear by Baal, then they shall be built up in the midst of my people. 17But if any nation will not listen, then I will completely uproot it and destroy it, says the LORD.

12.7–17: God's lament.✻ Using the first person pronoun, I, God laments the infidelity of *the beloved of my heart*. Described as a wild *lion,* God's beloved heritage has provoked divine hate, so punishment will follow. **14–17:** A prose comment reuses language of *plucking up* from Jeremiah's call (1.10). God seems to address the exiles directly by promising that those who destroy God's heritage will be *plucked from their land* and God will *pluck* the people of Judah from where they are and return them home, if they listen.

---

a Gk: Heb *to our future*   *b* Cn: Heb *Is the hyena, the bird of prey*   *c* Or *the trails*   *d* Heb *your*

Jeremiah's Confessions

Five poems in the book of Jeremiah are traditionally referred to as "confessions" or "complaints." They are intensely personal expressions of the prophet's✶ feelings, both as he speaks for God and as he suffers with his people. The five poems (11.18–12.6; 15.10–21; 17.14–18; 18.18–23; 20.7–13) are similar to psalms of lament,✶ which always contain complaints. Often they also contain requests for vengeance against enemies, a word of assurance, and a promise of praise. Jeremiah plays with these elements of lament, using some elements and dropping others. In all of his confessions, Jeremiah complains about his failure and rejection as a prophet. He says that he undertook his mission against his will and that it brings him nothing but pain. He prophesies only because God sends him; he is a true prophet (1.4–11), not a lying prophet who sends himself (23.21).

By the end of ch. 20, Jeremiah's sufferings and the sufferings of the nation overlap and mimic each other. Both nation and prophet face captivity. Symbolically, Jeremiah represents God as the prophet who must accuse and warn the nation. Yet he also represents the people, because his fate and his sufferings parallel theirs. The prophet's doubt, anger, and grief embody their sufferings. The people, however, also contribute to his suffering by rejecting his words. Thus they bring tragedy upon themselves—suffering that Jeremiah must also undergo, to the point where he wishes he had never been born.

13 Thus said the LORD to me, "Go and buy yourself a linen loincloth, and put it on your loins, but do not dip it in water." ²So I bought a loincloth according to the word of the LORD, and put it on my loins. ³And the word of the LORD came to me a second time, saying, ⁴"Take the loincloth that you bought and are wearing, and go now to the Euphrates,ᵃ and hide it there in a cleft of the rock." ⁵So I went, and hid it by the Euphrates,ᵇ as the LORD commanded me. ⁶And after many days the LORD said to me, "Go now to the Euphrates,ᵃ and take from there the loincloth that I commanded you to hide there." ⁷Then I went to the Euphrates,ᵃ and dug, and I took the loincloth from the place where I had hidden it. But now the loincloth was ruined; it was good for nothing. 8 Then the word of the LORD came to me: ⁹Thus says the LORD: Just so I will ruin the pride of Judah and the great pride of Jerusalem. ¹⁰This evil people, who refuse to hear my words, who stubbornly follow their own will and have gone after other gods to serve them and worship them, shall be like this loincloth, which is good for nothing. ¹¹For

as the loincloth clings to one's loins, so I made the whole house of Israel and the whole house of Judah cling to me, says the LORD, in order that they might be for me a people, a name, a praise, and a glory. But they would not listen.

13.1–27: The nation's pride. In this chapter Jeremiah performs a symbolic act (vv. 1–11), interprets a symbolic event (vv. 12–14), and in poetry again announces exile (vv. 15–27). The theme of the nation's false pride runs throughout the chapter. **1–11:** Jeremiah receives a divine command to purchase a loincloth and *hide it in a cleft of the rock* (v. 4). The results of his action symbolize his prophetic message. The loincloth is ruined by its exposure to the elements. **8–11:** Jeremiah's words explain the action. Judah is supposed to *cling* to God but instead has been full of pride and has refused to listen; hence, the nation will come to ruin.

12 You shall speak to them this word: Thus says the LORD, the God of Israel: Every wine-jar should be filled with wine. And they

ᵃ Or to Parah; Heb perath   ᵇ Or by Parah; Heb perath

will say to you, "Do you think we do not know that every wine-jar should be filled with wine?" 13Then you shall say to them: Thus says the LORD: I am about to fill all the inhabitants of this land—the kings who sit on David's throne, the priests, the prophets, and all the inhabitants of Jerusalem—with drunkenness. 14And I will dash them one against another, parents and children together, says the LORD. I will not pity or spare or have compassion when I destroy them.

13.12–14: In a second symbolic event to occur in the future, God interprets actions to be performed by the people, not by Jeremiah. The filling of *wine-jars* signifies not feasting, as readers might expect, but *drunkenness* that is destructive of the people and the land. These verses seem to provide the punishment for the pride named in Jeremiah's symbolic action of hiding the loincloth. This wine-drinking episode points forward to 25.15–29, when all the nations drink from the cup of destruction.

15 Hear and give ear; do not be haughty,
  for the LORD has spoken.
16 Give glory to the LORD your God
  before he brings darkness,
and before your feet stumble
  on the mountains at twilight;
while you look for light,
  he turns it into gloom
  and makes it deep darkness.
17 But if you will not listen,
  my soul will weep in secret for your
    pride;
my eyes will weep bitterly and run down
    with tears,
because the LORD's flock has been
    taken captive.

18 Say to the king and the queen mother:
  "Take a lowly seat,
for your beautiful crown
  has come down from your head."a
19 The towns of the Negeb are shut up
  with no one to open them;
all Judah is taken into exile,
  wholly taken into exile.

20 Lift up your eyes and see
  those who come from the north.

Where is the flock that was given you,
  your beautiful flock?
21 What will you say when they set as head
    over you
those whom you have trained
  to be your allies?
Will not pangs take hold of you,
  like those of a woman in labor?
22 And if you say in your heart,
  "Why have these things come upon
    me?"
it is for the greatness of your iniquity
  that your skirts are lifted up,
  and you are violated.
23 Can Ethiopiansb change their skin
  or leopards their spots?
Then also you can do good
  who are accustomed to do evil.
24 I will scatter youc like chaff
  driven by the wind from the desert.
25 This is your lot,
  the portion I have measured out to
    you, says the LORD,
because you have forgotten me
  and trusted in lies.
26 I myself will lift up your skirts over your
    face,
  and your shame will be seen.
27 I have seen your abominations,
  your adulteries and neighings, your
    shameless prostitutions
  on the hills of the countryside.
Woe to you, O Jerusalem!
  How long will it be
  before you are made clean?

13.15–27: Jeremiah warns the people against their pride and urges them to listen. 17: If they do not, his response will be to *weep* at their captivity as God weeps (9.1). 18–19: The *queen mother,* that is, the mother of the king, will be brought low because the invasion and exile are already underway. 20: The enemy from the north is coming. 22–27: According to the Hebrew text, God addresses Jerusalem, personified* again as female, with charges that her infidelity will result in her violation. God will be the one to lift her skirts, that is, to rape her. This shocking language uses the image of a raped woman to de-

a Gk Syr Vg: Meaning of Heb uncertain
b Or *Nubians;* Heb *Cushites*   c Heb *them*

scribe the invasion of the city, directed and accomplished by God.

14 The word of the LORD that came to Jeremiah concerning the drought:

2 Judah mourns
　　and her gates languish;
　they lie in gloom on the ground,
　　and the cry of Jerusalem goes up.
3 Her nobles send their servants
　　　for water;
　　they come to the cisterns,
　they find no water,
　　they return with their vessels empty.
　They are ashamed and dismayed
　　and cover their heads,
4 because the ground is cracked.
　　Because there has been no rain on
　　　　the land
　the farmers are dismayed;
　　they cover their heads.
5 Even the doe in the field forsakes her
　　　newborn fawn
　　because there is no grass.
6 The wild asses stand on the bare
　　　heights,[a]
　　they pant for air like jackals;
　their eyes fail
　　because there is no herbage.

7 Although our iniquities testify
　　　against us,
　　act, O LORD, for your name's sake;
　our apostasies indeed are many,
　　and we have sinned against you.
8 O hope of Israel,
　　its savior in time of trouble,
　why should you be like a stranger in the
　　　land,
　　like a traveler turning aside for the
　　　night?
9 Why should you be like someone
　　　confused,
　　like a mighty warrior who cannot give
　　　help?
　Yet you, O LORD, are in the midst of us,
　　and we are called by your name;
　　do not forsake us!

10 Thus says the LORD concerning
　　　this people:

Truly they have loved to wander,
　　they have not restrained their feet;
　therefore the LORD does not
　　　accept them,
　　now he will remember their iniquity
　　and punish their sins.

14.1–22: Drought and wound. This chapter contains two poems, one concerning a drought (vv. 1–10) and one concerning the wounds of war (vv. 17–22), with prose comment (vv. 11–16) between them. Though an actual drought may lie behind the first poem, it stands here as a image of the destruction of the creation caused by the nations' sinfulness. **3:** The earth and the animals are affected by the people's idolatry* as they return to empty *cisterns,* instead of to the "fountain of living water" (2.13). **8–9:** The people speak in the language of worship, asking why God has forsaken them. **10:** God describes again their *wandering,* as they turn to other gods.

11 The LORD said to me: Do not pray for the welfare of this people. 12Although they fast, I do not hear their cry, and although they offer burnt offering and grain offering, I do not accept them; but by the sword, by famine, and by pestilence I consume them. 13 Then I said: "Ah, Lord GOD! Here are the prophets saying to them, 'You shall not see the sword, nor shall you have famine, but I will give you true peace in this place.'" 14And the LORD said to me: The prophets are prophesying lies in my name; I did not send them, nor did I command them or speak to them. They are prophesying to you a lying vision, worthless divination, and the deceit of their own minds. 15Therefore thus says the LORD concerning the prophets who prophesy in my name though I did not send them, and who say, "Sword and famine shall not come on this land": By sword and famine those prophets shall be consumed. 16And the people to whom they prophesy shall be thrown out into the streets of Jerusalem, victims of famine and sword. There shall be no one to bury them—themselves, their wives, their sons, and their daughters. For I will pour out their wickedness upon them.

a Or *the trails*

14.11–16: In this prose comment we again hear God commanding Jeremiah not to intercede on behalf of the people because their case is beyond hope. Jeremiah stands in contrast to false prophets who preach lies to the people. This conflict suggests that the audience of the book is offered competing interpretations from its religious leaders. Jeremiah is the only prophet sent by God.

17 You shall say to them this word:
    Let my eyes run down with tears night
        and day,
        and let them not cease,
    for the virgin daughter—my people—is
        struck down with a crushing
        blow,
        with a very grievous wound.
18 If I go out into the field,
        look—those killed by the sword!
    And if I enter the city,
        look—those sick with*a* famine!
    For both prophet and priest ply their
        trade throughout the land,
        and have no knowledge.

19 Have you completely rejected Judah?
        Does your heart loathe Zion?
    Why have you struck us down
        so that there is no healing for us?
    We look for peace, but find no good;
        for a time of healing, but there is
        terror instead.
20 We acknowledge our wickedness,
        O LORD,
        the iniquity of our ancestors,
        for we have sinned against you.
21 Do not spurn us, for your name's sake;
        do not dishonor your glorious
        throne;
    remember and do not break your
        covenant with us.
22 Can any idols of the nations bring rain?
        Or can the heavens give showers?
    Is it not you, O LORD our God?
    We set our hope on you,
        for it is you who do all this.

14.17–22. 17: Jeremiah weeps at the woundedness of the people, portrayed as *the virgin daughter*, grievously wounded by *a crushing blow.* **19–22:** The people

use language of worship to protest God's neglect of them and to ask why there is no *healing* and no *rain.* The people's voice probably represents the voice of the exiles, expressing repentance and hope in the same style as the children in 3.22–25.

15 Then the LORD said to me: Though Moses and Samuel stood before me, yet my heart would not turn toward this people. Send them out of my sight, and let them go! 2And when they say to you, "Where shall we go?" you shall say to them: Thus says the LORD:

Those destined for pestilence, to
        pestilence,
    and those destined for the sword, to
        the sword;
    those destined for famine, to famine,
        and those destined for captivity, to
        captivity.

3And I will appoint over them four kinds of destroyers, says the LORD: the sword to kill, the dogs to drag away, and the birds of the air and the wild animals of the earth to devour and destroy. 4I will make them a horror to all the kingdoms of the earth because of what King Manasseh son of Hezekiah of Judah did in Jerusalem.

5 Who will have pity on you, O Jerusalem,
        or who will bemoan you?
    Who will turn aside
        to ask about your welfare?
6 You have rejected me, says the LORD,
        you are going backward;
    so I have stretched out my hand against
        you and destroyed you—
        I am weary of relenting.
7 I have winnowed them with a
        winnowing fork
        in the gates of the land;
    I have bereaved them, I have destroyed
        my people;
        they did not turn from their ways.
8 Their widows became more numerous
        than the sand of the seas;
    I have brought against the mothers of
        youths
        a destroyer at noonday;

---

a Heb *look—the sicknesses of*

I have made anguish and terror
     fall upon her suddenly.
9 She who bore seven has languished;
     she has swooned away;
     her sun went down while it was yet
         day;
     she has been shamed and disgraced.
And the rest of them I will give to the
         sword
     before their enemies,
                 says the LORD.

15.1–16.21: No future, yet a future. 15.1: Jeremiah cannot intercede with God for this sinful people because their infidelity places them beyond hope. Even the great mediators of the past, *Moses and Samuel,* could not get God to change the divine mind. These refusals by God to hear the prophet also indicate to the exilic audience that Jeremiah did not fail to prevent the nation's fall. Rather, they had sinned and God had no choice but to punish them. **2–3:** Poetry moves from the mythic description of the foe of the north to a more natural description of invasion and destruction. The culprit in this verse is King Manasseh, (2 Kings 21.10–15), who was famous for his idolatry.* **5–9:** God laments over female Jerusalem, describes the disasters ahead, and accepts full responsibility for bringing calamity upon her. But the poem indicates that God has punished her only after becoming *weary of relenting* (v. 6). The poem defends God from charges of cruelty.

10 Woe is me, my mother, that you ever bore me, a man of strife and contention to the whole land! I have not lent, nor have I borrowed, yet all of them curse me. 11 The LORD said: Surely I have intervened in your life*a* for good, surely I have imposed enemies on you in a time of trouble and in a time of distress.*b* 12 Can iron and bronze break iron from the north?

13 Your wealth and your treasures I will give as plunder, without price, for all your sins, throughout all your territory. 14 I will make you serve your enemies in a land that you do not know, for in my anger a fire is kindled that shall burn forever.
15 O LORD, you know;
     remember me and visit me,
     and bring down retribution for me on
         my persecutors.

In your forbearance do not take
     me away;
     know that on your account I suffer
         insult.
16 Your words were found, and I
         ate them,
     and your words became to me a joy
     and the delight of my heart;
     for I am called by your name,
         O LORD, God of hosts.
17 I did not sit in the company of
         merrymakers,
     nor did I rejoice;
     under the weight of your hand I
         sat alone,
     for you had filled me with
         indignation.
18 Why is my pain unceasing,
     my wound incurable,
     refusing to be healed?
Truly, you are to me like a deceitful
         brook,
     like waters that fail.
19 Therefore thus says the LORD:
If you turn back, I will take you back,
     and you shall stand before me.
If you utter what is precious, and not
         what is worthless,
     you shall serve as my mouth.
It is they who will turn to you,
     not you who will turn to them.
20 And I will make you to this people
     a fortified wall of bronze;
     they will fight against you,
     but they shall not prevail over you,
     for I am with you
     to save you and deliver you,
                 says the LORD.
21 I will deliver you out of the hand of the
         wicked,
     and redeem you from the grasp of the
         ruthless.

15.10–21: Jeremiah's second confession. See sidebar on p. 1047. **10:** Jeremiah lamentsh is calling to announce the coming tragedy to the community. **15:** He addresses God directly to complain that he has been faithful, taking the divine words into himself like food.

a Heb *intervened with you*   *b* Meaning of Heb uncertain

17: He stayed away from community life. 18: Like the people, Jeremiah's wound is *incurable,* for God is unreliable. 19–21: God replies that Jeremiah must *turn to* God, just as Jeremiah has asked the people to do (4.2). Then God will be with him and rescue him.

16

The word of the LORD came to me: ²You shall not take a wife, nor shall you have sons or daughters in this place. ³For thus says the LORD concerning the sons and daughters who are born in this place, and concerning the mothers who bear them and the fathers who beget them in this land: ⁴They shall die of deadly diseases. They shall not be lamented, nor shall they be buried; they shall become like dung on the surface of the ground. They shall perish by the sword and by famine, and their dead bodies shall become food for the birds of the air and for the wild animals of the earth.

5 For thus says the LORD: Do not enter the house of mourning, or go to lament, or bemoan them; for I have taken away my peace from this people, says the LORD, my steadfast love and mercy. ⁶Both great and small shall die in this land; they shall not be buried, and no one shall lament for them; there shall be no gashing, no shaving of the head for them. ⁷No one shall break bread*a* for the mourner, to offer comfort for the dead; nor shall anyone give them the cup of consolation to drink for their fathers or their mothers. ⁸You shall not go into the house of feasting to sit with them, to eat and drink. ⁹For thus says the LORD of hosts, the God of Israel: I am going to banish from this place, in your days and before your eyes, the voice of mirth and the voice of gladness, the voice of the bridegroom and the voice of the bride.

16.1–21: Jeremiah's celibacy. Several voices debate the meaning of exile. **1–9:** The first is the voice of God, who commands Jeremiah not to take a wife and not to beget children. Jeremiah's isolation from the community becomes even stronger. Yet his life becomes a symbolic act, a sign of what will happen to the people in exile. Normal life will be over. There will be no marriages, and that means there will be no children. Domestic life is over and the people have no future.

10 And when you tell this people all these words, and they say to you, "Why has the LORD pronounced all this great evil against us? What is our iniquity? What is the sin that we have committed against the LORD our God?" ¹¹then you shall say to them: It is because your ancestors have forsaken me, says the LORD, and have gone after other gods and have served and worshiped them, and have forsaken me and have not kept my law; ¹²and because you have behaved worse than your ancestors, for here you are, every one of you, following your stubborn evil will, refusing to listen to me. ¹³Therefore I will hurl you out of this land into a land that neither you nor your ancestors have known, and there you shall serve other gods day and night, for I will show you no favor.

14 Therefore, the days are surely coming, says the LORD, when it shall no longer be said, "As the LORD lives who brought the people of Israel up out of the land of Egypt," ¹⁵but "As the LORD lives who brought the people of Israel up out of the land of the north and out of all the lands where he had driven them." For I will bring them back to their own land that I gave to their ancestors.

16.10–15. 10–13: God quotes the people, who ask questions at the very heart of the book. Why has this happened? Exile has happened because of their sin and infidelity. **14–15:** Divine promises of a hopeful future addressed to the survivors of the nation's fall interrupt announcements of exile.

16 I am now sending for many fishermen, says the LORD, and they shall catch them; and afterward I will send for many hunters, and they shall hunt them from every mountain and every hill, and out of the clefts of the rocks. ¹⁷For my eyes are on all their ways; they are not hidden from my presence, nor is their iniquity concealed from my sight. ¹⁸And*b* I will doubly repay their iniquity and their sin, because they have polluted my land with the carcasses of their detestable idols, and have filled my inheritance with their abominations.

a Two Mss Gk: MT *break for them*   *b* Gk: Heb *And first*

19 O Lord, my strength and my
　　　　stronghold,
　　my refuge in the day of trouble,
to you shall the nations come
　from the ends of the earth and say:
　Our ancestors have inherited nothing
　　　but lies,
　worthless things in which there is no
　　　profit.
20 Can mortals make for themselves gods?
　　Such are no gods!

21 "Therefore I am surely going to teach
them, this time I am going to teach them my
power and my might, and they shall know
that my name is the Lord."

16.16–21. 16–18: God's punishment here may be
against the enemies who have invaded the land and
polluted it with idols. 19–20: A worshipping voice addresses God in the style of the children's speech (3.22–
25), expressing loyalty and repentance. This speech
provides a model of piety for the exiles to follow.

17 The sin of Judah is written with an
iron pen; with a diamond point it is
engraved on the tablet of their hearts, and
on the horns of their altars, 2while their children remember their altars and their sacred
poles,ᵃ beside every green tree, and on the
high hills, 3on the mountains in the open
country. Your wealth and all your treasures
I will give for spoil as the price of your sinᵇ
throughout all your territory. 4By your own
act you shall lose the heritage that I gave you,
and I will make you serve your enemies in a
land that you do not know, for in my anger
a fire is kindledᶜ that shall burn forever.

5 Thus says the Lord:
　Cursed are those who trust in
　　　mere mortals
　　and make mere flesh their strength,
　whose hearts turn away from
　　　the Lord.
6 They shall be like a shrub in
　　　the desert,
　and shall not see when relief comes.
They shall live in the parched places of
　　　the wilderness,
　in an uninhabited salt land.

7 Blessed are those who trust in
　　　the Lord,
　whose trust is the Lord.
8 They shall be like a tree planted
　　　by water,
　sending out its roots by the stream.
It shall not fear when heat comes,
　and its leaves shall stay green;
in the year of drought it is not anxious,
　and it does not cease to bear fruit.

9 The heart is devious above all else;
　it is perverse—
　who can understand it?
10 I the Lord test the mind
　and search the heart,
to give to all according to their ways,
　according to the fruit of their doings.

11 Like the partridge hatching what it did
　　　not lay,
　so are all who amass wealth unjustly;
in mid-life it will leave them,
　and at their end they will prove to be
　　　fools.

12 O glorious throne, exalted from the
　　　beginning,
　shrine of our sanctuary!
13 O hope of Israel! O Lord!
　All who forsake you shall be put to
　　　shame;
　those who turn away from youᵈ shall be
　　　recorded in the underworld,ᵉ
　for they have forsaken the fountain of
　　　living water, the Lord.

17.1–27: True worship. Many voices combine in this
chapter. 1–4: In prose accusation, God accuses the
people of Judah of idolatry* and promises that they
will be exiled. 5–8: In language reminiscent of Ps 1,
God announces the cursed fate of those who trust in
themselves, and the blessed condition of those who
trust in God. 12–13: The voice of worship addressed
to God reappears and speaks about the foolishness of
abandoning the fountain of living water (2.13).

---

a Heb Asherim　　b Cn: Heb spoil your high places for sin
c Two Mss Theodotion: you kindled　　d Heb me
e Or in the earth

14 Heal me, O LORD, and I shall be healed;
  save me, and I shall be saved;
  for you are my praise.
15 See how they say to me,
  "Where is the word of the LORD?
  Let it come!"
16 But I have not run away from being a
    shepherd[a] in your service,
  nor have I desired the fatal day.
  You know what came from my lips;
  it was before your face.
17 Do not become a terror to me;
  you are my refuge in the day
    of disaster;
18 Let my persecutors be shamed,
  but do not let me be shamed;
  let them be dismayed,
  but do not let me be dismayed;
  bring on them the day of disaster;
  destroy them with double destruction!

17.14–18: Jeremiah's third confession. See sidebar on p. 1047. Jeremiah is less accusatory of God here than in the previous confession and asks for healing of his wound. **15:** He quotes his enemies, who doubt that he speaks the word of God because it has not yet come true. He asks God to take vengeance against them.

19 Thus said the LORD to me: Go and stand in the People's Gate, by which the kings of Judah enter and by which they go out, and in all the gates of Jerusalem, 20and say to them: Hear the word of the LORD, you kings of Judah, and all Judah, and all the inhabitants of Jerusalem, who enter by these gates. 21Thus says the LORD: For the sake of your lives, take care that you do not bear a burden on the sabbath day or bring it in by the gates of Jerusalem. 22And do not carry a burden out of your houses on the sabbath or do any work, but keep the sabbath day holy, as I commanded your ancestors. 23Yet they did not listen or incline their ear; they stiffened their necks and would not hear or receive instruction.

24 But if you listen to me, says the LORD, and bring in no burden by the gates of this city on the sabbath day, but keep the sabbath day holy and do no work on it, 25then there shall enter by the gates of this city kings[b] who sit on the throne of David, riding in chariots and on horses, they and their officials, the people of Judah and the inhabitants of Jerusalem; and this city shall be inhabited forever. 26And people shall come from the towns of Judah and the places around Jerusalem, from the land of Benjamin, from the Shephelah, from the hill country, and from the Negeb, bringing burnt offerings and sacrifices, grain offerings and frankincense, and bringing thank offerings to the house of the LORD. 27But if you do not listen to me, to keep the sabbath day holy, and to carry in no burden through the gates of Jerusalem on the sabbath day, then I will kindle a fire in its gates; it shall devour the palaces of Jerusalem and shall not be quenched.

17.19–27: Sabbath sermon. In this prose passage, God directs Jeremiah to announce to the leadership the absolute necessity of keeping sabbath law. They are not to carry burdens or do work, and they must heed divine commands. If they fail, then Jerusalem will be destroyed by fire. This sermon explains again that the Exile* did not occur because of God's cruelty or forgetfulness but resulted from the community's failure to be faithful.

Captivity

Chs. 18–20: These chapters mark a climax* in the first part of the book and are more closely woven than previous sections. In them the threats of captivity and disaster come to a symbolic fulfillment. After relentless efforts by God and Jeremiah to bring the nation to repentance, punishment comes upon them.

---

18 The word that came to Jeremiah from the LORD: 2"Come, go down to the potter's house, and there I will let you hear my words." 3So I went down to the potter's house, and there he was working at his wheel. 4The vessel he was making of clay was spoiled in the potter's hand, and he reworked it into another vessel, as seemed good to him.

5 Then the word of the LORD came to me: 6Can I not do with you, O house of Israel, just as this potter has done? says the LORD.

---

a Meaning of Heb uncertain   b Cn: Heb *kings and officials*

Just like the clay in the potter's hand, so are you in my hand, O house of Israel. 7At one moment I may declare concerning a nation or a kingdom, that I will pluck up and break down and destroy it, 8but if that nation, concerning which I have spoken, turns from its evil, I will change my mind about the disaster that I intended to bring on it. 9And at another moment I may declare concerning a nation or a kingdom that I will build and plant it, 10but if it does evil in my sight, not listening to my voice, then I will change my mind about the good that I had intended to do to it. 11Now, therefore, say to the people of Judah and the inhabitants of Jerusalem: Thus says the LORD: Look, I am a potter shaping evil against you and devising a plan against you. Turn now, all of you from your evil way, and amend your ways and your doings.

12 But they say, "It is no use! We will follow our own plans, and each of us will act according to the stubbornness of our evil will."

18.1–12: The potter. Prose narrative* describes Jeremiah's visit to the potter. The potter makes a vessel that he dislikes, so he destroys it and starts again. **11:** This action becomes a symbol of God's plan for Israel and occasions a final invitation to repent. **12:** The people adamantly refuse to repent.

~~~~~~

13 Therefore thus says the LORD:
　　Ask among the nations:
　　Who has heard the like of this?
　　The virgin Israel has done
　　　a most horrible thing.
14 Does the snow of Lebanon leave
　　　the crags of Sirion?[a]
　　Do the mountain[b] waters run dry,[c]
　　　the cold flowing streams?
15 But my people have forgotten me,
　　　they burn offerings to a delusion;
　　they have stumbled[d] in their ways,
　　　in the ancient roads,
　　and have gone into bypaths,
　　　not the highway,
16 making their land a horror,
　　　a thing to be hissed at forever.
　　All who pass by it are horrified
　　　and shake their heads.

17 Like the wind from the east,
　　　I will scatter them before the enemy.
　　I will show them my back, not my face,
　　　in the day of their calamity.

18.13–17: God's response. God laments their idolatry* and turns from them.

~~~~~~

18 Then they said, "Come, let us make plots against Jeremiah—for instruction shall not perish from the priest, nor counsel from the wise, nor the word from the prophet. Come, let us bring charges against him,[e] and let us not heed any of his words."

19 Give heed to me, O LORD,
　　　and listen to what my adversaries say!
20 Is evil a recompense for good?
　　　Yet they have dug a pit for my life.
　　Remember how I stood before you
　　　to speak good for them,
　　　to turn away your wrath from them.
21 Therefore give their children over to
　　　　famine;
　　hurl them out to the power of
　　　　the sword,
　　let their wives become childless and
　　　　widowed.
　　May their men meet death by
　　　　pestilence,
　　　their youths be slain by the sword in
　　　　battle.
22 May a cry be heard from their houses,
　　　when you bring the marauder
　　　　suddenly upon them!
　　For they have dug a pit to catch me,
　　　and laid snares for my feet.
23 Yet you, O LORD, know
　　　all their plotting to kill me.
　　Do not forgive their iniquity,
　　　do not blot out their sin from your
　　　　sight.
　　Let them be tripped up before you;
　　　deal with them while you are angry.

18.18–23: Jeremiah's fourth confession. See sidebar on p. 1047. **18:** Enemies of Jeremiah speak in a prose comment that illustrates the community's failure to re-

a Cn: Heb *of the field*　　*b* Cn: Heb *foreign*
c Cn: Heb *Are . . . plucked up?*　　*d* Gk Syr Vg: Heb *they made them stumble*　　*e* Heb *strike him with the tongue*

pent. **19–20:** Jeremiah reminds God of how faithful Jeremiah has been to his prophetic mission. **21–23:** He asks God to punish the enemies who try to kill him. The prophet's* enemies are the enemies of God because they refuse to hear the divine word that the prophet claims to speak.

18.18–23: God's response...

19 Thus said the LORD: Go and buy a potter's earthenware jug. Take with you[a] some of the elders of the people and some of the senior priests, 2and go out to the valley of the son of Hinnom at the entry of the Potsherd Gate, and proclaim there the words that I tell you. 3You shall say: Hear the word of the LORD, O kings of Judah and inhabitants of Jerusalem. Thus says the LORD of hosts, the God of Israel: I am going to bring such disaster upon this place that the ears of everyone who hears of it will tingle. 4Because the people have forsaken me, and have profaned this place by making offerings in it to other gods whom neither they nor their ancestors nor the kings of Judah have known, and because they have filled this place with the blood of the innocent, 5and gone on building the high places of Baal to burn their children in the fire as burnt offerings to Baal, which I did not command or decree, nor did it enter my mind; 6therefore the days are surely coming, says the LORD, when this place shall no more be called Topheth, or the valley of the son of Hinnom, but the valley of Slaughter. 7And in this place I will make void the plans of Judah and Jerusalem, and will make them fall by the sword before their enemies, and by the hand of those who seek their life. I will give their dead bodies for food to the birds of the air and to the wild animals of the earth. 8And I will make this city a horror, a thing to be hissed at; everyone who passes by it will be horrified and will hiss because of all its disasters. 9And I will make them eat the flesh of their sons and the flesh of their daughters, and all shall eat the flesh of their neighbors in the siege, and in the distress with which their enemies and those who seek their life afflict them.

10 Then you shall break the jug in the sight of those who go with you, 11and shall say to them: Thus says the LORD of hosts:

So will I break this people and this city, as one breaks a potter's vessel, so that it can never be mended. In Topheth they shall bury until there is no more room to bury. 12Thus will I do to this place, says the LORD, and to its inhabitants, making this city like Topheth. 13And the houses of Jerusalem and the houses of the kings of Judah shall be defiled like the place of Topheth—all the houses upon whose roofs offerings have been made to the whole host of heaven, and libations have been poured out to other gods. 14 When Jeremiah came from Topheth, where the LORD had sent him to prophesy, he stood in the court of the LORD's house and said to all the people: 15Thus says the LORD of hosts, the God of Israel: I am now bringing upon this city and upon all its towns all the disaster that I have pronounced against it, because they have stiffened their necks, refusing to hear my words.

19.1–15: The broken pot. Jeremiah performs a symbolic action in which he breaks an earthenware jug in front of the elders and priests to represent the nation. He summarizes their idolatries, their sins, and their refusals to listen. **15:** Then he announces the fulfillment of the long promised disaster.

20 Now the priest Pashhur son of Immer, who was chief officer in the house of the LORD, heard Jeremiah prophesying these things. 2Then Pashhur struck the prophet Jeremiah, and put him in the stocks that were in the upper Benjamin Gate of the house of the LORD. 3The next morning when Pashhur released Jeremiah from the stocks, Jeremiah said to him, The LORD has named you not Pashhur but "Terror-allaround." 4For thus says the LORD: I am making you a terror to yourself and to all your friends; and they shall fall by the sword of their enemies while you look on. And I will give all Judah into the hand of the king of Babylon; he shall carry them captive to Babylon, and shall kill them with the sword. 5I will give all the wealth of this city, all its gains, all its prized belongings, and all the treasures of the kings of Judah into the hand

a Syr Tg Compare Gk: Heb lacks *take with you*

of their enemies, who shall plunder them, and seize them, and carry them to Babylon. 6And you, Pashhur, and all who live in your house, shall go into captivity, and to Babylon you shall go; there you shall die, and there you shall be buried, you and all your friends, to whom you have prophesied falsely.

20.1–6: Jeremiah's captivity. The book does not yet report the invasion of Jerusalem but, instead, portrays the disaster symbolically. Jeremiah himself is captured in the Temple* by the high priest. **4–6:** That event becomes the occasion for Jeremiah's announcement that *Babylon,* mentioned for the first time in the book, will invade and destroy Judah and that the high priest and his supporters will go into captivity.

7 O LORD, you have enticed me,
    and I was enticed;
  you have overpowered me,
    and you have prevailed.
  I have become a laughingstock all day
        long;
    everyone mocks me.
8 For whenever I speak, I must cry out,
    I must shout, "Violence and
        destruction!"
  For the word of the LORD has become
        for me
    a reproach and derision all day long.
9 If I say, "I will not mention him,
    or speak any more in his name,"
  then within me there is something like a
        burning fire
    shut up in my bones;
  I am weary with holding it in,
    and I cannot.
10 For I hear many whispering:
    "Terror is all around!
  Denounce him! Let us denounce him!"
    All my close friends
    are watching for me to stumble.
  "Perhaps he can be enticed,
    and we can prevail against him,
    and take our revenge on him."
11 But the LORD is with me like a dread
        warrior;
    therefore my persecutors will stumble,
    and they will not prevail.
  They will be greatly shamed,
    for they will not succeed.

Their eternal dishonor
    will never be forgotten.
12 O LORD of hosts, you test the righteous,
    you see the heart and the mind;
  let me see your retribution upon them,
    for to you I have committed
        my cause.

13 Sing to the LORD;
    praise the LORD!
  For he has delivered the life of
        the needy
    from the hands of evildoers.

20.7–13: Jeremiah's fifth confession. See sidebar on p. 1047. Jeremiah blamesh is captivity on God, who has given him words of terror to announce. **9:** Jeremiah tried to withhold his message of violence, but it was like fire: He could not hold it in. Jeremiah's message is not his own but is from God alone. **11–13:** Jeremiah remembers God is with him and that the word will be accomplished.

14 Cursed be the day
    on which I was born!
  The day when my mother bore me,
    let it not be blessed!
15 Cursed be the man
    who brought the news to my father,
        saying,
  "A child is born to you, a son,"
    making him very glad.
16 Let that man be like the cities
    that the LORD overthrew without pity;
  let him hear a cry in the morning
    and an alarm at noon,
17 because he did not kill me in the womb;
    so my mother would have been my
        grave,
    and her womb forever great.
18 Why did I come forth from the womb
    to see toil and sorrow,
    and spend my days in shame?

20.14–18: A curse. Jeremiah curses the day of his birth, like Job (Job 3). This curse closes the section on the covenant's* destruction that was begun by the curse against the nation in ch. 11. Jeremiah's curse speaks of the tragedy of his mission to announce disaster so that he wishes he had never been born. If his life represents that of the people, his captivity, the fulfillment of his word, and his curse enact and bring about their captivity.

THE INVASION'S AFTERMATH

Chs. 21–25: These loosely connected chapters assume that the nation has already been invaded by Babylon. So far, the book has presented captivity only in symbolic terms, but the invasion is described more realistically in 21.1–10. These chapters focus on survival in the battle's aftermath. Prose narratives* offer advice to the survivors (21.1–10; 24.1–10). Poems explain how the invasion happened by blaming kings and prophets (21.11–23.40). National survival is promised (25.1–14) and international justice foretold (25.15–38). The voice of a narrator is more prominent than in previous chapters, and these chapters refer more directly to historical dates and persons than do earlier chapters.

21 This is the word that came to Jeremiah from the LORD, when King Zedekiah sent to him Pashhur son of Malchiah and the priest Zephaniah son of Maaseiah, saying, 2"Please inquire of the LORD on our behalf, for King Nebuchadrezzar of Babylon is making war against us; perhaps the LORD will perform a wonderful deed for us, as he has often done, and will make him withdraw from us."

3 Then Jeremiah said to them: 4Thus you shall say to Zedekiah: Thus says the LORD, the God of Israel: I am going to turn back the weapons of war that are in your hands and with which you are fighting against the king of Babylon and against the Chaldeans who are besieging you outside the walls; and I will bring them together into the center of this city. 5I myself will fight against you with outstretched hand and mighty arm, in anger, in fury, and in great wrath. 6And I will strike down the inhabitants of this city, both human beings and animals; they shall die of a great pestilence. 7Afterward, says the LORD, I will give King Zedekiah of Judah, and his servants, and the people in this city—those who survive the pestilence, sword, and famine—into the hands of King Nebuchadrezzar of Babylon, into the hands of their enemies, into the hands of those who seek their lives. He shall strike them down with the edge of the sword; he shall not pity them, or spare them, or have compassion.

8 And to this people you shall say: Thus says the LORD: See, I am setting before you the way of life and the way of death. 9Those who stay in this city shall die by the sword, by famine, and by pestilence; but those who go out and surrender to the Chaldeans who are besieging you shall live and shall have their lives as a prize of war. 10For I have set my face against this city for evil and not for good, says the LORD: it shall be given into the hands of the king of Babylon, and he shall burn it with fire.

21.1–10: The attack. 1–2: Jeremiah presents a prophecy to messengers sent to him by *King Zedekiah* of Judah. Zedekiah hopes that God will send the Babylonians and their king, Nebuchadrezzar, away as in the past (Isa 36–37). **3–7:** But instead of sending the Babylonians (also called the *Chaldeans*) away, God will bring them into the city and fight against Judah. **8–9:** In language that appears also in Deut 30.11–10, the text urges them to "choose life." To live, they must surrender to Babylon.

Kings and prophets*
21.11–23.8: The leaders, royal and religious, receive blame for corruption, for injustice, and for turning away from God. Earlier chapters focused on failures of the whole community, but here the leaders alone fail and lead the nation to ruin.

11 To the house of the king of Judah say: Hear the word of the LORD, 12O house of David! Thus says the LORD:

Execute justice in the morning,
  and deliver from the hand of the
    oppressor
  anyone who has been robbed,
or else my wrath will go forth like fire,
  and burn, with no one to quench it,
  because of your evil doings.

13 See, I am against you, O inhabitant of
    the valley,
  O rock of the plain,
                              says the LORD;
  you who say, "Who can come down
    against us,
  or who can enter our places of refuge?"

14 I will punish you according to the fruit
        of your doings,
                          says the LORD;
    I will kindle a fire in its forest,
        and it shall devour all that is
        around it.

22 Thus says the LORD: Go down to the
    house of the king of Judah, and
speak there this word, 2and say: Hear the
word of the LORD, O King of Judah sitting
on the throne of David—you, and your servants, and your people who enter these
gates. 3Thus says the LORD: Act with justice
and righteousness, and deliver from the
hand of the oppressor anyone who has been
robbed. And do no wrong or violence to the
alien, the orphan, and the widow, or shed
innocent blood in this place. 4For if you will
indeed obey this word, then through the
gates of this house shall enter kings who sit
on the throne of David, riding in chariots and
on horses, they, and their servants, and their
people. 5But if you will not heed these
words, I swear by myself, says the LORD, that
this house shall become a desolation. 6For
thus says the LORD concerning the house of
the king of Judah:

21.11–22.6a: Justice. 21.11–14: The poem addresses
the kings by the title *house of David,* referring to all
the kings who occupied the Davidic throne (1 Sam 7).
The role of the king is to administer justice. If the kings
fail, then the fire of divine wrath will destroy them.
22.1–6a: A prose passage elaborates on the obligations of the kings to do justice for the afflicted.

    You are like Gilead to me,
        like the summit of Lebanon;
    but I swear that I will make you
        a desert,
        an uninhabited city.*a*
7   I will prepare destroyers against you,
        all with their weapons;
    they shall cut down your choicest cedars
        and cast them into the fire.
    8 And many nations will pass by this city,
and all of them will say one to another, "Why
has the LORD dealt in this way with that
great city?" 9And they will answer, "Because
they abandoned the covenant of the LORD

their God, and worshiped other gods and
served them."

10 Do not weep for him who is dead,
        nor bemoan him;
    weep rather for him who goes away,
        for he shall return no more
        to see his native land.
    11 For thus says the LORD concerning
Shallum son of King Josiah of Judah, who
succeeded his father Josiah, and who went
away from this place: He shall return here
no more, 12but in the place where they have
carried him captive he shall die, and he shall
never see this land again.

13 Woe to him who builds his house by
        unrighteousness,
        and his upper rooms by injustice;
    who makes his neighbors work for
        nothing,
        and does not give them their wages;
14 who says, "I will build myself a spacious
        house
        with large upper rooms,"
    and who cuts out windows for it,
        paneling it with cedar,
        and painting it with vermilion.
15 Are you a king
        because you compete in cedar?
    Did not your father eat and drink
        and do justice and righteousness?
        Then it was well with him.
16 He judged the cause of the poor
        and needy;
        then it was well.
    Is not this to know me?
        says the LORD.
17 But your eyes and heart
        are only on your dishonest gain,
        for shedding innocent blood,
        and for practicing oppression and
        violence.
    18 Therefore thus says the LORD con-
cerning King Jehoiakim son of Josiah of
Judah:
    They shall not lament for him, saying,
        "Alas, my brother!" or "Alas, sister!"

a Cn: Heb *uninhabited cities*

They shall not lament for him, saying,
    "Alas, lord!" or "Alas, his majesty!"
19 With the burial of a donkey he shall be
        buried—
    dragged off and thrown out beyond
        the gates of Jerusalem.

20 Go up to Lebanon, and cry out,
    and lift up your voice in Bashan;
  cry out from Abarim,
    for all your lovers are crushed.
21 I spoke to you in your prosperity,
    but you said, "I will not listen."
This has been your way from
      your youth,
  for you have not obeyed my voice.
22 The wind shall shepherd all your
      shepherds,
    and your lovers shall go into
      captivity;
  then you will be ashamed and dismayed
    because of all your wickedness.
23 O inhabitant of Lebanon,
    nested among the cedars,
how you will groan[a] when pangs come
      upon you,
    pain as of a woman in labor!

24 As I live, says the LORD, even if King Coniah son of Jehoiakim of Judah were the signet ring on my right hand, even from there I would tear you off 25 and give you into the hands of those who seek your life, into the hands of those of whom you are afraid, even into the hands of King Nebuchadrezzar of Babylon and into the hands of the Chaldeans. 26 I will hurl you and the mother who bore you into another country, where you were not born, and there you shall die. 27 But they shall not return to the land to which they long to return.

28 Is this man Coniah a despised broken
      pot,
    a vessel no one wants?
Why are he and his offspring hurled out
    and cast away in a land that they do
      not know?
29 O land, land, land,
    hear the word of the LORD!
30 Thus says the LORD:
Record this man as childless,

a man who shall not succeed in
    his days;
for none of his offspring shall succeed
    in sitting on the throne of David,
    and ruling again in Judah.

22.6b–30: Fate of kings and nation. Verse 6 connects all these poems to kings. **7–9:** Punishment will come upon them and the city will be destroyed. **10–11:** *King Josiah* and his son Jehoahaz, also known as *Shallum*, both meet tragic fates. Josiah dies in battle (2 Kings 23.28–30), but sadder still is the fate of Jehoahaz, who is exiled from the land. **13–19:** This poem contrasts good King Josiah with his son, the bad King Jehoiakim. Josiah is a true king because he does justice; his son exploits the people for his own benefit. **20–23:** These verses address an unidentified female ("you" is feminine in the Hebrew text) who is sent outside Israel to neighboring *Lebanon*. This location is puzzling, but the woman seems to be God's unfaithful wife, who has refused to listen. **24–30:** God promises to hurl into Babylonian exile King Jehoiakim's son, King Jehoiachin, here called *Coniah*. **30:** With him, kingship will end.

23 Woe to the shepherds who destroy and scatter the sheep of my pasture! says the LORD. 2 Therefore thus says the LORD, the God of Israel, concerning the shepherds who shepherd my people: It is you who have scattered my flock, and have driven them away, and you have not attended to them. So I will attend to you for your evil doings, says the LORD. 3 Then I myself will gather the remnant of my flock out of all the lands where I have driven them, and I will bring them back to their fold, and they shall be fruitful and multiply. 4 I will raise up shepherds over them who will shepherd them, and they shall not fear any longer, or be dismayed, nor shall any be missing, says the LORD.

5 The days are surely coming, says the LORD, when I will raise up for David a righteous Branch, and he shall reign as king and deal wisely, and shall execute justice and righteousness in the land. 6 In his days Judah will be saved and Israel will live in safety.

a Gk Vg Syr: Heb *will be pitied*

And this is the name by which he will be called: "The LORD is our righteousness."

7 Therefore, the days are surely coming, says the LORD, when it shall no longer be said, "As the LORD lives who brought the people of Israel up out of the land of Egypt," 8but "As the LORD lives who brought out and led the offspring of the house of Israel out of the land of the north and out of all the lands where he*a* had driven them." Then they shall live in their own land.

23.1–8: Restoration. In these prose verses, God promises restoration to kings, portrayed by the traditional figure of the shepherd. If the readers of the book were already in exile, these promises of future Davidic kingship would not contradict Jeremiah's prophecy of invasion. Those events would already have occurred. The audience awaits a new future promised here. The prophecies of doom explain in a variety of ways why things have come to this tragic situation.

9 Concerning the prophets:
  My heart is crushed within me,
    all my bones shake;
  I have become like a drunkard,
    like one overcome by wine,
  because of the LORD
    and because of his holy words.
10 For the land is full of adulterers;
    because of the curse the land
        mourns,
  and the pastures of the wilderness are
        dried up.
  Their course has been evil,
    and their might is not right.
11 Both prophet and priest are ungodly;
  even in my house I have found their
    wickedness,
                says the LORD.
12 Therefore their way shall be to them
  like slippery paths in the darkness,
  into which they shall be driven and
    fall;
  for I will bring disaster upon them
    in the year of their punishment,
               says the LORD.
13 In the prophets of Samaria
  I saw a disgusting thing:
  they prophesied by Baal
    and led my people Israel astray.

14 But in the prophets of Jerusalem
  I have seen a more shocking thing:
  they commit adultery and walk in
    lies;
  they strengthen the hands of
    evildoers,
  so that no one turns from wickedness;
  all of them have become like Sodom
    to me,
  and its inhabitants like Gomorrah.
15 Therefore thus says the LORD of hosts
    concerning the prophets:
  "I am going to make them eat
    wormwood,
  and give them poisoned water
    to drink;
  for from the prophets of Jerusalem
    ungodliness has spread throughout
      the land."

16 Thus says the LORD of hosts: Do not listen to the words of the prophets who prophesy to you; they are deluding you. They speak visions of their own minds, not from the mouth of the LORD. 17They keep saying to those who despise the word of the LORD, "It shall be well with you"; and to all who stubbornly follow their own stubborn hearts, they say, "No calamity shall come upon you."

23.9–40: Prophets. As a group of leaders, the prophets* failed to be true to their calling to speak the word of God. **9–11:** God laments over their infidelity. **13–14:** The prophets of the northern kingdom of *Samaria* were *shocking* in their worship of *Baal,* * but the prophets of Judah were even worse, like the two cities destroyed for their sinfulness (Gen 19).

18 For who has stood in the council
    of the LORD
  so as to see and to hear his word?
  Who has given heed to his word
    so as to proclaim it?
19 Look, the storm of the LORD!
    Wrath has gone forth,
  a whirling tempest;
  it will burst upon the head of
    the wicked.

a Gk: Heb I

20 The anger of the LORD will not
    turn back
    until he has executed and
      accomplished
    the intents of his mind.
In the latter days you will understand it
    clearly.

21 I did not send the prophets,
    yet they ran;
I did not speak to them,
    yet they prophesied.

22 But if they had stood in my council,
    then they would have proclaimed my
      words to my people,
and they would have turned them from
    their evil way,
    and from the evil of their doings.

23.18–22: The true prophet is one who goes before God, *in the council of the LORD.* These prophets God did not send, and they did not speak God's words; they are false prophets. By implication, only Jeremiah is a true prophet.

23 Am I a God near by, says the LORD, and not a God far off? 24Who can hide in secret places so that I cannot see them? says the LORD. Do I not fill heaven and earth? says the LORD. 25I have heard what the prophets have said who prophesy lies in my name, saying, "I have dreamed, I have dreamed!" 26How long? Will the hearts of the prophets ever turn back—those who prophesy lies, and who prophesy the deceit of their own heart? 27They plan to make my people forget my name by their dreams that they tell one another, just as their ancestors forgot my name for Baal. 28Let the prophet who has a dream tell the dream, but let the one who has my word speak my word faithfully. What has straw in common with wheat? says the LORD. 29Is not my word like fire, says the LORD, and like a hammer that breaks a rock in pieces? 30See, therefore, I am against the prophets, says the LORD, who steal my words from one another. 31See, I am against the prophets, says the LORD, who use their own tongues and say, "Says the LORD." 32See, I am against those who prophesy lying dreams, says the LORD, and who tell

them, and who lead my people astray by their lies and their recklessness, when I did not send them or appoint them; so they do not profit this people at all, says the LORD.

33 When this people, or a prophet, or a priest asks you, "What is the burden of the LORD?" you shall say to them, "You are the burden,ª and I will cast you off, says the LORD." 34And as for the prophet, priest, or the people who say, "The burden of the LORD," I will punish them and their households. 35Thus shall you say to one another, among yourselves, "What has the LORD answered?" or "What has the LORD spoken?" 36But "the burden of the LORD" you shall mention no more, for the burden is everyone's own word, and so you pervert the words of the living God, the LORD of hosts, our God. 37Thus you shall ask the prophet, "What has the LORD answered you?" or "What has the LORD spoken?" 38But if you say, "the burden of the LORD," thus says the LORD: Because you have said these words, "the burden of the LORD," when I sent to you, saying, You shall not say, "the burden of the LORD," 39therefore, I will surely lift you upᵇ and cast you away from my presence, you and the city that I gave to you and your ancestors. 40And I will bring upon you everlasting disgrace and perpetual shame, which shall not be forgotten.

23.23–40: These prose verses continue to discredit the other prophets who have led the people astray. **33–40:** A play on words makes the same attack on the prophets. The word translated *burden* can also mean "oracle*" or "prophetic poem." The prophets who ask for an oracle or message from God learn that they are God's *burden.*

24 The LORD showed me two baskets of figs placed before the temple of the LORD. This was after King Nebuchadrezzar of Babylon had taken into exile from Jerusalem King Jeconiah son of Jehoiakim of Judah, together with the officials of Judah, the artisans, and the smiths, and had brought them to Babylon. 2One basket had very good

a Gk Vg: Heb *What burden*   *b* Heb Mss Gk Vg: MT *forget you* figs, like first-ripe figs, but the other basket had very bad figs, so bad that they could not be eaten. [3] And the LORD said to me, "What do you see, Jeremiah?" I said, "Figs, the good figs very good, and the bad figs very bad, so bad that they cannot be eaten."

[4] Then the word of the LORD came to me: [5] Thus says the LORD, the God of Israel: Like these good figs, so I will regard as good the exiles from Judah, whom I have sent away from this place to the land of the Chaldeans. [6] I will set my eyes upon them for good, and I will bring them back to this land. I will build them up, and not tear them down; I will plant them, and not pluck them up. [7] I will give them a heart to know that I am the LORD; and they shall be my people and I will be their God, for they shall return to me with their whole heart.

[8] But thus says the LORD: Like the bad figs that are so bad they cannot be eaten, so will I treat King Zedekiah of Judah, his officials, the remnant of Jerusalem who remain in this land, and those who live in the land of Egypt. [9] I will make them a horror, an evil thing, to all the kingdoms of the earth—a disgrace, a byword, a taunt, and a curse in all the places where I shall drive them. [10] And I will send sword, famine, and pestilence upon them, until they are utterly destroyed from the land that I gave to them and their ancestors.

24.1–10: Figs. Jerusalem has been invaded, King Jehoiachin is in captivity, and King Zedekiah has been appointed in his place. Jeremiah has a vision of *two baskets of figs.* One symbolizes survivors in Babylon; the other stands for those who have stayed in Judah or escaped to Egypt. The first basket is good; the second is rotten. The message for the survivors is that to survive they must cooperate with Babylon. Only then will they have a future.

Babylon's fall
Ch. 25: This chapter closes off the first major division of the book by reaching back to ch. 1. At last, Jeremiah acts as "prophet to the nations" (1.5, 10).

25 The word that came to Jeremiah concerning all the people of Judah, in the fourth year of King Jehoiakim son of Jo-

siah of Judah (that was the first year of King Nebuchadrezzar of Babylon), [2] which the prophet Jeremiah spoke to all the people of Judah and all the inhabitants of Jerusalem: [3] For twenty-three years, from the thirteenth year of King Josiah son of Amon of Judah, to this day, the word of the LORD has come to me, and I have spoken persistently to you, but you have not listened. [4] And though the LORD persistently sent you all his servants the prophets, you have neither listened nor inclined your ears to hear [5] when they said, "Turn now, everyone of you, from your evil way and wicked doings, and you will remain upon the land that the LORD has given to you and your ancestors from of old and forever; [6] do not go after other gods to serve and worship them, and do not provoke me to anger with the work of your hands. Then I will do you no harm." [7] Yet you did not listen to me, says the LORD, and so you have provoked me to anger with the work of your hands to your own harm.

[8] Therefore thus says the LORD of hosts: Because you have not obeyed my words, [9] I am going to send for all the tribes of the north, says the LORD, even for King Nebuchadrezzar of Babylon, my servant, and I will bring them against this land and its inhabitants, and against all these nations around; I will utterly destroy them, and make them an object of horror and of hissing, and an everlasting disgrace.[a] [10] And I will banish from them the sound of mirth and the sound of gladness, the voice of the bridegroom and the voice of the bride, the sound of the millstones and the light of the lamp. [11] This whole land shall become a ruin and a waste, and these nations shall serve the king of Babylon seventy years. [12] Then after seventy years are completed, I will punish the king of Babylon and that nation, the land of the Chaldeans, for their iniquity, says the LORD, making the land an everlasting waste. [13] I will bring upon that land all the words that I have uttered against it, everything written in this book, which Jeremiah prophesied against all the nations. [14] For many nations and great

a Gk Compare Syr: Heb *and everlasting desolations*

kings shall make slaves of them also; and I will repay them according to their deeds and the work of their hands.

25.1–14: Invaders will be punished. 1: A narrator dates the chapter to the rules of the Judahite *King Je-hoiakim* and the Babylonian *King Nebuchadrezzar.* That date, 605 BCE, indicates that Jeremiah has proph-esied the fall of Judah to Babylon well in advance of events. His prophecy of the fall of Babylon will, there-fore, prove equally reliable. **3–7:** Jeremiah summarizes his career and the people's refusal to listen to his words. This refusal provoked divine anger. **8–14:** God presents the consequences of not listening. **9:** The *tribes of the north,* now identified as Babylon, will be God's agent of destruction. God calls the Babylonian king *my servant.* As divine agents, the Babylonians will destroy life on an international scale. **11:** Judah will serve Babylon for 70 years. This number may simply mean "a long time," for the Exile* lasted only 50 years. **14:** After that time God will punish Babylon.

~~~~~~~~~~

15 For thus the LORD, the God of Israel, said to me: Take from my hand this cup of the wine of wrath, and make all the nations to whom I send you drink it. ¹⁶They shall drink and stagger and go out of their minds because of the sword that I am sending among them.

17 So I took the cup from the LORD's hand, and made all the nations to whom the LORD sent me drink it: ¹⁸Jerusalem and the towns of Judah, its kings and officials, to make them a desolation and a waste, an ob-ject of hissing and of cursing, as they are to-day; ¹⁹Pharaoh king of Egypt, his servants, his officials, and all his people; ²⁰all the mixed people;ᵃ all the kings of the land of Uz; all the kings of the land of the Philis-tines—Ashkelon, Gaza, Ekron, and the rem-nant of Ashdod; ²¹Edom, Moab, and the Ammonites; ²²all the kings of Tyre, all the kings of Sidon, and the kings of the coast-land across the sea; ²³Dedan, Tema, Buz, and all who have shaven temples; ²⁴all the kings of Arabia and all the kings of the mixed peoplesᵃ that live in the desert; ²⁵all the kings of Zimri, all the kings of Elam, and all the kings of Media; ²⁶all the kings of the north, far and near, one after another, and all the kingdoms of the world that are on the face of the earth. And after them the king of Sheshachᵇ shall drink.

27 Then you shall say to them, Thus says the LORD of hosts, the God of Israel: Drink, get drunk and vomit, fall and rise no more, because of the sword that I am sending among you.

28 And if they refuse to accept the cup from your hand to drink, then you shall say to them: Thus says the LORD of hosts: You must drink! ²⁹See, I am beginning to bring disaster on the city that is called by my name, and how can you possibly avoid punishment? You shall not go unpunished, for I am sum-moning a sword against all the inhabitants of the earth, says the LORD of hosts.

25.15–29: Cup of wrath. A symbolic action makes the prophecy of vv. 8–14 concrete. God commands Jere-miah to act as a wine steward. But instead of serving a joyous feast, Jeremiah serves a cup of wrath to the kings of major nations and city-states around Judah. **26:** The final king to drink is the king of Babylon, here called *Sheshach.* All must drink of God's punishment. In the symbolic sphere, Judah and its enemies have already exchanged places. All that remains is for his-torical events to unfold.

~~~~~~~~~~

30 You, therefore, shall prophesy against them all these words, and say to them:
       The LORD will roar from on high,
           and from his holy habitation utter his
               voice;
       he will roar mightily against his fold,
           and shout, like those who tread
               grapes,
           against all the inhabitants of
               the earth.
31 The clamor will resound to the ends of
           the earth,
       for the LORD has an indictment
           against the nations;
       he is entering into judgment with all
           flesh,
       and the guilty he will put to
           the sword,
                       says the LORD.

---

a Meaning of Heb uncertain   *b Sheshach* is a cryptogram for *Babel,* Babylon

32 Thus says the LORD of hosts:
    See, disaster is spreading
        from nation to nation,
    and a great tempest is stirring
        from the farthest parts of the earth!

33 Those slain by the LORD on that day shall extend from one end of the earth to the other. They shall not be lamented, or gathered, or buried; they shall become dung on the surface of the ground.

34 Wail, you shepherds, and cry out;
    roll in ashes, you lords of the flock,
    for the days of your slaughter have
        come—and your dispersions,ᵃ
    and you shall fall like a choice vessel.

35 Flight shall fail the shepherds,
    and there shall be no escape for the
        lords of the flock.

36 Hark! the cry of the shepherds,
    and the wail of the lords of the flock!
    For the LORD is despoiling their
        pasture,

37 and the peaceful folds are devastated,
    because of the fierce anger of
        the LORD.

38 Like a lion he has left his covert;
    for their land has become a waste
    because of the cruel sword,
        and because of his fierce anger.

25.30–38: The lion. God is a roaring *lion* who will devour the nations that have destroyed Judah.

HOW THE NATION WILL SURVIVE

Chs. 26–52: The first "book" (chs. 1–25) accused Judah of infidelity, promised destruction and exile, and defended God from accusations of injustice. The second "book" (chs. 26–52) presents stories and poems that reveal how to survive the period after the nation's fall to Babylon. No longer is repentance to avert the disaster the primary concern. The book's audience lives with the community's failure to repent. They themselves must repent and endure. Jeremiah appears here as a model of faithful endurance. Jeremiah's companion Baruch also appears in this part of the book. Baruch has traditionally been named as the writer of stories about Jeremiah, particularly in chs. 37–45. The exilic period was a time of great conflict about how to survive. This book insists that survival requires continued submission to Babylon, repentance, and obedi-

ence as set out in the book of Jeremiah. **Chs. 26–29: Prophetic discord.** These chapters set forth disputes about which prophetic vision of the future will ensure the nation's survival.

---

26 At the beginning of the reign of King Jehoiakim son of Josiah of Judah, this word came from the LORD: ²Thus says the LORD: Stand in the court of the LORD's house, and speak to all the cities of Judah that come to worship in the house of the LORD; speak to them all the words that I command you; do not hold back a word. ³It may be that they will listen, all of them, and will turn from their evil way, that I may change my mind about the disaster that I intend to bring on them because of their evil doings. ⁴You shall say to them: Thus says the LORD: If you will not listen to me, to walk in my law that I have set before you, ⁵and to heed the words of my servants the prophets whom I send to you urgently—though you have not heeded— ⁶then I will make this house like Shiloh, and I will make this city a curse for all the nations of the earth.

7 The priests and the prophets and all the people heard Jeremiah speaking these words in the house of the LORD. ⁸And when Jeremiah had finished speaking all that the LORD had commanded him to speak to all the people, then the priests and the prophets and all the people laid hold of him, saying, "You shall die! ⁹Why have you prophesied in the name of the LORD, saying, 'This house shall be like Shiloh, and this city shall be desolate, without inhabitant'?" And all the people gathered around Jeremiah in the house of the LORD.

10 When the officials of Judah heard these things, they came up from the king's house to the house of the LORD and took their seat in the entry of the New Gate of the house of the LORD. ¹¹Then the priests and the prophets said to the officials and to all the people, "This man deserves the sentence of death because he has prophesied against this city, as you have heard with your own ears."

12 Then Jeremiah spoke to all the offi-

a Meaning of Heb uncertain

cials and all the people, saying, "It is the LORD who sent me to prophesy against this house and this city all the words you have heard. 13 Now therefore amend your ways and your doings, and obey the voice of the LORD your God, and the LORD will change his mind about the disaster that he has pronounced against you. 14 But as for me, here I am in your hands. Do with me as seems good and right to you. 15 Only know for certain that if you put me to death, you will be bringing innocent blood upon yourselves and upon this city and its inhabitants, for in truth the LORD sent me to you to speak all these words in your ears."

16 Then the officials and all the people said to the priests and the prophets, "This man does not deserve the sentence of death, for he has spoken to us in the name of the LORD our God." 17 And some of the elders of the land arose and said to all the assembled people, 18 "Micah of Moresheth, who prophesied during the days of King Hezekiah of Judah, said to all the people of Judah: 'Thus says the LORD of hosts,

Zion shall be plowed as a field;
Jerusalem shall become a heap
of ruins,
and the mountain of the house a
wooded height.'

19 Did King Hezekiah of Judah and all Judah actually put him to death? Did he not fear the LORD and entreat the favor of the LORD, and did not the LORD change his mind about the disaster that he had pronounced against them? But we are about to bring great disaster on ourselves!"

20 There was another man prophesying in the name of the LORD, Uriah son of Shemaiah from Kiriath-jearim. He prophesied against this city and against this land in words exactly like those of Jeremiah. 21 And when King Jehoiakim, with all his warriors and all the officials, heard his words, the king sought to put him to death; but when Uriah heard of it, he was afraid and fled and escaped to Egypt. 22 Then King Jehoiakim sent*a* Elnathan son of Achbor and men with him to Egypt, 23 and they took Uriah from Egypt and brought him to King Jehoiakim, who struck him down with the sword and

threw his dead body into the burial place of the common people.

24 But the hand of Ahikam son of Shaphan was with Jeremiah so that he was not given over into the hands of the people to be put to death.

26.1–24: Jeremiah on trial. This chapter shows that Jeremiah faced great conflict but that he is the true prophet★ and, hence, is to be heeded. **1–6:** The chapter refers to Jeremiah's Temple★ sermon (7.1–8.3) and summarizes it. What is of interest here, however, is the community's response to the sermon. Some accept it; priests, prophets, and King Jehoiakim reject it. Some of the leaders put Jeremiah on trial. **12:** Jeremiah responds to charges by claiming that it was God *who sent me*. The trial concludes with a declaration of Jeremiah's innocence. **17–23:** Some elders present examples of other prophets who spoke judgments against Jerusalem. **18–23:** *King Hezekiah* received the message of the prophet *Micah,* whereas the current king, Jehoiakim, rejected the words of the prophet *Uriah* and had him killed. **24:** Mysteriously, *Ahikam* rescues Jeremiah from death. The story blames the king for rejecting the prophetic word and invites the book's readers to join Jeremiah's supporters. It presents Jeremiah as a model of fidelity who, while in the hands of captors, remains faithful and is rescued from peril.

Yokes

Chs. 27–28: Jeremiah's conflict with other prophetic groups is the subject of these two chapters. Three stories increasingly narrow the conflict from an international disagreement to a personal dispute between two prophets.

27 In the beginning of the reign of King Zedekiah*b* son of Josiah of Judah, this word came to Jeremiah from the LORD. 2 Thus the LORD said to me: Make yourself a yoke of straps and bars, and put them on your neck. 3 Send word*c* to the king of Edom, the king of Moab, the king of the Ammonites, the king of Tyre, and the king of Sidon by the hand of the envoys who have come to Jerusalem to King Zedekiah of Judah. 4 Give them this charge for their masters: Thus says the LORD of hosts, the God of Israel: This is

a Heb adds *men to Egypt*   *b* Another reading is *Jehoiakim*   *c* Cn: Heb *send them* what you shall say to your masters: ⁵It is I who by my great power and my outstretched arm have made the earth, with the people and animals that are on the earth, and I give it to whomever I please. ⁶Now I have given all these lands into the hand of King Nebuchadnezzar of Babylon, my servant, and I have given him even the wild animals of the field to serve him. ⁷All the nations shall serve him and his son and his grandson, until the time of his own land comes; then many nations and great kings shall make him their slave.

8 But if any nation or kingdom will not serve this king, Nebuchadnezzar of Babylon, and put its neck under the yoke of the king of Babylon, then I will punish that nation with the sword, with famine, and with pestilence, says the LORD, until I have completed its*a* destruction by his hand. ⁹You, therefore, must not listen to your prophets, your diviners, your dreamers,*b* your soothsayers, or your sorcerers, who are saying to you, "You shall not serve the king of Babylon." ¹⁰For they are prophesying a lie to you, with the result that you will be removed far from your land; I will drive you out, and you will perish. ¹¹But any nation that will bring its neck under the yoke of the king of Babylon and serve him, I will leave on its own land, says the LORD, to till it and live there.

27.1–11: Jeremiah tells the nations that God has placed their lands under the control of Babylon and Nebuchadnezzar, *my servant* (v. 6). Their prophets have a contrary view. 11: Those who refuse to serve Babylon will be put under the *yoke*.

12 I spoke to King Zedekiah of Judah in the same way: Bring your necks under the yoke of the king of Babylon, and serve him and his people, and live. ¹³Why should you and your people die by the sword, by famine, and by pestilence, as the LORD has spoken concerning any nation that will not serve the king of Babylon? ¹⁴Do not listen to the words of the prophets who are telling you not to serve the king of Babylon, for they are prophesying a lie to you. ¹⁵I have not sent them, says the LORD, but they are prophesying

falsely in my name, with the result that I will drive you out and you will perish, you and the prophets who are prophesying to you.

16 Then I spoke to the priests and to all this people, saying, Thus says the LORD: Do not listen to the words of your prophets who are prophesying to you, saying, "The vessels of the LORD's house will soon be brought back from Babylon," for they are prophesying a lie to you. ¹⁷Do not listen to them; serve the king of Babylon and live. Why should this city become a desolation? ¹⁸If indeed they are prophets, and if the word of the LORD is with them, then let them intercede with the LORD of hosts, that the vessels left in the house of the LORD, in the house of the king of Judah, and in Jerusalem may not go to Babylon. ¹⁹For thus says the LORD of hosts concerning the pillars, the sea, the stands, and the rest of the vessels that are left in this city, ²⁰which King Nebuchadnezzar of Babylon did not take away when he took into exile from Jerusalem to Babylon King Jeconiah son of Jehoiakim of Judah, and all the nobles of Judah and Jerusalem— ²¹thus says the LORD of hosts, the God of Israel, concerning the vessels left in the house of the LORD, in the house of the king of Judah, and in Jerusalem: ²²They shall be carried to Babylon, and there they shall stay, until the day when I give attention to them, says the LORD. Then I will bring them up and restore them to this place.

27.12–22: The prophets of Judah also oppose the true word of God in a dispute about the Temple* vessels. These sacred items had been deported to Babylon in 597 BCE, and the prophets expect them to be restored to Judah quickly, implying that Babylonian rule will not last long.

28 In that same year, at the beginning of the reign of King Zedekiah of Judah, in the fifth month of the fourth year, the prophet Hananiah son of Azzur, from Gibeon, spoke to me in the house of the LORD, in the presence of the priests and all the people, saying, ²"Thus says the LORD of hosts, the God of Israel: I have broken the

a Heb *their*   *b* Gk Syr Vg: Heb *dreams*

yoke of the king of Babylon. ³Within two years I will bring back to this place all the vessels of the LORD's house, which King Nebuchadnezzar of Babylon took away from this place and carried to Babylon. ⁴I will also bring back to this place King Jeconiah son of Jehoiakim of Judah, and all the exiles from Judah who went to Babylon, says the LORD, for I will break the yoke of the king of Babylon."

5 Then the prophet Jeremiah spoke to the prophet Hananiah in the presence of the priests and all the people who were standing in the house of the LORD; ⁶and the prophet Jeremiah said, "Amen! May the LORD do so; may the LORD fulfill the words that you have prophesied, and bring back to this place from Babylon the vessels of the house of the LORD, and all the exiles. ⁷But listen now to this word that I speak in your hearing and in the hearing of all the people. ⁸The prophets who preceded you and me from ancient times prophesied war, famine, and pestilence against many countries and great kingdoms. ⁹As for the prophet who prophesies peace, when the word of that prophet comes true, then it will be known that the LORD has truly sent the prophet."

10 Then the prophet Hananiah took the yoke from the neck of the prophet Jeremiah, and broke it. ¹¹And Hananiah spoke in the presence of all the people, saying, "Thus says the LORD: This is how I will break the yoke of King Nebuchadnezzar of Babylon from the neck of all the nations within two years." At this, the prophet Jeremiah went his way.

12 Sometime after the prophet Hananiah had broken the yoke from the neck of the prophet Jeremiah, the word of the LORD came to Jeremiah: ¹³Go, tell Hananiah, Thus says the LORD: You have broken wooden bars only to forge iron bars in place of them! ¹⁴For thus says the LORD of hosts, the God of Israel: I have put an iron yoke on the neck of all these nations so that they may serve King Nebuchadnezzar of Babylon, and they shall indeed serve him; I have even given him the wild animals. ¹⁵And the prophet Jeremiah said to the prophet Hananiah, "Listen, Hananiah, the LORD has not sent you, and you made this people trust in a lie. ¹⁶There-

fore thus says the LORD: I am going to send you off the face of the earth. Within this year you will be dead, because you have spoken rebellion against the LORD."

17 In that same year, in the seventh month, the prophet Hananiah died.

28.1–17: The conflict of prophetic messages narrows down to a conflict between two prophets of Judah, *Hananiah* and *Jeremiah*. In competing symbolic actions, the two men wear *yokes* to enact and make concrete the prophetic messages. Jeremiah wears a wooden yoke to signify captivity by Babylon. **10:** Hananiah breaks Jeremiah's yoke as an attempt to say the opposite. **12–14:** Jeremiah returns later with an unbreakable *iron yoke*. **17:** Hananiah's death a year later indicates that he was a false prophet preaching his own word, not divine revelation (Deut 18.20).

29 These are the words of the letter that the prophet Jeremiah sent from Jerusalem to the remaining elders among the exiles, and to the priests, the prophets, and all the people, whom Nebuchadnezzar had taken into exile from Jerusalem to Babylon. ²This was after King Jeconiah, and the queen mother, the court officials, the leaders of Judah and Jerusalem, the artisans, and the smiths had departed from Jerusalem. ³The letter was sent by the hand of Elasah son of Shaphan and Gemariah son of Hilkiah, whom King Zedekiah of Judah sent to Babylon to King Nebuchadnezzar of Babylon. It said: ⁴Thus says the LORD of hosts, the God of Israel, to all the exiles whom I have sent into exile from Jerusalem to Babylon: ⁵Build houses and live in them; plant gardens and eat what they produce. ⁶Take wives and have sons and daughters; take wives for your sons, and give your daughters in marriage, that they may bear sons and daughters; multiply there, and do not decrease. ⁷But seek the welfare of the city where I have sent you into exile, and pray to the LORD on its behalf, for in its welfare you will find your welfare. ⁸For thus says the LORD of hosts, the God of Israel: Do not let the prophets and the diviners who are among you deceive you, and do not listen to the dreams that they dream,ᵃ ⁹for

ᵃ Cn: Heb *your dreams that you cause to dream*

it is a lie that they are prophesying to you in my name; I did not send them, says the LORD.

10 For thus says the LORD: Only when Babylon's seventy years are completed will I visit you, and I will fulfill to you my promise and bring you back to this place. [11] For surely I know the plans I have for you, says the LORD, plans for your welfare and not for harm, to give you a future with hope. [12] Then when you call upon me and come and pray to me, I will hear you. [13] When you search for me, you will find me; if you seek me with all your heart, [14] I will let you find me, says the LORD, and I will restore your fortunes and gather you from all the nations and all the places where I have driven you, says the LORD, and I will bring you back to the place from which I sent you into exile.

15 Because you have said, "The LORD has raised up prophets for us in Babylon,"— [16] Thus says the LORD concerning the king who sits on the throne of David, and concerning all the people who live in this city, your kinsfolk who did not go out with you into exile: [17] Thus says the LORD of hosts, I am going to let loose on them sword, famine, and pestilence, and I will make them like rotten figs that are so bad they cannot be eaten. [18] I will pursue them with the sword, with famine, and with pestilence, and will make them a horror to all the kingdoms of the earth, to be an object of cursing, and horror, and hissing, and a derision among all the nations where I have driven them, [19] because they did not heed my words, says the LORD, when I persistently sent to you my servants the prophets, but they[a] would not listen, says the LORD. [20] But now, all you exiles whom I sent away from Jerusalem to Babylon, hear the word of the LORD: [21] Thus says the LORD of hosts, the God of Israel, concerning Ahab son of Kolaiah and Zedekiah son of Maaseiah, who are prophesying a lie to you in my name: I am going to deliver them into the hand of King Nebuchadrezzar of Babylon, and he shall kill them before your eyes. [22] And on account of them this curse shall be used by all the exiles from Judah in Babylon: "The LORD make you like

Zedekiah and Ahab, whom the king of Babylon roasted in the fire," [23] because they have perpetrated outrage in Israel and have committed adultery with their neighbors' wives, and have spoken in my name lying words that I did not command them; I am the one who knows and bears witness, says the LORD.

24 To Shemaiah of Nehelam you shall say: [25] Thus says the LORD of hosts, the God of Israel: In your own name you sent a letter to all the people who are in Jerusalem, and to the priest Zephaniah son of Maaseiah, and to all the priests, saying, [26] The LORD himself has made you priest instead of the priest Jehoiada, so that there may be officers in the house of the LORD to control any madman who plays the prophet, to put him in the stocks and the collar. [27] So now why have you not rebuked Jeremiah of Anathoth who plays the prophet for you? [28] For he has actually sent to us in Babylon, saying, "It will be a long time; build houses and live in them, and plant gardens and eat what they produce."

29 The priest Zephaniah read this letter in the hearing of the prophet Jeremiah. [30] Then the word of the LORD came to Jeremiah: [31] Send to all the exiles, saying, Thus says the LORD concerning Shemaiah of Nehelam: Because Shemaiah has prophesied to you, though I did not send him, and has led you to trust in a lie, [32] therefore thus says the LORD: I am going to punish Shemaiah of Nehelam and his descendants; he shall not have anyone living among this people to see[b] the good that I am going to do to my people, says the LORD, for he has spoken rebellion against the LORD.

29.1–32: Letters. From Jerusalem, Jeremiah writes letters to the exiles and responds to a letter about him. The letters to the exiles present Jeremiah as the authority about the exiles' survival. **3:** Supporters of Jeremiah serve as couriers. The exiles are not to resist Babylonian rule, but to live there in normal domestic relations and to seek the welfare of the city where they are held captive. **10:** After 70 years, probably symbolizing a long time, their relationship with God will be

a Syr: Heb *you*   b Gk: Heb *and he shall not see*

restored, and they will return to their land. **21–23:** Two false prophets among the exiles, *Ahab* and *Zedekiah*, will die like Hananiah under the deuteronomistic* curse (Deut 18.20). **24–32:** *Shemaiah*, one of the exiles, writes to the high priest in Jerusalem that he should silence Jeremiah. Jeremiah curses him as a false prophet, one like Hananiah.

Little book of consolation

Chs. 30–33: These chapters combine poetry (chs. 30–31) and prose (chs. 32–33) to depict a harmonious, idealized future for Israel and Judah. The placement of these chapters of hope and healing toward the center of the book is puzzling. Stories and poems of accusation and conflict surround them as if to temper the hope the chapters create. This structure may reflect the situation of the exilic audience, for whom escape from captivity remains a distant possibility. The chapters create a vision of what lies ahead, but they do not present a program for escape. Instead, they create unimagined possibilities that may help the community to endure for a new day.

Chs. 30–31: Restoration. The poems create a vision of a future nation in which northern and southern kingdoms are restored and reunited in Jerusalem. Some of the poems collected address male Jacob/Israel. Jacob is a name used for the northern kingdom of Israel, and also the name of the ancestor of all the twelve tribes (Gen 29–30). Other poems address female figures representing Judah and Zion,* or Rachel, one of Jacob's wives and mother of a northern and southern tribe. These names bring together both northern and southern kingdoms.

---

30 The word that came to Jeremiah from the LORD: ²Thus says the LORD, the God of Israel: Write in a book all the words that I have spoken to you. ³For the days are surely coming, says the LORD, when I will restore the fortunes of my people, Israel and Judah, says the LORD, and I will bring them back to the land that I gave to their ancestors and they shall take possession of it.

4 These are the words that the LORD spoke concerning Israel and Judah:

5 Thus says the LORD:

We have heard a cry of panic,
   of terror, and no peace.
6 Ask now, and see,
   can a man bear a child?

Why then do I see every man
   with his hands on his loins like a
      woman in labor?
Why has every face turned pale?
7 Alas! that day is so great
   there is none like it;
it is a time of distress for Jacob;
   yet he shall be rescued from it.

8 On that day, says the LORD of hosts, I will break the yoke from off his*a* neck, and I will burst his*a* bonds, and strangers shall no more make a servant of him. ⁹But they shall serve the LORD their God and David their king, whom I will raise up for them.

10 But as for you, have no fear, my servant
      Jacob, says the LORD,
   and do not be dismayed, O Israel;
for I am going to save you from
      far away,
   and your offspring from the land of
      their captivity.
Jacob shall return and have quiet and
      ease,
   and no one shall make him afraid.
11 For I am with you, says the LORD, to
      save you;
   I will make an end of all the nations
      among which I scattered you,
      but of you I will not make an end.
   I will chastise you in just measure,
      and I will by no means leave you
      unpunished.

30.1–11. 2: God's command that Jeremiah write these words in *a book* makes it possible for Jeremiah to communicate with the exiles even though he is not with them. **5–7:** Images of panic and pain describe the *distress for Jacob.* **8–11:** Without explanation, hope replaces terror. God will remove the yoke of servitude from them, restore relationship with them, and raise up a king for them.

---

12 For thus says the LORD:
   Your hurt is incurable,
      your wound is grievous.
13 There is no one to uphold your cause,
   no medicine for your wound,
      no healing for you.

a Cn: Heb *your*

14 All your lovers have forgotten you;
  they care nothing for you;
for I have dealt you the blow of
    an enemy,
  the punishment of a merciless foe,
because your guilt is great,
  because your sins are so numerous.
15 Why do you cry out over your hurt?
  Your pain is incurable.
Because your guilt is great,
  because your sins are so numerous,
I have done these things to you.
16 Therefore all who devour you shall be
    devoured,
  and all your foes, everyone of them,
    shall go into captivity;
those who plunder you shall be
    plundered,
  and all who prey on you I will make a
    prey.
17 For I will restore health to you,
  and your wounds I will heal,
          says the LORD,
because they have called you an outcast:
  "It is Zion; no one cares for her!"

30.12–17: In a poetic movement similar to vv. 5–11, this poem also moves unexpectedly from desperation to salvation, but the images shift from panic to wound-edness and healing. The one addressed is daughter Zion, God's unfaithful wife (2.1–3.25). God now pities her in her abandonment.

18 Thus says the LORD:
  I am going to restore the fortunes of the
    tents of Jacob,
  and have compassion on his
    dwellings;
the city shall be rebuilt upon its mound,
  and the citadel set on its rightful site.
19 Out of them shall come thanksgiving,
  and the sound of merrymakers.
I will make them many, and they shall
    not be few;
  I will make them honored, and they
    shall not be disdained.
20 Their children shall be as of old,
  their congregation shall be
    established before me;
and I will punish all who oppress
    them.

21 Their prince shall be one of their own,
  their ruler shall come from their
    midst;
I will bring him near, and he shall
    approach me,
  for who would otherwise dare to
    approach me?
          says the LORD.
22 And you shall be my people,
  and I will be your God.

23 Look, the storm of the LORD!
  Wrath has gone forth,
a whirling*a* tempest;
  it will burst upon the head of
    the wicked.
24 The fierce anger of the LORD will not
    turn back
  until he has executed and
    accomplished
  the intents of his mind.
In the latter days you will understand
    this.

30.18–24. 18–22: God speaks to Jacob and refers also to Jerusalem, the city that will be rebuilt. Both northern and southern kingdoms are reunited in a poetic out-burst concerning thanksgiving and new life. 23–24: The national tragedy receives a summary interpreta-tion. Divine *wrath* will one day end, and the audience will understand it in the future.

31 At that time, says the LORD, I will be the God of all the families of Israel, and they shall be my people.
2 Thus says the LORD:
  The people who survived the sword
    found grace in the wilderness;
  when Israel sought for rest,
3   the LORD appeared to him*b* from far
    away.*c*
  I have loved you with an everlasting
    love;
  therefore I have continued my
    faithfulness to you.
4 Again I will build you, and you shall be
    built,
  O virgin Israel!

a One Ms: Meaning of MT uncertain   *b* Gk: Heb *me*
c Or *to him long ago*

Again you shall take*ᵃ* your tambourines,
  and go forth in the dance of the
    merrymakers.
5 Again you shall plant vineyards
  on the mountains of Samaria;
the planters shall plant,
  and shall enjoy the fruit.
6 For there shall be a day when sentinels
    will call
  in the hill country of Ephraim:
"Come, let us go up to Zion,
  to the LORD our God."

7 For thus says the LORD:
Sing aloud with gladness for Jacob,
  and raise shouts for the chief of the
    nations;
proclaim, give praise, and say,
  "Save, O LORD, your people,
  the remnant of Israel."

8 See, I am going to bring them from the
    land of the north,
  and gather them from the farthest
    parts of the earth,
among them the blind and the lame,
  those with child and those in labor,
    together;
  a great company, they shall return
    here.
9 With weeping they shall come,
  and with consolationsᵇ I will lead
    them back,
I will let them walk by brooks
    of water,
  in a straight path in which they shall
    not stumble;
for I have become a father to Israel,
  and Ephraim is my firstborn.

10 Hear the word of the LORD, O nations,
  and declare it in the coastlands far
    away;
say, "He who scattered Israel will
    gather him,
  and will keep him as a shepherd a
    flock."
11 For the LORD has ransomed Jacob,
  and has redeemed him from hands
    too strong for him.
12 They shall come and sing aloud on the
    height of Zion,

and they shall be radiant over the
    goodness of the LORD,
over the grain, the wine, and the oil,
  and over the young of the flock and
    the herd;
their life shall become like a watered
    garden,
  and they shall never languish again.
13 Then shall the young women rejoice in
    the dance,
  and the young men and the old shall
    be merry.
I will turn their mourning into joy,
  I will comfort them, and give them
    gladness for sorrow.
14 I will give the priests their fill of fatness,
  and my people shall be satisfied with
    my bounty,
                                says the LORD.

31.1–14: Return. All Israel, both north and south, will
be reunited. **3–4:** Survivors will return, covenant* will
be restored, and God will take back wife Israel, now
called a *virgin*, no longer a harlot. She will be like Miriam, leading the dance (Ex 15.20–21). **9:** Echoing the
children's return (3.22–25), God takes them back and
promises to be *a father* to them. **10–14:** Everyone in
the society will participate in life that will be fertile and
joyous on Zion.*

15 Thus says the LORD:
A voice is heard in Ramah,
  lamentation and bitter weeping.
Rachel is weeping for her children;
  she refuses to be comforted for her
    children,
  because they are no more.
16 Thus says the LORD:
Keep your voice from weeping,
  and your eyes from tears;
for there is a reward for your work,
                                says the LORD:
  they shall come back from the land of
    the enemy;
17 there is hope for your future,
                                says the LORD:
  your children shall come back to their
    own country.

a Or *adorn yourself with*   *b* Gk Compare Vg Tg: Heb
supplications

18 Indeed I heard Ephraim pleading:
"You disciplined me, and I took the
      discipline;
   I was like a calf untrained.
Bring me back, let me come back,
   for you are the LORD my God.
19 For after I had turned away I repented;
   and after I was discovered, I struck
      my thigh;
   I was ashamed, and I was dismayed
      because I bore the disgrace of my
      youth."
20 Is Ephraim my dear son?
   Is he the child I delight in?
As often as I speak against him,
   I still remember him.
Therefore I am deeply moved for him;
   I will surely have mercy on him,
                        says the LORD.

21 Set up road markers for yourself,
   make yourself guideposts;
consider well the highway,
   the road by which you went.
Return, O virgin Israel,
   return to these your cities.
22 How long will you waver,
   O faithless daughter?
For the LORD has created a new thing
   on the earth:
   a woman encompasses*a man.

23 Thus says the LORD of hosts, the God
of Israel: Once more they shall use these
words in the land of Judah and in its towns
when I restore their fortunes:
   "The LORD bless you, O abode of
      righteousness,
   O holy hill!"
24And Judah and all its towns shall live there
together, and the farmers and those who
wander*b* with their flocks.
25 I will satisfy the weary,
   and all who are faint I will replenish.
26 Thereupon I awoke and looked, and
my sleep was pleasant to me.
27 The days are surely coming, says the
LORD, when I will sow the house of Israel
and the house of Judah with the seed of humans and the seed of animals. 28And just as
I have watched over them to pluck up and

break down, to overthrow, destroy, and bring
evil, so I will watch over them to build and
to plant, says the LORD. 29In those days they
shall no longer say:
   "The parents have eaten sour grapes,
      and the children's teeth are set on
      edge."
30But all shall die for their own sins; the
teeth of everyone who eats sour grapes shall
be set on edge.

31.15–30: Rachel's comfort. Rachel (Gen 27–35),
perhaps symbolizing God's first wife (3.7–11), weeps
for her lost children and receives the breathtaking
news that they will return. **18–20:** Her son, actually her
grandson, repents like the children (3.22–25), and
God receives him back. **21–22:** God addresses wife Israel and asks how long it will be before she repents.
The poem ends with a puzzling claim that God has
done a new thing: *A woman encompasses a man*, perhaps an image of Rachel embracing her returning
child. **23–26:** The woman may be Jerusalem encompassing the people returning from exile. **27–28:** Perhaps wife Rachel encompasses a man sexually to give
birth to a new generation.

---

31 The days are surely coming, says the
LORD, when I will make a new covenant with
the house of Israel and the house of Judah.
32It will not be like the covenant that I made
with their ancestors when I took them by the
hand to bring them out of the land of
Egypt—a covenant that they broke, though
I was their husband,*c* says the LORD. 33But
this is the covenant that I will make with the
house of Israel after those days, says the
LORD: I will put my law within them, and I
will write it on their hearts; and I will be their
God, and they shall be my people. 34No
longer shall they teach one another, or say
to each other, "Know the LORD," for they
shall all know me, from the least of them to
the greatest, says the LORD; for I will forgive
their iniquity, and remember their sin no
more.

35 Thus says the LORD,
   who gives the sun for light by day

---

a Meaning of Heb uncertain   *b* Cn Compare Syr Vg
Tg: Heb *and they shall wander*   *c* Or *master*

and the fixed order of the moon and
the stars for light by night,
who stirs up the sea so that its waves
roar—
the LORD of hosts is his name:
36 If this fixed order were ever to cease
from my presence, says the LORD,
then also the offspring of Israel would
cease
to be a nation before me forever.

37 Thus says the LORD:
If the heavens above can be measured,
and the foundations of the earth
below can be explored,
then I will reject all the offspring
of Israel
because of all they have done,
says the LORD.

38 The days are surely coming, says the
LORD, when the city shall be rebuilt for the
LORD from the tower of Hananel to the Corner Gate. 39 And the measuring line shall go
out farther, straight to the hill Gareb, and
shall then turn to Goah. 40 The whole valley
of the dead bodies and the ashes, and all the
fields as far as the Wadi Kidron, to the corner of the Horse Gate toward the east, shall
be sacred to the LORD. It shall never again
be uprooted or overthrown.

31.31–40: New covenant.* The poems about the
restored family are followed by a brief but potent
claim that there will be a new way of relating within
the covenant family. God will make a new covenant
with them. God and Israel will live in renewed fidelity.
34: Everyone *from the least to the greatest* will know
God. 35–40: The cosmos itself and the fixed order of
creation will be a sign of that fidelity, and Jerusalem
will be *rebuilt* and never *overthrown.*

A changed future
Chs. 32–33: In these two narrative chapters, Jeremiah
buys a field and offers prayers that signify a hopeful
future for the exiles. Jeremiah purchases a field during
an imprisonment that occurs while Babylon is invading
Jerusalem. During an invasion, land is worthless.
Helped by his companion Baruch (v. 12), Jeremiah redeems the land of his cousin as expected by law. The
foolishness of that purchase stands as a promise that

life will resume in the land. Jeremiah, captive like the
exilic audience, is a model of obedient hopefulness in
the face of tragedy.

32 The word that came to Jeremiah
from the LORD in the tenth year of
King Zedekiah of Judah, which was the eighteenth year of Nebuchadrezzar. 2 At that time
the army of the king of Babylon was besieging Jerusalem, and the prophet Jeremiah was
confined in the court of the guard that was
in the palace of the king of Judah, 3 where
King Zedekiah of Judah had confined him.
Zedekiah had said, "Why do you prophesy
and say: Thus says the LORD: I am going to
give this city into the hand of the king of
Babylon, and he shall take it; 4 King Zedekiah
of Judah shall not escape out of the hands of
the Chaldeans, but shall surely be given into
the hands of the king of Babylon, and shall
speak with him face to face and see him eye
to eye; 5 and he shall take Zedekiah to Babylon, and there he shall remain until I attend
to him, says the LORD; though you fight
against the Chaldeans, you shall not succeed?"

6 Jeremiah said, The word of the LORD
came to me: 7 Hanamel son of your uncle
Shallum is going to come to you and say,
"Buy my field that is at Anathoth, for the
right of redemption by purchase is yours."
8 Then my cousin Hanamel came to me in
the court of the guard, in accordance with
the word of the LORD, and said to me, "Buy
my field that is at Anathoth in the land of
Benjamin, for the right of possession and redemption is yours; buy it for yourself." Then
I knew that this was the word of the LORD.

9 And I bought the field at Anathoth from
my cousin Hanamel, and weighed out the
money to him, seventeen shekels of silver.
10 I signed the deed, sealed it, got witnesses,
and weighed the money on scales. 11 Then I
took the sealed deed of purchase, containing
the terms and conditions, and the open copy;
12 and I gave the deed of purchase to Baruch
son of Neriah son of Mahseiah, in the presence of my cousin Hanamel, in the presence
of the witnesses who signed the deed of purchase, and in the presence of all the Judeans
who were sitting in the court of the guard.

13 In their presence I charged Baruch, saying, 14 Thus says the LORD of hosts, the God of Israel: Take these deeds, both this sealed deed of purchase and this open deed, and put them in an earthenware jar, in order that they may last for a long time. 15 For thus says the LORD of hosts, the God of Israel: Houses and fields and vineyards shall again be bought in this land.

16 After I had given the deed of purchase to Baruch son of Neriah, I prayed to the LORD, saying: 17 Ah Lord GOD! It is you who made the heavens and the earth by your great power and by your outstretched arm! Nothing is too hard for you. 18 You show steadfast love to the thousandth generation,[a] but repay the guilt of parents into the laps of their children after them, O great and mighty God whose name is the LORD of hosts, 19 great in counsel and mighty in deed; whose eyes are open to all the ways of mortals, rewarding all according to their ways and according to the fruit of their doings. 20 You showed signs and wonders in the land of Egypt, and to this day in Israel and among all humankind, and have made yourself a name that continues to this very day. 21 You brought your people Israel out of the land of Egypt with signs and wonders, with a strong hand and outstretched arm, and with great terror; 22 and you gave them this land, which you swore to their ancestors to give them, a land flowing with milk and honey; 23 and they entered and took possession of it. But they did not obey your voice or follow your law; of all you commanded them to do, they did nothing. Therefore you have made all these disasters come upon them. 24 See, the siege ramps have been cast up against the city to take it, and the city, faced with sword, famine, and pestilence, has been given into the hands of the Chaldeans who are fighting against it. What you spoke has happened, as you yourself can see. 25 Yet you, O Lord GOD, have said to me, "Buy the field for money and get witnesses"—though the city has been given into the hands of the Chaldeans.

26 The word of the LORD came to Jeremiah: 27 See, I am the LORD, the God of all flesh; is anything too hard for me? 28 Therefore, thus says the LORD: I am going to give this city into the hands of the Chaldeans and into the hand of King Nebuchadrezzar of Babylon, and he shall take it. 29 The Chaldeans who are fighting against this city shall come, set it on fire, and burn it, with the houses on whose roofs offerings have been made to Baal and libations have been poured out to other gods, to provoke me to anger. 30 For the people of Israel and the people of Judah have done nothing but evil in my sight from their youth; the people of Israel have done nothing but provoke me to anger by the work of their hands, says the LORD. 31 This city has aroused my anger and wrath, from the day it was built until this day, so that I will remove it from my sight 32 because of all the evil of the people of Israel and the people of Judah that they did to provoke me to anger—they, their kings and their officials, their priests and their prophets, the citizens of Judah and the inhabitants of Jerusalem. 33 They have turned their backs to me, not their faces; though I have taught them persistently, they would not listen and accept correction. 34 They set up their abominations in the house that bears my name, and defiled it. 35 They built the high places of Baal in the valley of the son of Hinnom, to offer up their sons and daughters to Molech, though I did not command them, nor did it enter my mind that they should do this abomination, causing Judah to sin.

36 Now therefore thus says the LORD, the God of Israel, concerning this city of which you say, "It is being given into the hand of the king of Babylon by the sword, by famine, and by pestilence": 37 See, I am going to gather them from all the lands to which I drove them in my anger and my wrath and in great indignation; I will bring them back to this place, and I will settle them in safety. 38 They shall be my people, and I will be their God. 39 I will give them one heart and one way, that they may fear me for all time, for their own good and the good of their children after them. 40 I will make an everlasting covenant with them, never to draw back from

a Or to thousands

doing good to them; and I will put the fear of me in their hearts, so that they may not turn from me. ⁴¹I will rejoice in doing good to them, and I will plant them in this land in faithfulness, with all my heart and all my soul.

42 For thus says the LORD: Just as I have brought all this great disaster upon this people, so I will bring upon them all the good fortune that I now promise them. ⁴³Fields shall be bought in this land of which you are saying, It is a desolation, without human beings or animals; it has been given into the hands of the Chaldeans. ⁴⁴Fields shall be bought for money, and deeds shall be signed and sealed and witnessed, in the land of Benjamin, in the places around Jerusalem, and in the cities of Judah, of the hill country, of the Shephelah, and of the Negeb; for I will restore their fortunes, says the LORD.

32.1–44. 16–25: Jeremiah's prayer elaborates on the theme of hopefulness, asking God to see the invasion as it occurs. 26–42: God replies to Jeremiah that there is a future. 38: The covenant* will be renewed. 42: The one who brought the disaster will bring a new future.

33 The word of the LORD came to Jeremiah a second time, while he was still confined in the court of the guard: ²Thus says the LORD who made the earth,ᵃ the LORD who formed it to establish it—the LORD is his name: ³Call to me and I will answer you, and will tell you great and hidden things that you have not known. ⁴For thus says the LORD, the God of Israel, concerning the houses of this city and the houses of the kings of Judah that were torn down to make a defense against the siege ramps and before the sword:ᵇ ⁵The Chaldeans are coming in to fightᶜ and to fill them with the dead bodies of those whom I shall strike down in my anger and my wrath, for I have hidden my face from this city because of all their wickedness. ⁶I am going to bring it recovery and healing; I will heal them and reveal to them abundanceᵇ of prosperity and security. ⁷I will restore the fortunes of Judah and the fortunes of Israel, and rebuild them as they were at first. ⁸I will cleanse them

from all the guilt of their sin against me, and I will forgive all the guilt of their sin and rebellion against me. ⁹And this cityᵈ shall be to me a name of joy, a praise and a glory before all the nations of the earth who shall hear of all the good that I do for them; they shall fear and tremble because of all the good and all the prosperity I provide for it.

10 Thus says the LORD: In this place of which you say, "It is a waste without human beings or animals," in the towns of Judah and the streets of Jerusalem that are desolate, without inhabitants, human or animal, there shall once more be heard ¹¹the voice of mirth and the voice of gladness, the voice of the bridegroom and the voice of the bride, the voices of those who sing, as they bring thank offerings to the house of the LORD:

"Give thanks to the LORD of hosts,
　for the LORD is good,
　for his steadfast love endures
　　forever!"

For I will restore the fortunes of the land as at first, says the LORD.

12 Thus says the LORD of hosts: In this place that is waste, without human beings or animals, and in all its towns there shall again be pasture for shepherds resting their flocks. ¹³In the towns of the hill country, of the Shephelah, and of the Negeb, in the land of Benjamin, the places around Jerusalem, and in the towns of Judah, flocks shall again pass under the hands of the one who counts them, says the LORD.

14 The days are surely coming, says the LORD, when I will fulfill the promise I made to the house of Israel and the house of Judah. ¹⁵In those days and at that time I will cause a righteous Branch to spring up for David; and he shall execute justice and righteousness in the land. ¹⁶In those days Judah will be saved and Jerusalem will live in safety. And this is the name by which it will be called: "The LORD is our righteousness."

17 For thus says the LORD: David shall never lack a man to sit on the throne of the house of Israel, ¹⁸and the levitical priests

ᵃ Gk: Heb it　ᵇ Meaning of Heb uncertain
ᶜ Cn: Heb *They are coming in to fight against the Chaldeans*　ᵈ Heb *And it*

shall never lack a man in my presence to offer burnt offerings, to make grain offerings, and to make sacrifices for all time.

19 The word of the LORD came to Jeremiah: 20Thus says the LORD: If any of you could break my covenant with the day and my covenant with the night, so that day and night would not come at their appointed time, 21only then could my covenant with my servant David be broken, so that he would not have a son to reign on his throne, and my covenant with my ministers the Levites. 22Just as the host of heaven cannot be numbered and the sands of the sea cannot be measured, so I will increase the offspring of my servant David, and the Levites who minister to me.

23 The word of the LORD came to Jeremiah: 24Have you not observed how these people say, "The two families that the LORD chose have been rejected by him," and how they hold my people in such contempt that they no longer regard them as a nation? 25Thus says the LORD: Only if I had not established my covenant with day and night and the ordinances of heaven and earth, 26would I reject the offspring of Jacob and of my servant David and not choose any of his descendants as rulers over the offspring of Abraham, Isaac, and Jacob. For I will restore their fortunes, and will have mercy upon them.

33.1–26: Restoration. The restored relationship between God and the people is illustrated here. **3:** God invites Jeremiah to make requests. **6:** God assures the people of *healing* and *prosperity*. **14–16:** God promises to restore the kingship and the priesthood and to reunite the peoples of Israel and Judah.

A good king and a bad community
Chs. 34–35: These two chapters contrast the failure of the king and people to obey God's word (ch. 34) with the exemplary fidelity of a small group of people called Rechabites (ch. 35). The former group faces the dire consequences of infidelity, and the latter group gains a future because of fidelity. Both stories are set during the Babylonian invasion, but the behavior they describe concerns consequences in the exilic present.

34 The word that came to Jeremiah from the LORD, when King Nebuchadrezzar of Babylon and all his army and all the kingdoms of the earth and all the peoples under his dominion were fighting against Jerusalem and all its cities: 2Thus says the LORD, the God of Israel: Go and speak to King Zedekiah of Judah and say to him: Thus says the LORD: I am going to give this city into the hand of the king of Babylon, and he shall burn it with fire. 3And you yourself shall not escape from his hand, but shall surely be captured and handed over to him; you shall see the king of Babylon eye to eye and speak with him face to face; and you shall go to Babylon. 4Yet hear the word of the LORD, O King Zedekiah of Judah! Thus says the LORD concerning you: You shall not die by the sword; 5you shall die in peace. And as spices were burned*a* for your ancestors, the earlier kings who preceded you, so they shall burn spices*b* for you and lament for you, saying, "Alas, lord!" For I have spoken the word, says the LORD.

6 Then the prophet Jeremiah spoke all these words to Zedekiah king of Judah, in Jerusalem, 7when the army of the king of Babylon was fighting against Jerusalem and against all the cities of Judah that were left, Lachish and Azekah; for these were the only fortified cities of Judah that remained.

8 The word that came to Jeremiah from the LORD, after King Zedekiah had made a covenant with all the people in Jerusalem to make a proclamation of liberty to them— 9that all should set free their Hebrew slaves, male and female, so that no one should hold another Judean in slavery. 10And they obeyed, all the officials and all the people who had entered into the covenant that all would set free their slaves, male or female, so that they would not be enslaved again; they obeyed and set them free. 11But afterward they turned around and took back the male and female slaves they had set free, and brought them again into subjection as slaves. 12The word of the LORD came to Jeremiah from the LORD: 13Thus says the LORD, the God of Israel: I myself made a covenant with

a Heb *as there was burning*   *b* Heb *shall burn*

your ancestors when I brought them out of the land of Egypt, out of the house of slavery, saying, [14]"Every seventh year each of you must set free any Hebrews who have been sold to you and have served you six years; you must set them free from your service." But your ancestors did not listen to me or incline their ears to me. [15]You yourselves recently repented and did what was right in my sight by proclaiming liberty to one another, and you made a covenant before me in the house that is called by my name; [16]but then you turned around and profaned my name when each of you took back your male and female slaves, whom you had set free according to their desire, and you brought them again into subjection to be your slaves. [17]Therefore, thus says the LORD: You have not obeyed me by granting a release to your neighbors and friends; I am going to grant a release to you, says the LORD—a release to the sword, to pestilence, and to famine. I will make you a horror to all the kingdoms of the earth. [18]And those who transgressed my covenant and did not keep the terms of the covenant that they made before me, I will make like*a* the calf when they cut it in two and passed between its parts: [19]the officials of Judah, the officials of Jerusalem, the eunuchs, the priests, and all the people of the land who passed between the parts of the calf [20]shall be handed over to their enemies and to those who seek their lives. Their corpses shall become food for the birds of the air and the wild animals of the earth. [21]And as for King Zedekiah of Judah and his officials, I will hand them over to their enemies and to those who seek their lives, to the army of the king of Babylon, which has withdrawn from you. [22]I am going to command, says the LORD, and will bring them back to this city; and they will fight against it, and take it, and burn it with fire. The towns of Judah I will make a desolation without inhabitant.

34.1–22: Jerusalem is under attack. 6–7: Only the fortress cities of *Lachish* and *Azekah* have not fallen to the Babylonians. The times are dire. 8–10: Zedekiah proclaims the freedom of Judean slaves, according to the law and God's command (Deut 15.12–14). At first all the people followed, but then they changed their minds, so they will go into slavery. 18–20: They will be cut up like a sacrificial animal in a covenant* offering.

~~~~~~~~~~

35 The word that came to Jeremiah from the LORD in the days of King Jehoiakim son of Josiah of Judah: [2]Go to the house of the Rechabites, and speak with them, and bring them to the house of the LORD, into one of the chambers; then offer them wine to drink. [3]So I took Jaazaniah son of Jeremiah son of Habazziniah, and his brothers, and all his sons, and the whole house of the Rechabites. [4]I brought them to the house of the LORD into the chamber of the sons of Hanan son of Igdaliah, the man of God, which was near the chamber of the officials, above the chamber of Maaseiah son of Shallum, keeper of the threshold. [5]Then I set before the Rechabites pitchers full of wine, and cups; and I said to them, "Have some wine." [6]But they answered, "We will drink no wine, for our ancestor Jonadab son of Rechab commanded us, 'You shall never drink wine, neither you nor your children; [7]nor shall you ever build a house, or sow seed; nor shall you plant a vineyard, or even own one; but you shall live in tents all your days, that you may live many days in the land where you reside.' [8]We have obeyed the charge of our ancestor Jonadab son of Rechab in all that he commanded us, to drink no wine all our days, ourselves, our wives, our sons, or our daughters, [9]and not to build houses to live in. We have no vineyard or field or seed; [10]but we have lived in tents, and have obeyed and done all that our ancestor Jonadab commanded us. [11]But when King Nebuchadrezzar of Babylon came up against the land, we said, 'Come, and let us go to Jerusalem for fear of the army of the Chaldeans and the army of the Arameans.' That is why we are living in Jerusalem."

12 Then the word of the LORD came to Jeremiah: [13]Thus says the LORD of hosts, the God of Israel: Go and say to the people of Judah and the inhabitants of Jerusalem, Can you not learn a lesson and obey my words?

---

a Cn: Heb lacks *like*

says the LORD. 14The command has been carried out that Jonadab son of Rechab gave to his descendants to drink no wine; and they drink none to this day, for they have obeyed their ancestor's command. But I myself have spoken to you persistently, and you have not obeyed me. 15I have sent to you all my servants the prophets, sending them persistently, saying, "Turn now everyone of you from your evil way, and amend your doings, and do not go after other gods to serve them, and then you shall live in the land that I gave to you and your ancestors." But you did not incline your ear or obey me. 16The descendants of Jonadab son of Rechab have carried out the command that their ancestor gave them, but this people has not obeyed me. 17Therefore, thus says the LORD, the God of hosts, the God of Israel: I am going to bring on Judah and on all the inhabitants of Jerusalem every disaster that I have pronounced against them; because I have spoken to them and they have not listened, I have called to them and they have not answered.

18 But to the house of the Rechabites Jeremiah said: Thus says the LORD of hosts, the God of Israel: Because you have obeyed the command of your ancestor Jonadab, and kept all his precepts, and done all that he commanded you, 19therefore thus says the LORD of hosts, the God of Israel: Jonadab son of Rechab shall not lack a descendant to stand before me for all time.

35.1–19: The *Rechabites,* by contrast, are faithful to their traditions. Little is certain about the identity of the Rechabites. 8–10: They refrained from drinking wine and owning houses or land in the tradition of their ancestor, *Jonadab son of Rechab.* They exemplify true obedience, as shown in 2 Kings 10.15–27, where Jonadab assists King Jehu in purging Baal worship from the land.

36 In the fourth year of King Jehoiakim son of Josiah of Judah, this word came to Jeremiah from the LORD: 2Take a scroll and write on it all the words that I have spoken to you against Israel and Judah and all the nations, from the day I spoke to you, from the days of Josiah until today. 3It may be that when the house of Judah hears of all the disasters that I intend to do to them, all of them may turn from their evil ways, so that I may forgive their iniquity and their sin.

4 Then Jeremiah called Baruch son of Neriah, and Baruch wrote on a scroll at Jeremiah's dictation all the words of the LORD that he had spoken to him. 5And Jeremiah ordered Baruch, saying, "I am prevented from entering the house of the LORD; 6so you go yourself, and on a fast day in the hearing of the people in the LORD's house you shall read the words of the LORD from the scroll that you have written at my dictation. You shall read them also in the hearing of all the people of Judah who come up from their towns. 7It may be that their plea will come before the LORD, and that all of them will turn from their evil ways, for great is the anger and wrath that the LORD has pronounced against this people." 8And Baruch son of Neriah did all that the prophet Jeremiah ordered him about reading from the scroll the words of the LORD in the LORD's house.

9 In the fifth year of King Jehoiakim son of Josiah of Judah, in the ninth month, all the people in Jerusalem and all the people who came from the towns of Judah to Jerusalem proclaimed a fast before the LORD. 10Then, in the hearing of all the people, Baruch read the words of Jeremiah from the scroll, in the house of the LORD, in the chamber of Gemariah son of Shaphan the secretary, which was in the upper court, at the entry of the New Gate of the LORD's house.

11 When Micaiah son of Gemariah son of Shaphan heard all the words of the LORD from the scroll, 12he went down to the king's house, into the secretary's chamber; and all the officials were sitting there: Elishama the secretary, Delaiah son of Shemaiah, Elnathan son of Achbor, Gemariah son of Shaphan, Zedekiah son of Hananiah, and all the officials. 13And Micaiah told them all the words that he had heard, when Baruch read the scroll in the hearing of the people. 14Then all the officials sent Jehudi son of Nethaniah son of Shelemiah son of Cushi to say to Baruch, "Bring the scroll that you read in the hearing of the people, and come." So Baruch son of Neriah took the scroll in his

hand and came to them. ¹⁵And they said to him, "Sit down and read it to us." So Baruch read it to them. ¹⁶When they heard all the words, they turned to one another in alarm, and said to Baruch, "We certainly must report all these words to the king." ¹⁷Then they questioned Baruch, "Tell us now, how did you write all these words? Was it at his dictation?" ¹⁸Baruch answered them, "He dictated all these words to me, and I wrote them with ink on the scroll." ¹⁹Then the officials said to Baruch, "Go and hide, you and Jeremiah, and let no one know where you are."

20 Leaving the scroll in the chamber of Elishama the secretary, they went to the court of the king; and they reported all the words to the king. ²¹Then the king sent Jehudi to get the scroll, and he took it from the chamber of Elishama the secretary; and Jehudi read it to the king and all the officials who stood beside the king. ²²Now the king was sitting in his winter apartment (it was the ninth month), and there was a fire burning in the brazier before him. ²³As Jehudi read three or four columns, the king*ᵃ* would cut them off with a penknife and throw them into the fire in the brazier, until the entire scroll was consumed in the fire that was in the brazier. ²⁴Yet neither the king, nor any of his servants who heard all these words, was alarmed, nor did they tear their garments. ²⁵Even when Elnathan and Delaiah and Gemariah urged the king not to burn the scroll, he would not listen to them. ²⁶And the king commanded Jerahmeel the king's son and Seraiah son of Azriel and Shelemiah son of Abdeel to arrest the secretary Baruch and the prophet Jeremiah. But the LORD hid them.

27 Now, after the king had burned the scroll with the words that Baruch wrote at Jeremiah's dictation, the word of the LORD came to Jeremiah: ²⁸Take another scroll and write on it all the former words that were in the first scroll, which King Jehoiakim of Judah has burned. ²⁹And concerning King Jehoiakim of Judah you shall say: Thus says the LORD, You have dared to burn this scroll, saying, Why have you written in it that the king of Babylon will certainly come and destroy this land, and will cut off from it hu-

man beings and animals? ³⁰Therefore thus says the LORD concerning King Jehoiakim of Judah: He shall have no one to sit upon the throne of David, and his dead body shall be cast out to the heat by day and the frost by night. ³¹And I will punish him and his offspring and his servants for their iniquity; I will bring on them, and on the inhabitants of Jerusalem, and on the people of Judah, all the disasters with which I have threatened them—but they would not listen.

32 Then Jeremiah took another scroll and gave it to the secretary Baruch son of Neriah, who wrote on it at Jeremiah's dictation all the words of the scroll that King Jehoiakim of Judah had burned in the fire; and many similar words were added to them.

36.1–32: Two scrolls. This chapter has many parallels with ch. 26, including strong indictments of King Jehoiakim. Baruch, Jeremiah's scribe,★ continues the prophet's★ message by writing it and by proclaiming it. **2–8:** *Baruch* is a reliable proclaimer of Jeremiah's message of repentance, written by divine command on a *scroll.* **9–19:** Supporters of Jeremiah hear Baruch's reading of the scroll and send him and Jeremiah into hiding. **20–26:** In a dramatic scene, the scroll is read to the king, who cuts it up and burns it as it is being read. The king's action is a symbolic attempt to destroy the uncontrollable power of the word by making it disappear. **27–32:** But the prophetic word cannot be erased; Jeremiah dictates another version and adds more words to it. Jehoiakim, therefore, is responsible for the fall of the nation, for he would not listen.

BARUCH'S ACCOUNT

Chs. 37–45: Baruch is described as the author of these stories about Jeremiah and other survivors of the Babylonian invasion (45.1). Perhaps these chapters represent the additional words of the second scroll (36.32). The chapters show the exilic audience how to survive suffering brought on by invasion and its aftermath. They describe how the prophetic word was rejected, was fulfilled, and how it created conflict among survivors. Jeremiah himself appears as an example of fidelity. He is imprisoned and rescued twice, escapes with his life, and becomes a model of faithful survival.

a Heb *he*

Prison and release
Chs. 37–39: These chapters are all set during the reign of Zedekiah, who is as unaccepting of the prophetic word as his predecessor Jehoiakim.

37 Zedekiah son of Josiah, whom King Nebuchadrezzar of Babylon made king in the land of Judah, succeeded Coniah son of Jehoiakim. 2But neither he nor his servants nor the people of the land listened to the words of the LORD that he spoke through the prophet Jeremiah.

3 King Zedekiah sent Jehucal son of Shelemiah and the priest Zephaniah son of Maaseiah to the prophet Jeremiah saying, "Please pray for us to the LORD our God." 4Now Jeremiah was still going in and out among the people, for he had not yet been put in prison. 5Meanwhile, the army of Pharaoh had come out of Egypt; and when the Chaldeans who were besieging Jerusalem heard news of them, they withdrew from Jerusalem.

6 Then the word of the LORD came to the prophet Jeremiah: 7Thus says the LORD, God of Israel: This is what the two of you shall say to the king of Judah, who sent you to me to inquire of me: Pharaoh's army, which set out to help you, is going to return to its own land, to Egypt. 8And the Chaldeans shall return and fight against this city; they shall take it and burn it with fire. 9Thus says the LORD: Do not deceive yourselves, saying, "The Chaldeans will surely go away from us," for they will not go away. 10Even if you defeated the whole army of Chaldeans who are fighting against you, and there remained of them only wounded men in their tents, they would rise up and burn this city with fire.

11 Now when the Chaldean army had withdrawn from Jerusalem at the approach of Pharaoh's army, 12Jeremiah set out from Jerusalem to go to the land of Benjamin to receive his share of property*a* among the people there. 13When he reached the Benjamin Gate, a sentinel there named Irijah son of Shelemiah son of Hananiah arrested the prophet Jeremiah saying, "You are deserting to the Chaldeans." 14And Jeremiah said, "That is a lie; I am not deserting to the Chaldeans." But Irijah would not listen to him, and arrested Jeremiah and brought him to the officials. 15The officials were enraged at Jeremiah, and they beat him and imprisoned him in the house of the secretary Jonathan, for it had been made a prison. 16Thus Jeremiah was put in the cistern house, in the cells, and remained there many days.

17 Then King Zedekiah sent for him, and received him. The king questioned him secretly in his house, and said, "Is there any word from the LORD?" Jeremiah said, "There is!" Then he said, "You shall be handed over to the king of Babylon." 18Jeremiah also said to King Zedekiah, "What wrong have I done to you or your servants or this people, that you have put me in prison? 19Where are your prophets who prophesied to you, saying, 'The king of Babylon will not come against you and against this land'? 20Now please hear me, my lord king: be good enough to listen to my plea, and do not send me back to the house of the secretary Jonathan to die there." 21So King Zedekiah gave orders, and they committed Jeremiah to the court of the guard; and a loaf of bread was given him daily from the bakers' street, until all the bread of the city was gone. So Jeremiah remained in the court of the guard.

37.1–21: In ch. 37, the king consults with Jeremiah twice, at the beginning and end of the chapter. The consultations frame Jeremiah's imprisonment. This arrangement suggests that the king is attempting to squeeze a favorable word from Jeremiah. 37.3–10: Zedekiah's hope is that the power struggles between Egypt and Pharaoh will reduce Babylonian power and avert disaster. Jeremiah says no. 11–16: In a series of abusive acts toward the prophet, officials imprison him, as if they could imprison the word. 17–21: Secretly, the king tries to persuade Jeremiah to give him hope, but the prophet faithfully repeats his message of doom and escapes with his life.

38 Now Shephatiah son of Mattan, Gedaliah son of Pashhur, Jucal son of Shelemiah, and Pashhur son of Malchiah heard the words that Jeremiah was saying to all the people, 2Thus says the LORD, Those

a Meaning of Heb uncertain

who stay in this city shall die by the sword, by famine, and by pestilence; but those who go out to the Chaldeans shall live; they shall have their lives as a prize of war, and live. ³Thus says the LORD, This city shall surely be handed over to the army of the king of Babylon and be taken. ⁴Then the officials said to the king, "This man ought to be put to death, because he is discouraging the soldiers who are left in this city, and all the people, by speaking such words to them. For this man is not seeking the welfare of this people, but their harm." ⁵King Zedekiah said, "Here he is; he is in your hands; for the king is powerless against you." ⁶So they took Jeremiah and threw him into the cistern of Malchiah, the king's son, which was in the court of the guard, letting Jeremiah down by ropes. Now there was no water in the cistern, but only mud, and Jeremiah sank in the mud.

7 Ebed-melech the Ethiopian,^a a eunuch in the king's house, heard that they had put Jeremiah into the cistern. The king happened to be sitting at the Benjamin Gate, ⁸So Ebed-melech left the king's house and spoke to the king, ⁹"My lord king, these men have acted wickedly in all they did to the prophet Jeremiah by throwing him into the cistern to die there of hunger, for there is no bread left in the city." ¹⁰Then the king commanded Ebed-melech the Ethiopian,^a "Take three men with you from here, and pull the prophet Jeremiah up from the cistern before he dies." ¹¹So Ebed-melech took the men with him and went to the house of the king, to a wardrobe of^b the storehouse, and took from there old rags and worn-out clothes, which he let down to Jeremiah in the cistern by ropes. ¹²Then Ebed-melech the Ethiopian^a said to Jeremiah, "Just put the rags and clothes between your armpits and the ropes." Jeremiah did so. ¹³Then they drew Jeremiah up by the ropes and pulled him out of the cistern. And Jeremiah remained in the court of the guard.

Jeremiah's imprisonment because he will not offer a hopeful message. Jeremiah sinks into the mud. **7–13:** An African, Ebed-melech, whose name means "servant of the king," dramatically rescues Jeremiah from death. In contrast to the king and his advisers, Ebed-melech shows true obedience.

14 King Zedekiah sent for the prophet Jeremiah and received him at the third entrance of the temple of the LORD. The king said to Jeremiah, "I have something to ask you; do not hide anything from me." ¹⁵Jeremiah said to Zedekiah, "If I tell you, you will put me to death, will you not? And if I give you advice, you will not listen to me." ¹⁶So King Zedekiah swore an oath in secret to Jeremiah, "As the LORD lives, who gave us our lives, I will not put you to death or hand you over to these men who seek your life."

17 Then Jeremiah said to Zedekiah, "Thus says the LORD, the God of hosts, the God of Israel, If you will only surrender to the officials of the king of Babylon, then your life shall be spared, and this city shall not be burned with fire, and you and your house shall live. ¹⁸But if you do not surrender to the officials of the king of Babylon, then this city shall be handed over to the Chaldeans, and they shall burn it with fire, and you yourself shall not escape from their hand." ¹⁹King Zedekiah said to Jeremiah, "I am afraid of the Judeans who have deserted to the Chaldeans, for I might be handed over to them and they would abuse me." ²⁰Jeremiah said, "That will not happen. Just obey the voice of the LORD in what I say to you, and it shall go well with you, and your life shall be spared. ²¹But if you are determined not to surrender, this is what the LORD has shown me— ²²a vision of all the women remaining in the house of the king of Judah being led out to the officials of the king of Babylon and saying,

'Your trusted friends have seduced you
    and have overcome you;
Now that your feet are stuck in
    the mud,
    they desert you.'

38.1–28: This story does not flow smoothly from the previous chapter. There Jeremiah was in prison, but here he is preaching freely to the people. **1–6:** He urges the people to surrender to Babylon to save their lives *as the prize of war* (v. 2). The king again allows

a Or *Nubian;* Heb *Cushite*   *b* Cn: Heb *to under*

23All your wives and your children shall be led out to the Chaldeans, and you yourself shall not escape from their hand, but shall be seized by the king of Babylon; and this city shall be burned with fire."

24 Then Zedekiah said to Jeremiah, "Do not let anyone else know of this conversation, or you will die. 25If the officials should hear that I have spoken with you, and they should come and say to you, 'Just tell us what you said to the king; do not conceal it from us, or we will put you to death. What did the king say to you?' 26then you shall say to them, 'I was presenting my plea to the king not to send me back to the house of Jonathan to die there.' " 27All the officials did come to Jeremiah and questioned him; and he answered them in the very words the king had commanded. So they stopped questioning him, for the conversation had not been overheard. 28And Jeremiah remained in the court of the guard until the day that Jerusalem was taken.

38.14–28: The king again consults with Jeremiah, who proclaims the king's capture. In this vision, the king changes places with Jeremiah: The king is *stuck in the mud.*

---

39 In the ninth year of King Zedekiah of Judah, in the tenth month, King Nebuchadrezzar of Babylon and all his army came against Jerusalem and besieged it; 2in the eleventh year of Zedekiah, in the fourth month, on the ninth day of the month, a breach was made in the city. 3When Jerusalem was taken,a all the officials of the king of Babylon came and sat in the middle gate: Nergal-sharezer, Samgar-nebo, Sarsechim the Rabsaris, Nergal-sharezer the Rabmag, with all the rest of the officials of the king of Babylon. 4When King Zedekiah of Judah and all the soldiers saw them, they fled, going out of the city at night by way of the king's garden through the gate between the two walls; and they went toward the Arabah. 5But the army of the Chaldeans pursued them, and overtook Zedekiah in the plains of Jericho; and when they had taken him, they brought him up to King Nebuchadrezzar of Babylon, at Riblah, in the land of Hamath; and he

passed sentence on him. 6The king of Babylon slaughtered the sons of Zedekiah at Riblah before his eyes; also the king of Babylon slaughtered all the nobles of Judah. 7He put out the eyes of Zedekiah, and bound him in fetters to take him to Babylon. 8The Chaldeans burned the king's house and the houses of the people, and broke down the walls of Jerusalem. 9Then Nebuzaradan the captain of the guard exiled to Babylon the rest of the people who were left in the city, those who had deserted to him, and the people who remained. 10Nebuzaradan the captain of the guard left in the land of Judah some of the poor people who owned nothing, and gave them vineyards and fields at the same time.

11 King Nebuchadrezzar of Babylon gave command concerning Jeremiah through Nebuzaradan, the captain of the guard, saying, 12"Take him, look after him well and do him no harm, but deal with him as he may ask you." 13So Nebuzaradan the captain of the guard, Nebushazban the Rabsaris, Nergal-sharezer the Rabmag, and all the chief officers of the king of Babylon sent 14and took Jeremiah from the court of the guard. They entrusted him to Gedaliah son of Ahikam son of Shaphan to be brought home. So he stayed with his own people.

15 The word of the LORD came to Jeremiah while he was confined in the court of the guard: 16Go and say to Ebed-melech the Ethiopian:b Thus says the LORD of hosts, the God of Israel: I am going to fulfill my words against this city for evil and not for good, and they shall be accomplished in your presence on that day. 17But I will save you on that day, says the LORD, and you shall not be handed over to those whom you dread. 18For I will surely save you, and you shall not fall by the sword; but you shall have your life as a prize of war, because you have trusted in me, says the LORD.

39.1–18: In straightforward prose, this chapter recounts the Babylonian invasion of Jerusalem and its

---

a This clause has been transposed from 38.28
b Or *Nubian;* Heb *Cushite*

consequences for Zedekiah and Jeremiah. The narrative's major interest is not the siege but the king's cowardice, escape, and capture, and Jeremiah's release. **3:** Babylonian officials have taken possession of the city and sit at the gate to govern. **9:** After Zedekiah and his family meet a horrible fate, the Babylonian captain distributes occupied land to the poor, perhaps to gain their support. **11–18:** Jeremiah gains Babylonian favor and is released to the protection of Gedaliah, the Judean governor appointed by Babylonians to replace the king. Jeremiah's release has symbolic meaning. He is a model of obedience in captivity, and he returns home as exiles hope to do. **18:** Because he trusts, he gains his life *as a prize of war*.

Chaos

Chs. 40–41: These chapters describe events in Judah after the invasion.

40 The word that came to Jeremiah from the LORD after Nebuzaradan the captain of the guard had let him go from Ramah, when he took him bound in fetters along with all the captives of Jerusalem and Judah who were being exiled to Babylon. ²The captain of the guard took Jeremiah and said to him, "The LORD your God threatened this place with this disaster; ³and now the LORD has brought it about, and has done as he said, because all of you sinned against the LORD and did not obey his voice. Therefore this thing has come upon you. ⁴Now look, I have just released you today from the fetters on your hands. If you wish to come with me to Babylon, come, and I will take good care of you; but if you do not wish to come with me to Babylon, you need not come. See, the whole land is before you; go wherever you think it good and right to go. ⁵If you remain,ᵃ then return to Gedaliah son of Ahikam son of Shaphan, whom the king of Babylon appointed governor of the towns of Judah, and stay with him among the people; or go wherever you think it right to go." So the captain of the guard gave him an allowance of food and a present, and let him go. ⁶Then Jeremiah went to Gedaliah son of Ahikam at Mizpah, and stayed with him among the people who were left in the land.

7 When all the leaders of the forces in the open country and their troops heard that the king of Babylon had appointed Gedaliah son of Ahikam governor in the land, and had committed to him men, women, and children, those of the poorest of the land who had not been taken into exile to Babylon, ⁸they went to Gedaliah at Mizpah—Ishmael son of Nethaniah, Johanan son of Kareah, Seraiah son of Tanhumeth, the sons of Ephai the Netophathite, Jezaniah son of the Maacathite, they and their troops. ⁹Gedaliah son of Ahikam son of Shaphan swore to them and their troops, saying, "Do not be afraid to serve the Chaldeans. Stay in the land and serve the king of Babylon, and it shall go well with you. ¹⁰As for me, I am staying at Mizpah to represent you before the Chaldeans who come to us; but as for you, gather wine and summer fruits and oil, and store them in your vessels, and live in the towns that you have taken over." ¹¹Likewise, when all the Judeans who were in Moab and among the Ammonites and in Edom and in other lands heard that the king of Babylon had left a remnant in Judah and had appointed Gedaliah son of Ahikam son of Shaphan as governor over them, ¹²then all the Judeans returned from all the places to which they had been scattered and came to the land of Judah, to Gedaliah at Mizpah; and they gathered wine and summer fruits in great abundance.

13 Now Johanan son of Kareah and all the leaders of the forces in the open country came to Gedaliah at Mizpah ¹⁴and said to him, "Are you at all aware that Baalis king of the Ammonites has sent Ishmael son of Nethaniah to take your life?" But Gedaliah son of Ahikam would not believe them. ¹⁵Then Johanan son of Kareah spoke secretly to Gedaliah at Mizpah, "Please let me go and kill Ishmael son of Nethaniah, and no one else will know. Why should he take your life, so that all the Judeans who are gathered around you would be scattered, and the remnant of Judah would perish?" ¹⁶But Gedaliah son of Ahikam said to Johanan son of Kareah, "Do not do such a thing, for you are telling a lie about Ishmael."

a Syr: Meaning of Heb uncertain

40.1–16. 1–6: The Babylonian captain allows Jeremiah to remain in the land, even though Jeremiah had described those who stayed in Judah as bad figs (ch. 24). 7–12: Under Gedaliah's governance there is peace in the land, and survivors are urged to submit to Babylon. 13–16: A plot against Gedaliah is reported to him, but Gedaliah cannot believe that Ishmael, a member of the royal family, would be capable of such disloyalty.

41 In the seventh month, Ishmael son of Nethaniah son of Elishama, of the royal family, one of the chief officers of the king, came with ten men to Gedaliah son of Ahikam, at Mizpah. As they ate bread together there at Mizpah, ²Ishmael son of Nethaniah and the ten men with him got up and struck down Gedaliah son of Ahikam son of Shaphan with the sword and killed him, because the king of Babylon had appointed him governor in the land. ³Ishmael also killed all the Judeans who were with Gedaliah at Mizpah, and the Chaldean soldiers who happened to be there.

4 On the day after the murder of Gedaliah, before anyone knew of it, ⁵eighty men arrived from Shechem and Shiloh and Samaria, with their beards shaved and their clothes torn, and their bodies gashed, bringing grain offerings and incense to present at the temple of the LORD. ⁶And Ishmael son of Nethaniah came out from Mizpah to meet them, weeping as he came. As he met them, he said to them, "Come to Gedaliah son of Ahikam." ⁷When they reached the middle of the city, Ishmael son of Nethaniah and the men with him slaughtered them, and threw them*ᵃ* into a cistern. ⁸But there were ten men among them who said to Ishmael, "Do not kill us, for we have stores of wheat, barley, oil, and honey hidden in the fields." So he refrained, and did not kill them along with their companions.

9 Now the cistern into which Ishmael had thrown all the bodies of the men whom he had struck down was the large cisternᵇ that King Asa had made for defense against King Baasha of Israel; Ishmael son of Nethaniah filled that cistern with those whom he had killed. ¹⁰Then Ishmael took captive all the rest of the people who were in Mizpah, the king's daughters and all the people who were left at Mizpah, whom Nebuzaradan, the captain of the guard, had committed to Gedaliah son of Ahikam. Ishmael son of Nethaniah took them captive and set out to cross over to the Ammonites.

11 But when Johanan son of Kareah and all the leaders of the forces with him heard of all the crimes that Ishmael son of Nethaniah had done, ¹²they took all their men and went to fight against Ishmael son of Nethaniah. They came upon him at the great pool that is in Gibeon. ¹³And when all the people who were with Ishmael saw Johanan son of Kareah and all the leaders of the forces with him, they were glad. ¹⁴So all the people whom Ishmael had carried away captive from Mizpah turned around and came back, and went to Johanan son of Kareah. ¹⁵But Ishmael son of Nethaniah escaped from Johanan with eight men, and went to the Ammonites. ¹⁶Then Johanan son of Kareah and all the leaders of the forces with him took all the rest of the people whom Ishmael son of Nethaniah had carried away captiveᶜ from Mizpah after he had slain Gedaliah son of Ahikam—soldiers, women, children, and eunuchs, whom Johanan brought back from Gibeon.ᵈ ¹⁷And they set out, and stopped at Geruth Chimham near Bethlehem, intending to go to Egypt ¹⁸because of the Chaldeans; for they were afraid of them, because Ishmael son of Nethaniah had killed Gedaliah son of Ahikam, whom the king of Babylon had made governor over the land.

41.1–18: During a meal, Ishmael and ten men massacre Gedaliah and everyone with him, as well as pilgrims on their way to the Temple.⋆ They desecrate their bodies by dumping them into a cistern and take the remaining survivors as hostages. Johanan, one of the Judeans, gathers forces and rescues the hostages. The bloodbath gives the Judeans reason to fear the Chaldeans and sets off the events narrated in the next chapters.

a Syr: Heb lacks *and threw them*; compare verse 9
b Gk: Heb *whom he had killed by the hand of Gedaliah*
c Cn: Heb *whom he recovered from Ishmael son of Nethaniah*   d Meaning of Heb uncertain

Emigration to Egypt

Chs. 42–44: Jeremiah is an ally of Babylon and an opponent of Egypt in the international power struggles that afflict Judah at this time. These chapters reflect anti-Egyptian viewpoints. They accuse survivors who go to Egypt of refusing to listen and engaging in idolatry.* Paradoxically, Jeremiah and his scribe* Baruch are also forced into exile.

42 Then all the commanders of the forces, and Johanan son of Kareah and Azariah*a* son of Hoshaiah, and all the people from the least to the greatest, approached ²the prophet Jeremiah and said, "Be good enough to listen to our plea, and pray to the LORD your God for us—for all this remnant. For there are only a few of us left out of many, as your eyes can see. ³Let the LORD your God show us where we should go and what we should do." ⁴The prophet Jeremiah said to them, "Very well! I am going to pray to the LORD your God as you request, and whatever the LORD answers you I will tell you; I will keep nothing back from you." ⁵They in their turn said to Jeremiah, "May the LORD be a true and faithful witness against us if we do not act according to everything that the LORD your God sends us through you. ⁶Whether it is good or bad, we will obey the voice of the LORD our God to whom we are sending you, in order that it may go well with us when we obey the voice of the LORD our God."

7 At the end of ten days the word of the LORD came to Jeremiah. ⁸Then he summoned Johanan son of Kareah and all the commanders of the forces who were with him, and all the people from the least to the greatest, ⁹and said to them, "Thus says the LORD, the God of Israel, to whom you sent me to present your plea before him: ¹⁰If you will only remain in this land, then I will build you up and not pull you down; I will plant you, and not pluck you up; for I am sorry for the disaster that I have brought upon you. ¹¹Do not be afraid of the king of Babylon, as you have been; do not be afraid of him, says the LORD, for I am with you, to save you and to rescue you from his hand. ¹²I will grant you mercy, and he will have mercy on you

and restore you to your native soil. ¹³But if you continue to say, 'We will not stay in this land,' thus disobeying the voice of the LORD your God ¹⁴and saying, 'No, we will go to the land of Egypt, where we shall not see war, or hear the sound of the trumpet, or be hungry for bread, and there we will stay,' ¹⁵then hear the word of the LORD, O remnant of Judah. Thus says the LORD of hosts, the God of Israel: If you are determined to enter Egypt and go to settle there, ¹⁶then the sword that you fear shall overtake you there, in the land of Egypt; and the famine that you dread shall follow close after you into Egypt; and there you shall die. ¹⁷All the people who have determined to go to Egypt to settle there shall die by the sword, by famine, and by pestilence; they shall have no remnant or survivor from the disaster that I am bringing upon them.

18 "For thus says the LORD of hosts, the God of Israel: Just as my anger and my wrath were poured out on the inhabitants of Jerusalem, so my wrath will be poured out on you when you go to Egypt. You shall become an object of execration and horror, of cursing and ridicule. You shall see this place no more. ¹⁹The LORD has said to you, O remnant of Judah, Do not go to Egypt. Be well aware that I have warned you today ²⁰that you have made a fatal mistake. For you yourselves sent me to the LORD your God, saying, 'Pray for us to the LORD our God, and whatever the LORD our God says, tell us and we will do it.' ²¹So I have told you today, but you have not obeyed the voice of the LORD your God in anything that he sent me to tell you. ²²Be well aware, then, that you shall die by the sword, by famine, and by pestilence in the place where you desire to go and settle."

42.1–22: Survivors of Ishmael's attack go to Jeremiah to make intercession on their behalf. Should they go to Egypt? They promise to obey his word. **10:** Jeremiah replies that they must *remain* in Judah. Then God will *rebuild* them after the *disaster,* for which God has repented. **18–22:** There is no escape from Babylon.

a Gk: Heb *Jezaniah*

43

When Jeremiah finished speaking to all the people all these words of the LORD their God, with which the LORD their God had sent him to them, 2Azariah son of Hoshaiah and Johanan son of Kareah and all the other insolent men said to Jeremiah, "You are telling a lie. The LORD our God did not send you to say, 'Do not go to Egypt to settle there'; 3but Baruch son of Neriah is inciting you against us, to hand us over to the Chaldeans, in order that they may kill us or take us into exile in Babylon." 4So Johanan son of Kareah and all the commanders of the forces and all the people did not obey the voice of the LORD, to stay in the land of Judah. 5But Johanan son of Kareah and all the commanders of the forces took all the remnant of Judah who had returned to settle in the land of Judah from all the nations to which they had been driven— 6the men, the women, the children, the princesses, and everyone whom Nebuzaradan the captain of the guard had left with Gedaliah son of Ahikam son of Shaphan; also the prophet Jeremiah and Baruch son of Neriah. 7And they came into the land of Egypt, for they did not obey the voice of the LORD. And they arrived at Tahpanhes.

8 Then the word of the LORD came to Jeremiah in Tahpanhes: 9Take some large stones in your hands, and bury them in the clay pavement[a] that is at the entrance to Pharaoh's palace in Tahpanhes. Let the Judeans see you do it, 10and say to them, Thus says the LORD of hosts, the God of Israel: I am going to send and take my servant King Nebuchadrezzar of Babylon, and he[b] will set his throne above these stones that I have buried, and he will spread his royal canopy over them. 11He shall come and ravage the land of Egypt, giving

> those who are destined for pestilence, to
>   pestilence,
> and those who are destined for
>   captivity, to captivity,
> and those who are destined for the
>   sword, to the sword.

12He[c] shall kindle a fire in the temples of the gods of Egypt; and he shall burn them and carry them away captive; and he shall pick clean the land of Egypt, as a shepherd picks his cloak clean of vermin; and he shall depart from there safely. 13He shall break the obelisks of Heliopolis, which is in the land of Egypt; and the temples of the gods of Egypt he shall burn with fire.

43.1–13: *Johanan,* the hero of ch. 42, turns insolent and accuses Jeremiah of lying and Baruch of inciting him. Both are forced into Egyptian exile against their will. They escape none of the pain of the exiles in Babylon, for they too leave their homeland as captives. **8–13:** Jeremiah directs a symbolic action of burying stones. Nebuchadrezzar will come and set up his rule there and destroy Egyptian deities.

44

The word that came to Jeremiah for all the Judeans living in the land of Egypt, at Migdol, at Tahpanhes, at Memphis, and in the land of Pathros, 2Thus says the LORD of hosts, the God of Israel: You yourselves have seen all the disaster that I have brought on Jerusalem and on all the towns of Judah. Look at them; today they are a desolation, without an inhabitant in them, 3because of the wickedness that they committed, provoking me to anger, in that they went to make offerings and serve other gods that they had not known, neither they, nor you, nor your ancestors. 4Yet I persistently sent to you all my servants the prophets, saying, "I beg you not to do this abominable thing that I hate!" 5But they did not listen or incline their ear, to turn from their wickedness and make no offerings to other gods. 6So my wrath and my anger were poured out and kindled in the towns of Judah and in the streets of Jerusalem; and they became a waste and a desolation, as they still are today. 7And now thus says the LORD God of hosts, the God of Israel: Why are you doing such great harm to yourselves, to cut off man and woman, child and infant, from the midst of Judah, leaving yourselves without a remnant? 8Why do you provoke me to anger with the works of your hands, making offerings to other gods in the land of Egypt where you have come to settle? Will you be

a Meaning of Heb uncertain   *b* Gk Syr: Heb I
c Gk Syr Vg: Heb I

cut off and become an object of cursing and ridicule among all the nations of the earth? 9Have you forgotten the crimes of your ancestors, of the kings of Judah, of their*a* wives, your own crimes and those of your wives, which they committed in the land of Judah and in the streets of Jerusalem? 10They have shown no contrition or fear to this day, nor have they walked in my law and my statutes that I set before you and before your ancestors.

44.1–30: Idolatry.* Jeremiah delivers a final prophetic message to Judeans living in Egypt. **1–6:** The fall of Judah and Jerusalem was caused by the people's failure to listen. Those who escaped to Egypt will suffer a similar fate, if they do not leave idolatry aside.

11 Therefore thus says the LORD of hosts, the God of Israel: I am determined to bring disaster on you, to bring all Judah to an end. 12I will take the remnant of Judah who are determined to come to the land of Egypt to settle, and they shall perish, everyone; in the land of Egypt they shall fall; by the sword and by famine they shall perish; from the least to the greatest, they shall die by the sword and by famine; and they shall become an object of execration and horror, of cursing and ridicule. 13I will punish those who live in the land of Egypt, as I have punished Jerusalem, with the sword, with famine, and with pestilence, 14so that none of the remnant of Judah who have come to settle in the land of Egypt shall escape or survive or return to the land of Judah. Although they long to go back to live there, they shall not go back, except some fugitives.

15 Then all the men who were aware that their wives had been making offerings to other gods, and all the women who stood by, a great assembly, all the people who lived in Pathros in the land of Egypt, answered Jeremiah: 16"As for the word that you have spoken to us in the name of the LORD, we are not going to listen to you. 17Instead, we will do everything that we have vowed, make offerings to the queen of heaven and pour out libations to her, just as we and our ancestors, our kings and our officials, used to do in the towns of Judah and in the streets of Jerusa-

lem. We used to have plenty of food, and prospered, and saw no misfortune. 18But from the time we stopped making offerings to the queen of heaven and pouring out libations to her, we have lacked everything and have perished by the sword and by famine." 19And the women said,*b* "Indeed we will go on making offerings to the queen of heaven and pouring out libations to her; do you think that we made cakes for her, marked with her image, and poured out libations to her without our husbands' being involved?"

20 Then Jeremiah said to all the people, men and women, all the people who were giving him this answer: 21"As for the offerings that you made in the towns of Judah and in the streets of Jerusalem, you and your ancestors, your kings and your officials, and the people of the land, did not the LORD remember them? Did it not come into his mind? 22The LORD could no longer bear the sight of your evil doings, the abominations that you committed; therefore your land became a desolation and a waste and a curse, without inhabitant, as it is to this day. 23It is because you burned offerings, and because you sinned against the LORD and did not obey the voice of the LORD or walk in his law and in his statutes and in his decrees, that this disaster has befallen you, as is still evident today."

24 Jeremiah said to all the people and all the women, "Hear the word of the LORD, all you Judeans who are in the land of Egypt, 25Thus says the LORD of hosts, the God of Israel: You and your wives have accomplished in deeds what you declared in words, saying, 'We are determined to perform the vows that we have made, to make offerings to the queen of heaven and to pour out libations to her.' By all means, keep your vows and make your libations! 26Therefore hear the word of the LORD, all you Judeans who live in the land of Egypt: Lo, I swear by my great name, says the LORD, that my name shall no longer be pronounced on the lips of

a Heb *his*   *b* Compare Syr: Heb lacks *And the women said* any of the people of Judah in all the land of Egypt, saying, 'As the Lord GOD lives.' 27I am going to watch over them for harm and not for good; all the people of Judah who are in the land of Egypt shall perish by the sword and by famine, until not one is left. 28And those who escape the sword shall return from the land of Egypt to the land of Judah, few in number; and all the remnant of Judah, who have come to the land of Egypt to settle, shall know whose words will stand, mine or theirs! 29This shall be the sign to you, says the LORD, that I am going to punish you in this place, in order that you may know that my words against you will surely be carried out: 30Thus says the LORD, I am going to give Pharaoh Hophra, king of Egypt, into the hands of his enemies, those who seek his life, just as I gave King Zedekiah of Judah into the hand of King Nebuchadrezzar of Babylon, his enemy who sought his life."

44.15–30: Worship of the queen of heaven exemplifies the idolatry of the exiles. Jeremiah had accused the Judean families of worshipping this astral deity in the Temple sermon (7.1–8.3). Here Jeremiah accuses the women as central participants in this worship. The women, however, speak from their experience. When they stopped worshipping the goddess, their world fell apart. **26:** Because of its idolatry, the believing community will disappear in Egypt. They have no future because they turned from God.

45 The word that the prophet Jeremiah spoke to Baruch son of Neriah, when he wrote these words in a scroll at the dictation of Jeremiah, in the fourth year of King Jehoiakim son of Josiah of Judah: 2Thus says the LORD, the God of Israel, to you, O Baruch: 3You said, "Woe is me! The LORD has added sorrow to my pain; I am weary with my groaning, and I find no rest." 4Thus you shall say to him, "Thus says the LORD: I am going to break down what I have built, and pluck up what I have planted—that is, the whole land. 5And you, do you seek great things for yourself? Do not seek them; for I am going to bring disaster upon all flesh, says the LORD; but I will give you your life as a prize of war in every place to which you may go."

45.1–5: Baruch's role. Chapter 45 brings the Baruch account to a close and also concludes chs. 26–44. **2–3:** Baruch utters a lament* of sorrow, pain, and weariness that follows curses upon his own people in ch. 44. **4:** God replies through Jeremiah with language used frequently throughout the book, *I am going to break down and pluck up the whole land.* **5:** Suffering cannot be avoided, but Baruch will survive. He will gain *his life as a prize of war.* With Baruch's lament and the divine response to it, the main part of the book ends on a somber note. Baruch is a weary survivor who is promised only his life. The idealized vision of chs. 30–33 is far from sight. But according to chs. 37–45, Jeremiah, Baruch, Ebed-melech, and a remnant survive. Survivors must obey Jeremiah's prophetic message as conveyed in this book.

ORACLES* AGAINST THE NATIONS

Chs. 46–51: These poems, confirming the survival of those who wait in obedient faithfulness, consist of a collection of prophetic poems in judgment against Israel's enemies. Their location at the end of the book gives meaning to Jeremiah's title "prophet* to the nations" (1.5, 10). God's voice in these poems announces that foreign nations had been instruments of divine punishment of Israel and Judah, but soon tables will turn to create a new future. These oracles address Israel's neighbors first (chs. 46–49) and close with oracles against Babylon (chs. 50–51).

46 The word of the LORD that came to the prophet Jeremiah concerning the nations.

2 Concerning Egypt, about the army of Pharaoh Neco, king of Egypt, which was by the river Euphrates at Carchemish and which King Nebuchadrezzar of Babylon defeated in the fourth year of King Jehoiakim son of Josiah of Judah:

3 Prepare buckler and shield,
    and advance for battle!
4 Harness the horses;
    mount the steeds!
  Take your stations with your helmets,
    whet your lances,
    put on your coats of mail!
5 Why do I see them terrified?
    They have fallen back;
  their warriors are beaten down,

and have fled in haste.
They do not look back—
    terror is all around!
                        says the LORD.
6 The swift cannot flee away,
    nor can the warrior escape;
in the north by the river Euphrates
    they have stumbled and fallen.

7 Who is this, rising like the Nile,
    like rivers whose waters surge?
8 Egypt rises like the Nile,
    like rivers whose waters surge.
It said, Let me rise, let me cover the
        earth,
    let me destroy cities and their
        inhabitants.
9 Advance, O horses,
    and dash madly, O chariots!
Let the warriors go forth:
    Ethiopia*a* and Put who carry
        the shield,
    the Ludim, who draw*b* the bow.
10 That day is the day of the Lord GOD of
        hosts,
    a day of retribution,
    to gain vindication from his foes.
The sword shall devour and be sated,
    and drink its fill of their blood.
For the Lord GOD of hosts holds
        a sacrifice
in the land of the north by the river
        Euphrates.
11 Go up to Gilead, and take balm,
    O virgin daughter Egypt!
In vain you have used many
        medicines;
    there is no healing for you.
12 The nations have heard of your shame,
    and the earth is full of your cry;
for warrior has stumbled against
        warrior;
    both have fallen together.

46.1–25: Against Egypt. These poems bring to poetic
fulfillment Jeremiah's prophecies to the Judean remnant that escaped to Egypt (chs. 43–44). Babylon will
destroy their safe haven. 2: The date of the first poem
in the *fourth year of Jehoiakim* sets this prophecy in
the years when Babylon destroyed Egyptian power in
the region. This means that Jeremiah's word of the de-

struction of Egypt came much earlier than the events
themselves. For survivors in exile, the date indicates
that God's plans have long been in place and that
there is hope for the future. **3–12:** A battle scene, similar to scenes of the cosmic battle with the foe from
the north in chs. 4–6 and 8–10, opens the poem. God
calls troops to prepare for war. **7–12:** The Nile River,
famous for its flooding, resembles the rise and fall of
Egypt. Egypt cannot possible defend itself since, in this
poetic vision, the enemy is divine.

---

13 The word that the LORD spoke to the
prophet Jeremiah about the coming of King
Nebuchadrezzar of Babylon to attack the
land of Egypt:
14 Declare in Egypt, and proclaim
        in Migdol;
    proclaim in Memphis and Tahpanhes;
Say, "Take your stations and be ready,
    for the sword shall devour those
        around you."
15 Why has Apis fled?*c*
    Why did your bull not stand?
    —because the LORD thrust
        him down.
16 Your multitude stumbled*d* and fell,
    and one said to another,*e*
"Come, let us go back to our
        own people
    and to the land of our birth,
    because of the destroying sword."
17 Give Pharaoh, king of Egypt, the name
    "Braggart who missed his chance."

18 As I live, says the King,
    whose name is the LORD of hosts,
one is coming
    like Tabor among the mountains,
    and like Carmel by the sea.
19 Pack your bags for exile,
    sheltered daughter Egypt!
For Memphis shall become a waste,
    a ruin, without inhabitant.

20 A beautiful heifer is Egypt—
    a gadfly from the north lights upon
        her.

a Or Nubia; Heb Cush   *b* Cn: Heb who grasp,
who draw   *c* Gk: Heb Why was it swept away
d Gk: Meaning of Heb uncertain   *e* Gk: Heb and fell
one to another and they said

21 Even her mercenaries in her midst
        are like fatted calves;
    they too have turned and fled
            together,
        they did not stand;
    for the day of their calamity has come
            upon them,
        the time of their punishment.

22 She makes a sound like a snake gliding
            away;
    for her enemies march in force,
    and come against her with axes,
        like those who fell trees.

23 They shall cut down her forest,
                            says the LORD,
        though it is impenetrable,
    because they are more numerous
            than locusts;
        they are without number.

24 Daughter Egypt shall be put to shame;
        she shall be handed over to a people
            from the north.

25 The LORD of hosts, the God of Israel,
said: See, I am bringing punishment upon
Amon of Thebes, and Pharaoh, and Egypt
and her gods and her kings, upon Pharaoh
and those who trust in him. 26I will hand
them over to those who seek their life, to
King Nebuchadrezzar of Babylon and his officers. Afterward Egypt shall be inhabited as
in the days of old, says the LORD.

27 But as for you, have no fear, my servant
            Jacob,
        and do not be dismayed, O Israel;
    for I am going to save you from
            far away,
        and your offspring from the land of
            their captivity.
    Jacob shall return and have quiet and
            ease,
        and no one shall make him afraid.

28 As for you, have no fear, my servant
            Jacob,
                            says the LORD,
        for I am with you.
    I will make an end of all the nations
        among which I have banished you,
    but I will not make an end of you!

I will chastise you in just measure,
    and I will by no means leave you
        unpunished.

46.13–28. 13: A prose comment identifies the human enemy as Nebuchadrezzar, King of Babylon. **14–25:** The battle, however, is really between *Apis,* the bull-god of Egypt, and the God of Israel. **17:** Egypt's king is here called *Braggart* because he boasts about power he never really had. **20–24:** Female metaphors* describe Egypt's vulnerability and shame. Egypt's crimes are pride and false claims to power, but the poem assures the exiles that its God rules the nations. **27–28:** God addresses Israel with words of comfort. Israel is to put aside fear. In their exile God will sustain them and punish their enemies.

47 The word of the LORD that came to
    the prophet Jeremiah concerning the
Philistines, before Pharaoh attacked Gaza:

2 Thus says the LORD:
    See, waters are rising out of the north
        and shall become an overflowing
            torrent;
    they shall overflow the land and all that
            fills it,
        the city and those who live in it.
    People shall cry out,
        and all the inhabitants of the land
            shall wail.

3 At the noise of the stamping of the
            hoofs of his stallions,
        at the clatter of his chariots, at the
            rumbling of their wheels,
    parents do not turn back for children,
        so feeble are their hands,

4 because of the day that is coming
        to destroy all the Philistines,
    to cut off from Tyre and Sidon
        every helper that remains.
    For the LORD is destroying the
            Philistines,
        the remnant of the coastland
            of Caphtor.

5 Baldness has come upon Gaza,
        Ashkelon is silenced.
    O remnant of their power!ᵃ
        How long will you gash yourselves?

a Gk: Heb *their valley*

6 Ah, sword of the LORD!
　　How long until you are quiet?
　Put yourself into your scabbard,
　　rest and be still!
7 How can it[a] be quiet,
　　when the LORD has given it
　　　an order?
　Against Ashkelon and against the
　　seashore—
　　there he has appointed it.

47.1–7: Against the Philistines. There are historical difficulties with this poem, since Philistia was not a major enemy of Israel during this time. Though its city-states along the seacoast continued for a long time, they ceased to exist as a larger unity during the Babylonian period. In the poetic world of this poem, however, God is the enemy bringing an attacker. **6–7:** The poem ends with the "song of the sword" in which the poet addresses God's weapon and begs it to be still, but the sword is unable to deny God's commands.

---

48 Concerning Moab.

Thus says the LORD of hosts, the God of Israel:
　Alas for Nebo, it is laid waste!
　　Kiriathaim is put to shame, it
　　　is taken;
　the fortress is put to shame and broken
　　down;
2　the renown of Moab is no more.
　In Heshbon they planned evil against
　　her:
　"Come, let us cut her off from being
　　a nation!"
　You also, O Madmen, shall be brought
　　to silence;[b]
　the sword shall pursue you.

3 Hark! a cry from Horonaim,
　　"Desolation and great destruction!"
4 "Moab is destroyed!"
　　her little ones cry out.
5 For at the ascent of Luhith
　　they go[c] up weeping bitterly;
　for at the descent of Horonaim
　　they have heard the distressing cry of
　　anguish.
6 Flee! Save yourselves!
　　Be like a wild ass[d] in the desert!

7 Surely, because you trusted in your
　　strongholds[e] and your treasures,
　you also shall be taken;
　Chemosh shall go out into exile,
　　with his priests and his attendants.
8 The destroyer shall come upon every
　　town,
　　and no town shall escape;
　the valley shall perish,
　　and the plain shall be destroyed,
　　as the LORD has spoken.

9 Set aside salt for Moab,
　　for she will surely fall;
　her towns shall become a desolation,
　　with no inhabitant in them.

10 Accursed is the one who is slack in doing the work of the LORD; and accursed is the one who keeps back the sword from bloodshed.

11　Moab has been at ease from his youth,
　　settled like wine[f] on its dregs;
　he has not been emptied from vessel to
　　vessel,
　　nor has he gone into exile;
　therefore his flavor has remained
　　and his aroma is unspoiled.
12 Therefore, the time is surely coming, says the LORD, when I shall send to him decanters to decant him, and empty his vessels, and break his[g] jars in pieces. 13 Then Moab shall be ashamed of Chemosh, as the house of Israel was ashamed of Bethel, their confidence.

48.1–47: Against Moab. This long poem concerns a traditional and bitter enemy and neighbor of Israel. **1–2:** God announces an invasion of Moab, whereupon a voice cries in alarm. Moab's sin is arrogance arising from its wealth and power. **7:** *Chemosh* was the chief God of Moab. **11–12:** Because Moab was known for its production of grapes, the poem describes Moab's complacency in terms of *wine* about to be poured out.

---

14 How can you say, "We are heroes
　　and mighty warriors"?

a Gk Vg: Heb *you*　　*b* The place-name *Madmen* sounds like the Hebrew verb *to be silent*　　*c* Cn: Heb *he goes*
d Gk Aquila: Heb *like Aroer*　　*e* Gk: Heb *works*
f Heb lacks *like wine*　　*g* Gk Aquila: Heb *their*

15 The destroyer of Moab and his towns
        has come up,
    and the choicest of his young men
        have gone down to slaughter,
    says the King, whose name is the
        LORD of hosts.
16 The calamity of Moab is near at hand
    and his doom approaches swiftly.
17 Mourn over him, all you his neighbors,
    and all who know his name;
    say, "How the mighty scepter is broken,
        the glorious staff!"

18 Come down from glory,
        and sit on the parched ground,
        enthroned daughter Dibon!
    For the destroyer of Moab has come up
        against you;
    he has destroyed your strongholds.
19 Stand by the road and watch,
        you inhabitant of Aroer!
    Ask the man fleeing and the woman
        escaping;
    say, "What has happened?"
20 Moab is put to shame, for it is broken
        down;
    wail and cry!
    Tell it by the Arnon,
        that Moab is laid waste.

21 Judgment has come upon the ta-
bleland, upon Holon, and Jahzah, and
Mephaath, 22 and Dibon, and Nebo, and
Beth-diblathaim, 23 and Kiriathaim, and
Beth-gamul, and Beth-meon, 24 and Kerioth,
and Bozrah, and all the towns of the land of
Moab, far and near. 25 The horn of Moab is
cut off, and his arm is broken, says the LORD.

26 Make him drunk, because he magnified himself against the LORD; let Moab wallow in his vomit; he too shall become a
laughingstock. 27 Israel was a laughingstock
for you, though he was not caught among
thieves; but whenever you spoke of him you
shook your head!

48.14–27. 18–20: God warns the capital city, *Dibon*,
addressed as a woman, that she too is under attack.
21–27: The cities of Moab are about to be destroyed.

28 Leave the towns, and live on the rock,
        O inhabitants of Moab!
    Be like the dove that nests
        on the sides of the mouth of a gorge.
29 We have heard of the pride of Moab—
        he is very proud—
    of his loftiness, his pride, and his
        arrogance,
    and the haughtiness of his heart.
30 I myself know his insolence, says the
        LORD;
    his boasts are false,
    his deeds are false.
31 Therefore I wail for Moab;
    I cry out for all Moab;
    for the people of Kir-heres I mourn.
32 More than for Jazer I weep for you,
        O vine of Sibmah!
    Your branches crossed over the sea,
        reached as far as Jazer;[a]
    upon your summer fruits and
        your vintage
    the destroyer has fallen.
33 Gladness and joy have been taken away
        from the fruitful land of Moab;
    I have stopped the wine from the wine
        presses;
    no one treads them with shouts of joy;
    the shouting is not the shout of joy.

48.28–33. 28–30: God next addresses the residents
of Moab, urging them to flee and accusing them of
false pride. **31–33:** Surprisingly, God wails for Moab.

34 Heshbon and Elealeh cry out;[b] as far
as Jahaz they utter their voice, from Zoar to
Horonaim and Eglath-shelishiyah. For even
the waters of Nimrim have become desolate.
35 And I will bring to an end in Moab, says
the LORD, those who offer sacrifice at a high
place and make offerings to their gods.
36 Therefore my heart moans for Moab like
a flute, and my heart moans like a flute for
the people of Kir-heres; for the riches they
gained have perished.

37 For every head is shaved and every
beard cut off; on all the hands there are
gashes, and on the loins sackcloth. 38 On all

---

a Two Mss and Isa 16.8: MT *the sea of Jazer*
b Cn: Heb *From the cry of Heshbon to Elealeh*

the housetops of Moab and in the squares there is nothing but lamentation; for I have broken Moab like a vessel that no one wants, says the LORD. ³⁹How it is broken! How they wail! How Moab has turned his back in shame! So Moab has become a derision and a horror to all his neighbors.

⁴⁰ For thus says the LORD:
Look, he shall swoop down like
        an eagle,
    and spread his wings against Moab;
⁴¹ the towns^a shall be taken
    and the strongholds seized.
The hearts of the warriors of Moab, on
        that day,
    shall be like the heart of a woman in
        labor.
⁴² Moab shall be destroyed as a people,
    because he magnified himself against
        the LORD.
⁴³ Terror, pit, and trap
    are before you, O inhabitants
        of Moab!
                        says the LORD.
⁴⁴ Everyone who flees from the terror
    shall fall into the pit,
and everyone who climbs out of the pit
    shall be caught in the trap.
For I will bring these things^b
    upon Moab
    in the year of their punishment,
                        says the LORD.

⁴⁵ In the shadow of Heshbon
    fugitives stop exhausted;
for a fire has gone out from Heshbon,
    a flame from the house of Sihon;
it has destroyed the forehead of Moab,
    the scalp of the people of tumult.^c
⁴⁶ Woe to you, O Moab!
    The people of Chemosh have
        perished,
for your sons have been taken captive,
    and your daughters into captivity.
⁴⁷ Yet I will restore the fortunes of Moab
    in the latter days, says the LORD.
Thus far is the judgment on Moab.

48.47: Even more surprising, the poem closes with a divine promise to restore Moab.

49 Concerning the Ammonites.

Thus says the LORD:
    Has Israel no sons?
        Has he no heir?
    Why then has Milcom dispossessed
        Gad,
        and his people settled in its towns?
² Therefore, the time is surely coming,
        says the LORD,
    when I will sound the battle alarm
        against Rabbah of the Ammonites;
    it shall become a desolate mound,
        and its villages shall be burned with
            fire;
    then Israel shall dispossess those who
        dispossessed him,
        says the LORD.

³ Wail, O Heshbon, for Ai is laid waste!
    Cry out, O daughters^d of Rabbah!
Put on sackcloth,
    lament, and slash yourselves with
        whips!^e
For Milcom shall go into exile,
    with his priests and his attendants.
⁴ Why do you boast in your strength?
    Your strength is ebbing,
O faithless daughter.
    You trusted in your treasures,
        saying,
    "Who will attack me?"
⁵ I am going to bring terror upon you,
    says the Lord GOD of hosts,
    from all your neighbors,
and you will be scattered, each
        headlong,
    with no one to gather the fugitives.
6 But afterward I will restore the fortunes
    of the Ammonites, says the LORD.

49.1–39: Against many nations. 1–6: The history of relations between Israel and their neighbors, the *Ammonites,* was bitter (40.13–41.3). They will be punished for land-grabbing, but God will finally restore them as well.

a Or *Kerioth*   *b* Gk Syr: Heb *bring upon it*   *c* Or *of Shaon*   *d* Or *villages*   *e* Cn: Meaning of Heb uncertain

7 Concerning Edom.

Thus says the LORD of hosts:
Is there no longer wisdom in Teman?
Has counsel perished from
the prudent?
Has their wisdom vanished?
8 Flee, turn back, get down low,
inhabitants of Dedan!
For I will bring the calamity of Esau
upon him,
the time when I punish him.
9 If grape-gatherers came to you,
would they not leave gleanings?
If thieves came by night,
even they would pillage only what
they wanted.
10 But as for me, I have stripped
Esau bare,
I have uncovered his hiding places,
and he is not able to conceal himself.
His offspring are destroyed,
his kinsfolk
and his neighbors; and he is
no more.
11 Leave your orphans, I will keep them
alive;
and let your widows trust in me.

12 For thus says the LORD: If those who
do not deserve to drink the cup still have to
drink it, shall you be the one to go unpunished? You shall not go unpunished; you
must drink it. 13 For by myself I have sworn,
says the LORD, that Bozrah shall become an
object of horror and ridicule, a waste, and an
object of cursing; and all her towns shall be
perpetual wastes.
14 I have heard tidings from the LORD,
and a messenger has been sent
among the nations:
"Gather yourselves together and come
against her,
and rise up for battle!"
15 For I will make you least among the
nations,
despised by humankind.
16 The terror you inspire
and the pride of your heart have
deceived you,
you who live in the clefts of the rock,a
who hold the height of the hill.

Although you make your nest as high as
the eagle's,
from there I will bring you down,
says the LORD.
17 Edom shall become an object of
horror; everyone who passes by it will be
horrified and will hiss because of all its disasters. 18 As when Sodom and Gomorrah
and their neighbors were overthrown, says
the LORD, no one shall live there, nor shall
anyone settle in it. 19 Like a lion coming
up from the thickets of the Jordan against
a perennial pasture, I will suddenly chase
Edomb away from it; and I will appoint over
it whomever I choose.c For who is like
me? Who can summon me? Who is the shepherd who can stand before me? 20 Therefore
hear the plan that the LORD has made
against Edom and the purposes that he has
formed against the inhabitants of Teman:
Surely the little ones of the flock shall be
dragged away; surely their fold shall be appalled at their fate. 21 At the sound of their
fall the earth shall tremble; the sound of
their cry shall be heard at the Red Sea.d
22 Look, he shall mount up and swoop down
like an eagle, and spread his wings against
Bozrah, and the heart of the warriors of
Edom in that day shall be like the heart of a
woman in labor.

49.7–22: The Edomites are Israel's neighbors and the
descendants of Jacob's brother, Esau (Gen 36). 7–10:
God will bring calamity upon them and leave only a
remnant of orphans and widows with no future. Their
sin is never named.

23 Concerning Damascus.

Hamath and Arpad are confounded,
for they have heard bad news;
they melt in fear, they are troubled like
the seae
that cannot be quiet.
24 Damascus has become feeble, she
turned to flee,
and panic seized her;

a Or of Sela b Heb him c Or and I will single out
the choicest of his rams: Meaning of Heb uncertain
d Or Sea of Reeds e Cn: Heb there is trouble in the sea

anguish and sorrows have taken hold of
her,
as of a woman in labor.
25 How the famous city is forsaken,[a]
the joyful town![b]
26 Therefore her young men shall fall in
her squares,
and all her soldiers shall be destroyed
in that day,
says the LORD of hosts.
27 And I will kindle a fire at the wall of
Damascus,
and it shall devour the strongholds of
Ben-hadad.

28 Concerning Kedar and the kingdoms
of Hazor that King Nebuchadrezzar of Babylon defeated.

Thus says the LORD:
Rise up, advance against Kedar!
Destroy the people of the east!
29 Take their tents and their flocks,
their curtains and all their goods;
carry off their camels for yourselves,
and a cry shall go up: "Terror is all
around!"
30 Flee, wander far away, hide in
deep places,
O inhabitants of Hazor!
says the LORD.
For King Nebuchadrezzar of Babylon
has made a plan against you
and formed a purpose against you.

31 Rise up, advance against a nation at ease,
that lives secure,
says the LORD,
that has no gates or bars,
that lives alone.
32 Their camels shall become booty,
their herds of cattle a spoil.
I will scatter to every wind
those who have shaven temples,
and I will bring calamity
against them from every side,
says the LORD.
33 Hazor shall become a lair of jackals,
an everlasting waste;
no one shall live there,
nor shall anyone settle in it.

49.23–33. 23–27: *Damascus,* the capital of Syria, will
be destroyed. Again no sin is identified. **28–33:** *Kedar*
and *Hazor,* cities in the north, will be attacked by Nebuchadrezzar and their people will be dispersed.

34 The word of the LORD that came to
the prophet Jeremiah concerning Elam, at
the beginning of the reign of King Zedekiah
of Judah.
35 Thus says the LORD of hosts: I am going to break the bow of Elam, the mainstay
of their might; 36and I will bring upon Elam
the four winds from the four quarters of
heaven; and I will scatter them to all these
winds, and there shall be no nation to which
the exiles from Elam shall not come. 37I will
terrify Elam before their enemies, and before
those who seek their life; I will bring disaster
upon them, my fierce anger, says the LORD.
I will send the sword after them, until I have
consumed them; 38and I will set my throne
in Elam, and destroy their king and officials,
says the LORD.
39 But in the latter days I will restore the
fortunes of Elam, says the LORD.

49.34–39: Elam will be destroyed in a cosmic upheaval, but God will restore their fortunes.

Against Babylon

Chs. 50–51: These poems form a suitable conclusion
to the book. In them the punisher is punished, the
destroyer is destroyed, and the inflictor of pain receives
pain. Although earlier parts of the book interpreted
Babylon as an agent of God to punish Judah, these
poems see Babylon as the aggressor who oppressed
Israel. They portray God as a warrior who sets right the
world's injustices and restores the victims' well-being.
The exiles receive a vision of a future in which they will
be released from their captivity, but there is not yet
energy for wild hope and dancing (chs. 30–33).

50 The word that the LORD spoke concerning Babylon, concerning the
land of the Chaldeans, by the prophet
Jeremiah:
2 Declare among the nations
and proclaim,

*a Vg: Heb is not forsaken b Syr Vg Tg: Heb the town
of my joy*

set up a banner and proclaim,
　do not conceal it, say:
Babylon is taken,
　Bel is put to shame,
　Merodach is dismayed.
Her images are put to shame,
　her idols are dismayed.

3 For out of the north a nation has come up against her; it shall make her land a desolation, and no one shall live in it; both human beings and animals shall flee away.

4 In those days and in that time, says the LORD, the people of Israel shall come, they and the people of Judah together; they shall come weeping as they seek the LORD their God. ⁵They shall ask the way to Zion, with faces turned toward it, and they shall come and join*a* themselves to the LORD by an everlasting covenant that will never be forgotten.

6 My people have been lost sheep; their shepherds have led them astray, turning them away on the mountains; from mountain to hill they have gone, they have forgotten their fold. ⁷All who found them have devoured them, and their enemies have said, "We are not guilty, because they have sinned against the LORD, the true pasture, the LORD, the hope of their ancestors."

8 Flee from Babylon, and go out of the land of the Chaldeans, and be like male goats leading the flock. ⁹For I am going to stir up and bring against Babylon a company of great nations from the land of the north; and they shall array themselves against her; from there she shall be taken. Their arrows are like the arrows of a skilled warrior who does not return empty-handed. ¹⁰Chaldea shall be plundered; all who plunder her shall be sated, says the LORD.

11 Though you rejoice, though you exult,
　O plunderers of my heritage,
though you frisk about like a heifer on
　　the grass,
　and neigh like stallions,
12 your mother shall be utterly shamed,

and she who bore you shall
　be disgraced.
Lo, she shall be the last of the nations,
　a wilderness, dry land, and a desert.
13 Because of the wrath of the LORD she
　　shall not be inhabited,
　but shall be an utter desolation;
everyone who passes by Babylon shall
　　be appalled
　and hiss because of all her wounds.
14 Take up your positions around Babylon,
　　all you that bend the bow;
shoot at her, spare no arrows,
　for she has sinned against the LORD.
15 Raise a shout against her from all sides,
　"She has surrendered;
her bulwarks have fallen,
　her walls are thrown down."
For this is the vengeance of the LORD:
　take vengeance on her,
　do to her as she has done.
16 Cut off from Babylon the sower,
　　and the wielder of the sickle in time
　　　of harvest;
because of the destroying sword
　all of them shall return to their own
　　　people,
　and all of them shall flee to their own
　　　land.

17 Israel is a hunted sheep driven away by lions. First the king of Assyria devoured it, and now at the end King Nebuchadrezzar of Babylon has gnawed its bones. ¹⁸Therefore, thus says the LORD of hosts, the God of Israel: I am going to punish the king of Babylon and his land, as I punished the king of Assyria. ¹⁹I will restore Israel to its pasture, and it shall feed on Carmel and in Bashan, and on the hills of Ephraim and in Gilead its hunger shall be satisfied. ²⁰In those days and at that time, says the LORD, the iniquity of Israel shall be sought, and there shall be none; and the sins of Judah, and none shall be found; for I will pardon the remnant that I have spared.

50.1–20: God's declaration of celebration opens the poem. The phrases express deep feeling in a few

a Gk: Heb *toward it. Come! They shall join*

words. Babylon is taken and her gods are shamed. The agent of destruction is the mythic foe from the north. **4–10:** The fate of Babylon is connected to the fate of Israel, for the coming attack on Babylon will signal the return of Israel and Judah. They will come weeping to seal the covenant* with God. **11–16:** The plunderers will be destroyed; God commands the army to take position. According to this poetry, the victory is already won, so the celebration may begin. **17–20:** God reinterprets Israel's history as a series of attacks upon lost sheep. They are helpless, even if sinners, and they will be pardoned.

21 Go up to the land of Merathaim;*
    go up against her,
and attack the inhabitants of Pekod*
    and utterly destroy the last of them,*
        says the LORD;
    do all that I have commanded you.
22 The noise of battle is in the land,
    and great destruction!
23 How the hammer of the whole earth
    is cut down and broken!
How Babylon has become
    a horror among the nations!
24 You set a snare for yourself and you
       were caught, O Babylon,
    but you did not know it;
you were discovered and seized,
    because you challenged the LORD.
25 The LORD has opened his armory,
    and brought out the weapons of
       his wrath,
for the Lord GOD of hosts has a task
      to do
    in the land of the Chaldeans.
26 Come against her from every
       quarter;
    open her granaries;
pile her up like heaps of grain, and
      destroy her utterly;
    let nothing be left of her.
27 Kill all her bulls,
    let them go down to the slaughter.
Alas for them, their day has come,
    the time of their punishment!

28 Listen! Fugitives and refugees from the land of Babylon are coming to declare in Zion the vengeance of the LORD our God, vengeance for his temple.

29 Summon archers against Babylon, all who bend the bow. Encamp all around her; let no one escape. Repay her according to her deeds; just as she has done, do to her—for she has arrogantly defied the LORD, the Holy One of Israel. 30 Therefore her young men shall fall in her squares, and all her soldiers shall be destroyed on that day, says the LORD.

31 I am against you, O arrogant one,
    says the Lord GOD of hosts;
for your day has come,
    the time when I will punish you.
32 The arrogant one shall stumble and fall,
    with no one to raise him up,
and I will kindle a fire in his cities,
    and it will devour everything around
      him.

33 Thus says the LORD of hosts: The people of Israel are oppressed, and so too are the people of Judah; all their captors have held them fast and refuse to let them go. 34 Their Redeemer is strong; the LORD of hosts is his name. He will surely plead their cause, that he may give rest to the earth, but unrest to the inhabitants of Babylon.

50.21–34: The battle preparations continue and become more vivid. **23–24:** Babylon, the *hammer of the whole earth*, will be cut down despite its great power, for the enemy is God. **28:** Fugitives escape from the city and run to Zion* to announce the changed state of affairs. **31–32:** God accuses Babylon of exceeding its divine commission to punish Judah: Babylon has gone berserk in its violence. Interpretation of international events has turned upside down in this book. Here Israel and Judah are oppressed people, not guilty people. They have a future, and the enemy will be punished for excesses. **34:** *Their Redeemer* will buy back the captives and give rest to the whole earth.

35 A sword against the Chaldeans, says the
    LORD,
  and against the inhabitants of
      Babylon,
  and against her officials and
      her sages!

a Or *of Double Rebellion*   *b* Or *of Punishment*
c Tg: Heb *destroy after them*

36 A sword against the diviners,
    so that they may become fools!
A sword against her warriors,
    so that they may be destroyed!
37 A sword against her*a* horses and against
        her*a* chariots,
    and against all the foreign troops in
        her midst,
    so that they may become women!
A sword against all her treasures,
    that they may be plundered!
38 A drought*b* against her waters,
    that they may be dried up!
For it is a land of images,
    and they go mad over idols.

39 Therefore wild animals shall live with hyenas in Babylon,*c* and ostriches shall inhabit her; she shall never again be peopled, or inhabited for all generations. 40 As when God overthrew Sodom and Gomorrah and their neighbors, says the LORD, so no one shall live there, nor shall anyone settle in her.

41 Look, a people is coming from
        the north;
    a mighty nation and many kings
    are stirring from the farthest parts of
        the earth.
42 They wield bow and spear,
    they are cruel and have no mercy.
The sound of them is like the roaring
        sea;
    they ride upon horses,
set in array as a warrior for battle,
    against you, O daughter Babylon!

43 The king of Babylon heard news
        of them,
    and his hands fell helpless;
anguish seized him,
    pain like that of a woman in labor.

44 Like a lion coming up from the thickets of the Jordan against a perennial pasture, I will suddenly chase them away from her; and I will appoint over her whomever I choose.*d* For who is like me? Who can summon me? Who is the shepherd who can

stand before me? 45 Therefore hear the plan that the LORD has made against Babylon, and the purposes that he has formed against the land of the Chaldeans: Surely the little ones of the flock shall be dragged away; surely their*e* fold shall be appalled at their fate. 46 At the sound of the capture of Babylon the earth shall tremble, and her cry shall be heard among the nations.

50.35–46: A curse-like poem about the *sword* gloats over the reversal of circumstances about to take place. It is as if chanting words about the sword would activate thrusts into the heart of Babylon. Five times the poem brings the sword against some element of Babylonian society. The last verse shifts to drought. The reason for the attack is Babylon's idolatry. ⋆ 41–46: The people from the north approach; they are cruel, noisy, and arrayed for battled against daughter Babylon. The agent of destruction is God, coming like a lion, coming with a plan that will make the earth tremble.

51 Thus says the LORD:
I am going to stir up a destructive
        wind*f*
    against Babylon
    and against the inhabitants of Leb-
        qamai;*g*
2 and I will send winnowers to Babylon,
    and they shall winnow her.
They shall empty her land
    when they come against her from
        every side
    on the day of trouble.
3 Let not the archer bend his bow,
    and let him not array himself in his
        coat of mail.
Do not spare her young men;
    utterly destroy her entire army.
4 They shall fall down slain in the land of
        the Chaldeans,
    and wounded in her streets.
5 Israel and Judah have not been
        forsaken
    by their God, the LORD of hosts,

a Cn: Heb *his*   *b* Another reading is *A sword*
c Heb lacks *in Babylon*   *d* Or *and I will single out the choicest of her rams*: Meaning of Heb uncertain
e Syr Gk Tg Compare 49.20: Heb lacks *their*   *f* Or *stir up the spirit of a destroyer*   *g* *Leb-qamai* is a cryptogram for *Kasdim*, Chaldea

though their land is full of guilt
    before the Holy One of Israel.

6 Flee from the midst of Babylon,
    save your lives, each of you!
Do not perish because of her guilt,
    for this is the time of the LORD's
        vengeance;
    he is repaying her what is due.
7 Babylon was a golden cup in the LORD's
        hand,
    making all the earth drunken;
    the nations drank of her wine,
    and so the nations went mad.
8 Suddenly Babylon has fallen and
        is shattered;
    wail for her!
Bring balm for her wound;
    perhaps she may be healed.
9 We tried to heal Babylon,
    but she could not be healed.
Forsake her, and let each of us go
        to our own country;
for her judgment has reached up
        to heaven
    and has been lifted up even to the
        skies.
10 The LORD has brought forth our
        vindication;
    come, let us declare in Zion
    the work of the LORD our God.

11 Sharpen the arrows!
    Fill the quivers!
The LORD has stirred up the spirit of the
kings of the Medes, because his purpose
concerning Babylon is to destroy it, for that
is the vengeance of the LORD, vengeance for
his temple.
12 Raise a standard against the walls of
        Babylon;
    make the watch strong;
post sentinels;
    prepare the ambushes;
for the LORD has both planned and done
    what he spoke concerning the
        inhabitants of Babylon.
13 You who live by mighty waters,
    rich in treasures,
your end has come,
    the thread of your life is cut.

14 The LORD of hosts has sworn by himself:
    Surely I will fill you with troops like a
        swarm of locusts,
    and they shall raise a shout of victory
        over you.

51.1–64: Flee. The opposing futures of Babylon and Israel continue to echo each other in this chapter. However, for the first time God orders the exiles to flee from Babylon and return to Zion.* God's power dominates these passages to show that God is the sovereign of history. Out of nothing God will create a future that will overturn systems of domination. **1–5:** Speaking in the first person, God plans the siege of Babylon. *I am going to stir up a . . . wind. . . . I will send winnowers.** God is bringing about cosmic upheaval that will destroy Babylonian power. **5:** Despite their guilt, God has not abandoned Israel and Judah. **6–10:** The exiles must flee. Urgent appeals to them to escape from the vengeance about to engulf Babylon open the poem. **8:** Babylon has been like a golden cup in God's hand but now has fallen. A voice calls for healing balm, but it is too late. **9:** The exiles *tried to heal Babylon* but they could not, so they flee to Zion to declare God's work. **11–14:** War preparations continue. God orders armies to make their weapons ready and to *prepare ambushes.* The *Medes,* an empire of the time, will destroy Babylon.

15 It is he who made the earth by
        his power,
    who established the world by
        his wisdom,
    and by his understanding stretched out
        the heavens.
16 When he utters his voice there is a
        tumult of waters in the heavens,
    and he makes the mist rise from the
        ends of the earth.
He makes lightnings for the rain,
    and he brings out the wind from his
        storehouses.
17 Everyone is stupid and without
        knowledge;
    goldsmiths are all put to shame by
        their idols;
    for their images are false,
    and there is no breath in them.
18 They are worthless, a work of delusion;
    at the time of their punishment they
        shall perish.

19 Not like these is the LORD,^a the portion
    of Jacob,
    for he is the one who formed
      all things,
    and Israel is the tribe of his inheritance;
      the LORD of hosts is his name.

20 You are my war club, my weapon of
      battle:
    with you I smash nations;
    with you I destroy kingdoms;
21 with you I smash the horse and its rider;
    with you I smash the chariot and the
      charioteer;
22 with you I smash man and woman;
    with you I smash the old man and the
      boy;
    with you I smash the young man and
      the girl;
23   with you I smash shepherds and their
      flocks;
    with you I smash farmers and
      their teams;
    with you I smash governors and
      deputies.

51.15–23. 15–19: A hymn, perhaps representing the voice of the exiles, praises the Creator, wise and understanding, who made the earth and maintains its natural processes. Compared to the Creator, the *idols* are worthless. They are the lifeless gods of the *goldsmith*. 20–23: Eight times the Creator says to his weapons or his armies, *I smash with you*, creating a rhythmic beat of destruction. Smashed will be nations, peoples, animals, and rulers.

24 I will repay Babylon and all the inhabitants of Chaldea before your very eyes for all the wrong that they have done in Zion, says the LORD.

25 I am against you, O destroying
      mountain,
                 says the LORD,
    that destroys the whole earth;
    I will stretch out my hand against you,
    and roll you down from the crags,
    and make you a burned-out
      mountain.
26 No stone shall be taken from you for a
      corner

and no stone for a foundation,
    but you shall be a perpetual waste,
      says the LORD.
27 Raise a standard in the land,
    blow the trumpet among the nations;
prepare the nations for war against her,
    summon against her the kingdoms,
      Ararat, Minni, and Ashkenaz;
appoint a marshal against her,
    bring up horses like bristling locusts.
28 Prepare the nations for war against her,
    the kings of the Medes, with their
      governors and deputies,
    and every land under their dominion.
29 The land trembles and writhes,
    for the LORD's purposes against
      Babylon stand,
to make the land of Babylon a
      desolation,
    without inhabitant.
30 The warriors of Babylon have given up
      fighting,
    they remain in their strongholds;
their strength has failed,
    they have become women;
    her buildings are set on fire,
    her bars are broken.
31 One runner runs to meet another,
    and one messenger to meet another,
to tell the king of Babylon
    that his city is taken from end to end:
32 the fords have been seized,
    the marshes have been burned with
      fire,
    and the soldiers are in panic.
33 For thus says the LORD of hosts, the
      God of Israel:
Daughter Babylon is like a threshing
      floor
    at the time when it is trodden;
yet a little while
    and the time of her harvest
      will come.

51.24–33: War preparations continue and God promises Babylon, *the destroying mountain,* that it will be attacked.

a Heb lacks *the* LORD

34 "King Nebuchadrezzar of Babylon has
         devoured me,
     he has crushed me;
 he has made me an empty vessel,
     he has swallowed me like a monster;
 he has filled his belly with my
         delicacies,
     he has spewed me out.
35 May my torn flesh be avenged on
         Babylon,"
     the inhabitants of Zion shall say.
 "May my blood be avenged on the
     inhabitants of Chaldea,"
     Jerusalem shall say.
36 Therefore thus says the LORD:
 I am going to defend your cause
     and take vengeance for you.
 I will dry up her sea
     and make her fountain dry;
37 and Babylon shall become a heap
         of ruins,
     a den of jackals,
 an object of horror and of hissing,
     without inhabitant.

38 Like lions they shall roar together;
     they shall growl like lions' whelps.
39 When they are inflamed, I will set out
         their drink
     and make them drunk, until they
         become merry
 and then sleep a perpetual sleep
     and never wake, says the LORD.
40 I will bring them down like lambs to the
         slaughter,
     like rams and goats.

41 How Sheshach[a] is taken,
     the pride of the whole earth seized!
 How Babylon has become
     an object of horror among the
         nations!
42 The sea has risen over Babylon;
     she has been covered by its
         tumultuous waves.
43 Her cities have become an object
         of horror,
     a land of drought and a desert,
 a land in which no one lives,
     and through which no mortal
         passes.

44 I will punish Bel in Babylon,
     and make him disgorge what he has
         swallowed.
 The nations shall no longer stream to him;
     the wall of Babylon has fallen.

51.34–44: More accusations describing Nebuchadrezzar's violence against the people of Zion accumulate. Babylon and its God, Bel, will be drunk and engorged. The superpower is ugly and out of control with its destruction of others.

~~~~~~

45 Come out of her, my people!
     Save your lives, each of you,
     from the fierce anger of the LORD!
46 Do not be fainthearted or fearful
     at the rumors heard in the land—
 one year one rumor comes,
     the next year another,
 rumors of violence in the land
     and of ruler against ruler.

47 Assuredly, the days are coming
     when I will punish the images
         of Babylon;
 her whole land shall be put to shame,
     and all her slain shall fall in
         her midst.
48 Then the heavens and the earth,
     and all that is in them,
 shall shout for joy over Babylon;
     for the destroyers shall come against
         them out of the north,
                 says the LORD.
49 Babylon must fall for the slain of Israel,
     as the slain of all the earth have
         fallen because of Babylon.
50 You survivors of the sword,
     go, do not linger!
 Remember the LORD in a distant land,
     and let Jerusalem come into your
         mind:
51 We are put to shame, for we have heard
         insults;
     dishonor has covered our face,
 for aliens have come
     into the holy places of the
         LORD's house.

a Sheshach is a cryptogram for Babel, Babylon

52 Therefore the time is surely coming,
      says the LORD,
      when I will punish her idols,
   and through all her land
      the wounded shall groan.
53 Though Babylon should mount up to
      heaven,
   and though she should fortify her
      strong height,
   from me destroyers would come upon
      her,
      says the LORD.

54 Listen!—a cry from Babylon!
      A great crashing from the land of the
      Chaldeans!
55 For the LORD is laying Babylon waste,
      and stilling her loud clamor.
   Their waves roar like mighty waters,
      the sound of their clamor resounds;
56 for a destroyer has come against her,
      against Babylon;
   her warriors are taken,
      their bows are broken;
   for the LORD is a God of recompense,
      he will repay in full.
57 I will make her officials and her sages
      drunk,
      also her governors, her deputies, and
      her warriors;
   they shall sleep a perpetual sleep and
      never wake,
      says the King, whose name is the
      LORD of hosts.

58 Thus says the LORD of hosts:
   The broad wall of Babylon
      shall be leveled to the ground,
   and her high gates
      shall be burned with fire.
   The peoples exhaust themselves for
      nothing,
   and the nations weary themselves
      only for fire.[a]

51.45–58: Again God calls the exiles to depart and save themselves. **46:** They must overcome their fears, which are being caused by rumors among them. In the future God will destroy Babylon. **47–48:** The cosmos will participate in the celebration. **50:** It is urgent that the exiles should *not linger* but remember that God is in Jerusalem. **50–58:** An imaginative portrayal of the attack ends the poetry of the book. There is a *cry,* smashing, *crashing,* for the destroyer has come against Babylon. Her leaders will be *drunk, asleep, never to wake.*

~~~~~~~~~~

59 The word that the prophet Jeremiah commanded Seraiah son of Neriah son of Mahseiah, when he went with King Zedekiah of Judah to Babylon, in the fourth year of his reign. Seraiah was the quartermaster. 60Jeremiah wrote in a[b] scroll all the disasters that would come on Babylon, all these words that are written concerning Babylon. 61And Jeremiah said to Seraiah: "When you come to Babylon, see that you read all these words, 62and say, 'O LORD, you yourself threatened to destroy this place so that neither human beings nor animals shall live in it, and it shall be desolate forever.' 63When you finish reading this scroll, tie a stone to it, and throw it into the middle of the Euphrates, 64and say, 'Thus shall Babylon sink, to rise no more, because of the disasters that I am bringing on her.' "[c]
   Thus far are the words of Jeremiah.

51.59–64: In a symbolic act written in prose, Baruch's brother, Seraiah, goes to Babylon under Jeremiah's directions. There Seraiah is to read the scroll containing prophecies against Babylon aloud, attach a stone to the scroll, and sink it in the Euphrates River. Like the sinking scroll, so will Babylon sink from its high position. This symbolic act embodies the divine will. It needs only to come to fulfillment.

THE END

Ch. 52: The prose conclusion to the book reports the end of national life in Judah, but neither God nor Jeremiah appear in it. The purpose of this bleak report may be to describe the fulfillment of Jeremiah's prophetic word. The setting is the Exile,* when Babylonian defeat is far from sight. The chapter is nearly identical to the account of Judah's fall that concludes the book of Kings (2 Kings 24.18–25.30). The narrative* divides into six short scenes.

---

a Gk Syr Compare Hab 2.13: Heb *and the nations for fire, and they are weary*   b Or *one*   c Gk: Heb *on her. And they shall weary themselves*

52 Zedekiah was twenty-one years old when he began to reign; he reigned eleven years in Jerusalem. His mother's name was Hamutal daughter of Jeremiah of Libnah. ²He did what was evil in the sight of the LORD, just as Jehoiakim had done. ³Indeed, Jerusalem and Judah so angered the LORD that he expelled them from his presence.

Zedekiah rebelled against the king of Babylon. ⁴And in the ninth year of his reign, in the tenth month, on the tenth day of the month, King Nebuchadrezzar of Babylon came with all his army against Jerusalem, and they laid siege to it; they built siegeworks against it all around. ⁵So the city was besieged until the eleventh year of King Zedekiah. ⁶On the ninth day of the fourth month the famine became so severe in the city that there was no food for the people of the land. ⁷Then a breach was made in the city wall;ᵃ and all the soldiers fled and went out from the city by night by the way of the gate between the two walls, by the king's garden, though the Chaldeans were all around the city. They went in the direction of the Arabah. ⁸But the army of the Chaldeans pursued the king, and overtook Zedekiah in the plains of Jericho; and all his army was scattered, deserting him. ⁹Then they captured the king, and brought him up to the king of Babylon at Riblah in the land of Hamath, and he passed sentence on him. ¹⁰The king of Babylon killed the sons of Zedekiah before his eyes, and also killed all the officers of Judah at Riblah. ¹¹He put out the eyes of Zedekiah, and bound him in fetters, and the king of Babylon took him to Babylon, and put him in prison until the day of his death.

12 In the fifth month, on the tenth day of the month—which was the nineteenth year of King Nebuchadrezzar, king of Babylon—Nebuzaradan the captain of the bodyguard who served the king of Babylon, entered Jerusalem. ¹³He burned the house of the LORD, the king's house, and all the houses of Jerusalem; every great house he burned down. ¹⁴All the army of the Chaldeans, who were with the captain of the guard, broke down all the walls around Jerusalem. ¹⁵Nebuzaradan the captain of the guard carried into exile some of the poorest of the people and the rest of the people who were left in the city and the deserters who had defected to the king of Babylon, together with the rest of the artisans. ¹⁶But Nebuzaradan the captain of the guard left some of the poorest people of the land to be vinedressers and tillers of the soil.

52.1–16. 1–3: Kings Jehoiakim and Zedekiah angered God, and Judah and Jerusalem *were expelled from his presence.* **4–11:** Zedekiah's failed escape and the tragedy of his capture and imprisonment and death suggest the possible fate awaiting Judah. **12–16:** The people are deported and divided with the poor remaining in the land.

---

17 The pillars of bronze that were in the house of the LORD, and the stands and the bronze sea that were in the house of the LORD, the Chaldeans broke in pieces, and carried all the bronze to Babylon. ¹⁸They took away the pots, the shovels, the snuffers, the basins, the ladles, and all the vessels of bronze used in the temple service. ¹⁹The captain of the guard took away the small bowls also, the firepans, the basins, the pots, the lampstands, the ladles, and the bowls for libation, both those of gold and those of silver. ²⁰As for the two pillars, the one sea, the twelve bronze bulls that were under the sea, and the stands,ᵇ which King Solomon had made for the house of the LORD, the bronze of all these vessels was beyond weighing. ²¹As for the pillars, the height of the one pillar was eighteen cubits, its circumference was twelve cubits; it was hollow and its thickness was four fingers. ²²Upon it was a capital of bronze; the height of the capital was five cubits; latticework and pomegranates, all of bronze, encircled the top of the capital. And the second pillar had the same, with pomegranates. ²³There were ninety-six pomegranates on the sides; all the pomegranates encircling the latticework numbered one hundred.

24 The captain of the guard took the chief priest Seraiah, the second priest Zeph-

---

ᵃ Heb lacks *wall*   ᵇ Cn: Heb *that were under the stands* aniah, and the three guardians of the threshold; 25 and from the city he took an officer who had been in command of the soldiers, and seven men of the king's council who were found in the city; the secretary of the commander of the army who mustered the people of the land; and sixty men of the people of the land who were found inside the city. 26 Then Nebuzaradan the captain of the guard took them, and brought them to the king of Babylon at Riblah. 27 And the king of Babylon struck them down, and put them to death at Riblah in the land of Hamath. So Judah went into exile out of its land.

28 This is the number of the people whom Nebuchadrezzar took into exile: in the seventh year, three thousand twenty-three Judeans; 29 in the eighteenth year of Nebuchadrezzar he took into exile from Jerusalem eight hundred thirty-two persons; 30 in the twenty-third year of Nebuchadrezzar, Nebuzaradan the captain of the guard took into exile of the Judeans seven hundred forty-five persons; all the persons were four thousand six hundred.

31 In the thirty-seventh year of the exile of King Jehoiachin of Judah, in the twelfth month, on the twenty-fifth day of the month, King Evil-merodach of Babylon, in the year he began to reign, showed favor to King Jehoiachin of Judah and brought him out of prison; 32 he spoke kindly to him, and gave him a seat above the seats of the other kings who were with him in Babylon. 33 So Jehoiachin put aside his prison clothes, and every day of his life he dined regularly at the king's table. 34 For his allowance, a regular daily allowance was given him by the king of Babylon, as long as he lived, up to the day of his death.

52.17–34. 17–23: The capture of the sacred Temple* vessels by the Babylonians underscores the end of worship life in the land. **28–30:** The numbers of exiles are provided, but their historical accuracy is in doubt. **31–34:** King Jehoiachin, also imprisoned in Babylon, survives and is restored to the table, though not yet released. The scene of the king's survival may offer a glimmer of hope to exiles for whom the king's survival with dignity may show the way to the future. This book has been about survival in the face of overwhelming catastrophe. If Jeremiah's words of judgment were fulfilled, then his words of hope will triumph as well.

LAMENTATIONS

Introduction

In five powerful, moving poems, Lamentations grieves for the destruction of Jerusalem in 586 BCE by the Babylonian armies. It is like many of the Psalms of lament★ in its mood and style, and it often speaks in general terms of the destruction, using metaphors★ and images that focus more on the feelings provoked by the calamity than on the events themselves. It shares with the Deuteronomistic★ History and some of the prophets★ the dominant conviction that suffering is an indication of God's displeasure, and yet other voices emerge—protests that the community suffers for the sins of its ancestors, that some of those who suffer (especially children) are innocent, and that the punishment may be unjustifiably harsh. The first four poems are acrostics,★ the first lines or stanzas beginning with the letters of the alphabet★ in sequence; the last poem has twenty-two lines, one for each letter of the Hebrew alphabet.

After the destruction of the Second Temple★ in 70 CE, Lamentations became part of the liturgy★ for the Ninth of Ab, the date of the Temple's fall. Hence, the book is found in the Jewish Bible with the "Megilloth" or festivalscrolls.★ See sidebar on p. 1113. The Christian canon,★ following the Septuagint,★ places the book after Jeremiah, whose strong expressions of emotion gained him the reputation of "the weeping prophet." The shifts in voices and styles, as well as the various acrostic techniques, lead most scholars to conclude that the book is a compilation of various materials, brought together to serve as a community liturgy of lament.

READING GUIDE

Lamentations is most helpfully read as an emotional response to suffering. How do these poems evoke our empathy with physical, emotional, and religious trauma—what it is to survive war, famine, the death of children, the rape of women, and the loss of the nation's religious and political center? How do the various voices (Jerusalem, a feminine voice; another individual "I," probably the poet; the community, in the plural "we") respond to tragedy?

1 First lament of the poet and the city
2 Second lament of the poet and the city
3 Miscellaneous laments
4 Third lament of the poet and the city
5 The community laments

1 How lonely sits the city
   that once was full of people!
How like a widow she has become,
   she that was great among the nations!
She that was a princess among the
     provinces
   has become a vassal.

2 She weeps bitterly in the night,
   with tears on her cheeks;

among all her lovers
   she has no one to comfort her;
all her friends have dealt treacherously
    with her,
   they have become her enemies.

3 Judah has gone into exile with suffering
   and hard servitude;
she lives now among the nations,
   and finds no resting place;

Acrostic Poems

Many of the stylistic elements of ancient Hebrew poetry remain unclear. One formal technique, however, is self-evident: The practice of beginning each line of a poem with the letters of the Hebrew alphabet in order (there are twenty-two letters in the Hebrew alphabet). This formal technique is called an *acrostic;* in English (and other languages) acrostic poems often use the first letters of a line to spell out a word or name, or to create some other pattern. Hebrew acrostics always follow the alphabetical pattern.

In the Bible, the following poems are acrostics: Psalms 9–10, 25, 34, 37, 111, 112, 119, 145; Proverbs 31.10–31; Lamentations; Nahum 1.2–8 (or possibly 2–10—the lines are disordered and the acrostic is incomplete); and Sirach 57.13–30. Of these texts, Psalms 34, 37, 112, 119, Proverbs 31, and Sirach 57 belong to the wisdom traditions of ancient Israel. It is possible that the acrostic pattern was a device used in schools, to aid in the memorization of a lengthy passage.

It might seem that an acrostic would be highly artificial, even possibly incoherent, since the beginning word of each line is in some sense a separate alphabetic entity, chosen for a reason other than meaning. We should compare this pattern, however, to the use of rhyme in English poetry: A rhyme is a pattern based on similarity of sound, and the aesthetic enjoyment of rhymed poetry is partly dependent on our observation of the poet's art in combining patterns of sound and meaning. Acrostic poems might have provided the same kind of pleasure. To test this supposition, try reading Psalms 9–10 or Lamentations 1 or 3. Do they appear to be arbitrary collections of lines, or do they present a strong sense of coherence? At a minimum, we can say that the acrostic form allows the poet an opportunity to work systematically through an idea or form, all the way "from A to Z," as we say in English. In the case of Lamentations, each chapter of which is composed entirely according to the acrostic pattern, the form provides a powerful structure by means of which to express the complaints and laments of the grieving people. In these chapters, the acrostic pattern is far more than a simple device to aid memorization.

The pattern not only structures but also limits and channels the deep feelings of grief and loss. Every society creates forms of behavior that help people to express their sorrow, and to come to terms with it. These forms of behavior put limits, sometimes even time limits, upon a period of mourning. The acrostics in Lamentations function in a similar way: By using the limits and regularity of the alphabet, they create a literary structure that sets boundaries upon the expression of grief and, in doing so, helps the reader move to a discernment of the hopeful words expressed in the center of the book, Lam 3.22–33.

---

her pursuers have all overtaken her
   in the midst of her distress.

4 The roads to Zion mourn,
   for no one comes to the festivals;
all her gates are desolate,
   her priests groan;

her young girls grieve,*
   and her lot is bitter.

5 Her foes have become the masters,
   her enemies prosper,

a Meaning of Heb uncertain

because the LORD has made her suffer
  for the multitude of her
    transgressions;
her children have gone away,
  captives before the foe.

6 From daughter Zion has departed
  all her majesty.
Her princes have become like stags
  that find no pasture;
they fled without strength
  before the pursuer.

7 Jerusalem remembers,
  in the days of her affliction and
    wandering,
all the precious things
  that were hers in days of old.
When her people fell into the hand of
  the foe,
  and there was no one to help her,
the foe looked on mocking
  over her downfall.

8 Jerusalem sinned grievously,
  so she has become a mockery;
all who honored her despise her,
  for they have seen her nakedness;
she herself groans,
  and turns her face away.

9 Her uncleanness was in her skirts;
  she took no thought of her future;
her downfall was appalling,
  with none to comfort her.
"O LORD, look at my affliction,
  for the enemy has triumphed!"

10 Enemies have stretched out their hands
  over all her precious things;
she has even seen the nations
  invade her sanctuary,
those whom you forbade
  to enter your congregation.

1.1–11a: A poet laments Jerusalem. As in many prophetic books (Hosea, Jeremiah, Ezekiel), Jerusalem is
personified* as a woman. In a striking series of contrasts, she who was great is now destitute like a *widow;*
once a princess, she is now a *vassal,* the underling in
a political relationship. 2: Political allies are called Je-

rusalem's *lovers* (Hos 2.7). 3: *Exile,* the conquering
strategy of the neo-Babylonian empire, involved moving large groups of people out of their homelands into
new locations. 4: Public activities (*festivals* and *gates,*
where people gather) have ceased. *Priests* and *young
girls* are among the many categories of people that
the book shows as suffering. 5: The book repeatedly
claims that *the LORD has made her suffer.* 8–10: *Nakedness* may have a sexual connotation (Lev 18.6).
Uncleanness refers to menstruation (Lev 15.16–24).
These conditions intensify her shame, considered by
the author to be as significant as physical suffering. The
immediate mention of *precious things* and the invasion of *her sanctuary,* while on the surface referring to
the Temple,* may have sexual connotations as well.

11 All her people groan
  as they search for bread;
they trade their treasures for food
  to revive their strength.
Look, O LORD, and see
  how worthless I have become.

12 Is it nothing to you,^a all you who
    pass by?
  Look and see
if there is any sorrow like my sorrow,
  which was brought upon me,
which the LORD inflicted
  on the day of his fierce anger.

13 From on high he sent fire;
  it went deep into my bones;
he spread a net for my feet;
  he turned me back;
he has left me stunned,
  faint all day long.

14 My transgressions were bound^a into a
    yoke;
  by his hand they were fastened
    together;
they weigh on my neck,
  sapping my strength;
the Lord handed me over
  to those whom I cannot withstand.

15 The LORD has rejected
  all my warriors in the midst of me;

a Meaning of Heb uncertain

he proclaimed a time against me
　to crush my young men;
the Lord has trodden as in a wine press
　the virgin daughter Judah.

16　For these things I weep;
　my eyes flow with tears;
for a comforter is far from me,
　one to revive my courage;
my children are desolate,
　for the enemy has prevailed.

17　Zion stretches out her hands,
　but there is no one to comfort her;
the LORD has commanded against Jacob
　that his neighbors should become his
　　foes;
Jerusalem has become
　a filthy thing among them.

18　The LORD is in the right,
　for I have rebelled against his word;
but hear, all you peoples,
　and behold my suffering;
my young women and young men
　have gone into captivity.

19　I called to my lovers
　but they deceived me;
my priests and elders
　perished in the city
while seeking food
　to revive their strength.

20　See, O LORD, how distressed I am;
　my stomach churns,
my heart is wrung within me,
　because I have been very rebellious.
In the street the sword bereaves;
　in the house it is like death.

21　They heard how I was groaning,
　with no one to comfort me.
All my enemies heard of my trouble;
　they are glad that you have done it.
Bring on the day you have announced,
　and let them be as I am.

22　Let all their evil doing come before you;
　and deal with them

as you have dealt with me
　because of all my transgressions;
for my groans are many
　and my heart is faint.

1.11b–22: Jerusalem herself speaks. The speaker changes at the end of v. 11, as the woman Jerusalem speaks in the first person. She repeats themes of the first speaker: She is shamed, and the devastation is punishment from God. **13–15:** *Net, fire:* Punishments are described generically (Ps 10.9; Isa 63.3). The weight of Israel's sin is compared to a *yoke* worn by captives of war (Isa 9.4). **16:** The lack of a *comforter* is a repeated theme of the book. **17:** The voice shifts back to third person briefly. *Zion** (the mountain on which Jerusalem is set), *Jacob* (the ancestor of the Israelites), and *Jerusalem* are used as synonyms. *Filthy thing* is the menstrual *uncleanness* of 1.9. **18:** The voice of Jerusalem returns, acknowledging her sin yet lamenting the pain she has experienced. **20:** Jerusalem's lament* resembles that of Jeremiah (Jer 8.18–9.1). **21–22:** Again concerned with being shamed in the face of others, Jerusalem asks that they, too, be treated according to their deeds. *Day you have announced* refers to the Day of the LORD, envisioned as a day of vindication against enemies (Isa 13.6–16).

2 How the Lord in his anger
　has humiliated*a* daughter Zion!
He has thrown down from heaven to
　　earth
　the splendor of Israel;
he has not remembered his footstool
　in the day of his anger.

2　The Lord has destroyed without mercy
　all the dwellings of Jacob;
in his wrath he has broken down
　the strongholds of daughter Judah;
he has brought down to the ground in
　　dishonor
　the kingdom and its rulers.

3　He has cut down in fierce anger
　all the might of Israel;
he has withdrawn his right hand from
　　them
　in the face of the enemy;

a Meaning of Heb uncertain

he has burned like a flaming fire
in Jacob,
consuming all around.

4 He has bent his bow like an enemy,
with his right hand set like a foe;
he has killed all in whom we
took pride
in the tent of daughter Zion;
he has poured out his fury like fire.

5 The Lord has become like an enemy;
he has destroyed Israel.
He has destroyed all its palaces,
laid in ruins its strongholds,
and multiplied in daughter Judah
mourning and lamentation.

6 He has broken down his booth like a
garden,
he has destroyed his tabernacle;
the LORD has abolished in Zion
festival and sabbath,
and in his fierce indignation has
spurned
king and priest.

7 The Lord has scorned his altar,
disowned his sanctuary;
he has delivered into the hand of the
enemy
the walls of her palaces;
a clamor was raised in the house of the
LORD
as on a day of festival.

8 The LORD determined to lay in ruins
the wall of daughter Zion;
he stretched the line;
he did not withhold his hand from
destroying;
he caused rampart and wall to lament;
they languish together.

9 Her gates have sunk into the ground;
he has ruined and broken her bars;
her king and princes are among
the nations;
guidance is no more,
and her prophets obtain
no vision from the LORD.

10 The elders of daughter Zion
sit on the ground in silence;
they have thrown dust on their heads
and put on sackcloth;
the young girls of Jerusalem
have bowed their heads to
the ground.

2.1–10. The poet on God's great anger. The poet describes the severity of God's punishment: Jerusalem is destroyed and humiliated. **1:** *Footstool:* The Temple (Ps 99.5). **2:** *Without mercy:* Without restraint. In a series of reversals, the great are brought down *to the ground.* **3–5:** God's *right hand,* his weapon hand, does not defend Israel but draws a bow against her like an enemy (Ex 15.6–12). **6–7:** *Booth, tabernacle*:* The Temple, which along with *festival, king,* and *priest* embodies the religious core of the nation, centered in Jerusalem and linked with the monarchy (2 Sam 7). **8–10:** *Stretched the line:* Apparently a step in destroying a building (2 Kings 21.13). God has broken down the very features intended to protect Jerusalem: *wall, gates* and *ramparts* (used for defense during military attacks). The listing of groups within the city underscores the totality of the destruction. *Dust* and *sackcloth** (v. 10) are typical gestures of mourning.

11 My eyes are spent with weeping;
my stomach churns;
my bile is poured out on the ground
because of the destruction of
my people,
because infants and babes faint
in the streets of the city.

12 They cry to their mothers,
"Where is bread and wine?"
as they faint like the wounded
in the streets of the city,
as their life is poured out
on their mothers' bosom.

13 What can I say for you, to what
compare you,
O daughter Jerusalem?
To what can I liken you, that I may
comfort you,
O virgin daughter Zion?
For vast as the sea is your ruin;
who can heal you?

14 Your prophets have seen for you
  false and deceptive visions;
 they have not exposed your iniquity
  to restore your fortunes,
 but have seen oracles for you
  that are false and misleading.

15 All who pass along the way
  clap their hands at you;
 they hiss and wag their heads
  at daughter Jerusalem;
 "Is this the city that was called
  the perfection of beauty,
  the joy of all the earth?"

16 All your enemies
  open their mouths against you;
 they hiss, they gnash their teeth,
  they cry: "We have devoured her!
 Ah, this is the day we longed for;
  at last we have seen it!"

17 The Lord has done what he purposed,
  he has carried out his threat;
 as he ordained long ago,
  he has demolished without pity;
 he has made the enemy rejoice
    over you,
  and exalted the might of your foes.

18 Cry aloud[a] to the Lord!
  O wall of daughter Zion!
 Let tears stream down like a torrent
  day and night!
 Give yourself no rest,
  your eyes no respite!

19 Arise, cry out in the night,
  at the beginning of the watches!
 Pour out your heart like water
  before the presence of the Lord!
 Lift your hands to him
  for the lives of your children,
 who faint for hunger
  at the head of every street.

2.11–19: The poet continues his lament. 11: Both the *stomach* (also 1.20) and *bile* refer to the seat of emotions (Jer 4.19); bile in addition means "bitterness" (from the taste of the digestive substance secreted from the gallbladder). 14: *False prophets** gave

unwarranted messages of comfort (Jer 14.13–16). 15–16: Jerusalem suffers not only the famine of children but also the taunts of enemies (Jer 19.8). 17: *As he ordained long ago* may refer to the teaching of the pre-exilic prophets, for whom destruction of the nation as punishment for sin was a common motif.* 18–19: The poet urges Jerusalem to petition God.

20 Look, O Lord, and consider!
  To whom have you done this?
 Should women eat their offspring,
  the children they have borne?
 Should priest and prophet be killed
  in the sanctuary of the Lord?

21 The young and the old are lying
  on the ground in the streets;
 my young women and my young men
  have fallen by the sword;
 in the day of your anger you have killed
    them,
  slaughtering without mercy.

22 You invited my enemies from all around
  as if for a day of festival;
 and on the day of the anger of the Lord
  no one escaped or survived;
 those whom I bore and reared
  my enemy has destroyed.

2.20–22: Jerusalem petitions God. The stark picture of women eating their own children and the death of the young raises this question: Has God punished too severely?

3 I am one who has seen affliction
  under the rod of God's[b] wrath;
2 he has driven and brought me
  into darkness without any light;
3 against me alone he turns his hand,
  again and again, all day long.

4 He has made my flesh and my skin
    waste away,
  and broken my bones;
5 he has besieged and enveloped me
  with bitterness and tribulation;
6 he has made me sit in darkness
  like the dead of long ago.

a Cn: Heb *Their heart cried*   *b* Heb *his*

7 He has walled me about so that I
     cannot escape;
  he has put heavy chains on me;
8 though I call and cry for help,
  he shuts out my prayer;
9 he has blocked my ways with hewn
     stones,
  he has made my paths crooked.

10 He is a bear lying in wait for me,
   a lion in hiding;
11 he led me off my way and tore me to
      pieces;
   he has made me desolate;
12 he bent his bow and set me
   as a mark for his arrow.

13 He shot into my vitals
   the arrows of his quiver;
14 I have become the laughingstock of all
      my people,
   the object of their taunt-songs all day
      long.
15 He has filled me with bitterness,
   he has sated me with wormwood.

16 He has made my teeth grind on gravel,
   and made me cower in ashes;
17 my soul is bereft of peace;
   I have forgotten what happiness is;
18 so I say, "Gone is my glory,
   and all that I had hoped for from the
      LORD."

19 The thought of my affliction and my
      homelessness
   is wormwood and gall!
20 My soul continually thinks of it
   and is bowed down within me.
21 But this I call to mind,
   and therefore I have hope:

22 The steadfast love of the LORD never
      ceases,*a*
   his mercies never come to an end;
23 they are new every morning;
   great is your faithfulness.
24 "The LORD is my portion," says my
      soul,
   "therefore I will hope in him."

3.1–66: Multiple responses to suffering. Speakers and moods shift throughout this chapter, making a neat outline difficult. Has the material been adjusted to fit the acrostic* pattern? Does the jarring style mimic the dissociation of trauma? **1–24: An individual lament.** Like other individual laments (Ps 38; 22), this section includes nonspecific complaints of suffering (vv. 1–19) and a statement of confidence in God (vv. 21–24). Identified neither with the poet who has spoken previously nor with Woman Zion, the speaker is an individual male (Heb., "geber"). He explicitly blames God for his troubles, comparing God to a wild animal (v. 10) and an enemy warrior (vv. 12–13). His troubles are not outlined but are compared to *heavy chains* (v. 7) and *gravel* to the teeth (v. 16). **15:** *Wormwood* (also v. 19) is a bitter-tasting plant (Jer 9.14). **19:** *Gall:* Bile (see comment on 2.1). **21–24:** Statement of confidence, a feature of the individual lament.

25 The LORD is good to those who wait for
      him,
   to the soul that seeks him.
26 It is good that one should wait quietly
   for the salvation of the LORD.
27 It is good for one to bear
   the yoke in youth,
28 to sit alone in silence
   when the Lord has imposed it,
29 to put one's mouth to the dust
   (there may yet be hope),
30 to give one's cheek to the smiter,
   and be filled with insults.

31 For the Lord will not
   reject forever.
32 Although he causes grief, he will have
      compassion
   according to the abundance of his
      steadfast love;
33 for he does not willingly afflict
   or grieve anyone.

34 When all the prisoners of the land
   are crushed under foot,
35 when human rights are perverted
   in the presence of the Most High,
36 when one's case is subverted
   —does the Lord not see it?

a Syr Tg: Heb LORD, *we are not cut off*

Megilloth in Jewish Liturgy

While Song of Solomon, Ruth, Lamentations, Ecclesiastes, and Esther originated in different times and places, today they are clustered together in the last section of the Jewish canon called the Writings. This arrangement reflects how the books are used: Each is read at one of the five pilgrimage festivals of Judaism, and their organization in the canon follows the order of the festivals.

Song of Solomon. By the turn of the era some Jewish interpreters were reading Song of Solomon as an allegory of God's love for Israel. For that reason, the book was eventually incorporated into the celebration of Passover, a spring festival that commemorates through the eating of symbolic foods the liberation of the Israelites from bondage in Egypt. The book's springtime references also fit appropriately with Passover's March–April setting.

Ruth. Shavuot, also known as the Feast of Weeks or Pentecost, was originally an agricultural festival, celebrating the end of the barley harvest and the beginning of the wheat harvest. Later it was given a historical connection: Based on Ex 19.1, Moses was said to have received the Law on Mt. Sinai at Shavuot. Both the agricultural and historical themes link with Ruth, since the book mentions harvest and since, according to Jewish tradition, Ruth represents a faithful convert.

Lamentations. Because of the book's concern with the destruction of Jerusalem by the Babylonian armies in 586 BCE, it is read at services on the Ninth of Ab, a day of mourning the loss of both the First and Second Temples (the latter destroyed by the Romans in 70 CE), as well as the exile of the Jewish community from Spain in 1492.

Ecclesiastes. Ecclesiastes' connection with its festival is not an obvious one: The book's insistence that persons should enjoy life links it with Sukkot (also Feast of Booths), which the Israelites are commanded to celebrate in Deut 16.15.

Esther. Of all the Megilloth, Esther has the clearest festival connection, since the book itself serves to explain and to encourage the observance of the festival of Purim. In modern Purim festivals, the book is read and children often dress up as its principal characters. The carnival-like atmosphere of modern Purim practices also finds obvious connections with the sumptuous banqueting in the book of Esther.

---

37 Who can command and have it done,
    if the Lord has not ordained it?
38 Is it not from the mouth of the Most
        High
    that good and bad come?
39 Why should any who draw breath
        complain
    about the punishment of their sins?

40 Let us test and examine our ways,
    and return to the LORD.

41 Let us lift up our hearts as well as our
        hands
    to God in heaven.
42 We have transgressed and rebelled,
    and you have not forgiven.

43 You have wrapped yourself with anger
        and pursued us,
    killing without pity;
44 you have wrapped yourself with a cloud
    so that no prayer can pass through.

45 You have made us filth and rubbish
    among the peoples.

46 All our enemies
    have opened their mouths against us;
47 panic and pitfall have come upon us,
    devastation and destruction.
48 My eyes flow with rivers of tears
    because of the destruction of
    my people.

49 My eyes will flow without ceasing,
    without respite,
50 until the LORD from heaven
    looks down and sees.
51 My eyes cause me grief
    at the fate of all the young women in
    my city.

3.25–51. 25–41: A teaching on God's goodness. In a jarring shift, this section at the center of the book offers beautiful statements of God's mercy, faithfulness, and compassion (vv. 22–33) and teaches silence in the face of suffering. Because some passages appear to contradict material that comes before and after (v. 39: Why should anyone complain?), these verses are often considered a later addition to the book. They function, however, to balance the community's expression of suffering with the book's insistent theme that God is justifiably punishing Judah for its sins. **40–41:** Because God has acted justly, Judah must examine its own wrongs. **42–51: A communal lament.** While beginning with recognition of guilt, the section also complains that God has refused to forgive (vv. 42, 44). Further complaints follow. The shame of defeat and enemy taunts, mentioned earlier in the book, is repeated. **48:** While the speaker shifts to "I" the theme remains the fate of the city.

52 Those who were my enemies without
        cause
    have hunted me like a bird;
53 they flung me alive into a pit
    and hurled stones on me;
54 water closed over my head;
    I said, "I am lost."

55 I called on your name, O LORD,
    from the depths of the pit;
56 you heard my plea, "Do not close your
    ear

to my cry for help, but give
    me relief!"
57 You came near when I called on you;
    you said, "Do not fear!"

58 You have taken up my cause, O Lord,
    you have redeemed my life.
59 You have seen the wrong done to me,
        O LORD;
    judge my cause.
60 You have seen all their malice,
    all their plots against me.

61 You have heard their taunts, O LORD,
    all their plots against me.
62 The whispers and murmurs of my
        assailants
    are against me all day long.
63 Whether they sit or rise—see,
    I am the object of their taunt-songs.

64 Pay them back for their deeds, O LORD,
    according to the work of their hands!
65 Give them anguish of heart;
    your curse be on them!
66 Pursue them in anger and destroy them
    from under the LORD's heavens.

3.52–66: A psalm of praise. As in 3.1–24, the individual catalogues his complaints generally and metaphorically: *like a bird*, v. 52; *pit*, vv. 53, 55 (Ps 7.15; 9.10). As in a psalm of thanksgiving (Ps 31), God is reported to have answered the prayer. **52:** *Without cause:* Strikingly different from the assumption of guilt (vv. 22–39). **59–66: Complaint about enemies.** Although the preceding verses suggest that God has already responded to the individual's plea, the speaker explicitly calls for God to punish enemies (1.21–22).

4 How the gold has grown dim,
    how the pure gold is changed!
  The sacred stones lie scattered
    at the head of every street.

2 The precious children of Zion,
    worth their weight in fine gold—
  how they are reckoned as earthen pots,
    the work of a potter's hands!

3 Even the jackals offer the breast
    and nurse their young,

but my people has become cruel,
like the ostriches in the wilderness.

4 The tongue of the infant sticks
to the roof of its mouth for thirst;
the children beg for food,
but no one gives them anything.

5 Those who feasted on delicacies
perish in the streets;
those who were brought up in purple
cling to ash heaps.

6 For the chastisement*a* of my people has
been greater
than the punishment*b* of Sodom,
which was overthrown in a moment,
though no hand was laid on it.*c*

7 Her princes were purer than snow,
whiter than milk;
their bodies were more ruddy
than coral,
their hair*c* like sapphire.*d*

8 Now their visage is blacker than soot;
they are not recognized in the streets.
Their skin has shriveled on their bones;
it has become as dry as wood.

9 Happier were those pierced by
the sword
than those pierced by hunger,
whose life drains away, deprived
of the produce of the field.

10 The hands of compassionate women
have boiled their own children;
they became their food
in the destruction of my people.

famine (5.10; Job 30.30). **10:** In a dramatic reversal,
once compassionate mothers eat rather than feed their
young.

11 The LORD gave full vent to his wrath;
he poured out his hot anger,
and kindled a fire in Zion
that consumed its foundations.

12 The kings of the earth did not believe,
nor did any of the inhabitants of the
world,
that foe or enemy could enter
the gates of Jerusalem.

13 It was for the sins of her prophets
and the iniquities of her priests,
who shed the blood of the righteous
in the midst of her.

14 Blindly they wandered through
the streets,
so defiled with blood
that no one was able
to touch their garments.

15 "Away! Unclean!" people shouted
at them;
"Away! Away! Do not touch!"
So they became fugitives and
wanderers;
it was said among the nations,
"They shall stay here no longer."

16 The LORD himself has scattered them,
he will regard them no more;
no honor was shown to the priests,
no favor to the elders.

4.1–10: Jerusalem's changed fortunes. The poet portrays a world upside down, where all that is normal has vanished. **2–4:** Children, once treasured, are as fragile as clay pots, and scarce food is not given to them. *Ostriches* have the reputation of neglecting their young (Job 39.13–18). **5–8:** *Purple*, due to the costliness of its dye, was worn by royalty. The once privileged class now starves. **6:** *Sodom:* See Gen 19.24–25. **9:** Quick death would be better than the slow torture of famine. **8:** *Black* skin is a description of

4.11–16: God's anger has debased Zion.* **12:** The poet assumes that other nations along with Israel (Ps 48) believed in the invincibility of Jerusalem. **13:** *Prophets* and *priests*, as the primary leaders of the people, are blamed for the bloodshed of war. **14–15:** *Defiled with blood* and *unclean* refer to the purity laws of Leviticus.

a Or *iniquity*   *b* Or *sin*   *c* Meaning of Heb uncertain   *d* Or *lapis lazuli*

17 Our eyes failed, ever watching
    vainly for help;
  we were watching eagerly
    for a nation that could not save.

18 They dogged our steps
    so that we could not walk in
      our streets;
  our end drew near; our days were
    numbered;
  for our end had come.

19 Our pursuers were swifter
    than the eagles in the heavens;
  they chased us on the mountains,
    they lay in wait for us in the
      wilderness.

20 The LORD's anointed, the breath of our
    life,
  was taken in their pits—
  the one of whom we said, "Under his
    shadow
  we shall live among the nations."

21 Rejoice and be glad, O daughter Edom,
    you that live in the land of Uz;
  but to you also the cup shall pass;
    you shall become drunk and strip
      yourself bare.

22 The punishment of your iniquity,
      O daughter Zion, is
    accomplished,
  he will keep you in exile no longer;
  but your iniquity, O daughter Edom, he
    will punish,
  he will uncover your sins.

5 Remember, O LORD, what has
    befallen us;
  look, and see our disgrace!

2 Our inheritance has been turned over to
    strangers,
  our homes to aliens.

3 We have become orphans, fatherless;
  our mothers are like widows.

4 We must pay for the water we drink;
  the wood we get must be bought.

5 With a yoke*a* on our necks we are hard
    driven;
  we are weary, we are given no rest.

6 We have made a pact with*b* Egypt and
    Assyria,
  to get enough bread.

7 Our ancestors sinned; they are
    no more,
  and we bear their iniquities.

8 Slaves rule over us;
  there is no one to deliver us from
    their hand.

9 We get our bread at the peril of
    our lives,
  because of the sword in the
    wilderness.

10 Our skin is black as an oven
  from the scorching heat of famine.

11 Women are raped in Zion,
  virgins in the towns of Judah.

12 Princes are hung up by their hands;
  no respect is shown to the elders.

13 Young men are compelled to grind,
  and boys stagger under loads
    of wood.

14 The old men have left the city gate,
  the young men their music.

15 The joy of our hearts has ceased;
  our dancing has been turned
    to mourning.

16 The crown has fallen from our head;
  woe to us, for we have sinned!

17 Because of this our hearts are sick,
  because of these things our eyes have
    grown dim:

18 because of Mount Zion, which
    lies desolate;
  jackals prowl over it.

4.17–22. 17–20: The final days of the city. The poet describes the fall of Jerusalem (2 Kings 25), as she loses any hope of protection. The *nation that could not save* is likely Egypt (Jer 44.30). LORD's *anointed**** is the king, who is described in exalted terms. 21–22: **Call for punishment of Edom.** Various biblical accounts complain that Edom gloated over Jerusalem's fall (Obadiah; Ps 137). The poet calls for the punishment and self-humiliation of Edom. 22: *Punishment . . . accomplished* may suggest that the book is written after the traumatic events described.

a Symmachus: Heb lacks *With a yoke*   *b* Heb *have given the hand to*

5.1–22: A community lament. This final poem follows the stylistic features of the communal laments of the Psalms (Ps 44; 79). A long description of misery and specific losses offers a glimpse into a conquered country: Babylonian conquerors force young and old into labor (vv. 5, 13); food and water are scarce (vv. 4, 6, 9, 10); *women are raped* (v. 11); and the once civilized city is now a haunt of *jackals* (v. 18). **7:** *We bear their iniquities:* Is the community accepting the guilt of their forebears or complaining that it is punished for sins not its own? **14–18:** All joy (*music, dancing*, public gathering at the *city gate*) has ceased.

19 But you, O LORD, reign forever;
   your throne endures to all generations.

20 Why have you forgotten us completely?
      Why have you forsaken us these many
         days?
21 Restore us to yourself, O LORD, that we
      may be restored;
   renew our days as of old—
22 unless you have utterly rejected us,
      and are angry with us beyond
         measure.

5.19–22: The poem ends on a poignant note. God's power is undisputed, though God's care is questioned. The community asks that its broken relationship with God be healed, but fears that God's anger may be yet too great.

EZEKIEL

Introduction

Ezekiel presents some of the most theologically challenging and dynamic material among the prophetic books of the Hebrew Bible. It wrestles with the problem of the Babylonian exile in a manner not unlike the modern problem of the Shoah or Holocaust: Why did God allow Jerusalem and the Temple* to be destroyed, and why did God allow the people of Israel to be carried away into exile? In arguing that God made a deliberate decision to destroy the Temple in order to purify Israel, Ezekiel draws upon his own priestly background in which sacrifice at the altar of the Temple is an essential element in self-purification, which aids in restoring one's relationship with God. The book develops its ideas in two major sections: Chs. 1–32 focus on God's plans to punish both Israel (chs. 1–24) and a select group of nations that would fall to Babylon (chs. 25–32); chs. 33–48 focus on God's plans to restore a purified Israel (chs. 33–39) with the Jerusalem Temple at the center of Israel and all creation (chs. 40–48).

Ezekiel was a Zadokite priest, a descendant of Zadok, one of the priests of David (2 Sam 15.24–29) who was also the priest who anointed* Solomon (1 Kings 1). The Zadokites were priests at the Jerusalem Temple from that point forward until the Exile.* Ezekiel was exiled to Babylonia together with King Jehoiachin in 597 BCE. He began his prophetic career five years later at the age of thirty (593 BCE) with a vision in which "the glory of the LORD" appeared to him in the form of a divine throne chariot, from which God instructed him to speak. Ezekiel's prophetic career continued for over 20 years and culminated in his vision of the restored Jerusalem Temple. His last oracle* with a specified date is from 571 BCE (29.17–21). The book was originally written in an effort to explain the Babylonian exile and to prepare the exiled Judahite community for its return to Jerusalem. Ezekiel's "visions of God" prompted the composition of much apocalyptic* and mystical literature. These kinds of writings—both Jewish and early Christian—were attempts to grapple with persecution and sufferings, such as threats to the Second Temple, its fall in 70 CE, and the destruction of Judea in 132–135 CE. Because Ezekiel attempts to describe God, a dangerous task, the Mishnah (the basic collection of religious and community regulations in Judaism) requires that readers be knowledgeable in Jewish tradition (m Hagigah 2.1). The book was nearly withdrawn from circulation until the rabbinic sage Hananiah ben Hezekiah resolved its contradictions with the Torah* (b Shabbat 13b; b Hagigah 13a; b Menahot 45a—all references to the Mishnah). The modern city of Tel Aviv is named for Ezekiel's home in Babylonia (3.15), and the prophet's notion of "the hidden face of God" (39.21–29) plays a major role in contemporary discussion of the Holocaust.

READING GUIDE

Ezekiel's visions of "the glory of the LORD" constitute a literary envelope for the book in which God condemns Jerusalem to destruction and departs from the Temple (chs. 1–11) and then returns to the restored Temple once the people and land of Israel and the city of Jerusalem are purified (chs. 40–48). Ezekiel engages in a great deal of symbolic action, such as taking a sword to his own hair (ch. 5), or refusing to mourn at the death of his wife (24.15–27), to illustrate and actualize God's message. He is very familiar with earlier tradition, such as the Exodus and

Wilderness traditions (Exodus; Numbers), the Priestly sacrificial regulations and Holiness Code (Lev 1–16; 17–26), and the prophecies of Isaiah and Jeremiah. He employs them throughout his own writings to discuss Israel's history (chs. 16; 20), Jerusalem's destruction as purifying sacrifice (chs. 9–11), individual moral responsibility (ch. 18), the downfall of Egypt (ch. 31), the character of the Davidic prince (ch. 34), and the restoration of Israel with "a new heart" and "a new spirit" (11.14–21; 36.16–38). He is concerned throughout the book with protecting the sanctity of God's holy name (36.21) and frequently uses a self-identification formula, "I am the LORD" (36.38), to validate his oracles. The prophecy concerning the valley of the dry bones (ch. 37) underlies Jewish and Christian beliefs concerning resurrection, and the oracle concerning Gog of Magog represents an early apocalyptic scenario of judgment against Israel's enemies. Because Ezekiel's vision of the restored Temple does not correspond to the Second Temple (515 BCE–70 CE), it is generally considered in Jewish tradition to be a portrayal of third Temple to be built at the time of the messiah.★

INTRODUCTION TO EZEKIEL'S PROPHECY

1.1–3.15: The introduction includes a superscription in 1.1–3, which identifies the prophet★ and his historical context, and an account of his inaugural vision in 1.4–3.15, in which God commissions him to speak. Compare the call narratives★ of Moses (Ex 3) or Isaiah (Isa 6).

1 In the thirtieth year, in the fourth month, on the fifth day of the month, as I was among the exiles by the river Chebar, the heavens were opened, and I saw visions of God. ²On the fifth day of the month (it was the fifth year of the exile of King Jehoiachin), ³the word of the LORD came to the priest Ezekiel son of Buzi, in the land of the Chaldeans by the river Chebar; and the hand of the LORD was on him there.

1.1–3: Superscription. See Isa 1.1; Jer 1.3. **1:** Some understand *the thirtieth year* as the thirtieth year after the prophet's call, the thirtieth year after Josiah's reform, the year of Jehoiachin's exile, or the date of the book's composition. It probably refers to Ezekiel's age at the time of his call. Ezekiel is a priest (1.3), and the age of priestly service begins at thirty (Num 4.3, compare Num 8.23–25) and concludes at fifty. Apart from the reference to the twenty-seventh year in 29.17, the dated oracles of the book extend from the fifth (1.2) to the twenty-fifth year of the Exile★ (40.1), so that the book correlates Ezekiel's prophetic oracles with the 20 years of active priestly service. *The river Chebar:* A canal by Nippur, a Babylonian city. **2:** *The fifth year of*

the exile of King Jehoiachin: 593 BCE. **3:** *Buzi* is otherwise unknown. Had he not been exiled, Ezekiel would have served as a Zadokite priest in the Temple.★

4 As I looked, a stormy wind came out of the north: a great cloud with brightness around it and fire flashing forth continually, and in the middle of the fire, something like gleaming amber. ⁵In the middle of it was something like four living creatures. This was their appearance: they were of human form. ⁶Each had four faces, and each of them had four wings. ⁷Their legs were straight, and the soles of their feet were like the sole of a calf's foot; and they sparkled like burnished bronze. ⁸Under their wings on their four sides they had human hands. And the four had their faces and their wings thus: ⁹their wings touched one another; each of them moved straight ahead, without turning as they moved. ¹⁰As for the appearance of their faces: the four had the face of a human being, the face of a lion on the right side, the face of an ox on the left side, and the face of an eagle; ¹¹such were their faces. Their wings were spread out above; each creature had two wings, each of which touched the wing of another, while two covered their bodies. ¹²Each moved straight ahead; wherever the spirit would go, they went, without turning as they went. ¹³In the middle of*ᵃ* the living creatures there was

a Gk OL: Heb *And the appearance of*

something that looked like burning coals of fire, like torches moving to and fro among the living creatures; the fire was bright, and lightning issued from the fire. ¹⁴The living creatures darted to and fro, like a flash of lightning.

15 As I looked at the living creatures, I saw a wheel on the earth beside the living creatures, one for each of the four of them.ᵃ ¹⁶As for the appearance of the wheels and their construction: their appearance was like the gleaming of beryl; and the four had the same form, their construction being something like a wheel within a wheel. ¹⁷When they moved, they moved in any of the four directions without veering as they moved. ¹⁸Their rims were tall and awesome, for the rims of all four were full of eyes all around. ¹⁹When the living creatures moved, the wheels moved beside them; and when the living creatures rose from the earth, the wheels rose. ²⁰Wherever the spirit would go, they went, and the wheels rose along with them; for the spirit of the living creatures was in the wheels. ²¹When they moved, the others moved; when they stopped, the others stopped; and when they rose from the earth, the wheels rose along with them; for the spirit of the living creatures was in the wheels.

22 Over the heads of the living creatures there was something like a dome, shining like crystal,ᵇ spread out above their heads. ²³Under the dome their wings were stretched out straight, one toward another; and each of the creatures had two wings covering its body. ²⁴When they moved, I heard the sound of their wings like the sound of mighty waters, like the thunder of the Almighty,ᶜ a sound of tumult like the sound of an army; when they stopped, they let down their wings. ²⁵And there came a voice from above the dome over their heads; when they stopped, they let down their wings.

26 And above the dome over their heads there was something like a throne, in appearance like sapphire;ᵈ and seated above the likeness of a throne was something that seemed like a human form. ²⁷Upward from what appeared like the loins I saw something like gleaming amber, something that looked

like fire enclosed all around; and downward from what looked like the loins I saw something that looked like fire, and there was a splendor all around. ²⁸Like the bow in a cloud on a rainy day, such was the appearance of the splendor all around. This was the appearance of the likeness of the glory of the LORD.

1.4–28a: The inaugural vision. The imagery of God's throne chariot (compare 1 Chr 28.18; Ps 18.10) is based on the most holy place in the Temple where the ark of the covenant* is kept under the cherubim* (1 Kings 6; see also Ex 25.10–22; 37.1–9). **4:** Wind, cloud, and fire appear frequently in theophanies* (Ex 19; 1 Kings 19). **5–12:** *Like:* The vision is only a proximate human attempt to describe the divine presence. The *four living creatures* are the cherubim that surround the ark. Exodus 25.18–22; 37.7–9; and 1 Kings 6.23–28; 2 Chr 3.10–14 each mentioned only two, but this passage combines the totals. Composite human/animal winged creatures are well represented throughout the ancient Near East as guardians of thrones, city gates, and temples. The number four presupposes the four horns of the Temple altar (Ex 27.2; 38.2; Zech 2.1–4; 1.18–21), which represent the four "winds" or cardinal directions, indicating God's presence in the Temple at the center of creation. The four faces represent the divine qualities of intelligence (human), royalty (lion), strength (ox), and mobility (eagle). **13–14:** The *burning coals of fire:* The sacrificial altar of the Temple (Ex 27.1–8; 38.1–7) or the incense altars (Ex 30.1–10; 37.5–28). **15–21:** The *wheels* contribute to the imagery of divine motion in all four directions. They are based on the image of the cart that carried the ark of the covenant from Philistia to Jerusalem (1 Sam 6; 2 Sam 6) and the rings that held the poles by which the Levites carried the ark (Ex 25.12–15; 30.4–5). The *wheel within a wheel:* A wheel with a hub. **22–25:** *Dome shining like crystal,* see Gen 1.6–8, which uses "firmament" or "dome" to symbolize the distinction between heaven and earth. *The sound of mighty waters:* The vision is both auditory and visual. **26–28a:** Compare 1 Sam 4.4; 2 Sam 6.2; 1 Chr 13.6, "the ark of the covenant of the LORD of Hosts, who is enthroned on the cherubim." *Sapphire:* See Ex 24.10. Ezekiel attempts to describe God in hu-

---

a Heb *of their faces*   *b* Gk: Heb *like the awesome crystal*   *c* Traditional rendering of Heb *Shaddai*
d Or *lapis lazuli*

man terms, but the imagery is inadequate. *Gleaming amber* and *fire* convey the power and incorporeality of the divine presence. The rainbow symbolizes God's covenant with creation (Gen 9.8–17). *The glory of the Lord:* God's presence (Ex 16.6–7; 40.34–38).

When I saw it, I fell on my face, and I heard the voice of someone speaking.

2 He said to me: O mortal,[a] stand up on your feet, and I will speak with you. ²And when he spoke to me, a spirit entered into me and set me on my feet; and I heard him speaking to me. ³He said to me, Mortal, I am sending you to the people of Israel, to a nation[b] of rebels who have rebelled against me; they and their ancestors have transgressed against me to this very day. ⁴The descendants are impudent and stubborn. I am sending you to them, and you shall say to them, "Thus says the Lord God." ⁵Whether they hear or refuse to hear (for they are a rebellious house), they shall know that there has been a prophet among them. ⁶And you, O mortal, do not be afraid of them, and do not be afraid of their words, though briers and thorns surround you and you live among scorpions; do not be afraid of their words, and do not be dismayed at their looks, for they are a rebellious house. ⁷You shall speak my words to them, whether they hear or refuse to hear; for they are a rebellious house.

8 But you, mortal, hear what I say to you; do not be rebellious like that rebellious house; open your mouth and eat what I give you. ⁹I looked, and a hand was stretched out to me, and a written scroll was in it. ¹⁰He spread it before me; it had writing on the front and on the back, and written on it were words of lamentation and mourning and woe.

3 He said to me, O mortal, eat what is offered to you; eat this scroll, and go, speak to the house of Israel. ²So I opened my mouth, and he gave me the scroll to eat. ³He said to me, Mortal, eat this scroll that I give you and fill your stomach with it. Then I ate it; and in my mouth it was as sweet as honey.

4 He said to me: Mortal, go to the house of Israel and speak my very words to them. ⁵For you are not sent to a people of obscure speech and difficult language, but to the house of Israel— ⁶not to many peoples of obscure speech and difficult language, whose words you cannot understand. Surely, if I sent you to them, they would listen to you. ⁷But the house of Israel will not listen to you, for they are not willing to listen to me; because all the house of Israel have a hard forehead and a stubborn heart. ⁸See, I have made your face hard against their faces, and your forehead hard against their foreheads. ⁹Like the hardest stone, harder than flint, I have made your forehead; do not fear them or be dismayed at their looks, for they are a rebellious house. ¹⁰He said to me: Mortal, all my words that I shall speak to you receive in your heart and hear with your ears; ¹¹then go to the exiles, to your people, and speak to them. Say to them, "Thus says the Lord God"; whether they hear or refuse to hear.

12 Then the spirit lifted me up, and as the glory of the Lord rose[c] from its place, I heard behind me the sound of loud rumbling; ¹³it was the sound of the wings of the living creatures brushing against one another, and the sound of the wheels beside them, that sounded like a loud rumbling. ¹⁴The spirit lifted me up and bore me away; I went in bitterness in the heat of my spirit, the hand of the Lord being strong upon me. ¹⁵I came to the exiles at Tel-abib, who lived by the river Chebar.[d] And I sat there among them, stunned, for seven days.

1.28b–3.15: The commissioning of Ezekiel. 1.28b: *A voice of someone speaking:* Compare 1 Kings 19.12. **2.1–2:** God addresses Ezekiel as *mortal*, literally, "son of adam," ninety-three times in the book. Adam means "human" in Hebrew, and "son of adam" conveys Ezekiel's mortal status in contrast to God. The *spirit* (literally, "wind") of the Lord prepares Ezekiel to serve as a prophet* (see 1 Sam 10.6, 10; 1 Kings 18.12). **2.3–7:** The charge of Israel's rebellion against God is a constant theme throughout the prophets to

a Or *son of man*; Heb *ben adam* (and so throughout the book when Ezekiel is addressed)   b Syr: Heb *to nations*
c Cn: Heb *and blessed be the glory of the Lord*
d Two Mss Syr: Heb *Chebar, and to where they lived.* Another reading is *Chebar, and I sat where they sat*

justify Israel's suffering as an act of divine punishment. Habakkuk and Job question this theology but ultimately defend God's righteousness. The messenger formula, *Thus says the Lord GOD,* indicates Ezekiel's role as God's representative. **2.8–3.3:** Ezekiel eats the scroll to internalize the divine message. The scroll represents the Torah* scroll stored in the ark of the covenant and read to the people (Deut 31.9–13, 24–27; Neh 8–10). Although the scroll is inscribed with *words of lamentation and mourning and woe,* Ezekiel states that it was *as sweet as honey* (compare Jer 15.16). **4–11:** *Many peoples of obscure speech and difficult language:* Many peoples were incorporated into the Assyrian and Babylonian empires (Isa 33.19). God stresses that the message is for Israel, not the nations. **12–15:** *Tel-abib,* "hill of barley," may derive from the Babylonian expression "til abubi," "hill of the flood"; Babylonia is prone to flooding in the spring.

EZEKIEL'S INITIAL ORACLES AND SYMBOLIC ACTIONS

3.16–7.27: These oracles* and symbolic actions are concerned with the destruction of Jerusalem and fall of the land of Israel.

16 At the end of seven days, the word of the LORD came to me: ¹⁷Mortal, I have made you a sentinel for the house of Israel; whenever you hear a word from my mouth, you shall give them warning from me. ¹⁸If I say to the wicked, "You shall surely die," and you give them no warning, or speak to warn the wicked from their wicked way, in order to save their life, those wicked persons shall die for their iniquity; but their blood I will require at your hand. ¹⁹But if you warn the wicked, and they do not turn from their wickedness, or from their wicked way, they shall die for their iniquity; but you will have saved your life. ²⁰Again, if the righteous turn from their righteousness and commit iniquity, and I lay a stumbling block before them, they shall die; because you have not warned them, they shall die for their sin, and their righteous deeds that they have done shall not be remembered; but their blood I will require at your hand. ²¹If, however, you warn the righteous not to sin, and they do not sin, they shall surely live, because they took warning; and you will have saved your life.

22 Then the hand of the LORD was upon me there; and he said to me, Rise up, go out into the valley, and there I will speak with you. ²³So I rose up and went out into the valley; and the glory of the LORD stood there, like the glory that I had seen by the river Chebar; and I fell on my face. ²⁴The spirit entered into me, and set me on my feet; and he spoke with me and said to me: Go, shut yourself inside your house. ²⁵As for you, mortal, cords shall be placed on you, and you shall be bound with them, so that you cannot go out among the people; ²⁶and I will make your tongue cling to the roof of your mouth, so that you shall be speechless and unable to reprove them; for they are a rebellious house. ²⁷But when I speak with you, I will open your mouth, and you shall say to them, "Thus says the Lord GOD"; let those who will hear, hear; and let those who refuse to hear, refuse; for they are a rebellious house.

3.16–27. 16–21: God describes Ezekiel's role as the *sentinel* or "watchman" for Israel, who is responsible for the lives and moral guidance of the people (Jer 6.17; Hos 9.8; compare Isa 21.6). Like sentinels posted on city walls to watch for danger (2 Sam 18.24; 2 Kings 9.17), gatekeepers are appointed from among the priests to guard the Temple (1 Chr 26). This role, which is developed more fully in ch. 33, is consistent with ch. 18. The prophet's responsibility is presented in four cases. **22–27:** Ezekiel's isolation resembles that of Moses, who spoke directly to God in the tent of meeting (Ex 33.7–34.35; Num 11), and the high priest, who appears alone before God and the ark at Yom Kippur or the Day of Atonement* (Lev 16). Ezekiel's dumbness derives from his priestly role. The priests perform their duties on the altar in silence (Lev 16).

4 And you, O mortal, take a brick and set it before you. On it portray a city, Jerusalem; ²and put siegeworks against it, and build a siege wall against it, and cast up a ramp against it; set camps also against it, and plant battering rams against it all around. ³Then take an iron plate and place it as an iron wall between you and the city; set your face toward it, and let it be in a state of siege, and press the siege against it. This is a sign for the house of Israel.

4 Then lie on your left side, and place the punishment of the house of Israel upon it; you shall bear their punishment for the number of the days that you lie there. ⁵For I assign to you a number of days, three hundred ninety days, equal to the number of the years of their punishment; and so you shall bear the punishment of the house of Israel. ⁶When you have completed these, you shall lie down a second time, but on your right side, and bear the punishment of the house of Judah; forty days I assign you, one day for each year. ⁷You shall set your face toward the siege of Jerusalem, and with your arm bared you shall prophesy against it. ⁸See, I am putting cords on you so that you cannot turn from one side to the other until you have completed the days of your siege.

4.1–8: Prophets perform symbolic actions to dramatize their statements and enable them to take effect (Isa 20; Jer 13; 19). Ezekiel builds a model of Jerusalem under siege. The action draws upon the imagery of Jer 1.18. The background of *three hundred and ninety* and *forty* is not entirely certain, and the Septuagint* (the Greek version of the Hebrew Bible) contains entirely different figures. If one counts backwards from the destruction of the Temple* in 587 BCE, the total of 430 years points to the time of the establishment of the united monarchy of Israel under Saul in 1017 BCE. Counting forward 390 years from that date takes one to 627 BCE, the twelfth year of Josiah's reign, the year in which his reforms begin (2 Chr 34.3; compare 2 Kings 22.3). Josiah failed in his attempt to reunite Israel and Judah. The remaining 40 years accounts for the time between the beginning of Josiah's reform and the destruction of Jerusalem.

9 And you, take wheat and barley, beans and lentils, millet and spelt; put them into one vessel, and make bread for yourself. During the number of days that you lie on your side, three hundred ninety days, you shall eat it. ¹⁰The food that you eat shall be twenty shekels a day by weight; at fixed times you shall eat it. ¹¹And you shall drink water by measure, one-sixth of a hin; at fixed times you shall drink. ¹²You shall eat it as a barley-cake, baking it in their sight on human dung. ¹³The LORD said, "Thus shall the people of Israel eat their bread, unclean, among the nations to which I will drive them." ¹⁴Then I said, "Ah Lord GOD! I have never defiled myself; from my youth up until now I have never eaten what died of itself or was torn by animals, nor has carrion flesh come into my mouth." ¹⁵Then he said to me, "See, I will let you have cow's dung instead of human dung, on which you may prepare your bread."

16 Then he said to me, Mortal, I am going to break the staff of bread in Jerusalem; they shall eat bread by weight and with fearfulness; and they shall drink water by measure and in dismay. ¹⁷Lacking bread and water, they will look at one another in dismay, and waste away under their punishment.

4.9–17: Ezekiel uses a variety of grains to demonstrate that there is insufficient grain to make an entire loaf. *Twenty shekels:** About ten ounces. *One-sixth of a hin:* About two-thirds of a quart. In order to demonstrate the difficult conditions of the coming siege, God commands Ezekiel to bake bread using human dung as fuel. When he protests that this is a breach of priestly purity, God allows him to use cow's dung. **16–17:** See Isa 3.1.

5 And you, O mortal, take a sharp sword; use it as a barber's razor and run it over your head and your beard; then take balances for weighing, and divide the hair. ²One third of the hair you shall burn in the fire inside the city, when the days of the siege are completed; one third you shall take and strike with the sword all around the city;ᵃ and one third you shall scatter to the wind, and I will unsheathe the sword after them. ³Then you shall take from these a small number, and bind them in the skirts of your robe. ⁴From these, again, you shall take some, throw them into the fire and burn them up; from there a fire will come out against all the house of Israel.

5.1–4: The *sword* or *barber's razor* (Isa 7.20) symbolizes the weapons of the Babylonians. One third of the hair is burned to represent those who die when the city is burned; one third is struck with the sword to symbolize those killed around the city; and one third

ᵃ Heb *it*

is scattered to symbolize those who escape only to be pursued by the Babylonians. Some of the hair is burned once again to symbolize the suffering of the people.

〜〜〜〜〜〜〜〜〜〜〜〜〜〜〜〜〜〜

5 Thus says the Lord GOD: This is Jerusalem; I have set her in the center of the nations, with countries all around her. 6But she has rebelled against my ordinances and my statutes, becoming more wicked than the nations and the countries all around her, rejecting my ordinances and not following my statutes. 7Therefore thus says the Lord GOD: Because you are more turbulent than the nations that are all around you, and have not followed my statutes or kept my ordinances, but have acted according to the ordinances of the nations that are all around you; 8therefore thus says the Lord GOD: I, I myself, am coming against you; I will execute judgments among you in the sight of the nations. 9And because of all your abominations, I will do to you what I have never yet done, and the like of which I will never do again. 10Surely, parents shall eat their children in your midst, and children shall eat their parents; I will execute judgments on you, and any of you who survive I will scatter to every wind. 11Therefore, as I live, says the Lord GOD, surely, because you have defiled my sanctuary with all your detestable things and with all your abominations—therefore I will cut you down;*a* my eye will not spare, and I will have no pity. 12One third of you shall die of pestilence or be consumed by famine among you; one third shall fall by the sword around you; and one third I will scatter to every wind and will unsheathe the sword after them.

13 My anger shall spend itself, and I will vent my fury on them and satisfy myself; and they shall know that I, the LORD, have spoken in my jealousy, when I spend my fury on them. 14Moreover I will make you a desolation and an object of mocking among the nations around you, in the sight of all that pass by. 15You shall be*b* a mockery and a taunt, a warning and a horror, to the nations around you, when I execute judgments on you in anger and fury, and with furious punishments—I, the LORD, have spoken—

16when I loose against you*c* my deadly arrows of famine, arrows for destruction, which I will let loose to destroy you, and when I bring more and more famine upon you, and break your staff of bread. 17I will send famine and wild animals against you, and they will rob you of your children; pestilence and bloodshed shall pass through you; and I will bring the sword upon you. I, the LORD, have spoken.

5.5–17: God sums up the theology of punishment that Ezekiel's symbolic actions illustrate. Charging that Israel acts like the nations (see 1 Sam 8.4–5) by defiling the Temple, God states that the people will suffer war and exile, and will perish by pestilence, famine, and sword. God's threat to make Israel *a desolation and an object of mocking among the nations* and to unleash famine, wild animals, etc., against the people recalls threats made in Jer 24.9–10 (see also Deut 28.37; 1 Kings 9.7).

Ezekiel's oracles* against the land of Israel Chs. 6–7: Ezekiel does not distinguish between Israel and Judah, but addresses the entire land and people of Israel arrayed around the Temple (Num 2; Ezek 48). The most holy place serves as the sacred center of the Temple, the Jerusalem Temple as the sacred center of Israel, and Israel as sacred center of the world.

---

6 The word of the LORD came to me: 2O mortal, set your face toward the mountains of Israel, and prophesy against them, 3and say, You mountains of Israel, hear the word of the Lord GOD! Thus says the Lord GOD to the mountains and the hills, to the ravines and the valleys: I, I myself will bring a sword upon you, and I will destroy your high places. 4Your altars shall become desolate, and your incense stands shall be broken; and I will throw down your slain in front of your idols. 5I will lay the corpses of the people of Israel in front of their idols; and I will scatter your bones around your altars. 6Wherever you live, your towns shall be waste and your high places ruined, so that your altars will be waste and ruined,*d* your

a Another reading is I will withdraw   *b* Gk Syr Vg Tg: Heb It shall be   *c* Heb them   *d* Syr Vg Tg: Heb and be made guilty idols broken and destroyed, your incense stands cut down, and your works wiped out. [7] The slain shall fall in your midst; then you shall know that I am the LORD.

8 But I will spare some. Some of you shall escape the sword among the nations and be scattered through the countries. [9] Those of you who escape shall remember me among the nations where they are carried captive, how I was crushed by their wanton heart that turned away from me, and their wanton eyes that turned after their idols. Then they will be loathsome in their own sight for the evils that they have committed, for all their abominations. [10] And they shall know that I am the LORD; I did not threaten in vain to bring this disaster upon them.

6.1–14: Oracle against the mountains of Israel. *The mountains of Israel:* The homeland of Israel in the hills of Samaria and Judah. **1–7:** Ezekiel identifies the cause of punishment in the various altars and high places* where the people worship, which compromise the sanctity of the land. As a Zadokite priest, Ezekiel holds that legitimate worship of God must take place only in the Jerusalem Temple (Deut 12). The scattering of dead corpses around the altars renders the land impure (Num 19; see also Lev 21.10–12). The prophet* employs the prophetic "proof saying," *then you shall know that I am the LORD,* throughout the book to identify God as the source of the prophet's words (Ex 20.2; Lev 19.3–4; see also Ex 3.13–22; Deut 5.6). **8–10:** Ezekiel relies on Isaiah's concept of a remnant of Israel (Isa 4.2–6; 6.13; 10.20–23) to demonstrate God's power to destroy and punish.

~~~~~~~

11 Thus says the Lord GOD: Clap your hands and stamp your foot, and say, Alas for all the vile abominations of the house of Israel! For they shall fall by the sword, by famine, and by pestilence. [12] Those far off shall die of pestilence; those nearby shall fall by the sword; and any who are left and are spared shall die of famine. Thus I will spend my fury upon them. [13] And you shall know that I am the LORD, when their slain lie among their idols around their altars, on every high hill, on all the mountain tops, under every green tree, and under every leafy oak, wherever they offered pleasing odor to all their idols. [14] I will stretch out my hand

against them, and make the land desolate and waste, throughout all their settlements, from the wilderness to Riblah.[a] Then they shall know that I am the LORD.

6.11–14: Ezekiel returns to the imagery of sword, pestilence, and famine (5.1–17) to tie his oracles against Israel to the fate of Jerusalem. *Altars, on every high hill, on all the mountain tops, under every green tree, and under every leafy oak:* A common formulaic description of pagan worship (Deut 12.2; 1 Kings 14.23; Jer 2.20). The *wilderness* designates the Negeb desert in southern Judah, and *Riblah* ("Diblah" in Hebrew; the Hebrew letters "resh" and "dalet" are similar and sometimes confused) is in Syria (2 Kings 23.33).

~~~~~~~

7 The word of the LORD came to me: [2] You, O mortal, thus says the Lord GOD to the land of Israel:
An end! The end has come
    upon the four corners of the land.
[3] Now the end is upon you,
    I will let loose my anger upon you;
    I will judge you according to your ways,
        I will punish you for all your
            abominations.
[4] My eye will not spare you, I will have no
            pity.
    I will punish you for your ways,
        while your abominations are among
            you.
Then you shall know that I am the LORD.
    [5] Thus says the Lord GOD:
    Disaster after disaster! See, it comes.
[6]   An end has come, the end has come.
    It has awakened against you; see,
        it comes!
[7] Your doom[b] has come to you,
        O inhabitant of the land.
    The time has come, the day is near—
        of tumult, not of reveling on the
            mountains.
[8] Soon now I will pour out my wrath
            upon you;
    I will spend my anger against you.
    I will judge you according to your ways,
        and punish you for all your
            abominations.

----

a Another reading is *Diblah*   *b* Meaning of Heb uncertain

9 My eye will not spare; I will have no
    pity.
    I will punish you according to your
        ways,
    while your abominations are among
        you.
Then you shall know that it is I the LORD
who strike.

7.1–27: Ezekiel's prophecy of the end. Ezekiel's three
oracles draw upon the "Day of the LORD" traditions to
announce the "end" of Israel (Am 5.18–20; 8.1–14;
Isa 2.6–22; 13). The "Day of the LORD" functioned
originally as an announcement of God's defense of Israel, but various prophets reconfigured it as an announcement of God's punishment of Israel. **7.1–4:** The
first oracle announces the end of Israel. *End* is drawn
from Amos's prophecy against Bethel (Am 8.1–3),
which includes the imagery of dead bodies scattered
about the altar as in 6.1–7. The *four corners of the land*
indicates the complete destruction of the land and rehearses the four cardinal directions that underlie the
symbolism of the four living creatures in ch. 1 (see Isa
11.12). **5–9:** Ezekiel again employs the statement *the
end has come*, but he shifts his language to that of the
"Day of the LORD" traditions.

---

10 See, the day! See, it comes!
    Your doom*a* has gone out.
    The rod has blossomed, pride has
        budded.
11 Violence has grown into a rod
        of wickedness.
    None of them shall remain,
    not their abundance, not their
        wealth;
    no pre-eminence among them.*a*
12 The time has come, the day draws near;
    let not the buyer rejoice, nor the
        seller mourn,
    for wrath is upon all their multitude.
13 For the sellers shall not return to what has
been sold as long as they remain alive. For
the vision concerns all their multitude; it
shall not be revoked. Because of their
iniquity, they cannot maintain their lives.*a*
14 They have blown the horn and made
        everything ready;
    but no one goes to battle,
    for my wrath is upon all their
        multitude.

15 The sword is outside, pestilence and
        famine are inside;
    those in the field die by the sword;
    those in the city—famine and
        pestilence devour them.
16 If any survivors escape,
    they shall be found on the mountains
    like doves of the valleys,
    all of them moaning over their iniquity.
17 All hands shall grow feeble,
    all knees turn to water.
18 They shall put on sackcloth,
    horror shall cover them.
    Shame shall be on all faces,
    baldness on all their heads.
19 They shall fling their silver into the
        streets,
    their gold shall be treated as unclean.
Their silver and gold cannot save them on
the day of the wrath of the LORD. They shall
not satisfy their hunger or fill their stomachs
with it. For it was the stumbling block of
their iniquity. 20From their*b* beautiful ornament, in which they took pride, they made
their abominable images, their detestable
things; therefore I will make of it an unclean
thing to them.
21 I will hand it over to strangers
        as booty,
    to the wicked of the earth as plunder;
    they shall profane it.
22 I will avert my face from them,
    so that they may profane my
        treasured*c* place;
    the violent shall enter it,
    they shall profane it.
23 Make a chain!*a*
    For the land is full of bloody crimes;
    the city is full of violence.
24 I will bring the worst of the nations
    to take possession of their houses.
    I will put an end to the arrogance of the
        strong,
    and their holy places shall be
        profaned.
25 When anguish comes, they will seek
        peace,
    but there shall be none.

---

a Meaning of Heb uncertain   *b* Syr Symmachus:
Heb *its*   *c* Or *secret*

26 Disaster comes upon disaster,
　　rumor follows rumor;
　they shall keep seeking a vision from the
　　　prophet;
　instruction shall perish from the
　　　priest,
　and counsel from the elders.
27 The king shall mourn,
　　the prince shall be wrapped in despair,
　　and the hands of the people of the
　　　land shall tremble.
　According to their way I will deal with
　　　them;
　according to their own judgments I
　　　will judge them.
And they shall know that I am the LORD.

7.10–27: The third oracle elaborates the imagery of the land's destruction in the "Day of the LORD." **10–11:** The blossoming rod represents Aaron's rod, which designates Levi as the priestly tribe (Num 17), but Jeremiah, a priest descended from Eli (1 Sam 1–3), employs it as a sign of Judah's punishment (Jer 1.11–12). The silver almond-shaped cap, recently discovered by archeologists in Jerusalem, once adorned the rod of a priest. The budding *pride* also translates as "insolence," indicating Ezekiel's view that the priestly rod is now employed for the punishment of Israel, just as Moses' rod punished Egypt (Ex 7–11). **12–13:** Normal life will end. **14–17:** Ezekiel again takes up the imagery of sword, pestilence, and famine (chs. 5–6). **18–21:** Compare Isa 2.6–21, which anticipates that people will throw away their silver and gold idols on the "Day of the LORD." **22:** God's intention to hide the divine face raises tremendous theological problems. God's *treasured place* was the most holy place in the Temple. **23–27:** The leaders are responsible for the punishment.

EZEKIEL'S VISION OF JERUSALEM'S DESTRUCTION

Chs. 8–11: Ezekiel portrays the destruction of Jerusalem as a priestly sacrifice that cleanses the city from impurity.

---

8 In the sixth year, in the sixth month, on the fifth day of the month, as I sat in my house, with the elders of Judah sitting before me, the hand of the Lord GOD fell upon me there. 2I looked, and there was a figure that looked like a human being;*a* below what appeared to be its loins it was fire, and above the loins it was like the appearance of brightness, like gleaming amber. 3It stretched out the form of a hand, and took me by a lock of my head; and the spirit lifted me up between earth and heaven, and brought me in visions of God to Jerusalem, to the entrance of the gateway of the inner court that faces north, to the seat of the image of jealousy, which provokes to jealousy. 4And the glory of the God of Israel was there, like the vision that I had seen in the valley.

5 Then God*b* said to me, "O mortal, lift up your eyes now in the direction of the north." So I lifted up my eyes toward the north, and there, north of the altar gate, in the entrance, was this image of jealousy. 6He said to me, "Mortal, do you see what they are doing, the great abominations that the house of Israel are committing here, to drive me far from my sanctuary? Yet you will see still greater abominations."

7 And he brought me to the entrance of the court; I looked, and there was a hole in the wall. 8Then he said to me, "Mortal, dig through the wall"; and when I dug through the wall, there was an entrance. 9He said to me, "Go in, and see the vile abominations that they are committing here." 10So I went in and looked; there, portrayed on the wall all around, were all kinds of creeping things, and loathsome animals, and all the idols of the house of Israel. 11Before them stood seventy of the elders of the house of Israel, with Jaazaniah son of Shaphan standing among them. Each had his censer in his hand, and the fragrant cloud of incense was ascending. 12Then he said to me, "Mortal, have you seen what the elders of the house of Israel are doing in the dark, each in his room of images? For they say, 'The LORD does not see us, the LORD has forsaken the land.'" 13He said also to me, "You will see still greater abominations that they are committing."

8.1–18: The impurity of the Temple. * **1–4:** *The sixth year:* 592 BCE. Ezekiel returns to the imagery of his in-

a Gk: Heb *like fire*　*b* Heb *he*

Describing the Indescribable

The book of Ezekiel contains a number of visions: descriptions in imagery, sounds and sights of realities that are outside ordinary experience (like the vision of the divine throne chariot in ch. 1) or of events that the prophet★ did not witness directly (like the vision of worship in the Jerusalem Temple★ in ch. 8). These visions, which go "behind the scenes" to show divine realities in human terms, had a great influence on later writings. Ezekiel may have influenced the book of Daniel in its visions concerning the course and meaning of world history. It also influenced later books, such as 1 Enoch,★ a Jewish pseudepigraphical★ work from the first century BCE that contains visions concerning the hidden secrets of both the divine and earthly realms; the book of Revelation in the New Testament, which uses visions to express the persecution and suffering of the early Christian church and its significance in human history; and the rabbinic "Heikhalot" ("palaces") literature, in which mystics "ascend" through the seven heavenly "palaces" to encounter the presence of God.

　　All of these works try to describe matters that are beyond normal human experience, but of course they must work within the limits of human language and experience to do this. This may explain why the images and descriptions seem so fanciful and sometimes even bizarre. As we read Ezekiel and these other writings, we should bear in mind that the writers may have been compelled to try to describe things that are indescribable, and that their language—gemstones and fire, scrolls that are eaten, and creatures with the head of a lion and the wings of an eagle—takes human vocabulary close to the breaking point. We are not meant to believe in these word pictures literally, but they function as metaphors★ that stimulate our imaginations and help us recognize that spiritual truths can be as real and as vivid as physical ones.

augural vision to describe a human-like being. The imagery of *fire* and *brightness like gleaming amber* describes a being that cannot be defined in earthly terms. *The entrance of the gateway of the inner court that faces north* places the prophet at the entry of the most sacred areas of the Temple. *The glory of the God of Israel:* The throne chariot of ch. 1 is present. **5–6:** The *image of jealousy:* North of the altar was a pagan idol placed in the Temple precincts. **7–13:** Mention of *the seventy elders of the house of Israel* and *Jaazaniah son of Shaphan* indicates that the highest leadership of the nation is involved in pagan worship inside the Temple. Shaphan played a major role in Josiah's reform (2 Kings 22); his sons Ahikam, Elasah, and Gemariah, and grandson Micaiah supported Jeremiah (Jer 26; 29; 36). The claim that *the LORD has forsaken the land* indicates the belief that God could not protect Jerusalem from Babylon.

14 Then he brought me to the entrance of the north gate of the house of the LORD; women were sitting there weeping for Tammuz. 15Then he said to me, "Have you seen this, O mortal? You will see still greater abominations than these."

16 And he brought me into the inner court of the house of the LORD; there, at the entrance of the temple of the LORD, between the porch and the altar, were about twenty-five men, with their backs to the temple of the LORD, and their faces toward the east, prostrating themselves to the sun toward the east. 17Then he said to me, "Have you seen this, O mortal? Is it not bad enough that the house of Judah commits the abominations done here? Must they fill the land with violence, and provoke my anger still further? See, they are putting the branch to their nose! 18Therefore I will act in wrath; my eye will not spare, nor will I have pity; and though they cry in my hearing with a loud voice, I will not listen to them."

8.14–18. 14–15: Women weep for *Tammuz,* the Babylonian vegetation god who dies at the onset of the dry season and must be brought back to life to inaugurate the rains. **16–18:** Ezekiel sees twenty-five men engaged in sun worship. The sun god Shamash was the Babylonian god of law and justice.

9 Then he cried in my hearing with a loud voice, saying, "Draw near, you executioners of the city, each with his destroying weapon in his hand." ²And six men came from the direction of the upper gate, which faces north, each with his weapon for slaughter in his hand; among them was a man clothed in linen, with a writing case at his side. They went in and stood beside the bronze altar.

3 Now the glory of the God of Israel had gone up from the cherub on which it rested to the threshold of the house. The LORD called to the man clothed in linen, who had the writing case at his side; ⁴and said to him, "Go through the city, through Jerusalem, and put a mark on the foreheads of those who sigh and groan over all the abominations that are committed in it." ⁵To the others he said in my hearing, "Pass through the city after him, and kill; your eye shall not spare, and you shall show no pity. ⁶Cut down old men, young men and young women, little children and women, but touch no one who has the mark. And begin at my sanctuary." So they began with the elders who were in front of the house. ⁷Then he said to them, "Defile the house, and fill the courts with the slain. Go!" So they went out and killed in the city. ⁸While they were killing, and I was left alone, I fell prostrate on my face and cried out, "Ah Lord GOD! will you destroy all who remain of Israel as you pour out your wrath upon Jerusalem?" ⁹He said to me, "The guilt of the house of Israel and Judah is exceedingly great; the land is full of bloodshed and the city full of perversity; for they say, 'The LORD has forsaken the land, and the LORD does not see.' ¹⁰As for me, my eye will not spare, nor will I have pity, but I will bring down their deeds upon their heads."

11 Then the man clothed in linen, with the writing case at his side, brought back

word, saying, "I have done as you commanded me."

9.1–11: The slaughter of Jerusalem. Sacrificial slaughter at the altar of the Temple portrays the killing of the people of Jerusalem. **1–2:** The *six men* come from the upper gate to the north with weapons in their hands to begin the slaughter. The Babylonian army would have entered Judah from the north (see Jer 1.13–16). The *man clothed in linen* wears the apparel of a priest who serves at the altar (Ex 28.39; Lev 6.10) and carries a *writing case* to record the sacrifices. The *bronze altar* had been moved to the north by Ahaz to accommodate an Assyrian altar (2 Kings 16.14). **3–11:** The living beings are now named *cherubim.** God commands that a *mark* (the ancient Hebrew letter "taw," translated "mark," looks like an X) be placed on the foreheads of *those who sigh and groan over all the abominations,* to protect them from death. A mark on the doorpost protects the Israelites from God's plague against the Egyptians (Ex 12.23). All who lack the mark are to die, defiling the sanctuary. Ezekiel attempts to intercede as Moses did (Ex 32.1–14; Num 14), but God states that the people believe that God lacks power.

The LORD's Departure from Jerusalem
Chs. 10–11: God's throne chariot will return in 43.1–12 when the city is purified and the Temple reestablished.

10 Then I looked, and above the dome that was over the heads of the cherubim there appeared above them something like a sapphire,ᵃ in form resembling a throne. ²He said to the man clothed in linen, "Go within the wheelwork underneath the cherubim; fill your hands with burning coals from among the cherubim, and scatter them over the city." He went in as I looked on. ³Now the cherubim were standing on the south side of the house when the man went in; and a cloud filled the inner court. ⁴Then the glory of the LORD rose up from the cherub to the threshold of the house; the house was filled with the cloud, and the court was full of the brightness of the glory of the LORD. ⁵The sound of the wings of the cherubim was heard as far as the outer court,

a Or *lapis lazuli*

like the voice of God Almighty*a* when he speaks.

6 When he commanded the man clothed in linen, "Take fire from within the wheelwork, from among the cherubim," he went in and stood beside a wheel. 7And a cherub stretched out his hand from among the cherubim to the fire that was among the cherubim, took some of it and put it into the hands of the man clothed in linen, who took it and went out. 8The cherubim appeared to have the form of a human hand under their wings.

9 I looked, and there were four wheels beside the cherubim, one beside each cherub; and the appearance of the wheels was like gleaming beryl. 10And as for their appearance, the four looked alike, something like a wheel within a wheel. 11When they moved, they moved in any of the four directions without veering as they moved; but in whatever direction the front wheel faced, the others followed without veering as they moved. 12Their entire body, their rims, their spokes, their wings, and the wheels—the wheels of the four of them—were full of eyes all around. 13As for the wheels, they were called in my hearing "the wheelwork." 14Each one had four faces: the first face was that of the cherub, the second face was that of a human being, the third that of a lion, and the fourth that of an eagle.

15 The cherubim rose up. These were the living creatures that I saw by the river Chebar. 16When the cherubim moved, the wheels moved beside them; and when the cherubim lifted up their wings to rise up from the earth, the wheels at their side did not veer. 17When they stopped, the others stopped, and when they rose up, the others rose up with them; for the spirit of the living creatures was in them.

18 Then the glory of the LORD went out from the threshold of the house and stopped above the cherubim. 19The cherubim lifted up their wings and rose up from the earth in my sight as they went out with the wheels beside them. They stopped at the entrance of the east gate of the house of the LORD; and the glory of the God of Israel was above them.

20 These were the living creatures that I saw underneath the God of Israel by the river Chebar; and I knew that they were cherubim. 21Each had four faces, each four wings, and underneath their wings something like human hands. 22As for what their faces were like, they were the same faces whose appearance I had seen by the river Chebar. Each one moved straight ahead.

10.1–22: God commands the *man clothed in linen* to take *burning coals from among the cherubim and scatter them over the city.* Much like the sin offerings presented in the Temple (Lev 4–5), the purpose of the sacrifice is to purify Jerusalem from its iniquity and impurity so that it can be reestablished at a later time (chs. 40–48). God's presence is signified by the *cloud* (Ex 19.9; 1 Kings 8.10–11) and *brightness of the glory of the LORD* as it moves about the Temple complex. Because of the sanctity of the throne chariot or ark, the man clothed in linen is unable to approach, and a cherub hands him the fire (2 Sam 6.6–11). Ezekiel's detailed description of the cherubim* and the wheels differs from ch. 1 in that one of their four faces is a cherub rather than an ox. Many medieval commentators speculate that the face of the cherub might encompass the four individual faces. *The glory of the LORD* above *the entrance of the east gate of the house of the LORD* is the main or processional entrance to the Temple (Ps 24.7–9; 118.19–20).

11 The spirit lifted me up and brought me to the east gate of the house of the LORD, which faces east. There, at the entrance of the gateway, were twenty-five men; among them I saw Jaazaniah son of Azzur, and Pelatiah son of Benaiah, officials of the people. 2He said to me, "Mortal, these are the men who devise iniquity and who give wicked counsel in this city; 3they say, 'The time is not near to build houses; this city is the pot, and we are the meat.' 4Therefore prophesy against them; prophesy, O mortal."

5 Then the spirit of the LORD fell upon me, and he said to me, "Say, Thus says the LORD: This is what you think, O house of Israel; I know the things that come into your mind. 6You have killed many in this city, and have filled its streets with the slain. 7There-

a Traditional rendering of Heb *El Shaddai*

fore thus says the Lord GOD: The slain whom you have placed within it are the meat, and this city is the pot; but you shall be taken out of it. 8You have feared the sword; and I will bring the sword upon you, says the Lord GOD. 9I will take you out of it and give you over to the hands of foreigners, and execute judgments upon you. 10You shall fall by the sword; I will judge you at the border of Israel. And you shall know that I am the LORD. 11This city shall not be your pot, and you shall not be the meat inside it; I will judge you at the border of Israel. 12Then you shall know that I am the LORD, whose statutes you have not followed, and whose ordinances you have not kept, but you have acted according to the ordinances of the nations that are around you."

13 Now, while I was prophesying, Pelatiah son of Benaiah died. Then I fell down on my face, cried with a loud voice, and said, "Ah Lord GOD! will you make a full end of the remnant of Israel?"

11.1–25: Ezekiel prophesies both judgment and restoration for the people. **1–4:** The *spirit* or "wind" transports Ezekiel to the east gate of the Temple where he sees twenty-five officials, probably those worshipping the sun in 8.16. Their statement, "*The time is not near to build houses,*" rejects Jeremiah's call to build and to plant (Jer 1.10; 31.28). The statement, "*This city is the pot, and we are the meat,*" indicates their belief that Jerusalem is to be sacrificed (24.1–14). **5–13:** God instructs Ezekiel to hold the twenty-five leaders responsible for the deaths of the people in Jerusalem. In stating that the dead will become the meat, and the city the pot, Ezekiel turns their statement against them, but indicates that they will be excluded because the sacrifice of the city is meant to purify Jerusalem. He alludes to their fear of foreign invaders and again turns their fears against them by stating that they will die at the borders of Israel (see 2 Kings 25.18–21; Jer 52.24–27). The immediate death of *Pelatiah son of Benaiah* confirms Ezekiel's word (compare Am 7.10–17; Jer 27–28).

14 Then the word of the LORD came to me: 15Mortal, your kinsfolk, your own kin, your fellow exiles,*a* the whole house of Israel, all of them, are those of whom the inhabitants of Jerusalem have said, "They have gone far from the LORD; to us this land is given for a possession." 16Therefore say: Thus says the Lord GOD: Though I removed them far away among the nations, and though I scattered them among the countries, yet I have been a sanctuary to them for a little while*b* in the countries where they have gone. 17Therefore say: Thus says the Lord GOD: I will gather you from the peoples, and assemble you out of the countries where you have been scattered, and I will give you the land of Israel. 18When they come there, they will remove from it all its detestable things and all its abominations. 19I will give them one*c* heart, and put a new spirit within them; I will remove the heart of stone from their flesh and give them a heart of flesh, 20so that they may follow my statutes and keep my ordinances and obey them. Then they shall be my people, and I will be their God. 21But as for those whose heart goes after their detestable things and their abominations,*d* I will bring their deeds upon their own heads, says the Lord GOD.

22 Then the cherubim lifted up their wings, with the wheels beside them; and the glory of the God of Israel was above them. 23And the glory of the LORD ascended from the middle of the city, and stopped on the mountain east of the city. 24The spirit lifted me up and brought me in a vision by the spirit of God into Chaldea, to the exiles. Then the vision that I had seen left me. 25And I told the exiles all the things that the LORD had shown me.

11.14–25. 14–21: God claims to be *a sanctuary to them for a little while:* God's presence in the world, rather than the Temple's presence in Jerusalem, ensures their future. God promises to gather the people from exile, to give them *the land of Israel,* and to purify the people from abominations in a manner characteristic of priestly purification. The promise of *one heart* (some manuscripts read "a new heart") and *a new spirit within them* takes up a theme from Jeremiah (Jer 32.39; see also Ezek 18.31; 36.26) concerning a new

---

a Gk Syr: Heb *people of your kindred*   *b* Or *to some extent*   *c* Another reading is *a new*   *d* Cn: Heb *And to the heart of their detestable things and their abominations their heart goes* covenant* in which God's Torah* is written upon their hearts (Jer 31.33–34; see also Ezek 16.59–63). *"They shall be my people, and I will be their God"* is a formulation that characterizes the covenant between God and Israel/Judah (14.11; 36.28; 37.23; Jer 7.23; 31.33; 32.38; Hos 2.23; Zech 8.8). **22–24:** Ezekiel is returned to *Chaldea* (Babylonia) to report to the exiles.

12 The word of the LORD came to me: ²Mortal, you are living in the midst of a rebellious house, who have eyes to see but do not see, who have ears to hear but do not hear; ³for they are a rebellious house. Therefore, mortal, prepare for yourself an exile's baggage, and go into exile by day in their sight; you shall go like an exile from your place to another place in their sight. Perhaps they will understand, though they are a rebellious house. ⁴You shall bring out your baggage by day in their sight, as baggage for exile; and you shall go out yourself at evening in their sight, as those do who go into exile. ⁵Dig through the wall in their sight, and carry the baggage through it. ⁶In their sight you shall lift the baggage on your shoulder, and carry it out in the dark; you shall cover your face, so that you may not see the land; for I have made you a sign for the house of Israel.

7 I did just as I was commanded. I brought out my baggage by day, as baggage for exile, and in the evening I dug through the wall with my own hands; I brought it out in the dark, carrying it on my shoulder in their sight.

8 In the morning the word of the LORD came to me: ⁹Mortal, has not the house of Israel, the rebellious house, said to you, "What are you doing?" ¹⁰Say to them, "Thus says the Lord GOD: This oracle concerns the prince in Jerusalem and all the house of Israel in it." ¹¹Say, "I am a sign for you: as I have done, so shall it be done to them; they shall go into exile, into captivity." ¹²And the prince who is among them shall lift his baggage on his shoulder in the dark, and shall go out; he*a* shall dig through the wall and carry it through; he shall cover his face, so that he may not see the land with his eyes. ¹³I will spread my net over him, and he shall be caught in my snare; and I will bring him

to Babylon, the land of the Chaldeans, yet he shall not see it; and he shall die there. ¹⁴I will scatter to every wind all who are around him, his helpers and all his troops; and I will unsheathe the sword behind them. ¹⁵And they shall know that I am the LORD, when I disperse them among the nations and scatter them through the countries. ¹⁶But I will let a few of them escape from the sword, from famine and pestilence, so that they may tell of all their abominations among the nations where they go; then they shall know that I am the LORD.

17 The word of the LORD came to me: ¹⁸Mortal, eat your bread with quaking, and drink your water with trembling and with fearfulness; ¹⁹and say to the people of the land, Thus says the Lord GOD concerning the inhabitants of Jerusalem in the land of Israel: They shall eat their bread with fearfulness, and drink their water in dismay, because their land shall be stripped of all it contains, on account of the violence of all those who live in it. ²⁰The inhabited cities shall be laid waste, and the land shall become a desolation; and you shall know that I am the LORD.

12.1–20: Symbolic actions concerning the Exile.* **12.1–7:** The first represents the exile of the house of Israel. God calls Israel *a rebellious house,* but adds *who have eyes to see, but do not see, who have ears to hear, but do not hear,* apparently in reference to Isa 6.9–10. Ezekiel is to prepare his baggage, dig through the wall, and depart with his face covered so that all may see that the exile of Israel is taking place. *I have made you a sign for the house of Israel* (compare Isa 7.14; 8.18). **8–16:** Ezekiel's action provokes questions. He relates the symbolic action to the exile of the Davidic king, which strikes at the foundation of Judean identity and the promise of God's protection of Jerusalem and the house of David (2 Sam 7; Ps 89; 132). Some understand *prince* as a reference to Zedekiah, who served as the Babylonian-appointed regent while Jehoiachin was in exile. Ezekiel's scenario of the prince's escape and capture reflects Zedekiah's capture near Jericho and blinding at Riblah prior to imprisonment in Babylon (2 Kings 25.1–7; Jer 52.4–11).

a Gk Syr: Heb *they*

17–20: Eating meals in fear dramatizes the realities of exile.

Oracles concerning prophets* and prophecy
12.21–14.11: Ezekiel's oracles* affirm the imminent fulfillment of God's visions and challenge those prophets and prophetesses who proclaim false messages of peace.

21 The word of the LORD came to me: 22 Mortal, what is this proverb of yours about the land of Israel, which says, "The days are prolonged, and every vision comes to nothing"? 23 Tell them therefore, "Thus says the Lord GOD: I will put an end to this proverb, and they shall use it no more as a proverb in Israel." But say to them, The days are near, and the fulfillment of every vision. 24 For there shall no longer be any false vision or flattering divination within the house of Israel. 25 But I the LORD will speak the word that I speak, and it will be fulfilled. It will no longer be delayed; but in your days, O rebellious house, I will speak the word and fulfill it, says the Lord GOD.

26 The word of the LORD came to me: 27 Mortal, the house of Israel is saying, "The vision that he sees is for many years ahead; he prophesies for distant times." 28 Therefore say to them, Thus says the Lord GOD: None of my words will be delayed any longer, but the word that I speak will be fulfilled, says the Lord GOD.

12.21–28. 21–25: Ezekiel responds to those who claim that his visions will not be fulfilled. *Proverb* here refers to a common saying among the people. *Vision* refers to both visual and auditory experience (see Isa 2.1). **26–27:** Ezekiel responds to the charge that his visions will be fulfilled only in the distant future by stating that they are about to be realized.

13 The word of the LORD came to me: 2 Mortal, prophesy against the prophets of Israel who are prophesying; say to those who prophesy out of their own imagination: "Hear the word of the LORD!" 3 Thus says the Lord GOD, Alas for the senseless prophets who follow their own spirit, and have seen nothing! 4 Your prophets have been like jackals among ruins, O Israel. 5 You have not gone up into the breaches, or repaired a wall for the house of Israel, so that it might stand in battle on the day of the LORD. 6 They have envisioned falsehood and lying divination; they say, "Says the LORD," when the LORD has not sent them, and yet they wait for the fulfillment of their word! 7 Have you not seen a false vision or uttered a lying divination, when you have said, "Says the LORD," even though I did not speak?

8 Therefore thus says the Lord GOD: Because you have uttered falsehood and envisioned lies, I am against you, says the Lord GOD. 9 My hand will be against the prophets who see false visions and utter lying divinations; they shall not be in the council of my people, nor be enrolled in the register of the house of Israel, nor shall they enter the land of Israel; and you shall know that I am the Lord GOD. 10 Because, in truth, because they have misled my people, saying, "Peace," when there is no peace; and because, when the people build a wall, these prophets*a* smear whitewash on it. 11 Say to those who smear whitewash on it that it shall fall. There will be a deluge of rain,*b* great hailstones will fall, and a stormy wind will break out. 12 When the wall falls, will it not be said to you, "Where is the whitewash you smeared on it?" 13 Therefore thus says the Lord GOD: In my wrath I will make a stormy wind break out, and in my anger there shall be a deluge of rain, and hailstones in wrath to destroy it. 14 I will break down the wall that you have smeared with whitewash, and bring it to the ground, so that its foundation will be laid bare; when it falls, you shall perish within it; and you shall know that I am the LORD. 15 Thus I will spend my wrath upon the wall, and upon those who have smeared it with whitewash; and I will say to you, The wall is no more, nor those who smeared it— 16 the prophets of Israel who prophesied concerning Jerusalem and saw visions of peace for it, when there was no peace, says the Lord GOD.

17 As for you, mortal, set your face against the daughters of your people, who prophesy out of their own imagination;

a Heb *they*　*b* Heb *rain and you*

prophesy against them [18]and say, Thus says the Lord GOD: Woe to the women who sew bands on all wrists, and make veils for the heads of persons of every height, in the hunt for human lives! Will you hunt down lives among my people, and maintain your own lives? [19]You have profaned me among my people for handfuls of barley and for pieces of bread, putting to death persons who should not die and keeping alive persons who should not live, by your lies to my people, who listen to lies.

20 Therefore thus says the Lord GOD: I am against your bands with which you hunt lives;[a] I will tear them from your arms, and let the lives go free, the lives that you hunt down like birds. [21]I will tear off your veils, and save my people from your hands; they shall no longer be prey in your hands; and you shall know that I am the LORD. [22]Because you have disheartened the righteous falsely, although I have not disheartened them, and you have encouraged the wicked not to turn from their wicked way and save their lives; [23]therefore you shall no longer see false visions or practice divination; I will save my people from your hand. Then you will know that I am the LORD.

13.1–23: Ezekiel must condemn prophets who announce peace (compare Jer 27–28). **1–7:** Ezekiel charges the prophets with false prophecy, claiming that they *prophesy out of their own imagination* rather than speak the word of God. He compares them to jackals who live in the ruins of others rather than do something useful. **8–16:** God is against those prophets who announce *"Peace" when there is no peace*. Much like Hananiah in Jer 27–28, prophets of peace would have relied upon the Davidic tradition of God's promise of security for the monarchy and Jerusalem. Ezekiel compares these prophecies to a wall that is *whitewashed* and then destroyed by rain, hail, and wind. Walls made of sun-dried brick are frequently destroyed by heavy rain and wind. **17–23:** Ezekiel then condemns the women who prophesy falsely and practice divination. Miriam (Ex 15.20–21), Deborah (Judg 4–5), and Huldah (2 Kings 22) demonstrate that female prophets appeared in both Israel and Judah. He points to the divinatory side of their activities in which they employ wristbands and veils (see Moses' veil in Ex 34.29–35), and he indicates that they are paid for their

services in barley and bread. Prophecy was a profession in the ancient world (1 Sam 9.7, but contrast Am 7.10–17). The false prophetesses and diviners apparently play a role in deciding capital cases in which a person's life is at stake. God will tear the bands from their hands and let the lives of such people go free like birds. Birds were frequently employed in divination in the ancient world (see Isa 8.19).

~~~~~~~~~~

14 Certain elders of Israel came to me and sat down before me. [2]And the word of the LORD came to me: [3]Mortal, these men have taken their idols into their hearts, and placed their iniquity as a stumbling block before them; shall I let myself be consulted by them? [4]Therefore speak to them, and say to them, Thus says the Lord GOD: Any of those of the house of Israel who take their idols into their hearts and place their iniquity as a stumbling block before them, and yet come to the prophet—I the LORD will answer those who come with the multitude of their idols, [5]in order that I may take hold of the hearts of the house of Israel, all of whom are estranged from me through their idols.

6 Therefore say to the house of Israel, Thus says the Lord GOD: Repent and turn away from your idols; and turn away your faces from all your abominations. [7]For any of those of the house of Israel, or of the aliens who reside in Israel, who separate themselves from me, taking their idols into their hearts and placing their iniquity as a stumbling block before them, and yet come to a prophet to inquire of me by him, I the LORD will answer them myself. [8]I will set my face against them; I will make them a sign and a byword and cut them off from the midst of my people; and you shall know that I am the LORD.

9 If a prophet is deceived and speaks a word, I, the LORD, have deceived that prophet, and I will stretch out my hand against him, and will destroy him from the midst of my people Israel. [10]And they shall bear their punishment—the punishment of the inquirer and the punishment of the prophet shall be the same— [11]so that the

a Gk Syr: Heb *lives for birds*

house of Israel may no longer go astray from me, nor defile themselves any more with all their transgressions. Then they shall be my people, and I will be their God, says the Lord GOD.

14.1–11: Ezekiel must contend with competition from other prophets. God states that the elders *have taken their idols into their hearts,* apparently a reference to their consulting pagan diviners or a charge that other Judean prophets are false. The coarse term for *idols,* literally "dung balls," demonstrates Ezekiel's disdain for such persons. In response to those who consult idols or false prophets, God states, "*I, the LORD, will answer him myself,*" and claims to deliberately deceive the false prophets so that they will be destroyed (1 Kings 22). The covenant* formula (see comment on 11.14–21) *they shall be my people, and I will be their God* conveys God's intention to convince the people to remain loyal.

12 The word of the LORD came to me: 13Mortal, when a land sins against me by acting faithlessly, and I stretch out my hand against it, and break its staff of bread and send famine upon it, and cut off from it human beings and animals, 14even if Noah, Daniel,ᵃ and Job, these three, were in it, they would save only their own lives by their righteousness, says the Lord GOD. 15If I send wild animals through the land to ravage it, so that it is made desolate, and no one may pass through because of the animals; 16even if these three men were in it, as I live, says the Lord GOD, they would save neither sons nor daughters; they alone would be saved, but the land would be desolate. 17Or if I bring a sword upon that land and say, "Let a sword pass through the land," and I cut off human beings and animals from it; 18though these three men were in it, as I live, says the Lord GOD, they would save neither sons nor daughters, but they alone would be saved. 19Or if I send a pestilence into that land, and pour out my wrath upon it with blood, to cut off humans and animals from it; 20even if Noah, Daniel,ᵃ and Job were in it, as I live, says the Lord GOD, they would save neither son nor daughter; they would save only their own lives by their righteousness.

21 For thus says the Lord GOD: How much more when I send upon Jerusalem my four deadly acts of judgment, sword, famine, wild animals, and pestilence, to cut off humans and animals from it! 22Yet, survivors shall be left in it, sons and daughters who will be brought out; they will come out to you. When you see their ways and their deeds, you will be consoled for the evil that I have brought upon Jerusalem, for all that I have brought upon it. 23They shall console you, when you see their ways and their deeds; and you shall know that it was not without cause that I did all that I have done in it, says the Lord GOD.

14.12–23: Concerning individual righteousness. After stating that God deceives false prophets and leads them to destruction, Ezekiel claims that people are responsible for their own moral action and safety from punishment. **12–20:** *Noah, Daniel, and Job* were exemplary righteous persons who had the capacity to save others. Noah saved his family during the flood (Gen 6–9), and Job saved his three friends who spoke wrongly about God (Job 42.7–9). Daniel and his friends saved only themselves by their righteousness (Dan 1; 3; 6), but in the Canaanite legend* of Aqhat, the righteous Dan-El saves his son Aqhat from death. Dan-El in Ezekiel is spelled according to the Canaanite pattern (see note a). **21–23:** The same punishments are applied to Jerusalem.

15 The word of the LORD came to me: 2 O mortal, how does the wood of the vine surpass all other wood— the vine branch that is among the trees of the forest? 3 Is wood taken from it to make anything? Does one take a peg from it on which to hang any object? 4 It is put in the fire for fuel; when the fire has consumed both ends of it and the middle of it is charred, is it useful for anything? 5 When it was whole it was used for nothing;

ᵃ Or, as otherwise read, *Danel*

Using Allegory

Allegory* is a form of extended comparison in which familiar objects or persons stand for ideals, concepts, or other ideas that cannot be seen or touched, such as love, faith, or righteousness. Although allegory is not a popular form in most present-day literature, we occasionally encounter allegory in everyday life. One allegorical figure that is familiar to the modern reader is the statue of Justice sometimes seen in courthouses or other settings. This is a sculpture of a beautiful woman, wearing a blindfold and holding balancing scales in one hand and a sword in the other. The woman's beauty symbolizes the appeal of justice to our admiration of what is right and fair. The blindfold symbolizes that justice makes no distinctions between persons, and therefore takes no account of the differences in importance between people seeking justice. The balance scales symbolize the open, public application of the rules of fairness. The sword symbolizes the penalties that justice can impose. These allegorical elements tell us something about our ideals of justice and righteousness in the contemporary world.

When Ezekiel uses the technique of allegorical comparison, as he does many times in this book, he is trying to make the concepts and ideals of faithfulness, purity, and worship real to the imaginations of his hearers or readers. Although some of his ideas and images are strange to us, with a little thought we, too, can see Ezekiel's vision of a just and holy society.

---

how much less—when the fire has
    consumed it,
and it is charred—
    can it ever be used for anything!
6 Therefore thus says the Lord GOD: Like the wood of the vine among the trees of the forest, which I have given to the fire for fuel, so I will give up the inhabitants of Jerusalem. 7I will set my face against them; although they escape from the fire, the fire shall still consume them; and you shall know that I am the LORD, when I set my face against them. 8And I will make the land desolate, because they have acted faithlessly, says the Lord GOD.

15.1–8: The allegory* of the useless vine. Ezekiel uses rhetorical* questions to compare the inhabitants of Jerusalem to the wood of a vine, which is entirely useless except for burning (see Judg 9.7–21). **2:** The wood of the vine does not surpass any other wood. **3:** It cannot be used to make anything, since vine branches are twisted and weak. **4–5:** Even when burned, the charred ends are useless. **6–8:** Like useless vine branches, Jerusalem will be burned.

---

16 The word of the LORD came to me: 2Mortal, make known to Jerusalem her abominations, 3and say, Thus says the Lord GOD to Jerusalem: Your origin and your birth were in the land of the Canaanites; your father was an Amorite, and your mother a Hittite. 4As for your birth, on the day you were born your navel cord was not cut, nor were you washed with water to cleanse you, nor rubbed with salt, nor wrapped in cloths. 5No eye pitied you, to do any of these things for you out of compassion for you; but you were thrown out in the open field, for you were abhorred on the day you were born.

16.1–63: The allegory of Jerusalem as God's adulterous wife. Compare Hosea's marriage to Gomer, whom he charged with harlotry to symbolize Israel's unfaithfulness to God (Hos 1–3; compare Jer 2–3). **1–5:** Ezekiel portrays Jerusalem as an unwanted baby who, like many female babies in pre-industrial cultures, is cast off to die as an economic liability. *Your father was an Amorite, and your mother a Hittite:* Ezekiel believes that a mixture of Amorite or Syrian peoples and Hittites or Anatolian peoples populated Canaan before Israel emerged. Jerusalem was in Canaanite (Jebusite) hands prior to David's conquest. The Jebusite population was never destroyed.

6 I passed by you, and saw you flailing about in your blood. As you lay in your blood, I said to you, "Live!" [a] and grow up [a] like a plant of the field." You grew up and became tall and arrived at full womanhood; [b] your breasts were formed, and your hair had grown; yet you were naked and bare.

8 I passed by you again and looked on you; you were at the age for love. I spread the edge of my cloak over you, and covered your nakedness: I pledged myself to you and entered into a covenant with you, says the Lord GOD, and you became mine. 9 Then I bathed you with water and washed off the blood from you, and anointed you with oil. 10 I clothed you with embroidered cloth and with sandals of fine leather; I bound you in fine linen and covered you with rich fabric. [c] 11 I adorned you with ornaments: I put bracelets on your arms, a chain on your neck, 12 a ring on your nose, earrings in your ears, and a beautiful crown upon your head. 13 You were adorned with gold and silver, while your clothing was of fine linen, rich fabric, [c] and embroidered cloth. You had choice flour and honey and oil for food. You grew exceedingly beautiful, fit to be a queen. 14 Your fame spread among the nations on account of your beauty, for it was perfect because of my splendor that I had bestowed on you, says the Lord GOD.

16.6–14: God commands the abandoned infant to live but does nothing to care for her. She grows up like a plant but remains naked. *I spread the edge of my cloak over you, and covered your nakedness* indicates God's intent to marry the young woman (Ruth 3.9). Only after taking Jerusalem in marriage does God wash the blood from her and clothe her. The description of fine clothing, jewelry, and food (see Isa 3.18–23) demonstrates God's generosity to the unwanted Jerusalem.

15 But you trusted in your beauty, and played the whore because of your fame, and lavished your whorings on any passer-by. [d] 16 You took some of your garments, and made for yourself colorful shrines, and on them played the whore; nothing like this has ever been or ever shall be. [c] 17 You also took your beautiful jewels of my gold and my silver that I had given you, and made for yourself male images, and with them played the whore; 18 and you took your embroidered garments to cover them, and set my oil and my incense before them. 19 Also my bread that I gave you—I fed you with choice flour and oil and honey—you set it before them as a pleasing odor; and so it was, says the Lord GOD. 20 You took your sons and your daughters, whom you had borne to me, and these you sacrificed to them to be devoured. As if your whorings were not enough! 21 You slaughtered my children and delivered them up as an offering to them. 22 And in all your abominations and your whorings you did not remember the days of your youth, when you were naked and bare, flailing about in your blood.

23 After all your wickedness (woe, woe to you! says the Lord GOD), 24 you built yourself a platform and made yourself a lofty place in every square; 25 at the head of every street you built your lofty place and prostituted your beauty, offering yourself to every passer-by, and multiplying your whoring. 26 You played the whore with the Egyptians, your lustful neighbors, multiplying your whoring, to provoke me to anger. 27 Therefore I stretched out my hand against you, reduced your rations, and gave you up to the will of your enemies, the daughters of the Philistines, who were ashamed of your lewd behavior. 28 You played the whore with the Assyrians, because you were insatiable; you played the whore with them, and still you were not satisfied. 29 You multiplied your whoring with Chaldea, the land of merchants; and even with this you were not satisfied.

30 How sick is your heart, says the Lord GOD, that you did all these things, the deeds of a brazen whore; 31 building your platform at the head of every street, and making your lofty place in every square! Yet you were not like a whore, because you scorned payment.

a Gk Syr: Heb *Live! I made you a myriad*   *b* Cn: Heb *ornament of ornaments*   *c* Meaning of Heb uncertain   *d* Heb adds *let it be his*

32Adulterous wife, who receives strangers instead of her husband! 33Gifts are given to all whores; but you gave your gifts to all your lovers, bribing them to come to you from all around for your whorings. 34So you were different from other women in your whorings: no one solicited you to play the whore; and you gave payment, while no payment was given to you; you were different.

16.15–34: God's charge that Jerusalem used the gifts to become a whore is a way to describe religious unfaithfulness. The metaphor* then shifts to political alliances with foreign nations. Israel allied itself with Egypt during the reigns of Solomon (1 Kings 3.1) and later Hoshea (2 Kings 17.4). Following Israel's destruction in 722/1 BCE, Assyria granted Philistia control of Israelite and Judean territory in the coastal plain. Israel made an alliance with Assyria during the reign of Menahem (2 Kings 15.17–22), and Judah turned to Assyria during the reign of Ahaz (2 Kings 16). Hezekiah established relations with Babylon (2 Kings 20; Isa 39). **30–34:** Ezekiel charges that Jerusalem pays her lovers. Ahaz's "bribe" to Tiglath-pileser (2 Kings 16.8) would be a case in point. When Nebuchadnezzar first conquered Jerusalem, he stripped the Temple of its wealth (2 Kings 24.10–17).

35 Therefore, O whore, hear the word of the LORD: 36Thus says the Lord GOD, Because your lust was poured out and your nakedness uncovered in your whoring with your lovers, and because of all your abominable idols, and because of the blood of your children that you gave to them, 37therefore, I will gather all your lovers, with whom you took pleasure, all those you loved and all those you hated; I will gather them against you from all around, and will uncover your nakedness to them, so that they may see all your nakedness. 38I will judge you as women who commit adultery and shed blood are judged, and bring blood upon you in wrath and jealousy. 39I will deliver you into their hands, and they shall throw down your platform and break down your lofty places; they shall strip you of your clothes and take your beautiful objects and leave you naked and bare. 40They shall bring up a mob against you, and they shall stone you and cut you to pieces with their swords. 41They shall burn your houses and execute judgments on you in the sight of many women; I will stop you from playing the whore, and you shall also make no more payments. 42So I will satisfy my fury on you, and my jealousy shall turn away from you; I will be calm, and will be angry no longer. 43Because you have not remembered the days of your youth, but have enraged me with all these things; therefore, I have returned your deeds upon your head, says the Lord GOD.

16.35–43: God states that all of Jerusalem's lovers, the nations with whom she was allied, will come to punish her. Deuteronomy 22.22–24 requires that an adulteress be stoned to death.

Have you not committed lewdness beyond all your abominations? 44See, everyone who uses proverbs will use this proverb about you, "Like mother, like daughter." 45You are the daughter of your mother, who loathed her husband and her children; and you are the sister of your sisters, who loathed their husbands and their children. Your mother was a Hittite and your father an Amorite. 46Your elder sister is Samaria, who lived with her daughters to the north of you; and your younger sister, who lived to the south of you, is Sodom with her daughters. 47You not only followed their ways, and acted according to their abominations; within a very little time you were more corrupt than they in all your ways. 48As I live, says the Lord GOD, your sister Sodom and her daughters have not done as you and your daughters have done. 49This was the guilt of your sister Sodom: she and her daughters had pride, excess of food, and prosperous ease, but did not aid the poor and needy. 50They were haughty, and did abominable things before me; therefore I removed them when I saw it. 51Samaria has not committed half your sins; you have committed more abominations than they, and have made your sisters appear righteous by all the abominations that you have committed. 52Bear your disgrace, you also, for you have brought about for your sisters a more favorable judgment; because of your sins in which you acted more abominably than they, they are more in the right than you. So be ashamed, you also, and bear your disgrace, for you have made your sisters appear righteous.

16.44–52: In charging that Jerusalem is like her mother *who loathed her husband and her children,* God points to the sexual *abominations* of the nations who possessed the land before Israel (Lev 18.24–30; 20.23; Gen 15.16). God compares Jerusalem to Samaria, the elder sister to the north, and Sodom, the younger sister to the south. According to biblical tradition (2 Kings 17; Gen 18–19), both cities were destroyed for their sins, but God states that Jerusalem's sins are even worse.

53 I will restore their fortunes, the fortunes of Sodom and her daughters and the fortunes of Samaria and her daughters, and I will restore your own fortunes along with theirs, 54in order that you may bear your disgrace and be ashamed of all that you have done, becoming a consolation to them. 55As for your sisters, Sodom and her daughters shall return to their former state, Samaria and her daughters shall return to their former state, and you and your daughters shall return to your former state. 56Was not your sister Sodom a byword in your mouth in the day of your pride, 57before your wickedness was uncovered? Now you are a mockery to the daughters of Aram*a* and all her neighbors, and to the daughters of the Philistines, those all around who despise you. 58You must bear the penalty of your lewdness and your abominations, says the LORD.

16.53–58: God intends to *restore the fortunes* of both Sodom and Samaria and their *daughters,* a reference to cities allied with each. In addition, God will restore Jerusalem. God intends to punish or cleanse Israel from sins much like sacrifice at the altar. Jerusalem has become a mockery to *Aram* (some manuscripts read "Edom") and Philistia, Judah's surviving neighbors.

59 Yes, thus says the Lord GOD: I will deal with you as you have done, you who have despised the oath, breaking the covenant; 60yet I will remember my covenant with you in the days of your youth, and I will establish with you an everlasting covenant. 61Then you will remember your ways, and be

ashamed when I*b* take your sisters, both your elder and your younger, and give them to you as daughters, but not on account of my*c* covenant with you. 62I will establish my covenant with you, and you shall know that I am the LORD, 63in order that you may remember and be confounded, and never open your mouth again because of your shame, when I forgive you all that you have done, says the Lord GOD.

16.59–63: *The everlasting covenant** with Jerusalem alludes to God's eternal protection for Jerusalem and the house of David (2 Sam 7; Isa 55.3) which may be compared to Jeremiah's new covenant (Jer 31.31–34). God *remembers* the covenant; only Judah is charged with *breaking* (literally, "transgressing") it. Jerusalem, not God, is charged with violating the "eternal covenant," according to which Jerusalem is destroyed. Samaria and Sodom were sisters, but they will become Jerusalem's daughters, indicating Jerusalem's premier status. *I will establish my covenant with you, and you shall know that I am the LORD* restates the covenant formula (compare Hos 2.20).

17 The word of the LORD came to me: 2O mortal, propound a riddle, and speak an allegory to the house of Israel. 3Say: Thus says the Lord GOD:

A great eagle, with great wings and long　pinions,
　rich in plumage of many colors,
　　came to the Lebanon.
　He took the top of the cedar,
4　broke off its topmost shoot;
　he carried it to a land of trade,
　　set it in a city of merchants.
5 Then he took a seed from the land,
　　placed it in fertile soil;
　a plant*d* by abundant waters,
　he set it like a willow twig.
6 It sprouted and became a vine
　　spreading out, but low;
　its branches turned toward him,
　　its roots remained where it stood.
　So it became a vine;
　　it brought forth branches,
　　put forth foliage.

a Another reading is *Edom*　　*b* Syr: Heb *you*
c Heb lacks *my*　　*d* Meaning of Heb uncertain

7 There was another great eagle,
    with great wings and much plumage.
And see! This vine stretched out
    its roots toward him;
it shot out its branches toward him,
    so that he might water it.
From the bed where it was planted
8   it was transplanted
to good soil by abundant waters,
    so that it might produce branches
    and bear fruit
    and become a noble vine.
9 Say: Thus says the Lord GOD:
    Will it prosper?
Will he not pull up its roots,
    cause its fruit to rot*a* and wither,
    its fresh sprouting leaves to fade?
No strong arm or mighty army will be
      needed
    to pull it from its roots.
10 When it is transplanted, will it thrive?
When the east wind strikes it,
    will it not utterly wither,
    wither on the bed where it grew?

17.1–24: The allegory* of the eagles, the vine, and the cedar. The allegory describes Jehoiachin's exile to Babylon, the installation of Zedekiah as king, and Zedekiah's demise when he revolted against Babylon. **1–2:** God instructs Ezekiel to speak *a riddle* and *an allegory.* **3–10:** The allegory proceeds in three stages. The first describes an eagle, later identified as Nebuchadnezzar, who breaks off the top shoot of the cedar and carries it *to a land of trade* and *a city of merchants.* Lebanon was known for "the cedars of Lebanon" (Ps 104.16), but the Davidic palace in Jerusalem, since it was built with cedar, is called the "House of the Forest of Lebanon" (1 Kings 7.2; Isa 22.9). The *topmost shoot* therefore symbolizes the Davidic monarch Jehoiachin (Isa 11.1); and the *land of trade* is Babylon (16.29). The seed that becomes a vine is Zedekiah. The *great eagle* is the Egyptian Pharaoh Psammetichus II, to whom Zedekiah turned for support in his revolt against Nebuchadnezzar (Jer 27). The rhetorical questions portray the destruction of the vine.

---

11 Then the word of the LORD came to me: 12 Say now to the rebellious house: Do you not know what these things mean? Tell them: The king of Babylon came to Jerusalem, took its king and its officials, and

brought them back with him to Babylon. 13 He took one of the royal offspring and made a covenant with him, putting him under oath (he had taken away the chief men of the land), 14 so that the kingdom might be humble and not lift itself up, and that by keeping his covenant it might stand. 15 But he rebelled against him by sending ambassadors to Egypt, in order that they might give him horses and a large army. Will he succeed? Can one escape who does such things? Can he break the covenant and yet escape? 16 As I live, says the Lord GOD, surely in the place where the king resides who made him king, whose oath he despised, and whose covenant with him he broke—in Babylon he shall die. 17 Pharaoh with his mighty army and great company will not help him in war, when ramps are cast up and siege walls built to cut off many lives. 18 Because he despised the oath and broke the covenant, because he gave his hand and yet did all these things, he shall not escape. 19 Therefore thus says the Lord GOD: As I live, I will surely return upon his head my oath that he despised, and my covenant that he broke. 20 I will spread my net over him, and he shall be caught in my snare; I will bring him to Babylon and enter into judgment with him there for the treason he has committed against me. 21 All the pick*b* of his troops shall fall by the sword, and the survivors shall be scattered to every wind; and you shall know that I, the LORD, have spoken.

17.11–21: The allegory is explained in detail. God identifies with the Babylonian king by referring to Zedekiah's revolt against Babylon as *the treason that he has committed against me.*

22 Thus says the Lord GOD:
    I myself will take a sprig
    from the lofty top of a cedar;
    I will set it out.
    I will break off a tender one
    from the topmost of its young twigs;
    I myself will plant it
    on a high and lofty mountain.

a Meaning of Heb uncertain   *b* Another reading is *fugitives*

23 On the mountain height of Israel
    I will plant it,
  in order that it may produce boughs and
        bear fruit,
    and become a noble cedar.
  Under it every kind of bird will live;
    in the shade of its branches
        will nest
    winged creatures of every kind.
24 All the trees of the field shall know
    that I am the LORD.
  I bring low the high tree,
    I make high the low tree;
  I dry up the green tree
    and make the dry tree flourish.
  I the LORD have spoken;
    I will accomplish it.

17.22–24: God employs the allegory of the cedar to promise the restoration of the Davidic monarchy (Isa 11.1–10; Jer 23.5–6; 33.15).

〜〜〜〜〜〜〜〜〜〜〜〜〜〜〜

18 The word of the LORD came to me: 2What do you mean by repeating this proverb concerning the land of Israel, "The parents have eaten sour grapes, and the children's teeth are set on edge"? 3As I live, says the Lord GOD, this proverb shall no more be used by you in Israel. 4Know that all lives are mine; the life of the parent as well as the life of the child is mine: it is only the person who sins that shall die.

18.1–32: Concerning the responsibility of the individual. The prophet* disputes the view that Israel's punishment is due to the sins of past generations (see Ex 20.5). **1–4:** The opposing view is quoted as a proverb, *"The parents have eaten sour grapes, and the children's teeth are set on edge"* (see Jer 31.29–30).

〜〜〜〜〜〜〜〜〜〜〜〜〜〜〜

5 If a man is righteous and does what is lawful and right— 6if he does not eat upon the mountains or lift up his eyes to the idols of the house of Israel, does not defile his neighbor's wife or approach a woman during her menstrual period, 7does not oppress anyone, but restores to the debtor his pledge, commits no robbery, gives his bread to the hungry and covers the naked with a garment, 8does not take advance or accrued interest, withholds his hand from iniquity, executes

true justice between contending parties, 9follows my statutes, and is careful to observe my ordinances, acting faithfully—such a one is righteous; he shall surely live, says the Lord GOD.

18.5–9: Ezekiel describes four cases. The first is a *righteous man*, whose actions are described in accordance with provisions from the Holiness Code (Lev 17–26): *eat upon the mountains,* eat meat without disposing of blood properly at the Temple* (Lev 17; 19.26); *lift up his eyes to the idols of the house of Israel,* improper worship of God (see Ex 20.4–6; Lev 19.4); *defile his neighbor's wife,* adultery (Lev 20.10; see also 19.20–22); *approach a woman during her menstrual period* (Lev 15.19–24); *does not oppress anyone,* economic oppression is unholy (Lev 19.13); *restores to the debtor his pledge* and *covers the naked with a garment,* a person's only cloak could be taken in pledge for a loan, but it had to be returned if the debtor needed it (Ex 22.25–27); *does not take advance or accrued interest* (Ex 22.25; Lev 25.35–38); *executes true justice between contending parties,* in a court of law (Lev 19.15–19). The righteous person will live.

〜〜〜〜〜〜〜〜〜〜〜〜〜〜〜

10 If he has a son who is violent, a shedder of blood, 11who does any of these things (though his father*a* does none of them), who eats upon the mountains, defiles his neighbor's wife, 12oppresses the poor and needy, commits robbery, does not restore the pledge, lifts up his eyes to the idols, commits abomination, 13takes advance or accrued interest; shall he then live? He shall not. He has done all these abominable things; he shall surely die; his blood shall be upon himself.

14 But if this man has a son who sees all the sins that his father has done, considers, and does not do likewise, 15who does not eat upon the mountains or lift up his eyes to the idols of the house of Israel, does not defile his neighbor's wife, 16does not wrong anyone, exacts no pledge, commits no robbery, but gives his bread to the hungry and covers the naked with a garment, 17withholds his hand from iniquity,*b* takes no advance or accrued interest, observes my ordinances, and

---

a Heb *he*   *b* Gk: Heb *the poor*

follows my statutes; he shall not die for his father's iniquity; he shall surely live. 18As for his father, because he practiced extortion, robbed his brother, and did what is not good among his people, he dies for his iniquity.

19 Yet you say, "Why should not the son suffer for the iniquity of the father?" When the son has done what is lawful and right, and has been careful to observe all my statutes, he shall surely live. 20The person who sins shall die. A child shall not suffer for the iniquity of a parent, nor a parent suffer for the iniquity of a child; the righteousness of the righteous shall be his own, and the wickedness of the wicked shall be his own.

21 But if the wicked turn away from all their sins that they have committed and keep all my statutes and do what is lawful and right, they shall surely live; they shall not die. 22None of the transgressions that they have committed shall be remembered against them; for the righteousness that they have done they shall live. 23Have I any pleasure in the death of the wicked, says the Lord GOD, and not rather that they should turn from their ways and live? 24But when the righteous turn away from their righteousness and commit iniquity and do the same abominable things that the wicked do, shall they live? None of the righteous deeds that they have done shall be remembered; for the treachery of which they are guilty and the sin they have committed, they shall die.

25 Yet you say, "The way of the Lord is unfair." Hear now, O house of Israel: Is my way unfair? Is it not your ways that are unfair? 26When the righteous turn away from their righteousness and commit iniquity, they shall die for it; for the iniquity that they have committed they shall die. 27Again, when the wicked turn away from the wickedness they have committed and do what is lawful and right, they shall save their life. 28Because they considered and turned away from all the transgressions that they had committed, they shall surely live; they shall not die. 29Yet the house of Israel says, "The way of the Lord is unfair." O house of Israel, are my ways unfair? Is it not your ways that are unfair?

30 Therefore I will judge you, O house of Israel, all of you according to your ways, says the Lord GOD. Repent and turn from all your transgressions; otherwise iniquity will be your ruin.[a] 31Cast away from you all the transgressions that you have committed against me, and get yourselves a new heart and a new spirit! Why will you die, O house of Israel? 32For I have no pleasure in the death of anyone, says the Lord GOD. Turn, then, and live.

18.10–32. 10–13: The son of a righteous person who sins is responsible and will die. **14–18:** The son of a sinner who does right will be spared. **19–20:** Ezekiel's opponents contend that the son is guilty for the sins of the father, but Ezekiel states that only the person who commits sins will be punished for them. **21–24:** A new principle enters the debate. Ezekiel contends that a wicked person who repents will be saved, but a righteous person who sins will be condemned. **25–29:** Ezekiel restates the preceding principle about repentance. **30–32:** *A new heart and a new spirit* (see 11.19; Jer 31.31–34; 32.36–41).

19 As for you, raise up a lamentation for the princes of Israel, 2and say:
What a lioness was your mother
　　among lions!
She lay down among young lions,
　　rearing her cubs.
3 She raised up one of her cubs;
　　he became a young lion,
and he learned to catch prey;
　　he devoured humans.
4 The nations sounded an alarm against
　　him;
　　he was caught in their pit;
and they brought him with hooks
　　to the land of Egypt.
5 When she saw that she was
　　thwarted,
　　that her hope was lost,
she took another of her cubs
　　and made him a young lion.
6 He prowled among the lions;
　　he became a young lion,
and he learned to catch prey;
　　he devoured people.

a Or *so that they shall not be a stumbling block of iniquity to you*

7 And he ravaged their strongholds,[a]
    and laid waste their towns;
    the land was appalled, and all in it,
    at the sound of his roaring.
8 The nations set upon him
    from the provinces all around;
    they spread their net over him;
    he was caught in their pit.
9 With hooks they put him in a cage,
    and brought him to the king
        of Babylon;
    they brought him into custody,
    so that his voice should be heard
        no more
    on the mountains of Israel.
10 Your mother was like a vine in
        a vineyard[b]
    transplanted by the water,
    fruitful and full of branches
        from abundant water.
11 Its strongest stem became
        a ruler's scepter;[c]
    it towered aloft
        among the thick boughs;
    it stood out in its height
        with its mass of branches.
12 But it was plucked up in fury,
    cast down to the ground;
    the east wind dried it up;
    its fruit was stripped off,
    its strong stem was withered;
        the fire consumed it.
13 Now it is transplanted into
        the wilderness,
    into a dry and thirsty land.
14 And fire has gone out from its stem,
    has consumed its branches and fruit,
    so that there remains in it no strong
        stem,
    no scepter for ruling.

This is a lamentation, and it is used as a
lamentation.

**19.1–14: Two allegories concerning the demise of
the monarchy.** Ezekiel laments the demise of the Davidic monarchy with two allegories styled as dirges or
songs of mourning. **1:** *Raise up a lamentation for the
princes of Israel:* Hebrew poetry typically had three
stressed syllables in each line. The lament,* however,
used a three-stress line followed by a two-stress line.

The poems use the 3/2 stress pattern (called "qinah")
of the funeral lament. Ezekiel refers to the kings as
"princes," thereby expressing the king's diminished
status in relation to the priests (34.24; 45.7–8). **2–9:**
The lion symbolizes the tribe of Judah and the royal
house of David (Gen 49.8–12). *A lioness was your
mother* refers to Judah or all Israel. Note the identification of Israel as the bride of God in Hosea (Hos 1–3),
Jeremiah (Jer 2–3), and Ezekiel (ch. 16). The first cub
who is *brought . . . with hooks to the land of Egypt* is
Jehoahaz, who was exiled to Egypt by Pharaoh Necho
after Josiah's death (2 Kings 23.31–34; 2 Chr 36.1–4).
The second cub who *learned to catch prey* and *devoured people* would be Jehoiakim, whom Pharaoh
Necho placed on the throne after exiling Jehoahaz.
Jeremiah condemns Jehoiakim for his injustice (Jer
21.11–22.19). *And brought him to the king of Babylon; they brought him into custody:* Jehoiachin, who
was exiled to Babylon following Jehoiakim's failed revolt (2 Kings 24.8–17; 2 Chr 36.9–10). **10–14:** This
poem employs the imagery of the vine (see chs. 15;
17; compare Isa 5.1–7). It is impossible to identify the
poem's imagery with specific individuals or countries
(see Isa 10.5–11.16; 1.29–31; 6.13). *The east wind
dried it up:* The "Sharab" or "Hamsin," a dry desert
wind like the Santa Ana winds of southern California,
is frequently employed as a symbol of God's power (Ex
14.21; 15.8–10; Isa 11.15). *Now it is transplanted into
the wilderness:* Jehoiachin's exile.

---

20 In the seventh year, in the fifth
    month, on the tenth day of the
month, certain elders of Israel came to consult the LORD, and sat down before me.
2 And the word of the LORD came to me:
3 Mortal, speak to the elders of Israel, and say
to them: Thus says the Lord GOD: Why are
you coming? To consult me? As I live, says
the Lord GOD, I will not be consulted by you.
4 Will you judge them, mortal, will you judge
them? Then let them know the abominations
of their ancestors, 5 and say to them: Thus
says the Lord GOD: On the day when I chose
Israel, I swore to the offspring of the house
of Jacob—making myself known to them in
the land of Egypt—I swore to them, saying,
I am the LORD your God. 6 On that day I
swore to them that I would bring them out

---

a Heb *his widows*   b Cn: Heb *in your blood*
c Heb *Its strongest stems became rulers' scepters*

of the land of Egypt into a land that I had searched out for them, a land flowing with milk and honey, the most glorious of all lands. 7And I said to them, Cast away the detestable things your eyes feast on, every one of you, and do not defile yourselves with the idols of Egypt; I am the LORD your God. 8But they rebelled against me and would not listen to me; not one of them cast away the detestable things their eyes feasted on, nor did they forsake the idols of Egypt.

Then I thought I would pour out my wrath upon them and spend my anger against them in the midst of the land of Egypt. 9But I acted for the sake of my name, that it should not be profaned in the sight of the nations among whom they lived, in whose sight I made myself known to them in bringing them out of the land of Egypt. 10So I led them out of the land of Egypt and brought them into the wilderness. 11I gave them my statutes and showed them my ordinances, by whose observance everyone shall live. 12Moreover I gave them my sabbaths, as a sign between me and them, so that they might know that I the LORD sanctify them. 13But the house of Israel rebelled against me in the wilderness; they did not observe my statutes but rejected my ordinances, by whose observance everyone shall live; and my sabbaths they greatly profaned.

Then I thought I would pour out my wrath upon them in the wilderness, to make an end of them. 14But I acted for the sake of my name, so that it should not be profaned in the sight of the nations, in whose sight I had brought them out. 15Moreover I swore to them in the wilderness that I would not bring them into the land that I had given them, a land flowing with milk and honey, the most glorious of all lands, 16because they rejected my ordinances and did not observe my statutes, and profaned my sabbaths; for their heart went after their idols. 17Nevertheless my eye spared them, and I did not destroy them or make an end of them in the wilderness.

20.1–44: Ezekiel's assessment of Israel's past and future. Ezekiel's overview of Israel's history in the wilderness provides a basis for projecting a future in which Israel will be returned to the wilderness and purged. **1–2:** *The seventh year . . . fifth month . . . tenth day:* August 14, 591 BCE. **3–4:** God refuses to answer the elders and instead calls upon Ezekiel to judge them. **5–32:** God rehearses the history of Israel's rebellion during the Exodus and Wilderness periods (see Ps 106). **5–6:** *I chose Israel:* God uses royal language (see 2 Sam 6.21; 1 Kings 8.16) to prepare the reader for God's role as king (v. 33). *I am the LORD your God. . . . I would bring them out of the land of Egypt:* See Ex 20.2. **7–8:** Apostasy in Egypt: Ex 14.10–12; Josh 24.14; Ps 106.7. **9:** *I acted for the sake of my name:* A key issue in Ezekiel (20.14, 22; 36.22; compare Ex 15.3; 32.12). **10–26:** Apostasy in the wilderness: Ex 32–34; Num 14; 25. **11–12:** The sabbath is the foundational sign of the covenant* (Ex 20.8–11; 31.12–17). **13–17:** The rebellion of the first generation is the golden calf incident (Ex 32–34) and the reaction to the report of the spies (Num 13–14) in which Moses persuaded God not to destroy the entire people (Ex 33.12–33; Num 14.13–25).

18 I said to their children in the wilderness, Do not follow the statutes of your parents, nor observe their ordinances, nor defile yourselves with their idols. 19I the LORD am your God; follow my statutes, and be careful to observe my ordinances, 20and hallow my sabbaths that they may be a sign between me and you, so that you may know that I the LORD am your God. 21But the children rebelled against me; they did not follow my statutes, and were not careful to observe my ordinances, by whose observance everyone shall live; they profaned my sabbaths.

Then I thought I would pour out my wrath upon them and spend my anger against them in the wilderness. 22But I withheld my hand, and acted for the sake of my name, so that it should not be profaned in the sight of the nations, in whose sight I had brought them out. 23Moreover I swore to them in the wilderness that I would scatter them among the nations and disperse them through the countries, 24because they had not executed my ordinances, but had rejected my statutes and profaned my sabbaths, and their eyes were set on their ancestors' idols. 25Moreover I gave them statutes that were not good and ordinances by which they could not live. 26I defiled them through their very gifts, in their offering up all their firstborn, in order that I might horrify them, so that they might know that I am the LORD.

20.18–26: Following Israel's rebellion at the report of the spies, God condemned the people to death in the wilderness (Num 14.26–38). The rebellion of the second generation refers to acts of apostasy following the incident of the spies (Meribah, Num 20; Baal of Peor, Num 25).

27 Therefore, mortal, speak to the house of Israel and say to them, Thus says the Lord GOD: In this again your ancestors blasphemed me, by dealing treacherously with me. 28 For when I had brought them into the land that I swore to give them, then wherever they saw any high hill or any leafy tree, there they offered their sacrifices and presented the provocation of their offering; there they sent up their pleasing odors, and there they poured out their drink offerings. 29 (I said to them, What is the high place to which you go? So it is called Bamah*a* to this day.) 30 Therefore say to the house of Israel, Thus says the Lord GOD: Will you defile yourselves after the manner of your ancestors and go astray after their detestable things? 31 When you offer your gifts and make your children pass through the fire, you defile yourselves with all your idols to this day. And shall I be consulted by you, O house of Israel? As I live, says the Lord GOD, I will not be consulted by you.

32 What is in your mind shall never happen—the thought, "Let us be like the nations, like the tribes of the countries, and worship wood and stone."

20.27–32: Apostasy in the land of Israel. 32: *Let us be like the nations:* See Deut 17.14; 1 Sam 8.4–5 concerning the institution of kingship.

33 As I live, says the Lord GOD, surely with a mighty hand and an outstretched arm, and with wrath poured out, I will be king over you. 34 I will bring you out from the peoples and gather you out of the countries where you are scattered, with a mighty hand and an outstretched arm, and with wrath poured out; 35 and I will bring you into the

wilderness of the peoples, and there I will enter into judgment with you face to face. 36 As I entered into judgment with your ancestors in the wilderness of the land of Egypt, so I will enter into judgment with you, says the Lord GOD. 37 I will make you pass under the staff, and will bring you within the bond of the covenant. 38 I will purge out the rebels among you, and those who transgress against me; I will bring them out of the land where they reside as aliens, but they shall not enter the land of Israel. Then you shall know that I am the LORD.

39 As for you, O house of Israel, thus says the Lord GOD: Go serve your idols, everyone of you now and hereafter, if you will not listen to me; but my holy name you shall no more profane with your gifts and your idols.

40 For on my holy mountain, the mountain height of Israel, says the Lord GOD, there all the house of Israel, all of them, shall serve me in the land; there I will accept them, and there I will require your contributions and the choicest of your gifts, with all your sacred things. 41 As a pleasing odor I will accept you, when I bring you out from the peoples, and gather you out of the countries where you have been scattered; and I will manifest my holiness among you in the sight of the nations. 42 You shall know that I am the LORD, when I bring you into the land of Israel, the country that I swore to give to your ancestors. 43 There you shall remember your ways and all the deeds by which you have polluted yourselves; and you shall loathe yourselves for all the evils that you have committed. 44 And you shall know that I am the LORD, when I deal with you for my name's sake, not according to your evil ways, or corrupt deeds, O house of Israel, says the Lord GOD.

20.33–44: God returns Israel to the wilderness to purge and restore the nation. **33:** *I will be king over you:* One of God's fundamental claims. **35:** *Wilderness of the peoples* associates Israel's exile among the nations with the wilderness tradition. **37:** *Pass under the staff:* Be counted to determine the offering due to

a That is *High Place*

God (see Lev 27.32). **40–44:** *My holy mountain:* the Jerusalem Temple.

45[a] The word of the LORD came to me: 46Mortal, set your face toward the south, preach against the south, and prophesy against the forest land in the Negeb; 47say to the forest of the Negeb, Hear the word of the LORD: Thus says the Lord GOD, I will kindle a fire in you, and it shall devour every green tree in you and every dry tree; the blazing flame shall not be quenched, and all faces from south to north shall be scorched by it. 48All flesh shall see that I the LORD have kindled it; it shall not be quenched. 49Then I said, "Ah Lord GOD! they are saying of me, 'Is he not a maker of allegories?'"

20.45–49: A prophecy against the Negeb. The Negeb is the desert region of southern Judah from which spies were sent into Canaan (Num 13.17, 22) prior to the rebellion in the wilderness. *South* designates the location of the Edomites (25.13), who are condemned for assisting Babylon in Judah's destruction (25.12–14).

21[b] The word of the LORD came to me: 2Mortal, set your face toward Jerusalem and preach against the sanctuaries; prophesy against the land of Israel 3and say to the land of Israel, Thus says the LORD: I am coming against you, and will draw my sword out of its sheath, and will cut off from you both righteous and wicked. 4Because I will cut off from you both righteous and wicked, therefore my sword shall go out of its sheath against all flesh from south to north; 5and all flesh shall know that I the LORD have drawn my sword out of its sheath; it shall not be sheathed again. 6Moan therefore, mortal; moan with breaking heart and bitter grief before their eyes. 7And when they say to you, "Why do you moan?" you shall say, "Because of the news that has come. Every heart will melt and all hands will be feeble, every spirit will faint and all knees will turn to water. See, it comes and it will be fulfilled," says the Lord GOD.

21.1–32: Oracles concerning God's sword. These oracles* may have accompanied a symbolic action in-

volving a sword (5.1–4; 14.21). **1–7:** Ezekiel speaks toward the Jerusalem sanctuary as the holy center of the nation.

8 And the word of the LORD came to me: 9Mortal, prophesy and say: Thus says the Lord; Say:
A sword, a sword is sharpened,
    it is also polished;
10 it is sharpened for slaughter,
    honed to flash like lightning!
How can we make merry?
    You have despised the rod,
    and all discipline.[c]
11 The sword[d] is given to be polished,
    to be grasped in the hand;
it is sharpened, the sword is polished,
    to be placed in the slayer's hand.
12 Cry and wail, O mortal,
    for it is against my people;
it is against all Israel's princes;
    they are thrown to the sword,
    together with my people.
    Ah! Strike the thigh!
13For consider: What! If you despise the rod, will it not happen?[c] says the Lord GOD.
14 And you, mortal, prophesy;
    strike hand to hand.
Let the sword fall twice, thrice;
    it is a sword for killing.
A sword for great slaughter—
    it surrounds them;
15 therefore hearts melt
    and many stumble.
At all their gates I have set
    the point[e] of the sword.
Ah! It is made for flashing,
    it is polished[e] for slaughter.
16 Attack to the right!
    Engage to the left!
    —wherever your edge is directed.
17 I too will strike hand to hand,
    I will satisfy my fury;
    I the LORD have spoken.

21.8–17: Ezekiel's song of the sword. *You have despised the rod:* A rod might normally be used for dis-

a Ch 21.1 in Heb   *b* Ch 21.6 in Heb   *c* Meaning of Heb uncertain   *d* Heb *It*   *e* Tg: Heb *wrapped up* cipline (Prov 10.13; 22.15), but now a deadly instrument is required.

18 The word of the LORD came to me: 19Mortal, mark out two roads for the sword of the king of Babylon to come; both of them shall issue from the same land. And make a signpost, make it for a fork in the road leading to a city; 20mark out the road for the sword to come to Rabbah of the Ammonites or to Judah and to*a* Jerusalem the fortified. 21For the king of Babylon stands at the parting of the way, at the fork in the two roads, to use divination; he shakes the arrows, he consults the teraphim,*b* he inspects the liver. 22Into his right hand comes the lot for Jerusalem, to set battering rams, to call out for slaughter, for raising the battle cry, to set battering rams against the gates, to cast up ramps, to build siege towers. 23But to them it will seem like a false divination; they have sworn solemn oaths; but he brings their guilt to remembrance, bringing about their capture.

24 Therefore thus says the Lord GOD: Because you have brought your guilt to remembrance, in that your transgressions are uncovered, so that in all your deeds your sins appear—because you have come to remembrance, you shall be taken in hand.*c*
25 As for you, vile, wicked prince of Israel,
   you whose day has come,
   the time of final punishment,
26 thus says the Lord GOD:
Remove the turban, take off the crown;
   things shall not remain as they are.
Exalt that which is low,
   abase that which is high.
27 A ruin, a ruin, a ruin—
   I will make it!
(Such has never occurred.)
Until he comes whose right it is;
   to him I will give it.

28 As for you, mortal, prophesy, and say, Thus says the Lord GOD concerning the Ammonites, and concerning their reproach; say:
A sword, a sword! Drawn for slaughter,
   polished to consume,*d* to flash like
      lightning.
29 Offering false visions for you,
   divining lies for you,
they place you over the necks

of the vile, wicked ones—
   those whose day has come,
      the time of final punishment.
30 Return it to its sheath!
In the place where you were created,
   in the land of your origin,
      I will judge you.
31 I will pour out my indignation upon
      you,
   with the fire of my wrath
      I will blow upon you.
I will deliver you into brutish hands,
   those skillful to destroy.
32 You shall be fuel for the fire,
   your blood shall enter the earth;
you shall be remembered no more,
   for I the LORD have spoken.

21.18–32: The sword of Babylon. 18–23: When the Babylonian king reaches a fork in the road, he employs divination to decide which route to take. His alternatives are Jerusalem and Rabbah, the capital of Ammon. Ammon is one of Judah's allies in revolt against Babylon (Jer 27.3). Jerusalem is a former ally of Babylon (2 Kings 20.12–19; Isa 39), but Judah's revolt justifies the protracted siege. *He shakes the arrows, he consults the teraphim, he inspects the liver:* Common techniques of divination. *Teraphim* are household or clan★ gods (Gen 31.19; Judg 17.5; 18.17, 20). **24–27:** The *vile, wicked prince* is Zedekiah. **28–32:** The sword will be wielded against Ammon, but it will be destroyed in Babylon where it was created.

22 The word of the LORD came to me: 2You, mortal, will you judge, will you judge the bloody city? Then declare to it all its abominable deeds. 3You shall say, Thus says the Lord GOD: A city! Shedding blood within itself; its time has come; making its idols, defiling itself. 4You have become guilty by the blood that you have shed, and defiled by the idols that you have made; you have brought your day near, the appointed time of your years has come. Therefore I have made you a disgrace before the nations, and a mockery to all the countries. 5Those who are near and those who are far from you will mock you, you infamous one, full of tumult.

a Gk Syr: Heb *Judah in*   *b* Or *the household gods*
c Or *be taken captive*   *d* Cn: Heb *to contain*

6 The princes of Israel in you, everyone according to his power, have been bent on shedding blood. 7Father and mother are treated with contempt in you; the alien residing within you suffers extortion; the orphan and the widow are wronged in you. 8You have despised my holy things, and profaned my sabbaths. 9In you are those who slander to shed blood, those in you who eat upon the mountains, who commit lewdness in your midst. 10In you they uncover their fathers' nakedness; in you they violate women in their menstrual periods. 11One commits abomination with his neighbor's wife; another lewdly defiles his daughter-in-law; another in you defiles his sister, his father's daughter. 12In you, they take bribes to shed blood; you take both advance interest and accrued interest, and make gain of your neighbors by extortion; and you have forgotten me, says the Lord GOD.

13 See, I strike my hands together at the dishonest gain you have made, and at the blood that has been shed within you. 14Can your courage endure, or can your hands remain strong in the days when I shall deal with you? I the LORD have spoken, and I will do it. 15I will scatter you among the nations and disperse you through the countries, and I will purge your filthiness out of you. 16And I[a] shall be profaned through you in the sight of the nations; and you shall know that I am the LORD.

22.1–31: **Oracles against Jerusalem.** Compare Isa 1.2–31. **2–16:** Ezekiel's preoccupation with blood derives from his role as a priest, which requires the proper treatment of blood since it is sacred (Lev 17). The crimes listed here derive especially from the Holiness Code in Lev 17–26: *shedding blood* (Lev 19.26; Gen 9.1–7); contempt against parents (Lev 20.9; Ex 21.17); extortion of the aliens, orphans, and widows (Lev 19.33–34; Ex 22.21–22; Deut 14.29); *holy things . . . sabbaths* (Lev 19.30); *slander* (Lev 19.16); *uncover father's nakedness* (Lev 18.8; 20.11); relations with menstruating women (Lev 18.19); incest (Lev 18; 20); bribery (Lev 19.15); interest on loans (Lev 25.36–37); extortion of a neighbor (Lev 19.15–18, 35–36).

17 The word of the LORD came to me: 18Mortal, the house of Israel has become dross to me; all of them, silver,[b] bronze, tin, iron, and lead. In the smelter they have become dross. 19Therefore thus says the Lord GOD: Because you have all become dross, I will gather you into the midst of Jerusalem. 20As one gathers silver, bronze, iron, lead, and tin into a smelter, to blow the fire upon them in order to melt them; so I will gather you in my anger and in my wrath, and I will put you in and melt you. 21I will gather you and blow upon you with the fire of my wrath, and you shall be melted within it. 22As silver is melted in a smelter, so you shall be melted in it; and you shall know that I the LORD have poured out my wrath upon you.

23 The word of the LORD came to me: 24Mortal, say to it: You are a land that is not cleansed, not rained upon in the day of indignation. 25Its princes[c] within it are like a roaring lion tearing the prey; they have devoured human lives; they have taken treasure and precious things; they have made many widows within it. 26Its priests have done violence to my teaching and have profaned my holy things; they have made no distinction between the holy and the common, neither have they taught the difference between the unclean and the clean, and they have disregarded my sabbaths, so that I am profaned among them. 27Its officials within it are like wolves tearing the prey, shedding blood, destroying lives to get dishonest gain. 28Its prophets have smeared whitewash on their behalf, seeing false visions and divining lies for them, saying, "Thus says the Lord GOD," when the LORD has not spoken. 29The people of the land have practiced extortion and committed robbery; they have oppressed the poor and needy, and have extorted from the alien without redress. 30And I sought for anyone among them who would repair the wall and stand in the breach before me on behalf of the land, so that I would not destroy it; but I found no one. 31Therefore I have poured out my indignation upon them; I have consumed them with the fire of my wrath; I have returned their conduct upon their heads, says the Lord GOD.

a Gk Syr Vg: Heb *you* b Transposed from the end of the verse; compare verse 20 c Gk: Heb *indignation*.
25*A conspiracy of its prophets*

22.17–31. 17–22: Just as precious metals are smelted to remove dross, Israel will be purified in fire to remove its sins and impurities (Isa 1.21–26). **23–31:** The prophet* names all classes of people in Jerusalem, including *its princes, its priests, its officials, its prophets,* and *the people of the land.*

23 The word of the LORD came to me: 2Mortal, there were two women, the daughters of one mother; 3they played the whore in Egypt; they played the whore in their youth; their breasts were caressed there, and their virgin bosoms were fondled. 4Oholah was the name of the elder and Oholibah the name of her sister. They became mine, and they bore sons and daughters. As for their names, Oholah is Samaria, and Oholibah is Jerusalem.

5 Oholah played the whore while she was mine; she lusted after her lovers the Assyrians, warriors*a* 6clothed in blue, governors and commanders, all of them handsome young men, mounted horsemen. 7She bestowed her favors upon them, the choicest men of Assyria all of them; and she defiled herself with all the idols of everyone for whom she lusted. 8She did not give up her whorings that she had practiced since Egypt; for in her youth men had lain with her and fondled her virgin bosom and poured out their lust upon her. 9Therefore I delivered her into the hands of her lovers, into the hands of the Assyrians, for whom she lusted. 10These uncovered her nakedness; they seized her sons and her daughters; and they killed her with the sword. Judgment was executed upon her, and she became a byword among women.

23.1–49: Oholah and Oholibah. Presupposing the portrayal of Israel as God's wife (compare Hos 1–3; Jer 2–3), Ezekiel employs the metaphor* of harlotry to describe Samaria and Jerusalem (see ch. 16). *Oholah,* "her tent," refers to Samaria. The name *Oholah* alludes to the presence of God who dwells in a tent (according to the Exodus and Wilderness traditions; compare 2 Sam 7.6). *Oholibah,* "my tent is in her," refers to Jerusalem and to the presence of the Temple.* **5–10:** Oholah's or Samaria's relations with the officers of Assyria presuppose its earlier alliance with Assyria

under the Jehu dynasty,* specifically, Menahem (2 Kings 15.17–22), and Hoshea (2 Kings 17.1–6). Ezekiel portrays this alliance as harlotry and argues that it led to Israel's destruction.

11 Her sister Oholibah saw this, yet she was more corrupt than she in her lusting and in her whorings, which were worse than those of her sister. 12She lusted after the Assyrians, governors and commanders, warriors*a* clothed in full armor, mounted horsemen, all of them handsome young men. 13And I saw that she was defiled; they both took the same way. 14But she carried her whorings further; she saw male figures carved on the wall, images of the Chaldeans portrayed in vermilion, 15with belts around their waists, with flowing turbans on their heads, all of them looking like officers—a picture of Babylonians whose native land was Chaldea. 16When she saw them she lusted after them, and sent messengers to them in Chaldea. 17And the Babylonians came to her into the bed of love, and they defiled her with their lust; and after she defiled herself with them, she turned from them in disgust. 18When she carried on her whorings so openly and flaunted her nakedness, I turned in disgust from her, as I had turned from her sister. 19Yet she increased her whorings, remembering the days of her youth, when she played the whore in the land of Egypt 20and lusted after her paramours there, whose members were like those of donkeys, and whose emission was like that of stallions. 21Thus you longed for the lewdness of your youth, when the Egyptians*b* fondled your bosom and caressed*c* your young breasts.

23.11–21: Ezekiel charges that Oholibah, Jerusalem, was even worse than her sister in pursuing both the Assyrians and the Chaldeans or Babylonians (see Jer 3.6–10, 11). King Ahaz of Judah requested Assyrian assistance against Israel in the Syro-Ephraimitic War (2 Kings 16), and Hezekiah later made an alliance with Babylon against Assyria (2 Kings 20.11–19; Isa 39). The reference to relations with Egypt may recall Solo-

a Meaning of Heb uncertain   *b* Two Mss: MT *from Egypt*   *c* Cn: Heb *for the sake of* mon's early alliance with Egypt (1 Kings 3.1) and Jehoiakim's support from Pharaoh Neco prior to his turn to Babylon (2 Kings 23.31–24.7).

22 Therefore, O Oholibah, thus says the Lord GOD: I will rouse against you your lovers from whom you turned in disgust, and I will bring them against you from every side: ²³the Babylonians and all the Chaldeans, Pekod and Shoa and Koa, and all the Assyrians with them, handsome young men, governors and commanders all of them, officers and warriors,^a all of them riding on horses. ²⁴They shall come against you from the north^b with chariots and wagons and a host of peoples; they shall set themselves against you on every side with buckler, shield, and helmet, and I will commit the judgment to them, and they shall judge you according to their ordinances. ²⁵I will direct my indignation against you, in order that they may deal with you in fury. They shall cut off your nose and your ears, and your survivors shall fall by the sword. They shall seize your sons and your daughters, and your survivors shall be devoured by fire. ²⁶They shall also strip you of your clothes and take away your fine jewels. ²⁷So I will put an end to your lewdness and your whoring brought from the land of Egypt; you shall not long for them, or remember Egypt any more. ²⁸For thus says the Lord GOD: I will deliver you into the hands of those whom you hate, into the hands of those from whom you turned in disgust; ²⁹and they shall deal with you in hatred, and take away all the fruit of your labor, and leave you naked and bare, and the nakedness of your whorings shall be exposed. Your lewdness and your whorings ³⁰have brought this upon you, because you played the whore with the nations, and polluted yourself with their idols. ³¹You have gone the way of your sister; therefore I will give her cup into your hand. ³²Thus says the Lord GOD:

You shall drink your sister's cup,
    deep and wide;
you shall be scorned and derided,
    it holds so much.
³³ You shall be filled with drunkenness
    and sorrow.

A cup of horror and desolation

is the cup of your sister Samaria;
³⁴ you shall drink it and drain it out,
    and gnaw its sherds,
    and tear out your breasts;

for I have spoken, says the Lord GOD. ³⁵Therefore thus says the Lord GOD: Because you have forgotten me and cast me behind your back, therefore bear the consequences of your lewdness and whorings.

22.22–35: Ezekiel declares that Oholibah's *lovers*, the Babylonians and their allies, will conquer Jerusalem. *Pekod* (see Jer 50.21), *Shoa*, and *Koa* are Aramean tribes allied with Babylon. Drinking from the sister's cup is a common motif* in Judean prophecy (Isa 51.17, 22; Jer 25.15–29; 51.7; Hab 2.16).

36 The LORD said to me: Mortal, will you judge Oholah and Oholibah? Then declare to them their abominable deeds. ³⁷For they have committed adultery, and blood is on their hands; with their idols they have committed adultery; and they have even offered up to them for food the children whom they had borne to me. ³⁸Moreover this they have done to me: they have defiled my sanctuary on the same day and profaned my sabbaths. ³⁹For when they had slaughtered their children for their idols, on the same day they came into my sanctuary to profane it. This is what they did in my house.

40 They even sent for men to come from far away, to whom a messenger was sent, and they came. For them you bathed yourself, painted your eyes, and decked yourself with ornaments; ⁴¹you sat on a stately couch, with a table spread before it on which you had placed my incense and my oil. ⁴²The sound of a raucous multitude was around her, with many of the rabble brought in drunken from the wilderness; and they put bracelets on the arms^c of the women, and beautiful crowns upon their heads.

43 Then I said, Ah, she is worn out with adulteries, but they carry on their sexual acts with her. ⁴⁴For they have gone in to her, as one goes in to a whore. Thus they went in to Oholah and to Oholibah, wanton women.

a Compare verses 6 and 12: Heb *officers and called ones*
b Gk: Meaning of Heb uncertain   c Heb *hands*

45But righteous judges shall declare them guilty of adultery and of bloodshed; because they are adulteresses and blood is on their hands.

46 For thus says the Lord GOD: Bring up an assembly against them, and make them an object of terror and of plunder. 47The assembly shall stone them and with their swords they shall cut them down; they shall kill their sons and their daughters, and burn up their houses. 48Thus will I put an end to lewdness in the land, so that all women may take warning and not commit lewdness as you have done. 49They shall repay you for your lewdness, and you shall bear the penalty for your sinful idolatry; and you shall know that I am the Lord GOD.

22.36–49: *They have defiled my sanctuary and profaned my sabbaths:* See ch. 8. *They even sent for men to come from far away* is a reference to Judean attempts to find allies (compare Jer 27.3). The sisters' punishment reflects that of an adulterous woman (Lev 20.10) or a person who profanes God (Lev 20.2–5). *So that all women may take warning and not commit lewdness:* Ezekiel is frequently accused of misogyny.

24 In the ninth year, in the tenth month, on the tenth day of the month, the word of the LORD came to me: 2Mortal, write down the name of this day, this very day. The king of Babylon has laid siege to Jerusalem this very day. 3And utter an allegory to the rebellious house and say to them, Thus says the Lord GOD:

Set on the pot, set it on,
    pour in water also;
4 put in it the pieces,
    all the good pieces, the thigh and the shoulder;
    fill it with choice bones.
5 Take the choicest one of the flock,
    pile the logs[a] under it;
    boil its pieces,[b]
    seethe[c] also its bones in it.

6 Therefore thus says the Lord GOD:
Woe to the bloody city,
    the pot whose rust is in it,
    whose rust has not gone out of it!

Empty it piece by piece,
    making no choice at all.[d]
7 For the blood she shed is inside it;
    she placed it on a bare rock;
    she did not pour it out on the ground,
    to cover it with earth.
8 To rouse my wrath, to take vengeance,
    I have placed the blood she shed
    on a bare rock,
    so that it may not be covered.
9Therefore thus says the Lord GOD:
Woe to the bloody city!
    I will even make the pile great.
10 Heap up the logs, kindle the fire;
    boil the meat well, mix in the spices,
    let the bones be burned.
11 Stand it empty upon the coals,
    so that it may become hot, its copper glow,
    its filth melt in it, its rust be consumed.
12 In vain I have wearied myself;[e]
    its thick rust does not depart.
    To the fire with its rust![f]
13 Yet, when I cleansed you in your filthy lewdness,
    you did not become clean from your filth;
    you shall not again be cleansed
    until I have satisfied my fury upon you.
14I the LORD have spoken; the time is coming, I will act. I will not refrain, I will not spare, I will not relent. According to your ways and your doings I will judge you, says the Lord GOD.

24.1–14: **The allegory* of the pot.** As a Temple priest, Ezekiel's duties include tending to pots used to cook sacrificial meat (1 Sam 2.12–17). Like Jeremiah (a priest descended from Eli), he employs activities from his own life as symbolic means to express God's word (see Jer 1.13). **1–2:** *The ninth year . . . the tenth month . . . the tenth day:* January 15, 588 BCE, apparently the day on which Nebuchadnezzar begins the siege of Jerusalem. **3–5:** *The thigh and the shoulder,*

a Compare verse 10: Heb *the bones*   b Two Mss: Heb *its boilings*   c Cn: Heb *its bones seethe*   d Heb *piece, no lot has fallen on it*   e Cn: Meaning of Heb uncertain   f Meaning of Heb uncertain the choice offerings (Num 18.12), including the breast and thigh (Ex 29.26–28; Lev 7.28–36; 10.12–15; Num 18.18; Gen 32.32), are given to the priests. **6–8:** The imagery of the corroded bottom of the pot symbolizes the bloody crimes of Jerusalem. Blood is sacred and must be covered when shed (Lev 17.13–16; Gen 9.1–7). **9–14:** As a cauldron is cleansed by fire, Ezekiel calls for the "cleansing" of Jerusalem by fire.

15 The word of the LORD came to me: 16Mortal, with one blow I am about to take away from you the delight of your eyes; yet you shall not mourn or weep, nor shall your tears run down. 17Sigh, but not aloud; make no mourning for the dead. Bind on your turban, and put your sandals on your feet; do not cover your upper lip or eat the bread of mourners.*a* 18So I spoke to the people in the morning, and at evening my wife died. And on the next morning I did as I was commanded.

19 Then the people said to me, "Will you not tell us what these things mean for us, that you are acting this way?" 20Then I said to them: The word of the LORD came to me: 21Say to the house of Israel, Thus says the Lord GOD: I will profane my sanctuary, the pride of your power, the delight of your eyes, and your heart's desire; and your sons and your daughters whom you left behind shall fall by the sword. 22And you shall do as I have done; you shall not cover your upper lip or eat the bread of mourners.*a* 23Your turbans shall be on your heads and your sandals on your feet; you shall not mourn or weep, but you shall pine away in your iniquities and groan to one another. 24Thus Ezekiel shall be a sign to you; you shall do just as he has done. When this comes, then you shall know that I am the Lord GOD.

25 And you, mortal, on the day when I take from them their stronghold, their joy and glory, the delight of their eyes and their heart's affection, and also*b* their sons and their daughters, 26on that day, one who has escaped will come to you to report to you the news. 27On that day your mouth shall be opened to the one who has escaped, and you shall speak and no longer be silent. So you shall be a sign to them; and they shall know that I am the LORD.

24.15–27: The death of Ezekiel's wife. The death of Ezekiel's wife symbolizes the destruction of Jerusalem (see Isa 7; 8; Jer 16; Hos 1–3). **15–18:** Ezekiel's action draws upon priestly sanctity to symbolize the inability of God and the people of Judah to mourn the loss of Jerusalem when in exile. Priests may not come into contact with the dead (Lev 21.1–12), and the high priest may not mourn for the dead (Lev 21.10–12; compare 10.1–7). **19–24:** *I will profane my sanctuary:* Only the priests could enter the most holy place. The people are to be fully dressed, with turbans and sandals, as they go into exile. **25–27:** During the Temple service, the priests officiated in silence. When the Temple is destroyed, Ezekiel will be able to speak again.

EZEKIEL'S ORACLES CONCERNING THE NATIONS

Chs. 25–32: Like other prophetic books (Isa 13–23; Jer 46–51), Ezekiel contains a section of oracles concerning foreign nations, which are intended to demonstrate God's power throughout the world. The nations included here, Ammon, Moab, Edom, Philistia, Tyre, and Egypt, would all be considered as targets of the Babylonian empire, although Egypt was never taken. Ezekiel identifies the projected expansion of Babylonia as an act of God.

25 The word of the LORD came to me: 2Mortal, set your face toward the Ammonites and prophesy against them. 3Say to the Ammonites, Hear the word of the Lord GOD: Thus says the Lord GOD, Because you said, "Aha!" over my sanctuary when it was profaned, and over the land of Israel when it was made desolate, and over the house of Judah when it went into exile; 4therefore I am handing you over to the people of the east for a possession. They shall set their encampments among you and pitch their tents in your midst; they shall eat your fruit, and they shall drink your milk. 5I will make Rabbah a pasture for camels and Ammon a fold for flocks. Then you shall know that I am the LORD. 6For thus says the Lord GOD: Because you have clapped your hands and stamped your feet and rejoiced with all the malice within you against the land of Israel,

a Vg Tg: Heb *of men*   *b* Heb lacks *and also*

7therefore I have stretched out my hand against you, and will hand you over as plunder to the nations. I will cut you off from the peoples and will make you perish out of the countries; I will destroy you. Then you shall know that I am the LORD.

25.1–7: The oracle concerning Ammon. The Babylonians employed Ammonites against Judah (2 Kings 24.1–2). Later, the Ammonites joined Judah in an anti-Babylonian coalition (Jer 27.3). Ammon was located east of the Jordan River. *Rabbah*, the site of present-day Amman, Jordan, was the capital. The Ammonites are condemned in part for mocking the destruction of the Jerusalem Temple. *The people of the east* are nomadic Arab tribes from the northern Arabian desert who moved into Ammon and Moab following their destruction by Babylonia.

8 Thus says the Lord GOD: Because Moabᵃ said, The house of Judah is like all the other nations, 9therefore I will lay open the flank of Moab from the townsᵇ on its frontier, the glory of the country, Beth-jeshimoth, Baal-meon, and Kiriathaim. 10I will give it along with Ammon to the people of the east as a possession. Thus Ammon shall be remembered no more among the nations, 11and I will execute judgments upon Moab. Then they shall know that I am the LORD.

25.8–11: The oracle concerning Moab. Like Ammon, the Moabites assisted the Babylonians against Judah (2 Kings 24.1–2) and later joined the anti-Babylonian coalition (Jer 27.3). Moab was located east of the southern portion of the Dead Sea.

12 Thus says the Lord GOD: Because Edom acted revengefully against the house of Judah and has grievously offended in taking vengeance upon them, 13therefore thus says the Lord GOD, I will stretch out my hand against Edom, and cut off from it humans and animals, and I will make it desolate; from Teman even to Dedan they shall fall by the sword. 14I will lay my vengeance upon Edom by the hand of my people Israel; and they shall act in Edom according to my anger and according to my wrath; and they shall know my vengeance, says the Lord GOD.

25.12–14: The oracle concerning Edom. Edom symbolizes God's wrath, perhaps because of its role in the destruction of the Jerusalem Temple (Ps 137.7; Lam 4.21–22; Ob 1–14). It was located southeast of the Dead Sea and sometimes encroached upon southern Judean territories. Edom's ancestor, Esau, was Jacob's twin brother (Gen 25–35).

15 Thus says the Lord GOD: Because with unending hostilities the Philistines acted in vengeance, and with malice of heart took revenge in destruction; 16therefore thus says the Lord GOD, I will stretch out my hand against the Philistines, cut off the Cherethites, and destroy the rest of the seacoast. 17I will execute great vengeance on them with wrathful punishments. Then they shall know that I am the LORD, when I lay my vengeance on them.

25.15–17: The oracle concerning Philistia. Philistia was occupied by Assyria during the eighth and seventh centuries BCE and was turned into an industrial center for the production of olive oil. It is not clear what action they took against Judah in the sixth century. Philistia was located along the Mediterranean coast, west and south of the hill country of Judah. *Cherethites*, the Cretans, were ancestors of the Philistines.

Oracles concerning Tyre and its rulers
Chs. 26–28: Tyre, the preeminent maritime power of the ancient world, joined Judah in revolt against Babylon (Jer 27.3). The Phoenician city of Tyre was an island until its conquest in 332 BCE by Alexander the Great, who built an earthen corridor through the water to assault the city by land. Shortly after his conquest of Jerusalem, Nebuchadnezzar laid siege to Tyre for 13 years but was never able to conquer it.

26 In the eleventh year, on the first day of the month, the word of the LORD came to me: 2Mortal, because Tyre said concerning Jerusalem,

"Aha, broken is the gateway of
    the peoples;
  it has swung open to me;
I shall be replenished,
    now that it is wasted,"

ᵃ Gk Old Latin: Heb *Moab and Seir*   ᵇ Heb *towns from its towns*

³therefore, thus says the Lord GOD:
   See, I am against you, O Tyre!
   I will hurl many nations against you,
      as the sea hurls its waves.
⁴ They shall destroy the walls of Tyre
      and break down its towers.
   I will scrape its soil from it
      and make it a bare rock.
⁵ It shall become, in the midst of the sea,
      a place for spreading nets.
I have spoken, says the Lord GOD.
   It shall become plunder for the nations,
⁶   and its daughter-towns in the country
      shall be killed by the sword.
Then they shall know that I am the LORD.

26.1–21: Four oracles concerning the destruction of Tyre. 1: *The eleventh year . . . the first day of the month:* 587 BCE, shortly after the fall of Jerusalem. **2–6:** Ezekiel's indictment and sentencing of Tyre presupposes that the city was a commercial rival to Judah. *Gateway of the peoples,* literally "gateways," indicates Judah's role in controlling inland trade routes. *Bare rock* ("sela'" or "rock" in Hebrew) plays upon the Hebrew name "Sor" (*Tyre*), which means "rock." *Daughter-towns* designates nearby towns that were subsidiary to Tyre.

~~~~

7 For thus says the Lord GOD: I will bring against Tyre from the north King Nebuchadrezzar of Babylon, king of kings, together with horses, chariots, cavalry, and a great and powerful army.
⁸ Your daughter-towns in the country
      he shall put to the sword.
   He shall set up a siege wall against you,
      cast up a ramp against you,
      and raise a roof of shields
         against you.
⁹ He shall direct the shock of his
      battering rams against
         your walls
   and break down your towers with his
      axes.
¹⁰ His horses shall be so many
      that their dust shall cover you.
   At the noise of cavalry, wheels,
         and chariots
      your very walls shall shake,
   when he enters your gates
      like those entering a breached city.

11 With the hoofs of his horses
      he shall trample all your streets.
   He shall put your people to
         the sword,
      and your strong pillars shall fall to the
         ground.
12 They will plunder your riches
      and loot your merchandise;
   they shall break down your walls
      and destroy your fine houses.
   Your stones and timber and soil
      they shall cast into the water.
13 I will silence the music of your songs;
      the sound of your lyres shall be
         heard no more.
14 I will make you a bare rock;
      you shall be a place for
         spreading nets.
   You shall never again be rebuilt,
      for I the LORD have spoken,
      says the Lord GOD.

26.7–14: *Nebuchadrezzar:* The Akkadian (the semitic language of ancient Mesopotamia) name is frequently mispronounced in Hebrew as Nebuchadnezzar (Dan 1.1). Ezekiel's description presupposes the tactics and weapons of land warfare, which were useless against an island state.

~~~~

15 Thus says the Lord GOD to Tyre: Shall not the coastlands shake at the sound of your fall, when the wounded groan, when slaughter goes on within you? ¹⁶Then all the princes of the sea shall step down from their thrones; they shall remove their robes and strip off their embroidered garments. They shall clothe themselves with trembling, and shall sit on the ground; they shall tremble every moment, and be appalled at you. ¹⁷And they shall raise a lamentation over you, and say to you:
   How you have vanished*a* from the seas,
      O city renowned,
   once mighty on the sea,
      you and your inhabitants,*b*
   who imposed your*c* terror
      on all the mainland!*d*

---

a Gk OL Aquila: Heb *have vanished, O inhabited one,*
b Heb *it and its inhabitants*   *c* Heb *their*
d Cn: Heb *its inhabitants*

18 Now the coastlands tremble
    on the day of your fall;
  the coastlands by the sea
    are dismayed at your passing.

19 For thus says the Lord GOD: When I make you a city laid waste, like cities that are not inhabited, when I bring up the deep over you, and the great waters cover you, 20then I will thrust you down with those who descend into the Pit, to the people of long ago, and I will make you live in the world below, among primeval ruins, with those who go down to the Pit, so that you will not be inhabited or have a place*a* in the land of the living. 21I will bring you to a dreadful end, and you shall be no more; though sought for, you will never be found again, says the Lord GOD.

26.15–21. 15–18: *Princes of the sea* is an allusion to Tyre's trading partners and allies. *They shall raise a lamentation:* The poem is composed in the "qinah" meter, characteristic of laments★ (see comment on 19.1). **19–21:** Ezekiel employs mythological language to portray Tyre's fall. *I bring up the deep over you* reverses the imagery of creation in which dry land emerges from the waters (Gen 1). *Descend into the Pit:* Descent into the underworld at death (see 32.17–22; Isa 24.22; Ps 63.9; 139.15) was a characteristic motif★ of Babylonian mythology in which the fertility god Tammuz had to be rescued from the underworld each year by the goddess Ishtar.

---

27 The word of the LORD came to me: 2Now you, mortal, raise a lamentation over Tyre, 3and say to Tyre, which sits at the entrance to the sea, merchant of the peoples on many coastlands, Thus says the Lord GOD:

  O Tyre, you have said,
    "I am perfect in beauty."
4 Your borders are in the heart of the
      seas;
    your builders made perfect
      your beauty.
5 They made all your planks
    of fir trees from Senir;
  they took a cedar from Lebanon
    to make a mast for you.
6 From oaks of Bashan
    they made your oars;

they made your deck of pines*b*
  from the coasts of Cyprus,
    inlaid with ivory.
7 Of fine embroidered linen from Egypt
    was your sail,
    serving as your ensign;
  blue and purple from the coasts
      of Elishah
    was your awning.
8 The inhabitants of Sidon and Arvad
    were your rowers;
  skilled men of Zemer*c* were within
      you,
    they were your pilots.
9 The elders of Gebal and its artisans
      were within you,
    caulking your seams;
  all the ships of the sea with their
      mariners were within you,
    to barter for your wares.
10 Paras*d* and Lud and Put
    were in your army,
    your mighty warriors;
  they hung shield and helmet in you;
    they gave you splendor.
11 Men of Arvad and Helech*e*
    were on your walls all around;
    men of Gamad were at your towers.
  They hung their quivers all around your
      walls;
    they made perfect your beauty.

27.1–36: Lamentation over Tyre. The "qinah" meter appears in vv. 3–9, 25–36 (see comment on 19.1). **3–9:** Ezekiel portrays Tyre as a well-built ship, which symbolizes the way in which Tyre achieved wealth through maritime trade. *Senir:* Mt. Hermon in northern Israel (Deut 3.9). *Bashan:* The region east of the Sea of Galilee. *Elishah:* Cyprus. *Arvad:* Phoenicia. *Zemer* means "Tyre" in Hebrew. *Gebal:* Byblos. **10–11:** Tyre's defenders include mercenary troops. *Paras:* Persia. *Lud:* Lydia. *Put:* Libya. *Helech* means "your army" in Hebrew. *Gamad* is uncertain.

---

12 Tarshish did business with you out of the abundance of your great wealth; silver, iron, tin, and lead they exchanged for your

---

a Gk: Heb *I will give beauty*   b Or *boxwood*
c Cn Compare Gen 10.18: Heb *your skilled men, O Tyre*
d Or *Persia*   e Or *and your army*

wares. ¹³Javan, Tubal, and Meshech traded with you; they exchanged human beings and vessels of bronze for your merchandise. ¹⁴Beth-togarmah exchanged for your wares horses, war horses, and mules. ¹⁵The Rhodians*a* traded with you; many coastlands were your own special markets; they brought you in payment ivory tusks and ebony. ¹⁶Edom*b* did business with you because of your abundant goods; they exchanged for your wares turquoise, purple, embroidered work, fine linen, coral, and rubies. ¹⁷Judah and the land of Israel traded with you; they exchanged for your merchandise wheat from Minnith, millet,*c* honey, oil, and balm. ¹⁸Damascus traded with you for your abundant goods—because of your great wealth of every kind—wine of Helbon, and white wool. ¹⁹Vedan and Javan from Uzal*c* entered into trade for your wares; wrought iron, cassia, and sweet cane were bartered for your merchandise. ²⁰Dedan traded with you in saddlecloths for riding. ²¹Arabia and all the princes of Kedar were your favored dealers in lambs, rams, and goats; in these they did business with you. ²²The merchants of Sheba and Raamah traded with you; they exchanged for your wares the best of all kinds of spices, and all precious stones, and gold. ²³Haran, Canneh, Eden, the merchants of Sheba, Asshur, and Chilmad traded with you. ²⁴These traded with you in choice garments, in clothes of blue and embroidered work, and in carpets of colored material, bound with cords and made secure; in these they traded with you.*d* ²⁵The ships of Tarshish traveled for you in your trade.

27.12–25a: A prose section contains a catalogue of Tyre's extensive commercial relations. *Tarshish:* Tartessos in southern Spain. *Javan:* Ionians or Greeks. *Tubal and Meshech:* Asia Minor. *Beth-togarmah:* Armenia. *Rhodians* (Greek) means Dedanites in Hebrew. *Edom:* Some read "Aram," but v. 14 makes this unlikely. *Turquoise, purple:* Phoenicia was known for trade in purple dye derived from shellfish. Phoenicia (Gk., "Phoinikos") and Canaan mean "purple." *Minnith:* in Ammonite territory (Judg 11.33). *Helbon:* Thirteen miles north of Damascus. *Vedan and Javan from Uzal:* Uzal is Sana in Yemen. *Dedan:* In central Arabia. *Kedar:* In Arabia. *Sheba:* In Arabia or Ethiopia. *Haran,*

Canneh, Eden: Cities in Syria. *Asshur:* Assyria. *Chilmad:* Media.

~~~~~~~~~~~~~~~~~~

So you were filled and heavily laden
  in the heart of the seas.
²⁶ Your rowers have brought you
  into the high seas.
The east wind has wrecked you
  in the heart of the seas.
²⁷ Your riches, your wares, your
    merchandise,
  your mariners and your pilots,
  your caulkers, your dealers in
    merchandise,
  and all your warriors within you,
with all the company
  that is with you,
sink into the heart of the seas
  on the day of your ruin.
²⁸ At the sound of the cry of your pilots
  the countryside shakes,
²⁹ and down from their ships
  come all that handle the oar.
The mariners and all the pilots
  of the sea
  stand on the shore
³⁰ and wail aloud over you,
  and cry bitterly.
They throw dust on their heads
  and wallow in ashes;
³¹ they make themselves bald for you,
  and put on sackcloth,
and they weep over you in bitterness of
  soul,
  with bitter mourning.
³² In their wailing they raise a lamentation
  for you,
  and lament over you:
"Who was ever destroyed*e* like Tyre
  in the midst of the sea?
³³ When your wares came from the seas,
  you satisfied many peoples;
with your abundant wealth and
    merchandise
  you enriched the kings of the earth.
³⁴ Now you are wrecked by the seas,
  in the depths of the waters;

---

a Gk: Heb *The Dedanites*   *b* Another reading is *Aram*
c Meaning of Heb uncertain   *d* Cn: Heb *in your market*   *e* Tg Vg: Heb *like silence*

your merchandise and all your crew
　　have sunk with you.
35 All the inhabitants of the coastlands
　　are appalled at you;
　　and their kings are horribly afraid,
　　　their faces are convulsed.
36 The merchants among the peoples hiss
　　　　at you;
　　you have come to a dreadful end
　　and shall be no more forever."

27.25b–36: The lament resumes with a description of
Tyre as a ship sinking by *the east wind,* a symbol of
God's power (Ex 14.21).

28

The word of the LORD came to me:
2 Mortal, say to the prince of Tyre,
Thus says the Lord GOD:
　　Because your heart is proud
　　and you have said, "I am a god;
　　I sit in the seat of the gods,
　　　in the heart of the seas,"
　　yet you are but a mortal, and no god,
　　though you compare your mind
　　　with the mind of a god.
3 You are indeed wiser than Daniel;[a]
　　no secret is hidden from you;
4 by your wisdom and your
　　　understanding
　　you have amassed wealth
　　　for yourself,
　　and have gathered gold and silver
　　into your treasuries.
5 By your great wisdom in trade
　　you have increased your wealth,
　　and your heart has become proud in
　　　your wealth.
6 Therefore thus says the Lord GOD:
　　Because you compare your mind
　　with the mind of a god,
7 therefore, I will bring strangers
　　　against you,
　　the most terrible of the nations;
　　they shall draw their swords against the
　　　beauty of your wisdom
　　and defile your splendor.
8 They shall thrust you down to the Pit,
　　and you shall die a violent death
　　in the heart of the seas.
9 Will you still say, "I am a god,"
　　in the presence of those who kill you,

though you are but a mortal, and no god,
　　in the hands of those who wound you?
10 You shall die the death of the
　　　uncircumcised
　　by the hand of foreigners;
　　for I have spoken, says the Lord GOD.

11　Moreover the word of the LORD came
to me: 12 Mortal, raise a lamentation over the
king of Tyre, and say to him, Thus says the
Lord GOD:
　　You were the signet of perfection,[b]
　　full of wisdom and perfect in beauty.
13 You were in Eden, the garden of God;
　　every precious stone was your
　　　covering,
　　carnelian, chrysolite, and moonstone,
　　beryl, onyx, and jasper,
　　sapphire,[c] turquoise, and emerald;
　　　and worked in gold were your settings
　　and your engravings.[b]
　　On the day that you were created
　　they were prepared.
14 With an anointed cherub as guardian I
　　　placed you;[b]
　　you were on the holy mountain
　　　of God;
　　you walked among the stones of fire.
15 You were blameless in your ways
　　from the day that you were created,
　　until iniquity was found in you.
16 In the abundance of your trade
　　you were filled with violence, and you
　　　sinned;
　　so I cast you as a profane thing from
　　　the mountain of God,
　　and the guardian cherub drove you
　　　out
　　from among the stones of fire.
17 Your heart was proud because of your
　　　beauty;
　　you corrupted your wisdom for the
　　　sake of your splendor.
　　I cast you to the ground;
　　I exposed you before kings,
　　to feast their eyes on you.
18 By the multitude of your iniquities,
　　in the unrighteousness of your trade,
　　you profaned your sanctuaries.

a Or, as otherwise read, *Danel*　　*b* Meaning of Heb
uncertain　　*c* Or *lapis lazuli*

So I brought out fire from within you;
    it consumed you,
and I turned you to ashes on the earth
    in the sight of all who saw you.
19 All who know you among the peoples
    are appalled at you;
  you have come to a dreadful end
    and shall be no more forever.

28.1–19: Oracles concerning the rulers of Tyre.
1–10: Self-deification, a frequent claim of ancient
Near Eastern rulers. *You are indeed wiser than Daniel:*
Ezekiel apparently holds the Tyrian king in high regard
and compares him to Daniel (Heb., Dan El), the wise
ruler of Canaanite mythology who stands behind the
figure of Daniel in biblical tradition (14.12–20). Ezekiel
charges that the king has overstepped his bounds. The
mythological language of descent into the sea and the
Pit reappears. *The uncircumcised** are non-Israelites
(see Gen 17). *11–19: Signet:* A sign of royal authority.
Ezekiel employs the imagery of the Garden of Eden
story to describe the Tyrian king's downfall. The
prophet* charges the king with corrupt trade practices.

20 The word of the LORD came to me:
21Mortal, set your face toward Sidon, and
prophesy against it, 22and say, Thus says the
Lord GOD:

  I am against you, O Sidon,
    and I will gain glory in your midst.
  They shall know that I am the LORD
    when I execute judgments in it,
    and manifest my holiness in it;
23 for I will send pestilence into it,
    and bloodshed into its streets;
  and the dead shall fall in its midst,
    by the sword that is against it on
      every side.
  And they shall know that I am the LORD.
24 The house of Israel shall no longer
find a pricking brier or a piercing thorn
among all their neighbors who have treated
them with contempt. And they shall know
that I am the Lord GOD.

28.20–24: Oracle* concerning Sidon. Another Phoenician port city, 25 miles north of Tyre. Sidon joined
the revolt (Jer 27.3) and probably fell to Nebuchadnezzar.

25 Thus says the Lord GOD: When I
gather the house of Israel from the peoples
among whom they are scattered, and manifest my holiness in them in the sight of the
nations, then they shall settle on their own
soil that I gave to my servant Jacob. 26They
shall live in safety in it, and shall build
houses and plant vineyards. They shall live
in safety, when I execute judgments upon all
their neighbors who have treated them with
contempt. And they shall know that I am the
LORD their God.

28.25–26: Oracle of blessing for Israel. Once the
nations that treated Israel with contempt are destroyed, the exiles will return to the land of Israel sworn
to Jacob (Gen 28; 35) to manifest God's holiness in the
world. *And they shall know that I am the LORD their
God:* The self-identification formula.

Seven oracles concerning Egypt and its rulers
Chs. 29–32: Egypt played a major role in instigating
the revolt against its enemy Babylon. When Pharaoh
Hophra attempted to relieve Jerusalem from the Babylonian siege in 588 BCE, he was repulsed (Jer 37;
44.30; see also Jer 32).

29 In the tenth year, in the tenth
month, on the twelfth day of the
month, the word of the LORD came to me:
2Mortal, set your face against Pharaoh king
of Egypt, and prophesy against him and
against all Egypt; 3speak, and say, Thus says
the Lord GOD:

  I am against you,
    Pharaoh king of Egypt,
  the great dragon sprawling
    in the midst of its channels,
  saying, "My Nile is my own;
    I made it for myself."
4 I will put hooks in your jaws,
    and make the fish of your channels
      stick to your scales.
  I will draw you up from your channels,
    with all the fish of your channels
      sticking to your scales.
5 I will fling you into the wilderness,
    you and all the fish of your
      channels;
  you shall fall in the open field,
    and not be gathered and buried.

To the animals of the earth and to the
> birds of the air
I have given you as food.
6 Then all the inhabitants of Egypt shall
> know
> that I am the LORD
because you*a* were a staff of reed
> to the house of Israel;
7 when they grasped you with the hand,
> you broke,
and tore all their shoulders;
and when they leaned on you,
> you broke,
and made all their legs unsteady.*b*

8 Therefore, thus says the Lord GOD: I
will bring a sword upon you, and will cut off
from you human being and animal; 9and the
land of Egypt shall be a desolation and a
waste. Then they shall know that I am the
LORD.

Because you*c* said, "The Nile is mine, and
I made it," 10therefore, I am against you, and
against your channels, and I will make the
land of Egypt an utter waste and desolation,
from Migdol to Syene, as far as the border
of Ethiopia.*d* 11No human foot shall pass
through it, and no animal foot shall pass
through it; it shall be uninhabited forty
years. 12I will make the land of Egypt a desolation among desolated countries; and her
cities shall be a desolation forty years among
cities that are laid waste. I will scatter the
Egyptians among the nations, and disperse
them among the countries.

13 Further, thus says the Lord GOD: At
the end of forty years I will gather the Egyptians from the peoples among whom they
were scattered; 14and I will restore the fortunes of Egypt, and bring them back to the
land of Pathros, the land of their origin; and
there they shall be a lowly kingdom. 15It
shall be the most lowly of the kingdoms, and
never again exalt itself above the nations;
and I will make them so small that they will
never again rule over the nations. 16The
Egyptians*e* shall never again be the reliance
of the house of Israel; they will recall their
iniquity, when they turned to them for aid.
Then they shall know that I am the Lord
GOD.

29.1–16: The first oracle concerning Egypt. 1–3a: *In
the tenth year . . . tenth month . . . the twelfth day:*
January 7, 587 BCE. **3b–7:** Ezekiel addresses Pharaoh,
probably Hophra, after his failed attempt to rescue Jerusalem. *The great dragon:* Egypt is compared to a
dragon in Isa 11.15, which employs the imagery of the
seven-headed Leviathan* (Lothan) of Canaanite mythology, and in Isa 30.7 to the sea dragon Rahab (see
also Isa 51.9–10; Job 9.13; 26.12–13; Ps 89.9–10). The
Nile River is the source of Egypt's life. *A staff of reed to
the house of Israel* symbolizes an unreliable support
(compare Isa 36.6; 2 Kings 18.21). **8–12:** Egypt's judgment results from Pharaoh's claim that the Nile is his
and not God's (28.2). *From Migdol to Syene:* Cities
that define the northern and southern borders of
Egypt. *Forty years:* Forty is a common number for a
complete and lengthy period of time (Num 14.33;
Judg 3.31; 1 Kings 2.11). **13–16:** Like Israel after it had
been punished (28.25–26), Egypt will be restored to
its land as a minor kingdom. The prophet clearly has
in mind Egypt's failure to aid Israel in its time of need.
Pathros: Upper Egypt, the southern portion of the
kingdom. In Egypt, "up" is south (upstream on the
Nile) and "down" is north (downstream on the Nile).

17 In the twenty-seventh year, in the first
month, on the first day of the month, the
word of the LORD came to me: 18Mortal,
King Nebuchadrezzar of Babylon made his
army labor hard against Tyre; every head was
made bald and every shoulder was rubbed
bare; yet neither he nor his army got anything from Tyre to pay for the labor that he
had expended against it. 19Therefore thus
says the Lord GOD: I will give the land of
Egypt to King Nebuchadrezzar of Babylon;
and he shall carry off its wealth and despoil
it and plunder it; and it shall be the wages
for his army. 20I have given him the land of
Egypt as his payment for which he labored,
because they worked for me, says the Lord
GOD.

21 On that day I will cause a horn to
sprout up for the house of Israel, and I will
open your lips among them. Then they shall
know that I am the LORD.

---

a Gk Syr Vg: Heb *they*   *b* Syr: Heb *stand*   *c* Gk Syr
Vg: Heb *he*   *d* Or *Nubia;* Heb *Cush*   *e* Heb *It*

29.17–21: The second oracle concerning Egypt. *The twenty-seventh year . . . the first month . . . the first day:* April 26, 571 BCE. Ezekiel refers to Nebuchadnezzar's failure to conquer Tyre as a basis for his campaign against Egypt. Following the conclusion of his siege against Tyre in 573 BCE, Nebuchadnezzar attacked Egypt in 668 BCE but failed to conquer the land. *A horn . . . for the house of Israel* refers to the restoration of the Davidic monarchy in the aftermath of Egypt's collapse (see Isa 11.1–16; Ps 132.17).

30

The word of the LORD came to me: 2Mortal, prophesy, and say, Thus says the Lord GOD:
Wail, "Alas for the day!"
3   For a day is near,
    the day of the LORD is near;
    it will be a day of clouds,
    a time of doom*a* for the nations.
4 A sword shall come upon Egypt,
    and anguish shall be in Ethiopia,*b*
    when the slain fall in Egypt,
    and its wealth is carried away,
    and its foundations are torn down.
5 Ethiopia,*b* and Put, and Lud, and all Arabia, and Libya,*c* and the people of the allied land*d* shall fall with them by the sword.

6 Thus says the LORD:
    Those who support Egypt shall fall,
    and its proud might shall come down;
    from Migdol to Syene
    they shall fall within it by the sword,
    says the Lord GOD.
7 They shall be desolated among other
        desolated countries,
    and their cities shall lie among cities
        laid waste.
8 Then they shall know that I am
        the LORD,
    when I have set fire to Egypt,
    and all who help it are broken.
9 On that day, messengers shall go out from me in ships to terrify the unsuspecting Ethiopians;*e* and anguish shall come upon them on the day of Egypt's doom;*f* for it is coming!

30.1–19: The third oracle concerning Egypt. 1: This section contains four oracles. **2–5:** God instructs Eze-

kiel to lament for Egypt and Ethiopia. Egypt was ruled by an Ethiopian dynasty* during the late seventh and early sixth centuries BCE (see Isa 20). The prophet employs the "Day of the LORD" motif* (Am 5.18–20; Isa 2.6–21; 13; 34; Zeph 1.2–18; 2.1–3). *Put and Lud:* See comments on 27.10–11. **6–9:** This oracle* draws on the "Day of the LORD" materials in Isaiah. *Proud might shall come down:* Isa 2.6–21. *Messengers shall go out:* Isa 18.1–2.

10 Thus says the Lord GOD:
    I will put an end to the hordes of Egypt,
    by the hand of King Nebuchadrezzar
        of Babylon.
11 He and his people with him, the most
        terrible of the nations,
    shall be brought in to destroy the land;
    and they shall draw their swords against
        Egypt,
    and fill the land with the slain.
12 I will dry up the channels,
    and will sell the land into the hand of
        evildoers;
    I will bring desolation upon the land
        and everything in it
    by the hand of foreigners;
    I the LORD have spoken.

13 Thus says the Lord GOD:
    I will destroy the idols
    and put an end to the images
        in Memphis;
    there shall no longer be a prince in the
        land of Egypt;
    so I will put fear in the land of Egypt.
14 I will make Pathros a desolation,
    and will set fire to Zoan,
    and will execute acts of judgment on
        Thebes.
15 I will pour my wrath upon Pelusium,
    the stronghold of Egypt,
    and cut off the hordes of Thebes.
16 I will set fire to Egypt;
    Pelusium shall be in great agony;
    Thebes shall be breached,
    and Memphis face adversaries by day.

a Heb lacks *of doom*   *b* Or *Nubia;* Heb *Cush*
c Compare Gk Syr Vg: Heb *Cub*   *d* Meaning of Heb uncertain   *e* Or *Nubians;* Heb *Cush*   *f* Heb *the day of Egypt*

17 The young men of On and of Pi-beseth
      shall fall by the sword;
      and the cities themselves[a] shall go
      into captivity.
18 At Tehaphnehes the day shall be dark,
      when I break there the dominion of
      Egypt,
      and its proud might shall come to an end;
      the city[b] shall be covered by a cloud,
      and its daughter-towns shall go into
      captivity.
19 Thus I will execute acts of judgment on
      Egypt.
      Then they shall know that I am the
      LORD.

30.10–19. 10–12: *Dry up the channels:* Isa 19.1–15.
13–19: Ezekiel cites Egyptian place names to demon-
strate that destruction will encompass the entire land.
Memphis: The early capital south of Cairo. *Zoan:* Also
called Rameses, Tanis, and Avaris, the site where the
Hebrew slaves worked in the Nile Delta (Ps 78.12, 43;
Ex 1.11). *Thebes:* Egypt's capital throughout much of
Israel's history. *Pelusium:* Near Zoan in the northeast-
ern Delta. *On:* Heliopolis, six miles northeast of Cairo.
Pi-beseth: Bubastis in the eastern Delta. *Tehaphnehes:*
By the north shore of the Gulf of Suez.

20 In the eleventh year, in the first
month, on the seventh day of the month, the
word of the LORD came to me: 21Mortal, I
have broken the arm of Pharaoh king of
Egypt; it has not been bound up for healing
or wrapped with a bandage, so that it may
become strong to wield the sword. 22There-
fore thus says the Lord GOD: I am against
Pharaoh king of Egypt, and will break his
arms, both the strong arm and the one that
was broken; and I will make the sword fall
from his hand. 23I will scatter the Egyptians
among the nations, and disperse them
throughout the lands. 24I will strengthen the
arms of the king of Babylon, and put my
sword in his hand; but I will break the arms
of Pharaoh, and he will groan before him
with the groans of one mortally wounded. 25I
will strengthen the arms of the king of Babylon, but the arms of Pharaoh shall fall. And
they shall know that I am the LORD, when I
put my sword into the hand of the king of
Babylon. He shall stretch it out against the

land of Egypt, 26and I will scatter the Egyptians among the nations and disperse them
throughout the countries. Then they shall
know that I am the LORD.

30.20–26: The fourth oracle concerning Pharaoh. *In
the eleventh year . . . the first month . . . the seventh
day:* April 29, 587 BCE. The *broken arm* of Pharaoh
refers to Nebuchadnezzar's defeat of Hophra, who attempted to relieve Jerusalem in 588 BCE (Jer 37.5). The
prophet anticipates an even more devastating defeat
of Egypt.

31 In the eleventh year, in the third
      month, on the first day of the month,
the word of the LORD came to me: 2Mortal,
say to Pharaoh king of Egypt and to his
hordes:
      Whom are you like in your greatness?
3   Consider Assyria, a cedar of Lebanon,
      with fair branches and forest shade,
      and of great height,
      its top among the clouds.[c]
4 The waters nourished it,
      the deep made it grow tall,
   making its rivers flow[d]
      around the place it was planted,
   sending forth its streams
      to all the trees of the field.
5 So it towered high
      above all the trees of the field;
   its boughs grew large
      and its branches long,
      from abundant water in its shoots.
6 All the birds of the air
      made their nests in its boughs;
   under its branches all the animals of the
      field
      gave birth to their young;
   and in its shade
      all great nations lived.
7 It was beautiful in its greatness,
      in the length of its branches;
   for its roots went down
      to abundant water.
8 The cedars in the garden of God could
      not rival it,
      nor the fir trees equal its boughs;

a Heb *and they*   b Heb *she*   c Gk: Heb *thick boughs*
d Gk: Heb *rivers going*

the plane trees were as nothing
compared with its branches;
no tree in the garden of God
was like it in beauty.
9 I made it beautiful
with its mass of branches,
the envy of all the trees of Eden
that were in the garden of God.

10 Therefore thus says the Lord GOD:
Because it[a] towered high and set its top
among the clouds,[b] and its heart was proud
of its height, 11I gave it into the hand of the
prince of the nations; he has dealt with it as
its wickedness deserves. I have cast it out.
12Foreigners from the most terrible of the
nations have cut it down and left it. On the
mountains and in all the valleys its branches
have fallen, and its boughs lie broken in all
the watercourses of the land; and all the peoples of the earth went away from its shade
and left it.

13 On its fallen trunk settle
all the birds of the air,
and among its boughs lodge
all the wild animals.
14All this is in order that no trees by the
waters may grow to lofty height or set their
tops among the clouds,[b] and that no trees
that drink water may reach up to them in
height.

For all of them are handed over to death,
to the world below;
along with all mortals,
with those who go down to the Pit.

15 Thus says the Lord GOD: On the day
it went down to Sheol I closed the deep over
it and covered it; I restrained its rivers, and
its mighty waters were checked. I clothed
Lebanon in gloom for it, and all the trees of
the field fainted because of it. 16I made the
nations quake at the sound of its fall, when
I cast it down to Sheol with those who go
down to the Pit; and all the trees of Eden,
the choice and best of Lebanon, all that were
well watered, were consoled in the world below. 17They also went down to Sheol with it,
to those killed by the sword, along with its
allies,[e] those who lived in its shade among
the nations.

18 Which among the trees of Eden was
like you in glory and in greatness? Now you

shall be brought down with the trees of Eden
to the world below; you shall lie among the
uncircumcised, with those who are killed by
the sword. This is Pharaoh and all his horde,
says the Lord GOD.

31.1–18: The fifth oracle concerning Pharaoh. The
imagery of a fallen cedar of Lebanon portrays Pharaoh's downfall. **1:** *In the eleventh year . . . the third
month . . . the first day:* June 21, 587 BCE. **2–9:** See
Isaiah's portrayal of the Assyrian monarch as a tall tree
that is to be felled (Isa 10.5–34) and the tradition of
the well-watered tree in the Garden of Eden that plays
a role in the downfall of Adam and Eve (Gen 2–3). **10–
14:** Because of its height and arrogance, the tree is cut
down (Isa 2.6–21; 10.5–34). *The prince of the nations:*
Literally, "the ram of the nations," Nebuchadnezzar.
The Babylonians boasted of the trees they took from
Lebanon. *Pit:* The underworld (Isa 14.3–23). **15–18:**
Sheol: * The Hebrew name for the underworld.

32 In the twelfth year, in the twelfth
month, on the first day of the month,
the word of the LORD came to me: 2Mortal,
raise a lamentation over Pharaoh king of
Egypt, and say to him:
You consider yourself a lion among the
nations,
but you are like a dragon in the seas;
you thrash about in your streams,
trouble the water with your feet,
and foul your[d] streams.
3 Thus says the Lord GOD:
In an assembly of many peoples
I will throw my net over you;
and I[e] will haul you up in
my dragnet.
4 I will throw you on the ground,
on the open field I will fling you,
and will cause all the birds of the air to
settle on you,
and I will let the wild animals of the
whole earth gorge themselves
with you.
5 I will strew your flesh on the
mountains,
and fill the valleys with your carcass.[f]

a Syr Vg: Heb *you*   b Gk: Heb *thick boughs*
c Heb *its arms*   d Heb *their*   e Gk Vg: Heb *they*
f Symmachus Syr Vg: Heb *your height*

6 I will drench the land with your flowing
　　blood
　　up to the mountains,
　　and the watercourses will be filled
　　　　with you.
7 When I blot you out, I will cover the
　　heavens,
　　and make their stars dark;
　　I will cover the sun with a cloud,
　　and the moon shall not give its light.
8 All the shining lights of the heavens
　　I will darken above you,
　　and put darkness on your land,
　　　　says the Lord GOD.
9 I will trouble the hearts of many peoples,
　　as I carry you captive[a] among the
　　　　nations,
　　into countries you have not known.
10 I will make many peoples appalled at
　　　　you;
　　their kings shall shudder because of
　　　　you,
　　When I brandish my sword before them,
　　they shall tremble every moment
　　for their lives, each one of them,
　　on the day of your downfall.
11 For thus says the Lord GOD:
　　The sword of the king of Babylon shall
　　　　come against you.
12 I will cause your hordes to fall
　　by the swords of mighty ones,
　　all of them most terrible among the
　　　　nations.
　　They shall bring to ruin the pride of
　　　　Egypt,
　　and all its hordes shall perish.
13 I will destroy all its livestock
　　from beside abundant waters;
　　and no human foot shall trouble them
　　　　any more,
　　nor shall the hoofs of cattle trouble
　　　　them.
14 Then I will make their waters clear,
　　and cause their streams to run like
　　　　oil, says the Lord GOD.
15 When I make the land of Egypt desolate
　　and when the land is stripped of all
　　　　that fills it,
　　when I strike down all who live in it,
　　then they shall know that I am the
　　　　LORD.

16 This is a lamentation; it shall
　　be chanted.
　　The women of the nations shall chant
　　　　it.
　　Over Egypt and all its hordes they shall
　　　　chant it,
　　says the Lord GOD.

**32.1–16: Ezekiel's sixth oracle concerning Pharaoh
and Egypt. 1:** *In the twelfth year . . . the twelfth
month . . . the first day:* March 3, 586 BCE. **2–15:** The
portrayal of Pharaoh's defeat by God draws upon the
mythological traditions of God's defeat of the sea
dragon Leviathan* at creation (Isa 11.15; 27.1; Ps
74.12–17; 104.7–9; Job 38.8–11; Ex 15). The motif of
darkness recalls the plague of darkness against Egypt
(Ex 10.21–29) and the "Day of the LORD" traditions
(Joel 2.1–2; 3.15; Zeph 1.15). *The sword of the King
of Babylon:* Nebuchadnezzar. The nations will witness
God's victory (Ex 15.13–18). **16:** Women served as
mourners in the ancient Near East (Jer 9.17–18).

17 In the twelfth year, in the first
month,[b] on the fifteenth day of the month,
the word of the LORD came to me:
18 Mortal, wail over the hordes of Egypt,
　　and send them down,
　　with Egypt[c] and the daughters of
　　　　majestic nations,
　　to the world below,
　　with those who go down to the Pit.
19 "Whom do you surpass in beauty?
　　Go down! Be laid to rest with the
　　　　uncircumcised!"
20 They shall fall among those who are killed
by the sword. Egypt[d] has been handed over
to the sword; carry away both it and its
hordes. 21 The mighty chiefs shall speak of
them, with their helpers, out of the midst of
Sheol: "They have come down, they lie still,
the uncircumcised, killed by the sword."

22 Assyria is there, and all its company,
their graves all around it, all of them killed,
fallen by the sword. 23 Their graves are set in
the uttermost parts of the Pit. Its company
is all around its grave, all of them killed,
fallen by the sword, who spread terror in the
land of the living.

a Gk: Heb *bring your destruction*　　　*b* Gk: Heb lacks *in
the first month*　　*c* Heb *it*　　*d* Heb *It*

24 Elam is there, and all its hordes around its grave; all of them killed, fallen by the sword, who went down uncircumcised into the world below, who spread terror in the land of the living. They bear their shame with those who go down to the Pit. 25 They have made Elam*a* a bed among the slain with all its hordes, their graves all around it, all of them uncircumcised, killed by the sword; for terror of them was spread in the land of the living, and they bear their shame with those who go down to the Pit; they are placed among the slain.

26 Meshech and Tubal are there, and all their multitude, their graves all around them, all of them uncircumcised, killed by the sword; for they spread terror in the land of the living. 27 And they do not lie with the fallen warriors of long ago*b* who went down to Sheol with their weapons of war, whose swords were laid under their heads, and whose shields*c* are upon their bones; for the terror of the warriors was in the land of the living. 28 So you shall be broken and lie among the uncircumcised, with those who are killed by the sword.

29 Edom is there, its kings and all its princes, who for all their might are laid with those who are killed by the sword; they lie with the uncircumcised, with those who go down to the Pit.

30 The princes of the north are there, all of them, and all the Sidonians, who have gone down in shame with the slain, for all the terror that they caused by their might; they lie uncircumcised with those who are killed by the sword, and bear their shame with those who go down to the Pit.

31 When Pharaoh sees them, he will be consoled for all his hordes—Pharaoh and all his army, killed by the sword, says the Lord GOD. 32 For he*d* spread terror in the land of the living; therefore he shall be laid to rest among the uncircumcised, with those who are slain by the sword—Pharaoh and all his multitude, says the Lord GOD.

32.17–32: Ezekiel's seventh oracle concerning Egypt. 17: *In the twelfth year . . . the first month . . . the fifteenth day:* April 27, 586 BCE. 18: God instructs Ezekiel to wail for Egypt as its people descend into the

underworld. 19–32: Egypt will join the nations that have been destroyed. *Assyria* was conquered by Babylon and Media during the period 627–609 BCE. *Elam* was destroyed by the Assyrians in the mid seventh century BCE. *Meshech and Tubal:* Two unidentified kingdoms in Asia Minor that perhaps were taken by Assyria. *Edom* was conquered by Babylon. *The princes of the north:* probably the Phoenicians.

ORACLES AND VISIONS OF RESTORATION

Chs. 33–48: After the fall of Jerusalem (33.21–22), the book emphasizes restoration for Israel (chs. 33–39) and the Temple* (chs. 40–48). **Chs. 33–39: Oracles of restoration for Israel.** News of Jerusalem's fall enables Ezekiel to speak (3.22–27). Many attribute Ezekiel's earlier silence to prophetic practice, but his priestly identity calls for him to serve at the altar in silence. After the fall of the Temple, he can speak.

33 The word of the LORD came to me: 2 O Mortal, speak to your people and say to them, If I bring the sword upon a land, and the people of the land take one of their number as their sentinel; 3 and if the sentinel sees the sword coming upon the land and blows the trumpet and warns the people; 4 then if any who hear the sound of the trumpet do not take warning, and the sword comes and takes them away, their blood shall be upon their own heads. 5 They heard the sound of the trumpet and did not take warning; their blood shall be upon themselves. But if they had taken warning, they would have saved their lives. 6 But if the sentinel sees the sword coming and does not blow the trumpet, so that the people are not warned, and the sword comes and takes any of them, they are taken away in their iniquity, but their blood I will require at the sentinel's hand.

7 So you, mortal, I have made a sentinel for the house of Israel; whenever you hear a word from my mouth, you shall give them warning from me. 8 If I say to the wicked, "O wicked ones, you shall surely die," and you do not speak to warn the wicked to turn from their ways, the wicked shall die in their

a Heb *it* *b* Gk Old Latin: Heb *of the uncircumcised* *c* Cn: Heb *iniquities* *d* Cn: Heb *I* iniquity, but their blood I will require at your hand. 9But if you warn the wicked to turn from their ways, and they do not turn from their ways, the wicked shall die in their iniquity, but you will have saved your life.

10 Now you, mortal, say to the house of Israel, Thus you have said: "Our transgressions and our sins weigh upon us, and we waste away because of them; how then can we live?" 11Say to them, As I live, says the Lord GOD, I have no pleasure in the death of the wicked, but that the wicked turn from their ways and live; turn back, turn back from your evil ways; for why will you die, O house of Israel? 12And you, mortal, say to your people, The righteousness of the righteous shall not save them when they transgress; and as for the wickedness of the wicked, it shall not make them stumble when they turn from their wickedness; and the righteous shall not be able to live by their righteousness*a* when they sin. 13Though I say to the righteous that they shall surely live, yet if they trust in their righteousness and commit iniquity, none of their righteous deeds shall be remembered; but in the iniquity that they have committed they shall die. 14Again, though I say to the wicked, "You shall surely die," yet if they turn from their sin and do what is lawful and right— 15if the wicked restore the pledge, give back what they have taken by robbery, and walk in the statutes of life, committing no iniquity— they shall surely live, they shall not die. 16None of the sins that they have committed shall be remembered against them; they have done what is lawful and right, they shall surely live.

17 Yet your people say, "The way of the Lord is not just," when it is their own way that is not just. 18When the righteous turn from their righteousness, and commit iniquity, they shall die for it.*b* 19And when the wicked turn from their wickedness, and do what is lawful and right, they shall live by it.*b* 20Yet you say, "The way of the Lord is not just." O house of Israel, I will judge all of you according to your ways!

21 In the twelfth year of our exile, in the tenth month, on the fifth day of the month, someone who had escaped from Jerusalem came to me and said, "The city has fallen." 22Now the hand of the LORD had been upon me the evening before the fugitive came; but he had opened my mouth by the time the fugitive came to me in the morning; so my mouth was opened, and I was no longer unable to speak.

23 The word of the LORD came to me: 24Mortal, the inhabitants of these waste places in the land of Israel keep saying, "Abraham was only one man, yet he got possession of the land; but we are many; the land is surely given us to possess." 25Therefore say to them, Thus says the Lord GOD: You eat flesh with the blood, and lift up your eyes to your idols, and shed blood; shall you then possess the land? 26You depend on your swords, you commit abominations, and each of you defiles his neighbor's wife; shall you then possess the land? 27Say this to them, Thus says the Lord GOD: As I live, surely those who are in the waste places shall fall by the sword; and those who are in the open field I will give to the wild animals to be devoured; and those who are in strongholds and in caves shall die by pestilence. 28I will make the land a desolation and a waste, and its proud might shall come to an end; and the mountains of Israel shall be so desolate that no one will pass through. 29Then they shall know that I am the LORD, when I have made the land a desolation and a waste because of all their abominations that they have committed.

30 As for you, mortal, your people who talk together about you by the walls, and at the doors of the houses, say to one another, each to a neighbor, "Come and hear what the word is that comes from the LORD." 31They come to you as people come, and they sit before you as my people, and they hear your words, but they will not obey them. For flattery is on their lips, but their heart is set on their gain. 32To them you are like a singer of love songs,*c* one who has a beautiful voice and plays well on an instrument; they hear what you say, but they will not do it. 33When this comes—and come it will!—

a Heb *by it*   *b* Heb *them*   *c* Cn: Heb *like a love song* then they shall know that a prophet has been among them.

33.1–33: Ezekiel's responsibilities as Israel's sentinel. In keeping with the role of the priest to observe God's requirements for Temple service, the prophet* now stands as *sentinel* or "watchman" on behalf of the people so that they will observe God's requirements. **1–9:** God establishes the analogy between the role of the prophet and that of a sentinel who stands watch over a city. The sentinel is not responsible for the fate of the people if he warns them, but he is fully responsible if he does not. The passage presupposes that the threat of death for the wicked can be reversed if they change their ways. **10–20:** See 18.21–32 on individual moral responsibility. Ezekiel debates with those who believe that past righteousness can deliver someone who commits sin later in life and vice versa. **21–22:** *In the twelfth year . . . in the tenth month . . . the fifth day:* January 19, 585 BCE. The prophet first receives word of the Temple's fall, and now speaks freely. **23–29:** Ezekiel counters the claim that *the inhabitants of these waste places,* desert nomads, will take control of the land. Ezekiel argues that they will be destroyed because they do not observe God's requirements for holy life in the land (Lev 17–18). **30–33:** God charges that people come to hear Ezekiel but will not do as he says.

34 The word of the LORD came to me: ²Mortal, prophesy against the shepherds of Israel: prophesy, and say to them—to the shepherds: Thus says the Lord GOD: Ah, you shepherds of Israel who have been feeding yourselves! Should not shepherds feed the sheep? ³You eat the fat, you clothe yourselves with the wool, you slaughter the fatlings; but you do not feed the sheep. ⁴You have not strengthened the weak, you have not healed the sick, you have not bound up the injured, you have not brought back the strayed, you have not sought the lost, but with force and harshness you have ruled them. ⁵So they were scattered, because there was no shepherd; and scattered, they became food for all the wild animals. ⁶My sheep were scattered, they wandered over all the mountains and on every high hill; my sheep were scattered over all the face of the earth, with no one to search or seek for them.

7 Therefore, you shepherds, hear the word of the LORD: ⁸As I live, says the Lord GOD, because my sheep have become a prey, and my sheep have become food for all the wild animals, since there was no shepherd; and because my shepherds have not searched for my sheep, but the shepherds have fed themselves, and have not fed my sheep; ⁹therefore, you shepherds, hear the word of the LORD: ¹⁰Thus says the Lord GOD, I am against the shepherds; and I will demand my sheep at their hand, and put a stop to their feeding the sheep; no longer shall the shepherds feed themselves. I will rescue my sheep from their mouths, so that they may not be food for them.

11 For thus says the Lord GOD: I myself will search for my sheep, and will seek them out. ¹²As shepherds seek out their flocks when they are among their scattered sheep, so I will seek out my sheep. I will rescue them from all the places to which they have been scattered on a day of clouds and thick darkness. ¹³I will bring them out from the peoples and gather them from the countries, and will bring them into their own land; and I will feed them on the mountains of Israel, by the watercourses, and in all the inhabited parts of the land. ¹⁴I will feed them with good pasture, and the mountain heights of Israel shall be their pasture; there they shall lie down in good grazing land, and they shall feed on rich pasture on the mountains of Israel. ¹⁵I myself will be the shepherd of my sheep, and I will make them lie down, says the Lord GOD. ¹⁶I will seek the lost, and I will bring back the strayed, and I will bind up the injured, and I will strengthen the weak, but the fat and the strong I will destroy. I will feed them with justice.

17 As for you, my flock, thus says the Lord GOD: I shall judge between sheep and sheep, between rams and goats: ¹⁸Is it not enough for you to feed on the good pasture, but you must tread down with your feet the rest of your pasture? When you drink of clear water, must you foul the rest with your feet? ¹⁹And must my sheep eat what you have trodden with your feet, and drink what you have fouled with your feet?

20 Therefore, thus says the Lord GOD to

them: I myself will judge between the fat sheep and the lean sheep. 21 Because you pushed with flank and shoulder, and butted at all the weak animals with your horns until you scattered them far and wide, 22 I will save my flock, and they shall no longer be ravaged; and I will judge between sheep and sheep.

23 I will set up over them one shepherd, my servant David, and he shall feed them: he shall feed them and be their shepherd. 24 And I, the LORD, will be their God, and my servant David shall be prince among them; I, the LORD, have spoken.

25 I will make with them a covenant of peace and banish wild animals from the land, so that they may live in the wild and sleep in the woods securely. 26 I will make them and the region around my hill a blessing; and I will send down the showers in their season; they shall be showers of blessing. 27 The trees of the field shall yield their fruit, and the earth shall yield its increase. They shall be secure on their soil; and they shall know that I am the LORD, when I break the bars of their yoke, and save them from the hands of those who enslaved them. 28 They shall no more be plunder for the nations, nor shall the animals of the land devour them; they shall live in safety, and no one shall make them afraid. 29 I will provide for them a splendid vegetation so that they shall no more be consumed with hunger in the land, and no longer suffer the insults of the nations. 30 They shall know that I, the LORD their God, am with them, and that they, the house of Israel, are my people, says the Lord GOD. 31 You are my sheep, the sheep of my pasture[a] and I am your God, says the Lord GOD.

34.1–31: Oracle concerning Israel's leaders or "shepherds": Ezekiel contends that Israel's leaders have acted improperly and must be replaced. **1–10:** The image of the shepherd commonly portrays monarchs in ancient Near Eastern literature (David, 1 Sam 16.11; 17). God charges that the *shepherds* have not taken care of the "flock" so that they are *scattered* or sent into exile. *Ah:* Literally, "woe!" **11–16:** God acts as the *shepherd* (Ps 23) who will return the people who have been scattered. *The fat and the strong* will

be destroyed because they neglected the people. **17–31:** Ezekiel portrays the leaders as stronger sheep who trample the pasture and dirty the water that others must use. God's rule will be manifested in the establishment of a Davidic *prince. A covenant* of peace:* The idyllic situation for those whom God will return to the land. Contrary to those who assert that "the inhabitants of the waste places" will take over the land (33.23–29), Ezekiel maintains that God will protect the people of Israel. The references to trees and animals together with the threat of enemies (see Lev 26) recall God's role as creator of the natural world and protector in the human world. *You are my sheep . . . and I am your God:* A variation of the covenant formula (11.20; 14.11).

~~~~~~~~~~~~~~~~~~~~~~~~~~~~~~~

35 The word of the LORD came to me: 2 Mortal, set your face against Mount Seir, and prophesy against it, 3 and say to it, Thus says the Lord GOD:

I am against you, Mount Seir;
I stretch out my hand against you
to make you a desolation and a waste.
4 I lay your towns in ruins;
you shall become a desolation,
and you shall know that I am
the LORD.

5 Because you cherished an ancient enmity, and gave over the people of Israel to the power of the sword at the time of their calamity, at the time of their final punishment; 6 therefore, as I live, says the Lord GOD, I will prepare you for blood, and blood shall pursue you; since you did not hate bloodshed, bloodshed shall pursue you. 7 I will make Mount Seir a waste and a desolation; and I will cut off from it all who come and go. 8 I will fill its mountains with the slain; on your hills and in your valleys and in all your watercourses those killed with the sword shall fall. 9 I will make you a perpetual desolation, and your cities shall never be inhabited. Then you shall know that I am the LORD.

10 Because you said, "These two nations and these two countries shall be mine, and we will take possession of them,"—although the LORD was there— 11 therefore, as I live, says the Lord GOD, I will deal with you ac-

---

a Gk OL: Heb *pasture, you are people*

cording to the anger and envy that you showed because of your hatred against them; and I will make myself known among you,[a] when I judge you. 12You shall know that I, the LORD, have heard all the abusive speech that you uttered against the mountains of Israel, saying, "They are laid desolate, they are given us to devour." 13And you magnified yourselves against me with your mouth, and multiplied your words against me; I heard it. 14Thus says the Lord GOD: As the whole earth rejoices, I will make you desolate. 15As you rejoiced over the inheritance of the house of Israel, because it was desolate, so I will deal with you; you shall be desolate, Mount Seir, and all Edom, all of it. Then they shall know that I am the LORD.

35.1–36. 15: Edom and Israel. Ezekiel delivers contrasting oracles* concerning judgment against Edom (Isa 34; Jer 49.7–22) and restoration for Israel. The oracles presuppose Edom's actions against Jerusalem at the time of the Babylonian assault (Ob 11–14; Ps 137.7–9). **35.1–15:** The prophecy concerning Edom begins with an initial oracle in vv. 3–4, followed by "proof sayings" in vv. 5–9, 10–13 that establish the grounds for punishment. **1–2a:** *Mount Seir:* The mountain range extending south from the Dead Sea and east of the Arabah that was Edom's homeland (Gen 36.8; Num 24.18; compare Gen 33.16). **2b–4:** The initial oracle calls for Edom's destruction. **5–9:** The first "proof saying" indicates that Edom played a role in Israel's destruction. *Ancient enmity* may allude to the feud between Esau and Jacob or the long history of conflict between Israel and Edom (Num 20.14–21). **10–13:** *These two nations and these two countries:* In addition to the conflict between Esau and Jacob, there is a tradition of God's self-revelation from Seir (Deut 33.2; Judg 5.4). **14–15:** Edom disappeared following the sixth century when it was overrun by nomads who later became known as the Nabateans.

36 And you, mortal, prophesy to the mountains of Israel, and say: O mountains of Israel, hear the word of the LORD. 2Thus says the Lord GOD: Because the enemy said of you, "Aha!" and, "The ancient heights have become our possession," 3therefore prophesy, and say: Thus says the Lord GOD: Because they made you desolate indeed, and crushed you from all sides, so

that you became the possession of the rest of the nations, and you became an object of gossip and slander among the people; 4therefore, O mountains of Israel, hear the word of the Lord GOD: Thus says the Lord GOD to the mountains and the hills, the watercourses and the valleys, the desolate wastes and the deserted towns, which have become a source of plunder and an object of derision to the rest of the nations all around; 5therefore thus says the Lord GOD: I am speaking in my hot jealousy against the rest of the nations, and against all Edom, who, with wholehearted joy and utter contempt, took my land as their possession, because of its pasture, to plunder it. 6Therefore prophesy concerning the land of Israel, and say to the mountains and hills, to the watercourses and valleys, Thus says the Lord GOD: I am speaking in my jealous wrath, because you have suffered the insults of the nations; 7therefore thus says the Lord GOD: I swear that the nations that are all around you shall themselves suffer insults.

8 But you, O mountains of Israel, shall shoot out your branches, and yield your fruit to my people Israel; for they shall soon come home. 9See now, I am for you; I will turn to you, and you shall be tilled and sown; 10and I will multiply your population, the whole house of Israel, all of it; the towns shall be inhabited and the waste places rebuilt; 11and I will multiply human beings and animals upon you. They shall increase and be fruitful; and I will cause you to be inhabited as in your former times, and will do more good to you than ever before. Then you shall know that I am the LORD. 12I will lead people upon you—my people Israel—and they shall possess you, and you shall be their inheritance. No longer shall you bereave them of children.

13 Thus says the Lord GOD: Because they say to you, "You devour people, and you bereave your nation of children," 14therefore you shall no longer devour people and no longer bereave your nation of children, says the Lord GOD; 15and no longer will I let you hear the insults of the nations, no longer

a Gk: Heb *them*

shall you bear the disgrace of the peoples; and no longer shall you cause your nation to stumble, says the Lord GOD.

36.1–15: The oracle concerning the restoration of the mountains of Israel is a deliberate contrast with that against Mount Seir. **2:** God begins by citing Edom's intentions to take control of Israel. **3–12:** The oracle presupposes the depopulation and desolation of the entire land, which must now be replenished. *The rest of the nations:* Edom elsewhere is a symbol for nations that threaten Israel (Isa 34; 63.1–6). *They shall increase and be fruitful:* See Gen 1.22, 28; 9.7. **13–15:** The prophet accuses the mountains of devouring people.

~~~~~~~~~~~~~~~~~~~~~~~~~~~~~~~~~~~~~~~

16 The word of the LORD came to me: 17 Mortal, when the house of Israel lived on their own soil, they defiled it with their ways and their deeds; their conduct in my sight was like the uncleanness of a woman in her menstrual period. 18 So I poured out my wrath upon them for the blood that they had shed upon the land, and for the idols with which they had defiled it. 19 I scattered them among the nations, and they were dispersed through the countries; in accordance with their conduct and their deeds I judged them. 20 But when they came to the nations, wherever they came, they profaned my holy name, in that it was said of them, "These are the people of the LORD, and yet they had to go out of his land." 21 But I had concern for my holy name, which the house of Israel had profaned among the nations to which they came.

22 Therefore say to the house of Israel, Thus says the Lord GOD: It is not for your sake, O house of Israel, that I am about to act, but for the sake of my holy name, which you have profaned among the nations to which you came. 23 I will sanctify my great name, which has been profaned among the nations, and which you have profaned among them; and the nations shall know that I am the LORD, says the Lord GOD, when through you I display my holiness before their eyes. 24 I will take you from the nations, and gather you from all the countries, and bring you into your own land. 25 I will sprinkle clean water upon you, and you shall be clean from all your uncleannesses, and from

all your idols I will cleanse you. 26 A new heart I will give you, and a new spirit I will put within you; and I will remove from your body the heart of stone and give you a heart of flesh. 27 I will put my spirit within you, and make you follow my statutes and be careful to observe my ordinances. 28 Then you shall live in the land that I gave to your ancestors; and you shall be my people, and I will be your God. 29 I will save you from all your uncleannesses, and I will summon the grain and make it abundant and lay no famine upon you. 30 I will make the fruit of the tree and the produce of the field abundant, so that you may never again suffer the disgrace of famine among the nations. 31 Then you shall remember your evil ways, and your dealings that were not good; and you shall loathe yourselves for your iniquities and your abominable deeds. 32 It is not for your sake that I will act, says the Lord GOD; let that be known to you. Be ashamed and dismayed for your ways, O house of Israel.

33 Thus says the Lord GOD: On the day that I cleanse you from all your iniquities, I will cause the towns to be inhabited, and the waste places shall be rebuilt. 34 The land that was desolate shall be tilled, instead of being the desolation that it was in the sight of all who passed by. 35 And they will say, "This land that was desolate has become like the garden of Eden; and the waste and desolate and ruined towns are now inhabited and fortified." 36 Then the nations that are left all around you shall know that I, the LORD, have rebuilt the ruined places, and replanted that which was desolate; I, the LORD, have spoken, and I will do it.

37 Thus says the Lord GOD: I will also let the house of Israel ask me to do this for them: to increase their population like a flock. 38 Like the flock for sacrifices,*a* like the flock at Jerusalem during her appointed festivals, so shall the ruined towns be filled with flocks of people. Then they shall know that I am the LORD.

36.16–38: The purification of Israel. Ezekiel portrays the restoration of Israel as a process of purifying sacrifice (chs. 8–11). **16–21:** The prophet initially employs

a Heb *flock of holy things*

the imagery of menstrual blood to portray the impurity of the land. According to priestly thought, blood is the seat of life and holiness, and, hence, requires special care (Gen 9.1–6; Lev 17). Like men who have bodily discharges (Lev 15.1–18), menstruating women are considered unclean (Lev 15.19–30) and require purification. The exile of the people profanes God's name. **22–32:** In order to reclaim God's name, Israel must be restored. God intends to purify Israel with clean water, which is the standard procedure for purification in such cases (Lev 15.7, 11–12; see also Lev 14.5–6, 50–52; Num 19.17). Once the land and people are cleansed, God will provide *a new heart* and *a new spirit* (11.19; 18.31; Jer 31.31–34) that will prompt the people to live a holy life in accordance with God's commandments. The covenant formula (v. 28) signifies the restoration of Israel's relationship with God and the fertility of the land. **33–36:** Replenishing of the land to resemble *the garden of Eden* (Gen 2–3) reveals God to the nations (Ex 15.13–18). **37–38:** The imagery of restoration is related to that of the sacrificial sheep that fill Jerusalem during festivals.

37 The hand of the LORD came upon me, and he brought me out by the spirit of the LORD and set me down in the middle of a valley; it was full of bones. ²He led me all around them; there were very many lying in the valley, and they were very dry. ³He said to me, "Mortal, can these bones live?" I answered, "O Lord GOD, you know." ⁴Then he said to me, "Prophesy to these bones, and say to them: O dry bones, hear the word of the LORD. ⁵Thus says the Lord GOD to these bones: I will cause breath*a* to enter you, and you shall live. ⁶I will lay sinews on you, and will cause flesh to come upon you, and cover you with skin, and put breath*a* in you, and you shall live; and you shall know that I am the LORD."

7 So I prophesied as I had been commanded; and as I prophesied, suddenly there was a noise, a rattling, and the bones came together, bone to its bone. ⁸I looked, and there were sinews on them, and flesh had come upon them, and skin had covered them; but there was no breath in them. ⁹Then he said to me, "Prophesy to the breath, prophesy, mortal, and say to the breath:*b* Thus says the Lord GOD: Come from the four winds, O breath,*b* and breathe

upon these slain, that they may live." ¹⁰I prophesied as he commanded me, and the breath came into them, and they lived, and stood on their feet, a vast multitude.

11 Then he said to me, "Mortal, these bones are the whole house of Israel. They say, 'Our bones are dried up, and our hope is lost; we are cut off completely.' ¹²Therefore prophesy, and say to them, Thus says the Lord GOD: I am going to open your graves, and bring you up from your graves, O my people; and I will bring you back to the land of Israel. ¹³And you shall know that I am the LORD, when I open your graves, and bring you up from your graves, O my people. ¹⁴I will put my spirit within you, and you shall live, and I will place you on your own soil; then you shall know that I, the LORD, have spoken and will act, says the LORD."

37.1–14: The valley of dry bones. Ezekiel's vision of dry bones symbolizes the restoration of the people of Israel. Many assume that it is based upon his observation of a battlefield filled with the bones of dead soldiers. The vision plays upon priestly concepts of purity, in that a priest must have no contact with the dead (Lev 21.1–12; those who do have contact with a corpse are defiled for a period of seven days, Num 19.10b–22). Since such impurity is the epitome of defilement in priestly thought, this image of new life is a very powerful metaphor* for the restoration and purification of Israel. **1–10:** God instructs him to prophesy. *Valley*, or "plain" is the location of his initial visions (1.22–27). *Breath:* Literally "wind." **11–14:** Resurrection symbolizes the restoration of Israel to its own land (see Isa 26.19; Dan 12.1–4).

15 The word of the LORD came to me: ¹⁶Mortal, take a stick and write on it, "For Judah, and the Israelites associated with it"; then take another stick and write on it, "For Joseph (the stick of Ephraim) and all the house of Israel associated with it"; ¹⁷and join them together into one stick, so that they may become one in your hand. ¹⁸And when your people say to you, "Will you not show us what you mean by these?" ¹⁹say to them, Thus says the Lord GOD: I am about to take the stick of Joseph (which is in the hand of Ephraim) and the tribes of Israel associated

a Or *spirit*   *b* Or *wind* or *spirit*

with it; and I will put the stick of Judah upon it,[a] and make them one stick, in order that they may be one in my hand. 20When the sticks on which you write are in your hand before their eyes, 21then say to them, Thus says the Lord GOD: I will take the people of Israel from the nations among which they have gone, and will gather them from every quarter, and bring them to their own land. 22I will make them one nation in the land, on the mountains of Israel; and one king shall be king over them all. Never again shall they be two nations, and never again shall they be divided into two kingdoms. 23They shall never again defile themselves with their idols and their detestable things, or with any of their transgressions. I will save them from all the apostasies into which they have fallen,[b] and will cleanse them. Then they shall be my people, and I will be their God.

24 My servant David shall be king over them; and they shall all have one shepherd. They shall follow my ordinances and be careful to observe my statutes. 25They shall live in the land that I gave to my servant Jacob, in which your ancestors lived; they and their children and their children's children shall live there forever; and my servant David shall be their prince forever. 26I will make a covenant of peace with them; it shall be an everlasting covenant with them; and I will bless[c] them and multiply them, and will set my sanctuary among them forevermore. 27My dwelling place shall be with them; and I will be their God, and they shall be my people. 28Then the nations shall know that I the LORD sanctify Israel, when my sanctuary is among them forevermore.

37.15–28: The two sticks. Ezekiel's symbolic action represents the unification of Israel and Judah under the rule of a Davidic king. See Isa 11, which also employs the image of a growing tree to symbolize the unification of Israel and Judah under a Davidic king. **15–19:** God instructs Ezekiel to write the names *Judah* and *Joseph* on two *sticks* (see Num 17.1–13). *Judah* is the southern kingdom, and *Joseph* is the father of *Ephraim*, the central tribe of the northern kingdom, Israel. *Stick:* Literally "tree" or "wood." **20–27:** Just as one gathers sticks for a fire (Isa 27.11), God will gather the exiles to establish them as one nation. Ezekiel

draws upon the tradition of permanent Davidic rule (2 Sam 7; Ps 89; 132), the eternal *covenant★ of peace* granted to the priest Phineas the son of Eleazar and grandson of Aaron (Num 25.10–13; see also Ezek 34.25), and the role of the Temple★ as the center of both Israel and all creation (Ex 40; see also Gen 2.1–3).

The Gog and Magog oracles
Chs. 38–39 Ezekiel's oracles against Gog, ruler from the land of Magog, express an apocalyptic★ drama of God's victory over the nations that threaten Israel. The original identity of *Gog* is uncertain, although some have identified him with Gyges, a seventh-century BCE ruler of Lydia in Asia Minor. The land of *Magog* appears together with *Meshech*, *Tubal*, *Gomer* (Cimmerians in central Asia Minor), and Togarmah (compare *Beth-togarmah*, in Armenia), apparently lands in Asia Minor and Greece. Ezekiel's oracles, however, draw upon Isaiah's prophecies concerning the downfall of a Mesopotamian ruler (Isa 14) and Jeremiah's prophecies concerning a "foe from the north" (Jer 2–3). The original identity of Gog matters little as later interpreters have understood him to be a trans-national symbol of evil, much like Edom and Egypt (for example, Isa 34; 63.1–6; Mal 1.2–5; Ex 15) or chaos monsters such as Leviathan★ or Behemoth★ (Ps 74; 104; Job 38–41).

---

38 The word of the LORD came to me: 2Mortal, set your face toward Gog, of the land of Magog, the chief prince of Meshech and Tubal. Prophesy against him 3and say: Thus says the Lord GOD: I am against you, O Gog, chief prince of Meshech and Tubal; 4I will turn you around and put hooks into your jaws, and I will lead you out with all your army, horses and horsemen, all of them clothed in full armor, a great company, all of them with shield and buckler, wielding swords. 5Persia, Ethiopia,[d] and Put are with them, all of them with buckler and helmet; 6Gomer and all its troops; Beth-togarmah from the remotest parts of the north with all its troops—many peoples are with you. 7 Be ready and keep ready, you and all the companies that are assembled around you,

---

[a] Heb *I will put them upon it*   [b] Another reading is *from all the settlements in which they have sinned*   [c] Tg: Heb *give*   [d] Or *Nubia*; Heb *Cush*

and hold yourselves in reserve for them. 8After many days you shall be mustered; in the latter years you shall go against a land restored from war, a land where people were gathered from many nations on the mountains of Israel, which had long lain waste; its people were brought out from the nations and now are living in safety, all of them. 9You shall advance, coming on like a storm; you shall be like a cloud covering the land, you and all your troops, and many peoples with you.

10 Thus says the Lord GOD: On that day thoughts will come into your mind, and you will devise an evil scheme. 11You will say, "I will go up against the land of unwalled villages; I will fall upon the quiet people who live in safety, all of them living without walls, and having no bars or gates"; 12to seize spoil and carry off plunder; to assail the waste places that are now inhabited, and the people who were gathered from the nations, who are acquiring cattle and goods, who live at the center*a* of the earth. 13Sheba and Dedan and the merchants of Tarshish and all its young warriors*b* will say to you, "Have you come to seize spoil? Have you assembled your horde to carry off plunder, to carry away silver and gold, to take away cattle and goods, to seize a great amount of booty?"

14 Therefore, mortal, prophesy, and say to Gog: Thus says the Lord GOD: On that day when my people Israel are living securely, you will rouse yourself*c* 15and come from your place out of the remotest parts of the north, you and many peoples with you, all of them riding on horses, a great horde, a mighty army; 16you will come up against my people Israel, like a cloud covering the earth. In the latter days I will bring you against my land, so that the nations may know me, when through you, O Gog, I display my holiness before their eyes.

Sheba: Southern Arabia. *Dedan:* Rhodes. *Tarshish:* Tartessos in Spain. **14–16:** God portrays Gog's advance with a mighty army against Israel. *In the latter days* normally refers to the future, and many believe the expression to have eschatological* meaning. The nations' knowledge of God draws upon earlier traditions (for example, Ex 15; Isa 2.1–4; Mic 4.1–5; Ps 46–48) in which the nations recognize God's power and sovereignty.

17 Thus says the Lord GOD: Are you he of whom I spoke in former days by my servants the prophets of Israel, who in those days prophesied for years that I would bring you against them? 18On that day, when Gog comes against the land of Israel, says the Lord GOD, my wrath shall be aroused. 19For in my jealousy and in my blazing wrath I declare: On that day there shall be a great shaking in the land of Israel; 20the fish of the sea, and the birds of the air, and the animals of the field, and all creeping things that creep on the ground, and all human beings that are on the face of the earth, shall quake at my presence, and the mountains shall be thrown down, and the cliffs shall fall, and every wall shall tumble to the ground. 21I will summon the sword against Gog*d* in*e* all my mountains, says the Lord GOD; the swords of all will be against their comrades. 22With pestilence and bloodshed I will enter into judgment with him; and I will pour down torrential rains and hailstones, fire and sulfur, upon him and his troops and the many peoples that are with him. 23So I will display my greatness and my holiness and make myself known in the eyes of many nations. Then they shall know that I am the LORD.

38.17–23: God portrays the defeat of Gog as a cosmic event that was announced by the prophets.* *On that day* is a formula that appears throughout Isaiah 1–39 (Isa 4.2; 7.18, 20, 21, 23). The cosmic dimensions of the defeat appear in the quaking of the land, including *the fish of the sea, the birds of the air, the animals of the field, all creeping things,* and *all human beings,* which alludes to the created order as described in Gen 1. Likewise, the defeat of Gog by the sword and natural

38.1–16. 1–9: God's initial instructions to Ezekiel present Gog as the leader of a host of nations that threaten Israel, a well-known motif* in the tradition about Zion* as an invincible fortress (see Ps 2; 46–48). *Persia, Ethiopia,* and *Put* (Libya) are distant lands from throughout the ancient Near Eastern world. **10–13:** God portrays Gog's intentions to plunder nations.

a Heb *navel*   *b* Heb *young lions*   *c* Gk: Heb *will you not know?*   *d* Heb *him*   *e* Heb *to* or *for* elements, such as *torrential rains, hailstones, fire,* and *sulphur,* appeal to God's role as creator as well as to the tradition about the destruction of Sodom and Gomorrah (Gen 18–19). Recognition by the nations is the object of God's action.

39 And you, mortal, prophesy against Gog, and say: Thus says the Lord GOD: I am against you, O Gog, chief prince of Meshech and Tubal! [2]I will turn you around and drive you forward, and bring you up from the remotest parts of the north, and lead you against the mountains of Israel. [3]I will strike your bow from your left hand, and will make your arrows drop out of your right hand. [4]You shall fall upon the mountains of Israel, you and all your troops and the peoples that are with you; I will give you to birds of prey of every kind and to the wild animals to be devoured. [5]You shall fall in the open field; for I have spoken, says the Lord GOD. [6]I will send fire on Magog and on those who live securely in the coastlands; and they shall know that I am the LORD.

7 My holy name I will make known among my people Israel; and I will not let my holy name be profaned any more; and the nations shall know that I am the LORD, the Holy One in Israel. [8]It has come! It has happened, says the Lord GOD. This is the day of which I have spoken.

9 Then those who live in the towns of Israel will go out and make fires of the weapons and burn them—bucklers and shields, bows and arrows, handpikes and spears—and they will make fires of them for seven years. [10]They will not need to take wood out of the field or cut down any trees in the forests, for they will make their fires of the weapons; they will despoil those who despoiled them, and plunder those who plundered them, says the Lord GOD.

11 On that day I will give to Gog a place for burial in Israel, the Valley of the Travelers[a] east of the sea; it shall block the path of the travelers, for there Gog and all his horde will be buried; it shall be called the Valley of Hamon-gog.[b] [12]Seven months the house of Israel shall spend burying them, in order to cleanse the land! [13]All the people of the land shall bury them; and it will bring them honor on the day that I show my glory, says the Lord GOD. [14]They will set apart men to pass through the land regularly and bury any invaders[c] who remain on the face of the land, so as to cleanse it; for seven months they shall make their search. [15]As the searchers[c] pass through the land, anyone who sees a human bone shall set up a sign by it, until the buriers have buried it in the Valley of Hamon-gog.[b] [16](A city Hamonah[d] is there also.) Thus they shall cleanse the land.

39.1–16: Unburied corpses on the mountains recall the imagery of the vision of dry bones (37.1–14), the death of the Babylonian king in the open (Isa 14.3–23), and the defeat of Assyria on the mountains of Israel (Isa 14.24–27). The victory fires that burn for seven years throughout the land recall the seven-year sabbatical agricultural and economic cycle (Lev 25.1–7; Ex 23.10–11; 21.1–6; Deut 15.1–18). The burial of Gog constitutes the final stage of the cleansing of the land of Israel prior to its restoration. *The Valley of the Travelers* or the "Valley of those who pass by" is apparently a wordplay on the Valley of Abarim east of the Dead Sea. Hebrew for "travelers, passersby" is "ha'obrim." *The Valley of Hamon-gog,* "the valley of the horde of Gog," is a wordplay on the Valley of Hinnom, southwest of Jerusalem, which was known for idolatry,* the burning of children, and dead bodies (2 Kings 23.10; Jer 7.30–34). The seven months of burial purify the land so that God's *glory* or presence may appear. *Hamonah:* "horde."

17 As for you, mortal, thus says the Lord GOD: Speak to the birds of every kind and to all the wild animals: Assemble and come, gather from all around to the sacrificial feast that I am preparing for you, a great sacrificial feast on the mountains of Israel, and you shall eat flesh and drink blood. [18]You shall eat the flesh of the mighty, and drink the blood of the princes of the earth—of rams, of lambs, and of goats, of bulls, all of them fatlings of Bashan. [19]You shall eat fat until you are filled, and drink blood until you are drunk, at the sacrificial feast that I am preparing for you. [20]And you shall be filled at

a Or *of the Abarim*   b That is, *the Horde of Gog*
c Heb *travelers*   d That is *The Horde*

my table with horses and charioteers,^a with warriors and all kinds of soldiers, says the Lord GOD.

21 I will display my glory among the nations; and all the nations shall see my judgment that I have executed, and my hand that I have laid on them. 22The house of Israel shall know that I am the LORD their God, from that day forward. 23And the nations shall know that the house of Israel went into captivity for their iniquity, because they dealt treacherously with me. So I hid my face from them and gave them into the hand of their adversaries, and they all fell by the sword. 24I dealt with them according to their uncleanness and their transgressions, and hid my face from them.

25 Therefore thus says the Lord GOD: Now I will restore the fortunes of Jacob, and have mercy on the whole house of Israel; and I will be jealous for my holy name. 26They shall forget^b their shame, and all the treachery they have practiced against me, when they live securely in their land with no one to make them afraid, 27when I have brought them back from the peoples and gathered them from their enemies' lands, and through them have displayed my holiness in the sight of many nations. 28Then they shall know that I am the LORD their God because I sent them into exile among the nations, and then gathered them into their own land. I will leave none of them behind; 29and I will never again hide my face from them, when I pour out my spirit upon the house of Israel, says the Lord GOD.

39.17–29: The feast of the birds and wild animals recalls the covenant* curses (for example, Deut 28.16–44) in which Israel is fed to the birds and animals, but they are now applied to Israel's enemies (Lev 26.22; Deut 28.26). The *sacrificial feast* reverses the imagery of the banquet on Zion* (Isa 25.6–10). These actions enable God to display the divine glory to the nations. *I hid my face from them* raises the question of God's injustice. *Restore the fortunes of Jacob* recalls God's promise to remember the covenant* with Jacob (Lev 26.40–45) if the people confess their iniquity.

**The vision of the restored Temple in Jerusalem
Chs. 40–48:** See God's promises (37.24–38) to make a covenant of peace with Israel and to place the sanc-

tuary among them forever. This vision provides a literary and conceptual envelope for the book that complements the visions of God's departure and the Temple's destruction in chs. 1–11 with one of the Temple's restorations and God's return. Ezekiel 40.1–43.12 relates instruction concerning the building of the Temple and the return of God's glory; 43.13–47.12 provides instruction concerning the associated structures and activities of the Temple complex; and 47.13–48.35 guides the reestablishment of the land and people of Israel around the Temple.

---

40 In the twenty-fifth year of our exile, at the beginning of the year, on the tenth day of the month, in the fourteenth year after the city was struck down, on that very day, the hand of the LORD was upon me, and he brought me there. 2He brought me, in visions of God, to the land of Israel, and set me down upon a very high mountain, on which was a structure like a city to the south. 3When he brought me there, a man was there, whose appearance shone like bronze, with a linen cord and a measuring reed in his hand; and he was standing in the gateway. 4The man said to me, "Mortal, look closely and listen attentively, and set your mind upon all that I shall show you, for you were brought here in order that I might show it to you; declare all that you see to the house of Israel."

40.1–43.12: The Temple* and the return of God's glory. 40.1–4: The date in v. 1 is April 28, 573 BCE. Ezekiel's visions began at the age of 30 in the fifth year of the Exile (1.1–3). After 20 years, Ezekiel would be ready to retire from priestly service at the age of 50 (Num 4.3; 8.23–25). Ezekiel is transported to Mt. Zion, the site of the First Temple. The city of Jerusalem is immediately to the south. Ezekiel's guide recalls the bronze-colored creatures that supported God's throne chariot (1.5–14; 8.2). The *linen cord* and the *measuring reed* enable the guide to instruct Ezekiel in the dimensions of the Temple structures.

5 Now there was a wall all around the outside of the temple area. The length of the measuring reed in the man's hand was six long cubits, each being a cubit and a hand-

---

a Heb *chariots*   *b* Another reading is *They shall bear* breadth in length; so he measured the thickness of the wall, one reed; and the height, one reed. [6]Then he went into the gateway facing east, going up its steps, and measured the threshold of the gate, one reed deep.[a] There were [7]recesses, and each recess was one reed wide and one reed deep; and the space between the recesses, five cubits; and the threshold of the gate by the vestibule of the gate at the inner end was one reed deep. [8]Then he measured the inner vestibule of the gateway, one cubit. [9]Then he measured the vestibule of the gateway, eight cubits; and its pilasters, two cubits; and the vestibule of the gate was at the inner end. [10]There were three recesses on either side of the east gate; the three were of the same size; and the pilasters on either side were of the same size. [11]Then he measured the width of the opening of the gateway, ten cubits; and the width of the gateway, thirteen cubits. [12]There was a barrier before the recesses, one cubit on either side; and the recesses were six cubits on either side. [13]Then he measured the gate from the back[b] of the one recess to the back[b] of the other, a width of twenty-five cubits, from wall to wall.[c] [14]He measured[d] also the vestibule, twenty cubits; and the gate next to the pilaster on every side of the court.[e] [15]From the front of the gate at the entrance to the end of the inner vestibule of the gate was fifty cubits. [16]The recesses and their pilasters had windows, with shutters[e] on the inside of the gateway all around, and the vestibules also had windows on the inside all around; and on the pilasters were palm trees.

[17]Then he brought me into the outer court; there were chambers there, and a pavement, all around the court; thirty chambers fronted on the pavement. [18]The pavement ran along the side of the gates, corresponding to the length of the gates; this was the lower pavement. [19]Then he measured the distance from the inner front of[f] the lower gate to the outer front of the inner court, one hundred cubits.[g]

20 Then he measured the gate of the outer court that faced north—its depth and width. [21]Its recesses, three on either side, and its pilasters and its vestibule were of the same size as those of the first gate; its depth was fifty cubits, and its width twenty-five cubits. [22]Its windows, its vestibule, and its palm trees were of the same size as those of the gate that faced toward the east. Seven steps led up to it; and its vestibule was on the inside.[h] [23]Opposite the gate on the north, as on the east, was a gate to the inner court; he measured from gate to gate, one hundred cubits.

24 Then he led me toward the south, and there was a gate on the south; and he measured its pilasters and its vestibule; they had the same dimensions as the others. [25]There were windows all around in it and in its vestibule, like the windows of the others; its depth was fifty cubits, and its width twenty-five cubits. [26]There were seven steps leading up to it; its vestibule was on the inside.[h] It had palm trees on its pilasters, one on either side. [27]There was a gate on the south of the inner court; and he measured from gate to gate toward the south, one hundred cubits.

40.5–47: The Temple walls, gates, and courtyards. 5: *Six long cubits:* over ten feet or three meters. A long cubit is about 518 millimeters or 20.68 inches. **5–16:** The *east gate* is the main gate of the Temple complex, which faces east toward the sun. It is built according to the basic pattern of the fortified Solomonic gates at Gezer, Hazor, and Megiddo, with an initial *threshold* built into the wall, followed by three recessed chambers, an inner threshold, and the *vestibule. Pilaster:* A projecting column that may have served as a door jamb. Windows provide light for the recessed chambers and the vestibule.

40.17–27. 17–19: The thirty chambers that line the *outer court* were used by the Levites for various activities (Jer 35.2–4; Neh 13.4–14). **20–27:** The gates for the outer court to the north and south are similar to the east gate. There is no west gate; the Temple occupies the western side of the compound. Each of the

a Heb *deep, and one threshold, one reed deep*
b Gk: Heb *roof*   c Heb *opening facing opening*
d Heb *made*   e Meaning of Heb uncertain
f Compare Gk: Heb *from before*   g Heb adds *the east and the north*   h Gk: Heb *before them*

three gates faces a corresponding gate to the inner court.

28 Then he brought me to the inner court by the south gate, and he measured the south gate; it was of the same dimensions as the others. 29 Its recesses, its pilasters, and its vestibule were of the same size as the others; and there were windows all around in it and in its vestibule; its depth was fifty cubits, and its width twenty-five cubits. 30 There were vestibules all around, twenty-five cubits deep and five cubits wide. 31 Its vestibule faced the outer court, and palm trees were on its pilasters, and its stairway had eight steps.

32 Then he brought me to the inner court on the east side, and he measured the gate; it was of the same size as the others. 33 Its recesses, its pilasters, and its vestibule were of the same dimensions as the others; and there were windows all around in it and in its vestibule; its depth was fifty cubits, and its width twenty-five cubits. 34 Its vestibule faced the outer court, and it had palm trees on its pilasters, on either side; and its stairway had eight steps.

35 Then he brought me to the north gate, and he measured it; it had the same dimensions as the others. 36 Its recesses, its pilasters, and its vestibule were of the same size as the others;*a* and it had windows all around. Its depth was fifty cubits, and its width twenty-five cubits. 37 Its vestibule*b* faced the outer court, and it had palm trees on its pilasters, on either side; and its stairway had eight steps.

38 There was a chamber with its door in the vestibule of the gate,*c* where the burnt offering was to be washed. 39 And in the vestibule of the gate were two tables on either side, on which the burnt offering and the sin offering and the guilt offering were to be slaughtered. 40 On the outside of the vestibule*d* at the entrance of the north gate were two tables; and on the other side of the vestibule of the gate were two tables. 41 Four tables were on the inside, and four tables on the outside of the side of the gate, eight tables, on which the sacrifices were to be slaughtered. 42 There were also four tables of

hewn stone for the burnt offering, a cubit and a half long, and one cubit and a half wide, and one cubit high, on which the instruments were to be laid with which the burnt offerings and the sacrifices were slaughtered. 43 There were pegs, one handbreadth long, fastened all around the inside. And on the tables the flesh of the offering was to be laid.

44 On the outside of the inner gateway there were chambers for the singers in the inner court, one*e* at the side of the north gate facing south, the other at the side of the east gate facing north. 45 He said to me, "This chamber that faces south is for the priests who have charge of the temple, 46 and the chamber that faces north is for the priests who have charge of the altar; these are the descendants of Zadok, who alone among the descendants of Levi may come near to the LORD to minister to him." 47 He measured the court, one hundred cubits deep, and one hundred cubits wide, a square; and the altar was in front of the temple.

40.28–47. 28–37: The south, east, and north gates to the inner court are similar to those for the outer court. 38–43: Chambers were built by the vestibule of the gate to prepare sacrificial animals for the *burnt offering* (Lev 1.3–17), the *sin offering* (Lev 4.1–5.13), and the *guilt offering* (Lev 5.14–6.7). 44–47: Chambers were placed by the sides of the north and east (LXX* reads "south") for the priests who had charge of the Temple and the altar.

48 Then he brought me to the vestibule of the temple and measured the pilasters of the vestibule, five cubits on either side; and the width of the gate was fourteen cubits; and the sidewalls of the gate were three cubits*f* on either side. 49 The depth of the vestibule was twenty cubits, and the width twelve*g* cubits; ten steps led up*h* to it; and

a One Ms: Compare verses 29 and 33: MT lacks *were of the same size as the others* *b* Gk Vg Compare verses 26, 31, 34: Heb *pilasters* *c* Cn: Heb *at the pilasters of the gates* *d* Cn: Heb *to him who goes up* *e* Heb lacks *one* *f* Gk: Heb *and the width of the gate was three cubits* *g* Gk: Heb *eleven* *h* Gk: Heb *and by steps that went up* there were pillars beside the pilasters on either side.

41 Then he brought me to the nave, and measured the pilasters; on each side six cubits was the width of the pilasters.*a* ²The width of the entrance was ten cubits; and the sidewalls of the entrance were five cubits on either side. He measured the length of the nave, forty cubits, and its width, twenty cubits. ³Then he went into the inner room and measured the pilasters of the entrance, two cubits; and the width of the entrance, six cubits; and the sidewalls*b* of the entrance, seven cubits. ⁴He measured the depth of the room, twenty cubits, and its width, twenty cubits, beyond the nave. And he said to me, This is the most holy place.

40.48–41.26: The Temple. 40.48–41.4: The Temple is constructed according to a three-room pattern, like that of Solomon's Temple (1 Kings 6) and other examples of temples and royal palaces from Canaan and Syria. The three rooms are the *vestibule* (35 feet by 21 feet), an entry or reception room; the *nave* (71 feet by 25 feet), the main hall where the Temple furnishings are placed; and the *inner room* (35 feet by 35 feet), also known as the most holy place, God's throne room which houses the ark of the covenant. Ezekiel does not enter the *inner room* since this is restricted to the high priest on Yom Kippur or the Day of Atonement★ (Lev 16). *Pillars:* Like those of Solomon's Temple (1 Kings 7.15–22).

---

5 Then he measured the wall of the temple, six cubits thick; and the width of the side chambers, four cubits, all around the temple. ⁶The side chambers were in three stories, one over another, thirty in each story. There were offsets*c* all around the wall of the temple to serve as supports for the side chambers, so that they should not be supported by the wall of the temple. ⁷The passageway*d* of the side chambers widened from story to story; for the structure was supplied with a stairway all around the temple. For this reason the structure became wider from story to story. One ascended from the bottom story to the uppermost story by way of the middle one. ⁸I saw also that the temple had a raised platform all around; the foundations of the side chambers measured a full reed of six long cubits. ⁹The thickness of the outer wall of the side chambers was five cubits; and the free space between the side chambers of the temple ¹⁰and the chambers of the court was a width of twenty cubits all around the temple on every side. ¹¹The side chambers opened onto the area left free, one door toward the north, and another door toward the south; and the width of the part that was left free was five cubits all around.

41.5–11: Three stories of chambers with thirty chambers each line the walls of the Temple. They have an independent support structure so that they are not supported by the Temple itself. A *stairway* provides access to the upper stories. The supports and stairways occupy more space on the lower stories so that each story is progressively larger. *Raised platform:* The "foundations of the earth" (Mic 6.2; Isa 24.18; Jer 31.37; Ps 82.5).

12 The building that was facing the temple yard on the west side was seventy cubits wide; and the wall of the building was five cubits thick all around, and its depth ninety cubits.

13 Then he measured the temple, one hundred cubits deep; and the yard and the building with its walls, one hundred cubits deep; ¹⁴also the width of the east front of the temple and the yard, one hundred cubits.

15 Then he measured the depth of the building facing the yard at the west, together with its galleries*e* on either side, one hundred cubits.

The nave of the temple and the inner room and the outer*f* vestibule ¹⁶were paneled,*g* and, all around, all three had windows with recessed*h* frames. Facing the threshold the temple was paneled with wood all around, from the floor up to the windows (now the windows were covered), ¹⁷to the space above the door, even to the inner room, and on the outside. And on all the walls all around in

a Compare Gk: Heb *tent*   *b* Gk: Heb *width*
c Gk Compare 1 Kings 6.6: Heb *they entered*
d Cn: Heb *it was surrounded*   *e* Cn: Meaning of Heb uncertain   *f* Gk: Heb *of the court*   *g* Gk: Heb *the thresholds*   *h* Cn Compare Gk 1 Kings 6.4: Meaning of Heb uncertain

the inner room and the nave there was a pattern.[a] 18It was formed of cherubim and palm trees, a palm tree between cherub and cherub. Each cherub had two faces: 19a human face turned toward the palm tree on the one side, and the face of a young lion turned toward the palm tree on the other side. They were carved on the whole temple all around; 20from the floor to the area above the door, cherubim and palm trees were carved on the wall.[b]

21 The doorposts of the nave were square. In front of the holy place was something resembling 22an altar of wood, three cubits high, two cubits long, and two cubits wide;[c] its corners, its base,[d] and its walls were of wood. He said to me, "This is the table that stands before the LORD." 23The nave and the holy place had each a double door. 24The doors had two leaves apiece, two swinging leaves for each door. 25On the doors of the nave were carved cherubim and palm trees, such as were carved on the walls; and there was a canopy of wood in front of the vestibule outside. 26And there were recessed windows and palm trees on either side, on the sidewalls of the vestibule.[e]

41.12–26. 12–15a: The unidentified building is behind the Temple to the west. **41.15b–26:** The interior decoration of the Temple. *Paneled,* Greek (compare v. 16 and 1 Kings 6.9; 7.3, 7). Hebrew reads "thresholds." The *cherubim** and *palm trees* carved into the paneling of the interior walls represent images from the garden of Eden (see 1 Kings 6.29). Unlike the cherubim who bear the throne chariot, these have only two faces, a human and a young lion. *Something resembling an altar of wood:* The table for the presentation of rows of "the bread of the Presence" (Ex 25.23–30; Lev 24.5–9; 1 Kings 7.48).

42 Then he led me out into the outer court, toward the north, and he brought me to the chambers that were opposite the temple yard and opposite the building on the north. 2The length of the building that was on the north side[f] was[g] one hundred cubits, and the width fifty cubits. 3Across the twenty cubits that belonged to the inner court, and facing the pavement that belonged to the outer court, the chambers rose[h] gallery[i] by gallery[i] in three stories. 4In front of the chambers was a passage on the inner side, ten cubits wide and one hundred cubits deep,[j] and its[k] entrances were on the north. 5Now the upper chambers were narrower, for the galleries[i] took more away from them than from the lower and middle chambers in the building. 6For they were in three stories, and they had no pillars like the pillars of the outer[l] court; for this reason the upper chambers were set back from the ground more than the lower and the middle ones. 7There was a wall outside parallel to the chambers, toward the outer court, opposite the chambers, fifty cubits long. 8For the chambers on the outer court were fifty cubits long, while those opposite the temple were one hundred cubits long. 9At the foot of these chambers ran a passage that one entered from the east in order to enter them from the outer court. 10The width of the passage[m] was fixed by the wall of the court.

On the south[n] also, opposite the vacant area and opposite the building, there were chambers 11with a passage in front of them; they were similar to the chambers on the north, of the same length and width, with the same exits[o] and arrangements and doors. 12So the entrances of the chambers to the south were entered through the entrance at the head of the corresponding passage, from the east, along the matching wall.[i]

13 Then he said to me, "The north chambers and the south chambers opposite the vacant area are the holy chambers, where the priests who approach the LORD shall eat the most holy offerings; there they shall deposit the most holy offerings—the grain offering, the sin offering, and the guilt offering—for the place is holy. 14When the priests enter the holy place, they shall not go

a Heb *measures*   b Cn Compare verse 25: Heb *and the wall*   c Gk: Heb lacks *two cubits wide*
d Gk: Heb *length*   e Cn: Heb *vestibule. And the side chambers of the temple and the canopies*   f Gk: Heb *door*   g Gk: Heb *before the length*   h Heb lacks *the chambers rose*   i Meaning of Heb uncertain
j Gk Syr: Heb *a way of one cubit*   k Heb *their*
l Gk: Heb lacks *outer*   m Heb lacks *of the passage*
n Gk: Heb *east*   o Heb *and all their exits*

out of it into the outer court without laying there the vestments in which they minister, for these are holy; they shall put on other garments before they go near to the area open to the people."

42.1–14: Chambers are built in three stories along the walls that define the outer and inner courts. The priests use them to store and eat *the grain offering* (Lev 2.1–16), *the sin offering* (Lev 4.1–5.13), and *the guilt offering* (Lev 5.14–6.7). The priests must leave their holy vestments in these chambers before entering the outer court.

15 When he had finished measuring the interior of the temple area, he led me out by the gate that faces east, and measured the temple area all around. 16He measured the east side with the measuring reed, five hundred cubits by the measuring reed. 17Then he turned and measured[a] the north side, five hundred cubits by the measuring reed. 18Then he turned and measured[a] the south side, five hundred cubits by the measuring reed. 19Then he turned to the west side and measured, five hundred cubits by the measuring reed. 20He measured it on the four sides. It had a wall around it, five hundred cubits long and five hundred cubits wide, to make a separation between the holy and the common.

42.15–20: The Temple complex is a 500-cubit square (861.63 feet). The outer wall marks the separation between the holy Temple and the profane world.

43 Then he brought me to the gate, the gate facing east. 2And there, the glory of the God of Israel was coming from the east; the sound was like the sound of mighty waters; and the earth shone with his glory. 3The[b] vision I saw was like the vision that I had seen when he came to destroy the city, and[c] like the vision that I had seen by the river Chebar; and I fell upon my face. 4As the glory of the LORD entered the temple by the gate facing east, 5the spirit lifted me up, and brought me into the inner court; and the glory of the LORD filled the temple.

6 While the man was standing beside me, I heard someone speaking to me out of the temple. 7He said to me: Mortal, this is the place of my throne and the place for the soles of my feet, where I will reside among the people of Israel forever. The house of Israel shall no more defile my holy name, neither they nor their kings, by their whoring, and by the corpses of their kings at their death.[d] 8When they placed their threshold by my threshold and their doorposts beside my doorposts, with only a wall between me and them, they were defiling my holy name by their abominations that they committed; therefore I have consumed them in my anger. 9Now let them put away their idolatry and the corpses of their kings far from me, and I will reside among them forever.

10 As for you, mortal, describe the temple to the house of Israel, and let them measure the pattern; and let them be ashamed of their iniquities. 11When they are ashamed of all that they have done, make known to them the plan of the temple, its arrangement, its exits and its entrances, and its whole form—all its ordinances and its entire plan and all its laws; and write it down in their sight, so that they may observe and follow the entire plan and all its ordinances. 12This is the law of the temple: the whole territory on the top of the mountain all around shall be most holy. This is the law of the temple.

43.1–12: The Divine Presence (chs. 1; 8–11) returns to the Temple complex through the east gate from which it had earlier departed (10.19). Ezekiel recalls his inaugural vision and reports that he is transported to the inner court where he sees *the glory of the LORD* filling the Temple (Ex 40.34–35; 1 Kings 8.10–13). God informs him that this will be *the place of my throne* (see 1 Chr 28.2; Ps 132.7; Isa 60.13; Lam 2.1). *The corpses of their kings* refers to burials of kings near the Temple (1 Kings 2.10; 11.43; 2 Kings 21.18, 26). God instructs Ezekiel to teach the people the plan for the Temple. *This is the law of the temple: Law* (Hebrew "torah") is more properly translated "instruction"; the statement summarizes God's instructions concerning the Temple.

a Gk: Heb *measuring reed all around. He measured*
b Gk: Heb *Like the vision*   c Syr: Heb *and the visions*
d Or *on their high places*

The Temple complex and its activities

43.13–47.12: Instructions concerning structures associated with the Temple and regulations concerning Temple rituals and practice.

13 These are the dimensions of the altar by cubits (the cubit being one cubit and a handbreadth): its base shall be one cubit high,*a* and one cubit wide, with a rim of one span around its edge. This shall be the height of the altar: 14From the base on the ground to the lower ledge, two cubits, with a width of one cubit; and from the smaller ledge to the larger ledge, four cubits, with a width of one cubit; 15and the altar hearth, four cubits; and from the altar hearth projecting upward, four horns. 16The altar hearth shall be square, twelve cubits long by twelve wide. 17The ledge also shall be square, fourteen cubits long by fourteen wide, with a rim around it half a cubit wide, and its surrounding base, one cubit. Its steps shall face east.

18 Then he said to me: Mortal, thus says the Lord GOD: These are the ordinances for the altar: On the day when it is erected for offering burnt offerings upon it and for dashing blood against it, 19you shall give to the levitical priests of the family of Zadok, who draw near to me to minister to me, says the Lord GOD, a bull for a sin offering. 20And you shall take some of its blood, and put it on the four horns of the altar, and on the four corners of the ledge, and upon the rim all around; thus you shall purify it and make atonement for it. 21You shall also take the bull of the sin offering, and it shall be burnt in the appointed place belonging to the temple, outside the sacred area.

22 On the second day you shall offer a male goat without blemish for a sin offering; and the altar shall be purified, as it was purified with the bull. 23When you have finished purifying it, you shall offer a bull without blemish and a ram from the flock without blemish. 24You shall present them before the LORD, and the priests shall throw salt on them and offer them up as a burnt offering to the LORD. 25For seven days you shall provide daily a goat for a sin offering; also a bull and a ram from the flock, without

blemish, shall be provided. 26Seven days shall they make atonement for the altar and cleanse it, and so consecrate it. 27When these days are over, then from the eighth day onward the priests shall offer upon the altar your burnt offerings and your offerings of well-being; and I will accept you, says the Lord GOD.

43.13–27: The altar is a four-level stepped structure, like a Mesopotamian ziggurat (a type of pyramid). The *base*, literally "bosom of the earth" (signifying the placement of the altar at the center of the earth), is 18 cubits square. The *lower ledge* is 16 cubits square. The upper ledge is 14 cubits square. The *altar hearth* ("ha-har'el" in Hebrew, "mountain of God" or "God appeared"; compare Ariel of Isa 29.1) has *four horns* (see Ex 27.2; 29.12; 1 Kings 1.50–51; Zech 2.1–4). The height of the structure is 10 cubits. Its steps face toward the east gate. The seven-day consecration of the altar is performed at Sukkot (Booths; 1 Kings 8.65–66; Ezra 3.1–7; but compare Num 7) and is analogous to the ordination* of priests (Ex 29.1–37; Lev 8). The purification of the altar with blood is analogous to the sprinkling of blood on the priests at their ordination (Ex 29.16), on the altar at Yom Kippur to make atonement* for the people (Lev 16.18–19), and on the people to seal the covenant* (Ex 24.1–8). *Salt* is also offered with grain offerings (Lev 2.13; Num 18.19).

44 Then he brought me back to the outer gate of the sanctuary, which faces east; and it was shut. 2The LORD said to me: This gate shall remain shut; it shall not be opened, and no one shall enter by it; for the LORD, the God of Israel, has entered by it; therefore it shall remain shut. 3Only the prince, because he is a prince, may sit in it to eat food before the LORD; he shall enter by way of the vestibule of the gate, and shall go out by the same way.

4 Then he brought me by way of the north gate to the front of the temple; and I looked, and lo! the glory of the LORD filled the temple of the LORD; and I fell upon my face. 5The LORD said to me: Mortal, mark well, look closely, and listen attentively to all that I shall tell you concerning all the ordinances

a Gk: Heb lacks *high*

of the temple of the LORD and all its laws; and mark well those who may be admitted to*a* the temple and all those who are to be excluded from the sanctuary. 6 Say to the rebellious house,*b* to the house of Israel, Thus says the Lord GOD: O house of Israel, let there be an end to all your abominations 7 in admitting foreigners, uncircumcised in heart and flesh, to be in my sanctuary, profaning my temple when you offer to me my food, the fat and the blood. You*c* have broken my covenant with all your abominations. 8 And you have not kept charge of my sacred offerings; but you have appointed foreigners*d* to act for you in keeping my charge in my sanctuary.

9 Thus says the Lord GOD: No foreigner, uncircumcised in heart and flesh, of all the foreigners who are among the people of Israel, shall enter my sanctuary. 10 But the Levites who went far from me, going astray from me after their idols when Israel went astray, shall bear their punishment. 11 They shall be ministers in my sanctuary, having oversight at the gates of the temple, and serving in the temple; they shall slaughter the burnt offering and the sacrifice for the people, and they shall attend on them and serve them. 12 Because they ministered to them before their idols and made the house of Israel stumble into iniquity, therefore I have sworn concerning them, says the Lord GOD, that they shall bear their punishment. 13 They shall not come near to me, to serve me as priest, nor come near any of my sacred offerings, the things that are most sacred; but they shall bear their shame, and the consequences of the abominations that they have committed. 14 Yet I will appoint them to keep charge of the temple, to do all its chores, all that is to be done in it.

44.1–46.24: Regulations concerning the Temple. 44.1–3: The east gate remains closed because God enters the Temple through the east gate. The king eats here. **4–14:** Those who have engaged in idolatry* or abominations are to be excluded from the Temple. Foreigners shall not enter (Lev 22.25; compare Isa 56.3–8). Deuteronomy 18.6–8 allows Levites to serve at the altar, but they are disenfranchised here for idolatrous behavior and allowed to perform only second-

ary service. The passage may presuppose the judgment leveled against the house of Eli (1 Sam 2) or inappropriate Levitical service at the high places* mentioned throughout 1–2 Kings.

15 But the levitical priests, the descendants of Zadok, who kept the charge of my sanctuary when the people of Israel went astray from me, shall come near to me to minister to me; and they shall attend me to offer me the fat and the blood, says the Lord GOD. 16 It is they who shall enter my sanctuary, it is they who shall approach my table, to minister to me, and they shall keep my charge. 17 When they enter the gates of the inner court, they shall wear linen vestments; they shall have nothing of wool on them, while they minister at the gates of the inner court, and within. 18 They shall have linen turbans on their heads, and linen undergarments on their loins; they shall not bind themselves with anything that causes sweat. 19 When they go out into the outer court to the people, they shall remove the vestments in which they have been ministering, and lay them in the holy chambers; and they shall put on other garments, so that they may not communicate holiness to the people with their vestments. 20 They shall not shave their heads or let their locks grow long; they shall only trim the hair of their heads. 21 No priest shall drink wine when he enters the inner court. 22 They shall not marry a widow, or a divorced woman, but only a virgin of the stock of the house of Israel, or a widow who is the widow of a priest. 23 They shall teach my people the difference between the holy and the common, and show them how to distinguish between the unclean and the clean. 24 In a controversy they shall act as judges, and they shall decide it according to my judgments. They shall keep my laws and my statutes regarding all my appointed festivals, and they shall keep my sabbaths holy. 25 They shall not defile themselves by going near to a dead person; for father or mother, however, and for son or daughter, and for brother or unmarried sister they may defile them-

a Cn: Heb *the entrance of*   *b* Gk: Heb lacks *house*
c Gk Syr Vg: Heb *They*   *d* Heb lacks *foreigners*

selves. 26After he has become clean, they shall count seven days for him. 27On the day that he goes into the holy place, into the inner court, to minister in the holy place, he shall offer his sin offering, says the Lord God.

28 This shall be their inheritance: I am their inheritance; and you shall give them no holding in Israel; I am their holding. 29They shall eat the grain offering, the sin offering, and the guilt offering; and every devoted thing in Israel shall be theirs. 30The first of all the first fruits of all kinds, and every offering of all kinds from all your offerings, shall belong to the priests; you shall also give to the priests the first of your dough, in order that a blessing may rest on your house. 31The priests shall not eat of anything, whether bird or animal, that died of itself or was torn by animals.

44.15–31: The Levites of the Zadokite line (1 Kings 2.26–27) shall enter the sanctuary and serve at the altar. They shall wear only linen (Ex 28.39); they shall not wear holy garments outside of the inner court (42.14); they shall trim their hair, but not shave it (Lev 21.5); they shall not drink wine in the inner court (Lev 10.9); they shall marry only virgins or the widows of other priests (Lev 21.7, 13–14); they shall instruct the people concerning holiness and purity (Lev 10.10–11; Deut 33.8–10; Hag 2.10–13); they shall act as judges (Ex 22.9; Deut 17.8–9; 19.17; 21.1–5); they shall observe the festivals (Lev 23; Num 28–29; Deut 16); they shall avoid contact with the dead and mourning, except for parents and siblings (Lev 21.1–3; Num 19); they shall receive no inheritance other than a share of the first fruits and offerings at the Temple (Num 18; Lev 27.28–29); and they shall not eat meat that was not properly slaughtered (Lev 22.8).

45 When you allot the land as an inheritance, you shall set aside for the Lord a portion of the land as a holy district, twenty-five thousand cubits long and twenty[a] thousand cubits wide; it shall be holy throughout its entire extent. 2Of this, a square plot of five hundred by five hundred cubits shall be for the sanctuary, with fifty cubits for an open space around it. 3In the holy district you shall measure off a section twenty-five thousand cubits long and ten thousand wide, in which shall be the sanctuary, the most holy place. 4It shall be a holy portion of the land; it shall be for the priests, who minister in the sanctuary and approach the Lord to minister to him; and it shall be both a place for their houses and a holy place for the sanctuary. 5Another section, twenty-five thousand cubits long and ten thousand cubits wide, shall be for the Levites who minister at the temple, as their holding for cities to live in.[b]

6 Alongside the portion set apart as the holy district you shall assign as a holding for the city an area five thousand cubits wide, and twenty-five thousand cubits long; it shall belong to the whole house of Israel.

7 And to the prince shall belong the land on both sides of the holy district and the holding of the city, alongside the holy district and the holding of the city, on the west and on the east, corresponding in length to one of the tribal portions, and extending from the western to the eastern boundary 8of the land. It is to be his property in Israel. And my princes shall no longer oppress my people; but they shall let the house of Israel have the land according to their tribes.

9 Thus says the Lord God: Enough, O princes of Israel! Put away violence and oppression, and do what is just and right. Cease your evictions of my people, says the Lord God.

10 You shall have honest balances, an honest ephah, and an honest bath.[c] 11The ephah and the bath shall be of the same measure, the bath containing one-tenth of a homer, and the ephah one-tenth of a homer; the homer shall be the standard measure. 12The shekel shall be twenty gerahs. Twenty shekels, twenty-five shekels, and fifteen shekels shall make a mina for you.

45.1–12. 1–9: The size and distribution of the holy district in the land for the use of the priests, the Levites, Israel, and the prince. According to the Hebrew text of v. 1 ("ten thousand cubits wide"), the combined land area is a 25,000-cubit square. The priestly portion includes the area for the sanctuary. The Levites' por-

a Gk: Heb ten   b Gk: Heb as their holding, twenty chambers   c A Heb measure of volume tion equals that of the priests, but the portion for the rest of Israel is half of that. The portion of the *prince* is not included in the *holy district* or *city;* he may not evict Israel. **10–12:** Holiness in the Temple requires just, standardized measures (Lev 19.35–36; Deut 25.13–16; compare Am 8.5; Mic 6.10–11; Prov 11.1; 20.10). The *homer* equals 6.524 bushels; the *ephah* is a dry measure that equals 20.878 quarts; the *bath* is a liquid measure that equals 6.073 gallons; the *shekel** is a measure of weight equivalent to 176.29 grains; 50 *shekels* constitute a *mina* equivalent to 20.148 ounces.

13 This is the offering that you shall make: one-sixth of an ephah from each homer of wheat, and one-sixth of an ephah from each homer of barley, [14]and as the fixed portion of oil,[a] one-tenth of a bath from each cor (the cor,[b] like the homer, contains ten baths); [15]and one sheep from every flock of two hundred, from the pastures of Israel. This is the offering for grain offerings, burnt offerings, and offerings of well-being, to make atonement for them, says the Lord GOD. [16]All the people of the land shall join with the prince in Israel in making this offering. [17]But this shall be the obligation of the prince regarding the burnt offerings, grain offerings, and drink offerings, at the festivals, the new moons, and the sabbaths, all the appointed festivals of the house of Israel: he shall provide the sin offerings, grain offerings, the burnt offerings, and the offerings of well-being, to make atonement for the house of Israel.

45.13–17: The people pay percentages of wheat (1.5%), barley (1.5%), oil (1%), and sheep (.5%) as a tax for the *grain offerings* (Lev 2); the *burnt offerings* (Lev 1); and the *offerings of well-being* (Lev 3). *All the people of the land shall join with the prince in Israel in making this offering* indicates that they pay their tax to the prince. The prince in turn is obligated to provide the *sin offerings* (Lev 4.1–5.13), the *grain offerings* (Lev 2), the *burnt offerings* (Lev 1), and the *offerings of well-being* (Lev 3) on behalf of the people at all festivals, new moons,* sabbaths, and appointed festivals.

18 Thus says the Lord GOD: In the first month, on the first day of the month, you shall take a young bull without blemish, and purify the sanctuary. [19]The priest shall take

some of the blood of the sin offering and put it on the doorposts of the temple, the four corners of the ledge of the altar, and the posts of the gate of the inner court. [20]You shall do the same on the seventh day of the month for anyone who has sinned through error or ignorance; so you shall make atonement for the temple.

21 In the first month, on the fourteenth day of the month, you shall celebrate the festival of the passover, and for seven days unleavened bread shall be eaten. [22]On that day the prince shall provide for himself and all the people of the land a young bull for a sin offering. [23]And during the seven days of the festival he shall provide as a burnt offering to the LORD seven young bulls and seven rams without blemish, on each of the seven days; and a male goat daily for a sin offering. [24]He shall provide as a grain offering an ephah for each bull, an ephah for each ram, and a hin of oil to each ephah. [25]In the seventh month, on the fifteenth day of the month and for the seven days of the festival, he shall make the same provision for sin offerings, burnt offerings, and grain offerings, and for the oil.

45.18–25: Observance of Passover* and Sukkot (Booths). **18–20:** The blood of a *sin offering* purifies the Temple, altar, and inner court on the first day of the first month. The animal blood atones for an individual who has sinned inadvertently. Note the smearing of blood on the doorposts at the Exodus (Ex 12.21–28). **21–25:** Many regard this as a festival calendar,* but it merely specifies the obligation of the prince to provide offerings for Passover (Ex 23.15; Lev 23.4–8; Deut 16.1–8) and Sukkot (Ex 23.16; Lev 23.33–36; Deut 16.13–15).

46 Thus says the Lord GOD: The gate of the inner court that faces east shall remain closed on the six working days; but on the sabbath day it shall be opened and on the day of the new moon it shall be opened. [2]The prince shall enter by the vestibule of the gate from outside, and shall take his stand by the post of the gate. The priests shall offer his burnt offering and his offer-

a Cn: Heb *oil, the bath the oil*   *b* Vg: Heb *homer*

ings of well-being, and he shall bow down at the threshold of the gate. Then he shall go out, but the gate shall not be closed until evening. ³The people of the land shall bow down at the entrance of that gate before the LORD on the sabbaths and on the new moons. ⁴The burnt offering that the prince offers to the LORD on the sabbath day shall be six lambs without blemish and a ram without blemish; ⁵and the grain offering with the ram shall be an ephah, and the grain offering with the lambs shall be as much as he wishes to give, together with a hin of oil to each ephah. ⁶On the day of the new moon he shall offer a young bull without blemish, and six lambs and a ram, which shall be without blemish; ⁷as a grain offering he shall provide an ephah with the bull and an ephah with the ram, and with the lambs as much as he wishes, together with a hin of oil to each ephah. ⁸When the prince enters, he shall come in by the vestibule of the gate, and he shall go out by the same way.

9 When the people of the land come before the LORD at the appointed festivals, whoever enters by the north gate to worship shall go out by the south gate; and whoever enters by the south gate shall go out by the north gate: they shall not return by way of the gate by which they entered, but shall go out straight ahead. ¹⁰When they come in, the prince shall come in with them; and when they go out, he shall go out.

46.1–18: Regulations concerning offerings and property for the prince and the people. 1–8: The east gate is opened on sabbaths and new moons so that the prince may enter to present his offerings. The prince *shall take his stand by the post of the gate* (see 2 Kings 11.14) and bow down at the *threshold of the gate*. The people bow down at the same gate entrance. See Num 28.9–15 for sabbath and new moon sacrifices. **9–10:** The people enter by the north and south gates, but exit by the opposite gates for efficient crowd management. *Appointed festivals* in v. 9 should read "appointed times."

---

11 At the festivals and the appointed seasons the grain offering with a young bull shall be an ephah, and with a ram an ephah, and with the lambs as much as one wishes

to give, together with a hin of oil to an ephah. ¹²When the prince provides a freewill offering, either a burnt offering or offerings of well-being as a freewill offering to the LORD, the gate facing east shall be opened for him; and he shall offer his burnt offering or his offerings of well-being as he does on the sabbath day. Then he shall go out, and after he has gone out the gate shall be closed.

13 He shall provide a lamb, a yearling, without blemish, for a burnt offering to the LORD daily; morning by morning he shall provide it. ¹⁴And he shall provide a grain offering with it morning by morning regularly, one-sixth of an ephah, and one-third of a hin of oil to moisten the choice flour, as a grain offering to the LORD; this is the ordinance for all time. ¹⁵Thus the lamb and the grain offering and the oil shall be provided, morning by morning, as a regular burnt offering.

16 Thus says the Lord GOD: If the prince makes a gift to any of his sons out of his inheritance,ᵃ it shall belong to his sons, it is their holding by inheritance. ¹⁷But if he makes a gift out of his inheritance to one of his servants, it shall be his to the year of liberty; then it shall revert to the prince; only his sons may keep a gift from his inheritance. ¹⁸The prince shall not take any of the inheritance of the people, thrusting them out of their holding; he shall give his sons their inheritance out of his own holding, so that none of my people shall be dispossessed of their holding.

46.11–18. 11–15: The freewill and *daily* offerings of the prince are specified (Lev 22.18–23, vow or freewill offering; Num 28.3–8, daily offering). **16–18:** The prince may pass property on to his sons, but property passed to servants reverts to the prince at the jubilee year (Lev 25.8–17). The prince may not pass property of the people to his own sons.

---

19 Then he brought me through the entrance, which was at the side of the gate, to the north row of the holy chambers for the priests; and there I saw a place at the extreme western end of them. ²⁰He said to me, "This is the place where the priests shall boil

ᵃ Gk: Heb *it is his inheritance*

the guilt offering and the sin offering, and where they shall bake the grain offering, in order not to bring them out into the outer court and so communicate holiness to the people."

21 Then he brought me out to the outer court, and led me past the four corners of the court; and in each corner of the court there was a court— 22in the four corners of the court were small*a* courts, forty cubits long and thirty wide; the four were of the same size. 23On the inside, around each of the four courts*b* was a row of masonry, with hearths made at the bottom of the rows all around. 24Then he said to me, "These are the kitchens where those who serve at the temple shall boil the sacrifices of the people."

46.19–24: Areas for the preparation of sacrifices for consumption by the priests are located in the northwestern area of the inner court. Kitchens for the people are located at the four corners of the outer court.

---

47 Then he brought me back to the entrance of the temple; there, water was flowing from below the threshold of the temple toward the east (for the temple faced east); and the water was flowing down from below the south end of the threshold of the temple, south of the altar. 2Then he brought me out by way of the north gate, and led me around on the outside to the outer gate that faces toward the east;*c* and the water was coming out on the south side.

3 Going on eastward with a cord in his hand, the man measured one thousand cubits, and then led me through the water; and it was ankle-deep. 4Again he measured one thousand, and led me through the water; and it was knee-deep. Again he measured one thousand, and led me through the water; and it was up to the waist. 5Again he measured one thousand, and it was a river that I could not cross, for the water had risen; it was deep enough to swim in, a river that could not be crossed. 6He said to me, "Mortal, have you seen this?"

Then he led me back along the bank of the river. 7As I came back, I saw on the bank of the river a great many trees on the one side and on the other. 8He said to me, "This water flows toward the eastern region and goes down into the Arabah; and when it enters the sea, the sea of stagnant waters, the water will become fresh. 9Wherever the river goes,*d* every living creature that swarms will live, and there will be very many fish, once these waters reach there. It will become fresh; and everything will live where the river goes. 10People will stand fishing beside the sea*e* from En-gedi to En-eglaim; it will be a place for the spreading of nets; its fish will be of a great many kinds, like the fish of the Great Sea. 11But its swamps and marshes will not become fresh; they are to be left for salt. 12On the banks, on both sides of the river, there will grow all kinds of trees for food. Their leaves will not wither nor their fruit fail, but they will bear fresh fruit every month, because the water for them flows from the sanctuary. Their fruit will be for food, and their leaves for healing."

47.1–12: Once the Temple is reestablished, water streams up from *below the threshold of the temple to the east* to water the land of Israel. This indicates the role of the Temple as the center of creation (the Garden of Eden, Gen 2.10–14; Ps 46.4). The course of the water reflects that of the Gihon spring (compare the Edenic river, Gen 2.10, 13), and emerges east of the city of David where its waters flow south into the Siloam pool (see 1 Kings 1.32–40; Isa 7.3; 2 Chr 32.4). The water flows into the Jordan Valley and eventually into the *Arabah* (the Jordan rift where the Dead Sea is located) to transform the waters of the Dead Sea into fresh water that supports fish and fruit trees (see Gen 2.1–14).

The reestablishment of the land and people of Israel
47.13–48.35: The reconstruction of the Temple and the resulting renewal of creation provide the basis for the reestablishment of the land and people of Israel.

---

13 Thus says the Lord GOD: These are the boundaries by which you shall divide the

---

a Gk Syr Vg: Meaning of Heb uncertain   *b* Heb *the four of them*   *c* Meaning of Heb uncertain   *d* Gk Syr Vg Tg: Heb *the two rivers go*   *e* Heb *it* land for inheritance among the twelve tribes of Israel. Joseph shall have two portions. [14]You shall divide it equally; I swore to give it to your ancestors, and this land shall fall to you as your inheritance.

15 This shall be the boundary of the land: On the north side, from the Great Sea by way of Hethlon to Lebo-hamath, and on to Zedad,[a] [16]Berothah, Sibraim (which lies between the border of Damascus and the border of Hamath), as far as Hazer-hatticon, which is on the border of Hauran. [17]So the boundary shall run from the sea to Hazarenon, which is north of the border of Damascus, with the border of Hamath to the north.[b] This shall be the north side.

18 On the east side, between Hauran and Damascus; along the Jordan between Gilead and the land of Israel; to the eastern sea and as far as Tamar.[c] This shall be the east side.

19 On the south side, it shall run from Tamar as far as the waters of Meribath-kadesh, from there along the Wadi of Egypt[d] to the Great Sea. This shall be the south side.

20 On the west side, the Great Sea shall be the boundary to a point opposite Lebo-hamath. This shall be the west side.

21 So you shall divide this land among you according to the tribes of Israel. [22]You shall allot it as an inheritance for yourselves and for the aliens who reside among you and have begotten children among you. They shall be to you as citizens of Israel; with you they shall be allotted an inheritance among the tribes of Israel. [23]In whatever tribe aliens reside, there you shall assign them their inheritance, says the Lord GOD.

47.13–23: The boundaries of the land are an idealized portrayal of the greatest extent of the Davidic kingdom and that of Jeroboam II (2 Sam 8.5–12; 2 Kings 14.25; compare Num 34). The northern border runs from the Mediterranean east to *Hazar-enon*, between Hamath (modern Hama) to the north and Damascus to the south (Num 34.7–9); the eastern border runs south through the Jordan Valley to *Tamar* just south of the Dead Sea (Num 34.10–12); the southern border runs through the Negeb to the *Wadi* of Egypt (modern *Wadi el-Arish* in the northeastern Sinai peninsula; see Num 34.3–5); the western border runs along the

Mediterranean coast (Num 34.6). *The aliens who reside among you* (Hebrew "gerim," or "sojourners," later considered converts in post-biblical Hebrew) live according to the same laws as Israelites (Lev 19.34; Num 15.29).

~~~~~~~~

48 These are the names of the tribes: Beginning at the northern border, on the Hethlon road,[e] from Lebo-hamath, as far as Hazar-enon (which is on the border of Damascus, with Hamath to the north), and[f] extending from the east side to the west,[g] Dan, one portion. [2]Adjoining the territory of Dan, from the east side to the west, Asher, one portion. [3]Adjoining the territory of Asher, from the east side to the west, Naphtali, one portion. [4]Adjoining the territory of Naphtali, from the east side to the west, Manasseh, one portion. [5]Adjoining the territory of Manasseh, from the east side to the west, Ephraim, one portion. [6]Adjoining the territory of Ephraim, from the east side to the west, Reuben, one portion. [7]Adjoining the territory of Reuben, from the east side to the west, Judah, one portion.

8 Adjoining the territory of Judah, from the east side to the west, shall be the portion that you shall set apart, twenty-five thousand cubits in width, and in length equal to one of the tribal portions, from the east side to the west, with the sanctuary in the middle of it. [9]The portion that you shall set apart for the LORD shall be twenty-five thousand cubits in length, and twenty[h] thousand in width. [10]These shall be the allotments of the holy portion: the priests shall have an allotment measuring twenty-five thousand cubits on the northern side, ten thousand cubits in width on the western side, ten thousand in width on the eastern side, and twenty-five thousand in length on the southern side, with the sanctuary of the LORD in the middle of it. [11]This shall be for the consecrated priests, the descendants[i] of Zadok, who kept my charge, who did not go astray when the

a Gk: Heb *Lebo-zedad*, [16]*Hamath*   b Meaning of Heb uncertain   c Compare Syr: Heb *you shall measure*
d Heb lacks *of Egypt*   e Compare 47.15: Heb *by the side of the way*   f Cn: Heb *and they shall be his*
g Gk Compare verses 2–8: Heb *the east side the west*
h Compare 45.1: Heb *ten*   i One Ms Gk: Heb *of the descendants*

people of Israel went astray, as the Levites did. ¹²It shall belong to them as a special portion from the holy portion of the land, a most holy place, adjoining the territory of the Levites. ¹³Alongside the territory of the priests, the Levites shall have an allotment twenty-five thousand cubits in length and ten thousand in width. The whole length shall be twenty-five thousand cubits and the width twenty*a* thousand. ¹⁴They shall not sell or exchange any of it; they shall not transfer this choice portion of the land, for it is holy to the LORD.

15 The remainder, five thousand cubits in width and twenty-five thousand in length, shall be for ordinary use for the city, for dwellings and for open country. In the middle of it shall be the city; ¹⁶and these shall be its dimensions: the north side four thousand five hundred cubits, the south side four thousand five hundred, the east side four thousand five hundred, and the west side four thousand five hundred. ¹⁷The city shall have open land: on the north two hundred fifty cubits, on the south two hundred fifty, on the east two hundred fifty, on the west two hundred fifty. ¹⁸The remainder of the length alongside the holy portion shall be ten thousand cubits to the east, and ten thousand to the west, and it shall be alongside the holy portion. Its produce shall be food for the workers of the city. ¹⁹The workers of the city, from all the tribes of Israel, shall cultivate it. ²⁰The whole portion that you shall set apart shall be twenty-five thousand cubits square, that is, the holy portion together with the property of the city.

21 What remains on both sides of the holy portion and of the property of the city shall belong to the prince. Extending from the twenty-five thousand cubits of the holy portion to the east border, and westward from the twenty-five thousand cubits to the west border, parallel to the tribal portions, it shall belong to the prince. The holy portion with the sanctuary of the temple in the middle of it, ²²and the property of the Levites and of the city, shall be in the middle of that which belongs to the prince. The portion of the prince shall lie between the territory of Judah and the territory of Benjamin.

48.1–35: The tribes are assigned equal portions of land arrayed along the length of the land from north to south. **1–7:** The northern tribes are listed from north to south as Dan, Asher, Naphtali, Manasseh, Ephraim, Reuben, Judah. **8–22:** The "holy district," or levitical allotment (45.1–9), is defined in detail. The priests are placed in the north, and the sanctuary is assigned to their portion; the Levites are placed to the south of the priests; and the portion reserved for Israel, which contains *the city* (Jerusalem), is placed to the south of the Levites. The portion allotted to the *prince* is on either side of the "holy district."

23 As for the rest of the tribes: from the east side to the west, Benjamin, one portion. ²⁴Adjoining the territory of Benjamin, from the east side to the west, Simeon, one portion. ²⁵Adjoining the territory of Simeon, from the east side to the west, Issachar, one portion. ²⁶Adjoining the territory of Issachar, from the east side to the west, Zebulun, one portion. ²⁷Adjoining the territory of Zebulun, from the east side to the west, Gad, one portion. ²⁸And adjoining the territory of Gad to the south, the boundary shall run from Tamar to the waters of Meribath-kadesh, from there along the Wadi of Egypt*b* to the Great Sea. ²⁹This is the land that you shall allot as an inheritance among the tribes of Israel, and these are their portions, says the Lord GOD.

30 These shall be the exits of the city: On the north side, which is to be four thousand five hundred cubits by measure, ³¹three gates, the gate of Reuben, the gate of Judah, and the gate of Levi, the gates of the city being named after the tribes of Israel. ³²On the east side, which is to be four thousand five hundred cubits, three gates, the gate of Joseph, the gate of Benjamin, and the gate of Dan. ³³On the south side, which is to be four thousand five hundred cubits by measure, three gates, the gate of Simeon, the gate of Issachar, and the gate of Zebulun. ³⁴On the west side, which is to be four thousand five hundred cubits, three gates,*c* the gate of Gad, the gate of Asher, and the gate of Naphtali. ³⁵The circumference of the city

a Gk: Heb *ten*　　*b* Heb lacks *of Egypt*　　*c* One Ms Gk Syr: MT *their gates three* shall be eighteen thousand cubits. And the name of the city from that time on shall be, The LORD is There.

48.23–35. 23–29: The southern tribes are listed from north to south as Benjamin, Simeon, Issachar, Zebulun, and Gad. 30–35: There are three gates allotted to the tribes on each side of the square city. The northern gates include Reuben, Judah, and Levi; the eastern gates include Joseph, Benjamin, and Dan; the southern gates include Simeon, Issachar, and Zebulun; and the western gates include Gad, Asher, and Naphtali. The name of the city is *The LORD is There* ("yhwh shammah") to signify the return of God's presence (see Isa 60.14; Jer 30.11).

DANIEL

Introduction

Daniel, the only example of an apocalyptic* book in the Hebrew Bible, appears among the Kethubim* ("Writings") of the Tanakh,* the Jewish version of the Bible, and among the Prophetic Books of the Christian First or Old Testament. Apocalyptic books are generally pseudonymous* or anonymous compositions, such as 1 Enoch,* 2 Baruch, or Revelation, in which a heavenly mediator reveals the future to a human being by means of an other-worldly journey or a review of world history. Apocalyptic literature is generally narrative* in form and employs various other-worldly images or motifs,* such as cosmic war, astronomical calculation, angels, mythological beings, and representations of God or other divine figures. Through a series of visions and dreams that provide a sweeping overview of world history from the Babylonian exile to the Hellenistic* period, Daniel is shown the impending downfall of the Seleucid* Syrian tyrant Antiochus IV Epiphanes* (175–163 BCE) and the emergence of God's kingdom, an independent Jewish state centered around the Jerusalem Temple.*

Although Daniel is initially portrayed as a Jewish exile in the court of the Babylonian King Nebuchadnezzar, the book clearly was not written during the sixth century BCE. Daniel is not a historical figure in Judah from this period, but his image is drawn from that of the legendary* sage and ruler of Canaanite mythology, Dan-El, who saves his son Aqhat from death in the fourteenth-century BCE Ugaritic tablets. Apocalyptic literature frequently employs well-known figures from the past, such as Enoch, Moses, or Ezra. Dan-El was known in Judah as early as the sixth century BCE (Ezek 14.14; 28.3). The literary history of the book is complicated and not well understood. It is written in two languages, Hebrew (1.1–2.4a; 8.1–12.13) and Aramaic* (2.4b–7.28), although these two portions do not correspond to its present literary structure. The tales in chs. 1–6 appear to have been composed in wisdom circles during the fourth or third centuries BCE to address the difficulties that Jews faced when living in the Diaspora.* As indicated by the precise historical knowledge conveyed in Daniel's final vision (chs. 10–12), the full form of the book was composed between 167 BCE, when Antiochus IV desecrated the Temple in Jerusalem, and 164 BCE, when Judah the Maccabee and his warriors rededicated the Temple, thereby inaugurating the festival of Hanukkah. The book supports the Maccabean revolt by positing a succession of four world empires, including Babylonia, Media, Persia, and Greece-Macedonia (see Nebuchadnezzar's dream, ch. 2; and the vision of the four beasts, ch. 7). The succession culminates in the emergence of the Seleucid Syrian empire and the rule of Antiochus IV, who is represented by the "little [horn]" with "human eyes . . . and a mouth speaking arrogantly" in 7.8 and "a contemptible person on whom royal majesty had not been conferred" in 11.21. Following his demise in battle, the anticipated Maccabean victory is symbolized by the deliverance of Daniel's people and the bringing of the dead to life (11.40–12.4). In later periods, Daniel has been read as an apocalyptic vision of the end of time. The Greek versions of Daniel in the Septuagint* and Theodotion contain additional chapters within the body of the work or added at the beginning or end of the book. These additional chapters, which appear separately in the Apocrypha* of Protestant Bibles, include the Prayer of Azariah and the Song of the Three Young Jews; Susanna; and Bel and the Dragon.

READING GUIDE

The book of Daniel is made up of two major sections. Chs. 1–6 presents six tales of Daniel and his companions in the Diaspora. Daniel appears as the epitome of a wise man, completely faithful to God and observant of Jewish tradition even in Babylonian exile. His wisdom and piety enable him to understand the will of God, to interpret it correctly to those around him, and to deliver himself and his companions from various threats. The tales employ these motifs to demonstrate that God will support those who adhere to Jewish identity and practice even when living outside of the land of Israel. They thereby establish both God's and Daniel's credibility as the basis for the visions that follow. The four visions of chs. 7–12 convey the major thrust of the book, insofar as the surveys of world history and the chronological calculations are designed to demonstrate the coming downfall of Antiochus IV and the emergence of the kingdom of God as a preordained divine act revealed to Daniel centuries before.

TALES CONCERNING DANIEL IN EXILE

Chs. 1–6: The tales establish Daniel's credibility as a righteous Jew whose God-given wisdom enables him to overcome the challenges of exile and to point to God's redemption of Jews from foreign domination.

1 In the third year of the reign of King Jehoiakim of Judah, King Nebuchadnezzar of Babylon came to Jerusalem and besieged it. ²The Lord let King Jehoiakim of Judah fall into his power, as well as some of the vessels of the house of God. These he brought to the land of Shinar,ᵃ and placed the vessels in the treasury of his gods.

1.1–21: Four young Jews in the Babylonian court. This tale establishes the theme of adherence to Jewish identity and practice by pointing to the success, wisdom, and good health of four young Jewish men who decline the delicacies and wine of the Babylonian king in order to observe Jewish dietary laws. **1–2:** *The third year of the reign of King Jehoiakim* was 606 BCE. Nebuchadnezzar assumed the throne of Babylon in 605 BCE, after he defeated Egypt and brought Judah under his rule. He besieged Jerusalem in 597 BCE during the reign of Jehoiachin (2 Kings 24.1–16) and again in 587 BCE during the regency of Zedekiah (2 Kings 25.1–7). *Shinar:* the location of Babylon (Gen 10.10; 11.2; Zech 5.11).

3 Then the king commanded his palace master Ashpenaz to bring some of the Israelites of the royal family and of the nobility,

⁴young men without physical defect and handsome, versed in every branch of wisdom, endowed with knowledge and insight, and competent to serve in the king's palace; they were to be taught the literature and language of the Chaldeans. ⁵The king assigned them a daily portion of the royal rations of food and wine. They were to be educated for three years, so that at the end of that time they could be stationed in the king's court. ⁶Among them were Daniel, Hananiah, Mishael, and Azariah, from the tribe of Judah. ⁷The palace master gave them other names: Daniel he called Belteshazzar, Hananiah he called Shadrach, Mishael he called Meshach, and Azariah he called Abednego.

1.3–7: The Babylonians trained persons from subject nations to serve in their courts. *Palace master:* Literally, "chief eunuch." *Chaldeans:* Aramaic-speaking Neo-Babylonians, used in Daniel for wise men. Daniel and his companions were given Babylonian names.

8 But Daniel resolved that he would not defile himself with the royal rations of food and wine; so he asked the palace master to allow him not to defile himself. ⁹Now God allowed Daniel to receive favor and compassion from the palace master. ¹⁰The palace master said to Daniel, "I am afraid of my lord the king; he has appointed your food and your drink. If he should see you in poorer condition than the other young men of your

ᵃ Gk Theodotion: Heb adds *to the house of his own gods*

own age, you would endanger my head with the king." 11Then Daniel asked the guard whom the palace master had appointed over Daniel, Hananiah, Mishael, and Azariah: 12"Please test your servants for ten days. Let us be given vegetables to eat and water to drink. 13You can then compare our appearance with the appearance of the young men who eat the royal rations, and deal with your servants according to what you observe." 14So he agreed to this proposal and tested them for ten days. 15At the end of ten days it was observed that they appeared better and fatter than all the young men who had been eating the royal rations. 16So the guard continued to withdraw their royal rations and the wine they were to drink, and gave them vegetables. 17To these four young men God gave knowledge and skill in every aspect of literature and wisdom; Daniel also had insight into all visions and dreams.

18 At the end of the time that the king had set for them to be brought in, the palace master brought them into the presence of Nebuchadnezzar, 19and the king spoke with them. And among them all, no one was found to compare with Daniel, Hananiah, Mishael, and Azariah; therefore they were stationed in the king's court. 20In every matter of wisdom and understanding concerning which the king inquired of them, he found them ten times better than all the magicians and enchanters in his whole kingdom. 21And Daniel continued there until the first year of King Cyrus.

1.8–21. 8–17: The *royal rations of food and wine* are not kosher* and therefore are unsuitable for Jews (Lev 11; Deut 14). Dream interpretation* is a mark of wisdom (Gen 40–41).**18–21:** God grants *wisdom and understanding* to those who adhere to divine requirements. *The first year of King Cyrus* was 539 BCE.

2 In the second year of Nebuchadnezzar's reign, Nebuchadnezzar dreamed such dreams that his spirit was troubled and his sleep left him. 2So the king commanded that the magicians, the enchanters, the sorcerers, and the Chaldeans be summoned to tell the king his dreams. When they came in and stood before the king, 3he said to them, "I have had such a dream that my spirit is troubled by the desire to understand it." 4The Chaldeans said to the king (in Aramaic),[a] "O king, live forever! Tell your servants the dream, and we will reveal the interpretation." 5The king answered the Chaldeans, "This is a public decree: if you do not tell me both the dream and its interpretation, you shall be torn limb from limb, and your houses shall be laid in ruins. 6But if you do tell me the dream and its interpretation, you shall receive from me gifts and rewards and great honor. Therefore tell me the dream and its interpretation." 7They answered a second time, "Let the king first tell his servants the dream, then we can give its interpretation." 8The king answered, "I know with certainty that you are trying to gain time, because you see I have firmly decreed: 9if you do not tell me the dream, there is but one verdict for you. You have agreed to speak lying and misleading words to me until things take a turn. Therefore, tell me the dream, and I shall know that you can give me its interpretation." 10The Chaldeans answered the king, "There is no one on earth who can reveal what the king demands! In fact no king, however great and powerful, has ever asked such a thing of any magician or enchanter or Chaldean. 11The thing that the king is asking is too difficult, and no one can reveal it to the king except the gods, whose dwelling is not with mortals."

12 Because of this the king flew into a violent rage and commanded that all the wise men of Babylon be destroyed. 13The decree was issued, and the wise men were about to be executed; and they looked for Daniel and his companions, to execute them. 14Then Daniel responded with prudence and discretion to Arioch, the king's chief executioner, who had gone out to execute the wise men of Babylon; 15he asked Arioch, the royal official, "Why is the decree of the king so urgent?" Arioch then explained the matter to Daniel. 16So Daniel went in and requested that the king give him

---

a The text from this point to the end of chapter 7 is in Aramaic time and he would tell the king the interpretation.

2.1–49: Nebuchadnezzar's dream. This tale demonstrates God's superiority and Daniel's incomparable wisdom. **1–16:** Nebuchadnezzar's impossible demand prepares the reader for Daniel's role as a supremely competent interpreter in chs. 7–12. Dream and omen interpretation were widely practiced in Babylonia. **1:** *The second year of Nebuchadnezzar's reign* was 603 BCE. Daniel appears before his training is complete (1.1, 5). **4:** From 2.4b through 7.28 the text is written in Aramaic.* While Hebrew is a west Semitic language, Aramaic is an east Semitic language, originating in northern Aram (Syria), that was employed extensively throughout the Near East from the seventh or eighth century BCE until the emergence of Islam in the seventh century CE.

17 Then Daniel went to his home and informed his companions, Hananiah, Mishael, and Azariah, 18and told them to seek mercy from the God of heaven concerning this mystery, so that Daniel and his companions with the rest of the wise men of Babylon might not perish. 19Then the mystery was revealed to Daniel in a vision of the night, and Daniel blessed the God of heaven.

20 Daniel said:

"Blessed be the name of God from age
　　　to age,
　　for wisdom and power are his.
21 He changes times and seasons,
　　deposes kings and sets up kings;
　　he gives wisdom to the wise
　　and knowledge to those who have
　　　understanding.
22 He reveals deep and hidden things;
　　he knows what is in the darkness,
　　and light dwells with him.
23 To you, O God of my ancestors,
　　I give thanks and praise,
　　for you have given me wisdom
　　　and power,
　　and have now revealed to me what we
　　　asked of you,
　　for you have revealed to us what the
　　　king ordered."

2.17–23: *A vision of the night:* Compare 1 Sam 3; 2 Sam 7.4. **18:** *The God of heaven:* A Persian title for the Jewish deity (Ezra 1.2; 5.11; Neh 1.4; 2.4). **20–23:** A song of praise thanking God for the dream (compare Neh 9.5; Hab 3.4).

24 Therefore Daniel went to Arioch, whom the king had appointed to destroy the wise men of Babylon, and said to him, "Do not destroy the wise men of Babylon; bring me in before the king, and I will give the king the interpretation." 25 Then Arioch quickly brought Daniel before the king and said to him: "I have found among the exiles from Judah a man who can tell the king the interpretation." 26The king said to Daniel, whose name was Belteshazzar, "Are you able to tell me the dream that I have seen and its interpretation?" 27Daniel answered the king, "No wise men, enchanters, magicians, or diviners can show to the king the mystery that the king is asking, 28but there is a God in heaven who reveals mysteries, and he has disclosed to King Nebuchadnezzar what will happen at the end of days. Your dream and the visions of your head as you lay in bed were these: 29To you, O king, as you lay in bed, came thoughts of what would be hereafter, and the revealer of mysteries disclosed to you what is to be. 30But as for me, this mystery has not been revealed to me because of any wisdom that I have more than any other living being, but in order that the interpretation may be known to the king and that you may understand the thoughts of your mind.

31 "You were looking, O king, and lo! there was a great statue. This statue was huge, its brilliance extraordinary; it was standing before you, and its appearance was frightening. 32The head of that statue was of fine gold, its chest and arms of silver, its middle and thighs of bronze, 33its legs of iron, its feet partly of iron and partly of clay. 34As you looked on, a stone was cut out, not by human hands, and it struck the statue on its feet of iron and clay and broke them in pieces. 35Then the iron, the clay, the bronze, the silver, and the gold, were all broken in pieces and became like the chaff of the summer threshing floors; and the wind carried them away, so that not a trace of them could be found. But the stone that struck the

statue became a great mountain and filled the whole earth.

2.24–35. 31–33: Colossi, giant statues of gods or rulers, were erected throughout the Hellenistic* world to demonstrate Greek power. The five parts of the statue symbolize the succession of empires that would rule Judea prior to the kingdom of God: Babylon, Media, Persia, Greece, and the Hellenistic Ptolemaic* and Seleucid* dynasties.* The decreasing value of the materials symbolizes historical decline. The mixture of iron and clay in the feet represents the mixed Greek and indigenous ancestry of the Ptolemaic and Seleucid dynasties, as well as the weakness of their rule. 34: *A stone was cut out, not by human hands:* An act of God.

36 "This was the dream; now we will tell the king its interpretation. 37You, O king, the king of kings—to whom the God of heaven has given the kingdom, the power, the might, and the glory, 38into whose hand he has given human beings, wherever they live, the wild animals of the field, and the birds of the air, and whom he has established as ruler over them all—you are the head of gold. 39After you shall arise another kingdom inferior to yours, and yet a third kingdom of bronze, which shall rule over the whole earth. 40And there shall be a fourth kingdom, strong as iron; just as iron crushes and smashes everything,[a] it shall crush and shatter all these. 41As you saw the feet and toes partly of potter's clay and partly of iron, it shall be a divided kingdom; but some of the strength of iron shall be in it, as you saw the iron mixed with the clay. 42As the toes of the feet were part iron and part clay, so the kingdom shall be partly strong and partly brittle. 43As you saw the iron mixed with clay, so will they mix with one another in marriage,[b] but they will not hold together, just as iron does not mix with clay. 44And in the days of those kings the God of heaven will set up a kingdom that shall never be destroyed, nor shall this kingdom be left to another people. It shall crush all these kingdoms and bring them to an end, and it shall stand forever; 45just as you saw that a stone was cut from the mountain not by hands, and that it crushed the iron, the bronze, the clay, the silver, and the gold. The great God has informed the king what shall be hereafter. The dream is certain, and its interpretation trustworthy."

46 Then King Nebuchadnezzar fell on his face, worshiped Daniel, and commanded that a grain offering and incense be offered to him. 47The king said to Daniel, "Truly, your God is God of gods and Lord of kings and a revealer of mysteries, for you have been able to reveal this mystery!" 48Then the king promoted Daniel, gave him many great gifts, and made him ruler over the whole province of Babylon and chief prefect over all the wise men of Babylon. 49Daniel made a request of the king, and he appointed Shadrach, Meshach, and Abednego over the affairs of the province of Babylon. But Daniel remained at the king's court.

2.36–49. 44: *The God of heaven will set up a kingdom:* An independent Jewish state under God, understood by later interpreters as an eschatological* kingdom of God. 46–49: The pagan king acknowledges God (see Ex 15.14–16; Isa 45.14–17).

3 King Nebuchadnezzar made a golden statue whose height was sixty cubits and whose width was six cubits; he set it up on the plain of Dura in the province of Babylon. 2Then King Nebuchadnezzar sent for the satraps, the prefects, and the governors, the counselors, the treasurers, the justices, the magistrates, and all the officials of the provinces, to assemble and come to the dedication of the statue that King Nebuchadnezzar had set up. 3So the satraps, the prefects, and the governors, the counselors, the treasurers, the justices, the magistrates, and all the officials of the provinces, assembled for the dedication of the statue that King Nebuchadnezzar had set up. When they were standing before the statue that Nebuchadnezzar had set up, 4the herald proclaimed aloud, "You are commanded, O peoples, nations, and languages, 5that when you hear the sound of the horn, pipe, lyre, trigon,

a Gk Theodotion Syr Vg: Aram adds *and like iron that crushes*   b Aram *by human seed* harp, drum, and entire musical ensemble, you are to fall down and worship the golden statue that King Nebuchadnezzar has set up. 6Whoever does not fall down and worship shall immediately be thrown into a furnace of blazing fire." 7Therefore, as soon as all the peoples heard the sound of the horn, pipe, lyre, trigon, harp, drum, and entire musical ensemble, all the peoples, nations, and languages fell down and worshiped the golden statue that King Nebuchadnezzar had set up.

8 Accordingly, at this time certain Chaldeans came forward and denounced the Jews. 9They said to King Nebuchadnezzar, "O king, live forever! 10You, O king, have made a decree, that everyone who hears the sound of the horn, pipe, lyre, trigon, harp, drum, and entire musical ensemble, shall fall down and worship the golden statue, 11and whoever does not fall down and worship shall be thrown into a furnace of blazing fire. 12There are certain Jews whom you have appointed over the affairs of the province of Babylon: Shadrach, Meshach, and Abednego. These pay no heed to you, O king. They do not serve your gods and they do not worship the golden statue that you have set up."

13 Then Nebuchadnezzar in furious rage commanded that Shadrach, Meshach, and Abednego be brought in; so they brought those men before the king. 14Nebuchadnezzar said to them, "Is it true, O Shadrach, Meshach, and Abednego, that you do not serve my gods and you do not worship the golden statue that I have set up? 15Now if you are ready when you hear the sound of the horn, pipe, lyre, trigon, harp, drum, and entire musical ensemble to fall down and worship the statue that I have made, well and good.*a* But if you do not worship, you shall immediately be thrown into a furnace of blazing fire, and who is the god that will deliver you out of my hands?"

16 Shadrach, Meshach, and Abednego answered the king, "O Nebuchadnezzar, we have no need to present a defense to you in this matter. 17If our God whom we serve is able to deliver us from the furnace of blazing fire and out of your hand, O king, let him deliver us.*b* 18But if not, be it known to you, O king, that we will not serve your gods and we will not worship the golden statue that you have set up."

3.1–30: The fiery furnace: The narrative* promotes adherence to Jewish identity and religion by demonstrating that God protects the righteous. **1–18:** Antiochus IV (175–163 BCE) erected a statue of Zeus in the Jerusalem Temple* and demanded that Jews worship Greek gods or be put to death (1 Macc 1.41–64; 2 Macc 6.1–11). His nickname, Epiphanes,* "manifest god," indicates that he expected worship as a god. Worship of national gods was generally understood as a sign of loyalty, but Jews are monotheistic and do not worship pagan gods. Charges of disloyalty prompted many anti-Jewish actions in the Greco-Roman and medieval periods and continue to underlie modern anti-Semitism.

19 Then Nebuchadnezzar was so filled with rage against Shadrach, Meshach, and Abednego that his face was distorted. He ordered the furnace heated up seven times more than was customary, 20and ordered some of the strongest guards in his army to bind Shadrach, Meshach, and Abednego and to throw them into the furnace of blazing fire. 21So the men were bound, still wearing their tunics,*c* their trousers,*c* their hats, and their other garments, and they were thrown into the furnace of blazing fire. 22Because the king's command was urgent and the furnace was so overheated, the raging flames killed the men who lifted Shadrach, Meshach, and Abednego. 23But the three men, Shadrach, Meshach, and Abednego, fell down, bound, into the furnace of blazing fire.

24 Then King Nebuchadnezzar was astonished and rose up quickly. He said to his counselors, "Was it not three men that we threw bound into the fire?" They answered the king, "True, O king." 25He replied, "But I see four men unbound, walking in the middle of the fire, and they are not hurt; and the fourth has the appearance of a

a Aram lacks *well and good*   *b* Or *If our God whom we serve is able to deliver us, he will deliver us from the furnace of blazing fire and out of your hand, O king.*
c Meaning of Aram word uncertain

god."[a] 26Nebuchadnezzar then approached the door of the furnace of blazing fire and said, "Shadrach, Meshach, and Abednego, servants of the Most High God, come out! Come here!" So Shadrach, Meshach, and Abednego came out from the fire. 27And the satraps, the prefects, the governors, and the king's counselors gathered together and saw that the fire had not had any power over the bodies of those men; the hair of their heads was not singed, their tunics[b] were not harmed, and not even the smell of fire came from them. 28Nebuchadnezzar said, "Blessed be the God of Shadrach, Meshach, and Abednego, who has sent his angel and delivered his servants who trusted in him. They disobeyed the king's command and yielded up their bodies rather than serve and worship any god except their own God. 29Therefore I make a decree: Any people, nation, or language that utters blasphemy against the God of Shadrach, Meshach, and Abednego shall be torn limb from limb, and their houses laid in ruins; for there is no other god who is able to deliver in this way." 30Then the king promoted Shadrach, Meshach, and Abednego in the province of Babylon.

3.19–30: The description of the fiery furnace is full of exaggeration, preparing the reader for the great miracle. **25:** The presence of a fourth man who *has the appearance of a god* (literally, *a son of the gods*) signifies divine intervention to save the young men (see v. 28). The pagan king acknowledges God's power and decrees destruction for nations that challenge God.

4[c] King Nebuchadnezzar to all peoples, nations, and languages that live throughout the earth: May you have abundant prosperity! 2The signs and wonders that the Most High God has worked for me I am pleased to recount.
3 How great are his signs,
    how mighty his wonders!
His kingdom is an everlasting kingdom,
    and his sovereignty is from generation
        to generation.

4.1–37: Nebuchadnezzar's madness. Using the form of an epistle or public proclamation, this chapter dem-

onstrates God's power over pagan rulers. **1–2:** A typical epistolary introduction. *All peoples, nations, and languages that live throughout the earth:* Mesopotamian rulers generally claimed rule over the entire world. The motif* prepares the reader to recognize God's universal sovereignty. **3:** Again, Nebuchadnezzar acknowledges God.

4[d] I, Nebuchadnezzar, was living at ease in my home and prospering in my palace. 5I saw a dream that frightened me; my fantasies in bed and the visions of my head terrified me. 6So I made a decree that all the wise men of Babylon should be brought before me, in order that they might tell me the interpretation of the dream. 7Then the magicians, the enchanters, the Chaldeans, and the diviners came in, and I told them the dream, but they could not tell me its interpretation. 8At last Daniel came in before me—he who was named Belteshazzar after the name of my god, and who is endowed with a spirit of the holy gods[e]—and I told him the dream: 9"O Belteshazzar, chief of the magicians, I know that you are endowed with a spirit of the holy gods[e] and that no mystery is too difficult for you. Hear[f] the dream that I saw; tell me its interpretation.
10[g]Upon my bed this is what I saw;
    there was a tree at the center of the
        earth,
    and its height was great.
11 The tree grew great and strong,
    its top reached to heaven,
    and it was visible to the ends of the
        whole earth.
12 Its foliage was beautiful,
    its fruit abundant,
    and it provided food for all.
The animals of the field found shade
        under it,
    the birds of the air nested in
        its branches,
    and from it all living beings
        were fed.

a Aram *a son of the gods*   b Meaning of Aram word uncertain   c Ch 3.31 in Aram   d Ch 4.1 in Aram   e Or *a holy, divine spirit*   f Theodotion: Aram *The visions of*   g Theodotion Syr Compare Gk: Aram adds *The visions of my head*

13 "I continued looking, in the visions of my head as I lay in bed, and there was a holy watcher, coming down from heaven. 14He cried aloud and said:

'Cut down the tree and chop off
     its branches,
   strip off its foliage and scatter its fruit.
Let the animals flee from beneath it
   and the birds from its branches.
15 But leave its stump and roots in the
     ground,
   with a band of iron and bronze,
   in the tender grass of the field.
Let him be bathed with the dew
     of heaven,
   and let his lot be with the animals of
     the field
   in the grass of the earth.
16 Let his mind be changed from that of a
     human,
   and let the mind of an animal be
     given to him.
   And let seven times pass over him.
17 The sentence is rendered by decree of
     the watchers,
   the decision is given by order of the
     holy ones,
in order that all who live may know
   that the Most High is sovereign over
     the kingdom of mortals;
he gives it to whom he will
   and sets over it the lowliest of human
     beings.'

18 "This is the dream that I, King Nebuchadnezzar, saw. Now you, Belteshazzar, declare the interpretation, since all the wise men of my kingdom are unable to tell me the interpretation. You are able, however, for you are endowed with a spirit of the holy gods."[a]

***

4.4–18: There are no extra-biblical accounts of Nebuchadnezzar's madness. The Babylonian king Nabonidus (556–539 BCE) lived in the Arabian desert while his son Belshazzar ruled in his stead. **8:** *Named Belteshazzar after the name of my god:* Belteshazzar means "protect his life" and is styled to resemble the name Bel, a title for the Babylonian city god, Marduk. **10–17:** The *tree at the center of the earth:* Ancient Near Eastern mythology frequently employs the image of a

cosmic tree (see Gen 2–3). See also Isa 10.5–34; Ezek 31, which portray Assyrian and Egyptian rulers as trees that will be cut down and sent to the netherworld. **13:** *Holy watcher:* A celestial being (1 Enoch* 1.5; 20.1; Jubilees 4.15). **15:** *Stump and roots in the ground:* See Isa 6.13; 11.1. **16:** *Let his mind be changed:* The motif is derived from Nabonidus, but also presupposes Babylonian traditions of Enkidu, the primal man of the Gilgamesh* epic, who lived among the animals before he was civilized by a woman.

***

19 Then Daniel, who was called Belteshazzar, was severely distressed for a while. His thoughts terrified him. The king said, "Belteshazzar, do not let the dream or the interpretation terrify you." Belteshazzar answered, "My lord, may the dream be for those who hate you, and its interpretation for your enemies! 20The tree that you saw, which grew great and strong, so that its top reached to heaven and was visible to the end of the whole earth, 21whose foliage was beautiful and its fruit abundant, and which provided food for all, under which animals of the field lived, and in whose branches the birds of the air had nests— 22it is you, O king! You have grown great and strong. Your greatness has increased and reaches to heaven, and your sovereignty to the ends of the earth. 23And whereas the king saw a holy watcher coming down from heaven and saying, 'Cut down the tree and destroy it, but leave its stump and roots in the ground, with a band of iron and bronze, in the grass of the field; and let him be bathed with the dew of heaven, and let his lot be with the animals of the field, until seven times pass over him'— 24this is the interpretation, O king, and it is a decree of the Most High that has come upon my lord the king: 25You shall be driven away from human society, and your dwelling shall be with the wild animals. You shall be made to eat grass like oxen, you shall be bathed with the dew of heaven, and seven times shall pass over you, until you have learned that the Most High has sovereignty over the kingdom of mortals, and gives it to whom he will. 26As it was commanded to leave the stump and roots of the tree, your

***

a Or *a holy, divine spirit*

kingdom shall be re-established for you from the time that you learn that Heaven is sovereign. 27Therefore, O king, may my counsel be acceptable to you: atone for*a* your sins with righteousness, and your iniquities with mercy to the oppressed, so that your prosperity may be prolonged."

4.19–27: Nebuchadnezzar's greatness, symbolized by his monumental building programs, was well-known throughout the ancient world.

~~~~~~~~~~~~~~~~~~~~~~~~~~~~~~~~~~~

28 All this came upon King Nebuchadnezzar. 29At the end of twelve months he was walking on the roof of the royal palace of Babylon, 30and the king said, "Is this not magnificent Babylon, which I have built as a royal capital by my mighty power and for my glorious majesty?" 31While the words were still in the king's mouth, a voice came from heaven: "O King Nebuchadnezzar, to you it is declared: The kingdom has departed from you! 32You shall be driven away from human society, and your dwelling shall be with the animals of the field. You shall be made to eat grass like oxen, and seven times shall pass over you, until you have learned that the Most High has sovereignty over the kingdom of mortals and gives it to whom he will." 33Immediately the sentence was fulfilled against Nebuchadnezzar. He was driven away from human society, ate grass like oxen, and his body was bathed with the dew of heaven, until his hair grew as long as eagles' feathers and his nails became like birds' claws.

34 When that period was over, I, Nebuchadnezzar, lifted my eyes to heaven, and my reason returned to me.

I blessed the Most High,
    and praised and honored the one who
        lives forever.
For his sovereignty is an everlasting
        sovereignty,
    and his kingdom endures from
        generation to generation.
35 All the inhabitants of the earth are
        accounted as nothing,
    and he does what he wills with the
        host of heaven
    and the inhabitants of the earth.

There is no one who can stay his hand
    or say to him, "What are you doing?"
36At that time my reason returned to me; and my majesty and splendor were restored to me for the glory of my kingdom. My counselors and my lords sought me out, I was re-established over my kingdom, and still more greatness was added to me. 37Now I, Nebuchadnezzar, praise and extol and honor the King of heaven,
    for all his works are truth,
        and his ways are justice;
    and he is able to bring low
        those who walk in pride.

4.28–37. 28–33: The prediction of the dream is fulfilled. 34–37: Nebuchadnezzar is restored when he acknowledges God's universal sovereignty.

~~~~~~~~~~~~~~~~~~~~~~~~~~~~~~~~~~~

5 King Belshazzar made a great festival for a thousand of his lords, and he was drinking wine in the presence of the thousand.

2 Under the influence of the wine, Belshazzar commanded that they bring in the vessels of gold and silver that his father Nebuchadnezzar had taken out of the temple in Jerusalem, so that the king and his lords, his wives, and his concubines might drink from them. 3So they brought in the vessels of gold and silver*b* that had been taken out of the temple, the house of God in Jerusalem, and the king and his lords, his wives, and his concubines drank from them. 4They drank the wine and praised the gods of gold and silver, bronze, iron, wood, and stone.

5 Immediately the fingers of a human hand appeared and began writing on the plaster of the wall of the royal palace, next to the lampstand. The king was watching the hand as it wrote. 6Then the king's face turned pale, and his thoughts terrified him. His limbs gave way, and his knees knocked together. 7The king cried aloud to bring in the enchanters, the Chaldeans, and the diviners; and the king said to the wise men of Babylon, "Whoever can read this writing and tell me its interpretation shall be clothed in

---

a Aram *break off*   *b* Theodotion Vg: Aram lacks *and silver* purple, have a chain of gold around his neck, and rank third in the kingdom." 8Then all the king's wise men came in, but they could not read the writing or tell the king the interpretation. 9Then King Belshazzar became greatly terrified and his face turned pale, and his lords were perplexed.

10 The queen, when she heard the discussion of the king and his lords, came into the banqueting hall. The queen said, "O king, live forever! Do not let your thoughts terrify you or your face grow pale. 11There is a man in your kingdom who is endowed with a spirit of the holy gods.[a] In the days of your father he was found to have enlightenment, understanding, and wisdom like the wisdom of the gods. Your father, King Nebuchadnezzar, made him chief of the magicians, enchanters, Chaldeans, and diviners,[b] 12because an excellent spirit, knowledge, and understanding to interpret dreams, explain riddles, and solve problems were found in this Daniel, whom the king named Belteshazzar. Now let Daniel be called, and he will give the interpretation."

5.1–31: Belshazzar's feast. This narrative* demonstrates the punishment of arrogant and sacrilegious rulers. **1:** Belshazzar was not king of Babylon, but served as regent in place of his father Nabonidus. **2–4:** Nebuchadnezzar was not Belshazzar's father (see comment on v. 1). Nebuchadnezzar's son Amel-Marduk (Evil-merodach, 2 Kings 25.27–30; Jer 52.31–34) ruled in 562–560 BCE and was assassinated by his brother-in-law. The use of holy Temple* vessels (see 2 Kings 24.13; 2 Chr 36.10) for drinking praise to the gods constitutes sacrilege like that of Antiochus IV (1 Macc 1.41–50; 2 Macc 5.15–6.11). **5–12:** *The fingers of a human hand:* A supernatural response to Belshazzar's sacrilege. Both the servants and the king demonstrate their incompetence until *the queen* reminds them of Daniel.

---

13 Then Daniel was brought in before the king. The king said to Daniel, "So you are Daniel, one of the exiles of Judah, whom my father the king brought from Judah? 14I have heard of you that a spirit of the gods[c] is in you, and that enlightenment, understanding, and excellent wisdom are found in you. 15Now the wise men, the enchanters, have

been brought in before me to read this writing and tell me its interpretation, but they were not able to give the interpretation of the matter. 16But I have heard that you can give interpretations and solve problems. Now if you are able to read the writing and tell me its interpretation, you shall be clothed in purple, have a chain of gold around your neck, and rank third in the kingdom."

17 Then Daniel answered in the presence of the king, "Let your gifts be for yourself, or give your rewards to someone else! Nevertheless I will read the writing to the king and let him know the interpretation. 18O king, the Most High God gave your father Nebuchadnezzar kingship, greatness, glory, and majesty. 19And because of the greatness that he gave him, all peoples, nations, and languages trembled and feared before him. He killed those he wanted to kill, kept alive those he wanted to keep alive, honored those he wanted to honor, and degraded those he wanted to degrade. 20But when his heart was lifted up and his spirit was hardened so that he acted proudly, he was deposed from his kingly throne, and his glory was stripped from him. 21He was driven from human society, and his mind was made like that of an animal. His dwelling was with the wild asses, he was fed grass like oxen, and his body was bathed with the dew of heaven, until he learned that the Most High God has sovereignty over the kingdom of mortals, and sets over it whomever he will. 22And you, Belshazzar his son, have not humbled your heart, even though you knew all this! 23You have exalted yourself against the Lord of heaven! The vessels of his temple have been brought in before you, and you and your lords, your wives and your concubines have been drinking wine from them. You have praised the gods of silver and gold, of bronze, iron, wood, and stone, which do not see or hear or know; but the God in whose power is your very breath, and to whom belong all your ways, you have not honored.

24 "So from his presence the hand was sent and this writing was inscribed. 25And

a Or *a holy, divine spirit*   *b* Aram adds *the king your father*   *c* Or *a divine spirit* this is the writing that was inscribed: MENE, MENE, TEKEL, and PARSIN. 26This is the interpretation of the matter: MENE, God has numbered the days of[a] your kingdom and brought it to an end; 27TEKEL, you have been weighed on the scales and found wanting; 28PERES,[b] your kingdom is divided and given to the Medes and Persians."

29 Then Belshazzar gave the command, and Daniel was clothed in purple, a chain of gold was put around his neck, and a proclamation was made concerning him that he should rank third in the kingdom.

30 That very night Belshazzar, the Chaldean king, was killed. 31[c]And Darius the Mede received the kingdom, being about sixty-two years old.

5.13–31. 13–29: Daniel chides Belshazzar for his arrogance, unlike "his father" Nebuchadnezzar, prior to interpreting the writing. The words are Aramaic* nouns for units of weight: "mené," a mina; "tequel," a shekel;* "parsin," a half mina. Daniel reads them as verbs: "menah," to number; "teqal," to weigh; and "peras," to divide. The root "prs" also serves as the base for the name Persia. **30:** Nabonidus fled Babylon at the approach of the Persian army. There is no evidence that Belshazzar was killed. **31:** *Darius the Mede* is not historical. Babylon submitted to Cyrus of Persia in 539. A Persian military commander and relative of the royal family, Darius, took the throne when Cyrus's son Cambyses was assassinated in 522 BCE. The Medes were part of the Persian empire, and various prophecies asserted that Babylon would fall to them (Isa 13.17–22; 21.1–10; Jer 51.11, 28).

6 It pleased Darius to set over the kingdom one hundred twenty satraps, stationed throughout the whole kingdom, 2and over them three presidents, including Daniel; to these the satraps gave account, so that the king might suffer no loss. 3Soon Daniel distinguished himself above all the other presidents and satraps because an excellent spirit was in him, and the king planned to appoint him over the whole kingdom. 4So the presidents and the satraps tried to find grounds for complaint against Daniel in connection with the kingdom. But they could find no grounds for complaint or any corruption, because he was faithful, and no negligence or

corruption could be found in him. 5The men said, "We shall not find any ground for complaint against this Daniel unless we find it in connection with the law of his God."

6 So the presidents and satraps conspired and came to the king and said to him, "O King Darius, live forever! 7All the presidents of the kingdom, the prefects and the satraps, the counselors and the governors are agreed that the king should establish an ordinance and enforce an interdict, that whoever prays to anyone, divine or human, for thirty days, except to you, O king, shall be thrown into a den of lions. 8Now, O king, establish the interdict and sign the document, so that it cannot be changed, according to the law of the Medes and the Persians, which cannot be revoked." 9Therefore King Darius signed the document and interdict.

10 Although Daniel knew that the document had been signed, he continued to go to his house, which had windows in its upper room open toward Jerusalem, and to get down on his knees three times a day to pray to his God and praise him, just as he had done previously. 11The conspirators came and found Daniel praying and seeking mercy before his God. 12Then they approached the king and said concerning the interdict, "O king! Did you not sign an interdict, that anyone who prays to anyone, divine or human, within thirty days except to you, O king, shall be thrown into a den of lions?" The king answered, "The thing stands fast, according to the law of the Medes and Persians, which cannot be revoked." 13Then they responded to the king, "Daniel, one of the exiles from Judah, pays no attention to you, O king, or to the interdict you have signed, but he is saying his prayers three times a day."

14 When the king heard the charge, he was very much distressed. He was determined to save Daniel, and until the sun went down he made every effort to rescue him. 15Then the conspirators came to the king and said to him, "Know, O king, that it is a

---

a Aram lacks *the days of*   b The singular of *Parsin*
c Ch 6.1 in Aram

law of the Medes and Persians that no interdict or ordinance that the king establishes
can be changed."

16 Then the king gave the command, and
Daniel was brought and thrown into the
den of lions. The king said to Daniel, "May
your God, whom you faithfully serve, deliver
you!" 17A stone was brought and laid on the
mouth of the den, and the king sealed it
with his own signet and with the signet of
his lords, so that nothing might be changed
concerning Daniel. 18Then the king went to
his palace and spent the night fasting; no
food was brought to him, and sleep fled from
him.

19 Then, at break of day, the king got up
and hurried to the den of lions. 20When he
came near the den where Daniel was, he
cried out anxiously to Daniel, "O Daniel, servant of the living God, has your God whom
you faithfully serve been able to deliver you
from the lions?" 21Daniel then said to the
king, "O king, live forever! 22My God sent
his angel and shut the lions' mouths so that
they would not hurt me, because I was found
blameless before him; and also before you,
O king, I have done no wrong." 23Then the
king was exceedingly glad and commanded
that Daniel be taken up out of the den. So
Daniel was taken up out of the den, and no
kind of harm was found on him, because he
had trusted in his God. 24The king gave a
command, and those who had accused Daniel were brought and thrown into the den of
lions—they, their children, and their wives.
Before they reached the bottom of the den
the lions overpowered them and broke all
their bones in pieces.

25 Then King Darius wrote to all peoples
and nations of every language throughout
the whole world: "May you have abundant
prosperity! 26I make a decree, that in all my
royal dominion people should tremble and
fear before the God of Daniel:

For he is the living God,
    enduring forever.
His kingdom shall never be destroyed,
    and his dominion has no end.
27 He delivers and rescues,
    he works signs and wonders in heaven
        and on earth;

for he has saved Daniel
    from the power of the lions."
28So this Daniel prospered during the reign
of Darius and the reign of Cyrus the Persian.

6.1–28: Daniel in the lions' den. This narrative demonstrates God's protection of righteous Jews from foreign monarchs who demand worship of pagan gods
and themselves. **1–9:** Darius I (522–486 BCE) organized
the Persian empire into twenty "satrapies," administered by officials called *satraps.* See Esth 1.1; 8.9. Daniel's success as *president,* an otherwise unknown position, prompts a plot to bring him down by playing
upon his religious piety. Darius is persuaded to demand worship of himself as a god, much like Antiochus
IV Epiphanes, "manifest god." *So that it cannot be
revoked:* Once signed with the royal signet, Persian
laws could not be revoked, even by the king. **10–18:**
Judaism requires three set times for prayer: morning,
afternoon, and evening (see Ps 55.17; Jdt 9.1). The
narrative portrays Darius as a victim of the plot since
he intended no harm to Daniel. Cyrus authorized the
building of the Second Temple* (2 Chr 36.22–23; Ezra
1.1–4), which was completed during the reign of Darius (Ezra 6). Darius calls upon God to save Daniel, and
attempts to do so himself. **22:** God sends an *angel* to
protect the righteous Daniel from the lions (compare
3.19–30). **24:** The families of criminals are punished as
well to deter crime (Num 16.23–33; Josh 7.24; 2 Sam
21.6, 9; Esth 9–13). **25–27:** Darius's announcement of
the kingdom of God serves the fundamental purpose
of the book: to point to the establishment of an independent Jewish kingdom identified as the kingdom
of God. **28:** Cyrus (539–530 BCE) preceded his son
Cambyses (530–522 BCE) and Darius I (522–486 BCE)
as ruler of Babylon.

DANIEL'S VISIONS CONCERNING THE COMING KINGDOM OF GOD

Chs. 7–12: The visions point to the establishment of
the kingdom of God as the primary theme of the book.
Scholars generally agree that these chapters were written in the mid second century BCE to support the Maccabean revolt against Seleucid* Syria. With the fall of
Seleucid Syria, the kingdom of God would be realized
as an independent Jewish state centered around the
Jerusalem Temple.*

7 In the first year of King Belshazzar of
Babylon, Daniel had a dream and visions

of his head as he lay in bed. Then he wrote down the dream:*a* 2I,*b* Daniel, saw in my vision by night the four winds of heaven stirring up the great sea, 3and four great beasts came up out of the sea, different from one another. 4The first was like a lion and had eagles' wings. Then, as I watched, its wings were plucked off, and it was lifted up from the ground and made to stand on two feet like a human being; and a human mind was given to it. 5Another beast appeared, a second one, that looked like a bear. It was raised up on one side, had three tusks*c* in its mouth among its teeth and was told, "Arise, devour many bodies!" 6After this, as I watched, another appeared, like a leopard. The beast had four wings of a bird on its back and four heads; and dominion was given to it. 7After this I saw in the visions by night a fourth beast, terrifying and dreadful and exceedingly strong. It had great iron teeth and was devouring, breaking in pieces, and stamping what was left with its feet. It was different from all the beasts that preceded it, and it had ten horns. 8I was considering the horns, when another horn appeared, a little one coming up among them; to make room for it, three of the earlier horns were plucked up by the roots. There were eyes like human eyes in this horn, and a mouth speaking arrogantly.

7.1–28: The vision of the four beasts. This narrative* points to God's overthrow of Antiochus IV. **1–8:** *First year of Belshazzar:* Belshazzar's regency began in 554 BCE. Daniel's vision draws upon creation traditions, which portray God's defeat of the sea or a sea dragon as the basis for the created world order (Ps 74.13–17; 89.9–10; Isa 27.1; 51.9–10; compare Gen 1; Ex 15). Here, the chaos monsters emerge from the sea to overturn creation. *The four winds* refer to the four cardinal directions, the universal context of *the four beasts,* which represent a succession of empires (ch. 2). The *lion* with *eagles' wings* is Babylon, which employed such figures extensively in art. The *bear* with *three tusks* (literally, "ribs") in its mouth is Media. The *leopard* with *four wings* and *four heads* is Persia, which ruled most of the Near Eastern world. The *beast* with *iron teeth* is the Greek-Macedonian empire of Alexander the Great. *The ten horns* represent the ten rulers of the Seleucid empire, who used horns as symbols of

their power. *The little horn* with *eyes . . . and a mouth speaking arrogantly* is Antiochus IV, who claimed to be a god and usurped the throne following the assassination of his brother, Seleucus IV.

〰〰〰〰〰〰〰〰〰〰〰〰〰〰〰〰〰〰〰〰〰〰

　9 As I watched,
　　thrones were set in place,
　　and an Ancient One*d* took his
　　　　throne,
　　his clothing was white as snow,
　　and the hair of his head like
　　　　pure wool;
　　his throne was fiery flames,
　　and its wheels were burning fire.
　10 A stream of fire issued
　　and flowed out from his presence.
　　A thousand thousands served him,
　　and ten thousand times ten thousand
　　　　stood attending him.
　　The court sat in judgment,
　　and the books were opened.
　11I watched then because of the noise of the arrogant words that the horn was speaking. And as I watched, the beast was put to death, and its body destroyed and given over to be burned with fire. 12As for the rest of the beasts, their dominion was taken away, but their lives were prolonged for a season and a time. 13As I watched in the night visions,
　　I saw one like a human being*e*
　　coming with the clouds of heaven.
　　And he came to the Ancient One*f*
　　and was presented before him.
　14 To him was given dominion
　　and glory and kingship,
　　that all peoples, nations, and languages
　　should serve him.
　　His dominion is an everlasting dominion
　　that shall not pass away,
　　and his kingship is one
　　that shall never be destroyed.

7.9–14. 9: *An Ancient One* (literally, "One Ancient of Days"): God. The portrayal of the divine court builds upon traditions in 1 Kings 22; Isa 6; Ezek 1; Ps 82;

a Q Ms Theodotion: MT adds *the beginning of the words; he said*　　*b* Theodotion: Aram *Daniel answered and said, "I*　　*c* Or *ribs*　　*d* Aram *an Ancient of Days*　*e* Aram *one like a son of man*　　*f* Aram *the Ancient of Days*

Job 1. **13:** *One like a human being:* Literally, "one like a son of man" (compare "mortal," literally, "son of man/adam," in Ezek 2.1), a designation for a human being, in this case a messiah* figure who will rule the world as king.

15 As for me, Daniel, my spirit was troubled within me,*ª* and the visions of my head terrified me. ¹⁶I approached one of the attendants to ask him the truth concerning all this. So he said that he would disclose to me the interpretation of the matter: ¹⁷"As for these four great beasts, four kings shall arise out of the earth. ¹⁸But the holy ones of the Most High shall receive the kingdom and possess the kingdom forever—forever and ever."

19 Then I desired to know the truth concerning the fourth beast, which was different from all the rest, exceedingly terrifying, with its teeth of iron and claws of bronze, and which devoured and broke in pieces, and stamped what was left with its feet; ²⁰and concerning the ten horns that were on its head, and concerning the other horn, which came up and to make room for which three of them fell out—the horn that had eyes and a mouth that spoke arrogantly, and that seemed greater than the others. ²¹As I looked, this horn made war with the holy ones and was prevailing over them, ²²until the Ancient One*ᵇ* came; then judgment was given for the holy ones of the Most High, and the time arrived when the holy ones gained possession of the kingdom.

23 This is what he said: "As for the fourth beast,

there shall be a fourth kingdom
  on earth
that shall be different from all the
  other kingdoms;
it shall devour the whole earth,
  and trample it down, and break it to
    pieces.
²⁴ As for the ten horns,
  out of this kingdom ten kings
    shall arise,
  and another shall arise after them.
This one shall be different from the
    former ones,
  and shall put down three kings.

²⁵ He shall speak words against the Most
    High,
  shall wear out the holy ones of the
    Most High,
  and shall attempt to change the
    sacred seasons and the law;
  and they shall be given into his power
    for a time, two times,*ᶜ* and half a
      time.
²⁶ Then the court shall sit in judgment,
  and his dominion shall be taken away,
    to be consumed and totally destroyed.
²⁷ The kingship and dominion
  and the greatness of the kingdoms
    under the whole heaven
  shall be given to the people of the
    holy ones of the Most High;
  their kingdom shall be an everlasting
    kingdom,
  and all dominions shall serve and
    obey them."

28 Here the account ends. As for me, Daniel, my thoughts greatly terrified me, and my face turned pale; but I kept the matter in my mind.

7.15–28. 16: *One of the attendants:* An angel. **18:** *The holy ones of the Most High* are either angels or human beings, both of whom were believed to be fighting Antiochus. The Judean revolt was led by the Hasmonean* priestly family, and the service of priests in the Temple* was believed to reflect that of the angels in heaven. **25:** *Shall attempt to change the sacred seasons and the law:* Antiochus banned the observance of sabbath and Torah* (1 Macc 1.41–50; 2 Macc 6.1–11), thus challenging the Jewish concept of creation, which is grounded in the sabbath as part of the created world order (Gen 2.1–3; Ex 31.12–17; compare Prov 8.22–36). *A time, two times, and half a time:* Three and a half years. Antiochus's persecution is of limited duration.

8 In the third year of the reign of King Belshazzar a vision appeared to me, Daniel, after the one that had appeared to me at first. ²In the vision I was looking and saw myself in Susa the capital, in the province of Elam,*ᵈ*

a Aram *troubled in its sheath*   *b* Aram *the Ancient of Days*   *c* Aram *a time, times*   *d* Gk Theodotion: MT Q Ms repeat *in the vision I was looking* and I was by the river Ulai.*³I looked up and saw a ram standing beside the river.*ᵇ It had two horns. Both horns were long, but one was longer than the other, and the longer one came up second. ⁴I saw the ram charging westward and northward and southward. All beasts were powerless to withstand it, and no one could rescue from its power; it did as it pleased and became strong.

5 As I was watching, a male goat appeared from the west, coming across the face of the whole earth without touching the ground. The goat had a horn* between its eyes. ⁶It came toward the ram with the two horns that I had seen standing beside the river,*ᵇ and it ran at it with savage force. ⁷I saw it approaching the ram. It was enraged against it and struck the ram, breaking its two horns. The ram did not have power to withstand it; it threw the ram down to the ground and trampled upon it, and there was no one who could rescue the ram from its power. ⁸Then the male goat grew exceedingly great; but at the height of its power, the great horn was broken, and in its place there came up four prominent horns toward the four winds of heaven.

9 Out of one of them came another*ᵈ horn, a little one, which grew exceedingly great toward the south, toward the east, and toward the beautiful land. ¹⁰It grew as high as the host of heaven. It threw down to the earth some of the host and some of the stars, and trampled on them. ¹¹Even against the prince of the host it acted arrogantly; it took the regular burnt offering away from him and overthrew the place of his sanctuary. ¹²Because of wickedness, the host was given over to it together with the regular burnt offering;*ᵉ it cast truth to the ground, and kept prospering in what it did. ¹³Then I heard a holy one speaking, and another holy one said to the one that spoke, "For how long is this vision concerning the regular burnt offering, the transgression that makes desolate, and the giving over of the sanctuary and host to be trampled?"*ᵉ ¹⁴And he answered him,*ᶠ "For two thousand three hundred evenings and mornings; then the sanctuary shall be restored to its rightful state."

8.1–27: The vision of the ram and the goat. A second vision surveys Greece's defeat of Persia and points to the downfall of Antiochus IV. The language of the book reverts to Hebrew (see 2.4b). *1–4: Third year of Belshazzar:* 552 BCE. *Susa*, located in the province of *Elam* by the River *Ulai* in modern Iran, was the winter capital of the Persian empire. The *ram* with *two horns* is the combined Persian-Median empire. *5:* The *male goat* with a *horn* is the empire of Alexander, who swept through Persia in 333–330 BCE. Alexander died in 323 BCE, and his empire split into separate kingdoms. *9–14: Another horn, a little one:* Antiochus IV, who attempted to extend his power to the south and east, including *the beautiful land* of Israel. Alexander defiled *the Temple*★ by turning it into a sanctuary for Zeus. *Two thousand three hundred evenings and mornings:* or 1,150 days, approximately three years and two months (see 7.25; 12.7), the time of Antiochus's persecution (1 Macc 1.54–4.52).

15 When I, Daniel, had seen the vision, I tried to understand it. Then someone appeared standing before me, having the appearance of a man, ¹⁶and I heard a human voice by the Ulai, calling, "Gabriel, help this man understand the vision." ¹⁷So he came near where I stood; and when he came, I became frightened and fell prostrate. But he said to me, "Understand, O mortal,*ᵍ that the vision is for the time of the end."

18 As he was speaking to me, I fell into a trance, face to the ground; then he touched me and set me on my feet. ¹⁹He said, "Listen, and I will tell you what will take place later in the period of wrath; for it refers to the appointed time of the end. ²⁰As for the ram that you saw with the two horns, these are the kings of Media and Persia. ²¹The male goat*ʰ is the king of Greece, and the great horn between its eyes is the first king. ²²As for the horn that was broken, in place of which four others arose, four kingdoms shall arise from his*ⁱ nation, but not with his power.

a Or *the Ulai Gate*   *b* Or *gate*   *c* Theodotion: Gk one horn; Heb *a horn of vision*   *d* Cn Compare 7.8: Heb *one*   *e* Meaning of Heb uncertain   *f* Gk Theodotion Syr Vg: Heb *me*   *g* Heb *son of man*   *h* Or *shaggy male goat*   *i* Gk Theodotion Vg: Heb *the*

23 At the end of their rule,
    when the transgressions have reached
      their full measure,
    a king of bold countenance shall arise,
      skilled in intrigue.
24 He shall grow strong in power,*
    shall cause fearful destruction,
    and shall succeed in what he does.
    He shall destroy the powerful
    and the people of the holy ones.
25 By his cunning
    he shall make deceit prosper under
      his hand,
    and in his own mind he shall
      be great.
    Without warning he shall destroy many
    and shall even rise up against the
      Prince of princes.
    But he shall be broken, and not by
      human hands.

26 The vision of the evenings and the mornings that has been told is true. As for you, seal up the vision, for it refers to many days from now."

27 So I, Daniel, was overcome and lay sick for some days; then I arose and went about the king's business. But I was dismayed by the vision and did not understand it.

8.15–27: The archangel Gabriel serves as the messenger to humanity in 8.15–26; 9.21–27; Lk 1.11–20. In 1 Enoch* 9 he intercedes on behalf of God's people and destroys the wicked. In Islam, he reveals the Quran to Muhammed. **17–18:** *The* (appointed) *time of the end:* The end of Antiochus's persecution. **25:** *Not by human hands:* God will act. **26:** *Seal up the vision:* Although given to Daniel in the sixth century, it will be realized in the second century (compare Isa 8.16; 29.11–12; 30.8; 34.16–17).

---

9 In the first year of Darius son of Ahasuerus, by birth a Mede, who became king over the realm of the Chaldeans— 2in the first year of his reign, I, Daniel, perceived in the books the number of years that, according to the word of the LORD to the prophet Jeremiah, must be fulfilled for the devastation of Jerusalem, namely, seventy years.

3 Then I turned to the Lord God, to seek an answer by prayer and supplication with fasting and sackcloth and ashes. 4I prayed to the LORD my God and made confession, saying,

"Ah, Lord, great and awesome God, keeping covenant and steadfast love with those who love you and keep your commandments, 5we have sinned and done wrong, acted wickedly and rebelled, turning aside from your commandments and ordinances. 6We have not listened to your servants the prophets, who spoke in your name to our kings, our princes, and our ancestors, and to all the people of the land.

7 "Righteousness is on your side, O Lord, but open shame, as at this day, falls on us, the people of Judah, the inhabitants of Jerusalem, and all Israel, those who are near and those who are far away, in all the lands to which you have driven them, because of the treachery that they have committed against you. 8Open shame, O LORD, falls on us, our kings, our officials, and our ancestors, because we have sinned against you. 9To the Lord our God belong mercy and forgiveness, for we have rebelled against him, 10and have not obeyed the voice of the LORD our God by following his laws, which he set before us by his servants the prophets.

11 "All Israel has transgressed your law and turned aside, refusing to obey your voice. So the curse and the oath written in the law of Moses, the servant of God, have been poured out upon us, because we have sinned against you. 12He has confirmed his words, which he spoke against us and against our rulers, by bringing upon us a calamity so great that what has been done against Jerusalem has never before been done under the whole heaven. 13Just as it is written in the law of Moses, all this calamity has come upon us. We did not entreat the favor of the LORD our God, turning from our iniquities and reflecting on his* fidelity. 14So the LORD kept watch over this calamity until he brought it upon us. Indeed, the LORD our God is right in all that he has done; for we have disobeyed his voice.

a Theodotion and one Gk Ms: Heb repeats (from 8.22) *but not with his power*   *b* Heb *your*

15 "And now, O Lord our God, who brought your people out of the land of Egypt with a mighty hand and made your name renowned even to this day—we have sinned, we have done wickedly. 16 O Lord, in view of all your righteous acts, let your anger and wrath, we pray, turn away from your city Jerusalem, your holy mountain; because of our sins and the iniquities of our ancestors, Jerusalem and your people have become a disgrace among all our neighbors. 17 Now therefore, O our God, listen to the prayer of your servant and to his supplication, and for your own sake, Lord,*a* let your face shine upon your desolated sanctuary. 18 Incline your ear, O my God, and hear. Open your eyes and look at our desolation and the city that bears your name. We do not present our supplication before you on the ground of our righteousness, but on the ground of your great mercies. 19 O Lord, hear; O Lord, forgive; O Lord, listen and act and do not delay! For your own sake, O my God, because your city and your people bear your name!"

9.1–27: The seventy weeks. This chapter applies Jeremiah's prophecy of a 70-year exile (Jer 25.11, 12; 29.10) together with the calculation of the jubilee year (Lev 25.8–17; "seven weeks of years") to predict the end of Antiochus's persecution. **1:** *Ahasuerus:* The Hebrew name for the Persian ruler Xerxes (see Esth 1.1; Ezra 4.6). Xerxes I (486–465 BCE) was the son of Darius I, and Xerxes II (425 BCE) was the son of Artaxerxes I (465–425 BCE). Darius II (423–405 BCE) was the son of Xerxes II, and Darius III (336–330 BCE), the son of Arses (338–336 BCE), was the last ruler of Persia; he was assassinated shortly after Alexander's final defeat of the Persian army. **2–19:** *Prayer and supplication:* Daniel employs a form of communal confession and petition (compare Ezra 9.6–15; Neh 1.5–11; 9.6–37). **11:** *The curse and the oath written in the law of Moses:* See Lev 26.14–45; Deut 28.15–68; 29.10–29.

20 While I was speaking, and was praying and confessing my sin and the sin of my people Israel, and presenting my supplication before the LORD my God on behalf of the holy mountain of my God— 21 while I was speaking in prayer, the man Gabriel, whom I had seen before in a vision, came to me in swift flight at the time of the evening sacri-

fice. 22 He came*b* and said to me, "Daniel, I have now come out to give you wisdom and understanding. 23 At the beginning of your supplications a word went out, and I have come to declare it, for you are greatly beloved. So consider the word and understand the vision:

24 "Seventy weeks are decreed for your people and your holy city: to finish the transgression, to put an end to sin, and to atone for iniquity, to bring in everlasting righteousness, to seal both vision and prophet, and to anoint a most holy place.*c* 25 Know therefore and understand: from the time that the word went out to restore and rebuild Jerusalem until the time of an anointed prince, there shall be seven weeks; and for sixty-two weeks it shall be built again with streets and moat, but in a troubled time. 26 After the sixty-two weeks, an anointed one shall be cut off and shall have nothing, and the troops of the prince who is to come shall destroy the city and the sanctuary. Its*d* end shall come with a flood, and to the end there shall be war. Desolations are decreed. 27 He shall make a strong covenant with many for one week, and for half of the week he shall make sacrifice and offering cease; and in their place*e* shall be an abomination that desolates, until the decreed end is poured out upon the desolator."

9.20–27. 24: *Seventy weeks:* Gabriel interprets Jeremiah's 70 years as "70 weeks of years" by applying the calculation of the jubilee year at "seven weeks of years" (Lev 25.8; see also 2 Chr 36.21). From 167 BCE, the total of 490 years would place the beginning of the calculation in 657 BCE during the reign of Manasseh, whose evil deeds prompted God to destroy Jerusalem and the Temple* (2 Kings 21.10–15). Gabriel's interpretation* points to the Maccabean revolt as the time when the punishment of Jerusalem would end. **25–26:** *Seven weeks:* Many claim that this is the 49 years that passed from the destruction of the Temple in 587 BCE to 538 BCE when Sheshbazzar laid the foundation for the Second Temple (Ezra 1.1–11; 5.13–16). The remaining *sixty-two weeks* or 434 years points to

a Theodotion Vg Compare Syr: Heb *for the Lord's sake*
b Gk Syr: Heb *He made to understand*   *c* Or *thing or one*   *d* Or *His*   *e* Cn: Meaning of Heb uncertain

104 BCE as the time of fulfillment, which goes beyond the period of the Maccabean revolt. *An anointed* one shall be cut off:* Antiochus removed the high priest Onias III, who was subsequently murdered (2 Macc 4.3–34). *The troops of the prince who is to come:* Antiochus sacked Jerusalem in 167 BCE following his humiliating withdrawal from Egypt. **27:** *He shall make a strong covenant* with many for one week:* Antiochus appointed Jason and then Menelaus as high priests in the Temple (2 Macc 4).

Daniel's vision of Antiochus's fall

Chs. 10–12: The culmination of the book describes the onset of the vision in 10.1–11.1; an overview of history from the fall of Persia to the projected fall of Antiochus IV in 11.2–12.4; and a conclusion that attempts to calculate the realization of the vision in 12.5–13. The author's description of historical events is accurate through 11.39, but the portrayal of Antiochus's demise in 11.40–12.4 is fictitious. The author wrote between December, 167 BCE, when the Temple* was desecrated, and December, 164 BCE, when it was rededicated by Judah the Maccabee.

---

10 In the third year of King Cyrus of Persia a word was revealed to Daniel, who was named Belteshazzar. The word was true, and it concerned a great conflict. He understood the word, having received understanding in the vision.

2 At that time I, Daniel, had been mourning for three weeks. 3I had eaten no rich food, no meat or wine had entered my mouth, and I had not anointed myself at all, for the full three weeks. 4On the twenty-fourth day of the first month, as I was standing on the bank of the great river (that is, the Tigris), 5I looked up and saw a man clothed in linen, with a belt of gold from Uphaz around his waist. 6His body was like beryl, his face like lightning, his eyes like flaming torches, his arms and legs like the gleam of burnished bronze, and the sound of his words like the roar of a multitude. 7I, Daniel, alone saw the vision; the people who were with me did not see the vision, though a great trembling fell upon them, and they fled and hid themselves. 8So I was left alone to see this great vision. My strength left me, and my complexion grew deathly pale, and I retained no strength. 9Then I heard the sound of his words; and when I heard the sound of his words, I fell into a trance, face to the ground.

10.1–11.1: The onset of Daniel's vision. Compare Ezekiel's vision (Ezek 1). **10.1:** *The third year of King Cyrus of Persia:* 536 BCE, 70 years after the date in 1.1 (see 9.24). **2–4:** Acts of self-denial are typical preparations for trances and other forms of mystical experience. **5:** *Twenty-fourth day of the month:* The 24th of Nissan, one day following the conclusion of Passover.* **5–6:** *A man clothed in linen:* An angel dressed as a priest and gleaming like the cherubim* of Ezekiel's vision (see Ezek 9.2; 40.3). *Uphaz:* See Jer 10.9. **7–9:** *Trance:* See Gen 2.21; 15.2.

10 But then a hand touched me and roused me to my hands and knees. 11He said to me, "Daniel, greatly beloved, pay attention to the words that I am going to speak to you. Stand on your feet, for I have now been sent to you." So while he was speaking this word to me, I stood up trembling. 12He said to me, "Do not fear, Daniel, for from the first day that you set your mind to gain understanding and to humble yourself before your God, your words have been heard, and I have come because of your words. 13But the prince of the kingdom of Persia opposed me twenty-one days. So Michael, one of the chief princes, came to help me, and I left him there with the prince of the kingdom of Persia,*a* 14and have come to help you understand what is to happen to your people at the end of days. For there is a further vision for those days."

15 While he was speaking these words to me, I turned my face toward the ground and was speechless. 16Then one in human form touched my lips, and I opened my mouth to speak, and said to the one who stood before me, "My lord, because of the vision such pains have come upon me that I retain no strength. 17How can my lord's servant talk with my lord? For I am shaking,*b* no strength remains in me, and no breath is left in me."

18 Again one in human form touched me and strengthened me. 19He said, "Do not

a Gk Theodotion: Heb *I was left there with the kings of Persia*   *b* Gk: Heb *from now* fear, greatly beloved, you are safe. Be strong and courageous!" When he spoke to me, I was strengthened and said, "Let my lord speak, for you have strengthened me." 20Then he said, "Do you know why I have come to you? Now I must return to fight against the prince of Persia, and when I am through with him, the prince of Greece will come. 21But I am to tell you what is inscribed in the book of truth. There is no one with me who contends against these princes except Michael, your prince. 1As for me, in the first year of Darius the Mede, I stood up to support and strengthen him.

10.10–11.1. 10–14: In ancient Near Eastern mythology, conflict among the nations often involves conflict among their gods. *The prince of Persia:* The angel or god of Persia. *Twenty-one days:* The duration of Daniel's fasting in v. 3. *Michael:* The archangel who protects the Jewish people (10.21; 12.1; see also Jude 9; Rev 12.7). **15–17:** Daniel speaks after his lips are touched (Isa 6.5–7; Ex 4.10–17; Ezek 3.26–27). *One in human form:* An angel. **10.18–11.1:** The angel, perhaps Michael, points to conflicts with Persia and Greece which are described in detail.

2 "Now I will announce the truth to you. Three more kings shall arise in Persia. The fourth shall be far richer than all of them, and when he has become strong through his riches, he shall stir up all against the kingdom of Greece. 3Then a warrior king shall arise, who shall rule with great dominion and take action as he pleases. 4And while still rising in power, his kingdom shall be broken and divided toward the four winds of heaven, but not to his posterity, nor according to the dominion with which he ruled; for his kingdom shall be uprooted and go to others besides these.

5 "Then the king of the south shall grow strong, but one of his officers shall grow stronger than he and shall rule a realm greater than his own realm. 6After some years they shall make an alliance, and the daughter of the king of the south shall come to the king of the north to ratify the agreement. But she shall not retain her power, and his offspring shall not endure. She shall

be given up, she and her attendants and her child and the one who supported her.

"In those times 7a branch from her roots shall rise up in his place. He shall come against the army and enter the fortress of the king of the north, and he shall take action against them and prevail. 8Even their gods, with their idols and with their precious vessels of silver and gold, he shall carry off to Egypt as spoils of war. For some years he shall refrain from attacking the king of the north; 9then the latter shall invade the realm of the king of the south, but will return to his own land.

11.2–12.4: Daniel's vision of history. Egypt did not attack Antiochus after 167 BCE. He died of tuberculosis in 164 or 163 BCE following campaigns in Armenia and Elymais (Elam). **2:** The three Persian kings are uncertain. **3–4:** Alexander, whose empire was divided after his death in 323 BCE. **5–6:** *The king of the south:* Ptolemy I (305–282 BCE), founder of the Ptolemaic* dynasty* of Egypt. *One of his officers:* Seleucus I (305–281 BCE), founder of the Syrian Seleucid* dynasty. Ptolemy II's (282–246 BCE) daughter Berenice married Antiochus II (261–247 BCE), but the alliance failed after Berenice, her child, and Antiochus II were murdered. **7–9:** Berenice's brother, Ptolemy III (246–222 BCE), invaded Syria to avenge her death, but he was repulsed by Seleucus II (246–225 BCE). **10:** *His sons:* Seleucus III (225–223 BCE) and Antiochus III (223–187 BCE).

10 "His sons shall wage war and assemble a multitude of great forces, which shall advance like a flood and pass through, and again shall carry the war as far as his fortress. 11Moved with rage, the king of the south shall go out and do battle against the king of the north, who shall muster a great multitude, which shall, however, be defeated by his enemy. 12When the multitude has been carried off, his heart shall be exalted, and he shall overthrow tens of thousands, but he shall not prevail. 13For the king of the north shall again raise a multitude, larger than the former, and after some years*a* he shall advance with a great army and abundant supplies.

a Heb *and at the end of the times years*

14 "In those times many shall rise against the king of the south. The lawless among your own people shall lift themselves up in order to fulfill the vision, but they shall fail. 15 Then the king of the north shall come and throw up siegeworks, and take a well-fortified city. And the forces of the south shall not stand, not even his picked troops, for there shall be no strength to resist. 16 But he who comes against him shall take the actions he pleases, and no one shall withstand him. He shall take a position in the beautiful land, and all of it shall be in his power. 17 He shall set his mind to come with the strength of his whole kingdom, and he shall bring terms of peace*a* and perform them. In order to destroy the kingdom,*b* he shall give him a woman in marriage; but it shall not succeed or be to his advantage. 18 Afterward he shall turn to the coastlands, and shall capture many. But a commander shall put an end to his insolence; indeed,*c* he shall turn his insolence back upon him. 19 Then he shall turn back toward the fortresses of his own land, but he shall stumble and fall, and shall not be found.

11.10–19. 11–12: Ptolemy IV (222–204 BCE) defeated Antiochus III at Raphia but failed to capitalize on his victory. 13–19: Antiochus III defeated Ptolemy V (204–180 BCE) in 200 BCE, taking control of the Sinai (and Judea). He later gave his daughter Cleopatra I to Ptolemy V in marriage.

20 "Then shall arise in his place one who shall send an official for the glory of the kingdom; but within a few days he shall be broken, though not in anger or in battle. 21 In his place shall arise a contemptible person on whom royal majesty had not been conferred; he shall come in without warning and obtain the kingdom through intrigue. 22 Armies shall be utterly swept away and broken before him, and the prince of the covenant as well. 23 And after an alliance is made with him, he shall act deceitfully and become strong with a small party. 24 Without warning he shall come into the richest parts*d* of the province and do what none of his predecessors had ever done, lavishing plunder, spoil, and wealth on them. He shall devise plans against strongholds, but only for a time. 25 He shall stir up his power and determination against the king of the south with a great army, and the king of the south shall wage war with a much greater and stronger army. But he shall not succeed, for plots shall be devised against him 26 by those who eat of the royal rations. They shall break him, his army shall be swept away, and many shall fall slain. 27 The two kings, their minds bent on evil, shall sit at one table and exchange lies. But it shall not succeed, for there remains an end at the time appointed. 28 He shall return to his land with great wealth, but his heart shall be set against the holy covenant. He shall work his will, and return to his own land.

11.20–28: The initial reign of Antiochus IV, who usurped the throne following the assassination of his brother Seleucus IV (187–175 BCE). His initial campaigns against Ptolemy VI (180–145 BCE) were successful.

29 "At the time appointed he shall return and come into the south, but this time it shall not be as it was before. 30 For ships of Kittim shall come against him, and he shall lose heart and withdraw. He shall be enraged and take action against the holy covenant. He shall turn back and pay heed to those who forsake the holy covenant. 31 Forces sent by him shall occupy and profane the temple and fortress. They shall abolish the regular burnt offering and set up the abomination that makes desolate. 32 He shall seduce with intrigue those who violate the covenant; but the people who are loyal to their God shall stand firm and take action. 33 The wise among the people shall give understanding to many; for some days, however, they shall fall by sword and flame, and suffer captivity and plunder. 34 When they fall victim, they shall receive a little help, and many shall join them insincerely. 35 Some of the wise shall fall, so that they may be refined, purified, and cleansed,*e* until the time of the

a Gk: Heb *kingdom, and upright ones with him*
b Heb *it*　　*c* Meaning of Heb uncertain　　*d* Or *among the richest men*　　*e* Heb *made them white*

end, for there is still an interval until the time appointed.

36 "The king shall act as he pleases. He shall exalt himself and consider himself greater than any god, and shall speak horrendous things against the God of gods. He shall prosper until the period of wrath is completed, for what is determined shall be done. 37He shall pay no respect to the gods of his ancestors, or to the one beloved by women; he shall pay no respect to any other god, for he shall consider himself greater than all. 38He shall honor the god of fortresses instead of these; a god whom his ancestors did not know he shall honor with gold and silver, with precious stones and costly gifts. 39He shall deal with the strongest fortresses by the help of a foreign god. Those who acknowledge him he shall make more wealthy, and shall appoint them as rulers over many, and shall distribute the land for a price.

11.29–39: Following his forced withdrawal from Egypt, Antiochus sacked and occupied Jerusalem in 167 BCE, profaned the Temple,* and proscribed the practice of Judaism. 30: *Kittim:* Originally Greeks or Cypriots (Gen 10.4; Ezek 27.6), later Romans. 34: *A little help:* The Maccabean revolt. 36: Antiochus called himself Epiphanes,* "manifest god." 37–39: Antiochus set aside the worship of Tammuz-Adonis in favor of Zeus Olympus, whose statue he placed in the Temple (1 Macc 1.54–59).

40 "At the time of the end the king of the south shall attack him. But the king of the north shall rush upon him like a whirlwind, with chariots and horsemen, and with many ships. He shall advance against countries and pass through like a flood. 41He shall come into the beautiful land, and tens of thousands shall fall victim, but Edom and Moab and the main part of the Ammonites shall escape from his power. 42He shall stretch out his hand against the countries, and the land of Egypt shall not escape. 43He shall become ruler of the treasures of gold and of silver, and all the riches of Egypt; and the Libyans and the Ethiopians*a* shall follow in his train. 44But reports from the east and the north shall alarm him, and he shall go

out with great fury to bring ruin and complete destruction to many. 45He shall pitch his palatial tents between the sea and the beautiful holy mountain. Yet he shall come to his end, with no one to help him.

11.40–45: The scenario presented here did not take place. *The beautiful land:* Israel.

12 "At that time Michael, the great prince, the protector of your people, shall arise. There shall be a time of anguish, such as has never occurred since nations first came into existence. But at that time your people shall be delivered, everyone who is found written in the book. 2Many of those who sleep in the dust of the earth*b* shall awake, some to everlasting life, and some to shame and everlasting contempt. 3Those who are wise shall shine like the brightness of the sky,*c* and those who lead many to righteousness, like the stars forever and ever. 4But you, Daniel, keep the words secret and the book sealed until the time of the end. Many shall be running back and forth, and evil*d* shall increase."

12.1–4: Michael calls upon Daniel to remain silent about the vision until its fulfillment. 2: Resurrection of the righteous (Isa 26.19; Ezek 37). 3: *Like the brightness of the sky:* The Hebrew word "zohar" ("brightness") from this verse serves as the title of the Zohar, the primary mystical work of Judaism.

5 Then I, Daniel, looked, and two others appeared, one standing on this bank of the stream and one on the other. 6One of them said to the man clothed in linen, who was upstream, "How long shall it be until the end of these wonders?" 7The man clothed in linen, who was upstream, raised his right hand and his left hand toward heaven. And I heard him swear by the one who lives forever that it would be for a time, two times, and half a time,*e* and that when the shattering of the power of the holy people comes to an end, all these things would be accom-

a Or *Nubians;* Heb *Cushites*   b Or *the land of dust*
c Or *dome*   d Cn Compare Gk: Heb *knowledge*
e Heb *a time, times, and a half*

plished. [8]I heard but could not understand; so I said, "My lord, what shall be the outcome of these things?" [9]He said, "Go your way, Daniel, for the words are to remain secret and sealed until the time of the end. [10]Many shall be purified, cleansed, and refined, but the wicked shall continue to act wickedly. None of the wicked shall understand, but those who are wise shall understand. [11]From the time that the regular burnt offering is taken away and the abomination that desolates is set up, there shall be one thousand two hundred ninety days. [12]Happy are those who persevere and attain the thousand three hundred thirty-five days. [13]But you, go your way,[a] and rest; you shall rise for your reward at the end of the days."

12.5–13: The realization of the vision. This section attempts to calculate the time when the vision will be realized. **5–6:** *Two others:* Angels. **7:** *A time, two times, and half a time:* Three and a half years, the approximate time from the desecration of the Temple* in 167 BCE to its rededication in 164 BCE (see 7.25). **11:** *One thousand two hundred ninety days:* An attempt to specify the figure in v. 7. **12:** *Thousand three hundred thirty-five days:* A second attempt to specify this figure. **13:** *The end of days:* The end of the period outlined in the vision (see 8.17; 9.26; 11.6, 13, 35, 40; 12.4, 9).

a Gk Theodotion: Heb adds *to the end*

HOSEA

Introduction

Hosea's central concern is Israel's loyalty to its God. He denounces Israel for worshipping other gods, in particular the Canaanite god Baal,* and pleads with Israel to return to the faithful worship of its God alone. To gain his audience's attention and to make his message vivid, Hosea used the metaphor* of marriage to describe Israel's relationship to God. God is pictured as a husband and Israel as his faithless and promiscuous wife. Israel, the disloyal wife, is urged to repent and return to her husband. The marriage metaphor is enacted by Hosea himself in chs. 1–3, when Hosea marries Gomer, described as a prostitute (2.2) and an adulteress (3.1). And Hosea uses the marriage metaphor repeatedly in the speeches in chs. 4–14, which make up the bulk of the book. A prophet* fond of metaphors, Hosea also compares Israel's disloyalty to a barren tree (9.13–17), a stubborn heifer (4.16; 10.11–15), and a rebellious son (11.1–7).

Hosea's prophecy can be divided into two parts, the first a collection of narratives* in chs. 1–3 that describes Israel's disloyalty in terms of Hosea's faithless wife. Narratives about prophets, such as these, typically take up less space in a prophetic book than the prophet's speeches themselves, and they frequently describe prophets acting out the message they wish to deliver. The second and larger part of Hosea is a collection of prophetic speeches (chs. 4–14) that condemn Israel's deceit, predict God's punishment, and express hope for Israel's renewal. It is difficult to know where one speech ends and the next begins, but a dominant pattern can be detected in which indictments of sin are followed by sentences of judgment. In the brief speech that begins this collection, for example, an indictment listing Israel's crimes (4.1–2) is followed by a sentence describing God's punishment (4.3). Much less common are speeches predicting Israel's restoration (11.8–11). Hosea's own speeches may have been supplemented at points by later editors who wished to relate Hosea's message to the southern kingdom of Judah or to the Judeans in exile (11.10–11).

Hosea lived and prophesied in the northern kingdom of Israel, also called Ephraim, at the time of the divided monarchy when Israel and Judah were separate kingdoms. Hosea was the only native northerner among the prophets, the rest of whom all lived in or came from Judah. His career covered the last 30 years of the kingdom of Israel (750–721 BCE), when Israel was under the constant threat of Assyrian imperialism and was wracked by a series of violent coups in its own capital, Samaria. Hosea deplores the internal political violence of this period (7.5–7) and Israel's attempt to protect itself by international alliances (7.11), and he believes Israel's impending doom in the face of Assyrian expansion to be God's punishment for its social and religious corruption.

Hosea is especially critical of the religious scene in Israelite society during this period. His frequent references to Baal (2.8, 13, 16) indicate that many Israelites had turned from their own God to worship this Canaanite deity. This attraction to Baal-worship among the Israelites was an old and continual problem, as the contest between Elijah and the prophets of Baal a century earlier shows (2 Kings 17–19). The Israelites believed that Baal, like Israel's own God, could deliver the rains and agricultural productivity on which their economy and survival depended. The calves that Hosea criticizes (8.5–6), though possibly pedestals or throne images for Israel's God, are also associated with Baal in this period, and Hosea regards them as idols of Baal.

Hosea begins a collection of twelve short prophetic books, often called the Minor Prophets because of their brief length when compared to the longer books of Isaiah, Jeremiah, and Ezekiel. These twelve books are arranged roughly in chronological order, starting with eighth-century prophets, as Hosea, Amos, and Micah are explicitly identified. The collection then moves to prophets of the seventh century and concludes with those of the sixth.

READING GUIDE

One key to understanding Hosea involves recognizing the variety of ways in which the image of marital infidelity is employed to picture Israel's religious disloyalty. Catching the basic point of the comparison and its shock value is more important than reconstructing the actual details of Hosea's marriage, which still elude scholars. It is also important to notice how much of Hosea's message of faithlessness is directed against abuses in Israelite religion: its priesthood, its rituals, its sacred sites and altars, and its basic integrity.

1 The word of the LORD that came to Hosea son of Beeri, in the days of Kings Uzziah, Jotham, Ahaz, and Hezekiah of Judah, and in the days of King Jeroboam son of Joash of Israel.

1.1: Title. The reigns of these Judean kings span almost a hundred years (783–687 BCE), while the reign of the single Israelite king mentioned, Jeroboam, lasts for only 41 of these years (786–746). Since Hosea's speeches are directed to Israel in particular and reflect events leading up to its fall to Assyria in 721 BCE, it is peculiar that the six kings who followed Jeroboam to the throne of Israel during this time are not mentioned here.

2 When the LORD first spoke through Hosea, the LORD said to Hosea, "Go, take for yourself a wife of whoredom and have children of whoredom, for the land commits great whoredom by forsaking the LORD." 3 So he went and took Gomer daughter of Diblaim, and she conceived and bore him a son. 4 And the LORD said to him, "Name him Jezreel;[a] for in a little while I will punish the house of Jehu for the blood of Jezreel, and I will put an end to the kingdom of the house of Israel. 5 On that day I will break the bow of Israel in the valley of Jezreel."

6 She conceived again and bore a daughter. Then the LORD said to him, "Name her Lo-ruhamah,[b] for I will no longer have pity on the house of Israel or forgive them. 7 But I will have pity on the house of Judah, and I will save them by the LORD their God; I will not save them by bow, or by sword, or by war, or by horses, or by horsemen."

8 When she had weaned Lo-ruhamah, she conceived and bore a son. 9 Then the LORD said, "Name him Lo-ammi,[c] for you are not my people and I am not your God."[d]

10[e] Yet the number of the people of Israel shall be like the sand of the sea, which can be neither measured nor numbered; and in the place where it was said to them, "You are not my people," it shall be said to them, "Children of the living God." 11 The people of Judah and the people of Israel shall be gathered together, and they shall appoint for themselves one head; and they shall take possession of[f] the land, for great shall be the day of Jezreel.

2 [g] Say to your brother,[h] Ammi,[i] and to your sister,[j] Ruhamah.[k]

1.2–2.1: Hosea marries the prostitute Gomer. In chs. 1 and 3 Hosea acts out the message he wishes to convey to Israel: Just as the wife he marries has been promiscuous, seeking out other lovers, so Israel has been unfaithful to its LORD, seeking out other gods to worship. **1.2:** *Whoredom* translates the common Hebrew term for prostitution. **4:** Hosea's first son *Jezreel* is named after the broad valley in northern Israel where

a That is *God sows*   b That is *Not pitied*   c That is *Not my people*   d Heb *I am not yours*   e Ch 2.1 in Heb   f Heb *rise up from*   g Ch 2.3 in Heb   h Gk: Heb *brothers*   i That is *My people*   j Gk Vg: Heb *sisters*   k That is *Pitied*

Jehu led a bloody coup (2 Kings 9.14–10.11), establishing a dynasty* in which Jeroboam, Hosea's contemporary, was the fourth king. The name symbolizes the imminent end of that dynasty, which occurred during Hosea's career when Jeroboam's son Zechariah was assassinated in 745 BCE. **6–9:** The names of Hosea's daughter, *Lo-ruhamah* ("Not pitied"), and second son, *Lo-ammi* ("Not my people"), symbolize

Mαp   **Kingdom of Israel in Hosea's time**

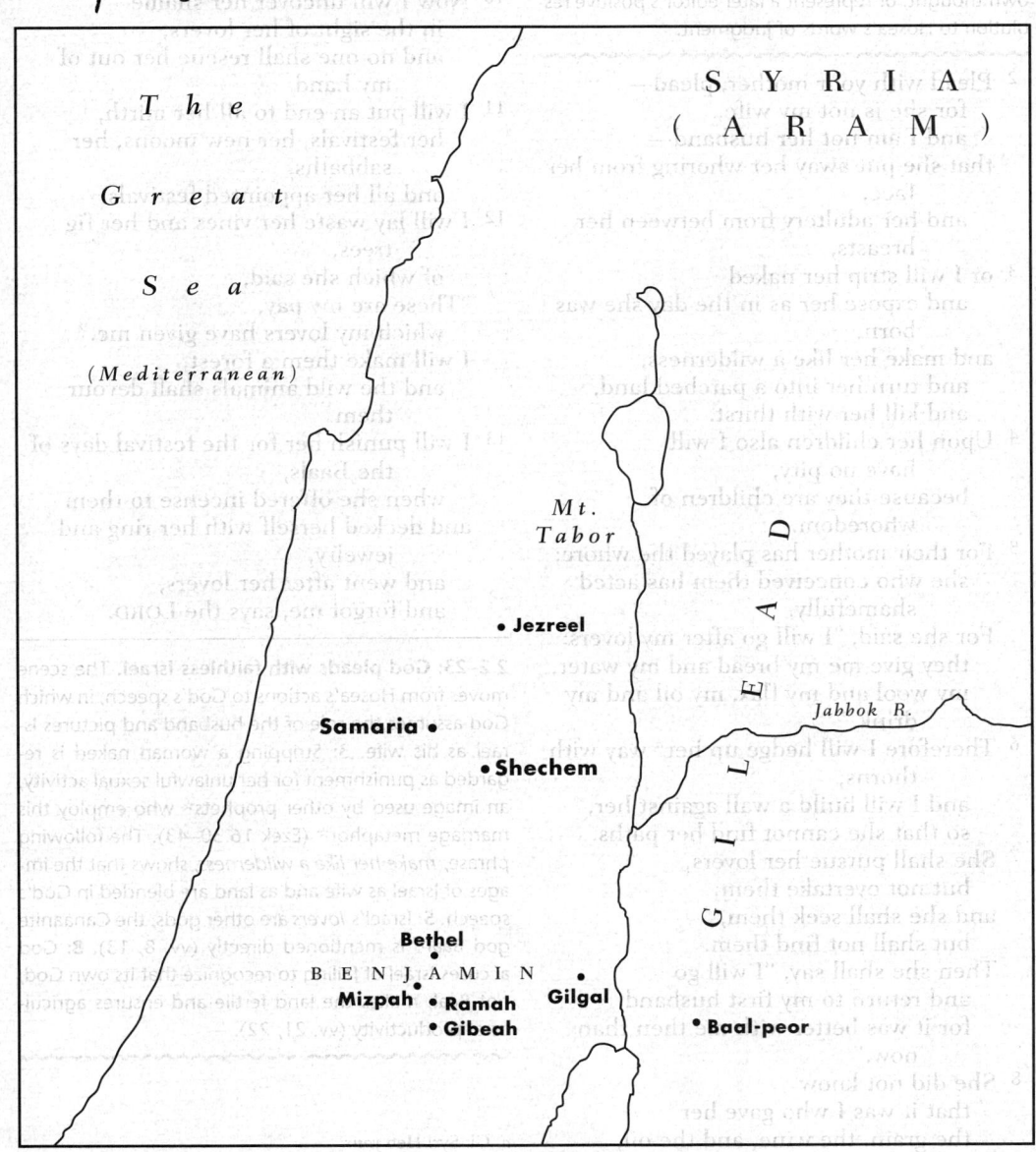

God's rejection of Israel for its faithlessness. **7:** Scholars disagree whether references to the southern kingdom of *Judah* here and elsewhere in Hosea are from Hosea himself or from later Judean editors who wished to relate Hosea's message to their own time and place. **1.10–2.1:** The marked shift to future salvation here, in which the meanings of Hosea's children's names are reversed to their positive counterparts, may either reflect the tension between despair and hope in Hosea's own thought, or represent a later editor's positive resolution to Hosea's words of judgment.

2 Plead with your mother, plead—
   for she is not my wife,
   and I am not her husband—
that she put away her whoring from her
      face,
   and her adultery from between her
      breasts,
3 or I will strip her naked
   and expose her as in the day she was
      born,
and make her like a wilderness,
   and turn her into a parched land,
   and kill her with thirst.
4 Upon her children also I will
      have no pity,
   because they are children of
      whoredom.
5 For their mother has played the whore;
   she who conceived them has acted
      shamefully.
For she said, "I will go after my lovers;
   they give me my bread and my water,
   my wool and my flax, my oil and my
      drink."
6 Therefore I will hedge up her*a* way with
      thorns;
   and I will build a wall against her,
   so that she cannot find her paths.
7 She shall pursue her lovers,
   but not overtake them;
and she shall seek them,
   but shall not find them.
Then she shall say, "I will go
   and return to my first husband,
   for it was better with me then than
      now."
8 She did not know
   that it was I who gave her
   the grain, the wine, and the oil,

and who lavished upon her silver
   and gold that they used for Baal.
9 Therefore I will take back
   my grain in its time,
   and my wine in its season;
and I will take away my wool and my
      flax,
   which were to cover her
      nakedness.
10 Now I will uncover her shame
   in the sight of her lovers,
   and no one shall rescue her out of
      my hand.
11 I will put an end to all her mirth,
   her festivals, her new moons, her
      sabbaths,
   and all her appointed festivals.
12 I will lay waste her vines and her fig
      trees,
   of which she said,
"These are my pay,
   which my lovers have given me."
I will make them a forest,
   and the wild animals shall devour
      them.
13 I will punish her for the festival days of
      the Baals,
   when she offered incense to them
and decked herself with her ring and
      jewelry,
   and went after her lovers,
   and forgot me, says the LORD.

2.2–23: God pleads with faithless Israel. The scene moves from Hosea's actions to God's speech, in which God assumes the role of the husband and pictures Israel as his wife. **3:** Stripping a woman naked is regarded as punishment for her unlawful sexual activity, an image used by other prophets* who employ this marriage metaphor* (Ezek 16.30–43). The following phrase, *make her like a wilderness,* shows that the images of Israel as wife and as land are blended in God's speech. **5:** Israel's *lovers* are other gods; the Canaanite god Baal* is mentioned directly (vv. 8, 13). **8:** God accuses Israel of failing to recognize that its own God, not Baal, makes the land fertile and ensures agricultural productivity (vv. 21, 22).

a Gk Syr: Heb *your*

14 Therefore, I will now allure her,
    and bring her into the wilderness,
    and speak tenderly to her.
15 From there I will give her her
        vineyards,
    and make the Valley of Achor a door
        of hope.
    There she shall respond as in the days
        of her youth,
    as at the time when she came out of
        the land of Egypt.
16On that day, says the LORD, you will call
me, "My husband," and no longer will you
call me, "My Baal."*a* 17For I will remove the
names of the Baals from her mouth, and they
shall be mentioned by name no more. 18I
will make for you*b* a covenant on that day
with the wild animals, the birds of the air,
and the creeping things of the ground; and I
will abolish*c* the bow, the sword, and war
from the land; and I will make you lie down
in safety. 19And I will take you for my wife
forever; I will take you for my wife in righteousness and in justice, in steadfast love,
and in mercy. 20I will take you for my wife
in faithfulness; and you shall know the
LORD.
21 On that day I will answer, says the
        LORD,
    I will answer the heavens
        and they shall answer the earth;
22 and the earth shall answer the grain,
        the wine, and the oil,
    and they shall answer Jezreel;*d*
23   and I will sow him*e* for myself in the
        land.
    And I will have pity on Lo-ruhamah,*f*
        and I will say to Lo-ammi,*g* "You are
        my people";
    and he shall say, "You are my God."

2.14–23. 14–15: References to *the wilderness, the Valley of Achor,* and *the land of Egypt* recall Israel's deliverance from slavery in Egypt (Ex 1–15), its journey
through the wilderness (Ex 16—Num 36), and its entrance into Canaan (Josh 7.24–26). **16:** Hosea plays on
the multiple meanings of the Hebrew word "ba'al": It
can be used as a common noun meaning "husband"
or "master" or as the name of the Canaanite god
Baal.

3 The LORD said to me again, "Go, love a
  woman who has a lover and is an adulteress, just as the LORD loves the people of
Israel, though they turn to other gods and
love raisin cakes." 2So I bought her for fifteen shekels of silver and a homer of barley
and a measure of wine.*h* 3And I said to her,
"You must remain as mine for many days;
you shall not play the whore, you shall not
have intercourse with a man, nor I with you."
4For the Israelites shall remain many days
without king or prince, without sacrifice or
pillar, without ephod or teraphim. 5After-
ward the Israelites shall return and seek the
LORD their God, and David their king; they
shall come in awe to the LORD and to his
goodness in the latter days.

3.1–5: Hosea marries an adulteress. The details of
this account are so sketchy that it is difficult to decide
whether it describes (1) Hosea's first marriage to
Gomer in ch. 1, but from the first- rather than third-
person perspective; (2) Hosea's marriage to a second
woman; or (3) Hosea's remarriage to Gomer. In any
case, the point of his symbolic act is clear: Israel has
been an unfaithful wife but God desires her return. **1:**
While Hosea connects *raisin cakes* with worship of
other gods (as does Isa 16.7), they are also associated
with legitimate Israelite worship (2 Sam 6.19). **2:** The
nature of Hosea's transaction is unclear. Payment was
made in ancient Israel for women slaves (Ex 21.7–11)
and for wives (Ex 22.16–17), but this amount is not
mentioned elsewhere, and the narrative* does not
identify the recipient of the payment. **4:** Hosea predicts
a coming judgment in which Israel will lose both political and religious leadership. The *ephod** (Ex 28.4)
and the *teraphim* (Judg 17.5; Zech 10.2) are both associated with priestly activity. **5:** The reference to *David their king* may indicate that Hosea looked forward
to the reunification of Israel and Judah under a single
king (1.11), since David had once ruled over a united
kingdom (2 Sam 5; alternatively, it may represent the
perspective of a later editor from the southern kingdom of Judah, over which David's descendants ruled
for its entire history.

---

a That is, *"My master"*   *b* Heb *them*   *c* Heb *break*
d That is *God sows*   *e* Cn: Heb *her*   *f* That is *Not
pitied*   *g* That is *Not my people*   *h* Gk: Heb *a homer
of barley and a lethech of barley*

Prophets and Gender

Hosea's primary image for Israel's disloyalty to God is the wife who is unfaithful to her husband and has become a prostitute. One reason Hosea chose this image is the fact that his audience was primarily male—the men held the power and wealth in ancient patriarchal societies such as biblical Israel. For these men, faithless wives were a stinging shame. And by comparing the men's behavior to faithless wives, Hosea wanted to shock them so they would see the seriousness of their crimes. The image of the faithless wife gave Hosea a forceful means of criticizing the abuses of Israel's male elite. The problem of the image is that it connects disloyalty and sin with women in particular, a connection that must be clearly rejected in order to keep such an image from being used to disparage and mistreat women.

4 Hear the word of the LORD, O people
  of Israel;
  for the LORD has an indictment
    against the inhabitants
    of the land.
  There is no faithfulness or loyalty,
    and no knowledge of God in the land.
2 Swearing, lying, and murder,
    and stealing and adultery break out;
    bloodshed follows bloodshed.
3 Therefore the land mourns,
    and all who live in it languish;
  together with the wild animals
    and the birds of the air,
    even the fish of the sea are perishing.

4 Yet let no one contend,
    and let none accuse,
    for with you is my contention,
      O priest.*a*
5 You shall stumble by day;
    the prophet also shall stumble with
      you by night,
    and I will destroy your mother.
6 My people are destroyed for lack of
      knowledge;
    because you have rejected knowledge,
    I reject you from being a priest to me.
  And since you have forgotten the law of
      your God,
    I also will forget your children.

7 The more they increased,
    the more they sinned against me;
    they changed*b* their glory into shame.

8 They feed on the sin of my people;
    they are greedy for their iniquity.
9 And it shall be like people, like priest;
    I will punish them for their ways,
    and repay them for their deeds.
10 They shall eat, but not be satisfied;
    they shall play the whore, but not
      multiply;
  because they have forsaken the LORD
    to devote themselves to
      11whoredom.

4.1–19: God puts Israel on trial. The language of this section puts God's accusations against Israel into the context of a legal proceeding initiated by an *indictment* (v. 1) describing the allegations against Israel. The judicial sentence that will follow (5.1–6.3) is already anticipated here (vv. 3, 6, 9–10). **2:** This list of crimes is similar to those outlawed in the ten commandments (Ex 20.7, 13–16). **4–10:** God prosecutes Israel's priests. **6:** The *law* (Heb., "torah") is the basis for Israel's life and worship.

  Wine and new wine
    take away the understanding.
12 My people consult a piece of wood,
    and their divining rod gives
      them oracles.
  For a spirit of whoredom has led them
      astray,
    and they have played the whore,
      forsaking their God.

a Cn: Meaning of Heb uncertain   *b* Ancient Heb tradition: MT *I will change*

13 They sacrifice on the tops of the
            mountains,
      and make offerings upon the hills,
   under oak, poplar, and terebinth,
      because their shade is good.

   Therefore your daughters play
            the whore,
      and your daughters-in-law commit
            adultery.
14 I will not punish your daughters when
            they play the whore,
      nor your daughters-in-law when they
            commit adultery;
   for the men themselves go aside with
            whores,
      and sacrifice with temple prostitutes;
   thus a people without understanding
            comes to ruin.

15 Though you play the whore, O Israel,
      do not let Judah become guilty.
   Do not enter into Gilgal,
      or go up to Beth-aven,
      and do not swear, "As the
            LORD lives."
16 Like a stubborn heifer,
      Israel is stubborn;
   can the LORD now feed them
      like a lamb in a broad pasture?

17 Ephraim is joined to idols—
      let him alone.
18 When their drinking is ended, they
            indulge in sexual orgies;
      they love lewdness more than their
            glory.[a]
19 A wind has wrapped them[b] in its wings,
      and they shall be ashamed because of
            their altars.[c]

4.11–19: God prosecutes Israel for heretical worship,
employing the image of prostitution introduced in chs.
1–3. 13: Since mountains (Mt. Sinai and Mt. Zion*)
and trees (Josh 24.26) are associated with authentic
Israelite worship, Hosea appears to be criticizing the
worship of other gods at these sites (as in Deut 12.2)
rather than these natural features themselves. 14: The
term *temple prostitutes* translates the Hebrew word
"qedeshot," literally "holy women." Partly because of
the images of prostitution in the context, scholars have

suggested that these women may have been practicing ritual sex in sacred fertility rites. But the Hebrew
term does not suggest this in itself, and there is very
little concrete evidence of such practices in the biblical
world. 15: *Gilgal* likely refers to a religious sanctuary
marking the site near Jericho where Israel entered Canaan (Josh 4.19–20). *Beth-aven*, literally "house of
worthlessness," appears to be a scornful name for
Bethel ("house of God"), one of the key northern religious shrines (1 Kings 12.26–30).

5 Hear this, O priests!
      Give heed, O house of Israel!
   Listen, O house of the king!
      For the judgment pertains to you;
   for you have been a snare at Mizpah,
      and a net spread upon Tabor,
2 and a pit dug deep in Shittim;[d]
      but I will punish all of them.

3 I know Ephraim,
      and Israel is not hidden from me;
   for now, O Ephraim, you have played
            the whore;
   Israel is defiled.
4 Their deeds do not permit them
      to return to their God.
   For the spirit of whoredom is within
            them,
      and they do not know the LORD.

5 Israel's pride testifies against him;
      Ephraim[e] stumbles in his guilt;
   Judah also stumbles with them.
6 With their flocks and herds they shall
            go
      to seek the LORD,
   but they will not find him;
      he has withdrawn from them.
7 They have dealt faithlessly with the
            LORD;
      for they have borne illegitimate
            children.
   Now the new moon shall devour them
      along with their fields.

5.1–6.3: God sentences Israel. An extended judgment speech describing God's punishment of Israel

a Cn Compare Gk: Meaning of Heb uncertain
b Heb her   c Gk Syr: Heb sacrifices   d Cn: Meaning
of Heb uncertain   e Heb Israel and Ephraim

follows the indictment of ch. 4. **5.1–7: God reviews Israel's sins. 1:** Hosea does not explain the crimes of *Mizpah,* a town in southern Israel, or of *Tabor,* a mountain in the Jezreel Valley in northern Israel. **7:** The *new moon** marked the beginning of the month and of religious observances in Israel (Isa 1.13, Am 8.5).

8 Blow the horn in Gibeah,
   the trumpet in Ramah.
  Sound the alarm at Beth-aven;
   look behind you, Benjamin!
9 Ephraim shall become a desolation
   in the day of punishment;
  among the tribes of Israel
   I declare what is sure.
10 The princes of Judah have become
   like those who remove the landmark;
  on them I will pour out
   my wrath like water.
11 Ephraim is oppressed, crushed in
     judgment,
  because he was determined to go
     after vanity.*ᵃ*
12 Therefore I am like maggots to
     Ephraim,
  and like rottenness to the house of
     Judah.
13 When Ephraim saw his sickness,
   and Judah his wound,
  then Ephraim went to Assyria,
   and sent to the great king.*ᵇ*
  But he is not able to cure you
   or heal your wound.
14 For I will be like a lion to Ephraim,
   and like a young lion to the house of
     Judah.
  I myself will tear and go away;
   I will carry off, and no one shall rescue.
15 I will return again to my place
   until they acknowledge their guilt and
     seek my face.
  In their distress they will beg
     my favor:

6 "Come, let us return to the LORD;
   for it is he who has torn, and he will
     heal us;
  he has struck down, and he will bind
     us up.
2 After two days he will revive us;
   on the third day he will raise us up,
   that we may live before him.

3 Let us know, let us press on to know
     the LORD;
  his appearing is as sure as the dawn;
  he will come to us like the showers,
   like the spring rains that water the
     earth."
4 What shall I do with you, O Ephraim?
   What shall I do with you, O Judah?
  Your love is like a morning cloud,
   like the dew that goes away early.
5 Therefore I have hewn them by the
     prophets,
   I have killed them by the words of my
     mouth,
  and my*ᶜ* judgment goes forth as the
     light.
6 For I desire steadfast love and not
     sacrifice,
   the knowledge of God rather than
     burnt offerings.

5.8–6.3. 5.8–15: God summons the guilty to announce the sentence. **8:** Why Hosea sounds the alarm in *Gibeah, Ramah,* and *Beth-aven,* all cities in the southern part of Israel occupied by the tribe of *Benjamin,* is not entirely clear. **13:** Hosea criticizes Israel for trying to save itself by an alliance with *Assyria,* the imperial power threatening Israel in Hosea's time. Two of Israel's kings, Menahem (2 Kings 15.19–20) and Hoshea (2 Kings 17.3), paid tribute to Assyria to remain in power. **6.1–3:** Hosea anticipates Israel's response to judgment: Only after it is punished will it try to change its ways.

7 But at*ᵈ* Adam they transgressed the
     covenant;
   there they dealt faithlessly with me.
8 Gilead is a city of evildoers,
   tracked with blood.
9 As robbers lie in wait*ᵉ* for someone,
   so the priests are banded together;*ᶠ*
  they murder on the road to Shechem,
   they commit a monstrous crime.
10 In the house of Israel I have seen a
     horrible thing;

a Gk: Meaning of Heb uncertain
b Cn: Heb *to a king who will contend*
c Gk Syr: Heb *your*   *d* Cn: Heb *like*
e Cn: Meaning of Heb uncertain
f Syr: Heb *are a company*

Ephraim's whoredom is there, Israel
is defiled.

11 For you also, O Judah, a harvest
is appointed.

6.4–11: Israel's disloyalty. God emphasizes Israel's lack of covenant* loyalty (v. 7), concluding with the image of prostitution (v. 10) that runs through the book. **6:** *Steadfast love* translates the Hebrew word "ḥesed," which describes loyalty to a relationship. Hosea's emphasis on right behavior rather than empty ritual is characteristic of prophetic thought (Am 5.21–24). **7–10:** The violent crime described here cannot be identified. *Adam* may refer to a city near the Jordan River (Josh 3.16). *Gilead*, located east of the Jordan, was the home of a band of men who assassinated Israel's king, Pekahiah (2 Kings 15.25). *Shechem*, Israel's first capital, was one of its most important cities.

When I would restore the fortunes of
my people,
7 ¹when I would heal Israel,
the corruption of Ephraim is revealed,
and the wicked deeds of Samaria;
for they deal falsely,
the thief breaks in,
and the bandits raid outside.
2 But they do not consider
that I remember all their wickedness.
Now their deeds surround them,
they are before my face.
3 By their wickedness they make the king
glad,
and the officials by their treachery.
4 They are all adulterers;
they are like a heated oven,
whose baker does not need to stir the
fire,
from the kneading of the dough until
it is leavened.
5 On the day of our king the officials
became sick with the heat of wine;
he stretched out his hand with
mockers.
6 For they are kindled*a* like an oven, their
heart burns within them;
all night their anger smolders;
in the morning it blazes like a flaming
fire.

7 All of them are hot as an oven,
and they devour their rulers.
All their kings have fallen;
none of them calls upon me.

7.1–16: Israel's political crimes. This speech focuses on the corruption of Israel's ruling elite by criticizing political intrigue at home (vv. 1–7) and alliances abroad (vv. 8–16). **1:** *Samaria* was Israel's capital through most of its history. **4–7:** Employing the image of a blazing oven, Hosea denounces the court officials responsible for numerous assassinations in Samaria. Four of the last six kings of Israel were killed in office.

8 Ephraim mixes himself with
the peoples;
Ephraim is a cake not turned.
9 Foreigners devour his strength,
but he does not know it;
gray hairs are sprinkled upon him,
but he does not know it.
10 Israel's pride testifies against*b* him;
yet they do not return to the LORD
their God,
or seek him, for all this.

11 Ephraim has become like a dove,
silly and without sense;
they call upon Egypt, they go
to Assyria.
12 As they go, I will cast my net over them;
I will bring them down like birds of
the air;
I will discipline them according to the
report made to their assembly.*c*
13 Woe to them, for they have strayed
from me!
Destruction to them, for they have
rebelled against me!
I would redeem them,
but they speak lies against me.

14 They do not cry to me from the heart,
but they wail upon their beds;
they gash themselves for grain
and wine;
they rebel against me.

a Gk Syr: Heb *brought near*   *b* Or *humbles*
c Meaning of Heb uncertain

Chart   The politics behind the prophet

King of Israel	Dates (BCE)	Path to Power	Historical Records
Jeroboam II	786–746	Son of Joash	2 Kings 14.23–29
Zechariah	746–745	Son of Jeroboam II	2 Kings 15.8–12
Shallum	745	Killed Zechariah	2 Kings 15.13–16
Menahem	745–738	Killed Shallum	2 Kings 15.17–22
Pekahiah	738–737	Son of Menahem	2 Kings 15.23–26
Pekah	737–732	Killed Pekahiah	2 Kings 15.25–27

15 It was I who trained and strengthened
    their arms,
  yet they plot evil against me.
16 They turn to that which does not profit;*a*
    they have become like a
      defective bow;
  their officials shall fall by the sword
    because of the rage of their tongue.
  So much for their babbling in the land
    of Egypt.

7.8–16. 11: Israel's foreign policy appears to have vacillated between alliances with *Egypt* and *Assyria*, the two great superpowers in whose sphere of influence Israel found itself. The history of Israel in 2 Kings mentions Israel's cooperation with Assyria (as explained in the comment on 5.13) and with Egypt (2 Kings 17.4) during Hosea's career. **14:** Gashing the body appears to be associated with earnest appeals to a deity, whether to Israel's God (Jer 41.5) or to Baal★ (1 Kings 18.28).

8 Set the trumpet to your lips!
  One like a vulture*b* is over the house
    of the LORD,
  because they have broken my covenant,
    and transgressed my law.
2 Israel cries to me,
  "My God, we—Israel—know you!"
3 Israel has spurned the good;
  the enemy shall pursue him.

4 They made kings, but not through me;
  they set up princes, but without my
    knowledge.
  With their silver and gold they made
    idols
  for their own destruction.
5 Your calf is rejected, O Samaria.
  My anger burns against them.
  How long will they be incapable of
    innocence?
6   For it is from Israel,
  an artisan made it;
    it is not God.
  The calf of Samaria
    shall be broken to pieces.*c*

8.1–9.9: Israel's religious crimes. Hosea criticizes Israel's religious practices, blaming Israel for worshipping images (8.4–6), participating in empty rituals (8.13), following other gods (9.1), and persecuting the prophets★ (9.7–8). **8.4:** By accusing Israel of making kings without God's knowledge, Hosea may refer to the installation of kings through violent palace uprisings rather than through proper religious and prophetic legitimation (7.1–7). **5–6:** The calf was a prominent religious image in Israel from its beginnings when its first king, Jeroboam I, set up calves in the religious sanctuaries at Bethel and Dan (1 Kings 12.28–30). They may have been considered pedestals or throne images for God, as were the cherubim★ in the Jerusalem Temple★ (1 Kings 6.23–28, 8.10–11), rather than images of God or idols. But both Hosea and Israel's historian (1 Kings 12.28) regard these calves as idols.

a Cn: Meaning of Heb uncertain   *b* Meaning of Heb uncertain   *c* Or *shall go up in flames*

The Canaanite God Baal

The god Baal,★ whom Hosea sees as the main rival of Israel's God, was a prominent Canaanite deity. He is known not only from the Bible, where he is presented in a negative light, but also from ancient texts found at Ugarit, a Canaanite city north of Israel where Baal was worshipped. In these texts, Baal is pictured with many of the same attributes as Israel's God. Baal is associated with the storm and with its accompanying phenomena—thunder, lightning, and rain—and is considered the source of the land's fertility, just as Israel's God is (Hosea 2.8–9, 21–23). Baal is described as riding the clouds, just as Israel's God does (Ps 68.4; Deut 33.26). And both deities appear to be associated with calf iconography. Thus, it is not hard to understand why Baal would have had particular appeal to the people of Israel and why Hosea is so insistent that Israel not replace its allegiance to its own God with devotion to Baal.

7 For they sow the wind,
     and they shall reap the whirlwind.
   The standing grain has no heads,
     it shall yield no meal;
   if it were to yield,
     foreigners would devour it.
8 Israel is swallowed up;
     now they are among the nations
     as a useless vessel.
9 For they have gone up to Assyria,
     a wild ass wandering alone;
   Ephraim has bargained for lovers.
10 Though they bargain with the
       nations,
   I will now gather them up.
   They shall soon writhe
     under the burden of kings
       and princes.

11 When Ephraim multiplied altars to
       expiate sin,
   they became to him altars for
       sinning.
12 Though I write for him the multitude of
       my instructions,
   they are regarded as a strange thing.
13 Though they offer choice sacrifices,*a*
     though they eat flesh,
     the LORD does not accept them.
   Now he will remember their iniquity,
     and punish their sins;
   they shall return to Egypt.

14 Israel has forgotten his Maker,
     and built palaces;
   and Judah has multiplied fortified
       cities;
   but I will send a fire upon his cities,
     and it shall devour his strongholds.

9 Do not rejoice, O Israel!
     Do not exult*b* as other nations do;
   for you have played the whore,
       departing from your God.
   You have loved a prostitute's pay
     on all threshing floors.
2 Threshing floor and wine vat shall not
       feed them,
   and the new wine shall fail them.
3 They shall not remain in the land of the
     LORD;
   but Ephraim shall return to Egypt,
   and in Assyria they shall eat unclean
       food.

4 They shall not pour drink offerings of
       wine to the LORD,
   and their sacrifices shall not please
       him.
   Such sacrifices shall be like mourners'
       bread;
   all who eat of it shall be defiled;

a Cn: Meaning of Heb uncertain   *b* Gk: Heb *To
exultation*

for their bread shall be for their hunger
      only;
  it shall not come to the house of the
      LORD.

8.7–9.4. 8.13: When Hosea describes Israel's punishment as a *return to Egypt,* he reverses the Exodus
(2.15; 9.3; Ex 1–15), in which God delivered Israel
from slavery. **9.1:** Since *threshing* floors* are sites for
worship (2 Sam 24.24–25), Hosea denounces Israel's
worship of Baal* there. The *prostitute's pay* to which
he refers is likely the grain harvest Israel attributed to
Baal rather than to God (2.8). **4:** *Mourners' bread* may
be translated literally in two ways: either "bread of sorrow," referring to bread eaten in exile (9.3), or "bread
of idolatry,*" referring to Israel's sacrifices that God
has rejected.

5 What will you do on the day of
      appointed festival,
    and on the day of the festival of the
      LORD?
6 For even if they escape destruction,
    Egypt shall gather them,
    Memphis shall bury them.
  Nettles shall possess their precious
      things of silver;[a]
    thorns shall be in their tents.

7 The days of punishment have come,
    the days of recompense have come;
    Israel cries,[b]
  "The prophet is a fool,
    the man of the spirit is mad!"
  Because of your great iniquity,
    your hostility is great.
8 The prophet is a sentinel for my God
      over Ephraim,
  yet a fowler's snare is on all his ways,
    and hostility in the house of his God.
9 They have deeply corrupted themselves
    as in the days of Gibeah;
  he will remember their iniquity,
    he will punish their sins.

9.5–9. 6: *Memphis* is a prominent Egyptian city
known for its pyramids, tombs, and burial grounds. **9:**
Hosea's reference here and in 10.9 to the corruption
in *Gibeah* may refer to the intertribal conflict and the
crimes that led to it (Judg 19–21).

10 Like grapes in the wilderness,
    I found Israel.
  Like the first fruit on the fig tree,
    in its first season,
    I saw your ancestors.
  But they came to Baal-peor,
    and consecrated themselves to a thing
      of shame,
    and became detestable like the thing
      they loved.
11 Ephraim's glory shall fly away like a
      bird—
    no birth, no pregnancy, no
      conception!
12 Even if they bring up children,
    I will bereave them until no one is
      left.
  Woe to them indeed
    when I depart from them!
13 Once I saw Ephraim as a young palm
      planted in a lovely meadow,[a]
    but now Ephraim must lead out his
      children for slaughter.
14 Give them, O LORD—
    what will you give?
  Give them a miscarrying womb
    and dry breasts.

15 Every evil of theirs began at Gilgal;
    there I came to hate them.
  Because of the wickedness of
      their deeds
    I will drive them out of my house.
  I will love them no more;
    all their officials are rebels.
16 Ephraim is stricken,
    their root is dried up,
    they shall bear no fruit.
  Even though they give birth,
    I will kill the cherished offspring of
      their womb.
17 Because they have not listened to him,
    my God will reject them;
    they shall become wanderers among
      the nations.

9.10–11.7: Images of a rebellious people. With a series of images taken from Israel's agricultural and fam-

a Meaning of Heb uncertain   b Cn Compare Gk: Heb
shall know

ily context—grapes and figs, a young palm tree, a vine, a female calf, a son—Hosea highlights Israel's past potential and present waywardness. **9.10–12:** The comparison of Israel to *grapes* and *figs* begins with images of fertility and a new harvest and concludes with images of infertility and barrenness. **10:** *Baal-peor* is a site east of the Jordan where the Israelites once worshipped Baal (Num 25.1–5). **13–17:** Israel is compared to a *young palm* with great potential (v. 13) whose roots dry up and whose fruit fails (v. 16). **15:** *Gilgal*, the site where Israel entered Canaan (Josh 4.19–20), is criticized by Hosea for its false worship (4.15). **17:** Hosea refers here and elsewhere (5.13–14; 10.14) to Israelites deported by conquering countries, a practice of the Assyrians described also by Israel's historian (2 Kings 15.29; 17.6).

10 Israel is a luxuriant vine
       that yields its fruit.
  The more his fruit increased
       the more altars he built;
  as his country improved,
       he improved his pillars.
2 Their heart is false;
       now they must bear their guilt.
  The LORD *a* will break down
       their altars,
  and destroy their pillars.

3 For now they will say:
       "We have no king,
  for we do not fear the LORD,
       and a king—what could he do for us?"
4 They utter mere words;
       with empty oaths they make
         covenants;
  so litigation springs up like poisonous
         weeds
  in the furrows of the field.
5 The inhabitants of Samaria tremble
       for the calf *b* of Beth-aven.
  Its people shall mourn for it,
       and its idolatrous priests shall wail *c*
         over it,
       over its glory that has departed from it.
6 The thing itself shall be carried to
         Assyria
  as tribute to the great king. *d*
  Ephraim shall be put to shame,
       and Israel shall be ashamed of his
         idol. *e*

7 Samaria's king shall perish
       like a chip on the face of the waters.
8 The high places of Aven, the sin
         of Israel,
       shall be destroyed.
  Thorn and thistle shall grow up
       on their altars.
  They shall say to the mountains, Cover
         us,
       and to the hills, Fall on us.

10.1–8: The comparison of Israel to a vine begins with images of bountiful fruit (v. 1) and concludes with images of thorns and thistles (v. 8). **1–2:** *Pillars* were common installations in Israelite sanctuaries (Gen 28.18–22). **3:** The people's words, *"We have no king,"* could anticipate the end of Israel and its kingship; or they could mean that Israel has rejected the rule of God, its divine king (1 Sam 8.4–8), as the following line seems to indicate. **5:** For Hosea's view of Israel's calves, compare 13.2 and 8.5–6 (see comment at 8.5–6). **8:** *The high places* of Aven* (literally, "worthlessness") are the sites of Israel's false worship (4.13).

9 Since the days of Gibeah you have
         sinned, O Israel;
       there they have continued.
  Shall not war overtake them in
         Gibeah?
10 I will come *f* against the wayward
         people to punish them;
  and nations shall be gathered against
         them
  when they are punished *g* for their
         double iniquity.

11 Ephraim was a trained heifer
       that loved to thresh,
  and I spared her fair neck;
  but I will make Ephraim break the
         ground;
       Judah must plow;
  Jacob must harrow for himself.
12 Sow for yourselves righteousness;
       reap steadfast love;
  break up your fallow ground;

a Heb *he*   *b* Gk Syr: Heb *calves*   *c* Cn: Heb *exult*
d Cn: Heb *to a king who will contend*   *e* Cn: Heb
counsel   *f* Cn Compare Gk: Heb *In my desire*
g Gk: Heb *bound*

for it is time to seek the LORD,
    that he may come and rain
        righteousness upon you.

13 You have plowed wickedness,
        you have reaped injustice,
        you have eaten the fruit of lies.
    Because you have trusted in
            your power
        and in the multitude of your
            warriors,
14 therefore the tumult of war shall rise
        against your people,
    and all your fortresses shall
            be destroyed,
    as Shalman destroyed Beth-arbel on the
            day of battle
        when mothers were dashed in pieces
            with their children.
15 Thus it shall be done to you, O Bethel,
        because of your great wickedness.
    At dawn the king of Israel
        shall be utterly cut off.

11 When Israel was a child, I loved him,
        and out of Egypt I called my son.
2 The more I[a] called them,
        the more they went from me;[b]
    they kept sacrificing to the Baals,
        and offering incense to idols.

3 Yet it was I who taught Ephraim to
            walk,
        I took them up in my[c] arms;
    but they did not know that I healed
            them.
4 I led them with cords of human
            kindness,
        with bands of love.
    I was to them like those
        who lift infants to their cheeks.[d]
    I bent down to them and fed them.

5 They shall return to the land of Egypt,
        and Assyria shall be their king,
    because they have refused to return
            to me.
6 The sword rages in their cities,
        it consumes their oracle-priests,
        and devours because of their
            schemes.

7 My people are bent on turning away
            from me.
    To the Most High they call,
        but he does not raise them up at all.[e]

10.9–11.7. 10.9–15: Israel is compared to a female calf
(v. 11), once obedient but now plowing wickedness.
9: For Hosea's criticism of *Gibeah*, see 9.9. **14:** Neither
Shalman nor *Beth-arbel* can be positively identified,
though some have suggested that *Shalman* is a shortened form of Shalmaneser V, who imprisoned Israel's
last king, Hoshea, and laid siege to Samaria (2 Kings
17.3–5). **15:** *Bethel* was one of Israel's major religious
sanctuaries. **11.1–7:** Israel is compared to a son who,
though loved and raised with kindness, is stubborn
and rebellious.

8 How can I give you up, Ephraim?
        How can I hand you over, O Israel?
    How can I make you like Admah?
        How can I treat you like Zeboiim?
    My heart recoils within me;
        my compassion grows warm
            and tender.
9 I will not execute my fierce anger;
        I will not again destroy Ephraim;
    for I am God and no mortal,
        the Holy One in your midst,
        and I will not come in wrath.[e]

10 They shall go after the LORD,
        who roars like a lion;
    when he roars,
        his children shall come trembling
            from the west.
11 They shall come trembling like birds
            from Egypt,
        and like doves from the land of
            Assyria;
    and I will return them to their homes,
        says the LORD.

11.8–11: A promise of restoration. The tone shifts
from judgment to salvation: God shows compassion
for Israel and promises to return its people to their
homes. **8:** *Admah* and *Zeboiim* are cities which, like
Sodom and Gomorrah, symbolize wickedness (Deut

---

a Gk: Heb *they*   b Gk: Heb *them*   c Gk Syr Vg:
Heb *his*   d Or *who ease the yoke on their jaws*
e Meaning of Heb uncertain

29.23). **10:** This image of Israel returning *trembling from the west* assumes an exilic context and suggests that vv. 10–11 may have been added by a later Judean editor.

~~~~~~~~~~~~~~~~~~~~~~~~~~~~~~

12^a Ephraim has surrounded me with lies,
    and the house of Israel with deceit;
but Judah still walks^b with God,
    and is faithful to the Holy One.^c

12 Ephraim herds the wind,
    and pursues the east wind all day
        long;
they multiply falsehood and violence;
    they make a treaty with Assyria,
    and oil is carried to Egypt.

2 The LORD has an indictment against
        Judah,
    and will punish Jacob according to his
        ways,
    and repay him according to his deeds.
3 In the womb he tried to supplant his
        brother,
    and in his manhood he strove with
        God.
4 He strove with the angel and prevailed,
    he wept and sought his favor;
    he met him at Bethel,
    and there he spoke with him.^c
5 The LORD the God of hosts,
    the LORD is his name!
6 But as for you, return to your God,
    hold fast to love and justice,
    and wait continually for your God.

7 A trader, in whose hands are false
        balances,
    he loves to oppress.
8 Ephraim has said, "Ah, I am rich,
    I have gained wealth for myself;
in all of my gain
    no offense has been found in me
    that would be sin."^d
9 I am the LORD your God
    from the land of Egypt;
I will make you live in tents again,
    as in the days of the appointed
        festival.

God's acts of salvation and Israel's acts of rebellion. **12.3a:** Hosea describes the birth of Israel's ancestor Jacob (later renamed Israel) who struggled with *his brother* Esau in their mother's womb (Gen 25.21–26). **3b–4a:** Israel's ancestor Jacob *strove with God* at the Jabbok River when he returned home to meet Esau (Gen 32.22–32). **4b:** God appeared to Israel's ancestor Jacob at *Bethel* in a dream (Gen 28.10–22). **9:** Hosea recalls Israel's deliverance from slavery in *Egypt* and its journey through the wilderness.

~~~~~~~~~~~~~~~~~~~~~~~~~~~~~~

10 I spoke to the prophets;
    it was I who multiplied visions,
    and through the prophets I will bring
        destruction.
11 In Gilead^e there is iniquity,
    they shall surely come to nothing.
In Gilgal they sacrifice bulls,
    so their altars shall be like
        stone heaps
    on the furrows of the field.
12 Jacob fled to the land of Aram,
    there Israel served for a wife,
    and for a wife he guarded sheep.^f
13 By a prophet the LORD brought Israel
        up from Egypt,
    and by a prophet he was guarded.
14 Ephraim has given bitter offense,
    so his Lord will bring his crimes down
        on him
    and pay him back for his insults.

13 When Ephraim spoke, there was
        trembling;
    he was exalted in Israel;
    but he incurred guilt through Baal
        and died.
2 And now they keep on sinning
    and make a cast image for
        themselves,
    idols of silver made according to their
        understanding,
    all of them the work of artisans.
"Sacrifice to these," they say.^g
    People are kissing calves!
3 Therefore they shall be like the morning
        mist
    or like the dew that goes away early,

---

a Ch 12.1 in Heb   b Heb *roams or rules*   c Gk Syr: Heb *us*   d Meaning of Heb uncertain   e Compare Syr: Heb *Gilead*   f Heb lacks *sheep*   g Cn Compare Gk: Heb *To these they say sacrifices of people*

11.12–13.16: The history of a rebellious people. Hosea recalls major events in Israel's past to illustrate

like chaff that swirls from the threshing
floor
or like smoke from a window.

4 Yet I have been the LORD your God
ever since the land of Egypt;
you know no God but me,
and besides me there is no savior.
5 It was I who fed[a] you in the
wilderness,
in the land of drought.
6 When I fed[b] them, they were satisfied;
they were satisfied, and their heart
was proud;
therefore they forgot me.
7 So I will become like a lion to them,
like a leopard I will lurk beside the
way.
8 I will fall upon them like a bear robbed
of her cubs,
and will tear open the covering
of their heart;
there I will devour them like a lion,
as a wild animal would mangle them.

9 I will destroy you, O Israel;
who can help you?[c]
10 Where now is[d] your king, that he may
save you?
Where in all your cities are your rulers,
of whom you said,
"Give me a king and rulers"?
11 I gave you a king in my anger,
and I took him away in my wrath.

12 Ephraim's iniquity is bound up;
his sin is kept in store.
13 The pangs of childbirth come for him,
but he is an unwise son;
for at the proper time he does not
present himself
at the mouth of the womb.

14 Shall I ransom them from the power of
Sheol?
Shall I redeem them from Death?
O Death, where are[e] your plagues?
O Sheol, where is[e] your destruction?
Compassion is hidden from my eyes.

15 Although he may flourish among
rushes,[f]
the east wind shall come, a blast from
the LORD,
rising from the wilderness;
and his fountain shall dry up,
his spring shall be parched.
It shall strip his treasury
of every precious thing.
16[g] Samaria shall bear her guilt,
because she has rebelled against her
God;
they shall fall by the sword,
their little ones shall be dashed in
pieces,
and their pregnant women
ripped open.

12.10–13.16. 12.11: For Hosea's view of *Gilead* and
Gilgal, compare 4.15, 6.8. 12: *The land of Aram* was
the territory to which Israel's ancestor Jacob fled from
his brother Esau's anger (Gen 27.41–45; 29.1–30). 13:
The prophet to whom Hosea refers is Moses, who led
Israel out of Egypt (Deut 34.10–12). 13.4: Hosea's idea
that Israel learned to know its God in Egypt appears to
be based on the tradition that the name of God was
revealed to Israel there (Ex 3.13–15). 5–6: After delivering Israel from Egypt, God fed them manna in the
wilderness (Num 11.7–9). 11: Hosea may share the
viewpoint of the author of 1 Sam 8.6–8, who saw Israel's request for a king as a rejection of God's rule.
14: *Sheol** was a shadowy realm inhabited by the
dead (Ps 6.5). 16: Hosea anticipates Israel's end with
a vivid image of the fall of its capital, *Samaria*.

14 Return, O Israel, to the LORD your
God,
for you have stumbled because of
your iniquity.
2 Take words with you
and return to the LORD;
say to him,
"Take away all guilt;
accept that which is good,
and we will offer
the fruit[h] of our lips.

a Gk Syr: Heb *knew*   b Cn: Heb *according to their
pasture*   c Gk Syr: Heb *for in me is your help*
d Gk Syr Vg: Heb *I will be*   e Gk Syr: Heb *I will be*
f Or *among brothers*   g Ch 14.1 in Heb   h Gk Syr:
Heb *bulls*

3 Assyria shall not save us;
    we will not ride upon horses;
    we will say no more, 'Our God,'
      to the work of our hands.
    In you the orphan finds mercy."

14.1–3: A call for repentance. Hosea urges Israel to turn from reliance on other nations to reliance on its God. **3:** To *ride upon horses* is to trust military strength more than God's protection.

4 I will heal their disloyalty;
    I will love them freely,
    for my anger has turned from them.
5 I will be like the dew to Israel;
    he shall blossom like the lily,
    he shall strike root like the forests of
      Lebanon.[a]
6 His shoots shall spread out;
    his beauty shall be like the olive tree,
    and his fragrance like that of
      Lebanon.
7 They shall again live beneath
      my[b] shadow,
    they shall flourish as a garden;[c]
    they shall blossom like the vine,

their fragrance shall be like the wine
      of Lebanon.

8 O Ephraim, what have I[d] to do with
      idols?
    It is I who answer and look after you.[e]
  I am like an evergreen cypress;
    your faithfulness[f] comes from me.
9 Those who are wise understand these
      things;
    those who are discerning know them.
  For the ways of the LORD are right,
    and the upright walk in them,
    but transgressors stumble in them.

14.4–9: A second promise of restoration. In the spirit of 11.8–11, God promises to restore Israel to faithfulness and well-being. **5:** The *forests of Lebanon* were legendary* for their magnificence (Ps 104.16). **9:** The concluding verse in Hosea shares the vocabulary and perspective of the book of Proverbs (10.29) and is likely a conclusion added by Israel's sages.

a Cn: Heb *like Lebanon*   b Heb *his*   c Cn: Heb *they shall grow grain*   d Or *What more has Ephraim*   e Heb *him*   f Heb *your fruit*

JOEL

Introduction

Joel is unique among the prophets★ in his focus on a natural catastrophe, a widespread and destructive locust plague. Interpreting the plague as divine judgment on Jerusalem, the prophet calls on the people to mourn their predicament (1.5–20) and tells the priests to declare a solemn assembly to repent and ask for God's forgiveness (2.1–17). Then he predicts that God will restore the land to its former prosperity (2.18–27). Two concluding sections that do not mention the locusts, a prediction of the outpouring of God's spirit (2.28–32) and of the political renewal of Jerusalem (3.1–21), are either Joel's visions of the future set in motion by the plague or additions to Joel by a later editor.

No clear historical references in chs. 1–2 connect this plague to a precise period in Jerusalem's history. Such plagues were not uncommon (Am 7.1–3), and understanding the seriousness of these ancient plagues is more important for reading Joel than knowing the exact date of this particular plague. Because the vision of Jerusalem's political renewal in ch. 3 was composed after Jerusalem was destroyed and its citizens exiled, many believe all of Joel was written at this time, perhaps as late as the fourth or fifth centuries BCE. Editors placed Joel between Hosea and Amos, two eighth-century prophets, either because a tradition held that the plague happened in this period or because parts of Joel are so much like Amos (see Joel 3.16a; Amos 1.2a).

READING GUIDE

To appreciate the danger of the crisis Joel faced, the modern reader must recover a sense of the terrible destructiveness of a locust infestation for a pre-industrial agricultural society that lives year to year by its harvests. The key issue for reading the book as a whole is deciding whether the locust plague in 1.1–2.27 is the prelude to the religious and political renewal predicted in 2.28–3.21 or whether these two parts of Joel arise from different experiences in Jerusalem's history.

1 The word of the LORD that came to Joel son of Pethuel:

2 Hear this, O elders,
    give ear, all inhabitants of the land!
Has such a thing happened in
        your days,
    or in the days of your ancestors?
3 Tell your children of it,
    and let your children tell their
        children,
    and their children another generation.

4 What the cutting locust left,
    the swarming locust has eaten.

What the swarming locust left,
    the hopping locust has eaten,
and what the hopping locust left,
    the destroying locust has eaten.

1.1–4: The locust plague. Joel introduces the locust plague as one unparalleled in the living memory of his people (compare 2.2). **4:** The four terms for locust here and in 2.25 may refer to stages in the growth of the locust. The meanings of the Hebrew terms are unclear, and the translations, *cutting locust,* etc., are only suggestions.

---

5 Wake up, you drunkards, and weep;
    and wail, all you wine-drinkers,

The Desert Locust

The desert locust, known to scientists as "Schistocerca americana, subspecies gregaria," is a distant cousin of the American grasshopper. It lives and breeds in the great desert stretching from the Sahara in Africa to the Arabian Peninsula, including the Sinai and Judean deserts. In the right conditions, it multiplies rapidly, crowds into dense swarms, and sweeps into neighboring fertile areas, where it eats its own weight in green food each day. A swarm of desert locusts in Somaliland in 1957 was estimated to include 16 billion locusts and to weigh 50,000 tons. The desert locust's threat to Middle Eastern societies is recorded in the earliest human records and continues into the present, where it is monitored and combated by the United Nations Food and Agriculture Organization's Emergency Center for Locust Operations.

over the sweet wine,
  for it is cut off from your mouth.
6 For a nation has invaded my land,
  powerful and innumerable;
its teeth are lions' teeth,
  and it has the fangs of a lioness.
7 It has laid waste my vines,
  and splintered my fig trees;
it has stripped off their bark and thrown
  it down;
  their branches have turned white.

8 Lament like a virgin dressed in
  sackcloth
  for the husband of her youth.
9 The grain offering and the drink
    offering are cut off
  from the house of the LORD.
The priests mourn,
  the ministers of the LORD.
10 The fields are devastated,
  the ground mourns;
for the grain is destroyed,
  the wine dries up,
  the oil fails.

11 Be dismayed, you farmers,
  wail, you vinedressers,
over the wheat and the barley;
  for the crops of the field are ruined.
12 The vine withers,
  the fig tree droops.
Pomegranate, palm, and apple—
  all the trees of the field are dried up;

surely, joy withers away
  among the people.

13 Put on sackcloth and lament,
  you priests;
wail, you ministers of the altar.
Come, pass the night in sackcloth,
  you ministers of my God!
Grain offering and drink offering
  are withheld from the house of
  your God.

14 Sanctify a fast,
  call a solemn assembly.
Gather the elders
  and all the inhabitants of the land
to the house of the LORD your God,
  and cry out to the LORD.

15 Alas for the day!
For the day of the LORD is near,
  and as destruction from the Almighty[a]
  it comes.
16 Is not the food cut off
  before our eyes,
joy and gladness
  from the house of our God?

17 The seed shrivels under the clods,[b]
  the storehouses are desolate;

a Traditional rendering of Heb Shaddai   b Meaning of Heb uncertain

the granaries are ruined
  because the grain has failed.
18 How the animals groan!
  The herds of cattle wander about
because there is no pasture for them;
  even the flocks of sheep are
    dazed.*a*

19 To you, O LORD, I cry.
  For fire has devoured
    the pastures of the wilderness,
  and flames have burned
    all the trees of the field.
20 Even the wild animals cry to you
  because the watercourses are
    dried up,
  and fire has devoured
    the pastures of the wilderness.

1.5–20: The call to mourning. Joel summons three groups into mourning: consumers of wine (vv. 5–10), farmers (vv. 11–12), and priests (vv. 13–18). Then he cries out to God himself (vv. 19–20). **6:** *A nation has invaded my land* begins an extended metaphor,* by which Joel compares the incoming locust swarms to an invading army (compare 2.2, 4–11, 25). **7:** *Their branches have turned white:* In this and other vivid details of decimated vegetation, Joel's description matches that of eyewitnesses of Jerusalem's last great locust plague in 1915. **15:** *The day of the LORD* is a prophetic theme that reappears throughout Joel (2.1, 11, 31; 3.14). **19:** Joel uses the metaphor of *fire* together with the metaphor of an army for the devouring locust (compare 2.3).

~~~~~~~~~~~~~~~~~~~~~~

2 Blow the trumpet in Zion;
  sound the alarm on my holy
    mountain!
Let all the inhabitants of the land
    tremble,
  for the day of the LORD is coming,
    it is near—
2 a day of darkness and gloom,
  a day of clouds and thick
    darkness!
Like blackness spread upon the
    mountains
  a great and powerful army comes;
their like has never been from of old,
  nor will be again after them
    in ages to come.

3 Fire devours in front of them,
  and behind them a flame burns.
Before them the land is like the garden
    of Eden,
  but after them a desolate wilderness,
    and nothing escapes them.

4 They have the appearance of horses,
  and like war-horses they charge.
5 As with the rumbling of chariots,
  they leap on the tops of the
    mountains,
like the crackling of a flame of fire
  devouring the stubble,
like a powerful army
  drawn up for battle.

6 Before them peoples are in anguish,
  all faces grow pale.*b*
7 Like warriors they charge,
  like soldiers they scale the wall.
Each keeps to its own course,
  they do not swerve from*c* their paths.
8 They do not jostle one another,
  each keeps to its own track;
they burst through the weapons
  and are not halted.
9 They leap upon the city,
  they run upon the walls;
they climb up into the houses,
  they enter through the windows like
    a thief.
10 The earth quakes before them,
  the heavens tremble.
The sun and the moon are darkened,
  and the stars withdraw their shining.
11 The LORD utters his voice
  at the head of his army;
how vast is his host!
  Numberless are those who obey his
    command.
Truly the day of the LORD is great;
  terrible indeed—who can endure it?

12 Yet even now, says the LORD,
  return to me with all your heart,

a Compare Gk Syr Vg: Meaning of Heb uncertain
b Meaning of Heb uncertain   *c* Gk Syr Vg: Heb *they do not take a pledge along*

with fasting, with weeping, and with
  mourning;
13 rend your hearts and not
    your clothing.
  Return to the LORD, your God,
    for he is gracious and merciful,
    slow to anger, and abounding in
      steadfast love,
    and relents from punishing.
14 Who knows whether he will not turn
    and relent,
    and leave a blessing behind him,
  a grain offering and a drink offering
    for the LORD, your God?

15 Blow the trumpet in Zion;
    sanctify a fast;
  call a solemn assembly;
16   gather the people.
  Sanctify the congregation;
    assemble the aged;
  gather the children,
    even infants at the breast.
  Let the bridegroom leave his room,
    and the bride her canopy.
17 Between the vestibule and the altar
    let the priests, the ministers of the
      LORD, weep.
  Let them say, "Spare your people,
    O LORD,
    and do not make your heritage a
      mockery,
    a byword among the nations.
  Why should it be said among the
    peoples,
  'Where is their God?' "

2.1–17: The call to repentance. 1–3: Turning again
to the priests whom he had just addressed (1.13–18),
Joel directs them to *blow the trumpet in Zion** (a synonym for Jerusalem), assembling all the people to ask
for God's forgiveness (vv. 15–17). **2**: *Darkness* and
clouds are traditional images associated with the day
of the LORD, but they may also refer here to the dense
swarms of locusts that can obscure the sun. **4–11**: Joel
develops in detail his comparison of the locust swarms
with an invading army. **13**: *Rend your hearts and not
your clothing:* While not abandoning ritual—he directs the priests to lead the people in a liturgy* of repentance—Joel sees genuine religion as a matter of

inner renewal, as is common among the prophets. Like
other prophets, Joel regards disasters like this as acts
of divine judgment that require repentance, but unlike
them, he does not describe the particular sins that he
believes have brought on this punishment. *Gracious
and merciful . . .* : This is an adaptation of a traditional
description of God (Ex 34.6–7; Jon 4.2).

18 Then the LORD became jealous for his
    land,
    and had pity on his people.
19 In response to his people the LORD said:
  I am sending you
    grain, wine, and oil,
    and you will be satisfied;
  and I will no more make you
    a mockery among the nations.
20 I will remove the northern army far
    from you,
    and drive it into a parched and
      desolate land,
  its front into the eastern sea,
    and its rear into the western sea;
  its stench and foul smell will rise up.
    Surely he has done great things!

21 Do not fear, O soil;
    be glad and rejoice,
    for the LORD has done great things!
22 Do not fear, you animals of the field,
    for the pastures of the wilderness are
      green;
  the tree bears its fruit,
    the fig tree and vine give their full
      yield.

23 O children of Zion, be glad
    and rejoice in the LORD your God;
  for he has given the early rain*a* for your
    vindication,
  he has poured down for you abundant
    rain,
    the early and the later rain, as before.
24 The threshing floors shall be full
    of grain,
  the vats shall overflow with wine
    and oil.

a Meaning of Heb uncertain

The Day of the LORD

Appearing five times in Joel (1.15; 2.1, 11, 31; 3.14), this expression is used in the Bible for a decisive divine act in human affairs. In its earliest occurrence, Amos uses it to describe an act of God's judgment on Israel (5.18–20). But since Amos implies that his audience believed this expression referred to an act of God's salvation, scholars think *the day of the LORD* originally had a positive meaning, describing God's victory on Israel's behalf. In some cases, in fact, this phrase is used for God's judgment on the nations and restoration of Judah (Ob 15–21; Zech 14.1–9). Scholars disagree whether *the day of the LORD* is used both ways in Joel—for judgment in 1.15; 2.1, 11 and for salvation in 2.31; 3.14—or whether all uses point toward the final salvation described in ch. 3.

25 I will repay you for the years
    that the swarming locust has eaten,
  the hopper, the destroyer, and the
      cutter,
    my great army, which I sent against
        you.
26 You shall eat in plenty and be
      satisfied,
  and praise the name of the LORD
      your God,
  who has dealt wondrously with you.
And my people shall never again be put
    to shame.
27 You shall know that I am in the midst
      of Israel,
  and that I, the LORD, am your God
      and there is no other.
And my people shall never again be put
    to shame.

your sons and your daughters shall
    prophesy,
  your old men shall dream dreams,
  and your young men shall see visions.
29 Even on the male and female slaves,
    in those days, I will pour out
      my spirit.

30 I will show portents in the heavens and on the earth, blood and fire and columns of smoke. ³¹The sun shall be turned to darkness, and the moon to blood, before the great and terrible day of the LORD comes. ³²Then everyone who calls on the name of the LORD shall be saved; for in Mount Zion and in Jerusalem there shall be those who escape, as the LORD has said, and among the survivors shall be those whom the LORD calls.

2.18–27: God's renewal of the land. Joel anticipates new harvests to replace those the locusts have destroyed. Each crop ruined in 1.1–2.17 is to be restored. **20:** *The northern army* in Hebrew is simply "the northerner," used for the locust here because it is a traditional designation of the enemy, since enemies invaded from the north, or because the locusts themselves came in from the north, as did the first swarms in the 1915 plague in Jerusalem. The *eastern sea* is the Dead Sea and the *western sea* is the Mediterranean Sea.

2.28–32: The outpouring of God's spirit. In the Hebrew Bible, these verses constitute a new chapter: 3.1–5. **28–29:** In the future, the prophetic gift will be spread among all people. **30–32:** *The day of the LORD* is pictured with traditional images of darkness as a day of judgment on Jerusalem, which only a few will survive. Whether these few are those who survived the locusts (which are not mentioned here) or the survivors of the destruction of Jerusalem in 586 BCE is not stated.

28ᵃ Then afterward
    I will pour out my spirit on all flesh;

3 ᵇFor then, in those days and at that time, when I restore the fortunes of Judah and Jerusalem, ²I will gather all the nations and

a Ch 3.1 in Heb   *b* Ch 4.1 in Heb

bring them down to the valley of Jehoshaphat, and I will enter into judgment with them there, on account of my people and my heritage Israel, because they have scattered them among the nations. They have divided my land, ³and cast lots for my people, and traded boys for prostitutes, and sold girls for wine, and drunk it down.

4 What are you to me, O Tyre and Sidon, and all the regions of Philistia? Are you paying me back for something? If you are paying me back, I will turn your deeds back upon your own heads swiftly and speedily. ⁵For you have taken my silver and my gold, and have carried my rich treasures into your temples.ᵃ ⁶You have sold the people of Judah and Jerusalem to the Greeks, removing them far from their own border. ⁷But now I will rouse them to leave the places to which you have sold them, and I will turn your deeds back upon your own heads. ⁸I will sell your sons and your daughters into the hand of the people of Judah, and they will sell them to the Sabeans, to a nation far away; for the LORD has spoken.

9 Proclaim this among the nations:
Prepare war,ᵇ
   stir up the warriors.
Let all the soldiers draw near,
   let them come up.
¹⁰ Beat your plowshares into swords,
   and your pruning hooks into spears;
   let the weakling say, "I am a warrior."

¹¹ Come quickly,ᶜ
   all you nations all around,
   gather yourselves there.
Bring down your warriors, O LORD.
¹² Let the nations rouse themselves,
   and come up to the valley of
      Jehoshaphat;
for there I will sit to judge
   all the neighboring nations.

¹³ Put in the sickle,
   for the harvest is ripe.
Go in, tread,
   for the wine press is full.
The vats overflow,
   for their wickedness is great.

¹⁴ Multitudes, multitudes,
   in the valley of decision!
For the day of the LORD is near
   in the valley of decision.
¹⁵ The sun and the moon are darkened,
   and the stars withdraw their shining.

¹⁶ The LORD roars from Zion,
   and utters his voice from Jerusalem,
   and the heavens and the earth shake.
But the LORD is a refuge for his
     people,
   a stronghold for the people of Israel.

¹⁷ So you shall know that I, the LORD
     your God,
   dwell in Zion, my holy mountain.
And Jerusalem shall be holy,
   and strangers shall never again pass
     through it.

¹⁸ In that day
the mountains shall drip sweet wine,
   the hills shall flow with milk,
and all the stream beds of Judah
   shall flow with water;
a fountain shall come forth from the
     house of the LORD
   and water the Wadi Shittim.

¹⁹ Egypt shall become a desolation
   and Edom a desolate wilderness,
because of the violence done to the
     people of Judah,
   in whose land they have shed
     innocent blood.
²⁰ But Judah shall be inhabited forever,
   and Jerusalem to all generations.
²¹ I will avenge their blood, and I will not
     clear the guilty,ᵈ
   for the LORD dwells in Zion.

3.1–21: Judgment on the nations and the restoration of Jerusalem. In the Hebrew Bible, these verses are 4.1–21. This poem does not mention the locusts, but takes as its backdrop the fall of Jerusalem in 586 BCE and the exile of its people (vv. 2, 5). It follows the

---

a Or *palaces*   *b* Heb *sanctify war*   *c* Meaning of Heb uncertain   *d* Gk Syr: Heb *I will hold innocent their blood that I have not held innocent* traditional structure of hymns, such as Ex 15.1–18 and Zech 14.1–21, which celebrate the victory of God the warrior over Israel's enemies. The threat to divine rule (vv. 1–8) brings God into a battle (vv. 9–14) that shakes the cosmos (vv. 15–16). Victorious, God is enthroned on his holy mountain (v. 17), making the world fertile (v. 18) and saving his people (vv. 19–21). **2:** *Jehoshaphat* is a symbolic—rather than an actual, geographical—place, meaning "the LORD has judged." **4:** *Tyre* and *Sidon,* cities on the Mediterra-nean coast north of Judah, and *Philistia* to the south are accused of participating in Judah's destruction and deporting its people. **8:** The *Sabeans* may be inhabitants of southern Arabia. **10:** This verse reverses the image of peace in Isa 2.4 and Mic 4.3. **19:** *Egypt,* sometimes ally and sometimes enemy, and *Edom,* elsewhere accused of participating in Jerusalem's destruction (Ob 8–14), are both counted here among the nations judged when Jerusalem is restored.

AMOS

Introduction

Amos is Israel's prophet* of social justice, proclaiming that true religion consists not just of ritual observances but in a moral life based on fair and equitable treatment of all members of society, powerful and powerless alike. This concern for justice lies at the heart of Israel's prophetic movement, but no other prophet expresses it with more passion and substance. Amos demands justice in all areas of society—political (6.10), judicial (5.10, 12), and economic (8.4–6)—and mercilessly attacks Israel's elite for their abuse of power (4.1, 6.1). He believes Israel's religious assemblies, sacred music, and elaborate sacrifices are pointless without principled and ethical behavior in daily affairs (5.21–24). And he regards the demise of Israelite society as the inevitable outcome of its internal corruption and injustices (5.6–7). The power of social justice in the imagination of Western society derives in large part from Israel's prophets and from Amos's passionate appeals in particular.

The book of Amos contains one brief narrative* about an event in his career (7.10–17) and several reports of his visions (7.1–9; 8.1–3; 9.1–4), but the book is primarily made up of short judgment speeches with a simple two-part structure: an indictment listing Israel's sins, and a sentence of judgment prescribing God's punishment for these sins. This structure is clearly visible, for example, in Amos's speech to the priest Amaziah at Bethel, in which Amos indicts Amaziah for restricting prophetic speech (7.16) and announces the divine sentence punishing Amaziah and his family (7.17). While judgment speeches against Israel predominate, the book of Amos actually begins with a series of judgment speeches, with this same two-part structure, directed against Israel's neighbors (1.3–2.5).

Although Amos reports his visions in the first person (8.1–3), the narrative about Amos's career (7.10–17) and the book's title (1.1) describe Amos in the third person, indicating that Amos's speeches were collected and passed down by his followers. Some contend that almost everything in Amos should be traced back to the prophet himself, while others think that Amos's followers have edited the collection of his speeches and added to them. Such additions are identified in particular with those texts that appear to update Amos's speeches against the northern kingdom of Israel with speeches that reflect the perspective of the southern kingdom of Judah, such as those that name Jerusalem and Judah (1.2; 2.4–5) and that predict the fall of the northern sanctuary of Bethel (3.13–14), which rivaled Judah's sanctuary in Jerusalem. Almost all scholars maintain that the oracle* of salvation for the royal family of David with which the book concludes (9.11–15) is a later addition, since it contrasts so strongly with the atmosphere of judgment that pervades the rest of the book.

Amos preached against the northern kingdom during the reign of Jeroboam II (1.1, 7.11) and is the first of Israel's prophets to have his speeches preserved in a collection bearing his name. Jeroboam's long 41-year reign (786–746 BCE) is presented in the accounts of Israel's history as a time of strength and expansion for Israel (2 Kings 14.23–29), a favorable portrait confirmed by Amos's repeated references to the prodigious wealth in its capital, Samaria (3.15; 5.11; 6.1, 4–6). Indeed, archaeologists have recovered from the ancient city of Samaria in this period examples of the fine ivory carvings of which Amos spoke (3.15; 6.4). During such an era of political and economic stability and growth, Amos's harsh criticism of Israelite society and his expectation that its injustices would soon bring it down must have seemed exaggerated and outlandish to his audience (5.18; 6.6). A mere 25 years after Jeroboam's death, however, Amos's predictions came true when Samaria fell to Assyrian armies.

READING GUIDE

Amos must be read as an anthology of short, independent speeches rather than as a book with a single thesis developed from beginning to end. Since his editors did not mark the beginnings and ends of these speeches, the reader must make an effort to identify them, keeping in mind the typical two-part speech form: indictment of sins followed by announcement of punishment. The reader must also be aware that Amos (and other prophets) composed speeches in a poetic form based on verse units of two parallel lines: "But let justice roll down like waters,/ and righteousness like an ever-flowing stream" (5.24). Keeping these two features of Amos's work in mind can help make sense of a book that might otherwise appear disorganized and repetitious.

1 The words of Amos, who was among the shepherds of Tekoa, which he saw concerning Israel in the days of King Uzziah of Judah and in the days of King Jeroboam son of Joash of Israel, two years*a* before the earthquake.
2 And he said:
The LORD roars from Zion,
 and utters his voice from Jerusalem;
the pastures of the shepherds wither,
 and the top of Carmel dries up.

1.1–2: Introduction. Prophetic books customarily begin with data about their authors. **1:** Amos preached during the reigns of *King Uzziah of Judah* (783–742 BCE) and *King Jeroboam of Israel* (786–746), and he owned sheep and orchards (7.14). Though from *Tekoa*, a town in Judah, Amos preached primarily to Judah's northern neighbor, Israel (2.6). **2:** *Jerusalem* and *Zion** are both names of the capital city of Judah. *Carmel* is a mountain range near the Mediterranean coast in Israel.

---

3 Thus says the LORD:
For three transgressions of Damascus,
 and for four, I will not revoke the
  punishment;*b*
because they have threshed Gilead
 with threshing sledges of iron.
4 So I will send a fire on the house
  of Hazael,
 and it shall devour the strongholds of
  Ben-hadad.

5 I will break the gate bars of Damascus,
 and cut off the inhabitants from the
  Valley of Aven,
 and the one who holds the scepter from
  Beth-eden;
 and the people of Aram shall go into
  exile to Kir,
          says the LORD.

6 Thus says the LORD:
For three transgressions of Gaza,
 and for four, I will not revoke the
  punishment;*b*
because they carried into exile entire
  communities,
 to hand them over to Edom.
7 So I will send a fire on the wall
  of Gaza,
 fire that shall devour its strongholds.
8 I will cut off the inhabitants from
  Ashdod,
 and the one who holds the scepter
  from Ashkelon;
I will turn my hand against Ekron,
 and the remnant of the Philistines
  shall perish,
          says the Lord GOD.

1.3–2.5: Judgments on Israel's neighbors. In typical two-part judgment speeches, containing indictments

a Or during two years   b Heb cause it to return

and sentences, Amos announces divine judgment on seven of Israel's closest neighbors (see map on page 1182). The indictments in each case involve acts of brutality against neighboring peoples. The repetition of *for three transgressions . . . and for four* in each indictment is a poetic convention meaning simply "several." The image of *fire* in each sentence predicts the violent destruction of the cities indicted. The phrase *says the* LORD, which begins and ends these speeches, identifies them as divine oracles* and the prophet* as a divine spokesperson. **3–5:** *Damascus* is the capital of the kingdom of Aram northeast of Israel, and *Hazael* and *Ben-hadad* are two of its kings. *Gilead* refers to Israelite territories east of the Jordan. The location of *Kir*, which Amos regarded as the original home of the Arameans (9.7), is uncertain. **6–8:** *Gaza, Ashdod, Ashkelon,* and *Ekron* are major Philistine cities southwest of Israel on the Mediterranean coast. *Edom*, to which both *Gaza* and *Tyre* (1.9–10) deported people, is Israel's neighbor southeast of the Dead Sea.

9 Thus says the LORD:
For three transgressions of Tyre,
    and for four, I will not revoke the
        punishment;[a]
because they delivered entire
        communities over to Edom,
    and did not remember the covenant
        of kinship.
10 So I will send a fire on the wall
        of Tyre,
    fire that shall devour its strongholds.

11 Thus says the LORD:
For three transgressions of Edom,
    and for four, I will not revoke the
        punishment;[a]
because he pursued his brother with the
        sword
    and cast off all pity;
he maintained his anger perpetually,[b]
    and kept his wrath[c] forever.
12 So I will send a fire on Teman,
    and it shall devour the strongholds of
        Bozrah.

13 Thus says the LORD:
For three transgressions of the
        Ammonites,
    and for four, I will not revoke the
        punishment;[a]

because they have ripped open pregnant
        women in Gilead
    in order to enlarge their territory.
14 So I will kindle a fire against the wall of
        Rabbah,
    fire that shall devour its strongholds,
with shouting on the day of battle,
    with a storm on the day of the
        whirlwind;
15 then their king shall go into exile,
    he and his officials together,
                    says the LORD.

2 Thus says the LORD:
For three transgressions of Moab,
    and for four, I will not revoke the
        punishment;[a]
because he burned to lime
    the bones of the king of Edom.
2 So I will send a fire on Moab,
    and it shall devour the strongholds of
        Kerioth,
and Moab shall die amid uproar,
    amid shouting and the sound of the
        trumpet;
3 I will cut off the ruler from its midst,
    and will kill all its officials with him,
                    says the LORD.

4 Thus says the LORD:
For three transgressions of Judah,
    and for four, I will not revoke the
        punishment;[a]
because they have rejected the law of
        the LORD,
    and have not kept his statutes,
but they have been led astray by the
        same lies
    after which their ancestors walked.
5 So I will send a fire on Judah,
    and it shall devour the strongholds of
        Jerusalem.

1.9–2.5. 1.9–10: *Tyre* is a Phoenician city on the Mediterranean coast northwest of Israel. **11–12:** *Edom* is Israel's neighbor to the southeast, and *Teman* and *Bozrah* are two of its major cities. Edom's *brother* may refer to either Israel or Judah (Ob 8–12). **13–15:** The

a Heb *cause it to return*   *b* Syr Vg: Heb *and his anger tore perpetually*   *c* Gk Syr Vg: Heb *and his wrath kept*

``They sell the righteous for silver''

With this phrase, Amos strikes at the heart of Israel's guilt (2.6, 8.6). He criticizes not just an abuse here and an injustice there, but an economic system that condones the accumulation of great wealth in the hands of a few (6.1–6) and the growth in the gap between rich and poor (5.11). In Israel's traditional economy, families supported themselves by farming their ancestral lands, as Amos himself may have done (1.1; 7.14–15). But as the wealthy imposed heavy taxes (2.8; 5.11), took collateral for themselves (2.8), and cheated customers in the marketplace (8.5), the poor were eventually forced off of their lands and reduced to debt-slavery, where they were bought and sold by the rich. Such an economic system was intolerable, according to Amos, for a society that had itself been once freed from slavery (2.10; 3.1).

Ammonites, Israel's neighbors to the east, are accused, as is Damascus (1.3), of crimes against the Israelites in *Gilead*. 2.1–3: *Moab*, located southeast of Israel, is accused of crimes against its southern neighbor *Edom*. 4–5: *Judah*, like Israel to follow (2.6–16), is criticized not for crimes against its neighbors, but for crimes within its own society against God's *law*.

Israelite audience into agreement with him, only to shock them with a concluding speech listing their own sins, even more numerous than those of their neighbors. 6–8: Amos's indictment begins with Israel's mistreatment of its poor (vv. 6b–7a), in particular, the sale of humans into slavery when they were unable to pay their debts (8.6). *Garments taken in pledge* (Ex 22.26–27; Deut 24.12–13) and *fines* refer to objects and money taken unfairly from the poor by the rich.

6 Thus says the LORD:
  For three transgressions of Israel,
    and for four, I will not revoke the
      punishment;*a*
  because they sell the righteous
    for silver,
    and the needy for a pair of sandals—
7 they who trample the head of the poor
    into the dust of the earth,
  and push the afflicted out of the
      way;
  father and son go in to the same girl,
    so that my holy name is profaned;
8 they lay themselves down beside every
      altar
    on garments taken in pledge;
  and in the house of their God
    they drink
  wine bought with fines they
      imposed.

9 Yet I destroyed the Amorite
      before them,
    whose height was like the height of
      cedars,
    and who was as strong as oaks;
  I destroyed his fruit above,
    and his roots beneath.
10 Also I brought you up out of the land of
      Egypt,
  and led you forty years in
      the wilderness,
    to possess the land of the Amorite.
11 And I raised up some of your children
      to be prophets
  and some of your youths to be
      nazirites.*b*
    Is it not indeed so, O people
      of Israel?
      says the LORD.

2.6–16: Judgment on Israel. This judgment speech concludes the series of speeches directed against Israel's neighbors. By starting with judgments against Israel's neighbors, Amos may have intended to lure his

a Heb *cause it to return*   *b* That is, *those separated* or *those consecrated*

12 But you made the nazirites*a* drink wine,
   and commanded the prophets,
      saying, "You shall not prophesy."

13 So, I will press you down in your place,
      just as a cart presses down
   when it is full of sheaves.*b*

14 Flight shall perish from the swift,
   and the strong shall not retain their
         strength,
   nor shall the mighty save their lives;

15 those who handle the bow shall
         not stand,
      and those who are swift of foot shall
            not save themselves,
      nor shall those who ride horses save
            their lives;

16 and those who are stout of heart among
            the mighty
      shall flee away naked in that day,
                              says the LORD.

2.9–16. 9–12: A brief historical summary stresses Israel's stubbornness by contrasting it with God's acts of salvation on Israel's behalf. **13–16:** The judgment imposed for Israel's crimes will bring an end to Israel's strongest defenses: its fastest runners, its strongest warriors, its most skilled archers, and its best horsemen.

3 Hear this word that the LORD has spoken against you, O people of Israel, against the whole family that I brought up out of the land of Egypt:

2 You only have I known
      of all the families of the earth;
   therefore I will punish you
      for all your iniquities.

3 Do two walk together
      unless they have made an appointment?

4 Does a lion roar in the forest,
      when it has no prey?
   Does a young lion cry out from its den,
      if it has caught nothing?

5 Does a bird fall into a snare on
            the earth,
      when there is no trap for it?
   Does a snare spring up from
            the ground,
      when it has taken nothing?

6 Is a trumpet blown in a city,
      and the people are not afraid?
   Does disaster befall a city,
      unless the LORD has done it?

7 Surely the Lord GOD does nothing,
      without revealing his secret
         to his servants the prophets.

8 The lion has roared;
      who will not fear?
   The Lord GOD has spoken;
      who can but prophesy?

3.1–8: The power of prophets. After a brief description of Israel's past salvation and future punishment (vv. 1–2), Amos begins a speech composed entirely of rhetorical* questions (vv. 3–8). With the first questions, Amos gains the audience's agreement on obvious issues in order to convince them of his real claim: When prophets speak, their words are the words of God (vv. 7–8).

9 Proclaim to the strongholds in Ashdod,
      and to the strongholds in the land of
            Egypt,
   and say, "Assemble yourselves on
         Mount*c* Samaria,
      and see what great tumults are
            within it,
      and what oppressions are in
            its midst."

10 They do not know how to do right, says
            the LORD,
      those who store up violence and
            robbery in their strongholds.

11 Therefore thus says the Lord GOD:
   An adversary shall surround the land,
      and strip you of your defense;
      and your strongholds shall be
            plundered.

12 Thus says the LORD: As the shepherd rescues from the mouth of the lion two legs, or a piece of an ear, so shall the people of Israel who live in Samaria be rescued, with the corner of a couch and part*b* of a bed.

3.9–12: Judgment on Samaria. Amos invites representatives from *Ashdod*, a Philistine city (1.8), and

---

a That is, *those separated* or *those consecrated*
b Meaning of Heb uncertain   *c* Gk Syr: Heb *the mountains of*

from *Egypt* to observe the *oppressions* of the poor on *Mount Samaria*, the capital of Israel. This indictment (vv. 9–10) is followed by God's sentence: Samaria's *strongholds shall be plundered* by an invading army (v. 11). The metaphor* of the plundering *lion* in v. 12 emphasizes how little will remain in Samaria after the enemy strikes.

13 Hear, and testify against the house of
          Jacob,
     says the Lord GOD, the God of hosts:
14 On the day I punish Israel for its
          transgressions,
      I will punish the altars of Bethel,
   and the horns of the altar shall
          be cut off
      and fall to the ground.
15 I will tear down the winter house as
          well as the summer house;
      and the houses of ivory shall perish,
   and the great houses*a* shall come
          to an end,
                    says the LORD.

3.13–15: Judgment on Bethel. Located in the southern part of Israel, *Bethel,* together with Dan in the north, was one of Israel's major religious centers. The judgment against Israel's houses (v. 15) that follows the judgment on Bethel contains an implicit criticism of the rich. Israel's wealthiest citizens built *winter houses* in the Jordan valley to escape the cold winter climate in the mountains of Samaria, and they made furniture inlaid with ivory for their homes (6.4).

4   Hear this word, you cows of Bashan
          who are on Mount Samaria,
     who oppress the poor, who crush the
          needy,
      who say to their husbands, "Bring
          something to drink!"
2   The Lord GOD has sworn by his holiness:
      The time is surely coming upon you,
   when they shall take you away with
          hooks,
      even the last of you with fishhooks.
3   Through breaches in the wall you shall
          leave,
      each one straight ahead;
   and you shall be flung out into
          Harmon,*b*
                    says the LORD.

4   Come to Bethel—and transgress;
          to Gilgal—and multiply transgression;
     bring your sacrifices every morning,
          your tithes every three days;
5   bring a thank offering of leavened
          bread,
      and proclaim freewill offerings,
          publish them;
      for so you love to do, O people
          of Israel!
                    says the Lord GOD.

6   I gave you cleanness of teeth in all your
          cities,
      and lack of bread in all your places,
   yet you did not return to me,
                    says the LORD.

7   And I also withheld the rain from you
          when there were still three months to
          the harvest;
      I would send rain on one city,
          and send no rain on another city;
      one field would be rained upon,
          and the field on which it did not rain
          withered;
8   so two or three towns wandered to one
          town
          to drink water, and were not satisfied;
      yet you did not return to me,
                    says the LORD.

9   I struck you with blight and mildew;
          I laid waste*c* your gardens and your
          vineyards;
      the locust devoured your fig trees and
          your olive trees;
   yet you did not return to me,
                    says the LORD.

10 I sent among you a pestilence after the
          manner of Egypt;
      I killed your young men with the sword;
   I carried away your horses;*d*
          and I made the stench of your camp
          go up into your nostrils;
      yet you did not return to me,
                    says the LORD.

a Or *many houses*   *b* Meaning of Heb uncertain
c Cn: Heb *the multitude of*   *d* Heb *with the captivity of your horses*

11 I overthrew some of you,
    as when God overthrew Sodom and
       Gomorrah,
    and you were like a brand snatched
       from the fire;
yet you did not return to me,
                says the LORD.

12 Therefore thus I will do to you,
    O Israel;
    because I will do this to you,
    prepare to meet your God, O Israel!

13 For lo, the one who forms the
       mountains, creates the wind,
    reveals his thoughts to mortals,
makes the morning darkness,
    and treads on the heights of
       the earth—
the LORD, the God of hosts, is
       his name!

and that which marched out a hundred
    shall have ten left.[a]

4 For thus says the LORD to the house of
       Israel:
Seek me and live;
5   but do not seek Bethel,
    and do not enter into Gilgal
       or cross over to Beer-sheba;
for Gilgal shall surely go into exile,
    and Bethel shall come to nothing.

6 Seek the LORD and live,
    or he will break out against the house
       of Joseph like fire,
    and it will devour Bethel, with no one
       to quench it.
7 Ah, you that turn justice to
       wormwood,
    and bring righteousness to
       the ground!

4.1–13. 1–3: Judgment on Samaria's elite women. In his indictment of their oppression of the poor (v. 1), Amos compares Israel's leading women to cattle grazing in Israel's prime pasture land, *Bashan*. The sentence for these women (vv. 2–3) is deportation, though the location of *Harmon* is uncertain. **4–13: Israel's stubbornness.** After criticizing the rituals practiced at two of Israel's religious centers, *Bethel* and *Gilgal* (vv. 4–5), perhaps because he judged them hypocritical, Amos lists a series of divine judgments that have failed to convince Israel of its injustices: famine (v. 6), drought (vv. 7–8), plant diseases and predators (v. 9), disease and death for Israel's army (v. 10), and defeat (v. 11). With the term *therefore*, which characteristically links indictments to sentences, Amos introduces God's judgment (vv. 12–13) for Israel's repeated refusal to reform.

5.1–27: A lament over Israel. Within a lament* anticipating Israel's fall (vv. 1–3, 16–20), Amos indicts Israel for its injustices (vv. 10–13, 21–27) and pleads with Israel to seek God in order to avoid disaster (vv. 4–7, 14–15). **1–3:** Amos begins his lament by describing the conquest of Israel as if it had already happened. **4–7:** In his opening appeal to seek God, Amos criticizes the worship (v. 5) of those who are not just (v. 7). **5:** *Beer-sheba*, a southern religious center with old associations with the northern kingdom of Israel (1 Sam 8.2; 1 Kings 19.3), is mentioned here alongside two northern centers, *Bethel* and *Gilgal*, which Amos criticizes elsewhere (4.4). **6:** *Joseph*, father of the ancestors of the two most powerful northern tribes (Ephraim and Manasseh), is employed by Amos as a synonym for Israel.

5 Hear this word that I take up over you
   in lamentation, O house of Israel:
2 Fallen, no more to rise,
    is maiden Israel;
forsaken on her land,
    with no one to raise her up.

3 For thus says the Lord GOD:
The city that marched out a thousand
    shall have a hundred left,

8 The one who made the Pleiades
       and Orion,
    and turns deep darkness into
       the morning,
    and darkens the day into night,
who calls for the waters of the sea,
    and pours them out on the surface of
       the earth,
the LORD is his name,

a Heb adds *to the house of Israel*

The Great Sea
(Mediterranean)

Mt. Carmel

The Negeb

Damascus

SYRIA
(ARAM)

Tyre

Dan

BASHAN

ISRAEL

Samaria

Bethel

Gilgal

Ekron

Ashdod

Jerusalem

Ashkelon

PHILISTIA

JUDAH

Tekoa

Gaza

Beer-sheba

Sea
of
the
Arabah
(Salt Sea)

GILEAD

AMMON

MOAB

EDOM

Map | Israel and environs in the time of Amos

9 who makes destruction flash out against
　　the strong,
　so that destruction comes upon the
　　fortress.

10 They hate the one who reproves in the
　　gate,
　and they abhor the one who speaks
　　the truth.
11 Therefore because you trample on the
　　poor
　and take from them levies of grain,
　you have built houses of hewn stone,
　　but you shall not live in them;
　you have planted pleasant vineyards,
　　but you shall not drink their wine.
12 For I know how many are your
　　transgressions,
　and how great are your sins—
　you who afflict the righteous, who take
　　a bribe,
　and push aside the needy in the gate.
13 Therefore the prudent will keep silent in
　　such a time;
　for it is an evil time.

5.8–13. 8–9: Hymns such as this one praising God's
power occur at several points in Amos (4.13; 9.5–6).
10–13: Amos indicts Israel for judicial and economic
abuses. Israel's judges heard and settled disputes at *the
gate* of the city (vv. 10, 12). *Levies of grain* are taxes
imposed by creditors or landlords on poor farmers.

14 Seek good and not evil,
　　that you may live;
　and so the LORD, the God of hosts, will
　　be with you,
　just as you have said.
15 Hate evil and love good,
　　and establish justice in the gate;
　it may be that the LORD, the God
　　of hosts,
　will be gracious to the remnant of
　　Joseph.

16 Therefore thus says the LORD, the God
　　of hosts, the Lord:
　In all the squares there shall be
　　wailing;
　and in all the streets they shall say,
　　"Alas! alas!"

They shall call the farmers to
　　mourning,
　and those skilled in lamentation, to
　　wailing;
17 in all the vineyards there shall
　　be wailing,
　for I will pass through the midst of
　　you,
　　　　　　　　　says the LORD.

18 Alas for you who desire the day of
　　the LORD!
　Why do you want the day of
　　the LORD?
　It is darkness, not light;
19 　as if someone fled from a lion,
　　and was met by a bear;
　or went into the house and rested a
　　hand against the wall,
　and was bitten by a snake.
20 Is not the day of the LORD darkness,
　　not light,
　and gloom with no brightness in it?

21 I hate, I despise your festivals,
　　and I take no delight in your solemn
　　　assemblies.
22 Even though you offer me your burnt
　　offerings and grain offerings,
　I will not accept them;
　and the offerings of well-being of your
　　fatted animals
　I will not look upon.
23 Take away from me the noise of your
　　songs;
　I will not listen to the melody of your
　　harps.
24 But let justice roll down like waters,
　　and righteousness like an ever-flowing
　　　stream.

5.14–24. 14–15: Amos's appeal to seek God by living
justly (vv. 4–7) is resumed. **16–20:** Amos continues his
lament begun in vv. 1–3. The *day of the LORD* (vv. 18,
20) is a decisive act of God in human affairs. Although
Amos's audience believed it would be a day of salvation, Amos saw it as a day of judgment. **21–24:** This is
Amos's classic statement about the meaninglessness of
worship (vv. 21–23) if it is practiced by those who do
not do justice in their daily affairs (v. 24).

25 Did you bring to me sacrifices and offerings the forty years in the wilderness,
O house of Israel? 26You shall take up Sakkuth your king, and Kaiwan your star-god,
your images,ᵃ which you made for yourselves; 27therefore I will take you into exile
beyond Damascus, says the LORD, whose
name is the God of hosts.

5.25–27: In what may be an editorial addition, Israel
is blamed for idolatry. ★ *Sakkuth* and *Kaiwan* are titles
for Saturn, an astral deity in Mesopotamia. *Damascus*
is the capital of the kingdom of Aram, northeast of
Israel (1.3).

6 Alas for those who are at ease in Zion,
  and for those who feel secure on
    Mount Samaria,
  the notables of the first of the nations,
  to whom the house of Israel
    resorts!
2 Cross over to Calneh, and see;
  from there go to Hamath the great;
  then go down to Gath of the
    Philistines.
  Are you betterᵇ than these kingdoms?
  Or is yourᶜ territory greater than
    theirᵈ territory,
3 O you that put far away the evil day,
  and bring near a reign of violence?

4 Alas for those who lie on beds of ivory,
  and lounge on their couches,
  and eat lambs from the flock,
  and calves from the stall;
5 who sing idle songs to the sound
    of the harp,
  and like David improvise on
    instruments of music;
6 who drink wine from bowls,
  and anoint themselves with the finest
    oils,
  but are not grieved over the ruin of
    Joseph!
7 Therefore they shall now be the first to
    go into exile,
  and the revelry of the loungers shall
    pass away.

8 The Lord GOD has sworn by himself
  (says the LORD, the God of hosts):

I abhor the pride of Jacob
  and hate his strongholds;
  and I will deliver up the city and all
    that is in it.

9 If ten people remain in one house, they
shall die. 10And if a relative, one who burns
the dead,ᵉ shall take up the body to bring it
out of the house, and shall say to someone
in the innermost parts of the house, "Is anyone else with you?" the answer will come,
"No." Then the relativeᶠ shall say, "Hush!
We must not mention the name of the
LORD."

11 See, the LORD commands,
  and the great house shall be shattered
    to bits,
  and the little house to pieces.
12 Do horses run on rocks?
  Does one plow the sea with oxen?ᵍ
  But you have turned justice
    into poison
  and the fruit of righteousness into
    wormwood—
13 you who rejoice in Lo-debar,ʰ
  who say, "Have we not by our own
    strength
  taken Karnaimⁱ for ourselves?"
14 Indeed, I am raising up against you a
    nation,
  O house of Israel, says the LORD, the
    God of hosts,
  and they shall oppress you from
    Lebo-hamath
  to the Wadi Arabah.

6.1–14: Judgment on Samaria's elite men. In this
judgment speech, Amos indicts Israel's leaders for excessive wealth and complacency (vv. 1–6) and announces a sentence that includes the conquest of Samaria and deportation of its leaders (vv. 7–14). **2:**
Calneh and *Hamath* are capital cities of important Syrian city-states. **6:** *Joseph* is a synonym for Israel (5.6).
13: *Lo-debar* and *Karnaim* are cities east of the Jordan
that may have been brought under Israelite control

---

a Heb *your images, your star-god*   *b* Or *Are they better*
c Heb *their*   *d* Heb *your*   *e* Or *who makes a burning
for him*   *f* Heb *he*   *g* Or *Does one plow them with
oxen*   *h* Or *in a thing of nothingness*   *i* Or *horns*

during Amos's career by the conquests of Jeroboam II (2 Kings 14.25). **14:** *Lebo-hamath* and the *Wadi* Arabah* are the northern and southern boundaries established for the kingdom of Israel by Jeroboam II (2 Kings 14.25); they are used here by Amos to depict Israel in its entirety.

7 This is what the Lord GOD showed me: he was forming locusts at the time the latter growth began to sprout (it was the latter growth after the king's mowings). ²When they had finished eating the grass of the land, I said,

"O Lord GOD, forgive, I beg you!
How can Jacob stand?
He is so small!"
³ The LORD relented concerning this;
"It shall not be," said the LORD.

4 This is what the Lord GOD showed me: the Lord GOD was calling for a shower of fire,ª and it devoured the great deep and was eating up the land. ⁵Then I said,

"O Lord GOD, cease, I beg you!
How can Jacob stand?
He is so small!"
6 The LORD relented concerning this;
"This also shall not be," said the Lord
GOD.

7 This is what he showed me: the Lord was standing beside a wall built with a plumb line, with a plumb line in his hand. ⁸And the LORD said to me, "Amos, what do you see?" And I said, "A plumb line." Then the Lord said,

"See, I am setting a plumb line
in the midst of my people Israel;
I will never again pass them by;
9 the high places of Isaac shall be made
desolate,
and the sanctuaries of Israel shall be
laid waste,
and I will rise against the house of
Jeroboam with the sword."

7.1–9: Amos's visions. In three separate visions—a locust plague (vv. 1–3); a fire storm (vv. 4–6); and a wall and plumb line (vv. 7–9)—God shows Amos judgments that will befall Israel. After the first two visions, Amos asks God to reconsider, and the punishment is

withheld. *Jacob* is used as a synonym for Israel in these two visions.

10 Then Amaziah, the priest of Bethel, sent to King Jeroboam of Israel, saying, "Amos has conspired against you in the very center of the house of Israel; the land is not able to bear all his words. ¹¹For thus Amos has said,

'Jeroboam shall die by the sword,
and Israel must go into exile
away from his land.'"
¹²And Amaziah said to Amos, "O seer, go, flee away to the land of Judah, earn your bread there, and prophesy there; ¹³but never again prophesy at Bethel, for it is the king's sanctuary, and it is a temple of the kingdom."

14 Then Amos answered Amaziah, "I amᵇ no prophet, nor a prophet's son; but I amᵇ a herdsman, and a dresser of sycamore trees, ¹⁵and the LORD took me from following the flock, and the LORD said to me, 'Go, prophesy to my people Israel.'

16 "Now therefore hear the word of the
LORD.
You say, 'Do not prophesy against Israel,
and do not preach against the house
of Isaac.'
17 Therefore thus says the LORD:
'Your wife shall become a prostitute in
the city,
and your sons and your daughters
shall fall by the sword,
and your land shall be parceled out by
line;
you yourself shall die in an
unclean land,
and Israel shall surely go into exile
away from its land.'"

7.10–17: Amos preaches at Bethel. This is the only narrative* in Amos describing an event in Amos's career and a specific setting in which he preached. Upon hearing Amos's unfavorable prediction about *Jeroboam*, king of Israel, *Amaziah*, priest of Bethel, responds in two ways: He sends word to Jeroboam in Samaria (vv. 10–11), and he banishes Amos from Bethel, one of Israel's major religious centers (vv. 12–13). Amaziah appears to claim that Amos, from the

a Or for a judgment by fire   b Or was

Judean town of Tekoa (1.1), should earn his living as a prophet* in his own country of Judah ("*earn your bread there*," v. 12), and stay out of Israel's affairs. When Amos responds that he is not a prophet but a shepherd and a farmer (v. 14), he may mean that he is not earning his living as a (professional) prophet at all, but rather communicating an unexpected but genuine divine revelation.

8 This is what the Lord GOD showed me—a basket of summer fruit.[a] 2 He said, "Amos, what do you see?" And I said, "A basket of summer fruit."[a] Then the LORD said to me,

"The end[b] has come upon my people Israel;
    I will never again pass them by.
3 The songs of the temple[c] shall become wailings in that day,"
        says the Lord GOD;
    "the dead bodies shall be many,
        cast out in every place. Be silent!"

8.1–3: Amos's visions continued. Like the visions described in 7.1–9, this vision reveals a coming judgment on Israel. **2:** The meaning of this vision is based on the similarity in Hebrew between the words for *summer fruit* ("qayits") and *end* ("qets").

4 Hear this, you that trample on the needy,
    and bring to ruin the poor of the land,
5 saying, "When will the new moon be over
    so that we may sell grain;
and the sabbath,
    so that we may offer wheat for sale?
We will make the ephah small and the shekel great,
    and practice deceit with false balances,
6 buying the poor for silver
    and the needy for a pair of sandals,
    and selling the sweepings of the wheat."

7 The LORD has sworn by the pride of Jacob:
    Surely I will never forget any of their deeds.

8 Shall not the land tremble on this account,
    and everyone mourn who lives in it,
and all of it rise like the Nile,
    and be tossed about and sink again,
        like the Nile of Egypt?

9 On that day, says the Lord GOD,
    I will make the sun go down at noon,
    and darken the earth in broad daylight.
10 I will turn your feasts into mourning,
    and all your songs into lamentation;
I will bring sackcloth on all loins,
    and baldness on every head;
I will make it like the mourning for an only son,
    and the end of it like a bitter day.

11 The time is surely coming, says the Lord GOD,
    when I will send a famine on the land;
not a famine of bread, or a thirst for water,
    but of hearing the words of the LORD.
12 They shall wander from sea to sea,
    and from north to east;
they shall run to and fro, seeking the word of the LORD,
    but they shall not find it.
13 In that day the beautiful young women and the young men
    shall faint for thirst.
14 Those who swear by Ashimah of Samaria,
    and say, "As your god lives, O Dan,"
and, "As the way of Beer-sheba lives"—
    they shall fall, and never rise again.

8.4–14: Judgment on Israel's businessmen. In this judgment speech, Amos indicts Israel's merchants for economic abuses (vv. 4–6), and announces a sentence of widespread devastation (vv. 7–14). **5:** The *new moon** and the *sabbath* are religious holidays (Isa 1.13; Hos 2.11) considered an annoyance by merchants who cannot make a profit during their obser-

a Heb *qayits*   b Heb *qets*   c Or *palace*

vance. The *ephah* is used to measure an amount of grain by capacity, and the *shekel*★ is used to measure an amount of grain by weight. Reducing the *ephah* and enlarging the *shekel* are thus two ways merchants can cheat their customers. **14:** The Hebrew text rendered *Ashimah* here means literally "guilt," thus, "the guilt of Samaria." However, scholars have altered the Hebrew slightly to read either "Ashimah," a Syrian deity (2 Kings 17.30), or Asherah,★ a Canaanite deity (1 Kings 16.33). Amos's mention of Israel's capital, *Samaria*, together with one of its major religious centers, *Dan*, and a southern center visited by northerners, *Beer-sheba* (5.5), includes within God's judgment the political and religious leaders of Israel.

9 I saw the LORD standing beside*ᵃ* the altar, and he said:
   Strike the capitals until the thresholds shake,
      and shatter them on the heads of all the people;*ᵇ*
   and those who are left I will kill with the sword;
      not one of them shall flee away,
      not one of them shall escape.

2 Though they dig into Sheol,
      from there shall my hand take them;
   though they climb up to heaven,
      from there I will bring them down.
3 Though they hide themselves on the top of Carmel,
      from there I will search out and take them;
   and though they hide from my sight at the bottom of the sea,
      there I will command the sea-serpent, and it shall bite them.
4 And though they go into captivity in front of their enemies,
      there I will command the sword, and it shall kill them;
   and I will fix my eyes on them
      for harm and not for good.

9.1–4: Amos's visions concluded. Like Amos's other visions (7.1–9; 8.1–3), this vision shows Amos God's coming judgment, but the judgment predicted here is the harshest and most complete of them all. **2:** *Sheol*★ is the abode of the dead.

5 The Lord, GOD of hosts,
      he who touches the earth and it melts,
         and all who live in it mourn,
      and all of it rises like the Nile,
      and sinks again, like the Nile of Egypt;
6 who builds his upper chambers in the heavens,
      and founds his vault upon the earth;
   who calls for the waters of the sea,
      and pours them out upon the surface of the earth—
      the LORD is his name.

7 Are you not like the Ethiopians*ᶜ* to me,
      O people of Israel? says the LORD.
   Did I not bring Israel up from the land of Egypt,
      and the Philistines from Caphtor and the Arameans from Kir?
8 The eyes of the Lord GOD are upon the sinful kingdom,
      and I will destroy it from the face of the earth
      —except that I will not utterly destroy the house of Jacob,
                              says the LORD.

9 For lo, I will command,
      and shake the house of Israel among all the nations
   as one shakes with a sieve,
      but no pebble shall fall to the ground.
10 All the sinners of my people shall die by the sword,
      who say, "Evil shall not overtake or meet us."

9.5–10: Master of the universe. Amos describes God's power over creation (vv. 5–6) and world history (vv. 7–10). **7:** *Caphtor* is likely Crete, while the location of *Kir* is uncertain. Just as God directed Israel's migration from Egypt (3.1), so God has directed the affairs of other nations.

11 On that day I will raise up
      the booth of David that is fallen,
   and repair its*ᵈ* breaches,

a Or *on*   *b* Heb *all of them*   *c* Or *Nubians*; Heb
Cushites   *d* Gk: Heb *their*

and raise up its[a] ruins,
and rebuild it as in the days of old;
12 in order that they may possess the
remnant of Edom
and all the nations who are called by
my name,
says the LORD who does this.

13 The time is surely coming, says
the LORD,
when the one who plows shall
overtake the one who reaps,
and the treader of grapes the one who
sows the seed;
the mountains shall drip sweet wine,
and all the hills shall flow with it.
14 I will restore the fortunes of my people
Israel,
and they shall rebuild the ruined
cities and inhabit them;
they shall plant vineyards and drink
their wine,
and they shall make gardens and eat
their fruit.

15 I will plant them upon their land,
and they shall never again be
plucked up
out of the land that I have
given them,
says the LORD your God.

9.11–15: Vision of renewal. These images of restoration, because they are unparalleled in the rest of
Amos and contrast so sharply with his expectation of
judgment, are widely regarded as a later addition to
Amos's prophecies. **11:** The ruined state of the *booth
of David,* a reference to the Davidic monarchy that
ruled Judah, appears to place this speech after the fall
of Jerusalem in 587 BCE. This image also suggests that
this text was written from the perspective of Judah, the
southern kingdom, rather than from the perspective
of the northern kingdom which Amos addressed. It
anticipates the return of the Babylonian exiles to rebuild their ruined country.

a Gk: Heb *his*

OBADIAH

Introduction

The book of Obadiah is unique among the prophetic* books because it contains only a single speech, and that speech is directed not against Israel or Judah but against a neighboring nation, Edom. Central to Obadiah's speech is a sense of betrayal, expressed most directly in vv. 8–14, which describe the Edomites entering Jerusalem, looting it, and mistreating its people, all the while gloating over Jerusalem's misfortunes. God's judgment of Edom, predicted in the verses that precede and follow, is viewed as fair punishment for the Edomites' disloyalty to their Israelite neighbors. Though relations between the Israelites and Edomites were often marked by conflict over the years (2 Kings 8.20–22; 14.7), Israel believed the two peoples were closely related as descendants of the two brothers, Jacob and Esau (Gen 25–33). While rivalry is already present in these stories of their ancestors, it is resolved by reconciliation rather than revenge and betrayal (Gen 33).

Though this speech is not dated by reference to particular kings or events, it appears to have been composed sometime after the Babylonians destroyed Jerusalem in 587 BCE. Following Jerusalem's fall, the Edomites moved in and took advantage of Judah's weakness, taking booty and betraying its survivors (vv. 11, 14; Ps 137.7). The parallel themes of Edom's fall and Judah's rise with which the book ends (vv. 15–21) anticipate the return of the Judean exiles from Babylon and their resettlement of Judah and the surrounding areas.

READING GUIDE

Readers should attend to the structure of this book. Obadiah's judgment speech against Edom begins with the sentence imposed for Edom's crimes (vv. 1–7), then provides the indictment listing the crimes for which this sentence is imposed (vv. 8–14), and concludes by returning to the sentence itself (vv. 15–21). This final sentence for Edom is woven together with expectations for Judah's renewal.

1 The vision of Obadiah.

Thus says the Lord GOD concerning
  Edom:
We have heard a report from the LORD,
  and a messenger has been sent
    among the nations:
"Rise up! Let us rise against it
    for battle!"
2 I will surely make you least among the
    nations;
  you shall be utterly despised.
3 Your proud heart has deceived you,
  you that live in the clefts of
    the rock,ᵃ
  whose dwelling is in the heights.

You say in your heart,
  "Who will bring me down to
    the ground?"
4 Though you soar aloft like the eagle,
  though your nest is set among the
    stars,
  from there I will bring you down,
    says the LORD.
5 If thieves came to you,
  if plunderers by night
  —how you have been destroyed!—
  would they not steal only what they
    wanted?

a Or *clefts of Sela*

If grape-gatherers came to you,
would they not leave gleanings?
6 How Esau has been pillaged,
his treasures searched out!
7 All your allies have deceived you,
they have driven you to the border;
your confederates have prevailed
against you;
those who ate*a* your bread have set a
trap for you—
there is no understanding of it.
8 On that day, says the LORD,
I will destroy the wise out of Edom,
and understanding out of
Mount Esau.
9 Your warriors shall be shattered,
O Teman,
so that everyone from Mount Esau
will be cut off.
10 For the slaughter and violence done to
your brother Jacob,
shame shall cover you,
and you shall be cut off forever.
11 On the day that you stood aside,
on the day that strangers carried off
his wealth,
and foreigners entered his gates
and cast lots for Jerusalem,
you too were like one of them.
12 But you should not have gloated*b* over*c*
your brother
on the day of his misfortune;
you should not have rejoiced over the
people of Judah
on the day of their ruin;
you should not have boasted
on the day of distress.
13 You should not have entered the gate of
my people
on the day of their calamity;
you should not have joined in the
gloating over Judah's*d* disaster
on the day of his calamity;
you should not have looted his goods
on the day of his calamity.
14 You should not have stood at
the crossings
to cut off his fugitives;
you should not have handed over his
survivors
on the day of distress.

1–7: The fall of Edom. Obadiah announces the sentence for Edom's crimes. **1:** This *messenger* is a member of the heavenly council sent to announce God's plans. **3:** *The clefts of the rock* refer to the mountain range, rising sharply to the east of the Jordan rift valley, on which Edom was located. **6:** *Esau*, the ancestor of the Edomites (Gen 25.30), is used by Obadiah as a synonym for Edom. **7:** *Those who ate your bread* are the allies mentioned earlier in the verse. Alliances were sealed by covenant* meals (Gen 31.44–46). **8–14: Edom's betrayal of Judah.** Obadiah lists the details of Edom's exploitation of Judah following Babylon's destruction of Jerusalem (587 BCE). **9:** *Teman* is either a synonym for Edom or the name of a section or city in Edom. *Mount Esau* may be a particular Edomite mountain or the mountain range on which Edom was located. **10:** *Jacob*, the *brother* of Edom's ancestor Esau (Gen 25.24–26), is used by Obadiah to represent the citizens of Jerusalem and Judah. **11:** *Jerusalem* is the capital of Judah.

15 For the day of the LORD is near against
all the nations.
As you have done, it shall be done
to you;
your deeds shall return on your own
head.
16 For as you have drunk on my
holy mountain,
all the nations around you shall drink;
they shall drink and gulp down,*e*
and shall be as though they had never
been.
17 But on Mount Zion there shall be those
that escape,
and it shall be holy;
and the house of Jacob shall take
possession of those who
dispossessed them.
18 The house of Jacob shall be a fire,
the house of Joseph a flame,
and the house of Esau stubble;
they shall burn them and
consume them,
and there shall be no survivor of the
house of Esau;
for the LORD has spoken.

a Cn: Heb lacks *those who ate*   b Heb *But do not gloat*
(and similarly through verse 14)   c Heb *on the day of*
d Heb *his*   e Meaning of Heb uncertain

19 Those of the Negeb shall possess Mount
　　　Esau,
　　and those of the Shephelah the land
　　　　of the Philistines;
　　they shall possess the land of Ephraim
　　　　and the land of Samaria,
　　and Benjamin shall possess Gilead.
20 The exiles of the Israelites who are in
　　　Halah*a*
　　shall possess*b* Phoenicia as far
　　　　as Zarephath;
　　and the exiles of Jerusalem who are in
　　　Sepharad
　　shall possess the towns of the Negeb.
21 Those who have been saved*c* shall go
　　　up to Mount Zion
　　to rule Mount Esau;
　　and the kingdom shall be the LORD's.

15–21: Edom's end and Judah's renewal. Obadiah weaves together the themes of Edom's judgment and Judah's salvation. **18:** *The house of Jacob* and *the house of Joseph* refer to the southern kingdom of Judah or the Israelite people as a whole, while *the house of Esau* refers to Edom. **19–20:** Listed here are the territories Obadiah expects to be resettled when Judah is restored: *the Negeb,* south of Judah; *Mount Esau,* the territory of Edom southeast of Judah; *the Shephelah,* the foothills west of Judah; *the land of the Philistines* on the Mediterranean coast west of Judah; *Ephraim* and its capital *Samaria,* the old northern kingdom of Israel; and *Phoenicia* and its city *Zarephath,* on the Mediterranean coast northwest of Judah.

a Cn: Heb *in this army*　　*b* Cn: Meaning of Heb uncertain　　*c* Or *Saviors*

JONAH

Introduction

The book of Jonah is unlike other prophetic books in that it contains a short story about a prophet* rather than a collection of prophetic speeches. Furthermore, Jonah is active not in his own country but in Nineveh, a great Assyrian city feared and hated by the Israelites, who more than once suffered at the hands of its conquering soldiers (2 Kings 18.9–16; Nah 3.1–4). Because the wicked Ninevites repent and are saved, though Jonah is displeased, the story has traditionally been understood to teach God's universal salvation, criticizing at the same time those who think salvation is limited to Israel alone. The story also emphasizes related themes: the importance of human repentance and the depth of divine compassion. In addition, the narrative also contrasts the frailty of the prophet with the power of the prophet's message (Jer 1.4–10).

Jonah has been unusually difficult to place into a particular historical setting. A Jonah son of Amittai (1.1) is mentioned by Israel's historian as an eighth-century prophet (2 Kings 14.25), which accounts for the book of Jonah's position together with other eighth-century prophets, such as Amos and Micah, among the twelve Minor Prophets. But these two prophets have nothing in common, and most scholars have preferred a post-exilic date (sixth to fourth centuries) for the book of Jonah, on the basis of its language and major themes. Nineveh was an important Assyrian city until its fall near the end of the seventh century (612 BCE), but it may well have remained a powerful symbol of the enemy among Israel's later prophets and storytellers.

READING GUIDE

The book of Jonah is full of humor and irony.* The author repeatedly undercuts the reader's expectations. Jonah is commanded to go in one direction and instead goes in the opposite direction; the sailors are more devout than the prophet; Jonah is disappointed when his mission succeeds; and he is more concerned about a plant than about a populous city. To appreciate the artistry of the story and its major themes most fully, the reader should watch for these and other ironies and humorous reversals.

1 Now the word of the LORD came to Jonah son of Amittai, saying, 2 "Go at once to Nineveh, that great city, and cry out against it; for their wickedness has come up before me." 3 But Jonah set out to flee to Tarshish from the presence of the LORD. He went down to Joppa and found a ship going to Tarshish; so he paid his fare and went on board, to go with them to Tarshish, away from the presence of the LORD.

4 But the LORD hurled a great wind upon the sea, and such a mighty storm came upon the sea that the ship threatened to break up. 5 Then the mariners were afraid, and each cried to his god. They threw the cargo that was in the ship into the sea, to lighten it for them. Jonah, meanwhile, had gone down into the hold of the ship and had lain down, and was fast asleep. 6 The captain came and said to him, "What are you doing sound asleep? Get up, call on your god! Perhaps the god will spare us a thought so that we do not perish."

7 The sailors*a* said to one another, "Come, let us cast lots, so that we may know on whose account this calamity has come

a Heb *They*

upon us." So they cast lots, and the lot fell on Jonah. 8Then they said to him, "Tell us why this calamity has come upon us. What is your occupation? Where do you come from? What is your country? And of what people are you?" 9"I am a Hebrew," he replied. "I worship the LORD, the God of heaven, who made the sea and the dry land." 10Then the men were even more afraid, and said to him, "What is this that you have done!" For the men knew that he was fleeing from the presence of the LORD, because he had told them so.

11 Then they said to him, "What shall we do to you, that the sea may quiet down for us?" For the sea was growing more and more tempestuous. 12He said to them, "Pick me up and throw me into the sea; then the sea will quiet down for you; for I know it is because of me that this great storm has come upon you." 13Nevertheless the men rowed hard to bring the ship back to land, but they could not, for the sea grew more and more stormy against them. 14Then they cried out to the LORD, "Please, O LORD, we pray, do not let us perish on account of this man's life. Do not make us guilty of innocent blood; for you, O LORD, have done as it pleased you." 15So they picked Jonah up and threw him into the sea; and the sea ceased from its raging. 16Then the men feared the LORD even more, and they offered a sacrifice to the LORD and made vows.

17ᵃ But the LORD provided a large fish to swallow up Jonah; and Jonah was in the belly of the fish three days and three nights.

2 Then Jonah prayed to the LORD his God from the belly of the fish, 2saying,

"I called to the LORD out of my distress,
    and he answered me;
out of the belly of Sheol I cried,
    and you heard my voice.
3 You cast me into the deep,
    into the heart of the seas,
    and the flood surrounded me;
all your waves and your billows
    passed over me.
4 Then I said, 'I am driven away
    from your sight;
howᵇ shall I look again
    upon your holy temple?'
5 The waters closed in over me;
    the deep surrounded me;
weeds were wrapped around my head
6   at the roots of the mountains.
I went down to the land
    whose bars closed upon me forever;
yet you brought up my life from
        the Pit,
    O LORD my God.
7 As my life was ebbing away,
    I remembered the LORD;
and my prayer came to you,
    into your holy temple.
8 Those who worship vain idols
    forsake their true loyalty.
9 But I with the voice of thanksgiving
    will sacrifice to you;
what I have vowed I will pay.
    Deliverance belongs to the LORD!"
10Then the LORD spoke to the fish, and it spewed Jonah out upon the dry land.

1.1–17: Jonah flees from God. The book of Jonah begins, as do other prophetic books, with the phrase *the word of the LORD came to . . .* (1.1; Hos 1.1), but unlike other prophets, Jonah embarks on an elaborate plan to escape his calling. The motif★ of descent runs through the narrative★ of Jonah's attempt to escape (vv. 3, 5, 15). **3:** *Tarshish* is a site of uncertain location on the Mediterranean coast west of Israel (Isa 23.1), in the opposite direction from Nineveh to the east. *Joppa* is an ancient Mediterranean port city, just south of modern Tel Aviv. **4:** Israel's God is frequently associated with the thunderstorm (Ex 19.16–17; Ps 18.7–15).

2.1–10: Jonah's prayer. Jonah's prayer, an appeal to God in poetic form, may be a traditional text taken over by the narrator to represent Jonah's petition. It is composed in the form of a lament,★ a common psalm type in which the worshipper pleads for God's help in a time of great distress (Ps 3, 5, 7). **2:** The lament opens with an address, in which the worshipper calls out to God. *Sheol*★ is the land of the dead. **3–6:** The description of distress follows the opening address. The image of deep waters swallowing the worshipper is common in such descriptions of distress (Ps 69.1–2, 14–15).

a Ch 2.1 in Heb   *b* Theodotion: Heb *surely*

The *holy temple* refers to the Temple* in Jerusalem. 7: A petition to God follows the description of distress. 8–9: Laments customarily end, as does this one, with the worshipper anticipating God's aid and promising to thank God by presenting a sacrifice at the Temple.

through humor and irony Nineveh's total response to Jonah's preaching.

3 The word of the LORD came to Jonah a second time, saying, 2"Get up, go to Nineveh, that great city, and proclaim to it the message that I tell you." 3So Jonah set out and went to Nineveh, according to the word of the LORD. Now Nineveh was an exceedingly large city, a three days' walk across. 4Jonah began to go into the city, going a day's walk. And he cried out, "Forty days more, and Nineveh shall be overthrown!" 5And the people of Nineveh believed God; they proclaimed a fast, and everyone, great and small, put on sackcloth.

6 When the news reached the king of Nineveh, he rose from his throne, removed his robe, covered himself with sackcloth, and sat in ashes. 7Then he had a proclamation made in Nineveh: "By the decree of the king and his nobles: No human being or animal, no herd or flock, shall taste anything. They shall not feed, nor shall they drink water. 8Human beings and animals shall be covered with sackcloth, and they shall cry mightily to God. All shall turn from their evil ways and from the violence that is in their hands. 9Who knows? God may relent and change his mind; he may turn from his fierce anger, so that we do not perish."

10 When God saw what they did, how they turned from their evil ways, God changed his mind about the calamity that he had said he would bring upon them; and he did not do it.

4 But this was very displeasing to Jonah, and he became angry. 2He prayed to the LORD and said, "O LORD! Is not this what I said while I was still in my own country? That is why I fled to Tarshish at the beginning; for I knew that you are a gracious God and merciful, slow to anger, and abounding in steadfast love, and ready to relent from punishing. 3And now, O LORD, please take my life from me, for it is better for me to die than to live." 4And the LORD said, "Is it right for you to be angry?" 5Then Jonah went out of the city and sat down east of the city, and made a booth for himself there. He sat under it in the shade, waiting to see what would become of the city.

6 The LORD God appointed a bush,ᵃ and made it come up over Jonah, to give shade over his head, to save him from his discomfort; so Jonah was very happy about the bush. 7But when dawn came up the next day, God appointed a worm that attacked the bush, so that it withered. 8When the sun rose, God prepared a sultry east wind, and the sun beat down on the head of Jonah so that he was faint and asked that he might die. He said, "It is better for me to die than to live."

9 But God said to Jonah, "Is it right for you to be angry about the bush?" And he said, "Yes, angry enough to die." 10Then the LORD said, "You are concerned about the bush, for which you did not labor and which you did not grow; it came into being in a night and perished in a night. 11And should I not be concerned about Nineveh, that great city, in which there are more than a hundred and twenty thousand persons who do not know their right hand from their left, and also many animals?"

3.1–10: The Ninevites repent and are saved. An irony* that underlies the response of the people of Nineveh to Jonah's preaching is that, while the people of Israel and Judah seldom respond to their own prophets by repenting (Hos 9.7; Am 4.6–12), these wicked enemies repent immediately. 6: *Sackcloth** and *ashes* are traditional signs of mourning and repentance (Joel 1.13; Isa 58.5). 7–8: By including Nineveh's *animals* in the rituals of fasting, wearing sackcloth, and praying to God, the narrator emphasizes

4.1–11: God's lesson to Jonah. In the final episode of Jonah's story, the prophet's self-interest is contrasted with God's compassion for others, even for those people considered enemies of Israel and Judah. 2: When Jonah says "*You are a gracious God and merciful,*" he

a Heb *qiqayon*, possibly *the castor bean plant*

is quoting an ancient Israelite creedal statement affirming God's compassion for the repentant and judgment on the unrepentant (Ex 34.6–7; Joel 2.13). **6:** The castor bean, the best suggestion for the Hebrew "qiqayon" (rendered here *bush*), is a perennial herb whose oil was used in antiquity for medicine and as fuel for oil lamps. Its large leaves could provide a modest amount of shade. **11:** The final phrase of the story, *many animals*, recalls the repentance of the animals in 3.7–8 and, not without a bit of humor and irony, emphasizes again the extent of God's compassion.

MICAH

Introduction

The book of Micah is a collection of two distinct kinds of prophetic speeches. One kind of speech is the judgment speech that indicts its listeners for the crimes they have committed and sentences them to an appropriate punishment. Such judgment speeches, found in chs. 1–3, 6, and 7.17, focus on Samaria, the capital of the northern kingdom of Israel; on Jerusalem, the capital of the southern kingdom of Judah; and on their ruling elite. Rulers, judges, priests, and prophets★ are accused of corruption and of mistreating and misleading their people (3.1, 5, 11). The other kind of address is the salvation speech. Such speeches, found in chs. 4–5, and 7.8–20, describe the misfortune their listeners have experienced and predict a period of renewal and restoration for them. The misfortune described in these speeches is most often the exile of Israelites that followed the fall of Samaria and Jerusalem (4.6, 10; 5.8). And the prediction of renewal anticipates the restoration of Jerusalem as a religious and political center (4.2, 7, 13; 7.11). Both kinds of speeches may have been delivered by a single prophet who predicted both judgment and the salvation that would follow it. The character of these speeches, however, suggests that they arose in two different historical contexts.

The judgment speeches in the book of Micah (chs. 1–3, 6; 7.1–7) come from a period in which both Samaria and Jerusalem were threatened by the imperial expansion of the Assyrian empire (1.6–9). Such was the case during the period assigned in the book's title (1.1) to Micah's prophetic career, the latter part of the eighth century BCE marked by the reigns of the Judean kings Jotham (742–735), Ahaz (735–715), and Hezekiah (715–687). Therefore these speeches are widely regarded as those of the prophet Micah, after whom the book was named. They were delivered to a ruling elite that was both corrupt and complacent, unaware of the grave danger in which they and their people lived (3.11–12). The salvation speeches (chs. 4–5; 7.8–20), by contrast, are addressed to people in exile and express many of the themes—the shame of defeat (4.11), life among the nations (5.7), divine forgiveness (7.18), return to Judah (4.6), the restoration of Jerusalem (4.8; 7.11), and judgment on the nations (4.13; 7.10)—of other exilic literature (Isa 40–55). Therefore it may be best to understand these parts of Micah as supplements added in the sixth century by those who preserved Micah's prophecy, in order to link Micah's message to a new era.

READING GUIDE

Like many other prophetic books, Micah must be read as an anthology of short speeches rather than as a unified narrative★ or as a single, continuous argument. In Micah's case, it is especially important to distinguish the judgment speeches from the salvation speeches and to keep their distinct historical contexts in mind.

1 The word of the LORD that came to Micah of Moresheth in the days of Kings Jotham, Ahaz, and Hezekiah of Judah, which he saw concerning Samaria and Jerusalem.

1.1: Title. Micah's home is the small village of *Moresheth*, southwest of Jerusalem in the southern kingdom of Judah, but his speeches are directed to *Samaria* and *Jerusalem*, capital cities of the north and the south.

~~~~~~~~~~~~~~~~~~~~~~~~~~~~

2 Hear, you peoples, all of you;
    listen, O earth, and all that is in it;
  and let the Lord GOD be a witness
      against you,
    the Lord from his holy temple.
3 For lo, the LORD is coming out of his
      place,
    and will come down and tread upon
      the high places of the earth.
4 Then the mountains will melt under
      him
    and the valleys will burst open,
  like wax near the fire,
    like waters poured down a
      steep place.
5 All this is for the transgression of Jacob
    and for the sins of the house of Israel.
  What is the transgression of Jacob?
    Is it not Samaria?
  And what is the high place[a] of Judah?
    Is it not Jerusalem?
6 Therefore I will make Samaria a heap in
      the open country,
    a place for planting vineyards.
  I will pour down her stones into
      the valley,
    and uncover her foundations.
7 All her images shall be beaten to pieces,
    all her wages shall be burned with
      fire,
  and all her idols I will lay waste;
  for as the wages of a prostitute she
      gathered them,
    and as the wages of a prostitute they
      shall again be used.

8 For this I will lament and wail;
    I will go barefoot and naked;
  I will make lamentation like the jackals,
    and mourning like the ostriches.

9 For her wound[b] is incurable.
    It has come to Judah;
  it has reached to the gate of my people,
    to Jerusalem.

1.2–9: Judgment on Samaria and Jerusalem. Micah's opening speech focuses on his primary audience: the ruling elite in the capitals of Israel and Judah. **3–4:** Divine appearances so powerful that they throw nature into disarray are common at the beginning of prophetic books (Am 1.2; Nah 1.3–5). **5:** *Samaria* and *Jerusalem* are viewed as the centers of corruption in their respective kingdoms. **6–7:** The end of *Samaria*, forecast here, occurred during Micah's career in 721 BCE when the Assyrians conquered Israel. **9:** A threat to *Jerusalem*, but not its end, is described.

~~~~~~~~~~~~~~~~~~~~~~~~~~~~

10 Tell it not in Gath,
    weep not at all;
  in Beth-leaphrah
    roll yourselves in the dust.
11 Pass on your way,
    inhabitants of Shaphir,
    in nakedness and shame;
  the inhabitants of Zaanan
    do not come forth;
  Beth-ezel is wailing
    and shall remove its support from you.
12 For the inhabitants of Maroth
    wait anxiously for good,
  yet disaster has come down from
      the LORD
    to the gate of Jerusalem.
13 Harness the steeds to the chariots,
    inhabitants of Lachish;
  it was the beginning of sin
    to daughter Zion,
  for in you were found
    the transgressions of Israel.
14 Therefore you shall give parting gifts
    to Moresheth-gath;
  the houses of Achzib shall be
      a deception
    to the kings of Israel.
15 I will again bring a conqueror upon you,
    inhabitants of Mareshah;
  the glory of Israel
    shall come to Adullam.

---

a Heb *what are the high places*   *b* Gk Syr Vg: Heb *wounds*

The Assyrian Invasion

The invasion of Judah by Sennacherib of Assyria, described in 1.10–16, is also documented in other ancient sources. Additional perspective is supplied by the following accounts, one from Israel's historians (2 Kings 18.13–16) and another from an Assyrian source.

As to Hezekiah, the Jew, he did not submit to my yoke, I laid siege to 46 of his strong cities, walled forts and to the countless small villages in their vicinity, and conquered (them) by means of well-stamped (earth-)ramps, and battering-rams brought (thus) near (to the walls) (combined with) the attack by foot soldiers, (using) mines, breeches as well as sapper work. I drove out (of them) 200,150 people, young and old, male and female, horses, mules, donkeys, camels, big and small cattle beyond counting, and considered (them) booty. Himself I made a prisoner in Jerusalem, his royal residence, like a bird in a cage. I surrounded him with earthwork in order to molest those who were leaving his city's gate. His towns which I had plundered, I took away from his country and gave them (over) to Mitini, king of Ashdod, Padi, king of Ekron, and Sillibel, king of Gaza. Thus I reduced his country, but I still increased the tribute and the *katrû*-presents (due) to me (as his) overlord which I imposed (later) upon him beyond the former tribute, to be delivered annually.—From the Annals of Sennacherib

In the fourteenth year of King Hezekiah, King Sennacherib of Assyria came up against all the fortified cities of Judah and captured them. King Hezekiah of Judah sent to the king of Assyria at Lachish, saying, "I have done wrong; withdraw from me; whatever you impose on me I will bear." The king of Assyria demanded of King Hezekiah of Judah three hundred talents of silver and thirty talents of gold. Hezekiah gave him all the silver that was found in the house of the LORD and in the treasuries of the king's house. At that time Hezekiah stripped the gold from the doors of the temple of the LORD, and from the doorposts that King Hezekiah of Judah had overlaid and gave it of the king of Assyria.—2 Kings 18.13–16 (NRSV)

¹⁶ Make yourselves bald and cut off your
    hair
  for your pampered children;
make yourselves as bald as the eagle,
  for they have gone from you
    into exile.

1.10–16: A lament* over the invasion of Judah. This speech may have been composed in response to the invasion in 701 BCE of the Assyrian King Sennacherib, who conquered *Lachish* (v. 13) together with other cities and towns in the Judean foothills in the vicinity of Micah's own village *Moresheth-gath* (v. 14; see sidebar above). Among the towns Micah lists as bearing the brunt of the Assyrian attack, *Beth-ezel* (v. 11), *Lachish* (v. 13), *Moresheth-gath* and *Achzib* (v. 14), and *Mareshah* and *Adullam* (v. 15) have all been identified with sites in the Judean foothills (see map on p.

1260), and the other places mentioned were likely situated in this vicinity as well.

2 Alas for those who devise wickedness
  and evil deeds*a* on their beds!
When the morning dawns, they
    perform it,
  because it is in their power.
² They covet fields, and seize them;
  houses, and take them away;
they oppress householder and house,
  people and their inheritance.
³ Therefore thus says the LORD:
  Now, I am devising against this family
    an evil

a Cn: Heb *work evil*

from which you cannot remove your
    necks;
and you shall not walk haughtily,
    for it will be an evil time.
4 On that day they shall take up a taunt
       song against you,
    and wail with bitter lamentation,
and say, "We are utterly ruined;
    the LORD *a* alters the inheritance of
       my people;
how he removes it from me!
    Among our captors *b* he parcels out
       our fields."
5 Therefore you will have no one to cast
       the line by lot
    in the assembly of the LORD.

2.1–5: Judgment for economic crimes. The theme of
this speech is the exploitation of the poor by the rich.
1–2: The indictment blames the wealthy for seizing
fields unfairly, including the ancestral *inheritance*
which was not to leave a family's possession. **3–5:** The
sentence imposes a punishment that suits the crime:
The wealthy will lose their own *fields* and others will
divide them among themselves.

6 "Do not preach"—thus they preach—
    "one should not preach of such things;
    disgrace will not overtake us."
7 Should this be said, O house of Jacob?
    Is the LORD's patience exhausted?
    Are these his doings?
Do not my words do good
    to one who walks uprightly?
8 But you rise up against my people *c* as
       an enemy;
    you strip the robe from the peaceful, *d*
from those who pass by trustingly
    with no thought of war.
9 The women of my people you drive out
    from their pleasant houses;
from their young children you take away
    my glory forever.
10 Arise and go;
    for this is no place to rest,
because of uncleanness that destroys
    with a grievous destruction. *e*
11 If someone were to go about uttering
       empty falsehoods,
    saying, "I will preach to you of wine
       and strong drink,"

such a one would be the preacher for
    this people!

2.6–11: The true prophets' message rejected. Opposition to prophets* such as Micah who pronounce
judgment arises from the belief that a disaster is un-
thinkable: "*Disgrace will not overtake us*" (v. 6; 3.5,
11). **9:** Micah tells the male elite (*you* is a masculine
plural form in Hebrew) that *women* and *children* will
bear the punishment for their sins. **11:** False prophets
dull the senses like liquor.

12 I will surely gather all of you, O Jacob,
    I will gather the survivors of Israel;
    I will set them together
       like sheep in a fold,
like a flock in its pasture;
    it will resound with people.
13 The one who breaks out will go up
       before them;
    they will break through and pass the
       gate,
    going out by it.
Their king will pass on before them,
    the LORD at their head.

2.12–13: Salvation for the survivors. This brief
speech, describing returning exiles as a flock of sheep
led by the LORD, is characteristic of the later, exilic parts
of Micah (4.6–8) and of other exilic literature (Isa
40.10–11). It is likely a supplement added to Micah's
own speeches.

3 And I said:
    Listen, you heads of Jacob
       and rulers of the house of Israel!
    Should you not know justice?—
2   you who hate the good and love the
       evil,
    who tear the skin off my people, *f*
       and the flesh off their bones;
3 who eat the flesh of my people,
    flay their skin off them,
break their bones in pieces,
    and chop them up like meat *g* in a
       kettle,
    like flesh in a caldron.

a Heb *he*   *b* Cn: Heb *the rebellious*   *c* Cn: Heb *But*
yesterday my people rose   *d* Cn: Heb *from before a*
garment   *e* Meaning of Heb uncertain   *f* Heb *from*
them   *g* Gk: Heb *as*

[3.4–3.5]

4 Then they will cry to the LORD,
   but he will not answer them;
   he will hide his face from them at that
      time,
   because they have acted wickedly.

5 Thus says the LORD concerning
      the prophets
   who lead my people astray,
   who cry "Peace"
   when they have something to eat,

■▸▸■

Map The Assyrian conquest of southwestern Judah

but declare war against those
  who put nothing into their mouths.
6 Therefore it shall be night to you,
    without vision,
  and darkness to you, without
    revelation.
The sun shall go down upon
    the prophets,
  and the day shall be black over
    them;
7 the seers shall be disgraced,
  and the diviners put to shame;
they shall all cover their lips,
  for there is no answer from God.
8 But as for me, I am filled with power,
  with the spirit of the LORD,
  and with justice and might,
to declare to Jacob his transgression
  and to Israel his sin.

9 Hear this, you rulers of the house of
    Jacob
  and chiefs of the house of Israel,
who abhor justice
  and pervert all equity,
10 who build Zion with blood
  and Jerusalem with wrong!
11 Its rulers give judgment for a bribe,
  its priests teach for a price,
  its prophets give oracles for money;
yet they lean upon the LORD and say,
  "Surely the LORD is with us!
  No harm shall come upon us."
12 Therefore because of you
  Zion shall be plowed as a field;
Jerusalem shall become a heap of ruins,
  and the mountain of the house a
    wooded height.

3.1–12: Judgment on the ruling elite. Chapter 3 is composed of three typical judgment speeches, each with an indictment of crimes and a sentence of punishment for them, directed at political and religious leaders. The theme introduced in Micah's opening speech, that the corruption of Israel and Judah stems from the highest levels of power in its capital cities, continues here. **1–4:** The first judgment speech, directed to political officials, includes an indictment (vv.1–3), accusing them of devouring their people by their injustices, and a sentence (v. 4), according to which they are abandoned by God. **5–8:** The second

judgment speech, directed to false *prophets*, indicts them for accepting bribes to give favorable prophecies (v. 5). The sentence by which they are blocked from receiving further revelations (vv. 6–7) is contrasted with Micah's own power to preach (v. 8). **9–12:** The third judgment speech indicts Jerusalem's political and religious leaders alike: its political *rulers*, its *priests*, and its *prophets* (vv. 9–11). The sentence Micah announces, the fall of *Jerusalem* (v. 12), sets him off from his contemporary Isaiah, who thought Jerusalem would be threatened but not conquered (Isa 29.1–8). Jerusalem in fact survived the Assyrian invasion and did not fall during Micah's career. Nearly a hundred years later, when the prophet Jeremiah also predicted the fall of Jerusalem and was about to be sentenced to death for his prediction, Micah's prophecy was recalled in Jeremiah's defense (Jer 26.16–19).

4 In days to come
  the mountain of the LORD's house
shall be established as the highest of the
    mountains,
  and shall be raised up above
    the hills.
Peoples shall stream to it,
2   and many nations shall come
    and say:
"Come, let us go up to the mountain of
    the LORD,
  to the house of the God of Jacob;
that he may teach us his ways
  and that we may walk in his paths."
For out of Zion shall go forth
    instruction,
  and the word of the LORD
    from Jerusalem.
3 He shall judge between many peoples,
  and shall arbitrate between strong
    nations far away;
they shall beat their swords into
    plowshares,
  and their spears into pruning
    hooks;
nation shall not lift up sword against
    nation,
  neither shall they learn war
    any more;
4 but they shall all sit under their own
    vines and under their own fig
    trees,
  and no one shall make them afraid;

for the mouth of the LORD of hosts
　　has spoken.

5 For all the peoples walk,
　　each in the name of its god,
but we will walk in the name of the
　　　LORD our God
　　forever and ever.

4.1–5: God rules from Jerusalem. This begins a new
collection of speeches (chs. 4–5) that announce salvation rather than judgment. They stress the return of
the Israelite exiles and the restoration of Jerusalem to
its former power and prestige. This same speech, celebrating God's rule over the nations in an era of universal disarmament, is preserved also among the
speeches of Micah's contemporary Isaiah (2.1–5). **1:**
The *mountain* on which the Temple* in Jerusalem is
located is in reality overshadowed by higher peaks in
the vicinity.

---

6 In that day, says the LORD,
　　I will assemble the lame
and gather those who have been driven
　　　away,
　　and those whom I have afflicted.
7 The lame I will make the remnant,
　　and those who were cast off, a strong
　　　nation;
and the LORD will reign over them in
　　　Mount Zion
　　now and forevermore.

8 And you, O tower of the flock,
　　hill of daughter Zion,
to you it shall come,
　　the former dominion shall come,
　　the sovereignty of daughter
　　　Jerusalem.

9 Now why do you cry aloud?
　　Is there no king in you?
Has your counselor perished,
　　that pangs have seized you like a
　　　woman in labor?
10 Writhe and groan,*a* O daughter Zion,
　　like a woman in labor;
for now you shall go forth from
　　　the city
　　and camp in the open country;
　　you shall go to Babylon.

There you shall be rescued,
　　there the LORD will redeem you
　　from the hands of your enemies.
11 Now many nations
　　are assembled against you,
saying, "Let her be profaned,
　　and let our eyes gaze upon Zion."
12 But they do not know
　　the thoughts of the LORD;
they do not understand his plan,
　　that he has gathered them as sheaves
　　　to the threshing floor.
13 Arise and thresh,
　　O daughter Zion,
for I will make your horn iron
　　and your hoofs bronze;
you shall beat in pieces many peoples,
　　and shall*b* devote their gain to the
　　　LORD,
　　their wealth to the Lord of the whole
　　　earth.

5 *c*Now you are walled around with
　　　a wall;*d*
　　siege is laid against us;
with a rod they strike the ruler of Israel
　　upon the cheek.

4.6–5.1: God gathers the exiles to Jerusalem. 6: This
characterization of the returning exiles as *lame* recalls
other exilic descriptions of them as similarly disabled
(Zeph 3.19–20; Isa 35.5–10). **8:** The phrase *former dominion* looks back to the time of the prophet Micah
when Jerusalem was capital of an independent kingdom. **9–10:** The image of *a woman in labor*, commonly used to describe excruciating pain, is also employed by Jeremiah to describe the suffering of the
exiles (30.1–7). **10:** *Babylon* is the Mesopotamian city
to which Jerusalem's leaders were deported when the
city fell to the Babylonians in 587 BCE. **13:** The image
of an ox threshing* grain is used to describe God's
judgment of the nations that have oppressed and exiled the Israelites (Isa 41.14–16).

2*e*But you, O Bethlehem of Ephrathah,
　　who are one of the little clans
　　　of Judah,

a Meaning of Heb uncertain　　*b* Gk Syr Tg: Heb *and
I will*　　*c* Ch 4.14 in Heb　　*d* Cn Compare Gk:
Meaning of Heb uncertain　　*e* Ch 5.1 in Heb

from you shall come forth for me
　　one who is to rule in Israel,
　whose origin is from of old,
　　from ancient days.
3 Therefore he shall give them up until
　　the time
　when she who is in labor has brought
　　forth;
　then the rest of his kindred shall
　　return
　　to the people of Israel.
4 And he shall stand and feed his flock in
　　the strength of the LORD,
　in the majesty of the name of the
　　LORD his God.
　And they shall live secure, for now he
　　shall be great
　to the ends of the earth;
5 and he shall be the one of peace.

5.2–5a: A new ruler. 2: By associating the new ruler over a restored Israel with *Bethlehem*, David's home town, and with *Ephrathah*, David's clan* (1 Sam 17.12), the author announces that the coming ruler will revive the dynasty* of David, which ruled in Jerusalem before it fell to the Babylonians in 587 BCE.

　If the Assyrians come into our land
　　and tread upon our soil,*
　we will raise against them seven
　　shepherds
　　and eight installed as rulers.
6 They shall rule the land of Assyria with
　　the sword,
　and the land of Nimrod with the
　　drawn sword;*
　they* shall rescue us from the Assyrians
　if they come into our land
　or tread within our border.
7 Then the remnant of Jacob,
　　surrounded by many peoples,
　shall be like dew from the LORD,
　　like showers on the grass,
　which do not depend upon people
　　or wait for any mortal.
8 And among the nations the remnant of
　　Jacob,
　　surrounded by many peoples,
　shall be like a lion among the animals of
　　the forest,

like a young lion among the flocks of
　　sheep,
　which, when it goes through,
　　treads down
　and tears in pieces, with no one to
　　deliver.
9 Your hand shall be lifted up over your
　　adversaries,
　and all your enemies shall be cut off.

10 In that day, says the LORD,
　　I will cut off your horses from among
　　you
　　and will destroy your chariots;
11 and I will cut off the cities of your
　　land
　　and throw down all your strongholds;
12 and I will cut off sorceries from your
　　hand,
　　and you shall have no more
　　soothsayers;
13 and I will cut off your images
　　and your pillars from among you,
　and you shall bow down no more
　　to the work of your hands;
14 and I will uproot your sacred poles*
　　from among you
　　and destroy your towns.
15 And in anger and wrath I will execute
　　vengeance
　on the nations that did not obey.

5.5b–15: Israel will be restored and its oppressors punished. 5–6: The *Assyrians* conquered the northern kingdom of Israel with its capital Samaria in 721 BCE. *Nimrod* was a legendary Assyrian ruler (Gen 10.8–12). **10–15:** It is unclear whether this judgment is intended for Israel or its enemies: The pronoun *you* appears to refer to Israel as it does in v. 9 and the content is typical of judgments on Israel, but the context of Israel's restoration and the reference to Israel's enemies in vv. 9 and 15 imply that this judgment is directed to them.

6 Hear what the LORD says:
　Rise, plead your case before
　　the mountains,
　　and let the hills hear your voice.

a Gk: Heb *in our palaces*　　*b* Cn: Heb *in its entrances*
c Heb *he*　　*d* Heb *Asherim*

2 Hear, you mountains, the controversy of
the LORD,
and you enduring foundations of the
earth;
for the LORD has a controversy with his
people,
and he will contend with Israel.

3 "O my people, what have I done
to you?
In what have I wearied you? Answer
me!
4 For I brought you up from the land of
Egypt,
and redeemed you from the house of
slavery;
and I sent before you Moses,
Aaron, and Miriam.
5 O my people, remember now what King
Balak of Moab devised,
what Balaam son of Beor answered
him,
and what happened from Shittim
to Gilgal,
that you may know the saving acts of
the LORD."

6 "With what shall I come before
the LORD,
and bow myself before God on
high?
Shall I come before him with
burnt offerings,
with calves a year old?
7 Will the LORD be pleased with
thousands of rams,
with ten thousands of rivers of oil?
Shall I give my firstborn for my
transgression,
the fruit of my body for the sin of my
soul?"
8 He has told you, O mortal, what
is good;
and what does the LORD require
of you
but to do justice, and to love kindness,
and to walk humbly with your God?

message to Israel as a lawsuit brought against the people. **1:** Elements of nature, like the *mountains* here,
are often called to witness solemn announcements
(1.2; Deut 32.1). **4:** *Moses, Aaron,* and *Miriam* were
Israel's leaders at the time of the exodus from *Egypt*
(Ex 4.10–17; 15.20–21). **5:** *King Balak of Moab* paid
Balaam son of Beor to curse the Israelites before they
entered Canaan, but God intervened (Num 22). The
Israelites passed *from Shittim to Gilgal* when they
crossed the Jordan River to enter the land of Canaan
(Josh 3–4). **6–8:** Like other prophets* (Am 5.21–24),
Micah asserts that religious rituals are meaningless
without the pursuit of justice in all areas of life (see
sidebar on p. 1265).

9 The voice of the LORD cries to the city
(it is sound wisdom to fear
your name):
Hear, O tribe and assembly of the
city![a]
10 Can I forget[b] the treasures of
wickedness in the house of the
wicked,
and the scant measure that is
accursed?
11 Can I tolerate wicked scales
and a bag of dishonest weights?
12 Your[c] wealthy are full of violence;
your[d] inhabitants speak lies,
with tongues of deceit in
their mouths.
13 Therefore I have begun[e] to strike you
down,
making you desolate because of your
sins.
14 You shall eat, but not be satisfied,
and there shall be a gnawing hunger
within you;
you shall put away, but not save,
and what you save, I will hand over to
the sword.
15 You shall sow, but not reap;
you shall tread olives, but not anoint
yourselves with oil;
you shall tread grapes, but not drink
wine.

6.1–8: God demands justice above all. This speech,
beginning the second collection from the eighth-
century prophet Micah (6.1–7.7), describes God's

a Cn Compare Gk: Heb *tribe, and who has appointed it
yet?*   *b* Cn: Meaning of Heb uncertain
c Heb *Whose*   *d* Heb *whose*   *e* Gk Syr Vg: Heb *have
made sick*

"What does the LORD require of you?"

Micah 6.8 is a concise summary of prophetic thought, based on three important Hebrew terms. The first, "mishpat," *justice*, is the basic word used by Israel's prophets to describe the fairness and equality they believed should govern all social relationships (Isa 1.27; Am 5.24). The second, "hesed," usually translated *kindness* (as here) or "mercy," is better translated "loyalty" or "integrity," since the word describes fulfilling one's social obligations responsibly. The third, "hatsnea' lekhet," *to walk humbly*, describes a way of life directly opposed to the exploitation of power that Micah sees as the root of the corruption and injustice in his society (1.5; 3.11; 7.3).

16 For you have kept the statutes of Omri^a
 and all the works of the house
  of Ahab,
 and you have followed their counsels.
 Therefore I will make you a desolation,
  and your^b inhabitants an object
   of hissing;
 so you shall bear the scorn of
  my people.

6.9–16: Judgment on Israel's businessmen. Micah resumes his attack on Israel's leadership, indicting its wealthy citizens for cheating the poor (vv. 9–12) and imposing a sentence by which they will be unable to enjoy the profits they have earned unfairly (vv. 13–16). **11:** Merchants use false *weights* to shortchange customers (Am 8.5). **16:** *Omri* and *Ahab* were the first two kings of a dynasty that ruled Samaria for 131 years (876–745 BCE).

7 Woe is me! For I have become like
  one who,
 after the summer fruit has
   been gathered,
 after the vintage has been gleaned,
 finds no cluster to eat;
  there is no first-ripe fig for which I
   hunger.
2 The faithful have disappeared from the
   land,
 and there is no one left who
   is upright;
 they all lie in wait for blood,
  and they hunt each other with nets.
3 Their hands are skilled to do evil;

 the official and the judge ask for a
   bribe,
 and the powerful dictate what
   they desire;
 thus they pervert justice.^c
4 The best of them is like a brier,
  the most upright of them a
   thorn hedge.
 The day of their^d sentinels, of their^d
   punishment, has come;
 now their confusion is at hand.
5 Put no trust in a friend,
  have no confidence in a loved one;
 guard the doors of your mouth
  from her who lies in your embrace;
6 for the son treats the father with
   contempt,
 the daughter rises up against
   her mother,
 the daughter-in-law against her
   mother-in-law;
 your enemies are members of your
   own household.
7 But as for me, I will look to the LORD,
 I will wait for the God of my
   salvation;
 my God will hear me.

7.1–7: "The powerful dictate what they desire" (v. 3). From the opening speech, in which Micah singles out for criticism the capitals of Israel and Judah, to this concluding speech (7.8–20 is an exilic supple-

a Gk Syr Vg Tg: Heb *the statutes of Omri are kept*
b Heb *its*   c Cn: Heb *they weave it*   d Heb *your*

ment), the abuse of power is a central concern in Micah's message. In this speech, Micah laments the spread of corruption from the powerful (vv. 1–4) to friend and family (vv. 5–6).

8 Do not rejoice over me, O my enemy;
when I fall, I shall rise;
when I sit in darkness,
the LORD will be a light to me.
9 I must bear the indignation of
the LORD,
because I have sinned against him,
until he takes my side
and executes judgment for me.
He will bring me out to the light;
I shall see his vindication.
10 Then my enemy will see,
and shame will cover her who said
to me,
"Where is the LORD your God?"
My eyes will see her downfall;[a]
now she will be trodden down
like the mire of the streets.

11 A day for the building of your walls!
In that day the boundary shall be far
extended.
12 In that day they will come to you
from Assyria to[b] Egypt,
and from Egypt to the River,
from sea to sea and from mountain to
mountain.
13 But the earth will be desolate
because of its inhabitants,
for the fruit of their doings.

14 Shepherd your people with your staff,
the flock that belongs to you,
which lives alone in a forest
in the midst of a garden land;
let them feed in Bashan and Gilead
as in the days of old.
15 As in the days when you came out of
the land of Egypt,
show us[c] marvelous things.

16 The nations shall see and be ashamed
of all their might;
they shall lay their hands on
their mouths;
their ears shall be deaf;
17 they shall lick dust like a snake,
like the crawling things of the earth;
they shall come trembling out of their
fortresses;
they shall turn in dread to the LORD
our God,
and they shall stand in fear of you.

18 Who is a God like you, pardoning
iniquity
and passing over the transgression
of the remnant of your[d] possession?
He does not retain his anger forever,
because he delights in showing
clemency.
19 He will again have compassion upon us;
he will tread our iniquities under foot.
You will cast all our[e] sins
into the depths of the sea.
20 You will show faithfulness to Jacob
and unswerving loyalty to Abraham,
as you have sworn to our ancestors
from the days of old.

7.8–20: Israel is pardoned and restored. Like the speeches in chs. 4–5, this speech addresses the plight of the exiles after the fall of Jerusalem in 587 BCE. 11: *The building of your walls* anticipates the reconstruction of Jerusalem. 12: The surrounding nations will recognize Jerusalem's new stature (4.1–5). 14: *Bashan* and *Gilead*, east of the Jordan, were prime pasture land. 15: The return from Babylonian captivity is viewed as a second Exodus, an event as significant as the first deliverance from slavery (Isa 51.9–11).

a Heb lacks *downfall*   b One Ms: MT *Assyria and cities of*   c Cn: Heb *I will show him*   d Heb *his*   e Gk Syr Vg Tg: Heb *their*

NAHUM

Introduction

Like the speeches of the prophet* Obadiah, Nahum's speeches are directed entirely to one of Israel's neighbors rather than to Israel itself. The object of Nahum's speeches is Nineveh, the capital city of the Assyrian empire for almost a hundred years, and the subject of his speeches is God's judgment on this city for its cruel treatment of its neighbors. Feelings of anger and vengeance run through the book (1.2, 6) together with a delight in the complete devastation of the city (3.19). Yet behind these emotions lies a belief in God's just government of world affairs. Assyria was an ancient superpower that had dominated its smaller, weaker neighbors through policies of colonial expansion and heavy taxation. Thus its demise was viewed by citizens of its satellite countries, such as Israel and Judah, as just punishment for its oppressive exploitation (2.10–13) and as a time of new freedom (1.12–13) and economic and religious revival (1.15; 2.2).

Nineveh, an ancient and powerful Assyrian city, became capital of the Assyrian empire during the reign of Sennacherib (704–681 BCE). It was, thereafter, the chief Assyrian city and a symbol of the empire itself, until it fell to the armies of the Medes and the Babylonians in 612 BCE. It was not long before Nineveh's fall that these speeches predicting its end were likely composed by the prophet Nahum. This distinguishes Nahum from the eighth-century prophets, Hosea, Amos, and Micah, who precede him in the collection of Minor Prophets, and it makes him a contemporary of Habakkuk and Zephaniah, who follow.

READING GUIDE

The strong emotions and extended descriptions of destruction in Nahum are best understood if the reader keeps in mind that Nahum was a citizen of a country that had been cruelly oppressed as a result of Nineveh's colonial ambitions.

1 An oracle concerning Nineveh. The book of the vision of Nahum of Elkosh.

2 A jealous and avenging God is
    the LORD,
  the LORD is avenging and wrathful;
  the LORD takes vengeance on his
    adversaries
  and rages against his enemies.
3 The LORD is slow to anger but great in
    power,
  and the LORD will by no means clear
    the guilty.

His way is in whirlwind and storm,
  and the clouds are the dust of
    his feet.

4 He rebukes the sea and makes it dry,
  and he dries up all the rivers;
  Bashan and Carmel wither,
  and the bloom of Lebanon fades.
5 The mountains quake before him,
  and the hills melt;
  the earth heaves before him,
  the world and all who live in it.

1.1–5. 1: **Title.** The location of the Judean town *Elkosh* is unknown. **2–8: God's terrifying power.** These verses make up an incomplete acrostic* poem, in which each two-line verse unit begins with the succeeding letter of the Hebrew alphabet.* **2:** The emphasis on the *vengeance* and *wrath* of God at the beginning of Nahum is related to the book's central theme: God's judgment of Nineveh for its cruelties.

3: God often appears in the form of a thunderstorm (Ex 19.16–17; Ps 77.17–18). **4:** The traditional enemy of the storm god in ancient Near Eastern mythology is the *sea* (alias river), a tradition reflected at points in biblical thought (Ps 89.9–10; Hab 3.8, 15). **4–5:** God's appearance shakes the world of nature (Am 1.2; Mic 1.3–4). *Bashan,* the highlands east of the Jordan, *Carmel,* the mountain range touching the Mediterranean Sea in northern Israel, and *Lebanon,* the coastal range north of Israel, were famous for their elevation and natural vegetation.

6 Who can stand before his indignation?
   Who can endure the heat of
     his anger?
His wrath is poured out like fire,
   and by him the rocks are broken in
     pieces.
7 The LORD is good,
   a stronghold in a day of trouble;
he protects those who take refuge
     in him,
8   even in a rushing flood.
He will make a full end of his
     adversaries,^a
and will pursue his enemies into
     darkness.
9 Why do you plot against the LORD?
   He will make an end;
   no adversary will rise up twice.
10 Like thorns they are entangled,
   like drunkards they are drunk;
   they are consumed like dry straw.
11 From you one has gone out
   who plots evil against the LORD,
   one who counsels wickedness.

12 Thus says the LORD,
   "Though they are at full strength
     and many,^b
   they will be cut off and pass away.
Though I have afflicted you,
   I will afflict you no more.
13 And now I will break off his yoke
     from you
   and snap the bonds that bind you."
14 The LORD has commanded
     concerning you:
   "Your name shall be perpetuated no
     longer;

from the house of your gods I will
     cut off
   the carved image and the cast image.
I will make your grave, for you
     are worthless."

15^c Look! On the mountains the feet of one
   who brings good tidings,
   who proclaims peace!
Celebrate your festivals, O Judah,
   fulfill your vows,
for never again shall the wicked
     invade you;
   they are utterly cut off.

2 A shatterer^d has come up against you.
   Guard the ramparts;
   watch the road;
gird your loins;
   collect all your strength.

1.9–15: Nineveh will be judged and Judah restored. The audience shifts repeatedly in this brief speech from Nineveh to Judah and back again. **9:** Nahum addresses the Ninevites (*you* is masculine plural in Hebrew). **10:** *Thorns* (Isa 34.13), *drunkards* (Lam 4.21), and *stubble* (Ob 18) are all images used for enemies whom God punishes. **11:** Nahum addresses the city of Nineveh (*you* is now feminine singular) and describes its king as *one who has gone out.* **12–13:** While *you* is still feminine singular in form, Nahum is now addressing Judah, describing its new freedom from Assyrian control as a release from imprisonment. **14:** Nahum turns to address the Assyrian king (*you* is now masculine singular). **15:** The poem concludes with words of hope to *Judah,* delivered by a member of the heavenly court.

2 (For the LORD is restoring the majesty
     of Jacob,
   as well as the majesty of Israel,
though ravagers have ravaged them
   and ruined their branches.)

3 The shields of his warriors are red;
   his soldiers are clothed in crimson.
The metal on the chariots flashes
   on the day when he musters them;
   the chargers^e prance.

a Gk: Heb *of her place*   b Meaning of Heb uncertain
c Ch 2.1 in Heb   d Cn: Heb *scatterer*
e Cn Compare Gk Syr: Heb *cypresses*

4 The chariots race madly through the
        streets,
    they rush to and fro through
        the squares;
    their appearance is like torches,
        they dart like lightning.
5 He calls his officers;
        they stumble as they come forward;
    they hasten to the wall,
        and the mantelet*a* is set up.
6 The river gates are opened,
        the palace trembles.
7 It is decreed*a* that the city*b* be exiled,
        its slave women led away,
    moaning like doves
        and beating their breasts.
8 Nineveh is like a pool
        whose waters*c* run away.
    "Halt! Halt!"—
        but no one turns back.
9 "Plunder the silver,
        plunder the gold!
    There is no end of treasure!
        An abundance of every precious
            thing!"

2.1–3.7: Nineveh is attacked. The detailed descriptions of a military assault on Nineveh and of battles in
its streets anticipate the imminent end of the city. **2.1:**
The *shatterer* (or "scatterer"; see note *d*) is the enemy
army attacking Nineveh. **2:** This verse appears to be
out of place, as the parentheses added by the translators indicate. It describes the restoration of Judah,
interrupting the narrative* of the attack on Nineveh.
It probably once followed 1.15 or is a later scribal addition. **3–5:** The description of the army attacking Nineveh continues from v. 1. **5:** The Hebrew term translated by *mantelet* is a noun from the root, "weave,"
and may be a woven shield to protect soldiers in battle.
6: These *river gates* controlled a network of canals that
brought water into Nineveh from the Tigris and Khoser
rivers nearby. They appear to have been opened by
the enemy to flood the city (v. 8).

---

10 Devastation, desolation, and
            destruction!
        Hearts faint and knees tremble,
    all loins quake,
        all faces grow pale!
11 What became of the lions' den,
        the cave*d* of the young lions,

where the lion goes,
        and the lion's cubs, with no one to
            disturb them?
12 The lion has torn enough for
            his whelps
    and strangled prey for his lionesses;
        he has filled his caves with prey
            and his dens with torn flesh.

13 See, I am against you, says the LORD
of hosts, and I will burn your*e* chariots in
smoke, and the sword shall devour your
young lions; I will cut off your prey from the
earth, and the voice of your messengers shall
be heard no more.

3 Ah! City of bloodshed,
        utterly deceitful, full of booty—
        no end to the plunder!
2 The crack of whip and rumble of wheel,
        galloping horse and bounding
            chariot!
3 Horsemen charging,
        flashing sword and glittering spear,
    piles of dead,
        heaps of corpses,
    dead bodies without end—
        they stumble over the bodies!
4 Because of the countless debaucheries
            of the prostitute,
        gracefully alluring, mistress
            of sorcery,
    who enslaves*f* nations through her
            debaucheries,
        and peoples through her sorcery,
5 I am against you,
        says the LORD of hosts,
        and will lift up your skirts over your
            face;
    and I will let nations look on your
            nakedness
        and kingdoms on your shame.
6 I will throw filth at you
        and treat you with contempt,
        and make you a spectacle.
7 Then all who see you will shrink from
            you and say,

---

a Meaning of Heb uncertain   *b* Heb *it*
c Cn Compare Gk: Heb *a pool, from the days that she has
become, and they*   *d* Cn: Heb *pasture*   *e* Heb *her*
f Heb *sells*

"Nineveh is devastated; who will
 bemoan her?"
Where shall I seek comforters
 for you?

2.10–3.7. 2.11–13: The *lion* is frequently used in the
Bible as an image for a king and a royal family (Ezek
19.2–7), in this case for the king of Nineveh filling his
caves with plundered prey. **3.1:** The *City of bloodshed*
is Nineveh. **4–7:** Nahum now takes up the image of a
prostitute to describe Nineveh. *Nakedness* and the accompanying *shame* are traditional punishments for
promiscuous behavior (Isa 47.3; Jer 13.26).

8 Are you better than Thebes[a]
 that sat by the Nile,
with water around her,
 her rampart a sea,
 water her wall?
9 Ethiopia[b] was her strength,
 Egypt too, and that without limit;
 Put and the Libyans were her[c]
 helpers.

10 Yet she became an exile,
 she went into captivity;
even her infants were dashed
 in pieces
 at the head of every street;
lots were cast for her nobles,
 all her dignitaries were bound
 in fetters.
11 You also will be drunken,
 you will go into hiding;[d]
you will seek
 a refuge from the enemy.
12 All your fortresses are like fig trees
 with first-ripe figs—
if shaken they fall
 into the mouth of the eater.
13 Look at your troops:
 they are women in your midst.
The gates of your land
 are wide open to your foes;
 fire has devoured the bars of
 your gates.

14 Draw water for the siege,
 strengthen your forts;
trample the clay,
 tread the mortar,
 take hold of the brick mold!
15 There the fire will devour you,
 the sword will cut you off.
 It will devour you like the locust.

Multiply yourselves like the locust,
 multiply like the grasshopper!
16 You increased your merchants
 more than the stars of the heavens.
 The locust sheds its skin and
 flies away.
17 Your guards are like grasshoppers,
 your scribes like swarms[d] of locusts
settling on the fences
 on a cold day—
when the sun rises, they fly away;
 no one knows where they have gone.

18 Your shepherds are asleep,
 O king of Assyria;
 your nobles slumber.
Your people are scattered on the
 mountains
 with no one to gather them.
19 There is no assuaging your hurt,
 your wound is mortal.
 All who hear the news about you
 clap their hands over you.
 For who has ever escaped
 your endless cruelty?

3.8–19: Nineveh's fate is sealed. **8:** *Thebes* was the
capital of Upper Egypt which, though heavily defended, was destroyed by the Assyrians in 663 BCE. **9:**
Put is a North African people associated with *Egypt*
and *Ethiopia* (Jer 46.8–9). **19:** Nahum's final verse
summarizes the image of Nineveh held by all who had
suffered as a result of its imperial ambitions.

---

a Heb *No-amon*   b Or *Nubia*; Heb *Cush*
c Gk: Heb *your*   d Meaning of Heb uncertain

HABAKKUK

Introduction

The prophet* Habakkuk is primarily concerned about believing in God's just rule over a world that appears to be overwhelmingly unjust. In this regard, he is more like Job and the psalmists who lament undeserved suffering than he is like Israel's other prophets. The book of Habakkuk is organized as a dialogue between the prophet and God, in which Habakkuk twice challenges God's power and plan. To Habakkuk's first complaint about injustices in Judean society (1.2–4), God promises that the guilty will be punished by invading Chaldeans (1.5–11). To Habakkuk's second complaint that the Chaldeans themselves are corrupt (1.12–2.1), God assures Habakkuk that his rule is reliable, and God calls for the righteous to be steadfast (2.2–4). Following this dialogue, a series of sayings describes the suicidal nature of tyranny (2.5–20), confirming the inevitable and just end of oppressive power. The book's concluding hymn (ch. 3) has been interpreted variously as the full description of Habakkuk's vision (2.2), as Habakkuk's prayer that this vision be fulfilled, and as a hymn that later editors added to Habakkuk's speeches to further resolve the dilemma they raise. In any case, the theophany* in this hymn (3.3–15) draws heavily on ancient traditions in which God establishes order in the cosmos by conquering chaos, symbolized by raging seas.

Habakkuk's initial proclamation about injustices in Judean society (1.2–4) and God's announcement of the Chaldean invasion (1.5–11) probably occurred during the violent reign of Jehoiakim (609–598 BCE; 2 Kings 23.36–24.7) before the first Babylonian (Chaldean) invasion of Judah in 597 BCE. Habakkuk's second complaint, and perhaps the arrangement of the dialogues as a whole, logically arises from his firsthand experience of the Babylonians between their first invasion (597) and their final conquest of Judah and destruction of Jerusalem (587). The hymn in ch. 3 may be a very old victory hymn added by Habakkuk's editors after the fall of Jerusalem to reemphasize God's universal rule.

READING GUIDE

The dialogue between Habakkuk and God around which the book is organized can best be followed if the reader keeps in mind the major concern that drives it: believing in God's just rule in an unjust world.

1 The oracle that the prophet Habakkuk
saw.

2 O LORD, how long shall I cry for help,
and you will not listen?
Or cry to you "Violence!"
and you will not save?
3 Why do you make me see wrongdoing
and look at trouble?
Destruction and violence are before me;
strife and contention arise.

4 So the law becomes slack
and justice never prevails.
The wicked surround the righteous—
therefore judgment comes forth
perverted.

1.1–4. 1: **Title.** The customary information about family, home, and date are not provided for Habakkuk. **2–4: Habakkuk's opening complaint: Judean corruption.** Habakkuk draws attention to crimes in his society, not by an indictment as is customary for Israel's prophets* (Mic 3.9–12), but by a lament.* His lament begins, as do laments in the Psalms (3, 13), with an address to God (v. 2) followed by a description of distress (vv. 3–4). **3:** *Destruction* (or "plunder") and *violence* are used by other prophets (Am 3.10; Ezek 45.9) to describe the ruthless accumulation of wealth. *Strife* and *contention* describe a breakdown in Judah's legal and judicial systems.

5 Look at the nations, and see!
  Be astonished! Be astounded!
  For a work is being done in your days
    that you would not believe if you were
      told.
6 For I am rousing the Chaldeans,
    that fierce and impetuous nation,
  who march through the breadth of the
      earth
    to seize dwellings not their own.
7 Dread and fearsome are they;
    their justice and dignity proceed from
      themselves.
8 Their horses are swifter than leopards,
    more menacing than wolves at dusk;
    their horses charge.
  Their horsemen come from far away;
    they fly like an eagle swift to devour.
9 They all come for violence,
    with faces pressing^a forward;
    they gather captives like sand.
10 At kings they scoff,
    and of rulers they make sport.
  They laugh at every fortress,
    and heap up earth to take it.
11 Then they sweep by like the wind;
    they transgress and become guilty;
    their own might is their god!

1.5–11: God's response: a Chaldean invasion. God announces to Habakkuk that Judah's injustices will be punished by means of a foreign nation that will depose its current leadership. **6:** The *Chaldeans* are the Neo-Babylonians, who rose to prominence in the ancient Near East during the reign of Nebuchadnezzar II (605–562 BCE). **8:** The typical ancient Near Eastern military machine was built around horse-drawn chariots and cavalry.

12 Are you not from of old,
    O LORD my God, my Holy One?
  You^b shall not die.

O LORD, you have marked them for
    judgment;
  and you, O Rock, have established
    them for punishment.
13 Your eyes are too pure to behold evil,
    and you cannot look on wrongdoing;
  why do you look on the treacherous,
    and are silent when the wicked
      swallow
    those more righteous than they?
14 You have made people like the fish of
      the sea,
    like crawling things that have
      no ruler.
15 The enemy^c brings all of them up with
      a hook;
  he drags them out with his net,
    he gathers them in his seine;
    so he rejoices and exults.
16 Therefore he sacrifices to his net
    and makes offerings to his seine;
  for by them his portion is lavish,
    and his food is rich.
17 Is he then to keep on emptying his net,
    and destroying nations without
      mercy?

1.12–2.1: Habakkuk's second complaint: Chaldean corruption. In his second complaint—probably composed after the Babylonians invaded Judah in 597, replaced its king, deported its leading citizens, and collected tribute (2 Kings 24)—Habakkuk claims that the very instruments of God's *judgment* (v. 12), the Babylonians, are themselves *wicked* (v. 13). **16:** When the Babylonian enemy *sacrifices to his net*, he is worshipping his own military armaments. **1.17–2.1:** Habakkuk wonders whether the Babylonians' injustices will go unpunished (1.17) or whether God will respond (2.1).

2 I will stand at my watchpost,
    and station myself on the rampart;
  I will keep watch to see what he will say
      to me,
    and what he^d will answer concerning
      my complaint.

a Meaning of Heb uncertain   *b* Ancient Heb tradition:
MT *We*   *c* Heb *He*   *d* Syr: Heb *I*

2 Then the LORD answered me and said:
Write the vision;
 make it plain on tablets,
  so that a runner may read it.
3 For there is still a vision for the
  appointed time;
 it speaks of the end, and does not lie.
If it seems to tarry, wait for it;
 it will surely come, it will not delay.
4 Look at the proud!
 Their spirit is not right in them,
 but the righteous live by their faith.[a]
5 Moreover, wealth[b] is treacherous;
 the arrogant do not endure.
They open their throats wide as Sheol;
 like Death they never have enough.
They gather all nations for themselves,
 and collect all peoples as their own.

2.2–4: God's response: God's rule is reliable. 2: God
tells Habakkuk to record his revelation so that the
prophet as God's messenger can carry and announce
it to the people. **3:** God emphasizes the reliability of
Habakkuk's revelation. **4:** This verse may contain the
content of Habakkuk's revelation or instructions about
waiting for it. The main point is that *the righteous live
by their faith.* "Faithfulness" (see note *a*) is a better
translation, since the Hebrew "emunah" means "firmness, steadfastness," or "fidelity."

~~~~~~~~~~~~~~~~~~~~~~~~~~~~~~~~~~~~

6 Shall not everyone taunt such people
and, with mocking riddles, say about them,
 "Alas for you who heap up what is not
  your own!"
 How long will you load yourselves
  with goods taken in pledge?
7 Will not your own creditors suddenly
  rise,
 and those who make you tremble
  wake up?
 Then you will be booty for them.
8 Because you have plundered many
  nations,
 all that survive of the peoples shall
  plunder you—
because of human bloodshed, and
 violence to the earth,
 to cities and all who live in them.

9 "Alas for you who get evil gain for your
  houses,

 setting your nest on high
  to be safe from the reach of harm!"
10 You have devised shame for your house
 by cutting off many peoples;
 you have forfeited your life.
11 The very stones will cry out from the
  wall,
 and the plaster[c] will respond from
  the woodwork.

12 "Alas for you who build a town by
  bloodshed,
 and found a city on iniquity!"
13 Is it not from the LORD of hosts
 that peoples labor only to feed the
  flames,
 and nations weary themselves for
  nothing?
14 But the earth will be filled
 with the knowledge of the glory of
  the LORD,
 as the waters cover the sea.

15 "Alas for you who make your neighbors
  drink,
 pouring out your wrath[d] until they
  are drunk,
 in order to gaze on their
  nakedness!"
16 You will be sated with contempt instead
  of glory.
 Drink, you yourself, and stagger![e]
 The cup in the LORD's right hand
 will come around to you,
 and shame will come upon
  your glory!
17 For the violence done to Lebanon will
  overwhelm you;
 the destruction of the animals will
  terrify you—[f]
because of human bloodshed and
  violence to the earth,
 to cities and all who live in them.

18 What use is an idol
 once its maker has shaped it—
 a cast image, a teacher of lies?

a Or *faithfulness*   *b* Other Heb Mss read *wine*
c Or *beam*   *d* Or *poison*   *e* Q Ms Gk: MT *be
uncircumcised*   *f* Gk Syr: Meaning of Heb uncertain

For its maker trusts in what has been
made,
though the product is only an idol
that cannot speak!
19 Alas for you who say to the wood,
"Wake up!"
to silent stone, "Rouse yourself!"
Can it teach?
See, it is gold and silver plated,
and there is no breath in it at all.

20 But the LORD is in his holy temple;
let all the earth keep silence before
him!

**2.5–20: Five proverbial sayings about the fall of ty-
rants.** These sayings all claim that oppressors, like the
Babylonians, will be suitably judged (1.17). In each
saying, all of which except the last begin with "Alas,"
the tyrant experiences a reversal of fortune, as if imperial power has within it the seeds of its own destruction. **5:** The introduction to these sayings describes the
insatiable greed of the tyrant. *Sheol** is the realm of
the dead. **6–8:** Stolen wealth will itself be stolen. The
Hebrew term translated *creditors* may also mean
"debtors," a double meaning intended here. **9–11:**
Security will be lost in the very strongholds built to
ensure it. **12–14:** The greatest efforts of tyrants are
only fuel for the fire. **15–17:** Honor gained by shaming
others will itself turn to shame. **18–20:** False gods will
fall silent.

3 A prayer of the prophet Habakkuk according to Shigionoth.

2 O LORD, I have heard of your renown,
and I stand in awe, O LORD, of your
work.
In our own time revive it;
in our own time make it known;
in wrath may you remember mercy.
3 God came from Teman,
the Holy One from Mount Paran.
                                         Selah

His glory covered the heavens,
and the earth was full of his praise.
4 The brightness was like the sun;
rays came forth from his hand,
where his power lay hidden.
5 Before him went pestilence,
and plague followed close behind.

6 He stopped and shook the earth;
he looked and made the
nations tremble.
The eternal mountains were shattered;
along his ancient pathways
the everlasting hills sank low.
7 I saw the tents of Cushan under
affliction;
the tent-curtains of the land of
Midian trembled.
8 Was your wrath against the rivers,[a]
O LORD?
Or your anger against the rivers,[a]
or your rage against the sea,[b]
when you drove your horses,
your chariots to victory?
9 You brandished your naked bow,
sated[c] were the arrows at your
command.[d]   *Selah*
You split the earth with rivers.
10 The mountains saw you, and writhed;
a torrent of water swept by;
the deep gave forth its voice.
The sun[e] raised high its hands;
11 the moon[f] stood still in its exalted
place,
at the light of your arrows
speeding by,
at the gleam of your flashing spear.
12 In fury you trod the earth,
in anger you trampled nations.
13 You came forth to save your people,
to save your anointed.
You crushed the head of the
wicked house,
laying it bare from foundation
to roof.[d]   *Selah*
14 You pierced with their[g] own arrows the
head[h] of his warriors,[i]
who came like a whirlwind to
scatter us,[j]
gloating as if ready to devour the poor
who were in hiding.
15 You trampled the sea with your horses,
churning the mighty waters.

---

a Or *against River*   b Or *against Sea*   c Cn: Heb
oaths   d Meaning of Heb uncertain   e Heb *It*
f Heb *sun, moon*   g Heb *his*   h Or *leader*
i Vg Compare Gk Syr: Meaning of Heb uncertain
j Heb *me*

16 I hear, and I tremble within;
    my lips quiver at the sound.
Rottenness enters into my bones,
    and my steps tremble[a] beneath me.
I wait quietly for the day of calamity
    to come upon the people who
        attack us.

17 Though the fig tree does not blossom,
    and no fruit is on the vines;
though the produce of the olive fails,
    and the fields yield no food;
though the flock is cut off from the fold,
    and there is no herd in the stalls,

18 yet I will rejoice in the LORD;
    I will exult in the God of my
        salvation.

19 GOD, the Lord, is my strength;
    he makes my feet like the feet of a
        deer,
    and makes me tread upon the
        heights.[b]

To the leader: with stringed[c]
    instruments.

3.1–19: A hymn praising God's rule. This hymn describes a theophany,* a direct appearance of God (vv. 3–15), placed in a framework describing the poet's response to it (vv. 2, 16–19). **1:** Though attributing the hymn to Habakkuk, the title contains a musical notation, *according to Shigionoth* (a Hebrew word no longer understood), which is found elsewhere only in Ps 7. Other features of ch. 3 found elsewhere only in the Psalms—the term *Selah* (vv. 3, 9, 13; a Hebrew word no longer understood) and the musical notations in v. 19—suggest that this hymn may once have existed as a psalm, independent of the prophetic book

that it now concludes. **2:** The hymn's introduction and conclusion (vv. 16–19) are composed in the first-person perspective of the poet. **3–15:** The theophany describes God's march into battle (vv. 3–7) and conquest of his enemies (vv. 8–15). **3:** *Teman* and *Mount Paran* refer to a sacred mountain in the southern desert, perhaps to be identified with Mount Sinai (Horeb) and where God appeared to Moses and Israel (Ex 19; Deut 33.2–3). **5:** *Pestilence* and *plague* are divine figures in antiquity; they may be part of the heavenly armies God leads into battle. **7:** *Cushan* and *Midian* are inhabitants of the southern desert where God's march begins. They are shaken together with nature (v. 6) when God appears. **8:** The forces of chaos that challenge God's rule of the world are personified* in ancient mythology as Sea and River, as they may be here (see the alternative translations in notes a and b). By describing God's enemies here and in v. 15 as *sea* and *river*, the poet claims that God conquers chaotic forces in both cosmic and historical realms. **10–11:** The *sun* and *moon* are heavenly figures who are members of God's armies, like pestilence and plague (v. 5), or are simply startled by God's appearance together with the rest of nature. **13:** The *anointed** is Israel's military or political leader. As note d indicates, the Hebrew text of the second half of this verse is difficult. It may also be understood as *laying bare* the body of the *wicked* (Sea/River) from buttocks to neck, thus describing God's defeat of the powers of cosmic chaos as well as Israel's historical enemies. **16–19:** The conclusion resumes the first-person perspective of the introduction (v.2), describing the poet's own awe at God's appearance (v. 16) and joy because of God's victory and rule (vv. 18–19).

---

a Cn Compare Gk: Meaning of Heb uncertain
b Heb *my heights*   c Heb *my stringed*

ZEPHANIAH

Introduction

Most distinctive about Zephaniah is the absolute devastation that characterizes his images of God's punishment of the people of Judah and Jerusalem. Like most other prophets,✶ Zephaniah calls attention to the crimes of Judah's leaders, their corruption and idolatry✶ (1.4–9; 3.1–7). And like other prophets, he anticipates and announces an impending disaster brought on Judah by God to punish it for its crimes (1.2–2.3). But Zephaniah's description of this disaster, called by him "the day of the LORD," is unmatched in its intensity. The disaster is so sweeping and unbounded that nothing can survive it (1.2–3, 18). Two other kinds of material found in Zephaniah are typical of prophetic books. One is a collection of judgment speeches against Judah's neighbors (2.4–15; Am 1.3–2.3); the other is a speech announcing the restoration of Judah and the return of its exiles (3.8–20; Mic 4.6–13).

The title of Zephaniah's prophecy places his ministry during the reign of Josiah, who governed the southern kingdom of Judah during 640–609 BCE, not long before its fall in 587 BCE. Zephaniah's protest against the worship of other gods and his condemnation of foreign practices (1.4–9) may indicate that he preached during the height of Assyrian influence in the early years of Josiah's reign, before Josiah initiated the reforms recorded by Israel's historians (1 Kings 22.1–23.30). Such a date would make Zephaniah a contemporary of Jeremiah, who also predicted the fall of Judah and Jerusalem (Jer 7). The conclusion of the book of Zephaniah (3.8–20), if not from Zephaniah himself, was added by editors after Judah's fall to announce hope for its survivors and exiles.

READING GUIDE

Zephaniah's criticism of Jerusalem (3.1–7) is directly related to his announcement of judgment on Judah and Jerusalem (1.2–2.3). Supplementing this core of the book are judgments on the nations (2.4–15) and an announcement of Judah's renewal (3.8–20).

1 The word of the LORD that came to Zephaniah son of Cushi son of Gedaliah son of Amariah son of Hezekiah, in the days of King Josiah son of Amon of Judah.

1.1: Title. *Josiah* governed the southern kingdom of Judah during 640–609 BCE (2 Kings 22.1–23.30). *Hezekiah,* Zephaniah's great-great-grandfather, may be the earlier Judean king who governed from 715–687 (2 Kings 18–20).

2 I will utterly sweep away everything
    from the face of the earth, says
      the LORD.
3 I will sweep away humans and animals;
    I will sweep away the birds of the air

and the fish of the sea.
    I will make the wicked stumble.ᵃ
    I will cut off humanity
      from the face of the earth, says
        the LORD.
4 I will stretch out my hand against
      Judah,
    and against all the inhabitants of
      Jerusalem;
and I will cut off from this place every
      remnant of Baal
    and the name of the idolatrous
      priests;ᵇ

a Cn: Heb *sea, and those who cause the wicked to stumble*   *b* Compare Gk: Heb *the idolatrous priests with the priests*

5 those who bow down on the roofs
    to the host of the heavens;
those who bow down and swear to
    the LORD,
    but also swear by Milcom;*a*
6 those who have turned back from
    following the LORD,
    who have not sought the LORD or
    inquired of him.

7 Be silent before the Lord GOD!
    For the day of the LORD is at hand;
the LORD has prepared a sacrifice,
    he has consecrated his guests.
8 And on the day of the LORD's sacrifice
I will punish the officials and the king's
    sons
    and all who dress themselves in
    foreign attire.
9 On that day I will punish
    all who leap over the threshold,
who fill their master's house
    with violence and fraud.

10 On that day, says the LORD,
    a cry will be heard from the Fish Gate,
a wail from the Second Quarter,
    a loud crash from the hills.
11 The inhabitants of the Mortar wail,
    for all the traders have perished;
    all who weigh out silver are cut off.
12 At that time I will search Jerusalem
    with lamps,
    and I will punish the people
who rest complacently*b* on their dregs,
    those who say in their hearts,
"The LORD will not do good,
    nor will he do harm."
13 Their wealth shall be plundered,
    and their houses laid waste.
Though they build houses,
    they shall not inhabit them;
though they plant vineyards,
    they shall not drink wine from them.

14 The great day of the LORD is near,
    near and hastening fast;
the sound of the day of the LORD
    is bitter,
the warrior cries aloud there.

15 That day will be a day of wrath,
    a day of distress and anguish,
    a day of ruin and devastation,
    a day of darkness and gloom,
    a day of clouds and thick darkness,
16   a day of trumpet blast and battle
    cry
against the fortified cities
    and against the lofty battlements.

17 I will bring such distress upon people
    that they shall walk like the blind;
    because they have sinned against
    the LORD,
their blood shall be poured out
    like dust,
    and their flesh like dung.
18 Neither their silver nor their gold
    will be able to save them
    on the day of the LORD's wrath;
in the fire of his passion
    the whole earth shall be consumed;
for a full, a terrible end
    he will make of all the inhabitants of
    the earth.

2 Gather together, gather,
    O shameless nation,
2 before you are driven away
    like the drifting chaff,*c*
before there comes upon you
    the fierce anger of the LORD,
before there comes upon you
    the day of the LORD's wrath.
3 Seek the LORD, all you humble of the
    land,
    who do his commands;
seek righteousness, seek humility;
    perhaps you may be hidden
    on the day of the LORD's wrath.
4 For Gaza shall be deserted,
    and Ashkelon shall become a
    desolation;
Ashdod's people shall be driven out at
    noon,
    and Ekron shall be uprooted.

a Gk Mss Syr Vg: Heb *Malcam* (or, *their king*)
b Heb *who thicken*   *c* Cn Compare Gk Syr: Heb *before
a decree is born; like chaff a day has passed away*

1.2–2.3: The day of the Lord: Judah is judged.
Though Zephaniah does include in this speech an indictment of Judah's sins (1.4–9), as is customary in prophetic judgment speeches, he emphasizes the sentence, God's punishment on Judah and its people. **1.2–3:** This is one of the most desolate images of judgment in prophetic literature (Jer 4.23–26). **4:** *Jerusalem*, the capital city of *Judah*, is singled out for further criticism in 3.1–7. With this mention of *Baal*,* the Canaanite god who is the major rival of Judah's God (Hos 2), Zephaniah begins the indictment of Judah's crimes, focusing on its rejection of Yahweh and its worship of other gods (vv. 4–9). **5:** *The host of the heavens* are the sun, moon, planets, and stars, the worship of which became widespread in Judah under Assyrian influence (2 Kings 21.3–5). *Milcom* is the god of the Ammonites (2.8; 2 Kings 23.13). **7:** Zephaniah introduces the theme of *the day of the LORD* for God's judgment on Judah, a theme that carries this judgment speech forward to its conclusion in 2.3. God's *sacrifice* is not the customary animal sacrifice but God's enemies (Jer 46.10), in this case the people of Judah themselves. **9:** Those *who leap over the threshhold* may be priests practicing a ritual associated with the Philistine god Dagon (1 Sam 5.5). **10:** *The Fish Gate* is located in the north wall of Jerusalem (Neh 12.39). *The Second Quarter* is a district in Jerusalem near the Temple* complex (2 Kings 22.14). **11:** *The Mortar* is Jerusalem's business district. **12:** The phrase "who thicken (note *b; or rest complacently) on their dregs"* may be translated: "Who are as undisturbed as the sediment of wine." **18:** While the picture of destruction in this verse appears to include the entire world, Zephaniah's concern is Judah in particular, as the preceding and following verses show. **2.1–3:** Zephaniah's judgment speech concludes with an appeal to Judah (*shameless nation*, v. 1) to *seek the LORD* and reform in order to avert disaster (Am 5.6, 14–15).

5 Ah, inhabitants of the seacoast,
  you nation of the Cherethites!
 The word of the LORD is against you,
  O Canaan, land of the Philistines;
 and I will destroy you until no
    inhabitant is left.
6 And you, O seacoast, shall be pastures,
  meadows for shepherds
  and folds for flocks.
7 The seacoast shall become the
    possession

of the remnant of the house of Judah,
  on which they shall pasture,
 and in the houses of Ashkelon
  they shall lie down at evening.
 For the LORD their God will be mindful
    of them
  and restore their fortunes.

8 I have heard the taunts of Moab
  and the revilings of the Ammonites,
 how they have taunted my people
  and made boasts against
    their territory.
9 Therefore, as I live, says the LORD of
    hosts,
  the God of Israel,
 Moab shall become like Sodom
  and the Ammonites like Gomorrah,
 a land possessed by nettles and salt pits,
  and a waste forever.
 The remnant of my people shall plunder
    them,
  and the survivors of my nation shall
    possess them.
10 This shall be their lot in return for their
    pride,
  because they scoffed and boasted
 against the people of the LORD
    of hosts.
11 The LORD will be terrible against them;
  he will shrivel all the gods of
    the earth,
 and to him shall bow down,
  each in its place,
 all the coasts and islands of
    the nations.

12 You also, O Ethiopians,[a]
  shall be killed by my sword.

13 And he will stretch out his hand against
    the north,
  and destroy Assyria;
 and he will make Nineveh a desolation,
  a dry waste like the desert.
14 Herds shall lie down in it,
  every wild animal;[b]

a Or *Nubians;* Heb *Cushites*   *b* Tg Compare Gk:
Heb *nation*

the desert owl[a] and the screech owl[a]
  shall lodge on its capitals;
the owl[b] shall hoot at the window,
  the raven[c] croak on the threshold;
  for its cedar work will be laid bare.

15 Is this the exultant city
  that lived secure,
that said to itself,
  "I am, and there is no one else"?
What a desolation it has become,
  a lair for wild animals!
Everyone who passes by it
  hisses and shakes the fist.

2.4–15: The nations are judged. The lengthy speech describing Judah's judgment is followed by a collection of shorter speeches describing judgment on four of Judah's neighbors: Philistia (vv. 4–7), Moab and Ammon (vv. 8–11), Ethiopia (v. 12), and Assyria (vv. 13–15). **4:** *Gaza, Ashkelon, Ashdod,* and *Ekron* are major cities of Philistia, Judah's neighbor on the Mediterranean coast. **5:** *Cherethites* is a synonym for, or a subgroup of, the Philistines, who are associated with Crete, part of the larger Aegean area from which the Philistines came. **8:** *Moab* and *Ammon* are Judah's neighbors east of the Jordan River. **9:** *Sodom* and *Gomorrah* were destroyed by God in a fierce firestorm (Gen 19.12–29) and therefore represent divine judgment. **13:** *Assyria,* with its capital in *Nineveh,* is an ancient Near Eastern superpower that destroyed the northern kingdom of Israel in 721 BCE and dominated the southern kingdom of Judah for a century before Zephaniah's career. **15:** *The exultant city* is Nineveh. The images of its fall here mirror those in the speeches of Nahum.

3 Ah, soiled, defiled,
    oppressing city!
2 It has listened to no voice;
    it has accepted no correction.
  It has not trusted in the LORD;
    it has not drawn near to its God.

3 The officials within it
    are roaring lions;
  its judges are evening wolves
    that leave nothing until the morning.
4 Its prophets are reckless,
    faithless persons;
  its priests have profaned what is sacred,
    they have done violence to the law.

5 The LORD within it is righteous;
    he does no wrong.
  Every morning he renders his
      judgment,
    each dawn without fail;
  but the unjust knows no shame.

6 I have cut off nations;
    their battlements are in ruins;
  I have laid waste their streets
    so that no one walks in them;
  their cities have been made desolate,
    without people, without inhabitants.
7 I said, "Surely the city[d] will fear me,
    it will accept correction;
  it will not lose sight[e]
    of all that I have brought upon it."
  But they were the more eager
    to make all their deeds corrupt.

3.1–7: Jerusalem is indicted. The sins listed here, together with those in 1.4–9, are the basis for the devastating judgment described in 1.2–2.3. **1:** The *oppressing city* is Jerusalem, Judah's capital. **3–4:** While Zephaniah's first indictment of Judah's sins focuses on the worship of other gods (1.4–9), this indictment focuses, as do those of Micah (4.6–8), on Judah's political and religious leadership. **7:** *The city* is Jerusalem.

8 Therefore wait for me, says the LORD,
    for the day when I arise as a witness.
  For my decision is to gather nations,
    to assemble kingdoms,
  to pour out upon them my indignation,
    all the heat of my anger;
  for in the fire of my passion
    all the earth shall be consumed.

9 At that time I will change the speech of
      the peoples
    to a pure speech,
  that all of them may call on the name of
      the LORD
    and serve him with one accord.
10 From beyond the rivers of Ethiopia[f]
    my suppliants, my scattered ones,
    shall bring my offering.

---

a Meaning of Heb uncertain   b Cn: Heb *a voice*
c Gk Vg: Heb *desolation*   d Heb *it*   e Gk Syr: Heb
its dwelling will not be cut off   f Or *Nubia;* Heb *Cush*

11 On that day you shall not be put
  to shame
 because of all the deeds by which you
  have rebelled against me;
 for then I will remove from your midst
  your proudly exultant ones,
 and you shall no longer be haughty
  in my holy mountain.
12 For I will leave in the midst of you
  a people humble and lowly.
 They shall seek refuge in the name of
  the LORD—
13   the remnant of Israel;
 they shall do no wrong
  and utter no lies,
 nor shall a deceitful tongue
  be found in their mouths.
 Then they will pasture and lie down,
  and no one shall make them afraid.

14 Sing aloud, O daughter Zion;
  shout, O Israel!
 Rejoice and exult with all your heart,
  O daughter Jerusalem!
15 The LORD has taken away the
   judgments against you,
  he has turned away your enemies.
 The king of Israel, the LORD, is in your
   midst;
  you shall fear disaster no more.
16 On that day it shall be said to
   Jerusalem:
 Do not fear, O Zion;
  do not let your hands grow weak.
17 The LORD, your God, is in your midst,
  a warrior who gives victory;
 he will rejoice over you with gladness,
  he will renew you*a* in his love;
 he will exult over you with
   loud singing

18   as on a day of festival.*b*
 I will remove disaster from you,*c*
  so that you will not bear reproach
   for it.
19 I will deal with all your oppressors
   at that time.
 And I will save the lame
  and gather the outcast,
 and I will change their shame
   into praise
  and renown in all the earth.
20 At that time I will bring you home,
  at the time when I gather you;
 for I will make you renowned
   and praised
  among all the peoples of the earth,
 when I restore your fortunes
  before your eyes, says the LORD.

3.8–20: Judah is restored. A major shift occurs here in the book of Zephaniah from the criticism of Judah and announcement of its destruction (1.2–2.3; 3.1–7) to the anticipation of its renewal. Either Zephaniah himself looked forward to a new era after Judah's fall, or this speech was added by Zephaniah's editors after Judah's fall to provide hope to its exiles. The speech shares numerous images with literature composed during and after the Exile* (after 587 BCE). **9:** The expectation of the conversion of the nations is characteristic of exilic literature (Isa 55.4–5; Mic 4.1–2). **11:** *My holy mountain* is the Temple* mount in Jerusalem. **19–20:** The return of Judah's exiles, often pictured as *lame* and *outcast*, was a widespread hope during the Exile and afterwards (Isa 35.5–10; Mic 4.6–8).

---

a Gk Syr: Heb *he will be silent*   *b* Gk Syr: Meaning of Heb uncertain   *c* Cn: Heb *I will remove from you; they were*

HAGGAI

Introduction

Haggai's main concern is the reconstruction of the Temple* in Jerusalem, which was reduced to ruins when Nebuchadnezzar conquered and destroyed Jerusalem in 587 BCE (2 Kings 25). His messages, all delivered in the fall of 520 BCE, make a single point: Judah's poor harvests and depressed economy stem from the people's disregard for their religious life, at the center of which is the Temple. By reconstructing the Temple and its ritual practices the people will again experience the divine blessing of agricultural bounty. The belief that God, preeminently present in the Temple, blessed the righteous with plenty was deeply imbedded in Israelite thought (Ps 36.5–9; Joel 2.18–27).

Haggai, together with Zechariah and Malachi whose prophecies conclude the Minor Prophets, lived in the post-exilic era, the period following the fall of Jerusalem (587 BCE) and the Babylonian exile (587–538), when the entire Near East was under Persian rule.* The policies of the first Persian monarch, Cyrus, allowed exiles to return to their homelands and govern their affairs with some autonomy (see the texts of Cyrus's decree). Many of the events of this era are recorded in the books of Ezra and Nehemiah. It appears from Haggai's speeches, dating to the second year of the reign of Persia's third king Darius (520 BCE), that exiles returning to Judah had rebuilt their own homes (1.4) but—nearly 20 years after Cyrus had allowed their return—had not yet begun the reconstruction of the Temple. This effort, begun as a result of Haggai's preaching (1.12–15), was completed five years later in 515 BCE (Ezra 5.1–2; 6.1–22).

READING GUIDE

The context and mood of Haggai's audience is entirely different from the audience of the pre-exilic prophets* who preceded him, a fact that must be kept in mind when reading his speeches. Whereas earlier prophets spoke to a powerful Israelite and Judean elite who were smug and complacent, Haggai addresses a people who have returned to a ruined land, are no longer in control of their own affairs, and often question whether the renewal of their homeland is a realistic possibility.

1 In the second year of King Darius, in the sixth month, on the first day of the month, the word of the LORD came by the prophet Haggai to Zerubbabel son of Shealtiel, governor of Judah, and to Joshua son of Jehozadak, the high priest: ²Thus says the LORD of hosts: These people say the time has not yet come to rebuild the LORD's house. ³Then the word of the LORD came by the prophet Haggai, saying: ⁴Is it a time for you yourselves to live in your paneled houses, while this house lies in ruins? ⁵Now therefore thus says the LORD of hosts: Consider how you have fared. ⁶You have sown much, and harvested little; you eat, but you never have enough; you drink, but you never have your fill; you clothe yourselves, but no one is warm; and you that earn wages earn wages to put them into a bag with holes.

7 Thus says the LORD of hosts: Consider how you have fared. ⁸Go up to the hills and bring wood and build the house, so that I may take pleasure in it and be honored, says the LORD. ⁹You have looked for much, and, lo, it came to little; and when you brought it home, I blew it away. Why? says the LORD

The Decree of Cyrus

After Cyrus, ruler of the Persian empire, conquered Babylon, he issued a decree that allowed exiles to return to their homelands. Two descriptions of that decree, one Cyrus's own text from the Cyrus Cylinder, and one the biblical text from Ezra 1.2–4, are reprinted here.

(As to the region) from . . . as far as Ashur and Susa, Agade, Eshnunna, the towns Zamban, Me-Turnu, Der as well as the region of the Gutians, I returned to (these) sacred cities on the other side of the Tigris, the sanctuaries of which have been ruins for a long time, the images which (used) to live therein and established for them permanent sanctuaries. I (also) gathered all their (former) inhabitants and returned (to them) their habitations.—From the Cyrus Cylinder

"Thus says King Cyrus of Persia: The LORD, the God of heaven, has given me all the kingdoms of the earth, and he has charged me to build him a house at Jerusalem in Judah. Any of those among you who are of his people—may their God be with them!—are now permitted to go up to Jerusalem in Judah, and rebuild the house of the LORD, the God of Israel—he is the God who is in Jerusalem; and let all survivors, in whatever place they reside, be assisted by the people of their place with silver and gold, with goods and with animals, besides freewill offerings for the house of God in Jerusalem."—Ezra 1.2–4 (NRSV)

---

of hosts. Because my house lies in ruins, while all of you hurry off to your own houses. 10Therefore the heavens above you have withheld the dew, and the earth has withheld its produce. 11And I have called for a drought on the land and the hills, on the grain, the new wine, the oil, on what the soil produces, on human beings and animals, and on all their labors.

12 Then Zerubbabel son of Shealtiel, and Joshua son of Jehozadak, the high priest, with all the remnant of the people, obeyed the voice of the LORD their God, and the words of the prophet Haggai, as the LORD their God had sent him; and the people feared the LORD. 13Then Haggai, the messenger of the LORD, spoke to the people with the LORD's message, saying, I am with you, says the LORD. 14And the LORD stirred up the spirit of Zerubbabel son of Shealtiel, governor of Judah, and the spirit of Joshua son of Jehozadak, the high priest, and the spirit of all the remnant of the people; and they came and worked on the house of the LORD of hosts, their God, 15on the twenty-fourth day of the month, in the sixth month.

1.1–15a: The charge to rebuild the Temple.✲ Haggai's first speech directs those who have returned to Jerusalem from exile to begin reconstruction of the Temple. **1:** *King Darius* (522–486) is the third monarch of the Persian empire, of which Judah became a province when the Persian king Cyrus conquered Babylon in 538 BCE. The *second year* of Darius's reign is 520 BCE. *Zerubbabel*, grandson of Jehoiachin ("Jeconiah"; 1 Chr 3.16–19), the king of Judah exiled to Babylon in 597 BCE (2 Kings 24.8–17; 25.27–30), had returned to Judah with other exiles (Ezra 2.1–2; see sidebar above). *Joshua's* grandfather Seraiah, chief priest of Jerusalem, was killed when Jerusalem was conquered by the Babylonians (2 Kings 25.18–21), and Joshua's father, *Jehozadak*, was deported to Babylon (1 Chr 6.14–15). **12:** *The remnant of the people* refers to those who had returned to Judah from Babylonian exile (Jer 43.5; see sidebar above).

2 In the second year of King Darius, 1in the seventh month, on the twenty-first day of the month, the word of the LORD came by the prophet Haggai, saying: 2Speak now to Zerubbabel son of Shealtiel, governor of Judah, and to Joshua son of Jehozadak,

the high priest, and to the remnant of the people, and say, ³Who is left among you that saw this house in its former glory? How does it look to you now? Is it not in your sight as nothing? ⁴Yet now take courage, O Zerubbabel, says the LORD; take courage, O Joshua, son of Jehozadak, the high priest; take courage, all you people of the land, says the LORD; work, for I am with you, says the LORD of hosts, ⁵according to the promise that I made you when you came out of Egypt. My spirit abides among you; do not fear. ⁶For thus says the LORD of hosts: Once again, in a little while, I will shake the heavens and the earth and the sea and the dry land; ⁷and I will shake all the nations, so that the treasure of all nations shall come, and I will fill this house with splendor, says the LORD of hosts. ⁸The silver is mine, and the gold is mine, says the LORD of hosts. ⁹The latter splendor of this house shall be greater than the former, says the LORD of hosts; and in this place I will give prosperity, says the LORD of hosts.

1.15b–2.9: The vision of the new Temple's glory. Haggai encourages those whose first efforts at reconstruction of the Temple* seem insignificant. **2.3:** *Its former glory* recalls the splendor of Solomon's Temple (1 Kings 6), which was destroyed when Jerusalem fell to the Babylonians in 587 BCE (2 Kings 25.9, 13–17). **4:** The *people of the land* may refer to those who had remained in Judah after its conquest by Babylon. **5:** Haggai reminds the people that God delivered them from slavery in *Egypt* (Ex 1–15). **6–7:** Descriptions of Judah's restoration are often accompanied by images of the cosmos in disarray (Isa 51.6) and of the nations bringing tribute to Jerusalem (Isa 45.14).

10 On the twenty-fourth day of the ninth month, in the second year of Darius, the word of the LORD came by the prophet Haggai, saying: ¹¹Thus says the LORD of hosts: Ask the priests for a ruling: ¹²If one carries consecrated meat in the fold of one's garment, and with the fold touches bread, or stew, or wine, or oil, or any kind of food, does it become holy? The priests answered, "No." ¹³Then Haggai said, "If one who is unclean by contact with a dead body touches any of these, does it become unclean?" The priests

answered, "Yes, it becomes unclean." ¹⁴Haggai then said, So is it with this people, and with this nation before me, says the LORD; and so with every work of their hands; and what they offer there is unclean. ¹⁵But now, consider what will come to pass from this day on. Before a stone was placed upon a stone in the LORD's temple, ¹⁶how did you fare?ᵃ When one came to a heap of twenty measures, there were but ten; when one came to the wine vat to draw fifty measures, there were but twenty. ¹⁷I struck you and all the products of your toil with blight and mildew and hail; yet you did not return to me, says the LORD. ¹⁸Consider from this day on, from the twenty-fourth day of the ninth month. Since the day that the foundation of the LORD's temple was laid, consider: ¹⁹Is there any seed left in the barn? Do the vine, the fig tree, the pomegranate, and the olive tree still yield nothing? From this day on I will bless you.

2.10–19: The promise of agricultural bounty. Haggai announces that God will bless the people's work on the Temple by granting them good harvests. **12:** The point of this priestly decision is that holiness cannot be transferred (from *consecrated meat* carried home to eat; Lev 6.26–27; 7.16–17). **13:** The point of this priestly decision is that uncleanness can be transferred (from a "corpse" through a person to other objects; Num 5.1–4). **14:** Both of these previous questions (vv. 12–13) simply set up Haggai's point in this verse: Without a proper worship space, uncleanness has tainted all that the people have done.

20 The word of the LORD came a second time to Haggai on the twenty-fourth day of the month: ²¹Speak to Zerubbabel, governor of Judah, saying, I am about to shake the heavens and the earth, ²²and to overthrow the throne of kingdoms; I am about to destroy the strength of the kingdoms of the nations, and overthrow the chariots and their riders; and the horses and their riders shall fall, every one by the sword of a comrade. ²³On that day, says the LORD of hosts, I will take you, O Zerubbabel my servant, son of Shealtiel, says the LORD, and make you

a Gk: Heb *since they were*

like a signet ring; for I have chosen you, says the LORD of hosts.

2.20–23: The promise to Zerubbabel. The focus shifts from the reconstruction of the Temple to the installation of Zerubbabel as Judah's leader. **21–22:** Descriptions of Judah's restoration are often accompanied by references to the conquest of other nations

(Joel 3). **23:** While *Zerubbabel* is only a governor of Judah (1.1; 2.21) under Persian authority, he is a member of the Davidic family that had ruled Jerusalem (see comment on 1.1), and Haggai may be announcing a greater role for him. Both *my servant* (2 Sam 7.5) and *signet ring* (Jer 22.24) may be royal images anticipating a revival of the Davidic dynasty.*

ZECHARIAH

Introduction

Zechariah, together with his contemporary Haggai, lived in a time of great crisis, the period following the destruction of Jerusalem (587 BCE) and the exile of its leading citizens to Babylon (587–538). Twenty years after the new Persian monarch Cyrus allowed exiles to return to their homelands, Zechariah spoke to those who had returned to the ruins of Judah and Jerusalem, encouraging them not to lose hope. His words of hope emphasize God's control of history and God's plans to restore the fortunes of Judah. In a series of eight visions, which make up the core of Zechariah's prophecy, these themes are elaborated in detail (see sidebar on p. 1290). The first and last visions describe God's universal rule along with the heavenly emissaries who carry out God's plans in the world (1.7–17; 6.1–8). The intervening visions announce the restoration and purification of Judah (1.18–2.5; 5.1–11) and the establishment of a new government in which leadership will be shared by priestly and political officials (chs. 3–4). The aim of these visions is to give the people of Judah confidence in the future and a new religious and political structure within which to build their future. Framing these visions are two speeches (1.1–6; 7.1–8.23) in which Zechariah urges his listeners to build a society more principled and just than their ancestors'.

Appended to the visions and speeches of Zechariah are two prophetic collections (chs. 9–11 and 12–14) that differ in style and content and are believed to have been composed by another prophetic figure or group. These collections lack the specific references to dates and people present in chs. 1–8, are composed in different literary forms and styles, and reflect a crisis in leadership and internal Judean conflicts absent in Zechariah's messages. Two themes dominate chs. 9–14, one unique to this section of the book, the other shared with chs. 1–8. Unique to chs. 9–14 is a criticism of Judah's political leaders, described as shepherds, and of Judah's proph-ets.✶ Judah's leaders are blamed for exploiting their people (11.4–17) and its prophets for preach-ing lies (13.1–6). Shared with chs. 1–8 is a vision of Judah's restoration, detailed in several lengthy speeches (chs. 9, 10, 12, 14).

The historical period in which Zechariah spoke can be determined precisely by the dates prefixed to the book's major sections (1.1, 7; 7.1). These speeches were all delivered between the years 520 and 518 BCE, the second to the fourth years of rule by the Persian monarch Darius. This was about 20 years after the Persian king Cyrus had conquered Babylon (538 BCE) and issued a decree repatriating exiles and supporting their return to their homelands (see sidebar on p. 1282). Urged by the great exilic prophet Second Isaiah (Isa 40–55), many Judean exiles took this opportunity to return home from Babylon and to begin the reconstruction of Jerusalem and its environs (Ezra 1–5). But the land lay in ruins (2.1–4), and the future did not look bright for those who returned (8.6). In such difficult circumstances Zechariah and his contemporary Haggai spoke, both to instill hope and to urge the people to begin the concrete process of re-building their cities and institutions.

The context of the supplements to Zechariah, chs. 9–14, cannot be determined as precisely as the prophecies of Zechariah themselves, since they contain no specific dates or references to identifiable people or events. They certainly reflect the same general environment in Judah during the post-exilic period. The crisis in leadership they address (11.4–17; 13.1–6), however, may place these supplements later than chs. 1–8, in a time when the sanctified leadership expected by Zechariah (chs. 3–4) had become corrupt and exploitive.

READING GUIDE

Zechariah should be read as a book in two parts: the visions and speeches of the prophet after whom the book is named (chs. 1–8), and the speeches of an anonymous prophetic figure or group added at a later time (chs. 9–12). Zechariah's own prophecies are best understood when the careful design of his visions, which progressively narrows the reader's focus from the world to Jerusalem, is kept in mind (see sidebar, p. 1290).

1 In the eighth month, in the second year of Darius, the word of the LORD came to the prophet Zechariah son of Berechiah son of Iddo, saying: ²The LORD was very angry with your ancestors. ³Therefore say to them, Thus says the LORD of hosts: Return to me, says the LORD of hosts, and I will return to you, says the LORD of hosts. ⁴Do not be like your ancestors, to whom the former prophets proclaimed, "Thus says the LORD of hosts, Return from your evil ways and from your evil deeds." But they did not hear or heed me, says the LORD. ⁵Your ancestors, where are they? And the prophets, do they live forever? ⁶But my words and my statutes, which I commanded my servants the prophets, did they not overtake your ancestors? So they repented and said, "The LORD of hosts has dealt with us according to our ways and deeds, just as he planned to do."

1.1–6: Zechariah's opening speech. Zechariah's visions (1.7–6.8) are introduced and concluded (chs. 7–8) by speeches in which Zechariah urges his listeners to embrace the social responsibilities and just behavior preached by the prophets* before him. **1:** Zechariah's opening and closing speeches (1.1; 7.1), together with his visions (1.7), are dated. The *second year of Darius* (522–486 BCE) is 520 BCE, the same year in which Haggai preached (Hag 1.1; 2.1, 10). **4:** The *former prophets* are Zechariah's predecessors who preached before the fall of Jerusalem. Zechariah quotes words similar to Jeremiah's (Jer 25.5).

---

7 On the twenty-fourth day of the eleventh month, the month of Shebat, in the second year of Darius, the word of the LORD came to the prophet Zechariah son of Bere-

chiah son of Iddo; and Zechariah*a* said, ⁸In the night I saw a man riding on a red horse! He was standing among the myrtle trees in the glen; and behind him were red, sorrel, and white horses. ⁹Then I said, "What are these, my lord?" The angel who talked with me said to me, "I will show you what they are." ¹⁰So the man who was standing among the myrtle trees answered, "They are those whom the LORD has sent to patrol the earth." ¹¹Then they spoke to the angel of the LORD who was standing among the myrtle trees, "We have patrolled the earth, and lo, the whole earth remains at peace." ¹²Then the angel of the LORD said, "O LORD of hosts, how long will you withhold mercy from Jerusalem and the cities of Judah, with which you have been angry these seventy years?" ¹³Then the LORD replied with gracious and comforting words to the angel who talked with me. ¹⁴So the angel who talked with me said to me, Proclaim this message: Thus says the LORD of hosts; I am very jealous for Jerusalem and for Zion. ¹⁵And I am extremely angry with the nations that are at ease; for while I was only a little angry, they made the disaster worse. ¹⁶Therefore, thus says the LORD, I have returned to Jerusalem with compassion; my house shall be built in it, says the LORD of hosts, and the measuring line shall be stretched out over Jerusalem. ¹⁷Proclaim further: Thus says the LORD of hosts: My cities shall again overflow with prosperity; the LORD will again comfort Zion and again choose Jerusalem.

a Heb *and he*

1.7–17: The first vision: The heavenly horsemen and God's plans for Jerusalem. This is the first of eight visions that make up the core of Zechariah's prophecy. **7:** The chronological notice dates the entire vision complex three months later than Zechariah's opening speech, or early in 519 BCE. **8:** These horsemen are God's heavenly patrol, keeping watch over the world's affairs (v. 10). The significance of the horses' colors is uncertain, but the number four represents totality. **11:** *Peace* in this case is undesirable, since the plight of Jerusalem remains unchanged. **12:** The Babylonian exile lasted only 50 years (587–538 BCE), not *seventy*, but Jeremiah mentions a 70-year period of servitude to Babylon (Jer 25.11–12), to which Zechariah may be referring. **16:** The rebuilding of the Temple★ is the central concern of Zechariah's contemporary Haggai.

18[a] And I looked up and saw four horns. 19I asked the angel who talked with me, "What are these?" And he answered me, "These are the horns that have scattered Judah, Israel, and Jerusalem." 20Then the LORD showed me four blacksmiths. 21And I asked, "What are they coming to do?" He answered, "These are the horns that scattered Judah, so that no head could be raised; but these have come to terrify them, to strike down the horns of the nations that lifted up their horns against the land of Judah to scatter its people."[b]

1.18–21: The second vision: The four horns and Judah's security. 18: The *horn*, a symbol of power (Ps 18.2), represents the strength of the nations that have conquered and exiled the Israelite people. The number four probably represents totality rather than specific countries. **20–21:** The *four blacksmiths* strike off the horns, thus putting an end to the power of the nations to dominate Judah.

2 [c]I looked up and saw a man with a measuring line in his hand. 2Then I asked, "Where are you going?" He answered me, "To measure Jerusalem, to see what is its width and what is its length." 3Then the angel who talked with me came forward, and another angel came forward to meet him, 4and said to him, "Run, say to that young man: Jerusalem shall be inhabited like villages without walls, because of the multitude of people and animals in it. 5For I will be a wall of fire all around it, says the LORD, and I will be the glory within it."

2.1–5: The third vision: The measuring line and Jerusalem's resettlement. 1: The *man with a measuring line* is a surveyor making preparations for rebuilding Jerusalem. **5:** God, not its walls (v. 4), will protect Jerusalem.

6 Up, up! Flee from the land of the north, says the LORD; for I have spread you abroad like the four winds of heaven, says the LORD. 7Up! Escape to Zion, you that live with daughter Babylon. 8For thus said the LORD of hosts (after his glory[d] sent me) regarding the nations that plundered you: Truly, one who touches you touches the apple of my eye.[e] 9See now, I am going to raise[f] my hand against them, and they shall become plunder for their own slaves. Then you will know that the LORD of hosts has sent me. 10Sing and rejoice, O daughter Zion! For lo, I will come and dwell in your midst, says the LORD. 11Many nations shall join themselves to the LORD on that day, and shall be my people; and I will dwell in your midst. And you shall know that the LORD of hosts has sent me to you. 12The LORD will inherit Judah as his portion in the holy land, and will again choose Jerusalem.

13 Be silent, all people, before the LORD; for he has roused himself from his holy dwelling.

2.6–13: A charge to the exiles. A brief speech, urging Judah's exiles to return from exile in Babylon, interrupts the sequence of visions. **7:** Babylon is the city to which the majority of Judah's exiles were deported (2 Kings 24.14–15; 25.11–12). **10:** *Daughter Zion*★ is Jerusalem.

3 Then he showed me the high priest Joshua standing before the angel of the LORD, and Satan[g] standing at his right hand to accuse him. 2And the LORD said to Satan,[g] "The LORD rebuke you, O Satan![g] The

---

a Ch 2.1 in Heb   b Heb it   c Ch 2.5 in Heb
d Cn: Heb *after glory he*   e Heb *his eye*   f Or *wave*
g Or *the Accuser;* Heb *the Adversary*

LORD who has chosen Jerusalem rebuke you! Is not this man a brand plucked from the fire?" ³Now Joshua was dressed with filthy clothes as he stood before the angel. ⁴The angel said to those who were standing before him, "Take off his filthy clothes." And to him he said, "See, I have taken your guilt away from you, and I will clothe you with festal apparel." ⁵And I said, "Let them put a clean turban on his head." So they put a clean turban on his head and clothed him with the apparel; and the angel of the LORD was standing by.

6 Then the angel of the LORD assured Joshua, saying ⁷"Thus says the LORD of hosts: If you will walk in my ways and keep my requirements, then you shall rule my house and have charge of my courts, and I will give you the right of access among those who are standing here. ⁸Now listen, Joshua, high priest, you and your colleagues who sit before you! For they are an omen of things to come: I am going to bring my servant the Branch. ⁹For on the stone that I have set before Joshua, on a single stone with seven facets, I will engrave its inscription, says the LORD of hosts, and I will remove the guilt of this land in a single day. ¹⁰On that day, says the LORD of hosts, you shall invite each other to come under your vine and fig tree."

3.1–10: The fourth vision: Joshua's installation as high priest. This vision may have been a later addition to the vision sequence; it does not open with the question and answer exchange between Zechariah and the interpreting angel that begins the other visions. **1:** The term *Satan* does not refer to the prince of evil familiar from early Christian writings. It is a common noun, not a name, in Hebrew and means "adversary" or "accuser" (see note *g*), that member of God's heavenly court designated to bring cases against individuals (Job 1.6). **2:** *A brand plucked from the fire* refers to someone who has survived God's judgment of Israel and Judah (Am 4.11). **3–5:** The reclothing of Joshua symbolizes his sanctification for priestly office (Lev 8.6–9). **7:** *My house* is the Temple* in Jerusalem. **8:** *My servant* and *the Branch* are royal titles used of the Davidic dynasty* (2 Sam 7.5; Jer 23.5) and may be used here of Zerubbabel (4.6–10a; Hag 2.23), governor of Judah and a member of the Davidic family. **9:**

The seven-faceted *stone* and its *inscription* are images of royalty (2 Sam 12.30; 2 Kings 11.12).

4 The angel who talked with me came again, and wakened me, as one is wakened from sleep. ²He said to me, "What do you see?" And I said, "I see a lampstand all of gold, with a bowl on the top of it; there are seven lamps on it, with seven lips on each of the lamps that are on the top of it. ³And by it there are two olive trees, one on the right of the bowl and the other on its left." ⁴I said to the angel who talked with me, "What are these, my lord?" ⁵Then the angel who talked with me answered me, "Do you not know what these are?" I said, "No, my lord." ⁶He said to me, "This is the word of the LORD to Zerubbabel: Not by might, nor by power, but by my spirit, says the LORD of hosts. ⁷What are you, O great mountain? Before Zerubbabel you shall become a plain; and he shall bring out the top stone amid shouts of 'Grace, grace to it!'"

8 Moreover the word of the LORD came to me, saying, ⁹"The hands of Zerubbabel have laid the foundation of this house; his hands shall also complete it. Then you will know that the LORD of hosts has sent me to you. ¹⁰For whoever has despised the day of small things shall rejoice, and shall see the plummet in the hand of Zerubbabel.

"These seven are the eyes of the LORD, which range through the whole earth." ¹¹Then I said to him, "What are these two olive trees on the right and the left of the lampstand?" ¹²And a second time I said to him, "What are these two branches of the olive trees, which pour out the oilᵃ through the two golden pipes?" ¹³He said to me, "Do you not know what these are?" I said, "No, my lord." ¹⁴Then he said, "These are the two anointed ones who stand by the Lord of the whole earth."

4.1–14: The fifth vision: The golden lampstand and Judah's leadership. This vision may originally have been the central vision in a seven-vision sequence. **2:** The *lampstand* (Heb., "menorah") in the Temple* is unusually elaborate and difficult to describe, though it

a Cn: Heb *gold*

is related to the lampstand in the tabernacle* (Ex 25.31–37). The *bowl* may have contained the oil for the lamps, and the *lips* held the lamps' wicks. **3:** Images of *trees* adorned the walls of Solomon's Temple (1 Kings 6.29). **6–10a:** This speech to *Zerubbabel,* encouraging him in the rebuilding of the Temple (Hag 2.1–4; Ezra 5.1–2), interrupts the vision narrative* and may be a later addition. **10b:** The vision narrative resumes with the explanation that the seven lamps represent God's *eyes,* watching the entire *earth.* **14:** The *anointed** ones, symbolized in the vision by the two olive trees (vv. 3, 11), represent Judah's leadership, shared by a religious figure (the high priest Joshua; 3.1–10) and by a political figure (Zerubbabel; 4.6–10a).

5 Again I looked up and saw a flying scroll. ²And he said to me, "What do you see?" I answered, "I see a flying scroll; its length is twenty cubits, and its width ten cubits." ³Then he said to me, "This is the curse that goes out over the face of the whole land; for everyone who steals shall be cut off according to the writing on one side, and everyone who swears falsely*a* shall be cut off according to the writing on the other side. ⁴I have sent it out, says the LORD of hosts, and it shall enter the house of the thief, and the house of anyone who swears falsely by my name; and it shall abide in that house and consume it, both timber and stones."

5.1–4: The sixth vision: The flying scroll and social justice. The scroll's flight indicates that the power of its message covers the whole land. **3–4:** The two crimes mentioned in the scroll's text are theft and deceit in official transactions (*swearing falsely*), two of the ten commandments (Ex 20.7, 15). Why these two are singled out is not stated, but they represent the elimination of corruption from Judean society, the theme of the next vision as well.

5 Then the angel who talked with me came forward and said to me, "Look up and see what this is that is coming out." ⁶I said, "What is it?" He said, "This is a basket*b* coming out." And he said, "This is their iniquity*c* in all the land." ⁷Then a leaden cover was lifted, and there was a woman sitting in the basket!*b* ⁸And he said, "This is Wickedness." So he thrust her back into the basket,*b* and

pressed the leaden weight down on its mouth. ⁹Then I looked up and saw two women coming forward. The wind was in their wings; they had wings like the wings of a stork, and they lifted up the basket*b* between earth and sky. ¹⁰Then I said to the angel who talked with me, "Where are they taking the basket?"*b* ¹¹He said to me, "To the land of Shinar, to build a house for it; and when this is prepared, they will set the basket*b* down there on its base."

5.5–11: The seventh vision: The basket and Judah's purification. 6: *Basket* translates the Hebrew term "ephah," a unit of measure. **8:** *Wickedness* is a general term referring to corruption and unrighteousness in general. **11:** The removal of the basket containing wickedness to *Shinar,* a name for the plain in which Babylon was located (Gen 11.1–9), symbolizes the elimination of wickedness from Judean society.

6 And again I looked up and saw four chariots coming out from between two mountains—mountains of bronze. ²The first chariot had red horses, the second chariot black horses, ³the third chariot white horses, and the fourth chariot dappled gray*d* horses. ⁴Then I said to the angel who talked with me, "What are these, my lord?" ⁵The angel answered me, "These are the four winds*e* of heaven going out, after presenting themselves before the Lord of all the earth. ⁶The chariot with the black horses goes toward the north country, the white ones go toward the west country,*f* and the dappled ones go toward the south country." ⁷When the steeds came out, they were impatient to get off and patrol the earth. And he said, "Go, patrol the earth." So they patrolled the earth. ⁸Then he cried out to me, "Lo, those who go toward the north country have set my spirit at rest in the north country."

6.1–8: The eighth vision: The heavenly chariots and international peace. In this, Zechariah's final vision, as in his first vision (1.7–17), the world is at peace, but

---

a The word *falsely* added from verse 4　*b* Heb *ephah*
c Gk Compare Syr: Heb *their eye*　*d* Compare Gk:
Meaning of Heb uncertain　*e* Or *spirits*　*f* Cn: Heb
go after them

The Design of Zechariah's Visions

Zechariah's visions are organized by a concentric structure to draw the reader's attention from the universal to the particular, from the perspective of God to the realities of life in Judah. The first and last visions describe the world from the perspective of God and God's heavenly emissaries (1.7–17; 6.1–8). The second and third visions (1.18–2.5), together with the sixth and seventh visions (5.1–11), narrow the reader's focus to the restoration of Judah and Jerusalem. And the two visions at the center of the design describe the officials who will preside over a renewed Jerusalem (chs. 3–4). If ch. 3 is a later addition as some claim, the concentric pattern is even more balanced and focused on the two anointed* leaders of the people.

- • **1.1–17** The first vision: The heavenly horsemen and God's plans for Jerusalem
  - • **1.18–21** The second vision: The four horns and Judah's security
    - • **2.1–5** The third vision: The measuring line and Jerusalem's resettlement
      - • **[3.1–10** The fourth vision: Joshua's installation as high priest]
        - • **4.1–14** The fifth vision: The golden lampstand and Judah's leadership
      - • **5.1–4** The sixth vision: The flying scroll and social justice
    - • **5.5–11** The seventh vision: The basket and Judah's purification
  - • **6.1–8** The eighth vision: The heavenly chariots and international peace

now that peace includes the restoration of Judah and Jerusalem among the nations. **1–3:** These four chariots parallel the four horsemen in Zechariah's first vision (1.8–10) and represent God's heavenly patrol (v. 7) assigned to watch over the world's affairs. *Mountains* signify the abode of the gods in antiquity (Ps 48.1). **8:** The chariot patrol that sets God's *spirit at rest in the north country* thereby establishes the security of Judah on the international scene. It was from the north that Judah's enemies attacked (Jer 6.22), and it was from the north that Judah's exiles returned from captivity in Babylon (Jer 3.18).

9 The word of the LORD came to me: [10]Collect silver and gold[a] from the exiles— from Heldai, Tobijah, and Jedaiah—who have arrived from Babylon; and go the same day to the house of Josiah son of Zephaniah. [11]Take the silver and gold and make a crown,[b] and set it on the head of the high priest Joshua son of Jehozadak; [12]say to him: Thus says the LORD of hosts: Here is a man whose name is Branch: for he shall branch out in his place, and he shall build the temple of the LORD. [13]It is he that shall build

the temple of the LORD; he shall bear royal honor, and shall sit upon his throne and rule. There shall be a priest by his throne, with peaceful understanding between the two of them. [14]And the crown[c] shall be in the care of Heldai,[d] Tobijah, Jedaiah, and Josiah[e] son of Zephaniah, as a memorial in the temple of the LORD.

15 Those who are far off shall come and help to build the temple of the LORD; and you shall know that the LORD of hosts has sent me to you. This will happen if you diligently obey the voice of the LORD your God.

6.9–15: A charge to the high priest Joshua. This speech, placed between Zechariah's last vision and his concluding speech (chs. 7–8) may be an editorial addition. **10:** *Josiah* is a priestly figure, whose father *Zephaniah* was killed alongside Joshua's grandfather

a Cn Compare verse 11: Heb lacks *silver and gold*
b Gk Mss Syr Tg: Heb *crowns*   *c* Gk Syr: Heb *crowns*
d Syr Compare verse 10: Heb *Helem*   *e* Syr Compare
verse 10: Heb *Hen*

Seraiah when Jerusalem was conquered (2 Kings 25.18–21). **11–13:** While this speech is directed to *Joshua*, its content seems more suitable for Zerubbabel. In 3.8 the *Branch* is not Joshua but an individual presented to him. In 4.6–10 Zerubbabel, not Joshua, is commissioned as the Temple* builder. Moreover, the Hebrew text does not say that *a crown* but that (two?) crowns were made (see note *b*), perhaps for both the royal figure and the priest mentioned in v. 13. It appears almost as if a speech once directed to Judah's political leader has been redirected to its religious leader. In any case, the concept of a leadership shared between religious and political figures found elsewhere in Zechariah (4.14) is present here too.

7 In the fourth year of King Darius, the word of the LORD came to Zechariah on the fourth day of the ninth month, which is Chislev. ²Now the people of Bethel had sent Sharezer and Regem-melech and their men, to entreat the favor of the LORD, ³and to ask the priests of the house of the LORD of hosts and the prophets, "Should I mourn and practice abstinence in the fifth month, as I have done for so many years?" ⁴Then the word of the LORD of hosts came to me: ⁵Say to all the people of the land and the priests: When you fasted and lamented in the fifth month and in the seventh, for these seventy years, was it for me that you fasted? ⁶And when you eat and when you drink, do you not eat and drink only for yourselves? ⁷Were not these the words that the LORD proclaimed by the former prophets, when Jerusalem was inhabited and in prosperity, along with the towns around it, and when the Negeb and the Shephelah were inhabited?

7.1–14: A charge to live justly. Zechariah's concluding speech is divided into two parts: an appeal—with an eye on the past—to create a just society (ch. 7), and a promise—with an eye on the future—of renewal and celebration (ch. 8). **1:** This speech is dated two years later (518 BCE) than Zechariah's opening speech (1.1). **2:** *Bethel* is 10 miles north of Jerusalem. **3:** *Prophets** were often asked for divine instructions (Ezek 8.1; 14.1). The period of mourning in the *fifth month*, about which the envoys ask Zechariah, may have commemorated the destruction of the Temple in the fifth month (2 Kings 25.8–9). **5:** *Seventy years* appears to refer to the Exile,* though the Exile was

shorter (see comment on 1.12). **7:** Zechariah refers to the period before Jerusalem's fall in 587 BCE.

8 The word of the LORD came to Zechariah, saying: ⁹Thus says the LORD of hosts: Render true judgments, show kindness and mercy to one another; ¹⁰do not oppress the widow, the orphan, the alien, or the poor; and do not devise evil in your hearts against one another. ¹¹But they refused to listen, and turned a stubborn shoulder, and stopped their ears in order not to hear. ¹²They made their hearts adamant in order not to hear the law and the words that the LORD of hosts had sent by his spirit through the former prophets. Therefore great wrath came from the LORD of hosts. ¹³Just as, when I*ᵃ* called, they would not hear, so, when they called, I would not hear, says the LORD of hosts, ¹⁴and I scattered them with a whirlwind among all the nations that they had not known. Thus the land they left was desolate, so that no one went to and fro, and a pleasant land was made desolate.

7.8–11: By responding to a question about mourning rituals (v. 3) with a charge to create a just society, Zechariah appears to side with his predecessors, the former prophets (v. 7), who claimed that religious rituals were meaningless apart from the practice of justice in all areas of life (Am 5.21–24). This same concern is also present in Zechariah's sixth and seventh visions (5.1–11). Throughout this speech Zechariah uses his ancestors who disobeyed as a lesson for his own audience.

8 The word of the LORD of hosts came to me, saying: ²Thus says the LORD of hosts: I am jealous for Zion with great jealousy, and I am jealous for her with great wrath. ³Thus says the LORD: I will return to Zion, and will dwell in the midst of Jerusalem; Jerusalem shall be called the faithful city, and the mountain of the LORD of hosts shall be called the holy mountain. ⁴Thus says the LORD of hosts: Old men and old women shall again sit in the streets of Jerusalem, each with staff in hand because of

a Heb *he*

their great age. 5And the streets of the city shall be full of boys and girls playing in its streets. 6Thus says the LORD of hosts: Even though it seems impossible to the remnant of this people in these days, should it also seem impossible to me, says the LORD of hosts? 7Thus says the LORD of hosts: I will save my people from the east country and from the west country; 8and I will bring them to live in Jerusalem. They shall be my people and I will be their God, in faithfulness and in righteousness.

9 Thus says the LORD of hosts: Let your hands be strong—you that have recently been hearing these words from the mouths of the prophets who were present when the foundation was laid for the rebuilding of the temple, the house of the LORD of hosts. 10For before those days there were no wages for people or for animals, nor was there any safety from the foe for those who went out or came in, and I set them all against one another. 11But now I will not deal with the remnant of this people as in the former days, says the LORD of hosts. 12For there shall be a sowing of peace; the vine shall yield its fruit, the ground shall give its produce, and the skies shall give their dew; and I will cause the remnant of this people to possess all these things. 13Just as you have been a cursing among the nations, O house of Judah and house of Israel, so I will save you and you shall be a blessing. Do not be afraid, but let your hands be strong.

14 For thus says the LORD of hosts: Just as I purposed to bring disaster upon you, when your ancestors provoked me to wrath, and I did not relent, says the LORD of hosts, 15so again I have purposed in these days to do good to Jerusalem and to the house of Judah; do not be afraid. 16These are the things that you shall do: Speak the truth to one another, render in your gates judgments that are true and make for peace, 17do not devise evil in your hearts against one another, and love no false oath; for all these are things that I hate, says the LORD.

18 The word of the LORD of hosts came to me, saying: 19Thus says the LORD of hosts: The fast of the fourth month, and the fast of the fifth, and the fast of the seventh,

and the fast of the tenth, shall be seasons of joy and gladness, and cheerful festivals for the house of Judah: therefore love truth and peace.

20 Thus says the LORD of hosts: Peoples shall yet come, the inhabitants of many cities; 21the inhabitants of one city shall go to another, saying, "Come, let us go to entreat the favor of the LORD, and to seek the LORD of hosts; I myself am going." 22Many peoples and strong nations shall come to seek the LORD of hosts in Jerusalem, and to entreat the favor of the LORD. 23Thus says the LORD of hosts: In those days ten men from nations of every language shall take hold of a Jew, grasping his garment and saying, "Let us go with you, for we have heard that God is with you."

8.1–23: A promise of restoration. In this second part of his final speech, Zechariah includes many of the typical themes of post-exilic prophecy: the renewal of Jerusalem (vv. 2–5), the return of the exiles (vv. 6–8), the rebuilding of the Temple (vv. 9–13), and the respect of the nations (vv. 20–23). 6: The *remnant* refers to the exiles who are returning to Judah (vv. 7–8; Hag 1.12). To these returnees the process of reconstruction *seems impossible* (4.10; Hag 2.3). 9: Laying the Temple's foundation is described in Hag 1.12–14 and Ezra 5.1–2. 10: The difficult times described here appear to reflect those mentioned by Haggai (1.2–11). 17: *False oaths* are a major concern in Zechariah's sixth vision (5.1–4). 19: Though not addressed directly to those who had asked Zechariah about mourning rituals (7.3), this speech instructs the people to substitute festivals of celebration for fasting. 22–23: The conversion of the nations is a common theme in the post-exilic period (Isa 60.1–7; Mic 4.1–4).

9

An Oracle.

The word of the LORD is against the
　　　land of Hadrach
　　and will rest upon Damascus.
　For to the LORD belongs the capital*a* of
　　　Aram,*b*
　　as do all the tribes of Israel;

a Heb *eye*　*b* Cn: Heb *of Adam* (or *of humankind*)

2 Hamath also, which borders on it,
    Tyre and Sidon, though they are very
        wise.
3 Tyre has built itself a rampart,
    and heaped up silver like dust,
    and gold like the dirt of the streets.
4 But now, the Lord will strip it of its
        possessions
    and hurl its wealth into the sea,
    and it shall be devoured by fire.

5 Ashkelon shall see it and be afraid;
    Gaza too, and shall writhe in anguish;
    Ekron also, because its hopes
        are withered.
    The king shall perish from Gaza;
    Ashkelon shall be uninhabited;
6 a mongrel people shall settle in Ashdod,
    and I will make an end of the pride of
        Philistia.
7 I will take away its blood from
        its mouth,
    and its abominations from between
        its teeth;
    it too shall be a remnant for our God;
    it shall be like a clan in Judah,
    and Ekron shall be like the Jebusites.
8 Then I will encamp at my house as a
        guard,
    so that no one shall march to and fro;
    no oppressor shall again overrun them,
    for now I have seen with my
        own eyes.

9.1–17: The divine warrior* defends Judah. This
chapter begins the second part of Zechariah, which,
because of its differences in style and content, appears
to have been composed later than chs. 1–8 and to
have been added to the prophecies of Zechariah. The
title *An Oracle** (9.1; 12.1) divides these supplementary speeches into two collections, chs. 9–11 and
12–14. **1–8:** God marches from north to south, defeating Judah's traditional enemies and taking up
residence in Jerusalem. **1–2a:** *Hadrach, Damascus,* and
Hamath are important Aramean cities north of Israel
and Judah. **2b–4:** *Tyre* and *Sidon* are important Phoenician cities on the Mediterranean coast northwest of
Judah. Tyre's legendary* wisdom and wealth are described in Ezek 28. **5–7:** *Ashkelon, Gaza, Ekron,* and
Ashdod are important Philistine cities on the Mediterranean coast west of Judah. The *Jebusites* (v. 7) were

defeated by David when he conquered Jerusalem
(2 Sam 5.6–10). **8:** Following victory, the divine warrior is enthroned in his temple (Ps 29.9–11).

9 Rejoice greatly, O daughter Zion!
    Shout aloud, O daughter Jerusalem!
    Lo, your king comes to you;
        triumphant and victorious is he,
    humble and riding on a donkey,
        on a colt, the foal of a donkey.
10 He*a* will cut off the chariot
        from Ephraim
    and the war-horse from Jerusalem;
    and the battle bow shall be cut off,
    and he shall command peace to the
        nations;
    his dominion shall be from sea to sea,
    and from the River to the ends of the
        earth.

11 As for you also, because of the blood of
        my covenant with you,
    I will set your prisoners free from the
        waterless pit.
12 Return to your stronghold, O prisoners
        of hope;
    today I declare that I will restore to
        you double.
13 For I have bent Judah as my bow;
    I have made Ephraim its arrow.
    I will arouse your sons, O Zion,
        against your sons, O Greece,
    and wield you like a warrior's sword.

14 Then the LORD will appear over them,
    and his arrow go forth like lightning;
    the Lord GOD will sound the trumpet
    and march forth in the whirlwinds of
        the south.
15 The LORD of hosts will protect them,
    and they shall devour and tread down
        the slingers;*b*
    they shall drink their blood*c* like wine,
    and be full like a bowl,
    drenched like the corners of the altar.

16 On that day the LORD their God will
        save them

a Gk: Heb I   b Cn: Heb *the slingstones*
c Gk: Heb *shall drink*

for they are the flock of his people;
for like the jewels of a crown
they shall shine on his land.
17 For what goodness and beauty are his!
Grain shall make the young
men flourish,
and new wine the young women.

9.9–17. 9: While God may be referred to as *king* in late prophetic literature (Zeph 3.14–15), a human *king* reviving the Davidic dynasty★ may be intended here (Jer 23.5–6; Hag 2.20–23). The Davidic king from the tribe of Judah referred to in Gen 49.10–11 is pictured with a *donkey,* the traditional transportation for gods and kings in antiquity. **10:** *Ephraim* is a name for the northern kingdom of Israel (Hos 5.5). International *peace* is a typical element in visions of the future (Mic 4.3–4). **11:** The exilic prophet★ Second Isaiah also combines God's remembrance of the covenant★ with God's liberation of the exiles (Isa 42.6–7). **13:** *Greece* (Heb., "Javan") is one of the lands to which Judeans were exiled (Isa 66.18–20; Joel 3.6).

~~~~~~~~~~~~~~~~~~~~~~

10 Ask rain from the LORD
in the season of the spring rain,
from the LORD who makes the storm
clouds,
who gives showers of rain to you,[a]
the vegetation in the field
to everyone.
2 For the teraphim[b] utter nonsense,
and the diviners see lies;
the dreamers tell false dreams,
and give empty consolation.
Therefore the people wander like
sheep;
they suffer for lack of a shepherd.

3 My anger is hot against the shepherds,
and I will punish the leaders;[c]
for the LORD of hosts cares for his
flock, the house of Judah,
and will make them like his proud
war-horse.
4 Out of them shall come the
cornerstone,
out of them the tent peg,
out of them the battle bow,
out of them every commander.
5 Together they shall be like warriors in
battle,

trampling the foe in the mud of the
streets;
they shall fight, for the LORD is with
them,
and they shall put to shame the riders
on horses.

10.1–12: God gathers the exiles. This speech continues the theme of restoration in the previous oracle★ by focusing on God's work of returning the exiles of Israel and Judah. **2:** *Teraphim* are objects or images used in worship (Judg 17.5) and were condemned by some writers (2 Kings 23.24). Here the main concern seems to be that all media of revelation have become silent. **3:** It is uncertain whether these *shepherds,* the people's *leaders,* are rulers of foreign countries oppressing Judah (Jer 12.10) or Judah's own rulers who have become corrupt (Isa 56.11), like those denigrated in 11.4–6. In either case, they will be punished so God can restore *the house of Judah.*

~~~~~~~~~~~~~~~~~~~~~~

6 I will strengthen the house of Judah,
and I will save the house of Joseph.
I will bring them back because I have
compassion on them,
and they shall be as though I had not
rejected them;
for I am the LORD their God and I
will answer them.
7 Then the people of Ephraim shall
become like warriors,
and their hearts shall be glad as with
wine.
Their children shall see it and rejoice,
their hearts shall exult in the LORD.

8 I will signal for them and gather them in,
for I have redeemed them,
and they shall be as numerous as they
were before.
9 Though I scattered them among
the nations,
yet in far countries they shall
remember me,
and they shall rear their children and
return.
10 I will bring them home from the land of
Egypt,
and gather them from Assyria;

a Heb *them*   *b* Or *household gods*   *c* Or *male goats*

I will bring them to the land of Gilead
  and to Lebanon,
until there is no room for them.
11 They*a* shall pass through the sea of
    distress,
  and the waves of the sea shall be
    struck down,
  and all the depths of the Nile
    dried up.
The pride of Assyria shall be laid low,
  and the scepter of Egypt shall depart.
12 I will make them strong in the LORD,
  and they shall walk in his name,
                              says the LORD.

10.6–12. 6–7: The *house of Joseph* and *Ephraim* are references to the northern kingdom of Israel. **10:** *Egypt* and *Assyria* are two of the countries to which Israelites were exiled (2 Kings 17.5–6; 25.26). *Gilead* and *Lebanon* are territories to the north of Israel.

11 Open your doors, O Lebanon,
  so that fire may devour your cedars!
2 Wail, O cypress, for the cedar
    has fallen,
  for the glorious trees are ruined!
Wail, oaks of Bashan,
  for the thick forest has been felled!
3 Listen, the wail of the shepherds,
  for their glory is despoiled!
Listen, the roar of the lions,
  for the thickets of the Jordan
    are destroyed!

11.1–3: God brings down wicked rulers. As in 10.3, the details are too few to indicate whether these *shepherds* (v. 3) are leaders of foreign nations, such as those God defeats in the previous verses (10.11–12), or leaders of Judah, such as those criticized in the following verses (11.4–6). The *cedars* and *cypress* of Lebanon and *the oaks of Bashan*, legendary* forests, are symbolic of the great and powerful.

4 Thus said the LORD my God: Be a shepherd of the flock doomed to slaughter. 5Those who buy them kill them and go unpunished; and those who sell them say, "Blessed be the LORD, for I have become rich"; and their own shepherds have no pity on them. 6For I will no longer have pity on the inhabitants of the earth, says the LORD.

I will cause them, every one, to fall each into the hand of a neighbor, and each into the hand of the king; and they shall devastate the earth, and I will deliver*b* no one from their hand.

7 So, on behalf of the sheep merchants, I became the shepherd of the flock doomed to slaughter. I took two staffs; one I named Favor, the other I named Unity, and I tended the sheep. 8In one month I disposed of the three shepherds, for I had become impatient with them, and they also detested me. 9So I said, "I will not be your shepherd. What is to die, let it die; what is to be destroyed, let it be destroyed; and let those that are left devour the flesh of one another!" 10I took my staff Favor and broke it, annulling the covenant that I had made with all the peoples. 11So it was annulled on that day, and the sheep merchants, who were watching me, knew that it was the word of the LORD. 12I then said to them, "If it seems right to you, give me my wages; but if not, keep them." So they weighed out as my wages thirty shekels of silver. 13Then the LORD said to me, "Throw it into the treasury"*b*—this lordly price at which I was valued by them. So I took the thirty shekels of silver and threw them into the treasury*b* in the house of the LORD. 14Then I broke my second staff Unity, annulling the family ties between Judah and Israel.

15 Then the LORD said to me: Take once more the implements of a worthless shepherd. 16For I am now raising up in the land a shepherd who does not care for the perishing, or seek the wandering,*c* or heal the maimed, or nourish the healthy,*d* but devours the flesh of the fat ones, tearing off even their hoofs.
17 Oh, my worthless shepherd,
  who deserts the flock!
May the sword strike his arm
  and his right eye!
Let his arm be completely withered,
  his right eye utterly blinded!

---

a Gk: Heb *He* *b* Syr: Heb *it to the potter*
c Syr Compare Gk Vg: Heb *the youth* *d* Meaning of Heb uncertain

11.4–17: The prophet satirizes Judah's corrupt leaders. In this first-person narrative,* an anonymous prophet acts out the corrupt practices of Judah's leaders in order to expose and denounce them. **5:** *Their own shepherds* are Judah's leaders, who *buy* and *kill them,* that is, their own people symbolized as sheep. **7:** The *sheep merchants* are Judah's leaders, buying and selling their people (v. 5). The names of the *two staffs,* Favor (or "pleasantness") and *Unity,* reflect the goals of the good shepherd for the sheep. **8:** The identity of the *three shepherds* is unknown. **9:** Having disposed of the three shepherds (v. 8), the prophet apparently becomes impatient with the people themselves. **10:** Breaking the staffs of *Favor* and *Unity* (v. 14) consigns the flock, the people of Judah, to a time of trouble and conflict. **12–13:** The reason for the amount of the wages and their deposit in the Temple* is uncertain. Donations of about this amount were made to the Temple to "redeem" people devoted to Temple service from their obligation (Lev 27.1–8). On the other hand, the prophet may, by placing tainted money in the Temple's treasuries, want to indict the Temple and its leaders as corrupt. **14:** The prophet abandons hope for the reunion of the old northern kingdom of *Israel* and southern kingdom of *Judah,* which traced their origins back to a single ancestor, Jacob (Gen 49). **15–17:** The prophet anticipates, by dressing up a second time as a shepherd (v. 4), the arrival of another corrupt leader.

12

An Oracle.

The word of the LORD concerning Israel: Thus says the LORD, who stretched out the heavens and founded the earth and formed the human spirit within: ²See, I am about to make Jerusalem a cup of reeling for all the surrounding peoples; it will be against Judah also in the siege against Jerusalem. ³On that day I will make Jerusalem a heavy stone for all the peoples; all who lift it shall grievously hurt themselves. And all the nations of the earth shall come together against it. ⁴On that day, says the LORD, I will strike every horse with panic, and its rider with madness. But on the house of Judah I will keep a watchful eye, when I strike every horse of the peoples with blindness. ⁵Then the clans of Judah shall say to themselves, "The inhabi-

tants of Jerusalem have strength through the LORD of hosts, their God."

6 On that day I will make the clans of Judah like a blazing pot on a pile of wood, like a flaming torch among sheaves; and they shall devour to the right and to the left all the surrounding peoples, while Jerusalem shall again be inhabited in its place, in Jerusalem.

7 And the LORD will give victory to the tents of Judah first, that the glory of the house of David and the glory of the inhabitants of Jerusalem may not be exalted over that of Judah. ⁸On that day the LORD will shield the inhabitants of Jerusalem so that the feeblest among them on that day shall be like David, and the house of David shall be like God, like the angel of the LORD, at their head. ⁹And on that day I will seek to destroy all the nations that come against Jerusalem.

12.1–9: Judah defeats the nations. This text, like ch. 9, describes Judah's defense against its neighboring nations. **1:** The title *An Oracle* marks the beginning of the second collection of speeches in chs. 9–14. **2:** The *cup of reeling,* a traditional image of judgment, renders the enemy drunk and senseless (Isa 51.17–22). **6:** The *flaming torch,* another traditional image of judgment, consumes the enemy, pictured as sheaves or stubble (Ob 18). **7:** *The house of David* refers to a revival of the Davidic dynasty* which ruled from Jerusalem before its fall in 587 BCE.

10 And I will pour out a spirit of compassion and supplication on the house of David and the inhabitants of Jerusalem, so that, when they look on the one*ᵃ* whom they have pierced, they shall mourn for him, as one mourns for an only child, and weep bitterly over him, as one weeps over a firstborn. ¹¹On that day the mourning in Jerusalem will be as great as the mourning for Hadad-rimmon in the plain of Megiddo. ¹²The land shall mourn, each family by itself; the family of the house of David by itself, and their wives by themselves; the family of the house of Nathan by itself, and their wives by themselves; ¹³the family of the house of Levi by

---

a Heb *on me*

itself, and their wives by themselves; the family of the Shimeites by itself, and their wives by themselves; ¹⁴and all the families that are left, each by itself, and their wives by themselves.

12.10–14: Mourning in Jerusalem. 10: The identification of the object of mourning, *the one whom they have pierced,* is uncertain; but due to the wide extent of the mourning and the leading role of the house of David in it (vv. 10, 12), the person mourned may have been a member of the royal family. **11:** *Hadad-rimmon* is the name of the Syrian storm god, a figure like Baal,* the Canaanite storm god. If taken as the name of a place named after his deity *in the plain of Megiddo,* however, this may be a reference to the mourning for the Judean king, Josiah, who was killed by the Egyptians in the plain of Megiddo and mourned by all of Judah and Jerusalem (2 Chr 35.20–25). **13:** *Levi* and *Shimei* are priestly families.

13 On that day a fountain shall be opened for the house of David and the inhabitants of Jerusalem, to cleanse them from sin and impurity. 2 On that day, says the LORD of hosts, I will cut off the names of the idols from the land, so that they shall be remembered no more; and also I will remove from the land the prophets and the unclean spirit. ³And if any prophets appear again, their fathers and mothers who bore them will say to them, "You shall not live, for you speak lies in the name of the LORD"; and their fathers and their mothers who bore them shall pierce them through when they prophesy. ⁴On that day the prophets will be ashamed, every one, of their visions when they prophesy; they will not put on a hairy mantle in order to deceive, ⁵but each of them will say, "I am no prophet, I am a tiller of the soil; for the land has been my possession*a* since my youth." ⁶And if anyone asks them, "What are these wounds on your chest?"*b* the answer will be "The wounds I received in the house of my friends."

⁷ "Awake, O sword, against my shepherd,
     against the man who is my associate,"
            says the LORD of hosts.

Strike the shepherd, that the sheep may
     be scattered;
I will turn my hand against
     the little ones.
⁸ In the whole land, says the LORD,
     two-thirds shall be cut off
     and perish,
     and one-third shall be left alive.
⁹ And I will put this third into the fire,
     refine them as one refines silver,
     and test them as gold is tested.
They will call on my name,
     and I will answer them.
I will say, "They are my people";
     and they will say, "The LORD is
     our God."

13.1–9: God removes false prophets and leaders. This text, like 11.4–17, focuses on corruption within Judah itself, especially among its leaders. **2–3:** The prophets whose writings have been preserved in the Bible often find themselves in conflict with other prophets preaching opposite messages (Jer 14.14; Ezek 13.1–7). Here the prophet accuses his opponents of preaching *lies in the name of the LORD* and announces God's judgment on them. *The unclean spirit* (or "breath") is the source of the prophets' false inspiration or revelation (1 Kings 22.19–23). **7:** The judgment on Judah's *shepherd* resumes the criticism of Judah's leadership in 11.4–17. **8–9:** The division of Judah into thirds for punishment is reminiscent of Ezekiel's prophecy (5.1–12). But here the prophet concentrates on a third that, though punished, will survive and renew their relationship to God.

14 See, a day is coming for the LORD, when the plunder taken from you will be divided in your midst. ²For I will gather all the nations against Jerusalem to battle, and the city shall be taken and the houses looted and the women raped; half the city shall go into exile, but the rest of the people shall not be cut off from the city. ³Then the LORD will go forth and fight against those nations as when he fights on a day of battle. ⁴On that day his feet shall

---

a Cn: Heb *for humankind has caused me to possess*
b Heb *wounds between your hands*

stand on the Mount of Olives, which lies before Jerusalem on the east; and the Mount of Olives shall be split in two from east to west by a very wide valley; so that one half of the Mount shall withdraw northward, and the other half southward. [5]And you shall flee by the valley of the LORD's mountain,[a] for the valley between the mountains shall reach to Azal;[b] and you shall flee as you fled from the earthquake in the days of King Uzziah of Judah. Then the LORD my God will come, and all the holy ones with him.

14.1–21: God defeats the nations and restores Jerusalem. Speeches such as this one describing the defense and restoration of Jerusalem in the context of God's intervention against the neighboring nations that have oppressed it are common in the period after the Exile,* as chs. 9, 10, and 12 illustrate (Isa 59.15–20; Joel 3). **1:** The *plunder* once taken from Jerusalem will be returned. **2:** This is the only verse in the chapter that describes judgment, rather than restoration, for Jerusalem. The prophet either anticipates a coming judgment on Jerusalem's corrupt leadership (11.4–17; 13.2–9) or recalls the fall of Jerusalem in 587 BCE. **4–5:** The citizens of Jerusalem will escape God's attack on the nations by fleeing east through a great rift in the Mount of Olives, which in reality towers over the city of Jerusalem.

---

6 On that day there shall not be[c] either cold or frost.[d] [7]And there shall be continuous day (it is known to the LORD), not day and not night, for at evening time there shall be light.

8 On that day living waters shall flow out from Jerusalem, half of them to the eastern sea and half of them to the western sea; it shall continue in summer as in winter.

14.8: The upwelling of Jerusalem's Gihon spring with abundant water is a common theme in visions of the future (Ezek 47.1–12; Joel 3.18).

---

9 And the LORD will become king over all the earth; on that day the LORD will be one and his name one.

10 The whole land shall be turned into a plain from Geba to Rimmon south of Jerusalem. But Jerusalem shall remain aloft on its site from the Gate of Benjamin to the place of the former gate, to the Corner Gate, and from the Tower of Hananel to the king's wine presses. [11]And it shall be inhabited, for never again shall it be doomed to destruction; Jerusalem shall abide in security.

12 This shall be the plague with which the LORD will strike all the peoples that wage war against Jerusalem: their flesh shall rot while they are still on their feet; their eyes shall rot in their sockets, and their tongues shall rot in their mouths. [13]On that day a great panic from the LORD shall fall on them, so that each will seize the hand of a neighbor, and the hand of the one will be raised against the hand of the other; [14]even Judah will fight at Jerusalem. And the wealth of all the surrounding nations shall be collected—gold, silver, and garments in great abundance. [15]And a plague like this plague shall fall on the horses, the mules, the camels, the donkeys, and whatever animals may be in those camps.

16 Then all who survive of the nations that have come against Jerusalem shall go up year after year to worship the King, the LORD of hosts, and to keep the festival of booths.[e] [17]If any of the families of the earth do not go up to Jerusalem to worship the King, the LORD of hosts, there will be no rain upon them. [18]And if the family of Egypt do not go up and present themselves, then on them shall[f] come the plague that the LORD inflicts on the nations that do not go up to keep the festival of booths.[e] [19]Such shall be the punishment of Egypt and the punishment of all the nations that do not go up to keep the festival of booths.[e]

14.16: The surrounding nations will make an annual pilgrimage to worship Israel's God in Jerusalem (8.22–23) in the fall for *the festival of booths*, a festival commemorating the autumn harvest (Deut 16.13–15).

---

a Heb *my mountains*   *b* Meaning of Heb uncertain
c Cn: Heb *there shall not be light*   *d* Compare Gk Syr
Vg Tg: Meaning of Heb uncertain   *e* Or *tabernacles;*
Heb *succoth*   *f* Gk Syr: Heb *shall not*

20 On that day there shall be inscribed on the bells of the horses, "Holy to the LORD." And the cooking pots in the house of the LORD shall be as holy as[a] the bowls in front of the altar; 21and every cooking pot in Jerusalem and Judah shall be sacred to the LORD of hosts, so that all who sacrifice may come and use them to boil the flesh of the sacrifice. And there shall no longer be trad-ers[b] in the house of the LORD of hosts on that day.

14.20–21: The holiness of the Temple's most sacred precincts will spread to all of Jerusalem.

a Heb *shall be like*   b Or *Canaanites*

MALACHI

Introduction

Malachi is primarily concerned about a lack of devotion and seriousness in Judah's Temple* worship and about a lack of fidelity in Judah's social relationships. The prophet* addresses these issues in a series of disputations, in which he often quotes his audience. He blames the Temple priesthood for its impure offerings (1.6–2.3) and improper teachings (2.4–9) and Judah's people for their meager contributions (3.6–12). Furthermore, he blames the people for a lack of faithfulness in family relations, in particular marriage (2.10–16), and in obligations to the poor and powerless (3.5). In his concern for social fidelity and justice, Malachi stands in the tradition of the pre-exilic prophets, such as Amos and Micah, who preached against injustice and the abuse of power. In his concern for proper worship in a sanctified temple, Malachi shares the concerns of other post-exilic prophets, such as Haggai and Zechariah. Malachi also expresses the post-exilic expectation of a great day of salvation when the righteous are restored and the wicked punished (4.1–3).

Since the book of Malachi contains no references to dates or to identifiable contemporary people or events, it is difficult to identify its precise social and historical setting. The mention of a governor (1.8; Hag 1.1) places it in the post-exilic period, together with Haggai and Zechariah which precede it, following the return to Judah of the Babylonian exiles. Because of a sense of disillusionment in Malachi's audience (1.2, 17) and a failure of leadership in the Temple and society (1.6–2.9), Malachi may have preached at a time later than Haggai and Zechariah (1–8), who initiated the reconstruction of the Temple and who had a positive view of Judah's new leadership.

READING GUIDE

If Malachi preached to a people disillusioned with early hopes of the restoration of their homeland (1.2, 17; 3.14–15), he faced a daunting challenge that must be kept in mind while reading his speeches. How does a people remain faithful when its efforts seem fruitless?

1 An oracle. The word of the LORD to Israel by Malachi.*

2 I have loved you, says the LORD. But you say, "How have you loved us?" Is not Esau Jacob's brother? says the LORD. Yet I have loved Jacob ³but I have hated Esau; I have made his hill country a desolation and his heritage a desert for jackals. ⁴If Edom says, "We are shattered but we will rebuild the ruins," the LORD of hosts says: They may build, but I will tear down, until they are called the wicked country, the people with whom the LORD is angry forever. ⁵Your own eyes shall see this, and you shall say, "Great is the LORD beyond the borders of Israel!"

1.1–5. 1: Title. Malachi, meaning "my messenger" (see note a), is either the name of an individual or a title selected for the author of this prophetic collection on the basis of 3.1. **2–5: Edom's ruins.** For those who think their modest efforts at the reconstruction of Judah do not reflect God's presence or love, the uninhabited ruins of their neighbor Edom are a stark reminder of God's real absence and anger. **2:** *Esau,* Edom's ancestor, was the *brother* of *Jacob,* Israel's an-

a Or by my messenger

cestor (Gen 25.21–34). **3–4:** God's destruction of Edom is viewed elsewhere as punishment for Edom's participation in the sacking of Jerusalem when it was conquered by the Babylonians (Obadiah; Ps 137.7–8).

6 A son honors his father, and servants their master. If then I am a father, where is the honor due me? And if I am a master, where is the respect due me? says the LORD of hosts to you, O priests, who despise my name. You say, "How have we despised your name?" 7By offering polluted food on my altar. And you say, "How have we polluted it?"*a* By thinking that the LORD's table may be despised. 8When you offer blind animals in sacrifice, is that not wrong? And when you offer those that are lame or sick, is that not wrong? Try presenting that to your governor; will he be pleased with you or show you favor? says the LORD of hosts. 9And now implore the favor of God, that he may be gracious to us. The fault is yours. Will he show favor to any of you? says the LORD of hosts. 10Oh, that someone among you would shut the temple*b* doors, so that you would not kindle fire on my altar in vain! I have no pleasure in you, says the LORD of hosts, and I will not accept an offering from your hands. 11For from the rising of the sun to its setting my name is great among the nations, and in every place incense is offered to my name, and a pure offering; for my name is great among the nations, says the LORD of hosts. 12But you profane it when you say that the Lord's table is polluted, and the food for it*c* may be despised. 13"What a weariness this is," you say, and you sniff at me,*d* says the LORD of hosts. You bring what has been taken by violence or is lame or sick, and this you bring as your offering! Shall I accept that from your hand? says the LORD. 14Cursed be the cheat who has a male in the flock and vows to give it, and yet sacrifices to the Lord what is blemished; for I am a great King, says the LORD of hosts, and my name is reverenced among the nations.

2 And now, O priests, this command is for you. 2If you will not listen, if you will not lay it to heart to give glory to my name, says the LORD of hosts, then I will send the curse on you and I will curse your blessings; indeed

I have already cursed them,*e* because you do not lay it to heart. 3I will rebuke your offspring, and spread dung on your faces, the dung of your offerings, and I will put you out of my presence.*f*

4 Know, then, that I have sent this command to you, that my covenant with Levi may hold, says the LORD of hosts. 5My covenant with him was a covenant of life and well-being, which I gave him; this called for reverence, and he revered me and stood in awe of my name. 6True instruction was in his mouth, and no wrong was found on his lips. He walked with me in integrity and uprightness, and he turned many from iniquity. 7For the lips of a priest should guard knowledge, and people should seek instruction from his mouth, for he is the messenger of the LORD of hosts. 8But you have turned aside from the way; you have caused many to stumble by your instruction; you have corrupted the covenant of Levi, says the LORD of hosts, 9and so I make you despised and abased before all the people, inasmuch as you have not kept my ways but have shown partiality in your instruction.

1.6–2.9: The priests' sins. Making up a third of the entire book, this accusation singles out two priestly sins: making improper offerings (1.6–2.3) and giving improper instruction (2.4–9). **1.8:** Priestly (Lev 1.3; 22.17–25) and deuteronomic (Deut 15.19–23) laws prohibit the sacrifice of blemished animals, Deuteronomy specifically forbidding the *lame* and *blind*. **2.4:** *Levi* is the ancestor of Israel's priestly families (1 Chr 6.1–48). **8:** Priests were responsible for teaching and *instruction*. Micah also blames priests for abusing their teaching office (3.11).

10 Have we not all one father? Has not one God created us? Why then are we faithless to one another, profaning the covenant of our ancestors? 11Judah has been faithless, and abomination has been committed in Israel and in Jerusalem; for Judah has profaned the sanctuary of the LORD, which he loves, and has married the daughter of a for-

a Gk: Heb *you*   *b* Heb lacks *temple*   *c* Compare Syr Tg: Heb *its fruit, its food*   *d* Another reading is *at it* *e* Heb *it*   *f* Cn Compare Gk Syr: Heb *and he shall bear you to it* eign god. 12May the LORD cut off from the tents of Jacob anyone who does this—any to witness[a] or answer, or to bring an offering to the LORD of hosts.

13 And this you do as well: You cover the LORD's altar with tears, with weeping and groaning because he no longer regards the offering or accepts it with favor at your hand. 14You ask, "Why does he not?" Because the LORD was a witness between you and the wife of your youth, to whom you have been faithless, though she is your companion and your wife by covenant. 15Did not one God make her?[b] Both flesh and spirit are his.[c] And what does the one God[d] desire? Godly offspring. So look to yourselves, and do not let anyone be faithless to the wife of his youth. 16For I hate[e] divorce, says the LORD, the God of Israel, and covering one's garment with violence, says the LORD of hosts. So take heed to yourselves and do not be faithless.

~~~~

2.10–16: Judah's unfaithfulness. This speech is either a criticism of idolatry,★ by means of the metaphor★ of unfaithfulness in marriage, or, more likely, a criticism of unfaithful marriage relationships themselves. **10–12:** Judean men have been *faithless* by marrying foreign women, *the daughter of a foreign god* (v. 11). The prohibition against marrying foreign women appears to stem from the concern that the husband will abandon worship of Israel's God (Ex 34.16; 1 Kings 11.1–2). **13–16:** Judean men have also been *faithless* by divorcing their wives. While deuteronomic law provides stipulations for divorce (Deut 24.1–4), this speech appears to be more critical of it.

~~~~

17 You have wearied the LORD with your words. Yet you say, "How have we wearied him?" By saying, "All who do evil are good in the sight of the LORD, and he delights in them." Or by asking, "Where is the God of justice?"

3 See, I am sending my messenger to prepare the way before me, and the Lord whom you seek will suddenly come to his temple. The messenger of the covenant in whom you delight—indeed, he is coming, says the LORD of hosts. 2But who can endure the day of his coming, and who can stand when he appears?

For he is like a refiner's fire and like fullers' soap; 3he will sit as a refiner and purifier of silver, and he will purify the descendants of Levi and refine them like gold and silver, until they present offerings to the LORD in righteousness.[f] 4Then the offering of Judah and Jerusalem will be pleasing to the LORD as in the days of old and as in former years.

5 Then I will draw near to you for judgment; I will be swift to bear witness against the sorcerers, against the adulterers, against those who swear falsely, against those who oppress the hired workers in their wages, the widow and the orphan, against those who thrust aside the alien, and do not fear me, says the LORD of hosts.

~~~~

2.17–3.5: God's judgment. Malachi announces a divine judgment as a response to those who weary God by complaining that the wicked prosper (v. 17). **3.1:** The identity of the *messenger* is not stated, though the conclusion to Malachi connects him with the prophet★ Elijah (4.5). **3:** The first group singled out for judgment is the *descendants of Levi*, the priests who have been making improper *offerings* (see 1.6–2.9). **5:** *The adulterers* judged here may be the faithless Judeans (2.10–16). By describing God's judgment against those who *oppress* the poor and powerless, including *the widow and the orphan*, Malachi takes up the theme of social justice preached by Israel's pre-exilic prophets (Isa 1.17).

~~~~

6 For I the LORD do not change; therefore you, O children of Jacob, have not perished. 7Ever since the days of your ancestors you have turned aside from my statutes and have not kept them. Return to me, and I will return to you, says the LORD of hosts. But you say, "How shall we return?"

8 Will anyone rob God? Yet you are robbing me! But you say, "How are we robbing you?" In your tithes and offerings! 9You are cursed with a curse, for you are robbing me—the whole nation of you! 10Bring the full tithe into the storehouse, so that there

a Cn Compare Gk: Heb *arouse*   b Or *Has he not made one?*   c Cn: Heb *and a remnant of spirit was his*   d Heb *he*   e Cn: Heb *he hates*   f Or *right offerings to the LORD* may be food in my house, and thus put me to the test, says the LORD of hosts; see if I will not open the windows of heaven for you and pour down for you an overflowing blessing. ¹¹I will rebuke the locust* for you, so that it will not destroy the produce of your soil; and your vine in the field shall not be barren, says the LORD of hosts. ¹²Then all nations will count you happy, for you will be a land of delight, says the LORD of hosts.

3.6–12: Judah's miserliness. Just as Judah's priests are not fulfilling their obligations for proper worship at the Temple★ (1.6–2.3), so Judah's people are not fulfilling theirs. They are not bringing to the Temple the *full tithes* (v. 10) of their produce required by Israelite law (Lev 27.30–33; Deut 14.22–29). **10:** The connection between proper worship and divine blessing in Malachi's message mirrors Haggai's thought (Hag 1.9–10).

13 You have spoken harsh words against me, says the LORD. Yet you say, "How have we spoken against you?" ¹⁴You have said, "It is vain to serve God. What do we profit by keeping his command or by going about as mourners before the LORD of hosts? ¹⁵Now we count the arrogant happy; evildoers not only prosper, but when they put God to the test they escape."

16 Then those who revered the LORD spoke with one another. The LORD took note and listened, and a book of remembrance was written before him of those who revered the LORD and thought on his name. ¹⁷They shall be mine, says the LORD of hosts, my special possession on the day when I act, and I will spare them as parents spare their children who serve them. ¹⁸Then once more you shall see the difference between the righteous and the wicked, between one who serves God and one who does not serve him.

4 ᵇSee, the day is coming, burning like an oven, when all the arrogant and all evildoers will be stubble; the day that comes shall burn them up, says the LORD of hosts, so that it will leave them neither root nor branch. ²But for you who revere my name the sun of righteousness shall rise, with healing in its wings. You shall go out leaping like calves from the stall. ³And you shall tread down the wicked, for they will be ashes under the soles of your feet, on the day when I act, says the LORD of hosts.

4 Remember the teaching of my servant Moses, the statutes and ordinances that I commanded him at Horeb for all Israel.

5 Lo, I will send you the prophet Elijah before the great and terrible day of the LORD comes. ⁶He will turn the hearts of parents to their children and the hearts of children to their parents, so that I will not come and strike the land with a curse.ᶜ

3.13–4.6: God's judgment of the wicked and salvation of the righteous. The announcement of God's judgment, like the announcement in 2.17–3.5, is made in response to those who believe that there is no justice, that the wicked prosper while the righteous do not (vv. 13–15). Such a concern was not unique to Malachi's audience, as the books of Job (21.28–31) and Ecclesiastes (7.15) illustrate. **3.16:** The *book of remembrance* is unique to Malachi, though it is based on older traditions (Ex 32.32; Ps 69.28). **4.2:** *The sun of righteousness* is a title for God, who is elsewhere described with solar imagery (Ps 4.6; 84.11). **4:** This event is summarized in Deut 5–6. **5:** The expectation of the return of *Elijah* may be related to the tradition that he did not die but was taken up into heaven (2 Kings 2.11–12). The phrase *"I will send . . . "* associates him with God's messenger, mentioned in 3.1.

---

a Heb *devourer*   b Ch 4.1–6 are Ch 3.19–24 in Heb
c Or *a ban of utter destruction*

THE APOCRYPHAL/DEUTEROCANONICAL BOOKS OF THE OLD TESTAMENT

New Revised
Standard Version

THE APOCRYPHAL/
DEUTEROCANONICAL BOOKS

The title of this section of the New Revised Standard Version Bible translation is a combination of the title of these books in the Protestant traditions, where they are known as the Apocrypha* or "hidden things," and the title in the Orthodox Christian and Roman Catholic traditions, where the are regarded as Deuterocanonical* or a "second [part of the] canon,"* in the official list of biblical books. For an account of the origins of these books and the different ways these various traditions understand them as sacred books, see the essay on the "Biblical Canon" on 26–40.

These writings were produced, for the most part, by the Jewish community during what is known as the Second Temple* period, the time roughly from the late fifth century BCE until the destruction of the Second Temple by the Romans in 70 CE. This means that they are later than most of the books in the Hebrew Bible or the Protestant Old Testament, although Daniel is generally regarded as from this time period. Because of these origins, most of the books of the Apocrypha either were written in Greek or translated into Greek for the Jewish community who were living outside of Israel. After the Babylonian invasion of Jerusalem in 586 BCE, Jewish communities were located all around the eastern Mediterranean region, in Mesopotamia (modern Iraq), Persia (modern Iran), Egypt (particularly Alexandria), and Asia Minor (modern Turkey). When Alexander the Great (356–323 BCE) conquered these regions, Greek became the common language of the people, used for trade and communication across the empire. The books now in the Apocrypha shared in this language world and so circulated among Jews in their Greek form. The early followers of Jesus understood these Greek texts to be sacred texts, along with the books of Hebrew Scripture.*

This collection of books contains a wide variety of kinds of literature. This variety can even be found within individual books. Baruch, for example, contains many of the different literary forms discussed below.

Short Stories

(See "Short Stories" on 674 for a discussion of this type of literature.)

Short stories in the Apocrypha include Tobit, Judith, Esther, Susanna (among the Additions to Daniel), and Bel and the Dragon (also among the Additions to Daniel). The book of 3 Maccabees, though longer than these other examples, also belongs in this category. With the exception of Susanna, which is set exclusively among the Jewish community, these stories narrate the lives of faithful Jews who are living among communities of non-Jews. They explore the various strategies Jews adopted to live among other groups, from assimilation (as in Esth) to outright opposition (as in Bel and 3 Macc).

Histories

(See "Historical Literature" on 311–314 for a discussion of this type of literature.)

There are several historical works in this collection: the books of 1 and 2 Maccabees and 1 Esdras. First Maccabees is a fairly straightforward account of the Seleucid* persecution of the Jews and the resulting revolt, under the leadership of Judas "the Maccabee" ("Hammer"). Second Maccabees covers the same events, but with much more rhetorical flair, in order to draw readers into the events and their significance for them. First Esdras (except for chapters 3, 4, and the beginning of 5) is a summary of the end of 2 Chronicles, all of Ezra, and part of Nehemiah. The first part of Baruch (1.1–14) is also a historical narrative.*

Wisdom Literature*

(See "Wisdom Literature" on 730–732 for a discussion of this type of literature.)

Two works in the Apocrypha can be understood as part of the Hebrew wisdom tradition: the Wisdom of Solomon and the Wisdom of Jesus son of Sirach, or Ecclesiasticus. Sirach was originally written in Hebrew and follows the forms of wisdom in the book of Proverbs. The Wisdom of Solomon is less formally related to Proverbs—it does not use the proverb form, for example. But its links to the wisdom tradition are clear, as the idea of Wisdom is central to its contents. The Wisdom of Solomon, even more than Sirach, was influenced by Greek philosophical literature and ideas. The book of 4 Maccabees takes the form of a Greek philosophical diatribe* or speech. It features examples of the faithful behavior of Jews who were martyred during the persecutions of the Maccabean period and meditates on the meaning of martyrdom for its community of readers. A wisdom poem is also found in Baruch (3.9–4.4).

Psalms and Psalmlike Poems

(See "Hebrew Poetry" on 730–731 for a discussion of this type of literature.)

The Prayer of Manasseh, the Prayer of Azariah, and the Song of the Three Jews (among the Additions to Daniel), and Psalm 151 show the influence of the canonical* book of Psalms. Manasseh follows the form of a lament;* the two psalmlike additions to Daniel are perhaps intended for use in worship. Psalm 151 is a brief celebration of the heroism of David. Baruch contains three poetical or prayerlike compositions: a penitential prayer (1.15–3.8); a wisdom poem (3.9–4.4); and a poem invoking and praising Jerusalem/Zion (4.5–5.9).

Letters

(See "Epistles," on 1887–1889 for a discussion of this type of literature.)

The Letter of Jeremiah (also sometimes printed as the sixth chapter of Baruch) is an exhortation* to faithfulness that purports to be from the prophet Jeremiah to Jews in the Exile.*

Apocalyptic* Literature

(See "Apocalyptic Literature" on 2057–2059 for a discussion of this type of literature.)

The book of 2 Esdras is an example of apocalyptic writing, the "unveiling" or revelation of the meaning of history as seen from the heavenly perspective.

TOBIT

Introduction

The books of Tobit, Judith, the Greek version of Esther, the expanded form of Daniel, and *Joseph and Aseneth** are the only ancient Jewish novels* known to have survived. Tobit is an entertaining work that recounts the intertwined stories of Tobit and his future daughter-in-law, Sarah. Their respective problems—Tobit has become blind and each of Sarah's seven successive husbands has died on his wedding night before the marriage can be consummated—are solved by the intervention of the angel Raphael, who comes to them in the guise of one of their kinsmen. Tobit, although set at the time of the fall of the northern kingdom of Israel (late eighth century BCE), was likely written much later, about third to second century BCE, in Hebrew or Aramaic. It contains many references to Persian lands, and though it may not have been written in the east, it has an eastern orientation. Many extended Jewish families, including the Tobiad family, engaged in commerce across the boundaries from west to east, and some may be reflected in this work's central characters.

The book can be divided into three parts: (1) Tobit's piety is demonstrated by his courage in burying the corpses of dead Jews in violation of a royal decree (ch. 1); (2) Tobit's and Sarah's problems are resolved through the intervention of the angel Raphael (chs. 2–12); and (3) Tobit pronounces his deathbed prayers and testament (chs. 13–14). The three parts may not have been written by the same hand, but they fit together as a satisfying three-part novel for the Jewish audience in the Greco-Roman period.

The book communicates a charming piety, in that family and religious values are paramount. Very little tension is created as to whether their problems will be solved (3.16), but the reader is thoroughly entertained by discovering precisely how the plot will proceed. In addition, the author utilizes humor and irony* to create a comic tone throughout, making the happy ending seem inevitable.

1 This book tells the story of Tobit son of Tobiel son of Hananiel son of Aduel son of Gabael son of Raphael son of Raguel of the descendants[a] of Asiel, of the tribe of Naphtali, 2who in the days of King Shalmaneser[b] of the Assyrians was taken into captivity from Thisbe, which is to the south of Kedesh Naphtali in Upper Galilee, above Asher toward the west, and north of Phogor.

1.1–2: Introduction. Tobit is identified by genealogy,* and the story is dated to the period of the fall of the ten northern tribes of Israel in 722 BCE, when many Israelites were deported to Assyria (2 Kings 17.1–6). The meanings of most of the names in this book are significant for the story. *Tobit* is probably from the Hebrew Tobiah ("God is my good"), from which is also derived the name of Tobit's son Tobias. **2:** *Thisbe* may be Thebez (Judg 9.50–57); *Asher* is probably Hazor.

3 I, Tobit, walked in the ways of truth and righteousness all the days of my life. I performed many acts of charity for my kindred and my people who had gone with me in exile to Nineveh in the land of the Assyri-

a Other ancient authorities lack *of Raphael son of Raguel of the descendants*   b Gk *Enemessaros* ans. ⁴When I was in my own country, in the land of Israel, while I was still a young man, the whole tribe of my ancestor Naphtali deserted the house of David and Jerusalem. This city had been chosen from among all the tribes of Israel, where all the tribes of Israel should offer sacrifice and where the temple, the dwelling of God, had been consecrated and established for all generations forever.

5 All my kindred and our ancestral house of Naphtali sacrificed to the calf*ᵃ* that King Jeroboam of Israel had erected in Dan and on all the mountains of Galilee. ⁶But I alone went often to Jerusalem for the festivals, as it is prescribed for all Israel by an everlasting decree. I would hurry off to Jerusalem with the first fruits of the crops and the firstlings of the flock, the tithes of the cattle, and the first shearings of the sheep. ⁷I would give these to the priests, the sons of Aaron, at the altar; likewise the tenth of the grain, wine, olive oil, pomegranates, figs, and the rest of the fruits to the sons of Levi who ministered at Jerusalem. Also for six years I would save up a second tenth in money and go and distribute it in Jerusalem. ⁸A third tenth*ᵇ* I would give to the orphans and widows and to the converts who had attached themselves to Israel. I would bring it and give it to them in the third year, and we would eat it according to the ordinance decreed concerning it in the law of Moses and according to the instructions of Deborah, the mother of my father Tobiel,*ᶜ* for my father had died and left me an orphan. ⁹When I became a man I married a woman,*ᵈ* a member of our own family, and by her I became the father of a son whom I named Tobias.

10 After I was carried away captive to Assyria and came as a captive to Nineveh, everyone of my kindred and my people ate the food of the Gentiles, ¹¹but I kept myself from eating the food of the Gentiles. ¹²Because I was mindful of God with all my heart, ¹³the Most High gave me favor and good standing with Shalmaneser,*ᵉ* and I used to buy everything he needed. ¹⁴Until his death I used to go into Media, and buy for him there. While in the country of Media I left bags of silver worth ten talents in trust with Gabael, the brother of Gabri. ¹⁵But when Shalmaneser*ᵉ* died, and his son Sennacherib reigned in his place, the highways into Media became unsafe and I could no longer go there.

1.3–15: Tobit is deported to Assyria and rises in the court of Shalmaneser. Beginning at 1.3 the text is narrated in the first person, but at 3.7 it shifts to the third person without explanation. **6–15:** Even after deportation, Tobit makes the required offerings in Jerusalem and keeps kosher* (that is, observes the traditional Jewish food laws). God rewards him by causing him to rise in the court of Shalmaneser. **9:** Tobit marries his kinswoman, according to the preferred practice of endogamy, or marrying within the extended family (4.12–13). **14:** *Ten talents* of silver, about 750 pounds, or a huge sum of money. **15:** Here and elsewhere, the account of the Assyrian kings contains some inaccuracies; Shalmaneser had died earlier, succeeded by Sargon and Sennacherib.

~~~

16 In the days of Shalmaneser*ᵉ* I performed many acts of charity to my kindred, those of my tribe. ¹⁷I would give my food to the hungry and my clothing to the naked; and if I saw the dead body of any of my people thrown out behind the wall of Nineveh, I would bury it. ¹⁸I also buried any whom King Sennacherib put to death when he came fleeing from Judea in those days of judgment that the king of heaven executed upon him because of his blasphemies. For in his anger he put to death many Israelites; but I would secretly remove the bodies and bury them. So when Sennacherib looked for them he could not find them. ¹⁹Then one of the Ninevites went and informed the king about me, that I was burying them; so I hid myself. But when I realized that the king knew about me and that I was being searched for to be put to death, I was afraid and ran away. ²⁰Then all my property was confiscated; nothing was left to me that was not taken into the royal treasury except my wife Anna and my son Tobias.

---

a Other ancient authorities read *heifer*   *b* *A third tenth* added from other ancient authorities   *c* Lat: Gk *Hananiel*   *d* Other ancient authorities add *Anna*   *e* Gk *Enemessaros*

21 But not forty[a] days passed before two of Sennacherib's[b] sons killed him, and they fled to the mountains of Ararat, and his son Esar-haddon[c] reigned after him. He appointed Ahikar, the son of my brother Hanael[d] over all the accounts of his kingdom, and he had authority over the entire administration. 22Ahikar interceded for me, and I returned to Nineveh. Now Ahikar was chief cupbearer, keeper of the signet, and in charge of administration of the accounts under King Sennacherib of Assyria; so Esar-haddon[c] reappointed him. He was my nephew and so a close relative.

1.16–22: Tobit's charitable acts land him in trouble.
The Jewish practice of burying the dead was different from many other ancient near eastern cultures, but this prohibition by Sennacherib is meant to dishonor the bodies of enemies. **19–22:** The character of *Ahikar*★ is borrowed from the popular ancient "Story of Ahikar." In this story Ahikar, prime minister to the king of Assyria, adopts his orphaned nephew, Nadab, as his own son in order to instruct him. Betrayed by his ungrateful nephew, Ahikar is condemned to death. The nephew, however, is found out and punished, and Ahikar is returned to his former position. The motifs★ of Tobit's disgrace, fall, and vindication at court are mirrored in this ancient near eastern tale, and also in Gen 37–50, Esther, Dan 3 and 6, and Bel and the Dragon. **20:** *Anna* in Hebrew means "grace."

2 Then during the reign of Esar-haddon[c] I returned home, and my wife Anna and my son Tobias were restored to me. At our festival of Pentecost, which is the sacred festival of weeks, a good dinner was prepared for me and I reclined to eat. 2When the table was set for me and an abundance of food placed before me, I said to my son Tobias, "Go, my child, and bring whatever poor person you may find of our people among the exiles in Nineveh, who is wholeheartedly mindful of God,[e] and he shall eat together with me. I will wait for you, until you come back." 3So Tobias went to look for some poor person of our people. When he had returned he said, "Father!" And I replied, "Here I am, my child." Then he went on to say, "Look, father, one of our own people has been murdered and thrown into the market place, and

now he lies there strangled." 4Then I sprang up, left the dinner before even tasting it, and removed the body[f] from the square[g] and laid it[f] in one of the rooms until sunset when I might bury it.[f] 5When I returned, I washed myself and ate my food in sorrow. 6Then I remembered the prophecy of Amos, how he said against Bethel,[h]

"Your festivals shall be turned into
    mourning,
    and all your songs into lamentation."
And I wept.

7 When the sun had set, I went and dug a grave and buried him. 8And my neighbors laughed and said, "Is he still not afraid? He has already been hunted down to be put to death for doing this, and he ran away; yet here he is again burying the dead!" 9That same night I washed myself and went into my courtyard and slept by the wall of the courtyard; and my face was uncovered because of the heat. 10I did not know that there were sparrows on the wall; their fresh droppings fell into my eyes and produced white films. I went to physicians to be healed, but the more they treated me with ointments the more my vision was obscured by the white films, until I became completely blind. For four years I remained unable to see. All my kindred were sorry for me, and Ahikar took care of me for two years before he went to Elymais.

2.1–10: Tobit is restored but becomes blind. Tobit's righteousness and charity are constant and may even seem excessive. **1:** *Pentecost*★ is Shavuot or Festival of Weeks (Lev 23.15–21; Acts 2.1). **4:** Tobit cannot bury the corpse on a religious holiday and also cannot sleep in the house (v. 9) because contact with a corpse would render him ritually unclean. **6:** Amos 8.10. **7:** Burial, like charity, kinfolk, and blessing, is a recurring motif★ in this work. The constant repetition, even overuse, of some of these terms is probably intended to create a lighthearted tone. **9–10:** It is not clear whether Tobit's blindness is caused by the supposedly

a Other ancient authorities read either *forty-five* or *fifty*
b Gk *his*　*c* Gk *Sacherdonos*　*d* Other authorities read *Hananael*　*e* Lat: Gk *wholeheartedly mindful*
f Gk *him*　*g* Other ancient authorities lack *from the square*　*h* Other ancient authorities read *against Bethlehem*

Chart **The parallel problems of Tobit and Sarah**

Tobit's piety (2.1–7)	Sarah's innocence (3.14)
Tobit's problem: blindness (2.9–10) →	Sarah's problem: demon (3.8a)
Tobit reproached (2.14b) ←	Sarah reproached (3.7, 8b–9)
Tobit's prayer (3.1–6)	Sarah's prayer (3.10–15)

natural effects of the bird droppings, by the demon Asmodeus (3.8), or by God to put a divine plan into motion.

11 At that time, also, my wife Anna earned money at women's work. 12 She used to send what she made to the owners and they would pay wages to her. One day, the seventh of Dystrus, when she cut off a piece she had woven and sent it to the owners, they paid her full wages and also gave her a young goat for a meal. 13 When she returned to me, the goat began to bleat. So I called her and said, "Where did you get this goat? It is surely not stolen, is it? Return it to the owners; for we have no right to eat anything stolen." 14 But she said to me, "It was given to me as a gift in addition to my wages." But I did not believe her, and told her to return it to the owners. I became flushed with anger against her over this. Then she replied to me, "Where are your acts of charity? Where are your righteous deeds? These things are known about you!"[a]

2.11–14: Tobit reproves Anna and is reproved by her. A seemingly unrelated plot development actually serves to demonstrate the limits of Tobit's charity and also to dramatize his personal suffering (see chart).

3 Then with much grief and anguish of heart I wept, and with groaning began to pray:
2 "You are righteous, O Lord,
  and all your deeds are just;
all your ways are mercy and truth;
  you judge the world.[b]
3 And now, O Lord, remember me
  and look favorably upon me.

Do not punish me for my sins
  and for my unwitting offenses
  and those that my ancestors
    committed before you.
They sinned against you,
4   and disobeyed your commandments.
So you gave us over to plunder, exile,
    and death,
  to become the talk, the byword, and
    an object of reproach
  among all the nations among whom
    you have dispersed us.
5 And now your many judgments are true
  in exacting penalty from me for my
    sins.
For we have not kept your
    commandments
  and have not walked in accordance
    with truth before you.
6 So now deal with me as you will;
  command my spirit to be taken from
    me,
  so that I may be released from the
    face of the earth and become
    dust.
For it is better for me to die than to
    live,
  because I have had to listen to
    undeserved insults,
  and great is the sorrow within me.
Command, O Lord, that I be released
    from this distress;
  release me to go to the eternal home,
  and do not, O Lord, turn your face
    away from me.

a Or to you; Gk with you   b Other ancient authorities read you render true and righteous judgment forever

For it is better for me to die
　　than to see so much distress in my
　　　life
　　and to listen to insults."

3.1–6: Tobit prays for death. Tobit's prayer is typical of the penitential prayers of late biblical texts (Neh 9; Dan 9.4–19; Bar 1.15–3.8), even where there is no apparent sin (Prayer of Azariah). Tobit concludes it, however, by asking for death. Is he overreacting to his affliction (as 5.10 implies), or is he broken in spirit because he feels God has forsaken him?

7 On the same day, at Ecbatana in Media, it also happened that Sarah, the daughter of Raguel, was reproached by one of her father's maids. ⁸For she had been married to seven husbands, and the wicked demon Asmodeus had killed each of them before they had been with her as is customary for wives. So the maid said to her, "You are the one who kills*ᵃ* your husbands! See, you have already been married to seven husbands and have not borne the name of*ᵇ* a single one of them. ⁹Why do you beat us? Because your husbands are dead? Go with them! May we never see a son or daughter of yours!"

10 On that day she was grieved in spirit and wept. When she had gone up to her father's upper room, she intended to hang herself. But she thought it over and said, "Never shall they reproach my father, saying to him, 'You had only one beloved daughter but she hanged herself because of her distress.' And I shall bring my father in his old age down in sorrow to Hades. It is better for me not to hang myself, but to pray the Lord that I may die and not listen to these reproaches anymore." ¹¹At that same time, with hands outstretched toward the window, she prayed and said,

"Blessed are you, merciful God!
　　Blessed is your name forever;
　　let all your works praise you forever.
12 And now, Lord,*ᶜ* I turn my face to
　　　you,
　　and raise my eyes toward you.
13 Command that I be released from the
　　　earth
　　and not listen to such reproaches any
　　　more.

14 You know, O Master, that I am
　　innocent
　　of any defilement with a man,
15 and that I have not disgraced my name
　　or the name of my father in the land
　　　of my exile.
I am my father's only child;
　　he has no other child to be his heir;
　　and he has no close relative or other
　　　kindred
　　for whom I should keep myself as
　　　wife.
Already seven husbands of mine have
　　died.
Why should I still live?
But if it is not pleasing to you, O Lord,
　　to take my life,
　　hear me in my disgrace."

3.7–15: Far away, Sarah suffers a similar fate. Sarah's suffering has been at the hands of the *demon Asmodeus,* but like Tobit, she is also reproved by a member of her household. While protesting her innocence, she also prays for death. **8:** *Asmodeus,* probably to be identified with "Aeshma Daeva," an archdemon in Persian lore.

16 At that very moment, the prayers of both of them were heard in the glorious presence of God. ¹⁷So Raphael was sent to heal both of them: Tobit, by removing the white films from his eyes, so that he might see God's light with his eyes; and Sarah, daughter of Raguel, by giving her in marriage to Tobias son of Tobit, and by setting her free from the wicked demon Asmodeus. For Tobias was entitled to have her before all others who had desired to marry her. At the same time that Tobit returned from the courtyard into his house, Sarah daughter of Raguel came down from her upper room.

3.16–17: Tobit's and Sarah's prayers are heard in heaven. The solutions to both their problems are announced, seemingly undercutting any suspense in the story. However, the interest now revolves around how the angel *Raphael* ("God has healed") will resolve the

---

a Other ancient authorities read *strangles*　*b* Other ancient authorities read *have had no benefit from*
c Other ancient authorities lack *Lord*

problems, and how the two unrelated plotlines will become intertwined. In addition, here and elsewhere the author creates irony* by providing the reader important information about the incidents of the story that the protagonists do not have; the reader in effect has an omniscient perspective.

4 That same day Tobit remembered the money that he had left in trust with Gabael at Rages in Media, 2and he said to himself, "Now I have asked for death. Why do I not call my son Tobias and explain to him about the money before I die?" 3Then he called his son Tobias, and when he came to him he said, "My son, when I die,*a* give me a proper burial. Honor your mother and do not abandon her all the days of her life. Do whatever pleases her, and do not grieve her in anything. 4Remember her, my son, because she faced many dangers for you while you were in her womb. And when she dies, bury her beside me in the same grave.

5 "Revere the Lord all your days, my son, and refuse to sin or to transgress his commandments. Live uprightly all the days of your life, and do not walk in the ways of wrongdoing; 6for those who act in accordance with truth will prosper in all their activities. To all those who practice righteousness*b* 7give alms from your possessions, and do not let your eye begrudge the gift when you make it. Do not turn your face away from anyone who is poor, and the face of God will not be turned away from you. 8If you have many possessions, make your gift from them in proportion; if few, do not be afraid to give according to the little you have. 9So you will be laying up a good treasure for yourself against the day of necessity. 10For almsgiving delivers from death and keeps you from going into the Darkness. 11Indeed, almsgiving, for all who practice it, is an excellent offering in the presence of the Most High.

12 "Beware, my son, of every kind of fornication. First of all, marry a woman from among the descendants of your ancestors; do not marry a foreign woman, who is not of your father's tribe; for we are the descendants of the prophets. Remember, my son, that Noah, Abraham, Isaac, and Jacob, our ancestors of old, all took wives from among their kindred. They were blessed in their children, and their posterity will inherit the land. 13So now, my son, love your kindred, and in your heart do not disdain your kindred, the sons and daughters of your people, by refusing to take a wife for yourself from among them. For in pride there is ruin and great confusion. And in idleness there is loss and dire poverty, because idleness is the mother of famine.

14 "Do not keep over until the next day the wages of those who work for you, but pay them at once. If you serve God you will receive payment. Watch yourself, my son, in everything you do, and discipline yourself in all your conduct. 15And what you hate, do not do to anyone. Do not drink wine to excess or let drunkenness go with you on your way. 16Give some of your food to the hungry, and some of your clothing to the naked. Give all your surplus as alms, and do not let your eye begrudge your giving of alms. 17Place your bread on the grave of the righteous, but give none to sinners. 18Seek advice from every wise person and do not despise any useful counsel. 19At all times bless the Lord God, and ask him that your ways may be made straight and that all your paths and plans may prosper. For none of the nations has understanding, but the Lord himself will give them good counsel; but if he chooses otherwise, he casts down to deepest Hades. So now, my child, remember these commandments, and do not let them be erased from your heart.

4.1–19: Tobit, thinking he is about to die, delivers his testament to his son. **1:** *Money* deposited earlier (1.14) must be recovered so that Tobit can face death. *Gabael* means "God is exalted." **3–19:** Tobit's testament is a combination of general wisdom precepts (e.g., v. 5) and motifs* specific to the story: burial, marriage to a kinswoman, and charity. Interestingly, Tobit's situation appears to contradict his own advice

a Lat   *b* The text of codex Sinaiticus goes directly from verse 6 to verse 19, reading *To those who practice righteousness* 19*the Lord will give good counsel.* In order to fill the lacuna verses 7 to 18 are derived from other ancient authorities

(vv. 6–7). **15**: The Golden Rule is found in many cultures in this negative form, but the positive form (Mt 7.12; Lk 6.31) is rarer.

~~~~~~

20 "And now, my son, let me explain to you that I left ten talents of silver in trust with Gabael son of Gabrias, at Rages in Media. 21 Do not be afraid, my son, because we have become poor. You have great wealth if you fear God and flee from every sin and do what is good in the sight of the Lord your God."

5 Then Tobias answered his father Tobit, "I will do everything that you have commanded me, father; 2 but how can I obtain the money*a* from him, since he does not know me and I do not know him? What evidence*b* am I to give him so that he will recognize and trust me, and give me the money? Also, I do not know the roads to Media, or how to get there." 3 Then Tobit answered his son Tobias, "He gave me his bond and I gave him my bond. I*c* divided his in two; we each took one part, and I put one with the money. And now twenty years have passed since I left this money in trust. So now, my son, find yourself a trustworthy man to go with you, and we will pay him wages until you return. But get back the money from Gabael."*d*

4.20–5.3: Tobit tells Tobias how to recover the money. The trip to retrieve the silver will set in motion the main events of the story. The next few chapters will include travel, adventure, demons, angels, magic, and love, the staples of exciting storytelling.

~~~~~~

4 So Tobias went out to look for a man to go with him to Media, someone who was acquainted with the way. He went out and found the angel Raphael standing in front of him; but he did not perceive that he was an angel of God. 5 Tobias*e* said to him, "Where do you come from, young man?" "From your kindred, the Israelites," he replied, "and I have come here to work." Then Tobias*f* said to him, "Do you know the way to go to Media?" 6 "Yes," he replied, "I have been there many times; I am acquainted with it and know all the roads. I have often traveled to Media, and would stay with our kinsman Gabael who lives in Rages of Media. It is a

journey of two days from Ecbatana to Rages; for it lies in a mountainous area, while Ecbatana is in the middle of the plain." 7 Then Tobias said to him, "Wait for me, young man, until I go in and tell my father; for I do need you to travel with me, and I will pay you your wages." 8 He replied, "All right, I will wait; but do not take too long."

9 So Tobias*f* went in to tell his father Tobit and said to him, "I have just found a man who is one of our own Israelite kindred!" He replied, "Call the man in, my son, so that I may learn about his family and to what tribe he belongs, and whether he is trustworthy enough to go with you."

10 Then Tobias went out and called him, and said, "Young man, my father is calling for you." So he went in to him, and Tobit greeted him first. He replied, "Joyous greetings to you!" But Tobit retorted, "What joy is left for me any more? I am a man without eyesight; I cannot see the light of heaven, but I lie in darkness like the dead who no longer see the light. Although still alive, I am among the dead. I hear people but I cannot see them." But the young man*f* said, "Take courage; the time is near for God to heal you; take courage." Then Tobit said to him, "My son Tobias wishes to go to Media. Can you accompany him and guide him? I will pay your wages, brother." He answered, "I can go with him and I know all the roads, for I have often gone to Media and have crossed all its plains, and I am familiar with its mountains and all of its roads."

11 Then Tobit*f* said to him, "Brother, of what family are you and from what tribe? Tell me, brother." 12 He replied, "Why do you need to know my tribe?" But Tobit*f* said, "I want to be sure, brother, whose son you are and what your name is." 13 He replied, "I am Azariah, the son of the great Hananiah, one of your relatives." 14 Then Tobit said to him, "Welcome! God save you, brother. Do not feel bitter toward me, brother, because I wanted to be sure about your ancestry. It turns out that you are a kinsman, and

a Gk it   *b* Gk sign   *c* Other authorities read *He*
d Gk *from him*   *e* Gk *He*   *f* Gk *he*

Novel

The terms novel* and romance* are often used by scholars to describe the fanciful and entertaining prose narratives* from the ancient world. A novel is a fictional story in prose. The increase in education in the ancient world during the third and second centuries BCE (see Sirach 51.23–26) created a literate class, and novels arose in various cultures as a new form of diversion and entertainment. Ancient Greek novels, often called romances as well, feature stereotyped plots that involve the separation and reunion of lovers: A handsome hero and beautiful heroine, engaged or newly married, are separated and tested during a series of adventures, but remain faithful to each other and are eventually reunited to live happily ever after. The storylines are often complicated and involve various marvelous occurrences, including the intervention of gods and goddesses to protect the protagonists. Jewish novels generally portray extended families rather than the nuclear family of husband and wife, and in many cases (Judith, Esther, Susanna, *Joseph and Aseneth,** and to some extent, Tobit) the heroine is at the center of the action. Her challenge is not to be reunited with her husband but to overcome the obstacles to Jews or to her religious life.

of good and noble lineage. For I knew Hananiah and Nathan,[a] the two sons of Shemeliah,[b] and they used to go with me to Jerusalem and worshiped with me there, and were not led astray. Your kindred are good people; you come of good stock. Hearty welcome!"

15 Then he added, "I will pay you a drachma a day as wages, as well as expenses for yourself and my son. So go with my son, 16and[c] I will add something to your wages." Raphael[d] answered, "I will go with him; so do not fear. We shall leave in good health and return to you in good health, because the way is safe." 17So Tobit[e] said to him, "Blessings be upon you, brother."

Then he called his son and said to him, "Son, prepare supplies for the journey and set out with your brother. May God in heaven bring you safely there and return you in good health to me; and may his angel, my son, accompany you both for your safety."

Before he went out to start his journey, he kissed his father and mother. Tobit then said to him, "Have a safe journey."

18 But his mother[f] began to weep, and said to Tobit, "Why is it that you have sent my child away? Is he not the staff of our hand as he goes in and out before us? 19Do not

heap money upon money, but let it be a ransom for our child. 20For the life that is given to us by the Lord is enough for us." 21Tobit[d] said to her, "Do not worry; our child will leave in good health and return to us in good health. Your eyes will see him on the day when he returns to you in good health. Say no more! Do not fear for them, my sister. 22For a good angel will accompany him; his journey will be successful, and he will come back in good health." 1So she stopped weeping.

6

5.4–6.1a: **The angel Raphael is hired to guide Tobias.** There is irony* and humor in the interviews with Raphael. Tobit and Tobias are brusque with Raphael, pressing to learn his identity, while the audience knows he is an angel. It is also significant that, with the exception of the Assyrian kings, every character in the book is related to Tobit, even Raphael in his human guise. **17a:** The irony continues when Tobit prays for an angel to accompany them. **17b–21:** Although Anna wisely counsels caution, Tobit now expresses a more

a Other ancient authorities read *Jathan* or *Nathaniah*
b Other ancient authorities read *Shemaiah*
c Other ancient authorities add *when you return safely*
d Gk *He*   e Gk *he*   f Other ancient authorities add *Anna*

optimistic outlook. The section of the story set in Nineveh thus concludes on a reassuring, rather than suspenseful, note.

The young man went out and the angel went with him; 2and the dog came out with him and went along with them. So they both journeyed along, and when the first night overtook them they camped by the Tigris river. 3Then the young man went down to wash his feet in the Tigris river. Suddenly a large fish leaped up from the water and tried to swallow the young man's foot, and he cried out. 4But the angel said to the young man, "Catch hold of the fish and hang on to it!" So the young man grasped the fish and drew it up on the land. 5Then the angel said to him, "Cut open the fish and take out its gall, heart, and liver. Keep them with you, but throw away the intestines. For its gall, heart, and liver are useful as medicine." 6So after cutting open the fish the young man gathered together the gall, heart, and liver; then he roasted and ate some of the fish, and kept some to be salted.

The two continued on their way together until they were near Media.*a* 7Then the young man questioned the angel and said to him, "Brother Azariah, what medicinal value is there in the fish's heart and liver, and in the gall?" 8He replied, "As for the fish's heart and liver, you must burn them to make a smoke in the presence of a man or woman afflicted by a demon or evil spirit, and every affliction will flee away and never remain with that person any longer. 9And as for the gall, anoint a person's eyes where white films have appeared on them; blow upon them, upon the white films, and the eyes*b* will be healed."

6.1b–9: On their way Raphael instructs Tobias in the exorcising of demons. Tobias is very quickly plunged into the world of magic and danger, and in the process, the reader learns how the *fish* will provide the means to solve the protagonists' problems. The information given the reader once again removes some of the suspense as to the role of the fish organs, yet at the same time, it gives the reader insights into how the lives of Tobit and Sarah will become intertwined. **2:** The *dog* that accompanies them, although serving little narrative purpose, is a common folktale motif* and may suggest a faithful traveling companion for an important quest.

---

10 When he entered Media and already was approaching Ecbatana,*c* 11Raphael said to the young man, "Brother Tobias." "Here I am," he answered. Then Raphael*d* said to him, "We must stay this night in the home of Raguel. He is your relative, and he has a daughter named Sarah. 12He has no male heir and no daughter except Sarah only, and you, as next of kin to her, have before all other men a hereditary claim on her. Also it is right for you to inherit her father's possessions. Moreover, the girl is sensible, brave, and very beautiful, and her father is a good man." 13He continued, "You have every right to take her in marriage. So listen to me, brother; tonight I will speak to her father about the girl, so that we may take her to be your bride. When we return from Rages we will celebrate her marriage. For I know that Raguel can by no means keep her from you or promise her to another man without incurring the penalty of death according to the decree of the book of Moses. Indeed he knows that you, rather than any other man, are entitled to marry his daughter. So now listen to me, brother, and tonight we shall speak concerning the girl and arrange her engagement to you. And when we return from Rages we will take her and bring her back with us to your house."

14 Then Tobias said in answer to Raphael, "Brother Azariah, I have heard that she already has been married to seven husbands and that they died in the bridal chamber. On the night when they went in to her, they would die. I have heard people saying that it was a demon that killed them. 15It does not harm her, but it kills anyone who desires to approach her. So now, since I am the only son my father has, I am afraid that I may die and bring my father's and mother's life down to their grave, grieving for me—and they have no other son to bury them."

---

a Other ancient authorities read *Ecbatana*   *b* Gk *they*
c Other ancient authorities read *Rages*   *d* Gk *he*

16 But Raphael[a] said to him, "Do you not remember your father's orders when he commanded you to take a wife from your father's house? Now listen to me, brother, and say no more about this demon. Take her. I know that this very night she will be given to you in marriage. 17When you enter the bridal chamber, take some of the fish's liver and heart, and put them on the embers of the incense. An odor will be given off; 18the demon will smell it and flee, and will never be seen near her any more. Now when you are about to go to bed with her, both of you must first stand up and pray, imploring the Lord of heaven that mercy and safety may be granted to you. Do not be afraid, for she was set apart for you before the world was made. You will save her, and she will go with you. I presume that you will have children by her, and they will be as brothers to you. Now say no more!" When Tobias heard the words of Raphael and learned that she was his kinswoman,[b] related through his father's lineage, he loved her very much, and his heart was drawn to her.

6.10–18: Raphael plays matchmaker for Tobias and Sarah. 12: Under the Jewish law of levirate marriage* (Deut 25.5–10; compare Gen 38), if a husband died and left no heirs, the nearest male relative was to marry the widow in order to produce heirs for the deceased. More distant relatives could marry the widow if there were no closer relatives, or if the closer relatives waived their right to marry her (compare Ruth 3–4). **13–15:** Tobias has heard of the demon who kills Sarah's husbands, but he points out the need to bury his parents as an overriding concern. The constant references to death and burial are probably intended as comic exaggeration; they begin in ch. 1 and reach a climax* in 8.9b–21. **16–18:** Raphael assures Tobias that choosing a kinswoman is also his father's wish, and that it will result in a happy marriage.

7 Now when they[c] entered Ecbatana, Tobias[a] said to him, "Brother Azariah, take me straight to our brother Raguel." So he took him to Raguel's house, where they found him sitting beside the courtyard door. They greeted him first, and he replied, "Joyous greetings, brothers; welcome and good health!" Then he brought them into his house. 2He said to his wife Edna, "How much the young man resembles my kinsman Tobit!" 3Then Edna questioned them, saying, "Where are you from, brothers?" They answered, "We belong to the descendants of Naphtali who are exiles in Nineveh." 4She said to them, "Do you know our kinsman Tobit?" And they replied, "Yes, we know him." Then she asked them, "Is he[d] in good health?" 5They replied, "He is alive and in good health." And Tobias added, "He is my father!" 6At that Raguel jumped up and kissed him and wept. 7He also spoke to him as follows, "Blessings on you, my child, son of a good and noble father![e] O most miserable of calamities that such an upright and beneficent man has become blind!" He then embraced his kinsman Tobias and wept. 8His wife Edna also wept for him, and their daughter Sarah likewise wept. 9Then Raguel[a] slaughtered a ram from the flock and received them very warmly.

7.1–9a: Tobias and Raphael proceed to the home of Raguel, Edna, and Sarah. 1: *Brothers*, in both Aramaic and Greek, can mean kinsmen. It is often used in Tobit, as family relations are emphasized. Note also *sister* for wife at vv. 11, 15, and 8.4.

When they had bathed and washed themselves and had reclined to dine, Tobias said to Raphael, "Brother Azariah, ask Raguel to give me my kinswoman[b] Sarah." 10But Raguel overheard it and said to the lad, "Eat and drink, and be merry tonight. For no one except you, brother, has the right to marry my daughter Sarah. Likewise I am not at liberty to give her to any other man than yourself, because you are my nearest relative. But let me explain to you the true situation more fully, my child. 11I have given her to seven men of our kinsmen, and all died on the night when they went in to her. But now, my child, eat and drink, and the Lord will act on behalf of you both." But Tobias said, "I will neither eat nor drink anything until you set-

a Gk *he* b Gk *sister* c Other ancient authorities read *he* d Other ancient authorities add *alive and* e Other ancient authorities add *When he heard that Tobit had lost his sight, he was stricken with grief and wept. Then he said,*

[1318] APOCRYPHA

tle the things that pertain to me." So Raguel said, "I will do so. She is given to you in accordance with the decree in the book of Moses, and it has been decreed from heaven that she be given to you. Take your kinswoman;[a] from now on you are her brother and she is your sister. She is given to you from today and forever. May the Lord of heaven, my child, guide and prosper you both this night and grant you mercy and peace." [12]Then Raguel summoned his daughter Sarah. When she came to him he took her by the hand and gave her to Tobias,[b] saying, "Take her to be your wife in accordance with the law and decree written in the book of Moses. Take her and bring her safely to your father. And may the God of heaven prosper your journey with his peace." [13]Then he called her mother and told her to bring writing material; and he wrote out a copy of a marriage contract, to the effect that he gave her to him as wife according to the decree of the law of Moses. [14]Then they began to eat and drink.

[15] Raguel called his wife Edna and said to her, "Sister, get the other room ready, and take her there." [16]So she went and made the bed in the room as he had told her, and brought Sarah[c] there. She wept for her daughter.[c] Then, wiping away the tears,[d] she said to her, "Take courage, my daughter; the Lord of heaven grant you joy[e] in place of your sorrow. Take courage, my daughter." Then she went out.

7.9b–16: A marriage is arranged between Tobias and Sarah. 10: Raguel is bound by the levirate* law to have his daughter marry Tobias (see comment on 6.12). 11: The marriage of Tobias and Sarah is arranged contractually between Tobias and Raguel according to Jewish law, but Raguel also warns Tobias that his predecessors have died.

〰〰〰〰〰〰〰〰〰〰〰〰〰〰

8 When they had finished eating and drinking they wanted to retire; so they took the young man and brought him into the bedroom. [2]Then Tobias remembered the words of Raphael, and he took the fish's liver and heart out of the bag where he had them and put them on the embers of the incense. [3]The odor of the fish so repelled the demon

that he fled to the remotest parts[f] of Egypt. But Raphael followed him, and at once bound him there hand and foot.

4 When the parents[g] had gone out and shut the door of the room, Tobias got out of bed and said to Sarah,[c] "Sister, get up, and let us pray and implore our Lord that he grant us mercy and safety." [5]So she got up, and they began to pray and implore that they might be kept safe. Tobias[h] began by saying,

"Blessed are you, O God of our
        ancestors,
    and blessed is your name in all
        generations forever.
Let the heavens and the whole creation
    bless you forever.
[6] You made Adam, and for him you made
        his wife Eve
    as a helper and support.
    From the two of them the human
        race has sprung.
You said, 'It is not good that the man
        should be alone;
    let us make a helper for him like
        himself.'
[7] I now am taking this kinswoman of
        mine,
    not because of lust,
    but with sincerity.
Grant that she and I may find mercy
    and that we may grow old
        together."

[8]And they both said, "Amen, Amen." [9]Then they went to sleep for the night.

8.1–9a: Tobias and Sarah consummate their marriage. 1–3: Because Tobias is appropriately prepared, the *demon* is easily exorcised. The struggle between Raphael and the demon, and the subsequent binding, are typical ways of describing the conflict of supernatural figures, but the description of the procedure is also humorous here. 5–7: Tobias and Sarah sanctify their marriage with a blessing that recalls the first marriage, that of Adam and Eve. In this scene, the dramatic center of the story, the importance of marriage and the

a Gk *sister*   b Gk *him*   c Gk *her*   d Other ancient authorities read *the tears of her daughter*   e Other ancient authorities read *favor*   f Or *fled through the air to the parts*   g Gk *they*   h Gk *He* solidifying of the extended family is affirmed. From this point on, the problems of the story begin to be resolved.

~~~~~~~

But Raguel arose and called his servants to him, and they went and dug a grave, ¹⁰for he said, "It is possible that he will die and we will become an object of ridicule and derision." ¹¹When they had finished digging the grave, Raguel went into his house and called his wife, ¹²saying, "Send one of the maids and have her go in to see if he is alive. But if he is dead, let us bury him without anyone knowing it." ¹³So they sent the maid, lit a lamp, and opened the door; and she went in and found them sound asleep together. ¹⁴Then the maid came out and informed them that he was alive and that nothing was wrong. ¹⁵So they blessed the God of heaven, and Raguel^a said,

"Blessed are you, O God, with every
    pure blessing;
let all your chosen ones bless you.^b
Let them bless you forever.
¹⁶ Blessed are you because you have made
    me glad.
It has not turned out as I expected,
but you have dealt with us according
    to your great mercy.
¹⁷ Blessed are you because you had
    compassion
on two only children.
Be merciful to them, O Master, and
    keep them safe;
bring their lives to fulfillment
in happiness and mercy."

¹⁸Then he ordered his servants to fill in the grave before daybreak.

19 After this he asked his wife to bake many loaves of bread; and he went out to the herd and brought two steers and four rams and ordered them to be slaughtered. So they began to make preparations. ²⁰Then he called for Tobias and swore on oath to him in these words:^c "You shall not leave here for fourteen days, but shall stay here eating and drinking with me; and you shall cheer up my daughter, who has been depressed. ²¹Take at once half of what I own and return in safety to your father; the other half will be yours when my wife and I die. Take courage, my child. I am your father and Edna is your mother, and we belong to you as well as to your wife^d now and forever. Take courage, my child."

8.9b–21: Raguel and Edna expect to bury another son-in-law but are surprised. In this humorous scene, Raguel wants Tobias buried quickly before anyone finds out that he has died. **15–17:** Raguel greets the good news with a heartfelt *blessing*. **18–21:** The filling in of the grave represents the end of the ordeal for Sarah's family, and Raguel can now celebrate a truly joyful wedding feast. His benevolence is indicated by his generous overtures to Tobias.

~~~~~~~

9 Then Tobias called Raphael and said to him, ²"Brother Azariah, take four servants and two camels with you and travel to Rages. Go to the home of Gabael, give him the bond, get the money, and then bring him with you to the wedding celebration. ⁴For you know that my father must be counting the days, and if I delay even one day I will upset him very much. ³You are witness to the oath Raguel has sworn, and I cannot violate his oath."^e ⁵So Raphael with the four servants and two camels went to Rages in Media and stayed with Gabael. Raphael^f gave him the bond and informed him that Tobit's son Tobias had married and was inviting him to the wedding celebration. So Gabael^g got up and counted out to him the money bags, with their seals intact; then they loaded them on the camels.^h ⁶In the morning they both got up early and went to the wedding celebration. When they came into Raguel's house they found Tobias reclining at table. He sprang up and greeted Gabael,ⁱ who wept and blessed him with the words, "Good and noble son of a father good and noble, upright and generous! May the Lord grant the blessing of heaven to you and your wife, and to your wife's father and mother. Blessed be God, for I see in Tobias the very image of my cousin Tobit."

^a Gk *they*   ^b Other ancient authorities lack this line   ^c Other ancient authorities read *Tobias and said to him*   ^d Gk *sister*   ^e In other ancient authorities verse 3 precedes verse 4   ^f Gk *He*   ^g Gk *he*   ^h Other ancient authorities lack *on the camels*   ⁱ Gk *him*

9.1–6: Tobias sends Raphael on ahead to retrieve the deposited money. 2: It is part of the fairytale-like tone of the text that Tobias trusts Raphael to retrieve the fortune on deposit with Gabael. **6:** Gabael greets Tobias enthusiastically. All of the characters are part of one extended family and they act accordingly.

10 Now, day by day, Tobit kept counting how many days Tobias[a] would need for going and for returning. And when the days had passed and his son did not appear, 2he said, "Is it possible that he has been detained? Or that Gabael has died, and there is no one to give him the money?" 3And he began to worry. 4His wife Anna said, "My child has perished and is no longer among the living." And she began to weep and mourn for her son, saying, 5"Woe to me, my child, the light of my eyes, that I let you make the journey." 6But Tobit kept saying to her, "Be quiet and stop worrying, my dear;[b] he is all right. Probably something unexpected has happened there. The man who went with him is trustworthy and is one of our own kin. Do not grieve for him, my dear;[b] he will soon be here." 7She answered him, "Be quiet yourself! Stop trying to deceive me! My child has perished." She would rush out every day and watch the road her son had taken, and would heed no one.[c] When the sun had set she would go in and mourn and weep all night long, getting no sleep at all.

10.1–7a: Tobit and Anna wait anxiously for Tobias and Raphael to return. Because the reader knows that Tobias is happily married, the suffering of Tobit and Anna has an ironic poignance. The opposite situation occurs in Judg 5.28–30, where a mother celebrates her son's victories, unaware that he has been killed. The disagreement here between Tobit and Anna mirrors the disagreement in ch. 2, although in this case the reader knows that they are about to be made exceedingly happy.

Now when the fourteen days of the wedding celebration had ended that Raguel had sworn to observe for his daughter, Tobias came to him and said, "Send me back, for I know that my father and mother do not believe that they will see me again. So I beg of you, father, to let me go so that I may return to my own father. I have already explained to you how I left him." 8But Raguel said to Tobias, "Stay, my child, stay with me; I will send messengers to your father Tobit and they will inform him about you." 9But he said, "No! I beg you to send me back to my father." 10So Raguel promptly gave Tobias his wife Sarah, as well as half of all his property: male and female slaves, oxen and sheep, donkeys and camels, clothing, money, and household goods. 11Then he saw them safely off; he embraced Tobias[d] and said, "Farewell, my child; have a safe journey. The Lord of heaven prosper you and your wife Sarah, and may I see children of yours before I die." 12Then he kissed his daughter Sarah and said to her, "My daughter, honor your father-in-law and your mother-in-law,[e] since from now on they are as much your parents as those who gave you birth. Go in peace, daughter, and may I hear a good report about you as long as I live." Then he bade them farewell and let them go. Then Edna said to Tobias, "My child and dear brother, the Lord of heaven bring you back safely, and may I live long enough to see children of you and of my daughter Sarah before I die. In the sight of the Lord I entrust my daughter to you; do nothing to grieve her all the days of your life. Go in peace, my child. From now on I am your mother and Sarah is your beloved wife.[b] May we all prosper together all the days of our lives." Then she kissed them both and saw them safely off. 13Tobias parted from Raguel with happiness and joy, praising the Lord of heaven and earth, King over all, because he had made his journey a success. Finally, he blessed Raguel and his wife Edna, and said, "I have been commanded by the Lord to honor you all the days of my life."[f]

10.7b–13: Tobias asks leave to return home. Raguel generously provides the dowry for his daughter and

a Gk *he*   b Gk *sister*   c Other ancient authorities read *and she would eat nothing*   d Gk *him*   e Other ancient authorities lack parts of *Then . . . mother-in-law*   f Lat: Meaning of Gk uncertain

Joseph and Aseneth

*Joseph and Aseneth,** a story about Joseph in Egypt, takes as its point of departure the account of Joseph and his brothers in Egypt in Gen 37–50. Aseneth, the beautiful but haughty daughter of an Egyptian priest, falls in love with Joseph, is converted by a heavenly messenger to belief in Joseph's God, and is married to him. As in the Greek romances, the protagonists here are both extravagantly beautiful, pious, and modest. Aseneth's conversion is accompanied by a meal consisting of the honey of heaven, which gives her eternal life. Despite an evil plot between Pharaoh's jealous son and two of Joseph's brothers, Joseph and Aseneth overcome all obstacles and Joseph, with Aseneth as his wife, becomes the ruler of Egypt when Pharaoh dies.

cements the bonds between the two branches of the extended family.

11 When they came near to Kaserin, which is opposite Nineveh, Raphael said, 2"You are aware of how we left your father. 3Let us run ahead of your wife and prepare the house while they are still on the way." 4As they went on together Raphael*a* said to him, "Have the gall ready." And the dog*b* went along behind them.

5 Meanwhile Anna sat looking intently down the road by which her son would come. 6When she caught sight of him coming, she said to his father, "Look, your son is coming, and the man who went with him!"

7 Raphael said to Tobias, before he had approached his father, "I know that his eyes will be opened. 8Smear the gall of the fish on his eyes; the medicine will make the white films shrink and peel off from his eyes, and your father will regain his sight and see the light."

9 Then Anna ran up to her son and threw her arms around him, saying, "Now that I have seen you, my child, I am ready to die." And she wept. 10Then Tobit got up and came stumbling out through the courtyard door. Tobias went up to him, 11with the gall of the fish in his hand, and holding him firmly, he blew into his eyes, saying, "Take courage, father." With this he applied the medicine on his eyes, 12and it made them smart.*c* 13Next, with both his hands he peeled off the white films from the corners of his eyes. Then To-

bit*a* saw his son and*d* threw his arms around him, 14and he wept and said to him, "I see you, my son, the light of my eyes!" Then he said,

"Blessed be God,
    and blessed be his great name,
    and blessed be all his holy angels.
May his holy name be blessed*e*
    throughout all the ages.
15 Though he afflicted me,
    he has had mercy upon me.*f*
    Now I see my son Tobias!"

So Tobit went in rejoicing and praising God at the top of his voice. Tobias reported to his father that his journey had been successful, that he had brought the money, that he had married Raguel's daughter Sarah, and that she was, indeed, on her way there, very near to the gate of Nineveh.

11.1–15: Tobias and Raphael return and cure Tobit's blindness. In a romance* such as this, the distinction between magic and religion becomes less relevant. It was God who made the fish available in 6.1b–9, and Raphael who explained its usefulness to Tobias (8.1–9a). Working in tandem, God and Raphael have manipulated events toward a happy ending. **14–15:** Tobit begins a series of blessings, which becomes a common motif* at this point in the narrative.

---

a Gk *he*   *b* Codex Sinaiticus reads *And the Lord*
c Lat: Meaning of Gk uncertain   *d* Other ancient authorities lack *saw his son and*   *e* Codex Sinaiticus reads *May his great name be upon us and blessed be all the angels*   *f* Lat: Gk lacks this line

16 Then Tobit, rejoicing and praising God, went out to meet his daughter-in-law at the gate of Nineveh. When the people of Nineveh saw him coming, walking along in full vigor and with no one leading him, they were amazed. 17Before them all, Tobit acknowledged that God had been merciful to him and had restored his sight. When Tobit met Sarah the wife of his son Tobias, he blessed her saying, "Come in, my daughter, and welcome. Blessed be your God who has brought you to us, my daughter. Blessed be your father and your mother, blessed be my son Tobias, and blessed be you, my daughter. Come in now to your home, and welcome, with blessing and joy. Come in, my daughter." So on that day there was rejoicing among all the Jews who were in Nineveh. 18Ahikar and his nephew Nadab were also present to share Tobit's joy. With merriment they celebrated Tobias's wedding feast for seven days, and many gifts were given to him.*a*

11.16–18: Tobit meets his daughter-in-law, Sarah. The general celebration is extended further, encompassing the *Jews* who reside in *Nineveh*. The term "Jews" is normally applied to the residents of Judah from the time of the exile on, but here this term is inappropriately used of an earlier period.

12 When the wedding celebration was ended, Tobit called his son Tobias and said to him, "My child, see to paying the wages of the man who went with you, and give him a bonus as well." 2He replied, "Father, how much shall I pay him? It would do no harm to give him half of the possessions brought back with me. 3For he has led me back to you safely, he cured my wife, he brought the money back with me, and he healed you. How much extra shall I give him as a bonus?" 4Tobit said, "He deserves, my child, to receive half of all that he brought back." 5So Tobias*b* called him and said, "Take for your wages half of all that you brought back, and farewell."

12.1–5: Tobit and Tobias decide to pay Raphael. Since the amount of money on deposit in Rages was so large, the payment of half to Raphael would be very generous. It is part of the mood of celebration for all the blessings the family has received.

6 Then Raphael*b* called the two of them privately and said to them, "Bless God and acknowledge him in the presence of all the living for the good things he has done for you. Bless and sing praise to his name. With fitting honor declare to all people the deeds*c* of God. Do not be slow to acknowledge him. 7It is good to conceal the secret of a king, but to acknowledge and reveal the works of God, and with fitting honor to acknowledge him. Do good and evil will not overtake you. 8Prayer with fasting*d* is good, but better than both is almsgiving with righteousness. A little with righteousness is better than wealth with wrongdoing.*e* It is better to give alms than to lay up gold. 9For almsgiving saves from death and purges away every sin. Those who give alms will enjoy a full life, 10but those who commit sin and do wrong are their own worst enemies.

11 "I will now declare the whole truth to you and will conceal nothing from you. Already I have declared it to you when I said, 'It is good to conceal the secret of a king, but to reveal with due honor the works of God.' 12So now when you and Sarah prayed, it was I who brought and read*f* the record of your prayer before the glory of the Lord, and likewise whenever you would bury the dead. 13And that time when you did not hesitate to get up and leave your dinner to go and bury the dead, 14I was sent to you to test you. And at the same time God sent me to heal you and Sarah your daughter-in-law. 15I am Raphael, one of the seven angels who stand ready and enter before the glory of the Lord."

16 The two of them were shaken; they fell face down, for they were afraid. 17But he said to them, "Do not be afraid; peace be with you. Bless God forevermore. 18As for me, when I was with you, I was not acting on my own will, but by the will of God. Bless

a Other ancient authorities lack parts of this sentence
b Gk *he* *c* Gk *words*; other ancient authorities read *words of the deeds* *d* Codex Sinaiticus *with sincerity*
e Lat *f* Lat: Gk lacks *and read*

him each and every day; sing his praises. ¹⁹Although you were watching me, I really did not eat or drink anything—but what you saw was a vision. ²⁰So now get up from the ground,ᵃ and acknowledge God. See, I am ascending to him who sent me. Write down all these things that have happened to you." And he ascended. ²¹Then they stood up, and could see him no more. ²²They kept blessing God and singing his praises, and they acknowledged God for these marvelous deeds of his, when an angel of God had appeared to them.

12.6–22: Raphael gives parting instructions and reveals his identity. 7–10: Raphael's instructions emphasize *almsgiving*, as did Tobit's at 4.6–11. The implication of this is that God has rewarded Tobit for his earlier acts of charity. **20:** *Write down all these things that have happened to you:* The present text of Tobit, which begins in the first person, is presumed to be the result of this command.

13 Then Tobitᵇ said:
"Blessed be God who lives forever,
because his kingdomᶜ lasts throughout all ages.
² For he afflicts, and he shows mercy;
he leads down to Hades in the lowest regions of the earth,
and he brings up from the great abyss,ᵈ
and there is nothing that can escape his hand.
³ Acknowledge him before the nations,
O children of Israel;
for he has scattered you among them.
⁴ He has shown you his greatness even there.
Exalt him in the presence of every living being,
because he is our Lord and he is our God;
he is our Father and he is God forever.
⁵ He will afflictᵉ you for your iniquities,
but he will again show mercy on all of you.
He will gather you from all the nations

among whom you have been scattered.
⁶ If you turn to him with all your heart
and with all your soul,
to do what is true before him,
then he will turn to you
and will no longer hide his face from you.
So now see what he has done for you;
acknowledge him at the top of your voice.
Bless the Lord of righteousness,
and exalt the King of the ages.ᶠ
In the land of my exile I acknowledge him,
and show his power and majesty to a nation of sinners:
'Turn back, you sinners, and do what is right before him;
perhaps he may look with favor upon you and show you mercy.'
⁷ As for me, I exalt my God,
and my soul rejoices in the King of heaven.
⁸ Let all people speak of his majesty,
and acknowledge him in Jerusalem.
⁹ O Jerusalem, the holy city,
he afflictedᵍ you for the deeds of your hands,ʰ
but will again have mercy on the children of the righteous.
¹⁰ Acknowledge the Lord, for he is good,ⁱ
and bless the King of the ages,
so that his tentʲ may be rebuilt in you in joy.
May he cheer all those within you who are captives,
and love all those within you who are distressed,
to all generations forever.
¹¹ A bright light will shine to all the ends of the earth;

a Other ancient authorities read *now bless the Lord on earth*   *b* Gk *he*   *c* Other ancient authorities read *forever, and his kingdom*   *d* Gk *from destruction*   *e* Other ancient authorities read *He afflicted*   *f* The lacuna in codex Sinaiticus, verses 6b to 10a, is filled in from other ancient authorities   *g* Other ancient authorities read *will afflict*   *h* Other ancient authorities read *your children*   *i* Other ancient authorities read *Lord worthily*   *j* Or *tabernacle*

many nations will come to you from
        far away,
the inhabitants of the remotest parts of
        the earth to your holy name,
bearing gifts in their hands for the
        King of heaven.
Generation after generation will give
        joyful praise in you;
the name of the chosen city will
        endure forever.
12 Cursed are all who speak a harsh word
        against you;
cursed are all who conquer you
        and pull down your walls,
all who overthrow your towers
        and set your homes on fire.
But blessed forever will be all who
        revere you.ᵃ
13 Go, then, and rejoice over the children
        of the righteous,
for they will be gathered together
        and will praise the Lord of the ages.
14 Happy are those who love you,
        and happy are those who rejoice in
        your prosperity.
Happy also are all people who grieve
        with you
because of your afflictions;
for they will rejoice with you
        and witness all your glory forever.
15 My soul blessesᵇ the Lord, the great
        King!
16   For Jerusalem will be builtᶜ as his
        house for all ages.
How happy I will be if a remnant of my
        descendants should survive
to see your glory and acknowledge the
        King of heaven.
The gates of Jerusalem will be built with
        sapphire and emerald,
and all your walls with precious
        stones.
The towers of Jerusalem will be built
        with gold,
and their battlements with pure gold.
The streets of Jerusalem will be paved
        with ruby and with stones of Ophir.
17 The gates of Jerusalem will sing hymns
        of joy,
and all her houses will cry,
        'Hallelujah!

Blessed be the God of Israel!'
        and the blessed will bless the holy
        name forever and ever."

13.1–17: Tobit's hymn of praise. It is possible that chs. 13–14 (except for 14.1–2) were not originally part of the story of Tobit but were added at different times. Although the hymn provides a fitting celebration to the happy ending of the story and emphasizes the motif* of "blessing," it does not refer to any of the incidents of the story.

14 So ended Tobit's words of praise.
2 Tobitᵈ died in peace when he was one hundred twelve years old, and was buried with great honor in Nineveh. He was sixty-twoᵉ years old when he lost his eyesight, and after regaining it he lived in prosperity, giving alms and continually blessing God and acknowledging God's majesty.
3 When he was about to die, he called his son Tobias and the seven sons of Tobiasᶠ and gave this command: "My son, take your children 4 and hurry off to Media, for I believe the word of God that Nahum spoke about Nineveh, that all these things will take place and overtake Assyria and Nineveh. Indeed, everything that was spoken by the prophets of Israel, whom God sent, will occur. None of all their words will fail, but all will come true at their appointed times. So it will be safer in Media than in Assyria and Babylon. For I know and believe that whatever God has said will be fulfilled and will come true; not a single word of the prophecies will fail. All of our kindred, inhabitants of the land of Israel, will be scattered and taken as captives from the good land; and the whole land of Israel will be desolate, even Samaria and Jerusalem will be desolate. And the temple of God in it will be burned to the ground, and it will be desolate for a while.ᵍ
5 "But God will again have mercy on them, and God will bring them back into the

a Other ancient authorities read *who build you up*
b Or *O my soul, bless*   c Other ancient authorities add
for a city   d Gk *He*   e Other ancient authorities
read *fifty-eight*   f Lat: Gk lacks *and the seven sons of
Tobias*   g Lat: Other ancient authorities read *of God
will be in distress and will be burned for a while*

land of Israel; and they will rebuild the temple of God, but not like the first one until the period when the times of fulfillment shall come. After this they all will return from their exile and will rebuild Jerusalem in splendor; and in it the temple of God will be rebuilt, just as the prophets of Israel have said concerning it. 6Then the nations in the whole world will all be converted and worship God in truth. They will all abandon their idols, which deceitfully have led them into their error; 7and in righteousness they will praise the eternal God. All the Israelites who are saved in those days and are truly mindful of God will be gathered together; they will go to Jerusalem and live in safety forever in the land of Abraham, and it will be given over to them. Those who sincerely love God will rejoice, but those who commit sin and injustice will vanish from all the earth. 8,9So now, my children, I command you, serve God faithfully and do what is pleasing in his sight. Your children are also to be commanded to do what is right and to give alms, and to be mindful of God and to bless his name at all times with sincerity and with all their strength. So now, my son, leave Nineveh; do not remain here. 10On whatever day you bury your mother beside me, do not stay overnight within the confines of the city. For I see that there is much wickedness within it, and that much deceit is practiced within it, while the people are without shame. See, my son, what Nadab did to Ahikar who had reared him. Was he not, while still alive, brought down into the earth? For God repaid him to his face for this shameful treatment. Ahikar came out into the light, but Nadab went into the eternal darkness, because he tried to kill Ahikar. Because he gave alms, Ahikar*a* escaped the fatal trap that Nadab had set for him, but Nadab fell into it him-

self, and was destroyed. 11So now, my children, see what almsgiving accomplishes, and what injustice does—it brings death! But now my breath fails me."

Then they laid him on his bed, and he died; and he received an honorable funeral. 12When Tobias's mother died, he buried her beside his father. Then he and his wife and children*b* returned to Media and settled in Ecbatana with Raguel his father-in-law. 13He treated his parents-in-law*c* with great respect in their old age, and buried them in Ecbatana of Media. He inherited both the property of Raguel and that of his father Tobit. 14He died highly respected at the age of one hundred seventeen*d* years. 15Before he died he heard*e* of the destruction of Nineveh, and he saw its prisoners being led into Media, those whom King Cyaxares*f* of Media had taken captive. Tobias*g* praised God for all he had done to the people of Nineveh and Assyria; before he died he rejoiced over Nineveh, and he blessed the Lord God forever and ever. Amen.*h*

14.1–15: The testament of Tobit. Unlike the first testament of Tobit (ch. 4), this one does not relate to the story directly but predicts future events and has parallels to Zech 8.20–23 and Isa 40–55. It does not emphasize coexistence in the Diaspora* as the rest of the book does but instead envisions a renewal of Jewish life in Jerusalem. **10:** *What Nadab did to Ahikar:* See comments on 1.19–22.

a Gk *he*; other ancient authorities read *Manasses*
b Codex Sinaiticus lacks *and children* c Gk *them*
d Other authorities read other numbers e Codex Sinaiticus reads *saw and heard* f Cn: Codex Sinaiticus *Ahikar*; other ancient authorities read *Nebuchadnezzar and Ahasuerus* g Gk *He* h Other ancient authorities lack *Amen*

JUDITH

Introduction

Judith is one of the most developed examples of the Jewish novelistic★ literature of antiquity (see introduction to Tobit). It is the rousing story of the young Jewish woman Judith, who through her bravery saves her village and, ultimately, Jerusalem. Though the style is typical of other Jewish novels of the period (Daniel and Esther with their Apocryphal★ additions, Tobit, and *Joseph and Aseneth*★), the central theme is also similar to biblical stories that depict a warrior killed by a woman, such as Judg 4–5, 9, and 2 Sam 20.14–22.

The story, probably written in Hebrew in about the middle of the second century BCE, is set in a much earlier period. The historical setting, however, seems to be intentionally blurred, since Assyria, the imperial power that threatens Israel, is here headed by Nebuchadnezzar, who was actually king of the Neo-Babylonian empire. The two worst empires in Jewish history—Assyria had conquered the northern part of Israel and the Neo-Babylonians the southern, or Judah— have been merged to create a fictitious "evil empire."

Judith is very carefully structured. It is divisible into two acts of about equal length: the growing threat of the Assyrian army, commanded by Holofernes (chs. 1–7), and the response to that threat, which is focused on one woman in one Jewish village, Bethulia (chs. 8–12; see chart on page 22). The overarching symbolic opposition that governs the entire drama, however, is that between the "lord" Nebuchadnezzar, whose servant is his general Holofernes, and the Lord God, whose servant is Judith. This theme in Judith may be derived from the depiction of Nicanor and his claim to be "sovereign on earth" in 2 Macc 15.1–5. There are also other parallels to the defeat of Nicanor (see comments).

Although the Book of Judith requires twelve chapters of preparation before reaching the climactic★ decapitation scene, the author uses many effective narrative★ techniques to create excitement and a sense of the impending threat along the way. The geographical references, for example, often strung together, communicate the idea of a world at war and the immensity of Nebuchadnezzar's threat. The descriptions of the mustering of the troops and their movements likewise make for a very vivid, almost cinematic drama, and the path of destruction of the invading armies can be seen as descending inexorably upon Israel and, even more dramatically, on the small mountain town of Bethulia, which means "virgin."

No fragment of the Book of Judith was found at Qumran, and it is not quoted or alluded to in Philo, Josephus, or the New Testament, but Judith is mentioned in First Clement 55.3–4, an early Christian text. The story, retaining its appeal over the centuries, has been retold in various versions and has inspired many works of art.

1 It was the twelfth year of the reign of Nebuchadnezzar, who ruled over the Assyrians in the great city of Nineveh. In those days Arphaxad ruled over the Medes in Ecbatana. ²He built walls around Ecbatana with hewn stones three cubits thick and six cubits long; he made the walls seventy cubits high and fifty cubits wide. ³At its gates he raised towers one hundred cubits high and sixty cubits wide at the foundations. ⁴He made its gates seventy cubits high and forty cubits wide to allow his armies to march out in force and his infantry to form their ranks. ⁵Then King Nebuchadnezzar made war

against King Arphaxad in the great plain that is on the borders of Ragau. 6There rallied to him all the people of the hill country and all those who lived along the Euphrates, the Tigris, and the Hydaspes, and, on the plain, Arioch, king of the Elymeans. Thus, many nations joined the forces of the Chaldeans.*a*

1.1–6: Nebuchadnezzar declares war against Arphaxad of Media. *Nebuchadnezzar* reigned over the Neo-Babylonian empire, not the *Assyrians*, from 605–562 BCE; his father, Nabopolassar, had destroyed the Assyrian capital in 612 BCE. The Assyrians may have been seen as equivalent to Syrians, or the Greek/Seleucid rulers from whom the Maccabees won their independence. *Arphaxad* is a fictional king. **6:** *Chaldeans* is another name for the Neo-Babylonians. The import of this reference is unclear, since Nebuchadnezzar is here associated with the Assyrians.

~~~

7 Then Nebuchadnezzar, king of the Assyrians, sent messengers to all who lived in Persia and to all who lived in the west, those who lived in Cilicia and Damascus, Lebanon and Antilebanon, and all who lived along the seacoast, 8and those among the nations of Carmel and Gilead, and Upper Galilee and the great plain of Esdraelon, 9and all who were in Samaria and its towns, and beyond the Jordan as far as Jerusalem and Bethany and Chelous and Kadesh and the river of Egypt, and Tahpanhes and Raamses and the whole land of Goshen, 10even beyond Tanis and Memphis, and all who lived in Egypt as far as the borders of Ethiopia. 11But all who lived in the whole region disregarded the summons of Nebuchadnezzar, king of the Assyrians, and refused to join him in the war; for they were not afraid of him, but regarded him as only one man.*b* So they sent back his messengers empty-handed and in disgrace.

12 Then Nebuchadnezzar became very angry with this whole region, and swore by his throne and kingdom that he would take revenge on the whole territory of Cilicia and Damascus and Syria, that he would kill with his sword also all the inhabitants of the land of Moab, and the people of Ammon, and all Judea, and every one in Egypt, as far as the coasts of the two seas.

13 In the seventeenth year he led his forces against King Arphaxad and defeated him in battle, overthrowing the whole army of Arphaxad and all his cavalry and all his chariots. 14Thus he took possession of his towns and came to Ecbatana, captured its towers, plundered its markets, and turned its glory into disgrace. 15He captured Arphaxad in the mountains of Ragau and struck him down with his spears, thus destroying him once and for all. 16Then he returned to Nineveh, he and all his combined forces, a vast body of troops; and there he and his forces rested and feasted for one hundred twenty days.

1.7–16: The rising threat of Nebuchadnezzar and his response to the nations who spurn him. The geographical expanse of the area threatened by Nebuchadnezzar is emphasized. The area is larger than either the Assyrian or Babylonian empires, but corresponds to lands ruled by the later Persian and Greek empires. **13–16:** The easy victory of Nebuchadnezzar over the great *Arphaxad* of *Ecbatana* demonstrates the threat that looms over smaller nations. This episode concludes with Nebuchadnezzar's celebration and a temporary pause in the action. A number of these pauses will occur throughout the novel,* framing the scenes of dramatic action and allowing for a more deliberate pacing of the story.

~~~

2 In the eighteenth year, on the twenty-second day of the first month, there was talk in the palace of Nebuchadnezzar, king of the Assyrians, about carrying out his revenge on the whole region, just as he had said. 2He summoned all his ministers and all his nobles and set before them his secret plan and recounted fully, with his own lips, all the wickedness of the region.*c* 3They decided that every one who had not obeyed his command should be destroyed.

4 When he had completed his plan, Nebuchadnezzar, king of the Assyrians, called Holofernes, the chief general of his army, second only to himself, and said to him, 5"Thus says the Great King, the lord of the whole earth: Leave my presence and take with you men confident in their strength,

a Syr: Gk *Cheleoudites*   *b* Or *a man*   *c* Meaning of Gk uncertain one hundred twenty thousand foot soldiers and twelve thousand cavalry. 6March out against all the land to the west, because they disobeyed my orders. 7Tell them to prepare earth and water, for I am coming against them in my anger, and will cover the whole face of the earth with the feet of my troops, to whom I will hand them over to be plundered. 8Their wounded shall fill their ravines and gullies, and the swelling river shall be filled with their dead. 9I will lead them away captive to the ends of the whole earth. 10You shall go and seize all their territory for me in advance. They must yield themselves to you, and you shall hold them for me until the day of their punishment. 11But to those who resist show no mercy, but hand them over to slaughter and plunder throughout your whole region. 12For as I live, and by the power of my kingdom, what I have spoken I will accomplish by my own hand. 13And you—take care not to transgress any of your lord's commands, but carry them out exactly as I have ordered you; do it without delay."

2.1–13: Nebuchadnezzar plots the destruction of all the nations that opposed him. 5–13: The grandiose language characterizes Nebuchadnezzar as one who has divine pretensions, and his orders to his *general Holofernes* sound much like God commissioning a prophet. There is an irony* here in Nebuchadnezzar's calling himself "lord." This term is used often for Nebuchadnezzar over the next chapters, extending the ironic theme further and bringing to mind the question: Who is Lord? There are parallels in the text to a real military campaign of a later period, that of Artaxerxes III Ochus of Persia in the middle of the fourth century BCE, who had in his army officers named Holofernes and Bagoas.

HOLOFERNES BEGINS THE CAMPAIGN TO DESTROY THE DISOBEDIENT NATIONS

2.14–3.10: This section of the narrative* begins a tightly structured arc of rising and falling action (see chart on following page).

14 So Holofernes left the presence of his lord, and summoned all the commanders, generals, and officers of the Assyrian army.

15He mustered the picked troops by divisions as his lord had ordered him to do, one hundred twenty thousand of them, together with twelve thousand archers on horseback, 16and he organized them as a great army is marshaled for a campaign. 17He took along a vast number of camels and donkeys and mules for transport, and innumerable sheep and oxen and goats for food; 18also ample rations for everyone, and a huge amount of gold and silver from the royal palace.

19 Then he set out with his whole army, to go ahead of King Nebuchadnezzar and to cover the whole face of the earth to the west with their chariots and cavalry and picked foot soldiers. 20Along with them went a mixed crowd like a swarm of locusts, like the dust*a* of the earth—a multitude that could not be counted.

21 They marched for three days from Nineveh to the plain of Bectileth, and camped opposite Bectileth near the mountain that is to the north of Upper Cilicia. 22From there Holofernes*b* took his whole army, the infantry, cavalry, and chariots, and went up into the hill country. 23He ravaged Put and Lud, and plundered all the Rassisites and the Ishmaelites on the border of the desert, south of the country of the Chelleans. 24Then he followed*c* the Euphrates and passed through Mesopotamia and destroyed all the fortified towns along the brook Abron, as far as the sea. 25He also seized the territory of Cilicia, and killed everyone who resisted him. Then he came to the southern borders of Japheth, facing Arabia. 26He surrounded all the Midianites, and burned their tents and plundered their sheepfolds. 27Then he went down into the plain of Damascus during the wheat harvest, and burned all their fields and destroyed their flocks and herds and sacked their towns and ravaged their lands and put all their young men to the sword.

28 So fear and dread of him fell upon all the people who lived along the seacoast, at Sidon and Tyre, and those who lived in Sur and Ocina and all who lived in Jamnia.

a Gk *sand*   *b* Gk *he*   *c* Or *crossed*

Chart Structure of the narrative* of Judith

First half

A   Campaign against disobedient nations; the people surrender (2.14–3.10)
B   Israel is "greatly terrified"; Joakim prepares for war (4.1–15)
C   Holofernes talks with Achior; Achior is expelled (5.1–6.13)
C' Achior is received in Bethulia; Achior talks with the people (6.14–21)
B' Holofernes prepares for war; Israel is "greatly terrified" (7.1–5)
A' Campaign against Bethulia; the people want to surrender (7.6–32)

Second half

A   Introduction of Judith (8.1–8)
B   Judith plans to save Israel (8.9–10.8)
C   Judith and her maid leave Bethulia (10.9–10)
D   Judith overcomes Holofernes (10.11–13.10a)
C' Judith and her maid return to Bethulia (13.10b–11)
B' Judith plans to destroy Israel's enemy (13.12–16.20)
A' Conclusion about Judith (16.21–25)

Those who lived in Azotus and Ascalon feared him greatly.

3 They therefore sent messengers to him to sue for peace in these words: 2"We, the servants of Nebuchadnezzar, the Great King, lie prostrate before you. Do with us whatever you will. 3See, our buildings and all our land and all our wheat fields and our flocks and herds and all our encampments*a* lie before you; do with them as you please. 4Our towns and their inhabitants are also your slaves; come and deal with them as you see fit."

5 The men came to Holofernes and told him all this. 6Then he went down to the seacoast with his army and stationed garrisons in the fortified towns and took picked men from them as auxiliaries. 7These people and all in the countryside welcomed him with garlands and dances and tambourines. 8Yet he demolished all their shrines*b* and cut down their sacred groves; for he had been commissioned to destroy all the gods of the land, so that all nations should worship Nebuchadnezzar alone, and that all their dialects and tribes should call upon him as a god.

9 Then he came toward Esdraelon, near

Dothan, facing the great ridge of Judea; 10he camped between Geba and Scythopolis, and remained for a whole month in order to collect all the supplies for his army.

2.28–3.10: The people of the seacoast surrender. The total capitulation of the other nations is dramatically presented in order to show how attractive this option would be. **3.8:** Nebuchadnezzar's destruction of other people's religious establishments and insistence on being worshipped *as a god* indicate the threat that awaits the people of Judea as well. Nebuchadnezzar intends a religious persecution in addition to the destruction of armies and political institutions. The demand of foreign kings to be worshipped as gods is also found in Dan 3.4–5; 6.7. **9–10:** Another pause in the action occurs as Holofernes camps for a *month* to *collect supplies*. This pause increases the sense of the mounting danger.

4 When the Israelites living in Judea heard of everything that Holofernes, the general of Nebuchadnezzar, the king of the Assyrians, had done to the nations, and how he had plundered and destroyed all their tem-

a Gk *all the sheepfolds of our tents*   b Syr: Gk *borders* ples, 2they were therefore greatly terrified at his approach; they were alarmed both for Jerusalem and for the temple of the Lord their God. 3For they had only recently returned from exile, and all the people of Judea had just now gathered together, and the sacred vessels and the altar and the temple had been consecrated after their profanation. 4So they sent word to every district of Samaria, and to Kona, Beth-horon, Belmain, and Jericho, and to Choba and Aesora, and the valley of Salem. 5They immediately seized all the high hilltops and fortified the villages on them and stored up food in preparation for war—since their fields had recently been harvested.

6 The high priest, Joakim, who was in Jerusalem at the time, wrote to the people of Bethulia and Betomesthaim, which faces Esdraelon opposite the plain near Dothan, 7ordering them to seize the mountain passes, since by them Judea could be invaded; and it would be easy to stop any who tried to enter, for the approach was narrow, wide enough for only two at a time to pass.

4.1–7: Israel prepares for attack. Of all the nations only Israel fortifies against Holofernes. The preparations show the resolve of the Israelites, but not their military resources. **3:** This verse describes not the situation under the Assyrians, nor under Nebuchadnezzar, king of the Babylonians at the beginning of the sixth century, but the return from exile under Cyrus of Persia nearer the end of the sixth century. It is also likely that the reconsecration of the Temple* after the Maccabean revolt is in mind (1 Macc 4.36–51). The author intentionally associates recent events in Jewish history with the ancient past of the story.

8 So the Israelites did as they had been ordered by the high priest Joakim and the senate of the whole people of Israel, in session at Jerusalem. 9And every man of Israel cried out to God with great fervor, and they humbled themselves with much fasting. 10They and their wives and their children and their cattle and every resident alien and hired laborer and purchased slave—they all put sackcloth around their waists. 11And all the Israelite men, women, and children living at Jerusalem prostrated themselves before the temple and put ashes on their heads and spread out their sackcloth before the Lord. 12They even draped the altar with sackcloth and cried out in unison, praying fervently to the God of Israel not to allow their infants to be carried off and their wives to be taken as booty, and the towns they had inherited to be destroyed, and the sanctuary to be profaned and desecrated to the malicious joy of the Gentiles.

13 The Lord heard their prayers and had regard for their distress; for the people fasted many days throughout Judea and in Jerusalem before the sanctuary of the Lord Almighty. 14The high priest Joakim and all the priests who stood before the Lord and ministered to the Lord, with sackcloth around their loins, offered the daily burnt offerings, the votive offerings, and freewill offerings of the people. 15With ashes on their turbans, they cried out to the Lord with all their might to look with favor on the whole house of Israel.

4.8–15: Israel prays, fasts. 8–10: The *senate* ("gerousia"), or Sanhedrin, is also an anachronism,* since it came into being long after the period described. The internal determination of the people is shown by their outward supplications and fasts, which make use of the rituals of mourning. **10:** *Sackcloth,* the material of which funeral shrouds were made, was the garment of ritualized grief, whether of mourning, penitence, or protest (Neh 9.1; Esth 4.1). A humorous element is also added, however: Even the *cattle* wear sackcloth!

5 It was reported to Holofernes, the general of the Assyrian army, that the people of Israel had prepared for war and had closed the mountain passes and fortified all the high hilltops and set up barricades in the plains. 2In great anger he called together all the princes of Moab and the commanders of Ammon and all the governors of the coastland, 3and said to them, "Tell me, you Canaanites, what people is this that lives in the hill country? What towns do they inhabit? How large is their army, and in what does their power and strength consist? Who rules over them as king and leads their army? 4And why have they alone, of all who live in the west, refused to come out and meet me?"

5 Then Achior, the leader of all the Ammonites, said to him, "May my lord please listen to a report from the mouth of your servant, and I will tell you the truth about this people that lives in the mountain district near you. No falsehood shall come from your servant's mouth. 6These people are descended from the Chaldeans. 7At one time they lived in Mesopotamia, because they did not wish to follow the gods of their ancestors who were in Chaldea. 8Since they had abandoned the ways of their ancestors, and worshiped the God of heaven, the God they had come to know, their ancestors*a* drove them out from the presence of their gods. So they fled to Mesopotamia, and lived there for a long time. 9Then their God commanded them to leave the place where they were living and go to the land of Canaan. There they settled, and grew very prosperous in gold and silver and very much livestock. 10When a famine spread over the land of Canaan they went down to Egypt and lived there as long as they had food. There they became so great a multitude that their race could not be counted. 11So the king of Egypt became hostile to them; he exploited them and forced them to make bricks. 12They cried out to their God, and he afflicted the whole land of Egypt with incurable plagues. So the Egyptians drove them out of their sight. 13Then God dried up the Red Sea before them, 14and he led them by the way of Sinai and Kadesh-barnea. They drove out all the people of the desert, 15and took up residence in the land of the Amorites, and by their might destroyed all the inhabitants of Heshbon; and crossing over the Jordan they took possession of all the hill country. 16They drove out before them the Canaanites, the Perizzites, the Jebusites, the Shechemites, and all the Gergesites, and lived there a long time.

17 "As long as they did not sin against their God they prospered, for the God who hates iniquity is with them. 18But when they departed from the way he had prescribed for them, they were utterly defeated in many battles and were led away captive to a foreign land. The temple of their God was razed to the ground, and their towns were occupied by their enemies. 19But now they have returned to their God, and have come back from the places where they were scattered, and have occupied Jerusalem, where their sanctuary is, and have settled in the hill country, because it was uninhabited.

20 "So now, my master and lord, if there is any oversight in this people and they sin against their God and we find out their offense, then we can go up and defeat them. 21But if they are not a guilty nation, then let my lord pass them by; for their Lord and God will defend them, and we shall become the laughingstock of the whole world."

22 When Achior had finished saying these things, all the people standing around the tent began to complain; Holofernes' officers and all the inhabitants of the seacoast and Moab insisted that he should be cut to pieces. 23They said, "We are not afraid of the Israelites; they are a people with no strength or power for making war. 24Therefore let us go ahead, Lord Holofernes, and your vast army will swallow them up."

5.1–24: Holofernes gathers information about Israel. The preparation for war is now seen from the enemy's side. **2:** *Moab* and *Ammon* were the traditional enemies of Israel (Judg 3.12–30; 2 Sam 10). Note also the "Edomites" at 7.8. **5–21:** Ironically, it is *Achior, the leader of all the Ammonites,* who describes the Jews by recounting their history. The character of Achior is probably influenced by the popular legendary* figure of Ahikar,* who advised the Assyrian kings. A copy of his story was found in the Jewish colony at Elephantine in Egypt. **17–21:** The lesson that Achior draws from Israel's history is that as long as Israelites are faithful to God and *do not sin,* they are invincible. The pattern of Israel's sin/punishment/repentance/salvation is found in Deut 28–32 and reappears in a number of texts in the late biblical period (Bar 1.15–3.8). **22–24:** Achior had said (v. 5) that he would tell the "truth about this people," but the truth is met here by Holofernes' desire to kill the messenger. Truth, and its opposite, deceit, will be an important issue later. Achior's prophecy against Holofernes functions in a way similar to Balaam's prophecy against Balak in Num 22–24.

a Gk *they*

6 When the disturbance made by the people outside the council had died down, Holofernes, the commander of the Assyrian army, said to Achior[a] in the presence of all the foreign contingents: 2 "Who are you, Achior and you mercenaries of Ephraim, to prophesy among us as you have done today and tell us not to make war against the people of Israel because their God will defend them? What god is there except Nebuchadnezzar? He will send his forces and destroy them from the face of the earth. Their God will not save them; 3 we the king's[b] servants will destroy them as one man. They cannot resist the might of our cavalry. 4 We will overwhelm them;[c] their mountains will be drunk with their blood, and their fields will be full of their dead. Not even their footprints will survive our attack; they will utterly perish. So says King Nebuchadnezzar, lord of the whole earth. For he has spoken; none of his words shall be in vain.

5 "As for you, Achior, you Ammonite mercenary, you have said these words in a moment of perversity; you shall not see my face again from this day until I take revenge on this race that came out of Egypt. 6 Then at my return the sword of my army and the spear[d] of my servants shall pierce your sides, and you shall fall among their wounded. 7 Now my slaves are going to take you back into the hill country and put you in one of the towns beside the passes. 8 You will not die until you perish along with them. 9 If you really hope in your heart that they will not be taken, then do not look downcast! I have spoken, and none of my words shall fail to come true."

10 Then Holofernes ordered his slaves, who waited on him in his tent, to seize Achior and take him away to Bethulia and hand him over to the Israelites. 11 So the slaves took him and led him out of the camp into the plain, and from the plain they went up into the hill country and came to the springs below Bethulia. 12 When the men of the town saw them,[e] they seized their weapons and ran out of the town to the top of the hill, and all the slingers kept them from coming up by throwing stones at them. 13 So having taken shelter below the hill, they bound

Achior and left him lying at the foot of the hill, and returned to their master.

6.1–13: Holofernes banishes Achior to Bethulia to die with the Israelites. 2–4: Holofernes makes a strong contrast between the two sides by saying *Nebuchadnezzar* is *god*. Holofernes speaks as a prophet for Nebuchadnezzar. **5–9:** *You shall not see my face again:* The reader will learn that Holofernes' words are true, but not in the way that he thinks. Verses 8–9 continue Holofernes' ironic prophecy. **10–11:** *Bethulia*, which means "virgin," is likely a fictitious town, but its description shows similarities to Shechem.

---

14 Then the Israelites came down from their town and found him; they untied him and brought him into Bethulia and placed him before the magistrates of their town, 15 who in those days were Uzziah son of Micah, of the tribe of Simeon, and Chabris son of Gothoniel, and Charmis son of Melchiel. 16 They called together all the elders of the town, and all their young men and women ran to the assembly. They set Achior in the midst of all their people, and Uzziah questioned him about what had happened. 17 He answered and told them what had taken place at the council of Holofernes, and all that he had said in the presence of the Assyrian leaders, and all that Holofernes had boasted he would do against the house of Israel. 18 Then the people fell down and worshiped God, and cried out:

19 "O Lord God of heaven, see their arrogance, and have pity on our people in their humiliation, and look kindly today on the faces of those who are consecrated to you."

20 Then they reassured Achior, and praised him highly. 21 Uzziah took him from the assembly to his own house and gave a banquet for the elders; and all that night they called on the God of Israel for help.

6.14–21: Bethulia receives Achior and hears his story. Achior's recognition of God's relationship to Israel has made him a sympathetic ally.

---

a Other ancient authorities add *and to all the Moabites*
b Gk *his*   *c* Other ancient authorities add *with it*
d Lat Syr: Gk *people*   *e* Other ancient authorities add *on the top of the hill*

7 The next day Holofernes ordered his whole army, and all the allies who had joined him, to break camp and move against Bethulia, and to seize the passes up into the hill country and make war on the Israelites. ²So all their warriors marched off that day; their fighting forces numbered one hundred seventy thousand infantry and twelve thousand cavalry, not counting the baggage and the foot soldiers handling it, a very great multitude. ³They encamped in the valley near Bethulia, beside the spring, and they spread out in breadth over Dothan as far as Balbaim and in length from Bethulia to Cyamon, which faces Esdraelon.

4 When the Israelites saw their vast numbers, they were greatly terrified and said to one another, "They will now strip clean the whole land; neither the high mountains nor the valleys nor the hills will bear their weight." ⁵Yet they all seized their weapons, and when they had kindled fires on their towers, they remained on guard all that night.

6 On the second day Holofernes led out all his cavalry in full view of the Israelites in Bethulia. ⁷He reconnoitered the approaches to their town, and visited the springs that supplied their water; he seized them and set guards of soldiers over them, and then returned to his army.

8 Then all the chieftains of the Edomites and all the leaders of the Moabites and the commanders of the coastland came to him and said, ⁹"Listen to what we have to say, my lord, and your army will suffer no losses. ¹⁰This people, the Israelites, do not rely on their spears but on the height of the mountains where they live, for it is not easy to reach the tops of their mountains. ¹¹Therefore, my lord, do not fight against them in regular formation, and not a man of your army will fall. ¹²Remain in your camp, and keep all the men in your forces with you; let your servants take possession of the spring of water that flows from the foot of the mountain, ¹³for this is where all the people of Bethulia get their water. So thirst will destroy them, and they will surrender their town. Meanwhile, we and our people will go up to the tops of the nearby mountains and camp there to keep watch to see that no one

gets out of the town. ¹⁴They and their wives and children will waste away with famine, and before the sword reaches them they will be strewn about in the streets where they live. ¹⁵Thus you will pay them back with evil, because they rebelled and did not receive you peaceably."

16 These words pleased Holofernes and all his attendants, and he gave orders to do as they had said. ¹⁷So the army of the Ammonites moved forward, together with five thousand Assyrians, and they encamped in the valley and seized the water supply and the springs of the Israelites. ¹⁸And the Edomites and Ammonites went up and encamped in the hill country opposite Dothan; and they sent some of their men toward the south and the east, toward Egrebeh, which is near Chusi beside the Wadi Mochmur. The rest of the Assyrian army encamped in the plain, and covered the whole face of the land. Their tents and supply trains spread out in great number, and they formed a vast multitude.

7.1–18: Holofernes advances on Bethulia and prepares for a siege. 2–3: The armies of Holofernes are impressive; their movements are described with geographical details. **4:** The sight *terrifies the Israelites*, which makes the later discussion of surrender all the more compelling. **8:** *Edomites:* See comment on 5.2.

19 The Israelites then cried out to the Lord their God, for their courage failed, because all their enemies had surrounded them, and there was no way of escape from them. ²⁰The whole Assyrian army, their infantry, chariots, and cavalry, surrounded them for thirty-four days, until all the water containers of every inhabitant of Bethulia were empty; ²¹their cisterns were going dry, and on no day did they have enough water to drink, for their drinking water was rationed. ²²Their children were listless, and the women and young men fainted from thirst and were collapsing in the streets of the town and in the gateways; they no longer had any strength.

23 Then all the people, the young men, the women, and the children, gathered around Uzziah and the rulers of the town

and cried out with a loud voice, and said before all the elders, 24"Let God judge between you and us! You have done us a great injury in not making peace with the Assyrians. 25For now we have no one to help us; God has sold us into their hands, to be strewn before them in thirst and exhaustion. 26Now summon them and surrender the whole town as booty to the army of Holofernes and to all his forces. 27For it would be better for us to be captured by them.*ª We shall indeed become slaves, but our lives will be spared, and we shall not witness our little ones dying before our eyes, and our wives and children drawing their last breath. 28We call to witness against you heaven and earth and our God, the Lord of our ancestors, who punishes us for our sins and the sins of our ancestors; do today the things that we have described!"

29 Then great and general lamentation arose throughout the assembly, and they cried out to the Lord God with a loud voice. 30But Uzziah said to them, "Courage, my brothers and sisters!*ᵇ Let us hold out for five days more; by that time the Lord our God will turn his mercy to us again, for he will not forsake us utterly. 31But if these days pass by, and no help comes for us, I will do as you say."

32 Then he dismissed the people to their various posts, and they went up on the walls and towers of their town. The women and children he sent home. In the town they were in great misery.

7.19–32: Faced with certain destruction, the citizens of Bethulia press to surrender. Three positions are presented in regard to Holofernes' threat: resistance, for which the citizens had earlier been preparing; capitulation, or complete surrender, which they now embrace as an option; and a third, moderate position advocated by Uzziah, which is to wait *for five days more* to see whether God will deliver them. **32:** A momentary pause occurs, as the people return to their *posts* and *homes, in great misery*. On this note the first half of the book ends.

8 Now in those days Judith heard about these things: she was the daughter of Merari son of Ox son of Joseph son of Oziel son of Elkiah son of Ananias son of Gideon son of Raphain son of Ahitub son of Elijah son of Hilkiah son of Eliab son of Nathanael son of Salamiel son of Sarasadai son of Israel. 2Her husband Manasseh, who belonged to her tribe and family, had died during the barley harvest. 3For as he stood overseeing those who were binding sheaves in the field, he was overcome by the burning heat, and took to his bed and died in his town Bethulia. So they buried him with his ancestors in the field between Dothan and Balamon. 4Judith remained as a widow for three years and four months 5at home where she set up a tent for herself on the roof of her house. She put sackcloth around her waist and dressed in widow's clothing. 6She fasted all the days of her widowhood, except the day before the sabbath and the sabbath itself, the day before the new moon and the day of the new moon, and the festivals and days of rejoicing of the house of Israel. 7She was beautiful in appearance, and was very lovely to behold. Her husband Manasseh had left her gold and silver, men and women slaves, livestock, and fields; and she maintained this estate. 8No one spoke ill of her, for she feared God with great devotion.

8.1–8: Judith hears about the assembly's decision. Judith is the very model of the pious Jewish woman. Her name in Hebrew, "yehudit," is the feminine form of "yehudi," which means Judean or Jew. She is given an impressive-sounding genealogy,* the longest for any woman in the Bible, although many of the names are unknown. The death of her husband, Manasseh, of sunstroke is surprisingly "unheroic," in contrast to Judith's role. **4–6:** Judith's period of mourning is far longer than usual, longer than prescribed by Jewish law. She also *fasts on all days* except those on which fasting is not allowed. **7–8:** Her beauty, wealth, and piety are above average, giving her some of the qualities of a folktale heroine.

9 When Judith heard the harsh words spoken by the people against the ruler, because they were faint for lack of water, and when she heard all that Uzziah said to them,

---

a Other ancient authorities add *than to die of thirst*
b Gk *Courage, brothers*

and how he promised them under oath to surrender the town to the Assyrians after five days, [10]she sent her maid, who was in charge of all she possessed, to summon Uzziah and[a] Chabris and Charmis, the elders of her town. [11]They came to her, and she said to them:

"Listen to me, rulers of the people of Bethulia! What you have said to the people today is not right; you have even sworn and pronounced this oath between God and you, promising to surrender the town to our enemies unless the Lord turns and helps us within so many days. [12]Who are you to put God to the test today, and to set yourselves up in the place of[b] God in human affairs? [13]You are putting the Lord Almighty to the test, but you will never learn anything! [14]You cannot plumb the depths of the human heart or understand the workings of the human mind; how do you expect to search out God, who made all these things, and find out his mind or comprehend his thought? No, my brothers, do not anger the Lord our God. [15]For if he does not choose to help us within these five days, he has power to protect us within any time he pleases, or even to destroy us in the presence of our enemies. [16]Do not try to bind the purposes of the Lord our God; for God is not like a human being, to be threatened, or like a mere mortal, to be won over by pleading. [17]Therefore, while we wait for his deliverance, let us call upon him to help us, and he will hear our voice, if it pleases him.

[18]"For never in our generation, nor in these present days, has there been any tribe or family or people or town of ours that worships gods made with hands, as was done in days gone by. [19]That was why our ancestors were handed over to the sword and to pillage, and so they suffered a great catastrophe before our enemies. [20]But we know no other god but him, and so we hope that he will not disdain us or any of our nation. [21]For if we are captured, all Judea will be captured and our sanctuary will be plundered; and he will make us pay for its desecration with our blood. [22]The slaughter of our kindred and the captivity of the land and the desolation of our inheritance—all this he will bring on our heads among the Gentiles, wherever we

serve as slaves; and we shall be an offense and a disgrace in the eyes of those who acquire us. [23]For our slavery will not bring us into favor, but the Lord our God will turn it to dishonor.

[24]"Therefore, my brothers, let us set an example for our kindred, for their lives depend upon us, and the sanctuary—both the temple and the altar—rests upon us. [25]In spite of everything let us give thanks to the Lord our God, who is putting us to the test as he did our ancestors. [26]Remember what he did with Abraham, and how he tested Isaac, and what happened to Jacob in Syrian Mesopotamia, while he was tending the sheep of Laban, his mother's brother. [27]For he has not tried us with fire, as he did them, to search their hearts, nor has he taken vengeance on us; but the Lord scourges those who are close to him in order to admonish them."

8.9–27: Judith upbraids the citizens for their lack of resolve. Judith objects to both the townspeople's desire to capitulate and Uzziah's moderate position of waiting five days. **10:** *Maid:* This unnamed servant will be granted a large role by Judith. **12–13:** To *put God to the test* would violate the injunction of Deut 6.16. **14:** *To search out God* cannot be done directly (Job 28.12–28), but observance of Jewish law was seen as a means of receiving God's revelation (Sir 24.23; Bar 3.15–4.1). Judith counsels continued resistance and absolute trust in God's help. **25–27:** God puts *those who are close to him* to the test, not the other way around.

---

[28] Then Uzziah said to her, "All that you have said was spoken out of a true heart, and there is no one who can deny your words. [29]Today is not the first time your wisdom has been shown, but from the beginning of your life all the people have recognized your understanding, for your heart's disposition is right. [30]But the people were so thirsty that they compelled us to do for them what we have promised, and made us take an oath that we cannot break. [31]Now since you are a God-fearing woman, pray for us, so that

---

a Other ancient authorities lack *Uzziah and* (see verses 28 and 35) b Or *above* the Lord may send us rain to fill our cisterns. Then we will no longer feel faint from thirst."

32 Then Judith said to them, "Listen to me. I am about to do something that will go down through all generations of our descendants. 33 Stand at the town gate tonight so that I may go out with my maid; and within the days after which you have promised to surrender the town to our enemies, the Lord will deliver Israel by my hand. 34 Only, do not try to find out what I am doing; for I will not tell you until I have finished what I am about to do."

35 Uzziah and the rulers said to her, "Go in peace, and may the Lord God go before you, to take vengeance on our enemies." 36 So they returned from the tent and went to their posts.

8.28–36: Uzziah acknowledges the wisdom of Judith's words, and she promises to take action. 29: Judith is known for her *wisdom*. **31–33:** Although Uzziah only asks her to pray for rain, Judith promises something far greater. The reader is not told what that is, but is alerted that *the Lord will deliver Israel by* her *hand*, thus building suspense. The giving of rain would have been a miracle from God, but Judith will also take matters into her own hands.

9 Then Judith prostrated herself, put ashes on her head, and uncovered the sackcloth she was wearing. At the very time when the evening incense was being offered in the house of God in Jerusalem, Judith cried out to the Lord with a loud voice, and said,

2 "O Lord God of my ancestor Simeon, to whom you gave a sword to take revenge on those strangers who had torn off a virgin's clothing[a] to defile her, and exposed her thighs to put her to shame, and polluted her womb to disgrace her; for you said, 'It shall not be done'—yet they did it; 3 so you gave up their rulers to be killed, and their bed, which was ashamed of the deceit they had practiced, was stained with blood, and you struck down slaves along with princes, and princes on their thrones. 4 You gave up their wives for booty and their daughters to captivity, and all their booty to be divided among your beloved children who burned with zeal for you and abhorred the pollution of their blood and called on you for help. O God, my God, hear me also, a widow.

5 "For you have done these things and those that went before and those that followed. You have designed the things that are now, and those that are to come. What you had in mind has happened; 6 the things you decided on presented themselves and said, 'Here we are!' For all your ways are prepared in advance, and your judgment is with foreknowledge.

7 "Here now are the Assyrians, a greatly increased force, priding themselves in their horses and riders, boasting in the strength of their foot soldiers, and trusting in shield and spear, in bow and sling. They do not know that you are the Lord who crushes wars; the Lord is your name. 8 Break their strength by your might, and bring down their power in your anger; for they intend to defile your sanctuary, and to pollute the tabernacle where your glorious name resides, and to break off the horns[b] of your altar with the sword. 9 Look at their pride, and send your wrath upon their heads. Give to me, a widow, the strong hand to do what I plan. 10 By the deceit of my lips strike down the slave with the prince and the prince with his servant; crush their arrogance by the hand of a woman.

11 "For your strength does not depend on numbers, nor your might on the powerful. But you are the God of the lowly, helper of the oppressed, upholder of the weak, protector of the forsaken, savior of those without hope. 12 Please, please, God of my father, God of the heritage of Israel, Lord of heaven and earth, Creator of the waters, King of all your creation, hear my prayer! 13 Make my deceitful words bring wound and bruise on those who have planned cruel things against your covenant, and against your sacred house, and against Mount Zion, and against the house your children possess. 14 Let your whole nation and every tribe know and understand that you are God, the God of all

a Cn: Gk *loosed her womb*   *b* Syr: Gk *horn*

power and might, and that there is no other who protects the people of Israel but you alone!"

9.1–14: Judith's prayer scene. As in other prayer scenes, Judith takes on the rituals of mourning (see comments on 4.8–15). **2–4:** Judith begins by invoking *my ancestor Simeon,* who avenged the rape of his sister Dinah by Shechem (Gen 34). Biblical tradition had condemned this vengeance as excessive or foolhardy (Gen 34.30; 49.5–7). Judith, however, perceived it as an occasion of heroism and conquest. **10:** Judith explicitly says that she will use *deceit* to *crush their arrogance by the hand of a woman* (11.5, 11–15). This is in ironic* contrast to Achior's insistence that he will speak only the truth (5.5). Judith is prepared to leave her cherished virtues behind to save her people. Many have objected to her use of deceit and sexual wiles, while others argue that she is justified by the threat to the Temple* and her people. In the biblical tradition, compare Ex 20.16 and Prov 6.16–19, which condemn lying, with Gen 27, 29, 31, 38, Ex 2, and Josh 2, where lying is used to advance the welfare of the patriarchs and matriarchs. In most of these cases, women are portrayed as deceiving others. Judith likewise creates a moral dilemma that engages both the fantasies and the reservations of the audience. **13:** Esther 9.1–2.

10 When Judith[a] had stopped crying out to the God of Israel, and had ended all these words, 2she rose from where she lay prostrate. She called her maid and went down into the house where she lived on sabbaths and on her festal days. 3She removed the sackcloth she had been wearing, took off her widow's garments, bathed her body with water, and anointed herself with precious ointment. She combed her hair, put on a tiara, and dressed herself in the festive attire that she used to wear while her husband Manasseh was living. 4She put sandals on her feet, and put on her anklets, bracelets, rings, earrings, and all her other jewelry. Thus she made herself very beautiful, to entice the eyes of all the men who might see her. 5She gave her maid a skin of wine and a flask of oil, and filled a bag with roasted grain, dried fig cakes, and fine bread;[b] then she wrapped up all her dishes and gave them to her to carry.

6 Then they went out to the town gate of Bethulia and found Uzziah standing there with the elders of the town, Chabris and Charmis. 7When they saw her transformed in appearance and dressed differently, they were very greatly astounded at her beauty and said to her, 8"May the God of our ancestors grant you favor and fulfill your plans, so that the people of Israel may glory and Jerusalem may be exalted." She bowed down to God.

9 Then she said to them, "Order the gate of the town to be opened for me so that I may go out and accomplish the things you have just said to me." So they ordered the young men to open the gate for her, as she requested. 10When they had done this, Judith went out, accompanied by her maid. The men of the town watched her until she had gone down the mountain and passed through the valley, where they lost sight of her.

10.1–10: Judith puts her plan into motion. Judith addressed God wearing sackcloth,* but now she temporarily comes out of mourning and beautifies herself. By implication, this is part of her deceit, but Judith is dedicating her act to God (v. 8). A similar sequence of beautification/prayer/action is found at Esther 15 in the Apocrypha.* **5:** Judith packs kosher* food to eat while with Holofernes. Vegetables were the safest possible kosher food in the Diaspora,* because meat might have come from an animal sacrificed to other gods (Dan 1.8–15).

11 As the women[c] were going straight on through the valley, an Assyrian patrol met her 12and took her into custody. They asked her, "To what people do you belong, and where are you coming from, and where are you going?" She replied, "I am a daughter of the Hebrews, but I am fleeing from them, for they are about to be handed over to you to be devoured. 13I am on my way to see Holofernes the commander of your army, to give him a true report; I will show him a way by which he can go and capture all the hill country without losing one of his men, captured or slain."

---

a Gk *she*　b Other ancient authorities add *and cheese*
c Gk *they*

14 When the men heard her words, and observed her face—she was in their eyes marvelously beautiful—they said to her, 15 "You have saved your life by hurrying down to see our lord. Go at once to his tent; some of us will escort you and hand you over to him. 16 When you stand before him, have no fear in your heart, but tell him what you have just said, and he will treat you well."

17 They chose from their number a hundred men to accompany her and her maid, and they brought them to the tent of Holofernes. 18 There was great excitement in the whole camp, for her arrival was reported from tent to tent. They came and gathered around her as she stood outside the tent of Holofernes, waiting until they told him about her. 19 They marveled at her beauty and admired the Israelites, judging them by her. They said to one another, "Who can despise these people, who have women like this among them? It is not wise to leave one of their men alive, for if we let them go they will be able to beguile the whole world!"

20 Then the guards of Holofernes and all his servants came out and led her into the tent. 21 Holofernes was resting on his bed under a canopy that was woven with purple and gold, emeralds and other precious stones. 22 When they told him of her, he came to the front of the tent, with silver lamps carried before him. 23 When Judith came into the presence of Holofernes[a] and his servants, they all marveled at the beauty of her face. She prostrated herself and did obeisance to him, but his slaves raised her up.

10.11–23: Judith impresses the guards, and is taken to Holofernes. 13: Judith, like Achior, says that she will give a *true report*, but unlike Achior, she will actually use deceit. However, the words that follow are partly true, and are very similar to what Achior said in ch. 5. 15–16: Here and elsewhere, the references to Holofernes or Nebuchadnezzar as *lord* can also be understood as referring to God, often in a humorous way. The benevolent protection of *our lord*, for instance, is more appropriately said of God than of Holofernes. 20–22: Holofernes' tent is marked by the luxury of a palace.

11 Then Holofernes said to her, "Take courage, woman, and do not be afraid in your heart, for I have never hurt anyone who chose to serve Nebuchadnezzar, king of all the earth. 2 Even now, if your people who live in the hill country had not slighted me, I would never have lifted my spear against them. They have brought this on themselves. 3 But now tell me why you have fled from them and have come over to us. In any event, you have come to safety. Take courage! You will live tonight and ever after. 4 No one will hurt you. Rather, all will treat you well, as they do the servants of my lord King Nebuchadnezzar."

5 Judith answered him, "Accept the words of your slave, and let your servant speak in your presence. I will say nothing false to my lord this night. 6 If you follow out the words of your servant, God will accomplish something through you, and my lord will not fail to achieve his purposes. 7 By the life of Nebuchadnezzar, king of the whole earth, and by the power of him who has sent you to direct every living being! Not only do human beings serve him because of you, but also the animals of the field and the cattle and the birds of the air will live, because of your power, under Nebuchadnezzar and all his house. 8 For we have heard of your wisdom and skill, and it is reported throughout the whole world that you alone are the best in the whole kingdom, the most informed and the most astounding in military strategy.

9 "Now as for Achior's speech in your council, we have heard his words, for the people of Bethulia spared him and he told them all he had said to you. 10 Therefore, lord and master, do not disregard what he said, but keep it in your mind, for it is true. Indeed our nation cannot be punished, nor can the sword prevail against them, unless they sin against their God.

11 "But now, in order that my lord may not be defeated and his purpose frustrated, death will fall upon them, for a sin has overtaken them by which they are about to pro-

---

a Gk *him*

voke their God to anger when they do what is wrong. 12Since their food supply is exhausted and their water has almost given out, they have planned to kill their livestock and have determined to use all that God by his laws has forbidden them to eat. 13They have decided to consume the first fruits of the grain and the tithes of the wine and oil, which they had consecrated and set aside for the priests who minister in the presence of our God in Jerusalem—things it is not lawful for any of the people even to touch with their hands. 14Since even the people in Jerusalem have been doing this, they have sent messengers there in order to bring back permission from the council of the elders. 15When the response reaches them and they act upon it, on that very day they will be handed over to you to be destroyed.

16 "So when I, your slave, learned all this, I fled from them. God has sent me to accomplish with you things that will astonish the whole world wherever people shall hear about them. 17Your servant is indeed God-fearing and serves the God of heaven night and day. So, my lord, I will remain with you; but every night your servant will go out into the valley and pray to God. He will tell me when they have committed their sins. 18Then I will come and tell you, so that you may go out with your whole army, and not one of them will be able to withstand you. 19Then I will lead you through Judea, until you come to Jerusalem; there I will set your throne.ᵃ You will drive them like sheep that have no shepherd, and no dog will so much as growl at you. For this was told me to give me foreknowledge; it was announced to me, and I was sent to tell you."

20 Her words pleased Holofernes and all his servants. They marveled at her wisdom and said, 21"No other woman from one end of the earth to the other looks so beautiful or speaks so wisely!" 22Then Holofernes said to her, "God has done well to send you ahead of the people, to strengthen our hands and bring destruction on those who have despised my lord. 23You are not only beautiful in appearance, but wise in speech. If you do as you have said, your God shall be my God, and you shall live in the palace of King Neb-

uchadnezzar and be renowned throughout the whole world."

11.1–23: Judith's dialogue with Holofernes. 5–8: Judith tells half-truths here by flattering the man she despises (see comment on 9.10). There is also a double meaning in Judith's words (vv. 6, 16). **11–19:** Although it is preposterous that Holofernes would have believed her story, in the world of the narrative* it becomes believable. **19:** Judith's words here are a clever combination of "whole truth" and "deceit"; she will indeed *lead* him *through Judea . . . to Jerusalem,* and *no dog will . . . growl* at him, but it will be because he is dead. **22:** Another double meaning.

12 Then he commanded them to bring her in where his silver dinnerware was kept, and ordered them to set a table for her with some of his own delicacies, and with some of his own wine to drink. 2But Judith said, "I cannot partake of them, or it will be an offense; but I will have enough with the things I brought with me." 3Holofernes said to her, "If your supply runs out, where can we get you more of the same? For none of your people are here with us." 4Judith replied, "As surely as you live, my lord, your servant will not use up the supplies I have with me before the Lord carries out by my hand what he has determined."

5 Then the servants of Holofernes brought her into the tent, and she slept until midnight. Toward the morning watch she got up 6and sent this message to Holofernes: "Let my lord now give orders to allow your servant to go out and pray." 7So Holofernes commanded his guards not to hinder her. She remained in the camp three days. She went out each night to the valley of Bethulia, and bathed at the spring in the camp.ᵇ 8After bathing, she prayed the Lord God of Israel to direct her way for the triumph of hisᶜ people. 9Then she returned purified and stayed in the tent until she ate her food toward evening.

12.1–9: Judith establishes a daily schedule of withdrawal and prayer. Judith has carefully plotted her

ᵃ Or *chariot* ᵇ Other ancient authorities lack *in the camp* ᶜ Other ancient authorities read *her* activities. She has her own food in a pouch and has arranged that early each morning she will go out with her maid to pray. **4:** Judith uses irony* and half-truths in a humorous way (see comment on 9.10). **7–9:** Her *bathing* has the effect of a cleansing ritual. At about the time that Judith was written, the "mikveh" (ritual bath) was becoming more popular among Jews.

10 On the fourth day Holofernes held a banquet for his personal attendants only, and did not invite any of his officers. 11He said to Bagoas, the eunuch who had charge of his personal affairs, "Go and persuade the Hebrew woman who is in your care to join us and to eat and drink with us. 12For it would be a disgrace if we let such a woman go without having intercourse with her. If we do not seduce her, she will laugh at us."

13 So Bagoas left the presence of Holofernes, and approached her and said, "Let this pretty girl not hesitate to come to my lord to be honored in his presence, and to enjoy drinking wine with us, and to become today like one of the Assyrian women who serve in the palace of Nebuchadnezzar." 14Judith replied, "Who am I to refuse my lord? Whatever pleases him I will do at once, and it will be a joy to me until the day of my death." 15So she proceeded to dress herself in all her woman's finery. Her maid went ahead and spread for her on the ground before Holofernes the lambskins she had received from Bagoas for her daily use in reclining.

16 Then Judith came in and lay down. Holofernes' heart was ravished with her and his passion was aroused, for he had been waiting for an opportunity to seduce her from the day he first saw her. 17So Holofernes said to her, "Have a drink and be merry with us!" 18Judith said, "I will gladly drink, my lord, because today is the greatest day in my whole life." 19Then she took what her maid had prepared and ate and drank before him. 20Holofernes was greatly pleased with her, and drank a great quantity of wine, much more than he had ever drunk in any one day since he was born.

12.10–20: Holofernes invites Judith to a banquet.
12–14: Holofernes' intentions with Judith are made

explicit: She is invited to become a courtesan. Judith appears to agree, but the audience knows that her words can be understood in two ways. Throughout, Judith manipulates Holofernes and controls him to her own ends. **16–20:** Presumably, it is because of Judith's suggestiveness in v. 18 that Holofernes drinks to excess in v. 20. It is ironic, then, that Holofernes thinks he will deceive her (v. 16).

13 When evening came, his slaves quickly withdrew. Bagoas closed the tent from outside and shut out the attendants from his master's presence. They went to bed, for they all were weary because the banquet had lasted so long. 2But Judith was left alone in the tent, with Holofernes stretched out on his bed, for he was dead drunk.

3 Now Judith had told her maid to stand outside the bedchamber and to wait for her to come out, as she did on the other days; for she said she would be going out for her prayers. She had said the same thing to Bagoas. 4So everyone went out, and no one, either small or great, was left in the bedchamber. Then Judith, standing beside his bed, said in her heart, "O Lord God of all might, look in this hour on the work of my hands for the exaltation of Jerusalem. 5Now indeed is the time to help your heritage and to carry out my design to destroy the enemies who have risen up against us."

6 She went up to the bedpost near Holofernes' head, and took down his sword that hung there. 7She came close to his bed, took hold of the hair of his head, and said, "Give me strength today, O Lord God of Israel!" 8Then she struck his neck twice with all her might, and cut off his head. 9Next she rolled his body off the bed and pulled down the canopy from the posts. Soon afterward she went out and gave Holofernes' head to her maid, 10who placed it in her food bag.

13.1–10a: Judith beheads Holofernes. The story has developed slowly until now, but this central scene is told in a few verses. The scene is reminiscent of Jael's execution of Sisera (Judg 4–5), but the villain here is more humorous and less tragic. Judith's prayer (vv. 4–5) is short and unsentimental. **9–10a:** Holofernes comes to an unheroic end: He has collapsed in a stupor on the bed where he had hoped to ravish Judith, and when he is beheaded, his body is rolled by her onto the floor, and his *head* is concealed in a *food bag.*

Then the two of them went out together, as they were accustomed to do for prayer. They passed through the camp, circled around the valley, and went up the mountain to Bethulia, and came to its gates. [11]From a distance Judith called out to the sentries at the gates, "Open, open the gate! God, our God, is with us, still showing his power in Israel and his strength against our enemies, as he has done today!"

12 When the people of her town heard her voice, they hurried down to the town gate and summoned the elders of the town. [13]They all ran together, both small and great, for it seemed unbelievable that she had returned. They opened the gate and welcomed them. Then they lit a fire to give light, and gathered around them. [14]Then she said to them with a loud voice, "Praise God, O praise him! Praise God, who has not withdrawn his mercy from the house of Israel, but has destroyed our enemies by my hand this very night!"

15 Then she pulled the head out of the bag and showed it to them, and said, "See here, the head of Holofernes, the commander of the Assyrian army, and here is the canopy beneath which he lay in his drunken stupor. The Lord has struck him down by the hand of a woman. [16]As the Lord lives, who has protected me in the way I went, I swear that it was my face that seduced him to his destruction, and that he committed no sin with me, to defile and shame me."

17 All the people were greatly astonished. They bowed down and worshiped God, and said with one accord, "Blessed are you our God, who have this day humiliated the enemies of your people."

18 Then Uzziah said to her, "O daughter, you are blessed by the Most High God above all other women on earth; and blessed be the Lord God, who created the heavens and the earth, who has guided you to cut off the head of the leader of our enemies. [19]Your praise[a] will never depart from the hearts of those who remember the power of God. [20]May God grant this to be a perpetual honor to you, and may he reward you with blessings, because you risked your own life when our nation was brought low, and you averted our ruin, walking in the straight path before our God." And all the people said, "Amen. Amen."

13.10b–20: Judith and her maid return to Bethulia. All the earlier plans now find their completion: Judith and her maid can proceed out of the camp unhindered, just as they have every morning. **15:** When Judas Maccabeus defeated Nicanor in 161 BCE, he exhibited the head and arm of Nicanor in Jerusalem (1 Macc 7.47–49; 2 Macc 15.30–36). This also resulted in a celebration (Jdt 15.8–16.25). **18–20:** Uzziah's blessing of Judith is like Deborah's blessing of Jael (Judg 5.24) and Melchizedek's blessing of Abraham (Gen 14.19–20). It is further noted that the memory of Judith's deed will live on as a *perpetual honor.*

14 Then Judith said to them, "Listen to me, my friends. Take this head and hang it upon the parapet of your wall. [2]As soon as day breaks and the sun rises on the earth, each of you take up your weapons, and let every able-bodied man go out of the town; set a captain over them, as if you were going down to the plain against the Assyrian outpost; only do not go down. [3]Then they will seize their arms and go into the camp and rouse the officers of the Assyrian army. They will rush into the tent of Holofernes and will not find him. Then panic will come over them, and they will flee before you. [4]Then you and all who live within the borders of Israel will pursue them and cut them down in their tracks. [5]But before you do all this, bring Achior the Ammonite to me so that he may see and recognize the man who despised the house of Israel and sent him to us as if to his death."

6 So they summoned Achior from the house of Uzziah. When he came and saw the head of Holofernes in the hand of one of the men in the assembly of the people, he fell down on his face in a faint. [7]When they

a Other ancient authorities read *hope*

raised him up he threw himself at Judith's feet, and did obeisance to her, and said, "Blessed are you in every tent of Judah! In every nation those who hear your name will be alarmed. 8 Now tell me what you have done during these days."

So Judith told him in the presence of the people all that she had done, from the day she left until the moment she began speaking to them. 9 When she had finished, the people raised a great shout and made a joyful noise in their town. 10 When Achior saw all that the God of Israel had done, he believed firmly in God. So he was circumcised, and joined the house of Israel, remaining so to this day.

11 As soon as it was dawn they hung the head of Holofernes on the wall. Then they all took their weapons, and they went out in companies to the mountain passes. 12 When the Assyrians saw them they sent word to their commanders, who then went to the generals and the captains and to all their other officers. 13 They came to Holofernes' tent and said to the steward in charge of all his personal affairs, "Wake up our lord, for the slaves have been so bold as to come down against us to give battle, to their utter destruction."

14 So Bagoas went in and knocked at the entry of the tent, for he supposed that he was sleeping with Judith. 15 But when no one answered, he opened it and went into the bedchamber and found him sprawled on the floor dead, with his head missing. 16 He cried out with a loud voice and wept and groaned and shouted, and tore his clothes. 17 Then he went to the tent where Judith had stayed, and when he did not find her, he rushed out to the people and shouted, 18 "The slaves have tricked us! One Hebrew woman has brought disgrace on the house of King Nebuchadnezzar. Look, Holofernes is lying on the ground, and his head is missing!"

19 When the leaders of the Assyrian army heard this, they tore their tunics and were greatly dismayed, and their loud cries and shouts rose up throughout the camp.

14.1–19: Judith initiates a military victory over the Assyrian forces. 13–19: The Assyrians at first con-

temptuously refer to the Israelites as *slaves*, and the term is repeated in surprise when they find Holofernes dead (v. 18). This emphasizes the irony* and humor of the situation, as the "slaves" have outsmarted the mighty Assyrians.

15 When the men in the tents heard it, they were amazed at what had happened. 2 Overcome with fear and trembling, they did not wait for one another, but with one impulse all rushed out and fled by every path across the plain and through the hill country. 3 Those who had camped in the hills around Bethulia also took to flight. Then the Israelites, everyone that was a soldier, rushed out upon them. 4 Uzziah sent men to Betomasthaim*a* and Choba and Kola, and to all the frontiers of Israel, to tell what had taken place and to urge all to rush out upon the enemy to destroy them. 5 When the Israelites heard it, with one accord they fell upon the enemy,*b* and cut them down as far as Choba. Those in Jerusalem and all the hill country also came, for they were told what had happened in the camp of the enemy. The men in Gilead and in Galilee outflanked them with great slaughter, even beyond Damascus and its borders. 6 The rest of the people of Bethulia fell upon the Assyrian camp and plundered it, acquiring great riches. 7 And the Israelites, when they returned from the slaughter, took possession of what remained. Even the villages and towns in the hill country and in the plain got a great amount of booty, since there was a vast quantity of it.

15.1–7: The Assyrians, in mortal fear, are put to flight. Once again, the story of Judith requires the willful suspension of disbelief. The pattern of the narrative,* however, is similar to that found in the Zion* psalms, such as Ps 48: The nations attack Jerusalem (Ps 48.4); God strikes the nations with panic (48.5–7); Jerusalem is delivered (48.8–11); victory is celebrated (48.12–14). 5–7: The revenge and taking of *booty* are paralleled in Esth 9.1–19 and in the concept of the ban* or holy war* in ancient Israel (Deut 20.10–18).

---

a Other ancient authorities add *and Bebai*   *b* Gk *them*

8 Then the high priest Joakim and the elders of the Israelites who lived in Jerusalem came to witness the good things that the Lord had done for Israel, and to see Judith and to wish her well. 9When they met her, they all blessed her with one accord and said to her, "You are the glory of Jerusalem, you are the great boast of Israel, you are the great pride of our nation! 10You have done all this with your own hand; you have done great good to Israel, and God is well pleased with it. May the Almighty Lord bless you forever!" And all the people said, "Amen."

11 All the people plundered the camp for thirty days. They gave Judith the tent of Holofernes and all his silver dinnerware, his beds, his bowls, and all his furniture. She took them and loaded her mules and hitched up her carts and piled the things on them.

12 All the women of Israel gathered to see her, and blessed her, and some of them performed a dance in her honor. She took ivy-wreathed wands in her hands and distributed them to the women who were with her; 13and she and those who were with her crowned themselves with olive wreaths. She went before all the people in the dance, leading all the women, while all the men of Israel followed, bearing their arms and wearing garlands and singing hymns.

15.8–13: The people celebrate. 12–13: It was customary for *women* to *dance* as they sang the victory songs (Ex 15.20–21; 1 Sam 18.6–7).

14 Judith began this thanksgiving before all Israel, and all the people loudly sang this song of praise. 1And Judith said,

16 Begin a song to my God with tambourines,
sing to my Lord with cymbals.
Raise to him a new psalm;[a]
exalt him, and call upon his name.
2 For the Lord is a God who crushes wars;
he sets up his camp among his people;
he delivered me from the hands of my pursuers.
3 The Assyrian came down from the mountains of the north;

he came with myriads of his warriors;
their numbers blocked up the wadis,
and their cavalry covered the hills.
4 He boasted that he would burn up my territory,
and kill my young men with the sword,
and dash my infants to the ground,
and seize my children as booty,
and take my virgins as spoil.
5 But the Lord Almighty has foiled them
by the hand of a woman.[b]
6 For their mighty one did not fall by the hands of the young men,
nor did the sons of the Titans strike him down,
nor did tall giants set upon him;
but Judith daughter of Merari
with the beauty of her countenance
undid him.

7 For she put away her widow's clothing
to exalt the oppressed in Israel.
She anointed her face with perfume;
8 she fastened her hair with a tiara
and put on a linen gown to beguile him.
9 Her sandal ravished his eyes,
her beauty captivated his mind,
and the sword severed his neck!
10 The Persians trembled at her boldness,
the Medes were daunted at her daring.

11 Then my oppressed people shouted;
my weak people cried out,[c] and the enemy[d] trembled;
they lifted up their voices, and the enemy[d] were turned back.
12 Sons of slave-girls pierced them through
and wounded them like the children of fugitives;
they perished before the army of my Lord.

---

a Other ancient authorities read *a psalm and praise*
b Other ancient authorities add *he has confounded them*
c Other ancient authorities read *feared*   d Gk *they*

13 I will sing to my God a new song:
     O Lord, you are great and glorious,
        wonderful in strength, invincible.
14 Let all your creatures serve you,
        for you spoke, and they were made.
     You sent forth your spirit,[a] and it
        formed them;[b]
        there is none that can resist your
           voice.
15 For the mountains shall be shaken to
        their foundations with the
        waters;
     before your glance the rocks shall
        melt like wax.
     But to those who fear you
        you show mercy.
16 For every sacrifice as a fragrant offering
        is a small thing,
     and the fat of all whole burnt
        offerings to you is a very little
        thing;
     but whoever fears the Lord is great
        forever.
17 Woe to the nations that rise up against
        my people!
     The Lord Almighty will take
        vengeance on them in the day of
        judgment;
     he will send fire and worms into their
        flesh;
     they shall weep in pain forever.

15.14–16.17: Judith's victory song. Compare the
hymn of praise found near the end of Tobit. Judith's
song is similar to the victory song of Moses at Ex 15
and of Deborah at Judg 5.

18 When they arrived at Jerusalem, they
worshiped God. As soon as the people were
purified, they offered their burnt offerings,
their freewill offerings, and their gifts. [19]Ju-
dith also dedicated to God all the possessions of Holofernes, which the people had
given her; and the canopy that she had taken
for herself from his bedchamber she gave as
a votive offering. [20]For three months the
people continued feasting in Jerusalem before the sanctuary, and Judith remained with
them.

21 After this they all returned home to
their own inheritances. Judith went to Bethulia, and remained on her estate. For the
rest of her life she was honored throughout
the whole country. [22]Many desired to marry
her, but she gave herself to no man all the
days of her life after her husband Manasseh
died and was gathered to his people. [23]She
became more and more famous, and grew
old in her husband's house, reaching the age
of one hundred five. She set her maid free.
She died in Bethulia, and they buried her in
the cave of her husband Manasseh; [24]and
the house of Israel mourned her for seven
days. Before she died she distributed her
property to all those who were next of kin to
her husband Manasseh, and to her own
nearest kindred. [25]No one ever again spread
terror among the Israelites during the lifetime of Judith, or for a long time after her
death.

16.18–25: Conclusion. 21–25: Typically, the hero or
heroine of legend* does not rejoin society; so also Judith withdraws to *her estate, frees* her *maid,* and dispenses her wealth. Her courage protects the *Israelites*
long *after her death.*

---

a Or breath   b Other ancient authorities read *they
were created*

Note. The deuterocanonical portions of the Book of Esther are several additional passages found in the Greek translation of the Hebrew Book of Esther, a translation that differs also in other respects from the Hebrew text (the latter is translated in the NRSV Old Testament). The disordered chapter numbers come from the displacement of the additions to the end of the canonical Book of Esther by Jerome in his Latin translation and from the subsequent division of the Bible into chapters by Stephen Langton, who numbered the additions consecutively as though they formed a direct continuation of the Hebrew text. So that the additions may be read in their proper context, the whole of the Greek version is here translated, though certain familiar names are given according to their Hebrew rather than their Greek form; for example, Mordecai and Vashti instead of Mardocheus and Astin. The order followed is that of the Greek text, but the chapter and verse numbers conform to those of the King James or Authorized Version. The additions, conveniently indicated by the letters A–F, are located as follows: A, before 1.1; B, after 3.13; C and D, after 4.17; E, after 8.12; F, after 10.3.

ESTHER (The Greek Version Containing the Additional Chapters)

Introduction

Of the three known versions of the book of Esther, the Septuagint★ (or Greek version) is the longest. Accepted as canon★ by Roman Catholics and Orthodox Christians, it differs in several ways from the Hebrew version (the Masoretic text★): It includes pious prayers and the contents of edicts; the names of the characters appear in the original language in their Greek forms (Mardocheus for Hebrew Mordecai; Astin for Hebrew Vasthi; Artaxerxes for Hebrew Ahasuerus; and different names for the eunuchs); and there are occasional internal differences. Earlier scholarship believed a Greek translator working from the Masoretic text added this material to make the text more explicitly religious, since the Hebrew version does not mention the name of God. More recent theories, however, suggest that the Septuagint may preserve an equally old alternative version of the book. In either case, a comparison of the Hebrew and Greek versions offers a glimpse of different writers and different religious communities.

The colophon★ (an inscription detailing authorship) that closes the book places it in the Hellenistic★ period, when the Jewish people struggled to maintain their identity in a world increasingly influenced by Greek culture. Not surprisingly, then, Greek Esther addresses the issue of Jewish identity more directly than does the Hebrew: Esther keeps God's laws (2.20); the Persians who align themselves with the Jews become circumcised (8.17); and the king calls Jewish laws "righteous" (16.15). As in other narratives★ of the Apocrypha★ and deuterocanonical books★ (Tobit, Susanna, Judith), characters are exemplary role models.

READING GUIDE

Readers are well served by first reading Hebrew Esther and then considering the differing details and flavor of the Greek. In this way, the effect of the additions becomes evident: The prophecy and fulfillment scheme that frames the book (Additions A and F) shows God as directing events; the texts of the king's edicts (Additions B and E) portray him as religious and powerful; the prayers of Mordecai and Esther (Addition C) establish their motives as religious; and the expanded drama in Esther's encounter with the king (Addition D) underscores her bravery and cunning.

ADDITION A

11 *a* 2In the second year of the reign of Artaxerxes the Great, on the first day of Nisan, Mordecai son of Jair son of Shimei*b* son of Kish, of the tribe of Benjamin, had a dream. 3He was a Jew living in the city of Susa, a great man, serving in the court of the king. 4He was one of the captives whom King Nebuchadnezzar of Babylon had brought from Jerusalem with King Jeconiah of Judea. And this was his dream: 5Noises*c* and confusion, thunders and earthquake, tumult on the earth! 6Then two great dragons came forward, both ready to fight, and they roared terribly. 7At their roaring every nation prepared for war, to fight against the righteous nation. 8It was a day of darkness and gloom, of tribulation and distress, affliction and great tumult on the earth! 9And the whole righteous nation was troubled; they feared the evils that threatened them,*d* and were ready to perish. 10Then they cried out to God; and at their outcry, as though from a tiny spring, there came a great river, with abundant water; 11light came, and the sun rose, and the lowly were exalted and devoured those held in honor.

12 Mordecai saw in this dream what God had determined to do, and after he awoke he had it on his mind, seeking all day to understand it in every detail.

11.2–12: Mordecai's dream. Greek Esther opens a year before the Hebrew with more focus on *Mordecai* as hero of the tale. **3:** Mordecai's official connection to the royal *court* is lacking in Hebrew. **4:** The Greek makes clear that Mordecai, not his ancestor Kish, was taken into captivity by the Babylonians; living several generations after the Babylonian destruction, he would have been a very old man. **5:** Similar in style to Dan 7–14, the vision reveals that events to come follow God's plan. **6:** As explained at the end of the book,

the *two great dragons* are Mordecai and Haman. **10:** The *tiny spring* turning to a *great river* is Esther. **12:** Unlike in the Hebrew, *God* is explicitly and frequently mentioned.

12 Now Mordecai took his rest in the courtyard with Gabatha and Tharra, the two eunuchs of the king who kept watch in the courtyard. 2He overheard their conversation and inquired into their purposes, and learned that they were preparing to lay hands on King Artaxerxes; and he informed the king concerning them. 3Then the king examined the two eunuchs, and after they had confessed it, they were led away to execution. 4The king made a permanent record of these things, and Mordecai wrote an account of them. 5And the king ordered Mordecai to serve in the court, and rewarded him for these things. 6But Haman son of Hammedatha, a Bougean, who was in great honor with the king, determined to injure Mordecai and his people because of the two eunuchs of the king.

END OF ADDITION A

12.1–6: A plot against the king. In contrast to the plot described in 2.21–23, *Mordecai* rather than Esther *informs the king* and is *rewarded* immediately. By linking *Haman's* hatred of Mordecai to the plot of the *eunuchs,* this addition portrays Haman as an enemy of the state; it also changes the chronology of the Hebrew, with Mordecai proving his loyalty before Esther is made queen. In 16.10 called a Macedonian and in Hebrew an Agagite, Haman is here called a *Bougean,* meaning unclear.

1 It was after this that the following things happened in the days of Artaxerxes, the

a Chapters 11.2—12.6 correspond to chapter A 1–17 in some translations.   *b* Gk *Semeios*   *c* Or *Voices*
d Gk *their own evils*

same Artaxerxes who ruled over one hundred twenty-seven provinces from India to Ethiopia.*a* 2In those days, when King Artaxerxes was enthroned in the city of Susa, 3in the third year of his reign, he gave a banquet for his Friends and other persons of various nations, the Persians and Median nobles, and the governors of the provinces. 4After this, when he had displayed to them the riches of his kingdom and the splendor of his bountiful celebration during the course of one hundred eighty days, 5at the end of the festivity*b* the king gave a drinking party for the people of various nations who lived in the city. This was held for six days in the courtyard of the royal palace, 6which was adorned with curtains of fine linen and cotton, held by cords of purple linen attached to gold and silver blocks on pillars of marble and other stones. Gold and silver couches were placed on a mosaic floor of emerald, mother-of-pearl, and marble. There were coverings of gauze, embroidered in various colors, with roses arranged around them. 7The cups were of gold and silver, and a miniature cup was displayed, made of ruby, worth thirty thousand talents. There was abundant sweet wine, such as the king himself drank. 8The drinking was not according to a fixed rule; but the king wished to have it so, and he commanded his stewards to comply with his pleasure and with that of the guests.

9 Meanwhile, Queen Vashti*c* gave a drinking party for the women in the palace where King Artaxerxes was.

1.1–9: Artaxerxes' banquet. The finery of the court is expanded beyond its Hebrew version. **8:** *Not according to a fixed rule:* The banquet is not normal custom but the initiative of the king.

10 On the seventh day, when the king was in good humor, he told Haman, Bazan, Tharra, Boraze, Zatholtha, Abataza, and Tharaba, the seven eunuchs who served King Artaxerxes, 11to escort the queen to him in order to proclaim her as queen and to place the diadem on her head, and to have her display her beauty to all the governors and the people of various nations, for she was indeed a beautiful woman. 12But Queen

Vashti*c* refused to obey him and would not come with the eunuchs. This offended the king and he became furious. 13He said to his Friends, "This is how Vashti*c* has answered me.*d* Give therefore your ruling and judgment on this matter." 14Arkesaeus, Sarsathaeus, and Malesear, then the governors of the Persians and Medes who were closest to the king—Arkesaeus, Sarsathaeus, and Malesear, who sat beside him in the chief seats—came to him 15and told him what must be done to Queen Vashti*c* for not obeying the order that the king had sent her by the eunuchs. 16Then Muchaeus said to the king and the governors, "Queen Vashti*c* has insulted not only the king but also all the king's governors and officials" 17(for he had reported to them what the queen had said and how she had defied the king). "And just as she defied King Artaxerxes, 18so now the other ladies who are wives of the Persian and Median governors, on hearing what she has said to the king, will likewise dare to insult their husbands. 19If therefore it pleases the king, let him issue a royal decree, inscribed in accordance with the laws of the Medes and Persians so that it may not be altered, that the queen may no longer come into his presence; but let the king give her royal rank to a woman better than she. 20Let whatever law the king enacts be proclaimed in his kingdom, and thus all women will give honor to their husbands, rich and poor alike." 21This speech pleased the king and the governors, and the king did as Muchaeus had recommended. 22The king sent the decree into all his kingdom, to every province in its own language, so that in every house respect would be shown to every husband.

1.10–22: Vashti's dismissal. Here, *Haman* is identified as one of the *eunuchs.* **11:** While in the Hebrew the king wishes to display Vashti's beauty, here he seeks to *proclaim her queen;* the change makes his request less objectionable. **22:** *Respect . . . shown to every husband* is softer than the Hebrew: "Every man should be master in his own house."

---

a Other ancient authorities lack *to Ethiopia*   *b* Gk *marriage feast*   *c* Gk *Astin*   *d* Gk *Astin has said thus and so*

2 After these things, the king's anger abated, and he no longer was concerned about Vashti[a] or remembered what he had said and how he had condemned her. [2]Then the king's servants said, "Let beautiful and virtuous girls be sought out for the king. [3]The king shall appoint officers in all the provinces of his kingdom, and they shall select beautiful young virgins to be brought to the harem in Susa, the capital. Let them be entrusted to the king's eunuch who is in charge of the women, and let ointments and whatever else they need be given them. [4]And the woman who pleases the king shall be queen instead of Vashti."[a] This pleased the king, and he did so.

[5] Now there was a Jew in Susa the capital whose name was Mordecai son of Jair son of Shimei[b] son of Kish, of the tribe of Benjamin; [6]he had been taken captive from Jerusalem among those whom King Nebuchadnezzar of Babylon had captured. [7]And he had a foster child, the daughter of his father's brother, Aminadab, and her name was Esther. When her parents died, he brought her up to womanhood as his own. The girl was beautiful in appearance. [8]So, when the decree of the king was proclaimed, and many girls were gathered in Susa the capital in custody of Gai, Esther also was brought to Gai, who had custody of the women. [9]The girl pleased him and won his favor, and he quickly provided her with ointments and her portion of food,[c] as well as seven maids chosen from the palace; he treated her and her maids with special favor in the harem. [10]Now Esther had not disclosed her people or country, for Mordecai had commanded her not to make it known. [11]And every day Mordecai walked in the courtyard of the harem, to see what would happen to Esther.

[12] Now the period after which a girl was to go to the king was twelve months. During this time the days of beautification are completed—six months while they are anointing themselves with oil of myrrh, and six months with spices and ointments for women. [13]Then she goes in to the king; she is handed to the person appointed, and goes with him from the harem to the king's palace. [14]In the evening she enters and in the morning she departs to the second harem, where Gai the king's eunuch is in charge of the women; and she does not go in to the king again unless she is summoned by name.

[15] When the time was fulfilled for Esther daughter of Aminadab, the brother of Mordecai's father, to go in to the king, she neglected none of the things that Gai, the eunuch in charge of the women, had commanded. Now Esther found favor in the eyes of all who saw her. [16]So Esther went in to King Artaxerxes in the twelfth month, which is Adar, in the seventh year of his reign. [17]And the king loved Esther and she found favor beyond all the other virgins, so he put on her the queen's diadem. [18]Then the king gave a banquet lasting seven days for all his Friends and the officers to celebrate his marriage to Esther; and he granted a remission of taxes to those who were under his rule.

2.1–18: Esther becomes queen. The king's forgetting of Vashti (unlike his "remembering" her in the Hebrew) sparks the search for a new queen. **5:** *Mordecai* is introduced again, suggesting that 11.2–12 is a later addition to the book. **16:** While in Hebrew Esther's turn was in the month of Tebeth, here the month is *Adar* (the same on which the lot will fall). **18:** *The remission of taxes* indicates the king's good mood.

---

[19] Meanwhile Mordecai was serving in the courtyard. [20]Esther had not disclosed her country—such were the instructions of Mordecai; but she was to fear God and keep his laws, just as she had done when she was with him. So Esther did not change her mode of life.

[21] Now the king's eunuchs, who were chief bodyguards, were angry because of Mordecai's advancement, and they plotted to kill King Artaxerxes. [22]The matter became known to Mordecai, and he warned Esther, who in turn revealed the plot to the king. [23]He investigated the two eunuchs and hanged them. Then the king ordered a memorandum to be deposited in the royal library in praise of the goodwill shown by Mordecai.

a Gk *Astin*   *b* Gk *Semeios*   *c* Gk lacks *of food*

2.19–23: A second plot. 20: *Did not change her mode of life:* The clear statement that *Esther keeps* Jewish *law* is in keeping with the Greek version's religious theme. In this second plot (see 2.1–6), Mordecai sends word through Esther.

3 After these events King Artaxerxes promoted Haman son of Hammedatha, a Bougean, advancing him and granting him precedence over all the king's*a* Friends. [2] So all who were at court used to do obeisance to Haman,*b* for so the king had commanded to be done. Mordecai, however, did not do obeisance. [3] Then the king's courtiers said to Mordecai, "Mordecai, why do you disobey the king's command?" [4] Day after day they spoke to him, but he would not listen to them. Then they informed Haman that Mordecai was resisting the king's command. Mordecai had told them that he was a Jew. [5] So when Haman learned that Mordecai was not doing obeisance to him, he became furiously angry, [6] and plotted to destroy all the Jews under Artaxerxes' rule.

[7] In the twelfth year of King Artaxerxes Haman*c* came to a decision by casting lots, taking the days and the months one by one, to fix on one day to destroy the whole race of Mordecai. The lot fell on the fourteenth*d* day of the month of Adar.

[8] Then Haman*c* said to King Artaxerxes, "There is a certain nation scattered among the other nations in all your kingdom; their laws are different from those of every other nation, and they do not keep the laws of the king. It is not expedient for the king to tolerate them. [9] If it pleases the king, let it be decreed that they are to be destroyed, and I will pay ten thousand talents of silver into the king's treasury." [10] So the king took off his signet ring and gave it to Haman to seal the decree*e* that was to be written against the Jews. [11] The king told Haman, "Keep the money, and do whatever you want with that nation."

[12] So on the thirteenth day of the first month the king's secretaries were summoned, and in accordance with Haman's instructions they wrote in the name of King Artaxerxes to the magistrates and the governors in every province from India to Ethiopia. There were one hundred twenty-seven provinces in all, and the governors were addressed each in his own language. [13] Instructions were sent by couriers throughout all the empire of Artaxerxes to destroy the Jewish people on a given day of the twelfth month, which is Adar, and to plunder their goods.

3.1–13: Mordecai refuses to bow. 7: In Greek *the lot falls on 14th Adar;* in Hebrew, on 13th Adar. 8: *Their laws* likely refers to Mosaic law, seen by both Jews and gentiles* as a distinctive mark of Judaism.

ADDITION B

13 *f*This is a copy of the letter: "The Great King, Artaxerxes, writes the following to the governors of the hundred twenty-seven provinces from India to Ethiopia and to the officials under them:

[2] "Having become ruler of many nations and master of the whole world (not elated with presumption of authority but always acting reasonably and with kindness), I have determined to settle the lives of my subjects in lasting tranquility and, in order to make my kingdom peaceable and open to travel throughout all its extent, to restore the peace desired by all people.

[3] "When I asked my counselors how this might be accomplished, Haman—who excels among us in sound judgment, and is distinguished for his unchanging goodwill and steadfast fidelity, and has attained the second place in the kingdom— [4] pointed out to us that among all the nations in the world there is scattered a certain hostile people, who have laws contrary to those of every nation and continually disregard the ordinances of kings, so that the unifying of the kingdom that we honorably intend cannot be brought about. [5] We understand that this people, and it alone, stands constantly in opposition to every nation, perversely following a strange manner of life and laws, and is ill-disposed to our government, doing all the

a Gk *all his*   *b* Gk *him*   *c* Gk *he*   *d* Other ancient witnesses read *thirteenth;* see 8.12   *e* Gk lacks *the decree*   *f* Chapter 13.1–7 corresponds to chapter B 1–7 in some translations.

harm they can so that our kingdom may not attain stability.

6 "Therefore we have decreed that those indicated to you in the letters written by Haman, who is in charge of affairs and is our second father, shall all—wives and children included—be utterly destroyed by the swords of their enemies, without pity or restraint, on the fourteenth day of the twelfth month, Adar, of this present year, 7so that those who have long been hostile and remain so may in a single day go down in violence to Hades, and leave our government completely secure and untroubled hereafter."

 END OF ADDITION B

13.1–7: The king's letter. This addition portrays Artaxerxes as bombastic but less swayed by moods than in the Hebrew. The king desires peace, even if he lacks judgment about who is trustworthy. Here, he, not Haman, issues the *decree*. 5: *Strange manner of life and laws* may refer to the distinctive practices of the Torah,* including circumcision* and kosher* food laws. 7: *Hades,** the abode of the dead, is mentioned in Hellenistic* Jewish documents.

3 14Copies of the document were posted in every province, and all the nations were ordered to be prepared for that day. 15The matter was expedited also in Susa. And while the king and Haman caroused together, the city of Susa*a* was thrown into confusion.

4 When Mordecai learned of all that had been done, he tore his clothes, put on sackcloth, and sprinkled himself with ashes; then he rushed through the street of the city, shouting loudly: "An innocent nation is being destroyed!" 2He got as far as the king's gate, and there he stopped, because no one was allowed to enter the courtyard clothed in sackcloth and ashes. 3And in every province where the king's proclamation had been posted there was a loud cry of mourning and lamentation among the Jews, and they put on sackcloth and ashes. 4When the queen's*b* maids and eunuchs came and told her, she was deeply troubled by what she heard had happened, and sent some clothes to Mordecai to put on instead of sackcloth; but he would not consent. 5Then Esther sum-

moned Hachratheus, the eunuch who attended her, and ordered him to get accurate information for her from Mordecai.*c*

7 So Mordecai told him what had happened and how Haman had promised to pay ten thousand talents into the royal treasury to bring about the destruction of the Jews. 8He also gave him a copy of what had been posted in Susa for their destruction, to show to Esther; and he told him to charge her to go in to the king and plead for his favor in behalf of the people. "Remember," he said, "the days when you were an ordinary person, being brought up under my care—for Haman, who stands next to the king, has spoken against us and demands our death. Call upon the Lord; then speak to the king in our behalf, and save us from death."

9 Hachratheus went in and told Esther all these things. 10And she said to him, "Go to Mordecai and say, 11'All nations of the empire know that if any man or woman goes to the king inside the inner court without being called, there is no escape for that person. Only the one to whom the king stretches out the golden scepter is safe—and it is now thirty days since I was called to go to the king.'"

12 When Hachratheus delivered her entire message to Mordecai, 13Mordecai told him to go back and say to her, "Esther, do not say to yourself that you alone among all the Jews will escape alive. 14For if you keep quiet at such a time as this, help and protection will come to the Jews from another quarter, but you and your father's family will perish. Yet, who knows whether it was not for such a time as this that you were made queen?" 15Then Esther gave the messenger this answer to take back to Mordecai: 16"Go and gather all the Jews who are in Susa and fast on my behalf; for three days and nights do not eat or drink, and my maids and I will also go without food. After that I will go to the king, contrary to the law, even if I must die." 17So Mordecai went away and did what Esther had told him to do.

---

a Gk *the city*   *b* Gk *When her*   *c* Other ancient witnesses add *⁶So Hachratheus went out to Mordecai in the street of the city opposite the city gate.*

4.1–17: Mordecai seeks Esther's aid. Mordecai's plea is more dramatic than in the Hebrew: Here, he runs through the streets, and his words to Esther are recorded. **8:** Mordecai reminds Esther of her debt to him and advises her to *call on the Lord.*

ADDITION C

13 8 *a* Then Mordecai*b* prayed to the Lord, calling to remembrance all the works of the Lord.

9 He said, "O Lord, Lord, you rule as King over all things, for the universe is in your power and there is no one who can oppose you when it is your will to save Israel, 10for you have made heaven and earth and every wonderful thing under heaven. 11You are Lord of all, and there is no one who can resist you, the Lord. 12You know all things; you know, O Lord, that it was not in insolence or pride or for any love of glory that I did this, and refused to bow down to this proud Haman; 13for I would have been willing to kiss the soles of his feet to save Israel! 14But I did this so that I might not set human glory above the glory of God, and I will not bow down to anyone but you, who are my Lord; and I will not do these things in pride. 15And now, O Lord God and King, God of Abraham, spare your people; for the eyes of our foes are upon us*c* to annihilate us, and they desire to destroy the inheritance that has been yours from the beginning. 16Do not neglect your portion, which you redeemed for yourself out of the land of Egypt. 17Hear my prayer, and have mercy upon your inheritance; turn our mourning into feasting that we may live and sing praise to your name, O Lord; do not destroy the lips*d* of those who praise you."

18 And all Israel cried out mightily, for their death was before their eyes.

13.8–18: Mordecai's prayer. Not found in Hebrew, Mordecai's prayer with its frequent mention of God's name helps give the book a strong pious flavor. Mordecai explains his refusal: As a religious man, he does not bow to anyone (though others in the Hebrew Bible do, see 1 Sam 24.8). Similar to many psalms, the prayer alludes to the events of the Exodus and reminds

God that if the Jewish people perish there will be no one to offer divine praise.

14 Then Queen Esther, seized with deadly anxiety, fled to the Lord. 2She took off her splendid apparel and put on the garments of distress and mourning, and instead of costly perfumes she covered her head with ashes and dung, and she utterly humbled her body; every part that she loved to adorn she covered with her tangled hair. 3She prayed to the Lord God of Israel, and said: "O my Lord, you only are our king; help me, who am alone and have no helper but you, 4for my danger is in my hand. 5Ever since I was born I have heard in the tribe of my family that you, O Lord, took Israel out of all the nations, and our ancestors from among all their forebears, for an everlasting inheritance, and that you did for them all that you promised. 6And now we have sinned before you, and you have handed us over to our enemies 7because we glorified their gods. You are righteous, O Lord! 8And now they are not satisfied that we are in bitter slavery, but they have covenanted with their idols 9to abolish what your mouth has ordained, and to destroy your inheritance, to stop the mouths of those who praise you and to quench your altar and the glory of your house, 10to open the mouths of the nations for the praise of vain idols, and to magnify forever a mortal king.

11 "O Lord, do not surrender your scepter to what has no being; and do not let them laugh at our downfall; but turn their plan against them, and make an example of him who began this against us. 12Remember, O Lord; make yourself known in this time of our affliction, and give me courage, O King of the gods and Master of all dominion! 13Put eloquent speech in my mouth before the lion, and turn his heart to hate the man who is fighting against us, so that there may be an end of him and those who agree with him. 14But save us by your hand, and help me, who am alone and have no helper but

a Chapters 13.8—15.16 correspond to chapters C 1–30 and D 1–16 in some translations.   *b* Gk *he*
c Gk *for they are eying us*   *d* Gk *mouth*

you, O Lord. 15You have knowledge of all things, and you know that I hate the splendor of the wicked and abhor the bed of the uncircumcised and of any alien. 16You know my necessity—that I abhor the sign of my proud position, which is upon my head on days when I appear in public. I abhor it like a filthy rag, and I do not wear it on the days when I am at leisure. 17And your servant has not eaten at Haman's table, and I have not honored the king's feast or drunk the wine of libations. 18Your servant has had no joy since the day that I was brought here until now, except in you, O Lord God of Abraham. 19O God, whose might is over all, hear the voice of the despairing, and save us from the hands of evildoers. And save me from my fear!"

END OF ADDITION C

14.1–19: Esther's prayer. Dramatically humbling herself, Esther sets aside her role as queen. **6–10:** She attributes the Jews' present trouble to their worship of foreign gods, an idea shared with the deuteronomistic* history (Judges through Kings). Evil ones threaten the Temple* and insist on worship of a *mortal king,* a theme common to other Jewish literature of the period. **15–16:** *Abhor the bed:* In contrast to Esther's apparent acceptance of gentile* ways in Hebrew, in Greek, Esther is a pious Jewish woman, married to a gentile against her will. She takes no joy in royal trappings, even calling the crown a *filthy rag* (menstrual rag).

ADDITION D

15 On the third day, when she ended her prayer, she took off the garments in which she had worshiped, and arrayed herself in splendid attire. 2Then, majestically adorned, after invoking the aid of the all-seeing God and Savior, she took two maids with her; 3on one she leaned gently for support, 4while the other followed, carrying her train. 5She was radiant with perfect beauty, and she looked happy, as if beloved, but her heart was frozen with fear. 6When she had gone through all the doors, she stood before the king. He was seated on his royal throne, clothed in the full array of his majesty, all covered with gold and precious stones. He was most terrifying.

7 Lifting his face, flushed with splendor, he looked at her in fierce anger. The queen faltered, and turned pale and faint, and collapsed on the head of the maid who went in front of her. 8Then God changed the spirit of the king to gentleness, and in alarm he sprang from his throne and took her in his arms until she came to herself. He comforted her with soothing words, and said to her, 9"What is it, Esther? I am your husband.*a* Take courage; 10You shall not die, for our law applies only to our subjects.*b* Come near."

11 Then he raised the golden scepter and touched her neck with it; 12he embraced her, and said, "Speak to me." 13She said to him, "I saw you, my lord, like an angel of God, and my heart was shaken with fear at your glory. 14For you are wonderful, my lord, and your countenance is full of grace." 15And while she was speaking, she fainted and fell. 16Then the king was agitated, and all his servants tried to comfort her.

END OF ADDITION D

---

5 *e* 3The king said to her, "What do you wish, Esther? What is your request? It shall be given you, even to half of my kingdom." 4And Esther said, "Today is a special day for me. If it pleases the king, let him and Haman come to the dinner that I shall prepare today." 5Then the king said, "Bring Haman quickly, so that we may do as Esther desires." So they both came to the dinner that Esther had spoken about. 6While they were drinking wine, the king said to Esther, "What is it, Queen Esther? It shall be granted you." 7She said, "My petition and request is: 8if I have found favor in the sight of the king, let the king and Haman come to the dinner that I shall prepare them, and tomorrow I will do as I have done today."

15.1–5.8: Esther petitions the king. Esther is here more delicate than in Hebrew (leaning on two maids and fainting in fear), and God's presence is much more

---

a Gk *brother*   *b* Meaning of Gk uncertain
c In Greek, Chapter D replaces verses 1 and 2 in Hebrew.

9 So Haman went out from the king joyful and glad of heart. But when he saw Mordecai the Jew in the courtyard, he was filled with anger. [10]Nevertheless, he went home and summoned his friends and his wife Zosara. [11]And he told them about his riches and the honor that the king had bestowed on him, and how he had advanced him to be the first in the kingdom. [12]And Haman said, "The queen did not invite anyone to the dinner with the king except me; and I am invited again tomorrow. [13]But these things give me no pleasure as long as I see Mordecai the Jew in the courtyard." [14]His wife Zosara and his friends said to him, "Let a gallows be made, fifty cubits high, and in the morning tell the king to have Mordecai hanged on it. Then, go merrily with the king to the dinner." This advice pleased Haman, and so the gallows was prepared.

5.9–14: Haman's plot. Haman seeks to kill Mordecai immediately, unable to wait for the execution of the pogrom.*

6 That night the Lord took sleep from the king, so he gave orders to his secretary to bring the book of daily records, and to read to him. [2]He found the words written about Mordecai, how he had told the king about the two royal eunuchs who were on guard and sought to lay hands on King Artaxerxes. [3]The king said, "What honor or dignity did we bestow on Mordecai?" The king's servants said, "You have not done anything for him." [4]While the king was inquiring about the goodwill shown by Mordecai, Haman was in the courtyard. The king asked, "Who is in the courtyard?" Now Haman had come to speak to the king about hanging Mordecai on the gallows that he had prepared. [5]The servants of the king answered, "Haman is standing in the courtyard." And the king said, "Summon him." [6]Then the king said to Haman, "What shall I do for the person whom I wish to honor?" And Haman said to himself, "Whom would the king wish to honor more than me?" [7]So he said to the king, "For a person whom the king wishes to honor, [8]let the king's servants bring out the fine linen robe that the king has worn, and the horse on which the king rides, [9]and let both be given to one of the king's honored Friends, and let him robe the person whom the king loves and mount him on the horse, and let it be proclaimed through the open square of the city, saying, 'Thus shall it be done to everyone whom the king honors.'" [10]Then the king said to Haman, "You have made an excellent suggestion! Do just as you have said for Mordecai the Jew, who is on duty in the courtyard. And let nothing be omitted from what you have proposed." [11]So Haman got the robe and the horse; he put the robe on Mordecai and made him ride through the open square of the city, proclaiming, "Thus shall it be done to everyone whom the king wishes to honor." [12]Then Mordecai returned to the courtyard, and Haman hurried back to his house, mourning and with his head covered. [13]Haman told his wife Zosara and his friends what had befallen him. His friends and his wife said to him, "If Mordecai is of the Jewish people, and you have begun to be humiliated before him, you will surely fall. You will not be able to defend yourself, because the living God is with him."

6.1–13: Mordecai rewarded. In Greek, the king's sleeplessness is God's doing. **2:** This entry was made after the second plot against the king (2.23). **10:** The king's reference to *Mordecai the Jew* suggests that he does not know against which people Haman drafted the edict. **13:** Haman's *wife* and *friends* already know that Mordecai is a Jew (see 5.13); this prediction is likely intended for the reader.

14 While they were still talking, the eunuchs arrived and hurriedly brought Haman to the banquet that Esther had prepared.

7 [1]So the king and Haman went in to drink with the queen. [2]And the second day, as they were drinking wine, the king said, "What is it, Queen Esther? What is your petition and what is your request? It shall be granted to you, even to half of my kingdom." [3]She answered and said, "If I have found favor with the king, let my life

be granted me at my petition, and my people at my request. ⁴For we have been sold, I and my people, to be destroyed, plundered, and made slaves—we and our children—male and female slaves. This has come to my knowledge. Our antagonist brings shame on[a] the king's court." ⁵Then the king said, "Who is the person that would dare to do this thing?" ⁶Esther said, "Our enemy is this evil man Haman!" At this, Haman was terrified in the presence of the king and queen.

6.14–7.6: Esther's banquet. 4: Enslavement is one of the threats the Jewish people face; in Hebrew, Esther tells the king that she would have kept silent had her people "merely" been made slaves. Esther strategically argues that the plot *brings shame on the king's court.*

7 The king rose from the banquet and went into the garden, and Haman began to beg for his life from the queen, for he saw that he was in serious trouble. ⁸When the king returned from the garden, Haman had thrown himself on the couch, pleading with the queen. The king said, "Will he dare even assault my wife in my own house?" Haman, when he heard, turned away his face. ⁹Then Bugathan, one of the eunuchs, said to the king, "Look, Haman has even prepared a gallows for Mordecai, who gave information of concern to the king; it is standing at Haman's house, a gallows fifty cubits high." So the king said, "Let Haman be hanged on that." ¹⁰So Haman was hanged on the gallows he had prepared for Mordecai. With that the anger of the king abated.

7.7–10: Haman punished. 8: *Turned away his face* may be an interpretation* of the difficult Hebrew reading "they covered his face." **10:** The king's *anger abated,* though the text does not indicate at what point he became angry. Haman's *hanging on the gallows* he intended for Mordecai is another of the book's frequent reversals.

8 On that very day King Artaxerxes granted to Esther all the property of the persecutor[b] Haman. Mordecai was summoned by the king, for Esther had told the king[c] that

he was related to her. ²The king took the ring that had been taken from Haman, and gave it to Mordecai; and Esther set Mordecai over everything that had been Haman's.

3 Then she spoke once again to the king and, falling at his feet, she asked him to avert all the evil that Haman had planned against the Jews. ⁴The king extended his golden scepter to Esther, and she rose and stood before the king. ⁵Esther said, "If it pleases you, and if I have found favor, let an order be sent rescinding the letters that Haman wrote and sent to destroy the Jews in your kingdom. ⁶How can I look on the ruin of my people? How can I be safe if my ancestral nation[d] is destroyed?" ⁷The king said to Esther, "Now that I[e] have granted all of Haman's property to you and have hanged him on a tree because he acted against the Jews, what else do you request? ⁸Write in my name what you think best and seal it with my ring; for whatever is written at the king's command and sealed with my ring cannot be contravened."

9 The secretaries were summoned on the twenty-third day of the first month, that is, Nisan, in the same year; and all that he commanded with respect to the Jews was given in writing to the administrators and governors of the provinces from India to Ethiopia, one hundred twenty-seven provinces, to each province in its own language. ¹⁰The edict was written[f] with the king's authority and sealed with his ring, and sent out by couriers. ¹¹He ordered the Jews in every city to observe their own laws, to defend themselves, and to act as they wished against their opponents and enemies ¹²on a certain day, the thirteenth of the twelfth month, which is Adar, throughout all the kingdom of Artaxerxes.

8.1–12: The king's new edict. In yet more reversals, Esther receives Haman's property; Mordecai assumes Haman's position; Persian law now benefits the people whom it formerly threatened; and Jews are ordered to observe the very laws that once made them suspect.

---

a Gk *is not worthy of*   b Gk *slanderer*   c Gk *him*
d Gk *country*   e Gk *If I*   f Gk *It was written*

ADDITION E

16^a The following is a copy of this letter:

"The Great King, Artaxerxes, to the governors of the provinces from India to Ethiopia, one hundred twenty-seven provinces, and to those who are loyal to our government, greetings.

2 "Many people, the more they are honored with the most generous kindness of their benefactors, the more proud do they become, 3 and not only seek to injure our subjects, but in their inability to stand prosperity, they even undertake to scheme against their own benefactors. 4 They not only take away thankfulness from others, but, carried away by the boasts of those who know nothing of goodness, they even assume that they will escape the evil-hating justice of God, who always sees everything. 5 And often many of those who are set in places of authority have been made in part responsible for the shedding of innocent blood, and have been involved in irremediable calamities, by the persuasion of friends who have been entrusted with the administration of public affairs, 6 when these persons by the false trickery of their evil natures beguile the sincere goodwill of their sovereigns.

7 "What has been wickedly accomplished through the pestilent behavior of those who exercise authority unworthily can be seen, not so much from the more ancient records that we hand on, as from investigation of matters close at hand.^b 8 In the future we will take care to render our kingdom quiet and peaceable for all, 9 by changing our methods and always judging what comes before our eyes with more equitable consideration. 10 For Haman son of Hammedatha, a Macedonian (really an alien to the Persian blood, and quite devoid of our kindliness), having become our guest, 11 enjoyed so fully the goodwill that we have for every nation that he was called our father and was continually bowed down to by all as the person second to the royal throne. 12 But, unable to restrain his arrogance, he undertook to deprive us of our kingdom and our life,^c 13 and with intricate craft and deceit asked for the destruction of Mordecai, our savior and per-petual benefactor, and of Esther, the blameless partner of our kingdom, together with their whole nation. 14 He thought that by these methods he would catch us undefended and would transfer the kingdom of the Persians to the Macedonians.

15 "But we find that the Jews, who were consigned to annihilation by this thrice-accursed man, are not evildoers, but are governed by most righteous laws 16 and are children of the living God, most high, most mighty,^d who has directed the kingdom both for us and for our ancestors in the most excellent order.

17 "You will therefore do well not to put in execution the letters sent by Haman son of Hammedatha, 18 since he, the one who did these things, has been hanged at the gate of Susa with all his household—for God, who rules over all things, has speedily inflicted on him the punishment that he deserved.

19 "Therefore post a copy of this letter publicly in every place, and permit the Jews to live under their own laws. 20 And give them reinforcements, so that on the thirteenth day of the twelfth month, Adar, on that very day, they may defend themselves against those who attack them at the time of oppression. 21 For God, who rules over all things, has made this day to be a joy for his chosen people instead of a day of destruction for them.

22 "Therefore you shall observe this with all good cheer as a notable day among your commemorative festivals, 23 so that both now and hereafter it may represent deliverance for you^e and the loyal Persians, but that it may be a reminder of destruction for those who plot against us.

24 "Every city and country, without exception, that does not act accordingly shall be destroyed in wrath with spear and fire. It shall be made not only impassable for human beings, but also most hateful to wild animals and birds for all time.

END OF ADDITION E

a Chapter 16.1–24 corresponds to chapter E 1–24 in some translations.   b Gk matters beside (your) feet
c Gk our spirit   d Gk greatest   e Other ancient authorities read for us

16.1–24: The text of the edict. Since Esther was given authority to draft the edict (8.8), the lavish praise of the king may be Esther's strategic stroking of the king's ego rather than his own boasting. **5–9:** The king accepts responsibility only for being insufficiently careful about his "friends." **10:** Haman is revealed as a *Macedonian,* not really a *Persian.* Alexander the Great, who overthrew the Persian empire, was Macedonian, suggesting a political motive for Haman's plot. **15:** The very *laws* that were seen as problematic in 13.4 are here lauded as *righteous.* **16:** Elsewhere in the Bible foreign rulers appeal to the God of Israel (Ezra 1.2). **17:** The king advises people not to observe *the letters sent by Haman,* though they came in his own name (ch. 13). **24:** The threat of uninhabitable land, even *hateful to wild animals,* is a common curse in the ancient Near East.

8 13 "Let copies of the decree be posted conspicuously in all the kingdom, and let all the Jews be ready on that day to fight against their enemies."

14 So the messengers on horseback set out with all speed to perform what the king had commanded; and the decree was published also in Susa. 15 Mordecai went out dressed in the royal robe and wearing a gold crown and a turban of purple linen. The people in Susa rejoiced on seeing him. 16 And the Jews had light and gladness 17 in every city and province wherever the decree was published; wherever the proclamation was made, the Jews had joy and gladness, a banquet and a holiday. And many of the Gentiles were circumcised and became Jews out of fear of the Jews.

8.13–17: The decree is distributed. The Greek makes explicit that the Persians converted to Judaism, even undergoing circumcision.* The edict makes no mention of plunder, which is allowed in the Hebrew.

9 Now on the thirteenth day of the twelfth month, which is Adar, the decree written by the king arrived. 2 On that same day the enemies of the Jews perished; no one resisted, because they feared them. 3 The chief provincial governors, the princes, and the royal secretaries were paying honor to the Jews, because fear of Mordecai weighed upon them. 4 The king's decree required that Mordecai's name be held in honor throughout the kingdom.ᵃ 6 Now in the city of Susa the Jews killed five hundred people, 7 including Pharsannestain, Delphon, Phasga, 8 Pharadatha, Barea, Sarbacha, 9 Marmasima, Aruphaeus, Arsaeus, Zabutheus, 10 the ten sons of Haman son of Hammedatha, the Bougean, the enemy of the Jews—and they indulgedᵇ themselves in plunder.

11 That very day the number of those killed in Susa was reported to the king. 12 The king said to Esther, "In Susa, the capital, the Jews have destroyed five hundred people. What do you suppose they have done in the surrounding countryside? Whatever more you ask will be done for you." 13 And Esther said to the king, "Let the Jews be allowed to do the same tomorrow. Also, hang up the bodies of Haman's ten sons." 14 So he permitted this to be done, and handed over to the Jews of the city the bodies of Haman's sons to hang up. 15 The Jews who were in Susa gathered on the fourteenth and killed three hundred people, but took no plunder.

16 Now the other Jews in the kingdom gathered to defend themselves, and got relief from their enemies. They destroyed fifteen thousand of them, but did not engage in plunder. 17 On the fourteenth day they rested and made that same day a day of rest, celebrating it with joy and gladness. 18 The Jews who were in Susa, the capital, came together also on the fourteenth, but did not rest. They celebrated the fifteenth with joy and gladness. 19 On this account then the Jews who are scattered around the country outside Susa keep the fourteenth of Adar as a joyful holiday, and send presents of food to one another, while those who live in the large cities keep the fifteenth day of Adar as their joyful holiday, also sending presents to one another.

9.1–19: The Jews act on the edict. The Jews' victory is striking: *No one resisted,* though the picture is still

---

a Meaning of Gk uncertain. Some ancient authorities add verse 5, *So the Jews struck down all their enemies with the sword, killing and destroying them, and they did as they pleased to those who hated them.*   b Other ancient authorities read *did not indulge* one of self-defense. They take *plunder* in only one of the three episodes. The total of *fifteen thousand* for the third episode is smaller than the Hebrew 75,000.

20 Mordecai recorded these things in a book, and sent it to the Jews in the kingdom of Artaxerxes both near and far, 21telling them that they should keep the fourteenth and fifteenth days of Adar, 22for on these days the Jews got relief from their enemies. The whole month (namely, Adar), in which their condition had been changed from sorrow into gladness and from a time of distress to a holiday, was to be celebrated as a time for feasting*a* and gladness and for sending presents of food to their friends and to the poor.

23 So the Jews accepted what Mordecai had written to them 24—how Haman son of Hammedatha, the Macedonian,*b* fought against them, how he made a decree and cast lots*c* to destroy them, 25and how he went in to the king, telling him to hang Mordecai; but the wicked plot he had devised against the Jews came back upon himself, and he and his sons were hanged. 26Therefore these days were called "Purim," because of the lots (for in their language this is the word that means "lots"). And so, because of what was written in this letter, and because of what they had experienced in this affair and what had befallen them, Mordecai established this festival,*d* 27and the Jews took upon themselves, upon their descendants, and upon all who would join them, to observe it without fail.*e* These days of Purim should be a memorial and kept from generation to generation, in every city, family, and country. 28These days of Purim were to be observed for all time, and the commemoration of them was never to cease among their descendants.

29 Then Queen Esther daughter of Aminadab along with Mordecai the Jew wrote down what they had done, and gave full authority to the letter about Purim.*f* 31And Mordecai and Queen Esther established this decision on their own responsibility, pledging their own well-being to the plan.*e* 32Esther established it by a decree forever, and it was written for a memorial.

10 The king levied a tax upon his kingdom both by land and sea. 2And as for his power and bravery, and the wealth and glory of his kingdom, they were recorded in the annals of the kings of the Persians and the Medes. 3Mordecai acted with authority on behalf of King Artaxerxes and was great in the kingdom, as well as honored by the Jews. His way of life was such as to make him beloved to his whole nation.

10.1–3: Greatness of Artaxerxes and of Mordecai. While the book is named for Esther, *Mordecai* and *Artaxerxes* receive praise.

ADDITION F

4*g* And Mordecai said, "These things have come from God; 5for I remember the dream that I had concerning these matters, and none of them has failed to be fulfilled. 6There was the little spring that became a river, and there was light and sun and abundant water—the river is Esther, whom the king married and made queen. 7The two dragons are Haman and myself. 8The nations are those that gathered to destroy the name of the Jews. 9And my nation, this is Israel, who cried out to God and was saved. The Lord has saved his people; the Lord has rescued us from all these evils; God has done great signs and wonders, wonders that have never happened among the nations. 10For this purpose he made two lots, one for the people of God and one for all the nations, 11and these two lots came to the hour and moment and day of decision

a Gk *of weddings*   *b* Other ancient witnesses read *the Bougean*   *c* Gk *a lot*   *d* Gk *he established* (it)   *e* Meaning of Gk uncertain   *f* Verse 30 in Heb is lacking in Gk: *Letters were sent to all the Jews, to the one hundred twenty-seven provinces of the kingdom of Ahasuerus, in words of peace and truth.*   *g* Chapter 10.4–13 and 11.1 correspond to chapter F 1–11 in some translations.

before God and among all the nations. 12 And God remembered his people and vindicated his inheritance. 13 So they will observe these days in the month of Adar, on the fourteenth and fifteenth[a] of that month, with an assembly and joy and gladness before God, from generation to generation forever among his people Israel." 1 In the fourth year of the reign of Ptolemy and Cleopatra, Dositheus, who said that he was a priest and a Levite,[b] and his son Ptolemy brought to Egypt[c] the preceding Letter about Purim, which they said was authentic and had been translated by Lysimachus son of Ptolemy, one of the residents of Jerusalem.

END OF ADDITION F

10.4–13: Mordecai's dream fulfilled. The opening dream of the book is decoded, showing God's role in the events that have unfolded. **5:** *None of them has failed to be fulfilled.* Prophecy and fulfillment are common themes of late biblical literature. **10:** A new connection with *lots* is made: the differing fates of the Jews and the gentiles.*

11.1: Postscript. A colophon* (information at the end of the book indicating its translator or copier) gives the book authority. Egyptian history records several kings named *Ptolemy* with queens named *Cleopatra;* suggested dates range from 114 to 48 BCE.

a Other ancient authorities lack *and fifteenth*
b Or *priest, and Levitas*   c Cn: Gk *brought in*

THE WISDOM OF SOLOMON

Introduction

The Wisdom of Solomon was originally composed in Greek by a Hellenized✶ Jew who almost certainly lived in Alexandria, Egypt, somewhere around the turn of the first century CE. The pseudonymous✶ ascription of the work to King Solomon derives from the text's first-person perspective, in which the king describes his own passionate pursuit of wisdom (chs. 7–9). Many works of wisdom literature✶ are ascribed to Solomon, including Proverbs and the Song of Solomon, as well as later noncanonical collections of Jewish and Christian religious poetry. Indeed, the Wisdom of Solomon, like most wisdom literature, is written in poetic form and reflects a high degree of stylistic sophistication. Numerous rhetorical✶ devices offer clues to the reader regarding both the structure and the meaning of the work. Furthermore, the text reveals an assimilated knowledge of many Greek philosophical concepts. The Wisdom of Solomon, whose topics include the problem of theodicy,✶ immortality of the soul, and the perils of idolatry,✶ assumes a philosophical understanding of the world that is characteristic of Platonism,✶ particularly its middle period (first century BCE through the second century CE), which was heavily informed by Stoicism. The author does not engage in the sort of philosophical analysis characteristic of that other well-known Alexandrian Jewish writer, Philo,✶ with whom he shares many ideas. Rather than argue a point, this author attempts to exhort and inspire his readers to embrace wisdom through his rhetorical flair and homiletical✶ use of examples from biblical history.

The Jewish community of ancient Alexandria experienced some of the greatest successes of any Diaspora✶ community, as well as some of the most serious persecutions. Because the text's latter chapters, which elaborate upon the Exodus story, reflect profound animosity toward the Egyptians—far exceeding their negative role in the book of Exodus—Wisdom must have been composed in the wake of persecution. Although there is no consensus among scholars regarding the date, the language and style suggest the late first century BCE or early first century CE, during which time Alexandrian Jews faced several social and political challenges. Some have suggested that the anti-Jewish rioting that occurred during the reign of Emperor Caligula (37–41 CE) constitutes the most likely context for the work.

READING GUIDE

The Wisdom of Solomon divides into three parts. The first, chs. 1–6, introduces the reader to the primary theological issues of the work and includes a mini-narrative✶ about a righteous man unjustly accused of wrong-doing by a conspiracy of wicked, self-serving men. The second section, chs. 7–9, speaks through the voice of Solomon and provides extended musings on the nature of wisdom. Chapter 10, which marks the start of the final section, encompasses a striking poem on Wisdom's role in the lives of biblical heroes. The final chapters of the book (11–19) focus on the Exodus, using many details of the story as symbolic indications of God's respective judgment of the righteous and the wicked.

chs. 1–6 Exhortation✶ to righteousness
chs. 7–9 Solomon's wisdom
chs. 10–19 Lessons from Israel's history

1 Love righteousness, you rulers of the
      earth,
   think of the Lord in goodness
   and seek him with sincerity of heart;
2 because he is found by those who do
      not put him to the test,
   and manifests himself to those who do
      not distrust him.
3 For perverse thoughts separate people
      from God,
   and when his power is tested, it exposes
      the foolish;
4 because wisdom will not enter a
      deceitful soul,
   or dwell in a body enslaved to sin.
5 For a holy and disciplined spirit will flee
      from deceit,
   and will leave foolish thoughts behind,
   and will be ashamed at the approach of
      unrighteousness.

6 For wisdom is a kindly spirit,
   but will not free blasphemers from the
      guilt of their words;
   because God is witness of their inmost
      feelings,
   and a true observer of their hearts, and
      a hearer of their tongues.
7 Because the spirit of the Lord has filled
      the world,
   and that which holds all things together
      knows what is said,
8 therefore those who utter unrighteous
      things will not escape notice,
   and justice, when it punishes, will not
      pass them by.
9 For inquiry will be made into the
      counsels of the ungodly,
   and a report of their words will come to
      the Lord,
   to convict them of their lawless
      deeds;
10 because a jealous ear hears all things,
   and the sound of grumbling does not go
      unheard.
11 Beware then of useless grumbling,
   and keep your tongue from slander;
   because no secret word is without
      result,ᵃ
   and a lying mouth destroys the soul.

1.1–15: Opening exhortation* and warning. The text begins with an exhortation to the *rulers of the earth* to act justly. This exhortation is not an indication of the intended readership, however. Nothing in this opening section addresses the issue of governance or political justice. Rather, the appeal is personal and generic; it applies to individuals of any sort. **1:** *Rulers of the earth* is intended to impress the reader, as well as to convey the perspective of King Solomon (see also 6.1, 24–25). **2–7:** That God sees the evil in people's *hearts,* even when others cannot see it, is a common theme in wisdom literature* (for example, Sir 23.18–19). What is distinctive in Wisdom is the emphasis upon the internal, spiritual realm that exists within each person. Such an emphasis reflects the influence of Greek philosophy. **4:** The author assumes that human beings are composed of two parts, the *body* and the *soul.* (Such an assumption is different from the traditional view of the Hebrew Bible about the nature of human beings, in which the human person is understood as an integrated whole; souls and bodies cannot exist apart from one another.) Body/soul dualism* derives from a more fundamental dualism common in Platonic* thought: The substance of spiritual things is completely different from that of material things, that is, matter. A person's physical body consists of matter (see 11.17), while a soul exists as a non-material substance that is potentially imperishable. (See sidebar, "Immortality of the Soul," p. 1365.) **7:** *That which holds all things together* comes from Stoic* philosophy, which teaches that the universe is one rational world-soul, also known as the "logos." The Stoic's goal is to conform his individual soul to the world-soul.

12 Do not invite death by the error of your
      life,
   or bring on destruction by the works of
      your hands;
13 because God did not make death,
   and he does not delight in the death of
      the living.
14 For he created all things so that they
      might exist;
   the generative forcesᵇ of the world are
      wholesome,

ᵃ Or *will go unpunished*
ᵇ Or *the creatures*

and there is no destructive poison in
them,
and the dominion[a] of Hades is not on
earth.
15 For righteousness is immortal.

1.12–15: Wisdom's blend of biblical monotheism and
Greek dualism★ creates some implicit theological contradictions. **13:** When the author says *God did not
make death,* he seems very far removed from classic
Hebraic theology, which holds that nothing is beyond
the control of an all-powerful God (see Isa 45.7). The
story of Adam and Eve, in which God pronounces a
death sentence upon the first couple (Gen 2.17; 3.19),
would seem to contradict any understanding of God
that separated death from God's ken (see 2 Esd 3.7).
Although the author's view is unusual, it is dependent
upon a reading of Genesis found in the literature of
the time, a reading that understands God to have originally created humans as immortal creatures (see Wis
2.23; 2 Esd 8.59). Death becomes part of human life
only as a result of sin (2.24). Since human mortality
was not part of God's plan, death must come from
another source. **14:** Although *Hades*★ is personified
here (see 2 Esd 8.53; Rev 6.8), it refers to the realm of
the dead (Sheol★ is the Hebrew equivalent; see, for
example, Prov 7.27), a place devoid of the presence
of God.

---

16 But the ungodly by their words and
deeds summoned death;[b]
considering him a friend, they pined
away
and made a covenant with him,
because they are fit to belong to his
company.

2 For they reasoned unsoundly, saying to
themselves,
"Short and sorrowful is our life,
and there is no remedy when a life
comes to its end,
and no one has been known to return
from Hades.
2 For we were born by mere chance,
and hereafter we shall be as though we
had never been,
for the breath in our nostrils is smoke,
and reason is a spark kindled by the
beating of our hearts;
3 when it is extinguished, the body will
turn to ashes,

and the spirit will dissolve like empty
air.
4 Our name will be forgotten in time,
and no one will remember our works;
our life will pass away like the traces of
a cloud,
and be scattered like mist
that is chased by the rays of the sun
and overcome by its heat.
5 For our allotted time is the passing of a
shadow,
and there is no return from our death,
because it is sealed up and no one turns
back.

6 "Come, therefore, let us enjoy the good
things that exist,
and make use of the creation to the full
as in youth.
7 Let us take our fill of costly wine and
perfumes,
and let no flower of spring pass us by.
8 Let us crown ourselves with rosebuds
before they wither.
9 Let none of us fail to share in our
revelry;
everywhere let us leave signs of
enjoyment,
because this is our portion, and this
our lot.
10 Let us oppress the righteous poor man;
let us not spare the widow
or regard the gray hairs of the aged.
11 But let our might be our law of right,
for what is weak proves itself to be
useless.

1.16–2.11: Covenant★ **with death.** The author employs a rhetorical★ device from Hellenistic★ diatribe,★
a popular genre★ of the era intended for pedagogical
purposes. The diatribe typically included dialogue with
imaginary opponents. In this case the opponents represent those who deny that humans are immortal. **2.1:**
The sentiment that the author caricatures through the
voice of his imaginary opponents is found in wisdom
literature★ (see, for example, Eccl 1.1–11; 9.7–10). **2:**
Chance stands in contrast to the deliberate plan of
God. *The breath in our nostrils is smoke* mocks the

---

a Or *palace*   *b* Gk *him*

older Hebraic view that regards breath as an animating source of life (breath, wind, and spirit are all the same word in both Greek and Hebrew) that expires along with the body at death. **6–11:** Since human life has no lasting value, the opponents draw the conclusion that frivolous pursuits and the exploitation of weaker individuals is justified. Compare Prov 1.10–14.

12 "Let us lie in wait for the righteous man,
   because he is inconvenient to us and
         opposes our actions;
   he reproaches us for sins against the law,
   and accuses us of sins against our
         training.
13 He professes to have knowledge of God,
   and calls himself a child*a* of the Lord.
14 He became to us a reproof of our
         thoughts;
15 the very sight of him is a burden to us,
   because his manner of life is unlike that
         of others,
   and his ways are strange.
16 We are considered by him as something
         base,
   and he avoids our ways as unclean;
   he calls the last end of the righteous
         happy,
   and boasts that God is his father.
17 Let us see if his words are true,
   and let us test what will happen at the
         end of his life;
18 for if the righteous man is God's child,
   he will help him,
   and will deliver him from the hand of
         his adversaries.
19 Let us test him with insult and torture,
   so that we may find out how gentle
         he is,
   and make trial of his forbearance.
20 Let us condemn him to a shameful
         death,
   for, according to what he says, he will
         be protected."

2.12–20: The righteous man unjustly accused. This section continues to address the relationship between justice and immortality, but it takes on a narrative* quality. The imaginary opponents introduced in 2.1 now conspire against a hypothetical *righteous man.* Their primary motivation is to test whether or not he is truly a servant of God, as he claims. Like many a

prophet* in Israel's history, the righteous man has reproved the people. Instead of repenting, they take action against him and ultimately *condemn him to a shameful death* (v. 20). This scenario has echoes of the fourth servant song in Isa 52.13–53.12. Its resonance with the story of Jesus' crucifixion led some of the early church fathers to see this text, like the servant song, as a prediction of that event. **13:** *Child of the Lord* is another way of designating the righteous man (see also vv. 16–17); it is not a formal title.

21 Thus they reasoned, but they were led
         astray,
   for their wickedness blinded them,
22 and they did not know the secret
         purposes of God,
   nor hoped for the wages of holiness,
   nor discerned the prize for blameless
         souls;
23 for God created us for incorruption,
   and made us in the image of his own
         eternity,*b*
24 but through the devil's envy death
         entered the world,
   and those who belong to his company
         experience it.

3 But the souls of the righteous are in
      the hand of God,
   and no torment will ever touch them.
2 In the eyes of the foolish they seemed
         to have died,
   and their departure was thought to be a
         disaster,
3 and their going from us to be their
         destruction;
   but they are at peace.
4 For though in the sight of others they
         were punished,
   their hope is full of immortality.
5 Having been disciplined a little, they
         will receive great good,
   because God tested them and found
         them worthy of himself;
6 like gold in the furnace he tried them,
   and like a sacrificial burnt offering he
         accepted them.
7 In the time of their visitation they will
         shine forth,

a Or *servant*   *b* Other ancient authorities read *nature*

and will run like sparks through the
stubble.

8 They will govern nations and rule over
peoples,
and the Lord will reign over them
forever.

9 Those who trust in him will understand
truth,
and the faithful will abide with him in
love,
because grace and mercy are upon his
holy ones,
and he watches over his elect.[a]

10 But the ungodly will be punished as
their reasoning deserves,
those who disregarded the righteous[b]
and rebelled against the Lord;

11 for those who despise wisdom and
instruction are miserable.
Their hope is vain, their labors are
unprofitable,
and their works are useless.

12 Their wives are foolish, and their
children evil;

13 their offspring are accursed.
For blessed is the barren woman who is
undefiled,
who has not entered into a sinful
union;
she will have fruit when God examines
souls.

14 Blessed also is the eunuch whose hands
have done no lawless deed,
and who has not devised wicked things
against the Lord;
for special favor will be shown him for
his faithfulness,
and a place of great delight in the
temple of the Lord.

15 For the fruit of good labors is renowned,
and the root of understanding does not
fail.

16 But children of adulterers will not come
to maturity,
and the offspring of an unlawful union
will perish.

17 Even if they live long they will be held
of no account,
and finally their old age will be without
honor.

18 If they die young, they will have no
hope
and no consolation on the day of
judgment.

19 For the end of an unrighteous
generation is grievous.

2.21–3.13a: Moving beyond the narrative* of the hypothetical man, the author steps back into his own
voice in order to teach on the immortality of the soul.
Immortality for the righteous constitutes the solution
to the problem of injustice as portrayed in the example
of the righteous man. **2.23:** *Image of his own eternity*
derives from Gen 1.26. **2.24:** *The devil's envy* may reflect the interpretive tradition that came to see the serpent in the Garden of Eden story as an embodiment
of Satan. **3.2–3:** The author refers to the physical death
of the righteous as perceived by others. **5:** *Having been
disciplined a little* takes account of the suffering the
righteous one endured at the hands of the wicked
prior to being rewarded by God. **13:** *Their offspring
are accursed* reflects the common biblical notion that
accountability for actions can extend to future generations (see Sir 23.22–27).

4 Better than this is childlessness with
virtue,
for in the memory of virtue[c] is
immortality,
because it is known both by God and by
mortals.

2 When it is present, people imitate[d] it,
and they long for it when it has gone;
throughout all time it marches, crowned
in triumph,
victor in the contest for prizes that are
undefiled.

3 But the prolific brood of the ungodly
will be of no use,
and none of their illegitimate seedlings
will strike a deep root
or take a firm hold.

4 For even if they put forth boughs for a
while,
standing insecurely they will be shaken
by the wind,
and by the violence of the winds they
will be uprooted.

a Text of this line uncertain; omitted by some ancient
authorities. Compare 4.15   b Or *what is right*
c Gk *it*   d Other ancient authorities read *honor*

Immortality of the Soul

The soul's immortality is a central issue in the first half of the book of Wisdom. Virtually all the books contained in Hebrew Scripture assume that human life ends at death. During the Hellenistic★ period, many Jews came to believe in life after death. Generally speaking, there were two ways of thinking about post-mortem existence: resurrection of the body and immortality of the soul. New Testament texts assert belief in resurrection (for example, 1 Cor 15.12–58). Other Jewish texts outside the scriptural canon★ (such as the writings of Philo★) reflect belief in the immortality of the soul, much like Wisdom. There was no agreement on the issue. The author of Sirach states repeatedly and unequivocally that life ends at death (38.21–23; 41.1–4). Sirach may be two centuries earlier than Wisdom, but even in the first century CE, the Sadducees★ denied there was life after death (Matt 22.23–33; Acts 23.8). The debate is closely tied to the problem of theodicy,★ as is evident in the text of Wisdom. If righteous people can be unjustly accused and wrongly condemned to death, where is justice? Belief in life after death allows for the possibility that wrongs may be set right, which is exactly what is described in 3.1–9.

5 The branches will be broken off before
    they come to maturity,
and their fruit will be useless,
    not ripe enough to eat, and good for
      nothing.
6 For children born of unlawful unions
    are witnesses of evil against their parents
      when God examines them.*a*
7 But the righteous, though they die early,
      will be at rest.
8 For old age is not honored for length of
      time,
or measured by number of years;
9 but understanding is gray hair for
      anyone,
and a blameless life is ripe old age.

3.13b–4.6: Childlessness. The author offers an impassioned diatribe★ against the traditional devaluation of childlessness. The inability to bear children was typically regarded as a curse and was grounds for a husband to divorce his wife. In traditional Israelite religion, the continuation of one's family line through one's progeny constitutes a form of immortality. Because the author of the Wisdom of Solomon advocates a belief in immortality for righteous individuals, producing heirs becomes less important. **3.13b:** Exactly what is being referred to by *a sinful union* is not clear. Some interpreters speculate that married women (perhaps even with the encouragement of their husbands) would have had sexual relations with other men in order to increase their chances for conceiving. Whatever the motivation, the author has in mind extramarital relations throughout the passage (3.16; 4.6).

THE FATE OF THE RIGHTEOUS AND THE UNRIGHTEOUS

4.7–5.23: These verses continue the hypothetical scenario begun in 2.12–20 and constitute a commentary on it. Regardless of whether they were the victims of unjust machinations and untimely deaths, the righteous will ultimately be vindicated by God.

10 There were some who pleased God and
      were loved by him,
and while living among sinners were
      taken up.
11 They were caught up so that evil might
      not change their understanding
or guile deceive their souls.
12 For the fascination of wickedness
      obscures what is good,
and roving desire perverts the innocent
      mind.

a Gk *at their examination*

13 Being perfected in a short time, they
fulfilled long years;
14 for their souls were pleasing to the
Lord,
therefore he took them quickly from the
midst of wickedness.
15 Yet the peoples saw and did not
understand,
or take such a thing to heart,
that God's grace and mercy are with his
elect,
and that he watches over his holy ones.

16 The righteous who have died will
condemn the ungodly who are
living,
and youth that is quickly perfected[a] will
condemn the prolonged old age
of the unrighteous.
17 For they will see the end of the wise,
and will not understand what the Lord
purposed for them,
and for what he kept them safe.
18 The unrighteous[b] will see, and will have
contempt for them,
but the Lord will laugh them to scorn.
After this they will become dishonored
corpses,
and an outrage among the dead forever;
19 because he will dash them speechless to
the ground,
and shake them from the foundations;
they will be left utterly dry and barren,
and they will suffer anguish,
and the memory of them will perish.

4.7–19. 10: *Some who pleased God . . . were taken up*
is a reference to Enoch* from Gen 5.24. **11–15:** The
reason for Enoch's deathless ascension to heaven was
to protect him from exposure to *wickedness.* Compare
ch. 10, where Wisdom personified protects several biblical heroes from the wickedness of their generation.
18–19: The fate of the *unrighteous* consists of *dis-*
honor and permanent extinction (as opposed to the
later Christian idea of a life of eternal punishment in a
fiery hell).

~~~~~~~~~~~~~~~

20 They will come with dread when their
sins are reckoned up,
and their lawless deeds will convict
them to their face.

5 Then the righteous will stand with
great confidence
in the presence of those who have
oppressed them
and those who make light of their
labors.
2 When the unrighteous[c] see them, they
will be shaken with dreadful
fear,
and they will be amazed at the
unexpected salvation of the
righteous.
3 They will speak to one another in
repentance,
and in anguish of spirit they will groan,
and say,
4 "These are persons whom we once held
in derision
and made a byword of reproach—fools
that we were!
We thought that their lives were
madness
and that their end was without honor.
5 Why have they been numbered among
the children of God?
And why is their lot among the saints?
6 So it was we who strayed from the way
of truth,
and the light of righteousness did not
shine on us,
and the sun did not rise upon us.
7 We took our fill of the paths of
lawlessness and destruction,
and we journeyed through trackless
deserts,
but the way of the Lord we have not
known.
8 What has our arrogance profited us?
And what good has our boasted wealth
brought us?

9 "All those things have vanished like a
shadow,
and like a rumor that passes by;
10 like a ship that sails through the billowy
water,
and when it has passed no trace can be
found,
no track of its keel in the waves;

---

a Or *ended*   *b* Gk *They*   *c* Gk *they*

11 or as, when a bird flies through the air,
no evidence of its passage is found;
the light air, lashed by the beat of its
     pinions
and pierced by the force of its rushing
     flight,
is traversed by the movement of its
     wings,
and afterward no sign of its coming is
     found there;
12 or as, when an arrow is shot at a target,
the air, thus divided, comes together at
     once,
so that no one knows its pathway.
13 So we also, as soon as we were born,
     ceased to be,
and we had no sign of virtue to show,
but were consumed in our wickedness."
14 Because the hope of the ungodly is like
     thistledown[a] carried by the wind,
and like a light frost[b] driven away by a
     storm;
it is dispersed like smoke before the
     wind,
and it passes like the remembrance of a
     guest who stays but a day.
15 But the righteous live forever,
and their reward is with the Lord;
the Most High takes care of them.
16 Therefore they will receive a glorious
     crown
and a beautiful diadem from the hand
     of the Lord,
because with his right hand he will
     cover them,
and with his arm he will shield them.
17 The Lord[c] will take his zeal as his
     whole armor,
and will arm all creation to repel[d] his
     enemies;
18 he will put on righteousness as a
     breastplate,
and wear impartial justice as a helmet;
19 he will take holiness as an invincible
     shield,
20 and sharpen stern wrath for a sword,
and creation will join with him to fight
     against his frenzied foes.
21 Shafts of lightning will fly with true
     aim,

and will leap from the clouds to the
     target, as from a well-drawn
     bow,
22 and hailstones full of wrath will be
     hurled as from a catapult;
the water of the sea will rage against
     them,
and rivers will relentlessly overwhelm
     them;
23 a mighty wind will rise against them,
and like a tempest it will winnow them
     away.
Lawlessness will lay waste the whole
     earth,
and evildoing will overturn the thrones
     of rulers.

4.19–5.23: The author describes another stage in the fate of the righteous and unrighteous. He portrays a final judgment scene, which creates the opportunity for the unrighteous to perceive the error of their ways—though only after it is too late—and to acknowledge God's reward of the righteous. 5.4–13: As in 2.1–20, the author speaks in the voice of his imaginary opponents. 13: This comment sounds much like souls are predestined (see also 4.14), or perhaps are inherently good or evil (see 8.19–20). Nowhere, however, does the author seem conscious of the problem of free will and determinism implicitly introduced by such comments. If souls are inherently good or evil, why are they held accountable to judgment? 17–23: A final cosmic battle between the forces of good and evil is a common feature of apocalyptic* thought.

6 Listen therefore, O kings, and
     understand;
learn, O judges of the ends of the earth.
2 Give ear, you that rule over multitudes,
and boast of many nations.
3 For your dominion was given you from
     the Lord,
and your sovereignty from the Most
     High;
he will search out your works and
     inquire into your plans.
4 Because as servants of his kingdom you
     did not rule rightly,
or keep the law,

---

a Other ancient authorities read *dust*   b Other ancient
authorities read *spider's web*   c Gk He   d Or *punish*

or walk according to the purpose of God,

5 he will come upon you terribly and
    swiftly,
because severe judgment falls on those
    in high places.

6 For the lowliest may be pardoned in
    mercy,
but the mighty will be mightily tested.

7 For the Lord of all will not stand in awe
    of anyone,
or show deference to greatness;
because he himself made both small
    and great,
and he takes thought for all alike.

8 But a strict inquiry is in store for the
    mighty.

9 To you then, O monarchs, my words are
    directed,
so that you may learn wisdom and not
    transgress.

10 For they will be made holy who observe
    holy things in holiness,
and those who have been taught them
    will find a defense.

11 Therefore set your desire on my words;
long for them, and you will be
    instructed.

12 Wisdom is radiant and unfading,
and she is easily discerned by those who
    love her,
and is found by those who seek her.

13 She hastens to make herself known to
    those who desire her.

14 One who rises early to seek her will
    have no difficulty,
for she will be found sitting at the gate.

15 To fix one's thought on her is perfect
    understanding,
and one who is vigilant on her account
    will soon be free from care,

16 because she goes about seeking those
    worthy of her,
and she graciously appears to them in
    their paths,
and meets them in every thought.

17 The beginning of wisdom[a] is the most
    sincere desire for instruction,
and concern for instruction is love of
    her,

18 and love of her is the keeping of her
    laws,
and giving heed to her laws is assurance
    of immortality,

19 and immortality brings one near to God;

20 so the desire for wisdom leads to a
    kingdom.

21 Therefore if you delight in thrones and
    scepters, O monarchs over the
    peoples,
honor wisdom, so that you may reign
    forever.

22 I will tell you what wisdom is and how
    she came to be,
and I will hide no secrets from you,
but I will trace her course from the
    beginning of creation,
and make knowledge of her clear,
and I will not pass by the truth;

23 nor will I travel in the company of sickly
    envy,
for envy[b] does not associate with
    wisdom.

24 The multitude of the wise is the
    salvation of the world,
and a sensible king is the stability of any
    people.

25 Therefore be instructed by my words,
    and you will profit.

6.1–25: Exhortation* to wisdom. Following the description of the final judgment, the author makes clear that those rulers who currently have dominion over the earth are responsible for lawlessness and thereby more accountable to God's judgment. **1–2:** For the direct address to *kings* and rulers, see comment on 1.1. **12–21:** Descriptions of wisdom personified as a female figure, "Sophia," are common in wisdom literature* (see, for example, Prov 8; Sir 1.1–10; 24.1–22). Both the Greek word "sophia" and the Hebrew word "hokhma," meaning "wisdom," are feminine. **17–20:** These verses form a syllogistic chain called a "sorites,"* a Greek rhetorical* device that allows the author to link items incrementally—items that would not ordinarily seem connected. Thus, the simple desire for wisdom eventually *leads to a kingdom* (v. 20). **22–25:** These words introduce Solomon as the teacher of wisdom.

a Gk *Her beginning*   b Gk *this*

SOLOMON'S WISDOM

7.1–9.18: This section presents Solomon speaking autobiographically. Instead of explicit exhortations* to others to seek wisdom, Solomon offers himself as the paradigmatic wisdom-seeker.

7 I also am mortal, like everyone else,
    a descendant of the first-formed child
        of earth;
    and in the womb of a mother I was
        molded into flesh,
2   within the period of ten months,
        compacted with blood,
    from the seed of a man and the pleasure
        of marriage.
3   And when I was born, I began to
        breathe the common air,
    and fell upon the kindred earth;
    my first sound was a cry, as is true of
        all.
4   I was nursed with care in swaddling
        cloths.
5   For no king has had a different
        beginning of existence;
6   there is for all one entrance into life,
        and one way out.
7   Therefore I prayed, and understanding
        was given me;
    I called on God, and the spirit of
        wisdom came to me.
8   I preferred her to scepters and thrones,
    and I accounted wealth as nothing in
        comparison with her.
9   Neither did I liken to her any priceless
        gem,
    because all gold is but a little sand in
        her sight,
    and silver will be accounted as clay
        before her.
10 I loved her more than health and
        beauty,
    and I chose to have her rather than
        light,
    because her radiance never ceases.
11 All good things came to me along with
        her,
    and in her hands uncounted wealth.
12 I rejoiced in them all, because wisdom
        leads them;

but I did not know that she was their
    mother.
13 I learned without guile and I impart
        without grudging;
    I do not hide her wealth,
14 for it is an unfailing treasure for
        mortals;
    those who get it obtain friendship with
        God,
    commended for the gifts that come
        from instruction.
15 May God grant me to speak with
        judgment,
    and to have thoughts worthy of what I
        have received;
    for he is the guide even of wisdom
    and the corrector of the wise.
16 For both we and our words are in his
        hand,
    as are all understanding and skill in
        crafts.
17 For it is he who gave me unerring
        knowledge of what exists,
    to know the structure of the world and
        the activity of the elements;
18 the beginning and end and middle of
        times,
    the alternations of the solstices and the
        changes of the seasons,
19 the cycles of the year and the
        constellations of the stars,
20 the natures of animals and the tempers
        of wild animals,
    the powers of spirits*a* and the thoughts
        of human beings,
    the varieties of plants and the virtues of
        roots;
21 I learned both what is secret and what
        is manifest,
22 for wisdom, the fashioner of all things,
        taught me.

7.1–22a. 1: When Solomon calls himself *mortal*, he does not negate the claims for the immortality of the soul elsewhere in the book, but merely emphasizes that he was born an ordinary man. **5:** That *no king has had a different beginning of existence* argues against claims that kings were divine. Such claims had been

a Or *winds*

made by Hellenistic* rulers in Egypt and some of the early Roman emperors. **7–22:** Solomon had unparalleled wealth, which the author explains as a by-product of his wisdom. Upon his ascension to the throne, Solomon prayed to the Lord for "an understanding mind" so that he could govern Israel justly (see also 9.1–18). God was pleased with Solomon's noble prayer, so God rewarded the king with wisdom as well as riches and glory (see 1 Kings 3.5–14). **15–22:** Solomon's prayer for wisdom includes all categories of knowledge. **22a:** Sophia is elsewhere attested as God's agent of creation (see Prov 8.22–31).

> There is in her a spirit that is
> > intelligent, holy,
> unique, manifold, subtle,
> mobile, clear, unpolluted,
> distinct, invulnerable, loving the good,
> > keen,
> irresistible, 23beneficent, humane,
> steadfast, sure, free from anxiety,
> all-powerful, overseeing all,
> and penetrating through all spirits
> that are intelligent, pure, and altogether
> > subtle.
> 24 For wisdom is more mobile than any
> > motion;
> because of her pureness she pervades
> > and penetrates all things.
> 25 For she is a breath of the power of
> > God,
> and a pure emanation of the glory of the
> > Almighty;
> therefore nothing defiled gains entrance
> > into her.
> 26 For she is a reflection of eternal light,
> a spotless mirror of the working of God,
> and an image of his goodness.
> 27 Although she is but one, she can do all
> > things,
> and while remaining in herself, she
> > renews all things;
> in every generation she passes into holy
> > souls
> and makes them friends of God, and
> > prophets;
> 28 for God loves nothing so much as the
> > person who lives with wisdom.
> 29 She is more beautiful than the sun,
> and excels every constellation of the
> > stars.

> Compared with the light she is found to
> > be superior,
> 30 for it is succeeded by the night,
> but against wisdom evil does not
> > prevail.
> 8 She reaches mightily from one end of
> > the earth to the other,
> and she orders all things well.

7.22b–8.1: This extended description of the figure of wisdom is marked by its philosophical orientation. **7.24:** That Sophia *pervades and penetrates all things* makes her functionally equivalent to "the spirit of the Lord that holds all things together" in 1.7. **25:** *Emanation* was a Platonic* concept that became a technical term in Neoplatonic* cosmology and gnosticism*; it describes the manifestation of sub-deities from the original source of divinity. Its use here implies something beyond making abstract wisdom into a real manifestation of God's glory ("kabod" in Hebrew; see, for example, Ex 40.34–38) as appears in Sir 24.3–4. **26:** Although the author is by no means consistent, the view of Sophia as a separate being is further confirmed by reference to her as a *mirror* and an *image*. *Image* alludes to Gen 1.26–27. *Mirror* is used to describe Christ in Heb 1.3.

> 2 I loved her and sought her from my
> > youth;
> I desired to take her for my bride,
> and became enamored of her beauty.
> 3 She glorifies her noble birth by living
> > with God,
> and the Lord of all loves her.
> 4 For she is an initiate in the knowledge
> > of God,
> and an associate in his works.
> 5 If riches are a desirable possession in
> > life,
> what is richer than wisdom, the active
> > cause of all things?
> 6 And if understanding is effective,
> who more than she is fashioner of what
> > exists?
> 7 And if anyone loves righteousness,
> her labors are virtues;
> for she teaches self-control and
> > prudence,
> justice and courage;
> nothing in life is more profitable for
> > mortals than these.

8 And if anyone longs for wide
  experience,
  she knows the things of old, and infers
    the things to come;
  she understands turns of speech and
    the solutions of riddles;
  she has foreknowledge of signs and
    wonders
  and of the outcome of seasons and
    times.
9 Therefore I determined to take her to
    live with me,
  knowing that she would give me good
    counsel
  and encouragement in cares and
    grief.
10 Because of her I shall have glory among
    the multitudes
  and honor in the presence of the elders,
    though I am young.
11 I shall be found keen in judgment,
  and in the sight of rulers I shall be
    admired.
12 When I am silent they will wait for
    me,
  and when I speak they will give heed;
  if I speak at greater length,
  they will put their hands on their
    mouths.
13 Because of her I shall have
    immortality,
  and leave an everlasting remembrance
    to those who come after me.
14 I shall govern peoples,
  and nations will be subject to me;
15 dread monarchs will be afraid of me
    when they hear of me;
  among the people I shall show myself
    capable, and courageous in war.
16 When I enter my house, I shall find rest
    with her;
  for companionship with her has no
    bitterness,
  and life with her has no pain, but
    gladness and joy.
17 When I considered these things
    inwardly,
  and pondered in my heart
  that in kinship with wisdom there is
    immortality,

18 and in friendship with her, pure delight,
  and in the labors of her hands, unfailing
    wealth,
  and in the experience of her company,
    understanding,
  and renown in sharing her words,
  I went about seeking how to get her for
    myself.
19 As a child I was naturally gifted,
  and a good soul fell to my lot;
20 or rather, being good, I entered an
    undefiled body.

8.2–20. 2: Sophia is also called a *bride* in Sir 15.2, and in Sir 24.13–20 the figure of Wisdom sensuously describes her beautiful allure. 7: *Self-control, prudence, justice,* and *courage* are the four cardinal virtues of Greek ethics. 10–12: This description accurately reflects the description of Solomon in 1 Kings. 19–20: The dualistic understanding of *body* and *soul* seems to create a kind of schizophrenia. Is the self, the "I" of Solomon's discourse, to be identified with the body or the soul? The author comes down in favor of the soul when he says *I entered an undefiled body.* The statement implies that souls are preexistent, though this idea is not pursued in the text.

21 But I perceived that I would not possess
    wisdom unless God gave her to
    me—
  and it was a mark of insight to know
    whose gift she was—
  so I appealed to the Lord and implored
    him,
  and with my whole heart I said:
9 "O God of my ancestors and Lord of
    mercy,
  who have made all things by your
    word,
2 and by your wisdom have formed
    humankind
  to have dominion over the creatures you
    have made,
3 and rule the world in holiness and
    righteousness,
  and pronounce judgment in uprightness
    of soul,
4 give me the wisdom that sits by your
    throne,
  and do not reject me from among your
    servants.

5 For I am your servant[a] the son of your
   serving girl,
   a man who is weak and short-lived,
   with little understanding of judgment
   and laws;
6 for even one who is perfect among
   human beings
   will be regarded as nothing without the
   wisdom that comes from you.
7 You have chosen me to be king of your
   people
   and to be judge over your sons and
   daughters.
8 You have given command to build a
   temple on your holy mountain,
   and an altar in the city of your
   habitation,
   a copy of the holy tent that you
   prepared from the beginning.
9 With you is wisdom, she who knows
   your works
   and was present when you made the
   world;
   she understands what is pleasing in
   your sight
   and what is right according to your
   commandments.
10 Send her forth from the holy heavens,
   and from the throne of your glory send
   her,
   that she may labor at my side,
   and that I may learn what is pleasing to
   you.
11 For she knows and understands all
   things,
   and she will guide me wisely in my
   actions
   and guard me with her glory.
12 Then my works will be acceptable,
   and I shall judge your people justly,
   and shall be worthy of the throne[b] of
   my father.
13 For who can learn the counsel of God?
   Or who can discern what the Lord wills?
14 For the reasoning of mortals is
   worthless,
   and our designs are likely to fail;
15 for a perishable body weighs down the
   soul,
   and this earthy tent burdens the
   thoughtful[c] mind.

16 We can hardly guess at what is on
   earth,
   and what is at hand we find with labor;
   but who has traced out what is in the
   heavens?
17 Who has learned your counsel,
   unless you have given wisdom
   and sent your holy spirit from on high?
18 And thus the paths of those on earth
   were set right,
   and people were taught what pleases
   you,
   and were saved by wisdom."

8.21–9.18: See comment on 7.7–22. 9.8–10: Solomon is credited with building the Temple.* At the Temple's dedication, the Lord came and dwelt in it (1 Kings 8.10–13; 9.3). 15: *A perishable body weighs down the soul* because material reality is thought of as weighty, whereas spiritual reality is weightless.

WISDOM'S ROLE IN THE LIVES OF ISRAEL'S HEROES

10.1–21: This section recounts biblical history by highlighting the lives of seven heroes. The heroes are not named, but they are easily recognizable. Hero lists are found in other Jewish Hellenistic* texts, such as Sir 44–50, 1 Macc 2.51–60, and in the New Testament in Heb 11. (See also the chart of Hero Lists on pages 142–143.) This text focuses on Sophia's role in the heroes' lives and ultimately her role in guiding Israel generally. This focus is accomplished by means of anaphora,* a rhetorical* device in which the same word is repeated at the start of each new unit. (In this case the repeated catchword is not Sophia, but "she.") Anaphora is also employed in Heb 11. As is often the case with hero lists, Wis 10 is more than a list of exemplary figures; it is a review of history that seeks to explain the birth of Israel into a distinct nation. Wisdom not only guides Israel through history, she protects and separates God's holy people from wickedness.

---

10 Wisdom[d] protected the first-formed
   father of the world, when he
   alone had been created;
   she delivered him from his
   transgression,

---

a Gk *slave* b Gk *thrones* c Or *anxious*
d Gk *She*

2 and gave him strength to rule all
     things.
3 But when an unrighteous man departed
     from her in his anger,
he perished because in rage he killed
     his brother.
4 When the earth was flooded because of
     him, wisdom again saved it,
steering the righteous man by a paltry
     piece of wood.

5 Wisdom*a* also, when the nations in
     wicked agreement had been put
     to confusion,
recognized the righteous man and
     preserved him blameless before
     God,
and kept him strong in the face of his
     compassion for his child.

6 Wisdom*a* rescued a righteous man when
     the ungodly were perishing;
he escaped the fire that descended on
     the Five Cities.*b*
7 Evidence of their wickedness still
     remains:
a continually smoking wasteland,
plants bearing fruit that does not
     ripen,
and a pillar of salt standing as a
     monument to an unbelieving
     soul.
8 For because they passed wisdom by,
they not only were hindered from
     recognizing the good,
but also left for humankind a reminder
     of their folly,
so that their failures could never go
     unnoticed.

9 Wisdom rescued from troubles those
     who served her.
10 When a righteous man fled from his
     brother's wrath,
she guided him on straight paths;
she showed him the kingdom of God,
and gave him knowledge of holy
     things;
she prospered him in his labors,
and increased the fruit of his toil.

11 When his oppressors were covetous,
     she stood by him and made him rich.
12 She protected him from his enemies,
     and kept him safe from those who lay in
     wait for him;
in his arduous contest she gave him the
     victory,
so that he might learn that godliness is
     more powerful than anything
     else.

10.1–12. 1: The author begins with the first human,
Adam. **3–4:** The mention of Cain explains the reason
for the *flood* and creates the contrast between the
wicked and the *righteous,* who is Noah. **5:** Abraham
is set against the background of the Tower of Babel
story. Although Abraham only appears in Genesis after
Babel (Gen 12.1), later Jewish tradition understood
him as part of the Babel generation. **6–8:** Lot's story is
recounted in Gen 19.1–29. **9–12:** The author has in
mind several events from Jacob's life (Gen 27–32).

13 When a righteous man was sold,
     wisdom*c* did not desert him,
but delivered him from sin.
     She descended with him into the
     dungeon,
14 and when he was in prison she did not
     leave him,
until she brought him the scepter of a
     kingdom
and authority over his masters.
     Those who accused him she showed to
     be false,
and she gave him everlasting honor.

15 A holy people and blameless race
wisdom delivered from a nation of
     oppressors.
16 She entered the soul of a servant of the
     Lord,
and withstood dread kings with wonders
     and signs.
17 She gave to holy people the reward of
     their labors;
she guided them along a marvelous
     way,
and became a shelter to them by day,
and a starry flame through the night.

a Gk *She*   *b* Or *on Pentapolis*   *c* Gk *she*

18 She brought them over the Red Sea,
   and led them through deep waters;
19 but she drowned their enemies,
   and cast them up from the depth of the
      sea.
20 Therefore the righteous plundered the
      ungodly;
   they sang hymns, O Lord, to your holy
      name,
   and praised with one accord your
      defending hand;
21 for wisdom opened the mouths of those
      who were mute,
   and made the tongues of infants speak
      clearly.

10.13–21. 13–14: The story of Joseph is found in Gen 37–50. *Delivered him from sin* most likely refers to the attempted seduction by Potiphar's wife (Gen 39). 15: *A holy people and blameless race* refers to Israel, while the *nation of oppressors* is Egypt. 16: God calls Moses his *servant* in Num 12.6–8. 17–21: These verses refer to several events of the Exodus. The Exodus story functions to illustrate the fundamental contrast between Jews and gentiles* (particularly Egyptians), between Judaism and pagan idolatry,* in chs. 11–19.

GOD'S JUDGMENT

11.1–12.27: This section deals with God's actions toward Jews (the Israelites liberated from Egypt) and gentiles* (the Egyptians and the Canaanites).

11 Wisdom*a* prospered their works by the hand of a holy prophet.
2 They journeyed through an uninhabited
      wilderness,
   and pitched their tents in untrodden
      places.
3 They withstood their enemies and
      fought off their foes.
4 When they were thirsty, they called
      upon you,
   and water was given them out of flinty
      rock,
   and from hard stone a remedy for their
      thirst.
5 For through the very things by which
      their enemies were punished,
   they themselves received benefit in their
      need.

6 Instead of the fountain of an ever-
      flowing river,
   stirred up and defiled with blood
7 in rebuke for the decree to kill the
      infants,
   you gave them abundant water
      unexpectedly,
8 showing by their thirst at that time
   how you punished their enemies.
9 For when they were tried, though they
      were being disciplined in mercy,
   they learned how the ungodly were
      tormented when judged in wrath.
10 For you tested them as a parent*b* does
      in warning,
   but you examined the ungodly*c* as a
      stern king does in condemnation.
11 Whether absent or present, they were
      equally distressed,
12 for a twofold grief possessed them,
   and a groaning at the memory of what
      had occurred.
13 For when they heard that through their
      own punishments
   the righteous*d* had received benefit,
      they perceived it was the Lord's
      doing.
14 For though they had mockingly rejected
      him who long before had been
      cast out and exposed,
   at the end of the events they marveled
      at him,
   when they felt thirst in a different way
      from the righteous.

11.1–14: The author has in mind the wilderness experience. 1: Moses is called a *prophet** in Deut 18.15; 34.10. 4: *Water . . . out of flinty rock* comes from Ex 17.1–7. 5–14: The author contrasts the difficult circumstances of the Israelites with those of the Egyptians. God disciplined the Israelites *in mercy* (v. 9) when they were disobedient, while the Egyptians were punished as a form of *condemnation* (v. 10).

15 In return for their foolish and wicked
      thoughts,
   which led them astray to worship
      irrational serpents and worthless
      animals,

a Gk *She*   *b* Gk *a father*   *c* Gk *those*   *d* Gk *they*

you sent upon them a multitude of
irrational creatures to punish
them,
16 so that they might learn that one is
punished by the very things by
which one sins.
17 For your all-powerful hand,
which created the world out of formless
matter,
did not lack the means to send upon
them a multitude of bears, or
bold lions,
18 or newly-created unknown beasts full of
rage,
or such as breathe out fiery breath,
or belch forth a thick pall of smoke,
or flash terrible sparks from their eyes;
19 not only could the harm they did
destroy people,ᵃ
but the mere sight of them could kill by
fright.
20 Even apart from these, peopleᵇ could
fall at a single breath
when pursued by justice
and scattered by the breath of your
power.
But you have arranged all things by
measure and number and
weight.
21 For it is always in your power to show
great strength,
and who can withstand the might of
your arm?
22 Because the whole world before you is
like a speck that tips the scales,
and like a drop of morning dew that
falls on the ground.
23 But you are merciful to all, for you can
do all things,
and you overlook people's sins, so that
they may repent.
24 For you love all things that exist,
and detest none of the things that you
have made,
for you would not have made anything if
you had hated it.
25 How would anything have endured if
you had not willed it?
Or how would anything not called forth
by you have been preserved?

26 You spare all things, for they are yours,
O Lord, you who love the living.

12 For your immortal spirit is in all
things.
2 Therefore you correct little by little
those who trespass,
and you remind and warn them of the
things through which they sin,
so that they may be freed from
wickedness and put their trust in
you, O Lord.

11.15–12.2: These verses attempt to explain why God did not simply destroy the Egyptians, since Egypt not only still exists but has continued to oppress God's people in the author's time. 15: Other writers also ridicule Egyptian worship of animals (see, for example, Philo,* *Decalogue* 76–80). 17–20: Even frightening, destructive creatures are products of God's intended plan. See also 12.26–27. 17: *Formless matter* is the material out of which earthly reality is composed. In Greek cosmology, it is an eternal, uncreated substance; whether the author of Wisdom holds that view is not clear.

---

3 Those who lived long ago in your holy
land
4 you hated for their detestable practices,
their works of sorcery and unholy rites,
5 their merciless slaughterᶜ of children,
and their sacrificial feasting on human
flesh and blood.
These initiates from the midst of a
heathen cult,ᵈ
6 these parents who murder helpless lives,
you willed to destroy by the hands of
our ancestors,
7 so that the land most precious of all to
you
might receive a worthy colony of the
servantsᵉ of God.
8 But even these you spared, since they
were but mortals,
and sent waspsᶠ as forerunners of your
army
to destroy them little by little,

a Gk *them*   b Gk *they*   c Gk *slaughterers*
d Meaning of Gk uncertain   e Or *children*
f Or *hornets*

9 though you were not unable to give the
    ungodly into the hands of the
    righteous in battle,
  or to destroy them at one blow by dread
    wild animals or your stern word.
10 But judging them little by little you gave
    them an opportunity to repent,
  though you were not unaware that their
    origin*a* was evil
  and their wickedness inborn,
  and that their way of thinking would
    never change.
11 For they were an accursed race from
    the beginning,
  and it was not through fear of anyone
    that you left them unpunished
    for their sins.

12 For who will say, "What have you done?"
  or will resist your judgment?
  Who will accuse you for the destruction
    of nations that you made?
  Or who will come before you to plead as
    an advocate for the unrighteous?
13 For neither is there any god besides you,
    whose care is for all people,*b*
  to whom you should prove that you have
    not judged unjustly;
14 nor can any king or monarch confront
    you about those whom you have
    punished.
15 You are righteous and you rule all things
    righteously,
  deeming it alien to your power
  to condemn anyone who does not
    deserve to be punished.
16 For your strength is the source of
    righteousness,
  and your sovereignty over all causes you
    to spare all.
17 For you show your strength when people
    doubt the completeness of your
    power,
  and you rebuke any insolence among
    those who know it.*c*
18 Although you are sovereign in strength,
    you judge with mildness,
  and with great forbearance you govern
    us;
  for you have power to act whenever you
    choose.

19 Through such works you have taught
    your people
  that the righteous must be kind,
  and you have filled your children with
    good hope,
  because you give repentance for sins.
20 For if you punished with such great care
    and indulgence*d*
  the enemies of your servants*e* and those
    deserving of death,
  granting them time and opportunity to
    give up their wickedness,
21 with what strictness you have judged
    your children,
  to whose ancestors you gave oaths and
    covenants full of good promises!
22 So while chastening us you scourge our
    enemies ten thousand times
    more,
  so that, when we judge, we may meditate
    upon your goodness,
  and when we are judged, we may expect
    mercy.

23 Therefore those who lived unrighteously,
    in a life of folly,
  you tormented through their own
    abominations.
24 For they went far astray on the paths of
    error,
  accepting as gods those animals that
    even their enemies*f* despised;
  they were deceived like foolish
    infants.

a Or *nature*   *b* Or *all things*   *c* Meaning of Gk
uncertain   *d* Other ancient authorities lack *and
indulgence*; others read *and entreaty*   *e* Or *children*
f Gk *they*

25 Therefore, as though to children who
    cannot reason,
  you sent your judgment to mock them.
26 But those who have not heeded the
    warning of mild rebukes
  will experience the deserved judgment of
    God.
27 For when in their suffering they became
    incensed
  at those creatures that they had thought
    to be gods, being punished by
    means of them,
  they saw and recognized as the true God
    the one whom they had before
    refused to know.
  Therefore the utmost condemnation
    came upon them.

12.19–27. 19–22: God's *mercy* serves as a model of righteousness for Israel. **23–27:** The mention of the worship of *animals* indicates that the subject of God's punishment here is again the Egyptians. **27:** The author most likely has in mind the ten plagues.

13 For all people who were ignorant of
    God were foolish by nature;
  and they were unable from the good
    things that are seen to know the
    one who exists,
  nor did they recognize the artisan while
    paying heed to his works;
2 but they supposed that either fire or
    wind or swift air,
  or the circle of the stars, or turbulent
    water,
  or the luminaries of heaven were the
    gods that rule the world.
3 If through delight in the beauty of these
    things people assumed them to be
    gods,
  let them know how much better than
    these is their Lord,
  for the author of beauty created them.
4 And if people*a* were amazed at their
    power and working,
  let them perceive from them
  how much more powerful is the one who
    formed them.
5 For from the greatness and beauty of
    created things

comes a corresponding perception of
    their Creator.
6 Yet these people are little to be blamed,
  for perhaps they go astray
  while seeking God and desiring to find
    him.
7 For while they live among his works,
    they keep searching,
  and they trust in what they see, because
    the things that are seen are
    beautiful.
8 Yet again, not even they are to be
    excused;
9 for if they had the power to know so
    much
  that they could investigate the world,
  how did they fail to find sooner the Lord
    of these things?

13.1–9: Worship of creation, rather than creator. The beauty of the natural world reflects the plan of an intelligent mind—this is known as the argument from design, a proof for the existence of God used throughout the centuries. The argument in antiquity represents a well-known strategy for undermining nature worship in order to demonstrate that the invisible God lies behind the visible world; it appears in Stoic* writings, in Philo,* and in truncated form in Paul (Rom 1.18–25). **2:** Elements such as fire and water and celestial bodies were commonly viewed as deities. Even in Judaism, celestial bodies were sometimes conceived as subordinate deities or angelic beings, part of the heavenly host (see Ps 89.5–7; Sir 42.16–17).

AGAINST IDOLATRY*

13.10–15.19: While the worshippers of nature may be called foolish (13.1), the author intensifies his attack when he turns to idolaters. The author's rhetoric,* including the facetious tone, reflects classic Jewish polemic* against pagan religion. Such polemic becomes especially prominent after the Exile* (see, for example, Isa 44.9–20; 46.1–7; Bel and the Dragon) and was a favorite topic of Philo* (see, for example, *Decalogue* 52–81).

10 But miserable, with their hopes set on
    dead things, are those

a Gk *they*

who give the name "gods" to the works of
  human hands,
gold and silver fashioned with skill,
and likenesses of animals,
or a useless stone, the work of an
  ancient hand.
11 A skilled woodcutter may saw down a
  tree easy to handle
and skillfully strip off all its bark,
and then with pleasing workmanship
make a useful vessel that serves life's
  needs,
12 and burn the cast-off pieces of his
  work
to prepare his food, and eat his fill.
13 But a cast-off piece from among them,
  useful for nothing,
a stick crooked and full of knots,
he takes and carves with care in his
  leisure,
and shapes it with skill gained in
  idleness;[a]
he forms it in the likeness of a human
  being,
14 or makes it like some worthless animal,
giving it a coat of red paint and coloring
  its surface red
and covering every blemish in it with
  paint;
15 then he makes a suitable niche for it,
and sets it in the wall, and fastens it
  there with iron.
16 He takes thought for it, so that it may
  not fall,
because he knows that it cannot help
  itself,
for it is only an image and has need of
  help.
17 When he prays about possessions and
  his marriage and children,
he is not ashamed to address a lifeless
  thing.
18 For health he appeals to a thing that is
  weak;
for life he prays to a thing that is dead;
for aid he entreats a thing that is utterly
  inexperienced;
for a prosperous journey, a thing that
  cannot take a step;
19 for money-making and work and success
  with his hands

he asks strength of a thing whose hands
  have no strength.

14 Again, one preparing to sail and
  about to voyage over raging waves
calls upon a piece of wood more fragile
  than the ship that carries him.
2 For it was desire for gain that planned
  that vessel,
and wisdom was the artisan who built it;
3 but it is your providence, O Father, that
  steers its course,
because you have given it a path in the
  sea,
and a safe way through the waves,
4 showing that you can save from every
  danger,
so that even a person who lacks skill may
  put to sea.
5 It is your will that works of your wisdom
  should not be without effect;
therefore people trust their lives even to
  the smallest piece of wood,
and passing through the billows on a raft
  they come safely to land.
6 For even in the beginning, when
  arrogant giants were perishing,
the hope of the world took refuge on a
  raft,
and guided by your hand left to the
  world the seed of a new
  generation.
7 For blessed is the wood by which
  righteousness comes.

8 But the idol made with hands is
  accursed, and so is the one who
  made it—
he for having made it, and the perishable
  thing because it was named a god.
9 For equally hateful to God are the
  ungodly and their ungodliness;
10 for what was done will be punished
  together with the one who did it.
11 Therefore there will be a visitation also
  upon the heathen idols,
because, though part of what God
  created, they became an
  abomination,

a Other ancient authorities read *with intelligent skill*

snares for human souls
and a trap for the feet of the foolish.

12 For the idea of making idols was the
        beginning of fornication,
and the invention of them was the
        corruption of life;
13 for they did not exist from the
        beginning,
nor will they last forever.
14 For through human vanity they entered
        the world,
and therefore their speedy end has been
        planned.
15 For a father, consumed with grief at an
        untimely bereavement,
made an image of his child, who had
        been suddenly taken from him;
he now honored as a god what was once
        a dead human being,
and handed on to his dependents secret
        rites and initiations.
16 Then the ungodly custom, grown strong
        with time, was kept as a law,
and at the command of monarchs
        carved images were worshiped.
17 When people could not honor monarchs[a]
        in their presence, since they lived
        at a distance,
they imagined their appearance far
        away,
and made a visible image of the king
        whom they honored,
so that by their zeal they might flatter
        the absent one as though
        present.
18 Then the ambition of the artisan
        impelled
even those who did not know the king
        to intensify their worship.
19 For he, perhaps wishing to please his
        ruler,
skillfully forced the likeness to take
        more beautiful form,
20 and the multitude, attracted by the
        charm of his work,
now regarded as an object of worship
        the one whom shortly before they
        had honored as a human being.

21 And this became a hidden trap for
        humankind,
because people, in bondage to
        misfortune or to royal authority,
bestowed on objects of stone or wood
        the name that ought not to be
        shared.

13.10–14.21. 14.6–7: The discussion of the wood
from which idols as well as ships are made causes the
author to recall Noah's building of the ark, which indeed saved the human race. The point is to ridicule
idol worshippers who appeal to a tiny statue to save
them from a perilous sea voyage. Compare Let Jer 59.
12–13: See comment on vv. 22–31. **15–21:** This story
functions as a tale of the origins of idolatry.*

22 Then it was not enough for them to err
        about the knowledge of God,
but though living in great strife due to
        ignorance,
they call such great evils peace.
23 For whether they kill children in their
        initiations, or celebrate secret
        mysteries,
or hold frenzied revels with strange
        customs,
24 they no longer keep either their lives or
        their marriages pure,
but they either treacherously kill one
        another, or grieve one another by
        adultery,
25 and all is a raging riot of blood and
        murder, theft and deceit,
        corruption, faithlessness, tumult,
        perjury,
26 confusion over what is good,
        forgetfulness of favors,
defiling of souls, sexual perversion,
disorder in marriages, adultery, and
        debauchery.
27 For the worship of idols not to be
        named
is the beginning and cause and end of
        every evil.
28 For their worshipers[b] either rave in
        exultation,
or prophesy lies, or live unrighteously,
        or readily commit perjury;

_a_ Gk them   _b_ Gk they

29 for because they trust in lifeless idols
   they swear wicked oaths and expect to
      suffer no harm.
30 But just penalties will overtake them on
      two counts:
   because they thought wrongly about
         God in devoting themselves to
         idols,
   and because in deceit they swore
         unrighteously through contempt
         for holiness.
31 For it is not the power of the things by
      which people swear,^a
   but the just penalty for those who sin,
      that always pursues the transgression of
         the unrighteous.

14.22–31: Idolatry* was often viewed by Jewish writers as the sin that leads to all other sins (this theme pervades the *Biblical Antiquities* of Pseudo-Philo, a writer roughly contemporary with Wisdom). **22:** *They call such great evils peace* means that idol worship inverts the proper social order, which is what the author describes in vv. 23–29. **24–26:** Jews often stereotyped gentiles* as sexually licentious. The connection between idolatry and deviant sexual behavior can also be found in Paul (Rom 1.20–27).

15 But you, our God, are kind and
      true,
   patient, and ruling all things^b in
      mercy.
2 For even if we sin we are yours,
      knowing your power;
   but we will not sin, because we know
      that you acknowledge us as
      yours.
3 For to know you is complete
      righteousness,
   and to know your power is the root of
      immortality.
4 For neither has the evil intent of human
      art misled us,
   nor the fruitless toil of painters,
   a figure stained with varied colors,
5 whose appearance arouses yearning in
      fools,
   so that they desire^c the lifeless form of
      a dead image.
6 Lovers of evil things and fit for such
      objects of hope^d

are those who either make or desire or
      worship them.

7 A potter kneads the soft earth
   and laboriously molds each vessel for
      our service,
   fashioning out of the same clay
   both the vessels that serve clean uses
   and those for contrary uses, making all
      alike;
   but which shall be the use of each of
      them
   the worker in clay decides.
8 With misspent toil, these workers form
      a futile god from the same clay—
   these mortals who were made of earth a
      short time before
   and after a little while go to the earth
      from which all mortals are taken,
   when the time comes to return the
      souls that were borrowed.
9 But the workers are not concerned that
      mortals are destined to die
   or that their life is brief,
   but they compete with workers in gold
      and silver,
   and imitate workers in copper;
   and they count it a glorious thing to
      mold counterfeit gods.
10 Their heart is ashes, their hope is
      cheaper than dirt,
   and their lives are of less worth than
      clay,
11 because they failed to know the one
      who formed them
   and inspired them with active souls
   and breathed a living spirit into them.
12 But they considered our existence an
      idle game,
   and life a festival held for profit,
   for they say one must get money
      however one can, even by base
      means.
13 For these persons, more than all others,
      know that they sin
   when they make from earthy matter
      fragile vessels and carved
      images.

---

a Or *of the oaths people swear*   *b* Or *ruling the universe*
c Gk *and he desires*   *d* Gk *such hopes*

14 But most foolish, and more miserable
      than an infant,
   are all the enemies who oppressed your
      people.
15 For they thought that all their heathen
      idols were gods,
   though these have neither the use of
      their eyes to see with,
   nor nostrils with which to draw breath,
   nor ears with which to hear,
   nor fingers to feel with,
   and their feet are of no use for walking.
16 For a human being made them,
   and one whose spirit is borrowed
      formed them;
   for none can form gods that are like
      themselves.
17 People are mortal, and what they make
      with lawless hands is dead;
   for they are better than the objects they
      worship,
   since[a] they have life, but the idols[b]
      never had.

15.1–19. 5: Jewish writers frequently poke fun at the
deadness of idols, particularly in comparison to "the
living God" (see Bel and the Dragon; 1 Thess 1.9).
7–13: The focus shifts from wooden idols to earthenware figurines. The author emphasizes that the *clay*
used to form idols is the same substance from which
humans were created (see Gen 2.7). 14–17: The only
difference between idols and humans is that humans
have been animated by a soul; this alone highlights
the absurdity of venerating idols which have no spiritual component.

---

18 Moreover, they worship even the most
      hateful animals,
   which are worse than all others when
      judged by their lack of
      intelligence;
19 and even as animals they are not so
      beautiful in appearance that one
      would desire them,
   but they have escaped both the praise of
      God and his blessing.
16 Therefore those people[e] were
      deservedly punished through
      such creatures,
   and were tormented by a multitude of
      animals.

2 Instead of this punishment you showed
      kindness to your people,
   and you prepared quails to eat,
   a delicacy to satisfy the desire of
      appetite;
3 in order that those people, when they
      desired food,
   might lose the least remnant of appetite[d]
   because of the odious creatures sent to
      them,
   while your people,[e] after suffering want
      a short time,
   might partake of delicacies.
4 For it was necessary that upon those
      oppressors inescapable want
      should come,
   while to these others it was merely
      shown how their enemies were
      being tormented.

5 For when the terrible rage of wild
      animals came upon your people[e]
   and they were being destroyed by the
      bites of writhing serpents,
   your wrath did not continue to the end;
6 they were troubled for a little while as a
      warning,
   and received a symbol of deliverance to
      remind them of your law's
      command.
7 For the one who turned toward it was
      saved, not by the thing that was
      beheld,
   but by you, the Savior of all.
8 And by this also you convinced our
      enemies
   that it is you who deliver from every
      evil.
9 For they were killed by the bites of
      locusts and flies,
   and no healing was found for them,
   because they deserved to be punished
      by such things.
10 But your children were not conquered
      even by the fangs of venomous
      serpents,

---

a Other ancient authorities read *of which*   b Gk *but
they*   c Gk *they*   d Gk *loathed the necessary appetite*
e Gk *them*

for your mercy came to their help and
healed them.

11 To remind them of your oracles they
were bitten,
and then were quickly delivered,
so that they would not fall into deep
forgetfulness
and become unresponsive[a] to your
kindness.

12 For neither herb nor poultice cured
them,
but it was your word, O Lord, that heals
all people.

13 For you have power over life and death;
you lead mortals down to the gates of
Hades and back again.

14 A person in wickedness kills another,
but cannot bring back the departed
spirit,
or set free the imprisoned soul.

15 To escape from your hand is impossible;

16 for the ungodly, refusing to know you,
were flogged by the strength of your
arm,
pursued by unusual rains and hail and
relentless storms,
and utterly consumed by fire.

17 For—most incredible of all—in water,
which quenches all things,
the fire had still greater effect,
for the universe defends the righteous.

18 At one time the flame was restrained,
so that it might not consume the
creatures sent against the
ungodly,
but that seeing this they might know
that they were being pursued by the
judgment of God;

19 and at another time even in the midst of
water it burned more intensely
than fire,
to destroy the crops of the unrighteous
land.

20 Instead of these things you gave your
people food of angels,
and without their toil you supplied them
from heaven with bread ready to
eat,
providing every pleasure and suited to
every taste.

21 For your sustenance manifested your
sweetness toward your children;
and the bread, ministering[b] to the
desire of the one who took it,
was changed to suit everyone's liking.

22 Snow and ice withstood fire without
melting,
so that they might know that the crops
of their enemies
were being destroyed by the fire that
blazed in the hail
and flashed in the showers of rain;

23 whereas the fire,[c] in order that the
righteous might be fed,
even forgot its native power.

24 For creation, serving you who made it,
exerts itself to punish the unrighteous,
and in kindness relaxes on behalf of
those who trust in you.

25 Therefore at that time also, changed
into all forms,
it served your all-nourishing bounty,
according to the desire of those who
had need,[d]

26 so that your children, whom you loved,
O Lord, might learn
that it is not the production of crops
that feeds humankind
but that your word sustains those who
trust in you.

27 For what was not destroyed by fire
was melted when simply warmed by a
fleeting ray of the sun,

28 to make it known that one must rise
before the sun to give you
thanks,
and must pray to you at the dawning of
the light;

29 for the hope of an ungrateful person
will melt like wintry frost,
and flow away like waste water.

**16.1–29: The contrasting fate of the Egyptians and
the Israelites.** The author again compares the fate of
the Egyptians with that of the Israelites (compare Ex
11.7). God cared for the Israelites in the wilderness,
while the Egyptians were punished and left wanting.

a Meaning of Gk uncertain   b Gk and it, ministering
c Gk this   d Or who made supplication

Although there are several references to particular events of the Exodus story and wilderness experience, the chronology of the story is not followed. The author makes use of the Exodus as a singular, symbolic event, rather than as a sequential narrative.* **2:** The story of God's sending the *quails* is found in Num 11 (compare Ex 16.13). **5–14:** The story of the bronze *serpent* comes from Num 21.4–9. **7:** The people were not actually healed by the serpent, but by God. **9:** *Locusts and flies* refers to the plagues visited upon the Egyptians (Ex 8.20–24; 10.4–15). More plagues are referred to in vv. 16–19. **20–21:** In contrast to the torments inflicted upon their oppressors, the Israelites receive manna. That manna changed its taste according to each person's satisfaction is an interpretive tradition found also in rabbinic texts (compare Ex 16.15–21).

17 Great are your judgments and hard
    to describe;
  therefore uninstructed souls have gone
    astray.
2 For when lawless people supposed that
    they held the holy nation in their
    power,
  they themselves lay as captives of
    darkness and prisoners of long
    night,
  shut in under their roofs, exiles from
    eternal providence.
3 For thinking that in their secret sins
    they were unobserved
  behind a dark curtain of forgetfulness,
  they were scattered, terribly[a] alarmed,
  and appalled by specters.
4 For not even the inner chamber that
    held them protected them from
    fear,
  but terrifying sounds rang out around
    them,
  and dismal phantoms with gloomy faces
    appeared.
5 And no power of fire was able to give
    light,
  nor did the brilliant flames of the stars
  avail to illumine that hateful night.
6 Nothing was shining through to them
  except a dreadful, self-kindled fire,
  and in terror they deemed the things
    that they saw
  to be worse than that unseen
    appearance.

7 The delusions of their magic art lay
    humbled,
  and their boasted wisdom was scornfully
    rebuked.
8 For those who promised to drive off the
    fears and disorders of a sick soul
  were sick themselves with ridiculous
    fear.
9 For even if nothing disturbing
    frightened them,
  yet, scared by the passing of wild
    animals and the hissing of snakes
10 they perished in trembling fear,
  refusing to look even at the air, though
    it nowhere could be avoided.
11 For wickedness is a cowardly thing,
    condemned by its own testimony;[b]
  distressed by conscience, it has always
    exaggerated[c] the difficulties.
12 For fear is nothing but a giving up of
    the helps that come from reason;
13 and hope, defeated by this inward
    weakness,
  prefers ignorance of what causes the
    torment.
14 But throughout the night, which was
    really powerless
  and which came upon them from the
    recesses of powerless Hades,
  they all slept the same sleep,
15 and now were driven by monstrous
    specters,
  and now were paralyzed by their souls'
    surrender;
  for sudden and unexpected fear
    overwhelmed them.
16 And whoever was there fell down,
  and thus was kept shut up in a prison
    not made of iron;
17 for whether they were farmers or
    shepherds
  or workers who toiled in the wilderness,
  they were seized, and endured the
    inescapable fate;
  for with one chain of darkness they all
    were bound.

a Other ancient authorities read *unobserved, they were darkened behind a dark curtain of forgetfulness, terribly* b Meaning of Gk uncertain c Other ancient authorities read *anticipated*

18 Whether there came a whistling wind,
  or a melodious sound of birds in wide-
    spreading branches,
  or the rhythm of violently rushing water,
19 or the harsh crash of rocks hurled
    down,
  or the unseen running of leaping
    animals,
  or the sound of the most savage roaring
    beasts,
  or an echo thrown back from a hollow
    of the mountains,
  it paralyzed them with terror.
20 For the whole world was illumined with
    brilliant light,
  and went about its work unhindered,
21 while over those people alone heavy
    night was spread,
  an image of the darkness that was
    destined to receive them;
  but still heavier than darkness were they
    to themselves.

17.1–21: The author elaborates upon the plague of *darkness* (Ex 10.21–23) with great drama. The Egyptians' experience of darkness mimics Hades,* the realm of the dead.

18 But for your holy ones there was
    very great light.
  Their enemies*a* heard their voices but
    did not see their forms,
  and counted them happy for not having
    suffered,
2 and were thankful that your holy ones,*b*
    though previously wronged, were
    doing them no injury;
  and they begged their pardon for having
    been at variance with them.*b*
3 Therefore you provided a flaming pillar
    of fire
  as a guide for your people's*c* unknown
    journey,
  and a harmless sun for their glorious
    wandering.
4 For their enemies*d* deserved to be
    deprived of light and imprisoned
    in darkness,
  those who had kept your children
    imprisoned,
  through whom the imperishable light of

the law was to be given to the
    world.

18.1–4: The *darkness* that encompassed the Egyptians is contrasted with the light, *the flaming pillar of fire*, that guided the Israelites through the wilderness at night (Ex 13.21).

5 When they had resolved to kill the
    infants of your holy ones,
  and one child had been abandoned and
    rescued,
  you in punishment took away a
    multitude of their children;
  and you destroyed them all together by
    a mighty flood.
6 That night was made known beforehand
    to our ancestors,
  so that they might rejoice in sure
    knowledge of the oaths in which
    they trusted.
7 The deliverance of the righteous and
    the destruction of their enemies
  were expected by your people.
8 For by the same means by which you
    punished our enemies
  you called us to yourself and glorified us.
9 For in secret the holy children of good
    people offered sacrifices,
  and with one accord agreed to the
    divine law,
  so that the saints would share alike the
    same things,
  both blessings and dangers;
  and already they were singing the
    praises of the ancestors.*e*
10 But the discordant cry of their enemies
    echoed back,
  and their piteous lament for their
    children was spread abroad.
11 The slave was punished with the same
    penalty as the master,
  and the commoner suffered the same
    loss as the king;
12 and they all together, by the one form*f*
    of death,
  had corpses too many to count.

a Gk *They*   b Meaning of Gk uncertain   c Gk *their*
d Gk *those persons*   e Other ancient authorities read
dangers, the ancestors already leading the songs of praise
f Gk *name*

For the living were not sufficient even
    to bury them,
since in one instant their most valued
    children had been destroyed.
13 For though they had disbelieved
    everything because of their magic
    arts,
yet, when their firstborn were destroyed,
    they acknowledged your people
    to be God's child.
14 For while gentle silence enveloped all
    things,
and night in its swift course was now
    half gone,
15 your all-powerful word leaped from
    heaven, from the royal throne,
into the midst of the land that was
    doomed,
a stern warrior
16 carrying the sharp sword of your
    authentic command,
and stood and filled all things with
    death,
and touched heaven while standing on
    the earth.
17 Then at once apparitions in dreadful
    dreams greatly troubled them,
and unexpected fears assailed them;
18 and one here and another there, hurled
    down half dead,
made known why they were dying;
19 for the dreams that disturbed them
    forewarned them of this,
so that they might not perish without
    knowing why they suffered.

20 The experience of death touched also
    the righteous,
and a plague came upon the multitude
    in the desert,
but the wrath did not long continue.
21 For a blameless man was quick to act as
    their champion;
he brought forward the shield of his
    ministry,
prayer and propitiation by incense;
he withstood the anger and put an end
    to the disaster,
showing that he was your servant.
22 He conquered the wrath*a* not by
    strength of body,

not by force of arms,
but by his word he subdued the
    avenger,
appealing to the oaths and covenants
    given to our ancestors.
23 For when the dead had already fallen on
    one another in heaps,
he intervened and held back the wrath,
and cut off its way to the living.
24 For on his long robe the whole world
    was depicted,
and the glories of the ancestors were
    engraved on the four rows of
    stones,
and your majesty was on the diadem
    upon his head.
25 To these the destroyer yielded, these he*b*
    feared;
for merely to test the wrath was enough.

18.5–25: The author now describes the tenth plague, the slaying of the *firstborn* (Ex 12.29–30). **5:** Pharaoh's smiting of the firstborn males among the Hebrews (Ex 1.8–22) becomes the reason for God's infliction of the tenth plague. *Mighty flood* refers to the drowning of the Egyptians in the Red Sea (see Ex 14.26–31; 15.8). Again, the author conflates events in the story. **9:** The author most likely thinks of the Passover* lambs when he says the *people offered sacrifices* (Ex 12.1–28). **10:** *Discordant cry* alludes to Ex 11.6; 12.30. **14–19:** The author attempts to envision how God carried out the smiting of the firstborn. **20–25:** These verses refer to the story in Num 16.43–50 in which Aaron makes use of incense to atone for the people and thus stops the *plague.* In Numbers, the Lord is responsible for having inflicted the plague; here it is *the avenger* (v. 22), whose destructive power must come from another source.

19 But the ungodly were assailed to
    the end by pitiless anger,
for God*c* knew in advance even their
    future actions:
2 how, though they themselves had
    permitted*d* your people to depart
and hastily sent them out,
they would change their minds and
    pursue them.

a Cn: Gk *multitude*   *b* Other ancient authorities read *they*   *c* Gk *he*   *d* Other ancient authorities read *had changed their minds to permit*

3 For while they were still engaged in
        mourning,
    and were lamenting at the graves of
        their dead,
    they reached another foolish decision,
    and pursued as fugitives those whom
        they had begged and compelled
        to leave.
4 For the fate they deserved drew them
        on to this end,
    and made them forget what had
        happened,
    in order that they might fill up the
        punishment that their torments
        still lacked,
5 and that your people might experience[a]
        an incredible journey,
    but they themselves might meet a
        strange death.

6 For the whole creation in its nature was
        fashioned anew,
    complying with your commands,
    so that your children[b] might be kept
        unharmed.
7 The cloud was seen overshadowing the
        camp,
    and dry land emerging where water had
        stood before,
    an unhindered way out of the Red Sea,
    and a grassy plain out of the raging
        waves,
8 where those protected by your hand
        passed through as one nation,
    after gazing on marvelous wonders.
9 For they ranged like horses,
    and leaped like lambs,
    praising you, O Lord, who delivered
        them.
10 For they still recalled the events of their
        sojourn,
    how instead of producing animals the
        earth brought forth gnats,
    and instead of fish the river spewed out
        vast numbers of frogs.
11 Afterward they saw also a new kind[c] of
        birds,
    when desire led them to ask for
        luxurious food;
12 for, to give them relief, quails came up
        from the sea.

19.1–12: The drowning of the Egyptians in the Red
Sea is their final punishment in the Exodus story (Ex
14.26–31). 1: *God knew in advance* reminds the
reader that "God hardened Pharaoh's heart" (Ex 11.9–
10)—a perspective that fits well with the notion that
souls are inherently good or evil (see comment on
5.13). 2–5: If the Egyptians had not *changed their
minds* and *pursued* the Israelites, they would not have
drowned. 6–12: This poetic praise of the miracle of the
Red Sea echoes Ps 114. See also vv. 18–21.

13 The punishments did not come upon
        the sinners
    without prior signs in the violence of
        thunder,
    for they justly suffered because of their
        wicked acts;
    for they practiced a more bitter hatred
        of strangers.
14 Others had refused to receive strangers
        when they came to them,
    but these made slaves of guests who
        were their benefactors.
15 And not only so—but, while
        punishment of some sort will
        come upon the former
    for having received strangers with
        hostility,
16 the latter, having first received them
        with festal celebrations,
    afterward afflicted with terrible
        sufferings
    those who had already shared the same
        rights.
17 They were stricken also with loss of
        sight—
    just as were those at the door of the
        righteous man—
    when, surrounded by yawning darkness,
    all of them tried to find the way through
        their own doors.

19.13–17: The author likens the Egyptians' enslavement of Israel to the treatment of the travelers in
Sodom (Gen 19.1–11). Both stories illustrate hateful
treatment of foreigners, but the Egyptians' offense is
considered far worse.

a Other ancient authorities read *accomplish*
b Or *servants*   c Or *production*

18 For the elements changed*a* places with
　　　one another,
　as on a harp the notes vary the nature
　　　of the rhythm,
　while each note remains the same.*b*
　This may be clearly inferred from the
　　　sight of what took place.
19 For land animals were transformed into
　　　water creatures,
　and creatures that swim moved over to
　　　the land.
20 Fire even in water retained its normal
　　　power,
　and water forgot its fire-quenching
　　　nature.
21 Flames, on the contrary, failed to
　　　consume
　the flesh of perishable creatures that
　　　walked among them,
　nor did they melt*c* the crystalline, quick-
　　　melting kind of heavenly food.

19.18–21: God's miraculous manipulation of nature during the Exodus is likened to a new creation. **20–21:** *Fire even in water* recalls the "pillar of fire" that led the people through the Red Sea and all along their journey (Ex 13.21).

22 For in everything, O Lord, you have
　　　exalted and glorified your
　　　people,
　and you have not neglected to help
　　　them at all times and in all
　　　places.

19.22: The concluding doxology reflects the tendency in Jewish tradition to recall the Exodus as the ultimate paradigm of hope for liberation.

a Gk *changing*　　b Meaning of Gk uncertain
c Cn: Gk *nor could be melted*

ECCLESIASTICUS, OR THE WISDOM OF JESUS SON OF SIRACH

Introduction

The Wisdom of Jesus, son of Sirach (the Greek rendition of the Hebrew "Joshua ben Sira"), commonly known as Ecclesiasticus, or simply Sirach, is a collection of Hebrew wisdom teachings authored by a highly respected Jerusalem scribe★ about 180 BCE. (The Latin title "Ecclesiasticus," the "church book," points to its early use by Christians.) Ben Sira, as he is commonly called, was a wisdom teacher and may have been the founder of a wisdom school; he may also have been a priest. The manuscript tradition for Sirach is complex. This English translation depends primarily upon different and often fragmentary Hebrew texts as well as Greek manuscripts.

The prologue, which was added by Ben Sira's grandson when he translated his grandfather's work into Greek, provides the date and place of translation (Egypt, about 117 BCE) as well as his motivation for undertaking the task of translation: Having found a paucity of available instruction in Jewish wisdom in the Diaspora,★ he published Ben Sira's book in Greek for those *who wished to gain learning and are disposed to live according to the law.* Indeed, it is from this perspective that Sirach offers advice on such topics as money, talk, and relationships.

The context within which Ben Sira produced his book of instruction was that of Hellenistic★ Judaism. After the conquest of Alexander the Great in 333 BCE, the Mediterranean world was divided up among Alexander's generals into individual Hellenistic dynasties. Over the next several hundred years the influence of Greek culture upon local peoples was extensive. Jews in the land of Israel as well as the Diaspora debated the extent to which Judaism could accommodate Greek ideas and practices. Conversely, Hellenistic rulers differed in the extent to which they would accommodate Judaism. Shortly after Sirach was composed, a Seleucid king, Antiochus IV Epiphanes,★ tried to force radical Hellenization by setting up a statue of Zeus in the Temple★ and outlawing Jewish practices. This crisis resulted in the Maccabean revolt (167–164 BCE), recounted in the first and second books of Maccabees.

Significantly, Sirach does not reflect explicit antagonism toward Greek culture. In fact, this is one reason that scholars date Sirach prior to the Maccabean revolt. To be sure, Ben Sira praises the glories of Judaism, displaying unmitigated pride in his Jewish tradition, but there is no evidence that he feels the tradition is seriously threatened. His wisdom, rather, reflects a sophisticated blend of Jewish beliefs, generic practical advice, and Hellenized notions of ethical piety. That Sirach contains practical advice is not surprising; such advice is typical of wisdom literature.★ What makes Sirach unique is its heavy reliance upon Jewish scripture and tradition. In comparison to Proverbs, for instance, Sirach has far more resonance with the books of the Hebrew Bible, containing numerous quotations, allusions, images, and summaries of the various parts of Jewish scripture.

READING GUIDE

As in so much of wisdom literature, the teachings of Sirach are conveyed through poetry. Similar to Proverbs in particular, Sirach is a loosely structured collection of instructional poems and proverbial sayings. At times its organization will seem almost random to the reader. Ben Sira often addresses the same theme at different points in the book. There is, however, a clear finale in chs. 44–50, the Hymn in Praise of the Ancestors, in which Ben Sira eulogizes the great heroes of Israel's history.

Besides the general interest in wisdom, the one overriding theme to which the reader should attend is the pursuit of honor. Ben Sira's ethical advice is predicated upon a system of honor and shame. In fact, the words "honor" and "shame" appear frequently. Honor for Ben Sira consists of much more than reputation; it is a commodity traded between men and used to achieve social status. Furthermore, although honor is measured by the esteem of one's peers, the ultimate sign of honor comes from God: the legacy of a good name that will last forever.

	Prologue
1.1–42.14	The instruction of Ben Sira
42.15–43.33	Praise of God's works in creation
44.1–50.29	Praise of the ancestors
51.1–30	Prayer and final praise of Wisdom

THE PROLOGUE

Many great teachings have been given to us through the Law and the Prophets and the others[a] that followed them, and for these we should praise Israel for instruction and wisdom. Now, those who read the scriptures must not only themselves understand them, but must also as lovers of learning be able through the spoken and written word to help the outsiders. So my grandfather Jesus, who had devoted himself especially to the reading of the Law and the Prophets and the other books of our ancestors, and had acquired considerable proficiency in them, was himself also led to write something pertaining to instruction and wisdom, so that by becoming familiar also with his book[b] those who love learning might make even greater progress in living according to the law.

You are invited therefore to read it with goodwill and attention, and to be indulgent in cases where, despite our diligent labor in translating, we may seem to have rendered some phrases imperfectly. For what was originally expressed in Hebrew does not have exactly the same sense when translated into another language. Not only this book, but even the Law itself, the Prophecies, and the rest of the books differ not a little when read in the original.

When I came to Egypt in the thirty-eighth year of the reign of Euergetes and stayed for some time, I found opportunity for no little instruction.[c] It seemed highly necessary that I should myself devote some diligence and labor to the translation of this book. During that time I have applied my skill day and night to complete and publish the book for those living abroad who wished to gain learning and are disposed to live according to the law.

Prologue. The prologue was not part of the original text of Sirach, but was written by Ben Sira's grandson as a preface to the Greek translation he made of his grandfather's work. Its purpose is to explain the motivation for the translation as well as the difficulty involved in translating Hebrew into Greek. It includes the first attestation to the tripartite canon* of Hebrew sacred writings: *the Law and the Prophets* and the *other books.*

1 All wisdom is from the Lord,
  and with him it remains forever.
2 The sand of the sea, the drops of rain,
  and the days of eternity—who can
    count them?

a Or *other books*   b Gk *with these things*   c Other ancient authorities read *I found a copy affording no little instruction*

3 The height of heaven, the breadth of
the earth,
the abyss, and wisdom[a]—who can
search them out?
4 Wisdom was created before all other
things,
and prudent understanding from
eternity.[b]
6 The root of wisdom—to whom has it
been revealed?
Her subtleties—who knows them?[c]
8 There is but one who is wise, greatly to
be feared,
seated upon his throne—the Lord.
9 It is he who created her;
he saw her and took her measure;
he poured her out upon all his works,
10 upon all the living according to his gift;
he lavished her upon those who love
him.[d]

1.1–10: The creation of Wisdom. As in Prov 1–9 and
Job 28, Wisdom is personified as a divine woman. She
is here described as having been created by God like
other parts of creation. The description is not meant
to be taken literally, since wisdom is an eternal attribute of God (v. 1). As in these verses, wisdom literature*
often reflects a tension between God's unknowable
wisdom and, at the same time, its revelation to humans by God.

11 The fear of the Lord is glory and
exultation,
and gladness and a crown of
rejoicing.
12 The fear of the Lord delights the heart,
and gives gladness and joy and long
life.[e]
13 Those who fear the Lord will have a
happy end;
on the day of their death they will be
blessed.

14 To fear the Lord is the beginning of
wisdom;
she is created with the faithful in the
womb.
15 She made[f] among human beings an
eternal foundation,
and among their descendants she will
abide faithfully.

16 To fear the Lord is fullness of wisdom;
she inebriates mortals with her fruits;
17 she fills their[g] whole house with
desirable goods,
and their[g] storehouses with her
produce.
18 The fear of the Lord is the crown of
wisdom,
making peace and perfect health to
flourish.[h]
19 She rained down knowledge and
discerning comprehension,
and she heightened the glory of those
who held her fast.
20 To fear the Lord is the root of wisdom,
and her branches are long life.[i]

22 Unjust anger cannot be justified,
for anger tips the scale to one's ruin.
23 Those who are patient stay calm until
the right moment,
and then cheerfulness comes back to
them.
24 They hold back their words until the
right moment;
then the lips of many tell of their
good sense.

25 In the treasuries of wisdom are wise
sayings,
but godliness is an abomination to a
sinner.
26 If you desire wisdom, keep the
commandments,
and the Lord will lavish her upon you.

a Other ancient authorities read *the depth of the abyss*
b Other ancient authorities add as verse 5, *The source of
wisdom is God's word in the highest heaven, and her ways
are the eternal commandments.* c Other ancient
authorities add as verse 7, *The knowledge of wisdom—to
whom was it manifested? And her abundant experience—
who has understood it?* d Other ancient authorities add
*Love of the Lord is glorious wisdom; to those to whom he
appears he apportions her, that they may see him.*
e Other ancient authorities add *The fear of the Lord is a
gift from the Lord; also for love he makes firm paths.*
f Gk *made as a nest* g Other ancient authorities read
her h Other ancient authorities add *Both are gifts of
God for peace; glory opens out for those who love him. He
saw her and took her measure.* i Other ancient
authorities add as verse 21, *The fear of the Lord drives
away sins; and where it abides, it will turn away all anger.*

27 For the fear of the Lord is wisdom and
       discipline,
   fidelity and humility are his delight.

28 Do not disobey the fear of the Lord;
       do not approach him with a divided
           mind.
29 Do not be a hypocrite before others,
       and keep watch over your lips.
30 Do not exalt yourself, or you may fall
       and bring dishonor upon yourself.
   The Lord will reveal your secrets
       and overthrow you before the whole
           congregation,
   because you did not come in the fear of
       the Lord,
   and your heart was full of deceit.

1.11–30: The fear of the Lord. This section constitutes a twenty-two-line poem, a form appearing periodically in Sirach. (Twenty-two is the number of letters
in the Hebrew alphabet.*) Taking his cue from Ps
111.10, *To fear the Lord is the beginning of wisdom,*
which is quoted in v. 14, Ben Sira equates the possession of wisdom with *the fear of the Lord.* Since the
pursuit of wisdom is a common goal found across cultures, *the fear of the Lord* may be a way of specifying
what counts as Jewish wisdom. **11–20:** Since Ben Sira
does not entertain the possibility of an afterlife, the
rewards and blessings of wisdom are manifest in one's
earthly life; they include happiness, long life, and lack
of want. Such a perspective is comparable to that of
Deut 6. **26–27:** The teachings of Ben Sira deal mostly
with practical wisdom that could just as easily apply to
gentile* as well as Jewish men. The reference to the
commandments, which fills out meaning of *the fear of
the Lord,* helps maintain a connection between Ben
Sira's general instructions for living and the explicitly
Jewish teachings of the Torah* (see also 2.16; 38.34b–
39.1). **28–30:** One who lacks wisdom inevitably *disobeys God,* which results in *dishonor.* Ben Sira's ethical
teachings are predicated upon a system of honor and
shame (dishonor). Dishonor is not an internal feeling
of guilt but rather a diminishment of one's esteem in
the eyes of others. God's way of punishing anyone
guilty of secret transgressions is to expose and thereby
shame the culprit *before the whole congregation.*

2 My child, when you come to serve the
     Lord,
   prepare yourself for testing.ᵃ

2 Set your heart right and be steadfast,
       and do not be impetuous in time of
           calamity.
3 Cling to him and do not depart,
       so that your last days may be
           prosperous.
4 Accept whatever befalls you,
       and in times of humiliation be
           patient.
5 For gold is tested in the fire,
       and those found acceptable, in the
           furnace of humiliation.ᵇ
6 Trust in him, and he will help you;
       make your ways straight, and hope in
           him.

7 You who fear the Lord, wait for his
       mercy;
   do not stray, or else you may fall.
8 You who fear the Lord, trust in him,
       and your reward will not be lost.
9 You who fear the Lord, hope for good
       things,
   for lasting joy and mercy.ᶜ
10 Consider the generations of old and
       see:
   has anyone trusted in the Lord and
       been disappointed?
   Or has anyone persevered in the fear of
       the Lordᵈ and been forsaken?
   Or has anyone called upon him and
       been neglected?
11 For the Lord is compassionate and
       merciful;
   he forgives sins and saves in time of
       distress.

12 Woe to timid hearts and to slack hands,
       and to the sinner who walks a double
           path!
13 Woe to the fainthearted who have no
       trust!
   Therefore they will have no shelter.
14 Woe to you who have lost your nerve!
   What will you do when the Lord's
       reckoning comes?

ᵃ Or *trials*   ᵇ Other ancient authorities add *in sickness
and poverty put your trust in him*   ᶜ Other ancient
authorities add *For his reward is an everlasting gift with
joy.*   ᵈ Gk *of him*

15 Those who fear the Lord do not disobey
    his words,
    and those who love him keep his
    ways.
16 Those who fear the Lord seek to please
    him,
    and those who love him are filled
    with his law.
17 Those who fear the Lord prepare their
    hearts,
    and humble themselves before him.
18 Let us fall into the hands of the Lord,
    but not into the hands of mortals;
    for equal to his majesty is his mercy,
    and equal to his name are his works.[a]

2.1–18: Life's trials. While Ben Sira maintains that the good are always rewarded (2.10) and the evil punished (7.1–3), he recognizes that people of all types go through hard times. He explains such times as tests which God administers; fidelity to God means that one will ultimately be rewarded. **1:** *My child* is a pedagogical expression in Hellenistic* antiquity and appears throughout the text of Sirach. **10:** *Generations of old* may refer generically to anyone's ancestors, but the expression also foreshadows chs. 44–50, in which Ben Sira catalogues the great heroes of biblical history. **18:** To *fall into the hands* can have ominous connotations, meaning to fall to the enemy in battle, and is elsewhere contrasted with the safety of falling into God's hands (see 2 Sam 24.14; 1 Chr 21.13; compare Heb 10.31). Falling *into the hands of mortals* represents the fear of being shamed by one's community.

3 Listen to me your father, O children;
    act accordingly, that you may be kept
    in safety.
2 For the Lord honors a father above his
    children,
    and he confirms a mother's right over
    her children.
3 Those who honor their father atone for
    sins,
4   and those who respect their mother
    are like those who lay up
    treasure.
5 Those who honor their father will have
    joy in their own children,
    and when they pray they will be
    heard.

6 Those who respect their father will have
    long life,
    and those who honor[b] their mother
    obey the Lord;
7   they will serve their parents as their
    masters.[c]
8 Honor your father by word and deed,
    that his blessing may come upon
    you.
9 For a father's blessing strengthens the
    houses of the children,
    but a mother's curse uproots their
    foundations.
10 Do not glorify yourself by dishonoring
    your father,
    for your father's dishonor is no glory
    to you.
11 The glory of one's father is one's own
    glory,
    and it is a disgrace for children not to
    respect their mother.
12 My child, help your father in his old
    age,
    and do not grieve him as long as he
    lives;
13 even if his mind fails, be patient with
    him;
    because you have all your faculties do
    not despise him.
14 For kindness to a father will not be
    forgotten,
    and will be credited to you against
    your sins;
15 in the day of your distress it will be
    remembered in your favor;
    like frost in fair weather, your sins
    will melt away.
16 Whoever forsakes a father is like a
    blasphemer,
    and whoever angers a mother is
    cursed by the Lord.

3.1–16: Honor father and mother. These verses comprise a tightly structured poem dedicated to the commandment to honor one's father and mother (Ex

a Syr: Gk lacks this line   b Heb: Other ancient
authorities read *comfort*   c In other ancient authorities
this line is preceded by *Those who fear the Lord honor
their father,*

20.12; Deut 5.16). This is the only one of the ten commandments to which the author devotes such extensive attention. In its Pentateuchal* context, it is the only commandment that is immediately followed by the promise of a reward, "so that your days may be long," which is alluded to in v. 6. This poem in particular offers insight into the complex economy of the honor-shame system. *Fathers,* because of their parental status, have the right to be *honored* above their children (v. 2). Ben Sira's ethical system requires knowing one's place in the social order (3.21). Since honoring a father includes caring for him in old age, a son guarantees future honor for himself in his old age by maintaining due respect for his father even when the father has become enfeebled. Thus, humbling oneself when appropriate earns one credit toward future honor.

~~~~~~~~~~~~~~~~~~~~~~~~~~~~~~~~~~~~~

17 My child, perform your tasks with
      humility;ᵃ
   then you will be loved by those whom
      God accepts.
18 The greater you are, the more you must
      humble yourself;
   so you will find favor in the sight of
      the Lord.ᵇ
20 For great is the might of the Lord;
   but by the humble he is glorified.
21 Neither seek what is too difficult for
      you,
   nor investigate what is beyond your
      power.
22 Reflect upon what you have been
      commanded,
   for what is hidden is not your
      concern.
23 Do not meddle in matters that are
      beyond you,
   for more than you can understand
      has been shown you.
24 For their conceit has led many astray,
   and wrong opinion has impaired their
      judgment.
25 Without eyes there is no light;
   without knowledge there is no
      wisdom.ᶜ
26 A stubborn mind will fare badly at the
      end,
   and whoever loves danger will perish
      in it.

27 A stubborn mind will be burdened by
      troubles,
   and the sinner adds sin to sins.
28 When calamity befalls the proud, there
      is no healing,
   for an evil plant has taken root in
      him.
29 The mind of the intelligent appreciates
      proverbs,
   and an attentive ear is the desire of
      the wise.

3.17–31: Glory and humility. Although a cultivated man's goal is the accrual of honor, an attitude of *humility* must accompany his devotion to this goal. **20–22:** Lack of humility carries the danger of excessive pride. God, who naturally stands at the top of the hierarchy, possesses the greatest share of glory. God's glory is made manifest through the humility of mortals, which includes awareness of one's limitations in obtaining wisdom. **30–31:** These verses remind the reader that charitable acts help insure one's *future,* which can include calamity and dependence on the generosity of others (see 7.32–36). This theme connects the previous section to the one that follows.

~~~~~~~~~~~~~~~~~~~~~~~~~~~~~~~~~~~~~

30 As water extinguishes a blazing fire,
   so almsgiving atones for sin.
31 Those who repay favors give thought to
      the future;
   when they fall they will find support.

4 My child, do not cheat the poor of
      their living,
   and do not keep needy eyes waiting.
2 Do not grieve the hungry,
   or anger one in need.
3 Do not add to the troubles of the
      desperate,
   or delay giving to the needy.
4 Do not reject a suppliant in distress,
   or turn your face away from the poor.
5 Do not avert your eye from the needy,
   and give no one reason to curse you;
6 for if in bitterness of soul some should
      curse you,
   their Creator will hear their prayer.

---

a Heb: Gk *meekness*   *b* Other ancient authorities add as verse 19, *Many are lofty and renowned, but to the humble he reveals his secrets.*   *c* Heb: Other ancient authorities lack verse 25

7 Endear yourself to the congregation;
    bow your head low to the great.
8 Give a hearing to the poor,
    and return their greeting politely.
9 Rescue the oppressed from the
        oppressor;
    and do not be hesitant in giving a
        verdict.
10 Be a father to orphans,
    and be like a husband to their
        mother;
    you will then be like a son of the Most
        High,
    and he will love you more than does
        your mother.

4.1–10: Care for those in need. Care for those who of necessity depend upon the good will of others for their survival reflects a standard of ethical piety that is well-represented in the various parts of the biblical tradition: in legal texts (Deut 24.17–22); in the prophets* (Amos 2.6–7); and elsewhere in wisdom literature* (Job 29.12–20; Prov 19.17, though compare Prov 19.6–7; Sir 10.26–31). **9:** *Giving a verdict* implies that Ben Sira's school trained those who would likely become legal advisers and judges.

~~~~~

11 Wisdom teaches[a] her children
    and gives help to those who seek her.
12 Whoever loves her loves life,
    and those who seek her from early
        morning are filled with joy.
13 Whoever holds her fast inherits glory,
    and the Lord blesses the place she[b]
        enters.
14 Those who serve her minister to the
        Holy One;
    the Lord loves those who love her.
15 Those who obey her will judge the
        nations,
    and all who listen to her will live
        secure.
16 If they remain faithful, they will inherit
        her;
    their descendants will also obtain her.
17 For at first she will walk with them on
        tortuous paths;
    she will bring fear and dread upon
        them,
    and will torment them by her discipline
    until she trusts them,[c]

and she will test them with her
        ordinances.
18 Then she will come straight back to
        them again and gladden them,
    and will reveal her secrets to them.
19 If they go astray she will forsake them,
    and hand them over to their ruin.

4.11–19: The counsel of Wisdom. The author here focuses on how it is that Wisdom manifests herself in the work of human beings. **17:** Part of obtaining wisdom is enduring life's trials so as to be *disciplined* by them. Such a notion of education derives from the Greek concept of education known as "paideia." See comment on 6.18.

~~~~~

20 Watch for the opportune time, and
        beware of evil,
    and do not be ashamed to be yourself.
21 For there is a shame that leads to sin,
    and there is a shame that is glory and
        favor.
22 Do not show partiality, to your own
        harm,
    or deference, to your downfall.
23 Do not refrain from speaking at the
        proper moment,[d]
    and do not hide your wisdom.[e]
24 For wisdom becomes known through
        speech,
    and education through the words of
        the tongue.
25 Never speak against the truth,
    but be ashamed of your ignorance.
26 Do not be ashamed to confess your sins,
    and do not try to stop the current of a
        river.
27 Do not subject yourself to a fool,
    or show partiality to a ruler.
28 Fight to the death for truth,
    and the Lord God will fight for you.
29 Do not be reckless in your speech,
    or sluggish and remiss in your deeds.
30 Do not be like a lion in your home,
    or suspicious of your servants.

a Heb Syr: Gk *exalts*   *b* Or *he*   *c* Or *until they remain faithful in their heart*   *d* Heb: Gk *at a time of salvation*   *e* So some Gk Mss and Heb Syr Lat: Other Gk Mss lack *and do not hide your wisdom*

31 Do not let your hand be stretched out to
        receive
    and closed when it is time to give.

4.20–31: Shame and humility. There are two kinds of *shame,* one necessary and appropriate, the other dangerous and destructive. The first kind of shame is comparable to the contemporary understanding of modesty or humility. Modesty applies primarily to women and humility to men. In this context, where the author addresses male humility, he admonishes his students to ascertain their gifts as well as their limitations relative to others. In other words, they should know exactly where they stand in the social order, being ashamed of their ignorance (v. 25) if they stand before one who is more educated, but never subjecting themselves to one more ignorant (v. 27).

5 Do not rely on your wealth,
        or say, "I have enough."
  2 Do not follow your inclination and
        strength
    in pursuing the desires of your heart.
  3 Do not say, "Who can have power over
        me?"
    for the Lord will surely punish you.

  4 Do not say, "I sinned, yet what has
        happened to me?"
    for the Lord is slow to anger.
  5 Do not be so confident of forgiveness*a*
    that you add sin to sin.
  6 Do not say, "His mercy is great,
        he will forgive*b* the multitude of my
        sins,"
    for both mercy and wrath are with
        him,
    and his anger will rest on sinners.
  7 Do not delay to turn back to the Lord,
    and do not postpone it from day to
        day;
    for suddenly the wrath of the Lord will
        come upon you,
    and at the time of punishment you
        will perish.
  8 Do not depend on dishonest wealth,
    for it will not benefit you on the day
        of calamity.

  9 Do not winnow in every wind,
    or follow every path.*c*

10 Stand firm for what you know,
    and let your speech be consistent.
11 Be quick to hear,
    but deliberate in answering.
12 If you know what to say, answer your
        neighbor;
    but if not, put your hand over your
        mouth.
13 Honor and dishonor come from
        speaking,
    and the tongue of mortals may be
        their downfall.
14 Do not be called double-tongued*d*
    and do not lay traps with your tongue;
    for shame comes to the thief,
    and severe condemnation to the
        double-tongued.
15 In great and small matters cause no
        harm,*e*

6 1and do not become an enemy instead
        of a friend;
    for a bad name incurs shame and
        reproach;
    so it is with the double-tongued
        sinner.

  2 Do not fall into the grip of passion,*f*
    or you may be torn apart as by a bull.*g*
  3 Your leaves will be devoured and your
        fruit destroyed,
    and you will be left like a withered
        tree.
  4 Evil passion destroys those who have it,
    and makes them the laughingstock of
        their enemies.

5.1–6.4: The dangers of money, talk, and passion. Another twenty-two-line poem provides an overview of three topics of central importance throughout the text of Sirach: *wealth, speech,* and *desire.* All three have the potential to bring one to ruin. Wealth should not be gained by thievery (5.8, 14b). Speech must not be *double-tongued* (5.14), meaning it should never be deceitful or self-serving. **6.2–4:** These verses present

a Heb: Gk *atonement*   *b* Heb: Gk *he* (or *it*) *will atone for*   *c* Gk adds *so it is with the double-tongued sinner* (see 6.1)   *d* Heb: Gk *a slanderer*   *e* Heb Syr: Gk *be ignorant*   *f* Heb: Meaning of Gk uncertain *g* Meaning of Gk uncertain problems for translators because of some peculiar phraseology and variant readings among manuscripts. Nevertheless, the theme of unchecked passion is self-evident. While money and speech govern relations between men, desire constitutes the social force between men and women. While women are not explicitly in view, these verses serve as an overture to teachings that appear later about the dangers of women and the need for a man to exercise self-control (9.1–9).

5 Pleasant speech multiplies friends,
    and a gracious tongue multiplies
      courtesies.
6 Let those who are friendly with you be
      many,
    but let your advisers be one in a
      thousand.
7 When you gain friends, gain them
      through testing,
    and do not trust them hastily.
8 For there are friends who are such
      when it suits them,
    but they will not stand by you in time
      of trouble.
9 And there are friends who change into
      enemies,
    and tell of the quarrel to your
      disgrace.
10 And there are friends who sit at your
      table,
    but they will not stand by you in time
      of trouble.
11 When you are prosperous, they become
      your second self,
    and lord it over your servants;
12 but if you are brought low, they turn
      against you,
    and hide themselves from you.
13 Keep away from your enemies,
    and be on guard with your friends.
14 Faithful friends are a sturdy shelter:
    whoever finds one has found a
      treasure.
15 Faithful friends are beyond price;
    no amount can balance their worth.
16 Faithful friends are life-saving medicine;
    and those who fear the Lord will find
      them.
17 Those who fear the Lord direct their
    friendship aright,

for as they are, so are their neighbors
   also.

6.5–17: Friendship. Ben Sira begins by encouraging the pursuit of many friends, but immediately follows it with warnings about the dangers of friendship. By *friends,* Ben Sira means a man's peers. Because a man's friends are also his potential competitors in the pursuit of honor, this dynamic creates a situation of distrust between men. Thus, Ben Sira encourages extreme caution when taking a friend into one's confidence (vv. 6–7).

18 My child, from your youth choose
      discipline,
    and when you have gray hair you will
      still find wisdom.
19 Come to her like one who plows and
      sows,
    and wait for her good harvest.
    For when you cultivate her you will toil
      but little,
    and soon you will eat of her produce.
20 She seems very harsh to the
      undisciplined;
    fools cannot remain with her.
21 She will be like a heavy stone to test
      them,
    and they will not delay in casting her
      aside.
22 For wisdom is like her name;
    she is not readily perceived by many.
23 Listen, my child, and accept my
      judgment;
    do not reject my counsel.
24 Put your feet into her fetters,
    and your neck into her collar.
25 Bend your shoulders and carry her,
    and do not fret under her bonds.
26 Come to her with all your soul,
    and keep her ways with all your
      might.
27 Search out and seek, and she will
      become known to you;
    and when you get hold of her, do not
      let her go.
28 For at last you will find the rest she
      gives,
    and she will be changed into joy for
      you.

29 Then her fetters will become for you a
        strong defense,
     and her collar a glorious robe.
30 Her yoke[a] is a golden ornament,
        and her bonds a purple cord.
31 You will wear her like a glorious robe,
        and put her on like a splendid crown.[b]

32 If you are willing, my child, you can be
        disciplined,
     and if you apply yourself you will
        become clever.
33 If you love to listen you will gain
        knowledge,
     and if you pay attention you will
        become wise.
34 Stand in the company of the elders.
     Who is wise? Attach yourself to such
        a one.
35 Be ready to listen to every godly
        discourse,
     and let no wise proverbs escape you.
36 If you see an intelligent person, rise
        early to visit him;
     let your foot wear out his doorstep.
37 Reflect on the statutes of the Lord,
        and meditate at all times on his
        commandments.
     It is he who will give insight to[c] your
        mind,
     and your desire for wisdom will be
        granted.

6.18–37: Wisdom and education. The pursuit of wisdom divides into two stages: the first is a disciplined youth; the second, the accomplished status of having acquired maturity in wisdom. **18–27:** The first stage requires commitment and fidelity, because training for wisdom makes for a difficult path. **18:** *Discipline* ("paideia" in Greek) connotes both a broad notion of education and cultivation and physical chastisement in the training of children. **23–25:** The endurance of painful experiences is essential to acquiring wisdom. **28–31:** The results of discipline are the rewards of wisdom, enjoyed by the man who has matured in wisdom. While the *fetters* and the *yoke* symbolize the laborious burden that accompanies the pursuit of wisdom in stage one, in stage two they are compared to the priestly vestments (see 50.11), which symbolize unparalleled glory and honor (see 45.7–8, 12–13).

PROHIBITIONS, WARNINGS AND RESPONSIBILITIES

7.1–9.16: The teachings in this section cover a wide variety of topics. What holds these verses together is that the majority of them are stated as prohibitions: *Do not do . . .*

7 Do no evil, and evil will never overtake
        you.
2 Stay away from wrong, and it will turn
        away from you.
3 Do[d] not sow in the furrows of injustice,
        and you will not reap a sevenfold
        crop.

4 Do not seek from the Lord high office,
        or the seat of honor from the king.
5 Do not assert your righteousness before
        the Lord,
     or display your wisdom before the
        king.
6 Do not seek to become a judge,
        or you may be unable to root out
        injustice;
     you may be partial to the powerful,
        and so mar your integrity.
7 Commit no offense against the public,
        and do not disgrace yourself among
        the people.

8 Do not commit a sin twice;
     not even for one will you go
        unpunished.
9 Do not say, "He will consider the great
        number of my gifts,
     and when I make an offering to the
        Most High God, he will accept
        it."
10 Do not grow weary when you pray;
     do not neglect to give alms.
11 Do not ridicule a person who is
        embittered in spirit,
     for there is One who humbles and
        exalts.
12 Do not devise[e] a lie against your brother,
        or do the same to a friend.

a Heb: Gk *Upon her*   b Heb: Gk *crown of gladness*
c Heb: Gk *will confirm*   d Gk *My child, do*   e Heb:
Gk *plow*

13 Refuse to utter any lie,
for it is a habit that results in no good.
14 Do not babble in the assembly of the
elders,
and do not repeat yourself when you
pray.

15 Do not hate hard labor
or farm work, which was created by
the Most High.
16 Do not enroll in the ranks of sinners;
remember that retribution does not
delay.
17 Humble yourself to the utmost,
for the punishment of the ungodly is
fire and worms.*a*

18 Do not exchange a friend for money,
or a real brother for the gold of
Ophir.
19 Do not dismiss*b* a wise and good wife,
for her charm is worth more than
gold.
20 Do not abuse slaves who work faithfully,
or hired laborers who devote
themselves to their task.
21 Let your soul love intelligent slaves;*c*
do not withhold from them their
freedom.

22 Do you have cattle? Look after them;
if they are profitable to you, keep
them.
23 Do you have children? Discipline them,
and make them obedient*d* from their
youth.
24 Do you have daughters? Be concerned
for their chastity,*e*
and do not show yourself too
indulgent with them.
25 Give a daughter in marriage, and you
complete a great task;
but give her to a sensible man.
26 Do you have a wife who pleases you?*f*
Do not divorce her;
but do not trust yourself to one whom
you detest.

27 With all your heart honor your father,
and do not forget the birth pangs of
your mother.

28 Remember that it was of your parents*g*
you were born;
how can you repay what they have
given to you?

29 With all your soul fear the Lord,
and revere his priests.
30 With all your might love your Maker,
and do not neglect his ministers.
31 Fear the Lord and honor the priest,
and give him his portion, as you have
been commanded:
the first fruits, the guilt offering, the gift
of the shoulders,
the sacrifice of sanctification, and the
first fruits of the holy things.

32 Stretch out your hand to the poor,
so that your blessing may be complete.
33 Give graciously to all the living;
do not withhold kindness even from
the dead.
34 Do not avoid those who weep,
but mourn with those who mourn.
35 Do not hesitate to visit the sick,
because for such deeds you will be
loved.
36 In all you do, remember the end of your
life,
and then you will never sin.

7.1–36. 2: The Hebrew word translated here as *wrong*
functions as a synonym for evil, but the same term can
mean guilt or punishment. Thus, in Ben Sira's view,
there is a close correlation between doing evil and the
calamities that befall people. 4–7: Scholars debate
whether these verses point toward specific historical
circumstances or are general warnings against arrogant, self-serving endeavors. Since having legal authority is elsewhere stated as an appropriate aspiration
for the educated scribe* (compare 38.31–39.11), the
warning against seeking legal office is puzzling. Thus,
these verses may reflect a political climate in which
individuals seeking such status were too often tempted
to collude with foreign powers for their own gain. 14:
The proscription of repetition in prayer most likely re-

a Heb *for the expectation of mortals is worms*   *b* Heb:
Gk *deprive yourself of*   *c* Heb *Love a wise slave as
yourself*   *d* Gk *bend their necks*   *e* Gk *body*
f Heb Syr lack *who pleases you*   *g* Gk *them*

fers to mindless prattling. **15:** Since Ben Sira's intended audience consists of urban elites whose livelihood likely depended upon trade, he anticipates their arrogance by this warning. **17:** The difference between the Hebrew and the Greek is significant. The Greek text reflects a belief in life after death, which allows for post-mortem divine retribution. It is clear from other verses in Sirach that such a view is not consistent with Ben Sira's theology, which holds that God rewards the righteous and punishes the wicked in this life (see 41.9–13; 44.8–15). **18–21:** All those mentioned in these verses—*friends, wives,* and *slaves*—will be dealt with later in the text at greater length. **22–28:** As with 7.18–21, the statements here stress a householder's responsibility toward others, particularly those who depend directly upon him, like *daughters, wives,* and aging *parents.* **36:** When the author warns his reader to *remember the end of your life,* it is not because that is the moment of divine judgment, but because, at the end of one's life, one will either have earned a good name or it will be blotted out (41.11–13).

8 Do not contend with the powerful,
    or you may fall into their hands.
2 Do not quarrel with the rich,
    in case their resources outweigh
      yours;
    for gold has ruined many,
      and has perverted the minds of kings.
3 Do not argue with the loud of mouth,
    and do not heap wood on their fire.
4 Do not make fun of one who is ill-bred,
    or your ancestors may be insulted.
5 Do not reproach one who is turning
      away from sin;
    remember that we all deserve
      punishment.
6 Do not disdain one who is old,
    for some of us are also growing old.
7 Do not rejoice over anyone's death;
    remember that we must all die.
8 Do not slight the discourse of the sages,
    but busy yourself with their maxims;
    because from them you will learn
      discipline
    and how to serve princes.
9 Do not ignore the discourse of the aged,
    for they themselves learned from their
      parents;*a*

from them you learn how to understand
    and to give an answer when the need
      arises.
10 Do not kindle the coals of sinners,
    or you may be burned in their flaming
      fire.
11 Do not let the insolent bring you to your
      feet,
    or they may lie in ambush against
      your words.
12 Do not lend to one who is stronger than
      you;
    but if you do lend anything, count it
      as a loss.
13 Do not give surety beyond your means;
    but if you give surety, be prepared to
      pay.
14 Do not go to law against a judge,
    for the decision will favor him
      because of his standing.
15 Do not go traveling with the reckless,
    or they will be burdensome to you;
    for they will act as they please,
    and through their folly you will perish
      with them.
16 Do not pick a fight with the quick-
      tempered,
    and do not journey with them
      through lonely country,
    because bloodshed means nothing to
      them,
    and where no help is at hand, they
      will strike you down.
17 Do not consult with fools,
    for they cannot keep a secret.
18 In the presence of strangers do nothing
    that is to be kept secret,
    for you do not know what they will
      divulge.*b*
19 Do not reveal your thoughts to anyone,
    or you may drive away your
      happiness.*c*

8.1–19: This chapter addresses a man's relations with others over whom—unlike slaves and children—he has no control, such as other men who have money

a Or *ancestors*   *b* Or *it will bring forth*   *c* Heb: Gk *and let him not return a favor to you* and power. **12**: *One who is stronger than you* refers to someone of higher social status, one who possesses more honor. One of lesser status cannot easily demand repayment of a loan. **18–19**: Ben Sira is counseling his students toward practicing the appropriate kind of shame. Revealing private inclinations leaves one vulnerable to public disgrace.

9 Do not be jealous of the wife of your
    bosom,
  or you will teach her an evil lesson to
    your own hurt.
2 Do not give yourself to a woman
  and let her trample down your
    strength.
3 Do not go near a loose woman,
  or you will fall into her snares.
4 Do not dally with a singing girl,
  or you will be caught by her tricks.
5 Do not look intently at a virgin,
  or you may stumble and incur
    penalties for her.
6 Do not give yourself to prostitutes,
  or you may lose your inheritance.
7 Do not look around in the streets of a
    city,
  or wander about in its deserted
    sections.
8 Turn away your eyes from a shapely
    woman,
  and do not gaze at beauty belonging
    to another;
  many have been seduced by a woman's
    beauty,
  and by it passion is kindled like a
    fire.
9 Never dine with another man's wife,
  or revel with her at wine;
  or your heart may turn aside to her,
  and in blood*a* you may be plunged
    into destruction.
10 Do not abandon old friends,
  for new ones cannot equal them.
  A new friend is like new wine;
  when it has aged, you can drink it
    with pleasure.
11 Do not envy the success of sinners,
  for you do not know what their end
    will be like.

12 Do not delight in what pleases the
    ungodly;
  remember that they will not be held
    guiltless all their lives.
13 Keep far from those who have power to
    kill,
  and you will not be haunted by the
    fear of death.
  But if you approach them, make no
    misstep,
  or they may rob you of your life.
  Know that you are stepping among
    snares,
  and that you are walking on the city
    battlements.
14 As much as you can, aim to know your
    neighbors,
  and consult with the wise.
15 Let your conversation be with intelligent
    people,
  and let all your discussion be about
    the law of the Most High.
16 Let the righteous be your dinner
    companions,
  and let your glory be in the fear of the
    Lord.

9.1–16. 1–9: This section is the first of several in which Ben Sira warns of the dangers of women. Here he discusses a wide variety of types of women. **1–2**: The warning not to be *jealous of the wife of your bosom* can be interpreted in two ways: Either it means that a man should not display jealousy because a wife may become jealous in return, or it means that a man should not be too zealous for his wife (the same Hebrew word can mean jealous or zealous)—that is, he should not burn with passion for her. Given that the following verses address sexual passion, the latter interpretation* is preferred. **3–7**: Warnings about the seductive powers of women are common in wisdom literature* (compare Prov 2.16–19; 5.3–6, 7). Nevertheless, Sirach is extreme in its negative assessment of women (see, for example, 25.24; 42.14). **9**: The proscription against *dining with another man's wife* must be set within the Hellenistic* context in which, according to traditional Greek practice, well-heeled

a Heb: Gk *by your spirit*

wives do not dine with their husbands in public. **10–16:** General warnings.

17 A work is praised for the skill of the
    artisan;
    so a people's leader is proved wise by
       his words.
18 The loud of mouth are feared in their
    city,
    and the one who is reckless in speech
       is hated.

10 A wise magistrate educates his
    people,
    and the rule of an intelligent person
       is well ordered.
2 As the people's judge is, so are his
    officials;
    as the ruler of the city is, so are all its
       inhabitants.
3 An undisciplined king ruins his people,
    but a city becomes fit to live in
       through the understanding of its
       rulers.
4 The government of the earth is in the
    hand of the Lord,
    and over it he will raise up the right
       leader for the time.
5 Human success is in the hand of the
    Lord,
    and it is he who confers honor upon
       the lawgiver.[a]

6 Do not get angry with your neighbor for
    every injury,
    and do not resort to acts of insolence.
7 Arrogance is hateful to the Lord and to
    mortals,
    and injustice is outrageous to both.
8 Sovereignty passes from nation to
    nation
    on account of injustice and insolence
       and wealth.[b]
9 How can dust and ashes be proud?
    Even in life the human body decays.[c]
10 A long illness baffles the physician;[d]
    the king of today will die tomorrow.
11 For when one is dead
    he inherits maggots and vermin[e] and
       worms.
12 The beginning of human pride is to
    forsake the Lord;

    the heart has withdrawn from its
       Maker.
13 For the beginning of pride is sin,
    and the one who clings to it pours out
       abominations.
    Therefore the Lord brings upon them
       unheard-of calamities,
    and destroys them completely.
14 The Lord overthrows the thrones of
    rulers,
    and enthrones the lowly in their
       place.
15 The Lord plucks up the roots of the
    nations,[f]
    and plants the humble in their place.
16 The Lord lays waste the lands of the
    nations,
    and destroys them to the foundations
       of the earth.
17 He removes some of them and destroys
    them,
    and erases the memory of them from
       the earth.
18 Pride was not created for human beings,
    or violent anger for those born of
       women.

9.17–10.18: Rulers, power, and pride. 9.17–10.5: Comments about rulers should be interpreted against the complex political situation of the second century BCE. The general nature of the author's comments allows for a generic standard of measure in assessing a ruler's quality; whether foreign or Israelite, a good ruler is one who possesses wisdom. The statement in 10.4 that *the government of the earth is in the hand of the Lord* reflects the author's theological understanding of Israel's subjection to foreign rule. **10.6–18:** Although the author addressed the sin of pride earlier (3.17–31), here he explicitly relates pride to those who have political power. **14–16:** Memory of painful political turnover in the land of Israel must have been potent. Statements like these put the importance of political power in perspective. **17:** Being remembered is an honor of the utmost importance, as is made clear in the follow-

a Heb: Gk *scribe*   b Other ancient authorities add here or after verse 9a, *Nothing is more wicked than one who loves money, for such a person puts his own soul up for sale.*   c Heb: Meaning of Gk uncertain   d Heb Lat: Meaning of Gk uncertain   e Heb: Gk *wild animals*   f Other ancient authorities read *proud nations* ing section and in the hymn in praise of the ancestors (chs. 44–50).

19 Whose offspring are worthy of honor?
     Human offspring.
   Whose offspring are worthy of honor?
     Those who fear the Lord.
   Whose offspring are unworthy of honor?
     Human offspring.
   Whose offspring are unworthy of honor?
     Those who break the commandments.
20 Among family members their leader is
     worthy of honor,
   but those who fear the Lord are
     worthy of honor in his eyes.ᵃ
22 The rich, and the eminent, and the
     poor—
   their glory is the fear of the Lord.
23 It is not right to despise one who is
     intelligent but poor,
   and it is not proper to honor one who
     is sinful.
24 The prince and the judge and the ruler
     are honored,
   but none of them is greater than the
     one who fears the Lord.
25 Free citizens will serve a wise servant,
   and an intelligent person will not
     complain.

26 Do not make a display of your wisdom
     when you do your work,
   and do not boast when you are in
     need.
27 Better is the worker who has goods in
     plenty
   than the boaster who lacks bread.
28 My child, honor yourself with humility,
   and give yourself the esteem you
     deserve.
29 Who will acquit those who condemnᵇ
     themselves?
   And who will honor those who
     dishonor themselves?ᶜ
30 The poor are honored for their
     knowledge,
   while the rich are honored for their
     wealth.
31 One who is honored in poverty, how
     much more in wealth!

And one dishonored in wealth, how
   much more in poverty!

11 The wisdom of the humble lifts
     their heads high,
   and seats them among the great.
2 Do not praise individuals for their good
     looks,
   or loathe anyone because of
     appearance alone.
3 The bee is small among flying creatures,
   but what it produces is the best of
     sweet things.
4 Do not boast about wearing fine
     clothes,
   and do not exalt yourself when you
     are honored;
   for the works of the Lord are wonderful,
   and his works are concealed from
     humankind.
5 Many kings have had to sit on the
     ground,
   but one who was never thought of has
     worn a crown.
6 Many rulers have been utterly
     disgraced,
   and the honored have been handed
     over to others.

10.19–11.6: Who is deserving of honor? In contrast to the previous section which described the proud and powerful who seemingly possess honor but ultimately lack it, this section addresses those who genuinely deserve honor. **10.19:** The opening questions emphasize that *human offspring are worthy of honor* if they *fear the Lord*. **24:** The implication is that *the prince, the judge, and the ruler* should be honored not because of their professional station, but because they fear the Lord. **26–31:** These verses offer a more detailed look at the ironies that arise from the humble pursuit of honor. Verses 30–31 illustrate that while the accumulation of wealth should not count toward the accumulation of honor, in fact it does. Ben Sira points out that the same man will be more honored if he is rich than if he is poor. Such a sentiment seems to contrast with other of Ben Sira's teachings about the insignificance of wealth (11.14–28), but it may simply

a Other ancient authorities add as verse 21, *The fear of the Lord is the beginning of acceptance; obduracy and pride are the beginning of rejection.*   *b* Heb: Gk *sin against*   *c* Heb Lat: Gk *their own life* reflect reality and his pragmatic approach to life (13.21–24).

7 Do not find fault before you investigate;
　　examine first, and then criticize.
8 Do not answer before you listen,
　　and do not interrupt when another is
　　　speaking.
9 Do not argue about a matter that does
　　not concern you,
　　and do not sit with sinners when they
　　　judge a case.

10 My child, do not busy yourself with
　　many matters;
　　if you multiply activities, you will not
　　　be held blameless.
　If you pursue, you will not overtake,
　　and by fleeing you will not escape.
11 There are those who work and struggle
　　and hurry,
　　but are so much the more in want.
12 There are others who are slow and need
　　help,
　　who lack strength and abound in
　　　poverty;
　but the eyes of the Lord look kindly
　　upon them;
　he lifts them out of their lowly
　　condition
13 and raises up their heads
　　to the amazement of the many.

14 Good things and bad, life and death,
　　poverty and wealth, come from the
　　　Lord.ᵃ
17 The Lord's gift remains with the
　　devout,
　　and his favor brings lasting success.
18 One becomes rich through diligence
　　and self-denial,
　　and the reward allotted to him is this:
19 when he says, "I have found rest,
　　and now I shall feast on my goods!"
　he does not know how long it will be
　　until he leaves them to others and
　　　dies.

20 Stand by your agreement and attend to
　　it,
　　and grow old in your work.

21 Do not wonder at the works of a sinner,
　　but trust in the Lord and keep at your
　　　job;
　for it is easy in the sight of the Lord
　　to make the poor rich suddenly, in an
　　　instant.
22 The blessing of the Lord isᵇ the reward
　　of the pious,
　　and quickly God causes his blessing
　　　to flourish.
23 Do not say, "What do I need,
　　and what further benefit can be
　　　mine?"
24 Do not say, "I have enough,
　　and what harm can come to me
　　　now?"
25 In the day of prosperity, adversity is
　　forgotten,
　　and in the day of adversity, prosperity
　　　is not remembered.
26 For it is easy for the Lord on the day of
　　death
　　to reward individuals according to
　　　their conduct.
27 An hour's misery makes one forget past
　　delights,
　　and at the close of one's life one's
　　　deeds are revealed.
28 Call no one happy before his death;
　　by how he ends, a person becomes
　　　known.ᶜ

11.7–28: Piety and rewards. Ben Sira implicitly addresses the problem of theodicy* which is created by his theology, namely, if one is presumably rewarded in this life for being pious, why are there pious poor people (vv. 10–13)? Under a purely monotheist system of belief, in which there is no opposing evil force such as Satan, God must be responsible for *poverty* as well as *wealth* (v. 14; compare Eccl 8.10–14). Ben Sira recognizes that a one-to-one correspondence does not exist between wealth and piety or poverty and wickedness. Thus, for Ben Sira, poverty is not necessarily a sign of punishment (v. 12). One's reward may simply

---

a Other ancient authorities add as verses 15 and 16,
¹⁵*Wisdom, understanding, and knowledge of the law come from the Lord; affection and the ways of good works come from him.* ¹⁶*Error and darkness were created with sinners; evil grows old with those who take pride in malice.*
b Heb: Gk is in　　*c* Heb: Gk *and through his children a person becomes known*

be delayed (vv. 21–22, 26). Conversely, wealth obtained early in life does not necessarily constitute a reward. Thus, one is encouraged not to revel in one's prosperity, since the Lord can easily take it away (vv. 23–25, 27–28). A similar overall philosophy appears in Ecclesiastes.

RELATIONS WITH OTHER MEN

11.29–13.24: The overwhelming majority of verses in this section express profound suspicion of others. Such suspicion derives from the competitive social world in which men must function.

29 Do not invite everyone into your home,
    for many are the tricks of the crafty.
30 Like a decoy partridge in a cage, so is
      the mind of the proud,
    and like spies they observe your
      weakness;[a]
31 for they lie in wait, turning good into
      evil,
    and to worthy actions they attach
      blame.
32 From a spark many coals are kindled,
    and a sinner lies in wait to shed
      blood.
33 Beware of scoundrels, for they devise
      evil,
    and they may ruin your reputation
      forever.
34 Receive strangers into your home and
      they will stir up trouble for you,
    and will make you a stranger to your
      own family.

12 If you do good, know to whom you
      do it,
    and you will be thanked for your good
      deeds.
2 Do good to the devout, and you will be
      repaid—
    if not by them, certainly by the Most
      High.
3 No good comes to one who persists in
      evil
    or to one who does not give alms.
4 Give to the devout, but do not help the
      sinner.
5 Do good to the humble, but do not
      give to the ungodly;

hold back their bread, and do not give it
      to them,
    for by means of it they might subdue
      you;
    then you will receive twice as much evil
    for all the good you have done to
      them.
6 For the Most High also hates sinners
    and will inflict punishment on the
      ungodly.[b]
7 Give to the one who is good, but do not
      help the sinner.
8 A friend is not known[c] in prosperity,
    nor is an enemy hidden in adversity.
9 One's enemies are friendly[d] when one
      prospers,
    but in adversity even one's friend
      disappears.
10 Never trust your enemy,
    for like corrosion in copper, so is his
      wickedness.
11 Even if he humbles himself and walks
      bowed down,
    take care to be on your guard against
      him.
    Be to him like one who polishes a
      mirror,
    to be sure it does not become
      completely tarnished.
12 Do not put him next to you,
    or he may overthrow you and take
      your place.
    Do not let him sit at your right hand,
    or else he may try to take your own
      seat,
    and at last you will realize the truth of
      my words,
    and be stung by what I have said.
13 Who pities a snake charmer when he is
      bitten,
    or all those who go near wild
      animals?
14 So no one pities a person who
      associates with a sinner
    and becomes involved in the other's
      sins.

a Heb: Gk *downfall*   b Other ancient authorities add
and he is keeping them for the day of their punishment
c Other ancient authorities read *punished*   d Heb: Gk
grieved

15 He stands by you for a while,
　　but if you falter, he will not be there.
16 An enemy speaks sweetly with his lips,
　　but in his heart he plans to throw you
　　　　into a pit;
　　an enemy may have tears in his eyes,
　　but if he finds an opportunity he will
　　　　never have enough of your
　　　　blood.
17 If evil comes upon you, you will find
　　　　him there ahead of you;
　　pretending to help, he will trip you up.
18 Then he will shake his head, and clap
　　　　his hands,
　　and whisper much, and show his true
　　　　face.

13 Whoever touches pitch gets dirty,
and whoever associates with a
proud person becomes like him.
2 Do not lift a weight too heavy for you,
　　or associate with one mightier and
　　　　richer than you.
　　How can the clay pot associate with the
　　　　iron kettle?
　　The pot will strike against it and be
　　　　smashed.
3 A rich person does wrong, and even
　　　　adds insults;
　　a poor person suffers wrong, and
　　　　must add apologies.
4 A rich person[a] will exploit you if you
　　　　can be of use to him,
　　but if you are in need he will abandon
　　　　you.
5 If you own something, he will live with
　　　　you;
　　he will drain your resources without a
　　　　qualm.
6 When he needs you he will deceive you,
　　and will smile at you and encourage
　　　　you;
　　he will speak to you kindly and say,
　　　　"What do you need?"
7 He will embarrass you with his delicacies,
　　until he has drained you two or three
　　　　times,
　　and finally he will laugh at you.
　　Should he see you afterwards, he will
　　　　pass you by
　　and shake his head at you.

11.29–13.7. 12.8–12: For Ben Sira, it is not easy to distinguish between a friend and an enemy, because an unscrupulous person may act like a friend when it benefits him, but turn against his "friend" when one needs him most. 13–14: By keeping company with *sinners,* one is not only likely to commit sins oneself, but may face guilt by association, because people tend to judge others by the company they keep. 13.1–7: Rich men are inherently more powerful by virtue of their wealth. Therefore they can wantonly take advantage of others of inferior financial worth.

8 Take care not to be led astray
　　and humiliated when you are enjoying
　　　　yourself.[b]
9 When an influential person invites you,
　　be reserved,
　　and he will invite you more insistently.
10 Do not be forward, or you may be
　　　　rebuffed;
　　do not stand aloof, or you will be
　　　　forgotten.
11 Do not try to treat him as an equal,
　　or trust his lengthy conversations;
　　for he will test you by prolonged talk,
　　and while he smiles he will be
　　　　examining you.
12 Cruel are those who do not keep your
　　　　secrets;
　　they will not spare you harm or
　　　　imprisonment.
13 Be on your guard and very careful,
　　for you are walking about with your
　　　　own downfall.[c]
15 Every creature loves its like,
　　and every person the neighbor.
16 All living beings associate with their
　　　　own kind,
　　and people stick close to those like
　　　　themselves.
17 What does a wolf have in common with
　　　　a lamb?
　　No more has a sinner with the devout.
18 What peace is there between a hyena
　　　　and a dog?

a Gk He   b Other ancient authorities read *in your folly*
c Other ancient authorities add as verse 14, *When you hear these things in your sleep, wake up! During all your life love the Lord, and call on him for your salvation.*

And what peace between the rich and the poor?

19 Wild asses in the wilderness are the prey of lions;
   likewise the poor are feeding grounds for the rich.

20 Humility is an abomination to the proud;
   likewise the poor are an abomination to the rich.

21 When the rich person totters, he is supported by friends,
   but when the humble*a* falls, he is pushed away even by friends.

22 If the rich person slips, many come to the rescue;
   he speaks unseemly words, but they justify him.
   If the humble person slips, they even criticize him;
   he talks sense, but is not given a hearing.

23 The rich person speaks and all are silent;
   they extol to the clouds what he says.
   The poor person speaks and they say, "Who is this fellow?"
   And should he stumble, they even push him down.

24 Riches are good if they are free from sin;
   poverty is evil only in the opinion of the ungodly.

13.8–24. 8–13: Ben Sira cautions against being too easily impressed or too solicitous of more powerful men, precisely because it is typical of such men to take advantage of others. 15–20: Through the use of animal metaphors,* Ben Sira implies that people of disparate means are too dissimilar to have genuine relationships. 21–24: People tend to revere wealthy men, whether or not they are truly deserving of such respect. Conversely, people tend to despise or at best ignore the poor. Such a tendency makes those of meager means particularly vulnerable. Since those of lesser means are inevitably drawn toward those of greater means in the hopes of benefiting from such a relationship, they leave themselves open to exploitation. The essential message Ben Sira is trying to deliver resides in his warning to exercise extreme caution regarding hobnobbing with men of wealth and influence.

25 The heart changes the countenance, either for good or for evil.*b*

26 The sign of a happy heart is a cheerful face,
   but to devise proverbs requires painful thinking.

14 Happy are those who do not blunder with their lips,
   and need not suffer remorse for sin.

2 Happy are those whose hearts do not condemn them,
   and who have not given up their hope.

3 Riches are inappropriate for a small-minded person;
   and of what use is wealth to a miser?

4 What he denies himself he collects for others;
   and others will live in luxury on his goods.

5 If one is mean to himself, to whom will he be generous?
   He will not enjoy his own riches.

6 No one is worse than one who is grudging to himself;
   this is the punishment for his meanness.

7 If ever he does good, it is by mistake;
   and in the end he reveals his meanness.

8 The miser is an evil person;
   he turns away and disregards people.

9 The eye of the greedy person is not satisfied with his share;
   greedy injustice withers the soul.

10 A miser begrudges bread,
   and it is lacking at his table.

11 My child, treat yourself well, according to your means,
   and present worthy offerings to the Lord.

12 Remember that death does not tarry,
   and the decree*c* of Hades has not been shown to you.

a Other ancient authorities read *poor*   *b* Other ancient authorities add *and a glad heart makes a cheerful countenance*   *c* Heb Syr: Gk *covenant*

13 Do good to friends before you die,
   and reach out and give to them as
      much as you can.
14 Do not deprive yourself of a day's
      enjoyment;
   do not let your share of desired good
      pass by you.
15 Will you not leave the fruit of your
      labors to another,
   and what you acquired by toil to be
      divided by lot?
16 Give, and take, and indulge yourself,
      because in Hades one cannot look for
      luxury.
17 All living beings become old like a
      garment,
   for the decree[a] from of old is, "You
      must die!"
18 Like abundant leaves on a spreading
      tree
   that sheds some and puts forth others,
   so are the generations of flesh and
      blood:
   one dies and another is born.
19 Every work decays and ceases to exist,
   and the one who made it will pass
      away with it.

13.25–14.19: Responsible uses of wealth. 13.25–
14.2: Unlike the modern cultural perspective that distinguishes between the head and the heart, the *heart*
for Ben Sira is the locus of both desire and intellect.
14.3–10: Ben Sira lambastes the *miser*. It is clear from
these verses that, in distinction to many schools of
Greek philosophy, he does not wish to advocate an
ascetic lifestyle in which one refrains from any sort of
indulgence. In general, Ben Sira's ethical philosophy
resembles the popular Greek ethic of moderation first
articulated by Aristotle (see also 31.19–31). 11–19:
Again, the outlook here is comparable to the wisdom
philosophy found in Ecclesiastes.

20 Happy is the person who meditates on[b]
      wisdom
   and reasons intelligently,
21 who[c] reflects in his heart on her ways
   and ponders her secrets,
22 pursuing her like a hunter,
   and lying in wait on her paths;
23 who peers through her windows
   and listens at her doors;

24 who camps near her house
   and fastens his tent peg to her walls;
25 who pitches his tent near her,
   and so occupies an excellent lodging
      place;
26 who places his children under her
      shelter,
   and lodges under her boughs;
27 who is sheltered by her from the heat,
   and dwells in the midst of her glory.

15 Whoever fears the Lord will do
      this,
   and whoever holds to the law will
      obtain wisdom.[d]
2 She will come to meet him like a
      mother,
   and like a young bride she will
      welcome him.
3 She will feed him with the bread of
      learning,
   and give him the water of wisdom to
      drink.
4 He will lean on her and not fall,
   and he will rely on her and not be put
      to shame.
5 She will exalt him above his neighbors,
   and will open his mouth in the midst
      of the assembly.
6 He will find gladness and a crown of
      rejoicing,
   and will inherit an everlasting name.
7 The foolish will not obtain her,
   and sinners will not see her.
8 She is far from arrogance,
   and liars will never think of her.
9 Praise is unseemly on the lips of a
      sinner,
   for it has not been sent from the
      Lord.
10 For in wisdom must praise be uttered,
   and the Lord will make it prosper.
11 Do not say, "It was the Lord's doing
      that I fell away";
   for he does not do[e] what he hates.

a Heb: Gk *covenant*   *b* Other ancient authorities read
dies in   *c* The structure adopted in verses 21–27
follows the Heb   *d* Gk *her*   *e* Heb: Gk *you ought
not to do*

12 Do not say, "It was he who led me
astray";
for he has no need of the sinful.
13 The Lord hates all abominations;
such things are not loved by those
who fear him.
14 It was he who created humankind in the
beginning,
and he left them in the power of their
own free choice.
15 If you choose, you can keep the
commandments,
and to act faithfully is a matter of
your own choice.
16 He has placed before you fire and
water;
stretch out your hand for whichever
you choose.
17 Before each person are life and death,
and whichever one chooses will be
given.
18 For great is the wisdom of the Lord;
he is mighty in power and sees
everything;
19 his eyes are on those who fear him,
and he knows every human action.
20 He has not commanded anyone to be
wicked,
and he has not given anyone
permission to sin.

14.20–15.20: **The pursuit of wisdom.** The poem on
Woman Wisdom found in 14.20–15.10 divides into
two parts: 14.20–15.1, which describes the wisdom-
seeker's pursuit, and 15.2–10, which describes Wisdom's response. Both sections are highly metaphorical.* **14.20–15.1:** The imagery used—a *hunter lying
in wait*—is rather dramatic. The hunting metaphor,
particularly since it includes details like *peers through
her windows* and *fastens his tent peg to her walls,* connotes sexual desire (compare 26.12). It seems that Ben
Sira wishes to redirect male sexual desire away from
earthly women to Woman Wisdom (compare 9.7–8).
In modern Freudian terms, such redirection is referred
to as sublimation. **15.2–10:** The sexual innuendo continues in the second half of the poem, since Woman
Wisdom is described as a *mother* and a *bride.* **5–6:**
That *she will exalt him above his neighbors* and cause
him *to inherit an everlasting name* means that Woman
Wisdom brings honor upon the man who successfully
pursues her. **11–19:** In these verses wisdom is not por-

trayed as a woman, but as an attribute of the *Lord.*
Attention is turned back to the potential pursuer of
wisdom through the presentation of a hypothetical dialogue, in which the would-be pursuer makes excuses
for his failures by blaming God. **14–17:** Ben Sira admonishes this God-blamer from a perspective of free
will.

16 Do not desire a multitude of
worthless*a* children,
and do not rejoice in ungodly
offspring.
2 If they multiply, do not rejoice in them,
unless the fear of the Lord is in them.
3 Do not trust in their survival,
or rely on their numbers;*b*
for one can be better than a thousand,
and to die childless is better than to
have ungodly children.
4 For through one intelligent person a city
can be filled with people,
but through a clan of outlaws it
becomes desolate.
5 Many such things my eye has seen,
and my ear has heard things more
striking than these.
6 In an assembly of sinners a fire is
kindled,
and in a disobedient nation wrath
blazes up.
7 He did not forgive the ancient giants
who revolted in their might.
8 He did not spare the neighbors of Lot,
whom he loathed on account of their
arrogance.
9 He showed no pity on the doomed
nation,
on those dispossessed because of
their sins;*c*
10 or on the six hundred thousand foot
soldiers
who assembled in their stubbornness.*d*

---

a Heb: Gk *unprofitable*   *b* Other ancient authorities
add *For you will groan in untimely mourning, and will
know of their sudden end.*   *c* Other ancient authorities
add *All these things he did to the hard-hearted nations, and
by the multitude of his holy ones he was not appeased.*
d Other ancient authorities add *Chastising, showing
mercy, striking, healing, the Lord persisted in mercy and
discipline.*

11 Even if there were only one stiff-necked
        person,
    it would be a wonder if he remained
        unpunished.
    For mercy and wrath are with the Lord;[a]
        he is mighty to forgive—but he also
        pours out wrath.
12 Great as is his mercy, so also is his
        chastisement;
    he judges a person according to his or
        her deeds.
13 The sinner will not escape with plunder,
    and the patience of the godly will not
        be frustrated.
14 He makes room for every act of mercy;
    everyone receives in accordance with
        his or her deeds.[b]

17 Do not say, "I am hidden from the Lord,
    and who from on high has me in
        mind?
    Among so many people I am unknown,
        for what am I in a boundless
        creation?
18 Lo, heaven and the highest heaven,
    the abyss and the earth, tremble at
        his visitation![c]
19 The very mountains and the
        foundations of the earth
    quiver and quake when he looks upon
        them.
20 But no human mind can grasp this,
    and who can comprehend his ways?
21 Like a tempest that no one can see,
    so most of his works are concealed.[d]
22 Who is to announce his acts of justice?
    Or who can await them? For his
        decree[e] is far off."[f]
23 Such are the thoughts of one devoid of
        understanding;
    a senseless and misguided person
        thinks foolishly.

16.1–23: God and the culpability of human beings.
While the previous section covered the relationship
between the figure of Wisdom and human beings,
this section covers the relationship between the biblical God and the same human beings. **1–4:** There is a
strong biblical tradition that views many progeny as a
divine blessing (Gen 1.28; Deut 7.12–14), but Ben Sira
nuances such a view: Only descendants who are

ethically sound are desirable (see also Wis 4.1–3).
5–14: The author illustrates God's capacity to punish
sinners and reward righteous people by alluding to
various examples from biblical history. **6:** *An assembly
of sinners* is a reference to the rebellion of Korah
(Num 11.1–3). **7:** The *ancient giants* resulted from the
illicit union of sons of God and human women (Gen
6.1–4). **8:** The story of the destruction of *Lot's* city,
Sodom, is found in Gen 19. **11–14:** These and the preceding verses appear to address the problem of collective—versus individual—*punishment* or *mercy*, but
without solving the issue. **17–23:** The hypothetical dialogue of these verses parallels the one in 15.11–19.
Both portray the dialogue partner as theologically
incorrect.

THE LORD'S CREATION

16.24–17.32: Ben Sira's version of the creation story
makes use of various parts of the biblical tradition
and manifests his particular interests. The focus in
16.26–30 is on the creation of heavenly bodies, while
17.1–32 focuses on human beings.

---

24 Listen to me, my child, and acquire
        knowledge,
    and pay close attention to my words.
25 I will impart discipline precisely[g]
    and declare knowledge accurately.

26 When the Lord created[h] his works from
        the beginning,
    and, in making them, determined
        their boundaries,
27 he arranged his works in an eternal
        order,
    and their dominion[i] for all
        generations.
    They neither hunger nor grow weary,
        and they do not abandon their tasks.

---

a Gk *him*   b Other ancient authorities add [15]*The Lord
hardened Pharaoh so that he did not recognize him, in
order that his works might be known under heaven.* [16]*His
mercy is manifest to the whole of creation, and he divided
his light and darkness with a plumb line.*   c Other
ancient authorities add *The whole world past and present
is in his will.*   d Meaning of Gk uncertain: Heb Syr *If I
sin, no eye can see me, and if I am disloyal all in secret,
who is to know?*   e Heb *the decree:* Gk *the covenant*
f Other ancient authorities add *and a scrutiny for all
comes at the end*   g Gk *by weight*   h Heb: Gk *judged*
i Or *elements*

28 They do not crowd one another,
    and they never disobey his word.
29 Then the Lord looked upon the earth,
    and filled it with his good things.
30 With all kinds of living beings he
        covered its surface,
    and into it they must return.

16.24–29: Ben Sira perceives the created world as a perfectly ordered whole; nothing is superfluous or out of place (see 42.21–23). The Greeks typically understood the cosmos as a beautifully ordered structure imposed upon chaotic matter. Such a perspective meshed well with the biblical perspective of divine origin of the created *order*. Although the created world has a beginning, it apparently does not have an end for Ben Sira, but is *eternal*. Individual creatures, however, do expire (16.30–17.1; see also 17.30–32).

17 The Lord created human beings out
        of earth,
    and makes them return to it again.
2 He gave them a fixed number of days,
    but granted them authority over
        everything on the earth.*a*
3 He endowed them with strength like his
        own,*b*
    and made them in his own image.
4 He put the fear of them*c* in all living
        beings,
    and gave them dominion over beasts
        and birds.*d*
6 Discretion and tongue and eyes,
    ears and a mind for thinking he gave
        them.
7 He filled them with knowledge and
        understanding,
    and showed them good and evil.
8 He put the fear of him into*e* their
        hearts
    to show them the majesty of his
        works.*f*
10 And they will praise his holy name,
9   to proclaim the grandeur of his
        works.
11 He bestowed knowledge upon them,
    and allotted to them the law of life.*g*
12 He established with them an eternal
        covenant,
    and revealed to them his decrees.
13 Their eyes saw his glorious majesty,

and their ears heard the glory of his
        voice.
14 He said to them, "Beware of all evil."
    And he gave commandment to each
        of them concerning the neighbor.
15 Their ways are always known to him;
    they will not be hid from his eyes.*h*
17 He appointed a ruler for every nation,
    but Israel is the Lord's own portion.*i*
19 All their works are as clear as the sun
        before him,
    and his eyes are ever upon their ways.
20 Their iniquities are not hidden from
        him,
    and all their sins are before the Lord.*j*
22 One's almsgiving is like a signet ring
        with the Lord,*k*
    and he will keep a person's kindness
        like the apple of his eye.*l*
23 Afterward he will rise up and repay
        them,
    and he will bring their recompense on
        their heads.
24 Yet to those who repent he grants a
        return,
    and he encourages those who are
        losing hope.
25 Turn back to the Lord and forsake your
        sins;
    pray in his presence and lessen your
        offense.

---

a Lat: Gk *it*   *b* Lat: Gk *proper to them*   *c* Syr: Gk *him*   *d* Other ancient authorities add as verse 5, *They obtained the use of the five faculties of the Lord; as sixth he distributed to them the gift of mind, and as seventh, reason, the interpreter of one's faculties.*   *e* Other ancient authorities read *He set his eye upon*   *f* Other ancient authorities add *and he gave them to boast of his marvels forever*   *g* Other ancient authorities add *so that they may know that they who are alive now are mortal*   *h* Other ancient authorities add *¹⁶Their ways from youth tend toward evil, and they are unable to make for themselves hearts of flesh in place of their stony hearts. ¹⁷For in the division of the nations of the whole earth, he appointed*   *i* Other ancient authorities add as verse 18, *whom, being his firstborn, he brings up with discipline, and allotting to him the light of his love, he does not neglect him.*   *j* Other ancient authorities add as verse 21, *But the Lord, who is gracious and knows how they are formed, has neither left them nor abandoned them, but has spared them.*   *k* Gk *him*   *l* Other ancient authorities add *apportioning repentance to his sons and daughters*

26 Return to the Most High and turn away
　　from iniquity,*
　and hate intensely what he abhors.
27 Who will sing praises to the Most High
　　in Hades
　in place of the living who give thanks?
28 From the dead, as from one who does
　　not exist, thanksgiving has
　　ceased;
　those who are alive and well sing the
　　Lord's praises.
29 How great is the mercy of the Lord,
　and his forgiveness for those who
　　return to him!
30 For not everything is within human
　　capability,
　since human beings are not
　　immortal.
31 What is brighter than the sun? Yet it
　　can be eclipsed.
　So flesh and blood devise evil.
32 He marshals the host of the height of
　　heaven;
　but all human beings are dust and
　　ashes.

17.1–32. 1: This verse alludes to two complementary passages from Genesis, that *human beings* were *created out of the earth* (Gen 2.7) and therefore upon death they will *return to it* (Gen 3.19). 2: The life span of humans is finite; that is, they are not immortal (17.30), although they receive the privilege of having *authority over everything on the earth*. Human mortality may be related in Ben Sira's mind to the fact that flesh, which is made of matter, is by definition temporal and subject to decay. 3: *In his own image* comes directly from Gen 1.26–27. 4: That humans have *dominion over* all the earth's creatures derives from Gen 1.28. 6–7: In these verses and those that follow, the author begins to move beyond the Genesis story of origins. Here he describes five faculties of perception, three of which coincide with the senses: taste, sight, and hearing. *Discretion* refers to one's will, while presumably *a mind for thinking* refers to the analytical powers of reason. These faculties are mentioned because they are the tools through which humans achieve wisdom. 8–11: For Ben Sira, the creation story is not simply a tale of origins, but a source of knowledge about *the grandeur of his works,* which teaches the student of scripture to fear the Lord (1.11–27). 12–17: The author moves swiftly from creation to Sinai

and the giving of the Torah.* In so doing, Ben Sira connects the creation of the world to the creation of the people Israel as a distinct entity within the world. *Israel is the Lord's own portion* is drawn from Deut 32.8–9, a text that also refers to the Lord's division of the world into various nations. 26–28: The mention of praising God as a way to *return to the Most High* forms a transition to the following section.

18 He who lives forever created the
　　whole universe;
2　the Lord alone is just.*
4 To none has he given power to proclaim
　　his works;
　and who can search out his mighty
　　deeds?
5 Who can measure his majestic power?
　And who can fully recount his
　　mercies?
6 It is not possible to diminish or increase
　　them,
　nor is it possible to fathom the
　　wonders of the Lord.
7 When human beings have finished, they
　　are just beginning,
　and when they stop, they are still
　　perplexed.
8 What are human beings, and of what
　　use are they?
　What is good in them, and what is
　　evil?
9 The number of days in their life is great
　　if they reach one hundred years.*
10 Like a drop of water from the sea and a
　　grain of sand,
　so are a few years among the days of
　　eternity.
11 That is why the Lord is patient with
　　them
　and pours out his mercy upon them.
12 He sees and recognizes that their end is
　　miserable;

---

a Other ancient authorities add *for he will lead you out of darkness to the light of health.*　*b* Other ancient authorities add *and there is no other beside him; [3]he steers the world with the span of his hand, and all things obey his will; for he is king of all things by his power, separating among them the holy things from the profane.*　*c* Other ancient authorities add *but the death of each one is beyond the calculation of all*

therefore he grants them forgiveness
all the more.

13 The compassion of human beings is for
their neighbors,
but the compassion of the Lord is for
every living thing.
He rebukes and trains and teaches
them,
and turns them back, as a shepherd
his flock.

14 He has compassion on those who
accept his discipline
and who are eager for his precepts.

18.1–14: Praise God. The words of praise for God resemble many psalms. The poem contrasts the unsurpassed majesty of God with the puny stature of human beings, then resolves the chasm between them by stressing God's *compassion* for humans.

VERBAL RESTRAINT, CONTROL OF DESIRE, AND CAUTION IN ALL MATTERS.

18.15–22.26: The majority of teachings included in this section address matters of speech as they relate to various behaviors.

15 My child, do not mix reproach with your
good deeds,
or spoil your gift by harsh words.

16 Does not the dew give relief from the
scorching heat?
So a word is better than a gift.

17 Indeed, does not a word surpass a good
gift?
Both are to be found in a gracious
person.

18 A fool is ungracious and abusive,
and the gift of a grudging giver makes
the eyes dim.

19 Before you speak, learn;
and before you fall ill, take care of
your health.

20 Before judgment comes, examine
yourself;
and at the time of scrutiny you will
find forgiveness.

21 Before falling ill, humble yourself;
and when you have sinned, repent.

22 Let nothing hinder you from paying a
vow promptly,
and do not wait until death to be
released from it.

23 Before making a vow, prepare yourself;
do not be like one who puts the Lord
to the test.

24 Think of his wrath on the day of death,
and of the moment of vengeance
when he turns away his face.

25 In the time of plenty think of the time
of hunger;
in days of wealth think of poverty and
need.

26 From morning to evening conditions
change;
all things move swiftly before the
Lord.

27 One who is wise is cautious in
everything;
when sin is all around, one guards
against wrongdoing.

28 Every intelligent person knows wisdom,
and praises the one who finds her.

29 Those who are skilled in words become
wise themselves,
and pour forth apt proverbs.*a*

SELF-CONTROL *b*

30 Do not follow your base desires,
but restrain your appetites.

31 If you allow your soul to take pleasure
in base desire,
it will make you the laughingstock of
your enemies.

32 Do not revel in great luxury,
or you may become impoverished by
its expense.

33 Do not become a beggar by feasting
with borrowed money,
when you have nothing in your purse.*c*

19 The one who does this*d* will not
become rich;
one who despises small things will fail
little by little.

a Other ancient authorities add *Better is confidence in the one Lord than clinging with a dead heart to a dead one.* *b* This heading is included in the Gk text. *c* Other ancient authorities add *for you will be plotting against your own life* *d* Heb: Gk *A worker who is a drunkard*

2 Wine and women lead intelligent men
       astray,
   and the man who consorts with
       prostitutes is reckless.
3 Decay and worms will take possession
       of him,
   and the reckless person will be
       snatched away.

18.15–19.3. 18.19–26: One may prevent foolishness,
ill health, and indebtedness by anticipatory behavior.
While such advice is sound and practical, Ben Sira can
seem overly cautious: *In the time of plenty think of the
time of hunger.* 18.27–19.3: The world is a dangerous
place, and life requires constant vigilance in order to
avoid its many temptations.

〰️〰️〰️〰️〰️〰️〰️〰️

4 One who trusts others too quickly has a
       shallow mind,
   and one who sins does wrong to
       himself.
5 One who rejoices in wickedness*a* will
       be condemned,*b*
6 but one who hates gossip has less
       evil.
7 Never repeat a conversation,
   and you will lose nothing at all.
8 With friend or foe do not report it,
   and unless it would be a sin for you,
       do not reveal it;
9 for someone may have heard you and
       watched you,
   and in time will hate you.
10 Have you heard something? Let it die
       with you.
   Be brave, it will not make you burst!
11 Having heard something, the fool
       suffers birth pangs
   like a woman in labor with a child.
12 Like an arrow stuck in a person's
       thigh,
   so is gossip inside a fool.

13 Question a friend; perhaps he did not
       do it;
   or if he did, so that he may not do it
       again.
14 Question a neighbor; perhaps he did not
       say it;
   or if he said it, so that he may not
       repeat it.

15 Question a friend, for often it is slander;
   so do not believe everything you hear.
16 A person may make a slip without
       intending it.
   Who has not sinned with his tongue?
17 Question your neighbor before you
       threaten him;
   and let the law of the Most High take
       its course.*c*

19.4–17: Ben Sira sternly warns against the dangers of
gossip. Gossip constitutes a form of unbridled speech,
and speech, like money, wine, and women, must be
carefully circumscribed. Speech is a primary source of
honor and dishonor (5.13). Rather than repeat gossip,
vv. 13–17 suggest confronting any *friend* who has
been the subject of casual talk.

〰️〰️〰️〰️〰️〰️〰️〰️

20 The whole of wisdom is fear of the
       Lord,
   and in all wisdom there is the
       fulfillment of the law.*d*
22 The knowledge of wickedness is not
       wisdom,
   nor is there prudence in the counsel
       of sinners.
23 There is a cleverness that is detestable,
   and there is a fool who merely lacks
       wisdom.
24 Better are the God-fearing who lack
       understanding
   than the highly intelligent who
       transgress the law.
25 There is a cleverness that is exact but
       unjust,
   and there are people who abuse
       favors to gain a verdict.
26 There is the villain bowed down in
       mourning,
   but inwardly he is full of deceit.

---

a Other ancient authorities read *heart*   *b* Other
ancient authorities add *but one who withstands pleasures
crowns his life.* *6One who controls the tongue will live
without strife,*   *c* Other ancient authorities add *and do
not be angry.* *18The fear of the Lord is the beginning of
acceptance, and wisdom obtains his love.* *19The knowledge
of the Lord's commandments is life-giving discipline; and
those who do what is pleasing to him enjoy the fruit of the
tree of immortality.*   *d* Other ancient authorities add
and the knowledge of his omnipotence. *21When a slave says
to his master, "I will not act as you wish,"* even if later he
does it, he angers the one who supports him.*

27 He hides his face and pretends not to
hear,
　　but when no one notices, he will take
　　advantage of you.
28 Even if lack of strength keeps him from
sinning,
　　he will nevertheless do evil when he
　　finds the opportunity.
29 A person is known by his appearance,
　　and a sensible person is known when
　　first met, face to face.
30 A person's attire and hearty laughter,
　　and the way he walks, show what he is.

19.20–30: Ben Sira attempts to sort out the difference
between true wisdom and mere cleverness. He is clear
that true wisdom includes observance of the commandments (v. 20b). *Cleverness* translates the Greek
"panourgia," which means resourcefulness or know-
how. The point is that competence in the game of life
does not automatically make a man wise or God-fearing. Somewhat ironically, this section concludes with
the comment, *A person is known by his appearance.*
Elsewhere Ben Sira is more skeptical of appearances
(11.1–4).

20 There is a rebuke that is untimely,
　　and there is the person who is wise
　　enough to keep silent.
2 How much better it is to rebuke than to
fume!
3 And the one who admits his fault will
　　be kept from failure.
4 Like a eunuch lusting to violate a girl
　　is the person who does right under
　　compulsion.
5 Some people keep silent and are
　　thought to be wise,
　　while others are detested for being
　　talkative.
6 Some people keep silent because they
　　have nothing to say,
　　while others keep silent because they
　　know when to speak.
7 The wise remain silent until the right
　　moment,
　　but a boasting fool misses the right
　　moment.
8 Whoever talks too much is detested,
　　and whoever pretends to authority is
　　hated.*a*

9 There may be good fortune for a person
　　in adversity,
　　and a windfall may result in a loss.
10 There is the gift that profits you
nothing,
　　and the gift to be paid back double.
11 There are losses for the sake of glory,
　　and there are some who have raised
　　their heads from humble
　　circumstances.
12 Some buy much for little,
　　but pay for it seven times over.
13 The wise make themselves beloved by
　　only few words,*b*
　　but the courtesies of fools are wasted.
14 A fool's gift will profit you nothing,*c*
　　for he looks for recompense
　　sevenfold.*d*
15 He gives little and upbraids much;
　　he opens his mouth like a town crier.
　　Today he lends and tomorrow he asks it
　　back;
　　such a one is hateful to God and
　　humans.*e*
16 The fool says, "I have no friends,
　　and I get no thanks for my good
　　deeds.
　　Those who eat my bread are evil-
　　tongued."
17 How many will ridicule him, and how
　　often!*f*

20.1–17. 9–17: When Ben Sira says *a windfall may result in a loss,* his intent is not merely to warn his students about sudden reversals of fortune. Rather, he
wishes to stress that economic gain is only one aspect
in the pursuit of honor. What one does and says in
relation to such gains makes all the difference. Gift-
giving, for example, constitutes an important means
of exchanging honor and can therefore be used man-
ipulatively (see 18.15–18). One is a fool to assume that
receipt of a *gift* necessarily implies a personal gain,
since the giver may expect *back double.* Conversely,

a Other ancient authorities add *How good it is to show
repentance when you are reproved, for so you will escape
deliberate sin!*　*b* Heb: Gk by words　*c* Other ancient
authorities add *so it is with the envious who give under
compulsion*　*d* Syr: Gk *he has many eyes instead of one*
e Other ancient authorities lack *to God and humans*
f Other ancient authorities add *for he has not honestly
received what he has, and what he does not have is
unimportant to him*

one is also a fool who gives a gift and, eagerly anticipating a complementary response, makes nagging demands.

18 A slip on the pavement is better than a
　　slip of the tongue;
　　the downfall of the wicked will occur
　　　　just as speedily.
19 A coarse person is like an inappropriate
　　story,
　　continually on the lips of the
　　　　ignorant.
20 A proverb from a fool's lips will be
　　rejected,
　　for he does not tell it at the proper
　　　　time.

21 One may be prevented from sinning by
　　poverty;
　　so when he rests he feels no
　　　　remorse.
22 One may lose his life through shame,
　　or lose it because of human respect.*a*
23 Another out of shame makes promises
　　to a friend,
　　and so makes an enemy for nothing.

20.18–23. 21–23: *Poverty* can be a blessing because one may confront fewer temptations for lack of means. The point of vv. 22–23 is that one must not falsely assume a high status, or pretend to have means and thus *make promises to a friend* without being able to fulfill those promises.

24 A lie is an ugly blot on a person;
　　it is continually on the lips of the
　　　　ignorant.
25 A thief is preferable to a habitual liar,
　　but the lot of both is ruin.
26 A liar's way leads to disgrace,
　　and his shame is ever with him.

　　　　PROVERBIAL SAYINGS *b*
27 The wise person advances himself by his
　　words,
　　and one who is sensible pleases the
　　　　great.
28 Those who cultivate the soil heap up
　　their harvest,
　　and those who please the great atone
　　　　for injustice.

29 Favors and gifts blind the eyes of the
　　wise;
　　like a muzzle on the mouth they stop
　　　　reproofs.
30 Hidden wisdom and unseen treasure,
　　of what value is either?
31 Better are those who hide their folly
　　than those who hide their wisdom.*e*

20.24–31. 27–31: These verses highlight a paradox the successful sage is likely to confront. A wise man ascends to a position of authority because of his insights regarding truth and justice and his ability to articulate those insights well. The higher his position, however, the more likely that men of power and influence will corrupt him with *favors and gifts.*

21 Have you sinned, my child? Do so
　　no more,
　　but ask forgiveness for your past sins.
2 Flee from sin as from a snake;
　　for if you approach sin, it will bite
　　　　you.
　Its teeth are lion's teeth,
　　and can destroy human lives.
3 All lawlessness is like a two-edged
　　sword;
　　there is no healing for the wound it
　　　　inflicts.
4 Panic and insolence will waste away
　　riches;
　　thus the house of the proud will be
　　　　laid waste.*d*
5 The prayer of the poor goes from their
　　lips to the ears of God,*e*
　　and his judgment comes speedily.
6 Those who hate reproof walk in the
　　sinner's steps,
　　but those who fear the Lord repent in
　　　　their heart.
7 The mighty in speech are widely
　　known;
　　when they slip, the sensible person
　　　　knows it.

a Other ancient authorities read *his foolish look*
b This heading is included in the Gk text.　　*c* Other
ancient authorities add ³²*Unwearied endurance in seeking
the Lord is better than a masterless charioteer of one's own
life.*　　*d* Other ancient authorities read *uprooted*
e Gk *his ears*

8 Whoever builds his house with other
people's money
is like one who gathers stones for his
burial mound.[a]
9 An assembly of the wicked is like a
bundle of tow,
and their end is a blazing fire.
10 The way of sinners is paved with
smooth stones,
but at its end is the pit of Hades.
11 Whoever keeps the law controls his
thoughts,
and the fulfillment of the fear of the
Lord is wisdom.
12 The one who is not clever cannot be
taught,
but there is a cleverness that
increases bitterness.
13 The knowledge of the wise will increase
like a flood,
and their counsel like a life-giving
spring.
14 The mind[b] of a fool is like a broken jar;
it can hold no knowledge.
15 When an intelligent person hears a wise
saying,
he praises it and adds to it;
when a fool[c] hears it, he laughs at[d] it
and throws it behind his back.
16 A fool's chatter is like a burden on a
journey,
but delight is found in the speech of
the intelligent.
17 The utterance of a sensible person is
sought in the assembly,
and they ponder his words in their
minds.
18 Like a house in ruins is wisdom to a fool,
and to the ignorant, knowledge is talk
that has no meaning.
19 To a senseless person education is
fetters on his feet,
and like manacles on his right hand.
20 A fool raises his voice when he laughs,
but the wise[e] smile quietly.
21 To the sensible person education is like
a golden ornament,
and like a bracelet on the right arm.

21.1–21: These verses constitute another twenty-two-line poem. Here Ben Sira apparently begins a new section, as indicated by the address *my child*, but most of its contents elaborate upon the ethical teachings appearing in the prior chapters. **2:** The *snake* alludes to the serpent in Gen 3 who persuaded the first woman to disobey God's command. **10:** *Hades* is the Greek equivalent of Sheol; it is not a place of eternal damnation, but is rather the realm of all the dead. Its mention in relation to *sinners* is meant to emphasize the hasty death that awaits the unrepentant. **11:** *Fulfillment of the fear of the Lord* refers to the observance of Torah. Observing the divine law means that one conforms one's will to God's, thus alleviating the pull of tempting thoughts.

22 The foot of a fool rushes into a house,
but an experienced person waits
respectfully outside.
23 A boor peers into the house from the
door,
but a cultivated person remains
outside.
24 It is ill-mannered for a person to listen
at a door;
the discreet would be grieved by the
disgrace.
25 The lips of babblers speak of what is not
their concern,[f]
but the words of the prudent are
weighed in the balance.
26 The mind of fools is in their mouth,
but the mouth of the wise is in[g] their
mind.
27 When an ungodly person curses an
adversary,[h]
he curses himself.
28 A whisperer degrades himself
and is hated in his neighborhood.

22 The idler is like a filthy stone,
and every one hisses at his
disgrace.
2 The idler is like the filth of dunghills;

anyone that picks it up will shake it
    off his hand.

3 It is a disgrace to be the father of an
    undisciplined son,
    and the birth of a daughter is a loss.
4 A sensible daughter obtains a husband
    of her own,
    but one who acts shamefully is a grief
    to her father.
5 An impudent daughter disgraces father
    and husband,
    and is despised by both.
6 Like music in time of mourning is ill-
    timed conversation,
    but a thrashing and discipline are at
    all times wisdom."

21.22–22.6. 22.3–6: *An undisciplined son* in Ben Sira's
day means both one whose behavior lacks control and
one who has not been properly educated. Such children bring shame upon their parents. In 30.1–13 a
longer section on the importance of disciplining children appears. When Ben Sira says that *the birth of a
daughter is a loss,* he reflects the economic and cultural values of his day. A daughter was considered a
social and financial liability. See 42.9–14 for more extensive comments about daughters.

9 Whoever teaches a fool is like one who
    glues potsherds together,
    or who rouses a sleeper from deep
    slumber.
10 Whoever tells a story to a fool tells it to
    a drowsy man;
    and at the end he will say, "What is it?"
11 Weep for the dead, for he has left the
    light behind;
    and weep for the fool, for he has left
    intelligence behind.
    Weep less bitterly for the dead, for he is
    at rest;
    but the life of the fool is worse than
    death.
12 Mourning for the dead lasts seven days,
    but for the foolish or the ungodly it
    lasts all the days of their lives.

13 Do not talk much with a senseless
    person
    or visit an unintelligent person.[b]

Stay clear of him, or you may have
    trouble,
    and be spattered when he shakes
    himself off.
    Avoid him and you will find rest,
    and you will never be wearied by his
    lack of sense.
14 What is heavier than lead?
    And what is its name except "Fool"?
15 Sand, salt, and a piece of iron
    are easier to bear than a stupid
    person.
16 A wooden beam firmly bonded into a
    building
    is not loosened by an earthquake;
    so the mind firmly resolved after due
    reflection
    will not be afraid in a crisis.
17 A mind settled on an intelligent thought
    is like stucco decoration that makes a
    wall smooth.
18 Fences[c] set on a high place
    will not stand firm against the wind;
    so a timid mind with a fool's resolve
    will not stand firm against any fear.

22.9–18: Ben Sira describes the heavy liability engen-
dered by contact with fools. 12: When Ben Sira speaks
of *mourning . . . for the foolish,* which *lasts all the days
of their lives,* he refers to the mourning of the friends
and relatives of fools.

19 One who pricks the eye brings tears,
    and one who pricks the heart makes
    clear its feelings.
20 One who throws a stone at birds scares
    them away,
    and one who reviles a friend destroys
    a friendship.
21 Even if you draw your sword against a
    friend,
    do not despair, for there is a way
    back.

a Other ancient authorities add [7]*Children who are
brought up in a good life, conceal the lowly birth of their
parents.* [8]*Children who are disdainfully and boorishly
haughty stain the nobility of their kindred.*   b Other
ancient authorities add *For being without sense he will
despise everything about you*   c Other ancient
authorities read *Pebbles*

22 If you open your mouth against your
    friend,
    do not worry, for reconciliation is
      possible.
  But as for reviling, arrogance, disclosure
    of secrets, or a treacherous
    blow—
    in these cases any friend will take to
      flight.

23 Gain the trust of your neighbor in his
    poverty,
    so that you may rejoice with him in
      his prosperity.
  Stand by him in time of distress,
    so that you may share with him in his
      inheritance.[a]
24 The vapor and smoke of the furnace
    precede the fire;
    so insults precede bloodshed.
25 I am not ashamed to shelter a friend,
    and I will not hide from him.
26 But if harm should come to me because
    of him,
    whoever hears of it will beware of
      him.

27 Who will set a guard over my mouth,
    and an effective seal upon my lips,
    so that I may not fall because of them,
    and my tongue may not destroy me?

23

O Lord, Father and Master of my
    life,
    do not abandon me to their designs,
    and do not let me fall because of
      them!
2 Who will set whips over my thoughts,
    and the discipline of wisdom over my
      mind,
    so as not to spare me in my errors,
    and not overlook my[b] sins?
3 Otherwise my mistakes may be
    multiplied,
    and my sins may abound,
  and I may fall before my adversaries,
    and my enemy may rejoice over me.[c]
4 O Lord, Father and God of my life,
    do not give me haughty eyes,
5   and remove evil desire from me.
6 Let neither gluttony nor lust overcome
    me,

    and do not give me over to shameless
    passion.

22.27–23.6: Prayer for self-control. Ben Sira turns from addressing his students to addressing God, in what appears to be an exemplary prayer for deliverance from sinful thoughts. In Ben Sira's anthropology, human beings possess powerful desires that must be tightly controlled. The pursuit of wisdom requires not merely the acquisition of knowledge and the internalization of good manners, but the ability to maintain self-control at all times.

DISCIPLINE OF THE TONGUE [d]

7 Listen, my children, to instruction
    concerning the mouth;
    the one who observes it will never be
      caught.
8 Sinners are overtaken through their lips;
    by them the reviler and the arrogant
    are tripped up.
9 Do not accustom your mouth to oaths,
    nor habitually utter the name of the
      Holy One;
10 for as a servant who is constantly under
    scrutiny
    will not lack bruises,
  so also the person who always swears
    and utters the Name
    will never be cleansed[e] from sin.
11 The one who swears many oaths is full
    of iniquity,
    and the scourge will not leave his
      house.
  If he swears in error, his sin remains on
    him,
    and if he disregards it, he sins doubly;
  if he swears a false oath, he will not be
    justified,
    for his house will be filled with
      calamities.

23.7–11: Swearing. Taking an *oath* is a matter of the utmost seriousness. The foundation of Ben Sira's teaching is the commandment against taking the

a Other ancient authorities add *For one should not always despise restricted circumstances, or admire a rich person who is stupid.*   b Gk *their*   c Other ancient authorities add *From them the hope of your mercy is remote*   d This heading is included in the Gk text.   e Syr *be free*

Lord's name in vain (Ex 20.7; compare Ex 23.13), which refers not to foul language but to the cavalier invocation of God's name in swearing. To swear an oath using the divine name is to attract God's attention and implicate him in the matter. An oath can refer either to a recounting of past deeds, as in a legal context, or to a future deed, as in the case of a promise. As v. 11 implies, a vow in antiquity had an efficacy far greater than solemn words uttered in modern society. Compare the story of Jephthah's daughter in Judg 11.

12 There is a manner of speaking
     comparable to death;[a]
     may it never be found in the
         inheritance of Jacob!
     Such conduct will be far from the godly,
     and they will not wallow in sins.

13 Do not accustom your mouth to coarse,
         foul language,
     for it involves sinful speech.

14 Remember your father and mother
     when you sit among the great,
     or you may forget yourself in their
         presence,
     and behave like a fool through bad
         habit;
     then you will wish that you had never
         been born,
     and you will curse the day of your
         birth.

15 Those who are accustomed to using
         abusive language
     will never become disciplined as long
         as they live.

16 Two kinds of individuals multiply sins,
     and a third incurs wrath.
     Hot passion that blazes like a fire
     will not be quenched until it burns
         itself out;
     one who commits fornication with his
         near of kin
     will never cease until the fire burns
         him up.

17 To a fornicator all bread is sweet;
     he will never weary until he dies.

18 The one who sins against his marriage
         bed
     says to himself, "Who can see me?
     Darkness surrounds me, the walls hide
         me,
     and no one sees me. Why should I
         worry?
     The Most High will not remember
         sins."

19 His fear is confined to human eyes
     and he does not realize that the eyes
         of the Lord
     are ten thousand times brighter than
         the sun;
     they look upon every aspect of human
         behavior
     and see into hidden corners.

20 Before the universe was created, it was
         known to him,
     and so it is since its completion.

21 This man will be punished in the streets
         of the city,
     and where he least suspects it, he will
         be seized.

22 So it is with a woman who leaves her
         husband
     and presents him with an heir by
         another man.

23 For first of all, she has disobeyed the
         law of the Most High;
     second, she has committed an offense
         against her husband;
     and third, through her fornication she
         has committed adultery
     and brought forth children by another
         man.

24 She herself will be brought before the
         assembly,
     and her punishment will extend to
         her children.

25 Her children will not take root,
     and her branches will not bear fruit.

26 She will leave behind an accursed
         memory
     and her disgrace will never be blotted
         out.

27 Those who survive her will recognize
     that nothing is better than the fear of
         the Lord,
     and nothing sweeter than to heed the
         commandments of the Lord.[b]

a Other ancient authorities read *clothed about with death*   b Other ancient authorities add as verse 28, *It is a great honor to follow God, and to be received by him is long life.*

23.16–27: Sins of sexual nature. 16: *Two kinds . . . and a third* indicates a numerical proverb—a mnemonic device that aids in categorization (see also 25.1–2; 26.5–6). In this passage it is difficult to identify clearly three distinct kinds of sexually deviant persons. Most likely, the first two are briefly noted in v. 16 as *one who has hot passion* and one who commits incest. The description of the third, the *fornicator,* begins in v. 17 and is elaborated upon until v. 21. As indicated by v. 18, Ben Sira is concerned with the *adulterer* in particular. Ben Sira expands the biblical definition of adultery. Adultery is typically defined as sex with another man's wife (Lev 20.10; Deut 22.22); thus, a married man who has sex with an unmarried woman does not commit adultery. Here, however, the marital status of the woman is irrelevant—any married man who has sexual relations with any woman has sinned. This definition is consistent with Ben Sira's teachings about the need for control of sexual desire. **18–21:** In the honor-shame ethical system, deviant behavior must be publicly revealed for dishonor to fall upon the miscreant. Shame is not an internal, personal feeling, but a public humiliation. Because sexual relations occur in private, the adulterer thinks he is safe. Therefore, public exposure of sexual sin is itself a form of punishment. **22–27:** These verses clearly refer to an adulterous woman, but the focus is not her unbridled passion, but an *heir* produced *by another man.* One of the primary motivations for the sexual control of women is to ensure the paternity of the husband.

THE PRAISE OF WISDOM [a]

24 Wisdom praises herself,
  and tells of her glory in the midst of
    her people.
2 In the assembly of the Most High she
    opens her mouth,
  and in the presence of his hosts she
    tells of her glory:
3 "I came forth from the mouth of the
    Most High,
  and covered the earth like a mist.
4 I dwelt in the highest heavens,
  and my throne was in a pillar of
    cloud.
5 Alone I compassed the vault of heaven
  and traversed the depths of the
    abyss.
6 Over waves of the sea, over all the
    earth,

and over every people and nation I
    have held sway.[b]
7 Among all these I sought a resting
    place;
  in whose territory should I abide?
8 "Then the Creator of all things gave me
    a command,
  and my Creator chose the place for
    my tent.
He said, 'Make your dwelling in Jacob,
  and in Israel receive your
    inheritance.'
9 Before the ages, in the beginning, he
    created me,
  and for all the ages I shall not cease
    to be.
10 In the holy tent I ministered before
    him,
  and so I was established in Zion.
11 Thus in the beloved city he gave me a
    resting place,
  and in Jerusalem was my domain.
12 I took root in an honored people,
  in the portion of the Lord, his
    heritage.
13 "I grew tall like a cedar in Lebanon,
  and like a cypress on the heights of
    Hermon.
14 I grew tall like a palm tree in En-gedi,[c]
  and like rosebushes in Jericho;
  like a fair olive tree in the field,
    and like a plane tree beside water[d] I
      grew tall.
15 Like cassia and camel's thorn I gave
    forth perfume,
  and like choice myrrh I spread my
    fragrance,
  like galbanum, onycha, and stacte,
    and like the odor of incense in the
      tent.
16 Like a terebinth I spread out my
    branches,
  and my branches are glorious and
    graceful.

a This heading is included in the Gk text.   *b* Other ancient authorities read *I have acquired a possession*
c Other ancient authorities read *on the beaches*
d Other ancient authorities omit *beside water*

17 Like the vine I bud forth delights,
  and my blossoms become glorious
    and abundant fruit.*

19 "Come to me, you who desire me,
  and eat your fill of my fruits.
20 For the memory of me is sweeter than
    honey,
  and the possession of me sweeter
    than the honeycomb.
21 Those who eat of me will hunger for
    more,
  and those who drink of me will thirst
    for more.
22 Whoever obeys me will not be put to
    shame,
  and those who work with me will not
    sin."

23 All this is the book of the covenant of
    the Most High God,
  the law that Moses commanded us
  as an inheritance for the
    congregations of Jacob.*
25 It overflows, like the Pishon, with
    wisdom,
  and like the Tigris at the time of the
    first fruits.
26 It runs over, like the Euphrates, with
    understanding,
  and like the Jordan at harvest time.
27 It pours forth instruction like the Nile,*
  like the Gihon at the time of vintage.
28 The first man did not know wisdom*
    fully,
  nor will the last one fathom her.
29 For her thoughts are more abundant
    than the sea,
  and her counsel deeper than the great
    abyss.

30 As for me, I was like a canal from a
    river,
  like a water channel into a garden.
31 I said, "I will water my garden
    and drench my flower-beds."
  And lo, my canal became a river,
    and my river a sea.
32 I will again make instruction shine forth
    like the dawn,
  and I will make it clear from far away.

33 I will again pour out teaching like
    prophecy,
  and leave it to all future generations.
34 Observe that I have not labored for
    myself alone,
  but for all who seek wisdom.*

24.1–34: In praise of wisdom. 1–22: This twenty-two-line poem, whose theme and form resemble Prov 8, marks the approximate halfway point in Sirach. The first half of the text was similarly introduced by a poem on Wisdom personified (1.1–10; other descriptions of personified Wisdom appear at 4.11–19; 6.18–37; 14.20–15.10). This poem stands out because Wisdom herself is the speaker of the poem. **2:** She is pictured as standing in the divine realm, among the heavenly host (compare Ps 82; 103.19–22). **6b–8:** Wisdom offered herself to other peoples, but God chose to match Wisdom permanently with Israel (compare Deut 32.8–9). **10–12:** Wisdom is understood to dwell in the Jerusalem Temple.* God's presence, typically denoted as "glory," during the Exodus dwelt in the tent of meeting and then in the tabernacle* (Ex 13.21–22; 33.9–11; 40.34–38). The Hebrew word that describes God's glory, "kabod," is the same as the word for honor. Accordingly, Wisdom is God's glory, just as she is the source of honor for earthly men. **13–17:** The language Woman Wisdom uses to describe herself is sexually charged (see comments on 14.20–15.10). **21:** The metaphors* of *hunger* and *thirst* may remind the reader of Jesus' comments about himself in John 4.14 and 6.35; however, the imagery there has a function in diametrical opposition to the use here. **23–29:** Ben Sira again makes explicit the connection between Wisdom and Torah* (compare 1.11–30). Here, however, God's law is first referred to as *the book of the covenant,** which may indicate Ben Sira's intentional use of scripture as part of his wisdom teachings. **30–34:** Ben Sira speaks self-consciously as a wisdom teacher. He even carries over the metaphor of flowing water from Wisdom to himself when he calls himself a *canal.* Just as the prophet* is a mouthpiece

---

a Other ancient authorities add as verse 18, *I am the mother of beautiful love, of fear, of knowledge, and of holy hope; being eternal, I am given to all my children, to those who are named by him.*   b Other ancient authorities add as verse 24, *"Do not cease to be strong in the Lord, cling to him so that he may strengthen you; the Lord Almighty alone is God, and besides him there is no savior."*   c Syr: Gk *It makes instruction shine forth like light*   d Gk *her* for God, Ben Sira understands himself as a conduit for Wisdom.

25 ¹ I take pleasure in three things,
and they are beautiful in the sight
of God and of mortals:[a]
agreement among brothers and sisters,
friendship among neighbors,
and a wife and a husband who live in
harmony.
² I hate three kinds of people,
and I loathe their manner of life:
a pauper who boasts, a rich person who
lies,
and an old fool who commits
adultery.

³ If you gathered nothing in your youth,
how can you find anything in your old
age?
⁴ How attractive is sound judgment in the
gray-haired,
and for the aged to possess good
counsel!
⁵ How attractive is wisdom in the aged,
and understanding and counsel in the
venerable!
⁶ Rich experience is the crown of the
aged,
and their boast is the fear of the
Lord.

⁷ I can think of nine whom I would call
blessed,
and a tenth my tongue proclaims:
a man who can rejoice in his children;
a man who lives to see the downfall
of his foes.
⁸ Happy the man who lives with a
sensible wife,
and the one who does not plow with
ox and ass together.[b]
Happy is the one who does not sin with
the tongue,
and the one who has not served an
inferior.
⁹ Happy is the one who finds a friend,[c]
and the one who speaks to attentive
listeners.
¹⁰ How great is the one who finds
wisdom!

But none is superior to the one who
fears the Lord.
¹¹ Fear of the Lord surpasses everything;
to whom can we compare the one
who has it?[d]

25.1–11: Roles and relationships. Ben Sira makes use of numerical proverbs to name various kinds of people. With the exception of v. 2, he speaks of positive situations by using several beatitudes. The teachings that follow in the coming chapters cover different kinds of human interaction.

---

¹³ Any wound, but not a wound of the
heart!
Any wickedness, but not the
wickedness of a woman!
¹⁴ Any suffering, but not suffering from
those who hate!
And any vengeance, but not the
vengeance of enemies!
¹⁵ There is no venom[e] worse than a
snake's venom,[e]
and no anger worse than a woman's[f]
wrath.

25.13–15: These verses serve as a kind of introduction to the theme of good and bad wives in chs. 25, 26. They point out the potential pitfalls relations with women can bring.

---

¹⁶ I would rather live with a lion and a
dragon
than live with an evil woman.
¹⁷ A woman's wickedness changes her
appearance,
and darkens her face like that of a
bear.
¹⁸ Her husband sits[g] among the neighbors,
and he cannot help sighing[h] bitterly.
¹⁹ Any iniquity is small compared to a
woman's iniquity;
may a sinner's lot befall her!

a Syr Lat: Gk *In three things I was beautiful and I stood in beauty before the Lord and mortals.*   b Heb Syr: Gk lacks *and the one who does not plow with ox and ass together.*   c Lat Syr: Gk *good sense*   d Other ancient authorities add as verse 12, *The fear of the Lord is the beginning of love for him, and faith is the beginning of clinging to him.*   e Syr: Gk *head*   f Other ancient authorities read *an enemy's*   g Heb Syr: Gk *loses heart*   h Other ancient authorities read *and listening he sighs*

20 A sandy ascent for the feet of the
　　aged—
　　such is a garrulous wife to a quiet
　　　husband.
21 Do not be ensnared by a woman's
　　　beauty,
　　and do not desire a woman for her
　　　possessions.ᵃ
22 There is wrath and impudence and
　　　great disgrace
　　when a wife supports her husband.
23 Dejected mind, gloomy face,
　　and wounded heart come from an evil
　　　wife.
　　Drooping hands and weak knees
　　　come from the wife who does not
　　　make her husband happy.
24 From a woman sin had its beginning,
　　and because of her we all die.
25 Allow no outlet to water,
　　and no boldness of speech to an evil
　　　wife.
26 If she does not go as you direct,
　　separate her from yourself.

she will be granted among the
　　blessings of the man who fears
　　the Lord.
4 Whether rich or poor, his heart is
　　content,
　　and at all times his face is cheerful.
5 Of three things my heart is frightened,
　　and of a fourth I am in great fear:ᵇ
　　Slander in the city, the gathering of a
　　　mob,
　　and false accusation—all these are
　　　worse than death.
6 But it is heartache and sorrow when a
　　wife is jealous of a rival,
　　and a tongue-lashing makes it known
　　to all.
7 A bad wife is a chafing yoke;
　　taking hold of her is like grasping a
　　scorpion.
8 A drunken wife arouses great anger;
　　she cannot hide her shame.
9 The haughty stare betrays an unchaste
　　wife;
　　her eyelids give her away.

25.16–26: Ben Sira first describes the bad wife. He exceeds the author of Proverbs in his negative comments on the subject (see Prov 21.19; 25.24; 27.15–16). 17: The description of a *wicked woman's* altered *appearance* serves as a warning to young suitors. 19: This statement implies that women are inherently more sinful. 22: Ben Sira recognizes that a man may be tempted to marry a woman of greater means in order to increase his own wealth. Such an imbalance, however, may mean that the wife will control the family finances with the result that a man could find himself subject to his wife's authority, diminishing his honor. 24: The author's allusion to Gen 3 makes explicit the equation between Eve's disobedience and human mortality. 26: Ben Sira recommends divorcing a willful woman, which means that she must depart her husband's house (see Deut 24.1–4).

26.1–9: Ben Sira turns his attention to the *good wife*, then turns back to the *bad wife*. 1–4: In contrast to modern values of marriage, Ben Sira's image of a good marriage is one in which the wife enhances the welfare of her husband. 7: Once again Ben Sira uses an analogy to an undesirable creature to characterize the bad wife (see 25.15–17). 9: *The haughty stare* means a lustful eye (see 23.4), whereas the mention of *eyelids* probably refers to a woman's ability to provoke lust in others (Prov 6.25).

10 Keep strict watch over a headstrong
　　　daughter,
　　or else, when she finds liberty, she
　　　will make use of it.
11 Be on guard against her impudent eye,
　　and do not be surprised if she sins
　　　against you.
12 As a thirsty traveler opens his mouth
　　and drinks from any water near him,
　　so she will sit in front of every tent
　　　peg
　　and open her quiver to the arrow.

26 Happy is the husband of a good
　　wife;
　　the number of his days will be
　　doubled.
2 A loyal wife brings joy to her husband,
　　and he will complete his years in
　　　peace.
3 A good wife is a great blessing;

a Heb Syr: Other Gk authorities read *for her beauty*
b Syr: Meaning of Gk uncertain

26.10–12: The switch from discussion of the bad wife to *headstrong daughter* seems abrupt. Since the Hebrew is not preserved for this section and the Syriac* reads "wife" instead of "daughter," many scholars understand these verses in the original to have continued the discussion of the bad wife. They explain the appearance of "daughter" in the Greek as resulting from a confusion with 42.11 where the expression "headstrong daughter" also appears. **12:** *Tent peg* and *arrow* are euphemisms* for male genitalia (compare 14.24).

~~~~~~~~~~~~~~~~~~~~~~~~

13 A wife's charm delights her husband,
    and her skill puts flesh on his bones.
14 A silent wife is a gift from the Lord,
    and nothing is so precious as her self-
        discipline.
15 A modest wife adds charm to charm,
    and no scales can weigh the value of
        her chastity.
16 Like the sun rising in the heights of the
        Lord,
    so is the beauty of a good wife in her
        well-ordered home.
17 Like the shining lamp on the holy
        lampstand,
    so is a beautiful face on a stately
        figure.
18 Like golden pillars on silver bases,
    so are shapely legs and steadfast feet.

────────────────

Other ancient authorities add
        verses 19–27:
19 *My child, keep sound the bloom of your*
        youth,
    and do not give your strength to
        strangers.
20 *Seek a fertile field within the whole plain,*
    and sow it with your own seed, trusting
        in your fine stock.
21 *So your offspring will prosper,*
    and, having confidence in their good
        descent, will grow great.
22 *A prostitute is regarded as spittle,*
    and a married woman as a tower of
        death to her lovers.
23 *A godless wife is given as a portion to a*
        lawless man,
    but a pious wife is given to the man
        who fears the Lord.

24 *A shameless woman constantly acts*
        disgracefully,
    but a modest daughter will even be
        embarrassed before her husband.
25 *A headstrong wife is regarded as a dog,*
    but one who has a sense of shame will
        fear the Lord.
26 *A wife honoring her husband will seem*
        wise to all,
    but if she dishonors him in her pride
        she will be known to all as ungodly.
    Happy is the husband of a good wife;
    for the number of his years will be
        doubled.
27 *A loud-voiced and garrulous wife is like a*
        trumpet sounding the charge,
    and every person like this lives in the
        anarchy of war.

────────────────

26.19–27: These verses appear in later manuscripts. It is unclear whether they were part of the original text, although the teachings are consistent with the rest of Sirach. **19–22:** Ben Sira tries to dissuade young men from sexual affairs prior to marriage.

~~~~~~~~~~~~~~~~~~~~~~~~

28 At two things my heart is grieved,
    and because of a third anger comes
        over me:
    a warrior in want through poverty,
    intelligent men who are treated
        contemptuously,
    and a man who turns back from
        righteousness to sin—
    the Lord will prepare him for the
        sword!
29 A merchant can hardly keep from
        wrongdoing,
    nor is a tradesman innocent of sin.

27 Many have committed sin for gain,[a]
    and those who seek to get rich will
        avert their eyes.
2 As a stake is driven firmly into a fissure
        between stones,
    so sin is wedged in between selling
        and buying.
3 If a person is not steadfast in the fear of
        the Lord,
    his house will be quickly overthrown.

a Other ancient authorities read *a trifle*

4 When a sieve is shaken, the refuse
    appears;
  so do a person's faults when he
    speaks.
5 The kiln tests the potter's vessels;
  so the test of a person is in his
    conversation.
6 Its fruit discloses the cultivation of a
    tree;
  so a person's speech discloses the
    cultivation of his mind.
7 Do not praise anyone before he speaks,
  for this is the way people are tested.

8 If you pursue justice, you will attain it
  and wear it like a glorious robe.
9 Birds roost with their own kind,
  so honesty comes home to those who
    practice it.
10 A lion lies in wait for prey;
  so does sin for evildoers.

11 The conversation of the godly is always
    wise,
  but the fool changes like the moon.
12 Among stupid people limit your time,
  but among thoughtful people linger on.
13 The talk of fools is offensive,
  and their laughter is wantonly sinful.
14 Their cursing and swearing make one's
    hair stand on end,
  and their quarrels make others stop
    their ears.
15 The strife of the proud leads to
    bloodshed,
  and their abuse is grievous to hear.

16 Whoever betrays secrets destroys
    confidence,
  and will never find a congenial friend.
17 Love your friend and keep faith with
    him;
  but if you betray his secrets, do not
    follow after him.
18 For as a person destroys his enemy,
  so you have destroyed the friendship
    of your neighbor.
19 And as you allow a bird to escape from
    your hand,
  so you have let your neighbor go, and
    will not catch him again.

20 Do not go after him, for he is too far
    off,
  and has escaped like a gazelle from a
    snare.
21 For a wound may be bandaged,
  and there is reconciliation after
    abuse,
  but whoever has betrayed secrets is
    without hope.

22 Whoever winks the eye plots mischief,
  and those who know him will keep
    their distance.
23 In your presence his mouth is all
    sweetness,
  and he admires your words;
  but later he will twist his speech
  and with your own words he will trip
    you up.
24 I have hated many things, but him
    above all;
  even the Lord hates him.
25 Whoever throws a stone straight up
    throws it on his own head,
  and a treacherous blow opens up
    many wounds.
26 Whoever digs a pit will fall into it,
  and whoever sets a snare will be
    caught in it.
27 If a person does evil, it will roll back
    upon him,
  and he will not know where it came
    from.
28 Mockery and abuse issue from the
    proud,
  but vengeance lies in wait for them
    like a lion.
29 Those who rejoice in the fall of the
    godly will be caught in a snare,
  and pain will consume them before
    their death.

26.28–29.28: Relations with other men. 26.29–27.3:
Ben Sira again views the business arena as inherently
problematic. Although he does not counsel his students to refrain from buying and selling, he advises
extreme caution. The logic of this teaching is analogous to Ben Sira's teaching on women—women are
extremely dangerous and can lead to ruin, but he regards women and marriage as essential to existence.
4–7: These verses help to explain why such emphasis

is placed on correct *speech*. Speech represents the embodiment of one's wisdom. **16–21:** In a world where public knowledge of a person's shortcomings can bring dishonor upon the person and his entire household, privacy is essential. Thus, *confidence* between *friends* was especially valued. **22–29:** The author has harsh words for those who, lacking integrity, act duplicitously in order to take advantage of others.

30 Anger and wrath, these also are
         abominations,
      yet a sinner holds on to them.

28 The vengeful will face the Lord's
         vengeance,
      for he keeps a strict account of*a* their
         sins.

2 Forgive your neighbor the wrong he has
         done,
      and then your sins will be pardoned
         when you pray.
3 Does anyone harbor anger against
         another,
      and expect healing from the Lord?
4 If one has no mercy toward another like
         himself,
      can he then seek pardon for his own
         sins?
5 If a mere mortal harbors wrath,
      who will make an atoning sacrifice for
         his sins?
6 Remember the end of your life, and set
         enmity aside;
      remember corruption and death, and
         be true to the commandments.
7 Remember the commandments, and do
         not be angry with your neighbor;
      remember the covenant of the Most
         High, and overlook faults.

8 Refrain from strife, and your sins will be
         fewer;
      for the hot-tempered kindle strife,
9 and the sinner disrupts friendships
      and sows discord among those who
         are at peace.
10 In proportion to the fuel, so will the fire
         burn,
      and in proportion to the obstinacy, so
         will strife increase;*b*
   in proportion to a person's strength will
         be his anger,

and in proportion to his wealth he
      will increase his wrath.
11 A hasty quarrel kindles a fire,
      and a hasty dispute sheds blood.
12 If you blow on a spark, it will glow;
      if you spit on it, it will be put out;
      yet both come out of your mouth.

27.30–28.11: One's anger should never get out of control. **28.4–5:** One cannot expect forgiveness from God for one's *own sins* without also granting forgiveness to fellow human beings. While God's wrath can be appeased by prayer and sacrifice, no such method of atonement exists between humans. Thus, it is incumbent upon humans to show *mercy* to others. **7:** *The commandments,* not volatile emotions, regulate human interaction. The call to *remember the covenant** reminds the reader that God has repeatedly forgiven Israel for her sins. **11:** Ben Sira teaches that hostile emotions can potentially cause bloodshed, resulting in a violation of one of God's prime commandments; compare Mt 5.21–23.

13 Curse the gossips and the double-
         tongued,
      for they destroy the peace of many.
14 Slander*c* has shaken many,
      and scattered them from nation to
         nation;
   it has destroyed strong cities,
      and overturned the houses of the
         great.
15 Slander*c* has driven virtuous women
         from their homes,
      and deprived them of the fruit of
         their toil.
16 Those who pay heed to slander*d* will
         not find rest,
      nor will they settle down in peace.
17 The blow of a whip raises a welt,
      but a blow of the tongue crushes the
         bones.
18 Many have fallen by the edge of the
         sword,
      but not as many as have fallen
         because of the tongue.

a Other ancient authorities read *for he firmly establishes*
b Other ancient authorities read *burn*   *c* Gk A third
tongue   *d* Gk *it*

19 Happy is the one who is protected from
　　it,
20 who has not been exposed to its anger,
　who has not borne its yoke,
　　and has not been bound with its
　　　fetters.
21 For its yoke is a yoke of iron,
　　and its fetters are fetters of bronze;
22 its death is an evil death,
　　and Hades is preferable to it.
23 It has no power over the godly;
　they will not be burned in its flame.
24 Those who forsake the Lord will fall
　　into its power;
　it will burn among them and will not
　　be put out.
　It will be sent out against them like a
　　lion;
　like a leopard it will mangle them.
24a As you fence in your property with
　　thorns,
25b so make a door and a bolt for your
　　mouth.
24b As you lock up your silver and gold,
25a so make balances and scales for your
　　words.
26 Take care not to err with your tongue,[a]
　　and fall victim to one lying in wait.

28.12–26: Again Sirach warns of the evil that can result
from sinful speech (see 18.15–21.28). **12:** This metaphorical* proverb illustrates that talk has the potential
for both good and evil, though the subject of Ben Sira's
instruction in this section is the latter. **14:** *Slander* here
translates the Greek phrase the "third tongue" (see
note c). The designation arises from the three-way
damage caused by slander. Unlike a simple lie, slander
involves the slanderer, the hearers—who themselves
typically perpetuate the slander—and the one who has
been slandered. **17:** This saying runs contrary to the
childhood rhyme: "Sticks and stones may break my
bones, but words will never hurt me." Ben Sira's dire
warnings about the calamitous effects of slander reflect the tremendous power words have in his cultural
context (see comment on 23.7–11). **21:** In regard to
*Hades,** see the comment on 21.10. **22–23:** *Burned
in its flame* refers not to Hades, but to the destructive
power of slander. The metaphorical use of a burning
flame reminds the reader of the proverb that introduces this section.

29 The merciful lend to their
　　neighbors;
　by holding out a helping hand they
　　keep the commandments.
2 Lend to your neighbor in his time of
　　need;
　repay your neighbor when a loan falls
　　due.
3 Keep your promise and be honest with
　　him,
　　and on every occasion you will find
　　what you need.
4 Many regard a loan as a windfall,
　　and cause trouble to those who help
　　them.
5 One kisses another's hands until he gets
　　a loan,
　　and is deferential in speaking of his
　　neighbor's money;
　but at the time for repayment he
　　delays,
　　and pays back with empty promises,
　　and finds fault with the time.
6 If he can pay, his creditor[b] will hardly
　　get back half,
　　and will regard that as a windfall.
　If he cannot pay, the borrower[b] has
　　robbed the other of his money,
　　and he has needlessly made him an
　　enemy;
　he will repay him with curses and
　　reproaches,
　　and instead of glory will repay him
　　with dishonor.
7 Many refuse to lend, not because of
　　meanness,
　　but from fear[c] of being defrauded
　　needlessly.

8 Nevertheless, be patient with someone
　　in humble circumstances,
　　and do not keep him waiting for your
　　alms.
9 Help the poor for the commandment's
　　sake,
　　and in their need do not send them
　　away empty-handed.

a Gk *with it*　　*b* Gk *he*　　*c* Other ancient authorities
read *many refuse to lend, therefore, because of such
meanness; they are afraid*

10 Lose your silver for the sake of a
         brother or a friend,
      and do not let it rust under a stone
         and be lost.
11 Lay up your treasure according to the
         commandments of the Most
         High,
      and it will profit you more than gold.
12 Store up almsgiving in your treasury,
      and it will rescue you from every
         disaster;
13 better than a stout shield and a sturdy
         spear,
      it will fight for you against the
         enemy.

14 A good person will be surety for his
         neighbor,
      but the one who has lost all sense of
         shame will fail him.
15 Do not forget the kindness of your
         guarantor,
      for he has given his life for you.
16 A sinner wastes the property of his
         guarantor,
17 and the ungrateful person abandons
         his rescuer.
18 Being surety has ruined many who were
         prosperous,
      and has tossed them about like waves
         of the sea;
      it has driven the influential into exile,
      and they have wandered among
         foreign nations.
19 The sinner comes to grief through
         surety;
      his pursuit of gain involves him in
         lawsuits.
20 Assist your neighbor to the best of your
         ability,
      but be careful not to fall yourself.

29.1–20: The author takes up two related topics: the pitfalls of borrowed money and the righteousness of charity. Both lending and borrowing are sanctioned by Ben Sira (vv. 1–3), but his descriptions of what can go wrong lead to a sympathetic statement about those who refuse to lend. **8–13:** It is perhaps significant that Ben Sira chooses to sandwich a discussion of *almsgiving* between two sections on lending money (vv. 1–7, 14–20). He seems to recognize that failure to repay a

loan may be due to pecuniary circumstances and not merely willful disregard of the debt. However, since a borrower who defaults on a loan technically robs *the other of his money* (v. 6), almsgiving, which carries with it no expectation of repayment, may represent a superior way of aiding the needy. Furthermore, although charity results in some measure of financial loss, helping the poor is ultimately profitable (vv. 11–13). **14–20:** *Being surety* refers to a person who puts up collateral for another. In contrast to Proverbs (11.15; 17.18; 20.16), Ben Sira teaches that being surety is a worthy endeavor, but again, should only be undertaken with caution.

21 The necessities of life are water, bread,
         and clothing,
      and also a house to assure privacy.
22 Better is the life of the poor under their
         own crude roof
      than sumptuous food in the house of
         others.
23 Be content with little or much,
      and you will hear no reproach for
         being a guest.[a]
24 It is a miserable life to go from house to
         house;
      as a guest you should not open your
         mouth;
25 you will play the host and provide drink
         without being thanked,
      and besides this you will hear rude
         words like these:
26 "Come here, stranger, prepare the
         table;
      let me eat what you have there."
27 "Be off, stranger, for an honored guest
         is here;
      my brother has come for a visit, and I
         need the guest-room."
28 It is hard for a sensible person to bear
      scolding about lodging[b] and the
         insults of the moneylender.

29.21–28: While hospitality is a typical biblical virtue, Ben Sira sternly warns against dependence upon others' hospitality which can result in humiliation.

a Lat: Gk *reproach from your family;* other ancient authorities lack this line   *b* Or *scolding from the household*

CONCERNING CHILDREN [a]

30 He who loves his son will whip him
often,
so that he may rejoice at the way he
turns out.

2 He who disciplines his son will profit by
him,
and will boast of him among
acquaintances.

3 He who teaches his son will make his
enemies envious,
and will glory in him among his
friends.

4 When the father dies he will not seem
to be dead,
for he has left behind him one like
himself,

5 whom in his life he looked upon with
joy
and at death, without grief.

6 He has left behind him an avenger
against his enemies,
and one to repay the kindness of his
friends.

7 Whoever spoils his son will bind up his
wounds,
and will suffer heartache at every cry.

8 An unbroken horse turns out stubborn,
and an unchecked son turns out
headstrong.

9 Pamper a child, and he will terrorize
you;
play with him, and he will grieve
you.

10 Do not laugh with him, or you will have
sorrow with him,
and in the end you will gnash your
teeth.

11 Give him no freedom in his youth,
and do not ignore his errors.

12 Bow down his neck in his youth, [b]
and beat his sides while he is young,
or else he will become stubborn and
disobey you,
and you will have sorrow of soul from
him. [c]

13 Discipline your son and make his yoke
heavy, [d]
so that you may not be offended by
his shamelessness.

30.1–13: Disciplining children. Male children are primarily in view here. The sanction of physical punishment in the raising of sons is typical (Prov 13.24; 23.13–14). Also typical in the Hellenistic* context is the connection between discipline and education (see comment on 6.18). **13:** *So that you may not be offended by his shamelessness* means that out-of-control children constitute public humiliations to their father.

LIFE'S PLEASURES

30.14–31.11: As severe as some of Sirach's teachings may be, the author does not advocate the pursuit of asceticism. Ben Sira's students are not required to abstain from food, drink, or most other bodily pleasures.

14 Better off poor, healthy, and fit
than rich and afflicted in body.

15 Health and fitness are better than any
gold,
and a robust body than countless
riches.

16 There is no wealth better than health of
body,
and no gladness above joy of heart.

17 Death is better than a life of misery,
and eternal sleep[e] than chronic
sickness.

CONCERNING FOODS [f]

18 Good things poured out upon a mouth
that is closed
are like offerings of food placed upon
a grave.

19 Of what use to an idol is a sacrifice?
For it can neither eat nor smell.
So is the one punished by the Lord;

20 he sees with his eyes and groans
as a eunuch groans when embracing
a girl. [g]

a This heading is included in the Gk text.   b Other ancient authorities lack this line and the preceding line   c Other ancient authorities lack this line   d Heb: Gk *take pains with him*   e Other ancient authorities lack *eternal sleep*   f This heading is included in the Gk text; other ancient authorities place the heading before verse 16   g Other ancient authorities add *So is the person who does right under compulsion*

30.18–20: *A mouth that is closed* may refer to a dead person. Such an interpretation* is implied by the author's parody of the supposed consumption of sacrifices made to idols (biblical authors often poke fun at the deadness of idols: Ps 115.4–7; Bel and the Dragon; Wis 13). However, the image of *a eunuch . . . embracing a girl* suggests perhaps that *a mouth that is closed* refers to an ascetic or a person in mourning, or any person who willfully abstains from the consumption of desirable food and drink. Indeed, in vv. 21–25 the author encourages a joyful embrace of life.

21 Do not give yourself over to sorrow,
 and do not distress yourself deliberately.
22 A joyful heart is life itself,
 and rejoicing lengthens one's life span.
23 Indulge yourself*a* and take comfort,
 and remove sorrow far from you,
 for sorrow has destroyed many,
 and no advantage ever comes from it.
24 Jealousy and anger shorten life,
 and anxiety brings on premature old
 age.
25 Those who are cheerful and merry at
 table
 will benefit from their food.

31 Wakefulness over wealth wastes
 away one's flesh,
 and anxiety about it drives away sleep.
2 Wakeful anxiety prevents slumber,
 and a severe illness carries off sleep.*b*
3 The rich person toils to amass a
 fortune,
 and when he rests he fills himself
 with his dainties.
4 The poor person toils to make a meager
 living,
 and if ever he rests he becomes
 needy.
5 One who loves gold will not be justified;
 one who pursues money will be led
 astray*c* by it.
6 Many have come to ruin because of
 gold,
 and their destruction has met them
 face to face.
7 It is a stumbling block to those who are
 avid for it,

and every fool will be taken captive
 by it.
8 Blessed is the rich person who is found
 blameless,
 and who does not go after gold.
9 Who is he, that we may praise him?
 For he has done wonders among his
 people.
10 Who has been tested by it and been
 found perfect?
 Let it be for him a ground for
 boasting.
Who has had the power to transgress
 and did not transgress,
 and to do evil and did not do it?
11 His prosperity will be established,*d*
 and the assembly will proclaim his
 acts of charity.

31.1–11: Ben Sira characterizes the man who is obsessed with amassing and protecting his wealth as one who will be ruined by it. Yet, Ben Sira also believes that some wealthy men can and do remain God-fearing. The rich man who remains virtuous is more worthy of praise than others because he has faced far more temptation (compare 20.21–23).

BEHAVIOR AT BANQUETS AND THE ETHIC OF MODERATION

31.12–32.13: Formal banquets known as symposia were common among the elite in Hellenistic* society and were adopted by the upper echelons of ancient Jewish society. (The most famous such banquet is described by Plato in *The Symposium*.)

12 Are you seated at the table of the great?*e*
 Do not be greedy at it,
 and do not say, "How much food
 there is here!"
13 Remember that a greedy eye is a bad
 thing.
 What has been created more greedy
 than the eye?
 Therefore it sheds tears for any
 reason.

a Other ancient authorities read *Beguile yourself*
b Other ancient authorities read *sleep carries off a severe illness*   *c* Heb Syr: Gk *pursues destruction will be filled*
d Other ancient authorities add *because of this*   *e* Heb Syr: Gk *at a great table*

14 Do not reach out your hand for
        everything you see,
    and do not crowd your neighbor*a* at
        the dish.
15 Judge your neighbor's feelings by your
        own,
    and in every matter be thoughtful.
16 Eat what is set before you like a well
        brought-up person,*b*
    and do not chew greedily, or you will
        give offense.
17 Be the first to stop, as befits good
        manners,
    and do not be insatiable, or you will
        give offense.
18 If you are seated among many
        persons,
    do not help yourself*c* before they do.

19 How ample a little is for a well-
        disciplined person!
    He does not breathe heavily when in
        bed.
20 Healthy sleep depends on moderate
        eating;
    he rises early, and feels fit.
    The distress of sleeplessness and of
        nausea
    and colic are with the glutton.
21 If you are overstuffed with food,
    get up to vomit, and you will have
        relief.
22 Listen to me, my child, and do not
        disregard me,
    and in the end you will appreciate my
        words.
    In everything you do be moderate,*d*
    and no sickness will overtake you.
23 People bless the one who is liberal with
        food,
    and their testimony to his generosity
        is trustworthy.
24 The city complains of the one who is
        stingy with food,
    and their testimony to his stinginess
        is accurate.

25 Do not try to prove your strength by
        wine-drinking,
    for wine has destroyed many.

26 As the furnace tests the work of the
        smith,*e*
    so wine tests hearts when the insolent
        quarrel.
27 Wine is very life to human beings
    if taken in moderation.
    What is life to one who is without
        wine?
    It has been created to make people
        happy.
28 Wine drunk at the proper time and in
        moderation
    is rejoicing of heart and gladness of
        soul.
29 Wine drunk to excess leads to bitterness
        of spirit,
    to quarrels and stumbling.
30 Drunkenness increases the anger of a
        fool to his own hurt,
    reducing his strength and adding
        wounds.
31 Do not reprove your neighbor at a
        banquet of wine,
    and do not despise him in his
        merrymaking;
    speak no word of reproach to him,
    and do not distress him by making
        demands of him.

32 If they make you master of the
        feast, do not exalt yourself;
    be among them as one of their
        number.
    Take care of them first and then sit
        down;
2   when you have fulfilled all your
        duties, take your place,
    so that you may be merry along with
        them
    and receive a wreath for your
        excellent leadership.

31.12–31: Ben Sira's philosophy regarding eating and drinking is summed up by the comment in 22b: *In everything you do be moderate.* **25:** Drinking to excess and drinking contests in particular were expected occurrences at symposia.

a Gk *him*   *b* Heb: Gk *like a human being*
c Gk *reach out your hand*   *d* Heb Syr: Gk *industrious*
e Heb: Gk *tests the hardening of steel by dipping*

3 Speak, you who are older, for it is your
right,
but with accurate knowledge, and do
not interrupt the music.
4 Where there is entertainment, do not
pour out talk;
do not display your cleverness at the
wrong time.
5 A ruby seal in a setting of gold
is a concert of music at a banquet of
wine.
6 A seal of emerald in a rich setting of
gold
is the melody of music with good
wine.

7 Speak, you who are young, if you are
obliged to,
but no more than twice, and only if
asked.
8 Be brief; say much in few words;
be as one who knows and can still
hold his tongue.
9 Among the great do not act as their
equal;
and when another is speaking, do not
babble.

10 Lightning travels ahead of the thunder,
and approval goes before one who is
modest.
11 Leave in good time and do not be the
last;
go home quickly and do not linger.
12 Amuse yourself there to your heart's
content,
but do not sin through proud
speech.
13 But above all bless your Maker,
who fills you with his good gifts.

GOD, TORAH,* AND THE PURSUIT OF DISCIPLINE

32.14–33.18: This section includes general comments on choosing the right path and using good judgment. Many of the individual poetic units explicitly contrast those who fear the Lord with the sinner (see especially 33.14).

14 The one who seeks God[a] will accept his
discipline,
and those who rise early to seek him[b]
will find favor.
15 The one who seeks the law will be filled
with it,
but the hypocrite will stumble at it.
16 Those who fear the Lord will form true
judgments,
and they will kindle righteous deeds
like a light.
17 The sinner will shun reproof,
and will find a decision according to
his liking.
18 A sensible person will not overlook a
thoughtful suggestion;
an insolent[c] and proud person will
not be deterred by fear.[d]
19 Do nothing without deliberation,
but when you have acted, do not
regret it.
20 Do not go on a path full of hazards,
and do not stumble at an obstacle
twice.[e]
21 Do not be overconfident on a smooth[f]
road,
22 and give good heed to your paths.[g]
23 Guard[h] yourself in every act,
for this is the keeping of the
commandments.

32.1–13. 1: *Master of the feast,* an appointed host, was an honored position at a symposium. **3–9:** Mature adults were accorded the right to speak when they pleased (v. 3); younger company should only speak when spoken to (v. 7). Symposia dictated that the guests be seated according to rank. Relative age was a primary criterion for establishing rank. **4–5:** *Entertainment* was typical at these banquets. **13:** *Bless your Maker* is likely a reference to blessing the food or a grace after meals.

32.14–23. 14: The word *discipline* translates the Hebrew "musar" and the Greek "paideia." The same term appears at the end of the section in 33.18, where

a Heb: Gk *who fears the Lord*   b Other ancient
authorities lack *to seek him*   c Heb: Gk *alien*
d Meaning of Gk uncertain. Other ancient authorities
add *and after acting, with him, without deliberation*
e Heb: Gk *stumble on stony ground*   f Or *an
unexplored*   g Heb Syr: Gk *and beware of your children*
h Heb Syr: Gk *Trust*

it is translated as *instruction.* "Musar," therefore, constitutes a framing device called an *inclusio,** which helps the reader identify the primary theme of this unit. The sense of musar/paideia in this context reflects education, and not so much physical punishment. The author equates three pursuits: seeking God, the observance of Torah,* and the pursuit of study. **15:** *The one who seeks the law* means one who studies God's instruction contained in the Torah. Although the Hebrew word "Torah" is often translated *law,* it also means *instruction.* **16–19:** The person who studies is also the person who carefully deliberates important matters and confers with others. **23:** The study of Torah automatically implies keeping the commandments as well.

24 The one who keeps the law preserves
　　himself,[a]
　　and the one who trusts the Lord will
　　not suffer loss.

33 No evil will befall the one who fears
　　the Lord,
　　but in trials such a one will be
　　rescued again and again.
2 The wise will not hate the law,
　　but the one who is hypocritical about
　　it is like a boat in a storm.
3 The sensible person will trust in the law;
　　for such a one the law is as
　　dependable as a divine oracle.

4 Prepare what to say, and then you will
　　be listened to;
　　draw upon your training, and give
　　your answer.
5 The heart of a fool is like a cart wheel,
　　and his thoughts like a turning axle.
6 A mocking friend is like a stallion
　　that neighs no matter who the rider is.

7 Why is one day more important than
　　another,
　　when all the daylight in the year is
　　from the sun?
8 By the Lord's wisdom they were
　　distinguished,
　　and he appointed the different
　　seasons and festivals.
9 Some days he exalted and hallowed,
　　and some he made ordinary days.

10 All human beings come from the
　　ground,
　　and humankind[b] was created out of
　　the dust.
11 In the fullness of his knowledge the
　　Lord distinguished them
　　and appointed their different ways.
12 Some he blessed and exalted,
　　and some he made holy and brought
　　near to himself;
　　but some he cursed and brought low,
　　and turned them out of their place.
13 Like clay in the hand of the potter,
　　to be molded as he pleases,
　　so all are in the hand of their Maker,
　　to be given whatever he decides.

14 Good is the opposite of evil,
　　and life the opposite of death;
　　so the sinner is the opposite of the
　　godly.
15 Look at all the works of the Most High;
　　they come in pairs, one the opposite
　　of the other.

16 Now I was the last to keep vigil;
　　I was like a gleaner following the
　　grape-pickers;
17 by the blessing of the Lord I arrived
　　first,
　　and like a grape-picker I filled my
　　wine press.
18 Consider that I have not labored for
　　myself alone,
　　but for all who seek instruction.

33.7–18: Ben Sira compares contrasting elements in creation to humankind. **9–12:** All *days* and all peoples are God's creation, but just as holy days are distinguished from other days, some people are *blessed* while others are *cursed.* That Israel was blessed among the nations derives from God's promise to Abraham (Gen 12.2–3; 22.17–18). *Some he made holy and brought near to himself* could refer to Israel generally (Lev 20.22–26), or to the priestly class specifically, since priests alone may approach the sacrificial altar (Lev 22.1–3; Ezek 40.46). However, *some . . . brought low* does not likely designate Israelites without priestly

a Heb: Gk *who believes the law heeds the commandments*
b Heb: Gk *Adam*

status, but rather the Canaanites because of the reference to those who have been *turned . . . out of their place* (Ex 33.1–2). **15:** The notion that the *works* of God *come in pairs* is not a typical biblical idea. Greek philosophy and cosmology, however, are often characterized by binary opposition. **16–18:** The author deliberately assumes his own voice. The *last to keep vigil* probably designates Ben Sira as the latest in a series of renowned wisdom teachers, while *I arrived first* means that Ben Sira assumed the highest level of teacher. He may have been the head of a wisdom school, or may even have founded his own school. Verse 18 repeats what is said in 24.34.

19 Hear me, you who are great among the
        people,
    and you leaders of the congregation,
        pay heed!

20 To son or wife, to brother or friend,
        do not give power over yourself, as
            long as you live;
    and do not give your property to
            another,
        in case you change your mind and
            must ask for it.
21 While you are still alive and have breath
        in you,
    do not let anyone take your place.
22 For it is better that your children should
        ask from you
    than that you should look to the hand
        of your children.
23 Excel in all that you do;
    bring no stain upon your honor.
24 At the time when you end the days of
        your life,
    in the hour of death, distribute your
        inheritance.
25 Fodder and a stick and burdens for a
        donkey;
    bread and discipline and work for a
        slave.
26 Set your slave to work, and you will find
        rest;
    leave his hands idle, and he will seek
        liberty.
27 Yoke and thong will bow the neck,
    and for a wicked slave there are racks
        and tortures.

28 Put him to work, in order that he may
        not be idle,
29 for idleness teaches much evil.
30 Set him to work, as is fitting for him,
    and if he does not obey, make his
        fetters heavy.
    Do not be overbearing toward anyone,
        and do nothing unjust.
31 If you have but one slave, treat him like
        yourself,
    because you have bought him with
        blood.
    If you have but one slave, treat him like
        a brother,
    for you will need him as you need
        your life.
32 If you ill-treat him, and he leaves you
        and runs away,
33   which way will you go to seek him?

33.19–33: Property and slaves. 20–24: These verses emphasize the need for the male head of household to maintain control of everything in his charge. Effective domestic authority contributes to the acquisition of honor. **25–33:** *Slaves,* too, are completely subject to the master's authority. **30–33** Significantly, Ben Sira encourages householders with *but one slave* to treat them humanely, even as brothers. Similar considerations are never stated for women and children.

34 The senseless have vain and false
        hopes,
    and dreams give wings to fools.
2 As one who catches at a shadow and
        pursues the wind,
    so is anyone who believes in[a] dreams.
3 What is seen in dreams is but a
        reflection,
    the likeness of a face looking at
        itself.
4 From an unclean thing what can be
        clean?
    And from something false what can
        be true?
5 Divinations and omens and dreams are
        unreal,
    and like a woman in labor, the mind
        has fantasies.

a Syr: Gk *pays heed to*

6 Unless they are sent by intervention
　　from the Most High,
　　pay no attention to them.
7 For dreams have deceived many,
　　and those who put their hope in them
　　　have perished.
8 Without such deceptions the law will be
　　fulfilled,
　　and wisdom is complete in the mouth
　　　of the faithful.

34.1–8: Dreams. The author has little regard for *dreams*. He considers them products of fantasy. He recognizes that people use dreams as a form of *divination*, but himself regards them as unreal, *unless they are sent by intervention from the Most High*. Ben Sira does not, however, offer any criteria for determining whether a dream comes directly from God. The author is no doubt aware that dream interpretation* plays a positive role elsewhere in Hebrew scripture (Gen 40–41; Dan 2; 4).

9 An educated*a* person knows many
　　things,
　　and one with much experience knows
　　　what he is talking about.
10 An inexperienced person knows few
　　things,
11 　　but he that has traveled acquires
　　much cleverness.
12 I have seen many things in my travels,
　　and I understand more than I can
　　　express.
13 I have often been in danger of death,
　　but have escaped because of these
　　　experiences.

14 The spirit of those who fear the Lord
　　will live,
15 　　for their hope is in him who saves
　　them.
16 Those who fear the Lord will not be
　　timid,
　　or play the coward, for he is their
　　　hope.
17 Happy is the soul that fears the Lord!
18 　　To whom does he look? And who is
　　his support?
19 The eyes of the Lord are on those who
　　love him,
　　a mighty shield and strong support,

a shelter from scorching wind and a
　　shade from noonday sun,
　　a guard against stumbling and a help
　　　against falling.
20 He lifts up the soul and makes the eyes
　　sparkle;
　　he gives health and life and blessing.

34.9–15. 9–13: Travel. Travel becomes a positive value during the Hellenistic* period when it and the resultant exposure to other cultures becomes more commonplace. **13:** *In danger of death* additionally highlights how vulnerable a traveler can be. Thus, travelers become both knowledgeable about other peoples and adept at looking out for themselves with minimal resources. **15:** *Saves them* refers to salvation from tribulation.

21 If one sacrifices ill-gotten goods, the
　　offering is blemished;*b*
22 　　the gifts*c* of the lawless are not
　　acceptable.
23 The Most High is not pleased with the
　　offerings of the ungodly,
　　nor for a multitude of sacrifices does
　　　he forgive sins.
24 Like one who kills a son before his
　　father's eyes
　　is the person who offers a sacrifice
　　　from the property of the poor.
25 The bread of the needy is the life of the
　　poor;
　　whoever deprives them of it is a
　　　murderer.
26 To take away a neighbor's living is to
　　commit murder;
27 　　to deprive an employee of wages is to
　　shed blood.

34.21–35.26: Sacrifice. 34.21–27: Sacrifice as a form of worship is a public act of piety. Underlying the author's remarks here is the notion that some individuals might be motivated to offer sacrifices to gain the respect of peers. **21:** Ben Sira encourages his students to be generous (35.10–13), but offerings, particularly animal sacrifices, can be costly for the average person. Thus Ben Sira mixes his discussion of sacrifice with warnings about *ill-gotten goods;* the implication being

a Other ancient authorities read *A traveled*　*b* Other ancient authorities read *is made in mockery*　*c* Other ancient authorities read *mockeries* that elaborate sacrifices made to God will not benefit the worshipper if such sacrifices were obtained by unethical means. **23:** For other critiques of sacrifice as an ineffective panacea for God when offered by the unrepentant, see Isa 1.11–17; Jer 7.21–26; Hos 8.13. Overall, Ben Sira has a positive view of sacrifice.

28 When one builds and another tears
        down,
      what do they gain but hard work?
29 When one prays and another curses,
      to whose voice will the Lord listen?
30 If one washes after touching a corpse,
      and touches it again,
      what has been gained by washing?
31 So if one fasts for his sins,
      and goes again and does the same
        things,
    who will listen to his prayer?
      And what has he gained by humbling
        himself?

34.28–31: Each of the poetic units illustrates how working at cross-purposes nullifies one's endeavors. The ultimate point appears in v. 31: Ritual acts of piety are of no benefit if one continues to sin. **30:** Contact with a *corpse* causes ritual impurity (see Num 19.11). *Washing* is of no avail until seven days have passed.

35

1   The one who keeps the law makes
        many offerings;
2   one who heeds the commandments
        makes an offering of well-being.
3 The one who returns a kindness offers
      choice flour,
4   and one who gives alms sacrifices a
        thank offering.
5 To keep from wickedness is pleasing to
      the Lord,
      and to forsake unrighteousness is an
        atonement.
6 Do not appear before the Lord empty-
      handed,
7   for all that you offer is in fulfillment
        of the commandment.
8 The offering of the righteous enriches
      the altar,
      and its pleasing odor rises before the
        Most High.
9 The sacrifice of the righteous is
      acceptable,

and it will never be forgotten.
10 Be generous when you worship the
      Lord,
      and do not stint the first fruits of your
        hands.
11 With every gift show a cheerful face,
      and dedicate your tithe with gladness.
12 Give to the Most High as he has given
      to you,
      and as generously as you can afford.
13 For the Lord is the one who repays,
      and he will repay you sevenfold.
14 Do not offer him a bribe, for he will not
      accept it;
15   and do not rely on a dishonest
        sacrifice;
    for the Lord is the judge,
      and with him there is no partiality.
16 He will not show partiality to the poor;
      but he will listen to the prayer of one
        who is wronged.
17 He will not ignore the supplication of
      the orphan,
      or the widow when she pours out her
        complaint.
18 Do not the tears of the widow run down
      her cheek
19   as she cries out against the one who
        causes them to fall?
20 The one whose service is pleasing to the
      Lord will be accepted,
      and his prayer will reach to the
        clouds.
21 The prayer of the humble pierces the
      clouds,
      and it will not rest until it reaches its
        goal;
    it will not desist until the Most High
        responds
22   and does justice for the righteous,
        and executes judgment.
    Indeed, the Lord will not delay,
      and like a warrior*a* will not be patient
    until he crushes the loins of the
        unmerciful
23   and repays vengeance on the nations;
    until he destroys the multitude of the
        insolent,

a Heb: Gk and with them

and breaks the scepters of the
  unrighteous;
24 until he repays mortals according to
  their deeds,
  and the works of all according to their
    thoughts;
25 until he judges the case of his people
  and makes them rejoice in his mercy.
26 His mercy is as welcome in time of
  distress
  as clouds of rain in time of drought.

35.1–26. 1–9: Ethical action, in addition to sacrifice, can be a means of worshipping God. 5: Living a life of righteousness can even count as *atonement*. 10–13: Since Ben Sira encourages *generous* sacrifices, the reader can assume that acts of righteousness in no way supplant sacrificial offerings, but are rather a necessary accompaniment. 14–15: It is not difficult to imagine that sacrifices could be conceived of as *bribes*. Such an attitude, however, nullifies any sacrifice. 16–26: Ben Sira displays profound faith in the power of *prayer*. These verses prepare the reader for the prayer that follows.

36 Have mercy upon us, O God[a] of
  all,
2 and put all the nations in fear of you.
3 Lift up your hand against foreign
    nations
  and let them see your might.
4 As you have used us to show your
    holiness to them,
  so use them to show your glory to us.
5 Then they will know,[b] as we have
    known,
  that there is no God but you, O Lord.
6 Give new signs, and work other
    wonders;
7 make your hand and right arm
    glorious.
8 Rouse your anger and pour out your
    wrath;
9 destroy the adversary and wipe out
    the enemy.
10 Hasten the day, and remember the
    appointed time,[c]
  and let people recount your mighty
    deeds.
11 Let survivors be consumed in the fiery
    wrath,

and may those who harm your people
  meet destruction.
12 Crush the heads of hostile rulers
  who say, "There is no one but
    ourselves."
13 Gather all the tribes of Jacob,[d]
16 and give them their inheritance, as at
    the beginning.
17 Have mercy, O Lord, on the people
    called by your name,
  on Israel, whom you have named[e]
    your firstborn,
18 Have pity on the city of your sanctuary,[f]
  Jerusalem, the place of your dwelling.[g]
19 Fill Zion with your majesty,[h]
  and your temple[i] with your glory.
20 Bear witness to those whom you created
    in the beginning,
  and fulfill the prophecies spoken in
    your name.
21 Reward those who wait for you
  and let your prophets be found
    trustworthy.
22 Hear, O Lord, the prayer of your
    servants, according to your
    goodwill toward[j] your people,
  and all who are on the earth will know
    that you are the Lord, the God of the
      ages.

36.1–22: A prayer for Israel. The prayer reflects a political and theological perspective different from the rest of Sirach. Typical of wisdom literature,* Sirach generally does not contain teachings about the end times, but focuses on providing guidance for living out one's life in the world as it currently exists. This section of the text is a petition for the overturning of the present world. As such, it presages a time in Jewish history, immediately following the time of Ben Sira, when Hellenistic* rule reaches an intolerable level and results in the Maccabean revolt (see introduction). It is difficult to know whether Ben Sira prays generically for a

a Heb: Gk O *Master, the God*   b Heb: Gk *And let them know you*   c Other ancient authorities read *remember your oath*   d Owing to a dislocation in the Greek Mss of Sirach, the verse numbers 14 and 15 are not used in chapter 36, though no text is missing.   e Other ancient authorities read *you have likened to*   f Or *on your holy city*   g Heb: Gk *your rest*   h Heb Syr: Gk *the celebration of your wondrous deeds*   i Heb Syr: Gk Lat *people*   j Heb and two Gk witnesses: Lat and most Gk witnesses read *according to the blessing of Aaron for* utopian time in the distant future when all God's promises to Israel would be fulfilled, or whether Ben Sira prays more particularly for immediate deliverance from the foreign domination of the Seleucid dynasty.* Comments like *crush the heads of hostile rulers* and *gather all the tribes of Jacob and give them their inheritance* sound explicitly political. They call for the reestablishment of Israel as a nation distinct from other nations and for the return of Diaspora* Jews, so that Israel in general and Jerusalem in particular can be restored to glory. **1–5:** Part of the motivation for the reestablishment of Israel is to demonstrate Israel's preeminent creed (Deut 6.4)—that there is only one God, the God of Israel (see Isa 45.21–22; see also v. 22). **6–16:** Ben Sira, like other biblical authors before him, uses the Exodus story as a model for understanding future salvation (see, for example, Isa 43.14–17).

23 The stomach will take any food,
    yet one food is better than another.
24 As the palate tastes the kinds of game,
    so an intelligent mind detects false
        words.
25 A perverse mind will cause grief,
    but a person with experience will pay
        him back.
26 A woman will accept any man as a
    husband,
    but one girl is preferable to another.
27 A woman's beauty lights up a man's
        face,
    and there is nothing he desires more.
28 If kindness and humility mark her
        speech,
    her husband is more fortunate than
        other men.
29 He who acquires a wife gets his best
        possession,[a]
    a helper fit for him and a pillar of
        support.[b]
30 Where there is no fence, the property
        will be plundered;
    and where there is no wife, a man
        will become a fugitive and a
        wanderer.[c]
31 For who will trust a nimble robber
        that skips from city to city?
    So who will trust a man that has no
        nest,
    but lodges wherever night overtakes
        him?

36.23–37.31: Making choices. 36.23–31: Ben Sira urges his students to be discriminating when making important life decisions, particularly in choosing a wife. **29:** *A helper fit for him* is an allusion to the description of Eve in Gen 2.18, 20, 23. **30:** *A fugitive and a wanderer* is an allusion to Cain in Gen 4.12, 14.

37 Every friend says, "I too am a
        friend";
    but some friends are friends only in
        name.
2 Is it not a sorrow like that for death
        itself
    when a dear friend turns into an
        enemy?
3 O inclination to evil, why were you
        formed
    to cover the land with deceit?
4 Some companions rejoice in the
        happiness of a friend,
    but in time of trouble they are against
        him.
5 Some companions help a friend for
        their stomachs' sake,
    yet in battle they will carry his
        shield.
6 Do not forget a friend during the battle,[d]
    and do not be unmindful of him
        when you distribute your spoils.[e]

7 All counselors praise the counsel they
        give,
    but some give counsel in their own
        interest.
8 Be wary of a counselor,
    and learn first what is his interest,
    for he will take thought for himself.
    He may cast the lot against you
9   and tell you, "Your way is good,"
    and then stand aside to see what
        happens to you.
10 Do not consult the one who regards you
        with suspicion;
    hide your intentions from those who
        are jealous of you.
11 Do not consult with a woman about her
        rival

a Heb: Gk *enters upon a possession*   b Heb: Gk *rest*
c Heb: Gk *wander about and sigh*   d Heb: Gk *in your heart*   e Heb: Gk *him in your wealth*

or with a coward about war,
with a merchant about business
or with a buyer about selling,
with a miser about generosity*
or with the merciless about kindness,
with an idler about any work
or with a seasonal laborer about
completing his work,
with a lazy servant about a big task—
pay no attention to any advice they
give.

12 But associate with a godly person
whom you know to be a keeper of the
commandments,
who is like-minded with yourself,
and who will grieve with you if you
fail.

13 And heed[b] the counsel of your own
heart,
for no one is more faithful to you
than it is.

14 For our own mind sometimes keeps us
better informed
than seven sentinels sitting high on a
watchtower.

15 But above all pray to the Most High
that he may direct your way in truth.

16 Discussion is the beginning of every
work,
and counsel precedes every
undertaking.

17 The mind is the root of all conduct;

18 it sprouts four branches,[c]
good and evil, life and death;
and it is the tongue that continually
rules them.

19 Some people may be clever enough to
teach many,
and yet be useless to themselves.

20 A skillful speaker may be hated;
he will be destitute of all food,

21 for the Lord has withheld the gift of
charm,
since he is lacking in all wisdom.

22 If a person is wise to his own
advantage,
the fruits of his good sense will be
praiseworthy.[d]

23 A wise person instructs his own
people,

and the fruits of his good sense will
endure.

24 A wise person will have praise heaped
upon him,
and all who see him will call him
happy.

25 The days of a person's life are
numbered,
but the days of Israel are without
number.

26 One who is wise among his people will
inherit honor,[e]
and his name will live forever.

27 My child, test yourself while you live;
see what is bad for you and do not
give in to it.

28 For not everything is good for everyone,
and no one enjoys everything.

29 Do not be greedy for every delicacy,
and do not eat without restraint;

30 for overeating brings sickness,
and gluttony leads to nausea.

31 Many have died of gluttony,
but the one who guards against it
prolongs his life.

37.1–31. 7–15: While Ben Sira elsewhere holds up the counsel of a friend as essential to one's ethical development (32.18; 37.16), here he points out that those who offer counsel often have their own interest in mind. Specific examples appear in v. 11. **25–26:** These statements sum up Ben Sira's version of immortality: Individuals die, but the community continues; righteous individuals also expire, but their reputations live on. **27–31:** This short section constitutes another expression of Ben Sira's ethic of moderation (see 31.19–31).

38 Honor physicians for their services,
for the Lord created them;

2 for their gift of healing comes from the
Most High,
and they are rewarded by the king.

3 The skill of physicians makes them
distinguished,

a Heb: Gk gratitude   b Heb: Gk establish   c Heb:
Gk As a clue to changes of heart four kinds of destiny
appear   d Other ancient witnesses read trustworthy
e Other ancient authorities read confidence

and in the presence of the great they
are admired.

4 The Lord created medicines out of the
earth,
and the sensible will not despise them.

5 Was not water made sweet with a tree
in order that its*e* power might be
known?

6 And he gave skill to human beings
that he*b* might be glorified in his
marvelous works.

7 By them the physician*c* heals and takes
away pain;

8 the pharmacist makes a mixture from
them.
God's*d* works will never be finished;
and from him health*e* spreads over all
the earth.

9 My child, when you are ill, do not delay,
but pray to the Lord, and he will heal
you.

10 Give up your faults and direct your
hands rightly,
and cleanse your heart from all sin.

11 Offer a sweet-smelling sacrifice, and a
memorial portion of choice flour,
and pour oil on your offering, as
much as you can afford.*f*

12 Then give the physician his place, for
the Lord created him;
do not let him leave you, for you need
him.

13 There may come a time when recovery
lies in the hands of physicians,*g*

14 for they too pray to the Lord
that he grant them success in diagnosis*h*
and in healing, for the sake of
preserving life.

15 He who sins against his Maker,
will be defiant toward the physician.*i*

16 My child, let your tears fall for the dead,
and as one in great pain begin the
lament.
Lay out the body with due ceremony,
and do not neglect the burial.

17 Let your weeping be bitter and your
wailing fervent;
make your mourning worthy of the
departed,
for one day, or two, to avoid criticism;
then be comforted for your grief.

18 For grief may result in death,
and a sorrowful heart saps one's
strength.

19 When a person is taken away, sorrow is
over;
but the life of the poor weighs down
the heart.

20 Do not give your heart to grief;
drive it away, and remember your
own end.

21 Do not forget, there is no coming back;
you do the dead*j* no good, and you
injure yourself.

22 Remember his*k* fate, for yours is like it;
yesterday it was his,*l* and today it is
yours.

23 When the dead is at rest, let his
remembrance rest too,
and be comforted for him when his
spirit has departed.

38.1–15: Work of the physician. The rhetoric* of the passage indicates that at least some members of Ben Sira's audience would not have accepted the services of a doctor. Resistance to the intervention of a *physician* derives from the idea that medical treatment undermines the will of God. Ben Sira argues that doctors and healing herbs are part of God's creation. Furthermore, doctors do not supplant prayer and sacrifice in the healing process (vv. 9–13). **5:** *Water made sweet* refers to the miraculous transformation of the waters at Marah in Ex 15.22–25.

38.16–23: Death and mourning. The author recognizes that mourning is a means of exorcising grief as a well as a religious duty. He counsels against indulging grief too long, since inconsolable depression can cause harm. **17:** *One day, or two* seems a short time for mourning compared to the traditional seven days (Gen 50.10; Jdt 16.24; Sir 22.12). **21–23:** Since there is no hope of life after death, prolonged lament* does no good.

---

a Or *his*   *b* Or *they*   *c* Heb: Gk *he*   *d* Gk *His*
e Or *peace*   *f* Heb: Lat lacks *as much as you can afford;* Meaning of Gk uncertain   *g* Gk *in their hands*
h Heb: Gk *rest*   *i* Heb: Gk *may he fall into the hands of the physician*   *j* Gk *him*   *k* Heb: Gk *my*
l Heb: Gk *mine*

24 The wisdom of the scribe depends on
     the opportunity of leisure;
   only the one who has little business
     can become wise.
25 How can one become wise who handles
     the plow,
   and who glories in the shaft of a goad,
   who drives oxen and is occupied with
     their work,
   and whose talk is about bulls?
26 He sets his heart on plowing furrows,
   and he is careful about fodder for the
     heifers.
27 So it is with every artisan and master
     artisan
   who labors by night as well as by day;
   those who cut the signets of seals,
     each is diligent in making a great
     variety;
   they set their heart on painting a lifelike
     image,
   and they are careful to finish their
     work.
28 So it is with the smith, sitting by the
     anvil,
   intent on his iron-work;
   the breath of the fire melts his flesh,
   and he struggles with the heat of the
     furnace;
   the sound of the hammer deafens his
     ears,[a]
   and his eyes are on the pattern of the
     object.
   He sets his heart on finishing his
     handiwork,
   and he is careful to complete its
     decoration.
29 So it is with the potter sitting at his
     work
   and turning the wheel with his feet;
   he is always deeply concerned over his
     products,
   and he produces them in quantity.
30 He molds the clay with his arm
   and makes it pliable with his feet;
   he sets his heart to finish the glazing,
   and he takes care in firing[b] the kiln.

31 All these rely on their hands,
   and all are skillful in their own work.
32 Without them no city can be inhabited,

   and wherever they live, they will not
     go hungry.[c]
   Yet they are not sought out for the
     council of the people,[d]
33 nor do they attain eminence in the
     public assembly.
   They do not sit in the judge's seat,
   nor do they understand the decisions
     of the courts;
   they cannot expound discipline or
     judgment,
   and they are not found among the
     rulers.[e]
34 But they maintain the fabric of the
     world,
   and their concern is for[f] the exercise
     of their trade.

38.24–34a: Work of the laborer. The primary purpose of this poem praising those who work with their
hands is to set up a contrast between the *laborer* and
the *scribe,*★ who is praised in the following poem. **31–
34:** Ben Sira recognizes that artisans are essential to
society, but the honor accorded them is rightly limited. While they may be adept at their trade, they are
not purveyors of wisdom.

~~~~~~~~~~~~~~~~~~~

   How different the one who devotes
     himself
   to the study of the law of the Most
     High!
39 He seeks out the wisdom of all the
     ancients,
   and is concerned with prophecies;
2 he preserves the sayings of the famous
   and penetrates the subtleties of
     parables;
3 he seeks out the hidden meanings of
     proverbs
   and is at home with the obscurities of
     parables.
4 He serves among the great
   and appears before rulers;
   he travels in foreign lands
   and learns what is good and evil in
     the human lot.

a Cn: Gk *renews his ear*   b Cn: Gk *cleaning*   c Syr:
Gk *and people can neither live nor walk there*   d Most
ancient authorities lack this line   e Cn: Gk *among
parables*   f Syr: Gk *prayer is in*

5 He sets his heart to rise early
    to seek the Lord who made him,
    and to petition the Most High;
he opens his mouth in prayer
    and asks pardon for his sins.

6 If the great Lord is willing,
    he will be filled with the spirit of
        understanding;
he will pour forth words of wisdom of
        his own
    and give thanks to the Lord in prayer.
7 The Lord[a] will direct his counsel and
        knowledge,
    as he meditates on his mysteries.
8 He will show the wisdom of what he has
        learned,
    and will glory in the law of the Lord's
        covenant.
9 Many will praise his understanding;
    it will never be blotted out.
His memory will not disappear,
    and his name will live through all
        generations.
10 Nations will speak of his wisdom,
    and the congregation will proclaim
        his praise.
11 If he lives long, he will leave a name
        greater than a thousand,
    and if he goes to rest, it is enough[b]
        for him.

38.34b–39.11: The scribe.* In contrast to laborers,
the scribe is a student of Torah* and a seeker of wisdom. Ben Sira is a scribe, and it is likely that the wisdom school in which he taught was primarily a training
ground for scribes. 39.9–11: The glory of the scribe is
unsurpassed by any other profession. Becoming a
scribe is the surest way to create a lasting legacy for
oneself.

---

12 I have more on my mind to express;
    I am full like the full moon.
13 Listen to me, my faithful children, and
        blossom
    like a rose growing by a stream of
        water.
14 Send out fragrance like incense,
    and put forth blossoms like a lily.
Scatter the fragrance, and sing a hymn
        of praise;

bless the Lord for all his works.
15 Ascribe majesty to his name
    and give thanks to him with praise,
with songs on your lips, and with harps;
    this is what you shall say in
        thanksgiving:

16 "All the works of the Lord are very
        good,
    and whatever he commands will be
        done at the appointed time.
17 No one can say, 'What is this?' or 'Why
        is that?'—
    for at the appointed time all such
        questions will be answered.
At his word the waters stood in a heap,
    and the reservoirs of water at the
        word of his mouth.
18 When he commands, his every purpose
        is fulfilled,
    and none can limit his saving power.
19 The works of all are before him,
    and nothing can be hidden from his
        eyes.
20 From the beginning to the end of time
    he can see everything,
    and nothing is too marvelous for him.
21 No one can say, 'What is this?' or 'Why
        is that?'—
    for everything has been created for its
        own purpose.

22 "His blessing covers the dry land like a
        river,
    and drenches it like a flood.
23 But his wrath drives out the nations,
    as when he turned a watered land
        into salt.
24 To the faithful his ways are straight,
    but full of pitfalls for the wicked.
25 From the beginning good things were
        created for the good,
    but for sinners good things and bad.[c]
26 The basic necessities of human life
    are water and fire and iron and salt
and wheat flour and milk and honey,
    the blood of the grape and oil and
        clothing.

a Gk He himself   b Cn: Meaning of Gk uncertain
c Heb Lat: Gk sinners bad things

27 All these are good for the godly,
  but for sinners they turn into evils.

28 "There are winds created for vengeance,
  and in their anger they can dislodge
    mountains;*
  on the day of reckoning they will pour
    out their strength
  and calm the anger of their Maker.

29 Fire and hail and famine and pestilence,
  all these have been created for
    vengeance;
30 the fangs of wild animals and scorpions
    and vipers,
  and the sword that punishes the
    ungodly with destruction.

31 They take delight in doing his bidding,
  always ready for his service on
    earth;
  and when their time comes they
    never disobey his command."

32 So from the beginning I have been
    convinced of all this
  and have thought it out and left it in
    writing:
33 All the works of the Lord are good,
  and he will supply every need in its
    time.
34 No one can say, "This is not as good as
    that,"
  for everything proves good in its
    appointed time.
35 So now sing praise with all your heart
    and voice,
  and bless the name of the Lord.

39.12–35: Praise to God and creation. 12–15: The
vivid imagery conveys the effusive inclination of the
writer, who is bursting with *praise.* **16:** *All the works
of the Lord are very good* represents an allusion to
Gen 1, where God sees each component of creation
as good. Ben Sira admonishes anyone who attempts
to identify negative parts of God's creation (vv. 33–
34). **17–21:** Ben Sira's attitude here is reminiscent of
God's answer to Job (Job 38.1–42.6). Since nothing in
creation falls outside God's domain, questioning the
purpose of any element is a challenge to God's authority. **26:** Even the most *basic* elements in *human
life* can become a curse, as when God drowned the
earth with water in the time of Noah or when God

rained sulfur and fire upon Sodom and Gomorrah. **28–
30:** The items listed here evoke the ten plagues in Exodus. Even hated creatures and natural disasters serve
an important purpose.

40 Hard work was created for
  everyone,
  and a heavy yoke is laid on the
    children of Adam,
  from the day they come forth from their
    mother's womb
  until the day they return to*b* the
    mother of all the living.*c*
2 Perplexities and fear of heart are theirs,
  and anxious thought of the day of
    their death.
3 From the one who sits on a splendid
    throne
  to the one who grovels in dust and
    ashes,
4 from the one who wears purple and a
    crown
  to the one who is clothed in burlap,
5 there is anger and envy and trouble and
    unrest,
  and fear of death, and fury and strife.
  And when one rests upon his bed,
  his sleep at night confuses his mind.
6 He gets little or no rest;
  he struggles in his sleep as he did by
    day.*d*
  He is troubled by the visions of his
    mind
  like one who has escaped from the
    battlefield.
7 At the moment he reaches safety he
    wakes up,
  astonished that his fears were
    groundless.
8 To all creatures, human and animal,
  but to sinners seven times more,
9 come death and bloodshed and strife
    and sword,
  calamities and famine and ruin and
    plague.
10 All these were created for the wicked,
  and on their account the flood came.

a Heb Syr: Gk *can scourge mightily*   *b* Other Gk and
Lat authorities read *are buried in*   *c* Heb: Gk *of all*
d Arm: Meaning of Gk uncertain

11 All that is of earth returns to earth,
and what is from above returns above. *a*

12 All bribery and injustice will be blotted
out,
but good faith will last forever.

13 The wealth of the unjust will dry up like
a river,
and crash like a loud clap of thunder
in a storm.

14 As a generous person has cause to
rejoice,
so lawbreakers will utterly fail.

15 The children of the ungodly put out few
branches;
they are unhealthy roots on sheer
rock.

16 The reeds by any water or river bank
are plucked up before any grass;

17 but kindness is like a garden of blessings,
and almsgiving endures forever.

40.1–17: Human misery. The comments here apply to the human condition in general. Certain difficulties cannot be averted regardless of one's station in life (vv. 3–4). **1:** That all humans are destined to live a life filled with hard labor derives from Gen 3.17–19. **2–7:** Ben Sira's comments about human *anxiety* and *fear of death* offer a rare look into psychological perceptions in antiquity. He implies that anxiety could be avoided if human beings simply accepted the world as it is and the inevitability of death. **8–11:** Ben Sira addresses the problem of theodicy.* He admits that all people experience strife, but remains confident that it afflicts the ungodly *seven times more.* **12–17:** The scribe* reiterates his faith that justice prevails.

---

18 Wealth and wages make life sweet, *b*
but better than either is finding a
treasure.

19 Children and the building of a city
establish one's name,
but better than either is the one who
finds wisdom.
Cattle and orchards make one
prosperous; *c*
but a blameless wife is accounted
better than either.

20 Wine and music gladden the heart,
but the love of friends *d* is better than
either.

21 The flute and the harp make sweet
melody,
but a pleasant voice is better than
either.

22 The eye desires grace and beauty,
but the green shoots of grain more
than either.

23 A friend or companion is always
welcome,
but a sensible wife *e* is better than
either.

24 Kindred and helpers are for a time of
trouble,
but almsgiving rescues better than
either.

25 Gold and silver make one stand firm,
but good counsel is esteemed more
than either.

26 Riches and strength build up confidence,
but the fear of the Lord is better than
either.
There is no want in the fear of the Lord,
and with it there is no need to seek
for help.

27 The fear of the Lord is like a garden of
blessing,
and covers a person better than any
glory.

28 My child, do not lead the life of a
beggar;
it is better to die than to beg.

29 When one looks to the table of another,
one's way of life cannot be considered
a life.
One loses self-respect with another
person's food,
but one who is intelligent and well
instructed guards against that.

30 In the mouth of the shameless begging
is sweet,
but it kindles a fire inside him.

40.18–30: The joys and limitations of assets. 18–27: Ben Sira assesses the relative merits of numerous goods. The pursuit of wisdom supersedes even the es-

a Heb Syr: Gk Lat *from the waters returns to the sea*
b Heb: Gk *Life is sweet for the self-reliant worker*
c Heb Syr: Gk lacks *but better . . . prosperous*   *d* Heb:
Gk *wisdom*   *e* Heb Compare Syr: Gk *wife with her
husband*

tablishment of a good name. **28–30:** While possessions ultimately do not rank with the pursuit of wisdom
and the fear of the Lord, the total lack of possessions
is a disgrace. Some sort of estate, however humble, is
a necessity (compare 36.29–31).

41

1 O death, how bitter is the thought
of you
to the one at peace among
possessions,
who has nothing to worry about and is
prosperous in everything,
and still is vigorous enough to enjoy
food!
2 O death, how welcome is your sentence
to one who is needy and failing in
strength,
worn down by age and anxious about
everything;
to one who is contrary, and has lost
all patience!
3 Do not fear death's decree for you;
remember those who went before you
and those who will come after.
4 This is the Lord's decree for all flesh;
why then should you reject the will of
the Most High?
Whether life lasts for ten years or a
hundred or a thousand,
there are no questions asked in
Hades.

5 The children of sinners are abominable
children,
and they frequent the haunts of the
ungodly.
6 The inheritance of the children of
sinners will perish,
and on their offspring will be a
perpetual disgrace.
7 Children will blame an ungodly father,
for they suffer disgrace because of
him.
8 Woe to you, the ungodly,
who have forsaken the law of the
Most High God!
9 If you have children, calamity will be
theirs;
you will beget them only for groaning.
When you stumble, there is lasting joy;[a]
and when you die, a curse is your lot.

10 Whatever comes from earth returns to
earth;
so the ungodly go from curse to
destruction.

11 The human body is a fleeting thing,
but a virtuous name will never be
blotted out.[b]
12 Have regard for your name, since it will
outlive you
longer than a thousand hoards of
gold.
13 The days of a good life are numbered,
but a good name lasts forever.

14 My children, be true to your training
and be at peace;
hidden wisdom and unseen treasure—
of what value is either?
15 Better are those who hide their folly
than those who hide their wisdom.
16 Therefore show respect for my words;
for it is not good to feel shame in every
circumstance,
nor is every kind of abashment to be
approved.[c]

41.1–14: Death. Ben Sira's teachings here largely reiterate his instruction in the preceding chapter (see
40.1–11). **4:** The Lord's *decree for all flesh* alludes to
Gen 3.19. **5–10:** The notion that the sin of one generation not only brings calamity upon itself but also
upon succeeding generations was commonplace in
Jewish tradition. A critique of such lingering blame is
found in Jer 31.29–30. In Ben Sira's terms, it is not just
punishment that extends over generations, but dishonor. Children born to dishonored parents come into
the world with a tainted reputation. **11–14:** Once
again Ben Sira stresses the importance of *a good name*
(see 37.26; 39.9–11); it is Ben Sira's version of
immortality.

---

17 Be ashamed of sexual immorality,
before your father or mother;
and of a lie, before a prince or a
ruler;

a Heb: Meaning of Gk uncertain   *b* Heb: Gk *People
grieve over the death of the body, but the bad name of
sinners will be blotted out   c* Heb: Gk *and not
everything is confidently esteemed by everyone*

18 of a crime, before a judge or magistrate;
  and of a breach of the law, before the
    congregation and the people;
  of unjust dealing, before your partner or
    your friend;
19   and of theft, in the place where you
    live.
  Be ashamed of breaking an oath or
    agreement,ª
  and of leaning on your elbow at meals;
  of surliness in receiving or giving,
20   and of silence, before those who greet
    you;
  of looking at a prostitute,
21   and of rejecting the appeal of a
    relative;
  of taking away someone's portion or gift,
    and of gazing at another man's wife;
22 of meddling with his servant-girl—
    and do not approach her bed;
  of abusive words, before friends—
  and do not be insulting after making
    a gift.

42 Be ashamed of repeating what you
    hear,
  and of betraying secrets.
  Then you will show proper shame,
    and will find favor with everyone.

Of the following things do not be
    ashamed,
  and do not sin to save face:
2 Do not be ashamed of the law of the
    Most High and his covenant,
  and of rendering judgment to acquit
    the ungodly;
3 of keeping accounts with a partner or
    with traveling companions,
  and of dividing the inheritance of
    friends;
4 of accuracy with scales and weights,
    and of acquiring much or little;
5 of profit from dealing with merchants,
  and of frequent disciplining of
    children,
  and of drawing blood from the back
    of a wicked slave.
6 Where there is an untrustworthy wife, a
    seal is a good thing;
  and where there are many hands, lock
    things up.

7 When you make a deposit, be sure it is
    counted and weighed,
  and when you give or receive, put it
    all in writing.
8 Do not be ashamed to correct the stupid
    or foolish
  or the aged who are guilty of sexual
    immorality.
  Then you will show your sound training,
    and will be approved by all.

41.15–42.8: Shame. This section offers a summary of things of which one should and should not be ashamed. **41.17–42.1a:** When Ben Sira says *be ashamed of . . . ,* it means that shame prevents improper behavior. Of course, if a person enacts such behavior, then unwanted shame (dishonor) accrues to that person. **42.1b:** Ben Sira's list of items that should not inspire shame may well include activities that might, in fact, have caused people to feel shame. **6:** *Where there is an untrustworthy wife, a seal is a good thing* means that a man should keep his money and valuables locked up and inaccessible to his wife if he has any suspicions about her. **7:** All business exchanges should be precisely recorded *in writing,* the implication being that a man is not required to depend upon personal trust.

9 A daughter is a secret anxiety to her
    father,
  and worry over her robs him of sleep;
  when she is young, for fear she may not
    marry,
  or if married, for fear she may be
    disliked;
10 while a virgin, for fear she may be
    seduced
  and become pregnant in her father's
    house;
  or having a husband, for fear she may
    go astray,
  or, though married, for fear she may
    be barren.
11 Keep strict watch over a headstrong
    daughter,
  or she may make you a laughingstock
    to your enemies,
  a byword in the city and the assembly of*b*
    the people,

ª Heb: Gk *before the truth of God and the covenant*
b Heb: Meaning of Gk uncertain

and put you to shame in public
　　gatherings.[a]
See that there is no lattice in her room,
　　no spot that overlooks the approaches
　　　to the house.[b]
12 Do not let her parade her beauty before
　　any man,
　　or spend her time among married
　　　women;[c]
13 for from garments comes the moth,
　　and from a woman comes woman's
　　　wickedness.
14 Better is the wickedness of a man than
　　a woman who does good;
　　it is woman who brings shame and
　　　disgrace.

42.9–14: The dangers of daughters. Ben Sira mentioned his negative assessment of *daughters* earlier (22.3–6), but he makes a lengthy statement here. (Its placement in the text is somewhat peculiar.) At no stage of life does she contribute to her father's welfare. Since she will become part of her husband's family when she marries, she will not carry on the legacy of her father's family. A young girl is therefore viewed as a liability until she marries. A father must protect the virginity of his daughter, because otherwise her marriageability may be adversely affected. Even after marriage she remains a concern to her father. Since the possibility of divorce exists, a girl who does not please her husband can be returned to her father's house. **14:** The severity of this statement is unparalleled in biblical literature.

GOD'S WORKS IN CREATION

42.15–43.33: This section constitutes another poem in praise of the creator and his creation (see 39.12–35), only it focuses on the celestial bodies and cosmic forces. Praise given to God may also be a necessary prelude to the praise of Jewish heroes lauded in chs. 44–50.

---

15 I will now call to mind the works of the
　　Lord,
　　and will declare what I have seen.
　By the word of the Lord his works are
　　made;
　　and all his creatures do his will.[d]
16 The sun looks down on everything with
　　its light,

and the work of the Lord is full of his
　　glory.
17 The Lord has not empowered even his
　　holy ones
　　to recount all his marvelous works,
　which the Lord the Almighty has
　　established
　　so that the universe may stand firm in
　　　his glory.
18 He searches out the abyss and the
　　human heart;
　　he understands their innermost
　　　secrets.
　For the Most High knows all that may
　　be known;
　　he sees from of old the things that are
　　　to come.[e]
19 He discloses what has been and what is
　　to be,
　　and he reveals the traces of hidden
　　　things.
20 No thought escapes him,
　　and nothing is hidden from him.
21 He has set in order the splendors of his
　　wisdom;
　　he is from all eternity one and the
　　　same.
　Nothing can be added or taken away,
　　and he needs no one to be his
　　　counselor.
22 How desirable are all his works,
　　and how sparkling they are to see![f]
23 All these things live and remain forever;
　　each creature is preserved to meet a
　　　particular need.[g]
24 All things come in pairs, one opposite
　　the other,
　　and he has made nothing incomplete.
25 Each supplements the virtues of the
　　other.
　　Who could ever tire of seeing his
　　　glory?

42.15–25. 16–17: In other religious traditions around the Mediterranean, the *sun* was a god. The author's

---

a Heb: Gk to shame before the great multitude　　b Heb: Gk lacks See . . . house　　c Heb: Meaning of Gk uncertain　　d Syr Compare Heb: most Gk witnesses lack and all . . . will　　e Heb: Gk he sees the sign(s) of the age　　f Meaning of Gk uncertain　　g Heb: Gk forever for every need, and all are obedient comment that *the sun looks down on everything with its light* partly reflects the author's understanding of the sun (and other celestial bodies) as a semi-divine entity (see also 43.1–5). The reference to *holy ones*, which also means angels, includes heavenly bodies like the sun (see 43.8b). However, when Ben Sira says that *the Lord has not empowered even his holy ones,* he makes clear the subordinate status of such semi-divine beings (see Ps 89.5–7). The sun follows God's orders (43.5). **24:** For the notion that the created order is structured *in pairs,* see the comment on 33.15.

43 The pride of the higher realms is
the clear vault of the sky,
as glorious to behold as the sight of
the heavens.

2 The sun, when it appears, proclaims as
it rises
what a marvelous instrument it is, the
work of the Most High.

3 At noon it parches the land,
and who can withstand its burning
heat?

4 A man tending*a* a furnace works in
burning heat,
but three times as hot is the sun
scorching the mountains;
it breathes out fiery vapors,
and its bright rays blind the eyes.

5 Great is the Lord who made it;
at his orders it hurries on its course.

6 It is the moon that marks the changing
seasons,*b*
governing the times, their everlasting
sign.

7 From the moon comes the sign for
festal days,
a light that wanes when it completes
its course.

8 The new moon, as its name suggests,
renews itself;*c*
how marvelous it is in this change,
a beacon to the hosts on high,
shining in the vault of the heavens!

9 The glory of the stars is the beauty of
heaven,
a glittering array in the heights of the
Lord.

10 On the orders of the Holy One they
stand in their appointed places;
they never relax in their watches.

11 Look at the rainbow, and praise him
who made it;
it is exceedingly beautiful in its
brightness.

12 It encircles the sky with its glorious arc;
the hands of the Most High have
stretched it out.

13 By his command he sends the driving
snow
and speeds the lightnings of his
judgment.

14 Therefore the storehouses are opened,
and the clouds fly out like birds.

15 In his majesty he gives the clouds their
strength,
and the hailstones are broken in
pieces.

17a The voice of his thunder rebukes the
earth;

16 when he appears, the mountains
shake.
At his will the south wind blows;

17b so do the storm from the north and
the whirlwind.
He scatters the snow like birds flying
down,
and its descent is like locusts
alighting.

18 The eye is dazzled by the beauty of its
whiteness,
and the mind is amazed as it falls.

19 He pours frost over the earth like salt,
and icicles form like pointed thorns.

20 The cold north wind blows,
and ice freezes on the water;
it settles on every pool of water,
and the water puts it on like a
breastplate.

21 He consumes the mountains and burns
up the wilderness,
and withers the tender grass like fire.

22 A mist quickly heals all things;
the falling dew gives refreshment
from the heat.

a Other ancient authorities read *blowing upon*
b Heb: Meaning of Gk uncertain   *c* Heb: Gk *The month is named after the moon*

23 By his plan he stilled the deep
    and planted islands in it.
24 Those who sail the sea tell of its
    dangers,
    and we marvel at what we hear.
25 In it are strange and marvelous
    creatures,
    all kinds of living things, and huge
    sea-monsters.
26 Because of him each of his messengers
    succeeds,
    and by his word all things hold
    together.

43.1–26. 6–8: Ben Sira reflects on *the moon* as the primary agent of the calendar,★ which determines holy days. The use of a lunar calendar was subject to critique by other ancient Jewish writers, namely, the producers of the Dead Sea Scrolls and the author of the noncanonical work *Jubilees*. 14: *Storehouses* are where God keeps large-scale forces and elements of nature like wind, thunder, and snow (see vv. 14b–22). 23: That God *stilled the deep* alludes to mythic traditions about chaotic forces that God curtailed in the act of creation (Job 26.12). 25: Ancient Near Eastern myth told stories of *sea-monsters,* such as Leviathan★ and Rahab, who had to be defeated so as to establish order (Ps 89.10; 104.25–26). 26: The word here translated *messenger* could also be translated angel (from either the Greek or the Hebrew). Just as the celestial bodies were earlier called "holy ones" (42.17), all the forces present in creation are agents of God and therefore are his messengers. The ultimate coherence of creation is reflected in such statements as *by his word all things hold together,* or in v. 27, *He is the all.* Ben Sira may have been influenced by Stoic★ philosophy, which held that the entire universe is held together by one rational principle (designated the "logos," literally *word* in Greek, used in v. 26).

27 We could say more but could never say
    enough;
    let the final word be: "He is the all."
28 Where can we find the strength to
    praise him?
    For he is greater than all his works.
29 Awesome is the Lord and very great,
    and marvelous is his power.
30 Glorify the Lord and exalt him as much
    as you can,
    for he surpasses even that.

When you exalt him, summon all your
    strength,
    and do not grow weary, for you
    cannot praise him enough.
31 Who has seen him and can describe
    him?
    Or who can extol him as he is?
32 Many things greater than these lie
    hidden,
    for I[a] have seen but few of his works.
33 For the Lord has made all things,
    and to the godly he has given wisdom.

PRAISE OF THE HEROES

44.1–51.24: The final chapters of Sirach form a distinct unit in which Ben Sira sings the praises of Israel's heroes. It is the most well-known passage in Sirach and represents a kind of finale. With the exception of the last hero, Simon son of Onias, all the heroes are known from biblical literature. Thus this long poem of praise partly functions as a retelling of biblical history. Its primary function is to recall the legacy of these renowned men (no women are included on the list), because they illustrate what it means to be truly honored. They are the paradigmatic examples of Ben Sira's claim that "a good name lasts forever" (41.13).

HYMN IN HONOR OF OUR ANCESTORS [b]

44 Let us now sing the praises of
    famous men,
    our ancestors in their generations.
2 The Lord apportioned to them[c] great
    glory,
    his majesty from the beginning.
3 There were those who ruled in their
    kingdoms,
    and made a name for themselves by
    their valor;
    those who gave counsel because they
    were intelligent;
    those who spoke in prophetic oracles;
4 those who led the people by their
    counsels
    and by their knowledge of the
    people's lore;
    they were wise in their words of
    instruction;

a Heb: Gk *we*   *b* This title is included in the Gk text.
c Heb: Gk *created*

Hero Lists

Embedded in many Jewish texts from the Hellenistic period are lists of biblical heroes. Sirach 44–50 is the most comprehensive of such hero catalogues. These catalogues serve as compilations of exemplary figures meant to inspire others or persuade them to emulate the heroes' behavior. In many cases, the hero catalogue also constitutes a recounting of biblical history, as Sirach 44–50 certainly does. Because the catalogues differ from one another, the authors of the respective texts obviously made choices about whom to include or omit. The inclusions and omissions often reveal the author's particular perspective on biblical history and the relative contributions of different biblical figures. For example, the main body of the list in

Sir 44–50	1 Macc 2.51–60	Wis 10	4 Macc 16.16–23	4 Macc 18.11–19
		Adam (Cain)		Abel (Cain)
Noah		Noah		
Abraham	Abraham	Abraham	Abraham	
Isaac		Isaac	Isaac	Isaac
		Lot		
Jacob		Jacob		
	Joseph	Joseph		Joseph
Moses		Moses		
Aaron				
Phinehas	Phinehas			Phinehas
Joshua	Joshua			
Caleb	Caleb			
the judges				
Samuel				
(Saul)				
Nathan				
David	David			
Solomon				
(Rehoboam)				
(Jeroboam)				
Elijah	Elijah			
Elisha				
Hezekiah				
Isaiah				
Josiah				
kings				
Jeremiah				
Ezekiel				
Job				
Prophets	Hananiah		Daniel	Hananiah
Zerubbabel	Azariah		Hananiah	Azariah
Jeshua	Mishael		Azariah	Mishael
Nehemiah	Daniel		Mishael	Daniel
				Isaiah
				David
				Solomon
				Ezekiel
				Moses

Sirach does not include Joseph (see, however, Sir 49.15 and the note there). This exclusion is most likely due to Ben Sira's interest in heroes who held national office in Israel. Because Joseph's only claim to political office was in Egypt, the author omits him. The chart below places a sampling of hero catalogues in parallel columns in order to make their similarities and differences more transparent. A few heroes appear in parentheses because they are listed only in passing, usually in conjunction with the hero named above them. It includes a listing from the Covenant of Damascus (CD), a Dead Sea Scroll text.

CD 2–3	2 Esdras (4 Ezra) 7.105–111	Acts 7	Heb 11
mighty heroes			
Watchers			Abel
sons of Watchers			Enoch
sons of Noah			Noah
Abraham	Abraham	Abraham	Abraham
			Sarah
Isaac		Isaac	Isaac
Jacob		Jacob	Jacob
		12 patriarchs	(Esau)
sons of Jacob		Joseph	Joseph
sons in Egypt	Moses	Moses	Moses
		(Aaron)	the people
			Rahab
	Joshua	Joshua	
			Gideon
	Samuel		Barak
			Samson
			Jephthah
kings	David	David	David
	Solomon	Solomon	Samuel
	Elijah		
	Hezekiah		
		prophets	prophets
			women
mighty heroes	many others		others

5 those who composed musical tunes,
 or put verses in writing;
6 rich men endowed with resources,
 living peacefully in their homes—
7 all these were honored in their
 generations,
 and were the pride of their times.
8 Some of them have left behind a name,
 so that others declare their praise.
9 But of others there is no memory;
 they have perished as though they
 had never existed;
 they have become as though they had
 never been born,
 they and their children after them.
10 But these also were godly men,
 whose righteous deeds have not been
 forgotten;
11 their wealth will remain with their
 descendants,
 and their inheritance with their
 children's children.*a*
12 Their descendants stand by the
 covenants;
 their children also, for their sake.
13 Their offspring will continue forever,
 and their glory will never be blotted
 out.
14 Their bodies are buried in peace,
 but their name lives on generation
 after generation.
15 The assembly declares*b* their wisdom,
 and the congregation proclaims their
 praise.

44.1–15: The writer first speaks generically of men of the past as an introduction to the hymn. The men whom Ben Sira finds worthy of praise are typically Israel's leaders, those who hold religious and political office. Although Ben Sira does not mention it explicitly in the introduction, the offices held by the heroes are sanctioned by special *covenants.** **7:** The men praised enjoyed honor and renown in their own time. **9–15:** Ben Sira's mention of those not remembered is striking. Given the comment in v. 10, *these also were godly men,* he does not refer to wicked, undeserving people, but rather the ordinary members of the Israelite community. Although no one publicly sings their praises, their legacy does continue in *their descendants,* who presumably preserve the family name (v. 14).

16 Enoch pleased the Lord and was taken
 up,
 an example of repentance to all
 generations.
17 Noah was found perfect and righteous;
 in the time of wrath he kept the race
 alive;*c*
 therefore a remnant was left on the
 earth
 when the flood came.
18 Everlasting covenants were made with
 him
 that all flesh should never again be
 blotted out by a flood.

44.16–18. 16: This verse only appears in later manuscripts, indicating that it was not part of the original text of Sirach. *Enoch,** a minor character in primeval biblical history (Gen 5.24), became a figure of intense theological speculation in the centuries after Sirach. Enoch is mentioned again in Sir 49.14. **17–18:** The story of *Noah* and *the flood* is found in Gen 6–9. Noah is the first to receive a *covenant** from God, symbolized by the rainbow (Gen 9.8–17).

19 Abraham was the great father of a
 multitude of nations,
 and no one has been found like him
 in glory.
20 He kept the law of the Most High,
 and entered into a covenant
 with him;
 he certified the covenant in his flesh,
 and when he was tested he proved
 faithful.
21 Therefore the Lord*d* assured him with
 an oath
 that the nations would be blessed
 through his offspring;
 that he would make him as numerous as
 the dust of the earth,
 and exalt his offspring like the stars,
 and give them an inheritance from sea
 to sea
 and from the Euphrates*e* to the ends
 of the earth.

a Heb Compare Lat Syr: Meaning of Gk uncertain
b Heb: Gk *Peoples declare*   *c* Heb: Gk *was taken in exchange*   *d* Gk *he*   *e* Syr: Heb Gk *River*

22 To Isaac also he gave the same assurance
　　for the sake of his father Abraham.
　The blessing of all people and the
　　　covenant
23 　he made to rest on the head of Jacob;
　he acknowledged him with his blessings,
　　and gave him his inheritance;
　he divided his portions,
　　and distributed them among twelve
　　　tribes.

44.19–23a. 19–21: Abraham's saga is recounted in Gen 12.1–25.11. **19:** *Abraham* was considered the quintessential father of the people of Israel, but he was also designated *the father of a multitude of nations* by God in Gen 17.5–6. **20:** *He kept the law of the Most High:* Although Abraham precedes Moses and the giving of the Torah,* Jewish tradition is that Abraham lived a Torah-observant life. The *covenant** between God and Abraham is manifest in the rite of circumcision* (Gen 17.9–14). *When he was tested* refers to Abraham's aborted sacrifice of Isaac. **21:** The covenant God makes with Abraham includes three promises: *that the nations would be blessed* (Gen 12.3; 22.15–18), that his descendants would be *as numerous as the dust of the earth* (Gen 13.16; 22.17), and that Abraham's own people would have a glorious *inheritance* (Gen 12.2; 13.14–17). **22–23:** The text passes quickly over *Isaac* and *Jacob;* not much can be said of their leadership roles.

~~~~~~~~~~~~~~~~~~~~~~~~~~~~~~~~~~~

From his descendants the Lord[a]
　　brought forth a godly man,
　who found favor in the sight of all

45 [1] and was beloved by God and
　　people,
　Moses, whose memory is blessed.
2 He made him equal in glory to the holy
　　ones,
　and made him great, to the terror of
　　his enemies.
3 By his words he performed swift
　　miracles;[b]
　the Lord[a] glorified him in the
　　presence of kings.
　He gave him commandments for his
　　people,
　and revealed to him his glory.
4 For his faithfulness and meekness he
　　consecrated him,
　choosing him out of all humankind.

5 He allowed him to hear his voice,
　and led him into the dark cloud,
　and gave him the commandments face
　　to face,
　the law of life and knowledge,
　so that he might teach Jacob the
　　covenant,
　and Israel his decrees.

44.23b–45.5: Because *Moses* himself is an agent of salvation, *he is equal in glory to the holy ones* (45.2; see also 42.17; 43.26). **3:** Moses rivaled Pharaoh's magicians (Ex 7), but the author is most likely thinking of all the various *miracles* God performed through Moses. **4–5:** Moses' unparalleled glory is also due to his being the facilitator of the covenant* given at Sinai, when God gave the people the Torah* (Ex 20.1–34.27). *Face to face* refers to Moses' reputation as the only one to have seen God (Ex 3; 33.11; 34.29–35; Deut 34.10).

~~~~~~~~~~~~~~~~~~~~~~~~~~~~~~~~~~~

6 He exalted Aaron, a holy man like
　　Moses[c]
　who was his brother, of the tribe of
　　Levi.
7 He made an everlasting covenant with
　　him,
　and gave him the priesthood of the
　　people.
　He blessed him with stateliness,
　　and put a glorious robe on him.
8 He clothed him in perfect splendor,
　　and strengthened him with the
　　　symbols of authority,
　the linen undergarments, the long
　　robe, and the ephod.
9 And he encircled him with
　　pomegranates,
　with many golden bells all around,
　to send forth a sound as he walked,
　　to make their ringing heard in the
　　　temple
　　as a reminder to his people;
10 with the sacred vestment, of gold and
　　violet
　and purple, the work of an
　　embroiderer;
　with the oracle of judgment, Urim and
　　Thummim;

a Gk he　　*b* Heb: Gk *caused signs to cease*　　*c* Gk *him*

11 with twisted crimson, the work of an
   artisan;
 with precious stones engraved like
   seals,
   in a setting of gold, the work of a
     jeweler,
 to commemorate in engraved letters
   each of the tribes of Israel;
12 with a gold crown upon his turban,
   inscribed like a seal with "Holiness,"
 a distinction to be prized, the work of
   an expert,
 a delight to the eyes, richly adorned.
13 Before him such beautiful things did
   not exist.
 No outsider ever put them on,
 but only his sons
 and his descendants in perpetuity.
14 His sacrifices shall be wholly burned
   twice every day continually.
15 Moses ordained him,
   and anointed him with holy oil;
 it was an everlasting covenant for him
 and for his descendants as long as the
   heavens endure,
 to minister to the Lord[a] and serve as
   priest
 and bless his people in his name.
16 He chose him out of all the living
   to offer sacrifice to the Lord,
 incense and a pleasing odor as a
   memorial portion,
 to make atonement for the[b] people.
17 In his commandments he gave him
   authority and statutes and[c]
     judgments,
 to teach Jacob the testimonies,
 and to enlighten Israel with his law.
18 Outsiders conspired against him,
   and envied him in the wilderness,
 Dathan and Abiram and their
   followers
 and the company of Korah, in wrath
   and anger.
19 The Lord saw it and was not pleased,
   and in the heat of his anger they were
     destroyed;
 he performed wonders against them
   to consume them in flaming fire.
20 He added glory to Aaron
   and gave him a heritage;

 he allotted to him the best of the first
   fruits,
 and prepared bread of first fruits in
   abundance;
21 for they eat the sacrifices of the Lord,
   which he gave to him and his
     descendants.
22 But in the land of the people he has no
   inheritance,
 and he has no portion among the
   people;
 for the Lord[d] himself is his[e] portion
   and inheritance.

45.6–22: *Aaron*, the first official priest, receives more
attention than any other hero. This is the primary reason that many scholars suspect that Ben Sira was a
priest, even though he never claims priestly status for
himself in the text. **7:** The *covenant** here refers to the
promise of a perpetual priesthood given in Ex 29.9;
40.15. **8–13:** Priestly garments and accoutrements are
described in Ex 28. **17:** A significant portion of the divine law applies exclusively to priests (Lev 21–22). **18.**
The rebellion of *Korah* is found in Num 16.1–17.15.
20–22: Because the priests enjoy religious privileges,
including receiving the tithes and *eating the sacrifices,*
they have *no land portion* like the other tribes
(Num 18).

23 Phinehas son of Eleazar ranks third in
   glory
   for being zealous in the fear of the
     Lord,
 and standing firm, when the people
   turned away,
   in the noble courage of his soul;
 and he made atonement for Israel.
24 Therefore a covenant of friendship was
   established with him,
   that he should be leader of the
     sanctuary and of his people,
 that he and his descendants should
   have
   the dignity of the priesthood forever.
25 Just as a covenant was established with
   David
   son of Jesse of the tribe of Judah,

a Gk *him*   b Other ancient authorities read *his* or *your*
c Heb: Gk *authority in covenants of*   d Gk *he*
e Other ancient authorities read *your*

that the king's heritage passes only from
son to son,
so the heritage of Aaron is for his
descendants alone.

26 And now bless the Lord
who has crowned you with glory.^a
May the Lord^b grant you wisdom of mind
to judge his people with justice,
so that their prosperity may not vanish,
and that their glory may endure
through all their generations.

45.23–26: *Phinehas,* whose story is told in Num 25, took it upon himself to root out impurity so that the community would not be punished. Like Aaron, Phinehas was a priest and was granted a special *covenant** of peace (Num 25.10–13). **23:** *Third in glory* presumably refers to Phinehas as third in the priestly line after Aaron and Eleazar (Num 25.10). **25:** The comparison with the Davidic covenant serves to elevate the status of the priestly covenant to the same level.

46 Joshua son of Nun was mighty in war,
and was the successor of Moses in
the prophetic office.
He became, as his name implies,
a great savior of God's^c elect,
to take vengeance on the enemies that
rose against them,
so that he might give Israel its
inheritance.
2 How glorious he was when he lifted his
hands
and brandished his sword against the
cities!
3 Who before him ever stood so firm?
For he waged the wars of the Lord.
4 Was it not through him that the sun
stood still
and one day became as long as two?
5 He called upon the Most High, the
Mighty One,
when enemies pressed him on every
side,
and the great Lord answered him
with hailstones of mighty power.
6 He overwhelmed that nation in battle,
and on the slope he destroyed his
opponents,

so that the nations might know his
armament,
that he was fighting in the sight of
the Lord;
for he was a devoted follower of the
Mighty One.
7 And in the days of Moses he proved his
loyalty,
he and Caleb son of Jephunneh:
they opposed the congregation,^d
restrained the people from sin,
and stilled their wicked grumbling.
8 And these two alone were spared
out of six hundred thousand infantry,
to lead the people^e into their
inheritance,
the land flowing with milk and honey.
9 The Lord gave Caleb strength,
which remained with him in his old
age,
so that he went up to the hill country,
and his children obtained it for an
inheritance,
10 so that all the Israelites might see
how good it is to follow the Lord.

46.1–10: *Joshua* first appears in Num 11.28, but his story mostly spans the book of Joshua. **1:** Joshua was designated Moses' successor by a laying on of hands (Deut 34.9). *Prophetic office* derives from Deut. 34.10, where Moses is proclaimed the greatest prophet* who ever lived. *As his name implies* refers to the etymology of Joshua; it comes from the Hebrew root meaning "save" or "rescue." **4:** Joshua 10.12–13 says *the sun stood still.* **5–6:** Joshua's honored memory rests on his reputation as a military leader, because he is the one who fought "the peoples of the land" in order to settle the Israelites. **7–8:** In Num 14, God decides that, with the exception of Joshua and *Caleb,* none of the adult members of Israel will enter the land. **8–9:** *Inheritance* refers primarily to the land.

11 The judges also, with their respective
names,
whose hearts did not fall into idolatry
and who did not turn away from the
Lord—
may their memory be blessed!

---

^a Heb: Gk lacks *And . . . glory*   ^b Gk *he*   ^c Gk *his*
^d Other ancient authorities read *the enemy*   ^e Gk *them*

12 May their bones send forth new life
    from where they lie,
    and may the names of those who have
        been honored
    live again in their children!

46.11–12: After the death of Joshua and before the establishment of the monarchy, several different *judges* ruled over Israel. The period was notorious for *idolatry★* and strife.

13 Samuel was beloved by his Lord;
    a prophet of the Lord, he established
        the kingdom
    and anointed rulers over his people.
14 By the law of the Lord he judged the
        congregation,
    and the Lord watched over Jacob.
15 By his faithfulness he was proved to be
    a prophet,
    and by his words he became known
        as a trustworthy seer.
16 He called upon the Lord, the Mighty
        One,
    when his enemies pressed him on
        every side,
    and he offered in sacrifice a suckling
        lamb.
17 Then the Lord thundered from heaven,
    and made his voice heard with a
        mighty sound;
18 he subdued the leaders of the enemy*
    and all the rulers of the Philistines.
19 Before the time of his eternal sleep,
    Samuel* bore witness before the
        Lord and his anointed:
    "No property, not so much as a pair of
        shoes,
    have I taken from anyone!"
    And no one accused him.
20 Even after he had fallen asleep, he
        prophesied
    and made known to the king his death,
    and lifted up his voice from the ground
    in prophecy, to blot out the
        wickedness of the people.

46.13–20: *Samuel* was known both as a *prophet★* (1 Sam 3.20) and a *judge* (1 Sam 7.15–17). His most influential legacy in Israelite history is his establishment of the monarchy (1 Sam 8–12), but most of the ac-

complishments listed by Ben Sira deal with his piety and prophecy. **20:** After Samuel's death, Saul engages the services of a woman capable of necromancy and Samuel's spirit is conjured up (1 Sam 28).

47 After him Nathan rose up
    to prophesy in the days of David.
2 As the fat is set apart from the offering
        of well-being,
    so David was set apart from the
        Israelites.
3 He played with lions as though they
        were young goats,
    and with bears as though they were
        lambs of the flock.
4 In his youth did he not kill a giant,
    and take away the people's disgrace,
    when he whirled the stone in the sling
    and struck down the boasting
        Goliath?
5 For he called on the Lord, the Most
        High,
    and he gave strength to his right arm
    to strike down a mighty warrior,
    and to exalt the power* of his people.
6 So they glorified him for the tens of
        thousands he conquered,
    and praised him for the blessings
        bestowed by the Lord,
    when the glorious diadem was given
        to him.
7 For he wiped out his enemies on every
        side,
    and annihilated his adversaries the
        Philistines;
    he crushed their power* to our own
        day.
8 In all that he did he gave thanks
    to the Holy One, the Most High,
        proclaiming his glory;
    he sang praise with all his heart,
    and he loved his Maker.
9 He placed singers before the altar,
    to make sweet melody with their
        voices.*
10 He gave beauty to the festivals,
    and arranged their times throughout
        the year,*

---

a Heb: Gk *leaders of the people of Tyre*   *b* Gk *he*
c Gk *horn*   *d* Other ancient authorities add *and daily they sing his praises*   *e* Gk *to completion*

while they praised God's[a] holy name,
  and the sanctuary resounded from
    early morning.
11 The Lord took away his sins,
  and exalted his power[b] forever;
he gave him a covenant of kingship
  and a glorious throne in Israel.

47.1–11: No other king enjoyed the affection of the people like *David*. **2:** God rejected Saul and chose David (1 Sam 16.1–14). **4–5:** The story of David and *Goliath* occurs in 1 Sam 17. **8–10:** In later tradition, David became known as the author of the psalms. The author of Chronicles, who recounts the history of the monarchy but writes from a later time than the author of 1 Samuel, describes David as having instituted regular worship of the Lord in the sanctuary (1 Chr 16). Ben Sira's comments reflect that tradition. **11:** By *his sins* Ben Sira most likely means David's sin with Bathsheba and the concomitant killing of her husband, Uriah (2 Sam 11.1–12.23). For God's *covenant** with David, see 1 Sam 5.1–5; 7.1–17.

12 After him a wise son rose up
  who because of him lived in
    security:[c]
13 Solomon reigned in an age of peace,
  because God made all his borders
    tranquil,
so that he might build a house in his
  name
and provide a sanctuary to stand
  forever.
14 How wise you were when you were
  young!
  You overflowed like the Nile[d] with
    understanding.
15 Your influence spread throughout the
  earth,
  and you filled it with proverbs having
    deep meaning.
16 Your fame reached to far-off islands,
  and you were loved for your peaceful
    reign.
17 Your songs, proverbs, and parables,
  and the answers you gave astounded
    the nations.
18 In the name of the Lord God,
  who is called the God of Israel,
you gathered gold like tin
  and amassed silver like lead.

19 But you brought in women to lie at your
    side,
  and through your body you were
    brought into subjection.
20 You stained your honor,
  and defiled your family line,
so that you brought wrath upon your
  children,
  and they were grieved[e] at your folly,
21 because the sovereignty was divided
  and a rebel kingdom arose out of
    Ephraim.
22 But the Lord will never give up his
    mercy,
  or cause any of his works to perish;
he will never blot out the descendants
  of his chosen one,
  or destroy the family line of him who
    loved him.
So he gave a remnant to Jacob,
  and to David a root from his own
    family.

47.12–22: *Solomon's* character presents a complex case for the author. In spite of the fact that Solomon was renowned for his wisdom, he acted dishonorably and foolishly. **12:** When Ben Sira says *because of him*, he refers to David (1 Kings 11.12). **13:** The *house* Solomon built was the Temple* that David had aspired to build (1 Kings 5–8). **14–17:** Solomon was famous for his *wisdom* (see, for example, 1 Kings 4.29–34) and was believed to be the author of Proverbs and the Song of Solomon, as well as many other noncanonical wisdom writings. **18:** He amassed great wealth (1 Kings 10.14–25). **19–20:** Solomon's primary sin from Ben Sira's perspective was his sexual licentiousness, through which he was *brought into subjection* (compare 33.20). For the writer of 1 Kings, Solomon's sin lay with his foreign wives and his wayward religious practices (1 Kings 11.1–8). **21:** Solomon's sin ultimately resulted in the division of the Davidic kingdom (1 Kings 11.9–13). **22:** Because of the Lord's love for David and the promise of an eternal covenant,* the Davidic family line would never be destroyed. The messianic expectation that characterized post-biblical Judaism derived partly from belief in the eternal covenant God made with David.

---

a Gk *his*   b Gk *horn*   c Heb: Gk *in a broad place*
d Heb: Gk *a river*   e Other ancient authorities read
I was grieved

23 Solomon rested with his ancestors,
  and left behind him one of his sons,
broad in*a* folly and lacking in sense,
  Rehoboam, whose policy drove the
    people to revolt.
Then Jeroboam son of Nebat led Israel
  into sin
  and started Ephraim on its sinful
    ways.
24 Their sins increased more and more,
  until they were exiled from their land.
25 For they sought out every kind of
    wickedness,
  until vengeance came upon them.

47.23–25: The divided kingdom is composed of Israel in the north and Judah in the south. The northern kingdom was destroyed by the Assyrians. (The south was spared from the Assyrians but later defeated by the Babylonians.)

48 Then Elijah arose, a prophet like
    fire,
  and his word burned like a torch.
2 He brought a famine upon them,
  and by his zeal he made them few in
    number.
3 By the word of the Lord he shut up the
    heavens,
  and also three times brought down
    fire.
4 How glorious you were, Elijah, in your
    wondrous deeds!
  Whose glory is equal to yours?
5 You raised a corpse from death
  and from Hades, by the word of the
    Most High.
6 You sent kings down to destruction,
  and famous men, from their sickbeds.
7 You heard rebuke at Sinai
  and judgments of vengeance at
    Horeb.
8 You anointed kings to inflict retribution,
  and prophets to succeed you.*b*
9 You were taken up by a whirlwind of
    fire,
  in a chariot with horses of fire.
10 At the appointed time, it is written, you
    are destined*c*
  to calm the wrath of God before it
    breaks out in fury,

to turn the hearts of parents to their
    children,
  and to restore the tribes of Jacob.
11 Happy are those who saw you
  and were adorned*d* with your love!
  For we also shall surely live.*e*

48.1–11: *Elijah* prophesied in the northern kingdom of Israel during the reign of Ahab. **2–7:** Elijah is most famous for the many miracles he performed as an agent of God. **3:** Ben Sira alludes to the three attempts by Ahab's successor, Ahaziah, to capture Elijah (2 Kings 1.9–16). **5:** For Elijah's resurrection of the widow's son, see 1 Kings 17.17–24. **9:** Elijah never suffered death, but ascended to heaven by means of a *whirlwind* (2 Kings 2.9–13). **10:** Elijah's return is prophesied in Mal 4.5–6.

12 When Elijah was enveloped in the
    whirlwind,
  Elisha was filled with his spirit.
  He performed twice as many signs,
    and marvels with every utterance of
      his mouth.*f*
  Never in his lifetime did he tremble
    before any ruler,
  nor could anyone intimidate him at
    all.
13 Nothing was too hard for him,
  and when he was dead, his body
    prophesied.
14 In his life he did wonders,
  and in death his deeds were
    marvelous.

48.12–14: *Elisha* was Elijah's successor (2 Kings 2.9–15). **13:** The touch of Elisha's *dead body* brings another man back to life in 2 Kings 13.20–21.

15 Despite all this the people did not
    repent,
  nor did they forsake their sins,
until they were carried off as plunder
    from their land,
  and were scattered over all the earth.

a Heb (with a play on the name Rehoboam) Syr: Gk *the people's*   b Heb: Gk *him*   c Heb: Gk *are for reproofs*   d Other ancient authorities read *and have died*   e Text and meaning of Gk uncertain   f Heb: Gk lacks *He performed . . . mouth*

The people were left very few in
    number,
  but with a ruler from the house of
    David.
16 Some of them did what was right,
  but others sinned more and more.

48.15–16: The author refers to the demise of the
northern kingdom, "when the king of Assyria . . .
carried the Israelites away to Assyria" (2 Kings 17.6).
The final events leading up to the Assyrian exile as
well as a summary of the people's sins are recounted
in 2 Kings 17.1–23. Although the Assyrians capture
many cities in the southern kingdom of Judah, Jerusalem and the Davidic line survive the siege (2 Kings
18–19).

---

17 Hezekiah fortified his city,
  and brought water into its midst;
  he tunneled the rock with iron tools,
  and built cisterns for the water.
18 In his days Sennacherib invaded the
    country;
  he sent his commander*a* and
    departed;
  he shook his fist against Zion,
  and made great boasts in his
    arrogance.
19 Then their hearts were shaken and their
    hands trembled,
  and they were in anguish, like women
    in labor.
20 But they called upon the Lord who is
    merciful,
  spreading out their hands toward
    him.
  The Holy One quickly heard them from
    heaven,
  and delivered them through Isaiah.
21 The Lord*b* struck down the camp of the
    Assyrians,
  and his angel wiped them out.
22 For Hezekiah did what was pleasing to
    the Lord,
  and he kept firmly to the ways of his
    ancestor David,
  as he was commanded by the prophet
    Isaiah,
  who was great and trustworthy in his
    visions.

23 In Isaiah's*c* days the sun went
    backward,
  and he prolonged the life of the king.
24 By his dauntless spirit he saw the
    future,
  and comforted the mourners in Zion.
25 He revealed what was to occur to the
    end of time,
  and the hidden things before they
    happened.

48.17–25: King *Hezekiah* of Judah is credited with saving Jerusalem from the siege of the Assyrian king, Sennacherib (2 Kings 18–19). Historical memory regards
Hezekiah as one of the few kings *who did what was
right* (Sir 48.16; 2 Kings 18.3–8). **17:** Hezekiah built
the tunnel of Siloam in order to insure the water supply
for the people during the siege (2 Kings 20.20). **20:**
Hezekiah's prayer to the Lord for deliverance from the
Assyrians is in 2 Kings 19.15–19. **22:** *Isaiah the
prophet** was Hezekiah's principal adviser. **23:** The *sun
went backward* as a sign to Hezekiah that he would
recover from illness (2 Kings 20.1–11). **24–25:** By these
words Ben Sira evokes not so much the stories told in
2 Kings, but the biblical book of Isaiah.

---

49 The name*d* of Josiah is like blended
    incense
  prepared by the skill of the perfumer;
  his memory*e* is as sweet as honey to
    every mouth,
  and like music at a banquet of wine.
2 He did what was right by reforming the
    people,
  and removing the wicked
    abominations.
3 He kept his heart fixed on the Lord;
  in lawless times he made godliness
    prevail.

49.1–3: Like Hezekiah, *Josiah* is remembered as a righteous king. In 2 Kings 22–23 Josiah discovered a "book
of the law" in the Temple* (2 Kings 22.8). The discovery inspired Josiah to renew the covenant,* which,
for a short time, led to a religious reform characterized
by exclusive worship of the Lord.

---

a Other ancient authorities add *from Lachish*   *b* Gk He
c Gk *his*   *d* Heb: Gk *memory*   *e* Heb: Gk *it*

4 Except for David and Hezekiah and
    Josiah,
  all of them were great sinners,
  for they abandoned the law of the Most
    High;
  the kings of Judah came to an end.
5 They*a gave their power to others,
  and their glory to a foreign nation,
6 who set fire to the chosen city of the
    sanctuary,
  and made its streets desolate,
  as Jeremiah had foretold.*b
7 For they had mistreated him,
  who even in the womb had been
    consecrated a prophet,
  to pluck up and ruin and destroy,
  and likewise to build and to plant.

49.4–7. 4–6a: In spite of Josiah's reform, the cumulative effect of the sins of the monarchy led to the destruction of Jerusalem by the Babylonians. **6b–7:** *Jeremiah* predicts the inevitability of Jerusalem's fall in judgment oracles* found in Jer 1–25. Although Jeremiah was commissioned by God before birth (Jer 1.5), his prophecies made him unpopular in his own time and were the source of his persecution.

---

8 It was Ezekiel who saw the vision of
    glory,
  which God*c showed him above the
    chariot of the cherubim.
9 For God*d also mentioned Job
  who held fast to all the ways of
    justice.*e
10 May the bones of the Twelve Prophets
    send forth new life from where they
    lie,
  for they comforted the people of Jacob
    and delivered them with confident
    hope.

49.8–10. 8: *Ezekiel's vision* of God's *chariot* can be found in Ezekiel 1. **49.9:** *Job* is mentioned in Ezek 14.14, 20. **49.10:** *The Twelve Prophets* include Hosea, Joel, Amos, Obadiah, Jonah, Micah, Nahum, Habakkuk, Zephaniah, Haggai, Zechariah, and Malachi, all of whose books were assembled in one collection in the Hebrew canon* known as the Book of the Twelve. The expression *May the bones . . . send forth new life* appears at 26.12.

11 How shall we magnify Zerubbabel?
  He was like a signet ring on the right
    hand,
12 and so was Jeshua son of Jozadak;
  in their days they built the house
  and raised a temple*f holy to the Lord,
    destined for everlasting glory.
13 The memory of Nehemiah also is
    lasting;
  he raised our fallen walls,
  and set up gates and bars,
  and rebuilt our ruined houses.

49.11–13: Ben Sira recalls the names of those who made possible the building of the Second Temple.* *Zerubbabel* was a Davidic ruler sanctioned by the Persians, who defeated the Babylonians and thus ended forced exile. *Jeshua son of Jozadak* was the first man called a high priest (Hag 1.1; Zech 6.11–14). *Nehemiah*, who lived slightly later than the two previous figures, rebuilt the city walls (Neh 2.11–6.16).

---

14 Few have*g ever been created on earth
    like Enoch,
  for he was taken up from the earth.
15 Nor was anyone ever born like Joseph;*h
  even his bones were cared for.
16 Shem and Seth and Enosh were
    honored,*i
  but above every other created living
    being was Adam.

49.14–16: These verses mention other heroes out of chronological sequence and appear awkward within the overall structure of the hymn. Some scholars understandably suspect these verses are a later addition, but all manuscripts contain some version of them.

---

50 The leader of his brothers and the
    pride of his people*j
  was the high priest, Simon son of
    Onias,
  who in his life repaired the house,
  and in his time fortified the temple.

---

a Heb *He*   b Gk *by the hand of Jeremiah*   c Gk *He*
d Gk *he*   e Heb Compare Syr: Meaning of Gk
uncertain   f Other ancient authorities read *people*
g Heb Syr: Gk *No one has*   h Heb Syr: Gk adds *the
leader of his brothers, the support of the people*   i Heb:
Gk *Shem and Seth were honored by people*   j Heb Syr:
Gk lacks this line. Compare 49.15

2 He laid the foundations for the high
　　double walls,
　　the high retaining walls for the
　　　temple enclosure.
3 In his days a water cistern was dug,^a
　　a reservoir like the sea in
　　　circumference.
4 He considered how to save his people
　　from ruin,
　　and fortified the city against siege.
5 How glorious he was, surrounded by the
　　people,
　　as he came out of the house of the
　　　curtain.
6 Like the morning star among the clouds,
　　like the full moon at the festal
　　　season;^a
7 like the sun shining on the temple of
　　the Most High,
　　like the rainbow gleaming in splendid
　　　clouds;
8 like roses in the days of first fruits,
　　like lilies by a spring of water,
　　like a green shoot on Lebanon on a
　　　summer day;
9 like fire and incense in the censer,
　　like a vessel of hammered gold
　　studded with all kinds of precious
　　　stones;
10 like an olive tree laden with fruit,
　　and like a cypress towering in the
　　　clouds.
11 When he put on his glorious robe
　　and clothed himself in perfect
　　　splendor,
　when he went up to the holy altar,
　　he made the court of the sanctuary
　　　glorious.
12 When he received the portions from the
　　hands of the priests,
　as he stood by the hearth of the altar
　with a garland of brothers around him,
　　he was like a young cedar on
　　　Lebanon
　surrounded by the trunks of palm
　　　trees.
13 All the sons of Aaron in their splendor
　　held the Lord's offering in their hands
　before the whole congregation of
　　　Israel.

14 Finishing the service at the altars,^b
　　and arranging the offering to the
　　　Most High, the Almighty,
15 he held out his hand for the cup
　　and poured a drink offering of the
　　　blood of the grape;
　he poured it out at the foot of the
　　　altar,
　　a pleasing odor to the Most High, the
　　　king of all.
16 Then the sons of Aaron shouted;
　　they blew their trumpets of
　　　hammered metal;
　　they sounded a mighty fanfare
　　as a reminder before the Most High.
17 Then all the people together quickly
　　fell to the ground on their faces
　to worship their Lord,
　　the Almighty, God Most High.

18 Then the singers praised him with their
　　voices
　　in sweet and full-toned melody.^c
19 And the people of the Lord Most High
　　offered
　　their prayers before the Merciful
　　　One,
　until the order of worship of the Lord
　　was ended,
　　and they completed his ritual.
20 Then Simon^d came down and raised his
　　hands
　　over the whole congregation of
　　　Israelites,
　to pronounce the blessing of the Lord
　　with his lips,
　　and to glory in his name;
21 and they bowed down in worship a
　　second time,
　　to receive the blessing from the Most
　　　High.

22 And now bless the God of all,
　　who everywhere works great
　　　wonders,
　who fosters our growth from birth,
　　and deals with us according to his
　　　mercy.

a Heb: Meaning of Gk uncertain　　*b* Other ancient
authorities read *altar*　　*c* Other ancient authorities read
in sweet melody throughout the house　　*d* Gk *he*

23 May he give us[a] gladness of heart,
 and may there be peace in our[b]
 days
 in Israel, as in the days of old.
24 May he entrust to us his mercy,
 and may he deliver us in our[c] days!

50.1–24. 1–21: *Simon Son of Onias,* also known as Simon II, held the office of *high priest* just before and during the time of Ben Sira. The description of Simon in his priestly visage (vv. 5–13) is similar to Aaron in 45.6–13. After Zerubbabel, the Davidic line seems to disappear. Religious and political authority gradually merged in the office of the high priest. These verses may have functioned as a kind of eulogy for Simon. **20–21:** The hymn praising the ancestors concludes with the final hero blessing the people, a role priests typically play (Num 6.22–27). **22–24:** Ben Sira offers his own benediction, another clue that he probably was a member of the priestly class.

---

25 Two nations my soul detests,
 and the third is not even a people:
26 Those who live in Seir,[d] and the
 Philistines,
 and the foolish people that live in
 Shechem.

50.25–26: This saying refers to Israel's neighbors. Perhaps its placement here reflects the author's attempt to reassert the distinctiveness of Israel.

---

27 Instruction in understanding and
 knowledge
 I have written in this book,
 Jesus son of Eleazar son of Sirach[e] of
 Jerusalem,
 whose mind poured forth wisdom.
28 Happy are those who concern
 themselves with these things,
 and those who lay them to heart will
 become wise.
29 For if they put them into practice, they
 will be equal to anything,
 for the fear[f] of the Lord is their
 path.

50.27–29: These verses amount to a colophon* or postscript, in which the author gives his full name and states his purpose in producing this book.

PRAYER OF JESUS SON OF SIRACH[g]

51 I give you thanks, O Lord and King,
 and praise you, O God my Savior.
 I give thanks to your name,
2 for you have been my protector and
 helper
 and have delivered me from destruction
 and from the trap laid by a slanderous
 tongue,
 from lips that fabricate lies.
 In the face of my adversaries
 you have been my helper ³and
 delivered me,
 in the greatness of your mercy and of
 your name,
 from grinding teeth about to devour me,
 from the hand of those seeking my
 life,
 from the many troubles I endured,
4 from choking fire on every side,
 and from the midst of fire that I had
 not kindled,
5 from the deep belly of Hades,
 from an unclean tongue and lying
 words—
6   the slander of an unrighteous tongue
 to the king.
 My soul drew near to death,
 and my life was on the brink of Hades
 below.
7 They surrounded me on every side,
 and there was no one to help me;
 I looked for human assistance,
 and there was none.
8 Then I remembered your mercy,
 O Lord,
 and your kindness[h] from of old,
 for you rescue those who wait for you
 and save them from the hand of their
 enemies.
9 And I sent up my prayer from the earth,
 and begged for rescue from death.
10 I cried out, "Lord, you are my Father;[i]
 do not forsake me in the days of
 trouble,

a Other ancient authorities read *you*   *b* Other ancient authorities read *your*   *c* Other ancient authorities read *his*   *d* Heb Compare Lat: Gk *on the mountain of Samaria*   *e* Heb: Meaning of Gk uncertain   *f* Heb: Other ancient authorities read *light*   *g* This title is included in the Gk text.   *h* Other ancient authorities read *work*   *i* Heb: Gk *the Father of my lord*

when there is no help against the
    proud.
11 I will praise your name continually,
    and will sing hymns of
        thanksgiving."
My prayer was heard,
12   for you saved me from destruction
    and rescued me in time of trouble.
For this reason I thank you and praise
        you,
    and I bless the name of the Lord.

Heb adds:

Give thanks to the LORD, for he is good,
    for his mercy endures forever;

Give thanks to the God of praises,
    for his mercy endures forever;

Give thanks to the guardian of Israel,
    for his mercy endures forever;

Give thanks to him who formed all
        things,
    for his mercy endures forever;

Give thanks to the redeemer of Israel,
    for his mercy endures forever;

Give thanks to him who gathers the
        dispersed of Israel,
    for his mercy endures forever;

Give thanks to him who rebuilt his city
        and his sanctuary,
    for his mercy endures forever;

Give thanks to him who makes a horn to
        sprout for the house of David,
    for his mercy endures forever;

Give thanks to him who has chosen the
        sons of Zadok to be priests,
    for his mercy endures forever;

Give thanks to the shield of Abraham,
    for his mercy endures forever;

Give thanks to the rock of Isaac,
    for his mercy endures forever;

Give thanks to the mighty one of Jacob,
    for his mercy endures forever;

Give thanks to him who has chosen Zion,
    for his mercy endures forever;

Give thanks to the King of the kings of
        kings,
    for his mercy endures forever;

He has raised up a horn for his people,
    praise for all his loyal ones.

For the children of Israel, the people
        close to him.
    Praise the LORD!

13 While I was still young, before I went
        on my travels,
    I sought wisdom openly in my prayer.
14 Before the temple I asked for her,
    and I will search for her until the
        end.

15 From the first blossom to the ripening
        grape
    my heart delighted in her;
my foot walked on the straight path;
    from my youth I followed her steps.

16 I inclined my ear a little and received
        her,
    and I found for myself much
        instruction.
17 I made progress in her;
    to him who gives wisdom I will give
        glory.

18 For I resolved to live according to
        wisdom,[a]
    and I was zealous for the good,
    and I shall never be disappointed.
19 My soul grappled with wisdom,[a]
    and in my conduct I was strict;[b]

I spread out my hands to the heavens,
    and lamented my ignorance of her.
20 I directed my soul to her,
    and in purity I found her.

a Gk *her*   *b* Meaning of Gk uncertain

With her I gained understanding from
the first;
therefore I will never be forsaken.

21 My heart was stirred to seek her;
therefore I have gained a prize
possession.

22 The Lord gave me my tongue as a
reward,
and I will praise him with it.

23 Draw near to me, you who are
uneducated,
and lodge in the house of
instruction.

24 Why do you say you are lacking in these
things,*a*
and why do you endure such great
thirst?

25 I opened my mouth and said,
Acquire wisdom*b* for yourselves
without money.

26 Put your neck under her*c* yoke,
and let your souls receive
instruction;
it is to be found close by.

27 See with your own eyes that I have
labored but little
and found for myself much serenity.

28 Hear but a little of my instruction,
and through me you will acquire
silver and gold.*d*

29 May your soul rejoice in God's*e* mercy,
and may you never be ashamed to
praise him.

30 Do your work in good time,
and in his own time God*f* will give
you your reward.

51.1–30: Prayers. A prayer of thanksgiving and another praise of Wisdom conclude the text of Sirach.
Because it follows the postscript, some scholars have
doubted the authenticity of this chapter. Manuscript
evidence, however, as well as its thematic consistency
with the rest of Sirach, provide good grounds for viewing this section as original. The hymn of thanksgiving
inserted in the middle of the chapter appears in the
Hebrew text, but not in the other ancient versions. Its
absence in some versions indicates that it was probably
added later. In addition to the manuscript evidence,
there are other reasons for seeing the hymn as secondary. It is modeled on Ps 136 and contains certain
phrases frequently found in texts produced by the
Dead Sea sect,* notably *the sons of Zadok.* The sect
of Jews associated with the Dead Sea are also known
to have authored many hymns of thanksgiving. **13–
30:** This final praise of Wisdom takes an autobiographical perspective. Since it begins with the author's youth
and speaks of rewards gained, it serves to inspire the
prospective student of Wisdom.

a Cn Compare Heb Syr: Meaning of Gk uncertain
b Heb: Gk lacks *wisdom* *c* Heb: other ancient
authorities read *the* *d* Syr Compare Heb: Gk *Get
instruction with a large sum of silver, and you will gain by
it much gold.* *e* Gk *his* *f* Gk *he*

BARUCH

Introduction

Baruch is a compilation of several writings attributed to the scribe of Jeremiah (Jer 32.9–15; chs. 36, 45). The book was not likely written by Baruch, however, because it exhibits later theological views and is influenced by later literature. It was more than likely composed in Hebrew in Palestine sometime during the second to first centuries BCE.

The book is divisible into four parts: introduction (1.1–14), penitential prayer (1.15–3.8), wisdom poem (3.9–4.4), and Zion⋆ poem (4.5–5.9). Each of the major sections is indebted to earlier biblical literature. The introduction has affinities with Ezra and Nehemiah. The penitential prayer is similar to Dan 9.4–19 and is perhaps based on it. The wisdom poem, which addresses the problem of finding the wisdom of God, is similar to Sir 24 and Job 28. The Zion poem has been influenced by Isa 40–66 and Deut 28–32. Despite many similar motifs,⋆ the parts were probably composed by different authors. For example, the divine name in the introduction and penitential prayer is generally "Lord," while in the wisdom poem it is "God," and in the Zion poem, "the Everlasting."

Although each of the parts of Baruch may pale in comparison to the earlier biblical literature, it provides a valuable insight into the everyday piety of Jews in the second or first century BCE, when it was likely written. The author contrasts the negative view of Israel's past sin with the optimistic vision of the community's returning to a proper praise of God. Penitence is the means of moving from the sinfulness of the past to the obedience and praise of the restored community. The theme of return in the Zion poem provides a celebratory conclusion to the work.

1 These are the words of the book that Baruch son of Neriah son of Mahseiah son of Zedekiah son of Hasadiah son of Hilkiah wrote in Babylon, 2in the fifth year, on the seventh day of the month, at the time when the Chaldeans took Jerusalem and burned it with fire.

3 Baruch read the words of this book to Jeconiah son of Jehoiakim, king of Judah, and to all the people who came to hear the book, 4and to the nobles and the princes, and to the elders, and to all the people, small and great, all who lived in Babylon by the river Sud.

5 Then they wept, and fasted, and prayed before the Lord; 6they collected as much money as each could give, 7and sent it to Jerusalem to the high priest[a] Jehoiakim son of Hilkiah son of Shallum, and to the priests, and to all the people who were present with him in Jerusalem. 8At the same time, on the tenth day of Sivan, Baruch[b] took the vessels of the house of the Lord, which had been carried away from the temple, to return them to the land of Judah—the silver vessels that Zedekiah son of Josiah, king of Judah, had made, 9after King Nebuchadnezzar of Babylon had carried away from Jerusalem Jeconiah and the princes and the prisoners and the nobles and the people of the land, and brought them to Babylon.

10 They said: Here we send you money; so buy with the money burnt offerings and sin offerings and incense, and prepare a grain offering, and offer them on the altar of the Lord our God; 11and pray for the life of King Nebuchadnezzar of Babylon, and for the life of his son Belshazzar, so that their days on earth may be like the days of heaven. 12The Lord will give us strength, and light to

a Gk the priest   b Gk he

our eyes; we shall live under the protection[a] of King Nebuchadnezzar of Babylon, and under the protection of his son Belshazzar, and we shall serve them many days and find favor in their sight. [13]Pray also for us to the Lord our God, for we have sinned against the Lord our God, and to this day the anger of the Lord and his wrath have not turned away from us. [14]And you shall read aloud this scroll that we are sending you, to make your confession in the house of the Lord on the days of the festivals and at appointed seasons.

1.1–14: Introduction. *All the people* are charged to hear the book, just as "all the people" heard the renewal of the law in Neh 8, and in both cases this charge is followed by a long penitential prayer. Baruch also gathers the Temple* vessels to return them to Jerusalem (Ezra 1). The piety of the exiled community is taken as a model for the Jews of the Diaspora* during the time when the work was written. Zechariah 7.2–5 also indicates that the anniversary of the fall of the Temple was marked by mourning. **10–11:** The Jews remaining in Jerusalem were enjoined to *pray for the life of King Nebuchadnezzar,* even though he destroyed the Temple. This is an extension of Jeremiah's advice to live peacefully under Nebuchadnezzar (Jer 29), but it also reflects the later practice of praying for the Persian king and his children (Ezra 6.10). Daniel also shows a willingness to live peacefully under Nebuchadnezzar (Dan 1–4). **11:** *Belshazzar* was actually the son of Nabonidus, but Baruch may have been influenced by the text of Dan 5.2, where the same mistake is found.

---

15 And you shall say: The Lord our God is in the right, but there is open shame on us today, on the people of Judah, on the inhabitants of Jerusalem, [16]and on our kings, our rulers, our priests, our prophets, and our ancestors, [17]because we have sinned before the Lord. [18]We have disobeyed him, and have not heeded the voice of the Lord our God, to walk in the statutes of the Lord that he set before us. [19]From the time when the Lord brought our ancestors out of the land of Egypt until today, we have been disobedient to the Lord our God, and we have been negligent, in not heeding his voice. [20]So to this day there have clung to us the calamities

and the curse that the Lord declared through his servant Moses at the time when he brought our ancestors out of the land of Egypt to give to us a land flowing with milk and honey. [21]We did not listen to the voice of the Lord our God in all the words of the prophets whom he sent to us, [22]but all of us followed the intent of our own wicked hearts by serving other gods and doing what is evil in the sight of the Lord our God.

2 So the Lord carried out the threat he spoke against us: against our judges who ruled Israel, and against our kings and our rulers and the people of Israel and Judah. [2]Under the whole heaven there has not been done the like of what he has done in Jerusalem, in accordance with the threats that were[b] written in the law of Moses. [3]Some of us ate the flesh of their sons and others the flesh of their daughters. [4]He made them subject to all the kingdoms around us, to be an object of scorn and a desolation among all the surrounding peoples, where the Lord has scattered them. [5]They were brought down and not raised up, because our nation[c] sinned against the Lord our God, in not heeding his voice.

6 The Lord our God is in the right, but there is open shame on us and our ancestors this very day. [7]All those calamities with which the Lord threatened us have come upon us. [8]Yet we have not entreated the favor of the Lord by turning away, each of us, from the thoughts of our wicked hearts. [9]And the Lord has kept the calamities ready, and the Lord has brought them upon us, for the Lord is just in all the works that he has commanded us to do. [10]Yet we have not obeyed his voice, to walk in the statutes of the Lord that he set before us.

11 And now, O Lord God of Israel, who brought your people out of the land of Egypt with a mighty hand and with signs and wonders and with great power and outstretched arm, and made yourself a name that continues to this day, [12]we have sinned, we have been ungodly, we have done wrong, O Lord our God, against all your ordinances. [13]Let

---

a Gk *in the shadow*   b Gk *in accordance with what is*
c Gk *because we*

your anger turn away from us, for we are left, few in number, among the nations where you have scattered us. [14]Hear, O Lord, our prayer and our supplication, and for your own sake deliver us, and grant us favor in the sight of those who have carried us into exile; [15]so that all the earth may know that you are the Lord our God, for Israel and his descendants are called by your name.

16 O Lord, look down from your holy dwelling, and consider us. Incline your ear, O Lord, and hear; [17]open your eyes, O Lord, and see, for the dead who are in Hades, whose spirit has been taken from their bodies, will not ascribe glory or justice to the Lord; [18]but the person who is deeply grieved, who walks bowed and feeble, with failing eyes and famished soul, will declare your glory and righteousness, O Lord.

19 For it is not because of any righteous deeds of our ancestors or our kings that we bring before you our prayer for mercy, O Lord our God. [20]For you have sent your anger and your wrath upon us, as you declared by your servants the prophets, saying: [21]Thus says the Lord: Bend your shoulders and serve the king of Babylon, and you will remain in the land that I gave to your ancestors. [22]But if you will not obey the voice of the Lord and will not serve the king of Babylon, [23]I will make to cease from the towns of Judah and from the region around Jerusalem the voice of mirth and the voice of gladness, the voice of the bridegroom and the voice of the bride, and the whole land will be a desolation without inhabitants.

24 But we did not obey your voice, to serve the king of Babylon; and you have carried out your threats, which you spoke by your servants the prophets, that the bones of our kings and the bones of our ancestors would be brought out of their resting place; [25]and indeed they have been thrown out to the heat of day and the frost of night. They perished in great misery, by famine and sword and pestilence. [26]And the house that is called by your name you have made as it is today, because of the wickedness of the house of Israel and the house of Judah.

27 Yet you have dealt with us, O Lord our God, in all your kindness and in all your great compassion, [28]as you spoke by your servant Moses on the day when you commanded him to write your law in the presence of the people of Israel, saying, [29]"If you will not obey my voice, this very great multitude will surely turn into a small number among the nations, where I will scatter them. [30]For I know that they will not obey me, for they are a stiff-necked people. But in the land of their exile they will come to themselves [31]and know that I am the Lord their God. I will give them a heart that obeys and ears that hear; [32]they will praise me in the land of their exile, and will remember my name [33]and turn from their stubbornness and their wicked deeds; for they will remember the ways of their ancestors, who sinned before the Lord. [34]I will bring them again into the land that I swore to give to their ancestors, to Abraham, Isaac, and Jacob, and they will rule over it; and I will increase them, and they will not be diminished. [35]I will make an everlasting covenant with them to be their God and they shall be my people; and I will never again remove my people Israel from the land that I have given them."

3 O Lord Almighty, God of Israel, the soul in anguish and the wearied spirit cry out to you. [2]Hear, O Lord, and have mercy, for we have sinned before you. [3]For you are enthroned forever, and we are perishing forever. [4]O Lord Almighty, God of Israel, hear now the prayer of the people[a] of Israel, the children of those who sinned before you, who did not heed the voice of the Lord their God, so that calamities have clung to us. [5]Do not remember the iniquities of our ancestors, but in this crisis remember your power and your name. [6]For you are the Lord our God, and it is you, O Lord, whom we will praise. [7]For you have put the fear of you in our hearts so that we would call upon your name; and we will praise you in our exile, for we have put away from our hearts all the iniquity of our ancestors who sinned against you. [8]See, we are today in our exile where you have scattered us, to be reproached and cursed and punished for all the iniquities of

a Gk dead

our ancestors, who forsook the Lord our God.

1.15–3.8: Penitential prayer. God's punishment is seen as a result of Israel's sin (Neh 9; Dan 9.4–19). The pattern of sin/punishment/repentance/salvation found in Deut 28–32 influences this passage and a number of other texts of the period (Jdt 5). **2.11–3.8:** The recitation of the mighty acts of God was a standard part of the renewal of the covenant (Ex 19.3–6; Deut 6.12; Josh 24), but here it is incorporated into the confession of sins. The contrast of God's gracious act and Israel's ungrateful response is sharply drawn. **17–18:** The *dead who are in Hades* cannot praise God (Ps 30.9; 88.10–12), but the truly penitent worshiper, who is *deeply grieved*, can. **21–35:** The author here interweaves a number of passages from Jeremiah (7.34; 8.1; 24.7; 27.9–12; 31.33; 32.36; 36.30). Jeremiah's message to *serve the king of Babylon* is restated, but the author may have in mind here peaceful coexistence with world governments of his or her own time.

9 Hear the commandments of life,
        O Israel;
    give ear, and learn wisdom!
10 Why is it, O Israel, why is it that you
        are in the land of your enemies,
    that you are growing old in a foreign
        country,
    that you are defiled with the dead,
11   that you are counted among those in
        Hades?
12 You have forsaken the fountain of
        wisdom.
13 If you had walked in the way of God,
    you would be living in peace
        forever.
14 Learn where there is wisdom,
    where there is strength,
    where there is understanding,
    so that you may at the same time
        discern
    where there is length of days, and
        life,
    where there is light for the eyes, and
        peace.
15 Who has found her place?
    And who has entered her
        storehouses?

16 Where are the rulers of the nations,
    and those who lorded it over the
        animals on earth;
17 those who made sport of the birds of
        the air,
    and who hoarded up silver and gold
    in which people trust,
    and there is no end to their getting;
18 those who schemed to get silver, and
        were anxious,
    but there is no trace of their works?
19 They have vanished and gone down to
        Hades,
    and others have arisen in their place.
20 Later generations have seen the light of
        day,
    and have lived upon the earth;
    but they have not learned the way to
        knowledge,
    nor understood her paths,
    nor laid hold of her.
21 Their descendants have strayed far from
        her*a* way.
22 She has not been heard of in Canaan,
    or seen in Teman;
23 the descendants of Hagar, who seek for
        understanding on the earth,
    the merchants of Merran and
        Teman,
    the story-tellers and the seekers for
        understanding,
    have not learned the way to wisdom,
    or given thought to her paths.
24 O Israel, how great is the house of
        God,
    how vast the territory that he
        possesses!
25 It is great and has no bounds;
    it is high and immeasurable.
26 The giants were born there, who were
        famous of old,
    great in stature, expert in war.
27 God did not choose them,
    or give them the way to knowledge;
28 so they perished because they had no
        wisdom,
    they perished through their folly.

a Other ancient authorities read *their*

29 Who has gone up into heaven, and
        taken her,
    and brought her down from the
        clouds?
30 Who has gone over the sea, and found
        her,
    and will buy her for pure gold?
31 No one knows the way to her,
        or is concerned about the path to her.
32 But the one who knows all things knows
        her,
    he found her by his understanding.
    The one who prepared the earth for all
        time
    filled it with four-footed creatures;
33 the one who sends forth the light, and it
        goes;
    he called it, and it obeyed him,
        trembling;
34 the stars shone in their watches, and
        were glad;
    he called them, and they said, "Here
        we are!"
    They shone with gladness for him
        who made them.
35 This is our God;
    no other can be compared to him.
36 He found the whole way to knowledge,
    and gave her to his servant Jacob
    and to Israel, whom he loved.
37 Afterward she appeared on earth
    and lived with humankind.

4 She is the book of the commandments
        of God,
    the law that endures forever.
    All who hold her fast will live,
        and those who forsake her will die.
2 Turn, O Jacob, and take her;
    walk toward the shining of her light.
3 Do not give your glory to another,
    or your advantages to an alien people.
4 Happy are we, O Israel,
    for we know what is pleasing to God.

3.9–4.4: A poem about God's wisdom. This section
is very similar to Prov 8–9, Job 28, Wis 7.15–22, and
especially Sir 24. However, unlike these, it lacks the role
of wisdom in creation, and includes the theme of Israel's exile as punishment found in the penitential
prayer above (see comment on 1.15–3.8). 9: Compare

Deut 30.19. The command to *hear* is similar both to
the giving of the law in Deut 4.1, 5.1, and 6.4 and to
the call of wisdom or the wise teacher in Prov 1.8, 9.1–
6, and Sir 51.23–25. The parallelism* of the two lines
here implies a relationship between God's *commandments* and *wisdom*, but the full nature of the relationship does not become clear until the end of the poem.
15–37: *Who has found her place?* See Job 28.12–28.
The *rulers of the nations,* despite their worldly achievements, will pass away. In the author's view, other
nations have no means of finding the wisdom of God;
Canaan and *Teman* were famous for their wisdom
(Ezek 28.4; Jer 49.7), but along with the others are not
able to find true wisdom. Even the *giants,* who had
divine origins (Gen 6.1–4), were unable to find wisdom. **4.1–4**: God alone, who commands the obedience of the heavens, gave wisdom to Israel, and it is
identified with *the book of the commandments of
God,* that is, the law (Sir 24.23). Job does not state
explicitly that wisdom can be found in the law, but
rather in "the fear of the Lord" (Job 28.28; Prov 9.10).

THE ZION* POEM

4.5–5.9: This poetic section borrows much from Isa
40–66 and Deut 28–32. The central theme, as in the
previous sections, is that the Jews of the exile looked
back on their sin and, through penitence, could look
forward to a return to God.

5 Take courage, my people,
    who perpetuate Israel's name!
6 It was not for destruction
    that you were sold to the nations,
    but you were handed over to your
        enemies
    because you angered God.
7 For you provoked the one who made you
    by sacrificing to demons and not to
        God.
8 You forgot the everlasting God, who
        brought you up,
    and you grieved Jerusalem, who reared
        you.
9 For she saw the wrath that came upon
        you from God,
    and she said:
    Listen, you neighbors of Zion,
        God has brought great sorrow upon me;
10 for I have seen the exile of my sons and
        daughters,

which the Everlasting brought upon
them.

11 With joy I nurtured them,
but I sent them away with weeping
and sorrow.

12 Let no one rejoice over me, a widow
and bereaved of many;
I was left desolate because of the sins of
my children,
because they turned away from the
law of God.

13 They had no regard for his statutes;
they did not walk in the ways of God's
commandments,
or tread the paths his righteousness
showed them.

14 Let the neighbors of Zion come;
remember the capture of my sons and
daughters,
which the Everlasting brought upon
them.

15 For he brought a distant nation against
them,
a nation ruthless and of a strange
language,
which had no respect for the aged
and no pity for a child.

16 They led away the widow's beloved sons,
and bereaved the lonely woman of her
daughters.

17 But I, how can I help you?

18 For he who brought these calamities
upon you
will deliver you from the hand of your
enemies.

19 Go, my children, go;
for I have been left desolate.

20 I have taken off the robe of peace
and put on sackcloth for my
supplication;
I will cry to the Everlasting all my
days.

21 Take courage, my children, cry to God,
and he will deliver you from the
power and hand of the enemy.

22 For I have put my hope in the
Everlasting to save you,
and joy has come to me from the
Holy One,

because of the mercy that will soon
come to you
from your everlasting savior.[a]

23 For I sent you out with sorrow and
weeping,
but God will give you back to me with
joy and gladness forever.

24 For as the neighbors of Zion have now
seen your capture,
so they soon will see your salvation by
God,
which will come to you with great glory
and with the splendor of the
Everlasting.

25 My children, endure with patience the
wrath that has come upon you
from God.
Your enemy has overtaken you,
but you will soon see their
destruction
and will tread upon their necks.

26 My pampered children have traveled
rough roads;
they were taken away like a flock
carried off by the enemy.

27 Take courage, my children, and cry to
God,
for you will be remembered by the
one who brought this upon you.

28 For just as you were disposed to go
astray from God,
return with tenfold zeal to seek him.

29 For the one who brought these
calamities upon you
will bring you everlasting joy with
your salvation.

**4.9–29: Zion,* representing Jerusalem, is personi-
fied as a grieving widow.** This section is heavily indebted to Isa 51.17–20 and Lam 1.1; 2.19–22, but it
is longer, somewhat more simplistic in its imagery, and
ultimately less artistic as poetry of grief. However, this
poem addresses the needs of a different audience and
situation. Many of Baruch's earlier motifs* are present
here, especially the explanation of God's punishment
as recompense for forsaking the *law of God* (vv. 12–
13). The description of the destruction is borrowed in

a Or from the Everlasting, your savior

part from Deut 28.49–50. **20:** *Sackcloth* is the garment of mourning. **21–29:** As before, images of destruction are followed by predictions of deliverance. **24–25:** The neighboring nations witnessed Israel's oppression; now they will bear witness to the *salvation by God,* and Israel *will tread upon their necks.* In Second Isaiah (Isa 40–55), it is Cyrus of Persia who will defeat other nations (Isa 45.1), and they will witness God's restoration of Israel. The triumphant tone, except in regard to Babylon, is usually a metaphor for the reverence of other nations (Isa 55.4–5) and does not imply their destruction and rule by Israel. However, in Third Isaiah (Isa 56–66), as here, the military triumph of Israel is emphasized (Isa 63).

30 Take courage, O Jerusalem,
    for the one who named you will
       comfort you.
31 Wretched will be those who mistreated
       you
    and who rejoiced at your fall.
32 Wretched will be the cities that your
       children served as slaves;
    wretched will be the city that received
       your offspring.
33 For just as she rejoiced at your fall
    and was glad for your ruin,
    so she will be grieved at her own
       desolation.
34 I will take away her pride in her great
       population,
    and her insolence will be turned to
       grief.
35 For fire will come upon her from the
       Everlasting for many days,
    and for a long time she will be
       inhabited by demons.

36 Look toward the east, O Jerusalem,
    and see the joy that is coming to you
       from God.
37 Look, your children are coming, whom
       you sent away;
    they are coming, gathered from east
       and west,
    at the word of the Holy One,
       rejoicing in the glory of God.

5 Take off the garment of your sorrow
       and affliction, O Jerusalem,
    and put on forever the beauty of the
       glory from God.
2 Put on the robe of the righteousness
       that comes from God;
    put on your head the diadem of the
       glory of the Everlasting;
3 for God will show your splendor
       everywhere under heaven.
4 For God will give you evermore the name,
    "Righteous Peace, Godly Glory."

5 Arise, O Jerusalem, stand upon the
       height;
    look toward the east,
    and see your children gathered from
       west and east
    at the word of the Holy One,
       rejoicing that God has remembered
       them.
6 For they went out from you on foot,
    led away by their enemies;
    but God will bring them back to you,
       carried in glory, as on a royal throne.
7 For God has ordered that every high
       mountain and the everlasting
       hills be made low
    and the valleys filled up, to make level
       ground,
    so that Israel may walk safely in the
       glory of God.
8 The woods and every fragrant tree
    have shaded Israel at God's command.
9 For God will lead Israel with joy,
    in the light of his glory,
    with the mercy and righteousness
       that come from him.

4.30–5.9: Jerusalem is addressed and assured of deliverance. Isaiah 40–66 is especially influential in this section; at some points the poetry is nearly identical. The fall of Babylon as part of Israel's vindication is based on Isa 43.14 and ch. 47, but it is quite different from the tone of Bar 1.11–12. **36–37:** As in Isaiah, Jerusalem looks forward to the return of her children.

THE LETTER OF JEREMIAH

Introduction

In ancient Judaism there was a sizable literature of writings in the name of Jeremiah and his scribe* Baruch (see Lamentations and Baruch). The Letter of Jeremiah, written in about third to second century BCE, purports to be the letter that Jeremiah wrote to the exiles who were deported by King Nebuchadnezzar to Babylon in 597 BCE (Jer 29.1). It is not a real letter—it lacks the typical beginning and end of an ancient letter—but rather a moral exhortation* that takes on the authority of Jeremiah. Its genre* is like other hortatory* letters that may have been read as sermons, such as Letter to the Hebrews, 1 and 2 Peter, and letters of some of the early Christian apostolic fathers.

The Letter of Jeremiah, like Daniel and Baruch, assumes a setting in the Exile* to address issues of Jews in the Greco-Roman period. It takes up the specific problem of Jews worshipping foreign idols. This theme is found in early Old Testament texts, but in later biblical literature it often takes on a satirical tone (Jer 10.3–5; Isa 44.9–20; Wis 13.10–19; Bel and the Dragon).

READING GUIDE

The Letter of Jeremiah can be divided into ten short sections (6.1–7, 8–16, 17–23, 24–29, 30–40a, 40b–44, 45–52, 53–56, 57–65, 66–69), the last nine of which conclude with a similar refrain:

vv. 16, 23, 29   they are not gods, so do not fear them
vv. 40, 44, 52, 56   why must anyone think that they are gods?
vv. 65, 69   they are not gods, so do not fear them

This creates a repetitive and rambling argument that has been criticized by modern scholars, but the arrangement becomes more meaningful if it is read as an oral sermon. The text becomes a cyclical meditation on the illusory nature of idols, which repeats the message over and over to bring the hearer to the inevitable conclusion that belief in idols is absurd (vv. 70–71).

The Letter of Jeremiah was probably written in Hebrew, although the earliest known fragment, discovered at Qumran, is in Greek. Although it was rarely quoted in ancient Judaism or Christianity, it evidently influenced the early Christian *Apology of Aristides*. In some ancient and modern versions of the Bible, it is printed as the sixth chapter of Baruch; consequently, it is often, as here, numbered accordingly. Although it originally had no connection with Baruch, it can be read as a further expression of many of the same themes.

6 ^aA copy of a letter that Jeremiah sent to those who were to be taken to Babylon as exiles by the king of the Babylonians, to give them the message that God had commanded him.

2 Because of the sins that you have committed before God, you will be taken to Babylon as exiles by Nebuchadnezzar, king of the Babylonians. 3Therefore when you have come to Babylon you will remain there for many years, for a long time, up to seven gen-

a The King James Version (like the Latin Vulgate) prints The Letter of Jeremiah as Chapter 6 of the Book of Baruch, and the chapter and verse numbers are here retained. In the Greek Septuagint, the Letter is separated from Baruch by the Book of Lamentations.

erations; after that I will bring you away from there in peace. ⁴Now in Babylon you will see gods made of silver and gold and wood, which people carry on their shoulders, and which cause the heathen to fear. ⁵So beware of becoming at all like the foreigners or of letting fear for these gods*ᵃ* possess you ⁶when you see the multitude before and behind them worshiping them. But say in your heart, "It is you, O Lord, whom we must worship." ⁷For my angel is with you, and he is watching over your lives.

6.1–7: The basic issue is stated: the folly of idol worship. The text is introduced as the letter that *Jeremiah* sent to *Babylon* after the first deportation of Jews in 597 BCE, on the model of the letter described in Jer 29.1. At times the speaker appears to be God (vv. 3, 7), but as a prophet, Jeremiah can pronounce God's own words (Jer 25.12–13). **2–3:** The Exile* is seen as punishment for the sins of the people (Bar 1.15–3.8; Prayer of Azariah). It is unclear why it is said that the recipients will stay in *Babylon* for *seven generations,* since Cyrus of Persia allowed Jews to return sixty years later. However, seven generations is an indefinite number of years that may connote the continuing experience of Jews in the various nations of the Diaspora,* a metaphorical* exile. **4–7:** The prohibition of images and idols was an ancient Israelite belief (Ex 20.4), and later texts posed the problem of refusing to worship them (Dan 4; Jdt 3.8). Jews are urged to contrast the idols with their strict monotheism, lack of images, and trust in God's *angel* to watch over them (Gen 48.16; Ex 23.20; 32.34; Tob 5; Dan 12.1).

8 Their tongues are smoothed by the carpenter, and they themselves are overlaid with gold and silver; but they are false and cannot speak. ⁹People*ᵇ* take gold and make crowns for the heads of their gods, as they might for a girl who loves ornaments. ¹⁰Sometimes the priests secretly take gold and silver from their gods and spend it on themselves, ¹¹or even give some of it to the prostitutes on the terrace. They deck their gods*ᵉ* out with garments like human beings—these gods of silver and gold and wood ¹²that cannot save themselves from rust and corrosion. When they have been dressed in purple robes, ¹³their faces are wiped because of the dust from the temple, which is

thick upon them. ¹⁴One of them holds a scepter, like a district judge, but is unable to destroy anyone who offends it. ¹⁵Another has a dagger in its right hand, and an ax, but cannot defend itself from war and robbers. ¹⁶From this it is evident that they are not gods; so do not fear them.

6.8–16: Idols are decorated by human beings. The making of idols is ridiculed in detail, as a way of exposing their natural, rather than supernatural, origins. The materials are even put to multiple purposes, often mundane or sinful. Jews, and later Christians, assumed that those who worship idols lose sight of the distinction between the material and the god worshipped. **11:** In the biblical tradition (Deut 23.17–18; 1 Kings 14.24) and elsewhere (Herodotus, *Histories* 1.199), it is often asserted that *prostitutes* were present at the temples of foreign cults for the worshippers who came there. It is not certain whether such cult prostitutes* really existed or whether this is a polemical* exaggeration. **14–15:** The author probably had in mind depictions of deities with *scepters* and *axes,* which would have been familiar to the audience, and of gods carried in religious processions (Isa 46.7).

17 For just as someone's dish is useless when it is broken, ¹⁸so are their gods when they have been set up in the temples. Their eyes are full of the dust raised by the feet of those who enter. And just as the gates are shut on every side against anyone who has offended a king, as though under sentence of death, so the priests make their temples secure with doors and locks and bars, in order that they may not be plundered by robbers. ¹⁹They light more lamps for them than they light for themselves, though their gods*ᵈ* can see none of them. ²⁰They are*ᵉ* just like a beam of the temple, but their hearts, it is said, are eaten away when crawling creatures from the earth devour them and their robes. They do not notice ²¹when their faces have been blackened by the smoke of the temple. ²²Bats, swallows, and birds alight on their bodies and heads; and so do cats. ²³From this you will know that they are not gods; so do not fear them.

---

a Gk *for them*   *b* Gk *They*   *c* Gk *them*   *d* Gk *they*
e Gk *It is*

6.17–23: Idols are protected, but to no avail. The satire continues with more comparisons to the everyday world: Gods are like broken dishes; they must be locked up to protect them from robbers; they are befouled by animals; and so on.

24 As for the gold that they wear for beauty—it[a] will not shine unless someone wipes off the tarnish; for even when they were being cast, they did not feel it. 25They are bought without regard to cost, but there is no breath in them. 26Having no feet, they are carried on the shoulders of others, revealing to humankind their worthlessness. And those who serve them are put to shame 27because, if any of these gods falls[b] to the ground, they themselves must pick it up. If anyone sets it upright, it cannot move itself; and if it is tipped over, it cannot straighten itself. Gifts are placed before them just as before the dead. 28The priests sell the sacrifices that are offered to these gods[c] and use the money themselves. Likewise their wives preserve some of the meat[d] with salt, but give none to the poor or helpless. 29Sacrifices to them may even be touched by women in their periods or at childbirth. Since you know by these things that they are not gods, do not fear them.

6.24–29: The priests and their wives are guilty of moral and ritual errors. 27: 1 Sam 5.1–5. **29:** Jewish identity and ritual purity in the Diaspora* were often emphasized by the avoidance of contact with *women in their periods or at childbirth.*

30 For how can they be called gods? Women serve meals for gods of silver and gold and wood; 31and in their temples the priests sit with their clothes torn, their heads and beards shaved, and their heads uncovered. 32They howl and shout before their gods as some do at a funeral banquet. 33The priests take some of the clothing of their gods[e] to clothe their wives and children. 34Whether one does evil to them or good, they will not be able to repay it. They cannot set up a king or depose one. 35Likewise they are not able to give either wealth or money; if one makes a vow to them and does not keep it, they will not require it. 36They cannot save anyone from death or rescue the weak from the strong. 37They cannot restore sight to the blind; they cannot rescue one who is in distress. 38They cannot take pity on a widow or do good to an orphan. 39These things that are made of wood and overlaid with gold and silver are like stones from the mountain, and those who serve them will be put to shame. 40Why then must anyone think that they are gods, or call them gods?

6.30–40a: Despite people's reverence, the idols are impotent. 35–38: In the Diaspora,* the foreign *gods* would have been attractive as benevolent deities who would aid the suppliant. It is probably the appeal of the foreign gods as alleged providers of health or wealth that is being countered here.

Besides, even the Chaldeans themselves dishonor them; for when they see someone who cannot speak, they bring Bel and pray that the mute may speak, as though Bel[f] were able to understand! 41Yet they themselves cannot perceive this and abandon them, for they have no sense. 42And the women, with cords around them, sit along the passageways, burning bran for incense. 43When one of them is led off by one of the passers-by and is taken to bed by him, she derides the woman next to her, because she was not as attractive as herself and her cord was not broken. 44Whatever is done for these idols[g] is false. Why then must anyone think that they are gods, or call them gods?

6.40b–44: Even the Chaldeans do not show proper respect. The *Chaldeans,* or Babylonians, worshiped *Bel* (Marduk) as their chief god (Isa 46.1). Cult prostitutes* are described again here (see comment on 6.11).

45 They are made by carpenters and goldsmiths; they can be nothing but what the ar-

a Lat Syr: Gk *they*　　b Gk *if they fall*　　c Gk *to them*
d Gk *of them*　　e Gk *some of their clothing*　　f Gk *he*
g Gk *them*

tisans wish them to be. [46]Those who make them will certainly not live very long themselves; [47]how then can the things that are made by them be gods? They have left only lies and reproach for those who come after. [48]For when war or calamity comes upon them, the priests consult together as to where they can hide themselves and their gods.[a] [49]How then can one fail to see that these are not gods, for they cannot save themselves from war or calamity? [50]Since they are made of wood and overlaid with gold and silver, it will afterward be known that they are false. [51]It will be manifest to all the nations and kings that they are not gods but the work of human hands, and that there is no work of God in them. [52]Who then can fail to know that they are not gods?[b]

6.45–52: Idols are impotent to save themselves or others. This section and the next two repeat the same arguments from before. The oral, sermonic nature of the writing would have allowed for a reprise of the main themes, but here they are pressed further in some respects.

53 For they cannot set up a king over a country or give rain to people. [54]They cannot judge their own cause or deliver one who is wronged, for they have no power; [55]they are like crows between heaven and earth. When fire breaks out in a temple of wooden gods overlaid with gold or silver, their priests will flee and escape, but the gods[c] will be burned up like timbers. [56]Besides, they can offer no resistance to king or enemy. Why then must anyone admit or think that they are gods?

6.53–56: Previous arguments are repeated. The idols are even less able to protect themselves from *fire* than are *their priests.*

57 Gods made of wood and overlaid with silver and gold are unable to save themselves from thieves or robbers. [58]Anyone who can will strip them of their gold and silver and of the robes they wear, and go off with this booty, and they will not be able to help themselves. [59]So it is better to be a king who shows his courage, or a household utensil

that serves its owner's need, than to be these false gods; better even the door of a house that protects its contents, than these false gods; better also a wooden pillar in a palace, than these false gods.

60 For sun and moon and stars are bright, and when sent to do a service, they are obedient. [61]So also the lightning, when it flashes, is widely seen; and the wind likewise blows in every land. [62]When God commands the clouds to go over the whole world, they carry out his command. [63]And the fire sent from above to consume mountains and woods does what it is ordered. But these idols[d] are not to be compared with them in appearance or power. [64]Therefore one must not think that they are gods, nor call them gods, for they are not able either to decide a case or to do good to anyone. [65]Since you know then that they are not gods, do not fear them.

66 They can neither curse nor bless kings; [67]they cannot show signs in the heavens for the nations, or shine like the sun or give light like the moon. [68]The wild animals are better than they are, for they can flee to shelter and help themselves. [69]So we have no evidence whatever that they are gods; therefore do not fear them.

6.57–69. 57–65: Idols cannot be compared to God. A *king* is more powerful than idols, but even a *household utensil* is more useful, and the *door of a house* is better able to *protect its contents.* The comparisons thus reduce idols even further; the result, though repetitive, is also comical. The net result of all the examples that have been brought forth is to lead to the conclusion that the reverence of idols is absurd. **60–63:** Celestial phenomena are superior to idols, but even they are *obedient* to *God* (Job 28.24–26; Ps 8.3–4; Bar 3.33–34). **66–69:** Summary comparisons of idols.

70 Like a scarecrow in a cucumber bed, which guards nothing, so are their gods of wood, overlaid with gold and silver. [71]In the same way, their gods of wood, overlaid with

---

a Gk *them*   *b* Meaning of Gk uncertain   *c* Gk *they*
d Gk *these things*

gold and silver, are like a thornbush in a garden on which every bird perches; or like a corpse thrown out in the darkness. [72] From the purple and linen[a] that rot upon them you will know that they are not gods; and they will finally be consumed themselves, and be a reproach in the land. [73] Better, therefore, is someone upright who has no idols; such a person will be far above reproach.

6.70–73: Final comparisons and conclusion. 70: Jer 10.5. **70–71:** A humorous comparison leads to the possibility of idols becoming ritually polluted *like a corpse.* **73:** The sermon ends with the main exhortation* and the philosophical lesson that is to be carried into everyday life.

a Cn: Gk *marble,* Syr *silk*

THE PRAYER OF AZARIAH
AND THE SONG OF THE THREE JEWS

Introduction

The Prayer of Azariah and the Song of the Three Young Jews are placed between Dan 3.23 and 3.24 in two Greek versions of Daniel (Septuagint★ and Theodotion) and in the Latin Vulgate.★ They therefore constitute part of the Roman Catholic version of Daniel, but they appear only in the Apocrypha★ of Protestant Bibles and do not appear in Jewish Bibles at all. The Prayer of Azariah is a typical form of the national or communal lament,★ which appeals to God for mercy in a time of crisis, and the Song of the Three Young Jews is a typical psalm of praise, extolling God as creator.

The Prayer of Azariah was probably composed in the mid-second century BCE, about the same time as the visions of Dan 7–12, to call for deliverance from Antiochus IV. The Song of the Three Young Jews was likely composed in the third to second centuries BCE, perhaps for use in the Temple★ liturgy.★ Both were originally written in either Hebrew or Aramaic★ and later translated.

READING GUIDE

Although neither piece was originally composed as part of Daniel, they are best read in light of that context, as they highlight the piety of the three young men in keeping with the tales of Dan 1–6.

(Additions to Daniel, inserted between 3.23 and 3.24)
1 They[a] walked around in the midst of the flames, singing hymns to God and blessing the Lord. 2 Then Azariah stood still in the fire and prayed aloud:

1.1–2: Narrative★ introduction. These verses tie the following poetic material into the narrative context of Dan 3.23. Only Azariah speaks in the version of Theodotion, whereas all three youths speak in the Septuagint.★

---

3 "Blessed are you, O Lord, God of our
  ancestors, and worthy of praise;
  and glorious is your name forever!
4 For you are just in all you have done;
  all your works are true and your ways
    right,
  and all your judgments are true.
5 You have executed true judgments in all
    you have brought upon us

and upon Jerusalem, the holy city of
    our ancestors;
  by a true judgment you have brought
    all this upon us because of our
    sins.
6 For we have sinned and broken your law
    in turning away from you;
  in all matters we have sinned
    grievously.
7 We have not obeyed your
    commandments,
  we have not kept them or done what
    you have commanded us for our
    own good.
8 So all that you have brought upon us,
  and all that you have done to us,
    you have done by a true judgment.

---

a That is, Hananiah, Mishael, and Azariah (Dan 2.17), the original names of Shadrach, Meshach, and Abednego (Dan 1.6–7)

9 You have handed us over to our
      enemies, lawless and hateful
      rebels,
   and to an unjust king, the most
      wicked in all the world.
10 And now we cannot open our mouths;
   we, your servants who worship you,
      have become a shame and a
      reproach.
11 For your name's sake do not give us up
      forever,
   and do not annul your covenant.
12   Do not withdraw your mercy from us,
   for the sake of Abraham your beloved
      and for the sake of your servant Isaac
      and Israel your holy one,
13 to whom you promised
   to multiply their descendants like the
      stars of heaven
   and like the sand on the shore of the
      sea.
14 For we, O Lord, have become fewer
      than any other nation,
   and are brought low this day in all the
      world because of our sins.
15 In our day we have no ruler, or prophet,
      or leader,
   no burnt offering, or sacrifice, or
      oblation, or incense,
   no place to make an offering before
      you and to find mercy.
16 Yet with a contrite heart and a humble
      spirit may we be accepted,
17   as though it were with burnt offerings
      of rams and bulls,
   or with tens of thousands of fat
      lambs;
   such may our sacrifice be in your
      sight today,
   and may we unreservedly follow you,[a]
   for no shame will come to those who
      trust in you.
18 And now with all our heart we follow
      you;
   we fear you and seek your presence.
19 Do not put us to shame,
   but deal with us in your patience
   and in your abundant mercy.
20 Deliver us in accordance with your
      marvelous works,
   and bring glory to your name, O Lord.

21 Let all who do harm to your servants be
      put to shame;
   let them be disgraced and deprived of
      all power,
   and let their strength be broken.
22 Let them know that you alone are the
      Lord God,
   glorious over the whole world."

1.3–22: Azariah's prayer. The prayer includes various elements of the communal or national lament* form of the psalms (Ps 44; 74; 79; 80; see Neh 9; Dan 9.4–20; Bar 1.15–3.8). **3–4:** Introductory invocation of God and God's righteous attributes. **5–10:** A confession of sin that acknowledges God's justice in bringing about punishment. **9:** *An unjust king,* Nebuchadnezzar or Antiochus IV. **11–22:** An appeal for God to show *mercy* and to restore the *covenant.* **11:** *For your name's sake,* Ezek 20.13–17; 36.22–23; see also Ex 32.11–15; Num 14.13–19. **12–13:** The psalmist cites the covenant with *Abraham* as the basis for the appeal (Gen 22.17).

23 Now the king's servants who threw them in kept stoking the furnace with naphtha, pitch, tow, and brushwood. 24 And the flames poured out above the furnace forty-nine cubits, 25 and spread out and burned those Chaldeans who were caught near the furnace. 26 But the angel of the Lord came down into the furnace to be with Azariah and his companions, and drove the fiery flame out of the furnace, 27 and made the inside of the furnace as though a moist wind were whistling through it. The fire did not touch them at all and caused them no pain or distress.

1.23–27: The stoking of the furnace. This brief prose interlude continues the hyperbole* of the Daniel narrative* to enhance the miraculous deliverance of the three young men.

28 Then the three with one voice praised and glorified and blessed God in the furnace:
29 "Blessed are you, O Lord, God of our
      ancestors,
   and to be praised and highly exalted
      forever;

a Meaning of Gk uncertain

30 And blessed is your glorious, holy name,
   and to be highly praised and highly
   exalted forever.
31 Blessed are you in the temple of your
   holy glory,
   and to be extolled and highly glorified
   forever.
32 Blessed are you who look into the
   depths from your throne on the
   cherubim,
   and to be praised and highly exalted
   forever.
33 Blessed are you on the throne of your
   kingdom,
   and to be extolled and highly exalted
   forever.
34 Blessed are you in the firmament of
   heaven,
   and to be sung and glorified forever.

35 "Bless the Lord, all you works of the
   Lord;
   sing praise to him and highly exalt
   him forever.
36 Bless the Lord, you heavens;
   sing praise to him and highly exalt
   him forever.
37 Bless the Lord, you angels of the Lord;
   sing praise to him and highly exalt
   him forever.
38 Bless the Lord, all you waters above the
   heavens;
   sing praise to him and highly exalt
   him forever.
39 Bless the Lord, all you powers of the
   Lord;
   sing praise to him and highly exalt
   him forever.
40 Bless the Lord, sun and moon;
   sing praise to him and highly exalt
   him forever.
41 Bless the Lord, stars of heaven;
   sing praise to him and highly exalt
   him forever.

42 "Bless the Lord, all rain and dew;
   sing praise to him and highly exalt
   him forever.
43 Bless the Lord, all you winds;
   sing praise to him and highly exalt
   him forever.

44 Bless the Lord, fire and heat;
   sing praise to him and highly exalt
   him forever.
45 Bless the Lord, winter cold and summer
   heat;
   sing praise to him and highly exalt
   him forever.
46 Bless the Lord, dews and falling snow;
   sing praise to him and highly exalt
   him forever.
47 Bless the Lord, nights and days;
   sing praise to him and highly exalt
   him forever.
48 Bless the Lord, light and darkness;
   sing praise to him and highly exalt
   him forever.
49 Bless the Lord, ice and cold;
   sing praise to him and highly exalt
   him forever.
50 Bless the Lord, frosts and snows;
   sing praise to him and highly exalt
   him forever.
51 Bless the Lord, lightnings and clouds;
   sing praise to him and highly exalt
   him forever.

52 "Let the earth bless the Lord;
   let it sing praise to him and highly
   exalt him forever.
53 Bless the Lord, mountains and hills;
   sing praise to him and highly exalt
   him forever.
54 Bless the Lord, all that grows in the
   ground;
   sing praise to him and highly exalt
   him forever.
55 Bless the Lord, seas and rivers;
   sing praise to him and highly exalt
   him forever.
56 Bless the Lord, you springs;
   sing praise to him and highly exalt
   him forever.
57 Bless the Lord, you whales and all that
   swim in the waters;
   sing praise to him and highly exalt
   him forever.
58 Bless the Lord, all birds of the air;
   sing praise to him and highly exalt
   him forever.
59 Bless the Lord, all wild animals and
   cattle;

sing praise to him and highly exalt
   him forever.

60 "Bless the Lord, all people on earth;
   sing praise to him and highly exalt
      him forever.
61 Bless the Lord, O Israel;
   sing praise to him and highly exalt
      him forever.
62 Bless the Lord, you priests of the Lord;
   sing praise to him and highly exalt
      him forever.
63 Bless the Lord, you servants of the Lord;
   sing praise to him and highly exalt
      him forever.
64 Bless the Lord, spirits and souls of the
      righteous;
   sing praise to him and highly exalt
      him forever.
65 Bless the Lord, you who are holy and
      humble in heart;
   sing praise to him and highly exalt
      him forever.

66 "Bless the Lord, Hananiah, Azariah, and
      Mishael;
   sing praise to him and highly exalt
      him forever.
For he has rescued us from Hades and
   saved us from the power*a* of death,

and delivered us from the midst of
   the burning fiery furnace;
from the midst of the fire he has
   delivered us.
67 Give thanks to the Lord, for he is
      good,
   for his mercy endures forever.
68 All who worship the Lord, bless the God
      of gods,
   sing praise to him and give thanks to
      him,
   for his mercy endures forever."

1.28–68: The Song of the Three Young Jews. This psalm of praise extols God as creator of the universe (see Ps 96; 97; 136; 148). There is an overall progression from heaven to earth. **28:** Narrative* introduction. **29–34:** A royal enthronement hymn that directly addresses God. The ark in the holy of holies in the Temple* portrays God's *throne* in heaven (1 Sam 4.4; 2 Sam 6.2; 1 Kings 6.23–28; Ps 18.7–15; 68.33–35). **35–41:** Praise from the creatures of heaven. **42–51:** Praise from the elements of heaven that affect the earth. **52–59:** Praise from the creatures of the earth. **60–68:** Praise from human beings, including *Hananiah, Azariah, and Mishael.* **67–68:** Ps 136.1–3.

a Gk hand

SUSANNA (Chapter 13 of the Greek Version of Daniel)

Introduction

Susanna appears as Dan 13 in the Greek Septuagint★ and Latin Vulgate★ versions and prior to Dan 1 in the Greek version of Theodotion. It is therefore part of the Roman Catholic book of Daniel, but it appears in the Apocrypha★ of Protestant Bibles and does not appear in Jewish Bibles. Susanna is a typical example of Jewish novelistic★ literature during the Second Temple★ period (see Esther; Tobit; Judith). It is intended to promote adherence to Jewish tradition and observance by portraying the vindication of a righteous woman against attempted rape and false charges of adultery.

Susanna was composed independently of the book of Daniel during the second century BCE. Despite the Greek puns of vv. 54–55 and 58–59, there is evidence that Susanna was composed in Hebrew. The implicit critique of community officials is common in folk literature of the time, but it may have been directed against those Jewish leaders who cooperated with the Seleucid★ dynasty,★ which ruled Judea prior to the Maccabean revolt that restored Jewish rule.

READING GUIDE

Although Daniel's appearance at the end of Susanna explains its inclusion as part of the Greek and Latin versions of Daniel, Susanna is best read as a separate short story with its own developing plot. Its portrayal of Susanna as a righteous and educated woman who stands up for her own rights lends itself easily to feminist interpretation.

1 There was a man living in Babylon whose name was Joakim. ²He married the daughter of Hilkiah, named Susanna, a very beautiful woman and one who feared the Lord. ³Her parents were righteous, and had trained their daughter according to the law of Moses. ⁴Joakim was very rich, and had a fine garden adjoining his house; the Jews used to come to him because he was the most honored of them all.

1.1–4: Introduction. The narrative introduces *Susanna* as a beautiful, pious, and righteous woman, trained in Torah and living in the Babylonian exile.★ The names of her husband, *Joakim,* and her father, *Hilkiah,* are the names of a king of Judah (Jehoiakim, 2 Kings 24.15) and a high priest under Josiah (2 Kings 22.4), and accentuate her high status. The name *Susanna* derives from the Hebrew "Shoshanna" (lily),

which appears in Song 2.1 as a symbol of beauty and sexuality.

---

5 That year two elders from the people were appointed as judges. Concerning them the Lord had said: "Wickedness came forth from Babylon, from elders who were judges, who were supposed to govern the people." ⁶These men were frequently at Joakim's house, and all who had a case to be tried came to them there.

7 When the people left at noon, Susanna would go into her husband's garden to walk. ⁸Every day the two elders used to see her, going in and walking about, and they began to lust for her. ⁹They suppressed their consciences and turned away their eyes from looking to Heaven or remembering their duty to administer justice. ¹⁰Both were over-

whelmed with passion for her, but they did not tell each other of their distress, ¹¹for they were ashamed to disclose their lustful desire to seduce her. ¹²Day after day they watched eagerly to see her.

13 One day they said to each other, "Let us go home, for it is time for lunch." So they both left and parted from each other. ¹⁴But turning back, they met again; and when each pressed the other for the reason, they confessed their lust. Then together they arranged for a time when they could find her alone.

1.5–14: The two wicked elders. The two elders notice Susanna and begin to stalk her. *5: Wickedness came forth from Babylon . . . :* The source of the quotation is unknown (see Jer 23.14–15; 29.20–23; Isa 48.20–23; 51.4).

---

15 Once, while they were watching for an opportune day, she went in as before with only two maids, and wished to bathe in the garden, for it was a hot day. ¹⁶No one was there except the two elders, who had hidden themselves and were watching her. ¹⁷She said to her maids, "Bring me olive oil and ointments, and shut the garden doors so that I can bathe." ¹⁸They did as she told them: they shut the doors of the garden and went out by the side doors to bring what they had been commanded; they did not see the elders, because they were hiding.

19 When the maids had gone out, the two elders got up and ran to her. ²⁰They said, "Look, the garden doors are shut, and no one can see us. We are burning with desire for you; so give your consent, and lie with us. ²¹If you refuse, we will testify against you that a young man was with you, and this was why you sent your maids away."

22 Susanna groaned and said, "I am completely trapped. For if I do this, it will mean death for me; if I do not, I cannot escape your hands. ²³I choose not to do it; I will fall into your hands, rather than sin in the sight of the Lord."

24 Then Susanna cried out with a loud voice, and the two elders shouted against her. ²⁵And one of them ran and opened the garden doors. ²⁶When the people in the house heard the shouting in the garden, they rushed in at the side door to see what had happened to her. ²⁷And when the elders told their story, the servants felt very much ashamed, for nothing like this had ever been said about Susanna.

1.15–27: The attempted seduction. The action of the elders borders on rape because they threaten Susanna with blackmail. Adultery requires the death penalty, but an engaged woman who cries for help is considered innocent (Lev 20.10; Deut 22.22–24).

---

28 The next day, when the people gathered at the house of her husband Joakim, the two elders came, full of their wicked plot to have Susanna put to death. In the presence of the people they said, ²⁹"Send for Susanna daughter of Hilkiah, the wife of Joakim." ³⁰So they sent for her. And she came with her parents, her children, and all her relatives.

31 Now Susanna was a woman of great refinement and beautiful in appearance. ³²As she was veiled, the scoundrels ordered her to be unveiled, so that they might feast their eyes on her beauty. ³³Those who were with her and all who saw her were weeping.

34 Then the two elders stood up before the people and laid their hands on her head. ³⁵Through her tears she looked up toward Heaven, for her heart trusted in the Lord. ³⁶The elders said, "While we were walking in the garden alone, this woman came in with two maids, shut the garden doors, and dismissed the maids. ³⁷Then a young man, who was hiding there, came to her and lay with her. ³⁸We were in a corner of the garden, and when we saw this wickedness we ran to them. ³⁹Although we saw them embracing, we could not hold the man, because he was stronger than we, and he opened the doors and got away. ⁴⁰We did, however, seize this woman and asked who the young man was, ⁴¹but she would not tell us. These things we testify."

Because they were elders of the people and judges, the assembly believed them and condemned her to death.

1.28–41: The trial of Susanna. The two elders falsely accuse Susanna of adultery with a young man. The elders' story appears to draw upon the motifs* of the narrative* of the attempted seduction of Joseph by Potiphar's wife (Gen 39). Susanna's unveiling reflects various statements that one of the punishments for a woman accused of adultery is to be stripped (Ezek 16.37–39; Hos 2.3–10).

42 Then Susanna cried out with a loud voice, and said, "O eternal God, you know what is secret and are aware of all things before they come to be; ⁴³you know that these men have given false evidence against me. And now I am to die, though I have done none of the wicked things that they have charged against me!"

44 The Lord heard her cry. ⁴⁵Just as she was being led off to execution, God stirred up the holy spirit of a young lad named Daniel, ⁴⁶and he shouted with a loud voice, "I want no part in shedding this woman's blood!"

47 All the people turned to him and asked, "What is this you are saying?" ⁴⁸Taking his stand among them he said, "Are you such fools, O Israelites, as to condemn a daughter of Israel without examination and without learning the facts? ⁴⁹Return to court, for these men have given false evidence against her."

50 So all the people hurried back. And the rest of theᵃ elders said to him, "Come, sit among us and inform us, for God has given you the standing of an elder." ⁵¹Daniel said to them, "Separate them far from each other, and I will examine them."

52 When they were separated from each other, he summoned one of them and said to him, "You old relic of wicked days, your sins have now come home, which you have committed in the past, ⁵³pronouncing unjust judgments, condemning the innocent and acquitting the guilty, though the Lord said, 'You shall not put an innocent and righteous person to death.' ⁵⁴Now then, if you really saw this woman, tell me this: Under what tree did you see them being intimate with each other?" He answered, "Under a mastic tree."ᵇ ⁵⁵And Daniel said, "Very well!

This lie has cost you your head, for the angel of God has received the sentence from God and will immediately cutᵇ you in two."

56 Then, putting him to one side, he ordered them to bring the other. And he said to him, "You offspring of Canaan and not of Judah, beauty has beguiled you and lust has perverted your heart. ⁵⁷This is how you have been treating the daughters of Israel, and they were intimate with you through fear; but a daughter of Judah would not tolerate your wickedness. ⁵⁸Now then, tell me: Under what tree did you catch them being intimate with each other?" He answered, "Under an evergreen oak."ᶜ ⁵⁹Daniel said to him, "Very well! This lie has cost you also your head, for the angel of God is waiting with his sword to splitᶜ you in two, so as to destroy you both."

60 Then the whole assembly raised a great shout and blessed God, who saves those who hope in him. ⁶¹And they took action against the two elders, because out of their own mouths Daniel had convicted them of bearing false witness; they did to them as they had wickedly planned to do to their neighbor. ⁶²Acting in accordance with the law of Moses, they put them to death. Thus innocent blood was spared that day.

63 Hilkiah and his wife praised God for their daughter Susanna, and so did her husband Joakim and all her relatives, because she was found innocent of a shameful deed. ⁶⁴And from that day onward Daniel had a great reputation among the people.

1.42–64: Daniel rescues Susanna. A full investigation is required in a case of false testimony. A false witness receives the penalty intended for the accused (Deut 19.15–21). The two elders give different stories under cross-examination. The sentencing employs puns in Greek. **54–55:** *A mastic tree:* Greek, "schinon." *Cut you:* Greek, "schisei sou." **58–59:** *An evergreen oak:* Greek, "prinon." *Split you:* Greek, "kataprisei se."

a Gk lacks *rest of the*   b The Greek words for *mastic tree* and *cut* are similar, thus forming an ironic wordplay
c The Greek words for *evergreen oak* and *split* are similar, thus forming an ironic wordplay

BEL AND THE DRAGON

(Chapter 14 of the Greek Version of Daniel)

Introduction

Bel and the Dragon appears at the end of the Greek and Latin versions of Daniel, as ch. 13 in Theodotion and as ch. 14 in the Septuagint⋆ and Vulgate.⋆ It is part of the Roman Catholic book of Daniel and the Apocrypha⋆ of Protestant Bibles, but it does not appear in Jewish Bibles. It appears to be a combination of two originally separate satirical narratives⋆ concerning Bel (vv. 1–22) and the Dragon or Serpent (vv. 23–42). It appears to draw upon the narratives concerning Nebuchadnezzar's statue in Dan 3 and Daniel in the lions' den in Dan 6, but its primary intention is to parody idol worship (see Isa 44.9–20).

Both narratives seem to presuppose a Hebrew or Aramaic⋆ original that was later translated into Greek. The sympathetic portrayal of Cyrus and the lampooning of the Babylonian cult suggests that the narratives⋆ were composed in the early second century BCE, prior to the suppression of Judaism by Antiochus IV.

READING GUIDE

Bel and the Dragon was not originally a part of Daniel, but when read with Dan 3 and 6, its humorous portrayal of Daniel's actions reminds readers that satire and laughter are also expressions of piety.

1 When King Astyages was laid to rest with his ancestors, Cyrus the Persian succeeded to his kingdom. 2 Daniel was a companion of the king, and was the most honored of all his Friends.

1.1–2: Introduction. *King Astyages,* the maternal grandfather of Cyrus, ruled the Medes from 585–550 BCE. Following his death, *Cyrus* of Persia (550–530 BCE) took the kingdom by force. He was designated as King of Babylon by the priests of Marduk (Bel) in 539 BCE.

---

3 Now the Babylonians had an idol called Bel, and every day they provided for it twelve bushels of choice flour and forty sheep and six measures*a* of wine. 4 The king revered it and went every day to worship it. But Daniel worshiped his own God.

So the king said to him, "Why do you not worship Bel?" 5 He answered, "Because I do not revere idols made with hands, but the living God, who created heaven and earth and has dominion over all living creatures."

6 The king said to him, "Do you not think that Bel is a living god? Do you not see how much he eats and drinks every day?" 7 And Daniel laughed, and said, "Do not be deceived, O king, for this thing is only clay inside and bronze outside, and it never ate or drank anything."

8 Then the king was angry and called the priests of Bel*b* and said to them, "If you do not tell me who is eating these provisions, you shall die. 9 But if you prove that Bel is eating them, Daniel shall die, because he has spoken blasphemy against Bel." Daniel said to the king, "Let it be done as you have said."

10 Now there were seventy priests of Bel,

a A little more than fifty gallons   *b* Gk *his priests* besides their wives and children. So the king went with Daniel into the temple of Bel. [11] The priests of Bel said, "See, we are now going outside; you yourself, O king, set out the food and prepare the wine, and shut the door and seal it with your signet. [12] When you return in the morning, if you do not find that Bel has eaten it all, we will die; otherwise Daniel will, who is telling lies about us." [13] They were unconcerned, for beneath the table they had made a hidden entrance, through which they used to go in regularly and consume the provisions. [14] After they had gone out, the king set out the food for Bel. Then Daniel ordered his servants to bring ashes, and they scattered them throughout the whole temple in the presence of the king alone. Then they went out, shut the door and sealed it with the king's signet, and departed. [15] During the night the priests came as usual, with their wives and children, and they ate and drank everything.

16 Early in the morning the king rose and came, and Daniel with him. [17] The king said, "Are the seals unbroken, Daniel?" He answered, "They are unbroken, O king." [18] As soon as the doors were opened, the king looked at the table, and shouted in a loud voice, "You are great, O Bel, and in you there is no deceit at all!"

19 But Daniel laughed and restrained the king from going in. "Look at the floor," he said, "and notice whose footprints these are." [20] The king said, "I see the footprints of men and women and children."

21 Then the king was enraged, and he arrested the priests and their wives and children. They showed him the secret doors through which they used to enter to consume what was on the table. [22] Therefore the king put them to death, and gave Bel over to Daniel, who destroyed it and its temple.

1.3–22: Daniel exposes the priests of Bel. *Bel*, a variant of Baal,* is a title commonly ascribed to Marduk, the city god of Babylon and head of the Babylonian pantheon (Isa 46.1; Jer 50.2). Herodotus describes the statue of Bel in Babylon as an 18-foot-tall, solid gold figure of a man. Like other deities in the ancient world, Bel was offered large quantities of food and drink (see Num 28–29), which supported the priests. People in

the ancient world were well aware that food offered to gods was eaten by the priests or used for other purposes, but this narrative* is intended to satirize the pagan worship of idols (see Isa 44.9–20). The temple of Bel in Babylon was destroyed by Xerxes in 486 BCE.

---

23 Now in that place[a] there was a great dragon, which the Babylonians revered. [24] The king said to Daniel, "You cannot deny that this is a living god; so worship him." [25] Daniel said, "I worship the Lord my God, for he is the living God. [26] But give me permission, O king, and I will kill the dragon without sword or club." The king said, "I give you permission."

27 Then Daniel took pitch, fat, and hair, and boiled them together and made cakes, which he fed to the dragon. The dragon ate them, and burst open. Then Daniel said, "See what you have been worshiping!"

28 When the Babylonians heard about it, they were very indignant and conspired against the king, saying, "The king has become a Jew; he has destroyed Bel, and killed the dragon, and slaughtered the priests." [29] Going to the king, they said, "Hand Daniel over to us, or else we will kill you and your household." [30] The king saw that they were pressing him hard, and under compulsion he handed Daniel over to them.

1.23–30: Daniel kills the dragon. The presence of a revered dragon in the temple of Bel conveys the satirical intent of the story. Marduk (Bel) won his place at the head of the pantheon by killing Tiamat, the chaos dragon of the deep, and by splitting her body in two to create heaven and earth. The feeding of the dragon until it bursts is comedic, as the dragon idol cannot possibly eat. Cyrus was known as a friend to the Jews (Isa 44.28; 45.1; 2 Chr 36.22–23; Ezra 1.1–4).

---

31 They threw Daniel into the lions' den, and he was there for six days. [32] There were seven lions in the den, and every day they had been given two human bodies and two sheep; but now they were given nothing, so that they would devour Daniel.

33 Now the prophet Habakkuk was in Judea; he had made a stew and had broken

---

a Other ancient authorities lack *in that place*

bread into a bowl, and was going into the field to take it to the reapers. ³⁴But the angel of the Lord said to Habakkuk, "Take the food that you have to Babylon, to Daniel, in the lions' den." ³⁵Habakkuk said, "Sir, I have never seen Babylon, and I know nothing about the den." ³⁶Then the angel of the Lord took him by the crown of his head and carried him by his hair; with the speed of the wind" he set him down in Babylon, right over the den.

37 Then Habakkuk shouted, "Daniel, Daniel! Take the food that God has sent you." ³⁸Daniel said, "You have remembered me, O God, and have not forsaken those who love you." ³⁹So Daniel got up and ate. And the angel of God immediately returned Habakkuk to his own place.

40 On the seventh day the king came to mourn for Daniel. When he came to the den

he looked in, and there sat Daniel! ⁴¹The king shouted with a loud voice, "You are great, O Lord, the God of Daniel, and there is no other besides you!" ⁴²Then he pulled Daniel* out, and threw into the den those who had attempted his destruction, and they were instantly eaten before his eyes.

1.31–42: Daniel in the lions' den. See Dan 6. The prophet* Habakkuk appears in the narrative,* perhaps because he waits for a vision of the end in which the righteous will be redeemed (Hab 2.1–4). His mode of transportation resembles those of Ezekiel (Ezek 8.1); Elijah (1 Kings 18.12; 2 Kings 2.16–18); and Elisha (2 Kings 5.26). **41:** The pagan king acknowledges God.

a Or by the power of his spirit   b Gk him

1 MACCABEES

Introduction

First Maccabees is a historical chronicle* of an important period in Jewish history: the attempt by the Syrian king Antiochus to suppress traditional Jewish worship in Jerusalem, in 167 BCE, and the ensuing Maccabean revolt, that led to a century of Jewish independence. The tone is straightforward and factual. Consequently, it conveys an impression of greater reliability than does 2 Maccabees, which gives a more colorful account of the same period. This impression may be misleading. While 1 Maccabees is an important historical source, it embodies a particular interpretation of the events in question. The story is told so as to glorify the Maccabees, or the Hasmonean house, as the dynasty* established by the Maccabees is called. The Maccabees are viewed as "the family of those men through whom deliverance was given to Israel" (5.62). Their slogan, as articulated by Mattathias in 2.27, is to be zealous for the law and support the covenant.* Not all Jews, however, either then or later, agreed that militant action was the right way to express zeal for the law. Different perspectives on the same material can be found in Daniel, which has little place for human militancy, and in 2 Maccabees, where the martyrs* who submit to death are just as important as the Maccabean rebels.

First Maccabees begins by recounting the events that led up to the persecution and continues with the history of the revolt, down to the death of Simon Maccabee and the rise to power of John Hyrcanus in 134 BCE. The book was probably written during the reign of Hyrcanus (134–104 BCE), but certainly before the conquest of Judea by the Romans in 63 BCE. This was a turbulent period in Jewish history. Apocalyptic* literature, such as we find in Daniel, became prominent during the time of persecution. Apocalyptic literature is literature that reports revelations about the heavenly world and about the future. Typically, it predicts the end of this world and the judgment of the dead. It takes its name from the Apocalypse* of John in the New Testament.

After the success of the Maccabees we find the emergence of different sects* in Judaism: Pharisees,* Sadducees,* and Essenes.* The movement that produced the Dead Sea Scrolls was probably identical with the Essenes, and for much of its early history it was highly critical of the Hasmoneans (the Maccabean dynasty). In this context, 1 Maccabees represents the point of view of the ruling family. The book simply ignores many of the issues that dominate other writings of the time: issues of purity, interest in angels, and eschatological* hopes for a radical change in the course of history. But the silence of the book on these issues is itself a theological position. The focus of 1 Maccabees is on politics, power, and the establishment of a Jewish state.

First Maccabees was almost certainly written in Hebrew, although it has only survived in Greek and translations based on the Greek. Remarkably, it was not accepted into the canon* of Hebrew Scriptures,* a fact that may reflect the ambivalence of the rabbis toward the legacy of the Maccabees. The book did, however, find a place in the Greek scriptures (the Septuagint*) and consequently in the Christian Bible, in the Catholic Orthodox traditions. It is ironic that a book that describes the militant defense of Judaism should owe its preservation primarily to Christians.

READING GUIDE

First Maccabees raises fundamental questions about the religious justification of violence and nationalism. Mattathias, father of the Maccabees, invokes the precedent of Phinehas from

Num 25, who showed his zeal for the law by killing an apostate Israelite with a spear. In the case of the Maccabees, militant zeal was successful, and so seemed to win divine approval. Some two centuries later, the same model of zeal was used by Jewish revolutionaries (Zealots⋆) against Rome. This time the results were catastrophic. It is clear even from 1 Maccabees that not all Jews supported the tactics of the Maccabees. Yet these tactics have remained an influential model both for the modern state of Israel and for some strands of Christian liberation theology.

First Maccabees provides no easy answers. History is intrinsically ambiguous, and no two situations are exactly alike. Nonetheless, reflection on the past can help us understand the motives for human actions and appreciate their variable results.

1.1–10	Introductory review of Hellenistic⋆ history
1.11–2.70	The persecution under Antiochus Epiphanes⋆
3.1–9.22	The career of Judas Maccabee
9.23–12.53	The career of Jonathan Maccabee
13.1–16.22	The career of Simon Maccabee

1 After Alexander son of Philip, the Macedonian, who came from the land of Kittim, had defeated[a] King Darius of the Persians and the Medes, he succeeded him as king. (He had previously become king of Greece.) 2He fought many battles, conquered strongholds, and put to death the kings of the earth. 3He advanced to the ends of the earth, and plundered many nations. When the earth became quiet before him, he was exalted, and his heart was lifted up. 4He gathered a very strong army and ruled over countries, nations, and princes, and they became tributary to him.

5 After this he fell sick and perceived that he was dying. 6So he summoned his most honored officers, who had been brought up with him from youth, and divided his kingdom among them while he was still alive. 7And after Alexander had reigned twelve years, he died.

8 Then his officers began to rule, each in his own place. 9They all put on crowns after his death, and so did their descendants after them for many years; and they caused many evils on the earth.

10 From them came forth a sinful root, Antiochus Epiphanes, son of King Antiochus; he had been a hostage in Rome. He began to reign in the one hundred thirty-seventh year of the kingdom of the Greeks.[b]

1.1–10: Alexander the Great. 1: Alexander set out from Macedonia in 334 BCE. *The land of Kittim* can refer to any western land. The name comes from Citium in Cyprus. Here the land is Greece. In Dan 11.30 and in the Dead Sea Scrolls the Kittim are the Romans. **8:** *His officers began to rule:* Different generals ruled over Greece, Asia Minor, Syria, and Egypt. Palestine was ruled by the Ptolemies⋆ of Egypt from 301 to 198 BCE. Then it passed into the control of the Seleucid dynasty⋆ of Syria. At first Antiochus III ("the Great") was benevolent to the Jews, but when the Seleucids⋆ were defeated by Rome at Magnesia in 190 BCE, they had to pay a heavy tribute and were subsequently in constant need of funds. **10:** *Antiochus Epiphanes:* Antiochus IV. Epiphanes⋆ means "god made manifest." He had been a hostage in Rome after the battle of Magnesia. He came to the throne in 175 BCE (= year 137 of the Seleucid era, which began in 312 BCE) after the deaths of Seleucus IV (187–175) and his infant son.

11 In those days certain renegades came out from Israel and misled many, saying, "Let us go and make a covenant with the Gentiles around us, for since we separated from them many disasters have come upon us." 12This proposal pleased them, 13and some of the people eagerly went to the king, who authorized them to observe the ordi-

a Gk adds *and he defeated*   b 175 B.C.

nances of the Gentiles. ¹⁴So they built a gymnasium in Jerusalem, according to Gentile custom, ¹⁵and removed the marks of circumcision, and abandoned the holy covenant. They joined with the Gentiles and sold themselves to do evil.

16 When Antiochus saw that his kingdom was established, he determined to become king of the land of Egypt, in order that he might reign over both kingdoms. ¹⁷So he invaded Egypt with a strong force, with chariots and elephants and cavalry and with a large fleet. ¹⁸He engaged King Ptolemy of Egypt in battle, and Ptolemy turned and fled before him, and many were wounded and fell. ¹⁹They captured the fortified cities in the land of Egypt, and he plundered the land of Egypt.

1.11–19: The Hellenistic* reform. 11: *Renegades:* this episode is described in much greater detail in 2 Macc 4.7–22. **14:** The *gymnasium* was a distinctive symbol of Greek culture. It was primarily a place for physical exercise, but it was also often a center of education. **15:** The *marks of circumcision** became an embarrassment because it was the Greek custom to exercise nude. **16:** Epiphanes* invaded Egypt twice. The first invasion, in 169 BCE, was successful. First Maccabees omits the second invasion (168 BCE), which ended in humiliation at the hands of a Roman official.

20 After subduing Egypt, Antiochus returned in the one hundred forty-third year.ᵃ He went up against Israel and came to Jerusalem with a strong force. ²¹He arrogantly entered the sanctuary and took the golden altar, the lampstand for the light, and all its utensils. ²²He took also the table for the bread of the Presence, the cups for drink offerings, the bowls, the golden censers, the curtain, the crowns, and the gold decoration on the front of the temple; he stripped it all off. ²³He took the silver and the gold, and the costly vessels; he took also the hidden treasures that he found. ²⁴Taking them all, he went into his own land.

He shed much blood,
    and spoke with great arrogance.
25 Israel mourned deeply in every
    community,
26   rulers and elders groaned,

    young women and young men became
      faint,
    the beauty of the women faded.
27 Every bridegroom took up the lament;
    she who sat in the bridal chamber
      was mourning.
28 Even the land trembled for its
      inhabitants,
    and all the house of Jacob was
      clothed with shame.

29 Two years later the king sent to the cities of Judah a chief collector of tribute, and he came to Jerusalem with a large force. ³⁰Deceitfully he spoke peaceable words to them, and they believed him; but he suddenly fell upon the city, dealt it a severe blow, and destroyed many people of Israel. ³¹He plundered the city, burned it with fire, and tore down its houses and its surrounding walls. ³²They took captive the women and children, and seized the livestock. ³³Then they fortified the city of David with a great strong wall and strong towers, and it became their citadel. ³⁴They stationed there a sinful people, men who were renegades. These strengthened their position; ³⁵they stored up arms and food, and collecting the spoils of Jerusalem they stored them there, and became a great menace,

36 for the citadelᵇ became an ambush
    against the sanctuary,
    an evil adversary of Israel at all times.
37 On every side of the sanctuary they
    shed innocent blood;
    they even defiled the sanctuary.
38 Because of them the residents of
    Jerusalem fled;
    she became a dwelling of strangers;
    she became strange to her offspring,
    and her children forsook her.
39 Her sanctuary became desolate like a
    desert;
    her feasts were turned into mourning,
    her sabbaths into a reproach,
    her honor into contempt.
40 Her dishonor now grew as great as her
    glory;
    her exaltation was turned into
      mourning.

a 169 B.C.   *b* Gk *it*

41 Then the king wrote to his whole kingdom that all should be one people, 42and that all should give up their particular customs. 43All the Gentiles accepted the command of the king. Many even from Israel gladly adopted his religion; they sacrificed to idols and profaned the sabbath. 44And the king sent letters by messengers to Jerusalem and the towns of Judah; he directed them to follow customs strange to the land, 45to forbid burnt offerings and sacrifices and drink offerings in the sanctuary, to profane sabbaths and festivals, 46to defile the sanctuary and the priests, 47to build altars and sacred precincts and shrines for idols, to sacrifice swine and other unclean animals, 48and to leave their sons uncircumcised. They were to make themselves abominable by everything unclean and profane, 49so that they would forget the law and change all the ordinances. 50He added,ᵃ "And whoever does not obey the command of the king shall die."

51 In such words he wrote to his whole kingdom. He appointed inspectors over all the people and commanded the towns of Judah to offer sacrifice, town by town. 52Many of the people, everyone who forsook the law, joined them, and they did evil in the land; 53they drove Israel into hiding in every place of refuge they had.

54 Now on the fifteenth day of Chislev, in the one hundred forty-fifth year,ᵇ they erected a desolating sacrilege on the altar of burnt offering. They also built altars in the surrounding towns of Judah, 55and offered incense at the doors of the houses and in the streets. 56The books of the law that they found they tore to pieces and burned with fire. 57Anyone found possessing the book of the covenant, or anyone who adhered to the law, was condemned to death by decree of the king. 58They kept using violence against Israel, against those who were found month after month in the towns. 59On the twenty-fifth day of the month they offered sacrifice on the altar that was on top of the altar of burnt offering. 60According to the decree, they put to death the women who had their children circumcised, 61and their families and those who circumcised them; and they hung the infants from their mothers' necks.

62 But many in Israel stood firm and were resolved in their hearts not to eat unclean food. 63They chose to die rather than to be defiled by food or to profane the holy covenant; and they did die. 64Very great wrath came upon Israel.

1.20–64: The persecution. 20: After his successful invasion of Egypt, Epiphanes* plundered the Temple* of Jerusalem, simply to replenish his funds. (This is also reported by Josephus, *Against Apion* 2.83–84. Second Maccabees 5.11–21 confuses this incident with an attack on Jerusalem after the second campaign.) **24–28:** 1 Maccabees interjects a poetic lament* here and on several other occasions throughout the narrative.* **29:** The sequence of events is unclear, because 1 Maccabees fails to mention Epiphanes' second invasion of Egypt. Second Maccabees 5 makes clear that the expedition of the "collector of tribute" was a punitive expedition, after the second invasion. Fighting had broken out between two Jewish factions in Jerusalem, and the king thought that Judea was in revolt. **33:** The fortified *City of David* became known as the Akra. It became the stronghold of a colony of Syrian soldiers in the heart of Jerusalem. **42:** The claim of 1 Maccabees that the king tried to make all peoples *give up their particular customs* is not supported by any other source, and it is contradicted by other evidence about his policies. The edict was only directed against Jews, and may even have been restricted to the land of Israel. Religious persecution of this sort was highly unusual in the ancient world, and the reason for Epiphanes' edict is far from clear. It is clear from 2 Maccabees, however, that there was a violent dispute between Jewish factions, and some scholars suspect that the suppression of traditional worship was encouraged by some of the "renegades" (such as the High Priest Menelaus) who wanted to adopt gentile* ways. **54:** The *desolating sacrilege* ("the abomination of desolation") was probably a "horned" Syrian altar, superimposed on the altar of sacrifice in the Temple, but some scholars think it was an idol. **60:** Further vivid examples of persecution can be found in 2 Maccabees.

2 In those days Mattathias son of John son of Simeon, a priest of the family of Joarib, moved from Jerusalem and settled in Modein. 2He had five sons, John surnamed Gaddi, 3Simon called Thassi, 4Judas called

ᵃ Gk lacks *He added*   ᵇ 167 B.C.

Maccabeus, [5]Eleazar called Avaran, and Jonathan called Apphus. [6]He saw the blasphemies being committed in Judah and Jerusalem, [7]and said,

"Alas! Why was I born to see this,
the ruin of my people, the ruin of the holy city,
and to live there when it was given over to the enemy,
the sanctuary given over to aliens?
[8] Her temple has become like a person without honor;[a]
[9] her glorious vessels have been carried into exile.
Her infants have been killed in her streets,
her youths by the sword of the foe.
[10] What nation has not inherited her palaces[b]
and has not seized her spoils?
[11] All her adornment has been taken away;
no longer free, she has become a slave.
[12] And see, our holy place, our beauty, and our glory have been laid waste;
the Gentiles have profaned them.
[13]   Why should we live any longer?"

[14] Then Mattathias and his sons tore their clothes, put on sackcloth, and mourned greatly.

[15] The king's officers who were enforcing the apostasy came to the town of Modein to make them offer sacrifice. [16]Many from Israel came to them; and Mattathias and his sons were assembled. [17]Then the king's officers spoke to Mattathias as follows: "You are a leader, honored and great in this town, and supported by sons and brothers. [18]Now be the first to come and do what the king commands, as all the Gentiles and the people of Judah and those that are left in Jerusalem have done. Then you and your sons will be numbered among the Friends of the king, and you and your sons will be honored with silver and gold and many gifts."

[19] But Mattathias answered and said in a loud voice: "Even if all the nations that live under the rule of the king obey him, and have chosen to obey his commandments, everyone of them abandoning the religion of their ancestors, [20]I and my sons and my brothers will continue to live by the covenant of our ancestors. [21]Far be it from us to desert the law and the ordinances. [22]We will not obey the king's words by turning aside from our religion to the right hand or to the left."

[23] When he had finished speaking these words, a Jew came forward in the sight of all to offer sacrifice on the altar in Modein, according to the king's command. [24]When Mattathias saw it, he burned with zeal and his heart was stirred. He gave vent to righteous anger; he ran and killed him on the altar. [25]At the same time he killed the king's officer who was forcing them to sacrifice, and he tore down the altar. [26]Thus he burned with zeal for the law, just as Phinehas did against Zimri son of Salu.

[27] Then Mattathias cried out in the town with a loud voice, saying: "Let every one who is zealous for the law and supports the covenant come out with me!" [28]Then he and his sons fled to the hills and left all that they had in the town.

[29] At that time many who were seeking righteousness and justice went down to the wilderness to live there, [30]they, their sons, their wives, and their livestock, because troubles pressed heavily upon them. [31]And it was reported to the king's officers, and to the troops in Jerusalem the city of David, that those who had rejected the king's command had gone down to the hiding places in the wilderness. [32]Many pursued them, and overtook them; they encamped opposite them and prepared for battle against them on the sabbath day. [33]They said to them, "Enough of this! Come out and do what the king commands, and you will live." [34]But they said, "We will not come out, nor will we do what the king commands and so profane the sabbath day." [35]Then the enemy[c] quickly attacked them. [36]But they did not answer them or hurl a stone at them or block up their hiding places, [37]for they said, "Let us all die in our innocence; heaven and earth testify for us that you are killing us unjustly." [38]So they attacked them on the sabbath, and

a Meaning of Gk uncertain   b Other ancient authorities read *has not had a part in her kingdom*   c Gk *they*

they died, with their wives and children and livestock, to the number of a thousand persons.

39 When Mattathias and his friends learned of it, they mourned for them deeply. 40And all said to their neighbors: "If we all do as our kindred have done and refuse to fight with the Gentiles for our lives and for our ordinances, they will quickly destroy us from the earth." 41So they made this decision that day: "Let us fight against anyone who comes to attack us on the sabbath day; let us not all die as our kindred died in their hiding places."

42 Then there united with them a company of Hasideans, mighty warriors of Israel, all who offered themselves willingly for the law. 43And all who became fugitives to escape their troubles joined them and reinforced them. 44They organized an army, and struck down sinners in their anger and renegades in their wrath; the survivors fled to the Gentiles for safety. 45And Mattathias and his friends went around and tore down the altars; 46they forcibly circumcised all the uncircumcised boys that they found within the borders of Israel. 47They hunted down the arrogant, and the work prospered in their hands. 48They rescued the law out of the hands of the Gentiles and kings, and they never let the sinner gain the upper hand.

2.1–70: Mattathias. *Mattathias* is not mentioned in 2 Maccabees. His prominence here has the effect of exalting the whole family, not just Judas. 20: When the Syrians had first conquered Jerusalem, the Jews had been given the right to follow their ancestral laws. This right was very widely recognized in the Hellenistic* and Roman worlds. 26: In Num 25, Phinehas shows his zeal by driving his spear through an Israelite man and Midianite woman in the act of intercourse. For this God gave him a covenant* of perpetual priesthood. He became the prototypical Zealot* whose example legitimated religious violence. 29–38: The fate of the people in the wilderness highlights the dilemma of the observant Jew. Strict observance of the law forbids fighting on the sabbath. The Maccabees resolved this dilemma by making an exception in the case of this commandment. 37: The reference to *heaven and earth* is an allusion to Deut 32, in which the Lord promises that he will avenge the blood of his servants. This

allusion suggests that those who died did so in the belief that God would act to avenge them. A similar belief is found in the contemporary non-canonical* book, the *Testament of Moses*. 42: Little is known about the *Hasideans*, except that they were "mighty warriors" who later became the first to make peace (7.13). Some scholars think that they were the predecessors of both the Pharisees* and the Essenes,* but this is not certain.

49 Now the days drew near for Mattathias to die, and he said to his sons: "Arrogance and scorn have now become strong; it is a time of ruin and furious anger. 50Now, my children, show zeal for the law, and give your lives for the covenant of our ancestors.

51 "Remember the deeds of the ancestors, which they did in their generations; and you will receive great honor and an everlasting name. 52Was not Abraham found faithful when tested, and it was reckoned to him as righteousness? 53Joseph in the time of his distress kept the commandment, and became lord of Egypt. 54Phinehas our ancestor, because he was deeply zealous, received the covenant of everlasting priesthood. 55Joshua, because he fulfilled the command, became a judge in Israel. 56Caleb, because he testified in the assembly, received an inheritance in the land. 57David, because he was merciful, inherited the throne of the kingdom forever. 58Elijah, because of great zeal for the law, was taken up into heaven. 59Hananiah, Azariah, and Mishael believed and were saved from the flame. 60Daniel, because of his innocence, was delivered from the mouth of the lions.

61 "And so observe, from generation to generation, that none of those who put their trust in him will lack strength. 62Do not fear the words of sinners, for their splendor will turn into dung and worms. 63Today they will be exalted, but tomorrow they will not be found, because they will have returned to the dust, and their plans will have perished. 64My children, be courageous and grow strong in the law, for by it you will gain honor.

65 "Here is your brother Simeon who, I know, is wise in counsel; always listen to him; he shall be your father. 66Judas Mac-

cabeus has been a mighty warrior from his youth; he shall command the army for you and fight the battle against the peoples.[a] [67]You shall rally around you all who observe the law, and avenge the wrong done to your people. [68]Pay back the Gentiles in full, and obey the commands of the law."

69 Then he blessed them, and was gathered to his ancestors. [70]He died in the one hundred forty-sixth year[b] and was buried in the tomb of his ancestors at Modein. And all Israel mourned for him with great lamentation.

2.49–70: The chapter concludes with a death-bed testament of Mattathias, recalling the heroes of biblical history and endorsing Judas as his successor.

〜〜〜〜〜〜〜〜〜〜〜〜〜〜〜〜〜〜〜〜〜〜〜〜

3 Then his son Judas, who was called Maccabeus, took command in his place. [2]All his brothers and all who had joined his father helped him; they gladly fought for Israel.

3 He extended the glory of his people.
  Like a giant he put on his breastplate;
  he bound on his armor of war and
      waged battles,
  protecting the camp by his sword.
4 He was like a lion in his deeds,
  like a lion's cub roaring for prey.
5 He searched out and pursued those who
      broke the law;
  he burned those who troubled his
      people.
6 Lawbreakers shrank back for fear of
      him;
  all the evildoers were confounded;
  and deliverance prospered by his
      hand.
7 He embittered many kings,
  but he made Jacob glad by his deeds,
  and his memory is blessed forever.
8 He went through the cities of Judah;
  he destroyed the ungodly out of the
      land;[c]
  thus he turned away wrath from
      Israel.
9 He was renowned to the ends of the
      earth;
  he gathered in those who were
      perishing.

10 Apollonius now gathered together Gentiles and a large force from Samaria to fight against Israel. [11]When Judas learned of it, he went out to meet him, and he defeated and killed him. Many were wounded and fell, and the rest fled. [12]Then they seized their spoils; and Judas took the sword of Apollonius, and used it in battle the rest of his life.

13 When Seron, the commander of the Syrian army, heard that Judas had gathered a large company, including a body of faithful soldiers who stayed with him and went out to battle, [14]he said, "I will make a name for myself and win honor in the kingdom. I will make war on Judas and his companions, who scorn the king's command." [15]Once again a strong army of godless men went up with him to help him, to take vengeance on the Israelites.

16 When he approached the ascent of Beth-horon, Judas went out to meet him with a small company. [17]But when they saw the army coming to meet them, they said to Judas, "How can we, few as we are, fight against so great and so strong a multitude? And we are faint, for we have eaten nothing today." [18]Judas replied, "It is easy for many to be hemmed in by few, for in the sight of Heaven there is no difference between saving by many or by few. [19]It is not on the size of the army that victory in battle depends, but strength comes from Heaven. [20]They come against us in great insolence and lawlessness to destroy us and our wives and our children, and to despoil us; [21]but we fight for our lives and our laws. [22]He himself will crush them before us; as for you, do not be afraid of them."

23 When he finished speaking, he rushed suddenly against Seron and his army, and they were crushed before him. [24]They pursued them[d] down the descent of Beth-horon to the plain; eight hundred of them fell, and the rest fled into the land of the Philistines. [25]Then Judas and his brothers began to be feared, and terror fell on the Gentiles all around them. [26]His fame reached the king,

---

a Or of the people   *b 166 B.C.*   *c Gk it*   *d Other ancient authorities read him* and the Gentiles talked of the battles of Judas.

3.1–4.61: The early victories of Judas. 3.3: The picture of the giant dressing for battle recalls the portrayal of the divine warrior* in Isa 59.16–19. It is typical of 1 Maccabees to look to a human warrior for deliverance. 10: *Apollonius* was the "collector of tribute" who had attacked Jerusalem in 1 Macc 1.29 (compare 2 Macc 5.24). 18–19: The idea that God can give victory to the few over the many is a popular biblical motif.* Compare the story of Gideon in Judg 7, or 1 Sam 14.6: "Nothing can hinder the Lord from saving by many or by few." 25: The *terror* that fell on the gentiles* recalls the fear that fell on the nations at the time of the Exodus and conquest (compare Ex 15.15–16; Josh 5.1).

27 When King Antiochus heard these reports, he was greatly angered; and he sent and gathered all the forces of his kingdom, a very strong army. 28 He opened his coffers and gave a year's pay to his forces, and ordered them to be ready for any need. 29 Then he saw that the money in the treasury was exhausted, and that the revenues from the country were small because of the dissension and disaster that he had caused in the land by abolishing the laws that had existed from the earliest days. 30 He feared that he might not have such funds as he had before for his expenses and for the gifts that he used to give more lavishly than preceding kings. 31 He was greatly perplexed in mind; then he determined to go to Persia and collect the revenues from those regions and raise a large fund.

32 He left Lysias, a distinguished man of royal lineage, in charge of the king's affairs from the river Euphrates to the borders of Egypt. 33 Lysias was also to take care of his son Antiochus until he returned. 34 And he turned over to Lysias*a* half of his forces and the elephants, and gave him orders about all that he wanted done. As for the residents of Judea and Jerusalem, 35 Lysias was to send a force against them to wipe out and destroy the strength of Israel and the remnant of Jerusalem; he was to banish the memory of them from the place, 36 settle aliens in all their territory, and distribute their land by

lot. 37 Then the king took the remaining half of his forces and left Antioch his capital in the one hundred and forty-seventh year.*b* He crossed the Euphrates river and went through the upper provinces.

38 Lysias chose Ptolemy son of Dorymenes, and Nicanor and Gorgias, able men among the Friends of the king, 39 and sent with them forty thousand infantry and seven thousand cavalry to go into the land of Judah and destroy it, as the king had commanded. 40 So they set out with their entire force, and when they arrived they encamped near Emmaus in the plain. 41 When the traders of the region heard what was said to them, they took silver and gold in immense amounts, and fetters,*c* and went to the camp to get the Israelites for slaves. And forces from Syria and the land of the Philistines joined with them.

42 Now Judas and his brothers saw that misfortunes had increased and that the forces were encamped in their territory. They also learned what the king had commanded to do to the people to cause their final destruction. 43 But they said to one another, "Let us restore the ruins of our people, and fight for our people and the sanctuary." 44 So the congregation assembled to be ready for battle, and to pray and ask for mercy and compassion.

45 Jerusalem was uninhabited like a
    wilderness;
  not one of her children went in or
    out.
The sanctuary was trampled down,
  and aliens held the citadel;
  it was a lodging place for the
    Gentiles.
Joy was taken from Jacob;
  the flute and the harp ceased to play.

46 Then they gathered together and went to Mizpah, opposite Jerusalem, because Israel formerly had a place of prayer in Mizpah. 47 They fasted that day, put on sackcloth and sprinkled ashes on their heads, and tore their clothes. 48 And they opened the book of the law to inquire into those matters about which the Gentiles consulted the like-

a Gk *him*   *b* 165 B.C.   *c* Syr: Gk Mss, Vg *slaves* nesses of their gods. [49]They also brought the vestments of the priesthood and the first fruits and the tithes, and they stirred up the nazirites*a* who had completed their days; [50]and they cried aloud to Heaven, saying,

"What shall we do with these?
  Where shall we take them?
[51] Your sanctuary is trampled down and
      profaned,
  and your priests mourn in
      humiliation.
[52] Here the Gentiles are assembled against
      us to destroy us;
  you know what they plot against us.
[53] How will we be able to withstand them,
  if you do not help us?"

54 Then they sounded the trumpets and gave a loud shout. [55]After this Judas appointed leaders of the people, in charge of thousands and hundreds and fifties and tens. [56]Those who were building houses, or were about to be married, or were planting a vineyard, or were fainthearted, he told to go home again, according to the law. [57]Then the army marched out and encamped to the south of Emmaus.

58 And Judas said, "Arm yourselves and be courageous. Be ready early in the morning to fight with these Gentiles who have assembled against us to destroy us and our sanctuary. [59]It is better for us to die in battle than to see the misfortunes of our nation and of the sanctuary. [60]But as his will in heaven may be, so shall he do."

4 Now Gorgias took five thousand infantry and one thousand picked cavalry, and this division moved out by night [2]to fall upon the camp of the Jews and attack them suddenly. Men from the citadel were his guides. [3]But Judas heard of it, and he and his warriors moved out to attack the king's force in Emmaus [4]while the division was still absent from the camp. [5]When Gorgias entered the camp of Judas by night, he found no one there, so he looked for them in the hills, because he said, "These men are running away from us."

6 At daybreak Judas appeared in the plain with three thousand men, but they did not have armor and swords such as they desired. [7]And they saw the camp of the Gentiles, strong and fortified, with cavalry all around it; and these men were trained in war. [8]But Judas said to those who were with him, "Do not fear their numbers or be afraid when they charge. [9]Remember how our ancestors were saved at the Red Sea, when Pharaoh with his forces pursued them. [10]And now, let us cry to Heaven, to see whether he will favor us and remember his covenant with our ancestors and crush this army before us today. [11]Then all the Gentiles will know that there is one who redeems and saves Israel."

12 When the foreigners looked up and saw them coming against them, [13]they went out from their camp to battle. Then the men with Judas blew their trumpets [14]and engaged in battle. The Gentiles were crushed, and fled into the plain, [15]and all those in the rear fell by the sword. They pursued them to Gazara, and to the plains of Idumea, and to Azotus and Jamnia; and three thousand of them fell. [16]Then Judas and his force turned back from pursuing them, [17]and he said to the people, "Do not be greedy for plunder, for there is a battle before us; [18]Gorgias and his force are near us in the hills. But stand now against our enemies and fight them, and afterward seize the plunder boldly."

19 Just as Judas was finishing this speech, a detachment appeared, coming out of the hills. [20]They saw that their army*b* had been put to flight, and that the Jews*b* were burning the camp, for the smoke that was seen showed what had happened. [21]When they perceived this, they were greatly frightened, and when they also saw the army of Judas drawn up in the plain for battle, [22]they all fled into the land of the Philistines. [23]Then Judas returned to plunder the camp, and they seized a great amount of gold and silver, and cloth dyed blue and sea purple, and great riches. [24]On their return they sang hymns and praises to Heaven—"For he is good, for his mercy endures forever." [25]Thus Israel had a great deliverance that day.

3.27–4.25. 3.41: It was common practice in the ancient world to sell people captured in battle into *slav-*

a That is *those separated* or *those consecrated*
b Gk *they*

ery. See Joel 3.6 where Tyre and Sidon are accused of selling Judeans to the Greeks. See also 2 Macc 8.10. **47:** Judas is careful to observe ritual as well as military preparation for battle. **51:** The desecration of the Temple* is portrayed as the main motivating factor. **55:** Judas appointed leaders, just as Moses did (Deut 1.15). He also sent home those who were preoccupied or fainthearted (Deut 20.5–8). **4.1–5:** Judas outmaneuvered his opponent. **9:** The victory is not attributed to superior tactics, however, but to the miraculous power of God. **24:** The refrain is from Psalm 136. It is also sung on the occasion of the rebuilding of the Temple in Ezra 3.11.

26 Those of the foreigners who escaped went and reported to Lysias all that had happened. ²⁷When he heard it, he was perplexed and discouraged, for things had not happened to Israel as he had intended, nor had they turned out as the king had ordered. ²⁸But the next year he mustered sixty thousand picked infantry and five thousand cavalry to subdue them. ²⁹They came into Idumea and encamped at Beth-zur, and Judas met them with ten thousand men.

30 When he saw that their army was strong, he prayed, saying, "Blessed are you, O Savior of Israel, who crushed the attack of the mighty warrior by the hand of your servant David, and gave the camp of the Philistines into the hands of Jonathan son of Saul, and of the man who carried his armor. ³¹Hem in this army by the hand of your people Israel, and let them be ashamed of their troops and their cavalry. ³²Fill them with cowardice; melt the boldness of their strength; let them tremble in their destruction. ³³Strike them down with the sword of those who love you, and let all who know your name praise you with hymns."

4.33: The Maccabees view the killing of their enemies as a manifestation of their love for God.

34 Then both sides attacked, and there fell of the army of Lysias five thousand men; they fell in action.ᵃ ³⁵When Lysias saw the rout of his troops and observed the boldness that inspired those of Judas, and how ready they were either to live or to die nobly, he withdrew to Antioch and enlisted mercenar-

ies in order to invade Judea again with an even larger army.

36 Then Judas and his brothers said, "See, our enemies are crushed; let us go up to cleanse the sanctuary and dedicate it." ³⁷So all the army assembled and went up to Mount Zion. ³⁸There they saw the sanctuary desolate, the altar profaned, and the gates burned. In the courts they saw bushes sprung up as in a thicket, or as on one of the mountains. They saw also the chambers of the priests in ruins. ³⁹Then they tore their clothes and mourned with great lamentation; they sprinkled themselves with ashes ⁴⁰and fell face down on the ground. And when the signal was given with the trumpets, they cried out to Heaven.

41 Then Judas detailed men to fight against those in the citadel until he had cleansed the sanctuary. ⁴²He chose blameless priests devoted to the law, ⁴³and they cleansed the sanctuary and removed the defiled stones to an unclean place. ⁴⁴They deliberated what to do about the altar of burnt offering, which had been profaned. ⁴⁵And they thought it best to tear it down, so that it would not be a lasting shame to them that the Gentiles had defiled it. So they tore down the altar, ⁴⁶and stored the stones in a convenient place on the temple hill until a prophet should come to tell what to do with them. ⁴⁷Then they took unhewnᵇ stones, as the law directs, and built a new altar like the former one. ⁴⁸They also rebuilt the sanctuary and the interior of the temple, and consecrated the courts. ⁴⁹They made new holy vessels, and brought the lampstand, the altar of incense, and the table into the temple. ⁵⁰Then they offered incense on the altar and lit the lamps on the lampstand, and these gave light in the temple. ⁵¹They placed the bread on the table and hung up the curtains. Thus they finished all the work they had undertaken.

52 Early in the morning on the twenty-fifth day of the ninth month, which is the month of Chislev, in the one hundred forty-eighth year,ᶜ ⁵³they rose and offered

ᵃ Or and some fell on the opposite side ᵇ Gk whole
ᶜ 164 B.C.

sacrifice, as the law directs, on the new altar of burnt offering that they had built. 54At the very season and on the very day that the Gentiles had profaned it, it was dedicated with songs and harps and lutes and cymbals. 55All the people fell on their faces and worshiped and blessed Heaven, who had prospered them. 56So they celebrated the dedication of the altar for eight days, and joyfully offered burnt offerings; they offered a sacrifice of well-being and a thanksgiving offering. 57They decorated the front of the temple with golden crowns and small shields; they restored the gates and the chambers for the priests, and fitted them with doors. 58There was very great joy among the people, and the disgrace brought by the Gentiles was removed.

59 Then Judas and his brothers and all the assembly of Israel determined that every year at that season the days of dedication of the altar should be observed with joy and gladness for eight days, beginning with the twenty-fifth day of the month of Chislev.

60 At that time they fortified Mount Zion with high walls and strong towers all around, to keep the Gentiles from coming and trampling them down as they had done before. 61Judas[a] stationed a garrison there to guard it; he also fortified Beth-zur to guard it, so that the people might have a stronghold that faced Idumea.

4.36–61: The high point of Judas's career is the purification of the Temple.* This is the event commemorated in the Jewish festival of Hanukkah (see 4.59). **4.46:** *Until a prophet should come:* Prophecy was thought to have ceased in the Persian period. The expectation of a prophet* here looks to the distant future. Compare the prophet like Moses (Deut 18.15) or the idea that Elijah would return (Mal 4.5). **4.47:** *Unhewn stones:* See Ex 20.25; Josh 8.31. On the fortifications of Mt. Zion,* see Ps 48.3.

5 When the Gentiles all around heard that the altar had been rebuilt and the sanctuary dedicated as it was before, they became very angry, 2and they determined to destroy the descendants of Jacob who lived among them. So they began to kill and destroy among the people. 3But Judas made war on the descendants of Esau in Idumea, at Akrabattene, because they kept lying in wait for Israel. He dealt them a heavy blow and humbled them and despoiled them. 4He also remembered the wickedness of the sons of Baean, who were a trap and a snare to the people and ambushed them on the highways. 5They were shut up by him in their[b] towers; and he encamped against them, vowed their complete destruction, and burned with fire their towers and all who were in them. 6Then he crossed over to attack the Ammonites, where he found a strong band and many people, with Timothy as their leader. 7He engaged in many battles with them, and they were crushed before him; he struck them down. 8He also took Jazer and its villages; then he returned to Judea.

9 Now the Gentiles in Gilead gathered together against the Israelites who lived in their territory, and planned to destroy them. But they fled to the stronghold of Dathema, 10and sent to Judas and his brothers a letter that said, "The Gentiles around us have gathered together to destroy us. 11They are preparing to come and capture the stronghold to which we have fled, and Timothy is leading their forces. 12Now then, come and rescue us from their hands, for many of us have fallen, 13and all our kindred who were in the land of Tob have been killed; the enemy[c] have captured their wives and children and goods, and have destroyed about a thousand persons there."

14 While the letter was still being read, other messengers, with their garments torn, came from Galilee and made a similar report; 15they said that the people of Ptolemais and Tyre and Sidon, and all Galilee of the Gentiles,[d] had gathered together against them "to annihilate us." 16When Judas and the people heard these messages, a great assembly was called to determine what they should do for their kindred who were in distress and were being attacked by enemies.[e] 17Then Judas said to his brother Simon, "Choose your men and go and rescue your kindred in Galilee; Jonathan my brother and

a Gk He   b Gk her   c Gk they   d Gk aliens
e Gk them

I will go to Gilead." [18]But he left Joseph, son of Zechariah, and Azariah, a leader of the people, with the rest of the forces, in Judea to guard it; [19]and he gave them this command, "Take charge of this people, but do not engage in battle with the Gentiles until we return." [20]Then three thousand men were assigned to Simon to go to Galilee, and eight thousand to Judas for Gilead.

21 So Simon went to Galilee and fought many battles against the Gentiles, and the Gentiles were crushed before him. [22]He pursued them to the gate of Ptolemais; as many as three thousand of the Gentiles fell, and he despoiled them. [23]Then he took the Jews[a] of Galilee and Arbatta, with their wives and children, and all they possessed, and led them to Judea with great rejoicing.

24 Judas Maccabeus and his brother Jonathan crossed the Jordan and made three days' journey into the wilderness. [25]They encountered the Nabateans, who met them peaceably and told them all that had happened to their kindred in Gilead: [26]"Many of them have been shut up in Bozrah and Bosor, in Alema and Chaspho, Maked and Carnaim"—all these towns were strong and large— [27]"and some have been shut up in the other towns of Gilead; the enemy[b] are getting ready to attack the strongholds tomorrow and capture and destroy all these people in a single day."

28 Then Judas and his army quickly turned back by the wilderness road to Bozrah; and he took the town, and killed every male by the edge of the sword; then he seized all its spoils and burned it with fire. [29]He left the place at night, and they went all the way to the stronghold of Dathema.[c] [30]At dawn they looked out and saw a large company, which could not be counted, carrying ladders and engines of war to capture the stronghold, and attacking the Jews within.[d] [31]So Judas saw that the battle had begun and that the cry of the town went up to Heaven, with trumpets and loud shouts, [32]and he said to the men of his forces, "Fight today for your kindred!" [33]Then he came up behind them in three companies, who sounded their trumpets and cried aloud in prayer. [34]And when the army of Timothy realized that it

was Maccabeus, they fled before him, and he dealt them a heavy blow. As many as eight thousand of them fell that day.

35 Next he turned aside to Maapha,[e] and fought against it and took it; and he killed every male in it, plundered it, and burned it with fire. [36]From there he marched on and took Chaspho, Maked, and Bosor, and the other towns of Gilead.

5.1–68: Gathering the scattered Jews. 1: Compare the opposition to the rebuilding of the Temple* after the Exile* (Ezra 4). **23:** The gathering in of Jews from outlying areas where they were beleaguered fulfills the promises of Ezek 39.27 and Jer 31.10 ("he who scattered Israel will gather him"). **35:** The ruthlessness of Judas, killing every male, and razing the cities, recalls the "herem" or ban* of the period of the conquest (Josh 6.21).

---

37 After these things Timothy gathered another army and encamped opposite Raphon, on the other side of the stream. [38]Judas sent men to spy out the camp, and they reported to him, "All the Gentiles around us have gathered to him; it is a very large force. [39]They also have hired Arabs to help them, and they are encamped across the stream, ready to come and fight against you." And Judas went to meet them.

40 Now as Judas and his army drew near to the stream of water, Timothy said to the officers of his forces, "If he crosses over to us first, we will not be able to resist him, for he will surely defeat us. [41]But if he shows fear and camps on the other side of the river, we will cross over to him and defeat him." [42]When Judas approached the stream of water, he stationed the officers[f] of the army at the stream and gave them this command, "Permit no one to encamp, but make them all enter the battle." [43]Then he crossed over against them first, and the whole army followed him. All the Gentiles were defeated before him, and they threw away their arms and fled into the sacred precincts at Carnaim. [44]But he took the town and burned

---

a Gk *those* b Gk *they* c Gk lacks *of Dathema*. See verse 9 d Gk *and they were attacking them* e Other ancient authorities read *Alema* f Or *scribes* the sacred precincts with fire, together with all who were in them. Thus Carnaim was conquered; they could stand before Judas no longer.

45 Then Judas gathered together all the Israelites in Gilead, the small and the great, with their wives and children and goods, a very large company, to go to the land of Judah. 46 So they came to Ephron. This was a large and very strong town on the road, and they could not go around it to the right or to the left; they had to go through it. 47 But the people of the town shut them out and blocked up the gates with stones. 48 Judas sent them this friendly message, "Let us pass through your land to get to our land. No one will do you harm; we will simply pass by on foot." But they refused to open to him. 49 Then Judas ordered proclamation to be made to the army that all should encamp where they were. 50 So the men of the forces encamped, and he fought against the town all that day and all the night, and the town was delivered into his hands. 51 He destroyed every male by the edge of the sword, and razed and plundered the town. Then he passed through the town over the bodies of the dead.

52 Then they crossed the Jordan into the large plain before Beth-shan. 53 Judas kept rallying the laggards and encouraging the people all the way until he came to the land of Judah. 54 So they went up to Mount Zion with joy and gladness, and offered burnt offerings, because they had returned in safety; not one of them had fallen.

55 Now while Judas and Jonathan were in Gilead and their[a] brother Simon was in Galilee before Ptolemais, 56 Joseph son of Zechariah, and Azariah, the commanders of the forces, heard of their brave deeds and of the heroic war they had fought. 57 So they said, "Let us also make a name for ourselves; let us go and make war on the Gentiles around us." 58 So they issued orders to the men of the forces that were with them and marched against Jamnia. 59 Gorgias and his men came out of the town to meet them in battle. 60 Then Joseph and Azariah were routed, and were pursued to the borders of Judea; as many as two thousand of the peo-

ple of Israel fell that day. 61 Thus the people suffered a great rout because, thinking to do a brave deed, they did not listen to Judas and his brothers. 62 But they did not belong to the family of those men through whom deliverance was given to Israel.

63 The man Judas and his brothers were greatly honored in all Israel and among all the Gentiles, wherever their name was heard. 64 People gathered to them and praised them.

65 Then Judas and his brothers went out and fought the descendants of Esau in the land to the south. He struck Hebron and its villages and tore down its strongholds and burned its towers on all sides. 66 Then he marched off to go into the land of the Philistines, and passed through Marisa.[b] 67 On that day some priests, who wished to do a brave deed, fell in battle, for they went out to battle unwisely. 68 But Judas turned aside to Azotus in the land of the Philistines; he tore down their altars, and the carved images of their gods he burned with fire; he plundered the towns and returned to the land of Judah.

5.37–68. 48–51: The destruction of Ephron for refusing passage recalls the encounter of Moses with the Amorites in Num 21.21–30. **55–62:** Two other Jewish commanders fail in their excursion because they do not belong to the family of the Maccabees. Divine favor is not given equally to all Jews. **65–68:** The final expedition in this chapter is not for the purpose of rescuing Jews but of tearing down altars and images. Deuteronomy 12.2–3 had commanded such violence in the land of Israel, but Judas carries it out even in the land of the Philistines.

6 King Antiochus was going through the upper provinces when he heard that Elymais in Persia was a city famed for its wealth in silver and gold. 2 Its temple was very rich, containing golden shields, breastplates, and weapons left there by Alexander son of Philip, the Macedonian king who first reigned over the Greeks. 3 So he came and tried to take the city and plunder it, but he could not because his plan had become

a Gk his   b Other ancient authorities read Samaria

known to the citizens ⁴and they withstood him in battle. So he fled and in great disappointment left there to return to Babylon.

5 Then someone came to him in Persia and reported that the armies that had gone into the land of Judah had been routed; ⁶that Lysias had gone first with a strong force, but had turned and fled before the Jews;ᵃ that the Jewsᵇ had grown strong from the arms, supplies, and abundant spoils that they had taken from the armies they had cut down; ⁷that they had torn down the abomination that he had erected on the altar in Jerusalem; and that they had surrounded the sanctuary with high walls as before, and also Beth-zur, his town.

8 When the king heard this news, he was astounded and badly shaken. He took to his bed and became sick from disappointment, because things had not turned out for him as he had planned. ⁹He lay there for many days, because deep disappointment continually gripped him, and he realized that he was dying. ¹⁰So he called all his Friends and said to them, "Sleep has departed from my eyes and I am downhearted with worry. ¹¹I said to myself, 'To what distress I have come! And into what a great flood I now am plunged! For I was kind and beloved in my power.' ¹²But now I remember the wrong I did in Jerusalem. I seized all its vessels of silver and gold, and I sent to destroy the inhabitants of Judah without good reason. ¹³I know that it is because of this that these misfortunes have come upon me; here I am, perishing of bitter disappointment in a strange land."

14 Then he called for Philip, one of his Friends, and made him ruler over all his kingdom. ¹⁵He gave him the crown and his robe and the signet, so that he might guide his son Antiochus and bring him up to be king. ¹⁶Thus King Antiochus died there in the one hundred forty-ninth year.ᵉ ¹⁷When Lysias learned that the king was dead, he set up Antiochus the king'sᵈ son to reign. Lysiasᵉ had brought him up from boyhood; he named him Eupator.

cabean books. The other two are in 2 Macc 1.11–17 and 9.1–29. First Maccabees 6 agrees with 2 Macc 1 that Epiphanes was trying to rob a temple, but differs in attributing his death to remorse over what he had done in Jerusalem. Second Maccabees 9 goes further, in claiming that Epiphanes repented on his deathbed and wanted to become a Jew. First Maccabees assumes that the death of the king is divine punishment for what he did in Jerusalem.

18 Meanwhile the garrison in the citadel kept hemming Israel in around the sanctuary. They were trying in every way to harm them and strengthen the Gentiles. ¹⁹Judas therefore resolved to destroy them, and assembled all the people to besiege them. ²⁰They gathered together and besieged the citadelᶠ in the one hundred fiftieth year;ᵍ and he built siege towers and other engines of war. ²¹But some of the garrison escaped from the siege and some of the ungodly Israelites joined them. ²²They went to the king and said, "How long will you fail to do justice and to avenge our kindred? ²³We were happy to serve your father, to live by what he said, and to follow his commands. ²⁴For this reason the sons of our people besieged the citadelʰ and became hostile to us; moreover, they have put to death as many of us as they have caught, and they have seized our inheritances. ²⁵It is not against us alone that they have stretched out their hands; they have also attacked all the lands on their borders. ²⁶And see, today they have encamped against the citadel in Jerusalem to take it; they have fortified both the sanctuary and Beth-zur; ²⁷unless you quickly prevent them, they will do still greater things, and you will not be able to stop them."

28 The king was enraged when he heard this. He assembled all his Friends, the commanders of his forces and those in authority.ⁱ ²⁹Mercenary forces also came to him from other kingdoms and from islands of the seas. ³⁰The number of his forces was one hundred thousand foot soldiers, twenty

---

6.1–17: The death of Epiphanes.* There are three distinct accounts of the death of Epiphanes in the Mac-

a Gk them   b Gk they   c 163 B.C.   d Gk his
e Gk He   f Gk it   g 162 B.C.   h Meaning of Gk uncertain   i Gk those over the reins

thousand horsemen, and thirty-two elephants accustomed to war. [31] They came through Idumea and encamped against Beth-zur, and for many days they fought and built engines of war; but the Jews[a] sallied out and burned these with fire, and fought courageously.

6.18–63: The first defeat. 30: The victory of the Syrian army at Beth-zechariah was due to superior numbers and the presence of elephants, the tanks of their day. First Maccabees offers no theological explanation for the defeat. Instead, it highlights the bravery of Eleazar, one of the Maccabee brothers, who gives his life in the hope of killing the king.

---

[32] Then Judas marched away from the citadel and encamped at Beth-zechariah, opposite the camp of the king. [33] Early in the morning the king set out and took his army by a forced march along the road to Beth-zechariah, and his troops made ready for battle and sounded their trumpets. [34] They offered the elephants the juice of grapes and mulberries, to arouse them for battle. [35] They distributed the animals among the phalanxes; with each elephant they stationed a thousand men armed with coats of mail, and with brass helmets on their heads; and five hundred picked horsemen were assigned to each beast. [36] These took their position beforehand wherever the animal was; wherever it went, they went with it, and they never left it. [37] On the elephants[b] were wooden towers, strong and covered; they were fastened on each animal by special harness, and on each were four[c] armed men who fought from there, and also its Indian driver. [38] The rest of the cavalry were stationed on either side, on the two flanks of the army, to harass the enemy while being themselves protected by the phalanxes. [39] When the sun shone on the shields of gold and brass, the hills were ablaze with them and gleamed like flaming torches.

[40] Now a part of the king's army was spread out on the high hills, and some troops were on the plain, and they advanced steadily and in good order. [41] All who heard the noise made by their multitude, by the marching of the multitude and the clanking of their

arms, trembled, for the army was very large and strong. [42] But Judas and his army advanced to the battle, and six hundred of the king's army fell. [43] Now Eleazar, called Avaran, saw that one of the animals was equipped with royal armor. It was taller than all the others, and he supposed that the king was on it. [44] So he gave his life to save his people and to win for himself an everlasting name. [45] He courageously ran into the midst of the phalanx to reach it; he killed men right and left, and they parted before him on both sides. [46] He got under the elephant, stabbed it from beneath, and killed it; but it fell to the ground upon him and he died. [47] When the Jews[a] saw the royal might and the fierce attack of the forces, they turned away in flight.

[48] The soldiers of the king's army went up to Jerusalem against them, and the king encamped in Judea and at Mount Zion. [49] He made peace with the people of Beth-zur, and they evacuated the town because they had no provisions there to withstand a siege, since it was a sabbatical year for the land. [50] So the king took Beth-zur and stationed a guard there to hold it. [51] Then he encamped before the sanctuary for many days. He set up siege towers, engines of war to throw fire and stones, machines to shoot arrows, and catapults. [52] The Jews[a] also made engines of war to match theirs, and fought for many days. [53] But they had no food in storage,[d] because it was the seventh year; those who had found safety in Judea from the Gentiles had consumed the last of the stores. [54] Only a few men were left in the sanctuary; the rest scattered to their own homes, for the famine proved too much for them.

[55] Then Lysias heard that Philip, whom King Antiochus while still living had appointed to bring up his son Antiochus to be king, [56] had returned from Persia and Media with the forces that had gone with the king, and that he was trying to seize control of the government. [57] So he quickly gave orders to

a Gk *they*   *b* Gk *them*   *c* Cn: Some authorities read *thirty*; others *thirty-two*   *d* Other ancient authorities read *in the sanctuary* withdraw, and said to the king, to the commanders of the forces, and to the troops, "Daily we grow weaker, our food supply is scant, the place against which we are fighting is strong, and the affairs of the kingdom press urgently on us. 58 Now then let us come to terms with these people, and make peace with them and with all their nation. 59 Let us agree to let them live by their laws as they did before; for it was on account of their laws that we abolished that they became angry and did all these things."

60 The speech pleased the king and the commanders, and he sent to the Jews[a] an offer of peace, and they accepted it. 61 So the king and the commanders gave them their oath. On these conditions the Jews[b] evacuated the stronghold. 62 But when the king entered Mount Zion and saw what a strong fortress the place was, he broke the oath he had sworn and gave orders to tear down the wall all around. 63 Then he set off in haste and returned to Antioch. He found Philip in control of the city, but he fought against him, and took the city by force.

6.32–63. 49: The land was left fallow in the sabbatical year (Lev 25.11). First Maccabees does not comment on the theological anomaly that observance of this law placed the Jews at a disadvantage in warfare. 55–63: There is no suggestion of divine intervention to prevent the capture of the Temple. * Contrast the story of the siege of Jerusalem by Sennacherib in 2 Kings 19.35; Isa 37.36.

7 In the one hundred fifty-first year[c] Demetrius son of Seleucus set out from Rome, sailed with a few men to a town by the sea, and there began to reign. 2 As he was entering the royal palace of his ancestors, the army seized Antiochus and Lysias to bring them to him. 3 But when this act became known to him, he said, "Do not let me see their faces!" 4 So the army killed them, and Demetrius took his seat on the throne of his kingdom.

5 Then there came to him all the renegade and godless men of Israel; they were led by Alcimus, who wanted to be high priest. 6 They brought to the king this accusation against the people: "Judas and his brothers have destroyed all your Friends, and have driven us out of our land. 7 Now then send a man whom you trust; let him go and see all the ruin that Judas[d] has brought on us and on the land of the king, and let him punish them and all who help them."

8 So the king chose Bacchides, one of the king's Friends, governor of the province Beyond the River; he was a great man in the kingdom and was faithful to the king. 9 He sent him, and with him he sent the ungodly Alcimus, whom he made high priest; and he commanded him to take vengeance on the Israelites. 10 So they marched away and came with a large force into the land of Judah; and he sent messengers to Judas and his brothers with peaceable but treacherous words. 11 But they paid no attention to their words, for they saw that they had come with a large force.

12 Then a group of scribes appeared in a body before Alcimus and Bacchides to ask for just terms. 13 The Hasideans were first among the Israelites to seek peace from them, 14 for they said, "A priest of the line of Aaron has come with the army, and he will not harm us." 15 Alcimus[e] spoke peaceable words to them and swore this oath to them, "We will not seek to injure you or your friends." 16 So they trusted him; but he seized sixty of them and killed them in one day, in accordance with the word that was written,

17 "The flesh of your faithful ones and
        their blood
     they poured out all around Jerusalem,
     and there was no one to bury them."
18 Then the fear and dread of them fell on all the people, for they said, "There is no truth or justice in them, for they have violated the agreement and the oath that they swore."

19 Then Bacchides withdrew from Jerusalem and encamped in Beth-zaith. And he sent and seized many of the men who had deserted to him,[f] and some of the people, and killed them and threw them into a great pit. 20 He placed Alcimus in charge of the

a Gk them   b Gk they   c 161 B.C.   d Gk he
e Gk He   f Or many of his men who had deserted

country and left with him a force to help him; then Bacchides went back to the king.

7.1–20: Alcimus and the Hasideans. 1: The arrival of Demetrius, son of Seleucus IV, was an advantage to the Jews, since henceforth Syrian power was divided between the rival claimants to the throne. **14:** As 2 Maccabees shows, the high priesthood was a bone of contention throughout this period. Menelaus, the high priest in the time of persecution, whom 1 Maccabees does not even mention, was not a member of the high priestly family. The Hasideans were prepared to accept Alcimus because of his priestly lineage. The Maccabees, however, saw that he had come with a large force (v. 11) and so did not trust him. **17:** The poetic interjection is an inexact quotation from Ps 79.3.

~~~~~~

21 Alcimus struggled to maintain his high priesthood, 22and all who were troubling their people joined him. They gained control of the land of Judah and did great damage in Israel. 23And Judas saw all the wrongs that Alcimus and those with him had done among the Israelites; it was more than the Gentiles had done. 24So Judas*a* went out into all the surrounding parts of Judea, taking vengeance on those who had deserted and preventing those in the city*b* from going out into the country. 25When Alcimus saw that Judas and those with him had grown strong, and realized that he could not withstand them, he returned to the king and brought malicious charges against them.

26 Then the king sent Nicanor, one of his honored princes, who hated and detested Israel, and he commanded him to destroy the people. 27So Nicanor came to Jerusalem with a large force, and treacherously sent to Judas and his brothers this peaceable message, 28"Let there be no fighting between you and me; I shall come with a few men to see you face to face in peace." 29 So he came to Judas, and they greeted one another peaceably; but the enemy were preparing to kidnap Judas. 30It became known to Judas that Nicanor*a* had come to him with treacherous intent, and he was afraid of him and would not meet him again. 31When Nicanor learned that his plan had been disclosed, he went out to meet Judas in

battle near Caphar-salama. 32About five hundred of the army of Nicanor fell, and the rest*c* fled into the city of David.

33 After these events Nicanor went up to Mount Zion. Some of the priests from the sanctuary and some of the elders of the people came out to greet him peaceably and to show him the burnt offering that was being offered for the king. 34But he mocked them and derided them and defiled them and spoke arrogantly, 35and in anger he swore this oath, "Unless Judas and his army are delivered into my hands this time, then if I return safely I will burn up this house." And he went out in great anger. 36At this the priests went in and stood before the altar and the temple; they wept and said,

37 "You chose this house to be called by
        your name,
    and to be for your people a house of
        prayer and supplication.
38 Take vengeance on this man and on his
        army,
    and let them fall by the sword;
    remember their blasphemies,
    and let them live no longer."

39 Now Nicanor went out from Jerusalem and encamped in Beth-horon, and the Syrian army joined him. 40Judas encamped in Adasa with three thousand men. Then Judas prayed and said, 41"When the messengers from the king spoke blasphemy, your angel went out and struck down one hundred eighty-five thousand of the Assyrians.*d* 42So also crush this army before us today; let the rest learn that Nicanor*a* has spoken wickedly against the sanctuary, and judge him according to this wickedness."

43 So the armies met in battle on the thirteenth day of the month of Adar. The army of Nicanor was crushed, and he himself was the first to fall in the battle. 44When his army saw that Nicanor had fallen, they threw down their arms and fled. 45The Jews*c* pursued them a day's journey, from Adasa as far as Gazara, and as they followed they kept sounding the battle call on the trumpets. 46People came out of all the surrounding vil-

a Gk he   *b* Gk and they were prevented   *c* Gk they
d Gk of them

Timeline

The Hellenistic Kingdoms were parts of Alexander the Great's empire, which broke apart at his death in 323 BCE. The revolt of the Jewish people under the Maccabees followed the beginning of the reign of Antiochus IV in 175 BCE. The timeline outlines the history of the Hellenistic Kingdoms preceding the revolt and then the events in Palestine itself.

The Hellenistic Kingdoms

Egypt: the Ptolemies		Syria: the Seleucids	
BCE		BCE	
323–285	Ptolemy I Soter	312/11–280	Seleucus I
285–246	Ptolemy II Philadelphus.	280–261	Antiochus I
	Philadelphus gave his daughter	261–246	Antiochus II
	Berenice in marriage to		
	Antiochus II. She was later put		
	aside and murdered.		
246–221	Ptolemy III Euergetes	246–226	Seleucus II
221–203	Ptolemy IV Philopator	226–223	Seleucus III
203–181	Ptolemy V Epiphanes	223–187	Antiochus III the Great
	198 Palestine passed from the Ptolemies to the Seleucids		
	197 Antiochus gave his daughter Cleopatra in marriage to Ptolemy V		
181–146	Ptolemy VI Philometor	187–175	Seleucus IV
		175–164	Antiochus IV Epiphanes

The Maccabean Period

BCE

- 175   Death of Seleucus IV. He is succeeded by his brother Antiochus IV Epiphanes.
- 175/74   Jason obtains the high priesthood by bribery and begins the Hellenistic Reform.
- 172   Menelaus outbids Jason for the priesthood.
- 170   Murder of Onias III, the legitimate high priest.
- 170/69   Antiochus Epiphanes' first invasion of Egypt.
- 169   Jason tries to recapture Jerusalem but fails to hold it, and again goes into exile. Antiochus plunders the Temple in Jerusalem.
- 168   Antiochus' second invasion of Egypt. He is forced to withdraw by a Roman ultimatum.
- 167   Appollonius massacres Jews in Jerusalem. The citadel Akra is fortified. Antiochus bans the Jewish law. The persecution begins. The "abomination of desolation" is placed on the altar in the Temple. The rebellion also gets underway.
- 165   Nicanor and Gorgias defeated at Emmaus.
- 164   Lysias, repulsed at Beth-zur, makes a settlement with the Jews. End of the persecution. Death of Antiochus Epiphanes. Purification of the Temple.
- 163   Lysias, accompanied by Antiochus V, defeats Judas at Beth-zechariah.
- 163   Menelaus deposed and executed by Antiochus V. Alcimus is appointed high priest.
- 162   Demetrius I, son of Seleucus IV, claims to be king. Antiochus V and Lysias are murdered.
- 161   Defeat of Nicanor by Judas at Adasa. Embassy of the Jews to Rome.
- 160   Judas defeated and killed by Bacchides at Elasa.
- 152   Alexander Balas, son of Antiochus IV, claims to be king. He appoints Jonathan Maccabee high priest.
- 150   Demetrius I is killed in battle against Alexander Balas.

The Maccabean Period (continued)

BCE	
147	Demetrius II claims the throne.
145	Deaths of Alexander Balas and Ptolemy VI Philometor of Egypt.
145	Antiochus VI, son of Alexander Balas, is proclaimed king by Trypho.
143	Jonathan sends envoys to Rome and Sparta. Jonathan is captured by Trypho and subsequently murdered.
142	Simon is declared high priest. Death of Antiochus VI.
141	The Akra garrison is disbanded.
139	Demetrius II captured by the Parthians.
138	Antiochus VII Sidetes becomes king. Simon's sons, John and Judas, defeat the king's general in battle.
134	Simon and two of his sons are murdered at Jericho by his son-in-law, Ptolemy. John Hyrcanus becomes leader of the Jews.

Source: J. J. Collins, *Daniel, 1–2 Maccabees*, Michael Glazier, Inc., 1981.

lages of Judea, and they outflanked the enemy[a] and drove them back to their pursuers,[b] so that they all fell by the sword; not even one of them was left. [47] Then the Jews[c] seized the spoils and the plunder; they cut off Nicanor's head and the right hand that he had so arrogantly stretched out, and brought them and displayed them just outside Jerusalem. [48] The people rejoiced greatly and celebrated that day as a day of great gladness. [49] They decreed that this day should be celebrated each year on the thirteenth day of Adar. [50] So the land of Judah had rest for a few days.

7.21–50: The defeat of Nicanor. 23: The evil done by Alcimus and other renegade Jews exceeds that of the gentiles.* **26:** Despite the statement that Nicanor was sent *to destroy the people,* it is clear that he had Jewish allies. **33–42:** Nicanor is portrayed as a figure in the tradition of Sennacherib, who blasphemes by threatening the Temple.* **47:** The display of Nicanor's head is shocking by modern sensibilities, but is a practice that has continued intermittently down to modern times, designed to terrorize the enemy and bolster the morale of one's own troops.

---

8 Now Judas heard of the fame of the Romans, that they were very strong and were well-disposed toward all who made an alliance with them, that they pledged friendship to those who came to them, [2] and that they were very strong. He had been told of their wars and of the brave deeds that they were doing among the Gauls, how they had defeated them and forced them to pay tribute, [3] and what they had done in the land of Spain to get control of the silver and gold mines there, [4] and how they had gained control of the whole region by their planning and patience, even though the place was far distant from them. They also subdued the kings who came against them from the ends of the earth, until they crushed them and inflicted great disaster on them; the rest paid them tribute every year. [5] They had crushed in battle and conquered Philip, and King Perseus of the Macedonians,[d] and the others who rose up against them. [6] They also had defeated Antiochus the Great, king of Asia, who went to fight against them with one hundred twenty elephants and with cavalry and chariots and a very large army. He was crushed by them; [7] they took him alive and decreed that he and those who would reign after him should pay a heavy tribute and give hostages and surrender some of their best provinces, [8] the countries of India, Media, and Lydia. These they took from him and gave to King Eumenes. [9] The Greeks planned to come and destroy them, [10] but this became known to them, and they sent a general against the Greeks[a] and attacked them. Many of them were wounded and fell, and

a Gk *them*   *b* Gk *these*   *c* Gk *they*   *d* Or *Kittim* the Romans[a] took captive their wives and children; they plundered them, conquered the land, tore down their strongholds, and enslaved them to this day. [11]The remaining kingdoms and islands, as many as ever opposed them, they destroyed and enslaved; [12]but with their friends and those who rely on them they have kept friendship. They have subdued kings far and near, and as many as have heard of their fame have feared them. [13]Those whom they wish to help and to make kings, they make kings, and those whom they wish they depose; and they have been greatly exalted. [14]Yet for all this not one of them has put on a crown or worn purple as a mark of pride, [15]but they have built for themselves a senate chamber, and every day three hundred twenty senators constantly deliberate concerning the people, to govern them well. [16]They trust one man each year to rule over them and to control all their land; they all heed the one man, and there is no envy or jealousy among them.

17 So Judas chose Eupolemus son of John son of Accos, and Jason son of Eleazar, and sent them to Rome to establish friendship and alliance, [18]and to free themselves from the yoke; for they saw that the kingdom of the Greeks was enslaving Israel completely. [19]They went to Rome, a very long journey; and they entered the senate chamber and spoke as follows: [20]"Judas, who is also called Maccabeus, and his brothers and the people of the Jews have sent us to you to establish alliance and peace with you, so that we may be enrolled as your allies and friends." [21]The proposal pleased them, [22]and this is a copy of the letter that they wrote in reply, on bronze tablets, and sent to Jerusalem to remain with them there as a memorial of peace and alliance:

23 "May all go well with the Romans and with the nation of the Jews at sea and on land forever, and may sword and enemy be far from them. [24]If war comes first to Rome or to any of their allies in all their dominion, [25]the nation of the Jews shall act as their allies wholeheartedly, as the occasion may indicate to them. [26]To the enemy that makes war they shall not give or supply grain, arms, money, or ships, just as Rome has decided;

and they shall keep their obligations without receiving any return. [27]In the same way, if war comes first to the nation of the Jews, the Romans shall willingly act as their allies, as the occasion may indicate to them. [28]And to their enemies there shall not be given grain, arms, money, or ships, just as Rome has decided; and they shall keep these obligations and do so without deceit. [29]Thus on these terms the Romans make a treaty with the Jewish people. [30]If after these terms are in effect both parties shall determine to add or delete anything, they shall do so at their discretion, and any addition or deletion that they may make shall be valid.

31 "Concerning the wrongs that King Demetrius is doing to them, we have written to him as follows, 'Why have you made your yoke heavy on our friends and allies the Jews? [32]If now they appeal again for help against you, we will defend their rights and fight you on sea and on land.'"

8.1–32: The treaty with Rome. 1–16: Rome is admired for its might and organization, despite the general hostility of 1 Maccabees toward the gentiles.* **7:** Antiochus the Great was not taken prisoner, but had to submit to the terms imposed by Rome. **9–11:** These verses are anachronistic.* They refer to the Roman conquest of Greece in 146 BCE, long after the death of Judas. **16:** The Romans chose two consuls, not one as stated here. **17:** *Eupolemus* is known as the author of a history of the Jews in Greek, of which fragments have survived. It is possible, but not certain, that *Jason* is Jason of Cyrene, whose work is condensed in 2 Maccabees. Since both of these authors wrote in Greek, they were presumably sympathetic to Hellenistic* culture. **23–32:** The authenticity of the letter is sometimes disputed, but it is probably genuine. The Romans promised little, and made no effort to intervene on behalf of the Jews, but they were gaining a potential foothold in the Near East. Judas gained some international recognition and moral support. The short-term results were harmless. When the Romans actually intervened in Judea a century later, the results were disastrous for the Jews.

9 When Demetrius heard that Nicanor and his army had fallen in battle, he sent

[a] Gk *they*

Bacchides and Alcimus into the land of Judah a second time, and with them the right wing of the army. [2]They went by the road that leads to Gilgal and encamped against Mesaloth in Arbela, and they took it and killed many people. [3]In the first month of the one hundred fifty-second year[a] they encamped against Jerusalem; [4]then they marched off and went to Berea with twenty thousand foot soldiers and two thousand cavalry.

5 Now Judas was encamped in Elasa, and with him were three thousand picked men. [6]When they saw the huge number of the enemy forces, they were greatly frightened, and many slipped away from the camp, until no more than eight hundred of them were left.

7 When Judas saw that his army had slipped away and the battle was imminent, he was crushed in spirit, for he had no time to assemble them. [8]He became faint, but he said to those who were left, "Let us get up and go against our enemies. We may have the strength to fight them." [9]But they tried to dissuade him, saying, "We do not have the strength. Let us rather save our own lives now, and let us come back with our kindred and fight them; we are too few." [10]But Judas said, "Far be it from us to do such a thing as to flee from them. If our time has come, let us die bravely for our kindred, and leave no cause to question our honor."

11 Then the army of Bacchides[b] marched out from the camp and took its stand for the encounter. The cavalry was divided into two companies, and the slingers and the archers went ahead of the army, as did all the chief warriors. [12]Bacchides was on the right wing. Flanked by the two companies, the phalanx advanced to the sound of the trumpets; and the men with Judas also blew their trumpets. [13]The earth was shaken by the noise of the armies, and the battle raged from morning until evening.

14 Judas saw that Bacchides and the strength of his army were on the right; then all the stouthearted men went with him, [15]and they crushed the right wing, and he pursued them as far as Mount Azotus. [16]When those on the left wing saw that the right wing was crushed, they turned and followed close behind Judas and his men. [17]The battle became desperate, and many on both sides were wounded and fell. [18]Judas also fell, and the rest fled.

19 Then Jonathan and Simon took their brother Judas and buried him in the tomb of their ancestors at Modein, [20]and wept for him. All Israel made great lamentation for him; they mourned many days and said,

21 "How is the mighty fallen,
     the savior of Israel!"

[22]Now the rest of the acts of Judas, and his wars and the brave deeds that he did, and his greatness, have not been recorded, but they were very many.

9.1–22: The death of Judas. 10: Judas meets his death fighting against superior numbers. There is no indication that he expected divine aid. Rather, he was concerned to defend his *honor*. There is no theological reflection on his death. His loss is not mitigated by any assertion of immortality. 21: The lament* for Judas recalls David's lament for Saul and Jonathan (2 Sam 1.27).

23 After the death of Judas, the renegades emerged in all parts of Israel; all the wrongdoers reappeared. [24]In those days a very great famine occurred, and the country went over to their side. [25]Bacchides chose the godless and put them in charge of the country. [26]They made inquiry and searched for the friends of Judas, and brought them to Bacchides, who took vengeance on them and made sport of them. [27]So there was great distress in Israel, such as had not been since the time that prophets ceased to appear among them.

28 Then all the friends of Judas assembled and said to Jonathan, [29]"Since the death of your brother Judas there has been no one like him to go against our enemies and Bacchides, and to deal with those of our nation who hate us. [30]Now therefore we have chosen you today to take his place as our ruler and leader, to fight our battle." [31]So Jonathan accepted the leadership at that time in place of his brother Judas.

32 When Bacchides learned of this, he

a 160 B.C.   *b* Gk lacks *of Bacchides*

tried to kill him. 33But Jonathan and his brother Simon and all who were with him heard of it, and they fled into the wilderness of Tekoa and camped by the water of the pool of Asphar. 34Bacchides found this out on the sabbath day, and he with all his army crossed the Jordan.

35 So Jonathan[a] sent his brother as leader of the multitude and begged the Nabateans, who were his friends, for permission to store with them the great amount of baggage that they had. 36But the family of Jambri from Medeba came out and seized John and all that he had, and left with it.

37 After these things it was reported to Jonathan and his brother Simon, "The family of Jambri are celebrating a great wedding, and are conducting the bride, a daughter of one of the great nobles of Canaan, from Nadabath with a large escort." 38Remembering how their brother John had been killed, they went up and hid under cover of the mountain. 39They looked out and saw a tumultuous procession with a great amount of baggage; and the bridegroom came out with his friends and his brothers to meet them with tambourines and musicians and many weapons. 40Then they rushed on them from the ambush and began killing them. Many were wounded and fell, and the rest fled to the mountain; and the Jews[b] took all their goods. 41So the wedding was turned into mourning and the voice of their musicians into a funeral dirge. 42After they had fully avenged the blood of their brother, they returned to the marshes of the Jordan.

43 When Bacchides heard of this, he came with a large force on the sabbath day to the banks of the Jordan. 44And Jonathan said to those with him, "Let us get up now and fight for our lives, for today things are not as they were before. 45For look! the battle is in front of us and behind us; the water of the Jordan is on this side and on that, with marsh and thicket; there is no place to turn. 46Cry out now to Heaven that you may be delivered from the hands of our enemies." 47So the battle began, and Jonathan stretched out his hand to strike Bacchides, but he eluded him and went to the rear. 48Then Jonathan and the men with him leaped into the Jordan and swam across to the other side, and the enemy[b] did not cross the Jordan to attack them. 49And about one thousand of Bacchides' men fell that day.

50 Then Bacchides[a] returned to Jerusalem and built strong cities in Judea: the fortress in Jericho, and Emmaus, and Bethhoron, and Bethel, and Timnath, and[c] Pharathon, and Tephon, with high walls and gates and bars. 51And he placed garrisons in them to harass Israel. 52He also fortified the town of Beth-zur, and Gazara, and the citadel, and in them he put troops and stores of food. 53And he took the sons of the leading men of the land as hostages and put them under guard in the citadel at Jerusalem.

9.23–73: The rise of Jonathan. 30: Jonathan is drafted as leader by popular acclaim. The emergence of a hero in a time of crisis recalls a familiar pattern in the Judges. Compare the manner in which Jephthah is drafted in Judg 11. But the spirit of the Lord does not fall on Jonathan, and his selection is due in part to the fact that he belongs to the family of the Maccabees. **34:** Bacchides attacks on the sabbath (see 1 Macc 2.32), but Jonathan is not restricted by the niceties of sabbath observance. **50:** Bacchides returned to Jerusalem because Jonathan's hit-and-run tactics made him too elusive.

54 In the one hundred and fifty-third year,[d] in the second month, Alcimus gave orders to tear down the wall of the inner court of the sanctuary. He tore down the work of the prophets! 55But he only began to tear it down, for at that time Alcimus was stricken and his work was hindered; his mouth was stopped and he was paralyzed, so that he could no longer say a word or give commands concerning his house. 56And Alcimus died at that time in great agony. 57When Bacchides saw that Alcimus was dead, he returned to the king, and the land of Judah had rest for two years.

58 Then all the lawless plotted and said, "See! Jonathan and his men are living in quiet and confidence. So now let us bring

a Gk he   b Gk they   c Some authorities omit and
d 159 B.C.

Bacchides back, and he will capture them all in one night." ⁵⁹And they went and consulted with him. ⁶⁰He started to come with a large force, and secretly sent letters to all his allies in Judea, telling them to seize Jonathan and his men; but they were unable to do it, because their plan became known. ⁶¹And Jonathan's men*a* seized about fifty of the men of the country who were leaders in this treachery, and killed them.

62 Then Jonathan with his men, and Simon, withdrew to Bethbasi in the wilderness; he rebuilt the parts of it that had been demolished, and they fortified it. ⁶³When Bacchides learned of this, he assembled all his forces, and sent orders to the men of Judea. ⁶⁴Then he came and encamped against Bethbasi; he fought against it for many days and made machines of war.

65 But Jonathan left his brother Simon in the town, while he went out into the country; and he went with only a few men. ⁶⁶He struck down Odomera and his kindred and the people of Phasiron in their tents. ⁶⁷Then he*b* began to attack and went into battle with his forces; and Simon and his men sallied out from the town and set fire to the machines of war. ⁶⁸They fought with Bacchides, and he was crushed by them. They pressed him very hard, for his plan and his expedition had been in vain. ⁶⁹So he was very angry at the renegades who had counseled him to come into the country, and he killed many of them. Then he decided to go back to his own land.

70 When Jonathan learned of this, he sent ambassadors to him to make peace with him and obtain release of the captives. ⁷¹He agreed, and did as he said; and he swore to Jonathan*c* that he would not try to harm him as long as he lived. ⁷²He restored to him the captives whom he had taken previously from the land of Judah; then he turned and went back to his own land, and did not come again into their territory. ⁷³Thus the sword ceased from Israel. Jonathan settled in Michmash and began to judge the people; and he destroyed the godless out of Israel.

the court of the gentiles* from the inner court. If so, his action was symbolic of tearing down the difference between Jew and gentile, the original program of the Hellenistic* reform. **56:** The death of Alcimus is presented as divine punishment for interfering with the Temple.* After this, the high priesthood was vacant for some years. **73:** The chapter ends with Jonathan established like one of the judges of old. *Michmash* was the village from which Jonathan son of Saul had driven the Philistines in 1 Sam 14.

10

In the one hundred sixtieth year*d* Alexander Epiphanes, son of Antiochus, landed and occupied Ptolemais. They welcomed him, and there he began to reign. ²When King Demetrius heard of it, he assembled a very large army and marched out to meet him in battle. ³Demetrius sent Jonathan a letter in peaceable words to honor him; ⁴for he said to himself, "Let us act first to make peace with him*e* before he makes peace with Alexander against us, ⁵for he will remember all the wrongs that we did to him and to his brothers and his nation." ⁶So Demetrius*f* gave him authority to recruit troops, to equip them with arms, and to become his ally; and he commanded that the hostages in the citadel should be released to him.

7 Then Jonathan came to Jerusalem and read the letter in the hearing of all the people and of those in the citadel. ⁸They were greatly alarmed when they heard that the king had given him authority to recruit troops. ⁹But those in the citadel released the hostages to Jonathan, and he returned them to their parents.

10 And Jonathan took up residence in Jerusalem and began to rebuild and restore the city. ¹¹He directed those who were doing the work to build the walls and encircle Mount Zion with squared stones, for better fortification; and they did so.

12 Then the foreigners who were in the strongholds that Bacchides had built fled; ¹³all of them left their places and went back to their own lands. ¹⁴Only in Beth-zur did some remain who had forsaken the law and

---

9.54–73. 54: It is not certain which *wall* Alcimus tore down, but it may have been the wall that separated

a Gk *they*   *b* Other ancient authorities read *they*
c Gk *him*   *d* 152 B.C.   *e* Gk *them*   *f* Gk *he*

the commandments, for it served as a place of refuge.

15 Now King Alexander heard of all the promises that Demetrius had sent to Jonathan, and he heard of the battles that Jonathan[a] and his brothers had fought, of the brave deeds that they had done, and of the troubles that they had endured. [16] So he said, "Shall we find another such man? Come now, we will make him our friend and ally." [17] And he wrote a letter and sent it to him, in the following words:

18 "King Alexander to his brother Jonathan, greetings. [19] We have heard about you, that you are a mighty warrior and worthy to be our friend. [20] And so we have appointed you today to be the high priest of your nation; you are to be called the king's Friend and you are to take our side and keep friendship with us." He also sent him a purple robe and a golden crown.

21 So Jonathan put on the sacred vestments in the seventh month of the one hundred sixtieth year,[b] at the festival of booths,[c] and he recruited troops and equipped them with arms in abundance. [22] When Demetrius heard of these things he was distressed and said, [23] "What is this that we have done? Alexander has gotten ahead of us in forming a friendship with the Jews to strengthen himself. [24] I also will write them words of encouragement and promise them honor and gifts, so that I may have their help." [25] So he sent a message to them in the following words:

"King Demetrius to the nation of the Jews, greetings. [26] Since you have kept your agreement with us and have continued your friendship with us, and have not sided with our enemies, we have heard of it and rejoiced. [27] Now continue still to keep faith with us, and we will repay you with good for what you do for us. [28] We will grant you many immunities and give you gifts.

29 "I now free you and exempt all the Jews from payment of tribute and salt tax and crown levies, [30] and instead of collecting the third of the grain and the half of the fruit of the trees that I should receive, I release them from this day and henceforth. I will not collect them from the land of Judah or from the three districts added to it from Samaria and Galilee, from this day and for all time. [31] Jerusalem and its environs, its tithes and its revenues, shall be holy and free from tax. [32] I release also my control of the citadel in Jerusalem and give it to the high priest, so that he may station in it men of his own choice to guard it. [33] And everyone of the Jews taken as a captive from the land of Judah into any part of my kingdom, I set free without payment; and let all officials cancel also the taxes on their livestock.

34 "All the festivals and sabbaths and new moons and appointed days, and the three days before a festival and the three after a festival—let them all be days of immunity and release for all the Jews who are in my kingdom. [35] No one shall have authority to exact anything from them or annoy any of them about any matter.

36 "Let Jews be enrolled in the king's forces to the number of thirty thousand men, and let the maintenance be given them that is due to all the forces of the king. [37] Let some of them be stationed in the great strongholds of the king, and let some of them be put in positions of trust in the kingdom. Let their officers and leaders be of their own number, and let them live by their own laws, just as the king has commanded in the land of Judah.

38 "As for the three districts that have been added to Judea from the country of Samaria, let them be annexed to Judea so that they may be considered to be under one ruler and obey no other authority than the high priest. [39] Ptolemais and the land adjoining it I have given as a gift to the sanctuary in Jerusalem, to meet the necessary expenses of the sanctuary. [40] I also grant fifteen thousand shekels of silver yearly out of the king's revenues from appropriate places. [41] And all the additional funds that the government officials have not paid as they did in the first years,[d] they shall give from now on for the service of the temple.[e] [42] Moreover, the five thousand shekels of silver that my officials[f] have received every year from the income

---

a Gk he b 152 B.C. c Or tabernacles
d Meaning of Gk uncertain e Gk house f Gk they

of the services of the temple, this too is canceled, because it belongs to the priests who minister there. [43]And all who take refuge at the temple in Jerusalem, or in any of its precincts, because they owe money to the king or are in debt, let them be released and receive back all their property in my kingdom.

[44] "Let the cost of rebuilding and restoring the structures of the sanctuary be paid from the revenues of the king. [45]And let the cost of rebuilding the walls of Jerusalem and fortifying it all around, and the cost of rebuilding the walls in Judea, also be paid from the revenues of the king."

10.1–89: Jonathan and the Syrian pretenders. 1: The arrival of Alexander Epiphanes* created a power struggle in the Seleucid empire and enabled Jonathan to play one pretender off against the other. **6:** Jonathan acknowledged the authority of the Syrian king when it worked to his advantage. **18:** Alexander made Jonathan a better offer: He appointed him high priest. Jonathan was not a legitimate high priest any more than Menelaus had been, but he accepted the office from a king whose own legitimacy was questionable. Many scholars think that Jonathan's acceptance of the high priesthood caused the Dead Sea sect* to break away from the Jerusalem Temple* and its cult, and that he is the figure who is called "The Wicked Priest" in the Pesher (commentary) on Habakkuk from the Dead Sea Scrolls. **25:** Demetrius responded with a grant of tax exemption. Jonathan was thus able to use his leverage to obtain advantages for his people. There is no question of Jewish independence at this point in the story.

---

[46] When Jonathan and the people heard these words, they did not believe or accept them, because they remembered the great wrongs that Demetrius[a] had done in Israel and how much he had oppressed them. [47]They favored Alexander, because he had been the first to speak peaceable words to them, and they remained his allies all his days. [48] Now King Alexander assembled large forces and encamped opposite Demetrius. [49]The two kings met in battle, and the army of Demetrius fled, and Alexander[b] pursued him and defeated them. [50]He pressed the battle strongly until the sun set, and on that day Demetrius fell.

[51] Then Alexander sent ambassadors to Ptolemy king of Egypt with the following message: [52]"Since I have returned to my kingdom and have taken my seat on the throne of my ancestors, and established my rule—for I crushed Demetrius and gained control of our country; [53]I met him in battle, and he and his army were crushed by us, and we have taken our seat on the throne of his kingdom— [54]now therefore let us establish friendship with one another; give me now your daughter as my wife, and I will become your son-in-law, and will make gifts to you and to her in keeping with your position."

[55] Ptolemy the king replied and said, "Happy was the day on which you returned to the land of your ancestors and took your seat on the throne of their kingdom. [56]And now I will do for you as you wrote, but meet me at Ptolemais, so that we may see one another, and I will become your father-in-law, as you have said." [57] So Ptolemy set out from Egypt, he and his daughter Cleopatra, and came to Ptolemais in the one hundred sixty-second year.[c] [58]King Alexander met him, and Ptolemy[a] gave him his daughter Cleopatra in marriage, and celebrated her wedding at Ptolemais with great pomp, as kings do.

[59] Then King Alexander wrote to Jonathan to come and meet him. [60]So he went with pomp to Ptolemais and met the two kings; he gave them and their Friends silver and gold and many gifts, and found favor with them. [61]A group of malcontents from Israel, renegades, gathered together against him to accuse him; but the king paid no attention to them. [62]The king gave orders to take off Jonathan's garments and to clothe him in purple, and they did so. [63]The king also seated him at his side; and he said to his officers, "Go out with him into the middle of the city and proclaim that no one is to bring charges against him about any matter, and let no one annoy him for any reason." [64]When his accusers saw the honor that was

---

a Gk he   *b* Other ancient authorities read *Alexander fled, and Demetrius*   *c* 150 B.C.

paid him, in accord with the proclamation, and saw him clothed in purple, they all fled. 65 Thus the king honored him and enrolled him among his chief[a] Friends, and made him general and governor of the province. 66 And Jonathan returned to Jerusalem in peace and gladness.

10.59: Jonathan freely accepts favors from gentile★ kings.

67 In the one hundred sixty-fifth year[b] Demetrius son of Demetrius came from Crete to the land of his ancestors. 68 When King Alexander heard of it, he was greatly distressed and returned to Antioch. 69 And Demetrius appointed Apollonius the governor of Coelesyria, and he assembled a large force and encamped against Jamnia. Then he sent the following message to the high priest Jonathan:

70 "You are the only one to rise up against us, and I have fallen into ridicule and disgrace because of you. Why do you assume authority against us in the hill country? 71 If you now have confidence in your forces, come down to the plain to meet us, and let us match strength with each other there, for I have with me the power of the cities. 72 Ask and learn who I am and who the others are that are helping us. People will tell you that you cannot stand before us, for your ancestors were twice put to flight in their own land. 73 And now you will not be able to withstand my cavalry and such an army in the plain, where there is no stone or pebble, or place to flee."

74 When Jonathan heard the words of Apollonius, his spirit was aroused. He chose ten thousand men and set out from Jerusalem, and his brother Simon met him to help him. 75 He encamped before Joppa, but the people of the city closed its gates, for Apollonius had a garrison in Joppa. 76 So they fought against it, and the people of the city became afraid and opened the gates, and Jonathan gained possession of Joppa.

77 When Apollonius heard of it, he mustered three thousand cavalry and a large army, and went to Azotus as though he were going farther. At the same time he advanced into the plain, for he had a large troop of cavalry and put confidence in it. 78 Jonathan[c] pursued him to Azotus, and the armies engaged in battle. 79 Now Apollonius had secretly left a thousand cavalry behind them. 80 Jonathan learned that there was an ambush behind him, for they surrounded his army and shot arrows at his men from early morning until late afternoon. 81 But his men stood fast, as Jonathan had commanded, and the enemy's[d] horses grew tired.

82 Then Simon brought forward his force and engaged the phalanx in battle (for the cavalry was exhausted); they were overwhelmed by him and fled, 83 and the cavalry was dispersed in the plain. They fled to Azotus and entered Beth-dagon, the temple of their idol, for safety. 84 But Jonathan burned Azotus and the surrounding towns and plundered them; and the temple of Dagon, and those who had taken refuge in it, he burned with fire. 85 The number of those who fell by the sword, with those burned alive, came to eight thousand.

10.84: The destruction of the temple of Dagon and those who had sought asylum there was in violation of all law and custom in the ancient world. Presumably, 1 Maccabees regards the action as justifiable because the temple was pagan. Even while Jonathan fraternizes with gentile★ kings, he is still represented as hostile to pagan religion.

86 Then Jonathan left there and encamped against Askalon, and the people of the city came out to meet him with great pomp.

87 He and those with him then returned to Jerusalem with a large amount of booty. 88 When King Alexander heard of these things, he honored Jonathan still more; 89 and he sent to him a golden buckle, such as it is the custom to give to the King's Kinsmen. He also gave him Ekron and all its environs as his possession.

11 Then the king of Egypt gathered great forces, like the sand by the seashore, and many ships; and he tried to get possession of Alexander's kingdom by trick-

a Gk first   b 147 B.C.   c Gk he   d Gk their

ery and add it to his own kingdom. ²He set out for Syria with peaceable words, and the people of the towns opened their gates to him and went to meet him, for King Alexander had commanded them to meet him, since he was Alexander's*a* father-in-law. ³But when Ptolemy entered the towns he stationed forces as a garrison in each town.

4 When he*b* approached Azotus, they showed him the burnt-out temple of Dagon, and Azotus and its suburbs destroyed, and the corpses lying about, and the charred bodies of those whom Jonathan*c* had burned in the war, for they had piled them in heaps along his route. ⁵They also told the king what Jonathan had done, to throw blame on him; but the king kept silent. ⁶Jonathan met the king at Joppa with pomp, and they greeted one another and spent the night there. ⁷And Jonathan went with the king as far as the river called Eleutherus; then he returned to Jerusalem.

8 So King Ptolemy gained control of the coastal cities as far as Seleucia by the sea, and he kept devising wicked designs against Alexander. ⁹He sent envoys to King Demetrius, saying, "Come, let us make a covenant with each other, and I will give you in marriage my daughter who was Alexander's wife, and you shall reign over your father's kingdom. ¹⁰I now regret that I gave him my daughter, for he has tried to kill me." ¹¹He threw blame on Alexander*d* because he coveted his kingdom. ¹²So he took his daughter away from him and gave her to Demetrius. He was estranged from Alexander, and their enmity became manifest.

13 Then Ptolemy entered Antioch and put on the crown of Asia. Thus he put two crowns on his head, the crown of Egypt and that of Asia. ¹⁴Now King Alexander was in Cilicia at that time, because the people of that region were in revolt. ¹⁵When Alexander heard of it, he came against him in battle. Ptolemy marched out and met him with a strong force, and put him to flight. ¹⁶So Alexander fled into Arabia to find protection there, and King Ptolemy was triumphant. ¹⁷Zabdiel the Arab cut off the head of Alexander and sent it to Ptolemy. ¹⁸But King Ptolemy died three days later, and his

troops in the strongholds were killed by the inhabitants of the strongholds. ¹⁹So Demetrius became king in the one hundred sixty-seventh year.*e*

20 In those days Jonathan assembled the Judeans to attack the citadel in Jerusalem, and he built many engines of war to use against it. ²¹But certain renegades who hated their nation went to the king and reported to him that Jonathan was besieging the citadel. ²²When he heard this he was angry, and as soon as he heard it he set out and came to Ptolemais; and he wrote Jonathan not to continue the siege, but to meet him for a conference at Ptolemais as quickly as possible.

23 When Jonathan heard this, he gave orders to continue the siege. He chose some of the elders of Israel and some of the priests, and put himself in danger, ²⁴for he went to the king at Ptolemais, taking silver and gold and clothing and numerous other gifts. And he won his favor. ²⁵Although certain renegades of his nation kept making complaints against him, ²⁶the king treated him as his predecessors had treated him; he exalted him in the presence of all his Friends. ²⁷He confirmed him in the high priesthood and in as many other honors as he had formerly had, and caused him to be reckoned among his chief*f* Friends. ²⁸Then Jonathan asked the king to free Judea and the three districts of Samaria*g* from tribute, and promised him three hundred talents. ²⁹The king consented, and wrote a letter to Jonathan about all these things; its contents were as follows:

30 "King Demetrius to his brother Jonathan and to the nation of the Jews, greetings. ³¹This copy of the letter that we wrote concerning you to our kinsman Lasthenes we have written to you also, so that you may know what it says. ³²'King Demetrius to his father Lasthenes, greetings. ³³We have determined to do good to the nation of the Jews, who are our friends and fulfill their obligations to us, because of the goodwill they show toward us. ³⁴We have confirmed as

---

a Gk *his*   *b* Other ancient authorities read *they*
c Gk *he*   *d* Gk *him*   *e* 145 B.C.   *f* Gk *first*
g Cn: Gk *the three districts and Samaria*

their possession both the territory of Judea and the three districts of Aphairema and Lydda and Rathamin; the latter, with all the region bordering them, were added to Judea from Samaria. To all those who offer sacrifice in Jerusalem we have granted release from[a] the royal taxes that the king formerly received from them each year, from the crops of the land and the fruit of the trees. 35 And the other payments henceforth due to us of the tithes, and the taxes due to us, and the salt pits and the crown taxes due to us—from all these we shall grant them release. 36 And not one of these grants shall be canceled from this time on forever. 37 Now therefore take care to make a copy of this, and let it be given to Jonathan and put up in a conspicuous place on the holy mountain.' "

38 When King Demetrius saw that the land was quiet before him and that there was no opposition to him, he dismissed all his troops, all of them to their own homes, except the foreign troops that he had recruited from the islands of the nations. So all the troops who had served under his predecessors hated him. 39 A certain Trypho had formerly been one of Alexander's supporters; he saw that all the troops were grumbling against Demetrius. So he went to Imalkue the Arab, who was bringing up Antiochus, the young son of Alexander, 40 and insistently urged him to hand Antiochus[b] over to him, to become king in place of his father. He also reported to Imalkue[b] what Demetrius had done and told of the hatred that the troops of Demetrius[c] had for him; and he stayed there many days.

41 Now Jonathan sent to King Demetrius the request that he remove the troops of the citadel from Jerusalem, and the troops in the strongholds; for they kept fighting against Israel. 42 And Demetrius sent this message back to Jonathan: "Not only will I do these things for you and your nation, but I will confer great honor on you and your nation, if I find an opportunity. 43 Now then you will do well to send me men who will help me, for all my troops have revolted." 44 So Jonathan sent three thousand stalwart men to him at Antioch, and when they came to the king, the king rejoiced at their arrival.

11.1–74: Dynastic struggles. 1: The king of Egypt in question was Ptolemy VI Philometor, who was known for his sympathy to the Jews, and who allowed the exiled High Priest Onias IV to build a temple at Leontopolis in Egypt. His campaign in Asia is of interest to 1 Maccabees, because it led to the death of Alexander Epiphanes,* who had been Jonathan's patron. **20:** The Syrian garrison in the Akra was still a thorn in the side of the Jews. Jonathan was not able to dislodge it.

45 Then the people of the city assembled within the city, to the number of a hundred and twenty thousand, and they wanted to kill the king. 46 But the king fled into the palace. Then the people of the city seized the main streets of the city and began to fight. 47 So the king called the Jews to his aid, and they all rallied around him and then spread out through the city; and they killed on that day about one hundred thousand. 48 They set fire to the city and seized a large amount of spoil on that day, and saved the king. 49 When the people of the city saw that the Jews had gained control of the city as they pleased, their courage failed and they cried out to the king with this entreaty: 50 "Grant us peace, and make the Jews stop fighting against us and our city." 51 And they threw down their arms and made peace. So the Jews gained glory in the sight of the king and of all the people in his kingdom, and they returned to Jerusalem with a large amount of spoil.

52 So King Demetrius sat on the throne of his kingdom, and the land was quiet before him. 53 But he broke his word about all that he had promised; he became estranged from Jonathan and did not repay the favors that Jonathan[d] had done him, but treated him very harshly.

54 After this Trypho returned, and with him the young boy Antiochus who began to reign and put on the crown. 55 All the troops that Demetrius had discharged gathered around him; they fought against Demetrius,[b] and he fled and was routed. 56 Trypho captured the elephants[e] and gained control

a Or Samaria, for all those who offer sacrifice in Jerusalem, in place of   b Gk him   c Gk his troops   d Gk he   e Gk animals of Antioch. 57 Then the young Antiochus wrote to Jonathan, saying, "I confirm you in the high priesthood and set you over the four districts and make you one of the king's Friends." 58 He also sent him gold plate and a table service, and granted him the right to drink from gold cups and dress in purple and wear a gold buckle. 59 He appointed Jonathan's*a* brother Simon governor from the Ladder of Tyre to the borders of Egypt.

60 Then Jonathan set out and traveled beyond the river and among the towns, and all the army of Syria gathered to him as allies. When he came to Askalon, the people of the city met him and paid him honor. 61 From there he went to Gaza, but the people of Gaza shut him out. So he besieged it and burned its suburbs with fire and plundered them. 62 Then the people of Gaza pleaded with Jonathan, and he made peace with them, and took the sons of their rulers as hostages and sent them to Jerusalem. And he passed through the country as far as Damascus.

63 Then Jonathan heard that the officers of Demetrius had come to Kadesh in Galilee with a large army, intending to remove him from office. 64 He went to meet them, but left his brother Simon in the country. 65 Simon encamped before Beth-zur and fought against it for many days and hemmed it in. 66 Then they asked him to grant them terms of peace, and he did so. He removed them from there, took possession of the town, and set a garrison over it.

67 Jonathan and his army encamped by the waters of Gennesaret. Early in the morning they marched to the plain of Hazor, 68 and there in the plain the army of the foreigners met him; they had set an ambush against him in the mountains, but they themselves met him face to face. 69 Then the men in ambush emerged from their places and joined battle. 70 All the men with Jonathan fled; not one of them was left except Mattathias son of Absalom and Judas son of Chalphi, commanders of the forces of the army. 71 Jonathan tore his clothes, put dust on his head, and prayed. 72 Then he turned back to the battle against the enemy*b* and routed them, and they fled. 73 When his men

who were fleeing saw this, they returned to him and joined him in the pursuit as far as Kadesh, to their camp, and there they encamped. 74 As many as three thousand of the foreigners fell that day. And Jonathan returned to Jerusalem.

11.45–74. 47: Jonathan sent troops to suppress a revolt against Demetrius in Antioch. Jewish soldiers often acted as mercenaries in the service of foreign kings. This action in turn often led to anti-Jewish sentiment on the part of the opponents of those kings. **71:** The chapter ends with a victory of Jonathan over the forces of Demetrius at Hazor in Galilee. In view of Jonathan's ruthless pursuit of "realpolitik," it is surprising to find that he turns the tide of battle by his prayer, but after all, he was the high priest. Although Jonathan was deeply immersed in Seleucid politics, 1 Maccabees gives the impression that the war is between Jews and gentiles,* and that God responds to the prayers of the Jews.

---

12 Now when Jonathan saw that the time was favorable for him, he chose men and sent them to Rome to confirm and renew the friendship with them. 2 He also sent letters to the same effect to the Spartans and to other places. 3 So they went to Rome and entered the senate chamber and said, "The high priest Jonathan and the Jewish nation have sent us to renew the former friendship and alliance with them." 4 And the Romans*c* gave them letters to the people in every place, asking them to provide for the envoys*b* safe conduct to the land of Judah.

5 This is a copy of the letter that Jonathan wrote to the Spartans: 6 "The high priest Jonathan, the senate of the nation, the priests, and the rest of the Jewish people to their brothers the Spartans, greetings. 7 Already in time past a letter was sent to the high priest Onias from Arius,*d* who was king among you, stating that you are our brothers, as the appended copy shows. 8 Onias welcomed the envoy with honor, and received the letter, which contained a clear declaration of alliance and friendship. 9 Therefore, though we have no need of these things, since we have

a Gk *his*   *b* Gk *them*   *c* Gk *they*   *d* Vg Compare verse 20: Gk *Darius* as encouragement the holy books that are in our hands, ¹⁰we have undertaken to send to renew our family ties and friendship with you, so that we may not become estranged from you, for considerable time has passed since you sent your letter to us. ¹¹We therefore remember you constantly on every occasion, both at our festivals and on other appropriate days, at the sacrifices that we offer and in our prayers, as it is right and proper to remember brothers. ¹²And we rejoice in your glory. ¹³But as for ourselves, many trials and many wars have encircled us; the kings around us have waged war against us. ¹⁴We were unwilling to annoy you and our other allies and friends with these wars, ¹⁵for we have the help that comes from Heaven for our aid, and so we were delivered from our enemies, and our enemies were humbled. ¹⁶We therefore have chosen Numenius son of Antiochus and Antipater son of Jason, and have sent them to Rome to renew our former friendship and alliance with them. ¹⁷We have commanded them to go also to you and greet you and deliver to you this letter from us concerning the renewal of our family ties. ¹⁸And now please send us a reply to this."

19 This is a copy of the letter that they sent to Onias: ²⁰"King Arius of the Spartans, to the high priest Onias, greetings. ²¹It has been found in writing concerning the Spartans and the Jews that they are brothers and are of the family of Abraham. ²²And now that we have learned this, please write us concerning your welfare; ²³we on our part write to you that your livestock and your property belong to us, and ours belong to you. We therefore command that our envoys*a* report to you accordingly."

12.1–23: Jews and Spartans. 1: Jonathan's embassy to Rome was presumably meant to seek recognition rather than actual aid. The claim of kinship with Sparta also shows that, at least in Jonathan's time, the Maccabees were by no means xenophobic.* Second Maccabees 5.9 also refers to the supposed kinship of Jews and Spartans. 9: The insistence that *we have no need of these things* can scarcely have been part of any actual correspondence between Jews and Spartans. It more probably reflects the reservations of the author of 1 Maccabees about Jewish-gentile* relations.19: It

is difficult to believe that a Spartan king would have written to a Jewish high priest saying that both peoples were descended from Abraham. The Spartan letter would seem to be a Jewish fiction. Other Jewish writers also concocted fanciful genealogies to establish relationships between Jews and the Hellenistic* world. One, Cleodemus Malchas, wrote that the sons of Abraham migrated to Libya and there joined with the Greek demi-god Heracles in a campaign. Heracles then allegedly married a daughter of one of the sons of Abraham. This episode shows again that the simple antithesis* of Jew and gentile that is projected in the early chapters of 1 Maccabees is not an accurate reflection of the realities of the Hellenistic* age.

24 Now Jonathan heard that the commanders of Demetrius had returned, with a larger force than before, to wage war against him. ²⁵So he marched away from Jerusalem and met them in the region of Hamath, for he gave them no opportunity to invade his own country. ²⁶He sent spies to their camp, and they returned and reported to him that the enemy*a* were being drawn up in formation to attack the Jews*b* by night. ²⁷So when the sun had set, Jonathan commanded his troops to be alert and to keep their arms at hand so as to be ready all night for battle, and he stationed outposts around the camp. ²⁸When the enemy heard that Jonathan and his troops were prepared for battle, they were afraid and were terrified at heart; so they kindled fires in their camp and withdrew.*c* ²⁹But Jonathan and his troops did not know it until morning, for they saw the fires burning. ³⁰Then Jonathan pursued them, but he did not overtake them, for they had crossed the Eleutherus river. ³¹So Jonathan turned aside against the Arabs who are called Zabadeans, and he crushed them and plundered them. ³²Then he broke camp and went to Damascus, and marched through all that region.

33 Simon also went out and marched through the country as far as Askalon and the neighboring strongholds. He turned aside to Joppa and took it by surprise, ³⁴for he had heard that they were ready to hand

a Gk *they*   *b* Gk *them*   *c* Other ancient authorities omit *and withdrew* over the stronghold to those whom Demetrius had sent. And he stationed a garrison there to guard it.

35 When Jonathan returned he convened the elders of the people and planned with them to build strongholds in Judea, 36to build the walls of Jerusalem still higher, and to erect a high barrier between the citadel and the city to separate it from the city, in order to isolate it so that its garrison*a* could neither buy nor sell. 37So they gathered together to rebuild the city; part of the wall on the valley to the east had fallen, and he repaired the section called Chaphenatha. 38Simon also built Adida in the Shephelah; he fortified it and installed gates with bolts.

39 Then Trypho attempted to become king in Asia and put on the crown, and to raise his hand against King Antiochus. 40He feared that Jonathan might not permit him to do so, but might make war on him, so he kept seeking to seize and kill him, and he marched out and came to Beth-shan. 41Jonathan went out to meet him with forty thousand picked warriors, and he came to Beth-shan. 42When Trypho saw that he had come with a large army, he was afraid to raise his hand against him. 43So he received him with honor and commended him to all his Friends, and he gave him gifts and commanded his Friends and his troops to obey him as they would himself. 44Then he said to Jonathan, "Why have you put all these people to so much trouble when we are not at war? 45Dismiss them now to their homes and choose for yourself a few men to stay with you, and come with me to Ptolemais. I will hand it over to you as well as the other strongholds and the remaining troops and all the officials, and will turn around and go home. For that is why I am here."

46 Jonathan*b* trusted him and did as he said; he sent away the troops, and they returned to the land of Judah. 47He kept with himself three thousand men, two thousand of whom he left in Galilee, while one thousand accompanied him. 48But when Jonathan entered Ptolemais, the people of Ptolemais closed the gates and seized him, and they killed with the sword all who had entered with him.

49 Then Trypho sent troops and cavalry into Galilee and the Great Plain to destroy all Jonathan's soldiers. 50But they realized that Jonathan had been seized and had perished along with his men, and they encouraged one another and kept marching in close formation, ready for battle. 51When their pursuers saw that they would fight for their lives, they turned back. 52So they all reached the land of Judah safely, and they mourned for Jonathan and his companions and were in great fear; and all Israel mourned deeply. 53All the nations around them tried to destroy them, for they said, "They have no leader or helper. Now therefore let us make war on them and blot out the memory of them from humankind."

12.24–53: The capture of Jonathan. Jonathan's remarkable success in the world of Hellenistic* politics ultimately led to his downfall. He was too powerful to be ignored by an ambitious climber like Trypho. His fatal mistake was unwarranted trust. The Pesher (commentary) on Habakkuk from the Dead Sea Scrolls says that God delivered the Wicked Priest into the hands of his enemies to destroy him. Many scholars think the reference is to Jonathan. If this is indeed the case, it gives an evaluation of Jonathan that is very different from that of 1 Maccabees. **53:** The chapter ends on a note of crisis, with the nations round about threatening to destroy Israel. This is, of course, a drastic oversimplification of the political situation of the day.

13 Simon heard that Trypho had assembled a large army to invade the land of Judah and destroy it, 2and he saw that the people were trembling with fear. So he went up to Jerusalem, and gathering the people together 3he encouraged them, saying to them, "You yourselves know what great things my brothers and I and the house of my father have done for the laws and the sanctuary; you know also the wars and the difficulties that my brothers and I have seen. 4By reason of this all my brothers have perished for the sake of Israel, and I alone am left. 5And now, far be it from me to spare my life in any time of distress, for I am not better than my brothers. 6But I will avenge my na-

a Gk *they*   *b* Gk *he*

tion and the sanctuary and your wives and children, for all the nations have gathered together out of hatred to destroy us."

7 The spirit of the people was rekindled when they heard these words, 8and they answered in a loud voice, "You are our leader in place of Judas and your brother Jonathan. 9Fight our battles, and all that you say to us we will do." 10So he assembled all the warriors and hurried to complete the walls of Jerusalem, and he fortified it on every side. 11He sent Jonathan son of Absalom to Joppa, and with him a considerable army; he drove out its occupants and remained there.

12 Then Trypho left Ptolemais with a large army to invade the land of Judah, and Jonathan was with him under guard. 13Simon encamped in Adida, facing the plain. 14Trypho learned that Simon had risen up in place of his brother Jonathan, and that he was about to join battle with him, so he sent envoys to him and said, 15"It is for the money that your brother Jonathan owed the royal treasury, in connection with the offices he held, that we are detaining him. 16Send now one hundred talents of silver and two of his sons as hostages, so that when released he will not revolt against us, and we will release him."

17 Simon knew that they were speaking deceitfully to him, but he sent to get the money and the sons, so that he would not arouse great hostility among the people, who might say, 18"It was because Simon*a* did not send him the money and the sons, that Jonathan*b* perished." 19So he sent the sons and the hundred talents, but Trypho*b* broke his word and did not release Jonathan.

20 After this Trypho came to invade the country and destroy it, and he circled around by the way to Adora. But Simon and his army kept marching along opposite him to every place he went. 21Now the men in the citadel kept sending envoys to Trypho urging him to come to them by way of the wilderness and to send them food. 22So Trypho got all his cavalry ready to go, but that night a very heavy snow fell, and he did not go because of the snow. He marched off and went into the land of Gilead. 23When he approached Baskama, he killed Jonathan, and he was

buried there. 24Then Trypho turned and went back to his own land.

25 Simon sent and took the bones of his brother Jonathan, and buried him in Modein, the city of his ancestors. 26All Israel bewailed him with great lamentation, and mourned him many days. 27And Simon built a monument over the tomb of his father and his brothers; he made it high so that it might be seen, with polished stone at the front and back. 28He also erected seven pyramids, opposite one another, for his father and mother and four brothers. 29For the pyramids*c* he devised an elaborate setting, erecting about them great columns, and on the columns he put suits of armor for a permanent memorial, and beside the suits of armor he carved ships, so that they could be seen by all who sail the sea. 30This is the tomb that he built in Modein; it remains to this day.

31 Trypho dealt treacherously with the young King Antiochus; he killed him 32and became king in his place, putting on the crown of Asia; and he brought great calamity on the land. 33But Simon built up the strongholds of Judea and walled them all around, with high towers and great walls and gates and bolts, and he stored food in the strongholds. 34Simon also chose emissaries and sent them to King Demetrius with a request to grant relief to the country, for all that Trypho did was to plunder. 35King Demetrius sent him a favorable reply to this request, and wrote him a letter as follows, 36"King Demetrius to Simon, the high priest and friend of kings, and to the elders and nation of the Jews, greetings. 37We have received the gold crown and the palm branch that you*d* sent, and we are ready to make a general peace with you and to write to our officials to grant you release from tribute. 38All the grants that we have made to you remain valid, and let the strongholds that you have built be your possession. 39We pardon any errors and offenses committed to this day, and cancel the crown tax that you owe; and whatever other tax has been col-

a Gk *I*   *b* Gk *he*   *c* Gk *For these*   *d* The word *you* in verses 37–40 is plural lected in Jerusalem shall be collected no longer. [40]And if any of you are qualified to be enrolled in our bodyguard,[a] let them be enrolled, and let there be peace between us."

13.1–53: The rise of Simon. In response to the threat of the nations, Simon offers himself as leader in place of his brothers. The emphasis falls on the family, which, with each successive member installed as leader, is on its way to becoming a dynasty.* The dynastic implications are strengthened by the construction of a family tomb in Modein (v. 25). **31:** The murder of Jonathan is followed by the murder of the young king, Antiochus. This shows the murderous character of Trypho. **35:** Still playing off one Syrian ruler against another, Simon obtains independence from Demetrius II.

[41] In the one hundred seventieth year[b] the yoke of the Gentiles was removed from Israel, [42]and the people began to write in their documents and contracts, "In the first year of Simon the great high priest and commander and leader of the Jews."

[43] In those days Simon[c] encamped against Gazara[d] and surrounded it with troops. He made a siege engine, brought it up to the city, and battered and captured one tower. [44]The men in the siege engine leaped out into the city, and a great tumult arose in the city. [45]The men in the city, with their wives and children, went up on the wall with their clothes torn, and they cried out with a loud voice, asking Simon to make peace with them; [46]they said, "Do not treat us according to our wicked acts but according to your mercy." [47]So Simon reached an agreement with them and stopped fighting against them. But he expelled them from the city and cleansed the houses in which the idols were located, and then entered it with hymns and praise. [48]He removed all uncleanness from it, and settled in it those who observed the law. He also strengthened its fortifications and built in it a house for himself. [49]Those who were in the citadel at Jerusalem were prevented from going in and out to buy and sell in the country. So they were very hungry, and many of them perished from famine. [50]Then they cried to Simon to make peace with them, and he did

so. But he expelled them from there and cleansed the citadel from its pollutions. [51]On the twenty-third day of the second month, in the one hundred seventy-first year,[e] the Jews[f] entered it with praise and palm branches, and with harps and cymbals and stringed instruments, and with hymns and songs, because a great enemy had been crushed and removed from Israel. [52]Simon[g] decreed that every year they should celebrate this day with rejoicing. He strengthened the fortifications of the temple hill alongside the citadel, and he and his men lived there. [53]Simon saw that his son John had reached manhood, and so he made him commander of all the forces; and he lived at Gazara.

13.41–53. 41: First Maccabees regards Simon's accession* to the high priesthood in the year 142 BCE (year 170 in the Seleucid era) as the time when the yoke of the gentile* was lifted. **50:** Simon succeeded in doing what Jonathan and Judas could not, expelling the Syrian garrison from the Akra. **53:** The emergence of John Hyrcanus as Simon's potential successor ensures the future of the dynasty.*

14 In the one hundred seventy-second year[h] King Demetrius assembled his forces and marched into Media to obtain help, so that he could make war against Trypho. [2]When King Arsaces of Persia and Media heard that Demetrius had invaded his territory, he sent one of his generals to take him alive. [3]The general[g] went and defeated the army of Demetrius, and seized him and took him to Arsaces, who put him under guard.

[4] The land[i] had rest all the days of
    Simon.
  He sought the good of his nation;
    his rule was pleasing to them,
    as was the honor shown him, all his
      days.
[5] To crown all his honors he took Joppa
    for a harbor,
    and opened a way to the isles of the
      sea.

---

a Or court   b 142 B.C.   c Gk he   d Cn: Gk Gaza
e 141 B.C.   f Gk they   g Gk He   h 140 B.C.
i Other ancient authorities add of Judah

6 He extended the borders of his nation,
   and gained full control of the country.
7 He gathered a host of captives;
   he ruled over Gazara and Beth-zur
      and the citadel,
   and he removed its uncleanness from it;
   and there was none to oppose him.
8 They tilled their land in peace;
   the ground gave its increase,
   and the trees of the plains their fruit.
9 Old men sat in the streets;
   they all talked together of good
      things,
   and the youths put on splendid
      military attire.
10 He supplied the towns with food,
   and furnished them with the means
      of defense,
   until his renown spread to the ends of
      the earth.
11 He established peace in the land,
   and Israel rejoiced with great joy.
12 All the people sat under their own vines
      and fig trees,
   and there was none to make them
      afraid.
13 No one was left in the land to fight
      them,
   and the kings were crushed in those
      days.
14 He gave help to all the humble among
      his people;
   he sought out the law,
   and did away with all the renegades
      and outlaws.
15 He made the sanctuary glorious,
   and added to the vessels of the
      sanctuary.

16 It was heard in Rome, and as far away as Sparta, that Jonathan had died, and they were deeply grieved. 17When they heard that his brother Simon had become high priest in his stead, and that he was ruling over the country and the towns in it, 18they wrote to him on bronze tablets to renew with him the friendship and alliance that they had established with his brothers Judas and Jonathan. 19And these were read before the assembly in Jerusalem.

20 This is a copy of the letter that the Spartans sent:

"The rulers and the city of the Spartans to the high priest Simon and to the elders and the priests and the rest of the Jewish people, our brothers, greetings. 21The envoys who were sent to our people have told us about your glory and honor, and we rejoiced at their coming. 22We have recorded what they said in our public decrees, as follows, 'Numenius son of Antiochus and Antipater son of Jason, envoys of the Jews, have come to us to renew their friendship with us. 23It has pleased our people to receive these men with honor and to put a copy of their words in the public archives, so that the people of the Spartans may have a record of them. And they have sent a copy of this to the high priest Simon.' "

24 After this Simon sent Numenius to Rome with a large gold shield weighing one thousand minas, to confirm the alliance with the Romans.ᵃ

14.1–24: **Simon's reign. 1:** The demise of Demetrius meant that there was no longer any established Seleucid ruler in a position to threaten Judea, but the claim that *the land had rest all the days of Simon* (v. 4) is undoubtedly an exaggeration. His reign is depicted as the fulfillment of prophecy. **8:** *The ground gave its increase:* See Lev 26.4; Ezek 34.27. **9:** *Old men sat in the streets:* See Zech 8.4. **12:** *All the people sat under their own vines:* See Mic 4.4. **15:** *The glorious sanctuary* completes the parallel with the golden age of Solomon. **16:** Simon renews the contacts with Rome and Sparta. **24:** The gift sent to Rome was very substantial for a small nation, indicating a strong desire on the part of Simon for friendship with Rome.

---

25 When the people heard these things they said, "How shall we thank Simon and his sons? 26For he and his brothers and the house of his father have stood firm; they have fought and repulsed Israel's enemies and established its freedom." 27So they made a record on bronze tablets and put it on pillars on Mount Zion.

This is a copy of what they wrote: "On the eighteenth day of Elul, in the one hundred seventy-second year,ᵇ which is the third year of the great high priest Simon, 28in Asara-

ᵃ Gk *them*   ᵇ 140 B.C.

mel,[a] in the great assembly of the priests and the people and the rulers of the nation and the elders of the country, the following was proclaimed to us:

29 "Since wars often occurred in the country, Simon son of Mattathias, a priest of the sons[b] of Joarib, and his brothers, exposed themselves to danger and resisted the enemies of their nation, in order that their sanctuary and the law might be preserved; and they brought great glory to their nation. 30Jonathan rallied the[c] nation, became their high priest, and was gathered to his people. 31When their enemies decided to invade their country and lay hands on their sanctuary, 32then Simon rose up and fought for his nation. He spent great sums of his own money; he armed the soldiers of his nation and paid them wages. 33He fortified the towns of Judea, and Beth-zur on the borders of Judea, where formerly the arms of the enemy had been stored, and he placed there a garrison of Jews. 34He also fortified Joppa, which is by the sea, and Gazara, which is on the borders of Azotus, where the enemy formerly lived. He settled Jews there, and provided in those towns[d] whatever was necessary for their restoration.

35 "The people saw Simon's faithfulness[e] and the glory that he had resolved to win for his nation, and they made him their leader and high priest, because he had done all these things and because of the justice and loyalty that he had maintained toward his nation. He sought in every way to exalt his people. 36In his days things prospered in his hands, so that the Gentiles were put out of the[e] country, as were also those in the city of David in Jerusalem, who had built themselves a citadel from which they used to sally forth and defile the environs of the sanctuary, doing great damage to its purity. 37He settled Jews in it and fortified it for the safety of the country and of the city, and built the walls of Jerusalem higher.

38 "In view of these things King Demetrius confirmed him in the high priesthood, 39made him one of his Friends, and paid him high honors. 40For he had heard that the Jews were addressed by the Romans as friends and allies and brothers, and that the Romans[f] had received the envoys of Simon with honor.

41 "The Jews and their priests have resolved that Simon should be their leader and high priest forever, until a trustworthy prophet should arise, 42and that he should be governor over them and that he should take charge of the sanctuary and appoint officials over its tasks and over the country and the weapons and the strongholds, and that he should take charge of the sanctuary, 43and that he should be obeyed by all, and that all contracts in the country should be written in his name, and that he should be clothed in purple and wear gold.

44 "None of the people or priests shall be permitted to nullify any of these decisions or to oppose what he says, or to convene an assembly in the country without his permission, or to be clothed in purple or put on a gold buckle. 45Whoever acts contrary to these decisions or rejects any of them shall be liable to punishment."

46 All the people agreed to grant Simon the right to act in accordance with these decisions. 47So Simon accepted and agreed to be high priest, to be commander and ethnarch of the Jews and priests, and to be protector of them all.[g] 48And they gave orders to inscribe this decree on bronze tablets, to put them up in a conspicuous place in the precincts of the sanctuary, 49and to deposit copies of them in the treasury, so that Simon and his sons might have them.

14.25–49: Simon's leadership. 25: The exaltation of Simon is completed by the edict of the people, declaring him to be high priest, ethnarch ("ruler of the people"), and commander for life. His mighty deeds and those of his family are listed, like those of the Lord in such biblical texts as Josh 24. This was the first time since the Babylonian exile that Judea was free of a gentile* military presence. **41:** Simon's high priesthood was confirmed *until a trustworthy prophet* *should arise.* As in 4.46, the prophet here is in the very

---

a This word resembles the Hebrew words for *the court of the people of God* or *the prince of the people of God*　b Meaning of Gk uncertain　　c Gk *their*　　d Gk *them* e Other ancient authorities read *conduct*　　f Gk *they* g Or *to preside over them all*

distant future. The passage emphasizes the permanence of Simon's reign.

THE RENEWED SYRIAN THREAT

15.1–16.10: But Simon's reign was not permanent.
The peace was interrupted in 138 BCE by the arrival of
Antiochus VII Sidetes, the younger brother of Deme-
trius II.

---

15 Antiochus, son of King Demetrius,
sent a letter from the islands of the
sea to Simon, the priest and ethnarch of the
Jews, and to all the nation; [2]its contents were
as follows: "King Antiochus to Simon the
high priest and ethnarch and to the nation
of the Jews, greetings. [3]Whereas certain
scoundrels have gained control of the kingdom of our ancestors, and I intend to lay
claim to the kingdom so that I may restore it
as it formerly was, and have recruited a host
of mercenary troops and have equipped war-
ships, [4]and intend to make a landing in the
country so that I may proceed against those
who have destroyed our country and those
who have devastated many cities in my kingdom, [5]now therefore I confirm to you all the
tax remissions that the kings before me have
granted you, and a release from all the other
payments from which they have released
you. [6]I permit you to mint your own coinage
as money for your country, [7]and I grant freedom to Jerusalem and the sanctuary. All the
weapons that you have prepared and the
strongholds that you have built and now hold
shall remain yours. [8]Every debt you owe to
the royal treasury and any such future debts
shall be canceled for you from henceforth
and for all time. [9]When we gain control
of our kingdom, we will bestow great honor
on you and your nation and the temple, so
that your glory will become manifest in all
the earth."

10 In the one hundred seventy-fourth
year[a] Antiochus set out and invaded the land
of his ancestors. All the troops rallied to him,
so that there were only a few with Trypho.
[11]Antiochus pursued him, and Trypho[b]
came in his flight to Dor, which is by the sea;
[12]for he knew that troubles had converged
on him, and his troops had deserted him.

[13]So Antiochus encamped against Dor, and
with him were one hundred twenty thousand
warriors and eight thousand cavalry. [14]He
surrounded the town, and the ships joined
battle from the sea; he pressed the town hard
from land and sea, and permitted no one to
leave or enter it.

15 Then Numenius and his companions
arrived from Rome, with letters to the kings
and countries, in which the following was
written: [16]"Lucius, consul of the Romans, to
King Ptolemy, greetings. [17]The envoys of the
Jews have come to us as our friends and allies to renew our ancient friendship and alliance. They had been sent by the high priest
Simon and by the Jewish people [18]and have
brought a gold shield weighing one thousand
minas. [19]We therefore have decided to write
to the kings and countries that they should
not seek their harm or make war against
them and their cities and their country, or
make alliance with those who war against
them. [20]And it has seemed good to us to accept the shield from them. [21]Therefore if
any scoundrels have fled to you from their
country, hand them over to the high priest
Simon, so that he may punish them according to their law."

22 The consul[c] wrote the same thing to
King Demetrius and to Attalus and Ariara-
thes and Arsaces, [23]and to all the countries,
and to Sampsames,[d] and to the Spartans,
and to Delos, and to Myndos, and to Sicyon,
and to Caria, and to Samos, and to Pamphylia, and to Lycia, and to Halicarnassus, and
to Rhodes, and to Phaselis, and to Cos, and
to Side, and to Aradus and Gortyna and
Cnidus and Cyprus and Cyrene. [24]They also
sent a copy of these things to the high priest
Simon.

25 King Antiochus besieged Dor for the
second time, continually throwing his forces
against it and making engines of war; and he
shut Trypho up and kept him from going out
or in. [26]And Simon sent to Antiochus[e] two
thousand picked troops, to fight for him, and
silver and gold and a large amount of military
equipment. [27]But he refused to receive

---

a 138 B.C.   *b* Gk *he*   *c* Gk *He*   *d* The name is
uncertain   *e* Gk *him*

them, and broke all the agreements he formerly had made with Simon, and became estranged from him. 28 He sent to him Athenobius, one of his Friends, to confer with him, saying, "You hold control of Joppa and Gazara and the citadel in Jerusalem; they are cities of my kingdom. 29 You have devastated their territory, you have done great damage in the land, and you have taken possession of many places in my kingdom. 30 Now then, hand over the cities that you have seized and the tribute money of the places that you have conquered outside the borders of Judea; 31 or else pay me five hundred talents of silver for the destruction that you have caused and five hundred talents more for the tribute money of the cities. Otherwise we will come and make war on you."

32 So Athenobius, the king's Friend, came to Jerusalem, and when he saw the splendor of Simon, and the sideboard with its gold and silver plate, and his great magnificence, he was amazed. When he reported to him the king's message, 33 Simon said to him in reply: "We have neither taken foreign land nor seized foreign property, but only the inheritance of our ancestors, which at one time had been unjustly taken by our enemies. 34 Now that we have the opportunity, we are firmly holding the inheritance of our ancestors. 35 As for Joppa and Gazara, which you demand, they were causing great damage among the people and to our land; for them we will give you one hundred talents."

15.1–35. 5: Sidetes confirmed the various concessions made by previous Syrian kings. 28: He demanded, however, that Simon give back the places he had taken by force. 33: Simon responded that he had only recovered the inheritance of his fathers.

~~~~~~

Athenobius[a] did not answer him a word, 36 but returned in wrath to the king and reported to him these words, and also the splendor of Simon and all that he had seen. And the king was very angry.

37 Meanwhile Trypho embarked on a ship and escaped to Orthosia. 38 Then the king made Cendebeus commander-in-chief of the coastal country, and gave him troops of infantry and cavalry. 39 He commanded him to encamp against Judea, to build up Kedron and fortify its gates, and to make war on the people; but the king pursued Trypho. 40 So Cendebeus came to Jamnia and began to provoke the people and invade Judea and take the people captive and kill them. 41 He built up Kedron and stationed horsemen and troops there, so that they might go out and make raids along the highways of Judea, as the king had ordered him.

16 John went up from Gazara and reported to his father Simon what Cendebeus had done. 2 And Simon called in his two eldest sons Judas and John, and said to them: "My brothers and I and my father's house have fought the wars of Israel from our youth until this day, and things have prospered in our hands so that we have delivered Israel many times. 3 But now I have grown old, and you by Heaven's[b] mercy are mature in years. Take my place and my brother's, and go out and fight for our nation, and may the help that comes from Heaven be with you."

4 So John[c] chose out of the country twenty thousand warriors and cavalry, and they marched against Cendebeus and camped for the night in Modein. 5 Early in the morning they started out and marched into the plain, where a large force of infantry and cavalry was coming to meet them; and a stream lay between them. 6 Then he and his army lined up against them. He saw that the soldiers were afraid to cross the stream, so he crossed over first; and when his troops saw him, they crossed over after him. 7 Then he divided the army and placed the cavalry in the center of the infantry, for the cavalry of the enemy were very numerous. 8 They sounded the trumpets, and Cendebeus and his army were put to flight; many of them fell wounded and the rest fled into the stronghold. 9 At that time Judas the brother of John was wounded, but John pursued them until Cendebeus[d] reached Kedron, which he had built. 10 They also fled into the towers that were in the fields of Azotus, and John[d] burned it with fire, and about two

---

a Gk He   b Gk his   c Other ancient authorities
read he   d Gk he

thousand of them fell. He then returned to Judea safely.

16.1–10: John Hyrcanus successfully repels the Syrian attack, but the episode shows that the young state is by no means secure.

11 Now Ptolemy son of Abubus had been appointed governor over the plain of Jericho; he had a large store of silver and gold, 12for he was son-in-law of the high priest. 13His heart was lifted up; he determined to get control of the country, and made treacherous plans against Simon and his sons, to do away with them. 14Now Simon was visiting the towns of the country and attending to their needs, and he went down to Jericho with his sons Mattathias and Judas, in the one hundred seventy-seventh year,ᵃ in the eleventh month, which is the month of Shebat. 15The son of Abubus received them treacherously in the little stronghold called Dok, which he had built; he gave them a great banquet, and hid men there. 16When Simon and his sons were drunk, Ptolemy and his men rose up, took their weapons, rushed in against Simon in the banquet hall and killed him and his two sons, as well as some of his servants. 17So he committed an act of great treachery and returned evil for good.

18 Then Ptolemy wrote a report about these things and sent it to the king, asking him to send troops to aid him and to turn over to him the towns and the country. 19He sent other troops to Gazara to do away with

John; he sent letters to the captains asking them to come to him so that he might give them silver and gold and gifts; 20and he sent other troops to take possession of Jerusalem and the temple hill. 21But someone ran ahead and reported to John at Gazara that his father and brothers had perished, and that "he has sent men to kill you also." 22When he heard this, he was greatly shocked; he seized the men who came to destroy him and killed them, for he had found out that they were seeking to destroy him.

23 The rest of the acts of John and his wars and the brave deeds that he did, and the building of the walls that he completed, and his achievements, 24are written in the annals of his high priesthood, from the time that he became high priest after his father.

16.11–24: The death of Simon. Like all his brothers, Simon met a violent death, treacherously murdered by his own son-in-law. His death was also ignominious, since he was drunk. This episode also recalls a statement about the Wicked Priest in the Pesher on Habakkuk from the Dead Sea Scrolls (column 11): "Its interpretation concerns the Priest whose shame has exceeded his glory because he . . . walked on paths of drunkenness to slake his thirst; but the cup of God's anger will engulf him."

The death of Simon is a somber conclusion to 1 Maccabees, but the survival of John Hyrcanus provides a note of hope for the future.

a 134 B.C.

2 MACCABEES

Introduction

Second Maccabees is an abridgment of a five-volume work by Jason of Cyrene. It covers the events leading up to the persecution under Antiochus Epiphanes,✶ and the course of the revolt down to the victory over Nicanor in 161 BCE (prior to the death of Judas). Unlike 1 Maccabees, the account is vivid and emotional, with frequent reference to miraculous and supernatural occurrences. A major feature of the book is the prominence accorded to the deaths of the martyrs.✶ Second Maccabees is often described as "tragic" or "pathetic" history writing, but this emotional quality is typical of much of Hellenistic✶ history writing, even in the case of the eminent historian Polybius, who criticized others for being too emotional. Miraculous episodes are not uncommon in Hellenistic historiography. While some of the episodes are fantastic, 2 Maccabees is also a valuable historical source and is superior to 1 Maccabees on some points.

The summary of Jason's work is introduced at 2.19 as "the story of Judas Maccabeus and his brothers, and the purification of the great temple,✶ and the dedication of the altar, and further the wars against Antiochus Epiphanes and his son Eupator, and the appearances which came from heaven." The preface in 2.19–32 and the conclusion in 15.37–39 are evidently the work of the person who abridged Jason's work. Other editorial comments can be found in 6.12–17, and probably in 4.17 and 5.17–20. The story of the martyrs in 2 Macc 7 may originally have been an independent story, but it is now well integrated into the theology of the book. Two letters found at the beginning of the book (1.1–2.18) are of separate origin.

Jason of Cyrene probably wrote soon after the last events he recorded (about 160 BCE, or shortly thereafter). The author may well have been the same Jason who was sent to Rome by Judas Maccabee (1 Macc 8.17). His companion, Eupolemus, also a historian, is mentioned in passing in 2 Macc 4.11. The context of the abridgment is indicated by the first letter in 2 Macc 1.1–9. This letter is dated to 124 BCE (the 188th year of the Seleucid era), and it is written to urge the Jews of Egypt to celebrate the festival of Hanukkah. The summary of Jason's history is appended to the letter to provide an explanation of the reason for the celebration. The summary was not necessarily compiled for this purpose; it has its own theological message. But it was evidently congenial to the promotion of the festival of Hanukkah.

The theological and literary context of 2 Maccabees is somewhat different from that of 1 Maccabees. Both Jason's work and the summary were written in Greek, and were more clearly steeped in Hellenistic culture than was the case with the originally Hebrew chronicle.✶ Jason of Cyrene presumably came from the Diaspora,✶ and the abridgment was found suitable for supporting an appeal to Diaspora Jews. Also, 2 Maccabees is not so closely bound to the Hasmonean dynasty,✶ the ruling family, as was the case with 1 Maccabees. Judas is the hero of the story, but there is no mention of Mattathias, and the story ends before the emergence of Jonathan and Simon as leaders.

READING GUIDE

Second Maccabees is structured as the account of a series of attacks on the Temple and its defense: 2 Macc 3; 4.1–10.9; 10.10–15.36. Yet "the Lord did not choose the nation for the sake of the holy place, but the place for the sake of the nation" (5.19). The society is of primary importance, and its welfare depends on observance of the law. The persecution of Antiochus Epiphanes* is in part a punishment for the sins of the Jews. It is overcome not only by the heroism of Judas Maccabee but also by the sacrificial deaths of the martyrs. Second Maccabees also attaches great importance to manifestations of aid from heaven. The theology of martyrdom is supported by a strong belief in resurrection, which was notably lacking in 1 Maccabees.

Like 1 Maccabees, 2 Maccabees raises questions about the use of violence and the justification of vengeance. The more prominent questions in this book, however, concern martyrdom, and even suicide in ch. 13. Was such sacrifice of life necessary, and should it be admired, as it is here? The questions concern the absolute claim of religious values in the face of death, and the power and danger of belief in the supernatural and the miraculous.

1 The Jews in Jerusalem and those in the land of Judea,

To their Jewish kindred in Egypt,

Greetings and true peace.

2 May God do good to you, and may he remember his covenant with Abraham and Isaac and Jacob, his faithful servants. 3 May he give you all a heart to worship him and to do his will with a strong heart and a willing spirit. 4 May he open your heart to his law and his commandments, and may he bring peace. 5 May he hear your prayers and be reconciled to you, and may he not forsake you in time of evil. 6 We are now praying for you here.

7 In the reign of Demetrius, in the one hundred sixty-ninth year,[a] we Jews wrote to you, in the critical distress that came upon us in those years after Jason and his company revolted from the holy land and the kingdom 8 and burned the gate and shed innocent blood. We prayed to the Lord and were heard, and we offered sacrifice and grain offering, and we lit the lamps and set out the loaves. 9 And now see that you keep the festival of booths in the month of Chislev, in the one hundred eighty-eighth year.[b]

1.1–9: The first letter. The purpose of the letter is to urge the Jews of Egypt to celebrate the festival of Hanukkah, to commemorate the rededication of the Temple* by Judas. **2:** The *covenant* with Abraham, Isaac, and Jacob* is the basis for unity between the different branches of Judaism. This should not be set over against the covenant with Moses, since the latter entails observance of the law and commandments (v. 4). **7:** An earlier letter had been sent to the Jews of Egypt in 143 BCE. The reference to *Jason and his company* agrees with 2 Maccabees in assigning primary responsibility for the upheavals to Jewish renegades. **8:** The letter takes the success of the Maccabean revolt as evidence that God heard the prayers and upheld the covenant.

10 The people of Jerusalem and of Judea and the senate and Judas,

To Aristobulus, who is of the family of the anointed priests, teacher of King Ptolemy, and to the Jews in Egypt,

Greetings and good health.

11 Having been saved by God out of grave dangers we thank him greatly for taking our

a 143 B.C. *b* 124 B.C.

side against the king,[a] [12]for he drove out those who fought against the holy city. [13]When the leader reached Persia with a force that seemed irresistible, they were cut to pieces in the temple of Nanea by a deception employed by the priests of the goddess[b] Nanea. [14]On the pretext of intending to marry her, Antiochus came to the place together with his Friends, to secure most of its treasures as a dowry. [15]When the priests of the temple of Nanea had set out the treasures and Antiochus had come with a few men inside the wall of the sacred precinct, they closed the temple as soon as he entered it. [16]Opening a secret door in the ceiling, they threw stones and struck down the leader and his men; they dismembered them and cut off their heads and threw them to the people outside. [17]Blessed in every way be our God, who has brought judgment on those who have behaved impiously.

18 Since on the twenty-fifth day of Chislev we shall celebrate the purification of the temple, we thought it necessary to notify you, in order that you also may celebrate the festival of booths and the festival of the fire given when Nehemiah, who built the temple and the altar, offered sacrifices.

19 For when our ancestors were being led captive to Persia, the pious priests of that time took some of the fire of the altar and secretly hid it in the hollow of a dry cistern, where they took such precautions that the place was unknown to anyone. [20]But after many years had passed, when it pleased God, Nehemiah, having been commissioned by the king of Persia, sent the descendants of the priests who had hidden the fire to get it. And when they reported to us that they had not found fire but only a thick liquid, he ordered them to dip it out and bring it. [21]When the materials for the sacrifices were presented, Nehemiah ordered the priests to sprinkle the liquid on the wood and on the things laid upon it. [22]When this had been done and some time had passed, and when the sun, which had been clouded over, shone out, a great fire blazed up, so that all marveled. [23]And while the sacrifice was being consumed, the priests offered prayer—the priests and everyone. Jonathan led, and the rest responded, as did Nehemiah. [24]The prayer was to this effect:

"O Lord, Lord God, Creator of all things, you are awe-inspiring and strong and just and merciful, you alone are king and are kind, [25]you alone are bountiful, you alone are just and almighty and eternal. You rescue Israel from every evil; you chose the ancestors and consecrated them. [26]Accept this sacrifice on behalf of all your people Israel and preserve your portion and make it holy. [27]Gather together our scattered people, set free those who are slaves among the Gentiles, look on those who are rejected and despised, and let the Gentiles know that you are our God. [28]Punish those who oppress and are insolent with pride. [29]Plant your people in your holy place, as Moses promised."

30 Then the priests sang the hymns. [31]After the materials of the sacrifice had been consumed, Nehemiah ordered that the liquid that was left should be poured on large stones. [32]When this was done, a flame blazed up; but when the light from the altar shone back, it went out. [33]When this matter became known, and it was reported to the king of the Persians that, in the place where the exiled priests had hidden the fire, the liquid had appeared with which Nehemiah and his associates had burned the materials of the sacrifice, [34]the king investigated the matter, and enclosed the place and made it sacred. [35]And with those persons whom the king favored he exchanged many excellent gifts. [36]Nehemiah and his associates called this "nephthar," which means purification, but by most people it is called naphtha.[c]

1.10–2.18: The second letter. This letter presents itself as having been sent in the time of Judas, but is generally regarded as inauthentic. It was probably inserted in the first century BCE. It is filled with legendary* details and has no historical value, but it attempts to reinforce the importance of Hanukkah by associating the festival not only with Judas but also with traditions about Nehemiah and even Solomon. **1.10:** *Aristobulus* is known as the author of an

---

a Cn: Gk *as those who array themselves against a king*
b Gk lacks *the goddess*　　c Gk *nephthai*

allegorical* commentary on the Torah.* The *Ptolemy* in question is Ptolemy VI Philomator, who was well disposed to the Jews. **13:** *The leader* is Antiochus Epiphanes.* This account of his death contradicts 2 Macc 9. **16:** Epiphanes was not actually killed in the raid on the Temple,* but Antiochus III (the Great) had been. **18:** Nehemiah did not build the Temple, and the captives had been taken to Babylon, not Persia. **21:** The sprinkling of the liquid on the wood recalls the story of Elijah in 1 Kings 18.33–35. **36:** *Naphtha:* petroleum.

2 One finds in the records that the prophet Jeremiah ordered those who were being deported to take some of the fire, as has been mentioned, [2] and that the prophet, after giving them the law, instructed those who were being deported not to forget the commandments of the Lord, or to be led astray in their thoughts on seeing the gold and silver statues and their adornment. [3] And with other similar words he exhorted them that the law should not depart from their hearts.

4 It was also in the same document that the prophet, having received an oracle, ordered that the tent and the ark should follow with him, and that he went out to the mountain where Moses had gone up and had seen the inheritance of God. [5] Jeremiah came and found a cave-dwelling, and he brought there the tent and the ark and the altar of incense; then he sealed up the entrance. [6] Some of those who followed him came up intending to mark the way, but could not find it. [7] When Jeremiah learned of it, he rebuked them and declared: "The place shall remain unknown until God gathers his people together again and shows his mercy. [8] Then the Lord will disclose these things, and the glory of the Lord and the cloud will appear, as they were shown in the case of Moses, and as Solomon asked that the place should be specially consecrated."

9 It was also made clear that being possessed of wisdom Solomon[a] offered sacrifice for the dedication and completion of the temple. [10] Just as Moses prayed to the Lord, and fire came down from heaven and consumed the sacrifices, so also Solomon prayed, and the fire came down and con-sumed the whole burnt offerings. [11] And Moses said, "They were consumed because the sin offering had not been eaten." [12] Likewise Solomon also kept the eight days.

13 The same things are reported in the records and in the memoirs of Nehemiah, and also that he founded a library and collected the books about the kings and prophets, and the writings of David, and letters of kings about votive offerings. [14] In the same way Judas also collected all the books that had been lost on account of the war that had come upon us, and they are in our possession. [15] So if you have need of them, send people to get them for you.

16 Since, therefore, we are about to celebrate the purification, we write to you. Will you therefore please keep the days? [17] It is God who has saved all his people, and has returned the inheritance to all, and the kingship and the priesthood and the consecration, [18] as he promised through the law. We have hope in God that he will soon have mercy on us and will gather us from everywhere under heaven into his holy place, for he has rescued us from great evils and has purified the place.

2.1–18. 4: Later Jewish writings often say that the Temple vessels had been hidden, because the idea of their desecration (as reported in Daniel) was too abhorrent. **8:** *Moses* and *Solomon* are invoked to reinforce the tradition of the sanctity of the holy place. **13:** There is no other evidence that Nehemiah founded a library or established a canon.* **14:** Some scholars credit Judas with forming the canon* of Hebrew Scriptures.* He does not appear, however, to have made judgments about the authority of texts, but simply to have collected books that were in danger of being lost. **16:** The letter concludes with an appeal to the Diaspora* Jews to join in celebrating the festival.

19 The story of Judas Maccabeus and his brothers, and the purification of the great temple, and the dedication of the altar, [20] and further the wars against Antiochus Epiphanes and his son Eupator, [21] and the appearances that came from heaven to those

a Gk *he*

who fought bravely for Judaism, so that though few in number they seized the whole land and pursued the barbarian hordes, 22and regained possession of the temple famous throughout the world, and liberated the city, and re-established the laws that were about to be abolished, while the Lord with great kindness became gracious to them— 23all this, which has been set forth by Jason of Cyrene in five volumes, we shall attempt to condense into a single book. 24For considering the flood of statistics involved and the difficulty there is for those who wish to enter upon the narratives of history because of the mass of material, 25we have aimed to please those who wish to read, to make it easy for those who are inclined to memorize, and to profit all readers. 26For us who have undertaken the toil of abbreviating, it is no light matter but calls for sweat and loss of sleep, 27just as it is not easy for one who prepares a banquet and seeks the benefit of others. Nevertheless, to secure the gratitude of many we will gladly endure the uncomfortable toil, 28leaving the responsibility for exact details to the compiler, while devoting our effort to arriving at the outlines of the condensation. 29For as the master builder of a new house must be concerned with the whole construction, while the one who undertakes its painting and decoration has to consider only what is suitable for its adornment, such in my judgment is the case with us. 30It is the duty of the original historian to occupy the ground, to discuss matters from every side, and to take trouble with details, 31but the one who recasts the narrative should be allowed to strive for brevity of expression and to forego exhaustive treatment. 32At this point therefore let us begin our narrative, without adding any more to what has already been said; for it would be foolish to lengthen the preface while cutting short the history itself.

2.19–32: Prologue. 21: *Appearances that came from heaven* were already part of Jason's history. **31:** The abbreviator claims license to take some liberties with the original, but gives little indication of the specific liberties taken.

3 While the holy city was inhabited in unbroken peace and the laws were strictly observed because of the piety of the high priest Onias and his hatred of wickedness, 2it came about that the kings themselves honored the place and glorified the temple with the finest presents, 3even to the extent that King Seleucus of Asia defrayed from his own revenues all the expenses connected with the service of the sacrifices.

4 But a man named Simon, of the tribe of Benjamin, who had been made captain of the temple, had a disagreement with the high priest about the administration of the city market. 5Since he could not prevail over Onias, he went to Apollonius of Tarsus,[a] who at that time was governor of Coelesyria and Phoenicia, 6and reported to him that the treasury in Jerusalem was full of untold sums of money, so that the amount of the funds could not be reckoned, and that they did not belong to the account of the sacrifices, but that it was possible for them to fall under the control of the king. 7When Apollonius met the king, he told him of the money about which he had been informed. The king[b] chose Heliodorus, who was in charge of his affairs, and sent him with commands to effect the removal of the reported wealth. 8Heliodorus at once set out on his journey, ostensibly to make a tour of inspection of the cities of Coelesyria and Phoenicia, but in fact to carry out the king's purpose.

9 When he had arrived at Jerusalem and had been kindly welcomed by the high priest of[c] the city, he told about the disclosure that had been made and stated why he had come, and he inquired whether this really was the situation. 10The high priest explained that there were some deposits belonging to widows and orphans, 11and also some money of Hyrcanus son of Tobias, a man of very prominent position, and that it totaled in all four hundred talents of silver and two hundred of gold. To such an extent the impious Simon had misrepresented the facts. 12And he said that it was utterly impossible that wrong should be done to those people who

---

a Gk *Apollonius son of Tharseas*   *b* Gk *He*   *c* Other ancient authorities read *and* had trusted in the holiness of the place and in the sanctity and inviolability of the temple that is honored throughout the whole world.

13 But Heliodorus, because of the orders he had from the king, said that this money must in any case be confiscated for the king's treasury. 14So he set a day and went in to direct the inspection of these funds.

There was no little distress throughout the whole city. 15The priests prostrated themselves before the altar in their priestly vestments and called toward heaven upon him who had given the law about deposits, that he should keep them safe for those who had deposited them. 16To see the appearance of the high priest was to be wounded at heart, for his face and the change in his color disclosed the anguish of his soul. 17For terror and bodily trembling had come over the man, which plainly showed to those who looked at him the pain lodged in his heart. 18People also hurried out of their houses in crowds to make a general supplication because the holy place was about to be brought into dishonor. 19Women, girded with sackcloth under their breasts, thronged the streets. Some of the young women who were kept indoors ran together to the gates, and some to the walls, while others peered out of the windows. 20And holding up their hands to heaven, they all made supplication. 21There was something pitiable in the prostration of the whole populace and the anxiety of the high priest in his great anguish.

22 While they were calling upon the Almighty Lord that he would keep what had been entrusted safe and secure for those who had entrusted it, 23Heliodorus went on with what had been decided. 24But when he arrived at the treasury with his bodyguard, then and there the Sovereign of spirits and of all authority caused so great a manifestation that all who had been so bold as to accompany him were astounded by the power of God, and became faint with terror. 25For there appeared to them a magnificently caparisoned horse, with a rider of frightening mien; it rushed furiously at Heliodorus and struck at him with its front hoofs. Its rider was seen to have armor and weapons of gold.

26Two young men also appeared to him, remarkably strong, gloriously beautiful and splendidly dressed, who stood on either side of him and flogged him continuously, inflicting many blows on him. 27When he suddenly fell to the ground and deep darkness came over him, his men took him up, put him on a stretcher, 28and carried him away—this man who had just entered the aforesaid treasury with a great retinue and all his bodyguard but was now unable to help himself. They recognized clearly the sovereign power of God.

29 While he lay prostrate, speechless because of the divine intervention and deprived of any hope of recovery, 30they praised the Lord who had acted marvelously for his own place. And the temple, which a little while before was full of fear and disturbance, was filled with joy and gladness, now that the Almighty Lord had appeared.

31 Some of Heliodorus's friends quickly begged Onias to call upon the Most High to grant life to one who was lying quite at his last breath. 32So the high priest, fearing that the king might get the notion that some foul play had been perpetrated by the Jews with regard to Heliodorus, offered sacrifice for the man's recovery. 33While the high priest was making an atonement, the same young men appeared again to Heliodorus dressed in the same clothing, and they stood and said, "Be very grateful to the high priest Onias, since for his sake the Lord has granted you your life. 34And see that you, who have been flogged by heaven, report to all people the majestic power of God." Having said this they vanished.

35 Then Heliodorus offered sacrifice to the Lord and made very great vows to the Savior of his life, and having bidden Onias farewell, he marched off with his forces to the king. 36He bore testimony to all concerning the deeds of the supreme God, which he had seen with his own eyes. 37When the king asked Heliodorus what sort of person would be suitable to send on another mission to Jerusalem, he replied, 38"If you have any enemy or plotter against your government, send him there, for you will get him back thoroughly flogged, if he survives

Looking at the Past

Legend, chronicle, and history are all ways of narrating the past. A *legend* is a popular story, often with a fantastic character. It may be based on an actual historical incident, or it may be entirely fictitious. In the context of religious literature, legends are meant to edify rather than to convey factual information. A *chronicle* is a factual account of events in the order in which they occurred. It usually reads as a simple sequence of events, without interpretative comments. *History* or *historiography*, like a chronicle, attempts to give an accurate account of the past, but includes discussions of causes and consequences. Historical writing normally involves the use of sources and the critical evaluation of evidence. Chronicles and legends, then, might serve as sources for the historian.

at all; for there is certainly some power of God about the place. ³⁹For he who has his dwelling in heaven watches over that place himself and brings it aid, and he strikes and destroys those who come to do it injury." ⁴⁰This was the outcome of the episode of Heliodorus and the protection of the treasury.

3.1–40: The legend* of Heliodorus. 1: The high priest in question was Onias III. **3:** Seleucus IV (187–175 BCE). **4:** Second Maccabees locates the origin of the troubles in a dispute about the city market, with the implication that the issue was the pursuit of wealth. **7:** *Heliodorus* was chancellor of the realm, a high-ranking officer of the emperor. **11:** Hyrcanus, son of Tobias, was sympathetic to the Ptolemies* but had been allowed to keep his funds in the Temple* for safe-keeping. **15:** The threat is not so much the loss of the funds as the violation of the sanctity of the Temple. **24:** The apparition of a deity in defense of a sanctuary was a well-known motif* in the Hellenistic* world. Several examples are found in the Lindos Chronicle,* an inscription from 99 BCE. Another parallel is found in 3 Macc 2. A biblical precedent for this kind of story can be found in Isa 37.36 and 2 Kings 19.35, in the destruction of the Assyrian king Sennacherib when he was threatening Jerusalem. **31:** Onias III is depicted as a saintly character, but also as one who was in no way rebellious against the king. **35:** The conversion of Heliodorus is entirely fictitious, but it is outdone in ch. 9 by the conversion of Antiochus Epiphanes.* In fact, Heliodorus went on to have the king assassinated in 175 BCE.

4 The previously mentioned Simon, who had informed about the money against*ᵃ* his own country, slandered Onias, saying that it was he who had incited Heliodorus and had been the real cause of the misfortune. ²He dared to designate as a plotter against the government the man who was the benefactor of the city, the protector of his compatriots, and a zealot for the laws. ³When his hatred progressed to such a degree that even murders were committed by one of Simon's approved agents, ⁴Onias recognized that the rivalry was serious and that Apollonius son of Menestheus,*ᵇ* and governor of Coelesyria and Phoenicia, was intensifying the malice of Simon. ⁵So he appealed to the king, not accusing his compatriots but having in view the welfare, both public and private, of all the people. ⁶For he saw that without the king's attention public affairs could not again reach a peaceful settlement, and that Simon would not stop his folly.

7 When Seleucus died and Antiochus, who was called Epiphanes, succeeded to the kingdom, Jason the brother of Onias obtained the high priesthood by corruption, ⁸promising the king at an interview*ᶜ* three hundred sixty talents of silver, and from another source of revenue eighty talents. ⁹In addition to this he promised to pay one hundred fifty more if permission were given to establish by his authority a gymnasium and

a Gk *and*   *b* Vg Compare verse 21: Meaning of Gk uncertain   *c* Or *by a petition* a body of youth for it, and to enroll the people of Jerusalem as citizens of Antioch. [10]When the king assented and Jason[a] came to office, he at once shifted his compatriots over to the Greek way of life.

11 He set aside the existing royal concessions to the Jews, secured through John the father of Eupolemus, who went on the mission to establish friendship and alliance with the Romans; and he destroyed the lawful ways of living and introduced new customs contrary to the law. [12]He took delight in establishing a gymnasium right under the citadel, and he induced the noblest of the young men to wear the Greek hat. [13]There was such an extreme of Hellenization and increase in the adoption of foreign ways because of the surpassing wickedness of Jason, who was ungodly and no true[b] high priest, [14]that the priests were no longer intent upon their service at the altar. Despising the sanctuary and neglecting the sacrifices, they hurried to take part in the unlawful proceedings in the wrestling arena after the signal for the discus-throwing, [15]disdaining the honors prized by their ancestors and putting the highest value upon Greek forms of prestige. [16]For this reason heavy disaster overtook them, and those whose ways of living they admired and wished to imitate completely became their enemies and punished them. [17]It is no light thing to show irreverence to the divine laws—a fact that later events will make clear.

18 When the quadrennial games were being held at Tyre and the king was present, [19]the vile Jason sent envoys, chosen as being Antiochian citizens from Jerusalem, to carry three hundred silver drachmas for the sacrifice to Hercules. Those who carried the money, however, thought best not to use it for sacrifice, because that was inappropriate, but to expend it for another purpose. [20]So this money was intended by the sender for the sacrifice to Hercules, but by the decision of its carriers it was applied to the construction of triremes.

21 When Apollonius son of Menestheus was sent to Egypt for the coronation[c] of Philometor as king, Antiochus learned that Philometor[a] had become hostile to his govern-

ment, and he took measures for his own security. Therefore upon arriving at Joppa he proceeded to Jerusalem. [22]He was welcomed magnificently by Jason and the city, and ushered in with a blaze of torches and with shouts. Then he marched his army into Phoenicia.

4.1–50: The Hellenistic* reform. 2: Second Maccabees is insistent that the previous well-being of the city was due to Onias's zeal for the law. **5:** It is disingenuous to say that Onias was *not accusing his compatriots,* but his accusations were probably justified. **7:** Jason was from the high priestly family, but in effect he bought the high priesthood. **9:** There has been extensive debate as to what it meant for the people of Jerusalem to be *citizens of Antioch.* Presumably Jason was constituting a new city, Antioch-at-Jerusalem, and not all the people were recognized as citizens. **10:** It is possible that Jason had a genuine desire to improve the lot of his people by adopting the *Greek way of life,* but he would hardly have paid such substantial sums of money if he did not stand to gain in return. **11:** The *existing royal concessions* had been granted by Antiochus III when he gained control of Jerusalem in 198 BCE. They guaranteed the Jews the right to live according to their ancestral laws. The mission to the Romans is reported in 1 Macc 8. **12:** The gymnasium is noted in 1 Macc 1.14. Second Maccabees neglects to mention that some Jews disguised the marks of their circumcision.* **16:** Second Maccabees sees the subsequent persecution and war as punishment for the adoption of Greek customs and neglect of traditional law. **22:** First Maccabees does not report that the king visited Jerusalem before his first invasion of Egypt, but says that he pillaged Jerusalem after the invasion.

23 After a period of three years Jason sent Menelaus, the brother of the previously mentioned Simon, to carry the money to the king and to complete the records of essential business. [24]But he, when presented to the king, extolled him with an air of authority, and secured the high priesthood for himself, outbidding Jason by three hundred talents of silver. [25]After receiving the king's orders he returned, possessing no qualification for the high priesthood, but having the hot temper

a Gk *he* *b* Gk lacks *true* *c* Meaning of Gk uncertain of a cruel tyrant and the rage of a savage wild beast. 26 So Jason, who after supplanting his own brother was supplanted by another man, was driven as a fugitive into the land of Ammon. 27 Although Menelaus continued to hold the office, he did not pay regularly any of the money promised to the king. 28 When Sostratus the captain of the citadel kept requesting payment—for the collection of the revenue was his responsibility—the two of them were summoned by the king on account of this issue. 29 Menelaus left his own brother Lysimachus as deputy in the high priesthood, while Sostratus left Crates, the commander of the Cyprian troops.

30 While such was the state of affairs, it happened that the people of Tarsus and of Mallus revolted because their cities had been given as a present to Antiochis, the king's concubine. 31 So the king went hurriedly to settle the trouble, leaving Andronicus, a man of high rank, to act as his deputy. 32 But Menelaus, thinking he had obtained a suitable opportunity, stole some of the gold vessels of the temple and gave them to Andronicus; other vessels, as it happened, he had sold to Tyre and the neighboring cities. 33 When Onias became fully aware of these acts, he publicly exposed them, having first withdrawn to a place of sanctuary at Daphne near Antioch. 34 Therefore Menelaus, taking Andronicus aside, urged him to kill Onias. Andronicus[a] came to Onias, and resorting to treachery, offered him sworn pledges and gave him his right hand; he persuaded him, though still suspicious, to come out from the place of sanctuary; then, with no regard for justice, he immediately put him out of the way. 35 For this reason not only Jews, but many also of other nations, were grieved and displeased at the unjust murder of the man. 36 When the king returned from the region of Cilicia, the Jews in the city[b] appealed to him with regard to the unreasonable murder of Onias, and the Greeks shared their hatred of the crime. 37 Therefore Antiochus was grieved at heart and filled with pity, and wept because of the moderation and good conduct of the deceased. 38 Inflamed with anger, he immediately stripped off the purple robe from Andronicus, tore off his clothes, and led him around the whole city to that very place where he had committed the outrage against Onias, and there he dispatched the bloodthirsty fellow. The Lord thus repaid him with the punishment he deserved.

39 When many acts of sacrilege had been committed in the city by Lysimachus with the connivance of Menelaus, and when report of them had spread abroad, the populace gathered against Lysimachus, because many of the gold vessels had already been stolen. 40 Since the crowds were becoming aroused and filled with anger, Lysimachus armed about three thousand men and launched an unjust attack, under the leadership of a certain Auranus, a man advanced in years and no less advanced in folly. 41 But when the Jews[c] became aware that Lysimachus was attacking them, some picked up stones, some blocks of wood, and others took handfuls of the ashes that were lying around, and threw them in wild confusion at Lysimachus and his men. 42 As a result, they wounded many of them, and killed some, and put all the rest to flight; the temple robber himself they killed close by the treasury.

43 Charges were brought against Menelaus about this incident. 44 When the king came to Tyre, three men sent by the senate presented the case before him. 45 But Menelaus, already as good as beaten, promised a substantial bribe to Ptolemy son of Dorymenes to win over the king. 46 Therefore Ptolemy, taking the king aside into a colonnade as if for refreshment, induced the king to change his mind. 47 Menelaus, the cause of all the trouble, he acquitted of the charges against him, while he sentenced to death those unfortunate men, who would have been freed uncondemned if they had pleaded even before Scythians. 48 And so those who had spoken for the city and the villages[d] and the holy vessels quickly suffered the unjust penalty. 49 Therefore even the Tyrians, showing their hatred of the crime, provided magnificently for their funeral. 50 But Menelaus, because of the greed

a Gk He   b Or in each city   c Gk they   d Other ancient authorities read the people of those in power, remained in office, growing in wickedness, having become the chief plotter against his compatriots.

4.23–50. 23: *Menelaus* was of the tribe of Benjamin (see 2 Macc 3.4) and therefore had no qualification for the high priesthood. **33–34:** The *place of sanctuary at Daphne* was almost certainly the temple of Apollo and Artemis. That a Jewish high priest should seek asylum there suggests that he was not such a zealot for the law as 2 Maccabees maintains. The murder of Onias III is also noted in Dan 9.26, but it is ignored in 1 Maccabees. **38:** *Andronicus* was actually executed for murdering the son of Seleucus IV. Second Maccabees regards his death as divine punishment for the murder of Onias. **47:** The *Scythians* were a byword for irrational cruelty in the Greek world. The fate of these emissaries does not fit the usual insistence in 2 Maccabees that people get their just deserts.

5 About this time Antiochus made his second invasion of Egypt. [2]And it happened that, for almost forty days, there appeared over all the city golden-clad cavalry charging through the air, in companies fully armed with lances and drawn swords— [3]troops of cavalry drawn up, attacks and counterattacks made on this side and on that, brandishing of shields, massing of spears, hurling of missiles, the flash of golden trappings, and armor of all kinds. [4]Therefore everyone prayed that the apparition might prove to have been a good omen.

5 When a false rumor arose that Antiochus was dead, Jason took no fewer than a thousand men and suddenly made an assault on the city. When the troops on the wall had been forced back and at last the city was being taken, Menelaus took refuge in the citadel. [6]But Jason kept relentlessly slaughtering his compatriots, not realizing that success at the cost of one's kindred is the greatest misfortune, but imagining that he was setting up trophies of victory over enemies and not over compatriots. [7]He did not, however, gain control of the government; in the end he got only disgrace from his conspiracy, and fled again into the country of the Ammonites. [8]Finally he met a miserable end. Accused[a] before Aretas the ruler of the Arabs, fleeing from city to city, pursued by everyone, hated as a rebel against the laws, and abhorred as the executioner of his country and his compatriots, he was cast ashore in Egypt. [9]There he who had driven many from their own country into exile died in exile, having embarked to go to the Lacedaemonians in hope of finding protection because of their kinship. [10]He who had cast out many to lie unburied had no one to mourn for him; he had no funeral of any sort and no place in the tomb of his ancestors.

11 When news of what had happened reached the king, he took it to mean that Judea was in revolt. So, raging inwardly, he left Egypt and took the city by storm. [12]He commanded his soldiers to cut down relentlessly everyone they met and to kill those who went into their houses. [13]Then there was massacre of young and old, destruction of boys, women, and children, and slaughter of young girls and infants. [14]Within the total of three days eighty thousand were destroyed, forty thousand in hand-to-hand fighting, and as many were sold into slavery as were killed.

15 Not content with this, Antiochus[b] dared to enter the most holy temple in all the world, guided by Menelaus, who had become a traitor both to the laws and to his country. [16]He took the holy vessels with his polluted hands, and swept away with profane hands the votive offerings that other kings had made to enhance the glory and honor of the place. [17]Antiochus was elated in spirit, and did not perceive that the Lord was angered for a little while because of the sins of those who lived in the city, and that this was the reason he was disregarding the holy place. [18]But if it had not happened that they were involved in many sins, this man would have been flogged and turned back from his rash act as soon as he came forward, just as Heliodorus had been, whom King Seleucus sent to inspect the treasury. [19]But the Lord did not choose the nation for the sake of the holy place, but the place for the sake of the nation. [20]Therefore the place itself shared in the misfortunes that befell the nation and afterward participated in its benefits; and

a Cn: Gk *Imprisoned*   *b* Gk *he*

what was forsaken in the wrath of the Almighty was restored again in all its glory when the great Lord became reconciled.

21 So Antiochus carried off eighteen hundred talents from the temple, and hurried away to Antioch, thinking in his arrogance that he could sail on the land and walk on the sea, because his mind was elated. [22]He left governors to oppress the people: at Jerusalem, Philip, by birth a Phrygian and in character more barbarous than the man who appointed him; [23]and at Gerizim, Andronicus; and besides these Menelaus, who lorded it over his compatriots worse than the others did. In his malice toward the Jewish citizens,[a] [24]Antiochus[b] sent Apollonius, the captain of the Mysians, with an army of twenty-two thousand, and commanded him to kill all the grown men and to sell the women and boys as slaves. [25]When this man arrived in Jerusalem, he pretended to be peaceably disposed and waited until the holy sabbath day; then, finding the Jews not at work, he ordered his troops to parade under arms. [26]He put to the sword all those who came out to see them, then rushed into the city with his armed warriors and killed great numbers of people.

27 But Judas Maccabeus, with about nine others, got away to the wilderness, and kept himself and his companions alive in the mountains as wild animals do; they continued to live on what grew wild, so that they might not share in the defilement.

5.1–27: The intervention of Antiochus. 2: Wonderful apparitions are frequently reported before important happenings throughout the Hellenistic* world. 5: According to 2 Maccabees, the occasion for the outbreak of violence was a false rumor that Antiochus Epiphanes* had been killed during his second invasion of Egypt. 8: The death of Jason is cited as evidence of divine retribution. 9: Lacedaemonians: Spartans. On their kinship with the Jews, see 1 Macc 12 and 14. 11: The idea that the king thought that Judea was in revolt is perhaps the most plausible explanation of his violent intervention in Jerusalem. His rage was also stirred up because he had been humiliated in Egypt; see Dan 11.30. 15: Second Maccabees locates the pillaging of the Temple* here, after the second revolt; 1 Macc 1.20 puts it after the first revolt. First Maccabees is thought

to preserve the more accurate account on this point. 17–18: Second Maccabees insists that these events are a (temporary) punishment for the sins of the Jews, and that otherwise Epiphanes* would have been turned back like Heliodorus. 21: The arrogance or hubris of the king before his fall fits a pattern common in both Greek tragedy and Hebrew scripture (for example, Isa 14; see also Dan 11.36, with reference to Antiochus Epiphanes). 23: Gerizim was the sacred mountain of the Samaritans, near Shechem. 24: For the attack of Apollonius, see 1 Macc 1.29. 27: Judas is introduced without reference to Mattathias.

6 Not long after this, the king sent an Athenian[c] senator[d] to compel the Jews to forsake the laws of their ancestors and no longer to live by the laws of God; [2]also to pollute the temple in Jerusalem and to call it the temple of Olympian Zeus, and to call the one in Gerizim the temple of Zeus-the-Friend-of-Strangers, as did the people who lived in that place.

3 Harsh and utterly grievous was the onslaught of evil. [4]For the temple was filled with debauchery and reveling by the Gentiles, who dallied with prostitutes and had intercourse with women within the sacred precincts, and besides brought in things for sacrifice that were unfit. [5]The altar was covered with abominable offerings that were forbidden by the laws. [6]People could neither keep the sabbath, nor observe the festivals of their ancestors, nor so much as confess themselves to be Jews.

7 On the monthly celebration of the king's birthday, the Jews[e] were taken, under bitter constraint, to partake of the sacrifices; and when a festival of Dionysus was celebrated, they were compelled to wear wreaths of ivy and to walk in the procession in honor of Dionysus. [8]At the suggestion of the people of Ptolemais[f] a decree was issued to the neighboring Greek cities that they should adopt the same policy toward the Jews and make them partake of the sacrifices, [9]and should kill those who did not choose to

a Or worse than the others did in his malice toward the Jewish citizens　　b Gk he　　c Other ancient authorities read Antiochian　　d Or Geron an Athenian　　e Gk they　　f Cn: Gk suggestion of the Ptolemies (or of Ptolemy) change over to Greek customs. One could see, therefore, the misery that had come upon them. [10] For example, two women were brought in for having circumcised their children. They publicly paraded them around the city, with their babies hanging at their breasts, and then hurled them down headlong from the wall. [11] Others who had assembled in the caves nearby, in order to observe the seventh day secretly, were betrayed to Philip and were all burned together, because their piety kept them from defending themselves, in view of their regard for that most holy day.

6.1–11: The religious persecution. 1: It is unclear whether the emissary is "an Athenian senator (or elder)" or "Geron the Athenian," or even "Athenaios, the elder." (The Greek word "geron" means elder.) Second Maccabees has no edict such as we find in 1 Macc 1.41. Neither does it state the reason for this interference in Jewish religion. 2: It was common in the Hellenistic* world to identify the deities of one culture with those of another. Zeus Olympius was presumably regarded as equivalent to "God Most High." The Letter of Aristeas,* a Jewish document written in Greek in the second century BCE, says that the Jews worship the same God, Zeus, as the Greeks, but by a different name. What is at issue here is not the suppression of all Jewish religion, but its translation and adaptation to Hellenistic categories. These reforms also applied to the Samaritans, but the Jewish historian Josephus* says that they took the initiative and asked for permission to change the name of their temple. 4: The *debauchery* in the temple has been taken to indicate that the cult introduced was of Syrian origin, like the old Canaanite cults condemned in the Bible. The Prophets* frequently allege that there was fornication and prostitution on the high places* of ancient Israel (for instance, Isa 57.7–8; Jer 3.6). Whether these prophetic critiques give a fair impression of the practice is now disputed. 5: The use of swine for sacrifice was especially offensive to Jews because swine (pigs) were regarded as ritually unclean (Lev 11.7). 6: Not only were new practices introduced, but traditional ones were suppressed. One could not *confess* to being a Jew, at least in the traditional sense of one who kept the Mosaic law. Gentiles* sometimes thought that Jewish worship was related to that of Dionysus, god of wine, because Jews drank wine in ritual celebrations. Third Maccabees 3 also reports an attempt by a king

(Ptolemy Philopator) to impose the worship of Dionysus on the Jews. The intention seems to have been to make the Jews conform to Greek norms. 11: For the massacre in a cave on the sabbath, see 1 Macc 2.29.

[12] Now I urge those who read this book not to be depressed by such calamities, but to recognize that these punishments were designed not to destroy but to discipline our people. [13] In fact, it is a sign of great kindness not to let the impious alone for long, but to punish them immediately. [14] For in the case of the other nations the Lord waits patiently to punish them until they have reached the full measure of their sins; but he does not deal in this way with us, [15] in order that he may not take vengeance on us afterward when our sins have reached their height. [16] Therefore he never withdraws his mercy from us. Although he disciplines us with calamities, he does not forsake his own people. [17] Let what we have said serve as a reminder; we must go on briefly with the story.

6.12–17: The theology of persecution. The abbreviator explains the persecution as divine discipline. God mercifully chastens the Jews before their sins get so great as to warrant utter destruction. A close parallel is found in Wis 12.22: "while chastening us, you scourge our enemies ten times more." The idea that Israel's misfortunes were punishment for sin was characteristic of deuteronomic theology in the Hebrew Bible, and the doctrine is often expounded by the Prophets.*

[18] Eleazar, one of the scribes in high position, a man now advanced in age and of noble presence, was being forced to open his mouth to eat swine's flesh. [19] But he, welcoming death with honor rather than life with pollution, went up to the rack of his own accord, spitting out the flesh, [20] as all ought to go who have the courage to refuse things that it is not right to taste, even for the natural love of life. [21] Those who were in charge of that unlawful sacrifice took the man aside because of their long acquaintance with him, and privately urged him to bring meat of his own providing, proper for him to use, and to pretend that he was eating the flesh of the sac-

rificial meal that had been commanded by the king, 22so that by doing this he might be saved from death, and be treated kindly on account of his old friendship with them. 23But making a high resolve, worthy of his years and the dignity of his old age and the gray hairs that he had reached with distinction, and his excellent life even from childhood, and moreover according to the holy God-given law, he declared himself quickly, telling them to send him to Hades.

24 "Such pretense is not worthy of our time of life," he said, "for many of the young might suppose that Eleazar in his ninetieth year had gone over to an alien religion, 25and through my pretense, for the sake of living a brief moment longer, they would be led astray because of me, while I defile and disgrace my old age. 26Even if for the present I would avoid the punishment of mortals, yet whether I live or die I will not escape the hands of the Almighty. 27Therefore, by bravely giving up my life now, I will show myself worthy of my old age 28and leave to the young a noble example of how to die a good death willingly and nobly for the revered and holy laws."

When he had said this, he went*a* at once to the rack. 29Those who a little before had acted toward him with goodwill now changed to ill will, because the words he had uttered were in their opinion sheer madness.*b* 30When he was about to die under the blows, he groaned aloud and said: "It is clear to the Lord in his holy knowledge that, though I might have been saved from death, I am enduring terrible sufferings in my body under this beating, but in my soul I am glad to suffer these things because I fear him."

31 So in this way he died, leaving in his death an example of nobility and a memorial of courage, not only to the young but to the great body of his nation.

6.18–31: The martyrdom* of Eleazar. 19: *Death with honor,* rather than life without it, was an ideal of Greek culture, beginning with Achilles in the Trojan war. Compare the decision of Judas Maccabee that led to his death in 1 Macc 9.10. **21:** Eleazar refuses any subterfuge that might save his life, partly for reasons of honor, and partly because of the example he would

set. **23:** To send him to *Hades** (the Greek netherworld, Hebrew Sheol*) is simply to kill him. Eleazar makes no profession of belief in an afterlife, unless it is implied in the statement, "Whether I live or die I will not escape the hands of the Almighty" (v. 26). He accepts his sufferings because of his fear of the Lord.

7 It happened also that seven brothers and their mother were arrested and were being compelled by the king, under torture with whips and thongs, to partake of unlawful swine's flesh. 2One of them, acting as their spokesman, said, "What do you intend to ask and learn from us? For we are ready to die rather than transgress the laws of our ancestors."

3 The king fell into a rage, and gave orders to have pans and caldrons heated. 4These were heated immediately, and he commanded that the tongue of their spokesman be cut out and that they scalp him and cut off his hands and feet, while the rest of the brothers and the mother looked on. 5When he was utterly helpless, the king*c* ordered them to take him to the fire, still breathing, and to fry him in a pan. The smoke from the pan spread widely, but the brothers*d* and their mother encouraged one another to die nobly, saying, 6"The Lord God is watching over us and in truth has compassion on us, as Moses declared in his song that bore witness against the people to their faces, when he said, 'And he will have compassion on his servants.' "*e*

7 After the first brother had died in this way, they brought forward the second for their sport. They tore off the skin of his head with the hair, and asked him, "Will you eat rather than have your body punished limb by limb?" 8He replied in the language of his ancestors and said to them, "No." Therefore he in turn underwent tortures as the first brother had done. 9And when he was at his last breath, he said, "You accursed wretch, you dismiss us from this present life, but the King of the universe will raise us up to an

---

a Other ancient authorities read *was dragged*
b Meaning of Gk uncertain   *c* Gk *he*   *d* Gk *they*
e Gk *slaves*

everlasting renewal of life, because we have died for his laws."

10 After him, the third was the victim of their sport. When it was demanded, he quickly put out his tongue and courageously stretched forth his hands, [11]and said nobly, "I got these from Heaven, and because of his laws I disdain them, and from him I hope to get them back again." [12]As a result the king himself and those with him were astonished at the young man's spirit, for he regarded his sufferings as nothing.

13 After he too had died, they maltreated and tortured the fourth in the same way. [14]When he was near death, he said, "One cannot but choose to die at the hands of mortals and to cherish the hope God gives of being raised again by him. But for you there will be no resurrection to life!"

15 Next they brought forward the fifth and maltreated him. [16]But he looked at the king,[a] and said, "Because you have authority among mortals, though you also are mortal, you do what you please. But do not think that God has forsaken our people. [17]Keep on, and see how his mighty power will torture you and your descendants!"

18 After him they brought forward the sixth. And when he was about to die, he said, "Do not deceive yourself in vain. For we are suffering these things on our own account, because of our sins against our own God. Therefore[b] astounding things have happened. [19]But do not think that you will go unpunished for having tried to fight against God!"

20 The mother was especially admirable and worthy of honorable memory. Although she saw her seven sons perish within a single day, she bore it with good courage because of her hope in the Lord. [21]She encouraged each of them in the language of their ancestors. Filled with a noble spirit, she reinforced her woman's reasoning with a man's courage, and said to them, [22]"I do not know how you came into being in my womb. It was not I who gave you life and breath, nor I who set in order the elements within each of you. [23]Therefore the Creator of the world, who shaped the beginning of humankind and devised the origin of all things, will in his mercy give life and breath back to you again, since you now forget yourselves for the sake of his laws."

24 Antiochus felt that he was being treated with contempt, and he was suspicious of her reproachful tone. The youngest brother being still alive, Antiochus[c] not only appealed to him in words, but promised with oaths that he would make him rich and enviable if he would turn from the ways of his ancestors, and that he would take him for his Friend and entrust him with public affairs. [25]Since the young man would not listen to him at all, the king called the mother to him and urged her to advise the youth to save himself. [26]After much urging on his part, she undertook to persuade her son. [27]But, leaning close to him, she spoke in their native language as follows, deriding the cruel tyrant: "My son, have pity on me. I carried you nine months in my womb, and nursed you for three years, and have reared you and brought you up to this point in your life, and have taken care of you.[d] [28]I beg you, my child, to look at the heaven and the earth and see everything that is in them, and recognize that God did not make them out of things that existed.[e] And in the same way the human race came into being. [29]Do not fear this butcher, but prove worthy of your brothers. Accept death, so that in God's mercy I may get you back again along with your brothers."

30 While she was still speaking, the young man said, "What are you[f] waiting for? I will not obey the king's command, but I obey the command of the law that was given to our ancestors through Moses. [31]But you,[g] who have contrived all sorts of evil against the Hebrews, will certainly not escape the hands of God. [32]For we are suffering because of our own sins. [33]And if our living Lord is angry for a little while, to rebuke and discipline us, he will again be reconciled with his own servants.[h] [34]But you, unholy wretch, you most defiled of all mortals, do not be elated in vain and puffed up by un-

---

a Gk at him   b Lat: Other ancient authorities lack Therefore   c Gk he   d Or have borne the burden of your education   e Or God made them out of things that did not exist   f The Gk here for you is plural   g The Gk here for you is singular   h Gk slaves certain hopes, when you raise your hand against the children of heaven. 35You have not yet escaped the judgment of the almighty, all-seeing God. 36For our brothers after enduring a brief suffering have drunk*a* of ever-flowing life, under God's covenant; but you, by the judgment of God, will receive just punishment for your arrogance. 37I, like my brothers, give up body and life for the laws of our ancestors, appealing to God to show mercy soon to our nation and by trials and plagues to make you confess that he alone is God, 38and through me and my brothers to bring to an end the wrath of the Almighty that has justly fallen on our whole nation."

39 The king fell into a rage, and handled him worse than the others, being exasperated at his scorn. 40So he died in his integrity, putting his whole trust in the Lord.

41 Last of all, the mother died, after her sons.

42 Let this be enough, then, about the eating of sacrifices and the extreme tortures.

7.1–42: The seven brothers. 1: *Seven* is a stock number; compare Taxo and his seven sons in the *Testament of Moses*. Josephus★ tells a story of a Galilean brigand with seven sons in *Antiquities* 14.429. Variants of the story of the mother with seven sons are found in rabbinic literature, set in Roman times. 3: The easily angered king is also a stock motif★ in ancient stories (see Daniel, 3 Maccabees). Some scholars have inferred from his presence that the story is set in Antioch, but this is not necessarily so. The story is a legend,★ and location is not an important consideration. 6: The quotation from the Song of Moses (Deut 32) sheds light on the motivation of the martyrs.★ The verse cited is Deut 32.36. Deuteronomy 32.43 promises that God "avenges the blood of his servants and takes vengeance on his adversaries." 9: The second brother introduces another consideration: the hope of resurrection. 11: The third brother gives the resurrection a very physical character: He hopes to get his limbs back. Such a physical view of resurrection is exceptional in Jewish texts of the second century BCE (Daniel, 1 Enoch★), most of which envisage a resurrection of the spirit. The physicality is required here because of the physical suffering of the youths. 14: Conversely, resurrection is denied to the tyrant. 17: The fifth son strikes a note of vengeance, anticipating the torture of

the king. 18: The sixth son reaffirms the deuteronomic doctrine that the suffering of the Jews is punishment for their own sins. 23: The mother grounds the hope for resurrection in the doctrine of creation. If God gave life once, he can do so again. 24: The king's promises to the youngest son are quite implausible, but underline the legendary★ character of the story. 28: This may be the earliest formulation in a Jewish context of the doctrine of creation out of nothing. The paradoxical advice, that one should accept death in order to gain life, is more typical of Greek than of Jewish thought. 32–33: The youngest son again reaffirms the doctrine of suffering as divine chastisement, in the confidence that it is *for a little while*. 38: The last son looks not only for vengeance, but for the king to recognize the true God, and to *bring an end to the wrath of the Almighty by the deaths of the brothers*.

8 Meanwhile Judas, who was also called Maccabeus, and his companions secretly entered the villages and summoned their kindred and enlisted those who had continued in the Jewish faith, and so they gathered about six thousand. 2They implored the Lord to look upon the people who were oppressed by all; and to have pity on the temple that had been profaned by the godless; 3to have mercy on the city that was being destroyed and about to be leveled to the ground; to hearken to the blood that cried out to him; 4to remember also the lawless destruction of the innocent babies and the blasphemies committed against his name; and to show his hatred of evil.

5 As soon as Maccabeus got his army organized, the Gentiles could not withstand him, for the wrath of the Lord had turned to mercy. 6Coming without warning, he would set fire to towns and villages. He captured strategic positions and put to flight not a few of the enemy. 7He found the nights most advantageous for such attacks. And talk of his valor spread everywhere.

8 When Philip saw that the man was gaining ground little by little, and that he was pushing ahead with more frequent successes, he wrote to Ptolemy, the governor of Coelesyria and Phoenicia, to come to the aid of the king's government. 9Then Ptolemy*b*

a Cn: Gk *fallen*   *b* Gk *he*

promptly appointed Nicanor son of Patroclus, one of the king's chief[a] Friends, and sent him, in command of no fewer than twenty thousand Gentiles of all nations, to wipe out the whole race of Judea. He associated with him Gorgias, a general and a man of experience in military service. 10 Nicanor determined to make up for the king the tribute due to the Romans, two thousand talents, by selling the captured Jews into slavery. 11 So he immediately sent to the towns on the seacoast, inviting them to buy Jewish slaves and promising to hand over ninety slaves for a talent, not expecting the judgment from the Almighty that was about to overtake him.

12 Word came to Judas concerning Nicanor's invasion; and when he told his companions of the arrival of the army, 13 those who were cowardly and distrustful of God's justice ran off and got away. 14 Others sold all their remaining property, and at the same time implored the Lord to rescue those who had been sold by the ungodly Nicanor before he ever met them, 15 if not for their own sake, then for the sake of the covenants made with their ancestors, and because he had called them by his holy and glorious name. 16 But Maccabeus gathered his forces together, to the number six thousand, and exhorted them not to be frightened by the enemy and not to fear the great multitude of Gentiles who were wickedly coming against them, but to fight nobly, 17 keeping before their eyes the lawless outrage that the Gentiles[b] had committed against the holy place, and the torture of the derided city, and besides, the overthrow of their ancestral way of life. 18 "For they trust to arms and acts of daring," he said, "but we trust in the Almighty God, who is able with a single nod to strike down those who are coming against us, and even, if necessary, the whole world."

19 Moreover, he told them of the occasions when help came to their ancestors; how, in the time of Sennacherib, when one hundred eighty-five thousand perished, 20 and the time of the battle against the Galatians that took place in Babylonia, when eight thousand Jews[c] fought along with four thousand Macedonians; yet when the Macedonians were hard pressed, the eight thousand, by the help that came to them from heaven, destroyed one hundred twenty thousand Galatians[d] and took a great amount of booty.

21 With these words he filled them with courage and made them ready to die for their laws and their country; then he divided his army into four parts. 22 He appointed his brothers also, Simon and Joseph and Jonathan, each to command a division, putting fifteen hundred men under each. 23 Besides, he appointed Eleazar to read aloud[e] from the holy book, and gave the watchword, "The help of God"; then, leading the first division himself, he joined battle with Nicanor.

24 With the Almighty as their ally, they killed more than nine thousand of the enemy, and wounded and disabled most of Nicanor's army, and forced them all to flee. 25 They captured the money of those who had come to buy them as slaves. After pursuing them for some distance, they were obliged to return because the hour was late. 26 It was the day before the sabbath, and for that reason they did not continue their pursuit. 27 When they had collected the arms of the enemy and stripped them of their spoils, they kept the sabbath, giving great praise and thanks to the Lord, who had preserved them for that day and allotted it to them as the beginning of mercy. 28 After the sabbath they gave some of the spoils to those who had been tortured and to the widows and orphans, and distributed the rest among themselves and their children. 29 When they had done this, they made common supplication and implored the merciful Lord to be wholly reconciled with his servants.[f]

30 In encounters with the forces of Timothy and Bacchides they killed more than twenty thousand of them and got possession of some exceedingly high strongholds, and they divided a very large amount of plunder, giving to those who had been tortured and to the orphans and widows, and also to the aged, shares equal to their own. 31 They col-

a Gk one of the first   b Gk they   c Gk lacks Jews
d Gk lacks Galatians   e Meaning of Gk uncertain
f Gk slaves

lected the arms of the enemy,[a] and carefully stored all of them in strategic places; the rest of the spoils they carried to Jerusalem. 32They killed the commander of Timothy's forces, a most wicked man, and one who had greatly troubled the Jews. 33While they were celebrating the victory in the city of their ancestors, they burned those who had set fire to the sacred gates, Callisthenes and some others, who had fled into one little house; so these received the proper reward for their impiety.[b]

34 The thrice-accursed Nicanor, who had brought the thousand merchants to buy the Jews, 35having been humbled with the help of the Lord by opponents whom he regarded as of the least account, took off his splendid uniform and made his way alone like a runaway slave across the country until he reached Antioch, having succeeded chiefly in the destruction of his own army! 36So he who had undertaken to secure tribute for the Romans by the capture of the people of Jerusalem proclaimed that the Jews had a Defender, and that therefore the Jews were invulnerable, because they followed the laws ordained by him.

8.1–36: The Maccabean revolt. 1: The story of the revolt begins halfway through the narrative* of 2 Maccabees. 3–5: The blood that has already been shed is a potent factor in the success of the revolt. Because of it, the *wrath of the Lord* had already *turned to mercy*. 10: Nicanor's plan to sell Jewish captives into *slavery* is also noted in 1 Macc 3.41. Second Maccabees skips over the early skirmishes so that the account of the war begins and ends with defeats of Nicanor (compare 2 Macc 15). 18: Not only is God able to give victory to a smaller force, but he can strike down the whole world by his power as Creator. The human army is scarcely necessary. 19–20: The case of *Sennacherib* is, of course, biblical (2 Kings 19.35; Isa 37.36), but the case of the Macedonians and Galatians is not. It is surprising to find this incident included as an instance of *when help came to their ancestors*. Perhaps the restriction to the ancestors was added by the abridger, and the original text simply listed examples of miraculous assistance, from whatever quarter. 22: In the list of Maccabean brothers, *Joseph* is apparently a mistake for John. Eleazar was also one of the brothers. 26: Second Maccabees claims that Judas observed the sab-

bath rest, although 1 Maccabees says that he waived that commandment. 33: On the burning of the gates, see 2 Macc 1.8, where it is attributed to Jason. 35: Nicanor, who had tried to enslave the Jews, fled like a runaway slave. In each case, the punishment fits the crime. 36: It is implausible that Nicanor proclaimed that the Jews had a divine defender. He shows little sign of such a belief when he reappears later in the story.

~~~~~~~~~~~~~~~~~~~~~

9 About that time, as it happened, Antiochus had retreated in disorder from the region of Persia. 2He had entered the city called Persepolis and attempted to rob the temples and control the city. Therefore the people rushed to the rescue with arms, and Antiochus and his army were defeated,[c] with the result that Antiochus was put to flight by the inhabitants and beat a shameful retreat. 3While he was in Ecbatana, news came to him of what had happened to Nicanor and the forces of Timothy. 4Transported with rage, he conceived the idea of turning upon the Jews the injury done by those who had put him to flight; so he ordered his charioteer to drive without stopping until he completed the journey. But the judgment of heaven rode with him! For in his arrogance he said, "When I get there I will make Jerusalem a cemetery of Jews."

5 But the all-seeing Lord, the God of Israel, struck him with an incurable and invisible blow. As soon as he stopped speaking he was seized with a pain in his bowels, for which there was no relief, and with sharp internal tortures— 6and that very justly, for he had tortured the bowels of others with many and strange inflictions. 7Yet he did not in any way stop his insolence, but was even more filled with arrogance, breathing fire in his rage against the Jews, and giving orders to drive even faster. And so it came about that he fell out of his chariot as it was rushing along, and the fall was so hard as to torture every limb of his body. 8Thus he who only a little while before had thought in his superhuman arrogance that he could command the waves of the sea, and had imagined

a Gk *their arms*   *b* Meaning of Gk uncertain   *c* Gk *they were defeated* that he could weigh the high mountains in a balance, was brought down to earth and carried in a litter, making the power of God manifest to all. 9And so the ungodly man's body swarmed with worms, and while he was still living in anguish and pain, his flesh rotted away, and because of the stench the whole army felt revulsion at his decay. 10Because of his intolerable stench no one was able to carry the man who a little while before had thought that he could touch the stars of heaven. 11Then it was that, broken in spirit, he began to lose much of his arrogance and to come to his senses under the scourge of God, for he was tortured with pain every moment. 12And when he could not endure his own stench, he uttered these words, "It is right to be subject to God; mortals should not think that they are equal to God."ᵃ

13 Then the abominable fellow made a vow to the Lord, who would no longer have mercy on him, stating 14that the holy city, which he was hurrying to level to the ground and to make a cemetery, he was now declaring to be free; 15and the Jews, whom he had not considered worth burying but had planned to throw out with their children for the wild animals and for the birds to eat, he would make, all of them, equal to citizens of Athens; 16and the holy sanctuary, which he had formerly plundered, he would adorn with the finest offerings; and all the holy vessels he would give back, many times over; and the expenses incurred for the sacrifices he would provide from his own revenues; 17and in addition to all this he also would become a Jew and would visit every inhabited place to proclaim the power of God. 18But when his sufferings did not in any way abate, for the judgment of God had justly come upon him, he gave up all hope for himself and wrote to the Jews the following letter, in the form of a supplication. This was its content:

19 "To his worthy Jewish citizens, Antiochus their king and general sends hearty greetings and good wishes for their health and prosperity. 20If you and your children are well and your affairs are as you wish, I am glad. As my hope is in heaven, 21I re-member with affection your esteem and goodwill. On my way back from the region of Persia I suffered an annoying illness, and I have deemed it necessary to take thought for the general security of all. 22I do not despair of my condition, for I have good hope of recovering from my illness, 23but I observed that my father, on the occasions when he made expeditions into the upper country, appointed his successor, 24so that, if anything unexpected happened or any unwelcome news came, the people throughout the realm would not be troubled, for they would know to whom the government was left. 25Moreover, I understand how the princes along the borders and the neighbors of my kingdom keep watching for opportunities and waiting to see what will happen. So I have appointed my son Antiochus to be king, whom I have often entrusted and commended to most of you when I hurried off to the upper provinces; and I have written to him what is written here. 26I therefore urge and beg you to remember the public and private services rendered to you and to maintain your present goodwill, each of you, toward me and my son. 27For I am sure that he will follow my policy and will treat you with moderation and kindness."

28 So the murderer and blasphemer, having endured the more intense suffering, such as he had inflicted on others, came to the end of his life by a most pitiable fate, among the mountains in a strange land. 29And Philip, one of his courtiers, took his body home; then, fearing the son of Antiochus, he withdrew to Ptolemy Philometor in Egypt.

9.1–29: The death of Antiochus Epiphanes.* 2: In contrast to the account in 2 Macc 1, this passage is correct that Epiphanes was not killed while robbing a temple, as Antiochus III had been. 4: Compare Dan 11.30, where Epiphanes vents on Jerusalem the frustration of his humiliation in Egypt. There is no evidence that he was preoccupied with the Jews in his last days. 8: The attempt to *command the waves of the sea* was a classic instance act of hubris or wildly excessive pride, associated with the Persian king Xerxes by the fifth-century tragedian Aeschylus. Only God could *weigh*

ᵃ Or *not think thoughts proper only to God*

the high mountains in a balance (Isa 40.11). **9:** Later Jewish tradition preserved a similar account of the death of Herod the Great. Mention of *worms* recalls Isa 66.24. **10:** See Dan 8.10, where Epiphanes is said to cast down some of the stars and trample them. The classic example of an attempt to rise above the stars is that of the king of Babylon in Isa 14. **15:** In the Greek world, Athens was revered, and so to be *equal to the citizens of Athens* was an honor. Yet the reforms initiated by an Athenian senator in 2 Macc 6.1 were not welcome in Jerusalem. **17:** The most fantastic part of Epiphanes' (fictitious) deathbed conversion is the promise that he would become a Jew. There was one notable case of conversion in the first century CE, involving the royal house of Adiabene, but the fantasy of royal conversion is often found in Jewish writings. Usually, however, the king in question stops short of becoming a Jew (compare Nebuchadnezzar in Dan 4). In the apocryphal★ story of Bel and the Dragon appended to the Book of Daniel, the Babylonians charge that "the king has become a Jew," but the charge is unfounded (Bel 28). **19:** The letter of Epiphanes may be authentic, or, more likely, may be a modification of an authentic letter. It makes no mention of his conversion and is not apologetic in tone. It cannot have been composed by the author of 2 Maccabees to fit the present context. It is essentially a letter of authorization for the succession of the monarchy to Antiochus V Eupator. **26–27:** In the context of 2 Maccabees, the reference to the *present good will* of the Jews and the claim that his policy had been one of *moderation and kindness,* are highly ironic. **29:** The chapter ends by reaffirming 2 Maccabees' favorite theme of divine retribution.

10 Now Maccabeus and his followers, the Lord leading them on, recovered the temple and the city; ²they tore down the altars that had been built in the public square by the foreigners, and also destroyed the sacred precincts. ³They purified the sanctuary, and made another altar of sacrifice; then, striking fire out of flint, they offered sacrifices, after a lapse of two years, and they offered incense and lighted lamps and set out the bread of the Presence. ⁴When they had done this, they fell prostrate and implored the Lord that they might never again fall into such misfortunes, but that, if they should ever sin, they might be disciplined by him with forbearance and not be

handed over to blasphemous and barbarous nations. ⁵It happened that on the same day on which the sanctuary had been profaned by the foreigners, the purification of the sanctuary took place, that is, on the twenty-fifth day of the same month, which was Chislev. ⁶They celebrated it for eight days with rejoicing, in the manner of the festival of booths, remembering how not long before, during the festival of booths, they had been wandering in the mountains and caves like wild animals. ⁷Therefore, carrying ivy-wreathed wands and beautiful branches and also fronds of palm, they offered hymns of thanksgiving to him who had given success to the purifying of his own holy place. ⁸They decreed by public edict, ratified by vote, that the whole nation of the Jews should observe these days every year. ⁹Such then was the end of Antiochus, who was called Epiphanes.

10.1–9: The purification of the Temple.★ 2: Compare the actions of Josiah in 2 Kings 23. **3:** Contrast the miraculous preservation of the fire in 2 Macc 1. The *lapse of two years* is incorrect; the interval had been three years (1 Macc 1.54; 4.52), but 2 Maccabees is correct in placing the rededication after the death of Epiphanes.★ **5:** First Maccabees 4.54 also claims that the Temple was rededicated on the same day that it had been profaned. **7:** The *ivy-wreathed wands* ("thyrsoi") were associated with the worship of Dionysus, which is ironic in view of the enforced worship of Dionysus in 2 Macc 6. **8:** The event is commemorated by the festival of Hanukkah.

10 Now we will tell what took place under Antiochus Eupator, who was the son of that ungodly man, and will give a brief summary of the principal calamities of the wars. ¹¹This man, when he succeeded to the kingdom, appointed one Lysias to have charge of the government and to be chief governor of Coelesyria and Phoenicia. ¹²Ptolemy, who was called Macron, took the lead in showing justice to the Jews because of the wrong that had been done to them, and attempted to maintain peaceful relations with them. ¹³As a result he was accused before Eupator by the king's Friends. He heard himself called a traitor at every turn, because he had abandoned Cyprus, which Philometor had entrusted to him, and had gone over to Antiochus Epiphanes. Unable to command the respect due his office,[a] he took poison and ended his life.

14 When Gorgias became governor of the region, he maintained a force of mercenaries, and at every turn kept attacking the Jews. 15Besides this, the Idumeans, who had control of important strongholds, were harassing the Jews; they received those who were banished from Jerusalem, and endeavored to keep up the war. 16But Maccabeus and his forces, after making solemn supplication and imploring God to fight on their side, rushed to the strongholds of the Idumeans. 17Attacking them vigorously, they gained possession of the places, and beat off all who fought upon the wall, and slaughtered those whom they encountered, killing no fewer than twenty thousand.

18 When at least nine thousand took refuge in two very strong towers well equipped to withstand a siege, 19Maccabeus left Simon and Joseph, and also Zacchaeus and his troops, a force sufficient to besiege them; and he himself set off for places where he was more urgently needed. 20But those with Simon, who were money-hungry, were bribed by some of those who were in the towers, and on receiving seventy thousand drachmas let some of them slip away. 21When word of what had happened came to Maccabeus, he gathered the leaders of the people, and accused these men of having sold their kindred for money by setting their enemies free to fight against them. 22Then he killed these men who had turned traitor, and immediately captured the two towers. 23Having success at arms in everything he undertook, he destroyed more than twenty thousand in the two strongholds.

24 Now Timothy, who had been defeated by the Jews before, gathered a tremendous force of mercenaries and collected the cavalry from Asia in no small number. He came on, intending to take Judea by storm. 25As he drew near, Maccabeus and his men sprinkled dust on their heads and girded their loins with sackcloth, in supplication to God. 26Falling upon the steps before the altar,

they implored him to be gracious to them and to be an enemy to their enemies and an adversary to their adversaries, as the law declares. 27And rising from their prayer they took up their arms and advanced a considerable distance from the city; and when they came near the enemy they halted. 28Just as dawn was breaking, the two armies joined battle, the one having as pledge of success and victory not only their valor but also their reliance on the Lord, while the other made rage their leader in the fight.

29 When the battle became fierce, there appeared to the enemy from heaven five resplendent men on horses with golden bridles, and they were leading the Jews. 30Two of them took Maccabeus between them, and shielding him with their own armor and weapons, they kept him from being wounded. They showered arrows and thunderbolts on the enemy, so that, confused and blinded, they were thrown into disorder and cut to pieces. 31Twenty thousand five hundred were slaughtered, besides six hundred cavalry.

32 Timothy himself fled to a stronghold called Gazara, especially well garrisoned, where Chaereas was commander. 33Then Maccabeus and his men were glad, and they besieged the fort for four days. 34The men within, relying on the strength of the place, kept blaspheming terribly and uttering wicked words. 35But at dawn of the fifth day, twenty young men in the army of Maccabeus, fired with anger because of the blasphemies, bravely stormed the wall and with savage fury cut down everyone they met. 36Others who came up in the same way wheeled around against the defenders and set fire to the towers; they kindled fires and burned the blasphemers alive. Others broke open the gates and let in the rest of the force, and they occupied the city. 37They killed Timothy, who was hiding in a cistern, and his brother Chaereas, and Apollophanes. 38When they had accomplished these things, with hymns and thanksgivings they blessed the Lord who shows great kindness to Israel and gives them the victory.

a Cn: Meaning of Gk uncertain

10.10–38: Gorgias and Timothy. 19: In 1 Macc 5.55–62 Joseph is accompanied by Azariah, and they fail because they do not belong to the Maccabean family. In 2 Maccabees, the problem is bribery. **22:** A causal connection is implied between the execution of the traitors and the capture of the towers; compare the capture of Ai in Josh 7–8. **29:** Heavenly apparitions play a crucial part in the battle. Angelic assistance is often claimed in apocalyptic* writings from this period such as Daniel. **32:** The capture of Gazara is attributed to Simon Maccabee, at a later date, in 1 Macc 13.43.

11 Very soon after this, Lysias, the king's guardian and kinsman, who was in charge of the government, being vexed at what had happened, ²gathered about eighty thousand infantry and all his cavalry and came against the Jews. He intended to make the city a home for Greeks, ³and to levy tribute on the temple as he did on the sacred places of the other nations, and to put up the high priesthood for sale every year. ⁴He took no account whatever of the power of God, but was elated with his ten thousands of infantry, and his thousands of cavalry, and his eighty elephants. ⁵Invading Judea, he approached Beth-zur, which was a fortified place about five stadia*ᵃ from Jerusalem, and pressed it hard.

⁶ When Maccabeus and his men got word that Lysias*ᵇ was besieging the strongholds, they and all the people, with lamentations and tears, prayed the Lord to send a good angel to save Israel. ⁷Maccabeus himself was the first to take up arms, and he urged the others to risk their lives with him to aid their kindred. Then they eagerly rushed off together. ⁸And there, while they were still near Jerusalem, a horseman appeared at their head, clothed in white and brandishing weapons of gold. ⁹And together they all praised the merciful God, and were strengthened in heart, ready to assail not only humans but the wildest animals or walls of iron. ¹⁰They advanced in battle order, having their heavenly ally, for the Lord had mercy on them. ¹¹They hurled themselves like lions against the enemy, and laid low eleven thousand of them and sixteen hundred cavalry, and forced all the rest to flee.

¹²Most of them got away stripped and wounded, and Lysias himself escaped by disgraceful flight.

13 As he was not without intelligence, he pondered over the defeat that had befallen him, and realized that the Hebrews were invincible because the mighty God fought on their side. So he sent to them ¹⁴and persuaded them to settle everything on just terms, promising that he would persuade the king, constraining him to be their friend.*ᵃ ¹⁵Maccabeus, having regard for the common good, agreed to all that Lysias urged. For the king granted every request in behalf of the Jews which Maccabeus delivered to Lysias in writing.

11.1–15: The defeat of Lysias. In 1 Macc 4.28–35 this battle is placed before the purification of the Temple,* and the letters cited in 2 Macc 11 support the earlier date. **3:** The priesthood had been virtually up for sale in the time of Jason and Menelaus, but this was never official policy. **8:** This apparition may also be reflected in 1 Enoch* 90.14. See also the apparition of "the captain of the army of the Lord" to Joshua in Josh 5.13–15. **13:** First Maccabees gives no indication that Lysias thought the Hebrews were invincible. He returns undaunted in 2 Macc 13. Second Maccabees never acknowledges the defeats of the Maccabees at Bethzechariah (1 Macc 6.32–47) or at Mount Azotus where Judas was killed (1 Macc 9.11–22).

16 The letter written to the Jews by Lysias was to this effect:

"Lysias to the people of the Jews, greetings. ¹⁷John and Absalom, who were sent by you, have delivered your signed communication and have asked about the matters indicated in it. ¹⁸I have informed the king of everything that needed to be brought before him, and he has agreed to what was possible. ¹⁹If you will maintain your goodwill toward the government, I will endeavor in the future to help promote your welfare. ²⁰And concerning such matters and their details, I have ordered these men and my representatives to confer with you. ²¹Farewell. The one hundred forty-eighth year,*ᶜ Dioscorinthius twenty-fourth."

ᵃ Meaning of Gk uncertain   ᵇ Gk *he*   ᶜ 164 B.C.

22 The king's letter ran thus:

"King Antiochus to his brother Lysias, greetings. 23 Now that our father has gone on to the gods, we desire that the subjects of the kingdom be undisturbed in caring for their own affairs. 24 We have heard that the Jews do not consent to our father's change to Greek customs, but prefer their own way of living and ask that their own customs be allowed them. 25 Accordingly, since we choose that this nation also should be free from disturbance, our decision is that their temple be restored to them and that they shall live according to the customs of their ancestors. 26 You will do well, therefore, to send word to them and give them pledges of friendship, so that they may know our policy and be of good cheer and go on happily in the conduct of their own affairs."

27 To the nation the king's letter was as follows:

"King Antiochus to the senate of the Jews and to the other Jews, greetings. 28 If you are well, it is as we desire. We also are in good health. 29 Menelaus has informed us that you wish to return home and look after your own affairs. 30 Therefore those who go home by the thirtieth of Xanthicus will have our pledge of friendship and full permission 31 for the Jews to enjoy their own food and laws, just as formerly, and none of them shall be molested in any way for what may have been done in ignorance. 32 And I have also sent Menelaus to encourage you. 33 Farewell. The one hundred forty-eighth year,a Xanthicus fifteenth."

34 The Romans also sent them a letter, which read thus:

"Quintus Memmius and Titus Manius, envoys of the Romans, to the people of the Jews, greetings. 35 With regard to what Lysias the kinsman of the king has granted you, we also give consent. 36 But as to the matters that he decided are to be referred to the king, as soon as you have considered them, send some one promptly so that we may make proposals appropriate for you. For we are on our way to Antioch. 37 Therefore make haste and send messengers so that we may have your judgment. 38 Farewell. The one hundred forty-eighth year,a Xanthicus fifteenth."

11.16–38: Four letters. The documents inserted here are authentic letters, but the chronology is confused. The first, third, and fourth letters are dated to the year 148 of the Seleucid era, or 165–164 BCE. The second letter is authored by Antiochus V Eupator after the death of Epiphanes.* **16:** This letter confirms the agreement reached with Lysias at the end of ch. 10. **22:** The letter of Eupator formally abandons the attempt to compel the Jews to follow a Greek way of life. Unfortunately, Eupator was murdered when Demetrius, son of Seleucus IV, arrived on the scene (1 Macc 7.1–4). **27:** The third letter documents an earlier attempt by Epiphanes to put an end to the persecution and war, at the urging of Menelaus. This letter, however, is only an amnesty. It does not include the provision for the restoration of the Temple* found in Eupator's letter (v. 25). **34:** This letter may represent the first contact between the Romans and the Jews. It implies recognition of the Jews as a people and sets the stage for the subsequent Jewish embassy to Rome (1 Macc 8).

12 When this agreement had been reached, Lysias returned to the king, and the Jews went about their farming.

2 But some of the governors in various places, Timothy and Apollonius son of Gennaeus, as well as Hieronymus and Demophon, and in addition to these Nicanor the governor of Cyprus, would not let them live quietly and in peace. 3 And the people of Joppa did so ungodly a deed as this: they invited the Jews who lived among them to embark, with their wives and children, on boats that they had provided, as though there were no ill will to the Jews;b 4 and this was done by public vote of the city. When they accepted, because they wished to live peaceably and suspected nothing, the people of Joppac took them out to sea and drowned them, at least two hundred. 5 When Judas heard of the cruelty visited on his compatriots, he gave orders to his men 6 and, calling upon God, the righteous judge, attacked the murderers of his kindred. He set fire to the harbor by night, burned the boats, and massacred those who had taken refuge there. 7 Then, because the city's gates were closed,

a 164 B.C.   b Gk to them   c Gk they

he withdrew, intending to come again and root out the whole community of Joppa. [8]But learning that the people in Jamnia meant in the same way to wipe out the Jews who were living among them, [9]he attacked the Jamnites by night and set fire to the harbor and the fleet, so that the glow of the light was seen in Jerusalem, thirty miles[a] distant.

12.1–9: The massacre at Joppa. 2: Second Maccabees is careful to point out that the Jews were willing to live quietly and at peace. **4:** The incident at Joppa, modern Tel Aviv, is one of the earliest outright attacks on a Jewish community in a Greek city. See 1 Macc 5.15, although Joppa is not explicitly mentioned there. **6:** Judas, characteristically, met fire with fire.

10 When they had gone more than a mile[b] from there, on their march against Timothy, at least five thousand Arabs with five hundred cavalry attacked them. [11]After a hard fight, Judas and his companions, with God's help, were victorious. The defeated nomads begged Judas to grant them pledges of friendship, promising to give him livestock and to help his people[c] in all other ways. [12]Judas, realizing that they might indeed be useful in many ways, agreed to make peace with them; and after receiving his pledges they went back to their tents.

13 He also attacked a certain town that was strongly fortified with earthworks[d] and walls, and inhabited by all sorts of Gentiles. Its name was Caspin. [14]Those who were within, relying on the strength of the walls and on their supply of provisions, behaved most insolently toward Judas and his men, railing at them and even blaspheming and saying unholy things. [15]But Judas and his men, calling upon the great Sovereign of the world, who without battering rams or engines of war overthrew Jericho in the days of Joshua, rushed furiously upon the walls. [16]They took the town by the will of God, and slaughtered untold numbers, so that the adjoining lake, a quarter of a mile[e] wide, appeared to be running over with blood.

17 When they had gone ninety-five miles[f] from there, they came to Charax, to the Jews who are called Toubiani. [18]They did not find Timothy in that region, for he had

by then left there without accomplishing anything, though in one place he had left a very strong garrison. [19]Dositheus and Sosipater, who were captains under Maccabeus, marched out and destroyed those whom Timothy had left in the stronghold, more than ten thousand men. [20]But Maccabeus arranged his army in divisions, set men[e] in command of the divisions, and hurried after Timothy, who had with him one hundred twenty thousand infantry and two thousand five hundred cavalry. [21]When Timothy learned of the approach of Judas, he sent off the women and the children and also the baggage to a place called Carnaim; for that place was hard to besiege and difficult of access because of the narrowness of all the approaches. [22]But when Judas's first division appeared, terror and fear came over the enemy at the manifestation to them of him who sees all things. In their flight they rushed headlong in every direction, so that often they were injured by their own men and pierced by the points of their own swords. [23]Judas pressed the pursuit with the utmost vigor, putting the sinners to the sword, and destroyed as many as thirty thousand.

24 Timothy himself fell into the hands of Dositheus and Sosipater and their men. With great guile he begged them to let him go in safety, because he held the parents of most of them, and the brothers of some, to whom no consideration would be shown. [25]And when with many words he had confirmed his solemn promise to restore them unharmed, they let him go, for the sake of saving their kindred.

26 Then Judas[g] marched against Carnaim and the temple of Atargatis, and slaughtered twenty-five thousand people. [27]After the rout and destruction of these, he marched also against Ephron, a fortified town where Lysias lived with multitudes of people of all nationalities.[d] Stalwart young men took their stand before the walls and made a vigorous defense; and great stores of war engines and missiles were there. [28]But

a Gk two hundred forty stadia   b Gk nine stadia
c Gk them   d Meaning of Gk uncertain   e Gk two
stadia   f Gk seven hundred fifty stadia   g Gk he

the Jews[a] called upon the Sovereign who with power shatters the might of his enemies, and they got the town into their hands, and killed as many as twenty-five thousand of those who were in it.

29 Setting out from there, they hastened to Scythopolis, which is seventy-five miles[b] from Jerusalem. 30 But when the Jews who lived there bore witness to the goodwill that the people of Scythopolis had shown them and their kind treatment of them in times of misfortune, 31 they thanked them and exhorted them to be well disposed to their race in the future also. Then they went up to Jerusalem, as the festival of weeks was close at hand.

32 After the festival called Pentecost, they hurried against Gorgias, the governor of Idumea, 33 who came out with three thousand infantry and four hundred cavalry. 34 When they joined battle, it happened that a few of the Jews fell. 35 But a certain Dositheus, one of Bacenor's men, who was on horseback and was a strong man, caught hold of Gorgias, and grasping his cloak was dragging him off by main strength, wishing to take the accursed man alive, when one of the Thracian cavalry bore down on him and cut off his arm; so Gorgias escaped and reached Marisa.

36 As Esdris and his men had been fighting for a long time and were weary, Judas called upon the Lord to show himself their ally and leader in the battle. 37 In the language of their ancestors he raised the battle cry, with hymns; then he charged against Gorgias's troops when they were not expecting it, and put them to flight.

38 Then Judas assembled his army and went to the city of Adullam. As the seventh day was coming on, they purified themselves according to the custom, and kept the sabbath there.

39 On the next day, as had now become necessary, Judas and his men went to take up the bodies of the fallen and to bring them back to lie with their kindred in the sepulchres of their ancestors. 40 Then under the tunic of each one of the dead they found sacred tokens of the idols of Jamnia, which the law forbids the Jews to wear. And it became

clear to all that this was the reason these men had fallen. 41 So they all blessed the ways of the Lord, the righteous judge, who reveals the things that are hidden; 42 and they turned to supplication, praying that the sin that had been committed might be wholly blotted out. The noble Judas exhorted the people to keep themselves free from sin, for they had seen with their own eyes what had happened as the result of the sin of those who had fallen. 43 He also took up a collection, man by man, to the amount of two thousand drachmas of silver, and sent it to Jerusalem to provide for a sin offering. In doing this he acted very well and honorably, taking account of the resurrection. 44 For if he were not expecting that those who had fallen would rise again, it would have been superfluous and foolish to pray for the dead. 45 But if he was looking to the splendid reward that is laid up for those who fall asleep in godliness, it was a holy and pious thought. Therefore he made atonement for the dead, so that they might be delivered from their sin.

12.10–45: The campaign against Timothy. 10: The death of Timothy was already reported in 2 Macc 10.37. The geography is also problematic, since it is implausible that Arab nomads would be within a few miles of Jamnia. 15: The parallel with the capture of Jericho emphasizes the role of divine aid. 22: *Terror and fear* also fell on the gentiles* at the time of the Exodus. 30: The case of Scythopolis (Bethshan) shows that Judas was not hostile to gentiles as such, but only to those who were hostile to the Jews. 31: Judas is careful to return to Jerusalem in time for the festival. 40: The implication is that only sinners are killed in battle (compare the explanation of military failure at Ai in Josh 7). Second Maccabees avoids the awkwardness of the death of Judas by terminating the narrative* before that point. 43: There is no indication in 1 Maccabees that Judas believed in resurrection. The sacrifices for the dead do not warrant the inference here. He may have offered the sacrifices to atone for sins, so that the army would not continue to be punished. The inferential character of the statement shows that Judas was not explicit about such a belief. 45: This

a Gk they b Gk six hundred stadia

is the earliest attestation of the idea that people could be delivered from their sins after death.

13 In the one hundred forty-ninth year*ᵃ* word came to Judas and his men that Antiochus Eupator was coming with a great army against Judea, ²and with him Lysias, his guardian, who had charge of the government. Each of them had a Greek force of one hundred ten thousand infantry, five thousand three hundred cavalry, twenty-two elephants, and three hundred chariots armed with scythes.

3 Menelaus also joined them and with utter hypocrisy urged Antiochus on, not for the sake of his country's welfare, but because he thought that he would be established in office. ⁴But the King of kings aroused the anger of Antiochus against the scoundrel; and when Lysias informed him that this man was to blame for all the trouble, he ordered them to take him to Beroea and to put him to death by the method that is customary in that place. ⁵For there is a tower there, fifty cubits high, full of ashes, and it has a rim running around it that on all sides inclines precipitously into the ashes. ⁶There they all push to destruction anyone guilty of sacrilege or notorious for other crimes. ⁷By such a fate it came about that Menelaus the lawbreaker died, without even burial in the earth. ⁸And this was eminently just; because he had committed many sins against the altar whose fire and ashes were holy, he met his death in ashes.

13.1–8: The death of Menelaus. The renewed campaign of Eupator and Lysias was presumably a response to the continued activity of Judas. **4:** Menelaus had been discredited by the failure of the peace he had negotiated. Many modern scholars agree with the assessment of Lysias that he was the cause of all the troubles. *Beroea* was the Seleucid name for Aleppo. **5:** Death by ashes was a Persian punishment. The victim either suffocated or was roasted. **8:** As usual, 2 Maccabees emphasizes that the punishment fits the crime.

9 The king with barbarous arrogance was coming to show the Jews things far worse than those that had been done*ᵇ* in his father's time. ¹⁰But when Judas heard of this, he ordered the people to call upon the Lord day and night, now if ever to help those who were on the point of being deprived of the law and their country and the holy temple, ¹¹and not to let the people who had just begun to revive fall into the hands of the blasphemous Gentiles. ¹²When they had all joined in the same petition and had implored the merciful Lord with weeping and fasting and lying prostrate for three days without ceasing, Judas exhorted them and ordered them to stand ready.

13 After consulting privately with the elders, he determined to march out and decide the matter by the help of God before the king's army could enter Judea and get possession of the city. ¹⁴So, committing the decision to the Creator of the world and exhorting his troops to fight bravely to the death for the laws, temple, city, country, and commonwealth, he pitched his camp near Modein. ¹⁵He gave his troops the watchword, "God's victory," and with a picked force of the bravest young men, he attacked the king's pavilion at night and killed as many as two thousand men in the camp. He stabbed*ᶜ* the leading elephant and its rider. ¹⁶In the end they filled the camp with terror and confusion and withdrew in triumph. ¹⁷This happened, just as day was dawning, because the Lord's help protected him.

18 The king, having had a taste of the daring of the Jews, tried strategy in attacking their positions. ¹⁹He advanced against Beth-zur, a strong fortress of the Jews, was turned back, attacked again,*ᵈ* and was defeated. ²⁰Judas sent in to the garrison whatever was necessary. ²¹But Rhodocus, a man from the ranks of the Jews, gave secret information to the enemy; he was sought for, caught, and put in prison. ²²The king negotiated a second time with the people in Beth-zur, gave pledges, received theirs, withdrew, attacked Judas and his men, was defeated; ²³he got word that Philip, who had been left in charge of the government, had revolted in Antioch; he was dismayed, called in the Jews, yielded and swore to observe all their

a 163 B.C.   *b* Or *the worst of the things that had been done*   *c* Meaning of Gk uncertain   *d* Or *faltered* rights, settled with them and offered sacrifice, honored the sanctuary and showed generosity to the holy place. 24He received Maccabeus, left Hegemonides as governor from Ptolemais to Gerar, 25and went to Ptolemais. The people of Ptolemais were indignant over the treaty; in fact they were so angry that they wanted to annul its terms.*ª 26Lysias took the public platform, made the best possible defense, convinced them, appeased them, gained their goodwill, and set out for Antioch. This is how the king's attack and withdrawal turned out.

13.9–26: The failure of Eupator's attack. This campaign is also described in 1 Macc 6.18–63, which acknowledges that Judas was defeated at Beth-zechariah. **10:** Second Maccabees emphasizes Judas's recourse to prayer. **15:** According to 1 Macc 6.43–44, Eleazar, brother of Judas, stabbed the elephant but lost his life in the process. **19–20:** According to 1 Macc 6.49 the people of Beth-zur surrendered because of lack of provisions. **22:** In 1 Maccabees, the defenders of Jerusalem were on the verge of capitulation. **23:** Both books of Maccabees agree that Eupator withdrew because of the revolt of Philip.

14 Three years later, word came to Judas and his men that Demetrius son of Seleucus had sailed into the harbor of Tripolis with a strong army and a fleet, 2and had taken possession of the country, having made away with Antiochus and his guardian Lysias.

3 Now a certain Alcimus, who had formerly been high priest but had willfully defiled himself in the times of separation,*ᵇ realized that there was no way for him to be safe or to have access again to the holy altar, 4and went to King Demetrius in about the one hundred fifty-first year,*ᶜ presenting to him a crown of gold and a palm, and besides these some of the customary olive branches from the temple. During that day he kept quiet. 5But he found an opportunity that furthered his mad purpose when he was invited by Demetrius to a meeting of the council and was asked about the attitude and intentions of the Jews. He answered:

6 "Those of the Jews who are called Hasideans, whose leader is Judas Maccabeus,

are keeping up war and stirring up sedition, and will not let the kingdom attain tranquility. 7Therefore I have laid aside my ancestral glory—I mean the high priesthood—and have now come here, 8first because I am genuinely concerned for the interests of the king, and second because I have regard also for my compatriots. For through the folly of those whom I have mentioned our whole nation is now in no small misfortune. 9Since you are acquainted, O king, with the details of this matter, may it please you to take thought for our country and our hard-pressed nation with the gracious kindness that you show to all. 10For as long as Judas lives, it is impossible for the government to find peace." 11When he had said this, the rest of the king's Friends,*ᵈ who were hostile to Judas, quickly inflamed Demetrius still more. 12He immediately chose Nicanor, who had been in command of the elephants, appointed him governor of Judea, and sent him off 13with orders to kill Judas and scatter his troops, and to install Alcimus as high priest of the great*ᵉ temple. 14And the Gentiles throughout Judea, who had fled before*ᵃ Judas, flocked to join Nicanor, thinking that the misfortunes and calamities of the Jews would mean prosperity for themselves.

15 When the Jews*ᶠ heard of Nicanor's coming and the gathering of the Gentiles, they sprinkled dust on their heads and prayed to him who established his own people forever and always upholds his own heritage by manifesting himself. 16At the command of the leader, they*ᵍ set out from there immediately and engaged them in battle at a village called Dessau.*ᵃ 17Simon, the brother of Judas, had encountered Nicanor, but had been temporarily*ʰ checked because of the sudden consternation created by the enemy. 18 Nevertheless Nicanor, hearing of the valor of Judas and his troops and their courage in battle for their country, shrank from deciding the issue by bloodshed. 19Therefore he sent Posidonius, Theodotus, and Matta-

---

a Meaning of Gk uncertain   *b* Other ancient authorities read *of mixing*   *c* 161 B.C.   *d* Gk *of the Friends*   *e* Gk *greatest*   *f* Gk *they*   *g* Gk *he*   *h* Other ancient authorities read *slowly* thias to give and receive pledges of friendship. 20When the terms had been fully considered, and the leader had informed the people, and it had appeared that they were of one mind, they agreed to the covenant. 21The leaders*a* set a day on which to meet by themselves. A chariot came forward from each army; seats of honor were set in place; 22Judas posted armed men in readiness at key places to prevent sudden treachery on the part of the enemy; so they duly held the consultation.

23 Nicanor stayed on in Jerusalem and did nothing out of the way, but dismissed the flocks of people that had gathered. 24And he kept Judas always in his presence; he was warmly attached to the man. 25He urged him to marry and have children; so Judas*b* married, settled down, and shared the common life.

26 But when Alcimus noticed their goodwill for one another, he took the covenant that had been made and went to Demetrius. He told him that Nicanor was disloyal to the government, since he had appointed that conspirator against the kingdom, Judas, to be his successor. 27The king became excited and, provoked by the false accusations of that depraved man, wrote to Nicanor, stating that he was displeased with the covenant and commanding him to send Maccabeus to Antioch as a prisoner without delay.

28 When this message came to Nicanor, he was troubled and grieved that he had to annul their agreement when the man had done no wrong. 29Since it was not possible to oppose the king, he watched for an opportunity to accomplish this by a stratagem. 30But Maccabeus, noticing that Nicanor was more austere in his dealings with him and was meeting him more rudely than had been his custom, concluded that this austerity did not spring from the best motives. So he gathered not a few of his men, and went into hiding from Nicanor. 31When the latter became aware that he had been cleverly outwitted by the man, he went to the great*c* and holy temple while the priests were offering the customary sacrifices, and commanded them to hand the man over. 32When they declared on oath that they did not know

where the man was whom he wanted, 33he stretched out his right hand toward the sanctuary, and swore this oath: "If you do not hand Judas over to me as a prisoner, I will level this shrine of God to the ground and tear down the altar, and build here a splendid temple to Dionysus."

34 Having said this, he went away. Then the priests stretched out their hands toward heaven and called upon the constant Defender of our nation, in these words: 35"O Lord of all, though you have need of nothing, you were pleased that there should be a temple for your habitation among us; 36so now, O holy One, Lord of all holiness, keep undefiled forever this house that has been so recently purified."

14.1–36: Alcimus and Nicanor. Second Maccabees ignores the slaughter of the Hasidim,* perhaps because it was a setback for the Jews. **6:** Second Maccabees identifies the Hasidim closely with Judas, and ignores that they were the first to make peace. A Hellenizer* like Alcimus may well have overlooked differences within the resistance movement. **12:** For the campaign of Nicanor, see 1 Macc 7.26–50. First Maccabees 7.27–32 claims that Nicanor was insincere; 2 Maccabees claims that he had genuine affectation for Judas. **26:** Second Maccabees typically places the blame on a Jewish renegade, in this case Alcimus, who forces Nicanor to resume hostilities. **33:** It is also typical of 2 Maccabees that the threat is focused on the Temple.* Thus the narrative* that began with the threat to the Temple by Heliodorus concludes with that by Nicanor.

37 A certain Razis, one of the elders of Jerusalem, was denounced to Nicanor as a man who loved his compatriots and was very well thought of and for his goodwill was called father of the Jews. 38In former times, when there was no mingling with the Gentiles, he had been accused of Judaism, and he had most zealously risked body and life for Judaism. 39Nicanor, wishing to exhibit the enmity that he had for the Jews, sent more than five hundred soldiers to arrest him; 40for he thought that by arresting*d* him

a *Gk* They   b *Gk* he   c *Gk greatest*   d Meaning of Gk uncertain he would do them an injury. 41When the troops were about to capture the tower and were forcing the door of the courtyard, they ordered that fire be brought and the doors burned. Being surrounded, Razis*a* fell upon his own sword, 42preferring to die nobly rather than to fall into the hands of sinners and suffer outrages unworthy of his noble birth. 43But in the heat of the struggle he did not hit exactly, and the crowd was now rushing in through the doors. He courageously ran up on the wall, and bravely threw himself down into the crowd. 44But as they quickly drew back, a space opened and he fell in the middle of the empty space. 45Still alive and aflame with anger, he rose, and though his blood gushed forth and his wounds were severe he ran through the crowd; and standing upon a steep rock, 46with his blood now completely drained from him, he tore out his entrails, took them in both hands and hurled them at the crowd, calling upon the Lord of life and spirit to give them back to him again. This was the manner of his death.

14.37–46: The suicide of Razis. 1: It is surprising that a traditionalist would be found among the elders during the high priesthood of Alcimus. 38: The *former times* were probably the years of persecution under Antiochus Epiphanes.* 41: Razis differs from the martyrs* in 2 Macc 7 by taking his own life. The most famous example of noble suicide in ancient Judaism is that of the Zealots* at Masada. There were biblical precedents, notably Saul and his armor-bearer in 1 Sam 31. 46: Razis dies in hope of resurrection, so his suicide was evidently not considered sinful.

15 When Nicanor heard that Judas and his troops were in the region of Samaria, he made plans to attack them with complete safety on the day of rest. 2When the Jews who were compelled to follow him said, "Do not destroy so savagely and barbarously, but show respect for the day that he who sees all things has honored and hallowed above other days," 3the thrice-accursed wretch asked if there were a sovereign in heaven who had commanded the keeping of the sabbath day. 4When they declared, "It is the living Lord himself, the Sov-

ereign in heaven, who ordered us to observe the seventh day," 5he replied, "But I am a sovereign also, on earth, and I command you to take up arms and finish the king's business." Nevertheless, he did not succeed in carrying out his abominable design.

6 This Nicanor in his utter boastfulness and arrogance had determined to erect a public monument of victory over Judas and his forces. 7But Maccabeus did not cease to trust with all confidence that he would get help from the Lord. 8He exhorted his troops not to fear the attack of the Gentiles, but to keep in mind the former times when help had come to them from heaven, and so to look for the victory that the Almighty would give them. 9Encouraging them from the law and the prophets, and reminding them also of the struggles they had won, he made them the more eager. 10When he had aroused their courage, he issued his orders, at the same time pointing out the perfidy of the Gentiles and their violation of oaths. 11He armed each of them not so much with confidence in shields and spears as with the inspiration of brave words, and he cheered them all by relating a dream, a sort of vision,*b* which was worthy of belief.

12 What he saw was this: Onias, who had been high priest, a noble and good man, of modest bearing and gentle manner, one who spoke fittingly and had been trained from childhood in all that belongs to excellence, was praying with outstretched hands for the whole body of the Jews. 13Then in the same fashion another appeared, distinguished by his gray hair and dignity, and of marvelous majesty and authority. 14And Onias spoke, saying, "This is a man who loves the family of Israel and prays much for the people and the holy city—Jeremiah, the prophet of God." 15Jeremiah stretched out his right hand and gave to Judas a golden sword, and as he gave it he addressed him thus: 16"Take this holy sword, a gift from God, with which you will strike down your adversaries."

17 Encouraged by the words of Judas, so noble and so effective in arousing valor and

a Gk he   *b* Meaning of Gk uncertain

awaking courage in the souls of the young, they determined not to carry on a campaign[a] but to attack bravely, and to decide the matter by fighting hand to hand with all courage, because the city and the sanctuary and the temple were in danger. 18Their concern for wives and children, and also for brothers and sisters[b] and relatives, lay upon them less heavily; their greatest and first fear was for the consecrated sanctuary. 19And those who had to remain in the city were in no little distress, being anxious over the encounter in the open country.

20 When all were now looking forward to the coming issue, and the enemy was already close at hand with their army drawn up for battle, the elephants[c] strategically stationed and the cavalry deployed on the flanks, 21Maccabeus, observing the masses that were in front of him and the varied supply of arms and the savagery of the elephants, stretched out his hands toward heaven and called upon the Lord who works wonders; for he knew that it is not by arms, but as the Lord[d] decides, that he gains the victory for those who deserve it. 22He called upon him in these words: "O Lord, you sent your angel in the time of King Hezekiah of Judea, and he killed fully one hundred eighty-five thousand in the camp of Sennacherib. 23So now, O Sovereign of the heavens, send a good angel to spread terror and trembling before us. 24By the might of your arm may these blasphemers who come against your holy people be struck down." With these words he ended his prayer.

25 Nicanor and his troops advanced with trumpets and battle songs, 26but Judas and his troops met the enemy in battle with invocations to God and prayers. 27So, fighting with their hands and praying to God in their hearts, they laid low at least thirty-five thousand, and were greatly gladdened by God's manifestation.

28 When the action was over and they were returning with joy, they recognized Nicanor, lying dead, in full armor. 29Then there was shouting and tumult, and they blessed the Sovereign Lord in the language of their ancestors. 30Then the man who was ever in body and soul the defender of his people, the man who maintained his youthful goodwill toward his compatriots, ordered them to cut off Nicanor's head and arm and carry them to Jerusalem. 31When he arrived there and had called his compatriots together and stationed the priests before the altar, he sent for those who were in the citadel. 32He showed them the vile Nicanor's head and that profane man's arm, which had been boastfully stretched out against the holy house of the Almighty. 33He cut out the tongue of the ungodly Nicanor and said that he would feed it piecemeal to the birds and would hang up these rewards of his folly opposite the sanctuary. 34And they all, looking to heaven, blessed the Lord who had manifested himself, saying, "Blessed is he who has kept his own place undefiled!" 35Judas[e] hung Nicanor's head from the citadel, a clear and conspicuous sign to everyone of the help of the Lord. 36And they all decreed by public vote never to let this day go unobserved, but to celebrate the thirteenth day of the twelfth month—which is called Adar in the Aramaic language—the day before Mordecai's day.

37 This, then, is how matters turned out with Nicanor, and from that time the city has been in the possession of the Hebrews. So I will here end my story.

15.1–37: The defeat of Nicanor. 1: Second Maccabees ignores the decision that the Maccabees had taken to fight on the sabbath. **7:** Judas's trust in the Lord is contrasted with the hubris of Nicanor. **12:** Onias III, the murdered high priest, was glorified in the early chapters of 2 Maccabees. By the time the book was written, however, the high priesthood had been usurped by the Maccabees. Second Maccabees nonetheless claims the support of the dead high priest. **14:** Jeremiah is included because of his association with the Temple★ at the time of the Babylonian attack, and because the sword is the dominant image in an oracle★ attributed to him in Jer 50.35–38. Ironically, Jeremiah, noted for his opposition to militant resistance, said that God would turn the swords of the defenders against themselves (Jer 21.4). First Enoch★ 90.19 also says that a sword was given to the Maccabees. **28:** The defeat of Nicanor was a major event, subsequently celebrated

---

a Or *to remain in camp*　　*b* Gk *for brothers*　　*c* Gk *animals*　　*d* Gk *he*　　*e* Gk *He* in a festival. **33:** His tongue was cut out because of his blasphemies against the Temple.

38 If it is well told and to the point, that is what I myself desired; if it is poorly done and mediocre, that was the best I could do. ³⁹For just as it is harmful to drink wine alone, or, again, to drink water alone, while wine mixed with water is sweet and delicious and enhances one's enjoyment, so also the style of the story delights the ears of those who read the work. And here will be the end.

15.37–39: The epilogue. The reference to enjoyment is jarring after the gory description of Nicanor's death. Second Maccabees ends on an upbeat note, before the death of Judas, ignoring the subsequent fluctuations in the fortunes of the Maccabees.

(b) The books from 1 Esdras through 3 Maccabees are recognized as Deuterocanonical Scripture by the Greek and the Russian Orthodox Churches. They are not so recognized by the Roman Catholic Church, but 1 Esdras and the Prayer of Manasseh (together with 2 Esdras) are placed in an appendix to the Latin Vulgate Bible.

1 ESDRAS

Introduction

First Esdras (also known as Esdras A or 3 Esdras) is a Greek version of biblical history from the celebration of Josiah's Passover* to the time of Ezra. First Esdras is canonical* for the Eastern Orthodox Church, but not for Protestants or Roman Catholics. Jerome condemned the book, but he translated it and placed it after the New Testament in the Vulgate. The relationship of 1 Esdras to canonical materials can be outlined as follows:

1 Esd 1.1–22	=	2 Chr 35.1–19
1 Esd 1.23–24	=	no canonical parallel
1 Esd 1.25–58	=	2 Chr 35.20–36.21
1 Esd 2.1–5a	=	2 Chr 36.22–23//Ezra 1.1–3a
1 Esd 2.5b–15	=	Ezra 1.3b–11
1 Esd 2.16–30	=	Ezra 4.7–24
1 Esd 3.1–5.6	=	no canonical parallel
1 Esd 5.7–73	=	Ezra 2.1–4.5
1 Esd 6.1–9.36	=	Ezra 5.1–10.44
1 Esd 9.37–55	=	Neh 7.73–8.13a

The most noticeable differences from the texts of Chronicles, Ezra, and Nehemiah are the inclusion of the Story of the Three Youths in 3.1–5.6 and the relocation of the verses equivalent to Ezra 4.7–24. The inclusion of Neh 7.73–8.12 immediately after Ezra 10 has led to the hypothesis* that 1 Esdras is a fragment of a translation of an earlier edition of the Chronicler's History (1 and 2 Chronicles; Ezra; Nehemiah), to which the Nehemiah Memoir (Neh 1.1–7.73a; 11.1–2; 12.31–43; 13.4–31) had not yet been added. First Esdras seems to be a fragment of a longer work because it ends in the middle of a sentence and begins in the middle of the account of Josiah. Another interpretation* of this book considers the present text to be a complete and independent work, consisting of excerpts from Chronicles, Ezra, and Nehemiah and the Story of the Three Youths that have been consciously crafted into a new literary entity. In this view, the abrupt beginning and incomplete final sentence would perhaps be the result of accidental damage to an early copy. The idea that 1 Esdras is a new literary entity has gained greater prominence as recent scholars have called into question whether there ever was a Chronicler's History consisting of all or parts of 1 and 2 Chronicles, Ezra, and Nehemiah. The underlying Hebrew/Aramaic* original that the Greek text of 1 Esdras is assumed to be translating is apparently older and shorter than the Masoretic* text, the standard text of the Hebrew Scriptures, which was put into final form by Jewish scholars at the end of the first century CE.

Because of the relative age of the underlying Hebrew text, it is probable that the book was composed as early as the second century BCE. Since it was used by Josephus in his account of the Persian period, it must have come into existence in any case no later than the mid first century CE. The addition in 1.23–24 helps to resolve the dilemma created by Josiah's premature death while the Story of the Three Youths highlights the role of Zerubbabel, a descendant of David, and explains why Darius was moved to support the building of the Temple.* Neither addition suggests a specific date of composition.

READING GUIDE

Our comments focus heavily, but not exclusively, on the materials not included in Chronicles, Ezra, and Nehemiah. By shifting Ezra 4.7–24 to an earlier location, the book partially unscrambles the confusion in this passage in its canonical location, which puts Artaxerxes I (464–424 BCE) before Darius I (522–486 BCE). In 1 Esdras Darius's efforts to stop the building of the Temple (1 Esd 2.16–30) now come before his permission for Zerubbabel to go ahead and rebuild the Temple in 1 Esd 3.1–5.6. Reading the Story of the Three Youths first will show the most dramatic change from Chronicles and Nehemiah.

1.1–58	The last kings of Judah
2.1–30	The early days of the return
3.1–5.6	The Story of the Three Youths
5.7–7.15	The rebuilding of the Temple
8.1–9.55	The mission of Ezra

1 Josiah kept the passover to his Lord in Jerusalem; he killed the passover lamb on the fourteenth day of the first month, ²having placed the priests according to their divisions, arrayed in their vestments, in the temple of the Lord. ³He told the Levites, the temple servants of Israel, that they should sanctify themselves to the Lord and put the holy ark of the Lord in the house that King Solomon, son of David, had built; ⁴and he said, "You need no longer carry it on your shoulders. Now worship the Lord your God and serve his people Israel; prepare yourselves by your families and kindred, ⁵in accordance with the directions of King David of Israel and the magnificence of his son Solomon. Stand in order in the temple according to the groupings of the ancestral houses of you Levites, who minister before your kindred the people of Israel, ⁶and kill the passover lamb and prepare the sacrifices for your kindred, and keep the passover according to the commandment of the Lord that was given to Moses."

7 To the people who were present Josiah gave thirty thousand lambs and kids, and three thousand calves; these were given from the king's possessions, as he promised, to the people and the priests and Levites. ⁸Hilkiah, Zechariah, and Jehiel,ᵃ the chief officers of the temple, gave to the priests for the passover two thousand six hundred sheep and three hundred calves. ⁹And Jeconiah and Shemaiah and his brother Nethanel, and Hashabiah and Ochiel and Joram, captains over thousands, gave the Levites for the passover five thousand sheep and seven hundred calves.

10 This is what took place. The priests and the Levites, having the unleavened bread, stood in proper order according to kindred ¹¹and the grouping of the ancestral houses, before the people, to make the offering to the Lord as it is written in the book of Moses; this they did in the morning. ¹²They roasted the passover lamb with fire, as required; and they boiled the sacrifices in bronze pots and caldrons, with a pleasing odor, ¹³and carried them to all the people. Afterward they prepared the passover for themselves and for their kindred the priests, the sons of Aaron, ¹⁴because the priests were offering the fat until nightfall; so the

a Gk Esyelus

Levites prepared it for themselves and for their kindred the priests, the sons of Aaron. ¹⁵The temple singers, the sons of Asaph, were in their place according to the arrangement made by David, and also Asaph, Zechariah, and Eddinus, who represented the king. ¹⁶The gatekeepers were at each gate; no one needed to interrupt his daily duties, for their kindred the Levites prepared the passover for them.

17 So the things that had to do with the sacrifices to the Lord were accomplished that day: the passover was kept ¹⁸and the sacrifices were offered on the altar of the Lord, according to the command of King Josiah. ¹⁹And the people of Israel who were present at that time kept the passover and the festival of unleavened bread seven days. ²⁰No passover like it had been kept in Israel since the times of the prophet Samuel; ²¹none of the kings of Israel had kept such a passover as was kept by Josiah and the priests and Levites and the people of Judah and all of Israel who were living in Jerusalem. ²²In the eighteenth year of the reign of Josiah this passover was kept.

1.1–22 (2 Chr 35.1–19): **Josiah's Passover.** It is not likely that this is the original beginning of the book since Josiah is not introduced and there is no date formula in v. 1 (see 2 Chr 34.8). **6:** The Levites killed the Passover lamb as they had at the time of Hezekiah (2 Chr 30.17). **12:** The Passover meal was both roasted and boiled (see Ex 12.8–9; Deut 16.7). **20:** No Passover had been held like this one since the time of Samuel the prophet (see 2 Kings 23.22). Its uniqueness apparently lay in the role of the Levites.

23 And the deeds of Josiah were upright in the sight of the Lord, for his heart was full of godliness. ²⁴In ancient times the events of his reign have been recorded—concerning those who sinned and acted wickedly toward the Lord beyond any other people or kingdom, and how they grieved the Lord^a deeply, so that the words of the Lord fell upon Israel.

1.23–24 (without canonical parallel): **Evaluation of Josiah.** In spite of the personal piety of Josiah, there were people during his reign who were more wicked

than any other people, with the result that God's word of judgment fell on Israel (1 Kings 13.2, 32, and 2 Kings 23.24–27 may have served as a source for this addition). These words resolve the theological difficulty in the accounts of Josiah, in both Kings and Chronicles, which cannot explain why the whole kingdom fell a few years after this great king died.

25 After all these acts of Josiah, it happened that Pharaoh, king of Egypt, went to make war at Carchemish on the Euphrates, and Josiah went out against him. ²⁶And the king of Egypt sent word to him saying, "What have we to do with each other, O king of Judea? ²⁷I was not sent against you by the Lord God, for my war is at the Euphrates. And now the Lord is with me! The Lord is with me, urging me on! Stand aside, and do not oppose the Lord."

28 Josiah, however, did not turn back to his chariot, but tried to fight with him, and did not heed the words of the prophet Jeremiah from the mouth of the Lord. ²⁹He joined battle with him in the plain of Megiddo, and the commanders came down against King Josiah. ³⁰The king said to his servants, "Take me away from the battle, for I am very weak." And immediately his servants took him out of the line of battle. ³¹He got into his second chariot; and after he was brought back to Jerusalem he died, and was buried in the tomb of his ancestors.

32 In all Judea they mourned for Josiah. The prophet Jeremiah lamented for Josiah, and the principal men, with the women,^b have made lamentation for him to this day; it was ordained that this should always be done throughout the whole nation of Israel. ³³These things are written in the book of the histories of the kings of Judea; and every one of the acts of Josiah, and his splendor, and his understanding of the law of the Lord, and the things that he had done before, and these that are now told, are recorded in the book of the kings of Israel and Judah.

34 The men of the nation took Jeconiah^c son of Josiah, who was twenty-three years

a Gk *him*   *b* Or *their wives*   *c* 2 Kings 23.30; 2 Chr 36.1 *Jehoahaz* old, and made him king in succession to his father Josiah. ³⁵He reigned three months in Judah and Jerusalem. Then the king of Egypt deposed him from reigning in Jerusalem, ³⁶and fined the nation one hundred talents of silver and one talent of gold. ³⁷The king of Egypt made his brother Jehoiakim king of Judea and Jerusalem. ³⁸Jehoiakim put the nobles in prison, and seized his brother Zarius and brought him back from Egypt.

1.25–38 (2 Chr 35.20–27): **The death of Josiah. 26–27:** Neco, *king of Egypt,* warns Josiah not to resist his march toward the Euphrates to shore up the reeling forces of the Assyrians. Since the Lord was with the Pharaoh, Josiah's attack on him would be an attack on the Lord as well. **28:** In 2 Chr 35.22 the words of Neco were said to come from the mouth of God; 1 Esdras adds that they were delivered by the prophet Jeremiah! By ignoring this prophetic word Josiah brought about his own premature death.

---

39 Jehoiakim was twenty-five years old when he began to reign in Judea and Jerusalem; he did what was evil in the sight of the Lord. ⁴⁰King Nebuchadnezzar of Babylon came up against him; he bound him with a chain of bronze and took him away to Babylon. ⁴¹Nebuchadnezzar also took some holy vessels of the Lord, and carried them away, and stored them in his temple in Babylon. ⁴²But the things that are reported about Jehoiakim,ᵃ and his uncleanness and impiety, are written in the annals of the kings.

43 His son Jehoiachinᵇ became king in his place; when he was made king he was eighteen years old, ⁴⁴and he reigned three months and ten days in Jerusalem. He did what was evil in the sight of the Lord. ⁴⁵A year later Nebuchadnezzar sent and removed him to Babylon, with the holy vessels of the Lord, ⁴⁶and made Zedekiah king of Judea and Jerusalem.

Zedekiah was twenty-one years old, and he reigned eleven years. ⁴⁷He also did what was evil in the sight of the Lord, and did not heed the words that were spoken by the prophet Jeremiah from the mouth of the Lord. ⁴⁸Although King Nebuchadnezzar had made him swear by the name of the Lord, he broke his oath and rebelled; he stiffened his neck and hardened his heart and transgressed the laws of the Lord, the God of Israel. ⁴⁹Even the leaders of the people and of the priests committed many acts of sacrilege and lawlessness beyond all the unclean deeds of all the nations, and polluted the temple of the Lord in Jerusalem—the temple that God had made holy. ⁵⁰The God of their ancestors sent his messenger to call them back, because he would have spared them and his dwelling place. ⁵¹But they mocked his messengers, and whenever the Lord spoke, they scoffed at his prophets, ⁵²until in his anger against his people because of their ungodly acts he gave command to bring against them the kings of the Chaldeans. ⁵³These killed their young men with the sword around their holy temple, and did not spare young man or young woman,ᶜ old man or child, for he gave them all into their hands. ⁵⁴They took all the holy vessels of the Lord, great and small, the treasure chests of the Lord, and the royal stores, and carried them away to Babylon. ⁵⁵They burned the house of the Lord, broke down the walls of Jerusalem, burned their towers with fire, ⁵⁶and utterly destroyed all its glorious things. The survivors he led away to Babylon with the sword, ⁵⁷and they were servants to him and to his sons until the Persians began to reign, in fulfillment of the word of the Lord by the mouth of Jeremiah, ⁵⁸saying, "Until the land has enjoyed its sabbaths, it shall keep sabbath all the time of its desolation until the completion of seventy years."

1.34–58 (2 Chr 36.1–21): **Josiah's royal successors and the final days of Jerusalem. 34:** Instead of *Jeconiah/Jehoiachin,* we would expect Jehoahaz, as in 2 Chr 36.1. **38:** *Jehoiakim* brought his brother *Zarius* back from Egypt, but according to the parallel text in 2 Chr 36.4, Neco took Jehoiakim's brother *Jehoahaz* down to Egypt. **43:** Instead of Jehoiakim in the Greek text, we would expect Jehoiachin, and NRSV so emends the text. **45:** After the Exile,★ the *holy vessels of the Lord* were returned to the Temple★ in Jerusalem. **48:** According to an addition in 1 Esdras, Zedekiah compounded his guilt known from 2 Chronicles (not

a Gk *him* *b* Gk *Jehoiakim* *c* Gk *virgin*

listening to the word of the Lord and violating an oath he had sworn to Nebuchadnezzar) by transgressing the *laws of the Lord, the God of Israel.* **58:** The devastated land enjoyed a sabbath rest during the Exile (see Lev 26.34–35). The Chronicler expected the Exile to last seventy years in fulfillment of the prophecy of Jeremiah (25.11; 29.10).

2 In the first year of Cyrus as king of the Persians, so that the word of the Lord by the mouth of Jeremiah might be accomplished— ²the Lord stirred up the spirit of King Cyrus of the Persians, and he made a proclamation throughout all his kingdom and also put it in writing:

3 "Thus says Cyrus king of the Persians: The Lord of Israel, the Lord Most High, has made me king of the world, ⁴and he has commanded me to build him a house at Jerusalem, which is in Judea. ⁵If any of you, therefore, are of his people, may your Lord be with you; go up to Jerusalem, which is in Judea, and build the house of the Lord of Israel— he is the Lord who dwells in Jerusalem— ⁶and let each of you, wherever you may live, be helped by the people of your place with gold and silver, ⁷with gifts and with horses and cattle, besides the other things added as votive offerings for the temple of the Lord that is in Jerusalem."

2.1–5a (2 Chr 36.22–23; Ezra 1.1–3a): **The proclamation of Cyrus.** The last two verses of 2 Chronicles and the first two verses and part of the third verse of Ezra say the same thing in almost identical words. This kind of repetition is called a doublet. Even though 1 Esdras is closely following the language in Chronicles and Ezra, the writer does not reproduce this doublet. This has led a number of scholars to propose that the books of Chronicles and at least part of the book of Ezra once comprised the Chronicler's history of Israel, from which the writer of 1 Esdras took his version. **2:** The author believes Cyrus was divinely inspired.

8 Then arose the heads of families of the tribes of Judah and Benjamin, and the priests and the Levites, and all whose spirit the Lord had stirred to go up to build the house in Jerusalem for the Lord; ⁹their neighbors helped them with everything, with silver and gold, with horses and cattle, and

with a very great number of votive offerings from many whose hearts were stirred.

10 King Cyrus also brought out the holy vessels of the Lord that Nebuchadnezzar had carried away from Jerusalem and stored in his temple of idols. ¹¹When King Cyrus of the Persians brought these out, he gave them to Mithridates, his treasurer, ¹²and by him they were given to Sheshbazzar,ᵃ the governor of Judea. ¹³The number of these was: one thousand gold cups, one thousand silver cups, twenty-nine silver censers, thirty gold bowls, two thousand four hundred ten silver bowls, and one thousand other vessels. ¹⁴All the vessels were handed over, gold and silver, five thousand four hundred sixty-nine, ¹⁵and they were carried back by Sheshbazzar with the returning exiles from Babylon to Jerusalem.

2.5b–15 (Ezra 1.3b–11): **The return led by Sheshbazzar. 12:** *Sheshbazzar,* though a Jew, has a Babylonian name, "May Shamash protect the father (of this child)." **15:** The return of the captured vessels to Jerusalem established continuity between the First and Second Temples,✴ just as the new Temple was set on the site of its predecessor (1 Esd 6.24; Ezra 6.3) and the altar was placed on its original foundations (1 Esd 5.50; Ezra 3.3).

16 In the time of King Artaxerxes of the Persians, Bishlam, Mithridates, Tabeel, Rehum, Beltethmus, the scribe Shimshai, and the rest of their associates, living in Samaria and other places, wrote him the following letter, against those who were living in Judea and Jerusalem:

17 "To King Artaxerxes our lord, your servants the recorder Rehum and the scribe Shimshai and the other members of their council, and the judges in Coelesyria and Phoenicia; ¹⁸Let it now be known to our lord the king that the Jews who came up from you to us have gone to Jerusalem and are building that rebellious and wicked city, repairing its market places and walls and laying the foundations for a temple. ¹⁹Now if this city is built and the walls finished, they will not only refuse to pay tribute but will even resist

ᵃ Gk *Sanabassaros*

kings. 20 Since the building of the temple is now going on, we think it best not to neglect such a matter, 21 but to speak to our lord the king, in order that, if it seems good to you, search may be made in the records of your ancestors. 22 You will find in the annals what has been written about them, and will learn that this city was rebellious, troubling both kings and other cities, 23 and that the Jews were rebels and kept setting up blockades in it from of old. That is why this city was laid waste. 24 Therefore we now make known to you, O lord and king, that if this city is built and its walls finished, you will no longer have access to Coelesyria and Phoenicia."

25 Then the king, in reply to the recorder Rehum, Beltethmus, the scribe Shimshai, and the others associated with them and living in Samaria and Syria and Phoenicia, wrote as follows:

26 "I have read the letter that you sent me. So I ordered search to be made, and it has been found that this city from of old has fought against kings, 27 that the people in it were given to rebellion and war, and that mighty and cruel kings ruled in Jerusalem and exacted tribute from Coelesyria and Phoenicia. 28 Therefore I have now issued orders to prevent these people from building the city and to take care that nothing more be done 29 and that such wicked proceedings go no further to the annoyance of kings."

30 Then, when the letter from King Artaxerxes was read, Rehum and the scribe Shimshai and their associates went quickly to Jerusalem, with cavalry and a large number of armed troops, and began to hinder the builders. And the building of the temple in Jerusalem stopped until the second year of the reign of King Darius of the Persians.

2.16–30 (Ezra 4.7–24): **Opposition to the Jews.** This passage consists of a letter to Artaxerxes in vv. 17–24, followed by the reply of the Persian king in vv. 26–29. These verses in their context in the book of Ezra justify the Jewish rejection of help from their neighbors (Ezra 4.3) since the subsequent behavior of the Samarians—fifty years later—proved that they had no positive interest in the restoration of Jerusalem. These hostile neighbors criticized the Jewish work on the city of Jerusalem and convinced Artaxerxes to put a stop to

it. 1 Esdras moved the passage to a different location so that Darius's stopping of the work on the Temple★ (v. 30) would precede the ringing endorsement of work on the Temple by Darius in 1 Esd 3.1–5.6. The text of Ezra 4.7–6.18 is written in Aramaic★ and is often referred to as the Aramaic Chronicle. **24:** *Coelesyria* (pronounced "seeli-Syria"). This term, which may be translated as "hollow Syria," includes the valley between the two mountain ranges running parallel to the Mediterranean coast west of Damascus. It is first attested in the fourth century BCE. It designated a large portion of the Eastern Mediterranean seaboard extending eastward toward the Euphrates in southern Syria (see Map 11 at back of book).

〜〜〜〜〜〜〜〜〜〜〜〜〜〜〜〜〜〜〜〜〜

3 Now King Darius gave a great banquet for all that were under him, all that were born in his house, and all the nobles of Media and Persia, 2 and all the satraps and generals and governors that were under him in the hundred twenty-seven satrapies from India to Ethiopia. 3 They ate and drank, and when they were satisfied they went away, and King Darius went to his bedroom; he went to sleep, but woke up again.

4 Then the three young men of the bodyguard, who kept guard over the person of the king, said to one another, 5 "Let each of us state what one thing is strongest; and to the one whose statement seems wisest, King Darius will give rich gifts and great honors of victory. 6 He shall be clothed in purple, and drink from gold cups, and sleep on a gold bed,*a* and have a chariot with gold bridles, and a turban of fine linen, and a necklace around his neck; 7 and because of his wisdom he shall sit next to Darius and shall be called Kinsman of Darius."

8 Then each wrote his own statement, and they sealed them and put them under the pillow of King Darius, 9 and said, "When the king wakes, they will give him the writing; and to the one whose statement the king and the three nobles of Persia judge to be wisest the victory shall be given according to what is written." 10 The first wrote, "Wine is strongest." 11 The second wrote, "The king is strongest." 12 The third wrote, "Women are

a Gk *on gold*

strongest, but above all things truth is victor."[a]

13 When the king awoke, they took the writing and gave it to him, and he read it. [14]Then he sent and summoned all the nobles of Persia and Media and the satraps and generals and governors and prefects, [15]and he took his seat in the council chamber, and the writing was read in their presence. [16]He said, "Call the young men, and they shall explain their statements." So they were summoned, and came in. [17]They said to them, "Explain to us what you have written."

3.1–17a: A contest among three young men. 2: The Persian Empire lasted from 550 to 330 BCE, when Alexander the Great conquered it. **3:** *He went to sleep, but woke up:* The king suffered from insomnia. **4–7:** The three youths decide to while away the hours with a contest about what is the strongest thing in the world, and they even decide which prizes Darius should offer to the winner! In his retelling of this story, Josephus has the king himself propose the contest and determine the rewards (*Antiquities of the Jews* 11.3.2, 35). **12:** The third young man proposes two answers: Women are the strongest, but even stronger is truth. This ambivalence suggests that the story may have developed and changed over the course of its history. **16–17:** The king's decision to let the men explain the reasons for their choices results in speeches defending their viewpoints.

Then the first, who had spoken of the strength of wine, began and said: [18]"Gentlemen, how is wine the strongest? It leads astray the minds of all who drink it. [19]It makes equal the mind of the king and the orphan, of the slave and the free, of the poor and the rich. [20]It turns every thought to feasting and mirth, and forgets all sorrow and debt. [21]It makes all hearts feel rich, forgets kings and satraps, and makes everyone talk in millions.[b] [22]When people drink they forget to be friendly with friends and kindred, and before long they draw their swords. [23]And when they recover from the wine, they do not remember what they have done. [24]Gentlemen, is not wine the strongest, since it forces people to do these things?" When he had said this, he stopped speaking.

3.17b–24: Wine is the strongest. 18–23: Alcohol affects thinking and emotions across social classes; it also makes people boast uncontrollably. Inebriated friends turn to violence, but forget everything when they sober up. **24:** Since wine makes people do irrational things, it must be the strongest thing in the world.

4 Then the second, who had spoken of the strength of the king, began to speak: [2]"Gentlemen, are not men strongest, who rule over land and sea and all that is in them? [3]But the king is stronger; he is their lord and master, and whatever he says to them they obey. [4]If he tells them to make war on one another, they do it; and if he sends them out against the enemy, they go, and conquer mountains, walls, and towers. [5]They kill and are killed, and do not disobey the king's command; if they win the victory, they bring everything to the king—whatever spoil they take and everything else. [6]Likewise those who do not serve in the army or make war but till the soil; whenever they sow and reap, they bring some to the king; and they compel one another to pay taxes to the king. [7]And yet he is only one man! If he tells them to kill, they kill; if he tells them to release, they release; [8]if he tells them to attack, they attack; if he tells them to lay waste, they lay waste; if he tells them to build, they build; [9]if he tells them to cut down, they cut down; if he tells them to plant, they plant. [10]All his people and his armies obey him. Furthermore, he reclines, he eats and drinks and sleeps, [11]but they keep watch around him, and no one may go away to attend to his own affairs, nor do they disobey him. [12]Gentlemen, why is not the king the strongest, since he is to be obeyed in this fashion?" And he stopped speaking.

4.1–12: The king is the strongest. 3: The king's superior strength emerges in his ability to order others around. **4–5:** People fight and lose their lives at the king's command and then turn over all the booty to him. **6:** Farmers pay taxes at the king's behest and use group pressure to bring compliance with the tax laws. **12:** The speech seems to flatter the king, but readers

a Or *but truth is victor over all things*   *b* Gk *talents* detect an implicit criticism of the king's autocratic power.

~~~~~~~~~~

13 Then the third, who had spoken of women and truth (and this was Zerubbabel), began to speak: 14"Gentlemen, is not the king great, and are not men many, and is not wine strong? Who is it, then, that rules them, or has the mastery over them? Is it not women? 15Women gave birth to the king and to every people that rules over sea and land. 16From women they came; and women brought up the very men who plant the vineyards from which comes wine. 17Women make men's clothes; they bring men glory; men cannot exist without women. 18If men gather gold and silver or any other beautiful thing, and then see a woman lovely in appearance and beauty, 19they let all those things go, and gape at her, and with open mouths stare at her, and all prefer her to gold or silver or any other beautiful thing. 20A man leaves his own father, who brought him up, and his own country, and clings to his wife. 21With his wife he ends his days, with no thought of his father or his mother or his country. 22Therefore you must realize that women rule over you!

"Do you not labor and toil, and bring everything and give it to women? 23A man takes his sword, and goes out to travel and rob and steal and to sail the sea and rivers; 24he faces lions, and he walks in darkness, and when he steals and robs and plunders, he brings it back to the woman he loves. 25A man loves his wife more than his father or his mother. 26Many men have lost their minds because of women, and have become slaves because of them. 27Many have perished, or stumbled, or sinned because of women. 28And now do you not believe me?

"Is not the king great in his power? Do not all lands fear to touch him? 29Yet I have seen him with Apame, the king's concubine, the daughter of the illustrious Bartacus; she would sit at the king's right hand 30and take the crown from the king's head and put it on her own, and slap the king with her left hand. 31At this the king would gaze at her with mouth agape. If she smiles at him, he laughs; if she loses her temper with him, he

flatters her, so that she may be reconciled to him. 32Gentlemen, why are not women strong, since they do such things?"

────────

4.13–32: Women are the strongest. 13: *Zerubbabel*, the only youth who is named, was also a renowned leader in the early post-exilic Jewish community (Ezra 3.2). 15–22: Women rule men because they give birth to them, raise them, and clothe them. Men fall in love with women and give them their money, or they leave their own country to be with their beloved and never look back. 23–26: Men engage in war or crime and turn their profits over to women. 27: The speaker seems to resent the power of women over individual men and blames them for men's sins. 28–32: Even the mighty king yields to his favorite concubine,* *Apame*, who toys with him and controls him. The king looks at her with open-mouthed amazement, just as commoners do with the women who control them (v. 19). This defense of women shows the folly of the second speaker's proposal about the strength of kings.

~~~~~~~~~~

33 Then the king and the nobles looked at one another; and he began to speak about truth: 34"Gentlemen, are not women strong? The earth is vast, and heaven is high, and the sun is swift in its course, for it makes the circuit of the heavens and returns to its place in one day. 35Is not the one who does these things great? But truth is great, and stronger than all things. 36The whole earth calls upon truth, and heaven blesses it. All God's works*a* quake and tremble, and with him there is nothing unrighteous. 37Wine is unrighteous, the king is unrighteous, women are unrighteous, all human beings are unrighteous, all their works are unrighteous, and all such things. There is no truth in them and in their unrighteousness they will perish. 38But truth endures and is strong forever, and lives and prevails forever and ever. 39With it there is no partiality or preference, but it does what is righteous instead of anything that is unrighteous or wicked. Everyone approves its deeds, 40and there is nothing unrighteous in its judgment. To it belongs the strength and the kingship and the power and the majesty of all the ages. Blessed be the God of truth!" 41When he

a Gk All the works

stopped speaking, all the people shouted and said, "Great is truth, and strongest of all!"

4.33–41: Truth is the strongest. 33: Just when Zerubbabel has apparently won the argument with his words about women, he makes a new proposal. **37:** Truth is the opposite of unrighteousness and mortality. **38:** Truth is everlasting. **39:** Truth might be defined as virtue, integrity, or steadfastness. Truth is an impartial judge. That is why Zerubbabel could tell the truth about the king in vv. 29–32. **40:** Truth has kingship, power, and majesty, which are ascribed to God in the doxological conclusion to the Lord's Prayer (see 1 Chr 29.11–13). **41:** Despite Zerubbabel's ambivalence, the crowd unanimously accepts his argument for the superiority of truth.

42 Then the king said to him, "Ask what you wish, even beyond what is written, and we will give it to you, for you have been found to be the wisest. You shall sit next to me, and be called my Kinsman." 43 Then he said to the king, "Remember the vow that you made on the day when you became king, to build Jerusalem, 44 and to send back all the vessels that were taken from Jerusalem, which Cyrus set apart when he began*a* to destroy Babylon, and vowed to send them back there. 45 You also vowed to build the temple, which the Edomites burned when Judea was laid waste by the Chaldeans. 46 And now, O lord the king, this is what I ask and request of you, and this befits your greatness. I pray therefore that you fulfill the vow whose fulfillment you vowed to the King of heaven with your own lips."

47 Then King Darius got up and kissed him, and wrote letters for him to all the treasurers and governors and generals and satraps, that they should give safe conduct to him and to all who were going up with him to build Jerusalem. 48 And he wrote letters to all the governors in Coelesyria and Phoenicia and to those in Lebanon, to bring cedar timber from Lebanon to Jerusalem, and to help him build the city. 49 He wrote in behalf of all the Jews who were going up from his kingdom to Judea, in the interest of their freedom, that no officer or satrap or governor or treasurer should forcibly enter their doors; 50 that all the country that they would occupy should be theirs without tribute; that the Idumeans should give up the villages of the Jews that they held; 51 that twenty talents a year should be given for the building of the temple until it was completed, 52 and an additional ten talents a year for burnt offerings to be offered on the altar every day, in accordance with the commandment to make seventeen offerings; 53 and that all who came from Babylonia to build the city should have their freedom, they and their children and all the priests who came. 54 He wrote also concerning their support and the priests' vestments in which*b* they were to minister. 55 He wrote that the support for the Levites should be provided until the day when the temple would be finished and Jerusalem built. 56 He wrote that land and wages should be provided for all who guarded the city. 57 And he sent back from Babylon all the vessels that Cyrus had set apart; everything that Cyrus had ordered to be done, he also commanded to be done and to be sent to Jerusalem.

4.42–57: Darius rewards Zerubbabel. 42: Zerubbabel not only wins the contest against his gentile* rivals, but he also ingratiates himself with the king. **43–46:** Zerubbabel uses the occasion of his victory to seek favors for the whole people, appealing to previous promises made by Cyrus and by Darius himself. **45:** Zerubbabel accuses the Edomites of burning the Temple* even though 1.55 (2 Chr 36.19) reports that the kings of the Chaldeans had done this. **47–57:** In his reply Darius combines excerpts from the decree of Cyrus (Ezra 1.2–4; 6.3–5), his own endorsement of that decree (Ezra 6.6–12), and Artaxerxes's commission of Nehemiah (Neh 2.5–8). Hence the focus shifts to rebuilding the city rather than just the Temple. Darius exempts the Jews from forcible entry of their property (4.49) and taxes (4.50) and expels the Idumeans (Edomites) from the land. **51–52:** Darius sets up annual grants for constructing the Temple and supporting the sacrificial system. He may have hoped that sacrifices would be made on his behalf (see 1 Esd 6.31; Ezra 6.10). There is no other biblical reference to *seventeen offerings*. **57:** The temple vessels provide symbolic continuity between the First and the Second Temples. Zerubbabel's predecessor Shesh-

a Cn: Gk *vowed*   *b* Gk *in what priestly vestments*

bazzar also brought back temple vessels to Jerusalem (1 Esd 2.14–15; Ezra 1.11; see 1 Esd 6.18–19; Ezra 5.14–15).

58 When the young man went out, he lifted up his face to heaven toward Jerusalem, and praised the King of heaven, saying, 59"From you comes the victory; from you comes wisdom, and yours is the glory. I am your servant. 60Blessed are you, who have given me wisdom; I give you thanks, O Lord of our ancestors."

61 So he took the letters, and went to Babylon and told this to all his kindred. 62And they praised the God of their ancestors, because he had given them release and permission 63to go up and build Jerusalem and the temple that is called by his name; and they feasted, with music and rejoicing, for seven days.

4.58–63: Prayer and praise. 48–50: The *young man* (Zerubbabel) praises God for giving him wisdom to win the contest. He identifies the *King of heaven* with the God of earlier generations. **61–63:** Zerubbabel's fellow exiles accept the news with joy and offer their own praises to God for seven days. Their response is more enthusiastic than one would expect from the canonical* account.

5 After this the heads of ancestral houses were chosen to go up, according to their tribes, with their wives and sons and daughters, and their male and female servants, and their livestock. 2And Darius sent with them a thousand cavalry to take them back to Jerusalem in safety, with the music of drums and flutes; 3all their kindred were making merry. And he made them go up with them.

4 These are the names of the men who went up, according to their ancestral houses in the tribes, over their groups: 5the priests, the descendants of Phinehas son of Aaron; Jeshua son of Jozadak son of Seraiah and Joakim son of Zerubbabel son of Shealtiel, of the house of David, of the lineage of Phares, of the tribe of Judah, 6who spoke wise words before King Darius of the Persians, in the second year of his reign, in the month of Nisan, the first month.

5.1–6: The leaders of the returning exiles. These verses form a transition to the materials drawn from Ezra in the next section. **5:** *Jeshua* was high priest in the early post-exilic period (see Ezra 3.2). We need to emend the genealogy* of Zerubbabel to read: Zerubbabel, the son of Shealtiel, son of Jehoiachin, of the house of David. The Book of Ezra does not put Zerubbabel in the line of David, perhaps because its author was willing to accept Persian rule and did not want to encourage political or military activities by loyalists of the royal house.

7 These are the Judeans who came up out of their sojourn in exile, whom King Nebuchadnezzar of Babylon had carried away to Babylon 8and who returned to Jerusalem and the rest of Judea, each to his own town. They came with Zerubbabel and Jeshua, Nehemiah, Seraiah, Resaiah, Eneneus, Mordecai, Beelsarus, Aspharasus, Reeliah, Rehum, and Baanah, their leaders.

9 The number of those of the nation and their leaders: the descendants of Parosh, two thousand one hundred seventy-two. The descendants of Shephatiah, four hundred seventy-two. 10The descendants of Arah, seven hundred fifty-six. 11The descendants of Pahath-moab, of the descendants of Jeshua and Joab, two thousand eight hundred twelve. 12The descendants of Elam, one thousand two hundred fifty-four. The descendants of Zattu, nine hundred forty-five. The descendants of Chorbe, seven hundred five. The descendants of Bani, six hundred forty-eight. 13The descendants of Bebai, six hundred twenty-three. The descendants of Azgad, one thousand three hundred twenty-two. 14The descendants of Adonikam, six hundred sixty-seven. The descendants of Bigvai, two thousand sixty-six. The descendants of Adin, four hundred fifty-four. 15The descendants of Ater, namely of Hezekiah, ninety-two. The descendants of Kilan and Azetas, sixty-seven. The descendants of Azaru, four hundred thirty-two. 16The descendants of Annias, one hundred one. The descendants of Arom. The descendants of Bezai, three hundred twenty-three. The descendants of Arsiphurith, one hundred twelve. 17The descendants of Baiterus, three

thousand five. The descendants of Bethlomon, one hundred twenty-three. [18]Those from Netophah, fifty-five. Those from Anathoth, one hundred fifty-eight. Those from Bethasmoth, forty-two. [19]Those from Kiriatharim, twenty-five. Those from Chephirah and Beeroth, seven hundred forty-three. [20]The Chadiasans and Ammidians, four hundred twenty-two. Those from Kirama and Geba, six hundred twenty-one. [21]Those from Macalon, one hundred twenty-two. Those from Betolio, fifty-two. The descendants of Niphish, one hundred fifty-six. [22]The descendants of the other Calamolalus and Ono, seven hundred twenty-five. The descendants of Jerechus, three hundred forty-five. [23]The descendants of Senaah, three thousand three hundred thirty.

24 The priests: the descendants of Jedaiah son of Jeshua, of the descendants of Anasib, nine hundred seventy-two. The descendants of Immer, one thousand and fifty-two. [25]The descendants of Pashhur, one thousand two hundred forty-seven. The descendants of Charme, one thousand seventeen.

26 The Levites: the descendants of Jeshua and Kadmiel and Bannas and Sudias, seventy-four. [27]The temple singers: the descendants of Asaph, one hundred twenty-eight. [28]The gatekeepers: the descendants of Shallum, the descendants of Ater, the descendants of Talmon, the descendants of Akkub, the descendants of Hatita, the descendants of Shobai, in all one hundred thirty-nine.

29 The temple servants: the descendants of Esau, the descendants of Hasupha, the descendants of Tabbaoth, the descendants of Keros, the descendants of Sua, the descendants of Padon, the descendants of Lebanah, the descendants of Hagabah, [30]the descendants of Akkub, the descendants of Uthai, the descendants of Ketab, the descendants of Hagab, the descendants of Subai, the descendants of Hana, the descendants of Cathua, the descendants of Geddur, [31]the descendants of Jairus, the descendants of Daisan, the descendants of Noeba, the descendants of Chezib, the descendants of Gazera, the descendants of Uzza, the de-

scendants of Phinoe, the descendants of Hasrah, the descendants of Basthai, the descendants of Asnah, the descendants of Maani, the descendants of Nephisim, the descendants of Acuph,[a] the descendants of Hakupha, the descendants of Asur, the descendants of Pharakim, the descendants of Bazluth, [32]the descendants of Mehida, the descendants of Cutha, the descendants of Charea, the descendants of Barkos, the descendants of Serar, the descendants of Temah, the descendants of Neziah, the descendants of Hatipha.

33 The descendants of Solomon's servants: the descendants of Assaphioth, the descendants of Peruda, the descendants of Jaalah, the descendants of Lozon, the descendants of Isdael, the descendants of Shephatiah, [34]the descendants of Agia, the descendants of Pochereth-hazzebaim, the descendants of Sarothie, the descendants of Masiah, the descendants of Gas, the descendants of Addus, the descendants of Subas, the descendants of Apherra, the descendants of Barodis, the descendants of Shaphat, the descendants of Allon.

35 All the temple servants and the descendants of Solomon's servants were three hundred seventy-two.

36 The following are those who came up from Tel-melah and Tel-harsha, under the leadership of Cherub, Addan, and Immer, [37]though they could not prove by their ancestral houses or lineage that they belonged to Israel: the descendants of Delaiah son of Tobiah, and the descendants of Nekoda, six hundred fifty-two.

38 Of the priests the following had assumed the priesthood but were not found registered: the descendants of Habaiah, the descendants of Hakkoz, and the descendants of Jaddus who had married Agia, one of the daughters of Barzillai, and was called by his name. [39]When a search was made in the register and the genealogy of these men was not found, they were excluded from serving as priests. [40]And Nehemiah and Attharias[b] told them not to share in the holy things un-

---

a Other ancient authorities read *Acub* or *Acum*
b Or *the governor*

til a high priest should appear wearing Urim and Thummim.*

41 All those of Israel, twelve or more years of age, besides male and female servants, were forty-two thousand three hundred sixty; 42 their male and female servants were seven thousand three hundred thirty-seven; there were two hundred forty-five musicians and singers. 43 There were four hundred thirty-five camels, and seven thousand thirty-six horses, two hundred forty-five mules, and five thousand five hundred twenty-five donkeys.

44 Some of the heads of families, when they came to the temple of God that is in Jerusalem, vowed that, to the best of their ability, they would erect the house on its site, 45 and that they would give to the sacred treasury for the work a thousand minas of gold, five thousand minas of silver, and one hundred priests' vestments.

46 The priests, the Levites, and some of the people* settled in Jerusalem and its vicinity; and the temple singers, the gatekeepers, and all Israel in their towns.

5.7–46 (Ezra 2.1–70; Neh 7.6–73a): **The list of those who returned from exile.** In its appearance in Ezra and Nehemiah, this list is a composite of a number of returns during the reigns of Cyrus and Cambyses, but in 1 Esdras it describes the return of Zerubbabel during the reign of Darius. While the list presupposes that the community in Palestine was composed almost entirely of Jews who had been in exile, this does not conform to historical fact. **9–23:** Laity. **24–25:** Priests. **26–35:** Levites and other Temple personnel. **26–35:** Those who could not document their ancestry. **40:** *Attharias* is a transliteration for a Persian word in the text meaning "governor." His identification with *Nehemiah* in 1 Esdras is mistaken.

---

47 When the seventh month came, and the Israelites were all in their own homes, they gathered with a single purpose in the square before the first gate toward the east. 48 Then Jeshua son of Jozadak, with his fellow priests, and Zerubbabel son of Shealtiel, with his kinsmen, took their places and prepared the altar of the God of Israel, 49 to offer burnt offerings upon it, in accordance with the directions in the book of Moses the man

of God. 50 And some joined them from the other peoples of the land. And they erected the altar in its place, for all the peoples of the land were hostile to them and were stronger than they; and they offered sacrifices at the proper times and burnt offerings to the Lord morning and evening. 51 They kept the festival of booths, as it is commanded in the law, and offered the proper sacrifices every day, 52 and thereafter the regular offerings and sacrifices on sabbaths and at new moons and at all the consecrated feasts. 53 And all who had made any vow to God began to offer sacrifices to God, from the new moon of the seventh month, though the temple of God was not yet built. 54 They gave money to the masons and the carpenters, and food and drink 55 and carts* to the Sidonians and the Tyrians, to bring cedar logs from Lebanon and convey them in rafts to the harbor of Joppa, according to the decree that they had in writing from King Cyrus of the Persians.

56 In the second year after their coming to the temple of God in Jerusalem, in the second month, Zerubbabel son of Shealtiel and Jeshua son of Jozadak made a beginning, together with their kindred and the levitical priests and all who had come back to Jerusalem from exile; 57 and they laid the foundation of the temple of God on the new moon of the second month in the second year after they came to Judea and Jerusalem. 58 They appointed the Levites who were twenty or more years of age to have charge of the work of the Lord. And Jeshua arose, and his sons and kindred and his brother Kadmiel and the sons of Jeshua Emadabun and the sons of Joda son of Iliadun, with their sons and kindred, all the Levites, pressing forward the work on the house of God with a single purpose.

So the builders built the temple of the Lord. 59 And the priests stood arrayed in their vestments, with musical instruments and trumpets, and the Levites, the sons of Asaph, with cymbals, 60 praising the Lord and blessing him, according to the directions of King

a Gk *Manifestation and Truth*   *b* Or *those who were of the people*   *c* Meaning of Gk uncertain

David of Israel; 61they sang hymns, giving thanks to the Lord, "For his goodness and his glory are forever upon all Israel." 62And all the people sounded trumpets and shouted with a great shout, praising the Lord for the erection of the house of the Lord. 63Some of the levitical priests and heads of ancestral houses, old men who had seen the former house, came to the building of this one with outcries and loud weeping, 64while many came with trumpets and a joyful noise, 65so that the people could not hear the trumpets because of the weeping of the people.

5.47–65 (Ezra 3.1–13): The altar and the foundation of the Temple.* 47: In Ezra the altar was set up in September, 538 BCE, but according to the new ordering of materials in 1 Esdras, the *seventh month* falls in the reign of Darius (522–486 BCE). This creates a tension with v. 57, where the foundation of the Temple is dated to the reign of Cyrus. The *square before the first gate,* not mentioned in Ezra, probably refers to the general area of the Temple. **51:** The *festival of booths* (Tabernacles) began on the 15th day of the month. **52:** The *sacrifices on sabbaths* are not mentioned in Ezra 3.5. This addition may reflect the heightened importance of the Sabbath at the time of 1 Esdras. **57:** The *foundation of the Temple* is dated to the reign of Cyrus here (see 1 Esd 5.73) and in Ezra 3.8 even though historically this happened during the reign of Darius, in 520 BCE. This new date implies the faithfulness of the exiles immediately after their return. The ceremony at the beginning of the repairs on the Temple recalls that of Solomon at the dedication of the Temple (1 Kings 8; 2 Chr 5–7) and of David when he brought the ark to Jerusalem (1 Chr 15–16). **63:** The First Temple had been destroyed in 586 BCE. **65:** The loud weeping of the people drowned out the sound of the trumpets, whereas in Ezra 3.13 the people could not distinguish between the shouts of joy and the shouts of weeping.

For the multitude sounded the trumpets loudly, so that the sound was heard far away; 66and when the enemies of the tribe of Judah and Benjamin heard it, they came to find out what the sound of the trumpets meant. 67They learned that those who had returned from exile were building the temple for the Lord God of Israel. 68So they approached Zerubbabel and Jeshua and the heads of the ancestral houses and said to them, "We will build with you. 69For we obey your Lord just as you do and we have been sacrificing to him ever since the days of King Esar-haddon[a] of the Assyrians, who brought us here." 70But Zerubbabel and Jeshua and the heads of the ancestral houses in Israel said to them, "You have nothing to do with us in building the house for the Lord our God, 71for we alone will build it for the Lord of Israel, as Cyrus, the king of the Persians, has commanded us." 72But the peoples of the land pressed hard[b] upon those in Judea, cut off their supplies, and hindered their building; 73and by plots and demagoguery and uprisings they prevented the completion of the building as long as King Cyrus lived. They were kept from building for two years, until the reign of Darius.

5.66–73 (Ezra 4.1–5): Interruption of the building of the Temple.* 66: The Jewish leaders did not accept the offers of help from the *enemies of the tribe of Judah and Benjamin,* who claimed to have been residents of Palestine since the time of *Esarhaddon* (680–669 BCE). **73:** According to Ezra 4.24, the building of the Temple ceased until the second year of Darius, about seventeen years (not *two years*) after it had been interrupted.

---

6 Now in the second year of the reign of Darius, the prophets Haggai and Zechariah son of Iddo prophesied to the Jews who were in Judea and Jerusalem; they prophesied to them in the name of the Lord God of Israel. 2Then Zerubbabel son of Shealtiel and Jeshua son of Jozadak began to build the house of the Lord that is in Jerusalem, with the help of the prophets of the Lord who were with them.

3At the same time Sisinnes the governor of Syria and Phoenicia and Sathrabuzanes and their associates came to them and said, 4"By whose order are you building this house and this roof and finishing all the other things? And who are the builders that are finishing these things?" 5Yet the elders of the Jews were dealt with kindly, for the providence of the Lord was over the captives;

a Gk *Asbasareth*   *b* Meaning of Gk uncertain

6they were not prevented from building until word could be sent to Darius concerning them and a report made.

7 A copy of the letter that Sisinnes the governor of Syria and Phoenicia, and Sathrabuzanes, and their associates the local rulers in Syria and Phoenicia, wrote and sent to Darius:

8 "To King Darius, greetings. Let it be fully known to our lord the king that, when we went to the country of Judea and entered the city of Jerusalem, we found the elders of the Jews, who had been in exile, 9building in the city of Jerusalem a great new house for the Lord, of hewn stone, with costly timber laid in the walls. 10These operations are going on rapidly, and the work is prospering in their hands and being completed with all splendor and care. 11Then we asked these elders, 'At whose command are you building this house and laying the foundations of this structure?' 12In order that we might inform you in writing who the leaders are, we questioned them and asked them for a list of the names of those who are at their head. 13They answered us, 'We are the servants of the Lord who created the heaven and the earth. 14The house was built many years ago by a king of Israel who was great and strong, and it was finished. 15But when our ancestors sinned against the Lord of Israel who is in heaven, and provoked him, he gave them over into the hands of King Nebuchadnezzar of Babylon, king of the Chaldeans; 16and they pulled down the house, and burned it, and carried the people away captive to Babylon. 17But in the first year that Cyrus reigned over the country of Babylonia, King Cyrus wrote that this house should be rebuilt. 18And the holy vessels of gold and of silver, which Nebuchadnezzar had taken out of the house in Jerusalem and stored in his own temple, these King Cyrus took out again from the temple in Babylon, and they were delivered to Zerubbabel and Sheshbazzar[a] the governor 19with the command that he should take all these vessels back and put them in the temple at Jerusalem, and that this temple of the Lord should be rebuilt on its site. 20Then this Sheshbazzar, after coming here, laid the foundations of the house

of the Lord that is in Jerusalem. Although it has been in process of construction from that time until now, it has not yet reached completion.' 21Now therefore, O king, if it seems wise to do so, let search be made in the royal archives of our lord[b] the king that are in Babylon; 22if it is found that the building of the house of the Lord in Jerusalem was done with the consent of King Cyrus, and if it is approved by our lord the king, let him send us directions concerning these things."

6.1–7.15 (Ezra 5.1–6.22 [5.1–6.18 are in Aramaic*]): **Completion of the Temple.* 1:** The phrase *second year of the reign of Darius* has been added to Ezra 5.1. **3:** *Sisinnes* and *Sathrabuzanes* are transliterations for Tattenai and Shetharbozenai in Ezra 5.3. Instead of *Syria and Phoenicia,* Ezra 5.3 reads "the province beyond the river." **8–22:** The letter from Sisinees and Sathrabuzanes to Darius asks him whether Cyrus and King Darius himself had approved the rebuilding of the Temple, and it quotes the Jews in their own defense in vv. 13–20. **14:** This *king of Israel* is Solomon. **15:** The elders willingly admit their responsibility for the destruction of the Temple. **17–19:** Cyrus authorized the rebuilding of the Temple and restored to Zerubbabel and Sheshbazzar the vessels that had been taken captive by Nebuchadnezzar (Ezra 5.14 mentions only Sheshbazzar). **22:** The king is asked whether Cyrus had originally authorized the rebuilding and whether Darius, the present Persian king, is willing to confirm that authorization.

23 Then Darius commanded that search be made in the royal archives that were deposited in Babylon. And in Ecbatana, the fortress that is in the country of Media, a scroll[c] was found in which this was recorded: 24"In the first year of the reign of King Cyrus, he ordered the building of the house of the Lord in Jerusalem, where they sacrifice with perpetual fire; 25its height to be sixty cubits and its width sixty cubits, with three courses of hewn stone and one course of new native timber; the cost to be paid from the treasury of King Cyrus; 26and that the holy vessels of the house of the Lord, both of gold and of silver, which Nebuchad-

a Gk *Sanabassarus*   b Other ancient authorities read *of Cyrus*   c Other authorities read *passage* nezzar took out of the house in Jerusalem and carried away to Babylon, should be restored to the house in Jerusalem, to be placed where they had been."

27 So Darius^a commanded Sisinnes the governor of Syria and Phoenicia, and Sathrabuzanes, and their associates, and those who were appointed as local rulers in Syria and Phoenicia, to keep away from the place, and to permit Zerubbabel, the servant of the Lord and governor of Judea, and the elders of the Jews to build this house of the Lord on its site. 28"And I command that it be built completely, and that full effort be made to help those who have returned from the exile of Judea, until the house of the Lord is finished; 29and that out of the tribute of Coelesyria and Phoenicia a portion be scrupulously given to these men, that is, to Zerubbabel the governor, for sacrifices to the Lord, for bulls and rams and lambs, 30and likewise wheat and salt and wine and oil, regularly every year, without quibbling, for daily use as the priests in Jerusalem may indicate, 31in order that libations may be made to the Most High God for the king and his children, and prayers be offered for their lives."

32 He commanded that if anyone should transgress or nullify any of the things herein written,^{b} a beam should be taken out of the house of the perpetrator, who then should be impaled upon it, and all property forfeited to the king.

33 "Therefore may the Lord, whose name is there called upon, destroy every king and nation that shall stretch out their hands to hinder or damage that house of the Lord in Jerusalem.

34 "I, King Darius, have decreed that it be done with all diligence as here prescribed."

6.23–34. 23: *Ecbatana* was the former Median capital that had been conquered by Cyrus in 550 BCE. It served as the summer residence for the Persian kings. **24–26:** A document in the Persian archives attests Cyrus's rebuilding decree and his order to return the temple vessels to Jerusalem. **27:** In Ezra 6.7 the governor of Judea is unnamed, and he is not given the title "servant of the Lord." The additions in 1 Esdras conform to its usual greater emphasis on Zerubbabel. **28:** Darius

gives his own endorsement to the rebuilding efforts. **29–31:** The king authorizes financial and material support for the sacrifices of the Temple in Jerusalem though his generosity is not without self-interest: The Jews are to pray for the king and his family. **32:** The king makes violation of his orders a capital crime.

7 Then Sisinnes the governor of Coelesyria and Phoenicia, and Sathrabuzanes, and their associates, following the orders of King Darius, 2supervised the holy work with very great care, assisting the elders of the Jews and the chief officers of the temple. 3The holy work prospered, while the prophets Haggai and Zechariah prophesied; 4and they completed it by the command of the Lord God of Israel. So with the consent of Cyrus and Darius and Artaxerxes, kings of the Persians, 5the holy house was finished by the twenty-third day of the month of Adar, in the sixth year of King Darius. 6And the people of Israel, the priests, the Levites, and the rest of those who returned from exile who joined them, did according to what was written in the book of Moses. 7They offered at the dedication of the temple of the Lord one hundred bulls, two hundred rams, four hundred lambs, 8and twelve male goats for the sin of all Israel, according to the number of the twelve leaders of the tribes of Israel; 9and the priests and the Levites stood arrayed in their vestments, according to kindred, for the services of the Lord God of Israel in accordance with the book of Moses; and the gatekeepers were at each gate.

10 The people of Israel who came from exile kept the passover on the fourteenth day of the first month, after the priests and the Levites were purified together. 11Not all of the returned captives were purified, but the Levites were all purified together,^{c} 12and they sacrificed the passover lamb for all the returned captives and for their kindred the priests and for themselves. 13The people of Israel who had returned from exile ate it, all those who had separated themselves from the abominations of the peoples of the land and sought the Lord. 14They also kept the

---

a Gk *he* b Other authorities read *stated above* or *added in writing* c Meaning of Gk uncertain festival of unleavened bread seven days, rejoicing before the Lord, [15]because he had changed the will of the king of the Assyrians concerning them, to strengthen their hands for the service of the Lord God of Israel.

7.1–15. 1–4: The Persian officials cooperated with the Jews, and the work on the Temple was finished successfully. Three factors played a role: the encouragement of the prophets; the command of God; and the consent of Cyrus, Darius, and Artaxerxes I (464–424 BCE). Artaxerxes ruled long after the completion of the Temple. Perhaps his provisions for the Temple at the time of Ezra led to the addition of his name here. **5:** Ezra 6.15 dates the completion of the Temple to the 3rd of Adar. 1 Esdras may have changed the date since the 3rd of Adar in 515 BCE fell on a sabbath. **9:** Ezra 6.18 lacks *the gatekeepers were at each gate*. **10:** At the rededication of the Temple in the time of Hezekiah and Josiah, Passover* was also observed (2 Chr 30.13–27; 35.1–19).

8 After these things, when Artaxerxes, the king of the Persians, was reigning, Ezra came, the son of Seraiah, son of Azariah, son of Hilkiah, son of Shallum, [2]son of Zadok, son of Ahitub, son of Amariah, son of Uzzi, son of Bukki, son of Abishua, son of Phineas, son of Eleazar, son of Aaron the high[a] priest. [3]This Ezra came up from Babylon as a scribe skilled in the law of Moses, which was given by the God of Israel; [4]and the king showed him honor, for he found favor before the king[b] in all his requests. [5]There came up with him to Jerusalem some of the people of Israel and some of the priests and Levites and temple singers and gatekeepers and temple servants, [6]in the seventh year of the reign of Artaxerxes, in the fifth month (this was the king's seventh year); for they left Babylon on the new moon of the first month and arrived in Jerusalem on the new moon of the fifth month, by the prosperous journey that the Lord gave them.[c] [7]For Ezra possessed great knowledge, so that he omitted nothing from the law of the Lord or the commandments, but taught all Israel all the ordinances and judgments.

8.1–7 (Ezra 7.1–10): **Ezra comes to Jerusalem.** In the seventh year of Artaxerxes (458 BCE), Ezra was sent to investigate the situation in Jerusalem on the basis of the law. **1–2:** Ezra's priestly genealogy.*

8 The following is a copy of the written commission from King Artaxerxes that was delivered to Ezra the priest and reader of the law of the Lord:

9 "King Artaxerxes to Ezra the priest and reader of the law of the Lord, greeting. [10]In accordance with my gracious decision, I have given orders that those of the Jewish nation and of the priests and Levites and others in our realm, those who freely choose to do so, may go with you to Jerusalem. [11]Let as many as are so disposed, therefore, leave with you, just as I and the seven Friends who are my counselors have decided, [12]in order to look into matters in Judea and Jerusalem, in accordance with what is in the law of the Lord, [13]and to carry to Jerusalem the gifts for the Lord of Israel that I and my Friends have vowed, and to collect for the Lord in Jerusalem all the gold and silver that may be found in the country of Babylonia, [14]together with what is given by the nation for the temple of their Lord that is in Jerusalem, both gold and silver for bulls and rams and lambs and what goes with them, [15]so as to offer sacrifices on the altar of their Lord that is in Jerusalem. [16]Whatever you and your kindred are minded to do with the gold and silver, perform it in accordance with the will of your God; [17]deliver the holy vessels of the Lord that are given you for the use of the temple of your God that is in Jerusalem. [18]And whatever else occurs to you as necessary for the temple of your God, you may provide out of the royal treasury.

19 "I, King Artaxerxes, have commanded the treasurers of Syria and Phoenicia that whatever Ezra the priest and reader of the law of the Most High God sends for, they shall take care to give him, [20]up to a hundred talents of silver, and likewise up to a hundred cors of wheat, a hundred baths of wine, and salt in abundance. [21]Let all things prescribed in the law of God be scrupulously fulfilled for the Most High God, so that

---

a Gk *the first*   *b* Gk *him*   *c* Other authorities add *for him* or *upon him* wrath may not come upon the kingdom of the king and his sons. 22You are also informed that no tribute or any other tax is to be laid on any of the priests or Levites or temple singers or gatekeepers or temple servants or persons employed in this temple, and that no one has authority to impose any tax on them.

23 "And you, Ezra, according to the wisdom of God, appoint judges and justices to judge all those who know the law of your God, throughout all Syria and Phoenicia; and you shall teach it to those who do not know it. 24All who transgress the law of your God or the law of the kingdom shall be strictly punished, whether by death or some other punishment, either fine or imprisonment."

8.8–24 (Ezra 7.11–26. [vv. 12–26 are written in Aramaic*]): **The king's letter of authorization.** Ezra is to bring Jews to Jerusalem, deliver gifts to the Temple,* inquire about the status of the law, appoint judges to administer the law, and teach the law to those who do not know it.

---

25 Then Ezra the scribe said,ᵃ "Blessed be the Lord alone, who put this into the heart of the king, to glorify his house that is in Jerusalem, 26and who honored me in the sight of the king and his counselors and all his Friends and nobles. 27I was encouraged by the help of the Lord my God, and I gathered men from Israel to go up with me."

28 These are the leaders, according to their ancestral houses and their groups, who went up with me from Babylon, in the reign of King Artaxerxes: 29Of the descendants of Phineas, Gershom. Of the descendants of Ithamar, Gamael. Of the descendants of David, Hattush son of Shecaniah. 30Of the descendants of Parosh, Zechariah, and with him a hundred fifty men enrolled. 31Of the descendants of Pahath-moab, Eliehoenai son of Zerahiah, and with him two hundred men. 32Of the descendants of Zattu, Shecaniah son of Jahaziel, and with him three hundred men. Of the descendants of Adin, Obed son of Jonathan, and with him two hundred fifty men. 33Of the descendants of Elam, Jeshaiah son of Gotholiah, and with him sev-

enty men. 34Of the descendants of Shephatiah, Zeraiah son of Michael, and with him seventy men. 35Of the descendants of Joab, Obadiah son of Jehiel, and with him two hundred twelve men. 36Of the descendants of Bani, Shelomith son of Josiphiah, and with him a hundred sixty men. 37Of the descendants of Bebai, Zechariah son of Bebai, and with him twenty-eight men. 38Of the descendants of Azgad, Johanan son of Hakkatan, and with him a hundred ten men. 39Of the descendants of Adonikam, the last ones, their names being Eliphelet, Jeuel, and Shemaiah, and with them seventy men. 40Of the descendants of Bigvai, Uthai son of Istalcurus, and with him seventy men.

41 I assembled them at the river called Theras, and we encamped there three days, and I inspected them. 42When I found there none of the descendants of the priests or of the Levites, 43I sent word to Eliezar, Iduel, Maasmas, 44Elnathan, Shemaiah, Jarib, Nathan, Elnathan, Zechariah, and Meshullam, who were leaders and men of understanding; 45I told them to go to Iddo, who was the leading man at the place of the treasury, 46and ordered them to tell Iddo and his kindred and the treasurers at that place to send us men to serve as priests in the house of our Lord. 47And by the mighty hand of our Lord they brought us competent men of the descendants of Mahli son of Levi, son of Israel, namely Sherebiahᵇ with his descendants and kinsmen, eighteen; 48also Hashabiah and Annunus and his brother Jeshaiah, of the descendants of Hananiah, and their descendants, twenty men; 49and of the temple servants, whom David and the leaders had given for the service of the Levites, two hundred twenty temple servants; the list of all their names was reported.

50 There I proclaimed a fast for the young men before our Lord, to seek from him a prosperous journey for ourselves and for our children and the livestock that were with us. 51For I was ashamed to ask the king for foot soldiers and cavalry and an escort to

---

ᵃ Other ancient authorities lack Then Ezra the scribe said   ᵇ Gk Asbebias keep us safe from our adversaries; 52for we had said to the king, "The power of our Lord will be with those who seek him, and will support them in every way." 53And again we prayed to our Lord about these things, and we found him very merciful.

54 Then I set apart twelve of the leaders of the priests, Sherebiah and Hashabiah, and ten of their kinsmen with them; 55and I weighed out to them the silver and the gold and the holy vessels of the house of our Lord, which the king himself and his counselors and the nobles and all Israel had given. 56I weighed and gave to them six hundred fifty talents of silver, and silver vessels worth a hundred talents, and a hundred talents of gold, 57and twenty golden bowls, and twelve bronze vessels of fine bronze that glittered like gold. 58And I said to them, "You are holy to the Lord, and the vessels are holy, and the silver and the gold are vowed to the Lord, the Lord of our ancestors. 59Be watchful and on guard until you deliver them to the leaders of the priests and the Levites, and to the heads of the ancestral houses of Israel, in Jerusalem, in the chambers of the house of our Lord." 60So the priests and the Levites who took the silver and the gold and the vessels that had been in Jerusalem carried them to the temple of the Lord.

61 We left the river Theras on the twelfth day of the first month; and we arrived in Jerusalem by the mighty hand of our Lord, which was upon us; he delivered us from every enemy on the way, and so we came to Jerusalem. 62When we had been there three days, the silver and the gold were weighed and delivered in the house of our Lord to the priest Meremoth son of Uriah; 63with him was Eleazar son of Phinehas, and with them were Jozabad son of Jeshua and Moeth son of Binnui,ᵃ the Levites. 64The whole was counted and weighed, and the weight of everything was recorded at that very time. 65And those who had returned from exile offered sacrifices to the Lord, the God of Israel, twelve bulls for all Israel, ninety-six rams, 66seventy-two lambs, and as a thank offering twelve male goats—all as a sacrifice to the Lord. 67They delivered the king's orders to the royal stewards and to the gover-

nors of Coelesyria and Phoenicia; and these officialsᵇ honored the people and the temple of the Lord.

8.25–90 (Ezra 7.27–9.15): **A narrative* about Ezra cast in the first person. 28–40** (Ezra 8.1–14): A list of those who were ready to return with Ezra. **42:** No priests or Levites were among those returning; Ezra 8.15 mentions only the absence of Levites. **47–48:** Thirty-eight Levites joined Ezra's group. **49:** Two hundred twenty Temple servants were also added. **54–60:** The inflated total of gifts demonstrates the glory of the Temple. **55:** The king and the people gave generously, just as at the dedication of Solomon's Temple (1 Chr 26.26). **65–66:** The numbers of the sacrifices are all multiples of twelve. They symbolize that the restoration community was all Israel, all twelve tribes.

68 After these things had been done, the leaders came to me and said, 69"The people of Israel and the rulers and the priests and the Levites have not put away from themselves the alien peoples of the land and their pollutions, the Canaanites, the Hittites, the Perizzites, the Jebusites, the Moabites, the Egyptians, and the Edomites. 70For they and their descendants have married the daughters of these people,ᶜ and the holy race has been mixed with the alien peoples of the land; and from the beginning of this matter the leaders and the nobles have been sharing in this iniquity."

71 As soon as I heard these things I tore my garments and my holy mantle, and pulled out hair from my head and beard, and sat down in anxiety and grief. 72And all who were ever moved atᵈ the word of the Lord of Israel gathered around me, as I mourned over this iniquity, and I sat grief-stricken until the evening sacrifice. 73Then I rose from my fast, with my garments and my holy mantle torn, and kneeling down and stretching out my hands to the Lord 74I said,

"O Lord, I am ashamed and confused before your face. 75For our sins have risen higher than our heads, and our mistakes have mounted up to heaven 76from the times

ᵃ Gk *Sabannus*   ᵇ Gk *they*   ᶜ Gk *their daughters*
ᵈ Or *zealous for*

of our ancestors, and we are in great sin to this day. 77Because of our sins and the sins of our ancestors, we with our kindred and our kings and our priests were given over to the kings of the earth, to the sword and exile and plundering, in shame until this day. 78And now in some measure mercy has come to us from you, O Lord, to leave to us a root and a name in your holy place, 79and to uncover a light for us in the house of the Lord our God, and to give us food in the time of our servitude. 80Even in our bondage we were not forsaken by our Lord, but he brought us into favor with the kings of the Persians, so that they have given us food 81and glorified the temple of our Lord, and raised Zion from desolation, to give us a stronghold in Judea and Jerusalem.

82 "And now, O Lord, what shall we say, when we have these things? For we have transgressed your commandments, which you gave by your servants the prophets, saying, 83'The land that you are entering to take possession of is a land polluted with the pollution of the aliens of the land, and they have filled it with their uncleanness. 84Therefore do not give your daughters in marriage to their descendants, and do not take their daughters for your descendants; 85do not seek ever to have peace with them, so that you may be strong and eat the good things of the land and leave it for an inheritance to your children forever.' 86And all that has happened to us has come about because of our evil deeds and our great sins. For you, O Lord, lifted the burden of our sins 87and gave us such a root as this; but we turned back again to transgress your law by mixing with the uncleanness of the peoples of the land. 88Were you not angry enough with us to destroy us without leaving a root or seed or name? 89O Lord of Israel, you are faithful; for we are left as a root to this day. 90See, we are now before you in our iniquities; for we can no longer stand in your presence because of these things."

91 While Ezra was praying and making his confession, weeping and lying on the ground before the temple, there gathered around him a very great crowd of men and women and youths from Jerusalem; for there was great weeping among the multitude. 92Then Shecaniah son of Jehiel, one of the men of Israel, called out, and said to Ezra, "We have sinned against the Lord, and have married foreign women from the peoples of the land; but even now there is hope for Israel. 93Let us take an oath to the Lord about this, that we will put away all our foreign wives, with their children, 94as seems good to you and to all who obey the law of the Lord. 95Rise up*a* and take action, for it is your task, and we are with you to take strong measures." 96Then Ezra rose up and made the leaders of the priests and Levites of all Israel swear that they would do this. And they swore to it.

8.68–9.36 (Ezra 9.1–10.44): **A dispute about mixed marriages. 70:** It is possible that the *alien peoples of the land* were Jews who had remained in Palestine during the Exile.* In any case, the leaders and nobles of the community were the chief culprits. **74–90: Ezra's prayer.** Ezra recounts the present and former sins of the community, telling how God has shown mercy to the community by restoring it and by giving the Jews favor with the Persian kings, who had glorified the Temple. The sin of intermarriage violates a number of Pentateuchal* and prophetic texts to which Ezra alludes, and this sin puts the whole community in jeopardy. **92:** *Shecaniah,* a lay person and apparently not guilty of intermarriage himself, led the people in a confession of their sins and called on Ezra to take action. **96:** Ezra put all the leaders under an oath.

9 Then Ezra set out and went from the court of the temple to the chamber of Jehohanan son of Eliashib, 2and spent the night there; and he did not eat bread or drink water, for he was mourning over the great iniquities of the multitude. 3And a proclamation was made throughout Judea and Jerusalem to all who had returned from exile that they should assemble at Jerusalem, 4and that if any did not meet there within two or three days, in accordance with the decision of the ruling elders, their livestock would be seized for sacrifice and the men

a Other ancient authorities read *as seems good to you."* *And all who obeyed the law of the Lord rose and said to Ezra,* 95"*Rise up* themselves[a] expelled from the multitude of those who had returned from the captivity.

5 Then the men of the tribe of Judah and Benjamin assembled at Jerusalem within three days; this was the ninth month, on the twentieth day of the month. 6All the multitude sat in the open square before the temple, shivering because of the bad weather that prevailed. 7Then Ezra stood up and said to them, "You have broken the law and married foreign women, and so have increased the sin of Israel. 8Now then make confession and give glory to the Lord the God of our ancestors, 9and do his will; separate yourselves from the peoples of the land and from your foreign wives."

10 Then all the multitude shouted and said with a loud voice, "We will do as you have said. 11But the multitude is great and it is winter, and we are not able to stand in the open air. This is not a work we can do in one day or two, for we have sinned too much in these things. 12So let the leaders of the multitude stay, and let all those in our settlements who have foreign wives come at the time appointed, 13with the elders and judges of each place, until we are freed from the wrath of the Lord over this matter."

14 Jonathan son of Asahel and Jahzeiah son of Tikvah[b] undertook the matter on these terms, and Meshullam and Levi and Shabbethai served with them as judges. 15And those who had returned from exile acted in accordance with all this.

16 Ezra the priest chose for himself the leading men of their ancestral houses, all of them by name; and on the new moon of the tenth month they began their sessions to investigate the matter. 17And the cases of the men who had foreign wives were brought to an end by the new moon of the first month.

9.1–17: The divorce of the foreign wives. 11: Because of the inclement weather and the large number of offenders, the people delegate the solution to a special investigative commission. **17:** The *new moon* of the first month* marked the end of the procedure, and the community was purified within about a year of Ezra's arrival (8.61).

18 Of the priests, those who were brought in and found to have foreign wives were: 19of the descendants of Jeshua son of Jozadak and his kindred, Maaseiah, Eliezar, Jarib, and Jodan. 20They pledged themselves to put away their wives, and to offer rams in expiation of their error. 21Of the descendants of Immer: Hanani and Zebadiah and Maaseiah and Shemaiah and Jehiel and Azariah. 22Of the descendants of Pashhur: Elioenai, Maaseiah, Ishmael, and Nathanael, and Gedaliah, and Salthas.

23 And of the Levites: Jozabad and Shimei and Kelaiah, who was Kelita, and Pethahiah and Judah and Jonah. 24Of the temple singers: Eliashib and Zaccur.[c] 25Of the gatekeepers: Shallum and Telem.[d]

26 Of Israel: of the descendants of Parosh: Ramiah, Izziah, Malchijah, Mijamin, and Eleazar, and Asibias, and Benaiah. 27Of the descendants of Elam: Mattaniah and Zechariah, Jezrielus and Abdi, and Jeremoth and Elijah. 28Of the descendants of Zamoth: Eliadas, Eliashib, Othoniah, Jeremoth, and Zabad and Zerdaiah. 29Of the descendants of Bebai: Jehohanan and Hananiah and Zabbai and Emathis. 30Of the descendants of Mani: Olamus, Mamuchus, Adaiah, Jashub, and Sheal and Jeremoth. 31Of the descendants of Addi: Naathus and Moossias, Laccunus and Naidus, and Bescaspasmys and Sesthel, and Belnuus and Manasseas. 32Of the descendants of Annan, Elionas and Asaias and Melchias and Sabbaias and Simon Chosamaeus. 33Of the descendants of Hashum: Mattenai and Mattattah and Zabad and Eliphelet and Manasseh and Shimei. 34Of the descendants of Bani: Jeremai, Momdius, Maerus, Joel, Mamdai and Bedeiah and Vaniah, Carabasion and Eliashib and Mamitanemus, Eliasis, Binnui, Elialis, Shimei, Shelemiah, Nethaniah. Of the descendants of Ezora: Shashai, Azarel, Azael, Samatus, Zambris, Joseph. 35Of the descendants of Nooma: Mazitias, Zabad, Iddo, Joel, Benaiah. 36All these had married foreign women, and they put them away together with their children.

a Gk *he himself*　　*b* Gk *Thocanos*　　*c* Gk *Bacchurus*
d Gk *Tolbanes*

9.18–36: A list of the priests, Levites, and laity who had intermarried. While the problem was serious, it involved a very small portion of the total population.

37 The priests and the Levites and the Israelites settled in Jerusalem and in the country. On the new moon of the seventh month, when the people of Israel were in their settlements, 38the whole multitude gathered with one accord in the open square before the east gate of the temple; 39they told Ezra the chief priest and reader to bring the law of Moses that had been given by the Lord God of Israel. 40So Ezra the chief priest brought the law, for all the multitude, men and women, and all the priests to hear the law, on the new moon of the seventh month. 41He read aloud in the open square before the gate of the temple from early morning until midday, in the presence of both men and women; and all the multitude gave attention to the law. 42Ezra the priest and reader of the law stood on the wooden platform that had been prepared; 43and beside him stood Mattathiah, Shema, Ananias, Azariah, Uriah, Hezekiah, and Baalsamus on his right, 44and on his left Pedaiah, Mishael, Malchijah, Lothasubus, Nabariah, and Zechariah. 45Then Ezra took up the book of the law in the sight of the multitude, for he had the place of honor in the presence of all. 46When he opened the law, they all stood erect. And Ezra blessed the Lord God Most High, the God of hosts, the Almighty, 47and the multitude answered, "Amen." They lifted up their hands, and fell to the ground and worshiped the Lord. 48Jeshua and Anniuth and Sherebiah, Jadinus, Akkub, Shabbethai, Hodiah, Maiannas and Kelita, Azariah and Jozabad, Hanan, Pelaiah, the Levites, taught the law of the Lord,*a* at the same time explaining what was read.

49 Then Attharates*b* said to Ezra the chief priest and reader, and to the Levites who were teaching the multitude, and to all, 50"This day is holy to the Lord"—now they were all weeping as they heard the law— 51"so go your way, eat the fat and drink the sweet, and send portions to those who have none; 52for the day is holy to the Lord; and do not be sorrowful, for the Lord will exalt you." 53The Levites commanded all the people, saying, "This day is holy; do not be sorrowful." 54Then they all went their way, to eat and drink and enjoy themselves, and to give portions to those who had none, and to make great rejoicing; 55because they were inspired by the words which they had been taught. And they came together.*c*

9.37–55 (Neh 7.73–8.13a): **Ezra reads the law.** The author of 1 Esdras probably knew the present arrangement of the books of Ezra and Nehemiah, though some scholars believe that his placement of Neh 8 right after Ezra 10 represents the original location for this chapter. **41:** The book from which Ezra read for some five or six hours was very likely a more or less final form of the Pentateuch.* **47:** By their *Amen* the people assented to the law. **49:** *Attharates* is a transliteration for the Persian word for governor. We should probably emend the text to have Ezra address the Levites, who were teaching the multitudes. **55:** The verse breaks off in mid-sentence, providing evidence for those who think 1 Esdras is a fragment, which originally ended with the equivalent of Neh 8.13–18 (see Josephus, *Antiquities of the Jews* 11.5.5, 157). The Feast of Booths celebrated on that day (Neh 8.17) was unparalleled since the days of Joshua (2 Chr 30.26; 35.18).

a Other ancient authorities add *and read the law of the Lord to the multitude*   b Or *the governor*   c The Greek text ends abruptly: compare Neh 8.13

THE PRAYER OF MANASSEH

Introduction

After a hymnic address that culminates with a celebration of God's *mercy* (v. 6; see *merciful* and *mercies* in vv. 6–7, as well as several synonyms), the prayer continues with a confession of *sin* and a plea for God to *forgive* (vv. 8–13d). It concludes with a celebration of God's *mercy* and a promise to *praise* God *continually* (vv. 8–15). It is similar in content and movement to Psalm 51, a prayer of confession attributed to King David.

The prayer is attributed to Manasseh, King of Judah from 687–642 BCE. Considered in some circles the worst of Judah's kings (2 Kings 21.9–18), Manasseh appears in a quite different light in 2 Chr 33.10–13. When exiled to Babylon by the Assyrians, he "humbled himself greatly" and "prayed" (2 Chr 33.12–13). Second Chronicles does not include the prayer. The Prayer of Manasseh purports to be this missing prayer, although it was probably written in Greek during the first century CE, 700 years after the time of Manasseh.

Since, according to 2 Kings 21.12, Manasseh was directly responsible for the destruction of Jerusalem that occurred in 587 BCE, the Prayer of Manasseh may have been meant as encouragement to Jews in the first century CE after the destruction of the Second Temple* in 70 CE. This is not certain, however, because the date of the work is disputed.

READING GUIDE

While its historical and social context is unclear, the Prayer of Manasseh clearly articulates the tension that characterizes the biblical portrayal of God. God holds sinners accountable (vv. 5, 10), yet promises *mercy* and *forgiveness* (vv. 6–7, 11, 13e–14). Notice the same tension in Ex 34.6–7, God's self-revelation to Moses.

1 O Lord Almighty,
  God of our ancestors,
  of Abraham and Isaac and Jacob
  and of their righteous offspring;
2 you who made heaven and earth
  with all their order;
3 who shackled the sea by your word of
    command,
  who confined the deep
  and sealed it with your terrible and
    glorious name;
4 at whom all things shudder,
  and tremble before your power,
5 for your glorious splendor cannot be
    borne,
  and the wrath of your threat to sinners
    is unendurable;
6 yet immeasurable and unsearchable
  is your promised mercy,

7 for you are the Lord Most High,
  of great compassion, long-suffering, and
    very merciful,
  and you relent at human suffering.
  O Lord, according to your great
    goodness
  you have promised repentance and
    forgiveness
  to those who have sinned against you,
  and in the multitude of your mercies
  you have appointed repentance for
    sinners,
  so that they may be saved. *a*
8 Therefore you, O Lord, God of the
    righteous,

---

a Other ancient authorities lack *O Lord, according . . . be saved*

have not appointed repentance for the
   righteous,
for Abraham and Isaac and Jacob, who
   did not sin against you,
but you have appointed repentance for
   me, who am a sinner.
9 For the sins I have committed are more
   in number than the sand of the
   sea;
my transgressions are multiplied,
   O Lord, they are multiplied!
I am not worthy to look up and see the
   height of heaven
because of the multitude of my iniquities.
10 I am weighted down with many an iron
   fetter,
so that I am rejected[a] because of my
   sins,
and I have no relief;
for I have provoked your wrath
and have done what is evil in your
   sight,
setting up abominations and multiplying
   offenses.
11 And now I bend the knee of my heart,
imploring you for your kindness.
12 I have sinned, O Lord, I have sinned,
and I acknowledge my transgressions.
13 I earnestly implore you,
forgive me, O Lord, forgive me!
Do not destroy me with my
   transgressions!
Do not be angry with me forever or
   store up evil for me;
do not condemn me to the depths of the
   earth.
For you, O Lord, are the God of those
   who repent,

14 and in me you will manifest your
   goodness;
for, unworthy as I am, you will save me
   according to your great mercy,
15 and I will praise you continually all the
   days of my life.
For all the host of heaven sings your
   praise,
and yours is the glory forever. Amen.

1.1–15. 1: The phrase, *God of our ancestors,* recalls
2 Chr 33.12, which inspired the prayer. **2–3:** God is
addressed as creator (Ps 115.15; 121.2). Verse 3 recalls
Gen 1.1–2, as well as other texts that suggest God has
controlled the chaotic waters (Job 38.8–11; Ps 74.13).
4–5a: *Shudder* and *tremble* are the language of theophany,* descriptions of God's appearing in the natural order (Ps 18.7–15; 97.3–5). **5b–6:** The presence
of God calls *sinners* to account, yet God has *promised
mercy.* The tension between *wrath* and *mercy* characterizes the whole Bible (see Ex 34.6–7). **7:** What
Manasseh needed and counted upon was *mercy,*
which is provided with several synonyms for emphasis.
The prayer begins to recall Psalm 51 at this point (see
also Ps 103.8–14, which recalls Ex 34.6–7). **8–13d:**
While *the righteous* do not need to repent, Manasseh
does (see Lk 5.32), as vv. 9–10, 12 make clear (see
2 Kings 21.1–9; 2 Chr 33.1–9). The confession is accompanied by an appeal to God's *kindness* (v. 11, see
Ps 51.1) and petitions God to *forgive* (v. 13; see Ps
51.2). **13e–15:** Returning the focus to God's *mercy,*
the prayer concludes with the promise to *praise,* an
act of submission to God and God's purposes (see
Ps 51.15–17).

a Other ancient authorities read *so that I cannot lift up
my head*

PSALM 151

Introduction

Neither a song of praise nor a prayer as are most of the 150 psalms (to which *the number* in the superscription apparently refers; see note *a*), it purports to be David's autobiographical reflection. The NRSV translation is based on a Greek text, and the poem appears following Psalm 150 in some Greek and late Syriac⋆ manuscripts. That the psalm was composed in Hebrew is suggested by the discovery of a Hebrew text of Psalm 151 at Qumran in the Dead Sea Scrolls. The Hebrew version is longer and more complex than the Greek version. The poem has been dated as early as the sixth century BCE, but it was probably written considerably later.

Because the date, authorship, and circumstances of origin are unknown, it is impossible to say anything specific about the historical and social contexts of Psalm 151. In general terms, it offers evidence of the piety that led earlier editors to attribute seventy-three psalms to David, including the association of thriteen psalms with specific episodes in David's life.

READING GUIDE

The two sections of the poem feature two events in David's life: his *anointing*⋆ by God's *messenger*, Samuel (vv. 1–5; see 1 Sam 16.1–13), and his defeat of the *Philistine* warrior, Goliath (vv. 6–7; see 1 Sam 17.19–54).

This psalm is ascribed to David as his own composition (though it is outside the number^a), after he had fought in single combat with Goliath.

1 I was small among my brothers,
  and the youngest in my father's house;
  I tended my father's sheep.

2 My hands made a harp;
  my fingers fashioned a lyre.

3 And who will tell my Lord?
  The Lord himself; it is he who hears.^b

4 It was he who sent his messenger^c
  and took me from my father's sheep,
  and anointed me with his anointing
  oil.

5 My brothers were handsome and tall,
  but the Lord was not pleased with
  them.

6 I went out to meet the Philistine,^d
  and he cursed me by his idols.

7 But I drew his own sword;
  I beheaded him, and took away
  disgrace from the people of
  Israel.

1.1–7. 1: The description corresponds to 1 Sam 16.11.
2: While not part of the story of David's *anointing*,⋆
1 Sam 16.23, 18.10 record that David played the lyre.
3–5: The apparent intent of v. 3 is to describe God's
unlikely choice of David, given the more impressive
qualifications of his brothers (v. 5; see 1 Sam 16.6–
10). 6–7: Verse 6 is based upon 1 Sam 17.43, and v. 7
upon 1 Sam 17.51.

a Other ancient authorities add *of the one hundred fifty* (psalms)   *b* Other ancient authorities add *everything*; others add *me*; others read *who will hear me*   *c* Or *angel*   *d* Or *foreigner*

3 MACCABEES

Introduction

Third Maccabees has nothing to do with the Maccabees. It is a story about the Jewish community in Egypt in the third century BCE, a melodramatic account of the danger that beset that community and its miraculous deliverance. While the story may preserve some historical details, it has a legendary* character. Its literary genre* resembles the story of Esther, or some of the stories in Dan 1–6. All these stories concern Jews outside the land of Israel (that is, in the Diaspora,* or scattering of the Jews in the gentile* world). In each of them, the Jews are endangered by hostile gentiles but are wonderfully delivered in the end. In this case, the story narrates three episodes involving Ptolemy IV Philopator, king of Egypt (221–204 BCE). The first is an introductory paragraph that describes how the king was saved from being assassinated by a Jew named Dositheus (1.1–5). The second episode tells of the king's unsuccessful attempt to enter the Jerusalem Temple* (1.6–2.24). The third episode concerns the king's persecution of the Jews of Egypt. This episode occupies the bulk of the book (2.25–6.15). The king is repeatedly thwarted by divine intervention and is eventually brought to his senses. The book concludes with a celebration of the deliverance of the Jews.

Unlike 1 and 2 Maccabees, 3 Maccabees was not included in the Latin Vulgate,* or in the canon* of the Roman Catholic Church. It is, however, regarded as canonical in Eastern Christianity.

Third Maccabees was written in Greek, most probably in Alexandria. It refers to the battle of Raphia (217 BCE) and so must have been written after that date, but it may have been written much later. The story of the persecution, the main episode in the book, is also found in Josephus, *Against Apion* 2.53–55, but according to Josephus, the Ptolemy in question was not Ptolemy IV Philopator but Ptolemy VIII Euergetes (who was known as Physcon, "pot-belly," 144–117 BCE). It appears, then, that 3 Maccabees incorporates elements of legend and folklore that were associated with different figures at various times. The book itself can scarcely have been written before the Roman era. There are parallels with 2 Maccabees and the Greek editions of Esther and Daniel, which would hardly have been possible before the first century BCE. A key factor in establishing the date of the book is the statement in 2.28 that the Jews should be reduced to the popular census (*laographia*) and slave condition. The only census that entailed a reduction in status for the Jews was associated with a poll tax introduced by the Emperor Augustus in 24/23 BCE. Citizens of Alexandria were not subject to this tax, but Egyptians and Jews were. Jews, who considered themselves on a par with the Alexandrians, and who despised the Egyptians, bitterly resented this tax. The issue of equality with the Alexandrians is mentioned in 3 Macc 2.30. If 3 Maccabees is alluding to the imposition of the poll tax, it cannot have been written before the Roman era.

Third Maccabees combines incidents that were probably originally independent. The combination here of a story of a threat to the Temple with the persecution of the Jews in Egypt may reflect the actual context in which the book was put together. In 38 CE the Emperor Caligula attempted to have his statue placed in the Temple in Jerusalem. At the same time, there was a riot against the Jews in Alexandria that has been described as the first pogrom* in history. (Our main account of these events is in the treatise on *The Embassy to Gaius* by the Jewish

Alexandrian philosopher, Philo★). The crises of the time of Caligula provide a plausible context for 3 Maccabees.

READING GUIDE

Much of the interest of 3 Maccabees lies in the picture it draws of life in the Jewish Diaspora★ in the Hellenistic★ and Roman periods. The Jews are loyal servants of the king, but also strict observers of the law. The Greeks are portrayed favorably, as sympathetic to the Jews. Problems arise because of the arrogance, and even madness, of the king. But much of the hostility in this book is directed against Jews who betray their religion. Equality with the Alexandrians should not be bought at the price of apostasy. Even the king eventually acknowledges that those who "transgressed the divine commandment for their belly's sake would never be well disposed to the king's estate either" (7.11) and gives permission for them to be slaughtered.

Third Maccabees may be taken to represent the faith of many Egyptian Jews in the early Roman period. They felt vulnerable to the whims of their rulers, but they were confident that God would deliver them. There is no mention here of resurrection or immortality, nor of any apocalyptic★ upheaval, even the overthrow of the king. Deliverance seemed possible within the framework of history and was compatible with gentile rule. This relatively optimistic view of life would eventually be shattered in the disasters that befell the Jewish community in connection with the revolts against Rome in 66 CE and especially in 115–117 CE, when the Jewish community in Alexandria was virtually wiped out.

1.1–5	The service of Dositheus in saving the king
1.6–2.24	The king's attempt to enter the Temple
2.25–6.15	The attack on Egyptian Jewry
6.16–7.23	The deliverance of the Jews

1 When Philopator learned from those who returned that the regions that he had controlled had been seized by Antiochus, he gave orders to all his forces, both infantry and cavalry, took with him his sister Arsinoë, and marched out to the region near Raphia, where the army of Antiochus was encamped. 2 But a certain Theodotus, determined to carry out the plot he had devised, took with him the best of the Ptolemaic arms that had been previously issued to him,[a] and crossed over by night to the tent of Ptolemy, intending single-handed to kill him and thereby end the war. 3 But Dositheus, known as the son of Drimylus, a Jew by birth who later changed his religion and apostatized from the ancestral traditions, had led the king away and arranged that a certain insignificant man should sleep in the tent; and so it turned out that this man incurred the vengeance meant for the king.[b] 4 When a bitter fight resulted, and matters were turning out rather in favor of Antiochus, Arsinoë went to the troops with wailing and tears, her locks all disheveled, and exhorted them to defend themselves and their children and wives bravely, promising to give them each two minas of gold if they won the battle. 5 And so it came about that the enemy was routed in the action, and many captives also were taken. 6 Now that he had foiled the plot, Ptolemy[c] decided to visit the neighboring cities and encourage them. 7 By doing this, and by endowing their sacred enclosures with gifts, he strengthened the morale of his subjects.

a Or the best of the Ptolemaic soldiers previously put under his command   b Gk that one   c Gk he

1.1–5: The battle of Raphia. *Raphia* was in Palestine, near Gaza, and was the scene of a battle between Ptolemy IV Philopator and Antiochus III (the Great) in 217 BCE. The Greek historian Polybius reports a plot to assassinate Ptolemy, but says nothing of Dositheus. The name *Dositheus* is a Greek equivalent of Nathaniel (both meaning "God has provided"), and is a typically Jewish name. The name occurs in a papyrus from around this time as that of a priest of the cult of Alexander, a very high position in Hellenistic* Egypt. The role of Dositheus here is very like that of Mordecai in Esth 2.21–23. It would seem that the author took a well-known Jewish name of this era and gave him a role in the story of Philopator similar to that of Mordecai in the story of Esther. The abruptness of this narrative* suggests that the author adapted it from a historical source. It shows the loyalty of the Jews to the king. It is ironic, however, that an act of loyalty sets in motion the chain of events that leads to persecution.

8 Since the Jews had sent some of their council and elders to greet him, to bring him gifts of welcome, and to congratulate him on what had happened, he was all the more eager to visit them as soon as possible. 9After he had arrived in Jerusalem, he offered sacrifice to the supreme God*a* and made thank offerings and did what was fitting for the holy place.*b* Then, upon entering the place and being impressed by its excellence and its beauty, 10he marveled at the good order of the temple, and conceived a desire to enter the sanctuary. 11When they said that this was not permitted, because not even members of their own nation were allowed to enter, not even all of the priests, but only the high priest who was pre-eminent over all— and he only once a year—the king was by no means persuaded. 12Even after the law had been read to him, he did not cease to maintain that he ought to enter, saying, "Even if those men are deprived of this honor, I ought not to be." 13And he inquired why, when he entered every other temple,*c* no one there had stopped him. 14And someone answered thoughtlessly that it was wrong to take that as a portent.*d* 15"But since this has happened," the king*e* said, "why should not I at least enter, whether they wish it or not?"

16 Then the priests in all their vestments prostrated themselves and entreated the supreme God*a* to aid in the present situation and to avert the violence of this evil design, and they filled the temple with cries and tears; 17those who remained behind in the city were agitated and hurried out, supposing that something mysterious was occurring. 18Young women who had been secluded in their chambers rushed out with their mothers, sprinkled their hair with dust,*f* and filled the streets with groans and lamentations. 19Those women who had recently been arrayed for marriage abandoned the bridal chambers*g* prepared for wedded union, and, neglecting proper modesty, in a disorderly rush flocked together in the city. 20Mothers and nurses abandoned even newborn children here and there, some in houses and some in the streets, and without a backward look they crowded together at the most high temple. 21Various were the supplications of those gathered there because of what the king was profanely plotting. 22In addition, the bolder of the citizens would not tolerate the completion of his plans or the fulfillment of his intended purpose. 23They shouted to their compatriots to take arms and die courageously for the ancestral law, and created a considerable disturbance in the holy place;*b* and being barely restrained by the old men and the elders,*h* they resorted to the same posture of supplication as the others. 24Meanwhile the crowd, as before, was engaged in prayer, 25while the elders near the king tried in various ways to change his arrogant mind from the plan that he had conceived. 26But he, in his arrogance, took heed of nothing, and began now to approach, determined to bring the aforesaid plan to a conclusion. 27When those who were around him observed this, they turned, together with our people, to call upon him who has all power to defend them in the present trouble and not to overlook this unlawful and haughty deed. 28The continuous, vehement, and concerted cry of the

a Gk *the greatest God*   *b* Gk *the place*   *c* Or *entered the temple precincts*   *d* Or *to boast of this*   *e* Gk *he* *f* Other ancient authorities add *and ashes*   *g* Or *the canopies*   *h* Other ancient authorities read *priests* crowds[a] resulted in an immense uproar; [29]for it seemed that not only the people but also the walls and the whole earth around echoed, because indeed all at that time[b] preferred death to the profanation of the place.

1.6–29: Ptolemy's visit. 9: In the Persian and Hellenistic* periods the God of the Jews is often venerated by gentiles* as *the supreme God,* or God Most High. The Jewish historian Josephus claims that Alexander the Great similarly visited Jerusalem and offered sacrifice. **10:** The king's *desire to enter the sanctuary* arises from his interest in architecture. Heliodorus, in 2 Macc 3, wanted to seize the temple treasure. The Roman general Pompey actually entered the holy of holies in 63 BCE. **11:** *Only the high priest* was allowed to enter; see Ex 30.10; Heb 9.7. **16:** The reaction of the priests is similar in 2 Macc 3. Similar incidents are reported by Josephus from the first century CE, when Pilate introduced standards into Jerusalem and when Caligula ordered the erection of his statue in the Temple.* **18:** On the confinement of virgins, see 2 Macc 3.19. **23:** The question of taking up *arms* is raised only to show the restraint of the Jewish elders. In fact, such a division of opinion was not unusual in the various crises that threatened the Jewish community.

2 Then the high priest Simon, facing the sanctuary, bending his knees and extending his hands with calm dignity, prayed as follows:[c] 2"Lord, Lord, king of the heavens, and sovereign of all creation, holy among the holy ones, the only ruler, almighty, give attention to us who are suffering grievously from an impious and profane man, puffed up in his audacity and power. 3For you, the creator of all things and the governor of all, are a just Ruler, and you judge those who have done anything in insolence and arrogance. 4You destroyed those who in the past committed injustice, among whom were even giants who trusted in their strength and boldness, whom you destroyed by bringing on them a boundless flood. 5You consumed with fire and sulfur the people of Sodom who acted arrogantly, who were notorious for their vices;[d] and you made them an example to those who should come afterward. 6You made known your mighty power by inflicting many and varied punishments on the audacious Pharaoh who had enslaved

your holy people Israel. 7And when he pursued them with chariots and a mass of troops, you overwhelmed him in the depths of the sea, but carried through safely those who had put their confidence in you, the Ruler over the whole creation. 8And when they had seen works of your hands, they praised you, the Almighty. 9You, O King, when you had created the boundless and immeasurable earth, chose this city and sanctified this place for your name, though you have no need of anything; and when you had glorified it by your magnificent manifestation,[e] you made it a firm foundation for the glory of your great and honored name. 10And because you love the house of Israel, you promised that if we should have reverses and tribulation should overtake us, you would listen to our petition when we come to this place and pray. 11And indeed you are faithful and true. 12And because oftentimes when our fathers were oppressed you helped them in their humiliation, and rescued them from great evils, 13see now, O holy King, that because of our many and great sins we are crushed with suffering, subjected to our enemies, and overtaken by helplessness. 14In our downfall this audacious and profane man undertakes to violate the holy place on earth dedicated to your glorious name. 15For your dwelling is the heaven of heavens, unapproachable by human beings. 16But because you graciously bestowed your glory on your people Israel, you sanctified this place. 17Do not punish us for the defilement committed by these men, or call us to account for this profanation, otherwise the transgressors will boast in their wrath and exult in the arrogance of their tongue, saying, 18'We have trampled down the house of the sanctuary as the houses of the abominations are trampled down.' 19Wipe away our sins and disperse our errors, and reveal your mercy at this hour. 20Speedily let your mercies overtake us, and put praises in the mouth of

---

a Other ancient authorities read *vehement cry of the assembled crowds*   *b* Other ancient authorities lack *at that time*   *c* Other ancient authorities lack verse 1   *d* Other ancient authorities read *secret in their vices*   *e* Or *epiphany* those who are downcast and broken in spirit, and give us peace."

2.1–20: The high priest's prayer. *Simon*, known as Simon the Just, is extolled in Sir 50. The prayer conforms to a type found in Ps 105 and 106, and in Ezra 9, Neh 9, Dan 9, and Bar 1.15–3.8. **4:** The destruction of the giants by the flood is inferred from the placement of Gen 6 before the story of Noah. **5:** Gen 19.24. **6:** Ex 5–12. The fate of the Pharaoh is especially appropriate here. **9:** Deut 12.13; 1 Kings 8.27–29. **17:** The boasting of the enemy is often invoked as a reason for divine action. See Ps 74.10, 18.

21 Thereupon God, who oversees all things, the first Father of all, holy among the holy ones, having heard the lawful supplication, scourged him who had exalted himself in insolence and audacity. 22He shook him on this side and that as a reed is shaken by the wind, so that he lay helpless on the ground and, besides being paralyzed in his limbs, was unable even to speak, since he was smitten*a* by a righteous judgment. 23Then both friends and bodyguards, seeing the severe punishment that had overtaken him, and fearing that he would lose his life, quickly dragged him out, panic-stricken in their exceedingly great fear. 24After a while he recovered, and though he had been punished, he by no means repented, but went away uttering bitter threats.

2.21–24: Divine intervention. 21: For God as *Father of all*, see Mal 2.10. **22:** Compare the punishment of Heliodorus in 2 Macc 3, which was administered by angels. **24:** Philopator differs from Heliodorus and from other gentile* kings punished by God (for example, Nebuchadnezzar in Dan 4) insofar as he does not repent.

25 When he arrived in Egypt, he increased in his deeds of malice, abetted by the previously mentioned drinking companions and comrades, who were strangers to everything just. 26He was not content with his uncounted licentious deeds, but even continued with such audacity that he framed evil reports in the various localities; and many of his friends, intently observing the king's purpose, themselves also followed his will. 27He

proposed to inflict public disgrace on the Jewish community,*b* and he set up a stone*c* on the tower in the courtyard with this inscription: 28"None of those who do not sacrifice shall enter their sanctuaries, and all Jews shall be subjected to a registration involving poll tax and to the status of slaves. Those who object to this are to be taken by force and put to death; 29those who are registered are also to be branded on their bodies by fire with the ivy-leaf symbol of Dionysus, and they shall also be reduced to their former limited status." 30In order that he might not appear to be an enemy of all, he inscribed below: "But if any of them prefer to join those who have been initiated into the mysteries, they shall have equal citizenship with the Alexandrians."

31 Now some, however, with an obvious abhorrence of the price to be exacted for maintaining the religion of their city,*d* readily gave themselves up, since they expected to enhance their reputation by their future association with the king. 32But the majority acted firmly with a courageous spirit and did not abandon their religion; and by paying money in exchange for life they confidently attempted to save themselves from the registration. 33They remained resolutely hopeful of obtaining help, and they abhorred those who separated themselves from them, considering them to be enemies of the Jewish nation,*b* and depriving them of companionship and mutual help.

2.25–33: The measures against the Jews. 25: The drinking companions have not been previously mentioned. Something may be lost from the beginning of the story. **28:** *Those who do not sacrifice* are only the Jews. In effect, this edict is a ban on synagogues.* The Greek word for *registration* here is especially associated with the poll tax introduced by Augustus in 24/23 BCE. The poll tax did not reduce Jews literally to *the status of slaves*, but it did involve a reduction in status that was deeply resented. **29:** The God of the Jews was often confused with Dionysus by the Greeks and Romans. See 2 Macc 6.7. The identification was argued by Plutarch, *Table-Talk* 4.6.1–2, who pointed to Jewish

a Other ancient authorities read *pierced*   *b* Gk *the nation*   *c* Gk *stele*   *d* Meaning of Gk uncertain ritual use of wine and the Festival of Tabernacles at the grape harvest and wine vintage in the fall. Philopator promoted the cult of Dionysus and attempted to regulate it. It is possible that he thought Judaism was a form of the cult of Dionysus and attempted to bring it into line with other observances of the cult, but 3 Maccabees is not a reliable historical witness. Branding was associated with the cult of Dionysus from ancient times. Slaves were also branded so that they could be easily identified. **30:** Philopator presents his initiative as an attempt to regulate Judaism by bringing it into line with a Greek cult, not to abolish it. Those who are properly initiated are not only left in peace, but given equal citizenship with the Alexandrians. The struggle for equal rights with the Alexandrians, however, only became an important issue in the Roman era. Jews as a class were never citizens of Alexandria. Citizenship would normally have required worship of pagan gods. Nonetheless, some observant Jews, such as Philo,* probably were citizens. Most Jews, however, probably wanted a status equal to citizenship, rather than actual citizenship. **31–33:** This verse must be read as a comment on the politics of Egyptian Judaism in the Roman period. Some upwardly mobile Jews, including Philo's nephew, Tiberius Julius Alexander, abandoned Judaism and became citizens. Others, like the author of 3 Maccabees, abhorred such apostasy. **32:** Those who acted firmly resemble the heroes in the time of persecution in Dan 11.32.

3 When the impious king comprehended this situation, he became so infuriated that not only was he enraged against those Jews who lived in Alexandria, but was still more bitterly hostile toward those in the countryside; and he ordered that all should promptly be gathered into one place, and put to death by the most cruel means. ²While these matters were being arranged, a hostile rumor was circulated against the Jewish nation by some who conspired to do them ill, a pretext being given by a report that they hindered others*ᵃ* from the observance of their customs. ³The Jews, however, continued to maintain goodwill and unswerving loyalty toward the dynasty; ⁴but because they worshiped God and conducted themselves by his law, they kept their separateness with respect to foods. For this reason they appeared hateful to some; ⁵but since they adorned their style of life with the good deeds of up-

right people, they were established in good repute with everyone. ⁶Nevertheless those of other races paid no heed to their good service to their nation, which was common talk among all; ⁷instead they gossiped about the differences in worship and foods, alleging that these people were loyal neither to the king nor to his authorities, but were hostile and greatly opposed to his government. So they attached no ordinary reproach to them.

8 The Greeks in the city, though wronged in no way, when they saw an unexpected tumult around these people and the crowds that suddenly were forming, were not strong enough to help them, for they lived under tyranny. They did try to console them, being grieved at the situation, and expected that matters would change; ⁹for such a great community ought not be left to its fate when it had committed no offense. ¹⁰And already some of their neighbors and friends and business associates had taken some of them aside privately and were pledging to protect them and to exert more earnest efforts for their assistance.

3.1–10: Slander against the Jews. 1: The attempt to gather those from the countryside is reminiscent of Philopator's attempt to regulate the cult of Dionysus, which required people from the interior of Egypt to come to Alexandria. **2:** The charge that Jews interfered with the religious observances of others is not otherwise found. The usual charges were "atheism," since the Jews did not worship the same gods as other people, and "inhospitality," because of their reluctance to mingle and intermarry. **4:** *Separateness with respect to foods* was often a source of offense, and Jewish apologists went to great lengths to give a satisfactory explanation (see Letter of Aristeas*). **7:** The Jews' loyalty to the king was questioned in Esther and Daniel, but in those cases the problem arises from conflict between courtiers. **8:** The most bitter enemies of the Jews in Alexandria were Greeks, or Greco-Egyptians. The Jews, however, wanted to be classified with the Greeks, as opposed to the Egyptians, and consequently the Greeks are favorably portrayed in Jewish writings of the period. Here those who slandered the

a Gk *them*

Jews are described enigmatically as *those of other races* (v. 6).

〜〜〜〜〜〜〜〜〜〜〜〜〜〜〜〜〜〜〜

11 Then the king, boastful of his present good fortune, and not considering the might of the supreme God,[a] but assuming that he would persevere constantly in his same purpose, wrote this letter against them:

12 "King Ptolemy Philopator to his generals and soldiers in Egypt and all its districts, greetings and good health:

13 "I myself and our government are faring well. 14When our expedition took place in Asia, as you yourselves know, it was brought to conclusion, according to plan, by the gods' deliberate alliance with us in battle, 15and we considered that we should not rule the nations inhabiting Coelesyria and Phoenicia by the power of the spear, but should cherish them with clemency and great benevolence, gladly treating them well. 16And when we had granted very great revenues to the temples in the cities, we came on to Jerusalem also, and went up to honor the temple of those wicked people, who never cease from their folly. 17They accepted our presence by word, but insincerely by deed, because when we proposed to enter their inner temple and honor it with magnificent and most beautiful offerings, 18they were carried away by their traditional arrogance, and excluded us from entering; but they were spared the exercise of our power because of the benevolence that we have toward all. 19By maintaining their manifest ill-will toward us, they become the only people among all nations who hold their heads high in defiance of kings and their own benefactors, and are unwilling to regard any action as sincere.

20 "But we, when we arrived in Egypt victorious, accommodated ourselves to their folly and did as was proper, since we treat all nations with benevolence. 21Among other things, we made known to all our amnesty toward their compatriots here, both because of their alliance with us and the myriad affairs liberally entrusted to them from the beginning; and we ventured to make a change, by deciding both to deem them worthy of Alexandrian citizenship and to make them participants in our regular religious rites.[b] 22But in their innate malice they took this in a contrary spirit, and disdained what is good. Since they incline constantly to evil, 23they not only spurn the priceless citizenship, but also both by speech and by silence they abominate those few among them who are sincerely disposed toward us; in every situation, in accordance with their infamous way of life, they secretly suspect that we may soon alter our policy. 24Therefore, fully convinced by these indications that they are ill-disposed toward us in every way, we have taken precautions so that, if a sudden disorder later arises against us, we shall not have these impious people behind our backs as traitors and barbarous enemies. 25Therefore we have given orders that, as soon as this letter arrives, you are to send to us those who live among you, together with their wives and children, with insulting and harsh treatment, and bound securely with iron fetters, to suffer the sure and shameful death that befits enemies. 26For when all of these have been punished, we are sure that for the remaining time the government will be established for ourselves in good order and in the best state. 27But those who shelter any of the Jews, whether old people or children or even infants, will be tortured to death with the most hateful torments, together with their families. 28Any who are willing to give information will receive the property of those who incur the punishment, and also two thousand drachmas from the royal treasury, and will be awarded their freedom.[c] 29Every place detected sheltering a Jew is to be made unapproachable and burned with fire, and shall become useless for all time to any mortal creature." 30The letter was written in the above form.

3.11–30: Ptolemy's first letter. 11: The king is accused of *hubris* (greatly excessive pride), an archetypal sin both in Hebrew prophecy (Isa 14; Ezek 27) and in Greek tragedy. **17:** The action against the Jews in Egypt is presented as a punishment for denying the

---

a Gk *the greatest God*   b Other ancient authorities read *partners of our regular priests*   c Gk *crowned with freedom* king access to the holy of holies. **21:** Antiochus IV Epiphanes* may also have thought that he was doing the Jews a favor by forcibly changing their rites. The account of the actions of Philopator may have Epiphanes in mind. **23:** Third Maccabees is at pains to show that citizenship was not an ultimate good for the Jews of Alexandria. **25:** The king orders a virtual genocide of the Jews that goes far beyond the persecution of Antiochus Epiphanes. It should be noted, however, that there is no racial theory underlying the hostility toward the Jews in Hellenistic* Egypt, so it is not accurate to call it antisemitism.

4 In every place, then, where this decree arrived, a feast at public expense was arranged for the Gentiles with shouts and gladness, for the inveterate enmity that had long ago been in their minds was now made evident and outspoken. ²But among the Jews there was incessant mourning, lamentation, and tearful cries; everywhere their hearts were burning, and they groaned because of the unexpected destruction that had suddenly been decreed for them. ³What district or city, or what habitable place at all, or what streets were not filled with mourning and wailing for them? ⁴For with such a harsh and ruthless spirit were they being sent off, all together, by the generals in the several cities, that at the sight of their unusual punishments, even some of their enemies, perceiving the common object of pity before their eyes, reflected on the uncertainty of life and shed tears at the most miserable expulsion of these people. ⁵For a multitude of grayheaded old men, sluggish and bent with age, was being led away, forced to march at a swift pace by the violence with which they were driven in such a shameful manner. ⁶And young women who had just entered the bridal chamber*a* to share married life exchanged joy for wailing, their myrrh-perfumed hair sprinkled with ashes, and were carried away unveiled, all together raising a lament instead of a wedding song, as they were torn by the harsh treatment of the heathen.*b* ⁷In bonds and in public view they were violently dragged along as far as the place of embarkation. ⁸Their husbands, in the prime of youth, their necks encircled with ropes instead of garlands, spent the re-

maining days of their marriage festival in lamentations instead of good cheer and youthful revelry, seeing death immediately before them.*c* ⁹They were brought on board like wild animals, driven under the constraint of iron bonds; some were fastened by the neck to the benches of the boats, others had their feet secured by unbreakable fetters, ¹⁰and in addition they were confined under a solid deck, so that, with their eyes in total darkness, they would undergo treatment befitting traitors during the whole voyage.

11 When these people had been brought to the place called Schedia, and the voyage was concluded as the king had decreed, he commanded that they should be enclosed in the hippodrome that had been built with a monstrous perimeter wall in front of the city, and that was well suited to make them an obvious spectacle to all coming back into the city and to those from the city*d* going out into the country, so that they could neither communicate with the king's forces nor in any way claim to be inside the circuit of the city.*e* ¹²And when this had happened, the king, hearing that the Jews' compatriots from the city frequently went out in secret to lament bitterly the ignoble misfortune of their kindred, ¹³ordered in his rage that these people be dealt with in precisely the same fashion as the others, not omitting any detail of their punishment. ¹⁴The entire race was to be registered individually, not for the hard labor that has been briefly mentioned before, but to be tortured with the outrages that he had ordered, and at the end to be destroyed in the space of a single day. ¹⁵The registration of these people was therefore conducted with bitter haste and zealous intensity from the rising of the sun until its setting, coming to an end after forty days but still uncompleted.

16 The king was greatly and continually filled with joy, organizing feasts in honor of

a Or *the canopy*   *b* Other ancient authorities read *as though torn by heathen whelps*   *c* Gk *seeing Hades already lying at their feet*   *d* Gk *those of them*   *e* Or *claim protection of the walls*; meaning of Gk uncertain all his idols, with a mind alienated from truth and with a profane mouth, praising speechless things that are not able even to communicate or to come to one's help, and uttering improper words against the supreme God.[a] 17But after the previously mentioned interval of time the scribes declared to the king that they were no longer able to take the census of the Jews because of their immense number, 18though most of them were still in the country, some still residing in their homes, and some at the place;[b] the task was impossible for all the generals in Egypt. 19After he had threatened them severely, charging that they had been bribed to contrive a means of escape, he was clearly convinced about the matter 20when they said and proved that both the paper[c] and the pens they used for writing had already given out. 21But this was an act of the invincible providence of him who was aiding the Jews from heaven.

4.1–21: The imprisonment of the Jews. 1: There is *inveterate enmity* between the Jews and the gentiles* despite the goodwill of the Greeks, noted in ch. 3. 4: The emotional account is characteristic of Hellenistic* historiography. 11: The use of the *hippodrome* anticipates the Roman use of the circus for tormenting Christians. 12–13: It appears here that only the Jews from the countryside were originally condemned, while their city brethren only aroused the king's wrath by their sympathy. There is no apparent reason why this should be so. It may be that this feature of the story reflects a source about the registration of devotees of Dionysus, since only those from the countryside were required to be registered. 14: The entire race was to be registered, even though it was about to be exterminated. The arrangement seems highly unrealistic. In 7.22, however, the Jews recover their property in accordance with the registration. 20: The impracticality of the registration is underlined when the pens and paper give out. Third Maccabees regards this development as a sign of divine providence, anticipating the greater deliverance that is to come.

5 Then the king, completely inflexible, was filled with overpowering anger and wrath; so he summoned Hermon, keeper of the elephants, 2and ordered him on the following day to drug all the elephants—five

hundred in number—with large handfuls of frankincense and plenty of unmixed wine, and to drive them in, maddened by the lavish abundance of drink, so that the Jews might meet their doom. 3When he had given these orders he returned to his feasting, together with those of his Friends and of the army who were especially hostile toward the Jews. 4And Hermon, keeper of the elephants, proceeded faithfully to carry out the orders. 5The servants in charge of the Jews[d] went out in the evening and bound the hands of the wretched people and arranged for their continued custody through the night, convinced that the whole nation would experience its final destruction. 6For to the Gentiles it appeared that the Jews were left without any aid, 7because in their bonds they were forcibly confined on every side. But with tears and a voice hard to silence they all called upon the Almighty Lord and Ruler of all power, their merciful God and Father, praying 8that he avert with vengeance the evil plot against them and in a glorious manifestation rescue them from the fate now prepared for them. 9So their entreaty ascended fervently to heaven.

10 Hermon, however, when he had drugged the pitiless elephants until they had been filled with a great abundance of wine and satiated with frankincense, presented himself at the courtyard early in the morning to report to the king about these preparations. 11But the Lord[e] sent upon the king a portion of sleep, that beneficence that from the beginning, night and day, is bestowed by him who grants it to whomever he wishes. 12And by the action of the Lord he was overcome by so pleasant and deep a sleep[f] that he quite failed in his lawless purpose and was completely frustrated in his inflexible plan. 13Then the Jews, since they had escaped the appointed hour, praised their holy God and again implored him who is easily reconciled to show the might of his all-powerful hand to the arrogant Gentiles. 14 But now, since it was nearly the mid-

a Gk *the greatest God*   *b* Other ancient authorities read *on the way*   *c* Or *paper factory*   *d* Gk *them*   *e* Gk *he*   *f* Other ancient authorities add *from evening until the ninth hour* dle of the tenth hour, the person who was in charge of the invitations, seeing that the guests were assembled, approached the king and nudged him. 15 And when he had with difficulty roused him, he pointed out that the hour of the banquet was already slipping by, and he gave him an account of the situation. 16 The king, after considering this, returned to his drinking, and ordered those present for the banquet to recline opposite him. 17 When this was done he urged them to give themselves over to revelry and to make the present*a* portion of the banquet joyful by celebrating all the more. 18 After the party had been going on for some time, the king summoned Hermon and with sharp threats demanded to know why the Jews had been allowed to remain alive through the present day. 19 But when he, with the corroboration of the king's*b* Friends, pointed out that while it was still night he had carried out completely the order given him, 20 the king,*c* possessed by a savagery worse than that of Phalaris, said that the Jews*d* were benefited by today's sleep, "but," he added, "tomorrow without delay prepare the elephants in the same way for the destruction of the lawless Jews!" 21 When the king had spoken, all those present readily and joyfully with one accord gave their approval, and all went to their own homes. 22 But they did not so much employ the duration of the night in sleep as in devising all sorts of insults for those they thought to be doomed.

5.1–51: **The trampling by the elephants. 1:** The name *Hermon* recalls Haman, archenemy of the Jews in the book of Esther. **2:** It made little sense to *drug all the elephants.* War elephants were trained to trample and would be difficult to control if drunk. The number *500* is an exaggeration. Philopator had only 73 elephants at the battle of Raphia. It has been suggested that the frankincense and wine were given as part of a Dionysiac ritual, but this is not stated in the text. **3:** Jews were often prominent in the army in the Ptolemaic period, but their prominence could easily give rise to resentment. **12:** The king fails initially because he sleeps through the appointed hour. **20:** Phalaris, tyrant of Agrigentum in the sixth century, was legendary* for his cruelty.

23 Then, as soon as the cock had crowed in the early morning, Hermon, having equipped*e* the animals, began to move them along in the great colonnade. 24 The crowds of the city had been assembled for this most pitiful spectacle and they were eagerly waiting for daybreak. 25 But the Jews, at their last gasp—since the time had run out—stretched their hands toward heaven and with most tearful supplication and mournful dirges implored the supreme God*f* to help them again at once. 26 The rays of the sun were not yet shed abroad, and while the king was receiving his Friends, Hermon arrived and invited him to come out, indicating that what the king desired was ready for action. 27 But he, on receiving the report and being struck by the unusual invitation to come out—since he had been completely overcome by incomprehension—inquired what the matter was for which this had been so zealously completed for him. 28 This was the act of God who rules over all things, for he had implanted in the king's mind a forgetfulness of the things he had previously devised. 29 Then Hermon and all the king's Friends*g* pointed out that the animals and the armed forces were ready, "O king, according to your eager purpose."*h* 30 But at these words he was filled with an overpowering wrath, because by the providence of God his whole mind had been deranged concerning these matters; and with a threatening look he said, 31 "If your parents or children were present, I would have prepared them to be a rich feast for the savage animals instead of the Jews, who give me no ground for complaint and have exhibited to an extraordinary degree a full and firm loyalty to my ancestors. 32 In fact you would have been deprived of life instead of these, if it were not for an affection arising from our nurture in common and your usefulness." 33 So Hermon suffered an unexpected and dangerous threat, and his eyes wavered and his face fell.

---

a Other ancient authorities read *delayed* (Gk *untimely*)
b Gk *his*   *c* Gk *he*   *d* Gk *they*   *e* Or *armed*
f Gk *the greatest God*   *g* Gk *all the Friends*
h Other ancient authorities read *pointed to the beasts and the armed forces, saying, "They are ready, O king, according to your eager purpose."*

34The king's Friends one by one sullenly slipped away and dismissed*a* the assembled people to their own occupations. 35Then the Jews, on hearing what the king had said, praised the manifest Lord God, King of kings, since this also was his aid that they had received.

36 The king, however, reconvened the party in the same manner and urged the guests to return to their celebrating. 37After summoning Hermon he said in a threatening tone, "How many times, you poor wretch, must I give you orders about these things? 38Equip*b* the elephants now once more for the destruction of the Jews tomorrow!" 39But the officials who were at table with him, wondering at his instability of mind, remonstrated as follows: 40"O king, how long will you put us to the test, as though we are idiots, ordering now for a third time that they be destroyed, and again revoking your decree in the matter?*c* 41As a result the city is in a tumult because of its expectation; it is crowded with masses of people, and also in constant danger of being plundered."

42 At this the king, a Phalaris in everything and filled with madness, took no account of the changes of mind that had come about within him for the protection of the Jews, and he firmly swore an irrevocable oath that he would send them to death*d* without delay, mangled by the knees and feet of the animals, 43and would also march against Judea and rapidly level it to the ground with fire and spear, and by burning to the ground the temple inaccessible to him*e* would quickly render it forever empty of those who offered sacrifices there. 44Then the Friends and officers departed with great joy, and they confidently posted the armed forces at the places in the city most favorable for keeping guard.

45 Now when the animals had been brought virtually to a state of madness, so to speak, by the very fragrant draughts of wine mixed with frankincense and had been equipped with frightful devices, the elephant keeper 46entered at about dawn into the courtyard—the city now being filled with countless masses of people crowding their way into the hippodrome—and urged the king on to the matter at hand. 47So he, when he had filled his impious mind with a deep rage, rushed out in full force along with the animals, wishing to witness, with invulnerable heart and with his own eyes, the grievous and pitiful destruction of the aforementioned people.

48 When the Jews saw the dust raised by the elephants going out at the gate and by the following armed forces, as well as by the trampling of the crowd, and heard the loud and tumultuous noise, 49they thought that this was their last moment of life, the end of their most miserable suspense, and giving way to lamentation and groans they kissed each other, embracing relatives and falling into one another's arms*f*—parents and children, mothers and daughters, and others with babies at their breasts who were drawing their last milk. 50Not only this, but when they considered the help that they had received before from heaven, they prostrated themselves with one accord on the ground, removing the babies from their breasts, 51and cried out in a very loud voice, imploring the Ruler over every power to manifest himself and be merciful to them, as they stood now at the gates of death.*d*

5.23–51. 28: The king fails a second time because of forgetfulness. Again, 3 Maccabees gives a naturalistic explanation and then interprets it as an act of divine providence. 33: Hermon is himself the victim of the king's whims. 43: Ptolemy VII Lathyrus did invade Judea in the time of Alexander Jannaeus in the first century BCE. Around the same time Queen Cleopatra III was dissuaded from invading by a Jewish general, Ananias, from the land of Onias at Leontopolis, on the grounds that she would incur the enmity of Jews everywhere.

6 Then a certain Eleazar, famous among the priests of the country, who had attained a ripe old age and throughout his life had been adorned with every virtue, directed the elders around him to stop calling upon the holy God, and he prayed as follows:

a Other ancient authorities read *he dismissed*
b Or Arm   *c* Other ancient authorities read *when the matter is in hand*   *d* Gk *Hades*   *e* Gk *us*   *f* Gk *falling upon their necks*

2 "King of great power, Almighty God Most High, governing all creation with mercy, 3 look upon the descendants of Abraham, O Father, upon the children of the sainted Jacob, a people of your consecrated portion who are perishing as foreigners in a foreign land. 4 Pharaoh with his abundance of chariots, the former ruler of this Egypt, exalted with lawless insolence and boastful tongue, you destroyed together with his arrogant army by drowning them in the sea, manifesting the light of your mercy on the nation of Israel. 5 Sennacherib exulting in his countless forces, oppressive king of the Assyrians, who had already gained control of the whole world by the spear and was lifted up against your holy city, speaking grievous words with boasting and insolence, you, O Lord, broke in pieces, showing your power to many nations. 6 The three companions in Babylon who had voluntarily surrendered their lives to the flames so as not to serve vain things, you rescued unharmed, even to a hair, moistening the fiery furnace with dew and turning the flame against all their enemies. 7 Daniel, who through envious slanders was thrown down into the ground to lions as food for wild animals, you brought up to the light unharmed. 8 And Jonah, wasting away in the belly of a huge, sea-born monster, you, Father, watched over and restored[a] unharmed to all his family. 9 And now, you who hate insolence, all-merciful and protector of all, reveal yourself quickly to those of the nation of Israel[b]—who are being outrageously treated by the abominable and lawless Gentiles.

10 "Even if our lives have become entangled in impieties in our exile, rescue us from the hand of the enemy, and destroy us, Lord, by whatever fate you choose. 11 Let not the vain-minded praise their vanities[c] at the destruction of your beloved people, saying, 'Not even their god has rescued them.' 12 But you, O Eternal One, who have all might and all power, watch over us now and have mercy on us who by the senseless insolence of the lawless are being deprived of life in the manner of traitors. 13 And let the Gentiles cower today in fear of your invincible might, O honored One, who have power to save the nation of Jacob. 14 The whole throng of infants and their parents entreat you with tears. 15 Let it be shown to all the Gentiles that you are with us, O Lord, and have not turned your face from us; but just as you have said, 'Not even when they were in the land of their enemies did I neglect them,' so accomplish it, O Lord."

6.1–15: The prayer of Eleazar. 1: The name Eleazar was popular in Hellenistic* Judaism. It is the name of the high priest in the Letter of Aristeas,* and of a martyr* in 2 Macc 6 and 4 Macc 5–6. Here Eleazar is *one of the priests,* but he is also aged, like the Eleazar of the Maccabean books. His prayer recalls tyrants who were humbled by God and acts of miraculous deliverance: *Pharaoh* (Ex 14), *Sennacherib* (2 Kings 18–19), the youths in *the fiery furnace* (Dan 3), *Daniel* in the lions' den (Dan 6), *Jonah* in the belly of the whale. **10:** This is the only suggestion in 3 Maccabees that the persecution may be a punishment for sin. **11:** For the boasting of the gentiles,* see 3 Macc 2.17. **15:** *Just as you have said:* Lev 26.44. Not all Diaspora* Jews thought they were living in the land of their enemies. Philo* claimed that Jews "severally hold that land as their fatherland in which they were born and reared" (*Against Flaccus* 46).

16 Just as Eleazar was ending his prayer, the king arrived at the hippodrome with the animals and all the arrogance of his forces. 17 And when the Jews observed this they raised great cries to heaven so that even the nearby valleys resounded with them and brought an uncontrollable terror upon the army. 18 Then the most glorious, almighty, and true God revealed his holy face and opened the heavenly gates, from which two glorious angels of fearful aspect descended, visible to all but the Jews. 19 They opposed the forces of the enemy and filled them with confusion and terror, binding them with immovable shackles. 20 Even the king began to shudder bodily, and he forgot his sullen insolence. 21 The animals turned back upon the armed forces following them and began trampling and destroying them.

---

a Other ancient authorities read *rescued and restored;* others, *mercifully restored*   b Other ancient authorities read *to the saints of Israel*   c Or *bless their vain gods*

22 Then the king's anger was turned to pity and tears because of the things that he had devised beforehand. 23For when he heard the shouting and saw them all fallen headlong to destruction, he wept and angrily threatened his Friends, saying, 24"You are committing treason and surpassing tyrants in cruelty; and even me, your benefactor, you are now attempting to deprive of dominion and life by secretly devising acts of no advantage to the kingdom. 25Who has driven from their homes those who faithfully kept our country's fortresses, and foolishly gathered every one of them here? 26Who is it that has so lawlessly encompassed with outrageous treatment those who from the beginning differed from[a] all nations in their goodwill toward us and often have accepted willingly the worst of human dangers? 27Loose and untie their unjust bonds! Send them back to their homes in peace, begging pardon for your former actions![b] 28Release the children of the almighty and living God of heaven, who from the time of our ancestors until now has granted an unimpeded and notable stability to our government." 29These then were the things he said; and the Jews, immediately released, praised their holy God and Savior, since they now had escaped death.

30 Then the king, when he had returned to the city, summoned the official in charge of the revenues and ordered him to provide to the Jews both wines and everything else needed for a festival of seven days, deciding that they should celebrate their rescue with all joyfulness in that same place in which they had expected to meet their destruction. 31Accordingly those disgracefully treated and near to death,[c] or rather, who stood at its gates, arranged for a banquet of deliverance instead of a bitter and lamentable death, and full of joy they apportioned to celebrants the place that had been prepared for their destruction and burial. 32They stopped their chanting of dirges and took up the song of their ancestors, praising God, their Savior and worker of wonders.[d] Putting an end to all mourning and wailing, they formed choruses[e] as a sign of peaceful joy. 33Likewise also the king, after convening a great banquet to celebrate these events, gave thanks to heaven unceasingly and lavishly for the unexpected rescue that he[f] had experienced. 34Those who had previously believed that the Jews would be destroyed and become food for birds, and had joyfully registered them, groaned as they themselves were overcome by disgrace, and their fire-breathing boldness was ignominiously[g] quenched.

35 The Jews, as we have said before, arranged the aforementioned choral group[h] and passed the time in feasting to the accompaniment of joyous thanksgiving and psalms. 36And when they had ordained a public rite for these things in their whole community and for their descendants, they instituted the observance of the aforesaid days as a festival, not for drinking and gluttony, but because of the deliverance that had come to them through God. 37Then they petitioned the king, asking for dismissal to their homes. 38So their registration was carried out from the twenty-fifth of Pachon to the fourth of Epeiph,[i] for forty days; and their destruction was set for the fifth to the seventh of Epeiph,[j] the three days 39on which the Lord of all most gloriously revealed his mercy and rescued them all together and unharmed. 40Then they feasted, being provided with everything by the king, until the fourteenth day,[k] on which also they made the petition for their dismissal. 41The king granted their request at once and wrote the following letter for them to the generals in the cities, magnanimously expressing his concern:

6.16–41: The reversal of fortune. 16: The story reaches its climax* as the king enters the *hippodrome*. **18:** *Two angels* also appeared in the story of Heliodorus in 2 Macc 3. **21:** If the elephants were indeed drunk, it would not be surprising that they would turn back on those behind them, but the story emphasizes the role of divine providence. See Dan 3, where the fire from the furnace burns some of the executioners.

a Or *excelled above* b Other ancient authorities read *revoking your former commands* c Gk *Hades*
d Other ancient authorities read *praising Israel and the wonder-working God; or praising Israel's Savior, the wonder-working God* e Or *dances* f Other ancient authorities read *they* g Other ancient authorities read *completely* h Or *dance* i July 7—August 15
j August 16—18 k August 25

24: Ptolemy puts the blame on his advisers, although he himself had taken the initiative. The courtiers are genuinely to blame in Esther and Daniel. **28:** It is a standard feature of such stories that the king recognizes the God of the Jews as the true God. See Dan 2.47; 4.34–35. In 2 Macc 9, Antiochus Epiphanes* declares his intention to become a Jew. **30:** The provision for a festival recalls the institution of Purim in Esth 9. Josephus also says that the deliverance from the elephants was "the origin of the well-known feast which the Jews of Alexandria keep, with good reason, on this day" (*Against Apion* 2.55). We have no other evidence for this feast. It may be that the story of the elephants was meant to relate the festival of Purim to the history of the Jews in Egypt.

7 "King Ptolemy Philopator to the generals in Egypt and all in authority in his government, greetings and good health: 2 "We ourselves and our children are faring well, the great God guiding our affairs according to our desire. 3 Certain of our friends, frequently urging us with malicious intent, persuaded us to gather together the Jews of the kingdom in a body and to punish them with barbarous penalties as traitors; 4 for they declared that our government would never be firmly established until this was accomplished, because of the ill-will that these people had toward all nations. 5 They also led them out with harsh treatment as slaves, or rather as traitors, and, girding themselves with a cruelty more savage than that of Scythian custom, they tried without any inquiry or examination to put them to death. 6 But we very severely threatened them for these acts, and in accordance with the clemency that we have toward all people we barely spared their lives. Since we have come to realize that the God of heaven surely defends the Jews, always taking their part as a father does for his children, 7 and since we have taken into account the friendly and firm goodwill that they had toward us and our ancestors, we justly have acquitted them of every charge of whatever kind. 8 We also have ordered all people to return to their own homes, with no one in any place*a* doing them harm at all or reproaching them for the irrational things that have happened. 9 For you should know that if we devise any evil

against them or cause them any grief at all, we always shall have not a mortal but the Ruler over every power, the Most High God, in everything and inescapably as an antagonist to avenge such acts. Farewell."

7.1–9: Ptolemy's second letter. This letter formalizes what the king had said in ch. 6. **3:** Again, the blame is placed on the friends of the king. **5:** The Scythians were synonymous with cruelty; see 2 Macc 4.47. **6:** The *God of heaven,* or the *Most High God* (v. 9), was a common pagan designation for the God of the Jews in the Persian and Hellenistic* periods. **9:** Compare the association of God with the king and Mt. Zion* in Ps 2.

10 On receiving this letter the Jews*b* did not immediately hurry to make their departure, but they requested of the king that at their own hands those of the Jewish nation who had willfully transgressed against the holy God and the law of God should receive the punishment they deserved. 11 They declared that those who for the belly's sake had transgressed the divine commandments would never be favorably disposed toward the king's government. 12 The king*c* then, admitting and approving the truth of what they said, granted them a general license so that freely, and without royal authority or supervision, they might destroy those everywhere in his kingdom who had transgressed the law of God. 13 When they had applauded him in fitting manner, their priests and the whole multitude shouted the Hallelujah and joyfully departed. 14 And so on their way they punished and put to a public and shameful death any whom they met of their compatriots who had become defiled. 15 In that day they put to death more than three hundred men; and they kept the day as a joyful festival, since they had destroyed the profaners. 16 But those who had held fast to God even to death and had received the full enjoyment of deliverance began their departure from the city, crowned with all sorts of very fragrant flowers, joyfully and loudly giving thanks to the one God of their ancestors, the

---

a Other ancient authorities read *way*   b Gk *they*
c Gk *He*

eternal Savior[a] of Israel, in words of praise and all kinds of melodious songs.

7.10–16: Revenge on the apostates. 10: At the end of the Book of Esther, the Jews took vengeance on their gentile* enemies and slew thousands. In 3 Maccabees, there is no vengeance against gentiles, and the king accepts no blame. The vengeance of the Jews is directed primarily against Jews who voluntarily transgressed the law, even though they did so under duress. **12:** The king agrees that such people cannot be trusted, and more than 300 of them are put to death.

17 When they had arrived at Ptolemais, called "rose-bearing" because of a characteristic of the place, the fleet waited for them, in accordance with the common desire, for seven days. [18]There they celebrated their deliverance,[b] for the king had generously provided all things to them for their journey until all of them arrived at their own houses. [19]And when they had all landed in peace with appropriate thanksgiving, there too in like manner they decided to observe these days as a joyous festival during the time of their stay. [20]Then, after inscribing them as holy on a pillar and dedicating a place of prayer at the site of the festival, they departed unharmed, free, and overjoyed, since at the king's command they had all of them

been brought safely by land and sea and river to their own homes. [21]They also possessed greater prestige among their enemies, being held in honor and awe; and they were not subject at all to confiscation of their belongings by anyone. [22]Besides, they all recovered all of their property, in accordance with the registration, so that those who held any of it restored it to them with extreme fear.[c] So the supreme God perfectly performed great deeds for their deliverance. [23]Blessed be the Deliverer of Israel through all times! Amen.

7.17–23: The departure. 17: The story ends with the return of the Jews to their homes. The *Ptolemais* in question was "Ptolemais at the harbor" near modern Cairo. **18:** The provisions supplied by the king recall the "plundering of the Egyptians" in the Exodus (Ex 12.35–36). Foreign kings often provided generously for Jewish groups in the Second Temple* period; see Ezra 1.4. **20:** The *place of prayer* is presumably a synagogue.* **22:** The registration proves to have had a providential purpose, since it enables the Jews to recover their property. **23:** The book concludes with the praise of the *Deliverer of Israel.*

---

a Other ancient authorities read *the holy Savior*; others, *the holy one*   *b* Gk they made a cup of deliverance   *c* Other ancient authorities read *with a very large supplement*

(c) The following book is included in the Slavonic Bible as 3 Esdras, but is not found in the Greek. It is included in the Appendix to the Latin Vulgate Bible as 4 Esdras.

2 ESDRAS

Introduction

Second Esdras is a composite book, containing three works of different origins. The central part of the book, chs. 3–14, is usually referred to as 4 Ezra. Fourth Ezra is an apocalypse,★ a narrative★ in which an angel transmits to a human character revelations concerning the divine plan of history and the supernatural world. It was probably written in Hebrew by a Jew from Judea, in about 100 CE. It was translated into Greek before the end of the second century and was preserved only by Christians. Although both the Hebrew and Greek versions (except for a few verses of the Greek) have been lost, 4 Ezra is preserved in eight different translations from the Greek. The Latin and Syriac★ translations are generally considered to be the most accurate reflections of the original text. Although 4 Ezra appears in many early biblical manuscripts of the Eastern Christian churches (often preceding or following the canonical★ books of Ezra and Nehemiah), it is no longer regarded as canonical scripture in any church except the Armenian, where its canonical status is debated.

Chapters 1–2, which scholars now call 5 Ezra, and 15–16, called 6 Ezra, are later works that were attached to 4 Ezra only in the Latin versions. The combination of 4, 5, and 6 Ezra, which appears under the title 4 Esdras in the appendix to the Vulgate,★ is now called 2 Esdras and is considered part of the Apocrypha★ by both Protestants and Roman Catholics. Both 5 and 6 Ezra appear to be Christian compositions in their current form, although some scholars believe that they were originally Jewish compositions that were substantially revised by Christian editors. Sixth Ezra was composed in Greek, some time after 260 CE, probably in the eastern part of the Roman Empire. It was probably not intended to be an appendix to 4 Ezra, but if it had its own introduction, this was removed when it was translated into Latin and joined to 4 Ezra. Fifth Ezra gives no clue as to its place of origin, but it was written either in Greek or Latin sometime between 130 and 250 CE, with most scholars favoring a date around 150. Fifth Ezra also circulated independently of 4 Ezra, and was connected to 4 Ezra sometime after 6 Ezra. Nevertheless, the author of 5 Ezra may have known 4 Ezra, and it is possible to read 5 Ezra as an early Christian response to issues raised by 4 Ezra. The genre★ of both 5 and 6 Ezra is best described as oracular★ (containing statements attributed to God) or prophetic (resembling the prophets★ of the Hebrew Bible) rather than apocalyptic,★ although both look forward to the end of the world. Fifth Ezra contains a brief apocalypse (2.42–48), however. The two Latin text families of 2 Esdras differ the most for 5 Ezra, and some of the variant readings presented in the textual notes probably reflect the original text of 5 Ezra.

The author of 4 Ezra gives expression to a "crisis of faith" that was provoked by the destruction of the Second Temple★ by the Romans in 70 CE. Other Jewish texts written in response to this catastrophic event (such as 2 Baruch and the Apocalypse of Abraham) reflect a similar mood of anguish and theological doubt. Fourth Ezra, however, poses a more serious challenge to theodicy★ than any other Jewish writing except Job. The author of 4 Ezra even calls into question the central Jewish belief in the covenant★ between God and Israel, although in the end he seems to affirm this belief. The author of 5 Ezra, on the other hand, takes the position that the covenant has been revoked from Israel and transferred to "another people," presumably the Christians. Fifth Ezra seems to come from a Christian community that feels the need to separate itself from its Jewish background or surroundings. Sixth Ezra appears to have been written during a period of intense persecution of the author's community by the Romans.

READING GUIDE
Fourth Ezra (chs. 3–14) should be read separately from 5 and 6 Ezra, and preferably first. It is divided into seven episodes, traditionally referred to as visions, which can be read one at a time (see outline). The first three episodes take the form of dialogues between Ezra and the angel Uriel. Each begins with Ezra lamenting* the fate of Israel, after which the angel engages in a theological dispute with him, then makes predictions about the coming end of time. The first two dialogues closely parallel each other, while the much longer third dialogue contains several rounds of dispute followed by predictions. The reader will notice that Ezra never fully accepts the angel's answers to his questions in the course of the dialogues. The fourth episode, which begins with a lament and a dialogue (this time between Ezra and a mourning woman) and ends with a vision, marks a turning point in the book. In the fifth and sixth episodes, Ezra receives visions and accepts the angel's interpretation* of them without argument or complaint. In the final episode, Ezra gladly accepts his commission as leader and comforter of his people, comparable to Moses. Although at the end Ezra appears reconciled to the fate of Israel, the author has left the reader with many unanswered questions. In particular, the nationalistic triumph predicted in the visions of chs. 11–13 is hard to reconcile with the angel's insistence in the dialogues on individual responsibility for salvation.

In reading 5 Ezra, the reader may wish to contrast the author's views of the covenant,* law, and salvation with those expressed in 4 Ezra. It is important to bear in mind the historical consequences of the Christian claim that the Jews forfeited the covenant through their sins. Similarly, in reading 6 Ezra, one could think of modern parallels to the hatred and thirst for revenge expressed here. What sort of circumstances give rise to such delight in destruction?

2 Esd 1–2 (5 Ezra)
- 1.4–2.32   Oracles of the Lord
- 2.32–48   Ezra's address to the nations and apocalyptic vision

2 Esd 3–14 (4 Ezra)
- 3.1–5.20   First dialogue
- 5.21–6.35   Second dialogue
- 6.36–9.26   Third dialogue
- 9.27–10.59   Dialogue and vision of the mourning woman
- 11.1–12.51   Vision of the eagle
- 13.1–58   Vision of the man from the sea
- 14.1–48   Ezra's commission and scribal activity

2 Esd 15–16 (6 Ezra) Oracles of the Lord

Comprising what is sometimes called
5 Ezra (chapters 1–2), 4 Ezra
(chapters 3–14), and 6 Ezra
(chapters 15–16)

1 The book[a] of the prophet Ezra son of
Seraiah, son of Azariah, son of Hilkiah,
son of Shallum, son of Zadok, son of Ahitub,
[2]son of Ahijah, son of Phinehas, son of Eli,
son of Amariah, son of Azariah, son of
Meraimoth, son of Arna, son of Uzzi, son of
Borith, son of Abishua, son of Phinehas, son
of Eleazar, [3]son of Aaron, of the tribe of
Levi, who was a captive in the country of the
Medes in the reign of Artaxerxes, king of the
Persians.[b]

1.1–3: Attribution. These verses were added to 5 Ezra
when it was placed before 4 Ezra. **1:** *The prophet*★
Ezra: The biblical Ezra was not a prophet, but a scribe★
and priest. The tradition that he was also a prophet is
found in 12.42. Ezra's genealogy★ (list of ancestors) is
similar, but not identical, to those found in Ezra 7.1–5
and 1 Esd 8.1–2. **3:** *In the reign of Artaxerxes:* Ezra
probably lived during the reign of Artaxerxes I (465–
24 BCE), but these prophecies were written in his name
centuries later.

---

4 The word of the Lord came to me, saying, [5]"Go, declare to my people their evil
deeds, and to their children the iniquities
that they have committed against me, so that
they may tell[c] their children's children [6]that
the sins of their parents have increased in
them, for they have forgotten me and have
offered sacrifices to strange gods. [7]Was it
not I who brought them out of the land of
Egypt, out of the house of bondage? But they
have angered me and despised my counsels.
[8]Now you, pull out the hair of your head and
hurl[d] all evils upon them, for they have not
obeyed my law—they are a rebellious people.
[9]How long shall I endure them, on whom I
have bestowed such great benefits? [10]For
their sake I have overthrown many kings; I
struck down Pharaoh with his servants and
all his army. [11]I destroyed all nations before
them, and scattered in the east the peoples
of two provinces,[e] Tyre and Sidon; I killed
all their enemies.

12 "But speak to them and say, Thus says
the Lord: [13]Surely it was I who brought you

through the sea, and made safe highways for
you where there was no road; I gave you Moses as leader and Aaron as priest; [14]I provided light for you from a pillar of fire, and
did great wonders among you. Yet you have
forgotten me, says the Lord.

15 "Thus says the Lord Almighty:[f] The
quails were a sign to you; I gave you camps
for your protection, and in them you complained. [16]You have not exulted in my name
at the destruction of your enemies, but to
this day you still complain.[g] [17]Where are the
benefits that I bestowed on you? When you
were hungry and thirsty in the wilderness,
did you not cry out to me, [18]saying, 'Why
have you led us into this wilderness to kill
us? It would have been better for us to serve
the Egyptians than to die in this wilderness.'
[19]I pitied your groanings and gave you
manna for food; you ate the bread of angels.
[20]When you were thirsty, did I not split the
rock so that waters flowed in abundance?
Because of the heat I clothed you with the
leaves of trees.[h] [21]I divided fertile lands
among you; I drove out the Canaanites, the
Perizzites, and the Philistines[i] before you.
What more can I do for you? says the Lord.
[22]Thus says the Lord Almighty:[f] When you
were in the wilderness, at the bitter stream,
thirsty and blaspheming my name, [23]I did
not send fire on you for your blasphemies,
but threw a tree into the water and made the
stream sweet.

1.4–23: Israel's sins and God's mercy. 5–7: Like the
prophets★ of the Hebrew Scriptures,★ Ezra is called by
God to denounce the people of Israel for their sins, and
to remind them of all that God has done for them.

---

a Other ancient authorities read *The second book*
b Other ancient authorities, which place chapters 1 and
2 after 16.78, lack verses 1–3 and begin the chapter: *The
word of the Lord that came to Ezra son of Chusi in the days
of King Nebuchadnezzar, saying,* "Go,   *c* Other ancient
authorities read *nourish*   *d* Other ancient authorities
read *and shake out*   *e* Other ancient authorities read
*Did I not destroy the city of Bethsaida because of you, and
to the south burn two cities . . . ?*   *f* Other ancient
authorities lack *Almighty*   *g* Other ancient authorities
read verse 16, *Your pursuer with his army I sank in the
sea, but still the people complain also concerning their own
destruction.*   *h* Other ancient authorities read *I made
for you trees with leaves*   *i* Other ancient authorities
read *Perizzites and their children*

8: In Ezra 9.3, Ezra pulls out some of his hair and his beard in a traditional sign of mourning, because of the faithlessness of the Israelites. **11:** This verse is obscure, but the point is clear: in the past, God took Israel's side against their enemies. **13–23:** God contrasts his merciful actions for Israel's sake (drawn from Exodus and Numbers) with the people's lack of faith and gratitude.

24 "What shall I do to you, O Jacob? You, Judah, would not obey me. I will turn to other nations and will give them my name, so that they may keep my statutes. ²⁵Because you have forsaken me, I also will forsake you. When you beg mercy of me, I will show you no mercy. ²⁶When you call to me, I will not listen to you; for you have defiled your hands with blood, and your feet are swift to commit murder. ²⁷It is not as though you had forsaken me; you have forsaken yourselves, says the Lord.

28 "Thus says the Lord Almighty: Have I not entreated you as a father entreats his sons or a mother her daughters or a nurse her children, ²⁹so that you should be my people and I should be your God, and that you should be my children and I should be your father? ³⁰I gathered you as a hen gathers her chicks under her wings. But now, what shall I do to you? I will cast you out from my presence. ³¹When you offer oblations to me, I will turn my face from you; for I have rejected your*ᵃ* festal days, and new moons, and circumcisions of the flesh.*ᵇ* ³²I sent you my servants the prophets, but you have taken and killed them and torn their bodies*ᶜ* in pieces; I will require their blood of you, says the Lord.*ᵈ*

33 "Thus says the Lord Almighty: Your house is desolate; I will drive you out as the wind drives straw; ³⁴and your sons will have no children, because with you*ᵉ* they have neglected my commandment and have done what is evil in my sight. ³⁵I will give your houses to a people that will come, who without having heard me will believe. Those to whom I have shown no signs will do what I have commanded. ³⁶They have seen no prophets, yet will recall their former state.*ᶠ* ³⁷I call to witness the gratitude of the people that is to come, whose children rejoice with gladness;*ᵍ* though they do not see me with bodily eyes, yet with the spirit they will believe the things I have said.

1.24–34: God's rejection of Israel. 24: *Other nations:* Other ancient authorities read "another nation." **26:** The author may have experienced violent conflicts between Jews and Christians, which could have motivated him to write this anti-Jewish tract. **27:** He emphasizes the self-destructive nature of Israel's disobedience. **28–29:** God has done everything in his power to preserve the covenant.* **30:** *As a hen:* Compare Mt 23.37 (Lk 13.34). **31:** God's rejection of superficial displays of piety is a common theme among the Hebrew prophets.* **32:** Although the theme of Israel's mistreatment of the prophets appears in 2 Chr 36.15–16, the closest parallel to this verse is Lk 11.49–51 (Mt 23.34–35). **33:** *Your house* refers to the Temple*; compare Mt 23.38. Note the numerous parallels between this passage and Mt 23.29–39.

38 "And now, father,*ʰ* look with pride and see the people coming from the east; ³⁹to them I will give as leaders Abraham, Isaac, and Jacob, and Hosea and Amos and Micah and Joel and Obadiah and Jonah ⁴⁰and Nahum and Habakkuk, Zephaniah, Haggai, Zechariah and Malachi, who is also called the messenger of the Lord.*ⁱ*

1.35–40: The transfer of Israel's privileges. 35: The benefits of the covenant* will be taken from Israel and given to *a people that will come,* presumably the

---

a Other ancient authorities read *I have not commanded for you*   *b* Other ancient authorities lack *of the flesh*   *c* Other ancient authorities read *the bodies of the apostles*   *d* Other ancient authorities add *Thus says the Lord Almighty: Recently you also laid hands on me, crying out before the judge's seat for him to deliver me to you. You took me as a sinner, not as a father who freed you from slavery, and you delivered me to death by hanging me on the tree; these are the things you have done. Therefore, says the Lord, let my Father and his angels return and judge between you and me; if I have not kept the commandment of the Father, if I have not nourished you, if I have not done the things my Father commanded, I will contend in judgment with you, says the Lord.*   *e* Other ancient authorities lack *with you*   *f* Other ancient authorities read *their iniquities*   *g* Other ancient authorities read *The apostles bear witness to the coming people with joy*   *h* Other ancient authorities read *brother*   *i* Other ancient authorities read *and Jacob, Elijah and Enoch, Zechariah and Hosea, Amos, Joel, Micah, Obadiah, Zephaniah,* ⁴⁰*Nahum, Jonah, Mattia (or Mattathias), Habakkuk, and twelve angels with flowers*

Christians. **36:** The verse is obscure, but clearly a contrast with v. 32 is intended. **38:** *The people coming from the east:* This verse may allude to a Jewish tradition about the return of the ten lost tribes of Israel from far in the east (compare 13.39–50), but if so, the motif* has been given a new meaning by the Christian author. **39–40:** The patriarchs of Genesis and the minor prophets* are symbolic of the spiritual heritage of Israel which is to be handed over to the Christians; compare Lk 13.28–29.

2 "Thus says the Lord: I brought this people out of bondage, and I gave them commandments through my servants the prophets; but they would not listen to them, and made my counsels void. ²The mother who bore them*ª* says to them, 'Go, my children, because I am a widow and forsaken. ³I brought you up with gladness; but with mourning and sorrow I have lost you, because you have sinned before the Lord God and have done what is evil in my sight.*ᵇ* ⁴But now what can I do for you? For I am a widow and forsaken. Go, my children, and ask for mercy from the Lord.' ⁵Now I call upon you, father, as a witness in addition to the mother of the children, because they would not keep my covenant, ⁶so that you may bring confusion on them and bring their mother to ruin, so that they may have no offspring. ⁷Let them be scattered among the nations; let their names be blotted out from the earth, because they have despised my covenant.

2.1–7: Israel reproached by mother and father. 2–4: *The mother who bore them* is Jerusalem, elsewhere personified as a mother bereft of her children (compare 10.41–49 and Bar 4.8–16). **5–6:** God's addressing Ezra as *father* here and in 1.38 does not have a precedent in the Hebrew prophets.* God seems to be asking Ezra to act out the punitive side of God's relationship with Israel and Jerusalem, in contrast to the nurturing side presented in 1.28–30.

8 "Woe to you, Assyria, who conceal the unrighteous within you! O wicked nation, remember what I did to Sodom and Gomorrah, ⁹whose land lies in lumps of pitch and heaps of ashes.*ᶜ* That is what I will do to those who have not listened to me, says the Lord Almighty."

2.8–9: Woe to Assyria. *Assyria* is likely a code name for Rome, but the meaning and relevance of this oracle* are obscure. It may be that the author sees Roman policies toward Jews *(the unrighteous)* as being more tolerant than those toward Christians. *Sodom and Gomorrah:* See Gen 19.24–28.

10 Thus says the Lord to Ezra: "Tell my people that I will give them the kingdom of Jerusalem, which I was going to give to Israel. ¹¹Moreover, I will take back to myself their glory, and will give to these others the everlasting habitations, which I had prepared for Israel.*ᵈ* ¹²The tree of life shall give them fragrant perfume, and they shall neither toil nor become weary. ¹³Go*ᵉ* and you will receive; pray that your days may be few, that they may be shortened. The kingdom is already prepared for you; be on the watch! ¹⁴Call, O call heaven and earth to witness: I set aside evil and created good; for I am the Living One, says the Lord.

15 "Mother, embrace your children; bring them up with gladness, as does a dove; strengthen their feet, because I have chosen you, says the Lord. ¹⁶And I will raise up the dead from their places, and bring them out from their tombs, because I recognize my name in them. ¹⁷Do not fear, mother of children, for I have chosen you, says the Lord. ¹⁸I will send you help, my servants Isaiah and Jeremiah. According to their counsel I have consecrated and prepared for you twelve trees loaded with various fruits, ¹⁹and the same number of springs flowing with milk and honey, and seven mighty mountains on which roses and lilies grow; by these I will fill your children with joy.

20 "Guard the rights of the widow, secure justice for the ward, give to the needy, defend the orphan, clothe the naked, ²¹care for the injured and the weak, do not ridicule the lame, protect the maimed, and let the blind have a vision of my splendor. ²²Protect the old and the young within your walls. ²³When

a Other ancient authorities read *They begat for themselves a mother who* *b* Other ancient authorities read *in his sight* *c* Other ancient authorities read *Gomorrah, whose land descends to hell* *d* Lat for those *e* Other ancient authorities read *Seek* you find any who are dead, commit them to the grave and mark it,[a] and I will give you the first place in my resurrection. 24Pause and be quiet, my people, because your rest will come.

25 "Good nurse, nourish your children; strengthen their feet. 26Not one of the servants[b] whom I have given you will perish, for I will require them from among your number. 27Do not be anxious, for when the day of tribulation and anguish comes, others shall weep and be sorrowful, but you shall rejoice and have abundance. 28The nations shall envy you, but they shall not be able to do anything against you, says the Lord. 29My power will protect[c] you, so that your children may not see hell.[d]

30 "Rejoice, O mother, with your children, because I will deliver you, says the Lord. 31Remember your children that sleep, because I will bring them out of the hiding places of the earth, and will show mercy to them; for I am merciful, says the Lord Almighty. 32Embrace your children until I come, and proclaim mercy to them; because my springs run over, and my grace will not fail."

33 I, Ezra, received a command from the Lord on Mount Horeb to go to Israel. When I came to them they rejected me and refused the Lord's commandment. 34Therefore I say to you, O nations that hear and understand, "Wait for your shepherd; he will give you everlasting rest, because he who will come at the end of the age is close at hand. 35Be ready for the rewards of the kingdom, because perpetual light will shine on you forevermore. 36Flee from the shadow of this age, receive the joy of your glory; I publicly call on my savior to witness.[e] 37Receive what the Lord has entrusted to you and be joyful, giving thanks to him who has called you to the celestial kingdoms. 38Rise, stand erect and see the number of those who have been sealed at the feast of the Lord. 39Those who have departed from the shadow of this age have received glorious garments from the Lord. 40Take again your full number, O Zion, and close the list of your people who are clothed in white, who have fulfilled the law of the Lord. 41The number of your children, whom you desired, is now complete; implore the Lord's authority that your people, who have been called from the beginning, may be made holy."

2.10–32: Encouragement for the church. 10: For the remainder of 5 Ezra, *my people* refers to the Christians, and the focus shifts from Israel's past to the present life and future redemption of the church. Although the phrase *the kingdom of Jerusalem* is not found elsewhere, the idea that the Kingdom of God to be established at the end of time will resemble Jerusalem is widespread in both Jewish and Christian literature (compare Rev 21.2). **12:** Another feature common to Jewish and Christian descriptions of the world to come is access to *the tree of life* (compare 8.52; Rev 22.2), which was denied to Adam and Eve after the Fall (Gen 3.24). **15–16:** *Mother* now refers to the church, rather than to the earthly Jerusalem. **17–19:** It is unclear whether the *12 trees, 12 springs,* and *7 mountains* are symbols for present aids to the church (like the prophecies of Isaiah and Jeremiah) or features of the heavenly kingdom. **20–24:** The church is charged to look after its most vulnerable members, including the *dead*. **25–32:** God will have *mercy* on all Christians, living and dead, on the day of judgment (compare 1 Thess 4.13–18).

2.33–41: Ezra's exhortation* to the church. 33: *On Mount Horeb:* The attempt to connect Ezra to Moses, who received his call on Mount Horeb (Ex 3.1), is also found in ch. 14, where the people of Israel apparently do accept Ezra's authority. **34:** Here, Ezra prophesies to the Christians, those who *hear and understand,* concerning the imminent return of their *shepherd,* Jesus. **38–40:** The idea that a predetermined number of righteous people must die before the coming of the Kingdom is found in both Jewish and Christian apocalypses* (compare 4.35–37; Rev 6.9–11). The righteous are also *sealed* and *clothed in white* in Rev 7.4, 9. **41:** *The number . . . is now complete:* Other ancient authorities read "Since formerly you desired your children to come, complete their number." Depending on which reading is original, the author is either emphasizing that the end of the world is immi-

a Or *seal it;* or *mark them and commit them to the grave*
b Or *slaves*   c Lat *hands will cover*   d Lat *Gehenna*
e Other ancient authorities read *I testify that my savior has been commissioned by the Lord*

nent or encouraging the church to accept martyr-dom* as the way to hasten it.

42 I, Ezra, saw on Mount Zion a great multitude that I could not number, and they all were praising the Lord with songs. 43 In their midst was a young man of great stature, taller than any of the others, and on the head of each of them he placed a crown, but he was more exalted than they. And I was held spellbound. 44 Then I asked an angel, "Who are these, my lord?" 45 He answered and said to me, "These are they who have put off mortal clothing and have put on the immortal, and have confessed the name of God. Now they are being crowned, and receive palms." 46 Then I said to the angel, "Who is that young man who is placing crowns on them and putting palms in their hands?" 47 He answered and said to me, "He is the Son of God, whom they confessed in the world." So I began to praise those who had stood valiantly for the name of the Lord.ᵃ 48 Then the angel said to me, "Go, tell my people how great and how many are the wonders of the Lord God that you have seen."

2.42–48: Ezra's vision. 42: *Mount Zion* is the hill in Jerusalem on which the Temple* stood; in v. 40, however, it refers to the church. **43:** *A young man of great stature:* Jesus is described as being exceptionally tall in a Christian apocalypse* of the second century, *The Shepherd of Hermas** (IX.6.1). **44:** The presence of an *angel* acting as an interpreter confirms that this section of 5 Ezra is a brief apocalypse.* **45–47:** *Crowns* and *palms* were symbols of victory that came to be associated with Christian martyrdom*; compare Rev 2.10. **48:** In contrast to 1.5, Ezra is commissioned at the end of 5 Ezra to convey good news to God's people. Compare the whole vision to Rev 7.9–17.

3 In the thirtieth year after the destruction of the city, I was in Babylon—I, Salathiel, who am also called Ezra. I was troubled as I lay on my bed, and my thoughts welled up in my heart, 2 because I saw the desolation of Zion and the wealth of those who lived in Babylon. 3 My spirit was greatly agitated, and I began to speak anxious words to the Most High, and said, 4 "O sovereign

Lord, did you not speak at the beginning when you plantedᵇ the earth—and that without help—and commanded the dustᶜ 5 and it gave you Adam, a lifeless body? Yet he was the creation of your hands, and you breathed into him the breath of life, and he was made alive in your presence. 6 And you led him into the garden that your right hand had planted before the earth appeared. 7 And you laid upon him one commandment of yours; but he transgressed it, and immediately you appointed death for him and for his descendants. From him there sprang nations and tribes, peoples and clans without number. 8 And every nation walked after its own will; they did ungodly things in your sight and rejected your commands, and you did not hinder them. 9 But again, in its time you brought the flood upon the inhabitants of the world and destroyed them. 10 And the same fate befell all of them: just as death came upon Adam, so the flood upon them. 11 But you left one of them, Noah with his household, and all the righteous who have descended from him.

3.1–3: Setting. 1: *In the thirtieth year:* Compare Ezek 1.1. Fourth Ezra claims to have been written, like Ezekiel, during the Babylonian Exile*; that is, 30 years after the destruction of the First Temple* (587/6 BCE), rather than after that of the Second Temple (70 CE). *I, Salathiel:* Salathiel is the Greek form of Hebrew Shealtiel, a minor biblical figure (Ezra 3.2; Neh 12.1) who fits the fictional date better than Ezra, who lived about a century later. The name Salathiel is not used in the rest of the book, however, and it is clear from ch. 14 that the narrator is meant to be the scribe* Ezra.

12 "When those who lived on earth began to multiply, they produced children and peoples and many nations, and again they began to be more ungodly than were their ancestors. 13 And when they were committing iniquity in your sight, you chose for yourself one of them, whose name was Abraham; 14 you loved him, and to him alone you re-

a Other ancient authorities read *to praise and glorify the Lord*   b Other ancient authorities read *formed*   c Syr Ethiop: Lat *people* or *world* vealed the end of the times, secretly by night. [15]You made an everlasting covenant with him, and promised him that you would never forsake his descendants; and you gave him Isaac, and to Isaac you gave Jacob and Esau. [16]You set apart Jacob for yourself, but Esau you rejected; and Jacob became a great multitude. [17]And when you led his descendants out of Egypt, you brought them to Mount Sinai. [18]You bent down the heavens and shook[a] the earth, and moved the world, and caused the depths to tremble, and troubled the times. [19]Your glory passed through the four gates of fire and earthquake and wind and ice, to give the law to the descendants of Jacob, and your commandment to the posterity of Israel.

[20] "Yet you did not take away their evil heart from them, so that your law might produce fruit in them. [21]For the first Adam, burdened with an evil heart, transgressed and was overcome, as were also all who were descended from him. [22]Thus the disease became permanent; the law was in the hearts of the people along with the evil root; but what was good departed, and the evil remained. [23]So the times passed and the years were completed, and you raised up for yourself a servant, named David. [24]You commanded him to build a city for your name, and there to offer you oblations from what is yours. [25]This was done for many years; but the inhabitants of the city transgressed, [26]in everything doing just as Adam and all his descendants had done, for they also had the evil heart. [27]So you handed over your city to your enemies.

[28] "Then I said in my heart, Are the deeds of those who inhabit Babylon any better? Is that why it has gained dominion over Zion? [29]For when I came here I saw ungodly deeds without number, and my soul has seen many sinners during these thirty years.[b] And my heart failed me, [30]because I have seen how you endure those who sin, and have spared those who act wickedly, and have destroyed your people, and protected your enemies, [31]and have not shown to anyone how your way may be comprehended.[c] Are the deeds of Babylon better than those of Zion? [32]Or has another nation known you besides Israel? Or what tribes have so believed the covenants as these tribes of Jacob? [33]Yet their reward has not appeared and their labor has borne no fruit. For I have traveled widely among the nations and have seen that they abound in wealth, though they are unmindful of your commandments. [34]Now therefore weigh in a balance our iniquities and those of the inhabitants of the world; and it will be found which way the turn of the scale will incline. [35]When have the inhabitants of the earth not sinned in your sight? Or what nation has kept your commandments so well? [36]You may indeed find individuals who have kept your commandments, but nations you will not find."

3.4–36: Ezra laments* the destruction of Jerusalem. Ezra begins his complaint against God with a summary of biblical history. Such summaries typically blame Israel for the destruction that has come upon them (for example, Ps 106; Neh 9; and also 1.4–23, above), but here Ezra draws a different conclusion. **4–11:** The stories of Gen 1–9 exemplify humanity's inherent sinfulness. **12:** Genesis 10–11 deal with the division of humanity into *many nations.* **13–16:** Beginning with *Abraham* in Gen 12, God chooses one nation and makes a *covenant** with them. *You revealed the end of the times:* The author believes (perhaps based on Gen 15.12–16) that Abraham received secret revelations similar to those Ezra will receive as the book progresses. **18–19:** The reactions of the natural world to the theophany* at Sinai are signs both of God's universal power and of the significance of the law for Israel. **20–22:** Although the law was intended to benefit the people of Israel, they were unable to keep it, because of the *evil heart* (inclination to sin) inherited from *Adam.* Ezra's view that the law is incompatible with the inherent sinfulness of humanity (compare Rom 5.12–13) is the core of his complaint against God. **23–27:** The immediate cause of Ezra's mourning is the destruction of Jerusalem, the city of David. **28–31:** The author expects his audience to identify *Babylon* with the Roman Empire; he is really asking how God, the ruler of the world, can allow the Romans to dominate the Jewish people. **32–36:** Ezra does not deny that Israel has sinned, but he questions God's justice in hold-

---

a Syr Ethiop Arab 1 Georg: Lat *set fast*   b Ethiop Arab 1 Arm: Lat Syr *in this thirtieth year*   c Syr; compare Ethiop: Lat *how this way should be forsaken* ing them to a higher standard than other peoples, since they share the burden of the "evil heart."

4 Then the angel that had been sent to me, whose name was Uriel, answered ²and said to me, "Your understanding has utterly failed regarding this world, and do you think you can comprehend the way of the Most High?" ³Then I said, "Yes, my lord." And he replied to me, "I have been sent to show you three ways, and to put before you three problems. ⁴If you can solve one of them for me, then I will show you the way you desire to see, and will teach you why the heart is evil."

5 I said, "Speak, my lord."

And he said to me, "Go, weigh for me the weight of fire, or measure for me a blast ª of wind, or call back for me the day that is past."

6 I answered and said, "Who of those that have been born can do that, that you should ask me about such things?"

7 And he said to me, "If I had asked you, 'How many dwellings are in the heart of the sea, or how many streams are at the source of the deep, or how many streams are above the firmament, or which are the exits of Hades, or which are the entrances ᵇ of paradise?' ⁸perhaps you would have said to me, 'I never went down into the deep, nor as yet into Hades, neither did I ever ascend into heaven.' ⁹But now I have asked you only about fire and wind and the day—things that you have experienced and from which you cannot be separated, and you have given me no answer about them." ¹⁰He said to me, "You cannot understand the things with which you have grown up; ¹¹how then can your mind comprehend the way of the Most High? And how can one who is already worn out ᶜ by the corrupt world understand incorruption?" ᵈ When I heard this, I fell on my face ᵉ ¹²and said to him, "It would have been better for us not to be here than to come here and live in ungodliness, and to suffer and not understand why."

13 He answered me and said, "I went into a forest of trees of the plain, and they made a plan ¹⁴and said, 'Come, let us go and make war against the sea, so that it may re-cede before us and so that we may make for ourselves more forests.' ¹⁵In like manner the waves of the sea also made a plan and said, 'Come, let us go up and subdue the forest of the plain so that there also we may gain more territory for ourselves.' ¹⁶But the plan of the forest was in vain, for the fire came and consumed it; ¹⁷likewise also the plan of the waves of the sea was in vain, ᶠ for the sand stood firm and blocked it. ¹⁸If now you were a judge between them, which would you undertake to justify, and which to condemn?"

19 I answered and said, "Each made a foolish plan, for the land has been assigned to the forest, and the locale of the sea a place to carry its waves."

20 He answered me and said, "You have judged rightly, but why have you not judged so in your own case? ²¹For as the land has been assigned to the forest and the sea to its waves, so also those who inhabit the earth can understand only what is on the earth, and he who is ᵍ above the heavens can understand what is above the height of the heavens."

22 Then I answered and said, "I implore you, my lord, why ʰ have I been endowed with the power of understanding? ²³For I did not wish to inquire about the ways above, but about those things that we daily experience: why Israel has been given over to the Gentiles in disgrace; why the people whom you loved has been given over to godless tribes, and the law of our ancestors has been brought to destruction and the written covenants no longer exist. ²⁴We pass from the world like locusts, and our life is like a mist, ⁱ and we are not worthy to obtain mercy. ²⁵But what will he do for his ʲ name that is invoked over us? It is about these things that I have asked."

a Syr Ethiop Arab 1 Arab 2 Georg *a measure*
b Syr Compare Ethiop Arab 2 Arm: Lat lacks *of Hades, or which are the entrances*   c Meaning of Lat uncertain
d Syr Ethiop *the way of the incorruptible?*   e Syr Ethiop Arab 1: Meaning of Lat uncertain   f Lat lacks *was in vain*   g Or *those who are*   h Syr Ethiop Arm: Meaning of Lat uncertain   i Syr Ethiop Arab Georg: Lat *a trembling*   j Ethiop adds *holy*

4.1–25: The limits of human knowledge. The angel *Uriel,* appearing suddenly, does not answer Ezra's questions, but rebukes him for presuming to understand the divine plan. **3–6:** He makes impossible requests to impress upon Ezra the limitations of humanity. **7:** Compare Job 38.16–18. **11:** The angel draws a firm line between the scope of human knowledge (*the corrupt world*) and the divine realm (*incorruption*). **13–21:** The parable* illustrates the folly of overreaching one's limits. **22–25:** Ezra does not dispute that there are things he cannot hope to understand, but he refuses to accept that the reason for his people's suffering is one of those things.

26 He answered me and said, "If you are alive, you will see, and if you live long,ᵃ you will often marvel, because the age is hurrying swiftly to its end. ²⁷It will not be able to bring the things that have been promised to the righteous in their appointed times, because this age is full of sadness and infirmities. ²⁸For the evil about whichᵇ you ask me has been sown, but the harvest of it has not yet come. ²⁹If therefore that which has been sown is not reaped, and if the place where the evil has been sown does not pass away, the field where the good has been sown will not come. ³⁰For a grain of evil seed was sown in Adam's heart from the beginning, and how much ungodliness it has produced until now—and will produce until the time of threshing comes! ³¹Consider now for yourself how much fruit of ungodliness a grain of evil seed has produced. ³²When heads of grain without number are sown, how great a threshing floor they will fill!"

33 Then I answered and said, "How long?ᵇ When will these things be? Why are our years few and evil?" ³⁴He answered me and said, "Do not be in a greater hurry than the Most High. You, indeed, are in a hurry for yourself,ᶜ but the Highest is in a hurry on behalf of many. ³⁵Did not the souls of the righteous in their chambers ask about these matters, saying, 'How long are we to remain here?ᵈ And when will the harvest of our reward come?' ³⁶And the archangel Jeremiel answered and said, 'When the number of those like yourselves is completed;ᵉ for he has weighed the age in the balance, ³⁷and

measured the times by measure, and numbered the times by number; and he will not move or arouse them until that measure is fulfilled.' "

38 Then I answered and said, "But, O sovereign Lord, all of us also are full of ungodliness. ³⁹It is perhaps on account of us that the time of threshing is delayed for the righteous—on account of the sins of those who inhabit the earth."

40 He answered me and said, "Go and ask a pregnant woman whether, when her nine months have been completed, her womb can keep the fetus within her any longer."

41 And I said, "No, lord, it cannot."

He said to me, "In Hades the chambers of the souls are like the womb. ⁴²For just as a woman who is in labor makes haste to escape the pangs of birth, so also do these places hasten to give back those things that were committed to them from the beginning. ⁴³Then the things that you desire to see will be disclosed to you."

44 I answered and said, "If I have found favor in your sight, and if it is possible, and if I am worthy, ⁴⁵show me this also: whether more time is to come than has passed, or whether for us the greater part has gone by. ⁴⁶For I know what has gone by, but I do not know what is to come."

47 And he said to me, "Stand at my right side, and I will show you the interpretation of a parable."

48 So I stood and looked, and lo, a flaming furnace passed by before me, and when the flame had gone by I looked, and lo, the smoke remained. ⁴⁹And after this a cloud full of water passed before me and poured down a heavy and violent rain, and when the violent rainstorm had passed, drops still remained in the cloud.ᶠ

50 He said to me, "Consider it for yourself; for just as the rain is more than the drops, and the fire is greater than the smoke,

a Syr: Lat *live*   *b* Syr Ethiop: Meaning of Lat uncertain   *c* Syr Ethiop Arab Arm: Meaning of Lat uncertain   *d* Syr Ethiop Arab 2 Georg: Lat *How long do I hope thus?*   *e* Syr Ethiop Arab 2: Lat *number of seeds is completed for you*   *f* Lat *in it* so the quantity that passed was far greater; but drops and smoke remained."

51 Then I prayed and said, "Do you think that I shall live until those days? Or who will be alive in those days?"

52 He answered me and said, "Concerning the signs about which you ask me, I can tell you in part; but I was not sent to tell you concerning your life, for I do not know.

4.26–52: The end of the age. The angel responds to Ezra's distress about Israel's present situation with a series of eschatological* predictions (concerning the end of the present age or world). The idea that there are two ages or worlds—the present one, which is coming to an end, and a future one, which will be perfect and eternal—is fundamental to this book and to apocalyptic* literature in general. **26–32:** Ezra should not expect to see the righteous rewarded in this age, which is incurably sinful and sorrowful as a result of Adam's sin. The metaphor* of sowing and harvesting is somewhat mixed: while the *time of threshing** (v. 30) evidently refers to the day of judgment, the *grain of evil seed* (v. 30) seems to refer to the "evil heart" and the *fruit of ungodliness* (v. 31) could mean either sinful deeds or sinful people. **35–37:** Many apocalypses share the belief that the *souls of the righteous* dead are stored in chambers or treasuries until the day of judgment, which will come when a predetermined number of righteous souls has been reached. Compare 2.38–41. **38–39:** Ezra assumes that no one now living is righteous, so he worries that the judgment may never come. **40–43:** The angel's response, which does not address Ezra's assumption, suggests that the time of the judgment is also predetermined. *In Hades** simply means underground; for the analogy, compare 5.48–50. **47–50:** A striking feature of Uriel's speeches is the frequent use of *parables** or analogies based on natural occurrences, in this case enhanced by a visual demonstration. **52:** Although Ezra has not asked about any *signs,* the angel may be responding to his implied question about *what is to come* (v. 46). Note that even the angel's knowledge is limited.

---

5 "Now concerning the signs: lo, the days are coming when those who inhabit the earth shall be seized with great terror,[a] and the way of truth shall be hidden, and the land shall be barren of faith. 2Unrighteousness shall be increased beyond what you yourself

see, and beyond what you heard of formerly. 3And the land that you now see ruling shall be a trackless waste, and people shall see it desolate. 4But if the Most High grants that you live, you shall see it thrown into confusion after the third period;[b]

and the sun shall suddenly begin to
    shine at night,
    and the moon during the day.
5 Blood shall drip from wood,
    and the stone shall utter its voice;
    the peoples shall be troubled,
    and the stars shall fall.[c]

6And one shall reign whom those who inhabit the earth do not expect, and the birds shall fly away together; 7and the Dead Sea[d] shall cast up fish; and one whom the many do not know shall make his voice heard by night, and all shall hear his voice.[e] 8There shall be chaos also in many places, fire shall often break out, the wild animals shall roam beyond their haunts, and menstruous women shall bring forth monsters. 9Salt waters shall be found in the sweet, and all friends shall conquer one another; then shall reason hide itself, and wisdom shall withdraw into its chamber, 10and it shall be sought by many but shall not be found, and unrighteousness and unrestraint shall increase on earth. 11One country shall ask its neighbor, 'Has righteousness, or anyone who does right, passed through you?' And it will answer, 'No.' 12At that time people shall hope but not obtain; they shall labor, but their ways shall not prosper. 13These are the signs that I am permitted to tell you, and if you pray again, and weep as you do now, and fast for seven days, you shall hear yet greater things than these."

5.1–12: The signs of the end. The idea that the approach of the end of the age will be signaled by terrible or unnatural occurrences is a common apocalyptic* motif.* Compare Mk 13.3–27. **3:** *The land that you*

---

a Syr Ethiop: Meaning of Lat uncertain   b Literally *after the third;* Ethiop *after three months;* Arm *after the third vision;* Georg *after the third day*   c Ethiop Compare Syr and Arab: Meaning of Lat uncertain   d Lat *Sea of Sodom*   e Cn: Lat *fish; and it shall make its voice heard by night, which the many have not known, but all shall hear its voice.*

now see ruling probably refers to the Roman Empire. That the author looks forward to the destruction of Rome becomes obvious in the fifth episode. **4:** *After the third period:* Although this phrase seems out of place here, the division of time into periods is another apocalyptic commonplace. **6:** The motif of an "unexpected king" (who is depicted as a violent despot in other Jewish apocalypses) appears in Dan 11.21, and may be in the background of the Christian idea of the Antichrist. **7:** There is no clear identification or parallel for the figure who *shall make his voice heard by night.* **9–10:** Wisdom, often personified, threatens in Prov 1.24–31 to withdraw from the people who have rejected her; compare Bar 3.9–19.

14 Then I woke up, and my body shuddered violently, and my soul was so troubled that it fainted. 15But the angel who had come and talked with me held me and strengthened me and set me on my feet.

16 Now on the second night Phaltiel, a chief of the people, came to me and said, "Where have you been? And why is your face sad? 17Or do you not know that Israel has been entrusted to you in the land of their exile? 18Rise therefore and eat some bread, and do not forsake us, like a shepherd who leaves the flock in the power of savage wolves."

19 Then I said to him, "Go away from me and do not come near me for seven days; then you may come to me." He heard what I said and left me. 20So I fasted seven days, mourning and weeping, as the angel Uriel had commanded me.

5.13–20: Conclusion of the first episode. Brief narrative* interludes conclude each of the seven episodes. They report on Ezra's reactions to the previous episode, establish the time interval and location for the one following, and usually include instructions by the angel relating to fasting or eating. Only this interlude and the one between the fifth and sixth episodes (12.40–50) relate conversations with fellow exiles. **16:** No person named *Phaltiel* who lived during the Exile* or in Ezra's time is known from the Bible. **17–18:** Ezra's leadership of his people in exile is the context for the revelations given to him.

21 After seven days the thoughts of my heart were very grievous to me again. 22Then my soul recovered the spirit of understanding, and I began once more to speak words in the presence of the Most High. 23I said, "O sovereign Lord, from every forest of the earth and from all its trees you have chosen one vine, 24and from all the lands of the world you have chosen for yourself one region,*a* and from all the flowers of the world you have chosen for yourself one lily, 25and from all the depths of the sea you have filled for yourself one river, and from all the cities that have been built you have consecrated Zion for yourself, 26and from all the birds that have been created you have named for yourself one dove, and from all the flocks that have been made you have provided for yourself one sheep, 27and from all the multitude of peoples you have gotten for yourself one people; and to this people, whom you have loved, you have given the law that is approved by all. 28And now, O Lord, why have you handed the one over to the many, and dishonored*b* the one root beyond the others, and scattered your only one among the many? 29And those who opposed your promises have trampled on those who believed your covenants. 30If you really hate your people, they should be punished at your own hands."

5.21–30: God's choice of Israel. Ezra's second prayer of lament* begins with a symbolic poem about Israel's status as God's chosen people, using images familiar from the prophets* and Psalms. **27:** The giving of *the law* is seen as the ultimate sign of God's love for Israel. **28–30:** Recent events, however, make Ezra wonder if God still loves Israel, or has actually come to *hate his people.*

31 When I had spoken these words, the angel who had come to me on a previous night was sent to me. 32He said to me, "Listen to me, and I will instruct you; pay attention to me, and I will tell you more."

33 Then I said, "Speak, my lord." And he said to me, "Are you greatly disturbed in mind over Israel? Or do you love him more than his Maker does?"

34 I said, "No, my lord, but because of my

a Ethiop: Lat *pit* 　 *b* Syr Ethiop Arab: Lat *prepared*

grief I have spoken; for every hour I suffer agonies of heart, while I strive to understand the way of the Most High and to search out some part of his judgment."

35 He said to me, "You cannot." And I said, "Why not, my lord? Why then was I born? Or why did not my mother's womb become my grave, so that I would not see the travail of Jacob and the exhaustion of the people of Israel?" 36 He said to me, "Count up for me those who have not yet come, and gather for me the scattered raindrops, and make the withered flowers bloom again for me; 37open for me the closed chambers, and bring out for me the winds shut up in them, or show me the picture of a voice; and then I will explain to you the travail that you ask to understand."ᵃ

38 I said, "O sovereign Lord, who is able to know these things except him whose dwelling is not with mortals? 39As for me, I am without wisdom, and how can I speak concerning the things that you have asked me?"

40 He said to me, "Just as you cannot do one of the things that were mentioned, so you cannot discover my judgment, or the goal of the love that I have promised to my people."

5.31–40: God's love is beyond human comprehension. The second dispute between Ezra and Uriel closely parallels the first (4.1–25) in form, but the angel picks up the theme of divine love from Ezra's lament* and combines it with the earlier theme of the limits of human knowledge. **35:** Once again, the impossibility of understanding God's ways drives Ezra to despair (compare 4.12). **40:** *My judgment:* Uriel often speaks for God in the first person. God's *love* for his people is directed toward a particular *goal* or end, which will be hidden from mortals until the time of the final judgment.

THE TIMING OF THE END

5.41–6.10: The second set of eschatological* predictions covers essentially the same content as 4.26–52.

---

41 I said, "Yet, O Lord, you have charge of those who are alive at the end, but what will those do who lived before me, or we, ourselves, or those who come after us?"

42 He said to me, "I shall liken my judgment to a circle;ᵇ just as for those who are last there is no slowness, so for those who are first there is no haste."

43 Then I answered and said, "Could you not have created at one time those who have been and those who are and those who will be, so that you might show your judgment the sooner?"

44 He replied to me and said, "The creation cannot move faster than the Creator, nor can the world hold at one time those who have been created in it."

45 I said, "How have you said to your servant that youᶜ will certainly give life at one time to your creation? If therefore all creatures will live at one timeᵈ and the creation will sustain them, it might even now be able to support all of them present at one time."

46 He said to me, "Ask a woman's womb, and say to it, 'If you bear tenᵉ children, why one after another?' Request it therefore to produce ten at one time."

47 I said, "Of course it cannot, but only each in its own time."

48 He said to me, "Even so I have given the womb of the earth to those who from time to time are sown in it. 49For as an infant does not bring forth, and a woman who has become old does not bring forth any longer, so I have made the same rule for the world that I created."

5.41–49. 41: Ezra mistakenly assumes that only *those who are alive at the end* will be judged. **42:** The angel's cryptic response indicates that chronological order has no bearing on the *judgment:* All who ever lived will be judged simultaneously. **46–49:** The analogy between *a mother's womb* and the *earth* (compare 4.40–43) illustrates that creation is an ongoing process that cannot be rushed.

---

50 Then I inquired and said, "Since you have now given me the opportunity, let me speak before you. Is our mother, of whom

---

ᵃ Lat *see*　ᵇ Or *crown*　ᶜ Syr Ethiop Arab 1:
Meaning of Lat uncertain　ᵈ Lat lacks *If . . . one time*
ᵉ Syr Ethiop Arab 2 Arm: Meaning of Lat uncertain

you have told me, still young? Or is she now approaching old age?"

51 He replied to me, "Ask a woman who bears children, and she will tell you. 52 Say to her, 'Why are those whom you have borne recently not like those whom you bore before, but smaller in stature?' 53 And she herself will answer you, 'Those born in the strength of youth are different from those born during the time of old age, when the womb is failing.' 54 Therefore you also should consider that you and your contemporaries are smaller in stature than those who were before you, 55 and those who come after you will be smaller than you, as born of a creation that already is aging and passing the strength of youth."

56 I said, "I implore you, O Lord, if I have found favor in your sight, show your servant through whom you will visit your creation."

6 He said to me, "At the beginning of the circle of the earth, before*a* the portals of the world were in place, and before the assembled winds blew, 2 and before the rumblings of thunder sounded, and before the flashes of lightning shone, and before the foundations of paradise were laid, 3 and before the beautiful flowers were seen, and before the powers of movements*b* were established, and before the innumerable hosts of angels were gathered together, 4 and before the heights of the air were lifted up, and before the measures of the firmaments were named, and before the footstool of Zion was established, 5 and before the present years were reckoned and before the imaginations of those who now sin were estranged, and before those who stored up treasures of faith were sealed— 6 then I planned these things, and they were made through me alone and not through another; just as the end shall come through me alone and not through another."

7 I answered and said, "What will be the dividing of the times? Or when will be the end of the first age and the beginning of the age that follows?"

8 He said to me, "From Abraham to Isaac,*c* because from him were born Jacob and Esau, for Jacob's hand held Esau's heel from the beginning. 9 Now Esau is the end of this age, and Jacob is the beginning of the age that follows. 10 The beginning of a person is the hand, and the end of a person is the heel;*d* seek for nothing else, Ezra, between the heel and the hand, Ezra!"

5.50–6.10. 50–55: It was a popular belief in the ancient world that the people of earlier generations had been bigger and better than those of recent ones. The idea that the successive children of one mother decline in size, however, has no known parallel and no scientific support. **5.56–6.6:** Ezra's question about who will execute the judgment on creation evokes a poetic response by the angel to the effect that God alone is the creator and judge of the world. Compare Prov 8.22–31. **8–10:** The symbolic language of this prediction alludes to an eschatological* interpretation* of Gen 25.26 in which *Esau* is identified with the Roman Empire and *Jacob* with the messianic kingdom of Israel. In other words, the end of this age will coincide with the fall of Rome and the beginning of the new age with the immediate appearance of the messiah.* This timing conflicts somewhat with eschatological scenarios elsewhere in the book (7.26–33, 113; 12.31–34), in which the messianic kingdom is the last stage of the present age and the day of judgment ushers in the new age.

11 I answered and said, "O sovereign Lord, if I have found favor in your sight, 12 show your servant the last of your signs of which you showed me a part on a previous night."

13 He answered and said to me, "Rise to your feet and you will hear a full, resounding voice. 14 And if the place where you are standing is greatly shaken 15 while the voice is speaking, do not be terrified; because the word concerns the end, and the foundations of the earth will understand 16 that the speech concerns them. They will tremble and be shaken, for they know that their end must be changed."

17 When I heard this, I got to my feet and

a Meaning of Lat uncertain: Compare Syr *The beginning by the hand of humankind, but the end by my own hands. For as before the land of the world existed there, and before;* Ethiop: *At first by the Son of Man, and afterwards I myself. For before the earth and the lands were created, and before*   *b* Or *earthquakes*   *c* Other ancient authorities read *to Abraham*   *d* Syr: Meaning of Lat uncertain listened; a voice was speaking, and its sound was like the sound of mighty*a* waters. 18It said, "The days are coming when I draw near to visit the inhabitants of the earth, 19and when I require from the doers of iniquity the penalty of their iniquity, and when the humiliation of Zion is complete. 20When the seal is placed upon the age that is about to pass away, then I will show these signs: the books shall be opened before the face of the firmament, and all shall see my judgment*b* together. 21Children a year old shall speak with their voices, and pregnant women shall give birth to premature children at three and four months, and these shall live and leap about. 22Sown places shall suddenly appear unsown, and full storehouses shall suddenly be found to be empty; 23the trumpet shall sound aloud, and when all hear it, they shall suddenly be terrified. 24At that time friends shall make war on friends like enemies, the earth and those who inhabit it shall be terrified, and the springs of the fountains shall stand still, so that for three hours they shall not flow.

25 "It shall be that whoever remains after all that I have foretold to you shall be saved and shall see my salvation and the end of my world. 26And they shall see those who were taken up, who from their birth have not tasted death; and the heart of the earth's*c* inhabitants shall be changed and converted to a different spirit. 27For evil shall be blotted out, and deceit shall be quenched; 28faithfulness shall flourish, and corruption shall be overcome, and the truth, which has been so long without fruit, shall be revealed."

6.11–28: A voice from heaven foretells the end. In response to Ezra's request for further signs of the end (a continuation of those given in 5.1–12), the angel prepares him to hear God's own voice. 14–16: In the Bible, the *shaking of the earth* accompanies theophanies* and is often a sign of God's anger; see Ps 18.7; Nah 1.5. 17:. *Like the sound of mighty waters:* Compare Ezek 43.2. 20: *When the seal is placed:* A seal, placed either on a scroll or a container, signifies completion. *The books shall be opened:* The idea that everyone's deeds are recorded in heavenly books that will be opened on the day of judgment is common to many apocalypses*; compare Dan 7.10; Rev 20.12.

21–24: These "signs," even more than those in 5.1–12, signify a reversal of the natural order at the time of the judgment. 25: *Whoever remains:* It becomes clear later in the book (9.7–12) that only the righteous will survive the "signs," which will bring about the destruction of sinners. 26: *Those who were taken up:* Enoch* (Gen 5.24) and Elijah (2 Kings 2.11), according to traditional interpretation,* were taken up into heaven alive and thus never died, and Ezra is promised the same end in 14.9.

29 While he spoke to me, little by little the place where I was standing began to rock to and fro.*d* 30And he said to me, "I have come to show you these things this night.*e* 31If therefore you will pray again and fast again for seven days, I will again declare to you greater things than these,*f* 32because your voice has surely been heard by the Most High; for the Mighty One has seen your uprightness and has also observed the purity that you have maintained from your youth. 33Therefore he sent me to show you all these things, and to say to you: 'Believe and do not be afraid! 34Do not be quick to think vain thoughts concerning the former times; then you will not act hastily in the last times.'"

35 Now after this I wept again and fasted seven days in the same way as before, in order to complete the three weeks that had been prescribed for me. 36Then on the eighth night my heart was troubled within me again, and I began to speak in the presence of the Most High. 37My spirit was greatly aroused, and my soul was in distress.

6.29–35: Conclusion of the second episode. 31–34: This is the first of several assurances by Uriel that God considers Ezra a righteous person. 35: *Three weeks:* Compare Dan 10. 2–3; this is the first indication that Ezra had already *fasted* for a week before the beginning of the first episode.

38 I said, "O Lord, you spoke at the beginning of creation, and said on the first day, 'Let heaven and earth be made,' and your

a Lat *many*   *b* Syr: Lat lacks *my judgment*   *c* Syr Compare Ethiop Arab 1 Arm: Lat lacks *earth's*   *d* Syr Ethiop Compare Arab Arm: Meaning of Lat uncertain   *e* Syr Compare Ethiop: Meaning of Lat uncertain   *f* Syr Ethiop Arab 1 Arm: Lat adds *by day* word accomplished the work. ³⁹Then the spirit was blowing, and darkness and silence embraced everything; the sound of human voices was not yet there.ª ⁴⁰Then you commanded a ray of light to be brought out from your store-chambers, so that your works could be seen.

41 "Again, on the second day, you created the spirit of the firmament, and commanded it to divide and separate the waters, so that one part might move upward and the other part remain beneath. ⁴²"On the third day you commanded the waters to be gathered together in a seventh part of the earth; six parts you dried up and kept so that some of them might be planted and cultivated and be of service before you. ⁴³For your word went forth, and at once the work was done. ⁴⁴Immediately fruit came forth in endless abundance and of varied appeal to the taste, and flowers of inimitable color, and odors of inexpressible fragrance. These were made on the third day.

45 "On the fourth day you commanded the brightness of the sun, the light of the moon, and the arrangement of the stars to come into being; ⁴⁶and you commanded them to serve humankind, about to be formed.

47 "On the fifth day you commanded the seventh part, where the water had been gathered together, to bring forth living creatures, birds, and fishes; and so it was done. ⁴⁸The dumb and lifeless water produced living creatures, as it was commanded, so that therefore the nations might declare your wondrous works.

49 "Then you kept in existence two living creatures;ᵇ the one you called Behemothᶜ and the name of the other Leviathan. ⁵⁰And you separated one from the other, for the seventh part where the water had been gathered together could not hold them both. ⁵¹And you gave Behemothᶜ one of the parts that had been dried up on the third day, to live in it, where there are a thousand mountains; ⁵²but to Leviathan you gave the seventh part, the watery part; and you have kept them to be eaten by whom you wish, and when you wish.

53 "On the sixth day you commanded the earth to bring forth before you cattle, wild animals, and creeping things; ⁵⁴and over these you placed Adam, as ruler over all the works that you had made; and from him we have all come, the people whom you have chosen.

55 "All this I have spoken before you, O Lord, because you have said that it was for us that you created this world.ᵈ ⁵⁶As for the other nations that have descended from Adam, you have said that they are nothing, and that they are like spittle, and you have compared their abundance to a drop from a bucket. ⁵⁷And now, O Lord, these nations, which are reputed to be as nothing, domineer over us and devour us. ⁵⁸But we your people, whom you have called your firstborn, only begotten, zealous for you,ᵉ and most dear, have been given into their hands. ⁵⁹If the world has indeed been created for us, why do we not possess our world as an inheritance? How long will this be so?"

6.36–59: Creation for the sake of Israel. Like the first two dialogues, the third begins with a prayer that seems to praise God at first, but ends with a complaint about the fate of Israel. Ezra's first prayer began with the creation of Adam (like Gen 2), but here he follows the creation account of Gen 1. **46:** Ezra emphasizes that all of creation was for the sake of *humankind,* a notion already implied in Gen 1. **49–52:** This passage elaborates on the reference to "the great sea monsters" in Gen 1.21. Traditions about Leviathan* and other sea monsters are scattered throughout the Bible (for example, Ps 74.14; Isa 27.1). A post-biblical tradition held that Leviathan and Behemoth* would be devoured by the righteous in a great banquet at the end of the age. **54:** Here *Adam* is presented as the ancestor of Israel, whereas Ezra's first prayer emphasizes that Adam was the father of all humanity. **55:** The notion that creation was for Israel's sake is not found in the Bible. **56:** On the other hand, the belief that *other nations* are relatively unimportant to God is biblical. Ezra is quoting from the Septuagint* version of Isa 40.15, which ends ". . . and they shall be counted as spittle." **57–59:** Ezra's initial question is still unan-

a Syr Ethiop: Lat *was not yet from you*   b Syr Ethiop: Lat *two souls*   c Other Lat authorities read *Enoch*
d Syr Ethiop Arab 2: Lat *the firstborn world* Compare Arab 1 *first world*   e Meaning of Lat uncertain

swered: Why has God allowed other nations to defeat and dispossess his chosen people?

7 When I had finished speaking these words, the angel who had been sent to me on the former nights was sent to me again. ²He said to me, "Rise, Ezra, and listen to the words that I have come to speak to you."

3 I said, "Speak, my lord." And he said to me, "There is a sea set in a wide expanse so that it is deep and vast, ⁴but it has an entrance set in a narrow place, so that it is like a river. ⁵If there are those who wish to reach the sea, to look at it or to navigate it, how can they come to the broad part unless they pass through the narrow part? ⁶Another example: There is a city built and set on a plain, and it is full of all good things; ⁷but the entrance to it is narrow and set in a precipitous place, so that there is fire on the right hand and deep water on the left. ⁸There is only one path lying between them, that is, between the fire and the water, so that only one person can walk on the path. ⁹If now the city is given to someone as an inheritance, how will the heir receive the inheritance unless by passing through the appointed danger?"

10 I said, "That is right, lord." He said to me, "So also is Israel's portion. ¹¹For I made the world for their sake, and when Adam transgressed my statutes, what had been made was judged. ¹²And so the entrances of this world were made narrow and sorrowful and toilsome; they are few and evil, full of dangers and involved in great hardships. ¹³But the entrances of the greater world are broad and safe, and yield the fruit of immortality. ¹⁴Therefore unless the living pass through the difficult and futile experiences, they can never receive those things that have been reserved for them. ¹⁵Now therefore why are you disturbed, seeing that you are to perish? Why are you moved, seeing that you are mortal? ¹⁶Why have you not considered in your mind what is to come, rather than what is now present?"

17 Then I answered and said, "O sovereign Lord, you have ordained in your law that the righteous shall inherit these things, but that the ungodly shall per-

ish. ¹⁸The righteous, therefore, can endure difficult circumstances while hoping for easier ones; but those who have done wickedly have suffered the difficult circumstances and will never see the easier ones."

19 He said to me, "You are not a better judge than the Lord,ᵃ or wiser than the Most High! ²⁰Let many perish who are now living, rather than that the law of God that is set before them be disregarded! ²¹For the Lordᵇ strictly commanded those who came into the world, when they came, what they should do to live, and what they should observe to avoid punishment. ²²Nevertheless they were not obedient, and spoke against him;

they devised for themselves vain
        thoughts,
23   and proposed to themselves wicked
        frauds;
    they even declared that the Most High
        does not exist,
    and they ignored his ways.
24 They scorned his law,
        and denied his covenants;
    they have been unfaithful to his
        statutes,
    and have not performed his works.

²⁵That is the reason, Ezra, that empty things are for the empty, and full things are for the full.

7.1–25: This world of trials. 3–9: The two parables* suggest that this world presents many obstacles to reaching the world to come. **11–12:** The angel seems to confirm Ezra's belief that this *world* was *made* for Israel, but he reminds him that it is inevitably a miserable place, as a result of *Adam's sin.* **14:** By his use of *the living,* Uriel extends the scope of the discussion from Israel to humanity in general. **15–16:** He urges Ezra to set his sights on the next world, which is the only inheritance worth possessing (compare 6.59). **17–18:** The angel has succeeded in shifting the terms of the discussion from Israel vs. other nations to *righteous* vs. sinners. For most of the third dialogue, Ezra pleads the cause of sinful humanity, only occasionally recalling his particular concern for Israel. **20:** This is the first and clearest statement of the rather harsh position that Uriel maintains throughout the third dialogue. **21:**

a Other ancient authorities read *God;* Ethiop Georg *the only One*   *b* Other ancient authorities read *God*

Those who came into the world: Uriel maintains that God's law is binding on all humanity; compare Sir 15.17–20. **25:** Uriel rephrases his point—that people will get exactly what they deserve—in the form of a proverb.

26 "For indeed the time will come, when the signs that I have foretold to you will come to pass, that the city that now is not seen shall appear,[a] and the land that now is hidden shall be disclosed. 27 Everyone who has been delivered from the evils that I have foretold shall see my wonders. 28 For my son the Messiah[b] shall be revealed with those who are with him, and those who remain shall rejoice four hundred years. 29 After those years my son the Messiah shall die, and all who draw human breath.[c] 30 Then the world shall be turned back to primeval silence for seven days, as it was at the first beginnings, so that no one shall be left. 31 After seven days the world that is not yet awake shall be roused, and that which is corruptible shall perish. 32 The earth shall give up those who are asleep in it, and the dust those who rest there in silence; and the chambers shall give up the souls that have been committed to them. 33 The Most High shall be revealed on the seat of judgment, and compassion shall pass away, and patience shall be withdrawn.[d] 34 Only judgment shall remain, truth shall stand, and faithfulness shall grow strong. 35 Recompense shall follow, and the reward shall be manifested; righteous deeds shall awake, and unrighteous deeds shall not sleep.[e] 36 The pit[f] of torment shall appear, and opposite it shall be the place of rest; and the furnace of hell[g] shall be disclosed, and opposite it the paradise of delight. 37 Then the Most High will say to the nations that have been raised from the dead, 'Look now, and understand whom you have denied, whom you have not served, whose commandments you have despised. 38 Look on this side and on that; here are delight and rest, and there are fire and torments.' Thus he will[h] speak to them on the day of judgment— 39 a day that has no sun or moon or stars, 40 or cloud or thunder or lightning, or wind or water or air, or darkness or evening or morning, 41 or summer or spring or heat

or winter[i] or frost or cold, or hail or rain or dew, 42 or noon or night, or dawn or shining or brightness or light, but only the splendor of the glory of the Most High, by which all shall see what has been destined. 43 It will last as though for a week of years. 44 This is my judgment and its prescribed order; and to you alone I have shown these things."

7.26–44: The day of judgment. This predictive section provides the most complete account of the eschatological* events in the book, but its primary focus is the judgment. **26:** *The city that now is not seen:* The author believes in a heavenly Jerusalem that will appear on earth when the messiah* comes; see 10.27, 50–54 and 13.36, and compare Rev 21.2. **27:** See 6.25. **28:** *My son the Messiah:* Although the words "my son" are lacking from some versions, they are used of the messiah in ch. 13 (but see comment on 13.32). A much more active role is assigned to the messiah in chs. 11–13. *Those who are with him:* Also mentioned in 13.52, these may be the same people as "those who were taken up" in 6.26 (see 14.9 for the connection). **29:** Elsewhere in the book it is implied that the messianic kingdom will come to an end, but this is the only explicit mention of the death of the messiah in this or any other Jewish apocalypse.* **30–31:** *Primeval silence:* See 6.39. It will take seven days to complete the destruction of this world, as long as it took to create it. **32:** *The chambers:* see comment on 4.35–37. *The souls* will rejoin their resurrected bodies prior to the judgment. **36:** See comment on 7.102–105. **37:** Again, Uriel implies that people of all nations will be held accountable for failing to believe in and obey God. **43:** *A week of years:* The judgment "day" will take seven years—another parallel to the seven days of creation. Apocalypses often reckon time in "weeks" of years; see Dan 9.24.

45 I answered and said, "O sovereign Lord, I said then and[j] I say now: Blessed are those who are alive and keep your com-

---

[a] Arm: Lat Syr *that the bride shall appear, even the city appearing*   [b] Syr Arab 1: Ethiop *my Messiah*; Arab 2 *the Messiah*; Arm *the Messiah of God*; Lat *my son Jesus*   [c] Arm *all who have continued in faith and in patience*   [d] Lat *shall gather together*   [e] The passage from verse 36 to verse 105, formerly missing, has been restored to the text   [f] Syr Ethiop: Lat *place*   [g] Lat Syr Ethiop *Gehenna*   [h] Syr Ethiop Arab 1: Lat *you shall*   [i] Or *storm*   [j] Syr: Lat *And I answered, "I said then, O Lord, and*

mandments! 46 But what of those for whom I prayed? For who among the living is there that has not sinned, or who is there among mortals that has not transgressed your covenant? 47 And now I see that the world to come will bring delight to few, but torments to many. 48 For an evil heart has grown up in us, which has alienated us from God,ᵃ and has brought us into corruption and the ways of death, and has shown us the paths of perdition and removed us far from life— and that not merely for a few but for almost all who have been created."

49 He answered me and said, "Listen to me, Ezra,ᵇ and I will instruct you, and will admonish you once more. 50 For this reason the Most High has made not one world but two. 51 Inasmuch as you have said that the righteous are not many but few, while the ungodly abound, hear the explanation for this.

52 "If you have just a few precious stones, will you add to them lead and clay?"ᶜ 53 I said, "Lord, how could that be?" 54 And he said to me, "Not only that, but ask the earth and she will tell you; defer to her, and she will declare it to you. 55 Say to her, 'You produce gold and silver and bronze, and also iron and lead and clay; 56 but silver is more abundant than gold, and bronze than silver, and iron than bronze, and lead than iron, and clay than lead.' 57 Judge therefore which things are precious and desirable, those that are abundant or those that are rare?"

58 I said, "O sovereign Lord, what is plentiful is of less worth, for what is more rare is more precious."

59 He answered me and said, "Consider within yourselfᵈ what you have thought, for the person who has what is hard to get rejoices more than the person who has what is plentiful. 60 So also will be the judgmentᵉ that I have promised; for I will rejoice over the few who shall be saved, because it is they who have made my glory to prevail now, and through them my name has now been honored. 61 I will not grieve over the great number of those who perish; for it is they who are now like a mist, and are similar to a flame and smoke—they are set on fire and burn hotly, and are extinguished."

7.45–61: **The few and the many. 45–47:** Ezra resumes the protest he took up in 7.17–78: What good to the mass of humanity is the promise of a future reward for the righteous? *48:* At the root of his distress is his belief that the *evil heart,* inherited from Adam, makes obedience to the law impossible or nearly so (see 3.20–22). *50: For this reason:* Because sinners predominate in this world, God has created another world for the righteous. *52–59:* To Uriel, the probability that only a very few persons will be saved is in accord with a law of nature: Precious things are rare. *61: Mist* and *smoke* are common biblical images for the fate of the wicked; for example, Ps 37.20; Hos 13.3.

62 I replied and said, "O earth, what have you brought forth, if the mind is made out of the dust like the other created things? 63 For it would have been better if the dust itself had not been born, so that the mind might not have been made from it. 64 But now the mind grows with us, and therefore we are tormented, because we perish and we know it. 65 Let the human race lament, but let the wild animals of the field be glad; let all who have been born lament, but let the cattle and the flocks rejoice. 66 It is much better with them than with us; for they do not look for a judgment, and they do not know of any torment or salvation promised to them after death. 67 What does it profit us that we shall be preserved alive but cruelly tormented? 68 For all who have been born are entangled inᶠ iniquities, and are full of sins and burdened with transgressions. 69 And if after death we were not to come into judgment, perhaps it would have been better for us."

70 He answered me and said, "When the Most High made the world and Adam and all who have come from him, he first prepared the judgment and the things that pertain to the judgment. 71 But now, understand from your own words—for you have said that the mind grows with us. 72 For this reason, therefore, those who live on earth

a Cn: Lat Syr Ethiop *from these*   b Syr Arab 1 Georg: Lat Ethiop lack *Ezra*   c Arab 1: Meaning of Lat Syr Ethiop uncertain   d Syr Ethiop Arab 1: Meaning of Lat uncertain   e Syr Arab 1: Lat *creation*   f Syr *defiled with* shall be tormented, because though they had understanding, they committed iniquity; and though they received the commandments, they did not keep them; and though they obtained the law, they dealt unfaithfully with what they received. 73 What, then, will they have to say in the judgment, or how will they answer in the last times? 74 How long the Most High has been patient with those who inhabit the world!—and not for their sake, but because of the times that he has foreordained."

7.62–74: The burden of conscience. 62–68: The angel's impassivity about the fate of humanity drives Ezra to address the earth in despair. How can a person live with the knowledge that he faces judgment and almost certain punishment after death? **70:** Uriel reminds him that the judgment is part of the plan of creation. **72–73:** Human beings were given a mind (or conscience) to enable them to keep the commandments; if they sin, it is their own fault. **74:** God has allowed this age to continue as long as it has, not out of pity on humanity, but because it was his plan to do so.

75 I answered and said, "If I have found favor in your sight, O Lord, show this also to your servant: whether after death, as soon as everyone of us yields up the soul, we shall be kept in rest until those times come when you will renew the creation, or whether we shall be tormented at once?"

76 He answered me and said, "I will show you that also, but do not include yourself with those who have shown scorn, or number yourself among those who are tormented. 77 For you have a treasure of works stored up with the Most High, but it will not be shown to you until the last times. 78 Now concerning death, the teaching is: When the decisive decree has gone out from the Most High that a person shall die, as the spirit leaves the body to return again to him who gave it, first of all it adores the glory of the Most High. 79 If it is one of those who have shown scorn and have not kept the way of the Most High, who have despised his law and hated those who fear God— 80 such spirits shall not enter into habitations, but shall immediately wander about in torments,

always grieving and sad, in seven ways. 81 The first way, because they have scorned the law of the Most High. 82 The second way, because they cannot now make a good repentance so that they may live. 83 The third way, they shall see the reward laid up for those who have trusted the covenants of the Most High. 84 The fourth way, they shall consider the torment laid up for themselves in the last days. 85 The fifth way, they shall see how the habitations of the others are guarded by angels in profound quiet. 86 The sixth way, they shall see how some of them will cross over[a] into torments. 87 The seventh way, which is worse[b] than all the ways that have been mentioned, because they shall utterly waste away in confusion and be consumed with shame,[c] and shall wither with fear at seeing the glory of the Most High in whose presence they sinned while they were alive, and in whose presence they are to be judged in the last times.

88 "Now this is the order of those who have kept the ways of the Most High, when they shall be separated from their mortal body.[d] 89 During the time that they lived in it,[e] they laboriously served the Most High, and withstood danger every hour so that they might keep the law of the Lawgiver perfectly. 90 Therefore this is the teaching concerning them: 91 First of all, they shall see with great joy the glory of him who receives them, for they shall have rest in seven orders. 92 The first order, because they have striven with great effort to overcome the evil thought that was formed with them, so that it might not lead them astray from life into death. 93 The second order, because they see the perplexity in which the souls of the ungodly wander and the punishment that awaits them. 94 The third order, they see the witness that he who formed them bears concerning them, that throughout their life they kept the law with which they were entrusted. 95 The fourth order, they understand the rest that they now enjoy, being gathered into their chambers and guarded by angels in profound quiet, and the glory waiting for them in the

a Cn: Meaning of Lat uncertain   b Lat Syr Ethiop greater   c Syr Ethiop: Meaning of Lat uncertain   d Lat *the corruptible vessel* last days. 96 The fifth order, they rejoice that they have now escaped what is corruptible and shall inherit what is to come; and besides they see the straits and toil*a* from which they have been delivered, and the spacious liberty that they are to receive and enjoy in immortality. 97 The sixth order, when it is shown them how their face is to shine like the sun, and how they are to be made like the light of the stars, being incorruptible from then on. 98 The seventh order, which is greater than all that have been mentioned, because they shall rejoice with boldness, and shall be confident without confusion, and shall be glad without fear, for they press forward to see the face of him whom they served in life and from whom they are to receive their reward when glorified. 99 This is the order of the souls of the righteous, as henceforth is announced;*b* and the previously mentioned are the ways of torment that those who would not give heed shall suffer hereafter."

100 Then I answered and said, "Will time therefore be given to the souls, after they have been separated from the bodies, to see what you have described to me?"

101 He said to me, "They shall have freedom for seven days, so that during these seven days they may see the things of which you have been told, and afterwards they shall be gathered in their habitations."

7.75–101: The experience of the soul after death. *75:* Ezra wants to know if the punishment of sinners begins immediately when they die, or only after the judgment. *76–77:* Although Uriel repeatedly assures Ezra that he is counted among the righteous, Ezra continues to consider himself a sinner. To Uriel, righteousness consists in having accumulated good works, whereas Ezra defines it as being free from sin. *78:* For the idea that *the spirit returns* to God at death, see Eccl 12.7; Wis 15.8. *80:* While the souls of the righteous will rest in *habitations* under the earth until the judgment (see 4.35–42), those of the wicked are condemned to *wander in torment* until the end of the age. The *seven ways* are different reasons for the grieving of the wicked, rather than successive stages of punishment. *81–87:* Although the physical "torments" of sinners are reserved for the judgment, anticipation of their punishment and envy of the righteous will make

their wanderings miserable. *88–89:* The author views the body as a container for the true person, which is the soul or spirit (see Wis 9.15). Nevertheless, his description of the judgment includes a bodily resurrection (see 7.32–38). *91–98:* The *seven orders* of the righteous do not exactly parallel the seven ways of the wicked, but they clearly reflect the same complex of ideas about the judgment. *97: Like the light of the stars:* Compare Dan 12.3. In the Bible, the stars are sometimes identified with angels (for example, Job 38.7), and in other apocalypses* the righteous are promised that they will dwell with the angels. *100–101:* These verses must refer to righteous souls only; they will be given *seven days* to observe the wanderings of the ungodly before coming to rest in their chambers.

~~~~~~~~~~~~~

102 I answered and said, "If I have found favor in your sight, show further to me, your servant, whether on the day of judgment the righteous will be able to intercede for the ungodly or to entreat the Most High for them— 103 fathers for sons or sons for parents, brothers for brothers, relatives for their kindred, or friends for those who are most dear."

104 He answered me and said, "Since you have found favor in my sight, I will show you this also. The day of judgment is decisive*c* and displays to all the seal of truth. Just as now a father does not send his son, or a son his father, or a master his servant, or a friend his dearest friend, to be ill*d* or sleep or eat or be healed in his place, 105 so no one shall ever pray for another on that day, neither shall anyone lay a burden on another;*e* for then all shall bear their own righteousness and unrighteousness."

36 106 I answered and said, "How then do we find that first Abraham prayed for the people of Sodom, and Moses for our ancestors who sinned in the desert, 37 107 and Joshua after him for Israel in the days of Achan, 38 108 and Samuel in the days of Saul,*f* and David for the plague, and Solomon for those at the dedication, 39 109 and Elijah for those who received the rain, and

a Syr Ethiop: Lat *fullness*   *b* Syr: Meaning of Lat uncertain   *c* Lat *bold*   *d* Syr Ethiop Arm: Lat *to understand*   *e* Syr Ethiop: Lat lacks *on that . . . another* *f* Syr Ethiop Arab 1: Lat Arab 2 Arm lack *in the days of Saul* for the one who was dead, that he might live, 40 *110* and Hezekiah for the people in the days of Sennacherib, and many others prayed for many? 41 *111* So if now, when corruption has increased and unrighteousness has multiplied, the righteous have prayed for the ungodly, why will it not be so then as well?"

42 *112* He answered me and said, "This present world is not the end; the full glory does not*a* remain in it;*b* therefore those who were strong prayed for the weak. 43 *113* But the day of judgment will be the end of this age and the beginning*c* of the immortal age to come, in which corruption has passed away, 44 *114* sinful indulgence has come to an end, unbelief has been cut off, and righteousness has increased and truth has appeared. 45 *115* Therefore no one will then be able to have mercy on someone who has been condemned in the judgment, or to harm*d* someone who is victorious."

7.102–115: No prayers on judgment day. *102–105:* Since the angel's insistence that *no one can pray for another* at the judgment ran counter to Christian doctrine, the entire page containing vv. *36–105* was cut from an early Latin manuscript. The chapter and verse numbering was based on this cut version, and only later was the missing passage recovered from other versions. Hence the exceptional length of ch. 7 and the double verse numbering for the rest of the chapter. *106–111:* Ezra cites biblical precedents for prayer on behalf of sinners. *Abraham:* Gen 18.23–33; *Moses:* Ex 32.11–14; *Joshua:* Josh 7.6–9; *Samuel:* 1 Sam 7.8–9; *David:* 2 Sam 24.17, 25; *Solomon:* 1 Kings 8.22–53; *Elijah:* 1 Kings 18.36–45 and 17.20–22; *Hezekiah:* 2 Kings 19.15–19. *112–115:* Uriel's response reiterates his point that the world to come is not for sinners, so there will be *no mercy in the judgment* (compare 7.33–34).

---

46 *116* I answered and said, "This is my first and last comment: it would have been better if the earth had not produced Adam, or else, when it had produced him, had restrained him from sinning. 47 *117* For what good is it to all that they live in sorrow now and expect punishment after death? 48 *118* O Adam, what have you done? For though it was you who sinned, the fall was not yours alone, but ours also who are your descendants. 49 *119* For what good is it to us, if an immortal time has been promised to us, but we have done deeds that bring death? 50 *120* And what good is it that an everlasting hope has been promised to us, but we have miserably failed? 51 *121* Or that safe and healthful habitations have been reserved for us, but we have lived wickedly? 52 *122* Or that the glory of the Most High will defend those who have led a pure life, but we have walked in the most wicked ways? 53 *123* Or that a paradise shall be revealed, whose fruit remains unspoiled and in which are abundance and healing, but we shall not enter it 54 *124* because we have lived in perverse ways?*e* 55 *125* Or that the faces of those who practiced self-control shall shine more than the stars, but our faces shall be blacker than darkness? 56 *126* For while we lived and committed iniquity we did not consider what we should suffer after death."

57 *127* He answered and said, "This is the significance of the contest that all who are born on earth shall wage: 58 *128* if they are defeated they shall suffer what you have said, but if they are victorious they shall receive what I have said.*f* 59 *129* For this is the way of which Moses, while he was alive, spoke to the people, saying, 'Choose life for yourself, so that you may live!' 60 *130* But they did not believe him or the prophets after him, or even myself who have spoken to them. 61 *131* Therefore there shall not be*g* grief at their destruction, so much as joy over those to whom salvation is assured."

62 *132* I answered and said, "I know, O Lord, that the Most High is now called merciful, because he has mercy on those who have not yet come into the world; 63 *133* and gracious, because he is gracious to those who turn in repentance to his law; 64 *134* and patient, because he shows patience toward those who have sinned, since they are his own creatures; 65 *135* and bountiful, because he would rather give than take

a Lat lacks *not*　*b* Or *the glory does not continuously abide in it*　*c* Syr Ethiop: Lat lacks *the beginning*
d Syr Ethiop: Lat *overwhelm*　*e* Cn: Lat Syr *places*
f Syr Ethiop Arab 1: Lat *what I say*　*g* Syr: Lat *there was not*

away;[a] 66 136 and abundant in compassion, because he makes his compassions abound more and more to those now living and to those who are gone and to those yet to come— 67 137 for if he did not make them abound, the world with those who inhabit it would not have life— 68 138 and he is called the giver, because if he did not give out of his goodness so that those who have committed iniquities might be relieved of them, not one ten-thousandth of humankind could have life; 69 139 and the judge, because if he did not pardon those who were created by his word and blot out the multitude of their sins,[b] 70 140 there would probably be left only very few of the innumerable multitude."

8 He answered me and said, "The Most High made this world for the sake of many, but the world to come for the sake of only a few. 2But I tell you a parable, Ezra. Just as, when you ask the earth, it will tell you that it provides a large amount of clay from which earthenware is made, but only a little dust from which gold comes, so is the course of the present world. 3Many have been created, but only a few shall be saved."

7.116–8.3: Conflicting views of the judgment. *116–126:* Ezra recapitulates his point of view: Sin is universal, inherited from Adam, and therefore the promises of the world to come can only sharpen the sorrow of life in this world. *127–131:* Uriel insists, quoting from Deut 30.19, that salvation has always been promised only to those who choose to live according to God's law. *132–140:* Ezra expresses his belief in God's mercy through a word-by-word commentary on Ex 34.6–7, a passage frequently quoted in Jewish prayers. The style of the commentary resembles a rabbinic midrash. * **8.1–3:** The angel's only response is to remind Ezra of the illustration from nature that he used earlier (7.52–61) to justify the destruction of the many.

---

4 I answered and said, "Then drink your fill of understanding,[c] O my soul, and drink wisdom, O my heart. 5For not of your own will did you come into the world,[d] and against your will you depart, for you have been given only a short time to live. 6O Lord above us, grant to your servant that we may pray before you, and give us a seed for our heart and cultivation of our understanding

so that fruit may be produced, by which every mortal who bears the likeness[e] of a human being may be able to live. 7For you alone exist, and we are a work of your hands, as you have declared. 8And because you give life to the body that is now fashioned in the womb, and furnish it with members, what you have created is preserved amid fire and water, and for nine months the womb[f] endures your creature that has been created in it. 9But that which keeps and that which is kept shall both be kept by your keeping.[d] And when the womb gives up again what has been created in it, 10you have commanded that from the members themselves (that is, from the breasts) milk, the fruit of the breasts, should be supplied, 11so that what has been fashioned may be nourished for a time; and afterwards you will still guide it in your mercy. 12You have nurtured it in your righteousness, and instructed it in your law, and reproved it in your wisdom. 13You put it to death as your creation, and make it live as your work. 14If then you will suddenly and quickly[g] destroy what with so great labor was fashioned by your command, to what purpose was it made? 15And now I will speak out: About all humankind you know best; but I will speak about your people, for whom I am grieved, 16and about your inheritance, for whom I lament, and about Israel, for whom I am sad, and about the seed of Jacob, for whom I am troubled. 17Therefore I will pray before you for myself and for them, for I see the failings of us who inhabit the earth; 18and now also[h] I have heard of the swiftness of the judgment that is to come. 19Therefore hear my voice and understand my words, and I will speak before you."

The beginning of the words of Ezra's prayer,[i] before he was taken up. He said: 20"O Lord, you who inhabit eternity,[j] whose eyes are exalted[k] and whose upper chambers are in the air, 21whose throne is beyond mea-

---

a Or *he is ready to give according to requests*
b Lat *contempts*　　c Syr: Lat *Then release understanding*
d Syr: Meaning of Lat uncertain　　e Syr: Lat *place*
f Lat *what you have formed*　　g Syr: Lat *will with a light command*　　h Syr: Lat *but*　　i Syr Ethiop; Lat *beginning of Ezra's words*　　j Or *you who abide forever*
k Another Lat text reads *whose are the highest heavens*

sure and whose glory is beyond comprehension, before whom the hosts of angels stand trembling 22and at whose command they are changed to wind and fire,*a* whose word is sure and whose utterances are certain, whose command is strong and whose ordinance is terrible, 23whose look dries up the depths and whose indignation makes the mountains melt away, and whose truth is established*b* forever— 24hear, O Lord, the prayer of your servant, and give ear to the petition of your creature; attend to my words. 25For as long as I live I will speak, and as long as I have understanding I will answer. 26O do not look on the sins of your people, but on those who serve you in truth. 27Do not take note of the endeavors of those who act wickedly, but of the endeavors of those who have kept your covenants amid afflictions. 28Do not think of those who have lived wickedly in your sight, but remember those who have willingly acknowledged that you are to be feared. 29Do not will the destruction of those who have the ways of cattle, but regard those who have gloriously taught your law.*c* 30Do not be angry with those who are deemed worse than wild animals, but love those who have always put their trust in your glory. 31For we and our ancestors have passed our lives in ways that bring death;*d* but it is because of us sinners that you are called merciful. 32For if you have desired to have pity on us, who have no works of righteousness, then you will be called merciful. 33For the righteous, who have many works laid up with you, shall receive their reward in consequence of their own deeds. 34But what are mortals, that you are angry with them; or what is a corruptible race, that you are so bitter against it? 35For in truth there is no one among those who have been born who has not acted wickedly; among those who have existed*e* there is no one who has not done wrong. 36For in this, O Lord, your righteousness and goodness will be declared, when you are merciful to those who have no store of good works."

8.4–36: Ezra's prayers for mercy. Unable to accept Uriel's hard-line position, Ezra decides to appeal directly to God. **4–5:** To show his exasperation with the

angel, he first addresses himself, in much the same way that he invoked the earth in 7.62. **6:** Ezra seems to be praying for a reversal of the situation described in 3.20–22. *Who bears the likeness of a human being:* The original probably read, "who bears the likeness of Adam"; the name Adam means "human being" in Hebrew. **7–12:** The author views pregnancy and child-rearing as creative acts of God. **13–14:** Ezra cannot believe that God would *create* so many people only to *destroy* them. **15:** He gives up on his appeal for the mass of humanity and reverts to his earlier concern with the fate of Israel. **19:** *The beginning . . . He said:* This heading is present in all the extant versions, but it appears to have been added to the original text. For the idea that Ezra was *taken up* to heaven, see 14.9 and comment on 14.48. **20–36:** Although influenced by the prayers of confession found in Ezra 9, Neh 9, and Dan 9, Ezra's prayer is more a petition for mercy than an acknowledgment of guilt. **20–23:** The prayer begins with praise of God's might. **24–30:** Like the biblical intercessors he named in 7.106–111, Ezra pleads the cause of his people. **31–33:** God's reputation for mercy (compare 7.132–140) rests on his treatment of sinners; the righteous have no need of mercy. **34:** Compare Job 7.17–18; Ps 8.4. **35–36:** Although Ezra continues to define righteousness as freedom from sin, he acknowledges Uriel's claim that some people have a *store of good works* (see 7.76–77).

37 He answered me and said, "Some things you have spoken rightly, and it will turn out according to your words. 38For indeed I will not concern myself about the fashioning of those who have sinned, or about their death, their judgment, or their destruction; 39but I will rejoice over the creation of the righteous, over their pilgrimage also, and their salvation, and their receiving their reward. 40As I have spoken, therefore, so it shall be.

41 "For just as the farmer sows many seeds in the ground and plants a multitude of seedlings, and yet not all that have been sown will come up*f* in due season, and not all that were planted will take root; so also

a Syr: Lat *they whose service takes the form of wind and fire* *b* Arab 2: Other authorities read *truth bears witness* *c* Syr *have received the brightness of your law* *d* Syr Ethiop: Meaning of Lat uncertain *e* Syr: Meaning of Lat uncertain *f* Syr Ethiop *will live;* Lat *will be saved* those who have been sown in the world will not all be saved."

42 I answered and said, "If I have found favor in your sight, let me speak. 43 If the farmer's seed does not come up, because it has not received your rain in due season, or if it has been ruined by too much rain, it perishes.*a* 44 But people, who have been formed by your hands and are called your own image because they are made like you, and for whose sake you have formed all things—have you also made them like the farmer's seed? 45 Surely not, O Lord*b* above! But spare your people and have mercy on your inheritance, for you have mercy on your own creation."

46 He answered me and said, "Things that are present are for those who live now, and things that are future are for those who will live hereafter. 47 For you come far short of being able to love my creation more than I love it. But you have often compared yourself*c* to the unrighteous. Never do so! 48 But even in this respect you will be praiseworthy before the Most High, 49 because you have humbled yourself, as is becoming for you, and have not considered yourself to be among the righteous. You will receive the greatest glory, 50 for many miseries will affect those who inhabit the world in the last times, because they have walked in great pride. 51 But think of your own case, and inquire concerning the glory of those who are like yourself, 52 because it is for you that paradise is opened, the tree of life is planted, the age to come is prepared, plenty is provided, a city is built, rest is appointed,*d* goodness is established and wisdom perfected beforehand. 53 The root of evil*e* is sealed up from you, illness is banished from you, and death*f* is hidden; Hades has fled and corruption has been forgotten;*g* 54 sorrows have passed away, and in the end the treasure of immortality is made manifest. 55 Therefore do not ask any more questions about the great number of those who perish. 56 For when they had opportunity to choose, they despised the Most High, and were contemptuous of his law, and abandoned his ways. 57 Moreover, they have even trampled on his righteous ones, 58 and said in their hearts that there is

no God—though they knew well that they must die. 59 For just as the things that I have predicted await*h* you, so the thirst and torment that are prepared await them. For the Most High did not intend that anyone should be destroyed; 60 but those who were created have themselves defiled the name of him who made them, and have been ungrateful to him who prepared life for them now. 61 Therefore my judgment is now drawing near; 62 I have not shown this to all people, but only to you and a few like you."

8.37–62: Final dispute. 37–40: Completely ignoring the emotional intensity of Ezra's appeal, Uriel reaffirms that God has no interest in sinners. **41:** He uses the familiar analogy of *sowing* to imply that God does not have as much invested in the creation of human life as Ezra supposes. **42–45:** For the first time, Ezra finds fault with one of the angel's analogies, arguing that humanity is created in God's own image (Gen 1.26–27). He again appeals directly to God for *mercy.* **46–62:** Uriel does not even acknowledge Ezra's point; he simply recapitulates his own points, beginning with the doctrine of the two worlds. **47–51:** More emphatically than above (*7.76–77*), he assures Ezra of his own salvation. **52:** Compare *7.119–125.* **53–54:** Compare *7.113–114. The root of evil* is equivalent to the "evil heart"; see 3.22. **56–58:** Compare *7.22–24.* **59–60:** God is not to blame for the destruction of the many; human beings choose their own fates (compare *7.72, 129–131*). **62:** *A few like you:* The revelations of the dialogues are to be shared only with other righteous persons. Later in the book, Ezra is told to keep his visions secret from all but the wise: 12.37–38; 14.26, 46–47.

Then I answered and said, 63 "O Lord, you have already shown me a great number of the signs that you will do in the last times, but you have not shown me when you will do them."

9 He answered me and said, "Measure carefully in your mind, and when you see that some of the predicted signs have oc-

a Cn: Compare Syr Arab 1 Arm Georg 2: Meaning of Lat uncertain   *b* Ethiop Arab Compare Syr: Lat lacks O Lord   *c* Syr Ethiop: Lat *brought yourself near*   *d* Syr Ethiop: Lat *allowed*   *e* Lat lacks *of evil*   *f* Syr Ethiop Arm: Lat lacks *death*   *g* Syr: Lat *Hades and corruption have fled into oblivion;* or *corruption has fled into Hades to be forgotten*   *h* Syr: Lat *will receive* curred, [2]then you will know that it is the very time when the Most High is about to visit the world that he has made. [3]So when there shall appear in the world earthquakes, tumult of peoples, intrigues of nations, wavering of leaders, confusion of princes, [4]then you will know that it was of these that the Most High spoke from the days that were of old, from the beginning. [5]For just as with everything that has occurred in the world, the beginning is evident,[a] and the end manifest; [6]so also are the times of the Most High: the beginnings are manifest in wonders and mighty works, and the end in penalties[b] and in signs.

[7] "It shall be that all who will be saved and will be able to escape on account of their works, or on account of the faith by which they have believed, [8]will survive the dangers that have been predicted, and will see my salvation in my land and within my borders, which I have sanctified for myself from the beginning. [9]Then those who have now abused my ways shall be amazed, and those who have rejected them with contempt shall live in torments. [10]For as many as did not acknowledge me in their lifetime, though they received my benefits, [11]and as many as scorned my law while they still had freedom, and did not understand but despised it[c] while an opportunity of repentance was still open to them, [12]these must in torment acknowledge it[c] after death. [13]Therefore, do not continue to be curious about how the ungodly will be punished; but inquire how the righteous will be saved, those to whom the age belongs and for whose sake the age was made."[d]

14 I answered and said, [15]"I said before, and I say now, and will say it again: there are more who perish than those who will be saved, [16]as a wave is greater than a drop of water."

17 He answered me and said, "As is the field, so is the seed; and as are the flowers, so are the colors; and as is the work, so is the product; and as is the farmer, so is the threshing floor. [18]For there was a time in this age when I was preparing for those who now exist, before the world was made for them to live in, and no one opposed me then, for no one existed; [19]but now those who have been created in this world, which is supplied both with an unfailing table and an inexhaustible pasture,[e] have become corrupt in their ways. [20]So I considered my world, and saw that it was lost. I saw that my earth was in peril because of the devices of those who[f] had come into it. [21]And I saw and spared some[g] with great difficulty, and saved for myself one grape out of a cluster, and one plant out of a great forest.[h] [22]So let the multitude perish that has been born in vain, but let my grape and my plant be saved, because with much labor I have perfected them.

8.63–9.22: The purpose of the signs. In spite of Ezra's question, this discourse is less specific about the timing of *the signs* than those at the end of the first two dialogues. The emphasis is on their punitive purpose (see comment on 6.25). **9.2:** *To visit* often connotes punishment; compare 5.56. **3:** Compare Mk 13.7–8. **5–6:** The text of these verses is corrupt, but Uriel may be likening the world to a living being, in that it has a clear *beginning* and *end*. **7:** Throughout the book, *faith* and good *works* are assumed to go hand in hand; therefore, the author is probably not suggesting that these are two alternative paths to salvation. **8:** The survivors of the signs will enjoy the earthly rewards of the messianic kingdom (compare 7.27–28; 12.34) prior to the day of judgment. **9–12:** The terrible signs that will bring about the death of the ungodly who are living at the time of the end will be only a foretaste of the punishments that await them after the judgment. **15–16:** Ezra has accepted the fact that only a few will be saved, but his feelings about it remain the same. **17–20:** In life as in agriculture, results depend on both materials and effort. God gave humanity the materials for success in this world, but they have nearly destroyed the earth along with themselves. **21–22:** The imagery (compare 5.23) suggests the biblical notion that God will spare only a tiny remnant of Israel (see Isa 17.4–6; Am 3.12). The concept of a remnant, however, contradicts what Uriel has been saying all along about the righteous saving themselves, and about Israel having no privileged status.

a Syr: Ethiop *is in the word;* Meaning of Lat uncertain *b* Syr: Lat Ethiop *in effects*   *c* Or *me*   *d* Syr: Lat *saved, and whose is the age and for whose sake the age was made and when*   *e* Cn: Lat *law*   *f* Cn: Lat *devices that*   *g* Lat *them*   *h* Syr Ethiop Arab 1: Lat *tribe*

23 "Now, if you will let seven days more pass—do not, however, fast during them, [24]but go into a field of flowers where no house has been built, and eat only of the flowers of the field, and taste no meat and drink no wine, but eat only flowers— [25]and pray to the Most High continually, then I will come and talk with you."

26 So I went, as he directed me, into the field that is called Ardat;[a] there I sat among the flowers and ate of the plants of the field, and the nourishment they afforded satisfied me. [27]After seven days, while I lay on the grass, my heart was troubled again as it was before. [28]Then my mouth was opened, and I began to speak before the Most High, and said, [29]"O Lord, you showed yourself among us, to our ancestors in the wilderness when they came out from Egypt and when they came into the untrodden and unfruitful wilderness; [30]and you said, 'Hear me, O Israel, and give heed to my words, O descendants of Jacob. [31]For I sow my law in you, and it shall bring forth fruit in you, and you shall be glorified through it forever.' [32]But though our ancestors received the law, they did not keep it and did not observe the[b] statutes; yet the fruit of the law did not perish—for it could not, because it was yours. [33]Yet those who received it perished, because they did not keep what had been sown in them. [34]Now this is the general rule that, when the ground has received seed, or the sea a ship, or any dish food or drink, and when it comes about that what was sown or what was launched or what was put in is destroyed, [35]they are destroyed, but the things that held them remain; yet with us it has not been so. [36]For we who have received the law and sinned will perish, as well as our hearts that received it; [37]the law, however, does not perish but survives in its glory."

9.23–26: Conclusion of the third episode. Uriel's instructions to Ezra partly parallel those following the first two dialogues, but they signal a change in his location and the nature of his *fast*.

9.27–37: Ezra's final complaint. The fourth episode begins, like the first three, with a prayer of lament.* 31: Compare 3.20. 32–33: Ezra seems resigned to Uriel's point that the law is more precious to God than

the persons who fail to keep it; see 7.20. 34–37: Nevertheless, this order of priorities still does not make sense to Ezra, as his rather awkward analogy demonstrates.

38 When I said these things in my heart, I looked around,[c] and on my right I saw a woman; she was mourning and weeping with a loud voice, and was deeply grieved at heart; her clothes were torn, and there were ashes on her head. [39]Then I dismissed the thoughts with which I had been engaged, and turned to her [40]and said to her, "Why are you weeping, and why are you grieved at heart?"

41 She said to me, "Let me alone, my lord, so that I may weep for myself and continue to mourn, for I am greatly embittered in spirit and deeply distressed."

42 I said to her, "What has happened to you? Tell me."

43 And she said to me, "Your servant was barren and had no child, though I lived with my husband for thirty years. [44]Every hour and every day during those thirty years I prayed to the Most High, night and day. [45]And after thirty years God heard your servant, and looked upon my low estate, and considered my distress, and gave me a son. I rejoiced greatly over him, I and my husband and all my neighbors;[d] and we gave great glory to the Mighty One. [46]And I brought him up with much care. [47]So when he grew up and I came to take a wife for him, I set a day for the marriage feast.

9.38–10.28: Vision of the mourning woman. Ezra is unaware that the *woman* he suddenly sees is a vision sent to console him. 9.39–40: For a moment, her grief makes him forget his own. 43–46: The beginning of her story reflects the common biblical motif* of a *barren* woman whose prayers for a *child* are eventually rewarded; see especially 1 Sam 1.

10 "But it happened that when my son entered his wedding chamber, he fell down and died. [2]So all of us put out our lamps, and all my neighbors[d] attempted to

a Syr Ethiop *Arpad*; Arm *Ardab*   b Lat *my*
c Syr Arab Arm: Lat *I looked about me with my eyes*
d Literally *all my citizens*

console me; I remained quiet until the evening of the second day. ³But when all of them had stopped consoling me, encouraging me to be quiet, I got up in the night and fled, and I came to this field, as you see. ⁴And now I intend not to return to the town, but to stay here; I will neither eat nor drink, but will mourn and fast continually until I die."

5 Then I broke off the reflections with which I was still engaged, and answered her in anger and said, ⁶"You most foolish of women, do you not see our mourning, and what has happened to us? ⁷For Zion, the mother of us all, is in deep grief and great distress. ⁸It is most appropriate to mourn now, because we are all mourning, and to be sorrowful, because we are all sorrowing; you are sorrowing for one son, but we, the whole world, for our mother.ᵃ ⁹Now ask the earth, and she will tell you that it is she who ought to mourn over so many who have come into being upon her. ¹⁰From the beginning all have been born of her, and others will come; and, lo, almost all goᵇ to perdition, and a multitude of them will come to doom. ¹¹Who then ought to mourn the more, she who lost so great a multitude, or you who are grieving for one alone? ¹²But if you say to me, 'My lamentation is not like the earth's, for I have lost the fruit of my womb, which I brought forth in pain and bore in sorrow; ¹³but it is with the earth according to the way of the earth—the multitude that is now in it goes as it came'; ¹⁴then I say to you, 'Just as you brought forth in sorrow, so the earth also has from the beginning given her fruit, that is, humankind, to him who made her.' ¹⁵Now, therefore, keep your sorrow to yourself, and bear bravely the troubles that have come upon you. ¹⁶For if you acknowledge the decree of God to be just, you will receive your son back in due time, and will be praised among women. ¹⁷Therefore go into the town to your husband."

18 She said to me, "I will not do so; I will not go into the city, but I will die here."

19 So I spoke again to her, and said, ²⁰"Do not do that, but let yourself be persuaded—for how many are the adversities of Zion?—and be consoled because of the sorrow of Jerusalem. ²¹For you see how our sanctuary has been laid waste, our altar thrown down, our temple destroyed; ²²our harp has been laid low, our song has been silenced, and our rejoicing has been ended; the light of our lampstand has been put out, the ark of our covenant has been plundered, our holy things have been polluted, and the name by which we are called has been almost profaned; our childrenᶜ have suffered abuse, our priests have been burned to death, our Levites have gone into exile, our virgins have been defiled, and our wives have been ravished; our righteous menᵈ have been carried off, our little ones have been cast out, our young men have been enslaved and our strong men made powerless. ²³And, worst of all, the seal of Zion has been deprived of its glory, and given over into the hands of those that hate us. ²⁴Therefore shake off your great sadness and lay aside your many sorrows, so that the Mighty One may be merciful to you again, and the Most High may give you rest, a respite from your troubles."

25 While I was talking to her, her face suddenly began to shine exceedingly; her countenance flashed like lightning, so that I was too frightened to approach her, and my heart was terrified. Whileᵉ I was wondering what this meant, ²⁶she suddenly uttered a loud and fearful cry, so that the earth shook at the sound. ²⁷When I looked up, the woman was no longer visible to me, but a city was being built,ᶠ and a place of huge foundations showed itself. I was afraid, and cried with a loud voice and said, ²⁸"Where is the angel Uriel, who came to me at first? For it was he who brought me into this overpowering bewilderment; my end has become corruption, and my prayer a reproach."

10.1–28. 2: Putting out the lights and sitting for a full day in silence were Jewish mourning customs of the period. **6–11:** The woman's loss seems trivial to Ezra compared to the destruction of Jerusalem (described

a Compare Syr: Meaning of Lat uncertain   *b* Literally *walk*   *c* Ethiop *free men*   *d* Syr *our seers*   *e* Syr Ethiop Arab 1: Lat lacks *I was too . . . terrified. While*   *f* Lat: Syr Ethiop Arab 1 Arab 2 Arm *but there was an established city* in vv. 21–24) and the doom of the majority of humankind. **16:** Ezra, who has resisted Uriel's claims about divine justice, now presents the acknowledgment of God's justice as the key to salvation. **20:** In the ancient world, to *console* someone meant to persuade them that their troubles were not so bad. **23:** It is uncertain what the author means by *the seal of Zion.*★ **25:** The woman's transformation bears some resemblance to Jesus' transfiguration (Mt 17.2–8 and parallels). **27:** The city Ezra sees is the heavenly Jerusalem (see comment on 7.26).

〰〰〰〰〰〰〰〰

29 While I was speaking these words, the angel who had come to me at first came to me, and when he saw me ^{30}lying there like a corpse, deprived of my understanding, he grasped my right hand and strengthened me and set me on my feet, and said to me, ^{31}"What is the matter with you? And why are you troubled? And why are your understanding and the thoughts of your mind troubled?"

32 I said, "It was because you abandoned me. I did as you directed, and went out into the field, and lo, what I have seen and can still see, I am unable to explain."

33 He said to me, "Stand up like a man, and I will instruct you."

34 I said, "Speak, my lord; only do not forsake me, so that I may not die before my time.^{a} ^{35}For I have seen what I did not know, and I hear^b what I do not understand ^{36}—or is my mind deceived, and my soul dreaming? ^{37}Now therefore I beg you to give your servant an explanation of this bewildering vision."

38 He answered me and said, "Listen to me, and I will teach you, and tell you about the things that you fear; for the Most High has revealed many secrets to you. ^{39}He has seen your righteous conduct, and that you have sorrowed continually for your people and mourned greatly over Zion. ^{40}This therefore is the meaning of the vision. ^{41}The woman who appeared to you a little while ago, whom you saw mourning and whom you began to console ^{42}(you do not now see the form of a woman, but there appeared to you a city being built)^c ^{43}and who told you about the misfortune of her son—this is the interpretation: ^{44}The woman whom you saw is Zion, which you now behold as a city being

built.^{d} ^{45}And as for her telling you that she was barren for thirty years, the reason is that there were three thousand^e years in the world before any offering was offered in it.^{f} ^{46}And after three thousand^g years Solomon built the city, and offered offerings; then it was that the barren woman bore a son. ^{47}And as for her telling you that she brought him up with much care, that was the period of residence in Jerusalem. ^{48}And as for her saying to you, 'My son died as he entered his wedding chamber,' and that misfortune had overtaken her,^{h} this was the destruction that befell Jerusalem. ^{49}So you saw her likeness, how she mourned for her son, and you began to console her for what had happened.^{i} ^{50}For now the Most High, seeing that you are sincerely grieved and profoundly distressed for her, has shown you the brilliance of her glory, and the loveliness of her beauty. ^{51}Therefore I told you to remain in the field where no house had been built, ^{52}for I knew that the Most High would reveal these things to you. ^{53}Therefore I told you to go into the field where there was no foundation of any building, ^{54}because no work of human construction could endure in a place where the city of the Most High was to be revealed.

――――――――――

10.29–54: Vision of the mourning woman interpreted. 30: Ezra's bewilderment is a typical apocalyptic★ motif★; compare Dan 8.17; Rev 1.17. **38–39:** The revelations Ezra has received are a reward not only for righteousness (compare 6.31–32), but also for his *mourning over Zion,*★ which Uriel had earlier criticized (5.33, 40). **41–44:** The irony★ of Ezra's attempt to *console* the woman becomes clear as her identity is revealed. **45–46:** It is uncertain whether she represents the physical Mount Zion or the heavenly Jerusalem, imagined as existing since the creation of the world. In either case, the author dates creation 3,000 years before Solomon's building of the earthly Jerusalem (represented by her son). Jerusalem was traditionally established by David (compare 3.24; 2 Sam 5.7),

a Syr Ethiop Arab: Lat *die to no purpose* b Other ancient authorities read *have heard* c Lat: Syr Ethiop Arab 1 Arab 2 Arm *an established city* d Cn: Lat *an established city* e Most Lat Mss read *three* f Cn: Lat Syr Arab Arm *her* g Syr Ethiop Arab Arm: Lat *three* h Or *him* i Most Lat Mss and Arab 1 add *These were the things to be opened to you* but it was Solomon who built the Temple* (1 Kings 6–7). **49–50:** The purpose of the vision was to console Ezra with the knowledge that Zion will be restored at the end of days.

~~~~~~~~~~~~

55 "Therefore do not be afraid, and do not let your heart be terrified; but go in and see the splendor or*ᵃ* the vastness of the building, as far as it is possible for your eyes to see it, ⁵⁶and afterward you will hear as much as your ears can hear. ⁵⁷For you are more blessed than many, and you have been called to be with*ᵇ* the Most High as few have been. ⁵⁸But tomorrow night you shall remain here, ⁵⁹and the Most High will show you in those dream visions what the Most High will do to those who inhabit the earth in the last days."

So I slept that night and the following one, as he had told me.

10.55–59: Conclusion of the fourth episode. 55–56: The visionary city is no mere mirage; Uriel urges Ezra to explore it fully, with the implication that he will receive further explanations. **57:** See 14.9. **58–59:** This time Ezra only has to wait one day for the next revelation, which will be the first to take the form of a *dream.*

~~~~~~~~~~~~

11 On the second night I had a dream: I saw rising from the sea an eagle that had twelve feathered wings and three heads. ²I saw it spread its wings over*ᶜ* the whole earth, and all the winds of heaven blew upon it, and the clouds were gathered around it.*ᵈ* ³I saw that out of its wings there grew opposing wings; but they became little, puny wings. ⁴But its heads were at rest; the middle head was larger than the other heads, but it too was at rest with them. ⁵Then I saw that the eagle flew with its wings, and it reigned over the earth and over those who inhabit it. ⁶And I saw how all things under heaven were subjected to it, and no one spoke against it—not a single creature that was on the earth. ⁷Then I saw the eagle rise upon its talons, and it uttered a cry to its wings, saying, ⁸"Do not all watch at the same time; let each sleep in its own place, and watch in its turn; ⁹but let the heads be reserved for the last."

10 I looked again and saw that the voice did not come from its heads, but from the middle of its body. ¹¹I counted its rival wings, and there were eight of them. ¹²As I watched, one wing on the right side rose up, and it reigned over all the earth. ¹³And after a time its reign came to an end, and it disappeared, so that even its place was no longer visible. Then the next wing rose up and reigned, and it continued to reign a long time. ¹⁴While it was reigning its end came also, so that it disappeared like the first. ¹⁵And a voice sounded, saying to it, ¹⁶"Listen to me, you who have ruled the earth all this time; I announce this to you before you disappear. ¹⁷After you no one shall rule as long as you have ruled, not even half as long."

18 Then the third wing raised itself up, and held the rule as the earlier ones had done, and it also disappeared. ¹⁹And so it went with all the wings; they wielded power one after another and then were never seen again. ²⁰I kept looking, and in due time the wings that followed*ᵉ* also rose up on the right*ᶠ* side, in order to rule. There were some of them that ruled, yet disappeared suddenly; ²¹and others of them rose up, but did not hold the rule.

22 And after this I looked and saw that the twelve wings and the two little wings had disappeared, ²³and nothing remained on the eagle's body except the three heads that were at rest and six little wings. ²⁴As I kept looking I saw that two little wings separated from the six and remained under the head that was on the right side; but four remained in their place. ²⁵Then I saw that these little wings*ᵍ* planned to set themselves up and hold the rule. ²⁶As I kept looking, one was set up, but suddenly disappeared; ²⁷a second also, and this disappeared more quickly than the first. ²⁸While I continued to look the two that remained were planning between themselves to reign

---

a Other ancient authorities read *and*　　*b* Or *been named by*　　*c* Arab 2 Arm: Lat Syr Ethiop *in*　　*d* Syr: Compare Ethiop Arab: Lat lacks *the clouds* and *around it*　　*e* Syr Arab 2 *the little wings*　　*f* Some Ethiop Mss read *left*　　*g* Syr: Lat *underwings* together; 29and while they were planning, one of the heads that were at rest (the one that was in the middle) suddenly awoke; it was greater than the other two heads. 30And I saw how it allied the two heads with itself, 31and how the head turned with those that were with it and devoured the two little wings*a* that were planning to reign. 32Moreover this head gained control of the whole earth, and with much oppression dominated its inhabitants; it had greater power over the world than all the wings that had gone before.

33 After this I looked again and saw the head in the middle suddenly disappear, just as the wings had done. 34But the two heads remained, which also in like manner ruled over the earth and its inhabitants. 35And while I looked, I saw the head on the right side devour the one on the left.

11.1–35: **Vision of the eagle.** The eagle was a symbol of the Roman Empire displayed on their battle standards. **1–2:** Compare Dan 7.1–3. **5–6:** In the first century CE, the Romans ruled over most of the world known to the author. **9:** Based on what is said about them in vv. 30–35, the three *heads* are generally identified with the emperors Vespasian (69–79 CE), Titus (79–81) and Domitian (81–96). Vespasian and Titus were successive leaders of the Roman war against the Jews (66–73) before becoming emperors. The vision must have originally been written during the reign of Domitian, although it appears to have been updated after his death (see comment on 12.1–3). **10:** *The voice* is that of Rome as a whole. **16–17:** The second wing represents Augustus, whose reign (27 BCE–14 CE) was by far the longest of any of the first-century emperors. Julius Caesar (who died in 44 BCE) is being counted as the first emperor. **18–22:** It is difficult to identify the remaining wings and *little wings* because the vision was updated rather clumsily after the Roman Empire had lasted well beyond Domitian's death. **25–29:** Six men attempted to rule in the chaotic period between the death of Nero and the accession★ of Vespasian (68–69 CE). **30–31:** Titus and Domitian were Vespasian's sons. **35:** Domitian was rumored to have had Titus killed.

36 Then I heard a voice saying to me, "Look in front of you and consider what you see." 37When I looked, I saw what seemed

to be a lion roused from the forest, roaring; and I heard how it uttered a human voice to the eagle, and spoke, saying, 38"Listen and I will speak to you. The Most High says to you, 39'Are you not the one that remains of the four beasts that I had made to reign in my world, so that the end of my times might come through them? 40You, the fourth that has come, have conquered all the beasts that have gone before; and you have held sway over the world with great terror, and over all the earth with grievous oppression; and for so long you have lived on the earth with deceit.*b* 41You have judged the earth, but not with truth, 42for you have oppressed the meek and injured the peaceable; you have hated those who tell the truth, and have loved liars; you have destroyed the homes of those who brought forth fruit, and have laid low the walls of those who did you no harm. 43Your insolence has come up before the Most High, and your pride to the Mighty One. 44The Most High has looked at his times; now they have ended, and his ages have reached completion. 45Therefore you, eagle, will surely disappear, you and your terrifying wings, your most evil little wings, your malicious heads, your most evil talons, and your whole worthless body, 46so that the whole earth, freed from your violence, may be refreshed and relieved, and may hope for the judgment and mercy of him who made it.'"

12 While the lion was saying these words to the eagle, I looked 2and saw that the remaining head had disappeared. The two wings that had gone over to it rose up and*c* set themselves up to reign, and their reign was brief and full of tumult. 3When I looked again, they were already vanishing. The whole body of the eagle was burned, and the earth was exceedingly terrified.

11.36–12.3a: **A lion defeats the eagle.** *The lion* (identified as the messiah★ in 12.31–32) was a favorite messianic symbol, drawn from Gen 49.9 (compare Rev 5.5). **39–40:** *The four beasts* is an allusion to Dan

a Syr: Lat *underwings*   *b* Syr Arab Arm: Lat Ethiop *The fourth came, however, and conquered . . . and held sway . . . and for so long lived*   *c* Ethiop: Lat lacks *rose up and*

7.4–8. In Daniel, the fourth beast represents the empire of the Greeks, so the author of 4 Ezra is reinterpreting Daniel's vision for his own times. **43:** Compare Dan 7.8, 11. **45–46:** The destruction of the Roman Empire will coincide with the end of the age; compare 6.7–10. **12.1–3:** If these verses were added to the vision after the death of Domitian, it is likely that they were written near the beginning of the reign of Trajan (98–117 CE). Since Nerva was emperor only from 96 to 98, Trajan might have been expected to be similarly short-lived.

~~~~~~

Then I woke up in great perplexity of mind and great fear, and I said to my spirit, 4"You have brought this upon me, because you search out the ways of the Most High. 5I am still weary in mind and very weak in my spirit, and not even a little strength is left in me, because of the great fear with which I have been terrified tonight. 6Therefore I will now entreat the Most High that he may strengthen me to the end."

7 Then I said, "O sovereign Lord, if I have found favor in your sight, and if I have been accounted righteous before you beyond many others, and if my prayer has indeed come up before your face, 8strengthen me and show me, your servant, the interpretation and meaning of this terrifying vision so that you may fully comfort my soul. 9For you have judged me worthy to be shown the end of the times and the last events of the times."

10 He said to me, "This is the interpretation of this vision that you have seen: 11The eagle that you saw coming up from the sea is the fourth kingdom that appeared in a vision to your brother Daniel. 12But it was not explained to him as I now explain to you or have explained it. 13The days are coming when a kingdom shall rise on earth, and it shall be more terrifying than all the kingdoms that have been before it. 14And twelve kings shall reign in it, one after another. 15But the second that is to reign shall hold sway for a longer time than any other one of the twelve. 16This is the interpretation of the twelve wings that you saw.

17 "As for your hearing a voice that spoke, coming not from the eagle's*a* heads but from the midst of its body, this is the interpretation: 18In the midst of*b* the time of that kingdom great struggles shall arise, and it shall be in danger of falling; nevertheless it shall not fall then, but shall regain its former power.*c* 19As for your seeing eight little wings*d* clinging to its wings, this is the interpretation: 20Eight kings shall arise in it, whose times shall be short and their years swift; 21two of them shall perish when the middle of its time draws near; and four shall be kept for the time when its end approaches, but two shall be kept until the end.

22 "As for your seeing three heads at rest, this is the interpretation: 23In its last days the Most High will raise up three kings,*e* and they*f* shall renew many things in it, and shall rule the earth 24and its inhabitants more oppressively than all who were before them. Therefore they are called the heads of the eagle, 25because it is they who shall sum up his wickedness and perform his last actions. 26As for your seeing that the large head disappeared, one of the kings*g* shall die in his bed, but in agonies. 27But as for the two who remained, the sword shall devour them. 28For the sword of one shall devour him who was with him; but he also shall fall by the sword in the last days.

29 "As for your seeing two little wings*h* passing over to*i* the head which was on the right side, 30this is the interpretation: It is these whom the Most High has kept for the eagle's*a* end; this was the reign which was brief and full of tumult, as you have seen.

31 "And as for the lion whom you saw rousing up out of the forest and roaring and speaking to the eagle and reproving him for his unrighteousness, and as for all his words that you have heard, 32this is the Messiah*j* whom the Most High has kept until the end of days, who will arise from the offspring of David, and will come and speak*k* with them. He will denounce them for their ungodliness and for their wickedness, and will display before them their contemptuous dealings. 33For first he will bring them alive before his

a Lat *his*   b Syr Arm: Lat *After*   c Ethiop Arab 1 Arm: Lat Syr *its beginning*   d Syr: Lat *underwings* e Syr Ethiop Arab Arm: Lat *kingdoms*   f Syr Ethiop Arm: Lat *he*   g Lat *them*   h Arab 1: Lat *underwings* i Syr Ethiop: Lat lacks *to*   j Literally *anointed one* k Syr: Lat lacks *of days . . . and speak* judgment seat, and when he has reproved them, then he will destroy them. 34But in mercy he will set free the remnant of my people, those who have been saved throughout my borders, and he will make them joyful until the end comes, the day of judgment, of which I spoke to you at the beginning. 35This is the dream that you saw, and this is its interpretation. 36And you alone were worthy to learn this secret of the Most High. 37Therefore write all these things that you have seen in a book, put it*a* in a hidden place; 38and you shall teach them to the wise among your people, whose hearts you know are able to comprehend and keep these secrets. 39But as for you, wait here seven days more, so that you may be shown whatever it pleases the Most High to show you." Then he left me.

12.3b–39: Vision of the eagle and the lion interpreted. 4: Ezra, disturbed by the vision, takes up Uriel's reproach of 4.10–11 against himself. **7–9:** He has finally accepted, however, that his righteousness makes him worthy of special revelations. **11–12:** Here the author acknowledges his reinterpretation of Dan 7. **14–21:** The interpretation* provides no new information to help in identifying the wings and winglets. **18:** See comment on 11.25–29. **23:** Note the author's belief that God controls all events of history. **27–28:** See comment on 11.35. Domitian, like Titus, did in fact meet a violent end; but since this was quite predictable, these verses could have been written before his death. **29–30:** Compare comment at 12.1–3. In the vision, the lion appears before the brief reign of these two little wings. **32–34:** *The Messiah★:* Compare 7.28–29 and 13.25–52. Only here is he described as being from the family of David. His judgment of the Romans is quite separate from the final judgment by God. **37–38:** Compare 8.62; Dan 12.4.

40 When all the people heard that the seven days were past and I had not returned to the city, they all gathered together, from the least to the greatest, and came to me and spoke to me, saying, 41"How have we offended you, and what harm have we done you, that you have forsaken us and sit in this place? 42For of all the prophets you alone are left to us, like a cluster of grapes from the vintage, and like a lamp in a dark place, and

like a haven for a ship saved from a storm. 43Are not the disasters that have befallen us enough? 44Therefore if you forsake us, how much better it would have been for us if we also had been consumed in the burning of Zion. 45For we are no better than those who died there." And they wept with a loud voice.

Then I answered them and said, 46"Take courage, O Israel; and do not be sorrowful, O house of Jacob; 47for the Most High has you in remembrance, and the Mighty One has not forgotten you in your struggle. 48As for me, I have neither forsaken you nor withdrawn from you; but I have come to this place to pray on account of the desolation of Zion, and to seek mercy on account of the humiliation of our*b* sanctuary. 49Now go to your homes, every one of you, and after these days I will come to you." 50So the people went into the city, as I told them to do. 51But I sat in the field seven days, as the angel*c* had commanded me; and I ate only of the flowers of the field, and my food was of plants during those days.

12.40–51: Conclusion of the fifth episode. The interlude between the two dream visions, though longer, resembles the interlude between the first and second dialogues (5.13–20). **40:** In fact, nine days (counting inclusively) have passed since Ezra went out to the field of Ardat (9.26–27); *the seven days* he was commanded to wait in the previous verse are still to come (see v. 51). **42:** See comment on 1.1. **43–44:** The people's despair recalls that of Ezra in 5.35. **46–48:** Ezra's words of comfort contradict Uriel's conviction that God's mercy toward Israel is a thing of the past (*7.131*). On the other hand, they are consistent with the message of the preceding vision and especially the one that follows: God will send the messiah★ to save the remnant of Israel (12.34; 13.48–49).

1 3 After seven days I dreamed a dream in the night. 2And lo, a wind arose from the sea and stirred up*d* all its waves. 3As I kept looking the wind made something like the figure of a man come up out of the heart of the sea. And I saw*e* that this man

a Ethiop Arab 1 Arab 2 Arm: Lat Syr *them*   *b* Syr Ethiop: Lat *your*   *c* Literally *he*   *d* Other ancient authorities read *I saw a wind arise from the sea and stir up*   *e* Syr: Lat lacks *the wind . . . I saw* flew[a] with the clouds of heaven; and wherever he turned his face to look, everything under his gaze trembled, [4]and whenever his voice issued from his mouth, all who heard his voice melted as wax melts[b] when it feels the fire.

5 After this I looked and saw that an innumerable multitude of people were gathered together from the four winds of heaven to make war against the man who came up out of the sea. [6]And I looked and saw that he carved out for himself a great mountain, and flew up on to it. [7]And I tried to see the region or place from which the mountain was carved, but I could not.

8 After this I looked and saw that all who had gathered together against him, to wage war with him, were filled with fear, and yet they dared to fight. [9]When he saw the onrush of the approaching multitude, he neither lifted his hand nor held a spear or any weapon of war; [10]but I saw only how he sent forth from his mouth something like a stream of fire, and from his lips a flaming breath, and from his tongue he shot forth a storm of sparks.[c] [11]All these were mingled together, the stream of fire and the flaming breath and the great storm, and fell on the onrushing multitude that was prepared to fight, and burned up all of them, so that suddenly nothing was seen of the innumerable multitude but only the dust of ashes and the smell of smoke. When I saw it, I was amazed.

12 After this I saw the same man come down from the mountain and call to himself another multitude that was peaceable. [13]Then many people[d] came to him, some of whom were joyful and some sorrowful; some of them were bound, and some were bringing others as offerings.

13.1–13: Vision of the man. 2–3: As in 11.1–2, the image of *a wind stirring* up the sea is taken from Dan 7.2. But here the figure who rises from the sea is based on the "one like a son of man" of Dan 7.13. **3–4:** The man's supernatural powers recall biblical depictions of God as a warrior; for example, Ps 18.7–15 and 68.1–4. **5:** Compare Ps 2.1–2; Ezek 38.14–16. *The four winds of heaven* means the four directions of the compass. **6–7:** Compare Dan 2.34–35. **9–10:** The man has no need for ordinary weapons; compare the descrip-

tion of the ideal king in Isa 11.4, a passage often interpreted as referring to the messiah.* **12–13:** These verses reflect the traditional belief that the gentiles* will eventually turn to the Lord and help the exiles of Israel to return to Jerusalem. See Isa 45.20–24; 66.18–21.

~~~~~~~~~~~~~~~~~~~

Then I woke up in great terror, and prayed to the Most High, and said, [14]"From the beginning you have shown your servant these wonders, and have deemed me worthy to have my prayer heard by you; [15]now show me the interpretation of this dream also. [16]For as I consider it in my mind, alas for those who will be left in those days! And still more, alas for those who are not left! [17]For those who are not left will be sad [18]because they understand the things that are reserved for the last days, but cannot attain them. [19]But alas for those also who are left, and for that very reason! For they shall see great dangers and much distress, as these dreams show. [20]Yet it is better[e] to come into these things,[f] though incurring peril, than to pass from the world like a cloud, and not to see what will happen in the last days."

He answered me and said, [21]"I will tell you the interpretation of the vision, and I will also explain to you the things that you have mentioned. [22]As for what you said about those who survive, and concerning those who do not survive,[g] this is the interpretation: [23]The one who brings the peril at that time will protect those who fall into peril, who have works and faith toward the Almighty. [24]Understand therefore that those who are left are more blessed than those who have died.

25 "This is the interpretation of the vision: As for your seeing a man come up from the heart of the sea, [26]this is he whom the Most High has been keeping for many ages, who will himself deliver his creation; and he will direct those who are left. [27]And as for your seeing wind and fire and a storm coming out of his mouth, [28]and as for his not

---

a Syr Ethiop Arab Arm: Lat *grew strong*   *b* Syr: Lat *burned as the earth rests*   *c* Meaning of Lat uncertain   *d* Lat Syr Arab 2 literally *the faces of many people*   *e* Ethiop Compare Arab 2: Lat *easier*   *f* Syr: Lat *this*   *g* Syr Arab 1: Lat lacks *and . . . not survive* holding a spear or weapon of war, yet destroying the onrushing multitude that came to conquer him, this is the interpretation: ²⁹The days are coming when the Most High will deliver those who are on the earth. ³⁰And bewilderment of mind shall come over those who inhabit the earth. ³¹They shall plan to make war against one another, city against city, place against place, people against people, and kingdom against kingdom. ³²When these things take place and the signs occur that I showed you before, then my Son will be revealed, whom you saw as a man coming up from the sea.^a

33 "Then, when all the nations hear his voice, all the nations shall leave their own lands and the warfare that they have against one another; ³⁴and an innumerable multitude shall be gathered together, as you saw, wishing to come and conquer him. ³⁵But he shall stand on the top of Mount Zion. ³⁶And Zion shall come and be made manifest to all people, prepared and built, as you saw the mountain carved out without hands. ³⁷Then he, my Son, will reprove the assembled nations for their ungodliness (this was symbolized by the storm), ³⁸and will reproach them to their face with their evil thoughts and the torments with which they are to be tortured (which were symbolized by the flames), and will destroy them without effort by means of the law^b (which was symbolized by the fire).

13.14–55: Vision of the man interpreted. 16–19: The sight of the destruction of a great multitude (13.11) causes Ezra to lapse for a moment into his earlier despair; compare 7.47–48; 9.15–16. **20:** He corrects himself, however: It is better to live through the "signs of the end" than to die ignorant of the divine plan of history. **23:** *Works and faith:* See comment on 9.7; compare 7.77. **26:** Although the word "messiah*" is not used in this chapter, that is clearly the identity of the figure described; compare 12.31–34. **27–28:** These verses anticipate the interpretation* of vv. 9–11, which does not actually come until vv. 37–38. **30–31:** Compare 9.3–4. **32:** Compare 7.28. *My Son:* Variant readings suggest that the original Hebrew may have designated the messiah as "my servant," which came to be translated "my son" through an ambiguity in the Greek. On the other hand, both

vision and interpretation allude to Ps 2, in which God calls the king "my son." **33–34:** See comment on 13.5. **35:** Compare Ps 2.6. **36:** Compare 7.26. *Without hands:* Although these words do not occur in 13.6–7, they are also taken from Dan 2.34–35. **37–38:** The divine warrior* images of the vision are interpreted as symbols of less violent judicial actions.

39 "And as for your seeing him gather to himself another multitude that was peaceable, ⁴⁰these are the nine^c tribes that were taken away from their own land into exile in the days of King Hoshea, whom Shalmaneser, king of the Assyrians, made captives; he took them across the river, and they were taken into another land. ⁴¹But they formed this plan for themselves, that they would leave the multitude of the nations and go to a more distant region, where no human beings had ever lived, ⁴²so that there at least they might keep their statutes that they had not kept in their own land. ⁴³And they went in by the narrow passages of the Euphrates river. ⁴⁴For at that time the Most High performed signs for them, and stopped the channels of the river until they had crossed over. ⁴⁵Through that region there was a long way to go, a journey of a year and a half; and that country is called Arzareth.^d

46 "Then they lived there until the last times; and now, when they are about to come again, ⁴⁷the Most High will stop^e the channels of the river again, so that they may be able to cross over. Therefore you saw the multitude gathered together in peace. ⁴⁸But those who are left of your people, who are found within my holy borders, shall be saved.^f ⁴⁹Therefore when he destroys the multitude of the nations that are gathered together, he will defend the people who remain. ⁵⁰And then he will show them very many wonders."

51 I said, "O sovereign Lord, explain this to me: Why did I see the man coming up from the heart of the sea?"

52 He said to me, "Just as no one can explore or know what is in the depths of the

a Syr and most Lat Mss lack *from the sea*   *b* Syr: Lat *effort and the law*   *c* Other Lat Mss *ten;* Syr Ethiop Arab 1 Arm *nine and a half*   *d* That is *Another Land*   *e* Syr: Lat *stops*   *f* Syr: Lat lacks *shall be saved* sea, so no one on earth can see my Son or those who are with him, except in the time of his day.ᵃ ⁵³This is the interpretation of the dream that you saw. And you alone have been enlightened about this, ⁵⁴because you have forsaken your own ways and have applied yourself to mine, and have searched out my law; ⁵⁵for you have devoted your life to wisdom, and called understanding your mother. ⁵⁶Therefore I have shown you these things; for there is a reward laid up with the Most High. For it will be that after three more days I will tell you other things, and explain weighty and wondrous matters to you."

57 Then I got up and walked in the field, giving great glory and praise to the Most High for the wonders that he doesᵇ from time to time, ⁵⁸and because he governs the times and whatever things come to pass in their seasons. And I stayed there three days.

13.39–47: This long digression reflects speculations current in the author's time about what became of the "ten lost tribes of Israel" (see 2 Kings 17.18, 23). **40:** The number *nine* (variant nine and a half) may represent the author's attempt to correct the tradition: The tribe of Levi obviously did not all go into exile, since they continued to serve in the Jerusalem Temple.* **44:** This miracle recalls the parting of the Red Sea (Ex 14) and the Jordan River (Josh 3). **48–50:** See comment on 9.8. **51–52:** Whereas in Dan 7.2–3 *the sea* symbolizes chaos or evil, for our author it simply represents mystery*; compare 4.7. *Those who are with him:* See comment on 7.28.

13.56–58: Conclusion of the sixth episode. 56: Ezra is told to wait *three days* before the next and last revelation, bringing the total of his days of solitude and fasting or abstinence to forty (see comment on 6.35). Moses fasted forty days on Mount Sinai while receiving the law (Ex 34.28); in the next episode Ezra is presented as a second Moses. Compare also Elijah's forty-day fast on the mountain of the Lord (1 Kings 19.8). **57–58:** Note how dramatically Ezra's attitude toward God has changed.

14 On the third day, while I was sitting under an oak, suddenly a voice came out of a bush opposite me and said, "Ezra, Ezra!" ²And I answered, "Here I am, Lord," and I rose to my feet. ³Then he said to me,

"I revealed myself in a bush and spoke to Moses when my people were in bondage in Egypt; ⁴and I sent him and ledᶜ my people out of Egypt; and I led him up on Mount Sinai, where I kept him with me many days. ⁵I told him many wondrous things, and showed him the secrets of the times and declared to himᵈ the end of the times. Then I commanded him, saying, ⁶'These words you shall publish openly, and these you shall keep secret.' ⁷And now I say to you: ⁸Lay up in your heart the signs that I have shown you, the dreams that you have seen, and the interpretations that you have heard; ⁹for you shall be taken up from among humankind, and henceforth you shall live with my Son and with those who are like you, until the times are ended. ¹⁰The age has lost its youth, and the times begin to grow old. ¹¹For the age is divided into twelve parts, and nineᵉ of its parts have already passed, ¹²as well as half of the tenth part; so two of its parts remain, besides half of the tenth part.ᶠ ¹³Now therefore, set your house in order, and reprove your people; comfort the lowly among them, and instruct those that are wise.ᵍ And now renounce the life that is corruptible, ¹⁴and put away from you mortal thoughts; cast away from you the burdens of humankind, and divest yourself now of your weak nature; ¹⁵lay to one side the thoughts that are most grievous to you, and hurry to escape from these times. ¹⁶For evils worse than those that you have now seen happen shall take place hereafter. ¹⁷For the weaker the world becomes through old age, the more shall evils be increased upon its inhabitants. ¹⁸Truth shall go farther away, and falsehood shall come near. For the eagleʰ that you saw in the vision is already hurrying to come."

14.1–18: The Lord speaks to Ezra. 1–2: Compare Ex 3.4. **4–6:** The author believes that *on Mount Sinai* Moses received, in addition to the law, *secret* revelations

ᵃ Syr: Ethiop *except when his time and his day have come.* Lat lacks *his*   ᵇ Lat *did*   ᶜ Syr Arab 1 Arab 2 *he led*   ᵈ Syr Ethiop Arab Arm: Lat lacks *declared to him*   ᵉ Cn: Lat Ethiop *ten*   ᶠ Syr lacks verses 11, 12: Ethiop *For the world is divided into ten parts, and has come to the tenth, and half of the tenth remains. Now . . .*   ᵍ Lat lacks *and . . . wise*   ʰ Syr Ethiop Arab Arm: Meaning of Lat uncertain pertaining to the *end times;* compare 3.13–34. **9:** Ezra will be *taken up* to heaven to become one of the companions of the messiah*; see comments on 6.26; 7.28. **10:** Compare 5.50–55. **11–12:** This is the book's only numerical reckoning of the time remaining to the end, and the actual numbers differ among the versions. Compare Dan 12.7. **13:** Ezra's responsibility toward the people of Israel in general is simply to *comfort* them, as he did in 12.46–49. He is to share the apocalyptic* secrets only with a few *who are wise;* compare 12.37–38. **14–15:** In preparation for his assumption into heaven, Ezra must put aside his concern for sinful humanity. **16–18:** He will be spared from witnessing the deterioration of the world prior to the end; compare 5.1–12.

19 Then I answered and said, "Let me speak*a* in your presence, Lord. 20For I will go, as you have commanded me, and I will reprove the people who are now living; but who will warn those who will be born hereafter? For the world lies in darkness, and its inhabitants are without light. 21For your law has been burned, and so no one knows the things which have been done or will be done by you. 22If then I have found favor with you, send the holy spirit into me, and I will write everything that has happened in the world from the beginning, the things that were written in your law, so that people may be able to find the path, and that those who want to live in the last days may do so."

23 He answered me and said, "Go and gather the people, and tell them not to seek you for forty days. 24But prepare for yourself many writing tablets, and take with you Sarea, Dabria, Selemia, Ethanus, and Asiel—these five, who are trained to write rapidly; 25and you shall come here, and I will light in your heart the lamp of understanding, which shall not be put out until what you are about to write is finished. 26And when you have finished, some things you shall make public, and some you shall deliver in secret to the wise; tomorrow at this hour you shall begin to write."

27 Then I went as he commanded me, and I gathered all the people together, and said, 28"Hear these words, O Israel. 29At first our ancestors lived as aliens in Egypt, and they were liberated from there 30and re-

ceived the law of life, which they did not keep, which you also have transgressed after them. 31Then land was given to you for a possession in the land of Zion; but you and your ancestors committed iniquity and did not keep the ways that the Most High commanded you. 32And since he is a righteous judge, in due time he took from you what he had given. 33And now you are here, and your people*b* are farther in the interior.*c* 34If you, then, will rule over your minds and discipline your hearts, you shall be kept alive, and after death you shall obtain mercy. 35For after death the judgment will come, when we shall live again; and then the names of the righteous shall become manifest, and the deeds of the ungodly shall be disclosed. 36But let no one come to me now, and let no one seek me for forty days."

37 So I took the five men, as he commanded me, and we proceeded to the field, and remained there. 38And on the next day a voice called me, saying, "Ezra, open your mouth and drink what I give you to drink." 39So I opened my mouth, and a full cup was offered to me; it was full of something like water, but its color was like fire. 40I took it and drank; and when I had drunk it, my heart poured forth understanding, and wisdom increased in my breast, for my spirit retained its memory, 41and my mouth was opened and was no longer closed. 42Moreover, the Most High gave understanding to the five men, and by turns they wrote what was dictated, using characters that they did not know.*d* They sat forty days; they wrote during the daytime, and ate their bread at night. 43But as for me, I spoke in the daytime and was not silent at night. 44So during the forty days, ninety-four*e* books were written. 45And when the forty days were ended, the Most High spoke to me, saying, "Make public the twenty-four*f* books that you wrote first, and let the worthy and the unworthy read them; 46but keep the seventy that were written last, in order to give them to the wise

a Most Lat Mss lack *Let me speak*   *b* Lat *brothers*
c Syr Ethiop Arm: Lat *are among you*   *d* Syr Compare
Ethiop Arab 2 Arm: Meaning of Lat uncertain
e Syr Ethiop Arab 1 Arm: Meaning of Lat uncertain
f Syr Arab 1: Lat lacks *twenty-four*

among your people. [47]For in them is the spring of understanding, the fountain of wisdom, and the river of knowledge." [48]And I did so.[a]

14.19–48: The restoration of the Scriptures. 21: For the idea that the law was destroyed along with Jerusalem, compare 4.23. Here, *law* seems to mean the Scriptures as a whole. **23:** *Forty days* : See comment on 13.56. **24:** The names of Ezra's five assistants or disciples are all biblical, but do not belong to figures from Ezra's time. **27–35:** Ezra's speech to the people reflects Uriel's teaching about the law and judgment. Nevertheless, he conceals the fact that few will be saved, presenting the judgment as an instance of God's mercy (contrast 7.33). **38–41:** The fiery liquid represents inspiration; compare Ezek 2.8–3.3 and Rev 10.8–11. **42:** His assistants apparently require a lesser form of inspiration in order to write in an unfamiliar alphabet.★ The present Hebrew alphabet was taken over from Aramaic★ in Ezra's time. **44–46:** The *twenty-four books* are the canonical★ Jewish Scriptures (traditionally, the twelve minor prophets★ are counted as one book), but the *seventy that were written last* cannot be identified with any known books. Probably they represent apocalyptic★ works known to the author, who counted himself among the wise persons who are worthy to know God's secrets. **47:** For the imagery, compare Sir 24.23–31; there, however, it is the law that overflows with wisdom. **48:** The text preserved in note *a* probably reflects the original ending of 4 Ezra, since his assumption to heaven was promised in 14.9. These lines would have been removed when 6 Ezra was added to 4 Ezra in the Latin text (see introduction).

15 [b]Speak in the ears of my people the words of the prophecy that I will put in your mouth, says the Lord, [2]and cause them to be written on paper; for they are trustworthy and true. [3]Do not fear the plots against you, and do not be troubled by the unbelief of those who oppose you. [4]For all unbelievers shall die in their unbelief.[c]

15.1–4: Command to prophesy. Sixth Ezra begins abruptly, as if it were simply a continuation of God's instructions to Ezra in 14.45–48. Since it was probably composed independently of 4 Ezra, its own introduc-

tion may have been removed to make for a smoother transition.

[5] Beware, says the Lord, I am bringing evils upon the world, the sword and famine, death and destruction, [6]because iniquity has spread throughout every land, and their harmful doings have reached their limit. [7]Therefore, says the Lord, [8]I will be silent no longer concerning their ungodly acts that they impiously commit, neither will I tolerate their wicked practices. Innocent and righteous blood cries out to me, and the souls of the righteous cry out continually. [9]I will surely avenge them, says the Lord, and will receive to myself all the innocent blood from among them. [10]See, my people are being led like a flock to the slaughter; I will not allow them to live any longer in the land of Egypt, [11]but I will bring them out with a mighty hand and with an uplifted arm, and will strike Egypt with plagues, as before, and will destroy all its land.

[12] Let Egypt mourn, and its foundations, because of the plague of chastisement and castigation that the Lord will bring upon it. [13]Let the farmers that till the ground mourn, because their seed shall fail to grow[d] and their trees shall be ruined by blight and hail and by a terrible tempest. [14]Alas for the world and for those who live in it! [15]For the sword and misery draw near them, and nation shall rise up to fight against nation, with swords in their hands. [16]For there shall be unrest among people; growing strong against one another, they shall in their might have no respect for their king or the chief of their leaders. [17]For a person will desire to go into a city, and shall not be able to do so. [18]Because of their pride the cities shall be in confusion, the houses shall be destroyed, and

a Syr adds *in the seventh year of the sixth week, five thousand years and three months and twelve days after creation. At that time Ezra was caught up, and taken to the place of those who are like him, after he had written all these things. And he was called the scribe of the knowledge of the Most High for ever and ever. Ethiop Arab 1 Arm* have a similar ending   *b* Chapters 15 and 16 (except 15.57–59, which has been found in Greek) are extant only in Lat   *c* Other ancient authorities add *and all who believe shall be saved by their faith*   *d* Lat lacks *to grow* people shall be afraid. ¹⁹People shall have no pity for their neighbors, but shall make an assault upon*a* their houses with the sword, and plunder their goods, because of hunger for bread and because of great tribulation.

20 See how I am calling together all the kings of the earth to turn to me, says God, from the rising sun and from the south, from the east and from Lebanon; to turn and repay what they have given them. ²¹Just as they have done to my elect until this day, so I will do, and will repay into their bosom. Thus says the Lord God: ²²My right hand will not spare the sinners, and my sword will not cease from those who shed innocent blood on earth. ²³And a fire went forth from his wrath, and consumed the foundations of the earth and the sinners, like burnt straw. ²⁴Alas for those who sin and do not observe my commandments, says the Lord;*b* ²⁵I will not spare them. Depart, you faithless children! Do not pollute my sanctuary. ²⁶For God*c* knows all who sin against him; therefore he will hand them over to death and slaughter. ²⁷Already calamities have come upon the whole earth, and you shall remain in them; God*c* will not deliver you, because you have sinned against him.

15.5–27: Impending doom for sinners. The prophecies of 6 Ezra are motivated by the belief that the end of the world is at hand; many of the calamities predicted in 15.5–16.34 recall the "signs" of the end in 4 Ezra 5.1–13 and 6.17–24. **10:** *My people:* It is generally assumed that the author and his audience, who were evidently suffering persecution, were Christians, but it is possible that 6 Ezra, like 4 Ezra, was a Jewish composition. *Egypt* is probably just a symbol for oppressive rulers, but it may have been the actual location of the author's community. **20–22:** The *kings of the earth* are the primary target of God's vengeance, because they have caused *innocent blood* to be shed. **24–27:** No one who has broken the commandments will go unpunished, however.

---

28 What a terrifying sight, appearing from the east! ²⁹The nations of the dragons of Arabia shall come out with many chariots, and from the day that they set out, their hissing shall spread over the earth, so that all

who hear them will fear and tremble. ³⁰Also the Carmonians, raging in wrath, shall go forth like wild boars*d* from the forest, and with great power they shall come and engage them in battle, and with their tusks they shall devastate a portion of the land of the Assyrians with their teeth. ³¹And then the dragons,*e* remembering their origin, shall become still stronger; and if they combine in great power and turn to pursue them, ³²then these shall be disorganized and silenced by their power, and shall turn and flee.*f* ³³And from the land of the Assyrians an enemy in ambush shall attack them and destroy one of them, and fear and trembling shall come upon their army, and indecision upon their kings.

34 See the clouds from the east, and from the north to the south! Their appearance is exceedingly threatening, full of wrath and storm. ³⁵They shall clash against one another and shall pour out a heavy tempest on the earth, and their own tempest;*g* and there shall be blood from the sword as high as a horse's belly ³⁶and a man's thigh and a camel's hock. ³⁷And there shall be fear and great trembling on the earth; those who see that wrath shall be horror-stricken, and they shall be seized with trembling. ³⁸After that, heavy storm clouds shall be stirred up from the south, and from the north, and another part from the west. ³⁹But the winds from the east shall prevail over the cloud that was*h* raised in wrath, and shall dispel it; and the tempest*g* that was to cause destruction by the east wind shall be driven violently toward the south and west. ⁴⁰Great and mighty clouds, full of wrath and tempest, shall rise and destroy all the earth and its inhabitants, and shall pour out upon every high and lofty place*i* a terrible tempest, ⁴¹fire and hail and flying swords and floods of water, so that all the fields and all the streams shall be filled with the abundance of those waters. ⁴²They shall destroy cities and walls, mountains and

a Cn: Lat *shall empty*   *b* Other ancient authorities read *God*   *c* Other ancient authorities read *the Lord*   *d* Other ancient authorities lack *like wild boars*   *e* Cn: Lat *dragon*   *f* Other ancient authorities read *turn their face to the north*   *g* Meaning of Lat uncertain   *h* Literally *that he*   *i* Or *eminent person* hills, trees of the forests, and grass of the meadows, and their grain. ⁴³They shall go on steadily to Babylon and blot it out. ⁴⁴They shall come to it and surround it; they shall pour out on it the tempest*a* and all its fury;*b* then the dust and smoke shall reach the sky, and all who are around it shall mourn for it. ⁴⁵And those who survive shall serve those who have destroyed it.

15.28–45: Visions of terror from the east. 28–33: The first of the two visions is believed to be a symbolic description of a battle between the forces of Odenathus of Palmyra (the dragons of Arabia) and Shapur I of Persia (the Carmonians) which took place in the Roman province of Syria (Assyria) in 260–261 CE. If this interpretation* is correct, the author of 6 Ezra must have written sometime after that date. For the style, compare Dan 8 and 11. **34–45:** The symbolic language of the second vision is much less specific, suggesting that the events it predicts had not yet taken place when it was written. **43:** Babylon is almost certainly a code name for Rome (compare 3.28–36 and Rev 18). Evidently, the author anticipated the destruction of Rome by an army from the east.

46 And you, Asia, who share in the splendor of Babylon and the glory of her person— ⁴⁷woe to you, miserable wretch! For you have made yourself like her; you have decked out your daughters for prostitution to please and glory in your lovers, who have always lusted after you. ⁴⁸You have imitated that hateful one in all her deeds and devices.*c* Therefore God*d* says, ⁴⁹I will send evils upon you: widowhood, poverty, famine, sword, and pestilence, bringing ruin to your houses, bringing destruction and death. ⁵⁰And the glory of your strength shall wither like a flower when the heat shall rise that is sent upon you. ⁵¹You shall be weakened like a wretched woman who is beaten and wounded, so that you cannot receive your mighty lovers. ⁵²Would I have dealt with you so violently, says the Lord, ⁵³if you had not killed my chosen people continually, exulting and clapping your hands and talking about their death when you were drunk? 54 Beautify your face! ⁵⁵The reward of a prostitute is in your lap; therefore you shall receive your recompense. ⁵⁶As you will do to

my chosen people, says the Lord, so God will do to you, and will hand you over to adversities. ⁵⁷Your children shall die of hunger, and you shall fall by the sword; your cities shall be wiped out, and all your people who are in the open country shall fall by the sword. ⁵⁸Those who are in the mountains and highlands*e* shall perish of hunger, and they shall eat their own flesh in hunger for bread and drink their own blood in thirst for water. ⁵⁹Unhappy above all others, you shall come and suffer fresh miseries. ⁶⁰As they pass by they shall crush the hateful*f* city, and shall destroy a part of your land and abolish a portion of your glory, when they return from devastated Babylon. ⁶¹You shall be broken down by them like stubble,*g* and they shall be like fire to you. ⁶²They shall devour you and your cities, your land and your mountains; they shall burn with fire all your forests and your fruitful trees. ⁶³They shall carry your children away captive, plunder your wealth, and mar the glory of your countenance.

15.46–63: Woe to Asia. Asia probably refers to the Roman province of Asia Minor (modern Turkey); it is condemned for adopting many of the customs of its conqueror. **47–48:** The cities (daughters) of Asia Minor were adorned with many temples to the Roman gods. Prostitution is a common metaphor* for the worship of foreign gods in the Hebrew Bible; compare also Rev 17.4–6. **52–59:** Some scholars locate the author's persecuted community in Asia Minor because of the bitterness of these verses. **60:** The nation that destroys Rome will also wipe out Asia on its way back to the east.

16 Woe to you, Babylon and Asia! Woe to you, Egypt and Syria! ²Bind on sackcloth and cloth of goats' hair,*h* and wail for your children, and lament for them; for

---

a Meaning of Lat uncertain   *b* Other ancient authorities add *until they destroy it to its foundations*   *c* Other ancient authorities read *devices, and you have followed after that one about to gratify her magnates and leaders so that you may be made proud and be pleased by her fornications*   *d* Other ancient authorities read *the Lord*   *e* Gk: Lat omits *and highlands*   *f* Another reading is *idle* or *unprofitable*   *g* Other ancient authorities read *like dry straw*   *h* Other ancient authorities lack *cloth of goats' hair* your destruction is at hand. ³The sword has been sent upon you, and who is there to turn it back? ⁴A fire has been sent upon you, and who is there to quench it? ⁵Calamities have been sent upon you, and who is there to drive them away? ⁶Can one drive off a hungry lion in the forest, or quench a fire in the stubble once it has started to burn?ᵃ ⁷Can one turn back an arrow shot by a strong archer? ⁸The Lord God sends calamities, and who will drive them away? ⁹Fire will go forth from his wrath, and who is there to quench it? ¹⁰He will flash lightning, and who will not be afraid? He will thunder, and who will not be terrified? ¹¹The Lord will threaten, and who will not be utterly shattered at his presence? ¹²The earth and its foundations quake, the sea is churned up from the depths, and its waves and the fish with them shall be troubled at the presence of the Lord and the glory of his power. ¹³For his right hand that bends the bow is strong, and his arrows that he shoots are sharp and when they are shot to the ends of the world will not miss once. ¹⁴Calamities are sent forth and shall not return until they come over the earth. ¹⁵The fire is kindled, and shall not be put out until it consumes the foundations of the earth. ¹⁶Just as an arrow shot by a mighty archer does not return, so the calamities that are sent upon the earth shall not return. ¹⁷Alas for me! Alas for me! Who will deliver me in those days?

16.1–17: The inescapable divine retribution. 1: The four places named represent the extent of the Roman Empire. **2–5:** Although to *bind on sackcloth** can be a sign of mourning or repentance (compare Jon 3.5–10), the author does not expect God to forgive his enemies. **6–11:** Compare Am 3.3–8, a similar series of rhetorical* questions intended to illustrate that what the prophet* predicts will inevitably occur. **17:** The author apparently counts himself among the sinners who will be punished in the end, an interesting parallel to 4 Ezra.

---

18 The beginning of sorrows, when there shall be much lamentation; the beginning of famine, when many shall perish; the beginning of wars, when the powers shall be terrified; the beginning of calamities, when all

shall tremble. What shall they do, when the calamities come? ¹⁹Famine and plague, tribulation and anguish are sent as scourges for the correction of humankind. ²⁰Yet for all this they will not turn from their iniquities, or ever be mindful of the scourges. ²¹Indeed, provisions will be so cheap upon earth that people will imagine that peace is assured for them, and then calamities shall spring up on the earth—the sword, famine, and great confusion. ²²For many of those who live on the earth shall perish by famine; and those who survive the famine shall die by the sword. ²³And the dead shall be thrown out like dung, and there shall be no one to console them; for the earth shall be left desolate, and its cities shall be demolished. ²⁴No one shall be left to cultivate the earth or to sow it. ²⁵The trees shall bear fruit, but who will gather it? ²⁶The grapes shall ripen, but who will tread them? For in all places there shall be great solitude; ²⁷a person will long to see another human being, or even to hear a human voice. ²⁸For ten shall be left out of a city; and two, out of the field, those who have hidden themselves in thick groves and clefts in the rocks. ²⁹Just as in an olive orchard three or four olives may be left on every tree, ³⁰or just as, when a vineyard is gathered, some clusters may be leftᵇ by those who search carefully through the vineyard, ³¹so in those days three or four shall be left by those who search their houses with the sword. ³²The earth shall be left desolate, and its fields shall be plowed up,ᶜ and its roads and all its paths shall bring forth thorns, because no sheep will go along them. ³³Virgins shall mourn because they have no bridegrooms; women shall mourn because they have no husbands; their daughters shall mourn, because they have no help. ³⁴Their bridegrooms shall be killed in war, and their husbands shall perish of famine.

16.18–34: The devastation of humankind. 18: The *calamities* will begin suddenly. **19–20:** Sinners will re-

---

a Other ancient authorities read *fire when dry straw has been set on fire*   *b* Other ancient authorities read *a cluster may remain exposed*   *c* Other ancient authorities read *be for briers* fuse to believe that God is punishing them until it is too late for them to repent (compare Am 4.6–12). **21:** Disaster will strike when it is least expected; compare 1 Thess 5.3. **28:** Compare Am 5.3. **29–31:** For the idea that only a tiny fraction of humanity will be spared from final destruction, compare 9.21; for the image, see Isa 17.6. **32:** Compare Isa 5.6. **33–34:** Compare Jer 7.34.

〰〰〰〰〰〰〰〰〰〰〰〰〰〰〰〰

35 Listen now to these things, and understand them, you who are servants of the Lord. 36This is the word of the Lord; receive it and do not disbelieve what the Lord says.ᵃ 37The calamities draw near, and are not delayed. 38Just as a pregnant woman, in the ninth month when the time of her delivery draws near, has great pains around her womb for two or three hours beforehand, but when the child comes forth from the womb, there will not be a moment's delay, 39so the calamities will not delay in coming upon the earth, and the world will groan, and pains will seize it on every side.

40 Hear my words, O my people; prepare for battle, and in the midst of the calamities be like strangers on the earth. 41Let the one who sells be like one who will flee; let the one who buys be like one who will lose; 42let the one who does business be like one who will not make a profit; and let the one who builds a house be like one who will not live in it; 43let the one who sows be like one who will not reap; so also the one who prunes the vines, like one who will not gather the grapes; 44those who marry, like those who will have no children; and those who do not marry, like those who are widowed. 45Because of this, those who labor, labor in vain; 46for strangers shall gather their fruits, and plunder their goods, overthrow their houses, and take their children captive; for in captivity and famine they will produce their children.ᵇ 47Those who conduct business, do so only to have it plundered; the more they adorn their cities, their houses and possessions, and their persons, 48the more angry I will be with them for their sins, says the Lord. 49Just as a respectable and virtuous woman abhors a prostitute, 50so righteousness shall abhor iniquity, when she decks herself out, and shall accuse her to her face

when he comes who will defend the one who searches out every sin on earth.

─────────────────

16.35–52: Exhortation* to righteousness. For the remainder of the book, the author urges his own community to avoid sin and the concerns of the world that is soon going to end. **37–39:** Compare 4.40–42; Mk 13.8. **40:** *Strangers on the earth:* Compare Heb 11.13–16. **41–48:** One should not set any store in the affairs of the world, both because they will come to nothing and because they are tainted with sin. **50:** *When he comes* refers to the messiah* (or to Jesus' second coming), and *the one who searches out every sin on earth* is God.

〰〰〰〰〰〰〰〰〰〰〰〰〰〰〰〰

51 Therefore do not be like her or her works. 52For in a very short time iniquity will be removed from the earth, and righteousness will reign over us. 53Sinners must not say that they have not sinned;ᶜ for Godᵈ will burn coals of fire on the head of everyone who says, "I have not sinned before God and his glory." 54The Lordᵉ certainly knows everything that people do; he knows their imaginations and their thoughts and their hearts. 55He said, "Let the earth be made," and it was made, and "Let the heaven be made," and it was made. 56At his word the stars were fixed in their places, and he knows the number of the stars. 57He searches the abyss and its treasures; he has measured the sea and its contents; 58he has confined the sea in the midst of the waters;ᶠ and by his word he has suspended the earth over the water. 59He has spread out the heaven like a dome and made it secure upon the waters; 60he has put springs of water in the desert, and pools on the tops of the mountains, so as to send rivers from the heights to water the earth. 61He formed human beings and put a heart in the midst of each body, and gave each person breath and life and understanding 62and the spiritᵍ of Almighty

---

a Cn: Lat *do not believe the gods of whom the Lord speaks*   *b* Other ancient authorities read *therefore those who are married may know that they will produce children for captivity and famine*   *c* Other ancient authorities add *or the unjust done injustice*   *d* Lat *for he*   *e* Other ancient authorities read *Lord God*   *f* Other ancient authorities read *confined the world between the waters and the waters*   *g* Or *breath*

God,[a] who surely made all things and searches out hidden things in hidden places. [63]He knows your imaginations and what you think in your hearts! Woe to those who sin and want to hide their sins! [64]The Lord will strictly examine all their works, and will make a public spectacle of all of you. [65]You shall be put to shame when your sins come out before others, and your own iniquities shall stand as your accusers on that day. [66]What will you do? Or how will you hide your sins before the Lord and his glory? [67]Indeed, God[b] is the judge; fear him! Cease from your sins, and forget your iniquities, never to commit them again; so God[b] will lead you forth and deliver you from all tribulation.

16.53–67: Nothing is hidden from God. 53: A sinner who refuses to confess has no hope of forgiveness; compare 1 Jn 1.8–10. **55–62:** Compare 6.38–54. Here, the point is that nothing in the world is beyond God's knowledge. **61–62:** *Understanding* is here associated with the divine spirit (or *breath;* see Gen 2.7) that animates human beings; contrast with 7.62. **63:** Therefore every thought is known to God. **67:** God will forgive those who repent and stop sinning.

68 The burning wrath of a great multitude is kindled over you; they shall drag some of you away and force you to eat what was sacrificed to idols. [69]And those who consent to eat shall be held in derision and contempt, and shall be trampled under foot. [70]For in many places[c] and in neighboring cities there shall be a great uprising against those who fear the Lord. [71]They shall[d] be like maniacs, sparing no one, but plundering and destroying those who continue to fear the Lord.[e] [72]For they shall destroy and plunder their

goods, and drive them out of house and home. [73]Then the tested quality of my elect shall be manifest, like gold that is tested by fire.

74 Listen, my elect ones, says the Lord; the days of tribulation are at hand, but I will deliver you from them. [75]Do not fear or doubt, for God[b] is your guide. [76]You who keep my commandments and precepts, says the Lord God, must not let your sins weigh you down, or your iniquities prevail over you. [77]Woe to those who are choked by their sins and overwhelmed by their iniquities! They are like a field choked with underbrush and its path[f] overwhelmed with thorns, so that no one can pass through. [78]It is shut off and given up to be consumed by fire.

16.68–78: The test of persecution. 68: *Force you to eat what was sacrificed to idols:* Pagan rulers sometimes required universal participation in their sacrifices, which Jews and Christians alike regarded as an abomination; see 2 Macc 6.7–9; Acts 21.25. **70–72:** The extreme persecution described here may reflect the author's fears rather than actual events. **73:** Persecutions are part of God's plan, intended to test who is truly faithful; compare Zech 13.9. **74:** Nevertheless, God will not allow the elect to be tested for too long. **76–78:** Therefore, they must keep away from sin until the final judgment. If 6 Ezra is a Christian composition, the imagery here may have been drawn from the two sower parables* found together in Mt 13; see especially Mt 13.22, 30, 40–42.

a Other ancient authorities read *of the Lord Almighty*
b Other ancient authorities read *the Lord*   c Meaning of Lat uncertain   d Other ancient authorities read *For people, because of their misfortunes, shall*   e Other ancient authorities read *fear God*   f Other ancient authorities read *seed*

4 MACCABEES

Introduction

Fourth Maccabees is a rhetorical★ treatment of the thesis formally stated in 1.1: "whether devout reason is sovereign over the emotions," a thesis that the author declares to be "most philosophical." The opening section of the book, 1.1–3.18, is a fairly abstract, rhetorical discussion of the nature of reason, the emotions, and the relation between them. Thereafter, the author focuses on the example of the Maccabean martyrs.★ The story of the martyrs is told, but the narrative★ element is always subordinate to the philosophical issue. The discussion of the martyrs has many characteristics of an encomium★ or panegyric, a speech in praise of the dead. Many scholars have accordingly classified the book as a sermon, or as a funeral oration. There is reference to "the present occasion" in 1.10 and 3.19. These features, however, are conventions of the rhetorical schools of Greek and Roman antiquity. Students were trained to write speeches as if they were for specific occasions. There is a reference to the tomb of the martyrs at 17.8, and it is possible that the speech was actually delivered as a commemorative oration. It is probably simpler, however, to suppose that it was written in the form of such an oration, as a philosophical and ethical tract. Fourth Maccabees was never canonical,★ but it was included in important biblical manuscripts and was often cited by the church fathers. It appealed to Christians because it was an exposition in praise of martyrdom.

Fourth Maccabees was most probably written in the second half of the first century CE. In 4.2, Cilicia is treated as part of the administrative region of Syria; this was only the case between 20 and 54 CE. Fourth Maccabees can scarcely have been written before this time, but it could have been written later. There is no other indication of the precise date. Neither is there any clear indication of the place of composition. Some scholars tend to ascribe all Jewish works that are written in Greek to Alexandria, which had the most famous and literate Jewish community outside Israel. But there is no specific indication of Alexandrian origin here. Many scholars locate the book in Antioch, because there was a Christian cult of the martyrs there that goes back at least to the fourth century CE. The book could conceivably have been written in Jerusalem, but there is no evidence for any work that presupposes this level of Greek education and was written in the land of Israel. A Diaspora★ origin is virtually certain.

The cultural context of 4 Maccabees is highly Hellenized,★ to a degree that is paralleled among the Jewish writings from antiquity only in the writings of Philo★ and the Wisdom of Solomon. The author must surely have had a good Greek education in the gymnasium. After 50 CE, such an education would have been difficult to obtain in Alexandria. The author is well versed in Greek philosophy and rhetoric.★ Nonetheless, he remains a strictly observant Jew. The distinctive character of the book lies in the attempt to defend strict observance of the law within the categories of Greek philosophy.

READING GUIDE

Fourth Maccabees has sometimes been classified as Stoic★ in its philosophy, but more recent commentators have recognized that it is highly eclectic. Reason is virtually equated with obedience to the law: "Reason is the mind that with sound logic prefers the life of wisdom. Wisdom, next, is the knowledge of divine and human matters and the causes of these. This in turn is education in the law, by which we learn divine matters reverently and human affairs to our advantage" (1.15–17). The equation of wisdom and the law is merely asserted. The thrust of the argument is that it is possible to be faithful to the law even in the face of torture and death. This would seem to argue for the possibility, and admirability, of self-control rather than of reason.

Fourth Maccabees seeks to buttress the reasonableness of observing the law in two ways. One is the doctrine of retribution. The martyrs* look forward to "blessed eternity" (17.18; compare 15.3). By contrast, the persecutor "will deservedly undergo from the divine justice eternal torment by fire." There is no reference to bodily resurrection. While the exact nature of afterlife is not discussed, it is compatible with the immortality of the soul. The other consideration, however, is even more basic in 4 Maccabees: the inherent nobility of virtue. The second brother asks the tyrant: "Do you not think that you are being tortured more than I, as you see the arrogant design of your tyranny being defeated by our endurance for the sake of religion? I lighten my pain by the joys that come from virtue, but you suffer torture by the threats that come from impiety" (9.30–32). Self-control is good in itself. Virtue is not dependent on secondary effects. Observance of the law is a virtue insofar as it leads to control of the passions.

1.1–12	Introduction and statement of thesis
1.13–3.18	Theoretical discussion
3.19–4.26	The background of the persecution
5.1–7.23	The martyrdom* of Eleazar
8.1–14.10	The martyrdom of the seven brothers
14.11–17.6	The martyrdom of the mother
17.7–18.24	A final encomium*

1 The subject that I am about to discuss is most philosophical, that is, whether devout reason is sovereign over the emotions. So it is right for me to advise you to pay earnest attention to philosophy. ²For the subject is essential to everyone who is seeking knowledge, and in addition it includes the praise of the highest virtue—I mean, of course, rational judgment. ³If, then, it is evident that reason rules over those emotions that hinder self-control, namely, gluttony and lust, ⁴it is also clear that it masters the emotions that hinder one from justice, such as malice, and those that stand in the way of courage, namely anger, fear, and pain. ⁵Some might perhaps ask, "If reason rules the emotions, why is it not sovereign over forgetfulness and ignorance?" Their attempt at argument is ridiculous!ᵃ ⁶For reason does not rule its own emotions, but those that are opposed to justice, courage, and self-control;ᵇ and it is not for the purpose of destroying them, but so that one may not give way to them.

1.1–6: Statement of the thesis. 1: The role of *reason* in controlling the passions was brilliantly expressed by Plato in the "Phaedrus" through the image of a charioteer with two horses. Self-control was also very important in Stoic* philosophy. **2–4:** *Rational judgment, self-control, justice,* and *courage* constitute one of several formulations of the four cardinal *virtues* in Platonic and Stoic philosophy. **5:** Rhetorical* handbooks encourage orators to use imaginary debate partners to sharpen the discussion. The objection raised here is repeated at 2.24. It raises two possible counter-arguments: that reason cannot control the emotions, since it cannot control *forgetfulness and ignorance;* and that

a Or *They are attempting to make my argument ridiculous!* b Other ancient authorities add *and rational judgment* to master the emotions is to eliminate them. The author dismisses both objections out of hand.

7 I could prove to you from many and various examples that reason[a] is dominant over the emotions, 8but I can demonstrate it best from the noble bravery of those who died for the sake of virtue, Eleazar and the seven brothers and their mother. 9All of these, by despising sufferings that bring death, demonstrated that reason controls the emotions. 10On this anniversary[b] it is fitting for me to praise for their virtues those who, with their mother, died for the sake of nobility and goodness, but I would also call them blessed for the honor in which they are held. 11All people, even their torturers, marveled at their courage and endurance, and they became the cause of the downfall of tyranny over their nation. By their endurance they conquered the tyrant, and thus their native land was purified through them. 12I shall shortly have an opportunity to speak of this; but, as my custom is, I shall begin by stating my main principle, and then I shall turn to their story, giving glory to the all-wise God.

1.7–12: The choice of examples. 10: The focus on the martyrs* seems to be required in part by the supposed occasion of the oration, whether this is an actual commemoration or a literary fiction. **11:** The author credits the martyrs with *conquering the tyrant* (see Rev 12.10–11) and purifying the land. The emphasis in this book, however, is on the personal virtue of the martyrs.

13 Our inquiry, accordingly, is whether reason is sovereign over the emotions. 14We shall decide just what reason is and what emotion is, how many kinds of emotions there are, and whether reason rules over all these. 15Now reason is the mind that with sound logic prefers the life of wisdom. 16Wisdom, next, is the knowledge of divine and human matters and the causes of these. 17This, in turn, is education in the law, by which we learn divine matters reverently and human affairs to our advantage. 18Now the kinds of wisdom are rational judgment, justice, courage, and self-control. 19Rational judgment is supreme over all of these, since

by means of it reason rules over the emotions. 20The two most comprehensive types[c] of the emotions are pleasure and pain; and each of these is by nature concerned with both body and soul. 21The emotions of both pleasure and pain have many consequences. 22Thus desire precedes pleasure and delight follows it. 23Fear precedes pain and sorrow comes after. 24Anger, as a person will see by reflecting on this experience, is an emotion embracing pleasure and pain. 25In pleasure there exists even a malevolent tendency, which is the most complex of all the emotions. 26In the soul it is boastfulness, covetousness, thirst for honor, rivalry, and malice; 27in the body, indiscriminate eating, gluttony, and solitary gormandizing.

28 Just as pleasure and pain are two plants growing from the body and the soul, so there are many offshoots of these plants,[d] 29each of which the master cultivator, reason, weeds and prunes and ties up and waters and thoroughly irrigates, and so tames the jungle of habits and emotions. 30For reason is the guide of the virtues, but over the emotions it is sovereign.

1.13–30a: Definitions. 16: This definition of *wisdom* may have originated with the Stoics* but was a philosophical commonplace in antiquity. **17:** The identification of wisdom with the Law of Moses was made in Sir 24. It would not have been acknowledged by any non-Jewish philosopher. **18:** The *kinds of wisdom* are the cardinal virtues. **20:** *Pleasure* is taken to imply desire and delight, while *pain* implies fear and sorrow. **24:** The author goes on to refine the understanding of the emotions in greater detail than is required by his subsequent argument.

Observe now, first of all, that rational judgment is sovereign over the emotions by virtue of the restraining power of self-control. 31Self-control, then, is dominance over the desires. 32Some desires are mental, others are physical, and reason obviously rules over both. 33Otherwise, how is it that when we are attracted to forbidden foods we

a Other ancient authorities read *devout reason*
b Gk *At this time*   c Or *sources*   d Other ancient authorities read *these emotions*

abstain from the pleasure to be had from them? Is it not because reason is able to rule over appetites? I for one think so. [34]Therefore when we crave seafood and fowl and animals and all sorts of foods that are forbidden to us by the law, we abstain because of domination by reason. [35]For the emotions of the appetites are restrained, checked by the temperate mind, and all the impulses of the body are bridled by reason.

1.30b–2.23: Examples of the power of reason. The examples are drawn from Jewish law and tradition. **1.30:** *Self-control* in this passage is often translated as "temperance." **33–34:** In Greek tradition, self-control was often exemplified by restraint in eating. Fourth Maccabees finds here a rationale for the Jewish food laws (Lev 11.1–31; Deut 14.3–21). Other Hellenistic* Jewish writers had defended these laws by allegorical* interpretation.* (For instance, the Letter of Aristeas* says that birds forbidden by the Jewish food laws symbolize oppression and violence, while animals that chew the cud symbolize memory, etc.). Fourth Maccabees dispenses with such rationalizations and defends the food laws as exercises in the Greek virtue of self-control.

---

2 And why is it amazing that the desires of the mind for the enjoyment of beauty are rendered powerless? [2]It is for this reason, certainly, that the temperate Joseph is praised, because by mental effort[a] he overcame sexual desire. [3]For when he was young and in his prime for intercourse, by his reason he nullified the frenzy[b] of the passions. [4]Not only is reason proved to rule over the frenzied urge of sexual desire, but also over every desire.[c] [5]Thus the law says, "You shall not covet your neighbor's wife or anything that is your neighbor's." [6]In fact, since the law has told us not to covet, I could prove to you all the more that reason is able to control desires.

Just so it is with the emotions that hinder one from justice. [7]Otherwise how could it be that someone who is habitually a solitary gormandizer, a glutton, or even a drunkard can learn a better way, unless reason is clearly lord of the emotions? [8]Thus, as soon as one adopts a way of life in accordance with the law, even though a lover of money, one is

forced to act contrary to natural ways and to lend without interest to the needy and to cancel the debt when the seventh year arrives. [9]If one is greedy, one is ruled by the law through reason so that one neither gleans the harvest nor gathers the last grapes from the vineyard.

In all other matters we can recognize that reason rules the emotions. [10]For the law prevails even over affection for parents, so that virtue is not abandoned for their sakes. [11]It is superior to love for one's wife, so that one rebukes her when she breaks the law. [12]It takes precedence over love for children, so that one punishes them for misdeeds. [13]It is sovereign over the relationship of friends, so that one rebukes friends when they act wickedly. [14]Do not consider it paradoxical when reason, through the law, can prevail even over enmity. The fruit trees of the enemy are not cut down, but one preserves the property of enemies from marauders and helps raise up what has fallen.[d]

[15]It is evident that reason rules even[e] the more violent emotions: lust for power, vainglory, boasting, arrogance, and malice. [16]For the temperate mind repels all these malicious emotions, just as it repels anger—for it is sovereign over even this. [17]When Moses was angry with Dathan and Abiram, he did nothing against them in anger, but controlled his anger by reason. [18]For, as I have said, the temperate mind is able to get the better of the emotions, to correct some, and to render others powerless. [19]Why else did Jacob, our most wise father, censure the households of Simeon and Levi for their irrational slaughter of the entire tribe of the Shechemites, saying, "Cursed be their anger"? [20]For if reason could not control anger, he would not have spoken thus. [21]Now when God fashioned human beings, he planted in them emotions and inclinations, [22]but at the same time he enthroned the mind among the senses as a sacred governor over them all. [23]To the mind he gave the law; and one who lives subject to this will

a Other ancient authorities add *in reasoning*
b Or *gadfly*   c Or *all covetousness*   d Or *the beasts that have fallen*   e Other ancient authorities read *through*

rule a kingdom that is temperate, just, good, and courageous.

2.1–23. 2: In the Testaments of the Twelve Patriarchs,* a Christian work that embodies much Jewish tradition, each of the patriarchs exemplifies a virtue, either by positive or negative example. *Joseph* exemplifies self-control. For the biblical story, see Gen 39. 6: The reasoning is circular, since the author takes the rational character of the law as axiomatic. 8: The law on *lending without interest* applies only to lending to Jews (Ex 22.25; Lev 25.36; Deut 23.20). This also holds for the remission of *debt* (Deut 15.1–3). 9: The *gleanings** of *the harvest* were to be left for the poor and the alien (Lev 19.9–10). 10: Reverence for *parents* ranks immediately after reverence for God in Jewish tradition (Lev 19.2–3). In contrast, family ties are downgraded in the New Testament: "Whoever loves father or mother more than me is not worthy of me, and whoever loves son or daughter more than me is not worthy of me" (Mt 10.37–38; compare Lk 14.26). The point in 4 Maccabees is that the law takes precedence over all other obligations. 14: For the *fruit trees:* Deut 20.19–20; for raising up *what has fallen:* Ex 23.4–5. 17: In Num 16.1–35 *Moses* appeals to the Lord, who causes the ground to open under Korah and his associates. This would seem to be a dubious example of rational restraint. 19: *Jacob's* rebuke of *Simeon* and *Levi* (Gen 34.30; 49.7) is a better example. 21: According to Jewish tradition, God gave humanity two *inclinations,* one good and one bad, but the evil inclination can be controlled. Compare Sir 15.14–15: "It was he who created humanity in the beginning and left them in the power of their inclination. If you choose, you can keep the commandments, and to act faithfully is a matter of your own choice." The Middle Stoics* (Panaetius, Posidonius) also taught that the emotions were innate and could be controlled but not eradicated. 23a: Compare Sir 17.11: "He bestowed knowledge upon them, and allotted them the law of life." 23b: Compare Wis 6.20: "The desire for a kingdom leads to a kingdom." The Stoics taught that the wise man who lives according to reason is the only true king, as he controls the only things over which a person has real power.

---

24 How is it then, one might say, that if reason is master of the emotions, it does not control forgetfulness and ignorance? 3 ¹But this argument is entirely ridiculous; for it is evident that reason rules not over its own emotions, but over those of the body. ²No one of us*a* can eradicate that kind of desire, but reason can provide a way for us not to be enslaved by desire. ³No one of us can eradicate anger from the mind, but reason can help to deal with anger. ⁴No one of us can eradicate malice, but reason can fight at our side so that we are not overcome by malice. ⁵For reason does not uproot the emotions but is their antagonist.

6 Now this can be explained more clearly by the story of King David's thirst. ⁷David had been attacking the Philistines all day long, and together with the soldiers of his nation had killed many of them. ⁸Then when evening fell, he*b* came, sweating and quite exhausted, to the royal tent, around which the whole army of our ancestors had encamped. ⁹Now all the rest were at supper, ¹⁰but the king was extremely thirsty, and though springs were plentiful there, he could not satisfy his thirst from them. ¹¹But a certain irrational desire for the water in the enemy's territory tormented and inflamed him, undid and consumed him. ¹²When his guards complained bitterly because of the king's craving, two staunch young soldiers, respecting*c* the king's desire, armed themselves fully, and taking a pitcher climbed over the enemy's ramparts. ¹³Eluding the sentinels at the gates, they went searching throughout the enemy camp ¹⁴and found the spring, and from it boldly brought the king a drink. ¹⁵But David,*d* though he was burning with thirst, considered it an altogether fearful danger to his soul to drink what was regarded as equivalent to blood. ¹⁶Therefore, opposing reason to desire, he poured out the drink as an offering to God. ¹⁷For the temperate mind can conquer the drives of the emotions and quench the flames of frenzied desires; ¹⁸it can overthrow bodily agonies even when they are extreme, and by nobility of reason spurn all domination by the emotions.

2.24–3.18: King David's thirst. 2.24: The author repeats the question from 1.5, again insisting that reason

a Gk *you*   *b* Other ancient authorities read *he hurried and*   *c* Or *embarrassed because of*   *d* Gk *he* does not rule over its own emotions, and does not eradicate emotions but controls them. **6:** For *King David's thirst,* see 2 Sam 23.13–17; 1 Chr 11.15–19. **8:** The details of the story are embellished. **10:** Second Samuel makes no reference to *plentiful springs,* nor to complaints of the guards (v. 12). **11:** The Greek terms here reflect technical Stoic* discussions of the working of the emotions. **18:** The reference to *bodily agonies* anticipates the stories of the martyrs.*

~~~~~~~~~~~~~~~~~~~~~~~~~~~~~

19 The present occasion now invites us to a narrative demonstration of temperate reason.

20 At a time when our ancestors were enjoying profound peace because of their observance of the law and were prospering, so that even Seleucus Nicanor, king of Asia, had both appropriated money to them for the temple service and recognized their commonwealth— 21 just at that time certain persons attempted a revolution against the public harmony and caused many and various disasters.

4 Now there was a certain Simon, a political opponent of the noble and good man, Onias, who then held the high priesthood for life. When despite all manner of slander he was unable to injure Onias in the eyes of the nation, he fled the country with the purpose of betraying it. 2 So he came to Apollonius, governor of Syria, Phoenicia, and Cilicia, and said, 3 "I have come here because I am loyal to the king's government, to report that in the Jerusalem treasuries there are deposited tens of thousands in private funds, which are not the property of the temple but belong to King Seleucus." 4 When Apollonius learned the details of these things, he praised Simon for his service to the king and went up to Seleucus to inform him of the rich treasure. 5 On receiving authority to deal with this matter, he proceeded quickly to our country accompanied by the accursed Simon and a very strong military force. 6 He said that he had come with the king's authority to seize the private funds in the treasury. 7 The people indignantly protested his words, considering it outrageous that those who had committed deposits to the sacred treasury should be deprived of them, and did all that they could to prevent

it. 8 But, uttering threats, Apollonius went on to the temple. 9 While the priests together with women and children were imploring God in the temple to shield the holy place that was being treated so contemptuously, 10 and while Apollonius was going up with his armed forces to seize the money, angels on horseback with lightning flashing from their weapons appeared from heaven, instilling in them great fear and trembling. 11 Then Apollonius fell down half dead in the temple area that was open to all, stretched out his hands toward heaven, and with tears begged the Hebrews to pray for him and propitiate the wrath of the heavenly army. 12 For he said that he had committed a sin deserving of death, and that if he were spared he would praise the blessedness of the holy place before all people. 13 Moved by these words, the high priest Onias, although otherwise he had scruples about doing so, prayed for him so that King Seleucus would not suppose that Apollonius had been overcome by human treachery and not by divine justice. 14 So Apollonius,[a] having been saved beyond all expectations, went away to report to the king what had happened to him.

15 When King Seleucus died, his son Antiochus Epiphanes succeeded to the throne, an arrogant and terrible man, 16 who removed Onias from the priesthood and appointed Onias's[b] brother Jason as high priest. 17 Jason[c] agreed that if the office were conferred on him he would pay the king three thousand six hundred sixty talents annually. 18 So the king appointed him high priest and ruler of the nation. 19 Jason[c] changed the nation's way of life and altered its form of government in complete violation of the law, 20 so that not only was a gymnasium constructed at the very citadel[d] of our native land, but also the temple service was abolished. 21 The divine justice was angered by these acts and caused Antiochus himself to make war on them. 22 For when he was warring against Ptolemy in Egypt, he heard that a rumor of his death had spread and that the people of Jerusalem had rejoiced greatly. He speedily marched against them, 23 and af-

a Gk *he*   *b* Gk *his*   *c* Gk *He*   *d* Or *high place* ter he had plundered them he issued a decree that if any of them were found observing the ancestral law they should die. 24When, by means of his decrees, he had not been able in any way to put an end to the people's observance of the law, but saw that all his threats and punishments were being disregarded 25—even to the extent that women, because they had circumcised their sons, were thrown headlong from heights along with their infants, though they had known beforehand that they would suffer this— 26when, I say, his decrees were despised by the people, he himself tried through torture to compel everyone in the nation to eat defiling foods and to renounce Judaism.

3.19–4.26: The background of the persecution. 3.19: The style of the book changes at this point from philosophical argument to narrative.* **3.20:** See 3 Macc 3.1–3. The author has confused Seleucus I Nicator (mistakenly called Nicanor, the name of the adversary of Judas Maccabee), who reigned from 305/4 until 281/0 BCE, with Seleucus IV Philopator (187–175 BCE). **4.2:** In 2 Maccabees, Heliodorus is the Syrian official in question. *Apollonius* appears later in another attack on Jerusalem in 2 Macc 5.24–6. The combination of *Syria, Phoenicia,* and *Cilicia* in one administrative district is anachronistic.* They were only so combined in 20–54 CE. In 2 Macc 4.4 Apollonius is governor only of Coelesyria and Phoenicia. **4.3:** The reference to *tens of thousands* shows the author's tendency to exaggeration. **13:** *Onias's* scruples are not noted in 2 Maccabees. **14:** Unlike Heliodorus, Apollonius does not offer sacrifice or give testimony to the power of the Lord. **15:** *Antiochus Epiphanes** was the brother, not the son, of Seleucus IV. **17:** According to 2 Macc 4.8, Jason offered the king 360 talents from one source and 80 from another. Fourth Maccabees multiplies the first number by ten. **21:** No other source is so explicit in saying that God caused Antiochus Epiphanes* to *make war* on the Jews, but 2 Maccabees also views the persecution as punishment for sin. **22:** It is clear from 2 Maccabees that fighting had already broken out in Jerusalem before the king intervened. **25:** See 1 Macc 1.60–61; 2 Macc 6.10.

5 The tyrant Antiochus, sitting in state with his counselors on a certain high place, and with his armed soldiers standing around him, 2ordered the guards to seize

each and every Hebrew and to compel them to eat pork and food sacrificed to idols. 3If any were not willing to eat defiling food, they were to be broken on the wheel and killed. 4When many persons had been rounded up, one man, Eleazar by name, leader of the flock, was brought[a] before the king. He was a man of priestly family, learned in the law, advanced in age, and known to many in the tyrant's court because of his philosophy.[b]

5 When Antiochus saw him he said, 6"Before I begin to torture you, old man, I would advise you to save yourself by eating pork, 7for I respect your age and your gray hairs. Although you have had them for so long a time, it does not seem to me that you are a philosopher when you observe the religion of the Jews. 8When nature has granted it to us, why should you abhor eating the very excellent meat of this animal? 9It is senseless not to enjoy delicious things that are not shameful, and wrong to spurn the gifts of nature. 10It seems to me that you will do something even more senseless if, by holding a vain opinion concerning the truth, you continue to despise me to your own hurt. 11Will you not awaken from your foolish philosophy, dispel your futile reasonings, adopt a mind appropriate to your years, philosophize according to the truth of what is beneficial, 12and have compassion on your old age by honoring my humane advice? 13For consider this: if there is some power watching over this religion of yours, it will excuse you from any transgression that arises out of compulsion."

5.1–6.35: The martyrdom* of Eleazar. 5.1: *Antiochus* was not said to be personally present at the martyrdom of Eleazar in 2 Macc 5.18–31. Fourth Maccabees emphasizes the central, public location of the martyrdoms. **4:** In 2 Maccabees, *Eleazar* was an aged scribe* in high position. Here he is a *priest* and a well-known *philosopher*. His death may then be compared to the deaths of philosophers in Greek and Roman tradition. **7:** As Antiochus poses the question, the issue is whether one can be both a philosopher and an observant Jew. **8:** The reference to *nature* recalls the Stoic*

a *Or was the first of the flock to be brought*   b *Other ancient authorities read his advanced age* ideal, "to live in harmony with nature." **9:** The idea that one should *enjoy delicious things* is vaguely Epicurean.* See also the speech of the unrighteous in Wis 2. **13:** Antiochus even attempts to relieve Eleazar's scruples by reminding him of divine mercy.

14 When the tyrant urged him in this fashion to eat meat unlawfully, Eleazar asked to have a word. 15When he had received permission to speak, he began to address the people as follows: 16"We, O Antiochus, who have been persuaded to govern our lives by the divine law, think that there is no compulsion more powerful than our obedience to the law. 17Therefore we consider that we should not transgress it in any respect. 18Even if, as you suppose, our law were not truly divine and we had wrongly held it to be divine, not even so would it be right for us to invalidate our reputation for piety. 19Therefore do not suppose that it would be a petty sin if we were to eat defiling food; 20to transgress the law in matters either small or great is of equal seriousness, 21for in either case the law is equally despised. 22You scoff at our philosophy as though living by it were irrational, 23but it teaches us self-control, so that we master all pleasures and desires, and it also trains us in courage, so that we endure any suffering willingly; 24it instructs us in justice, so that in all our dealings we act impartially,*a* and it teaches us piety, so that with proper reverence we worship the only living God.

25 "Therefore we do not eat defiling food; for since we believe that the law was established by God, we know that in the nature of things the Creator of the world in giving us the law has shown sympathy toward us. 26He has permitted us to eat what will be most suitable for our lives,*b* but he has forbidden us to eat meats that would be contrary to this. 27It would be tyrannical for you to compel us not only to transgress the law, but also to eat in such a way that you may deride us for eating defiling foods, which are most hateful to us. 28But you shall have no such occasion to laugh at me, 29nor will I transgress the sacred oaths of my ancestors concerning the keeping of the law, 30not even if you gouge out my eyes and burn my entrails.

31I am not so old and cowardly as not to be young in reason on behalf of piety. 32Therefore get your torture wheels ready and fan the fire more vehemently! 33I do not so pity my old age as to break the ancestral law by my own act. 34I will not play false to you, O law that trained me, nor will I renounce you, beloved self-control. 35I will not put you to shame, philosophical reason, nor will I reject you, honored priesthood and knowledge of the law. 36You, O king,*c* shall not defile the honorable mouth of my old age, nor my long life lived lawfully. 37My ancestors will receive me as pure, as one who does not fear your violence even to death. 38You may tyrannize the ungodly, but you shall not dominate my religious principles, either by words or through deeds."

5.14–38. 16: The Stoics* also governed their lives by *divine law,* but they understood it very differently. **20:** The idea that *to transgress the law in matters either small or great is of equal seriousness* is typical of traditional Jewish attitudes to the law. **23–24:** Regardless of its divine origin (which the author most certainly upholds) the law is justified as a philosophy of *self-control,* which also teaches *justice* and *piety.* **25:** The belief in creation is crucial to Eleazar's argument. There can be no discrepancy between the law of the creator and the law of nature. The Stoics also believed that nature, in constituting the individual human being, was well-disposed and sympathetic. **34:** Eleazar's loyalty is directed as much to virtue of *self-control* as to the ancestral *law,* because he virtually identifies the two. **37:** The statement that *my ancestors will receive me* does not necessarily imply a belief in an afterlife, but it should be so understood in the context of 4 Maccabees. **38:** Piety is the safeguard of inner freedom.

6 When Eleazar in this manner had made eloquent response to the exhortations of the tyrant, the guards who were standing by dragged him violently to the instruments of torture. 2First they stripped the old man, though he remained adorned with the gracefulness of his piety. 3After they had tied his arms on each side they flogged him, 4while

a Or so that we hold in balance all our habitual inclinations b Or souls c Gk lacks O king a herald who faced him cried out, "Obey the king's commands!" 5But the courageous and noble man, like a true Eleazar, was unmoved, as though being tortured in a dream; 6yet while the old man's eyes were raised to heaven, his flesh was being torn by scourges, his blood flowing, and his sides were being cut to pieces. 7Although he fell to the ground because his body could not endure the agonies, he kept his reason upright and unswerving. 8One of the cruel guards rushed at him and began to kick him in the side to make him get up again after he fell. 9But he bore the pains and scorned the punishment and endured the tortures. 10Like a noble athlete the old man, while being beaten, was victorious over his torturers; 11in fact, with his face bathed in sweat, and gasping heavily for breath, he amazed even his torturers by his courageous spirit.

12 At that point, partly out of pity for his old age, 13partly out of sympathy from their acquaintance with him, partly out of admiration for his endurance, some of the king's retinue came to him and said, 14"Eleazar, why are you so irrationally destroying yourself through these evil things? 15We will set before you some cooked meat; save yourself by pretending to eat pork."

16 But Eleazar, as though more bitterly tormented by this counsel, cried out: 17"Never may we, the children of Abraham,a think so basely that out of cowardice we feign a role unbecoming to us! 18For it would be irrational if having lived in accordance with truth up to old age and having maintained in accordance with law the reputation of such a life, we should now change our course 19and ourselves become a pattern of impiety to the young by setting them an example in the eating of defiling food. 20It would be shameful if we should survive for a little while and during that time be a laughingstock to all for our cowardice, 21and be despised by the tyrant as unmanly by not contending even to death for our divine law. 22Therefore, O children of Abraham, die nobly for your religion! 23And you, guards of the tyrant, why do you delay?"

24 When they saw that he was so courageous in the face of the afflictions, and that

he had not been changed by their compassion, the guards brought him to the fire. 25There they burned him with maliciously contrived instruments, threw him down, and poured stinking liquids into his nostrils. 26When he was now burned to his very bones and about to expire, he lifted up his eyes to God and said, 27"You know, O God, that though I might have saved myself, I am dying in burning torments for the sake of the law. 28Be merciful to your people, and let our punishment suffice for them. 29Make my blood their purification, and take my life in exchange for theirs." 30After he said this, the holy man died nobly in his tortures; even in the tortures of death he resisted, by virtue of reason, for the sake of the law.

31 Admittedly, then, devout reason is sovereign over the emotions. 32For if the emotions had prevailed over reason, we would have testified to their domination. 33But now that reason has conquered the emotions, we properly attribute to it the power to govern. 34It is right for us to acknowledge the dominance of reason when it masters even external agonies. It would be ridiculous to deny it.b 35I have proved not only that reason has mastered agonies, but also that it masters pleasures and in no respect yields to them.

6.1–35. 10: The metaphor* of the athletic contest, a favorite device in Hellenistic* moral exhortation,* is widely used by Hellenistic Jewish writers such as Philo.* It is also used in the New Testament (1 Cor 9.24–27; 1 Tim 4.7; 6.12) 15: In 2 Macc 5, the offer of subterfuge is made and rejected before the torture begins. 18–19: Eleazar's refusal is based in part on the integrity of his own life and in part on the example he would set. 28–29: The last words of Eleazar introduce a different rationale for his death: His suffering is a vicarious sacrifice for his people. Compare the servant of the Lord in Isa 53. This is an important parallel to the understanding of the death of Jesus as an atoning sacrifice in the New Testament. See Mk 10.45. 31–35: The author concludes that the example of Eleazar proves his thesis that reason can control the emotions.

a Or O children of Abraham   b Syr: Meaning of Gk uncertain

The Philosophy of Philo

Judaism was influenced by Greek philosophy in the Hellenistic★ period. This influence was most clearly in evidence in Alexandria in the work of Philo★ (30 BCE to 45 CE). Philo is regarded as an exponent of Middle Platonism,★ which combined insights from Platonism and Stoicism.★ References to his thought are found in the Wisdom of Solomon and in Fourth Maccabees. The Jewish writers borrowed the Stoic concept of the Logos, as a rational world soul, but they also affirmed the Platonic idea of the transcendence of God and the immortality of the soul. Philo and other Hellenistic Jewish authors interpreted the Jewish scriptures in philosophical terms by using the method of allegorical★ interpretation,★ which was developed by Alexandrian scholars in their interpretation of Homer. So, for example, the Jewish dietary laws were interpreted as lessons that one should abstain from vice and excess. This method of interpretation later played a fundamental part in the development of Christian theology as it allowed people to believe that Plato and Moses were really saying the same thing, or that Plato was "Moses speaking Greek."

7 For like a most skillful pilot, the reason of our father Eleazar steered the ship of religion over the sea of the emotions, 2and though buffeted by the stormings of the tyrant and overwhelmed by the mighty waves of tortures, 3in no way did he turn the rudder of religion until he sailed into the haven of immortal victory. 4No city besieged with many ingenious war machines has ever held out as did that most holy man. Although his sacred life was consumed by tortures and racks, he conquered the besiegers with the shield of his devout reason. 5For in setting his mind firm like a jutting cliff, our father Eleazar broke the maddening waves of the emotions. 6O priest, worthy of the priesthood, you neither defiled your sacred teeth nor profaned your stomach, which had room only for reverence and purity, by eating defiling foods. 7O man in harmony with the law and philosopher of divine life! 8Such should be those who are administrators of the law, shielding it with their own blood and noble sweat in sufferings even to death. 9You, father, strengthened our loyalty to the law through your glorious endurance, and you did not abandon the holiness that you praised, but by your deeds you made your words of divine*a* philosophy credible. 10O aged man, more powerful than tortures;

O elder, fiercer than fire; O supreme king over the passions, Eleazar! 11For just as our father Aaron, armed with the censer, ran through the multitude of the people and conquered the fiery*b* angel, 12so the descendant of Aaron, Eleazar, though being consumed by the fire, remained unmoved in his reason. 13Most amazing, indeed, though he was an old man, his body no longer tense and firm,*c* his muscles flabby, his sinews feeble, he became young again 14in spirit through reason; and by reason like that of Isaac he rendered the many-headed rack ineffective. 15O man of blessed age and of venerable gray hair and of law-abiding life, whom the faithful seal of death has perfected!

16 If, therefore, because of piety an aged man despised tortures even to death, most certainly devout reason is governor of the emotions. 17Some perhaps might say, "Not all have full command of their emotions, because not all have prudent reason." 18But as many as attend to religion with a whole heart, these alone are able to control the passions of the flesh, 19since they believe that they, like our patriarchs Abraham and Isaac and Jacob, do not die to God, but live to God.

a Other ancient authorities lack *divine*   *b* Other ancient authorities lack *fiery*   *c* Gk *the tautness of the body already loosed*

20No contradiction therefore arises when some persons appear to be dominated by their emotions because of the weakness of their reason. 21What person who lives as a philosopher by the whole rule of philosophy, and trusts in God, 22and knows that it is blessed to endure any suffering for the sake of virtue, would not be able to overcome the emotions through godliness? 23For only the wise and courageous are masters of their emotions.

7.1–23: Encomium* for Eleazar. 1: The comparison of the wise man to a *ship's pilot* was common in Hellenistic* philosophy. **4:** Comparison to a besieged *city* was characteristic of Stoicism.* See also 1 QH 11.6–7 where the Qumran hymnist compares himself to a boat in the depths of the sea and to a *besieged city*. **6:** Contrast Mk 7.15: It is not what goes in to a person that *defiles,* but what comes out. **7:** By living in *harmony with the law,* Eleazar fulfills the ideals of both Stoicism and Judaism. **11:** The reference is to Num 16.46–50, where *Aaron* atones for the people after the death of Korah and his companions. The point of analogy here is that Eleazar also atones for the people. Aaron did not suffer in this context. **14:** The reference is to the Akedah, or sacrifice of *Isaac.* Genesis 22 says nothing of Isaac's understanding of his near-sacrifice, but later tradition held that he offered himself willingly. Fourth Maccabees, with the Biblical Antiquities of Pseudo-Philo,* is one of the earliest witnesses to the view that Isaac's sacrifice was voluntary and meritorious. **19:** Belief in an afterlife is crucial to the reasoning of the martyrs.* Compare Wis 3. For the belief that *Abraham, Isaac, and Jacob* are living, see Mk 12.26. For the expression *live to God,* see Rom 6.10; Gal 2.19.

8 For this is why even the very young, by following a philosophy in accordance with devout reason, have prevailed over the most painful instruments of torture. 2For when the tyrant was conspicuously defeated in his first attempt, being unable to compel an aged man to eat defiling foods, then in violent rage he commanded that others of the Hebrew captives be brought, and that any who ate defiling food would be freed after eating, but if any were to refuse, they would be tortured even more cruelly.

3 When the tyrant had given these orders, seven brothers—handsome, modest, noble, and accomplished in every way—were brought before him along with their aged mother. 4When the tyrant saw them, grouped about their mother as though a chorus, he was pleased with them. And struck by their appearance and nobility, he smiled at them, and summoned them nearer and said, 5"Young men, with favorable feelings I admire each and every one of you, and greatly respect the beauty and the number of such brothers. Not only do I advise you not to display the same madness as that of the old man who has just been tortured, but I also exhort you to yield to me and enjoy my friendship. 6Just as I am able to punish those who disobey my orders, so I can be a benefactor to those who obey me. 7Trust me, then, and you will have positions of authority in my government if you will renounce the ancestral tradition of your national life. 8Enjoy your youth by adopting the Greek way of life and by changing your manner of living. 9But if by disobedience you rouse my anger, you will compel me to destroy each and every one of you with dreadful punishments through tortures. 10Therefore take pity on yourselves. Even I, your enemy, have compassion for your youth and handsome appearance. 11Will you not consider this, that if you disobey, nothing remains for you but to die on the rack?"

12 When he had said these things, he ordered the instruments of torture to be brought forward so as to persuade them out of fear to eat the defiling food. 13When the guards had placed before them wheels and joint-dislocators, rack and hooks[a] and catapults[b] and caldrons, braziers and thumbscrews and iron claws and wedges and bellows, the tyrant resumed speaking: 14"Be afraid, young fellows; whatever justice you revere will be merciful to you when you transgress under compulsion."

8.1–14: Introduction of the seven brothers. 2: The king fluctuates between *violent rage* and apparent benevolence. Compare Dan 1, where Jewish captives also

a Meaning of Gk uncertain   b Here and elsewhere in 4 Macc an instrument of torture refuse to eat *defiling food,* but without the threat of torture. **3:** What follows is an elaboration of 2 Macc 7. The older story does not describe the attributes of the youths, but see Dan 1.4. **5:** The *beauty* of the youths conforms to a Greek ideal. The *number* seven is the traditional Hebrew ideal of a family blessed by God (see 1 Sam 2.5). The *friendship* of the king entailed a position at the royal court. There is perhaps a suggestion of erotic attraction on the part of the king. **6:** To be a *benefactor* brought great honor in the Hellenistic★ world. Some of the Ptolemies★ of Egypt added the title Benefactor (Euergetes) to their names. **8:** Compare the speech of the wicked in Wis 2.6: "Let us enjoy the good things that exist, and make use of the creation to the full as in youth." The *Greek way of life* was what Antiochus Epiphanes★ had attempted to impose in Jerusalem. **14:** See 5.13. A just God should not hold anyone guilty who sinned under duress.

15 But when they had heard the inducements and saw the dreadful devices, not only were they not afraid, but they also opposed the tyrant with their own philosophy, and by their right reasoning nullified his tyranny. 16Let us consider, on the other hand, what arguments might have been used if some of them had been cowardly and unmanly. Would they not have been the following? 17"O wretches that we are and so senseless! Since the king has summoned and exhorted us to accept kind treatment if we obey him, 18why do we take pleasure in vain resolves and venture upon a disobedience that brings death? 19O men and brothers, should we not fear the instruments of torture and consider the threats of torments, and give up this vain opinion and this arrogance that threatens to destroy us? 20Let us take pity on our youth and have compassion on our mother's age; 21and let us seriously consider that if we disobey we are dead! 22Also, divine justice will excuse us for fearing the king when we are under compulsion. 23Why do we banish ourselves from this most pleasant life and deprive ourselves of this delightful world? 24Let us not struggle against compulsion*a* or take hollow pride in being put to the rack. 25Not even the law itself would arbitrarily put us to death for fearing the instruments of torture. 26Why does such contentiousness excite us and such a fatal stubbornness

please us, when we can live in peace if we obey the king?"

8.15–26: Invalid arguments. 16: The author uses the rhetorical★ device of entertaining hypothetical *arguments* that might be used for a contrary position. These arguments correspond fairly closely to those of the king in the preceding section.

27 But the youths, though about to be tortured, neither said any of these things nor even seriously considered them. 28For they were contemptuous of the emotions and sovereign over agonies, 29so that as soon as the tyrant had ceased counseling them to eat defiling food, all with one voice together, as from one mind, said:

9 "Why do you delay, O tyrant? For we are ready to die rather than transgress our ancestral commandments; 2we are obviously putting our forebears to shame unless we should practice ready obedience to the law and to Moses*b* our counselor. 3Tyrant and counselor of lawlessness, in your hatred for us do not pity us more than we pity ourselves.*c* 4For we consider this pity of yours, which insures our safety through transgression of the law, to be more grievous than death itself. 5You are trying to terrify us by threatening us with death by torture, as though a short time ago you learned nothing from Eleazar. 6And if the aged men of the Hebrews because of their religion lived piously*d* while enduring torture, it would be even more fitting that we young men should die despising your coercive tortures, which our aged instructor also overcame. 7Therefore, tyrant, put us to the test; and if you take our lives because of our religion, do not suppose that you can injure us by torturing us. 8For we, through this severe suffering and endurance, shall have the prize of virtue and shall be with God, on whose account we suffer; 9but you, because of your bloodthirstiness toward us, will deservedly undergo from the divine justice eternal torment by fire."

a Or *fate*   *b* Other ancient authorities read *knowledge*
c Meaning of Gk uncertain   *d* Other ancient authorities read *died*

8.27–9.9: The reply of the youths. 8.29: The youths speak *with one voice* like a Greek chorus. **9.3:** *Pity* that leads to neglect of the law is really *hatred.* **6:** See Heb 11.35–37. Some Hebrew prophets,* such as Isaiah, were believed to have been martyred.* The *aged instructor* is Eleazar. Fourth Maccabees relates the figures in the story more closely than was the case in 2 Maccabees. **8:** See 7.19. **9:** Hell *fire* becomes the standard punishment of the damned in the Hellenistic* period, such as in the Dead Sea Scrolls. It has no basis in the Hebrew Bible. Isaiah 66.24 says of the dead bodies of those who rebel against God that "their worm shall not die, their fire shall not be quenched." But it is not suggested that the rebels will be alive to feel the torment of the fire.

10 When they had said these things, the tyrant was not only indignant, as at those who are disobedient, but also infuriated, as at those who are ungrateful. 11Then at his command the guards brought forward the eldest, and having torn off his tunic, they bound his hands and arms with thongs on each side. 12When they had worn themselves out beating him with scourges, without accomplishing anything, they placed him upon the wheel. 13When the noble youth was stretched out around this, his limbs were dislocated, 14and with every member disjointed he denounced the tyrant, saying, 15"Most abominable tyrant, enemy of heavenly justice, savage of mind, you are mangling me in this manner, not because I am a murderer, or as one who acts impiously, but because I protect the divine law." 16And when the guards said, "Agree to eat so that you may be released from the tortures," 17he replied, "You abominable lackeys, your wheel is not so powerful as to strangle my reason. Cut my limbs, burn my flesh, and twist my joints; 18through all these tortures I will convince you that children of the Hebrews alone are invincible where virtue is concerned." 19While he was saying these things, they spread fire under him, and while fanning the flames[a] they tightened the wheel further. 20The wheel was completely smeared with blood, and the heap of coals was being quenched by the drippings of gore, and pieces of flesh were falling off the axles of the machine. 21Although the ligaments joining his bones were already severed, the courageous youth, worthy of Abraham, did not groan, 22but as though transformed by fire into immortality, he nobly endured the rackings. 23"Imitate me, brothers," he said. "Do not leave your post in my struggle[b] or renounce our courageous family ties. 24Fight the sacred and noble battle for religion. Thereby the just Providence of our ancestors may become merciful to our nation and take vengeance on the accursed tyrant." 25When he had said this, the saintly youth broke the thread of life.

9.10–25: The torture of the first brother. 11: In 2 Macc 7, the tongue of the first brother is cut out. Here his torture is different, but he retains the use of his tongue. **22:** The word translated *immortality* is more accurately rendered "incorruptibility." Compare Phil 3.21; 1 Cor 15.51–53; 2 Cor 3.18. According to Wis 2.23, God created humanity for incorruption, but death entered the world through the devil's envy. **25:** The deaths of the martyrs* may trigger divine vengeance. See Deut 32.35–36. This comes to pass in 2 Macc 8.5.

26 While all were marveling at his courageous spirit, the guards brought in the next eldest, and after fitting themselves with iron gauntlets having sharp hooks, they bound him to the torture machine and catapult. 27Before torturing him, they inquired if he were willing to eat, and they heard his noble decision.[c] 28These leopard-like beasts tore out his sinews with the iron hands, flayed all his flesh up to his chin, and tore away his scalp. But he steadfastly endured this agony and said, 29"How sweet is any kind of death for the religion of our ancestors!" 30To the tyrant he said, "Do you not think, you most savage tyrant, that you are being tortured more than I, as you see the arrogant design of your tyranny being defeated by our endurance for the sake of religion? 31I lighten my pain by the joys that come from virtue, 32but you suffer torture by the threats that

a Meaning of Gk uncertain　*b* Other ancient authorities read *post forever*　*c* Other ancient authorities read *having heard his noble decision, they tore him to shreds* come from impiety. You will not escape, you most abominable tyrant, the judgments of the divine wrath."

9.26–32: The second brother. 29: The Latin poet Horace said that it was sweet and proper to die for one's country. The second brother echoes this sentiment, but substitutes *religion* for country. **31–32:** The king is liable to two kinds of punishment: the knowledge of his own *impiety* and the prospect of *divine judgment*.

10 When he too had endured a glorious death, the third was led in, and many repeatedly urged him to save himself by tasting the meat. [2]But he shouted, "Do you not know that the same father begot me as well as those who died, and the same mother bore me, and that I was brought up on the same teachings? [3]I do not renounce the noble kinship that binds me to my brothers."[a] [5]Enraged by the man's boldness, they disjointed his hands and feet with their instruments, dismembering him by prying his limbs from their sockets, [6]and breaking his fingers and arms and legs and elbows. [7]Since they were not able in any way to break his spirit,[b] they abandoned the instruments[c] and scalped him with their fingernails in a Scythian fashion. [8]They immediately brought him to the wheel, and while his vertebrae were being dislocated by this, he saw his own flesh torn all around and drops of blood flowing from his entrails. [9]When he was about to die, he said, [10]"We, most abominable tyrant, are suffering because of our godly training and virtue, [11]but you, because of your impiety and bloodthirstiness, will undergo unceasing torments."

[12] When he too had died in a manner worthy of his brothers, they dragged in the fourth, saying, [13]"As for you, do not give way to the same insanity as your brothers, but obey the king and save yourself." [14]But he said to them, "You do not have a fire hot enough to make me play the coward. [15]No—by the blessed death of my brothers, by the eternal destruction of the tyrant, and by the everlasting life of the pious, I will not renounce our noble family ties. [16]Contrive tortures, tyrant, so that you may learn from them that I am a brother to those who have just now been tortured." [17]When he heard this, the bloodthirsty, murderous, and utterly abominable Antiochus gave orders to cut out his tongue. [18]But he said, "Even if you remove my organ of speech, God hears also those who are mute. [19]See, here is my tongue; cut it off, for in spite of this you will not make our reason speechless. [20]Gladly, for the sake of God, we let our bodily members be mutilated. [21]God will visit you swiftly, for you are cutting out a tongue that has been melodious with divine hymns."

10.1–21: The third and fourth brothers. 5: *Boldness* was especially characteristic of Cynic* philosophers. **7:** The cruelty of the Scythians was also noted in 2 Macc 4.47 and 3 Macc 7.5. **10:** In 2 Macc 7.18 the sixth brother says that the martyrs* suffered for their own sins, or the sins of their people. Here they are said to *suffer* as a test of their *virtue*. **11:** The eternal *torments* of the king contrast with the ephemeral suffering of the martyrs. **17:** The descriptions of the king become more extreme as the story progresses. The *tongue* of the third brother was also cut out in 2 Macc 7, where he expressed his hope that he would get it back. Fourth Maccabees appears to envision the resurrection in less physical terms.

11 When he too died, after being cruelly tortured, the fifth leaped up, saying, [2]"I will not refuse, tyrant, to be tortured for the sake of virtue. [3]I have come of my own accord, so that by murdering me you will incur punishment from the heavenly justice for even more crimes. [4]Hater of virtue, hater of humankind, for what act of ours are you destroying us in this way? [5]Is it because[d] we revere the Creator of all things and live according to his virtuous law? [6]But these deeds deserve honors, not tortures."[e] [9]While he was saying these things, the guards bound him and dragged him to the catapult; [10]they

a Other ancient authorities add verse 4, *So if you have any instrument of torture, apply it to my body; for you cannot touch my soul, even if you wish."* b Gk *to strangle him* c Other ancient authorities read *they tore off his skin* d Other ancient authorities read *Or does it seem evil to you that* e Other authorities add verses 7 and 8, *[7]If you but understood human feelings and had hope of salvation from God— [8]but, as it is, you are a stranger to God and persecute those who serve him."*

tied him to it on his knees, and fitting iron clamps on them, they twisted his back[a] around the wedge on the wheel,[b] so that he was completely curled back like a scorpion, and all his members were disjointed. 11 In this condition, gasping for breath and in anguish of body, 12 he said, "Tyrant, they are splendid favors that you grant us against your will, because through these noble sufferings you give us an opportunity to show our endurance for the law."

13 When he too had died, the sixth, a mere boy, was led in. When the tyrant inquired whether he was willing to eat and be released, he said, 14 "I am younger in age than my brothers, but I am their equal in mind. 15 Since to this end we were born and bred, we ought likewise to die for the same principles. 16 So if you intend to torture me for not eating defiling foods, go on torturing!" 17 When he had said this, they led him to the wheel. 18 He was carefully stretched tight upon it, his back was broken, and he was roasted[c] from underneath. 19 To his back they applied sharp spits that had been heated in the fire, and pierced his ribs so that his entrails were burned through. 20 While being tortured he said, "O contest befitting holiness, in which so many of us brothers have been summoned to an arena of sufferings for religion, and in which we have not been defeated! 21 For religious knowledge, O tyrant, is invincible. 22 I also, equipped with nobility, will die with my brothers, 23 and I myself will bring a great avenger upon you, you inventor of tortures and enemy of those who are truly devout. 24 We six boys have paralyzed your tyranny. 25 Since you have not been able to persuade us to change our mind or to force us to eat defiling foods, is not this your downfall? 26 Your fire is cold to us, and the catapults painless, and your violence powerless. 27 For it is not the guards of the tyrant but those of the divine law that are set over us; therefore, unconquered, we hold fast to reason."

The opportunity to *exhibit endurance* is considered a good in itself, even apart from its reward in the hereafter. **13:** The youth of the *sixth* brother is emphasized because young children were not expected to have such self-control. **14:** The *mind* of a youth can reach maturity before the body. **20:** For the motif* of the *contest,* see 6.10. **25:** The failure of the king is his *downfall,* since it shows that he will never succeed in his design.

12 When he too, thrown into the caldron, had died a blessed death, the seventh and youngest of all came forward. 2 Even though the tyrant had been vehemently reproached by the brothers, he felt strong compassion for this child when he saw that he was already in fetters. He summoned him to come nearer and tried to persuade him, saying, 3 "You see the result of your brothers' stupidity, for they died in torments because of their disobedience. 4 You too, if you do not obey, will be miserably tortured and die before your time, 5 but if you yield to persuasion you will be my friend and a leader in the government of the kingdom." 6 When he had thus appealed to him, he sent for the boy's mother to show compassion on her who had been bereaved of so many sons and to influence her to persuade the surviving son to obey and save himself. 7 But when his mother had exhorted him in the Hebrew language, as we shall tell a little later, 8 he said, "Let me loose, let me speak to the king and to all his friends that are with him." 9 Extremely pleased by the boy's declaration, they freed him at once. 10 Running to the nearest of the braziers, 11 he said, "You profane tyrant, most impious of all the wicked, since you have received good things and also your kingdom from God, were you not ashamed to murder his servants and torture on the wheel those who practice religion? 12 Because of this, justice has laid up for you intense and eternal fire and tortures, and these throughout all time[d] will never let you go. 13 As a man, were you not ashamed, you most savage beast, to cut out the tongues of

---

11.1–27: The fifth and sixth brothers. 3: The fifth brother volunteers for torture in order to increase the ultimate punishment of the king. **4:** So far from being a benefactor (8.6), the king is a *hater of mankind.* **12:**

a Gk *loins*   *b* Meaning of Gk uncertain   *c* Other ancient authorities add *by fire*   *d* Gk *throughout the whole age* men who have feelings like yours and are made of the same elements as you, and to maltreat and torture them in this way? [14]Surely they by dying nobly fulfilled their service to God, but you will wail bitterly for having killed without cause the contestants for virtue." [15]Then because he too was about to die, he said, [16]"I do not desert the excellent example[a] of my brothers, [17]and I call on the God of our ancestors to be merciful to our nation;[b] [18]but on you he will take vengeance both in this present life and when you are dead." [19]After he had uttered these imprecations, he flung himself into the braziers and so ended his life.[c]

12.1–19: The seventh brother. 2: Even the king is moved by the youth of the last brother. 5: The promise that if the child complied he would become a *leader* in the *kingdom* seems absurd in view of his youth. 6: The youth of the child provides an occasion to vary the pattern by calling in the *mother*. 7: She speaks in Hebrew so that the king will not understand. 9: The torturers are very willing to believe the apparent submission. 18: For the appeal to divine *vengeance*, see 9.25. 19: Fourth Maccabees alters the account of 2 Maccabees to allow the seventh brother to commit suicide. This was considered a more noble death in antiquity, especially among the Stoics.* Compare Razis in 2 Macc 14.37–46 and the mass suicide of defenders of Masada in 74 CE. (Masada was the last outpost in the Jewish revolt against Rome, which began in 66 CE and was essentially ended in 70 CE when the Jerusalem Temple* was destroyed.)

13 Since, then, the seven brothers despised sufferings even unto death, everyone must concede that devout reason is sovereign over the emotions. [2]For if they had been slaves to their emotions and had eaten defiling food, we would say that they had been conquered by these emotions. [3]But in fact it was not so. Instead, by reason, which is praised before God, they prevailed over their emotions. [4]The supremacy of the mind over these cannot be overlooked, for the brothers[d] mastered both emotions and pains. [5]How then can one fail to confess the sovereignty of right reason over emotion in those who were not turned back by fiery agonies? [6]For just as towers jutting out over harbors hold back the threatening waves and make it calm for those who sail into the inner basin, [7]so the seven-towered right reason of the youths, by fortifying the harbor of religion, conquered the tempest of the emotions. [8]For they constituted a holy chorus of religion and encouraged one another, saying, [9]"Brothers, let us die like brothers for the sake of the law; let us imitate the three youths in Assyria who despised the same ordeal of the furnace. [10]Let us not be cowardly in the demonstration of our piety." [11]While one said, "Courage, brother," another said, "Bear up nobly," [12]and another reminded them, "Remember whence you came, and the father by whose hand Isaac would have submitted to being slain for the sake of religion." [13]Each of them and all of them together looking at one another, cheerful and undaunted, said, "Let us with all our hearts consecrate ourselves to God, who gave us our lives,[e] and let us use our bodies as a bulwark for the law. [14]Let us not fear him who thinks he is killing us, [15]for great is the struggle of the soul and the danger of eternal torment lying before those who transgress the commandment of God. [16]Therefore let us put on the full armor of self-control, which is divine reason. [17]For if we so die,[f] Abraham and Isaac and Jacob will welcome us, and all the fathers will praise us." [18]Those who were left behind said to each of the brothers who were being dragged away, "Do not put us to shame, brother, or betray the brothers who have died before us."

[19] You are not ignorant of the affection of family ties, which the divine and all-wise Providence has bequeathed through the fathers to their descendants and which was implanted in the mother's womb. [20]There each of the brothers spent the same length of time and was shaped during the same period of time; and growing from the same blood and through the same life, they were brought to the light of day. [21]When they were born after

a Other ancient authorities read *the witness*   b Other ancient authorities read *my race*   c Gk *and so gave up*; other ancient authorities read *gave up his spirit* or *his soul*   d Gk *they*   e Or *souls*   f Other ancient authorities read *suffer* an equal time of gestation, they drank milk from the same fountains. From such embraces brotherly-loving souls are nourished; 22and they grow stronger from this common nurture and daily companionship, and from both general education and our discipline in the law of God.

23 Therefore, when sympathy and brotherly affection had been so established, the brothers were the more sympathetic to one another. 24Since they had been educated by the same law and trained in the same virtues and brought up in right living, they loved one another all the more. 25A common zeal for nobility strengthened their goodwill toward one another, and their concord, 26because they could make their brotherly love more fervent with the aid of their religion. 27But although nature and companionship and virtuous habits had augmented the affection of family ties, those who were left endured for the sake of religion, while watching their brothers being maltreated and tortured to death.

14 Furthermore, they encouraged them to face the torture, so that they not only despised their agonies, but also mastered the emotions of brotherly love. 2 O reason,*a* more royal than kings and freer than the free! 3O sacred and harmonious concord of the seven brothers on behalf of religion! 4None of the seven youths proved coward or shrank from death, 5but all of them, as though running the course toward immortality, hastened to death by torture. 6Just as the hands and feet are moved in harmony with the guidance of the mind, so those holy youths, as though moved by an immortal spirit of devotion, agreed to go to death for its sake. 7O most holy seven, brothers in harmony! For just as the seven days of creation move in choral dance around religion, 8so these youths, forming a chorus, encircled the sevenfold fear of tortures and dissolved it. 9Even now, we ourselves shudder as we hear of the suffering of these young men; they not only saw what was happening, not only heard the direct word of threat, but also bore the sufferings patiently, and in agonies of fire at that. 10What could be more excruciatingly painful than this? For the power of fire is intense and swift, and it consumed their bodies quickly.

13.1–14.10: Reflections on the death of the brothers. 13.1: The author returns to his main theme by drawing the conclusion about the sovereignty of *reason*. 9: The *three youths* in Dan 3 were in Babylon, not Assyria. 12: Fourth Maccabees is one of the earliest witnesses to the view that Isaac willingly consented to be sacrificed by Abraham; see 7.14 above. 14: Compare Mt 10.28; Lk 12.4: "Do not fear those who kill the body but cannot kill the soul; rather fear him who can destroy both soul and body in hell." 15: There are two contests in progress, one between the king and the Jews but another, greater one for the salvation of the soul. 17: See 5.37; Luke 16.22. 19: The *affection of family ties* was both an asset and an obstacle in the context of martyrdom.* The brothers could strengthen each other, but their natural desire to preserve each other had to be overcome. The nature of family affections was often discussed by the Stoics.* 24: In this case the affection of the brothers was trained by the law. 14.2: The direct address to reason is an example of the rhetorical* device of apostrophe. 3: The orator shifts immediately into an encomium* of the seven brothers. 5: For the metaphor* of the athletic contest, see the comment on 6.10. Compare 1 Cor 9.24–27. 7: The number *seven* often had mystical associations in antiquity.

11 Do not consider it amazing that reason had full command over these men in their tortures, since the mind of woman despised even more diverse agonies, 12for the mother of the seven young men bore up under the rackings of each one of her children. 13 Observe how complex is a mother's love for her children, which draws everything toward an emotion felt in her inmost parts. 14Even unreasoning animals, as well as human beings, have a sympathy and parental love for their offspring. 15For example, among birds, the ones that are tame protect their young by building on the housetops, 16and the others, by building in precipitous chasms and in holes and tops of trees, hatch the nestlings and ward off the intruder. 17If they are not able to keep the intruder*b* away, they do what they can to help their young by

a Or O minds   *b* Gk it

flying in circles around them in the anguish of love, warning them with their own calls. [18]And why is it necessary to demonstrate sympathy for children by the example of unreasoning animals, [19]since even bees at the time for making honeycombs defend themselves against intruders and, as though with an iron dart, sting those who approach their hive and defend it even to the death? [20]But sympathy for her children did not sway the mother of the young men; she was of the same mind as Abraham.

14.11–20: Maternal affection. 11: Women were commonly believed to have weaker rational powers and stronger passions than men, but the Stoics★ and Cynics★ held that women had equal capacity for reason. **13–20:** Maternal affection is presented as an instinctual emotion that must be controlled by reason. **20:** Abraham was willing to sacrifice his son Isaac (Gen 22).

---

15 O reason of the children, tyrant over the emotions! O religion, more desirable to the mother than her children! [2]Two courses were open to this mother, that of religion, and that of preserving her seven sons for a time, as the tyrant had promised. [3]She loved religion more, the religion that preserves them for eternal life according to God's promise.[a] [4]In what manner might I express the emotions of parents who love their children? We impress upon the character of a small child a wondrous likeness both of mind and of form. Especially is this true of mothers, who because of their birth pangs have a deeper sympathy toward their offspring than do the fathers. [5]Considering that mothers are the weaker sex and give birth to many, they are more devoted to their children.[b] [6]The mother of the seven boys, more than any other mother, loved her children. In seven pregnancies she had implanted in herself tender love toward them, [7]and because of the many pains she suffered with each of them she had sympathy for them; [8]yet because of the fear of God she disdained the temporary safety of her children. [9]Not only so, but also because of the nobility of her sons and their ready obedience to the law, she felt a greater tenderness

toward them. [10]For they were righteous and self-controlled and brave and magnanimous, and loved their brothers and their mother, so that they obeyed her even to death in keeping the ordinances.

11 Nevertheless, though so many factors influenced the mother to suffer with them out of love for her children, in the case of none of them were the various tortures strong enough to pervert her reason. [12]But each child separately and all of them together the mother urged on to death for religion's sake. [13]O sacred nature and affection of parental love, yearning of parents toward offspring, nurture and indomitable suffering by mothers! [14]This mother, who saw them tortured and burned one by one, because of religion did not change her attitude. [15]She watched the flesh of her children being consumed by fire, their toes and fingers scattered[c] on the ground, and the flesh of the head to the chin exposed like masks.

16 O mother, tried now by more bitter pains than even the birth pangs you suffered for them! [17]O woman, who alone gave birth to such complete devotion! [18]When the firstborn breathed his last, it did not turn you aside, nor when the second in torments looked at you piteously nor when the third expired; [19]nor did you weep when you looked at the eyes of each one in his tortures gazing boldly at the same agonies, and saw in their nostrils the signs of the approach of death. [20]When you saw the flesh of children burned upon the flesh of other children, severed hands upon hands, scalped heads upon heads, and corpses fallen on other corpses, and when you saw the place filled with many spectators of the torturings, you did not shed tears. [21]Neither the melodies of sirens nor the songs of swans attract the attention of their hearers as did the voices of the children in torture calling to their mother. [22]How great and how many torments the mother then suffered as her sons were tortured on the wheel and with the hot irons! [23]But de-

---

a Gk according to God   *b* Or For to the degree that mothers are weaker and the more children they bear, the more they are devoted to their children.   *c* Or quivering vout reason, giving her heart a man's courage in the very midst of her emotions, strengthened her to disregard, for the time, her parental love.

24 Although she witnessed the destruction of seven children and the ingenious and various rackings, this noble mother disregarded all these[a] because of faith in God. 25For as in the council chamber of her own soul she saw mighty advocates—nature, family, parental love, and the rackings of her children— 26this mother held two ballots, one bearing death and the other deliverance for her children. 27She did not approve the deliverance that would preserve the seven sons for a short time, 28but as the daughter of God-fearing Abraham she remembered his fortitude.

29 O mother of the nation, vindicator of the law and champion of religion, who carried away the prize of the contest in your heart! 30O more noble than males in steadfastness, and more courageous than men in endurance! 31Just as Noah's ark, carrying the world in the universal flood, stoutly endured the waves, 32so you, O guardian of the law, overwhelmed from every side by the flood of your emotions and the violent winds, the torture of your sons, endured nobly and withstood the wintry storms that assail religion.

15.1–32: **Praise of the mother. 1:** The mother's choice is between her religion and her sons. **3:** The choice is mitigated by the promise that religion preserves the sons for *eternal life.* **4:** The discussion of parental affection reflects Stoic understanding of psychology. The *sympathy* is grounded in natural likeness. **5:** The author exploits the common idea that women are the *weaker sex* in order to heighten the praise of the mother in this case. **9:** Her natural affection was strengthened by admiration of their piety. **10:** The virtues of the sons resemble the cardinal virtues of the Stoics.* **21:** The *melodies of sirens* tempted Odysseus in the course of his return from Troy. The mother exhibits the Stoic virtue of "apathy," lack of emotion. **23:** Her courage is described as a *man's courage.* The Jewish philosopher, Philo* of Alexandria, also taught that women could become male by virtue of their reason and moral excellence. **28:** For *Abraham,* see 14.20. **29:** She is *mother of the nation* because of the role she

plays in overcoming Antiochus. The metaphor* of the *contest* appears repeatedly in 4 Maccabees; see 6.10. **30:** In the climactic conclusion of the praise, she not only equals men but surpasses them.

16 If, then, a woman, advanced in years and mother of seven sons, endured seeing her children tortured to death, it must be admitted that devout reason is sovereign over the emotions. 2Thus I have demonstrated not only that men have ruled over the emotions, but also that a woman has despised the fiercest tortures. 3The lions surrounding Daniel were not so savage, nor was the raging fiery furnace of Mishael so intensely hot, as was her innate parental love, inflamed as she saw her seven sons tortured in such varied ways. 4But the mother quenched so many and such great emotions by devout reason.

5 Consider this also: If this woman, though a mother, had been fainthearted, she would have mourned over them and perhaps spoken as follows: 6"O how wretched am I and many times unhappy! After bearing seven children, I am now the mother of none! 7O seven childbirths all in vain, seven profitless pregnancies, fruitless nurturings and wretched nursings! 8In vain, my sons, I endured many birth pangs for you, and the more grievous anxieties of your upbringing. 9Alas for my children, some unmarried, others married and without offspring.[b] I shall not see your children or have the happiness of being called grandmother. 10Alas, I who had so many and beautiful children am a widow and alone, with many sorrows.[c] 11And when I die, I shall have none of my sons to bury me."

16.1–11: **Invalid arguments. 1:** The author returns to his main thesis. **3:** For the *lions:* Dan 6; for the *furnace:* Dan 3. **5:** As in the case of the brothers, the author proposes invalid arguments that might have influenced the mother, but did not.

12 Yet that holy and God-fearing mother did not wail with such a lament for any of

---

a Other ancient authorities read *having bidden them farewell, surrendered them* b Gk *without benefit* c Or *much to be pitied* them, nor did she dissuade any of them from dying, nor did she grieve as they were dying. ¹³On the contrary, as though having a mind like adamant and giving rebirth for immortality to the whole number of her sons, she implored them and urged them on to death for the sake of religion. ¹⁴O mother, soldier of God in the cause of religion, elder and woman! By steadfastness you have conquered even a tyrant, and in word and deed you have proved more powerful than a man. ¹⁵For when you and your sons were arrested together, you stood and watched Eleazar being tortured, and said to your sons in the Hebrew language, ¹⁶"My sons, noble is the contest to which you are called to bear witness for the nation. Fight zealously for our ancestral law. ¹⁷For it would be shameful if, while an aged man endures such agonies for the sake of religion, you young men were to be terrified by tortures. ¹⁸Remember that it is through God that you have had a share in the world and have enjoyed life, ¹⁹and therefore you ought to endure any suffering for the sake of God. ²⁰For his sake also our father Abraham was zealous to sacrifice his son Isaac, the ancestor of our nation; and when Isaac saw his father's hand wielding a knife[a] and descending upon him, he did not cower. ²¹Daniel the righteous was thrown to the lions, and Hananiah, Azariah, and Mishael were hurled into the fiery furnace and endured it for the sake of God. ²²You too must have the same faith in God and not be grieved. ²³It is unreasonable for people who have religious knowledge not to withstand pain."

24 By these words the mother of the seven encouraged and persuaded each of her sons to die rather than violate God's commandment. ²⁵They knew also that those who die for the sake of God live to God, as do Abraham and Isaac and Jacob and all the patriarchs.

17 Some of the guards said that when she also was about to be seized and put to death she threw herself into the flames so that no one might touch her body.

16.12–17.1: The speech of the mother and her suicide. 16: The exhortation* to fight zealously for our ancestral law was also the exhortation of Mattathias in 1 Macc 2, but it seems less appropriate here since the sons are not in a position to fight. 18: Obligations to God outweigh all others. 20: The story of the sacrifice of Isaac (Gen 22) has been invoked several times (7.14; 13.12). Here, the mother says only that Isaac did not cower. The other allusions indicate that he offered himself willingly. 21: The stories in Dan 3 and 6 have already been alluded to in 16.3. 23: The conclusion abruptly shifts back from religious to philosophical considerations, reinterpreting the actions of the biblical figures as examples of Stoic* virtue. 25: The argument is undergirded, however, by an appeal to immortality that is not typical of Stoic philosophy. The phrase "live in God" was already used in 7.19. 17.1: In addition to its intrinsic nobility, the suicide of the mother has the advantage of preserving her purity by allowing no one to touch her body.

2 O mother, who with your seven sons nullified the violence of the tyrant, frustrated his evil designs, and showed the courage of your faith! ³Nobly set like a roof on the pillars of your sons, you held firm and unswerving against the earthquake of the tortures. ⁴Take courage, therefore, O holy-minded mother, maintaining firm an enduring hope in God. ⁵The moon in heaven, with the stars, does not stand so august as you, who, after lighting the way of your star-like seven sons to piety, stand in honor before God and are firmly set in heaven with them. ⁶For your children were true descendants of father Abraham.[b]

17.2–6: Final praise of the mother. 5: The martyrs* are star-like in heaven like the martyrs in Dan 12.3. In Semitic tradition, the stars were the host of heaven or the angels. In Greek tradition, also, the stars were gods, and many people believed in astral immortality (the idea that souls became stars after death). Fourth Maccabees shows little interest in bodily resurrection, and evidently thought instead in terms of immortality with the stars.

7 If it were possible for us to paint the history of your religion as an artist might,

---

a Gk sword   b Gk For your childbearing was from Abraham the father; other ancient authorities read For . . . Abraham the servant would not those who first beheld it have shuddered as they saw the mother of the seven children enduring their varied tortures to death for the sake of religion? 8Indeed it would be proper to inscribe on their tomb these words as a reminder to the people of our nation:*a*

9 "Here lie buried an aged priest and an aged woman and seven sons, because of the violence of the tyrant who wished to destroy the way of life of the Hebrews. 10They vindicated their nation, looking to God and enduring torture even to death."

11 Truly the contest in which they were engaged was divine, 12for on that day virtue gave the awards and tested them for their endurance. The prize was immortality in endless life. 13Eleazar was the first contestant, the mother of the seven sons entered the competition, and the brothers contended. 14The tyrant was the antagonist, and the world and the human race were the spectators. 15Reverence for God was victor and gave the crown to its own athletes. 16Who did not admire the athletes of the divine*b* legislation? Who were not amazed?

17 The tyrant himself and all his council marveled at their*c* endurance, 18because of which they now stand before the divine throne and live the life of eternal blessedness. 19For Moses says, "All who are consecrated are under your hands." 20These, then, who have been consecrated for the sake of God,*d* are honored, not only with this honor, but also by the fact that because of them our enemies did not rule over our nation, 21the tyrant was punished, and the homeland purified—they having become, as it were, a ransom for the sin of our nation. 22And through the blood of those devout ones and their death as an atoning sacrifice, divine Providence preserved Israel that previously had been mistreated.

23 For the tyrant Antiochus, when he saw the courage of their virtue and their endurance under the tortures, proclaimed them to his soldiers as an example for their own endurance, 24and this made them brave and courageous for infantry battle and siege, and he ravaged and conquered all his enemies.

17.7–18.24: Concluding encomium.* 17.8: The reference to the *tomb* suggests that at least the conclusion, if not the whole book, is conceived as a funeral oration. 9: The conflict is viewed as between two ways of life. Greek funeral orations from the Persian wars of the fifth century also view the threat as an attempt to destroy a *way of life.* 11: The metaphor* of the *contest* is invoked yet again; see 6.10. 19: Deuteronomy 33.3 is cited according to the Greek translation or Septuagint.* 21: The idea that the martyrs* were *a ransom for the sin* of the nation was already found in 6.29; see Mk 10.45. 22: The atoning power of blood is paralleled in Rom 3.21–26. Fourth Maccabees is arguably the closest Jewish parallel to the understanding of the death of Jesus as an atoning sacrifice. 23: There is of course no basis for the story that Antiochus held the martyrs up *as an example.* 24: The idea that the example of the martyrs led to the success of Antiochus's forces is paradoxical. The author is focusing only on the universal admiration for their behavior.

18 O Israelite children, offspring of the seed of Abraham, obey this law and exercise piety in every way, 2knowing that devout reason is master of all emotions, not only of sufferings from within, but also of those from without.

3 Therefore those who gave over their bodies in suffering for the sake of religion were not only admired by mortals, but also were deemed worthy to share in a divine inheritance. 4Because of them the nation gained peace, and by reviving observance of the law in the homeland they ravaged the enemy. 5The tyrant Antiochus was both punished on earth and is being chastised after his death. Since in no way whatever was he able to compel the Israelites to become pagans and to abandon their ancestral customs, he left Jerusalem and marched against the Persians.

6 The mother of seven sons expressed also these principles to her children: 7"I was a pure virgin and did not go outside my father's house; but I guarded the rib from which woman was made.*e* 8No seducer cor-

---

a Or *as a memorial to the heroes of our people*   *b* Other ancient authorities read *true*   *c* Other ancient authorities add *virtue and*   *d* Other ancient authorities lack *for the sake of God*   *e* Gk *the rib that was built* rupted me on a desert plain, nor did the destroyer, the deceitful serpent, defile the purity of my virginity. 9In the time of my maturity I remained with my husband, and when these sons had grown up their father died. A happy man was he, who lived out his life with good children, and did not have the grief of bereavement. 10While he was still with you, he taught you the law and the prophets. 11He read to you about Abel slain by Cain, and Isaac who was offered as a burnt offering, and about Joseph in prison. 12He told you of the zeal of Phinehas, and he taught you about Hananiah, Azariah, and Mishael in the fire. 13He praised Daniel in the den of the lions and blessed him. 14He reminded you of the scripture of Isaiah, which says, 'Even though you go through the fire, the flame shall not consume you.' 15He sang to you songs of the psalmist David, who said, 'Many are the afflictions of the righteous.' 16He recounted to you Solomon's proverb, 'There is a tree of life for those who do his will.' 17He confirmed the query of Ezekiel, 'Shall these dry bones live?' 18For he did not forget to teach you the song that Moses taught, which says, 19'I kill and I make alive: this is your life and the length of your days.' "

20 O bitter was that day—and yet not bitter—when that bitter tyrant of the Greeks quenched fire with fire in his cruel caldrons, and in his burning rage brought those seven sons of the daughter of Abraham to the catapult and back again to more*a* tortures, 21pierced the pupils of their eyes and cut out their tongues, and put them to death with various tortures. 22For these crimes divine justice pursued and will pursue the accursed tyrant. 23But the sons of Abraham with their victorious mother are gathered together into the chorus of the fathers, and have received pure and immortal*b* souls from God, 24to whom be glory forever and ever. Amen.

18.1–24. 1: The author returns yet again to his main theme of the sovereignty of reason over the passions. **3:** The benefits of martyrdom* are three-fold: personal immortality, revival of the nation, and punishment of the tyrant in both this life and in the next. **6:** The concluding words of the mother summarize the Jewish way of life as the author sees it. The mother guarded her purity. The father taught his children the scriptures, with special reference to the examples of Isaac, Joseph, and Daniel and his companions, all of which have been cited before. **14:** The reference is to Isa 43.2. **15:** Ps 34.19. **16:** Prov 3.18. **17:** Ezek 37.2–3. **19:** Deut 32.9; 30.20. **23:** The book ends with an affirmation of the immortality of the martyrs.

a Other ancient authorities read *to all his*   *b* Other ancient authorities read *victorious*

THE NEW COVENANT COMMONLY CALLED
THE NEW TESTAMENT OF OUR LORD
AND SAVIOR JESUS CHRIST

New Revised
Standard Version

NEW TESTAMENT NARRATIVES: THE GOSPELS AND ACTS

The Gospels

The English word "gospel" comes from two Old English words: gōd (pronounced "goad" and meaning "good") and spel ("story" or "message"). The Old English is an exact translation of the Greek word, *euangelion*, also a composite noun meaning "good" (*eu*) "message" (*angelion*). The root meaning of the noun is a reminder that the word "gospel" did not originally mean a narrative* composition that tells the story of Jesus but was much more closely linked to the activity of proclaiming a message. In Paul, for example, the act of proclaiming the good news is at the heart of its usage (e.g., 1 Cor 9.12, 14, 18, 23). Paul uses the noun *euangelion* and the verb from which it is derived (*euangelizomai*) to characterize his missionary activity among his communities. Yet even in Paul, there are occasions when "gospel" seems to have a more fixed content (Rom 1.1–6; 1 Cor 15.1–11).

The noun "gospel" only appears in two of the four canonical* Gospels, Matthew and Mark. In most of its occurrences, it is used by characters in the story, either John the Baptist or Jesus, to describe their own ministries of proclamation (Mt 24.14, 26.13; Mk 1.14, 15; 8.35, 10.29, 13.10, 14.9), much like Paul's use of the term in his letters. A more ambiguous usage is the very opening line of Mark (1.1), "The beginning of the good news [*euangelion*] of Jesus Christ, the Son of God." If we read the word "gospel" here in light of the other canonical uses of the term, then this may simply be the author's announcement that what follows is a proclamation of the good news, with no intention of indicating anything about literary form and composition. But given the influence of Mark's story of Jesus on subsequent writings—for example, all of the other Gospels essentially follow the narrative order established by Mark—it also seems likely that the author of Mark uses this noun self-consciously to name the type of story that follows. In Mark 1.1, we see the transition from "gospel" as something that is proclaimed orally, to "gospel" as something that is written and subsequently read: from a message that is announced—to a narrative (a story with a beginning, middle, and end) that is in fixed form.

A general outline of all four canonical Gospels is remarkably similar: stories of Jesus' teaching, punctuated with a few accounts of Jesus' miracles, followed by a more extensive narrative of the arrest and crucifixion of Jesus. Mark contains neither birth stories nor resurrection stories, perhaps evidence of its self-understanding as written proclamation—its emphasis remains on the good news of the kingdom of God breaking into history and ordinary life through the life and death of Jesus (Mk 1.14–15). Matthew and Luke are more intentional about creating a story with a clear beginning and end, as they begin their Gospels with birth narratives and conclude them with extensive resurrection narratives. John provides a middle term between these two approaches to gospel writing. It contains no birth narratives and so, like Mark, seems closer to the idea of the gospel as the written proclamation of the good news of the life and death of Jesus. Like Matthew and Luke, however, it does end with extensive resurrection narratives.

This basic gospel outline suggests that the ancient literary genre* to which the gospels are most similar is that of ancient biography (as found, for instance, in Plutarch's *Lives*). This genre designation fits Matthew and Luke better than it fits Mark and John, but the similarities among all four Gospels suggest that to some degree, each of them can be understood as self-consciously telling the story of the life of a famous man. To designate the Gospels alongside ancient biographies is most helpful in providing a category for understanding how ancient readers might have understood these texts. Ancient biography was a very different genre from contemporary biography, which attempts to amass facts and exhaustive details to reconstruct a picture of someone's life. Rather ancient biography, as Plutarch's *Lives* demonstrates, was written to hold up the person's life as a model to emulate or as an example of necessary social virtues.

The precise relationship among all four Gospels is complex, and the understanding of how they relate is not easy to resolve. Mark, Matthew, and Luke (the so-called Synoptic Gospels,* because they can be "viewed together") not only share the same broad outline but also tell many of the same stories in very similar ways (see synoptic problem,* for a discussion of the relationship of Mark, Matthew, and Luke). John's presentation of the stories is more distinctive than that found in the other three canonical Gospels, but there is nonetheless a remarkable overlap of content in telling the story of Jesus' life and ministry in all four Gospels. All narrate healings of a paralytic and of a blind man, and narrate the feeding of the five thousand. All four contain stories of John the Baptist, the call of the first disciples, and Jesus' ministry with women; and all contain conflict stories between Jesus and the religious leaders of his time. Each Gospel gives its own interpretation to these shared events, so it is important to note John's distinctiveness but also not to overstate it.

The shared traditions and stories across all four Gospels have led scholars to assume that the written gospel form is the last stage of a process that has its roots in oral storytelling and preaching. Certain kinds of stories and story forms dominate the narration of Jesus' ministry in the Gospels.

MIRACLE STORIES

All four Gospels contain many stories that demonstrate that the power of God as revealed in Jesus can overturn conventional expectations about the natural world. These miracles fall into several categories: nature miracles, exorcisms, miraculous provision of food and drink, and healing stories.

Nature miracles

Jesus' stilling of the storm (Mt 8.23–27; Mk 4.35–41; Lk 8.22–25) and walking on water (Mt 14.22–27; Mk 6.47–52; Jn 6.16–21) fit into this category. In these stories, God's power as revealed in Jesus is shown to be stronger even than the forces of nature.

Exorcisms

In these stories, Jesus meets someone who is possessed by a demon or evil spirit (Mt 8.28–34, 17.14–21; Mk 1.21–28, 5.1–20, 9.14–29; Lk 8.26–39, 9.37–42). These stories focus on the confrontation between Jesus and the demon, and the result of the story—that the demon is expelled from the person—points to the power of cosmic good over cosmic evil. John contains no exorcisms.

Miraculous provision of food and drink

All four Gospels narrate the story of Jesus' feeding of the five thousand with bread and fish (Mt 14.13–21; Mk 6.34–44; Lk 9.10–17; Jn 6.1–13). Mark and Matthew include a second miraculous feeding of the multitudes with bread and fish (Mt 15.32–39; Mk 8.1–10). John also narrates a second bread- and fish-feeding miracle, in which the emphasis falls on the disciples' miraculous catch of fish at Jesus' instruction (Jn 21.1–14; cf. the great catch of fish in Luke 5.4–7). The miracle of the superabundance of good wine from water at the wedding at Cana (Jn 2.1–11) also belongs in this category. These miracle stories all reveal God's power to provide more than people need or even know they want.

HEALING STORIES

The majority of miracles in all four Gospels fall into this category. Jesus heals a wide range of physical conditions, from paralysis (Mt 9.1–8; Mk 2.1–12; Lk 5.17–26; Jn 5.1–18) to hemor-rhaging (Mt 9.20–22; Mk 5.21–34; Lk 8.43–48) to blindness (Mt 20.29–34; Mk 10.46–52; Lk 18.35–43; Jn 9.1–41). The basic form of a healing miracle is the same—Jesus is made aware of a situation of physical need (Mk 1.30), he heals the person (1.31a), there is corroboration that the healing took place (1.31b). But within that common form, all four Gospels work significant variations on the healing story. In some, the healing occurs early in the story and serves to spur a conflict between Jesus and the religious authorities (Jn 5.1–18, 19ff.). In others, the healing is a test of faith, either of the person who needs healing (Mt 9.27–31) or of someone who comes to Jesus on their behalf (Jn 4.46–53). And in still others, Jesus' initiative in offering healing takes center stage, becoming more central than the person's situation of need (Jn 9.1–12). Each of the healing stories shows God's power and will for life and wholeness in the world.

There are a few miracle stories in which Jesus brings a person back from the dead (Mk 5.35–43; Lk 7.11–17; Jn 11.1–42). These stories show that God's power for life, as demonstrated in the healing stories, knows no limits.

TEACHING STORIES

The other key element in the Gospels' presentation of the life and ministry of Jesus is his teach-ing stories. Like the miracle stories, teaching stories, too, fall into several general categories.

Parables*

Parables are short stories, using figurative language, told by Jesus to invite his listeners to reas-sess their understanding of where God is known in the world. Jesus teaches in parables in all four Gospels, although the form is used sparingly in John (the only full parable is in Jn 10.1–6). The subject matter of the parables is drawn from nature (e.g., the parable of the mustard seed, Mk 4.30–32), from common human experience (e.g., the parable of the lost coin, Lk 15.8–10), or may relate more complex stories (e.g., the prodigal son, Lk 15.11–32; the workers in the vine-yard, Mt 20.1–16) that invert conventional assumptions about how the characters will act.

Because parables use figurative language, they are not designed to be easily understood. Many scholars have argued that parables are intentionally designed not to be understood. By using them as a teaching tool, Jesus is constantly challenging and unsettling his audiences. The difficulty of interpreting parables is explicitly named by Jesus in many places in the Gospels (e.g., Mk 4.10–12). Yet their interpretive difficulty notwithstanding, parables are among the favorite Gospel texts, because their story world and vivid language continually stimulate the imagination to envision God in new ways.

CONTROVERSY STORIES

Jesus' teaching in all four Gospels is marked by deliberate and intentional questioning of Jesus by the religious authorities and of Jesus' questioning of the authorities' positions. Most of these stories end with a teaching by Jesus that often summarizes the subject and point of the controversy. For example, Mark 2.15–28 is a series of three controversy stories. In the first (vv. 15–17), the scribes challenge Jesus for eating with tax collectors and sinners, which provokes Jesus to say, "I have come to call not the righteous but sinners." In the second, many people question why Jesus' disciples do not fast, which leads to an extended teaching on the appropriate time for fasting (vv. 19–20) and new practices (vv. 21–23). The third controversy is triggered by Jesus' disciples picking grain on the Sabbath (2.23–24). This controversy provides Jesus with the opportunity to provide a fresh interpretation of scripture (vv. 25–26) and to offer a new teaching on the meaning and purpose of the Sabbath (v. 27). The teaching with which Jesus concludes in a controversy story often introduces a fresh point of conflict.

In controversy stories, Jesus' skill and knowledge as a teacher is highlighted because he engages in disputes with the most learned religious leaders of his day. Through controversy stories, the Gospels are able to show the reader Jesus' authority as a teacher.

CORRECTION STORIES

The religious authorities are, in effect Jesus' "partners" in both conversation and debates in these controversy stories. Correction stories show another side of Jesus' teaching. In these stories, Jesus' conversation partners are normally his own disciples and followers. Here, Jesus teaches by correcting the mistaken view of his disciples and followers. Correction stories also often end with a teaching or a pronouncement, and like the religious authorities in controversy stories, Jesus' followers do not always accept or agree with Jesus' pronouncement.

Correction stories occur in all four Gospels: the discussion among Jesus' disciples about who is the greatest (Mt 20.17–19; Mk 10.35–45; Lk 18.31–34); disputes among Jesus' disciples about the identity of the Son of Man (Mt 8.18–20; Jn 6.60–71); and about the nature of discipleship (Lk 9.59–62).

"I AM" SAYINGS

The "I am" sayings are a distinctive element of Jesus' teaching found in the Gospel of John. These sayings share characteristics with parables and the pronouncements (teachings) that conclude controversy and correction stories. Like parables, the "I am" sayings use highly figurative language: the bread of life (Jn. 6.35; cf. 6.51), light of the world (8.12; 9.5), gate for the sheep (10.7, 9), good shepherd (10.11, 14), true vine (15.1, 5). These figurative sayings, like the parables, invite Jesus' listeners to look at him and the way God is known in him in new ways.

Yet these "I am" sayings also can occur in John as the teaching that summarizes the point of a controversy (8.12; 6.51) or as a correction to the views of his followers ("I am the resurrection and the life," 11.25; "I am the way and the truth and the life," 14.6). Looked at in this way, while the form of Jesus' teaching may be distinctive in the "I am" sayings, the context and nature of Jesus' teaching in John is consistent with his teaching in the Synoptic Gospels.

PASSION NARRATIVES

In each of the four canonical Gospels, the longest continuous unit of storytelling is the passion narrative—the story of Jesus' arrest, trial, and crucifixion. In the passion narratives, the narrative units build on one another in a way that is not the case in the narration of Jesus' life and ministry, heightening the tension as the story moves toward Jesus' death. Each of the Gospels has its own distinctive emphasis as it tells the story of Jesus' death (see comments on each of the four Gospels), but they agree about the basic contours of the last days of Jesus' life.

RESURRECTION NARRATIVES

Unlike the passion narratives, resurrection stories vary widely from Gospel to Gospel. The original ending of Mark contains no resurrection stories, although later tradition added them and they have found their way into the manuscript tradition (Mk 16.9–20).

The Acts of the Apostles

The other narrative book in the New Testament is the Acts of the Apostles. Acts is widely understood to be a sequel to the Gospel of Luke, in which the Gospel writer explicitly links the story of the life and death of Jesus to the story of the rise of the church. Matthew and John end with stories that look to the life of the church (Mt 28 ; Jn 21), but Luke is the only Gospel that has a full-blown sequel. Paul's letters also give the New Testament reader important access to the early years of the church, as do the other epistolary writings (letters). But Acts is the only complete New Testament narrative of the first years of the early church, from the period after the ministry of Jesus through the missionary activities of Paul and other early followers.

The author of Luke and Acts is quite explicit in directing the reader to understand the two books as a part of a single literary composition. The author refers explicitly to "the first book" at the beginning of Acts (Acts 1.1), and addresses the same named reader, Theophilus (Lk 1.3; Acts 1.1), in both books. The order of books in the New Testament canon can make it difficult for the contemporary reader to recognize the seamless continuity between Luke and Acts, since the canon groups all four Gospels together and so separates Luke from Acts. One challenge in reading Acts is to re-create its original unity with the Gospel of Luke.

Just as ancient biography is a helpful category for understanding how their first readers would have recognized and understood the literary genre of the Gospels, ancient historiography (history writing) is a helpful category for understanding the story form of Acts. To read Acts as historiography locates Acts with two different examples of historical literature: the histories of Greek and Roman literature (e.g., Herodotus, Tacitus, Suetonius) and the historical literature of the Hebrew Bible (see essay on "Historical Literature," 311–314). In ancient historiography, as in ancient biography, the rhetorical* force of the events being narrated was an essential part of the storytelling, not simply recording the events that occurred.

Acts shares with other narratives the key characteristic of having a beginning, a middle, and an end. Its beginning is quite definite: following the prologue to Theophilus, the story opens with resurrection appearances of Jesus and his departure to heaven (ascension). The middle of the story is also definite, built around the gift of the Holy Spirit at Pentecost, the stories of the early church leaders, and the increase in those joining the movement. The end, by contrast, is actually "open-ended": the story of Acts ends with Paul in Rome under Roman guard, awaiting trial. The indefiniteness of this ending, the non-ending of the narrative end, is best read as deliberate. Unlike the life of Jesus Christ as narrated in the Gospels, the account of the spread of Christianity does not end with Paul in Rome but continues (as Luke knew) well beyond that. Luke is saying, in effect, "The book is ending, but the story is not over."

THE GOSPEL ACCORDING TO
MATTHEW

Introduction

This Gospel, the favorite of the early church, offers a carefully crafted account of Jesus' birth, mission, and passion. Beginning with a genealogy★ that anchors Jesus in Jewish history, the text develops the story of a messiah★ who faithfully upholds the Torah,★ fulfills prophecy, and establishes the model of leadership through service.

The Gospel is neatly organized for teaching purposes. Following the infancy accounts, baptism,★ and temptation, which securely connect Jesus to the scriptures of Israel, the evangelist presents five extended speeches interspersed with controversy accounts and healings. The best known, the Sermon on the Mount (chs. 5–7) combines blessings and teachings to convey the radical nature of Jesus' message. The second discourse (ch. 10) offers missionary instructions as well as warnings of the persecutions that will accompany proclamation of the good news. The parables★ collected in ch. 13 describe the kingdom of heaven as a time and a place of great joy, if only those with ears to hear can grasp the message. Rules for ecclesial organization comprise ch. 18, and chs. 24–25 prophesy the apocalyptic★ consummation of history and the final judgment.

Such literary artistry provides one of several hints that the evangelist was a scribe★ (see 13.52), capable of combining traditional material into a coherent narrative.★ Scribal training may also account for the Gospel's extensive use of fulfillment citations: Along with numerous allusions, Matthew directly quotes scripture forty times and offers several statements, called "fulfillment citations" or "formula citations," which proclaim Jesus' "fulfillment" of a passage from scripture (2.17–18, 23; 4.14b–16; 8.17; 12.18–21; 13.35; 21.4–5; 27.9–10). Finally, perhaps scribal training underlies Matthew's depiction of Jesus as a new Moses: Both, as infants, escape a death ordered by political leaders; both sojourn in Egypt; both give instructions from a mountain; and both face people not always receptive to their message.

In Matthew the emphasis on Jewish history, the use of the expression "kingdom of heaven" rather than "kingdom of God" (which marks Jewish avoidance of the sacred name), the preservation of the Laws of Torah, and the lack of explanation for Jewish practices such as ritual washing prior to eating all suggest a setting among Jews who proclaimed Jesus the messiah. Possibilities for the place of writing range from Syria to Galilee to the Transjordan. Stressing Torah observance, the evangelist is unclear about the extent to which the commandments (Heb., "mitzvot") should be followed by gentile★ believers in the church. In part, this lack of clarity results from the Gospel's view of salvation-history: Before the cross, Jesus comes only to the "lost sheep of the house of Israel" (10.6; 15.24); in the Great Commission of 28.16–20, the mission is extended to "all nations" (28.19).

Although the evangelist urges that Pharisaic teachings be followed (23.2), the Gospel also reflects, frequently through harsh polemic,★ the church's separation from the synagogue.★ Whether Matthew should be considered "anti-Jewish" remains an area of debate. Scholars who view the evangelist as Jewish and still within the synagogue system frequently classify the polemical language as typical disputation between members of the same group. Others even propose that Matthew's polemic has the same setting and effect as the excoriations of Israel delivered by the prophets.* Those who see the Gospel as reflecting a majority gentile audience and as having separated from the synagogue are more likely to see the text as anti-Jewish. Regardless of its historical circumstances, the Gospel of Matthew, with its infamous line attributed to the Jerusalem crowd, "His blood be on us and on our children" (27.25), has tragically served as a warrant for violence against Jews. Given Matthew's insistence on higher righteousness—"righteousness" is a key Matthean term—and love of neighbor, likely the evangelist would be horrified by such actions taken in the Gospel's name.

Along with establishing its tense relationship to Jews who did not accept the gospel message, Matthew also reveals the Christian community's process of developing an internal identity. Of the four canonical* Gospels, Matthew's is the only one to use the term "church" (Gk. "ekklesia") and the only one to proclaim Peter the "rock" who holds the keys to the kingdom. This concern for institutional organization, coupled with the evangelist's use of sources, interest in the gentile mission, awareness of the destruction of the Jerusalem Temple* in 70 CE (see Mt 22.7), and self-definition in relation to the synagogue, suggests a compositional date sometime toward the end of the first century. Economically, the church may have been comparatively well off. Only in Matthew is Joseph of Arimathea explicitly designated "rich" (27.57). Whereas Luke has Jesus announce, "Blessed are you who are poor" and "Blessed are you who are hungry now" (Lk 6.20–21), the Sermon on the Mount proclaims, "Blessed are the poor in spirit" and "Blessed are those who hunger and thirst for righteousness" (Mt 5.3, 6).

READING GUIDE

There are many ways of outlining Matthew's Gospel. One model divides the text at 4.17 and 16.21, where the expression "from that time on, Jesus began to . . ." appears. This division emphasizes the preparation for his ministry, his mission, and his passion. Alternatively, the Gospel may be seen as composed of twelve sections: This model, which is listed below, highlights the literary precision of interspersing the five teaching discourses with narrative material.

1.1–4.22	Son of David and Son of God
4.23–7.29	Sermon on the Mount
8.1–9.34	Healings and controversies
9.35–10.42	Missionary instructions
11.1–12.50	Conflict intensifies
13.1–53	Parables* of the kingdom
13.54–17.27	Opposition and acceptance
18.1–35	The church community
19.1–22.46	The authority of Jesus
23.1–25.46	Judgments present and future
26.1–27.66	Passion and crucifixion
28.1–20	Resurrection

1 An account of the genealogy*a* of Jesus the Messiah,*b* the son of David, the son of Abraham.

2 Abraham was the father of Isaac, and Isaac the father of Jacob, and Jacob the father of Judah and his brothers, 3and Judah

a Or birth   *b* Or Jesus Christ

the father of Perez and Zerah by Tamar, and Perez the father of Hezron, and Hezron the father of Aram, [4]and Aram the father of Aminadab, and Aminadab the father of Nahshon, and Nahshon the father of Salmon, [5]and Salmon the father of Boaz by Rahab, and Boaz the father of Obed by Ruth, and Obed the father of Jesse, [6]and Jesse the father of King David.

And David was the father of Solomon by the wife of Uriah, [7]and Solomon the father of Rehoboam, and Rehoboam the father of Abijah, and Abijah the father of Asaph,[a] [8]and Asaph[a] the father of Jehoshaphat, and Jehoshaphat the father of Joram, and Joram the father of Uzziah, [9]and Uzziah the father of Jotham, and Jotham the father of Ahaz, and Ahaz the father of Hezekiah, [10]and Hezekiah the father of Manasseh, and Manasseh the father of Amos,[b] and Amos[b] the father of Josiah, [11]and Josiah the father of Jechoniah and his brothers, at the time of the deportation to Babylon.

12 And after the deportation to Babylon: Jechoniah was the father of Salathiel, and Salathiel the father of Zerubbabel, [13]and Zerubbabel the father of Abiud, and Abiud the father of Eliakim, and Eliakim the father of Azor, [14]and Azor the father of Zadok, and Zadok the father of Achim, and Achim the father of Eliud, [15]and Eliud the father of Eleazar, and Eleazar the father of Matthan, and Matthan the father of Jacob, [16]and Jacob the father of Joseph the husband of Mary, of whom Jesus was born, who is called the Messiah.[c]

17 So all the generations from Abraham to David are fourteen generations; and from David to the deportation to Babylon, fourteen generations; and from the deportation to Babylon to the Messiah,[c] fourteen generations.

1.1–4.22: Son of David and Son of God. 1.1–17 (Lk 3.23–28). **1:** *Account of the genealogy,* literally, "Book of genesis." *Christ* is the Greek for the Hebrew term "mashiach," "anointed* one." *Son of David* is a messianic title. References to Abraham (3.9; 8.11; 22.32) have universalistic import. **3:** On Tamar, Rahab, Ruth, the wife of Uriah, and Mary, see sidebar, "Women in the Genealogy," p. 1669. **6:** Luke's

genealogy* goes through David's son Nathan, not Solomon. **11:** See 2 Kings 24.8–16. **16:** Joseph is the legal father. **17:** The last division contains thirteen names.

~~~~~~~~~~~~~~~~~~~~~~

18 Now the birth of Jesus the Messiah[d] took place in this way. When his mother Mary had been engaged to Joseph, but before they lived together, she was found to be with child from the Holy Spirit. [19]Her husband Joseph, being a righteous man and unwilling to expose her to public disgrace, planned to dismiss her quietly. [20]But just when he had resolved to do this, an angel of the Lord appeared to him in a dream and said, "Joseph, son of David, do not be afraid to take Mary as your wife, for the child conceived in her is from the Holy Spirit. [21]She will bear a son, and you are to name him Jesus, for he will save his people from their sins." [22]All this took place to fulfill what had been spoken by the Lord through the prophet:
23 "Look, the virgin shall conceive and
　　bear a son,
　　and they shall name him Emmanuel,"
which means, "God is with us." [24]When Joseph awoke from sleep, he did as the angel of the Lord commanded him; he took her as his wife, [25]but had no marital relations with her until she had borne a son;[e] and he named him Jesus.

1.18–2.23 (Lk 1.26–2.40). **19:** Joseph's righteousness may refer to his unwillingness to shame Mary, or to his decision to divorce her. **20:** Like his namesake in Genesis, Joseph dreams. Dreams are a Matthean motif.* See 2.13. **21:** *Jesus,* the Greek form for Joshua, means "the Lord saves" or "Yahweh helps"; allusions to Moses' successor are likely. **23:** See Isa 7.14; Matthew cites the Septuagint*; the Hebrew refers to an already pregnant "young woman." **25:** Later claims for Mary's perpetual virginity are not noted.

~~~~~~~~~~~~~~~~~~~~~~

2 In the time of King Herod, after Jesus was born in Bethlehem of Judea, wise men[f] from the East came to Jerusalem,

a Other ancient authorities read *Asa*　　*b* Other ancient authorities read *Amon*　　*c* Or *the Christ*　　*d* Or *Jesus Christ*　　*e* Other ancient authorities read *her firstborn son*　　*f* Or *astrologers;* Gk *magi*

■▲▲■

Women in the Genealogy

Matthew's genealogy* names five women (Tamar, Rahab, Ruth, the wife of Uriah, and Mary), all of whom display a righteousness that, at a quick glance, might be regarded as scandalous. Tamar seduced her father-in-law, Judah, and he in turn proclaimed her "more righteous" than he for her actions (Gen 38.26). Rahab was the prostitute from Jericho who aided Joshua's spies (Josh 2, 6). Ruth, already suspect because of her Moabite origins (Gen 19), had an unexpected and sexually suggestive meeting with Boaz late one night at the threshing* floor (Ruth 3). Bathsheba, identified as Uriah's wife, was brought by King David to the palace for an adulterous act (2 Sam 11–12). She later worked to assure that her son, Solomon, would become king when David died (1 Kings 1.15–31). Tamar, Rahab, and Ruth, as well as Bathsheba, all display a higher righteousness than the men with whom they are associated: They take action; they are guilty of neither crime nor sin.

Joseph, hearing of Mary's pregnancy and being a "righteous man," resolves to divorce her quietly. It is not clear whether his righteousness demands that he divorce her (divorcing a woman pregnant by another man would be the "right" thing to do), or whether his righteousness compels him to divorce her quietly and so spare her additional public humiliation. Informed by a dream that the conception is in accord with Isa 7.14 (Matthew offers the Greek wording of "parthenos," virgin, rather than the Hebrew wording "almah," young woman), he marries her and thereby becomes the child's legal father. Joseph, like the other unexpected people named in the genealogy, engages in an act that may appear scandalous, but is, like the proclamation of a crucified messiah,* a sign of the workings of heaven.

■▲▲■

2 asking, "Where is the child who has been born king of the Jews? For we observed his star at its rising,*a* and have come to pay him homage." 3 When King Herod heard this, he was frightened, and all Jerusalem with him; 4 and calling together all the chief priests and scribes of the people, he inquired of them where the Messiah*b* was to be born. 5 They told him, "In Bethlehem of Judea; for so it has been written by the prophet:

6 'And you, Bethlehem, in the land
　　of Judah,
　are by no means least among the
　　rulers of Judah;
　for from you shall come a ruler
　　who is to shepherd*c* my
　　people Israel.'"

2.1–6. 1: *Wise men* (lit. Magi) were astrologers or magicians (compare Acts 8, 13). **2:** *King of the Jews* (or Judeans) reappears as the sign on the cross (27.37). See Num 24.17; Bar Cochba (Aramaic* "Son of the Star") was the title given to the Jewish leader of the

132–135 CE revolt against Rome. **3:** Matthew has anti-Jerusalem and anti-leadership biases. The Jerusalem leaders do not know their own scriptures. **6:** Mic 5.2.

7 Then Herod secretly called for the wise men*d* and learned from them the exact time when the star had appeared. 8 Then he sent them to Bethlehem, saying, "Go and search diligently for the child; and when you have found him, bring me word so that I may also go and pay him homage." 9 When they had heard the king, they set out; and there, ahead of them, went the star that they had seen at its rising,*a* until it stopped over the place where the child was. 10 When they saw that the star had stopped,*e* they were overwhelmed with joy. 11 On entering the house, they saw the child with Mary his mother; and they knelt down and paid him homage. Then, opening their treasure chests, they of-

---

a Or *in the East*　　*b* Or *the Christ*　　*c* Or *rule*
d Or *astrologers;* Gk *magi*　　*e* Gk *saw the star*

fered him gifts of gold, frankincense, and myrrh. 12And having been warned in a dream not to return to Herod, they left for their own country by another road.

13 Now after they had left, an angel of the Lord appeared to Joseph in a dream and said, "Get up, take the child and his mother, and flee to Egypt, and remain there until I tell you; for Herod is about to search for the child, to destroy him." 14Then Joseph[a] got up, took the child and his mother by night, and went to Egypt, 15and remained there until the death of Herod. This was to fulfill what had been spoken by the Lord through the prophet, "Out of Egypt I have called my son."

16 When Herod saw that he had been tricked by the wise men,[b] he was infuriated, and he sent and killed all the children in and around Bethlehem who were two years old or under, according to the time that he had learned from the wise men.[b] 17Then was fulfilled what had been spoken through the prophet Jeremiah:
18 "A voice was heard in Ramah,
    wailing and loud lamentation,
  Rachel weeping for her children;
    she refused to be consoled, because
      they are no more."

19 When Herod died, an angel of the Lord suddenly appeared in a dream to Joseph in Egypt and said, 20"Get up, take the child and his mother, and go to the land of Israel, for those who were seeking the child's life are dead." 21Then Joseph[a] got up, took the child and his mother, and went to the land of Israel. 22But when he heard that Archelaus was ruling over Judea in place of his father Herod, he was afraid to go there. And after being warned in a dream, he went away to the district of Galilee. 23There he made his home in a town called Nazareth, so that what had been spoken through the prophets might be fulfilled, "He will be called a Nazorean."

posed in 6 CE, was replaced by Roman governors (including Pontius Pilate). His brother Antipas ruled the Galilee. **23:** An otherwise unattested quotation.

3 In those days John the Baptist appeared in the wilderness of Judea, proclaiming, 2"Repent, for the kingdom of heaven has come near."[c] 3This is the one of whom the prophet Isaiah spoke when he said,
"The voice of one crying out in
      the wilderness:
  'Prepare the way of the Lord,
    make his paths straight.' "
4Now John wore clothing of camel's hair with a leather belt around his waist, and his food was locusts and wild honey. 5Then the people of Jerusalem and all Judea were going out to him, and all the region along the Jordan, 6and they were baptized by him in the river Jordan, confessing their sins.

7 But when he saw many Pharisees and Sadducees coming for baptism, he said to them, "You brood of vipers! Who warned you to flee from the wrath to come? 8Bear fruit worthy of repentance. 9Do not presume to say to yourselves, 'We have Abraham as our ancestor'; for I tell you, God is able from these stones to raise up children to Abraham. 10Even now the ax is lying at the root of the trees; every tree therefore that does not bear good fruit is cut down and thrown into the fire.

11 "I baptize you with[d] water for repentance, but one who is more powerful than I is coming after me; I am not worthy to carry his sandals. He will baptize you with[d] the Holy Spirit and fire. 12His winnowing fork is in his hand, and he will clear his threshing floor and will gather his wheat into the granary; but the chaff he will burn with unquenchable fire."

3.1–12 (Mk 1.1–8; Lk 3.1–18; Jn 1.6–8, 19–28). **2:** John and Jesus (4.17) proclaim the same message. **3:** Many first-century Jews believed Elijah would announce the messianic age (Mal 3.1; 4.5–6). **4–6:** The ascetic description contrasts Herodian luxury. "Baptizo" (Gk.) means "dip" or "immerse." Matthew does

---

2.7–23. 13: Jesus is a new Moses, and Herod is another Pharaoh **15:** See Hos 11.1. **16:** The "slaughter of the innocents" evokes Ex 1. **18:** See Jer 31.15. Rachel, who yearned for children and died in childbirth, is buried near Bethlehem (Gen 35.16–20). **22:** *Archelaus,* de-

a Gk *he*   *b* Or *astrologers;* Gk *magi*   *c* Or *is at hand*
d Or *in*

not note the baptism* was for forgiveness (Mk 1.4). **7:** *Pharisees** and *Sadducees** is an unlikely combination; Matthew may be reflecting a united Jewish leadership. **9:** "Stone" and "son" sound similar in Aramaic.* **10:** John anticipates the last judgment. **11–12:** See Lk 12.49. John is the forerunner of the final Judge.

13 Then Jesus came from Galilee to John at the Jordan, to be baptized by him. ¹⁴John would have prevented him, saying, "I need to be baptized by you, and do you come to me?" ¹⁵But Jesus answered him, "Let it be so now; for it is proper for us in this way to fulfill all righteousness." Then he consented. ¹⁶And when Jesus had been baptized, just as he came up from the water, suddenly the heavens were opened to him and he saw the Spirit of God descending like a dove and alighting on him. ¹⁷And a voice from heaven said, "This is my Son, the Beloved,ᵃ with whom I am well pleased."

3.13–17 (Mk 1.9–11; Lk 3.21–22; Jn 1.31–34). **15:** Jesus' first words express authority and echo Matthew's concerns for righteousness and fulfillment. **17:** Combines Ps 2.7 and Isa 42.1; the announcement is to all present (contrast Mark).

4 Then Jesus was led up by the Spirit into the wilderness to be tempted by the devil. ²He fasted forty days and forty nights, and afterwards he was famished. ³The tempter came and said to him, "If you are the Son of God, command these stones to become loaves of bread." ⁴But he answered, "It is written,

'One does not live by bread alone,
   but by every word that comes from
      the mouth of God.'"

5 Then the devil took him to the holy city and placed him on the pinnacle of the temple, ⁶saying to him, "If you are the Son of God, throw yourself down; for it is written,

'He will command his angels concerning
   you,'
   and 'On their hands they will bear
      you up,
   so that you will not dash your foot
      against a stone.'"

⁷Jesus said to him, "Again it is written, 'Do not put the Lord your God to the test.'"

8 Again, the devil took him to a very high mountain and showed him all the kingdoms of the world and their splendor; ⁹and he said to him, "All these I will give you, if you will fall down and worship me." ¹⁰Jesus said to him, "Away with you, Satan! for it is written,

'Worship the Lord your God,
   and serve only him.'"

¹¹Then the devil left him, and suddenly angels came and waited on him.

4.1–11 (Mk 1.12–13; Lk 4.1–13). The temptation recollects the Israelites in the wilderness after crossing the sea (Ex 14–32). **1:** "Testing" or "tempting" is used elsewhere only of the leaders (16.1; 19.3; 22.18, 35), where Jesus also responds with scriptural citation. **2:** Forty days alludes to Moses (Ex 34.28; Deut 9.9); Jesus' fasting prefigures church practice (6.16–18; 9.14–15). **4:** Cites Deut 8.3. **6:** Ps 91.11–12. **7:** Deut 6.16. **10:** Deut 6.13. Luke reverses the last two temptations: Matthew's version emphasizes universal authority (see 28.18); Luke's emphasizes Jerusalem. **11:** Jesus receives for his fidelity what the Devil had offered in temptation.

12 Now when Jesusᵇ heard that John had been arrested, he withdrew to Galilee. ¹³He left Nazareth and made his home in Capernaum by the sea, in the territory of Zebulun and Naphtali, ¹⁴so that what had been spoken through the prophet Isaiah might be fulfilled:

15 "Land of Zebulun, land of Naphtali,
   on the road by the sea, across the
      Jordan, Galilee of the Gentiles—
16 the people who sat in darkness
   have seen a great light,
   and for those who sat in the region and
      shadow of death
   light has dawned."

¹⁷From that time Jesus began to proclaim, "Repent, for the kingdom of heaven has come near."ᶜ

4.12–17 (Mk 1.14–15; Lk 4.14–15): The mission opens in Galilee, where the Great Commission (28.16–20) will occur. **12:** *Arrested* (lit. "handed over") is used for Judas's betrayal and the divine delivering of Jesus (see Isa 53.6). *Withdrew,* typical of Jesus' response to danger (see 12.15; 14.13). **13:** *Capernaum,* home to Peter

a Or *my beloved Son*   *b* Gk *he*   *c* Or *is at hand*

Gospels

Although today we speak of a Gospel (Gk., "euangellion," good news, glad tidings) as if it were a biography of Jesus, this is not what the term meant to first-century Greek speakers. They would have thought of secular announcements, such as a decrease in taxes. Adapting the secular term, the church proclaimed the good news of Jesus (see Mk 1.14; 1 Cor 15.3; Rom 1.3–5). Of the four canonical★ Gospels, only those by Matthew (4.23; 9.35; 24.14) and Mark (1.1, 14–15; 8.35; 10.29; 14.9) actually use the term. For Matthew, the good news is primarily that of the kingdom of heaven; for Mark, the content of the good news is the person and story of Jesus.

Other texts produced by early Christians were also known as Gospels; these include the Gospels of Thomas,★ Peter, and Mary, as well as the Gospel of Truth and the Gospel According to the Hebrews. Unlike the canonical accounts, which present narratives★ depicting a ministry in Galilee, a journey to Jerusalem, conflicts with Temple★ officials, Roman crucifixion, and resurrection, these other Gospels emphasize Jesus' sayings and claims of his divine nature. For example, the Gospel of Thomas presents over 100 statements attributed to Jesus; some match comments in the canonical Gospels and others are unique. Thomas has no continuous narrative, and it contains no commentary on Jesus' death or resurrection.

---

and Andrew, will be Jesus' own city (9.1). **15–16:** Isa 9.1–2. Matthew emphasizes Galilee's gentile★ connection; here the Great Commission (28.19) begins. **17:** Summarizes Jesus' message; *repent* reflects the Hebrew "Tshuva," "return" or "change direction."

18 As he walked by the Sea of Galilee, he saw two brothers, Simon, who is called Peter, and Andrew his brother, casting a net into the sea—for they were fishermen. [19]And he said to them, "Follow me, and I will make you fish for people." [20]Immediately they left their nets and followed him. [21]As he went from there, he saw two other brothers, James son of Zebedee and his brother John, in the boat with their father Zebedee, mending their nets, and he called them. [22]Immediately they left the boat and their father, and followed him.

23 Jesus[a] went throughout Galilee, teaching in their synagogues and proclaiming the good news[b] of the kingdom and curing every disease and every sickness among the people. [24]So his fame spread throughout all Syria, and they brought to him all the sick,

those who were afflicted with various diseases and pains, demoniacs, epileptics, and paralytics, and he cured them. [25]And great crowds followed him from Galilee, the Decapolis, Jerusalem, Judea, and from beyond the Jordan.

4.18–25. 18–22 (Mk 1.16–20; Lk 5.1–11; Jn 1.35–42): The abrupt calling of the disciples is common in Hellenistic★ and Hebrew stories (see 1 Kings 19.19–21). **23–25:** Only Jesus teaches and proclaims. **23–24:** *Good news* is "gospel." *Their synagogues*★ need not indicate alienation; Jesus restricts his mission to Israel (10.5b–6; 15.24).

THE SERMON ON THE MOUNT

5.1–7.29: The Sermon on the Mount, evoking Moses on Sinai, contains material scattered throughout Mark and Luke as well as sayings unique to Matthew. Luke 6.17 presents much of this material in the "Sermon on the Plain."

a Gk He *b* Gk *gospel*

5 When Jesus*a* saw the crowds, he went up the mountain; and after he sat down, his disciples came to him. 2Then he began to speak, and taught them, saying:

3 "Blessed are the poor in spirit, for theirs is the kingdom of heaven.

4 "Blessed are those who mourn, for they will be comforted.

5 "Blessed are the meek, for they will inherit the earth.

6 "Blessed are those who hunger and thirst for righteousness, for they will be filled.

7 "Blessed are the merciful, for they will receive mercy.

8 "Blessed are the pure in heart, for they will see God.

9 "Blessed are the peacemakers, for they will be called children of God.

10 "Blessed are those who are persecuted for righteousness' sake, for theirs is the kingdom of heaven.

11 "Blessed are you when people revile you and persecute you and utter all kinds of evil against you falsely*b* on my account. 12Rejoice and be glad, for your reward is great in heaven, for in the same way they persecuted the prophets who were before you.

5.3–12 (Lk 6.17, 20–23): The Beatitude (Gk. "makarios," "fortunate, happy") form appears in prophetic and wisdom literature.★ **3:** *Poor in spirit* appears in the Qumran Scrolls (1QS 14.7). **5:** See Ps 37.11. **6:** See Isa 55.1–2. **9:** *Peacemakers* implies active engagement, not passivity. **10:** On persecution, see 1 Pet 3.14.

~~~~~~~

13 "You are the salt of the earth; but if salt has lost its taste, how can its saltiness be restored? It is no longer good for anything, but is thrown out and trampled under foot.

14 "You are the light of the world. A city built on a hill cannot be hid. 15No one after lighting a lamp puts it under the bushel basket, but on the lampstand, and it gives light to all in the house. 16In the same way, let your light shine before others, so that they may see your good works and give glory to your Father in heaven.

17 "Do not think that I have come to abolish the law or the prophets; I have come not to abolish but to fulfill. 18For truly I tell you, until heaven and earth pass away, not one letter,*c* not one stroke of a letter, will pass from the law until all is accomplished. 19Therefore, whoever breaks*d* one of the least of these commandments, and teaches others to do the same, will be called least in the kingdom of heaven; but whoever does them and teaches them will be called great in the kingdom of heaven. 20For I tell you, unless your righteousness exceeds that of the scribes and Pharisees, you will never enter the kingdom of heaven.

5.13–20. 13–16 (Mk 9.49–50; Lk 14.34–35): *Salt* loses taste by admixture, becoming impure. **14:** Reflects Isaiah's imperative (2.2–5; 42.6; 49.6) to be a light to the nations. **17–20:** "*Law* and *prophets*★" frames the Sermon (see 7.12); law is Torah★ (Pentateuch★); the prophetic writings contain history (Joshua–2 Kings) and oracles★ (Isaiah–Malachi). **19:** Jesus does not abrogate but intensifies Torah. **20:** Scribes★ and Pharisees★ epitomize *righteousness* (see 23.2); Jesus' followers must be even more righteous.

~~~~~~~

21 "You have heard that it was said to those of ancient times, 'You shall not murder'; and 'whoever murders shall be liable to judgment.' 22But I say to you that if you are angry with a brother or sister,*e* you will be liable to judgment; and if you insult*f* a brother or sister,*g* you will be liable to the council; and if you say, 'You fool,' you will be liable to the hell*h* of fire. 23So when you are offering your gift at the altar, if you remember that your brother or sister*i* has something against you, 24leave your gift there before the altar and go; first be reconciled to your brother or sister,*i* and then come and offer your gift. 25Come to terms quickly with your accuser while you are on the way to court*j* with him, or your accuser may hand you over to the judge, and the judge to the guard, and you will be thrown into prison.

---

a Gk *he*   *b* Other ancient authorities lack *falsely*
c Gk *one iota*   *d* Or *annuls*   *e* Gk *a brother*; other ancient authorities add *without cause*   *f* Gk *say Raca to* (an obscure term of abuse)   *g* Gk *a brother*
h Gk *Gehenna*   *i* Gk *your brother*   *j* Gk lacks *to court*

26 Truly I tell you, you will never get out until you have paid the last penny.

27 "You have heard that it was said, 'You shall not commit adultery.' 28 But I say to you that everyone who looks at a woman with lust has already committed adultery with her in his heart. 29 If your right eye causes you to sin, tear it out and throw it away; it is better for you to lose one of your members than for your whole body to be thrown into hell.[a] 30 And if your right hand causes you to sin, cut it off and throw it away; it is better for you to lose one of your members than for your whole body to go into hell.[a]

31 "It was also said, 'Whoever divorces his wife, let him give her a certificate of divorce.' 32 But I say to you that anyone who divorces his wife, except on the ground of unchastity, causes her to commit adultery; and whoever marries a divorced woman commits adultery.

33 "Again, you have heard that it was said to those of ancient times, 'You shall not swear falsely, but carry out the vows you have made to the Lord.' 34 But I say to you, Do not swear at all, either by heaven, for it is the throne of God, 35 or by the earth, for it is his footstool, or by Jerusalem, for it is the city of the great King. 36 And do not swear by your head, for you cannot make one hair white or black. 37 Let your word be 'Yes, Yes' or 'No, No'; anything more than this comes from the evil one.[b]

38 "You have heard that it was said, 'An eye for an eye and a tooth for a tooth.' 39 But I say to you, Do not resist an evildoer. But if anyone strikes you on the right cheek, turn the other also; 40 and if anyone wants to sue you and take your coat, give your cloak as well; 41 and if anyone forces you to go one mile, go also the second mile. 42 Give to everyone who begs from you, and do not refuse anyone who wants to borrow from you.

cause of abuse of the practice or because of a particular concern for the economic fate of the woman; indeed, Jewish women had marriage contracts that gave them some financial compensation in cases of divorce. *Unchastity* (Gk. "porneia"), an exception recorded only by Matthew, may refer to incestuous marriages contracted by gentile* converts (see Lev 17–18), to any sexual crime, or to adultery; see Mt 19.9. **33–37:** See Lev 19.12; Num 30.2; Deut 23.21; Mt 23.16–20. **38–42** (Lk 6.29–30): May refer to forms of social protest, the active response of a disempowered people (*right cheek* implies backhanded blows; nakedness in the court is not desirable; Romans permitted conscription of a person for a set distance; going the extra miles could compromise the soldier's ability or preserve another from the burden). **38:** See Ex 21.23–24; Lev 24.19–20; Deut 19.21. Rabbinic sources also argue against such retaliation.

43 "You have heard that it was said, 'You shall love your neighbor and hate your enemy.' 44 But I say to you, Love your enemies and pray for those who persecute you, 45 so that you may be children of your Father in heaven; for he makes his sun rise on the evil and on the good, and sends rain on the righteous and on the unrighteous. 46 For if you love those who love you, what reward do you have? Do not even the tax collectors do the same? 47 And if you greet only your brothers and sisters,[c] what more are you doing than others? Do not even the Gentiles do the same? 48 Be perfect, therefore, as your heavenly Father is perfect.

5.43–48 (Lk 6.27–28, 32–36): *Love your enemies* responds to the one antithesis* not first recorded in Torah.* **43:** Appears in the Qumran Scrolls (1 QS 1.9–10). **46–47:** *Gentiles** and *tax collectors* are both outsiders to Matthew's community and those who are to be evangelized (see 9.9; 18.17; 28.19). **48:** Perfection (Deut 18.13; see Matt 19.21), commanded only in Matthew (Lk 6.36 requires "mercy"), suggests integrity and purity of heart.

6 "Beware of practicing your piety before others in order to be seen by them; for then you have no reward from your Father in heaven.

5.21–42: The antitheses* insist that behavior match intent. **21:** Reflects Ex 20.13; Deut 5.17. **23–24:** Matthew presumes the validity of Temple* sacrifice. **27:** Reflects Ex 20.14; Deut 5.18. **29–30** (Mk 9.43–48): The comment on physical mutilation is hyperbolic.* **31–32** (Mk 10.11–12; Lk 16.18): Jesus forbids divorce (see Mal 2.14–16) on the basis of Gen 2.24, not be-

a Gk *Gehenna*   b Or *evil*   c Gk *your brothers*

2 "So whenever you give alms, do not sound a trumpet before you, as the hypocrites do in the synagogues and in the streets, so that they may be praised by others. Truly I tell you, they have received their reward. ³But when you give alms, do not let your left hand know what your right hand is doing, ⁴so that your alms may be done in secret; and your Father who sees in secret will reward you.ᵃ

5 "And whenever you pray, do not be like the hypocrites; for they love to stand and pray in the synagogues and at the street corners, so that they may be seen by others. Truly I tell you, they have received their reward. ⁶But whenever you pray, go into your room and shut the door and pray to your Father who is in secret; and your Father who sees in secret will reward you.ᵃ

7 "When you are praying, do not heap up empty phrases as the Gentiles do; for they think that they will be heard because of their many words. ⁸Do not be like them, for your Father knows what you need before you ask him.

6.1–7: Pious practice continues Matthew's emphasis on harmonizing intent and action. Matthew denounces shows of piety and those who preach but do not practice (23.3–12). **2:** Almsgiving is a major aspect of Jewish piety. **3–4:** Recipients of alms should neither suffer embarrassment in the presence of the giver nor be in a position where reciprocation is expected. **7:** "Gentiles*" are those outside the church.

9 "Pray then in this way:
   Our Father in heaven,
      hallowed be your name.
10   Your kingdom come.
      Your will be done,
         on earth as it is in heaven.
11   Give us this day our daily bread.ᵇ
12   And forgive us our debts,
      as we also have forgiven
      our debtors.
13   And do not bring us to the time of
      trial,ᶜ
      but rescue us from the evil one.ᵈ
¹⁴For if you forgive others their trespasses, your heavenly Father will also forgive you;

¹⁵but if you do not forgive others, neither will your Father forgive your trespasses.

6.9–15. 9–13 (Lk 11.2–4): The Lord's Prayer is the center of the sermon. **9:** The address is typical for Jewish prayers. **10:** Anticipates Jesus' prayer in Gethsemane (26.42). **11:** *Daily* may mean "for tomorrow"; if so, the prayer expresses hope for the eschatological* banquet along with the concern for basic human needs. **12:** An economic ideal of giving without expectation of return. **13:** On testing, see 26.42. **14–15:** Responsibilities of believers: See 18.35.

16 "And whenever you fast, do not look dismal, like the hypocrites, for they disfigure their faces so as to show others that they are fasting. Truly I tell you, they have received their reward. ¹⁷But when you fast, put oil on your head and wash your face, ¹⁸so that your fasting may be seen not by others but by your Father who is in secret; and your Father who sees in secret will reward you.ᵃ

19 "Do not store up for yourselves treasures on earth, where moth and rustᵉ consume and where thieves break in and steal; ²⁰but store up for yourselves treasures in heaven, where neither moth nor rustᵉ consumes and where thieves do not break in and steal. ²¹For where your treasure is, there your heart will be also.

22 "The eye is the lamp of the body. So, if your eye is healthy, your whole body will be full of light; ²³but if your eye is unhealthy, your whole body will be full of darkness. If then the light in you is darkness, how great is the darkness!

24 "No one can serve two masters; for a slave will either hate the one and love the other, or be devoted to the one and despise the other. You cannot serve God and wealth.ᶠ

25 "Therefore I tell you, do not worry about your life, what you will eat or what you will drink,ᵍ or about your body, what you will wear. Is not life more than food, and the

ᵃ Other ancient authorities add *openly*   ᵇ Or *our bread for tomorrow*   ᶜ Or *us into temptation*   ᵈ Or *from evil.* Other ancient authorities add, in some form, *For the kingdom and the power and the glory are yours forever. Amen.*   ᵉ Gk *eating*   ᶠ Gk *mammon*
ᵍ Other ancient authorities lack *or what you will drink*

body more than clothing? 26Look at the birds of the air; they neither sow nor reap nor gather into barns, and yet your heavenly Father feeds them. Are you not of more value than they? 27And can any of you by worrying add a single hour to your span of life?*ª 28And why do you worry about clothing? Consider the lilies of the field, how they grow; they neither toil nor spin, 29yet I tell you, even Solomon in all his glory was not clothed like one of these. 30But if God so clothes the grass of the field, which is alive today and tomorrow is thrown into the oven, will he not much more clothe you—you of little faith? 31Therefore do not worry, saying, 'What will we eat?' or 'What will we drink?' or 'What will we wear?' 32For it is the Gentiles who strive for all these things; and indeed your heavenly Father knows that you need all these things. 33But strive first for the kingdom of God*ᵇ and his*ᶜ righteousness, and all these things will be given to you as well.

6.16–33. 16–18: The Greek contains a pun: They make their faces disappear in order to appear to fast. Matthew will continue to associate Pharisees★ with hypocrisy. Fasting is a form of Jewish piety. **22–23** (Lk 11.34–36): Reflects the sermon's themes of sight and appearance. **24** (Lk 16.13): More economic admonitions; "mammon" is the Aramaic★ term for wealth (see 19.16–30). **25–33** (Lk 12.22–31): A redefinition of human needs and desires. **33:** If the economic admonitions of the sermon are practiced, such need would be eliminated.

---

34 "So do not worry about tomorrow, for tomorrow will bring worries of its own. Today's trouble is enough for today.

7 "Do not judge, so that you may not be judged. 2For with the judgment you make you will be judged, and the measure you give will be the measure you get. 3Why do you see the speck in your neighbor's*ᵈ eye, but do not notice the log in your own eye? 4Or how can you say to your neighbor,*ᵉ 'Let me take the speck out of your eye,' while the log is in your own eye? 5You hypocrite, first take the log out of your own eye, and then you will see clearly to take the speck out of your neighbor's*ᵈ eye.

6 "Do not give what is holy to dogs; and do not throw your pearls before swine, or they will trample them under foot and turn and maul you.

7 "Ask, and it will be given you; search, and you will find; knock, and the door will be opened for you. 8For everyone who asks receives, and everyone who searches finds, and for everyone who knocks, the door will be opened. 9Is there anyone among you who, if your child asks for bread, will give a stone? 10Or if the child asks for a fish, will give a snake? 11If you then, who are evil, know how to give good gifts to your children, how much more will your Father in heaven give good things to those who ask him!

12 "In everything do to others as you would have them do to you; for this is the law and the prophets.

7.1–12. 1–5 (Mk 4.24; Lk 6.37–38; 41–42): Appropriate practice: Matthew's warnings against scribes★ and Pharisees★ (ch. 23) apply to everyone. **6:** Believers should not force the gospel on those unwilling to listen. **7–11** (Lk 11.9–13): Repeats the sermon's emphasis on trust in divine benevolence. **12** (Lk 6.31): The Golden Rule has numerous parallels (see Tob 4.15). Jesus' contemporary, the Pharisee Rabbi Hillel, stated the principle as "What is hateful to you, do not do to your fellow. That is the Law and the Prophets★; the rest is commentary, go and learn."

---

13 "Enter through the narrow gate; for the gate is wide and the road is easy*ᶠ that leads to destruction, and there are many who take it. 14For the gate is narrow and the road is hard that leads to life, and there are few who find it.

15 "Beware of false prophets, who come to you in sheep's clothing but inwardly are ravenous wolves. 16You will know them by their fruits. Are grapes gathered from thorns, or figs from thistles? 17In the same way, every good tree bears good fruit, but the bad tree bears bad fruit. 18A good tree cannot bear bad fruit, nor can a bad tree bear good fruit. 19Every tree that does not bear good

---

a Or add one cubit to your height   b Other ancient authorities lack of God   c Or its   d Gk brother's   e Gk brother   f Other ancient authorities read for the road is wide and easy fruit is cut down and thrown into the fire. 20Thus you will know them by their fruits.

21 "Not everyone who says to me, 'Lord, Lord,' will enter the kingdom of heaven, but only the one who does the will of my Father in heaven. 22On that day many will say to me, 'Lord, Lord, did we not prophesy in your name, and cast out demons in your name, and do many deeds of power in your name?' 23Then I will declare to them, 'I never knew you; go away from me, you evildoers.'

24 "Everyone then who hears these words of mine and acts on them will be like a wise man who built his house on rock. 25The rain fell, the floods came, and the winds blew and beat on that house, but it did not fall, because it had been founded on rock. 26And everyone who hears these words of mine and does not act on them will be like a foolish man who built his house on sand. 27The rain fell, and the floods came, and the winds blew and beat against that house, and it fell—and great was its fall!"

28 Now when Jesus had finished saying these things, the crowds were astounded at his teaching, 29for he taught them as one having authority, and not as their scribes.

7.13–29. 13–14 (Lk 13.23–24): Warnings against complacency and misplaced security. **15–20** (Lk 6.43–45; 13.6–9): Matthew consistently requires proper action (see 7.21). **21–23**: Warnings against hypocrisy; throughout the sermon, Jesus insists that appearance, intent, and action correspond. **24–27** (Lk 6.47–49): Wisdom sayings that anticipate the parables.* **28–29:** *Authority* is a Matthean motif*; on scribal teaching, see Mk 1.22.

GALILEAN MISSION

8.1–9.38: These two chapters describe Jesus' teaching and healing during his ministry in Galilee.

---

8 When Jesus*a* had come down from the mountain, great crowds followed him; 2and there was a leper*b* who came to him and knelt before him, saying, "Lord, if you choose, you can make me clean." 3He stretched out his hand and touched him, saying, "I do choose. Be made clean!" Immediately his leprosy*b* was cleansed. 4Then Jesus

said to him, "See that you say nothing to anyone; but go, show yourself to the priest, and offer the gift that Moses commanded, as a testimony to them."

5 When he entered Capernaum, a centurion came to him, appealing to him 6and saying, "Lord, my servant is lying at home paralyzed, in terrible distress." 7And he said to him, "I will come and cure him." 8The centurion answered, "Lord, I am not worthy to have you come under my roof; but only speak the word, and my servant will be healed. 9For I also am a man under authority, with soldiers under me; and I say to one, 'Go,' and he goes, and to another, 'Come,' and he comes, and to my slave, 'Do this,' and the slave does it." 10When Jesus heard him, he was amazed and said to those who followed him, "Truly I tell you, in no one*c* in Israel have I found such faith. 11I tell you, many will come from east and west and will eat with Abraham and Isaac and Jacob in the kingdom of heaven, 12while the heirs of the kingdom will be thrown into the outer darkness, where there will be weeping and gnashing of teeth." 13And to the centurion Jesus said, "Go; let it be done for you according to your faith." And the servant was healed in that hour.

8.1–13: 2–4 (Mk 1.40–44; Lk 5.12–14): Leprosy (see Lev 13–14) refers to various skin diseases. Lepers required priestly sanction to reenter society. **5–13** (Lk 7.1–10; Jn 4.46–53): The gentile* centurion. Verse 7 may be read as a question—Shall I heal him?—anticipating a negative answer. Elsewhere Jesus restricts his mission to Jews (10.5b–6), and prior to the resurrection he displays reluctance at extending it to gentiles (15.24). **8:** Matthew's Jesus never enters a gentile's home (contrast Mk 7). **9:** Centurions command between 50 and 100 soldiers; here the centurion admits his helplessness and faith in Jesus' power. **11:** May refer to Diaspora* Jews or to gentiles. **12:** *Heirs* (lit. sons) of the kingdom refers in v. 13 to Jesus' followers: Even those inside the church may forfeit salvation through improper action and belief.

---

a Gk *he*   *b* The terms *leper* and *leprosy* can refer to several diseases   *c* Other ancient authorities read *Truly I tell you, not even*

14 When Jesus entered Peter's house, he saw his mother-in-law lying in bed with a fever; 15he touched her hand, and the fever left her, and she got up and began to serve him. 16That evening they brought to him many who were possessed with demons; and he cast out the spirits with a word, and cured all who were sick. 17This was to fulfill what had been spoken through the prophet Isaiah, "He took our infirmities and bore our diseases."

18 Now when Jesus saw great crowds around him, he gave orders to go over to the other side. 19A scribe then approached and said, "Teacher, I will follow you wherever you go." 20And Jesus said to him, "Foxes have holes, and birds of the air have nests; but the Son of Man has nowhere to lay his head." 21Another of his disciples said to him, "Lord, first let me go and bury my father." 22But Jesus said to him, "Follow me, and let the dead bury their own dead."

8.14–22. 14–15 (Mk 1.30–31; Lk 4.38–39): Peter's mother-in-law "serves"; the term derives from the Greek term for "deacon." Peter's wife is not mentioned. **15–17** (Mk 1.32–34; Lk 4.40–41): Another fulfillment citation; prior to the Gospels, this passage, like many other fulfillment citations, was not viewed as referring to the messiah.* **17:** See Isa 53.4. Matthew lacks Mark's commands for the demons' silence. **18–22** (Mk 4.35; Lk 8.22; 9.57–60): Itinerancy marks Jesus' mission and that of his followers (see ch. 10). **19:** *Teacher* is used by those who are not disciples; in Matthew, Jesus calls disciples; followers do not apply for the position. **20:** *Son of Man* means "human being" (Ezek 37), but it also carries divine connotations (Dan 7.13–14). **21–22:** Jesus' saying shocks; nothing, not even one's own family, takes precedence over service to him.

23 And when he got into the boat, his disciples followed him. 24A windstorm arose on the sea, so great that the boat was being swamped by the waves; but he was asleep. 25And they went and woke him up, saying, "Lord, save us! We are perishing!" 26And he said to them, "Why are you afraid, you of little faith?" Then he got up and rebuked the winds and the sea; and there was a dead calm. 27They were amazed, saying, "What sort of man is this, that even the winds and the sea obey him?"

28 When he came to the other side, to the country of the Gadarenes,*a* two demoniacs coming out of the tombs met him. They were so fierce that no one could pass that way. 29Suddenly they shouted, "What have you to do with us, Son of God? Have you come here to torment us before the time?" 30Now a large herd of swine was feeding at some distance from them. 31The demons begged him, "If you cast us out, send us into the herd of swine." 32And he said to them, "Go!" So they came out and entered the swine; and suddenly, the whole herd rushed down the steep bank into the sea and perished in the water. 33The swineherds ran off, and on going into the town, they told the whole story about what had happened to the demoniacs. 34Then the whole town came out to meet Jesus; and when they saw him, they begged

9 him to leave their neighborhood. 1And after getting into a boat he crossed the sea and came to his own town.

8.23–34. 23–27: Stilling the storm. See comment on Mk 4.35–41 (Lk 8.22–24). **28–34** (Mk 5.1–20; Lk 8.26–39): The Gadarene exorcism occurs in Gadara, a gentile* city six miles from the Sea of Galilee; Gadara was the capital of Perea. Matthew typically doubles the number of those Jesus heals and presents a shorter version of Mark's account. Mark's references to "Legion" are absent.

2 And just then some people were carrying a paralyzed man lying on a bed. When Jesus saw their faith, he said to the paralytic, "Take heart, son; your sins are forgiven." 3Then some of the scribes said to themselves, "This man is blaspheming." 4But Jesus, perceiving their thoughts, said, "Why do you think evil in your hearts? 5For which is easier, to say, 'Your sins are forgiven,' or to say, 'Stand up and walk'? 6But so that you may know that the Son of Man has authority on earth to forgive sins"—he then said to the paralytic—"Stand up, take your bed and go to your home." 7And he stood up and went to his home. 8When the crowds saw it, they

a Other ancient authorities read *Gergesenes*; others, *Gerasenes* were filled with awe, and they glorified God, who had given such authority to human beings.

9 As Jesus was walking along, he saw a man called Matthew sitting at the tax booth; and he said to him, "Follow me." And he got up and followed him.

10 And as he sat at dinner[a] in the house, many tax collectors and sinners came and were sitting[b] with him and his disciples. 11When the Pharisees saw this, they said to his disciples, "Why does your teacher eat with tax collectors and sinners?" 12But when he heard this, he said, "Those who are well have no need of a physician, but those who are sick. 13Go and learn what this means, 'I desire mercy, not sacrifice.' For I have come to call not the righteous but sinners."

9.1–13. 1–8 (Mk 2.1–12; Lk 5.17–26): The paralytic's healing increases religious opposition to Jesus; the charge is blasphemy. Forgiveness of sins, a divine prerogative, traditionally followed repentance, but here the man does not explicitly repent. The saying in 9.6 appears in a different setting in Jn 5.8; it may have been originally preserved apart from a story. **9–13** (Mk 2.13–17; Lk 5.27–32): Matthew, the tax collector, is called Levi in Mk 2.14. Tax collectors and sinners are those who deliberately transgress divine commands. **12:** A Hellenistic* proverb. **13:** Cites Hos 6.6 (see Mt 2.7). The point for both Hosea and Matthew is emphasis rather than contrast; sacrifice has value, but it is meaningless without mercy.

14 Then the disciples of John came to him, saying, "Why do we and the Pharisees fast often,[c] but your disciples do not fast?" 15And Jesus said to them, "The wedding guests cannot mourn as long as the bridegroom is with them, can they? The days will come when the bridegroom is taken away from them, and then they will fast. 16No one sews a piece of unshrunk cloth on an old cloak, for the patch pulls away from the cloak, and a worse tear is made. 17Neither is new wine put into old wineskins; otherwise, the skins burst, and the wine is spilled, and the skins are destroyed; but new wine is put into fresh wineskins, and so both are preserved."

18 While he was saying these things to them, suddenly a leader of the synagogue[d] came in and knelt before him, saying, "My daughter has just died; but come and lay your hand on her, and she will live." 19And Jesus got up and followed him, with his disciples. 20Then suddenly a woman who had been suffering from hemorrhages for twelve years came up behind him and touched the fringe of his cloak, 21for she said to herself, "If I only touch his cloak, I will be made well." 22Jesus turned, and seeing her he said, "Take heart, daughter; your faith has made you well." And instantly the woman was made well. 23When Jesus came to the leader's house and saw the flute players and the crowd making a commotion, 24he said, "Go away; for the girl is not dead but sleeping." And they laughed at him. 25But when the crowd had been put outside, he went in and took her by the hand, and the girl got up. 26And the report of this spread throughout that district.

9.14–26. 14–17 (Mk 2.18–22; Lk 5.33–39): On Fasting, see comment on 6.16–18. Despite acknowledging Jesus at the baptism,* John retains his own disciples. **17:** Matthew affirms both old and new commandments (see 5.16). **18–26** (Mk 5.21–43; Lk 8.40–56): The woman and the child share gender and an implicit foreshadowing of the cross: Like the woman, Jesus will bleed; like the child, he will die; and like both, he will be restored to life. **18:** Unlike Mark, Matthew makes clear the child is dead. Matthew shows no concern for ritual impurity for either the hemorrhaging woman or the corpse. **20:** *Hemorrhages* were probably uterine. For *fringe*, see Num 15.38–40; Deut. 22.12. **22:** *Made well* could also be translated "saved." Jesus praises the woman's faith.

27 As Jesus went on from there, two blind men followed him, crying loudly, "Have mercy on us, Son of David!" 28When he entered the house, the blind men came to him; and Jesus said to them, "Do you believe that I am able to do this?" They said to him, "Yes, Lord." 29Then he touched their eyes and said, "According to your faith let it be done

a Gk reclined　　b Gk were reclining　　c Other ancient authorities lack *often*　　d Gk lacks *of the synagogue* to you." 30And their eyes were opened. Then Jesus sternly ordered them, "See that no one knows of this." 31But they went away and spread the news about him throughout that district.

32 After they had gone away, a demoniac who was mute was brought to him. 33And when the demon had been cast out, the one who had been mute spoke; and the crowds were amazed and said, "Never has anything like this been seen in Israel." 34But the Pharisees said, "By the ruler of the demons he casts out the demons."*a*

9.27–34: In the Gospels illness is frequently a metaphor* for spiritual ignorance. The healing of the two blind men is similar to 20.29–34; Matthew typically doubles the number of those Jesus heals. **30–31:** The messianic secret (see sidebar on p. 52). **32–34:** A healing similar to 12.22–24 (Lk 11.14–15). **34:** The Pharisees* doubt not Jesus' power but its source; they are therefore both spiritually ignorant and unable to recognize Satan.

35 Then Jesus went about all the cities and villages, teaching in their synagogues, and proclaiming the good news of the kingdom, and curing every disease and every sickness. 36When he saw the crowds, he had compassion for them, because they were harassed and helpless, like sheep without a shepherd. 37Then he said to his disciples, "The harvest is plentiful, but the laborers are few; 38therefore ask the Lord of the harvest to send out laborers into his harvest."

9.35–38: *The harvest* is a common reference for the final judgment. Jesus continues his compassionate mission to Israel; the focus of this mission is intensified in 10.6 and remains in place even at the Great Commission (see 28.19).

10 Then Jesus*b* summoned his twelve disciples and gave them authority over unclean spirits, to cast them out, and to cure every disease and every sickness. 2These are the names of the twelve apostles: first, Simon, also known as Peter, and his brother Andrew; James son of Zebedee, and his brother John; 3Philip and Bartholomew; Thomas and Matthew the tax collector;

James son of Alphaeus, and Thaddaeus;*c* 4Simon the Cananaean, and Judas Iscariot, the one who betrayed him.

10.1–11.1: The second or "missionary" discourse. 10.1–4 (Mk 6.7; 3.13–19; Lk 9.1; 6.12–16): Matthew neither recounted the calling of twelve nor previously noted this number. Only here are they called *apostles*★ (Gk., "ones sent out"). The disciples receive authority (v. 1) but do not participate in a mission until after Jesus' resurrection; unlike Mark and Luke, Matthew portrays no mission of either the twelve (Mark) or the seventy (Luke). On Peter, see comment on 16.18. **4:** *Cananean* refers to one who is "zealous"; in the war of 66–70 CE and subsequently, it came to refer to an anti-Roman agitator. If Simon is a political rebel, he does not express such concerns in the Gospel.

5 These twelve Jesus sent out with the following instructions: "Go nowhere among the Gentiles, and enter no town of the Samaritans, 6but go rather to the lost sheep of the house of Israel. 7As you go, proclaim the good news, 'The kingdom of heaven has come near.'*d* 8Cure the sick, raise the dead, cleanse the lepers,*e* cast out demons. You received without payment; give without payment. 9Take no gold, or silver, or copper in your belts, 10no bag for your journey, or two tunics, or sandals, or a staff; for laborers deserve their food. 11Whatever town or village you enter, find out who in it is worthy, and stay there until you leave. 12As you enter the house, greet it. 13If the house is worthy, let your peace come upon it; but if it is not worthy, let your peace return to you. 14If anyone will not welcome you or listen to your words, shake off the dust from your feet as you leave that house or town. 15Truly I tell you, it will be more tolerable for the land of Sodom and Gomorrah on the day of judgment than for that town.

10.5b–15: Missionary instructions. 5b–6: Unique to Matthew (see 15.24); corresponds to Jesus' activity (see Rom 15.8) and ends with the Great Commission. The people of Israel are heirs to the divine promises;

a Other ancient authorities lack this verse   *b* Gk *he*
c Other ancient authorities read *Lebbaeus*, or *Lebbaeus called Thaddaeus*   *d* Or *is at hand*   *e* The terms *leper* and *leprosy* can refer to several diseases

the end of the Gospel does not mark their removal from divine favor but instead marks the placing of the gentiles* on equal footing. **7–15** (Mk 6.8–11; Lk 9.2–5; 10.3–12). **7–8:** Reflects Jesus' works in Mt 8–9; the disciples will do what Jesus has done. **9–10:** Resembles instructions for Cynic* philosophers; Mk 6.8–11 permits staff and sandals. **10:** Missionaries should be supported (see 1 Cor 9.14). **11–15:** Admonishes Christian householders to receive itinerant missionaries, as does the Didache* 11–13.

16 "See, I am sending you out like sheep into the midst of wolves; so be wise as serpents and innocent as doves. [17]Beware of them, for they will hand you over to councils and flog you in their synagogues; [18]and you will be dragged before governors and kings because of me, as a testimony to them and the Gentiles. [19]When they hand you over, do not worry about how you are to speak or what you are to say; for what you are to say will be given to you at that time; [20]for it is not you who speak, but the Spirit of your Father speaking through you. [21]Brother will betray brother to death, and a father his child, and children will rise against parents and have them put to death; [22]and you will be hated by all because of my name. But the one who endures to the end will be saved. [23]When they persecute you in one town, flee to the next; for truly I tell you, you will not have gone through all the towns of Israel before the Son of Man comes.

10.16–23: Missionary warnings. Matthew frames the eschatological* concerns of Mk 13 in terms of daily life; what for Mark signals the final judgment for Matthew indicates the daily fate of those who proclaim Jesus. **17:** Flogging is punishment for violation of Torah* (Deut 25.1–3); such discipline (no longer practiced) was meant to keep one inside the system rather than to excommunicate. "Handed over" is used of the suffering servant (Isa 53.6) and of Jesus (17.22; 20.18–19; 26.2). **18:** Reflects the post-Easter community's fate. **19–20:** Matthew's only reference to the disciples' having the Spirit. **21–22:** Interprets Mic 7.6 in terms of the last judgment (see also 1 Enoch 100.2). **23:** The mission to Israel does not cease.

24 "A disciple is not above the teacher, nor a slave above the master; [25]it is enough for the disciple to be like the teacher, and the slave like the master. If they have called the master of the house Beelzebul, how much more will they malign those of his household!

26 "So have no fear of them; for nothing is covered up that will not be uncovered, and nothing secret that will not become known. [27]What I say to you in the dark, tell in the light; and what you hear whispered, proclaim from the housetops. [28]Do not fear those who kill the body but cannot kill the soul; rather fear him who can destroy both soul and body in hell.*[a] [29]Are not two sparrows sold for a penny? Yet not one of them will fall to the ground apart from your Father. [30]And even the hairs of your head are all counted. [31]So do not be afraid; you are of more value than many sparrows.

32 "Everyone therefore who acknowledges me before others, I also will acknowledge before my Father in heaven; [33]but whoever denies me before others, I also will deny before my Father in heaven.

34 "Do not think that I have come to bring peace to the earth; I have not come to bring peace, but a sword.

35　For I have come to set a man against
　　　his father,
　and a daughter against her mother,
　and a daughter-in-law against her
　　　mother-in-law;
36　and one's foes will be members of one's
　　　own household.

[37]Whoever loves father or mother more than me is not worthy of me; and whoever loves son or daughter more than me is not worthy of me; [38]and whoever does not take up the cross and follow me is not worthy of me. [39]Those who find their life will lose it, and those who lose their life for my sake will find it.

40 "Whoever welcomes you welcomes me, and whoever welcomes me welcomes the one who sent me. [41]Whoever welcomes a prophet in the name of a prophet will receive a prophet's reward; and whoever welcomes a righteous person in the name of a righteous person will receive the reward of

a Gk *Gehenna*

the righteous; ⁴²and whoever gives even a cup of cold water to one of these little ones in the name of a disciple—truly I tell you, none of these will lose their reward."

10.24–42: Community exhortations.* 25: Matthew supports an egalitarian community in terms of leadership, although the language is male-centered; it is not clear that Matthew expected women to be leaders in the church. **26–27:** See Lk 12.2–9. **16–39:** Members of Matthew's church are to proclaim their faith through their actions and attitudes. Membership will be seen as well through the strife confession will cause, as believers are forced to choose between church and family (see Lk 12.51–53). **28–31:** See 6.26–33. **32–33:** Anticipates vv. 40–42. **35:** See Mic 7.6. **37:** Lk 14.26 intensifies the call by adding *wife* to the list of those less important than Jesus and his church. **38:** Matthew's first reference to the cross. **42:** *Little ones* refers to disciples (see 18.1–14). **40–42:** See 18.6; 25.31–46.

11 Now when Jesus had finished instructing his twelve disciples, he went on from there to teach and proclaim his message in their cities.

2 When John heard in prison what the Messiah*ᵃ* was doing, he sent word by his*ᵇ* disciples ³and said to him, "Are you the one who is to come, or are we to wait for another?" ⁴Jesus answered them, "Go and tell John what you hear and see: ⁵the blind receive their sight, the lame walk, the lepers*ᶜ* are cleansed, the deaf hear, the dead are raised, and the poor have good news brought to them. ⁶And blessed is anyone who takes no offense at me."

7 As they went away, Jesus began to speak to the crowds about John: "What did you go out into the wilderness to look at? A reed shaken by the wind? ⁸What then did you go out to see? Someone*ᵈ* dressed in soft robes? Look, those who wear soft robes are in royal palaces. ⁹What then did you go out to see? A prophet?*ᵉ* Yes, I tell you, and more than a prophet. ¹⁰This is the one about whom it is written,

'See, I am sending my messenger ahead
        of you,
    who will prepare your way
        before you.'

¹¹Truly I tell you, among those born of women no one has arisen greater than John the Baptist; yet the least in the kingdom of heaven is greater than he. ¹²From the days of John the Baptist until now the kingdom of heaven has suffered violence,*ᶠ* and the violent take it by force. ¹³For all the prophets and the law prophesied until John came; ¹⁴and if you are willing to accept it, he is Elijah who is to come. ¹⁵Let anyone with ears*ᵍ* listen!

16 "But to what will I compare this generation? It is like children sitting in the marketplaces and calling to one another,
¹⁷ 'We played the flute for you, and you
            did not dance;
    we wailed, and you did not mourn.'
¹⁸For John came neither eating nor drinking, and they say, 'He has a demon'; ¹⁹the Son of Man came eating and drinking, and they say, 'Look, a glutton and a drunkard, a friend of tax collectors and sinners!' Yet wisdom is vindicated by her deeds."*ʰ*

11.1–19. 1: Matthew recounts no mission; the instructions apply to the time of the church. **2–19** (Lk 7.18–35; 16.16): **John and Elijah.** The account interprets the baptism* scene. **2:** John was imprisoned by Herod Antipas at Machaerus. **3:** John may be asking about Jesus' messianic status, or about the type of messiah* he is. Jesus does not conform to popular expectations. *The one who is to come* is the messiah. **4–5:** See Isa 29.18–19; 35.5–6; Lk 4.18–19. **6:** Take offense is "skandalizein," to stumble over. **7:** The reed was a Herodian symbol; John's mission is contrasted with secular royalty and equated with Elijah's role. **10:** Mal 3.1 (see Mk 1.2). **11–14:** Not Jesus' disciple, John represents the border between insiders and outsiders, as Elijah represents the transition between this age and the age to come.

20 Then he began to reproach the cities in which most of his deeds of power had been done, because they did not repent. ²¹"Woe to you, Chorazin! Woe to you, Beth-

a Or *the Christ* *b* Other ancient authorities read *two of his* *c* The terms *leper* and *leprosy* can refer to several diseases *d* Or *Why then did you go out? To see someone* *e* Other ancient authorities read *Why then did you go out? To see a prophet?* *f* Or *has been coming violently* *g* Other ancient authorities add *to hear* *h* Other ancient authorities read *children* saida! For if the deeds of power done in you had been done in Tyre and Sidon, they would have repented long ago in sackcloth and ashes. 22But I tell you, on the day of judgment it will be more tolerable for Tyre and Sidon than for you. 23And you, Capernaum,

will you be exalted to heaven?

No, you will be brought down

to Hades.

For if the deeds of power done in you had been done in Sodom, it would have remained until this day. 24But I tell you that on the day of judgment it will be more tolerable for the land of Sodom than for you."

25 At that time Jesus said, "I thank*a* you, Father, Lord of heaven and earth, because you have hidden these things from the wise and the intelligent and have revealed them to infants; 26yes, Father, for such was your gracious will.*b* 27All things have been handed over to me by my Father; and no one knows the Son except the Father, and no one knows the Father except the Son and anyone to whom the Son chooses to reveal him.

28 "Come to me, all you that are weary and are carrying heavy burdens, and I will give you rest. 29Take my yoke upon you, and learn from me; for I am gentle and humble in heart, and you will find rest for your souls. 30For my yoke is easy, and my burden is light."

12 At that time Jesus went through the grainfields on the sabbath; his disciples were hungry, and they began to pluck heads of grain and to eat. 2When the Pharisees saw it, they said to him, "Look, your disciples are doing what is not lawful to do on the sabbath." 3He said to them, "Have you not read what David did when he and his companions were hungry? 4He entered the house of God and ate the bread of the Presence, which it was not lawful for him or his companions to eat, but only for the priests. 5Or have you not read in the law that on the sabbath the priests in the temple break the sabbath and yet are guiltless? 6I tell you, something greater than the temple is here. 7But if you had known what this means, 'I desire mercy and not sacrifice,' you would not have condemned the guiltless. 8For the Son of Man is lord of the sabbath."

9 He left that place and entered their synagogue; 10a man was there with a withered hand, and they asked him, "Is it lawful to cure on the sabbath?" so that they might accuse him. 11He said to them, "Suppose one of you has only one sheep and it falls into a pit on the sabbath; will you not lay hold of it and lift it out? 12How much more valuable is a human being than a sheep! So it is lawful to do good on the sabbath." 13Then he said to the man, "Stretch out your hand." He stretched it out, and it was restored, as sound as the other. 14But the Pharisees went out and conspired against him, how to destroy him.

11.16–30: Wisdom sayings. Jesus speaks as the representative of Sophia (wisdom), a manifestation of the divine on earth (see Prov 1–9; Wis 7.1–8, 21). **18–19** (Lk 7.33): These are insults; the charges against Jesus recollect the rebellious son (Deut 21.20). Lk 7.35 speaks of Wisdom's children; Matthew of her deeds. **20–24:** "Woe oracles*" are common prophetic formulations. Matthew records no events leading to these condemnations and does not mention the Galilean cities of Chorazin and Bethsaida elsewhere. Missing entirely from the Gospel tradition are references to the larger Galilean cities of Tiberias and Sepphoris. Tyre, Sidon, and Sodom are proverbial symbols of gentile* evil. **25–30** (Lk 10.21–22): The image of Jesus as Wisdom continues (11.19; see Sir 51.23–30), with typical reversal of expectations; the innocent and simple surpass the wise in wisdom. **28–30:** Jesus suggests he fulfills the role of Torah.*

12.1–14: Sabbath Controversies. Jesus participates in Judaism's ongoing discussion about how to celebrate the day of rest (see Mk 2.23–28; Lk 6.1–5). **2:** Represents the Pharisees'* interpretation* of Ex 20.8–11. **3–4:** See 1 Sam 21.1–6; Lev 24.5–9. **6:** *Something greater* is not (just) Jesus but also divine mercy. **7:** See comment on 9.13. **8:** The verse has two meanings: Jesus is the authoritative interpreter of the sabbath, but any "son of man" (that is, any human being) is also the one the sabbath is to serve. **9–14** (Mk 3.1–6; Lk 6.6–11): See comment on Mk 3.1–6.

a Or *praise*   *b* Or *for so it was well-pleasing in your sight*

15 When Jesus became aware of this, he departed. Many crowds[a] followed him, and he cured all of them, 16and he ordered them not to make him known. 17This was to fulfill what had been spoken through the prophet Isaiah:

18 "Here is my servant, whom I
        have chosen,
    my beloved, with whom my soul is
        well pleased.
    I will put my Spirit upon him,
        and he will proclaim justice to the
            Gentiles.
19 He will not wrangle or cry aloud,
        nor will anyone hear his voice in the
            streets.
20 He will not break a bruised reed
        or quench a smoldering wick
    until he brings justice to victory.
21   And in his name the Gentiles will
        hope."

12.15–21 (Mk 3.7–12; Lk 6.17–19; 4.40): **More ful-fillment citations. 18–21:** See Isa 42.1–4. The term for *Gentiles** can also be translated, here and else-where in Matthew, as "nations." In the Hebrew of Isa-iah's text, the *servant* may be read as a reference to the nation of Israel rather than to an individual; the last line mentions not "gentiles" but "coastlands."

22 Then they brought to him a demoniac who was blind and mute; and he cured him, so that the one who had been mute could speak and see. 23All the crowds were amazed and said, "Can this be the Son of David?" 24But when the Pharisees heard it, they said, "It is only by Beelzebul, the ruler of the de-mons, that this fellow casts out the demons." 25He knew what they were thinking and said to them, "Every kingdom divided against it-self is laid waste, and no city or house divided against itself will stand. 26If Satan casts out Satan, he is divided against himself; how then will his kingdom stand? 27If I cast out demons by Beelzebul, by whom do your own exorcists[b] cast them out? Therefore they will be your judges. 28But if it is by the Spirit of God that I cast out demons, then the king-dom of God has come to you. 29Or how can one enter a strong man's house and plunder his property, without first tying up the strong

man? Then indeed the house can be plun-dered. 30Whoever is not with me is against me, and whoever does not gather with me scatters. 31Therefore I tell you, people will be forgiven for every sin and blasphemy, but blasphemy against the Spirit will not be for-given. 32Whoever speaks a word against the Son of Man will be forgiven, but whoever speaks against the Holy Spirit will not be for-given, either in this age or in the age to come.

33 "Either make the tree good, and its fruit good; or make the tree bad, and its fruit bad; for the tree is known by its fruit. 34You brood of vipers! How can you speak good things, when you are evil? For out of the abundance of the heart the mouth speaks. 35The good person brings good things out of a good treasure, and the evil person brings evil things out of an evil treasure. 36I tell you, on the day of judgment you will have to give an account for every careless word you utter; 37for by your words you will be justified, and by your words you will be condemned."

38 Then some of the scribes and Phari-sees said to him, "Teacher, we wish to see a sign from you." 39But he answered them, "An evil and adulterous generation asks for a sign, but no sign will be given to it except the sign of the prophet Jonah. 40For just as Jonah was three days and three nights in the belly of the sea monster, so for three days and three nights the Son of Man will be in the heart of the earth. 41The people of Nin-eveh will rise up at the judgment with this generation and condemn it, because they re-pented at the proclamation of Jonah, and see, something greater than Jonah is here! 42The queen of the South will rise up at the judgment with this generation and condemn it, because she came from the ends of the earth to listen to the wisdom of Solomon, and see, something greater than Solomon is here!

12.22–42. 22–37 (Mk 3.20–30; Lk 11.14–23): **Jesus' authority.** Here begins Matthew's longest exact cor-respondence to Marcan order. **24:** *Son of David* is a royal messianic title, which Matthew had already em-phasized in the genealogy.* **24:** The Pharisees* do not

---

a Other ancient authorities lack *crowds*   b Gk *sons*

deny Jesus' miracles, but they fear his popularity. Beelzebul* is a pagan god (see 2 Kings 1.2). **27:** The first century witnessed many pagan as well as Jewish and Christian exorcists. **28–29:** The binding of Satan at the end-time appears throughout Jewish writings at this time. **31:** The unpardonable sin is probably the refusal to acknowledge divine power; it likely also refers, for Matthew, to the rejection of the church's Spirit-filled missionaries. **33–36:** See 7.16–20; Mk 7.14–23; Lk 6.43–45. **38–42:** See Lk 11.16, 29–32. **38:** *Teacher* is used only by unbelievers. **39:** Implicitly contains the sign of the conversion of the gentiles.* **41–42:** The Pharisees* recall the prediction after the crucifixion (see 27.62–66). **42:** The Queen of Sheba (1 Kings 10.1–10; 2 Chr 9.1–9).

43 "When the unclean spirit has gone out of a person, it wanders through waterless regions looking for a resting place, but it finds none. 44Then it says, 'I will return to my house from which I came.' When it comes, it finds it empty, swept, and put in order. 45Then it goes and brings along seven other spirits more evil than itself, and they enter and live there; and the last state of that person is worse than the first. So will it be also with this evil generation."

46 While he was still speaking to the crowds, his mother and his brothers were standing outside, wanting to speak to him. 47Someone told him, "Look, your mother and your brothers are standing outside, wanting to speak to you."[a] 48But to the one who had told him this, Jesus[b] replied, "Who is my mother, and who are my brothers?" 49And pointing to his disciples, he said, "Here are my mother and my brothers! 50For whoever does the will of my Father in heaven is my brother and sister and mother."

12.43–50. 43–45 (Lk 11.24–26): **Lapsed faith.** Matthew consistently requires proper action to accompany confession; protestations of repentance not followed by consistent action result in a worse situation for the lapsed believer. **46–50** (Mk 3.31–35; Lk 8.19–21): **Jesus' true family.** The concern for lapsed faith is ironic* in light of the immediate reference to Jesus' mother, the first reference to her since the nativity story. Jesus replaces biological kin with the family of faith.

13 That same day Jesus went out of the house and sat beside the sea. 2Such great crowds gathered around him that he got into a boat and sat there, while the whole crowd stood on the beach. 3And he told them many things in parables, saying: "Listen! A sower went out to sow. 4And as he sowed, some seeds fell on the path, and the birds came and ate them up. 5Other seeds fell on rocky ground, where they did not have much soil, and they sprang up quickly, since they had no depth of soil. 6But when the sun rose, they were scorched; and since they had no root, they withered away. 7Other seeds fell among thorns, and the thorns grew up and choked them. 8Other seeds fell on good soil and brought forth grain, some a hundredfold, some sixty, some thirty. 9Let anyone with ears[c] listen!"

10 Then the disciples came and asked him, "Why do you speak to them in parables?" 11He answered, "To you it has been given to know the secrets[d] of the kingdom of heaven, but to them it has not been given. 12For to those who have, more will be given, and they will have an abundance; but from those who have nothing, even what they have will be taken away. 13The reason I speak to them in parables is that 'seeing they do not perceive, and hearing they do not listen, nor do they understand.' 14With them indeed is fulfilled the prophecy of Isaiah that says:

'You will indeed listen, but never understand,
 and you will indeed look, but never perceive.
15 For this people's heart has grown dull,
 and their ears are hard of hearing,
 and they have shut their eyes;
 so that they might not look with their eyes,
 and listen with their ears,
 and understand with their heart and turn—
 and I would heal them.'

16But blessed are your eyes, for they see, and your ears, for they hear. 17Truly I tell you,

a Other ancient authorities lack verse 47   b Gk he
c Other ancient authorities add *to hear*   d Or *mysteries*

many prophets and righteous people longed to see what you see, but did not see it, and to hear what you hear, but did not hear it.

18 "Hear then the parable of the sower. ¹⁹When anyone hears the word of the kingdom and does not understand it, the evil one comes and snatches away what is sown in the heart; this is what was sown on the path. ²⁰As for what was sown on rocky ground, this is the one who hears the word and immediately receives it with joy; ²¹yet such a person has no root, but endures only for a while, and when trouble or persecution arises on account of the word, that person immediately falls away.*ᵃ* ²²As for what was sown among thorns, this is the one who hears the word, but the cares of the world and the lure of wealth choke the word, and it yields nothing. ²³But as for what was sown on good soil, this is the one who hears the word and understands it, who indeed bears fruit and yields, in one case a hundredfold, in another sixty, and in another thirty."

24 He put before them another parable: "The kingdom of heaven may be compared to someone who sowed good seed in his field; ²⁵but while everybody was asleep, an enemy came and sowed weeds among the wheat, and then went away. ²⁶So when the plants came up and bore grain, then the weeds appeared as well. ²⁷And the slaves of the householder came and said to him, 'Master, did you not sow good seed in your field? Where, then, did these weeds come from?' ²⁸He answered, 'An enemy has done this.' The slaves said to him, 'Then do you want us to go and gather them?' ²⁹But he replied, 'No; for in gathering the weeds you would uproot the wheat along with them. ³⁰Let both of them grow together until the harvest; and at harvest time I will tell the reapers, Collect the weeds first and bind them in bundles to be burned, but gather the wheat into my barn.' "

thew's concerns about lapsing faith. **24–30:** In society and in the church, good and evil exist together; the final judgment separates them (25.31–46).

31 He put before them another parable: "The kingdom of heaven is like a mustard seed that someone took and sowed in his field; ³²it is the smallest of all the seeds, but when it has grown it is the greatest of shrubs and becomes a tree, so that the birds of the air come and make nests in its branches."

33 He told them another parable: "The kingdom of heaven is like yeast that a woman took and mixed in with*ᵇ* three measures of flour until all of it was leavened."

34 Jesus told the crowds all these things in parables; without a parable he told them nothing. ³⁵This was to fulfill what had been spoken through the prophet:*ᶜ*

"I will open my mouth to speak
    in parables;
I will proclaim what has been hidden
    from the foundation of the
    world."*ᵈ*

36 Then he left the crowds and went into the house. And his disciples approached him, saying, "Explain to us the parable of the weeds of the field." ³⁷He answered, "The one who sows the good seed is the Son of Man; ³⁸the field is the world, and the good seed are the children of the kingdom; the weeds are the children of the evil one, ³⁹and the enemy who sowed them is the devil; the harvest is the end of the age, and the reapers are angels. ⁴⁰Just as the weeds are collected and burned up with fire, so will it be at the end of the age. ⁴¹The Son of Man will send his angels, and they will collect out of his kingdom all causes of sin and all evildoers, ⁴²and they will throw them into the furnace of fire, where there will be weeping and gnashing of teeth. ⁴³Then the righteous will shine like the sun in the kingdom of their Father. Let anyone with ears*ᵉ* listen!

44 "The kingdom of heaven is like treasure hidden in a field, which someone found

---

13.1–52 (Mk 4.1–34; Lk 8.4–18; 13.18–21): **The third or parable ✶ discourse.** See sidebar, "Parables," p. 1687. **11:** Understanding is a divine gift (11.25–30; 16.17). **13:** The crowds are already imperceptive; contrast Mark, where parables make them so. **14–15:** See Isa 6.9–10. **18–23:** The interpretation reinforces Mat-

a Gk *stumbles*   *b* Gk *hid in*   *c* Other ancient authorities read *the prophet Isaiah*   *d* Other ancient authorities lack *of the world*   *e* Other ancient authorities add *to hear*

Parables

Parables★ use conventional images to disturb complacent existence; in shaking up one's worldview, they force reconsideration of what is normally considered safe, desirable, and honorable. While today the parables have become so domesticated that "pearl of great price" (Mt 13.45–46; Thomas★ 76) and "good Samaritan" (Luke 10.30–35) are conventional expressions for, respectively, a major business opportunity and a person who helps fix a flat tire, such uncontroversial, banal readings miss the point.

Jesus' parables are found in the Synoptic Gospels★ and, often in a parallel form, in the Gospel of Thomas (but not in the Gospel of John). He adapted the genre★—already known in the scriptural tradition (such as Nathan's parable of the ewe lamb in 1 Sam 12.1–4) and not uncommon in Rabbinic literature—to provide teachings about the kingdom of heaven. These teachings reveal a kingdom of such enormous worth that everything must be dedicated toward it: the pearl, the treasure in the field (Mt 13.44; Thomas 109). The parables show a divine grace that works in unexpected ways: the laborers in the vineyard (Mt 20.1–15). They tell about small, hidden, ignominious beginnings that reap surprising results: the leaven (Mt 13.33; Lk 13.20; Thomas 96); the mustard seed (Mt 13.31, 32; Mk 4.30–32; Lk 13.18–19; Thomas 20). And they teach of a final judgment in which some are chosen and some are not: the harvest (Mk 4.26–29; Thomas 21); the weeds and the wheat (Mt 13.24–30; Thomas 57). Although the images are mundane rather than apocalyptic,★ the kingdom they present is not clearly and unequivocally present. It is simultaneously a daily revelation and a promise for the future.

and hid; then in his joy he goes and sells all that he has and buys that field.

45 "Again, the kingdom of heaven is like a merchant in search of fine pearls; 46on finding one pearl of great value, he went and sold all that he had and bought it.

47 "Again, the kingdom of heaven is like a net that was thrown into the sea and caught fish of every kind; 48when it was full, they drew it ashore, sat down, and put the good into baskets but threw out the bad. 49So it will be at the end of the age. The angels will come out and separate the evil from the righteous 50and throw them into the furnace of fire, where there will be weeping and gnashing of teeth.

51 "Have you understood all this?" They answered, "Yes." 52And he said to them, "Therefore every scribe who has been trained for the kingdom of heaven is like the master of a household who brings out of his treasure what is new and what is old." 53When Jesus had finished these parables, he left that place.

13.31–53. 31–32 (Lk 13.18–19): Mustard produces small bushes; the parable★ is exaggerated irony.★ 33 (Lk 13.20–21): *Yeast* traditionally symbolizes decay; the woman underhandedly "hides" dough. Jesus' references to the kingdom highlight what is traditionally unwanted, unimpressive, and devalued; the kingdom resists conventional explanation or example. Sowing and baking suggest separate gender roles. 35: See Ps 78. 37: Unbelief is caused by Satan. 44–46: Unexpected, even questionable behavior indicates total dedication and urgency (12.29; Lk 16.1–13). 45–46: The Gnostic★ "Hymn of the Pearl" uses this image of the precious gem (Gk., "Margarita") to symbolize knowledge about salvation. 47–48: Dragnets are several hundred feet wide. 51–52: *Trained*, literally, "discipled." The scribe,★ trained in interpretation★ of Torah,★ may be the evangelist's self-portrait;

new and old coexist, just as do Jesus' teaching and Torah.

~~~~~~~~~~~~~~~~~~~~

54 He came to his hometown and began to teach the people*a* in their synagogue, so that they were astounded and said, "Where did this man get this wisdom and these deeds of power? ⁵⁵Is not this the carpenter's son? Is not his mother called Mary? And are not his brothers James and Joseph and Simon and Judas? ⁵⁶And are not all his sisters with us? Where then did this man get all this?" ⁵⁷And they took offense at him. But Jesus said to them, "Prophets are not without honor except in their own country and in their own house." ⁵⁸And he did not do many deeds of power there, because of their unbelief.

13.54–58 (Mk 6.1–6; Lk 4.16–30): **Rejection in Nazareth.** The unnamed hometown is Nazareth; Jesus will not return there. **55–56:** Mark depicts Jesus as an artisan (Gk., "tekton"). Later church tradition suggests the siblings are cousins. On James, see Gal 1.19. **58:** Matthew changes Mark's "inability" to a matter of Jesus' volition.

~~~~~~~~~~~~~~~~~~~~

14 At that time Herod the ruler*b* heard reports about Jesus; ²and he said to his servants, "This is John the Baptist; he has been raised from the dead, and for this reason these powers are at work in him." ³For Herod had arrested John, bound him, and put him in prison on account of Herodias, his brother Philip's wife,*c* ⁴because John had been telling him, "It is not lawful for you to have her." ⁵Though Herod*d* wanted to put him to death, he feared the crowd, because they regarded him as a prophet. ⁶But when Herod's birthday came, the daughter of Herodias danced before the company, and she pleased Herod ⁷so much that he promised on oath to grant her whatever she might ask. ⁸Prompted by her mother, she said, "Give me the head of John the Baptist here on a platter." ⁹The king was grieved, yet out of regard for his oaths and for the guests, he commanded it to be given; ¹⁰he sent and had John beheaded in the prison. ¹¹The head was brought on a platter and given to the girl, who brought it to her mother. ¹²His disciples

came and took the body and buried it; then they went and told Jesus.

14.1–12 (Mk 6.14–29; Lk 9.7–9): **The death of John the Baptist.** The story is told in retrospect. Herod and Herodias parallel Ahab and Jezebel; John is equated with their opponent Elijah. **3:** Herodias had been married to Antipas's half-brother; the relationship was incestuous (Lev 18.16; 20.21). **5:** Matthew's Herod more actively seeks John's death; Mk 6.17–28 emphasizes that Herod is manipulated by Herodias. **6:** Josephus* names the daughter Salome. She is a young girl (Gr., "Korasion"), not a physically mature woman, as she is often depicted in movies. Her dance is not described as lewd. Josephus confirms that Herod Antipas executed the Baptist, but he presents the execution as a preemptive strike lest John's rousing sermons incite the people to rebellion.

13 Now when Jesus heard this, he withdrew from there in a boat to a deserted place by himself. But when the crowds heard it, they followed him on foot from the towns. ¹⁴When he went ashore, he saw a great crowd; and he had compassion for them and cured their sick. ¹⁵When it was evening, the disciples came to him and said, "This is a deserted place, and the hour is now late; send the crowds away so that they may go into the villages and buy food for themselves." ¹⁶Jesus said to them, "They need not go away; you give them something to eat." ¹⁷They replied, "We have nothing here but five loaves and two fish." ¹⁸And he said, "Bring them here to me." ¹⁹Then he ordered the crowds to sit down on the grass. Taking the five loaves and the two fish, he looked up to heaven, and blessed and broke the loaves, and gave them to the disciples, and the disciples gave them to the crowds. ²⁰And all ate and were filled; and they took up what was left over of the broken pieces, twelve baskets full. ²¹And those who ate were about five thousand men, besides women and children.

14.13–21 (Mk 6.30–44; Lk 9.10–17; Jn 6.1–13): **Feeding the 5,000.** Notice the contrast between the

a Gk them   *b* Gk tetrarch   *c* Other ancient authorities read *his brother's wife*   *d* Gk he wilderness feeding and Antipas's dinner party. Sea crossing, wilderness setting, hungry crowds, and miraculous food remind one of Israel's Sinai experience and Elisha's miraculous meal (2 Kings 4.42–44). The scene also prefigures the last supper and the messianic banquet. **21:** Matthew makes special note of women and children.

22 Immediately he made the disciples get into the boat and go on ahead to the other side, while he dismissed the crowds. 23And after he had dismissed the crowds, he went up the mountain by himself to pray. When evening came, he was there alone, 24but by this time the boat, battered by the waves, was far from the land,*a* for the wind was against them. 25And early in the morning he came walking toward them on the sea. 26But when the disciples saw him walking on the sea, they were terrified, saying, "It is a ghost!" And they cried out in fear. 27But immediately Jesus spoke to them and said, "Take heart, it is I; do not be afraid."

28 Peter answered him, "Lord, if it is you, command me to come to you on the water." 29He said, "Come." So Peter got out of the boat, started walking on the water, and came toward Jesus. 30But when he noticed the strong wind,*b* he became frightened, and beginning to sink, he cried out, "Lord, save me!" 31Jesus immediately reached out his hand and caught him, saying to him, "You of little faith, why did you doubt?" 32When they got into the boat, the wind ceased. 33And those in the boat worshiped him, saying, "Truly you are the Son of God."

34 When they had crossed over, they came to land at Gennesaret. 35After the people of that place recognized him, they sent word throughout the region and brought all who were sick to him, 36and begged him that they might touch even the fringe of his cloak; and all who touched it were healed.

14.22–36 (Mk 6.45–52; Jn 6.15–21): **Stilling the storm. 24:** The boat, likely symbolizing the church, is *battered.* The sea is a symbol of chaos. **25–27:** In earlier scripture, only the Deity walks on the sea (Job 9.8; 38.16; Ps 77.19; Isa 43.16, etc.). The "I am" language is filled with divine connotations (Ex 3.13–15). **28:** Peter's question recalls Satan's temptation (4.3). **31:**

Doubt connotes vacillation, not lack of belief (see 28.17). **33:** Unlike Mark (6.52), Matthew portrays comprehending disciples.

15 Then Pharisees and scribes came to Jesus from Jerusalem and said, 2"Why do your disciples break the tradition of the elders? For they do not wash their hands before they eat." 3He answered them, "And why do you break the commandment of God for the sake of your tradition? 4For God said,*c* 'Honor your father and your mother,' and, 'Whoever speaks evil of father or mother must surely die.' 5But you say that whoever tells father or mother, 'Whatever support you might have had from me is given to God,'*d* then that person need not honor the father.*e* 6So, for the sake of your tradition, you make void the word*f* of God. 7You hypocrites! Isaiah prophesied rightly about you when he said:

8 'This people honors me with their lips,
　　but their hearts are far from me;
9 in vain do they worship me,
　　teaching human precepts as
　　　　doctrines.' "

10 Then he called the crowd to him and said to them, "Listen and understand: 11it is not what goes into the mouth that defiles a person, but it is what comes out of the mouth that defiles." 12Then the disciples approached and said to him, "Do you know that the Pharisees took offense when they heard what you said?" 13He answered, "Every plant that my heavenly Father has not planted will be uprooted. 14Let them alone; they are blind guides of the blind.*g* And if one blind person guides another, both will fall into a pit." 15But Peter said to him, "Explain this parable to us." 16Then he said, "Are you also still without understanding? 17Do you not see that whatever goes into the mouth enters the stomach, and goes out into the sewer? 18But what comes out of the mouth proceeds from the heart, and this is what defiles.

---

a Other ancient authorities read *was out on the sea*　*b* Other ancient authorities read *the wind*　*c* Other ancient authorities read *commanded, saying*　*d* Or *is an offering*　*e* Other ancient authorities add *or the mother*　*f* Other ancient authorities read *law;* others, *commandment*　*g* Other ancient authorities lack *of the blind*

19For out of the heart come evil intentions, murder, adultery, fornication, theft, false witness, slander. 20These are what defile a person, but to eat with unwashed hands does not defile."

15.1–20 (Mk 7.1–23): **Competing traditions. 1–2:** Handwashing maintains a holy state. The Pharisees* may have adapted priestly regulations (Ex 30.17–21; Lev 22.4–7) in extending the sanctity of the Temple* altar to the domestic table. **4:** See Ex 20.12; Deut 5.16. **5:** A practice unmentioned in Jewish sources. **7–9:** See Isa 60.21 (Septuagint*). **11:** Establishes priority, not abrogation, of dietary regulations (compare Mk 7.19); it is unlikely that Jesus proclaimed all foods clean, as the accounts in Gal 2 and Acts 10, 15 confirm. One early Jewish view was that while Jews adhered to biblical dietary commands, gentiles* were only forbidden from blood, strangled meat, and meat offered to idols (see also Acts 15.20).

21 Jesus left that place and went away to the district of Tyre and Sidon. 22Just then a Canaanite woman from that region came out and started shouting, "Have mercy on me, Lord, Son of David; my daughter is tormented by a demon." 23But he did not answer her at all. And his disciples came and urged him, saying, "Send her away, for she keeps shouting after us." 24He answered, "I was sent only to the lost sheep of the house of Israel." 25But she came and knelt before him, saying, "Lord, help me." 26He answered, "It is not fair to take the children's food and throw it to the dogs." 27She said, "Yes, Lord, yet even the dogs eat the crumbs that fall from their masters' table." 28Then Jesus answered her, "Woman, great is your faith! Let it be done for you as you wish." And her daughter was healed instantly.

15.21–28 (Mk 7.24–30): **The Canaanite woman. 22:** Canaanites were the native inhabitants of the land promised to Abraham's descendants (compare Mk 7.26, where the woman is given the elite designation "a Greek, a Syrophoenician by birth"). The woman employs a Jewish, not Canaanite, reference to David. Jesus does not (again contrast Mark) enter a gentile* home. **26:** Repeats 10.6; the reference to *dogs* is an insult. As in 8.5–11, Jesus heals a gentile reluctantly, after conversation, at a distance, and in light of faith.

Her success, guaranteed by her faith, is anticipated by the presence of Canaanites (Rahab and, possibly, Tamar) in Jesus' genealogy.*

---

29 After Jesus had left that place, he passed along the Sea of Galilee, and he went up the mountain, where he sat down. 30Great crowds came to him, bringing with them the lame, the maimed, the blind, the mute, and many others. They put them at his feet, and he cured them, 31so that the crowd was amazed when they saw the mute speaking, the maimed whole, the lame walking, and the blind seeing. And they praised the God of Israel.

32 Then Jesus called his disciples to him and said, "I have compassion for the crowd, because they have been with me now for three days and have nothing to eat; and I do not want to send them away hungry, for they might faint on the way." 33The disciples said to him, "Where are we to get enough bread in the desert to feed so great a crowd?" 34Jesus asked them, "How many loaves have you?" They said, "Seven, and a few small fish." 35Then ordering the crowd to sit down on the ground, 36he took the seven loaves and the fish; and after giving thanks he broke them and gave them to the disciples, and the disciples gave them to the crowds. 37And all of them ate and were filled; and they took up the broken pieces left over, seven baskets full. 38Those who had eaten were four thousand men, besides women and children. 39After sending away the crowds, he got into the boat and went to the region of Magadan.ᵃ

15.29–39. 29–31 (Mk 7.31–37): **Feeding the 4,000.** Unlike Mark, Matthew does not clearly suggest gentile* crowds. **32–39** (Mk 8.1–10): A doublet of 14.13–21. Again Matthew notes the presence of women and children; therefore, the crowd was much larger than 4,000. **39:** *Magadan* is not known.

16 The Pharisees and Sadducees came, and to test Jesusᵇ they asked him to show them a sign from heaven. 2He an-

a Other ancient authorities read *Magdala* or *Magdalan*
b Gk *him*

swered them, "When it is evening, you say, 'It will be fair weather, for the sky is red.' [3]And in the morning, 'It will be stormy today, for the sky is red and threatening.' You know how to interpret the appearance of the sky, but you cannot interpret the signs of the times.[a] [4]An evil and adulterous generation asks for a sign, but no sign will be given to it except the sign of Jonah." Then he left them and went away.

[5] When the disciples reached the other side, they had forgotten to bring any bread. [6]Jesus said to them, "Watch out, and beware of the yeast of the Pharisees and Sadducees." [7]They said to one another, "It is because we have brought no bread." [8]And becoming aware of it, Jesus said, "You of little faith, why are you talking about having no bread? [9]Do you still not perceive? Do you not remember the five loaves for the five thousand, and how many baskets you gathered? [10]Or the seven loaves for the four thousand, and how many baskets you gathered? [11]How could you fail to perceive that I was not speaking about bread? Beware of the yeast of the Pharisees and Sadducees!" [12]Then they understood that he had not told them to beware of the yeast of bread, but of the teaching of the Pharisees and Sadducees.

16.1–12. **1–4** (Mk 8.11–13; Lk 11.16, 29; 12.54–56): **Demands for signs.** This account is a doublet of 12.38–40. **1:** The pairing of Sadducees* and Pharisees* is unusual and likely not historical (see 3.7). "Testing" recalls 4.1–11. **4:** See comment on 12.40. In John's Gospel, Jesus performs "signs" in order to bring people to belief. **5–12** (Mk 8.14–21; Lk 12.1): **Warnings against Pharisees.** Yeast is a traditional symbol of evil and decay (see 13.33). Matthew elsewhere commends Pharisaic teaching but not practice (23.2). The polemic* may be the result of competition between Matthew's church and the local synagogue.* **12:** Unlike in Mk 8.16–17, the disciples comprehend Jesus' teachings.

13 Now when Jesus came into the district of Caesarea Philippi, he asked his disciples, "Who do people say that the Son of Man is?" [14]And they said, "Some say John the Baptist, but others Elijah, and still others Jeremiah or one of the prophets." [15]He said to them,

"But who do you say that I am?" [16]Simon Peter answered, "You are the Messiah,[b] the Son of the living God." [17]And Jesus answered him, "Blessed are you, Simon son of Jonah! For flesh and blood has not revealed this to you, but my Father in heaven. [18]And I tell you, you are Peter,[c] and on this rock[d] I will build my church, and the gates of Hades will not prevail against it. [19]I will give you the keys of the kingdom of heaven, and whatever you bind on earth will be bound in heaven, and whatever you loose on earth will be loosed in heaven." [20]Then he sternly ordered the disciples not to tell anyone that he was[e] the Messiah.[b]

16.13–20 (Mk 8.27–33; Lk 9.18–22): **Peter's confession.** Caesarea Philippi, formerly Paneas, was on the border between Jewish and gentile* territory and had a large temple built by Herod the Great and dedicated to Caesar Augustus; see comment on Mk 8.27. **17–19:** Unique to Matthew and consistent with Matthew's particular interest in church structure and community organization. **17:** Jesus addresses Peter directly. *Revealed* (Gk., "apokalypto") suggests divine disclosure. **18:** Peter (Gk., "Petros") means "rock" or "stone" (Gk., "petra"), as in "petrified." In Aramaic,* both nouns are pronounced "Kepha" (see Gal 2.9, Cephas). *Church* (Gk., "ekklesia") appears in the Gospels only here and 18.17. **19:** *Keys* represent teaching and administrative authority (Isa 22.20–25). *Bind* and *loose* in rabbinic literature mean, respectively, forbid and permit.

21 From that time on, Jesus began to show his disciples that he must go to Jerusalem and undergo great suffering at the hands of the elders and chief priests and scribes, and be killed, and on the third day be raised. [22]And Peter took him aside and began to rebuke him, saying, "God forbid it, Lord! This must never happen to you." [23]But he turned and said to Peter, "Get behind me, Satan! You are a stumbling block to me; for you are setting your mind not on divine things but on human things."

24 Then Jesus told his disciples, "If any want to become my followers, let them deny

a Other ancient authorities lack [2]*When it is . . . of the times*   *b* Or *the Christ*   *c* Gk *Petros*   *d* Gk *petra*   *e* Other ancient authorities add *Jesus* themselves and take up their cross and follow me. 25For those who want to save their life will lose it, and those who lose their life for my sake will find it. 26For what will it profit them if they gain the whole world but forfeit their life? Or what will they give in return for their life?

27 "For the Son of Man is to come with his angels in the glory of his Father, and then he will repay everyone for what has been done. 28Truly I tell you, there are some standing here who will not taste death before they see the Son of Man coming in his kingdom."

16.21–28: Passion predictions (17.22–23; 20.17–19; 26.2). **21:** The first of four predictions. Jesus' death is divinely willed. **23:** *Get behind me* is also a discipleship posture (see 4.19). While the cross is a *stumbling block* (Gk., "skandalon") to those outside the church, Peter here is the stumbling block for refusing to accept it. **24–28** (Mk 8.34–9.1; Lk 9.23–27): The true disciples will follow their master; Jesus predicts not just his passion, but theirs. **27:** Matthew emphasizes action, not (empty) confession. **27–28:** Likely refers to the parousia,★ the return of Jesus to judge the world (see 1 Thess 4.15–18), although Mt 28.20 suggests that Jesus never leaves his church.

17 Six days later, Jesus took with him Peter and James and his brother John and led them up a high mountain, by themselves. 2And he was transfigured before them, and his face shone like the sun, and his clothes became dazzling white. 3Suddenly there appeared to them Moses and Elijah, talking with him. 4Then Peter said to Jesus, "Lord, it is good for us to be here; if you wish, I*a* will make three dwellings*b* here, one for you, one for Moses, and one for Elijah." 5While he was still speaking, suddenly a bright cloud overshadowed them, and from the cloud a voice said, "This is my Son, the Beloved;*c* with him I am well pleased; listen to him!" 6When the disciples heard this, they fell to the ground and were overcome by fear. 7But Jesus came and touched them, saying, "Get up and do not be afraid." 8And when they looked up, they saw no one except Jesus himself alone.

9 As they were coming down the moun-

tain, Jesus ordered them, "Tell no one about the vision until after the Son of Man has been raised from the dead." 10And the disciples asked him, "Why, then, do the scribes say that Elijah must come first?" 11He replied, "Elijah is indeed coming and will restore all things; 12but I tell you that Elijah has already come, and they did not recognize him, but they did to him whatever they pleased. So also the Son of Man is about to suffer at their hands." 13Then the disciples understood that he was speaking to them about John the Baptist.

17.1–13. 1–8: The transfiguration (Mk 9.2–8; 9.28–36). The transfiguration (Gk., "metamorphoo-mai," to undergo metamorphosis) repeats baptismal★ themes. Matthew again connects Jesus to Moses and John to Elijah. Moses, Elijah, and Jesus, all initially rejected by their people, advocated Torah,★ performed miracles, experienced mountaintop theophanies,★ and survived death. **5:** The heavenly voice echoes the baptism.★ The scene also anticipates the resurrection; see 28.1–10. **9–13: Elijah's return.** See Mk 9.9–13 and comment on 9.9.

14 When they came to the crowd, a man came to him, knelt before him, 15and said, "Lord, have mercy on my son, for he is an epileptic and he suffers terribly; he often falls into the fire and often into the water. 16And I brought him to your disciples, but they could not cure him." 17Jesus answered, "You faithless and perverse generation, how much longer must I be with you? How much longer must I put up with you? Bring him here to me." 18And Jesus rebuked the demon,*d* and it*e* came out of him, and the boy was cured instantly. 19Then the disciples came to Jesus privately and said, "Why could we not cast it out?" 20He said to them, "Because of your little faith. For truly I tell you, if you have faith the size of a*f* mustard seed, you will say to this mountain, 'Move from here to there,' and it will move; and nothing will be impossible for you."*g*

a Other ancient authorities read *we*   b Or *tents*
c Or *my beloved Son*   d Gk *it* or *him*
e Gk *the demon*   f Gk *faith as a grain of*   g Other ancient authorities add verse 21, *But this kind does not come out except by prayer and fasting*

22 As they were gathering[a] in Galilee, Jesus said to them, "The Son of Man is going to be betrayed into human hands, 23and they will kill him, and on the third day he will be raised." And they were greatly distressed.

24 When they reached Capernaum, the collectors of the temple tax[b] came to Peter and said, "Does your teacher not pay the temple tax?"[b] 25He said, "Yes, he does." And when he came home, Jesus spoke of it first, asking, "What do you think, Simon? From whom do kings of the earth take toll or tribute? From their children or from others?" 26When Peter[c] said, "From others," Jesus said to him, "Then the children are free. 27However, so that we do not give offense to them, go to the sea and cast a hook; take the first fish that comes up; and when you open its mouth, you will find a coin;[d] take that and give it to them for you and me."

17.14–27. 14–21 (Mk 9.14–29; Lk 9.37–42): **The epileptic child. 15:** See 15.22; 20.30–31. The child is literally "moonstruck." Here and elsewhere, Jesus frequently heals children; "children" will become a metaphor* for members of the church. **20:** See 21.21–22. **22–23** (Mk 9.30–32; Lk 9.43–45): **The second passion prediction. 22:** "Betray" is better translated "hand over"; the passive voice suggests divine initiative. Although Judas remains culpable, Jesus' death is part of the divine plan for salvation. **24–27:** Paying the half-shekel* tax for Temple* upkeep, derived from Neh 10.32–39 (see Ex 30.11–16), was debated in Second Temple Judaism: Some believed it should be paid annually; others argued for a one-time donation. After 70 CE, Rome imposed the humiliating two-drachma tax (the "Fiscus Iudaicus") on Jews for the upkeep of a temple to Jupiter. **26:** Jesus advises payment for the sake of community peace.

---

18 At that time the disciples came to Jesus and asked, "Who is the greatest in the kingdom of heaven?" 2He called a child, whom he put among them, 3and said, "Truly I tell you, unless you change and become like children, you will never enter the kingdom of heaven. 4Whoever becomes humble like this child is the greatest in the kingdom of heaven. 5Whoever welcomes one such child in my name welcomes me.

6 "If any of you put a stumbling block before one of these little ones who believe in me, it would be better for you if a great millstone were fastened around your neck and you were drowned in the depth of the sea. 7Woe to the world because of stumbling blocks! Occasions for stumbling are bound to come, but woe to the one by whom the stumbling block comes!

8 "If your hand or your foot causes you to stumble, cut it off and throw it away; it is better for you to enter life maimed or lame than to have two hands or two feet and to be thrown into the eternal fire. 9And if your eye causes you to stumble, tear it out and throw it away; it is better for you to enter life with one eye than to have two eyes and to be thrown into the hell[e] of fire.

10 "Take care that you do not despise one of these little ones; for, I tell you, in heaven their angels continually see the face of my Father in heaven.[f] 12What do you think? If a shepherd has a hundred sheep, and one of them has gone astray, does he not leave the ninety-nine on the mountains and go in search of the one that went astray? 13And if he finds it, truly I tell you, he rejoices over it more than over the ninety-nine that never went astray. 14So it is not the will of your[g] Father in heaven that one of these little ones should be lost.

15 "If another member of the church[h] sins against you,[i] go and point out the fault when the two of you are alone. If the member listens to you, you have regained that one.[j] 16But if you are not listened to, take one or two others along with you, so that every word may be confirmed by the evidence of two or three witnesses. 17If the member refuses to listen to them, tell it to the church; and if the offender refuses to listen even to the church, let such a one be to you as a Gentile and a tax collector. 18Truly I tell you, whatever you bind on earth will be bound in heaven, and whatever

a Other ancient authorities read *living*
b Gk *didrachma*   c Gk *he*   d Gk *stater;* the stater was worth two didrachmas   e Gk *Gehenna*
f Other ancient authorities add verse 11, *For the Son of Man came to save the lost*   g Other ancient authorities read *my*   h Gk *If your brother*   i Other ancient authorities lack *against you*   j Gk *the brother*

you loose on earth will be loosed in heaven. ¹⁹Again, truly I tell you, if two of you agree on earth about anything you ask, it will be done for you by my Father in heaven. ²⁰For where two or three are gathered in my name, I am there among them."

21 Then Peter came and said to him, "Lord, if another member of the church^a sins against me, how often should I forgive? As many as seven times?" ²²Jesus said to him, "Not seven times, but, I tell you, seventy-seven^b times.

23 "For this reason the kingdom of heaven may be compared to a king who wished to settle accounts with his slaves. ²⁴When he began the reckoning, one who owed him ten thousand talents^c was brought to him; ²⁵and, as he could not pay, his lord ordered him to be sold, together with his wife and children and all his possessions, and payment to be made. ²⁶So the slave fell on his knees before him, saying, 'Have patience with me, and I will pay you everything.' ²⁷And out of pity for him, the lord of that slave released him and forgave him the debt. ²⁸But that same slave, as he went out, came upon one of his fellow slaves who owed him a hundred denarii;^d and seizing him by the throat, he said, 'Pay what you owe.' ²⁹Then his fellow slave fell down and pleaded with him, 'Have patience with me, and I will pay you.' ³⁰But he refused; then he went and threw him into prison until he would pay the debt. ³¹When his fellow slaves saw what had happened, they were greatly distressed, and they went and reported to their lord all that had taken place. ³²Then his lord summoned him and said to him, 'You wicked slave! I forgave you all that debt because you pleaded with me. ³³Should you not have had mercy on your fellow slave, as I had mercy on you?' ³⁴And in anger his lord handed him over to be tortured until he would pay his entire debt. ³⁵So my heavenly Father will also do to every one of you, if you do not forgive your brother or sister^e from your heart."

Jesus' followers; children are typically seen as without power, without economic resources, dependent, and without progeny. **6–9:** See 5.29–30; Mk 9.42–48; Lk 17.1–2). **11–14** (Lk 15.3–7): Verse 11 was likely inserted by scribes★ familiar with Lk 19.10. **12:** The *sheep* is not the most valuable (as in Gospel of Thomas★ 107) but requires rescue because it is lost. **17:** Gentiles★ and tax collectors are objects of missionary endeavors (see 9.11; 11.19); those excommunicated from the church immediately become those to be invited in. **18:** Extends Peter's commission (16.19) to the church. **21–22** (Lk 17.4): Forgiveness is not antithetical★ to church discipline. **23–35:** Slaves could own slaves and, in some cases, could purchase freedom. **24:** A talent of silver equals 6,000 drachmas; 10,000 (Gk., "myrias," hence "myriad") is extreme; the debt is unpayable. Matthew allegorically★ associates the king with God, although the king may be seen here as a human ruler who goes back on his original amnesty. The lesson is then on human forgiveness, not divine mercy. **25:** See Lev 25.39.

19

When Jesus had finished saying these things, he left Galilee and went to the region of Judea beyond the Jordan. ²Large crowds followed him, and he cured them there.

3 Some Pharisees came to him, and to test him they asked, "Is it lawful for a man to divorce his wife for any cause?" ⁴He answered, "Have you not read that the one who made them at the beginning 'made them male and female,' ⁵and said, 'For this reason a man shall leave his father and mother and be joined to his wife, and the two shall become one flesh'? ⁶So they are no longer two, but one flesh. Therefore what God has joined together, let no one separate." ⁷They said to him, "Why then did Moses command us to give a certificate of dismissal and to divorce her?" ⁸He said to them, "It was because you were so hard-hearted that Moses allowed you to divorce your wives, but from the beginning it was not so. ⁹And I say to you, whoever divorces his wife, except for

---

18.1–35: The fourth or ecclesial discourse. 1–5: See Mk 9.33–37; Lk 9.46–48. *Little ones* (vv. 6, 10, 14) are

a Gk if my brother   b Or seventy times seven
c A talent was worth more than fifteen years' wages of a laborer   d The denarius was the usual day's wage for a laborer   e Gk brother

unchastity, and marries another commits adultery."ᵃ

10 His disciples said to him, "If such is the case of a man with his wife, it is better not to marry." ¹¹But he said to them, "Not everyone can accept this teaching, but only those to whom it is given. ¹²For there are eunuchs who have been so from birth, and there are eunuchs who have been made eunuchs by others, and there are eunuchs who have made themselves eunuchs for the sake of the kingdom of heaven. Let anyone accept this who can."

19.1–12 (Mk 10.1–12): **Marriage and divorce. 1:** Jesus travels east of the Jordan to avoid Samaria (see 10.5). **3:** First-century Jewish debates on divorce usually concerned cause, not legitimacy. The Baptist, according to Mt 14.3–4, was executed for objecting to Herod Antipas's marriage to Herodias. Josephus adds that in order to marry Herodias, Herod divorced his Nabatean wife. In 5.32 and 19.4–6, Jesus' concern is scriptural (Gen 1.17; 2.24), not the state of divorced Jewish women. **7:** See Deut 24.1–4. **9:** On unchastity, see comment on 5.32. **11–12:** Endorses voluntary celibacy (see 1 Cor 7.1–9).

13 Then little children were being brought to him in order that he might lay his hands on them and pray. The disciples spoke sternly to those who brought them; ¹⁴but Jesus said, "Let the little children come to me, and do not stop them; for it is to such as these that the kingdom of heaven belongs." ¹⁵And he laid his hands on them and went on his way.

16 Then someone came to him and said, "Teacher, what good deed must I do to have eternal life?" ¹⁷And he said to him, "Why do you ask me about what is good? There is only one who is good. If you wish to enter into life, keep the commandments." ¹⁸He said to him, "Which ones?" And Jesus said, "You shall not murder; You shall not commit adultery; You shall not steal; You shall not bear false witness; ¹⁹Honor your father and mother; also, You shall love your neighbor as yourself." ²⁰The young man said to him, "I have kept all these;ᵇ what do I still lack?" ²¹Jesus said to him, "If you wish to be perfect, go, sell your possessions, and give the money

ᶜ to the poor, and you will have treasure in heaven; then come, follow me." ²²When the young man heard this word, he went away grieving, for he had many possessions.

23 Then Jesus said to his disciples, "Truly I tell you, it will be hard for a rich person to enter the kingdom of heaven. ²⁴Again I tell you, it is easier for a camel to go through the eye of a needle than for someone who is rich to enter the kingdom of God." ²⁵When the disciples heard this, they were greatly astounded and said, "Then who can be saved?" ²⁶But Jesus looked at them and said, "For mortals it is impossible, but for God all things are possible."

27 Then Peter said in reply, "Look, we have left everything and followed you. What then will we have?" ²⁸Jesus said to them, "Truly I tell you, at the renewal of all things, when the Son of Man is seated on the throne of his glory, you who have followed me will also sit on twelve thrones, judging the twelve tribes of Israel. ²⁹And everyone who has left houses or brothers or sisters or father or mother or children or fields, for my name's sake, will receive a hundredfold,ᵈ and will inherit eternal life. ³⁰But many who are first will be last, and the last will be first.

19.13–30. 13–15 (Mk 10.13–16; Lk 18.15–17): **Blessing children.** See comment on 18.1–10. **16–30** (Mk 10.17–31; Lk 18.18–30): **The rich young man.** Matthew describes Jesus' questioner as *young;* Mark has *rich;* Luke has *ruler.* **17:** Jesus rejects any personal honor. **18–19:** See Ex 20.12–16; Deut 5.16–20; Jesus consistently upholds Torah.* **21:** See comment on 5.48. **24:** The point is impossibility, not difficulty; see comment on Mk 10.25. **27:** See comment on Mark 10.28. **28:** Some Jewish groups expected the ingathering of the exiles during the messianic age. **30:** See 20.16; Mk 10.31; Lk 13.30). Again, Jesus replaces the value of name, position, wealth, and legacy with the kingdom of heaven.

ᵃ Other ancient authorities read *except on the ground of unchastity, causes her to commit adultery;* others add at the end of the verse *and he who marries a divorced woman commits adultery*   ᵇ Other ancient authorities add *from my youth*   ᶜ Gk lacks *the money*   ᵈ Other ancient authorities read *manifold*

20 "For the kingdom of heaven is like a landowner who went out early in the morning to hire laborers for his vineyard. [2]After agreeing with the laborers for the usual daily wage,*a* he sent them into his vineyard. [3]When he went out about nine o'clock, he saw others standing idle in the marketplace; [4]and he said to them, 'You also go into the vineyard, and I will pay you whatever is right.' So they went. [5]When he went out again about noon and about three o'clock, he did the same. [6]And about five o'clock he went out and found others standing around; and he said to them, 'Why are you standing here idle all day?' [7]They said to him, 'Because no one has hired us.' He said to them, 'You also go into the vineyard.' [8]When evening came, the owner of the vineyard said to his manager, 'Call the laborers and give them their pay, beginning with the last and then going to the first.' [9]When those hired about five o'clock came, each of them received the usual daily wage.*a* [10]Now when the first came, they thought they would receive more; but each of them also received the usual daily wage.*a* [11]And when they received it, they grumbled against the landowner, [12]saying, 'These last worked only one hour, and you have made them equal to us who have borne the burden of the day and the scorching heat.' [13]But he replied to one of them, 'Friend, I am doing you no wrong; did you not agree with me for the usual daily wage?*a* [14]Take what belongs to you and go; I choose to give to this last the same as I give to you. [15]Am I not allowed to do what I choose with what belongs to me? Or are you envious because I am generous?'*b* [16]So the last will be first, and the first will be last."*c*

20.1–16: Unexpected payment. Jesus' parables,* as well as divine grace, continue to challenge conventional views.

17 While Jesus was going up to Jerusalem, he took the twelve disciples aside by themselves, and said to them on the way, [18]"See, we are going up to Jerusalem, and the Son of Man will be handed over to the chief priests and scribes, and they will condemn him to death; [19]then they will hand him over to the Gentiles to be mocked and flogged and crucified; and on the third day he will be raised."

20 Then the mother of the sons of Zebedee came to him with her sons, and kneeling before him, she asked a favor of him. [21]And he said to her, "What do you want?" She said to him, "Declare that these two sons of mine will sit, one at your right hand and one at your left, in your kingdom." [22]But Jesus answered, "You do not know what you are asking. Are you able to drink the cup that I am about to drink?"*d* They said to him, "We are able." [23]He said to them, "You will indeed drink my cup, but to sit at my right hand and at my left, this is not mine to grant, but it is for those for whom it has been prepared by my Father."

24 When the ten heard it, they were angry with the two brothers. [25]But Jesus called them to him and said, "You know that the rulers of the Gentiles lord it over them, and their great ones are tyrants over them. [26]It will not be so among you; but whoever wishes to be great among you must be your servant, [27]and whoever wishes to be first among you must be your slave; [28]just as the Son of Man came not to be served but to serve, and to give his life a ransom for many."

29 As they were leaving Jericho, a large crowd followed him. [30]There were two blind men sitting by the roadside. When they heard that Jesus was passing by, they shouted, "Lord,*e* have mercy on us, Son of David!" [31]The crowd sternly ordered them to be quiet; but they shouted even more loudly, "Have mercy on us, Lord, Son of David!" [32]Jesus stood still and called them, saying, "What do you want me to do for you?" [33]They said to him, "Lord, let our eyes be opened." [34]Moved with compassion, Jesus touched their eyes. Immediately they regained their sight and followed him.

20.17–34. 17–19 (Mk 10.32–34; Lk 18.31–34): **The third passion prediction.** This passage specifies cru-

a Gk *a denarius*　*b* Gk *is your eye evil because I am good?*　*c* Other ancient authorities add *for many are called but few are chosen*　*d* Other ancient authorities add *or to be baptized with the baptism that I am baptized with?*　*e* Other ancient authorities lack *Lord* cifixion (see 10.38; 16.24). **20–28** (Mk 10.35–45; Lk 22.24–27): **Evils of competition**. Mark assigns the question of personal exaltation directly to James and John. The "mother of the sons of Zebedee," named only by Matthew, witnesses the crucifixion (27.56). **22:** The *cup* symbolizes suffering, rejection, and violent death, including that ordained by God (see Martyrdom of Isaiah★ 5.13). Jesus thus predicts that the brothers will suffer violent death. **28:** *Ransom* can mean "rescue" or "deliver"; Matthew asserts, but does not explain, the saving function of Jesus' death. *Many* means "all" (in contrast to "a few"); see comment on Mk 10.45. **29–34** (Mk 10.46–52; Lk 18.35–43): **The blind men of Jericho**. A doublet of 9.27–31. **30:** Matthew doubles Mark's individual Bartimaeus. On *Son of David,* see comment on Mk 10.47. The title has particular import as Jesus prepares to enter David's city, Jerusalem.

21.1–11 (Mk 1.1–11; Lk 19.28–38; Jn 12.12–18): **Preparations for Jerusalem**. In Matthew (and Mark), this is Jesus' first entry into Jerusalem: Luke and John depict earlier visits. Although this event is traditionally called "Palm Sunday," palms are mentioned only in John; in Matthean chronology, the entry occurs on Monday. **2–3:** See comment on Mk 11.2. **4–5:** The ninth fulfillment citation, from Isa 62.11; Zech 9.9. **7:** Matthew takes literally Zechariah's poetic reference to two donkeys. **9:** *Hosanna,*★ originally a plea for salvation, became a festive shout. The citation comes from Ps 118.25–26, the last Hallel Psalm sung at Passover.★ *One who comes* has messianic connotations.

21 When they had come near Jerusalem and had reached Bethphage, at the Mount of Olives, Jesus sent two disciples, 2saying to them, "Go into the village ahead of you, and immediately you will find a donkey tied, and a colt with her; untie them and bring them to me. 3If anyone says anything to you, just say this, 'The Lord needs them.' And he will send them immediately.*a*" 4This took place to fulfill what had been spoken through the prophet, saying,

5 "Tell the daughter of Zion,
　Look, your king is coming to you,
　　humble, and mounted on a donkey,
　　　and on a colt, the foal of a donkey."

6The disciples went and did as Jesus had directed them; 7they brought the donkey and the colt, and put their cloaks on them, and he sat on them. 8A very large crowd*b* spread their cloaks on the road, and others cut branches from the trees and spread them on the road. 9The crowds that went ahead of him and that followed were shouting,

"Hosanna to the Son of David!
　Blessed is the one who comes in the
　　name of the Lord!
　Hosanna in the highest heaven!"

10When he entered Jerusalem, the whole city was in turmoil, asking, "Who is this?" 11The crowds were saying, "This is the prophet Jesus from Nazareth in Galilee."

12 Then Jesus entered the temple*c* and drove out all who were selling and buying in the temple, and he overturned the tables of the money changers and the seats of those who sold doves. 13He said to them, "It is written,

'My house shall be called a house
　of prayer';
but you are making it a den
　of robbers."

14 The blind and the lame came to him in the temple, and he cured them. 15But when the chief priests and the scribes saw the amazing things that he did, and heard*d* the children crying out in the temple, "Hosanna to the Son of David," they became angry 16and said to him, "Do you hear what these are saying?" Jesus said to them, "Yes; have you never read,

'Out of the mouths of infants and
　nursing babies
　you have prepared praise for
　　yourself'?"

17He left them, went out of the city to Bethany, and spent the night there.

18 In the morning, when he returned to the city, he was hungry. 19And seeing a fig tree by the side of the road, he went to it and found nothing at all on it but leaves. Then he said to it, "May no fruit ever come from you again!" And the fig tree withered at once. 20When the disciples saw it, they were amazed, saying, "How did the fig tree wither

a Or 'The Lord needs them and will send them back immediately.'　*b* Or Most of the crowd　*c* Other ancient authorities add of God　*d* Gk lacks heard at once?" 21 Jesus answered them, "Truly I tell you, if you have faith and do not doubt, not only will you do what has been done to the fig tree, but even if you say to this mountain, 'Be lifted up and thrown into the sea,' it will be done. 22 Whatever you ask for in prayer with faith, you will receive."

21.12–22. 12–17 (Mk 11.11, 15–19; Lk 19.45–48; Jn 2.13–25): **The Temple* protest. 12–13:** The activity occurs in the Court of the Gentiles.* Selling animals and exchanging coins (many with pagan symbols) for Tyrian shekels* were necessary in order for pilgrims to participate in Temple worship. Matthew does not condemn Temple worship per se (5.23; 12.5–6; 17.24; 23.16–20), but Jesus becomes the new site of divine presence. **13:** *Den of robbers* indicates not dishonesty in the Temple system (see Jer 7.1–11) but a haven for those who sin elsewhere. **14:** Jesus casts out insiders and welcomes the sick. **15:** The leaders are more concerned with the children's acclamation than with Jesus' actions. **16:** Ps 8.2. **18–22** (Mk 11.12–14; 20.25): **The fig tree.** Matthew condenses Mark's two-stage account into an instantaneous miracle. The tree may symbolize Jerusalem and the Temple. **19:** *Fruit* connotes proper action. **21–22:** See 17.20.

---

23 When he entered the temple, the chief priests and the elders of the people came to him as he was teaching, and said, "By what authority are you doing these things, and who gave you this authority?" 24 Jesus said to them, "I will also ask you one question; if you tell me the answer, then I will also tell you by what authority I do these things. 25 Did the baptism of John come from heaven, or was it of human origin?" And they argued with one another, "If we say, 'From heaven,' he will say to us, 'Why then did you not believe him?' 26 But if we say, 'Of human origin,' we are afraid of the crowd; for all regard John as a prophet." 27 So they answered Jesus, "We do not know." And he said to them, "Neither will I tell you by what authority I am doing these things.

28 "What do you think? A man had two sons; he went to the first and said, 'Son, go and work in the vineyard today.' 29 He answered, 'I will not'; but later he changed his mind and went. 30 The father*ᵃ* said to the second and said the same; and he answered,

'I go, sir'; but he did not go. 31 Which of the two did the will of his father?" They said, "The first." Jesus said to them, "Truly I tell you, the tax collectors and the prostitutes are going into the kingdom of God ahead of you. 32 For John came to you in the way of righteousness and you did not believe him, but the tax collectors and the prostitutes believed him; and even after you saw it, you did not change your minds and believe him.

21.23–32 (Mk 11.27–33; Lk 20.1–8; Jn 2.18–22): **Temple* teaching.** While Jesus teaches in the Temple, the chief priests and elders will later plot his death (26.3). **23–24:** Jesus' opponents seek to trap him with a question, and Jesus responds in kind. *Authority* is a Matthean theme (7.29; 8.9; 9.8; 10.1; 28.17). **28–32:** The parable* of the two sons is unique to Matthew. Consistent with the Gospel's themes, the parable emphasizes the importance of deeds (see 7.21–23) and denigrates empty promises. The Sadducees* and Pharisees* heard John the Baptist (3.5–7) but rejected his teaching. **32:** Tax collectors and prostitutes place themselves deliberately outside the communal standards of righteousness.

---

33 "Listen to another parable. There was a landowner who planted a vineyard, put a fence around it, dug a wine press in it, and built a watchtower. Then he leased it to tenants and went to another country. 34 When the harvest time had come, he sent his slaves to the tenants to collect his produce. 35 But the tenants seized his slaves and beat one, killed another, and stoned another. 36 Again he sent other slaves, more than the first; and they treated them in the same way. 37 Finally he sent his son to them, saying, 'They will respect my son.' 38 But when the tenants saw the son, they said to themselves, 'This is the heir; come, let us kill him and get his inheritance.' 39 So they seized him, threw him out of the vineyard, and killed him. 40 Now when the owner of the vineyard comes, what will he do to those tenants?" 41 They said to him, "He will put those wretches to a miserable death, and lease the vineyard to other tenants who will give him the produce at the harvest time."

a Gk *He*

42 Jesus said to them, "Have you never read in the scriptures:

'The stone that the builders rejected
    has become the cornerstone;ᵃ
  this was the Lord's doing,
    and it is amazing in our eyes'?

⁴³Therefore I tell you, the kingdom of God will be taken away from you and given to a people that produces the fruits of the kingdom.ᵇ ⁴⁴The one who falls on this stone will be broken to pieces; and it will crush anyone on whom it falls."ᶜ

45 When the chief priests and the Pharisees heard his parables, they realized that he was speaking about them. ⁴⁶They wanted to arrest him, but they feared the crowds, because they regarded him as a prophet.

21.33–46 (Mk 12.1–12; Lk 20.9–19): **The parable* of the vineyard.** The vineyard symbolizes Israel (Isa 5.1–7). **34:** *Produce* is "fruits," Matthew's term for good works. *Slaves* likely represent the prophets.* **39:** The son's death corresponds to that of Jesus (27.32); the parable makes sense with this allegorical* meaning, while on a literal level, the father's action in sending the son is foolishness at best. **40–41:** The *tenants* are, allegorically, the chief priests and elders; the *other tenants* are the Jews and gentiles* of Matthew's church. **42:** See Ps 118.22–23 (Septuagint*).

22 Once more Jesus spoke to them in parables, saying: ²"The kingdom of heaven may be compared to a king who gave a wedding banquet for his son. ³He sent his slaves to call those who had been invited to the wedding banquet, but they would not come. ⁴Again he sent other slaves, saying, 'Tell those who have been invited: Look, I have prepared my dinner, my oxen and my fat calves have been slaughtered, and everything is ready; come to the wedding banquet.' ⁵But they made light of it and went away, one to his farm, another to his business, ⁶while the rest seized his slaves, mistreated them, and killed them. ⁷The king was enraged. He sent his troops, destroyed those murderers, and burned their city. ⁸Then he said to his slaves, 'The wedding is ready, but those invited were not worthy. ⁹Go therefore into the main streets, and invite everyone you find to the wedding banquet.' ¹⁰Those slaves went out into the streets and gathered all whom they found, both good and bad; so the wedding hall was filled with guests.

11 "But when the king came in to see the guests, he noticed a man there who was not wearing a wedding robe, ¹²and he said to him, 'Friend, how did you get in here without a wedding robe?' And he was speechless. ¹³Then the king said to the attendants, 'Bind him hand and foot, and throw him into the outer darkness, where there will be weeping and gnashing of teeth.' ¹⁴For many are called, but few are chosen."

22.1–14 (see Lk 14.15–24; see Gospel of Thomas* 64): **The parable of the marriage feast.** Refusing a royal invitation constitutes rebellion (2 Sam 10.4). **11–13:** New clothing represents a new identity (see Rom 13.12–14; Rev 3.4). **14:** *Chosen* (Gk., "elektos") means accepted at final judgment.

15 Then the Pharisees went and plotted to entrap him in what he said. ¹⁶So they sent their disciples to him, along with the Herodians, saying, "Teacher, we know that you are sincere, and teach the way of God in accordance with truth, and show deference to no one; for you do not regard people with partiality. ¹⁷Tell us, then, what you think. Is it lawful to pay taxes to the emperor, or not?" ¹⁸But Jesus, aware of their malice, said, "Why are you putting me to the test, you hypocrites? ¹⁹Show me the coin used for the tax." And they brought him a denarius. ²⁰Then he said to them, "Whose head is this, and whose title?" ²¹They answered, "The emperor's." Then he said to them, "Give therefore to the emperor the things that are the emperor's, and to God the things that are God's." ²²When they heard this, they were amazed; and they left him and went away.

23 The same day some Sadducees came to him, saying there is no resurrection;ᵈ and they asked him a question, saying, ²⁴"Teacher, Moses said, 'If a man dies childless, his brother shall marry the widow, and raise up children for his brother.' ²⁵Now

---

a Or *keystone*   *b* Gk *the fruits of it*   *c* Other ancient authorities lack verse 44   *d* Other ancient authorities read *who say that there is no resurrection* there were seven brothers among us; the first married, and died childless, leaving the widow to his brother. 26The second did the same, so also the third, down to the seventh. 27Last of all, the woman herself died. 28In the resurrection, then, whose wife of the seven will she be? For all of them had married her."

29 Jesus answered them, "You are wrong, because you know neither the scriptures nor the power of God. 30For in the resurrection they neither marry nor are given in marriage, but are like angels*a* in heaven. 31And as for the resurrection of the dead, have you not read what was said to you by God, 32'I am the God of Abraham, the God of Isaac, and the God of Jacob'? He is God not of the dead, but of the living." 33And when the crowd heard it, they were astounded at his teaching.

22.15–33 (Mk 12.13–17; Lk 20.20–26): **Paying taxes. 16:** *Herodians* are supporters of Rome (see Mk 3.6). The Roman head-tax was instituted in 6 CE to indicate Judea's status as a Roman province. Roman coinage usually contained Caesar's portrait and an inscription proclaiming his divinity; Jesus apparently does not carry money (see 6.24). Jesus' enigmatic answer satisfies both pro- and anti-Roman factions: For pro-Roman factions, the line appears to support payment of taxes; for those who believe everything belongs to God, the line supports their protest against Roman presence. **23–33** (Mk 12.18–27; Lk 20.27–40): **Angelic bodies.** On levirate marriage* (Latin, "levir," brother-in-law) see Deut 25.5–6, Gen 38, Ruth 3 (Tamar and Ruth also appear in Matthew's genealogy*). The rationale of the practice is to continue the family name. **32:** See Ex 3.6. Jesus envisages the resurrected body to be without sexual desire or the desire for procreation (see also 1 Cor 15).

---

34 When the Pharisees heard that he had silenced the Sadducees, they gathered together, 35and one of them, a lawyer, asked him a question to test him. 36"Teacher, which commandment in the law is the greatest?" 37He said to him, " 'You shall love the Lord your God with all your heart, and with all your soul, and with all your mind.' 38This is the greatest and first commandment. 39And a second is like it: 'You shall love your neighbor as yourself.' 40On these two commandments hang all the law and the prophets."

41 Now while the Pharisees were gathered together, Jesus asked them this question: 42"What do you think of the Messiah?*b* Whose son is he?" They said to him, "The son of David." 43He said to them, "How is it then that David by the Spirit*c* calls him Lord, saying,

44 'The Lord said to my Lord,
  "Sit at my right hand,
    until I put your enemies under your
      feet" '?

45If David thus calls him Lord, how can he be his son?" 46No one was able to give him an answer, nor from that day did anyone dare to ask him any more questions.

22.34–46. 34–40 (Mk 28.34; Lk 10.25–28): **The great commandment.** Rabbinic authorities in antiquity also discussed which commandments summarized the others (see comment on 7.12). **37:** The first commandment (Deut 6.4–9), Deut 11.18–20, and Ex 13.9 are contained in the "tefillin" (phylacteries) worn by Jewish men (and, today, some women). *Love* is a verbal form of the Greek noun "agape." **41–46:** Son of David. See comment on Mk 12.35–37 (Lk 20.41–44).

23 Then Jesus said to the crowds and to his disciples, 2"The scribes and the Pharisees sit on Moses' seat; 3therefore, do whatever they teach you and follow it; but do not do as they do, for they do not practice what they teach. 4They tie up heavy burdens, hard to bear,*d* and lay them on the shoulders of others; but they themselves are unwilling to lift a finger to move them. 5They do all their deeds to be seen by others; for they make their phylacteries broad and their fringes long. 6They love to have the place of honor at banquets and the best seats in the synagogues, 7and to be greeted with respect in the marketplaces, and to have people call them rabbi. 8But you are not to be called rabbi, for you have one teacher, and you are all students.*e* 9And call no one your father

a Other ancient authorities add *of God*   *b* Or *Christ*   *c* Gk *in spirit*   *d* Other ancient authorities lack *hard to bear*   *e* Gk *brothers* on earth, for you have one Father—the one in heaven. 10Nor are you to be called instructors, for you have one instructor, the Messiah.*a* 11The greatest among you will be your servant. 12All who exalt themselves will be humbled, and all who humble themselves will be exalted.

13 "But woe to you, scribes and Pharisees, hypocrites! For you lock people out of the kingdom of heaven. For you do not go in yourselves, and when others are going in, you stop them.*b* 15Woe to you, scribes and Pharisees, hypocrites! For you cross sea and land to make a single convert, and you make the new convert twice as much a child of hell*c* as yourselves.

16 "Woe to you, blind guides, who say, 'Whoever swears by the sanctuary is bound by nothing, but whoever swears by the gold of the sanctuary is bound by the oath.' 17You blind fools! For which is greater, the gold or the sanctuary that has made the gold sacred? 18And you say, 'Whoever swears by the altar is bound by nothing, but whoever swears by the gift that is on the altar is bound by the oath.' 19How blind you are! For which is greater, the gift or the altar that makes the gift sacred? 20So whoever swears by the altar, swears by it and by everything on it; 21and whoever swears by the sanctuary, swears by it and by the one who dwells in it; 22and whoever swears by heaven, swears by the throne of God and by the one who is seated upon it.

23 "Woe to you, scribes and Pharisees, hypocrites! For you tithe mint, dill, and cummin, and have neglected the weightier matters of the law: justice and mercy and faith. It is these you ought to have practiced without neglecting the others. 24You blind guides! You strain out a gnat but swallow a camel!

25 "Woe to you, scribes and Pharisees, hypocrites! For you clean the outside of the cup and of the plate, but inside they are full of greed and self-indulgence. 26You blind Pharisee! First clean the inside of the cup,*d* so that the outside also may become clean.

27 "Woe to you, scribes and Pharisees, hypocrites! For you are like whitewashed tombs, which on the outside look beautiful, but inside they are full of the bones of the dead and of all kinds of filth. 28So you also on the outside look righteous to others, but inside you are full of hypocrisy and lawlessness.

29 "Woe to you, scribes and Pharisees, hypocrites! For you build the tombs of the prophets and decorate the graves of the righteous, 30and you say, 'If we had lived in the days of our ancestors, we would not have taken part with them in shedding the blood of the prophets.' 31Thus you testify against yourselves that you are descendants of those who murdered the prophets. 32Fill up, then, the measure of your ancestors. 33You snakes, you brood of vipers! How can you escape being sentenced to hell?*c* 34Therefore I send you prophets, sages, and scribes, some of whom you will kill and crucify, and some you will flog in your synagogues and pursue from town to town, 35so that upon you may come all the righteous blood shed on earth, from the blood of righteous Abel to the blood of Zechariah son of Barachiah, whom you murdered between the sanctuary and the altar. 36Truly I tell you, all this will come upon this generation.

23.1–36: Woes against Pharisees* and scribes.* Matthew defines the church and its members in contrast to synagogues* and its leaders. **2:** *Moses' seat* represents synagogue teaching and administrative authority. **5:** On *phylacteries*, see comment on 22.37; *fringes,* see comment on 9.20. **13–36:** The seven "woe oracles*" all concern self-definition and self-regulation; Jesus' pronouncements against the Pharisees also function as Matthew's warnings to church members. **15:** Refers either to a gentile* mission or to Pharisaic attempts to convince other Jews of their teachings. **16–22:** Suggests 5.33–37. **23–24** (Lk 11.42): *Camel* and *gnat* sound similar in Aramaic.* **25–26:** See Lk 11.39–41. **27–28** (Lk 11.44): Tombs were *whitewashed* to prevent accidental contact and so impurity (Num 19.11–22); contact with a corpse prevented immediate entry into the Temple.* **29–32** (Lk 11.47–

a Or *the Christ*   *b* Other authorities add here (or after verse 12) verse 14, *Woe to you, scribes and Pharisees, hypocrites! For you devour widows' houses and for the sake of appearance you make long prayers; therefore you will receive the greater condemnation*   *c* Gk *Gehenna*
d Other ancient authorities add *and of the plate*

48): Only one such murder (2 Chr 24.20–22) appears in Scripture; pseudepigraphical* texts from the Hellenistic* period recount others, as Jews began to develop the martyrdom* as a literary form. **34–36** (Lk 11.49–51): On Zechariah, see 2 Chr 24.20–22; with Abel (Gen 4.8), he frames Hebrew (biblical) history. Matthew connects this Zechariah with the prophet* (Zech 1.1).

37 "Jerusalem, Jerusalem, the city that kills the prophets and stones those who are sent to it! How often have I desired to gather your children together as a hen gathers her brood under her wings, and you were not willing! 38See, your house is left to you, desolate.*a 39For I tell you, you will not see me again until you say, 'Blessed is the one who comes in the name of the Lord.'"

23.37–39 (Lk 13.34–35): **The lament* over Jerusalem.** This passage reflects the destruction of the Temple* in 70 CE **38:** The *house* is the Temple. **39:** Cites Ps 118.26, perhaps here a reference to Jesus' return in the final judgment, which is the theme of the next two chapters.

24 As Jesus came out of the temple and was going away, his disciples came to point out to him the buildings of the temple. 2Then he asked them, "You see all these, do you not? Truly I tell you, not one stone will be left here upon another; all will be thrown down."

3 When he was sitting on the Mount of Olives, the disciples came to him privately, saying, "Tell us, when will this be, and what will be the sign of your coming and of the end of the age?" 4Jesus answered them, "Beware that no one leads you astray. 5For many will come in my name, saying, 'I am the Messiah!'b and they will lead many astray. 6And you will hear of wars and rumors of wars; see that you are not alarmed; for this must take place, but the end is not yet. 7For nation will rise against nation, and kingdom against kingdom, and there will be faminesc and earthquakes in various places: 8all this is but the beginning of the birth pangs.

24.1–25.46: The fifth or eschatological* discourse. 24.1–3 (Mk 13.1–2; Lk 21.5–7): Jesus leaves the

Temple* for the last time; only his disciples accompany him. **2:** The Kotel or Western (Wailing) wall of Herod's Temple remains one of Judaism's sacred sites. **3:** The Mount of Olives suggests the "eschaton" (see Zech 14.4). Matthew associates the destruction of Jerusalem in 70 CE during the first Jewish revolt against Rome with conventional motifs* concerning the end of the age.

9 "Then they will hand you over to be tortured and will put you to death, and you will be hated by all nations because of my name. 10Then many will fall away,d and they will betray one another and hate one another. 11And many false prophets will arise and lead many astray. 12And because of the increase of lawlessness, the love of many will grow cold. 13But the one who endures to the end will be saved. 14And this good newse of the kingdom will be proclaimed throughout the world, as a testimony to all the nations; and then the end will come.

15 "So when you see the desolating sacrilege standing in the holy place, as was spoken of by the prophet Daniel (let the reader understand), 16then those in Judea must flee to the mountains; 17the one on the housetop must not go down to take what is in the house; 18the one in the field must not turn back to get a coat. 19Woe to those who are pregnant and to those who are nursing infants in those days! 20Pray that your flight may not be in winter or on a sabbath. 21For at that time there will be great suffering, such as has not been from the beginning of the world until now, no, and never will be. 22And if those days had not been cut short, no one would be saved; but for the sake of the elect those days will be cut short. 23Then if anyone says to you, 'Look! Here is the Messiah!'b or 'There he is!'—do not believe it. 24For false messiahsf and false prophets will appear and produce great signs and omens, to lead astray, if possible, even the elect. 25Take note, I have told you beforehand. 26So, if they say to you, 'Look! He is in the wilderness,' do not go out. If they say, 'Look!

a Other ancient authorities lack *desolate* b Or the *Christ* c Other ancient authorities add *and pestilences* d Or *stumble* e Or *gospel* f Or *christs*

He is in the inner rooms,' do not believe it. 27For as the lightning comes from the east and flashes as far as the west, so will be the coming of the Son of Man. 28Wherever the corpse is, there the vultures will gather.

29 "Immediately after the suffering of those days

the sun will be darkened,
　and the moon will not give its light;
the stars will fall from heaven,
　and the powers of heaven will
　　be shaken.

30Then the sign of the Son of Man will appear in heaven, and then all the tribes of the earth will mourn, and they will see 'the Son of Man coming on the clouds of heaven' with power and great glory. 31And he will send out his angels with a loud trumpet call, and they will gather his elect from the four winds, from one end of heaven to the other.

32 "From the fig tree learn its lesson: as soon as its branch becomes tender and puts forth its leaves, you know that summer is near. 33So also, when you see all these things, you know that he*a* is near, at the very gates. 34Truly I tell you, this generation will not pass away until all these things have taken place. 35Heaven and earth will pass away, but my words will not pass away.

36 "But about that day and hour no one knows, neither the angels of heaven, nor the Son,*b* but only the Father. 37For as the days of Noah were, so will be the coming of the Son of Man. 38For as in those days before the flood they were eating and drinking, marrying and giving in marriage, until the day Noah entered the ark, 39and they knew nothing until the flood came and swept them all away, so too will be the coming of the Son of Man. 40Then two will be in the field; one will be taken and one will be left. 41Two women will be grinding meal together; one will be taken and one will be left. 42Keep awake therefore, for you do not know on what day*c* your Lord is coming. 43But understand this: if the owner of the house had known in what part of the night the thief was coming, he would have stayed awake and would not have let his house be broken into. 44Therefore you also must be ready, for the Son of Man is coming at an unexpected hour.

45 "Who then is the faithful and wise slave, whom his master has put in charge of his household, to give the other slaves*d* their allowance of food at the proper time? 46Blessed is that slave whom his master will find at work when he arrives. 47Truly I tell you, he will put that one in charge of all his possessions. 48But if that wicked slave says to himself, 'My master is delayed,' 49and he begins to beat his fellow slaves, and eats and drinks with drunkards, 50the master of that slave will come on a day when he does not expect him and at an hour that he does not know. 51He will cut him in pieces*e* and put him with the hypocrites, where there will be weeping and gnashing of teeth.

24.4–51 (Mk 13.3–37; Lk 21.8–36): Combines apocalyptic* sayings with seven admonitions encouraging vigilance until Jesus' return. 4–8: Wars, famines, earthquakes, and persecution are typical apocalyptic motifs* (see Dan 2.28–29). 9: Persecution is the result of Christian confession. 13–14: Persecution does not preclude mission. For 24.14 see 28.19; Matthew here explains the delay of the final judgment. 15: *Desolating sacrilege,* see comment on Mark 13.14. 20: *On a sabbath* may indicate dispensation to transgress Torah* observance, or that the flight would distinguish church members from their Torah-observant neighbors. 29–31: Cites Isa 13.10; 34.4; Ezek 32.7; Joel 2.10–11; Zeph 1.15. 34–36: Matthew expects the end time within the present generation but resists providing an end-time calendar. To a great extent, the Jewish war fulfilled many of these predictions. 37–39 (Lk 17.26–27); 40–41 (Lk 17.34–35): Life continues with traditional gender roles, before judgment occurs. 43–51: See Lk 12.39–46. 43–44: Presents a scandalous image: Jesus is pictured as breaking and entering (1 Thess 5.2; Rev 3.3). 51: Matthew's expression for damnation.

25 "Then the kingdom of heaven will be like this. Ten bridesmaids*f* took their lamps and went to meet the bridegroom.*g* 2Five of them were foolish, and five were wise. 3When the foolish took their lamps, they took no oil with them; 4but the

---

a Or it　　*b* Other ancient authorities lack *nor the Son*
c Other ancient authorities read *at what hour*
d Gk *to give them*　　*e* Or *cut him off*　　*f* Gk *virgins*
g Other ancient authorities add *and the bride*

wise took flasks of oil with their lamps. ⁵As the bridegroom was delayed, all of them became drowsy and slept. ⁶But at midnight there was a shout, 'Look! Here is the bridegroom! Come out to meet him.' ⁷Then all those bridesmaids*ᵃ* got up and trimmed their lamps. ⁸The foolish said to the wise, 'Give us some of your oil, for our lamps are going out.' ⁹But the wise replied, 'No! there will not be enough for you and for us; you had better go to the dealers and buy some for yourselves.' ¹⁰And while they went to buy it, the bridegroom came, and those who were ready went with him into the wedding banquet; and the door was shut. ¹¹Later the other bridesmaids*ᵃ* came also, saying, 'Lord, lord, open to us.' ¹²But he replied, 'Truly I tell you, I do not know you.' ¹³Keep awake therefore, for you know neither the day nor the hour.*ᵇ*

25.1–13: The parable* of the ten bridesmaids. This story about *bridesmaids* (Gk., "parthenoi," virgins) is unique to Matthew. The wedding time recollects the midnight thief (24.43). The *bridegroom* is Jesus (9.15; 22.1–3); there is no bride. Perhaps best interpreted allegorically,* the *oil* represents the wise bridesmaids' righteous action; this cannot be shared.

14 "For it is as if a man, going on a journey, summoned his slaves and entrusted his property to them; ¹⁵to one he gave five talents,*ᶜ* to another two, to another one, to each according to his ability. Then he went away. ¹⁶The one who had received the five talents went off at once and traded with them, and made five more talents. ¹⁷In the same way, the one who had the two talents made two more talents. ¹⁸But the one who had received the one talent went off and dug a hole in the ground and hid his master's money. ¹⁹After a long time the master of those slaves came and settled accounts with them. ²⁰Then the one who had received the five talents came forward, bringing five more talents, saying, 'Master, you handed over to me five talents; see, I have made five more talents.' ²¹His master said to him, 'Well done, good and trustworthy slave; you have been trustworthy in a few things, I will put you in charge of many things; enter into the

joy of your master.' ²²And the one with the two talents also came forward, saying, 'Master, you handed over to me two talents; see, I have made two more talents.' ²³His master said to him, 'Well done, good and trustworthy slave; you have been trustworthy in a few things, I will put you in charge of many things; enter into the joy of your master.' ²⁴Then the one who had received the one talent also came forward, saying, 'Master, I knew that you were a harsh man, reaping where you did not sow, and gathering where you did not scatter seed; ²⁵so I was afraid, and I went and hid your talent in the ground. Here you have what is yours.' ²⁶But his master replied, 'You wicked and lazy slave! You knew, did you, that I reap where I did not sow, and gather where I did not scatter? ²⁷Then you ought to have invested my money with the bankers, and on my return I would have received what was my own with interest. ²⁸So take the talent from him, and give it to the one with the ten talents. ²⁹For to all those who have, more will be given, and they will have an abundance; but from those who have nothing, even what they have will be taken away. ³⁰As for this worthless slave, throw him into the outer darkness, where there will be weeping and gnashing of teeth.'

25.14–30 (Lk 19.12–27): **The parable* of the talents.** For *talent,* see comment on 18.24. **17:** Church living requires action and risk, not passivity. **26:** The master's response shocks; like the parables in ch. 13, this account subverts conventional expectations of behavior and response.

31 "When the Son of Man comes in his glory, and all the angels with him, then he will sit on the throne of his glory. ³²All the nations will be gathered before him, and he will separate people one from another as a shepherd separates the sheep from the goats, ³³and he will put the sheep at his right hand and the goats at the left. ³⁴Then the king will say to those at his right hand, 'Come, you that are blessed by my Father, inherit the

a Gk *virgins*   *b* Other ancient authorities add *in which the Son of Man is coming*   *c* A talent was worth more than fifteen years' wages of a laborer kingdom prepared for you from the foundation of the world; ³⁵for I was hungry and you gave me food, I was thirsty and you gave me something to drink, I was a stranger and you welcomed me, ³⁶I was naked and you gave me clothing, I was sick and you took care of me, I was in prison and you visited me.' ³⁷Then the righteous will answer him, 'Lord, when was it that we saw you hungry and gave you food, or thirsty and gave you something to drink? ³⁸And when was it that we saw you a stranger and welcomed you, or naked and gave you clothing? ³⁹And when was it that we saw you sick or in prison and visited you?' ⁴⁰And the king will answer them, 'Truly I tell you, just as you did it to one of the least of these who are members of my family,^a you did it to me.' ⁴¹Then he will say to those at his left hand, 'You that are accursed, depart from me into the eternal fire prepared for the devil and his angels; ⁴²for I was hungry and you gave me no food, I was thirsty and you gave me nothing to drink, ⁴³I was a stranger and you did not welcome me, naked and you did not give me clothing, sick and in prison and you did not visit me.' ⁴⁴Then they also will answer, 'Lord, when was it that we saw you hungry or thirsty or a stranger or naked or sick or in prison, and did not take care of you?' ⁴⁵Then he will answer them, 'Truly I tell you, just as you did not do it to one of the least of these, you did not do it to me.' ⁴⁶And these will go away into eternal punishment, but the righteous into eternal life."

25.31–46: The judgment. The depiction of the return of Jesus combines the Gospel's various messianic* titles: Son of Man, king, lord, shepherd, "one who comes." 32: Nations is often interpreted to mean just gentiles,* but there are no compelling reasons to see Jews as excluded from the terms of the judgment. 40 (10.42): The least may be all the needy, but Matthew emphasizes the treatment of missionaries. 46: Eternal life is synonymous with inheriting the kingdom mentioned in 25.34.

26 When Jesus had finished saying all these things, he said to his disciples, ²"You know that after two days the Passover is coming, and the Son of Man will be handed over to be crucified."

³ Then the chief priests and the elders of the people gathered in the palace of the high priest, who was called Caiaphas, ⁴and they conspired to arrest Jesus by stealth and kill him. ⁵But they said, "Not during the festival, or there may be a riot among the people."

⁶ Now while Jesus was at Bethany in the house of Simon the leper,^b ⁷a woman came to him with an alabaster jar of very costly ointment, and she poured it on his head as he sat at the table. ⁸But when the disciples saw it, they were angry and said, "Why this waste? ⁹For this ointment could have been sold for a large sum, and the money given to the poor." ¹⁰But Jesus, aware of this, said to them, "Why do you trouble the woman? She has performed a good service for me. ¹¹For you always have the poor with you, but you will not always have me. ¹²By pouring this ointment on my body she has prepared me for burial. ¹³Truly I tell you, wherever this good news^c is proclaimed in the whole world, what she has done will be told in remembrance of her."

26.1–13. 2–5 (Mk 14.1–2; Lk 22.1–2; Jn 11.47–53): Jesus' death. The prediction specifies Passover,* the Jewish festival of freedom from Egyptian slavery (Ex 12.1–20). 3: Caiaphas, son-in-law of Annas, held his position by Roman appointment. 5: The population of Jerusalem increased tenfold at pilgrimage festivals; given the Roman occupation and the presence of Roman soldiers on the Temple* mount, tensions among the Jewish pilgrims celebrating liberation from Egyptian slavery were high. 6–13 (Mk 14.3–9): The anointing woman. John 12.1–8 sets a similar scene at the home of Martha and Mary and identifies the woman anointing* Jesus as Mary; Lk 7.36–50 is set at the home of Simon the Pharisee;* his unnamed woman is identified as a "sinner." In Matthew the unidentified woman anoints Jesus in preparation for his burial; therefore, (against Mk 16.1) the women at the tomb do not come to anoint the body. 10: Good service is literally "good works" (see 5.16). 11: See Deut 15.11.

¹⁴ Then one of the twelve, who was called Judas Iscariot, went to the chief priests ¹⁵and said, "What will you give me if

^a Gk these my brothers　　^b The terms leper and leprosy can refer to several diseases　　^c Or gospel

I betray him to you?" They paid him thirty pieces of silver. 16And from that moment he began to look for an opportunity to betray him.

17 On the first day of Unleavened Bread the disciples came to Jesus, saying, "Where do you want us to make the preparations for you to eat the Passover?" 18He said, "Go into the city to a certain man, and say to him, 'The Teacher says, My time is near; I will keep the Passover at your house with my disciples.' " 19So the disciples did as Jesus had directed them, and they prepared the Passover meal.

20 When it was evening, he took his place with the twelve;[a] 21and while they were eating, he said, "Truly I tell you, one of you will betray me." 22And they became greatly distressed and began to say to him one after another, "Surely not I, Lord?" 23He answered, "The one who has dipped his hand into the bowl with me will betray me. 24The Son of Man goes as it is written of him, but woe to that one by whom the Son of Man is betrayed! It would have been better for that one not to have been born." 25Judas, who betrayed him, said, "Surely not I, Rabbi?" He replied, "You have said so."

26 While they were eating, Jesus took a loaf of bread, and after blessing it he broke it, gave it to the disciples, and said, "Take, eat; this is my body." 27Then he took a cup, and after giving thanks he gave it to them, saying, "Drink from it, all of you; 28for this is my blood of the[b] covenant, which is poured out for many for the forgiveness of sins. 29I tell you, I will never again drink of this fruit of the vine until that day when I drink it new with you in my Father's kingdom."

26.14–29. 14–16 (Mk 14.10–11; Lk 22.3–6): **Betrayal plans**. Judas's action was announced in 10.4. **15:** Judas's greed, noted only by Matthew, contrasts with the woman's generosity (26.7). Matthew provides no other motivation for Judas's handing over of Jesus; Luke and John both suggest Satanic possession. Ironically,* the story of Judas will also be remembered (see 26.13). On the *thirty pieces of silver,* see Zech 11.12–13 (Ex 21.32). **17–29** (Mk 14.12–25; Lk 22.7–23; Jn 13.21–30; see also 1 Cor 10.16; 11.23–26): **The**

last supper. 17: Thursday; *Passover*** preparations included finding a place in Jerusalem to eat the Passover meal (the "Seder"), removing leaven, obtaining a lamb (the "Passover") sacrificed in the Temple,* roasting it, and eating it along with other traditional foods, such as unleavened bread (matzo) and bitter herbs. Scholars debate whether the last supper was a Passover Seder, as it is in the Synoptic Gospels,* or whether it occurred during the general time of Passover, as it does in the Gospel of John. **20:** Jewish days begin at sunset (see Gen 1). **24:** See comment on Mk 14.21. **25:** Unlike Mark, Matthew reveals that Jesus knew Judas's role. *Rabbi* is not used by Jesus' followers. **27:** *Cup* suggests Jesus' giving his life (20.22; 26.39). The idea of literally consuming human flesh and blood is abhorrent to Jewish sensibilities and contrary to Jewish law.

---

30 When they had sung the hymn, they went out to the Mount of Olives.

31 Then Jesus said to them, "You will all become deserters because of me this night; for it is written,

'I will strike the shepherd,
   and the sheep of the flock will
      be scattered.'

32But after I am raised up, I will go ahead of you to Galilee." 33Peter said to him, "Though all become deserters because of you, I will never desert you." 34Jesus said to him, "Truly I tell you, this very night, before the cock crows, you will deny me three times." 35Peter said to him, "Even though I must die with you, I will not deny you." And so said all the disciples.

26.30–35 (Mk 14.26–31; Lk 22.31–34, 39; Jn 14.31; 18.1; 13.36–38): **Mount of Olives. 30:** Seder meals traditionally include the singing of the Hallel Psalms (113–118); this is the only indication, aside from time references, that the supper is a Passover* meal. **31:** Cites Zech 13.7. **35:** The disciples will fail but repent (28.16). Mark also anticipates a resurrection appearance in Galilee, but only Matthew actually provides it; Luke and John set their appearances in Jerusalem.

---

36 Then Jesus went with them to a place called Gethsemane; and he said to his dis-

---

a Other ancient authorities add *disciples*   b Other ancient authorities add *new*

The Synoptic Problem

The Gospels of Matthew, Mark, and Luke are known as the "Synoptics" (from the Greek term for "see together") because they share substantial amounts of similar material, presented with the same wording and in the same order. Scholars have for more than two-hundred years been debating the relationship among the three texts, however. The North African Church Father, Augustine, proposed that the Gospels were composed in canonical* order. First Matthew, then Mark, Luke, and finally, as a summary of the Synoptics, John. Theologically helpful, this theory is structurally unlikely. The agreements in wording and order among the Synoptics do indicate that Mark is the middle term. Either Mark is a combination and summary of Matthew and Luke or, as most scholars theorize today, Mark wrote first and Matthew and Luke independently used his Gospel.

If this latter view is correct, then the solution to the "Synoptic problem*" is not yet complete. Matthew and Luke share a substantial amount of material—mostly consisting of sayings rather than narrative,* such as the debates between Jesus and Satan at the Temptation, the Beatitudes, and the Lord's Prayer—that is absent from Mark's Gospel. To account for this material, scholars have hypothesized a second source, designated Q (from the German term "Quelle," or source) that may underlie Matthew and Luke. Primarily "sayings" material, Q appears to lack a passion narrative.

ciples, "Sit here while I go over there and pray." 37 He took with him Peter and the two sons of Zebedee, and began to be grieved and agitated. 38 Then he said to them, "I am deeply grieved, even to death; remain here, and stay awake with me." 39 And going a little farther, he threw himself on the ground and prayed, "My Father, if it is possible, let this cup pass from me; yet not what I want but what you want." 40 Then he came to the disciples and found them sleeping; and he said to Peter, "So, could you not stay awake with me one hour? 41 Stay awake and pray that you may not come into the time of trial;ᵃ the spirit indeed is willing, but the flesh is weak." 42 Again he went away for the second time and prayed, "My Father, if this cannot pass unless I drink it, your will be done." 43 Again he came and found them sleeping, for their eyes were heavy. 44 So leaving them again, he went away and prayed for the third time, saying the same words. 45 Then he came to the disciples and said to them, "Are you still sleeping and taking your rest? See, the hour is at hand, and the Son of Man is betrayed

into the hands of sinners. 46 Get up, let us be going. See, my betrayer is at hand."

26.36–46 (Mk 14.32–42; Lk 22.40–46): **Agony in Gethsemane**. The Synoptics identify the setting as Gethsemane, while John calls it a "garden." **37:** The three who sleep had witnessed the transfiguration (17.1) and claimed willingness to drink Jesus' cup (20.22; 26.33). **40:** *Stay awake* recollects 24.42.

47 While he was still speaking, Judas, one of the twelve, arrived; with him was a large crowd with swords and clubs, from the chief priests and the elders of the people. 48 Now the betrayer had given them a sign, saying, "The one I will kiss is the man; arrest him." 49 At once he came up to Jesus and said, "Greetings, Rabbi!" and kissed him. 50 Jesus said to him, "Friend, do what you are here to do." Then they came and laid hands on Jesus and arrested him. 51 Suddenly, one of those with Jesus put his hand on his sword, drew it, and struck the slave of the high

ᵃ Or *into temptation*

priest, cutting off his ear. 52 Then Jesus said to him, "Put your sword back into its place; for all who take the sword will perish by the sword. 53 Do you think that I cannot appeal to my Father, and he will at once send me more than twelve legions of angels? 54 But how then would the scriptures be fulfilled, which say it must happen in this way?" 55 At that hour Jesus said to the crowds, "Have you come out with swords and clubs to arrest me as though I were a bandit? Day after day I sat in the temple teaching, and you did not arrest me. 56 But all this has taken place, so that the scriptures of the prophets may be fulfilled." Then all the disciples deserted him and fled.

26.47–56 (Mk 14.43–52; Lk 22.47–53; Jn 18.2–11): **The arrest. 51:** Matthew specifies the sword-owner is a disciple (Mark is not explicit; John identifies him as Peter). Jesus argues against retaliation (see 5.38–39, 43–48). **53:** *Twelve legions* indicates 72,000 soldiers. **55:** *Bandit* is used by Josephus for those who resisted Roman rule (see 27.38, 44). Hints of Roman political concerns underlie the story and provide some historical explanation for why Jesus dies on a Roman cross under a political title. **56:** Unlike Mark, Matthew redeems the disciples with the Great Commission.

57 Those who had arrested Jesus took him to Caiaphas the high priest, in whose house the scribes and the elders had gathered. 58 But Peter was following him at a distance, as far as the courtyard of the high priest; and going inside, he sat with the guards in order to see how this would end. 59 Now the chief priests and the whole council were looking for false testimony against Jesus so that they might put him to death, 60 but they found none, though many false witnesses came forward. At last two came forward 61 and said, "This fellow said, 'I am able to destroy the temple of God and to build it in three days.' " 62 The high priest stood up and said, "Have you no answer? What is it that they testify against you?" 63 But Jesus was silent. Then the high priest said to him, "I put you under oath before the living God, tell us if you are the Messiah,*a* the Son of God." 64 Jesus said to him, "You have said so. But I tell you,

From now on you will see the
    Son of Man
  seated at the right hand of Power
  and coming on the clouds of heaven."
65 Then the high priest tore his clothes and said, "He has blasphemed! Why do we still need witnesses? You have now heard his blasphemy. 66 What is your verdict?" They answered, "He deserves death." 67 Then they spat in his face and struck him; and some slapped him, 68 saying, "Prophesy to us, you Messiah!*a* Who is it that struck you?"

69 Now Peter was sitting outside in the courtyard. A servant-girl came to him and said, "You also were with Jesus the Galilean." 70 But he denied it before all of them, saying, "I do not know what you are talking about." 71 When he went out to the porch, another servant-girl saw him, and she said to the bystanders, "This man was with Jesus of Nazareth."*b* 72 Again he denied it with an oath, "I do not know the man." 73 After a little while the bystanders came up and said to Peter, "Certainly you are also one of them, for your accent betrays you." 74 Then he began to curse, and he swore an oath, "I do not know the man!" At that moment the cock crowed. 75 Then Peter remembered what Jesus had said: "Before the cock crows, you will deny me three times." And he went out and wept bitterly.

26.57–75: **The trial.** The Gospel accounts contain numerous legal irregularities; see comment on Mk 14.53–72. **59:** Matthew adds *false* (see Mk 14.55) to emphasize the leaders' hypocrisy. **63, 67:** Jesus' silence and suffering reflects Isaiah's suffering servant (Isa 53.7; 50.6). **63–64:** Jesus responds indirectly and thus is consistent with his forbidding of oaths (5.33–37; 23.16–22). **64:** See Dan 7.13; Ps 110.1. **65:** Tearing garments is a sign of mourning; the tearing of priestly garments is forbidden (Lev 10.6; 21.10). **67:** Matthew intensifies the condemnation of the chief priests and elders. **68:** The arrest and Peter's denial prove Jesus' prophetic abilities even as the tormentors mockingly ask him to demonstrate them.

27 When morning came, all the chief priests and the elders of the people

a Or *Christ*   *b* Gk *the Nazorean*

conferred together against Jesus in order to bring about his death. ²They bound him, led him away, and handed him over to Pilate the governor.

3 When Judas, his betrayer, saw that Jesus*ᵃ* was condemned, he repented and brought back the thirty pieces of silver to the chief priests and the elders. ⁴He said, "I have sinned by betraying innocent*ᵇ* blood." But they said, "What is that to us? See to it yourself." ⁵Throwing down the pieces of silver in the temple, he departed; and he went and hanged himself. ⁶But the chief priests, taking the pieces of silver, said, "It is not lawful to put them into the treasury, since they are blood money." ⁷After conferring together, they used them to buy the potter's field as a place to bury foreigners. ⁸For this reason that field has been called the Field of Blood to this day. ⁹Then was fulfilled what had been spoken through the prophet Jeremiah,*ᶜ* "And they took*ᵈ* the thirty pieces of silver, the price of the one on whom a price had been set,*ᵉ* on whom some of the people of Israel had set a price, ¹⁰and they gave*ᶠ* them for the potter's field, as the Lord commanded me."

27.1–10. 1–2 (Mk 15.1; Lk 23.1; Jn 18.28–32): **Pilate's involvement.** The Roman governor came from Caesarea to Jerusalem at Passover.* **3–10** (Acts 1.16–20): **Judas's death.** A scene unique to Matthew, Judas's death evokes the suicide of Ahithophel, who betrayed David (2 Sam 17). According to Acts, Judas dies a much less dignified death. In both accounts, the death is linked to the purchase of a *field* for the burial of foreigners. **9–10:** See Zech 11.12–13; Jer 18.1–3; 32.6–15.

---

11 Now Jesus stood before the governor; and the governor asked him, "Are you the King of the Jews?" Jesus said, "You say so." ¹²But when he was accused by the chief priests and elders, he did not answer. ¹³Then Pilate said to him, "Do you not hear how many accusations they make against you?" ¹⁴But he gave him no answer, not even to a single charge, so that the governor was greatly amazed.

15 Now at the festival the governor was accustomed to release a prisoner for the crowd, anyone whom they wanted. ¹⁶At that time they had a notorious prisoner, called Jesus*ᵍ* Barabbas. ¹⁷So after they had gathered, Pilate said to them, "Whom do you want me to release for you, Jesus*ᵍ* Barabbas or Jesus who is called the Messiah?"*ʰ* ¹⁸For he realized that it was out of jealousy that they had handed him over. ¹⁹While he was sitting on the judgment seat, his wife sent word to him, "Have nothing to do with that innocent man, for today I have suffered a great deal because of a dream about him." ²⁰Now the chief priests and the elders persuaded the crowds to ask for Barabbas and to have Jesus killed. ²¹The governor again said to them, "Which of the two do you want me to release for you?" And they said, "Barabbas." ²²Pilate said to them, "Then what should I do with Jesus who is called the Messiah?"*ʰ* All of them said, "Let him be crucified!" ²³Then he asked, "Why, what evil has he done?" But they shouted all the more, "Let him be crucified!"

24 So when Pilate saw that he could do nothing, but rather that a riot was beginning, he took some water and washed his hands before the crowd, saying, "I am innocent of this man's blood;*ⁱ* see to it yourselves." ²⁵Then the people as a whole answered, "His blood be on us and on our children!" ²⁶So he released Barabbas for them; and after flogging Jesus, he handed him over to be crucified.

27 Then the soldiers of the governor took Jesus into the governor's headquarters,*ʲ* and they gathered the whole cohort around him. ²⁸They stripped him and put a scarlet robe on him, ²⁹and after twisting some thorns into a crown, they put it on his head. They put a reed in his right hand and knelt before him and mocked him, saying, "Hail, King of the Jews!" ³⁰They spat on him, and took the reed and struck him on the head. ³¹After mocking him, they stripped him of the robe and put his own clothes on him. Then they led him away to crucify him.

a Gk *he*   *b* Other ancient authorities read *righteous*
c Other ancient authorities read *Zechariah* or *Isaiah*
d Or *I took*   *e* Or *the price of the precious One*
f Other ancient authorities read *I gave*   *g* Other
ancient authorities lack *Jesus*   *h* Or *the Christ*
i Other ancient authorities read *this righteous blood,* or
this righteous man's blood   *j* Gk *the praetorium*

27.11–31. 11–26 (Mk 15.2–15; Lk 23.2–25; Jn 18.29–19.16): **The condemnation. 11:** Pilate's question is political: Is Jesus king? *Jews* could be translated "Judeans." **14:** See 26.62; Mk 14.61; Lk 23.9. **15–26** (Mk 15.1–5; Lk 23.2–5; Jn 18.38–40; 19.4–16). **15:** This custom of releasing a prisoner is unattested outside of Mark and Matthew. **16:** *Barabbas* is Aramaic* for "son of the father"; his first name given in many early manuscripts is "Jesus." Matthew thus explicitly contrasts the Jesus of crime with the Jesus of peace; symbolically, the innocent one will die so that the guilty can go free. **19:** Pilate's *wife* resembles Joseph and the Magi. **25:** Likely refers to the devastation caused by the destruction of Jerusalem in 70 CE; sadly, some Christians interpret the verse, unique to Matthew and consistent with the Gospel's negative view of Jerusalem, as indicating collective, eternal Jewish guilt. **27–31** (Mk 15.16–20; Lk 23.11; Jn 19.1–3): **The mocking.** The mocking ironically* attests to Jesus' messianic kingship. *Cohorts* contain five hundred soldiers. The Roman soldiers intensify the tortures begun by the Sanhedrin* leaders.

32 As they went out, they came upon a man from Cyrene named Simon; they compelled this man to carry his cross. 33And when they came to a place called Golgotha (which means Place of a Skull), 34they offered him wine to drink, mixed with gall; but when he tasted it, he would not drink it. 35And when they had crucified him, they divided his clothes among themselves by casting lots;*a* 36then they sat down there and kept watch over him. 37Over his head they put the charge against him, which read, "This is Jesus, the King of the Jews."

38 Then two bandits were crucified with him, one on his right and one on his left. 39Those who passed by derided*b* him, shaking their heads 40and saying, "You who would destroy the temple and build it in three days, save yourself! If you are the Son of God, come down from the cross." 41In the same way the chief priests also, along with the scribes and elders, were mocking him, saying, 42"He saved others; he cannot save himself.*c* He is the King of Israel; let him come down from the cross now, and we will believe in him. 43He trusts in God; let God deliver him now, if he wants to; for he said,

'I am God's Son.' " 44The bandits who were crucified with him also taunted him in the same way.

27.32–44 (Mk 15.21–32; Lk 23.26, 33–43; Jn 19.17–24): **Jesus' crucifixion. 32:** *Cyrene,* modern Libya, had a sizable Jewish population; the stranger Simon's conscripted labor contrasts with the disciple Simon's absence. **33:** *Golgotha* (Latin, "Calvaria") means "place of the skull." The location is unknown. **34:** *Gall* echoes Ps 69.21; Mark's narcotic becomes in Matthew a cruel drink. **35–46:** The crucifixion throughout suggests Ps 22. **37:** The titulus, which could be translated also "King of the Judeans," is both mockery and confession (see comment on 27.42). **38:** *Bandits* could refer to anti-Roman revolutionaries. Unlike in Luke, there is no "good thief"; Jesus has no friends at the cross. **42:** *Israel* indicates that Jesus' kingdom is not merely Judea. The presence of chief priests at the place of death is unlikely.

45 From noon on, darkness came over the whole land*d* until three in the afternoon. 46And about three o'clock Jesus cried with a loud voice, "Eli, Eli, lema sabachthani?" that is, "My God, my God, why have you forsaken me?" 47When some of the bystanders heard it, they said, "This man is calling for Elijah." 48At once one of them ran and got a sponge, filled it with sour wine, put it on a stick, and gave it to him to drink. 49But the others said, "Wait, let us see whether Elijah will come to save him."*e* 50Then Jesus cried again with a loud voice and breathed his last.*f* 51At that moment the curtain of the temple was torn in two, from top to bottom. The earth shook, and the rocks were split. 52The tombs also were opened, and many bodies of the saints who had fallen asleep were raised. 53After his resurrection they came out of the tombs and entered the holy city and appeared to many. 54Now when the centurion and those with him, who were keeping watch over Jesus, saw the earthquake and what took place,

a Other ancient authorities add *in order that what had been spoken through the prophet might be fulfilled, "They divided my clothes among themselves, and for my clothing they cast lots."* *b* Or *blasphemed* *c* Or *is he unable to save himself?* *d* Or *earth* *e* Other ancient authorities add *And another took a spear and pierced his side, and out came water and blood* *f* Or *gave up his spirit* they were terrified and said, "Truly this man was God's Son!"[a]

55 Many women were also there, looking on from a distance; they had followed Jesus from Galilee and had provided for him. 56Among them were Mary Magdalene, and Mary the mother of James and Joseph, and the mother of the sons of Zebedee.

27.45–56 (Mk 15.33–41, 56; Lk 23.44–49; Jn 19.28–37): **Jesus' death. 46:** See Ps 22.1; the psalm ends with universal redemption. Matthew recounts the Hebrew, Mark the Aramaic.* *Eli* sounds like *Elijah*, who was the expected herald of the messianic age (see Mal. 3). The crowds do not realize Elijah has come (11.14; 17.10–13). **51:** The *curtain* depicted the zodiac; as at the baptism,* the heavens open. **52:** Anticipates the general resurrection. **54:** The portents, not Jesus' suffering (as in Mark), convert the Roman executioners. **56:** Matthew's first reference to the group of women. *Mary the mother of James and Joseph* is seen by some traditions to be Jesus' mother, but this would be an odd identification. The presence of the mother of the sons of Zebedee highlights the absence of her sons.

57 When it was evening, there came a rich man from Arimathea, named Joseph, who was also a disciple of Jesus. 58He went to Pilate and asked for the body of Jesus; then Pilate ordered it to be given to him. 59So Joseph took the body and wrapped it in a clean linen cloth 60and laid it in his own new tomb, which he had hewn in the rock. He then rolled a great stone to the door of the tomb and went away. 61Mary Magdalene and the other Mary were there, sitting opposite the tomb.

62 The next day, that is, after the day of Preparation, the chief priests and the Pharisees gathered before Pilate 63and said, "Sir, we remember what that impostor said while he was still alive, 'After three days I will rise again.' 64Therefore command the tomb to be made secure until the third day; otherwise his disciples may come and steal him away, and tell the people, 'He has been raised from the dead,' and the last deception would be worse than the first." 65Pilate said to them, "You have a guard[b] of soldiers; go, make it as secure as you can."[c] 66So they went with the

guard and made the tomb secure by sealing the stone.

27.57–65 (Mk 15.42–47; Lk 23.50–56; Jn 19.38–42): **The burial. 57:** Only Matthew identifies *Joseph* as rich; he is not a Sanhedrin* member (as in Mark) but a *disciple.* Consistent for Matthew as well, he is not from the faithless city, Jerusalem. **58–59:** Burial of those killed, especially by oppressive governments, is a revered act in Judaism (see Tobit). **61:** Only the women keep vigil. **62–65:** The only reference to *Pharisees** in Synoptic Passion accounts. Ironically,* the Pharisees remember what Jesus' disciples first reject and then appear to forget. *Sir* (Gk., "kyrios," Lord) is used by the disciples to address Jesus. For the prediction, see 12.38–42.

28 After the sabbath, as the first day of the week was dawning, Mary Magdalene and the other Mary went to see the tomb. 2And suddenly there was a great earthquake; for an angel of the Lord, descending from heaven, came and rolled back the stone and sat on it. 3His appearance was like lightning, and his clothing white as snow. 4For fear of him the guards shook and became like dead men. 5But the angel said to the women, "Do not be afraid; I know that you are looking for Jesus who was crucified. 6He is not here; for he has been raised, as he said. Come, see the place where he[d] lay. 7Then go quickly and tell his disciples, 'He has been raised from the dead,[e] and indeed he is going ahead of you to Galilee; there you will see him.' This is my message for you." 8So they left the tomb quickly with fear and great joy, and ran to tell his disciples. 9Suddenly Jesus met them and said, "Greetings!" And they came to him, took hold of his feet, and worshiped him. 10Then Jesus said to them, "Do not be afraid; go and tell my brothers to go to Galilee; there they will see me."

28.1–10 (Mk 16.1–8; Lk 24.1–11; Jn 20.1–20): **The resurrected Jesus. 2:** The *angel* replaces Mark's "young man." In contrast to Mark's account, the

a Or *a son of God*   b Or *Take a guard*   c Gk *you know how*   d Other ancient authorities read *the Lord*   e Other ancient authorities lack *from the dead* women neither come to anoint* the body nor worry about the stone. Their brave presence at a tomb of a crucified man that was guarded by Pilate's soldiers was politically dangerous; women too were crucified by Rome. **7–10:** The women are commissioned as missionaries; unlike in Mark's account, they fulfill their mission. Matthew sets no resurrection accounts in Jerusalem (on Galilee, see 4.12–17). **10:** *Brothers* indicates reconciliation with the eleven, absent since 26.56.

11 While they were going, some of the guard went into the city and told the chief priests everything that had happened. 12After the priests*a* had assembled with the elders, they devised a plan to give a large sum of money to the soldiers, 13telling them, "You must say, 'His disciples came by night and stole him away while we were asleep.' 14If this comes to the governor's ears, we will satisfy him and keep you out of trouble." 15So they took the money and did as they were directed. And this story is still told among the Jews to this day.

16 Now the eleven disciples went to Galilee, to the mountain to which Jesus had directed them. 17When they saw him, they worshiped him; but some doubted. 18And Jesus came and said to them, "All authority in heaven and on earth has been given to me. 19Go therefore and make disciples of all nations, baptizing them in the name of the Father and of the Son and of the Holy Spirit, 20and teaching them to obey everything that I have commanded you. And remember, I am with you always, to the end of the age."*b*

28.11–20. 11–15: The bribe. The guards parallel the actions of the women. **13:** The leaders ironically* spread the rumor of the event the guards at the tomb were to prevent. **15:** Matthew's only use of *Jews* or, perhaps, "Judeans." The evangelist indicates what those Jews outside the church said about the Gospel's resurrection proclamation. **16–20** (1 Cor 15.5–6; Jn 21.1–23; Lk 24.11): **The Great Commission. 17:** *Worship* indicates prostration (not done prior to the crucifixion). *Doubt* (found elsewhere only at 14.31) suggests the disciples are not perfect believers, a comfort to Matthew's church. **18–19:** The change in Jesus' status now prompts a mission to gentiles* (see 10.5b; 15.24), but the mission to Jews (10.6) is not revoked. **20:** The disciples are now commissioned to teach. Jesus' last words, precluding an ascension, recollect 1.23; 18.20. The Gospel is framed with the promise of "God with us."

a Gk *they*　b Other ancient authorities add *Amen*

THE GOSPEL ACCORDING TO

MARK

Introduction

Mark, the earliest continuous narrative* of Jesus' life known to have survived, depicts neither a miraculous birth nor a glorious resurrection appearance, but rather leadership that derives from service, power in suffering, and glory in death.

The story of the healing of the blind man of Bethsaida (Mk 8.22–26) serves as a paradigm for the Gospel. After his first ministrations, Jesus asks the man, "Can you see anything?" The man responds, "I can see people, but they look like trees, walking." Only after Jesus lays his hands on the man a second time is clarity of vision achieved. In a similar manner, Mark's Gospel neatly divides into two sections. The first eight chapters present a Jesus who speaks in parables,* who uses the enigmatic self-designation "Son of Man," who frequently orders those aware of his identity as Son of God or of his powers to heal to remain silent, and who is misunderstood by his Galilean community, his family, and even his disciples. Something momentous is happening, but the meaning of his person and mission is shrouded in secrecy and parable.

Clarity comes midway through the narrative. "Immediately" (one of the Gospel's favorite words) after the Bethsaida healing, Jesus asks his disciples about his identity. Following Peter's insight that Jesus is not John the Baptist, or Elijah, or one of the prophets,* but is in fact the messiah* (8.28–30), Jesus finally speaks "quite openly" (8.32): "Then he began to teach them that the Son of Man must undergo great suffering, and be rejected by the elders, the chief priests, and the scribes,* and be killed, and after three days rise again" (8.31). The remainder of the Gospel, the "passion narrative," details both the resistance to and the fulfillment of this prediction.

Peter rebukes Jesus; he and his fellow disciples cannot accept that the Lord's anointed would suffer and die. This failure of appropriate theology corresponds to their later failures in action: One disciple betrays Jesus (14.17–21); three others are unable to support him in Gethsemane (14.28–50); all desert him at the arrest (14.50); and Peter denies him (ch. 14). The women followers from Galilee (15.40–41) similarly fail in their intention to anoint* his body (16.1), and they flee from the tomb not to proclaim the resurrection but in silence and in fear (16.8). But some do recognize the meaning of Jesus' identity. The woman at the house of Simon the leper anoints his body for burial (14.8), and the centurion at the cross, upon seeing Jesus breathe his last, proclaims, "Truly this man was God's Son" (15.39).

Unlike the other canonical* Gospels, Mark records no resurrection appearances. The young man at the tomb reminds the women that Jesus had promised to return to his followers (16.7, see 14.28), but the reconciliation recorded in Mt 16.20 is missing in the earliest manuscripts of Mark's Gospel. The early church added to Mark's original conclusion at 16.8 several resurrection appearances, but the Gospel may better be appreciated with its abrupt ending (see sidebar, "The Ending of Mark," on p. 1743). Like the two-stage healing in Bethsaida, Peter's incomplete recognition of Jesus' identity, and even the cry of dereliction, "My God, my God, why have you forsaken me?" which Jesus utters from the cross, there is a second part to the story, unrecounted but well known to Mark's community. The blind man eventually sees; Peter will, as the other Gospels,

Acts, and Paul's letters tell us, become an apostle✶ of the early church; Psalm 22, with which Jesus' cry begins, ends with a celebration of redemption.

The evangelist's decision to record the words and deeds of Jesus in narrative form, as opposed to saying collections or miracle lists, and the emphasis on Jesus' victory through suffering both suggest the needs of the congregation to which the Gospel was addressed. For a community undergoing persecution, or struggling with delay of the return of the "Son of Man," or facing alternative interpretations of Jesus' life and mission, the narrative provides guidance: Followers of Jesus will suffer, as he did; the Son will come like a thief in the night, so believers should remain steadfast and be prepared; Jesus is not some demi-god or miracle worker to be confused with or even compared to such figures as, respectively, Asclepius or Apollonius of Tyana. He is the one whose death ransoms many (10.45).

The identity of the author is not provided in the earliest manuscripts, although the church father Eusebius records a tradition that this Gospel was written by (John) Mark, Peter's companion (Acts 12, 15; 1 Pet 5.13). The narrative reveals the evangelist to be a Greek-speaking Christian, using the Septuagint✶ (LXX), the Greek translation of the Hebrew Scriptures,✶ and writing for an audience to some extent unfamiliar with Jewish practices and with the Aramaic✶ language (5.41; 7.3–4, 34; 15.26). Both Rome and Alexandria are proposed in early sources as sites of composition; current research has also proposed Galilee or Southern Syria. Whether the Gospel indicates awareness of the destruction of the Jerusalem Temple✶ in 70 CE is unclear. Mark 13.2 predicts the fall of the Temple, but the statement could well have been Jesus' own prediction.

READING GUIDE

The shortest of the canonical Gospels and a narrative that presents more action than teaching, Mark is often read too quickly from beginning to end. Readers, especially those familiar with the Gospels of Matthew and Luke, may consequently miss Mark's particular interests, structure, and style. This deceptively simple Gospel divides thematically into two sections: Chs. 1–8 concentrate on the Galilean ministry and feature miracles, parables, and controversies with Pharisees.✶ Lacking the nativity accounts familiar from Matthew and Luke, Mark presents a mysterious Jesus who emerges in the context of John's baptism;✶ how he is the "Son of God" proclaimed by the voice from heaven is not made immediately clear. However, his activities, frequently punctuated with the expression "and immediately," convey a sense of urgency and newness. The break comes at 8.27–38, when instead of speaking in parables Jesus proclaims plainly the necessity of the passion. Chs. 9–16, in which the pace of the narrative slows, turn from enigmatic sayings and miraculous deeds to Jesus' suffering. Here misunderstanding of and opposition to his mission both increase: Many of his disciples will fail him and the Temple establishment, replacing the Pharisees as his chief antagonists, will seek his death. Only those outside his inner circle—the woman who anoints him, the centurion who guards the cross, and the reader of Mark's narrative—will understand the importance of his passion and death.

1.1–13	Beginning the ministry (baptism and temptation)
1.14–9.50	Galilean ministry (teachings, healings, controversies)
10.1–52	Journey to Jerusalem
11.1–15.47	Passion narrative
16.1–8	Resurrection narrative (16.9–20 are later additions)

John the Baptist

In all four canonical* Gospels, Jesus begins his adult activities with John's baptism.* However, each Gospel presents the baptism account in a different way. For Mark, John is a preacher of the end time who anchors the story of Jesus into the prophetic* traditions of Israel; this Gospel displays no difficulty in Jesus' submission to baptism for repentance. For Matthew, Jesus and John debate the appropriateness of the baptism; John yields to Jesus' insistence that the action is required "to fulfill all righteousness" (Mt 3.15). Luke depicts Jesus as superior to John even prior to their births (Lk 1.39–44) and describes the baptism in the passive voice rather than highlighting the Baptist's involvement ("when Jesus also had been baptized . . . ," Lk 3.21). In John's account, likely the latest of the four, John the Baptist is presented as a witness to Jesus, but the baptism is not depicted (Jn 1.29–34). The Gospels also indicate that John retained his disciples rather than, together with his followers, joining Jesus, and that John's disciples engaged in practices distinct from those of Jesus. The Gospels' increasing subordination of John to Jesus may well reflect conflict and debate between the two groups of followers.

The Jewish historian Josephus* corroborates the Gospels' testimony that John spoke about repentance and the remission of sins, that he gathered large crowds, and that he was executed by Herod Antipas. *Antiquities of the Jews* (Book 18) explains that John encouraged the Jews to lead righteous lives, to practice justice to others and piety toward God and, once they had so oriented their lives, to submit to John's baptism. The ritual act did not gain pardon for sins; rather, it was a consecration of the body which implied that the soul was already cleansed.

John's enormous popularity threatened the Galilean tetrarch, Herod Antipas. According to the Gospels, Herod arrested John because of the Baptist's condemnations of his marriage. Josephus provides background information. First, he notes that Herod's motivation was his fear that John's enormous popularity would eventually lead to sedition. Second, he states that by marrying Herodias, the wife of his half-brother, Herod rejected his own first wife, the daughter of Aretas, King of Nabataea. Understandably upset, Aretas waged war against Antipas and defeated his troops. According to Josephus, the destruction of Antipas's army appeared to many Jews to be divine vengeance for his execution of the Baptist.

---

1 The beginning of the good news*a* of Jesus Christ, the Son of God.*b* 2 As it is written in the prophet Isaiah,*c*

"See, I am sending my messenger ahead of you,*d*
    who will prepare your way;
3 the voice of one crying out in the
        wilderness:
    'Prepare the way of the Lord,
        make his paths straight,' "

4 John the baptizer appeared*e* in the wilderness, proclaiming a baptism of repentance for the forgiveness of sins. 5 And people from the whole Judean countryside and all the people of Jerusalem were going out to him, and were baptized by him in the river Jordan, confessing their sins. 6 Now John was clothed with camel's hair, with a leather belt around his waist, and he ate locusts and wild honey. 7 He proclaimed, "The one who is more powerful than I is coming after me; I am not worthy to stoop

a Or *gospel*   *b* Other ancient authorities lack *the Son of God*   *c* Other ancient authorities read *in the prophets*   *d* Gk *before your face*   *e* Other ancient authorities read *John was baptizing* down and untie the thong of his sandals. 8I have baptized you with[a] water; but he will baptize you with[a] the Holy Spirit."

1.1–8 (Mt 3.1–12; Lk 3.1–18; Jn 1.6–8, 19–28): **John the Baptist. 1:** *Good news* (Gk., "Euangellion") is the literal meaning of "gospel"; Mark is the only canonical* Gospel to have this self-designation. *Son of God* appears rarely; Son of Man is Jesus' self-designation. **2a:** See Mal 3.1. **3:** Isa 40.3 advised the Babylonian exiles to build a road to Jerusalem; Mark adapts the statement to locate John in the wilderness. **4:** *The wilderness* is a traditional place of renewal. See sidebars on "Gospels" (p. 1672) and "John the Baptist" (p. 1715).

9 In those days Jesus came from Nazareth of Galilee and was baptized by John in the Jordan. 10And just as he was coming up out of the water, he saw the heavens torn apart and the Spirit descending like a dove on him. 11And a voice came from heaven, "You are my Son, the Beloved;[b] with you I am well pleased."

12 And the Spirit immediately drove him out into the wilderness. 13He was in the wilderness forty days, tempted by Satan; and he was with the wild beasts; and the angels waited on him.

14 Now after John was arrested, Jesus came to Galilee, proclaiming the good news[c] of God,[d] 15and saying, "The time is fulfilled, and the kingdom of God has come near;[e] repent, and believe in the good news."[c]

1.9–15. 9–11 (Mt 3.13–17; Lk 3.21–22; Jn 1.31–34): **The baptism.** **9:** Mark neither records a Bethlehem birth and infancy account nor addresses the question of Jesus' sinlessness. **10:** With the rending of the Temple* veil, the heavens symbolically open again at the cross (15.38). **11:** The heavenly *voice* speaks directly to Jesus; in Matthew's account it makes a public proclamation. **12–13** (Mt 4.1–11; Lk 4.1–13): **The temptation. 12:** *Immediately* is a Marcan motif* expressing urgency. The wilderness setting, temptation, and forty days echo the Exodus and Moses' experiences on Sinai. **13:** Unlike his Hebrew ancestors, Jesus does not succumb to temptation in the wilderness; unlike Adam and Eve, he lives peacefully with animals and angels. **14–15** (Mt 4.12–17; Lk 4.14–15): **The good news.** Jesus begins his mission only after the Baptist is arrested by Herod Antipas; the two are not depicted

as rivals; rather, Jesus elaborates on John's message of repentance.

16 As Jesus passed along the Sea of Galilee, he saw Simon and his brother Andrew casting a net into the sea—for they were fishermen. 17And Jesus said to them, "Follow me and I will make you fish for people." 18And immediately they left their nets and followed him. 19As he went a little farther, he saw James son of Zebedee and his brother John, who were in their boat mending the nets. 20Immediately he called them; and they left their father Zebedee in the boat with the hired men, and followed him.

21 They went to Capernaum; and when the sabbath came, he entered the synagogue and taught. 22They were astounded at his teaching, for he taught them as one having authority, and not as the scribes. 23Just then there was in their synagogue a man with an unclean spirit, 24and he cried out, "What have you to do with us, Jesus of Nazareth? Have you come to destroy us? I know who you are, the Holy One of God." 25But Jesus rebuked him, saying, "Be silent, and come out of him!" 26And the unclean spirit, convulsing him and crying with a loud voice, came out of him. 27They were all amazed, and they kept on asking one another, "What is this? A new teaching—with authority! He[f] commands even the unclean spirits, and they obey him." 28At once his fame began to spread throughout the surrounding region of Galilee.

1.16–28. 16–20 (Mt 4.18–22; Lk 5.1–11; Jn 1.35–42). **The First Disciples.** Simon will be nicknamed "Peter" or "rock" (3.16). The four disciples are not peasants but boat owners from Capernaum, a mid-sized Galilean city. The Gospels never mention the larger cites of Sepphoris and Tiberias, although Sepphoris is just a few miles from Nazareth. The Sea of Galilee is also known as the Sea of Tiberias and Lake Gennesaret. **21–29** (Lk 4.33–37): **The Capernaum synagogue.** Synagogues are places of worship and assembly; visitors were welcome to teach. **22:** Scribes,* trained in

a Or in   *b* Or *my beloved Son*   *c* Or *gospel*
d Other ancient authorities read *of the kingdom*
e Or *is at hand*   *f* Or *A new teaching! With*
authority he

The Messianic Secret

Throughout the earlier parts of Mark's Gospel, Jesus commands secrecy regarding his healing activities and his messianic identity; demons, disciples, and individuals healed of diseases are all forbidden to speak. Although the recipients of the healings typically proclaim the good news of Jesus' activity despite the command, the demons and the disciples heed the injunction. Several theories have been proposed to explain this motif;* no one theory fully explains it, and most are not mutually exclusive.

Early in this century, W. Wrede suggested the motif was an invention of the early church. In his reconstruction, Jesus neither thought nor announced that he was the messiah;* when, after his crucifixion, his followers began to proclaim Jesus to be the Christ, they needed some explanation for why his identity had not been previously known: hence, the secrecy motif.

Contemporary explanations often focus on Mark's literary interests. The secrecy motif complements Jesus' other enigmatic traits: teaching in parables* and use of "Son of Man," a term with multiple meanings. By utilizing the commands to silence, the Gospel deflects emphasis from Jesus' miracles and onto his suffering. At the same time, however, the disobedience to the command by those healed indicated the impossibility of hiding the good news. In terms of narrative irony,* the motif points out diverse reactions to Jesus: The demons identify him, and his enemies recognize his power; only his closest followers, the twelve and the women from Galilee, fail to recognize the extent of his power and the means by which it is manifested. His true nature is proclaimed finally by the centurion at the cross: Seeing Jesus, die, the centurion correctly identifies him as "God's Son" (15.39).

Outside this pattern, Mk 5.1–20, the exorcism of the demoniac in Gerasa, not only lacks the motif but has Jesus command the healed man to proclaim the miracle. Perhaps this scene indicated some ethnic concern on the part of the evangelist: While Jesus' identity is not to be announced in Judea and Galilee, primarily Jewish areas, the proclamation is enjoined in the gentile* areas—indicated at the very least by the presence of pigs—of Decapolis.

interpretation* of Torah,* cited their teachers ("in the name of . . . "); Jesus speaks on his own authority. **24–25:** Demons recognize Jesus, but his disciples do not (3.11; 5.6–7). *Be silent* begins the messianic secret (see sidebar above, "The Messianic Secret").

29 As soon as they*a* left the synagogue, they entered the house of Simon and Andrew, with James and John. 30Now Simon's mother-in-law was in bed with a fever, and they told him about her at once. 31He came and took her by the hand and lifted her up. Then the fever left her, and she began to serve them.

32 That evening, at sundown, they brought to him all who were sick or possessed with demons. 33And the whole city was gathered around the door. 34And he cured many who were sick with various diseases, and cast out many demons; and he would not permit the demons to speak, because they knew him.

35 In the morning, while it was still very dark, he got up and went out to a deserted place, and there he prayed. 36And Simon and his companions hunted for him. 37When they found him, they said to him, "Everyone is searching for you." 38He answered, "Let us go on to the neighboring towns, so that I may proclaim the message there also; for that is what I came out to do." 39And he went throughout Galilee, pro-

a Other ancient authorities read *he*

claiming the message in their synagogues and casting out demons.

1.29–39. 30–31 (Mt 8.14–15; Lk 4.38–39): **Simon's mother-in-law.** His wife is not mentioned. **31:** Serve is from the Greek "Diakonein," from which we get the term "deacon." **32–39** (Mt 8.16–17; Lk 4.40–41): **Galilean mission. 32:** Sabbath ends at sundown. **35:** Jesus frequently withdraws for prayer. **39:** Jesus continues to teach and heal in synagogues.

~~~~~~~~~~

40 A leper[a] came to him begging him, and kneeling[b] he said to him, "If you choose, you can make me clean." [41] Moved with pity,[c] Jesus[d] stretched out his hand and touched him, and said to him, "I do choose. Be made clean!" [42] Immediately the leprosy[a] left him, and he was made clean. [43] After sternly warning him he sent him away at once, [44] saying to him, "See that you say nothing to anyone; but go, show yourself to the priest, and offer for your cleansing what Moses commanded, as a testimony to them." [45] But he went out and began to proclaim it freely, and to spread the word, so that Jesus[d] could no longer go into a town openly, but stayed out in the country; and people came to him from every quarter.

2 When he returned to Capernaum after some days, it was reported that he was at home. [2] So many gathered around that there was no longer room for them, not even in front of the door; and he was speaking the word to them. [3] Then some people[e] came, bringing to him a paralyzed man, carried by four of them. [4] And when they could not bring him to Jesus because of the crowd, they removed the roof above him; and after having dug through it, they let down the mat on which the paralytic lay. [5] When Jesus saw their faith, he said to the paralytic, "Son, your sins are forgiven." [6] Now some of the scribes were sitting there, questioning in their hearts, [7] "Why does this fellow speak in this way? It is blasphemy! Who can forgive sins but God alone?" [8] At once Jesus perceived in his spirit that they were discussing these questions among themselves; and he said to them, "Why do you raise such questions in your hearts? [9] Which is easier, to say to the paralytic, 'Your sins are forgiven,' or to

say, 'Stand up and take your mat and walk'? [10] But so that you may know that the Son of Man has authority on earth to forgive sins"—he said to the paralytic— [11] "I say to you, stand up, take your mat and go to your home." [12] And he stood up, and immediately took the mat and went out before all of them; so that they were all amazed and glorified God, saying, "We have never seen anything like this!"

1.40–2.12. 40–44 (Mt 8.2–4; Lk 5.12–14): **The leper.** Leprosy referred to a variety of skin diseases; clean indicates both healing and ritual purity required for re-entry into society. Only priests could pronounce lepers clean; the leper does not obey Jesus' commands either for silence or for priestly pronouncement. **45:** Jesus' popularity as a healer interferes with his preaching. **2.1–12** (Mt 9.1–8; Lk 5.17–26): **The paralytic. 5:** Granting forgiveness of sins was a divine prerogative. **9:** The saying appears in a different context in Jn 5.8. **10:** The title Son of Man has both human ("mortal") (Ezek 37.3) and superhuman (Dan 7.13–14, 1 Enoch★ 37–71) connotations. Enigmatic like the parables,★ the title requires hearers to determine the meaning for themselves.

~~~~~~~~~~

13 Jesus[f] went out again beside the sea; the whole crowd gathered around him, and he taught them. [14] As he was walking along, he saw Levi son of Alphaeus sitting at the tax booth, and he said to him, "Follow me." And he got up and followed him.

15 And as he sat at dinner[g] in Levi's[h] house, many tax collectors and sinners were also sitting[i] with Jesus and his disciples—for there were many who followed him. [16] When the scribes of[j] the Pharisees saw that he was eating with sinners and tax collectors, they said to his disciples, "Why does he eat[k] with tax collectors and sinners?" [17] When Jesus heard this, he said to them, "Those who are well have no need of a physician, but those who are sick; I have come to call not the righteous but sinners."

a The terms leper and leprosy can refer to several diseases   b Other ancient authorities lack kneeling   c Other ancient authorities read anger   d Gk he   e Gk they   f Gk He   g Gk reclined   h Gk his   i Gk reclining   j Other ancient authorities read and   k Other ancient authorities add and drink

2.13–17 (Mt 9.9–13; Lk 5.27–32): **Tax collectors and sinners.** *Levi* is called Matthew in Mt 9.9. Tax collectors were despised as Roman collaborators and extortionists. *Sinners* are those who deliberately place themselves apart from observance of Torah;* Mark does not see all people as in a sinful state. **16:** *Pharisees** were a branch of Judaism dedicated to interpreting biblical law, likely including the extension of the sanctity of the Temple* to the home (including the table); rivals of the early followers of Jesus, they are frequently negatively depicted in Christian texts.

18 Now John's disciples and the Pharisees were fasting; and people*a* came and said to him, "Why do John's disciples and the disciples of the Pharisees fast, but your disciples do not fast?" 19 Jesus said to them, "The wedding guests cannot fast while the bridegroom is with them, can they? As long as they have the bridegroom with them, they cannot fast. 20 The days will come when the bridegroom is taken away from them, and then they will fast on that day.

21 "No one sews a piece of unshrunk cloth on an old cloak; otherwise, the patch pulls away from it, the new from the old, and a worse tear is made. 22 And no one puts new wine into old wineskins; otherwise, the wine will burst the skins, and the wine is lost, and so are the skins; but one puts new wine into fresh wineskins."*b*

2.18–22 (Mt 9.14–17; Lk 5.33–39): **New practices.** Although John acknowledged Jesus' worthiness, he retained his own disciples. Fasting, a traditional form of Jewish piety, is adopted by Jesus' followers after the crucifixion (2.20). **19:** Bridegroom and wedding imagery suggest times of exceptional joy. **21–22:** Jesus' gospel represents the new wine; neither old nor new teachings are lost.

23 One sabbath he was going through the grainfields; and as they made their way his disciples began to pluck heads of grain. 24 The Pharisees said to him, "Look, why are they doing what is not lawful on the sabbath?" 25 And he said to them, "Have you never read what David did when he and his companions were hungry and in need of food? 26 He entered the house of God, when

Abiathar was high priest, and ate the bread of the Presence, which it is not lawful for any but the priests to eat, and he gave some to his companions." 27 Then he said to them, "The sabbath was made for humankind, and not humankind for the sabbath; 28 so the Son of Man is lord even of the sabbath."

2.23–28 (Mt 12.1–8; Lk 6.1–5): **Lord of the sabbath.** It is unlikely Pharisees* spied on people in grainfields; the complaint against the disciples, but not Jesus, suggests conflicts between church and synagogue.* **25:** Citing scripture to interpret scripture is typical of Jesus', and rabbinic, teaching. Abiathar's father Ahimelech was high priest when David ate consecrated bread (1 Sam 21.1–6; 2 Sam 15.35). **27:** Also a rabbinic teaching.

3 Again he entered the synagogue, and a man was there who had a withered hand. 2 They watched him to see whether he would cure him on the sabbath, so that they might accuse him. 3 And he said to the man who had the withered hand, "Come forward." 4 Then he said to them, "Is it lawful to do good or to do harm on the sabbath, to save life or to kill?" But they were silent. 5 He looked around at them with anger; he was grieved at their hardness of heart and said to the man, "Stretch out your hand." He stretched it out, and his hand was restored. 6 The Pharisees went out and immediately conspired with the Herodians against him, how to destroy him.

3.1–6 (Mt 12.9–14; Lk 6.6–11): **Sabbath healing.** Rabbinic law mandates that preservation of life overrules all commandments ("Mitzvoth"). **5:** Jesus does not touch the man and therefore cannot be charged with working. **6:** *Herodians* are connected with the royal family; Herod Antipas has been foreshadowed as an enemy (1.14).

7 Jesus departed with his disciples to the sea, and a great multitude from Galilee followed him; 8 hearing all that he was doing, they came to him in great numbers from Judea, Jerusalem, Idumea, beyond the Jordan,

a Gk *they*   *b* Other ancient authorities lack *but one puts new wine into fresh wineskins* and the region around Tyre and Sidon. ⁹He told his disciples to have a boat ready for him because of the crowd, so that they would not crush him; ¹⁰for he had cured many, so that all who had diseases pressed upon him to touch him. ¹¹Whenever the unclean spirits saw him, they fell down before him and shouted, "You are the Son of God!" ¹²But he sternly ordered them not to make him known.

13 He went up the mountain and called to him those whom he wanted, and they came to him. ¹⁴And he appointed twelve, whom he also named apostles,ᵃ to be with him, and to be sent out to proclaim the message, ¹⁵and to have authority to cast out demons. ¹⁶So he appointed the twelve:ᵇ Simon (to whom he gave the name Peter); ¹⁷James son of Zebedee and John the brother of James (to whom he gave the name Boanerges, that is, Sons of Thunder); ¹⁸and Andrew, and Philip, and Bartholomew, and Matthew, and Thomas, and James son of Alphaeus, and Thaddaeus, and Simon the Cananaean, ¹⁹and Judas Iscariot, who betrayed him.

3.7–19. 7–12 (Mt 12.15–21; Lk 6.17–19): **Public healings. 8:** The sites listed are areas with predominantly Jewish populations. **13–19** (Mt 10.2–4; Lk 6.12–16): **The twelve disciples.** The *twelve* symbolically represent the tribes of Israel; Gospel variations in the names of the twelve suggest the number was of greater import than the individuals. *Apostle,*★ a Greek term for messenger, is a special category of disciple. **16:** The name *Peter* comes from the Greek "petra," meaning "rock" (as in "petrified"). **17:** *James* and *John* elsewhere express turbulent personalities (Lk 9.54–55). **18:** Cananaeans were anti-Roman revolutionaries. **19:** Mark does not provide Judas a motive; until the passion, Judas appears as a loyal disciple.

Then he went home; ²⁰and the crowd came together again, so that they could not even eat. ²¹When his family heard it, they went out to restrain him, for people were saying, "He has gone out of his mind." ²²And the scribes who came down from Jerusalem said, "He has Beelzebul, and by the ruler of the demons he casts out demons." ²³And he called them to him, and spoke to them in parables, "How can Satan cast out Satan? ²⁴If a kingdom is divided against itself, that kingdom cannot stand. ²⁵And if a house is divided against itself, that house will not be able to stand. ²⁶And if Satan has risen up against himself and is divided, he cannot stand, but his end has come. ²⁷But no one can enter a strong man's house and plunder his property without first tying up the strong man; then indeed the house can be plundered.

28 "Truly I tell you, people will be forgiven for their sins and whatever blasphemies they utter; ²⁹but whoever blasphemes against the Holy Spirit can never have forgiveness, but is guilty of an eternal sin"— ³⁰for they had said, "He has an unclean spirit."

31 Then his mother and his brothers came; and standing outside, they sent to him and called him. ³²A crowd was sitting around him; and they said to him, "Your mother and your brothers and sistersᶜ are outside, asking for you." ³³And he replied, "Who are my mother and my brothers?" ³⁴And looking at those who sat around him, he said, "Here are my mother and my brothers! ³⁵Whoever does the will of God is my brother and sister and mother."

3.20–35 (Mt 12.22–37; Lk 11.14–23): **Rejections.** Jesus' family doubts his sanity, and he replaces the biological family with the family of faith. **22:** *Beelzebul*★ refers to a false god (2 Kings 1.2) or demon. The scribes★ accept Jesus' power but question the source of his authority; they ironically charge Jesus the exorcist with being possessed. **23:** *Parables*★ (see sidebar on p. 1687); Mark does not present parables until 4.3.

4 Again he began to teach beside the sea. Such a very large crowd gathered around him that he got into a boat on the sea and sat there, while the whole crowd was beside the sea on the land. ²He began to teach them many things in parables, and in his teaching he said to them: ³"Listen! A sower went out to sow. ⁴And as he sowed, some seed fell on

---

ᵃ Other ancient authorities lack *whom he also named apostles* ᵇ Other ancient authorities lack *So he appointed the twelve* ᶜ Other ancient authorities lack *and sisters* the path, and the birds came and ate it up. [5]Other seed fell on rocky ground, where it did not have much soil, and it sprang up quickly, since it had no depth of soil. [6]And when the sun rose, it was scorched; and since it had no root, it withered away. [7]Other seed fell among thorns, and the thorns grew up and choked it, and it yielded no grain. [8]Other seed fell into good soil and brought forth grain, growing up and increasing and yielding thirty and sixty and a hundredfold." [9]And he said, "Let anyone with ears to hear listen!"

[10] When he was alone, those who were around him along with the twelve asked him about the parables. [11]And he said to them, "To you has been given the secret[a] of the kingdom of God, but for those outside, everything comes in parables; [12]in order that

    'they may indeed look, but not perceive,
      and may indeed listen, but not
        understand;
    so that they may not turn again and be
        forgiven.' "

[13] And he said to them, "Do you not understand this parable? Then how will you understand all the parables? [14]The sower sows the word. [15]These are the ones on the path where the word is sown: when they hear, Satan immediately comes and takes away the word that is sown in them. [16]And these are the ones sown on rocky ground: when they hear the word, they immediately receive it with joy. [17]But they have no root, and endure only for a while; then, when trouble or persecution arises on account of the word, immediately they fall away.[b] [18]And others are those sown among the thorns: these are the ones who hear the word, [19]but the cares of the world, and the lure of wealth, and the desire for other things come in and choke the word, and it yields nothing. [20]And these are the ones sown on the good soil: they hear the word and accept it and bear fruit, thirty and sixty and a hundredfold."

[21] He said to them, "Is a lamp brought in to be put under the bushel basket, or under the bed, and not on the lampstand? [22]For there is nothing hidden, except to be disclosed; nor is anything secret, except to come to light. [23]Let anyone with ears to hear

listen!" [24]And he said to them, "Pay attention to what you hear; the measure you give will be the measure you get, and still more will be given you. [25]For to those who have, more will be given; and from those who have nothing, even what they have will be taken away."

[26] He also said, "The kingdom of God is as if someone would scatter seed on the ground, [27]and would sleep and rise night and day, and the seed would sprout and grow, he does not know how. [28]The earth produces of itself, first the stalk, then the head, then the full grain in the head. [29]But when the grain is ripe, at once he goes in with his sickle, because the harvest has come."

[30] He also said, "With what can we compare the kingdom of God, or what parable will we use for it? [31]It is like a mustard seed, which, when sown upon the ground, is the smallest of all the seeds on earth; [32]yet when it is sown it grows up and becomes the greatest of all shrubs, and puts forth large branches, so that the birds of the air can make nests in its shade."

[33] With many such parables he spoke the word to them, as they were able to hear it; [34]he did not speak to them except in parables, but he explained everything in private to his disciples.

4.1–34 (Mt 13; Lk 8.4–18; 13.18–21): **Teaching in parables.*** **4–5:** The description is of "broadcast sowing" rather than of a wasteful or inept farmer. Allegorical* interpretation* makes *the seed* both *the word* and the ones who receive it (4.14–20). **12:** Adapted from Isa 6.9–10; those outside the new family of faith will not understand parables (see also 4.33). **13:** The disciples frequently do not understand (see sidebar on p. 1725). **21–22:** Jesus' now-hidden identity will be disclosed. **25:** Reversal of status is a hallmark of Jesus' teaching (Mt 7.2; 13.12; Lk 6.38). **26–27:** The enigmatic parables present a kingdom growing slowly but inexorably. **29:** *Harvest* connotes the final judgment (Joel 3.13). **31:** Mustard seeds (see Mt 13.31–32; Lk 13.18–19) are tiny, as are mustard bushes; the description of the bush as a shade tree is jarring.

a Or *mystery*   b Or *stumble*

35 On that day, when evening had come, he said to them, "Let us go across to the other side." 36 And leaving the crowd behind, they took him with them in the boat, just as he was. Other boats were with him. 37 A great windstorm arose, and the waves beat into the boat, so that the boat was already being swamped. 38 But he was in the stern, asleep on the cushion; and they woke him up and said to him, "Teacher, do you not care that we are perishing?" 39 He woke up and rebuked the wind, and said to the sea, "Peace! Be still!" Then the wind ceased, and there was a dead calm. 40 He said to them, "Why are you afraid? Have you still no faith?" 41 And they were filled with great awe and said to one another, "Who then is this, that even the wind and the sea obey him?"

4.35–41 (Mt 8.18, 23–27; Lk 8.22–25): **Stilling the storm.** Controlling nature is a contemporary sign of divine authority; similar tales of sleeping during storms are told of Dionysius. The disciples' fear and doubt anticipate the state of Jesus' followers at the crucifixion.

5 They came to the other side of the sea, to the country of the Gerasenes.ᵃ 2 And when he had stepped out of the boat, immediately a man out of the tombs with an unclean spirit met him. 3 He lived among the tombs; and no one could restrain him any more, even with a chain; 4 for he had often been restrained with shackles and chains, but the chains he wrenched apart, and the shackles he broke in pieces; and no one had the strength to subdue him. 5 Night and day among the tombs and on the mountains he was always howling and bruising himself with stones. 6 When he saw Jesus from a distance, he ran and bowed down before him; 7 and he shouted at the top of his voice, "What have you to do with me, Jesus, Son of the Most High God? I adjure you by God, do not torment me." 8 For he had said to him, "Come out of the man, you unclean spirit!" 9 Then Jesusᵇ asked him, "What is your name?" He replied, "My name is Legion; for we are many." 10 He begged him earnestly not to send them out of the country. 11 Now there on the hillside a great herd of swine was feeding; 12 and the unclean spiritsᶜ

begged him, "Send us into the swine; let us enter them." 13 So he gave them permission. And the unclean spirits came out and entered the swine; and the herd, numbering about two thousand, rushed down the steep bank into the sea, and were drowned in the sea.

14 The swineherds ran off and told it in the city and in the country. Then people came to see what it was that had happened. 15 They came to Jesus and saw the demoniac sitting there, clothed and in his right mind, the very man who had had the legion; and they were afraid. 16 Those who had seen what had happened to the demoniac and to the swine reported it. 17 Then they began to beg Jesusᵈ to leave their neighborhood. 18 As he was getting into the boat, the man who had been possessed by demons begged him that he might be with him. 19 But Jesusᵇ refused, and said to him, "Go home to your friends, and tell them how much the Lord has done for you, and what mercy he has shown you." 20 And he went away and began to proclaim in the Decapolis how much Jesus had done for him; and everyone was amazed.

5.1–20 (Mt 8.28–34; Lk 8.26–39): **The Gerasene demoniac.** Gerasa is in the Decapolis, a league of ten cities with mixed Jewish and gentile* populations. 6–7: Again, demons recognize Jesus' identity (1.24) while disciples and family members frequently do not. 9: A *legion* (a Latin term) consisted of four to six thousand soldiers in the Roman army; the name given to demons suggests negative views of the empire. 17: Fear stems from both Jesus' extraordinary powers and the threat of additional economic loss. 19: Rather than command secrecy, Jesus mandates a proclamation; the announcement is made in the Decapolis rather than the primarily Jewish Galilee or Judea.

21 When Jesus had crossed again in the boatᵉ to the other side, a great crowd gathered around him; and he was by the sea. 22 Then one of the leaders of the synagogue named Jairus came and, when he saw him, fell at his feet 23 and begged him repeatedly, "My little daughter is at the point of death.

a Other ancient authorities read *Gergesenes*; others, *Gadarenes* b Gk *he* c Gk *they* d Gk *him*
e Other ancient authorities lack *in the boat*

Come and lay your hands on her, so that she may be made well, and live." 24So he went with him.

And a large crowd followed him and pressed in on him. 25Now there was a woman who had been suffering from hemorrhages for twelve years. 26She had endured much under many physicians, and had spent all that she had; and she was no better, but rather grew worse. 27She had heard about Jesus, and came up behind him in the crowd and touched his cloak, 28for she said, "If I but touch his clothes, I will be made well." 29Immediately her hemorrhage stopped; and she felt in her body that she was healed of her disease. 30Immediately aware that power had gone forth from him, Jesus turned about in the crowd and said, "Who touched my clothes?" 31And his disciples said to him, "You see the crowd pressing in on you; how can you say, 'Who touched me?' " 32He looked all around to see who had done it. 33But the woman, knowing what had happened to her, came in fear and trembling, fell down before him, and told him the whole truth. 34He said to her, "Daughter, your faith has made you well; go in peace, and be healed of your disease."

35 While he was still speaking, some people came from the leader's house to say, "Your daughter is dead. Why trouble the teacher any further?" 36But overhearing*a* what they said, Jesus said to the leader of the synagogue, "Do not fear, only believe." 37He allowed no one to follow him except Peter, James, and John, the brother of James. 38When they came to the house of the leader of the synagogue, he saw a commotion, people weeping and wailing loudly. 39When he had entered, he said to them, "Why do you make a commotion and weep? The child is not dead but sleeping." 40And they laughed at him. Then he put them all outside, and took the child's father and mother and those who were with him, and went in where the child was. 41He took her by the hand and said to her, "Talitha cum," which means, "Little girl, get up!" 42And immediately the girl got up and began to walk about (she was twelve years of age). At this they were overcome with amazement. 43He strictly ordered

them that no one should know this, and told them to give her something to eat.

5.21–43 (Mt 9.18–26; Lk 8.40–56): **Two women healed. 25:** The *hemorrhages* are likely vaginal or uterine bleeding. **28:** She may have regarded Jesus as a magician. **31:** The disciples again fail to understand (4.41; 6.37, 52). **34:** *Made well* is the same term as "saved." For Mark, faith is the prerequisite for healing. **41:** The Aramaic* may have sounded to Mark's Greek audience like a magical incantation. **42:** The girl's age matches the years of the woman's illness; the girl is on the verge of menarche and marriage; the woman can now bear children. Mark frames one story with the other so that they become mutually informing; the same rhetorical* technique appears in 6.7–30: The disciples' mission frames the Baptist's death.

6 He left that place and came to his hometown, and his disciples followed him. 2On the sabbath he began to teach in the synagogue, and many who heard him were astounded. They said, "Where did this man get all this? What is this wisdom that has been given to him? What deeds of power are being done by his hands! 3Is not this the carpenter, the son of Mary*b* and brother of James and Joses and Judas and Simon, and are not his sisters here with us?" And they took offense*c* at him. 4Then Jesus said to them, "Prophets are not without honor, except in their hometown, and among their own kin, and in their own house." 5And he could do no deed of power there, except that he laid his hands on a few sick people and cured them. 6And he was amazed at their unbelief.

6.1–6 (Mt 13.54–58; Lk 4.16–30): **Rejection at home. 1:** The *hometown* is likely Nazareth (see 1.9), although Jesus and the twelve appear to be based in Capernaum (2.1). **3:** *Carpenter* (Gk., "tekton") is an artisan. Joseph's fate is not recorded. **4:** A proverbial saying. **5:** Lack of faith prevents miracles (according to Mt 13.58, Jesus is unwilling, not unable).

Then he went about among the villages teaching. 7He called the twelve and began to

a Or *ignoring*; other ancient authorities read *hearing*
b Other ancient authorities read *son of the carpenter and of Mary* *c* Or *stumbled*

send them out two by two, and gave them authority over the unclean spirits. 8He ordered them to take nothing for their journey except a staff; no bread, no bag, no money in their belts; 9but to wear sandals and not to put on two tunics. 10He said to them, "Wherever you enter a house, stay there until you leave the place. 11If any place will not welcome you and they refuse to hear you, as you leave, shake off the dust that is on your feet as a testimony against them." 12So they went out and proclaimed that all should repent. 13They cast out many demons, and anointed with oil many who were sick and cured them.

6.7–13 (Mt 10.1, 9–11; Lk 9.1–6): **Missionary instructions. 7:** Contrasts with Matthew's lack of mission and Luke's concern that the twelve remain with Jesus as witnesses. **8:** The disciples take even less than Cynics (traveling Greco-Roman philosophers who urged audiences to divest themselves of all social conventions and to live according to nature) and are completely dependent upon those who receive them. **12–13:** Repentance repeats the original message of Jesus and John, as teaching, exorcism, and healing show the disciples in Jesus' role. Recounting John's death (6.14–29) in the context of the mission, Mark indicates the dangers Jesus' followers face.

14 King Herod heard of it, for Jesus'[a] name had become known. Some were[b] saying, "John the baptizer has been raised from the dead; and for this reason these powers are at work in him." 15But others said, "It is Elijah." And others said, "It is a prophet, like one of the prophets of old." 16But when Herod heard of it, he said, "John, whom I beheaded, has been raised."

17 For Herod himself had sent men who arrested John, bound him, and put him in prison on account of Herodias, his brother Philip's wife, because Herod[c] had married her. 18For John had been telling Herod, "It is not lawful for you to have your brother's wife." 19And Herodias had a grudge against him, and wanted to kill him. But she could not, 20for Herod feared John, knowing that he was a righteous and holy man, and he protected him. When he heard him, he was greatly perplexed;[d] and yet he liked to listen

to him. 21But an opportunity came when Herod on his birthday gave a banquet for his courtiers and officers and for the leaders of Galilee. 22When his daughter Herodias[e] came in and danced, she pleased Herod and his guests; and the king said to the girl, "Ask me for whatever you wish, and I will give it." 23And he solemnly swore to her, "Whatever you ask me, I will give you, even half of my kingdom." 24She went out and said to her mother, "What should I ask for?" She replied, "The head of John the baptizer." 25Immediately she rushed back to the king and requested, "I want you to give me at once the head of John the Baptist on a platter." 26The king was deeply grieved; yet out of regard for his oaths and for the guests, he did not want to refuse her. 27Immediately the king sent a soldier of the guard with orders to bring John's[a] head. He went and beheaded him in the prison, 28brought his head on a platter, and gave it to the girl. Then the girl gave it to her mother. 29When his disciples heard about it, they came and took his body, and laid it in a tomb.

6.14–29 (Mt 14.1–12; Lk 9.7–9): **The death of John.** Herod Antipas, the son of Herod the Great (see Mt 2) was tetrarch, not king, of Galilee and Perea. **16:** Mark recounts the Baptist's death as a flashback. **18:** Marriage of one woman to two living brothers is forbidden (Lev 18.16; 20.21). **22:** Josephus* names the daughter Salome. *Girl* is the term describing Jairus's twelve-year-old daughter (5.42). There is an implicit contrast between the ruler Jairus's family and that of the tetrarch Antipas: One receives life; the other brings death. **24–26** (vv. 19–20): Mark seeks to exonerate Antipas. **29:** John's disciples prove more loyal than the twelve.

30 The apostles gathered around Jesus, and told him all that they had done and taught. 31He said to them, "Come away to a deserted place all by yourselves and rest a while." For many were coming and going, and they had no leisure even to eat. 32And they went away in the boat to a deserted place by themselves. 33Now many saw them

---

a Gk *his*   b Other ancient authorities read *He was*
c Gk *he*   d Other ancient authorities read *he did many things*   e Other ancient authorities read *the daughter of Herodias herself*

The Problem of the Disciples

Mark's portrait of the twelve is highly problematic. On the one hand, they come when Jesus calls them; they do not hesitate to leave their boats, their property, and their families (1.16–20; 2.14; 10.28). They successfully complete their first mission, during which they perform exorcisms, anoint* the sick with oil, and heal (6.12–13, 30).

On the other hand, they consistently fail to understand Jesus' teachings, exhortations,* and desires. As early as 1.37 they interrupt Jesus, who has withdrawn from the crowds for prayer and solitude. Verse 4.13 recounts Jesus' impatience for their lack of understanding of the parables.* In 4.40, following the calming of the storm, Jesus asks, "Why are you afraid? Have you still no faith?" Upon the healing of the woman with the hemorrhages, they chide Jesus: "You see the crowd pressing in on you; how can you say, 'Who touched me?'" (5.31).The disciples are unable to recognize Jesus' identity in the stilling of the storm (6.51–52); as Mark states, "They were utterly astounded, for they did not understand about the loaves, but their hearts were hardened." In 7.17–18, confused by Jesus' discussion of dietary regulations, the twelve ask Jesus about his parable. Jesus responds, "Then do you also fail to understand?" Following the miraculous feedings of first 5,000 and then 4,000, the disciples worry in 8.16, "We have no bread."

In the latter half of the Gospel, the failure of the twelve intensifies. They are unable to accept the passion predictions; they have insufficient faith to heal the epileptic child (9.18–19, 28–29); without warrant they reprove the exorcist who heals in Jesus' name (9.38–41); they attempt to prevent children from approaching Jesus (10.13–16); they yearn for positions of honor rather than service (10.35–40); and they display anger with each other (10.41–44). Judas betrays Jesus, Peter denies him, and the last collective action of the disciples in the Gospel is to forsake Jesus by fleeing from Gethsemane (14.50). Even the women who follow him from Galilee come to anoint the body: Had they known of, or believed in, the resurrection, this would not have been necessary. The last sentence of the original Gospel ends with the women fleeing from the tomb: "they said nothing to anyone, for they were afraid" (16.8).

Scholars debate the meaning of Mark's depiction of Jesus' followers. Apparently, both Mark and Luke found it disturbing, since in their Gospels the disciples are more faithful and more understanding. Perhaps Mark wanted the twelve to represent the range of believers: Members of Mark's community may have doubted, denied Jesus under pressure of persecution, or failed to grasp the need for service. Perhaps Mark wanted readers first to identify with the disciples and then, finally, to reject their misperceptions of Jesus' nature and mission.

going and recognized them, and they hurried there on foot from all the towns and arrived ahead of them. 34As he went ashore, he saw a great crowd; and he had compassion for them, because they were like sheep without a shepherd; and he began to teach them many things. 35When it grew late, his disciples came to him and said, "This is a deserted place, and the hour is now very late; 36send them away so that they may go into the surrounding country and villages and buy something for themselves to eat." 37But he answered them, "You give them something to eat." They said to him, "Are we to go and buy two hundred denarii*a* worth of bread, and give it to them to eat?" 38And he said to

a The denarius was the usual day's wage for a laborer

them, "How many loaves have you? Go and see." When they had found out, they said, "Five, and two fish." 39Then he ordered them to get all the people to sit down in groups on the green grass. 40So they sat down in groups of hundreds and of fifties. 41Taking the five loaves and the two fish, he looked up to heaven, and blessed and broke the loaves, and gave them to his disciples to set before the people; and he divided the two fish among them all. 42And all ate and were filled; 43and they took up twelve baskets full of broken pieces and of the fish. 44Those who had eaten the loaves numbered five thousand men.

6.30–44 (Mt 14.13–21; Lk 9.10–17; Jn 6.1–13): **Feeding the 5,000. 34:** *Sheep without a shepherd* is a proverbial saying (Num 27.17; 1 Kings 22.17; Ezek 34.5) which here suggests both John's death and Herod's ineptitude. Mark does not provide the content of Jesus' teaching. **37:** The disciples again misperceive (see sidebar on previous page). **41:** The description, echoing Elisha's miracle (2 Kings 4.42–44), provides no hint that the people shared their own food.

---

45 Immediately he made his disciples get into the boat and go on ahead to the other side, to Bethsaida, while he dismissed the crowd. 46After saying farewell to them, he went up on the mountain to pray.

47 When evening came, the boat was out on the sea, and he was alone on the land. 48When he saw that they were straining at the oars against an adverse wind, he came towards them early in the morning, walking on the sea. He intended to pass them by. 49But when they saw him walking on the sea, they thought it was a ghost and cried out; 50for they all saw him and were terrified. But immediately he spoke to them and said, "Take heart, it is I; do not be afraid." 51Then he got into the boat with them and the wind ceased. And they were utterly astounded, 52for they did not understand about the loaves, but their hearts were hardened.

53 When they had crossed over, they came to land at Gennesaret and moored the boat. 54When they got out of the boat, people at once recognized him, 55and rushed about that whole region and began to bring

the sick on mats to wherever they heard he was. 56And wherever he went, into villages or cities or farms, they laid the sick in the marketplaces, and begged him that they might touch even the fringe of his cloak; and all who touched it were healed.

6.45–56. 45–52 (Mt 14.22–36; Jn 6.15–21): **Walking on water. 45:** *Bethsaida* is a village north of the Sea of Galilee. **48:** The time is "the fourth watch," 3:00–6:00 a.m. **49:** A false vision of the resurrection. **52:** The disciples' misperception increases (see sidebar on previous page). **53–56: General healings.** Fringes (Num 15.38–40; Deut 22.12; Mt 9.20) remind Jewish wearers of divine commandments (Torah*).

---

7 Now when the Pharisees and some of the scribes who had come from Jerusalem gathered around him, 2they noticed that some of his disciples were eating with defiled hands, that is, without washing them. 3(For the Pharisees, and all the Jews, do not eat unless they thoroughly wash their hands,[a] thus observing the tradition of the elders; 4and they do not eat anything from the market unless they wash it;[b] and there are also many other traditions that they observe, the washing of cups, pots, and bronze kettles.[c]) 5So the Pharisees and the scribes asked him, "Why do your disciples not live[d] according to the tradition of the elders, but eat with defiled hands?" 6He said to them, "Isaiah prophesied rightly about you hypocrites, as it is written,

'This people honors me with their lips,
    but their hearts are far from me;
7 in vain do they worship me,
    teaching human precepts as
        doctrines.'
8You abandon the commandment of God and hold to human tradition."

9 Then he said to them, "You have a fine way of rejecting the commandment of God in order to keep your tradition! 10For Moses said, 'Honor your father and your mother'; and, 'Whoever speaks evil of father or mother must surely die.' 11But you say that

---

a Meaning of Gk uncertain   b Other ancient authorities read *and when they come from the marketplace, they do not eat unless they purify themselves*   c Other ancient authorities add *and beds*   d Gk *walk* if anyone tells father or mother, 'Whatever support you might have had from me is Corban' (that is, an offering to God*a*)— 12then you no longer permit doing anything for a father or mother, 13thus making void the word of God through your tradition that you have handed on. And you do many things like this."

14 Then he called the crowd again and said to them, "Listen to me, all of you, and understand: 15there is nothing outside a person that by going in can defile, but the things that come out are what defile."*b*

17 When he had left the crowd and entered the house, his disciples asked him about the parable. 18He said to them, "Then do you also fail to understand? Do you not see that whatever goes into a person from outside cannot defile, 19since it enters, not the heart but the stomach, and goes out into the sewer?" (Thus he declared all foods clean.) 20And he said, "It is what comes out of a person that defiles. 21For it is from within, from the human heart, that evil intentions come: fornication, theft, murder, 22adultery, avarice, wickedness, deceit, licentiousness, envy, slander, pride, folly. 23All these evil things come from within, and they defile a person."

7.1–23 (Mt 15.1–20): **Pharisaic traditions. 1–4:** Likely writing to a gentile★ audience, Mark explains Pharisaic customs. *Tradition of the elders* interprets biblical law and provides direction for sanctifying daily life. **5:** The focus on disciples suggests debate between church and synagogue;★ Jesus' followers began to differentiate themselves from Jewish practices. **6–7:** Cites Isa. 29.13 from the Septuagint.★ **11:** *Corban* is property dedicated to the Temple;★ this particular practice is not recorded in any Jewish text. **19:** Mark interprets Jesus to mean that the Torah's★ dietary laws are abrogated (see Acts 10, 15; Gal 2 for alternative explanations for rescinding biblical commandments).

24 From there he set out and went away to the region of Tyre.*c* He entered a house and did not want anyone to know he was there. Yet he could not escape notice, 25but a woman whose little daughter had an unclean spirit immediately heard about him, and she came and bowed down at his feet.

26Now the woman was a Gentile, of Syrophoenician origin. She begged him to cast the demon out of her daughter. 27He said to her, "Let the children be fed first, for it is not fair to take the children's food and throw it to the dogs." 28But she answered him, "Sir,*d* even the dogs under the table eat the children's crumbs." 29Then he said to her, "For saying that, you may go—the demon has left your daughter." 30So she went home, found the child lying on the bed, and the demon gone.

31 Then he returned from the region of Tyre, and went by way of Sidon towards the Sea of Galilee, in the region of the Decapolis. 32They brought to him a deaf man who had an impediment in his speech; and they begged him to lay his hand on him. 33He took him aside in private, away from the crowd, and put his fingers into his ears, and he spat and touched his tongue. 34Then looking up to heaven, he sighed and said to him, "Ephphatha," that is, "Be opened." 35And immediately his ears were opened, his tongue was released, and he spoke plainly. 36Then Jesus*e* ordered them to tell no one; but the more he ordered them, the more zealously they proclaimed it. 37They were astounded beyond measure, saying, "He has done everything well; he even makes the deaf to hear and the mute to speak."

7.24–37. 24–30 (Mt 15.21–28): **The Syrophoenician woman.** The gentile★ woman's detailed identification may indicate her high social standing (contrast Mt 15.22). **27:** Jesus' mission is to the *children:* The reference likely is to Israel, as opposed to gentiles. **29:** In Matthew's account, Jesus rewards her faith; here he acknowledges her cleverness. The woman makes no confession concerning Jesus' messianic status; she may regard him as a wonder-worker. **31–37** (Mt 15.29–31): **Healings in the Decapolis. 32–35:** Jesus' actions resemble magical techniques; elsewhere he heals by word alone. **36:** Again the command to secrecy fails.

8 In those days when there was again a great crowd without anything to eat, he

a Gk lacks *to God*　　*b* Other ancient authorities add verse 16, "*Let anyone with ears to hear listen*"　　*c* Other ancient authorities add *and Sidon*　　*d* Or *Lord*; other ancient authorities prefix *Yes*　　*e* Gk *he* called his disciples and said to them, 2"I have compassion for the crowd, because they have been with me now for three days and have nothing to eat. 3If I send them away hungry to their homes, they will faint on the way— and some of them have come from a great distance." 4His disciples replied, "How can one feed these people with bread here in the desert?" 5He asked them, "How many loaves do you have?" They said, "Seven." 6Then he ordered the crowd to sit down on the ground; and he took the seven loaves, and after giving thanks he broke them and gave them to his disciples to distribute; and they distributed them to the crowd. 7They had also a few small fish; and after blessing them, he ordered that these too should be distributed. 8They ate and were filled; and they took up the broken pieces left over, seven baskets full. 9Now there were about four thousand people. And he sent them away. 10And immediately he got into the boat with his disciples and went to the district of Dalmanutha.*a*

11 The Pharisees came and began to argue with him, asking him for a sign from heaven, to test him. 12And he sighed deeply in his spirit and said, "Why does this generation ask for a sign? Truly I tell you, no sign will be given to this generation." 13And he left them, and getting into the boat again, he went across to the other side.

14 Now the disciples*b* had forgotten to bring any bread; and they had only one loaf with them in the boat. 15And he cautioned them, saying, "Watch out—beware of the yeast of the Pharisees and the yeast of Herod."*c* 16They said to one another, "It is because we have no bread." 17And becoming aware of it, Jesus said to them, "Why are you talking about having no bread? Do you still not perceive or understand? Are your hearts hardened? 18Do you have eyes, and fail to see? Do you have ears, and fail to hear? And do you not remember? 19When I broke the five loaves for the five thousand, how many baskets full of broken pieces did you collect?" They said to him, "Twelve." 20"And the seven for the four thousand, how many baskets full of broken pieces did you collect?" And they said to him, "Seven."

21Then he said to them, "Do you not yet understand?"

22 They came to Bethsaida. Some people*d* brought a blind man to him and begged him to touch him. 23He took the blind man by the hand and led him out of the village; and when he had put saliva on his eyes and laid his hands on him, he asked him, "Can you see anything?" 24And the man*e* looked up and said, "I can see people, but they look like trees, walking." 25Then Jesus*e* laid his hands on his eyes again; and he looked intently and his sight was restored, and he saw everything clearly. 26Then he sent him away to his home, saying, "Do not even go into the village."*f*

8.1–26. 1–10 (Mt 15.32–39): **Feeding the 4,000.** The account resembles 6.30–44, perhaps here for a gentile* crowd. **10:** *Dalmanutha* is otherwise unattested in ancient sources; other manuscripts read Magdala; Matthew has Magadan. **11–13** (Mt 12.38–40; 16.1–4): **Sign from heaven.** Matthew records that the only sign will be that of Jonah. **14–21** (Mt 16.5–12; Lk 12.1): **Yeast and bread. 15:** *Yeast* symbolizes corruption. *Herod* refers to Herod Antipas (6.14–29). **16–17:** The disciples mistake this symbol for real bread; their misperception continues; compare Mt 16.12 (see sidebar "Parables" on p. 1687). **22–26: The blind man.** The two-stage healing may signal the Gospel's message: During his ministry, Jesus is misperceived; after the resurrection, followers begin to see clearly (see 9.9).

---

27 Jesus went on with his disciples to the villages of Caesarea Philippi; and on the way he asked his disciples, "Who do people say that I am?" 28And they answered him, "John the Baptist; and others, Elijah; and still others, one of the prophets." 29He asked them, "But who do you say that I am?" Peter answered him, "You are the Messiah."*g* 30And he sternly ordered them not to tell anyone about him.

31 Then he began to teach them that the Son of Man must undergo great suffering,

a Other ancient authorities read *Mageda* or *Magdala*
b Gk *they*   *c* Other ancient authorities read *the Herodians*   *d* Gk *They*   *e* Gk *he*   *f* Other ancient authorities add *or tell anyone in the village*
g Or *the Christ*

and be rejected by the elders, the chief priests, and the scribes, and be killed, and after three days rise again. ³²He said all this quite openly. And Peter took him aside and began to rebuke him. ³³But turning and looking at his disciples, he rebuked Peter and said, "Get behind me, Satan! For you are setting your mind not on divine things but on human things."

34 He called the crowd with his disciples, and said to them, "If any want to become my followers, let them deny themselves and take up their cross and follow me. ³⁵For those who want to save their life will lose it, and those who lose their life for my sake, and for the sake of the gospel,ᵃ will save it. ³⁶For what will it profit them to gain the whole world and forfeit their life? ³⁷Indeed, what can they give in return for their life? ³⁸Those who are ashamed of me and of my wordsᵇ in this adulterous and sinful generation, of them the Son of Man will also be ashamed when he comes in the glory of his Father with the holy angels." ¹And he said to them, "Truly I tell you, there are some standing here who will not taste death until they see that the kingdom of God has come withᶜ power."

8.27–9.1. 27–33 (Mt 16.13–23; Lk 9.18–22): **Revelation at Caesarea Philippi.** Caesarea Philippi, in northern Galilee, borders Jewish and gentile★ areas. **29:** Messiah,★ a Hebrew term meaning "anointed,"★ is equivalent to the Greek term "Christ." **31:** First of three passion predictions (9.30–32; 10.33–34). **32–33:** Jesus speaks plainly of suffering but otherwise speaks in parables;★ Peter rejects the idea that the messiah will suffer and die. **8.34–9.1 (Mt 16.24–28; Lk 9.23–27): Discipleship.** Disciples must reject human standards and personal glory (8.32–33). **38:** Adulterous is prophetic★ language for idolatry★ and the international alliances that often accompany it (see Hosea). Verses 8.35 and 10.31 frame the internal section by emphasizing contrasts in values and the model of the little child. The same themes repeat in 10.35–45. **9.1:** Mark expects the "parousia,"★ the return of Jesus in judgment, during his generation.

2 Six days later, Jesus took with him Peter and James and John, and led them up a high mountain apart, by themselves. And he was transfigured before them, ³and his clothes became dazzling white, such as no oneᵈ on earth could bleach them. ⁴And there appeared to them Elijah with Moses, who were talking with Jesus. ⁵Then Peter said to Jesus, "Rabbi, it is good for us to be here; let us make three dwellings,ᵉ one for you, one for Moses, and one for Elijah." ⁶He did not know what to say, for they were terrified. ⁷Then a cloud overshadowed them, and from the cloud there came a voice, "This is my Son, the Beloved;ᶠ listen to him!" ⁸Suddenly when they looked around, they saw no one with them any more, but only Jesus.

9 As they were coming down the mountain, he ordered them to tell no one about what they had seen, until after the Son of Man had risen from the dead. ¹⁰So they kept the matter to themselves, questioning what this rising from the dead could mean. ¹¹Then they asked him, "Why do the scribes say that Elijah must come first?" ¹²He said to them, "Elijah is indeed coming first to restore all things. How then is it written about the Son of Man, that he is to go through many sufferings and be treated with contempt? ¹³But I tell you that Elijah has come, and they did to him whatever they pleased, as it is written about him."

9.2–13 (Mt 17.1–8; Lk 9.28–36): **The transfiguration.** Lacking resurrection appearances, Mark may intend the transfiguration to show Jesus' glorification. **9:** One explanation for messianic secrecy: Jesus' mission cannot be understood apart from cross and resurrection. **13:** Elijah was to herald the end of the age (see Mal 3.1; 4); Jesus' comment cryptically refers to the Baptist (see also 1 Kings 19).

14 When they came to the disciples, they saw a great crowd around them, and some scribes arguing with them. ¹⁵When the whole crowd saw him, they were immediately overcome with awe, and they ran forward to greet him. ¹⁶He asked them, "What are you arguing about with them?" ¹⁷Someone from the crowd answered him,

a Other ancient authorities read lose their life for the sake of the gospel　　b Other ancient authorities read and of mine　　c Or in　　d Gk no fuller　　e Or tents f Or my beloved Son

"Teacher, I brought you my son; he has a spirit that makes him unable to speak; ¹⁸and whenever it seizes him, it dashes him down; and he foams and grinds his teeth and becomes rigid; and I asked your disciples to cast it out, but they could not do so." ¹⁹He answered them, "You faithless generation, how much longer must I be among you? How much longer must I put up with you? Bring him to me." ²⁰And they brought the boy*ᵃ* to him. When the spirit saw him, immediately it convulsed the boy,*ᵃ* and he fell on the ground and rolled about, foaming at the mouth. ²¹Jesus*ᵇ* asked the father, "How long has this been happening to him?" And he said, "From childhood. ²²It has often cast him into the fire and into the water, to destroy him; but if you are able to do anything, have pity on us and help us." ²³Jesus said to him, "If you are able!—All things can be done for the one who believes." ²⁴Immediately the father of the child cried out,*ᶜ* "I believe; help my unbelief!" ²⁵When Jesus saw that a crowd came running together, he rebuked the unclean spirit, saying to it, "You spirit that keeps this boy from speaking and hearing, I command you, come out of him, and never enter him again!" ²⁶After crying out and convulsing him terribly, it came out, and the boy was like a corpse, so that most of them said, "He is dead." ²⁷But Jesus took him by the hand and lifted him up, and he was able to stand. ²⁸When he had entered the house, his disciples asked him privately, "Why could we not cast it out?" ²⁹He said to them, "This kind can come out only through prayer."*ᵈ*

9.14–29 (Mt 17.14–21; Lk 9.37–42): **The possessed child. 18:** The disciples fail to use appropriate prayer (9.29). **19:** Jesus rejects being perceived only as a miracle worker. **24:** The father's cry may speak to those in Mark's community who have undergone persecution. **29:** Healings arise from divine response, not human magic.

30 They went on from there and passed through Galilee. He did not want anyone to know it; ³¹for he was teaching his disciples, saying to them, "The Son of Man is to be betrayed into human hands, and they will kill

him, and three days after being killed, he will rise again." ³²But they did not understand what he was saying and were afraid to ask him.

33 Then they came to Capernaum; and when he was in the house he asked them, "What were you arguing about on the way?" ³⁴But they were silent, for on the way they had argued with one another who was the greatest. ³⁵He sat down, called the twelve, and said to them, "Whoever wants to be first must be last of all and servant of all." ³⁶Then he took a little child and put it among them; and taking it in his arms, he said to them, ³⁷"Whoever welcomes one such child in my name welcomes me, and whoever welcomes me welcomes not me but the one who sent me."

38 John said to him, "Teacher, we saw someone*ᵉ* casting out demons in your name, and we tried to stop him, because he was not following us." ³⁹But Jesus said, "Do not stop him; for no one who does a deed of power in my name will be able soon afterward to speak evil of me. ⁴⁰Whoever is not against us is for us. ⁴¹For truly I tell you, whoever gives you a cup of water to drink because you bear the name of Christ will by no means lose the reward.

9.30–41. 30–32 (Mt 17.22–23; Lk 9.43–45): **The second passion prediction.** See Mk 8.31; 10.33. The disciples still do not comprehend. **33–37** (Mt 18.1–5; Lk 9.46–48): **First and last.** The disciples recognize the subject of superiority was contrary to Jesus' insistence on selflessness. Children represent powerlessness; as divine "son," Jesus is also in the role of child. **38–41** (Lk 9.49–59): **The rival exorcist. 38:** *In your name* complements v. 37's *in my name.* **39–40** (Mt 12.30; Lk 11.23): Familiarity will eventually lead to faith. Mark's saying that those who are not against Jesus are for him is much more positive than Matthew and Luke's rendition.

42 "If any of you put a stumbling block before one of these little ones who believe in me,*ᶠ* it would be better for you if a great

a Gk *him*   *b* Gk *He*   *c* Other ancient authorities add *with tears*   *d* Other ancient authorities add *and fasting*   *e* Other ancient authorities add *who does not follow us*   *f* Other ancient authorities lack *in me* millstone were hung around your neck and you were thrown into the sea. 43 If your hand causes you to stumble, cut it off; it is better for you to enter life maimed than to have two hands and to go to hell,[a] to the unquenchable fire.[b] 45 And if your foot causes you to stumble, cut it off; it is better for you to enter life lame than to have two feet and to be thrown into hell.[a,b] 47 And if your eye causes you to stumble, tear it out; it is better for you to enter the kingdom of God with one eye than to have two eyes and to be thrown into hell,[a] 48 where their worm never dies, and the fire is never quenched.

49 "For everyone will be salted with fire.[c] 50 Salt is good; but if salt has lost its saltiness, how can you season it?[d] Have salt in yourselves, and be at peace with one another."

9.42–50. 42–48 (Mt 5.29–30; 18.6–9; Lk 17.1–2): **Warnings against stumbling blocks. 42:** *Little ones* (see comments on the "little child" in 9.33–37) are those who follow Jesus. **43–47:** The sayings express the radicality of Jesus' message. **48:** See Isa 66.24. **49–50** (Mt 5.13; Lk 14.34–35): *Salt* perhaps refers to sacrificial offerings and therefore to purification and integrity.

〰️〰️〰️〰️〰️〰️〰️〰️〰️

10 He left that place and went to the region of Judea and[e] beyond the Jordan. And crowds again gathered around him; and, as was his custom, he again taught them.

2 Some Pharisees came, and to test him they asked, "Is it lawful for a man to divorce his wife?" 3 He answered them, "What did Moses command you?" 4 They said, "Moses allowed a man to write a certificate of dismissal and to divorce her." 5 But Jesus said to them, "Because of your hardness of heart he wrote this commandment for you. 6 But from the beginning of creation, 'God made them male and female.' 7 'For this reason a man shall leave his father and mother and be joined to his wife,[f] 8 and the two shall become one flesh.' So they are no longer two, but one flesh. 9 Therefore what God has joined together, let no one separate."

10 Then in the house the disciples asked him again about this matter. 11 He said to them, "Whoever divorces his wife and marries another commits adultery against her; 12 and if she divorces her husband and marries another, she commits adultery."

13 People were bringing little children to him in order that he might touch them; and the disciples spoke sternly to them. 14 But when Jesus saw this, he was indignant and said to them, "Let the little children come to me; do not stop them; for it is to such as these that the kingdom of God belongs. 15 Truly I tell you, whoever does not receive the kingdom of God as a little child will never enter it." 16 And he took them up in his arms, laid his hands on them, and blessed them.

10.1–16. 1–12 (Mt 5.31–32; 19.1–12; Lk 16.18): **Marriage and divorce. 2:** Pharisees* accepted divorce but debated acceptable reasons for it. **3–4:** See Deut 24.1–4. **12:** Sources from the Diaspora* indicate Jewish women could and did sue for divorce. Some of the Dead Sea scrolls also forbid divorce, and certainly forbid polygamy, by appeal to Gen 2. Mark leaves open the possibility of separation, as long as no remarriage takes place. **13–16** (Mt 19.13–15; Lk 18.15–17): **Blessing children.** See 9.36; Mark continues to contrast the ideal of the little child with the behavior of the disciples.

〰️〰️〰️〰️〰️〰️〰️〰️〰️

17 As he was setting out on a journey, a man ran up and knelt before him, and asked him, "Good Teacher, what must I do to inherit eternal life?" 18 Jesus said to him, "Why do you call me good? No one is good but God alone. 19 You know the commandments: 'You shall not murder; You shall not commit adultery; You shall not steal; You shall not bear false witness; You shall not defraud; Honor your father and mother.'" 20 He said to him, "Teacher, I have kept all these since my youth." 21 Jesus, looking at him, loved him and said, "You lack one thing; go, sell what you own, and give the money[g] to the poor, and you will have treasure in heaven; then

---

a Gk *Gehenna*　b Verses 44 and 46 (which are identical with verse 48) are lacking in the best ancient authorities　c Other ancient authorities either add or substitute *and every sacrifice will be salted with salt*　d Or *how can you restore its saltiness?*　e Other ancient authorities lack *and*　f Other ancient authorities lack *and be joined to his wife*　g Gk lacks *the money* come, follow me." 22When he heard this, he was shocked and went away grieving, for he had many possessions.

23 Then Jesus looked around and said to his disciples, "How hard it will be for those who have wealth to enter the kingdom of God!" 24And the disciples were perplexed at these words. But Jesus said to them again, "Children, how hard it is*ᵃ* to enter the kingdom of God! 25It is easier for a camel to go through the eye of a needle than for someone who is rich to enter the kingdom of God." 26They were greatly astounded and said to one another,*ᵇ* "Then who can be saved?" 27Jesus looked at them and said, "For mortals it is impossible, but not for God; for God all things are possible."

28 Peter began to say to him, "Look, we have left everything and followed you." 29Jesus said, "Truly I tell you, there is no one who has left house or brothers or sisters or mother or father or children or fields, for my sake and for the sake of the good news,*ᶜ* 30who will not receive a hundredfold now in this age—houses, brothers and sisters, mothers and children, and fields, with persecutions—and in the age to come eternal life. 31But many who are first will be last, and the last will be first."

10.17–31 (Mt 19.16–30; Lk 18.18–30): **The rich man.** 18: Jesus insists all honor be directed to God. 19: See Ex 20.12–16; Deut 5.16–20. 21: Jesus recognizes the man's sincerity. 25: Riches distract and cause self-glorification. 28: Peter exaggerates: He retains his home in Capernaum (1.29). 30: Mark omits "fathers"; the new family does not place anyone as head of the household or patriarch. 31 (Mt 19.30; 20.16; Lk 13.30): See comment on 8.35.

---

32 They were on the road, going up to Jerusalem, and Jesus was walking ahead of them; they were amazed, and those who followed were afraid. He took the twelve aside again and began to tell them what was to happen to him, 33saying, "See, we are going up to Jerusalem, and the Son of Man will be handed over to the chief priests and the scribes, and they will condemn him to death; then they will hand him over to the Gentiles; 34they will mock him, and spit upon him,

and flog him, and kill him; and after three days he will rise again."

35 James and John, the sons of Zebedee, came forward to him and said to him, "Teacher, we want you to do for us whatever we ask of you." 36And he said to them, "What is it you want me to do for you?" 37And they said to him, "Grant us to sit, one at your right hand and one at your left, in your glory." 38But Jesus said to them, "You do not know what you are asking. Are you able to drink the cup that I drink, or be baptized with the baptism that I am baptized with?" 39They replied, "We are able." Then Jesus said to them, "The cup that I drink you will drink; and with the baptism with which I am baptized, you will be baptized; 40but to sit at my right hand or at my left is not mine to grant, but it is for those for whom it has been prepared."

41 When the ten heard this, they began to be angry with James and John. 42So Jesus called them and said to them, "You know that among the Gentiles those whom they recognize as their rulers lord it over them, and their great ones are tyrants over them. 43But it is not so among you; but whoever wishes to become great among you must be your servant, 44and whoever wishes to be first among you must be slave of all. 45For the Son of Man came not to be served but to serve, and to give his life a ransom for many."

10.32–45. 32–34 (Mt 20.17–19; Lk 18.31–34): **The third passion prediction. 32:** Fear marks the disciples throughout the rest of the gospel. 35–45 (Mt 20.20–28; Lk 22.24–27): **James and John.** The disciples have yet to learn Jesus' lessons of self-loss and humility; Matthew protects their role by assigning the question to their mother. 45: *Ransom* is paid to release captives and slaves; from whom or what Jesus' death purchases release (Satan? sin?) is not specified (see comment on Mt 20.28).

---

46 They came to Jericho. As he and his disciples and a large crowd were leaving Jer-

---

a Other ancient authorities add *for those who trust in riches*   *b* Other ancient authorities read *to him*   *c* Or *gospel* icho, Bartimaeus son of Timaeus, a blind beggar, was sitting by the roadside. [47]When he heard that it was Jesus of Nazareth, he began to shout out and say, "Jesus, Son of David, have mercy on me!" [48]Many sternly ordered him to be quiet, but he cried out even more loudly, "Son of David, have mercy on me!" [49]Jesus stood still and said, "Call him here." And they called the blind man, saying to him, "Take heart; get up, he is calling you." [50]So throwing off his cloak, he sprang up and came to Jesus. [51]Then Jesus said to him, "What do you want me to do for you?" The blind man said to him, "My teacher,[a] let me see again." [52]Jesus said to him, "Go; your faith has made you well." Immediately he regained his sight and followed him on the way.

10.46–52 (Mt 20.29–34; Lk 18.35–43): **Bartimaeus.** *Bartimaeus* means *son of Timaeus;* Mark explains the Aramaic* formulation. **47:** *Son of David* indicates Jesus' messianic kingship, which takes on heightened political implications as Jesus nears Jerusalem. **48:** Here the crowd ironically invokes the secrecy motif.*

11 When they were approaching Jerusalem, at Bethphage and Bethany, near the Mount of Olives, he sent two of his disciples [2]and said to them, "Go into the village ahead of you, and immediately as you enter it, you will find tied there a colt that has never been ridden; untie it and bring it. [3]If anyone says to you, 'Why are you doing this?' just say this, 'The Lord needs it and will send it back here immediately.' " [4]They went away and found a colt tied near a door, outside in the street. As they were untying it, [5]some of the bystanders said to them, "What are you doing, untying the colt?" [6]They told them what Jesus had said; and they allowed them to take it. [7]Then they brought the colt to Jesus and threw their cloaks on it; and he sat on it. [8]Many people spread their cloaks on the road, and others spread leafy branches that they had cut in the fields. [9]Then those who went ahead and those who followed were shouting,

"Hosanna!

Blessed is the one who comes in the name of the Lord!

[10] Blessed is the coming kingdom of our ancestor David!

Hosanna in the highest heaven!"

[11] Then he entered Jerusalem and went into the temple; and when he had looked around at everything, as it was already late, he went out to Bethany with the twelve.

11.1–11 (Mt 21.1–11; Lk 19.28–38; Jn 12.12–18): **Entering Jerusalem.** Mark does not specify whether Jesus had friends in Jerusalem or whether his command was based on foreknowledge. The *colt* recollects Zech 9.9 and thereby has messianic and royal implications. **10:** On *David,* see comment on 10.47.

[12] On the following day, when they came from Bethany, he was hungry. [13]Seeing in the distance a fig tree in leaf, he went to see whether perhaps he would find anything on it. When he came to it, he found nothing but leaves, for it was not the season for figs. [14]He said to it, "May no one ever eat fruit from you again." And his disciples heard it.

[15] Then they came to Jerusalem. And he entered the temple and began to drive out those who were selling and those who were buying in the temple, and he overturned the tables of the money changers and the seats of those who sold doves; [16]and he would not allow anyone to carry anything through the temple. [17]He was teaching and saying, "Is it not written,

'My house shall be called a house of prayer for all the nations'?

But you have made it a den of robbers."

[18]And when the chief priests and the scribes heard it, they kept looking for a way to kill him; for they were afraid of him, because the whole crowd was spellbound by his teaching. [19]And when evening came, Jesus and his disciples[b] went out of the city.

[20] In the morning as they passed by, they saw the fig tree withered away to its roots. [21]Then Peter remembered and said to him, "Rabbi, look! The fig tree that you cursed has withered." [22]Jesus answered them, "Have[c]

a Aramaic *Rabbouni*   b Gk *they:* other ancient authorities read *he*   c Other ancient authorities read "*If you have* faith in God. 23Truly I tell you, if you say to this mountain, 'Be taken up and thrown into the sea,' and if you do not doubt in your heart, but believe that what you say will come to pass, it will be done for you. 24So I tell you, whatever you ask for in prayer, believe that you have received*a* it, and it will be yours.

25 "Whenever you stand praying, forgive, if you have anything against anyone; so that your Father in heaven may also forgive you your trespasses."*b*

11.12–25. 12–14 (Mt 21.18–20; Lk 13.6–9): **Cursing the fig tree.** Mark may intend the tree to symbolize Jerusalem; its cursing and withering (11.20) frame Jesus' entry into the city. Like the tree, the city fails to bear fruit; much of Jerusalem was destroyed during the war against Rome in 66–70 CE. **15–19** (Mt 21.12–17; Lk 19.45–48; Jn 2.13–25): **The Temple* protest.** See comment on Mt 21.12–13. **17:** See Isa. 56.7; Jer 7.11. The *Temple* was a *house of prayer for all the nations;* the scene is set in the Court of the Gentiles.* **18:** The crowds support Jesus; the *chief priests* and *scribes* replace the Pharisees* as Jesus' opponents. **20–25:** **The dead fig tree.** The two-stage miracle (see 8.22–26) frames the entry into Jerusalem. **21:** *Rabbi* means "my teacher." **24–25:** Mark frequently highlights prayer (1.35; 9.29; 11.17); the verses echo the Lord's Prayer (see Mt. 6.9–13; Lk 11.2–4).

---

27 Again they came to Jerusalem. As he was walking in the temple, the chief priests, the scribes, and the elders came to him 28and said, "By what authority are you doing these things? Who gave you this authority to do them?" 29Jesus said to them, "I will ask you one question; answer me, and I will tell you by what authority I do these things. 30Did the baptism of John come from heaven, or was it of human origin? Answer me." 31They argued with one another, "If we say, 'From heaven,' he will say, 'Why then did you not believe him?' 32But shall we say, 'Of human origin'?"—they were afraid of the crowd, for all regarded John as truly a prophet. 33So they answered Jesus, "We do not know." And Jesus said to them, "Neither will I tell you by what authority I am doing these things."

11.27–33 (Mt 21.23–27; Lk 20.1–8; Jn 2.18–22): **Temple* teachings. 29:** Jesus answers a question with a question and so avoids his interlocutors' trap (see 12.13–17). Jesus speaks not on the authority of his teachers (see 1.22) but on his own.

12 Then he began to speak to them in parables. "A man planted a vineyard, put a fence around it, dug a pit for the wine press, and built a watchtower; then he leased it to tenants and went to another country. 2When the season came, he sent a slave to the tenants to collect from them his share of the produce of the vineyard. 3But they seized him, and beat him, and sent him away empty-handed. 4And again he sent another slave to them; this one they beat over the head and insulted. 5Then he sent another, and that one they killed. And so it was with many others; some they beat, and others they killed. 6He had still one other, a beloved son. Finally he sent him to them, saying, 'They will respect my son.' 7But those tenants said to one another, 'This is the heir; come, let us kill him, and the inheritance will be ours.' 8So they seized him, killed him, and threw him out of the vineyard. 9What then will the owner of the vineyard do? He will come and destroy the tenants and give the vineyard to others. 10Have you not read this scripture:

'The stone that the builders rejected
    has become the cornerstone;*c*
11 this was the Lord's doing,
    and it is amazing in our eyes'?"

12 When they realized that he had told this parable against them, they wanted to arrest him, but they feared the crowd. So they left him and went away.

12.1–12 (Mt 21.33–46; Lk 20.9–19): **The parable* of the vineyard.** In Isa 5.1–7 the *vineyard* represents Israel. **6:** *Beloved son* echoes the baptism* (1.11) and transfiguration (9.7). **7:** A reference to the cross is unavoidable. **10:** Cites Ps 118.22–23 (Septuagint*). **12:**

---

a Other ancient authorities read *are receiving*
b Other ancient authorities add verse 26, "*But if you do not forgive, neither will your Father in heaven forgive your trespasses.*"   *c* Or *keystone*

The chief priests, scribes,* and elders recognize they are the "tenants."

13 Then they sent to him some Pharisees and some Herodians to trap him in what he said. 14And they came and said to him, "Teacher, we know that you are sincere, and show deference to no one; for you do not regard people with partiality, but teach the way of God in accordance with truth. Is it lawful to pay taxes to the emperor, or not? 15Should we pay them, or should we not?" But knowing their hypocrisy, he said to them, "Why are you putting me to the test? Bring me a denarius and let me see it." 16And they brought one. Then he said to them, "Whose head is this, and whose title?" They answered, "The emperor's." 17Jesus said to them, "Give to the emperor the things that are the emperor's, and to God the things that are God's." And they were utterly amazed at him.

18 Some Sadducees, who say there is no resurrection, came to him and asked him a question, saying, 19"Teacher, Moses wrote for us that if a man's brother dies, leaving a wife but no child, the man^a shall marry the widow and raise up children for his brother. 20There were seven brothers; the first married and, when he died, left no children; 21and the second married the widow^b and died, leaving no children; and the third likewise; 22none of the seven left children. Last of all the woman herself died. 23In the resurrection^c whose wife will she be? For the seven had married her."

24 Jesus said to them, "Is not this the reason you are wrong, that you know neither the scriptures nor the power of God? 25For when they rise from the dead, they neither marry nor are given in marriage, but are like angels in heaven. 26And as for the dead being raised, have you not read in the book of Moses, in the story about the bush, how God said to him, 'I am the God of Abraham, the God of Isaac, and the God of Jacob'? 27He is God not of the dead, but of the living; you are quite wrong."

28 One of the scribes came near and heard them disputing with one another, and seeing that he answered them well, he asked him, "Which commandment is the first of all?" 29Jesus answered, "The first is, 'Hear, O Israel: the Lord our God, the Lord is one; 30you shall love the Lord your God with all your heart, and with all your soul, and with all your mind, and with all your strength.' 31The second is this, 'You shall love your neighbor as yourself.' There is no other commandment greater than these." 32Then the scribe said to him, "You are right, Teacher; you have truly said that 'he is one, and besides him there is no other'; 33and 'to love him with all the heart, and with all the understanding, and with all the strength,' and 'to love one's neighbor as oneself,'—this is much more important than all whole burnt offerings and sacrifices." 34When Jesus saw that he answered wisely, he said to him, "You are not far from the kingdom of God." After that no one dared to ask him any question.

12.13–17: **Paying taxes.** See comment on Mt 22.15–22 (Lk 20.20–26). **18–27: Angelic bodies.** See comment on Mt 22.23–33 (Lk 20.27–40). **28–34: The great commandment.** See comment on Mt 22.34–30 (Lk 10.25–28).

35 While Jesus was teaching in the temple, he said, "How can the scribes say that the Messiah^d is the son of David? 36David himself, by the Holy Spirit, declared,

'The Lord said to my Lord,

"Sit at my right hand,

until I put your enemies under your feet."'

37David himself calls him Lord; so how can he be his son?" And the large crowd was listening to him with delight.

38 As he taught, he said, "Beware of the scribes, who like to walk around in long robes, and to be greeted with respect in the marketplaces, 39and to have the best seats in the synagogues and places of honor at banquets! 40They devour widows' houses and for the sake of appearance say long prayers. They will receive the greater condemnation."

41 He sat down opposite the treasury, and watched the crowd putting money into

a Gk his brother   b Gk her   c Other ancient authorities add when they rise   d Or the Christ the treasury. Many rich people put in large sums. 42A poor widow came and put in two small copper coins, which are worth a penny. 43Then he called his disciples and said to them, "Truly I tell you, this poor widow has put in more than all those who are contributing to the treasury. 44For all of them have contributed out of their abundance; but she out of her poverty has put in everything she had, all she had to live on."

12.35–42. 35–37 (Mt 22.41–46; Lk 20.41–44): **Son of David. 35:** Although in danger from the priests, Jesus continues to teach in the Temple.* His question disturbs traditional beliefs in the Davidic (royal, political) messiah.* **36:** Psalm 110 is the most quoted passage from scripture. The crowds appear to appreciate Jesus' besting of the scribes.* **38–40** (Mt 23.1, 6; Lk 20.45–47): **Condemnation of the scribes.** Jesus condemns hypocrisy and self-aggrandizement; for Mark, the warnings should not be lost on Jesus' own followers. **41–44** (Lk 21.1–4): **The widow in the Temple.*** **41:** *Treasury* refers to "tzedakah" or charity boxes; the *widow* participates in an act of Jewish piety. **42:** The *coin* is a lepton; one hundred twenty leptons equal one denarius. Her deed evokes Jesus' promise that the one who gives all will obtain all (10.23–31) and anticipates the anointing* by the woman who also did what she could with what she had (14.3–9).

---

13 As he came out of the temple, one of his disciples said to him, "Look, Teacher, what large stones and what large buildings!" 2Then Jesus asked him, "Do you see these great buildings? Not one stone will be left here upon another; all will be thrown down."

13.1–2 (Mt 24.1–3; Lk 19.43–44; 21.5–7): **Predicting Jerusalem's destruction. 1:** The stones measured 38x18x12 feet. **2:** Scholars debate whether Mark knew of Jerusalem's destruction. One wall, the Western Wall or the "Kotel," remains standing from Herod's Temple;* the site is a sacred location for Jews.

---

3 When he was sitting on the Mount of Olives opposite the temple, Peter, James, John, and Andrew asked him privately, 4"Tell us, when will this be, and what will be the sign that all these things are about to be accomplished?" 5Then Jesus began to say to them, "Beware that no one leads you astray. 6Many will come in my name and say, 'I am he!'*a* and they will lead many astray. 7When you hear of wars and rumors of wars, do not be alarmed; this must take place, but the end is still to come. 8For nation will rise against nation, and kingdom against kingdom; there will be earthquakes in various places; there will be famines. This is but the beginning of the birth pangs.

9 "As for yourselves, beware; for they will hand you over to councils; and you will be beaten in synagogues; and you will stand before governors and kings because of me, as a testimony to them. 10And the good news*b* must first be proclaimed to all nations. 11When they bring you to trial and hand you over, do not worry beforehand about what you are to say; but say whatever is given you at that time, for it is not you who speak, but the Holy Spirit. 12Brother will betray brother to death, and a father his child, and children will rise against parents and have them put to death; 13and you will be hated by all because of my name. But the one who endures to the end will be saved.

14 "But when you see the desolating sacrilege set up where it ought not to be (let the reader understand), then those in Judea must flee to the mountains; 15the one on the housetop must not go down or enter the house to take anything away; 16the one in the field must not turn back to get a coat. 17Woe to those who are pregnant and to those who are nursing infants in those days! 18Pray that it may not be in winter. 19For in those days there will be suffering, such as has not been from the beginning of the creation that God created until now, no, and never will be. 20And if the Lord had not cut short those days, no one would be saved; but for the sake of the elect, whom he chose, he has cut short those days. 21And if anyone says to you at that time, 'Look! Here is the Messiah!'*c* or 'Look! There he is!'—do not believe it. 22False messiahs*d* and false prophets will appear and produce signs and omens, to lead astray, if possible, the elect.

---

a Gk I am　　*b* Gk gospel　　*c* Or the Christ
d Or christs

Apocalyptic

The term "apocalyptic"✶ derives from a Greek word meaning "to uncover, to reveal." It gives its name to the last book of the Christian canon,✶ the Book of Revelation, which is also known as the Apocalypse of John (see Rev 1.1). The name also extends to the type of literature associated with the Book of Revelation: Apocalyptic materials contain elements such as a pessimistic view of the present world, a dualistic outlook that divides people into the few to be saved and the many damned, tours of heaven and hell, descriptions of future cataclysms, cryptic signs in need of interpretation, and angels to provide such interpretation. Examples are found in the Hebrew Scriptures✶ (such as the latter half of the Book of Daniel) as well as in the Pseudepigrapha (1 Enoch,✶ 2 Baruch, 4 Ezra), the Dead Sea scrolls (1QM, the War of the Sons of Light against the Sons of Darkness), and the New Testament Apocrypha✶ (Apocalypse of Peter). Frequently the texts are ascribed to ancient worthies (Baruch, Ezra, Abraham, even Adam), who then "predict" the future.

Within the Gospel tradition, Mark 13—often called the Little Apocalypse to distinguish it from the Book of Revelation—contains several hallmarks of the genre:✶ predictions of destruction, heavenly portents, the gathering of the elect, etc. Matthew appropriates much of this material, but takes it out of its eschatological✶ or end-of-the-world context. What for Mark are signs of the end (persecution, family disintegration) are for Matthew indications that one is living according to Jesus' teaching.

Although the literature can be frightening, apocalyptic writing serves to encourage the group to which it is addressed. It urges steadfastness in the face of persecution, assures the reader of heavenly control over what appears to be a chaotic world, and offers the promise that, with the momentous entry of the divine into human history, the righteous will be rewarded and the wicked punished. Likely not all early readers took the signs literally; rather, they recognized the conventional aspects of the genre.

Apocalyptic literature is found, cross-culturally, among both groups that are persecuted and groups that perceive themselves to be fully disenfranchised, with no hope of affecting their future. Scholars debate whether Jesus was an apocalyptic prophet,✶ or whether his early followers added apocalyptic statements to the collections of his sayings. On the one hand, the parables✶ are not typically apocalyptic; they use quite mundane images to convey their points. On the other, Mk 13 and its parallels in Matthew and Luke, the writings of Paul (especially 1 Thessalonians), and quite likely the preaching of John the Baptist all suggest that apocalyptic thinking was part of Jesus' legacy.

---

23 But be alert; I have already told you everything.

24 "But in those days, after that suffering,

the sun will be darkened,

and the moon will not give its light,

25 and the stars will be falling

from heaven,

and the powers in the heavens will be shaken.

26 Then they will see 'the Son of Man coming in clouds' with great power and glory. 27 Then he will send out the angels, and gather his elect from the four winds, from the ends of the earth to the ends of heaven.

28 "From the fig tree learn its lesson: as soon as its branch becomes tender and puts forth its leaves, you know that summer is near. 29 So also, when you see these things

taking place, you know that he[a] is near, at the very gates. 30Truly I tell you, this generation will not pass away until all these things have taken place. 31Heaven and earth will pass away, but my words will not pass away.

32 "But about that day or hour no one knows, neither the angels in heaven, nor the Son, but only the Father. 33Beware, keep alert;[b] for you do not know when the time will come. 34It is like a man going on a journey, when he leaves home and puts his slaves in charge, each with his work, and commands the doorkeeper to be on the watch. 35Therefore, keep awake—for you do not know when the master of the house will come, in the evening, or at midnight, or at cockcrow, or at dawn, 36or else he may find you asleep when he comes suddenly. 37And what I say to you I say to all: Keep awake."

13.3–37 (Mt 10.16–25; 24.4–36; Lk 21.8–36): **Mark's little apocalypse.*** See sidebar, "Apocalyptic." **6:** *I am he* (Gk., "Ego eimi," literally, "I am,") are the divine words of self-identification from Ex 3. **14:** *Desolating sacrilege* (or "abomination of desolation"), in Dan 9.27; 11.31; 12.11, refers to the sacrifice of a pig on the Temple altar by Antiochus IV Epiphanes;* perhaps Mark refers to Caligula's unrealized threat of placing his statue in the Temple. **26:** The heavenly *Son of Man* also suggests Daniel's prophecy (Dan 7.13). **30:** See 9.1. **37:** The disciples fail to remain awake (14.32–42).

14 It was two days before the Passover and the festival of Unleavened Bread. The chief priests and the scribes were looking for a way to arrest Jesus[c] by stealth and kill him; 2for they said, "Not during the festival, or there may be a riot among the people."

3 While he was at Bethany in the house of Simon the leper,[d] as he sat at the table, a woman came with an alabaster jar of very costly ointment of nard, and she broke open the jar and poured the ointment on his head. 4But some were there who said to one another in anger, "Why was the ointment wasted in this way? 5For this ointment could have been sold for more than three hundred denarii,[e] and the money given to the poor." And they scolded her. 6But Jesus said, "Let her alone; why do you trouble her? She has performed a good service for me. 7For you always have the poor with you, and you can show kindness to them whenever you wish; but you will not always have me. 8She has done what she could; she has anointed my body beforehand for its burial. 9Truly I tell you, wherever the good news[f] is proclaimed in the whole world, what she has done will be told in remembrance of her."

14.1–9. 1–2 (Mt 26.2–5; Lk 22.1–2; Jn 11.47–53): **The plot to kill Jesus.** Mark does not make explicit why the leaders seek Jesus' death. Motives might include disruption of Temple* function; Jesus' popularity; his besting them in public dispute; his condemnations of their behavior; his political threat and implicit challenge to Rome; his messianic claim; or simply that events carry out the divine will. **3–9** (Mt 26.6–13; Lk 7.36–50; Jn 12.1–8): **The anointing woman. 3:** The anointing* is for burial (14.8); this woman succeeds where Jesus' female followers will fail (16.1). **7:** See Deut 15.11. Jesus reminds his followers that their responsibilities to *the poor* will not cease. **9:** Although her story is told, her name (unlike the women of 16.1) is not; see comment on 15.39.

10 Then Judas Iscariot, who was one of the twelve, went to the chief priests in order to betray him to them. 11When they heard it, they were greatly pleased, and promised to give him money. So he began to look for an opportunity to betray him.

12 On the first day of Unleavened Bread, when the Passover lamb is sacrificed, his disciples said to him, "Where do you want us to go and make the preparations for you to eat the Passover?" 13So he sent two of his disciples, saying to them, "Go into the city, and a man carrying a jar of water will meet you; follow him, 14and wherever he enters, say to the owner of the house, 'The Teacher asks, Where is my guest room where I may eat the Passover with my disciples?' 15He will show you a large room upstairs, furnished and ready. Make preparations for us there." 16So the disciples set out and went to the city, and found everything as he had told them; and they prepared the Passover meal.

a Or *it*   *b* Other ancient authorities add *and pray*   *c* Gk *him*   *d* The terms *leper* and *leprosy* can refer to several diseases   *e* The denarius was the usual day's wage for a laborer   *f* Or *gospel*

17 When it was evening, he came with the twelve. [18]And when they had taken their places and were eating, Jesus said, "Truly I tell you, one of you will betray me, one who is eating with me." [19]They began to be distressed and to say to him one after another, "Surely, not I?" [20]He said to them, "It is one of the twelve, one who is dipping bread[a] into the bowl[b] with me. [21]For the Son of Man goes as it is written of him, but woe to that one by whom the Son of Man is betrayed! It would have been better for that one not to have been born."

22 While they were eating, he took a loaf of bread, and after blessing it he broke it, gave it to them, and said, "Take; this is my body." [23]Then he took a cup, and after giving thanks he gave it to them, and all of them drank from it. [24]He said to them, "This is my blood of the[c] covenant, which is poured out for many. [25]Truly I tell you, I will never again drink of the fruit of the vine until that day when I drink it new in the kingdom of God."

14.10–25. 10–11 (Mt 26.14–16; Lk 22.3–6): **Judas.** Unlike Matthew (greed) and Luke and John (Satanic possession), Mark offers no motive for Judas's betrayal. Judas's identification as *one of the twelve* reinforces the disciples' failures of faith and nerve. **12–16** (Mt 26.17–19; Lk 22.7–13): **Supper preparations.** For Mark, the last supper is a Seder (Heb. for "order") meal. The *Passover** is the Paschal lamb, which would have been sacrificed in the Temple* that afternoon. **13–14:** Luke identifies the disciples as Peter and John. Carrying water jugs may have been women's work. **17–25** (Mt 26.21–25; Lk 22.14, 21–23; Jn 13.21–30): **The last supper.** Divine plan does not preclude human responsibility. To share food is to be of one family; Judas's treachery is thereby heightened. **22–25** (Mt 26.26–29; Lk 22.15–20; 1 Cor 10.16; 11.23–26): Jesus' language suggests Temple sacrifice and Jewish martyr* traditions (see 2 Macc). **25** (Lk 13.29): Perhaps Jesus is thinking of a heavenly, messianic banquet.

---

26 When they had sung the hymn, they went out to the Mount of Olives. [27]And Jesus said to them, "You will all become deserters; for it is written,

'I will strike the shepherd,
and the sheep will be scattered.'

[28]But after I am raised up, I will go before you to Galilee." [29]Peter said to him, "Even though all become deserters, I will not." [30]Jesus said to him, "Truly I tell you, this day, this very night, before the cock crows twice, you will deny me three times." [31]But he said vehemently, "Even though I must die with you, I will not deny you." And all of them said the same.

32 They went to a place called Gethsemane; and he said to his disciples, "Sit here while I pray." [33]He took with him Peter and James and John, and began to be distressed and agitated. [34]And he said to them, "I am deeply grieved, even to death; remain here, and keep awake." [35]And going a little farther, he threw himself on the ground and prayed that, if it were possible, the hour might pass from him. [36]He said, "Abba,[d] Father, for you all things are possible; remove this cup from me; yet, not what I want, but what you want." [37]He came and found them sleeping; and he said to Peter, "Simon, are you asleep? Could you not keep awake one hour? [38]Keep awake and pray that you may not come into the time of trial;[e] the spirit indeed is willing, but the flesh is weak." [39]And again he went away and prayed, saying the same words. [40]And once more he came and found them sleeping, for their eyes were very heavy; and they did not know what to say to him. [41]He came a third time and said to them, "Are you still sleeping and taking your rest? Enough! The hour has come; the Son of Man is betrayed into the hands of sinners. [42]Get up, let us be going. See, my betrayer is at hand."

43 Immediately, while he was still speaking, Judas, one of the twelve, arrived; and with him there was a crowd with swords and clubs, from the chief priests, the scribes, and the elders. [44]Now the betrayer had given them a sign, saying, "The one I will kiss is the man; arrest him and lead him away under guard." [45]So when he came, he went up to him at once and said, "Rabbi!" and kissed him. [46]Then they laid hands on him and arrested him. [47]But one of those who stood

a Gk lacks *bread*   b Other ancient authorities read *same bowl*   c Other ancient authorities add *new*   d Aramaic for *Father*   e Or *into temptation* near drew his sword and struck the slave of the high priest, cutting off his ear. 48Then Jesus said to them, "Have you come out with swords and clubs to arrest me as though I were a bandit? 49Day after day I was with you in the temple teaching, and you did not arrest me. But let the scriptures be fulfilled." 50All of them deserted him and fled.

51 A certain young man was following him, wearing nothing but a linen cloth. They caught hold of him, 52but he left the linen cloth and ran off naked.

14.26–52. 26–31 (Mt 26.30–35; Lk 22.39, 31–34): **Predictions of failure and victory. 26:** Seders end with the singing of the Hallel Psalms (Ps 115–118). **27:** Zech 13.7. **28** (see 16.7): The Gospel likely ended without recording resurrection appearances (see sidebar, "The Ending of Mark," p. 1743). **30–31:** Mark portrays the disciples' failures, not their redemption. **32–42** (Mt 26.36–46; Lk 22.40–46): **Grief in Gethsemane.** Jn 18.1 refers to a garden. **32:** Jesus frequently prays (1.35; 9.29; 11.17). **33:** The three sleeping disciples foreshadow the three women who fail at the tomb. **36:** *Abba* is *father* in Aramaic★ (Rom 8.15; Gal 4.6). **38:** *Time of trial* is, in Greek, "temptation." The Gospel does not encourage or glorify martyrdom.★ **43–52** (Mt 26.47–56; Lk 22.47–53; Jn 18.2–11): **The arrest. 44:** The sign of intimacy and peace becomes the means of handing Jesus over to the chief priests. **47:** Mark does not identify the sword-wielder. **50:** The last appearance of the disciples as a group highlights their failure. **51–52:** The *young man* is also not identified; some traditions speculate that he is Mark and the house of the last supper belonged to his mother (Acts 12.12); he may represent the newly baptized follower who strips off his old way of life and puts on another. Another "young man" appears in the tomb (16.5).

---

53 They took Jesus to the high priest; and all the chief priests, the elders, and the scribes were assembled. 54Peter had followed him at a distance, right into the courtyard of the high priest; and he was sitting with the guards, warming himself at the fire. 55Now the chief priests and the whole council were looking for testimony against Jesus to put him to death; but they found none. 56For many gave false testimony against him, and their testimony did not agree. 57Some stood up and gave false testimony

against him, saying, 58"We heard him say, 'I will destroy this temple that is made with hands, and in three days I will build another, not made with hands.' " 59But even on this point their testimony did not agree. 60Then the high priest stood up before them and asked Jesus, "Have you no answer? What is it that they testify against you?" 61But he was silent and did not answer. Again the high priest asked him, "Are you the Messiah,*a* the Son of the Blessed One?" 62Jesus said, "I am; and

'you will see the Son of Man
    seated at the right hand of the Power,'
    and 'coming with the clouds
        of heaven.' "

63Then the high priest tore his clothes and said, "Why do we still need witnesses? 64You have heard his blasphemy! What is your decision?" All of them condemned him as deserving death. 65Some began to spit on him, to blindfold him, and to strike him, saying to him, "Prophesy!" The guards also took him over and beat him.

14.53–65: Indictment of Caiaphas. The trial contains numerous legal irregularities (at night, on a holiday, without legitimate witnesses, etc.). **56–59:** The false witnesses ironically predict the truth of the Temple's★ destruction and Jesus' resurrection. **61–62:** Jesus attests unequivocally to his identity as the divine Son. His citation combines Dan 7.13 and Ps 110.1. **63:** Tearing clothes signals grief and mourning, and it may anticipate the tearing of the Temple curtain (15.38). With torn clothes and curtain, the priest cannot officiate in the Temple. **64:** *All* condemn Jesus, but Joseph of Arimathea, a member of the Sanhedrin,★ will beg Pilate for Jesus' body and entomb it (15.42–46). The verse continues the irregularities: Jesus has not clearly blasphemed; the penalty for blasphemy is stoning.

---

66 While Peter was below in the courtyard, one of the servant-girls of the high priest came by. 67When she saw Peter warming himself, she stared at him and said, "You also were with Jesus, the man from Nazareth." 68But he denied it, saying, "I do not know or understand what you are talking

a Or the Christ

about." And he went out into the forecourt.ᵃ Then the cock crowed.ᵇ ⁶⁹And the servant-girl, on seeing him, began again to say to the bystanders, "This man is one of them." ⁷⁰But again he denied it. Then after a little while the bystanders again said to Peter, "Certainly you are one of them; for you are a Galilean." ⁷¹But he began to curse, and he swore an oath, "I do not know this man you are talking about." ⁷²At that moment the cock crowed for the second time. Then Peter remembered that Jesus had said to him, "Before the cock crows twice, you will deny me three times." And he broke down and wept.

14.66–72 (Mt 26.69–75; Lk 22.54–71; Jn 18.25–27; and see Mk 14.30, 65): **Peter's betrayal. 70:** Perhaps *Peter* is identified by accent. **72:** Peter's last appearance is one of remorse.

15 As soon as it was morning, the chief priests held a consultation with the elders and scribes and the whole council. They bound Jesus, led him away, and handed him over to Pilate. ²Pilate asked him, "Are you the King of the Jews?" He answered him, "You say so." ³Then the chief priests accused him of many things. ⁴Pilate asked him again, "Have you no answer? See how many charges they bring against you." ⁵But Jesus made no further reply, so that Pilate was amazed.

6 Now at the festival he used to release a prisoner for them, anyone for whom they asked. ⁷Now a man called Barabbas was in prison with the rebels who had committed murder during the insurrection. ⁸So the crowd came and began to ask Pilate to do for them according to his custom. ⁹Then he answered them, "Do you want me to release for you the King of the Jews?" ¹⁰For he realized that it was out of jealousy that the chief priests had handed him over. ¹¹But the chief priests stirred up the crowd to have him release Barabbas for them instead. ¹²Pilate spoke to them again, "Then what do you wish me to doᶜ with the man you callᵈ the King of the Jews?" ¹³They shouted back, "Crucify him!" ¹⁴Pilate asked them, "Why, what evil has he done?" But they shouted all the more, "Crucify him!" ¹⁵So Pilate, wish-

ing to satisfy the crowd, released Barabbas for them; and after flogging Jesus, he handed him over to be crucified.

15.1–15 (Mt 27.1–2; Lk 23.1; Jn 18.28–32): **Trial before Pilate. 1:** See comment on Mt 27.1–2. **2–5** (Mt 27.11–14; Lk 23.2–5; Jn 18.29–19.16): *Pilate* has political concerns; Jesus responds indirectly and again (see 14.61) refuses to defend himself. **6–15** (Mt 27.15–26; Lk 23.18–25; Jn 18.38–40; 19.4–16). **6:** See comment on Mt 27.15. **7:** *Barabbas* means "son of the father." The insurrection, unidentified, suggests political rebellion. **15:** Pilate takes the expedient route; later Christian traditions will increasingly exonerate him and vilify the Jewish leaders and people.

16 Then the soldiers led him into the courtyard of the palace (that is, the governor's headquartersᵉ); and they called together the whole cohort. ¹⁷And they clothed him in a purple cloak; and after twisting some thorns into a crown, they put it on him. ¹⁸And they began saluting him, "Hail, King of the Jews!" ¹⁹They struck his head with a reed, spat upon him, and knelt down in homage to him. ²⁰After mocking him, they stripped him of the purple cloak and put his own clothes on him. Then they led him out to crucify him.

21 They compelled a passer-by, who was coming in from the country, to carry his cross; it was Simon of Cyrene, the father of Alexander and Rufus. ²²Then they brought Jesusᶠ to the place called Golgotha (which means the place of a skull). ²³And they offered him wine mixed with myrrh; but he did not take it. ²⁴And they crucified him, and divided his clothes among them, casting lots to decide what each should take.

25 It was nine o'clock in the morning when they crucified him. ²⁶The inscription of the charge against him read, "The King of the Jews." ²⁷And with him they crucified two bandits, one on his right and one on his left.ᵍ

a Or *gateway*   *b* Other ancient authorities lack *Then the cock crowed*   *c* Other ancient authorities read *what should I do*   *d* Other ancient authorities lack *the man you call*   *e* Gk *the praetorium*   *f* Gk *him*
g Other ancient authorities add verse 28, *And the scripture was fulfilled that says, "And he was counted among the lawless."*

29Those who passed by derided*a* him, shaking their heads and saying, "Aha! You who would destroy the temple and build it in three days, 30save yourself, and come down from the cross!" 31In the same way the chief priests, along with the scribes, were also mocking him among themselves and saying, "He saved others; he cannot save himself. 32Let the Messiah,*b* the King of Israel, come down from the cross now, so that we may see and believe." Those who were crucified with him also taunted him.

33 When it was noon, darkness came over the whole land*c* until three in the afternoon. 34At three o'clock Jesus cried out with a loud voice, "Eloi, Eloi, lema sabachthani?" which means, "My God, my God, why have you forsaken me?"*d* 35When some of the bystanders heard it, they said, "Listen, he is calling for Elijah." 36And someone ran, filled a sponge with sour wine, put it on a stick, and gave it to him to drink, saying, "Wait, let us see whether Elijah will come to take him down." 37Then Jesus gave a loud cry and breathed his last. 38And the curtain of the temple was torn in two, from top to bottom. 39Now when the centurion, who stood facing him, saw that in this way he*e* breathed his last, he said, "Truly this man was God's Son!"*f*

15.16–39. 16–20 (Mt 27.27–31; Lk 23.11; Jn 19.1–3; see Mic 5.1): **The mockery.** The cohort's action fulfills Jesus' mandate of kingship through weakness (10.41–45). **21–32** (Mt 27.32–44; Lk 23.33–43; Jn 19.17–24): **The crucifixion. 21–22:** See comment on Mt 27.32–33. **23:** *Wine mixed with myrrh* is a sedative. **24:** See Ps 22.18. **25–32:** See comment on Mt 27.37–44. **29:** Should be translated "blasphemed" rather than *derided;* the bystanders commit the crime for which Jesus, wrongly, is condemned by the chief priest. **31:** Ironically, Jesus saves others by not saving himself. **33–39** (Mt 27.45–56; Lk 23.44–48; Jn 19.25–30): **Jesus' death. 34–38:** See comment on Mt 27.45–56. **39:** The centurion understands what Peter did not (8.31–33).

40 There were also women looking on from a distance; among them were Mary Magdalene, and Mary the mother of James

the younger and of Joses, and Salome. 41These used to follow him and provided for him when he was in Galilee; and there were many other women who had come up with him to Jerusalem.

42 When evening had come, and since it was the day of Preparation, that is, the day before the sabbath, 43Joseph of Arimathea, a respected member of the council, who was also himself waiting expectantly for the kingdom of God, went boldly to Pilate and asked for the body of Jesus. 44Then Pilate wondered if he were already dead; and summoning the centurion, he asked him whether he had been dead for some time. 45When he learned from the centurion that he was dead, he granted the body to Joseph. 46Then Joseph*g* bought a linen cloth, and taking down the body,*h* wrapped it in the linen cloth, and laid it in a tomb that had been hewn out of the rock. He then rolled a stone against the door of the tomb. 47Mary Magdalene and Mary the mother of Joses saw where the body*h* was laid.

15.40–47. 40–41 (Mt 27.56; Lk 8.1–3): **Women disciples.** The first reference to *women* followers suggests women followed Jesus throughout his mission. **42–47** (Mt 27.57–61; Lk 23.50–56; Jn 19.38–42): **Jesus' burial.** Mk 14.55 implicates the "whole council" in Jesus' condemnation; *Joseph* may have repented. **44:** Crucifixion could take several days; Mark makes it clear that Jesus is really dead.

16 When the sabbath was over, Mary Magdalene, and Mary the mother of James, and Salome bought spices, so that they might go and anoint him. 2And very early on the first day of the week, when the sun had risen, they went to the tomb. 3They had been saying to one another, "Who will roll away the stone for us from the entrance to the tomb?" 4When they looked up, they saw that the stone, which was very large, had already been rolled back. 5As they entered the tomb, they saw a young man, dressed in

a Or *blasphemed*   *b* Or *the Christ*   *c* Or *earth*
d Other ancient authorities read *made me a reproach*
e Other ancient authorities add *cried out and*
f Or *a son of God*   *g* Gk *he*   *h* Gk *it*

The Ending of Mark

The earliest copies of the Gospel of Mark end with 16.8. The women, commissioned by the young man in the tomb to report the news of Jesus' resurrection to the disciples, flee in terror: "They said nothing to anyone, for they were afraid." Certainly the evangelist knew the tradition of resurrection appearances: Jesus' three predictions of his death (Mk 8.31; 9.31; 10.34) also foretell the resurrection; 14.28 locates the reunion of the resurrected Jesus and his followers in Galilee; and 16.7 echoes this notice. Consequently, a few scholars believe that the original ending to the Gospel was either lost, or that John 21 represents the ending of Mark.

However, the stories now found in Mk 16.9–20 do not appear to have been part of the original text: They differ in style and in emphasis from the rest of the Gospel, and it is in the account of the resurrection that the Synoptic* accounts, close throughout the passion, start to differ. Mark emphasizes Jesus' glory as manifested in suffering and servitude, not in signs and wonders. The ending of the Gospel with the fear of the women both complements the fear Mark's audience may have felt and suggests the inadequacy of the view of Jesus held by the twelve: a view that rejects the way of the cross. The longer ending's majestic resurrection accounts and emphasis on charismatic signs such as holding venomous snakes and drinking poison consequently create a jarring effect.

The followers of Jesus, likely in the early second century, found Mark's shocking ending inappropriate. The longer version, now comprising Mk 16.9–20, appears to derive from scenes found elsewhere in the Synoptic tradition: The identification of Mary as having been possessed by seven demons comes from Lk 8.3; Mk 16.12–13 suggests Luke's depiction of the appearance on the Emmaus road (Lk 24.12–35); Mk 16.14–18 draws upon Mt 28.16 (the disciples' doubt) and 28.19 (the great commission). The miraculous signs suggest scenes from Acts as well as the spiritual gifts recorded in 1 Corinthians. Finally, Mk 16.19–20 summarizes the ascension account of Acts 2.

---

a white robe, sitting on the right side; and they were alarmed. 6But he said to them, "Do not be alarmed; you are looking for Jesus of Nazareth, who was crucified. He has been raised; he is not here. Look, there is the place they laid him. 7But go, tell his disciples and Peter that he is going ahead of you to Galilee; there you will see him, just as he told you." 8So they went out and fled from the tomb, for terror and amazement had seized them; and they said nothing to anyone, for they were afraid.*

16.1–8 (Mt 28.1–10; Lk 24.1–11; Jn 20.1–10): **The empty tomb. 1:** The women are too late (see 14.3–9). **6–7:** Had the twelve not told the women about Jesus' prediction of resurrection (14.28)? **8:** The origi-

nal ending of Mark's Gospel (see sidebar, "The Ending of Mark").

~~~~~~~~~~~~~~~~~~~~~~~~~~~~~~~~~~~~~~

THE SHORTER ENDING OF MARK

[And all that had been commanded them they told briefly to those around Peter. And afterward Jesus himself sent out through them, from east to west, the sacred

---

a Some of the most ancient authorities bring the book to a close at the end of verse 8. One authority concludes the book with the shorter ending; others include the shorter ending and then continue with verses 9–20. In most authorities verses 9–20 follow immediately after verse 8, though in some of these authorities the passage is marked as being doubtful.

and imperishable proclamation of eternal salvation."⟧

THE LONGER ENDING OF MARK

9 ⟦Now after he rose early on the first day of the week, he appeared first to Mary Magdalene, from whom he had cast out seven demons. 10 She went out and told those who had been with him, while they were mourning and weeping. 11 But when they heard that he was alive and had been seen by her, they would not believe it.

12 After this he appeared in another form to two of them, as they were walking into the country. 13 And they went back and told the rest, but they did not believe them.

14 Later he appeared to the eleven themselves as they were sitting at the table; and he upbraided them for their lack of faith and stubbornness, because they had not believed those who saw him after he had risen.[b] 15 And he said to them, "Go into all the world and proclaim the good news[c] to the whole creation. 16 The one who believes and is baptized will be saved; but the one who does not believe will be condemned. 17 And these signs will accompany those who believe: by using my name they will cast out demons; they will speak in new tongues; 18 they will pick up snakes in their hands,[d] and if they

drink any deadly thing, it will not hurt them; they will lay their hands on the sick, and they will recover."

19 So then the Lord Jesus, after he had spoken to them, was taken up into heaven and sat down at the right hand of God. 20 And they went out and proclaimed the good news everywhere, while the Lord worked with them and confirmed the message by the signs that accompanied it."⟧

16.9–20: Resurrection accounts. The longer ending combines material from Matthew, Luke, and John as well as the account of the ascension in Acts 1. **17–18:** Emphasis on miracles conflicts with Mark's tendency to emphasize suffering.

a Other ancient authorities add *Amen*   *b* Other ancient authorities add, in whole or in part, *And they excused themselves, saying, "This age of lawlessness and unbelief is under Satan, who does not allow the truth and power of God to prevail over the unclean things of the spirits. Therefore reveal your righteousness now"—thus they spoke to Christ. And Christ replied to them, "The term of years of Satan's power has been fulfilled, but other terrible things draw near. And for those who have sinned I was handed over to death, that they may return to the truth and sin no more, that they may inherit the spiritual and imperishable glory of righteousness that is in heaven."*   *c* Or *gospel*   *d* Other ancient authorities lack *in their hands*

THE GOSPEL ACCORDING TO LUKE

Introduction

Luke is the third of the Synoptic Gospels.⋆ Early interpreters recognized that Matthew, Mark, and Luke were so closely related that they should be "seen together," as "synoptic" means in Greek. Luke is the first book of the larger work carried forward in the Acts of the Apostles (see Acts 1.1, "In the first book, Theophilus, I wrote about all that Jesus did and taught . . . "). Taken together, Luke-Acts is the largest work in the New Testament and the most consistently historical in its literary style. Luke-Acts does not claim to be a more accurate record than its sources or other Gospels, but the author announces qualifications to provide an "orderly account" in order to communicate the truth (1.1–4). The narrative⋆ declares the life and ministry of Jesus to be the fulfillment of "the law of Moses, the prophets,⋆ and the psalms" (see 1.1; 24.27, 32, 44). The appeals to Israel's scriptures bear witness to the "definite plan and foreknowledge of God," as the speeches of the apostles⋆ in Acts also attest explicitly (see Acts 2.22–24, 30–36; 3.18). God's "kingdom" or "rule" is not an abstract ideal or merely a heavenly future. The narrative of Luke-Acts tells what happened when Jesus the "anointed⋆ one" (Luke 2.11; 22.67; 23.2, 35, 39; 24.26, 46; Acts 2.31, 36; 3.20; 4.10: "messiah"⋆ in Hebrew or "Christ" in Greek) brought God's rule, will, and work into the history of Israel and the Roman order.

Later tradition named Luke as the author of this narrative and called it a "Gospel." The titles for the four Gospels were probably attached in the second century when they were collected and read next to each other. None of them identifies its author in the body of the account. None of the Gospels says when it was written (see aside to "the reader" in Mk 13.14, which may allude to the impending or just completed Roman destruction of the Temple⋆ in 70–73 CE). The Gospel according to Luke was probably written in the late first century, shortly after the destruction. Luke is focused on God's reign as inaugurated by Jesus the messiah within Israel.

READING GUIDE

From beginning to end, Luke is a literary masterpiece. It is a testimony to God's reign promised in the scriptures, inaugurated by the messiah, and vindicated by God. Following a formal prologue (1.1–4), chs. 1–2 announce God's visitation and redemption (1.68) in angelic declarations along with inspired hymns and prophetic⋆ oracles.⋆ They relate the births of John and Jesus in terms that are reminiscent of wonder children of Israel's past. Children of divine promise also confront God's people with divine judgment.

Chapters 3–21 tell the story of Jesus' mission and ministry in Israel, presenting him as the messianic protagonist in the story. Jesus is purposeful in word and deed. He calls forth disciples and provokes rejection from the beginning of his ministry. Then he "set his face to go to Jerusalem" (9.51) where powerful forces will stand against him.

The resolution of the story in chs. 22–24 moves through Jesus' trial, crucifixion, death, and resurrection. The reader must consider carefully who truly has authority and power in these scenes, while the narrative awaits God's final vindication.

1 Since many have undertaken to set down an orderly account of the events that have been fulfilled among us, [2]just as they were handed on to us by those who from the beginning were eyewitnesses and servants of the word, [3]I too decided, after investigating everything carefully from the very first,[a] to write an orderly account for you, most excellent Theophilus, [4]so that you may know the truth concerning the things about which you have been instructed.

1.1–4: Prologue. These four verses are one complex sentence, providing a formal introduction like those in Greek and Roman histories. The first two verses state the condition (*Since many have undertaken . . .*), and the last two the result (*I too decided . . .*). *Orderly account* (vv. 1, 3) means both writing a coherent narrative* and following the sequence of what happened. **1:** To say these events *have been fulfilled among us* is to affirm them as God's way of keeping the promises made in Israel's scriptures. **2:** The *servants of the word* probably interpreted the scriptures and proclaimed the word (4.20–21; Acts 1.21–22; 13.5; 26.16). **3:** *Theophilus* may have been a patron of the Christian community or of the writing of Luke and Acts, perhaps providing financial support (Acts 1.1). **4:** *The truth* here means the "firm basis" or "assurance," since Theophilus has already been *instructed,* perhaps as a Christian catechumen.

VISITATION OF THE LORD GOD OF ISRAEL

1.5–2.52: This story is told by means of two angelic announcements (annunciations) of special conceptions (1.5–25, John, and 1.26–38, Jesus), the mutual blessing of the mothers (1.39–56), two announced births (1.57–80; 2.1–40), and the return to the Temple* of the child Jesus (2.41–52). These stories echo the birth of Samuel, who anointed* David as

king of Israel (1 Sam 1–2; 16.13; see also Lk 3.21–22; Acts 10.37–38).

---

5 In the days of King Herod of Judea, there was a priest named Zechariah, who belonged to the priestly order of Abijah. His wife was a descendant of Aaron, and her name was Elizabeth. [6]Both of them were righteous before God, living blamelessly according to all the commandments and regulations of the Lord. [7]But they had no children, because Elizabeth was barren, and both were getting on in years.

8 Once when he was serving as priest before God and his section was on duty, [9]he was chosen by lot, according to the custom of the priesthood, to enter the sanctuary of the Lord and offer incense. [10]Now at the time of the incense offering, the whole assembly of the people was praying outside. [11]Then there appeared to him an angel of the Lord, standing at the right side of the altar of incense. [12]When Zechariah saw him, he was terrified; and fear overwhelmed him. [13]But the angel said to him, "Do not be afraid, Zechariah, for your prayer has been heard. Your wife Elizabeth will bear you a son, and you will name him John. [14]You will have joy and gladness, and many will rejoice at his birth, [15]for he will be great in the sight of the Lord. He must never drink wine or strong drink; even before his birth he will be filled with the Holy Spirit. [16]He will turn many of the people of Israel to the Lord their God. [17]With the spirit and power of Elijah he will go before him, to turn the hearts of parents to their children, and the disobedient to the wisdom of the righteous, to make

a Or for a long time

ready a people prepared for the Lord." [18]Zechariah said to the angel, "How will I know that this is so? For I am an old man, and my wife is getting on in years." [19]The angel replied, "I am Gabriel. I stand in the presence of God, and I have been sent to speak to you and to bring you this good news. [20]But now, because you did not believe my words, which will be fulfilled in their time, you will become mute, unable to speak, until the day these things occur."

21 Meanwhile the people were waiting for Zechariah, and wondered at his delay in the sanctuary. [22]When he did come out, he could not speak to them, and they realized that he had seen a vision in the sanctuary. He kept motioning to them and remained unable to speak. [23]When his time of service was ended, he went to his home.

24 After those days his wife Elizabeth conceived, and for five months she remained in seclusion. She said, [25]"This is what the Lord has done for me when he looked favorably on me and took away the disgrace I have endured among my people."

so?," is regarded as disbelief by Gabriel (see v. 20 and Gen 15.8; 17.17; 18.12–15, and contrast with Mary's question in v. 34). 20: His *mute* condition is a temporary sign of judgment, awaiting inspired speech (1.64–79; see also Acts 13.11). 25: Her pregnancy is *what the Lord has done for me* (see Sarah and Hannah in Gen 16.2; 1 Sam 1.1–18).

26 In the sixth month the angel Gabriel was sent by God to a town in Galilee called Nazareth, [27]to a virgin engaged to a man whose name was Joseph, of the house of David. The virgin's name was Mary. [28]And he came to her and said, "Greetings, favored one! The Lord is with you."[a] [29]But she was much perplexed by his words and pondered what sort of greeting this might be. [30]The angel said to her, "Do not be afraid, Mary, for you have found favor with God. [31]And now, you will conceive in your womb and bear a son, and you will name him Jesus. [32]He will be great, and will be called the Son of the Most High, and the Lord God will give to him the throne of his ancestor David. [33]He will reign over the house of Jacob forever, and of his kingdom there will be no end." [34]Mary said to the angel, "How can this be, since I am a virgin?"[b] [35]The angel said to her, "The Holy Spirit will come upon you, and the power of the Most High will overshadow you; therefore the child to be born[c] will be holy; he will be called Son of God. [36]And now, your relative Elizabeth in her old age has also conceived a son; and this is the sixth month for her who was said to be barren. [37]For nothing will be impossible with God." [38]Then Mary said, "Here am I, the servant of the Lord; let it be with me according to your word." Then the angel departed from her.

1.5–25: The announcement of John's birth. 5: *Herod*, "the Great," was an Idumean appointed king of the Jews by the Romans (see Mt 2; Lk 23.3, 12, 38). *Zechariah* and *Elizabeth* both have priestly lineage (1 Chr 24.1–19; Neh 12.4). **6:** *Righteous before God* means they observed the law (see Simeon and Anna in 2.25; Joseph of Arimathea in 23.50–51; Paul in Acts 24.16–18). **7:** In biblical history, God brought special blessing through children of once *barren* women (see Sarah and Isaac in Gen 16–21, and particularly Hannah and Samuel in 1 Sam 1–2). **9:** To be *chosen by lot* meant to be designated by God (see Acts 1.24–26). **10:** The *incense offering* was to be made in the morning and the evening (Ex 30.7–8). **11:** The *angel of the Lord* is God's messenger Gabriel (1.19; see also Dan 9.20–27). **12–13:** *Fear* in the presence of a divine manifestation is a sign of wisdom (Prov 1.7, see also Isa 6.5–6; Lk 1.65; 2.9; 5.26; 8.37; Acts 2.43; 5.5, 11; 19.17). **15:** Like Samuel (1 Sam 1.11), John's prophecy and spirit would not come from *wine or strong drink* (see also Hannah in 1 Sam 1.12–16), but from being *filled with the Holy Spirit* (see Acts 2.12–17). **17:** The *spirit and power of Elijah* means to call Israel to prepare for God's coming by repentance (see 3.3–17). **18:** Zechariah's question, *"How will I know that this is*

1.26–38: The announcement of Jesus' birth. 26: This is the *sixth month* of Elizabeth's miraculous pregnancy (see 1.24). **27:** Isa 7.14 prophesied that a *virgin* (Heb., "young woman") will bear a son (see Mt 1.22–23). **28:** To be a *favored one* is to be blessed by God and chosen for a special role (1.25, 30). **31:**

a Other ancient authorities add *Blessed are you among women*   b Gk *I do not know a man*   c Other ancient authorities add *of you*

Jesus is a form of the common Hebrew name Joshua ("he saves," see Mt 1.21). **32–33:** The angel declares Jesus' "greatness" as fulfillment of God's promises to *David* and his *kingdom* (Ps 2; Isa 9.6–7; 2 Sam 7.12–14). **34:** Mary's question, *"How can this be?"* is echoed as trust and wonder in her acceptance in v. 38, *"Let it be"* (compare 1.18). **35:** God's *Holy Spirit* and *power overshadow* Israel like a cloud to protect them from harm and shield them from God's holiness (Ex 19.16; 40.35; Lk 9.34). So also Mary is protected in a divine conception (see 2.48–49). **36:** Elizabeth's pregnancy *in her old age* is a confirming sign. **37:** *Nothing will be impossible with God* echoes God's word to Sarah's laughter about her pregnancy (Gen 18.11–15).

39 In those days Mary set out and went with haste to a Judean town in the hill country, ⁴⁰where she entered the house of Zechariah and greeted Elizabeth. ⁴¹When Elizabeth heard Mary's greeting, the child leaped in her womb. And Elizabeth was filled with the Holy Spirit ⁴²and exclaimed with a loud cry, "Blessed are you among women, and blessed is the fruit of your womb. ⁴³And why has this happened to me, that the mother of my Lord comes to me? ⁴⁴For as soon as I heard the sound of your greeting, the child in my womb leaped for joy. ⁴⁵And blessed is she who believed that there would be*ᵃ* a fulfillment of what was spoken to her by the Lord."

46 And Mary*ᵇ* said,

"My soul magnifies the Lord,
⁴⁷   and my spirit rejoices in God
        my Savior,
⁴⁸ for he has looked with favor on the
        lowliness of his servant.
    Surely, from now on all generations
        will call me blessed;
⁴⁹ for the Mighty One has done great
        things for me,
    and holy is his name.
⁵⁰ His mercy is for those who fear him
    from generation to generation.
⁵¹ He has shown strength with his arm;
    he has scattered the proud in the
        thoughts of their hearts.
⁵² He has brought down the powerful from
        their thrones,
    and lifted up the lowly;

⁵³ he has filled the hungry with
        good things,
    and sent the rich away empty.
⁵⁴ He has helped his servant Israel,
    in remembrance of his mercy,
⁵⁵ according to the promise he made to
        our ancestors,
    to Abraham and to his descendants
        forever."

56 And Mary remained with her about three months and then returned to her home.

1.39–56: Elizabeth and Mary meet and prophesy. 41–42: The unborn *child leaped in her womb* in anticipation of his role (see Gen 25.22), and his mother spoke as a prophet* (*filled with the Holy Spirit* and *with a loud cry*). Mary is *blessed* both in her faithfulness (1.45) and in her bearing Jesus (see Judg 5.24; Lk 11.27–28). **43:** Elizabeth's question to *the mother of my Lord* echoes recognition of King David (2 Sam 24.21) and recalls earlier messages about the Lord God (1.32, 45–47). **44–46:** *Joy* and *rejoicing* are signs of God's blessing (1.14; Acts 2.46). **46–55:** These verses are called Mary's "magnificat" because of the Latin translation of *my soul magnifies*. They closely parallel Hannah's song to God who rescues the poor (1 Sam 2). **47:** *God my Savior* anticipates Jesus' role as Savior (2.11). **48:** God's *favor* for Mary's *lowliness* is a sign of hope for all the lowly and hungry (1.52–53). **51–52:** The *strength with his arm* is a biblical image of God's action in history (Ex 6.6). The *proud* and the *powerful* will no longer hide deceitful hearts (see 2.35; 11.17). **54–55:** God's *remembrance* of *mercy* is a source of hope in trouble (Gen 8.1; 9.15) and trust in God's *promise* to bless *Abraham* (Gen 12.2–3; Acts 3.25).

---

57 Now the time came for Elizabeth to give birth, and she bore a son. ⁵⁸Her neighbors and relatives heard that the Lord had shown his great mercy to her, and they rejoiced with her.

59 On the eighth day they came to circumcise the child, and they were going to name him Zechariah after his father. ⁶⁰But his mother said, "No; he is to be called John." ⁶¹They said to her, "None of your relatives has this name." ⁶²Then they began

a Or *believed, for there will be*   *b* Other ancient authorities read *Elizabeth* motioning to his father to find out what name he wanted to give him. 63He asked for a writing tablet and wrote, "His name is John." And all of them were amazed. 64Immediately his mouth was opened and his tongue freed, and he began to speak, praising God. 65Fear came over all their neighbors, and all these things were talked about throughout the entire hill country of Judea. 66All who heard them pondered them and said, "What then will this child become?" For, indeed, the hand of the Lord was with him.

67 Then his father Zechariah was filled with the Holy Spirit and spoke this prophecy:
68 "Blessed be the Lord God of Israel,
for he has looked favorably on his
people and redeemed them.
69 He has raised up a mighty savior*a* for us
in the house of his servant David,
70 as he spoke through the mouth of his
holy prophets from of old,
71 that we would be saved from our
enemies and from the hand of all
who hate us.
72 Thus he has shown the mercy promised
to our ancestors,
and has remembered his
holy covenant,
73 the oath that he swore to our ancestor
Abraham,
to grant us 74that we, being rescued
from the hands of our enemies,
might serve him without fear, 75in
holiness and righteousness
before him all our days.
76 And you, child, will be called the
prophet of the Most High;
for you will go before the Lord to
prepare his ways,
77 to give knowledge of salvation to his
people
by the forgiveness of their sins.
78 By the tender mercy of our God,
the dawn from on high will break
upon*b* us,
79 to give light to those who sit in
darkness and in the shadow of
death,
to guide our feet into the way
of peace."

80 The child grew and became strong in spirit, and he was in the wilderness until the day he appeared publicly to Israel.

1.57–80: The birth and presentation of John. 59: Elizabeth and Zechariah are again fully observant of the law to circumcise* John on the eighth day (Gen 17.12; Lev 12.3). **62:** Motioning suggests they are coaxing a message from him in his limited means of communicating (1.22). **63–64:** Obedience to the angel's naming the child John (1.13) restores his speech and praise of God. **66–67:** "What then will this child become?" is a question of faith (see 1.18, 34), prompting Zechariah's answer in inspired prophecy. **68–79:** Zechariah's prophecy is sung in Christian worship as the "benedictus" ("Blessed be . . . "). Jewish prayers often pronounced a blessing on God for wonderful deeds (Ps 41.13; 72.18; 106.48). **69:** The savior promised here is literally the horn of salvation (see note a, see also 2.11) from which a Davidic king was anointed* (1 Sam 2.10; Ps 18.2; 132.17). **76:** John was the prophet* of the Most High to do the anointing* (see Acts 10.37–38), and Jesus was the Son of the Most High (1.32). **78:** The dawn from on high is a promise of liberation from the darkness of captivity (Mal 4.2; Ps 107.10; Is 42.7). **80:** Luke's "growth refrain" (the child grew . . .) echoes 1 Sam 2.21, 26 and is repeated twice for Jesus (Lk 2.40, 52).

2 In those days a decree went out from Emperor Augustus that all the world should be registered. 2This was the first registration and was taken while Quirinius was governor of Syria. 3All went to their own towns to be registered. 4Joseph also went from the town of Nazareth in Galilee to Judea, to the city of David called Bethlehem, because he was descended from the house and family of David. 5He went to be registered with Mary, to whom he was engaged and who was expecting a child. 6While they were there, the time came for her to deliver her child. 7And she gave birth to her firstborn son and wrapped him in bands of cloth, and laid him in a manger, because there was no place for them in the inn.

8 In that region there were shepherds living in the fields, keeping watch over their

---

a Gk a horn of salvation   *b* Other ancient authorities read has broken upon flock by night. [9]Then an angel of the Lord stood before them, and the glory of the Lord shone around them, and they were terrified. [10]But the angel said to them, "Do not be afraid; for see—I am bringing you good news of great joy for all the people: [11]to you is born this day in the city of David a Savior, who is the Messiah,[a] the Lord. [12]This will be a sign for you: you will find a child wrapped in bands of cloth and lying in a manger." [13]And suddenly there was with the angel a multitude of the heavenly host,[b] praising God and saying,

[14] "Glory to God in the highest heaven,
    and on earth peace among those
        whom he favors!"[c]

[15] When the angels had left them and gone into heaven, the shepherds said to one another, "Let us go now to Bethlehem and see this thing that has taken place, which the Lord has made known to us." [16]So they went with haste and found Mary and Joseph, and the child lying in the manger. [17]When they saw this, they made known what had been told them about this child; [18]and all who heard it were amazed at what the shepherds told them. [19]But Mary treasured all these words and pondered them in her heart. [20]The shepherds returned, glorifying and praising God for all they had heard and seen, as it had been told them.

2.1–20: The birth of Jesus. 1: Luke projects Jesus' birth against the background of the whole Roman order, *all the world,* while Matthew draws attention to King Herod's reign in Judea (Mt 2). *Augustus* was an honorary name of Gaius Octavius, who ruled as *emperor* from 31 BCE to 14 CE. **2:** This specific *registration* has proved hard to establish historically (see Acts 5.37), but the Romans regularly used this means to establish control of taxes, lands, and military conscription. **4:** *Bethlehem* was also King David's birthplace (1 Sam 16.1), and his origins tending sheep were legendary* (Ps 78.70–71). **8:** The Roman poet Virgil also proposed that the ideal ruler would be a shepherd of the people, born among simple shepherds (*Aeneid* 6.791 and the fourth *Eclogue*). **9:** The *glory of the Lord* is the blazing light of divine presence (Ex 16.10; 24.17). **11:** Caesar Augustus was also acclaimed as *Savior* and *Lord,* and Christians would later face consequences for confessing, "Jesus is Lord." But in this context these titles are as thoroughly Jewish and scriptural as the title *messiah** or "anointed* one" is for Israel's king. **12–20:** Without asking for confirmation (see Zechariah in 1.18), the *shepherds* are given the *sign* of the *child* in the *manger,* and they are exemplary in telling what they had *heard and seen* (see Acts 1.1–5).

---

21 After eight days had passed, it was time to circumcise the child; and he was called Jesus, the name given by the angel before he was conceived in the womb.

22 When the time came for their purification according to the law of Moses, they brought him up to Jerusalem to present him to the Lord 23(as it is written in the law of the Lord, "Every firstborn male shall be designated as holy to the Lord"), 24and they offered a sacrifice according to what is stated in the law of the Lord, "a pair of turtledoves or two young pigeons."

25 Now there was a man in Jerusalem whose name was Simeon;[d] this man was righteous and devout, looking forward to the consolation of Israel, and the Holy Spirit rested on him. 26It had been revealed to him by the Holy Spirit that he would not see death before he had seen the Lord's Messiah.[e] 27Guided by the Spirit, Simeon[f] came into the temple; and when the parents brought in the child Jesus, to do for him what was customary under the law, 28Simeon[g] took him in his arms and praised God, saying,

29 "Master, now you are dismissing your
        servant[h] in peace,
    according to your word;
30 for my eyes have seen your salvation,
31   which you have prepared in the
        presence of all peoples,
32 a light for revelation to the Gentiles
    and for glory to your people Israel."

33 And the child's father and mother were amazed at what was being said about him. 34Then Simeon[d] blessed them and said to his mother Mary, "This child is destined

---

a Or *the Christ*   *b* Gk *army*   *c* Other ancient authorities read *peace, goodwill among people*   *d* Gk *Symeon*   *e* Or *the Lord's Christ*   *f* Gk *In the Spirit, he*   *g* Gk *he*   *h* Gk *slave* for the falling and the rising of many in Israel, and to be a sign that will be opposed [35]so that the inner thoughts of many will be revealed—and a sword will pierce your own soul too."

36 There was also a prophet, Anna[a] the daughter of Phanuel, of the tribe of Asher. She was of a great age, having lived with her husband seven years after her marriage, [37]then as a widow to the age of eighty-four. She never left the temple but worshiped there with fasting and prayer night and day. [38]At that moment she came, and began to praise God and to speak about the child[b] to all who were looking for the redemption of Jerusalem.

39 When they had finished everything required by the law of the Lord, they returned to Galilee, to their own town of Nazareth. [40]The child grew and became strong, filled with wisdom; and the favor of God was upon him.

2.21–40: The circumcision* and presentation of Jesus. 21–24: In circumcising and naming Jesus on the *eighth* day and again at the *purification,* Joseph and Mary obey the law and the command of the *angel* (Lev 12.4–8; Lk 1.59; 2.39). **25:** The *consolation of Israel* and *the redemption of Jerusalem* (v. 38) are formal terms expressing the hope of the *righteous and devout* in God's promises to Israel (see also 23.50–51; 24.21). *Simeon* is emphatically credited with the presence of the Holy Spirit (vv. 25, 26, 27), and the major struggle or plot of Luke's story is disclosed in his two oracles.* **28–32:** Simeon's first oracle is a blessing of God, declaring the significance of the child in God's thoroughly positive purpose to fulfill Israel's calling (see Isa 49.6; 52.10) to be a *light to the Gentiles** (all non-Jewish peoples). Acts 1.6–8 also recalls Isa 49.6. **34:** Simeon's second oracle is a severe blessing of Jesus' human parents, declaring Jesus as *destined* or "set" by God for both judgment and hope in Israel because of the opposition this child will evoke as the *sign* (see also 2.12; Isa 8.18) of God's purpose. **35:** God's initiative will uncover people's *inner thoughts* or secret purposes, provoking suffering. **36–37:** *Anna's* credentials as a *prophet** and a *widow* (see Acts 2.18; 6.1) complement Simeon's.

---

41 Now every year his parents went to Jerusalem for the festival of the Passover.

[42]And when he was twelve years old, they went up as usual for the festival. [43]When the festival was ended and they started to return, the boy Jesus stayed behind in Jerusalem, but his parents did not know it. [44]Assuming that he was in the group of travelers, they went a day's journey. Then they started to look for him among their relatives and friends. [45]When they did not find him, they returned to Jerusalem to search for him. [46]After three days they found him in the temple, sitting among the teachers, listening to them and asking them questions. [47]And all who heard him were amazed at his understanding and his answers. [48]When his parents[c] saw him they were astonished; and his mother said to him, "Child, why have you treated us like this? Look, your father and I have been searching for you in great anxiety." [49]He said to them, "Why were you searching for me? Did you not know that I must be in my Father's house?"[d] [50]But they did not understand what he said to them. [51]Then he went down with them and came to Nazareth, and was obedient to them. His mother treasured all these things in her heart.

52 And Jesus increased in wisdom and in years,[e] and in divine and human favor.

2.41–52: The child Jesus in the Temple. This is the only story in the New Testament about Jesus' childhood beyond his birth. The apocryphal* "infancy Gospels" tell other stories which are thorough fictions. **41:** *Passover** (Ex 12.1–27) was a major occasion for pilgrimages to Jerusalem, and in Luke, Jesus does not return to Jerusalem until his last Passover (19.28–48; 22.1). **46:** Jesus' engagement with the teachers in the *temple** foreshadows later encounters where their opposition will be evident (20.20–21, 27–28, 39–40; 21.5–7; 22.53). **48–49:** Luke regards Joseph as Jesus' earthly father (*your father and I,* see also 2.27, 33, 41), but the evangelist is emphatic about God's agency in Jesus' conception so that Jesus is God's son and the Temple is his *Father's house* (see also 3.22–23). **52:** This concluding "growth refrain" again echoes 1 Samuel 2 and the story of John (1.80).

---

a Gk *Hanna*　　*b* Gk *him*　　*c* Gk *they*
d Or *be about my Father's interests?*　　*e* Or *in stature*

does not bear good fruit is cut down and thrown into the fire."

10 And the crowds asked him, "What then should we do?" [11]In reply he said to them, "Whoever has two coats must share with anyone who has none; and whoever has food must do likewise." [12]Even tax collectors came to be baptized, and they asked him, "Teacher, what should we do?" [13]He said to them, "Collect no more than the amount prescribed for you." [14]Soldiers also asked him, "And we, what should we do?" He said to them, "Do not extort money from anyone by threats or false accusation, and be satisfied with your wages."

15 As the people were filled with expectation, and all were questioning in their hearts concerning John, whether he might be the Messiah,[b] [16]John answered all of them by saying, "I baptize you with water; but one who is more powerful than I is coming; I am not worthy to untie the thong of his sandals. He will baptize you with[c] the Holy Spirit and fire. [17]His winnowing fork is in his hand, to clear his threshing floor and to gather the wheat into his granary; but the chaff he will burn with unquenchable fire."

18 So, with many other exhortations, he proclaimed the good news to the people. [19]But Herod the ruler,[a] who had been rebuked by him because of Herodias, his brother's wife, and because of all the evil things that Herod had done, [20]added to them all by shutting up John in prison.

THE INAUGURATION OF THE KINGDOM

3.1–9.50: After the extended overture provided in the first two chapters, the body of the story now begins. From this point, close parallels with the Gospel according to Mark probably indicate Luke's use of Mark as a source (see 1.1–2). Luke also shares smaller and larger blocks of material with Matthew, especially sayings (see Lk 6–7). This has suggested to scholars that both Luke and Matthew used a common sayings source, known as the "Q" document (the German word for "source" is Quelle). Luke's composition of this "orderly account" from these sources displays the literary art of Luke's witness to the "truth" in which the reader has already been instructed (1.3–4).

3 In the fifteenth year of the reign of Emperor Tiberius, when Pontius Pilate was governor of Judea, and Herod was ruler[a] of Galilee, and his brother Philip ruler[a] of the region of Ituraea and Trachonitis, and Lysanias ruler[a] of Abilene, [2]during the high priesthood of Annas and Caiaphas, the word of God came to John son of Zechariah in the wilderness. [3]He went into all the region around the Jordan, proclaiming a baptism of repentance for the forgiveness of sins, [4]as it is written in the book of the words of the prophet Isaiah,

"The voice of one crying out in
    the wilderness:
'Prepare the way of the Lord,
    make his paths straight.
[5] Every valley shall be filled,
    and every mountain and hill shall be
        made low,
    and the crooked shall be made
        straight,
    and the rough ways made smooth;
[6] and all flesh shall see the salvation of
        God.' "

7 John said to the crowds that came out to be baptized by him, "You brood of vipers! Who warned you to flee from the wrath to come? [8]Bear fruits worthy of repentance. Do not begin to say to yourselves, 'We have Abraham as our ancestor'; for I tell you, God is able from these stones to raise up children to Abraham. [9]Even now the ax is lying at the root of the trees; every tree therefore that

3.1–20: The voice in the wilderness. 1–2: These verses establish a "synchronism" in the mode of ancient historians, fixing the date of something by multiple associations with other dates of public record. *Tiberius* ruled the Roman empire from about 14–37 CE, and *Pontius Pilate* enforced Roman rule in *Judea*. *Herod* Antipas was a son of Herod the Great, but ruled only as a minor tetrarch (see note a) of *Galilee* in the north, although he asked the Romans to name him "king of the Jews" like his father (see 23.1–12). The Romans also controlled who was appointed to the *high priesthood,* since this was the most powerful religious, cultural, and financial role of the subjugated province (see 23.13–16). *The word of God came to*

a Gk *tetrarch*   *b* Or *the Christ*   *c* Or *in*

John in the midst of political realities as happened before with the prophet* Jeremiah (Jer 1.1–2). **3**: The *baptism** of repentance for the forgiveness of sins is a cleansing ritual to return a purified people, restored in the land by God as ancient Israel was led through the *Jordan* (Josh 3; Lk 7.29; 20.4–8; Acts 13.24). **4–6**: Luke's story lacks details about John's hair shirt, leather girdle, and diet (Mk 1.5–6), but emphasizes his role in announcing the Isaiah prophecy of Israel's return and restoration. **7–9**: A *brood* (Gk., offspring) *of vipers* depicts John's hearers as under judgment (see Gen 3.14), not as worthy heirs of the promises to *Abraham* (see Lk 1.55). **10**: *What then should we do?* is one of Luke's masterful questions emphasizing that repentance is more than a change of heart (see also vv. 12, 14; 10.25; 18.18; Acts 2.37; 16.30; 22.10). **15–17**: The Gospel according to John (Jn 1.19–34) is even more insistent that John disclaimed being the *Messiah.** *The Holy Spirit and fire* anticipates Pentecost,* where the *fire* of judgment is again announced (Acts 2.1–4, 19). **18–19**: The Jewish historian Josephus* also reports John's baptism* and preaching of righteousness and that *Herod* Antipas put John to death (*Ant.* 18.116–119).

21 Now when all the people were baptized, and when Jesus also had been baptized and was praying, the heaven was opened, ²²and the Holy Spirit descended upon him in bodily form like a dove. And a voice came from heaven, "You are my Son, the Beloved;*ᵃ* with you I am well pleased."*ᵇ*

3.21–23: Jesus' baptism. Christian tradition is clear that John baptized Jesus (Mt 3.13–17; Mk 1.9–11; Jn 1.29–34), and Luke does not deny it. But by first reporting John's imprisonment and not mentioning him in the baptism, Luke emphasizes that Jesus was anointed* as messiah* by the *Holy Spirit* (see Acts 10.37–38; Lk 4.18), as the "Spirit of the Lord" once confirmed the anointing of Saul and David (1 Sam 10.1, 9–10; 11.5–15; 16.13). The *voice from heaven* echoes the royal acclamations of Ps 2 and Isa 42.

23 Jesus was about thirty years old when he began his work. He was the son (as was thought) of Joseph son of Heli, ²⁴son of Matthat, son of Levi, son of Melchi, son of Jannai, son of Joseph, ²⁵son of Mattathias, son of Amos, son of Nahum, son of Esli, son of Naggai, ²⁶son of Maath, son of Mattathias,

son of Semein, son of Josech, son of Joda, ²⁷son of Joanan, son of Rhesa, son of Zerubbabel, son of Shealtiel,*ᶜ* son of Neri, ²⁸son of Melchi, son of Addi, son of Cosam, son of Elmadam, son of Er, ²⁹son of Joshua, son of Eliezer, son of Jorim, son of Matthat, son of Levi, ³⁰son of Simeon, son of Judah, son of Joseph, son of Jonam, son of Eliakim, ³¹son of Melea, son of Menna, son of Mattatha, son of Nathan, son of David, ³²son of Jesse, son of Obed, son of Boaz, son of Sala,*ᵈ* son of Nahshon, ³³son of Amminadab, son of Admin, son of Arni,*ᵉ* son of Hezron, son of Perez, son of Judah, ³⁴son of Jacob, son of Isaac, son of Abraham, son of Terah, son of Nahor, ³⁵son of Serug, son of Reu, son of Peleg, son of Eber, son of Shelah, ³⁶son of Cainan, son of Arphaxad, son of Shem, son of Noah, son of Lamech, ³⁷son of Methuselah, son of Enoch, son of Jared, son of Mahalaleel, son of Cainan, ³⁸son of Enos, son of Seth, son of Adam, son of God.

3.23–38: The genealogy of the messiah.** Lineage is important to royal legitimacy, and Luke was concerned to show the connections with the heritage of God's promises through *David* and *Abraham* (Acts 2.30; 3.25; 13.23–26). Matthew's account reaches back in three phases of 14 generations through the Exile* to David and to Abraham (Mt 1). In Luke's account, Jesus is Son of God in his conception (1.35; 3.23), through his royal ancestor David (1.32; 3.31), and finally through the paternity of *Adam, son of God* (3.38).

4 Jesus, full of the Holy Spirit, returned from the Jordan and was led by the Spirit in the wilderness, ²where for forty days he was tempted by the devil. He ate nothing at all during those days, and when they were over, he was famished. ³The devil said to him, "If you are the Son of God, command this stone to become a loaf of bread." ⁴Jesus answered him, "It is written, 'One does not live by bread alone.'"

a Or *my beloved Son*   *b* Other ancient authorities read *You are my Son, today I have begotten you*
c Gk *Salathiel*   *d* Other ancient authorities read *Salmon*   *e* Other ancient authorities read *Amminadab, son of Aram*; others vary widely

5 Then the devil[a] led him up and showed him in an instant all the kingdoms of the world. 6And the devil[a] said to him, "To you I will give their glory and all this authority; for it has been given over to me, and I give it to anyone I please. 7If you, then, will worship me, it will all be yours." 8Jesus answered him, "It is written,

'Worship the Lord your God,
　and serve only him.' "

9 Then the devil[a] took him to Jerusalem, and placed him on the pinnacle of the temple, saying to him, "If you are the Son of God, throw yourself down from here, 10for it is written,

'He will command his angels concerning
　you,
　to protect you,'

11and

'On their hands they will bear you up,
　so that you will not dash your foot
　　against a stone.' "

12Jesus answered him, "It is said, 'Do not put the Lord your God to the test.' " 13When the devil had finished every test, he departed from him until an opportune time.

4.1–13: The testing of the Son of God. Jesus' obedience to God is proved in terms well known from Israel's heritage. **1:** The *Holy Spirit* remains with God's anointed* (see 3.22). **2:** Moses and Elijah also fasted for *forty days* (Ex 34.28; Deut 9.9, 18; 1 Kings 19.8). **4–12:** Each of the three tests concludes with Jesus' quotation of Deuteronomy (v. 4, Deut 8.3; v. 8, Deut 6.13; v. 12, Deut 6.16). When tested, Jesus proves to be the faithful Son of God, even as Israel was proved unfaithful during 40 years in the wilderness (Deut 8.2–5). The *devil* rarely appears so directly in biblical narrative,* here (vv. 10–11) quoting Ps 91, which actually counsels trusting God, not testing. **13:** The devil's departure *until an opportune time* anticipates the "opportunity" to betray Jesus in 22.3–6.

~~~

14 Then Jesus, filled with the power of the Spirit, returned to Galilee, and a report about him spread through all the surrounding country. 15He began to teach in their synagogues and was praised by everyone.

16 When he came to Nazareth, where he had been brought up, he went to the synagogue on the sabbath day, as was his custom.

He stood up to read, 17and the scroll of the prophet Isaiah was given to him. He unrolled the scroll and found the place where it was written:

18 "The Spirit of the Lord is upon me,
　because he has anointed me
　　to bring good news to the poor.
He has sent me to proclaim release to
　the captives
　and recovery of sight to the blind,
　　to let the oppressed go free,
19　to proclaim the year of the Lord's
　　favor."

20And he rolled up the scroll, gave it back to the attendant, and sat down. The eyes of all in the synagogue were fixed on him. 21Then he began to say to them, "Today this scripture has been fulfilled in your hearing." 22All spoke well of him and were amazed at the gracious words that came from his mouth. They said, "Is not this Joseph's son?" 23He said to them, "Doubtless you will quote to me this proverb, 'Doctor, cure yourself!' And you will say, 'Do here also in your hometown the things that we have heard you did at Capernaum.' " 24And he said, "Truly I tell you, no prophet is accepted in the prophet's hometown. 25But the truth is, there were many widows in Israel in the time of Elijah, when the heaven was shut up three years and six months, and there was a severe famine over all the land; 26yet Elijah was sent to none of them except to a widow at Zarephath in Sidon. 27There were also many lepers[b] in Israel in the time of the prophet Elisha, and none of them was cleansed except Naaman the Syrian." 28When they heard this, all in the synagogue were filled with rage. 29They got up, drove him out of the town, and led him to the brow of the hill on which their town was built, so that they might hurl him off the cliff. 30But he passed through the midst of them and went on his way.

4.14–30: The messiah's* inaugural announcement. 14–15: Luke often writes brief summaries to introduce or conclude important stories, here heightening antic-

---

a Gk *he*　　*b* The terms *leper* and *leprosy* can refer to several diseases ipation of Jesus' reception in the *synagogue*★ in Nazareth. **16–21:** This is one of the most complete remaining descriptions of synagogue practice from the era before the Roman destruction of the Temple.★ In accord with the reading from Isa 61 and 58, *the Spirit of the Lord* authorizes the *anointed*★ ruler's speech (see also 3.22; 4.1, 14), and his program enacts God's care for the *poor* (1.52; 6.20; 7.22; 14.13, 21; 16.20, 22). The *year of the Lord's favor* is the time of "jubilee" and restoration (Lev 25.8–12). As Jesus *rolled up the scroll* while their *eyes were fixed on him,* the reader awaits his word and their verdict. **21–22:** Isaiah's prophecy is programmatic for Jesus *today. In your hearing* (literally, in your ears) indicates a truth prophetically declared whether or not they can "hear" it (Isa 6.9–13). Their question about *Joseph's son* reveals disbelief in Jesus as anointed ruler and Son of God (see Zechariah in 1.18–20). **23–27:** Jesus interprets their questioning as rejection with emphatic accusations: *"Doubtless you will quote . . . And you will say . . . Truly I tell you . . . But the truth is . . . "* He cites the precedents of *Elijah* and *Elisha* (1 King 17; 2 Kings 5) for judgment of Israel. **28–30:** Deut 18.20 prescribed death for false prophets,★ after their word does not prove true (see 7.22–23).

31 He went down to Capernaum, a city in Galilee, and was teaching them on the sabbath. ³²They were astounded at his teaching, because he spoke with authority. ³³In the synagogue there was a man who had the spirit of an unclean demon, and he cried out with a loud voice, ³⁴"Let us alone! What have you to do with us, Jesus of Nazareth? Have you come to destroy us? I know who you are, the Holy One of God." ³⁵But Jesus rebuked him, saying, "Be silent, and come out of him!" When the demon had thrown him down before them, he came out of him without having done him any harm. ³⁶They were all amazed and kept saying to one another, "What kind of utterance is this? For with authority and power he commands the unclean spirits, and out they come!" ³⁷And a report about him began to reach every place in the region.

38 After leaving the synagogue he entered Simon's house. Now Simon's mother-in-law was suffering from a high fever, and they asked him about her. ³⁹Then he stood over her and rebuked the fever, and it left her. Immediately she got up and began to serve them.

40 As the sun was setting, all those who had any who were sick with various kinds of diseases brought them to him; and he laid his hands on each of them and cured them. ⁴¹Demons also came out of many, shouting, "You are the Son of God!" But he rebuked them and would not allow them to speak, because they knew that he was the Messiah.ᵃ

42 At daybreak he departed and went into a deserted place. And the crowds were looking for him; and when they reached him, they wanted to prevent him from leaving them. ⁴³But he said to them, "I must proclaim the good news of the kingdom of God to the other cities also; for I was sent for this purpose." ⁴⁴So he continued proclaiming the message in the synagogues of Judea.ᵇ

4.31–44: Proclaiming the kingdom in Galilee and Judea. 31–37: In Israel's purity code, an *unclean demon* is the exact opposite of *the Holy One of God.* This encounter in the *synagogue*★ during *teaching* on the *sabbath* is provoked by an evil, unclean power that knows *Jesus of Nazareth* by name and status. Saving the man from *harm* still left Jesus open to accusation of violating the sabbath (see 6.9). **38:** This is the first mention of *Simon,* anticipating his call in 5.1–11. **41–42:** *Son of God* and *Messiah*★ (Gk., Christ, anointed★ one) are virtually the same titles in Luke. **43:** Jesus' determined *purpose* or mission is central in Luke's narrative★ (9.51, 53; 13.32–33).

5 Once while Jesusᶜ was standing beside the lake of Gennesaret, and the crowd was pressing in on him to hear the word of God, ²he saw two boats there at the shore of the lake; the fishermen had gone out of them and were washing their nets. ³He got into one of the boats, the one belonging to Simon, and asked him to put out a little way from the shore. Then he sat down and taught the crowds from the boat. ⁴When he had finished speaking, he said to Simon, "Put out into the deep water and let down your nets

---

a Or *the Christ*   *b* Other ancient authorities read *Galilee*   *c* Gk *he* for a catch." 5 Simon answered, "Master, we have worked all night long but have caught nothing. Yet if you say so, I will let down the nets." 6When they had done this, they caught so many fish that their nets were beginning to break. 7So they signaled their partners in the other boat to come and help them. And they came and filled both boats, so that they began to sink. 8But when Simon Peter saw it, he fell down at Jesus' knees, saying, "Go away from me, Lord, for I am a sinful man!" 9For he and all who were with him were amazed at the catch of fish that they had taken; 10and so also were James and John, sons of Zebedee, who were partners with Simon. Then Jesus said to Simon, "Do not be afraid; from now on you will be catching people." 11When they had brought their boats to shore, they left everything and followed him.

5.1–11: The call of Simon. This story resembles several biblical accounts of the call of a leader of Israel when the wonder and power of God is revealed in the midst of ordinary circumstances (Ex 3, Moses; Judg 6, Gideon; Isa 6, Isaiah). **1:** The *lake of Gennesaret* is another name for the sea of Galilee. **3:** Mk 4.1–2 and Mt 13.1–22 also report that Jesus teaches from a boat. **8:** Peter's sense that he is *a sinful man* expresses his fear in the presence of divine power. **10–11:** Matthew and Mark report the call of *Simon, James, and John* (plus Andrew) at the very beginning of Jesus' ministry (Mt 4.18–22; Mk 1.16–20).

12 Once, when he was in one of the cities, there was a man covered with leprosy.*a* When he saw Jesus, he bowed with his face to the ground and begged him, "Lord, if you choose, you can make me clean." 13Then Jesus*b* stretched out his hand, touched him, and said, "I do choose. Be made clean." Immediately the leprosy*a* left him. 14And he ordered him to tell no one. "Go," he said, "and show yourself to the priest, and, as Moses commanded, make an offering for your cleansing, for a testimony to them." 15But now more than ever the word about Jesus*c* spread abroad; many crowds would gather to hear him and to be cured of their diseases. 16But he would withdraw to deserted places and pray.

5.12–16: The cleansing of leprosy. 12: *Leprosy* included a complex variety of diseases, but the symptoms identified in Lev 13–14 were understood more in terms of ritual impurity than contagion, requiring exclusion from the community. In Nazareth (4.27), Jesus had cited the precedent of the prophet* Elisha's healing of a leper (2 Kings 5).

17 One day, while he was teaching, Pharisees and teachers of the law were sitting near by (they had come from every village of Galilee and Judea and from Jerusalem); and the power of the Lord was with him to heal.*d* 18Just then some men came, carrying a paralyzed man on a bed. They were trying to bring him in and lay him before Jesus;*e* 19but finding no way to bring him in because of the crowd, they went up on the roof and let him down with his bed through the tiles into the middle of the crowd*e* in front of Jesus. 20When he saw their faith, he said, "Friend,*f* your sins are forgiven you." 21Then the scribes and the Pharisees began to question, "Who is this who is speaking blasphemies? Who can forgive sins but God alone?" 22When Jesus perceived their questionings, he answered them, "Why do you raise such questions in your hearts? 23Which is easier, to say, 'Your sins are forgiven you,' or to say, 'Stand up and walk'? 24But so that you may know that the Son of Man has authority on earth to forgive sins"—he said to the one who was paralyzed—"I say to you, stand up and take your bed and go to your home." 25Immediately he stood up before them, took what he had been lying on, and went to his home, glorifying God. 26Amazement seized all of them, and they glorified God and were filled with awe, saying, "We have seen strange things today."

5.17–26: Forgiveness of sins and healing of paralysis. This healing story is the occasion for a dispute with the religious authorities on the interpretation* of the law. **17:** The *Pharisees* * and teachers of the law were

a The terms *leper* and *leprosy* can refer to several diseases   *b* Gk *he*   *c* Gk *him*   *d* Other ancient authorities read *was present to heal them*   *e* Gk *into the midst*   *f* Gk *Man* central figures in synagogues* in every community, calling Israel to observance of the Torah* (law of God given to Moses). **20–22:** Jesus both *saw* the *faith* of the crowd and *perceived* the *questionings* of *the scribes* and the Pharisees** as disbelief *in your hearts* (see 2.35). Questions were a customary method of teaching by prompting an answer from the law, but these questions accused Jesus of *blasphemy* (slandering God or God's name). **23:** Jesus' question also calls for interpretation*; *which is easier* means which is the "lighter" or the "heavier" matter according to the law. **24:** *The Son of Man* is the judge on the clouds of heaven at the end in Dan 7.13. Jesus claims that authority for himself *on earth.*

27 After this he went out and saw a tax collector named Levi, sitting at the tax booth; and he said to him, "Follow me." 28And he got up, left everything, and followed him.

29 Then Levi gave a great banquet for him in his house; and there was a large crowd of tax collectors and others sitting at the table*a* with them. 30The Pharisees and their scribes were complaining to his disciples, saying, "Why do you eat and drink with tax collectors and sinners?" 31Jesus answered, "Those who are well have no need of a physician, but those who are sick; 32I have come to call not the righteous but sinners to repentance."

33 Then they said to him, "John's disciples, like the disciples of the Pharisees, frequently fast and pray, but your disciples eat and drink." 34Jesus said to them, "You cannot make wedding guests fast while the bridegroom is with them, can you? 35The days will come when the bridegroom will be taken away from them, and then they will fast in those days." 36He also told them a parable: "No one tears a piece from a new garment and sews it on an old garment; otherwise the new will be torn, and the piece from the new will not match the old. 37And no one puts new wine into old wineskins; otherwise the new wine will burst the skins and will be spilled, and the skins will be destroyed. 38But new wine must be put into fresh wineskins. 39And no one after drinking old wine desires new wine, but says, 'The old is good.' "*b*

6 One sabbath*c* while Jesus*d* was going through the grainfields, his disciples plucked some heads of grain, rubbed them in their hands, and ate them. 2But some of the Pharisees said, "Why are you doing what is not lawful*e* on the sabbath?" 3Jesus answered, "Have you not read what David did when he and his companions were hungry? 4He entered the house of God and took and ate the bread of the Presence, which it is not lawful for any but the priests to eat, and gave some to his companions?" 5Then he said to them, "The Son of Man is lord of the sabbath."

6 On another sabbath he entered the synagogue and taught, and there was a man there whose right hand was withered. 7The scribes and the Pharisees watched him to see whether he would cure on the sabbath, so that they might find an accusation against him. 8Even though he knew what they were thinking, he said to the man who had the withered hand, "Come and stand here." He got up and stood there. 9Then Jesus said to them, "I ask you, is it lawful to do good or to do harm on the sabbath, to save life or to destroy it?" 10After looking around at all of them, he said to him, "Stretch out your hand." He did so, and his hand was restored. 11But they were filled with fury and discussed with one another what they might do to Jesus.

5.27–6.11: Conflicts about authority. 27–32: *Tax collectors* and *sinners* were Jews who were not regarded as *righteous* because they did not observe the law but often collaborated with the Roman order. They were considered ineligible to be disciples at the fellowship table with a teacher, drawing near to the law. Mk 2.13–17 and Mt 9.9–13 also emphasize Jesus' dramatic interpretation of who is invited to return to God (*repentance*). **33–39:** Jesus claims the freedom of the messiah,* or ruler of the end time. The *wedding* feast was a symbol of heaven. **35:** This verse has encouraged Christians to *fast* to prepare for the return of Christ when feasting will again replace fasting. **6.1–5:** The royal privileges that David exercised (1 Sam 21.1–6)

a Gk *reclining*   *b* Other ancient authorities read *better*; others lack verse 39   *c* Other ancient authorities read *On the second first sabbath*   *d* Gk *he*   *e* Other ancient authorities add *to do* are claimed by the messiah, Jesus. *The bread of the Presence* was holy or set apart for God. Jesus again uses the title *Son of Man* to declare his role and authority concerning God's law (5.24; Dan 7.13). **6–11:** The conflict about sabbath law escalates as the other teachers seek *an accusation.* Jesus' question, *is it lawful . . . on the sabbath,* is a classic question posed by Jewish teachers of the law: What kind of emergencies take precedence over sabbath practice?

12 Now during those days he went out to the mountain to pray; and he spent the night in prayer to God. 13And when day came, he called his disciples and chose twelve of them, whom he also named apostles: 14Simon, whom he named Peter, and his brother Andrew, and James, and John, and Philip, and Bartholomew, 15and Matthew, and Thomas, and James son of Alphaeus, and Simon, who was called the Zealot, 16and Judas son of James, and Judas Iscariot, who became a traitor.

17 He came down with them and stood on a level place, with a great crowd of his disciples and a great multitude of people from all Judea, Jerusalem, and the coast of Tyre and Sidon. 18They had come to hear him and to be healed of their diseases; and those who were troubled with unclean spirits were cured. 19And all in the crowd were trying to touch him, for power came out from him and healed all of them.

6.12–19: Preparing for Jesus' sayings. 12: Jesus often *prays* at significant points in the story (3.21; 5.16; 6.12; 9.18, 28–29; 11.1; 22.41, 44–45; 23.46). **13–16:** The *twelve* are significant as *apostles** who are sent as ambassadors of the mission and judges of the twelve tribes of Israel, which is why *Judas Iscariot* had to be replaced later (22.3–6, 30, 47–53; Acts 1.15–26). **17:** Jesus standing to teach from a *level place* compares with Matthew's description that he "went up the mountain" and "sat down." The gathering crowds from many regions anticipate a momentous event (5.17). **19:** The *power* to heal is again a sign of the presence of God's Spirit (4.1, 14; 5.17).

20 Then he looked up at his disciples and said:
"Blessed are you who are poor,
for yours is the kingdom of God.

21 "Blessed are you who are hungry now,
for you will be filled.
"Blessed are you who weep now,
for you will laugh.

22 "Blessed are you when people hate you, and when they exclude you, revile you, and defame you*a* on account of the Son of Man. 23Rejoice in that day and leap for joy, for surely your reward is great in heaven; for that is what their ancestors did to the prophets.
24 "But woe to you who are rich,
for you have received your
consolation.
25 "Woe to you who are full now,
for you will be hungry.
"Woe to you who are laughing now,
for you will mourn and weep.
26 "Woe to you when all speak well of you, for that is what their ancestors did to the false prophets.

27 "But I say to you that listen, Love your enemies, do good to those who hate you, 28bless those who curse you, pray for those who abuse you. 29If anyone strikes you on the cheek, offer the other also; and from anyone who takes away your coat do not withhold even your shirt. 30Give to everyone who begs from you; and if anyone takes away your goods, do not ask for them again. 31Do to others as you would have them do to you.

32 "If you love those who love you, what credit is that to you? For even sinners love those who love them. 33If you do good to those who do good to you, what credit is that to you? For even sinners do the same. 34If you lend to those from whom you hope to receive, what credit is that to you? Even sinners lend to sinners, to receive as much again. 35But love your enemies, do good, and lend, expecting nothing in return.*b* Your reward will be great, and you will be children of the Most High; for he is kind to the ungrateful and the wicked. 36Be merciful, just as your Father is merciful.

37 "Do not judge, and you will not be judged; do not condemn, and you will not be condemned. Forgive, and you will be for-

a Gk *cast out your name as evil* *b* Other ancient authorities read *despairing of no one* given; ³⁸give, and it will be given to you. A good measure, pressed down, shaken together, running over, will be put into your lap; for the measure you give will be the measure you get back."

39 He also told them a parable: "Can a blind person guide a blind person? Will not both fall into a pit? ⁴⁰A disciple is not above the teacher, but everyone who is fully qualified will be like the teacher. ⁴¹Why do you see the speck in your neighbor's*ᵃ* eye, but do not notice the log in your own eye? ⁴²Or how can you say to your neighbor,*ᵇ* 'Friend,*ᵇ* let me take out the speck in your eye,' when you yourself do not see the log in your own eye? You hypocrite, first take the log out of your own eye, and then you will see clearly to take the speck out of your neighbor's*ᵃ* eye.

43 "No good tree bears bad fruit, nor again does a bad tree bear good fruit; ⁴⁴for each tree is known by its own fruit. Figs are not gathered from thorns, nor are grapes picked from a bramble bush. ⁴⁵The good person out of the good treasure of the heart produces good, and the evil person out of evil treasure produces evil; for it is out of the abundance of the heart that the mouth speaks.

46 "Why do you call me 'Lord, Lord,' and do not do what I tell you? ⁴⁷I will show you what someone is like who comes to me, hears my words, and acts on them. ⁴⁸That one is like a man building a house, who dug deeply and laid the foundation on rock; when a flood arose, the river burst against that house but could not shake it, because it had been well built.*ᶜ* ⁴⁹But the one who hears and does not act is like a man who built a house on the ground without a foundation. When the river burst against it, immediately it fell, and great was the ruin of that house."

6.20–49: The address on the plain. These verses begin a section (6.20–8.3) that is without parallels in Mark. This section contains many sayings of Jesus that are largely shared with Matthew. Many scholars suggest Matthew and Luke may have drawn from a "Sayings Source," which is commonly called "Q" for the German word "Quelle." No copy of such a source has ever been found apart from the verses shared and close agreements of Matthew and Luke, along with

some parallels in the noncanonical Gospel of Thomas.* Luke's account does not glorify poverty, but stresses the contrast between the present need of the *poor* and their future abundance, while the *rich* who have plenty *now* will be deprived in the future. **20:** *Blessed* means favored by God, in this case because of God's particular care for the *poor* (4.18; 7.22–23). *The kingdom of God* is God's heavenly rule come to earth as announced in the reign of the messiah,* Jesus (see 4.18; 7.22; 17.20–21). **24:** Prophetic announcements of *woe* indicate divine judgment (10.13; 11.42–52; 17.1; 21.23; 22.22). **26:** *False prophets** are popular for telling people what they want to hear (Isa 30.10). **27–31:** This section ends with the "golden rule," but now radically applied to *enemies, abusers,* thieves, and *beggars.* These verses have often been misused to discourage oppressed people from seeking justice. **32–38:** The *credit* that *sinners* receive fits with usual standards of fair exchange which gentiles* and nonbelievers practice. The *children of the Most High* operate with the economy of *mercy* rather than fairness, relying on the reward systems of God's reign. **39–49:** Jesus directs these traditional warnings against hypocrisy to his own disciples (6.17, 40), emphasizing the obedience of *action* (v. 47).

IDENTIFYING THE MESSIAH* OF GOD

7.1–9.50: Jesus' mission moves beyond speaking to his disciples. His role is publicly tested.

---

7 After Jesus*ᵈ* had finished all his sayings in the hearing of the people, he entered Capernaum. ²A centurion there had a slave whom he valued highly, and who was ill and close to death. ³When he heard about Jesus, he sent some Jewish elders to him, asking him to come and heal his slave. ⁴When they came to Jesus, they appealed to him earnestly, saying, "He is worthy of having you do this for him, ⁵for he loves our people, and it is he who built our synagogue for us." ⁶And Jesus went with them, but when he was not far from the house, the centurion sent friends to say to him, "Lord, do not trouble yourself, for I am not worthy to have you come under my roof; ⁷therefore I did not presume to come to you. But only speak the

---

a Gk *brother's*   *b* Gk *brother*   *c* Other ancient authorities read *founded upon the rock*   *d* Gk *he* word, and let my servant be healed. 8For I also am a man set under authority, with soldiers under me; and I say to one, 'Go,' and he goes, and to another, 'Come,' and he comes, and to my slave, 'Do this,' and the slave does it." 9When Jesus heard this he was amazed at him, and turning to the crowd that followed him, he said, "I tell you, not even in Israel have I found such faith." 10When those who had been sent returned to the house, they found the slave in good health.

11 Soon afterwards*a* he went to a town called Nain, and his disciples and a large crowd went with him. 12As he approached the gate of the town, a man who had died was being carried out. He was his mother's only son, and she was a widow; and with her was a large crowd from the town. 13When the Lord saw her, he had compassion for her and said to her, "Do not weep." 14Then he came forward and touched the bier, and the bearers stood still. And he said, "Young man, I say to you, rise!" 15The dead man sat up and began to speak, and Jesus*b* gave him to his mother. 16Fear seized all of them; and they glorified God, saying, "A great prophet has risen among us!" and "God has looked favorably on his people!" 17This word about him spread throughout Judea and all the surrounding country.

18 The disciples of John reported all these things to him. So John summoned two of his disciples 19and sent them to the Lord to ask, "Are you the one who is to come, or are we to wait for another?" 20When the men had come to him, they said, "John the Baptist has sent us to you to ask, 'Are you the one who is to come, or are we to wait for another?'" 21Jesus*c* had just then cured many people of diseases, plagues, and evil spirits, and had given sight to many who were blind. 22And he answered them, "Go and tell John what you have seen and heard: the blind receive their sight, the lame walk, the lepers*d* are cleansed, the deaf hear, the dead are raised, the poor have good news brought to them. 23And blessed is anyone who takes no offense at me."

precedent in Elisha (2 Kings 5.1–14; Lk 4.27). **2–5:** The *centurion* is a "friend of Israel" (see also Acts 10.2). **11–17: The great prophet and God's visitation. 14:** *Touching the bier* would have made Jesus ritually unclean. **15:** Like Elijah (see 4.26), Jesus raised the widow's son and *gave him to his mother* (1 Kings 17.17–24; see also 2 Kings 4.18–37). **16:** *God has looked favorably on his people* is literally "God has visited his people," picking up the promising and fearsome theme of divine "visitation" (1.68; 19.44). **18–23: John's question. 19–20:** *The one who is to come* was announced by John (3.16), now answered in prophetic terms (Isa 29.18; 35.5–6; 61.1). **22:** Jesus has done what he announced at Nazareth (4.18).

～～～～～～～～～～～～

24 When John's messengers had gone, Jesus*b* began to speak to the crowds about John:*e* "What did you go out into the wilderness to look at? A reed shaken by the wind? 25What then did you go out to see? Someone*f* dressed in soft robes? Look, those who put on fine clothing and live in luxury are in royal palaces. 26What then did you go out to see? A prophet? Yes, I tell you, and more than a prophet. 27This is the one about whom it is written,

'See, I am sending my messenger ahead
          of you,
    who will prepare your way
          before you.'

28I tell you, among those born of women no one is greater than John; yet the least in the kingdom of God is greater than he." 29(And all the people who heard this, including the tax collectors, acknowledged the justice of God,*g* because they had been baptized with John's baptism. 30But by refusing to be baptized by him, the Pharisees and the lawyers rejected God's purpose for themselves.)

31 "To what then will I compare the people of this generation, and what are they like? 32They are like children sitting in the marketplace and calling to one another,

'We played the flute for you, and you
          did not dance;
    we wailed, and you did not weep.'

7.1–50: Jesus the prophet* of God. 1–10: Jesus' encounter with a trusting foreigner has prophetic

a Other ancient authorities read *Next day*   *b* Gk *he*
c Gk *He*   *d* The terms *leper* and *leprosy* can refer to several diseases   *e* Gk *him*   *f* Or *Why then did you go out? To see someone*   *g* Or *praised God*

33For John the Baptist has come eating no bread and drinking no wine, and you say, 'He has a demon'; 34the Son of Man has come eating and drinking, and you say, 'Look, a glutton and a drunkard, a friend of tax collectors and sinners!' 35Nevertheless, wisdom is vindicated by all her children."

7.24–35: The greatest prophet★ is surpassed. 26–28: John marks the end of the era of the great prophets, fulfilling Malachi's (3.1) prophecy (see Mt 11.14), and anticipating *the kingdom of God* inaugurated by Jesus (see also 16.16). **31:** *The people of this generation* (see 11.29–32, 50–51; 17.25) are under judgment, including those who thought they were protecting the law of God. **35:** God's *wisdom* is seen to prove who (*her children,* compare Mt 11.19, "her deeds") are truly faithful (see 11.49).

36 One of the Pharisees asked Jesus[a] to eat with him, and he went into the Pharisee's house and took his place at the table. 37And a woman in the city, who was a sinner, having learned that he was eating in the Pharisee's house, brought an alabaster jar of ointment. 38She stood behind him at his feet, weeping, and began to bathe his feet with her tears and to dry them with her hair. Then she continued kissing his feet and anointing them with the ointment. 39Now when the Pharisee who had invited him saw it, he said to himself, "If this man were a prophet, he would have known who and what kind of woman this is who is touching him—that she is a sinner." 40Jesus spoke up and said to him, "Simon, I have something to say to you." "Teacher," he replied, "speak." 41"A certain creditor had two debtors; one owed five hundred denarii,[b] and the other fifty. 42When they could not pay, he canceled the debts for both of them. Now which of them will love him more?" 43Simon answered, "I suppose the one for whom he canceled the greater debt." And Jesus[c] said to him, "You have judged rightly." 44Then turning toward the woman, he said to Simon, "Do you see this woman? I entered your house; you gave me no water for my feet, but she has bathed my feet with her tears and dried them with her hair. 45You gave me no kiss, but from the time I came in she has not stopped kiss-

ing my feet. 46You did not anoint my head with oil, but she has anointed my feet with ointment. 47Therefore, I tell you, her sins, which were many, have been forgiven; hence she has shown great love. But the one to whom little is forgiven, loves little." 48Then he said to her, "Your sins are forgiven." 49But those who were at the table with him began to say among themselves, "Who is this who even forgives sins?" 50And he said to the woman, "Your faith has saved you; go in peace."

7.36–50: The prophet★ who forgives sins. 36: The setting at Simon the *Pharisee's★* table again raises the question of who is included with the righteous (see ch. 14). **37–39:** This *woman in the city* may have been one of the "people of the land" whom the Pharisees regarded as a *sinner* (see also v. 39) for not properly observing the law (5.30–32; compare 7.29–30). The true *prophet* knows who is in God's favor or disfavor. **44–46:** *Footwashing, ointments,* and *kissing* are lavish displays of near eastern hospitality. **48–50:** Jesus' declarations display Jewish aversion to speaking directly of God, *your sins are forgiven, your faith has saved you,* but the scandal remains for the Pharisees. Only God can forgive sins (5.21–22).

8 Soon afterwards he went on through cities and villages, proclaiming and bringing the good news of the kingdom of God. The twelve were with him, 2as well as some women who had been cured of evil spirits and infirmities: Mary, called Magdalene, from whom seven demons had gone out, 3and Joanna, the wife of Herod's steward Chuza, and Susanna, and many others, who provided for them[d] out of their resources.

4 When a great crowd gathered and people from town after town came to him, he said in a parable: 5"A sower went out to sow his seed; and as he sowed, some fell on the path and was trampled on, and the birds of the air ate it up. 6Some fell on the rock; and as it grew up, it withered for lack of moisture. 7Some fell among thorns, and the thorns grew with it and choked it. 8Some fell into

a Gk *him*　　*b* The denarius was the usual day's wage for a laborer　　*c* Gk *he*　　*d* Other ancient authorities read *him* good soil, and when it grew, it produced a hundredfold." As he said this, he called out, "Let anyone with ears to hear listen!"

9 Then his disciples asked him what this parable meant. [10]He said, "To you it has been given to know the secrets[a] of the kingdom of God; but to others I speak[b] in parables, so that

'looking they may not perceive,
and listening they may not understand.'

11 "Now the parable is this: The seed is the word of God. [12]The ones on the path are those who have heard; then the devil comes and takes away the word from their hearts, so that they may not believe and be saved. [13]The ones on the rock are those who, when they hear the word, receive it with joy. But these have no root; they believe only for a while and in a time of testing fall away. [14]As for what fell among the thorns, these are the ones who hear; but as they go on their way, they are choked by the cares and riches and pleasures of life, and their fruit does not mature. [15]But as for that in the good soil, these are the ones who, when they hear the word, hold it fast in an honest and good heart, and bear fruit with patient endurance.

16 "No one after lighting a lamp hides it under a jar, or puts it under a bed, but puts it on a lampstand, so that those who enter may see the light. [17]For nothing is hidden that will not be disclosed, nor is anything secret that will not become known and come to light. [18]Then pay attention to how you listen; for to those who have, more will be given; and from those who do not have, even what they seem to have will be taken away."

19 Then his mother and his brothers came to him, but they could not reach him because of the crowd. [20]And he was told, "Your mother and your brothers are standing outside, wanting to see you." [21]But he said to them, "My mother and my brothers are those who hear the word of God and do it."

see also 23.49, 55). **4–8:** See also Mk 4.1–9; Mt 13.1–9. **9–10:** In accord with Isa 6, the knowledge of *the secrets of the kingdom of God* is both revealed and hidden because of divine judgment (see 19.42; Acts 13.40–41; 28.26–28). **11–15:** Luke identifies *the seed* as *the word of God*, revealing the will of God and emphasizing growth as active obedience (8.21). *Endurance* is not merely waiting, but withstanding persecution and rejection (21.12–19). **16–18:** The *secret* things Jesus taught are quickly public, never mere private pieties. **19–21:** Jesus' true kindred, like Abraham's children (3.7–9), are identified by fidelity, not bloodlines.

22 One day he got into a boat with his disciples, and he said to them, "Let us go across to the other side of the lake." So they put out, [23]and while they were sailing he fell asleep. A windstorm swept down on the lake, and the boat was filling with water, and they were in danger. [24]They went to him and woke him up, shouting, "Master, Master, we are perishing!" And he woke up and rebuked the wind and the raging waves; they ceased, and there was a calm. [25]He said to them, "Where is your faith?" They were afraid and amazed, and said to one another, "Who then is this, that he commands even the winds and the water, and they obey him?"

26 Then they arrived at the country of the Gerasenes,[c] which is opposite Galilee. [27]As he stepped out on land, a man of the city who had demons met him. For a long time he had worn[d] no clothes, and he did not live in a house but in the tombs. [28]When he saw Jesus, he fell down before him and shouted at the top of his voice, "What have you to do with me, Jesus, Son of the Most High God? I beg you, do not torment me"— [29]for Jesus[e] had commanded the unclean spirit to come out of the man. (For many times it had seized him; he was kept under guard and bound with chains and shackles, but he would break the bonds and be driven by the demon into the wilds.) [30]Jesus then asked

---

8.1–21: Jesus, proclaimer of the word of God. 1–3: These verses are a Lukan summary, concluding the section that began in 6.20 without parallels in Mark's Gospel. *Mary Magdalene and Joanna* are mentioned later among the first witnesses to the resurrection (24.10,

a Or *mysteries*   *b* Gk lacks *I speak*   *c* Other ancient authorities read *Gadarenes;* others, *Gergesenes*
d Other ancient authorities read *a man of the city who had had demons for a long time met him. He wore*
e Gk *he*

him, "What is your name?" He said, "Legion"; for many demons had entered him. [31]They begged him not to order them to go back into the abyss.

32 Now there on the hillside a large herd of swine was feeding; and the demons[a] begged Jesus[b] to let them enter these. So he gave them permission. [33]Then the demons came out of the man and entered the swine, and the herd rushed down the steep bank into the lake and was drowned.

34 When the swineherds saw what had happened, they ran off and told it in the city and in the country. [35]Then people came out to see what had happened, and when they came to Jesus, they found the man from whom the demons had gone sitting at the feet of Jesus, clothed and in his right mind. And they were afraid. [36]Those who had seen it told them how the one who had been possessed by demons had been healed. [37]Then all the people of the surrounding country of the Gerasenes[c] asked Jesus[b] to leave them; for they were seized with great fear. So he got into the boat and returned. [38]The man from whom the demons had gone begged that he might be with him; but Jesus[d] sent him away, saying, [39]"Return to your home, and declare how much God has done for you." So he went away, proclaiming throughout the city how much Jesus had done for him.

8.22–56: The commanding word of Jesus. 24: *Master* is the title of a person in authority (5.5; 8.45; 9.33, 49; 17.13). **25:** *"Who then is this?"* recalls the power of God over the forces of the deep (Ps 107.28–29). **26–39: The Gerasene demoniac. 27–28:** The lore about *demons* included anti-social behavior (*he wore no clothes*) and ritual impurity (*in the tombs*). His *shouting* is a power confrontation where the demoniac knows Jesus' name (*Son of the Most High God*, see 4.34, 41) and must reveal his, or at least the size of the horde (a Roman *Legion* was a troop of several thousand soldiers). **31–33:** The *abyss* is the bottomless pit reserved for God's enemies (Rev 9.1–11). *The swine* are unclean and suitable for demons, but water was their destruction (see 11.24, "waterless regions"). **37:** The people, *seized with great fear*, have seen but not believed (8.10).

40 Now when Jesus returned, the crowd welcomed him, for they were all waiting for him. [41]Just then there came a man named Jairus, a leader of the synagogue. He fell at Jesus' feet and begged him to come to his house, [42]for he had an only daughter, about twelve years old, who was dying.

As he went, the crowds pressed in on him. [43]Now there was a woman who had been suffering from hemorrhages for twelve years; and though she had spent all she had on physicians,[e] no one could cure her. [44]She came up behind him and touched the fringe of his clothes, and immediately her hemorrhage stopped. [45]Then Jesus asked, "Who touched me?" When all denied it, Peter[f] said, "Master, the crowds surround you and press in on you." [46]But Jesus said, "Someone touched me; for I noticed that power had gone out from me." [47]When the woman saw that she could not remain hidden, she came trembling; and falling down before him, she declared in the presence of all the people why she had touched him, and how she had been immediately healed. [48]He said to her, "Daughter, your faith has made you well; go in peace."

49 While he was still speaking, someone came from the leader's house to say, "Your daughter is dead; do not trouble the teacher any longer." [50]When Jesus heard this, he replied, "Do not fear. Only believe, and she will be saved." [51]When he came to the house, he did not allow anyone to enter with him, except Peter, John, and James, and the child's father and mother. [52]They were all weeping and wailing for her; but he said, "Do not weep; for she is not dead but sleeping." [53]And they laughed at him, knowing that she was dead. [54]But he took her by the hand and called out, "Child, get up!" [55]Her spirit returned, and she got up at once. Then he directed them to give her something to eat. [56]Her parents were astounded; but he ordered them to tell no one what had happened.

a Gk *they*   b Gk *him*   c Other ancient authorities read *Gadarenes*; others, *Gergesenes*   d Gk *he*   e Other ancient authorities lack *and though she had spent all she had on physicians*   f Other ancient authorities add *and those who were with him*

8.40–56: Jesus heals the afflicted and raises the dead. These two stories have already been woven together in Mark (Mk 5.21–43). The delay in healing *Jairus's daughter* means she is already dead when he arrives. **43–45:** Her chronic bleeding exceeded normal monthly flow and rendered her continually unclean and unable to *touch* anyone (Lev 15.19–30). **46:** The *power* to heal was the presence of the Spirit (4.14; 5.17). **48:** To call her *daughter* is to mark her restoration in the family of Israel (see 13.16) and connects with the child (8.49). **55:** To say *her spirit returned* is to emphasize that she had died (23.46).

9 Then Jesus*a* called the twelve together and gave them power and authority over all demons and to cure diseases, 2and he sent them out to proclaim the kingdom of God and to heal. 3He said to them, "Take nothing for your journey, no staff, nor bag, nor bread, nor money—not even an extra tunic. 4Whatever house you enter, stay there, and leave from there. 5Wherever they do not welcome you, as you are leaving that town shake the dust off your feet as a testimony against them." 6They departed and went through the villages, bringing the good news and curing diseases everywhere.

7 Now Herod the ruler*b* heard about all that had taken place, and he was perplexed, because it was said by some that John had been raised from the dead, 8by some that Elijah had appeared, and by others that one of the ancient prophets had arisen. 9Herod said, "John I beheaded; but who is this about whom I hear such things?" And he tried to see him.

9.1–50: Jesus, the Christ and chosen of God. 1–6: He authorizes the twelve. The *power and authority* of *the twelve* is directly tied to their commission as agents of *the kingdom of God* within Israel (see 6.13; 22.30). **3:** They are sent without the *staff* and *bag* of provisions for wandering philosophers (see 10.4–5). **5:** To *shake the dust off* is to declare freedom from responsibility (10.11; Acts 13.51). **7–9: He provokes Herod.** Herod's appearance is ominous (3.1), anticipating his threatening return in 13.31. The link with *Elijah* is again strong (7.26–27; 9.19).

10 On their return the apostles told Jesus*c* all they had done. He took them with him and withdrew privately to a city called Bethsaida. 11When the crowds found out about it, they followed him; and he welcomed them, and spoke to them about the kingdom of God, and healed those who needed to be cured.

12 The day was drawing to a close, and the twelve came to him and said, "Send the crowd away, so that they may go into the surrounding villages and countryside, to lodge and get provisions; for we are here in a deserted place." 13But he said to them, "You give them something to eat." They said, "We have no more than five loaves and two fish—unless we are to go and buy food for all these people." 14For there were about five thousand men. And he said to his disciples, "Make them sit down in groups of about fifty each." 15They did so and made them all sit down. 16And taking the five loaves and the two fish, he looked up to heaven, and blessed and broke them, and gave them to the disciples to set before the crowd. 17And all ate and were filled. What was left over was gathered up, twelve baskets of broken pieces.

9.10–17: He feeds the 5,000. This section agrees closely with Mark's sequence (see Mk 6.32–44). The feeding story is filled with reminders of God feeding Israel in the wilderness and Elijah feeding 100 men (2 Kings 4.42–44). It also anticipates the Passover* supper in Lk 22 (*taking the loaves*, he *blessed, broke, and gave*).

18 Once when Jesus*a* was praying alone, with only the disciples near him, he asked them, "Who do the crowds say that I am?" 19They answered, "John the Baptist; but others, Elijah; and still others, that one of the ancient prophets has arisen." 20He said to them, "But who do you say that I am?" Peter answered, "The Messiah*d* of God."

21 He sternly ordered and commanded them not to tell anyone, 22saying, "The Son of Man must undergo great suffering, and be rejected by the elders, chief priests, and scribes, and be killed, and on the third day be raised."

a Gk *he*   *b* Gk *tetrarch*   *c* Gk *him*
d Or *The Christ*

23 Then he said to them all, "If any want to become my followers, let them deny themselves and take up their cross daily and follow me. 24For those who want to save their life will lose it, and those who lose their life for my sake will save it. 25What does it profit them if they gain the whole world, but lose or forfeit themselves? 26Those who are ashamed of me and of my words, of them the Son of Man will be ashamed when he comes in his glory and the glory of the Father and of the holy angels. 27But truly I tell you, there are some standing here who will not taste death before they see the kingdom of God."

9.18–27: He is revealed as the messiah* and predicts his death. 20: The repeated question of who Jesus is (9.9, 18) receives the decisive answer of *Messiah of God* (see the demons in 4.41), and this royal title will be the charge for his execution (22.67; 23.35–37). 21–22: This is the first of several predictions Jesus makes of his death (9.43–45; 12.50; 13.33; 18.31–34). 26: The *Son of Man* is the judge at the end time (Dan 7.13).

28 Now about eight days after these sayings Jesus*a* took with him Peter and John and James, and went up on the mountain to pray. 29And while he was praying, the appearance of his face changed, and his clothes became dazzling white. 30Suddenly they saw two men, Moses and Elijah, talking to him. 31They appeared in glory and were speaking of his departure, which he was about to accomplish at Jerusalem. 32Now Peter and his companions were weighed down with sleep; but since they had stayed awake,*b* they saw his glory and the two men who stood with him. 33Just as they were leaving him, Peter said to Jesus, "Master, it is good for us to be here; let us make three dwellings,*c* one for you, one for Moses, and one for Elijah"—not knowing what he said. 34While he was saying this, a cloud came and overshadowed them; and they were terrified as they entered the cloud. 35Then from the cloud came a voice that said, "This is my Son, my Chosen;*d* listen to him!" 36When the voice had spoken, Jesus was found alone. And they kept silent and in those days told no one any of the things they had seen.

9.28–36: He is revealed as the chosen Son of God. *The mountain, the dazzling white clothes, Moses and Elijah, his glory, the cloud,* and *the voice from heaven* are all biblical dimensions of a divine appearance (epiphany*). 30: *Moses* and *Elijah* had miraculous endings of their lives. 31: Jesus' *departure* in Greek is his "exodus," which is something he will *accomplish at Jerusalem* (see his "baptism"* in 12.50). 33: The *dwellings* are the "tents" of the Jewish feast of booths (Deut 16.13).

37 On the next day, when they had come down from the mountain, a great crowd met him. 38Just then a man from the crowd shouted, "Teacher, I beg you to look at my son; he is my only child. 39Suddenly a spirit seizes him, and all at once he*e* shrieks. It convulses him until he foams at the mouth; it mauls him and will scarcely leave him. 40I begged your disciples to cast it out, but they could not." 41Jesus answered, "You faithless and perverse generation, how much longer must I be with you and bear with you? Bring your son here." 42While he was coming, the demon dashed him to the ground in convulsions. But Jesus rebuked the unclean spirit, healed the boy, and gave him back to his father. 43And all were astounded at the greatness of God.

While everyone was amazed at all that he was doing, he said to his disciples, 44"Let these words sink into your ears: The Son of Man is going to be betrayed into human hands." 45But they did not understand this saying; its meaning was concealed from them, so that they could not perceive it. And they were afraid to ask him about this saying.

46 An argument arose among them as to which one of them was the greatest. 47But Jesus, aware of their inner thoughts, took a little child and put it by his side, 48and said to them, "Whoever welcomes this child in my name welcomes me, and whoever welcomes me welcomes the one who sent me; for the least among all of you is the greatest."

49 John answered, "Master, we saw

a Gk he b Or but when they were fully awake
c Or tents d Other ancient authorities read my Beloved e Or it

someone casting out demons in your name, and we tried to stop him, because he does not follow with us." ⁵⁰But Jesus said to him, "Do not stop him; for whoever is not against you is for you."

9.37–50. 37–43: He heals a possessed boy. On the *only son*, see 7.12. **9.43b–50: He speaks firmly to his disciples. 45:** This verse emphasizes the disciples' inability to understand Jesus' predictions of suffering as due to God (*its meaning was concealed from them*, see Isa 6 cited in Lk 8.10). **46:** The *argument* about who was *greatest* is even more negatively recounted in Mk 9.33–37. **50:** Mk 9.38–41 has a fuller account of the strange exorcist.

THE WAY OF THE DETERMINED MESSIAH*

9.51–19.27: This section is an extended journey narrative* of the departure or "exodus" Jesus fulfilled by going to Jerusalem (9.31). Luke's repeated reminders that Jesus is on this journey reveal the literary significance of following him on the "way." This larger section is organized into a three-phase journey (9.51–13.21; 13.22–17.10; 17.11–19.27).

51 When the days drew near for him to be taken up, he set his face to go to Jerusalem. ⁵²And he sent messengers ahead of him. On their way they entered a village of the Samaritans to make ready for him; ⁵³but they did not receive him, because his face was set toward Jerusalem. ⁵⁴When his disciples James and John saw it, they said, "Lord, do you want us to command fire to come down from heaven and consume them?"ᵃ ⁵⁵But he turned and rebuked them. ⁵⁶Thenᵇ they went on to another village.

57 As they were going along the road, someone said to him, "I will follow you wherever you go." ⁵⁸And Jesus said to him, "Foxes have holes, and birds of the air have nests; but the Son of Man has nowhere to lay his head." ⁵⁹To another he said, "Follow me." But he said, "Lord, first let me go and bury my father." ⁶⁰But Jesusᶜ said to him, "Let the dead bury their own dead; but as for you, go and proclaim the kingdom of God." ⁶¹Another said, "I will follow you, Lord; but let me first say farewell to those at my home." ⁶²Jesus said to him, "No one who puts a

hand to the plow and looks back is fit for the kingdom of God."

9.51–13.21: Jesus faces toward Jerusalem. 9.51–62: He sets his face. 51: The prophet* Isaiah also *set his face* "like flint" (Isa 50.7), and Ezekiel was called to "set your face toward Jerusalem" in order to prophesy against the sanctuaries (Ezek 21.1–2). **52:** The *Samaritans* did not recognize the Temple* in Jerusalem (Jn 4.19–20). **54:** Elijah brought *fire down from heaven* to *consume* those who rejected his message. **58:** Here the *Son of Man* speaks of the human, suffering Jesus (9.22, 44), not the judge of the end (9.26) **59:** The *burial* of a *father* is a profound Jewish obligation (Gen 50.5; Tob 4.3).

10 After this the Lord appointed seventyᵈ others and sent them on ahead of him in pairs to every town and place where he himself intended to go. ²He said to them, "The harvest is plentiful, but the laborers are few; therefore ask the Lord of the harvest to send out laborers into his harvest. ³Go on your way. See, I am sending you out like lambs into the midst of wolves. ⁴Carry no purse, no bag, no sandals; and greet no one on the road. ⁵Whatever house you enter, first say, 'Peace to this house!' ⁶And if anyone is there who shares in peace, your peace will rest on that person; but if not, it will return to you. ⁷Remain in the same house, eating and drinking whatever they provide, for the laborer deserves to be paid. Do not move about from house to house. ⁸Whenever you enter a town and its people welcome you, eat what is set before you; ⁹cure the sick who are there, and say to them, 'The kingdom of God has come near to you.'ᵉ ¹⁰But whenever you enter a town and they do not welcome you, go out into its streets and say, ¹¹'Even the dust of your town that clings to our feet, we wipe off in protest against you. Yet know this: the kingdom of God has come near.'ᶠ ¹²I tell you, on that day it will

a Other ancient authorities add *as Elijah did*
b Other ancient authorities read *rebuked them, and said,* "You do not know what spirit you are of, ⁵⁶for the Son of Man has not come to destroy the lives of human beings but to save them." Then   c Gk *he*   d Other ancient authorities read *seventy-two*   e Or *is at hand for you*
f Or *is at hand*

be more tolerable for Sodom than for that town.

13 "Woe to you, Chorazin! Woe to you, Bethsaida! For if the deeds of power done in you had been done in Tyre and Sidon, they would have repented long ago, sitting in sackcloth and ashes. 14But at the judgment it will be more tolerable for Tyre and Sidon than for you. 15And you, Capernaum,

will you be exalted to heaven?

No, you will be brought down
to Hades.

16 "Whoever listens to you listens to me, and whoever rejects you rejects me, and whoever rejects me rejects the one who sent me."

17 The seventy*a* returned with joy, saying, "Lord, in your name even the demons submit to us!" 18He said to them, "I watched Satan fall from heaven like a flash of lightning. 19See, I have given you authority to tread on snakes and scorpions, and over all the power of the enemy; and nothing will hurt you. 20Nevertheless, do not rejoice at this, that the spirits submit to you, but rejoice that your names are written in heaven."

21 At that same hour Jesus*b* rejoiced in the Holy Spirit*c* and said, "I thank*d* you, Father, Lord of heaven and earth, because you have hidden these things from the wise and the intelligent and have revealed them to infants; yes, Father, for such was your gracious will.*e* 22All things have been handed over to me by my Father; and no one knows who the Son is except the Father, or who the Father is except the Son and anyone to whom the Son chooses to reveal him."

23 Then turning to the disciples, Jesus*b* said to them privately, "Blessed are the eyes that see what you see! 24For I tell you that many prophets and kings desired to see what you see, but did not see it, and to hear what you hear, but did not hear it."

Peace to this house is an official greeting, traditional from the time of King David (1 Sam 25.6). **8–12:** Unlike many approaching rulers, the coming of this *kingdom* is not coercive, but its consequences will be profound *on that day*, at the divine *judgment* (v. 14), as in God's destruction of *Sodom* (Gen 19.15–28). **15:** The prophetic* woe on *Capernaum* echoes Isa 14.11, 13–15. **16–20:** The divine authority of those who are sent derives from Jesus' identity (see also 10.22). The fall of *Satan* is a hope of the end time (Rev 12.7–9; 20.2–3). **21–23:** The presence of *the Holy Spirit* is the mark of *the Father's* reign. These verses became central to later Christian teaching of the holy Trinity. **23–24:** This saying presents the promise of the prophetic warning of Isa 6 (see 8.10).

25 Just then a lawyer stood up to test Jesus.*f* "Teacher," he said, "what must I do to inherit eternal life?" 26He said to him, "What is written in the law? What do you read there?" 27He answered, "You shall love the Lord your God with all your heart, and with all your soul, and with all your strength, and with all your mind; and your neighbor as yourself." 28And he said to him, "You have given the right answer; do this, and you will live."

29 But wanting to justify himself, he asked Jesus, "And who is my neighbor?" 30Jesus replied, "A man was going down from Jerusalem to Jericho, and fell into the hands of robbers, who stripped him, beat him, and went away, leaving him half dead. 31Now by chance a priest was going down that road; and when he saw him, he passed by on the other side. 32So likewise a Levite, when he came to the place and saw him, passed by on the other side. 33But a Samaritan while traveling came near him; and when he saw him, he was moved with pity. 34He went to him and bandaged his wounds, having poured oil and wine on them. Then he put him on his own animal, brought him to an inn, and took care of him. 35The next day he took out two denarii,*g* gave them to the innkeeper, and said, 'Take care of him;

10.1–24: He sends out seventy. 1: The *seventy* (or *seventy-two;* see note *a*) probably correspond to the seventy elders chosen by Moses from the twelve tribes (see 9.1–12), plus Eldad and Medad (Ex 24.1, 9; Num 11.16, 24–30). Early Christian missionaries regularly traveled *in pairs* (Acts 8.14; 15.32, 40). **2:** The *harvest* is the long-promised gathering of Israel (Isa 27.12). **5:**

a Other ancient authorities read *seventy-two*   *b* Gk *he*
c Other authorities read *in the spirit*   *d* Or *praise*
e Or *for so it was well-pleasing in your sight*   *f* Gk *him*
g The denarius was the usual day's wage for a laborer

and when I come back, I will repay you whatever more you spend.' ³⁶Which of these three, do you think, was a neighbor to the man who fell into the hands of the robbers?" ³⁷He said, "The one who showed him mercy." Jesus said to him, "Go and do likewise."

38 Now as they went on their way, he entered a certain village, where a woman named Martha welcomed him into her home. ³⁹She had a sister named Mary, who sat at the Lord's feet and listened to what he was saying. ⁴⁰But Martha was distracted by her many tasks; so she came to him and asked, "Lord, do you not care that my sister has left me to do all the work by myself? Tell her then to help me." ⁴¹But the Lord answered her, "Martha, Martha, you are worried and distracted by many things; ⁴²there is need of only one thing.ᵃ Mary has chosen the better part, which will not be taken away from her."

10.25–11.13: Jesus teaches the way of the kingdom. 10.25–42: On practicing God's law of love. 25: The *lawyer* is an interpreter of the scriptures (see also the ruler in 18.18). **27:** Jesus and the lawyer agree on combining Israel's great "Shema" on the *love* of *God* ("Hear O Israel": Deut 6.4–9) with Lev 19.18b on the love of the *neighbor*. **29:** Luke often notes the tendency of the "righteous" to *justify* themselves rather than God (16.15; 18.9–14, 18–30). **33–37:** The *Samaritan* is not called "good" in Luke (see 9.52; Acts 8). He observed the law by showing *mercy*. **38–39:** In Jn 11.1–12.8, *Martha* and *Mary* both engage in a discussion of the resurrection. Mary *listened* (Gk., heard his word) as a disciple (10.24).

11 He was praying in a certain place, and after he had finished, one of his disciples said to him, "Lord, teach us to pray, as John taught his disciples." ²He said to them, "When you pray, say:

Father,ᵇ hallowed be your name.
　　Your kingdom come.ᶜ
3　Give us each day our daily bread.ᵈ
4　And forgive us our sins,
　　　　for we ourselves forgive everyone
　　　　　　indebted to us.
　　And do not bring us to the time of
　　　　trial."ᵉ

5 And he said to them, "Suppose one of you has a friend, and you go to him at midnight and say to him, 'Friend, lend me three loaves of bread; ⁶for a friend of mine has arrived, and I have nothing to set before him.' ⁷And he answers from within, 'Do not bother me; the door has already been locked, and my children are with me in bed; I cannot get up and give you anything.' ⁸I tell you, even though he will not get up and give him anything because he is his friend, at least because of his persistence he will get up and give him whatever he needs.

9 "So I say to you, Ask, and it will be given you; search, and you will find; knock, and the door will be opened for you. ¹⁰For everyone who asks receives, and everyone who searches finds, and for everyone who knocks, the door will be opened. ¹¹Is there anyone among you who, if your child asks forᶠ a fish, will give a snake instead of a fish? ¹²Or if the child asks for an egg, will give a scorpion? ¹³If you then, who are evil, know how to give good gifts to your children, how much more will the heavenly Father give the Holy Spiritᵍ to those who ask him!"

11.1–13: On prayer. Luke's version of the kingdom prayer is briefer and less well known (see Mt 6.9–13). **2:** *Father* is a remarkably intimate word, expressing trust more than authority (see 11.13; Gal 4.6; Rom 8.15, compare Lk 22.24–30; Acts 4.24–26). **4:** The prayer to be protected from *the time of trial* points to the power of evil (see 8.13; 22.3, 28, 31, 40, 46). **8:** *Persistence* is unashamed (see 18.1–8), not necessarily polite. **9–10:** These verses are compact sayings in which God's activity is indirectly promised. **11–12:** *Snakes* and *scorpions* are *evil* scourges (10.19), not given by good fathers (11.2).

a Other ancient authorities read *few things are necessary, or only one*　b Other ancient authorities read *Our Father in heaven*　c A few ancient authorities read *Your Holy Spirit come upon us and cleanse us.* Other ancient authorities add *Your will be done, on earth as in heaven*　d Or *our bread for tomorrow*　e Or *us into temptation.* Other ancient authorities add *but rescue us from the evil one* (or *from evil*)　f Other ancient authorities add *bread, will give a stone; or if your child asks for*　g Other ancient authorities read *the Father give the Holy Spirit from heaven*

14 Now he was casting out a demon that was mute; when the demon had gone out, the one who had been mute spoke, and the crowds were amazed. 15But some of them said, "He casts out demons by Beelzebul, the ruler of the demons." 16Others, to test him, kept demanding from him a sign from heaven. 17But he knew what they were thinking and said to them, "Every kingdom divided against itself becomes a desert, and house falls on house. 18If Satan also is divided against himself, how will his kingdom stand? —for you say that I cast out the demons by Beelzebul. 19Now if I cast out the demons by Beelzebul, by whom do your exorcists*a* cast them out? Therefore they will be your judges. 20But if it is by the finger of God that I cast out the demons, then the kingdom of God has come to you. 21When a strong man, fully armed, guards his castle, his property is safe. 22But when one stronger than he attacks him and overpowers him, he takes away his armor in which he trusted and divides his plunder. 23Whoever is not with me is against me, and whoever does not gather with me scatters.

24 "When the unclean spirit has gone out of a person, it wanders through waterless regions looking for a resting place, but not finding any, it says, 'I will return to my house from which I came.' 25When it comes, it finds it swept and put in order. 26Then it goes and brings seven other spirits more evil than itself, and they enter and live there; and the last state of that person is worse than the first."

11.14–54: Jesus meets opposition. 11.14–26: Satan's kingdom. 15: *Beelzebul*⋆ is a variant of "Baal-zebub," the god of Ekron (2 Kings 1.2–6), whom Elijah defeated as a false god. **20:** In Ex 8.19, even the Egyptian magicians could tell that Moses accomplished the plagues by *the finger of God.* Jesus' words are a warning against "opposing God" (Acts 5.39; 11.17). **21–23:** The royal imagery expresses God's strength in the realm of a mighty foe (Isa 49.24–25). **24:** On *waterless regions,* see 8.33.

---

27 While he was saying this, a woman in the crowd raised her voice and said to him, "Blessed is the womb that bore you and the breasts that nursed you!" 28But he said, "Blessed rather are those who hear the word of God and obey it!"

29 When the crowds were increasing, he began to say, "This generation is an evil generation; it asks for a sign, but no sign will be given to it except the sign of Jonah. 30For just as Jonah became a sign to the people of Nineveh, so the Son of Man will be to this generation. 31The queen of the South will rise at the judgment with the people of this generation and condemn them, because she came from the ends of the earth to listen to the wisdom of Solomon, and see, something greater than Solomon is here! 32The people of Nineveh will rise up at the judgment with this generation and condemn it, because they repented at the proclamation of Jonah, and see, something greater than Jonah is here!

33 "No one after lighting a lamp puts it in a cellar,*b* but on the lampstand so that those who enter may see the light. 34Your eye is the lamp of your body. If your eye is healthy, your whole body is full of light; but if it is not healthy, your body is full of darkness. 35Therefore consider whether the light in you is not darkness. 36If then your whole body is full of light, with no part of it in darkness, it will be as full of light as when a lamp gives you light with its rays."

11.27–36: The word of God. 29: *The sign of Jonah* is Jesus, "a sign that will be opposed" (2.34). **31–32:** *The queen of the South* is the Queen of Sheba who like *the people of Nineveh* came to bless God and even *repent* (1 Kings 10.1–11; Jon 3.6–10). **32:** The faith of foreigners is again a judgment on *this generation* (see 4.24–27).

---

37 While he was speaking, a Pharisee invited him to dine with him; so he went in and took his place at the table. 38The Pharisee was amazed to see that he did not first wash before dinner. 39Then the Lord said to him, "Now you Pharisees clean the outside of the cup and of the dish, but inside you are

---

a Gk *sons*　　*b* Other ancient authorities add *or under the bushel basket* full of greed and wickedness. ⁴⁰You fools! Did not the one who made the outside make the inside also? ⁴¹So give for alms those things that are within; and see, everything will be clean for you.

42 "But woe to you Pharisees! For you tithe mint and rue and herbs of all kinds, and neglect justice and the love of God; it is these you ought to have practiced, without neglecting the others. ⁴³Woe to you Pharisees! For you love to have the seat of honor in the synagogues and to be greeted with respect in the marketplaces. ⁴⁴Woe to you! For you are like unmarked graves, and people walk over them without realizing it."

45 One of the lawyers answered him, "Teacher, when you say these things, you insult us too." ⁴⁶And he said, "Woe also to you lawyers! For you load people with burdens hard to bear, and you yourselves do not lift a finger to ease them. ⁴⁷Woe to you! For you build the tombs of the prophets whom your ancestors killed. ⁴⁸So you are witnesses and approve of the deeds of your ancestors; for they killed them, and you build their tombs. ⁴⁹Therefore also the Wisdom of God said, 'I will send them prophets and apostles, some of whom they will kill and persecute,' ⁵⁰so that this generation may be charged with the blood of all the prophets shed since the foundation of the world, ⁵¹from the blood of Abel to the blood of Zechariah, who perished between the altar and the sanctuary. Yes, I tell you, it will be charged against this generation. ⁵²Woe to you lawyers! For you have taken away the key of knowledge; you did not enter yourselves, and you hindered those who were entering."

53 When he went outside, the scribes and the Pharisees began to be very hostile toward him and to cross-examine him about many things, ⁵⁴lying in wait for him, to catch him in something he might say.

11.37–54: Woe to the Pharisees.* The passage includes six *woes,* three to the *Pharisees* for their concerns about externals and three to the *lawyers* (see 10.25), accusing them of misusing their authority. This is prophetic* speech from a teacher of Israel to his people. It has often been misused by gentile* Christians to justify themselves. **38:** *Washing* was required for ritual cleanliness, not mere hygiene. **42:** Jesus accuses them of being scrupulous only in *tithing* (giving one tenth, see Deut 14.22–29; 26.12–15; Lev 27.30–33) little things like seasonings. **44:** Even touching *unmarked graves* would make a person unclean (see 7.14; 8.54). **46:** The charge of *loading burdens hard to bear* is repeated in Acts 15.10. **49:** *The Wisdom of God* speaks in Prov 1.20–33; 8; and Wis 7 (see also Lk 7.35). **52:** *The key of knowledge* is probably the scriptures, made inaccessible by professionals. **54:** This fierce encounter concludes with an anticipation of the plot against Jesus (see 19.47; 20.19–20; 22.1–2).

12 Meanwhile, when the crowd gathered by the thousands, so that they trampled on one another, he began to speak first to his disciples, "Beware of the yeast of the Pharisees, that is, their hypocrisy. ²Nothing is covered up that will not be uncovered, and nothing secret that will not become known. ³Therefore whatever you have said in the dark will be heard in the light, and what you have whispered behind closed doors will be proclaimed from the housetops.

4 "I tell you, my friends, do not fear those who kill the body, and after that can do nothing more. ⁵But I will warn you whom to fear: fear him who, after he has killed, has authority*ᵃ* to cast into hell.*ᵇ* Yes, I tell you, fear him! ⁶Are not five sparrows sold for two pennies? Yet not one of them is forgotten in God's sight. ⁷But even the hairs of your head are all counted. Do not be afraid; you are of more value than many sparrows.

8 "And I tell you, everyone who acknowledges me before others, the Son of Man also will acknowledge before the angels of God; ⁹but whoever denies me before others will be denied before the angels of God. ¹⁰And everyone who speaks a word against the Son of Man will be forgiven; but whoever blasphemes against the Holy Spirit will not be forgiven. ¹¹When they bring you before the synagogues, the rulers, and the authorities, do not worry about how*ᶜ* you are to defend yourselves or what you are to say; ¹²for the Holy Spirit will teach you at that very hour what you ought to say."

a Or *power*   *b* Gk *Gehenna*   *c* Other ancient authorities add *or what*

12.1–13.21: Jesus calls for readiness and repentance. 12.1–12: Hidden and revealed. 1: Jesus' warning against *the yeast of the Pharisees** implies hidden impurity, invisible as *hypocrisy* (see Ex 12.14–20; see "unmarked graves" in Lk 11.44). **5:** *Hell* is literally "Gehenna"* (see note *b*, p. 1770), the valley outside Jerusalem where refuse was burned, including unclean bodies. **8–12:** Jewish visions of the last judgment (Dan 7) confront those who fail in their confession under trial with a more fearsome court (1 Jn 2.22–23). **10–12:** Believers often fear the "unforgivable sin" *against the Holy Spirit.* The contrast here is between active *blasphemy* (see 5.21), probably under threat or torture, and trust in the Holy Spirit to *teach* in a time of trial (Mk 13.11; Mt 10.20).

13 Someone in the crowd said to him, "Teacher, tell my brother to divide the family inheritance with me." 14But he said to him, "Friend, who set me to be a judge or arbitrator over you?" 15And he said to them, "Take care! Be on your guard against all kinds of greed; for one's life does not consist in the abundance of possessions." 16Then he told them a parable: "The land of a rich man produced abundantly. 17And he thought to himself, 'What should I do, for I have no place to store my crops?' 18Then he said, 'I will do this: I will pull down my barns and build larger ones, and there I will store all my grain and my goods. 19And I will say to my soul, Soul, you have ample goods laid up for many years; relax, eat, drink, be merry.' 20But God said to him, 'You fool! This very night your life is being demanded of you. And the things you have prepared, whose will they be?' 21So it is with those who store up treasures for themselves but are not rich toward God."

22 He said to his disciples, "Therefore I tell you, do not worry about your life, what you will eat, or about your body, what you will wear. 23For life is more than food, and the body more than clothing. 24Consider the ravens: they neither sow nor reap, they have neither storehouse nor barn, and yet God feeds them. Of how much more value are you than the birds! 25And can any of you by worrying add a single hour to your span of life?*a* 26If then you are not able to do so small a thing as that, why do you worry about

the rest? 27Consider the lilies, how they grow: they neither toil nor spin;*b* yet I tell you, even Solomon in all his glory was not clothed like one of these. 28But if God so clothes the grass of the field, which is alive today and tomorrow is thrown into the oven, how much more will he clothe you—you of little faith! 29And do not keep striving for what you are to eat and what you are to drink, and do not keep worrying. 30For it is the nations of the world that strive after all these things, and your Father knows that you need them. 31Instead, strive for his*c* kingdom, and these things will be given to you as well.

32 "Do not be afraid, little flock, for it is your Father's good pleasure to give you the kingdom. 33Sell your possessions, and give alms. Make purses for yourselves that do not wear out, an unfailing treasure in heaven, where no thief comes near and no moth destroys. 34For where your treasure is, there your heart will be also.

12.13–34. 13–21: The peril of wealth. This is one of several Lukan parables* using examples of immoral behavior (16.1–9; 18.1–8), pointing beyond concern for possessions. **19:** The *fool* talks to himself (*"Soul, . . . "*), advising the life of pleasure (Eccl 8.15) as if there were no God or judgment (Ps 14.1). **22–34: The security and treasure of the kingdom.** These sayings are largely shared with Mt 6.19–21, 25–34, reflecting a positive view of the world, even the need of *food* and *clothing.* The wealth of *Solomon* was legendary.* He was credited with not seeking it (1 Kings 3). *Worry* and *striving* are better focused on God's *kingdom,* which then proves to be a gift of the *Father's good pleasure* (see 11.13).

35 "Be dressed for action and have your lamps lit; 36be like those who are waiting for their master to return from the wedding banquet, so that they may open the door for him as soon as he comes and knocks. 37Blessed are those slaves whom the master finds alert when he comes; truly I tell you, he will fasten his belt and have them sit down to eat, and he will come and serve them. 38If he comes

a Or *add a cubit to your stature*   *b* Other ancient authorities read *Consider the lilies; they neither spin nor weave*   *c* Other ancient authorities read *God's* during the middle of the night, or near dawn, and finds them so, blessed are those slaves.

39 "But know this: if the owner of the house had known at what hour the thief was coming, he*a* would not have let his house be broken into. 40You also must be ready, for the Son of Man is coming at an unexpected hour."

41 Peter said, "Lord, are you telling this parable for us or for everyone?" 42And the Lord said, "Who then is the faithful and prudent manager whom his master will put in charge of his slaves, to give them their allowance of food at the proper time? 43Blessed is that slave whom his master will find at work when he arrives. 44Truly I tell you, he will put that one in charge of all his possessions. 45But if that slave says to himself, 'My master is delayed in coming,' and if he begins to beat the other slaves, men and women, and to eat and drink and get drunk, 46the master of that slave will come on a day when he does not expect him and at an hour that he does not know, and will cut him in pieces,*b* and put him with the unfaithful. 47That slave who knew what his master wanted, but did not prepare himself or do what was wanted, will receive a severe beating. 48But the one who did not know and did what deserved a beating will receive a light beating. From everyone to whom much has been given, much will be required; and from the one to whom much has been entrusted, even more will be demanded.

49 "I came to bring fire to the earth, and how I wish it were already kindled! 50I have a baptism with which to be baptized, and what stress I am under until it is completed! 51Do you think that I have come to bring peace to the earth? No, I tell you, but rather division! 52From now on five in one household will be divided, three against two and two against three; 53they will be divided:

father against son
    and son against father,
mother against daughter
    and daughter against mother,
mother-in-law against her daughter-in-
    law
    and daughter-in-law against mother-
    in-law."

54 He also said to the crowds, "When you see a cloud rising in the west, you immediately say, 'It is going to rain'; and so it happens. 55And when you see the south wind blowing, you say, 'There will be scorching heat'; and it happens. 56You hypocrites! You know how to interpret the appearance of earth and sky, but why do you not know how to interpret the present time?

57 "And why do you not judge for yourselves what is right? 58Thus, when you go with your accuser before a magistrate, on the way make an effort to settle the case,*c* or you may be dragged before the judge, and the judge hand you over to the officer, and the officer throw you in prison. 59I tell you, you will never get out until you have paid the very last penny."

12.35–59: Be ready! This is a collection of traditional sayings on watchfulness (see also Mt 24.42–51; 10.34–36; 16.2–3; 25.1–13; Mk 13.33–37; 14.38). In the context of Luke's story, they anticipate Jesus' "visitation" of Jerusalem (19.41–44) as well as the last judgment. **49:** *To bring fire to the earth* is literally "to hurl" fire as in the judgment Elijah invoked (1 Kings 18.36–40), but not yet (9.54). On Jesus' unfulfilled *wish,* see also 13.34; 22.42. **50:** For Jesus to be *under stress* is literally to be "constrained" in obedience until God inaugurates the *baptism** of fire (see 3.16; 24.49; Acts 1.5–8; 2.1–13). **51–53:** This *division* is the opposite of Gabriel's promise (1.17, but see also 2.34). **54–57:** People are able to predict the weather and to *judge what is right,* but miss the chance to repent in *the present time.*

---

13 At that very time there were some present who told him about the Galileans whose blood Pilate had mingled with their sacrifices. 2He asked them, "Do you think that because these Galileans suffered in this way they were worse sinners than all other Galileans? 3No, I tell you; but unless you repent, you will all perish as they did. 4Or those eighteen who were killed when the tower of Siloam fell on them—do you think that they were worse offenders than all the others living in Jerusalem? 5No, I tell you;

---

a Other ancient authorities add *would have watched and*
b Or *cut him off*   *c* Gk *settle with him*

but unless you repent, you will all perish just as they did."

6 Then he told this parable: "A man had a fig tree planted in his vineyard; and he came looking for fruit on it and found none. ⁷So he said to the gardener, 'See here! For three years I have come looking for fruit on this fig tree, and still I find none. Cut it down! Why should it be wasting the soil?' ⁸He replied, 'Sir, let it alone for one more year, until I dig around it and put manure on it. ⁹If it bears fruit next year, well and good; but if not, you can cut it down.' "

13.10–9. The time to repent. 1: The phrase *at that very time* links this section to the warnings of 12.49–59, ending each portion with a warning *unless you repent . . .* (vv. 3, 5), or *if not, you can cut it down* (v. 9). *Pilate* was famous for his violence against pilgrims in Jerusalem and disdain for *Galileans* (23.1–12). **4:** The fall of the *tower of Siloam* is otherwise unknown. Judgment also causes the innocent to suffer (see 19.41–44; 21.5–24). **6:** The *fig tree* and *vineyard* were common images for Israel (Jer 8.13; Hos 9.10; Mic 7.1).

~~~~~~

10 Now he was teaching in one of the synagogues on the sabbath. ¹¹And just then there appeared a woman with a spirit that had crippled her for eighteen years. She was bent over and was quite unable to stand up straight. ¹²When Jesus saw her, he called her over and said, "Woman, you are set free from your ailment." ¹³When he laid his hands on her, immediately she stood up straight and began praising God. ¹⁴But the leader of the synagogue, indignant because Jesus had cured on the sabbath, kept saying to the crowd, "There are six days on which work ought to be done; come on those days and be cured, and not on the sabbath day." ¹⁵But the Lord answered him and said, "You hypocrites! Does not each of you on the sabbath untie his ox or his donkey from the manger, and lead it away to give it water? ¹⁶And ought not this woman, a daughter of Abraham whom Satan bound for eighteen long years, be set free from this bondage on the sabbath day?" ¹⁷When he said this, all his opponents were put to shame; and the entire crowd was rejoicing at all the wonderful things that he was doing.

18 He said therefore, "What is the kingdom of God like? And to what should I compare it? ¹⁹It is like a mustard seed that someone took and sowed in the garden; it grew and became a tree, and the birds of the air made nests in its branches."

20 And again he said, "To what should I compare the kingdom of God? ²¹It is like yeast that a woman took and mixed in with*ᵃ* three measures of flour until all of it was leavened."

13.10–21. 10–17: The bent woman. This is the third controversy about *sabbath* observance (6.1–5; 6.6–11, see also 14.1–6), and Jesus is again teaching in a *synagogue*⋆ (4.14–30, 31–38, 44). **14–15:** Deut 5.13 and Ex 20.9–10 prohibited *work* on the *sabbath,* but Deut 22.1–4 commanded help for a neighbor's ox or donkey. Jesus' contemporaries debated what "work" was rightly prohibited and what was required. **16:** Jesus' argument takes a classic rabbinic form, "So much the more" should a *daughter of Abraham* deserve and require this special "work," healing (see 14.5). **18–21: The hidden kingdom.** These two parables⋆ of remarkable growth convey the living, dynamic sense of the *kingdom of God* fulfilling the promises (see Dan 4.10–12; Ezek 17.22–24; 31.2–9). **21:** *Yeast* is a surprising image because of its "uncleanness" (see 12.1).

~~~~~~

22 Jesus*ᵇ* went through one town and village after another, teaching as he made his way to Jerusalem. ²³Someone asked him, "Lord, will only a few be saved?" He said to them, ²⁴"Strive to enter through the narrow door; for many, I tell you, will try to enter and will not be able. ²⁵When once the owner of the house has got up and shut the door, and you begin to stand outside and to knock at the door, saying, 'Lord, open to us,' then in reply he will say to you, 'I do not know where you come from.' ²⁶Then you will begin to say, 'We ate and drank with you, and you taught in our streets.' ²⁷But he will say, 'I do not know where you come from; go away from me, all you evildoers!' ²⁸There will be weeping and gnashing of teeth when you see Abraham and Isaac and Jacob and

a Gk *hid in*   *b* Gk *He*

all the prophets in the kingdom of God, and you yourselves thrown out. 29Then people will come from east and west, from north and south, and will eat in the kingdom of God. 30Indeed, some are last who will be first, and some are first who will be last."

13.22–17.10: Jesus journeys toward Jerusalem. 13.22–30: He prophesies the end. 22: This verse reminds the reader of the journey Jesus began in 9.51–54 (see also 17.11). 24: *Strive* here means "be disciplined" in accord with the values of the kingdom. 26: *We ate and drank with you* implies intimate companionship 28: Luke includes *all the prophets*★ along with Israel's patriarchs *Abraham, Isaac, and Jacob* (Mt 8.11) who gather for God's promised banquet (Ex 24.9–11; Isa 25.6–8). 29: Scattered Israel will be gathered from *east and west . . .* (Isa 11.11–16; 60.1–22).

31 At that very hour some Pharisees came and said to him, "Get away from here, for Herod wants to kill you." 32He said to them, "Go and tell that fox for me,*a* 'Listen, I am casting out demons and performing cures today and tomorrow, and on the third day I finish my work. 33Yet today, tomorrow, and the next day I must be on my way, because it is impossible for a prophet to be killed outside of Jerusalem.' 34Jerusalem, Jerusalem, the city that kills the prophets and stones those who are sent to it! How often have I desired to gather your children together as a hen gathers her brood under her wings, and you were not willing! 35See, your house is left to you. And I tell you, you will not see me until the time comes when*b* you say, 'Blessed is the one who comes in the name of the Lord.' "

13.31–35: Jesus' lament★ for Jerusalem. This prophetic★ word is shared with Matthew (23.37–39). 31–32: *Herod* again represents a threat (3.19–20; 9.7–9; 23.6–12), and a *fox* is an insulting name, like "weasel." 32–33: These verses are filled with the prophetic force of Jesus' yearning, will, and intention: *I must be . . . because it is impossible* (see 12.50; 18.31). 34: Israel's scriptures warned against killing the prophets★ (2 Chr 24.20–22; Jer 26.20–23; Lk 11.50–51). 35: The phrase *until the time comes* anticipates Lk 19.38, when Ps 118.26 is recited by his disciples.

DINNER DISCOURSES

14.1–35: Dinner conversations were famous teaching settings in the Greek and Jewish worlds. In Jewish and Christian tradition, the banquet becomes a symbol for who is chosen or invited to the heavenly feast. Dinner discussions recur throughout this larger section (see 15.1; 17.10) until Jesus' journey to Jerusalem explicitly resumes in 17.11.

14 On one occasion when Jesus*c* was going to the house of a leader of the Pharisees to eat a meal on the sabbath, they were watching him closely. 2Just then, in front of him, there was a man who had dropsy. 3And Jesus asked the lawyers and Pharisees, "Is it lawful to cure people on the sabbath, or not?" 4But they were silent. So Jesus*c* took him and healed him, and sent him away. 5Then he said to them, "If one of you has a child*d* or an ox that has fallen into a well, will you not immediately pull it out on a sabbath day?" 6And they could not reply to this.

7 When he noticed how the guests chose the places of honor, he told them a parable. 8"When you are invited by someone to a wedding banquet, do not sit down at the place of honor, in case someone more distinguished than you has been invited by your host; 9and the host who invited both of you may come and say to you, 'Give this person your place,' and then in disgrace you would start to take the lowest place. 10But when you are invited, go and sit down at the lowest place, so that when your host comes, he may say to you, 'Friend, move up higher'; then you will be honored in the presence of all who sit at the table with you. 11For all who exalt themselves will be humbled, and those who humble themselves will be exalted."

12 He said also to the one who had invited him, "When you give a luncheon or a dinner, do not invite your friends or your brothers or your relatives or rich neighbors,

a Gk lacks *for me*   *b* Other ancient authorities lack *the time comes when*   *c* Gk *he*   *d* Other ancient authorities read *a donkey* in case they may invite you in return, and you would be repaid. 13But when you give a banquet, invite the poor, the crippled, the lame, and the blind. 14And you will be blessed, because they cannot repay you, for you will be repaid at the resurrection of the righteous."

15 One of the dinner guests, on hearing this, said to him, "Blessed is anyone who will eat bread in the kingdom of God!" 16Then Jesus*a* said to him, "Someone gave a great dinner and invited many. 17At the time for the dinner he sent his slave to say to those who had been invited, 'Come; for everything is ready now.' 18But they all alike began to make excuses. The first said to him, 'I have bought a piece of land, and I must go out and see it; please accept my regrets.' 19Another said, 'I have bought five yoke of oxen, and I am going to try them out; please accept my regrets.' 20Another said, 'I have just been married, and therefore I cannot come.' 21So the slave returned and reported this to his master. Then the owner of the house became angry and said to his slave, 'Go out at once into the streets and lanes of the town and bring in the poor, the crippled, the blind, and the lame.' 22And the slave said, 'Sir, what you ordered has been done, and there is still room.' 23Then the master said to the slave, 'Go out into the roads and lanes, and compel people to come in, so that my house may be filled. 24For I tell you,*b* none of those who were invited will taste my dinner.' "

14.1–24. 1–6: The meal with a *Pharisee★* is again a setting for dispute (7.36–50; 11.37–54) about the law. **2:** *Dropsy* is a condition of edema, or retention of bodily fluids, which was perceived as defiling (see also 8.43–48). **5:** Note *d* (p. 1774) indicates that the manuscripts differ on whether Jesus appealed to the precedent of the "ox and the donkey" or the "ox and the *child*." Even the most strict interpretations of Deut 22.4 would allow *sabbath* violations for the welfare of a child (see 13.16). **9–10:** Jesus' words reflect the traditional wisdom of Prov 25.6–7. **11:** Jesus places the exaltation and humbling in the context of his teaching (see 6.20–36). **12–14, 21b–24:** Jesus' inclusion of the *crippled, the lame, and the blind* challenges the purity code of Lev 21.17–23 in light of the judgment standards of the kingdom at the *resurrection of the righ-*

teous (see also 6.23, 35, 37–38). **23–24:** Jesus' mission continues to provoke a divided response in Israel (2.34; 3.8; Acts 13.46; 18.6; 28.23–28).

25 Now large crowds were traveling with him; and he turned and said to them, 26"Whoever comes to me and does not hate father and mother, wife and children, brothers and sisters, yes, and even life itself, cannot be my disciple. 27Whoever does not carry the cross and follow me cannot be my disciple. 28For which of you, intending to build a tower, does not first sit down and estimate the cost, to see whether he has enough to complete it? 29Otherwise, when he has laid a foundation and is not able to finish, all who see it will begin to ridicule him, 30saying, 'This fellow began to build and was not able to finish.' 31Or what king, going out to wage war against another king, will not sit down first and consider whether he is able with ten thousand to oppose the one who comes against him with twenty thousand? 32If he cannot, then, while the other is still far away, he sends a delegation and asks for the terms of peace. 33So therefore, none of you can become my disciple if you do not give up all your possessions.

34 "Salt is good; but if salt has lost its taste, how can its saltiness be restored?*c* 35It is fit neither for the soil nor for the manure pile; they throw it away. Let anyone with ears to hear listen!"

14.25–35: Counting the cost. This section presents three severe arguments, with illustrations, pressing to a conclusion for repentance from all who *hear* (v. 35b). **26, 27, 33:** *Whoever does not . . . cannot be my disciple.* Ex 32.25–29 and Deut 33.8–9 provide precedents from Israel's holy war★ traditions. Early Christian interpreters struggled with this passage, arguing against those who sought martyrdom,★ but recognizing that following Jesus could cost them their families, lives, and possessions. **35b:** See also 8.8, 10, 18.

15 Now all the tax collectors and sinners were coming near to listen to him. 2And the Pharisees and the scribes

---

a Gk *he*   *b* The Greek word for *you* here is plural
c Or *how can it be used for seasoning?*

were grumbling and saying, "This fellow welcomes sinners and eats with them."

3 So he told them this parable: 4"Which one of you, having a hundred sheep and losing one of them, does not leave the ninety-nine in the wilderness and go after the one that is lost until he finds it? 5When he has found it, he lays it on his shoulders and rejoices. 6And when he comes home, he calls together his friends and neighbors, saying to them, 'Rejoice with me, for I have found my sheep that was lost.' 7Just so, I tell you, there will be more joy in heaven over one sinner who repents than over ninety-nine righteous persons who need no repentance.

8 "Or what woman having ten silver coins,^a if she loses one of them, does not light a lamp, sweep the house, and search carefully until she finds it? 9When she has found it, she calls together her friends and neighbors, saying, 'Rejoice with me, for I have found the coin that I had lost.' 10Just so, I tell you, there is joy in the presence of the angels of God over one sinner who repents."

15.1–31: Love for the lost. 1–2: The discussions about table fellowship of ch. 14 continue with the complaint of the *Pharisees* and the scribes** about Jesus eating with *sinners,* that is, those who are not properly observant (see 5.30–32; 7.34, 39). In Luke's narrative,* the three parables* that follow respond to this criticism with God's profound compassion for the lost. 3–10: The stories of the lost sheep and lost coin follow virtually the same outline (compare Mt 18.12–14): *Which one/woman . . . having a hundred sheep/ten coins, losing one . . . does not leave/light, sweep, search . . . until he/she finds it? And when he/she has found it . . . he/she calls friends and neighbors saying, "Rejoice with me for I have found my sheep/coin." Just so I tell you.* The concern for the lost exceeds prudent wisdom (for example, leaving the *ninety-nine in the wilderness*), and the joy of *heaven* is also extravagant.

---

11 Then Jesus^b said, "There was a man who had two sons. 12The younger of them said to his father, 'Father, give me the share of the property that will belong to me.' So he divided his property between them. 13A few days later the younger son gathered all he had and traveled to a distant country, and

there he squandered his property in dissolute living. 14When he had spent everything, a severe famine took place throughout that country, and he began to be in need. 15So he went and hired himself out to one of the citizens of that country, who sent him to his fields to feed the pigs. 16He would gladly have filled himself with^c the pods that the pigs were eating; and no one gave him anything. 17But when he came to himself he said, 'How many of my father's hired hands have bread enough and to spare, but here I am dying of hunger! 18I will get up and go to my father, and I will say to him, "Father, I have sinned against heaven and before you; 19I am no longer worthy to be called your son; treat me like one of your hired hands."' 20So he set off and went to his father. But while he was still far off, his father saw him and was filled with compassion; he ran and put his arms around him and kissed him. 21Then the son said to him, 'Father, I have sinned against heaven and before you; I am no longer worthy to be called your son.'^d 22But the father said to his slaves, 'Quickly, bring out a robe—the best one—and put it on him; put a ring on his finger and sandals on his feet. 23And get the fatted calf and kill it, and let us eat and celebrate; 24for this son of mine was dead and is alive again; he was lost and is found!' And they began to celebrate.

25 "Now his elder son was in the field; and when he came and approached the house, he heard music and dancing. 26He called one of the slaves and asked what was going on. 27He replied, 'Your brother has come, and your father has killed the fatted calf, because he has got him back safe and sound.' 28Then he became angry and refused to go in. His father came out and began to plead with him. 29But he answered his father, 'Listen! For all these years I have been working like a slave for you, and I have never disobeyed your command; yet you have never given me even a young goat so that I might celebrate with my friends. 30But when this

a Gk *drachmas,* each worth about a day's wage for a laborer *b* Gk *he* *c* Other ancient authorities read *filled his stomach with* *d* Other ancient authorities add *Treat me like one of your hired servants* son of yours came back, who has devoured your property with prostitutes, you killed the fatted calf for him!' ³¹Then the father*ᵃ said to him, 'Son, you are always with me, and all that is mine is yours. ³²But we had to celebrate and rejoice, because this brother of yours was dead and has come to life; he was lost and has been found.' "

15.11–32: The parable* of the prodigal son. This is one of the most famous stories in the Bible. Like the stories of the lost sheep and coin, this is not a morality lesson, but a witness to the extravagant love of a father. **12:** Giving children their *share of the property* before death was regarded as imprudent (Sir 33.19–23). **15:** *Pigs* were especially shameful and unclean (Lev 11.7–8). **17–19, 21:** Was the son genuinely contrite ("*I am no longer worthy*") or merely desperate (see 16.3; 18.4)? The father ignores his practiced speech anyway. **20:** The father's *compassion* is the heart of the story, explaining his imprudent behavior in the presence of the slaves. **24:** The *celebration* when the *lost* is *found* is the same as in heaven (15.7, 10, 32), which is exactly the complaint against Jesus' table fellowship by those who scrupulously defend the moral order (15.1–2, 29–30). **25–32:** The *angry* complaints of *the elder son* hold the high ground of law and order, but lack the father's love. The father has not deprived him of any rights or love (v. 31).

16 Then Jesusᵃ said to the disciples, "There was a rich man who had a manager, and charges were brought to him that this man was squandering his property. ²So he summoned him and said to him, 'What is this that I hear about you? Give me an accounting of your management, because you cannot be my manager any longer.' ³Then the manager said to himself, 'What will I do, now that my master is taking the position away from me? I am not strong enough to dig, and I am ashamed to beg. ⁴I have decided what to do so that, when I am dismissed as manager, people may welcome me into their homes.' ⁵So, summoning his master's debtors one by one, he asked the first, 'How much do you owe my master?' ⁶He answered, 'A hundred jugs of olive oil.' He said to him, 'Take your bill, sit down quickly, and make it fifty.' ⁷Then he asked another, 'And how much do you owe?' He

replied, 'A hundred containers of wheat.' He said to him, 'Take your bill and make it eighty.' ⁸And his master commended the dishonest manager because he had acted shrewdly; for the children of this age are more shrewd in dealing with their own generation than are the children of light. ⁹And I tell you, make friends for yourselves by means of dishonest wealthᵇ so that when it is gone, they may welcome you into the eternal homes.ᶜ

16.1–31: The dangers of wealth. 1–9: Jesus' parable* again draws on an immoral example (see 15.11–23; 18.1–8). **1–7:** Charged with *squandering* his master's *property,* the manager uses his authority once more to his own advantage by discounting *his master's debtors.* **8–9:** The master's commendation of the shrewdness of the *dishonest manager* is ironic or bitter, like the final verdict on those who make *friends* by *dishonest wealth* (16.11; 6.24–26).

10 "Whoever is faithful in a very little is faithful also in much; and whoever is dishonest in a very little is dishonest also in much. ¹¹If then you have not been faithful with the dishonest wealth,ᵇ who will entrust to you the true riches? ¹²And if you have not been faithful with what belongs to another, who will give you what is your own? ¹³No slave can serve two masters; for a slave will either hate the one and love the other, or be devoted to the one and despise the other. You cannot serve God and wealth."ᵇ

14 The Pharisees, who were lovers of money, heard all this, and they ridiculed him. ¹⁵So he said to them, "You are those who justify yourselves in the sight of others; but God knows your hearts; for what is prized by human beings is an abomination in the sight of God.

16 "The law and the prophets were in effect until John came; since then the good news of the kingdom of God is proclaimed, and everyone tries to enter it by force.ᵈ ¹⁷But it is easier for heaven and earth to pass away, than for one stroke of a letter in the law to be dropped.

a Gk he   b Gk mammon   c Gk tents
d Or everyone is strongly urged to enter it

18 "Anyone who divorces his wife and marries another commits adultery, and whoever marries a woman divorced from her husband commits adultery.

16.10–18: These verses include a diverse collection of sayings (see Mt 6.24; 11.12–13; 5.18; 19.9), which Luke uses to emphasize Jesus' radical message concerning *wealth* (vv. 13–14), *self-justification* (v. 15), or evading the demands of the *law* (vv. 16–18). **14–15:** *The Pharisees** are treated as Jesus' adversaries at this point in the story (see also 18.9–14, but contrast Acts 15.5; 23.6–10). **16:** The contrast between the eras of the *law and the prophets** and the *proclaimed kingdom of God* again magnifies *John's* role (7.28) but also stresses the "constraint" or *force* on all to enter the kingdom (see translation problem reflected in note *d*). Jesus' purposeful mission confronts all with the force of God's rule.

---

19 "There was a rich man who was dressed in purple and fine linen and who feasted sumptuously every day. 20And at his gate lay a poor man named Lazarus, covered with sores, 21who longed to satisfy his hunger with what fell from the rich man's table; even the dogs would come and lick his sores. 22The poor man died and was carried away by the angels to be with Abraham.*a* The rich man also died and was buried. 23In Hades, where he was being tormented, he looked up and saw Abraham far away with Lazarus by his side.*b* 24He called out, 'Father Abraham, have mercy on me, and send Lazarus to dip the tip of his finger in water and cool my tongue; for I am in agony in these flames.' 25But Abraham said, 'Child, remember that during your lifetime you received your good things, and Lazarus in like manner evil things; but now he is comforted here, and you are in agony. 26Besides all this, between you and us a great chasm has been fixed, so that those who might want to pass from here to you cannot do so, and no one can cross from there to us.' 27He said, 'Then, father, I beg you to send him to my father's house— 28for I have five brothers—that he may warn them, so that they will not also come into this place of torment.' 29Abraham replied, 'They have Moses and the prophets; they should listen to them.' 30He said, 'No, father

Abraham; but if someone goes to them from the dead, they will repent.' 31He said to him, 'If they do not listen to Moses and the prophets, neither will they be convinced even if someone rises from the dead.' "

16.19–31: This story amplifies the reversal of values where "what is prized by human beings is an abomination in the sight of God" (v. 15). **22–23:** The poor man is given a name, *Lazarus,* and is accorded the highest dignity of a child of *Abraham* (3.8; see Gen 15.15; 47.30; Deut 31.16), which will place him at the head table with Abraham for the great feast (13.28–29). *Hades** is the lower (*he looked up*) realm of the dead (10.15). **29–31:** See also Jesus' commendation of *Moses and the prophets** after the resurrection (24.27, 32, 44–45).

---

17 Jesus*c* said to his disciples, "Occasions for stumbling are bound to come, but woe to anyone by whom they come! 2It would be better for you if a millstone were hung around your neck and you were thrown into the sea than for you to cause one of these little ones to stumble. 3Be on your guard! If another disciple*d* sins, you must rebuke the offender, and if there is repentance, you must forgive. 4And if the same person sins against you seven times a day, and turns back to you seven times and says, 'I repent,' you must forgive."

5 The apostles said to the Lord, "Increase our faith!" 6The Lord replied, "If you had faith the size of a*e* mustard seed, you could say to this mulberry tree, 'Be uprooted and planted in the sea,' and it would obey you.

7 "Who among you would say to your slave who has just come in from plowing or tending sheep in the field, 'Come here at once and take your place at the table'? 8Would you not rather say to him, 'Prepare supper for me, put on your apron and serve me while I eat and drink; later you may eat and drink'? 9Do you thank the slave for doing what was commanded? 10So you also, when you have done all that you were ordered to do, say, 'We are worthless slaves; we have done only what we ought to have done!' "

---

a Gk *to Abraham's bosom*   *b* Gk *in his bosom*
c Gk *He*   *d* Gk *your brother*   *e* Gk *faith as a grain of*

17.1–10: 1: Jesus' teaching is almost entirely directed to *his disciples* from this point until he arrives in Jerusalem (19.28). **2:** The *little ones* are Jesus' followers (see Mk 9.42; Mt 18.6–7, children). **4:** On forgiving *seven times,* compare Mt 18.21–22. **6:** The *mulberry tree* was known for its spreading root system. **10:** Jewish wisdom agreed: "If you have achieved much in the law, claim not merit for yourself; for this purpose you were created" (Aboth 2, 8).

11 On the way to Jerusalem Jesus*ᵃ* was going through the region between Samaria and Galilee. 12As he entered a village, ten lepers*ᵇ* approached him. Keeping their distance, 13they called out, saying, "Jesus, Master, have mercy on us!" 14When he saw them, he said to them, "Go and show yourselves to the priests." And as they went, they were made clean. 15Then one of them, when he saw that he was healed, turned back, praising God with a loud voice. 16He prostrated himself at Jesus'*ᶜ* feet and thanked him. And he was a Samaritan. 17Then Jesus asked, "Were not ten made clean? But the other nine, where are they? 18Was none of them found to return and give praise to God except this foreigner?" 19Then he said to him, "Get up and go on your way; your faith has made you well."

17.11–19.27: Jesus approaches Jerusalem. 11: Luke focuses again on the journey to *Jerusalem* (9.51; 13.31–35; 19.28). **12–14:** The *lepers* kept *their distance* as the law required (Lev 13.45–46) and also obediently sought approval by being cleansed of impurity by *the priests.* **16–18:** Luke again emphasizes the thanksgiving to *God* of the *Samaritan* (10.33) as a *foreigner* (see 4.27; 8.39–40). **19:** All the lepers were "made clean" or "healed" (vv. 14–15), but the *faith* that has made him *well* (lit., "saved") is the blessing of "seeing" (15; 10.23).

20 Once Jesus*ᵃ* was asked by the Pharisees when the kingdom of God was coming, and he answered, "The kingdom of God is not coming with things that can be observed; 21nor will they say, 'Look, here it is!' or 'There it is!' For, in fact, the kingdom of God is among*ᵈ* you."

22 Then he said to the disciples, "The days are coming when you will long to see one of the days of the Son of Man, and you will not see it. 23They will say to you, 'Look there!' or 'Look here!' Do not go, do not set off in pursuit. 24For as the lightning flashes and lights up the sky from one side to the other, so will the Son of Man be in his day.*ᵉ* 25But first he must endure much suffering and be rejected by this generation. 26Just as it was in the days of Noah, so too it will be in the days of the Son of Man. 27They were eating and drinking, and marrying and being given in marriage, until the day Noah entered the ark, and the flood came and destroyed all of them. 28Likewise, just as it was in the days of Lot: they were eating and drinking, buying and selling, planting and building, 29but on the day that Lot left Sodom, it rained fire and sulfur from heaven and destroyed all of them 30—it will be like that on the day that the Son of Man is revealed. 31On that day, anyone on the housetop who has belongings in the house must not come down to take them away; and likewise anyone in the field must not turn back. 32Remember Lot's wife. 33Those who try to make their life secure will lose it, but those who lose their life will keep it. 34I tell you, on that night there will be two in one bed; one will be taken and the other left. 35There will be two women grinding meal together; one will be taken and the other left."*ᶠ* 37Then they asked him, "Where, Lord?" He said to them, "Where the corpse is, there the vultures will gather."

17.20–37. 20–21: The *Pharisees*✱ were known more for preparing for God's reign through obedience to the law than for speculations about signs of the end. Jesus' statement about the *kingdom* being *among you* fits their view of the closeness of the law (Deut 30.11–14), but now it is the messiah✱ who is among them. **22–37:** *The days of the Son of Man* are the time of the last judgment of Dan 7, when the righteous will be vindicated (see also 21.27–28). **26–30:** *Noah* and *Lot* were known to have lived in times of great iniquity, bringing

a Gk he   *b* The terms *leper* and *leprosy* can refer to several diseases   *c* Gk his   *d* Or *within*   *e* Other ancient authorities lack *in his day*   *f* Other ancient authorities add verse 36, "*Two will be in the field; one will be taken and the other left.*"

the judgment of God on the earth (Gen 6, 18–19; see also Lk 10.12). **32:** *Lot's wife* "looked back" and was destroyed (9.62; Gen 19.26). **37:** *The vultures* (Lev 11.13) gathering over a *corpse* are a visible (17.22), grim sign of destruction when repentance is no longer possible.

18 Then Jesus*a* told them a parable about their need to pray always and not to lose heart. ²He said, "In a certain city there was a judge who neither feared God nor had respect for people. ³In that city there was a widow who kept coming to him and saying, 'Grant me justice against my opponent.' ⁴For a while he refused; but later he said to himself, 'Though I have no fear of God and no respect for anyone, ⁵yet because this widow keeps bothering me, I will grant her justice, so that she may not wear me out by continually coming.' *b* ⁶And the Lord said, "Listen to what the unjust judge says. ⁷And will not God grant justice to his chosen ones who cry to him day and night? Will he delay long in helping them? ⁸I tell you, he will quickly grant justice to them. And yet, when the Son of Man comes, will he find faith on earth?"

18.1–8. 3: God has special concern for justice for the *widow* (Deut 10.18; 24.17; 27.19; Ps 68.5). **4–6:** The *unjust judge* fails the standards of the law both with regard to *fear* of *God* and human *respect.* **7:** God's care for *his chosen ones* is stated in terms of a traditional Jewish argument from contrast, "so much the more." **8:** Perseverance in prayer will be needed until the end when *the Son of Man comes* (Dan 7.13; Lk 17.24, 30).

9 He also told this parable to some who trusted in themselves that they were righteous and regarded others with contempt: ¹⁰"Two men went up to the temple to pray, one a Pharisee and the other a tax collector. ¹¹The Pharisee, standing by himself, was praying thus, 'God, I thank you that I am not like other people: thieves, rogues, adulterers, or even like this tax collector. ¹²I fast twice a week; I give a tenth of all my income.' ¹³But the tax collector, standing far off, would not even look up to heaven, but was beating his breast and saying, 'God, be mer-

ciful to me, a sinner!' ¹⁴I tell you, this man went down to his home justified rather than the other; for all who exalt themselves will be humbled, but all who humble themselves will be exalted."

15 People were bringing even infants to him that he might touch them; and when the disciples saw it, they sternly ordered them not to do it. ¹⁶But Jesus called for them and said, "Let the little children come to me, and do not stop them; for it is to such as these that the kingdom of God belongs. ¹⁷Truly I tell you, whoever does not receive the kingdom of God as a little child will never enter it."

18 A certain ruler asked him, "Good Teacher, what must I do to inherit eternal life?" ¹⁹Jesus said to him, "Why do you call me good? No one is good but God alone. ²⁰You know the commandments: 'You shall not commit adultery; You shall not murder; You shall not steal; You shall not bear false witness; Honor your father and mother.'" ²¹He replied, "I have kept all these since my youth." ²²When Jesus heard this, he said to him, "There is still one thing lacking. Sell all that you own and distribute the money*c* to the poor, and you will have treasure in heaven; then come, follow me." ²³But when he heard this, he became sad; for he was very rich. ²⁴Jesus looked at him and said, "How hard it is for those who have wealth to enter the kingdom of God! ²⁵Indeed, it is easier for a camel to go through the eye of a needle than for someone who is rich to enter the kingdom of God."

26 Those who heard it said, "Then who can be saved?" ²⁷He replied, "What is impossible for mortals is possible for God."

18.9–27. 9–34: *Contempt* for *others* accompanies self-righteousness. **12:** The Pharisee* has exceeded the requirements of the law in tithing (Deut 14.22–23). **14:** To be *justified* is to be declared righteous by God rather than by self (18.9; 10.29; see Rom 3.21–26). **18:** The *ruler*'s question and its sequel comment (v. 21) are similar to the "lawyer's" in 10.25–37. **19:** God's goodness stands apart in the scriptures (Ps 34.8;

a Gk he   *b* Or so that she may not finally come and slap me in the face   *c* Gk lacks the money

106.1; 118.29; 1 Chr 16.34). **20:** *The commandments* define what is good in obedience to God's will (10.27–28; Deut 30.15–20). **22:** The pun on what the rich lack is their ability to leave what they have to *follow* in obedience. **27:** Luke again states that "nothing is *impossible* with God" (1.37).

〜〜〜〜〜〜〜〜

28 Then Peter said, "Look, we have left our homes and followed you." 29And he said to them, "Truly I tell you, there is no one who has left house or wife or brothers or parents or children, for the sake of the kingdom of God, 30who will not get back very much more in this age, and in the age to come eternal life."

31 Then he took the twelve aside and said to them, "See, we are going up to Jerusalem, and everything that is written about the Son of Man by the prophets will be accomplished. 32For he will be handed over to the Gentiles; and he will be mocked and insulted and spat upon. 33After they have flogged him, they will kill him, and on the third day he will rise again." 34But they understood nothing about all these things; in fact, what he said was hidden from them, and they did not grasp what was said.

35 As he approached Jericho, a blind man was sitting by the roadside begging. 36When he heard a crowd going by, he asked what was happening. 37They told him, "Jesus of Nazareth[a] is passing by." 38Then he shouted, "Jesus, Son of David, have mercy on me!" 39Those who were in front sternly ordered him to be quiet; but he shouted even more loudly, "Son of David, have mercy on me!" 40Jesus stood still and ordered the man to be brought to him; and when he came near, he asked him, 41"What do you want me to do for you?" He said, "Lord, let me see again." 42Jesus said to him, "Receive your sight; your faith has saved you." 43Immediately he regained his sight and followed him, glorifying God; and all the people, when they saw it, praised God.

18.28–43. 28–30: This section closely parallels Mk 10.23–31 and Mt 19.23–30 and recalls the sacrifices called for in 9.57–62. **31–34:** In close parallel with Mk 10.32–34 and Mt 20.17–19, Luke stresses the fulfillment of *everything that is written about the Son of*

Man by the prophets (see Acts 8.30–35; Isa 53). The *Gentiles*★ are non-Jews (Acts 4.25–26). **34:** This complex sentence states their lack of understanding from three perspectives (see "ignorance" in Acts 3.17–18). **35–43:** The *blind man* twice acclaims Jesus as *Son of David,* which is clearly a royal title, and Jesus fulfills the role for which he was anointed,★ giving sight to the blind (see 4.18 citing Isa 61.1 and 7.22 alluding to Isa 35.5).

〜〜〜〜〜〜〜〜

19 He entered Jericho and was passing through it. 2A man was there named Zacchaeus; he was a chief tax collector and was rich. 3He was trying to see who Jesus was, but on account of the crowd he could not, because he was short in stature. 4So he ran ahead and climbed a sycamore tree to see him, because he was going to pass that way. 5When Jesus came to the place, he looked up and said to him, "Zacchaeus, hurry and come down; for I must stay at your house today." 6So he hurried down and was happy to welcome him. 7All who saw it began to grumble and said, "He has gone to be the guest of one who is a sinner." 8Zacchaeus stood there and said to the Lord, "Look, half of my possessions, Lord, I will give to the poor; and if I have defrauded anyone of anything, I will pay back four times as much." 9Then Jesus said to him, "Today salvation has come to this house, because he too is a son of Abraham. 10For the Son of Man came to seek out and to save the lost."

19.1–10. 2–3: *Zacchaeus* is both a *tax collector,* to whom the Pharisees★ objected (see 15.1–2), and *rich.* The wealthy were at a disadvantage according to Jesus (18.24–25). His being *short* is only significant because he took unusual measures displaying faith (see also 7.36–50; 8.43–48). **8:** His actions are free, nondefensive, and exceeding even what the law required (Lev 5.16; Num 5.7; Ex 22.1). **9:** *A son of Abraham* is an heir to the promises (3.8; 13.16 (daughter); Gal 3.29).

〜〜〜〜〜〜〜〜

11 As they were listening to this, he went on to tell a parable, because he was near Jerusalem, and because they supposed that the

a Gk the Nazorean

kingdom of God was to appear immediately. ¹²So he said, "A nobleman went to a distant country to get royal power for himself and then return. ¹³He summoned ten of his slaves, and gave them ten pounds,ᵃ and said to them, 'Do business with these until I come back.' ¹⁴But the citizens of his country hated him and sent a delegation after him, saying, 'We do not want this man to rule over us.' ¹⁵When he returned, having received royal power, he ordered these slaves, to whom he had given the money, to be summoned so that he might find out what they had gained by trading. ¹⁶The first came forward and said, 'Lord, your pound has made ten more pounds.' ¹⁷He said to him, 'Well done, good slave! Because you have been trustworthy in a very small thing, take charge of ten cities.' ¹⁸Then the second came, saying, 'Lord, your pound has made five pounds.' ¹⁹He said to him, 'And you, rule over five cities.' ²⁰Then the other came, saying, 'Lord, here is your pound. I wrapped it up in a piece of cloth, ²¹for I was afraid of you, because you are a harsh man; you take what you did not deposit, and reap what you did not sow.' ²²He said to him, 'I will judge you by your own words, you wicked slave! You knew, did you, that I was a harsh man, taking what I did not deposit and reaping what I did not sow? ²³Why then did you not put my money into the bank? Then when I returned, I could have collected it with interest.' ²⁴He said to the bystanders, 'Take the pound from him and give it to the one who has ten pounds.' ²⁵(And they said to him, 'Lord, he has ten pounds!') ²⁶'I tell you, to all those who have, more will be given; but from those who have nothing, even what they have will be taken away. ²⁷But as for these enemies of mine who did not want me to be king over them—bring them here and slaughter them in my presence.' "

19.11–27. 11: The approach to *Jerusalem* anticipates a crisis in Jesus' royal role (see 19.28–47). 13: The *pound* is not a large amount, perhaps $20, but these funds were entrusted to the servants. 14, 27: The animosity of the *citizens* and their eventual punishment are recounted only in Luke's version of the story (see Mk 13.34; Mt 25.14–30; but see also

Lk 20.19). 22: On the *harsh* master, see 17.7–10. These images fit the way many oriental rulers and masters behaved (20.16). Will God do the same (Acts 2.36–39)?

JESUS' VISITATION IN JERUSALEM

19.28–21.38: Jesus' entry into Jerusalem marks a major new phase in the story (see 9.51).

28 After he had said this, he went on ahead, going up to Jerusalem.

29 When he had come near Bethphage and Bethany, at the place called the Mount of Olives, he sent two of the disciples, ³⁰saying, "Go into the village ahead of you, and as you enter it you will find tied there a colt that has never been ridden. Untie it and bring it here. ³¹If anyone asks you, 'Why are you untying it?' just say this, 'The Lord needs it.' " ³²So those who were sent departed and found it as he had told them. ³³As they were untying the colt, its owners asked them, "Why are you untying the colt?" ³⁴They said, "The Lord needs it." ³⁵Then they brought it to Jesus; and after throwing their cloaks on the colt, they set Jesus on it. ³⁶As he rode along, people kept spreading their cloaks on the road. ³⁷As he was now approaching the path down from the Mount of Olives, the whole multitude of the disciples began to praise God joyfully with a loud voice for all the deeds of power that they had seen, ³⁸saying,

"Blessed is the king
     who comes in the name of the Lord!
   Peace in heaven,
     and glory in the highest heaven!"
³⁹Some of the Pharisees in the crowd said to him, "Teacher, order your disciples to stop." ⁴⁰He answered, "I tell you, if these were silent, the stones would shout out."

19.28–40: The royal procession. Jesus' entry into Jerusalem is recounted in all four Gospels as an enactment of the royal entry of Zech 9.9. 29: These towns are close to Jerusalem. 31, 34: *"The Lord needs it"* is language of a military or royal requisition. 37: The

ᵃ The mina, rendered here by *pound*, was about three months' wages for a laborer *whole multitude of the disciples* is no mere crowd, but those who have *seen* (10.23). Their *praise* of *God* resounds with the angels, shepherds, and faithful in Israel (2.13, 20; 18.43). **38:** The citation of Ps 118 was anticipated in 13.35, and Luke specifically identifies "the one who comes" as *the king.* **39:** Luke is careful to emphasize that *some Pharisees,*✶ not all, sought to deter Jesus (see Acts 15.5). **40:** This verse can be translated as *the stones will shout,* a prophetic✶ warning about stones in a destruction (41–44; 21.6).

41 As he came near and saw the city, he wept over it, 42 saying, "If you, even you, had only recognized on this day the things that make for peace! But now they are hidden from your eyes. 43 Indeed, the days will come upon you, when your enemies will set up ramparts around you and surround you, and hem you in on every side. 44 They will crush you to the ground, you and your children within you, and they will not leave within you one stone upon another; because you did not recognize the time of your visitation from God."*a*

45 Then he entered the temple and began to drive out those who were selling things there; 46 and he said, "It is written,

'My house shall be a house of prayer';

but you have made it a den
of robbers."

47 Every day he was teaching in the temple. The chief priests, the scribes, and the leaders of the people kept looking for a way to kill him; 48 but they did not find anything they could do, for all the people were spellbound by what they heard.

19.41–48. 41–44: These verses offer a graphic description of siege warfare in a prophetic✶ declaration filled with Jeremiah's words predicting Jerusalem's first destruction by the neo-Babylonian empire (Jer 6.6–21; 8.18–21; 15.5; 23.38–40). **44:** *The time of your visitation from God* occurred when God's king Jesus arrived (1.68; 7.16). **45–46:** The elimination from the *temple*✶ of *those who were selling* was a prophetic hope (Zech 14.21), so that it could be restored as *a house of prayer* (Isa 56.7). **47–48:** Luke emphasizes the increasing official hostility to Jesus and the loyalty of *all the people* throughout chs. 20–22. These chapters parallel Mark 12–14 closely.

20 One day, as he was teaching the people in the temple and telling the good news, the chief priests and the scribes came with the elders 2 and said to him, "Tell us, by what authority are you doing these things? Who is it who gave you this authority?" 3 He answered them, "I will also ask you a question, and you tell me: 4 Did the baptism of John come from heaven, or was it of human origin?" 5 They discussed it with one another, saying, "If we say, 'From heaven,' he will say, 'Why did you not believe him?' 6 But if we say, 'Of human origin,' all the people will stone us; for they are convinced that John was a prophet." 7 So they answered that they did not know where it came from. 8 Then Jesus said to them, "Neither will I tell you by what authority I am doing these things."

9 He began to tell the people this parable: "A man planted a vineyard, and leased it to tenants, and went to another country for a long time. 10 When the season came, he sent a slave to the tenants in order that they might give him his share of the produce of the vineyard; but the tenants beat him and sent him away empty-handed. 11 Next he sent another slave; that one also they beat and insulted and sent away empty-handed. 12 And he sent still a third; this one also they wounded and threw out. 13 Then the owner of the vineyard said, 'What shall I do? I will send my beloved son; perhaps they will respect him.' 14 But when the tenants saw him, they discussed it among themselves and said, 'This is the heir; let us kill him so that the inheritance may be ours.' 15 So they threw him out of the vineyard and killed him. What then will the owner of the vineyard do to them? 16 He will come and destroy those tenants and give the vineyard to others." When they heard this, they said, "Heaven forbid!" 17 But he looked at them and said, "What then does this text mean:

'The stone that the builders rejected
   has become the cornerstone'?*b*

18 Everyone who falls on that stone will be broken to pieces; and it will crush anyone on whom it falls." 19 When the scribes and chief priests realized that he had told this parable

a Gk lacks *from God*   *b* Or *keystone*

against them, they wanted to lay hands on him at that very hour, but they feared the people.

20.1–21.4: Conflicts while teaching in the Temple. ★ **1–2:** This story follows a standard debate among Jewish interpreters, and the question of *authority* calls for the scriptural answers Luke has provided all along. **3–4:** In Luke's account (3.21–22), Jesus' *baptism*★ by *John* was emphatically *from heaven*. **5–8:** Their refusal to reply displays fear of *the people* and relieves Jesus from continuing debate. **9–19: The vineyard and the tenants.** This harsh *parable*★ has been misused by gentile★ Christians to justify violence against Jews. **9:** Isa 5.1–7 depicts Jerusalem as God's *vineyard,* under threat. **13–15:** To kill a *beloved son* is to provoke wrath (see Acts 2.37) **17:** This is another reference to Ps 118 (see 19.38). **19:** Jesus' parable *against them* is no more severe than many prophetic★ judgments against God's people, but they are alarming to any group tempted to think they are entitled or self-righteous (Rom 11.13–36). Note again their fear of *the people* (20.6).

20 So they watched him and sent spies who pretended to be honest, in order to trap him by what he said, so as to hand him over to the jurisdiction and authority of the governor. ²¹So they asked him, "Teacher, we know that you are right in what you say and teach, and you show deference to no one, but teach the way of God in accordance with truth. ²²Is it lawful for us to pay taxes to the emperor, or not?" ²³But he perceived their craftiness and said to them, ²⁴"Show me a denarius. Whose head and whose title does it bear?" They said, "The emperor's." ²⁵He said to them, "Then give to the emperor the things that are the emperor's, and to God the things that are God's." ²⁶And they were not able in the presence of the people to trap him by what he said; and being amazed by his answer, they became silent.

20.20–26. 20: This is the first mention of the Roman *governor* (see 23.1–25, especially 23.2 on "taxes to the emperor"). **21:** To *show deference* would mean to allow political influence to prevail over *truth*. **22:** *Lawful* means in accord with God's law as interpreted by Israel's teachers. **25:** Jesus' answer still leaves them with the question of whether all things belong to God

(Ps 24.1: see also Acts 4.19; 5.29). **26:** *The presence of the people* is again the context for this attempted trap.

27 Some Sadducees, those who say there is no resurrection, came to him ²⁸and asked him a question, "Teacher, Moses wrote for us that if a man's brother dies, leaving a wife but no children, the man*ᵃ* shall marry the widow and raise up children for his brother. ²⁹Now there were seven brothers; the first married, and died childless; ³⁰then the second ³¹and the third married her, and so in the same way all seven died childless. ³²Finally the woman also died. ³³In the resurrection, therefore, whose wife will the woman be? For the seven had married her."

34 Jesus said to them, "Those who belong to this age marry and are given in marriage; ³⁵but those who are considered worthy of a place in that age and in the resurrection from the dead neither marry nor are given in marriage. ³⁶Indeed they cannot die anymore, because they are like angels and are children of God, being children of the resurrection. ³⁷And the fact that the dead are raised Moses himself showed, in the story about the bush, where he speaks of the Lord as the God of Abraham, the God of Isaac, and the God of Jacob. ³⁸Now he is God not of the dead, but of the living; for to him all of them are alive." ³⁹Then some of the scribes answered, "Teacher, you have spoken well." ⁴⁰For they no longer dared to ask him another question.

41 Then he said to them, "How can they say that the Messiah*ᵇ* is David's son? ⁴²For David himself says in the book of Psalms,

'The Lord said to my Lord,
  "Sit at my right hand,
43   until I make your enemies your
        footstool." '

⁴⁴David thus calls him Lord; so how can he be his son?"

45 In the hearing of all the people he said to the*ᶜ* disciples, ⁴⁶"Beware of the scribes, who like to walk around in long robes, and love to be greeted with respect in the mar-

a Gk *his brother*   *b* Or *the Christ*   *c* Other ancient authorities read *his* ketplaces, and to have the best seats in the synagogues and places of honor at banquets. 47They devour widows' houses and for the sake of appearance say long prayers. They will receive the greater condemnation."

21 He looked up and saw rich people putting their gifts into the treasury; 2he also saw a poor widow put in two small copper coins. 3He said, "Truly I tell you, this poor widow has put in more than all of them; 4for all of them have contributed out of their abundance, but she out of her poverty has put in all she had to live on."

20.27–21.4: These disputes with the *Sadducees*★ with support from the *scribes*★ (v. 39) anticipate divisions between the Sadducees and the Pharisees★ concerning the *resurrection* in Acts 23.6–10; 24.15–21; 26.4–8. **27–33:** The case is clearly intended to ridicule belief in the resurrection. **28:** The obligation to marry a brother's widow is called levirate marriage★ (Deut 25.5–10; Gen 38.8; Ruth 3–4). **34–36:** This is one of the more complete New Testament statements about the altered bodily state of resurrection (see 1 Cor 15.35–57). **37–38:** Jesus is making an interpretive argument for the resurrection on the basis of God's word from the burning *bush* in Ex 3.6. **41–44:** Jesus pursues another interpretive argument, now on Ps 110. The appeal to Ps 110 will be taken further as testimony to the resurrection in Acts 2.29–36. "Son of David" is a crucial royal title in Luke (1.27, 32, 69; 2.4, 11; 6.3; 18.38–39) and in Acts (2.25–36). **45–47:** Jesus responds to several attempts (19.47–20.40) to entrap him in the presence of *the people* with a prophetic★ oracle★ denouncing *the scribes* (see Mt 23). **21.1–4:** The *widow* is again an example of faith (2.36–38; Acts 6.1–2), displaying a generosity from her *poverty* that warns the *rich* against false security (see 16.1–31).

---

5 When some were speaking about the temple, how it was adorned with beautiful stones and gifts dedicated to God, he said, 6"As for these things that you see, the days will come when not one stone will be left upon another; all will be thrown down."

7 They asked him, "Teacher, when will this be, and what will be the sign that this is about to take place?" 8And he said, "Beware that you are not led astray; for many will come in my name and say, 'I am he!'ᵃ and, 'The time is near!'ᵇ Do not go after them.

9 "When you hear of wars and insurrections, do not be terrified; for these things must take place first, but the end will not follow immediately." 10Then he said to them, "Nation will rise against nation, and kingdom against kingdom; 11there will be great earthquakes, and in various places famines and plagues; and there will be dreadful portents and great signs from heaven.

12 "But before all this occurs, they will arrest you and persecute you; they will hand you over to synagogues and prisons, and you will be brought before kings and governors because of my name. 13This will give you an opportunity to testify. 14So make up your minds not to prepare your defense in advance; 15for I will give you wordsᶜ and a wisdom that none of your opponents will be able to withstand or contradict. 16You will be betrayed even by parents and brothers, by relatives and friends; and they will put some of you to death. 17You will be hated by all because of my name. 18But not a hair of your head will perish. 19By your endurance you will gain your souls.

20 "When you see Jerusalem surrounded by armies, then know that its desolation has come near.ᵈ 21Then those in Judea must flee to the mountains, and those inside the city must leave it, and those out in the country must not enter it; 22for these are days of vengeance, as a fulfillment of all that is written. 23Woe to those who are pregnant and to those who are nursing infants in those days! For there will be great distress on the earth and wrath against this people; 24they will fall by the edge of the sword and be taken away as captives among all nations; and Jerusalem will be trampled on by the Gentiles, until the times of the Gentiles are fulfilled.

25 "There will be signs in the sun, the moon, and the stars, and on the earth distress among nations confused by the roaring of the sea and the waves. 26People will faint from fear and foreboding of what is coming upon the world, for the powers of the heavens will be shaken. 27Then they will see 'the

---

a Gk *I am*   *b* Or *at hand*   *c* Gk *a mouth*
d Or *is at hand*

Son of Man coming in a cloud' with power and great glory. 28 Now when these things begin to take place, stand up and raise your heads, because your redemption is drawing near."

21.5–28: Dire warnings at the Temple.* 5: *The temple* is a crucial place for teaching (2.46; 19.47; 20.1; 22.53; Acts 21.27–22.29). Jesus' words throughout this chapter, closely paralleled in Mk 13 and Mt 24, recall Jeremiah's dire oracles* about the first Temple prior to its destruction (Jer 7.1–15; 23.11). **8:** The Jewish historian Josephus* tells of prophets,* including one named Jesus who used Jeremiah's words, during the Roman siege (*War* 6.271–275; 285–315; 442). **9:** The destruction *must take place first* before *the end* because of God's will for the whole world (see 21.24). **11:** The destruction is depicted on a cosmic scale in the tradition of Jewish apocalyptic* (Isa 24–27; Rev 6). **12–19:** As in 12.11–12, Jesus predicts what later happens in Acts to the apostles* on trial before *kings and governors* (see also Acts 9.15–16: to suffer for the sake of *my name*). **13:** The *opportunity to testify* (Gk., "marturion") may be a faithful "witness" unto death (24.48; Acts 1.8; 2.32; 3.15; 5.32; 10.39, 41; 13.31; 22.15; 26.16). **19:** *Endurance* is a mark of faithfulness (8.15; 22.28–30). **20–24:** Jesus' words are filled with scriptural phrases from the first destruction, now directed toward the impending Roman siege (see also 13.34–35; 19.41–44) **22:** The *days of vengeance* is a scriptural phrase for God's wrath (Hos 9.7; Deut 32.35; Jer 46.10; 50.31). **24:** The *Gentiles** or non-Jewish nations are God's instruments of judgment, as in the Greek version of Zech 12.3: "I will make Jersualem to be a stone trodden down by all the Gentiles" (see Rev 11.2), but they will not dominate forever (Deut 32.26–27; Isa 45–47). **25–28:** The cosmic *signs* of the end of the world reflect the vision of the *Son of Man* in Daniel 7. **28:** The faithful continue to hope to see the *redemption* of Jerusalem (2.38).

29 Then he told them a parable: "Look at the fig tree and all the trees; 30 as soon as they sprout leaves you can see for yourselves and know that summer is already near. 31 So also, when you see these things taking place, you know that the kingdom of God is near. 32 Truly I tell you, this generation will not pass away until all things have taken place. 33 Heaven and earth will pass away, but my words will not pass away.

34 "Be on guard so that your hearts are not weighed down with dissipation and drunkenness and the worries of this life, and that day does not catch you unexpectedly, 35 like a trap. For it will come upon all who live on the face of the whole earth. 36 Be alert at all times, praying that you may have the strength to escape all these things that will take place, and to stand before the Son of Man."

37 Every day he was teaching in the temple, and at night he would go out and spend the night on the Mount of Olives, as it was called. 38 And all the people would get up early in the morning to listen to him in the temple.

21.29–38: In Luke, these words mark the end of Jesus' *teaching in the temple** which began in 19.28. Only Luke uses the parable* to emphasize that *the kingdom of God is near* (see 17.20–21). **34–36:** *That day* is the judgment day for *all on . . . the whole earth,* with the *Son of Man* as judge (Dan 7). **38:** Note again the loyalty of *all the people* (see 19.47–48).

22 Now the festival of Unleavened Bread, which is called the Passover, was near. 2 The chief priests and the scribes were looking for a way to put Jesus*a* to death, for they were afraid of the people.

3 Then Satan entered into Judas called Iscariot, who was one of the twelve; 4 he went away and conferred with the chief priests and officers of the temple police about how he might betray him to them. 5 They were greatly pleased and agreed to give him money. 6 So he consented and began to look for an opportunity to betray him to them when no crowd was present.

22.1–23.56 (Mk 14–15; Mt 26–27): **The tragic death of Jesus. 22.1–2:** These verses provide a transition into Luke's dramatic narrative* of Jesus' betrayal, trial, death, and resurrection. *Unleavened Bread* recalls the flight from Egypt, setting faithful Israelites apart (Ex 12.1–20). Luke alerts the reader to observe the differing roles played out in the story of struggle and death that follows. Those who were *looking for a way to put Jesus to death* also *were afraid of the people.* How did

a Gk *him*

various disciples behave? What roles did the rulers play? And finally, how was God's will accomplished? (See the interpretation* of these events in the sermons in Acts 2.22–36; 4.24–28; 10.36–41; 13.27–31). **3–6:** *Satan* (see 10.18) or "the devil" (4.1–13) finds an active conspirator in *Judas* (*he went away, . . . conferred, . . . consented and began to look for an opportunity*), *one of the twelve* (6.13; 22.29–30).

7 Then came the day of Unleavened Bread, on which the Passover lamb had to be sacrificed. ⁸So Jesus*ᵃ* sent Peter and John, saying, "Go and prepare the Passover meal for us that we may eat it." ⁹They asked him, "Where do you want us to make preparations for it?" ¹⁰"Listen," he said to them, "when you have entered the city, a man carrying a jar of water will meet you; follow him into the house he enters ¹¹and say to the owner of the house, 'The teacher asks you, "Where is the guest room, where I may eat the Passover with my disciples?" ' ¹²He will show you a large room upstairs, already furnished. Make preparations for us there." ¹³So they went and found everything as he had told them; and they prepared the Passover meal.

14 When the hour came, he took his place at the table, and the apostles with him. ¹⁵He said to them, "I have eagerly desired to eat this Passover with you before I suffer; ¹⁶for I tell you, I will not eat it*ᵇ* until it is fulfilled in the kingdom of God." ¹⁷Then he took a cup, and after giving thanks he said, "Take this and divide it among yourselves; ¹⁸for I tell you that from now on I will not drink of the fruit of the vine until the kingdom of God comes." ¹⁹Then he took a loaf of bread, and when he had given thanks, he broke it and gave it to them, saying, "This is my body, which is given for you. Do this in remembrance of me." ²⁰And he did the same with the cup after supper, saying, "This cup that is poured out for you is the new covenant in my blood.*ᶜ* ²¹But see, the one who betrays me is with me, and his hand is on the table. ²²For the Son of Man is going as it has been determined, but woe to that one by whom he is betrayed!" ²³Then they began to ask one another which one of them it could be who would do this.

22.7–23. 7: *Passover*★ (Mt 26.1–5; Mk 14.1–2; Jn 11.55) was a significant occasion because of the crowds in the city and because the feast symbolized Israel's freedom from oppression (Ex 12.1–20; Deut 16.1–8; Lev 23.5–6). **8–13:** Jesus again *sent* two disciples with advance notice of what they would find (19.29–32). **15:** Jesus' language, *I have eagerly desired*, echoes the determination he showed in setting his face to go to Jerusalem (9.53; 12.49–50; 13.33). **17–18:** Only Luke reports more than one *cup* (see also v. 20), consistent with Passover practice. The taking, blessing/*giving thanks,* breaking, and giving of the bread also reflects Jewish practice (see 24.30). **19–20:** To declare Jesus' *body given for* (lit., on behalf of) *you* and his *blood poured out for you* is to use the language of sacrifice, deeply reminiscent of the Passover (Ex 12.13–27) and the blood of the covenant★ God first made with Israel (Ex 24.8). The *new covenant* is promised in Jer 31.31. **22:** The suffering of *the Son of Man* is again *determined* in accord with God's plan (9.22, 44; 18.31; 24.7; see Acts 2.23; 10.42; 17.31), while the betrayer is held responsible for his action (22.48; see Acts 1.16).

24 A dispute also arose among them as to which one of them was to be regarded as the greatest. ²⁵But he said to them, "The kings of the Gentiles lord it over them; and those in authority over them are called benefactors. ²⁶But not so with you; rather the greatest among you must become like the youngest, and the leader like one who serves. ²⁷For who is greater, the one who is at the table or the one who serves? Is it not the one at the table? But I am among you as one who serves.

28 "You are those who have stood by me in my trials; ²⁹and I confer on you, just as my Father has conferred on me, a kingdom, ³⁰so that you may eat and drink at my table in my kingdom, and you will sit on thrones judging the twelve tribes of Israel.

31 "Simon, Simon, listen! Satan has demanded*ᵈ* to sift all of you like wheat, ³²but I have prayed for you that your own faith may

a Gk *he*　　b Other ancient authorities read *never eat it again*　　c Other ancient authorities lack, in whole or in part, verses 19b-20 (*which is given . . . in my blood*)　　d Or *has obtained permission* not fail; and you, when once you have turned back, strengthen your brothers." [33]And he said to him, "Lord, I am ready to go with you to prison and to death!" [34]Jesus[a] said, "I tell you, Peter, the cock will not crow this day, until you have denied three times that you know me."

35 He said to them, "When I sent you out without a purse, bag, or sandals, did you lack anything?" They said, "No, not a thing." [36]He said to them, "But now, the one who has a purse must take it, and likewise a bag. And the one who has no sword must sell his cloak and buy one. [37]For I tell you, this scripture must be fulfilled in me, 'And he was counted among the lawless'; and indeed what is written about me is being fulfilled." [38]They said, "Lord, look, here are two swords." He replied, "It is enough."

22.24–38. 24: The foolish argument about who is *the greatest* which began in 9.46 again prompts teaching. 30: In Israel's past, Moses appointed judges (Ex 18), rulers who led tribal Israel (see Judges). The *twelve* apostles* will be assigned *thrones* of judgment over Israel's *tribes* in Jesus' reign (9.1; Acts 1.17; Rev 7.4–8). 31–34: *Satan* tests Israel's newly appointed rulers, like *wheat* in a sieve (4.1–13; 22.40; Am 9.9). *Once you have turned back* anticipates Peter's repentance (22.61–62). 35–38: Only Luke tells this story about the *sword,* depicting Jesus' unusual need for equipment (contrast 10.4) for scriptural reasons. *Two swords are enough* to justify charges of *lawless* behavior against Jesus and thus fulfill the prophecy of Isa 53.12 (see 23.39–41).

---

39 He came out and went, as was his custom, to the Mount of Olives; and the disciples followed him. [40]When he reached the place, he said to them, "Pray that you may not come into the time of trial."[b] [41]Then he withdrew from them about a stone's throw, knelt down, and prayed, [42]"Father, if you are willing, remove this cup from me; yet, not my will but yours be done." [[43]Then an angel from heaven appeared to him and gave him strength. [44]In his anguish he prayed more earnestly, and his sweat became like great drops of blood falling down on the ground.][c] [45]When he got up from prayer, he came to the disciples and found them sleeping be-

cause of grief, [46]and he said to them, "Why are you sleeping? Get up and pray that you may not come into the time of trial."[b]

47 While he was still speaking, suddenly a crowd came, and the one called Judas, one of the twelve, was leading them. He approached Jesus to kiss him; [48]but Jesus said to him, "Judas, is it with a kiss that you are betraying the Son of Man?" [49]When those who were around him saw what was coming, they asked, "Lord, should we strike with the sword?" [50]Then one of them struck the slave of the high priest and cut off his right ear. [51]But Jesus said, "No more of this!" And he touched his ear and healed him. [52]Then Jesus said to the chief priests, the officers of the temple police, and the elders who had come for him, "Have you come out with swords and clubs as if I were a bandit? [53]When I was with you day after day in the temple, you did not lay hands on me. But this is your hour, and the power of darkness!"

22.39–53. 39: Gethsemane (see Mk 14.32; Mt 26.36) is a place on *the Mount of Olives,* opposite Jerusalem. 40–42: The prayer to avert the *time of trial* (see 11.4) is now replaced by obedience to the *will* of the *Father* (11.2) as the *cup* of divine purpose and passion, even wrath (Isa 51.17, 22; Jer 25.15, 17, 28; 49.12; Ps 11.6; 75.8; Ezek 23.31–33; Hab 2.16), cannot be evaded. 43–44: The *strength* the *angel* gives equips Jesus for this time of trial (see 4.10). These verses depict Jesus sweating profusely in athletic struggle (Gk., "agonia"), not merely mental *anguish* (see note *c*). 47–48: *Judas* is again actively *leading* a *crowd* of officials who are intent on capturing Jesus (see 22.4, 52). *The Son of Man* is the heavenly judge, who is betrayed at great peril (12.8–10; 21.27, 36; 22.22; Dan 7.13). 49–51: On the *sword,* see 22.36–38. Only Luke reports that Jesus *healed* the high priest's slave (see Mt 26.47–52; Mk 14.43–52). 53: *The power of darkness* is the dominion of evil (22.3) in which darkness reigns rather than light (1.79; Acts 26.18).

---

54 Then they seized him and led him away, bringing him into the high priest's house. But Peter was following at a distance. [55]When they had kindled a fire in the middle

---

a Gk *He*   *b* Or *into temptation*   *c* Other ancient authorities lack verses 43 and 44 of the courtyard and sat down together, Peter sat among them. 56Then a servant-girl, seeing him in the firelight, stared at him and said, "This man also was with him." 57But he denied it, saying, "Woman, I do not know him." 58A little later someone else, on seeing him, said, "You also are one of them." But Peter said, "Man, I am not!" 59Then about an hour later still another kept insisting, "Surely this man also was with him; for he is a Galilean." 60But Peter said, "Man, I do not know what you are talking about!" At that moment, while he was still speaking, the cock crowed. 61The Lord turned and looked at Peter. Then Peter remembered the word of the Lord, how he had said to him, "Before the cock crows today, you will deny me three times." 62And he went out and wept bitterly.

63 Now the men who were holding Jesus began to mock him and beat him; 64they also blindfolded him and kept asking him, "Prophesy! Who is it that struck you?" 65They kept heaping many other insults on him.

66 When day came, the assembly of the elders of the people, both chief priests and scribes, gathered together, and they brought him to their council. 67They said, "If you are the Messiah,a tell us." He replied, "If I tell you, you will not believe; 68and if I question you, you will not answer. 69But from now on the Son of Man will be seated at the right hand of the power of God." 70All of them asked, "Are you, then, the Son of God?" He said to them, "You say that I am." 71Then they said, "What further testimony do we need? We have heard it ourselves from his own lips!"

of the power of God) of the Son of Man (21.36) and declares his accusers' words and deeds bear witness to his true identity, probably by fulfilling the scriptures about opposing the messiah of God (Acts 4.25–28).

23 Then the assembly rose as a body and brought Jesusb before Pilate. 2They began to accuse him, saying, "We found this man perverting our nation, forbidding us to pay taxes to the emperor, and saying that he himself is the Messiah, a king."c 3Then Pilate asked him, "Are you the king of the Jews?" He answered, "You say so." 4Then Pilate said to the chief priests and the crowds, "I find no basis for an accusation against this man." 5But they were insistent and said, "He stirs up the people by teaching throughout all Judea, from Galilee where he began even to this place."

6 When Pilate heard this, he asked whether the man was a Galilean. 7And when he learned that he was under Herod's jurisdiction, he sent him off to Herod, who was himself in Jerusalem at that time. 8When Herod saw Jesus, he was very glad, for he had been wanting to see him for a long time, because he had heard about him and was hoping to see him perform some sign. 9He questioned him at some length, but Jesusd gave him no answer. 10The chief priests and the scribes stood by, vehemently accusing him. 11Even Herod with his soldiers treated him with contempt and mocked him; then he put an elegant robe on him, and sent him back to Pilate. 12That same day Herod and Pilate became friends with each other; before this they had been enemies.

13 Pilate then called together the chief priests, the leaders, and the people, 14and said to them, "You brought me this man as one who was perverting the people; and here I have examined him in your presence and have not found this man guilty of any of your charges against him. 15Neither has Herod, for he sent him back to us. Indeed, he has done nothing to deserve death. 16I will therefore have him flogged and release him."e

22.54–71. 54–55: The high priest's house was a palace or official residence. Unlike Judas, Peter is not an active conspirator, but following at a distance (at his peril: 22.33), he seeks to remain unidentified. 59: His speech or garb probably revealed Peter's Galilean origin. 61–62: Peter's grief as he remembered (22.34) is a display of repentance for unintended complicity in evil. 63–64: Brutal hazing of prisoners often preceded official interrogation. 66–71: The Jewish court focuses on the titles Messiah* and Son of God, royal roles (4.41; 23.35–38; 23.2) which only God could award. Jesus warns of the divine judgment (seated at the right hand

a Or the Christ   b Gk him   c Or is an anointed king   d Gk he   e Here, or after verse 19, other ancient authorities add verse 17, Now he was obliged to release someone for them at the festival

18 Then they all shouted out together, "Away with this fellow! Release Barabbas for us!" 19(This was a man who had been put in prison for an insurrection that had taken place in the city, and for murder.) 20Pilate, wanting to release Jesus, addressed them again; 21but they kept shouting, "Crucify, crucify him!" 22A third time he said to them, "Why, what evil has he done? I have found in him no ground for the sentence of death; I will therefore have him flogged and then release him." 23But they kept urgently demanding with loud shouts that he should be crucified; and their voices prevailed. 24So Pilate gave his verdict that their demand should be granted. 25He released the man they asked for, the one who had been put in prison for insurrection and murder, and he handed Jesus over as they wished.

23.1–25. 1–2: *Pilate* was the Roman governor who came to Jerusalem during Passover* to keep the peace (see 13.1; Acts 4.27). 3: Pilate focuses on the title *king of the Jews,* which only the Roman Senate could award. Jesus again interprets the accusation as a testimony to its truth (see 22.71). 5: The charge that *he stirs up the people* implies insurrection and implicates *the people* who have defended Jesus from the crowds of Temple* officials (see 19.47; 20.1, 6, 26; 21.38; 22.2, 52). 6–7: *Herod* Antipas (3.1, 19–20; 9.7–9; 13.31) sought his father's appointment as king of the Jews, but the Romans only made him tetrarch of Galilee and Perea. 11–12: Only Luke tells this cruel story with *Herod* himself participating in royal mockery and thus becoming *friends with Pilate* (23.15). 13–14: Pilate's reputation for violent disrespect for Jewish customs (13.1; Josephus,* *The Jewish War* 2.172–177) may suggest Luke thought he was taunting the *chief priests, the leaders, and the people,* accusing them of false *charges* as if they were the ones *perverting the people.* Like Peter (22.54–62), "the people" who protected Jesus (see 19.47–48) are now at risk themselves. They only add to Jesus' danger by being associated with him and will deny him three times (see 23.22–23, 27). (17) 18–19: The story of *Barabbas* is told in detail in Mk 15.6–15 and Mt 27.15–23, and later copies added v. 17 to make Luke's account complete (see note *e*, p. 1789). 25: Compared with Mk 15.15 and Mt 27.26, Luke's account emphasizes Pilate's responsibility for releasing one convicted of *insurrection and murder,* further violating Roman law by executing *Jesus*

whom he had declared innocent three times (23.22). The phrase *as they wished* sharpens the question of whose will is being done in this execution (see vv. 27–28).

26 As they led him away, they seized a man, Simon of Cyrene, who was coming from the country, and they laid the cross on him, and made him carry it behind Jesus. 27A great number of the people followed him, and among them were women who were beating their breasts and wailing for him. 28But Jesus turned to them and said, "Daughters of Jerusalem, do not weep for me, but weep for yourselves and for your children. 29For the days are surely coming when they will say, 'Blessed are the barren, and the wombs that never bore, and the breasts that never nursed.' 30Then they will begin to say to the mountains, 'Fall on us'; and to the hills, 'Cover us.' 31For if they do this when the wood is green, what will happen when it is dry?"

32 Two others also, who were criminals, were led away to be put to death with him. 33When they came to the place that is called The Skull, they crucified Jesus*a* there with the criminals, one on his right and one on his left. [34Then Jesus said, "Father, forgive them; for they do not know what they are doing."]*b* And they cast lots to divide his clothing. 35And the people stood by, watching; but the leaders scoffed at him, saying, "He saved others; let him save himself if he is the Messiah*c* of God, his chosen one!" 36The soldiers also mocked him, coming up and offering him sour wine, 37and saying, "If you are the King of the Jews, save yourself!" 38There was also an inscription over him,*d* "This is the King of the Jews."

39 One of the criminals who were hanged there kept deriding*e* him and saying, "Are you not the Messiah?*c* Save yourself and us!" 40But the other rebuked him, saying, "Do you not fear God, since you are under the same sentence of condemnation? 41And we

a Gk *him*   *b* Other ancient authorities lack the sentence *Then Jesus . . . what they are doing*
c Or *the Christ*   *d* Other ancient authorities add *written in Greek and Latin and Hebrew* (that is, *Aramaic*)
e Or *blaspheming*

indeed have been condemned justly, for we are getting what we deserve for our deeds, but this man has done nothing wrong." 42Then he said, "Jesus, remember me when you come into^a your kingdom." 43He replied, "Truly I tell you, today you will be with me in Paradise."

44 It was now about noon, and darkness came over the whole land^b until three in the afternoon, 45while the sun's light failed;^c and the curtain of the temple was torn in two. 46Then Jesus, crying with a loud voice, said, "Father, into your hands I commend my spirit." Having said this, he breathed his last. 47When the centurion saw what had taken place, he praised God and said, "Certainly this man was innocent."^d 48And when all the crowds who had gathered there for this spectacle saw what had taken place, they returned home, beating their breasts. 49But all his acquaintances, including the women who had followed him from Galilee, stood at a distance, watching these things.

than a miscarriage of Roman justice because of God's care for the righteous (Wis 2–3). **48–49:** On the anguished *beating their breasts* of the *crowds* and the *women,* see 23.27–31.

50 Now there was a good and righteous man named Joseph, who, though a member of the council, 51had not agreed to their plan and action. He came from the Jewish town of Arimathea, and he was waiting expectantly for the kingdom of God. 52This man went to Pilate and asked for the body of Jesus. 53Then he took it down, wrapped it in a linen cloth, and laid it in a rock-hewn tomb where no one had ever been laid. 54It was the day of Preparation, and the sabbath was beginning.^e 55The women who had come with him from Galilee followed, and they saw the tomb and how his body was laid. 56Then they returned, and prepared spices and ointments.

On the sabbath they rested according to the commandment.

23.26–49. 26: *Simon* is otherwise unknown (see also Mk 15.21; Mt 27.32). **27–28:** Jesus' death is clearly not the desire of *a great number of the people* or the faithful *women* (vv. 35, 48–49, 55). **28–31:** As in 19.41–44, only Luke relates Jesus' dire prophetic* oracle,* echoing Jeremiah's call to the "mourning women" to raise a dirge over Jerusalem (Jer 9.17–22). The cries to the *mountains* and the *hills* recall the destruction oracle of Hos 10.8. On the ominous image of the *green* and *dry* wood, see Ezek 20.47. **34:** The conviction that Israel and its rulers acted in "ignorance" will be crucial to the preaching of repentance in Acts 3.17. **35–38:** In echoes of Isa 42.1, Luke links the royal titles *Messiah* of God* and *King of the Jews* with Jesus' identity as the servant who suffers as *the chosen one* (9.35; Acts 3.13, 26; 4.27, 30; 8.30–35). **43:** *Paradise* is a biblical image of the garden of bliss (2 Cor 12.4; Rev 2.7). **44–45:** The *darkness* at midday and the tearing of the *curtain of the temple** separating the holy precincts (Ex 26.31–35, 37; 38.18) are cosmic signs, open to many interpretations (see Mk 15.37–38; Heb 9.6–28). **46:** Only Luke reports Jesus' dying word as the resignation of his *spirit* (see 3.22; 4.1; Acts 1.8; Ps 31.5), and "he expired" (lit. in Greek). **47:** When the *centurion* declares Jesus *innocent* (see Mk 15.39; Mt 27.54: "God's Son"), the word could also be translated "righteous." According to Jewish traditions, this death was more

23.50–56. 50–52: Otherwise unknown, *Joseph of Arimathea* is another Israelite who observed God's law (*good and righteous*) and hoped in God's promises (see Simeon and Anna in Lk 2.25–26, 37–38). **54:** *The day of Preparation* for the day of rest (24.56) was literally "shining forth" (see note *e: dawning*). perhaps as the *sabbath* candles were being lit at evening. **56:** *Spices and ointments* were administered to the dead (24.1; Jn 12.7; 19.40).

24 But on the first day of the week, at early dawn, they came to the tomb, taking the spices that they had prepared. 2They found the stone rolled away from the tomb, 3but when they went in, they did not find the body.^f 4While they were perplexed about this, suddenly two men in dazzling clothes stood beside them. 5The women^g were terrified and bowed their faces to the ground, but the men^h said to them, "Why do you look for the living among the dead? He

---

a Other ancient authorities read *in*   b Or *earth*
c Or *the sun was eclipsed.* Other ancient authorities read *the sun was darkened*   d Or *righteous*   e Gk *was dawning*   f Other ancient authorities add *of the Lord Jesus*   g Gk *They*   h Gk *but they*

is not here, but has risen.ᵃ ⁶Remember how he told you, while he was still in Galilee, ⁷that the Son of Man must be handed over to sinners, and be crucified, and on the third day rise again." ⁸Then they remembered his words, ⁹and returning from the tomb, they told all this to the eleven and to all the rest. ¹⁰Now it was Mary Magdalene, Joanna, Mary the mother of James, and the other women with them who told this to the apostles. ¹¹But these words seemed to them an idle tale, and they did not believe them. ¹²But Peter got up and ran to the tomb; stooping and looking in, he saw the linen cloths by themselves; then he went home, amazed at what had happened.ᵇ

24.1–53 (Mk 16; Mt 28): **Divine vindication and exaltation of Jesus, the messiah.*** **1–12** (Mk 16.1–8; Mt 28.1–8): **The empty tomb. 4:** The *two men in dazzling clothes* (see also 9.29) will later be identified as angels (24.23). **5–9:** Fear and homage express the women's awareness of divine messengers (1.12; 2.9). The reproof for misunderstanding will be repeated (24.25, 38, 44, 46). To understand God's ways, Israel is often called to *remember* (see Deut 7.18; 8.18; 24.9; 32.7); now Jesus' predictions of the *Son of Man*'s death and resurrection (see especially 9.22, 43–45; 12.50; 13.33; 18.31–34) are to be recalled. **10–12:** The witness of the *women* (see 8.1–3) is again emphasized in vv. 22–24 as well as the disbelief by the *apostles,*** including *Peter.*

13 Now on that same day two of them were going to a village called Emmaus, about seven milesᶜ from Jerusalem, ¹⁴and talking with each other about all these things that had happened. ¹⁵While they were talking and discussing, Jesus himself came near and went with them, ¹⁶but their eyes were kept from recognizing him. ¹⁷And he said to them, "What are you discussing with each other while you walk along?" They stood still, looking sad.ᵈ ¹⁸Then one of them, whose name was Cleopas, answered him, "Are you the only stranger in Jerusalem who does not know the things that have taken place there in these days?" ¹⁹He asked them, "What things?" They replied, "The things about Jesus of Nazareth,ᵉ who was a prophet mighty in deed and word before God and all the peo-

ple, ²⁰and how our chief priests and leaders handed him over to be condemned to death and crucified him. ²¹But we had hoped that he was the one to redeem Israel.ᶠ Yes, and besides all this, it is now the third day since these things took place. ²²Moreover, some women of our group astounded us. They were at the tomb early this morning, ²³and when they did not find his body there, they came back and told us that they had indeed seen a vision of angels who said that he was alive. ²⁴Some of those who were with us went to the tomb and found it just as the women had said; but they did not see him." ²⁵Then he said to them, "Oh, how foolish you are, and how slow of heart to believe all that the prophets have declared! ²⁶Was it not necessary that the Messiahᵍ should suffer these things and then enter into his glory?" ²⁷Then beginning with Moses and all the prophets, he interpreted to them the things about himself in all the scriptures.

28 As they came near the village to which they were going, he walked ahead as if he were going on. ²⁹But they urged him strongly, saying, "Stay with us, because it is almost evening and the day is now nearly over." So he went in to stay with them. ³⁰When he was at the table with them, he took bread, blessed and broke it, and gave it to them. ³¹Then their eyes were opened, and they recognized him; and he vanished from their sight. ³²They said to each other, "Were not our hearts burning within usʰ while he was talking to us on the road, while he was opening the scriptures to us?" ³³That same hour they got up and returned to Jerusalem; and they found the eleven and their companions gathered together. ³⁴They were saying, "The Lord has risen indeed, and he has appeared to Simon!" ³⁵Then they told what had happened on the road, and how he had been made known to them in the breaking of the bread.

a Other ancient authorities lack *He is not here, but has risen*　*b* Other ancient authorities lack verse 12　*c* Gk *sixty stadia;* other ancient authorities read *a hundred sixty stadia*　*d* Other ancient authorities read *walk along, looking sad?"*　*e* Other ancient authorities read *Jesus the Nazorean*　*f* Or *to set Israel free*　*g* Or *the Christ*　*h* Other ancient authorities lack *within us*

24.13–35: The way to Emmaus. This story is a masterpiece. Recalling Luke's whole narrative,* this story gives the reader privileged insight into events the participants in the drama only see later. **14–16:** They discuss *all these things that had happened,* but again not even Jesus' disciples on the journey (9.51–56) can "see" or understand (18.31–34). *Their eyes were kept from recognizing him,* because God has not yet revealed the risen messiah.* **19–20:** The disciples' question again prompts a witness to the meaning of what has happened (*"What things? . . . the things about Jesus . . . ";* see Acts 2.12; 4.7). On Jesus as *a prophet,* see Luke 7.11–17. **21:** Their hope echoes earlier voices in the story (2.25, 38; 23.51). *The third day* was anticipated in 9.22; 24.7. **23:** The *vision of angels* must refer to the two men in 24.4. **25–27:** To be *foolish* and *slow of heart* appears to be forgivable ignorance (3.15), compared with hardness of heart (Acts 28.26–28). The truth to be known lies in the interpretation of *all the scriptures* as attesting the necessity of the suffering of the *Messiah* (see 24.32, 44; Acts 2.23–32; 4.23–31). **30:** The phrasing (*he took bread, blessed, and broke it, and gave it*) recalls the last supper (22.19). **31:** This "remembrance" is a revelation of Jesus' presence (22.19; 24.35). **33–34:** The *eleven* remaining apostles* (Acts 1.12–26) have not received Jesus' instruction.

36 While they were talking about this, Jesus himself stood among them and said to them, "Peace be with you."[a] 37They were startled and terrified, and thought that they were seeing a ghost. 38He said to them, "Why are you frightened, and why do doubts arise in your hearts? 39Look at my hands and my feet; see that it is I myself. Touch me and see; for a ghost does not have flesh and bones as you see that I have." 40And when he had said this, he showed them his hands and his feet.[b] 41While in their joy they were disbelieving and still wondering, he said to them, "Have you anything here to eat?" 42They gave him a piece of broiled fish, 43and he took it and ate in their presence.

44 Then he said to them, "These are my words that I spoke to you while I was still with you—that everything written about me in the law of Moses, the prophets, and the psalms must be fulfilled." 45Then he opened their minds to understand the scriptures, 46and he said to them, "Thus it is written, that the Messiah[c] is to suffer and to rise from the dead on the third day, 47and that repentance and forgiveness of sins is to be proclaimed in his name to all nations, beginning from Jerusalem. 48You are witnesses[d] of these things. 49And see, I am sending upon you what my Father promised; so stay here in the city until you have been clothed with power from on high."

50 Then he led them out as far as Bethany, and, lifting up his hands, he blessed them. 51While he was blessing them, he withdrew from them and was carried up into heaven.[e] 52And they worshiped him, and[f] returned to Jerusalem with great joy; 53and they were continually in the temple blessing God.[g]

24.36–53: The messiah's* final appearance, commission, and departure. 36–37: Luke's story emphasizes both the awesome wonder of Jesus' appearance and the physical reality of his resurrected body (*flesh and bones,* see 20.34–36). **41:** *Disbelieving* for *joy* and *wondering* is more like Mary's faith than Zechariah's doubt at the beginning of the story (1.18–20, 28–38). **42–43:** *Broiled fish* are also mentioned in Jn 21.4–14, and Jesus' witnesses recall eating with him in Acts 10.41. **44–45:** *The law of Moses, the prophets,* and *the psalms* is a very inclusive catalog in a time probably before Israel's *scriptures* were gathered in a single book. **46–48:** This saying of Jesus is not literally *written* in any surviving version of Israel's scriptures. This is the testimony from the scriptures his *witnesses* are sent to make. **49–52:** The promise of the *Father* is the gift of the Holy Spirit at Pentecost* to be awaited in *Jerusalem* (Acts 1.4, 8; 2.33). **53:** The *temple* remains a crucial center for divine activity (1.9; 2.27, 37, 46; 20.1; Acts 3.1; 4.1; 6.13).

a Other ancient authorities lack *and said to them, "Peace be with you."*　　b Other ancient authorities lack verse 40　c Or *the Christ*　d Or *nations. Beginning from Jerusalem* [48]*you are witnesses*　e Other ancient authorities lack *and was carried up into heaven*　f Other ancient authorities lack *worshiped him, and*　g Other ancient authorities add *Amen*

THE GOSPEL ACCORDING TO JOHN

Introduction

From the time of Irenaeus (about 180 CE) tradition names John the son of Zebedee as the beloved disciple (13.23; 19.26–27; 20.1–10; 21.7, 20–24; perhaps also 1.35–40; 18.15–16; 19.35) and author of the Gospel. Irenaeus names him as author of the Epistles and Revelation also. Many scholars doubt this identification but agree that these books are derived from a common school, influenced by one dominant teacher. The same tradition locates the "Johannine literature" in Asia Minor, around Ephesus, a view that finds some support in the opening chapters of Revelation (9.22; 24.9), as does the use of the name John.

The story of the ministry of Jesus is set in "Palestine" between 26 and 30 CE but the Gospel was probably completed and published in the last decade of the first century CE. The Gospel thus has two contexts: the ministry of Jesus (26–30 CE); and the situation of the author and his community after the destruction of Jerusalem in 70 CE. There was growing antagonism between Jesus' believers and the synagogue,★ at least in John's region (9.22, 34; 12.42; 16.2; 20.19). This theme partly overlaps with the account of the antagonism toward Jesus by powerful Jewish leaders who instigated his arrest and execution by the Romans. Generally, *the Jews* denotes the Jewish leaders, and the term can be used interchangeably with the Pharisees★ (see comment on 9.18–23). Antagonism is often expressed in dualistic language, especially the opposition between the light and the darkness. This dualism★ is characteristic of some parts of the Dead Sea scrolls, reflecting the conflict of the community that produced the scrolls with the rest of Judaism.

The Gospel encourages the believer to make a courageous witness in the face of intimidation and threat. It offers hope and encouragement through the presence of the risen Jesus in the Spirit Paraclete (chs. 14–16).

READING GUIDE

The prologue (1.1–18) introduces the reader to the theological world in which John's story of Jesus makes sense. Matthew and Luke provide accounts of Jesus' genealogy★ and miraculous birth to begin the stories, but John goes back even farther. The story of Jesus is grounded in God's creative purpose that leads first to the creation of the world and then to the advent of Jesus into the world.

John's understanding of Jesus is built on the belief that Jesus is the divine Word made flesh (the incarnate Word). The Word comes from God and is God's agent in creation and the course of history. The Word becomes incarnate (human) in the life and ministry of Jesus, and this theme is dealt with predominantly in terms of the intimacy of the Father-Son relationship (1.18).

John 1.11–13 traces a mini-outline for the story of Jesus in John: Jesus brings an offer of new life with God (vv. 12–13), but not all people accept the revelation of God that Jesus brings (v. 11). The gospel narrative★ that follows contains stories of acceptance and rejection. John uses extended dialogues, metaphor,★ irony,★ and symbolic language as ways to draw readers into the story of Jesus, so that readers can make their own decisions about the Jesus portrayed in its pages. In telling these stories, John provides readers with their own experience of the revelation of God in Jesus (see 20.30–31) and thus places them in the same situation as the characters in the story.

PROLOGUE

1.1–18: This section is distinct in style and content: The Word is the subject of the prologue; Jesus is the subject of the rest of the Gospel. References to John the Baptist (vv. 6–8, 15) connect the prologue to the beginning of the story (1.19–36; see esp. 1.30). John's witness and the contrast of Jesus with Moses identify the incarnate Word with Jesus Christ (v. 17). Themes introduced in the prologue (light and darkness, witness, knowing, believing, truth, glory, born of the Spirit, the Father-Son relationship) are central to the Gospel. The prologue provides the reader with the theological perspective from which to read the story that follows. Most of the prologue is hymnic, marked by a poetic pattern in which a keyword at the end of one line is repeated at the beginning of the next.

1 In the beginning was the Word, and the Word was with God, and the Word was God. ²He was in the beginning with God. ³All things came into being through him, and without him not one thing came into being. What has come into being ⁴in him was life,ᵃ and the life was the light of all people. ⁵The light shines in the darkness, and the darkness did not overcome it.

6 There was a man sent from God, whose name was John. ⁷He came as a witness to testify to the light, so that all might believe through him. ⁸He himself was not the light, but he came to testify to the light. ⁹The true light, which enlightens everyone, was coming into the world.ᵇ

10 He was in the world, and the world came into being through him; yet the world did not know him. ¹¹He came to what was his own,ᶜ and his own people did not accept him. ¹²But to all who received him, who believed in his name, he gave power to become children of God, ¹³who were born, not of blood or of the will of the flesh or of the will of man, but of God.

14 And the Word became flesh and lived among us, and we have seen his glory, the glory as of a father's only son,ᵈ full of grace and truth. ¹⁵(John testified to him and cried out, "This was he of whom I said, 'He who comes after me ranks ahead of me because he was before me.' ") ¹⁶From his fullness we have all received, grace upon grace. ¹⁷The law indeed was given through Moses; grace and truth came through Jesus Christ. ¹⁸No one has ever seen God. It is God the only Son,ᵉ who is close to the Father's heart,ᶠ who has made him known.

1.1–18. 1–5: The relation of the Word to God and to creation. 1–2: Echoes Gen 1.1 and positions the story of Jesus as a rereading of the creation story. The Gospel speaks of God by telling the story of Jesus. *Word:* the active and revealing Word of God (Gen 1.1; Ps 33.6; Prov 8.22). In Judaism Word was identified with Torah.* The God-Word relationship is paradoxical: distinction (*with God*) and identity (*was God*). **6–8:** *John* is a *witness* to Jesus; his work is the same as

a Or ³*through him. And without him not one thing came into being that has come into being.* ⁴*In him was life*
b Or *He was the true light that enlightens everyone coming into the world*   c Or *to his own home*
d Or *the Father's only Son*   e Other ancient authorities read *It is an only Son, God,* or *It is the only Son*
f Gk *bosom*

the purpose of the Gospel (20.31). His witness is given in some detail (1.15, 19–23, 26–27, 29–34, 36; 3.27–30, 31–36). **9–11:** The *world* (used 78 times in the Gospel) is the stage for the appearance of the Word and the manifestation of the light. It is both "all things" created by the Word (1.3) and the place where the *darkness* occurs, part of the paradox that the world, which was created by the Word, rejects the Word. **12–13:** The name of God (the Father) is made known in the Word made flesh (the Son); compare 5.43; 10.25; 12.13, 28; 17.6, 11, 12, 26. Those who believe are born of God (see 3.3, 5). **14–18:** The Word enters into history. **14:** In the NT only the Johannine writings speak of the incarnation (see also 1 Jn 4.2; 2 Jn 7; compare Gal 4.4). The *Word* "tabernacles" in the *flesh* and reveals God's glory (compare 2.21–22 and see Ex 25.8; Ezek 37.27; Zech 2.10–11; Sir 24.8 for the dwelling of God and his glory with his people). *Only son:* the Word's unique relationship to the Father (*monogenes*, see 1.14, 18; 3.16, 18); see sidebar, "God's only Son," p. 1799. The *glory* recalls the revelation to Moses at the giving of the law (see Ex 33.18–34.8). **17:** Only here and in 17.3 is the double name "Jesus Christ" used. Elsewhere "Christ" is used in its meaning as "messiah"* (1.20, 25, 41; 4.25 and elsewhere). **18:** God is hidden but known through the Son.

THE WAY OF THE INCARNATE WORD IN THE WORLD

1.19–12.50: The public ministry of Jesus was divided into two parts: the search for the incarnate Word (1.19–4.54); and the rejection of the incarnate Word (5.1–12.50).

19 This is the testimony given by John when the Jews sent priests and Levites from Jerusalem to ask him, "Who are you?" 20 He confessed and did not deny it, but confessed, "I am not the Messiah."*a* 21 And they asked him, "What then? Are you Elijah?" He said, "I am not." "Are you the prophet?" He answered, "No." 22 Then they said to him, "Who are you? Let us have an answer for those who sent us. What do you say about yourself?" 23 He said,

"I am the voice of one crying out in the wilderness,

'Make straight the way of the Lord,' "

as the prophet Isaiah said.

24 Now they had been sent from the Pharisees. 25 They asked him, "Why then are you baptizing if you are neither the Messiah,*a* nor Elijah, nor the prophet?" 26 John answered them, "I baptize with water. Among you stands one whom you do not know, 27 the one who is coming after me; I am not worthy to untie the thong of his sandal." 28 This took place in Bethany across the Jordan where John was baptizing.

29 The next day he saw Jesus coming toward him and declared, "Here is the Lamb of God who takes away the sin of the world! 30 This is he of whom I said, 'After me comes a man who ranks ahead of me because he was before me.' 31 I myself did not know him; but I came baptizing with water for this reason, that he might be revealed to Israel." 32 And John testified, "I saw the Spirit descending from heaven like a dove, and it remained on him. 33 I myself did not know him, but the one who sent me to baptize with water said to me, 'He on whom you see the Spirit descend and remain is the one who baptizes with the Holy Spirit.' 34 And I myself have seen and have testified that this is the Son of God."*b*

1.19–4.54: The search for the incarnate Word (messiah*) is portrayed by a sequence of scenes. **1.19–28:** John's witness to the Jews. In response to *priests and Levites* (1.19, 24) John reveals his role and that of *the messiah*. The Jerusalem leadership will come to oppose Jesus; here they are faithful Jews awaiting the messiah. **20:** John answers the question, "Are you the Christ?" (1.41 and see note *a*) **21:** First-century messianic expectations were complex (compare Mk 6.14–16; 8.27–30). **21–23:** Isa 40.3 (see Mk 1.3). John is the witness to the coming one (see 1.7). **26–27:** Water baptism* contrasts with baptism of the Spirit (see Mk 1.8) explained in the next scene (1.33), but this does not answer the question. The coming one is among them but remains unknown; the hiddenness of the messiah accords with Jewish teaching. **28:** The location of this *Bethany* is unknown; contrast the Bethany of 11.1; 12.1. **29–34:** John's witness to Jesus. The Jews from Jerusalem are no longer present. The audience for John's words is the reader. **29:** John

a Or *the Christ*   *b* Other ancient authorities read *is God's chosen one* does not baptize Jesus or speak to him. *Lamb of God:* Lambs were not used as sin offerings, but the Gospel associates Jesus with the Passover★ lamb (19.14, 36). Also see Isa 53.7. **30:** See 1.15, 27. **33:** His water baptism is the sign that would reveal the coming one to Israel. *Spirit descend:* The other Gospels (see Mk 1.10) describe this as part of Jesus' baptism; here it is the sign that makes him known. **34:** *Son of God,* a Johannine phrase, replaces *Lamb of God.*

35 The next day John again was standing with two of his disciples, 36and as he watched Jesus walk by, he exclaimed, "Look, here is the Lamb of God!" 37The two disciples heard him say this, and they followed Jesus. 38When Jesus turned and saw them following, he said to them, "What are you looking for?" They said to him, "Rabbi" (which translated means Teacher), "where are you staying?" 39He said to them, "Come and see." They came and saw where he was staying, and they remained with him that day. It was about four o'clock in the afternoon. 40One of the two who heard John speak and followed him was Andrew, Simon Peter's brother. 41He first found his brother Simon and said to him, "We have found the Messiah" (which is translated Anointed*a*). 42He brought Simon*b* to Jesus, who looked at him and said, "You are Simon son of John. You are to be called Cephas" (which is translated Peter*c*).

43 The next day Jesus decided to go to Galilee. He found Philip and said to him, "Follow me." 44Now Philip was from Bethsaida, the city of Andrew and Peter. 45Philip found Nathanael and said to him, "We have found him about whom Moses in the law and also the prophets wrote, Jesus son of Joseph from Nazareth." 46Nathanael said to him, "Can anything good come out of Nazareth?" Philip said to him, "Come and see." 47When Jesus saw Nathanael coming toward him, he said of him, "Here is truly an Israelite in whom there is no deceit!" 48Nathanael asked him, "Where did you get to know me?" Jesus answered, "I saw you under the fig tree before Philip called you." 49Nathanael replied, "Rabbi, you are the Son of God! You are the King of Israel!" 50Jesus answered, "Do you believe because I told you that I saw you under the fig tree? You will see greater things than these." 51And he said to him, "Very truly, I tell you,*d* you will see heaven opened and the angels of God ascending and descending upon the Son of Man."

1.35–51. 35–42: Two disciples. 35: Two of John's disciples are the new audience. **37–38:** In contrast to the other Gospels (see Mk 1.16–20), the disciples of John took the initiative, seeking Jesus, not being called by him. **40–42:** *Andrew, Simon Peter's brother:* The less well-known brother appears first. John commonly uses the double name, *Simon Peter,* in Greek form though both go back to Semitic originals (Symeon and Kephas, see v. 42 and Gal 2.9, 11). The explanation of Simon's naming takes place after he is introduced. **43–51:** John has disappeared, but the two disciples (and Jesus and Peter) connect the preceding scene with this. **43–44:** *Philip* appears in 6.5–9; 12.21–22; 14.8. Like Andrew and Peter he is from Bethsaida (contrast Mk 1.21, 29). **45:** Andrew had found Simon; Philip now finds *Nathanael* (who only appears here and in 21.2). *Him about whom Moses* (see Deut 18.15, 18) *. . . and . . . the prophets★ wrote:* the messiah.★ The initiative of the disciples is asserted. *Son of Joseph:* Jesus was a common name. **47:** Israel (Jacob, Gen 32.28) was deceitful (Gen 27.34–36). **49:** Nathanael's confession, introduced by *Rabbi,* is minimal, acknowledging Jesus as the Davidic messiah (2 Sam 7.14; Ps 2.7; 89.26; compare Jn 12.13). The Gospel seeks to expand that vision. **50:** *Greater things:* See 5.20; 14.12. **51:** *You* is plural (see note d). *Angels . . . ascending and descending* might allude to Jacob's dream (Gen 28.12) or to the vision of the Son of Man (see 3.13), the heavenly king, upon whom the angels converge (Dan 7.13–14).

2 On the third day there was a wedding in Cana of Galilee, and the mother of Jesus was there. 2Jesus and his disciples had also been invited to the wedding. 3When the wine gave out, the mother of Jesus said to him, "They have no wine." 4And Jesus said to her, "Woman, what concern is that to you and to me? My hour has not yet come." 5His mother said to the servants, "Do whatever he tells you." 6Now standing there were six

a Or *Christ*   *b* Gk *him*   *c* From the word for *rock* in Aramaic (*kepha*) and Greek (*petra*), respectively
d Both instances of the Greek word for *you* in this verse are plural

stone water jars for the Jewish rites of purification, each holding twenty or thirty gallons. 7Jesus said to them, "Fill the jars with water." And they filled them up to the brim. 8He said to them, "Now draw some out, and take it to the chief steward." So they took it. 9When the steward tasted the water that had become wine, and did not know where it came from (though the servants who had drawn the water knew), the steward called the bridegroom 10and said to him, "Everyone serves the good wine first, and then the inferior wine after the guests have become drunk. But you have kept the good wine until now." 11Jesus did this, the first of his signs, in Cana of Galilee, and revealed his glory; and his disciples believed in him.

12 After this he went down to Capernaum with his mother, his brothers, and his disciples; and they remained there a few days.

2.1–12: The wedding at Cana. This story is found only in John. It is the first of two Cana signs (see 4.46–54), both of which are initiated by requests to Jesus. **1:** *The third day* links this incident to the four days of ch. 1. The miracle may be the first example of the "greater things" (1.50) which culminate in the exaltation of the Son of Man. *Cana* is a small town northwest of Nazareth. **4:** *Woman*, an abrupt address, is the only way Jesus greets his mother (compare 19.26). She is not named in this Gospel. *Hour*, elsewhere the time of Jesus' glorification, refers to Jesus' chosen time to act. **6–8:** Rites of purification included ritual cleansing of hands at meals. The quantity and size of the *stone jars* is unusual and emphasizes the extravagance of the sign. **11:** *The first:* See 4.54. Other signs are mentioned (2.23); they are important enough to be in the summary conclusion (20.30–31). Signs point to the presence of God, acting in Jesus. **12:** *Capernaum* is on the northern shore of the sea of Galilee (see 6.17, 24, 59). *Brothers:* See also 7.3–9. From this point Jesus travels with his disciples (see 3.22).

13 The Passover of the Jews was near, and Jesus went up to Jerusalem. 14In the temple he found people selling cattle, sheep, and doves, and the money changers seated at their tables. 15Making a whip of cords, he drove all of them out of the temple, both the sheep and the cattle. He also poured out the coins of the money changers and overturned their tables. 16He told those who were selling the doves, "Take these things out of here! Stop making my Father's house a marketplace!" 17His disciples remembered that it was written, "Zeal for your house will consume me." 18The Jews then said to him, "What sign can you show us for doing this?" 19Jesus answered them, "Destroy this temple, and in three days I will raise it up." 20The Jews then said, "This temple has been under construction for forty-six years, and will you raise it up in three days?" 21But he was speaking of the temple of his body. 22After he was raised from the dead, his disciples remembered that he had said this; and they believed the scripture and the word that Jesus had spoken.

2.13–22: Cleansing the Temple.* Compare Mt 21.12–17; Mk 11.15–19; Lk 19.45–48, where this story is placed during the last week of Jesus' life. **13:** *Passover*** of the Jews:* See sidebar on Jewish festivals, p. 1819. As many as 100,000 pilgrims *went up* to Jerusalem (in the hills of Judea) for this festival. **14:** Animals were sold for sacrifice, and *money changers* converted foreign coins to Temple currency for this purpose. **16:** See Zech 14.21. *Marketplace*, "house of trade," that is, a business. **17:** Ps 69.9. **18:** Compare 6.30 with this demand for a sign. **19–20:** Remodeling of the second Temple was begun by Herod the Great in 20 BCE and was not completed until the early 60s CE. **21:** Jesus' death and resurrection is the *sign.* (vv. 18–19). **22:** Only when the disciples remembered from the vantage point of the resurrection did they understand and believe. See 12.16; 14.25–26.

23 When he was in Jerusalem during the Passover festival, many believed in his name because they saw the signs that he was doing. 24But Jesus on his part would not entrust himself to them, because he knew all people 25and needed no one to testify about anyone; for he himself knew what was in everyone.

3 Now there was a Pharisee named Nicodemus, a leader of the Jews. 2He came to Jesus[a] by night and said to him, "Rabbi, we know that you are a teacher who has

a Gk *him*

God's Only Son

The Father-Son relationship is central to this presentation of the story of Jesus. For Jesus, God is characteristically spoken of as Father, especially "the Father who sent me" (more than twenty times), and Jesus is the one sent by the Father to make the Father known (3.16 and 4.34). Father-Son imagery for God and Jesus is John's distinctive language for speaking about how God is revealed in the incarnation.

come from God; for no one can do these signs that you do apart from the presence of God." ³Jesus answered him, "Very truly, I tell you, no one can see the kingdom of God without being born from above."ᵃ ⁴Nicodemus said to him, "How can anyone be born after having grown old? Can one enter a second time into the mother's womb and be born?" ⁵Jesus answered, "Very truly, I tell you, no one can enter the kingdom of God without being born of water and Spirit. ⁶What is born of the flesh is flesh, and what is born of the Spirit is spirit.ᵇ ⁷Do not be astonished that I said to you, 'Youᶜ must be born from above.'ᵈ ⁸The windᵇ blows where it chooses, and you hear the sound of it, but you do not know where it comes from or where it goes. So it is with everyone who is born of the Spirit." ⁹Nicodemus said to him, "How can these things be?" ¹⁰Jesus answered him, "Are you a teacher of Israel, and yet you do not understand these things?

11 "Very truly, I tell you, we speak of what we know and testify to what we have seen; yet youᵉ do not receive our testimony. ¹²If I have told you about earthly things and you do not believe, how can you believe if I tell you about heavenly things? ¹³No one has ascended into heaven except the one who descended from heaven, the Son of Man.ᶠ ¹⁴And just as Moses lifted up the serpent in the wilderness, so must the Son of Man be lifted up, ¹⁵that whoever believes in him may have eternal life.ᵍ

demus, mentioned here and in 7.45–52; 19.38–42, represents inadequate faith based on signs (2.23) and leaders who believe but fear to acknowledge Jesus openly (12.42–43). **2:** He comes out of the darkness (3.19–21; 11.10; 13.30) and into the light. His confession, like that of Nathanael (see 1.49), is introduced by *Rabbi*, indicating minimal understanding. Because the story of Nicodemus appears in installments, there is room for development. **3–8:** Jesus' response presumes that a question underlies the visit. Jesus makes three solemn pronouncements introduced by *Very truly* (vv. 3, 5, 11). Only here in John (vv. 3, 5) does Jesus speak of the *kingdom of God*. One can only enter by *being born* either *from above* or *anew* (note a). The Greek word for spirit ("pneuma") is also ambiguous (see note b). This is clarified in 5–8 (compare 1.12–13). The second "you" in v. 7 is plural, indicating it applies generally, not just to Nicodemus. See note c. **11–15:** The second "you" in v. 11, and all four occurrences in v. 12, are plural (see note e), perhaps suggesting words spoken to the reader by the narrator. **13–15:** The emphasis is on ascent: *The Son of Man must be lifted up* (see 1.51; 8.28; 12.32–34; compare Num 21.9; Isa 52.13), exalted to heaven by way of the cross. Jesus begins by speaking of the kingdom of God and concludes by speaking of eternal life (see also 4.14, 36; 5.24, 39; 6.27, 47, 54, 58; 17.2–3). The subject has not changed, but the language has moved from that of the common Jesus tradition to characteristic Johannine language. Nicodemus has disappeared; these words are addressed to the reader.

2.23–3.15: Jesus and Nicodemus. 23–25: A summary refers to *signs* and the resulting popular belief *in his name,* which Jesus did not trust. This introduces Nicodemus, a man impressed by signs (3.2). **3.1:** Nico-

a Or *born anew*   *b* The same Greek word means both *wind* and *spirit*   *c* The Greek word for *you* here is plural   *d* Or *anew*   *e* The Greek word for *you* here and in verse 12 is plural   *f* Other ancient authorities add *who is in heaven*   *g* Some interpreters hold that the quotation concludes with verse 15

16 "For God so loved the world that he gave his only Son, so that everyone who believes in him may not perish but may have eternal life.

17 "Indeed, God did not send the Son into the world to condemn the world, but in order that the world might be saved through him. [18]Those who believe in him are not condemned; but those who do not believe are condemned already, because they have not believed in the name of the only Son of God. [19]And this is the judgment, that the light has come into the world, and people loved darkness rather than light because their deeds were evil. [20]For all who do evil hate the light and do not come to the light, so that their deeds may not be exposed. [21]But those who do what is true come to the light, so that it may be clearly seen that their deeds have been done in God."[a]

3.16–21: First summary of the Gospel. 16–18: God's love is revealed in the *giving* of his unique son. Compare the use of *sent* in 5.36; 6.29, 57; 17.3, 8, 18, 21, 23, 25; 20.21; 1 Jn 4.10. The coming of the Son gives life; rejecting him brings death and condemnation (see 12.47–48). "Believing," a key term, is used 98 times. **19–21:** The coming of Jesus as the *light* of the world (see 1.4–5, 9–13; 8.12; 9.5) creates a situation of a judgment because people cannot avoid the choice of light or darkness. The point emphasizes the inevitability of choice, in which the person is revealed (compare 16.8) as born of God or as a child of darkness (the devil, see 8.43–47).

22 After this Jesus and his disciples went into the Judean countryside, and he spent some time there with them and baptized. [23]John also was baptizing at Aenon near Salim because water was abundant there; and people kept coming and were being baptized [24]—John, of course, had not yet been thrown into prison.

25 Now a discussion about purification arose between John's disciples and a Jew.[b] [26]They came to John and said to him, "Rabbi, the one who was with you across the Jordan, to whom you testified, here he is baptizing, and all are going to him." [27]John answered, "No one can receive anything except what has been given from heaven. [28]You yourselves are my witnesses that I said, 'I am not the Messiah,[c] but I have been sent ahead of him.' [29]He who has the bride is the bridegroom. The friend of the bridegroom, who stands and hears him, rejoices greatly at the bridegroom's voice. For this reason my joy has been fulfilled. [30]He must increase, but I must decrease."[d]

3.22–30: The witness of John reintroduced (compare 1.6–8, 15, 19–34, 36). **22:** Jesus travels with his disciples. Here (and in 3.26; 4.1) Jesus baptizes; this is qualified in 4.2. **23:** *Aenon near Salim* is an uncertain location in the Judean countryside. **24:** That John was *not yet* in prison contradicts Mk 1.14. **25:** Baptism* introduces a dispute about *purification* between the disciples of John (see 1.35, 37) and a Jew, or perhaps the Jews (see note *b*). **26:** *Testified:* See 1.19–34, 35–36. The report suggests that the crowds have turned from John to Jesus. The dispute about purification apparently causes Jesus to leave the area (4.1–3). **27:** John's words resemble Jesus' response to Pilate (19.11). **29–30:** Bride and bridegroom imagery is common in the Hebrew Scriptures* and elsewhere in the New Testament (Isa 62.5; Jer 2.2; Hos 2.16–20; Mk 2.19–20; Rev 19.6–8; 21.9–10). The *friend* is the best man whose *joy is fulfilled* (see 15.11; 16.24; 17.13; 1 Jn 1.4; 2 Jn 12) by seeing the bridegroom hold central place.

31 The one who comes from above is above all; the one who is of the earth belongs to the earth and speaks about earthly things. The one who comes from heaven is above all. [32]He testifies to what he has seen and heard, yet no one accepts his testimony. [33]Whoever has accepted his testimony has certified[e] this, that God is true. [34]He whom God has sent speaks the words of God, for he gives the Spirit without measure. [35]The Father loves the Son and has placed all things in his hands. [36]Whoever believes in the Son has eternal life; whoever disobeys the Son will not see life, but must endure God's wrath.

a Some interpreters hold that the quotation concludes with verse 15 *b* Other ancient authorities read *the Jews* *c* Or *the Christ* *d* Some interpreters hold that the quotation continues through verse 36 *e* Gk *set a seal to*

3.31–36: Second summary of the Gospel. John (no disciples are present) summarizes the Johannine gospel, echoing 3.12–13, 16–21, and presenting Jesus as the emissary from God. **31–32:** See 3.11–13; 8.23. **33:** To put *a seal to* a message is to confirm it (see note *e,* p. 1800). Perhaps the Spirit received by believers is the seal. **34:** As the emissary of God (see 3.17; 5.24, 36–38; 6.39; 8.16, 18, 42; 17.21, 23, 25; 20.21) Jesus gives the Spirit to those who receive his witness. **35:** The Father-Son relationship is the key to Jesus' authority as the revealer of God (5.20) (see sidebar, "God's only Son," p. 1799). **36:** *God's wrath,* see 5.29; 1 Jn 5.12.

4 Now when Jesus*ᵃ* learned that the Pharisees had heard, "Jesus is making and baptizing more disciples than John" ²— although it was not Jesus himself but his disciples who baptized— ³he left Judea and started back to Galilee. ⁴But he had to go through Samaria. ⁵So he came to a Samaritan city called Sychar, near the plot of ground that Jacob had given to his son Joseph. ⁶Jacob's well was there, and Jesus, tired out by his journey, was sitting by the well. It was about noon.

7 A Samaritan woman came to draw water, and Jesus said to her, "Give me a drink." ⁸(His disciples had gone to the city to buy food.) ⁹The Samaritan woman said to him, "How is it that you, a Jew, ask a drink of me, a woman of Samaria?" (Jews do not share things in common with Samaritans.)*ᵇ* ¹⁰Jesus answered her, "If you knew the gift of God, and who it is that is saying to you, 'Give me a drink,' you would have asked him, and he would have given you living water." ¹¹The woman said to him, "Sir, you have no bucket, and the well is deep. Where do you get that living water? ¹²Are you greater than our ancestor Jacob, who gave us the well, and with his sons and his flocks drank from it?" ¹³Jesus said to her, "Everyone who drinks of this water will be thirsty again, ¹⁴but those who drink of the water that I will give them will never be thirsty. The water that I will give will become in them a spring of water gushing up to eternal life." ¹⁵The woman said to him, "Sir, give me this water, so that I may never be thirsty or have to keep coming here to draw water."

16 Jesus said to her, "Go, call your husband, and come back." ¹⁷The woman answered him, "I have no husband." Jesus said to her, "You are right in saying, 'I have no husband'; ¹⁸for you have had five husbands, and the one you have now is not your husband. What you have said is true!" ¹⁹The woman said to him, "Sir, I see that you are a prophet. ²⁰Our ancestors worshiped on this mountain, but you*ᶜ* say that the place where people must worship is in Jerusalem." ²¹Jesus said to her, "Woman, believe me, the hour is coming when you will worship the Father neither on this mountain nor in Jerusalem. ²²You worship what you do not know; we worship what we know, for salvation is from the Jews. ²³But the hour is coming, and is now here, when the true worshipers will worship the Father in spirit and truth, for the Father seeks such as these to worship him. ²⁴God is spirit, and those who worship him must worship in spirit and truth." ²⁵The woman said to him, "I know that Messiah is coming" (who is called Christ). "When he comes, he will proclaim all things to us." ²⁶Jesus said to her, "I am he,*ᵈ* the one who is speaking to you."

27 Just then his disciples came. They were astonished that he was speaking with a woman, but no one said, "What do you want?" or, "Why are you speaking with her?" ²⁸Then the woman left her water jar and went back to the city. She said to the people, ²⁹"Come and see a man who told me everything I have ever done! He cannot be the Messiah,*ᵉ* can he?" ³⁰They left the city and were on their way to him.

4.1–42: Water and the quest for eternal life. 1–6: Transition. Baptism* introduces the theme of water . **1–3:** A *Jew* or *Jews* (in 3.25) become the *Pharisees** (in 4.1); Jesus' evasive action, the first sign of hostility (anticipated in 1.5, 10–11) explains his movement to the next scene, where the theme of water continues. **4:** The most direct route between Jerusalem and Galilee

a Other ancient authorities read *the Lord*   *b* Other ancient authorities lack this sentence   *c* The Greek word for *you* here and in verses 21 and 22 is plural   *d* Gk *I am*   *e* Or *the Christ* was *through Samaria.* **5–6:** *Sychar* is probably near Shechem (Gen 33.18–19) at modern Askar. *Jacob's well* is not mentioned in the Hebrew Scriptures.* *Noon* is not the normal time to draw water. Perhaps this encounter is humanly unlikely but divinely planned. **7–26: The quest for water at the well.** The story echoes meetings at a well from the Hebrew Scriptures: Abraham's servant in search of a wife for Isaac (Gen 24); Jacob and Rachel (Gen 29.1–30); Moses and the daughters of Ruel (Ex 2.15b–22), all stories about betrothals that are also quests. Jesus seeks refreshment; the woman comes for water, and her perception of who Jesus is grows (4.9, 12, 19, 25). **7–9:** Samaritans had been excluded from the rebuilding of the Jewish nation after the Exile* (2 Kings 17.24–34; Neh 9.2). Jewish purity laws made drinking vessels a critical issue. **10:** *Living water* bubbling from a spring symbolizes life-giving power (see 7.37–39). **11–15:** Compare 6.30–35. The woman misunderstood. Compare Nicodemus in 3.4, 9. Jesus clarifies his meaning; though the woman still does not fully understand, she requests the gift. Compare 6.34. **16–19:** Jesus' insight convinces her that he is a prophet* (compare 1.47–49). **20:** *This mountain:* Gerizim, where Samaritans once had a temple (Deut 11.26–30; 27.1–13; Josh 8.30–35). **21–24:** Because God is spirit, not tied to a particular place, the place is irrelevant. On *truth,* see 5.33; 8.32, 40, 44; 14.6, 17; 16.7, 13; 17.17, 19; 18.37, 38. **25–26:** The woman awaits the *messiah,** using the Jewish (not Samaritan) title. **27–30:** The attitude of the disciples reinforces the unusual aspect of Jesus' contact with the woman (see 4.9). She leaves without her water jar; she had found the life-giving water. **29–30:** The tentative question expresses uncertainty. Compare the first disciples who led others to Jesus (1.41–42, 45–51).

31 Meanwhile the disciples were urging him, "Rabbi, eat something." [32]But he said to them, "I have food to eat that you do not know about." [33]So the disciples said to one another, "Surely no one has brought him something to eat?" [34]Jesus said to them, "My food is to do the will of him who sent me and to complete his work. [35]Do you not say, 'Four months more, then comes the harvest'? But I tell you, look around you, and see how the fields are ripe for harvesting. [36]The reaper is already receiving[a] wages and is gathering fruit for eternal life, so that sower and reaper may rejoice together. [37]For here

the saying holds true, 'One sows and another reaps.' [38]I sent you to reap that for which you did not labor. Others have labored, and you have entered into their labor."

39 Many Samaritans from that city believed in him because of the woman's testimony, "He told me everything I have ever done." [40]So when the Samaritans came to him, they asked him to stay with them; and he stayed there two days. [41]And many more believed because of his word. [42]They said to the woman, "It is no longer because of what you said that we believe, for we have heard for ourselves, and we know that this is truly the Savior of the world."

4.31–42. 31–38: Jesus and the disciples. 31–34: The disciples talk to Jesus about food in a way that exposes their ignorance of his mission (see 6.27 and 5.17). **35–38:** The imagery moves from food to harvest, often an image of judgment, but here the gathering of the fruits of mission. *Others:* Probably a reference to Moses, the prophets,* and Jesus. **39–42: The harvest.** The woman was a provisional witness: Many believed because of her, but many more believed because of Jesus' word. This progress leads to the climactic Johannine confession, *This is truly the Savior of the world* (compare 3.16–17; 12.47; 1 Jn 4.14).

43 When the two days were over, he went from that place to Galilee [44](for Jesus himself had testified that a prophet has no honor in the prophet's own country). [45]When he came to Galilee, the Galileans welcomed him, since they had seen all that he had done in Jerusalem at the festival; for they too had gone to the festival.

46 Then he came again to Cana in Galilee where he had changed the water into wine. Now there was a royal official whose son lay ill in Capernaum. [47]When he heard that Jesus had come from Judea to Galilee, he went and begged him to come down and heal his son, for he was at the point of death. [48]Then Jesus said to him, "Unless you[b] see signs and wonders you will not believe." [49]The official said to him, "Sir, come down before my little boy dies." [50]Jesus said to

a Or [35]. . . *the fields are already ripe for harvesting.* [36]*The reaper is receiving*   *b* Both instances of the Greek word for *you* in this verse are plural him, "Go; your son will live." The man believed the word that Jesus spoke to him and started on his way. 51As he was going down, his slaves met him and told him that his child was alive. 52So he asked them the hour when he began to recover, and they said to him, "Yesterday at one in the afternoon the fever left him." 53The father realized that this was the hour when Jesus had said to him, "Your son will live." So he himself believed, along with his whole household. 54Now this was the second sign that Jesus did after coming from Judea to Galilee.

4.43–54. 43–45: Transition to Galilee (see 4.3). **44:** The proverb does not apply: The Galileans receive him (4.45; contrast Mk 6.4); Jerusalem is his *own country,* foreshadowing conflict (5.16, 18). **45:** See 2.13, 23. **46–54: The second Cana sign. 46–47:** The *royal official* probably served Herod Antipas. Capernaum to Cana was about eighteen miles. **48:** *You* is plural, addressing a wider group than the official. Jesus' statement poses a difficulty which the official had to overcome if his son were to be healed. **49–50:** His persistence was rewarded and progress of faith is implied (compare 4.42). **51–53:** Elaborate evidence confirms the healing. **54:** The two Cana signs are explicitly connected by opening and closing words.

THE REJECTION OF THE INCARNATE WORD

5.1–12.50: Jesus heals a man, provoking controversy with the Jewish leaders that continues through the rest of the Gospel. Chapters 5, 6, and 7 begin with the general phrase *after this,* indicating no tight connection among the events.

5 After this there was a festival of the Jews, and Jesus went up to Jerusalem. 2 Now in Jerusalem by the Sheep Gate there is a pool, called in Hebrew*a* Bethzatha,*b* which has five porticoes. 3In these lay many invalids—blind, lame, and paralyzed.*c* 5One man was there who had been ill for thirty-eight years. 6When Jesus saw him lying there and knew that he had been there a long time, he said to him, "Do you want to be made well?" 7The sick man answered him, "Sir, I have no one to put me into the pool when the water is stirred up; and while I am making my way, someone else

steps down ahead of me." 8Jesus said to him, "Stand up, take your mat and walk." 9At once the man was made well, and he took up his mat and began to walk.

Now that day was a sabbath. 10So the Jews said to the man who had been cured, "It is the sabbath; it is not lawful for you to carry your mat." 11But he answered them, "The man who made me well said to me, 'Take up your mat and walk.'" 12They asked him, "Who is the man who said to you, 'Take it up and walk'?" 13Now the man who had been healed did not know who it was, for Jesus had disappeared in*d* the crowd that was there. 14Later Jesus found him in the temple and said to him, "See, you have been made well! Do not sin any more, so that nothing worse happens to you." 15The man went away and told the Jews that it was Jesus who had made him well. 16Therefore the Jews started persecuting Jesus, because he was doing such things on the sabbath. 17But Jesus answered them, "My Father is still working, and I also am working." 18For this reason the Jews were seeking all the more to kill him, because he was not only breaking the sabbath, but was also calling God his own Father, thereby making himself equal to God.

5.1–47: Sabbath sign, controversy and witness. 1–18: Sabbath sign and controversy. 1–2: An unnamed festival is the occasion for a journey to Jerusalem. **3–9a:** The seriousness of the man's condition is emphasized, Jesus' action is described and evidence of the healing is provided. Jesus made the man "whole" (see 5.6, 11, 14, 15; 7.23). **9b:** Only now do we learn it *was the sabbath.* This transforms the account into a controversy story. **10–15:** *The Jews,* the "authorities" (compare the *Pharisees** in 9.13–14). On sabbath law, see Ex 20.8–11; 31.12–17; 35.2–3; Lev 23.3; Deut 5.12–13. Carrying a burden was work (see Neh 13.15–21; Jer 17.19–27) and therefore forbidden. On the connection of sin and misfortune, see 9.2. The man

---

a That is, *Aramaic*   *b* Other ancient authorities read *Bethesda,* others *Bethsaida*   *c* Other ancient authorities add, wholly or in part, *waiting for the stirring of the water;* *4for an angel of the Lord went down at certain seasons into the pool, and stirred up the water; whoever stepped in first after the stirring of the water was made well from whatever disease that person had.*   *d* Or *had left because of* healed by Jesus becomes an informer. **16:** This is the first act of persecution against Jesus. **17:** Asserting that God works on the sabbath was not controversial, but calling God *Father* and asserting his own continuing work on the sabbath was (see 5.18). This indicates the importance of *works* (see 4.32–34; 5.36; 6.28–29; 9.3–4; 10.25, 37–38; 14.10). **18:** Violent action against Jesus recurs (see 7.1, 19–20, 25; 8.37, 40, 59; 10.31–39).

19 Jesus said to them, "Very truly, I tell you, the Son can do nothing on his own, but only what he sees the Father doing; for whatever the Father*ᵃ* does, the Son does likewise. ²⁰The Father loves the Son and shows him all that he himself is doing; and he will show him greater works than these, so that you will be astonished. ²¹Indeed, just as the Father raises the dead and gives them life, so also the Son gives life to whomever he wishes. ²²The Father judges no one but has given all judgment to the Son, ²³so that all may honor the Son just as they honor the Father. Anyone who does not honor the Son does not honor the Father who sent him. ²⁴Very truly, I tell you, anyone who hears my word and believes him who sent me has eternal life, and does not come under judgment, but has passed from death to life.

25 "Very truly, I tell you, the hour is coming, and is now here, when the dead will hear the voice of the Son of God, and those who hear will live. ²⁶For just as the Father has life in himself, so he has granted the Son also to have life in himself; ²⁷and he has given him authority to execute judgment, because he is the Son of Man. ²⁸Do not be astonished at this; for the hour is coming when all who are in their graves will hear his voice ²⁹and will come out—those who have done good, to the resurrection of life, and those who have done evil, to the resurrection of condemnation.

30 "I can do nothing on my own. As I hear, I judge; and my judgment is just, because I seek to do not my own will but the will of him who sent me.

5.19–30: **The work of the Father and the Son.** *Very truly,* three times (vv. 19, 24, 25), emphasizes that the Father and the Son do the same work. **19–23:** The

Father's love for the Son is the basis of the equality and unity of action (compare 3.35; 10.17; 15.9; 17.23–24). The greater work is giving *life*. *Judgment,* understood in biblical tradition to be God's distinctive work, is delegated to the Son. **24:** The *I* saying asserts the unity of Jesus with the Father. **25–29:** The life-giving action of the Son is linked with the Father. As in v. 24 there is a transition to *judgment.* Perhaps v. 28 foreshadows the raising of Lazarus (11.38–44). *Resurrection* on the last day, see 6.39, 40, 44, 54; 11.24. *Son of Man,* see 1.51 and Dan 7.13. On the basis of *judgment,* see Dan 12.2. **30:** This *I* saying reasserts the unity of action of Jesus with the one *who sent me* (see 5.19–23; 8.15–16).

31 "If I testify about myself, my testimony is not true. ³²There is another who testifies on my behalf, and I know that his testimony to me is true. ³³You sent messengers to John, and he testified to the truth. ³⁴Not that I accept such human testimony, but I say these things so that you may be saved. ³⁵He was a burning and shining lamp, and you were willing to rejoice for a while in his light. ³⁶But I have a testimony greater than John's. The works that the Father has given me to complete, the very works that I am doing, testify on my behalf that the Father has sent me. ³⁷And the Father who sent me has himself testified on my behalf. You have never heard his voice or seen his form, ³⁸and you do not have his word abiding in you, because you do not believe him whom he has sent.

39 "You search the scriptures because you think that in them you have eternal life; and it is they that testify on my behalf. ⁴⁰Yet you refuse to come to me to have life. ⁴¹I do not accept glory from human beings. ⁴²But I know that you do not have the love of God in*ᵇ* you. ⁴³I have come in my Father's name, and you do not accept me; if another comes in his own name, you will accept him. ⁴⁴How can you believe when you accept glory from one another and do not seek the glory that comes from the one who alone is God? ⁴⁵Do not think that I will accuse you before the Father; your accuser is Moses, on whom you have set your hope. ⁴⁶If you believed Moses, you would believe me, for he wrote about

a Gk *that one*   *b* Or *among*

me. [47]But if you do not believe what he wrote, how will you believe what I say?"

5.31–47: Witnesses to Jesus. 31: Jewish law did not accept self-witness (see Deut 19.15). Contrast 8.13–18. **32–33:** *Another who testifies* may be John but is more likely God. The reference to John looks back to 1.19–28. **34–35:** The witness of John was for the sake of others (see 1.35–42 and compare 11.42; 12.30). **36–38:** More important than John was the witness of Jesus' *works* because the works of the Son are the works of the Father (see 5.17). God's testimony to Jesus could be in his works, or, in light of 5.39, 45–47, in the scriptures. But reference to the inaccessibility of God's voice and form recalls Ex 19.9–11. **39–40:** They fail to see that *the scriptures* witness to Jesus, who gives eternal life. **41–44:** Jesus may sound self-promoting, but he claims no glory for himself, only for the Father. **45–47:** Despite 5.27, Jesus is not the accuser: This is one role of Moses (in the law); another role is the witness to Jesus.

6 After this Jesus went to the other side of the Sea of Galilee, also called the Sea of Tiberias.[a] [2]A large crowd kept following him, because they saw the signs that he was doing for the sick. [3]Jesus went up the mountain and sat down there with his disciples. [4]Now the Passover, the festival of the Jews, was near. [5]When he looked up and saw a large crowd coming toward him, Jesus said to Philip, "Where are we to buy bread for these people to eat?" [6]He said this to test him, for he himself knew what he was going to do. [7]Philip answered him, "Six months' wages[b] would not buy enough bread for each of them to get a little." [8]One of his disciples, Andrew, Simon Peter's brother, said to him, [9]"There is a boy here who has five barley loaves and two fish. But what are they among so many people?" [10]Jesus said, "Make the people sit down." Now there was a great deal of grass in the place; so they[c] sat down, about five thousand in all. [11]Then Jesus took the loaves, and when he had given thanks, he distributed them to those who were seated; so also the fish, as much as they wanted. [12]When they were satisfied, he told his disciples, "Gather up the fragments left over, so that nothing may be lost." [13]So they gathered them up, and from the fragments

of the five barley loaves, left by those who had eaten, they filled twelve baskets. [14]When the people saw the sign that he had done, they began to say, "This is indeed the prophet who is to come into the world."

15 When Jesus realized that they were about to come and take him by force to make him king, he withdrew again to the mountain by himself.

16 When evening came, his disciples went down to the sea, [17]got into a boat, and started across the sea to Capernaum. It was now dark, and Jesus had not yet come to them. [18]The sea became rough because a strong wind was blowing. [19]When they had rowed about three or four miles,[d] they saw Jesus walking on the sea and coming near the boat, and they were terrified. [20]But he said to them, "It is I;[e] do not be afraid." [21]Then they wanted to take him into the boat, and immediately the boat reached the land toward which they were going.

6.1–71: The quest for eternal life and the bread of life. 1–15: Feeding the crowd. Compare Mt 14. 13–21; Mk 6.30–44; Lk 9.10–17. **1:** The narrative* might be more straightforward if ch. 6 followed ch. 4 (ch. 5 is set in Jerusalem). Jesus' movement is not from Jerusalem (from the south) but (presumably from Cana, on the west) *to the other* (eastern) *side of the Sea of Galilee*, also named the *Sea of Tiberias* after the city of that name, built in 20 CE in honor of Tiberias Caesar. The theme, however, follows from the search for eternal life in 5.39–40. **2:** The initiative of the *crowd* is stressed (4.46–54, see also 2.23). **3:** He retreats to an unnamed *mountain* to escape the crowd (compare 6.15). **4:** The connection to *Passover* is crucial for the story and the following discourse. **5–10:** Dialogues are characteristic of John (compare 1.40–45; 12.21–22). Philip reveals the magnitude of the task; Andrew's unlikely solution shows the magnitude of the sign. *Barley loaves*, the food of the poor (see 2 Kings 4.42–44). **11–13:** Jesus' action of taking the loaves, giving *thanks*, and distributing them looks eucharistic* but does not mention "breaking." ("Eucharist" is derived from the word translated *he had given thanks*. But Je-

---

a Gk *of Galilee of Tiberias*   b Gk *Two hundred denarii;* the denarius was the usual day's wage for a laborer   c Gk *the men*   d Gk *about twenty-five or thirty stadia*   e Gk *I am*

The ``I am'' Sayings in John's Gospel

A number of Jesus' sayings in John are commonly called the "I am" sayings. He says, "I am the bread of life" (6.35); "I am the light of the world" (8.12; 9.5); "I am the gate" (10.7, 9); "I am the good shepherd" (10.11, 14); "I am the resurrection and the life" (11.25); "I am the way, the truth, and the life" (14.6); and "I am the true vine" (15.1, 5). These sayings reinforce themes that are demonstrated in the signs and in Jesus' other statements. For instance, the feeding of the five thousand (ch. 6) and its accompanying explanation emphasize Jesus as the sustenance of his followers. Although some commentators have tried to find exact correspondences between the "I am" sayings, the signs, and Jesus' other speeches, it is probably better to look at these sayings as brief summaries of themes found throughout the Gospel.

sus also gave thanks for the fish.) *Gather up the fragments:* The sign was more than adequate. *Twelve baskets:* Probably the twelve had one each (see 6.67, 70, 71). **14–15:** The people attempt to *make* Jesus *king.* Josephus* tells of leaders who offered signs of coming deliverance in the desert. **16–21: Sea crossing** (Mt 14.22–27; Mk 6.45–52). The journey reinforces Jesus' rejection of the attempt to make him king and reveals the disciples' fearfulness and Jesus' control over nature.

THREE DIALOGUES

6.22–71: Three different groups interact with Jesus: the crowd from the feeding (vv. 22–40); the Jews in the synagogue* (vv. 41–59); and the disciples (vv. 60–71).

22 The next day the crowd that had stayed on the other side of the sea saw that there had been only one boat there. They also saw that Jesus had not got into the boat with his disciples, but that his disciples had gone away alone. 23 Then some boats from Tiberias came near the place where they had eaten the bread after the Lord had given thanks.*a* 24 So when the crowd saw that neither Jesus nor his disciples were there, they themselves got into the boats and went to Capernaum looking for Jesus.

25 When they found him on the other side of the sea, they said to him, "Rabbi, when did you come here?" 26 Jesus answered them, "Very truly, I tell you, you are looking for me, not because you saw signs, but because you ate your fill of the loaves. 27 Do

not work for the food that perishes, but for the food that endures for eternal life, which the Son of Man will give you. For it is on him that God the Father has set his seal." 28 Then they said to him, "What must we do to perform the works of God?" 29 Jesus answered them, "This is the work of God, that you believe in him whom he has sent." 30 So they said to him, "What sign are you going to give us then, so that we may see it and believe you? What work are you performing? 31 Our ancestors ate the manna in the wilderness; as it is written, 'He gave them bread from heaven to eat.' " 32 Then Jesus said to them, "Very truly, I tell you, it was not Moses who gave you the bread from heaven, but it is my Father who gives you the true bread from heaven. 33 For the bread of God is that which*b* comes down from heaven and gives life to the world." 34 They said to him, "Sir, give us this bread always."

35 Jesus said to them, "I am the bread of life. Whoever comes to me will never be hungry, and whoever believes in me will never be thirsty. 36 But I said to you that you have seen me and yet do not believe. 37 Everything that the Father gives me will come to me, and anyone who comes to me I will never drive away; 38 for I have come down from heaven, not to do my own will, but the will of him who sent me. 39 And this is the will of him who sent me, that I should lose nothing of

a Other ancient authorities lack *after the Lord had given thanks* *b* Or *he who* all that he has given me, but raise it up on the last day. 40This is indeed the will of my Father, that all who see the Son and believe in him may have eternal life; and I will raise them up on the last day."

6.22–40: The story of the crowd continues. *One boat confirms Jesus' unique sea crossing.* **23–24:** *Boats from Tiberias, on the southwestern shore, go to Capernaum, on the northern shore.* **25:** On seeking and finding, see 1.37–45; 7.33–34; 8.21; 13.33–36. **26:** Jesus questions their motives (contrast 6.2). **27–30:** The dialogue moves to another level: the *food of eternal life.* **31–34:** They appeal to their Exodus ancestors (*fathers,* compare 4.12, 20) who ate *manna* (Ex 16.15), *bread from heaven* (Ex 16.4; Ps 78.24). Jesus asserts that the bread from heaven is not manna, but the one who (see note *b,* p. 1806) comes down from heaven, giving life to the world. The crowd, in language reminiscent of the Samaritan woman (see 4.15), requests the true bread. **35–40:** The crowd has no opportunity to respond after v. 35, the first of the great *I am* sayings (see sidebar, "I am" sayings, p. 1806). *The last day* (see 6.39, 40, 44, 54; compare 11.24): Eternal life is manifest in resurrection, not judgment.

---

41 Then the Jews began to complain about him because he said, "I am the bread that came down from heaven." 42They were saying, "Is not this Jesus, the son of Joseph, whose father and mother we know? How can he now say, 'I have come down from heaven'?" 43Jesus answered them, "Do not complain among yourselves. 44No one can come to me unless drawn by the Father who sent me; and I will raise that person up on the last day. 45It is written in the prophets, 'And they shall all be taught by God.' Everyone who has heard and learned from the Father comes to me. 46Not that anyone has seen the Father except the one who is from God; he has seen the Father. 47Very truly, I tell you, whoever believes has eternal life. 48I am the bread of life. 49Your ancestors ate the manna in the wilderness, and they died. 50This is the bread that comes down from heaven, so that one may eat of it and not die. 51I am the living bread that came down from heaven. Whoever eats of this bread will live forever; and the bread that I will give for the life of the world is my flesh."

52 The Jews then disputed among themselves, saying, "How can this man give us his flesh to eat?" 53So Jesus said to them, "Very truly, I tell you, unless you eat the flesh of the Son of Man and drink his blood, you have no life in you. 54Those who eat my flesh and drink my blood have eternal life, and I will raise them up on the last day; 55for my flesh is true food and my blood is true drink. 56Those who eat my flesh and drink my blood abide in me, and I in them. 57Just as the living Father sent me, and I live because of the Father, so whoever eats me will live because of me. 58This is the bread that came down from heaven, not like that which your ancestors ate, and they died. But the one who eats this bread will live forever." 59He said these things while he was teaching in the synagogue at Capernaum.

60 When many of his disciples heard it, they said, "This teaching is difficult; who can accept it?" 61But Jesus, being aware that his disciples were complaining about it, said to them, "Does this offend you? 62Then what if you were to see the Son of Man ascending to where he was before? 63It is the spirit that gives life; the flesh is useless. The words that I have spoken to you are spirit and life. 64But among you there are some who do not believe." For Jesus knew from the first who were the ones that did not believe, and who was the one that would betray him. 65And he said, "For this reason I have told you that no one can come to me unless it is granted by the Father."

66 Because of this many of his disciples turned back and no longer went about with him. 67So Jesus asked the twelve, "Do you also wish to go away?" 68Simon Peter answered him, "Lord, to whom can we go? You have the words of eternal life. 69We have come to believe and know that you are the Holy One of God."*a* 70Jesus answered them, "Did I not choose you, the twelve? Yet one of you is a devil." 71He was speaking of Judas son of Simon Iscariot,*b* for he, though one of the twelve, was going to betray him.

a Other ancient authorities read *the Christ, the Son of the living God*　　*b* Other ancient authorities read *Judas Iscariot son of Simon;* others, *Judas son of Simon from Karyot* (Kerioth)

6.41–71. 41–59: Debate with and rejection by the Jews replaces the discussion with the crowd. **41–51: Dispute over origins. 41–42:** *Complain* recalls faithless Israel in the wilderness (see Ex 16.2; Num 14.2, 36; 17.6–15; Jn 6.43, 61; 7.12, 38). **43–44:** Jesus reiterates the role of the Father and his own role on the last day. **45:** Isa 54.13; those taught by *the Father* come to Jesus. **46:** Compare 1.18. **47–51:** Belief is one possible meaning of eating the *bread from . . . heaven* (see 6.35, 51, 54, 58). **52–59:** Dispute over eating *his flesh* leads to more provocation: They must also *drink Jesus' blood.* Jews were forbidden to drink blood (see Deut 12.16) because it contained life sacred to God. The language is eucharistic,* to be taken symbolically; the listeners misunderstand, adopting a crude physical meaning. **59:** The synagogue* is a reminder of Jesus' own Judaism. **60–71: Dispute with the disciples. 63:** *The words . . . are spirit and life:* Jesus explicitly rejects the crude physical interpretation. **64–65:** Although there is dissent among the disciples, as there was among the crowd and the Jews, *Jesus* and *the Father* offer the assurance that they are in control (see 6.37, 44, 71; 12.4–6; 13.2, 11, 18, 21–30; 18.2–5). **66–71:** Dissent had its impact even on the *twelve.* For Peter's confession, compare Mk 8.27–29. *Judas,* not Peter, is the *devil* (compare Mk 8.32). **71:** *Iscariot,* perhaps "man of Kerioth," a town of southern Judea (see note *b*, p. 1807).

THE FESTIVAL OF BOOTHS

7.1–52: See Lev 23.34–43; Deut 16.13–17; Neh 8.14–18. Also see sidebar, "Jewish Festivals in John's Gospel," p. 1819.

7 After this Jesus went about in Galilee. He did not wish*a* to go about in Judea because the Jews were looking for an opportunity to kill him. ²Now the Jewish festival of Booths*b* was near. ³So his brothers said to him, "Leave here and go to Judea so that your disciples also may see the works you are doing; ⁴for no one who wants*c* to be widely known acts in secret. If you do these things, show yourself to the world." ⁵(For not even his brothers believed in him.) ⁶Jesus said to them, "My time has not yet come, but your time is always here. ⁷The world cannot hate you, but it hates me because I testify against it that its works are evil. ⁸Go to the festival

yourselves. I am not*d* going to this festival, for my time has not yet fully come." ⁹After saying this, he remained in Galilee.

10 But after his brothers had gone to the festival, then he also went, not publicly but as it were*e* in secret. ¹¹The Jews were looking for him at the festival and saying, "Where is he?" ¹²And there was considerable complaining about him among the crowds. While some were saying, "He is a good man," others were saying, "No, he is deceiving the crowd." ¹³Yet no one would speak openly about him for fear of the Jews.

7.1–10: Setting. 1: *The Jews,* probably the Jewish authorities. **2:** *The Jewish festival* may signal that, although observed by Jesus, it was not observed by the Johannine believers (see 5.1; 6.4). **3–5:** Jesus' *brothers* were in the company of Jesus and his disciples (compare 2.12). Jesus appears to reject their suggestion, as he did that of their mother (see 2.3–4), yet both times does what he is asked. *Not even his brothers believed:* This needs to be balanced against their presence with the disciples. **6–10:** Jesus goes to Jerusalem in his own time and fashion. His *time* (see 2.4; 7.30 and 5.25, 28; 8.20; 12.23; 17.1) means the time of God's purpose. Jesus, present but hidden in Jerusalem, evokes the idea of the hidden messiah* (see 7.27; 7.1, 10; 11.54; 12.36).

---

14 About the middle of the festival Jesus went up into the temple and began to teach. ¹⁵The Jews were astonished at it, saying, "How does this man have such learning,*f* when he has never been taught?" ¹⁶Then Jesus answered them, "My teaching is not mine but his who sent me. ¹⁷Anyone who resolves to do the will of God will know whether the teaching is from God or whether I am speaking on my own. ¹⁸Those who speak on their own seek their own glory; but the one who seeks the glory of him who sent him is true, and there is nothing false in him.

19 "Did not Moses give you the law? Yet none of you keeps the law. Why are you looking for an opportunity to kill me?" ²⁰The crowd answered, "You have a demon! Who is trying to kill you?" ²¹Jesus answered them,

a Other ancient authorities read *was not at liberty*
b Or *Tabernacles*   *c* Other ancient authorities read *wants it*   *d* Other ancient authorities add *yet*
e Other ancient authorities lack *as it were*   *f* Or *this man know his letters*

"I performed one work, and all of you are astonished. 22Moses gave you circumcision (it is, of course, not from Moses, but from the patriarchs), and you circumcise a man on the sabbath. 23If a man receives circumcision on the sabbath in order that the law of Moses may not be broken, are you angry with me because I healed a man's whole body on the sabbath? 24Do not judge by appearances, but judge with right judgment."

25 Now some of the people of Jerusalem were saying, "Is not this the man whom they are trying to kill? 26And here he is, speaking openly, but they say nothing to him! Can it be that the authorities really know that this is the Messiah?*a* 27Yet we know where this man is from; but when the Messiah*a* comes, no one will know where he is from." 28Then Jesus cried out as he was teaching in the temple, "You know me, and you know where I am from. I have not come on my own. But the one who sent me is true, and you do not know him. 29I know him, because I am from him, and he sent me." 30Then they tried to arrest him, but no one laid hands on him, because his hour had not yet come. 31Yet many in the crowd believed in him and were saying, "When the Messiah*a* comes, will he do more signs than this man has done?"*b*

32 The Pharisees heard the crowd muttering such things about him, and the chief priests and Pharisees sent temple police to arrest him. 33Jesus then said, "I will be with you a little while longer, and then I am going to him who sent me. 34You will search for me, but you will not find me; and where I am, you cannot come." 35The Jews said to one another, "Where does this man intend to go that we will not find him? Does he intend to go to the Dispersion among the Greeks and teach the Greeks? 36What does he mean by saying, 'You will search for me and you will not find me' and 'Where I am, you cannot come'?"

***

7.11–52: At the feast. 11–12: *Complaining*, arguing or murmuring about him (compare 6.41). There were different groups: the Jewish leaders, 7.1, 11; divided *crowd(s)*, 7.12, 30–31, 40–44, 49; 8.30; 9.16; 10.19–21; the *Pharisees** and *chief priests* (who may be the leaders of 7.1, 11), 7.32, 45. Opinion of Jesus

was divided: (a) Jesus' goodness (5.6, 9, 14, 15; 7.23; 9.30–33); (b) Jesus as deceiver (5.9, 16, 18, 23–24; 7.45–52; 9.28, 34). **13:** *Fear of the Jews* suggests that they were powerful leaders (compare 9.22; 12.42; 19.38; 20.19). **14:** Jesus enters the *Temple** and exits only in 8.59. The secret visit has become public (compare 7.28). **15–18:** Jesus' integrity is shown by the selfless seeking of the Father's glory (compare 5.19, 30–31, 41–44 and 8.26–28; 12.43; 14.10). **19:** *Moses*, see 5.39, 45–47; *kill me*, see 5.16–18. **21:** *One work*, see 5.1–9. **22–24:** *Sabbath*, see Gen 17.9–14; Lev 12.3. If tradition allowed for *circumcision** on the sabbath, why not healing (literally "making whole")? The critics use a double standard (compare 8.15). **25–29:** Jesus' secret arrival in Jerusalem led to his dramatic appearance in the Temple (v. 14). The mystery* of his origin is now the subject of Jesus' teaching (see also 8.14; 9.29; 19.9). **30:** *His hour had not yet come:* a warning that the time of arrest and execution would come. **31:** The leaders are at times part of *the crowd*, at times distinguished from it, causing some confusion in the language. **32–36:** *Pharisees* alternates with *Jews* as the term for Jesus' opponents (see 7.45, 47; 8.13; 9.13, 15, 16, 40). *Chief priests*, see 12.10; 18.35; 16.6, 15. This context makes clear that *Jews* means "religious leaders," not all the people. A combination of *Pharisees* and *chief priests* acted to arrest Jesus, indicating a decision by the Sanhedrin,* the supreme Jewish political governing body (see 11.47). **33–36:** Jesus is still in the Temple. His audience includes *the Jews. A little while*, see 12.35; 13.33; 14.19; 16.16–19. The misunderstanding of going to the Diaspora* Jews among the Greeks (gentiles*) may foreshadow the mission to the nations (compare 12.20).

~~~~~~~~~~~~~~~~~~~~~~~~~~~~~~~~~~~~~

37 On the last day of the festival, the great day, while Jesus was standing there, he cried out, "Let anyone who is thirsty come to me, 38and let the one who believes in me drink. As*c* the scripture has said, 'Out of the believer's heart*d* shall flow rivers of living water.'" 39Now he said this about the Spirit, which believers in him were to receive; for as yet there was no Spirit,*e* because Jesus was not yet glorified.

40 When they heard these words, some

***

a Or *the Christ*   *b* Other ancient authorities read *is doing*   *c* Or *come to me and drink.* 38*The one who believes in me, as*   *d* Gk *out of his belly*   *e* Other ancient authorities read *for as yet the Spirit* (others, *Holy Spirit*) *had not been given* in the crowd said, "This is really the prophet." [41] Others said, "This is the Messiah."[a] But some asked, "Surely the Messiah[a] does not come from Galilee, does he? [42] Has not the scripture said that the Messiah[a] is descended from David and comes from Bethlehem, the village where David lived?" [43] So there was a division in the crowd because of him. [44] Some of them wanted to arrest him, but no one laid hands on him.

[45] Then the temple police went back to the chief priests and Pharisees, who asked them, "Why did you not arrest him?" [46] The police answered, "Never has anyone spoken like this!" [47] Then the Pharisees replied, "Surely you have not been deceived too, have you? [48] Has any one of the authorities or of the Pharisees believed in him? [49] But this crowd, which does not know the law—they are accursed." [50] Nicodemus, who had gone to Jesus[b] before, and who was one of them, asked, [51] "Our law does not judge people without first giving them a hearing to find out what they are doing, does it?" [52] They replied, "Surely you are not also from Galilee, are you? Search and you will see that no prophet is to arise from Galilee."

8 [[53] Then each of them went home, [1] while Jesus went to the Mount of Olives. [2] Early in the morning he came again to the temple. All the people came to him and he sat down and began to teach them. [3] The scribes and the Pharisees brought a woman who had been caught in adultery; and making her stand before all of them, [4] they said to him, "Teacher, this woman was caught in the very act of committing adultery. [5] Now in the law Moses commanded us to stone such women. Now what do you say?" [6] They said this to test him, so that they might have some charge to bring against him. Jesus bent down and wrote with his finger on the ground. [7] When they kept on questioning him, he straightened up and said to them, "Let anyone among you who is without sin be the first to throw a stone at her." [8] And once again he bent down and wrote on the ground.[c] [9] When they heard it, they went away, one by one, beginning with the elders; and Jesus was left alone with the woman standing before him. [10] Jesus straightened up and said to her, "Woman, where are they? Has no one condemned you?" [11] She said, "No one, sir."[d] And Jesus said, "Neither do I condemn you. Go your way, and from now on do not sin again."]][e]

7.37–52. 37–39: The last day of the feast is the moment for a dramatic pronouncement. At the feast the water from the rock (Num 20.2–13) was commemorated in a way that promised future blessings (Isa 44.3; 55.1). Jesus' saying relates this tradition to the outpouring of the Spirit to believers. *The one who believes in me:* see note c, p. 1809. The text is ambiguous but probably refers to the Spirit flowing from Jesus (4.10; 19.34), not the believer. *Scripture,* Isa 44.2–3 or Zech 14.8 (Zechariah was read at this festival). *Glorified,* the reality of Jesus' relation to the Father was revealed in his death and resurrection (see 12.23; 16.7 and comment on 1.14–18; compare Joel 2.28–29; Acts 2.14–21). **40–44:** The crowd continued to be divided. *The prophet,*✳ see 1.21, 25, 45; 6.14–15; *Messiah,*✳ see 1.20, 25, 41. **45–52:** The *police* do not attempt an *arrest* because of the effect of Jesus' teaching. The position of the *Pharisees*✳ is ironic:✳ *One of the authorities,* namely Nicodemus, has *gone to Jesus;* they hold the *crowd* in contempt for ignorance of the law, but they themselves ignore the law by condemning Jesus *without . . . a hearing.*

7.53–8.11: An early non-Johannine story (see note e). This interrupts 7.14–8.59 (entry into Temple✳ and exit). Though it is not clear where this originated, it is based on old tradition. **8.1–2:** Crowds of pilgrims at festivals often spent the night on the slopes of *the Mount of Olives* (compare Lk 21.37–38). **3:** *Scribes,*✳ often mentioned in the other Gospels, but only here in John. **5:** Both guilty parties (not only the woman) were condemned to death by Lev 20.10; Deut 22.22. **6:** The attempt is to put Jesus in a "no win" situation: Overlooking the sin means disobeying the law, and condemning the woman would weaken his popular support. What Jesus wrote is unknown. **7:** The witnesses were to cast the first stone, Deut 17.7. It may be significant that no guilty man is mentioned. **9:** El-

a Or *the Christ*   *b* Gk *him*   *c* Other ancient authorities add *the sins of each of them*   *d* Or *Lord*
e The most ancient authorities lack 7.53—8.11; other authorities add the passage here or after 7.36 or after 21.25 or after Luke 21.38, with variations of text; some mark the passage as doubtful.

ders, more likely "oldest." **10–11:** Jesus did not condemn her, but called on her not to sin again (compare 5.14). The story illustrates 3.17; 12.47.

~~~~~~~~~~~~~~~~~~~~~~~~~~~~~

12 Again Jesus spoke to them, saying, "I am the light of the world. Whoever follows me will never walk in darkness but will have the light of life." 13Then the Pharisees said to him, "You are testifying on your own behalf; your testimony is not valid." 14Jesus answered, "Even if I testify on my own behalf, my testimony is valid because I know where I have come from and where I am going, but you do not know where I come from or where I am going. 15You judge by human standards;*a* I judge no one. 16Yet even if I do judge, my judgment is valid; for it is not I alone who judge, but I and the Father*b* who sent me. 17In your law it is written that the testimony of two witnesses is valid. 18I testify on my own behalf, and the Father who sent me testifies on my behalf." 19Then they said to him, "Where is your Father?" Jesus answered, "You know neither me nor my Father. If you knew me, you would know my Father also." 20He spoke these words while he was teaching in the treasury of the temple, but no one arrested him, because his hour had not yet come.

21 Again he said to them, "I am going away, and you will search for me, but you will die in your sin. Where I am going, you cannot come." 22Then the Jews said, "Is he going to kill himself? Is that what he means by saying, 'Where I am going, you cannot come'?" 23He said to them, "You are from below, I am from above; you are of this world, I am not of this world. 24I told you that you would die in your sins, for you will die in your sins unless you believe that I am he."*c* 25They said to him, "Who are you?" Jesus said to them, "Why do I speak to you at all?*d* 26I have much to say about you and much to condemn; but the one who sent me is true, and I declare to the world what I have heard from him." 27They did not understand that he was speaking to them about the Father. 28So Jesus said, "When you have lifted up the Son of Man, then you will realize that I am he,*c* and that I do nothing on my own, but I speak these things as the Father in-

structed me. 29And the one who sent me is with me; he has not left me alone, for I always do what is pleasing to him." 30As he was saying these things, many believed in him.

31 Then Jesus said to the Jews who had believed in him, "If you continue in my word, you are truly my disciples; 32and you will know the truth, and the truth will make you free." 33They answered him, "We are descendants of Abraham and have never been slaves to anyone. What do you mean by saying, 'You will be made free'?"

34 Jesus answered them, "Very truly, I tell you, everyone who commits sin is a slave to sin. 35The slave does not have a permanent place in the household; the son has a place there forever. 36So if the Son makes you free, you will be free indeed. 37I know that you are descendants of Abraham; yet you look for an opportunity to kill me, because there is no place in you for my word. 38I declare what I have seen in the Father's presence; as for you, you should do what you have heard from the Father."*e*

8.12–59: Self-witness and controversy. 12–14: *Again* looks back to 7.37. Water and light are associated with the festival (see 1.4–5, 9; 3.19–21; 9.4–5; 11.9–10; 12.35–36, 46 on the theme). Jesus offered life-giving water and claimed to be *the light of the world.* Knowledge of his origin and destiny, of which *the Pharisees*★ were ignorant, made his testimony valid (see 7.27–29). **15–16:** The paradox expresses the idea that *judgment* brought about by his coming is the judgment of the one who sent him (see 5.30, 37; 8.29). **17–18:** Multiple *witnesses,* see Num 35.30; Deut 17.6; 19.15. **21–30:** The opponents do not know Jesus' origin or destiny. The crucifixion, being *lifted up* and glorified (3.14; 12.32, 34), is a revelatory event. **31–33:** The promise has two dimensions: Knowing *the truth* will make them *free,* and knowing *the truth* (the Son, 8.36) will make them *free.* **34:** They were slaves *to sin* (see Rom 6.15–23; 2 Peter 2.19). **35–36:** See Gen 21.9–10; Ex 21.2; Deut 15.12; compare Gal 4.1–7; Heb 3.5–6. A proverbial saying; the permanent status of the son (the heir) guarantees lasting freedom.

---

a Gk *according to the flesh*   *b* Other ancient authorities read *he*   *c* Gk I *am*   *d* Or *What I have told you from the beginning*   *e* Other ancient authorities read *you do what you have heard from your father*

37: The paradox: They are Abraham's seed, but they seek to kill Jesus (see 5.18; 7.1, 19–20, 25) which sets them at odds with Abraham (see 8.39–40). **38:** The contrast: Jesus does what he has *seen* from his father (God, compare 3.11–13, 32, 35; 5.19–20, 37) while the Jews do what they have *heard* from their *father* (the devil, and see note *e*, p. 1811, and 8.41, 44; 1 Jn 3.8, 10, 12).

39 They answered him, "Abraham is our father." Jesus said to them, "If you were Abraham's children, you would be doing*a* what Abraham did, 40but now you are trying to kill me, a man who has told you the truth that I heard from God. This is not what Abraham did. 41You are indeed doing what your father does." They said to him, "We are not illegitimate children; we have one father, God himself." 42Jesus said to them, "If God were your Father, you would love me, for I came from God and now I am here. I did not come on my own, but he sent me. 43Why do you not understand what I say? It is because you cannot accept my word. 44You are from your father the devil, and you choose to do your father's desires. He was a murderer from the beginning and does not stand in the truth, because there is no truth in him. When he lies, he speaks according to his own nature, for he is a liar and the father of lies. 45But because I tell the truth, you do not believe me. 46Which of you convicts me of sin? If I tell the truth, why do you not believe me? 47Whoever is from God hears the words of God. The reason you do not hear them is that you are not from God."

48 The Jews answered him, "Are we not right in saying that you are a Samaritan and have a demon?" 49Jesus answered, "I do not have a demon; but I honor my Father, and you dishonor me. 50Yet I do not seek my own glory; there is one who seeks it and he is the judge. 51Very truly, I tell you, whoever keeps my word will never see death." 52The Jews said to him, "Now we know that you have a demon. Abraham died, and so did the prophets; yet you say, 'Whoever keeps my word will never taste death.' 53Are you greater than our father Abraham, who died? The prophets also died. Who do you claim to be?" 54Jesus answered, "If I glorify myself, my glory is

nothing. It is my Father who glorifies me, he of whom you say, 'He is our God,' 55though you do not know him. But I know him; if I would say that I do not know him, I would be a liar like you. But I do know him and I keep his word. 56Your ancestor Abraham rejoiced that he would see my day; he saw it and was glad." 57Then the Jews said to him, "You are not yet fifty years old, and have you seen Abraham?"*b* 58Jesus said to them, "Very truly, I tell you, before Abraham was, I am." 59So they picked up stones to throw at him, but Jesus hid himself and went out of the temple.

8.39–59. 39–43: The attempt to kill him is not consistent with what Abraham did but reveals another line of descent (compare 1 Jn 3.7–10, 12). They claim to have *one father, God* (see Deut 32.6; Isa 63.16; 64.8). Their behavior betrays a different origin. **44:** *Liar,* see 8.55. This bitter language reflects later conflict between Christians and the synagogue* (see also 7.20; 8.48). **48–58:** The argument with the Jewish leaders elicits an escalating series of claims from Jesus: *I honor my Father; whoever keeps my word will never see death; it is my Father who glorifies me; I know the Father and I keep his word; Abraham rejoiced that he would see my day; before Abraham was, I am.* The opponents remain at the literal, earthbound level: *You are a Samaritan and have a demon; Abraham died; the prophets* died; you are not yet fifty years old.* **59:** Another attempt *to kill* Jesus (see comment on 5.18), by stoning, the traditional Jewish method of execution (see also 10.31; 11.8) for offenses such as blasphemy.

9 As he walked along, he saw a man blind from birth. 2His disciples asked him, "Rabbi, who sinned, this man or his parents, that he was born blind?" 3Jesus answered, "Neither this man nor his parents sinned; he was born blind so that God's works might be revealed in him. 4We*c* must work the works of him who sent me*d* while it is day; night is coming when no one can work. 5As long as I am in the world, I am the light of the world." 6When he had said this, he spat on the ground and made mud with the saliva

a Other ancient authorities read *If you are Abraham's children, then do* *b* Other ancient authorities read *has Abraham seen you?* *c* Other ancient authorities read *I* *d* Other ancient authorities read *us* and spread the mud on the man's eyes, 7 saying to him, "Go, wash in the pool of Siloam" (which means Sent). Then he went and washed and came back able to see. 8 The neighbors and those who had seen him before as a beggar began to ask, "Is this not the man who used to sit and beg?" 9 Some were saying, "It is he." Others were saying, "No, but it is someone like him." He kept saying, "I am the man." 10 But they kept asking him, "Then how were your eyes opened?" 11 He answered, "The man called Jesus made mud, spread it on my eyes, and said to me, 'Go to Siloam and wash.' Then I went and washed and received my sight." 12 They said to him, "Where is he?" He said, "I do not know."

13 They brought to the Pharisees the man who had formerly been blind. 14 Now it was a sabbath day when Jesus made the mud and opened his eyes. 15 Then the Pharisees also began to ask him how he had received his sight. He said to them, "He put mud on my eyes. Then I washed, and now I see." 16 Some of the Pharisees said, "This man is not from God, for he does not observe the sabbath." But others said, "How can a man who is a sinner perform such signs?" And they were divided. 17 So they said again to the blind man, "What do you say about him? It was your eyes he opened." He said, "He is a prophet."

18 The Jews did not believe that he had been blind and had received his sight until they called the parents of the man who had received his sight 19 and asked them, "Is this your son, who you say was born blind? How then does he now see?" 20 His parents answered, "We know that this is our son, and that he was born blind; 21 but we do not know how it is that now he sees, nor do we know who opened his eyes. Ask him; he is of age. He will speak for himself." 22 His parents said this because they were afraid of the Jews; for the Jews had already agreed that anyone who confessed Jesus[a] to be the Messiah[b] would be put out of the synagogue. 23 Therefore his parents said, "He is of age; ask him."

24 So for the second time they called the man who had been blind, and they said to him, "Give glory to God! We know that this man is a sinner." 25 He answered, "I do not know whether he is a sinner. One thing I do know, that though I was blind, now I see." 26 They said to him, "What did he do to you? How did he open your eyes?" 27 He answered them, "I have told you already, and you would not listen. Why do you want to hear it again? Do you also want to become his disciples?" 28 Then they reviled him, saying, "You are his disciple, but we are disciples of Moses. 29 We know that God has spoken to Moses, but as for this man, we do not know where he comes from." 30 The man answered, "Here is an astonishing thing! You do not know where he comes from, and yet he opened my eyes. 31 We know that God does not listen to sinners, but he does listen to one who worships him and obeys his will. 32 Never since the world began has it been heard that anyone opened the eyes of a person born blind. 33 If this man were not from God, he could do nothing." 34 They answered him, "You were born entirely in sins, and are you trying to teach us?" And they drove him out.

35 Jesus heard that they had driven him out, and when he found him, he said, "Do you believe in the Son of Man?"[c] 36 He answered, "And who is he, sir?[d] Tell me, so that I may believe in him." 37 Jesus said to him, "You have seen him, and the one speaking with you is he." 38 He said, "Lord,[d] I believe." And he worshiped him. 39 Jesus said, "I came into this world for judgment so that those who do not see may see, and those who do see may become blind." 40 Some of the Pharisees near him heard this and said to him, "Surely we are not blind, are we?" 41 Jesus said to them, "If you were blind, you would not have sin. But now that you say, 'We see,' your sin remains.

9.1–41: The healing of a blind man. Jesus, the light of the world, is manifest: The narrative* interprets the light as life-giving and judging in eight scenes. **Scene 1, 1–5: Jesus and the disciples.** The disciples assume that sin causes adversity (compare 5.14 and 8.11). Jesus rejects this view; adversity is an opportunity for the

a Gk *him*   b Or *the Christ*
c Other ancient authorities read *the Son of God*
d *Sir* and *Lord* translate the same Greek word

works of God (see 5.17). The coming *night* (see 13.30) will violently remove Jesus (the light of the world) by killing him. **Scene 2, 6–7: Jesus heals the blind man** (compare Mk 8.23). *The pool of Siloam* was fed by the spring of Gihon (see 2 Kings 20.20; 2 Chr 32.30; Isa 22.11). **Scene 3, 8–12: The man and his neighbors.** At this point the questioners are not opponents. The healed man's faith develops: **First stage of faith:** *the man called Jesus.* Compare with 5.12–13. **Scene 4, 13–17: The man and the Pharisees:** an interrogation to ascertain "the facts." **14:** A new "fact": It was the *sabbath* (compare 5.9; 5.16; also 7.21–24). **16:** Compare 5.9–10 and 5.14, 15. The Pharisees were divided (7.12). **17: Second stage of faith:** *He is a prophet,* not *the prophet* of 1.21, 25, 45; 6.14–15. **Scene 5, 18–23: The Jews and the parents.** The *Jews* (Pharisees, 9.13–17) are synagogue authorities, so the parents, themselves Jews, are *afraid of the Jews* (compare 7.13). Nobody has mentioned *the messiah.* Being *put out of the synagogue* is the situation of the Johannine believers (see 9.35; 12.42; 16.2). **Scene 6, 24–34: The Pharisees and the man: second interrogation. 28–34:** Disciples of Moses oppose disciples of Jesus and his unknown origin (compare 7.27–28; 8.14; 3.8). But God *does not listen to sinners* (Ps 34.15; 66.18; Isa 1.15; Prov 15.29). **Third stage of faith:** *from God.* The Jews assert the connection between sin and affliction (see 9.2–3) and cast the man out. **Scene 7, 9.35–39: Jesus and the man.** Jesus introduces the final, **Fourth stage of faith:** *Son of Man,* his chosen self-designation. Jesus' self-revelation ends with the man's confession of faith and worship. **Scene 8, 40–41: Jesus and the Pharisees.** The question implies a negative answer. Either they are blind but sin in refusing to acknowledge it, or they are not blind and sin willfully (see 15.22–24).

10 "Very truly, I tell you, anyone who does not enter the sheepfold by the gate but climbs in by another way is a thief and a bandit. ²The one who enters by the gate is the shepherd of the sheep. ³The gatekeeper opens the gate for him, and the sheep hear his voice. He calls his own sheep by name and leads them out. ⁴When he has brought out all his own, he goes ahead of them, and the sheep follow him because they know his voice. ⁵They will not follow a stranger, but they will run from him because they do not know the voice of strangers." ⁶Jesus used this figure of speech with them, but

they did not understand what he was saying to them.

7 So again Jesus said to them, "Very truly, I tell you, I am the gate for the sheep. ⁸All who came before me are thieves and bandits; but the sheep did not listen to them. ⁹I am the gate. Whoever enters by me will be saved, and will come in and go out and find pasture. ¹⁰The thief comes only to steal and kill and destroy. I came that they may have life, and have it abundantly.

11 "I am the good shepherd. The good shepherd lays down his life for the sheep. ¹²The hired hand, who is not the shepherd and does not own the sheep, sees the wolf coming and leaves the sheep and runs away—and the wolf snatches them and scatters them. ¹³The hired hand runs away because a hired hand does not care for the sheep. ¹⁴I am the good shepherd. I know my own and my own know me, ¹⁵just as the Father knows me and I know the Father. And I lay down my life for the sheep. ¹⁶I have other sheep that do not belong to this fold. I must bring them also, and they will listen to my voice. So there will be one flock, one shepherd. ¹⁷For this reason the Father loves me, because I lay down my life in order to take it up again. ¹⁸No one takes*ᵃ* it from me, but I lay it down of my own accord. I have power to lay it down, and I have power to take it up again. I have received this command from my Father."

19 Again the Jews were divided because of these words. ²⁰Many of them were saying, "He has a demon and is out of his mind. Why listen to him?" ²¹Others were saying, "These are not the words of one who has a demon. Can a demon open the eyes of the blind?"

10.1–21: Jesus' critique of the Pharisees* continues. Shepherd imagery was used of God and human rulers (Ps 80.1; Isa 40.10–11; Jer 23.1–6; Ezek 34.1–24; Zech 11.4–17; Jn 21.15–17; Acts 20.28–29). The double interpretation* (vv. 7–18) covers vv. 1–3a, the *gate,* and vv. 3b–5, *shepherd.* **1–6: The parable.* 1:** The *sheepfold* is a stone enclosure. **3–5:** Compare Num 27.16–17. *The gatekeeper:* perhaps John the Baptist (1.24–37). *Follow him . . . know his voice:* the sign of

ᵃ Other ancient authorities read *has taken*

the true leader. **7–10: First interpretation:** *the gate.* **7–8:** Jesus as *the gate* is in part undercut by v. 8. Those *who came before:* Israel's leaders (see Jer 23.1–6; Ezek 34.1–24); here, the Pharisees. *Thieves and bandits:* They had not cared for the people. **9–10:** The contrast of Jesus with the thieves is dramatic. Again, an identification with the shepherd (in v. 10b) makes best sense. **11–18: Second interpretation:** *the shepherd.* **11–13:** See Jn 15.13; compare 1 Sam 17.34–35. Unlike the thieves, *the hired hand* has a legitimate though subordinate role. **14–15:** The shepherd is the ideal leader (compare 14.20–21; 15.9; 17.21). **16:** *Other sheep:* other Jewish believers; or Jews of the dispersion (see Isa 56.8); or gentiles* (see 7.35; 11.52; 12.20–21, 32). *One flock,* a united community; *one shepherd* (see Ezek 34.23; 37.24), Jesus. **17–18:** *The father loves me* (see 3.35; 15.10): Jesus' self-giving mission is rooted in the Father-Son relationship. **19–21: Response.** The audience (*Pharisees* in 9.40), now *the Jews,* disagrees: demon possession (7.20) or curing the blind (9.25, 30, 32)?

22 At that time the festival of the Dedication took place in Jerusalem. It was winter, 23and Jesus was walking in the temple, in the portico of Solomon. 24So the Jews gathered around him and said to him, "How long will you keep us in suspense? If you are the Messiah,ᵃ tell us plainly." 25Jesus answered, "I have told you, and you do not believe. The works that I do in my Father's name testify to me; 26but you do not believe, because you do not belong to my sheep. 27My sheep hear my voice. I know them, and they follow me. 28I give them eternal life, and they will never perish. No one will snatch them out of my hand. 29What my Father has given me is greater than all else, and no one can snatch it out of the Father's hand.ᵇ 30The Father and I are one."

31 The Jews took up stones again to stone him. 32Jesus replied, "I have shown you many good works from the Father. For which of these are you going to stone me?" 33The Jews answered, "It is not for a good work that we are going to stone you, but for blasphemy, because you, though only a human being, are making yourself God." 34Jesus answered, "Is it not written in your law,ᶜ 'I said, you are gods'? 35If those to whom the word of God came were called 'gods'—and the scrip-

ture cannot be annulled— 36can you say that the one whom the Father has sanctified and sent into the world is blaspheming because I said, 'I am God's Son'? 37If I am not doing the works of my Father, then do not believe me. 38But if I do them, even though you do not believe me, believe the works, so that you may know and understandᵈ that the Father is in me and I am in the Father." 39Then they tried to arrest him again, but he escaped from their hands.

40 He went away again across the Jordan to the place where John had been baptizing earlier, and he remained there. 41Many came to him, and they were saying, "John performed no sign, but everything that John said about this man was true." 42And many believed in him there.

10.22–42. 22–39: Continuing conflict with the Jews. 22: Hanukkah, or the feast of lights, commemorating the *dedication* of the Temple* by Judas Maccabeus (164 BCE) after the desecration by Antiochus Epiphanes* (see 1 Macc 4.36–59), began on 25 Kislev and ran for 8 days (see sidebar, p. 154). **23:** *The portico of Solomon,* the covered walkway on the eastern side of the court of the gentiles* in the Temple.* **24–25:** *The Messiah:** see 1.41; 4.25–26; 7.25–31, 40–44; 9.22; 11.27; 12.34. Jesus had not explicitly told *the Jews,* but see 4.26 and 8.25 note d, p. 1811. On the witness of the *works,* see 5.36. **26–27:** See 10.3, 14, 16; 18.37. **28–30:** *Given* by the Father: See 6.35–40, 44–45; 17.2, 6, 9, 12. **31:** *The Jews took up stones again:* See 8.59; 7.30. **32–33:** Jesus appeals to his *many good works* (see 4.34; 5.17, 20; 9.4; 10.25, 36); *the Jews* see blasphemy (see 5.18; 10.33). **34–36:** Here (as in 12.34; 15.25) *law* means scripture, Ps 82.6. This is a type of Rabbinic argument: If something is true of the lesser, how much more is it justified of the greater. **37–38:** The goodness of his works is the starting place for those who find his claims difficult (compare 9.25–26, 30–33). **39–42:** Jesus' withdrawal (compare 7.1; 8.59; 11.54; 12.36) is a recognition of rejection. But *where John had been baptizing* (see 1.28), he finds acceptance.

a Or *the Christ*   *b* Other ancient authorities read *My Father who has given them to me is greater than all, and no one can snatch them out of the Father's hand.*   *c* Other ancient authorities read *in the law*   *d* Other ancient authorities lack *and understand*; others read *and believe*

LAZARUS: DEATH AND RESURRECTION

11.1–44: The raising of Lazarus foreshadows the resurrection of Jesus, but paradoxically also was a cause of the death of Jesus (see 11.46–53).

11 Now a certain man was ill, Lazarus of Bethany, the village of Mary and her sister Martha. ²Mary was the one who anointed the Lord with perfume and wiped his feet with her hair; her brother Lazarus was ill. ³So the sisters sent a message to Jesus,ª "Lord, he whom you love is ill." ⁴But when Jesus heard it, he said, "This illness does not lead to death; rather it is for God's glory, so that the Son of God may be glorified through it." ⁵Accordingly, though Jesus loved Martha and her sister and Lazarus, ⁶after having heard that Lazarusᵇ was ill, he stayed two days longer in the place where he was.

7 Then after this he said to the disciples, "Let us go to Judea again." ⁸The disciples said to him, "Rabbi, the Jews were just now trying to stone you, and are you going there again?" ⁹Jesus answered, "Are there not twelve hours of daylight? Those who walk during the day do not stumble, because they see the light of this world. ¹⁰But those who walk at night stumble, because the light is not in them." ¹¹After saying this, he told them, "Our friend Lazarus has fallen asleep, but I am going there to awaken him." ¹²The disciples said to him, "Lord, if he has fallen asleep, he will be all right." ¹³Jesus, however, had been speaking about his death, but they thought that he was referring merely to sleep. ¹⁴Then Jesus told them plainly, "Lazarus is dead. ¹⁵For your sake I am glad I was not there, so that you may believe. But let us go to him." ¹⁶Thomas, who was called the Twin,ᶜ said to his fellow disciples, "Let us also go, that we may die with him."

11.1–16: Context. 1: *Bethany* is on the eastern side of the Mount of Olives (11.18; 12.1), not to be confused with *Bethany beyond the Jordan* (1.28). **2:** *The one who anointed:** narrated in 12.1–8. *The Lord:* unusual language before the resurrection; see "my Lord" in 20.13. **3:** The message implies a request to come and

heal Lazarus, *he whom you love* (compare 11.5, 36; 13.1, 23; 19.26; 20.2; 21.7, 20). **4–6:** Jesus' control contrasts with his response at the tomb (vv. 35, 38). *God's glory* and the glorification of *the Son* take precedence (compare 2.11; 9.3; 11.40; 13.31–32; 14.13; 17.1). **6–8:** Jesus acts in God's time (2.3–4; 7.6). **9–10:** The time to act is now, a saying that recalls 9.4–5 (compare 8.12; 12.35–36). **11–15:** *Our friend* has the sense of one loved (see 11.3, 5, 36; compare 15.13, 14, 15). *Fallen asleep*, an early euphemism* for death. **16:** *Thomas* asks questions or expresses doubts that reveal the ignorance of the disciples (14.5) or bring about assurances from Jesus, as in the resurrection scene (20.24–29). He was also one of the seven disciples met by the risen Jesus on the seashore (21.2).

17 When Jesus arrived, he found that Lazarusᵇ had already been in the tomb four days. ¹⁸Now Bethany was near Jerusalem, some two milesᵈ away, ¹⁹and many of the Jews had come to Martha and Mary to console them about their brother. ²⁰When Martha heard that Jesus was coming, she went and met him, while Mary stayed at home. ²¹Martha said to Jesus, "Lord, if you had been here, my brother would not have died. ²²But even now I know that God will give you whatever you ask of him." ²³Jesus said to her, "Your brother will rise again." ²⁴Martha said to him, "I know that he will rise again in the resurrection on the last day." ²⁵Jesus said to her, "I am the resurrection and the life.ᵉ Those who believe in me, even though they die, will live, ²⁶and everyone who lives and believes in me will never die. Do you believe this?" ²⁷She said to him, "Yes, Lord, I believe that you are the Messiah,ᶠ the Son of God, the one coming into the world."

28 When she had said this, she went back and called her sister Mary, and told her privately, "The Teacher is here and is calling for you." ²⁹And when she heard it, she got up quickly and went to him. ³⁰Now Jesus had not yet come to the village, but was still at the place where Martha had met him. ³¹The Jews who were with her in the house,

ª Gk *him*   ᵇ Gk *he*   ᶜ Gk *Didymus*   ᵈ Gk *fifteen stadia*   ᵉ Other ancient authorities lack *and the life* ᶠ Or *the Christ* consoling her, saw Mary get up quickly and go out. They followed her because they thought that she was going to the tomb to weep there. 32When Mary came where Jesus was and saw him, she knelt at his feet and said to him, "Lord, if you had been here, my brother would not have died." 33When Jesus saw her weeping, and the Jews who came with her also weeping, he was greatly disturbed in spirit and deeply moved. 34He said, "Where have you laid him?" They said to him, "Lord, come and see." 35Jesus began to weep. 36So the Jews said, "See how he loved him!" 37But some of them said, "Could not he who opened the eyes of the blind man have kept this man from dying?"

38 Then Jesus, again greatly disturbed, came to the tomb. It was a cave, and a stone was lying against it. 39Jesus said, "Take away the stone." Martha, the sister of the dead man, said to him, "Lord, already there is a stench because he has been dead four days." 40Jesus said to her, "Did I not tell you that if you believed, you would see the glory of God?" 41So they took away the stone. And Jesus looked upward and said, "Father, I thank you for having heard me. 42I knew that you always hear me, but I have said this for the sake of the crowd standing here, so that they may believe that you sent me." 43When he had said this, he cried with a loud voice, "Lazarus, come out!" 44The dead man came out, his hands and feet bound with strips of cloth, and his face wrapped in a cloth. Jesus said to them, "Unbind him, and let him go."

11.17–44. 17–27: Jesus and Martha. 17: Jewish custom was to bury on the same day as death. After three days death was believed to be final. 19: *Many of the Jews,* not the Jewish leaders (compare 11.31, 45 and 8.31). Jewish mourning practices were elaborate. 20: Except for visiting the tomb, a family in mourning did not leave home during the first week. Martha must have left the house undetected (see 11.31). 21: *If you had been here* (see 11.4–7, 11–15, 21, 32, 37), Lazarus' death could have been avoided. It had a place in God's purpose (see 11.14–15). 22–27: Many Jews believed in a resurrection (and judgment) on the last day (5.27–29; 6.39, 44, 54; compare Dan 12.2). The "I am" saying affirms that resurrection and life overlap for the believer. For coming *into the world,* see 1.9–

10; 3.19; 17.18; 18.37. **28–37: Mary and Jesus. 31:** *The Jews* followed Mary and became the audience for the meeting of Jesus with Mary. **32:** *Knelt,* expressing petition. **33–36:** Jesus' deep emotional response balances his earlier detachment (11.6–7, 14–15). **38–44: Jesus and Lazarus.** Cave tombs with rolling stone seals were common at this time (compare 20.1). **41–44:** Address to God as *Father* characterizes the prayer of ch. 17 (vv. 1, 5, 11, 21, 24, 25). On binding and wrapping the body, see 20.6–7.

~~~~~~~~~~~~~~~~~~~~~~~~~~~~~~

45 Many of the Jews therefore, who had come with Mary and had seen what Jesus did, believed in him. 46But some of them went to the Pharisees and told them what he had done. 47So the chief priests and the Pharisees called a meeting of the council, and said, "What are we to do? This man is performing many signs. 48If we let him go on like this, everyone will believe in him, and the Romans will come and destroy both our holy place*a* and our nation." 49But one of them, Caiaphas, who was high priest that year, said to them, "You know nothing at all! 50You do not understand that it is better for you to have one man die for the people than to have the whole nation destroyed." 51He did not say this on his own, but being high priest that year he prophesied that Jesus was about to die for the nation, 52and not for the nation only, but to gather into one the dispersed children of God. 53So from that day on they planned to put him to death.

54 Jesus therefore no longer walked about openly among the Jews, but went from there to a town called Ephraim in the region near the wilderness; and he remained there with the disciples.

55 Now the Passover of the Jews was near, and many went up from the country to Jerusalem before the Passover to purify themselves. 56They were looking for Jesus and were asking one another as they stood in the temple, "What do you think? Surely he will not come to the festival, will he?" 57Now the chief priests and the Pharisees had given orders that anyone who knew where Jesus*b* was should let them know, so that they might arrest him.

a Or *our temple;* Greek *our place*   *b* Gk *he*

11.45–57: Consequences. 45: On seeing and believing, see 12.9–11 and compare 2.23. John 11.40 reverses the order. **46–48:** Informers (compare 5.15) reintroduce the Pharisees* (last mentioned in 9.40). Together with the chief priests they constitute the *council (Sanhedrin*),* the highest Jewish authority. The fears of Roman reprisal came to pass in the Roman destruction of Jerusalem in 70 CE. **49–52:** Though subject to the approval of the Roman governor, Caiaphas was high priest from 18 to 36 CE (compare 18.13). As head of the *Sanhedrin,* the high priest was a political and religious leader. *To gather into one* (compare 10.16; 12.32; 17.21, 22) might refer to Diaspora* Jews, or to people from all nations. **53:** The decision now taken was more formal than those of 5.18; 7.1, 19–20, 25; 8.37, 40, 59; 10.31–39. **54:** *Ephraim* might be the town near Bethel mentioned in 2 Sam 13.23; 1 Macc 11.34. **55–57:** *Passover* of the Jews* (compare 2.13; 6.4; 13.1; 18.28). Celebrating the Passover involved purification. Jesus' popularity with the pilgrims to the festival, who *sought* Jesus (compare 7.11), is contrasted with the malicious intent of the rulers and Pharisees who sought informers and plotted to arrest Jesus. This prepares the way for the account of Jesus' entry into Jerusalem (12.12–19).

12 Six days before the Passover Jesus came to Bethany, the home of Lazarus, whom he had raised from the dead. ²There they gave a dinner for him. Martha served, and Lazarus was one of those at the table with him. ³Mary took a pound of costly perfume made of pure nard, anointed Jesus' feet, and wiped them*a* with her hair. The house was filled with the fragrance of the perfume. ⁴But Judas Iscariot, one of his disciples (the one who was about to betray him), said, ⁵"Why was this perfume not sold for three hundred denarii*b* and the money given to the poor?" ⁶(He said this not because he cared about the poor, but because he was a thief; he kept the common purse and used to steal what was put into it.) ⁷Jesus said, "Leave her alone. She bought it*c* so that she might keep it for the day of my burial. ⁸You always have the poor with you, but you do not always have me."

9 When the great crowd of the Jews learned that he was there, they came not only because of Jesus but also to see Lazarus,

whom he had raised from the dead. ¹⁰So the chief priests planned to put Lazarus to death as well, ¹¹since it was on account of him that many of the Jews were deserting and were believing in Jesus.

12 The next day the great crowd that had come to the festival heard that Jesus was coming to Jerusalem. ¹³So they took branches of palm trees and went out to meet him, shouting,

"Hosanna!
 Blessed is the one who comes in
  the name of the Lord—
 the King of Israel!"

¹⁴Jesus found a young donkey and sat on it; as it is written:

15 "Do not be afraid, daughter of Zion.
 Look, your king is coming,
  sitting on a donkey's colt!"

¹⁶His disciples did not understand these things at first; but when Jesus was glorified, then they remembered that these things had been written of him and had been done to him. ¹⁷So the crowd that had been with him when he called Lazarus out of the tomb and raised him from the dead continued to testify.*d* ¹⁸It was also because they heard that he had performed this sign that the crowd went to meet him. ¹⁹The Pharisees then said to one another, "You see, you can do nothing. Look, the world has gone after him!"

12.1–19. 1–8: The anointing* at Bethany (Mk 14.3–9; Lk 7.37–38). **1:** *Passover,** see 11.55–57. *Bethany,* see 11.1. *Lazarus,* see 11.1–44. **2–3:** *Martha, Mary,* see 11.1. They prepared dinner: Martha served, Lazarus reclined with the company, and Mary anointed Jesus' feet. A *pound of . . . nard,* a large amount of perfumed ointment (compare Mk 14.3). **6:** *Common purse,* a money box. **7:** The anointing foreshadows Jesus' death and burial. Mary's anointing Jesus' feet foreshadows the footwashing in 13.1–20. **9–11: The plot against Lazarus** (compare 11.45–53). **9:** *The great crowd,* not the Jewish leaders (see 12.12; 11.19). **10–11:** See the decision to kill Jesus in 11.53. **12–19: The triumphal entry** (Mt 21.1–11; Mk 11.1–

a Gk *his feet* *b* Three hundred denarii would be nearly a year's wages for a laborer *c* Gk lacks *She bought it* *d* Other ancient authorities read *with him began to testify that he had called. . .from the dead*

Jewish Festivals in John's Gospel

John notes several Jewish festivals of which *Passover*★ (*Pesach*), commemorating the Exodus, on the fifteenth day of the month *Nisan* (March or April), is easily the most important (2.13, 23; 4.45; 6.4; 11.55; 12.1, 12, 20; 13.1, 29; 18.28, 39; 19.14). The majority of Passover references are associated directly or indirectly with the death of Jesus. According to John, Jesus died as the Passover lambs were slain. Other festivals mentioned are "Booths" or "Tabernacles" (*Sukkoth*) in October (7.1–14, 37); Dedication (*Hanukkah*), in December (10.22); and an unnamed festival (5.1). The festivals help to shape the structure of the Gospel and provide a rationale for Jesus' frequent visits to Jerusalem. The narrator refers to these as festivals *of the Jews*; (2.13; 5.1; 6.4; 7.2; 11.55; 19.42). Jesus, as a Jew, observes the festivals.

11; Lk 19.28–40). **12:** *The great crowd:* As many as 100,000 pilgrims came to the festival of Passover. *The next day* suggests that it might include the great crowd of vv. 9–11. **13:** Palm branches were symbols of national triumph and victory (2 Macc 10.7; 1 Macc 13.51). Psalm 118.25–26 is used at major festivals. *Hosanna*★ is a cry for help, "Save us." God and king in the quotation suggest a messianic★ understanding of *the King of Israel*. **14–15:** Zech 9.9. **16:** *When Jesus was glorified*, Jesus' departure to the Father was an act of revelation. **17–18:** The crowds of 12.9 and 12.12 overlap. **19:** The fears expressed by the Pharisees,★ *The world has gone after him!*, perhaps foreshadow the gentile★ mission (see 12.20–26).

20 Now among those who went up to worship at the festival were some Greeks. 21They came to Philip, who was from Bethsaida in Galilee, and said to him, "Sir, we wish to see Jesus." 22Philip went and told Andrew; then Andrew and Philip went and told Jesus. 23Jesus answered them, "The hour has come for the Son of Man to be glorified. 24Very truly, I tell you, unless a grain of wheat falls into the earth and dies, it remains just a single grain; but if it dies, it bears much fruit. 25Those who love their life lose it, and those who hate their life in this world will keep it for eternal life. 26Whoever serves me must follow me, and where I am, there will my servant be also. Whoever serves me, the Father will honor.

27 "Now my soul is troubled. And what should I say—'Father, save me from this hour'? No, it is for this reason that I have come to this hour. 28Father, glorify your name." Then a voice came from heaven, "I have glorified it, and I will glorify it again." 29The crowd standing there heard it and said that it was thunder. Others said, "An angel has spoken to him." 30Jesus answered, "This voice has come for your sake, not for mine. 31Now is the judgment of this world; now the ruler of this world will be driven out. 32And I, when I am lifted up from the earth, will draw all people*ᵃ* to myself." 33He said this to indicate the kind of death he was to die. 34The crowd answered him, "We have heard from the law that the Messiah*ᵇ* remains forever. How can you say that the Son of Man must be lifted up? Who is this Son of Man?" 35Jesus said to them, "The light is with you for a little longer. Walk while you have the light, so that the darkness may not overtake you. If you walk in the darkness, you do not know where you are going. 36While you have the light, believe in the light, so that you may become children of light."

12.20–36a. 20–26: Unfulfilled quest. Some Greeks seek Jesus, foreshadowing the mission to the nations or Diaspora★ Jews (see 7.35–36). **21–22:** *Philip* (see 1.43, 44) and *Andrew* (see 1.40–41) link Jesus' first disciples to this new mission. **23:** The *hour* of Jesus' glorification, his death and return to the Father (12.27–28, 31–33; contrast 2.4; 7.6, 30; 8.20) has now arrived. **24–26:** Abundant life-giving through

a Other ancient authorities read *all things*   *b* Or *the Christ* death interprets both Jesus' death and the service of the disciples (see 13.14–16; 15.18–21). **27–36a: Words overheard by the crowd: another Gospel summary.** Contrast the Gethsemane setting of Mk 14.33–36. Jesus affirms the Father's will as the hour of his death arrives. **31:** *The ruler of this world,* the devil (compare 14.30; 16.11) is *driven out,* a cosmic exorcism. **32:** *Lifted up* is a reference to Jesus' death (12.34) and ascent to the Father (3.14; 8.28); he will *draw all people* (see 6.44 and Jer 38.3). **34:** *The law,* scripture (compare10.34; 15.25). *The messiah* remains for ever* (see Ps 89.3–4, 19–21, 28–29, 35–37; 110.4; Isa 9.6–7; Dan 7.13–14). **35–36a:** *The light is with you a little longer* (see 7.33) signals the approaching darkness. The opportunity for belief was short.

After Jesus had said this, he departed and hid from them. 37Although he had performed so many signs in their presence, they did not believe in him. 38This was to fulfill the word spoken by the prophet Isaiah:

"Lord, who has believed our message,
    and to whom has the arm of the Lord
        been revealed?"
39And so they could not believe, because Isaiah also said,
40 "He has blinded their eyes
    and hardened their heart,
 so that they might not look with their
        eyes,
    and understand with their heart and
        turn—
    and I would heal them."
41Isaiah said this because*a* he saw his glory and spoke about him. 42Nevertheless many, even of the authorities, believed in him. But because of the Pharisees they did not confess it, for fear that they would be put out of the synagogue; 43for they loved human glory more than the glory that comes from God.

44 Then Jesus cried aloud: "Whoever believes in me believes not in me but in him who sent me. 45And whoever sees me sees him who sent me. 46I have come as light into the world, so that everyone who believes in me should not remain in the darkness. 47I do not judge anyone who hears my words and does not keep them, for I came not to judge the world, but to save the world. 48The one who rejects me and does not receive my

word has a judge; on the last day the word that I have spoken will serve as judge, 49for I have not spoken on my own, but the Father who sent me has himself given me a commandment about what to say and what to speak. 50And I know that his commandment is eternal life. What I speak, therefore, I speak just as the Father has told me."

12.36b–50. 36b–43: Summary concerning unbelief. 36b–37: Jesus withdrew and *hid* (compare 7.10; 8.59; 11.54) because the power of darkness was already at work. Elsewhere those who see *signs* believe (2.11, 23; 20.31); here, in spite of *many signs, they did not believe* (but see 12.42). **38–40:** Isa 53.1, Isa 6.10 (used in Mk 4.12) explain unbelief. The prince of this world has blinded them (compare 2 Cor 4.4; 1 Jn 2.11) to prevent God from healing them. **41:** Patriarchs and prophets* seeing Jesus and his time is found also in Jn 8.56–58. **42–43:** Exceptions to unbelief are Nicodemus (3.1–15; 7.48–52; 19.39) and Joseph of Arimathea (19.38). *Glory,* praise or approval by people or by God (compare 5.41–44). **44–50: Summary conclusion concerning signs, belief, and judgment.** Jesus solemnly summarizes (*he cried out and said,* compare 7.37) his public ministry. Belief in him is related to the one who sent him. Believers come out of the darkness, become children of light (12.36), and have eternal life.

THE TESTAMENT OF JESUS

13.1–17.26: The way of the incarnate Word with *his own.* Jesus' last words are his "testament" to his disciples, similar to Gen 48–49 and later works containing warnings and promises based on those chapters, like *The Testaments of the Twelve Patriarchs.** Jesus' testament comes during the last meal shared with his disciples, on the eve of Passover.* Jesus died the next day at the moment the Passover lambs were being slain.

13 Now before the festival of the Passover, Jesus knew that his hour had come to depart from this world and go to the Father. Having loved his own who were in the world, he loved them to the end. 2The devil had already put it into the heart of Judas son of Simon Iscariot to betray him. And during supper 3Jesus, knowing that the Father had given all things into his hands, and

a Other ancient witnesses read *when*

that he had come from God and was going to God, ⁴got up from the table,ᵃ took off his outer robe, and tied a towel around himself. ⁵Then he poured water into a basin and began to wash the disciples' feet and to wipe them with the towel that was tied around him. ⁶He came to Simon Peter, who said to him, "Lord, are you going to wash my feet?" ⁷Jesus answered, "You do not know now what I am doing, but later you will understand." ⁸Peter said to him, "You will never wash my feet." Jesus answered, "Unless I wash you, you have no share with me." ⁹Simon Peter said to him, "Lord, not my feet only but also my hands and my head!" ¹⁰Jesus said to him, "One who has bathed does not need to wash, except for the feet,ᵇ but is entirely clean. And youᶜ are clean, though not all of you." ¹¹For he knew who was to betray him; for this reason he said, "Not all of you are clean."

12 After he had washed their feet, had put on his robe, and had returned to the table, he said to them, "Do you know what I have done to you? ¹³You call me Teacher and Lord—and you are right, for that is what I am. ¹⁴So if I, your Lord and Teacher, have washed your feet, you also ought to wash one another's feet. ¹⁵For I have set you an example, that you also should do as I have done to you. ¹⁶Very truly, I tell you, servantsᵈ are not greater than their master, nor are messengers greater than the one who sent them. ¹⁷If you know these things, you are blessed if you do them. ¹⁸I am not speaking of all of you; I know whom I have chosen. But it is to fulfill the scripture, 'The one who ate my breadᵉ has lifted his heel against me.' ¹⁹I tell you this now, before it occurs, so that when it does occur, you may believe that I am he.ᶠ ²⁰Very truly, I tell you, whoever receives one whom I send receives me; and whoever receives me receives him who sent me."

own, ultimately, all believers. **2–3:** The narrator has already identified Judas as the betrayer (6.70–71). Jesus remains in control; his return to the Father is part of the divine plan (compare 16.28). **4–5:** *Wash the . . . feet*, normal hospitality after a journey, but usually performed by a slave or disciple. **6–11:** *You are clean* (see 15.3; 17.17, 19), but not Judas (see 6.64, 70–71; 13.2, 26–30; 17.12). **12–20: Interpreting the footwashing** as an enactment of the love command (13.34; 15.12–13). The *example* of the greater serving the less makes the command more forceful (13.34; 15.12; 17.18; 20.21). **18–20:** The treachery of Judas, forcefully portrayed at the meal that Jesus hosts (compare 13.10–11), is further emphasized by *scripture* (Psalm 41.9 and see Jn 13.26). *I am,* see note f. Here Jesus affirms he is the one sent by the Father.

21 After saying this Jesus was troubled in spirit, and declared, "Very truly, I tell you, one of you will betray me." ²²The disciples looked at one another, uncertain of whom he was speaking. ²³One of his disciples—the one whom Jesus loved—was reclining next to him; ²⁴Simon Peter therefore motioned to him to ask Jesus of whom he was speaking. ²⁵So while reclining next to Jesus, he asked him, "Lord, who is it?" ²⁶Jesus answered, "It is the one to whom I give this piece of bread when I have dipped it in the dish."ᵍ So when he had dipped the piece of bread, he gave it to Judas son of Simon Iscariot.ʰ ²⁷After he received the piece of bread,ⁱ Satan entered into him. Jesus said to him, "Do quickly what you are going to do." ²⁸Now no one at the table knew why he said this to him. ²⁹Some thought that, because Judas had the common purse, Jesus was telling him, "Buy what we need for the festival"; or, that he should give something to the poor. ³⁰So, after receiving the piece of bread, he immediately went out. And it was night.

31 When he had gone out, Jesus said, "Now the Son of Man has been glorified, and God has been glorified in him. ³²If God has

---

13.1–14.31: The first discourse and its setting. 13.1–11: Setting: The footwashing replaces the Lord's supper found at this meal in the other Gospels (compare Mt 26.17–30; Mk 14.12–26; Lk 22.7–23). Jesus' loving service is their example and motivation. **1:** *Before the festival,* the day before *Passover.** *To the end,* completely and until death (see 13.34; 15.12–13). *His* been glorified in him,^a God will also glorify him in himself and will glorify him at once. ³³Little children, I am with you only a little longer. You will look for me; and as I said to the Jews so now I say to you, 'Where I am going, you cannot come.' ³⁴I give you a new commandment, that you love one another. Just as I have loved you, you also should love one another. ³⁵By this everyone will know that you are my disciples, if you have love for one another."

36 Simon Peter said to him, "Lord, where are you going?" Jesus answered, "Where I am going, you cannot follow me now; but you will follow afterward." ³⁷Peter said to him, "Lord, why can I not follow you now? I will lay down my life for you." ³⁸Jesus answered, "Will you lay down your life for me? Very truly, I tell you, before the cock crows, you will have denied me three times.

13.21–38. 21–30: Betrayal foretold. Jesus is *troubled* a second time (compare 12.27). This is the first appearance of *the disciple whom Jesus loved* (see 19.26–27; 20.1–10; 21.7, 20–24). Peter needs his help. *Next to him,* literally "in his bosom" as Jesus was in the bosom of the Father (compare 1.18). *It was night:* Judas went out into the darkness (see 3.2; 9.4; 11.10; in the light of 1.4–5; 3.19–21; 8.12; 12.35–36) and his fate was sealed. **31–38: The meaning of Jesus' death and departure. 31–32:** See 12.23, 28; 17.1, 4–5; 1.14–18. **33:** *A little while,* see 7.33. *As I said to the Jews,* see 7.34–35; 8.21. He does not tell the disciples, "you will die in your sins" but *you will follow afterwards.* **34–35:** The new commandment (13.1; 15.12–13): They are to *love one another* (not, here, neighbors or enemies). **36–37:** Jesus gives his life for them, not the reverse as Peter affirms (see 13.6–10; compare 10.11, 15, 17–18; 15.13–14). **38:** The boast of 13.37 meets Jesus' prediction of the threefold denial (see 18.15–18, 25–27), which elicits the threefold word of restoration in the epilogue (21.15–19).

---

14 "Do not let your hearts be troubled. Believe^b in God, believe also in me. ²In my Father's house there are many dwelling places. If it were not so, would I have told you that I go to prepare a place for you?^c ³And if I go and prepare a place for you, I will come again and will take you to myself, so that where I am, there you may be also.

⁴And you know the way to the place where I am going."^d ⁵Thomas said to him, "Lord, we do not know where you are going. How can we know the way?" ⁶Jesus said to him, "I am the way, and the truth, and the life. No one comes to the Father except through me. ⁷If you know me, you will know^e my Father also. From now on you do know him and have seen him."

8 Philip said to him, "Lord, show us the Father, and we will be satisfied." ⁹Jesus said to him, "Have I been with you all this time, Philip, and you still do not know me? Whoever has seen me has seen the Father. How can you say, 'Show us the Father'? ¹⁰Do you not believe that I am in the Father and the Father is in me? The words that I say to you I do not speak on my own; but the Father who dwells in me does his works. ¹¹Believe me that I am in the Father and the Father is in me; but if you do not, then believe me because of the works themselves. ¹²Very truly, I tell you, the one who believes in me will also do the works that I do and, in fact, will do greater works than these, because I am going to the Father. ¹³I will do whatever you ask in my name, so that the Father may be glorified in the Son. ¹⁴If in my name you ask me^f for anything, I will do it.

15 "If you love me, you will keep^g my commandments. ¹⁶And I will ask the Father, and he will give you another Advocate,^h to be with you forever. ¹⁷This is the Spirit of truth, whom the world cannot receive, because it neither sees him nor knows him. You know him, because he abides with you, and he will be inⁱ you.

14.1–17. 1–14: Jesus the way to the Father. 1: An assurance forms an inclusio,* a passage defined by beginning and ending with the same word or phrase (see 14.27), *Do not let your hearts be troubled.* **2–3:** *I will come again,* a reference to a parousia* or second com-

---

a Other ancient authorities lack *If God has been glorified in him* b Or *You believe* c Or *If it were not so, I would have told you; for I go to prepare a place for you* d Other ancient authorities read *Where I am going you know, and the way you know* e Other ancient authorities read *If you had known me, you would have known* f Other ancient authorities lack *me* g Other ancient authorities read *me, keep* h Or *Helper* i Or *among* ing. **4–11: Misunderstanding of the way.** In Judaism the law is *the way* to God (compare Acts 9.2; 22.4; 24.14) and *the truth* (compare 1.14; 6.55; 8.31–32; 17.17; 18.37). As the way to the Father, Jesus was the life-giving truth (see 6.35, 48; 11.25). **8–10:** Jesus' central message is his relation to the Father. **13–14:** *In my name,* the request should be consistent with the character of Jesus. **15–17: The Spirit Paraclete promised to believers.** The Father, at the Son's request, gives the *Advocate* ("Paraclete," Comforter or Helper, a title used of the Spirit here and in 14.26; 15.26; 16.7, of Jesus in 1 Jn 2.1); he takes the place of Jesus. He is also called *Spirit of truth* (15.26; 16.13). Where the presence of the earthly Jesus (the incarnate Word) was temporary, the presence of the *Advocate* is *forever*.

18 "I will not leave you orphaned; I am coming to you. ¹⁹In a little while the world will no longer see me, but you will see me; because I live, you also will live. ²⁰On that day you will know that I am in my Father, and you in me, and I in you. ²¹They who have my commandments and keep them are those who love me; and those who love me will be loved by my Father, and I will love them and reveal myself to them." ²²Judas (not Iscariot) said to him, "Lord, how is it that you will reveal yourself to us, and not to the world?" ²³Jesus answered him, "Those who love me will keep my word, and my Father will love them, and we will come to them and make our home with them. ²⁴Whoever does not love me does not keep my words; and the word that you hear is not mine, but is from the Father who sent me.

25 "I have said these things to you while I am still with you. ²⁶But the Advocate,ᵃ the Holy Spirit, whom the Father will send in my name, will teach you everything, and remind you of all that I have said to you. ²⁷Peace I leave with you; my peace I give to you. I do not give to you as the world gives. Do not let your hearts be troubled, and do not let them be afraid. ²⁸You heard me say to you, 'I am going away, and I am coming to you.' If you loved me, you would rejoice that I am going to the Father, because the Father is greater than I. ²⁹And now I have told you this before it occurs, so that when it does occur, you may believe. ³⁰I will no longer talk much with you, for the ruler of this world is com-

ing. He has no power over me; ³¹but I do as the Father has commanded me, so that the world may know that I love the Father. Rise, let us be on our way.

14.18–31. 18–24: Jesus' presence promised to the believers. Jesus also promises his return (14.3, 28). Absent from the world (compare 7.33) he is present to his disciples through the Spirit. *Judas, not Iscariot:* Judas (Jude), after the Maccabean hero, was a popular name. **25–26: The Spirit as teacher** (compare 14.16–17; 15.26–27; 16.12–15; contrast 16.7–11). Jesus' partial teaching is contrasted with the complete teaching of the Spirit (16.12–15). The Spirit is given by the Father at Jesus' request (14.16), sent by the Father in Jesus' name (14.26), sent by Jesus from the Father (15.26), sent by Jesus (16.7). **27–31: Conclusion of first discourse.** Jesus' encounter with *the ruler of this world* marks the beginning of the crisis (see 12.31; 16.11; compare 13.2, 27). The discourse apparently ends when Jesus says *"Rise,"* but they do not depart until 18.1.

15 "I am the true vine, and my Father is the vinegrower. ²He removes every branch in me that bears no fruit. Every branch that bears fruit he prunesᵇ to make it bear more fruit. ³You have already been cleansedᵇ by the word that I have spoken to you. ⁴Abide in me as I abide in you. Just as the branch cannot bear fruit by itself unless it abides in the vine, neither can you unless you abide in me. ⁵I am the vine, you are the branches. Those who abide in me and I in them bear much fruit, because apart from me you can do nothing. ⁶Whoever does not abide in me is thrown away like a branch and withers; such branches are gathered, thrown into the fire, and burned. ⁷If you abide in me, and my words abide in you, ask for whatever you wish, and it will be done for you. ⁸My Father is glorified by this, that you bear much fruit and becomeᶜ my disciples. ⁹As the Father has loved me, so I have loved you; abide in my love. ¹⁰If you keep my commandments, you will abide in my love, just as I have kept my Father's commandments and abide in his love. ¹¹I have said these

a Or *Helper*   *b* The same Greek root refers to pruning and cleansing   *c* Or *be* things to you so that my joy may be in you, and that your joy may be complete.

12 "This is my commandment, that you love one another as I have loved you. 13 No one has greater love than this, to lay down one's life for one's friends. 14 You are my friends if you do what I command you. 15 I do not call you servants*a* any longer, because the servant*b* does not know what the master is doing; but I have called you friends, because I have made known to you everything that I have heard from my Father. 16 You did not choose me but I chose you. And I appointed you to go and bear fruit, fruit that will last, so that the Father will give you whatever you ask him in my name. 17 I am giving you these commands so that you may love one another.

15.1–16.4a: **Second elaboration of the discourse. 1–6: The vine** (Ps 80.8–16; Isa 5.1–7; 27.2–6; Jer 2.21). Jesus, not Israel, is the true vine, God's vine. Pruning symbolizes cleansing (see note *b*, p. 1823, and 13.10; 17.17, 19). **7–10:** *Abide in*, love and obey. The disciples' abiding in Jesus is patterned on Jesus' abiding in the Father. **11–17:** *These things*, the commandments (v. 10) become one commandment (v. 12; see 15.14, 17; 13.34–35).

---

18 "If the world hates you, be aware that it hated me before it hated you. 19 If you belonged to the world,*c* the world would love you as its own. Because you do not belong to the world, but I have chosen you out of the world—therefore the world hates you. 20 Remember the word that I said to you, 'Servants*d* are not greater than their master.' If they persecuted me, they will persecute you; if they kept my word, they will keep yours also. 21 But they will do all these things to you on account of my name, because they do not know him who sent me. 22 If I had not come and spoken to them, they would not have sin; but now they have no excuse for their sin. 23 Whoever hates me hates my Father also. 24 If I had not done among them the works that no one else did, they would not have sin. But now they have seen and hated both me and my Father. 25 It was to fulfill the word that is written in their law, 'They hated me without a cause.'

26 "When the Advocate*e* comes, whom I will send to you from the Father, the Spirit of truth who comes from the Father, he will testify on my behalf. 27 You also are to testify because you have been with me from the beginning.

16 "I have said these things to you to keep you from stumbling. 2 They will put you out of the synagogues. Indeed, an hour is coming when those who kill you will think that by doing so they are offering worship to God. 3 And they will do this because they have not known the Father or me. 4 But I have said these things to you so that when their hour comes you may remember that I told you about them.

15.18–16.4a: The *world*, humanity in its rejection of God and the one whom he sent (1.10–11; 5.23, 42–44; 7.28). Satan is *the ruler of this world* (12.31; 14.30; 16.11; 1 Jn 5.19); neither Jesus nor the disciples belong to it (3.31; 8.23; 17.14–16; compare 1 Jn 4.5–6), yet God loved it (3.16). The world's hatred arises from ignorance that comes from disobedience. Jesus quotes Ps 35.19; 69.4. *Their law*, scripture; not rejection of Jewish scripture but an assertion of Jesus' innocence according to the scriptures of those who hated him (see 10.34). **26–27:** The Spirit foreshadows the work of 16.7–15. *He will testify* (see 16.13) extends the metaphor* of the law court. *You also are to testify*, see 9.17, 25, 30, 33. For inspired testimony under persecution, see Mk 13.11. **16.1–4a:** To be *put out of the synagogues** echoes 9.22, 34; 12.42. *The hour is coming* (see 16.25) warns in detail of a future time of persecution for believers.

THIRD PRESENTATION OF THE DISCOURSE

16.4b–33: Although the discourse continues, this marks a new beginning.

"I did not say these things to you from the beginning, because I was with you. 5 But now I am going to him who sent me; yet none of you asks me, 'Where are you going?' 6 But because I have said these things to you, sorrow has filled your hearts. 7 Nevertheless I tell you the truth: it is to your advantage that

a Gk *slaves*   *b* Gk *slave*   *c* Gk *were of the world*
d Gk *Slaves*   *e* Or *Helper*

I go away, for if I do not go away, the Advocate* will not come to you; but if I go, I will send him to you. 8And when he comes, he will prove the world wrong about* sin and righteousness and judgment: 9about sin, because they do not believe in me; 10about righteousness, because I am going to the Father and you will see me no longer; 11about judgment, because the ruler of this world has been condemned.

16.4b–11. 4b–6: Jesus returns to the theme of his departure (see 14.1–8). Earlier Thomas asked where Jesus was going (14.5), and Peter had already asked, *Lord, where are you going?* (13.36). Here Jesus complains that *none of you asks me, "Where are you going?"* (16.5). Jesus had previously assured them he would not leave them *orphaned* (14.18). Here he stresses the expediency of his departure. **7–11: The Advocate and the world.** Jesus' departure is the means by which he is able to send the *Advocate* (see 14.16, 17, 26), either Jesus' renewed presence in the Spirit (14.18–19, 23) or the one who takes Jesus' place. In relation to the world the Advocate performs three tasks: (a) *He will prove the world wrong,* that is, convict by exposing. Just as the coming of the light exposed the sin of the world (3.19–21), so does the coming of the *Advocate.* (b) He will vindicate the *righteousness* of Jesus. (c) He will judge the world, a *judgment* (see 3.17–21; 5.24; 12.47–48) revealed when *the ruler of this world is condemned,* judged, cast out (see 12.31; 14.30).

12 "I still have many things to say to you, but you cannot bear them now. 13When the Spirit of truth comes, he will guide you into all the truth; for he will not speak on his own, but will speak whatever he hears, and he will declare to you the things that are to come. 14He will glorify me, because he will take what is mine and declare it to you. 15All that the Father has is mine. For this reason I said that he will take what is mine and declare it to you.

16 "A little while, and you will no longer see me, and again a little while, and you will see me." 17Then some of his disciples said to one another, "What does he mean by saying to us, 'A little while, and you will no longer see me, and again a little while, and you will see me'; and 'Because I am going to the Father'?" 18They said, "What does he

mean by this 'a little while'? We do not know what he is talking about." 19Jesus knew that they wanted to ask him, so he said to them, "Are you discussing among yourselves what I meant when I said, 'A little while, and you will no longer see me, and again a little while, and you will see me'? 20Very truly, I tell you, you will weep and mourn, but the world will rejoice; you will have pain, but your pain will turn into joy. 21When a woman is in labor, she has pain, because her hour has come. But when her child is born, she no longer remembers the anguish because of the joy of having brought a human being into the world. 22So you have pain now; but I will see you again, and your hearts will rejoice, and no one will take your joy from you. 23On that day you will ask nothing of me.* Very truly, I tell you, if you ask anything of the Father in my name, he will give it to you.* 24Until now you have not asked for anything in my name. Ask and you will receive, so that your joy may be complete.

16.12–15: The Spirit of truth and believers. Compare 14.17; 15.25–26. The Spirit teaches what the disciples were not ready to learn from Jesus, leading them into all the truth. Jesus is the source; the teaching is *whatever* [the Spirit] *hears* (compare Jesus in 8.26–28; 12.49; 14.10; 15.15; 17.7–8) and is dependent on Jesus. **16–24: The pain of loss will turn to joy.** *A little while,* both until his departure by death and from his death until his resurrection appearances and perhaps until his presence in the Spirit. *Going to the Father,* see 16.5, 10. **21:** *In labor . . . pain,* a metaphor* for times of trouble (Isa 13.8; 21.3; 26.17; Mic 4.9), especially eschatological* or end times (Mk 13.8; 1 Thess 5.3; Rev 12.1–6). **22:** *I will see you again,* at the resurrection (14.19–20). **23–24:** *On that day* the disciples will stand in a direct relation to God. **24:** Compare 14.13–14; 15.11, 16.

25 "I have said these things to you in figures of speech. The hour is coming when I will no longer speak to you in figures, but will tell you plainly of the Father. 26On that day you will ask in my name. I do not say to you that I will ask the Father on your behalf;

a Or *Helper*   *b* Or *convict the world of*   *c* Or *will ask me no question*   *d* Other ancient authorities read *Father, he will give it to you in my name*

²⁷for the Father himself loves you, because you have loved me and have believed that I came from God.ᵃ ²⁸I came from the Father and have come into the world; again, I am leaving the world and am going to the Father."

29 His disciples said, "Yes, now you are speaking plainly, not in any figure of speech! ³⁰Now we know that you know all things, and do not need to have anyone question you; by this we believe that you came from God." ³¹Jesus answered them, "Do you now believe? ³²The hour is coming, indeed it has come, when you will be scattered, each one to his home, and you will leave me alone. Yet I am not alone because the Father is with me. ³³I have said this to you, so that in me you may have peace. In the world you face persecution. But take courage; I have conquered the world!"

16.25–33: Peace in the midst of persecution. 25–28: *Figures of speech,* or parables* (see 10.6), are in contrast with plain speech (see 16.29). *The hour is coming* (contrast 16.2), a reference to *that day* (16.23, 26; see 14.20). Three things occur on that day: no more riddles but plain speech; direct asking of the Father in Jesus' name; and Jesus' return to the Father. **29–33:** The disciples affirm *that day* to be *now*. Jesus puts the affirmation of faith into question: This is not that day but the hour of testing (see 16.2). *You will be scattered,* see Zech 13.7; Mk 14.27, 50. The warning prepares the disciples for the test (see 13.19; 16.1, 4a). The third presentation of the discourse begins and ends with forewarning. Its purpose is to give *peace* (see 14.27) in the face of *persecution* (see 15.18–16.4a).

JESUS' GREAT DECLARATORY PRAYER

17.1–26: This passage sums up his teaching. It elaborates aspects of the prayer Jesus taught his disciples (Mt 6.9–13; Lk 11.2–4). The prayer for the mission focuses first on Jesus, then on the disciples, and finally on those who believe through the word of the disciples. Each depends on the one before it: Jesus is the foundation.

---

17 After Jesus had spoken these words, he looked up to heaven and said, "Father, the hour has come; glorify your Son so that the Son may glorify you, ²since you have given him authority over all people,ᵇ to give eternal life to all whom you have given him. ³And this is eternal life, that they may know you, the only true God, and Jesus Christ whom you have sent. ⁴I glorified you on earth by finishing the work that you gave me to do. ⁵So now, Father, glorify me in your own presence with the glory that I had in your presence before the world existed.

6 "I have made your name known to those whom you gave me from the world. They were yours, and you gave them to me, and they have kept your word. ⁷Now they know that everything you have given me is from you; ⁸for the words that you gave to me I have given to them, and they have received them and know in truth that I came from you; and they have believed that you sent me. ⁹I am asking on their behalf; I am not asking on behalf of the world, but on behalf of those whom you gave me, because they are yours. ¹⁰All mine are yours, and yours are mine; and I have been glorified in them. ¹¹And now I am no longer in the world, but they are in the world, and I am coming to you. Holy Father, protect them in your name that you have given me, so that they may be one, as we are one. ¹²While I was with them, I protected them in your name thatᶜ you have given me. I guarded them, and not one of them was lost except the one destined to be lost,ᵈ so that the scripture might be fulfilled. ¹³But now I am coming to you, and I speak these things in the world so that they may have my joy made complete in themselves.ᵉ ¹⁴I have given them your word, and the world has hated them because they do not belong to the world, just as I do not belong to the world. ¹⁵I am not asking you to take them out of the world, but I ask you to protect them from the evil one.ᶠ ¹⁶They do not belong to the world, just as I do not belong to the world. ¹⁷Sanctify them in the truth; your word is truth. ¹⁸As you have sent me into the world, so I have sent them into the world. ¹⁹And for their sakes I sanctify my-

a Other ancient authorities read *the Father*
b Gk *flesh*   *c* Other ancient authorities read *protected in your name those whom*   *d* Gk *except the son of destruction*   *e* Or *among themselves*   *f* Or *from evil*

self, so that they also may be sanctified in truth."

17.1–19. 1–5: Jesus' mission. This begins and concludes with petitions to God as *Father*. Jesus *glorified* (revealed) the Father by doing his will. Now everything depends on God's revealing himself in and through Jesus' death (12.23; 13.31–32). *Authority* (see 3.35; 5.20) is expressed in giving *eternal life* (see 6.37–39; 10.29). Knowing, like believing, is the way to eternal life (compare 17.8 and 25; see 3.16; 5.24; 20.31). Jesus had *finished the work* (see 4.34; 5.36) and now asked to return to his former glory. **6–19: The disciples' mission. 6–11a:** The opening declares what Jesus revealed to his disciples, establishes their belonging to both Jesus and the Father, affirms that *they have kept your word*, and recognizes that Jesus' departure leaves the disciples in the world. **11b:** Jesus prays not for the world (17.9) but for the integrity of the disciples in the world. *Holy Father* (compare *Righteous Father* in 17.25) expresses the concern that the disciples be kept from corruption (see 17.17). Jesus' sanctification is the basis of the disciples' sanctification (17.19). **12–13:** *Joy,* in the context of tribulation in the world, is the objective (see 15.11). **14–17:** The word in the world provokes hatred, whether toward Jesus or the disciples (see 8.23, 39–59; 9.22, 34; 15.18–16.4a). *Protect them from the evil one* and *sanctify them* recalls the Lord's Prayer (Mt 6.9 13). **18–19:** The disciples' mission is enabled by Jesus' sanctifying word and work.

20 "I ask not only on behalf of these, but also on behalf of those who will believe in me through their word, ²¹that they may all be one. As you, Father, are in me and I am in you, may they also be in us,ᵃ so that the world may believe that you have sent me. ²²The glory that you have given me I have given them, so that they may be one, as we are one, ²³I in them and you in me, that they may become completely one, so that the world may know that you have sent me and have loved them even as you have loved me. ²⁴Father, I desire that those also, whom you have given me, may be with me where I am, to see my glory, which you have given me because you loved me before the foundation of the world.

25 "Righteous Father, the world does not know you, but I know you; and these know that you have sent me. ²⁶I made your name

known to them, and I will make it known, so that the love with which you have loved me may be in them, and I in them."

17.20–26. 20–23: The mission of subsequent believers. 20: The Gospel has prepared the way for belief through the word of the disciples (see 1.35–51; 4.39; 20.29). **21–23:** The prayer for unity aims to continue the revelation from the Father in the Son to the disciples and on to those who heard them. Jesus asks *that they may be one* with the Father and the Son, united in belief, knowledge, and love. **24–26: The final petitions.** Jesus requests that the disciples may *see* and share the *glory* which he had before creation (see 17.5). *Righteous Father* expresses confidence in the love of the Father for the Son which is to be in the believers. Assurance is important because *the world does not know you* (1.10–11; 7.28; 15.18–16.4a; 17.14–16). The twofold mission witnesses to Jesus as the one sent by the Father and makes the love of the Father present in the lives of those who believe.

THE REJECTION AND GLORIFICATION OF THE INCARNATE WORD

18.1–19.42: The arrest, trial and crucifixion of Jesus.

18 After Jesus had spoken these words, he went out with his disciples across the Kidron valley to a place where there was a garden, which he and his disciples entered. ²Now Judas, who betrayed him, also knew the place, because Jesus often met there with his disciples. ³So Judas brought a detachment of soldiers together with police from the chief priests and the Pharisees, and they came there with lanterns and torches and weapons. ⁴Then Jesus, knowing all that was to happen to him, came forward and asked them, "Whom are you looking for?" ⁵They answered, "Jesus of Nazareth."ᵇ Jesus replied, "I am he."ᶜ Judas, who betrayed him, was standing with them. ⁶When Jesusᵈ said to them, "I am he,"ᵉ they stepped back and fell to the ground. ⁷Again he asked them, "Whom are you looking for?" And they said, "Jesus of Nazareth."ᵇ ⁸Jesus answered, "I told you that I am he.ᶜ So if you are look-

a Other ancient authorities read *be one in us*
b Gk *the Nazorean*   c Gk *I am*   d Gk *he*

ing for me, let these men go." 9This was to fulfill the word that he had spoken, "I did not lose a single one of those whom you gave me." 10Then Simon Peter, who had a sword, drew it, struck the high priest's slave, and cut off his right ear. The slave's name was Malchus. 11Jesus said to Peter, "Put your sword back into its sheath. Am I not to drink the cup that the Father has given me?"

12 So the soldiers, their officer, and the Jewish police arrested Jesus and bound him. 13First they took him to Annas, who was the father-in-law of Caiaphas, the high priest that year. 14Caiaphas was the one who had advised the Jews that it was better to have one person die for the people.

15 Simon Peter and another disciple followed Jesus. Since that disciple was known to the high priest, he went with Jesus into the courtyard of the high priest, 16but Peter was standing outside at the gate. So the other disciple, who was known to the high priest, went out, spoke to the woman who guarded the gate, and brought Peter in. 17The woman said to Peter, "You are not also one of this man's disciples, are you?" He said, "I am not." 18Now the slaves and the police had made a charcoal fire because it was cold, and they were standing around it and warming themselves. Peter also was standing with them and warming himself.

19 Then the high priest questioned Jesus about his disciples and about his teaching. 20Jesus answered, "I have spoken openly to the world; I have always taught in synagogues and in the temple, where all the Jews come together. I have said nothing in secret. 21Why do you ask me? Ask those who heard what I said to them; they know what I said." 22When he had said this, one of the police standing nearby struck Jesus on the face, saying, "Is that how you answer the high priest?" 23Jesus answered, "If I have spoken wrongly, testify to the wrong. But if I have spoken rightly, why do you strike me?" 24Then Annas sent him bound to Caiaphas the high priest.

25 Now Simon Peter was standing and warming himself. They asked him, "You are not also one of his disciples, are you?" He denied it and said, "I am not." 26One of the slaves of the high priest, a relative of the man whose ear Peter had cut off, asked, "Did I not see you in the garden with him?" 27Again Peter denied it, and at that moment the cock crowed.

18.1–27. 1–11: Betrayal and arrest. 1–3: The action resumes from 13.31. *The Kidron valley,* east of Jerusalem, separates the city from the Mount of Olives which, during Passover,* counted as part of the city. *Detachment,* a cohort, normally 600 Roman soldiers; it is unlikely that a full cohort is intended. Only in this Gospel are Pharisees* and Roman soldiers involved in the arrest of Jesus (contrast Mk 14.43–50). **4–8:** Jesus, *knowing* (see 13.1, 3; 19.28), remains in control at his arrest. **9:** Extraordinarily, the fulfillment formula is not used of scripture but of Jesus' word (see 17.12; compare 6.39). **10:** *Malchus:* Only John gives this name. **11:** *The cup* (Mk 14.36) may contain judgment and suffering or joy and salvation. Jesus accepts all that the Father gives him. **12–27: Jesus and Peter on trial.** The narrative* effectively alternates between Jesus and Peter. **12–14: Jesus before Annas.** *Officer,* a tribune, the commander of a cohort. *Annas,* deposed from the high priesthood by the Romans in 15 CE, remained influential. His sons were high priest before and after Caiaphas, who was his son-in-law. The Romans could manipulate the appointment. *Caiaphas . . . high priest that year:* This was not an annual appointment. **15–18: Peter before the servant girl.** The question implies a "No!" answer. Peter conforms to expectation, his *I am not* contrasting with Jesus' *I am* (vv. 5, 8). **19–24:** *High priest,* Annas (v. 24); the title is honorary. Jesus appeals to his open teaching (see Mk 14.49). **25–27: Peter before the servants.** A dramatic double denial; then *the cock crowed* (13.38).

JESUS BEFORE PILATE

18.28–19.16a: This trial is structured as a series of alternating scenes between Pilate and the Jewish leaders and Pilate and Jesus, interrupted only by a scene between the soldiers and Jesus.

---

28 Then they took Jesus from Caiaphas to Pilate's headquarters.*a* It was early in the morning. They themselves did not enter the headquarters,*a* so as to avoid ritual defile-

a Gk *the praetorium*

ment and to be able to eat the Passover. ²⁹So Pilate went out to them and said, "What accusation do you bring against this man?" ³⁰They answered, "If this man were not a criminal, we would not have handed him over to you." ³¹Pilate said to them, "Take him yourselves and judge him according to your law." The Jews replied, "We are not permitted to put anyone to death." ³²(This was to fulfill what Jesus had said when he indicated the kind of death he was to die.)

33 Then Pilate entered the headquarters^a again, summoned Jesus, and asked him, "Are you the King of the Jews?" ³⁴Jesus answered, "Do you ask this on your own, or did others tell you about me?" ³⁵Pilate replied, "I am not a Jew, am I? Your own nation and the chief priests have handed you over to me. What have you done?" ³⁶Jesus answered, "My kingdom is not from this world. If my kingdom were from this world, my followers would be fighting to keep me from being handed over to the Jews. But as it is, my kingdom is not from here." ³⁷Pilate asked him, "So you are a king?" Jesus answered, "You say that I am a king. For this I was born, and for this I came into the world, to testify to the truth. Everyone who belongs to the truth listens to my voice." ³⁸Pilate asked him, "What is truth?"

18.28–38a. 28–32: Jesus handed over to Pilate by the Jewish leaders. Pilate's *headquarters* in Jerusalem, the praetorium (see note *a*), contained his residence, barracks, and a court of judgment (19.13). His permanent residence was in Caesarea, but he moved to Jerusalem in case of trouble at Passover.* He was governor from 26 to 36 CE; an inscription at Caesarea confirms his presence. Entering a gentile* house where the law is not kept caused ritual defilement; hence the Jews remain outside while Jesus is inside. The statement that the Jews were *not permitted to put anyone to death* might not have applied in cases of Temple* infringements. 32: See 12.32–33. 33–38a: Pilate and Jesus. 33: Kingship is a political charge (6.14–15). Pilate sought to extract a confession. The leaders (*your own nation and the chief priests*), and not Pilate (*I am not a Jew, am I?*), are responsible for this charge. 36–38a: Jesus admits to the charge, though he redefines the terms. *Every one who belongs to the truth* (see

comment on 4.21–24) *listens to my voice* (compare.10.3, 5, 16, 27).

After he had said this, he went out to the Jews again and told them, "I find no case against him. ³⁹But you have a custom that I release someone for you at the Passover. Do you want me to release for you the King of the Jews?" ⁴⁰They shouted in reply, "Not this man, but Barabbas!" Now Barabbas was a bandit.

19 Then Pilate took Jesus and had him flogged. ²And the soldiers wove a crown of thorns and put it on his head, and they dressed him in a purple robe. ³They kept coming up to him, saying, "Hail, King of the Jews!" and striking him on the face. ⁴Pilate went out again and said to them, "Look, I am bringing him out to you to let you know that I find no case against him." ⁵So Jesus came out, wearing the crown of thorns and the purple robe. Pilate said to them, "Here is the man!" ⁶When the chief priests and the police saw him, they shouted, "Crucify him! Crucify him!" Pilate said to them, "Take him yourselves and crucify him; I find no case against him." ⁷The Jews answered him, "We have a law, and according to that law he ought to die because he has claimed to be the Son of God."

8 Now when Pilate heard this, he was more afraid than ever. ⁹He entered his headquarters^a again and asked Jesus, "Where are you from?" But Jesus gave him no answer. ¹⁰Pilate therefore said to him, "Do you refuse to speak to me? Do you not know that I have power to release you, and power to crucify you?" ¹¹Jesus answered him, "You would have no power over me unless it had been given you from above; therefore the one who handed me over to you is guilty of a greater sin." ¹²From then on Pilate tried to release him, but the Jews cried out, "If you release this man, you are no friend of the emperor. Everyone who claims to be a king sets himself against the emperor."

13 When Pilate heard these words, he brought Jesus outside and sat^b on the judge's bench at a place called The Stone Pavement,

---

a Gk *the praetorium*   *b* Or *seated him*

or in Hebrew*a* Gabbatha. 14Now it was the day of Preparation for the Passover; and it was about noon. He said to the Jews, "Here is your King!" 15They cried out, "Away with him! Away with him! Crucify him!" Pilate asked them, "Shall I crucify your King?" The chief priests answered, "We have no king but the emperor." 16Then he handed him over to them to be crucified.

18.38b–19.16a. 38b–40: Pilate and the Jewish authorities. Outside the Gospels there is no mention of the custom of releasing a prisoner at Passover.* *Barabbas*, unknown outside the Gospels, was a *bandit* (see 10.8), perhaps a "freedom fighter" opposed to Roman rule. **19.1–3: The soldiers and Jesus.** Though not guilty, Jesus was *flogged* as a condemned prisoner. *Crown of thorns*, with thorns turned outward to look like sun rays, and *purple*, the color of royal garments, were mockery based on the accusation of kingship. **4–7: Pilate presents Jesus to the Jewish authorities.** The leaders, not the crowd, call for Jesus to be crucified. **8–11: Pilate and Jesus.** *More afraid than ever:* A better, though difficult, translation is *he became afraid*. Even though Pilate's power originates from God, the fulfillment of the purpose of God does not excuse Pilate or, more especially, Judas. *The one who handed me over to you* could be Judas (18.2–3, 5) or Caiaphas (18.24, 28). *The greater sin:* Pilate is not altogether exonerated. **12–16a: Pilate and the Jews.** To claim to be king was treason against the emperor. **13:** The judgment of Jesus before Pilate is given a formal legal setting. The meaning of *Gabbatha* is obscure (see 19.17; contrast 1.38). **14:** *Preparation for the Passover,* the eve of Passover, 14th Nisan (see 18.28; 19.31, 42). The time, *noon*, the sixth hour, when the Passover lambs began to be slaughtered. **15:** There is deep irony* in the assertion, *We have no king but the emperor,* rather than confessing God as king. **16a:** Pilate hands Jesus over *to them,* that is, to the Roman soldiers (not to the Jews, see 19.13), to be crucified.

So they took Jesus; 17and carrying the cross by himself, he went out to what is called The Place of the Skull, which in Hebrew*a* is called Golgotha. 18There they crucified him, and with him two others, one on either side, with Jesus between them. 19Pilate also had an inscription written and put on the cross. It read, "Jesus of Nazareth,*b* the King of the Jews." 20Many of the Jews

read this inscription, because the place where Jesus was crucified was near the city; and it was written in Hebrew,*a* in Latin, and in Greek. 21Then the chief priests of the Jews said to Pilate, "Do not write, 'The King of the Jews,' but, 'This man said, I am King of the Jews.' " 22Pilate answered, "What I have written I have written." 23When the soldiers had crucified Jesus, they took his clothes and divided them into four parts, one for each soldier. They also took his tunic; now the tunic was seamless, woven in one piece from the top. 24So they said to one another, "Let us not tear it, but cast lots for it to see who will get it." This was to fulfill what the scripture says,

"They divided my clothes among themselves,
      and for my clothing they cast lots."
25And that is what the soldiers did.

Meanwhile, standing near the cross of Jesus were his mother, and his mother's sister, Mary the wife of Clopas, and Mary Magdalene. 26When Jesus saw his mother and the disciple whom he loved standing beside her, he said to his mother, "Woman, here is your son." 27Then he said to the disciple, "Here is your mother." And from that hour the disciple took her into his own home.

28 After this, when Jesus knew that all was now finished, he said (in order to fulfill the scripture), "I am thirsty." 29A jar full of sour wine was standing there. So they put a sponge full of the wine on a branch of hyssop and held it to his mouth. 30When Jesus had received the wine, he said, "It is finished." Then he bowed his head and gave up his spirit.

19.16b–30: Crucifixion. Note the theme of the fulfillment of scripture in 19.24, 28, 36–37. **17:** *Carrying his cross,* that is, the cross bar. *Golgotha* is Aramaic* for skull, perhaps because of the shape of the hill. **19:** An inscription of the charges was displayed. The Latin, "Iesus Nazarenus Rex Iudaeorum," provides the acronym "INRI." **20:** Jews spoke Greek and Hebrew or Aramaic; Romans spoke Latin. **21–22:** Jesus was executed as a political revolutionary, and Pilate is unwilling to appease the Jewish leaders. **23–24:** The

a That is, *Aramaic*   *b* Gk *the Nazorean*

clothes were divided among the four soldiers. They cast lots for the more valuable one-piece *tunic*. *Scripture*, Ps 22.18. **25:** There are probably four women, two identified by relationship and two by name. It is unlikely that the *sister* of the mother of Jesus would also be called Mary. *Mary Magdalene* is probably named after the town of Magdala on the western shore of the sea of Galilee. **26–27:** John does not name the mother of Jesus here or elsewhere (2.1–5, 12; 6.42; 19.25). She and the disciple Jesus loved, who is not named either (see on 13.23), are committed to each other's care. They are portrayed here as ideal disciples. **28–30: The death of Jesus.** *When Jesus knew*, see 13.1, 3; 18.4. *Fulfill the scripture . . . I am thirsty*, probably an allusion to Ps 22.15; perhaps the fulfilling of scripture by the provision of sour *wine* (see Ps 69.21). *Hyssop** was unsuitable for the task but was an important part of Passover* observance (see Ex 12.22), building the picture of Jesus as the Passover lamb. **30:** *He said, It is finished* (compare 4.34; 5.36; 17.4) . . . *and gave up his spirit:* He was in control until the end.

31 Since it was the day of Preparation, the Jews did not want the bodies left on the cross during the sabbath, especially because that sabbath was a day of great solemnity. So they asked Pilate to have the legs of the crucified men broken and the bodies removed. 32Then the soldiers came and broke the legs of the first and of the other who had been crucified with him. 33But when they came to Jesus and saw that he was already dead, they did not break his legs. 34Instead, one of the soldiers pierced his side with a spear, and at once blood and water came out. 35(He who saw this has testified so that you also may believe. His testimony is true, and he knows*a* that he tells the truth.) 36These things occurred so that the scripture might be fulfilled, "None of his bones shall be broken." 37And again another passage of scripture says, "They will look on the one whom they have pierced."

38 After these things, Joseph of Arimathea, who was a disciple of Jesus, though a secret one because of his fear of the Jews, asked Pilate to let him take away the body of Jesus. Pilate gave him permission; so he came and removed his body. 39Nicodemus, who had at first come to Jesus by night, also

came, bringing a mixture of myrrh and aloes, weighing about a hundred pounds. 40They took the body of Jesus and wrapped it with the spices in linen cloths, according to the burial custom of the Jews. 41Now there was a garden in the place where he was crucified, and in the garden there was a new tomb in which no one had ever been laid. 42And so, because it was the Jewish day of Preparation, and the tomb was nearby, they laid Jesus there.

19.31–42. 31–37: Death confirmed. 31: Death by crucifixion might take days; breaking the prisoners' legs would cause asphyxiation because they could not push themselves up to breathe. Deut 21.22–23 forbids bodies to hang overnight. The concern was intensified because the day following the *Preparation* (see 19.14) was not only a sabbath but also Passover.* **34:** The *blood and water* confirms Jesus' humanity (see 1 Jn 5.6). **35:** The witness might be the disciple Jesus loved. **36:** The first *scripture* might be a combination of three or four passages (Ex 12.10; compare Ex 12.46; see also Num 9.12; Ps 34.21). The second is Zech 12.10. **38–42: Burial.** *Arimathea*: a town northwest of Jerusalem. *Joseph of Arimathea* (compare Mk 15.43) was *a disciple . . . a secret one* (see 7.13; 9.22; 12.42; 20.19). *Nicodemus* (see 3.1–15; 7.48–52) was another, who first came to Jesus under cover of night but now is in the open. *Myrrh and aloes* would reduce the smell of decay. *A hundred* [Roman] *pounds,* about 34 kilograms, an extravagant quantity. The Passion begins in a garden (18.1) and ends at the garden tomb (19.41).

20 Early on the first day of the week, while it was still dark, Mary Magdalene came to the tomb and saw that the stone had been removed from the tomb. 2So she ran and went to Simon Peter and the other disciple, the one whom Jesus loved, and said to them, "They have taken the Lord out of the tomb, and we do not know where they have laid him." 3Then Peter and the other disciple set out and went toward the tomb. 4The two were running together, but the other disciple outran Peter and reached the tomb first. 5He bent down to look in and saw the linen wrappings lying there, but he did

a Or there is one who knows

not go in. 6Then Simon Peter came, following him, and went into the tomb. He saw the linen wrappings lying there, 7and the cloth that had been on Jesus' head, not lying with the linen wrappings but rolled up in a place by itself. 8Then the other disciple, who reached the tomb first, also went in, and he saw and believed; 9for as yet they did not understand the scripture, that he must rise from the dead. 10Then the disciples returned to their homes.

20.1–29: The risen Word and the empowerment of "his own." 1–10: At the tomb. 1: *First day,* Sunday. *Mary Magdalene* was also at the crucifixion (19.25). **2–4:** *Peter and the other disciple . . . whom Jesus loved* again appear together, to the disadvantage of Peter (13.23–25; 21.20–24; compare *the other disciple* in 18.15–16 and 20.8). **5–10:** Peter was *following* the disciple Jesus loved, possibly implying a subordinate position. *Yet they did not understand the scripture* (compare 2.22; 12.16) tends to weaken the importance of the belief of the other disciple.

11 But Mary stood weeping outside the tomb. As she wept, she bent over to look*a* into the tomb; 12and she saw two angels in white, sitting where the body of Jesus had been lying, one at the head and the other at the feet. 13They said to her, "Woman, why are you weeping?" She said to them, "They have taken away my Lord, and I do not know where they have laid him." 14When she had said this, she turned around and saw Jesus standing there, but she did not know that it was Jesus. 15Jesus said to her, "Woman, why are you weeping? Whom are you looking for?" Supposing him to be the gardener, she said to him, "Sir, if you have carried him away, tell me where you have laid him, and I will take him away." 16Jesus said to her, "Mary!" She turned and said to him in Hebrew,*b* "Rabbouni!" (which means Teacher). 17Jesus said to her, "Do not hold on to me, because I have not yet ascended to the Father. But go to my brothers and say to them, 'I am ascending to my Father and your Father, to my God and your God.' " 18Mary Magdalene went and announced to the disciples, "I have seen the Lord"; and she told them that he had said these things to her.

20.11–18. 11–13: Mary Magdalene and two angels. *Why are you weeping?* highlights Mary's response, which prepares for the meeting with Jesus. **14–18: Mary Magdalene and the risen Jesus.** Jesus' address, *Woman,* is characteristic (see 2.4; 4.21; 19.26). She only recognizes Jesus when he calls her by name. *Rabbouni,* a variant of Rabbi (see 1.38), perhaps not appropriate to the revelation of the risen Lord. *My Father and your Father . . . my God and your God,* Jesus mediates the revelation of God to believers (14.6) and makes direct access to God as Father possible. Mary's report to the disciples forms a bridge to the next scene.

19 When it was evening on that day, the first day of the week, and the doors of the house where the disciples had met were locked for fear of the Jews, Jesus came and stood among them and said, "Peace be with you." 20After he said this, he showed them his hands and his side. Then the disciples rejoiced when they saw the Lord. 21Jesus said to them again, "Peace be with you. As the Father has sent me, so I send you." 22When he had said this, he breathed on them and said to them, "Receive the Holy Spirit. 23If you forgive the sins of any, they are forgiven them; if you retain the sins of any, they are retained."

24 But Thomas (who was called the Twin*c*), one of the twelve, was not with them when Jesus came. 25So the other disciples told him, "We have seen the Lord." But he said to them, "Unless I see the mark of the nails in his hands, and put my finger in the mark of the nails and my hand in his side, I will not believe."

26 A week later his disciples were again in the house, and Thomas was with them. Although the doors were shut, Jesus came and stood among them and said, "Peace be with you." 27Then he said to Thomas, "Put your finger here and see my hands. Reach out your hand and put it in my side. Do not doubt but believe." 28Thomas answered him, "My Lord and my God!" 29Jesus said to him, "Have you believed because you have seen me? Blessed are those who have not seen and yet have come to believe."

a Gk lacks *to look*   *b* That is, *Aramaic*
c Gk *Didymus*

30 Now Jesus did many other signs in the presence of his disciples, which are not written in this book. 31But these are written so that you may come to believe[a] that Jesus is the Messiah,[b] the Son of God, and that through believing you may have life in his name.

20.19–31. 19–29: Jesus and the disciples. Two scenes depict Jesus' meeting with the disciples. **19–23:** A week later. *Peace be with you* recalls 14.27. *Hands* include the forearm, often nailed in crucifixion; *side* revealed the spear wound, positive identification. *As the Father has sent me* (3.16), *so I send you* (13.20; 17.18). *As*, "because" and "in the same way." *He breathed on them* (see Gen 2.7). *Receive the Holy Spirit* (see 14.15–16, 25–26; 15.26; 16.7–15), the meaning of the symbolic action. The authority to forgive sin is rooted in Jesus' mission (20.21; compare Mt 16.19; 18.18). **24–25:** *Thomas* the twin (Didymus), see 11.16; 14.5; 21.2. **26–29:** Invited to test the evidence, Thomas confesses without it. Jesus blesses *those who have not seen and yet . . . believe* (see 17.20–26). **30–31: Conclusion. 30:** The gospel narrative* is not a full chronicle* of everything Jesus did in his ministry. **31:** *These are written . . . that you may . . . believe* (see note d, p. 1832). The evangelist has told his story for the purpose of bringing his readers to faith in Jesus as the *messiah,** redefined as *Son of God*.

EPILOGUE: TYING UP LOOSE THREADS

21.1–25: The conclusion of 20.30–31, differences of language and style in ch. 21, and the setting in Galilee lead many scholars to conclude that ch. 21 is an appendix, added by followers. It accomplishes several tasks: (a) It combines resurrection appearances in Jerusalem (Lk 24.36–49) with an appearance in Galilee (foreshadowed in Mk 14.28; 16.10; Mt 28.10, but described only in Mt 28.16–20). (b) It ties John's Jerusalem orientation to the Galilean orientation of Mark and Matthew. (c) It reinstates Peter after his denial of Jesus and establishes his leadership role without displacing the disciple Jesus loved.

---

21 After these things Jesus showed himself again to the disciples by the Sea of Tiberias; and he showed himself in this way. 2Gathered there together were Simon Peter, Thomas called the Twin,[c] Nathanael of Cana in Galilee, the sons of Zebedee, and two others of his disciples. 3Simon Peter said to them, "I am going fishing." They said to him, "We will go with you." They went out and got into the boat, but that night they caught nothing.

4 Just after daybreak, Jesus stood on the beach; but the disciples did not know that it was Jesus. 5Jesus said to them, "Children, you have no fish, have you?" They answered him, "No." 6He said to them, "Cast the net to the right side of the boat, and you will find some." So they cast it, and now they were not able to haul it in because there were so many fish. 7That disciple whom Jesus loved said to Peter, "It is the Lord!" When Simon Peter heard that it was the Lord, he put on some clothes, for he was naked, and jumped into the sea. 8But the other disciples came in the boat, dragging the net full of fish, for they were not far from the land, only about a hundred yards[d] off.

9 When they had gone ashore, they saw a charcoal fire there, with fish on it, and bread. 10Jesus said to them, "Bring some of the fish that you have just caught." 11So Simon Peter went aboard and hauled the net ashore, full of large fish, a hundred fifty-three of them; and though there were so many, the net was not torn. 12Jesus said to them, "Come and have breakfast." Now none of the disciples dared to ask him, "Who are you?" because they knew it was the Lord. 13Jesus came and took the bread and gave it to them, and did the same with the fish. 14This was now the third time that Jesus appeared to the disciples after he was raised from the dead.

21.1–14: *Sea of Tiberias,* or Galilee, see 6.1. Jesus appears to seven disciples, though only three are named. *Simon Peter* (see 1.41–42); *Thomas . . . the Twin* (see 11.16; 14.5; 20.24–29); and *Nathanael from Cana of Galilee* (see 1.45–51). *The sons of Zebedee* are not otherwise mentioned in John, though the disciple Jesus loved was identified with John the brother of James by Irenaeus (about 180 CE) and, on the basis of 21.7, 20–24, was assumed to be the author of the Gospel.

---

a Other ancient authorities read *may continue to believe*
b Or *the Christ*   c Gk *Didymus*   d Gk *two hundred cubits*

Not Peter, but the *disciple Jesus loved,* recognizes *the Lord* (compare 20.8). Peter is *naked,* perhaps wearing only a loin cloth. He jumps into the sea to get to land quickly. Though Jesus already has *bread* and *fish* (see 6.9), he tells them to bring some of the catch. This is not a miracle of multiplication but a miraculous catch of *a hundred fifty-three,* a large number that may have symbolic meaning, though it is not clear. The sum of the numbers 1 to 17 is 153 (17 is the sum of 10 + 7, both of which indicate completeness and perfection). The catch might therefore symbolize the completeness of the mission. The miracle is accentuated by the untorn net. Jesus had presided over an evening meal on the night of his betrayal (13.1–38). Now he presides at a breakfast meal with eucharistic* overtones (21.13; see 6.11). Reference to the *third* resurrection appearance is consistent with 20.19, 26.

15 When they had finished breakfast, Jesus said to Simon Peter, "Simon son of John, do you love me more than these?" He said to him, "Yes, Lord; you know that I love you." Jesus said to him, "Feed my lambs." 16 A second time he said to him, "Simon son of John, do you love me?" He said to him, "Yes, Lord; you know that I love you." Jesus said to him, "Tend my sheep." 17 He said to him the third time, "Simon son of John, do you love me?" Peter felt hurt because he said to him the third time, "Do you love me?" And he said to him, "Lord, you know everything; you know that I love you." Jesus said to him, "Feed my sheep. 18 Very truly, I tell you, when you were younger, you used to fasten your own belt and to go wherever you wished. But when you grow old, you will stretch out your hands, and someone else will fasten a belt around you and take you where you do not wish to go." 19 (He said this to indicate the kind of death by which he would glorify God.) After this he said to him, "Follow me."

20 Peter turned and saw the disciple whom Jesus loved following them; he was the one who had reclined next to Jesus at the supper and had said, "Lord, who is it that is going to betray you?" 21 When Peter saw him, he said to Jesus, "Lord, what about him?" 22 Jesus said to him, "If it is my will that he remain until I come, what is that to you? Follow me!" 23 So the rumor spread in the community*a* that this disciple would not die. Yet Jesus did not say to him that he would not die, but, "If it is my will that he remain until I come, what is that to you?"*b*

24 This is the disciple who is testifying to these things and has written them, and we know that his testimony is true. 25 But there are also many other things that Jesus did; if every one of them were written down, I suppose that the world itself could not contain the books that would be written.

21.15–25. 15–19: Jesus and Simon Peter. *Simon son of John,* see 1.42. The threefold profession of love parallels the threefold denial (18.15–18; 25–27), indicating restoration. While the third question uses a different word for love in Greek than the first two, the text says *the third time,* indicating no substantial difference. John speaks of the Father's love for the Son using both Greek verbs for love (3.35; 5.20). Jesus also varies his language in calling on Peter to demonstrate his love: *Feed my lambs; Tend my sheep; Feed my sheep.* No variation in the task is meant. **18–19:** *Stretch out your hands,* a reference to Peter's crucifixion (see ch. 19 and 12.33). *Follow me* (see 12.25–26). **20–23:** On the relationship between Peter and the disciple Jesus loved, see 13.23–25. **24–25:** *We know that his testimony is true:* Others attest to his witness; this and v. 23 may imply the death of the disciple. The conclusion and perhaps all of ch. 21 come from those who received the disciple's witness; perhaps the disciple provided the substance of what finally was written by others, being the source of the Gospel rather than the direct author.

a Gk *among the brothers* *b* Other ancient authorities lack *what is that to you*

THE ACTS OF THE APOSTLES

Introduction

Acts is a sequel to the Gospel according to Luke (Acts 1.1: "In the first book . . . ," see introduction to Luke). The title, the Acts of the Apostles,★ which was probably added later, suggests parallels to accounts of the "acts" or "mighty deeds" of famous rulers and generals. After the fourth century when Christianity became the official religion of the empire, Acts was read as an account of the glorious Christian march from Jerusalem to Rome. Gentile★ Christianity was understood as the successor that surpassed Judaism, as the Roman Empire once succeeded Greece. But reading Acts as the story of a gentile triumph, told at the expense of the Jews, is to forget its Jewish Christian origins.

Acts proclaims Jesus as the messiah★ fulfilling the promises God made to Israel. Its historical origins probably lie in the decades following the Roman destruction of Jerusalem (70–73 CE). All Jews shared the scriptures, including the prophetic★ and historical books which were written following the first destruction by Nebuchadnezzar (586 BCE). What repentance was required for God to restore Israel following this second destruction? Even the Pharisees★ were divided. The vast majority argued for a repentance consisting of scrupulous observance of the law, separation from those who wanted to continue to fight against Rome, and exclusion of those who believed the messiah had come. On the other hand, Acts tells of "believers who belonged to the sect★ of the Pharisees" (15.5). To call them "Christian Pharisees" may obscure their particular Jewish tradition of practice and faith in the kingdom of God and the messiah. They believed Jesus was the messiah. The Hebrew word for "anointed★ one," "messiah," may fit them better than the Greek word "Christ." Acts notes that these "messianist Pharisees" argued for the necessity of observance of the law, even for gentile converts.

But the Jerusalem council disagreed, deciding not "to trouble those Gentiles that are turning to God" (15.19), so that Jews and gentiles alike "will be saved through the grace of the Lord Jesus" (15.11). The repentance required is a turning to "this Jesus God raised up" (2.32), and the restoration is "the rising of many in Israel" to be "a light for revelation to the Gentiles and for glory to your people Israel" (Lk 2.32–34), inaugurated by the resurrection of Jesus.

Acts is the story of Jesus' apostles and witnesses, emerging from within a divided Israel, laying claim to the scriptural promises, and moving into mission in the Jewish and gentile communities of the Roman empire. The "restoration of the kingdom to Israel" (1.6; 3.20) is interpreted to be the renewal of Israel's calling to "restore the survivors of Israel" to be "a light to the nations, that my salvation may reach to the end of the earth" (Isa 49.6).

Like the majority of Jews, these "messianists" or "Christians" (Acts 11.26) spoke Greek and read Israel's scriptures in the ancient Greek version known as the Septuagint★ (abbreviated LXX★ in the comments). They followed the map of synagogues★ spread over centuries through the Greco-Roman world, from Egypt through North Africa in the south, to Spain in the west, and Babylonia in the east. Their mission was first to gather Israel, and extending the mission to the gentiles required profoundly difficult decisions. The Book of Acts has surprisingly few stories in which the audience is exclusively gentile.

The apostles are thus agents of the vindicated and exalted messiah, Jesus. Their journeys are the mission of God, directed or guided by the Holy Spirit from Jerusalem throughout the regions of Judea and Samaria out into Asia Minor, back to the Temple✶ in Jerusalem, and on to Rome, albeit in chains. Their encounters with Jewish, Greek, and Roman cultures and authorities are defining moments for the Christian movement, requiring "boldness" from the witnesses and profound assurance from Israel's scriptures. The narrative✶ offers an affirmative verdict on this new "sect" (24.5, 14; 28.22) and a judgment against its adversaries in terms announced by the Pharisee Gamaliel, "If this plan or this undertaking is of human origin, it will fail; but if it is of God, you will not be able to overthrow them—in that case you may even be found fighting against God!" (5.38–39).

READING GUIDE

The geography of the journeys offers the most straightforward outline of the story of Acts. The opening verses (1.1–5) provide a simple summary of the themes of "the first book," and the first chapter sets the stage for the narrative. In his last words on earth, Jesus also presents the outline of the story to follow, linked to places (1.8). The apostles are also restored to "twelve," to judge Israel's twelve tribes in the kingdom (Lk 22.30; Acts 1.15–26; 26.7). They remain in Jerusalem not only until Pentecost✶ (2.1), but throughout the first section of their confrontational mission in Jerusalem, centered in the Temple. At the end of this section, they are "scattered throughout the countryside of Judea and Samaria" (8.1).

In the second major section of the narrative (8.2–15.35), the mission moves beyond Jerusalem throughout the regions of the eastern shore of the Mediterranean, primarily from Jerusalem to Antioch in Syria, with Barnabas going as far north as Tarsus "to look for Saul" (11.25). Crucial episodes confirm the distinctive Jewish character of this "Christian" movement (11.26), and these chapters set the stage for the gentile mission through the conversion of Saul (9.1–30), Peter's encounter with Cornelius (vv. 10–11), and Paul's first missionary journey (vv. 13–14), beginning in Antioch of Syria moving west as far as Antioch of Pisidia, and leading back to Jerusalem for the council (v. 15).

The third major section (15.36–21.16) is organized around two Pauline journeys. Both move as far west as Macedonia and Athens or Corinth, and both journeys end in Jerusalem. These journeys include crucial encounters with Hellenistic✶ religions and the Roman order in complex relationships with local Jewish communities. Like the leaders of the Temple earlier in the story, the synagogues of Asia Minor and Greece are confronted with the apostolic message "showing by the scriptures that the Messiah is Jesus" (18.28). Some gentiles hear. A few believe. But the Jewish and gentile opposition also increases.

The fourth major section (21.17–28.31) opens with Paul's arrival in Jerusalem, giving account to the elders (22.17–25), and his entry into the Temple (22.26), prompting trials before the Roman tribune in the presence of the chief priests and the Temple Sanhedrin✶ (22.26–23.10). Paul's journey to Rome begins (23.11) as he is spirited away to Caesarea in protective custody (23.11–35). Paul defends himself before the Roman procurators Felix and Festus, finally appealing to the emperor, and then before King Agrippa (24.1–26.32). After a perilous journey to Rome where his divine protection is demonstrated (27.1–28.15), Paul the Roman prisoner again preaches to local Jewish leaders, interpreting their disagreement and rejection in Isaiah's prophetic language of promise and warning that echoes through the whole of the narrative.

1 In the first book, Theophilus, I wrote about all that Jesus did and taught from the beginning 2until the day when he was taken up to heaven, after giving instructions through the Holy Spirit to the apostles whom he had chosen. 3After his suffering he presented himself alive to them by many convincing proofs, appearing to them during forty days and speaking about the kingdom of God. 4While staying*a* with them, he ordered them not to leave Jerusalem, but to wait there for the promise of the Father. "This," he said, "is what you have heard from me; 5for John baptized with water, but you will be baptized with*b* the Holy Spirit not many days from now."

6 So when they had come together, they asked him, "Lord, is this the time when you will restore the kingdom to Israel?" 7He replied, "It is not for you to know the times or periods that the Father has set by his own authority. 8But you will receive power when the Holy Spirit has come upon you; and you will be my witnesses in Jerusalem, in all Judea and Samaria, and to the ends of the earth." 9When he had said this, as they were watching, he was lifted up, and a cloud took him out of their sight. 10While he was going and they were gazing up toward heaven, suddenly two men in white robes stood by them. 11They said, "Men of Galilee, why do you stand looking up toward heaven? This Jesus, who has been taken up from you into heaven, will come in the same way as you saw him go into heaven."

1.1–26: Awaiting the promise. 1–11: The exaltation of Jesus. 1–5: These verses provide a resumption of the story as it ends in *the first book* of The Gospel according to Luke (see comments on Lk 1.1–4; 24.36–53) and anticipate the first episodes of Acts. **2:** *The apostles* whom he had chosen were specifically the twelve (Lk 6.13; 9.1; 22.30), now without Judas

(1.16–17). **3:** Luke 24 indicates that both physical signs and scriptural interpretation* are combined in these *convincing proofs,* entailing appearances and persuasive witness to *the kingdom of God* with Jesus attested as the messiah* of this dominion straight through Acts (28.31). **4:** *The promise of the Father* was given at Pentecost* (2.1–47; see v. 33). **5:** On the contrast between John's baptism* *with water* and the baptism *with the Holy Spirit,* see also Lk 3.16–17, 21–22; Acts 18.25; 19.2–6). **6:** Israel hoped God would accomplish the restoration in accord with prophetic* promises (Isa 49.6; Jer 29.14). **7:** The promised restoration is assumed, but *the times or periods that the Father has set* are not open to human knowledge, except that the kingdom is near (Mk 13.32; Lk 21.31). **8:** This *power* is a sign of divine authority (4.7), the agency of *the Holy Spirit,* not the apostles themselves, but their office is that of *witnesses* to Jesus' resurrection (1.22). *Jerusalem, all Judea and Samaria,* are the geographic locations of the opening chapters. *The ends of the earth* are prophetic symbols of Israel's renewed divine calling (Isa 49.6). **9:** The *cloud* is a sign of divine presence (Lk 9.34). **10:** The *two men* are again heavenly witnesses (Lk 24.4). **11:** In being *taken up* (1.22), Jesus accomplishes his "departure" (Lk 9.31) and is exalted by God to heavenly rule (Acts 7.56).

12 Then they returned to Jerusalem from the mount called Olivet, which is near Jerusalem, a sabbath day's journey away. 13When they had entered the city, they went to the room upstairs where they were staying, Peter, and John, and James, and Andrew, Philip and Thomas, Bartholomew and Matthew, James son of Alphaeus, and Simon the Zealot, and Judas son of*c* James. 14All these were constantly devoting themselves to prayer, together with certain women, including Mary the mother of Jesus, as well as his brothers.

a Or *eating*   *b* Or *by*   *c* Or *the brother of*

15 In those days Peter stood up among the believers[a] (together the crowd numbered about one hundred twenty persons) and said, [16]"Friends,[b] the scripture had to be fulfilled, which the Holy Spirit through David foretold concerning Judas, who became a guide for those who arrested Jesus— [17]for he was numbered among us and was allotted his share in this ministry." [18](Now this man acquired a field with the reward of his wickedness; and falling headlong,[c] he burst open in the middle and all his bowels gushed out. [19]This became known to all the residents of Jerusalem, so that the field was called in their language Hakeldama, that is, Field of Blood.) [20]"For it is written in the book of Psalms,

'Let his homestead become desolate,
    and let there be no one to live in it';
and
'Let another take his position of
    overseer.'

[21]So one of the men who have accompanied us during all the time that the Lord Jesus went in and out among us, [22]beginning from the baptism of John until the day when he was taken up from us—one of these must become a witness with us to his resurrection." [23]So they proposed two, Joseph called Barsabbas, who was also known as Justus, and Matthias. [24]Then they prayed and said, "Lord, you know everyone's heart. Show us which one of these two you have chosen [25]to take the place[d] in this ministry and apostleship from which Judas turned aside to go to his own place." [26]And they cast lots for them, and the lot fell on Matthias; and he was added to the eleven apostles.

1.12–26: Restoring the twelve. 13: On the named apostles,* see also Lk 6.13–16. 14: Luke again draws attention to the presence of the *women* at a critical occasion of God's action (Lk 8.1–3; 23.49; 23.5–10), specifically Jesus' mother *Mary* (Lk 1.35). 15–20: *Peter* again affirms that *the scripture had to be fulfilled* (Lk 24.25–26, 44–47), and his first speech in Acts is a scriptural testimony interpreting what has happened on the basis of Ps 69.25 (68.26: LXX*) and 109.8 (LXX 108). 16–18: On Judas' active conspiracy, see Lk 22.3–6, 47–48. On his death, compare Mt 27.5. 22: On the baptism* of John as Jesus' anointing* by God, see Lk

3.21–22; Acts 10.38). To be *a witness to his resurrection* (Gk., "martyr"*) will bring suffering and death even to those who were not "eyewitnesses" from the beginning (Lk 1.1; Acts 7; 24.14–21). 23: Neither *Joseph called Barsabbas* nor *Matthias* is ever mentioned again in the New Testament. 26: Casting *lots* was a traditional Jewish practice for discerning God's choice (Lev 16.8; Num 26.55; 33.54; Josh 19). The *eleven* must be restored to twelve because of Israel's twelve tribes (Lk 5.13; 9.1; 22.30; Acts 26.7).

2 When the day of Pentecost had come, they were all together in one place. [2]And suddenly from heaven there came a sound like the rush of a violent wind, and it filled the entire house where they were sitting. [3]Divided tongues, as of fire, appeared among them, and a tongue rested on each of them. [4]All of them were filled with the Holy Spirit and began to speak in other languages, as the Spirit gave them ability.

5 Now there were devout Jews from every nation under heaven living in Jerusalem. [6]And at this sound the crowd gathered and was bewildered, because each one heard them speaking in the native language of each. [7]Amazed and astonished, they asked, "Are not all these who are speaking Galileans? [8]And how is it that we hear, each of us, in our own native language? [9]Parthians, Medes, Elamites, and residents of Mesopotamia, Judea and Cappadocia, Pontus and Asia, [10]Phrygia and Pamphylia, Egypt and the parts of Libya belonging to Cyrene, and visitors from Rome, both Jews and proselytes, [11]Cretans and Arabs—in our own languages we hear them speaking about God's deeds of power." [12]All were amazed and perplexed, saying to one another, "What does this mean?" [13]But others sneered and said, "They are filled with new wine."

2.1–8.1: The witness in Jerusalem. 2.1–13 The promise of the Father given at Pentecost.* 1: *Pentecost* is the fiftieth day after Passover,* the popular Feast of Weeks* of early harvest (Ex 23.16; 34.22; Lev 23.15–21; Deut 16.9–12). 2: The *sound like the rush*

a Gk *brothers*   b Gk *Men, brothers*   c Or *swelling up*
d Other ancient authorities read *the share*

of a violent wind recalls the loud sounds of God's presence at Sinai (Ex 19.16–19, compare also 1 Kings 19.11–12). **3:** *Divided tongues,* distributed to each, anticipate the inspired speaking and hearing of vv. 4–13. *Fire* indicates divine presence (Gen 15.17; Ex 3.2; 13.21–22; 24.17), as promised (Lk 3.16). **4:** Luke often describes inspiration in terms of being *filled with the Holy Spirit* (Lk 1.15, 41, 67; Acts 4.8; 9.17; 13.9), now directly fulfilling Jesus' promise (Lk 24.49; Acts 1.4–5, 8). In Greek, *to speak in other languages* is literally "to speak in other tongues." **5:** *Devout Jews* were observant of the law (Lk 2.25; Acts 8.2; 22.12). **6:** In Greek, they hear "each in our own dialect" (v. 8). **9–11:** All of these groups represent Jewish (v. 5) communities, including gentiles* who had become Jews (*proselytes*) spread throughout the world, now gathered in Jerusalem. **11:** This is a miracle of both speech and hearing since they now hear *in our own languages* (Gk., "tongues"). The subject matter of inspired witness is *God's deeds of power* (Deut 11.3; Ps 70.19; Lk 1.46–55). **12–13:** *"What does this mean?"* is a faithful question in the midst of perplexity, prompting Peter's speech (see also Lk 1.29, 34). *"They are filled with new wine"* is a judgment intended to discredit their prophetic* speech (v. 15).

14 But Peter, standing with the eleven, raised his voice and addressed them, "Men of Judea and all who live in Jerusalem, let this be known to you, and listen to what I say. ¹⁵Indeed, these are not drunk, as you suppose, for it is only nine o'clock in the morning. ¹⁶No, this is what was spoken through the prophet Joel:

17 'In the last days it will be, God declares,
  that I will pour out my Spirit upon all
    flesh,
  and your sons and your daughters
    shall prophesy,
  and your young men shall see visions,
  and your old men shall
    dream dreams.
18 Even upon my slaves, both men and
    women,
  in those days I will pour out
    my Spirit;
  and they shall prophesy.
19 And I will show portents in the heaven
    above
  and signs on the earth below,
    blood, and fire, and smoky mist.

20 The sun shall be turned to darkness
    and the moon to blood,
  before the coming of the Lord's
    great and glorious day.
21 Then everyone who calls on the name of
    the Lord shall be saved.'

22 "You that are Israelites,ᵃ listen to what I have to say: Jesus of Nazareth,ᵇ a man attested to you by God with deeds of power, wonders, and signs that God did through him among you, as you yourselves know— ²³this man, handed over to you according to the definite plan and foreknowledge of God, you crucified and killed by the hands of those outside the law. ²⁴But God raised him up, having freed him from death,ᶜ because it was impossible for him to be held in its power. ²⁵For David says concerning him,
  'I saw the Lord always before me,
    for he is at my right hand so that I
      will not be shaken;
26 therefore my heart was glad, and my
    tongue rejoiced;
  moreover my flesh will live in hope.
27 For you will not abandon my soul to
    Hades,
  or let your Holy One experience
    corruption.
28 You have made known to me the ways
    of life;
  you will make me full of gladness
    with your presence.'

2.14–47: Peter's sermon at Pentecost.* **14–16:** Peter's speech directly answers the question, "What does this mean?" (v. 12) through an extended scriptural interpretation.* **17–21:** These verses correspond very closely to the book of Joel (2.28–32) as it survives in the Greek version known as the Septuagint (LXX*). *In the last days* (LXX: "afterward") could mean "at the end of time" or in the time before the restoration of the fortunes of Judah and Jerusalem (Joel 3.1; Acts 1.6–8). The pouring out of God's *Spirit* signifies the renewal of prophecy among men and women. Verses 22–39 will identify Jesus as the *"Lord"* in whose name salvation is given. **22:** *Israelites* (v. 29) includes all Jews who claim the promises God made to Israel. By means of the *deeds of power, wonders and signs* (Lk 24.19;

a Gk *Men, Israelites*   *b* Gk *the Nazorean*   *c* Gk *the pains of death*

Acts 10.38), Jesus is *attested* as the true prophet★ (Deut 18; Acts 3.22). **23:** Luke consistently attests that Jesus' death occurred through God's *definite plan and foreknowledge*, Israel's active complicity, and the direct agency of the gentiles,★ or *those outside the law* (4.27–28). **25–28:** *David* is regarded as the author of Ps 16.8–11. *Hades*★ is the realm of the dead (Lk 10.15; 16.23). The *Holy One* was Israel's anointed★ king, "set apart" for God.

~~~~~~~~~~~~~~~~~~~

29 "Fellow Israelites,*a* I may say to you confidently of our ancestor David that he both died and was buried, and his tomb is with us to this day. ³⁰Since he was a prophet, he knew that God had sworn with an oath to him that he would put one of his descendants on his throne. ³¹Foreseeing this, David*b* spoke of the resurrection of the Messiah,*c* saying,

'He was not abandoned to Hades,
    nor did his flesh experience
        corruption.'

³²This Jesus God raised up, and of that all of us are witnesses. ³³Being therefore exalted at*d* the right hand of God, and having received from the Father the promise of the Holy Spirit, he has poured out this that you both see and hear. ³⁴For David did not ascend into the heavens, but he himself says,

'The Lord said to my Lord,
    "Sit at my right hand,
35   until I make your enemies your
            footstool." '

³⁶Therefore let the entire house of Israel know with certainty that God has made him both Lord and Messiah,*e* this Jesus whom you crucified."

37 Now when they heard this, they were cut to the heart and said to Peter and to the other apostles, "Brothers,*a* what should we do?" ³⁸Peter said to them, "Repent, and be baptized every one of you in the name of Jesus Christ so that your sins may be forgiven; and you will receive the gift of the Holy Spirit. ³⁹For the promise is for you, for your children, and for all who are far away, everyone whom the Lord our God calls to him." ⁴⁰And he testified with many other arguments and exhorted them, saying, "Save yourselves from this corrupt generation." ⁴¹So those who welcomed his message were

baptized, and that day about three thousand persons were added. ⁴²They devoted themselves to the apostles' teaching and fellowship, to the breaking of bread and the prayers.

43 Awe came upon everyone, because many wonders and signs were being done by the apostles. ⁴⁴All who believed were together and had all things in common; ⁴⁵they would sell their possessions and goods and distribute the proceeds*f* to all, as any had need. ⁴⁶Day by day, as they spent much time together in the temple, they broke bread at home*g* and ate their food with glad and generous*h* hearts, ⁴⁷praising God and having the goodwill of all the people. And day by day the Lord added to their number those who were being saved.

———————————————

2.29–47. 29–31: Luke reads the psalms as Davidic prophecy (Lk 20.41–42; 24.44; Acts 1.16, 20; 4.25; 13.33–36). *David* was not speaking of himself, since he died and decayed, but spoke as a *prophet*★ of another anointed★ one or *Messiah*★ who would fulfill this promise. **32:** Witness is again focused on Jesus' resurrection (1.22). **33:** The dramatic displays of the *Holy Spirit* are signs that Jesus himself has *received from the Father the promise of the Holy Spirit*, and being *exalted at the right hand of God*, he has authority to inaugurate his reign. Along with Lk 10.21–22, this is a key passage in subsequent understandings of the Triune God. **34:** *David* is again cited as a prophet by quoting from Ps 110.1 (Lk 20.42–44). **36:** This verse is the rhetorical★ conclusion of Peter's speech. Jesus has been attested from scripture as God's *Lord and Messiah*, which is also to indict all who were involved in his crucifixion. **37:** To be *cut to the heart* is a profoundly physical response of contrition. *"What should we do?"* was also the distraught response of those convicted by John's preaching (Lk 3.10–14; see 10.25; 12.17; 16.3–4; 18.18). **38:** John also told people to *repent and be baptized* as a warning against "the wrath to come," but now that the messiah's reign has begun, forgiveness and *the gift of the Holy Spirit* are promised (Lk 3.7–9, 15–17). The *name of Jesus Christ* is divine agency and authority for the apostles★ (3.6, 16; 4.10, 12, 17–18, 30; 5.28, 40–41; 8.12; 9.16, 21, 27, 28; 16.18; 19.13, 17; 21.13; 22.16; 26.9). **39:** The

a Gk *Men, brothers*   *b* Gk *he*   *c* Or *the Christ*
d Or *by*   *e* Or *Christ*   *f* Gk *them*   *g* Or *from house to house*   *h* Or *sincere*

promise is the restoration of Israel and renewal of God's call (Isa 49.6; Acts 1.8; Isa 57.19). **40:** *This corrupt generation* is a biblical diagnosis (Deut 32.5; Ps 78.8; Lk 9.41; 11.29). **41:** On the *three thousand persons*, see also 2.47; 4.4; 5.14; 6.1, 7. **42:** This verse, which summarizes Luke's picture of the early movement, is elaborated in vv. 43–47. **44–46:** Luke seems to depict holding *all things in common* as a voluntary practice (see also 5.4). The *temple*★ remains the natural gathering place for prayer (see Acts 3–4, 5.20; 21.26).

3 One day Peter and John were going up to the temple at the hour of prayer, at three o'clock in the afternoon. ²And a man lame from birth was being carried in. People would lay him daily at the gate of the temple called the Beautiful Gate so that he could ask for alms from those entering the temple. ³When he saw Peter and John about to go into the temple, he asked them for alms. ⁴Peter looked intently at him, as did John, and said, "Look at us." ⁵And he fixed his attention on them, expecting to receive something from them. ⁶But Peter said, "I have no silver or gold, but what I have I give you; in the name of Jesus Christ of Nazareth,ᵃ stand up and walk." ⁷And he took him by the right hand and raised him up; and immediately his feet and ankles were made strong. ⁸Jumping up, he stood and began to walk, and he entered the temple with them, walking and leaping and praising God. ⁹All the people saw him walking and praising God, ¹⁰and they recognized him as the one who used to sit and ask for alms at the Beautiful Gate of the temple; and they were filled with wonder and amazement at what had happened to him.

11 While he clung to Peter and John, all the people ran together to them in the portico called Solomon's Portico, utterly astonished. ¹²When Peter saw it, he addressed the people, "You Israelites,ᵇ why do you wonder at this, or why do you stare at us, as though by our own power or piety we had made him walk? ¹³The God of Abraham, the God of Isaac, and the God of Jacob, the God of our ancestors has glorified his servantᶜ Jesus, whom you handed over and rejected in the presence of Pilate, though he had decided to release him. ¹⁴But you rejected the Holy and

Righteous One and asked to have a murderer given to you, ¹⁵and you killed the Author of life, whom God raised from the dead. To this we are witnesses. ¹⁶And by faith in his name, his name itself has made this man strong, whom you see and know; and the faith that is through Jesusᵈ has given him this perfect health in the presence of all of you.

3.1–26: The power of the prophet★ like Moses. 1: *The hour of prayer* was one of many daily observances, again reflecting Luke's attention to the practices of the Temple★ (Lk 1.8–10; 2.22–24, 37). **2:** The *lame* had a special place in Jesus' messianic priorities (Lk 7.22; 14.13, 21) in contrast to their exclusion in Lev 21.16–18. The *Beautiful Gate* could be any of several entrances to Jerusalem. **3:** Giving *alms* is a traditional Jewish obligation (Lk 11.41; 12.33; Acts 9.36; 10.2, 4, 31; 24.17). **4–5:** Peter's looking *intently* at the lame man not only contrasts with the tendency to avert the eyes from a beggar, but emphasizes the riveted gaze of an intense interchange (Lk 4.20; 22.56; Acts 1.10). **6:** Peter's command *in the name of Jesus Christ* (2.38) echoes Jesus' word to the paralyzed man in Lk 5.23. **8:** *Jumping up, walking, and leaping, and praising God* into the Temple marks this healing as a fulfillment of Israel's promised restoration like a leaping lame man in Isa. 35.1–10. **10–12:** *Wonder and amazement* and being *utterly astonished* are still short of understanding or belief at what has happened (Lk 4.36; 5.26; Acts 2.12), but they provide the occasion for Peter's message. **13–15:** The thorough identification with Israel (*the God of our ancestors*) marks this as prophetic speech among Jews. The oracles★ are structured as in 2.23–24.36, highlighting the conflict between "you" and "God": *God has glorified his servant Jesus, whom you handed over and rejected.* As *servant* (Acts 3.26; 4.25, 27, 30), *Holy* (Lk 1.35), and *Righteous* (Lk 23.47; see comment on Acts 7.52), Jesus is fulfilling a host of scriptural roles. The title *Author of life* is unusual (see 5.31, translated "Leader"), but clearly contrasts Jesus, the source of life, with those who deal in death. The *witnesses* are again focused on Jesus' resurrection (1.22). **16:** *Faith in his name* becomes the very agency of divine power (see 2.38, and contrast the misuse of Jesus' name by those who are not witnesses in 19.11–16).

---

a Gk *the Nazorean*   *b* Gk *Men, Israelites*   *c* Or *child*
d Gk *him*

17 "And now, friends,[a] I know that you acted in ignorance, as did also your rulers. [18]In this way God fulfilled what he had foretold through all the prophets, that his Messiah[b] would suffer. [19]Repent therefore, and turn to God so that your sins may be wiped out, [20]so that times of refreshing may come from the presence of the Lord, and that he may send the Messiah[c] appointed for you, that is, Jesus, [21]who must remain in heaven until the time of universal restoration that God announced long ago through his holy prophets. [22]Moses said, 'The Lord your God will raise up for you from your own people[a] a prophet like me. You must listen to whatever he tells you. [23]And it will be that everyone who does not listen to that prophet will be utterly rooted out of the people.' [24]And all the prophets, as many as have spoken, from Samuel and those after him, also predicted these days. [25]You are the descendants of the prophets and of the covenant that God gave to your ancestors, saying to Abraham, 'And in your descendants all the families of the earth shall be blessed.' [26]When God raised up his servant,[d] he sent him first to you, to bless you by turning each of you from your wicked ways."

3.17–26. 17: *Ignorance* is forgivable in Acts, at least until the opportunity to repent is given (17.30), although it is unlikely that the *rulers* will find this offer attractive. 18: Without citing a specific prophetic* passage, Luke again affirms that God's plan *that his Messiah* would suffer* had been *foretold through all the prophets* (Lk 24.25, 44–46; Acts 17.2–3; 3.24). 20: *The times of refreshing* recalls the cessation of suffering when God was obeyed (Ex 8.15). In language that echoes Moses' plea that someone else be sent (Ex 4.13), Jesus is identified as *the Messiah appointed for you.* 21: In Luke's narrative,* Jesus *must remain in heaven* for the sake of the completion of the divine plan (Lk 24.7, 26, 44; Acts 1.16, 22). Its necessity is grounded in the scriptures (*that God announced long ago through his holy prophets*), and the goal remains the fulfillment of God's promises to Israel of *universal restoration* (1.6–8). 22: In Deut 18.15–19, the prediction of the prophet like Moses is a test of true and false prophecy (see also Deut 34.10–12). Luke reads it as a direct testimony to the raising up of Jesus (Acts 7.37). 23: The warning that those who do not listen will be

utterly *rooted out* comes from Lev 23.29, intensifying the call to repentance. 25: Jewish traditions which called the people *descendants of the prophets* heightened the sense that they were able to decide these matters without professional interpreters. Luke again emphasizes the common theme in Genesis that promises to Abraham are Israel's calling by which *all the families of the earth shall be blessed* (Gen 12.3; 18.18; 22.18; 26.4; Acts 1.6–8). 26: Israel's repentance is meant for the blessing of the world (see also Gen 22.18: "because you obeyed my voice").

4 While Peter and John[e] were speaking to the people, the priests, the captain of the temple, and the Sadducees came to them, [2]much annoyed because they were teaching the people and proclaiming that in Jesus there is the resurrection of the dead. [3]So they arrested them and put them in custody until the next day, for it was already evening. [4]But many of those who heard the word believed; and they numbered about five thousand.

5 The next day their rulers, elders, and scribes assembled in Jerusalem, [6]with Annas the high priest, Caiaphas, John,[f] and Alexander, and all who were of the high-priestly family. [7]When they had made the prisoners[g] stand in their midst, they inquired, "By what power or by what name did you do this?" [8]Then Peter, filled with the Holy Spirit, said to them, "Rulers of the people and elders, [9]if we are questioned today because of a good deed done to someone who was sick and are asked how this man has been healed, [10]let it be known to all of you, and to all the people of Israel, that this man is standing before you in good health by the name of Jesus Christ of Nazareth,[h] whom you crucified, whom God raised from the dead. [11]This Jesus[i] is

'the stone that was rejected by you, the builders;

it has become the cornerstone.'[j]

[12]There is salvation in no one else, for there is no other name under heaven given among mortals by which we must be saved."

a Gk *brothers*   b Or *his Christ*   c Or *the Christ*
d Or *child*   e Gk *While they*   f Other ancient
authorities read *Jonathan*   g Gk *them*   h Gk *the
Nazorean*   i Gk *This*   j Or *keystone*

13 Now when they saw the boldness of Peter and John and realized that they were uneducated and ordinary men, they were amazed and recognized them as companions of Jesus. 14When they saw the man who had been cured standing beside them, they had nothing to say in opposition. 15So they ordered them to leave the council while they discussed the matter with one another. 16They said, "What will we do with them? For it is obvious to all who live in Jerusalem that a notable sign has been done through them; we cannot deny it. 17But to keep it from spreading further among the people, let us warn them to speak no more to anyone in this name." 18So they called them and ordered them not to speak or teach at all in the name of Jesus. 19But Peter and John answered them, "Whether it is right in God's sight to listen to you rather than to God, you must judge; 20for we cannot keep from speaking about what we have seen and heard." 21After threatening them again, they let them go, finding no way to punish them because of the people, for all of them praised God for what had happened. 22For the man on whom this sign of healing had been performed was more than forty years old.

4.1–22: Arrest and trial for the name. 1–2: As the major Jewish institution which the Romans allowed, the Temple* had its own officials and security force. Proclamation of *the resurrection . . . in Jesus* is regarded as a threat to the Temple, perhaps especially by the *Sadducees,** who did not believe in the resurrection (23.6–10). **4:** The *five thousand* believers indicates a substantial response (2.41; Lk 9.14). **5–6:** This list indicates the composition of the council or Sanhedrin* of the Temple (4.15; see Lk 19.47; 22.66), reflecting the succession in the high priesthood from Annas (6–15 CE) to Caiaphas (18–36 CE). **7:** The question of *power* or *name* is a challenge of the legitimacy of their authority (Lk 20.2). **8:** Luke emphasizes that the *rulers of the people and elders* are now confronted with the authority of *the Holy Spirit* (see also 2.4; 4.31; 6.5; 7.55; 9.17; 11.24; 13.9). **10:** This public trial is again an occasion for testimony to *all* Israel (2.14, 36) and another indictment for the crucifixion of the Messiah* (2.23–24; 3.14–15; 5.30–31; 7.51–53). **11:** Ps 118.22 is again (see Lk 20.17) used as a charge against the authorities. **12:** This is one of the most ex-

clusive statements about Jesus in the New Testament (see also Jn 14.6), again linking his roles as messiah and savior (see Lk 2.11). In Luke's narrative,* to be *saved* means physical, social, and spiritual well-being in life and death. **13:** Like contemporary preaching philosophers, the apostles* were known for their *boldness* in speech (4.29–31; 18.26; 28.31). **14:** In Lk 21.15, Jesus promised "words and a wisdom" which opponents could not contradict. **19–20:** As in Socrates' classic defense of his teaching before the court in Athens (*Apology* 29D), the apostles show deference to the court's judgment about what is *right in God's sight*, but take responsibility for what they must do themselves in continuing to *speak*, no matter what the consequences (5.29). **21:** As with Jesus (Lk 19.47–48; 20.19; 22.2), the officials are frustrated in their efforts to silence the apostles *because of the people*. **22:** This unusual healing was a *sign of healing* because it pointed to God's fulfillment of an ancient promise of restoration (3.8).

23 After they were released, they went to their friends[a] and reported what the chief priests and the elders had said to them. 24When they heard it, they raised their voices together to God and said, "Sovereign Lord, who made the heaven and the earth, the sea, and everything in them, 25it is you who said by the Holy Spirit through our ancestor David, your servant:[b]
'Why did the Gentiles rage,
    and the peoples imagine vain things?
26 The kings of the earth took their stand,
    and the rulers have gathered together
    against the Lord and against his
        Messiah.'[c]
27For in this city, in fact, both Herod and Pontius Pilate, with the Gentiles and the peoples of Israel, gathered together against your holy servant[b] Jesus, whom you anointed, 28to do whatever your hand and your plan had predestined to take place. 29And now, Lord, look at their threats, and grant to your servants[d] to speak your word with all boldness, 30while you stretch out your hand to heal, and signs and wonders are performed through the name of your holy servant[b] Jesus." 31When they had prayed,

a Gk *their own*   *b* Or *child*   *c* Or *his Christ*
d Gk *slaves*

the place in which they were gathered together was shaken; and they were all filled with the Holy Spirit and spoke the word of God with boldness.

4.23–5.16: The divine authority of the apostles.* 4.24: Their prayer to the *Sovereign Lord* invokes God's royal dominion (see also Lk 2.29) over *everything* (Acts 14.15; 17.24). 25–26: In the Psalms, God spoke through King *David* (Lk 24.44; Acts 1.16; 2.25, 30–31). Psalm 2 is about God's protection of the messiah* from those who *have gathered* to threaten his reign as ruler over the nations. 27: A direct link is made to the dire roles all these groups played in Jesus' trial, especially *Herod* (Lk 9.7–9; 13.31; 23.6–12) and *Pilate* (Lk 13.1; 23.1–25). Even the way they *gathered together* signaled the divine drama (see v. 26). As God's *holy servant*, Jesus is again in David's line (vv. 25, 31), *anointed** or "made messiah" at his baptism* (10.38). 28: Luke's conviction about what is *predestined* or "necessary" is grounded in the way the scriptures stated God's *plan* that had to be fulfilled (Lk 24.26, 44). 30: The figure of Moses as God's servant (3.26) again illumines the images of stretching out *your hand* in *signs and wonders* (Ex 3.20; 4.4; Acts 7.36). 31: The *shaking* of the place is another sign of divine presence (Acts 2.2).

32 Now the whole group of those who believed were of one heart and soul, and no one claimed private ownership of any possessions, but everything they owned was held in common. 33With great power the apostles gave their testimony to the resurrection of the Lord Jesus, and great grace was upon them all. 34There was not a needy person among them, for as many as owned lands or houses sold them and brought the proceeds of what was sold. 35They laid it at the apostles' feet, and it was distributed to each as any had need. 36There was a Levite, a native of Cyprus, Joseph, to whom the apostles gave the name Barnabas (which means "son of encouragement"). 37He sold a field that belonged to him, then brought the money, and laid it at the apostles' feet.

5 But a man named Ananias, with the consent of his wife Sapphira, sold a piece of property; 2with his wife's knowledge, he kept back some of the proceeds, and brought only a part and laid it at the apostles' feet. 3"An-anias," Peter asked, "why has Satan filled your heart to lie to the Holy Spirit and to keep back part of the proceeds of the land? 4While it remained unsold, did it not remain your own? And after it was sold, were not the proceeds at your disposal? How is it that you have contrived this deed in your heart? You did not lie to us[a] but to God!" 5Now when Ananias heard these words, he fell down and died. And great fear seized all who heard of it. 6The young men came and wrapped up his body,[b] then carried him out and buried him.

7 After an interval of about three hours his wife came in, not knowing what had happened. 8Peter said to her, "Tell me whether you and your husband sold the land for such and such a price." And she said, "Yes, that was the price." 9Then Peter said to her, "How is it that you have agreed together to put the Spirit of the Lord to the test? Look, the feet of those who have buried your husband are at the door, and they will carry you out." 10Immediately she fell down at his feet and died. When the young men came in they found her dead, so they carried her out and buried her beside her husband. 11And great fear seized the whole church and all who heard of these things.

12 Now many signs and wonders were done among the people through the apostles. And they were all together in Solomon's Portico. 13None of the rest dared to join them, but the people held them in high esteem. 14Yet more than ever believers were added to the Lord, great numbers of both men and women, 15so that they even carried out the sick into the streets, and laid them on cots and mats, in order that Peter's shadow might fall on some of them as he came by. 16A great number of people would also gather from the towns around Jerusalem, bringing the sick and those tormented by unclean spirits, and they were all cured.

4.32–5.16. 4.32–34: Luke's picture of *common* ownership expresses a vision of the practices of the community of the resurrection (see also 2.44–47; 24.15–16, 25). 35: On the distribution *as any had need*, see

a Gk *to men* b Meaning of Gk uncertain

6.1–2. **36**: *Barnabas* is identified as a *Levite* (they have no "allotment" in the land, Deut 14.29) and will provide a link to Paul's mission to *Cyprus* (Acts 11.19–20; 13.2–4; 21.16). **37**: His gift, *laid at the apostles'* feet, acknowledges their authority without coercion. **5.1–4**: The *consent* and *knowledge* of *Sapphira* disclose the conspiracy to *lie* which they *contrived*. *Satan* is associated with the premeditated character of such collusion (see Lk 22.3–6). **9**: They are not merely challenging apostolic authority, but putting *the Spirit of the Lord to the test*, as in Israel in the Exodus (see Ex 17.2, 7; Deut 6.16; Lk 4.12; 11.16; Acts 15.10). **11**: The *fear* is characteristic awe of divine activity (2.43; 19.17; Lk 1.12, 65; 2.9; 7.16; 8.37). This is the first mention of *the church* (Gk., "ekklesia"), meaning the "assembly" or "assembly of believers" (4.32), as Israel was also called in the Greek scriptures (Deut 4.10; 9.10; 18.16; 23.1–2). **12**: *Solomon's Portico* clearly puts them back in the Temple* (3.11; 5.25), in the presence of danger (4.1). **15**: The expectation that even *Peter's shadow* could heal is a remarkable testimony to the overshadowing power of the Most High (Lk 1.35; Acts 19.11–12). **16**: As in the early conflicts with Jesus over his healing, Luke emphasizes that *they were all cured* (Lk 6.19).

17 Then the high priest took action; he and all who were with him (that is, the sect of the Sadducees), being filled with jealousy, [18] arrested the apostles and put them in the public prison. [19] But during the night an angel of the Lord opened the prison doors, brought them out, and said, [20] "Go, stand in the temple and tell the people the whole message about this life." [21] When they heard this, they entered the temple at daybreak and went on with their teaching.

When the high priest and those with him arrived, they called together the council and the whole body of the elders of Israel, and sent to the prison to have them brought. [22] But when the temple police went there, they did not find them in the prison; so they returned and reported, [23] "We found the prison securely locked and the guards standing at the doors, but when we opened them, we found no one inside." [24] Now when the captain of the temple and the chief priests heard these words, they were perplexed about them, wondering what might be going on. [25] Then someone arrived and announced,

"Look, the men whom you put in prison are standing in the temple and teaching the people!" [26] Then the captain went with the temple police and brought them, but without violence, for they were afraid of being stoned by the people.

27 When they had brought them, they had them stand before the council. The high priest questioned them, [28] saying, "We gave you strict orders not to teach in this name,[a] yet here you have filled Jerusalem with your teaching and you are determined to bring this man's blood on us." [29] But Peter and the apostles answered, "We must obey God rather than any human authority.[b] [30] The God of our ancestors raised up Jesus, whom you had killed by hanging him on a tree. [31] God exalted him at his right hand as Leader and Savior that he might give repentance to Israel and forgiveness of sins. [32] And we are witnesses to these things, and so is the Holy Spirit whom God has given to those who obey him."

5.17–42: The trial of Israel. 17: Acts uses the word *sect** to mean a "division" or "school," including the *Sadducees** (see 23.1–10), the *Pharisees** (15.5; 26.5), and the Christians or followers of the messiah,* Jesus (24.5, 14; 28.22). *Jealousy* is more than petty envy, because the question of God's favor or promises is at stake in the conflicts among the "sects" (7.9; 17.5). **19**: On divinely initiated escapes from *prison*, see also 12.6–11; 16.26–31. **20**: The Temple* is the divinely ordained place for teaching *the people* (Lk 19.47; 20.1; 21.5–6, 38). *The whole message about this life* is another summary of the proclamation (4.1; 5.42; 13.26). **24**: Their being *perplexed* again creates the opportunity for interpretation.* **26**: On the fear of *the people*, see comment on 4.21. **28**: *To bring this man's blood on us* is to hold them accountable for Jesus' death (Gen 4.10–11; see Mt 27.24–25), as Peter did in 4.10–11. **29**: The high priests also claimed to speak with God's *authority*. **30**: Peter again indicts the rulers by contrasting God's raising Jesus and their involvement in his death (2.23–24; 3.13–15; 4.10). **31**: On Jesus as *Leader*, see 3.15. His role as *Savior* is full of scriptural and political associations since this is a title often used of rulers (see Lk 2.11; Acts 13.23; Isa 43.11).

a Other ancient authorities read *Did we not give you strict orders not to teach in this name?*   *b* Gk *than men*

Repentance and forgiveness of sins are both gifts, grounded in God's promises (Acts 2.38; 11.18).

~~~~~~

33 When they heard this, they were enraged and wanted to kill them. 34But a Pharisee in the council named Gamaliel, a teacher of the law, respected by all the people, stood up and ordered the men to be put outside for a short time. 35Then he said to them, "Fellow Israelites,ᵃ consider carefully what you propose to do to these men. 36For some time ago Theudas rose up, claiming to be somebody, and a number of men, about four hundred, joined him; but he was killed, and all who followed him were dispersed and disappeared. 37After him Judas the Galilean rose up at the time of the census and got people to follow him; he also perished, and all who followed him were scattered. 38So in the present case, I tell you, keep away from these men and let them alone; because if this plan or this undertaking is of human origin, it will fail; 39but if it is of God, you will not be able to overthrow them—in that case you may even be found fighting against God!"

They were convinced by him, 40and when they had called in the apostles, they had them flogged. Then they ordered them not to speak in the name of Jesus, and let them go. 41As they left the council, they rejoiced that they were considered worthy to suffer dishonor for the sake of the name. 42And every day in the temple and at homeᵇ they did not cease to teach and proclaim Jesus as the Messiah.ᶜ

5.33–42. 34: A Pharisee* could speak in the council with a different view of both resurrection (23.6–10) and inspiration than the Sadducees.* In Acts 22.3, Paul claimed that Gamaliel was his teacher in the law (see Lk 5.17). 36: Agreeing with Gamaliel about true and false prophets* (see also Deut 18.22), Josephus* reported that Theudas claimed to be a prophet who could lead his followers through the Jordan like Moses or Joshua (Antiquities 20.97–98). 37: Josephus (Antiquities 18.1–10; War 2.117–118; 7.252–258) confirms that Judas the Galilean led an abortive revolt against the Roman census. 39: Of course Luke regards opposition to the apostolic mission exactly as fighting against God (11.17). 40: Although they are released, they are not vindicated. The order against preaching

remains in force, backed with flogging (Lk 23.22). 42: The focus of their preaching in the Temple* (5.20–21) remains that Jesus is the Messiah* (2.36; 10.36–38; 17.3).

~~~~~~

6 Now during those days, when the disciples were increasing in number, the Hellenists complained against the Hebrews because their widows were being neglected in the daily distribution of food. 2And the twelve called together the whole community of the disciples and said, "It is not right that we should neglect the word of God in order to wait on tables.ᵈ 3Therefore, friends,ᵉ select from among yourselves seven men of good standing, full of the Spirit and of wisdom, whom we may appoint to this task, 4while we, for our part, will devote ourselves to prayer and to serving the word." 5What they said pleased the whole community, and they chose Stephen, a man full of faith and the Holy Spirit, together with Philip, Prochorus, Nicanor, Timon, Parmenas, and Nicolaus, a proselyte of Antioch. 6They had these men stand before the apostles, who prayed and laid their hands on them.

7 The word of God continued to spread; the number of the disciples increased greatly in Jerusalem, and a great many of the priests became obedient to the faith.

8 Stephen, full of grace and power, did great wonders and signs among the people. 9Then some of those who belonged to the synagogue of the Freedmen (as it was called), Cyrenians, Alexandrians, and others of those from Cilicia and Asia, stood up and argued with Stephen. 10But they could not withstand the wisdom and the Spiritᶠ with which he spoke. 11Then they secretly instigated some men to say, "We have heard him speak blasphemous words against Moses and God." 12They stirred up the people as well as the elders and the scribes; then they suddenly confronted him, seized him, and brought him before the council. 13They set up false witnesses who said, "This man never stops saying things against this holy place and the law; 14for we have heard him say

---

a Gk Men, Israelites   b Or from house to house
c Or the Christ   d Or keep accounts   e Gk brothers
f Or spirit

that this Jesus of Nazareth[a] will destroy this place and will change the customs that Moses handed on to us." [15]And all who sat in the council looked intently at him, and they saw that his face was like the face of an angel.

6.1–15: Stephen, the Hellenist,* prompts persecution. 1: The *Hellenists* were probably Greek-speaking Jews who belonged among the *disciples* or followers of Jesus (6.2, 7), along with the *Hebrews* who were Jews who spoke a dialect of Hebrew called Aramaic.* The *daily distribution* was given "to each as any had need," and the special needs of the *widows* had priority according to the law (Deut 10.18; 14.29; 26.12–13). **2:** *The twelve* apostles* (1.26) had a particular role in Israel (Lk 22.30), which required their service of *the word of God*, a synonym for God's own mission (4.31; 6.7; 8.14; 11.1; 12.24; 19.20). **3:** In Lk 9.1–10.1, the sending of the twelve is followed by the sending of the seventy, all still within Israel. These well-attested *seven* (compare 1.21–22) are assigned the *task* of serving the identified "need," which was central to the community (2.45; 4.35). **5:** Greek names were common among Jews throughout the empire. In addition to *Stephen, Philip* is the only one who plays a further role in the narrative* (8.5, 29, 40; 21.8–9) **6:** The *apostles'* prayer and laying on of hands (13.3) mark the confirmation of the Spirit's choice as much as did the casting of lots (1.26). **7:** This summary verse indicates the promising culmination of the early mission in *Jerusalem* (1.8), particularly with the inclusion of *many of the priests*. The conflicts that follow are not with priests who became disciples. **8:** Nothing is said of Stephen's serving the needs of the widows, but his *great wonders and signs* manifest the work of God through him as through the apostles (5.12). **9:** These specific *synagogues** for Greek-speaking Jews from throughout the empire are otherwise unknown. **10:** Hellenistic philosophers, including Greek-speaking Jews, were interested in *wisdom* (see 1 Cor 1.22), but this was an inspired display of "a wisdom that none could oppose" (Lk 21.15). **11–12:** The charges of blasphemy *against Moses and God* are contrived, as they were against Jesus (see Lk 20.19–20). The conspirators are the ones who *stir up the people* (see Lk 23.5). **13:** The prohibition of *false witnesses* is one of the ten commandments (Ex 20.16; Deut 19.16–18). The charge against Stephen is similar to that brought against Paul (21.28). The security of Israel was believed to rest on the sanctity of the law and the Temple.* **14:**

Luke only reports this charge against Jesus in this context (see Mk 14.58; 15.29; Mt 26.61; 27.40; Jn 2.19–21). **15:** Stephen's transformation with *his face like the face of an angel* was a warning of contending with God (see Dan 3.24–30).

---

7 Then the high priest asked him, "Are these things so?" [2]And Stephen replied: "Brothers[b] and fathers, listen to me. The God of glory appeared to our ancestor Abraham when he was in Mesopotamia, before he lived in Haran, [3]and said to him, 'Leave your country and your relatives and go to the land that I will show you.' [4]Then he left the country of the Chaldeans and settled in Haran. After his father died, God had him move from there to this country in which you are now living. [5]He did not give him any of it as a heritage, not even a foot's length, but promised to give it to him as his possession and to his descendants after him, even though he had no child. [6]And God spoke in these terms, that his descendants would be resident aliens in a country belonging to others, who would enslave them and mistreat them during four hundred years. [7]'But I will judge the nation that they serve,' said God, 'and after that they shall come out and worship me in this place.' [8]Then he gave him the covenant of circumcision. And so Abraham[c] became the father of Isaac and circumcised him on the eighth day; and Isaac became the father of Jacob, and Jacob of the twelve patriarchs.

[9] "The patriarchs, jealous of Joseph, sold him into Egypt; but God was with him, [10]and rescued him from all his afflictions, and enabled him to win favor and to show wisdom when he stood before Pharaoh, king of Egypt, who appointed him ruler over Egypt and over all his household. [11]Now there came a famine throughout Egypt and Canaan, and great suffering, and our ancestors could find no food. [12]But when Jacob heard that there was grain in Egypt, he sent our ancestors there on their first visit. [13]On the second visit Joseph made himself known to his brothers, and Joseph's family became known to Pharaoh. [14]Then Joseph sent and

a Gk *the Nazorean*   *b* Gk *Men, brothers*   *c* Gk *he* invited his father Jacob and all his relatives to come to him, seventy-five in all; [15]so Jacob went down to Egypt. He himself died there as well as our ancestors, [16]and their bodies[a] were brought back to Shechem and laid in the tomb that Abraham had bought for a sum of silver from the sons of Hamor in Shechem.

7.1–8.1: Stephen's witness. 7.1: The interrogation recalls Jesus' trial before the *high priest* (Lk 22.67) and Pilate (Lk 23.3). **2–50:**This extended retelling of stories from Genesis displays careful interpretations* of the Greek version known as the Septuagint* (LXX). As they are retold, the stories emphasize God's initiative and activity. **2:** *The God of glory* is an unusual title (Ps 29.3) for the Lord who *appeared to Abraham* in Gen 12.7. **3:** The quotation is from Gen 12.1. **5:** The contrast between present promise and future *possession* originates in Genesis (13.15; 17.8; 48.4). **6:** Israel knew what it was to be *resident aliens** (Gen 15.13; Ex 2.22; 18.3; Deut 23.7), even in their own land, because it belonged to God (Lev 25.23). **7:** The quotation of Gen 15.14 continues. **8:** *The covenant* of circumcision** is described in several passages in Genesis (17.10–14). On the *twelve patriarchs* and their relationship to the twelve apostles,* see Lk 22.30; Acts 1.26. **9:** Gen 37.11 also identifies their jealousy, closely connected with their hatred for Joseph's receiving their father's love (Gen 37.4; see Acts 5.17). Among all the stories of the patriarchs, Stephen's focus on Joseph highlights a divided Israel with God taking special care of Joseph, for *God was with him* (see Gen 39.2, 21, 23; and Peter in Acts 10.38). **11–16:** These verses are a condensed version of Gen 41–50.

---

17 "But as the time drew near for the fulfillment of the promise that God had made to Abraham, our people in Egypt increased and multiplied [18]until another king who had not known Joseph ruled over Egypt. [19]He dealt craftily with our race and forced our ancestors to abandon their infants so that they would die. [20]At this time Moses was born, and he was beautiful before God. For three months he was brought up in his father's house; [21]and when he was abandoned, Pharaoh's daughter adopted him and brought him up as her own son. [22]So Moses was instructed in all the wisdom of the Egyptians and was powerful in his words and deeds.

23 "When he was forty years old, it came into his heart to visit his relatives, the Israelites.[b] [24]When he saw one of them being wronged, he defended the oppressed man and avenged him by striking down the Egyptian. [25]He supposed that his kinsfolk would understand that God through him was rescuing them, but they did not understand. [26]The next day he came to some of them as they were quarreling and tried to reconcile them, saying, 'Men, you are brothers; why do you wrong each other?' [27]But the man who was wronging his neighbor pushed Moses[c] aside, saying, 'Who made you a ruler and a judge over us? [28]Do you want to kill me as you killed the Egyptian yesterday?' [29]When he heard this, Moses fled and became a resident alien in the land of Midian. There he became the father of two sons.

30 "Now when forty years had passed, an angel appeared to him in the wilderness of Mount Sinai, in the flame of a burning bush. [31]When Moses saw it, he was amazed at the sight; and as he approached to look, there came the voice of the Lord: [32]'I am the God of your ancestors, the God of Abraham, Isaac, and Jacob.' Moses began to tremble and did not dare to look. [33]Then the Lord said to him, 'Take off the sandals from your feet, for the place where you are standing is holy ground. [34]I have surely seen the mistreatment of my people who are in Egypt and have heard their groaning, and I have come down to rescue them. Come now, I will send you to Egypt.'

35 "It was this Moses whom they rejected when they said, 'Who made you a ruler and a judge?' and whom God now sent as both ruler and liberator through the angel who appeared to him in the bush. [36]He led them out, having performed wonders and signs in Egypt, at the Red Sea, and in the wilderness for forty years. [37]This is the Moses who said to the Israelites, 'God will raise up a prophet for you from your own people[d] as he raised me up.' [38]He is the one who was in the congregation in the wilderness with the angel who spoke to him at Mount Sinai, and with

a Gk *they*   *b* Gk *his brothers, the sons of Israel*
c Gk *him*   *d* Gk *your brothers*

our ancestors; and he received living oracles to give to us. 39Our ancestors were unwilling to obey him; instead, they pushed him aside, and in their hearts they turned back to Egypt, 40saying to Aaron, 'Make gods for us who will lead the way for us; as for this Moses who led us out from the land of Egypt, we do not know what has happened to him.' 41At that time they made a calf, offered a sacrifice to the idol, and reveled in the works of their hands. 42But God turned away from them and handed them over to worship the host of heaven, as it is written in the book of the prophets:

'Did you offer to me slain victims and
        sacrifices
    forty years in the wilderness,
        O house of Israel?
43 No; you took along the tent of
        Moloch,
    and the star of your god
        Rephan, the images that you made
            to worship;
    so I will remove you beyond Babylon.'

44 "Our ancestors had the tent of testimony in the wilderness, as God*a* directed when he spoke to Moses, ordering him to make it according to the pattern he had seen. 45Our ancestors in turn brought it in with Joshua when they dispossessed the nations that God drove out before our ancestors. And it was there until the time of David, 46who found favor with God and asked that he might find a dwelling place for the house of Jacob.*b* 47But it was Solomon who built a house for him. 48Yet the Most High does not dwell in houses made with human hands;*c* as the prophet says,

49 'Heaven is my throne,
        and the earth is my footstool.
    What kind of house will you build for
            me, says the Lord,
    or what is the place of my rest?
50 Did not my hand make all these things?'

7.17–50: The story of Moses to Solomon, from Exodus to Kings, is told in sequence (note times in vv. 20, 23, 26, 30, 36, 42, 45) and from within Israel (*our ancestors* in vv. 19, 32 38, 39, 44, 45), repeating the themes of the scriptural histories of God's fidelity and Israel's rejection. Like Moses' speech at the end of his life

(Deut 32–34), Stephen is citing Israel's history "in witness against you" (Deut 32.46), as a call to repentance. **22:** In the retelling of Ex 2 in many Jewish sources, Moses was famous for his mastery of the *wisdom of the Egyptians.* **25–27:** This interpretation★ of what *they did not understand* is consistent with Luke's emphasis on the "ignorance" that can be forgiven (3.17; 17.30). To push *Moses aside* is to reject him as *ruler and liberator* (v. 35). **30:** The appearance of the *angel in the flame of a burning bush* (Ex 3.2) was variously allegorized★ in many first-century interpretations. Like the Pharisees★ who were known to believe in angelic messengers, Stephen receives these accounts literally (see vv. 38, 53). **35:** The phrase *this Moses whom they rejected* (see also v. 37, *this is the Moses who said*) parallels *this Jesus whom you crucified* (2.36; see also 2.23, 32). **37:** Stephen invokes the crucial passage from Deut 18.15 that was used to identify Jesus as "the prophet★ like Moses" (3.22). **39:** *Our ancestors were unwilling to obey . . . pushed him aside* (see comment on v. 27). **40–41:** On the story of the *calf,* see Ex 32. **41:** *Idolatry★* is the most grievous sin in Israel, violating the first commandment. **42–43:** The *book of the prophets* may refer to a collection of the twelve minor prophets. The prophetic verdict of Amos 5.25–27 against Israel's idolatry is now cited not merely for exile beyond Damascus, but *beyond Babylon.* **44–48:** This scriptural argument turns against the Temple★ as God's *dwelling place,* because *the Most High does not dwell in houses made with human hands* (see v. 41 on idols and Paul's speech about temples in 17.24). **49–50:** This citation from Isa 66.1 further claims the whole creation as God's dwelling, made by *"my hand."* Ps 132.13–14, by contrast, affirms Zion★ as God's chosen habitation and resting place forever.

51 "You stiff-necked people, uncircumcised in heart and ears, you are forever opposing the Holy Spirit, just as your ancestors used to do. 52Which of the prophets did your ancestors not persecute? They killed those who foretold the coming of the Righteous One, and now you have become his betrayers and murderers. 53You are the ones that received the law as ordained by angels, and yet you have not kept it."

54 When they heard these things, they

a Gk *he*   *b* Other ancient authorities read *for the God of Jacob*   *c* Gk *with hands* became enraged and ground their teeth at Stephen.*a* 55 But filled with the Holy Spirit, he gazed into heaven and saw the glory of God and Jesus standing at the right hand of God. 56 "Look," he said, "I see the heavens opened and the Son of Man standing at the right hand of God!" 57 But they covered their ears, and with a loud shout all rushed together against him. 58 Then they dragged him out of the city and began to stone him; and the witnesses laid their coats at the feet of a young man named Saul. 59 While they were stoning Stephen, he prayed, "Lord Jesus, receive my spirit." 60 Then he knelt down and cried out in a loud voice, "Lord, do not hold this sin against them." When he had said

8 this, he died.*b* 1 And Saul approved of their killing him.

7.51–8.1. 51: The recitation now turns into a full indictment, addressed to *you stiff-necked people* (see Ex 33.3, 5) and *your ancestors*. The sin is *opposing the Holy Spirit* (see Gamaliel's warning in 5.39). 52: The accusation of persecuting and killing *the prophets*★ is traditional speech (Lk 6.23, 26; 11.47–52; 13.34) calling for repentance. It is dangerous if taken out of its prophetic context within Israel and used self-righteously by non-Jews (see Rom 11). In calling Jesus *the Righteous One*, Luke draws upon the prophetic and wisdom traditions (Wis 2.12–22) of the suffering righteous (see also Lk 23.47; Acts 3.14; 22.14). 55: Rejecting Stephen is again "opposing the Holy Spirit" (v. 51), as he is *filled with the Holy Spirit* (6.3, 10, 15). 56: The *heavens opened* at Jesus' baptism★ too (Lk 3.21) and in Peter's vision (10.11). *The Son of Man* (Dan 7.13) is clearly Jesus, usually "sitting at the right hand of the power of God" (Lk 2.69; Acts 2.33), but now *standing*, perhaps preparing to receive Stephen or to come "in his glory" (Lk 9.26). 57–58: Stoning is the punishment for blasphemy, which is also why *they covered their ears* (see 7.51). This is the first appearance of *Saul*, who appears as a leader since they *laid their coats at* his feet. 59–60: Stephen's giving up his *spirit* follows the pattern of Jesus' death in Luke 23.46, including the prayer for those who killed him (Lk 23.34). 8.1: *Saul approved* as a witness and was complicit in the murder (see Lk 11.48; Acts 22.20).

That day a severe persecution began against the church in Jerusalem, and all except the apostles were scattered throughout the countryside of Judea and Samaria. 2 Devout men buried Stephen and made loud lamentation over him. 3 But Saul was ravaging the church by entering house after house; dragging off both men and women, he committed them to prison.

8.2–15.35: Scattered throughout the countryside. 8.2–3: Scattered by persecution: The *severe persecution* (which lasts until 9.31) appears to be focused on the Hellenists.★ *The apostles*★ (6.2) were excepted. The mission moves beyond Jerusalem to *Judea and Samaria* in accord with the promise (1.8; see also 9.31). *Devout Jews* attended to proper burials (Lk 23.50; 9.59–60) with *lamentation* (Lk 23.27, 48). Acts 9.2; 22.4–5; 26.10 claim *Saul* acted under the high priest's authority. Jesus' word in Lk 21.12 identifies such persecution as within God's plan (see Acts 12.4; 16.23).

4 Now those who were scattered went from place to place, proclaiming the word. 5 Philip went down to the city*c* of Samaria and proclaimed the Messiah*d* to them. 6 The crowds with one accord listened eagerly to what was said by Philip, hearing and seeing the signs that he did, 7 for unclean spirits, crying with loud shrieks, came out of many who were possessed; and many others who were paralyzed or lame were cured. 8 So there was great joy in that city.

9 Now a certain man named Simon had previously practiced magic in the city and amazed the people of Samaria, saying that he was someone great. 10 All of them, from the least to the greatest, listened to him eagerly, saying, "This man is the power of God that is called Great." 11 And they listened eagerly to him because for a long time he had amazed them with his magic. 12 But when they believed Philip, who was proclaiming the good news about the kingdom of God and the name of Jesus Christ, they were baptized, both men and women. 13 Even Simon himself believed. After being baptized, he stayed constantly with Philip and was amazed when he saw the signs and great miracles that took place.

a Gk *him*   *b* Gk *fell asleep*   *c* Other ancient authorities read *a city*   *d* Or *the Christ*

14 Now when the apostles at Jerusalem heard that Samaria had accepted the word of God, they sent Peter and John to them. [15]The two went down and prayed for them that they might receive the Holy Spirit [16](for as yet the Spirit had not come[a] upon any of them; they had only been baptized in the name of the Lord Jesus). [17]Then Peter and John[b] laid their hands on them, and they received the Holy Spirit. [18]Now when Simon saw that the Spirit was given through the laying on of the apostles' hands, he offered them money, [19]saying, "Give me also this power so that anyone on whom I lay my hands may receive the Holy Spirit." [20]But Peter said to him, "May your silver perish with you, because you thought you could obtain God's gift with money! [21]You have no part or share in this, for your heart is not right before God. [22]Repent therefore of this wickedness of yours, and pray to the Lord that, if possible, the intent of your heart may be forgiven you. [23]For I see that you are in the gall of bitterness and the chains of wickedness." [24]Simon answered, "Pray for me to the Lord, that nothing of what you[c] have said may happen to me."

25 Now after Peter and John[d] had testified and spoken the word of the Lord, they returned to Jerusalem, proclaiming the good news to many villages of the Samaritans.

8.4–25: The mission in Samaria. 5: *Philip*, like Stephen, is a Hellenist,* appointed to wait on tables (6.1–6), but immediately makes a public witness. The mission in *Samaria* is significant to moving beyond Jerusalem, as Samaria was significant to Jesus' journey toward Jerusalem (Lk 9.51–56; 10.29–37). The message remains focused on Jesus as *Messiah*★ (see 2.36; 3.18; 4.26–27; 17.3). 6: The response of the *crowd* is comparable to that of the people in Jerusalem (2.43; 4.32–33) 7: This summary of healings recalls Jesus' ministry in Lk 7.21–22. *Loud shrieks* were characteristic of manifestations of demons (Lk 4.33, 41; 8.28; 9.39). 9–10: *Simon*, known in Christian stories as "Simon Magus" or "Simon the Magician," was infamous as a Samaritan heretic. Simon's claim that *he was someone great* and his acclamation as *the power of God that is called Great* are both blasphemy (Acts 12.22–23). 11: Luke consistently links *magic*, widely practiced through rituals, books, amulets, and spells,

with demonic forces (Acts 13.10; 19.13–20). 12–13: Believing *the good news* Philip proclaimed and being *baptized* was a turning away of repentance or conversion from the practices of Simon. *Signs* and *great miracles* were thus displays of God's power (Acts 2.43; 5.12; 6.8), not the magician's art. 14: The arrival of *the apostles*★ (8.1) signals the authorization of the office of *the word of God* that was entrusted to the twelve (see 6.2). 15–20: The confirming sign of receiving *the Holy Spirit* is *given through the apostles' hands*, but not finally controlled by the twelve (6.6; 11.1–18, 22; 19.1–7). Because of this story, buying a spiritual office with *money* became known as "simony." *May your silver perish with you* is a prophetic★ warning, calling for repentance, not a final verdict. 21–22: The *part or share* is divinely given (1.26). The repentance of the *heart* is marked with remorse (2.37), not scheming for personal advantage. 25: *Peter and John* bring the mission of the apostles to the *Samaritans*, confirming the work of the Hellenists.

26 Then an angel of the Lord said to Philip, "Get up and go toward the south[e] to the road that goes down from Jerusalem to Gaza." (This is a wilderness road.) [27]So he got up and went. Now there was an Ethiopian eunuch, a court official of the Candace, queen of the Ethiopians, in charge of her entire treasury. He had come to Jerusalem to worship [28]and was returning home; seated in his chariot, he was reading the prophet Isaiah. [29]Then the Spirit said to Philip, "Go over to this chariot and join it." [30]So Philip ran up to it and heard him reading the prophet Isaiah. He asked, "Do you understand what you are reading?" [31]He replied, "How can I, unless someone guides me?" And he invited Philip to get in and sit beside him. [32]Now the passage of the scripture that he was reading was this:

"Like a sheep he was led to the
    slaughter,
  and like a lamb silent before
    its shearer,
    so he does not open his mouth.
[33] In his humiliation justice was denied
    him.

a Gk *fallen*   *b* Gk *they*   *c* The Greek word for *you* and the verb *pray* are plural   *d* Gk *after they*   *e* Or *go at noon*

Who can describe his generation?
For his life is taken away from the
earth."

34The eunuch asked Philip, "About whom,
may I ask you, does the prophet say this,
about himself or about someone else?"
35Then Philip began to speak, and starting
with this scripture, he proclaimed to him the
good news about Jesus. 36As they were going
along the road, they came to some water; and
the eunuch said, "Look, here is water! What
is to prevent me from being baptized?"ᵃ
38He commanded the chariot to stop, and
both of them, Philip and the eunuch, went
down into the water, and Philipᵇ baptized
him. 39When they came up out of the water,
the Spirit of the Lord snatched Philip away;
the eunuch saw him no more, and went on
his way rejoicing. 40But Philip found himself
at Azotus, and as he was passing through the
region, he proclaimed the good news to all
the towns until he came to Caesarea.

8.26–40: The mission goes to Africa. 26: The instructions of *an angel of the Lord* (see Lk 1.11; see Acts
23.8–9) leave no doubt of God's agency in this episode. *Gaza* is south of Jerusalem on the route to Africa.
27: *Ethiopia* lies south of Egypt and had Jewish communities from at least the time of the Babylonian destruction (see Isa 11.11; Zeph 3.10). Oriental rulers often placed *eunuchs,* castrated slaves or servants, in
significant positions of trust. In Isa 56.3–5, the eunuch
and the foreigner are symbols of Israel's hope of restoration. **29:** Now *the Spirit* directs Philip, instead of
an angel (26). **30–31:** The ancients regularly *read*
aloud, although this remains an unusual setting for
eavesdropping. The two questions are again excellent
examples of Luke's depiction of teaching (see 2.7, 8,
12). **32–33:** *The passage of the scripture* is Isa 53.7–8
(in the Greek version) which points to God's servant
who suffered. In Acts, *his life is taken away from the
earth* (as the Greek version of Isa reads) points to Jesus'
exaltation (see Acts 1.22; 3.21). **34:** The Ethiopian's
question opens the discussion for witness. Scholars remain interested in the question for their understanding of Isaiah. **36:** The question proves to be an enduring concern for what is to *prevent* or obstruct entry
into the kingdom (see Lk 11.52; 18.16; Acts 10.47;
11.17). **39:** *Philip* is *snatched* as in a rapture or sudden
removal (see Ezek 11.24; 1 Kings 18.12; 2 Kings 2.16;
Lk 17.34–35). **40:** *Philip's* mission continues north of

Gaza along the coast from *Azotos* to *Caesarea,* where
he was later reported to have a house (see 21.8).

9 Meanwhile Saul, still breathing threats
and murder against the disciples of the
Lord, went to the high priest 2and asked him
for letters to the synagogues at Damascus,
so that if he found any who belonged to the
Way, men or women, he might bring them
bound to Jerusalem. 3Now as he was going
along and approaching Damascus, suddenly
a light from heaven flashed around him. 4He
fell to the ground and heard a voice saying
to him, "Saul, Saul, why do you persecute
me?" 5He asked, "Who are you, Lord?" The
reply came, "I am Jesus, whom you are persecuting. 6But get up and enter the city, and
you will be told what you are to do." 7The
men who were traveling with him stood
speechless because they heard the voice but
saw no one. 8Saul got up from the ground,
and though his eyes were open, he could see
nothing; so they led him by the hand and
brought him into Damascus. 9For three days
he was without sight, and neither ate nor
drank.

9.1–31: The call of Saul (see also 22.6–16; 26.12–18).
1–2: Saul's pursuit of *the disciples of the Lord* is confirmed by Paul's letters (1 Cor 15.9), but Luke's stress
on the active collaboration of the *high priest* and
Temple★ authorities (see also 9.14; 22.5; 26.10, 12)
raises questions whether they had such powers of ex-
tradition. The *letters to the synagogues★* were common means of introduction or recommendation (see
Acts 28.21; 2 Cor 3.1). Acts tells nothing more about
the mission to *Damascus* or "all the towns" (8.40). *The
Way* is a designation of the followers of Jesus used by
both members and adversaries (19.9, 23; 22.4; 24.14,
22). **3:** The *light from heaven* is a sign of divine presence (see Lk 2.9; 9.29; 10.18; 17.24; 24.4; Acts 22.6;
26.13). **4–5:** Repeating *Saul's* name recalls the call
story of Moses, also in a divine display (Ex 3; 1 Sam
3.4, 10), revealing that Saul is *persecuting* the Lord
Jesus in the persons of his followers (Lk 10.16). **7:** Acts'
three accounts of this event differ on who saw or heard
what (see 22.9; 26.13). **8:** Saul's temporary blindness

a Other ancient authorities add all or most of verse 37,
*And Philip said, "If you believe with all your heart, you
may." And he replied, "I believe that Jesus Christ is the Son
of God."* b Gk *he*

is probably a divine judgment (13.11, 17–18; Isa 6.9–10, cited in Acts 28.26–27). **9:** Saul was apparently fasting (v. 11; 13.1–3).

~~~~~~~~~~~~~~~~~~~~~~~~~~~~~~~~~~~~~

10 Now there was a disciple in Damascus named Ananias. The Lord said to him in a vision, "Ananias." He answered, "Here I am, Lord." ¹¹The Lord said to him, "Get up and go to the street called Straight, and at the house of Judas look for a man of Tarsus named Saul. At this moment he is praying, ¹²and he has seen in a vision*ᵃ* a man named Ananias come in and lay his hands on him so that he might regain his sight." ¹³But Ananias answered, "Lord, I have heard from many about this man, how much evil he has done to your saints in Jerusalem; ¹⁴and here he has authority from the chief priests to bind all who invoke your name." ¹⁵But the Lord said to him, "Go, for he is an instrument whom I have chosen to bring my name before Gentiles and kings and before the people of Israel; ¹⁶I myself will show him how much he must suffer for the sake of my name." ¹⁷So Ananias went and entered the house. He laid his hands on Saul*ᵇ* and said, "Brother Saul, the Lord Jesus, who appeared to you on your way here, has sent me so that you may regain your sight and be filled with the Holy Spirit." ¹⁸And immediately something like scales fell from his eyes, and his sight was restored. Then he got up and was baptized, ¹⁹and after taking some food, he regained his strength.

For several days he was with the disciples in Damascus, ²⁰and immediately he began to proclaim Jesus in the synagogues, saying, "He is the Son of God." ²¹All who heard him were amazed and said, "Is not this the man who made havoc in Jerusalem among those who invoked this name? And has he not come here for the purpose of bringing them bound before the chief priests?" ²²Saul became increasingly more powerful and confounded the Jews who lived in Damascus by proving that Jesus*ᶜ* was the Messiah.*ᵈ*

23 After some time had passed, the Jews plotted to kill him, ²⁴but their plot became known to Saul. They were watching the gates day and night so that they might kill him; ²⁵but his disciples took him by night and let

him down through an opening in the wall,*ᵉ* lowering him in a basket.

26 When he had come to Jerusalem, he attempted to join the disciples; and they were all afraid of him, for they did not believe that he was a disciple. ²⁷But Barnabas took him, brought him to the apostles, and described for them how on the road he had seen the Lord, who had spoken to him, and how in Damascus he had spoken boldly in the name of Jesus. ²⁸So he went in and out among them in Jerusalem, speaking boldly in the name of the Lord. ²⁹He spoke and argued with the Hellenists; but they were attempting to kill him. ³⁰When the believers*ᶠ* learned of it, they brought him down to Caesarea and sent him off to Tarsus.

31 Meanwhile the church throughout Judea, Galilee, and Samaria had peace and was built up. Living in the fear of the Lord and in the comfort of the Holy Spirit, it increased in numbers.

9.10–31. 10: *"Here I am, Lord"* is the response of a faithful Israelite to such a vision (1 Sam 3.4, 6; Acts 22.12). **11:** The heavenly directions get right down to the *street, house,* and *man,* by name (see also 10.32). **15:** As a *chosen instrument* or vessel (2 Cor 4.7), Saul is the bearer of Jesus' mission. The *Gentiles,** *kings,* and *the people of Israel* will be the audiences of Saul/Paul's mission, largely in that order (13.46–47; 26.2–23; 28.23–28). God's mission is never done with Israel (Lk 2.25, 29–32, 34). **16:** He *must suffer* because this is the way of Jesus' mission, necessitated by God's plan in the scriptures (Lk 9.22; 17.25; 22.37; 24.7, 26, 44; Acts 4.27–28). On suffering for the *name,* see Acts 5.41 and comment on 3.16. **17–18:** The restoration of *sight* was a sign of the fulfillment of prophetic* promises (Lk 7.22; Isa 29.18; 35.5–6). Saul's baptism* is closely linked with being *filled with the Holy Spirit* (see 2.38). **20–22:** Proclaiming Jesus to be *the Son of God* meant to prove him to be the *Messiah,** probably through scriptural argument (v. 22; Lk 1.32, 35; 3.22; 4.3, 9, 41; 22.67–70; Acts 10.38; 17.2–3). **25:** 2 Cor 11.33 also refers to this escape from *Damascus in a basket.* **26–28:** The larger group of *disciples* feared Saul until he was accepted by the twelve *apostles** (6.1–2; 15.4, 6, 22; on *Barnabas,* the "son of conso-

a Other ancient authorities lack *in a vision*   *b* Gk *him*
c Gk *that this*   *d* Or *the Christ*   *e* Gk *through*
the wall   *f* Gk *brothers*

lation," see 4.36). Speaking *boldly* is a sign of inspired witness (2.29; 4.13, 29, 31; 13.46; 14.3; 18.26; 19.8; 26.26). **29–30:** *The Hellenists* who were attempting to kill* Saul may belong to the same synagogues* as the Hellenists who were *believers* (see 6.1–6, 9) who again steal Saul away for his own safety (9.24–25; 23.23–24). **31:** This Lukan summary again marks the progress of the mission promised in 1.8 (see 8.1).

32 Now as Peter went here and there among all the believers,ᵃ he came down also to the saints living in Lydda. ³³There he found a man named Aeneas, who had been bedridden for eight years, for he was paralyzed. ³⁴Peter said to him, "Aeneas, Jesus Christ heals you; get up and make your bed!" And immediately he got up. ³⁵And all the residents of Lydda and Sharon saw him and turned to the Lord.

36 Now in Joppa there was a disciple whose name was Tabitha, which in Greek is Dorcas.ᵇ She was devoted to good works and acts of charity. ³⁷At that time she became ill and died. When they had washed her, they laid her in a room upstairs. ³⁸Since Lydda was near Joppa, the disciples, who heard that Peter was there, sent two men to him with the request, "Please come to us without delay." ³⁹So Peter got up and went with them; and when he arrived, they took him to the room upstairs. All the widows stood beside him, weeping and showing tunics and other clothing that Dorcas had made while she was with them. ⁴⁰Peter put all of them outside, and then he knelt down and prayed. He turned to the body and said, "Tabitha, get up." Then she opened her eyes, and seeing Peter, she sat up. ⁴¹He gave her his hand and helped her up. Then calling the saints and widows, he showed her to be alive. ⁴²This became known throughout Joppa, and many believed in the Lord. ⁴³Meanwhile he stayed in Joppa for some time with a certain Simon, a tanner.

9.32–43: Peter's acts of power. 32: Peter is on a circuit of oversight, moving *here and there among all the believers.* **33–35:** Compare Jesus' healing of the *paralyzed man* in Lk 5.17–26, including the command to *get up* and the *immediate* healing. In Acts the response of the *residents* is more evidently repentance

and faith as they *turned to the Lord* (8.6–8). **36:** The name *Tabitha* or *Dorcas* means gazelle (Song 2.9; 8.14). *Good works and acts of charity* were honored in Jewish tradition (Lk 11.41; 12.33; Acts 3.2; 10.2). **37:** Jewish practice required proper preparation of the body for burial, including washing (Lk 23.50–24.1). **39:** On *the widows,* see Lk 2.37; Acts 6.2; 9.41. **40:** *Peter's* words calling to *Tabitha* to *get up* echo Jesus' command to the little girl in Lk 8.54 (see also Mk 5.41, "Talitha cum"). **43:** The name of *Simon the Tanner* again gives particularity to the story (9.10, 33, 36; 10.1, 6).

10 In Caesarea there was a man named Cornelius, a centurion of the Italian Cohort, as it was called. ²He was a devout man who feared God with all his household; he gave alms generously to the people and prayed constantly to God. ³One afternoon at about three o'clock he had a vision in which he clearly saw an angel of God coming in and saying to him, "Cornelius." ⁴He stared at him in terror and said, "What is it, Lord?" He answered, "Your prayers and your alms have ascended as a memorial before God. ⁵Now send men to Joppa for a certain Simon who is called Peter; ⁶he is lodging with Simon, a tanner, whose house is by the seaside." ⁷When the angel who spoke to him had left, he called two of his slaves and a devout soldier from the ranks of those who served him, ⁸and after telling them everything, he sent them to Joppa.

10.1–11.18: God gives repentance to the gentiles.* 10.1: *Caesarea,* a coastal city built by Herod the Great as a Roman port, is a thoroughfare in Acts (8.40; 9.30; 12.19; 18.22; 21.8, 16; 23.23, 33; 25.1, 4, 6, 13). A *centurion* led 100 soldiers within a *cohort* of about 600. See also Jesus and the centurion in Lk 7.1–10. **2:** Being *devout* (10.7; see also Lk 2.25; Acts 2.5; 8.2; 22.12), fearing God (10.22, 35; 13.26; see also 13.43, 50; 16.14; 17.4, 17; 18.7) giving alms (see comment on 9.36), and praying (2.42–46) all marked him as righteous according to the law, although he was a gentile.* **3–4:** *Three o'clock* was the ninth hour of the day, the hour of prayer (3.1). Like Saul and Ananias (9.3, 10), Peter and *Cornelius* have a double *vision* of

ᵃ Gk *all of them*   ᵇ The name Tabitha in Aramaic and the name Dorcas in Greek mean *a gazelle* a heavenly messenger appearing in two places (10.3, 11–13). The centurion calls the angel *Lord*, addressing an authority (compare "the Lord Jesus" in 9.17). **5–6:** The name, *Simon Peter* (Lk 5.8; 6.14), and the place are again specific (see comment on 9.11). Whether the house of a *tanner* could ever have been anything but ritually unclean does not seem to be a problem.

9 About noon the next day, as they were on their journey and approaching the city, Peter went up on the roof to pray. 10He became hungry and wanted something to eat; and while it was being prepared, he fell into a trance. 11He saw the heaven opened and something like a large sheet coming down, being lowered to the ground by its four corners. 12In it were all kinds of four-footed creatures and reptiles and birds of the air. 13Then he heard a voice saying, "Get up, Peter; kill and eat." 14But Peter said, "By no means, Lord; for I have never eaten anything that is profane or unclean." 15The voice said to him again, a second time, "What God has made clean, you must not call profane." 16This happened three times, and the thing was suddenly taken up to heaven.

10.9–16: *Peter's* vision deals directly with the *profane or unclean* (see also his recounting in 11.5–11). **12–13:** In Lev 11.1–47, Israel was commanded to make a distinction among the *four-footed creatures*, not to gather *all kinds* together, particularly to *eat*. **15:** *"What God has made clean"* apparently now included creatures that had been identified as unclean according to the laws of Israel. The word *profane* means "vulgar" or "common" and could be used to refer to all the nations not chosen of God or set apart by their observance of the law as holy to God. **16:** Repeating the vision *three times* anticipates the difficulty of the concern (11.1–8; 15.1–2).

17 Now while Peter was greatly puzzled about what to make of the vision that he had seen, suddenly the men sent by Cornelius appeared. They were asking for Simon's house and were standing by the gate. 18They called out to ask whether Simon, who was called Peter, was staying there. 19While Peter was still thinking about the vision, the Spirit said to him, "Look, three*a* men are searching for you. 20Now get up, go down,

and go with them without hesitation; for I have sent them." 21So Peter went down to the men and said, "I am the one you are looking for; what is the reason for your coming?" 22They answered, "Cornelius, a centurion, an upright and God-fearing man, who is well spoken of by the whole Jewish nation, was directed by a holy angel to send for you to come to his house and to hear what you have to say." 23So Peter*b* invited them in and gave them lodging.

The next day he got up and went with them, and some of the believers*c* from Joppa accompanied him. 24The following day they came to Caesarea. Cornelius was expecting them and had called together his relatives and close friends. 25On Peter's arrival Cornelius met him, and falling at his feet, worshiped him. 26But Peter made him get up, saying, "Stand up; I am only a mortal." 27And as he talked with him, he went in and found that many had assembled; 28and he said to them, "You yourselves know that it is unlawful for a Jew to associate with or to visit a Gentile; but God has shown me that I should not call anyone profane or unclean. 29So when I was sent for, I came without objection. Now may I ask why you sent for me?"

30 Cornelius replied, "Four days ago at this very hour, at three o'clock, I was praying in my house when suddenly a man in dazzling clothes stood before me. 31He said, 'Cornelius, your prayer has been heard and your alms have been remembered before God. 32Send therefore to Joppa and ask for Simon, who is called Peter; he is staying in the home of Simon, a tanner, by the sea.' 33Therefore I sent for you immediately, and you have been kind enough to come. So now all of us are here in the presence of God to listen to all that the Lord has commanded you to say."

34 Then Peter began to speak to them: "I truly understand that God shows no partiality, 35but in every nation anyone who fears him and does what is right is acceptable to him. 36You know the message he sent to the

a One ancient authority reads *two*; others lack the word
b Gk *he*   *c* Gk *brothers*

people of Israel, preaching peace by Jesus Christ—he is Lord of all. ³⁷That message spread throughout Judea, beginning in Galilee after the baptism that John announced: ³⁸how God anointed Jesus of Nazareth with the Holy Spirit and with power; how he went about doing good and healing all who were oppressed by the devil, for God was with him. ³⁹We are witnesses to all that he did both in Judea and in Jerusalem. They put him to death by hanging him on a tree; ⁴⁰but God raised him on the third day and allowed him to appear, ⁴¹not to all the people but to us who were chosen by God as witnesses, and who ate and drank with him after he rose from the dead. ⁴²He commanded us to preach to the people and to testify that he is the one ordained by God as judge of the living and the dead. ⁴³All the prophets testify about him that everyone who believes in him receives forgiveness of sins through his name."

10.17–43. **19:** Since he was *still thinking about the vision,* Peter got his first signal of their presence directly from *the Spirit.* **20:** He was to go *without hesitation,* which meant no delay, distinctions, or objections (v. 29; Jas 2.4). **22:** Compare v. 2. **23:** *Peter's* hospitality already begins to diminish the boundary, unless it is assumed the "slaves" and "devout soldier" (v. 7) were Jews (v. 28). **25–26:** Worship here could simply mean acknowledgment of authority in oriental homage, but it could imply a blasphemous confusion of a *mortal* and God (14.15). **28:** The boundaries of what was lawful in relationships between Jews and gentiles* were drawn carefully in various Jewish traditions, but few were so strict as to prevent association or visits (see Jesus in Lk 7.7). **34:** In Deut 10.17, not showing *partiality* means dispensing justice fairly, without regard to social standing. The Christians saw this principle as lying behind God's readiness to receive gentiles who did righteous acts (vv. 4, 31; Rom 2.10–11). **36–43:** This is one of the most compact summaries of early Christian preaching. **36:** God's *message* to *the people of Israel* in *Jesus Christ* was *peace* (Lk 1.79; 2.14; 7.50; 8.48; 10.5–6; 19.38; 24.36). The acclamation, *"he is Lord of all,"* implies Jesus' exaltation (Acts 2.34–36). **37–38:** Jesus' *anointing,* * or being made messiah,* was God's work, after John's baptism* (Lk 2.20, 21–22). *God was with him* is a scriptural phrase emphasizing God's agency (Acts

7.9). **41:** *Chosen by God as witnesses* refers to those who were witnesses to the resurrection, especially the twelve apostles* (Lk 24.48; Acts 1.8, 22; 2.32; 3.15; 5.32). **42:** The *people* here are Israel. Jesus' role as ultimate *judge* is also underscored in 17.31. **43:** Luke continues the emphasis on *all the prophets* * (Lk 24.27, 44), now as ratifying the radical message of *forgiveness* for *everyone* through faith (Rom 3.21–26).

44 While Peter was still speaking, the Holy Spirit fell upon all who heard the word. ⁴⁵The circumcised believers who had come with Peter were astounded that the gift of the Holy Spirit had been poured out even on the Gentiles, ⁴⁶for they heard them speaking in tongues and extolling God. Then Peter said, ⁴⁷"Can anyone withhold the water for baptizing these people who have received the Holy Spirit just as we have?" ⁴⁸So he ordered them to be baptized in the name of Jesus Christ. Then they invited him to stay for several days.

10.44–48. **44:** *The Holy Spirit's* dramatic presence has been called the "Gentile* Pentecost,*" confirming the fulfillment of prophecy and the giving of repentance to gentiles as it was given to Israel in Acts 2 (11.15–17). **45:** *Even on the Gentiles* is an emphatic statement of God's initiative, reflecting Peter's reluctance, then perplexity, then obedience (vv. 14, 17, 20) with regard to the gentiles. **47:** Peter's question echoes the inquiry of the Ethiopian (8.36). *Just as we have* is again an emphatic reminder of God's giving repentance to Israel, confirmed by the *Holy Spirit* (2.1–4, 38–42; 8.17).

11 Now the apostles and the believers*ᵃ* who were in Judea heard that the Gentiles had also accepted the word of God. ²So when Peter went up to Jerusalem, the circumcised believers*ᵇ* criticized him, ³saying, "Why did you go to uncircumcised men and eat with them?" ⁴Then Peter began to explain it to them, step by step, saying, ⁵"I was in the city of Joppa praying, and in a trance I saw a vision. There was something like a large sheet coming down from heaven, being lowered by its four corners; and it

a Gk *brothers*   *b* Gk lacks *believers*

came close to me. 6As I looked at it closely I saw four-footed animals, beasts of prey, reptiles, and birds of the air. 7I also heard a voice saying to me, 'Get up, Peter; kill and eat.' 8But I replied, 'By no means, Lord; for nothing profane or unclean has ever entered my mouth.' 9But a second time the voice answered from heaven, 'What God has made clean, you must not call profane.' 10This happened three times; then everything was pulled up again to heaven. 11At that very moment three men, sent to me from Caesarea, arrived at the house where we were. 12The Spirit told me to go with them and not to make a distinction between them and us.ª These six brothers also accompanied me, and we entered the man's house. 13He told us how he had seen the angel standing in his house and saying, 'Send to Joppa and bring Simon, who is called Peter; 14he will give you a message by which you and your entire household will be saved.' 15And as I began to speak, the Holy Spirit fell upon them just as it had upon us at the beginning. 16And I remembered the word of the Lord, how he had said, 'John baptized with water, but you will be baptized with the Holy Spirit.' 17If then God gave them the same gift that he gave us when we believed in the Lord Jesus Christ, who was I that I could hinder God?" 18When they heard this, they were silenced. And they praised God, saying, "Then God has given even to the Gentiles the repentance that leads to life."

11.1–18. 1: The ratification by *the apostles** is needed, as in the Samaritan mission (8.14), now with controversy; see 15.4. **2–3:** So far in Acts, *the circumcised** *believers* appear to include all the Christians in *Jerusalem* since this is the beginning of *Peter's* mission to the gentiles, the *uncircumcised* (15.1–2). Eating *with* gentiles* risked mixing clean and unclean food or eating meat that had been sacrificed to idols when it was slaughtered (Gal 2.12–14; 1 Cor 10.14–32). **4–17:** The story of Acts 10 is rehearsed. **12:** *These six brothers* are "circumcised believers" (10.45). **17:** *God* is the primary agent of this mission (vv. 7, 9, 12, 13, 15, 18). To interfere is to *hinder* or oppose *God* (5.39). **18:** In Greek, the definite conclusion of the argument is signaled by the word *then*, and *God's* gift *to the Gentiles* is *the repentance that leads to life.* The opportunity to turn to God is itself a sign of divine mercy, not only a command (3.19–26; 5.31).

19 Now those who were scattered because of the persecution that took place over Stephen traveled as far as Phoenicia, Cyprus, and Antioch, and they spoke the word to no one except Jews. 20But among them were some men of Cyprus and Cyrene who, on coming to Antioch, spoke to the Hellenistsᵇ also, proclaiming the Lord Jesus. 21The hand of the Lord was with them, and a great number became believers and turned to the Lord. 22News of this came to the ears of the church in Jerusalem, and they sent Barnabas to Antioch. 23When he came and saw the grace of God, he rejoiced, and he exhorted them all to remain faithful to the Lord with steadfast devotion; 24for he was a good man, full of the Holy Spirit and of faith. And a great many people were brought to the Lord. 25Then Barnabas went to Tarsus to look for Saul, 26and when he had found him, he brought him to Antioch. So it was that for an entire year they met withᶜ the church and taught a great many people, and it was in Antioch that the disciples were first called "Christians."

27 At that time prophets came down from Jerusalem to Antioch. 28One of them named Agabus stood up and predicted by the Spirit that there would be a severe famine over all the world; and this took place during the reign of Claudius. 29The disciples determined that according to their ability, each would send relief to the believersᵈ living in Judea; 30this they did, sending it to the elders by Barnabas and Saul.

12 About that time King Herod laid violent hands upon some who belonged to the church. 2He had James, the brother of John, killed with the sword. 3After he saw that it pleased the Jews, he proceeded to arrest Peter also. (This was during the festival of Unleavened Bread.) 4When he had seized him, he put him in prison and handed him over to four squads of soldiers to guard

a Or *not to hesitate*   *b* Other ancient authorities read *Greeks*   *c* Or *were guests of*   *d* Gk *brothers* him, intending to bring him out to the people after the Passover. [5] While Peter was kept in prison, the church prayed fervently to God for him.

11.19–12.25: Peter's mission expands and ends. 19: The *persecution over Stephen* again accounts for the expanding mission (8.1), so far still limited to *Jews. Antioch* will be the base for Paul's mission (13.1; 14.26–15.2; 18.22). **20:** Since Luke contrasts them with the Jews, these *Hellenists*★ differ from the Greek-speaking Jews appointed to serve in Acts 6.1–6 (note *b*, p. 1857, indicates ancient manuscripts that simply called them *Greeks*). Like the Samaritans in Acts 8, they are not called gentiles.★ **22–24:** The embassy of *Barnabas* from *the church in Jerusalem* appears to be another official visitation (8.14), and his credentials as *a good man, full of the Holy Spirit and of faith* also recall his obedience to the apostles★ (4.36–37). **25–26:** Having once introduced *Saul* to the apostles (9.27), then having sent him from Damascus to *Tarsus, Barnabas* now brings him to *Antioch*. In Greek, the name *"Christians"* clearly links with *"the anointed*★ one"* (*"Christos"*) from the Hebrew *"messiah."*★ Among Jewish groups, the believers are the *"messianists"* or followers of the Messiah/Christ Jesus. **27–28:** Although they come from Jerusalem, these *prophets*★ do not appear to have apostolic authorization, but were accepted as having a special gift of the *Spirit* (see also 13.1; 21.10, *Agabus;* 1 Cor 12.28–29; 14.29, 32, 37; Eph 2.20; 3.5; 4.11). Referring to the *famine during the reign of Claudius* reminds the reader of the connection with events of public consequence (Lk 2.1; 3.1; Acts 5.36–37; 17.6; 18.2; 24.5; 26.26: "this was not done in a corner"). **29–30:** *Barnabas and Saul* are the agents of this ministry of *relief* (12.25; Rom 15.31; 2 Cor 8.4; 9.1, 12–13). **12.1:** This *King Herod* is Agrippa I, grandson of Herod the Great (Lk 1.5; see also Herod the ruler who imprisoned and beheaded John the Baptizer and interrogated Jesus: Lk 3.1, 19; 8.3; 9.7–9; 13.31; 23.7–15; Acts 4.27). **2:** *James* was one of the twelve and close to Jesus (Lk 5.10; 6.14; 8.51; 9.28, 54; Acts 1.13). **3–4:** *The Jews* whom this execution *pleased* in Luke's story are probably "the Judeans" who regarded the followers of Jesus as a threat to the Temple★ and its leadership. The *festival of Unleavened Bread* and *the Passover*★ are virtually identified in Luke's narrative,★ marking the time of Jesus' and Peter's arrest (Lk 22.1). **5:** The fervent prayers of *the church* hope for *God* to act.

[6] The very night before Herod was going to bring him out, Peter, bound with two chains, was sleeping between two soldiers, while guards in front of the door were keeping watch over the prison. [7] Suddenly an angel of the Lord appeared and a light shone in the cell. He tapped Peter on the side and woke him, saying, "Get up quickly." And the chains fell off his wrists. [8] The angel said to him, "Fasten your belt and put on your sandals." He did so. Then he said to him, "Wrap your cloak around you and follow me." [9] Peter[a] went out and followed him; he did not realize that what was happening with the angel's help was real; he thought he was seeing a vision. [10] After they had passed the first and the second guard, they came before the iron gate leading into the city. It opened for them of its own accord, and they went outside and walked along a lane, when suddenly the angel left him. [11] Then Peter came to himself and said, "Now I am sure that the Lord has sent his angel and rescued me from the hands of Herod and from all that the Jewish people were expecting."

[12] As soon as he realized this, he went to the house of Mary, the mother of John whose other name was Mark, where many had gathered and were praying. [13] When he knocked at the outer gate, a maid named Rhoda came to answer. [14] On recognizing Peter's voice, she was so overjoyed that, instead of opening the gate, she ran in and announced that Peter was standing at the gate. [15] They said to her, "You are out of your mind!" But she insisted that it was so. They said, "It is his angel." [16] Meanwhile Peter continued knocking; and when they opened the gate, they saw him and were amazed. [17] He motioned to them with his hand to be silent, and described for them how the Lord had brought him out of the prison. And he added, "Tell this to James and to the believers."[b] Then he left and went to another place.

12.6–17. 6: The details emphasize the intensity of the *watch*. **7–8:** *An angel of the Lord* again accomplishes a release from prison (5.19; Lk 4.18). **9:** *Peter* has been confounded by visions before (10.10, 17; 12.11). **10:**

a Gk He   *b* Gk *brothers*

The *gate* opening *of its own accord* is miraculous. **11:** Peter's verdict is a lucid declaration of the meaning of this rescue. **12–17:** These verses emphasize the fabulous character of the story. None of these common names can be decisively linked with persons known in the narrative. **17:** This *James* is probably "the Lord's brother," one of the leaders of the church in Jerusalem (Acts 15.13; Gal 1.19; 2.9).

18 When morning came, there was no small commotion among the soldiers over what had become of Peter. 19When Herod had searched for him and could not find him, he examined the guards and ordered them to be put to death. Then he went down from Judea to Caesarea and stayed there.

20 Now Herod*a* was angry with the people of Tyre and Sidon. So they came to him in a body; and after winning over Blastus, the king's chamberlain, they asked for a reconciliation, because their country depended on the king's country for food. 21On an appointed day Herod put on his royal robes, took his seat on the platform, and delivered a public address to them. 22The people kept shouting, "The voice of a god, and not of a mortal!" 23And immediately, because he had not given the glory to God, an angel of the Lord struck him down, and he was eaten by worms and died.

24 But the word of God continued to advance and gain adherents. 25Then after completing their mission Barnabas and Saul returned to*b* Jerusalem and brought with them John, whose other name was Mark.

12.18–25. 20: The exact political and economic relationships between *Herod* and *Tyre and Sidon* are otherwise unknown, but Josephus✶ also reports a dramatic account of Herod appearing in radiant garments of woven silver, being acclaimed a god, and dying suddenly (*Antiquities* 19.343–352). **22:** The acclamation of a ruler as *the voice of a god, and not of a mortal* is blasphemy (14.11–15). **23:** *An angel of the Lord* could be an agent of judgment (2 Kings 19.35) as well as rescue (12.7). **24–25:** These verses are another Lukan summary, emphasizing the growing effectiveness of *the word of God* (see 2.47; 4.4; 6.7; 9.31; 11.24) and the link between *Jerusalem* and the mission of the church at Antioch (11.27; 13.1).

13 Now in the church at Antioch there were prophets and teachers: Barnabas, Simeon who was called Niger, Lucius of Cyrene, Manaen a member of the court of Herod the ruler,*c* and Saul. 2While they were worshiping the Lord and fasting, the Holy Spirit said, "Set apart for me Barnabas and Saul for the work to which I have called them." 3Then after fasting and praying they laid their hands on them and sent them off.

4 So, being sent out by the Holy Spirit, they went down to Seleucia; and from there they sailed to Cyprus. 5When they arrived at Salamis, they proclaimed the word of God in the synagogues of the Jews. And they had John also to assist them. 6When they had gone through the whole island as far as Paphos, they met a certain magician, a Jewish false prophet, named Bar-Jesus. 7He was with the proconsul, Sergius Paulus, an intelligent man, who summoned Barnabas and Saul and wanted to hear the word of God. 8But the magician Elymas (for that is the translation of his name) opposed them and tried to turn the proconsul away from the faith. 9But Saul, also known as Paul, filled with the Holy Spirit, looked intently at him 10and said, "You son of the devil, you enemy of all righteousness, full of all deceit and villainy, will you not stop making crooked the straight paths of the Lord? 11And now listen—the hand of the Lord is against you, and you will be blind for a while, unable to see the sun." Immediately mist and darkness came over him, and he went about groping for someone to lead him by the hand. 12When the proconsul saw what had happened, he believed, for he was astonished at the teaching about the Lord.

13.1–14.28: Paul's first missionary journey among Jews and gentiles.✶ 13.1: These *prophets✶ and teachers* (11.27–28) are largely unknown (Rom 16.21?), except for *Barnabas* and *Saul* and a suggested link with *the court of Herod* (Lk 8.3). **2–4:** Other than through *fasting and prayer* (Lk 2.37; 5.33; Acts 14.23), Acts does not explain how *the Holy Spirit* spoke (16.6, 10), but the laying on of hands and sending them off

a Gk *he*   *b* Other ancient authorities read *from*
c Gk *tetrarch*

are acts of obedience to this call (6.6; 8.17–19; 9.17), so that they go, *sent out by the Holy Spirit.* **4–5:** *Seleucia* was the port for Antioch, and *Salamis,* the eastern port of *Cyprus.* Their first destination is *the synagogues* of the Jews* (Lk 4.15; Acts 6.9; 13.14; 14.1; 16.13, 16; 17.1, 10, 17; 18.4, 19, 26; 19.8). *John* is John Mark (12.25; 13.13). **6–7:** *Paphos* is on the western shore of Cyprus. This *magician* (8.9–13) is also judged to be a *false prophet* (11.27–28; Deut 18.22). *Bar-Jesus* or "Son of Joshua" was a fitting name for a prophet (see Jesus, son of Ananias, in Josephus,* *War* 6.300–309), now contending with an agent of Jesus the Messiah* for the hearing of the Roman *proconsul* (18.12). **8–9:** Both the *magician* and *Saul* are known by more than one name, and *Paul* will be the apostle's* (14.4, 14) name for the rest of the narrative.* **10–11:** This is the language of spiritual warfare (5.1– 11; 8.20–24), renaming him again as *son of the devil,* not son of Joshua, and accusing him of making the paths *crooked,* rather than *straight* (Isa 40.3–4; Lk 3.4– 5). **11:** Like Saul himself, Elymas is *blind for a while* and must be *led by the hand* (9.8–9; 22.11). **12:** The *proconsul* is confronted with two kinds of Jewish prophecy and *teaching* (13.1), and Paul demonstrated the power of the Holy Spirit (13.9).

13 Then Paul and his companions set sail from Paphos and came to Perga in Pamphylia. John, however, left them and returned to Jerusalem; [14]but they went on from Perga and came to Antioch in Pisidia. And on the sabbath day they went into the synagogue and sat down. [15]After the reading of the law and the prophets, the officials of the synagogue sent them a message, saying, "Brothers, if you have any word of exhortation for the people, give it." [16]So Paul stood up and with a gesture began to speak:

"You Israelites,[a] and others who fear God, listen. [17]The God of this people Israel chose our ancestors and made the people great during their stay in the land of Egypt, and with uplifted arm he led them out of it. [18]For about forty years he put up with[b] them in the wilderness. [19]After he had destroyed seven nations in the land of Canaan, he gave them their land as an inheritance [20]for about four hundred fifty years. After that he gave them judges until the time of the prophet Samuel. [21]Then they asked for a king; and God gave them Saul son of Kish, a man of

the tribe of Benjamin, who reigned for forty years. [22]When he had removed him, he made David their king. In his testimony about him he said, 'I have found David, son of Jesse, to be a man after my heart, who will carry out all my wishes.' [23]Of this man's posterity God has brought to Israel a Savior, Jesus, as he promised; [24]before his coming John had already proclaimed a baptism of repentance to all the people of Israel. [25]And as John was finishing his work, he said, 'What do you suppose that I am? I am not he. No, but one is coming after me; I am not worthy to untie the thong of the sandals[c] on his feet.'

13.13–25. 13–14: *Paul's* mission moves north to *Pamphylia* on the mainland. *John's* departure later caused divisions (15.38). **15:** As in Jesus' first address in a synagogue* where he read from Isaiah (Lk 4.14–30), Paul is invited to speak after *the reading of the law and the prophets** (15.21). To call them *brothers* meant to acknowledge them as belonging to *the people* of Israel. **16:** The worship of the synagogue apparently included Jews (*Israelites*) and *others who fear God* (13.26), some of whom were probably gentiles* and some converts (10.2; 13.43). **17:** Like Stephen, Paul focused on God's faithful promise and *Israel's* need to repent (7.23, 37, 42; 13.23, 24). God's *uplifted arm* is the means of salvation (Ex 6.1, 6; 32.11). **18:** On *forty years,* see 7.36. Paul does not mention Moses (unlike Stephen, 7.20–44), but dwells on God's forbearance (Deut 1.31). **19:** The *seven nations* are identified in Deut 7.1. **20–22:** The scriptural allusions of these verses point to Davidic kingship (see 1 Sam 10.21–24; 14.14; 15.23; 16.1), drawing on a verse from Isa 44.28 about Cyrus to speak of David *"who will carry out all my wishes."* **23:** On Jesus as *Israel's promised Savior,* see Lk 2.11; Acts 5.31. **24–25:** John's *baptism** is again carefully set before Jesus' *coming* (see comment on Lk 3.18–21; Acts 10.36–38).

26 "My brothers, you descendants of Abraham's family, and others who fear God, to us[d] the message of this salvation has been sent. [27]Because the residents of Jerusalem and their leaders did not recognize him or understand the words of the prophets that

a Gk *Men, Israelites*   *b* Other ancient authorities read *cared for*   *c* Gk *untie the sandals*   *d* Other ancient authorities read *you* are read every sabbath, they fulfilled those words by condemning him. 28Even though they found no cause for a sentence of death, they asked Pilate to have him killed. 29When they had carried out everything that was written about him, they took him down from the tree and laid him in a tomb. 30But God raised him from the dead; 31and for many days he appeared to those who came up with him from Galilee to Jerusalem, and they are now his witnesses to the people. 32And we bring you the good news that what God promised to our ancestors 33he has fulfilled for us, their children, by raising Jesus; as also it is written in the second psalm,

'You are my Son;
      today I have begotten you.'
34As to his raising him from the dead, no more to return to corruption, he has spoken in this way,

'I will give you the holy promises made
      to David.'
35Therefore he has also said in another psalm,

'You will not let your Holy One
      experience corruption.'
36For David, after he had served the purpose of God in his own generation, died,ᵃ was laid beside his ancestors, and experienced corruption; 37but he whom God raised up experienced no corruption. 38Let it be known to you therefore, my brothers, that through this man forgiveness of sins is proclaimed to you; 39by this Jesusᵇ everyone who believes is set free from all those sinsᶜ from which you could not be freed by the law of Moses. 40Beware, therefore, that what the prophets said does not happen to you:
41 'Look, you scoffers!
      Be amazed and perish,
for in your days I am doing a work,
      a work that you will never believe,
            even if someone tells you.' "

42 As Paul and Barnabasᵈ were going out, the people urged them to speak about these things again the next sabbath. 43When the meeting of the synagogue broke up, many Jews and devout converts to Judaism followed Paul and Barnabas, who spoke to them and urged them to continue in the grace of God.

13.26–43. 26: *The message of this salvation* is about the promised Savior, Jesus (v. 23), which is the *good news . . . God promised* (v. 32; 2.39). **27:** This verse is a prophetic* indictment, citing ignorance and misunderstanding of the scriptural promises against *the residents of Jerusalem and their leaders* (3.14–17; 7.51–53). **28:** This verse repeats the charge of 3.13. Acts 4.25–28 holds *Pilate* accountable (Lk 23.1–25). **29:** The phrase *everything that was written about him* echoes Jesus' words in Lk 22.37; 24.27, 44. **31–33:** The *witnesses to the people* (Lk 24.48; Acts 1.8) again focus on *Jesus'* resurrection (1.22; 2.32; 3.15). Verses from Ps 2 are also cited in 4.25–26 (see Heb 1.5; 5.5). **34–37:** The direct references to Isa 55.3 and Ps 16.10 rehearse the argument (2.25–31) that in his resurrection Jesus fulfilled the promises made to *David.* **38–39:** *Let it be known to you* is the language of solemn declaration (2.14; 4.10) announcing God's *forgiveness of sins* for *everyone who believes* in the same terms that Paul used in Romans to speak of "justification" or "being declared righteous" from sin by faith rather than *the law* (see Rom 2.13; 3.24–26; 4.2, 5; 5.1, 9; 8.30, 33). **40–41:** *The prophets* may again imply a collection of "the minor prophets" (7.42), including Hab 1.5, which is cited directly. **43:** Luke emphasizes the response of faith among *Jews and devout converts to Judaism* (see comments on 11.20; 13.16).

44 The next sabbath almost the whole city gathered to hear the word of the Lord.ᵉ 45But when the Jews saw the crowds, they were filled with jealousy; and blaspheming, they contradicted what was spoken by Paul. 46Then both Paul and Barnabas spoke out boldly, saying, "It was necessary that the word of God should be spoken first to you. Since you reject it and judge yourselves to be unworthy of eternal life, we are now turning to the Gentiles. 47For so the Lord has commanded us, saying,

'I have set you to be a light for
      the Gentiles,
so that you may bring salvation to the
      ends of the earth.' "
48 When the Gentiles heard this, they were glad and praised the word of the Lord; and as many as had been destined for eternal life became believers. 49Thus the word of the

ᵃ Gk *fell asleep*   ᵇ Gk *this*   ᶜ Gk *all*   ᵈ Gk *they*
ᵉ Other ancient authorities read *God*

Lord spread throughout the region. ⁵⁰But the Jews incited the devout women of high standing and the leading men of the city, and stirred up persecution against Paul and Barnabas, and drove them out of their region. ⁵¹So they shook the dust off their feet in protest against them, and went to Iconium. ⁵²And the disciples were filled with joy and with the Holy Spirit.

14 The same thing occurred in Iconium, where Paul and Barnabas*a* went into the Jewish synagogue and spoke in such a way that a great number of both Jews and Greeks became believers. ²But the unbelieving Jews stirred up the Gentiles and poisoned their minds against the brothers. ³So they remained for a long time, speaking boldly for the Lord, who testified to the word of his grace by granting signs and wonders to be done through them. ⁴But the residents of the city were divided; some sided with the Jews, and some with the apostles. ⁵And when an attempt was made by both Gentiles and Jews, with their rulers, to mistreat them and to stone them, ⁶the apostles*a* learned of it and fled to Lystra and Derbe, cities of Lycaonia, and to the surrounding country; ⁷and there they continued proclaiming the good news.

13.44–14.7. 13.44–45: On *jealousy*, see Acts 5.17; 7.9. Those who were *contradicting Paul* were probably also accusing him of *blaspheming* on the grounds of their scriptural arguments. 46–47: Their boldness is again inspired speech (4.13, 31; 9.27–28). Paul uses the promise from Isa 49.6 (see 1.6–8) as a prophetic* reproof and repeatedly declares his *turning to the Gentiles** (18.6; 28.28), but he never stops witnessing to Jews. 48: The phrase *as many as had been destined for eternal life* again alludes to "the definite plan" of God in the scriptures (2.23; 3.24). 49: On *the word of the Lord*, see 12.24; 13.44, 46. 50: *Persecution* again causes the mission to move ahead (8.1). 51: In Lk 10.11, Jesus warned his disciples about shaking *the dust off their feet*. 14.1: The mission in *Iconium* again begins in the *synagogue** (13.14). 4–5: In this passage (see also v. 14), Paul and Barnabas are called *the apostles,** a title otherwise reserved in Acts for "the twelve" (1.26). They are clearly Jewish, but are contrasted with *the Jews*, who must be those who hold a strict "Jewish" or "Judean" interpretation* of the faith of Israel

(15.1) as they divide the residents, apparently including *both Gentiles and Jews,* against Paul and Barnabas.

8 In Lystra there was a man sitting who could not use his feet and had never walked, for he had been crippled from birth. ⁹He listened to Paul as he was speaking. And Paul, looking at him intently and seeing that he had faith to be healed, ¹⁰said in a loud voice, "Stand upright on your feet." And the man*b* sprang up and began to walk. ¹¹When the crowds saw what Paul had done, they shouted in the Lycaonian language, "The gods have come down to us in human form!" ¹²Barnabas they called Zeus, and Paul they called Hermes, because he was the chief speaker. ¹³The priest of Zeus, whose temple was just outside the city,*c* brought oxen and garlands to the gates; he and the crowds wanted to offer sacrifice. ¹⁴When the apostles Barnabas and Paul heard of it, they tore their clothes and rushed out into the crowd, shouting, ¹⁵"Friends,*d* why are you doing this? We are mortals just like you, and we bring you good news, that you should turn from these worthless things to the living God, who made the heaven and the earth and the sea and all that is in them. ¹⁶In past generations he allowed all the nations to follow their own ways; ¹⁷yet he has not left himself without a witness in doing good— giving you rains from heaven and fruitful seasons, and filling you with food and your hearts with joy." ¹⁸Even with these words, they scarcely restrained the crowds from offering sacrifice to them.

19 But Jews came there from Antioch and Iconium and won over the crowds. Then they stoned Paul and dragged him out of the city, supposing that he was dead. ²⁰But when the disciples surrounded him, he got up and went into the city. The next day he went on with Barnabas to Derbe.

14.8–20. 8–10: *Paul's* healing of the man *crippled from birth* closely parallels Jesus' (Lk 5.17–26) and Peter's (Acts 3.1–10). 11–12: Greek tradition included stories of such visitations from the realm of the gods.

a Gk *they*   *b* Gk *he*   *c* Or *The priest of Zeus-Outside-the-City*   *d* Gk *Men*

Zeus was at the top of the assembly or Pantheon of the Gods. *Hermes* was the divine messenger with winged feet. **13:** Even rumors of a visit of *Zeus* could bring fame to a local *temple*. **14–15:** *The apostles★ Barnabas and Paul* (v. 4) respond just as Peter did to Cornelius (10.26) and as Herod did not when acclaimed divine (12.22). **15–17:** This is the first sermon in Acts to gentiles★ who may not know Jewish scriptural tradition, calling for "repentance" (*turn from these worthless things to the living God*) by a broad appeal to the order of creation (4.24; 17.24–31; Rom 1.18–25). **19:** The report of pursuing opponents from previous cities (13.50–14.5) will be repeated in 17.13 (see Gal 2.4–5; 5.11).

21 After they had proclaimed the good news to that city and had made many disciples, they returned to Lystra, then on to Iconium and Antioch. 22There they strengthened the souls of the disciples and encouraged them to continue in the faith, saying, "It is through many persecutions that we must enter the kingdom of God." 23And after they had appointed elders for them in each church, with prayer and fasting they entrusted them to the Lord in whom they had come to believe.

24 Then they passed through Pisidia and came to Pamphylia. 25When they had spoken the word in Perga, they went down to Attalia. 26From there they sailed back to Antioch, where they had been commended to the grace of God for the work*ᵃ* that they had completed. 27When they arrived, they called the church together and related all that God had done with them, and how he had opened a door of faith for the Gentiles. 28And they stayed there with the disciples for some time.

14.21–28. 22: The necessity of *persecutions* (Gk., "thlipsis," see 7.10–11; 11.19; 20.23) is revealed in persistent opposition to God's *kingdom* (9.16). **23:** *Elders* are now *appointed* as another class of leaders in addition to apostles and deacons (6.1–7; 11.30; 15.2, 4). **27:** The *Gentile* mission is identified as what *God had done* (11.17–18; 12.24; 13.47–48). The *door of faith* is a Pauline image (1 Cor 16.9; 2 Cor 2.12; Col 4.3).

15 Then certain individuals came down from Judea and were teaching the brothers, "Unless you are circumcised according to the custom of Moses, you cannot be saved." 2And after Paul and Barnabas had no small dissension and debate with them, Paul and Barnabas and some of the others were appointed to go up to Jerusalem to discuss this question with the apostles and the elders. 3So they were sent on their way by the church, and as they passed through both Phoenicia and Samaria, they reported the conversion of the Gentiles, and brought great joy to all the believers.*ᵇ* 4When they came to Jerusalem, they were welcomed by the church and the apostles and the elders, and they reported all that God had done with them. 5But some believers who belonged to the sect of the Pharisees stood up and said, "It is necessary for them to be circumcised and ordered to keep the law of Moses."

6 The apostles and the elders met together to consider this matter. 7After there had been much debate, Peter stood up and said to them, "My brothers,*ᶜ* you know that in the early days God made a choice among you, that I should be the one through whom the Gentiles would hear the message of the good news and become believers. 8And God, who knows the human heart, testified to them by giving them the Holy Spirit, just as he did to us; 9and in cleansing their hearts by faith he has made no distinction between them and us. 10Now therefore why are you putting God to the test by placing on the neck of the disciples a yoke that neither our ancestors nor we have been able to bear? 11On the contrary, we believe that we will be saved through the grace of the Lord Jesus, just as they will."

15.1–35: The assembly in Jerusalem. 1: These *individuals from Judea* are evidently Jews, perhaps like the "false believers secretly brought in" Paul faced in Gal 2.4 or perhaps the Christian Pharisees★ of 15.5. *The brothers* would normally be Jews, but these seem to be gentile★ believers (15.23). *Saved* means to be an heir of God's promises to Israel (v. 11, see 4.2), as demonstrated by observing the *custom* (Lk 1.9; 2.42; Acts

a Or *committed in the grace of God to the work*
b Gk *brothers*　　*c* Gk *Men, brothers*

6.14; 16.21; 21.21; 26.3; 28.17) of circumcision,* which Luke regards as what faithful Jews do (Lk 1.59; 2.21; Acts 7.8; 16.3). **3:** *The conversion of the Gentiles* is literally their "turning" or "repentance" (11.18; 14.15; 15.19). **5:** These *believers who belonged to the sect★ of the Pharisees★* are evidently Christians. It is not clear what their link might have been with "the circumcised believers" who traveled with Peter (10.45; 11.12). The word *sect★* means "group" or "party" without especially negative connotations (5.17; 24.5, 14; 26.5; 28.22). They taught that circumcision was *necessary* for salvation (15.1). **7–9:** *Peter* rehearses the story of *God's* action through him in chs. 10–11. The phrase *in the early days* points to Peter's precedence in the *Gentile* mission. The expression *cleansing their hearts by faith* addresses both the concern of what is unclean (10.15; 11.9) and recalls receiving the gift of the *Holy Spirit* "when we believed" (11.17). **10:** The word *therefore* marks the conclusion of the testimony, confronting them with the Pharisee Gamaliel's warning to avoid "fighting against God" (5.39) or *putting God to the test* (Lk 4.2; 11.16; Acts 5.9). The *yoke* was an image of the discipline or instruction of the law (Sir 51.6; Mt 11.29–30), but it could also represent bondage or a burden too heavy to *bear* (Gal 5.1; Mt 23.4). **11:** By Peter's *contrary* argument, *they* do not need to be circumcised like us, but *we will be saved . . . just as they will.*

12 The whole assembly kept silence, and listened to Barnabas and Paul as they told of all the signs and wonders that God had done through them among the Gentiles. 13After they finished speaking, James replied, "My brothers,ᵃ listen to me. 14Simeon has related how God first looked favorably on the Gentiles, to take from among them a people for his name. 15This agrees with the words of the prophets, as it is written,

16 'After this I will return,
and I will rebuild the dwelling of David,
which has fallen;
from its ruins I will rebuild it,
and I will set it up,
17 so that all other peoples may seek the Lord—
even all the Gentiles over whom my name has been called.
Thus says the Lord, who has been making these things 18known from long ago.'ᵇ

19Therefore I have reached the decision that we should not trouble those Gentiles who are turning to God, 20but we should write to them to abstain only from things polluted by idols and from fornication and from whatever has been strangledᶜ and from blood. 21For in every city, for generations past, Moses has had those who proclaim him, for he has been read aloud every sabbath in the synagogues."

15.12–21. 12: *The signs and wonders* confirm divine activity (2.43; 5.12; 8.6–7). **13:** *James,* "the brother of the Lord," emerges as the leader of the Jerusalem church (1.14; 12.17; 21.18; 1 Cor 15.7; Gal 1.19; 2.9, 12). **14:** The phrase *a people for his name* extends the meaning of the word "people," which is usually reserved for Israel and includes *the Gentiles* as "saved" (on *his name,* see also 2.21; 15.17) or "God's people." **16–17:** The citation from Amos 9.11–12 is another prophetic★ witness to God's long-standing intention for Israel's restoration to be a blessing to the *Gentiles* (1.6–8; Isa 49.6; Acts 3.25; Gen 12.3). **19–20:** James' solemn declaration is rehearsed with variations in 15.29 and 21.25. The edict requires no practices but only abstaining from things that were probably regarded as most offensive by Jewish Christians. *Things polluted by idols* could be far-reaching since the whole empire was full of religious practices and images (Acts 17.16), but in 15.29 and 21.25 the issue is more narrowly sacrifices to idols (1 Cor 8–10). *Fornication* probably meant all sexual impurity, but Jewish tradition also made a close link with idolatry★ (Wis 14.12). Things *strangled* and *blood* are probably allusions to Jewish convictions that the life of a creature is in its blood, which is to be poured out to God (Lev 17.10–13). **21:** The point seems to be that Jews, proselytes, and gentiles everywhere will recognize "these essentials" as appropriate (v. 28), without making circumcision★ a requirement for salvation.

22 Then the apostles and the elders, with the consent of the whole church, decided to choose men from among their membersᵈ and to send them to Antioch with Paul and Barnabas. They sent Judas called Barsabbas, and Silas, leaders among the brothers,

a Gk Men, brothers   *b* Other ancient authorities read *things. ¹⁸Known to God from of old are all his works.'*
c Other ancient authorities lack *and from whatever has been strangled*   *d* Gk *from among them*

23with the following letter: "The brothers, both the apostles and the elders, to the believers*a* of Gentile origin in Antioch and Syria and Cilicia, greetings. 24Since we have heard that certain persons who have gone out from us, though with no instructions from us, have said things to disturb you and have unsettled your minds,*b* 25we have decided unanimously to choose representatives*c* and send them to you, along with our beloved Barnabas and Paul, 26who have risked their lives for the sake of our Lord Jesus Christ. 27We have therefore sent Judas and Silas, who themselves will tell you the same things by word of mouth. 28For it has seemed good to the Holy Spirit and to us to impose on you no further burden than these essentials: 29that you abstain from what has been sacrificed to idols and from blood and from what is strangled*d* and from fornication. If you keep yourselves from these, you will do well. Farewell."

30 So they were sent off and went down to Antioch. When they gathered the congregation together, they delivered the letter. 31When its members*e* read it, they rejoiced at the exhortation. 32Judas and Silas, who were themselves prophets, said much to encourage and strengthen the believers.*a* 33After they had been there for some time, they were sent off in peace by the believers*a* to those who had sent them.*f* 35But Paul and Barnabas remained in Antioch, and there, with many others, they taught and proclaimed the word of the Lord.

15.22–35. 22: All the officials (see comment on 14.23) formally *choose* and *send* "prophets"★ (15.32; 11.27; 13.1) along with *Paul and Barnabas: Judas called Barsabbas* (see *Joseph called Barsabbas* in 1.23) and *Silas* (15.40–41; 16.19, 25, 29; 17.4, 10, 14–15; 18.5). **23–29:** James's letter recites the story of the council. **23:** On *the believers of Gentile origin*, see 15.1. **28:** The phrase *it has seemed good to the Holy Spirit and to us* is the formal language of declarations, confirming God's agency. **35:** Luke's summary concludes this section of the narrative.★

36 After some days Paul said to Barnabas, "Come, let us return and visit the believers*a* in every city where we proclaimed the word

of the Lord and see how they are doing." 37Barnabas wanted to take with them John called Mark. 38But Paul decided not to take with them one who had deserted them in Pamphylia and had not accompanied them in the work. 39The disagreement became so sharp that they parted company; Barnabas took Mark with him and sailed away to Cyprus. 40But Paul chose Silas and set out, the believers*a* commending him to the grace of the Lord. 41He went through Syria and Cilicia, strengthening the churches.

16 Paul*g* went on also to Derbe and to Lystra, where there was a disciple named Timothy, the son of a Jewish woman who was a believer; but his father was a Greek. 2He was well spoken of by the believers*a* in Lystra and Iconium. 3Paul wanted Timothy to accompany him; and he took him and had him circumcised because of the Jews who were in those places, for they all knew that his father was a Greek. 4As they went from town to town, they delivered to them for observance the decisions that had been reached by the apostles and elders who were in Jerusalem. 5So the churches were strengthened in the faith and increased in numbers daily.

6 They went through the region of Phrygia and Galatia, having been forbidden by the Holy Spirit to speak the word in Asia. 7When they had come opposite Mysia, they attempted to go into Bithynia, but the Spirit of Jesus did not allow them; 8so, passing by Mysia, they went down to Troas. 9During the night Paul had a vision: there stood a man of Macedonia pleading with him and saying, "Come over to Macedonia and help us." 10When he had seen the vision, we immediately tried to cross over to Macedonia, being convinced that God had called us to proclaim the good news to them.

15.36–22.29: The journeys of Paul. 15.36–16.10: The mission moves to Europe. 36–41: These verses

---

a Gk *brothers*   *b* Other ancient authorities add *saying, 'You must be circumcised and keep the law,'*   *c* Gk *men*   *d* Other ancient authorities lack *and from what is strangled*   *e* Gk *When they*   *f* Other ancient authorities add verse 34, *But it seemed good to Silas to remain there*   *g* Gk *He* resume the narrative* of Paul's travels (13.1–14.28), which had been interrupted by the Jerusalem council (15.1–35), and introduce his second missionary journey (15.39–18.22). **37:** According to Col 4.10, *John called Mark* was a relative of *Barnabas*. **38:** Mark's earlier departure (13.13) is now interpreted as a desertion. **40–41:** *Silas* and *Judas* were chosen earlier by the Jerusalem authorities to represent the agreement that validated the mission of Paul and Barnabas (15.27), and *Syria and Cilicia* were crucial areas for the message (15.23; Gal 1.21). **16.1:** *Derbe* and *Lystra* were the sites of the mission in 14.6–21. *Timothy* is also mentioned in 17.14–15; 18.5; 19.22; 20.4; Rom 16.21; 1 Cor 4.17; 16.10; Phil 1.1; 2.19; Col 1.1). **3–4:** *Timothy's* circumcision* is intended to make him acceptable as a Jew (v. 1: *son of a Jewish woman*), without compromising *the decisions . . . reached by the apostles* and *elders* about the gentiles* (15.19). **6–7:** *The Holy Spirit* and *the Spirit of Jesus* appear to be alternative terms for the same divine agency that is now redirecting the mission by preventing their plans (8.36; 10.47; 11.17). **9–10:** Once again a *vision* (10.3, 10; 11.5; 18.9) is a means of divine communication to cross a boundary, now beyond Asia Minor to *Macedonia* in Europe.

11 We set sail from Troas and took a straight course to Samothrace, the following day to Neapolis, 12 and from there to Philippi, which is a leading city of the district[a] of Macedonia and a Roman colony. We remained in this city for some days. 13 On the sabbath day we went outside the gate by the river, where we supposed there was a place of prayer; and we sat down and spoke to the women who had gathered there. 14 A certain woman named Lydia, a worshiper of God, was listening to us; she was from the city of Thyatira and a dealer in purple cloth. The Lord opened her heart to listen eagerly to what was said by Paul. 15 When she and her household were baptized, she urged us, saying, "If you have judged me to be faithful to the Lord, come and stay at my home." And she prevailed upon us.

16 One day, as we were going to the place of prayer, we met a slave-girl who had a spirit of divination and brought her owners a great deal of money by fortune-telling. 17 While she followed Paul and us, she would cry out, "These men are slaves of the Most High God, who proclaim to you[b] a way of salvation." 18 She kept doing this for many days. But Paul, very much annoyed, turned and said to the spirit, "I order you in the name of Jesus Christ to come out of her." And it came out that very hour.

19 But when her owners saw that their hope of making money was gone, they seized Paul and Silas and dragged them into the marketplace before the authorities. 20 When they had brought them before the magistrates, they said, "These men are disturbing our city; they are Jews 21 and are advocating customs that are not lawful for us as Romans to adopt or observe." 22 The crowd joined in attacking them, and the magistrates had them stripped of their clothing and ordered them to be beaten with rods. 23 After they had given them a severe flogging, they threw them into prison and ordered the jailer to keep them securely. 24 Following these instructions, he put them in the innermost cell and fastened their feet in the stocks.

16.11–40: The mission in Philippi. 12: Paul's letter to "all the saints in Christ Jesus who are in *Philippi*" (Phil 1.1) reveals his enduring bond with them. **13–14:** The *place of prayer* (see also 16.16) was clearly a gathering for Jewish worship *on the sabbath day,* whether or not it was a proper "synagogue,"* and *Lydia* was already *a worshiper of God,* whether Jewish or gentile.* *Thyatira* was in central Asia Minor, from which Paul had just come (Rev 2.18–29). *Purple* textiles were the clothing of the wealthy (Lk 16.19). To say *the Lord opened her heart to listen* is to suggest the miracle of faith (Lk 24.32–33, 45; contrast Acts 28.26–28). **15:** The merchant Lydia has sufficient means to support the mission (Lk 8.3), urging her hospitality as a sign of acceptance (Lk 19.5; 24.29). On the baptism* of *her household,* see also 10.24, 44–48; 11.14; 16.31–34. **16:** Her *spirit of divination* claimed links with the "Python spirit" of the serpent oracle* of Delphi. **17:** In Luke, *the Most High* is a biblical title for God (Lk 1.32, 35, 76; 6.35), but *the Most High God* is a phrase used in recognition by those possessed by a lesser spirit, provoking an exorcism (Lk 8.28–29). **19–22:** Her owners' only *hope* for her was in *making money* (8.14–24;

---

a Other authorities read *a city of the first district*
b Other ancient authorities read *to us*

19.23–40), and their accusations against the *Jews* for making *Romans adopt* unlawful customs may again allude to circumcision.* Their case is without merit on both grounds, but it stirs the *crowd* (compare Luke 23.1–25). **24**: The security measures recall Peter's imprisonment in 12.4.

25 About midnight Paul and Silas were praying and singing hymns to God, and the prisoners were listening to them. 26Suddenly there was an earthquake, so violent that the foundations of the prison were shaken; and immediately all the doors were opened and everyone's chains were unfastened. 27When the jailer woke up and saw the prison doors wide open, he drew his sword and was about to kill himself, since he supposed that the prisoners had escaped. 28But Paul shouted in a loud voice, "Do not harm yourself, for we are all here." 29The jailer*a* called for lights, and rushing in, he fell down trembling before Paul and Silas. 30Then he brought them outside and said, "Sirs, what must I do to be saved?" 31They answered, "Believe on the Lord Jesus, and you will be saved, you and your household." 32They spoke the word of the Lord*b* to him and to all who were in his house. 33At the same hour of the night he took them and washed their wounds; then he and his entire family were baptized without delay. 34He brought them up into the house and set food before them; and he and his entire household rejoiced that he had become a believer in God.

35 When morning came, the magistrates sent the police, saying, "Let those men go." 36And the jailer reported the message to Paul, saying, "The magistrates sent word to let you go; therefore come out now and go in peace." 37But Paul replied, "They have beaten us in public, uncondemned, men who are Roman citizens, and have thrown us into prison; and now are they going to discharge us in secret? Certainly not! Let them come and take us out themselves." 38The police reported these words to the magistrates, and they were afraid when they heard that they were Roman citizens; 39so they came and apologized to them. And they took them out and asked them to leave the city. 40After leaving the prison they went to Lydia's home;

and when they had seen and encouraged the brothers and sisters*c* there, they departed.

16.25–40. 25: *Praying and singing* invoke divine assistance in critical times (Lk 3.21; 6.12; 9.18, 28–29; 10.21–22; 11.1; 18.1–8; 22.32, 41–46; 23.46; Acts 1.14; 2.42, 47; 4.23–31; 6.4; 7.59–60; 9.11; 10.2, 9; 12.12; 13.2–3). **26–27**: Compare Peter's miraculous escapes in 5.19–20 and 12.6–10, leading to the execution of the guards in 12.19. **30**: Unlike Cornelius, this gentile* convert seems to have no previous knowledge of Israel's faith, but like the Jews in Jerusalem asks, *"What must I do to be saved?"* (2.37). **31**: Faith in *the Lord Jesus* Christ is the only requirement for salvation and baptism* of the *household* (10.44–48; 11.17–18; 15.8–9). **37–38**: Such *secret* dealings reveal their shameful character, even by Roman law (1 Thess 2.2), and *Roman citizens* had higher standards of protection against capricious actions. **40**: The story ends again in *Lydia's home* (vv. 14–15).

17 After Paul and Silas*d* had passed through Amphipolis and Apollonia, they came to Thessalonica, where there was a synagogue of the Jews. 2And Paul went in, as was his custom, and on three sabbath days argued with them from the scriptures, 3explaining and proving that it was necessary for the Messiah*e* to suffer and to rise from the dead, and saying, "This is the Messiah,*e* Jesus whom I am proclaiming to you." 4Some of them were persuaded and joined Paul and Silas, as did a great many of the devout Greeks and not a few of the leading women. 5But the Jews became jealous, and with the help of some ruffians in the marketplaces they formed a mob and set the city in an uproar. While they were searching for Paul and Silas to bring them out to the assembly, they attacked Jason's house. 6When they could not find them, they dragged Jason and some believers*c* before the city authorities,*f* shouting, "These people who have been turning the world upside down have come here also, 7and Jason has entertained them as guests. They are all acting contrary to the decrees of the emperor, saying that

a Gk He   *b* Other ancient authorities read *word of God*
c Gk *brothers*   *d* Gk *they*   *e* Or *the Christ*
f Gk *politarchs*

there is another king named Jesus." [8]The people and the city officials were disturbed when they heard this, [9]and after they had taken bail from Jason and the others, they let them go.

10 That very night the believers[a] sent Paul and Silas off to Beroea; and when they arrived, they went to the Jewish synagogue. [11]These Jews were more receptive than those in Thessalonica, for they welcomed the message very eagerly and examined the scriptures every day to see whether these things were so. [12]Many of them therefore believed, including not a few Greek women and men of high standing. [13]But when the Jews of Thessalonica learned that the word of God had been proclaimed by Paul in Beroea as well, they came there too, to stir up and incite the crowds. [14]Then the believers[a] immediately sent Paul away to the coast, but Silas and Timothy remained behind. [15]Those who conducted Paul brought him as far as Athens; and after receiving instructions to have Silas and Timothy join him as soon as possible, they left him.

17.1–15: Conflicts in Thessalonica and Beroea. 1–2: *As was his custom* like Jesus (Lk 4.16), Paul's mission again begins with *the Jews,* in a *synagogue,*＊ on a *sabbath* (16.13; 17.17). **3:** The scriptural interpretations＊ again focus on the *necessity* of the suffering of the *Messiah*＊ and that Jesus is the *Messiah* (2.32–36; 3.18–20; 4.26–7). **5:** Jealousy was also identified as the motive for earlier efforts by Jews to stir up opposition to the apostles＊ (5.17; 13.45), which is probably an echo of Deut 32.21 where God makes Israel jealous (see Rom 10.19). *Jason's house* is identified as a house of prayer or a "house church" (see Lydia in 16.15). **6:** *Turning the world upside down* meant rebellion against the Roman order (11.28; 21.38; 24.5). **7:** Calling Jesus "the messiah" sounded like he was being acclaimed a *king,* which either meant a pretender to the rule of the *emperor* or at least the crowning of a ruler without Roman authorization, grounds enough for an execution (Lk 23.2–3, 35–37). **9:** Unlike in Philippi, the officials use the legal means of *bail,* and Paul and Silas depart without a confrontation (16.36–39). **10:** *Beroea* is about 60 miles south of Thessalonica. **11–12:** Their scripture study *every day* is commended as a quest for the truth in contrast to the rabble in Thessalonica. The *Greek women and men* appear to be in the synagogue too.

~~~~~~~~~~~~~~~~~~~~~~

16 While Paul was waiting for them in Athens, he was deeply distressed to see that the city was full of idols. [17]So he argued in the synagogue with the Jews and the devout persons, and also in the marketplace[b] every day with those who happened to be there. [18]Also some Epicurean and Stoic philosophers debated with him. Some said, "What does this babbler want to say?" Others said, "He seems to be a proclaimer of foreign divinities." (This was because he was telling the good news about Jesus and the resurrection.) [19]So they took him and brought him to the Areopagus and asked him, "May we know what this new teaching is that you are presenting? [20]It sounds rather strange to us, so we would like to know what it means." [21]Now all the Athenians and the foreigners living there would spend their time in nothing but telling or hearing something new.

22 Then Paul stood in front of the Areopagus and said, "Athenians, I see how extremely religious you are in every way. [23]For as I went through the city and looked carefully at the objects of your worship, I found among them an altar with the inscription, 'To an unknown god.' What therefore you worship as unknown, this I proclaim to you. [24]The God who made the world and everything in it, he who is Lord of heaven and earth, does not live in shrines made by human hands, [25]nor is he served by human hands, as though he needed anything, since he himself gives to all mortals life and breath and all things. [26]From one ancestor[c] he made all nations to inhabit the whole earth, and he allotted the times of their existence and the boundaries of the places where they would live, [27]so that they would search for God[d] and perhaps grope for him and find him—though indeed he is not far from each one of us. [28]For 'In him we live and move and have our being'; as even some of your own poets have said,

'For we too are his offspring.'

a Gk *brothers*   b Or *civic center*; Gk *agora*
c Gk *From one*; other ancient authorities read *From one blood*   d Other ancient authorities read *the Lord*

29 Since we are God's offspring, we ought not to think that the deity is like gold, or silver, or stone, an image formed by the art and imagination of mortals. 30 While God has overlooked the times of human ignorance, now he commands all people everywhere to repent, 31 because he has fixed a day on which he will have the world judged in righteousness by a man whom he has appointed, and of this he has given assurance to all by raising him from the dead."

32 When they heard of the resurrection of the dead, some scoffed; but others said, "We will hear you again about this." 33 At that point Paul left them. 34 But some of them joined him and became believers, including Dionysius the Areopagite and a woman named Damaris, and others with them.

17.16–34: Paul in Athens. 16: Paul's distress at *idols* is a classic Jewish judgment (v. 28; Isa 41.21–24; 44.9–20; 45.1–25). 17: The *marketplace* (Gk., "agora") was where philosophers publicly encountered the people. 18: The *Epicureans*** were known for disbelief in religious traditions, and the *Stoics*** sought to protect good order and civil religion. No philosopher wanted to be called a *babbler*, and proclaiming *foreign divinities* was like the charge on which Socrates was executed. 19: The *Areopagus* was the site of Athenian trials. 20: Luke again introduces an apostolic speech with the question of *what it means* (2.12). 22–23: Paul appears to build a case against the philosophers, first by criticizing those who were *extremely religious* (superstitious) and second by telling them they worship *the unknown god* in ignorance (17.30). 24–25: Greek wisdom also could speak of the creator god as *not* needing *anything* from mortals (14.15). The critique of *shrines* was a favorite Jewish prophetic* theme (7.48–50). 25–26: These verses read like a commentary on Gen 1.24, 27–28; 2.7. 27: Greek philosophy was well acquainted with the *search for God*, even to trying to apprehend or touch God with the mind. 28: This unusual citation of the Greek *poet* Aratus imitates the way the scriptures of Israel are cited regularly. 29: See v. 16. 30: *Ignorance* is no longer an excuse when the truth is known (see 3.17). Repentance means the deep change of mind or heart, which the philosophers often called "conversion." 31–32: The *fixed day* is the last judgment (Lk 10.12; 12.46; 17.24, 30; Acts 2.20). The phrase *a man whom he has appointed* re-

calls the "human being" or "son of man" in Dan 7.13 to whom judgment is given by God (7.56). In Acts, the *resurrection* is the vindication of Jesus, demonstrating his role as judge in the end time, but it also prompts derision from the Greeks (24.2–21).

18 After this Paul*a* left Athens and went to Corinth. 2 There he found a Jew named Aquila, a native of Pontus, who had recently come from Italy with his wife Priscilla, because Claudius had ordered all Jews to leave Rome. Paul*b* went to see them, 3 and, because he was of the same trade, he stayed with them, and they worked together—by trade they were tentmakers. 4 Every sabbath he would argue in the synagogue and would try to convince Jews and Greeks.

5 When Silas and Timothy arrived from Macedonia, Paul was occupied with proclaiming the word,*c* testifying to the Jews that the Messiah*d* was Jesus. 6 When they opposed and reviled him, in protest he shook the dust from his clothes*e* and said to them, "Your blood be on your own heads! I am innocent. From now on I will go to the Gentiles." 7 Then he left the synagogue*f* and went to the house of a man named Titius*g* Justus, a worshiper of God; his house was next door to the synagogue. 8 Crispus, the official of the synagogue, became a believer in the Lord, together with all his household; and many of the Corinthians who heard Paul became believers and were baptized. 9 One night the Lord said to Paul in a vision, "Do not be afraid, but speak and do not be silent; 10 for I am with you, and no one will lay a hand on you to harm you, for there are many in this city who are my people." 11 He stayed there a year and six months, teaching the word of God among them.

12 But when Gallio was proconsul of Achaia, the Jews made a united attack on Paul and brought him before the tribunal. 13 They said, "This man is persuading people to worship God in ways that are contrary to the law." 14 Just as Paul was about to speak,

a Gk *he*   *b* Gk *He*   *c* Gk *with the word*   *d* Or *the Christ*   *e* Gk *reviled him, he shook out his clothes*   *f* Gk *left there*   *g* Other ancient authorities read *Titus*

Gallio said to the Jews, "If it were a matter of crime or serious villainy, I would be justified in accepting the complaint of you Jews; 15but since it is a matter of questions about words and names and your own law, see to it yourselves; I do not wish to be a judge of these matters." 16And he dismissed them from the tribunal. 17Then all of them[a] seized Sosthenes, the official of the synagogue, and beat him in front of the tribunal. But Gallio paid no attention to any of these things.

18.1–19.41: The mission in Corinth and Ephesus. 2: *Aquila and Priscilla* appear as partners in ministry with Paul in many contexts (18.18, 26; Rom 16.3; 1 Cor 16.19; 2 Tim 4.19). *Claudius's* edict expelling the Jews from *Rome* is dated around 49 CE. **3:** Like rabbis and philosophers who worked with their hands (1 Thess 2.9; 2 Thess 3.6–8; 1 Cor 4.12; 9.6), they practiced their *trade* of tentmaking to avoid becoming a burden to their hearers. **5:** The crucial message remains that *Jesus is the Messiah*★ (see 2.31–32; 3.18–20; 10.38–43; 18.28). **6:** To *shake the dust from his clothes* is a prophetic★ act of judgment (Lk 10.11; Acts 13.51), consistent with holding people responsible for their own lives or *blood* upon their heads (2 Sam 1.16; 1 Kings 2.33). Paul's second threat to *go to the Gentiles*★ (13.46; 28.28) is also prophetic reproach, but he soon returns to a synagogue★ (18.19). **8:** *Crispus* is probably the one mentioned by Paul in 1 Cor 1.14 as one of the few he *baptized*★. **9–10:** The *Lord* speaking in the *vision* must be the Lord Jesus, but perhaps through a messenger (9.10; 10.3; 16.9). *Do not be afraid . . . I am with you* is an assurance of divine presence (Isa 41.10; 43.5; Jer 1.8, 19; Mt 28.20). **12:** According to an inscription found in Corinth, *Gallio* was named *proconsul* by the Emperor Claudius in late 51 CE. **13:** Their charge against Paul is not general sedition (16.20–21; 17.7) but violation of *the law* of Israel. **14–17:** *Gallio* refuses to become involved in an intra-Jewish debate (24.20–22; 26.3).

18 After staying there for a considerable time, Paul said farewell to the believers[b] and sailed for Syria, accompanied by Priscilla and Aquila. At Cenchreae he had his hair cut, for he was under a vow. 19When they reached Ephesus, he left them there, but first he himself went into the synagogue and had a discussion with the Jews. 20When they asked him to stay longer, he declined; 21but on taking leave of them, he said, "I[c] will return to you, if God wills." Then he set sail from Ephesus.

22 When he had landed at Caesarea, he went up to Jerusalem[d] and greeted the church, and then went down to Antioch. 23After spending some time there he departed and went from place to place through the region of Galatia[e] and Phrygia, strengthening all the disciples.

24 Now there came to Ephesus a Jew named Apollos, a native of Alexandria. He was an eloquent man, well-versed in the scriptures. 25He had been instructed in the Way of the Lord; and he spoke with burning enthusiasm and taught accurately the things concerning Jesus, though he knew only the baptism of John. 26He began to speak boldly in the synagogue; but when Priscilla and Aquila heard him, they took him aside and explained the Way of God to him more accurately. 27And when he wished to cross over to Achaia, the believers[b] encouraged him and wrote to the disciples to welcome him. On his arrival he greatly helped those who through grace had become believers, 28for he powerfully refuted the Jews in public, showing by the scriptures that the Messiah[f] is Jesus.

18.18–28. 18: Paul appears to *cut his hair* at the beginning of taking a special *vow*, in contrast to shaving his head at the completion of the vow at the Temple★ (Num 6.1–21; Acts 21.24). **21:** As note *c* indicates, some ancient copies stress the necessity of Paul's journey to Jerusalem in terms similar to Jesus' mission (Lk 9.51–53; 13.33; Acts 19.21; 20.22). **22:** This brief visit appears significant only as a display of Paul's respect for the *church* in *Jerusalem*. **24–25:** *Apollos* introduces the scriptural interpretations★ associated with the Hellenistic★ Jewish traditions of *Alexandria* (1 Cor 1.12; 3.4–6, 22; 4.6; 16.12). The *baptism*★ *of John* is a preparation for the baptism of the Holy Spirit (Lk 3.16; Acts 1.5; 11.16; 19.3–5). **26:** *Priscilla and Aquila* are both teachers (18.2) of *the Way* (9.2; 16.17; 19.9;

a Other ancient authorities read *all the Greeks* *b* Gk *brothers* *c* Other ancient authorities read *I must at all costs keep the approaching festival in Jerusalem, but I* *d* Gk *went up* *e* Gk *the Galatian region* *f* Or *the Christ*

22.4; 24.22). **27:** 1 Cor 1–4 attests the impact of Apollos's mission in *Achaia*.

19 While Apollos was in Corinth, Paul passed through the interior regions and came to Ephesus, where he found some disciples. [2]He said to them, "Did you receive the Holy Spirit when you became believers?" They replied, "No, we have not even heard that there is a Holy Spirit." [3]Then he said, "Into what then were you baptized?" They answered, "Into John's baptism." [4]Paul said, "John baptized with the baptism of repentance, telling the people to believe in the one who was to come after him, that is, in Jesus." [5]On hearing this, they were baptized in the name of the Lord Jesus. [6]When Paul had laid his hands on them, the Holy Spirit came upon them, and they spoke in tongues and prophesied— [7]altogether there were about twelve of them.

8 He entered the synagogue and for three months spoke out boldly, and argued persuasively about the kingdom of God. [9]When some stubbornly refused to believe and spoke evil of the Way before the congregation, he left them, taking the disciples with him, and argued daily in the lecture hall of Tyrannus.*a* [10]This continued for two years, so that all the residents of Asia, both Jews and Greeks, heard the word of the Lord.

11 God did extraordinary miracles through Paul, [12]so that when the handkerchiefs or aprons that had touched his skin were brought to the sick, their diseases left them, and the evil spirits came out of them. [13]Then some itinerant Jewish exorcists tried to use the name of the Lord Jesus over those who had evil spirits, saying, "I adjure you by the Jesus whom Paul proclaims." [14]Seven sons of a Jewish high priest named Sceva were doing this. [15]But the evil spirit said to them in reply, "Jesus I know, and Paul I know; but who are you?" [16]Then the man with the evil spirit leaped on them, mastered them all, and so overpowered them that they fled out of the house naked and wounded. [17]When this became known to all residents of Ephesus, both Jews and Greeks, everyone was awestruck; and the name of the Lord Jesus was praised. [18]Also many of those who

became believers confessed and disclosed their practices. [19]A number of those who practiced magic collected their books and burned them publicly; when the value of these books*b* was calculated, it was found to come to fifty thousand silver coins. [20]So the word of the Lord grew mightily and prevailed.

19.1–20. 1–7: The distinctive messianic baptism* of the Way is again (see comment on 18.24–25) contrasted to other Jewish washings or baptisms of repentance, including *John's*. Baptism *in the name of the Lord Jesus* is accompanied by the laying on of hands and confirmed by the *Holy Spirit* as "the repentance that leads to life" (10.45–48; 11.15–18). **8–10:** This brief summary reports two years and three months in Ephesus. The stubborn refusal in the *synagogue** is another prophetic* diagnosis of hardening (7.51; 14.2; 28.26–28), explaining the move to the non-Jewish *lecture hall of Tyrannus* without recounting the argument there. **11:** *Miracles* are powerful acts, displaying divine presence (2.22; 4.33; 6.8; 8.13; 10.38). **12:** The use of physical means for healing was common Hellenistic* practice (5.15–16). **13–14:** The *itinerant Jewish exorcists* were probably not well regarded in the synagogues (13.6); their use of *the name of the Lord Jesus* was not informed by faith, and there is no record of a legitimate *high priest named Sceva*. **15:** The *evil spirits* were known for sassy talk (Lk 4.34; 8.28). **18–19:** The apostles' powerful acts are again sharply distinguished from *magic* (8.4–25; 13.4–12). **20:** The power that triumphs in the story is not the apostles' own, but *the word of the Lord*.

---

21 Now after these things had been accomplished, Paul resolved in the Spirit to go through Macedonia and Achaia, and then to go on to Jerusalem. He said, "After I have gone there, I must also see Rome." [22]So he sent two of his helpers, Timothy and Erastus, to Macedonia, while he himself stayed for some time longer in Asia.

23 About that time no little disturbance broke out concerning the Way. [24]A man named Demetrius, a silversmith who made

a Other ancient authorities read *of a certain Tyrannus, from eleven o'clock in the morning to four in the afternoon*
b Gk *them*

silver shrines of Artemis, brought no little business to the artisans. 25These he gathered together, with the workers of the same trade, and said, "Men, you know that we get our wealth from this business. 26You also see and hear that not only in Ephesus but in almost the whole of Asia this Paul has persuaded and drawn away a considerable number of people by saying that gods made with hands are not gods. 27And there is danger not only that this trade of ours may come into disrepute but also that the temple of the great goddess Artemis will be scorned, and she will be deprived of her majesty that brought all Asia and the world to worship her."

28 When they heard this, they were enraged and shouted, "Great is Artemis of the Ephesians!" 29The city was filled with the confusion; and people*a* rushed together to the theater, dragging with them Gaius and Aristarchus, Macedonians who were Paul's travel companions. 30Paul wished to go into the crowd, but the disciples would not let him; 31even some officials of the province of Asia,*b* who were friendly to him, sent him a message urging him not to venture into the theater. 32Meanwhile, some were shouting one thing, some another; for the assembly was in confusion, and most of them did not know why they had come together. 33Some of the crowd gave instructions to Alexander, whom the Jews had pushed forward. And Alexander motioned for silence and tried to make a defense before the people. 34But when they recognized that he was a Jew, for about two hours all of them shouted in unison, "Great is Artemis of the Ephesians!" 35But when the town clerk had quieted the crowd, he said, "Citizens of Ephesus, who is there that does not know that the city of the Ephesians is the temple keeper of the great Artemis and of the statue that fell from heaven?*c* 36Since these things cannot be denied, you ought to be quiet and do nothing rash. 37You have brought these men here who are neither temple robbers nor blasphemers of our*d* goddess. 38If therefore Demetrius and the artisans with him have a complaint against anyone, the courts are open, and there are proconsuls; let them bring charges there against one another. 39If

there is anything further*e* you want to know, it must be settled in the regular assembly. 40For we are in danger of being charged with rioting today, since there is no cause that we can give to justify this commotion." 41When he had said this, he dismissed the assembly.

19.21–41. 21: The themes of *resolve in the Spirit* and necessity for the journey (*"I must also see Rome"*) disclose divine direction (Lk 9.51–62; 13.31–35). **22:** On *Timothy,* see 16.1. *Erastus* is mentioned in Rom 16.23 and 2 Tim 4.20. **24:** *Artemis* was the famed hunter goddess, called Diana in Latin. **26:** Paul's prophetic* speech against idols *made with hands* (17.24) endangered whole guilds of workers. **28:** *Artemis of the Ephesians* was a title that reflected special patronage for the city. **29:** A theater in Ephesus seating 25,000 has been excavated. **31–33:** The *officials of the province of Asia* and the Jewish spokesman *Alexander* cannot protect Paul from the mob. **35:** The *town clerk* restores order with a recitation of the public piety of the Artemis cult. *The statue that fell from heaven* may have been a meteorite that was thought to be an image of the goddess. Even its coinage marked Ephesus as the *temple keeper.* **37:** *Temple robbers* were especially hated in antiquity because the temples marked the cultural integrity of the cities and often served as banks.

---

20 After the uproar had ceased, Paul sent for the disciples; and after encouraging them and saying farewell, he left for Macedonia. 2When he had gone through those regions and had given the believers*f* much encouragement, he came to Greece, 3where he stayed for three months. He was about to set sail for Syria when a plot was made against him by the Jews, and so he decided to return through Macedonia. 4He was accompanied by Sopater son of Pyrrhus from Beroea, by Aristarchus and Secundus from Thessalonica, by Gaius from Derbe, and by Timothy, as well as by Tychicus and Trophimus from Asia. 5They went ahead and were waiting for us in Troas; 6but we sailed from Philippi after the days of Unleavened Bread,

a Gk *they*   *b* Gk *some of the Asiarchs*   *c* Meaning of Gk uncertain   *d* Other ancient authorities read *your*
e Other ancient authorities read *about other matters*
f Gk *given them*

and in five days we joined them in Troas, where we stayed for seven days.

7 On the first day of the week, when we met to break bread, Paul was holding a discussion with them; since he intended to leave the next day, he continued speaking until midnight. 8There were many lamps in the room upstairs where we were meeting. 9A young man named Eutychus, who was sitting in the window, began to sink off into a deep sleep while Paul talked still longer. Overcome by sleep, he fell to the ground three floors below and was picked up dead. 10But Paul went down, and bending over him took him in his arms, and said, "Do not be alarmed, for his life is in him." 11Then Paul went upstairs, and after he had broken bread and eaten, he continued to converse with them until dawn; then he left. 12Meanwhile they had taken the boy away alive and were not a little comforted.

20.1–22.16: Going to Jerusalem. 20.1: The journey to *Macedonia* announced in 19.22 now resumes. **3:** A *plot . . . against him by the Jews* again prompts movement (9.24; 20.19; 23.30). **4:** Paul's companions gather from a variety of places, perhaps to bring an offering together to Jerusalem (20.16; 24.17; Rom 15.16; 2 Cor 9.1). **6–7:** The entourage observes the Jewish practice of *the days of Unleavened Bread,* which Luke identifies with Passover* (Lk 22.1), timing its travel by the Liturgical calendar* (20.18), but now breaking *bread* in Christian worship on *the first day of the week* (Lk 24.1; Acts 2.42, 46; 1 Cor 16.2; Rev 1.10). **9–10:** *Eutychus,* whose name means "good fortune," is unknown outside this story. Paul's discernment of whether the boy was *dead* or sleeping recalls Jesus' miraculous action with Jairus's daughter in Lk 8.52 and the actions of Elijah (1 Kings 17.17–24) and Elisha (2 Kings 4.32–37).

13 We went ahead to the ship and set sail for Assos, intending to take Paul on board there; for he had made this arrangement, intending to go by land himself. 14When he met us in Assos, we took him on board and went to Mitylene. 15We sailed from there, and on the following day we arrived opposite Chios. The next day we touched at Samos, and*a* the day after that we came to Miletus. 16For Paul had decided to sail past Ephesus, so that he might not have to spend time in Asia; he was eager to be in Jerusalem, if possible, on the day of Pentecost.

17 From Miletus he sent a message to Ephesus, asking the elders of the church to meet him. 18When they came to him, he said to them:

"You yourselves know how I lived among you the entire time from the first day that I set foot in Asia, 19serving the Lord with all humility and with tears, enduring the trials that came to me through the plots of the Jews. 20I did not shrink from doing anything helpful, proclaiming the message to you and teaching you publicly and from house to house, 21as I testified to both Jews and Greeks about repentance toward God and faith toward our Lord Jesus. 22And now, as a captive to the Spirit,*b* I am on my way to Jerusalem, not knowing what will happen to me there, 23except that the Holy Spirit testifies to me in every city that imprisonment and persecutions are waiting for me. 24But I do not count my life of any value to myself, if only I may finish my course and the ministry that I received from the Lord Jesus, to testify to the good news of God's grace.

25 "And now I know that none of you, among whom I have gone about proclaiming the kingdom, will ever see my face again. 26Therefore I declare to you this day that I am not responsible for the blood of any of you, 27for I did not shrink from declaring to you the whole purpose of God. 28Keep watch over yourselves and over all the flock, of which the Holy Spirit has made you overseers, to shepherd the church of God*c* that he obtained with the blood of his own Son.*d* 29I know that after I have gone, savage wolves will come in among you, not sparing the flock. 30Some even from your own group will come distorting the truth in order to entice the disciples to follow them. 31Therefore be alert, remembering that for three years I did not cease night or day to warn everyone with tears. 32And now I commend you to God and to the message of his grace, a mes-

a Other ancient authorities add *after remaining at Trogyllium*   *b* Or *And now, bound in the spirit*
c Other ancient authorities read *of the Lord*   *d* Or *with his own blood;* Gk *with the blood of his own Own*

sage that is able to build you up and to give you the inheritance among all who are sanctified. 33I coveted no one's silver or gold or clothing. 34You know for yourselves that I worked with my own hands to support myself and my companions. 35In all this I have given you an example that by such work we must support the weak, remembering the words of the Lord Jesus, for he himself said, 'It is more blessed to give than to receive.'"

36 When he had finished speaking, he knelt down with them all and prayed. 37There was much weeping among them all; they embraced Paul and kissed him, 38grieving especially because of what he had said, that they would not see him again. Then they brought him to the ship.

20.13–38. 16: *Pentecost* was a time for Jewish pilgrimage to *Jerusalem* (see comments on 2.9–11; 20.6–7). **17–18:** In Acts, *the elders of the church* are appointed locally with divine authority comparable to the apostles* (11.30; 14.23; 15.2, 4, 6, 22, 23; 16.4), and Paul's account of his ministry and farewell commendation in vv. 18–35 is addressed to *them*. **19:** The apostle's *trials* (Gk., "peirosmos"; see Lk 4.2; 1 Thess 3.5; Gal 4.14) are spiritual tests as well as human conflicts. *Humility and tears* are signs of a ministry like Jesus' (Lk 19.41–44; 22.24–27). **20:** *"I did not shrink"* is another way of claiming apostolic boldness (4.13; 9.27–28; 13.46; 19.8). **21:** On *both Jews and Greeks,* see 13.44–48; 14.27; 17.4, 11, 17; 18.5–6, 19; 19.8–10, 17). The content of the *repentance toward God* or "conversion" (Gk., "metanoia") proclaimed in Acts is specifically *faith toward our Lord Jesus* (2.38; 3.19; 5.31; 11.18; 17.30; 26.20). **22–23:** To be *captive to the Spirit* who *testifies to me in every city* is to be bound by God's determined purpose in suffering rather than power (see 19.21; 21.11). Paul's directed journey comes to a climax* in the Temple* in *Jerusalem* (Lk 9.51; 13.22, 33–34; 19.11, 28, 41–44). **24:** The journey or mission is an athletic *course* to finish (13.25; 1 Cor 9.24; Phil 3.14; 2 Tim 4.7). *The ministry . . . I received from the Lord Jesus* stands in contrast to Paul's earlier self-appointed mission (9.1, 15; 22.3–10; 26.9–18). **26:** To be *not responsible for the blood of any of you* means Paul has fulfilled his calling with regard to them and their lives (18.6). **28:** The elders of the congregation are entrusted with the office of *overseers* (Gk., "episkopos"), and *the church of God* is both local and a larger spiritual reality (1 Cor 1.2, "the

church of God that is in Corinth"). **29–31:** Paul's warning against *wolves* (Ezek 22.27; Lk 10.3) sounds an alert (Lk 12.37–39) against false teachers who distort *the truth* (Lk 9.41; Acts 13.10). **35:** This traditional saying is not otherwise attributed to *the Lord Jesus* (but see Lk 6.35–36, 38, 1 Clement 2.1). **36:** Paul *knelt down* and *prayed* as Jesus did following his farewell to his disciples (Lk 22.41; Acts 21.5–6).

21 When we had parted from them and set sail, we came by a straight course to Cos, and the next day to Rhodes, and from there to Patara.*a* 2When we found a ship bound for Phoenicia, we went on board and set sail. 3We came in sight of Cyprus; and leaving it on our left, we sailed to Syria and landed at Tyre, because the ship was to unload its cargo there. 4We looked up the disciples and stayed there for seven days. Through the Spirit they told Paul not to go on to Jerusalem. 5When our days there were ended, we left and proceeded on our journey; and all of them, with wives and children, escorted us outside the city. There we knelt down on the beach and prayed 6and said farewell to one another. Then we went on board the ship, and they returned home.

7 When we had finished*b* the voyage from Tyre, we arrived at Ptolemais; and we greeted the believers*c* and stayed with them for one day. 8The next day we left and came to Caesarea; and we went into the house of Philip the evangelist, one of the seven, and stayed with him. 9He had four unmarried daughters*d* who had the gift of prophecy. 10While we were staying there for several days, a prophet named Agabus came down from Judea. 11He came to us and took Paul's belt, bound his own feet and hands with it, and said, "Thus says the Holy Spirit, 'This is the way the Jews in Jerusalem will bind the man who owns this belt and will hand him over to the Gentiles.'" 12When we heard this, we and the people there urged him not to go up to Jerusalem. 13Then Paul answered, "What are you doing, weeping and breaking my heart? For I am ready not only

a Other ancient authorities add *and Myra*
b Or *continued*   *c* Gk *brothers*   *d* Gk *four daughters, virgins,*

to be bound but even to die in Jerusalem for the name of the Lord Jesus." [14]Since he would not be persuaded, we remained silent except to say, "The Lord's will be done."

15 After these days we got ready and started to go up to Jerusalem. [16]Some of the disciples from Caesarea also came along and brought us to the house of Mnason of Cyprus, an early disciple, with whom we were to stay.

21.1–16. 2: The earlier mission in *Phoenicia* was briefly mentioned in 11.19. 4: Taking their words literally would prevent Paul from going to *Jerusalem* (16.6–7), but the context makes clear this is a prophetic* warning (20.23; 21.12–14). 8: *Philip the evangelist* (6.3–6) arrived in *Caesarea* in 8.40 (see also 8.4–13, 26–39). 9: On women prophets, see 2.18. 10: On *Agabus the prophet*, see 11.27. 11: The use of Paul's *belt* as a symbol of his being *bound* by the *Holy Spirit* (20.22) has prophetic precedents (Jer 19.1–13; Ezek 4.1–17; Peter's belt in John 19.18–19). 13: *"I am ready . . . to die"* is a mature conviction in this passage (20.24; contrast Lk 22.33). *Jerusalem* is the place in prophetic tradition where God's prophets and apostles* meet the most intense opposition (see comments on Lk 11.49–51; 13.33–34). 14: Luke's entire narrative* is alive to the question of how *the Lord's will* is accomplished in the midst of rejection (see comments on Lk 22.42; 23.25; Acts 18.21). 15: The arrival in *Jerusalem* (v. 17) concludes this section of Paul's travel narrative, as also for Jesus in Lk 19.28.

---

17 When we arrived in Jerusalem, the brothers welcomed us warmly. [18]The next day Paul went with us to visit James; and all the elders were present. [19]After greeting them, he related one by one the things that God had done among the Gentiles through his ministry. [20]When they heard it, they praised God. Then they said to him, "You see, brother, how many thousands of believers there are among the Jews, and they are all zealous for the law. [21]They have been told about you that you teach all the Jews living among the Gentiles to forsake Moses, and that you tell them not to circumcise their children or observe the customs. [22]What then is to be done? They will certainly hear that you have come. [23]So do what we tell you. We have four men who are under a vow.

[24]Join these men, go through the rite of purification with them, and pay for the shaving of their heads. Thus all will know that there is nothing in what they have been told about you, but that you yourself observe and guard the law. [25]But as for the Gentiles who have become believers, we have sent a letter with our judgment that they should abstain from what has been sacrificed to idols and from blood and from what is strangled[a] and from fornication." [26]Then Paul took the men, and the next day, having purified himself, he entered the temple with them, making public the completion of the days of purification when the sacrifice would be made for each of them.

21.17–28.31: On trial for the promise. 21.17–25: The leaders of the church in Jerusalem receive Paul. 17–20: *The brothers* (15.1, 13) represent the broad assembly of believers who now received Paul *warmly*, and *James and the elders* join them in hearing about the mission *among the Gentiles** (15.12). But their concern is focused only on *how may thousands of believers* (2.41; 4.4; 6.7) *there are among the Jews, all zealous for the law* (15.21). 21: The false charge is literally that Paul is teaching *the Jews* apostasy from Moses. 23–24: On the *vow*, see Num 6.1–21 and Acts 18.18. 25: The agreement about the *Gentiles* (15.19–29) remains in force.

---

27 When the seven days were almost completed, the Jews from Asia, who had seen him in the temple, stirred up the whole crowd. They seized him, [28]shouting, "Fellow Israelites, help! This is the man who is teaching everyone everywhere against our people, our law, and this place; more than that, he has actually brought Greeks into the temple and has defiled this holy place." [29]For they had previously seen Trophimus the Ephesian with him in the city, and they supposed that Paul had brought him into the temple. [30]Then all the city was aroused, and the people rushed together. They seized Paul and dragged him out of the temple, and immediately the doors were shut. [31]While they were trying to kill him, word came to the tri-

---

a Other ancient authorities lack *and from what is strangled* bune of the cohort that all Jerusalem was in an uproar. 32Immediately he took soldiers and centurions and ran down to them. When they saw the tribune and the soldiers, they stopped beating Paul. 33Then the tribune came, arrested him, and ordered him to be bound with two chains; he inquired who he was and what he had done. 34Some in the crowd shouted one thing, some another; and as he could not learn the facts because of the uproar, he ordered him to be brought into the barracks. 35When Paul[a] came to the steps, the violence of the mob was so great that he had to be carried by the soldiers. 36The crowd that followed kept shouting, "Away with him!"

21.26–23.10: Conflicts in the Temple.* 26–28: In Luke-Acts, the *temple* was a place where Jesus and Stephen also testified in face of the extended provocation of adversaries (Lk 20.1–21.4; Acts 6.8–7.60; Acts 3.1–4.31), including charges of *teaching . . . against . . . this place* (6.13; Lk 21.5–6). **30–32:** Luke depicts a mob dragging Paul outside the sacred precincts to kill him as a *temple* defiler (see also Jesus in Lk 4.16–30 and Stephen in Acts 6–7), prompting the Roman army *tribune* (Claudius Lysias, 23.2) to call out his *cohort* of a thousand *soldiers* (see also Gallio in 18.12–17; 19.28–41).

37 Just as Paul was about to be brought into the barracks, he said to the tribune, "May I say something to you?" The tribune[b] replied, "Do you know Greek? 38Then you are not the Egyptian who recently stirred up a revolt and led the four thousand assassins out into the wilderness?" 39Paul replied, "I am a Jew, from Tarsus in Cilicia, a citizen of an important city; I beg you, let me speak to the people." 40When he had given him permission, Paul stood on the steps and motioned to the people for silence; and when there was a great hush, he addressed them in the Hebrew[c] language, saying:

22 "Brothers and fathers, listen to the defense that I now make before you."

2 When they heard him addressing them in Hebrew,[c] they became even more quiet. Then he said:

3 "I am a Jew, born in Tarsus in Cilicia, but brought up in this city at the feet of Gamaliel, educated strictly according to our ancestral law, being zealous for God, just as all of you are today. 4I persecuted this Way up to the point of death by binding both men and women and putting them in prison, 5as the high priest and the whole council of elders can testify about me. From them I also received letters to the brothers in Damascus, and I went there in order to bind those who were there and to bring them back to Jerusalem for punishment.

6 "While I was on my way and approaching Damascus, about noon a great light from heaven suddenly shone about me. 7I fell to the ground and heard a voice saying to me, 'Saul, Saul, why are you persecuting me?' 8I answered, 'Who are you, Lord?' Then he said to me, 'I am Jesus of Nazareth[d] whom you are persecuting.' 9Now those who were with me saw the light but did not hear the voice of the one who was speaking to me. 10I asked, 'What am I to do, Lord?' The Lord said to me, 'Get up and go to Damascus; there you will be told everything that has been assigned to you to do.' 11Since I could not see because of the brightness of that light, those who were with me took my hand and led me to Damascus.

12 "A certain Ananias, who was a devout man according to the law and well spoken of by all the Jews living there, 13came to me; and standing beside me, he said, 'Brother Saul, regain your sight!' In that very hour I regained my sight and saw him. 14Then he said, 'The God of our ancestors has chosen you to know his will, to see the Righteous One and to hear his own voice; 15for you will be his witness to all the world of what you have seen and heard. 16And now why do you delay? Get up, be baptized, and have your sins washed away, calling on his name.'

17 "After I had returned to Jerusalem and while I was praying in the temple, I fell into a trance 18and saw Jesus[e] saying to me, 'Hurry and get out of Jerusalem quickly, because they will not accept your testimony about me.' 19And I said, 'Lord, they themselves know that in every synagogue I im-

a Gk *he*   *b* Gk *He*   *c* That is, *Aramaic*
d Gk *the Nazorean*   *e* Gk *him*

prisoned and beat those who believed in you. 20And while the blood of your witness Stephen was shed, I myself was standing by, approving and keeping the coats of those who killed him.' 21Then he said to me, 'Go, for I will send you far away to the Gentiles.' "

21.37–22.21. 21.38: The *Egyptian* was a famous Jewish "prophet"* who led a rebellion in the era of Felix, around 54 CE (Josephus,* *War* 2.261–263; *Antiquities* 20.168–172). The *assassins* were cloak-and-dagger killers fighting Rome (Josephus, *War* 2.254–257; *Antiquities* 20.186–188). **40:** On *the Hebrew language*, see note c and 22.2. **22.1–22:** Like 26.1–23, this *defense* (Gk., "apologia") speech (see also 24.1–21) retells the story of Acts 9.1–31. **3:** *Gamaliel* has already appeared in 5.33–39, advocating that the council be restrained in its response to the apostles.* *Being zealous for God* is closely tied to strict observance of *our ancestral law* (see also "zealous for the law" in 21.20; Gal 1.14; Rom 10.2–4). **4:** *This Way* means the followers of Jesus as messiah* (9.2; 19.9, 23). **12–14:** *Ananias* is now credited with being *devout* according to the law (9.10), and he speaks for *the God of our ancestors* (9.17). For Jesus' identity as *the Righteous One*, see comments on Lk 23.47; Acts 3.14; 7.52. **17–18:** The story of Paul's *trance* in the *temple*,* only told here, recalls Peter's trance (10.10; 11.5) and echoes the call of Isaiah in the Temple (Isa 6.1–13). **21:** Paul's commission is now even more like Isaiah's "light to the gentiles*" (see comment on Acts 1.8), and the people of Israel are not mentioned (9.14).

22 Up to this point they listened to him, but then they shouted, "Away with such a fellow from the earth! For he should not be allowed to live." 23And while they were shouting, throwing off their cloaks, and tossing dust into the air, 24the tribune directed that he was to be brought into the barracks, and ordered him to be examined by flogging, to find out the reason for this outcry against him. 25But when they had tied him up with thongs,ᵃ Paul said to the centurion who was standing by, "Is it legal for you to flog a Roman citizen who is uncondemned?" 26When the centurion heard that, he went to the tribune and said to him, "What are you about to do? This man is a Roman citizen." 27The tribune came and asked Paul,ᵇ "Tell me, are you a Roman citizen?" And he

said, "Yes." 28The tribune answered, "It cost me a large sum of money to get my citizenship." Paul said, "But I was born a citizen." 29Immediately those who were about to examine him drew back from him; and the tribune also was afraid, for he realized that Paul was a Roman citizen and that he had bound him.

30 Since he wanted to find out what Paulᶜ was being accused of by the Jews, the next day he released him and ordered the chief priests and the entire council to meet. He brought Paul down and had him stand before them.

23 While Paul was looking intently at the council he said, "Brothers,ᵈ up to this day I have lived my life with a clear conscience before God." 2Then the high priest Ananias ordered those standing near him to strike him on the mouth. 3At this Paul said to him, "God will strike you, you whitewashed wall! Are you sitting there to judge me according to the law, and yet in violation of the law you order me to be struck?" 4Those standing nearby said, "Do you dare to insult God's high priest?" 5And Paul said, "I did not realize, brothers, that he was high priest; for it is written, 'You shall not speak evil of a leader of your people.' "

6 When Paul noticed that some were Sadducees and others were Pharisees, he called out in the council, "Brothers, I am a Pharisee, a son of Pharisees. I am on trial concerning the hope of the resurrectionᵉ of the dead." 7When he said this, a dissension began between the Pharisees and the Sadducees, and the assembly was divided. 8(The Sadducees say that there is no resurrection, or angel, or spirit; but the Pharisees acknowledge all three.) 9Then a great clamor arose, and certain scribes of the Pharisees' group stood up and contended, "We find nothing wrong with this man. What if a spirit or an angel has spoken to him?" 10When the dissension became violent, the tribune, fearing that they would tear Paul to pieces, ordered the soldiers to go down, take him by force, and bring him into the barracks.

a Or *up for the lashes*   b Gk *him*   c Gk *he*
d Gk *Men, brothers*   e Gk *concerning hope and resurrection*

22.22–23.10. 22.22: Compare the reaction of the crowd to this inclusive mission to Luke's account of Jesus in the synagogue* in Nazareth (Lk 4.16–30). 23: *Shouting* (7.57; 14.14), *throwing . . . cloaks* (14.14; 18.6), and *tossing dust* (13.51) are ritual acts to prevent the evil of Paul's words. 24: *Flogging* was a standard Roman method of interrogation. 25–27: This passage and 16.37–39 give a glimpse into Luke's understanding of the rights of Roman citizenship. 28: Since he bears the name of Claudius (23.26), *the tribune* probably purchased his citizenship during the reign of Claudius (41–54 CE). 30: The tribune's ability to order *the chief priests and the entire council to meet* discloses the thorough control of the Roman order. 23.1: *Living with a clear conscience before God* means fidelity to the law (23.3; 24.14–16). 2: In Jn 18.22, Jesus was also struck on the face for his answer to *the high priest*. 3: Paul invokes a biblical judgment (Deut 28.22) against the high priest for not obeying the *law* he was defending (7.53). 5: Paul's quotation of Ex 22.27 is a critique of any *"leader of your people"* who does not evidently obey the law. 6–9: The *hope of the resurrection* is a central issue (24.20–21), not merely a device to divide the crowd. Jesus also challenged the *Sadducees* on *the resurrection* with a scriptural argument the *Pharisees* and their scribes* accepted (Lk 22.27–40). 7: On the *dissension* within Israel, see also 14.4.

11 That night the Lord stood near him and said, "Keep up your courage! For just as you have testified for me in Jerusalem, so you must bear witness also in Rome."

12 In the morning the Jews joined in a conspiracy and bound themselves by an oath neither to eat nor drink until they had killed Paul. 13There were more than forty who joined in this conspiracy. 14They went to the chief priests and elders and said, "We have strictly bound ourselves by an oath to taste no food until we have killed Paul. 15Now then, you and the council must notify the tribune to bring him down to you, on the pretext that you want to make a more thorough examination of his case. And we are ready to do away with him before he arrives."

16 Now the son of Paul's sister heard about the ambush; so he went and gained entrance to the barracks and told Paul.

17Paul called one of the centurions and said, "Take this young man to the tribune, for he has something to report to him." 18So he took him, brought him to the tribune, and said, "The prisoner Paul called me and asked me to bring this young man to you; he has something to tell you." 19The tribune took him by the hand, drew him aside privately, and asked, "What is it that you have to report to me?" 20He answered, "The Jews have agreed to ask you to bring Paul down to the council tomorrow, as though they were going to inquire more thoroughly into his case. 21But do not be persuaded by them, for more than forty of their men are lying in ambush for him. They have bound themselves by an oath neither to eat nor drink until they kill him. They are ready now and are waiting for your consent." 22So the tribune dismissed the young man, ordering him, "Tell no one that you have informed me of this."

23 Then he summoned two of the centurions and said, "Get ready to leave by nine o'clock tonight for Caesarea with two hundred soldiers, seventy horsemen, and two hundred spearmen. 24Also provide mounts for Paul to ride, and take him safely to Felix the governor." 25He wrote a letter to this effect:

26 "Claudius Lysias to his Excellency the governor Felix, greetings. 27This man was seized by the Jews and was about to be killed by them, but when I had learned that he was a Roman citizen, I came with the guard and rescued him. 28Since I wanted to know the charge for which they accused him, I had him brought to their council. 29I found that he was accused concerning questions of their law, but was charged with nothing deserving death or imprisonment. 30When I was informed that there would be a plot against the man, I sent him to you at once, ordering his accusers also to state before you what they have against him.*"

31 So the soldiers, according to their instructions, took Paul and brought him during the night to Antipatris. 32The next day they let the horsemen go on with him, while they returned to the barracks. 33When they

a Other ancient authorities add *Farewell*

came to Caesarea and delivered the letter to the governor, they presented Paul also before him. 34On reading the letter, he asked what province he belonged to, and when he learned that he was from Cilicia, 35he said, "I will give you a hearing when your accusers arrive." Then he ordered that he be kept under guard in Herod's headquarters.*a*

23.11–35: Paul in protective custody. 11: This *night* vision introduces the last phase of the apostle's* journey toward *Rome.* **16–22:** *The son of Paul's sister* is known only from this story. **23–24:**The large numbers indicate a full military contingent. *Felix* was *the governor* in Palestine from 52 to 60 CE. **27:** Paul's status as a *Roman citizen* is again the source of his protection (16.37–38; 22.25–27). **29:** On *questions of their law,* see also 18.15; 25.8; 26.3. **31:** *Antipatris* was founded by Herod the Great on the road from Jerusalem to Caesarea. **34:** As with Pilate and Jesus (Lk 23.6–7), the governor involves Herod in a dispute about someone from his territory. **35:** *Herod's headquarters* (note *a:* praetorium) was a secure bastion.

24 Five days later the high priest Ananias came down with some elders and an attorney, a certain Tertullus, and they reported their case against Paul to the governor. 2When Paul*b* had been summoned, Tertullus began to accuse him, saying:

"Your Excellency,*c* because of you we have long enjoyed peace, and reforms have been made for this people because of your foresight. 3We welcome this in every way and everywhere with utmost gratitude. 4But, to detain you no further, I beg you to hear us briefly with your customary graciousness. 5We have, in fact, found this man a pestilent fellow, an agitator among all the Jews throughout the world, and a ringleader of the sect of the Nazarenes.*d* 6He even tried to profane the temple, and so we seized him.*e* 8By examining him yourself you will be able to learn from him concerning everything of which we accuse him."

9 The Jews also joined in the charge by asserting that all this was true.

10 When the governor motioned to him to speak, Paul replied:

"I cheerfully make my defense, knowing that for many years you have been a judge over this nation. 11As you can find out, it is not more than twelve days since I went up to worship in Jerusalem. 12They did not find me disputing with anyone in the temple or stirring up a crowd either in the synagogues or throughout the city. 13Neither can they prove to you the charge that they now bring against me. 14But this I admit to you, that according to the Way, which they call a sect, I worship the God of our ancestors, believing everything laid down according to the law or written in the prophets. 15I have a hope in God—a hope that they themselves also accept—that there will be a resurrection of both*f* the righteous and the unrighteous. 16Therefore I do my best always to have a clear conscience toward God and all people. 17Now after some years I came to bring alms to my nation and to offer sacrifices. 18While I was doing this, they found me in the temple, completing the rite of purification, without any crowd or disturbance. 19But there were some Jews from Asia—they ought to be here before you to make an accusation, if they have anything against me. 20Or let these men here tell what crime they had found when I stood before the council, 21unless it was this one sentence that I called out while standing before them, 'It is about the resurrection of the dead that I am on trial before you today.' "

24.1–26.32: Paul's testimony before governors and kings. 24.1: *Tertullus* presents a Roman legal argument (contrast Lk 10.25) on behalf of the *high priest,* but may not have been a Jew himself (24.9). **2:** Even cruel Roman rulers like Pilate (Lk 13.1; 23.1–24) were held responsible for keeping the *peace* ("pax Romana"). **3–4:** Excessive *gratitude* did not disguise the unrest and insurrections surrounding Felix's administration or his reputation for abuse of office. **5:** The charge that Paul is an *agitator* echoes what was said against Jesus before Pilate (Lk 23.2, 5, 14), but now

---

a Gk *praetorium*   *b* Gk *he*   *c* Gk lacks *Your Excellency*   *d* Gk *Nazoreans*   *e* Other ancient authorities add *and we would have judged him according to our law.* 7*But the chief captain Lysias came and with great violence took him out of our hands,* 8*commanding his accusers to come before you.*   *f* Other ancient authorities read *of the dead, both of* throughout the Roman *world* (Gk., "oikoumene"). This is the only instance in which the "Christians" (11.26) are called the *sect*✫ or party (28.22) of the *Nazarenes,* probably referring to followers of the messiah✫ from Nazareth (Lk 18.37). **6:** Profaning temples, a serious charge in any part of the Roman realm (19.35–37), was the specific cause of Paul's arrest (21.28). **10:** Paul's cheerful *defense* signifies his appreciation for Felix's knowledge (24.22) and more critically expresses his "hope in God" because he is on trial for the resurrection (22.15; 26.6–7). **12:** Jesus did dispute publicly in the *temple*✫ (Lk 19.47–21.38; 22.53). **14–15:** Paul defends *the Way* (see comment on 9.2) as a Jewish *sect* or party (23.6–9; 24.5) teaching the *resurrection* from *the law* and *the prophets*✫ (Lk 24.27, 44–48). **16:** A *clear conscience* is needed for the judgment (17.31; 24.25). **18–21:** See 21.17–22.10.

22 But Felix, who was rather well informed about the Way, adjourned the hearing with the comment, "When Lysias the tribune comes down, I will decide your case." ²³Then he ordered the centurion to keep him in custody, but to let him have some liberty and not to prevent any of his friends from taking care of his needs.

24 Some days later when Felix came with his wife Drusilla, who was Jewish, he sent for Paul and heard him speak concerning faith in Christ Jesus. ²⁵And as he discussed justice, self-control, and the coming judgment, Felix became frightened and said, "Go away for the present; when I have an opportunity, I will send for you." ²⁶At the same time he hoped that money would be given him by Paul, and for that reason he used to send for him very often and converse with him.

27 After two years had passed, Felix was succeeded by Porcius Festus; and since he wanted to grant the Jews a favor, Felix left Paul in prison.

24.22–27. 22: *Lysias* has already been quite clear in his judgment (23.29). **24:** *Drusilla,* the daughter of Herod Agrippa I, was criticized for "transgressing the ancestral laws" by leaving her husband to marry Felix (Josephus,✫ *Antiquities* 20.141–143). *Faith in Christ Jesus* again means the belief that Jesus is the messiah✫ (see comments on 2.31, 36; 10.38). **25–26:** Standard Hellenistic✫ ethical discourse on *justice and self-*

control becomes urgent when linked with Jewish and messianist convictions about *the coming judgment* (24.15). **27:** *Porcius Festus* became procurator around 59–60 CE. The idea of granting *the Jews a favor* (also 25.9) reflects the relationship of the Roman occupation force with Judean leadership.

25 Three days after Festus had arrived in the province, he went up from Caesarea to Jerusalem ²where the chief priests and the leaders of the Jews gave him a report against Paul. They appealed to him ³and requested, as a favor to them against Paul,ᵃ to have him transferred to Jerusalem. They were, in fact, planning an ambush to kill him along the way. ⁴Festus replied that Paul was being kept at Caesarea, and that he himself intended to go there shortly. ⁵"So," he said, "let those of you who have the authority come down with me, and if there is anything wrong about the man, let them accuse him."

6 After he had stayed among them not more than eight or ten days, he went down to Caesarea; the next day he took his seat on the tribunal and ordered Paul to be brought. ⁷When he arrived, the Jews who had gone down from Jerusalem surrounded him, bringing many serious charges against him, which they could not prove. ⁸Paul said in his defense, "I have in no way committed an offense against the law of the Jews, or against the temple, or against the emperor." ⁹But Festus, wishing to do the Jews a favor, asked Paul, "Do you wish to go up to Jerusalem and be tried there before me on these charges?" ¹⁰Paul said, "I am appealing to the emperor's tribunal; this is where I should be tried. I have done no wrong to the Jews, as you very well know. ¹¹Now if I am in the wrong and have committed something for which I deserve to die, I am not trying to escape death; but if there is nothing to their charges against me, no one can turn me over to them. I appeal to the emperor." ¹²Then Festus, after he had conferred with his council, replied, "You have appealed to the emperor; to the emperor you will go."

a Gk *him*

25.1–12. 1: *Caesarea* was the Roman city Herod the Great built on the Mediterranean, and *Jerusalem* was high in the Judean hills. **5:** *Those who have the authority* are the "leading men," probably linked closely with the Temple.★ **10:** Paul's innocence of the charges has been his defense to which the tribune (23.29) and narrator have agreed (25.7), but Festus's opinion (*as you very well know*) is so far (25.18–20, 26–27; 26.31–32) only indicated through Paul (contrast Pilate in Lk 23.13, 20, 22). **11–12:** Only Roman citizens could *appeal to the emperor* (16.37–38; 22.25–29).

13 After several days had passed, King Agrippa and Bernice arrived at Caesarea to welcome Festus. 14Since they were staying there several days, Festus laid Paul's case before the king, saying, "There is a man here who was left in prison by Felix. 15When I was in Jerusalem, the chief priests and the elders of the Jews informed me about him and asked for a sentence against him. 16I told them that it was not the custom of the Romans to hand over anyone before the accused had met the accusers face to face and had been given an opportunity to make a defense against the charge. 17So when they met here, I lost no time, but on the next day took my seat on the tribunal and ordered the man to be brought. 18When the accusers stood up, they did not charge him with any of the crimes*a* that I was expecting. 19Instead they had certain points of disagreement with him about their own religion and about a certain Jesus, who had died, but whom Paul asserted to be alive. 20Since I was at a loss how to investigate these questions, I asked whether he wished to go to Jerusalem and be tried there on these charges.*b* 21But when Paul had appealed to be kept in custody for the decision of his Imperial Majesty, I ordered him to be held until I could send him to the emperor." 22Agrippa said to Festus, "I would like to hear the man myself." "Tomorrow," he said, "you will hear him."

23 So on the next day Agrippa and Bernice came with great pomp, and they entered the audience hall with the military tribunes and the prominent men of the city. Then Festus gave the order and Paul was brought in. 24And Festus said, "King Agrippa and all here present with us, you see this man about whom the whole Jewish community petitioned me, both in Jerusalem and here, shouting that he ought not to live any longer. 25But I found that he had done nothing deserving death; and when he appealed to his Imperial Majesty, I decided to send him. 26But I have nothing definite to write to our sovereign about him. Therefore I have brought him before all of you, and especially before you, King Agrippa, so that, after we have examined him, I may have something to write— 27for it seems to me unreasonable to send a prisoner without indicating the charges against him."

25.13–27. 13: Herod *Agrippa* II, great-grandson of Herod the Great (Lk 1.5) and son of Agrippa I (Acts 12.1, 6, 20–23), and his sister *Bernice* pay the respects that client kings give to imperial representatives. **19:** Festus partially understands that the dispute is about the resurrection (23.6; 24.20). **21:** *His Imperial Majesty* is *the emperor* Nero. **24:** *The whole Jewish community* is a clear over statement. **26–27:** Festus's quest for *something* to *write* is comparable to Pilate's problem when he declared Jesus had done "nothing to deserve death"(Lk 23.15; but see 23.38).

26 Agrippa said to Paul, "You have permission to speak for yourself." Then Paul stretched out his hand and began to defend himself:

2 "I consider myself fortunate that it is before you, King Agrippa, I am to make my defense today against all the accusations of the Jews, 3because you are especially familiar with all the customs and controversies of the Jews; therefore I beg of you to listen to me patiently.

4 "All the Jews know my way of life from my youth, a life spent from the beginning among my own people and in Jerusalem. 5They have known for a long time, if they are willing to testify, that I have belonged to the strictest sect of our religion and lived as a Pharisee. 6And now I stand here on trial on account of my hope in the promise made by

a Other ancient authorities read *with anything*
b Gk *on them*

God to our ancestors, 7a promise that our twelve tribes hope to attain, as they earnestly worship day and night. It is for this hope, your Excellency,[a] that I am accused by Jews! 8Why is it thought incredible by any of you that God raises the dead?

9 "Indeed, I myself was convinced that I ought to do many things against the name of Jesus of Nazareth.[b] 10And that is what I did in Jerusalem; with authority received from the chief priests, I not only locked up many of the saints in prison, but I also cast my vote against them when they were being condemned to death. 11By punishing them often in all the synagogues I tried to force them to blaspheme; and since I was so furiously enraged at them, I pursued them even to foreign cities.

26.1–11. 1: In contrast to Jesus' silence before Agrippa I (Lk 23.7–12), *Paul stretched out his hand* in the presence of *Agrippa* II to silence the crowd like an orator (13.16; 19.33; 21.40). 3: *The customs and controversies of the Jews* either do not interest or confuse the Romans (18.14–17; 22.30; 23.10, 29; 25.19–20, 26). 5: Even as a follower of the Way, Paul continues to claim to be a true *Pharisee*★ (15.5). 6: To be *on trial on account of my hope in the promise* is also to be on trial for the resurrection (24.14–15). 7: The *promise that our twelve tribes hope to attain* is restoration (1.6; 3.21), which includes *worship day and night* as the goal (Lk 1.74–75) as well as a way to *attain* restoration. 8: *That God raises the dead* may or may not be *incredible* (17.32), but Paul presents Jesus' resurrection as God's way of keeping the promise "made to our ancestors" (26.6, 23). 9–18: This is the third account of Paul's transforming vision (9.1–22; 22.3–21). 10–11: Paul's casting *his vote against them* may refer to his approval of Stephen's death (8.1). To call them *the saints* whom he was trying to *force to blaspheme* is to adopt the point of view of the believers.

---

12 "With this in mind, I was traveling to Damascus with the authority and commission of the chief priests, 13when at midday along the road, your Excellency,[a] I saw a light from heaven, brighter than the sun, shining around me and my companions. 14When we had all fallen to the ground, I heard a voice saying to me in the Hebrew[c] language, 'Saul, Saul, why are you persecut-

ing me? It hurts you to kick against the goads.' 15I asked, 'Who are you, Lord?' The Lord answered, 'I am Jesus whom you are persecuting. 16But get up and stand on your feet; for I have appeared to you for this purpose, to appoint you to serve and testify to the things in which you have seen me[d] and to those in which I will appear to you. 17I will rescue you from your people and from the Gentiles—to whom I am sending you 18to open their eyes so that they may turn from darkness to light and from the power of Satan to God, so that they may receive forgiveness of sins and a place among those who are sanctified by faith in me.'

19 "After that, King Agrippa, I was not disobedient to the heavenly vision, 20but declared first to those in Damascus, then in Jerusalem and throughout the countryside of Judea, and also to the Gentiles, that they should repent and turn to God and do deeds consistent with repentance. 21For this reason the Jews seized me in the temple and tried to kill me. 22To this day I have had help from God, and so I stand here, testifying to both small and great, saying nothing but what the prophets and Moses said would take place: 23that the Messiah[e] must suffer, and that, by being the first to rise from the dead, he would proclaim light both to our people and to the Gentiles."

26.12–23. 13–14: Several details heighten the earlier accounts: *brighter than the sun; we had all fallen to the ground; a voice in the Hebrew language.* Kicking *against the goads* is the action of a stubborn resistance to divine prodding. 16: *To serve and testify* corresponds to the calling of ministers and witnesses (Lk 1.2; Acts 1.22; 2.32; 10.39, 41). 17–18: Paul's mission is again focused on *the Gentiles*★ (see 22.21 in contrast to 9.15) to bring them into the promises to Israel. The text echoes with the promises of light and forgiveness of Isa 42.7, 16, and Acts 2.38–39. *Satan* is directly mentioned in Lk 10.18; 11.18; 13.16; 22.3, 31; Acts 5.3. 20: Paul's account focuses on Palestine (1.8) with no mention of his mission in Asia Minor or Greece. 22: Like Jesus in Luke 24.27, 44 (see also Lk 16.31), Paul claims the fulfillment of *the prophets*★

a Gk O king   *b* Gk the Nazorean   *c* That is, Aramaic
d Other ancient authorities read *the things that you have seen*   *e* Or *the Christ*

and Moses. **23:** The necessity of the suffering of the *Messiah** is a central affirmation in the scriptural interpretation* of Luke and Acts (see comments on Lk 24.25–27; Acts 3.18). The promise of *light both to our people and to the Gentiles* is a thematic allusion to Isa 49.6 (see also 1.8; 13.47).

24 While he was making this defense, Festus exclaimed, "You are out of your mind, Paul! Too much learning is driving you insane!" 25But Paul said, "I am not out of my mind, most excellent Festus, but I am speaking the sober truth. 26Indeed the king knows about these things, and to him I speak freely; for I am certain that none of these things has escaped his notice, for this was not done in a corner. 27King Agrippa, do you believe the prophets? I know that you believe." 28Agrippa said to Paul, "Are you so quickly persuading me to become a Christian?"*a* 29Paul replied, "Whether quickly or not, I pray to God that not only you but also all who are listening to me today might become such as I am—except for these chains."

30 Then the king got up, and with him the governor and Bernice and those who had been seated with them; 31and as they were leaving, they said to one another, "This man is doing nothing to deserve death or imprisonment." 32Agrippa said to Festus, "This man could have been set free if he had not appealed to the emperor."

26.24–32. 24: Paul's *learning* is Jewish scriptural interpretation* (Mt 9.13). **26–27:** Like Cornelius (10.28), *King Agrippa* could be expected to know this much about the prophetic* tradition. **28:** The question is whether he can be *so quickly* persuaded by *Christian* scriptural interpretation. **31:** Like Jesus, who was declared innocent three times by Pilate with counsel (albeit absurd) from Herod Antipas (Lk 23.4, 14,22), Paul is exonerated by Lysias (23.29), Festus (23.25), and now by Felix with counsel from Herod Agrippa II. But neither was released.

27 When it was decided that we were to sail for Italy, they transferred Paul and some other prisoners to a centurion of the Augustan Cohort, named Julius. 2Embarking on a ship of Adramyttium that was about to set sail to the ports along the coast of Asia, we put to sea, accompanied by Aristarchus, a Macedonian from Thessalonica. 3The next day we put in at Sidon; and Julius treated Paul kindly, and allowed him to go to his friends to be cared for. 4Putting out to sea from there, we sailed under the lee of Cyprus, because the winds were against us. 5After we had sailed across the sea that is off Cilicia and Pamphylia, we came to Myra in Lycia. 6There the centurion found an Alexandrian ship bound for Italy and put us on board. 7We sailed slowly for a number of days and arrived with difficulty off Cnidus, and as the wind was against us, we sailed under the lee of Crete off Salmone. 8Sailing past it with difficulty, we came to a place called Fair Havens, near the city of Lasea.

9 Since much time had been lost and sailing was now dangerous, because even the Fast had already gone by, Paul advised them, 10saying, "Sirs, I can see that the voyage will be with danger and much heavy loss, not only of the cargo and the ship, but also of our lives." 11But the centurion paid more attention to the pilot and to the owner of the ship than to what Paul said. 12Since the harbor was not suitable for spending the winter, the majority was in favor of putting to sea from there, on the chance that somehow they could reach Phoenix, where they could spend the winter. It was a harbor of Crete, facing southwest and northwest.

13 When a moderate south wind began to blow, they thought they could achieve their purpose; so they weighed anchor and began to sail past Crete, close to the shore. 14But soon a violent wind, called the northeaster, rushed down from Crete.*b* 15Since the ship was caught and could not be turned head-on into the wind, we gave way to it and were driven. 16By running under the lee of a small island called Cauda*c* we were scarcely able to get the ship's boat under control. 17After hoisting it up they took measures*d* to undergird the ship; then, fearing that they would run on the Syrtis, they lowered the sea anchor and so were driven. 18We were being pounded by the storm so violently that on the

a Or *Quickly you will persuade me to play the Christian*
b Gk *it*   *c* Other ancient authorities read *Clauda*
d Gk *helps*

next day they began to throw the cargo overboard, [19]and on the third day with their own hands they threw the ship's tackle overboard. [20]When neither sun nor stars appeared for many days, and no small tempest raged, all hope of our being saved was at last abandoned.

[21] Since they had been without food for a long time, Paul then stood up among them and said, "Men, you should have listened to me and not have set sail from Crete and thereby avoided this damage and loss. [22]I urge you now to keep up your courage, for there will be no loss of life among you, but only of the ship. [23]For last night there stood by me an angel of the God to whom I belong and whom I worship, [24]and he said, 'Do not be afraid, Paul; you must stand before the emperor; and indeed, God has granted safety to all those who are sailing with you.' [25]So keep up your courage, men, for I have faith in God that it will be exactly as I have been told. [26]But we will have to run aground on some island."

27.1–28.31: Paul's journey to Rome. 27.1–28.15: This journey account is filled with nautical details, but less theological content than the rest of the Acts narrative.* 27.9–11: The Fast, or "Day of Atonement," appears to be only a calendar* reference for the late season (contrast 20.16). 17: The sea anchor provided drag but did not arrest the ship's movement. 21–25: I have faith in God echoes 24.15. Paul testifies that the safety of the journey depends on God's promise to him (23.11) rather than the ineptitude of their sailing. 26: Paul predicts the shipwreck on Malta (28.1).

---

[27] When the fourteenth night had come, as we were drifting across the sea of Adria, about midnight the sailors suspected that they were nearing land. [28]So they took soundings and found twenty fathoms; a little farther on they took soundings again and found fifteen fathoms. [29]Fearing that we might run on the rocks, they let down four anchors from the stern and prayed for day to come. [30]But when the sailors tried to escape from the ship and had lowered the boat into the sea, on the pretext of putting out anchors from the bow, [31]Paul said to the centurion and the soldiers, "Unless these men stay in the ship, you cannot be saved." [32]Then the soldiers cut away the ropes of the boat and set it adrift.

[33] Just before daybreak, Paul urged all of them to take some food, saying, "Today is the fourteenth day that you have been in suspense and remaining without food, having eaten nothing. [34]Therefore I urge you to take some food, for it will help you survive; for none of you will lose a hair from your heads." [35]After he had said this, he took bread; and giving thanks to God in the presence of all, he broke it and began to eat. [36]Then all of them were encouraged and took food for themselves. [37](We were in all two hundred seventy-six[a] persons in the ship.) [38]After they had satisfied their hunger, they lightened the ship by throwing the wheat into the sea.

[39] In the morning they did not recognize the land, but they noticed a bay with a beach, on which they planned to run the ship ashore, if they could. [40]So they cast off the anchors and left them in the sea. At the same time they loosened the ropes that tied the steering-oars; then hoisting the foresail to the wind, they made for the beach. [41]But striking a reef,[b] they ran the ship aground; the bow stuck and remained immovable, but the stern was being broken up by the force of the waves. [42]The soldiers' plan was to kill the prisoners, so that none might swim away and escape; [43]but the centurion, wishing to save Paul, kept them from carrying out their plan. He ordered those who could swim to jump overboard first and make for the land, [44]and the rest to follow, some on planks and others on pieces of the ship. And so it was that all were brought safely to land.

28 After we had reached safety, we then learned that the island was called Malta. [2]The natives showed us unusual kindness. Since it had begun to rain and was cold, they kindled a fire and welcomed all of us around it. [3]Paul had gathered a bundle of brushwood and was putting it on the fire, when a viper, driven out by the heat, fastened itself on his hand. [4]When the natives

---

a Other ancient authorities read seventy-six; others, about seventy-six   b Gk place of two seas saw the creature hanging from his hand, they said to one another, "This man must be a murderer; though he has escaped from the sea, justice has not allowed him to live." 5 He, however, shook off the creature into the fire and suffered no harm. 6 They were expecting him to swell up or drop dead, but after they had waited a long time and saw that nothing unusual had happened to him, they changed their minds and began to say that he was a god.

27.27–28.6. 27.33: Paul intervenes for the fourth time (vv. 10, 21, 31). 34: On the assurance that they will not *lose a hair from your heads,* see Lk 21.18; 12.7. 43–44: So *Paul* was saved, and so *all* were saved (27.24). 28.3: A *viper* (Lk 3.7) could refer to many varieties of snakes, which traditional lore regarded as representing spiritual forces. 4: *Justice* is viewed by the locals as a personified power executing vengeance on one who almost escaped (Am 5.19). 6: His power over snakes (Lk 10.18–19; Mk 16.18) makes them think he is a *god* (14.11–12).

7 Now in the neighborhood of that place were lands belonging to the leading man of the island, named Publius, who received us and entertained us hospitably for three days. 8 It so happened that the father of Publius lay sick in bed with fever and dysentery. Paul visited him and cured him by praying and putting his hands on him. 9 After this happened, the rest of the people on the island who had diseases also came and were cured. 10 They bestowed many honors on us, and when we were about to sail, they put on board all the provisions we needed.

11 Three months later we set sail on a ship that had wintered at the island, an Alexandrian ship with the Twin Brothers as its figurehead. 12 We put in at Syracuse and stayed there for three days; 13 then we weighed anchor and came to Rhegium. After one day there a south wind sprang up, and on the second day we came to Puteoli. 14 There we found believers*a* and were invited to stay with them for seven days. And so we came to Rome. 15 The believers*a* from there, when they heard of us, came as far as the Forum of Appius and Three Taverns to meet us. On seeing them, Paul thanked God and took courage.

28.7–15. 8–9: Paul's healing of the *fever* of Publius' father followed by the healing of the people recalls Jesus' healing of Peter's mother (Lk 4.38–40). 12–15: The last phases of the voyage lead from *Syracuse* on Sicily, to *Rhegium* on the toe of Italy, to dock at *Puteoli,* the great port of Naples. Then the group travels overland through places called *the Forum of Appius* and the *Three Taverns,* with Christian *believers* coming south from Rome *to meet us.*

16 When we came into Rome, Paul was allowed to live by himself, with the soldier who was guarding him.

17 Three days later he called together the local leaders of the Jews. When they had assembled, he said to them, "Brothers, though I had done nothing against our people or the customs of our ancestors, yet I was arrested in Jerusalem and handed over to the Romans. 18 When they had examined me, the Romans*b* wanted to release me, because there was no reason for the death penalty in my case. 19 But when the Jews objected, I was compelled to appeal to the emperor— even though I had no charge to bring against my nation. 20 For this reason therefore I have asked to see you and speak with you,*c* since it is for the sake of the hope of Israel that I am bound with this chain." 21 They replied, "We have received no letters from Judea about you, and none of the brothers coming here has reported or spoken anything evil about you. 22 But we would like to hear from you what you think, for with regard to this sect we know that everywhere it is spoken against."

23 After they had set a day to meet with him, they came to him at his lodgings in great numbers. From morning until evening he explained the matter to them, testifying to the kingdom of God and trying to convince them about Jesus both from the law of Moses and from the prophets. 24 Some were convinced by what he had said, while others refused to believe. 25 So they disagreed with each other; and as they were leaving, Paul made one further statement: "The Holy

a Gk brothers   b Gk they   c Or I have asked you to see me and speak with me

Spirit was right in saying to your ancestors through the prophet Isaiah,

26 'Go to this people and say,
  You will indeed listen, but never
      understand,
    and you will indeed look, but never
      perceive.
27 For this people's heart has grown dull,
    and their ears are hard of hearing,
      and they have shut their eyes;
    so that they might not look with
      their eyes,
    and listen with their ears,
  and understand with their heart and
      turn—
    and I would heal them.'

28 Let it be known to you then that this salvation of God has been sent to the Gentiles; they will listen."*

30 He lived there two whole years at his own expense* and welcomed all who came to him, 31 proclaiming the kingdom of God and teaching about the Lord Jesus Christ with all boldness and without hindrance.

28.16–31: Paul in Rome. 16: Chained (v. 20) to a *soldier*, Paul lives in *Rome* under house arrest for two years (v. 30). **17:** Paul takes the initiative to consult with *the local leaders of the Jews* (vv. 17–22), identifying with them as *brothers* (2.37; 15.13; 22.2; 23.6; 28.21) of *our people* and *our ancestors* (22.3; 24.14; 26.6). **18:** On the *Roman* desire to *release* Paul, see comment on 26.31. **19:** The objections of *the Jews* have been recounted in detail (20.27–29; 22.21–22; 23.1–10; 24.2–9; 25.2, 7, 15, 18–19, 24; 26.2–3). Paul's *appeal to the emperor* (25.11–12) is as a defendant, not bringing a *charge* or case against Israel. **20:**

Paul is not only defending himself but *the hope of Israel* for God's promised restoration (see 1.6; 3.21), inaugurated through the resurrection of the messiah,* Jesus (24.15–14, 21; 26.6–7, 16–18, 21–23). **21:** *Letters* often accompanied visits as official means of communication (9.2; 15.22–23). **22:** On the Way as a Jewish *sect** or "party," see 5.17; 15.5; 24.5, 14; 26.5. **23:** Paul's explanation is another extended interpretation* of Israel's scriptures (17.1–4; 18.4, 28; 19.8–9), that is, *Moses and the prophets** (see Lk 24.27, 44; Acts 3.22–24; 26.22). **24:** The divided response is characteristic of both gentile* and Jewish audiences (2.12–13; 14.1–2, 4; 17.32–34; 18.6–8; 21.20, 25), but to say they *refused to believe* is to make a prophetic judgment (compare 18.27). **25:** Isa 6.9–10 is cited as a reproof of *the Holy Spirit*, where God's promises are cited against Israel or a portion of Israel to call for repentance, never as a final verdict (see also Jesus in Lk 8.10; Acts 13.40–41; Rom 11.8). **28:** For a third time (13.46–47; 18.6), the *Gentile* mission is a warning to those in Israel who do not believe (Rom 9–11). Paul's mission does not display undivided *listening* among gentiles either. **29:** This verse is not recorded in the best manuscripts (note *a*), but echoes the divided response of verse 24. **30:** To live *at his own expense* may suggest enough freedom (v. 16) to practice his trade (18.3). *All who came to him* probably means both Jews and gentiles (vv. 24, 28). **31:** The *boldness* of apostolic witness (2.29; 4.13, 29, 31; 9.27–28; 13.46; 14.3; 18.26; 19.8) continues *without hindrance* in accord with God's promise (23.11), even in the midst of opposition and chains.

~~~

a Other ancient authorities add verse 29, *And when he had said these words, the Jews departed, arguing vigorously among themselves*   *b* Or *in his own hired dwelling*

LETTERS OR EPISTLES

The New Testament can roughly be divided into two general types of literature: narrative* and non-narrative (see "A Reader's Guide to the Books of the Bible," 17–25). Narrative books explicitly tell a story—the story of Jesus and the early disciples in the four Gospels, or the story of the early church in the Acts of the Apostles (see "Gospels and Acts," 1661–1665). While the narrative books of the New Testament receive the most attention from readers as possible sources for the life of Jesus, they are not the dominant literary form. Rather, epistles (letters) predominate; twenty-two of the twenty-seven books that make up the New Testament canon* are letters, and one book, that of Revelation, has many epistolary or letter-like features. Only the four Gospels and Acts are not structured as epistles.

That the letter is the dominant literary form in the New Testament reveals much about the history of early Christianity and its original social context. In its initial decades, Christianity was a missionary movement, with its early leaders moving from city to city in the ancient Mediterranean world to proclaim the work of God in Jesus Christ. The dominance of the epistle form in the New Testament canon means that the canon itself conveys to later readers not only the theological content of the early church but also its forms of communication. Later readers come closest to the experience of early Christians through the letters, since they are inseparable from the social contexts in which they were first written.

Like wisdom literature* (see "Hebrew Poetry and Wisdom Literature," 730–732), epistles are not unique to the biblical literature but are a literary form common to the ancient Mediterranean world. The early Christians' appropriation of this literary form for the missionary work of the early church shows the ease with which the first leaders made use of common cultural practices to accomplish their ends. Their use of a written form also points to the literacy level of the authors of the letters, as well as of at least some members of the communities to whom these letters were addressed.

At its most basic, a letter makes possible communication between two parties who are geographically separated from one another. Letters served a variety of purposes in the ancient Mediterranean world, ranging from formal communication between governmental envoys to the most personal and intimate correspondence between friends and loved ones. The majority of New Testament epistles come closest in form to Hellenistic* personal letters, although the influence of other types of epistles can also be seen (e.g., Hebrews, James, and 2 Peter resemble Hellenistic philosophical letters).

The basic form of the Hellenistic personal letter is:

- **Greeting**: from the letter writer [and companions] to the recipient [and companions].
- **Thanksgiving**: usually to the gods for the recipient of the letter.
- **Main body**: the purpose for which the letter is written.
- **Closing greetings and blessings**: to other members of the recipient's community, as well as a final appeal to the gods.

This form is most clearly followed by Paul in his letters, and attention to Paul's use of conventional letter elements heightens the reader's understanding of Paul's communication with his churches. First Corinthians, for example, contains all the standard features of a Hellenistic personal letter:

- **Greeting**: "Paul, called to be an apostle…to the church of God that is in Corinth… Grace to you and peace from God our Father and the Lord Jesus Christ," 1.1–3.

- **Thanksgiving**: "I give thanks to my God always for you because of the grace that has been given you in Christ Jesus," 1.4–9.
- **Main body**: "Now I appeal to you, brothers and sisters, by the name of the Lord Jesus Christ that all of you be in agreement," 1.10–16.18).
- **Closing greetings and blessings**: "The churches of Asia send greetings. . . . The grace of the Lord Jesus be with you. My love be with all of you in Christ Jesus" (16.19–24).

Because contemporary Bible readers encounter Paul's letters as part of a collection of letters that are included in the Christian canon, the letters are usually thought of first as sacred texts and only secondarily as an actual correspondence between Paul and fledgling Christian communities. Yet, as the outline of 1 Corinthians shows, Paul seems to have thought of his letters in the exact opposite way—his adherence to letter-writing conventions shows that for Paul, these writings were first and foremost a correspondence with communities from whom he was separated by time and distance. This can be seen especially in the instructions and greetings with which his letters conclude. Paul concludes 1 Corinthians with references to his upcoming travels (16.4–6), to other fellow missionaries (16.10–12), reflections on his current circumstances (16.17–18), as well as the conventional concluding greetings. For Paul, letter writing was a way of being present even in his absence, a way of staying in personal contact with a community that he was nurturing in the life of faith.

Close attention to the ways in which Paul varies the conventional epistle form shows that Paul built on his community's recognition of the common epistolary conventions when he communicated with them. His letter to the Galatians, for example, begins and ends conventionally—with opening greetings (1.1–5) and a closing blessing (6.18)—but most strikingly, this letter is missing the standard thanksgiving. The greeting is not followed by "I give thanks..." (in addition to 1 Cor, see, Rom 1.8–15; Eph 1.15–16; 1 Thess 1.2; 2 Thess 1.3; Philem 4–5). Instead, Paul writes, "I am astonished that you are so quickly deserting the one who called you in the grace of Christ" (Gal 1.6). The ancient letter-reader would notice the lack of a thanksgiving immediately. Here form and content cohere to underscore Paul's anger with the Galatians: what is said communicates Paul's displeasure, but to the reader of ancient epistles, Paul's dramatic departure from form also communicates his displeasure. Paul's anger with the Galatians and concern for the possible consequences of their actions overrides common epistolary practices.

Paul's letter to the Philippians plays with conventional epistolary practice and the reader's expectations in a quite different way. Like 1 Corinthians, Philippians opens with a greeting (1.1–2) and thanksgiving (1.3–5, "I thank my God every time I remember you, constantly praying with joy in every one of my prayers for all of you, because of your sharing in the gospel from the first day until now.") But in an epistolary turn that is the exact opposite of Paul's turn in Galatians, the reader of Philippians has a difficult time determining where the thanksgiving ends and the main body of the letter begins. Paul continues to share his thanks and joy in the Philippian community well into ch. 3 (for instance, 1.18–19, 25–26, 27–30; 2.12, 17–18; 3.1). Here again, form and content cohere to increase the impact of Paul's message, because those in Philippi who first received this letter would recognize how the outpouring of thanks and rejoicing overwhelms the conventional thanksgiving form and cannot be contained by it.

It is important, however, not to read all New Testament epistles as if they followed the personal letter form favored by Paul. Hebrews, for example, concludes with standard epistolary elements—final instructions (13.18–19), blessings (13.20–21, 25), and final greetings (13.22–24)—but these personal details do not set the tone for the correspondence as they do in Paul's letters. Rather, the emphasis in Hebrews is more on instruction and exhortation* than on personal, missionary correspondence. James opens with a standard epistolary greeting but contains no other elements of the epistolary form. The letter's named addressees ("the twelve tribes in the Dispersion") is more symbolic than community-specific, encompassing perhaps all new Christians as the new twelve tribes, further underscoring the difference in form between James and Paul's letters. Yet even given these differences, the early Christian practice of letter writing as missional activity has an impact on how James is composed.

Perhaps the New Testament book whose epistolary conventions are most overlooked is the book of Revelation. Revelation is recognized as the dominant example of apocalyptic* literature (see "Apocalyptic Literature," 2057–2059), but it also can be classified as an epistle. It is framed explicitly as a letter to the seven churches in Asia Minor (modern-day Turkey), with the conventional greeting form: "John to the seven churches that are in Asia: Grace to you and peace..." (1.4). Revelation also contains an opening thanksgiving, but unlike the thanksgivings in Paul's letters, John gives thanks and praise for Jesus Christ, rather than for the recipients of the letter (1.5–6). The opening address to seven churches may at first seem as generalized and symbolic as James's address to the twelve tribes, but the seven individual letters that follow in chs. 2 and 3 make clear that John has very specific communities in view. Each community has its own needs and its own failings, and even though the language of these letters is more visionary than that found in Paul's letters, they share in the personal, missional intent of those letters. John has the nurture of a community in the life of faith in view as he writes. John returns to the epistolary form at the end of Revelation, closing with a blessing that resembles Paul's closing blessings. Since many of Paul's letters (or those attributed to Paul) are addressed to the same region and in one case the same city (Ephesus) as those found in Revelation, it seems fair to assume that John's readers, like Paul's, would have known the letter form and its use by early Christians for the missional spread of the gospel.

THE LETTER OF PAUL TO THE
ROMANS

Introduction

Romans stands first among Paul's letters because it is the longest of them and probably has had the most influence. It was written relatively late in his ministry, probably in the late 50s CE toward the end of the 6 to 7 year period he spent traveling around the Aegean. During this time Paul started churches composed of both Jews and gentiles.* In these newly founded churches, questions arose about how Jews and gentiles were related to each other: How do Jews and gentiles relate to God, now that Christ has come? Do both groups become members of God's people the same way? What does it mean if gentiles are more receptive to the gospel than Jews? How should Jews and gentiles relate to each other "in Christ"? On what should they base their conduct? the law of Moses? the teachings of Christ? In Romans Paul deals with such practical questions that have arisen out of his ministry among the churches.

Paul had never visited Rome but, as ch. 16 makes clear, a number of his close acquaintances and co-workers were there. We are not certain when Christianity arrived at Rome, but by the time Paul writes, the church seems relatively well established. He is eager to visit (1.11) in order to extend his ministry farther westward and ultimately reach Spain (15.24, 28). Romans serves as his formal introduction to the church at Rome. It provides a strong, comprehensive statement of his understanding of the gospel of Christ. By sending the letter, probably through his co-worker Phoebe (16.1), Paul presents himself and his gospel to the church at Rome, which already had important symbolic significance for other Christians throughout the Mediterranean world.

READING GUIDE

Romans has a three-part structure. Chapters 1–8 may be read as an extended argument in which Paul develops themes introduced in the purpose statement in 1.16–17. The good news of Jesus Christ is seen as the effective means through which God's saving work occurs. It also reveals God's character as true and reliable. Paul begins by showing the universal human dilemma: Everyone, regardless of ethnic background, lives in the grip of sin (1.18–3.20). God's action in Christ provides a way out (3.21–26) by reintroducing faith as the single saving principle by which all human beings can relate to God. The principle of law, especially the Mosaic law, can no longer serve as the basis for salvation. Abraham serves as an example of saving faith (ch. 4), and what faith in Christ means is spelled out in chs. 5–8. The work of Christ is interpreted in light of Gen 1–3. Christ is presented as a second Adam who stands at the head of a new order of humanity (ch. 5). Living with Christ means dying with Christ (ch. 6). The limits of the law are presented in ch. 7. Christ introduces a new principle, or power: the Spirit who enables those in Christ to deal effectively with sin (ch. 8).

In chs. 9–11 Paul discusses how God's work in Christ relates to God's purpose for Israel. These chapters are sometimes read in isolation from the rest of the letter. In reality, the issues discussed in this section are closely connected with the whole letter.

Chapters 12–15 sketch a profile of what it means to live by faith. They deal with more general situations than is often the case in other Pauline letters such as 1 Corinthians. Chapter 14, for example, addresses the realities of living together in communities where the "weak" and "strong" must find ways of dealing with each other's strongly held beliefs and practices. From the middle of ch. 15 forward, Paul addresses concrete concerns of his ministry, especially his anxieties about going to Jerusalem and presenting the money he has collected for the "poor among the saints" there (15.26).

1 Paul, a servant*a* of Jesus Christ, called to be an apostle, set apart for the gospel of God, ²which he promised beforehand through his prophets in the holy scriptures, ³the gospel concerning his Son, who was descended from David according to the flesh ⁴and was declared to be Son of God with power according to the spirit*b* of holiness by resurrection from the dead, Jesus Christ our Lord, ⁵through whom we have received grace and apostleship to bring about the obedience of faith among all the Gentiles for the sake of his name, ⁶including yourselves who are called to belong to Jesus Christ,

7 To all God's beloved in Rome, who are called to be saints:

Grace to you and peace from God our Father and the Lord Jesus Christ.

8 First, I thank my God through Jesus Christ for all of you, because your faith is proclaimed throughout the world. ⁹For God, whom I serve with my spirit by announcing the gospel*c* of his Son, is my witness that without ceasing I remember you always in my prayers, ¹⁰asking that by God's will I may somehow at last succeed in coming to you. ¹¹For I am longing to see you so that I may share with you some spiritual gift to strengthen you— ¹²or rather so that we may be mutually encouraged by each other's faith, both yours and mine. ¹³I want you

to know, brothers and sisters,*d* that I have often intended to come to you (but thus far have been prevented), in order that I may reap some harvest among you as I have among the rest of the Gentiles. ¹⁴I am a debtor both to Greeks and to barbarians, both to the wise and to the foolish ¹⁵— hence my eagerness to proclaim the gospel to you also who are in Rome.

16 For I am not ashamed of the gospel; it is the power of God for salvation to everyone who has faith, to the Jew first and also to the Greek. ¹⁷For in it the righteousness of God is revealed through faith for faith; as it is written, "The one who is righteous will live by faith."*e*

1.1–17. 1–15: Greeting and prayer of thanksgiving. 1–7: Greeting. The writer *Paul* identifies himself and his mission as they relate to Christ and God. *Grace* and *peace* combine standard forms of gentile* and Jewish address. This greeting is longer than most because Paul is writing to a church he has not yet visited and he wants to align himself with early Christian belief (vv. 2–6). **8–15: Prayer of thanksgiving.** Opening thanksgivings in the Pauline letters often set the mood for the rest of the letter and signal key themes. Paul's mission to the *Gentiles* reflects a central concern of the letter (v. 13). There is no hint that he will reach Rome as a

a Gk *slave*　　*b* Or *Spirit*　　*c* Gk *my spirit in the gospel*
d Gk *brothers*　　*e* Or *The one who is righteous through faith will live*

prisoner, as Acts depicts (Acts 28). **16–17: Purpose.** These verses, which actually conclude the prayer of thanksgiving, summarize the main themes of the letter. *I am not ashamed* means "I have confidence in." The *gospel,* the good news about Jesus Christ, tells a story about God's saving activity. It stems from God and expresses God's power to transform human lives. It also reveals *the righteousness of God,* either God's character as one who is reliable and trustworthy or what is given by the God who sets things right. The proper response to God's action in Christ is *faith,* which is both the means (*through faith*) and the end (*for faith*) of life before God. The Old Testament quotation is a distinctive Pauline rendering based on Hab 2.4.

18 For the wrath of God is revealed from heaven against all ungodliness and wickedness of those who by their wickedness suppress the truth. ¹⁹For what can be known about God is plain to them, because God has shown it to them. ²⁰Ever since the creation of the world his eternal power and divine nature, invisible though they are, have been understood and seen through the things he has made. So they are without excuse; ²¹for though they knew God, they did not honor him as God or give thanks to him, but they became futile in their thinking, and their senseless minds were darkened. ²²Claiming to be wise, they became fools; ²³and they exchanged the glory of the immortal God for images resembling a mortal human being or birds or four-footed animals or reptiles.

24 Therefore God gave them up in the lusts of their hearts to impurity, to the degrading of their bodies among themselves, ²⁵because they exchanged the truth about God for a lie and worshiped and served the creature rather than the Creator, who is blessed forever! Amen.

26 For this reason God gave them up to degrading passions. Their women exchanged natural intercourse for unnatural, ²⁷and in the same way also the men, giving up natural intercourse with women, were consumed with passion for one another. Men committed shameless acts with men and received in their own persons the due penalty for their error.

28 And since they did not see fit to ac-

knowledge God, God gave them up to a debased mind and to things that should not be done. ²⁹They were filled with every kind of wickedness, evil, covetousness, malice. Full of envy, murder, strife, deceit, craftiness, they are gossips, ³⁰slanderers, God-haters,ᵃ insolent, haughty, boastful, inventors of evil, rebellious toward parents, ³¹foolish, faithless, heartless, ruthless. ³²They know God's decree, that those who practice such things deserve to die—yet they not only do them but even applaud others who practice them.

1.18–8.39: God's purpose and character revealed in Christ. 1.18–32: God's wrath against sinful humanity. Gentiles* are not mentioned specifically in 1.18–32, but they appear to be in view (see 1.30, *God-haters;* 2.14; 3.9). Paul thinks humanity can know God through creation. Yet rather than honoring God properly as creator, people devised inappropriate forms of worship: *images* of humans and animals (v. 23). Such worship is misguided because it gives honor to *mortal* things rather than exclusive honor to the *immortal God* (v. 23). Worshiping *creatures* instead of the *Creator* is here seen as the ultimate *lie.* Closely associated with idol worship were sexual practices regarded by Jews as impure and degrading to the body (vv. 24–25). Failure to acknowledge God leads to *debased* thinking and immoral behavior. The sins listed in vv. 29–31 mainly describe behavior that destroys meaningful relationships among friends and family, leading to chaos within society (1 Cor 6.10–11; Gal 5.19–21). Paul repeatedly emphasizes that *God gave them up . . .* (vv. 24, 26, 28), suggesting God's disgust with such arrogant, socially destructive behavior.

2 Therefore you have no excuse, whoever you are, when you judge others; for in passing judgment on another you condemn yourself, because you, the judge, are doing the very same things. ²You say,ᵇ "We know that God's judgment on those who do such things is in accordance with truth." ³Do you imagine, whoever you are, that when you judge those who do such things and yet do them yourself, you will escape the judgment of God? ⁴Or do you despise the riches of his kindness and forbearance and patience? Do

a Or *God-hated*   *b* Gk lacks *You say*

you not realize that God's kindness is meant to lead you to repentance? [5]But by your hard and impenitent heart you are storing up wrath for yourself on the day of wrath, when God's righteous judgment will be revealed. [6]For he will repay according to each one's deeds: [7]to those who by patiently doing good seek for glory and honor and immortality, he will give eternal life; [8]while for those who are self-seeking and who obey not the truth but wickedness, there will be wrath and fury. [9]There will be anguish and distress for everyone who does evil, the Jew first and also the Greek, [10]but glory and honor and peace for everyone who does good, the Jew first and also the Greek. [11]For God shows no partiality.

12 All who have sinned apart from the law will also perish apart from the law, and all who have sinned under the law will be judged by the law. [13]For it is not the hearers of the law who are righteous in God's sight, but the doers of the law who will be justified. [14]When Gentiles, who do not possess the law, do instinctively what the law requires, these, though not having the law, are a law to themselves. [15]They show that what the law requires is written on their hearts, to which their own conscience also bears witness; and their conflicting thoughts will accuse or perhaps excuse them [16]on the day when, according to my gospel, God, through Jesus Christ, will judge the secret thoughts of all.

2.1–16. 1–11: God's wrath against religious people. The language shifts to direct address, from *they* and *them* in 1.18–32 to *you. Whoever you are* (vv. 1, 3), literally, "O man!," is an open-ended charge against religious people who do the very things they condemn in others. Such people think God's *kindness* gives them slack rather than reason to change their lives (*repentance,* v. 4). Like those whom they condemn (1.18), they too will experience God's *wrath and fury* (v. 8; see 5.9; 12.19). *Day of wrath,* see Zeph. 1.14–16; Rev 6.17. At the final judgment, God will render impartial judgment. V. 6 quotes Ps 62.12; see Prov 24.12. Good and evil cut across ethnic lines (vv. 9–10). **12–16: Doing what the law requires. 12:** Experiencing the harsh effects of sin and developing a sense of moral accountability before God do not derive ex-

clusively from *the law* of Moses. This is something all people experience, both gentiles* who live *apart from the law* and Jews who live *under the law.* **16:** *The day of judgment,* 2 Cor 1.14; Phil 1.6, 10.

~~~~~~

17 But if you call yourself a Jew and rely on the law and boast of your relation to God [18]and know his will and determine what is best because you are instructed in the law, [19]and if you are sure that you are a guide to the blind, a light to those who are in darkness, [20]a corrector of the foolish, a teacher of children, having in the law the embodiment of knowledge and truth, [21]you, then, that teach others, will you not teach yourself? While you preach against stealing, do you steal? [22]You that forbid adultery, do you commit adultery? You that abhor idols, do you rob temples? [23]You that boast in the law, do you dishonor God by breaking the law? [24]For, as it is written, "The name of God is blasphemed among the Gentiles because of you."

25 Circumcision indeed is of value if you obey the law; but if you break the law, your circumcision has become uncircumcision. [26]So, if those who are uncircumcised keep the requirements of the law, will not their uncircumcision be regarded as circumcision? [27]Then those who are physically uncircumcised but keep the law will condemn you that have the written code and circumcision but break the law. [28]For a person is not a Jew who is one outwardly, nor is true circumcision something external and physical. [29]Rather, a person is a Jew who is one inwardly, and real circumcision is a matter of the heart—it is spiritual and not literal. Such a person receives praise not from others but from God.

2.17–29. 17–24: Inconsistent behavior condemned. 17–18: Jewish identity is closely linked to Torah* observance. **19:** Isa 42.6–7. **21–23:** These rhetorical* questions directly indict those who *boast in the law* yet flagrantly violate its teachings. Stealing and committing adultery are forbidden in the Decalogue (Ex 20.1–17; Deut 5.1–21). **24:** The quotation is based on the Greek version of Isa 52.5. See Ezek 36.20. **25–29: What really defines a person.** Gen 17.1–14 required male circumcision* as the sign of God's covenant* with Israel. It indicated willingness to observe Torah (Gal 5.3). *Uncircumcised* gentiles who fulfill the moral requirements of Torah are, in a *spiritual* sense, circumcised, and more commendable than Jews who violate Torah. *Circumcision★ . . . of the heart* suggests an obedient spirit (Deut 10.16; 30.6).

3 Then what advantage has the Jew? Or what is the value of circumcision? [2]Much, in every way. For in the first place the Jews[a] were entrusted with the oracles of God. [3]What if some were unfaithful? Will their faithlessness nullify the faithfulness of God? [4]By no means! Although everyone is a liar, let God be proved true, as it is written,

"So that you may be justified in your
words,
and prevail in your judging."[b]

[5]But if our injustice serves to confirm the justice of God, what should we say? That God is unjust to inflict wrath on us? (I speak in a human way.) [6]By no means! For then how could God judge the world? [7]But if through my falsehood God's truthfulness abounds to his glory, why am I still being condemned as a sinner? [8]And why not say (as some people slander us by saying that we say), "Let us do evil so that good may come"? Their condemnation is deserved!

9 What then? Are we any better off?[c] No, not at all; for we have already charged that all, both Jews and Greeks, are under the power of sin, [10]as it is written:

"There is no one who is righteous, not
even one;
[11] there is no one who has
understanding,
there is no one who seeks God.
[12] All have turned aside, together they
have become worthless;
there is no one who shows kindness,
there is not even one."
[13] "Their throats are opened graves;
they use their tongues to deceive."
"The venom of vipers is under their lips."
[14] "Their mouths are full of cursing and
bitterness."
[15] "Their feet are swift to shed blood;
[16] ruin and misery are in their paths,
[17] and the way of peace they have
not known."

[18] "There is no fear of God before their
eyes."

19 Now we know that whatever the law says, it speaks to those who are under the law, so that every mouth may be silenced, and the whole world may be held accountable to God. [20]For "no human being will be justified in his sight" by deeds prescribed by the law, for through the law comes the knowledge of sin.

3.1–20. 1–8: Answering Jewish objections. 2: Scripture contains the *oracles★ of God,* what God has spoken to Israel (Deut 4.7–8; Ps 147.15, 18–20). **3–7:** God's reliability is variously described as *faithfulness, justice, truthfulness.* **4:** One psalm finds humans unreliable (Ps 116.11), another regards God as an honest judge (Ps 51.4). **8:** This criticism is answered more fully in ch. 6. **9–20: No one has the moral advantage. 9:** *Jews and Greeks* include everyone (1.16). **10–18:** Various biblical quotations are grouped together to show that *all . . . are under the power of sin.* **10–12:** Eccl 7.20; Ps 14.1–3. **13:** Ps 5.9; 140.3. **14:** Ps 10.7. **15–17:** Isa 59.7–8; Prov 1.16. **18:** Ps 36.1. **20:** Ps 143.2; Gal 2.16.

21 But now, apart from law, the righteousness of God has been disclosed, and is attested by the law and the prophets, [22]the righteousness of God through faith in Jesus Christ[d] for all who believe. For there is no distinction, [23]since all have sinned and fall short of the glory of God; [24]they are now justified by his grace as a gift, through the redemption that is in Christ Jesus, [25]whom God put forward as a sacrifice of atonement[e] by his blood, effective through faith. He did this to show his righteousness, because in his divine forbearance he had passed over the sins previously committed; [26]it was to prove at the present time that he himself is righteous and that he justifies the one who has faith in Jesus.[f]

27 Then what becomes of boasting? It is excluded. By what law? By that of works? No, but by the law of faith. [28]For we hold that a person is justified by faith apart from works

a Gk *they*   b Gk *when you are being judged*
c Or *at any disadvantage?*   d Or *through the faith of Jesus Christ*   e Or *a place of atonement*   f Or *who has the faith of Jesus*

prescribed by the law. [29]Or is God the God of Jews only? Is he not the God of Gentiles also? Yes, of Gentiles also, [30]since God is one; and he will justify the circumcised on the ground of faith and the uncircumcised through that same faith. [31]Do we then overthrow the law by this faith? By no means! On the contrary, we uphold the law.

3.21–31. 21–26: Experiencing God's righteousness through Christ. 21: *The righteousness of God:* God's integrity and ability to set things right. **22, 26:** To have *faith in Jesus Christ* means Christ is the object of faith: Believers regard him as God's agent of *redemption* (v. 24). To have *the faith of Jesus Christ* (see notes *d* and *f*) means Christ is the example of faith: His fidelity reveals God's integrity and displays the type of faith for which believers should strive (Gal. 2.16, 20; 3.20). **27–31: Faith and law. 27:** *Boasting:* putting confidence in human achievement instead of divine power (1 Cor 1.29, 31). **28:** This verse compactly summarizes Paul's position (Gal 2.16). **28–30:** Two ways of being religious, or relating to God, are contrasted: through *works* of *the law* (of Moses) and *the law* (principle) *of faith.* Paul insists that Jews (*the circumcised*) and gentiles★ (*the uncircumcised*) relate to God the same way: *through . . . faith* (v. 30). **31:** *Overthrow the law* probably expresses the views of Paul's critics. His claim to *uphold the law* is developed in ch. 4.

4 What then are we to say was gained by[a] Abraham, our ancestor according to the flesh? [2]For if Abraham was justified by works, he has something to boast about, but not before God. [3]For what does the scripture say? "Abraham believed God, and it was reckoned to him as righteousness." [4]Now to one who works, wages are not reckoned as a gift but as something due. [5]But to one who without works trusts him who justifies the ungodly, such faith is reckoned as righteousness. [6]So also David speaks of the blessedness of those to whom God reckons righteousness apart from works:

7 "Blessed are those whose iniquities are forgiven,
     and whose sins are covered;
8 blessed is the one against whom the Lord will not reckon sin."

9 Is this blessedness, then, pronounced only on the circumcised, or also on the un-circumcised? We say, "Faith was reckoned to Abraham as righteousness." [10]How then was it reckoned to him? Was it before or after he had been circumcised? It was not after, but before he was circumcised. [11]He received the sign of circumcision as a seal of the righteousness that he had by faith while he was still uncircumcised. The purpose was to make him the ancestor of all who believe without being circumcised and who thus have righteousness reckoned to them, [12]and likewise the ancestor of the circumcised who are not only circumcised but who also follow the example of the faith that our ancestor Abraham had before he was circumcised.

13 For the promise that he would inherit the world did not come to Abraham or to his descendants through the law but through the righteousness of faith. [14]If it is the adherents of the law who are to be the heirs, faith is null and the promise is void. [15]For the law brings wrath; but where there is no law, neither is there violation.

4.1–15. 1–8: The example of Abraham. 3: Gen 15.6. **4–5:** *Righteousness* may be seen as an earned wage given to *one who works* or as a gift freely bestowed to the *one who trusts* in God who accepts sinners. **7–8:** Ps 32.1–2. **9–12: When Abraham received God's blessing.** The sequence of events in Genesis is critical to Paul's argument. Which was the more defining moment for Abraham? Faith (Gen 15.6) or circumcision★ (Gen 17.1–14)? Faith, since it came first. Thus, Abraham is better seen as the *ancestor of all who believe* (Jews and gentiles★) rather than the *ancestor of the circumcised* (Jews only). **13–15: God's promise through faith, not the Mosaic law. 13:** *The promise* of many descendants through Isaac experienced *through the righteousness of faith* is given in Genesis (15.1–6; 18.18; 22.15–18). It did not come *through the law* of Moses, which came much later. Since *the promise* is linked more closely to *faith* than it is to *the law,* it is best experienced not by *adherents of the law* but by those living in faith. **15:** Without *law,* there is no sense of *violation* (Gal 3.19).

16 For this reason it depends on faith, in order that the promise may rest on grace and be guaranteed to all his descendants, not

---

a Other ancient authorities read *say about*

only to the adherents of the law but also to those who share the faith of Abraham (for he is the father of all of us, [17] as it is written, "I have made you the father of many nations")—in the presence of the God in whom he believed, who gives life to the dead and calls into existence the things that do not exist. [18] Hoping against hope, he believed that he would become "the father of many nations," according to what was said, "So numerous shall your descendants be." [19] He did not weaken in faith when he considered his own body, which was already[a] as good as dead (for he was about a hundred years old), or when he considered the barrenness of Sarah's womb. [20] No distrust made him waver concerning the promise of God, but he grew strong in his faith as he gave glory to God, [21] being fully convinced that God was able to do what he had promised. [22] Therefore his faith[b] "was reckoned to him as righteousness." [23] Now the words, "it was reckoned to him," were written not for his sake alone, [24] but for ours also. It will be reckoned to us who believe in him who raised Jesus our Lord from the dead, [25] who was handed over to death for our trespasses and was raised for our justification.

4.16–25: Abraham's ability to trust. 16: *The promise of God's blessing is given in* grace *and received in* faith *to* all his descendants, *both Jews* (adherents of the law) *and gentiles* * (those who share the faith of Abraham). **17–19:** God's creative power is shown by giving life to Abraham's "dead" body and Sarah's barren womb. **17:** Gen 17.5. **18:** Gen 15.5. **19:** *Hundred years old,* Gen. 17.17. **20–21:** Unwavering trust characterizes *the faith of Abraham* (v. 16). **22:** Gen 15.6. **24–25:** To believe that God *raised Jesus . . . from the dead* requires faith like that of Abraham and Sarah. For them, receiving God's *righteousness* meant experiencing God as utterly reliable, as someone whose promises come true. God can be similarly experienced by those who believe that God gave life to the crucified Jesus. The language *handed over* and *raised* suggests a two-part confession.

5 Therefore, since we are justified by faith, we[c] have peace with God through our Lord Jesus Christ, [2] through whom we have

obtained access[d] to this grace in which we stand; and we[e] boast in our hope of sharing the glory of God. [3] And not only that, but we[e] also boast in our sufferings, knowing that suffering produces endurance, [4] and endurance produces character, and character produces hope, [5] and hope does not disappoint us, because God's love has been poured into our hearts through the Holy Spirit that has been given to us.

[6] For while we were still weak, at the right time Christ died for the ungodly. [7] Indeed, rarely will anyone die for a righteous person—though perhaps for a good person someone might actually dare to die. [8] But God proves his love for us in that while we still were sinners Christ died for us. [9] Much more surely then, now that we have been justified by his blood, will we be saved through him from the wrath of God.[f] [10] For if while we were enemies, we were reconciled to God through the death of his Son, much more surely, having been reconciled, will we be saved by his life. [11] But more than that, we even boast in God through our Lord Jesus Christ, through whom we have now received reconciliation.

5.1–11. 1–5: Peace with God through Christ. 1: Gal 2.16. *Peace* results where justice and righteousness prevail (Isa 32.16–18). **2:** To experience salvation as gift, not reward, is to *stand* in God's *grace* (1 Pet 5.12; Rom. 4.4–5). **2–3:** Boast is used positively here, meaning "take pride in" (Rom 3.27; 1 Cor 1.29). **3–4:** *Suffering* is properly understood within the larger perspective of resurrection *hope*. **5:** God's past actions provide the basis for *hope* (Ps 22.3–5). The *Holy Spirit* given to believers is the tangible expression of *God's love* (Titus 3.6). **6–11: Christ died for sinners. 6:** The *ungodly* live against God (Rom 4.5). **7:** It is hard enough to die for a generous, good-hearted person, even harder to die for a hard-hearted *righteous person*. **8:** Christ's death for *sinners* who are neither *good* nor *righteous* shows God's unusual love (Jn 3.16; 1 Jn 4.10). **9:** *His blood:* Jesus' death is understood as atoning sacrifice (Rom 3.25). **10–11:** Those yielding to the

a Other ancient authorities lack *already*
b Gk *Therefore it* c Other ancient authorities read *let us* d Other ancient authorities add *by faith*
e Or *let us* f Gk *the wrath*

power of sin become *enemies* of God (Rom 3.9–18). Christ's death reconciles sinful humanity with God (2 Cor 5.18–19; Col 1.21–22); through *his* resurrection *life,* believers experience similar hope of being *saved.* **11:** God now becomes the proper object of pride (1 Cor. 1.31).

12 Therefore, just as sin came into the world through one man, and death came through sin, and so death spread to all because all have sinned— ¹³sin was indeed in the world before the law, but sin is not reckoned when there is no law. ¹⁴Yet death exercised dominion from Adam to Moses, even over those whose sins were not like the transgression of Adam, who is a type of the one who was to come.

15 But the free gift is not like the trespass. For if the many died through the one man's trespass, much more surely have the grace of God and the free gift in the grace of the one man, Jesus Christ, abounded for the many. ¹⁶And the free gift is not like the effect of the one man's sin. For the judgment following one trespass brought condemnation, but the free gift following many trespasses brings justification. ¹⁷If, because of the one man's trespass, death exercised dominion through that one, much more surely will those who receive the abundance of grace and the free gift of righteousness exercise dominion in life through the one man, Jesus Christ.

18 Therefore just as one man's trespass led to condemnation for all, so one man's act of righteousness leads to justification and life for all. ¹⁹For just as by the one man's disobedience the many were made sinners, so by the one man's obedience the many will be made righteous. ²⁰But law came in, with the result that the trespass multiplied; but where sin increased, grace abounded all the more, ²¹so that, just as sin exercised dominion in death, so grace might also exercise dominion through justification*a* leading to eternal life through Jesus Christ our Lord.

5.12–21. 12–14: Sin, death, and law. 12: Tracing *sin* and *death* to *one man,* Adam, is based on Gen 3. Universal sin brings universal death (Rom 3.9). **13–14:** Adam's *sin* preceded the Mosaic *law* chronologically,

but *law* makes *sin* and its consequences specific, thus easier to deal with. *Adam* is seen as a *type* (a figure with important similarities) of Christ, *the one who was to come* (1 Cor. 15.45–47). **15–17: Adam and Christ.** *Free gift* translates different Greek words ("charisma," vv. 15a, 16b; "dorea," vv. 15b, 17; "dorema," v. 16), but they all refer to God's *free gift* of Christ, which is contrasted with *one man's* (Adam's) *trespass.* Both events are alike because they show how one person can affect many people. But they have very different effects. Adam's *trespass* brought *condemnation* (v. 16) and *death* (v. 17), whereas God's *free gift* of Christ brought *justification* (v. 16) and *life* (v. 17). **18–21: Law and grace. 18–19:** These verses summarize and extend the contrast of the previous section. **20–21:** The Mosaic *law came in* and made sin and its consequences clear (4.15). Trespasses *multiplied* because awareness of *sin increased.* Yet, the lethal effects of sin were exceeded by God's *grace* shown through *Jesus Christ our Lord.* This event revealed God's *righteousness* by proving God reliable and making real the prospect of *eternal life* (6.23).

6 What then are we to say? Should we continue in sin in order that grace may abound? ²By no means! How can we who died to sin go on living in it? ³Do you not know that all of us who have been baptized into Christ Jesus were baptized into his death? ⁴Therefore we have been buried with him by baptism into death, so that, just as Christ was raised from the dead by the glory of the Father, so we too might walk in newness of life.

6.1–4: Dying to sin. 1: Paul now answers his critics more fully (3.8). **2–4:** Through baptism,* believers ritually reenact Jesus' death and resurrection, experiencing the radical shift from death to life as moral renewal: death *to sin* and *newness of life* (Col 2.11–12).

5 For if we have been united with him in a death like his, we will certainly be united with him in a resurrection like his. ⁶We know that our old self was crucified with him so that the body of sin might be destroyed, and we might no longer be enslaved to sin. ⁷For whoever has died is freed from sin. ⁸But if we have died with Christ, we believe

a Or *righteousness*

that we will also live with him. ⁹We know that Christ, being raised from the dead, will never die again; death no longer has dominion over him. ¹⁰The death he died, he died to sin, once for all; but the life he lives, he lives to God. ¹¹So you also must consider yourselves dead to sin and alive to God in Christ Jesus.

12 Therefore, do not let sin exercise dominion in your mortal bodies, to make you obey their passions. ¹³No longer present your members to sin as instruments*a* of wickedness, but present yourselves to God as those who have been brought from death to life, and present your members to God as instruments*a* of righteousness. ¹⁴For sin will have no dominion over you, since you are not under law but under grace.

6.5–14. 5–11: Dying and living with Christ. 5–8: *With him:* Believers "enter" Christ's experience as co-participants (Gal 2.19–20). 10: *He died to sin:* In dying, Christ yielded to sin's power to kill. Christ's death occurred once; his new life with God is ongoing: *He lives to God.* 11: *Sin* and *God* represent opposing realities and loyalties. 12–14: Shifting loyalties. *Sin* may be an impersonal force, but it seriously competes with God for *dominion* over *mortal bodies.* 13: *Those . . . brought from death to life* have relived Christ's experience (v. 8). 14: Christ's death also represents a shift from *law* to *grace* (Jn 1.17).

15 What then? Should we sin because we are not under law but under grace? By no means! ¹⁶Do you not know that if you present yourselves to anyone as obedient slaves, you are slaves of the one whom you obey, either of sin, which leads to death, or of obedience, which leads to righteousness? ¹⁷But thanks be to God that you, having once been slaves of sin, have become obedient from the heart to the form of teaching to which you were entrusted, ¹⁸and that you, having been set free from sin, have become slaves of righteousness. ¹⁹I am speaking in human terms because of your natural limitations.*b* For just as you once presented your members as slaves to impurity and to greater and greater iniquity, so now present your members as slaves to righteousness for sanctification.

20 When you were slaves of sin, you were free in regard to righteousness. ²¹So what advantage did you then get from the things of which you now are ashamed? The end of those things is death. ²²But now that you have been freed from sin and enslaved to God, the advantage you get is sanctification. The end is eternal life. ²³For the wages of sin is death, but the free gift of God is eternal life in Christ Jesus our Lord.

6.15–23. 15–19: Choosing whom to obey. 15: For Paul's critics, exchanging *law* for *grace* encourages *sin* (3.8). 16–19: The widespread practice of slavery in antiquity informs Paul's discussion: Living as *slaves* meant obedient submission (Eph 6.5–9; Col 3.22–4.1). 20–23: Thinking long-term. 20: To be *free* is to be without obligation *to righteousness.* 21: Sin can cause physical *death* and ultimate separation from God (8.6, 13). 22: With changed loyalties comes a purer life, *sanctification* (1 Thess 4.3), and eventually *eternal life* with God (5.21).

7 Do you not know, brothers and sisters*c*—for I am speaking to those who know the law—that the law is binding on a person only during that person's lifetime? ²Thus a married woman is bound by the law to her husband as long as he lives; but if her husband dies, she is discharged from the law concerning the husband. ³Accordingly, she will be called an adulteress if she lives with another man while her husband is alive. But if her husband dies, she is free from that law, and if she marries another man, she is not an adulteress.

4 In the same way, my friends,*c* you have died to the law through the body of Christ, so that you may belong to another, to him who has been raised from the dead in order that we may bear fruit for God. ⁵While we were living in the flesh, our sinful passions, aroused by the law, were at work in our members to bear fruit for death. ⁶But now we are discharged from the law, dead to that which held us captive, so that we are slaves not under the old written code but in the new life of the Spirit.

a Or *weapons*   *b* Gk *the weakness of your flesh*
c Gk *brothers*

7　What then should we say? That the law is sin? By no means! Yet, if it had not been for the law, I would not have known sin. I would not have known what it is to covet if the law had not said, "You shall not covet." ⁸But sin, seizing an opportunity in the commandment, produced in me all kinds of covetousness. Apart from the law sin lies dead. ⁹I was once alive apart from the law, but when the commandment came, sin revived ¹⁰and I died, and the very commandment that promised life proved to be death to me. ¹¹For sin, seizing an opportunity in the commandment, deceived me and through it killed me. ¹²So the law is holy, and the commandment is holy and just and good.

13　Did what is good, then, bring death to me? By no means! It was sin, working death in me through what is good, in order that sin might be shown to be sin, and through the commandment might become sinful beyond measure.

7.1–13. 1–3: **Marriage and the law.** Whether *the* Jewish *law* (Ex 20.14; Deut 5.18) or Roman law is in view is not clear. The same principle holds for both: Laws governing marriage presuppose two living partners. The death of one partner (here, the husband) invalidates the law, leaving the other partner (the wife) free to marry. **4–6: Christ's death and the law.** *The law* of Moses is the first husband, the risen Christ the second husband. Paul's readers are the wife now *discharged from* the obligations *of the old written code.* Newly married to Christ, they *belong to another* and enjoy *the new life of the Spirit.* Generally, the analogy makes sense, but seems forced. V. 4 is difficult. **7–13: The value of the law. 7:** V. 5 seems to support this objection. By naming the sin, *the law* raises the sinner's consciousness. *To covet* is to want something that belongs to someone else (Ex 20.17; Deut 5.21). **8–11:** *Sin* takes on personal qualities, having power to seize and manipulate people and laws.

14　For we know that the law is spiritual; but I am of the flesh, sold into slavery under sin.ᵃ ¹⁵I do not understand my own actions. For I do not do what I want, but I do the very thing I hate. ¹⁶Now if I do what I do not want, I agree that the law is good. ¹⁷But in fact it is no longer I that do it, but sin that dwells within me. ¹⁸For I know that nothing good dwells within me, that is, in my flesh. I can will what is right, but I cannot do it. ¹⁹For I do not do the good I want, but the evil I do not want is what I do. ²⁰Now if I do what I do not want, it is no longer I that do it, but sin that dwells within me.

21　So I find it to be a law that when I want to do what is good, evil lies close at hand. ²²For I delight in the law of God in my inmost self, ²³but I see in my members another law at war with the law of my mind, making me captive to the law of sin that dwells in my members. ²⁴Wretched man that I am! Who will rescue me from this body of death? ²⁵Thanks be to God through Jesus Christ our Lord!

So then, with my mind I am a slave to the law of God, but with my flesh I am a slave to the law of sin.

7.14–25. **14–20: The struggle to do good.** *I am of the flesh:* Paul may be speaking of his own moral struggle or using "I" to express everyone's experience. *Sin that dwells within me* (vv. 17, 20) suggests an alien presence wreaking havoc in an unwilling host. **21–25: The war within us. 21:** *A law* here means "a rule." **22:** *The law of God* may be the Mosaic law (vv. 14, 16). **23:** Elsewhere the opposition is between flesh and Spirit (Gal 5.17). **25:** As before, *sin* and *God* are enemies (6.22).

8　There is therefore now no condemnation for those who are in Christ Jesus. ²For the law of the Spiritᵇ of life in Christ Jesus has set youᶜ free from the law of sin and of death. ³For God has done what the law, weakened by the flesh, could not do: by sending his own Son in the likeness of sinful flesh, and to deal with sin,ᵈ he condemned sin in the flesh, ⁴so that the just requirement of the law might be fulfilled in us, who walk not according to the flesh but according to the Spirit.ᵇ ⁵For those who live according to the flesh set their minds on the things of the flesh, but those who live according to the Spiritᵇ set their minds on the things of the Spirit.ᵇ ⁶To set the mind on the flesh is

ᵃ Gk *sold under sin*　　ᵇ Or *spirit*　　ᶜ Here the Greek word *you* is singular number; other ancient authorities read *me* or *us*　　ᵈ Or *and as a sin offering* death, but to set the mind on the Spirit^a is life and peace. 7For this reason the mind that is set on the flesh is hostile to God; it does not submit to God's law—indeed it cannot, 8and those who are in the flesh cannot please God.

9 But you are not in the flesh; you are in the Spirit,^{a} since the Spirit of God dwells in you. Anyone who does not have the Spirit of Christ does not belong to him. 10But if Christ is in you, though the body is dead because of sin, the Spirit^a is life because of righteousness. 11If the Spirit of him who raised Jesus from the dead dwells in you, he who raised Christ^b from the dead will give life to your mortal bodies also through^c his Spirit that dwells in you.

8.1–11. 1–8: Life in the Spirit. 1: *No condemnation:* Those *in Christ* no longer feel doomed (Jn 5.24). **2:** God's life-giving Spirit unleashed in Christ becomes a liberating *law,* replacing the Mosaic *law* that *sin* uses to produce *death* (7.5, 11). **3–4:** By sending Christ as *a sin offering* (note d on p. 1899), God met the *requirement of the law* (Lev 4–5). Recognizing what *the law . . . could not do,* however, God dealt with human sin (*sin in the flesh*) with a human sacrifice (*in the likeness of sinful flesh*). **5–8:** *Flesh* and *Spirit* represent opposing outlooks, with different lifestyles and consequences: *death* versus *life and peace* (Gal 5.16–26). **9–11: God, Christ, Spirit.** Paul now uses the plural form of *you* (8.2). His main focus may be group rather than individual identity. **9:** Having the *Spirit of Christ* becomes the distinguishing mark of Christian identity. **10:** *If Christ is in you:* Christ's pattern of "dying and rising" becomes part of us (Gal 2.19–20). Our *body* may be mortal because of Adam's *sin,* yet our *spirit* (note a) lives because of God's *righteousness* shown through Christ (5.18). **11:** God's *Spirit* living within us links our experience of the risen Christ with our hope of resurrection *life.*

---

12 So then, brothers and sisters,^{d} we are debtors, not to the flesh, to live according to the flesh— 13for if you live according to the flesh, you will die; but if by the Spirit you put to death the deeds of the body, you will live. 14For all who are led by the Spirit of God are children of God. 15For you did not receive a spirit of slavery to fall back into fear, but you have received a spirit of adoption. When we

cry, "Abba!^{e} Father!" 16it is that very Spirit bearing witness^f with our spirit that we are children of God, 17and if children, then heirs, heirs of God and joint heirs with Christ—if, in fact, we suffer with him so that we may also be glorified with him.

18 I consider that the sufferings of this present time are not worth comparing with the glory about to be revealed to us. 19For the creation waits with eager longing for the revealing of the children of God; 20for the creation was subjected to futility, not of its own will but by the will of the one who subjected it, in hope 21that the creation itself will be set free from its bondage to decay and will obtain the freedom of the glory of the children of God. 22We know that the whole creation has been groaning in labor pains until now; 23and not only the creation, but we ourselves, who have the first fruits of the Spirit, groan inwardly while we wait for adoption, the redemption of our bodies. 24For in^g hope we were saved. Now hope that is seen is not hope. For who hopes^h for what is seen? 25But if we hope for what we do not see, we wait for it with patience.

8.12–25. 12–17: Living as God's children. 12–13: Living *according to the flesh* leads to various forms of self-gratification, *deeds of the body.* **14:** This is especially true of Christ (8.3; Lk 4.1–13). **15–17:** In note e, the ability to *cry, "Abba! Father!"* derives from the *spirit of adoption.* The Spirit's co-testimony does not result from the prayer, as it does in the NRSV text. The prayer preserves the Aramaic* language of Jesus (Mk 14.36; Gal 4.6). **18–25: Present sufferings and future glory. 18:** *Sufferings* and *glory* develop 8.17. Believers share both experiences *with Christ.* **19–25:** *The creation* is the whole created order. **20:** *Subjected to futility:* The creation story is in view, especially Gen 3.17–19. **22:** The whole universe is viewed as a woman in labor, giving birth to new life (Gal 4.19). **23:** *First fruits of the Spirit:* In the Old Testament, what was harvested first were the "first fruits," an indication of

---

a Or *spirit*   *b* Other ancient authorities read *the Christ* or *Christ Jesus* or *Jesus Christ*   *c* Other ancient authorities read *on account of*   *d* Gk *brothers* *e* Aramaic for *Father*   *f* Or *15a spirit of adoption, by which we cry, "Abba! Father!"* *16The Spirit itself bears witness*   *g* Or *by*   *h* Other ancient authorities read *awaits* more to come (Ex 23.16). Similarly, the *Spirit* is understood here as a foretaste of the future glory. **24:** 2 Cor 4.18.

~~~~~~~~~~~~~~~~~~~~~~~~~~~~~~~~~~~~~~~

26 Likewise the Spirit helps us in our weakness; for we do not know how to pray as we ought, but that very Spirit intercedes[a] with sighs too deep for words. [27]And God,[b] who searches the heart, knows what is the mind of the Spirit, because the Spirit[c] intercedes for the saints according to the will of God.[d]

28 We know that all things work together for good[e] for those who love God, who are called according to his purpose. [29]For those whom he foreknew he also predestined to be conformed to the image of his Son, in order that he might be the firstborn within a large family.[f] [30]And those whom he predestined he also called; and those whom he called he also justified; and those whom he justified he also glorified.

31 What then are we to say about these things? If God is for us, who is against us? [32]He who did not withhold his own Son, but gave him up for all of us, will he not with him also give us everything else? [33]Who will bring any charge against God's elect? It is God who justifies. [34]Who is to condemn? It is Christ Jesus, who died, yes, who was raised, who is at the right hand of God, who indeed intercedes for us.[g] [35]Who will separate us from the love of Christ? Will hardship, or distress, or persecution, or famine, or nakedness, or peril, or sword? [36]As it is written,

> "For your sake we are being killed all
> day long;
> we are accounted as sheep to be
> slaughtered."

[37]No, in all these things we are more than conquerors through him who loved us. [38]For I am convinced that neither death, nor life, nor angels, nor rulers, nor things present, nor things to come, nor powers, [39]nor height, nor depth, nor anything else in all creation, will be able to separate us from the love of God in Christ Jesus our Lord.

8.26–39. 26–27: The Spirit as intercessor. 26: *Our weakness* is being unable to say what we need. *Inter-*

cedes: The Spirit pleads our case before God (Heb 7.25). **27:** Here God knows the Spirit as thoroughly as the human heart (Ps 139.1–6). Praying "in the Spirit" recognizes the Spirit's mediating role (Eph 6.18; Jude 20). **28–30: Being part of God's larger purpose. 28:** The alternate readings (note *e*) yield significant differences. The most believable of the three is: *In all things God works for good.* **29–30:** The people of God rather than individuals are in view. **31–39: More than conquerors.** Central to this triumphant finale is what God did in Christ (vv. 32, 34, 37, 39), aptly summarized in the final line: *the love of God in Christ Jesus our Lord.* **32:** Christ as God's sacrifice is in view (8.3). *Everything else* includes protective care from suffering (v. 35) and cosmic threats, present and future (vv. 37–39). **33:** *God's elect* are God's people (8.28–30). **36:** Ps 44.22.

~~~~~~~~~~~~~~~~~~~~~~~~~~~~~~~~~~~~~~~

9 I am speaking the truth in Christ—I am not lying; my conscience confirms it by the Holy Spirit— [2]I have great sorrow and unceasing anguish in my heart. [3]For I could wish that I myself were accursed and cut off from Christ for the sake of my own people,[h] my kindred according to the flesh. [4]They are Israelites, and to them belong the adoption, the glory, the covenants, the giving of the law, the worship, and the promises; [5]to them belong the patriarchs, and from them, according to the flesh, comes the Messiah,[i] who is over all, God blessed forever.[j] Amen.

6 It is not as though the word of God had failed. For not all Israelites truly belong to Israel, [7]and not all of Abraham's children are his true descendants; but "It is through Isaac that descendants shall be named for you." [8]This means that it is not the children of the flesh who are the children of God, but the children of the promise are counted as descendants. [9]For this is what the promise said, "About this time I will return and Sarah shall have a son." [10]Nor is that all; something similar happened to Rebecca when she had conceived children by one husband, our

a Other ancient authorities add *for us*   *b* Gk *the one* *c* Gk *he* or *it*   *d* Gk *according to God*   *e* Other ancient authorities read *God makes all things work together for good,* or *in all things God works for good* *f* Gk *among many brothers*   *g* Or *Is it Christ Jesus . . . for us?*   *h* Gk *my brothers*   *i* Or *the Christ* *j* Or *Messiah, who is God over all, blessed forever;* or *Messiah. May he who is God over all be blessed forever*

ancestor Isaac. [11]Even before they had been born or had done anything good or bad (so that God's purpose of election might continue, [12]not by works but by his call) she was told, "The elder shall serve the younger." [13]As it is written,

"I have loved Jacob,
    but I have hated Esau."

9.1–11.36: God's purpose for Israel. 9.1–5: Blessings belonging to Israel. 5: Here the NRSV retains the ambiguity of the Greek (see alternate translations in note *j*). Ordinarily, Paul uses such language of God rather than of Christ (1.25; 2 Cor 11.31). **6–13: Abraham's true descendants. 6–7:** The earlier distinction (2.28–29) between physical and spiritual pedigree is now stated differently. **7:** Gen 21.12. **8:** *Children of the promise* are gentiles* and Jews who, like Abraham, live by faith (4.16). **9:** Gen 18.10. **12:** Gen 25.23. Like Abraham, Rebecca lived by faith. **13:** Mal 1.2–3.

14 What then are we to say? Is there injustice on God's part? By no means! [15]For he says to Moses,

"I will have mercy on whom I have mercy,
    and I will have compassion on whom
        I have compassion."
[16]So it depends not on human will or exertion, but on God who shows mercy. [17]For the scripture says to Pharaoh, "I have raised you up for the very purpose of showing my power in you, so that my name may be proclaimed in all the earth." [18]So then he has mercy on whomever he chooses, and he hardens the heart of whomever he chooses.

19 You will say to me then, "Why then does he still find fault? For who can resist his will?" [20]But who indeed are you, a human being, to argue with God? Will what is molded say to the one who molds it, "Why have you made me like this?" [21]Has the potter no right over the clay, to make out of the same lump one object for special use and another for ordinary use? [22]What if God, desiring to show his wrath and to make known his power, has endured with much patience the objects of wrath that are made for destruction; [23]and what if he has done so in order to make known the riches of his glory for the objects of mercy, which he has prepared beforehand for glory— [24]including us

whom he has called, not from the Jews only but also from the Gentiles? [25]As indeed he says in Hosea,

"Those who were not my people I will
        call 'my people,'
    and her who was not beloved I will
        call 'beloved.' "
26 "And in the very place where it was said
        to them, 'You are not my people,'
    there they shall be called children of
        the living God."

9.14–26: God's freedom to choose. 14: Paul anticipates criticism of his logic (3.3–5). **15:** Ex 33.19. **16:** God does not require *human will or exertion* to show *mercy.* **17:** Ex 9.16. **19:** Paul's imaginary dialogue partner responds. **20–21:** The image of the potter and clay (drawn from Isa 29.16; 45.9) emphasizes God's sovereign power. **22–23:** God can show *wrath* or *mercy.* **25–26:** From both *Jews* and *Gentiles,** God can form a newly *beloved* people. **25:** Hos 2.25. **26:** Hos 1.10.

27 And Isaiah cries out concerning Israel, "Though the number of the children of Israel were like the sand of the sea, only a remnant of them will be saved; [28]for the Lord will execute his sentence on the earth quickly and decisively."[a] [29]And as Isaiah predicted,

"If the Lord of hosts had not left
        survivors[b] to us,
    we would have fared like Sodom
        and been made like Gomorrah."

30 What then are we to say? Gentiles, who did not strive for righteousness, have attained it, that is, righteousness through faith; [31]but Israel, who did strive for the righteousness that is based on the law, did not succeed in fulfilling that law. [32]Why not? Because they did not strive for it on the basis of faith, but as if it were based on works. They have stumbled over the stumbling stone, [33]as it is written,

"See, I am laying in Zion a stone that
        will make people stumble, a rock
        that will make them fall,
    and whoever believes in him[c] will not
        be put to shame."

a Other ancient authorities read *for he will finish his work and cut it short in righteousness, because the Lord will make the sentence shortened on the earth*
b Or *descendants*; Gk *seed*   *c* Or *trusts in it*

9.27–33. 27–29: A remnant will be saved. 27: Isa 10.22. 28: See Isa 28.22. 29: Isa 1.9. 30–33: Gentiles succeeded where Israel failed. *Faith,* the capacity to trust God (note *c*), not performance, is the critical difference (4.5). 33: Isa 28.16; Isa 8.14.

10 Brothers and sisters,[a] my heart's desire and prayer to God for them is that they may be saved. 2I can testify that they have a zeal for God, but it is not enlightened. 3For, being ignorant of the righteousness that comes from God, and seeking to establish their own, they have not submitted to God's righteousness. 4For Christ is the end of the law so that there may be righteousness for everyone who believes.

5 Moses writes concerning the righteousness that comes from the law, that "the person who does these things will live by them." 6But the righteousness that comes from faith says, "Do not say in your heart, 'Who will ascend into heaven?' " (that is, to bring Christ down) 7"or 'Who will descend into the abyss?' " (that is, to bring Christ up from the dead). 8But what does it say?

"The word is near you,
on your lips and in your heart"

(that is, the word of faith that we proclaim); 9because[b] if you confess with your lips that Jesus is Lord and believe in your heart that God raised him from the dead, you will be saved. 10For one believes with the heart and so is justified, and one confesses with the mouth and so is saved. 11The scripture says, "No one who believes in him will be put to shame." 12For there is no distinction between Jew and Greek; the same Lord is Lord of all and is generous to all who call on him. 13For, "Everyone who calls on the name of the Lord shall be saved."

10.1–13. 1–4: Paul's prayer for Israel. 1–2: Paul speaks of Israel (9.31–33). 3: *Righteousness that comes from God:* 1.16–17. 4: *The end of the law:* Christ either abolishes the law or is its goal, probably the latter (3.21–22). 5–13: Righteousness through faith. 5: Lev 18.5. The emphasis here is on living by doing. 6a: Deut 9.4. 6b: Deut 30.12. 7: Ps 107.26; see Deut 30.13. 8: Deut 30.14. *Faith* does not try to locate Christ "out there," but rather expresses an inner con-

viction believed *with the heart* and expressed *with your lips.* 10: What *the heart* believes, *the mouth* confesses. 11: Isa 28.16. 12: *No distinction:* Jews and gentiles[*] are justified the same way (3.30). 13: Joel 2.32.

14 But how are they to call on one in whom they have not believed? And how are they to believe in one of whom they have never heard? And how are they to hear without someone to proclaim him? 15And how are they to proclaim him unless they are sent? As it is written, "How beautiful are the feet of those who bring good news!" 16But not all have obeyed the good news;[c] for Isaiah says, "Lord, who has believed our message?" 17So faith comes from what is heard, and what is heard comes through the word of Christ.[d]

18 But I ask, have they not heard? Indeed they have; for

"Their voice has gone out to all
the earth,
and their words to the ends of the
world."

19Again I ask, did Israel not understand? First Moses says,

"I will make you jealous of those who
are not a nation;
with a foolish nation I will make you
angry."

20Then Isaiah is so bold as to say,

"I have been found by those who did
not seek me;
I have shown myself to those who did
not ask for me."

21But of Israel he says, "All day long I have held out my hands to a disobedient and contrary people."

10.14–21. 14–17: Hearing the gospel of Christ. 14–15: Being summoned is ultimately traceable to proclamation. 15: Isa 42.7; Nah 1.15. Proclaimers of God's *good news* are like messengers announcing battle victories. 16: Isa 53.1. 17: Abraham may be in view if *word of God* is read (see note *e*). 18–21: Israel's refusal to hear. The law, prophets,[*] and writings at-

a Gk *Brothers*   *b* Or *namely, that*   *c* Or *gospel*
d Or *about Christ;* other ancient authorities read
of God

test Israel's disobedience. **18**: Ps 19.4. **19**: Deut 32.21. **20**: Isa 65.1. **21**: Isa 65.2.

11 I ask, then, has God rejected his people? By no means! I myself am an Israelite, a descendant of Abraham, a member of the tribe of Benjamin. ²God has not rejected his people whom he foreknew. Do you not know what the scripture says of Elijah, how he pleads with God against Israel? ³"Lord, they have killed your prophets, they have demolished your altars; I alone am left, and they are seeking my life." ⁴But what is the divine reply to him? "I have kept for myself seven thousand who have not bowed the knee to Baal." ⁵So too at the present time there is a remnant, chosen by grace. ⁶But if it is by grace, it is no longer on the basis of works, otherwise grace would no longer be grace.ᵃ

7 What then? Israel failed to obtain what it was seeking. The elect obtained it, but the rest were hardened, ⁸as it is written,

"God gave them a sluggish spirit,
    eyes that would not see
    and ears that would not hear,
down to this very day."

⁹And David says,

"Let their table become a snare
        and a trap,
    a stumbling block and a retribution
        for them;
¹⁰ let their eyes be darkened so that they
        cannot see,
    and keep their backs forever bent."

11 So I ask, have they stumbled so as to fall? By no means! But through their stumblingᵇ salvation has come to the Gentiles, so as to make Israelᶜ jealous. ¹²Now if their stumblingᵇ means riches for the world, and if their defeat means riches for Gentiles, how much more will their full inclusion mean!

Christians. **8**: Deut 29.4; Isa 29.9–10. **9–10**: Ps 69.22–23. **10**: *Backs forever bent:* The blind walk stooped.

13 Now I am speaking to you Gentiles. Inasmuch then as I am an apostle to the Gentiles, I glorify my ministry ¹⁴in order to make my own peopleᵈ jealous, and thus save some of them. ¹⁵For if their rejection is the reconciliation of the world, what will their acceptance be but life from the dead! ¹⁶If the part of the dough offered as first fruits is holy, then the whole batch is holy; and if the root is holy, then the branches also are holy.

17 But if some of the branches were broken off, and you, a wild olive shoot, were grafted in their place to share the rich rootᵉ of the olive tree, ¹⁸do not boast over the branches. If you do boast, remember that it is not you that support the root, but the root that supports you. ¹⁹You will say, "Branches were broken off so that I might be grafted in." ²⁰That is true. They were broken off because of their unbelief, but you stand only through faith. So do not become proud, but stand in awe. ²¹For if God did not spare the natural branches, perhaps he will not spare you.ᶠ ²²Note then the kindness and the severity of God: severity toward those who have fallen, but God's kindness toward you, provided you continue in his kindness; otherwise you also will be cut off. ²³And even those of Israel,ᵍ if they do not persist in unbelief, will be grafted in, for God has the power to graft them in again. ²⁴For if you have been cut from what is by nature a wild olive tree and grafted, contrary to nature, into a cultivated olive tree, how much more will these natural branches be grafted back into their own olive tree.

11.1–12. 1–6: A remnant chosen by grace. 1: The objection of 3.1 is stated more emphatically. Paul offers himself as an example of an obedient Israelite (2 Cor 11.22). **2:** 1 Sam 12.22. **3:** 1 Kings 19.10, 14. **4:** 1 Kings 19.18. **5:** A portion of Israel has experienced God's righteousness as gift (5.15; 11.27). **7–12: Israel's refusal enables gentiles'* obedience. 7:** *The elect* are the faithful remnant of responsive Jewish

11.13–32: Paul speaks to gentiles. * The previous discussion has been an ongoing conversation with Israel

a Other ancient authorities add But if it is by works, it is no longer on the basis of grace, otherwise work would no longer be work   b Gk transgression   c Gk them   d Gk my flesh   e Other ancient authorities read the richness   f Other ancient authorities read neither will he spare you   g Gk lacks of Israel about Israel. **13–16: Effect of Paul's ministry on Israel. 13:** *Apostle** *to the Gentiles:* Paul so defines himself (1.5; Gal 2.8). **14:** Provoking Israel to jealousy fulfills Deut 32.21 (10.19). **15:** Israel's rejection can become the occasion for universal reconciliation. Israel's acceptance would show God's creative power (4.17). **16:** Both images emphasize the solidarity between Israel and the gentiles. **17–24: Lessons from the olive tree. 17:** Gentiles are the *wild olive shoot,* Israel the *root.* **18:** Jews earlier, now gentiles, are forbidden to *boast* (2.17–21). **20:** *Unbelief* is refusal to acknowledge Jesus as messiah.* **21:** Both Jews and gentiles can experience God's wrath (2.9–10). **22:** *Kindness* and *severity* represent God's two sides (9.22–24). **23:** *Of Israel* is an acceptable expansion (note *g* on p. 1905), since Israel's unbelief is clearly in view. **24:** Paul holds out hope for Israel.

25 So that you may not claim to be wiser than you are, brothers and sisters,ᵃ I want you to understand this mystery: a hardening has come upon part of Israel, until the full number of the Gentiles has come in. ²⁶And so all Israel will be saved; as it is written,

"Out of Zion will come the Deliverer;
    he will banish ungodliness
        from Jacob."
²⁷ "And this is my covenant with them,
    when I take away their sins."
²⁸As regards the gospel they are enemies of Godᵇ for your sake; but as regards election they are beloved, for the sake of their ancestors; ²⁹for the gifts and the calling of God are irrevocable. ³⁰Just as you were once disobedient to God but have now received mercy because of their disobedience, ³¹so they have now been disobedient in order that, by the mercy shown to you, they too may nowᶜ receive mercy. ³²For God has imprisoned all in disobedience so that he may be merciful to all.

33 O the depth of the riches and wisdom and knowledge of God! How unsearchable are his judgments and how inscrutable his ways!
³⁴ "For who has known the mind of the
        Lord?
    Or who has been his counselor?"
³⁵ "Or who has given a gift to him,
        to receive a gift in return?"
³⁶For from him and through him and to him

are all things. To him be the glory forever. Amen.

11.25–36. 25–32: How Israel will be saved. 25: *Part of Israel* implies the obedience of some Jews (11.5). **26:** The gentiles'* acceptance will prompt the full response of Israel. **26–27:** Isa 59.20–21; 27.9; Jer 31.33–34. **28:** *Enemies:* By refusing to submit to God's righteousness, Israel is at cross purposes with God (10.3–4). *Beloved* recalls the language of Hosea (9.25). **30:** Just as gentiles benefited from Israel's bad fortune, now Israel should benefit from the gentiles' good fortune. **32:** 3.9. **33–36: Concluding prayer: God's wisdom.** The *mystery** of God's workings (11.25) prompts this exuberant prayer acknowledging the depth of God's wisdom (1 Cor 2.7). **34:** Isa 40.13. **35:** See Job 41.11, Hebrew text (note *h*). **36:** 1 Cor 8.6; Col 1.16.

12 I appeal to you therefore, brothers and sisters,ᵃ by the mercies of God, to present your bodies as a living sacrifice, holy and acceptable to God, which is your spiritualᵈ worship. ²Do not be conformed to this world,ᵉ but be transformed by the renewing of your minds, so that you may discern what is the will of God—what is good and acceptable and perfect.ᶠ

3 For by the grace given to me I say to everyone among you not to think of yourself more highly than you ought to think, but to think with sober judgment, each according to the measure of faith that God has assigned. ⁴For as in one body we have many members, and not all the members have the same function, ⁵so we, who are many, are one body in Christ, and individually we are members one of another. ⁶We have gifts that differ according to the grace given to us: prophecy, in proportion to faith; ⁷ministry, in ministering; the teacher, in teaching; ⁸the exhorter, in exhortation; the giver, in generosity; the leader, in diligence; the compassionate, in cheerfulness.

12.1–15.13: Moral exhortation:* living by faith. 12.1–2: Renewed minds. 1: *Living sacrifice* recalls

ᵃ Gk *brothers*   ᵇ Gk lacks *of God*   ᶜ Other ancient authorities lack *now*   ᵈ Or *reasonable*   ᵉ Gk *age* ᶠ Or *what is the good and acceptable and perfect will of God*

Christ's example (3.25; 8.3). **2:** A changed outlook makes for clear moral vision (Col. 3.1–4). **3–8: Viewing ourselves properly. 3:** This caution against pride recalls earlier warnings (2.17; 3.27; 1 Cor 4.6). **4–7:** Now Paul suggests a remedy: An inflated self-image is offset by recognizing mutual need of each other's gifts (1 Cor 12.4–11).

9 Let love be genuine; hate what is evil, hold fast to what is good; 10love one another with mutual affection; outdo one another in showing honor. 11Do not lag in zeal, be ardent in spirit, serve the Lord.*a* 12Rejoice in hope, be patient in suffering, persevere in prayer. 13Contribute to the needs of the saints; extend hospitality to strangers.

14 Bless those who persecute you; bless and do not curse them. 15Rejoice with those who rejoice, weep with those who weep. 16Live in harmony with one another; do not be haughty, but associate with the lowly;*b* do not claim to be wiser than you are. 17Do not repay anyone evil for evil, but take thought for what is noble in the sight of all. 18If it is possible, so far as it depends on you, live peaceably with all. 19Beloved, never avenge yourselves, but leave room for the wrath of God;*c* for it is written, "Vengeance is mine, I will repay, says the Lord." 20No, "if your enemies are hungry, feed them; if they are thirsty, give them something to drink; for by doing this you will heap burning coals on their heads." 21Do not be overcome by evil, but overcome evil with good.

12.9–21. 9–13: Building community. These pieces of moral advice sketch a profile of sincere behavior tempered by genuine concern for others, both *saints* and *strangers* (1 Thess 4.9–12). **9:** Am 5.15. **12:** *Hope* and *suffering:* 5.1–5. **13:** Heb 13.2; 1 Pet 4.9. **14–21: Controlling our impulses.** This advice echoes Jewish morality and Jesus' teaching. **14:** Mt 5.44. **15:** Sir 7.34. **16:** Living *in harmony* is threatened by *haughty* attitudes; it ultimately occurs as a gift from God (15.5). **19:** Deut 32.35. **20:** Prov 25.21–22. **21:** Mt 5.39–41.

13 Let every person be subject to the governing authorities; for there is no authority except from God, and those authorities that exist have been instituted by God. 2Therefore whoever resists authority resists what God has appointed, and those who resist will incur judgment. 3For rulers are not a terror to good conduct, but to bad. Do you wish to have no fear of the authority? Then do what is good, and you will receive its approval; 4for it is God's servant for your good. But if you do what is wrong, you should be afraid, for the authority*d* does not bear the sword in vain! It is the servant of God to execute wrath on the wrongdoer. 5Therefore one must be subject, not only because of wrath but also because of conscience. 6For the same reason you also pay taxes, for the authorities are God's servants, busy with this very thing. 7Pay to all what is due them—taxes to whom taxes are due, revenue to whom revenue is due, respect to whom respect is due, honor to whom honor is due.

8 Owe no one anything, except to love one another; for the one who loves another has fulfilled the law. 9The commandments, "You shall not commit adultery; You shall not murder; You shall not steal; You shall not covet"; and any other commandment, are summed up in this word, "Love your neighbor as yourself." 10Love does no wrong to a neighbor; therefore, love is the fulfilling of the law.

11 Besides this, you know what time it is, how it is now the moment for you to wake from sleep. For salvation is nearer to us now than when we became believers; 12the night is far gone, the day is near. Let us then lay aside the works of darkness and put on the armor of light; 13let us live honorably as in the day, not in reveling and drunkenness, not in debauchery and licentiousness, not in quarreling and jealousy. 14Instead, put on the Lord Jesus Christ, and make no provision for the flesh, to gratify its desires.

13.1–14. 1–7: Duties to governing authorities. Paul's positive view of civil authority is paralleled in 1 Pet 2.13–17. **1–4:** In Jewish teaching, rulers ultimately derive their authority from God (Wis 6.1–3). **6–7:** *Taxes:* Mt 22.15–22. **8–10:** *Love's obligation.* **8:** Fol-

a Other ancient authorities read *serve the opportune time*
b Or *give yourselves to humble tasks*　　*c* Gk *the wrath*
d Gk *it*

lowing the Decalogue's commands expresses love (Gal 5.14). **9:** Deut 5.17–21; Ex 20.13–17. **9b:** Lev 19.18; Mt 22.34–40. **11–14: Being alert.** Such advice is usually given when the Lord's coming is expected soon. **11:** *Time:* 1 Cor 7.29; 1 Thess 5.6. **12:** In apocalyptic* thought, *darkness* and *light* define types of behavior (1 Thess 5.1–5; Eph 5.8–11). **13–14:** Preparation for the end requires moral living.

14 Welcome those who are weak in faith,*a* but not for the purpose of quarreling over opinions. ²Some believe in eating anything, while the weak eat only vegetables. ³Those who eat must not despise those who abstain, and those who abstain must not pass judgment on those who eat; for God has welcomed them. ⁴Who are you to pass judgment on servants of another? It is before their own lord that they stand or fall. And they will be upheld, for the Lord*b* is able to make them stand.

5 Some judge one day to be better than another, while others judge all days to be alike. Let all be fully convinced in their own minds. ⁶Those who observe the day, observe it in honor of the Lord. Also those who eat, eat in honor of the Lord, since they give thanks to God; while those who abstain, abstain in honor of the Lord and give thanks to God.

7 We do not live to ourselves, and we do not die to ourselves. ⁸If we live, we live to the Lord, and if we die, we die to the Lord; so then, whether we live or whether we die, we are the Lord's. ⁹For to this end Christ died and lived again, so that he might be Lord of both the dead and the living.

14.1–15.13: Dealing with differences. Here Paul offers instructions about what is required when people from different backgrounds with strongly held opinions try to live together as a community of faith (1 Cor 8–10). **1–6: What to eat and what holidays to observe. 1–2:** The *weak,* those with stricter views about what to eat, may be Jews or gentiles.* **2:** Those willing to eat *anything* reflect Paul's more open view about food laws (14.14; 1 Cor 8.8). **3:** God's acceptance of weak and strong requires mutual respect from both. **4:** *Their own lord* may be the principle they hold dear, or the way they understand what God requires. **5–6:** The *day* may be the sabbath or other Jewish holidays

gentiles did not observe (Gal 4.10; Col 2.16). For gentiles who did not observe the sabbath, *all days* were *alike.* Every day was a workday. **6:** Devotion to God can produce opposite religious practices. **7–9: Living for the Lord not for ourselves.** Being *the Lord's* makes living in isolation impossible. Christ's death and resurrection is a shared reality linking all Christians together, both *dead* and *living* (1 Cor 12.27).

10 Why do you pass judgment on your brother or sister?*c* Or you, why do you despise your brother or sister?*c* For we will all stand before the judgment seat of God.*d* ¹¹For it is written,

"As I live, says the Lord, every knee
shall bow to me,
and every tongue shall give praise to*e*
God."

¹²So then, each of us will be accountable to God.*f*

13 Let us therefore no longer pass judgment on one another, but resolve instead never to put a stumbling block or hindrance in the way of another.*g* ¹⁴I know and am persuaded in the Lord Jesus that nothing is unclean in itself; but it is unclean for anyone who thinks it unclean. ¹⁵If your brother or sister*c* is being injured by what you eat, you are no longer walking in love. Do not let what you eat cause the ruin of one for whom Christ died. ¹⁶So do not let your good be spoken of as evil. ¹⁷For the kingdom of God is not food and drink but righteousness and peace and joy in the Holy Spirit. ¹⁸The one who thus serves Christ is acceptable to God and has human approval. ¹⁹Let us then pursue what makes for peace and for mutual upbuilding. ²⁰Do not, for the sake of food, destroy the work of God. Everything is indeed clean, but it is wrong for you to make others fall by what you eat; ²¹it is good not to eat meat or drink wine or do anything that makes your brother or sister*c* stumble.*h* ²²The faith that you have, have as your own

a Or *conviction*   *b* Other ancient authorities read *for God*   *c* Gk *brother*   *d* Other ancient authorities read *of Christ*   *e* Or *confess*   *f* Other ancient authorities lack *to God*   *g* Gk *of a brother*   *h* Other ancient authorities add *or be upset or be weakened* conviction before God. Blessed are those who have no reason to condemn themselves because of what they approve. 23But those who have doubts are condemned if they eat, because they do not act from faith;[a] for whatever does not proceed from faith[a] is sin.[b]

14.10–23: Learning not to judge each other. 10: To judge others is to assume God's unique role (2 Cor 5.10). **11:** Isa 49.18; Jer 22.24; Ezek 5.11; Isa 45.23. **13:** This conclusion follows from vv. 11–12; see Mt 18.6–7. **14:** *In the Lord Jesus* may mean fidelity to Jesus' teaching (Mt 15.11; Acts 10.15). **15:** Paul echoes the advice he gives in 1 Cor 8.11–15. **17b:** These characterize life in the Spirit (ch. 8). **19:** *Peace* and *mutual upbuilding:* 1 Cor 14.12, 26. **20–22:** Paul consistently advises placing limits on personal liberty for the sake of others (1 Cor 8.9–13). **22–23:** Acting *from faith* requires clear convictions, free from lingering doubts and feelings of self-condemnation. A right act wrongly felt is wrong.

15 We who are strong ought to put up with the failings of the weak, and not to please ourselves. 2Each of us must please our neighbor for the good purpose of building up the neighbor. 3For Christ did not please himself; but, as it is written, "The insults of those who insult you have fallen on me." 4For whatever was written in former days was written for our instruction, so that by steadfastness and by the encouragement of the scriptures we might have hope. 5May the God of steadfastness and encouragement grant you to live in harmony with one another, in accordance with Christ Jesus, 6so that together you may with one voice glorify the God and Father of our Lord Jesus Christ.

7 Welcome one another, therefore, just as Christ has welcomed you, for the glory of God. 8For I tell you that Christ has become a servant of the circumcised on behalf of the truth of God in order that he might confirm the promises given to the patriarchs, 9and in order that the Gentiles might glorify God for his mercy. As it is written,

"Therefore I will confess[c] you among
    the Gentiles,
and sing praises to your name";

10and again he says,

"Rejoice, O Gentiles, with his people";

11and again,

"Praise the Lord, all you Gentiles,
    and let all the peoples praise him";

12and again Isaiah says,

"The root of Jesse shall come,
    the one who rises to rule
        the Gentiles;
    in him the Gentiles shall hope."

13May the God of hope fill you with all joy and peace in believing, so that you may abound in hope by the power of the Holy Spirit.

15.1–13. 1–6: Helping the weak. 1–2: The previous discussion is summarized well here. **3:** Ps 69.9. **4:** *Whatever was written in former days* refers to the previously quoted psalm, but applies to the Old Testament *scriptures* generally (1 Cor 10.11). **5:** The concluding prayer for harmony echoes earlier advice (12.16; Phil 2.2). **7–13: Concluding appeal. 7–8:** Christ's example influences Christian behavior (3.26; 2 Cor 8.9). **8:** *Servant of the circumcised* indicates Christ's service to Jews (Gal 4.4–5), whose *patriarchs* received the *promises* that gentiles* would receive God's blessing (4.13; 9.4). The following Old Testament quotations include gentiles in God's purpose. **9:** Ps 18.49; 2 Sam 22.50. **10:** Deut 32.43 (Hebrew text, see note a) **11:** Ps 117.1. **12:** Isa 11.10. **13:** Paul prays for the vision of 14.17 to be realized.

14 I myself feel confident about you, my brothers and sisters,[d] that you yourselves are full of goodness, filled with all knowledge, and able to instruct one another. 15Nevertheless on some points I have written to you rather boldly by way of reminder, because of the grace given me by God 16to be a minister of Christ Jesus to the Gentiles in the priestly service of the gospel of God, so that the offering of the Gentiles may be acceptable, sanctified by the Holy Spirit. 17In Christ Jesus, then, I have reason to boast of my work for God. 18For I will not venture to speak of anything except what Christ has accomplished[e] through me to win obedience from

a Or *conviction*   *b* Other authorities, some ancient, add here 16.25–27   *c* Or *thank*   *d* Gk *brothers*
e Gk *speak of those things that Christ has not accomplished*

the Gentiles, by word and deed, 19by the power of signs and wonders, by the power of the Spirit of God,*a* so that from Jerusalem and as far around as Illyricum I have fully proclaimed the good news*b* of Christ. 20Thus I make it my ambition to proclaim the good news,*b* not where Christ has already been named, so that I do not build on someone else's foundation, 21but as it is written,

"Those who have never been told of him shall see,
and those who have never heard of him shall understand."

22 This is the reason that I have so often been hindered from coming to you. 23But now, with no further place for me in these regions, I desire, as I have for many years, to come to you 24when I go to Spain. For I do hope to see you on my journey and to be sent on by you, once I have enjoyed your company for a little while. 25At present, however, I am going to Jerusalem in a ministry to the saints; 26for Macedonia and Achaia have been pleased to share their resources with the poor among the saints at Jerusalem. 27They were pleased to do this, and indeed they owe it to them; for if the Gentiles have come to share in their spiritual blessings, they ought also to be of service to them in material things. 28So, when I have completed this, and have delivered to them what has been collected,*c* I will set out by way of you to Spain; 29and I know that when I come to you, I will come in the fullness of the blessing*d* of Christ.

30 I appeal to you, brothers and sisters,*e* by our Lord Jesus Christ and by the love of the Spirit, to join me in earnest prayer to God on my behalf, 31that I may be rescued from the unbelievers in Judea, and that my ministry*f* to Jerusalem may be acceptable to the saints, 32so that by God's will I may come to you with joy and be refreshed in your company. 33The God of peace be with all of you.*g* Amen.

to his ministry as *priestly service* is unusual. **19:** *Signs and wonders* accompanied Paul's ministry (2 Cor 12.12). *Illyricum* was a Roman province across the Adriatic Sea from Italy. **21:** Isa 52.15. **22:** What *hindered* Paul is not known (1.13). **23:** *These regions* were probably the areas bordering the Aegean Sea. **24:** Hospitality would also include financial provision for his mission to *Spain* (see v. 28; 1 Cor 16.6). **25–26:** *Ministry to the saints* refers to the financial collection Paul had gathered for poor Christians in Jerusalem (1 Cor 16.1–4; 2 Cor 8–9). **27:** Paul applies the principle of reciprocity stated in Gal 6.6. **30–33: Paul's anxiety about the collection. 31:** *Unbelievers in Judea* are probably non-Christian Jews (1 Thess 2.15). Acts 21.17–36 relates Paul's arrival in Jerusalem and the controversy it causes among Jews, but omits the collection.

16 I commend to you our sister Phoebe, a deacon*h* of the church at Cenchreae, 2so that you may welcome her in the Lord as is fitting for the saints, and help her in whatever she may require from you, for she has been a benefactor of many and of myself as well.

3 Greet Prisca and Aquila, who work with me in Christ Jesus, 4and who risked their necks for my life, to whom not only I give thanks, but also all the churches of the Gentiles. 5Greet also the church in their house. Greet my beloved Epaenetus, who was the first convert*i* in Asia for Christ. 6Greet Mary, who has worked very hard among you. 7Greet Andronicus and Junia,*j* my relatives*k* who were in prison with me; they are prominent among the apostles, and they were in Christ before I was. 8Greet Ampliatus, my beloved in the Lord. 9Greet Urbanus, our co-worker in Christ, and my beloved Stachys. 10Greet Apelles, who is approved in Christ. Greet those who belong to the family of Aristobulus. 11Greet my relative*l* Herodion. Greet those in the Lord who belong to the family of Narcissus. 12Greet those workers

---

15.14–33: Paul's plans and anxieties. 14–29: Paul reflects on his own ministry. 14: Paul reaffirms his confidence in the Roman church (1.8; 1 Cor 1.5). **15–16:** *Grace given me* refers to Paul's call to be an apostle★ to the gentiles★ (1 Cor 15.10–11). Referring

a Other ancient authorities read *of the Spirit* or *of the Holy Spirit*   *b* Or *gospel*   *c* Gk *have sealed to them this fruit*   *d* Other ancient authorities add *of the gospel*   *e* Gk *brothers*   *f* Other ancient authorities read *my bringing of a gift*   *g* One ancient authority adds 16.25–27 here   *h* Or *minister*   *i* Gk *first fruits*   *j* Or *Junias*; other ancient authorities read *Julia*   *k* Or *compatriots*   *l* Or *compatriot* in the Lord, Tryphaena and Tryphosa. Greet the beloved Persis, who has worked hard in the Lord. 13Greet Rufus, chosen in the Lord; and greet his mother—a mother to me also. 14Greet Asyncritus, Phlegon, Hermes, Patrobas, Hermas, and the brothers and sisters*a* who are with them. 15Greet Philologus, Julia, Nereus and his sister, and Olympas, and all the saints who are with them. 16Greet one another with a holy kiss. All the churches of Christ greet you.

16.1–23: Concluding personal greetings and exhortations.★ **1–2: Phoebe commended 1:** *Deacon* (Gk., "diakonos"), or minister (see note *h* on p. 1910), is the same term used of Christ (15.8) and Paul (1 Cor 3.5). *Cenchreae* was a suburb of Corinth (Acts 18.18). **3–16: Paul sends his greetings. 3–5:** *Priscilla and Aquila:* Acts 18.2–3; 1 Cor 16.19. **5:** *Asia:* western Asia Minor. **7:** The feminine form *Junia* is preferred over the masculine form *Junias* (see note *j* on p. 1910). She is the only woman *among the apostles*★ in the New Testament. *My relatives* probably means fellow Jews. **8–16:** All the names listed are mentioned only here in the New Testament. Another *Rufus* is mentioned in Mk 15.21. The number of people Paul knows by name in the Roman church is remarkable. **16:** The *holy kiss* possibly originated in early Christian circles (1 Cor 16.20; 2 Cor 13.12). The *churches of Christ* in Achaia, where Paul was writing, are meant.

17 I urge you, brothers and sisters,*a* to keep an eye on those who cause dissensions and offenses, in opposition to the teaching that you have learned; avoid them. 18For such people do not serve our Lord Christ, but their own appetites,*b* and by smooth talk and flattery they deceive the hearts of the simple-minded. 19For while your obedience is known to all, so that I rejoice over you, I want you to be wise in what is good and guileless in what is evil. 20The God of peace will shortly crush Satan under your feet. The grace of our Lord Jesus Christ be with you.*c*

21 Timothy, my co-worker, greets you; so do Lucius and Jason and Sosipater, my relatives.*d*

22 I Tertius, the writer of this letter, greet you in the Lord.*e*

23 Gaius, who is host to me and to the whole church, greets you. Erastus, the city treasurer, and our brother Quartus, greet you.*f*

25 Now to God*g* who is able to strengthen you according to my gospel and the proclamation of Jesus Christ, according to the revelation of the mystery that was kept secret for long ages 26but is now disclosed, and through the prophetic writings is made known to all the Gentiles, according to the command of the eternal God, to bring about the obedience of faith— 27to the only wise God, through Jesus Christ, to whom*h* be the glory forever! Amen.*i*

16.17–27. 17–20: Warnings against troublemakers. 18: *Their own appetites,* literally "their own belly," are their own desires (Phil 3.19). *Smooth talk and flattery:* False teachers often have a way with words (Eph 5.6; Col 2.4). **19:** Paul's advice echoes Jesus' teaching (Mt 10.16). **20:** Paul expects God's final triumph soon (1 Cor 15.24). **21–23: Paul's co-workers send greetings. 21:** *Timothy* was Paul's long-time co-worker (Acts 16.1; 1 Cor 16.10–11). **22:** *Tertius* was Paul's secretary. **23:** Most likely, this is the *Gaius* of Corinth whom Paul baptized (1 Cor 1.14). **25–27: Benediction.** How the letter originally ended is unclear. For the different possibilities, see notes *g, h,* and *i.* **25–26:** The *mystery*★ . . . *kept secret for long ages* is God's vision of a universal community composed of both Jews and gentiles★ who live in obedient *faith* (Eph 3.1–6).

---

a Gk *brothers*   *b* Gk *their own belly*   *c* Other ancient authorities lack this sentence   *d* Or *compatriots*   *e* Or *I Tertius, writing this letter in the Lord, greet you*   *f* Other ancient authorities add verse 24, *The grace of our Lord Jesus Christ be with all of you. Amen.*   *g* Gk *the one*   *h* Other ancient authorities lack *to whom.* The verse then reads, *to the only wise God be the glory through Jesus Christ forever. Amen.*   *i* Other ancient authorities lack 16.25–27 or include it after 14.23 or 15.33; others put verse 24 after verse 27

THE FIRST LETTER OF PAUL TO
THE CORINTHIANS

Introduction

In 1 Corinthians Paul combines instruction with exhortation.* The church at Corinth had been started by Paul only a few years earlier, and much of the letter deals with questions that arose within the congregation as it sought to live out the demands of the gospel within an urban setting. But the letter does more than provide additional information from their founding apostle.* It also encourages the church to be more unified in its internal dealings and to put its leaders in proper perspective. They are asked to recognize Paul's unique authority and his right to instruct them about their faith, but also to see him and other figures, such as Apollos and Peter, as co-workers in a larger enterprise, in which God is the main player. First Corinthians may be seen as a pastoral letter addressing very practical questions of congregational life.

First Corinthians was written in the early 50s during Paul's extended period of mission and ministry in the Aegean region. Paul probably wrote the letter from Ephesus, a major city across the Aegean from Corinth. The letter in its present form may consist of shorter letters or notes sent on different occasions. Prior to the writing of the letter, Paul has received reports of friction among the members (1.11–12). He also knows of incidents that require his attention (5.1–2). He has received at least one written communication from the Corinthians asking for instruction and clarification about a number of points (7.1), and he has already written them at least once (5.9). Thus when we read 1 Corinthians we are joining a conversation that has been going on for some time.

READING GUIDE

The letter exhibits the standard features of a Pauline letter: opening greeting (1.1–3), thanksgiving (1.4–9), body of the letter (1.10–16.12), and benediction (16.13). Structurally, it divides into three parts. In the first section (1.10–4.21) Paul warns against divisions and quarrels, and he spells out what it means to be a "church of God" (1.2). The second section (chs. 5–6) deals with a case of serious sexual impropriety and internal legal disputes. The third section (chs. 7–16) takes up the Corinthians' questions. The repetition of "Now concerning . . . " (7.1; 8.1; 12.1; 16.1) suggests that Paul is taking up their concerns one by one and making a serious effort to provide thoughtful responses that would suffice until his next visit (11.34).

1 Paul, called to be an apostle of Christ Jesus by the will of God, and our brother Sosthenes,

2 To the church of God that is in Corinth, to those who are sanctified in Christ Jesus, called to be saints, together with all those who in every place call on the name of our Lord Jesus Christ, both their Lord*a* and ours:

3 Grace to you and peace from God our Father and the Lord Jesus Christ.

4 I give thanks to my*b* God always for you because of the grace of God that has been given you in Christ Jesus, 5for in every way you have been enriched in him, in speech and knowledge of every kind— 6just as the testimony of*c* Christ has been strengthened among you— 7so that you are not lacking in any spiritual gift as you wait for the revealing of our Lord Jesus Christ. 8He will also strengthen you to the end, so that you may be blameless on the day of our Lord Jesus Christ. 9God is faithful; by him you were called into the fellowship of his Son, Jesus Christ our Lord.

1.1–9. 1–3: Greeting. This opening greeting reflects the basic structure of greetings used in ancient letters. The writers of the letter (*Paul* and *Sosthenes*) address *the church of God that is in Corinth* and wish them *grace* and *peace,* standard forms of greeting among gentiles* and Jews. **4–9: Prayer of thanksgiving.** Paul's letters usually begin with an extended prayer (see Rom 1.8–15; Phil 1.3–11). In a reassuring tone, he introduces themes developed later in the letter. All, not just a few, have enough *speech and knowledge* to be confident of their faith (compare 8.1–3). Nor do only an elite few experience *spiritual gifts* (chs. 12–14). Everyone who has been strengthened by the *testimony of Christ,* the preaching about Christ, continues to be strengthened by God. The prayer looks forward to *the day of our Lord Jesus Christ,* when Christ would return (ch. 15; 16.22).

10 Now I appeal to you, brothers and sisters,*d* by the name of our Lord Jesus Christ, that all of you be in agreement and that there be no divisions among you, but that you be united in the same mind and the same purpose. 11For it has been reported to me by Chloe's people that there are quarrels among you, my brothers and sisters.*e* 12What I mean is that each of you says, "I belong to Paul," or "I belong to Apollos," or "I belong to Cephas," or "I belong to Christ." 13Has Christ been divided? Was Paul crucified for you? Or were you baptized in the name of Paul? 14I thank God*f* that I baptized none of you except Crispus and Gaius, 15so that no one can say that you were baptized in my name. 16(I did baptize also the household of Stephanas; beyond that, I do not know whether I baptized anyone else.) 17For Christ did not send me to baptize but to proclaim the gospel, and not with eloquent wisdom, so that the cross of Christ might not be emptied of its power.

1.10–17: Appeal for unity. Full *divisions* have not yet occurred, but *quarrels* have. *Chloe's people,* members of her household, are mentioned nowhere else. To *belong to* someone means looking only to that person for spiritual guidance. *Apollos* ministered to the Corinthian church after Paul's founding visit (3.5–6; Acts 18.24–19.1) and is now with Paul as he writes this letter (16.12). Whether *Cephas* (Peter) had actually been in Corinth or was only known by reputation is not clear. *Crispus* was a prominent synagogue* official (Acts 18.8), and *Gaius* hosted Paul and the Corinthian house church (Rom 16.23). The *household of Stephanas* later receives high praise from Paul for devoted service to the church (16.15–18).

18 For the message about the cross is foolishness to those who are perishing, but to us who are being saved it is the power of God. 19For it is written,

"I will destroy the wisdom of the wise,
    and the discernment of the discerning
        I will thwart."

20Where is the one who is wise? Where is the scribe? Where is the debater of this age? Has not God made foolish the wisdom of the world? 21For since, in the wisdom of God, the world did not know God through wisdom, God decided, through the foolishness of our proclamation, to save those

---

a Gk *theirs*   *b* Other ancient authorities lack *my*
c Or *to*   *d* Gk *brothers*   *e* Gk *my brothers*
f Other ancient authorities read *I am thankful*

who believe. 22For Jews demand signs and Greeks desire wisdom, 23but we proclaim Christ crucified, a stumbling block to Jews and foolishness to Gentiles, 24but to those who are the called, both Jews and Greeks, Christ the power of God and the wisdom of God. 25For God's foolishness is wiser than human wisdom, and God's weakness is stronger than human strength.

26 Consider your own call, brothers and sisters:*a* not many of you were wise by human standards,*b* not many were powerful, not many were of noble birth. 27But God chose what is foolish in the world to shame the wise; God chose what is weak in the world to shame the strong; 28God chose what is low and despised in the world, things that are not, to reduce to nothing things that are, 29so that no one*c* might boast in the presence of God. 30He is the source of your life in Christ Jesus, who became for us wisdom from God, and righteousness and sanctification and redemption, 31in order that, as it is written, "Let the one who boasts, boast in*d* the Lord."

1.18–31. 18–25: The cross, God's folly. Seen one way, the story of Christ's death, *the message about the cross,* seems foolish. Crucifixion was a shameful way for anyone to die, especially someone embodying God's hopes. *Jews* and *Greeks* represent two ways of knowing or relating to God—demanding *signs* and desiring *wisdom.* The one stresses dramatic displays of power by God, the other gradual, intuitive learning about God. The cross, however, locates God somewhere else, at the intersection of human *foolishness* and *weakness.* **26–31: The Corinthians themselves prove God's power and wisdom.** The Corinthians' own *call* shows God's capacity for upsetting human expectations. To *boast in the presence of God* suggests arrogant behavior (compare 4.6; 5.2). To *boast in the Lord* is to recognize God as the source of *life in Christ Jesus* (v. 31; compare Jer. 9.24).

2 When I came to you, brothers and sisters,*a* I did not come proclaiming the mystery*e* of God to you in lofty words or wisdom. 2For I decided to know nothing among you except Jesus Christ, and him crucified. 3And I came to you in weakness and in fear and in much trembling. 4My speech and my

proclamation were not with plausible words of wisdom,*f* but with a demonstration of the Spirit and of power, 5so that your faith might rest not on human wisdom but on the power of God.

6 Yet among the mature we do speak wisdom, though it is not a wisdom of this age or of the rulers of this age, who are doomed to perish. 7But we speak God's wisdom, secret and hidden, which God decreed before the ages for our glory. 8None of the rulers of this age understood this; for if they had, they would not have crucified the Lord of glory. 9But, as it is written,

"What no eye has seen, nor ear heard,
    nor the human heart conceived,
  what God has prepared for those who
        love him"—

10these things God has revealed to us through the Spirit; for the Spirit searches everything, even the depths of God. 11For what human being knows what is truly human except the human spirit that is within? So also no one comprehends what is truly God's except the Spirit of God. 12Now we have received not the spirit of the world, but the Spirit that is from God, so that we may understand the gifts bestowed on us by God. 13And we speak of these things in words not taught by human wisdom but taught by the Spirit, interpreting spiritual things to those who are spiritual.*g*

14 Those who are unspiritual*h* do not receive the gifts of God's Spirit, for they are foolishness to them, and they are unable to understand them because they are spiritually discerned. 15Those who are spiritual discern all things, and they are themselves subject to no one else's scrutiny.

16 "For who has known the mind
        of the Lord
    so as to instruct him?"
But we have the mind of Christ.

a Gk brothers   *b* Gk according to the flesh   *c* Gk no flesh   *d* Or of   *e* Other ancient authorities read testimony   *f* Other ancient authorities read the persuasiveness of wisdom   *g* Or interpreting spiritual things in spiritual language, or comparing spiritual things with spiritual   *h* Or natural

2.1–16. 1–5: Paul's preaching illustrates God's power. Here Paul recalls his founding visit (Acts 18.1–18). *Mystery* of God* is not a puzzle but something hidden that God can reveal (compare Rom 16.25–26). The alternate reading, *testimony of God,* suggests that God bears witness through Paul's preaching. *Jesus Christ, and him crucified* includes both Paul's preaching and manner of life (compare Gal 2.19–20). *Demonstration of the Spirit and of power:* Paul saw himself as a channel for the Holy Spirit exerting power (1 Thess 1.5; 2.13). **6–16: Wisdom for the mature.** Now Paul speaks of wisdom positively. *This age* and *the rulers of this age* refer to Paul's world and those who control it, probably heavenly forces rather than earthly rulers. **9:** *As it is written:* Paul mixes several Old Testament passages (Isa. 64.4; 52.15; 65.16). **14:** The *unspiritual* ("psychikos"), or "natural," person is a two-dimensional figure living in a three-dimensional world. **15:** The *spiritual* ("pneumatikos") person is guided by God's Spirit ("pnemua"). **16:** Isa 40.13. The *mind of Christ,* guided by God's Spirit, seeks *what is truly God's* (v. 11; Phil. 2.5–11).

3 And so, brothers and sisters,[a] I could not speak to you as spiritual people, but rather as people of the flesh, as infants in Christ. ²I fed you with milk, not solid food, for you were not ready for solid food. Even now you are still not ready, ³for you are still of the flesh. For as long as there is jealousy and quarreling among you, are you not of the flesh, and behaving according to human inclinations? ⁴For when one says, "I belong to Paul," and another, "I belong to Apollos," are you not merely human?

5 What then is Apollos? What is Paul? Servants through whom you came to believe, as the Lord assigned to each. ⁶I planted, Apollos watered, but God gave the growth. ⁷So neither the one who plants nor the one who waters is anything, but only God who gives the growth. ⁸The one who plants and the one who waters have a common purpose, and each will receive wages according to the labor of each. ⁹For we are God's servants, working together; you are God's field, God's building.

10 According to the grace of God given to me, like a skilled master builder I laid a foundation, and someone else is building on it.

Each builder must choose with care how to build on it. ¹¹For no one can lay any foundation other than the one that has been laid; that foundation is Jesus Christ. ¹²Now if anyone builds on the foundation with gold, silver, precious stones, wood, hay, straw— ¹³the work of each builder will become visible, for the Day will disclose it, because it will be revealed with fire, and the fire will test what sort of work each has done. ¹⁴If what has been built on the foundation survives, the builder will receive a reward. ¹⁵If the work is burned up, the builder will suffer loss; the builder will be saved, but only as through fire.

16 Do you not know that you are God's temple and that God's Spirit dwells in you?[b] ¹⁷If anyone destroys God's temple, God will destroy that person. For God's temple is holy, and you are that temple.

18 Do not deceive yourselves. If you think that you are wise in this age, you should become fools so that you may become wise. ¹⁹For the wisdom of this world is foolishness with God. For it is written,

"He catches the wise in their
    craftiness,"
²⁰and again,
"The Lord knows the thoughts of the
    wise,
    that they are futile."
²¹So let no one boast about human leaders. For all things are yours, ²²whether Paul or Apollos or Cephas or the world or life or death or the present or the future—all belong to you, ²³and you belong to Christ, and Christ belongs to God.

3.1–23. 1–9: Rightly viewing God's servants. 1: Like infants, *people of the flesh* think only of their own needs and self-interests. **2:** Heb 5.12–14. **3:** *Jealousy and quarreling* are among the desires of the flesh (Gal 5.20). **5–9:** The emphasis throughout is on God's initiative. **10–17: Paul as master builder. 10:** Paul experienced the *grace of God* when God called him (15.10–11; Rom 15.15–16). Starting churches was like laying the foundation of a building (Rom 15.20). **11:** Eph 2.19–22; Mt 16.18. **13:** The *Day* of judgment is

a Gk *brothers*   b In verses 16 and 17 the Greek word for *you* is plural often envisioned as destruction of the world by fire (Mal 4.1; 2 Thess 1.8). **16–17:** The building metaphor* now becomes specific: *God's temple. You* refers to the congregation. In 6.19–20 the individual's body is a temple. **18–23: Becoming truly wise. 19:** Job 5.12. **20:** Ps 94.11. **21:** Rather than following *human leaders* who claim to be wise, belonging *to Christ* gives them all they need.

4 Think of us in this way, as servants of Christ and stewards of God's mysteries. ²Moreover, it is required of stewards that they be found trustworthy. ³But with me it is a very small thing that I should be judged by you or by any human court. I do not even judge myself. ⁴I am not aware of anything against myself, but I am not thereby acquitted. It is the Lord who judges me. ⁵Therefore do not pronounce judgment before the time, before the Lord comes, who will bring to light the things now hidden in darkness and will disclose the purposes of the heart. Then each one will receive commendation from God.

6 I have applied all this to Apollos and myself for your benefit, brothers and sisters,ᵃ so that you may learn through us the meaning of the saying, "Nothing beyond what is written," so that none of you will be puffed up in favor of one against another. ⁷For who sees anything different in you?ᵇ What do you have that you did not receive? And if you received it, why do you boast as if it were not a gift?

8 Already you have all you want! Already you have become rich! Quite apart from us you have become kings! Indeed, I wish that you had become kings, so that we might be kings with you! ⁹For I think that God has exhibited us apostles as last of all, as though sentenced to death, because we have become a spectacle to the world, to angels and to mortals. ¹⁰We are fools for the sake of Christ, but you are wise in Christ. We are weak, but you are strong. You are held in honor, but we in disrepute. ¹¹To the present hour we are hungry and thirsty, we are poorly clothed and beaten and homeless, ¹²and we grow weary from the work of our own hands. When reviled, we bless; when persecuted, we endure; ¹³when slandered, we speak

kindly. We have become like the rubbish of the world, the dregs of all things, to this very day.

14 I am not writing this to make you ashamed, but to admonish you as my beloved children. ¹⁵For though you might have ten thousand guardians in Christ, you do not have many fathers. Indeed, in Christ Jesus I became your father through the gospel. ¹⁶I appeal to you, then, be imitators of me. ¹⁷For this reason I sentᵉ you Timothy, who is my beloved and faithful child in the Lord, to remind you of my ways in Christ Jesus, as I teach them everywhere in every church. ¹⁸But some of you, thinking that I am not coming to you, have become arrogant. ¹⁹But I will come to you soon, if the Lord wills, and I will find out not the talk of these arrogant people but their power. ²⁰For the kingdom of God depends not on talk but on power. ²¹What would you prefer? Am I to come to you with a stick, or with love in a spirit of gentleness?

4.1–21. 1–7: How to think of God's ministers. 1: More important than their personal characteristics is how ministers relate to *Christ* and *God. Servants* and *stewards* are roles defined by superiors. **3:** Some were sitting in judgment on Paul (9.3). **4:** *The Lord* establishes the true perspective for judging behavior (6.13). **5:** Paul expects the Lord's coming soon (1.7; 7.29, 31). Judgment is a time of unveiling secrets (Rom 2.16; see Lk 8.17). **6:** The meaning of the saying is uncertain; it may refer to 1.31. *Puffed up* suggests an inflated self-image that leads to boasting (3.21). **7:** The alternate rendering (note *b*) makes more sense. **8–13: The illusion of having already arrived. 8:** This ironic language applies to the "spiritual people" (3.1) who claim superior wisdom (6.5). **9–10:** *Apostles** are like prisoners of war, last in the victory parade, a *spectacle* to everyone. **11–12:** The missionary lives a vagabond's existence. **14–21: Paul appeals to his children. 14–15:** Starting churches was like having children (Gal 4.19; 1 Thess 2.11). **16:** As their father, Paul expected the church to imitate his behavior (11.1; Phil 3.17). **17:** *Timothy:* The alternate rendering *am sending* (note *c*) is preferred, since Timothy is apparently still

a Gk *brothers*　　b Or *Who makes you different from another?*　　c Or *am sending* with Paul (16.10–11). *My ways in Jesus Christ* are what Paul taught and how he behaved. **18–21:** *Arrogant behavior* is a root problem in the church (5.2; 13.4).

5 It is actually reported that there is sexual immorality among you, and of a kind that is not found even among pagans; for a man is living with his father's wife. ²And you are arrogant! Should you not rather have mourned, so that he who has done this would have been removed from among you?

3 For though absent in body, I am present in spirit; and as if present I have already pronounced judgment ⁴in the name of the Lord Jesus on the man who has done such a thing.ᵃ When you are assembled, and my spirit is present with the power of our Lord Jesus, ⁵you are to hand this man over to Satan for the destruction of the flesh, so that his spirit may be saved in the day of the Lord.ᵇ

6 Your boasting is not a good thing. Do you not know that a little yeast leavens the whole batch of dough? ⁷Clean out the old yeast so that you may be a new batch, as you really are unleavened. For our paschal lamb, Christ, has been sacrificed. ⁸Therefore, let us celebrate the festival, not with the old yeast, the yeast of malice and evil, but with the unleavened bread of sincerity and truth.

9 I wrote to you in my letter not to associate with sexually immoral persons— ¹⁰not at all meaning the immoral of this world, or the greedy and robbers, or idolaters, since you would then need to go out of the world. ¹¹But now I am writing to you not to associate with anyone who bears the name of brother or sisterᶜ who is sexually immoral or greedy, or is an idolater, reviler, drunkard, or robber. Do not even eat with such a one. ¹²For what have I to do with judging those outside? Is it not those who are inside that you are to judge? ¹³God will judge those outside. "Drive out the wicked person from among you."

dicate a formal procedure for disciplining wayward members (Mt 18.20). **4:** The alternate translation (note *a*) makes the offense even more serious. **5:** *Hand over to Satan:* Paul thinks *Satan* is still an active force (Rom 16.20). **6–7:** Removing leaven in preparation for Passover* provides the background for Paul's remarks here (Ex 12.14–20). Christ's death is seen as the lamb sacrificed at Passover (Ex 12.21–27; Rom 3.25). **8:** *Celebrate the festival:* The image of Passover observance is extended to Christian worship and practice. **9–13: Relating to immoral Christians. 9:** This previous letter is lost, unless it is preserved in 2 Cor 6.14–7.1. **11:** Refusing to *eat* with someone had great symbolic significance (Mt 9.10–13; Acts 11.3). **13:** Deut 17.7.

6 When any of you has a grievance against another, do you dare to take it to court before the unrighteous, instead of taking it before the saints? ²Do you not know that the saints will judge the world? And if the world is to be judged by you, are you incompetent to try trivial cases? ³Do you not know that we are to judge angels—to say nothing of ordinary matters? ⁴If you have ordinary cases, then, do you appoint as judges those who have no standing in the church? ⁵I say this to your shame. Can it be that there is no one among you wise enough to decide between one believerᶜ and another, ⁶but a believerᶜ goes to court against a believerᶜ—and before unbelievers at that?

7 In fact, to have lawsuits at all with one another is already a defeat for you. Why not rather be wronged? Why not rather be defrauded? ⁸But you yourselves wrong and defraud—and believersᵈ at that.

9 Do you not know that wrongdoers will not inherit the kingdom of God? Do not be deceived! Fornicators, idolaters, adulterers, male prostitutes, sodomites, ¹⁰thieves, the greedy, drunkards, revilers, robbers—none of these will inherit the kingdom of God. ¹¹And this is what some of you used to be. But you were washed, you were sanctified, you were justified in the name of the Lord Jesus Christ and in the Spirit of our God.

12 "All things are lawful for me," but not

5.1–13. 1–8: A case of sexual immorality. 1: *Sexual immorality* ("porneia") is a general term including a variety of sexual sins (6.13, 18). The Old Testament forbade sexual relations between son and stepmother (Lev 18.8). **3–5:** The language of these verses may in-

a Or *on the man who has done such a thing in the name of the Lord Jesus*　　b Other ancient authorities add *Jesus*　　c Gk *brother*　　d Gk *brothers* all things are beneficial. "All things are lawful for me," but I will not be dominated by anything. [13]"Food is meant for the stomach and the stomach for food,"[a] and God will destroy both one and the other. The body is meant not for fornication but for the Lord, and the Lord for the body. [14]And God raised the Lord and will also raise us by his power. [15]Do you not know that your bodies are members of Christ? Should I therefore take the members of Christ and make them members of a prostitute? Never! [16]Do you not know that whoever is united to a prostitute becomes one body with her? For it is said, "The two shall be one flesh." [17]But anyone united to the Lord becomes one spirit with him. [18]Shun fornication! Every sin that a person commits is outside the body; but the fornicator sins against the body itself. [19]Or do you not know that your body is a temple[b] of the Holy Spirit within you, which you have from God, and that you are not your own? [20]For you were bought with a price; therefore glorify God in your body.

6.1–20. 1–11: Dealing with internal disputes. 1: The *grievance* is not specified, but being *defrauded* suggests *lawsuits* involving money, perhaps rents or loans. **2:** In 5.12, *saints* judge each other. This probably refers to future judgment, when saints will *judge angels* (2 Pet 2.4). **5:** The question is sarcastic (4.8–10). **9–10:** Sins of sex and greed are prominent here, since chs. 5–6 address them (Rom 1.29–31; Gal 5.19–21). **11:** *Washed* (Titus 3.5), *sanctified* (2 Thess 2.13), and *justified* (Rom 3.24) are different ways of referring to their conversion. **12–20: Avoiding sexual sins. 12–13:** The slogans in quotation marks express the views of the "spiritual people" (3.1) who emphasize their freedom and independence. *Fornication* ("porneia," vv. 13, 18; 5.1) is sexual immorality of any kind. **14:** God's action in Christ governs Christian conduct (Rom 14.7–9). **15–16:** *Prostitute* ("porne") is a woman who practices sexual immorality as a profession. **16:** Gen 2.24. **19–20:** The individual's *body* is in view (compare 3.16–17). *Temple* ("naos") may be the Jerusalem Temple* (Mt 26.61) or a pagan shrine (Acts 17.24). **20:** *Bought with a price:* Christ purchased their freedom from slavery (7.23; Rom 6.17).

---

7 Now concerning the matters about which you wrote: "It is well for a man not to touch a woman." [2]But because of cases of sexual immorality, each man should have his own wife and each woman her own husband. [3]The husband should give to his wife her conjugal rights, and likewise the wife to her husband. [4]For the wife does not have authority over her own body, but the husband does; likewise the husband does not have authority over his own body, but the wife does. [5]Do not deprive one another except perhaps by agreement for a set time, to devote yourselves to prayer, and then come together again, so that Satan may not tempt you because of your lack of self-control. [6]This I say by way of concession, not of command. [7]I wish that all were as I myself am. But each has a particular gift from God, one having one kind and another a different kind.

8 To the unmarried and the widows I say that it is well for them to remain unmarried as I am. [9]But if they are not practicing self-control, they should marry. For it is better to marry than to be aflame with passion.

10 To the married I give this command—not I but the Lord—that the wife should not separate from her husband [11](but if she does separate, let her remain unmarried or else be reconciled to her husband), and that the husband should not divorce his wife.

12 To the rest I say—I and not the Lord—that if any believer[c] has a wife who is an unbeliever, and she consents to live with him, he should not divorce her. [13]And if any woman has a husband who is an unbeliever, and he consents to live with her, she should not divorce him. [14]For the unbelieving husband is made holy through his wife, and the unbelieving wife is made holy through her husband. Otherwise, your children would be unclean, but as it is, they are holy. [15]But if the unbelieving partner separates, let it be so; in such a case the brother or sister is not bound. It is to peace that God has called you.[d] [16]Wife, for all you know, you might save your husband. Husband, for all you know, you might save your wife.

---

a The quotation may extend to the word *other*
b Or *sanctuary*   c Gk *brother*   d Other ancient authorities read *us*

7.1–40: Questions about marriage. 1–7: Responsibilities within marriage. 1: Again, the quotation comes from the Corinthians. They probably asked, "Should married Christian couples stop having sexual intercourse?" **3:** *Conjugal rights:* Spouses should fulfill each other's sexual needs. **4:** Mutual ownership of each other's body is unusual. **5–6:** *Command:* Paul cannot quote the Old Testament or Jesus on the matter. **7:** *As I myself am:* Paul is unmarried (7.8). **8–9: Advice to the unmarried and widows.** *Self-control:* If they cannot control their sexual desires, they should marry. **10–11: Advice to the married.** *Command:* Jesus spoke directly to this question (Mk 10.11–12). *Separate* and *divorce* refer to the same action, not two stages of a divorce proceeding. **12–16: Advice to those with non-Christian spouses. 12:** *Not the Lord:* Jesus nowhere addressed this question. **12–13:** In view is a married couple where one spouse becomes a Christian. **14:** *Made holy:* The moral influence of the Christian spouse extends to the *unbelieving* spouse, thereby ensuring the spiritual welfare of the children. **15–16:** Compared with Jesus (Mt 19.3–9; Mk 10.10–12), Paul broadens the basis for divorce. **16:** The Greek is not as clear as the NRSV. It can be read *you might not save,* which would support his advice in v. 15.

17 However that may be, let each of you lead the life that the Lord has assigned, to which God called you. This is my rule in all the churches. [18]Was anyone at the time of his call already circumcised? Let him not seek to remove the marks of circumcision. Was anyone at the time of his call uncircumcised? Let him not seek circumcision. [19]Circumcision is nothing, and uncircumcision is nothing; but obeying the commandments of God is everything. [20]Let each of you remain in the condition in which you were called.

21 Were you a slave when called? Do not be concerned about it. Even if you can gain your freedom, make use of your present condition now more than ever.[a] [22]For whoever was called in the Lord as a slave is a freed person belonging to the Lord, just as whoever was free when called is a slave of Christ. [23]You were bought with a price; do not become slaves of human masters. [24]In whatever condition you were called, brothers and sisters,[b] there remain with God.

25 Now concerning virgins, I have no command of the Lord, but I give my opinion as one who by the Lord's mercy is trustworthy. [26]I think that, in view of the impending[c] crisis, it is well for you to remain as you are. [27]Are you bound to a wife? Do not seek to be free. Are you free from a wife? Do not seek a wife. [28]But if you marry, you do not sin, and if a virgin marries, she does not sin. Yet those who marry will experience distress in this life,[d] and I would spare you that. [29]I mean, brothers and sisters,[b] the appointed time has grown short; from now on, let even those who have wives be as though they had none, [30]and those who mourn as though they were not mourning, and those who rejoice as though they were not rejoicing, and those who buy as though they had no possessions, [31]and those who deal with the world as though they had no dealings with it. For the present form of this world is passing away.

7.17–31. 17–24: Paul's principle: remain as you are. Vv. 17, 20, and 24 state the principle informing Paul's advice in ch. 7. **17–20:** *Circumcision** signified being Jewish. *Remove the marks:* Some Jewish males underwent a surgical procedure to become *uncircumcised* (1 Macc 1.15). **19:** Paul's experience of Christ radically changed his view (Gal 5.6). **21–24:** V. 21 is ambiguous in Greek. The alternate rendering (note *a*) is possible, but the NRSV rendering is more consistent with his overall advice. **22:** Conversion to Christ redefines loyalties. **23:** *Bought with a price:* See comment on 6.20. **25–31: Advice to the unmarried. 25:** *Virgins* are probably young, unmarried women. *No command:* Paul cannot quote Jesus on the matter. *Trustworthy:* 4.2. **26–28:** *Impending crisis,* possibly *present crisis* (note *c*), probably refers to the soon expected return of the Lord (vv. 29, 31), which would be preceded by social and cosmic upheaval (Mk 13.4–8). **29–31:** Expecting the end soon created a sense of urgency that changed all relationships—domestic, personal, and economic. A world *passing away* does not make demands like a world thought to last forever.

32 I want you to be free from anxieties. The unmarried man is anxious about the affairs of the Lord, how to please the Lord; [33]but the married man is anxious about the

a Or *avail yourself of the opportunity*   *b* Gk *brothers*
c Or *present*   *d* Gk *in the flesh*

affairs of the world, how to please his wife, ³⁴and his interests are divided. And the unmarried woman and the virgin are anxious about the affairs of the Lord, so that they may be holy in body and spirit; but the married woman is anxious about the affairs of the world, how to please her husband. ³⁵I say this for your own benefit, not to put any restraint upon you, but to promote good order and unhindered devotion to the Lord.

36 If anyone thinks that he is not behaving properly toward his fiancée,ᵃ if his passions are strong, and so it has to be, let him marry as he wishes; it is no sin. Let them marry. ³⁷But if someone stands firm in his resolve, being under no necessity but having his own desire under control, and has determined in his own mind to keep her as his fiancée,ᵃ he will do well. ³⁸So then, he who marries his fiancéeᵃ does well; and he who refrains from marriage will do better.

39 A wife is bound as long as her husband lives. But if the husband dies,ᵇ she is free to marry anyone she wishes, only in the Lord. ⁴⁰But in my judgment she is more blessed if she remains as she is. And I think that I too have the Spirit of God.

7.32–40. 32–35: **Being free from anxiety.** Paul explains the basis for his advice in vv. 25–31. Marriage makes practical demands not directly concerned with *the affairs of the Lord.* Single people may focus exclusively on such things. 35: *Restraint:* Rather than discouraging marriage, Paul is encouraging *good order* and *devotion to the Lord.* 36–38: **Advice for those engaged to be married.** 36: Fiancée translates the Greek word for *virgin* ("parthenos"; see note a). It may refer to a father's engaged daughter. The Greek of vv. 36–38 is much less clear than the NRSV translation, which expresses one interpretation.* 38: *Refrains from marriage:* Paul's advice here is consistent with the rest of the chapter. 39–40: **Advice to widows.** This extends the advice of v. 8. The death of one married partner dissolves the marriage (Rom 7.1–3). 40: *Remains as she is:* Paul follows the principle expressed in vv. 17–24. *Spirit of God:* Paul claims prophetic* authority for his views (14.37).

---

8 Now concerning food sacrificed to idols: we know that "all of us possess knowledge." Knowledge puffs up, but love builds

up. ²Anyone who claims to know something does not yet have the necessary knowledge; ³but anyone who loves God is known by him.

4 Hence, as to the eating of food offered to idols, we know that "no idol in the world really exists," and that "there is no God but one." ⁵Indeed, even though there may be so-called gods in heaven or on earth—as in fact there are many gods and many lords— ⁶yet for us there is one God, the Father, from whom are all things and for whom we exist, and one Lord, Jesus Christ, through whom are all things and through whom we exist.

7 It is not everyone, however, who has this knowledge. Since some have become so accustomed to idols until now, they still think of the food they eat as food offered to an idol; and their conscience, being weak, is defiled. ⁸"Food will not bring us close to God."ᶜ We are no worse off if we do not eat, and no better off if we do. ⁹But take care that this liberty of yours does not somehow become a stumbling block to the weak. ¹⁰For if others see you, who possess knowledge, eating in the temple of an idol, might they not, since their conscience is weak, be encouraged to the point of eating food sacrificed to idols? ¹¹So by your knowledge those weak believers for whom Christ died are destroyed.ᵈ ¹²But when you thus sin against members of your family,ᵉ and wound their conscience when it is weak, you sin against Christ. ¹³Therefore, if food is a cause of their falling,ᶠ I will never eat meat, so that I may not cause one of themᵍ to fall.

8.1–11.1: **Instructions about eating food sacrificed to idols. 8.1–6: Balancing knowledge with love.** The quotations in vv. 1 and 4 express the views of the spiritually mature (3.1). 1: *Love builds up:* The edifying power of *love* ("agape") is further developed in chs. 12–14. 2: *Necessary knowledge:* Knowing often means not knowing (13.12). 6: Here Paul quotes a two-part confession acknowledging God as Creator and Christ as God's agent of creation (Rom 11.36; Col 1.16). 7–13: **Obligations to the weak.** 7: Gentile* converts are in view. 8: The quotation expresses the

---

a Gk *virgin*   *b* Gk *falls asleep*   *c* The quotation may extend to the end of the verse   *d* Gk *the weak brother . . . is destroyed*   *e* Gk *against the brothers* *f* Gk *my brother's falling*   *g* Gk *cause my brother* view of the spiritually mature: Food is food. If the quotation continues, it should read, "We are no worse off if we do eat, no better off if we do not eat." **9:** *Liberty* is the freedom that strong people have, based on their enlightened attitude. *Stumbling block:* Rom 14.30, 20–21. **11:** *Knowledge* without love has destructive power. **12:** *You sin against Christ* because the church is the body of Christ (12.27; see 6.15). **13:** Better to limit one's liberty than cause a weak Christian harm (Rom 14.20–21).

9 Am I not free? Am I not an apostle? Have I not seen Jesus our Lord? Are you not my work in the Lord? ²If I am not an apostle to others, at least I am to you; for you are the seal of my apostleship in the Lord.

3 This is my defense to those who would examine me. ⁴Do we not have the right to our food and drink? ⁵Do we not have the right to be accompanied by a believing wife,ᵃ as do the other apostles and the brothers of the Lord and Cephas? ⁶Or is it only Barnabas and I who have no right to refrain from working for a living? ⁷Who at any time pays the expenses for doing military service? Who plants a vineyard and does not eat any of its fruit? Or who tends a flock and does not get any of its milk?

8 Do I say this on human authority? Does not the law also say the same? ⁹For it is written in the law of Moses, "You shall not muzzle an ox while it is treading out the grain." Is it for oxen that God is concerned? ¹⁰Or does he not speak entirely for our sake? It was indeed written for our sake, for whoever plows should plow in hope and whoever threshes should thresh in hope of a share in the crop. ¹¹If we have sown spiritual good among you, is it too much if we reap your material benefits? ¹²If others share this rightful claim on you, do not we still more?

Nevertheless, we have not made use of this right, but we endure anything rather than put an obstacle in the way of the gospel of Christ. ¹³Do you not know that those who are employed in the temple service get their food from the temple, and those who serve at the altar share in what is sacrificed on the altar? ¹⁴In the same way, the Lord commanded that those who proclaim the gospel should get their living by the gospel.

15 But I have made no use of any of these rights, nor am I writing this so that they may be applied in my case. Indeed, I would rather die than that—no one will deprive me of my ground for boasting! ¹⁶If I proclaim the gospel, this gives me no ground for boasting, for an obligation is laid on me, and woe to me if I do not proclaim the gospel! ¹⁷For if I do this of my own will, I have a reward; but if not of my own will, I am entrusted with a commission. ¹⁸What then is my reward? Just this: that in my proclamation I may make the gospel free of charge, so as not to make full use of my rights in the gospel.

9.1–27: Paul limits his rights as an apostle.* 1–14: The apostle's right to be paid. 1–2: Paul experienced God's call to be an *apostle* in a vision of Christ (15.8; Gal 1.15–16). **3:** Paul's practice of refusing pay drew criticism. **7:** Everyday examples show that workers deserve pay. **8:** Scripture provides additional support (Deut 25.4). **12:** *Others:* Some ministers besides Paul have apparently received pay from the church. **13:** Established religious practice provides a third reason. **14:** Fourth, a command of *the Lord* Jesus supports the practice (Lk 10.7; Gal 6.6). **15–18: Paul gives up his right. 15:** *Boasting:* He preached the gospel free of charge. **16:** *Obligation:* He thought his call to the gentiles* required special measures. **18:** *Reward:* For Paul, preaching the gospel was its own reward.

19 For though I am free with respect to all, I have made myself a slave to all, so that I might win more of them. ²⁰To the Jews I became as a Jew, in order to win Jews. To those under the law I became as one under the law (though I myself am not under the law) so that I might win those under the law. ²¹To those outside the law I became as one outside the law (though I am not free from God's law but am under Christ's law) so that I might win those outside the law. ²²To the weak I became weak, so that I might win the weak. I have become all things to all people, that I might by all means save some. ²³I do it all for the sake of the gospel, so that I may share in its blessings.

24 Do you not know that in a race the runners all compete, but only one receives

---

a Gk *a sister as wife*

the prize? Run in such a way that you may win it. 25Athletes exercise self-control in all things; they do it to receive a perishable wreath, but we an imperishable one. 26So I do not run aimlessly, nor do I box as though beating the air; 27but I punish my body and enslave it, so that after proclaiming to others I myself should not be disqualified.

9.19–27. 19–23: Becoming a slave. 19: *Slave:* Along with apostle,* Paul uses *slave* as a self-designation (Phil 1.1). *Win* means to convert. 20: *Became as a Jew* is surprising, since Paul was born a Jew (Phil 3.5–6). *Those under the law* probably refers to Jewish Christians who continued to observe Torah.* Paul no longer lived *under the law* in the same way (Gal 4–5). 21: *Those outside the law* are gentiles.* *Christ's law:* Rom 8.2. 22: *The weak* are gentile Christians (8.7).

24–27: **Saying no to oneself.** Two athletic examples—runners and boxers—illustrate the importance of *self-control,* the ability to limit our desires (2 Pet 1.6). 27: *Punish my body* refers to the athlete's training.

10 I do not want you to be unaware, brothers and sisters,*a* that our ancestors were all under the cloud, and all passed through the sea, 2and all were baptized into Moses in the cloud and in the sea, 3and all ate the same spiritual food, 4and all drank the same spiritual drink. For they drank from the spiritual rock that followed them, and the rock was Christ. 5Neverthe-

a Gk *brothers*

Diagram   Hellenistic city plan showing places of worship, culture, and commerce less, God was not pleased with most of them, and they were struck down in the wilderness.

6 Now these things occurred as examples for us, so that we might not desire evil as they did. ⁷Do not become idolaters as some of them did; as it is written, "The people sat down to eat and drink, and they rose up to play." ⁸We must not indulge in sexual immorality as some of them did, and twenty-three thousand fell in a single day. ⁹We must not put Christ*ᵃ* to the test, as some of them did, and were destroyed by serpents. ¹⁰And do not complain as some of them did, and were destroyed by the destroyer. ¹¹These things happened to them to serve as an example, and they were written down to instruct us, on whom the ends of the ages have come. ¹²So if you think you are standing, watch out that you do not fall. ¹³No testing has overtaken you that is not common to everyone. God is faithful, and he will not let you be tested beyond your strength, but with the testing he will also provide the way out so that you may be able to endure it.

14 Therefore, my dear friends,*ᵇ* flee from the worship of idols. ¹⁵I speak as to sensible people; judge for yourselves what I say. ¹⁶The cup of blessing that we bless, is it not a sharing in the blood of Christ? The bread that we break, is it not a sharing in the body of Christ? ¹⁷Because there is one bread, we who are many are one body, for we all partake of the one bread. ¹⁸Consider the people of Israel;*ᶜ* are not those who eat the sacrifices partners in the altar? ¹⁹What do I imply then? That food sacrificed to idols is anything, or that an idol is anything? ²⁰No, I imply that what pagans sacrifice, they sacrifice to demons and not to God. I do not want you to be partners with demons. ²¹You cannot drink the cup of the Lord and the cup of demons. You cannot partake of the table of the Lord and the table of demons. ²²Or are we provoking the Lord to jealousy? Are we stronger than he?

drink: Israel's wilderness experience is reinterpreted in light of the Lord's supper (11.23–26). **6:** *Examples:* 10.11; Rom 15.4. **7–10:** These verses draw four lessons from the story. **7:** *Idolaters* recalls the golden calf incident (Ex 32); the quotation is from Ex 32.6. **8:** *Sexual immorality* recalls the Baal* of Peor incident (Num 25). **9:** Putting *the Lord* (Yahweh, not *Christ,* as in NRSV) *to the test* recalls the bronze serpent incident (Num 21). **10:** *Do not complain* recalls incidents in Ex 16; Num 14, 17. **11:** *Ends of the ages:* The "last days" had begun with Christ's resurrection (Acts 2). **13:** *God is faithful:* 1.9; 2 Cor 1.18. **14–22: Avoid worship of idols. 14:** Paul develops the first of the four lessons (10.7). **16–21:** Like other sacred meals eaten in honor of a deity, the Lord's supper unites the worshipper with Christ. Christians must choose between *the table of the Lord* (Jesus) and *the table of demons.* **22:** *Jealousy:* Deut 32.21; Ex 34.14.

23 "All things are lawful," but not all things are beneficial. "All things are lawful," but not all things build up. ²⁴Do not seek your own advantage, but that of the other. ²⁵Eat whatever is sold in the meat market without raising any question on the ground of conscience, ²⁶for "the earth and its fullness are the Lord's." ²⁷If an unbeliever invites you to a meal and you are disposed to go, eat whatever is set before you without raising any question on the ground of conscience. ²⁸But if someone says to you, "This has been offered in sacrifice," then do not eat it, out of consideration for the one who informed you, and for the sake of conscience— ²⁹I mean the other's conscience, not your own. For why should my liberty be subject to the judgment of someone else's conscience? ³⁰If I partake with thankfulness, why should I be denounced because of that for which I give thanks?

31 So, whether you eat or drink, or whatever you do, do everything for the glory of God. ³²Give no offense to Jews or to Greeks or to the church of God, ³³just as I try to please everyone in everything I do, not seeking my own advantage, but that of many, so

11 that they may be saved. ¹Be imitators of me, as I am of Christ.

10.1–22. 1–13: Israel's example. 2: *Baptized into Moses:* This unusual phrase reflects Christian retelling of the exodus story. It suggests that Israel participated with Moses in the exodus as Christians participate in Jesus' death and resurrection. **3:** *Spiritual food* and

a Other ancient authorities read *the Lord*   *b* Gk *my beloved*   *c* Gk *Israel according to the flesh*

10.23–11.1: What to do in a private setting. Paul resumes the discussion from 8.7–13. **10.23:** The quotations reflect the views of the strong (6.12–20). **24:** *Your own advantage:* The advice in 8.1b becomes concrete. **25:** This follows the principle stated in 8.8 (Rom 14.14, 20). **26:** The quotation is from Ps 24.1. **27:** The setting is a private home. **28:** This is probably the weak person speaking. The same advice is given in 8.13. **29:** *The other's conscience* is that of the weak person (8.10). **29b–30:** The questions do not logically follow. They sound like questions the strong would ask, defending their right to eat. **31:** *Glory of God:* Col 3.17. **33:** This briefly states the principle informing Paul's advice in chs. 8–10. **11.1:** *Imitators:* 4.16. Christ's example is elaborated in Phil 2.5–11.

2 I commend you because you remember me in everything and maintain the traditions just as I handed them on to you. ³But I want you to understand that Christ is the head of every man, and the husband*a* is the head of his wife,*b* and God is the head of Christ. ⁴Any man who prays or prophesies with something on his head disgraces his head, ⁵but any woman who prays or prophesies with her head unveiled disgraces her head—it is one and the same thing as having her head shaved. ⁶For if a woman will not veil herself, then she should cut off her hair; but if it is disgraceful for a woman to have her hair cut off or to be shaved, she should wear a veil. ⁷For a man ought not to have his head veiled, since he is the image and reflection*c* of God; but woman is the reflection*c* of man. ⁸Indeed, man was not made from woman, but woman from man. ⁹Neither was man created for the sake of woman, but woman for the sake of man. ¹⁰For this reason a woman ought to have a symbol of*d* authority on her head,*e* because of the angels. ¹¹Nevertheless, in the Lord woman is not independent of man or man independent of woman. ¹²For just as woman came from man, so man comes through woman; but all things come from God. ¹³Judge for yourselves: is it proper for a woman to pray to God with her head unveiled? ¹⁴Does not nature itself teach you that if a man wears long hair, it is degrading to him, ¹⁵but if a woman has long hair, it is her glory? For her hair is

given to her for a covering. ¹⁶But if anyone is disposed to be contentious—we have no such custom, nor do the churches of God.

11.2–34: Some instructions about worship: what to wear and how to observe the Lord's supper. 2–16: Advice about covering the head. 2: *Traditions* are teachings Paul had received from others (15.3; 2 Thess 2.15). **3:** *Head* may mean source (head of a river) rather than one with authority over another. For a similar hierarchy, see 3.22–23. **4–5:** *Prays or prophesies:* A worship setting is in view. No distinction is made between what men and women do (14.33b–36). **7–9:** Gen 1–2 informs Paul's remarks here. *Image and reflection of God* uses language from Gen 1.27. *Reflection of man:* According to Gen 2.18–25, the woman was created from man. *Reflection,* or *glory* (note *c;* Greek "doxa"), draws on the image of a reflecting light: Man reflects God's light, woman reflects man's light (Heb 1.3). **10:** The verse is very difficult. Possibly, "The woman ought to have authority over her own head" (see the alternate translation in note *e*). *Because of the angels* may recall Gen 6.2. **11–12:** For similar mutuality, see 7.2–4. **13–14:** *Nature:* Paul's remarks accept social and religious customs of his day.

17 Now in the following instructions I do not commend you, because when you come together it is not for the better but for the worse. ¹⁸For, to begin with, when you come together as a church, I hear that there are divisions among you; and to some extent I believe it. ¹⁹Indeed, there have to be factions among you, for only so will it become clear who among you are genuine. ²⁰When you come together, it is not really to eat the Lord's supper. ²¹For when the time comes to eat, each of you goes ahead with your own supper, and one goes hungry and another becomes drunk. ²²What! Do you not have homes to eat and drink in? Or do you show contempt for the church of God and humiliate those who have nothing? What should I say to you? Should I commend you? In this matter I do not commend you!

23 For I received from the Lord what I also handed on to you, that the Lord Jesus

a The same Greek word means *man* or *husband*
b Or *head of the woman*   *c* Or *glory*   *d* Gk lacks *a symbol of*   *e* Or *have freedom of choice regarding her head*

The First Eucharist

The Lord Jesus on the night when he was betrayed took a loaf of bread, and when he had given thanks, he broke it and said, "This is my body that is for you. Do this in remembrance of me." In the same way he took the cup also, after supper, saying, "This cup is the new covenant in my blood. Do this, as often as you drink it, in remembrance of me."—1 Cor 11.23–25

While they were eating, he took a loaf of bread, and after blessing it he broke it, gave it to them, and said, "Take, this is my body." Then he took a cup, and after giving thanks he gave it to them, and all of them drank from it. He said to them, "This is my blood of the covenant, which is poured out for many."—Mark 14.22–24

While they were eating, Jesus took a loaf of bread, and after blessing it he broke it, and gave it to the disciples, and said, "Take, eat; this is my body." Then he took a cup, and after giving thanks he gave it to them, saying, "Drink from it, all of you; for this is my blood of the covenant, which is poured out for many for the forgiveness of sins."—Matthew 26.26–28

Then he took a loaf of bread, and when he had given thanks, he broke it and gave it to them, saying, "This is my body, which is given for you. Do this in remembrance of me." And he did the same with the cup after supper, saying, "This cup that is poured out for you is the new covenant in my blood."—Luke 22.19–20

Give thanks in this way. First for the cup: "We give thanks to you, our Father, for the holy vine of David your servant, which you have made known to us through your servant, Jesus. To you be glory forever." And for the broken bread: "We give thanks to you, our Father, for the life and knowledge that you have made known to us through your servant, Jesus. To you be glory forever. As this broken bread was scattered on the hills, and was brought together and made one, so let your church be brought together into your kingdom from the ends of the earth. For yours is the glory and the power through Jesus Christ forever."—"The Teaching of the Twelve Apostles" (*The Didache**), ch. 9 (early second century CE)

We give thanks to you, O God, through your beloved son Jesus Christ . . . Who when he was being betrayed . . . took bread and gave thanks to you and said, "Take, eat; this is my body which is broken for you." In the same way also he took the cup, saying, "This is my blood which is shed for you. As often as you do this, do it in remembrance of me."—*The Apostolic Tradition* of Hippolytus (around 225 CE)

on the night when he was betrayed took a loaf of bread, 24and when he had given thanks, he broke it and said, "This is my body that is for[a] you. Do this in remembrance of me." 25In the same way he took the cup also, after supper, saying, "This cup is the new covenant in my blood. Do this, as often as you drink it, in remembrance of me." 26For as often as you eat this bread and drink the cup, you proclaim the Lord's death until he comes.

27 Whoever, therefore, eats the bread or drinks the cup of the Lord in an unworthy manner will be answerable for the body and blood of the Lord. 28Examine yourselves, and only then eat of the bread and drink of the cup. 29For all who eat and drink[b] without discerning the body,[c] eat and drink judg-

a Other ancient authorities read *is broken for*
b Other ancient authorities add *in an unworthy manner,*
c Other ancient authorities read *the Lord's body*

ment against themselves. ³⁰For this reason many of you are weak and ill, and some have died.ᵃ ³¹But if we judged ourselves, we would not be judged. ³²But when we are judged by the Lord, we are disciplinedᵇ so that we may not be condemned along with the world.

33 So then, my brothers and sisters,ᶜ when you come together to eat, wait for one another. ³⁴If you are hungry, eat at home, so that when you come together, it will not be for your condemnation. About the other things I will give instructions when I come.

11.17–34: The Lord's supper. 17–22: Being divided at worship. 18: They meet in Gaius's house (Rom 16.23). **18–19:** The *divisions* and *factions* are along social and economic lines. **22:** *Those who have not* are the poor, literally the "have-nots." **23–26: Recalling Jesus' words before his death. 23:** *From the Lord:* The story of the institution of the Eucharist* goes back to Christ. Paul's version is closest to Luke's account (Lk 22.14–23; Mt 26.26–29) and is the oldest recorded version. **24:** *In remembrance of me:* Lk 22.19. **25:** *After supper:* A meal is eaten between the bread and cup (Lk 22.20). The *cup* of wine symbolized the beginning of the *new covenant** that began with Christ's death (Jer 31.31–34; Ex 24.8). **26:** This verse adds Paul's interpretation* to the tradition he received. **27–34: Taking the supper seriously. 27:** To eat *in an unworthy manner* is to engage in the meal without thinking about what it really means. **28:** *Examine yourselves:* Remember the words *for you* (v. 24). **29:** *The body* is both the crucified Lord and the church gathered as *the Lord's body* (see note *c;* also, 12.27). **30:** Some have become sick and died because the church has not cared for them. **31–32:** Paul's warning is stern: Our behavior is *judged by the Lord,* and misbehavior is *disciplined* (Heb 12.5–7, 10). **33:** *Wait for one another:* Worship as one church, not many groups. **34:** Paul expects to visit them soon (16.5–9).

12 Now concerning spiritual gifts,ᵈ brothers and sisters,ᵉ I do not want you to be uninformed. ²You know that when you were pagans, you were enticed and led astray to idols that could not speak. ³Therefore I want you to understand that no one speaking by the Spirit of God ever says "Let Jesus be cursed!" and no one can say "Jesus is Lord" except by the Holy Spirit.

4 Now there are varieties of gifts, but the same Spirit; ⁵and there are varieties of services, but the same Lord; ⁶and there are varieties of activities, but it is the same God who activates all of them in everyone. ⁷To each is given the manifestation of the Spirit for the common good. ⁸To one is given through the Spirit the utterance of wisdom, and to another the utterance of knowledge according to the same Spirit, ⁹to another faith by the same Spirit, to another gifts of healing by the one Spirit, ¹⁰to another the working of miracles, to another prophecy, to another the discernment of spirits, to another various kinds of tongues, to another the interpretation of tongues. ¹¹All these are activated by one and the same Spirit, who allots to each one individually just as the Spirit chooses.

12.1–14.40: Instructions about spiritual gifts. 12.1–3: Establishing perspective. 1: The Corinthians had asked about "pneumatikoi," literally "spirituals," rendered as *spiritual gifts* or *spiritual persons* (note *d*). The same term is used in 3.1. **2:** Many in the church had non-Jewish backgrounds (6.9–11; 1 Thess 1.9–10). **3:** *"Let Jesus be cursed!"* What circumstances prompted anyone to say this is not clear. It could be based on Deut 21.23 (Gal 3.13). **4–11: The Spirit's many activities. 4–7:** Gifts ("charismata"), *services* ("diakoniai"), and *activities* ("energemata") are different ways of describing *manifestations of the Spirit.* Paul emphasizes their variety, their common source, and their intended purpose—to serve the *common good.* **8–10:** *Utterances of wisdom* and *knowledge* describe speech that informs and enlightens. *Faith, gifts of healing,* and *working of miracles* belong together. *Prophecy* is paired with *discernment of spirits,* the ability to evaluate prophetic* speech. *Various kinds of tongues* require *the interpretation* of tongues.* **11:** All are *spiritual* (v. 1) activities because their source is *the same Spirit.*

12 For just as the body is one and has many members, and all the members of the body, though many, are one body, so it is with Christ. ¹³For in the one Spirit we were

---

a Gk *fallen asleep*   *b* Or *When we are judged, we are being disciplined by the Lord*   *c* Gk *brothers*
d Or *spiritual persons*

all baptized into one body—Jews or Greeks, slaves or free—and we were all made to drink of one Spirit.

14 Indeed, the body does not consist of one member but of many. 15 If the foot would say, "Because I am not a hand, I do not belong to the body," that would not make it any less a part of the body. 16 And if the ear would say, "Because I am not an eye, I do not belong to the body," that would not make it any less a part of the body. 17 If the whole body were an eye, where would the hearing be? If the whole body were hearing, where would the sense of smell be? 18 But as it is, God arranged the members in the body, each one of them, as he chose. 19 If all were a single member, where would the body be? 20 As it is, there are many members, yet one body. 21 The eye cannot say to the hand, "I have no need of you," nor again the head to the feet, "I have no need of you." 22 On the contrary, the members of the body that seem to be weaker are indispensable, 23 and those members of the body that we think less honorable we clothe with greater honor, and our less respectable members are treated with greater respect; 24 whereas our more respectable members do not need this. But God has so arranged the body, giving the greater honor to the inferior member, 25 that there may be no dissension within the body, but the members may have the same care for one another. 26 If one member suffers, all suffer together with it; if one member is honored, all rejoice together with it.

27 Now you are the body of Christ and individually members of it. 28 And God has appointed in the church first apostles, second prophets, third teachers; then deeds of power, then gifts of healing, forms of assistance, forms of leadership, various kinds of tongues. 29 Are all apostles? Are all prophets? Are all teachers? Do all work miracles? 30 Do all possess gifts of healing? Do all speak in tongues? Do all interpret? 31 But strive for the greater gifts. And I will show you a still more excellent way.

one body (Gal 3.26–28). **14–26:** V. 14 states the basic theme of this section. **17–19:** The absurdity of the image makes its point. **20:** The main point is repeated (v. 12). **22–25:** The *weaker, less honorable, less respectable, inferior* members are the sexual organs, all *indispensable* and requiring *honor* and *respect*. They are compared with the *more respectable members,* the parts not covered with clothing. **24:** *God has so arranged:* Paul renders the Genesis creation story in greater detail. **26:** The body *suffers* and *rejoices* as a single organism (Rom 12.15). **27–31: The church as the body of Christ. 27:** This states v. 13 more fully. Their identity as *the body of Christ* does not appear to be self-evident to the Corinthians. **28:** The universal *church* is in view here (Eph 1.22–23). The first three groups are probably listed in ranked order (Eph 4.11–13). *Apostles,** literally "those sent," may refer to missionaries rather than the twelve apostles (15.5, 7). The roles and activities doubtless overlapped. **29–30:** These rhetorical* questions expand on v. 12.

13 If I speak in the tongues of mortals and of angels, but do not have love, I am a noisy gong or a clanging cymbal. 2 And if I have prophetic powers, and understand all mysteries and all knowledge, and if I have all faith, so as to remove mountains, but do not have love, I am nothing. 3 If I give away all my possessions, and if I hand over my body so that I may boast,[a] but do not have love, I gain nothing.

4 Love is patient; love is kind; love is not envious or boastful or arrogant 5 or rude. It does not insist on its own way; it is not irritable or resentful; 6 it does not rejoice in wrongdoing, but rejoices in the truth. 7 It bears all things, believes all things, hopes all things, endures all things.

8 Love never ends. But as for prophecies, they will come to an end; as for tongues, they will cease; as for knowledge, it will come to an end. 9 For we know only in part, and we prophesy only in part; 10 but when the complete comes, the partial will come to an end. 11 When I was a child, I spoke like a child, I thought like a child, I reasoned like a child; when I became an adult, I put an end to childish ways. 12 For now we see in a mirror,

12.12–31. **12–26: One body and many members. 13:** Through baptism,* people from many backgrounds and social levels become members of Christ's

a Other ancient authorities read *body to be burned*

dimly,*a* but then we will see face to face. Now I know only in part; then I will know fully, even as I have been fully known. 13And now faith, hope, and love abide, these three; and the greatest of these is love.

13.1–13: The way of love. The *I* in this chapter is Paul speaking out of his own experience, but its lofty, poetic tone extends Paul's own experience to everyone. **1–3: Religion requires love.** Each item mentioned relates to Paul's own experience: *tongues* (14.18); *prophetic*★ *powers* (14.37); *mysteries and knowledge* (2.6–13; 4.1; 15.51); *faith* (power to heal; Rom 15.18–19; 2 Cor 12.12); giving away *possessions* (4.11; 9.18); handing over his *body* (2 Cor 4.10–12). He uses *boast* in a positive sense (Rom 15.17). **4–7: Active love.** Paul sketches this profile of *love* with terms used of his own ministry: *patient and kind* (2 Cor 6.6); *not envious or boastful* (3.7, 21); *not arrogant or rude* (2 Cor 2.17; 4.1–2); *does not insist on its own way* (10.24, 33); not *irritable or resentful* (4.14); *does not rejoice in wrongdoing, but rejoices in the truth* (2 Cor 6.10; 11.29); *bears, believes, hopes, endures* (9.27; 2 Cor 6.3–10). **8–13: Love never ends. 9:** *In part:* For all their value, both knowledge and prophetic speech give an incomplete picture. **10:** *The complete* probably refers to the end time, when God is fully revealed (Rom 8.18–25). **12:** *In a mirror, dimly:* Paul compares life to looking in a mirror that yields an unclear image. Paul thinks of conversion as being *fully known* by God (8.3; Gal. 4.9). **13:** *These three* are difficult to separate (Col 1.4–5; 1 Thess 1.3).

14 Pursue love and strive for the spiritual gifts, and especially that you may prophesy. 2For those who speak in a tongue do not speak to other people but to God; for nobody understands them, since they are speaking mysteries in the Spirit. 3On the other hand, those who prophesy speak to other people for their upbuilding and encouragement and consolation. 4Those who speak in a tongue build up themselves, but those who prophesy build up the church. 5Now I would like all of you to speak in tongues, but even more to prophesy. One who prophesies is greater than one who speaks in tongues, unless someone interprets, so that the church may be built up.

6 Now, brothers and sisters,*b* if I come to you speaking in tongues, how will I benefit you unless I speak to you in some revelation or knowledge or prophecy or teaching? 7It is the same way with lifeless instruments that produce sound, such as the flute or the harp. If they do not give distinct notes, how will anyone know what is being played? 8And if the bugle gives an indistinct sound, who will get ready for battle? 9So with yourselves; if in a tongue you utter speech that is not intelligible, how will anyone know what is being said? For you will be speaking into the air. 10There are doubtless many different kinds of sounds in the world, and nothing is without sound. 11If then I do not know the meaning of a sound, I will be a foreigner to the speaker and the speaker a foreigner to me. 12So with yourselves; since you are eager for spiritual gifts, strive to excel in them for building up the church.

13 Therefore, one who speaks in a tongue should pray for the power to interpret. 14For if I pray in a tongue, my spirit prays but my mind is unproductive. 15What should I do then? I will pray with the spirit, but I will pray with the mind also; I will sing praise with the spirit, but I will sing praise with the mind also. 16Otherwise, if you say a blessing with the spirit, how can anyone in the position of an outsider say the "Amen" to your thanksgiving, since the outsider does not know what you are saying? 17For you may give thanks well enough, but the other person is not built up. 18I thank God that I speak in tongues more than all of you; 19nevertheless, in church I would rather speak five words with my mind, in order to instruct others also, than ten thousand words in a tongue.

14.1–40: Prophecy better than tongues. 1–5: Tongues and prophecy compared. 1: *Spiritual gifts* ("pneumatika"): 12.1. **2:** *Speak . . . to God:* Tongues are a form of prayer only God can understand. **3:** *Speak to other people:* Prophecy is proclamation other people can understand. **4:** *Themselves . . . church:* Tongues benefit the individual, prophecy the group. **5–6:** Paul prefers prophecy over tongues. **6–19: Tongues require interpretation.**★ **6:** Unlike *tongues*, these four types of speech can be understood without

a Gk *in a riddle* *b* Gk *brothers*

an interpreter. **7–8:** Music without *distinct notes* is only noise. **9–11:** Tongues are not foreign speech; they are *like* foreign speech—unintelligible without an interpreter. **12:** *Building up:* This restates the principle of 10.24, 33: Do my words benefit the group? **13:** Speaking and interpreting *a tongue* can be done by the same person (12.10). **14–17:** *In a tongue* is one way of praying. Only words prayed or sung *with the spirit* produce a group of worshipping individuals. Worship done with both spirit and *mind* creates a church. **18–19:** Since Paul himself can *speak in tongues* (13.1; 14.6), he knows their value and their limits.

20 Brothers and sisters,ᵃ do not be children in your thinking; rather, be infants in evil, but in thinking be adults. ²¹In the law it is written,

"By people of strange tongues
　　and by the lips of foreigners
　I will speak to this people;
　　yet even then they will not listen to
　　　me,"

says the Lord. ²²Tongues, then, are a sign not for believers but for unbelievers, while prophecy is not for unbelievers but for believers. ²³If, therefore, the whole church comes together and all speak in tongues, and outsiders or unbelievers enter, will they not say that you are out of your mind? ²⁴But if all prophesy, an unbeliever or outsider who enters is reproved by all and called to account by all. ²⁵After the secrets of the unbeliever's heart are disclosed, that person will bow down before God and worship him, declaring, "God is really among you."

26 What should be done then, my friends?ᵃ When you come together, each one has a hymn, a lesson, a revelation, a tongue, or an interpretation. Let all things be done for building up. ²⁷If anyone speaks in a tongue, let there be only two or at most three, and each in turn; and let one interpret. ²⁸But if there is no one to interpret, let them be silent in church and speak to themselves and to God. ²⁹Let two or three prophets speak, and let the others weigh what is said. ³⁰If a revelation is made to someone else sitting nearby, let the first person be silent. ³¹For you can all prophesy one by one, so that all may learn and all be encouraged. ³²And the spirits of prophets are subject to

the prophets, ³³for God is a God not of disorder but of peace.

(As in all the churches of the saints, ³⁴women should be silent in the churches. For they are not permitted to speak, but should be subordinate, as the law also says. ³⁵If there is anything they desire to know, let them ask their husbands at home. For it is shameful for a woman to speak in church.ᵇ ³⁶Or did the word of God originate with you? Or are you the only ones it has reached?)

37 Anyone who claims to be a prophet, or to have spiritual powers, must acknowledge that what I am writing to you is a command of the Lord. ³⁸Anyone who does not recognize this is not to be recognized. ³⁹So, my friends,ᶜ be eager to prophesy, and do not forbid speaking in tongues; ⁴⁰but all things should be done decently and in order.

14.20–40. 20–25: Worship outsiders can understand. 20: The issue is their level of maturity (13.11; Eph 4.14–15). **21:** Isa 28.11–12. Yahweh speaks to Israel using a foreign language (Assyrian), but without success. **22:** *Strange tongues* might be understandable to strangers, but not to God's people. Intelligible speech, *prophecy,* is better for them. **23–25:** As it turns out, even the *unbeliever* and *outsider* benefit more if they can understand what is said *when the whole church comes together.* Prophetic* proclamation can convict the *unbeliever's heart* and show God's presence within the church. The quotation is from Isa 45.14. **26–36: Suggestions for orderly worship. 26:** The variety of activities suggests unstructured worship. *Building up* restates the overarching principle (14.12). **27–28:** The restrictions on speaking *in a tongue* imply the individual's ability to control speech. Paul's instructions are consistent: no interpreter, no tongues (14.5, 13; see 12.10). **29–33:** Prophetic speech can also be controlled. Since it is understandable, it is weighed rather than interpreted. Chaotic worship fails to recognize the true nature of God (7.15; Rom 15.33). **33b–36:** The restrictions on women's speech are in parentheses because their location here is disputed (note *b*). The role of women in worship is discussed nowhere else in chs. 12–14. The instructions do not agree with Paul's earlier discussion in 11.2–16, where women pray and prophesy along with men. Many scholars

a Gk *brothers*　　*b* Other ancient authorities put verses 34–35 after verse 40　　*c* Gk *my brothers* doubt they were written by Paul and date them to a later period (1 Tim 2.11–12; Titus 2.5). **37–40: Concluding words. 37**: *Command of the Lord:* In what sense is not clear. Paul is not able to cite Christ's teaching as he does earlier (7.10; 9.14). **39**: *Be eager to prophesy:* He restates the point where the discussion began (14.1). *Do not forbid speaking in tongues:* He recognizes that some people will. Paul sees their dangers but also their potential value. **40**: His advice is grounded in God's character (14.33).

15 Now I would remind you, brothers and sisters,*a* of the good news*b* that I proclaimed to you, which you in turn received, in which also you stand, 2through which also you are being saved, if you hold firmly to the message that I proclaimed to you—unless you have come to believe in vain.

3 For I handed on to you as of first importance what I in turn had received: that Christ died for our sins in accordance with the scriptures, 4and that he was buried, and that he was raised on the third day in accordance with the scriptures, 5and that he appeared to Cephas, then to the twelve. 6Then he appeared to more than five hundred brothers and sisters*a* at one time, most of whom are still alive, though some have died.*c* 7Then he appeared to James, then to all the apostles. 8Last of all, as to one untimely born, he appeared also to me. 9For I am the least of the apostles, unfit to be called an apostle, because I persecuted the church of God. 10But by the grace of God I am what I am, and his grace toward me has not been in vain. On the contrary, I worked harder than any of them—though it was not I, but the grace of God that is with me. 11Whether then it was I or they, so we proclaim and so you have come to believe.

12 Now if Christ is proclaimed as raised from the dead, how can some of you say there is no resurrection of the dead? 13If there is no resurrection of the dead, then Christ has not been raised; 14and if Christ has not been raised, then our proclamation has been in vain and your faith has been in vain. 15We are even found to be misrepresenting God, because we testified of God that he raised Christ—whom he did not

raise if it is true that the dead are not raised. 16For if the dead are not raised, then Christ has not been raised. 17If Christ has not been raised, your faith is futile and you are still in your sins. 18Then those also who have died*c* in Christ have perished. 19If for this life only we have hoped in Christ, we are of all people most to be pitied.

20 But in fact Christ has been raised from the dead, the first fruits of those who have died.*c* 21For since death came through a human being, the resurrection of the dead has also come through a human being; 22for as all die in Adam, so all will be made alive in Christ. 23But each in his own order: Christ the first fruits, then at his coming those who belong to Christ. 24Then comes the end,*d* when he hands over the kingdom to God the Father, after he has destroyed every ruler and every authority and power. 25For he must reign until he has put all his enemies under his feet. 26The last enemy to be destroyed is death. 27For "God*e* has put all things in subjection under his feet." But when it says, "All things are put in subjection," it is plain that this does not include the one who put all things in subjection under him. 28When all things are subjected to him, then the Son himself will also be subjected to the one who put all things in subjection under him, so that God may be all in all.

15.1–58: Instructions about resurrection. 1–11: The tradition of Christ's resurrection. 2: *Being saved:* Conversion has lasting effects. **3**: *Handed on . . . received:* Paul uses language describing the transmission of sacred teaching (11.23). **3–5**: This is one of the earliest summaries of Christian preaching (Rom 1.1–4). *Died, buried, raised,* and *appeared* identify key moments of the passion story (Mk 14–16). *In accordance with the Scriptures* reflects Christian conviction that God was at work in these events (Isa 53; Hos 6.2). **5–11**: Women figure more prominently in the gospel appearance stories (Mt 28.1–10; Mk 16.1–8; Lk 23.55–24.12; Jn 20.1–18). Appearances to *more than five hundred* and *James* are distinctive elements

a Gk *brothers*   *b* Or *gospel*   *c* Gk *fallen asleep*
d Or *Then come the rest*   *e* Gk *he*

of this list. The *twelve* (v. 5) are distinguished from *all the apostles** (v.7). Paul places himself within the same tradition, even though his experience of the risen Lord was exceptional (Gal 1.13–17). **12–19: Some doubt the resurrection. 12:** The truth of Christ's resurrection is assumed throughout. *No resurrection of the dead:* Doubts could arise in different forms: no life at all after death; no resurrection of the body, only the soul; no future resurrection (it is already here). **13–14:** Denying resurrection in principle eliminates Christ's resurrection. **15:** Paul's credibility is at stake. **17–18:** The church's faith is also threatened. **19:** Christian preaching is about future hope, or nothing at all (Rom 5.5; 8.24–25). **20–28: Christ, Adam, and future resurrection. 20:** The faith of 15.3–5 is reaffirmed. *First fruits:* Christ's resurrection is like the beginning of harvest because more of the same follows (1 Thess 4.14). **21–22:** Like Adam, Christ stands at the beginning of a new order of humanity. The crucial difference: Adam introduced death, Christ life (Rom 5.12–17). **23–28:** The sequence of events outlined here emphasizes how *those who belong to Christ* share the experience of *Christ* (1 Thess 4.13–18 reflects different concerns). *The end* ("telos") is a better translation than *the rest* (see note *d* on p. 1930). It is the time when the risen Lord, finally triumphant over every other power, especially *death*, yields the reign to *God the Father*. The language of v. 25 is drawn from Ps 110.1. V. 27 draws on Ps 8.6, which Paul explains in vv. 27–28. He understands *his feet* to mean Christ's *feet*. Christ subjects everything (including death), then yields power to God to whom all, including Christ, are subject.

29 Otherwise, what will those people do who receive baptism on behalf of the dead? If the dead are not raised at all, why are people baptized on their behalf?

30 And why are we putting ourselves in danger every hour? 31 I die every day! That is as certain, brothers and sisters,[a] as my boasting of you—a boast that I make in Christ Jesus our Lord. 32 If with merely human hopes I fought with wild animals at Ephesus, what would I have gained by it? If the dead are not raised,

"Let us eat and drink,
   for tomorrow we die."
33 Do not be deceived:
"Bad company ruins good morals."
34 Come to a sober and right mind, and sin

no more; for some people have no knowledge of God. I say this to your shame.

35 But someone will ask, "How are the dead raised? With what kind of body do they come?" 36 Fool! What you sow does not come to life unless it dies. 37 And as for what you sow, you do not sow the body that is to be, but a bare seed, perhaps of wheat or of some other grain. 38 But God gives it a body as he has chosen, and to each kind of seed its own body. 39 Not all flesh is alike, but there is one flesh for human beings, another for animals, another for birds, and another for fish. 40 There are both heavenly bodies and earthly bodies, but the glory of the heavenly is one thing, and that of the earthly is another. 41 There is one glory of the sun, and another glory of the moon, and another glory of the stars; indeed, star differs from star in glory.

42 So it is with the resurrection of the dead. What is sown is perishable, what is raised is imperishable. 43 It is sown in dishonor, it is raised in glory. It is sown in weakness, it is raised in power. 44 It is sown a physical body, it is raised a spiritual body. If there is a physical body, there is also a spiritual body. 45 Thus it is written, "The first man, Adam, became a living being"; the last Adam became a life-giving spirit. 46 But it is not the spiritual that is first, but the physical, and then the spiritual. 47 The first man was from the earth, a man of dust; the second man is[b] from heaven. 48 As was the man of dust, so are those who are of the dust; and as is the man of heaven, so are those who are of heaven. 49 Just as we have borne the image of the man of dust, we will[c] also bear the image of the man of heaven.

15.29–49. 29–34: What we practice shows what we believe. 29: This practice is mentioned only here in the New Testament. Paul assumes the practice in order to draw the implication. **30:** He now appeals to his own practice: daily risking his life as an apostle.* **31:** *I die every day:* In his apostolic life, Paul reenacts the Christ-event (2 Cor 4.7–12). **32:** *Wild beasts at Ephesus* refers to Paul's opponents; the quotation is from Isa 22.13. **33:** Paul quotes a popular proverb traceable

---

a Gk *brothers*   *b* Other ancient authorities add *the Lord*
c Other ancient authorities read *let us*

to the Greek comic poet Menander (4th century BCE). **34:** Sin is easier when God is absent from the future. **35–41: Some examples from nature. 35:** An imaginary questioner asks what happens to the body. **36–38:** A grain of seed must "die" (be buried in the ground) before it rises from the earth in a different form as wheat (Jn 12.24). **39–41:** Nature presents different forms of life. *Glory* is brightness or radiance. **42–49: Nature helps explain resurrection. 42–44:** *Sown* and *raised* continue the image of the seed from vv. 36–38. The contrasting qualities underscore the differences in the forms of life before and after "burial." **45–49:** Gen 2.7. The *first Adam* received life; Christ, the *second Adam,* gives (resurrection) life. Adam and Christ represent different forms of life. All humans share Adam's dust. Those in Christ are *of heaven* and will eventually breathe his *life-giving spirit.*

50 What I am saying, brothers and sisters,[a] is this: flesh and blood cannot inherit the kingdom of God, nor does the perishable inherit the imperishable. [51]Listen, I will tell you a mystery! We will not all die,[b] but we will all be changed, [52]in a moment, in the twinkling of an eye, at the last trumpet. For the trumpet will sound, and the dead will be raised imperishable, and we will be changed. [53]For this perishable body must put on imperishability, and this mortal body must put on immortality. [54]When this perishable body puts on imperishability, and this mortal body puts on immortality, then the saying that is written will be fulfilled:

"Death has been swallowed up
        in victory."
[55] "Where, O death, is your victory?
        Where, O death, is your sting?"
[56]The sting of death is sin, and the power of sin is the law. [57]But thanks be to God, who gives us the victory through our Lord Jesus Christ.

58 Therefore, my beloved,[c] be steadfast, immovable, always excelling in the work of the Lord, because you know that in the Lord your labor is not in vain.

15.50–58: A vision of the future. 50: *Kingdom of God* refers to the heavenly reign Christ turns over to God (v. 24). It differs radically from life as we know it. **51:** *Mystery** signifies a hidden truth being unveiled (4.1). *We will not all die:* Those alive at the resurrection es-

cape death but not change. **52:** Trumpets summon God's people to worship (Num 10.2–10), to return from exile (Isa 27.13), and to gather for the end time (Mt 24.31; 1 Thess 4.16). **54–55:** The quotation combines Isa 25.8 and Hos 13.14. V. 55 speaks to the living and dead respectively. The living escape death; by rising the dead overcome death's sting. **56:** *Sin, death, law:* Adam's sin introduced humanity to death's sting (Rom 5.12). The sin that began with Adam continued to exercise its power through the Mosaic law (Rom 5.20; 7.6). Christ's death and resurrection broke the stranglehold of all three—sin, death, and law (Rom 8.2). **58:** *Not in vain:* Living in hope fuels life (Col 1.23).

16 Now concerning the collection for the saints: you should follow the directions I gave to the churches of Galatia. [2]On the first day of every week, each of you is to put aside and save whatever extra you earn, so that collections need not be taken when I come. [3]And when I arrive, I will send any whom you approve with letters to take your gift to Jerusalem. [4]If it seems advisable that I should go also, they will accompany me.

5 I will visit you after passing through Macedonia—for I intend to pass through Macedonia— [6]and perhaps I will stay with you or even spend the winter, so that you may send me on my way, wherever I go. [7]I do not want to see you now just in passing, for I hope to spend some time with you, if the Lord permits. [8]But I will stay in Ephesus until Pentecost, [9]for a wide door for effective work has opened to me, and there are many adversaries.

10 If Timothy comes, see that he has nothing to fear among you, for he is doing the work of the Lord just as I am; [11]therefore let no one despise him. Send him on his way in peace, so that he may come to me; for I am expecting him with the brothers.

12 Now concerning our brother Apollos, I strongly urged him to visit you with the other brothers, but he was not at all willing[d] to come now. He will come when he has the opportunity.

a Gk *brothers*   b Gk *fall asleep*   c Gk *beloved brothers*   d Or *it was not at all God's will for him*

13 Keep alert, stand firm in your faith, be courageous, be strong. 14Let all that you do be done in love.

15 Now, brothers and sisters,*a* you know that members of the household of Stephanas were the first converts in Achaia, and they have devoted themselves to the service of the saints; 16I urge you to put yourselves at the service of such people, and of everyone who works and toils with them. 17I rejoice at the coming of Stephanas and Fortunatus and Achaicus, because they have made up for your absence; 18for they refreshed my spirit as well as yours. So give recognition to such persons.

19 The churches of Asia send greetings. Aquila and Prisca, together with the church in their house, greet you warmly in the Lord. 20All the brothers and sisters*a* send greetings. Greet one another with a holy kiss.

21 I, Paul, write this greeting with my own hand. 22Let anyone be accursed who has no love for the Lord. Our Lord, come!*b* 23The grace of the Lord Jesus be with you. 24My love be with all of you in Christ Jesus.*c*

16.1–24. 1–4: Answering questions about the collection. 1: *Collection for the saints:* This was a major project for Paul during his ministry in the Aegean (2 Cor 8–9; Rom 15.25–29; Gal 2.10). **2:** *When I come:* In vv. 5–9 Paul explains his plans to visit them. **3:** *Jerusalem:* The collection was for poor Christians in Jerusalem (Rom 15.26). **5–9: Travel plans.** V. 8 confirms that Paul is writing from Ephesus. The churches he began in Philippi and Thessalonica were located in *Mac-*

edonia (Acts 16–17). *Send me on my way* suggests hospitality and financial assistance (Rom 15.22). *Pentecost*★ occurred in the spring, fifty days after Passover★ (Lev 23.15–21). **10–12: Paul's co-workers. 10–11:** *Timothy* was with Paul on his founding visit to Corinth (Acts 18.5). He may be the one delivering the letter to Corinth (see 4.17). The identity of *the brothers* is not known. **12:** *Apollos* was an important figure within the Corinthian church (1.12; 3.4–6, 22; 4.6). This picture is confirmed by Acts (18.27–19.1). At the time of this writing, he is with Paul in Ephesus. **13–14: Concluding advice.** These brief injunctions are all defined by *love* (ch. 13). **15–18: Commending valuable co-workers.** Paul himself baptized the *household of Stephanas* (1.16). Their conversion apparently preceded that of Crispus and Gaius (1.14). **16:** Leadership derives from service. **17:** They may have been the source of Paul's information for various issues (see 5.1). **19–24: Final greetings. 19:** *Churches of Asia* would include Ephesus primarily (Acts 19). As usual, *Aquila and Prisca* have established a house-church in Ephesus (Acts 18.2; Rom 16.3–5). **20:** *Holy kiss:* This practice of greeting at worship may have originated in Christian circles (Rom 16.16; 2 Cor 13.12). **21:** Paul's remark implies his use of a secretary for writing (or copying) the rest of the letter (Gal 6.11; Col 4.18). **22:** These words seem harsh, especially linked with *love for the Lord. Our Lord, come!* indicates Paul's eagerness for the end (see note *b*). **23–24:** The benediction, while brief, expresses important Pauline sentiments (see 2 Cor 13.13; Rom 16.20; 1 Thess 5.28).

---

a Gk *brothers*   *b* Gk *Marana tha.* These Aramaic words can also be read *Maran atha,* meaning *Our Lord has come*   *c* Other ancient authorities add *Amen*

THE SECOND LETTER OF PAUL TO THE CORINTHIANS

Introduction

Paul's second letter to the church at Corinth is a combination of shorter letters written over several months. Chs. 1–7 focus mostly on Paul's understanding of his apostolic ministry. Embedded within them is a short section that appears to have been composed separately (6.14–7.1). Chs. 8–9 deal with the collection for Christians in Jerusalem, a project of great importance for Paul. In chs. 10–13 Paul is on the defensive, answering charges brought against him by his opponents. It is difficult to determine the chronological order of these individual letters. Many scholars think chs. 10–13 were written first, shortly after Paul returned from a painful visit to the church in Corinth. Their polemical* tone suggests that they were written in the heat of controversy, or shortly thereafter. Chs. 1–7, by contrast, do not show as much anger. Instead, they begin on a note of great relief, which suggests that they were written after the crisis was over. The chapters on the collection may consist of shorter letters Paul sent to the church over a period of time encouraging them to contribute to the project. In spite of its uneven literary character, 2 Corinthians gives valuable insight into Paul's self-understanding as an apostle.*

After Paul sent 1 Corinthians, his situation in Ephesus worsened (2 Cor 1.8–11), and his plans to visit Corinth changed (1 Cor 16.5–8; 2 Cor 1.15–24). The situation in Corinth also changed. Other Christian missionaries arrived there and began working with the church. Their specific identity is unknown, but Paul clearly regarded them as rivals and saw them as a threat to the work he had done in Corinth (10.10–11; 11.4–6, 12–15, 22–23; 12.11). They may have accepted financial support from the church, thereby interfering with the Corinthians' plans to contribute to the collection fund for Jerusalem Christians. At some point, Paul decided to make a personal visit to Corinth to address a deteriorating situation (2.1–3). He made the trip, confronted an unnamed individual (2.5–11), and returned to Ephesus convinced that the trip had been a disaster. This prompted him to write chs. 10–13, sometimes called the "severe letter" (2.4). After sending it, he had to leave Ephesus without knowing how the letter had been received (2.12–13). But he heard from Titus, one of his co-workers who had been sent to Corinth, that the letter had hit the mark (7.5–16). This greatly relieved Paul and prompted him to write chs. 1–7. Echoes of the controversy are still heard in these chapters, but it is clearly past (3.1; 4.2). One of the controversy's benefits was that it caused him to reflect extensively on his own theology of ministry, which he details in 2.14–6.13.

READING GUIDE

Readers of 2 Corinthians will experience its literary unevenness. The NRSV translators have indicated the most obvious literary gaps with double spacing (1.2–3; 6.13–24; 7.1–2; 7.16–8.1; 9.15–10.1). One should also be alert to the change of mood in the letter. Parts of the letter are very polemical, especially chs. 10–13. Other parts are much more conciliatory in tone, especially chs. 1–7. The subject matter also changes. Chs. 8–9 focus exclusively on the collection, which is not mentioned in other parts of the letter. Part of the challenge in reading 2 Corinthians is to account for these changes in subject matter and tone. This requires some understanding of Paul's ongoing relationship with Corinth as reflected in 1 Corinthians and Acts.

1 Paul, an apostle of Christ Jesus by the will of God, and Timothy our brother,

To the church of God that is in Corinth, including all the saints throughout Achaia:

2 Grace to you and peace from God our Father and the Lord Jesus Christ.

3 Blessed be the God and Father of our Lord Jesus Christ, the Father of mercies and the God of all consolation, 4who consoles us in all our affliction, so that we may be able to console those who are in any affliction with the consolation with which we ourselves are consoled by God. 5For just as the sufferings of Christ are abundant for us, so also our consolation is abundant through Christ. 6If we are being afflicted, it is for your consolation and salvation; if we are being consoled, it is for your consolation, which you experience when you patiently endure the same sufferings that we are also suffering. 7Our hope for you is unshaken; for we know that as you share in our sufferings, so also you share in our consolation.

church. This has given way to *consolation* and a sense of relief that a severe crisis has passed.

8 We do not want you to be unaware, brothers and sisters,*a* of the affliction we experienced in Asia; for we were so utterly, unbearably crushed that we despaired of life itself. 9Indeed, we felt that we had received the sentence of death so that we would rely not on ourselves but on God who raises the dead. 10He who rescued us from so deadly a peril will continue to rescue us; on him we have set our hope that he will rescue us again, 11as you also join in helping us by your prayers, so that many will give thanks on our*b* behalf for the blessing granted us through the prayers of many.

12 Indeed, this is our boast, the testimony of our conscience: we have behaved in the world with frankness*c* and godly sincerity, not by earthly wisdom but by the grace of God—and all the more toward you. 13For we write you nothing other than what you can read and also understand; I hope you will understand until the end— 14as you have already understood us in part—that on the day of the Lord Jesus we are your boast even as you are our boast.

1.1–7. 1–2: Greeting. This greeting resembles other Pauline greetings (1 Thess 1.1; Phil 1.1–2). Timothy joins Paul in addressing the church. He had participated in the church's founding (1.19; Acts 18.5) and was well known to the church (1 Cor 4.17; 16.10–11). **3–7: Prayer of blessing.** Pauline letters usually open with a prayer of thanksgiving (Rom 1.8–15; 1 Cor 1.4–9). Here Paul uses the Jewish prayer of blessing ("berakah") found elsewhere in the New Testament (Eph 1.3–14; 1 Pet 1.3–9). Paul had recently experienced great *affliction* and *suffering* in his dealings with the

---

1.8–14: Paul's recent despair. *Affliction . . . in Asia:* The circumstances of this crisis are not known. It may refer to the riot described in Acts 19.23–41. **9:** *Sentence of death* need not mean legal punishment. It is

a Gk *brothers*   *b* Other ancient authorities read *your*
c Other ancient authorities read *holiness*

probably a figure of speech for a close shave with death. **12:** *Boast* here and in v. 14 is used in a positive sense, meaning "source of pride" (Phil 2.16). *Frankness,* sometimes rendered "simplicity," is being straightforward in one's dealings. **13–14:** *End . . . day of the Lord Jesus* refers to the time of Jesus' return (1 Cor 1.8; Phil 1.6).

15 Since I was sure of this, I wanted to come to you first, so that you might have a double favor;^a 16I wanted to visit you on my way to Macedonia, and to come back to you from Macedonia and have you send me on to Judea. 17Was I vacillating when I wanted to do this? Do I make my plans according to ordinary human standards,^b ready to say "Yes, yes" and "No, no" at the same time? 18As surely as God is faithful, our word to you has not been "Yes and No." 19For the Son of God, Jesus Christ, whom we proclaimed among you, Silvanus and Timothy and I, was not "Yes and No"; but in him it is always "Yes." 20For in him every one of God's promises is a "Yes." For this reason it is through him that we say the "Amen," to the glory of God. 21But it is God who establishes us with you in Christ and has anointed us, 22by putting his seal on us and giving us his Spirit in our hearts as a first installment.

1.15–22: Paul's change of plans. 15: *Double favor* refers to Paul's two planned visits. **16:** The route implied is Ephesus, Corinth (in Achaia), Macedonia (probably Thessalonica or Philippi), Corinth, Judea (1 Cor 16.5–8). The trip to *Judea* would be to deliver the collection for poor Christians in Jerusalem (Rom 15.25–26). **17–20:** To identify Christ as God's *"Yes"* reflects the conviction that God's promises have been fulfilled in him (Gal 3.14–16; Rom 15.8). **21–22:** *His Spirit* may be Christ's Spirit (Rom 8.9). *First installment* is a commercial term, "down payment," a gesture of good faith indicating the balance will follow (Rom 5.5; 8.23).

23 But I call on God as witness against me: it was to spare you that I did not come again to Corinth. 24I do not mean to imply that we lord it over your faith; rather, we are workers with you for your joy, because you 2 stand firm in the faith. 1So I made up my mind not to make you another pain-

ful visit. 2For if I cause you pain, who is there to make me glad but the one whom I have pained? 3And I wrote as I did, so that when I came, I might not suffer pain from those who should have made me rejoice; for I am confident about all of you, that my joy would be the joy of all of you. 4For I wrote you out of much distress and anguish of heart and with many tears, not to cause you pain, but to let you know the abundant love that I have for you.

5 But if anyone has caused pain, he has caused it not to me, but to some extent—not to exaggerate it—to all of you. 6This punishment by the majority is enough for such a person; 7so now instead you should forgive and console him, so that he may not be overwhelmed by excessive sorrow. 8So I urge you to reaffirm your love for him. 9I wrote for this reason: to test you and to know whether you are obedient in everything. 10Anyone whom you forgive, I also forgive. What I have forgiven, if I have forgiven anything, has been for your sake in the presence of Christ. 11And we do this so that we may not be outwitted by Satan; for we are not ignorant of his designs.

12 When I came to Troas to proclaim the good news of Christ, a door was opened for me in the Lord; 13but my mind could not rest because I did not find my brother Titus there. So I said farewell to them and went on to Macedonia.

1.23–2.13: A painful visit recalled. This visit apparently caused Paul to change the plans mentioned in 1.16. Instead of going from Ephesus to Corinth, he must have gone north to Troas, then on to Macedonia, where he is now writing (2.12–23). **2.2:** This person's identity is not known, but clearly the confrontation was painful for everyone involved—Paul, the person, the whole church (2.5–8). **3–4, 9:** This letter better describes chs. 10–13 than 1 Corinthians, which does not reflect such *distress, anguish,* and *tears.* It was apparently written from Ephesus after Paul returned from the painful visit to Corinth. **6–11:** How the unnamed person was punished *by the majority* is not clear. Perhaps the church excluded him from its presence or

a Other ancient authorities read *pleasure*
b Gk *according to the flesh*

simply reprimanded him. Paul's call for *love* and *forgiveness* and his remarks in v. 9 suggest that the church sided with Paul. **11:** Paul sees Satan as an active opponent (11.14; 12.7). **12–13:** Troas was located on the northwestern coast of Asia Minor. Titus probably delivered the "tearful letter" to Corinth.

14 But thanks be to God, who in Christ always leads us in triumphal procession, and through us spreads in every place the fragrance that comes from knowing him. 15For we are the aroma of Christ to God among those who are being saved and among those who are perishing; 16to the one a fragrance from death to death, to the other a fragrance from life to life. Who is sufficient for these things? 17For we are not peddlers of God's word like so many;*a* but in Christ we speak as persons of sincerity, as persons sent from God and standing in his presence.

3 Are we beginning to commend ourselves again? Surely we do not need, as some do, letters of recommendation to you or from you, do we? 2You yourselves are our letter, written on our*b* hearts, to be known and read by all; 3and you show that you are a letter of Christ, prepared by us, written not with ink but with the Spirit of the living God, not on tablets of stone but on tablets of human hearts.

2.14–6.13: Paul's understanding of ministry. 2.14–17: Ministers sent from God. The image is a victory march where the conquering general, along with his chief officers, leads his army in *triumphal procession,* the air filled with the burning of incense (1 Cor 4.9). The *aroma* signifies *life* to the victors, *death* to the conquered. **17:** *Peddlers of God's word:* Teachers traveling around the Roman world were frequently accused of being in it for the money (4.2). *Persons of sincerity* are people with pure motives (1.12). **3.1–3: Letters written on the heart.** *Letters of recommendation:* Acts 18.27. *A letter of Christ:* Christ whose Spirit lives within *human hearts* is the content of the letter (1.21–22). The image of God's message written on the heart is drawn from Jer 31.33. Paul's best *recommendation* is the church itself.

4 Such is the confidence that we have through Christ toward God. 5Not that we are competent of ourselves to claim anything as coming from us; our competence is from God, 6who has made us competent to be ministers of a new covenant, not of letter but of spirit; for the letter kills, but the Spirit gives life.

7 Now if the ministry of death, chiseled in letters on stone tablets,*c* came in glory so that the people of Israel could not gaze at Moses' face because of the glory of his face, a glory now set aside, 8how much more will the ministry of the Spirit come in glory? 9For if there was glory in the ministry of condemnation, much more does the ministry of justification abound in glory! 10Indeed, what once had glory has lost its glory because of the greater glory; 11for if what was set aside came through glory, much more has the permanent come in glory!

12 Since, then, we have such a hope, we act with great boldness, 13not like Moses, who put a veil over his face to keep the people of Israel from gazing at the end of the glory that*d* was being set aside. 14But their minds were hardened. Indeed, to this very day, when they hear the reading of the old covenant, that same veil is still there, since only in Christ is it set aside. 15Indeed, to this very day whenever Moses is read, a veil lies over their minds; 16but when one turns to the Lord, the veil is removed. 17Now the Lord is the Spirit, and where the Spirit of the Lord is, there is freedom. 18And all of us, with unveiled faces, seeing the glory of the Lord as though reflected in a mirror, are being transformed into the same image from one degree of glory to another; for this comes from the Lord, the Spirit.

3.4–18: Ministers of a new covenant. ★ Christ inaugurates the *new covenant* promised by Jeremiah (31.31–34; 1 Cor 11.25). It replaces the Mosaic law, which was written on *tablets of stone* (v. 3; Ex 31.18). For Paul, *letter* symbolizes this written law code, which he experienced as *death;* he found it suffocating (vv. 6, 7; Rom 7.9–10). By contrast, he experienced Christ's life-giving *Spirit* in the *new covenant* (v. 6; 1.21–22; 1 Cor 15.45). Thus its symbol was *spirit* ("pneuma"). Paul thinks of each covenant as a *minis-*

a Other ancient authorities read *like the others*
b Other ancient authorities read *your*   c Gk *on stones*
d Gk *of what*

try ("diakonia") in which one serves. The *old covenant* of Moses (v. 14) is described negatively: *death* (v. 7), *condemnation* (v. 9), fading *glory* (v.10), temporary (vv. 7, 11). The *new covenant* under Christ, by contrast, has positive features: *Spirit* (v. 8), *justification* (v. 9), *greater glory* (v. 10), *permanent* (v. 11). Paul's discussion draws on Ex 34.29–35, where God gives Moses the law at Sinai. *Glory* refers to the brightness of Moses' face (Ex 34.30) and throughout the section could be translated "radiance." But Paul experienced Christ as a more dazzling light, a *greater glory* (v. 10; 4.4, 6). For Paul, the veil that hid the face of Moses from the Israelites at Sinai now hides Moses' meaning when they read scripture (vv. 14–15). The death of Christ, however, removed the veil, thereby providing a clear view of God (v. 14). Turning to Christ in conversion (v. 16) gives one *freedom*—unobstructed access to God. Those who view God *with unveiled faces* gradually acquire God's glory as a gift of the Spirit (v. 18).

4 Therefore, since it is by God's mercy that we are engaged in this ministry, we do not lose heart. ²We have renounced the shameful things that one hides; we refuse to practice cunning or to falsify God's word; but by the open statement of the truth we commend ourselves to the conscience of everyone in the sight of God. ³And even if our gospel is veiled, it is veiled to those who are perishing. ⁴In their case the god of this world has blinded the minds of the unbelievers, to keep them from seeing the light of the gospel of the glory of Christ, who is the image of God. ⁵For we do not proclaim ourselves; we proclaim Jesus Christ as Lord and ourselves as your slaves for Jesus' sake. ⁶For it is the God who said, "Let light shine out of darkness," who has shone in our hearts to give the light of the knowledge of the glory of God in the face of Jesus Christ.

7 But we have this treasure in clay jars, so that it may be made clear that this extraordinary power belongs to God and does not come from us. ⁸We are afflicted in every way, but not crushed; perplexed, but not driven to despair; ⁹persecuted, but not forsaken; struck down, but not destroyed; ¹⁰always carrying in the body the death of Jesus, so that the life of Jesus may also be made visible in our bodies. ¹¹For while we live, we are always being given up to death for Jesus' sake, so that the life of Jesus may be made visible in our mortal flesh. ¹²So death is at work in us, but life in you.

13 But just as we have the same spirit of faith that is in accordance with scripture— "I believed, and so I spoke"—we also believe, and so we speak, ¹⁴because we know that the one who raised the Lord Jesus will raise us also with Jesus, and will bring us with you into his presence. ¹⁵Yes, everything is for your sake, so that grace, as it extends to more and more people, may increase thanksgiving, to the glory of God.

16 So we do not lose heart. Even though our outer nature is wasting away, our inner nature is being renewed day by day. ¹⁷For this slight momentary affliction is preparing us for an eternal weight of glory beyond all measure, ¹⁸because we look not at what can be seen but at what cannot be seen; for what can be seen is temporary, but what cannot be seen is eternal.

4.1–18. 1–6: Ministering under God's light. These remarks develop 2.17. To stand in God's presence can cause one to *lose heart*. **2:** Paul's language recalls ancient descriptions of false philosophers. Ministry carried out before God in public view requires higher standards than those found among religious impostors. **3:** *Veiled:* Paul admits his teaching can be difficult to understand (2 Pet 3.15–16). **4:** *God of this world* likely describes Satan (2.11; Jn 12.31). *Image of God:* As God's image, Christ reflects God's dazzling brilliance (3.18; Heb 1.3). **5:** The gospel is the message, ministers the messengers (Rom 10.9). **6:** The quotation draws on Gen 1.3 and Ps 112.4. Creation has been reenacted in Christ (5.17). **7–12: Embodying Jesus' death and life in ministry. 7:** *Treasure* refers to the gospel (4.3–4). Its source of power is God (Rom 1.16–17). **8–9:** This list of hardships echoes the opening prayer (1.3–7; 1 Cor 4.9–13). **10–11:** Paul's apostolic lifestyle models the message he preaches: He dies and rises with Christ (Rom 6.8). **12:** Paul's experience with death enables him to transmit life to his churches. **13–18: Ministering in the spirit of faith. 13:** Ps 115.1 in the Septuagint* (the ancient Greek translation of the Hebrew Scriptures*). *Spirit of faith* is the capacity to believe. **14:** What Christ experienced in his resurrection, ministers will experience along with their churches (Rom 8.11). **15:** *Grace* is spread by those who speak the faith they believe (v. 13). **16:** *Outer nature* and *inner nature* correspond to body and spirit (1 Cor 5.3; 7.34). Christ's Spirit renews the believer's spirit (3.18). **17:** *Eternal weight of glory* is the fullness of God's glory already revealed in Christ (3.18). **18:** This aptly summarizes Paul's understanding of hope (Rom 8.24–25; Heb 11.1–3).

5 For we know that if the earthly tent we live in is destroyed, we have a building from God, a house not made with hands, eternal in the heavens. 2For in this tent we groan, longing to be clothed with our heavenly dwelling— 3if indeed, when we have taken it off*a* we will not be found naked. 4For while we are still in this tent, we groan under our burden, because we wish not to be unclothed but to be further clothed, so that what is mortal may be swallowed up by life. 5He who has prepared us for this very thing is God, who has given us the Spirit as a guarantee.

6 So we are always confident; even though we know that while we are at home in the body we are away from the Lord— 7for we walk by faith, not by sight. 8Yes, we do have confidence, and we would rather be away from the body and at home with the Lord. 9So whether we are at home or away, we make it our aim to please him. 10For all of us must appear before the judgment seat of Christ, so that each may receive recompense for what has been done in the body, whether good or evil.

5.1–10: Looking to the future with confidence. The perishable body is compared to an *earthly tent* in Wis 9.15. *Building from God* may recall Mk 14.58, where Jesus' resurrected body is envisioned as a reconstructed temple *not made with hands*. Christ's resurrection gives the believer hope of inhabiting a similar dwelling. **2–4:** Mixing the image of inhabiting a building with putting on new clothing is awkward, but intelligible. *Taken it off:* This reading makes more sense than the alternative (note *a*). Dying is like shedding a tent. *Burden* recalls the afflictions in the list of hardships (4.8–9). Resurrection *life* swallows up *mortal* existence (1 Cor 15.42–57). **5–6:** God's raising Christ begins the preparation (4.14; 1.21–22) and establishes confidence (4.1). **7:** *Faith* in Christ's resurrection changes the way we "see" (4.13–15, 18). **8–9:** Phil

1.23–24. **10:** Resurrection faith establishes a time of accountability (Rom 14.10; 1 Cor 15.32–34).

11 Therefore, knowing the fear of the Lord, we try to persuade others; but we ourselves are well known to God, and I hope that we are also well known to your consciences. 12We are not commending ourselves to you again, but giving you an opportunity to boast about us, so that you may be able to answer those who boast in outward appearance and not in the heart. 13For if we are beside ourselves, it is for God; if we are in our right mind, it is for you. 14For the love of Christ urges us on, because we are convinced that one has died for all; therefore all have died. 15And he died for all, so that those who live might live no longer for themselves, but for him who died and was raised for them.

16 From now on, therefore, we regard no one from a human point of view;*b* even though we once knew Christ from a human point of view,*b* we know him no longer in that way. 17So if anyone is in Christ, there is a new creation: everything old has passed away; see, everything has become new! 18All this is from God, who reconciled us to himself through Christ, and has given us the ministry of reconciliation; 19that is, in Christ God was reconciling the world to himself,*c* not counting their trespasses against them, and entrusting the message of reconciliation to us. 20So we are ambassadors for Christ, since God is making his appeal through us; we entreat you on behalf of Christ, be reconciled to God. 21For our sake he made him to be sin who knew no sin, so that in him we might become the righteousness of God.

5.11–21: The ministry of reconciliation. 11: *Well known:* Nothing is hidden in ministry as defined in 4.2. **12–13:** The tone is defensive. Commending himself and being beside himself echo his opponents' criticisms (4.5; 10.12; 11.16). **14–15:** *Love of Christ:* Christ's love is meant (Rom 8.35; Gal 2.20), though love for Christ results. *Died for all:* Christ's death is a

---

a Other ancient authorities read *put it on*
b Gk *according to the flesh*   *c* Or *God was in Christ reconciling the world to himself*

sacrifice with universal benefit (Rom 18–19). *All have died:* We might expect, "All can live." But v. 15 explains: *No longer* to *live* for oneself is death to the self (Gal 2.20). **16:** *Human point of view:* What it means to see Christ this way is disputed: knowing merely the historical facts about Jesus? trying to understand Christ without seeing God's bigger story? failing to see Christ as the funnel of God's spirit? **17:** Christ is the sphere of God's *new creation* (4.5–6); to enter Christ is to experience old becoming new. **18–20:** God as the prime mover continues an earlier theme (2.14; 4.1; 5.5). *Reconciliation* makes enemies friends (Rom 5.10). *Ministry of reconciliation* continues God's work (6.1). **21:** Rom 8.3; Gal 3.13.

6 As we work together with him,^{a} we urge you also not to accept the grace of God in vain. ²For he says,

"At an acceptable time I have listened
to you,
and on a day of salvation I have
helped you."

See, now is the acceptable time; see, now is the day of salvation! ³We are putting no obstacle in anyone's way, so that no fault may be found with our ministry, ⁴but as servants of God we have commended ourselves in every way: through great endurance, in afflictions, hardships, calamities, ⁵beatings, imprisonments, riots, labors, sleepless nights, hunger; ⁶by purity, knowledge, patience, kindness, holiness of spirit, genuine love, ⁷truthful speech, and the power of God; with the weapons of righteousness for the right hand and for the left; ⁸in honor and dishonor, in ill repute and good repute. We are treated as impostors, and yet are true; ⁹as unknown, and yet are well known; as dying, and see—we are alive; as punished, and yet not killed; ¹⁰as sorrowful, yet always rejoicing; as poor, yet making many rich; as having nothing, and yet possessing everything.

11 We have spoken frankly to you Corinthians; our heart is wide open to you. ¹²There is no restriction in our affections, but only in yours. ¹³In return—I speak as to children—open wide your hearts also.

6.1–13: Working together with God. 1: 1 Cor 3.9 confirms *with him* as a correct rendering of the Greek (note *a*). **2:** Isa 49.8. **3:** This echoes the defensive tone

of chs. 10–13. **4:** *Servants of God* ("theou diakonoi") should be rendered "ministers of God" for consistency. **4–10:** Paul's list of commendations includes hardships (vv. 4b–5) and virtuous behavior (vv. 6–7) lived out among life's contradictions and puzzles (vv. 8–10). Many elements of this self-portrait are confirmed in Acts 13–28, as well as Paul's other descriptions of his ministry (1 Thess 2). The paradoxes of vv. 8–10 specify the ways he has embodied the dying and rising of Christ (4.10–12). **11–12:** This final appeal indicates the level of alienation Paul and the Corinthians had experienced (11.1–6). It continues in 7.2–4.

14 Do not be mismatched with unbelievers. For what partnership is there between righteousness and lawlessness? Or what fellowship is there between light and darkness? ¹⁵What agreement does Christ have with Beliar? Or what does a believer share with an unbeliever? ¹⁶What agreement has the temple of God with idols? For we^b are the temple of the living God; as God said,

"I will live in them and walk among
them,
and I will be their God,
and they shall be my people.
¹⁷ Therefore come out from them,
and be separate from them, says the
Lord,
and touch nothing unclean;
then I will welcome you,
¹⁸ and I will be your father,
and you shall be my sons and
daughters,
says the Lord Almighty."

7 Since we have these promises, beloved, let us cleanse ourselves from every defilement of body and of spirit, making holiness perfect in the fear of God.

6.14–7.1: Separating from evil. This section interrupts the train of thought (compare 7.2 and 6.13). Most likely it was a separate letter composed on another occasion. Some scholars think it is the "previous letter" of 1 Cor 5.9. **14:** Good and evil are seen as absolute opposites in separatist communities like Qumran and parts of early Christianity (1 Thess 5.4–5; Jn 3.19–21), but moral choices are often presented

a Gk *As we work together*   *b* Other ancient authorities read *you* as clearly opposed options (Deut 30.15–30; Mt 7.13–14). **15:** *Beliar,* also Belial, occurs often in non-biblical literature, especially that from Qumran, to describe the leader of the forces of darkness, Satan. It only occurs here in the New Testament. **16:** *Idols* and *temple* are incompatible (1 Cor 10.20–22). Combines Lev. 26.11–12 and Ezek 37.27. **17:** Combines Isa 52.11 and Ezek 20.34. **18:** Paraphrases 2 Sam 7.14, drawing on Isa 43.6 (see Jer 31.9). *Lord Almighty* reflects 2 Sam 7.8 (see Am 3.13). **7.1:** 1 Thess 4.1–6.

2 Make room in your hearts*ᵃ* for us; we have wronged no one, we have corrupted no one, we have taken advantage of no one. ³I do not say this to condemn you, for I said before that you are in our hearts, to die together and to live together. ⁴I often boast about you; I have great pride in you; I am filled with consolation; I am overjoyed in all our affliction.

5 For even when we came into Macedonia, our bodies had no rest, but we were afflicted in every way—disputes without and fears within. ⁶But God, who consoles the downcast, consoled us by the arrival of Titus, ⁷and not only by his coming, but also by the consolation with which he was consoled about you, as he told us of your longing, your mourning, your zeal for me, so that I rejoiced still more. ⁸For even if I made you sorry with my letter, I do not regret it (though I did regret it, for I see that I grieved you with that letter, though only briefly). ⁹Now I rejoice, not because you were grieved, but because your grief led to repentance; for you felt a godly grief, so that you were not harmed in any way by us. ¹⁰For godly grief produces a repentance that leads to salvation and brings no regret, but worldly grief produces death. ¹¹For see what earnestness this godly grief has produced in you, what eagerness to clear yourselves, what indignation, what alarm, what longing, what zeal, what punishment! At every point you have proved yourselves guiltless in the matter. ¹²So although I wrote to you, it was not on account of the one who did the wrong, nor on account of the one who was wronged, but in order that your zeal for us might be made known to you before God. ¹³In this we find comfort.

In addition to our own consolation, we rejoiced still more at the joy of Titus, because his mind has been set at rest by all of you. ¹⁴For if I have been somewhat boastful about you to him, I was not disgraced; but just as everything we said to you was true, so our boasting to Titus has proved true as well. ¹⁵And his heart goes out all the more to you, as he remembers the obedience of all of you, and how you welcomed him with fear and trembling. ¹⁶I rejoice, because I have complete confidence in you.

7.2–16: Paul rejoices over the church's repentance. 2: These charges explain his defense in 2.17 and 4.2. **3:** *I said before:* When is not certain; possibly 4.12. **5:** This resumes the discussion in 2.12–13. **6–7:** The *consolation* Paul received from Titus's good report about Corinth is expressed in the opening prayer (1.3–7). **8:** This is the "tearful letter" mentioned earlier (2.3–4, 9), probably chs. 10–13. **9–13:** *Godly grief,* literally "grief according to God," results in God's reconciling love (5.18–21). Either the congregation's *repentance* is in view—they finally sided with Paul (v. 12)—or the individual *who did the wrong* admitted it (2.7). This is one of the few times *repentance* occurs in Paul's letters (12.21; Rom 2.4). **13b–16:** These remarks confirm Titus's pivotal role in the crisis.

8 We want you to know, brothers and sisters,*ᵇ* about the grace of God that has been granted to the churches of Macedonia; ²for during a severe ordeal of affliction, their abundant joy and their extreme poverty have overflowed in a wealth of generosity on their part. ³For, as I can testify, they voluntarily gave according to their means, and even beyond their means, ⁴begging us earnestly for the privilege*ᶜ* of sharing in this ministry to the saints— ⁵and this, not merely as we expected; they gave themselves first to the Lord and, by the will of God, to us, ⁶so that we might urge Titus that, as he had already made a beginning, so he should also complete this generous undertaking*ᵈ* among you. ⁷Now as you excel in everything—in faith, in speech, in knowledge, in utmost eagerness, and in our love for you*ᵉ*—so we want you to excel also in this generous undertaking.*ᵈ*

a Gk lacks *in your hearts*　　*b* Gk *brothers*　　*c* Gk *grace*
d Gk *this grace*　　*e* Other ancient authorities read *your love for us*

8 I do not say this as a command, but I am testing the genuineness of your love against the earnestness of others. 9For you know the generous act^a of our Lord Jesus Christ, that though he was rich, yet for your sakes he became poor, so that by his poverty you might become rich. 10And in this matter I am giving my advice: it is appropriate for you who began last year not only to do something but even to desire to do something— 11now finish doing it, so that your eagerness may be matched by completing it according to your means. 12For if the eagerness is there, the gift is acceptable according to what one has—not according to what one does not have. 13I do not mean that there should be relief for others and pressure on you, but it is a question of a fair balance between 14your present abundance and their need, so that their abundance may be for your need, in order that there may be a fair balance. 15As it is written,

"The one who had much did not have too much,
and the one who had little did not have too little."

16 But thanks be to God who put in the heart of Titus the same eagerness for you that I myself have. 17For he not only accepted our appeal, but since he is more eager than ever, he is going to you of his own accord. 18With him we are sending the brother who is famous among all the churches for his proclaiming the good news;^{b} 19and not only that, but he has also been appointed by the churches to travel with us while we are administering this generous undertaking^c for the glory of the Lord himself^d and to show our goodwill. 20We intend that no one should blame us about this generous gift that we are administering, 21for we intend to do what is right not only in the Lord's sight but also in the sight of others. 22And with them we are sending our brother whom we have often tested and found eager in many matters, but who is now more eager than ever because of his great confidence in you. 23As for Titus, he is my partner and co-worker in your service; as for our brothers, they are messengers^e of the churches, the glory of Christ. 24Therefore openly before the churches, show them the proof of your love and of our reason for boasting about you.

8.1–9.15: The collection. 8.1–7: Macedonian generosity. 1: *Churches of Macedonia* probably means Philippi, Thessalonica, and Beroea. (Acts 16–17). 2: *Severe ordeal:* The founding of these churches had met stiff resistance (1 Thess 1.6; 3.1–5; Phil 1.29–30). 5–6: *Privilege* translates "charis," used several times in chs. 8–9, for the collection itself (vv. 6–7, note *d* on p .1941, v. 19, note *c*). Since it designates both God's generosity (8.1; 9.14) and Christ's *generous act* (8.9), it properly describes the collection as a concrete expression of good will toward others. 7: Earlier Paul commended their possession of these gifts (1 Cor 1.5–7). 8–15: Christ's generosity. 8: *Genuineness of your love* may be their love for Christ (5.14; Rom 12.9). 9: Christ is similarly portrayed in the early Christian hymn in Phil 2.5–11, where he also serves as an example for Christian behavior. 10–11: Paul had given instructions about the collection in 1 Cor 16.1–4. 12–14: The principle of *fair balance* can be expressed another way: Since Jews have bestowed a spiritual blessing on gentiles,* they are entitled to receive a physical blessing (financial support) from gentiles (Rom 15.27). 15: Ex 16.18.

8.16–24: Plans for collecting and delivering the funds. As Paul's *partner and co-worker* (v. 23), Titus played a key role in getting the collection started in Corinth (v. 6). 18–19: The identity of this famous preacher is unknown. Because of his eloquence and close association with Corinth, Apollos is a possibility (Acts 18.24–19.1; 1 Cor 1–4). 20–21: Whether the *blame* related to how the money was being collected and handled in transit, or how it was to be used, is not clear. As with many projects involving money, it was controversial (Rom 15.30–33). 22: Our *brother* is possibly Timothy (see comment on 1.1). 23: *Messengers* translates "apostoloi" (note *e*), literally "ones sent" for a particular purpose (Rom 16.7). 24: The other *churches* in Macedonia and Achaia are in view.

9 Now it is not necessary for me to write you about the ministry to the saints, 2for I know your eagerness, which is the subject

a Gk *the grace* *b* Or *the gospel* *c* Gk *this grace*
d Other ancient authorities lack *himself* *e* Gk *apostles*

of my boasting about you to the people of Macedonia, saying that Achaia has been ready since last year; and your zeal has stirred up most of them. ³But I am sending the brothers in order that our boasting about you may not prove to have been empty in this case, so that you may be ready, as I said you would be; ⁴otherwise, if some Macedonians come with me and find that you are not ready, we would be humiliated—to say nothing of you—in this undertaking.ᵃ ⁵So I thought it necessary to urge the brothers to go on ahead to you, and arrange in advance for this bountiful gift that you have promised, so that it may be ready as a voluntary gift and not as an extortion.

6 The point is this: the one who sows sparingly will also reap sparingly, and the one who sows bountifully will also reap bountifully. ⁷Each of you must give as you have made up your mind, not reluctantly or under compulsion, for God loves a cheerful giver. ⁸And God is able to provide you with every blessing in abundance, so that by always having enough of everything, you may share abundantly in every good work. ⁹As it is written,

"He scatters abroad, he gives to
　　the poor;
his righteousnessᵇ endures forever."

¹⁰He who supplies seed to the sower and bread for food will supply and multiply your seed for sowing and increase the harvest of your righteousness.ᵇ ¹¹You will be enriched in every way for your great generosity, which will produce thanksgiving to God through us; ¹²for the rendering of this ministry not only supplies the needs of the saints but also overflows with many thanksgivings to God. ¹³Through the testing of this ministry you glorify God by your obedience to the confession of the gospel of Christ and by the generosity of your sharing with them and with all others, ¹⁴while they long for you and pray for you because of the surpassing grace of God that he has given you. ¹⁵Thanks be to God for his indescribable gift!

brothers are those mentioned in 8.18, 22. **5:** *V gift:* It should be like Christ's gift (8.9). **6–15:** **to give. 6:** The proverb expresses general experience (Job 4.8; Prov. 11.24–25). **7:** The gift should be deliberate and voluntary (Philem 14). *God loves a cheerful giver:* This quotation is based on the Septuagint* version (the ancient Greek translation of the Hebrew Scriptures*) of Prov 22.8a (see Sir 35.9). **8:** God's generosity toward human beings is a recurrent biblical theme (Deut 30.9–10; Lk 1.53). For Paul, it especially enables human generosity. **9:** Ps 112.9. **10:** Based on Isa 55.10. **11–12:** The more blessings, the more prayers of thanksgiving offered. **13:** Willingness to give is seen as an expression (and test) of one's confession of faith. **14–15:** God's graciousness is the ultimate reason to give.

10 I myself, Paul, appeal to you by the meekness and gentleness of Christ—I who am humble when face to face with you, but bold toward you when I am away!— ²I ask that when I am present I need not show boldness by daring to oppose those who think we are acting according to human standards.ᶜ ³Indeed, we live as human beings,ᵈ but we do not wage war according to human standards;ᵉ ⁴for the weapons of our warfare are not merely human,ᵉ but they have divine power to destroy strongholds. We destroy arguments ⁵and every proud obstacle raised up against the knowledge of God, and we take every thought captive to obey Christ. ⁶We are ready to punish every disobedience when your obedience is complete.

7 Look at what is before your eyes. If you are confident that you belong to Christ, remind yourself of this, that just as you belong to Christ, so also do we. ⁸Now, even if I boast a little too much of our authority, which the Lord gave for building you up and not for tearing you down, I will not be ashamed of it. ⁹I do not want to seem as though I am trying to frighten you with my letters. ¹⁰For they say, "His letters are weighty and strong, but his bodily presence is weak, and his speech contemptible." ¹¹Let such people understand that what we say by letter when absent, we will also do when present.

9.1–15. 1–5: Paul explains the purpose of the delegation. 1: *Ministry to the saints* is another name for the collection (8.4, 20). **2:** *Last year:* 8.10. **3:** The

a Other ancient authorities add *of boasting*
b Or *benevolence*　　*c* Gk *according to the flesh*
d Gk *in the flesh*　　*e* Gk *fleshly*

12 We do not dare to classify or compare ourselves with some of those who commend themselves. But when they measure themselves by one another, and compare themselves with one another, they do not show good sense. 13 We, however, will not boast beyond limits, but will keep within the field that God has assigned to us, to reach out even as far as you. 14 For we were not overstepping our limits when we reached you; we were the first to come all the way to you with the good news^a of Christ. 15 We do not boast beyond limits, that is, in the labors of others; but our hope is that, as your faith increases, our sphere of action among you may be greatly enlarged, 16 so that we may proclaim the good news^a in lands beyond you, without boasting of work already done in someone else's sphere of action. 17 "Let the one who boasts, boast in the Lord." 18 For it is not those who commend themselves that are approved, but those whom the Lord commends.

11 I wish you would bear with me in a little foolishness. Do bear with me! 2 I feel a divine jealousy for you, for I promised you in marriage to one husband, to present you as a chaste virgin to Christ. 3 But I am afraid that as the serpent deceived Eve by its cunning, your thoughts will be led astray from a sincere and pure^b devotion to Christ. 4 For if someone comes and proclaims another Jesus than the one we proclaimed, or if you receive a different spirit from the one you received, or a different gospel from the one you accepted, you submit to it readily enough. 5 I think that I am not in the least inferior to these super-apostles. 6 I may be untrained in speech, but not in knowledge; certainly in every way and in all things we have made this evident to you.

7 Did I commit a sin by humbling myself so that you might be exalted, because I proclaimed God's good news^c to you free of charge? 8 I robbed other churches by accepting support from them in order to serve you. 9 And when I was with you and was in need, I did not burden anyone, for my needs were supplied by the friends^d who came from Macedonia. So I refrained and will continue to refrain from burdening you in any way. 10 As the truth of Christ is in me, this boast of mine will not be silenced in the regions of Achaia. 11 And why? Because I do not love you? God knows I do!

12 And what I do I will also continue to do, in order to deny an opportunity to those who want an opportunity to be recognized as our equals in what they boast about. 13 For such boasters are false apostles, deceitful workers, disguising themselves as apostles of Christ. 14 And no wonder! Even Satan disguises himself as an angel of light. 15 So it is not strange if his ministers also disguise themselves as ministers of righteousness. Their end will match their deeds.

10.1–13.10: Paul defends his ministry. 10.1–11: Taking the offensive. 1: The character of Christ figures prominently in chs. 10–13 (11.4; Mt 11.29). *Humble . . . bold:* Paul mimics his opponents' description of him (v. 10). **2–4:** *Human* translates "sarx," literally "flesh" (notes *c, d, e,* p. 1943). It denotes an outlook opposed to God and concerned primarily with oneself. **4–6:** The military imagery serves to draw the battle lines between Paul and his opponents. He sees the controversy as more than a battle of words; it is a conflict of a much higher order (Rom 13.12; Eph 6.10–17). **7:** Paul's fidelity to Christ was an issue. **8–9:** The source and nature of Paul's *authority* are concerns throughout this section (13.10). **10:** This identifies two important criticisms: inconsistent behavior (1.15–22) and poor speaking ability (4.2; 11.6). **12–18: Limits of self-promotion. 12:** *Commend themselves:* Paul was probably accused of making himself the center of his preaching (3.1–3; 4.5; 5.12). Now he criticizes his opponents for promoting themselves as a way of gaining favor. **13–16:** Paul regarded Achaia as the region God assigned him. He thinks the "super-apostles" (12.11) have invaded his territory. He preferred to work where no one else had been (Rom 15.20). **17:** Jer 9.23–24; see 1 Cor 1.31. **18:** Paul consistently defers to God's judgment (1 Cor 4.3–4).

11.1–15: Paul's love for the Corinthians. 1: *Foolishness:* This anticipates the fool's speech that follows (11.16–29). **2:** The image is a father whose daughter has deeply disappointed him. **3:** Gen 3.13. *Led astray*

---

^a Or *the gospel*   ^b Other ancient authorities lack *and pure*   ^c Gk *the gospel of God*   ^d Gk *brothers*

suggests sexual seduction. **4:** The opponents are obviously Christian. *Another Jesus* probably means an understanding of Christ completely different from Paul's, perhaps one emphasizing Jesus' miracle-working power and resurrection to the neglect of his human limitations and crucifixion. *Different spirit* is possibly a different understanding of the Holy Spirit. Their different gospel certainly placed them at odds with Paul (Gal 1.6–9). **5:** *Super-apostles:* This is doubtless Paul's label for his opponents (12.11). It need not refer to the twelve apostles,* but could be a derisive way of referring to competing missionaries. **6:** He echoes their criticisms of him. **7–9:** In keeping with the policy outlined in 1 Cor 9, he preached without pay. *Humbling myself* refers to working to support himself. *Other churches:* He received financial support from the Philippians (Phil 4.15). **11:** His opponents might have argued: If he loved you, he would accept your money. **12:** *Equals:* They wanted to have equal claim on the church. **13:** The language is unusually harsh. *Apostles* probably means "missionaries," rather than some of the twelve apostles (8.23; 12.11–13). **14–15:** Calling them ministers of Satan intensifies the criticism.

16 I repeat, let no one think that I am a fool; but if you do, then accept me as a fool, so that I too may boast a little. 17What I am saying in regard to this boastful confidence, I am saying not with the Lord's authority, but as a fool; 18since many boast according to human standards,*a* I will also boast. 19For you gladly put up with fools, being wise yourselves! 20For you put up with it when someone makes slaves of you, or preys upon you, or takes advantage of you, or puts on airs, or gives you a slap in the face. 21To my shame, I must say, we were too weak for that!

But whatever anyone dares to boast of—I am speaking as a fool—I also dare to boast of that. 22Are they Hebrews? So am I. Are they Israelites? So am I. Are they descendants of Abraham? So am I. 23Are they ministers of Christ? I am talking like a madman—I am a better one: with far greater labors, far more imprisonments, with countless floggings, and often near death. 24Five times I have received from the Jews the forty lashes minus one. 25Three times I was beaten with rods. Once I received a stoning. Three times I was shipwrecked; for a night

and a day I was adrift at sea; 26on frequent journeys, in danger from rivers, danger from bandits, danger from my own people, danger from Gentiles, danger in the city, danger in the wilderness, danger at sea, danger from false brothers and sisters;*b* 27in toil and hardship, through many a sleepless night, hungry and thirsty, often without food, cold and naked. 28And, besides other things, I am under daily pressure because of my anxiety for all the churches. 29Who is weak, and I am not weak? Who is made to stumble, and I am not indignant?

30 If I must boast, I will boast of the things that show my weakness. 31The God and Father of the Lord Jesus (blessed be he forever!) knows that I do not lie. 32In Damascus, the governor*c* under King Aretas guarded the city of Damascus in order to*d* seize me, 33but I was let down in a basket through a window in the wall,*e* and escaped from his hands.

11.16–33: A fool speaks! 18: They boast in self-achievements (10.2–4). **19:** This recalls Paul's description of the "spiritual people" in 1 Cor 4.10. **20:** They submit to the false apostles'* demands for money. **22:** These labels identify them as Jewish Christians. Unlike Paul's opponents in Galatia, they do not require circumcision* and observance of the law (Gal 5.2–6). **23:** *Ministers of Christ:* Their language is Christian (11.4). *Madman:* 5.13. **23–27:** This list of hardships is longer and more detailed than others (6.4–10). Acts 13–28 confirms many of these details. **24:** This indicates Paul was under synagogue* jurisdiction. **28:** *Anxiety:* This was especially seen in the way he awaited Titus's report (2.12–13; 7.5, 13; 1 Thess 2). **30–33:** This episode caps the list of hardships. **31:** The use of the oath underscores that the claims that follow will be hard to believe (Gal 1.20). **32–33:** This may be the escape referred to in Acts 9.23–25.

12 It is necessary to boast; nothing is to be gained by it, but I will go on to visions and revelations of the Lord. 21 know a person in Christ who fourteen years ago was caught up to the third heaven—whether

---

a Gk *according to the flesh*   *b* Gk *brothers*
c Gk *ethnarch*   *d* Other ancient authorities read *and wanted to*   *e* Gk *through the wall*

in the body or out of the body I do not know; God knows. ³And I know that such a person—whether in the body or out of the body I do not know; God knows— ⁴was caught up into Paradise and heard things that are not to be told, that no mortal is permitted to repeat. ⁵On behalf of such a one I will boast, but on my own behalf I will not boast, except of my weaknesses. ⁶But if I wish to boast, I will not be a fool, for I will be speaking the truth. But I refrain from it, so that no one may think better of me than what is seen in me or heard from me, ⁷even considering the exceptional character of the revelations. Therefore, to keep*a* me from being too elated, a thorn was given me in the flesh, a messenger of Satan to torment me, to keep me from being too elated.*b* ⁸Three times I appealed to the Lord about this, that it would leave me, ⁹but he said to me, "My grace is sufficient for you, for power*c* is made perfect in weakness." So, I will boast all the more gladly of my weaknesses, so that the power of Christ may dwell in me. ¹⁰Therefore I am content with weaknesses, insults, hardships, persecutions, and calamities for the sake of Christ; for whenever I am weak, then I am strong.

11 I have been a fool! You forced me to it. Indeed you should have been the ones commending me, for I am not at all inferior to these super-apostles, even though I am nothing. ¹²The signs of a true apostle were performed among you with utmost patience, signs and wonders and mighty works. ¹³How have you been worse off than the other churches, except that I myself did not burden you? Forgive me this wrong!

12.1–13. 1–10: Experiencing visions and revelations of the Lord. 1: Paul now moves to a different order of boasting. **2:** The *person in Christ* is surely Paul himself. *Fourteen years ago* would put it shortly after his conversion, probably in the 30s. **3:** The language suggests an ecstatic experience, in which he was taken *out of the body.* **4:** *Paradise* is where God dwells (Lk 23.43; Rev 2.7). Hearing unrepeatable things describes the *revelations* in greater detail (v. 1). What he saw is emphasized less. **5:** Such an experience enabled Paul to distinguish his ordinary self from the one *caught up* into heaven. **6–7:** In talking about such experiences, less is better. **7:** What this *thorn in the flesh* was no one knows, though many guesses have been made. *Messenger of Satan* is literally "angel of Satan." **8:** *The Lord* can be either God (1.2) or Christ (13.14). **9:** *Power of Christ:* Christ transmits the power he experienced in the resurrection (4.11; 1 Cor 6.14). **10:** *Weak . . . strong* expresses the paradox of the cross (1 Cor 1.25). **11–13: Concluding the fool's speech. 11:** *Super-apostles:* 11.5. *I am nothing:* Again Paul speaks sarcastically, mimicking the opponents (10.7). **12:** Paul occasionally refers to his wonder-working ability (Rom 15.19). It is developed much more fully in Acts. **13:** Their argument could have run: You were much closer to Philippi; they supported you financially (Phil 4.15).

14 Here I am, ready to come to you this third time. And I will not be a burden, because I do not want what is yours but you; for children ought not to lay up for their parents, but parents for their children. ¹⁵I will most gladly spend and be spent for you. If I love you more, am I to be loved less? ¹⁶Let it be assumed that I did not burden you. Nevertheless (you say) since I was crafty, I took you in by deceit. ¹⁷Did I take advantage of you through any of those whom I sent to you? ¹⁸I urged Titus to go, and sent the brother with him. Titus did not take advantage of you, did he? Did we not conduct ourselves with the same spirit? Did we not take the same steps?

19 Have you been thinking all along that we have been defending ourselves before you? We are speaking in Christ before God. Everything we do, beloved, is for the sake of building you up. ²⁰For I fear that when I come, I may find you not as I wish, and that you may find me not as you wish; I fear that there may perhaps be quarreling, jealousy, anger, selfishness, slander, gossip, conceit, and disorder. ²¹I fear that when I come again, my God may humble me before you, and that I may have to mourn over many who previously sinned and have not repented of the impurity, sexual immorality, and licentiousness that they have practiced.

a Other ancient authorities read *To keep*   *b* Other ancient authorities lack *to keep me from being too elated*   *c* Other ancient authorities read *my power*

12.14–21: Fatherly love and anxiety. 14: *Third time:* The founding visit (Acts 18) was followed by the painful visit (2.1), which prompted this severe letter. Writing from Macedonia, he is now ready to come a third time (13.1). *What is yours:* He did not want their money. The parent-child image extends through both letters (11.2; 1 Cor 4.14–15). **16:** *Crafty* explains his denials in 2.17 and 4.2. **17–18:** The sending of *Titus* and *the brother* described in 8.16–24 appears to be in view. *Taking advantage* could be applying pressure to participate in the collection. **19:** His self-defense has occurred under oath. *Building up* defines the purpose and limits of Paul's use of authority (10.8). **20:** Some of these vices of social disorder have been present for a long time (1 Cor 1–4). **21:** Sexual sins have not figured prominently in 2 Corinthians, although they are included in the warnings of 6.14–7.1. These fears may go back to the first letter (1 Cor 5, 7).

13 This is the third time I am coming to you. "Any charge must be sustained by the evidence of two or three witnesses." ²I warned those who sinned previously and all the others, and I warn them now while absent, as I did when present on my second visit, that if I come again, I will not be lenient— ³since you desire proof that Christ is speaking in me. He is not weak in dealing with you, but is powerful in you. ⁴For he was crucified in weakness, but lives by the power of God. For we are weak in him,ᵃ but in dealing with you we will live with him by the power of God.

5 Examine yourselves to see whether you are living in the faith. Test yourselves. Do you not realize that Jesus Christ is in you?—unless, indeed, you fail to meet the test! ⁶I hope you will find out that we have not failed. ⁷But we pray to God that you may not do anything wrong—not that we may appear to have met the test, but that you may do what is right, though we may seem to have failed. ⁸For we cannot do anything against the truth, but only for the truth. ⁹For we rejoice when we are weak and you are strong. This is what we pray for, that you may become perfect. ¹⁰So I write these things while I am away from you, so that when I come, I may not have to be severe in using the authority that the Lord has given me for building up and not for tearing down.

11 Finally, brothers and sisters,ᵇ farewell.ᶜ Put things in order, listen to my appeal,ᵈ agree with one another, live in peace; and the God of love and peace will be with you. ¹²Greet one another with a holy kiss. All the saints greet you.

13 The grace of the Lord Jesus Christ, the love of God, and the communion ofᵉ the Holy Spirit be with all of you.

13.1–13. 1–4: Final warnings. 1: *Third time:* 12.14; the quotation is from Deut 19.15. **2:** Paul resumes the tone of a stern father (1 Cor 4.18–21). **3:** Again, the tone is sarcastic. They could have asked: How do we know your apostolic call is legitimate? **4:** Like 4.7–12, Paul's lifestyle bears the stamp of Christ's death and resurrection. Defining the resurrection power as the power to discipline is a new wrinkle. **5–10: Parting advice. 5:** Such advice, taken seriously, makes them less vulnerable to the pressures of outside teachers. The presence of Christ within them should give them confidence to chart their own course (Rom 8.10). **6–9:** These are the words of an anxious father—self-doubts, fear that his children will never grow up, willingness to be weak as long as the children are strong. **10:** He closes with a father's threat (10.8; 12.19). **11–13: Farewell and benediction. 11:** Such advice brings harmony. **12:** The *holy kiss* was a form of liturgical greeting that may have originated in early Christian circles (Rom 16.16; 1 Cor 16.20). **13:** The trinitarian form of the benediction is distinctive.

a Other ancient authorities read *with him* b Gk *brothers* c Or *rejoice* d Or *encourage one another* e Or *and the sharing in*

THE LETTER OF PAUL TO THE
GALATIANS

Introduction

Some of Paul's most biting language occurs in this letter addressed to "the churches of Galatia" (1.2). He is put out with his readers because they are rejecting what he had taught them (3.1; 4.12–20), and even more put out with those teachers who are leading his churches astray. Paul charges them with "perverting the gospel of Christ" by insisting that gentiles✴ must observe the Mosaic law. In particular, they are requiring circumcision.✴ For Paul, the issues being fought over in Galatia have enormous consequences. The truth of the gospel he has preached through-out the eastern Mediterranean is at stake. If the other side is right, Christ's death was in vain.

Many of the themes addressed in Romans are treated here, but the focus is different. The role of the Mosaic law remains a central question, as does justification by faith. The example of Abraham figures centrally in the argument (3.6–18). New arguments also appear, such as the allegory✴ comparing Hagar and Sarah (4.21–31). More than in Romans, here the choice between law and gospel is seen as a choice between slavery and freedom (chs. 4–5). The tone is also more polemical✴ than Romans because Paul's apostleship has been directly attacked. He is much more defensive in Galatians and consequently devotes much of the opening chapters to personal concerns.

When Galatians was written is not certain. Many scholars think it was written about the same time as Romans, while Paul was in Corinth en route to Jerusalem with the collection for the poor Christians there. This view accounts for their similarity of theme but also for their differences in outlook. Galatians is directed to churches Paul himself had started (4.11–20). Other teachers who are sharply critical of Paul's work as an apostle✴ and his understanding of the gospel are now present in these churches. Fearing the Galatians will abandon his teachings and begin observing Torah,✴ Paul writes this angry letter denouncing the Galatians as weak and indecisive, and the new teachers as enemies of Christ.

READING GUIDE

The letter divides into three parts. The opening section (1.6–2.14) deals with personal matters—Paul's earlier life in Judaism, his apostolic call, his meeting with other Christian leaders in Jerusalem, and his confrontation with Peter in Antioch. The middle of the letter (2.15–4.31) is a tightly packed treatment of Paul's gospel in which he explains the effects of Christ's death on the Mosaic law. The last two chapters (5.1–6.18) move to more practical concerns. Here Paul explains the freedom Christ has brought. He gives moral teaching that sketches a profile of Christian behavior.

1 Paul an apostle—sent neither by human commission nor from human authorities, but through Jesus Christ and God the Father, who raised him from the dead— 2and all the members of God's family*a* who are with me,

To the churches of Galatia:

3 Grace to you and peace from God our Father and the Lord Jesus Christ, 4who gave himself for our sins to set us free from the present evil age, according to the will of our God and Father, 5to whom be the glory forever and ever. Amen.

6 I am astonished that you are so quickly deserting the one who called you in the grace of Christ and are turning to a different gospel— 7not that there is another gospel, but there are some who are confusing you and want to pervert the gospel of Christ. 8But even if we or an angel*b* from heaven should proclaim to you a gospel contrary to what we proclaimed to you, let that one be accursed! 9As we have said before, so now I repeat, if anyone proclaims to you a gospel contrary to what you received, let that one be accursed!

10 Am I now seeking human approval, or God's approval? Or am I trying to please people? If I were still pleasing people, I would not be a servant*c* of Christ.

11 For I want you to know, brothers and sisters,*d* that the gospel that was proclaimed by me is not of human origin; 12for I did not receive it from a human source, nor was I taught it, but I received it through a revelation of Jesus Christ.

1.1–12. 1–5: Greeting. 1: Paul's strong denial of the *human* origin of his apostleship (1.11–12) is a hint of the controversy that drives this letter. **4:** *Gave himself:* Christ's death is understood as a sin offering for others (Eph 5.2; Lev 4–5). **6–12: Paul defends his gospel.** Paul omits his normal opening prayer of thanksgiving for his readers, showing how angry he is with them (contrast 1 Cor 1.4–9). **6–7:** *Different gospel* refers to the views Paul opposes in the letter; mainly, that God requires gentile* Christians to observe the Mosaic law (4.21; 5.2–4). **8–9:** The use of a double curse is especially emphatic (1 Cor 16.22). **10:** The perspective of Paul's critics. **11–12:** *Human origin* renders "kata anthropon," literally "according to man," thus human. *Revelation of Jesus Christ:* Paul's understanding of the gospel occurred through a revelation whose content was Jesus Christ (v. 16).

13 You have heard, no doubt, of my earlier life in Judaism. I was violently persecuting the church of God and was trying to destroy it. 14I advanced in Judaism beyond many among my people of the same age, for I was far more zealous for the traditions of my ancestors. 15But when God, who had set me apart before I was born and called me through his grace, was pleased 16to reveal his Son to me,*e* so that I might proclaim him among the Gentiles, I did not confer with any human being, 17nor did I go up to Jerusalem to those who were already apostles before me, but I went away at once into Arabia, and afterwards I returned to Damascus.

a Gk *all the brothers*   *b* Or *a messenger*   *c* Gk *slave*
d Gk *brothers*   *e* Gk *in me*

18 Then after three years I did go up to Jerusalem to visit Cephas and stayed with him fifteen days; 19but I did not see any other apostle except James the Lord's brother. 20In what I am writing to you, before God, I do not lie! 21Then I went into the regions of Syria and Cilicia, 22and I was still unknown by sight to the churches of Judea that are in Christ; 23they only heard it said, "The one who formerly was persecuting us is now proclaiming the faith he once tried to destroy." 24And they glorified God because of me.

1.13–24: Paul recalls his past. 13: His role as persecutor was a key memory informing Paul's understanding of his apostleship (1 Cor 15.9; Acts 8.3). 14: His formal training as a Pharisee* is in view (Phil 3.5–6; Acts 22.3). 15: The language recalls Old Testament prophetic calls (Isa 49.1; Jer 1.5). 16: The experience changed Paul into the apostle* to the gentiles* (Rom 15.15–16; Acts 9.15). 17: Paul's autobiographical account differs slightly from the story of his call in Acts 9. In Acts 9.26–30; 22.17–21, Paul returns to *Jerusalem* immediately after his conversion. *Arabia* was a nearby region. The return *to Damascus* locates the events of v. 15 (Acts 9; 2 Cor 11.32–33). 18–19: This visit is sometimes identified with Acts 9.26–30, although Acts 9 mentions neither *Cephas* (Peter) nor *James*. 20: 2 Cor 11.31. 21: *Syria* is the region of Damascus; *Cilicia* is eastern Asia Minor. 22–23: This is difficult to harmonize with Acts 9.26–30.

2 Then after fourteen years I went up again to Jerusalem with Barnabas, taking Titus along with me. 2I went up in response to a revelation. Then I laid before them (though only in a private meeting with the acknowledged leaders) the gospel that I proclaim among the Gentiles, in order to make sure that I was not running, or had not run, in vain. 3But even Titus, who was with me, was not compelled to be circumcised, though he was a Greek. 4But because of false believers*a* secretly brought in, who slipped in to spy on the freedom we have in Christ Jesus, so that they might enslave us— 5we did not submit to them even for a moment, so that the truth of the gospel might always remain with you. 6And from those who were supposed to be acknowledged leaders (what they actually were makes no difference to me; God shows no partiality)—those leaders contributed nothing to me. 7On the contrary, when they saw that I had been entrusted with the gospel for the uncircumcised, just as Peter had been entrusted with the gospel for the circumcised 8(for he who worked through Peter making him an apostle to the circumcised also worked through me in sending me to the Gentiles), 9and when James and Cephas and John, who were acknowledged pillars, recognized the grace that had been given to me, they gave to Barnabas and me the right hand of fellowship, agreeing that we should go to the Gentiles and they to the circumcised. 10They asked only one thing, that we remember the poor, which was actually what I was*b* eager to do.

2.1–10: The Jerusalem summit meeting. 1: Acts 15 reports Paul and Barnabas's visit to the Jerusalem conference, but not the visit of Titus. The content of that meeting differs substantially from what Paul reports here. 2: *Revelation:* Paul felt compelled by God to go. 3: As an uncircumcised gentile,* *Titus* serves as the test case. 4: These *false brothers* (note *a*) remain unidentified. "Brothers" suggests they are Christians (Acts 15.5). 6: *Acknowledged leaders:* The Greek reads, "those who were supposed to be something." They appear to be different from those named in vv. 7–9. 7–8: How Paul came up with this division of labor is not clear. Acts presents Peter preaching both to Jews and gentiles, although Paul is mainly responsible for the gentile mission outside of Palestine. V. 8 refers to Paul's call (1.15–16). 9: *James* is probably the brother of Jesus, not the apostle* (Acts 15.13–21; 12.1–5). *Cephas* is Peter (v. 7). *John* is nowhere else mentioned by Paul; he is probably the apostle (Acts 3–4; Mt 4.21). James and Peter are mentioned in Acts 15; John is not. *Acknowledged pillars* may be sarcastic: "supposedly pillars." It nonetheless indicates their status as leaders. 10: Acts 15 does not mention the collection (see Acts 11.27–29). It figures prominently in Paul's letters (1 Cor 16.1–4; 2 Cor 8–9; Rom 15.25–27).

11 But when Cephas came to Antioch, I opposed him to his face, because he stood self-condemned; 12for until certain people

a Gk *false brothers* *b* Or *had been*

came from James, he used to eat with the Gentiles. But after they came, he drew back and kept himself separate for fear of the circumcision faction. 13And the other Jews joined him in this hypocrisy, so that even Barnabas was led astray by their hypocrisy. 14But when I saw that they were not acting consistently with the truth of the gospel, I said to Cephas before them all, "If you, though a Jew, live like a Gentile and not like a Jew, how can you compel the Gentiles to live like Jews?"*a*

15 We ourselves are Jews by birth and not Gentile sinners; 16yet we know that a person is justified*b* not by the works of the law but through faith in Jesus Christ.*c* And we have come to believe in Christ Jesus, so that we might be justified by faith in Christ,*d* and not by doing the works of the law, because no one will be justified by the works of the law. 17But if, in our effort to be justified in Christ, we ourselves have been found to be sinners, is Christ then a servant of sin? Certainly not! 18But if I build up again the very things that I once tore down, then I demonstrate that I am a transgressor. 19For through the law I died to the law, so that I might live to God. I have been crucified with Christ; 20and it is no longer I who live, but it is Christ who lives in me. And the life I now live in the flesh I live by faith in the Son of God,*e* who loved me and gave himself for me. 21I do not nullify the grace of God; for if justification*f* comes through the law, then Christ died for nothing.

2.11–14: Paul opposes Peter at Antioch. 11: When the Antioch visit occurred is not known. **12–13:** *This hypocrisy:* Eating with gentiles* indicated full acceptance. Refusing to do so implied their "uncleanness" before God. For Paul, gentile Christians were accepted by God. Their status before God did not change with the coming and going of conservative Jews. The *circumcision* faction,* literally "those of the circumcision," required gentile Christians to be circumcised (5.2–6). **14:** "How can you meet gentiles half way (not keep food laws), then require them to go the whole way (be circumcised)?" **15–21: Paul's gospel: We are justified through Christ, not the law. 15:** *Gentile sinners:* 1 Thess 4.5. **16:** *Reckoned as righteous* (by God) well expresses *justified* (note *b*); see Rom 3.21–26.

Faith in Jesus Christ: Christ is the object of our faith; we trust him as God's agent of redemption. *Faith of Jesus Christ* (note *d*): Christ's own faithfulness to God enables our salvation (Rom 3.22, 26). **17:** Does Christ serve sin's purpose by exposing us as sinners? **18:** What Paul *tore down* was Torah* observance as the only basis for relating to God. **19:** Paul found the demands of the law suffocating (Rom. 7.9–10). **19b–20:** *Crucified with Christ:* Paul reenacted Christ's death as a coparticipant. Like Christ, he experienced a death of the self (Rom 6.10). Now filled with the living Christ, his life exhibits faith defined by Christ—either trust placed in Christ or the pattern of faithfulness Christ himself displayed before God (note *e*). Christ's death exemplifies love for others (1.4; 2 Cor 5.14). **21:** This briefly states Paul's position.

3 You foolish Galatians! Who has bewitched you? It was before your eyes that Jesus Christ was publicly exhibited as crucified! 2The only thing I want to learn from you is this: Did you receive the Spirit by doing the works of the law or by believing what you heard? 3Are you so foolish? Having started with the Spirit, are you now ending with the flesh? 4Did you experience so much for nothing?—if it really was for nothing. 5Well then, does God*g* supply you with the Spirit and work miracles among you by your doing the works of the law, or by your believing what you heard?

3.1–5: Recalling the Galatians' conversion. 1: Paul's preaching and lifestyle *publicly* displayed Christ's crucifixion (1 Cor 2.1–2; 2 Cor 4.10–12). **2:** *Receive the Spirit:* The mark of genuine conversion is experiencing God's life-giving Spirit through Christ (Rom 8.9). **3:** *Flesh* and law are closely identified in Paul (Rom 8.3). **5:** *Work miracles* (literally "working powers") signified the presence of the Spirit (1 Cor 12.10).

6 Just as Abraham "believed God, and it was reckoned to him as righteousness," 7so, you see, those who believe are the descendants of Abraham. 8And the scripture, foreseeing that God would justify the Gentiles

a Some interpreters hold that the quotation extends into the following paragraph   *b* Or *reckoned as righteous;* and so elsewhere   *c* Or *the faith of Jesus Christ*   *d* Or *the faith of Christ*   *e* Or *by the faith of the Son of God*   *f* Or *righteousness*   *g* Gk *he* by faith, declared the gospel beforehand to Abraham, saying, "All the Gentiles shall be blessed in you." [9] For this reason, those who believe are blessed with Abraham who believed.

10 For all who rely on the works of the law are under a curse; for it is written, "Cursed is everyone who does not observe and obey all the things written in the book of the law." [11] Now it is evident that no one is justified before God by the law; for "The one who is righteous will live by faith." [a] [12] But the law does not rest on faith; on the contrary, "Whoever does the works of the law [b] will live by them." [13] Christ redeemed us from the curse of the law by becoming a curse for us—for it is written, "Cursed is everyone who hangs on a tree"— [14] in order that in Christ Jesus the blessing of Abraham might come to the Gentiles, so that we might receive the promise of the Spirit through faith.

15 Brothers and sisters, [c] I give an example from daily life: once a person's will [d] has been ratified, no one adds to it or annuls it. [16] Now the promises were made to Abraham and to his offspring; [e] it does not say, "And to offsprings," [f] as of many; but it says, "And to your offspring," [e] that is, to one person, who is Christ. [17] My point is this: the law, which came four hundred thirty years later, does not annul a covenant previously ratified by God, so as to nullify the promise. [18] For if the inheritance comes from the law, it no longer comes from the promise; but God granted it to Abraham through the promise.

3.6–18: God's promise to Abraham. This treatment of Abraham should be compared with Rom 4. **6:** Gen 15.6; see Rom 4.3. **7:** Abraham's true descendants are not the circumcised, but those who have faith like his (Rom 4.16). **8:** Gen 12.3; 18.18. **9:** *Those who believe,* both Jews and gentiles,* share Abraham's capacity for faith. **10:** Deut 27.26. The emphasis is on *all the things:* obligation to do everything the law says. Since this is impossible, the law is a *curse.* Romans omits this argument (see James 2.10). **11:** For Paul, faith as an alternative way of relating to God is expressed in Hab 2.4, however it is understood (see note *a*; Rom 1.17). **12:** Paul uses Lev 18.5 to show that the law is based

on doing, not believing (Rom 10.5). **13:** *The curse of the law* is not being able to do everything in the law (v. 10). A curse was needed to break the curse: Christ's death by crucifixion broke the law (Deut 21.23). **14:** *The blessing of Abraham* is God's promise to Abraham mentioned in v. 8. **15–18:** The illustration of the will is based on Gen 13.15; 17.8; 24.7. Paul sees the singular use of *offspring,* literally "seed" ("sperma") as significant. Since it is singular, it cannot refer to Abraham's many descendants. Rather it must refer to a single descendant of Abraham who made God's promise possible—Christ (v. 16). **17:** Ex 12.40. The covenant* with Abraham envisioned that through a single person the gentiles would be blessed. Since this was like a ratified will, the law that came later did not void the earlier agreement. This can only mean that the law was not the channel through which the promise was kept alive. The promise bypassed the law.

---

19 Why then the law? It was added because of transgressions, until the offspring [e] would come to whom the promise had been made; and it was ordained through angels by a mediator. [20] Now a mediator involves more than one party; but God is one.

21 Is the law then opposed to the promises of God? Certainly not! For if a law had been given that could make alive, then righteousness would indeed come through the law. [22] But the scripture has imprisoned all things under the power of sin, so that what was promised through faith in Jesus Christ [g] might be given to those who believe.

23 Now before faith came, we were imprisoned and guarded under the law until faith would be revealed. [24] Therefore the law was our disciplinarian until Christ came, so that we might be justified by faith. [25] But now that faith has come, we are no longer subject to a disciplinarian, [26] for in Christ Jesus you are all children of God through faith. [27] As many of you as were baptized into Christ have clothed yourselves with Christ. [28] There is no longer Jew or Greek, there is no longer slave or free, there is no longer male and female; for all of you are one in Christ Jesus. [29] And if you belong to Christ,

a Or *The one who is righteous through faith will live*
b Gk *does them*   *c* Gk *Brothers*   *d* Or *covenant* (as in verse 17)   *e* Gk *seed*   *f* Gk *seeds*   *g* Or *through the faith of Jesus Christ*

then you are Abraham's offspring,[a] heirs according to the promise.

3.19–29: Why the law was given. Paul shows similar concern to defend the law in Romans (Rom 7.7–12). **19–20:** *Because of transgressions:* This is a very difficult phrase: as a way of dealing with transgressions that could be dealt with no other way? as a way of naming our transgressions? *Ordained through angels by a mediator:* The particular event this refers to is unclear. Its intent is to show that the law expressed God's will indirectly. **21–22:** This would seem to follow from vv. 17–18 (Rom 3.31). As in Rom 7, *sin* is seen as a powerful, almost personal, force capable of using the law to its own advantage. *Faith in Jesus Christ:* See comments on 2.15–21. **23–29:** *Faith* refers to the way of faith, anticipated by Abraham but exemplified in Christ. **24:** *Disciplinarian* refers to a teacher responsible for a child's upbringing on behalf of the parents, a temporary role. **26:** *In Christ Jesus:* Believers now enjoy the status of full-fledged children who no longer need a surrogate parent. *Faith* marks the way one "enters" Christ. **27:** Through baptism★ believers "die and rise" with Christ, thereby entering the sphere where God's life-giving power is operative. So engulfed are they by Christ, it is like putting on a garment (Col 3.9–11). **28:** The elimination of ethnic, social, and gender distinctions derives from the oneness experienced in Christ (1 Cor 7.17–24). The language here is probably drawn from an early baptismal formula. **29:** This is the point toward which Paul has been building. God promised Abraham that gentiles★ would receive blessing through his "seed." This occurred with Christ, the seed of Abraham, who enabled Abraham's way of relating to God to become a reality—the way of faith. Those who respond to Christ in faith, both gentiles and Jews, become Abraham's children. Who, then, are Abraham's children? Jews alone? No. Everyone who shares the faith of Abraham. Christ, first, then those who exhibit faith like Christ.

4 My point is this: heirs, as long as they are minors, are no better than slaves, though they are the owners of all the property; ²but they remain under guardians and trustees until the date set by the father. ³So with us; while we were minors, we were enslaved to the elemental spirits[b] of the world. ⁴But when the fullness of time had come, God sent his Son, born of a woman, born under the law, ⁵in order to redeem those who were under the law, so that we might receive adoption as children. ⁶And because you are children, God has sent the Spirit of his Son into our[c] hearts, crying, "Abba![d] Father!" ⁷So you are no longer a slave but a child, and if a child then also an heir, through God.[e]

8 Formerly, when you did not know God, you were enslaved to beings that by nature are not gods. ⁹Now, however, that you have come to know God, or rather to be known by God, how can you turn back again to the weak and beggarly elemental spirits?[f] How can you want to be enslaved to them again? ¹⁰You are observing special days, and months, and seasons, and years. ¹¹I am afraid that my work for you may have been wasted.

4.1–11: No longer slaves, but children. 1: *Heirs:* Comparing life under the law to being a minor continues the illustration introduced in 3.15. *Slaves* introduces a second image, which is developed in chs. 4–5. **3:** *Elemental spirits of the world* (Gk., "ta stoicheia tou kosmou") is difficult. *Rudiments* (note b) captures the sense of "stoicheion" as something fundamental—elements or principles. These may perhaps be elementary forms of religion that were superseded by Christ, or the four elements (fire, air, water, earth) understood as heavenly forces. See 4.9. **4:** The language sounds confessional (Rom 8.3). Here Paul succinctly states what the gospel birth stories present more fully, especially Luke (Lk 1–2; Mt 1–2). Emphasized are Jesus' humanity and Jewishness. **5:** *Redeem,* literally "buy back," suggests buying the freedom of young slaves in order to adopt them as *children.* **6:** The reality of 3.26 is presupposed. *"Abba! Father!"* expresses Christ's obedient spirit (Mk 14.36; Rom 8.15). **7:** Being able to address God the way Jesus did signals the change in status from *slave* to *child.* **8:** This is typical language for living as gentiles★ (1 Thess 4.5). **9:** The difference between "knowing God" and "being known by God" is an important distinction for Paul. One borders on arrogance, the other sees knowledge as God's domain (1 Cor 13.12). *Weak and beggarly elemental spirits:* Jews criticized pagans for blindly submitting to forces with no real power. **10:** Given the

a Gk *seed*   *b* Or *the rudiments*   *c* Other ancient authorities read *your*   *d* Aramaic for *Father*
e Other ancient authorities read *an heir of God through Christ*   *f* Or *beggarly rudiments*

Galatians' attraction to the law, these are doubtless Jewish observances (5.4; Col 2.16). **11:** This reference to his founding visit triggers the following discussion.

12 Friends,[a] I beg you, become as I am, for I also have become as you are. You have done me no wrong. [13]You know that it was because of a physical infirmity that I first announced the gospel to you; [14]though my condition put you to the test, you did not scorn or despise me, but welcomed me as an angel of God, as Christ Jesus. [15]What has become of the goodwill you felt? For I testify that, had it been possible, you would have torn out your eyes and given them to me. [16]Have I now become your enemy by telling you the truth? [17]They make much of you, but for no good purpose; they want to exclude you, so that you may make much of them. [18]It is good to be made much of for a good purpose at all times, and not only when I am present with you. [19]My little children, for whom I am again in the pain of childbirth until Christ is formed in you, [20]I wish I were present with you now and could change my tone, for I am perplexed about you.

4.12–20: Paul recalls his founding visit. 12: Paul's meaning is not clear. Perhaps, "Come back over to me, just as I once came to you." **13–15:** His much discussed *physical infirmity* is not known. His reference to *eyes* may be a figure of speech expressing their generosity rather than an allusion to some health problem (v. 15; 2 Cor 12.7–8). **16:** This recalls his blunt speech (1.6–9; 3.1–5). **17:** The false teachers of 1.7 are in mind. *Exclude you:* They are charged with trying to cut the Galatians off from Paul, or possibly from Christ. **19–20:** Paul is now the anxious mother fretting over her children (1 Thess 2.7).

21 Tell me, you who desire to be subject to the law, will you not listen to the law? [22]For it is written that Abraham had two sons, one by a slave woman and the other by a free woman. [23]One, the child of the slave, was born according to the flesh; the other, the child of the free woman, was born through the promise. [24]Now this is an allegory: these women are two covenants. One woman, in fact, is Hagar, from Mount Sinai, bearing children for slavery. [25]Now Hagar is Mount Sinai in Arabia[b] and corresponds to the present Jerusalem, for she is in slavery with her children. [26]But the other woman corresponds to the Jerusalem above; she is free, and she is our mother. [27]For it is written,

"Rejoice, you childless one, you who
    bear no children,
  burst into song and shout, you who
    endure no birth pangs;
 for the children of the desolate woman
    are more numerous
  than the children of the one who is
    married."

[28]Now you,[c] my friends,[d] are children of the promise, like Isaac. [29]But just as at that time the child who was born according to the flesh persecuted the child who was born according to the Spirit, so it is now also. [30]But what does the scripture say? "Drive out the slave and her child; for the child of the slave will not share the inheritance with the child of the free woman." [31]So then, friends,[d] we are children, not of the slave

5 but of the free woman. [1]For freedom Christ has set us free. Stand firm, therefore, and do not submit again to a yoke of slavery.

4.21–5.1: The allegory* of Hagar and Sarah. The mother image of v. 19 is developed in the comparison of these two famous mothers (Gen 16–21). **4.21:** Attraction to the law requires an argument from the law. **23:** *Flesh:* Ishmael's birth occurred through human conniving. Jacob's birth fulfilled God's *promise* to Abraham and Sarah (Gen 17). **24–26:** In *allegory*, things referred to in a text are understood to have another, often deeper, meaning. Gen 16 describes Hagar as a slave-girl. Since Paul associates the Mosaic law with slavery (3.22; 4.3), Hagar can stand for *Mount Sinai,* where the law was given to Moses. It is now practiced in *present Jerusalem.* Sarah, by contrast, is *free.* She has no association with slavery (the Mosaic law), but instead symbolizes another reality, *Jerusalem above.* **27:** Isa 54.1. **28:** Those who have responded to God in faith (3.26) are *like Isaac,* Abraham's children. Now, as then, the two children fight: *flesh* (law)

a Gk *Brothers* b Other ancient authorities read *For Sinai is a mountain in Arabia* c Other ancient authorities read *we* d Gk *brothers* against *Spirit* (faith). **30:** Gen 21.10 gives scriptural basis for rejecting the Mosaic law. **31:** According to scripture, Abraham has two family lines, one leading through Hagar to slavery under the law, the other through Sarah to freedom as embodied in the promise. Paul urges the Galatians to trace their lineage through the latter. **5.1:** Since Christ is Abraham's promised *offspring* (3.16), he is the link to *freedom* represented by Sarah. To begin observing the Mosaic law is to switch bloodlines and revert to a *yoke of slavery.*

2 Listen! I, Paul, am telling you that if you let yourselves be circumcised, Christ will be of no benefit to you. ³Once again I testify to every man who lets himself be circumcised that he is obliged to obey the entire law. ⁴You who want to be justified by the law have cut yourselves off from Christ; you have fallen away from grace. ⁵For through the Spirit, by faith, we eagerly wait for the hope of righteousness. ⁶For in Christ Jesus neither circumcision nor uncircumcision counts for anything; the only thing that counts is faith working*ᵃ* through love.

7 You were running well; who prevented you from obeying the truth? ⁸Such persuasion does not come from the one who calls you. ⁹A little yeast leavens the whole batch of dough. ¹⁰I am confident about you in the Lord that you will not think otherwise. But whoever it is that is confusing you will pay the penalty. ¹¹But my friends,*ᵇ* why am I still being persecuted if I am still preaching circumcision? In that case the offense of the cross has been removed. ¹²I wish those who unsettle you would castrate themselves!

5.2–12: Why circumcision★ should be refused. Here Paul gets to the central issue that is dividing the community. The opposing teachers thought God required the gentile★ Christians in Galatia to be circumcised. **3:** Circumcision indicated willingness to live by Torah★ (Gen 17.9–14). The emphasis here is *entire law* (3.10). **4:** *Cut yourselves off* can be rendered, "You were estranged." To choose law is to abandon Christ, the symbol of God's *grace* (1.6, 15; 2.20–21; Rom 5.15). **5:** Rom 8.18–25. **6:** Christ redefines the meaning of ethnic identity (6.15; 1 Cor 7.19). *Faith working through love* is generally taken as "faith *made effective* (note a) through loving acts" (5.13–14). It could be

"faith that becomes effective by responding to Christ's love" (2.20). **7–8:** The call to follow the law does not come from God. **9:** 1 Cor 5.6. **10:** The curse of 1.6–9 will take effect. **11:** To convince the Galatians, the opposing teachers apparently argued that Paul approved of circumcision. **12:** Not only would circumcision hurt physically, it would also banish them under the law (Deut 23.1).

13 For you were called to freedom, brothers and sisters;*ᵇ* only do not use your freedom as an opportunity for self-indulgence,*ᶜ* but through love become slaves to one another. ¹⁴For the whole law is summed up in a single commandment, "You shall love your neighbor as yourself." ¹⁵If, however, you bite and devour one another, take care that you are not consumed by one another.

16 Live by the Spirit, I say, and do not gratify the desires of the flesh. ¹⁷For what the flesh desires is opposed to the Spirit, and what the Spirit desires is opposed to the flesh; for these are opposed to each other, to prevent you from doing what you want. ¹⁸But if you are led by the Spirit, you are not subject to the law. ¹⁹Now the works of the flesh are obvious: fornication, impurity, licentiousness, ²⁰idolatry, sorcery, enmities, strife, jealousy, anger, quarrels, dissensions, factions, ²¹envy,*ᵈ* drunkenness, carousing, and things like these. I am warning you, as I warned you before: those who do such things will not inherit the kingdom of God.

22 By contrast, the fruit of the Spirit is love, joy, peace, patience, kindness, generosity, faithfulness, ²³gentleness, and self-control. There is no law against such things. ²⁴And those who belong to Christ Jesus have crucified the flesh with its passions and desires. ²⁵If we live by the Spirit, let us also be guided by the Spirit. ²⁶Let us not become conceited, competing against one another, envying one another.

5.13–26: Living in freedom. Having just discussed what returning to slavery would mean (5.2–12), Paul now expounds on *freedom* (5.1). **13:** *Self-indulgence*

a Or *made effective*   *b* Gk *brothers*   *c* Gk *the flesh*
d Other ancient authorities add *murder*

captures the sense of *the flesh* ("sarx"; note *c* on p. 1955). Now the slave imagery is used positively: *Love* requires a new form of submission (Rom 6.15–19). **14:** Lev 19.18; Rom 13.8–10. **16–17:** *Spirit* and *flesh* define opposing spheres of life and loyalties (Rom 8.5–7). **18:** *The law* is associated with flesh (Rom 7). **19–21:** *Works of the flesh:* This vice list enumerates various forms of self-indulgence (v. 13; see Rom 1.29–31). Sexual sins head the list, followed by sins leading to social disorder, then personal excesses. *Kingdom of God* is God's future reign (1 Cor 6.9–10). **22–26:** *Fruit of the Spirit* is what living by the Spirit produces (2 Pet 1.5–7). **24:** The moral life is similarly described in Rom 6.6. **25–26:** Rom 8.5–8. Life in the Spirit recognizes different gifts and mutual need, thereby devaluing interpersonal rivalry (1 Cor 12).

6 My friends,*a* if anyone is detected in a transgression, you who have received the Spirit should restore such a one in a spirit of gentleness. Take care that you yourselves are not tempted. ²Bear one another's burdens, and in this way you will fulfill*b* the law of Christ. ³For if those who are nothing think they are something, they deceive themselves. ⁴All must test their own work; then that work, rather than their neighbor's work, will become a cause for pride. ⁵For all must carry their own loads.

6 Those who are taught the word must share in all good things with their teacher.

7 Do not be deceived; God is not mocked, for you reap whatever you sow. ⁸If you sow to your own flesh, you will reap corruption from the flesh; but if you sow to the Spirit, you will reap eternal life from the Spirit. ⁹So let us not grow weary in doing what is right, for we will reap at harvest time, if we do not give up. ¹⁰So then, whenever we have an opportunity, let us work for the good of all, and especially for those of the family of faith.

6.1–10: Moral exhortations.* **1:** Church discipline should seek to *restore,* not just punish (Mt 18.15–20; 1 Cor 5.1–8). Its overall tone is defined by 5.22–23. **2:** *The law of Christ* expresses the way of love (2.20). It produces mutual responsibility (Rom 15.1). **3:** Arrogance thrives on self-illusion (1 Cor 8.2). **4–5:** This expresses the other side of responsible behavior. **6:** Teachers are entitled to (financial) support from their students (1 Cor 9). **7–10:** V. 7 expresses popular wis-

dom (Job 4.8; Prov 22.8). **9:** *Harvest time* points to the final judgment (Mt 13.11–12).

11 See what large letters I make when I am writing in my own hand! ¹²It is those who want to make a good showing in the flesh that try to compel you to be circumcised—only that they may not be persecuted for the cross of Christ. ¹³Even the circumcised do not themselves obey the law, but they want you to be circumcised so that they may boast about your flesh. ¹⁴May I never boast of anything except the cross of our Lord Jesus Christ, by which*c* the world has been crucified to me, and I to the world. ¹⁵For*d* neither circumcision nor uncircumcision is anything; but a new creation is everything! ¹⁶As for those who will follow this rule—peace be upon them, and mercy, and upon the Israel of God.

17 From now on, let no one make trouble for me; for I carry the marks of Jesus branded on my body.

18 May the grace of our Lord Jesus Christ be with your spirit, brothers and sisters.*e* Amen.

6.11–18: Paul's closing appeal. 11: This reflects his customary practice (1 Cor 16.21). In his own handwriting, he summarizes themes already treated in the letter. **12:** He attacks the motives of his opponents (4.17–18). **13:** Criticizing their inconsistent practice recalls Rom 2.17–24. By "boasting" of the number of converts they have won, they violate Jer 9.23–24. **14:** Paul restates his central claim: The crucified Christ is his sole focus (1 Cor 2.2). The crucifixion marked two deaths: the collapse of the world that defined him (law) and the eclipse of the self-understanding that derived from that world. **15:** Ethnic identity no longer matters (3.26–28; 5.6; 1 Cor 7.19). What matters is participating in God's reordered universe brought about by Christ (2 Cor 5.17). **16:** *Israel of God* possibly refers to those who oppose him, but could be God's people as originally envisioned in the promise to Abraham: those who live by faith, both Jews and gentiles.* **17:** His apostolic life imprinted the crucifixion on his body (2 Cor 4.17).

a Gk *Brothers* *b* Other ancient authorities read *in this way fulfill* *c* Or *through whom* *d* Other ancient authorities add *in Christ Jesus* *e* Gk *brothers*

THE LETTER OF PAUL TO THE EPHESIANS

Introduction

Ephesians has traits in common with both a liturgy★ and a letter. It reads like a liturgy about the powerful and beneficent love of God in bringing Jews and gentiles★ into one body and in exalting that body to a cosmic level. Praise and thanksgiving celebrate God's predetermined plan of love in raising Christ from the dead, in placing him over all things, in sealing the church with the Holy Spirit, and in making Christ the head of the universal church, his body (1.3–23). The liturgical flavor is also found in the stirring call to arms against cosmic powers and a sonorous request for sustained alertness, prayer, and supplication with which Ephesians ends (6.10–20). The work also reads like a typical Hellenistic★ letter. Epistolary notices (1.1–2; 6.21–24) introduce and conclude the document, and its contents are reminiscent of other Pauline letters, especially important reminders of Paul's mission (3.1–21), and a set of exhortations★ toward unity and full stature in Christ (4.1–6.9).

As a letter, however, the work is puzzling in several respects. First, the earliest manuscripts lack the words "in Ephesus" (v. 1), so that it could have been written to Laodicea (thus supplying the letter mentioned in Col 4.6), or perhaps as a circular letter to several communities. As a result, the specific addressees are not certain, and not even the mention of gentiles (2.11; 3.1) among the recipients narrows the target. The inclusion of the words "in Ephesus" in later manuscripts and links with Colossians suggest a setting in Asia Minor, the location of Colossae, but the exact setting remains a conjecture.

Second, though it shares much with Colossians (similar openings and closings, twenty-nine words in common, similar rhetorical★ structure, and a similar set of household codes★), Ephesians lacks Colossians' specific concern about "heresy" (see the introduction to Colossians).

Third, there are questions about authorship and dating. Arguments for or against Paul's authorship each have their proponents, but the peculiar style, unique diction, and distinctive viewpoints of the letter lend more weight to a post-Pauline authorship. The proportion of words unique to this letter is greater than the number found in any of the undisputed letters. In addition, the letter extends the meaning of typical expressions from the undisputed letters in uncharacteristic ways; for example, the church is universal and Christ is the head of the body (1.22). As for its distinctive viewpoints, it assumes that the status of the gentiles in the church is a settled issue (3.6) and that Christians are already saved and resurrected with Christ. Accordingly, many scholars date the letter to early post-Pauline times (around 80 CE) when the hopes of a quick return of the risen Lord had faded. Again, because of the general character of the letter, the dating is uncertain.

READING GUIDE

Despite its puzzles, Ephesians appears to address Christians as they live in the interim between two great cosmic battles: one already performed by God (1.20–23) when all things were placed under Jesus' feet, and another to be held on that "evil day" when the church in its fullness as

Christ's body will fight in heavenly places (6.13). In between these battles, the universal church has been created for good works (2.10), and it accepts the unity of the body of Christ and grows toward full maturity. To accept that unity, the universal church must recognize the great pre-ordained mystery,* that is, the bringing together in Christ (1.10) of all social relations (between different ethnic groups and among those in households) in the exalted body of Christ. Paul has already played and continues to play a role in the universal church's growth toward full maturity (3.1–21). To reach full maturity, however, the church must walk a distinctive walk of love in keeping with its exalted status (4.6–9). The goal of the full maturity of the exalted church, moreover, is to attack the cosmic powers which still have an effect on the disobedient (or the unbelievers), that is, on those who are not a part of the household of God.

1.1–2	Epistolary opening
1.3–2.22	The battle before the exaltation
3.1–21	Paul's imprisonment and ministry
4.1–6.9	Walking in accord with the exaltation
6.10–20	The battle beyond the exaltation
6.21–24	Epistolary closing

1 Paul, an apostle of Christ Jesus by the will of God,

To the saints who are in Ephesus and are faithful*a* in Christ Jesus:

2 Grace to you and peace from God our Father and the Lord Jesus Christ.

1.1–2: The epistolary opening is typical for Paul's letters: identification of the letter's sender and recipients, followed by words of greeting.

---

3 Blessed be the God and Father of our Lord Jesus Christ, who has blessed us in Christ with every spiritual blessing in the heavenly places, 4just as he chose us in Christ*b* before the foundation of the world to be holy and blameless before him in love. 5He destined us for adoption as his children through Jesus Christ, according to the good pleasure of his will, 6to the praise of his glorious grace that he freely bestowed on us in the Beloved. 7In him we have redemption through his blood, the forgiveness of our trespasses, according to the riches of his grace 8that he lavished on us. With all wisdom and insight 9he has made known to us the mystery of his will, according to his good pleasure that he set forth in Christ, 10as a plan for the fullness of time, to gather up all things in him, things in heaven and things

on earth. 11In Christ we have also obtained an inheritance,*c* having been destined according to the purpose of him who accomplishes all things according to his counsel and will, 12so that we, who were the first to set our hope on Christ, might live for the praise of his glory. 13In him you also, when you had heard the word of truth, the gospel of your salvation, and had believed in him, were marked with the seal of the promised Holy Spirit; 14this*d* is the pledge of our inheritance toward redemption as God's own people, to the praise of his glory.

1.3–14: Praise to God. The repetitions of *praise* (vv. 6, 12, 14) divide the one Greek sentence into three parts (vv. 3–6, 7–12, 13–14). **3:** *Heavenly places* occurs nowhere else in the New Testament but Ephesians (1.20; 2.6; 3.10; 6.12). **5–6:** *Adoption,* a favorite concept for Paul (Gal 4.15; Rom 8.15, 23; 9.4); Paul never uses *beloved* to characterize Christ though later Christian writers, like Ignatius,* do. **7:** For Paul, *redemption* (a purchase payment) covers all of the believers' lives and is completed only at the second coming ("parousia*"). (See 3.24; 8.23; 1 Cor 1.30; see also 1 Cor 15.23.) Ephesians holds a similar view but never mentions parousia. **8:** *Wisdom* and *insight* emphasize

a Other ancient authorities lack *in Ephesus,* reading *saints who are also faithful*   *b* Gk *in him*   *c* Or *been made a heritage*   *d* Other ancient authorities read *who* adequate perception; the recipients should avoid deceit and spread truth (4.14, 25; 5.6; 6.14). **9:** *Mystery,** Colossians reserves this expression for Christ (Col 1.26–27; 2.2; 4.3); here it indicates God's reconciliation of all things, including Jews and gentiles* in the body of Christ (3.3–4, 9). **10:** *Gather up,* "head up": Jesus is head of the body and the church grows toward that head. **11:** Paul links adoption to *inheritance* (Gal 3.29; 4.7; Rom 8.17). **12–14:** *We, you* connects vv. 7–12 to 13–14, anticipating the direct address to gentiles in 2.1 and 3.1. A *seal* confirms authenticity; a *pledge* is a deposit against a full amount to be paid later; both are used similarly in Paul's undisputed letters (2 Cor 1.22; 5.5; Rom 8.23).

15 I have heard of your faith in the Lord Jesus and your love[a] toward all the saints, and for this reason 16I do not cease to give thanks for you as I remember you in my prayers. 17I pray that the God of our Lord Jesus Christ, the Father of glory, may give you a spirit of wisdom and revelation as you come to know him, 18so that, with the eyes of your heart enlightened, you may know what is the hope to which he has called you, what are the riches of his glorious inheritance among the saints, 19and what is the immeasurable greatness of his power for us who believe, according to the working of his great power. 20God[b] put this power to work in Christ when he raised him from the dead and seated him at his right hand in the heavenly places, 21far above all rule and authority and power and dominion, and above every name that is named, not only in this age but also in the age to come. 22And he has put all things under his feet and has made him the head over all things for the church, 23which is his body, the fullness of him who fills all in all.

1.15–23: A thanksgiving. 18: *Heart,* the seat of knowledge and understanding. Because of the *hope to which he has called you,* the church must live out its calling, as described in 4.1–3. **20–22:** *At the right hand,* the most honored position (Col 3–1); *under his feet,* a sign of victory; both quoted from Ps 110. **22:** Christ as *head* of the church (compare Col 1.18) is not found in the undisputed Pauline letters, which speak of local churches, not the universal church.

2 You were dead through the trespasses and sins 2in which you once lived, following the course of this world, following the ruler of the power of the air, the spirit that is now at work among those who are disobedient. 3All of us once lived among them in the passions of our flesh, following the desires of flesh and senses, and we were by nature children of wrath, like everyone else. 4But God, who is rich in mercy, out of the great love with which he loved us 5even when we were dead through our trespasses, made us alive together with Christ[c]—by grace you have been saved— 6and raised us up with him and seated us with him in the heavenly places in Christ Jesus, 7so that in the ages to come he might show the immeasurable riches of his grace in kindness toward us in Christ Jesus. 8For by grace you have been saved through faith, and this is not your own doing; it is the gift of God— 9not the result of works, so that no one may boast. 10For we are what he has made us, created in Christ Jesus for good works, which God prepared beforehand to be our way of life.

11 So then, remember that at one time you Gentiles by birth,[d] called "the uncircumcision" by those who are called "the circumcision"—a physical circumcision made in the flesh by human hands— 12remember that you were at that time without Christ, being aliens from the commonwealth of Israel, and strangers to the covenants of promise, having no hope and without God in the world. 13But now in Christ Jesus you who once were far off have been brought near by the blood of Christ. 14For he is our peace; in his flesh he has made both groups into one and has broken down the dividing wall, that is, the hostility between us. 15He has abolished the law with its commandments and ordinances, that he might create in himself one new humanity in place of the two, thus making peace, 16and might reconcile both groups to God in one body[e] through the cross, thus putting to death that hostility through it.[f] 17So he came and proclaimed

a Other ancient authorities lack *and your love*
b Gk *He*   c Other ancient authorities read *in Christ*
d Gk *in the flesh*   e Or *reconcile both of us in one body for God*   f Or *in him,* or *in himself*

peace to you who were far off and peace to those who were near; 18for through him both of us have access in one Spirit to the Father. 19So then you are no longer strangers and aliens, but you are citizens with the saints and also members of the household of God, 20built upon the foundation of the apostles and prophets, with Christ Jesus himself as the cornerstone.*a* 21In him the whole structure is joined together and grows into a holy temple in the Lord; 22in whom you also are built together spiritually*b* into a dwelling place for God.

2.1–22: God's reconciling grace. God saves humankind from enemy powers and Christ ends the enmity between Jews and gentiles.* **1–10:** Contrast between past walk (vv. 1–3) and present walk (4–10). **2:** *Lived,* literally "walked," connects the former walk (2.2) and the new way of walking in 2.10 (see 4.1, 17; 5.2, 8, 15). *Ruler of the power of the air,* Satan (4.27; 6.11–12). **3:** *Flesh,* fleshly disposition. **5–6:** *By grace you have been saved,* similar to Paul's language elsewhere, but he never views resurrection of believers as a present reality. **10:** The good works that the community does are possible because God has created them in Christ. The life they lead is the *way* (literally "walk," v. 1) God has made possible. **11–22:** Jews and gentiles are reconciled to God in the body of Christ. **12:** *Aliens,* those without knowledge (Col 1.21) **13:** The *far off . . . brought near* (also 2.17), possibly drawn from Isa 57.19. **14:** *Dividing wall,* possibly the Temple* barrier separating the court of the gentiles from the parts of the Temple open only to Jews. **18:** *Access,* the right of approach, as if to a king (3.12). **19:** *Household* of God: For the patriarchal writer, God is father over the social relations in the believers' family (1.3, 17; 2.18; 3.14; 4.6; 5.20; 6.23). **20:** Paul speaks of Christ as a foundation (1 Cor 3.10–15), but not *apostles** and *prophets.** *Cornerstone* or keystone, a messianic term (Isa 28.16, perhaps Ps 118.21–23).

3 This is the reason that I Paul am a prisoner for*c* Christ Jesus for the sake of you Gentiles— 2for surely you have already heard of the commission of God's grace that was given me for you, 3and how the mystery was made known to me by revelation, as I wrote above in a few words, 4a reading of which will enable you to perceive my understanding of the mystery of Christ. 5In former generations this mystery*d* was not made known to humankind, as it has now been revealed to his holy apostles and prophets by the Spirit; 6that is, the Gentiles have become fellow heirs, members of the same body, and sharers in the promise in Christ Jesus through the gospel.

7 Of this gospel I have become a servant according to the gift of God's grace that was given me by the working of his power. 8Although I am the very least of all the saints, this grace was given to me to bring to the Gentiles the news of the boundless riches of Christ, 9and to make everyone see*e* what is the plan of the mystery hidden for ages in*f* God who created all things; 10so that through the church the wisdom of God in its rich variety might now be made known to the rulers and authorities in the heavenly places. 11This was in accordance with the eternal purpose that he has carried out in Christ Jesus our Lord, 12in whom we have access to God in boldness and confidence through faith in him.*g* 13I pray therefore that you*h* may not lose heart over my sufferings for you; they are your glory.

14 For this reason I bow my knees before the Father,*i* 15from whom every family*j* in heaven and on earth takes its name. 16I pray that, according to the riches of his glory, he may grant that you may be strengthened in your inner being with power through his Spirit, 17and that Christ may dwell in your hearts through faith, as you are being rooted and grounded in love. 18I pray that you may have the power to comprehend, with all the saints, what is the breadth and length and height and depth, 19and to know the love of Christ that surpasses knowledge, so that you may be filled with all the fullness of God.

20 Now to him who by the power at work within us is able to accomplish abundantly far more than all we can ask or imagine, 21to him be glory in the church and in Christ Jesus to all generations, forever and ever. Amen.

a Or *keystone*　*b* Gk *in the Spirit*　*c* Or *of*
d Gk *it*　*e* Other ancient authorities read *to bring to light*　*f* Or *by*　*g* Or *the faith of him*　*h* Or *I*
i Other ancient authorities add *of our Lord Jesus Christ*
j Gk *fatherhood*

3.1–21: Paul's imprisonment and ministry. 1: The prayer (vv. 1, 14–21) is interrupted by vv. 2–13 (see Col 1.23–27) clarifying Paul's work on behalf of gentiles.* On Paul as prisoner, see 2 Cor 6.5; 11.23; Philem 1.9; Phil 1.13–14. **2:** *Commission,* a management or stewardship position. **3:** *As I wrote above,* uncertain, but possibly the mission to the gentiles (2.11–12) or Christ's revelation (1.9–10). **10:** The church manifests the wisdom of God's plan of reconciliation. **14–21:** The prayer resumes in a single sentence (vv. 14–19) and closes with a doxology (vv. 20–21). **14:** A play on *father* ("patera") and *family* ("patria"). **16–19:** The goal is the fullness of God by way of the love of Christ. **20–21:** The doxology recalls the emphasis on power and abundance (1.19–20; 2.7).

ETHICAL EXHORTATIONS*

4.1–6.20: This section contains exhortations to unity and full stature in Christ, admonitions against vice, encouragements to worship, and even household rules, in order to participate in the love of Christ. Much of this material is also in Col 3.1–4.6.

4 I therefore, the prisoner in the Lord, beg you to lead a life worthy of the calling to which you have been called, ²with all humility and gentleness, with patience, bearing with one another in love, ³making every effort to maintain the unity of the Spirit in the bond of peace. ⁴There is one body and one Spirit, just as you were called to the one hope of your calling, ⁵one Lord, one faith, one baptism, ⁶one God and Father of all, who is above all and through all and in all.

7 But each of us was given grace according to the measure of Christ's gift. ⁸Therefore it is said,

"When he ascended on high he made
　　captivity itself a captive;
he gave gifts to his people."

⁹(When it says, "He ascended," what does it mean but that he had also descended*ᵃ* into the lower parts of the earth? ¹⁰He who descended is the same one who ascended far above all the heavens, so that he might fill all things.) ¹¹The gifts he gave were that some would be apostles, some prophets, some evangelists, some pastors and teachers,

¹²to equip the saints for the work of ministry, for building up the body of Christ, ¹³until all of us come to the unity of the faith and of the knowledge of the Son of God, to maturity, to the measure of the full stature of Christ. ¹⁴We must no longer be children, tossed to and fro and blown about by every wind of doctrine, by people's trickery, by their craftiness in deceitful scheming. ¹⁵But speaking the truth in love, we must grow up in every way into him who is the head, into Christ, ¹⁶from whom the whole body, joined and knit together by every ligament with which it is equipped, as each part is working properly, promotes the body's growth in building itself up in love.

4.1–16: Maintain unity. Unity comes from the Spirit (vv. 1–6), and the diversity of gifts of the Spirit brings the church to maturity (vv. 7–16). **1:** *Calling,* see 1.18; 2.11. **2:** *Patience,* literally, the ability to endure the pressure of heat. **7–10:** Ps 68.18 explains the origin (Christ) and goal (Christ's filling) of Christian gifts. **11–16:** The *gifts* are essential for the church to reach maturity (contrasted with immaturity).

17 Now this I affirm and insist on in the Lord: you must no longer live as the Gentiles live, in the futility of their minds. ¹⁸They are darkened in their understanding, alienated from the life of God because of their ignorance and hardness of heart. ¹⁹They have lost all sensitivity and have abandoned themselves to licentiousness, greedy to practice every kind of impurity. ²⁰That is not the way you learned Christ! ²¹For surely you have heard about him and were taught in him, as truth is in Jesus. ²²You were taught to put away your former way of life, your old self, corrupt and deluded by its lusts, ²³and to be renewed in the spirit of your minds, ²⁴and to clothe yourselves with the new self, created according to the likeness of God in true righteousness and holiness.

25 So then, putting away falsehood, let all of us speak the truth to our neighbors, for we are members of one another. ²⁶Be angry but do not sin; do not let the sun go down on your anger, ²⁷and do not make room for

ᵃ Other ancient authorities add *first*

the devil. 28Thieves must give up stealing; rather let them labor and work honestly with their own hands, so as to have something to share with the needy. 29Let no evil talk come out of your mouths, but only what is useful for building up,ᵃ as there is need, so that your words may give grace to those who hear. 30And do not grieve the Holy Spirit of God, with which you were marked with a seal for the day of redemption. 31Put away from you all bitterness and wrath and anger and wrangling and slander, together with all malice, 32and be kind to one another, tenderhearted, forgiving one another, as God in Christ has

5 forgiven you.ᵇ 1Therefore be imitators of God, as beloved children, 2and live in love, as Christ loved usᶜ and gave himself up for us, a fragrant offering and sacrifice to God.

4.17–5.2: Old and new walks. (See 2.1–10.) The new walk, which avoids the walk of the gentiles★ (4.17a) with its futility, vices, opposition to instruction (4.17b–24), has practical implications (4.25–5.1). **17:** *Affirm and testify,* a pleonasm★ (deliberate repetition) drawn from legal language. **20:** *Learned . . . heard . . . taught,* instructions preceding baptism★. **22–24:** *Put away, clothe yourselves with the new self,* baptismal terms. **25–26:** *Speak the truth,* Zec 8–16; *be angry and sin not,* Ps 4.4. **1–2:** *Imitators of God,* never used by Paul, though he speaks of imitating Christ (1 Cor 11.1), himself (1 Thess 1.6; Phil 3.17) or others (Phil 3.17).

---

3 But fornication and impurity of any kind, or greed, must not even be mentioned among you, as is proper among saints. 4Entirely out of place is obscene, silly, and vulgar talk; but instead, let there be thanksgiving. 5Be sure of this, that no fornicator or impure person, or one who is greedy (that is, an idolater), has any inheritance in the kingdom of Christ and of God.

6 Let no one deceive you with empty words, for because of these things the wrath of God comes on those who are disobedient. 7Therefore do not be associated with them. 8For once you were darkness, but now in the Lord you are light. Live as children of light— 9for the fruit of the light is found in all that is good and right and true. 10Try to find out

what is pleasing to the Lord. 11Take no part in the unfruitful works of darkness, but instead expose them. 12For it is shameful even to mention what such people do secretly; 13but everything exposed by the light becomes visible, 14for everything that becomes visible is light. Therefore it says,

"Sleeper, awake!
    Rise from the dead,
    and Christ will shine on you."

5.3–14: Believers as children of light. 3–7: Paul (Gal 5.19–21; 1 Cor 6.9–10) uses the *vice* list, here expressing the former life of darkness (5.8). **8–14:** *Live* (walk) *as children of the light* (1 Thess 5.5) to influence the world through the church's character. **14:** The hymn's origin is unknown; it recalls Isa 60.1.

---

15 Be careful then how you live, not as unwise people but as wise, 16making the most of the time, because the days are evil. 17So do not be foolish, but understand what the will of the Lord is. 18Do not get drunk with wine, for that is debauchery; but be filled with the Spirit, 19as you sing psalms and hymns and spiritual songs among yourselves, singing and making melody to the Lord in your hearts, 20giving thanks to God the Father at all times and for everything in the name of our Lord Jesus Christ.

21 Be subject to one another out of reverence for Christ.

22 Wives, be subject to your husbands as you are to the Lord. 23For the husband is the head of the wife just as Christ is the head of the church, the body of which he is the Savior. 24Just as the church is subject to Christ, so also wives ought to be, in everything, to their husbands.

25 Husbands, love your wives, just as Christ loved the church and gave himself up for her, 26in order to make her holy by cleansing her with the washing of water by the word, 27so as to present the church to himself in splendor, without a spot or wrinkle or anything of the kind—yes, so that she may be holy and without blemish. 28In the

---

a Other ancient authorities read *building up faith*
b Other ancient authorities read *us*   *c* Other ancient authorities read *you*

same way, husbands should love their wives as they do their own bodies. He who loves his wife loves himself. 29For no one ever hates his own body, but he nourishes and tenderly cares for it, just as Christ does for the church, 30because we are members of his body.ᵃ 31"For this reason a man will leave his father and mother and be joined to his wife, and the two will become one flesh." 32This is a great mystery, and I am applying it to Christ and the church. 33Each of you, however, should love his wife as himself, and a wife should respect her husband.

6 Children, obey your parents in the Lord,ᵇ for this is right. 2"Honor your father and mother"—this is the first commandment with a promise: 3"so that it may be well with you and you may live long on the earth."

4 And, fathers, do not provoke your children to anger, but bring them up in the discipline and instruction of the Lord.

5 Slaves, obey your earthly masters with fear and trembling, in singleness of heart, as you obey Christ; 6not only while being watched, and in order to please them, but as slaves of Christ, doing the will of God from the heart. 7Render service with enthusiasm, as to the Lord and not to men and women, 8knowing that whatever good we do, we will receive the same again from the Lord, whether we are slaves or free.

9 And, masters, do the same to them. Stop threatening them, for you know that both of you have the same Master in heaven, and with him there is no partiality.

5.15–6.9: Strengthening believers. Contrasts (5.15–18) clarify the believers' walk; they are strengthened through worship with others (5.18–20) and mutual submission (5.21–6.9). **5.20:** On continuous thanks, see 1 Thess 5.18; Col 3.17. **5.21–6.9:** Household codes* governed social relations within an extended family. See Col 3.18–4.1. Ephesians expands on relations between husband and wife. **22–33:** Col 3.18–19. For the writer, the unity of the husband and wife, unlike the unity of Jews and gentiles,* does not result in equality. **6.1–4:** Col 3.20–21. **3:** Deut 5.16. **5–9:** Col 3.22–4.1. On slavery, see introduction to Philemon.

10 Finally, be strong in the Lord and in the strength of his power. 11Put on the whole armor of God, so that you may be able to stand against the wiles of the devil. 12For ourᶜ struggle is not against enemies of blood and flesh, but against the rulers, against the authorities, against the cosmic powers of this present darkness, against the spiritual forces of evil in the heavenly places. 13Therefore take up the whole armor of God, so that you may be able to withstand on that evil day, and having done everything, to stand firm. 14Stand therefore, and fasten the belt of truth around your waist, and put on the breastplate of righteousness. 15As shoes for your feet put on whatever will make you ready to proclaim the gospel of peace. 16With all of these,ᵈ take the shield of faith, with which you will be able to quench all the flaming arrows of the evil one. 17Take the helmet of salvation, and the sword of the Spirit, which is the word of God.

18 Pray in the Spirit at all times in every prayer and supplication. To that end keep alert and always persevere in supplication for all the saints. 19Pray also for me, so that when I speak, a message may be given to me to make known with boldness the mystery of the gospel,ᵉ 20for which I am an ambassador in chains. Pray that I may declare it boldly, as I must speak.

6.10–20: A call to arms and prayer for strength to proclaim truth. 14: Ephesians 4.25. **17:** *Helmet of salvation,* Isa 59.17. The *sword of the Spirit,* the word of God, the only offensive weapon. **18–20:** On the importance of prayer throughout Ephesians, see 1.15–23; 3.14–21. **20:** The *ambassador* is an envoy sent on behalf of another. *Chains* suggest dishonor. Yet the writer accepts the title and only asks for boldness.

21 So that you also may know how I am and what I am doing, Tychicus will tell you everything. He is a dear brother and a faithful minister in the Lord. 22I am sending him

ᵃ Other ancient authorities add *of his flesh and of his bones* ᵇ Other ancient authorities lack *in the Lord* ᶜ Other ancient authorities read *your* ᵈ Or *In all circumstances* ᵉ Other ancient authorities lack *of the gospel* to you for this very purpose, to let you know how we are, and to encourage your hearts.

23 Peace be to the whole community,[a] and love with faith, from God the Father and the Lord Jesus Christ. 24Grace be with all who have an undying love for our Lord Jesus Christ.[b]

6.21–24: Epistolary closing. 21: Tychicus, 4.7; 2 Tim 4.12; Titus 3.12; Acts 20.4–6. **22:** Col. 4.8.

[a] Gk *to the brothers*   [b] Other ancient authorities add *Amen*

THE LETTER OF PAUL TO THE PHILIPPIANS

Introduction

Philippians, a friendly and joyful letter, expresses themes of relinquishing one's status for others (2.6–11), presence and absence (1.27; 2.12, 24) and Paul's longing for this church (4.1), the oneness of thought and deeds (2.2; 4.2), and giving and receiving (4.15–19). Above all, it commends friendship. References to joy—present, desired, or expected (1.4, 18, 25; 2.2, 17–19, 29; 3.1; 4.1, 4, 10)—encourage a positive attitude about circumstances which otherwise appear sullen and sordid.

Located on the coast of northern Greece about ninety miles northeast of Thessalonica and named for Philip II, king of Macedonia (359–336 BCE), Philippi was a Roman colony heavily populated with war veterans. According to both Paul and Acts the church at Philippi was the first church Paul established in his mission to the gentiles★ of ancient Macedonia (Phil 4.15; 1 Thess 2.2; Acts 16.11–15). The relationship between Paul and this church was long and dear, for Paul mentions how often the community shared in a partnership with him (4.16; 2 Cor 8.2). The names in the letter (Epaphroditus, Euodia, Syntyche, and Clement) are Greek, and the two women appear to be quite prominent. Archaeological investigations have shown that women were leaders in some of the cults at Philippi. From Acts we know that one woman, Lydia, was Paul's first convert (Acts 16.4) at Philippi.

Paul assuredly wrote the letter from prison (1.7), but it is not clear where or why he wrote or whether it is a combination of several letters. He may have been in Rome, Caesarea, Ephesus, or Corinth. Depending on where it was written, it could date from 50 CE (Corinth); 54–57 CE (Ephesus); 58–60 CE (Caesarea); and the early sixties CE (Rome).

Philippians appears to some scholars to be a combination of letters because there is an apparent break at the beginning of ch. 3 and Paul only gives thanks for a gift at the end of the letter, although he has had ample opportunity before. These scholars would divide it into Letter 1 (4.10–20), Letter 2 (1.1–3.1; 4.4–7, 21–23), and Letter 3 (3.2–4.3; 4.8, 9). Against this division, however, are the similarity between 3:2–4 and the rest of the letter, the similar kinds of opposition in 1.28–29 and 3.2–4.3, themes of friendship and enmity throughout, and the echoes in the later thanks (a strategic postscript rather than an afterthought) of earlier themes such as joy (4.10; 1.4); gospel (4.5; 1.4); fruit (4.17; 1.11) and glory of God (4.20; 1.11).

How do the letter's many themes relate to its main purpose? Paul may be using the different themes to address two distinct but related problems: external intimidation and internal strife. Paul delicately offers a single solution, a new understanding of honor. The church will not be intimidated by outsiders if it behaves as if the prestige associated with the day of the Lord, when its members will gain true honor through their conformity to the body of Jesus' glory, is already the standard for their view of honor, or is the type of honor by which their lives are informed (3.20). The church will be unified if it lives, in accordance with this end-time orientation, in a "manner worthy of the gospel of Christ" (1.27), renouncing status distinctions and seeking each others' interests for God's glory (2.5–11).

READING GUIDE

Opening and closing words (1.1–2; 4 21–23) frame the insistence that the gospel of Christ rearranges the meaning of honor toward pleasing God. A thanksgiving (1.3–11) acknowledges the partnership of Paul and the church in defending and establishing the gospel and commends the orientation of their lives toward the day of Christ and the glory of God. Paul proclaims his joy in spreading the gospel and exalting Christ (1.12–26). The Philippians can solve their problems—external intimidation and internal strife—by living in accord with the gospel (1.27–30), but they must reason from the same mind (2.1–4). Several examples follow (2.5–4.7) as demonstrations of the reorientation, and a final section (4.8–20) asks for excellence through pleasing God in all situations.

1.1–2	Opening
1.3–11	Thanksgiving
1.12–26	Suffering for the gospel
1.27–30	Living worthy of the gospel
2.1–4	The proper mind
2.5–4.7	Examples of the gospel's reconfiguration of honor
4.8–20	Consistency in all situations
4.21–23	Closing

1 Paul and Timothy, servants*a* of Christ Jesus,

To all the saints in Christ Jesus who are in Philippi, with the bishops*b* and deacons:*c*

2 Grace to you and peace from God our Father and the Lord Jesus Christ.

1.1–2: Opening. 1: *Servants,* literally "slaves" ("douloi"), anticipates 2.7, "slave" ("doulou"), the form Jesus took in becoming a human being, and 2.22, Timothy "slaved" ("edouleusen") for the gospel. **2:** *Bishops and deacons,* leadership titles, either functions ("overseers" and "servers") or specific offices, like clergy today.

3 I thank my God every time I remember you, *4*constantly praying with joy in every one of my prayers for all of you, *5*because of your sharing in the gospel from the first day until now. *6*I am confident of this, that the one who began a good work among you will bring it to completion by the day of Jesus Christ. *7*It is right for me to think this way about all of you, because you hold me in your heart,*d* for all of you share in God's grace*e* with me, both in my imprisonment and in the defense and confirmation of the gospel.

*8*For God is my witness, how I long for all of you with the compassion of Christ Jesus. *9*And this is my prayer, that your love may overflow more and more with knowledge and full insight *10*to help you to determine what is best, so that in the day of Christ you may be pure and blameless, *11*having produced the harvest of righteousness that comes through Jesus Christ for the glory and praise of God.

1.3–11: Thanksgiving. Preview of the letter's themes. **6:** The *work* extends through life, emanating from God until consummation of the new age. *The day of Jesus Christ* (compare Amos 5.20; Zeph 1.15) refers to the return of Jesus (see 2 Cor 1.8). **7:** *Think* (2.2, 5; 3.15, 19; 4.2, 10), moral reasoning or correct disposition of the mind. *Heart,* one's inner life, not simply feelings. NRSV *share* is actually a noun, "partnership" between Paul and his audience. This is one of several compound words (1.17, 27; 2.2, 17–18, 25; 3.21; 4.3, 14) with a *syn*-prefix (meaning "with"), emphasizing unity. *Confirmation,* establishing the gospel in believers. **8:** Com-

a Gk slaves   *b* Or overseers   *c* Or overseers and helpers   *d* Or because I hold you in my heart   *e* Gk in grace passion, affection. **9:** *Knowledge* through experience of what really matters so that conduct brings glory and praise to God. **11:** *Harvest of righteousness,* apocalyptic* imagery that places present-day problems in the setting of the end-time.

～～～～～～～～～～～～～～～～～～～～～～～

12 I want you to know, beloved,*ᵃ* that what has happened to me has actually helped to spread the gospel, ¹³so that it has become known throughout the whole imperial guard*ᵇ* and to everyone else that my imprisonment is for Christ; ¹⁴and most of the brothers and sisters,*ᵃ* having been made confident in the Lord by my imprisonment, dare to speak the word*ᶜ* with greater boldness and without fear.

15 Some proclaim Christ from envy and rivalry, but others from goodwill. ¹⁶These proclaim Christ out of love, knowing that I have been put here for the defense of the gospel; ¹⁷the others proclaim Christ out of selfish ambition, not sincerely but intending to increase my suffering in my imprisonment. ¹⁸What does it matter? Just this, that Christ is proclaimed in every way, whether out of false motives or true; and in that I rejoice.

Yes, and I will continue to rejoice, ¹⁹for I know that through your prayers and the help of the Spirit of Jesus Christ this will turn out for my deliverance. ²⁰It is my eager expectation and hope that I will not be put to shame in any way, but that by my speaking with all boldness, Christ will be exalted now as always in my body, whether by life or by death. ²¹For to me, living is Christ and dying is gain. ²²If I am to live in the flesh, that means fruitful labor for me; and I do not know which I prefer. ²³I am hard pressed between the two: my desire is to depart and be with Christ, for that is far better; ²⁴but to remain in the flesh is more necessary for you. ²⁵Since I am convinced of this, I know that I will remain and continue with all of you for your progress and joy in faith, ²⁶so that I may share abundantly in your boasting in Christ Jesus when I come to you again.

─────────────────────────────

1.12–26: Suffering for the gospel. *Spread* (v. 12) and *progress* (v. 25) are the same word in Greek, unifying the two parts of the passage: Paul's joy in proclaiming

Christ despite his imprisonment (1.12–18a); and his joy in the exaltation of Christ in his body whether he lives or dies (1.18b–26). Everything else—love, envy, life, or death—is relative to this joy. Imprisonment (1.12–26) is an example of placing the needs of others above personal concerns. **12:** *Spread* or "progress," clearing (literally "cutting") a path for an army; see v. 25. **13:** *Whole imperial guard:* In Rome, "praetorium" (see note *b*) is the emperor's elite soldiers; in Asia Minor, it is the provincial residence of any Roman administrator. **16:** *Defense of the gospel,* the effort to convince outsiders of the gospel's values. **20:** *Put to shame,* made ashamed because of the paradox of good news about the shameful death of Jesus. Paul will not be ashamed because his circumstances exalt Christ whether he lives or dies.

～～～～～～～～～～～～～～～～～～～～～～～

27 Only, live your life in a manner worthy of the gospel of Christ, so that, whether I come and see you or am absent and hear about you, I will know that you are standing firm in one spirit, striving side by side with one mind for the faith of the gospel, ²⁸and are in no way intimidated by your opponents. For them this is evidence of their destruction, but of your salvation. And this is God's doing. ²⁹For he has graciously granted you the privilege not only of believing in Christ, but of suffering for him as well— ³⁰since you are having the same struggle that you saw I had and now hear that I still have.

─────────────────────────────

1.27–30: Living worthy of the gospel. 27: *Live your life,* literally "conduct life as a citizen" of heaven (3.20). *Worthy of the gospel of Christ,* that is, in a manner that does not seek one's own elevation above another (2.6–11). **29:** Paul suffers for the gospel to show that *suffering* is part of grace. **27–30:** A series of athletic or military images includes *striving side by side* (compare 4.3), *struggle* (the contest of defending the gospel to outsiders), and even *standing firm.*

─────────────────────────────

EXAMPLES OF THE GOSPEL'S RECONFIGURATION OF HONOR

2.1–4.7: Specific examples of Jesus (2.6–11), Timothy and Epaphroditus (2.19–3.1a) and Paul himself (3.1b–4.1a) express the frame of mind Paul com-

a Gk *brothers*   *b* Gk *whole praetorium*
c Other ancient authorities read *word of God*

mends before he exhorts the Philippians toward unity in the church (4.1b–7).

2 If then there is any encouragement in Christ, any consolation from love, any sharing in the Spirit, any compassion and sympathy, ²make my joy complete: be of the same mind, having the same love, being in full accord and of one mind. ³Do nothing from selfish ambition or conceit, but in humility regard others as better than yourselves. ⁴Let each of you look not to your own interests, but to the interests of others. ⁵Let the same mind be in you that was*a* in Christ Jesus,

6   who, though he was in the form of God,
      did not regard equality with God
        as something to be exploited,
7   but emptied himself,
      taking the form of a slave,
      being born in human likeness.
  And being found in human form,
8   he humbled himself
      and became obedient to the point of
        death—
      even death on a cross.
9   Therefore God also highly exalted him
      and gave him the name
      that is above every name,
10   so that at the name of Jesus
      every knee should bend,
      in heaven and on earth and under the
        earth,
11   and every tongue should confess
      that Jesus Christ is Lord,
      to the glory of God the Father.

2.1–11. 1–4: The proper mind. The Philippians must seek true honor, not their own glory. **1:** *If there is any encouragement in Christ . . .* , not an expression of doubt but a call for consideration. **2:** *Make my joy complete,* that is, more joy than he already has despite difficult circumstances; an appeal based on the common benefits he and his audience share as believers. **3:** Self-centered *ambition* seeks to elevate one's own status (1.15, 17); *conceit,* "empty glorying," is an improper motive when the goal of life is the "glory" of God (1.11; see 4.20). **6–11: A hymn on Jesus' unselfish disposition.** It is unclear whether Paul composed this hymn himself or is quoting it. The example of Jesus is central to the message he brings the Philip-

pians. Just as Jesus is described as a *slave* (v. 7), so are Paul and Timothy (1.1; 2.22). Just as Jesus submitted *to the point of death* (v. 8), so Epaphroditus moved "close to death" (2.30) for the sake of Christ. Voluntarily giving up privileges for the sake of others and to God's glory redefines conventional views of honor in which persons compete fiercely to gain more favor than their peers.

12 Therefore, my beloved, just as you have always obeyed me, not only in my presence, but much more now in my absence, work out your own salvation with fear and trembling; ¹³for it is God who is at work in you, enabling you both to will and to work for his good pleasure.

14 Do all things without murmuring and arguing, ¹⁵so that you may be blameless and innocent, children of God without blemish in the midst of a crooked and perverse generation, in which you shine like stars in the world. ¹⁶It is by your holding fast to the word of life that I can boast on the day of Christ that I did not run in vain or labor in vain. ¹⁷But even if I am being poured out as a libation over the sacrifice and the offering of your faith, I am glad and rejoice with all of you— ¹⁸and in the same way you also must be glad and rejoice with me.

2.12–18: Applying the hymn to life. Based on the honor of being a slave who brings glory to God, Paul commends efforts that seek to please God, oriented toward the day of Christ, for God began and would continue the work among the Philippians until it was completed on that day (1.6). **12:** *Work out* or "work forth" (that is, demonstrate) *salvation,* a work that is not yet complete. **15:** *Crooked and perverse generation* (Deut 32.5), in contrast to God's blameless children who shine like the stars. **16:** *Labor,* Paul's efforts in proclaiming the gospel, oriented to the day of Christ on which he can boast if his church holds fast. **17:** *Being poured out as a libation over the sacrifice,* Paul's present suffering for the gospel. Later, he views the Philippians' gift as a "sacrifice," that is, a financial hardship on behalf of the gospel (4.18).

19 I hope in the Lord Jesus to send Timothy to you soon, so that I may be cheered

a Or *that you have*

``Honor'' in Aristotle

In his *Ethics*, Aristotle discusses virtue, happiness, pleasure, and self-control. The ideal person is "great of soul," superior in wisdom and virtue, one for whom, therefore, humility would be an error. "The man who thinks himself worthy of less than he is really worthy of is unduly humble . . . and the man whose deserts are great would seem *most* unduly humble. . . . If, then, he deserves and claims great things, and above all the greatest things, he will be concerned with one thing in particular. . . . The greatest of (external goods) . . . which we render to the gods, and which people of position most aim at, and which is the prize appointed for the noblest deeds . . . is honor" (Book 4, ch. 3, translated by David Ross).

by news of you. 20I have no one like him who will be genuinely concerned for your welfare. 21All of them are seeking their own interests, not those of Jesus Christ. 22But Timothy's*a* worth you know, how like a son with a father he has served with me in the work of the gospel. 23I hope therefore to send him as soon as I see how things go with me; 24and I trust in the Lord that I will also come soon.

25 Still, I think it necessary to send to you Epaphroditus—my brother and co-worker and fellow soldier, your messenger*b* and minister to my need; 26for he has been longing for*c* all of you, and has been distressed because you heard that he was ill. 27He was indeed so ill that he nearly died. But God had mercy on him, and not only on him but on me also, so that I would not have one sorrow after another. 28I am the more eager to send him, therefore, in order that you may rejoice at seeing him again, and that I may be less anxious. 29Welcome him then in the Lord with all joy, and honor such people, 30because he came close to death for the work of Christ,*d* risking his life to make up for those services that you could not give me.

3 Finally, my brothers and sisters,*e* rejoice*f* in the Lord.

2.19–3.1a: Timothy and Epaphroditus: Examples of unselfishness. *Timothy* (2.19–24) and *Epaphroditus* (2.25–30), examples of unselfishness concerned with the whole church. **22:** *Timothy,* see Acts 16.1–3; 1 Cor 16.10–11; 1 Thess 3.1–6. **25:** *Epaphroditus,* see 4.18; Col 1.7; Philem 23. **29–30:** *Honor such people,* Paul

continues to redefine honor: Honor those who risk their lives for Christ (2.30). **1a:** *Finally,* a transition (also at 4.8).

To write the same things to you is not troublesome to me, and for you it is a safeguard.

2 Beware of the dogs, beware of the evil workers, beware of those who mutilate the flesh!*g* 3For it is we who are the circumcision, who worship in the Spirit of God*h* and boast in Christ Jesus and have no confidence in the flesh— 4even though I, too, have reason for confidence in the flesh.

If anyone else has reason to be confident in the flesh, I have more: 5circumcised on the eighth day, a member of the people of Israel, of the tribe of Benjamin, a Hebrew born of Hebrews; as to the law, a Pharisee; 6as to zeal, a persecutor of the church; as to righteousness under the law, blameless.

7 Yet whatever gains I had, these I have come to regard as loss because of Christ. 8More than that, I regard everything as loss because of the surpassing value of knowing Christ Jesus my Lord. For his sake I have suffered the loss of all things, and I regard them as rubbish, in order that I may gain Christ 9and be found in him, not having a righteousness of my own that comes from the law, but one that comes through faith in Christ,*i* the righteousness from God based

a Gk *his* *b* Gk *apostle* *c* Other ancient authorities read *longing to see* *d* Other ancient authorities read *of the Lord* *e* Gk *my brothers* *f* Or *farewell* *g* Gk *the mutilation* *h* Other ancient authorities read *worship God in spirit* *i* Or *through the faith of Christ* on faith. [10]I want to know Christ[a] and the power of his resurrection and the sharing of his sufferings by becoming like him in his death, [11]if somehow I may attain the resurrection from the dead.

[12] Not that I have already obtained this or have already reached the goal;[b] but I press on to make it my own, because Christ Jesus has made me his own. [13]Beloved,[c] I do not consider that I have made it my own;[d] but this one thing I do: forgetting what lies behind and straining forward to what lies ahead, [14]I press on toward the goal for the prize of the heavenly[e] call of God in Christ Jesus. [15]Let those of us then who are mature be of the same mind; and if you think differently about anything, this too God will reveal to you. [16]Only let us hold fast to what we have attained.

[17] Brothers and sisters,[e] join in imitating me, and observe those who live according to the example you have in us. [18]For many live as enemies of the cross of Christ; I have often told you of them, and now I tell you even with tears. [19]Their end is destruction; their god is the belly; and their glory is in their shame; their minds are set on earthly things. [20]But our citizenship[f] is in heaven, and it is from there that we are expecting a Savior, the Lord Jesus Christ. [21]He will transform the body of our humiliation[g] that it may be conformed to the body of his glory,[h] by the power that also enables him to make all things subject to himself. [1]Therefore, my brothers and sisters,[i] whom I love and long for, my joy and crown, stand firm in the Lord in this way, my beloved.

3.1b–4.1: The example of Paul. A transition (v. 1) and warning (v. 2) lead into Paul's renunciation of his advantages to counter any tendencies to arrogance (vv. 3–11). He commends perfection but notes, in a play on words, how perfect people (relatively speaking) know they have not reached perfection (vv. 12–16). Finally, while enemies of the cross have an earthly orientation, Paul commends a heavenly citizenship in which the believers await glorification in the future (3.17–4.1). **1:** *To write the same things,* probably about disunity; Paul positions the words he writes about his own life as a safeguard for the community's problems. **2:** *Beware,* repeated three times, or "watch

out for," warns about a possibility, not what already exists. Verses 2 and 18–19 likely refer to practices in the community, rather than actual opponents, that breed disunity. *Dogs* in ancient writing were examples of shameless greed. **3:** *Circumcision,** metaphorically,* God's people. **7:** *Regard* echoes 2.3, which commends church-members to "regard others better than themselves," and 2.6 which asserts that Jesus did not "regard equality with God as something to be exploited." **10:** *Becoming like* ("symmorphizomenos") Jesus, a link to 2.7, in which Jesus took on the "form" ("morphen") of a slave. **13–14:** The image is of running a race. **17:** *Imitation,* see 1 Cor 4.16; 11.1; 1 Thess 1.6. **20:** *Citizenship,* not political but heavenly. See Gal 4.26.

[2] I urge Euodia and I urge Syntyche to be of the same mind in the Lord. [3]Yes, and I ask you also, my loyal companion,[j] help these women, for they have struggled beside me in the work of the gospel, together with Clement and the rest of my co-workers, whose names are in the book of life.

[4] Rejoice[k] in the Lord always; again I will say, Rejoice.[k] [5]Let your gentleness be known to everyone. The Lord is near. [6]Do not worry about anything, but in everything by prayer and supplication with thanksgiving let your requests be made known to God. [7]And the peace of God, which surpasses all understanding, will guard your hearts and your minds in Christ Jesus.

4.2–7: Exhortations to overcome disunity and opposition. 2: *Be of the same mind:* The point of disagreement is unknown, but a number of the letter's key expressions *(same mind, struggled side by side, work of the gospel)* come together here. *Book of life,* see Ex 32.32; Ps 69.28; Dan 12.1. **4–7:** Brief exhortations to develop the right attitude; *guard,* a military term, describes God's peace.

[8] Finally, beloved,[l] whatever is true, whatever is honorable, whatever is just, whatever is pure, whatever is pleasing, what-

a Gk *him*   b Or *have already been made perfect*
c Gk *Brothers*   d Other ancient authorities read *my own yet*   e Gk *upward*   f Or *commonwealth*
g Or *our humble bodies*   h Or *his glorious body*
i Gk *my brothers*   j Or *loyal Syzygus*   k Or *Farewell*
l Gk *brothers*

ever is commendable, if there is any excellence and if there is anything worthy of praise, think about^a these things. ⁹Keep on doing the things that you have learned and received and heard and seen in me, and the God of peace will be with you.

10 I rejoice^b in the Lord greatly that now at last you have revived your concern for me; indeed, you were concerned for me, but had no opportunity to show it.^c ¹¹Not that I am referring to being in need; for I have learned to be content with whatever I have. ¹²I know what it is to have little, and I know what it is to have plenty. In any and all circumstances I have learned the secret of being well-fed and of going hungry, of having plenty and of being in need. ¹³I can do all things through him who strengthens me. ¹⁴In any case, it was kind of you to share my distress.

15 You Philippians indeed know that in the early days of the gospel, when I left Macedonia, no church shared with me in the matter of giving and receiving, except you alone. ¹⁶For even when I was in Thessalonica, you sent me help for my needs more than once. ¹⁷Not that I seek the gift, but I seek the profit that accumulates to your account. ¹⁸I have been paid in full and have more than enough; I am fully satisfied, now that I have received from Epaphroditus the gifts you sent, a fragrant offering, a sacrifice acceptable and pleasing to God. ¹⁹And my God will fully satisfy every need of yours according to his riches in glory in Christ Jesus. ²⁰To our God and Father be glory forever and ever. Amen.

4.8–20: A call for consistency in all situations. A brief, poetic passage commends right thinking and right action (vv. 8–9) and notes the proper attitude toward changing circumstances (vv. 10–20). **8–9:** The *whatever* statements indicate a series of attitudes for living that can help the community face any difficulty. **10:** *Revived your concern,* the Philippians maintained concern for Paul even when they could not express it. **10–13:** Paul's attitude resembles Cynic* and Stoic* discussions of his time, but he does not see the source of endurance in himself. Paul challenges the Philippians to learn the value of "humiliation," shunned by conventional society but reinforced elsewhere in the letter (2.3, 8; 3.21). **15–19:** The community never lacked concern for him (v. 10), even though he neither needed nor sought it. Their reward is from God. **16:** Paul never accepted gifts from a church while he was with them (see 1 Cor 9; 1 Thess 2.9; 2 Cor 8.1–5) **18:** On *sacrifice,* see 2.17.

21 Greet every saint in Christ Jesus. The friends^d who are with me greet you. ²²All the saints greet you, especially those of the emperor's household.

23 The grace of the Lord Jesus Christ be with your spirit.^e

4.21–23: Closing. Mutual greetings (compare 1 Cor 16.19–21; 1 Thess 5.26–27) and a blessing (compare Philemon). **22:** *The emperor's household,* the slaves of the emperor in Rome or the colonies.

a Gk *take account of*   *b* Gk *I rejoiced*   *c* Gk lacks *to show it*   *d* Gk *brothers*   *e* Other ancient authorities add *Amen*

THE LETTER OF PAUL TO THE
COLOSSIANS

Introduction

Colossians is a mixture of liturgical* elements (a prayer in 1.9–12, a hymn in 1.15–20, and baptismal* reminiscences in 3.1–4.6); typical features of letters (1.2; 4.17–18); and exhortations* on fidelity to correct teachings. True Christian maturity depends on fidelity to enduring spiritual wisdom and understanding, not to limited, human regulations and rituals that give only the appearance of wisdom (2.16–23). Furthermore, the true wisdom of the community's foundational teachings is the full, sufficient, and exclusive basis for its new life in Christ (2.9). The letter also shares much with Ephesians (see introduction to Ephesians), particularly the portrait of the cosmic lordship of Christ, the head of the church (1.18; see Eph 1.22). Where the letters agree, however, it is likely that Ephesians is commenting on Colossians.

The congregation at Colossae was gentile* (1.27; 2.13). It is uncertain where this letter was written: Manuscript variants suggest different locations, including Rome and Ephesus; although Paul's imprisonment is mentioned, no place is given (4.3, 10). Colossae was probably about 100 miles southeast of Ephesus in the upper Lycus River valley of southwestern Asia Minor (in Phrygia or modern-day Turkey), but its exact location is unknown because the city relocated after an earthquake (60–64 CE).

The authorship is also uncertain, although Paul is given as its author. There is no written evidence that Paul ever visited Colossae, and the church was likely established by Epaphras (1.7), a resident from that city (4.12). Moreover, despite similarities to several Pauline letters (Galatians, Romans, Philippians, 1 and 2 Corinthians, and Philemon), aspects of its style and theology suggest it is post-Pauline. There are many long sentences, like 1.3–8, which the NRSV breaks into five distinct sentences. It also contains many redundant expressions: 1.11–12 is a string of synonyms ("strengthened with all power," "endurance and patience," and "share in the inheritance"). Theologically, the letter presents hope as an object in heaven (1.5), not vigorous, assured expectation as in the undisputed Pauline letters (see 1 Thess 1.3). It never mentions the parousia,* the second coming of Christ.

The letter seems to have been written to fight a heresy that was gaining favor in Asia Minor. The letter says nothing positive about this philosophy, and the heretical teachings can only be known indirectly (mostly from 2.8–23). Even then, the exact meaning of "worship of angels" (2.18) is unclear: possibly angel worship as in some mystery religions* or possibly the angels' worship of God as in Jewish mysticism. It may also be that the letter does not attack a "heresy" at all, but simply threats from the general culture. In any case, it argues against two types of claims: cosmological and ritualistic. The cosmological contended that the vast powers that control the universe must be adored. The ritualistic required regulations about food and drink (2.16, 21) and special festivals and days (2.16). Against both the letter asserts that all that believers need is found in Christ.

READING GUIDE

To encourage fidelity to foundational teachings, Colossians recalls that the community had already grown based on them (1.3–23), contrasts true teaching to "human" teachings which merely appear to sustain growth (1.24–2.23), and urges the community to grow further in the new dominion which they have joined as a result of receiving the foundational teachings (3.1–4.6).

1.1–2	Epistolary opening
1.3–14	Prayers and God's redemption
1.15–2.19	Fidelity to the teachings about the hope
2.20–4.6	Practical implications of the hope
4.7–18	Epistolary closing

1 Paul, an apostle of Christ Jesus by the will of God, and Timothy our brother, 2 To the saints and faithful brothers and sisters*a* in Christ in Colossae:

Grace to you and peace from God our Father.

1.1–2: The epistolary opening. See 2 Cor 1.1; Gal 1.1. **1:** *Saints,* holy ones, believers (2 Cor 1.1; Rom 1.7; Phil 1.1; Eph 1.1).

---

3 In our prayers for you we always thank God, the Father of our Lord Jesus Christ, 4for we have heard of your faith in Christ Jesus and of the love that you have for all the saints, 5because of the hope laid up for you in heaven. You have heard of this hope before in the word of the truth, the gospel 6that has come to you. Just as it is bearing fruit and growing in the whole world, so it has been bearing fruit among yourselves from the day you heard it and truly comprehended the grace of God. 7This you learned from Epaphras, our beloved fellow servant.*b* He is a faithful minister of Christ on your*c* behalf, 8and he has made known to us your love in the Spirit.

9 For this reason, since the day we heard it, we have not ceased praying for you and asking that you may be filled with the knowledge of God's*d* will in all spiritual wisdom and understanding, 10so that you may lead lives worthy of the Lord, fully pleasing to him, as you bear fruit in every good work and as you grow in the knowledge of God. 11May you be made strong with all the strength that comes from his glorious power, and may you be prepared to endure everything with patience, while joyfully 12giving thanks to the Father, who has enabled*e* you*f* to share in the inheritance of the saints in the light. 13He has rescued us from the power of darkness and transferred us into the kingdom of his beloved Son, 14in whom we have redemption, the forgiveness of sins.*g*

1.3–14: Prayers and God's redemption. Two prayers (vv. 3–8, 9–12) reveal the basis of the community's growth in faith: God rescued the believers from the power of darkness and moved them into *the kingdom of his beloved son* (v. 13). **3–8:** Themes of growth and learning (1.28; 2.6; 3.10; 4.12) emphasize the fruitfulness of the gospel (v. 5) in increasing the knowledge of God's will (vv. 9–10) and in building the body of Christ (2.19). *Epaphras* (v. 7) taught hope linked to Christ, unlike the "heresy" which downplays Christ (see 2.18–19). **5:** *Hope,* no longer the firm expectation of God's promise but an object already available, *laid up* or stored up, though it awaits revelation. **6:** *Bearing fruit and growing* describes the gospel of God's grace. **7:** *Epaphras,* 4.12; Philem 23. **9–12:** A shift from past reception of the gospel to a fuller comprehension of God's will. **9:** *Knowledge . . . spiritual wisdom and understanding.* All three have practical implications. *Wisdom* (a favorite term; see 2.3, 23; 4.5) and *understanding* or insight are linked in the Hebrew Scriptures* or their Greek translation (see Deut 1.13,

a Gk *brothers*　　*b* Gk *slave*　　*c* Other ancient authorities read *our*　　*d* Gk *his*　　*e* Other ancient authorities read *called*　　*f* Other ancient authorities read *us*　　*g* Other ancient authorities add *through his blood*

15; 1 Kings 16.18; Isa 3.3). **10:** *Lead,* or conduct; see 2.6; 3.7–17; 4.5. **12:** *Inheritance,* share or allotment. **13–14:** This basic statement of belief recites what God has done.

be blameless before God if they are steadfast. **21:** *Estranged,* alienated or unfamiliar with something. See Eph. 2.12; 4.18.

15 He is the image of the invisible God, the firstborn of all creation; 16for in*a* him all things in heaven and on earth were created, things visible and invisible, whether thrones or dominions or rulers or powers—all things have been created through him and for him. 17He himself is before all things, and in*a* him all things hold together. 18He is the head of the body, the church; he is the beginning, the firstborn from the dead, so that he might come to have first place in everything. 19For in him all the fullness of God was pleased to dwell, 20and through him God was pleased to reconcile to himself all things, whether on earth or in heaven, by making peace through the blood of his cross.

21 And you who were once estranged and hostile in mind, doing evil deeds, 22he has now reconciled*b* in his fleshly body*c* through death, so as to present you holy and blameless and irreproachable before him— 23provided that you continue securely established and steadfast in the faith, without shifting from the hope promised by the gospel that you heard, which has been proclaimed to every creature under heaven. I, Paul, became a servant of this gospel.

1.15–23: A hymn to the universal Christ and comment on his redeeming work. Christ, the cosmic agent of creation, has reconciled creation's warring elements (vv. 15–20), and the reconciled must remain faithful to their early teachings to ensure maturity (vv. 21–23). **15–20:** The hymn's origin is unknown, but if not Christian it may be an adaptation from a Greek mystery religion,★ a Jewish text about the Son of Man and the end times, or a Hellenistic★ Jewish wisdom text like Prov 8.22–31 or Sir 24.1–22. It easily divides into two: Christ as the agent of creation (vv. 15–18a) and Christ as an agent of redemption (vv. 18b–20). **16:** Christ's role in creation is like the role of Wisdom (see Prov 8.22–26; Sir 24.9). **18:** *Head of the body,* see 2.19; Eph 1.22–23. **20:** *Reconcile,* restore to friendship from enmity. See 1.22; Rom 5.10; 1 Cor 7.11; 2 Cor 5.18–21; Eph 2.16. **21–23:** A direct exhortation★ to the recipients: God has reconciled them and they will

24 I am now rejoicing in my sufferings for your sake, and in my flesh I am completing what is lacking in Christ's afflictions for the sake of his body, that is, the church. 25I became its servant according to God's commission that was given to me for you, to make the word of God fully known, 26the mystery that has been hidden throughout the ages and generations but has now been revealed to his saints. 27To them God chose to make known how great among the Gentiles are the riches of the glory of this mystery, which is Christ in you, the hope of glory. 28It is he whom we proclaim, warning everyone and teaching everyone in all wisdom, so that we may present everyone mature in Christ. 29For this I toil and struggle with all the energy that he powerfully inspires within me.

2 For I want you to know how much I am struggling for you, and for those in Laodicea, and for all who have not seen me face to face. 2I want their hearts to be encouraged and united in love, so that they may have all the riches of assured understanding and have the knowledge of God's mystery, that is, Christ himself,*d* 3in whom are hidden all the treasures of wisdom and knowledge. 4I am saying this so that no one may deceive you with plausible arguments. 5For though I am absent in body, yet I am with you in spirit, and I rejoice to see your morale and the firmness of your faith in Christ.

6 As you therefore have received Christ Jesus the Lord, continue to live your lives*e* in him, 7rooted and built up in him and established in the faith, just as you were taught, abounding in thanksgiving.

8 See to it that no one takes you captive through philosophy and empty deceit, according to human tradition, according to the elemental spirits of the universe,*f* and not

a Or *by*   *b* Other ancient authorities read *you have now been reconciled*   *c* Gk *in the body of his flesh*
d Other ancient authorities read *of the mystery of God, both of the Father and of Christ*   *e* Gk *to walk*
f Or *the rudiments of the world*

according to Christ. ⁹For in him the whole fullness of deity dwells bodily, ¹⁰and you have come to fullness in him, who is the head of every ruler and authority. ¹¹In him also you were circumcised with a spiritual circumcision,ᵃ by putting off the body of the flesh in the circumcision of Christ; ¹²when you were buried with him in baptism, you were also raised with him through faith in the power of God, who raised him from the dead. ¹³And when you were dead in trespasses and the uncircumcision of your flesh, Godᵇ made youᶜ alive together with him, when he forgave us all our trespasses, ¹⁴erasing the record that stood against us with its legal demands. He set this aside, nailing it to the cross. ¹⁵He disarmedᵈ the rulers and authorities and made a public example of them, triumphing over them in it.

16　Therefore do not let anyone condemn you in matters of food and drink or of observing festivals, new moons, or sabbaths. ¹⁷These are only a shadow of what is to come, but the substance belongs to Christ. ¹⁸Do not let anyone disqualify you, insisting on self-abasement and worship of angels, dwellingᵉ on visions,ᶠ puffed up without cause by a human way of thinking,ᵍ ¹⁹and not holding fast to the head, from whom the whole body, nourished and held together by its ligaments and sinews, grows with a growth that is from God.

1.24–2.19: A personal witness and a warning. An autobiographical sketch describes the church's maturation (1.24–2.5) and leads to a warning against deviating from the truth (2.6–19). **1.24:** A certain amount of *suffering* is assumed to be necessary (see 1 Thess 3.3) before the end can arrive. *Completing . . . Christ's afflictions,* any suffering brings the end sooner. **26–27:** The *mystery*⋆ is *Christ in you,* the image of Christ growing in you. **29:** *Toil, struggle,* the effort to bring about the community's maturity. See 1 Thess 2.9. **2.6:** *Live your lives,* "conduct" your lives; see 1.10. **8–19:** The warning: Although the heresy appears as wisdom because of its ascetic and ritualistic practices, Christ's death and resurrection are sufficient to bring the believers' lives into the new dominion. **8:** *Takes you captive,* false teachers are like robbers or kidnappers. **11–12:** *Putting off, buried with him in baptism,*⋆ baptismal images joined with *spiritual circumcision*⋆

to describe entry into the new life (see Gal 3.27). **14:** *Record,* a note of debt. **15:** *Disarmed,* stripped of power. Roman emperors led captives in a public triumphal procession. **17:** *Shadow* and *substance,* a familiar contrast in Greek thought (see Plato's *Republic* 514a–518b). **18:** *Angels' worship,* worship offered to angels or worship offered by angels, probably the latter.

PRACTICAL IMPLICATIONS OF THE HOPE

2.20–4.6: Life with Christ governs regulations about food and drink and relations with other Christians, family members, and outsiders. An initial transition (2.20–23) reveals the practical implications of death with Christ. Another transition (3.1–4) commends the life raised with Christ, followed by a vice list (3.5–11), a virtue list (3.12–17), and household duties (3.18–4.6).

20　If with Christ you died to the elemental spirits of the universe,ʰ why do you live as if you still belonged to the world? Why do you submit to regulations, ²¹"Do not handle, Do not taste, Do not touch"? ²²All these regulations refer to things that perish with use; they are simply human commands and teachings. ²³These have indeed an appearance of wisdom in promoting self-imposed piety, humility, and severe treatment of the body, but they are of no value in checking self-indulgence.ⁱ

3 So if you have been raised with Christ, seek the things that are above, where Christ is, seated at the right hand of God. ²Set your minds on things that are above, not on things that are on earth, ³for you have died, and your life is hidden with Christ in God. ⁴When Christ who is yourʲ life is revealed, then you also will be revealed with him in glory.

5　Put to death, therefore, whatever in you is earthly: fornication, impurity, passion, evil desire, and greed (which is idolatry). ⁶On ac-

a Gk *a circumcision made without hands*　　*b* Gk *he*
c Other ancient authorities read *made us;* others, *made*
d Or *divested himself of*　　*e* Other ancient authorities read *not dwelling*　　*f* Meaning of Gk uncertain
g Gk *by the mind of his flesh*　　*h* Or *the rudiments of the world*　　*i* Or *are of no value, serving only to indulge the flesh*　　*j* Other authorities read *our*

count of these the wrath of God is coming on those who are disobedient.[a] 7These are the ways you also once followed, when you were living that life.[b] 8But now you must get rid of all such things—anger, wrath, malice, slander, and abusive[c] language from your mouth. 9Do not lie to one another, seeing that you have stripped off the old self with its practices 10and have clothed yourselves with the new self, which is being renewed in knowledge according to the image of its creator. 11In that renewal[d] there is no longer Greek and Jew, circumcised and uncircumcised, barbarian, Scythian, slave and free; but Christ is all and in all!

12 As God's chosen ones, holy and beloved, clothe yourselves with compassion, kindness, humility, meekness, and patience. 13Bear with one another and, if anyone has a complaint against another, forgive each other; just as the Lord[e] has forgiven you, so you also must forgive. 14Above all, clothe yourselves with love, which binds everything together in perfect harmony. 15And let the peace of Christ rule in your hearts, to which indeed you were called in the one body. And be thankful. 16Let the word of Christ[f] dwell in you richly; teach and admonish one another in all wisdom; and with gratitude in your hearts sing psalms, hymns, and spiritual songs to God.[g] 17And whatever you do, in word or deed, do everything in the name of the Lord Jesus, giving thanks to God the Father through him.

18 Wives, be subject to your husbands, as is fitting in the Lord. 19Husbands, love your wives and never treat them harshly.

20 Children, obey your parents in everything, for this is your acceptable duty in the Lord. 21Fathers, do not provoke your children, or they may lose heart. 22Slaves, obey your earthly masters[h] in everything, not only while being watched and in order to please them, but wholeheartedly, fearing the Lord.[h] 23Whatever your task, put yourselves into it, as done for the Lord and not for your masters,[i] 24since you know that from the Lord you will receive the inheritance as your reward; you serve[j] the Lord Christ. 25For the wrongdoer will be paid back for whatever wrong has been done, and there is no parti-

4 ality. 1Masters, treat your slaves justly and fairly, for you know that you also have a Master in heaven.

2 Devote yourselves to prayer, keeping alert in it with thanksgiving. 3At the same time pray for us as well that God will open to us a door for the word, that we may declare the mystery of Christ, for which I am in prison, 4so that I may reveal it clearly, as I should.

5 Conduct yourselves wisely toward outsiders, making the most of the time.[k] 6Let your speech always be gracious, seasoned with salt, so that you may know how you ought to answer everyone.

3.1–4.6. 3.1: *Right hand of God,* see Ps 110.1. **5–11:** On the use of vice lists in Paul, see Rom 1.29–31; Gal 5.19–21. Hellenistic* teachers often used vice and virtue lists to challenge their students. **11:** *Barbarian,* non-Greek. *Scythian,* a wild person; *no longer* will there be different ethnic groups, nor groups and subgroups. The author commends ethnic and class equality but not the equality of the sexes as found in Gal 3.28. **16:** See Eph 5.19. **3.18–4.1:** Household codes* governed life within the extended family. See Eph 5.22–6.9; 1 Tim 2.8–15; 6.1–2; Titus 2.1–10; 1 Pet 2.13–3.7. **5:** *Making the most of time,* see Eph 5.16. **6:** *Seasoned with salt,* carefully or wisely selected. See Mk 9.49–50; Mt 5.13.

7 Tychicus will tell you all the news about me; he is a beloved brother, a faithful minister, and a fellow servant[l] in the Lord. 8I have sent him to you for this very purpose, so that you may know how we are[m] and that he may encourage your hearts; 9he is coming with Onesimus, the faithful and beloved brother, who is one of you. They will tell you about everything here.

---

a Other ancient authorities lack *on those who are disobedient* (Gk *the children of disobedience*)
b Or *living among such people*   c Or *filthy*   d Gk *its creator, 11where*   e Other ancient authorities read *just as Christ*   f Other ancient authorities read *of God,* or *of the Lord*   g Other ancient authorities read *to the Lord*   h In Greek the same word is used for *master* and *Lord*   i Gk *not for men*   j Or *you are slaves of,* or *be slaves of*   k Or *opportunity*
l Gk *slave*   m Other authorities read *that I may know how you are*

10 Aristarchus my fellow prisoner greets you, as does Mark the cousin of Barnabas, concerning whom you have received instructions—if he comes to you, welcome him. [11]And Jesus who is called Justus greets you. These are the only ones of the circumcision among my co-workers for the kingdom of God, and they have been a comfort to me. [12]Epaphras, who is one of you, a servant[a] of Christ Jesus, greets you. He is always wrestling in his prayers on your behalf, so that you may stand mature and fully assured in everything that God wills. [13]For I testify for him that he has worked hard for you and for those in Laodicea and in Hierapolis. [14]Luke, the beloved physician, and Demas greet you. [15]Give my greetings to the brothers and sisters[b] in Laodicea, and to Nympha and the church in her house. [16]And when this letter has been read among you, have it read also in the church of the Laodiceans; and see that you read also the letter from Laodicea. [17]And say to Archippus, "See that you complete the task that you have received in the Lord."

18 I, Paul, write this greeting with my own hand. Remember my chains. Grace be with you.[c]

4.7–18: Epistolary closing. A reemphasis on the importance of maturity and commendation of persons firmly entrenched in the ethos of the new dominion. **7–10:** *Tychichus, Aristarchus,* see Acts 20.4. **14:** See Philem 23. **15:** *Nympha:* Some manuscripts treat Nympha as a female name, others as a male name, perhaps because of a scribe* who did not consider the possibility of a woman's owning a house, though the patronage of women in early Christianity is generally accepted. **16:** The *letter from Laodicea* is lost, though Marcion, an early Christian writer who died around 160 CE, thought it was our letter to the Ephesians. **17:** *Archippus,* see Philem 2. **18:** A scribe would have written the letter, with the author approving the dictation in his *own hand.*

a Gk *slave*   b Gk *brothers*   c Other ancient authorities add *Amen*

THE FIRST LETTER OF PAUL TO
THE **THESSALONIANS**

Introduction

First Thessalonians is Paul's earliest known letter. It is friendly and encouraging, filled with praise, affection, and expressions of family feeling. Paul commends the Thessalonians' steadfastness (1.3) and their mutual support and comfort (4.1, 9; 5.11). He remembers them with fondness (1.3; 3.6); he and they long for each other (2.17; 3.6). Images of kinship—father (1.1, 3; 2.11–12; 3.11, 13); sons (1.10; 5.5); children (2.7–8); and "brothers" (fourteen times)—are evoked throughout. Along with affection comes exhortation*: Chapters 4 and 5, and to an extent 1–3, urge the Thessalonians to act virtuously.

Thessalonica, the capital of the Roman province of Macedonia, was founded in 316 BCE by Cassander, one of Alexander's generals, and later annexed by Rome. It was a free city with a Greek, not Roman, legal system. Since it was on a major trade route, it flourished commercially, and the largely Greek population worked hard to keep its freedom, accommodating its Roman benefactors and including their deities in its religious life. Paul had formed the Thessalonian church after leaving Philippi, where he and others were "shamefully mistreated" (2.2; see Acts 17.1–4). His stay at Thessalonica was also difficult (2.2) and resulted in a painful separation (2.17), perhaps because his focus on the approaching end times directed the Thessalonians away from concerns about conventional prestige to the expectation of the end. Even worse, he was unable to return to the young congregation (2.18). After sending Timothy from Athens (3.1) to strengthen the community, Paul went to Corinth, where Timothy came with favorable news about the church's fidelity to his teachings and from which Paul probably wrote. Acts 18.11–17 suggests he arrived in Corinth before Gallio became proconsul, so he probably wrote around 50 or 51 CE (an inscription dates Gallio's arrival in Corinth between January and August of 51 CE).

READING GUIDE

The letter has a typical opening (1.1) and closing (5.23–28), and the main body encourages the young congregation to maintain its convictions of the imminent consummation of the new age at the day of the Lord (see 1 Thess 5.2) despite repeated afflictions. First, a brief thanksgiving reviews the community's founding moments (1.2–5). Second, Paul elaborates on the founding teachings and acknowledges the consistency of the community and its leaders in holding despite difficulties to belief in the Lord's coming (1.6–2.16). A third part (2.17–3.13) treats the most recent period of the community's difficulty, from the separation to the time of the letter's composition. This passage shows the dedication of both the missionaries and the congregation and implores God for aid in maintaining an ethic governed by an end-time orientation. Finally, Paul reinforces the end-time beliefs, though acknowledging that they demand the community's consistency in following the lifestyle of imminent expectation (4.1–5.22).

1.1	Epistolary opening
1.2–5	Thanksgiving

1 Paul, Silvanus, and Timothy,
To the church of the Thessalonians in God the Father and the Lord Jesus Christ: Grace to you and peace.

1.1: **Opening.** A typical greeting, although written in an extremely simple form (see Phil 1.1–2). **1:** *Silvanus,* Latin form of Silas, one of Paul's companions (Acts 15.22, 40; 17.4). *Timothy,* one of Paul's emissaries and a traveling companion (Rom 16.21; 1 Cor 4.17; 16.10; Phil 2.19). *Grace and peace,* likely a variation of the Jewish "mercy and peace" (see 2 Baruch 78.2, a late Jewish apocryphal writing, probably from the first century CE).

2 We always give thanks to God for all of you and mention you in our prayers, constantly ³remembering before our God and Father your work of faith and labor of love and steadfastness of hope in our Lord Jesus Christ. ⁴For we know, brothers and sisters*a* beloved by God, that he has chosen you, ⁵because our message of the gospel came to you not in word only, but also in power and in the Holy Spirit and with full conviction; just as you know what kind of persons we proved to be among you for your sake. ⁶And you became imitators of us and of the Lord, for in spite of persecution you received the word with joy inspired by the Holy Spirit, ⁷so that you became an example to all the believers in Macedonia and in Achaia. ⁸For the word of the Lord has sounded forth from you not only in Macedonia and Achaia, but in every place your faith in God has become known, so that we have no need to speak about it. ⁹For the people of those regions*b* report about us what kind of welcome we had among you, and how you turned to God from idols, to serve a living and true God, ¹⁰and to wait for his Son from heaven, whom he raised from the dead—Jesus, who rescues us from the wrath that is coming.

1.2–10. 2–5: Thanksgiving. Paul highlights his consistent prayers, signs of the congregation's ongoing life, and God's initiative in the effectiveness of the gospel and Paul's mission team. **3:** *Faith . . . love . . . hope,* see 5.8; Rom 5.1–5; 1 Cor 13.13; Gal 5.5–6. **4:** On the kinship expression *brothers and sisters,* see Deut 15.3. *Beloved by God,* see Deut 33.12. *Chosen,* see Deut 4.37; 7.6–8; 10.14–15; 14.2. **1.6–2.16: The suffering and endurance of the congregation.** Three sections depict how the Thessalonians suffered *with joy inspired by the Holy Spirit* (1.6–10), the endurance of the mission team (2.1–12), and what the Thessalonians suffered (2.13–16). **1.6–10: How the Thessalonians suffered. 6:** *Persecution* (3.3–4, 7), suffering or affliction, the woes that precede the consummation of the new age. **8:** *Sounded forth,* the Greek implies continuous spreading of the word. **9–10:** This may be a formal statement of belief. *Turned to God from idols* suggests, contrary to Acts 17.4, that the converts were gentiles.* See 2.14.

2 You yourselves know, brothers and sisters,*a* that our coming to you was not in vain, ²but though we had already suffered and been shamefully mistreated at Philippi, as you know, we had courage in our God to declare to you the gospel of God in spite of great opposition. ³For our appeal does not spring from deceit or impure motives or trickery, ⁴but just as we have been approved by God to be entrusted with the message of the gospel, even so we speak, not to please mortals, but to please God who tests our hearts. ⁵As you know and as God is our witness, we never came with words of flattery or with a pretext for greed; ⁶nor did we seek praise from mortals, whether from you or from others, ⁷though we might have made demands as apostles of Christ. But we were gentle*c* among you, like a nurse tenderly car-

---

a Gk *brothers*   *b* Gk *For they*   *c* Other ancient authorities read *infants* ing for her own children. ⁸So deeply do we care for you that we are determined to share with you not only the gospel of God but also our own selves, because you have become very dear to us.

9 You remember our labor and toil, brothers and sisters;ᵃ we worked night and day, so that we might not burden any of you while we proclaimed to you the gospel of God. ¹⁰You are witnesses, and God also, how pure, upright, and blameless our conduct was toward you believers. ¹¹As you know, we dealt with each one of you like a father with his children, ¹²urging and encouraging you and pleading that you lead a life worthy of God, who calls you into his own kingdom and glory.

2.1–12: The endurance of the mission team. Paul denounces false teachers and praises the mission team for building up the congregation. **2:** *Opposition,* a metaphor* of athletic struggle (Epictetus Diss, 1.24.1–2; 4 Macc 16.16). **4:** *God . . . tests our hearts,* see Gal 1.10; Prov 17.3. **7:** The Greek word "epioi," *gentle,* found in some manuscripts, differs from "nepioi," *infants,* by only the letter "n" (see note c on p. 1979). Paul rarely uses "infant" positively (see Rom 2.20; 1 Cor 3.1; 13.11; Gal 4.1, 3), so *gentle* is probably original. **11:** *Father . . . children,* see Gal 4.19–20; 1 Cor 4.14–21; 2 Cor 6.11–13. **12:** *Lead a life worthy* (Gal 5.16; Rom 13.13), "walk" a distinctive (holy) life even though the end time is not yet obvious to a world that is passing away (see 4.1–8). *Kingdom* of God, rare in Paul (see 1 Cor 4.20).

13 We also constantly give thanks to God for this, that when you received the word of God that you heard from us, you accepted it not as a human word but as what it really is, God's word, which is also at work in you believers. ¹⁴For you, brothers and sisters,ᵃ became imitators of the churches of God in Christ Jesus that are in Judea, for you suffered the same things from your own compatriots as they did from the Jews, ¹⁵who killed both the Lord Jesus and the prophets,ᵇ and drove us out; they displease God and oppose everyone ¹⁶by hindering us from speaking to the Gentiles so that they may be saved. Thus they have constantly been filling up the measure of their sins; but God's wrath has overtaken them at last.ᶜ

2.13–16: The suffering of the Thessalonians. The anti-Jewish tone is uncharacteristic of Paul, but there is no evidence that it was inserted later, and it is not directed toward all Jews. Debate and angry argument between Jews occur in Jewish writings of the time (see Josephus,* *Antiquities* 1.15.91; Philo,* *Cherubim** 17). Paul's point is his ministry's success despite opposition. The passage functions like a hinge in reminding the Thessalonians how they suffered in receiving the word (2.14; see 1.6) and in foreshadowing Paul's account of his separation from the community (2.17–3.13). **16:** *God's wrath,* perhaps an actual event, but given the survival of the Judean churches and the Thessalonians, more likely that God *at last* has prevented opponents (some Jews or some gentiles*) from destroying them.

17 As for us, brothers and sisters,ᵃ when, for a short time, we were made orphans by being separated from you—in person, not in heart—we longed with great eagerness to see you face to face. ¹⁸For we wanted to come to you—certainly I, Paul, wanted to again and again—but Satan blocked our way. ¹⁹For what is our hope or joy or crown of boasting before our Lord Jesus at his coming? Is it not you? ²⁰Yes, you are our glory and joy!

3 Therefore when we could bear it no longer, we decided to be left alone in Athens; ²and we sent Timothy, our brother and co-worker for God in proclaimingᵈ the gospel of Christ, to strengthen and encourage you for the sake of your faith, ³so that no one would be shaken by these persecutions. Indeed, you yourselves know that this is what we are destined for. ⁴In fact, when we were with you, we told you beforehand that we were to suffer persecution; so it turned out, as you know. ⁵For this reason, when I could bear it no longer, I sent to find out about your faith; I was afraid that somehow the tempter had tempted you and that our labor had been in vain.

---

a Gk *brothers*   *b* Other ancient authorities read *their own prophets*   *c* Or *completely* or *forever*   *d* Gk lacks *proclaiming*

6 But Timothy has just now come to us from you, and has brought us the good news of your faith and love. He has told us also that you always remember us kindly and long to see us—just as we long to see you. 7For this reason, brothers and sisters,*a* during all our distress and persecution we have been encouraged about you through your faith. 8For we now live, if you continue to stand firm in the Lord. 9How can we thank God enough for you in return for all the joy that we feel before our God because of you? 10Night and day we pray most earnestly that we may see you face to face and restore whatever is lacking in your faith.

11 Now may our God and Father himself and our Lord Jesus direct our way to you. 12And may the Lord make you increase and abound in love for one another and for all, just as we abound in love for you. 13And may he so strengthen your hearts in holiness that you may be blameless before our God and Father at the coming of our Lord Jesus with all his saints.

2.17–3.13: Separation and end-time orientation. Paul tells of his separation and turn from sorrow to joy: Because the church has survived, Paul will present them at the coming of the Lord as his joyful reward (2.17–20). Timothy's visit encourages the congregation and Paul (3.1–8). A third section (3.9–13) returns to the theme of joy, along with a prayer that the congregation will grow more in the present and will be found blameless at the Lord's coming. **3.8:** *Stand,* one of several military terms in this letter. **11–13:** A hinge between the previous mention of the Lord's coming (2.19) and later themes of love (3.4, 9–12), holiness (3.13; 4.3), and the Lord's coming (4.11; 5.11).

4 Finally, brothers and sisters,*a* we ask and urge you in the Lord Jesus that, as you learned from us how you ought to live and to please God (as, in fact, you are doing), you should do so more and more. 2For you know what instructions we gave you through the Lord Jesus. 3For this is the will of God, your sanctification: that you abstain from fornication; 4that each one of you know how to control your own body*b* in holiness and honor, 5not with lustful passion, like the Gentiles who do not know God; 6that no one

wrong or exploit a brother or sister*c* in this matter, because the Lord is an avenger in all these things, just as we have already told you beforehand and solemnly warned you. 7For God did not call us to impurity but in holiness. 8Therefore whoever rejects this rejects not human authority but God, who also gives his Holy Spirit to you.

9 Now concerning love of the brothers and sisters,*a* you do not need to have anyone write to you, for you yourselves have been taught by God to love one another; 10and indeed you do love all the brothers and sisters*a* throughout Macedonia. But we urge you, beloved,*a* to do so more and more, 11to aspire to live quietly, to mind your own affairs, and to work with your hands, as we directed you, 12so that you may behave properly toward outsiders and be dependent on no one.

4.1–12: Holy living toward each other and outsiders. 1: *Finally* marks the last large section of the letter. **4:** *Body,* literally "vessel," could also mean "wife."

13 But we do not want you to be uninformed, brothers and sisters,*a* about those who have died,*d* so that you may not grieve as others do who have no hope. 14For since we believe that Jesus died and rose again, even so, through Jesus, God will bring with him those who have died.*d* 15For this we declare to you by the word of the Lord, that we who are alive, who are left until the coming of the Lord, will by no means precede those who have died.*d* 16For the Lord himself, with a cry of command, with the archangel's call and with the sound of God's trumpet, will descend from heaven, and the dead in Christ will rise first. 17Then we who are alive, who are left, will be caught up in the clouds together with them to meet the Lord in the air; and so we will be with the Lord forever. 18Therefore encourage one another with these words.

5 Now concerning the times and the seasons, brothers and sisters,*a* you do not need to have anything written to you. 2For

a Gk *brothers*   b Or *how to take a wife for himself*
c Gk *brother*   d Gk *fallen asleep*

you yourselves know very well that the day of the Lord will come like a thief in the night. [3]When they say, "There is peace and security," then sudden destruction will come upon them, as labor pains come upon a pregnant woman, and there will be no escape! [4]But you, beloved,[a] are not in darkness, for that day to surprise you like a thief; [5]for you are all children of light and children of the day; we are not of the night or of darkness. [6]So then let us not fall asleep as others do, but let us keep awake and be sober; [7]for those who sleep sleep at night, and those who are drunk get drunk at night. [8]But since we belong to the day, let us be sober, and put on the breastplate of faith and love, and for a helmet the hope of salvation. [9]For God has destined us not for wrath but for obtaining salvation through our Lord Jesus Christ, [10]who died for us, so that whether we are awake or asleep we may live with him. [11]Therefore encourage one another and build up each other, as indeed you are doing.

4.13–5.11: The expectation of the end times. Paul shows the distinctiveness of a community expecting the Lord's coming. **4.16:** *God's trumpet,* see Ex 19.16, 19; Isa 27.13; Joel 2.1. **17:** *Meet,* a term used of a delegation going out to meet a ruler. **5.3:** *Labor pains,* see Jer 6.24; 13.21; 22.23; Hos 13.13; Mic 4.9. **5:** *Children of light,* an expression that occurs in the Dead Sea Scrolls (1 QS 1.9–10; 3.13). **8:** On military imagery, see Isa 59.17. **10:** *Who died for us,* an early formulation of belief about Christ.

12 But we appeal to you, brothers and sisters,[a] to respect those who labor among you, and have charge of you in the Lord and admonish you; [13]esteem them very highly in love because of their work. Be at peace among yourselves. [14]And we urge you, beloved,[a] to admonish the idlers, encourage the fainthearted, help the weak, be patient with all of them. [15]See that none of you repays evil for evil, but always seek to do good

to one another and to all. [16]Rejoice always, [17]pray without ceasing, [18]give thanks in all circumstances; for this is the will of God in Christ Jesus for you. [19]Do not quench the Spirit. [20]Do not despise the words of prophets,[b] [21]but test everything; hold fast to what is good; [22]abstain from every form of evil.

5.12–22: How the congregation should live. 12: *Those who . . . have charge of you,* "leaders" or patrons in the congregation who provided the means for the congregation to survive. **14:** *Idlers:* NRSV, perhaps influenced by 2 Thess 3.11, uses this specific noun rather than the more general "disorderly ones." It is not a comment about laziness, but about those who have not fully embraced the end-time orientation and need for holy living.

23 May the God of peace himself sanctify you entirely; and may your spirit and soul and body be kept sound[c] and blameless at the coming of our Lord Jesus Christ. [24]The one who calls you is faithful, and he will do this.

25 Beloved,[d] pray for us.

26 Greet all the brothers and sisters[a] with a holy kiss. [27]I solemnly command you by the Lord that this letter be read to all of them.[e]

28 The grace of our Lord Jesus Christ be with you.[f]

5.23–28: Epistolary closing. The passage is framed with a prayer or blessing form (5.23, 28) that reminds the congregation of the letter's themes: the survival of the community because of God's initiative (1.4; 2.12); sanctification (3.13; 4.3–4, 7–8); and the end time (1.10; 2.19; 3.13) which orients the community's life toward distinctive, blameless living. **24:** *One who calls,* an ongoing process, not a one-time event.

a Gk *brothers*   b Gk *despise prophecies*
c Or *complete*   d Gk *Brothers*   e Gk *to all the brothers*   f Other ancient authorities add *Amen*

THE SECOND LETTER OF PAUL TO
THE THESSALONIANS

Introduction

Second Thessalonians, though lacking the personal tone of 1 Thessalonians, expresses strong concern for the community's survival. Prayers, exhortations* to discipline, explanations of suffering, and attention to the community's thoughts and deeds (1.11), all give it a tone of encouragement.

It is uncertain if Paul wrote the letter. In favor of his authorship are similarities with 1 Thessalonians: simple headings (1 Thess 1.1; 2 Thess 1.2); repeated thanksgivings (1 Thess 1.2; 2.13; 3.9; 2 Thess 1.3; 2.13); and prayers (1 Thess 3.11; 2 Thess 2.16) following thanksgivings (1 Thess 3.9; 2 Thess 2.13). In addition, both letters rely on belief in the approaching end time. Yet these very similarities lead some interpreters to ask why Paul would want to imitate himself so closely in a second composition. Moreover, an end-time perspective is the ground of hope in 1 Thessalonians (1 Thess 4.13–18), while the ground of certainty in 2 Thessalonians is a certain authorized body of knowledge (see the emphasis on traditions in 2 Thess 2.15; 3.6). The need to authenticate and differentiate itself from other, non-genuine letters (3.17) is the strongest argument against Paul's authorship (that effort would not be necessary while an author remained alive). If the letter was not written by Paul, we cannot be certain about its time of composition.

Whoever wrote it, the letter encourages steadfastness, refutes enthusiasts, and commends true teaching as the church awaits the coming of Jesus. The letter refutes some members for spreading inaccurate information about the day of the Lord (2.1–12); others (or perhaps the same persons) are rebuked for refusing to work. The community, awaiting God's vindication, is commended for its firm grasp on "the truth" (2.10), the apostolic* tradition, in which it will witness effectively to others.

READING GUIDE

After a typical opening (1.1–2), the writer gives thanks for the congregation's steadfastness despite affliction (1.3–4) and comments on that affliction in light of the not yet present day of vindication (1.5–10). The writer couches teaching in the language of prayer (1.11–12), and then admonishes the community twice (2.1–12; 3.6–15) in order to correct misinformation that threatens the community's resolve and to challenge disruptive behavior that could fracture a unified faith. The letter closes with a typical Hellenistic* postscript (3.16–18).

1.1–2	Epistolary opening
1.3–10	Perseverance and future vindication
1.11–3.15	Admonitions against delusional thoughts and disruptive behavior
3.16–18	Epistolary closing

1 Paul, Silvanus, and Timothy,
To the church of the Thessalonians in God our Father and the Lord Jesus Christ:
2 Grace to you and peace from God our[a] Father and the Lord Jesus Christ.

1.1–2: Epistolary opening. The greeting is similar to 1 Thessalonians but longer. On *Silvanus* and *Timothy*, see 1 Thess 1.1.

3 We must always give thanks to God for you, brothers and sisters,[b] as is right, because your faith is growing abundantly, and the love of everyone of you for one another is increasing. 4Therefore we ourselves boast of you among the churches of God for your steadfastness and faith during all your persecutions and the afflictions that you are enduring.
5 This is evidence of the righteous judgment of God, and is intended to make you worthy of the kingdom of God, for which you are also suffering. 6For it is indeed just of God to repay with affliction those who afflict you, 7and to give relief to the afflicted as well as to us, when the Lord Jesus is revealed from heaven with his mighty angels 8in flaming fire, inflicting vengeance on those who do not know God and on those who do not obey the gospel of our Lord Jesus. 9These will suffer the punishment of eternal destruction, separated from the presence of the Lord and from the glory of his might, 10when he comes to be glorified by his saints and to be marveled at on that day among all who have believed, because our testimony to you was believed. 11To this end we always pray for you, asking that our God will make you worthy of his call and will fulfill by his power every good resolve and work of faith, 12so that the name of our Lord Jesus may be glorified in you, and you in him, according to the grace of our God and the Lord Jesus Christ.

1.3–12. 3–10: Perseverance and future vindication. This long sentence includes a thanksgiving (vv. 3–4) and a commentary on affliction (vv. 5–10). **3–4:** The thanksgiving report relates the community's progress and *steadfastness.* **4:** *Persecutions . . . afflictions,* both mean suffering, but the first, external suffering, is more specific. They may mean the woes of the end time; see Dan 12.1. **5–10:** These verses teach that suffering is a sign of being chosen and that those who suffer will be vindicated at the judgment. *That day* anticipates 2.1–12, which refutes those who think their recent afflictions mean that the "day of the Lord" has already appeared. **7–10:** Descriptions of God in the Hebrew Scriptures* and other Jewish writings now apply to Jesus (see the *angels* in Zech 14.5; 1 Enoch 1.9; *flaming fire* in Isa 66.15–16; *glorified* in Ps 89.7). **11–12: A prayer.** These verses are the letter's main teaching. *Resolve, work of faith* anticipate the refutations in 2.1–12 and 3.1–15. **12:** See Isaiah 66.5, but it is Jesus who will *be glorified.*

2 As to the coming of our Lord Jesus Christ and our being gathered together to him, we beg you, brothers and sisters,[b] 2not to be quickly shaken in mind or alarmed, either by spirit or by word or by letter, as though from us, to the effect that the day of the Lord is already here. 3Let no one deceive you in any way; for that day will not come unless the rebellion comes first and the lawless one[c] is revealed, the one destined for destruction.[d] 4He opposes and exalts himself above every so-called god or object of worship, so that he takes his seat in the temple of God, declaring himself to be God. 5Do you not remember that I told you these things when I was still with you? 6And you know what is now restraining him, so that he may be revealed when his time comes. 7For the mystery of lawlessness is already at work, but only until the one who now restrains it is removed. 8And then the lawless one will be revealed, whom the Lord Jesus[e] will destroy[f] with the breath of his mouth, annihilating him by the manifestation of his coming. 9The coming of the lawless one is apparent in the working of Satan, who uses all power, signs, lying wonders, 10and every kind of wicked deception for those who are perishing, because they refused to love the truth and so be saved. 11For

---

a Other ancient authorities read *the*   *b* Gk *brothers*
c Gk *the man of lawlessness*; other ancient authorities read *the man of sin*   *d* Gk *the son of destruction*
e Other ancient authorities lack *Jesus*   *f* Other ancient authorities read *consume*

this reason God sends them a powerful delusion, leading them to believe what is false, ¹²so that all who have not believed the truth but took pleasure in unrighteousness will be condemned.

13 But we must always give thanks to God for you, brothers and sisters*a* beloved by the Lord, because God chose you as the first fruits*b* for salvation through sanctification by the Spirit and through belief in the truth. ¹⁴For this purpose he called you through our proclamation of the good news,*c* so that you may obtain the glory of our Lord Jesus Christ. ¹⁵So then, brothers and sisters,*a* stand firm and hold fast to the traditions that you were taught by us, either by word of mouth or by our letter.

2.1–15: A refutation. False teaching about the day of the Lord is stated (vv. 1–2) and refuted (vv. 3–12). In contrast is thanksgiving for the different fate of believers (vv. 13–15), who hold on to the *truth* (v. 13), the *proclamation,* and the *traditions* (vv. 14–15). 3: *Lawless one,* perhaps a false prophet★ or one of the emperors. 6–7: The identity of the unknown one *restraining* the lawless one is impossible to determine, but the conflict between the two belongs to what must occur before the day of the Lord. 13: *We must always give thanks;* see 1.3. 15: *Stand firm,* see 1 Thess 3.8.

16 Now may our Lord Jesus Christ himself and God our Father, who loved us and through grace gave us eternal comfort and good hope, ¹⁷comfort your hearts and strengthen them in every good work and word.

2.16–17: Another prayer. As in 1.11–12, this prayer anticipates subsequent concerns, in this case God's role in strengthening the community (3.3) and "work" (3.8–12). 17: *Comfort your hearts,* see Isa 51.12; 61.2.

3 Finally, brothers and sisters,*a* pray for us, so that the word of the Lord may spread rapidly and be glorified everywhere, just as it is among you, ²and that we may be rescued from wicked and evil people; for not all have faith. ³But the Lord is faithful; he will strengthen you and guard you from the evil one.*d* ⁴And we have confidence in the Lord concerning you, that you are doing and will go on doing the things that we command. ⁵May the Lord direct your hearts to the love of God and to the steadfastness of Christ.

6 Now we command you, beloved,*a* in the name of our Lord Jesus Christ, to keep away from believers who are*e* living in idleness and not according to the tradition that they*f* received from us. ⁷For you yourselves know how you ought to imitate us; we were not idle when we were with you, ⁸and we did not eat anyone's bread without paying for it; but with toil and labor we worked night and day, so that we might not burden any of you. ⁹This was not because we do not have that right, but in order to give you an example to imitate. ¹⁰For even when we were with you, we gave you this command: Anyone unwilling to work should not eat. ¹¹For we hear that some of you are living in idleness, mere busybodies, not doing any work. ¹²Now such persons we command and exhort in the Lord Jesus Christ to do their work quietly and to earn their own living. ¹³Brothers and sisters,*g* do not be weary in doing what is right.

14 Take note of those who do not obey what we say in this letter; have nothing to do with them, so that they may be ashamed. ¹⁵Do not regard them as enemies, but warn them as believers.*h*

3.1–15: Commands and exhortations.★ Two sets of commands and encouragements to virtue (vv. 1–4 and 6–15) surround a prayer (v. 5). 1: *Finally,* the last section of the letter. 6–15: Commands and exhortations to the entire community (vv. 6–10) and to the offending figures in the congregation (vv. 11–12) precede a command on how to deal with the disobedient (vv. 13–15). 6: *In idleness* could also mean "in disorderliness." Apparently expecting the Lord to return very soon, some in the congregation stopped working.

---

a Gk *brothers*   *b* Other ancient authorities read *from the beginning*   *c* Or *through our gospel*   *d* Or *from evil*   *e* Gk *from every brother who is*   *f* Other ancient authorities read *you*   *g* Gk *Brothers*   *h* Gk *a brother*

16 Now may the Lord of peace himself give you peace at all times in all ways. The Lord be with all of you.

17 I, Paul, write this greeting with my own hand. This is the mark in every letter of mine; it is the way I write. [18] The grace of our Lord Jesus Christ be with all of you.[a]

3.16–18: Epistolary closing. *Peace* and *grace* for *all of you* suggests a desire to draw in the erring members. **17:** *With my own hand,* in light of 2.2, suggests that the writer feels a need to authenticate his letter.

a Other ancient authorities add *Amen*

THE FIRST LETTER OF PAUL TO
TIMOTHY

Introduction

First Timothy is the longest of the three Pastoral letters. It is concerned with worship in early Christian congregations, proper behavior, proper and improper worship practices, and the roles of the various ministers in the local church. It also combats some beliefs that the author regards as false teaching.

First Timothy asserts that it was written by Paul (1.1), but as noted in the sidebar on p. 1991, this is almost certainly not the case. It assumes that Paul left Timothy in Ephesus, a view that contrasts with the story in Acts. In Acts Paul sent Timothy and Erastus on to Macedonia (Greece) while he waited in Ephesus (Acts 19.22). The letter is written as if addressed to Timothy (1.2; 6.20), who elsewhere in the New Testament is a resident of Lystra (in Lycaonia, Acts 16.1), and one of Paul's companions (Acts 17.14–15; 18.5; 19.22; 20.4) and emissaries (1 Thess 3.2, 6; 1 Cor 4.17; 16.10; Phil 2.19, 23). Since Paul did not write the letter and it is addressed to a wider audience than just one man (see note a, p. 1993), the address to "Timothy" may be symbolic rather than literal. In this reading, Timothy may stand for the faithful in Ephesus (1.3). It is not possible to date the letter with any certainty.

The letter opposes those who teach a different doctrine (1.3; 6.3). The letter combats these teachings because they promote socially unacceptable behavior (4.1–5) and cause dissension (6.4) and apostasy, or a renouncing of the faith (4.1).

READING GUIDE

An opening (1.1–2) and closing (6.21b) hold together two larger parts: one that gives the background for the instructions (1.3–20); and the instructions themselves (2.1–6.21a). The background explains Timothy's task (1.3–11) and offers examples (1.12–20) to show the need for sound teaching. Instructions for the household of God (2.1–3.13; 5.1–6.2a) precede discourses on sound and unsound teachings (3.14–4.16; 6.2b–21a).

1.1–2	Epistolary opening
1.3–11	Timothy's task
1.12–20	Examples and counter-examples
2.1–6.21a	Instructions and sound teaching
6.21b	Epistolary closing

1 Paul, an apostle of Christ Jesus by the command of God our Savior and of Christ Jesus our hope,

2 To Timothy, my loyal child in the faith: Grace, mercy, and peace from God the Father and Christ Jesus our Lord.

1.1–2: Epistolary opening. The formal opening suggests a chain of command from God to Paul to Timothy. **1:** *Command,* literally "order placed upon," see Titus 1.3. *Savior* in Paul describes Jesus (see Phil 3.20); in the Pastorals *savior* describes both God (1 Tim 1.1; 2.3; 4.10; Titus 1.3; 2.10; 3.4) and Jesus (2 Tim 1.10;

Titus 1.4; 2.13; 3.6). **2:** *My loyal child* also describes Titus (Titus 1.4).

3 I urge you, as I did when I was on my way to Macedonia, to remain in Ephesus so that you may instruct certain people not to teach any different doctrine, [4]and not to occupy themselves with myths and endless genealogies that promote speculations rather than the divine training[a] that is known by faith. [5]But the aim of such instruction is love that comes from a pure heart, a good conscience, and sincere faith. [6]Some people have deviated from these and turned to meaningless talk, [7]desiring to be teachers of the law, without understanding either what they are saying or the things about which they make assertions.

8 Now we know that the law is good, if one uses it legitimately. [9]This means understanding that the law is laid down not for the innocent but for the lawless and disobedient, for the godless and sinful, for the unholy and profane, for those who kill their father or mother, for murderers, [10]fornicators, sodomites, slave traders, liars, perjurers, and whatever else is contrary to the sound teaching [11]that conforms to the glorious gospel of the blessed God, which he entrusted to me.

1.3–11: Timothy's task. Timothy is to teach against the false doctrine that encourages deviations from order (*training*) that promotes *good conscience*. These deviations include those who revel in speculative thought (v. 4), those who do not teach *love that comes from a pure heart* (v. 5), and those whose teaching does not conform to *the glorious gospel of the blessed God* (v. 11). **3:** *Instruct,* see 1.5,18; 4.11. **4:** *Training,* literally "household law." See 3.4–5, 12, 15; 5.13–14. **5:** *Conscience,* see 1.19. **9–11:** The vices roughly follow the order of the Ten Commandments.

---

12 I am grateful to Christ Jesus our Lord, who has strengthened me, because he judged me faithful and appointed me to his service, [13]even though I was formerly a blasphemer, a persecutor, and a man of violence. But I received mercy because I had acted ignorantly in unbelief, [14]and the grace of our Lord overflowed for me with the faith and love that are in Christ Jesus. [15]The saying is sure and worthy of full acceptance, that Christ Jesus came into the world to save sinners—of whom I am the foremost. [16]But for that very reason I received mercy, so that in me, as the foremost, Jesus Christ might display the utmost patience, making me an example to those who would come to believe in him for eternal life. [17]To the King of the ages, immortal, invisible, the only God, be honor and glory forever and ever.[b] Amen.

18 I am giving you these instructions, Timothy, my child, in accordance with the prophecies made earlier about you, so that by following them you may fight the good fight, [19]having faith and a good conscience. By rejecting conscience, certain persons have suffered shipwreck in the faith; [20]among them are Hymenaeus and Alexander, whom I have turned over to Satan, so that they may learn not to blaspheme.

1.12–20: Examples and counter-examples. The example of one in service of the gospel (vv. 12–17) contrasts with those who still need to be taught not to blaspheme (vv. 18–20). **12–17:** Autobiographical reflections begin with thanksgiving (v. 12) and end with praise (v. 17), anticipating the salvation of others (2.1–4) just as the writer was saved from ignorance because of the patience of Jesus. **15:** *The saying is sure,* see 3.1; 4.9. **18–20:** Referring to 1.3–11, a contrast between Timothy's character and the false teachers. **19:** *Shipwreck,* as if the teachers have steered off course. **20:** *Hymenaeus,* see 2 Tim 2.17. *Alexander,* see 2 Tim 4.14.

INSTRUCTIONS AND SOUND TEACHING

2.1–6.21a: Two lists of instructions (2.1–3.13; 5.1–6.2a) precede two explanations of the difference between sound and unsound teaching (3.14–4.16 and 6.2b–6.21a).

---

2 First of all, then, I urge that supplications, prayers, intercessions, and thanksgivings be made for everyone, [2]for kings and all who are in high positions, so that we may lead a quiet and peaceable life in all godliness and dignity. [3]This is right and is ac-

a Or *plan*   *b* Gk *to the ages of the ages*

ceptable in the sight of God our Savior, 4who desires everyone to be saved and to come to the knowledge of the truth. 5For

there is one God;
    there is also one mediator between
        God and humankind,
    Christ Jesus, himself human,
6   who gave himself a ransom for all

—this was attested at the right time. 7For this I was appointed a herald and an apostle (I am telling the truth,*ᵃ* I am not lying), a teacher of the Gentiles in faith and truth.

8 I desire, then, that in every place the men should pray, lifting up holy hands without anger or argument; 9also that the women should dress themselves modestly and decently in suitable clothing, not with their hair braided, or with gold, pearls, or expensive clothes, 10but with good works, as is proper for women who profess reverence for God. 11Let a woman*ᵇ* learn in silence with full submission. 12I permit no woman*ᵇ* to teach or to have authority over a man;*ᶜ* she is to keep silent. 13For Adam was formed first, then Eve; 14and Adam was not deceived, but the woman was deceived and became a transgressor. 15Yet she will be saved through childbearing, provided they continue in faith and love and holiness, with modesty.

3 The saying is sure:*ᵈ* whoever aspires to the office of bishop*ᵉ* desires a noble task. 2Now a bishop*ᶠ* must be above reproach, married only once,*ᵍ* temperate, sensible, respectable, hospitable, an apt teacher, 3not a drunkard, not violent but gentle, not quarrelsome, and not a lover of money. 4He must manage his own household well, keeping his children submissive and respectful in every way— 5for if someone does not know how to manage his own household, how can he take care of God's church? 6He must not be a recent convert, or he may be puffed up with conceit and fall into the condemnation of the devil. 7Moreover, he must be well thought of by outsiders, so that he may not fall into disgrace and the snare of the devil.

8 Deacons likewise must be serious, not double-tongued, not indulging in much wine, not greedy for money; 9they must hold fast to the mystery of the faith with a clear conscience. 10And let them first be tested; then, if they prove themselves blameless, let them serve as deacons. 11Women*ʰ* likewise must be serious, not slanderers, but temperate, faithful in all things. 12Let deacons be married only once,*ⁱ* and let them manage their children and their households well; 13for those who serve well as deacons gain a good standing for themselves and great boldness in the faith that is in Christ Jesus.

2.1–3.13: Worship and household conduct. The qualities of right worship (2.1–15) resemble those of a well-conducted household (3.1–13), both having as their goal the salvation of outsiders. **2.1–15: Worship.** The aim of worship is the salvation of all. **2:** *Godliness,* see 3.16; 4.7–8; 6.3, 5, 6, 11. **5–6:** This may be a formal statement of belief. **8:** *Lifting up holy hands,* see Ps. 113.4; 141.2; 143.6; 2 Macc 14.34. **11–12:** These troubling verses may reflect the same thinking as 1 Cor 14.34–35. **13–15:** A commentary on Gen 3.13, 16. **3.1–13: The households of leaders.** The household character of church leaders can determine their ability to hold office within the church. The list includes instructions about overseers (*bishops*) (vv. 2–7), *deacons* (vv. 8–10, 12–13) and deaconesses (v. 11).

14 I hope to come to you soon, but I am writing these instructions to you so that, 15if I am delayed, you may know how one ought to behave in the household of God, which is the church of the living God, the pillar and bulwark of the truth. 16Without any doubt, the mystery of our religion is great:

He*ʲ* was revealed in flesh,
    vindicated*ᵏ* in spirit,*ˡ*
    seen by angels,
    proclaimed among Gentiles,
    believed in throughout the world,
    taken up in glory.

---

a Other ancient authorities add *in Christ*   *b* Or *wife*
c Or *her husband*   *d* Some interpreters place these words at the end of the previous paragraph. Other ancient authorities read *The saying is commonly accepted*
e Or *overseer*   *f* Or *an overseer*   *g* Gk *the husband of one wife*   *h* Or *Their wives,* or *Women deacons*
i Gk *be husbands of one wife*   *j* Gk *Who;* other ancient authorities read *God;* others, *Which*
k Or *justified*   *l* Or *by the Spirit*

4 Now the Spirit expressly says that in later[a] times some will renounce the faith by paying attention to deceitful spirits and teachings of demons, 2through the hypocrisy of liars whose consciences are seared with a hot iron. 3They forbid marriage and demand abstinence from foods, which God created to be received with thanksgiving by those who believe and know the truth. 4For everything created by God is good, and nothing is to be rejected, provided it is received with thanksgiving; 5for it is sanctified by God's word and by prayer.

6 If you put these instructions before the brothers and sisters,[b] you will be a good servant[c] of Christ Jesus, nourished on the words of the faith and of the sound teaching that you have followed. 7Have nothing to do with profane myths and old wives' tales. Train yourself in godliness, 8for, while physical training is of some value, godliness is valuable in every way, holding promise for both the present life and the life to come. 9The saying is sure and worthy of full acceptance. 10For to this end we toil and struggle,[d] because we have our hope set on the living God, who is the Savior of all people, especially of those who believe.

11 These are the things you must insist on and teach. 12Let no one despise your youth, but set the believers an example in speech and conduct, in love, in faith, in purity. 13Until I arrive, give attention to the public reading of scripture,[e] to exhorting, to teaching. 14Do not neglect the gift that is in you, which was given to you through prophecy with the laying on of hands by the council of elders.[f] 15Put these things into practice, devote yourself to them, so that all may see your progress. 16Pay close attention to yourself and to your teaching; continue in these things, for in doing this you will save both yourself and your hearers.

3.14–4.16: Right behavior. Two exhortations* describe the behavior consistent with belief. An autobiographical aside, speaking of the writer's speedy return, equates *the church of the living God* with *the household of God* (3.14–16). Instructions on teaching and setting *an example* (4.1–16) focus on the issue of authority in the period between the writer's departure from Ephesus and his return. These exhortations also contrast right behavior with that of the deviating teachers, who practice self-control in ways that do not show the goodness of creation in the lives of believers as they seek to influence others. **4.1–2:** *In later times,* see 2 Tim 3.1–9. The false teachers are *liars* who cause others to *renounce the faith by paying attention to deceitful spirits.* **6:** *Put . . . before* in Greek is a form of the same word as "appointed" (1.12; 2.7). **11:** On Timothy's role as a teacher (4.11, 13, 16) or as one who has followed sound teaching (4.6), see 2 Tim 1.13. **14:** On Timothy's gift of *prophecy* through the *laying on of hands,* see 2 Tim 1.6.

5 Do not speak harshly to an older man,[g] but speak to him as to a father, to younger men as brothers, 2to older women as mothers, to younger women as sisters— with absolute purity.

3 Honor widows who are really widows. 4If a widow has children or grandchildren, they should first learn their religious duty to their own family and make some repayment to their parents; for this is pleasing in God's sight. 5The real widow, left alone, has set her hope on God and continues in supplications and prayers night and day; 6but the widow[h] who lives for pleasure is dead even while she lives. 7Give these commands as well, so that they may be above reproach. 8And whoever does not provide for relatives, and especially for family members, has denied the faith and is worse than an unbeliever.

9 Let a widow be put on the list if she is not less than sixty years old and has been married only once;[i] 10she must be well attested for her good works, as one who has brought up children, shown hospitality, washed the saints' feet, helped the afflicted, and devoted herself to doing good in every way. 11But refuse to put younger widows on the list; for when their sensual desires alienate them from Christ, they want to marry, 12and so they incur condemnation for having violated their first pledge. 13Besides that, they learn to be idle, gadding about from

a Or *the last*   *b* Gk *brothers*   *c* Or *deacon*
d Other ancient authorities read *suffer reproach*
e Gk *to the reading*   *f* Gk *by the presbytery*   *g* Or *an elder,* or *a presbyter*   *h* Gk *she*   *i* Gk *the wife of one husband*

The Pastoral Letters

First and Second Timothy and Titus, sometimes called "Pastoral Letters," are grouped together in order of length. Although they are now part of the canon (see "The Nature and Formation of the Biblical Canon," p. 26), early lists omitted some or all of them, and they were not accepted until about the last quarter of the second century CE. The Pastorals received this name because they were interpreted as providing Timothy and Titus with instructions for the pastoral ordering and care of their churches.

The three letters have a common, distinctive vocabulary that includes terms shared with ethical writings in popular Greek thought. The theological vocabulary of these letters speaks not of Jesus' second coming but of his epiphany✶ ("appearance," 1 Tim 6.14; Titus 2.13). By "righteousness" they mean not justification but moral uprightness (1 Tim 6.11; 2 Tim 2.22; 3.16; 4.8), and by "faith" not trust in God but a collection of traditions to be guarded (1 Tim 3.9; 2 Tim 1.13; 2.2; Titus 1.13).

The Pastorals present a picture of Paul that is somewhat at odds with the image of him that emerges from the undisputed letters. The support Paul expresses for women and their active roles in the community in the undisputed writings—those who accompanied him (Phil 4.2–3) or whom he praised (Rom 16.1–2)—is weakened in the household codes✶ of the Pastorals (1 Tim 2.11–15; Titus 2.3–5). Paul's endorsement of charismatic authority becomes instead Paul the final authority. Though Paul advised young widows to abstain from sexual passion (1 Cor 7.8), the Pastorals see marital intercourse as the best means of controlling sexual appetite (1 Tim 5.14). In Romans, Paul speaks of a westward mission, but not an eastern one as the Pastorals suppose. An eastern mission presupposes Paul's release from Roman imprisonment, followed by the mission and a second imprisonment, though Acts suggests only one (Acts 27; compare Acts 20).

It is unlikely that Paul wrote these letters. They are attributed to Paul in order to gain authority. This kind of writing, called "pseudonymous,"✶ occurs elsewhere in ancient literature, for instance, "Socrates's Apology," or the book of Daniel. The realistic touches about Paul or his colleagues (1 Tim 1.12–17; 2.7; 2 Tim 1.8–18; 4.6–8; Titus 1.5) are a part of this attribution.

---

house to house; and they are not merely idle, but also gossips and busybodies, saying what they should not say. ¹⁴So I would have younger widows marry, bear children, and manage their households, so as to give the adversary no occasion to revile us. ¹⁵For some have already turned away to follow Satan. ¹⁶If any believing woman[a] has relatives who are really widows, let her assist them; let the church not be burdened, so that it can assist those who are real widows.

17 Let the elders who rule well be considered worthy of double honor,[b] especially those who labor in preaching and teaching; ¹⁸for the scripture says, "You shall not muzzle an ox while it is treading out the grain," and, "The laborer deserves to be paid." ¹⁹Never accept any accusation against an elder except on the evidence of two or three witnesses. ²⁰As for those who persist in sin, rebuke them in the presence of all, so that the rest also may stand in fear. ²¹In the presence of God and of Christ Jesus and of the

a Other ancient authorities read believing man or woman; others, believing man   b Or compensation elect angels, I warn you to keep these instructions without prejudice, doing nothing on the basis of partiality. 22Do not ordain[a] anyone hastily, and do not participate in the sins of others; keep yourself pure.

23 No longer drink only water, but take a little wine for the sake of your stomach and your frequent ailments.

24 The sins of some people are conspicuous and precede them to judgment, while the sins of others follow them there. 25So also good works are conspicuous; and even when they are not, they cannot remain hidden.

6 Let all who are under the yoke of slavery regard their masters as worthy of all honor, so that the name of God and the teaching may not be blasphemed. 2Those who have believing masters must not be disrespectful to them on the ground that they are members of the church;[b] rather they must serve them all the more, since those who benefit by their service are believers and beloved.[c]

5.1–6.2a: Proper behavior to various people. Instructions on how to treat people of various ranks within the household of God: older men (vv. 1–2), *widows* (vv. 3–16), *elders* (vv. 17–21), and, after a brief digression (vv. 22–25), slaves (6.1–2a). **18:** *"The laborer deserves to be paid,"* see Lk 10.7. **19:** *The evidence of two or three witnesses,* see Deut. 17.6; 19.15.

~~~~~~~~~~~~~~~~

Teach and urge these duties. 3Whoever teaches otherwise and does not agree with the sound words of our Lord Jesus Christ and the teaching that is in accordance with godliness, 4is conceited, understanding nothing, and has a morbid craving for controversy and for disputes about words. From these come envy, dissension, slander, base suspicions, 5and wrangling among those who are depraved in mind and bereft of the truth, imagining that godliness is a means of gain.[d] 6Of course, there is great gain in godliness combined with contentment; 7for we brought nothing into the world, so that[e] we can take nothing out of it; 8but if we have food and clothing, we will be content with these. 9But those who want to be rich fall into temptation and are trapped by many

senseless and harmful desires that plunge people into ruin and destruction. 10For the love of money is a root of all kinds of evil, and in their eagerness to be rich some have wandered away from the faith and pierced themselves with many pains.

6.2b–10: Further exhortations. * A contrast between right behavior and that of the false teachers (see 4.1–16). **3–5:** One long sentence of standard phrases used to attack an opponent's motivation, in this case material gain. *Contentment,* see Phil 4.11. **6–10:** A proverbial treatment of self-sufficiency. **10:** *The love of money is a root of all kinds of evil:* Similar proverbs are known in Hellenistic* Jewish literature (Philo*) and Greco-Roman moral philosophy (Diogenes Laertius).

~~~~~~~~~~~~~~~~

11 But as for you, man of God, shun all this; pursue righteousness, godliness, faith, love, endurance, gentleness. 12Fight the good fight of the faith; take hold of the eternal life, to which you were called and for which you made[f] the good confession in the presence of many witnesses. 13In the presence of God, who gives life to all things, and of Christ Jesus, who in his testimony before Pontius Pilate made the good confession, I charge you 14to keep the commandment without spot or blame until the manifestation of our Lord Jesus Christ, 15which he will bring about at the right time—he who is the blessed and only Sovereign, the King of kings and Lord of lords. 16It is he alone who has immortality and dwells in unapproachable light, whom no one has ever seen or can see; to him be honor and eternal dominion. Amen.

17 As for those who in the present age are rich, command them not to be haughty, or to set their hopes on the uncertainty of riches, but rather on God who richly provides us with everything for our enjoyment. 18They are to do good, to be rich in good works, generous, and ready to share, 19thus storing up for themselves the treasure of a

---

a Gk *Do not lay hands on*   *b* Gk *are brothers*
c Or *since they are believers and beloved, who devote themselves to good deeds*   *d* Other ancient authorities add *Withdraw yourself from such people*   *e* Other ancient authorities read *world—it is certain that*
f Gk *confessed*

good foundation for the future, so that they may take hold of the life that really is life.

20 Timothy, guard what has been entrusted to you. Avoid the profane chatter and contradictions of what is falsely called knowledge; 21by professing it some have missed the mark as regards the faith.

Grace be with you.ᵃ

6.11–21a: Sound and unsound teaching. 11–16: Exhortations perhaps from a baptismal* or ordination liturgy,* used here as a contrast to the previous vices of 6.4–5. 17–19: Admonitions to wealthy persons. 20: Entrusted, literally "deposited" as one would deposit money. See 2 Tim 1.12, 14. 21b: Epistolary closing. The plural (literally, "you all," see note a) shows that the letter is addressed to a wider group.

a The Greek word for you here is plural; in other ancient authorities it is singular. Other ancient authorities add Amen.

THE SECOND LETTER OF PAUL TO TIMOTHY

Introduction

Second Timothy, in form similar to a last will and testament from a dying father, is a moving, stirring letter about impending death and hopes for the steadfast faithfulness of those left behind. Like the other Pastorals, it argues against false teachings and draws on traditional beliefs and proverbial sayings to make its argument. Yet unlike them, this is a personal exhortation* rather than a formal guide for ministers or a presentation of traditional teaching. Vivid images of hard work, models of leadership, and passionate personal defenses combine to make it a lively document.

The letter, addressed to Timothy (see introduction to 1 Timothy), is probably the latest of the Pastorals. It claims to be written from prison (1.16–17; 2.9; 4.16–17) and implies two trials or perhaps one trial in two parts: a successful, first defense without human aid; and a second defense in which the writer does not expect to succeed (4.16–18). The place of imprisonment is not known, but Ephesus is a good candidate for the letter's destination. The assumption of a second imprisonment after a first one in Rome, however, does not agree with Paul's own letters or Acts 20. Since the letter was not written by Paul, though it pretends to be, it cannot be dated with certainty.

READING GUIDE

Between the opening and closing (1.1–2; 4.19–22), the writer reminds the reader "to rekindle the gift of God" without shame (1.3–10) and encourages him (and others indirectly) to pass on the apostolic* teachings faithfully (1.11–4.18) in the present and beyond the writer's own fading future.

1.1–2	Epistolary opening
1.3–10	Reminders to rekindle God's gift
1.11–4.18	Passing on the apostolic teachings
4.19–22	Epistolary closing

1 Paul, an apostle of Christ Jesus by the will of God, for the sake of the promise of life that is in Christ Jesus,

2 To Timothy, my beloved child:

Grace, mercy, and peace from God the Father and Christ Jesus our Lord.

3 I am grateful to God—whom I worship with a clear conscience, as my ancestors did—when I remember you constantly in my prayers night and day. ⁴Recalling your tears, I long to see you so that I may be filled with joy. ⁵I am reminded of your sincere faith, a faith that lived first in your grandmother Lois and your mother Eunice and now, I am sure, lives in you. ⁶For this reason I remind you to rekindle the gift of God that is within you through the laying on of my hands; ⁷for God did not give us a spirit of cowardice, but

---

1.1–2: **Epistolary opening.** See 2 Cor 1.1; 1 Tim 1.1.
2: *Child,* see 2.1; 1 Tim 1.2. The repetition of *child* and *you* (in singular form: 2.1; 3.10, 14; 4.5) gives the tone of a last will.

rather a spirit of power and of love and of self-discipline.

8 Do not be ashamed, then, of the testimony about our Lord or of me his prisoner, but join with me in suffering for the gospel, relying on the power of God, 9who saved us and called us with a holy calling, not according to our works but according to his own purpose and grace. This grace was given to us in Christ Jesus before the ages began, 10but it has now been revealed through the appearing of our Savior Christ Jesus, who abolished death and brought life and immortality to light through the gospel. 11For this gospel I was appointed a herald and an apostle and a teacher,ᵃ 12and for this reason I suffer as I do. But I am not ashamed, for I know the one in whom I have put my trust, and I am sure that he is able to guard until that day what I have entrusted to him.ᵇ 13Hold to the standard of sound teaching that you have heard from me, in the faith and love that are in Christ Jesus. 14Guard the good treasure entrusted to you, with the help of the Holy Spirit living in us.

15 You are aware that all who are in Asia have turned away from me, including Phygelus and Hermogenes. 16May the Lord grant mercy to the household of Onesiphorus, because he often refreshed me and was not ashamed of my chain; 17when he arrived in Rome, he eagerlyᶜ searched for me and found me 18—may the Lord grant that he will find mercy from the Lord on that day! And you know very well how much service he rendered in Ephesus.

1.3–18. 3–10: Appeals to suffer for the gospel. 3–5: One sentence in Greek, this links the writer and his ancestors to Timothy and his *mother* and *grandmother. Conscience,* see 1 Tim 3.9. Timothy's *mother,* see Acts 16.1. *Sincere,* literally "without hypocrisy." **6–10:** A maxim against cowardice (see Sir 34.4) precedes a direct exhortation* against being ashamed of the gospel and a fragment of a hymn summarizing the gospel. **6:** *Rekindle,* the word implies continuous burning. *Laying on of . . . hands,* see 1 Tim 4.14. **7:** *Self-discipline,* not private rigor but God-given endurance. See Titus 1.8; 2.5–6. **8:** *Ashamed* in various forms (1.12, 16; 2.15) is a key theme: Believers must rely on the power of God to counter the shame and suffering

---

associated with the gospel. **10:** Elsewhere in the Pastorals (4.1; 1 Tim 6.14), *appearing* means Jesus' future coming; here, his incarnation. **1.11–4.18: Passing on the apostolic* teachings. 1.11–18: Serving the gospel.** Personal experiences (vv. 11, 15–18) illustrate perseverance (vv. 11–14). Onesiphorus is an example of one not ashamed of the gospel. In contrast, Phygelus and Hermogenes have turned away. **12:** *That day,* see 1.18; 4.8. **14:** *Treasure,* literally a deposit. **15:** *Asia,* a Roman province, western Asia Minor (modern Turkey). *Phygelus and Hermogenes,* unknown elsewhere. **17–18:** *Found . . . find,* a play on words.

2 You then, my child, be strong in the grace that is in Christ Jesus; 2and what you have heard from me through many witnesses entrust to faithful people who will be able to teach others as well. 3Share in suffering like a good soldier of Christ Jesus. 4No one serving in the army gets entangled in everyday affairs; the soldier's aim is to please the enlisting officer. 5And in the case of an athlete, no one is crowned without competing according to the rules. 6It is the farmer who does the work who ought to have the first share of the crops. 7Think over what I say, for the Lord will give you understanding in all things.

8 Remember Jesus Christ, raised from the dead, a descendant of David—that is my gospel, 9for which I suffer hardship, even to the point of being chained like a criminal. But the word of God is not chained. 10Therefore I endure everything for the sake of the elect, so that they may also obtain the salvation that is in Christ Jesus, with eternal glory. 11The saying is sure:
If we have died with him, we will also
    live with him;
12 if we endure, we will also reign with
        him;
    if we deny him, he will also deny us;
13 if we are faithless, he remains faithful—
    for he cannot deny himself.

2.1–26: Admonitions. 1–13: Work and endure for the gospel. A transition (vv. 1–2) leads into three proverbial images (vv. 3–7) and a brief statement of belief

---

a Other ancient authorities add *of the Gentiles*
b Or *what has been entrusted to me*   c Or *promptly*

(v. 8). Personal testimony to endurance (vv. 9–10) leads to a longer profession of belief (vv. 11–13). **1–2:** *Be strong* ("endynamou") recalls that God has granted believers a spirit of *power* ("dynameos," 1.7), and that believers should rely on the *power* ("dynamin," 1.8) of God; it anticipates that others will deny this *power* ("dynamin," 3.5) and that in the writer's first defense God gave him *strength* ("enedynamosen," 4.17). *Entrust* recalls "deposit" (*treasure*) of 1.14 and anticipates the contrast between true and false teaching (2.14–26; 4.2–4). **3–6:** Proverbial figures of a *soldier, athlete,* and *farmer,* vivid images of hard work under specified rules. The *soldier of Christ* seeks to *please . . . the enlisting officer.* The *athlete* runs to receive a crown *according to the rules.* The *farmer* who labors can expect *the first share of the crops.* See 1 Tim 5.18: "The laborer deserves to be paid." **8–10:** The writer's *gospel* links the glory of Jesus, the Davidic messiah,* with his death and resurrection; the believer relies upon God's power when suffering dishonor, since the result is eternal glory. **11–13:** A hymn encouraging endurance and faithfulness. *The saying is sure,* see 1 Tim 1.15; 1 Tim 3.1; 4.9; Titus 3.8.

14 Remind them of this, and warn them before God*a* that they are to avoid wrangling over words, which does no good but only ruins those who are listening. 15 Do your best to present yourself to God as one approved by him, a worker who has no need to be ashamed, rightly explaining the word of truth. 16 Avoid profane chatter, for it will lead people into more and more impiety, 17 and their talk will spread like gangrene. Among them are Hymenaeus and Philetus, 18 who have swerved from the truth by claiming that the resurrection has already taken place. They are upsetting the faith of some. 19 But God's firm foundation stands, bearing this inscription: "The Lord knows those who are his," and, "Let everyone who calls on the name of the Lord turn away from wickedness."

20 In a large house there are utensils not only of gold and silver but also of wood and clay, some for special use, some for ordinary. 21 All who cleanse themselves of the things I have mentioned*b* will become special utensils, dedicated and useful to the owner of the house, ready for every good work. 22 Shun youthful passions and pursue righteousness, faith, love, and peace, along with those who call on the Lord from a pure heart. 23 Have nothing to do with stupid and senseless controversies; you know that they breed quarrels. 24 And the Lord's servant*c* must not be quarrelsome but kindly to everyone, an apt teacher, patient, 25 correcting opponents with gentleness. God may perhaps grant that they will repent and come to know the truth, 26 and that they may escape from the snare of the devil, having been held captive by him to do his will.*d*

2.14–26: Warnings and encouragements. 14–19: *Wrangling over words* (see also v. 23; 1 Tim 6.4; Titus 3.9) and *profane chatter* (1 Tim 6.20) are opposed to the word of truth. **17:** *Gangrene,* a spreading death of tissue caused by obstruction of blood flow. *Hymenaeus* (see 1 Tim 1.20), *Philetus* (unknown elsewhere), models of false teaching. **19:** See Num 16.5, 26; Isa 26.13; Joel 3.5. Numbers 16 tells the story of Korah and his followers, who renounced their faith and from whom the people of God therefore separated themselves. **20–21:** *Utensils* will be judged not by their materials (*gold . . . silver . . . wood . . . clay*) but by the cleanliness that makes them *useful.* **22–26:** Warnings to all who are able to teach. *Lord's servant,* see Titus 1.1. *Shun . . . pursue,* see 1 Tim 6.10. *An apt teacher,* see 1 Tim 3.2.

3 You must understand this, that in the last days distressing times will come. 2 For people will be lovers of themselves, lovers of money, boasters, arrogant, abusive, disobedient to their parents, ungrateful, unholy, 3 inhuman, implacable, slanderers, profligates, brutes, haters of good, 4 treacherous, reckless, swollen with conceit, lovers of pleasure rather than lovers of God, 5 holding to the outward form of godliness but denying its power. Avoid them! 6 For among them are those who make their way into households and captivate silly women, overwhelmed by their sins and swayed by all kinds of desires, 7 who are always being instructed and can never arrive at a knowledge

a Other ancient authorities read *the Lord* *b* Gk *of these things* *c* Gk *slave* *d* Or *by him, to do his* (that is, God's) *will* of the truth. 8As Jannes and Jambres opposed Moses, so these people, of corrupt mind and counterfeit faith, also oppose the truth. 9But they will not make much progress, because, as in the case of those two men,*a* their folly will become plain to everyone.

10 Now you have observed my teaching, my conduct, my aim in life, my faith, my patience, my love, my steadfastness, 11my persecutions, and my suffering the things that happened to me in Antioch, Iconium, and Lystra. What persecutions I endured! Yet the Lord rescued me from all of them. 12Indeed, all who want to live a godly life in Christ Jesus will be persecuted. 13But wicked people and impostors will go from bad to worse, deceiving others and being deceived. 14But as for you, continue in what you have learned and firmly believed, knowing from whom you learned it, 15and how from childhood you have known the sacred writings that are able to instruct you for salvation through faith in Christ Jesus. 16All scripture is inspired by God and is*b* useful for teaching, for reproof, for correction, and for training in righteousness, 17so that everyone who belongs to God may be proficient, equipped for every good work.

3.1–17: Warnings of the end time and examples of endurance. 2–5: A list of vices similar to those in popular Greek writings. **6–9:** A denunciation of the folly of false teaching. *Silly women,* susceptible to false teaching because they are controlled by their desires, a problem later noted without the gender-specific designation (4.3). *Jannes and Jambres,* Pharaoh's magicians, not named in Ex 7.11 but in the Dead Sea Scrolls (Damascus Rule 5.17–19). **10–17:** Personal testimony in a virtue list (vv. 10–11), maxims (vv. 12–13) and admonitions (vv. 14–17) present the writer as a model teacher and sufferer. *Sacred writings,* Hellenistic* Judaism's name for the Jewish scriptures.

---

4 In the presence of God and of Christ Jesus, who is to judge the living and the dead, and in view of his appearing and his kingdom, I solemnly urge you: 2proclaim the message; be persistent whether the time is favorable or unfavorable; convince, rebuke, and encourage, with the utmost patience in teaching. 3For the time is coming when people will not put up with sound doctrine, but having itching ears, they will accumulate for themselves teachers to suit their own desires, 4and will turn away from listening to the truth and wander away to myths. 5As for you, always be sober, endure suffering, do the work of an evangelist, carry out your ministry fully.

6 As for me, I am already being poured out as a libation, and the time of my departure has come. 7I have fought the good fight, I have finished the race, I have kept the faith. 8From now on there is reserved for me the crown of righteousness, which the Lord, the righteous judge, will give me on that day, and not only to me but also to all who have longed for his appearing.

9 Do your best to come to me soon, 10for Demas, in love with this present world, has deserted me and gone to Thessalonica; Crescens has gone to Galatia,*c* Titus to Dalmatia. 11Only Luke is with me. Get Mark and bring him with you, for he is useful in my ministry. 12I have sent Tychicus to Ephesus. 13When you come, bring the cloak that I left with Carpus at Troas, also the books, and above all the parchments. 14Alexander the coppersmith did me great harm; the Lord will pay him back for his deeds. 15You also must beware of him, for he strongly opposed our message.

16 At my first defense no one came to my support, but all deserted me. May it not be counted against them! 17But the Lord stood by me and gave me strength, so that through me the message might be fully proclaimed and all the Gentiles might hear it. So I was rescued from the lion's mouth. 18The Lord will rescue me from every evil attack and save me for his heavenly kingdom. To him be the glory forever and ever. Amen.

4.1–18: Solemn closing exhortation.* 1: See 1 Tim 5.21. **6:** *Poured out as a libation,* an image of sacrifice; see Phil 2.17; Ex 29.40–41. **7–8:** *Race, crown,* athletic

---

a Gk lacks *two men*   *b* Or *Every scripture inspired by God is also*   *c* Other ancient authorities read *Gaul* images. *Fought the good fight,* either a military or an athletic image (see 2.2–5). **9–16:** The names in these verses also appear in Col 4.7, 10 ,14; Titus 3.12; Eph 6.21; Philem 24. *Parchments,* scrolls, a double emphasis since *books* were scrolls; a fair paraphrase would be: "also the books, especially the books." **14:** *Alexander,* perhaps the figure in 1 Tim 1.20. **16:** *First defense,* either the first of two trials or the first part of one trial. **17:** *The lion's mouth,* see Ps 22.21.

19 Greet Prisca and Aquila, and the household of Onesiphorus. 20 Erastus remained in Corinth; Trophimus I left ill in Miletus. 21 Do your best to come before winter. Eubulus sends greetings to you, as do

Pudens and Linus and Claudia and all the brothers and sisters. *a*

22 The Lord be with your spirit. Grace be with you. *b*

4.19–22: Epistolary closing. Greetings, a reminder, a benediction. **19:** *Priscilla and Aquila,* see Acts 18.2, 18; Rom 16.3; 1 Cor 16.19. *Erastus,* see Acts 19.22; it is uncertain if he is the Corinthian city official noted in Rom 16.23. *Trophimus,* see Acts 20.4; 21.29. **22:** The benediction includes single and plural blessings.

a Gk *all the brothers*   *b* The Greek word for *you* here is plural. Other ancient authorities add *Amen*

THE LETTER OF PAUL TO
TITUS

Introduction

Titus, the shortest of the Pastoral Letters (see sidebar, p. 1991), shares much with 1 Timothy. Both give qualifications for congregational leaders, though Titus only discusses the elder (1.6–10; see 1 Tim 3.1–13; 4.14; 5.17–22). Both include household instructions, in an attempt to address the effect of false teaching on families (2.1–15; see 2 Tim 2.15; 3.4–5, 12; 5.4, 8, 14). Both contrast the believer's former life with the present to encourage right behavior (2.11–14; 3.3–7; 1 Tim 1.12–16). And in both, the teachings that are opposed include divisive myths and genealogies* (1.14; 3.9; see 1 Tim 1.4).

There are few clues in the letter to its time and place of writing or its intended audience. It is attributed to Paul and purports to be addressed to Titus, a Greek who traveled with Paul (Gal 2.1, 3) and was one of his emissaries (2 Cor 2.13; 7.6–7, 13–16; 8.6, 16; 12.18; 2 Tim 4.10). Yet it is difficult to find time in Paul's life for a visit to Crete (just south of the Aegean Sea) before his Roman imprisonment (Acts 27.7–13). Nor does Acts tell us where Titus was when Paul passed through Crete as a prisoner (1.5). Those who see Paul as the author usually date the letter to the sixties, outside the narrative* of Acts, sometime between a first winter noted in Titus 3.12 and a second one noted in 2 Tim 4.21. Yet according to Acts 20, Paul does not expect to return East after his Roman imprisonment, a strong argument against Paul's authorship.

Whoever wrote it, the letter aims to ensure the stability of some new congregations on Crete. Titus therefore has two tasks: appointing "qualified" elders and eliminating rebellious, false teaching. The elders are to be appointed in every town (1.5) and must not exhibit the qualities of false teachers (1.6–9). False teachers are numerous; their teachings upset whole families; and greed is their driving motivation (1.10–15). To counter the effect on families, moreover, the letter gives a comprehensive set of household and civic admonitions (2.1–3.11), thus ensuring that the new believers in Crete exhibit—at all levels—the order, self-control, and good works expected of those who have been saved and look to eternal life (2.13; 3.7).

READING GUIDE

The letter's emphasis on teaching provides the clue to its division. After an opening (1.1–4), instructions on the appointment of elders contrast true and false teachers (1.5–16). The main section gives the content and motivation of the teaching and authority (2.1–3.11). A closing (3.12–15) gives personal notes, final commands, greetings, and a benediction.

1.1–4   Epistolary opening
1.5–16   Instructions on church order
2.1–3.11   Teachings on appropriate behavior
3.12–15   Epistolary closing

1 Paul, a servant*a* of God and an apostle of Jesus Christ, for the sake of the faith of God's elect and the knowledge of the truth that is in accordance with godliness, ²in the hope of eternal life that God, who never lies, promised before the ages began— ³in due time he revealed his word through the proclamation with which I have been entrusted by the command of God our Savior,

4 To Titus, my loyal child in the faith we share:

Grace*b* and peace from God the Father and Christ Jesus our Savior.

1.1–4: Epistolary opening. The longest opening in the Pastorals names the writer, the recipient, and God as agents of truth, preparing for the attack on the false teachers (1.12–14). **1:** *Servant,* literally "slave," *of God,* form the roots of this expression in the Hebrew Scriptures, see 2 Sam 7.5; Jer 7.25. In the undisputed letters Paul uses "servant of Christ" (Rom 1.1; Gal 1.10; Phil 1.1). **3:** *Command,* literally "order upon." The Greek word is related to other terms in the letter: "directed" (1.5); "submissive" (2.5, 9); "authority" (2.15); "subjected" (3.1). *Savior,* see 1.4; 2.10, 13; 3.4, 6; see also 2.11; 1 Tim 2.3; 4.10. **4:** *Loyal child,* see 1 Tim 1.2; 2 Tim 1.2; 2.1.

~~~~~

5 I left you behind in Crete for this reason, so that you should put in order what remained to be done, and should appoint elders in every town, as I directed you: ⁶someone who is blameless, married only once,*c* whose children are believers, not accused of debauchery and not rebellious. ⁷For a bishop,*d* as God's steward, must be blameless; he must not be arrogant or quick-tempered or addicted to wine or violent or greedy for gain; ⁸but he must be hospitable, a lover of goodness, prudent, upright, devout, and self-controlled. ⁹He must have a firm grasp of the word that is trustworthy in accordance with the teaching, so that he may be able both to preach with sound doctrine and to refute those who contradict it.

10 There are also many rebellious people, idle talkers and deceivers, especially those of the circumcision; ¹¹they must be silenced, since they are upsetting whole families by teaching for sordid gain what it is not right

to teach. ¹²It was one of them, their very own prophet, who said,

"Cretans are always liars, vicious brutes, lazy gluttons."

¹³That testimony is true. For this reason rebuke them sharply, so that they may become sound in the faith, ¹⁴not paying attention to Jewish myths or to commandments of those who reject the truth. ¹⁵To the pure all things are pure, but to the corrupt and unbelieving nothing is pure. Their very minds and consciences are corrupted. ¹⁶They profess to know God, but they deny him by their actions. They are detestable, disobedient, unfit for any good work.

1.5–16: Instructions on church order. The letter contrasts the elders and the false teachers: The false teachers are motivated by *sordid gain* (v. 11); the elders must not be *greedy for gain* (v. 7). The false teachers upset *whole families* (v. 11); the elders must be able to control their own families (v. 6). **5:** Paul, while a captive, spent time at *Crete* (Acts 27.7–15), but neither Acts nor his own letters says he started a mission there. Furthermore, after Crete Paul is taken on to Malta, not Nicopolos (Acts 28.1). **5–7:** *Elders* and *bishops* seem to be the same. **9:** The determination of *sound* (healthy or correct) *doctrine* is based on the reasoning of a community; see 1.13; 2.1, 2, 8; 1 Tim 1.10; 6.3; 2 Tim 1.13; 4.3. **12:** A stereotype attributed by some early Christians (Clement of Alexandria, Chrysostom, and Jerome) to Epimenides, a Cretan poet from the sixth century BCE. **16:** *Work,* see 1.16; 2.7, 14; 3.1, 8).

~~~~~

2 But as for you, teach what is consistent with sound doctrine. ²Tell the older men to be temperate, serious, prudent, and sound in faith, in love, and in endurance.

3 Likewise, tell the older women to be reverent in behavior, not to be slanderers or slaves to drink; they are to teach what is good, ⁴so that they may encourage the young women to love their husbands, to love their children, ⁵to be self-controlled, chaste, good managers of the household, kind, being submissive to their husbands, so that the word of God may not be discredited.

---

a Gk *slave*   *b* Other ancient authorities read *Grace, mercy,*   *c* Gk *husband of one wife*   *d* Or *an overseer*

6 Likewise, urge the younger men to be self-controlled. 7Show yourself in all respects a model of good works, and in your teaching show integrity, gravity, 8and sound speech that cannot be censured; then any opponent will be put to shame, having nothing evil to say of us.

9 Tell slaves to be submissive to their masters and to give satisfaction in every respect; they are not to talk back, 10not to pilfer, but to show complete and perfect fidelity, so that in everything they may be an ornament to the doctrine of God our Savior.

11 For the grace of God has appeared, bringing salvation to all,*a* 12training us to renounce impiety and worldly passions, and in the present age to live lives that are self-controlled, upright, and godly, 13while we wait for the blessed hope and the manifestation of the glory of our great God and Savior,*b* Jesus Christ. 14He it is who gave himself for us that he might redeem us from all iniquity and purify for himself a people of his own who are zealous for good deeds.

15 Declare these things; exhort and reprove with all authority.*c* Let no one look down on you.

2.1–3.11: Teachings on appropriate behavior. 2.1–15: Private behavior. The letter explains appropriate behavior and its motivation and gives a general reminder of Titus's authority. **2–10:** A domestic code: admonitions to older men (v. 2), older women (v. 3), young women (vv. 4–5), younger men, including Titus (vv. 6–8), and slaves (vv. 9–10). Absent is any admonition to masters. **2:** *Prudent* is related linguistically to words that are translated *self-controlled* in vv. 5, 6, 12. **12:** *Worldly passions,* see 3.3. **13:** The writer speaks not about the "coming" of Jesus, but about his *manifestation* or "appearing," words used to describe the appearance of an earthly ruler. **15:** *Let no one look down on you* (perhaps because of age, vv. 6, 7), see 1 Tim 4.12.

3 Remind them to be subject to rulers and authorities, to be obedient, to be ready for every good work, 2to speak evil of no one, to avoid quarreling, to be gentle, and to show every courtesy to everyone. 3For we ourselves were once foolish, disobedient, led astray, slaves to various passions and pleasures, passing our days in malice and envy, despicable, hating one another. 4But when the goodness and loving kindness of God our Savior appeared, 5he saved us, not because of any works of righteousness that we had done, but according to his mercy, through the water*d* of rebirth and renewal by the Holy Spirit. 6This Spirit he poured out on us richly through Jesus Christ our Savior, 7so that, having been justified by his grace, we might become heirs according to the hope of eternal life. 8The saying is sure.

I desire that you insist on these things, so that those who have come to believe in God may be careful to devote themselves to good works; these things are excellent and profitable to everyone. 9But avoid stupid controversies, genealogies, dissensions, and quarrels about the law, for they are unprofitable and worthless. 10After a first and second admonition, have nothing more to do with anyone who causes divisions, 11since you know that such a person is perverted and sinful, being self-condemned.

3.1–11: Public behavior. An explanation of expected behavior toward the authorities and other outsiders, its motivation, and a more extended reminder of Titus's authority. **1:** *Be subject to,* see 2.5, 9, where the word (or a related term) is translated "be submissive." See 1 Tim 2.11; 3.4. *Authorities,* see Rom 13.1–7; 1 Pet 2.13–17. **8:** *The saying is sure,* see 1 Tim 1.15; 3.1; 4.9; 2 Tim 2.11. **10:** *Divisions,* Greek "hairetikon," the word from which we get "heretic," is perhaps only a reference to 1.11, not to an unorthodox group as in later church history.

12 When I send Artemas to you, or Tychicus, do your best to come to me at Nicopolis, for I have decided to spend the winter there. 13Make every effort to send Zenas the lawyer and Apollos on their way, and see that they lack nothing. 14And let people learn to devote themselves to good works in order to meet urgent needs, so that they may not be unproductive.

a Or has appeared to all, bringing salvation   b Or of the great God and our Savior   c Gk commandment   d Gk washing

15 All who are with me send greetings to you. Greet those who love us in the faith. Grace be with all of you.ᵃ

3.12–15: Epistolary closing. 12: *Artemas, Tychicus,* those coming to Crete to replace Titus. *Tychicus,* see Acts 20.4; Eph 6.21; Col 4.7–9; 2 Tim 4.2. *Nicopolis,* possibly a city in Epirus on the western coast of Greece.

13: *Apollos,* see Acts 18.24–28; 19.1; 1 Cor 1.12; 3.4–9; 4, 6; 16.12. **15:** Though the letter is addressed to Titus, its use of the second person plural form (*all of you*) here suggests that it was intended for a wider audience.

a Other ancient authorities add *Amen*

THE LETTER OF PAUL TO PHILEMON

Introduction

The letter to Philemon is Paul's shortest and the only undisputed letter addressed to an individual. Despite its brevity, its clever wordplay, careful speech, and presentation of character give it a distinct, graceful tone. Furthermore, it is really more than a private letter to Philemon: The central portion directly addresses Philemon, but the number of persons addressed in vv. 3 and 25 shifts, and v. 1 names several persons along with the group that meets in Philemon's house.

Philemon resembles a letter of recommendation: A powerful person (who can grant favors) writes to another powerful person on behalf of someone less powerful. In Philemon, Paul wants a favor for Onesimus ("welcome him as you would me," v. 17; compare v. 20) and recalls a favor done for Philemon (v. 19).

It is uncertain where Philemon lived or where Paul was in prison (vv. 1, 9, 13, 22). Because Onesimus and Archippus (v. 2) are mentioned in Colossians (Col 4.9, 17), Philemon may have lived in Colossae. If so, then Ephesus (located, like Colossae, in Asia Minor) is likely the place from which Paul writes, rather than from Rome or Caesarea, both much more distant places where Paul was imprisoned. The date of writing would be about 55 CE.

The social circumstances that evoked the letter are clear—the practice of slavery—but the precise contours of those circumstances are not. Onesimus, a slave, was absent from the house of his master, Philemon. Had Onesimus taken money or valuables and run away? Had Philemon mistreated Onesimus? Was Onesimus looking for someone to plead for better treatment from Philemon? Or perhaps Onesimus had not run away. Perhaps he was carrying out a task for Philemon and it had taken longer than either of them had expected. Some slaves managed affairs for their masters. Paul may be addressing the possibility that the delay was costly for Philemon (v. 18). Furthermore, Paul's reference to Onesimus's uselessness (v. 11) could also refer to the short period ("a while") of unexpected absence, not the entire absence. The contrast in v. 11 then need not be "formerly" (as in the NSRV) versus "now" but "at the time [of the delay]" versus "now." During this time, Paul had converted Onesimus. Now, to explain the "delay" during which the conversion took place, Paul writes commending Onesimus's changed character and citing the change as the reason for the delay. Moreover, Onesimus now might be "useful" to Paul, though Paul will wait for Philemon to allow Onesimus to stay and will not coerce Philemon into generosity (v. 14).

READING GUIDE

Paul's requests show that the goal of the letter is to commend Onesimus, Philemon's slave. First, Paul quickly reestablishes relations with Philemon: Philemon has refreshed the hearts of many saints through the goodness of his love (v. 4). Next, Paul tells Philemon that Onesimus is a beloved brother, Paul's very heart (vv. 12, 16). Last, Paul makes his request: "Refresh my heart," that is, accept Onesimus (v. 20).

1 Paul, a prisoner of Christ Jesus, and Timothy our brother,[a]

To Philemon our dear friend and co-worker, 2to Apphia our sister,[b] to Archippus our fellow soldier, and to the church in your house:

3 Grace to you and peace from God our Father and the Lord Jesus Christ.

4 When I remember you[c] in my prayers, I always thank my God 5because I hear of your love for all the saints and your faith toward the Lord Jesus. 6I pray that the sharing of your faith may become effective when you perceive all the good that we[d] may do for Christ. 7I have indeed received much joy and encouragement from your love, because the hearts of the saints have been refreshed through you, my brother.

1–7: Opening and thanksgiving. Paul praises Philemon but does not mention Onesimus: He wants Philemon to act out of good will, so he establishes Philemon's good will at the start. Because he wants Philemon to accept Onesimus, Paul's very heart (v. 12), he praises Philemon's love. **1:** *Timothy,* see 1 Thess 3.1–6; 1 Cor 4.17; Phil 2.19–24. *Dear,* the Greek is the same as "beloved," used for Onesimus in vv. 5, 7, 9, 16. **2:** *Apphia our sister,* in the Lord. *Archippus,* see Col 4.17. *Fellow soldier,* see Phil 2.25. *Church in your house,* early Christians worshiped in private homes (Rom 16.5; 1 Cor 16.19; Col 4.15). **5:** *Love for all the saints,* extravagant praise so that Philemon will love the new saint, Onesimus. **6:** *The good,* see Rom 10.15; Phil 1.6; 1 Thess 5.15; Gal 6.10. **7:** *Hearts,* literally "inward parts."

---

8 For this reason, though I am bold enough in Christ to command you to do your duty, 9yet I would rather appeal to you on the basis of love—and I, Paul, do this as an old man, and now also as a prisoner of Christ Jesus.[e] 10I am appealing to you for my child, Onesimus, whose father I have become during my imprisonment. 11Formerly he was useless to you, but now he is indeed useful[f]

both to you and to me. 12I am sending him, that is, my own heart, back to you. 13I wanted to keep him with me, so that he might be of service to me in your place during my imprisonment for the gospel; 14but I preferred to do nothing without your consent, in order that your good deed might be voluntary and not something forced. 15Perhaps this is the reason he was separated from you for a while, so that you might have him back forever, 16no longer as a slave but more than a slave, a beloved brother—especially to me but how much more to you, both in the flesh and in the Lord.

8–16: Paul's appeal. 8: *For this reason,* a transition marks a new section. **9:** *Old man* could mean "ambassador," but likely refers to Paul's age. **10:** *My child,* a metaphor* for a convert. See 1 Cor 4.14, 17; Gal 4.19. **11:** *Useless . . . useful,* see introduction and note f. **15:** *He was separated,* a passive form, possibly suggesting God as the cause, underlining the point that the delay was beneficial.

---

17 So if you consider me your partner, welcome him as you would welcome me. 18If he has wronged you in any way, or owes you anything, charge that to my account. 19I, Paul, am writing this with my own hand: I will repay it. I say nothing about your owing me even your own self. 20Yes, brother, let me have this benefit from you in the Lord! Refresh my heart in Christ. 21Confident of your obedience, I am writing to you, knowing that you will do even more than I say.

22 One thing more—prepare a guest room for me, for I am hoping through your prayers to be restored to you.

23 Epaphras, my fellow prisoner in Christ

---

a Gk *the brother*   b Gk *the sister*   c From verse 4 through verse 21, *you* is singular   d Other ancient authorities read *you* (plural)   e Or *as an ambassador of Christ Jesus, and now also his prisoner*   f The name Onesimus means *useful* or (compare verse 20) *beneficial*

Jesus, sends greetings to you,^a ²⁴and so do Mark, Aristarchus, Demas, and Luke, my fellow workers.

25 The grace of the Lord Jesus Christ be with your spirit.^b

17–25: Request and closing. The letter opened in both private and public spheres and closes in the same way, with the greetings in vv. 24 and 25. **17:** *So,* a transitional word marking the start of the final section. **19:** *My own hand,* Paul probably dictated his letters to a scribe* (1 Cor 16.21; Gal 6.11), but here he writes

himself. **20:** *Benefit,* Greek "onaimen," similar to Onesimus; through this wordplay, Paul indirectly asks for Onesimus. **21:** *More than I say,* perhaps "more than I say obliquely"; Philemon must decide freely. **23–24:** *Epaphras,* see Col 1.7; 4.12. The others are mentioned in Col 4.10–17, which includes Jesus Justus as well. **25:** A similar benediction is found in Phil 4.23; Gal 6.18.

~~~~~~~~~~~~~~~~~~~~~~~~~~~~~~~~~~~~~

a Here *you* is singular   *b* Other ancient authorities add *Amen*

THE LETTER TO THE
HEBREWS

Introduction

Over time Paul the apostle★ was thought to be the author, and this document was placed at the end of his collected letters. Paul, after all, was a prodigious letter writer; but scholars now agree that he did not write Hebrews, nor is it a genuine letter, except for a few features at its end (13.20–25). The content, style, and viewpoint are not those of Paul, but of a highly educated person familiar with Greek philosophy, the scriptures, and allegorical★ logic. Hence the author is often compared to Philo★ of Alexandria, who in the same century writes in a similar manner about Israelite matters. The audience is often thought to be Israelites living in exile because use of the scriptures as an argument and extensive discussion of the Jerusalem Temple★ and cult are things that would make particular sense to those of Judean background. But scholars cannot be certain about identifying author, audience, or place of composition. The type of document seems to be a mixture of exhortation★ and argument, but in a manner totally unlike other New Testament letters.

READING GUIDE

Hebrews, which claims to be a "word of exhortation" (13.22) in the form of a letter (13.18–25), resembles ancient philosophical essay letters. That is, it is more like an extended presentation of a position or idea than it is like a piece of personal correspondence. It interweaves two themes: (1) the need to remain faithful and (2) the basis for steadfast faith as found in the description of Jesus' death as victim and priest. Jesus' faithfulness, his sharing of our mortal nature, and his obedience learned through suffering qualify him as the ideal model of perseverance and faithfulness. The structure of the document, then, consists of alternating presentation of the themes: (1) the examination of Jesus' death (2.10–18; 5.1–10; 7.1–10.18), and (2) the exhortation to faithfulness (2.1–4; 3.1–4.16; 5.11–6.19; 10.19–39; 12.1–29; 13.1–17). Overall, the argument goes as follows:

1. Comparison: superiority of Jesus to angels (1.1–14)
2. Exhortation: the example of Jesus (2.1–18)
3. Exhortation to faithfulness: the example of ancient Israel (3.1–4.13)
4. Main thesis: Jesus as suffering but faithful high priest (4.14–5.14)
5. Exhortation to mature understanding and faithfulness (6.1–20)
6. Comparison: superiority of Jesus' priesthood to that of Levites
   A. Jesus and Melchizedek (7.1–10, 15–22, 26–28)
   B. Old levitical priesthood (7.11–14, 23–25)
7. Comparison: superiority of the new covenant★ through Jesus (8.1–13)
8. Comparison: superiority of Jesus' sacrifice (9.1–22)
9. Comparison: superiority of Jesus' new temple (9.23–28)
10. Comparison: superiority of Jesus' obedience to material sacrifices (10.1–18)

11. Exhortation to faithfulness: hope in the promise
    A. Holding fast to the confession (10.19–39)
    B. Witnesses of faith and steadfastness and hope (11.1–39)
12. Exhortation to more general virtues
    A. Difficulties and discipline require courage (12.1–29)
    B. Community issues: love, marriage, and authority (13.1–19)
13. Letter closing: blessing and greetings (13.20–25)

Hebrews regularly uses the scriptures to interpret the role and status of Jesus and to encourage the believers. It cites individual verses of psalms as well as lengthy quotations, and is familiar with narrative* as well as legal materials. Scripture serves as the best argument to clarify Jesus' priesthood and to exhort to faithfulness (see chart below). While most New Testament documents understand the Bible as prophecy, Hebrews takes this process one step further by using the Bible to outline a religious system superior to any other.

Furthermore, the author regularly argues that Jesus is "better than" the most important and exalted persons or things in the Judean tradition. Jesus is superior to heavenly angels (1.5–14) and earthly worthies, such as Moses (3.1–6) and Aaron (5.1–10). His priesthood surpasses that of Levi (7.1–28), and his sacrifice that of the old order (9.1–14). The covenant he mediates is better than that of Israel (8.7–13; 9.15–22; 12.24).

The author applies to Jesus traditional concepts used to speak about a true deity. Gods in antiquity were named "immortals" in contrast to mortal men and women; they never die, but we do. Moreover, a true god must be both uncreated in the past and imperishable in the future. Just this sort of language is used of Jesus in two places. The author begins by describing Jesus as the one "through whom God created the worlds" (1.2). Because Jesus is not himself created, he must be "eternal in the past." Then, citing Ps 102.25, he affirms Jesus as the heavenly figure who "in the beginning . . . founded the earth, and the heavens are the work of your hands" (1.10); this echoes the sense of Jesus as uncreated or eternal in the past. Juxtaposed are statements proclaiming Jesus' imperishability. The earth and the heavens will perish and grow old like garments (1.10–11 / Ps 102.26–27); but Jesus will "remain . . . the same" and "your years will never

Chart Use of Scriptural Citations in Hebrews

Passage in Hebrews	Scripture cited	Topic
1.5–14	Ps 2.7; 97.7; 104.4; 102.25–27	descriptions of Christ's high status
2.6–8	Ps 8	scandal of the cross
3.7–11	Ps 95	exhortation to faithfulness
5.6; 6.20; 7.11, 17, 21	Ps 110.4	priest like Melchizedek
7.1–10	Gen 14.17–20	Abraham and Melchizedek
8.6–13	Jer 31.31–34	new covenant in Jesus
9.6–22	Lev 16–17	day of atonement

end" (1.11–12). Because Jesus is both eternal in the past and imperishable in the future, he is rightly called "God" (1.8 / Ps 45.6).

This same claim is made for Jesus when Melchizedek is declared as a type of Jesus' priesthood. Melchizedek is the priest who blessed Abraham (Gen 14; 18–20); he not only represents a different kind of priesthood in Israel, but his name indicates that he was also a king, both of which become important in understanding Jesus' exalted role and status. Levitical priests die and so do not continue in the priesthood; Jesus' priesthood is superior because he "continues forever" (7.24). What can be known about Melchizedek is understood to describe Jesus, the true priest. Of Melchizedek the author says: "Without father, without mother, without genealogy,☆ having neither beginning of days nor end of life" (7.3). When applied to Jesus ("[Melchizedek] resembling the Son of God, he remains a priest forever," 7.3b), this claims that the Son of God truly is uncreated in the past ("without father, mother, genealogy") and imperishable in the future ("neither beginning of days nor end of life"). Thus Jesus is indescribably superior to all other creatures, angels, Moses, Aaron, and Levi: He shares the qualities of the Deity.

Readers should expect two types of materials, both exhortation to faithfulness and celebration of Jesus' death. In reading chs. 7–10, we profit by consulting the notes to see what biblical document is cited or alluded to in regard to Jesus' death as priestly sacrifice. This material should be seen in combination with the comparison motif☆ in which Jesus is better than or superior to heavenly angels and earthly heroes. If Christ is so exalted and noble, then his death is less a scandal to his disciples (12.2) and more a model of obedience and faithfulness to follow.

1 Long ago God spoke to our ancestors in many and various ways by the prophets, 2but in these last days he has spoken to us by a Son,*a* whom he appointed heir of all things, through whom he also created the worlds. 3He is the reflection of God's glory and the exact imprint of God's very being, and he sustains*b* all things by his powerful word. When he had made purification for sins, he sat down at the right hand of the Majesty on high, 4having become as much superior to angels as the name he has inherited is more excellent than theirs.

5 For to which of the angels did God ever say,

"You are my Son;
today I have begotten you"?

Or again,

"I will be his Father,
and he will be my Son"?

6And again, when he brings the firstborn into the world, he says,

"Let all God's angels worship him."

7Of the angels he says,

"He makes his angels winds,
and his servants flames of fire."

8But of the Son he says,

"Your throne, O God, is*c* forever and ever,
and the righteous scepter is the scepter of your*d* kingdom.
9 You have loved righteousness and hated wickedness;
therefore God, your God, has anointed you
with the oil of gladness beyond your companions."

10And,

"In the beginning, Lord, you founded the earth,
and the heavens are the work of your hands;
11 they will perish, but you remain;
they will all wear out like clothing;
12 like a cloak you will roll them up,
and like clothing*e* they will be changed.
But you are the same,
and your years will never end."

---

a Or *the Son* b Or *bears along* c Or *God is your throne* d Other ancient authorities read *his* e Other ancient authorities lack *like clothing*

13But to which of the angels has he ever said,

"Sit at my right hand
    until I make your enemies a footstool
        for your feet"?

14Are not all angels*a* spirits in the divine service, sent to serve for the sake of those who are to inherit salvation?

1.1–14. 1–4: Jesus' excellence. Hebrews celebrates Jesus' past and future. **1–2:** Jesus enjoyed power to *create,* and in the future he will be *heir of all things.* **3:** As *reflection* and *imprint,* Jesus shares all that God is, especially eternity. **5–14: Scripture says.** Jesus' excellence is demonstrated by a chain of biblical citations· applied to him. **5:** Ps 2.7 and 2 Sam 7.14 declare Jesus' relationship to God as *Son* to *Father.* **6–7:** Deut 32.43 asserts that heavenly *angels* acknowledge Jesus' exalted status. **8–9:** Jesus is even called *God* according to Ps 104.4 because of his eternity: *forever and ever.* **10–12:** Scripture declares Jesus' divine character in terms of past eternity and future imperishability; his past eternity is noted: *in the beginning* (Ps 102.25–27). Because uncreated, Jesus will have no end. Created things, like clothing, wear out, but Jesus will *remain* and always be *the same.* **13–14:** The application of Ps 110.1 to Jesus confirms his exalted role as seated *at the right hand* of God (1.3) and being *superior to angels* (1.4).

2 Therefore we must pay greater attention to what we have heard, so that we do not drift away from it. 2For if the message declared through angels was valid, and every transgression or disobedience received a just penalty, 3how can we escape if we neglect so great a salvation? It was declared at first through the Lord, and it was attested to us by those who heard him, 4while God added his testimony by signs and wonders and various miracles, and by gifts of the Holy Spirit, distributed according to his will.

5 Now God*b* did not subject the coming world, about which we are speaking, to angels. 6But someone has testified somewhere,

"What are human beings that you are
    mindful of them,*c*
or mortals, that you care for them?*d*
7 You have made them for a little while
    lower*e* than the angels;
you have crowned them with glory
    and honor,*f*

8   subjecting all things under
        their feet."

Now in subjecting all things to them, God*b* left nothing outside their control. As it is, we do not yet see everything in subjection to them, 9but we do see Jesus, who for a little while was made lower*g* than the angels, now crowned with glory and honor because of the suffering of death, so that by the grace of God*h* he might taste death for everyone.

2.1–9. 1–4: Exhortation* to constancy. 1: Although Jesus did not change (1.10–12), the author worries that the disciples will *drift away* from the gospel. **2–3:** If Sinai's revelation carried sanctions, more come with the greater revelation in Jesus. **4:** Three legal proofs are given for the gospel's truth: the *Lord* declared it; eyewitnesses attest to it; and signs confirm it. **5–9: Jesus' exalted status.** When applied to Jesus, Ps 8.4–6 tells about his death (*for a little while lower than the angels*) and resurrection (*crowned . . . with glory and honor*). The psalm describes the disciples' plight, for they see things *lower,* that is, oppressive and chaotic. Yet the psalm celebrates how God *crowned* Jesus *with glory and honor,* the tangible sign of which is God's *subjecting all things* to Jesus. Jesus' suffering of death and being crowned with glory establishes him as one like us, our elder brother, pioneer of our salvation. He tasted *death for everyone.*

10 It was fitting that God,*b* for whom and through whom all things exist, in bringing many children to glory, should make the pioneer of their salvation perfect through sufferings. 11For the one who sanctifies and those who are sanctified all have one Father.*i* For this reason Jesus*b* is not ashamed to call them brothers and sisters,*j* 12saying,

"I will proclaim your name to my
    brothers and sisters,*j*
in the midst of the congregation I will
    praise you."
13And again,
"I will put my trust in him."

a Gk *all of them*   *b* Gk *he*   *c* Gk *What is man that you are mindful of him?*   *d* Gk *or the son of man that you care for him?* In the Hebrew of Psalm 8.4–6 both *man* and *son of man* refer to all humankind   *e* Or *them only a little lower*   *f* Other ancient authorities add *and set them over the works of your hands*   *g* Or *who was made a little lower*   *h* Other ancient authorities read *apart from God*   *i* Gk *are all of one*   *j* Gk *brothers*

And again,

"Here am I and the children whom God
has given me."

14 Since, therefore, the children share flesh and blood, he himself likewise shared the same things, so that through death he might destroy the one who has the power of death, that is, the devil, ¹⁵and free those who all their lives were held in slavery by the fear of death. ¹⁶For it is clear that he did not come to help angels, but the descendants of Abraham. ¹⁷Therefore he had to become like his brothers and sisters^a in every respect, so that he might be a merciful and faithful high priest in the service of God, to make a sacrifice of atonement for the sins of the people. ¹⁸Because he himself was tested by what he suffered, he is able to help those who are being tested.

2.10–18: Pioneer of salvation. Interpreting earthly suffering, the author talks about the salutary effects of Jesus' death. **10–13, 16–17:** Since only mortals die, Jesus' death shows his solidarity with his disciples who are his mortal *brothers and sisters*. **14–15:** Jesus' *death* is likened to a battle in which the dying one destroyed the cause of his death, the *devil* (Wis 2.23–24). **17–18:** Jesus' solidarity in death with his disciples equips him with mercy *and* faithfulness to be their ideal priestly intermediary.

---

3 Therefore, brothers and sisters,^a holy partners in a heavenly calling, consider that Jesus, the apostle and high priest of our confession, ²was faithful to the one who appointed him, just as Moses also "was faithful in all^b God's^c house." ³Yet Jesus^d is worthy of more glory than Moses, just as the builder of a house has more honor than the house itself. ⁴(For every house is built by someone, but the builder of all things is God.) ⁵Now Moses was faithful in all God's^c house as a servant, to testify to the things that would be spoken later. ⁶Christ, however, was faithful over God's^c house as a son, and we are his house if we hold firm^e the confidence and the pride that belong to hope.

3.1–6: Jesus, greater than Moses. Greater than angels (1.5–14) and superior to levitical priests (7.11–28), Jesus is also greater than Moses. **2:** The author's

exhortation* *to* faith means faithfulness and perseverance. **3–4:** Jesus' superiority to Moses in *glory* and *honor* is compared to that of a *builder* to the *house* he builds. **5–6:** Moses was only faithful as *servant* over God's house, whereas Jesus served as faithful *son*. Only by faithfulness can disciples belong to Jesus' *house*, a common metaphor* for the church: either as a building (1 Cor 3.16; Eph 2.19–22) or a household (1 Tim 3.15).

---

7 Therefore, as the Holy Spirit says,
"Today, if you hear his voice,
8 do not harden your hearts as in
the rebellion,
as on the day of testing in the
wilderness,
9 where your ancestors put me to the test,
though they had seen my works ¹⁰for
forty years.
Therefore I was angry with that
generation,
and I said, 'They always go astray in
their hearts,
and they have not known my ways.'
¹¹ As in my anger I swore,
'They will not enter my rest.' "
¹²Take care, brothers and sisters,^a that none of you may have an evil, unbelieving heart that turns away from the living God. ¹³But exhort one another every day, as long as it is called "today," so that none of you may be hardened by the deceitfulness of sin. ¹⁴For we have become partners of Christ, if only we hold our first confidence firm to the end. ¹⁵As it is said,
"Today, if you hear his voice,
do not harden your hearts as in
the rebellion."
¹⁶Now who were they who heard and yet were rebellious? Was it not all those who left Egypt under the leadership of Moses? ¹⁷But with whom was he angry forty years? Was it not those who sinned, whose bodies fell in the wilderness? ¹⁸And to whom did he swear that they would not enter his rest, if not to those who were disobedient? ¹⁹So we see that they were unable to enter because of unbelief.

---

a Gk *brothers*   b Other ancient authorities lack *all*
c Gk *his*   d Gk *this one*   e Other ancient authorities add *to the end*

4 Therefore, while the promise of entering his rest is still open, let us take care that none of you should seem to have failed to reach it. 2For indeed the good news came to us just as to them; but the message they heard did not benefit them, because they were not united by faith with those who listened.*a* 3For we who have believed enter that rest, just as God*b* has said,

"As in my anger I swore,

'They shall not enter my rest,' "

though his works were finished at the foundation of the world. 4For in one place it speaks about the seventh day as follows, "And God rested on the seventh day from all his works." 5And again in this place it says, "They shall not enter my rest." 6Since therefore it remains open for some to enter it, and those who formerly received the good news failed to enter because of disobedience, 7again he sets a certain day—"today"—saying through David much later, in the words already quoted,

"Today, if you hear his voice,
    do not harden your hearts."

8For if Joshua had given them rest, God*b* would not speak later about another day. 9So then, a sabbath rest still remains for the people of God; 10for those who enter God's rest also cease from their labors as God did from his. 11Let us therefore make every effort to enter that rest, so that no one may fall through such disobedience as theirs.

12 Indeed, the word of God is living and active, sharper than any two-edged sword, piercing until it divides soul from spirit, joints from marrow; it is able to judge the thoughts and intentions of the heart. 13And before him no creature is hidden, but all are naked and laid bare to the eyes of the one to whom we must render an account.

God knows the secrets of the heart (Rom 8.27; 1 Cor 4.5).

14 Since, then, we have a great high priest who has passed through the heavens, Jesus, the Son of God, let us hold fast to our confession. 15For we do not have a high priest who is unable to sympathize with our weaknesses, but we have one who in every respect has been tested*c* as we are, yet without sin. 16Let us therefore approach the throne of grace with boldness, so that we may receive mercy and find grace to help in time of need.

5 Every high priest chosen from among mortals is put in charge of things pertaining to God on their behalf, to offer gifts and sacrifices for sins. 2He is able to deal gently with the ignorant and wayward, since he himself is subject to weakness; 3and because of this he must offer sacrifice for his own sins as well as for those of the people. 4And one does not presume to take this honor, but takes it only when called by God, just as Aaron was.

5 So also Christ did not glorify himself in becoming a high priest, but was appointed by the one who said to him,

"You are my Son,
    today I have begotten you";

6as he says also in another place,

"You are a priest forever,
    according to the order of
        Melchizedek."

7 In the days of his flesh, Jesus*b* offered up prayers and supplications, with loud cries and tears, to the one who was able to save him from death, and he was heard because of his reverent submission. 8Although he was a Son, he learned obedience through what he suffered; 9and having been made perfect, he became the source of eternal salvation for all who obey him, 10having been designated by God a high priest according to the order of Melchizedek.

3.7–4.13: Exhortation* based on Ps 95.7–11. This exhortation applies five phrases from the psalm to the addressees' current situation. (1) *Today,* 3.13 and 4.7; (2) *do not harden your hearts,* 3.12–13; (3) *rebellion,* 3.15–16; (4) *angry,* 3.17; (5) *not enter my rest,* 3.18; 4.1–6, 8–11. The example of the Exodus generation, once blessed but later cursed, should remind hearers of the need for constant faithfulness (1 Cor 10.6–13; Jude 5). **4.12–13:** Another traditional warning is given:

4.14–5.10: Christ the perfect high priest. 4.14–16: The exhortation* to faithfulness is linked to Christ's

a Other ancient authorities read *it did not meet with faith in those who listened*   *b* Gk *he*   *c* Or *tempted* role as *high priest*. He is worthy of his role because, by sharing our trials, he gains access to God's throne. **5.1–4:** The *high priest*, who offers *sacrifice* for the people, qualifies for that role because of empathy with fellow sufferers and sinners. But he does not *presume* to take this role; it is only given by God. **5–6:** God's oaths in Ps 2.7 and Ps 110.4 prove that Jesus' priestly role is no false claim, but a divine appointment. **7–10:** Returning to 4.15 and 5.2, the author dramatizes Jesus' salvific faithfulness. His suffering led to his perfection, which then qualified him for the role of saving *high priest*.

11 About this*ᵃ* we have much to say that is hard to explain, since you have become dull in understanding. ¹²For though by this time you ought to be teachers, you need someone to teach you again the basic elements of the oracles of God. You need milk, not solid food; ¹³for everyone who lives on milk, being still an infant, is unskilled in the word of righteousness. ¹⁴But solid food is for the mature, for those whose faculties have been trained by practice to distinguish good from evil.

5.11–14: Children versus adults. The description of Christ's high priesthood is likened to *solid food* for the mature; in contrast, the audience is likened to *infants* who can only digest *milk*. This contrast between adults' and children's food is a common expression of correction (1 Cor 3.1–3; 1 Pet 2.2).

6 Therefore let us go on toward perfection,*ᵇ* leaving behind the basic teaching about Christ, and not laying again the foundation: repentance from dead works and faith toward God, ²instruction about baptisms, laying on of hands, resurrection of the dead, and eternal judgment. ³And we will do*ᶜ* this, if God permits. ⁴For it is impossible to restore again to repentance those who have once been enlightened, and have tasted the heavenly gift, and have shared in the Holy Spirit, ⁵and have tasted the goodness of the word of God and the powers of the age to come, ⁶and then have fallen away, since on their own they are crucifying again the Son of God and are holding him up to contempt. ⁷Ground that drinks up the rain falling on it repeatedly, and that produces a crop useful to those for whom it is cultivated, re-

ceives a blessing from God. ⁸But if it produces thorns and thistles, it is worthless and on the verge of being cursed; its end is to be burned over.

9 Even though we speak in this way, beloved, we are confident of better things in your case, things that belong to salvation. ¹⁰For God is not unjust; he will not overlook your work and the love that you showed for his sake*ᵈ* in serving the saints, as you still do. ¹¹And we want each one of you to show the same diligence so as to realize the full assurance of hope to the very end, ¹²so that you may not become sluggish, but imitators of those who through faith and patience inherit the promises.

6.1–12: Either progress or slip back. 1–3: While exhorting to *perfection*, the author identifies the instruction given new members: elementary *teaching about Christ, repentance*, conversion to the one God, *baptism,*★ and the doctrine of a *judgment* after death. **4–6:** The author warns that slipping back cannot be remedied (2 Pet 2.21–22), for subsequent loss of holiness cancels Jesus' crucifixion (2.14–18; 5.7–10). **7–8:** The contrast between productive and barren soil resembles Jesus' parable★ about kinds of soils (Mk 4.14–20). **9–12:** Balancing his warning, the author encourages by confirming the value of acts of mercy (Mt 22.39; 25.31–46). Thus *faith*fulness, linked with *love*, leads to the assurance of *hope*.

13 When God made a promise to Abraham, because he had no one greater by whom to swear, he swore by himself, ¹⁴saying, "I will surely bless you and multiply you." ¹⁵And thus Abraham,*ᵉ* having patiently endured, obtained the promise. ¹⁶Human beings, of course, swear by someone greater than themselves, and an oath given as confirmation puts an end to all dispute. ¹⁷In the same way, when God desired to show even more clearly to the heirs of the promise the unchangeable character of his purpose, he guaranteed it by an oath, ¹⁸so that through two unchangeable things, in which it is impossible that God would prove

a Or *him*   *b* Or *toward maturity*   *c* Other ancient authorities read *let us do*   *d* Gk *for his name*   *e* Gk *he* false, we who have taken refuge might be strongly encouraged to seize the hope set before us. [19]We have this hope, a sure and steadfast anchor of the soul, a hope that enters the inner shrine behind the curtain, [20]where Jesus, a forerunner on our behalf, has entered, having become a high priest forever according to the order of Melchizedek.

6.13–20: Value of God's oath. 13–15: The author introduces a pattern that will recur many times: God's *promise* and our patient faithfulness in waiting for its fulfillment, which is hope. *Abraham* (Gen 22.16–17) exemplifies this pattern perfectly here and in 11.8–12. **16:** It is a legal principle that the word of someone is confirmed when accompanied by an *oath*. **17–18:** Similarly, God's *promise* to Abraham's descendants is guaranteed by the *oath* that makes Jesus our high priest (7.20–21). **19:** *Hope* is the new word in the exhortation,* expressing faithfulness, patience in difficulty, and expectation of rewards after death (4.16; 6.2). **20:** Our hope of access to God rests entirely on Jesus' death as *high priest.*

7 This "King Melchizedek of Salem, priest of the Most High God, met Abraham as he was returning from defeating the kings and blessed him"; [2]and to him Abraham apportioned "one-tenth of everything." His name, in the first place, means "king of righteousness"; next he is also king of Salem, that is, "king of peace." [3]Without father, without mother, without genealogy, having neither beginning of days nor end of life, but resembling the Son of God, he remains a priest forever.

[4] See how great he is! Even[a] Abraham the patriarch gave him a tenth of the spoils. [5]And those descendants of Levi who receive the priestly office have a commandment in the law to collect tithes[b] from the people, that is, from their kindred,[c] though these also are descended from Abraham. [6]But this man, who does not belong to their ancestry, collected tithes[b] from Abraham and blessed him who had received the promises. [7]It is beyond dispute that the inferior is blessed by the superior. [8]In the one case, tithes are received by those who are mortal; in the other, by one of whom it is testified that he lives. [9]One might even say that Levi himself, who

receives tithes, paid tithes through Abraham, [10]for he was still in the loins of his ancestor when Melchizedek met him.

7.1–10: Melchizedek, Abraham, and Levi. The citation of Ps 110.4 in 5.6 announced Christ's priesthood. This section develops that theme. **1–3:** Although the Bible knows of two kinds of priests, Levi and his offspring and *Melchizedek* (Gen 14.17–20), the author now argues for Melchizedek's superiority in three ways: (1) Melchizedek received *tithes* even from the great patriarch *Abraham;* (2) his name declares him a *king* as well as a priest (Melchizedek means "king of righteousness" in Hebrew; *Salem* is a form of "shalom," peace); (3) he was eternal in the past and imperishable in the future, marks of a true deity. **4–8:** The significance of *tithes* (7.2) is argued to show Melchizedek's superiority over levitical priests. While the latter collect *tithes* from their own, Melchizedek took them from a stranger, even the great Abraham. Moreover, he *blessed* the heir of the great promise; but the one who blesses is *superior* to the one blessed. **9–10:** Since the cultural notion of fertility held that all of a man's descendants were present as minuscule potential human beings in his testicles, Levi, a future descendant of Abraham, was present in Abraham, and so Levi could be said to be paying tithes to Melchizedek when Abraham did.

---

11 Now if perfection had been attainable through the levitical priesthood—for the people received the law under this priesthood—what further need would there have been to speak of another priest arising according to the order of Melchizedek, rather than one according to the order of Aaron? [12]For when there is a change in the priesthood, there is necessarily a change in the law as well. [13]Now the one of whom these things are spoken belonged to another tribe, from which no one has ever served at the altar. [14]For it is evident that our Lord was descended from Judah, and in connection with that tribe Moses said nothing about priests. [15] It is even more obvious when another priest arises, resembling Melchizedek, [16]one who has become a priest, not through a legal requirement concerning physical descent,

a Other ancient authorities lack *Even*　　*b* Or *a tenth*
c Gk *brothers*

but through the power of an indestructible life. ¹⁷For it is attested of him,

> "You are a priest forever,
> according to the order of
> Melchizedek."

¹⁸There is, on the one hand, the abrogation of an earlier commandment because it was weak and ineffectual ¹⁹(for the law made nothing perfect); there is, on the other hand, the introduction of a better hope, through which we approach God.

20 This was confirmed with an oath; for others who became priests took their office without an oath, ²¹but this one became a priest with an oath, because of the one who said to him,

> "The Lord has sworn
> and will not change his mind,
> 'You are a priest forever' "—

²²accordingly Jesus has also become the guarantee of a better covenant.

23 Furthermore, the former priests were many in number, because they were prevented by death from continuing in office; ²⁴but he holds his priesthood permanently, because he continues forever. ²⁵Consequently he is able for all time to save[a] those who approach God through him, since he always lives to make intercession for them.

7.11–25. 11–14: Judah versus Levi. Continuing the comparison, the author claims that *perfection* (efficacy and duration) does not come from *levitical priesthood*, thus necessitating another priest. Since priesthood was hereditary, Jesus could not be a *levitical priest* because he is of the tribe of *Judah,* not Levi. But he qualifies to be a priest forever *according to the order of Melchizedek.* **15–25: Melchizedek versus Levi. 15–22:** Jesus the new *priest* does not receive his office by hereditary means, but because of an *indestructible life* (1.10–12), as Ps 110.4 states, "You are a priest *forever.*" The ineffectual levitical priesthood was replaced by a *better* hope, Christ's effectual priesthood. God *confirmed* Jesus' eternal priesthood by an oath. "The Lord has sworn. . . ." **23–25:** *Death* prevents Levites from functioning, whereas Jesus' priestly mediation is permanent because he lives *forever.*

---

26 For it was fitting that we should have such a high priest, holy, blameless, undefiled, separated from sinners, and exalted above the heavens. ²⁷Unlike the other[b] high priests, he has no need to offer sacrifices day after day, first for his own sins, and then for those of the people; this he did once for all when he offered himself. ²⁸For the law appoints as high priests those who are subject to weakness, but the word of the oath, which came later than the law, appoints a Son who has been made perfect forever.

7.26–28: Why Jesus is better. This summary of Jesus' superiority contrasts the Levites' daily sacrifices for sin with the single offering by the *blameless* Jesus that cancels others' sins. Once more priesthood by oath is superior to that established by hereditary laws (7.16–22).

---

8 Now the main point in what we are saying is this: we have such a high priest, one who is seated at the right hand of the throne of the Majesty in the heavens, ²a minister in the sanctuary and the true tent[c] that the Lord, and not any mortal, has set up. ³For every high priest is appointed to offer gifts and sacrifices; hence it is necessary for this priest also to have something to offer. ⁴Now if he were on earth, he would not be a priest at all, since there are priests who offer gifts according to the law. ⁵They offer worship in a sanctuary that is a sketch and shadow of the heavenly one; for Moses, when he was about to erect the tent,[c] was warned, "See that you make everything according to the pattern that was shown you on the mountain." ⁶But Jesus[d] has now obtained a more excellent ministry, and to that degree he is the mediator of a better covenant, which has been enacted through better promises. ⁷For if that first covenant had been faultless, there would have been no need to look for a second one.

8 God[e] finds fault with them when he says:

> "The days are surely coming, says the
> Lord,
> when I will establish a new covenant
> with the house of Israel
> and with the house of Judah;

---

a Or *able to save completely*   *b* Gk lacks *other*
c Or *tabernacle*   *d* Gk *he*   *e* Gk *He*

9 not like the covenant that I made with
      their ancestors,
   on the day when I took them by the
      hand to lead them out of the
      land of Egypt;
for they did not continue in
   my covenant,
   and so I had no concern for them,
      says the Lord.
10 This is the covenant that I will make
      with the house of Israel
   after those days, says the Lord:
   I will put my laws in their minds,
      and write them on their hearts,
   and I will be their God,
      and they shall be my people.
11 And they shall not teach one another
      or say to each other, 'Know the Lord,'
   for they shall all know me,
      from the least of them to the greatest.
12 For I will be merciful toward their
      iniquities,
   and I will remember their sins
      no more."
13 In speaking of "a new covenant," he has
made the first one obsolete. And what is
obsolete and growing old will soon
disappear.

8.1–13. 1–6: Topics to be developed. After summarizing Christ's status and role, the author lists three
themes to be developed: (1) *the true tent* in heaven,
(2) the priestly *sacrifice*, and (3) a *better covenant.**
His exposition begins with the last theme. **7–13: A better covenant.** Jeremiah's remarks on a *new covenant*
(Jer 31.31–34) are cited at great length. Although Jeremiah spoke about a renewed covenant, the author
reads him as predicting a *new* and better one to replace its aged and obsolete predecessor.

9 Now even the first covenant had regulations for worship and an earthly sanctuary. 2 For a tent* was constructed, the first
one, in which were the lampstand, the table,
and the bread of the Presence;* this is called
the Holy Place. 3 Behind the second curtain
was a tent* called the Holy of Holies. 4 In it
stood the golden altar of incense and the ark
of the covenant overlaid on all sides with
gold, in which there were a golden urn holding the manna, and Aaron's rod that budded,

and the tablets of the covenant; 5 above it
were the cherubim of glory overshadowing
the mercy seat.* Of these things we cannot
speak now in detail.

6 Such preparations having been made,
the priests go continually into the first tent*
to carry out their ritual duties; 7 but only the
high priest goes into the second, and he but
once a year, and not without taking the blood
that he offers for himself and for the sins
committed unintentionally by the people.
8 By this the Holy Spirit indicates that the
way into the sanctuary has not yet been disclosed as long as the first tent* is still standing. 9 This is a symbol* of the present time,
during which gifts and sacrifices are offered
that cannot perfect the conscience of the
worshiper, 10 but deal only with food and
drink and various baptisms, regulations for
the body imposed until the time comes to set
things right.

11 But when Christ came as a high priest
of the good things that have come,* then
through the greater and perfect* tent* (not
made with hands, that is, not of this creation), 12 he entered once for all into the Holy
Place, not with the blood of goats and calves,
but with his own blood, thus obtaining eternal redemption. 13 For if the blood of goats
and bulls, with the sprinkling of the ashes of
a heifer, sanctifies those who have been defiled so that their flesh is purified, 14 how
much more will the blood of Christ, who
through the eternal Spirit* offered himself
without blemish to God, purify our* conscience from dead works to worship the living God!

9.1–14. 1–5: The tent. The author distinguished in 8.5
the true "pattern" in heaven and its earthly "sketch";
here he simply catalogs the furnishings of the earthly
temple.* **6–14: Atonement sacrifice versus Christ's
sacrifice. 6–7:** The author turns from covenant* to
atonement sacrifices. He contrasts the daily offering of
ordinary sacrifices in the outer *tent* with the special
offering by the high priest who alone enters the *sec-

a Or tabernacle   b Gk the presentation of the loaves
c Or the place of atonement   d Gk parable
e Other ancient authorities read good things to come
f Gk more perfect   g Other ancient authorities read
Holy Spirit   h Other ancient authorities read your

ond tent once a year. **9–10:** This atonement sacrifice symbolizes the imperfection of the current system. **11–12:** In contrast, Christ's death is interpreted as the perfect atonement: (1) He entered the *perfect tent,* (2) *once for all,* (3) to offer the perfect sacrifice. **13–14:** Again in contrast, Jesus' *Spirit*-aided offering of his own *blood* effects an atonement better than animal sacrifices, which *purify* only *flesh.*

15 For this reason he is the mediator of a new covenant, so that those who are called may receive the promised eternal inheritance, because a death has occurred that redeems them from the transgressions under the first covenant.*a* ¹⁶Where a will*a* is involved, the death of the one who made it must be established. ¹⁷For a will*a* takes effect only at death, since it is not in force as long as the one who made it is alive. ¹⁸Hence not even the first covenant was inaugurated without blood. ¹⁹For when every commandment had been told to all the people by Moses in accordance with the law, he took the blood of calves and goats,*b* with water and scarlet wool and hyssop, and sprinkled both the scroll itself and all the people, ²⁰saying, "This is the blood of the covenant that God has ordained for you." ²¹And in the same way he sprinkled with the blood both the tent*c* and all the vessels used in worship. ²²Indeed, under the law almost everything is purified with blood, and without the shedding of blood there is no forgiveness of sins.

23 Thus it was necessary for the sketches of the heavenly things to be purified with these rites, but the heavenly things themselves need better sacrifices than these. ²⁴For Christ did not enter a sanctuary made by human hands, a mere copy of the true one, but he entered into heaven itself, now to appear in the presence of God on our behalf. ²⁵Nor was it to offer himself again and again, as the high priest enters the Holy Place year after year with blood that is not his own; ²⁶for then he would have had to suffer again and again since the foundation of the world. But as it is, he has appeared once for all at the end of the age to remove sin by the sacrifice of himself. ²⁷And just as it is appointed for mortals to die once, and after that the judgment, ²⁸so Christ, having

been offered once to bear the sins of many, will appear a second time, not to deal with sin, but to save those who are eagerly waiting for him.

9.15–28. 15–22: Play on words: covenant* and will. The same Greek word can be translated either as "will" or "covenant." **15–17:** Abraham's heirs stand to inherit God's *promised* legacy. Legal tradition declares that for a *will* to be valid a *death* must be proven, namely, Christ's. **18–22:** In regard to the second meaning, *covenant, blood* is required for a valid covenant, thus establishing a parallelism: *Will* requires *death* and *covenant* requires *blood.* **23–28: Better above. 23–25:** The argument about heavenly and earthly patterns (8.5) returns. Although animal sacrifices may purify earthly sanctuaries, the heavenly archetype needs better. Jesus, greater than levitical priests, enters God's true presence and offers the superior sacrifice of his blood. **26–28:** Since Christ's death has already *removed sin*, when he comes again, it will be to *save* his own, not to judge them.

10 Since the law has only a shadow of the good things to come and not the true form of these realities, it*d* can never, by the same sacrifices that are continually offered year after year, make perfect those who approach. ²Otherwise, would they not have ceased being offered, since the worshipers, cleansed once for all, would no longer have any consciousness of sin? ³But in these sacrifices there is a reminder of sin year after year. ⁴For it is impossible for the blood of bulls and goats to take away sins. ⁵Consequently, when Christ*e* came into the world, he said,

"Sacrifices and offerings you have not
        desired,
    but a body you have prepared for me;
  6 in burnt offerings and sin offerings
      you have taken no pleasure.
 7 Then I said, 'See, God, I have come to
        do your will, O God'
    (in the scroll of the book*f* it is
        written of me)."

a The Greek word used here means both *covenant* and *will*   *b* Other ancient authorities lack *and goats*
c Or *tabernacle*   *d* Other ancient authorities read *they*
e Gk *he*   *f* Meaning of Gk uncertain

8When he said above, "You have neither desired nor taken pleasure in sacrifices and offerings and burnt offerings and sin offerings" (these are offered according to the law), 9then he added, "See, I have come to do your will." He abolishes the first in order to establish the second. 10And it is by God's will[a] that we have been sanctified through the offering of the body of Jesus Christ once for all.

11 And every priest stands day after day at his service, offering again and again the same sacrifices that can never take away sins. 12But when Christ[b] had offered for all time a single sacrifice for sins, "he sat down at the right hand of God," 13and since then has been waiting "until his enemies would be made a footstool for his feet." 14For by a single offering he has perfected for all time those who are sanctified. 15And the Holy Spirit also testifies to us, for after saying,

16 "This is the covenant that I will make
        with them
    after those days, says the Lord:
    I will put my laws in their hearts,
        and I will write them on their minds,"
17he also adds,
    "I will remember[c] their sins and their
        lawless deeds no more."
18Where there is forgiveness of these, there is no longer any offering for sin.

10.1–18. 1–10: Sacrifice versus obedience. 1–4: Contrasts abound: *Shadows* are contrasted with *realities,* and the *law* concerning sacrifices with *the good things to come.* The annual offering of animals could not remove humankind's *sin.* **5–10:** The author argues from Ps 40.6–8 that God wants not animal sacrifices at all, but rather obedience. So God abolishes the shadowy first covenant* to establish the *second.* Jesus' obedience (5.8) becomes the model for our faithfulness. **11–18: Superior in effectiveness. 11–13:** Continuing the contrast, a levitical priest *stands* when repetitively offering ineffectual sacrifices, but Christ sits after offering once for all an effective sacrifice. Citing Ps 110.1, the author emphasizes Jesus' superiority to levitical priests: He sits at God's right hand and waits to have all *enemies* under his *feet.*

19 Therefore, my friends,[d] since we have confidence to enter the sanctuary by the blood of Jesus, 20by the new and living way that he opened for us through the curtain (that is, through his flesh), 21and since we have a great priest over the house of God, 22let us approach with a true heart in full assurance of faith, with our hearts sprinkled clean from an evil conscience and our bodies washed with pure water. 23Let us hold fast to the confession of our hope without wavering, for he who has promised is faithful. 24And let us consider how to provoke one another to love and good deeds, 25not neglecting to meet together, as is the habit of some, but encouraging one another, and all the more as you see the Day approaching.

26 For if we willfully persist in sin after having received the knowledge of the truth, there no longer remains a sacrifice for sins, 27but a fearful prospect of judgment, and a fury of fire that will consume the adversaries. 28Anyone who has violated the law of Moses dies without mercy "on the testimony of two or three witnesses." 29How much worse punishment do you think will be deserved by those who have spurned the Son of God, profaned the blood of the covenant by which they were sanctified, and outraged the Spirit of grace? 30For we know the one who said, "Vengeance is mine, I will repay." And again, "The Lord will judge his people." 31It is a fearful thing to fall into the hands of the living God.

10.19–31. 19–25: Exhortation.* Summarizing the benefit from Jesus' superiority, the author endorses three traditional virtues: *faith,* which is confidence, *hope* or faithful loyalty, and *love,* which considers the group's needs. **26–31: Warning. 26–27:** Dire warnings follow the exhortation: No remedy for sin remains, only *judgment* (Mk 3.28–30). **28–31:** Another comparison: If earthly justice according to Moses is fearsome (Deut 17.2–6), all the more is God's *vengeance* (Deut 32.35–36). Sin dishonors Jesus (*spurned the Son of God*) and pollutes his sacrifice (*profaned the blood*).

32 But recall those earlier days when, after you had been enlightened, you endured

a Gk by that will   b Gk this one   c Gk on their
minds and I will remember   d Gk Therefore, brothers

a hard struggle with sufferings, ³³sometimes being publicly exposed to abuse and persecution, and sometimes being partners with those so treated. ³⁴For you had compassion for those who were in prison, and you cheerfully accepted the plundering of your possessions, knowing that you yourselves possessed something better and more lasting. ³⁵Do not, therefore, abandon that confidence of yours; it brings a great reward. ³⁶For you need endurance, so that when you have done the will of God, you may receive what was promised. ³⁷For yet

"in a very little while,
    the one who is coming will come and
        will not delay;
³⁸ but my righteous one will live by faith.
    My soul takes no pleasure in anyone
        who shrinks back."

³⁹But we are not among those who shrink back and so are lost, but among those who have faith and so are saved.

10.32–39: Exhortation for faith. 32–35: A lengthy list of previous *sufferings* faithfully endured leads to an exhortation to further fidelity. **36–39:** The importance of *faith* is rooted in Hos 2.3–4. But *faith* has two meanings here: (1) belief in God's promises, and (2) *endurance* or faithfulness. Both meanings inform the exhortation to *faith* in ch. 11.

11 Now faith is the assurance of things hoped for, the conviction of things not seen. ²Indeed, by faith[a] our ancestors received approval. ³By faith we understand that the worlds were prepared by the word of God, so that what is seen was made from things that are not visible.[b]

4 By faith Abel offered to God a more acceptable[c] sacrifice than Cain's. Through this he received approval as righteous, God himself giving approval to his gifts; he died, but through his faith[d] he still speaks. ⁵By faith Enoch was taken so that he did not experience death; and "he was not found, because God had taken him." For it was attested before he was taken away that "he had pleased God." ⁶And without faith it is impossible to please God, for whoever would approach him must believe that he exists and that he rewards those who seek him. ⁷By

faith Noah, warned by God about events as yet unseen, respected the warning and built an ark to save his household; by this he condemned the world and became an heir to the righteousness that is in accordance with faith.

11.1–7. 1–3: Overture to faith. *Faith* may refer either to what is yet to come or to God's word of promise. Fundamentally, *faith* means acceptance of God's *word*. **4–7: First Examples.** (See chart of Heroes at Sirach 44.) Three ancient heroes either died faithfully or escaped death through faithfulness. *Abel*, by offering an *acceptable sacrifice*, was judged *righteous*. *Enoch** overcame death, according to Gen 5.21–24. *Noah*, heeding God's word of warning, escaped destruction.

8 By faith Abraham obeyed when he was called to set out for a place that he was to receive as an inheritance; and he set out, not knowing where he was going. ⁹By faith he stayed for a time in the land he had been promised, as in a foreign land, living in tents, as did Isaac and Jacob, who were heirs with him of the same promise. ¹⁰For he looked forward to the city that has foundations, whose architect and builder is God. ¹¹By faith he received power of procreation, even though he was too old—and Sarah herself was barren—because he considered him faithful who had promised.[e] ¹²Therefore from one person, and this one as good as dead, descendants were born, "as many as the stars of heaven and as the innumerable grains of sand by the seashore."

13 All of these died in faith without having received the promises, but from a distance they saw and greeted them. They confessed that they were strangers and foreigners on the earth, ¹⁴for people who speak in this way make it clear that they are seeking a homeland. ¹⁵If they had been thinking of the land that they had left behind, they would have had opportunity to return. ¹⁶But as it is, they desire a better country, that is, a heavenly one. Therefore God is

a Gk *by this*   *b* Or *was not made out of visible things*
c Gk *greater*   *d* Gk *through it*   *e* Or *By faith Sarah herself, though barren, received power to conceive, even when she was too old, because she considered him faithful who had promised.*

not ashamed to be called their God; indeed, he has prepared a city for them.

17 By faith Abraham, when put to the test, offered up Isaac. He who had received the promises was ready to offer up his only son, [18]of whom he had been told, "It is through Isaac that descendants shall be named for you." [19]He considered the fact that God is able even to raise someone from the dead—and figuratively speaking, he did receive him back. [20]By faith Isaac invoked blessings for the future on Jacob and Esau. [21]By faith Jacob, when dying, blessed each of the sons of Joseph, "bowing in worship over the top of his staff." [22]By faith Joseph, at the end of his life, made mention of the exodus of the Israelites and gave instructions about his burial.[a]

11.8–22. 8–16: God's faithfulness to Abraham. 8–9: This echoes the exhortation* of "entering into my rest" in 4.1–3, 8–11. *Abraham*, believing God's promise, journeyed to an unseen, but promised land. **11–12:** *Believing* God's promise of a son, Abraham believed that life could come from death. God, then, is *faithful* to those who believe his promises. **13–16:** The *faith* of these heroes lies in their trust in God's *promises*, while not seeing their fulfillment. They hoped for a better land than this earthly one, a hope validated by God's gift of a heavenly city. **17–22: Patriarchs' faith. 17–19:** Abraham's *faith* consisted both of obedience in sacrificing Isaac (Gen 22.1–10) and steadfast belief in God's promise of descendants through Isaac. It also explains Abraham's belief that *God is able to raise someone from the dead*, whether this refers to Abraham's sacrificing of Isaac (Gen 22) or to his aged body (Rom 4.17). **20–21:** In *blessing* their sons, Isaac and Jacob manifested *faith* that God would fulfill in them the divine promises. **22:** Joseph predicted the future for his sons, believing in God's faithfulness.

23 By faith Moses was hidden by his parents for three months after his birth, because they saw that the child was beautiful; and they were not afraid of the king's edict.[b] [24]By faith Moses, when he was grown up, refused to be called a son of Pharaoh's daughter, [25]choosing rather to share ill-treatment with the people of God than to enjoy the fleeting pleasures of sin. [26]He considered abuse suffered for the Christ[c] to be

greater wealth than the treasures of Egypt, for he was looking ahead to the reward. [27]By faith he left Egypt, unafraid of the king's anger; for he persevered as though[d] he saw him who is invisible. [28]By faith he kept the Passover and the sprinkling of blood, so that the destroyer of the firstborn would not touch the firstborn of Israel.[e]

29 By faith the people passed through the Red Sea as if it were dry land, but when the Egyptians attempted to do so they were drowned. [30]By faith the walls of Jericho fell after they had been encircled for seven days. [31]By faith Rahab the prostitute did not perish with those who were disobedient,[f] because she had received the spies in peace.

32 And what more should I say? For time would fail me to tell of Gideon, Barak, Samson, Jephthah, of David and Samuel and the prophets— [33]who through faith conquered kingdoms, administered justice, obtained promises, shut the mouths of lions, [34]quenched raging fire, escaped the edge of the sword, won strength out of weakness, became mighty in war, put foreign armies to flight. [35]Women received their dead by resurrection. Others were tortured, refusing to accept release, in order to obtain a better resurrection. [36]Others suffered mocking and flogging, and even chains and imprisonment. [37]They were stoned to death, they were sawn in two,[g] they were killed by the sword; they went about in skins of sheep and goats, destitute, persecuted, tormented— [38]of whom the world was not worthy. They wandered in deserts and mountains, and in caves and holes in the ground.

39 Yet all these, though they were commended for their faith, did not receive what was promised, [40]since God had provided something better so that they would not, apart from us, be made perfect.

11.23–40. 23–28: Moses escapes death. Moses' *faith* is illustrated by escaping death three times: (1) provi-

a Gk *his bones*   b Other ancient authorities add *By faith Moses, when he was grown up, killed the Egyptian, because he observed the humiliation of his people* (Gk *brothers*)   c Or *the Messiah*   d Or *because*   e Gk *would not touch them*   f Or *unbelieving*   g Other ancient authorities add *they were tempted* dential protection at birth, (2) escaping the king's anger, and (3) celebrating the *Passover*★ and escaping the *destroyer* by the lamb's blood. **29–31: Faith in divine protection.** With *faith* in God's protective word, the Israelites at the Red Sea were saved, while the Egyptians perished. In Jericho's collapse, Rahab saw her *faith* validated for sheltering Israelite spies. The faithful God controls both land and sea. **32–40: Faith in the face of death.** The final list of history's faithful ones demonstrates three different meanings of *faith*. The faith in God's promises by warriors, kings, and prophets★ brought victory or escape. Others showed *faith* in God's promise to raise the dead. Finally, in the face of torture and death, still others maintained *faith*, even though they did not experience God's promise.

12 Therefore, since we are surrounded by so great a cloud of witnesses, let us also lay aside every weight and the sin that clings so closely,*a* and let us run with perseverance the race that is set before us, ²looking to Jesus the pioneer and perfecter of our faith, who for the sake of*b* the joy that was set before him endured the cross, disregarding its shame, and has taken his seat at the right hand of the throne of God.

3 Consider him who endured such hostility against himself from sinners,*c* so that you may not grow weary or lose heart. ⁴In your struggle against sin you have not yet resisted to the point of shedding your blood. ⁵And you have forgotten the exhortation that addresses you as children—

"My child, do not regard lightly the
    discipline of the Lord,
  or lose heart when you are punished
    by him;
⁶ for the Lord disciplines those whom he
    loves,
  and chastises every child whom he
    accepts."
⁷Endure trials for the sake of discipline. God is treating you as children; for what child is there whom a parent does not discipline? ⁸If you do not have that discipline in which all children share, then you are illegitimate and not his children. ⁹Moreover, we had human parents to discipline us, and we respected them. Should we not be even more willing to be subject to the Father of spirits and live?

¹⁰For they disciplined us for a short time as seemed best to them, but he disciplines us for our good, in order that we may share his holiness. ¹¹Now, discipline always seems painful rather than pleasant at the time, but later it yields the peaceful fruit of righteousness to those who have been trained by it.

12 Therefore lift your drooping hands and strengthen your weak knees, ¹³and make straight paths for your feet, so that what is lame may not be put out of joint, but rather be healed.

14 Pursue peace with everyone, and the holiness without which no one will see the Lord. ¹⁵See to it that no one fails to obtain the grace of God; that no root of bitterness springs up and causes trouble, and through it many become defiled. ¹⁶See to it that no one becomes like Esau, an immoral and godless person, who sold his birthright for a single meal. ¹⁷You know that later, when he wanted to inherit the blessing, he was rejected, for he found no chance to repent,*d* even though he sought the blessing*e* with tears.

12.1–17. 1–12: Christ's example and new exhortation.★ **1–3:** In addition to the *cloud of witnesses* above, Jesus offers the ideal example. He despised the shame of the cross and was vindicated by God *at the right hand of the throne of God.* Thus he pioneered and perfected our faithfulness in God who raises the dead. **4–11:** The citation of Prov 3.11–12 provides the theme of the exhortation, *discipline*. Discipline by earthly parents is contrasted with that of the heavenly parent. Honor, perfection, and fruitfulness come from God's parental *discipline*. **13–17: Exhortation to advance.** The author issues several commands. As an example of what not to do, he cites *Esau*, who swapped future blessing for immediate satisfaction. As said earlier, there is no repentance for this (6.4–7).

18 You have not come to something*f* that can be touched, a blazing fire, and darkness, and gloom, and a tempest, ¹⁹and the sound

a Other ancient authorities read *sin that easily distracts* *b* Or *who instead of* *c* Other ancient authorities read *such hostility from sinners against themselves* *d* Or *no chance to change his father's mind* *e* Gk *it* *f* Other ancient authorities read *a mountain* of a trumpet, and a voice whose words made the hearers beg that not another word be spoken to them. 20(For they could not endure the order that was given, "If even an animal touches the mountain, it shall be stoned to death." 21Indeed, so terrifying was the sight that Moses said, "I tremble with fear.") 22But you have come to Mount Zion and to the city of the living God, the heavenly Jerusalem, and to innumerable angels in festal gathering, 23and to the assembly*a* of the firstborn who are enrolled in heaven, and to God the judge of all, and to the spirits of the righteous made perfect, 24and to Jesus, the mediator of a new covenant, and to the sprinkled blood that speaks a better word than the blood of Abel.

25 See that you do not refuse the one who is speaking; for if they did not escape when they refused the one who warned them on earth, how much less will we escape if we reject the one who warns from heaven! 26At that time his voice shook the earth; but now he has promised, "Yet once more I will shake not only the earth but also the heaven." 27This phrase, "Yet once more," indicates the removal of what is shaken—that is, created things—so that what cannot be shaken may remain. 28Therefore, since we are receiving a kingdom that cannot be shaken, let us give thanks, by which we offer to God an acceptable worship with reverence and awe; 29for indeed our God is a consuming fire.

12.18–29: A better covenant* and a better city. The exhortation* contrasts two covenants, represented by the old, earthly Sinai and the new, heavenly *Zion.* **18–21:** *Terrifying* events left Moses and the people fearful. Because touching the mountain meant *death* (Ex 19.12–15), access to God was limited. **22–24:** On the heavenly *Zion,* a civic festival is attended by *angels, firstborn, God, spirits of the righteous,* and *Jesus. God* will *judge,* and Jesus will testify to our purity because of his blood. **25–29:** Whereas Israel feared the word at Sinai, Jesus' word both purifies and comforts. The author contrasts those who reject past words of warning and so perish with those who hear a word of warning and act on this exhortation. The word of warning in Hag 2.6 talks of two "shakings," a past and future judgment. Valuing the reward of an ever-

lasting *kingdom,* believers will show great *reverence* to God.

~~~~~~

13 Let mutual love continue. 2Do not neglect to show hospitality to strangers, for by doing that some have entertained angels without knowing it. 3Remember those who are in prison, as though you were in prison with them; those who are being tortured, as though you yourselves were being tortured.*b* 4Let marriage be held in honor by all, and let the marriage bed be kept undefiled; for God will judge fornicators and adulterers. 5Keep your lives free from the love of money, and be content with what you have; for he has said, "I will never leave you or forsake you." 6So we can say with confidence,

"The Lord is my helper;
    I will not be afraid.
What can anyone do to me?"

7 Remember your leaders, those who spoke the word of God to you; consider the outcome of their way of life, and imitate their faith. 8Jesus Christ is the same yesterday and today and forever. 9Do not be carried away by all kinds of strange teachings; for it is well for the heart to be strengthened by grace, not by regulations about food,*c* which have not benefited those who observe them. 10We have an altar from which those who officiate in the tent*d* have no right to eat. 11For the bodies of those animals whose blood is brought into the sanctuary by the high priest as a sacrifice for sin are burned outside the camp. 12Therefore Jesus also suffered outside the city gate in order to sanctify the people by his own blood. 13Let us then go to him outside the camp and bear the abuse he endured. 14For here we have no lasting city, but we are looking for the city that is to come. 15Through him, then, let us continually offer a sacrifice of praise to God, that is, the fruit of lips that confess his name. 16Do not neglect to do good and to share what you have, for such sacrifices are pleasing to God.

17 Obey your leaders and submit to them, for they are keeping watch over your souls

a Or *angels, and to the festal gathering* 23*and assembly*
b Gk *were in the body*   *c* Gk *not by foods*
d Or *tabernacle*

and will give an account. Let them do this with joy and not with sighing—for that would be harmful to you.

13.1–17: Catalog of concluding exhortations.* **1–7:** Virtues such as *love, hospitality* after Abraham's example (Gen 18.1–8), and *honorable marriages,* and vices such as *love of money* are listed. To God, who spoke a word of *faithfulness* (Josh 1.5), we respond with a word of *confidence* (Ps 118.6). And to *leaders,* who *spoke the word of God,* we listen with *faithfulness.* **8:** Faithfulness is best characterized by *Jesus,* who will always remain the same. **9–10:** *Strange teachings* refers to dietary laws (9.10), that urge a purity independent of Jesus. **11–15:** Just as sin offerings are burned *outside the camp* and Christ, our perfect sin offering, died *outside the camp,* so persevering disciples may have to imitate his abuse and social distancing. The new and perfect *city* the audience awaits was described in 12.22–24. **16–17:** Disciples nonetheless offer sacrifice, albeit a *sacrifice of praise* or the sacrifice of doing *good* and sharing, none of which are sin offerings. Such offerings do not require a temple or sacrificial system or priestly clergy.

---

18 Pray for us; we are sure that we have a clear conscience, desiring to act honorably in all things. 19I urge you all the more to do this, so that I may be restored to you very soon.

20 Now may the God of peace, who brought back from the dead our Lord Jesus, the great shepherd of the sheep, by the blood of the eternal covenant, 21make you complete in everything good so that you may do his will, working among us*a* that which is pleasing in his sight, through Jesus Christ, to whom be the glory forever and ever. Amen.

22 I appeal to you, brothers and sisters,*b* bear with my word of exhortation, for I have written to you briefly. 23I want you to know that our brother Timothy has been set free; and if he comes in time, he will be with me when I see you. 24Greet all your leaders and all the saints. Those from Italy send you greetings. 25Grace be with all of you.*c*

13.18–25: Final messages. **18–19:** This is the only glimpse of the author in the document; it resembles similar requests in Paul's authentic letters (Rom 15.30). Sender and addressees are joined in a confederacy of prayer and patronage. **20–21:** This benediction summarizes many aspects of the way God and Christ are described: God raises *the dead* (1.3; 5.5) and Jesus' blood ratifies a *covenant** (10.11–18). **22–25:** The *word of exhortation** refers to both the encouragement to faithfulness and the argument about the surpassing worth of Jesus' sacrifice, blood, and priesthood. The fiction that Paul is the author extends to the news about Timothy's release and the *greetings* from *Italy,* the traditional place of Paul's final imprisonment.

---

a Other ancient authorities read *you*   *b* Gk *brothers*
c Other ancient authorities add *Amen*

THE LETTER OF JAMES

Introduction

The author claims to be "James, servant of the Lord" and sends this generic letter to "the twelve tribes in the Dispersion." Two issues need to be addressed. Despite tradition, scholars do not think that the author is the brother of Jesus (Mk 6.3) nor the overseer of the Jerusalem church (Acts 12.17; Gal 1.19). He writes fine Greek and uses rhetoric★ impressively; he is well educated in Judean and biblical traditions and can translate Semitic expressions into plausible Greek. This type of literacy seems most unlikely for a Galilean peasant. He addresses the audience as "the twelve tribes in the Dispersion," an identity that embraces the totality of the Christian church, just as Israel consisted of twelve tribes; the Christian Scriptures also consider the community as the new twelve tribes, who are governed by the twelve apostles★ (Mt 19.28; Lk 22.30). No other letter claims such a wide audience; 1 Peter only spoke of the exiles dispersed in Asia Minor (1.1). Yet, although we cannot know for sure the identity of the author and the specific audience addressed, the document contains many items that resemble typical pieces of moral exhortation★ in Greek writings.

READING GUIDE

Notice of sender, addressees, and greetings (1.1) are the only elements of typical New Testament letters here. The author reflects the world of the Greco-Roman philosophical tradition which composed both "moral epistles" (see Seneca) and "exhortatory letters" (see 1 Thess). Such letters, while addressed to a specific person, discussed various virtues and encouraged their performance. In addition to this general letter type, James is also characterized by small units loosely stitched together, a process typical of biblical wisdom literature.★ Nevertheless, readers sense that James enjoys a unity in other formal ways, such as the use of diatribal★ style that denounces opponents and sinners (2.1–13, 14–26; 3.1–13), "commonplaces," or adages and proverbial statements (3.1–5, 13–18; 4.10), and binary terms and images. The shape of the argument goes as follows.

1. Letter opening: author and addresses (1.1–2)
2. First exhortation
   A. The value of trials and testing (1.3–16)
   B. Miscellany of virtues (1.17–27)
   C. Partiality condemned (2.1–13)
   D. Wholeness of faith and works urged (2.14–26)
3. Second exhortation
   A. Holiness and control of the tongue (3.1–12)
   B. Factionalism and envy condemned (3.13–18)
   C. Wrong speech: speaking out of one's cravings (4.1–10)
   D. Wrong speech: speaking against another (4.11–12)
   E. Wrong speech: boasting in one's own power (4.13–17)
4. Third exhortation
   A. Folly of wealth (5.1–6)
   B. Patience urged (5.7–12)

5. Fourth exhortation
   A. Prayer and healing for group members (5.13–18)
   B. Conversion of erring members (5.19–20)

Cultural notions of "purity" help us to understand James. Purity and perfection mean "whole-ness," not division or mixture. Those who doubt when praying are "doubleminded" (1.6–8), thus unclean. Perfect religion means both justice to neighbor and maintaining oneself unstained (1.27). Wholeness means that "faith" requires "deeds" to be authentic (2.14–26). Failure to keep but one commandment corrupts the observance of all the rest (2.8–13). Purity refers also to well-guarded body orifices which prevent unclean things from entering and leaving the body. Hence control of the mouth looms large in James's sense of perfection (3.1–12; 4.11–12; 5.12).

1 James, a servant[a] of God and of the Lord Jesus Christ,
   To the twelve tribes in the Dispersion: Greetings.

2 My brothers and sisters,[b] whenever you face trials of any kind, consider it nothing but joy, 3because you know that the testing of your faith produces endurance; 4and let endurance have its full effect, so that you may be mature and complete, lacking in nothing.

5 If any of you is lacking in wisdom, ask God, who gives to all generously and un-grudgingly, and it will be given you. 6But ask in faith, never doubting, for the one who doubts is like a wave of the sea, driven and tossed by the wind; 7, 8for the doubter, being double-minded and unstable in every way, must not expect to receive anything from the Lord.

9 Let the believer[c] who is lowly boast in being raised up, 10and the rich in being brought low, because the rich will disappear like a flower in the field. 11For the sun rises with its scorching heat and withers the field; its flower falls, and its beauty perishes. It is the same way with the rich; in the midst of a busy life, they will wither away.

12 Blessed is anyone who endures temp-tation. Such a one has stood the test and will receive the crown of life that the Lord[d] has promised to those who love him. 13No one, when tempted, should say, "I am being tempted by God"; for God cannot be tempted by evil and he himself tempts no one. 14But one is tempted by one's own de-sire, being lured and enticed by it; 15then, when that desire has conceived, it gives birth to sin, and that sin, when it is fully grown, gives birth to death. 16Do not be deceived, my beloved.[e]

17 Every generous act of giving, with every perfect gift, is from above, coming down from the Father of lights, with whom there is no variation or shadow due to change.[f] 18In fulfillment of his own purpose he gave us birth by the word of truth, so that we would become a kind of first fruits of his creatures.

1.1–18. 1–8: Faith and faithfulness. James announces one of the letter's main themes, faith or faithfulness. 3–4: Faithfulness or endurance in trials leads to ma-turity; thus adult faith is pure and whole: complete, lacking in nothing. 5–7: Next, faith means petitioning God with wholeness of mind. Jewish purity concerns affirm what is whole, but shun what is of two kinds (doubt and faith; see Lev 19.19; Deut 22.9–11). This theme will be developed in 5.13–18. 9–11: Rise of poor, fall of rich. James repeats the tradition that the rich will fail and the lowly rise (Lk 1.51–52; 1 Cor 1.18–29). He likens the fate of the rich to that of desert flow-ers which quickly wither, thus echoing Jesus' parable* (Mk 4.5–6; 1 Pet 1.24–25). 12–18: Temptation and benefaction. 12: James honors with a victor's crown those who faithfully endure trials (2 Tim 4.8). 13–15: Whence come temptations? Not from God, but from human passions; the human life cycle (conception, birth, fully grown) demonstrates how even a small pol-

a Gk slave   b Gk brothers   c Gk brother
d Gk he; other ancient authorities read God   e Gk my
beloved brothers   f Other ancient authorities read
variation due to a shadow of turning

lution grows into total depravity. **17:** Again God's person and gifts are pure: with God there is no *variation,* and every *perfect* benefaction descends from God. **18:** *God,* who does not tempt, is our best benefactor, whose gift of *birth* comes through the preaching of the gospel. This is contrasted to the *birth* of evil in 1.15.

19 You must understand this, my beloved:[a] let everyone be quick to listen, slow to speak, slow to anger; ²⁰for your anger does not produce God's righteousness. ²¹Therefore rid yourselves of all sordidness and rank growth of wickedness, and welcome with meekness the implanted word that has the power to save your souls.

22 But be doers of the word, and not merely hearers who deceive themselves. ²³For if any are hearers of the word and not doers, they are like those who look at themselves[b] in a mirror; ²⁴for they look at themselves and, on going away, immediately forget what they were like. ²⁵But those who look into the perfect law, the law of liberty, and persevere, being not hearers who forget but doers who act—they will be blessed in their doing.

26 If any think they are religious, and do not bridle their tongues but deceive their hearts, their religion is worthless. ²⁷Religion that is pure and undefiled before God, the Father, is this: to care for orphans and widows in their distress, and to keep oneself unstained by the world.

1.19–27. 19–21: Ears and mouths. James introduces a topic that will receive detailed treatment in 3.5–12. Since holiness and *anger* cannot both abide in a pure heart, believers must uproot the weeds to make room for the *word* of God. **22–27: Ears, eyes, hands, mouth.** Continuing the body metaphor,* James encourages bodily wholeness, a basic Jewish purity concept. **22–23:** Wholeness requires ears that hear God's *word* to connect with hands acting on it. **25:** God's *law* does not constrain us, but is a *perfect* guide bringing *liberty,* not slavery to passion. **26–27:** James contrasts good and bad *religion* in terms of holiness. An uncontrolled tongue corrupts the whole person, but hands that care for the needy indicate *pure and undefiled* faith. True believers, moreover, keep themselves pure, *unstained by the world.*

2 My brothers and sisters,[c] do you with your acts of favoritism really believe in our glorious Lord Jesus Christ?[d] ²For if a person with gold rings and in fine clothes comes into your assembly, and if a poor person in dirty clothes also comes in, ³and if you take notice of the one wearing the fine clothes and say, "Have a seat here, please," while to the one who is poor you say, "Stand there," or, "Sit at my feet,"[e] ⁴have you not made distinctions among yourselves, and become judges with evil thoughts? ⁵Listen, my beloved brothers and sisters.[f] Has not God chosen the poor in the world to be rich in faith and to be heirs of the kingdom that he has promised to those who love him? ⁶But you have dishonored the poor. Is it not the rich who oppress you? Is it not they who drag you into court? ⁷Is it not they who blaspheme the excellent name that was invoked over you?

8 You do well if you really fulfill the royal law according to the scripture, "You shall love your neighbor as yourself." ⁹But if you show partiality, you commit sin and are convicted by the law as transgressors. ¹⁰For whoever keeps the whole law but fails in one point has become accountable for all of it. ¹¹For the one who said, "You shall not commit adultery," also said, "You shall not murder." Now if you do not commit adultery but if you murder, you have become a transgressor of the law. ¹²So speak and so act as those who are to be judged by the law of liberty. ¹³For judgment will be without mercy to anyone who has shown no mercy; mercy triumphs over judgment.

2.1–13. 1–7: Rich and poor again. Developing 1.9–11, James contrasts the group's reception of *poor* and *rich.* **1–4:** Favoritism to the wealthy cancels faith in the risen Lord, because it ignores the fact that Jesus, humbled and brought low, was exalted by God. **5:** *God* obviously does not evaluate as we do, for God chooses *the poor* to be rich (1 Cor 1.26–30). **6–7:** In James's world of opposites, the rich are the oppressors and the

a Gk *my beloved brothers*　　*b* Gk *at the face of his birth*
c Gk *My brothers*　　*d* Or *hold the faith of our glorious*
Lord Jesus Christ without acts of favoritism　　*e* Gk *Sit*
under my footstool　　*f* Gk *brothers*

poor their victims; by siding with the rich, they dishonor members of the group and thus *blaspheme* God's holy name. **8–13: Wholeness as purity. 8–9:** James presents two laws: the general *law* of love (Mk 12.28–33) and some specific commandments. *Love* means impartiality (2.1–8; Rom 10.12–13; Acts 10.34) and mercy. **10–11:** Twice he emphasizes the seriousness of failing to keep even one commandment: Perfection means being *accountable for all.* He interprets this in terms of Jewish purity: Failure is like pollution, corrupting what is good. **12–13:** Fearing lawlessness, he emphasizes God's *law of liberty.*

14 What good is it, my brothers and sisters,*ª* if you say you have faith but do not have works? Can faith save you? 15 If a brother or sister is naked and lacks daily food, 16 and one of you says to them, "Go in peace; keep warm and eat your fill," and yet you do not supply their bodily needs, what is the good of that? 17 So faith by itself, if it has no works, is dead.

18 But someone will say, "You have faith and I have works." Show me your faith apart from your works, and I by my works will show you my faith. 19 You believe that God is one; you do well. Even the demons believe—and shudder. 20 Do you want to be shown, you senseless person, that faith apart from works is barren? 21 Was not our ancestor Abraham justified by works when he offered his son Isaac on the altar? 22 You see that faith was active along with his works, and faith was brought to completion by the works. 23 Thus the scripture was fulfilled that says, "Abraham believed God, and it was reckoned to him as righteousness," and he was called the friend of God. 24 You see that a person is justified by works and not by faith alone. 25 Likewise, was not Rahab the prostitute also justified by works when she welcomed the messengers and sent them out by another road? 26 For just as the body without the spirit is dead, so faith without works is also dead.

2.14–26: Perfection of active faith. James performs here like a teacher. anticipating objections and answering them. **14–17:** Some object that *faith* alone counts; James counters that *faith* which does not feed the hungry and clothe the naked is *dead* or unclean.

Perfection, then, means wholeness: both faith and works. **18–20:** To those who boast of their *works,* James counters that *faith* can be manifested only by *works,* but without *works* it is useless. Mere understanding of God's supremacy counts for nothing, unless faithful obedience follows. **21–26:** As proof, James cites from the Bible male and female examples of perfect faith. *Abraham,* a righteous believer (Gen 15.6), showed perfect faithfulness by offering Isaac as a sacrifice (Gen 22); obedient actions brought *faith* to *completion. Rahab,* who extended hospitality to Israelite spies (Josh 2.1–12), is considered holy in spite of being a prostitute. In conclusion, James labels the position of *faith without works* as the ultimate pollution, death.

3 Not many of you should become teachers, my brothers and sisters,*ª* for you know that we who teach will be judged with greater strictness. 2 For all of us make many mistakes. Anyone who makes no mistakes in speaking is perfect, able to keep the whole body in check with a bridle. 3 If we put bits into the mouths of horses to make them obey us, we guide their whole bodies. 4 Or look at ships: though they are so large that it takes strong winds to drive them, yet they are guided by a very small rudder wherever the will of the pilot directs. 5 So also the tongue is a small member, yet it boasts of great exploits.

How great a forest is set ablaze by a small fire! 6 And the tongue is a fire. The tongue is placed among our members as a world of iniquity; it stains the whole body, sets on fire the cycle of nature,*ᵇ* and is itself set on fire by hell.*ᶜ* 7 For every species of beast and bird, of reptile and sea creature, can be tamed and has been tamed by the human species, 8 but no one can tame the tongue—a restless evil, full of deadly poison. 9 With it we bless the Lord and Father, and with it we curse those who are made in the likeness of God. 10 From the same mouth come blessing and cursing. My brothers and sisters,*ᵈ* this ought not to be so. 11 Does a spring pour forth from the same opening both fresh and brackish water? 12 Can a fig tree, my brothers

a Gk *brothers*   *b* Or *wheel of birth*   *c* Gk Gehenna
d Gk My *brothers*

and sisters,*a* yield olives, or a grapevine figs? No more can salt water yield fresh.

3.1–12: Unbridled tongue equals pollution. Echoing 1.19, James again urges control of bodily orifices. **2–4:** Perfection comes from making *no mistakes* with the tongue. He refers here to strong control of the mouth, noting how a mere *bridle* guides the horse, as a *rudder* does a ship. **5–6:** The destruction of a large forest by a tiny *fire* illustrates the power of an uncontrolled tongue. In the world of purity concerns, something so small as a tongue can *stain the whole body,* the way yeast was thought to corrupt flour. **7–8:** He likens the tongue to the one animal never tamed, the snake. Both contain poison in their mouths. **9–12:** Since holiness is wholeness, the mouth cannot speak both *blessing* and *cursing;* one cannot *bless* God and *curse* others. Wholeness applies to natural examples. Springs cannot yield both pure and brackish water; *fig trees* produce figs, not olives, and *grapevines* yield grapes, not figs.

13 Who is wise and understanding among you? Show by your good life that your works are done with gentleness born of wisdom. ¹⁴But if you have bitter envy and selfish ambition in your hearts, do not be boastful and false to the truth. ¹⁵Such wisdom does not come down from above, but is earthly, unspiritual, devilish. ¹⁶For where there is envy and selfish ambition, there will also be disorder and wickedness of every kind. ¹⁷But the wisdom from above is first pure, then peaceable, gentle, willing to yield, full of mercy and good fruits, without a trace of partiality or hypocrisy. ¹⁸And a harvest of righteousness is sown in peace for*b* those who make peace.

3.13–18: Evil envy. Continuing his juxtaposition of evil and good, James contrasts two types of wisdom: True *wisdom from above* is both practical and *pure;* it yields meekness, *peace,* and *mercy,* which are manifested in the practice of a good life. In contrast, false wisdom is *earthly, unspiritual,* and *devilish;* it manifests itself in highly aggressive behavior, such as *envy, ambition,* and *disorder.* One is reminded of the description of lowliness in 2.5.

4 Those conflicts and disputes among you, where do they come from? Do they not come from your cravings that are at war

within you? ²You want something and do not have it; so you commit murder. And you covet*c* something and cannot obtain it; so you engage in disputes and conflicts. You do not have, because you do not ask. ³You ask and do not receive, because you ask wrongly, in order to spend what you get on your pleasures. ⁴Adulterers! Do you not know that friendship with the world is enmity with God? Therefore whoever wishes to be a friend of the world becomes an enemy of God. ⁵Or do you suppose that it is for nothing that the scripture says, "God*d* yearns jealously for the spirit that he has made to dwell in us"? ⁶But he gives all the more grace; therefore it says,

"God opposes the proud,
    but gives grace to the humble."

⁷Submit yourselves therefore to God. Resist the devil, and he will flee from you. ⁸Draw near to God, and he will draw near to you. Cleanse your hands, you sinners, and purify your hearts, you double-minded. ⁹Lament and mourn and weep. Let your laughter be turned into mourning and your joy into dejection. ¹⁰Humble yourselves before the Lord, and he will exalt you.

4.1–10: Friendship with the world; hatred of God. **1–3:** In question-and-answer format, James describes the genesis of evil. *Conflicts* that spring from envy (3.14, 16) lead either to *murder* or covetousness. **4:** Using contrasts, he juxtaposes friendship with enmity, humility with pride, and God with the devil. Friends of the world are God's enemies, and God's friendship means enmity with the world. **5–6:** God's jealousy refers to God's desire to protect what is God's; it is the opposite of the "envy" in 3.16, which seeks to hurt another. Prov 3.34 proves that God resists the *proud* and enriches the *humble,* a theme found frequently in James. **7–8:** Using spatial metaphors,* James urges his addressees to flee from the devil and *draw near to God.* The path to purity means cleansing one's hands and purifying one's heart, being wholly in God's service. Impurity lies in being *double-minded,* or mixing contradictory things. **9–10:** A return to the theme of humility (v. 6), now with a strong call to repentance.

a Gk *my brothers*   *b* Or *by*   *c* Or *you murder and you covet*   *d* Gk *He*

11 Do not speak evil against one another, brothers and sisters.[a] Whoever speaks evil against another or judges another, speaks evil against the law and judges the law; but if you judge the law, you are not a doer of the law but a judge. 12There is one lawgiver and judge who is able to save and to destroy. So who, then, are you to judge your neighbor?

4.11–12: Evil speech again. Continuing 1.19 and 3.1–12, James resumes his censure of internal division (3.14–18; 4.1–2). Again, James focuses on wrong speech: *speak evil against one another* and *speak evil against the law and the judges*. Such people lack wholeness, judging the law but not doing it. This concludes with a reference to God, who both gave the law and will be its judge; see 2.8–13.

13 Come now, you who say, "Today or tomorrow we will go to such and such a town and spend a year there, doing business and making money." 14Yet you do not even know what tomorrow will bring. What is your life? For you are a mist that appears for a little while and then vanishes. 15Instead you ought to say, "If the Lord wishes, we will live and do this or that." 16As it is, you boast in your arrogance; all such boasting is evil. 17Anyone, then, who knows the right thing to do and fails to do it, commits sin.

5 Come now, you rich people, weep and wail for the miseries that are coming to you. 2Your riches have rotted, and your clothes are moth-eaten. 3Your gold and silver have rusted, and their rust will be evidence against you, and it will eat your flesh like fire. You have laid up treasure[b] for the last days. 4Listen! The wages of the laborers who mowed your fields, which you kept back by fraud, cry out, and the cries of the harvesters have reached the ears of the Lord of hosts. 5You have lived on the earth in luxury and in pleasure; you have fattened your hearts in a day of slaughter. 6You have condemned and murdered the righteous one, who does not resist you.

4.13–5.6: Pride of the rich. The criticism of the *rich* in 1.10–11 and 2.1–4 returns. **4.13–15:** Evil speech expresses arrogance focused on getting rich. In con-

trast, virtuous speech entrusts one's life and prosperity to God. **16–17:** *Boasting*, another form of evil speech, expresses pride. In a repeat of "faith and works" (2.14–26), wholeness is lost when someone *knows the right thing to do*, but *fails to do it*. **5.1–4:** Continuing his censure of the rich, James firsts devalues clothing and jewelry as corruptible (Mt 6.19–21). Then, echoing the popular saying that the wealthy are all thieves, he notes that they withhold *wages* from laborers. **5–6:** Finally, the fruits of injustice simply make the wealthy fat for judgment's *slaughter*, James's next topic.

7 Be patient, therefore, beloved,[a] until the coming of the Lord. The farmer waits for the precious crop from the earth, being patient with it until it receives the early and the late rains. 8You also must be patient. Strengthen your hearts, for the coming of the Lord is near.[c] 9Beloved,[d] do not grumble against one another, so that you may not be judged. See, the Judge is standing at the doors! 10As an example of suffering and patience, beloved,[a] take the prophets who spoke in the name of the Lord. 11Indeed we call blessed those who showed endurance. You have heard of the endurance of Job, and you have seen the purpose of the Lord, how the Lord is compassionate and merciful.

5.7–11: Patience unto judgment. The exhortation* to patience comes in two parts: vv. 7–8 and 10–11. Patience, moreover, awaits the great judgment, both its *coming* (vv. 7–8) and the appearance of the great *Judge*. **7:** James reflects agricultural patterns in the Middle East with the winter and the spring *rains*. **9:** The warning against judgments connects with similar remarks in 4.11–12 and echoes Mt 7.1–5. In Rev 3.20 Jesus the Judge *stands at the door*, although the *Judge* here is more likely God. **10–11:** Like the examples in 2.21–26, the prophets* exemplify *endurance* and faithfulness in difficult times. The premier example is *Job*. This is the only mention of Job in the New Testament.

12 Above all, my beloved,[a] do not swear, either by heaven or by earth or by any other oath, but let your "Yes" be yes and your "No"

---

a Gk brothers   b Or will eat your flesh, since you have stored up fire   c Or is at hand   d Gk Brothers be no, so that you may not fall under condemnation.

13 Are any among you suffering? They should pray. Are any cheerful? They should sing songs of praise. 14Are any among you sick? They should call for the elders of the church and have them pray over them, anointing them with oil in the name of the Lord. 15The prayer of faith will save the sick, and the Lord will raise them up; and anyone who has committed sins will be forgiven. 16Therefore confess your sins to one another, and pray for one another, so that you may be healed. The prayer of the righteous is powerful and effective. 17Elijah was a human being like us, and he prayed fervently that it might not rain, and for three years and six months it did not rain on the earth. 18Then he prayed again, and the heaven gave rain and the earth yielded its harvest.

19 My brothers and sisters,*a* if anyone among you wanders from the truth and is brought back by another, 20you should know that whoever brings back a sinner from wandering will save the sinner's*b* soul from death and will cover a multitude of sins.

5.12–20. 12–18: More on speech. 12: This simplification of oaths resembles Jesus' curtailment of them (Mt 5.34–37; 2 Cor 1.19–20). **13–14:** While some speech is controlled, other speech is urged at all times, such as prayer and *praise.* Prayer for the sick entails *anointing** by *elders.* **15–16:** The author may understand illness here as caused by sinfulness, because he encourages confession *of sins* and mutual *prayer* for healing. **16–18:** *Elijah* illustrates the claim about the *effective prayer of the righteous.* His first prayer stopped all rain (1 Kings 17.1), whereas his second prayer started it again (1 Kings 18.1). **19–20: Saving others.** In a world of social and geographical immobility, wandering suggested deviance. But good shepherding of the lost yields great rewards for both the lost sheep and the shepherd.

a Gk My brothers   *b Gk his*

THE FIRST LETTER OF PETER

Introduction

The author presents himself as the apostle* whom Jesus commissioned, "Peter," thus establishing his authority to speak (Mt 16.16–19; John 21.15–19). The addressees reside in no particular cities, as is the case with Paul's letters; they live throughout ancient Asia Minor, the region we now call Turkey. If the letter was composed at the outbreak in Rome of anti-Christian hatred associated with Nero, then it is possible that the historical "Peter" might be dictating this document in Rome to his secretary Sylvanus (5.12). But outside of Rome, there was no official persecution of Christians until much later. Nevertheless, the author seems to be speaking as though he were a high-ranking person in the church of Rome, which is called "Babylon" in 5.13. Current scholarship, however, thinks that the author writes on the occasion of the persecution in the provinces, which began under the emperor Trajan (97–117) and for which we have evidence in the letters of Pliny, the Roman governor of Asia Minor (*Letters* 10.96). As is the case with 2 Peter, Jude, and James, a later writer writes in the name, spirit, and teaching of an earlier authority. The addressees, moreover, are often called "exiles," indicating that the majority of them are peoples forced to leave their own lands and so lose any citizenship or benefit from being a native or local inhabitant. The author often refers to their "suffering," most probably meaning the social and economic hostility against Christians who could no longer support local deities or participate in civic festivals because of their Christian beliefs.

READING GUIDE

Three formal aspects, when noted, greatly aid in reading this document. First, Peter embodies the typical structure of ancient letters: opening (1.1–2), thanksgiving (1.3–9), body (1.10–5.11), and closing (5.12–14). Its epistolary type is that of a letter of exhortation.* Second, the body of the letter contains very interesting material. Some describe the document's contents as a baptismal* liturgy,* emphasizing new birth (1.3; 2.2), cleansing (1.22), and baptism (3.19–21). Others consider it as the script for a Christian Passover* because it emphasizes Christ's death and resurrection. But "exhortation" seems the best genre,* which stresses Christians' radical break with their past and their constancy in present troubles. Third, the letter contains an extended catalog of "household duties" stressing rights and obligations: Certain people endowed with authority have a right to lead and others, especially those of socially inferior positions, have a duty to obey. All should obey secular authority (2.13–17); slaves, their masters (2.18–25), and wives, their husbands (3.1–7). The duties of elders and young men finish the catalog (5.1–5). The letter is also structured around the pastoral meaning of the basic confession about Jesus, belief in his death, resurrection, and judgment. Death: All imitate Christ in their sufferings in innocence and humility (2.18–25; 3.15–18). Resurrection: They must live worthy of rising with him (1.3–5; 3.18–22). Judgment: If faithful, they will rejoice at the Day of Judgment (1.5, 17; 4.4–6, 13). The argument of the letter goes as follows.

1. Letter opening
   A. Author, addressees, thanksgiving (1.1–9)
   B. Fragility of the great inheritance: faithfulness urged (1.10–25)

2. Christ: model of rejection and exaltation (2.1–10)
3. Main exhortation: moral code of duties
   A. Duties to emperor and governors (2.11–17)
   B. Duties of slaves to masters (2.18–25)
   C. Duties of wives to husbands and husbands to wives (3.1–7)
   D. Duties of all group members (3.8–12)
   E. Duties of elders (5.1–5)
4. Christ: model of righteous suffering and exaltation (3.13–22)
5. Living in the end time
   A. Holiness (4.1–6)
   B. Mutual love and hospitality (4.7–11)
   C. Courage in the face of coming suffering (4.12–19)
6. Letter closing: final exhortation, note from secretary, and greetings (5.6–14)

1 Peter, an apostle of Jesus Christ,
To the exiles of the Dispersion in Pontus, Galatia, Cappadocia, Asia, and Bithynia, ²who have been chosen and destined by God the Father and sanctified by the Spirit to be obedient to Jesus Christ and to be sprinkled with his blood:

May grace and peace be yours in abundance.

3 Blessed be the God and Father of our Lord Jesus Christ! By his great mercy he has given us a new birth into a living hope through the resurrection of Jesus Christ from the dead, ⁴and into an inheritance that is imperishable, undefiled, and unfading, kept in heaven for you, ⁵who are being protected by the power of God through faith for a salvation ready to be revealed in the last time. ⁶In this you rejoice,ᵃ even if now for a little while you have had to suffer various trials, ⁷so that the genuineness of your faith—being more precious than gold that, though perishable, is tested by fire—may be found to result in praise and glory and honor when Jesus Christ is revealed. ⁸Although you have not seenᵇ him, you love him; and even though you do not see him now, you believe in him and rejoice with an indescribable and glorious joy, ⁹for you are receiving the outcome of your faith, the salvation of your souls.

1.1–9. 1–2: Letter opening. 1: Peter addresses Christians in Asia Minor, acknowledging their civil status as

exiles. 2: God their patron purifies them with the *blood* of Jesus, thus conferring worth on a valueless people. Patrons are high-ranking persons with great resources who enter into formal agreement with lower-ranking suppliants or clients; patrons bestow protection, food, and the like, while clients maintain strong loyalty to their patrons and give them praise and honor. Thus the Christian God bestows lavish divine gifts on God's clients, the Christian communities, but expects from them respect, exclusive allegiance, and praise. **3–9: Thanksgiving.** Most Christian letters begin with a thanksgiving; this one is Semitic in form (*Blessed be the God*; see 2 Cor 1.3–7). It introduces themes developed later (*new birth, inheritance,* suffering). **3–5:** Peter rehearses God's benefaction to these exiles, especially the promise of resurrection. **6–7:** Loyalty from God's clients in difficult circumstances brings *praise, glory, and honor* from their patron on judgment day.

10 Concerning this salvation, the prophets who prophesied of the grace that was to be yours made careful search and inquiry, ¹¹inquiring about the person or time that the Spirit of Christ within them indicated when it testified in advance to the sufferings destined for Christ and the subsequent glory. ¹²It was revealed to them that they were serving not themselves but you, in regard to the things that have now been announced to you through those who brought you good news by the Holy Spirit sent from heaven— things into which angels long to look!

a Or *Rejoice in this*   *b* Other ancient authorities read *known*

13 Therefore prepare your minds for action;[a] discipline yourselves; set all your hope on the grace that Jesus Christ will bring you when he is revealed. ¹⁴Like obedient children, do not be conformed to the desires that you formerly had in ignorance. ¹⁵Instead, as he who called you is holy, be holy yourselves in all your conduct; ¹⁶for it is written, "You shall be holy, for I am holy."

17 If you invoke as Father the one who judges all people impartially according to their deeds, live in reverent fear during the time of your exile. ¹⁸You know that you were ransomed from the futile ways inherited from your ancestors, not with perishable things like silver or gold, ¹⁹but with the precious blood of Christ, like that of a lamb without defect or blemish. ²⁰He was destined before the foundation of the world, but was revealed at the end of the ages for your sake. ²¹Through him you have come to trust in God, who raised him from the dead and gave him glory, so that your faith and hope are set on God.

1.10–21. 10–16: Good theology means good morals. Topics from the thanksgiving are developed: inheritance and suffering leading to glory. **10–11:** Prophets* confirm that suffering leads to future glory, a pattern applied to Jesus (2.22; Isa 53) and his disciples. **13–14:** Thus they should act like obedient children, avoiding desires and pursuing purity. **15–16:** Called by the holy God, they too must be holy, spotless or blameless (Lev 11.44–45). **17–21: Recalling conversion. 17:** Although blessed, they still face God's impartial judgment. **18–21:** Jesus' sacrificial death ransomed Christians; thus God works in them the process of death leading to glory.

22 Now that you have purified your souls by your obedience to the truth[b] so that you have genuine mutual love, love one another deeply[c] from the heart.[d] ²³You have been born anew, not of perishable but of imperishable seed, through the living and enduring word of God.[e] ²⁴For

"All flesh is like grass
    and all its glory like the flower
        of grass.
The grass withers,
    and the flower falls,

²⁵ but the word of the Lord endures
        forever."
That word is the good news that was announced to you.

2 Rid yourselves, therefore, of all malice, and all guile, insincerity, envy, and all slander. ²Like newborn infants, long for the pure, spiritual milk, so that by it you may grow into salvation— ³if indeed you have tasted that the Lord is good.

1.22–2.3: New birth, new behavior. Conversion to the "holy" God demands a holy life. **22–23:** The new birth (1.3) functions as part of the exhortation* to holy living. **23–25:** In contrast to a mortal world where things die (All flesh is like grass), in God's immortal world, the word of divine promises endures forever (vv. 10–11, 21). **2.1–2:** The addressees' new birth means death to previous sin, pursuit of spiritual milk which nourishes for endurance, and wisdom for valuing this noble state.

4 Come to him, a living stone, though rejected by mortals yet chosen and precious in God's sight, and ⁵like living stones, let yourselves be built[f] into a spiritual house, to be a holy priesthood, to offer spiritual sacrifices acceptable to God through Jesus Christ. ⁶For it stands in scripture:

"See, I am laying in Zion a stone,
    a cornerstone chosen and precious;
    and whoever believes in him[g] will not
        be put to shame."

⁷To you then who believe, he is precious; but for those who do not believe,

"The stone that the builders rejected
    has become the very head of
        the corner,"

⁸and

"A stone that makes them stumble,
    and a rock that makes them fall."

They stumble because they disobey the word, as they were destined to do.

9 But you are a chosen race, a royal priesthood, a holy nation, God's own people,[h] in

a Gk gird up the loins of your mind   b Other ancient
authorities add through the Spirit   c Or constantly
d Other ancient authorities read a pure heart
e Or through the word of the living and enduring God
f Or you yourselves are being built   g Or it
h Gk a people for his possession

order that you may proclaim the mighty acts of him who called you out of darkness into his marvelous light.

10 Once you were not a people,
     but now you are God's people;
once you had not received mercy,
     but now you have received mercy.

2.4–10: Holy temple in Christ. Suffering challenges belief in God's providence; Jesus' death, moreover, was shameful (Heb 12.2). Peter reinterprets Jesus' death according to Scripture and invites the addressees to reinterpret their own ambiguous situation. **4–8:** Despite death, Jesus is a *living stone;* although rejected, he is exalted. Thus he serves as *cornerstone* (Isa 28.16) and *head of the corner* (Ps 118.22) of an imperishable new temple.* Through crisis and deliverance, believers become like Christ, namely, *living stones* of a *spiritual house* and a *holy priesthood* (2.5, 9). **9–10:** They enjoy high status; once *not a people,* they are God's *chosen race* and God's *own people;* dishonored here, they *will not be put to shame* (v. 6) in God's kingdom.

11 Beloved, I urge you as aliens and exiles to abstain from the desires of the flesh that wage war against the soul. 12Conduct yourselves honorably among the Gentiles, so that, though they malign you as evildoers, they may see your honorable deeds and glorify God when he comes to judge.*a*

13 For the Lord's sake accept the authority of every human institution,*b* whether of the emperor as supreme, 14or of governors, as sent by him to punish those who do wrong and to praise those who do right. 15For it is God's will that by doing right you should silence the ignorance of the foolish. 16As servants*c* of God, live as free people, yet do not use your freedom as a pretext for evil. 17Honor everyone. Love the family of believers.*d* Fear God. Honor the emperor.

18 Slaves, accept the authority of your masters with all deference, not only those who are kind and gentle but also those who are harsh. 19For it is a credit to you if, being aware of God, you endure pain while suffering unjustly. 20If you endure when you are beaten for doing wrong, what credit is that? But if you endure when you do right and suffer for it, you have God's approval. 21For to

this you have been called, because Christ also suffered for you, leaving you an example, so that you should follow in his steps. 22 "He committed no sin,
     and no deceit was found in his mouth."
23When he was abused, he did not return abuse; when he suffered, he did not threaten; but he entrusted himself to the one who judges justly. 24He himself bore our sins in his body on the cross,*e* so that, free from sins, we might live for righteousness; by his wounds*f* you have been healed. 25For you were going astray like sheep, but now you have returned to the shepherd and guardian of your souls.

2.11–25. 11–17: Civic and family duties. Peter begins here a lengthy catalog of traditional duties, which are aspects of justice. Although *aliens and exiles,* disciples must act *honorably* like citizens. This means accepting *the authority* either of civic rulers, Roman emperor, local governors, or heads of families. Despite their social status as *servants,* they should *live as free people* by honoring and fearing those with political authority. **18–25: Slaves gaining honor.** Typical catalogs of duties address both masters and slaves (Eph 6.5–9; Col 4.1), but only slaves are mentioned here. **18–20:** Honorable behavior is expected, namely, accepting *authority* from good and evil masters alike. Unjust *suffering* for doing good, while shameful to others, is a credit to God (see *honorable* behavior in 2.12). **21–25:** Isa 53.9 says that Christ left an *example* of suffering unjustly but honorably. He forswore vengeance, the mark of honorable males in classical cultures; his *wounds healed* our sins. Slaves, then, belong to the flock of an honorable *shepherd and guardian,* who rewards them (5.4).

3 Wives, in the same way, accept the authority of your husbands, so that, even if some of them do not obey the word, they may be won over without a word by their wives' conduct, 2when they see the purity and reverence of your lives. 3Do not adorn yourselves outwardly by braiding your hair, and by wearing gold ornaments or fine clothing; 4rather, let your adornment be the inner self

a Gk *God on the day of visitation*   *b* Or *every institution ordained for human beings*   *c* Gk *slaves*   *d* Gk *Love the brotherhood*   *e* Or *carried up our sins in his body to the tree*   *f* Gk *bruise* with the lasting beauty of a gentle and quiet spirit, which is very precious in God's sight. [5]It was in this way long ago that the holy women who hoped in God used to adorn themselves by accepting the authority of their husbands. [6]Thus Sarah obeyed Abraham and called him lord. You have become her daughters as long as you do what is good and never let fears alarm you.

7 Husbands, in the same way, show consideration for your wives in your life together, paying honor to the woman as the weaker sex,[a] since they too are also heirs of the gracious gift of life—so that nothing may hinder your prayers.

8 Finally, all of you, have unity of spirit, sympathy, love for one another, a tender heart, and a humble mind. [9]Do not repay evil for evil or abuse for abuse; but, on the contrary, repay with a blessing. It is for this that you were called—that you might inherit a blessing. [10]For

"Those who desire life
　　and desire to see good days,
　let them keep their tongues from evil
　　and their lips from speaking deceit;
[11] let them turn away from evil and do
　　　good;
　　let them seek peace and pursue it.
[12] For the eyes of the Lord are on
　　　the righteous,
　　and his ears are open to their prayer.
　　But the face of the Lord is against those
　　　who do evil."

3.1–12. 1–7: **Wives and husbands. 1:** In this exposition of patriarchal authority, wives should *accept* their husbands' *authority*. **2–5:** Honorable behavior resides in a heightened sense of purity, which here means avoidance of expensive and seductive *adornment*. Instead of outward glitter (hair, jewelry, or clothing), wives should *adorn* themselves with inner virtue, such as a *gentle and quiet spirit*. As slaves imitate the example of the crucified Jesus, wives follow *Sarah's* example of obedience to *Abraham*. **7:** *Husbands* reciprocate by honoring their wives. Conjugal duties here reflect the ancient gender division of society, with males exercising authority in public, while females, considered weaker, showed obedience in private. **8–12: Something for everybody. 8–9:** Peter celebrates actions that bind the church together, such as *unity,* *love, tenderness,* and *humility:* There can be no envy or competition in the group, thus the deadly games of seeking honor are censured. Moreover, all vengeance is forsworn, as Jesus mandated (Mt 5.43–45) and Ps 34.12–16 confirms.

~~~~~~~~~~~~~~~~~~~~~~~~~~~~~~~~

13 Now who will harm you if you are eager to do what is good? [14]But even if you do suffer for doing what is right, you are blessed. Do not fear what they fear,[b] and do not be intimidated, [15]but in your hearts sanctify Christ as Lord. Always be ready to make your defense to anyone who demands from you an accounting for the hope that is in you; [16]yet do it with gentleness and reverence.[c] Keep your conscience clear, so that, when you are maligned, those who abuse you for your good conduct in Christ may be put to shame. [17]For it is better to suffer for doing good, if suffering should be God's will, than to suffer for doing evil. [18]For Christ also suffered[d] for sins once for all, the righteous for the unrighteous, in order to bring you[e] to God. He was put to death in the flesh, but made alive in the spirit, [19]in which also he went and made a proclamation to the spirits in prison, [20]who in former times did not obey, when God waited patiently in the days of Noah, during the building of the ark, in which a few, that is, eight persons, were saved through water. [21]And baptism, which this prefigured, now saves you—not as a removal of dirt from the body, but as an appeal to God for[f] a good conscience, through the resurrection of Jesus Christ, [22]who has gone into heaven and is at the right hand of God, with angels, authorities, and powers made subject to him.

3.13–22. 13–17: **Suffering well. 13–15:** All members are addressed in terms resembling the exhortation* to slaves in 2.18–25. Peter declares unjust suffering a blessing or honor (Mt 5.10–11) while enemies are put to *shame.* **16–17:** Although Christians forswear vengeance (3.9), they may prepare an appropriate *defense* (Mt 10.19–20) for some forms of civic trial. The best defense is a *clear conscience,* that is, respect for the values and actions thought by others to be honorable

a Gk *vessel*　　b Gk *their fear*　　c Or *respect*
d Other ancient authorities read *died*　　e Other ancient authorities read *us*　　f Or *a pledge to God from*

orable. **18–22: Christ as model.** While paralleling the example of Jesus in 2.21–22, these verses contain a traditional hymn about his death, vindication, and enthronement (see 1 Tim 3.16 for a similar structure). **18–19:** Christ models sinless suffering, emphasizing the good that comes from endurance. *Put to death*, Jesus was *made alive* by God; when vindicated, he rebuked the evil powers responsible for his death and the group's suffering. **20–21:** Peter interrupts with a reminder of baptism.* *Noah* and seven other persons escaped destruction in the flood, prefiguring *baptism*, spiritual washing and new birth. **22:** The hymn continues with mention of Jesus' resurrection and enthronement, when all heavenly spirits and powers obey him. Suffering like Christ, disciples experience a baptismal transformation from moral death to heavenly life, thus sharing in Jesus' resurrection. They also glory in Jesus' authority over the cosmos.

4 Since therefore Christ suffered in the flesh,*a* arm yourselves also with the same intention (for whoever has suffered in the flesh has finished with sin), 2 so as to live for the rest of your earthly life*b* no longer by human desires but by the will of God. 3 You have already spent enough time in doing what the Gentiles like to do, living in licentiousness, passions, drunkenness, revels, carousing, and lawless idolatry. 4 They are surprised that you no longer join them in the same excesses of dissipation, and so they blaspheme.*c* 5 But they will have to give an accounting to him who stands ready to judge the living and the dead. 6 For this is the reason the gospel was proclaimed even to the dead, so that, though they had been judged in the flesh as everyone is judged, they might live in the spirit as God does.

7 The end of all things is near;*d* therefore be serious and discipline yourselves for the sake of your prayers. 8 Above all, maintain constant love for one another, for love covers a multitude of sins. 9 Be hospitable to one another without complaining. 10 Like good stewards of the manifold grace of God, serve one another with whatever gift each of you has received. 11 Whoever speaks must do so as one speaking the very words of God; whoever serves must do so with the strength that God supplies, so that God may be glorified in all things through Jesus Christ. To him

belong the glory and the power forever and ever. Amen.

4.1–11. 1–6: The final judgment. The hymn about Jesus leads naturally to the Day of Judgment. **1–4:** Baptismal* transformation means the end of *life in the flesh* but the beginning of life according to the *will of God.* Conversion means a clear break with the ways of one's neighbors, who ridicule converts for their distinctive behavior (2.18–3.17). **5–6:** Judgment confronts all, good and bad, living and dead. Christ *proclaimed the gospel even to the dead* so that all may be saved. **7–11: Final judgment: ideal response.** The judgment mentioned above controls how we read vv. 7–11. **7–9:** Unlike their indulgent neighbors, Christians demonstrate disciplined lives whose purity validates their prayers. Avoiding indulgence, they *maintain constant love* and practice hospitality, thus putting others before themselves. **10–11:** God's gifts are a patron's benefaction to his clients. Conversely, clients offer *glory* or honor to their patron in the doxology.

12 Beloved, do not be surprised at the fiery ordeal that is taking place among you to test you, as though something strange were happening to you. 13 But rejoice insofar as you are sharing Christ's sufferings, so that you may also be glad and shout for joy when his glory is revealed. 14 If you are reviled for the name of Christ, you are blessed, because the spirit of glory,*e* which is the Spirit of God, is resting on you.*f* 15 But let none of you suffer as a murderer, a thief, a criminal, or even as a mischief maker. 16 Yet if any of you suffers as a Christian, do not consider it a disgrace, but glorify God because you bear this name. 17 For the time has come for judgment to begin with the household of God; if it begins with us, what will be the end for those who do not obey the gospel of God? 18 And

"If it is hard for the righteous
    to be saved,
    what will become of the ungodly and
        the sinners?"

a Other ancient authorities add *for us*; others, *for you*
b Gk *rest of the time in the flesh*   *c* Or *they malign you*
d Or *is at hand*   *e* Other ancient authorities add *and of power*   *f* Other ancient authorities add *On their part he is blasphemed, but on your part he is glorified*

¹⁹Therefore, let those suffering in accordance with God's will entrust themselves to a faithful Creator, while continuing to do good.

4.12–19: Suffering and the coming judgment. 12–14: Christians' suffering means *sharing Christ's sufferings;* as Jesus was vindicated, they will be *blessed,* honored, and glorified (Mt 5.11–12). **15–16:** Suffering should never be punishment for immorality (2.19–20). But dishonor for *the name* of *Christian* (Acts 11.26) means glory to God. **17–19:** *God's household* is held to a higher standard than unbelievers, as shown by Prov 11.31. The proper duty of clients who suffer is to honor their *faithful* patron with loyal trust (1 Cor 1.9; 1 Thess 5.24).

5 Now as an elder myself and a witness of the sufferings of Christ, as well as one who shares in the glory to be revealed, I exhort the elders among you ²to tend the flock of God that is in your charge, exercising the oversight,ᵃ not under compulsion but willingly, as God would have you do itᵇ—not for sordid gain but eagerly. ³Do not lord it over those in your charge, but be examples to the flock. ⁴And when the chief shepherd appears, you will win the crown of glory that never fades away. ⁵In the same way, you who are younger must accept the authority of the elders.ᶜ And all of you must clothe yourselves with humility in your dealings with one another, for

"God opposes the proud,
    but gives grace to the humble."

6 Humble yourselves therefore under the mighty hand of God, so that he may exalt you in due time. ⁷Cast all your anxiety on him, because he cares for you. ⁸Discipline yourselves, keep alert.ᵈ Like a roaring lion your adversary the devil prowls around, looking for someone to devour. ⁹Resist him, steadfast in your faith, for you know that your brothers and sistersᵉ in all the world are undergoing the same kinds of suffering. ¹⁰And after you have suffered for a little while, the God of all grace, who has called you to his eternal glory in Christ, will himself restore, support, strengthen, and establish you. ¹¹To him be the power forever and ever. Amen.

12 Through Silvanus, whom I consider a faithful brother, I have written this short letter to encourage you and to testify that this is the true grace of God. Stand fast in it. ¹³Your sister churchᶠ in Babylon, chosen together with you, sends you greetings; and so does my son Mark. ¹⁴Greet one another with a kiss of love.

Peace to all of you who are in Christ.ᵍ

5.1–14. 1–5: Household duties: elders. The last set of household duties addresses local leaders. **1–3:** Peter's authority to speak as *elder* rests on his *witness* of Christ's sufferings (Mt 26.40, 69–75) and vindication (1.1). Courageous, voluntary leadership which is not self-serving is needed (Mt 20.25–28). **4:** *Elders,* who are local shepherds, will be honored when the *chief shepherd* comes. **5:** Codes of duties, which address reciprocal pairs (wives and husbands, 3.1–7), link *elders* (5.1–4) with *younger* men. Characteristic of the subordinate member of the pairs, *young* men must have respect *for the authority of the elders.* **6–11: Final exhortations.＊ 6–7:** Peter applies Ps 55.22 to the church, echoing Jesus' words (Mt 23.12; Lk 14.11). **8–9:** The flock of the chief shepherd is attacked by a *roaring lion,* the devil (Ps 22.13; Lk 22.31). Fidelity comes from solidarity with comparable *suffering* of *brothers and sisters* elsewhere. **10–11:** As God vindicated Christ (1.11), so *the God of all grace* will surely *restore* or glorify those whom he has *called.* A doxology follows (4.11). **12–14: Letter closing. 12:** *Silvanus* writes as Peter's secretary (see 1 Cor 16.20). **13:** *Greetings* typically end letters. Greetings are sent from *Babylon,* a symbolic name that refers to the city-state Babylon which destroyed Jerusalem and carried its population into exile (Mt 1.11); Christians also used it to hide the name of their oppressor, the city-state of Rome (Rev 16.19; 17.5; 18.2, 10). It is, then, a symbolic place name. Still, it echoes the earlier mention of "exile in the Dispersion" (1.1) and "aliens and exiles" (2.11). Eusebius records that *Mark* was Peter's associate in Rome and the author of the second gospel (*E.H.* 2.15.1–2; 3.39.15). **14:** The *kiss of love* reminds the church of its identity as a family or household (see exhortations to love in 1.22; 2.17; 4.8).

---

a Other ancient authorities lack *exercising the oversight*
b Other ancient authorities lack *as God would have you do it*   c Or *of those who are older*   d Or *be vigilant*
e Gk *your brotherhood*   f Gk *She who is*   g Other ancient authorities add *Amen*

THE SECOND LETTER OF PETER

Introduction

The author presents himself as "Simeon Peter," who was an "apostle★ of Jesus," and who, according to gospel traditions, was commissioned by Jesus (Mt 16.16–18; 28.18–20). Although not the founder of this particular church (see 3.2), he claims authority to speak because he was an eyewitness to Jesus' transfiguration. He has received special revelations (1.12–15), especially about the Day of the Lord. Yet Peter is probably not the author because sections of the document suggest a much later time. First, he refers to "your apostles," implying that he comes late on the scene. Second, he mentions Paul's letters (3.15), which were not collected until the second century. Third, he speaks of "the other Scriptures" (3.16), which implies Christian writings that only later were canonized★ in this way. Fourth, most of ch. 2 is taken directly from Jude. The fine Greek vocabulary implies a formal education unlikely for a fisherman. Someone, then, other than Peter writes in the apostle's name.

READING GUIDE

Second Peter contains many conventions typical of ancient letters. It opens with notice of sender and addressees and continues with a greeting (1.1–2) and thanksgiving (1.3–10). The body of the letter provides an apology, or explanatory defense, to numerous slanders about God's final judgment: Taking up each slander, the author defends the authenticity of the prophecy of the second coming of Jesus (1.16–18); the inspiration of both prophecy and its interpretation (1.19–21); the fact of divine judgment as found in the Scriptures (2.1–3, 4–10; 3.4–7); and a denial of the argument of "delay" (3.8–9, 10–13). Typical of Christian letters, it concludes with an exhortation★ (3.17–18) and praise of God (3.18). The argument of the letter goes as follows.

1. Letter opening: author, addressees, God's benefaction (1.1–11)
2. Occasion of the letter: Peter's farewell address (1.12–15)
3. Reply to the first slander: prophecy of Jesus' coming defended (1.16–18)
4. Reply to the second slander: prophecy and interpretation defended (1.19–21)
5. Reply to the third slander
   A. Opponents deny the master's judgment (2.1–3)
   B. Defense of God's judgment from Scripture (2.4–10)
6. Shame on the opponents
   A. Beasts, lust, and greed (2.11–17)
   B. Hypocrisy and harm (2.18–22)
7. Reply to the fourth slander
   A. Opponents deny God's promise in a static world (3.1–4)
   B. Defense of the divine word of judgment (3.5–7)
8. Reply to the fifth slander
   A. Opponents cite God's delay of judgment to deny it (3.9)
   B. Delay a gift of mercy; unpredictable time of Jesus' return (3.8, 10–13)
9. Final exhortation and letter closing (3.14–18)

Because of the polemical* tone and argument, 2 Peter resembles an essay or literary letter. In addition to the letter form, the author employs another important genre,* the farewell address (1.12–15), a genre typical of the speeches of dying patriarchs and leaders (Lk 22.14–38; Acts 20.17–35). It generally contains a prediction of the leader's death, a prediction of future crises for those who remain, a legacy, and an exhortation to a particular virtue, in this case fidelity to the ancient tradition. These characteristic elements will be discussed below in 1.12–15.

1 Simeon*a* Peter, a servant*b* and apostle of Jesus Christ,

To those who have received a faith as precious as ours through the righteousness of our God and Savior Jesus Christ:*c*

2 May grace and peace be yours in abundance in the knowledge of God and of Jesus our Lord.

3 His divine power has given us everything needed for life and godliness, through the knowledge of him who called us by*d* his own glory and goodness. 4Thus he has given us, through these things, his precious and very great promises, so that through them you may escape from the corruption that is in the world because of lust, and may become participants of the divine nature. 5For this very reason, you must make every effort to support your faith with goodness, and goodness with knowledge, 6and knowledge with self-control, and self-control with endurance, and endurance with godliness, 7and godliness with mutual*e* affection, and mutual*e* affection with love. 8For if these things are yours and are increasing among you, they keep you from being ineffective and unfruitful in the knowledge of our Lord Jesus Christ. 9For anyone who lacks these things is nearsighted and blind, and is forgetful of the cleansing of past sins. 10Therefore, brothers and sisters,*f* be all the more eager to confirm your call and election, for if you do this, you will never stumble. 11For in this way, entry into the eternal kingdom of our Lord and Savior Jesus Christ will be richly provided for you.

Ex 32.13; David: 2 Sam 7.5). No specific place is addressed; instead the recipients are identified as all those who share a most valuable thing, such as *faith in God and Jesus* that is, correct faith. **3–10: Thanksgiving.** Letters often include "thanksgivings," which introduce themes to be developed. **3–4:** Peter singles out two blessings for praise: *everything needed for life and godliness* and *precious and very great promises.* **5–8:** Correct faith leads to purity, not corruption, and predicts a sharing in *the divine nature* in the afterlife. In support, Peter cites a chain of virtues that follow from correct faith (see Rom 5.1–5), thus illustrating the principle that "good doctrine leads to good behavior" and vice versa. Besides *faith, endurance (hope)* and *mutual affection,* virtues such as *knowledge, self-control,* and *godliness* point to topics developed later: correct doctrine, moral rectitude, and justice toward God.

12 Therefore I intend to keep on reminding you of these things, though you know them already and are established in the truth that has come to you. 13I think it right, as long as I am in this body,*g* to refresh your memory, 14since I know that my death*h* will come soon, as indeed our Lord Jesus Christ has made clear to me. 15And I will make every effort so that after my departure you may be able at any time to recall these things.

16 For we did not follow cleverly devised myths when we made known to you the power and coming of our Lord Jesus Christ, but we had been eyewitnesses of his majesty. 17For he received honor and glory from God the Father when that voice was conveyed to him by the Majestic Glory, saying, "This is

1.1–11. 1–2: Sender and addressees. The sender's name, *Simeon Peter,* is a rare Semitic variation of "Simon Peter" or simply "Peter." As *servant and apostle** he claims high status, for great Israelite figures were often called "servant of the Lord" (Moses:

a Other ancient authorities read *Simon*   *b* Gk *slave*   *c* Or *of our God and the Savior Jesus Christ*   *d* Other ancient authorities read *through*   *e* Gk *brotherly*   *f* Gk *brothers*   *g* Gk *tent*   *h* Gk *the putting off of my tent* my Son, my Beloved,ᵃ with whom I am well pleased." ¹⁸We ourselves heard this voice come from heaven, while we were with him on the holy mountain.

19 So we have the prophetic message more fully confirmed. You will do well to be attentive to this as to a lamp shining in a dark place, until the day dawns and the morning star rises in your hearts. ²⁰First of all you must understand this, that no prophecy of scripture is a matter of one's own interpretation, ²¹because no prophecy ever came by human will, but men and women moved by the Holy Spirit spoke from God.ᵇ

1.12–21. 12–15: Farewell address. Typical of farewell addresses, Peter announces his death. Such biblical forms generally have (1) announcement of death (1.14); (2) predictions of future crises (2.1–3; 3.1–7); (3) exhortation* to a specific virtue (1.4–11; 3.1–2); and (4) legacy (2.4–10; 3.8–10). This prediction echoes Jn 21.18–19, even as it confirms the tradition that Peter regularly received special revelations (Mt 16.16–17; 17.25–27). **16–21: Transfiguration.** Claiming to have been present at Jesus' transfiguration (Mt 17.1–8), Peter interprets that event as a prophecy of Jesus' return in glory. **16–18:** As an *eyewitness*, he claims a role that confirms his authority to explain and defend other prophecies about Jesus, such as his return to judge the world. **19–21:** He defends the inspiration of both the prophet* who receives prophecy and its interpreter. Prophecy is *fully confirmed*, or established, because God is its author (*This is my beloved Son*, note *a*), and God's Spirit inspires both prophet and interpreter. The prophecy *confirmed* is about the final judgment of the world. Christ, the *morning star* (Rev 22.16) brings light and hope, not fear.

2 But false prophets also arose among the people, just as there will be false teachers among you, who will secretly bring in destructive opinions. They will even deny the Master who bought them—bringing swift destruction on themselves. ²Even so, many will follow their licentious ways, and because of these teachersᶜ the way of truth will be maligned. ³And in their greed they will exploit you with deceptive words. Their condemnation, pronounced against them long ago, has not been idle, and their destruction is not asleep.

4 For if God did not spare the angels when they sinned, but cast them into hellᵈ and committed them to chainsᵉ of deepest darkness to be kept until the judgment; ⁵and if he did not spare the ancient world, even though he saved Noah, a herald of righteousness, with seven others, when he brought a flood on a world of the ungodly; ⁶and if by turning the cities of Sodom and Gomorrah to ashes he condemned them to extinctionᶠ and made them an example of what is coming to the ungodly;ᵍ ⁷and if he rescued Lot, a righteous man greatly distressed by the licentiousness of the lawless ⁸(for that righteous man, living among them day after day, was tormented in his righteous soul by their lawless deeds that he saw and heard), ⁹then the Lord knows how to rescue the godly from trial, and to keep the unrighteous under punishment until the day of judgment ¹⁰—especially those who indulge their flesh in depraved lust, and who despise authority.

2.1–10a. 1–3: First look at the opponents. Farewell addresses typically predict future crises (Acts 20.29–30), here, the advent of *false teachers*. **1–3:** When they *deny the Master*, they declare that God does not judge, a common deviant doctrine among Greeks and Judeans. One reason for thinking this is the observation of the slowness of judgment: It *is idle* or God sleeps (3.8–9). **4–10a: First response.** Responding to a denial of divine judgment, Peter cites proof from the Bible. **4–8:** *God did not spare* evil angels; God *saved Noah*, but *brought a flood on the ungodly*; God *rescued Lot*, but turned *Sodom and Gomorrah* to ashes. **9–10:** These examples prove that *the Lord knows how to rescue the godly* and *to keep the unrighteous until the day of judgment*. Besides God's judgment, the author also defends the belief in survival after death, when God's judgment will reward the good and requite the wicked.

---

a Other ancient authorities read *my beloved Son*
b Other ancient authorities read *but moved by the Holy Spirit saints of God spoke*   *c* Gk *because of them*
d Gk *Tartaros*   *e* Other ancient authorities read *pits*
f Other ancient authorities lack *to extinction*
g Other ancient authorities read *an example to those who were to be ungodly*

Bold and willful, they are not afraid to slander the glorious ones,[a] 11whereas angels, though greater in might and power, do not bring against them a slanderous judgment from the Lord.[b] 12These people, however, are like irrational animals, mere creatures of instinct, born to be caught and killed. They slander what they do not understand, and when those creatures are destroyed,[c] they also will be destroyed, 13suffering[d] the penalty for doing wrong. They count it a pleasure to revel in the daytime. They are blots and blemishes, reveling in their dissipation[e] while they feast with you. 14They have eyes full of adultery, insatiable for sin. They entice unsteady souls. They have hearts trained in greed. Accursed children! 15They have left the straight road and have gone astray, following the road of Balaam son of Bosor,[f] who loved the wages of doing wrong, 16but was rebuked for his own transgression; a speechless donkey spoke with a human voice and restrained the prophet's madness.

17 These are waterless springs and mists driven by a storm; for them the deepest darkness has been reserved. 18For they speak bombastic nonsense, and with licentious desires of the flesh they entice people who have just[g] escaped from those who live in error. 19They promise them freedom, but they themselves are slaves of corruption; for people are slaves to whatever masters them. 20For if, after they have escaped the defilements of the world through the knowledge of our Lord and Savior Jesus Christ, they are again entangled in them and overpowered, the last state has become worse for them than the first. 21For it would have been better for them never to have known the way of righteousness than, after knowing it, to turn back from the holy commandment that was passed on to them. 22It has happened to them according to the true proverb,

"The dog turns back to its own vomit,"

and,

"The sow is washed only to wallow in the mud."

insulting the angels who are predicted to accompany the divine judgment (Mt 24.30–31). More name-calling follows: *irrational animals, blots and blemishes, adulterous,* and *greedy.* He continually pronounces judgment on them *(caught and killed, will be destroyed, suffering the penalty for doing wrong)*—a judgment they deny. **15–16:** *Balaam* (Num 22) provides another biblical example of a "false prophet*" who was rebuked by his dumb donkey. **17–18:** More name-calling, but in terms of things that fail: *waterless springs* are all promise and no payoff. He accuses his opponents of base motives (first greed and now license) and argues that their doctrine cannot lead to moral integrity. **19–20:** In promising *freedom,* they proclaim freedom from fear of God's judgment and presumably God's law; but this perverse idea only leads to *slavery,* not freedom, and to *corruption,* not holiness. **21–22:** The opponents are likened to the most unclean animals in that culture, *dogs* and *sows;* after baptism* and purification, they return to their previous *vomit* and *mud.* The opponents' doctrine, then, only leads to a bad end—proof that it is wrong.

3 This is now, beloved, the second letter I am writing to you; in them I am trying to arouse your sincere intention by reminding you 2that you should remember the words spoken in the past by the holy prophets, and the commandment of the Lord and Savior spoken through your apostles. 3First of all you must understand this, that in the last days scoffers will come, scoffing and indulging their own lusts 4and saying, "Where is the promise of his coming? For ever since our ancestors died,[h] all things continue as they were from the beginning of creation!" 5They deliberately ignore this fact, that by the word of God heavens existed long ago and an earth was formed out of water and by means of water, 6through which the world of that time was deluged with water and perished. 7But by the same word the present

a Or *angels;* Gk *glories*   b Other ancient authorities read *before the Lord;* others lack the phrase   c Gk *in their destruction*   d Other ancient authorities read *receiving*   e Other ancient authorities read *love-feasts*   f Other ancient authorities read *Beor*   g Other ancient authorities read *actually*   h Gk *our fathers fell asleep*

2.10b–22: Assorted attacks. 11–14: Peter resorts to name-calling (*bold, willful*), accusing his opponents of heavens and earth have been reserved for fire, being kept until the day of judgment and destruction of the godless.

8 But do not ignore this one fact, beloved, that with the Lord one day is like a thousand years, and a thousand years are like one day. [9]The Lord is not slow about his promise, as some think of slowness, but is patient with you,[a] not wanting any to perish, but all to come to repentance. [10]But the day of the Lord will come like a thief, and then the heavens will pass away with a loud noise, and the elements will be dissolved with fire, and the earth and everything that is done on it will be disclosed.[b]

11 Since all these things are to be dissolved in this way, what sort of persons ought you to be in leading lives of holiness and godliness, [12]waiting for and hastening[c] the coming of the day of God, because of which the heavens will be set ablaze and dissolved, and the elements will melt with fire? [13]But, in accordance with his promise, we wait for new heavens and a new earth, where righteousness is at home.

3.1–13. 1–7: Another refutation. 1–2: Peter claims that this is his *second letter,* but 1 Peter can hardly be the earlier one because it shares so little of this author's vocabulary or themes. Moreover, by referring to what was said by *your apostles,** the author positions himself as a much later authority. This letter aims to remind the recipients of what their *holy prophets** and *Lord and Savior* said about the Day of the Lord, which is the crux of the conflict. **3–4:** Farewell addresses generally predict future crises; here scoffers ridicule the prophecy of Jesus' return. *"Where is the promise of his coming?"* Delay serves as their chief argument against Jesus' coming and God's judgment. **5–7:** The author refutes their scoffing by emphasizing the reliability of God's *word.* God's word created the world out of water and judged it (recall Noah, 2.5); that *same word* declares that God will judge *by fire* what is created. It was common to describe God's two basic powers as creative power at the world's beginning and executive power at its end. The Christian God is also confessed as having both powers, which the opponents here deny. **8–13: Challenge and riposte.** Peter challenges more scoffing statements from his opponents. **8–9:** The standard argument against divine judgment is its delay; sinners seem to escape, and faithful people

seem not to be rewarded. Peter refutes this in two ways: First, God's time is not our time, as Ps 90.4 indicates (*one day is like a thousand years*); moreover, God's "delay" is a gift of time for *repentance* (Rom 2.4–5) because God *does not want any to perish.* **10:** Yet the traditional prophecy of the Lord coming *like a thief* (1 Thess 5.2; Rev 3.3) reminds us that the exact time cannot be known. **11–13:** Correct theology leads to correct behavior; hence, all who await the world's dissolution and recreation will live upright lives guided by this truth. The idea of *new heavens and a new earth* reflects a technical idea in Greek philosophy called cosmic "regeneration" (see Mt 19.28). The Stoics,* for example, claimed that the world would dissolve in fire but then be recreated. A claim, then, is made that all right-thinking people accept the idea of the world's end.

14 Therefore, beloved, while you are waiting for these things, strive to be found by him at peace, without spot or blemish; [15]and regard the patience of our Lord as salvation. So also our beloved brother Paul wrote to you according to the wisdom given him, [16]speaking of this as he does in all his letters. There are some things in them hard to understand, which the ignorant and unstable twist to their own destruction, as they do the other scriptures. [17]You therefore, beloved, since you are forewarned, beware that you are not carried away with the error of the lawless and lose your own stability. [18]But grow in the grace and knowledge of our Lord and Savior Jesus Christ. To him be the glory both now and to the day of eternity. Amen.[d]

3.14–18: Letter closing. Once more, the true tradition about the coming judgment yields pastoral results in the reform of human lives. **14:** We are to be *without spot or blemish,* just as Paul regularly announced to his churches (1 Thess 3.13; Phil 2.15). **15–16:** The reference to *Paul* indicates that some of his letters are known, possibly even collected by this time. Our author admits that Paul's letters are *hard to understand;*

a Other ancient authorities read *on your account*
b Other ancient authorities read *will be burned up*
c Or *earnestly desiring*   *d* Other ancient authorities lack *Amen*

yet he cites them as support for God's *patience* or delay of judgment (Rom 2.4–5), Christian belief in a final judgment (Rom 14.10), the consequent need for spotlessness (1 Thess 3.11–13), and the coming of Christ like a thief in the night (1 Thess 5.2). **17–18:** The letter ends with a final exhortation* to shun the erroneous doctrine, which leads to lawlessness. The final doxology is addressed to Jesus, not God, which is very unusual.

THE FIRST LETTER OF JOHN

Introduction

The opening and closing greetings of a letter are lacking in 1 John, which reads more like a tract or homily. It is a self-consciously literary work, making many references to writing: "We are writing" (1.4); "I am writing" (2.1, 7, 8, 12, 13, 14, 21, 26; 5.13). Its theme is the meaning of the gospel (the Christian message) in the specific situation in which the author perceived the readers to be. There is a positive exposition of gospel truth (1.1–4), addressed in a warmly pastoral tone to the readers as "little children" (2.1, 18, 28; 3.18; 5.21) or "beloved" (2.7; 3.2, 21; 4.1, 7, 11). Fellow believers are brothers and sisters whom the readers are exhorted to love as members of the family of God, made children of God by the love of God (3.1–2). Love of one another is the key trait of the children of God (4.7–12, 20–21; 5.1–5). Yet there is a strident condemnation of those who oppose this position, so that 1 John is both warmly pastoral and sharply polemical* in tone (see 1.6, 8, 10; 2.4, 6, 9; 4.1–6, 20). This suggests that the purpose of the letter was to strengthen believers (supporters) by dealing sharply with the opponents (it was not written to them) so that believers might not be tempted to stray.

Language, style, and ideas suggest a connection with the Gospel of John. Tradition attributes these books to the same author. From the time of Irenaeus the author has been identified as John, the disciple Jesus loved. Although Irenaeus appeals to the antecedents of this tradition, we have no knowledge of it independently of him. For this reason, no confidence can be placed in Irenaeus' remarks. Similarities between the Gospel and 1 John suggest that they come from the same author, or at least from the same school. Scholars disagree about whether the Gospel was written first, at the same time as 1 John, or subsequently. The sequence affects the way each of the works is read. It is likely that the author of 1 John knew the tradition of the Gospel of John and made use of it, and that 2, 3 John were written at the same time as 1 John, to accompany it. The author of 2, 3 John describes himself as "the elder" probably not referring to his age but to his position of leadership in a Christian community or group of churches.

The Gospel was shaped over a long period of time, during which believers struggled with opponents in the synagogue* (see 9.22, 34; 12.42; 16.2), and the completed Gospel may have been published around the same time 1, 2, and 3 John were written, although it was decisively shaped somewhat earlier so that its tradition was available to the author of the letters. The tradition locating the Johannine literature in and around Ephesus is at least as plausible as any other suggestion.

First John has the character of a tract that nurtures supporters and opposes those who have withdrawn (2.18–19). The context of the letter is a serious crisis of schism in which a significant section of the community has withdrawn. While the schism reflects a leadership struggle, serious differences also divide the two groups. An understanding of the two groups can be built up by a cautious reading of the positions the author affirms and opposes. So serious is the schism in the eyes of the author that he presents it as evidence that "it is the last hour" (2.18). The situation differs greatly from the conflict with the synagogue, which is the dominant context of the Gospel. In the face of Jewish opposition the Gospel stresses the presence of God in Jesus, but 1 John stresses the reality and significance of the humanity of Jesus for believers against the refusal of the opponents to recognize this (4.1–6). Consistent with this is the pervasive and significant use of Jewish scripture in the Gospel and the absence of any quotation in 1 John, where the only reference related to scripture is to Cain, who slew his brother, (3.12). Our author asserts that this is evidence of being of "the evil one." By implication he asserts that the schismatics are children of the devil because they do not love the brethren (compare Jn 8.44).

The task of 1 John is to deal with the confusion caused by the schism. It was written to confirm that those who remained in the community were on the side of the truth and that the opponents had shown their error by their departure. A three-fold reworking of two tests to reveal those who are of the truth provides the substance of 1 John. The two tests concern the true confession of faith and the ethical evidence of the lives of the children of God.

READING GUIDE

The prologue (1.1–4) makes the reader aware from the beginning that 1 John has a close relationship to the Gospel. Other themes draw attention to shared characteristic language: light and darkness, truth, love, witness, knowing. While 1 John has an invitingly pastoral appeal, the reader should be alert to the polemical tone used when dealing with the assertions of opponents, in antithetical* statements and in the outline of what the opponents denied.

1.1–4	Prologue
1.5–2.27	Two tests of fellowship with God
2.28–4.6	The connection between the two tests
4.7–5.12	The inseparability of the two tests
5.13–21	Conclusion

1 We declare to you what was from the beginning, what we have heard, what we have seen with our eyes, what we have looked at and touched with our hands, concerning the word of life— ²this life was revealed, and we have seen it and testify to it, and declare to you the eternal life that was with the Father and was revealed to us— ³we declare to you what we have seen and heard so that you also may have fellowship with us; and truly our fellowship is with the Father and with his Son Jesus Christ. ⁴We are writing these things so that our*a* joy may be complete.

5 This is the message we have heard from him and proclaim to you, that God is light and in him there is no darkness at all. ⁶If we say that we have fellowship with him while we are walking in darkness, we lie and do not do what is true; ⁷but if we walk in the light as he himself is in the light, we have fellowship with one another, and the blood of Jesus his Son cleanses us from all sin. ⁸If we say that we have no sin, we deceive ourselves, and the truth is not in us. ⁹If we confess our sins, he who is faithful and just will forgive us our sins and cleanse us from all unrighteousness. ¹⁰If we say that we have not sinned, we make him a liar, and his word is not in us.

2 My little children, I am writing these things to you so that you may not sin. But if anyone does sin, we have an advocate with the Father, Jesus Christ the righteous; ²and he is the atoning sacrifice for our sins, and not for ours only but also for the sins of the whole world.

1.1–4 Prologue. Themes borrowed from Jn 1.1–18 emphasize the humanity of Jesus. **1:** *Word of life:* both message and person (Jn 1.1, 14). **2:** *Life was revealed* in the Word (see Jn 1.4); the Word dwells in and is the source of *eternal life:* see 2.25; 3.14–15; 5.11–13, 20; Jn 3.15. **3:** *Fellowship,* among believers, with the Father and the Son (see 1.6, 7; Jn 1.14–18; 3.16). **4:** *We are writing* (see 2.1, 7, 8, 12–14, 21, 25; 5.13) shows a self-consciously literary work.

a Other ancient authorities read *your*

1.5–2.27: Two tests. 1.5–2.17: The ethical test. Expressed as walking in the light, testing six of the seven assertions made by the opponents (1.6, 8, 10; 2.4, 6, 9; see 4.20). **1.5–2.2: Walking in the light: sin and sinlessness. 5:** *God is light:* see 4.8 and Jn 4.24. *Light* is the self-revealing character of God. **6–7:** *If we say:* a formula introducing the first three assertions (1.6, 8, 10) of the opponents. *Walking in the darkness* falsifies the claim because *God is light* (1.5; see Jn 3.19–21; 8.12; 11.9–10; 12.35–36). Lying (see 2.4) is opposed to *doing what is true* (see Jn 3.21). *The blood of Jesus* (see 5.6–8) *cleanses us from all sin,* (see 1.9; 2.2; 5.16–17) through sacrifice. **8–9:** *We have no sin:* self-deception (see 1.10). The way to deal with sin is not denial but confession. *Faithful and just:* better, "faithful and righteous" (see 2.1, 29; 3.7). **10:** *We have not sinned* perhaps refers to past behavior; it is unclear how this differs from the second assertion. **2.1–2:** The provision for one who sins is the presence of the *advocate,* elsewhere used only of the Holy Spirit (see Jn 14.16). Jesus is also the *atoning sacrifice* (see 4.10; Lev 16.16, 30) *for the sins of the whole world* (see 4.14; compare Jn 1.29).

3 Now by this we may be sure that we know him, if we obey his commandments. 4Whoever says, "I have come to know him," but does not obey his commandments, is a liar, and in such a person the truth does not exist; 5but whoever obeys his word, truly in this person the love of God has reached perfection. By this we may be sure that we are in him: 6whoever says, "I abide in him," ought to walk just as he walked.

7 Beloved, I am writing you no new commandment, but an old commandment that you have had from the beginning; the old commandment is the word that you have heard. 8Yet I am writing you a new commandment that is true in him and in you, because*a* the darkness is passing away and the true light is already shining. 9Whoever says, "I am in the light," while hating a brother or sister,*b* is still in the darkness. 10Whoever loves a brother or sister*c* lives in the light, and in such a person*d* there is no cause for stumbling. 11But whoever hates another believer*e* is in the darkness, walks in the darkness, and does not know the way

to go, because the darkness has brought on blindness.

12 I am writing to you, little children,
    because your sins are forgiven on
        account of his name.
13 I am writing to you, fathers,
    because you know him who is from
        the beginning.
    I am writing to you, young people,
    because you have conquered
        the evil one.
14 I write to you, children,
    because you know the Father.
    I write to you, fathers,
    because you know him who is from
        the beginning.
    I write to you, young people,
    because you are strong
    and the word of God abides in you,
        and you have overcome the
            evil one.

15 Do not love the world or the things in the world. The love of the Father is not in those who love the world; 16for all that is in the world—the desire of the flesh, the desire of the eyes, the pride in riches—comes not from the Father but from the world. 17And the world and its desire*f* are passing away, but those who do the will of God live forever.

2.3–17. 3–11: Walking in the light: love and obedience. A second group of three assertions is introduced by *whoever says* (2.4, 6, 9). **3–4:** Knowledge is tested by keeping the commandments. **5–6:** The one in whom the *love of God* reaches *perfection* truly exists (see 4.12, 17). Abiding is tested by conforming to the example of Jesus. Jesus' example conforms to his commandments. **7–8:** The love command (3.2, 21; 4.1, 7) is paradoxical since an *old command* becomes a *new commandment* (see Jn 13.34; 2 Jn 5). **9–11:** *I am in the light:* The evidence of being in the darkness is hating the brother (or sister); of being in the light is loving the other. **12–14: Reasons for writing.** Three groups are addressed twice, as *little children, fathers,* and *young people,* probably degrees of spiritual maturity. What is written to *little children* (v. 12) differs from

a Or *that*   *b* Gk *hating a brother*   *c* Gk *loves a brother*   *d* Or *in it*   *e* Gk *hates a brother*   *f* Or *the desire for it* what is written to *children* (v. 14). What is said of *fathers* is repeated exactly in the second address. An additional comment is made in the second address to *young people.* **13:** *Him who is from the beginning,* Jesus (contrast 1.1). *Conquered: overcome* in 2.14 (see 4.4; 5.4, 5; Jn 16.33). **14:** *Children,* parallel structure suggests the same group as *little children* in 2.12. *Children* and *father* form a natural pair. **15–17: True and false loves.** The *world,* the *flesh,* and the devil oppose God (4.4–6; 5.4–5, 19). God's love transforms the world; those who *love the world* are possessed by it. *Desire* is controlled or determined by its object.

18 Children, it is the last hour! As you have heard that antichrist is coming, so now many antichrists have come. From this we know that it is the last hour. ¹⁹They went out from us, but they did not belong to us; for if they had belonged to us, they would have remained with us. But by going out they made it plain that none of them belongs to us. ²⁰But you have been anointed by the Holy One, and all of you have knowledge.ᵃ ²¹I write to you, not because you do not know the truth, but because you know it, and you know that no lie comes from the truth. ²²Who is the liar but the one who denies that Jesus is the Christ?ᵇ This is the antichrist, the one who denies the Father and the Son. ²³No one who denies the Son has the Father; everyone who confesses the Son has the Father also. ²⁴Let what you heard from the beginning abide in you. If what you heard from the beginning abides in you, then you will abide in the Son and in the Father. ²⁵And this is what he has promised us,ᶜ eternal life.

26 I write these things to you concerning those who would deceive you. ²⁷As for you, the anointing that you received from him abides in you, and so you do not need anyone to teach you. But as his anointing teaches you about all things, and is true and is not a lie, and just as it has taught you, abide in him.ᵈ

2.18–27: Christological test: testing the false confession. 18–19: The antichrist and the last hour. *Children,* the whole community. *The last hour* (see 2 Thess 2.3–12) is signaled by the appearance of many *antichrists* (referred to only in 2.18, 22; 4.3; 2 Jn 7),

opponents from within the community who deny Jesus is the Christ (see 2.22; 4.3). **19–21:** The opponents were once members of the community. *Anointed,** see 2.27. *Holy One,* probably the Holy Spirit (Jn 14.26), but perhaps Jesus (Acts 3.14; 4.27) or God (Jn 17.11). *The truth,* the correct confession of Jesus as the Christ. **22–23:** The opponents denied that the human Jesus was the divine Christ (4.2–3; 2 Jn 7). *Everyone who confesses the Son has the Father:* Jesus reshapes the understanding of God (2 Jn 9). **24–26:** *What you heard:* the teaching; *abides . . . abide:* Appropriating the original message unites the believers with the Father and the Son. **27:** *Anointing* is a mark of knowledge and of new life.

28 And now, little children, abide in him, so that when he is revealed we may have confidence and not be put to shame before him at his coming.

29 If you know that he is righteous, you may be sure that everyone who does right has been born of him. ¹See what love the Father has given us, that we should be called children of God; and that is what we are. The reason the world does not know us is that it did not know him. ²Beloved, we are God's children now; what we will be has not yet been revealed. What we do know is this: when heᵈ is revealed, we will be like him, for we will see him as he is. ³And all who have this hope in him purify themselves, just as he is pure.

4 Everyone who commits sin is guilty of lawlessness; sin is lawlessness. ⁵You know that he was revealed to take away sins, and in him there is no sin. ⁶No one who abides in him sins; no one who sins has either seen him or known him. ⁷Little children, let no one deceive you. Everyone who does what is right is righteous, just as he is righteous. ⁸Everyone who commits sin is a child of the devil; for the devil has been sinning from the beginning. The Son of God was revealed for this purpose, to destroy the works of the devil. ⁹Those who have been born of God do not sin, because God's seed abides in them;ᵉ

a Other ancient authorities read *you know all things*
b Or *the Messiah* *c* Other ancient authorities read *you*
d Or *it* *e* Or *because the children of God abide in him*

they cannot sin, because they have been born of God. [10]The children of God and the children of the devil are revealed in this way: all who do not do what is right are not from God, nor are those who do not love their brothers and sisters.[a]

2.28–4.6: The relationship of the two tests. 2.28–3.24: Ethical test. 2.28–3.10: Who are the children of God? 2.28–3.3: *Little children . . . born of him . . . children of God:* The believers, like Jesus, see God as Father. *When he is revealed,* that is, at his *coming* (see 2.28), the children will be like the Son (compare 4.17). **4–10:** The letter apparently asserts the sinlessness of believers but elsewhere calls the claim of sinlessness a lie (1.6–2.2, 6). Only through the Son of God is freedom from sin possible. By distinguishing between *the children of God* and *the children of the devil,* the letter provides guidance to judge the believers' moral lives: *Children of the devil* neither act morally nor show love for others.

[11] For this is the message you have heard from the beginning, that we should love one another. [12]We must not be like Cain who was from the evil one and murdered his brother. And why did he murder him? Because his own deeds were evil and his brother's righteous. [13]Do not be astonished, brothers and sisters,[b] that the world hates you. [14]We know that we have passed from death to life because we love one another. Whoever does not love abides in death. [15]All who hate a brother or sister[a] are murderers, and you know that murderers do not have eternal life abiding in them. [16]We know love by this, that he laid down his life for us— and we ought to lay down our lives for one another. [17]How does God's love abide in anyone who has the world's goods and sees a brother or sister[e] in need and yet refuses help? [18] Little children, let us love, not in word or speech, but in truth and action. [19]And by this we will know that we are from the truth and will reassure our hearts before him [20]whenever our hearts condemn us; for God is greater than our hearts, and he knows everything. [21]Beloved, if our hearts do not condemn us, we have boldness before God; [22]and we receive from him whatever we ask,

because we obey his commandments and do what pleases him.

23 And this is his commandment, that we should believe in the name of his Son Jesus Christ and love one another, just as he has commanded us. [24]All who obey his commandments abide in him, and he abides in them. And by this we know that he abides in us, by the Spirit that he has given us.

3.11–24. 11–18: Love one another. The message which goes back to Jesus, the beginning, is *Love one another* (see 2.10; 3.23; 2 Jn 5; Jn 13.34–35). *Cain* (see Gen 4.1–16), this is the only reference to the Hebrew Scriptures* in the letter. *The evil one,* the devil (see 2.13–14; 3.8, 10; 5.18–19; Jn 8.44; 12.31; 14.30). Those who love are, paradoxically, hated by the world (compare 2.15–17). *God's love* in the believer's life is expressed in costly actions of practical help. **19–24: Love is the basis of confidence before God.** *By this we will know* (contrast the present tense in 2.3) is a reference to the future possibility of lack of assurance before God. The evidence of love will overcome an uncertain heart. Much of the letter tries to build up the believer's confidence. Keeping God's commandments is the means of abiding in him; receiving the Spirit is the evidence of abiding in him (see 4.1, 2, 6, 13; 5.6–8; Jn 14.15–17, 25–26; 16.7–15).

4 Beloved, do not believe every spirit, but test the spirits to see whether they are from God; for many false prophets have gone out into the world. [2]By this you know the Spirit of God: every spirit that confesses that Jesus Christ has come in the flesh is from God, [3]and every spirit that does not confess Jesus[d] is not from God. And this is the spirit of the antichrist, of which you have heard that it is coming; and now it is already in the world. [4]Little children, you are from God, and have conquered them; for the one who is in you is greater than the one who is in the world. [5]They are from the world; therefore what they say is from the world, and the world listens to them. [6]We are from God. Whoever knows God listens to us, and whoever is not from God does not listen to us.

a Gk *his brother*   *b* Gk *brothers*   *c* Gk *brother*
d Other ancient authorities read *does away with Jesus* (Gk *dissolves Jesus*)

From this we know the spirit of truth and the spirit of error.

4.1–6: The christological test of abiding in the Spirit. Inspired prophetic* speech is not enough. Believers must *test the spirits* to distinguish the *spirit of truth* from the *spirit of error* (4.6), the *spirit of the antichrist* (4.3), the spirit at work in *false prophets** (4.1), and the spirit of this world. The denial that *Jesus Christ has come in the flesh* manifests the antichrist (see 2.18). Those who know the Spirit of God *listen to us* (see Jn 8.42–47; 10.3–5, 14, 26–27), and *whoever listens to us* recognizes the spirit of truth (see Jn 14.17; 15.26; 16.13; compare 1 Jn 5.6). The "spirit of falsehood," the Jewish idiom for the Greek spirit of error, appears alongside the "spirit of truth" in the ancient Jewish texts from Qumran (Dead Sea scrolls).

7 Beloved, let us love one another, because love is from God; everyone who loves is born of God and knows God. 8 Whoever does not love does not know God, for God is love. 9 God's love was revealed among us in this way: God sent his only Son into the world so that we might live through him. 10 In this is love, not that we loved God but that he loved us and sent his Son to be the atoning sacrifice for our sins. 11 Beloved, since God loved us so much, we also ought to love one another. 12 No one has ever seen God; if we love one another, God lives in us, and his love is perfected in us.

13 By this we know that we abide in him and he in us, because he has given us of his Spirit. 14 And we have seen and do testify that the Father has sent his Son as the Savior of the world. 15 God abides in those who confess that Jesus is the Son of God, and they abide in God. 16 So we have known and believe the love that God has for us.

God is love, and those who abide in love abide in God, and God abides in them. 17 Love has been perfected among us in this: that we may have boldness on the day of judgment, because as he is, so are we in this world. 18 There is no fear in love, but perfect love casts out fear; for fear has to do with punishment, and whoever fears has not reached perfection in love. 19 We love[a] because he first loved us. 20 Those who say, "I love God," and hate their brothers or sisters,[b] are liars; for those who do not love a brother or sister[c] whom they have seen, cannot love God whom they have not seen. 21 The commandment we have from him is this: those who love God must love their brothers and sisters[a] also.

4.7–5.12: The inseparable connection between the two tests. 4.7–21: Ethical test: Love based on faith. God's love for us is the foundation of love for one another. **8–16:** The repetition of *God is love* in vv. 8 and 16 frames this section, emphasizing the theological foundation of ethics. **9–10:** Our knowledge of God comes from his Son, revealed (see 3.16; Jn 3.16) in the loving act of sending his Son as an *atoning sacrifice* (see 2.2). **11–12:** That loving act is the basis for behavior; our love for one another demonstrates the reality of the relationship with God. **13–16:** The argument moves at the intellectual level and in the realm of experience. The believers know and testify that *the Father has sent his Son as the Savior of the world;* they experience God abiding in them as they confess that *Jesus is the Son of God.* This knowledge and experience is found in the community. **17–18:** Living as Jesus lived, keeping his word, and conforming to his example are expressions of abiding in his love. This is the basis of confidence on the day of judgment (see 2.28). **19–21:** The believer's love has its source and model in God's foundational act of love. *Those who say* (literally, "If anyone says"), the final (seventh) assertion of the opponents. Love within the believers' community ratifies the claim to love God. The author does not deal with the command to love neighbor (see Mt 5.43; 19.19) or enemy (Mt 5.44).

5 Everyone who believes that Jesus is the Christ[d] has been born of God, and everyone who loves the parent loves the child. 2 By this we know that we love the children of God, when we love God and obey his commandments. 3 For the love of God is this, that we obey his commandments. And his commandments are not burdensome, 4 for whatever is born of God conquers the world. And this is the victory that conquers the world, our faith. 5 Who is it that conquers the world but the one who believes that Jesus is the Son of God?

a Other ancient authorities add *him;* others add *God*
b Gk *brothers*   c Gk *brother*   d Or *the Messiah*

6 This is the one who came by water and blood, Jesus Christ, not with the water only but with the water and the blood. And the Spirit is the one that testifies, for the Spirit is the truth. [7]There are three that testify:[a] [8]the Spirit and the water and the blood, and these three agree. [9]If we receive human testimony, the testimony of God is greater; for this is the testimony of God that he has testified to his Son. [10]Those who believe in the Son of God have the testimony in their hearts. Those who do not believe in God[b] have made him a liar by not believing in the testimony that God has given concerning his Son. [11]And this is the testimony: God gave us eternal life, and this life is in his Son. [12]Whoever has the Son has life; whoever does not have the Son of God does not have life.

5.1–12 Christological test: Faith is the basis of love. 1–3: Right faith is the test for the claim to be a child of God. So is love for the children of God (2.28–29; 3.1). **4–5:** *Faith,* far from being an intellectual abstraction, becomes the *victory that conquers the world.* **6:** *Water and blood,* perhaps a reference to baptism* and death, or to the effusion of water and blood at Jesus' death (Jn 19.34–35). According to Jn 15.26, *the Spirit is the one who testifies* and *the Spirit is the truth* (see 4.6). **9–10:** Those with correct faith have the testimony in their hearts, apparently an appeal to the witness of the Spirit (4.13). **11–12:** God's witness has two sides: the Son and the eternal life he brings. To know Christ is to know his benefits (see Jn 3.15–16, 36; 5.24).

~~~~~~

13 I write these things to you who believe in the name of the Son of God, so that you may know that you have eternal life.

14 And this is the boldness we have in him, that if we ask anything according to his will, he hears us. [15]And if we know that he hears us in whatever we ask, we know that we have obtained the requests made of him. [16]If you see your brother or sister[c] committing what is not a mortal sin, you will ask,

and God[d] will give life to such a one—to those whose sin is not mortal. There is sin that is mortal; I do not say that you should pray about that. [17]All wrongdoing is sin, but there is sin that is not mortal.

18 We know that those who are born of God do not sin, but the one who was born of God protects them, and the evil one does not touch them. [19]We know that we are God's children, and that the whole world lies under the power of the evil one. [20]And we know that the Son of God has come and has given us understanding so that we may know him who is true;[e] and we are in him who is true, in his Son Jesus Christ. He is the true God and eternal life.

21 Little children, keep yourselves from idols.[f]

5.13–21 Conclusion. 13: The beginning of the conclusion resembles Jn 20.31, with the most significant modification that believers may *know* that they have eternal life. In the face of the disturbing threat of the opponents, the assurance of believers has become the crucial issue. **16–17:** *Mortal sin,* leading to death or unforgivable (compare Mk 3.29). **18–20:** The letter concludes with three affirmations of knowledge. *We know . . . do not sin:* see 3.4–10. *We know* that *we are God's children,* see 4.4, 6. Over against this, the world lies in the power of *the evil one,* (see 3.12; 2.15–17; 5.4–5). *We know that the Son of God has come and has given us understanding* of the one *who is true.* Some texts (see note e) correctly interpret this as a reference to God, *the true God,* the Father (see Jn 17.3). **21:** *Idols:* God is the source of eternal life, but idols are lifeless and powerless. Opponents deal only with idols, not with the God who is true.

~~~~~~

a A few other authorities read (with variations) [7]*There are three that testify in heaven, the Father, the Word, and the Holy Spirit, and these three are one.* [8]*And there are three that testify on earth:*   *b* Other ancient authorities read *in the Son*   *c* Gk *your brother*   *d* Gk *he*   *e* Other ancient authorities read *know the true God*   *f* Other ancient authorities add *Amen*

THE SECOND LETTER OF JOHN

Introduction

The second and third letters of John have formal greetings and the author identifies himself as "the elder," which is probably a title of authority rather than an indication of age. There is a good case for seeing 2, 3 John as supporting letters sent with 1 John. The second letter is addressed to "the elect lady and her children," which is probably a symbolic reference to a neighboring church and its individual members. As a covering letter it briefly summarizes the main teaching of the first letter, crystallizing the two main points: the correctness of the confession of faith in Jesus Christ coming in the flesh, and the outworking of faith in love for one another. There is also a call for the readers to refuse hospitality to those who do not share the correct teaching (10–11).

READING GUIDE

1–3	Opening greeting
4–6	Commendation and call to love one another
7–9	Warning against the opponents, the deceivers
10–11	Warning against offering hospitality to the opponents
12–13	Final greetings

1 The elder to the elect lady and her children, whom I love in the truth, and not only I but also all who know the truth, ²because of the truth that abides in us and will be with us forever:

3 Grace, mercy, and peace will be with us from God the Father and from*a* Jesus Christ, the Father's Son, in truth and love.

4 I was overjoyed to find some of your children walking in the truth, just as we have been commanded by the Father. ⁵But now, dear lady, I ask you, not as though I were writing you a new commandment, but one we have had from the beginning, let us love one another. ⁶And this is love, that we walk according to his commandments; this is the commandment just as you have heard it from the beginning—you must walk in it.

7 Many deceivers have gone out into the world, those who do not confess that Jesus Christ has come in the flesh; any such person is the deceiver and the antichrist! ⁸Be on your guard, so that you do not lose what we*b* have worked for, but may receive a full re-

ward. ⁹Everyone who does not abide in the teaching of Christ, but goes beyond it, does not have God; whoever abides in the teaching has both the Father and the Son. ¹⁰Do not receive into the house or welcome anyone who comes to you and does not bring this teaching; ¹¹for to welcome is to participate in the evil deeds of such a person.

12 Although I have much to write to you, I would rather not use paper and ink; instead I hope to come to you and talk with you face to face, so that our joy may be complete.

13 The children of your elect sister send you their greetings.*c*

1–3: The opening greeting has a standard letter format: from A to B, greeting. The *elder* was an authoritative leader (see 1 Pet 5.1) addressing the *elect lady and her children,* a symbolic reference to a local church and its members (see v. 13). Such a greeting

---

a Other ancient authorities add *the Lord*   *b* Other ancient authorities read *you*   *c* Other ancient authorities add *Amen* often mentioned virtues of the persons addressed. Here the elder affirmed that he, and all who know the truth, truly love the addressees. The greeting, in the name of the Father and the Son, overlooks the Spirit (compare 1 Tim 1.2; 2 Tim 1.2) while stressing the reality of the relationship of the Father and the Son, again using the key themes of truth and love. **4–6:** Reference to *some* of the children walking in the truth may indirectly reveal that the schism of 1 Jn 2.19 had affected this community also. *The truth* may be a reference to the christological confession; the command, no longer new, was foundational for the community (see 1 Jn 2.7–8; 5.3; Jn 13.34). **7–9:** The *many deceiv-* *ers* are like the false prophets* and *antichrist* who deny the incarnation (see 1 Jn 2.18–23, 26; 3.7; 4.2–3, 6). The warning shows that the threat of the influence of the schismatics had not disappeared. Reference to going *beyond* the teaching of Christ suggests the schismatics were progressive in their teaching (see 1 Jn 1.1–4; 3.23). **10–11:** The warning against providing hospitality to the false teachers argues that to aid them is to assist in their mission (compare Tit 3.10). **12:** This conclusion is like that of 3 Jn 13–14. Stated preference for face-to-face contact is common. **13:** The elder greets his readers in the name of his own community.

THE THIRD LETTER OF JOHN

Introduction

The third letter is addressed to an individual named Gaius whom the author says he loves and who was perhaps a "disciple" of the author. This letter is about hospitality in the mission. It opposes the work of Diotrephes, possibly a rival elder, who may have sided with the opponents of the author and refused hospitality. It indicates that the opponents and their supporters had already withdrawn hospitality to our author and his supporters.

READING GUIDE

1	Opening greeting
2–4	Commendation for walking in the truth
5–8	Commendation for providing hospitality to missionaries
9–10	Critique of Diotrephes
11–12	Commendation of Demetrius
13–15	Final greeting

1 The elder to the beloved Gaius, whom I love in truth.

2 Beloved, I pray that all may go well with you and that you may be in good health, just as it is well with your soul. ³I was overjoyed when some of the friends*a* arrived and testified to your faithfulness to the truth, namely how you walk in the truth. ⁴I have no greater joy than this, to hear that my children are walking in the truth.

5 Beloved, you do faithfully whatever you do for the friends,*a* even though they are strangers to you; ⁶they have testified to your love before the church. You will do well to send them on in a manner worthy of God; ⁷for they began their journey for the sake of Christ,*b* accepting no support from non-believers.*c* ⁸Therefore we ought to support such people, so that we may become co-workers with the truth.

9 I have written something to the church; but Diotrephes, who likes to put himself first, does not acknowledge our authority. ¹⁰So if I come, I will call attention to what he is doing in spreading false charges against us. And not content with those charges, he refuses to welcome the friends,*a* and even prevents those who want to do so and expels them from the church.

11 Beloved, do not imitate what is evil but imitate what is good. Whoever does good is from God; whoever does evil has not seen God. ¹²Everyone has testified favorably about Demetrius, and so has the truth itself. We also testify for him,*d* and you know that our testimony is true.

13 I have much to write to you, but I would rather not write with pen and ink; ¹⁴instead I hope to see you soon, and we will talk together face to face.

15 Peace to you. The friends send you their greetings. Greet the friends there, each by name.

1: The opening and closing mark this as a genuine letter. *The elder* (see 2 Jn 1) addresses the *beloved* (see 2, 5, 11; 1 Jn 2.7; 3.2; 4.1, 7). *Gaius* was a common Roman name (see Acts 19.29; 20.4; Rom 16.3; 1 Cor 1.14). Just as the elder claimed to *truly love* the recipients of 2 John, he now affirms his genuine love for Gaius. **2:** Prayers for the well-being of the recipient often follow the greeting. **3–4:** The elder notes reports of the faithfulness of Gaius, to whom he refers as one of his children, probably a convert. Reference to *walking in the truth* (see 2 Jn 4) probably denotes the chris-

a Gk *brothers*   *b* Gk *for the sake of the name*
c Gk *the Gentiles*   *d* Gk lacks *for him*

tological confession of faith. **5–8:** Supporters of the elder reported the hospitality (see 2 Jn 10–11; Titus 3.13) shown by Gaius to the friends (literally *brothers,* see note *a*). Hospitality shown to the supporters of the elder is said to make those who gave it *co-workers with the truth* (compare 2 Jn 11). **9–10:** The critique of Diotrephes signals a leadership struggle with the elder. *I have written something to the church* is probably a reference to 1 John. Diotrephes obviously rejected the teaching of 1 John. He seems to have been a local leader with authority similar to that of the elder. Just as the elder counseled the refusal of hospitality to his opponents, so Diotrephes used his authority to enforce the refusal of hospitality to supporters of the elder, *the friends.* **11–12:** Whoever *does good is from God* (see 1 Jn 2.29; 3.10; Mt 7.15–20). Demetrius seems to have been a supporter of the elder. Perhaps his credentials were challenged by Diotrephes and now the elder calls all supporters to his aid. *Our testimony is true,* see Jn 5.31–37; 19.35; 21.24. **13–15:** The closing, like that of 2 Jn 12–13, asserts the priority of a face-to-face meeting over a lengthy letter (compare 1 Cor 16.19–20). The greeting of *peace,* the Jewish greeting, sets 3 John apart from 1 and 2 John, as do the reciprocal greetings from *friends* (rather than *children*).

THE LETTER OF JUDE

Introduction

The author identifies himself as Jude, "brother of James," who is presumably the brother of Jesus (Mk 6.3; Acts 15.13). Oddly, he does not claim Jesus as his kin, although Eusebius records legends about the grandsons of Jude "who is said to have been the brother, according to the flesh, of the Savior" (*H.E.* 3.19.1). His viewpoint reflects Judean interests as evidenced by the scriptural references and the obscure Israelite works cited (1 Enoch;* "Assumption of Moses"*). The level of literacy and the quality of Greek style are much higher than one would expect of a village peasant. The fiction that Jude is so highly connected by birth lends authority to the letter's message, since heretical persons who deny key elements of the group's faith would be outweighed by the word of a genuine authority such as Jude.

READING GUIDE

In terms of the typical structure of ancient letters, Jude begins with notice of sender, addressees, and greetings (vv. 1–2). No thanksgiving is given, as Jude plunges into the body of the letter: First, he petitions the recipients (vv. 3–4), then lays out an elaborate argument (vv. 5–16), and ends with a number of disclosures (vv. 17–23). The letter concludes with a doxology (vv. 24–25). Both the introduction and conclusion exhort the audience to faithfulness (vv. 3, 20–23). A number of triplets are found internally: accusations (v. 4); examples of punishment (vv. 5–7); another triple accusation (v. 8); another triple example of punishment (v. 11).

Jude exposes heretical doctrines, such as "denying the Lord," an error that rejects the belief that God will judge the world. Presumably the heretics claim that for true believers, the "end times" are already here (1 Cor 4.8; 2 Tim 2.17–18). Authentic Christians, the heretics claim, are those who have already been raised with Jesus, and so will not be subject to judgment. Moreover, because they are "spiritual," they are no longer concerned with matters of the body, earthly laws, or human authority. Against such, Jude argues that generations previously saved were subsequently condemned (vv. 5–7). From various places, Jude cites prophecies that "the Lord will judge" (vv. 8–9, 14–16). The argument of the letter goes as follows.

1. Letter opening: author, addressees, and blessing (1–3)
2. Letter body: the opponents' crimes and punishment
   A. Triple charges and punishment (4–7)
   B. Triple charges and prediction of punishment (8–9)
   C. Another charge (10)
   D. Triple examples of punished sinners (11)
   E. Multiple references to crimes and prediction of punishment (12–16)
3. Exhortation* to faithfulness
   A. Predictions of godless people infiltrating the group (17–19)
   B. Exhortation to faithfulness (20–23)
4. Letter closing: praise of God (24–25)

1 Jude,[a] a servant[b] of Jesus Christ and brother of James,

To those who are called, who are beloved[c] in[d] God the Father and kept safe for[d] Jesus Christ:

2 May mercy, peace, and love be yours in abundance.

3 Beloved, while eagerly preparing to write to you about the salvation we share, I find it necessary to write and appeal to you to contend for the faith that was once for all entrusted to the saints. [4]For certain intruders have stolen in among you, people who long ago were designated for this condemnation as ungodly, who pervert the grace of our God into licentiousness and deny our only Master and Lord, Jesus Christ.[e]

5 Now I desire to remind you, though you are fully informed, that the Lord, who once for all saved[f] a people out of the land of Egypt, afterward destroyed those who did not believe. [6]And the angels who did not keep their own position, but left their proper dwelling, he has kept in eternal chains in deepest darkness for the judgment of the great day. [7]Likewise, Sodom and Gomorrah and the surrounding cities, which, in the same manner as they, indulged in sexual immorality and pursued unnatural lust,[g] serve as an example by undergoing a punishment of eternal fire.

8 Yet in the same way these dreamers also defile the flesh, reject authority, and slander the glorious ones.[h] [9]But when the archangel Michael contended with the devil and disputed about the body of Moses, he did not dare to bring a condemnation of slander[i] against him, but said, "The Lord rebuke you!" [10]But these people slander whatever they do not understand, and they are destroyed by those things that, like irrational animals, they know by instinct. [11]Woe to them! For they go the way of Cain, and abandon themselves to Balaam's error for the sake of gain, and perish in Korah's rebellion. [12]These are blemishes[j] on your love-feasts, while they feast with you without fear, feeding themselves.[k] They are waterless clouds carried along by the winds; autumn trees without fruit, twice dead, uprooted; [13]wild waves of the sea, casting up the foam of their own shame; wandering stars, for whom the deepest darkness has been reserved forever.

1–13. 1–2: Letter opening. Jude is *servant,* not a slave but a figure of very high status such as Abraham, Moses, and David (Ex 32.13; 1 Sam 17.23). If *brother of James* (Acts 12.17; 15.12), then Jude is also kin of Jesus. He addresses no geographical church, which suggests that this is a general letter that could be read in any church. **3–4: Enter heretics.** Jude writes because *certain intruders* are abroad whose false doctrine (*deny our only Master and Lord*) leads to immorality (*pervert the grace of God into licentiousness*). He finds it necessary to exhort the addressees to *contend for the faith* that was delivered to the disciples in its fullness. He appeals, then, to the antiquity of an immutable tradition. **5–7: Refutation.** Jude cites three examples of divine judgment: Although God *saved* a people, God later *destroyed* those who proved unfaithful. Similarly, although many angels remained faithful, God imprisoned the angels who strayed. Sodom and Gomorrah illustrate divine judgment on immorality. Hence, if the intruders deny the sovereignty of God to judge, these examples rebut that error and serve as proof of the coming judgment. **8–9: What could be worse?** Jude claims that these intruders accept no laws concerning the body (*defile the flesh*) and reject all *authority,* even that of the angels who assist God's judgment. He cites an obscure document, the "Assumption of Moses,"* in which Michael the archangel confirmed God's sovereignty: *The Lord rebuke you.* This proves useful in support of the tradition about the Day of Judgment, which the intruders deny. **10–13: Precedents of punishment.** Just as three biblical examples were cited in vv. 5–7, so we find here three examples of deviants brought to judgment: Cain, Balaam, and Korah. In legend* *Cain* exemplified godlessness and envy; *Balaam* was willing to lead Israel astray and curse it (Num 22); *Korah* typified ambition and rebellion (Num 16.1–35). Besides accusing the intruders of parasitical corruption, they are compared to fleeting, empty natural phenomena such as *waterless clouds, uprooted trees,*

---

wild waves, and *wandering stars.* Their instability makes them perilous guides.

~~~~~~~~~~~~~~~~~~~~~~~~~~~~~~~~~~~~~

14 It was also about these that Enoch, in the seventh generation from Adam, prophesied, saying, "See, the Lord is coming*a* with ten thousands of his holy ones, ¹⁵to execute judgment on all, and to convict everyone of all the deeds of ungodliness that they have committed in such an ungodly way, and of all the harsh things that ungodly sinners have spoken against him." ¹⁶These are grumblers and malcontents; they indulge their own lusts; they are bombastic in speech, flattering people to their own advantage.

17 But you, beloved, must remember the predictions of the apostles of our Lord Jesus Christ; ¹⁸for they said to you, "In the last time there will be scoffers, indulging their own ungodly lusts." ¹⁹It is these worldly people, devoid of the Spirit, who are causing divisions. ²⁰But you, beloved, build yourselves up on your most holy faith; pray in the Holy Spirit; ²¹keep yourselves in the love of God; look forward to the mercy of our Lord Jesus Christ that leads to*b* eternal life. ²²And have mercy on some who are wavering; ²³save others by snatching them out of the fire; and have mercy on still others with fear, hating even the tunic defiled by their bodies.*c*

24 Now to him who is able to keep you from falling, and to make you stand without blemish in the presence of his glory with rejoicing, ²⁵to the only God our Savior, through Jesus Christ our Lord, be glory, majesty, power, and authority, before all time and now and forever. Amen.

───────────────────────────────

14–25. 14–16: Enoch★ to the rescue. Jude cites as authoritative a prophecy from 1 Enoch about the coming judgment. This popular document, although used by Second Temple Judeans and later Christian writers, was never judged to be canonical.★ Jude uses it here because it contains a full statement of the topic of God's judgment and contains many parallels with gospel traditions such as Mt 24.29–31. **17–23: Prediction of heretics too.** Another prediction announces that *scoffers* will come, the fulfillment of which bolsters Jude's repetition of predictions of the coming judgment. As the opponents lack faith, love, and especially hope, Jude encourages the church to *faithfulness, love,* and hope (*looking foward to the mercy of our Lord*). Far from abandoning the opponents, he urges the addressees to *have mercy on the wavering* and to *save others by snatching* them from a fiery judgment. **24–25: Letter closing.** A doxology concludes the letter, beginning with acknowledgment of both God's protection of the church and purification of the members. This demonstrates that right theology (confession of God's will and powers) leads to right morals. Supreme honor is paid to God: *glory, majesty, power,* and *authority,* similar to the hymn of praise in Rev 4.11. In contrast, the scoffers *deny* the powers of our *Master and Lord* (v. 4).

~~~~~~~~~~~~~~~~~~~~~~~~~~~~~~~~~~~~~

a Gk *came*   *b* Gk *Christ to*   *c* Gk *by the flesh.* The Greek text of verses 22–23 is uncertain at several points

APOCALYPTIC ⋆ LITERATURE

The English word "apocalypse"⋆ is a transliteration of the Greek word, *apokalypsis*, and the title of the book of Revelation in Greek. While popular usage assumes that the meaning of apocalypse is "the cataclysmic end of the world," the translation "revelation" (from the Latin word, *revelatio*) comes much closer to the true meaning of *apokalypsis*, whose literal translation is "unveiling." Apocalypse as unveiling is a reminder that in apocalyptic literature, form and content are intertwined because it is equally about the communication process of unveiling and the content that is unveiled. Apocalyptic literature reveals, or unveils, a fresh perspective on reality.

While the New Testament book of Revelation was the first book to receive the name "apocalypse," the name also refers to a type of literature of which Revelation is one example. Apocalyptic literature is found in the Old Testament, the Apocrypha,⋆ and the New Testament, making it one of the most versatile genres⋆ in biblical literature. By contrast to prophetic⋆ literature, for example, that is largely tied with particular periods in Israel's history (see "Prophetic Literature," 923), apocalyptic literature figures prominently in a wide range of historical periods and movements in Jewish and Christian literature. There are two canonical⋆ apocalypses, Revelation and Daniel (esp. chs. 7–12), as well as the "little apocalypses" of the Synoptic Gospels⋆ (Mt 24.4–36; Mk 13; Lk 21.8–36). In addition, there are apocalyptic elements in some of the canonical prophetic literature (for instance, Isa 24–27) and in some of Paul's letters (for example, 1 Thess). The book of 4 Ezra (2 Esdras 3–14) is an example of apocalyptic literature in the Apocrypha. In addition, apocalyptic literature is found extensively outside of the biblical canon: *Enoch*,⋆ 2 and 3 *Baruch, the Apocalypse of Abraham*, in the Dead Sea Scrolls, and in early Christian apocryphal books (for instance, *Apocalypse of Peter*).

All apocalypses are narratives⋆ and all involve the "revealing" of secrets of the heavenly or supernatural world to a human seer or prophet.⋆ The communication of what has been revealed is the subject matter of the written book. Key to apocalyptic literature is that the seer is able to cross the spatial and temporal divide between earth and heaven and between present and future. The vivid language and stories of apocalyptic narratives simultaneously illustrate how different the heavenly (supernatural) world is from the present, earthly (natural) world and how interconnected the two realms are.

Each apocalypse has its own distinctive perspectives and literary and theological goals, but there are also common traits that belong to the apocalyptic genre more generally.

Visions and Dreams

The seer receives the revealed secrets through dreams, visions, by being transported to heaven, or some combination of all three. The seer's claim to have received these secrets, which he now makes known, is central to apocalyptic literature. In Daniel 7, for example, first the fact of Daniel's dream is mentioned ("Daniel had a dream and visions of his head as he lay in bed.") and then Daniel's writing and communication of the dream is narrated ("Then he wrote down the dream: I, Daniel, saw in my vision..." [7.1–2]). In 4 Ezra (2 Esd), Ezra receives several visions (9.27–13.58) in which the supernatural world breaks into the present. In Revelation, John receives a vision through which he is able to see the heavenly throne room ("After this I looked, and there in heaven a door stood open! And the first voice...said...'Come up here.'" [Rev 4.1]). Through dreams and visions, the divide between the natural and supernatural realms become permeable, rather than impassable.

Imagery

Apocalyptic visions are highly symbolic, their narratives composed with images of unusual animals, dramatic use of numbers, and vivid visions of both the heavenly realm and a transformed earth. Daniel 7 is a vision of "the four winds of heaven stirring up the great sea, and four great beasts came up out of the sea, different from one another." Ezra sees "rising from the sea an eagle that had twelve feathered wings and three heads. I saw it spread its wings over the whole earth, and all the winds of heaven blew upon it." (2 Esd 11.1–2). John sees "four living creatures, full of eyes in front and behind" (Rev 4.6), the well-known four horses and riders (Rev 6–7), and several sets of seven angels. In each of these apocalypses the use of specific numbers and very vivid images work literarily to force the imagination of the reader to focus on the same thing the seer sees. The visions are not generalized but narrate each sensory detail of the seer's experience.

Apocalyptic literature also draws on common mythological imagery in its visions. The concrete representation of evil as a serpent, a beast, a dragon, or Satan himself engages a wellspring of mythology common to the Mediterranean world. The myth of heavenly combat (Dan 7.20; Rev 12) is a common mythological motif,* as are references to the constellations and the zodiac (e.g., Dan 8.10; Rev 12.1). The image of the woman clothed like the sun in Revelation 12 and the birth of her son may allude to the myth of Apollo.

The imagery of the visions also is replete with scriptural allusions. Creation imagery dominates in apocalyptic literature, images of the unsettling waters of chaos (Dan 7.2; 2 Esd 13.2–3; Rev 13.1) and images of a reclaimed garden of Eden (Rev 22.1–2). There are strong echoes of Ezekiel in Daniel, 2 Esdras, and Revelation, as all contain the image of the four living creatures (Ezek 1). The concentration of biblical imagery helps to underscore that the vision the seer is receiving is from heaven. The seer's visions take the shape of stories that would already be recognized by the reader of apocalyptic literature as belonging to the revealed word of God. These scriptural echoes help the reader to see the ways in which God is presiding over the cosmic drama narrated in the books.

Patterns

Another common element of apocalyptic literature is the use of highly structured patterns to convey the content of the visions. Daniel and 4 Ezra (2 Esdras 3–14), for example, contain highly structured symbolic reviews of history, in which ages and kingdoms are presented in numerical patterns, whose meaning is then interpreted by the angel mediator. Revelation contains a stylized presentation of the heavenly journey, in which numbers and patterns are repeated in a cyclical manner. In both types of patterns—the more linear and the cyclical—the patterns create a sense of order in what is otherwise perceived to be disorder and even chaos. For both Daniel and Revelation, the political climate at the time of the books can be understood as rendering invisible both God's presence in the world and God's plan for the world (see introductions to Dan, 1189 and Rev, 2060). The distinctive narrative patterns of apocalyptic literature render God's plans visible by exaggerating their orderliness in the midst of disorder.

Interpretation

The seers' visions and dreams always need interpretation.* Due to their symbolic and imagistic quality, their meaning is not self-evident to the seer/prophet. The role of interpreter is played by a heavenly mediator, most often an angel. Unlike in contemporary religion, where angels are most often thought of as guardian angels, in apocalyptic and biblical literature more generally angels are messengers of God's word (the English word "angel" is a transliteration of the Greek word *angellos*, which means "messenger"). Angels as divine messengers dominate apocalyptic literature.

In Daniel 7:15–24, for example, Daniel turns to one of the heavenly "attendants" (an angel) "to ask him the truth concerning all this. So he said that he would disclose to me the interpretation of the matter." Much of 2 Esdras is a dialogue between Ezra and an angel, and angels are John's constant companions and interpreters in Revelation. Like the concentration of biblical imagery, the presence of angelic mediators in apocalyptic literature also underscores that the visions are from God, since God's angel messengers are necessary to interpret them.

The Command to Write

Although the actual experience of the vision is attributed to an individual in apocalyptic literature, the vision has communal implications. The seer is the conduit of the vision of the heavenly world for a broader community, and the assumption that the seer is writing down his visions is an essential part of apocalyptic literature (Dan 8.26; Rev 1.11, 19; 21.5). What the seer does with what is written, however, varies. Daniel, for instance, is explicitly ordered by his angelic mediator to seal what he has written down and to "keep the words secret and the book sealed until the time of the end" (Dan 12.4, 9). In Revelation, in what seems a quite intentional contrast to Daniel, the angel says to John, "Do not seal up the words of the prophecy of this book, for the time is near" (Rev 22.10).

The drama and vivid imagery of apocalyptic literature are the literary means to communicate the "unveiling" that is the heart of apocalyptic. The conceit of apocalyptic literature is that the seer is given an opportunity to see into heaven and into God's large-scale plans for human history and creation in a way that is normally veiled to human perception. Apocalyptic literature takes away the veil that can make evil appear to be at best innocuous, at worst, merely ordinarily bad: the imagery of the beast in Revelation 13 is meant to alert the reader to the utterly abhorrent character of moral evil. This strategy helps the readers to reexamine their assumptions about how the world is ordered. The seers themselves are unsettled by their visions—Daniel becomes ill (Dan 8.27), John succumbs to tears (Rev 5.4). Apocalyptic literature is unsettling to readers because it was designed to be unsettling.

THE REVELATION TO JOHN

Introduction

The Apocalypse✶ of John is a symbolic vision report containing elaborate descriptions (of Jesus, of a trip to heaven, and of the agents of evil in the world) and dramatic actions. It is unique among biblical works in its scope and intensity, though it shares certain symbolic elements with other New Testament descriptions of the end times (2 Thess 2; Mk 13; Mt 24–25; Lk 21). It also has numerous affinities with visionary literature in the Hebrew Scriptures✶ (esp. Dan 6–12, but also Zech 9–14 and aspects of Ezekiel). The closest analogies, however, are in the numerous vision reports now known collectively as the pseudepigrapha,✶ a group of Jewish writings not in the Bible but often claiming to be written by some biblical person (for example, 1 Enoch,✶ 4 Ezra, Testament of Abraham).

Key traits of such visionary literature include the following:

1. The claim that a secret revelation has been given to some seer or prophet.✶
2. This revelation is imparted in a dream, a vision, or a transportation of the seer to heaven—often the three means are combined.
3. The revelation is usually mediated by some figure, such as an angel, who acts as guide and interpreter to the seer.
4. The revelation is usually not self-explanatory, but is encoded in a variety of esoteric symbols involving animals (often composites of different animals, with multiple heads), mythological figures, and numbers.
5. The revelation is often attributed to some figure who lived long before the time of the actual author: Isaiah, Moses, Enoch,✶ Daniel, Adam, Zephaniah, Peter, etc.

Revelation shares all these traits except the last; it is the only known example of a vision report that gives the actual author's name.

Most scholars accept a date around 95 CE, though a few maintain an earlier dating around 70. The late dating is supported by the testimony of the earliest commentators, especially Irenaeus (*Against Heresies* 5.30.3), as well as by data from the text of Revelation itself. Most persuasive is the use of the code name Babylon for Rome, suggesting that Rome has come to be seen as the second destroyer of Jerusalem as Babylon was the first. The argument for the earlier dating rests on allusions in the text, such as the ease with which 666 can be identified with Nero (see sidebar on p. 2080; comments on 13.11–18). The earlier dating would place it in the context of Nero's persecution of Christians at Rome (64–68 CE) and of the great Judean-Roman War (66–74 CE). Both may be right. The Apocalypse is a complex book, consisting of visions no doubt recorded over many years but probably edited and published in the present form near the end of the first century.

The naming of the churches addressed (1.4, 11) places the work squarely in the Hellenistic✶ (Greek-speaking), Roman cities along the Western coast of Asia Minor (modern-day Turkey). The author is identified as John, without further qualification. While tradition has long identified the author as John the son of Zebedee, one of Jesus' disciples, there is nothing in the text to suggest this, and one point makes the identification doubtful: The vision of the New Jerusalem

Chart The three basic stories in Revelation

	Story One	Story Two	Story Three
Place	Patmos	Heaven	Earth
Characters	Jesus as majestic human; John; Churches	Jesus as slain Lamb; Elders; Heavenly beings	Jesus as heavenly warrior; Dragon and beasts; Woman and her children
Action	Letter writing	Worship	War
John presented as	Secretary	Heavenly traveler	Seer/prophet★
Mythic paradigm	Theophany★	Throne vision	Holy war★
Chapters	1–3	4–11	12–22

shows it as founded on the twelve apostles,★ making them appear to be figures of the distant past (21.14).

The once universal view that Revelation was written in response to Roman persecution has now been largely abandoned, for there is simply no evidence of any such persecution in this region in the late first century. In fact, Revelation speaks very little about actual persecution (and names only one martyr,★ Antipas of Pergamum; 2.13); suffering is envisioned for the future. The historical and social context seems to be peace and prosperity, and the great temptation is not to renounce the faith (as it might be in a time of persecution) but to be seduced by the glamour and luxury of Greco-Roman culture.

There is no agreement on the best way to imagine the organization of the material in the Apocalypse; numerous possibilities can be argued depending on the focus. Most schemes concentrate on the four numbered series of seven visions (letters, seals, trumpets, and bowls), often adding other series of seven (unnumbered) visions. Here we will focus on the action of the story and see that action as occurring in three stages:

1. Jesus appears to John and dictates seven letters (1–3).
2. John is taken to heaven and sees how God's reign comes (4–11).
3. Satan attacks Jesus' followers but is finally defeated (12–22).

These three stories are in some ways self-contained units, but they share a common frame (a letter from John to the churches) and overlapping themes and characters (notably, the Lamb of story two appears repeatedly in story three).

READING GUIDE

Within these stories the major divisions are fairly clearly marked. We can note the following basic text segments.

Rev 1–3 The seven messages from the risen Jesus
- An opening address to the audience (1.1–11)
- A vision of Jesus (1.12–20) with seven messages (2–3)

Rev 4–11 The scenes of the heavenly court
- The liturgy★ of creation (4) and redemption (5)
- The unsealing of the scroll (6–7)
- The sounding of trumpets (8–11) and the proclamation of God's rule

Rev 12–22 The cosmic war
- The two signs in heaven: a woman pursued by a dragon (12–14)
  - The two beasts (13) and the army of the Lamb (14)
- The second sign in heaven: seven final plagues (15–16) with elaborate visions of two female figures: the prostitute (17–18) with accompanying scenes of judgment (19.1–21.8), and the bride (21.9–27) with accompanying scenes of restoration (22.1–5)
- A closing address to the audience (22.6–21)

1.1–11: The opening: orienting the audience. This section contains the basic markers to allow the reader to place this writing: It is first of all a revelation (a message from God), but also a letter (a message from a known person). See sidebar, "The Meaning of Apocalypse," p. 2071.

1 The revelation of Jesus Christ, which God gave him to show his servants*a* what must soon take place; he made*b* it known by sending his angel to his servant*c* John, ²who testified to the word of God and to the testimony of Jesus Christ, even to all that he saw.

3 Blessed is the one who reads aloud the words of the prophecy, and blessed are those who hear and who keep what is written in it; for the time is near.

4 John to the seven churches that are in Asia:

Grace to you and peace from him who is and who was and who is to come, and from the seven spirits who are before his throne, ⁵and from Jesus Christ, the faithful witness, the firstborn of the dead, and the ruler of the kings of the earth.

To him who loves us and freed*d* us from our sins by his blood, ⁶and made*b* us to be a kingdom, priests serving*e* his God and Father, to him be glory and dominion forever and ever. Amen.

⁷ Look! He is coming with the clouds;
    every eye will see him,

even those who pierced him;
    and on his account all the tribes of
      the earth will wail.
So it is to be. Amen.

8 "I am the Alpha and the Omega," says the Lord God, who is and who was and who is to come, the Almighty.

1.1–8. 1–3: As v. 3 indicates, the work is to be read aloud, thus the first voice one hears is that of the public reader. This voice announces that the *revelation* is *of Jesus Christ*, meaning that it both belongs to him and is about him. The revelation descends through the orders: God, Jesus, angel, John, churches. **4–7:** Suddenly the revelation genre★ is forced into the letter genre, as John speaks in his own voice. This is a standard letter opening, comparable to any of Paul's letters. **4–5a:** The *grace* has three sources: God, Jesus, and the Spirit, each described symbolically. God is described in a terse (and awkward) expression, literally: the being, the was, and the coming. One expects, but does not find, a future tense. The Spirit is symbolized as sevenfold, meaning perfect and complete. Jesus has three symbolic tags, referring respectively to his death, resurrection, and present reign. **5b–6:** This short doxology emphasizes two major themes of Revelation: *kingdom* (politics) and *priests* (religion); they are thoroughly intermixed in John's vision. **7:** This oracular★ announcement places Jesus' coming in the present tense, surrounded by his past suffering and future revelation. **8:** The voice of the Lord speaks next; God's title here echoes the Exodus story (Ex 3.14). John care-

a Gk *slaves*   *b* Gk *and he made*   *c* Gk *slave*
d Other ancient authorities read *washed*
e Gk *priests to*

fully avoids a future tense, instead describing God as "coming," a major theme (for example, 1.7; 3.11; 16.15; 21.2; 22.1, 7, 20).

9 I, John, your brother who share with you in Jesus the persecution and the kingdom and the patient endurance, was on the island called Patmos because of the word of God and the testimony of Jesus.[a] 10I was in the spirit[b] on the Lord's day, and I heard behind me a loud voice like a trumpet 11saying, "Write in a book what you see and send it to the seven churches, to Ephesus, to Smyrna, to Pergamum, to Thyatira, to Sardis, to Philadelphia, and to Laodicea." 12 Then I turned to see whose voice it was that spoke to me, and on turning I saw seven golden lampstands, 13and in the midst of the lampstands I saw one like the Son of Man, clothed with a long robe and with a golden sash across his chest. 14His head and his hair were white as white wool, white as snow; his eyes were like a flame of fire, 15his feet were like burnished bronze, refined as in a furnace, and his voice was like the sound of many waters. 16In his right hand he held seven stars, and from his mouth came a sharp, two-edged sword, and his face was like the sun shining with full force. 17 When I saw him, I fell at his feet as though dead. But he placed his right hand on me, saying, "Do not be afraid; I am the first and the last, 18and the living one. I was dead, and see, I am alive forever and ever; and I have the keys of Death and of Hades. 19Now write what you have seen, what is, and what is to take place after this. 20As for the mystery of the seven stars that you saw in my right hand, and the seven golden lampstands: the seven stars are the angels of the seven churches, and the seven lampstands are the seven churches.

1.9–20. 9–11: Voices on Patmos. John's choice of the title brother probably indicates a community that does not emphasize hierarchy. Persecution, kingdom, endurance is a very odd triad, since in ordinary understanding the time of persecution precedes the time of the kingdom; they do not overlap. Endurance is an active, not a passive quality; some would translate it "resistance." Patmos was a sparsely settled island in

John's day, not a penal colony as is often said. John's presence there could be the result of banishment (forced relocation by the government) or it could be voluntary, either to carry his testimony there or to use the relative isolation of Patmos to collect and edit his visions. 10: In the spirit probably indicates a trance-like state, but more importantly it is a claim that the vision is inspired. The Lord's day is, prosaically, Sunday, but poetically it refers to the day of Jesus' resurrection (past) and coming (future; compare the expression "day of the Lord" in Isa 13, Joel 2, or Zeph 1). John's particular expression could also be understood as the Imperial day, pointing to a contrast between Jesus and the emperor that will become increasingly pointed (see ch. 13). 12–20: The vision of Jesus. This relies heavily on the descriptions of heavenly realities in Dan 7–10, especially the Ancient One (Dan 7.9–10), together with elements from Zechariah (4.2), Ezekiel (43.2), and Isaiah (11.4; 49.2). The Son of Man figure is complex, with the basic meaning of human (contrasted with the beasts; see Dan 7.13). The description of the robe and sash mark the figure as royal or priestly. Holding the seven stars is a sign of control over destiny. The stars above correspond to the lampstands below, as the heavenly corresponds to the earthly. The sword is not in his hand (power, coercion) but in his mouth (word, testimony). 17–20: The commission from Jesus; see Dan 10.9. 20: John clearly explains the meaning of many of his symbols. The worldview is dualistic,✶ with a correspondence between what is above (stars and angels) and what is below (lamps and churches). In modern terms we might think of the inner spiritual reality of the everyday world.

2 "To the angel of the church in Ephesus write: These are the words of him who holds the seven stars in his right hand, who walks among the seven golden lampstands: 2 "I know your works, your toil and your patient endurance. I know that you cannot tolerate evildoers; you have tested those who claim to be apostles but are not, and have found them to be false. 3I also know that you are enduring patiently and bearing up for the sake of my name, and that you have not grown weary. 4But I have this against you, that you have abandoned the love you had at first. 5Remember then from what you have fallen; repent, and do the works you did at

a Or testimony to Jesus   b Or in the Spirit

first. If not, I will come to you and remove your lampstand from its place, unless you repent. 6Yet this is to your credit: you hate the works of the Nicolaitans, which I also hate. 7Let anyone who has an ear listen to what the Spirit is saying to the churches. To everyone who conquers, I will give permission to eat from the tree of life that is in the paradise of God.

2.1–7: The letter from the star holder to Ephesus: Love. Each letter is a unified composition that follows the general pattern: addressee, sender (described with traits from the vision in ch. 1), description of the present situation with statements of praise or warning, a promise to those who conquer, a refrain about hearing what the spirit says (with these last two items reversed in the first three letters). **1:** *Angel* means messenger and could refer to the leader of the local congregation, but more likely it refers to the heavenly counterpart (or inner reality) of the church, as in 1.20. See Dan 10.20–21. *Ephesus* was the leading commercial city of the area. **2:** *Endurance* is a quality John shares; see 1.9. *Apostles** are those who claim to be sent by Jesus; this is the first clue that the leadership of these churches is divided. **5:** *I will come* is actually a present tense: I am coming. **6:** *Nicolaitans* ("conqueror of people") are undefined in John's story, and no other ancient source gives us any reliable information about them. **7:** *Everyone who conquers* is the requirement for reward in each of the letters. *To eat* a sacred meal perhaps alludes to the Eucharist;* sacred meals were a common aspect of ancient temples. *The tree of life* is a multidimensional symbol, referring to the tree in Eden (Gen 2); Wisdom (Prov 3.18); and the tree of Artemis, the great goddess of Ephesus whose temple was one of the seven wonders of the ancient world. It may also refer to the cross of Jesus, the true tree of life. *Paradise* was a name both for Eden and for the temple enclosure of Artemis; for a connection with Jesus' cross, see Luke 23.43.

---

8 "And to the angel of the church in Smyrna write: These are the words of the first and the last, who was dead and came to life:

9 "I know your affliction and your poverty, even though you are rich. I know the slander on the part of those who say that they are Jews and are not, but are a synagogue of Satan. 10Do not fear what you are about to

suffer. Beware, the devil is about to throw some of you into prison so that you may be tested, and for ten days you will have affliction. Be faithful until death, and I will give you the crown of life. 11Let anyone who has an ear listen to what the Spirit is saying to the churches. Whoever conquers will not be harmed by the second death.

2.8–11: The letter from the sufferer to Smyrna: Do not fear tribulation. *Smyrna* was a city of great wealth that had been destroyed and rebuilt. Its riches amid poverty is contrasted with the poverty amid riches at Laodicea (3.17). **9:** *Slander* probably refers to Jewish refusal to recognize John's community as part of the Jewish community, thus exposing them to Roman suspicions as a new religious group. John engages in similar slander by calling them *those who say that they are Jews and are not.* *Synagogue** of Satan is not anti-Semitic in this situation since John himself is claiming to be Jewish, but it soon becomes so in Christian tradition. **10:** *Prison* was not a punishment in the Roman world, but a place of detention until punishment could be meted out. *Ten days* indicates a full and complete (ten) but relative short (days) time. For a ten-day mourning ritual connected with Smyrna, see *Iliad* 24.602ff. *Crown of life* refers to the garland given to victorious athletes. **11:** *Second death* is an idea that occurs only in Revelation (see also 20.6, 14; 21.8). It is the opposite of participating in the first resurrection and the same as the lake of fire.

---

12 "And to the angel of the church in Pergamum write: These are the words of him who has the sharp two-edged sword:

13 "I know where you are living, where Satan's throne is. Yet you are holding fast to my name, and you did not deny your faith in me*a* even in the days of Antipas my witness, my faithful one, who was killed among you, where Satan lives. 14But I have a few things against you: you have some there who hold to the teaching of Balaam, who taught Balak to put a stumbling block before the people of Israel, so that they would eat food sacrificed to idols and practice fornication. 15So you also have some who hold to the teaching of the Nicolaitans. 16Repent then. If not, I will come to you soon and make war against

a Or *deny my faith*

them with the sword of my mouth. [17]Let anyone who has an ear listen to what the Spirit is saying to the churches. To everyone who conquers I will give some of the hidden manna, and I will give a white stone, and on the white stone is written a new name that no one knows except the one who receives it.

2.12–17. The letter from the warrior to Pergamum: Resist evil. *Pergamum* was a strongly fortified, mountaintop city that had dominated this whole region until Rome's power prevailed. *Two-edged sword* is Jesus' word; see 1.16. **13:** It is no longer possible to decide what John meant by *Satan's throne,* but throne points to a political context. Nothing else is known about the martyr* *Antipas,* the only named martyr in this story. **14:** *Balaam* was an ancient prophet* who failed to curse Israel but still damaged the Israelites by counseling cultural accommodation; see Num 22–25. *Food sacrificed to idols* would encompass nearly all meat offered for public sale in a major city, since it would be dedicated to a god when butchered. *Fornication* is probably spiritual. **15:** On the *Nicolaitans* see 2.6. **16:** *I will come* is another present tense; see 2.5. **17:** *Manna* was the miraculous food that preserved Israel in the wilderness after the Exodus (Ex 16), perhaps now symbolic of the Eucharist;* see Jn 6. The meaning of the *white stone* remains obscure, though white is associated with victory in Revelation; juries voted with white and dark stones. The *new name* is a metaphor* for a changed person (Gen 32.24–28); that *no one knows* it shows that the change in the person is beyond ordinary understanding, see comment on 19.12.

18 "And to the angel of the church in Thyatira write: These are the words of the Son of God, who has eyes like a flame of fire, and whose feet are like burnished bronze:

19 "I know your works—your love, faith, service, and patient endurance. I know that your last works are greater than the first. [20]But I have this against you: you tolerate that woman Jezebel, who calls herself a prophet and is teaching and beguiling my servants[a] to practice fornication and to eat food sacrificed to idols. [21]I gave her time to repent, but she refuses to repent of her fornication. [22]Beware, I am throwing her on a bed, and those who commit adultery with her I am throwing into great distress, unless they repent of her doings; [23]and I will strike

her children dead. And all the churches will know that I am the one who searches minds and hearts, and I will give to each of you as your works deserve. [24]But to the rest of you in Thyatira, who do not hold this teaching, who have not learned what some call 'the deep things of Satan,' to you I say, I do not lay on you any other burden; [25]only hold fast to what you have until I come. [26]To everyone who conquers and continues to do my works to the end,

I will give authority over the nations;
[27] to rule[b] them with an iron rod,
    as when clay pots are shattered—

[28]even as I also received authority from my Father. To the one who conquers I will also give the morning star. [29]Let anyone who has an ear listen to what the Spirit is saying to the churches.

2.18–29: The letter from the Son of God to Thyatira: Hold fast. *Thyatira* was an inland commercial and manufacturing center with many trade guilds. It was also the home of an important temple of Apollo that was famous for its prophetic* oracles* given through a priestess known as the Sibyl. **20:** *Jezebel,* the ancient queen who sponsored the prophets* of Baal* against Elijah (1 Kings 18–22), is symbolic of John's opponent here; Jezebel is not her real name. On *fornication* and *food sacrificed to idols,* see 2.14. Paul's regulations were less strict than John's; see 1 Cor 8–10. **22:** *Adultery* is probably symbolic of worshipping other gods. **23:** *Her children* are her disciples. *Minds* is literally kidneys, the seat of emotions and feelings. The *heart* was the center of the will. **24:** The address *to the rest* reveals a division in the community. *The deep things of Satan* is clearly a local phrase at whose meaning we can only guess. Laying on them no *other burden* might echo the teaching older than Paul demanding abstention from sacrificed meat (Acts 15.28). **27:** The *iron rod* is a reference to the powers of Israel's king (Psalm 2.9). **28:** The *morning star* is Venus, but for John it is a symbol of Christ (22.16).

3 "And to the angel of the church in Sardis write: These are the words of him who has the seven spirits of God and the seven stars:

    "I know your works; you have a name of

a Gk *slaves*   *b* Or *to shepherd*

being alive, but you are dead. ²Wake up, and strengthen what remains and is on the point of death, for I have not found your works perfect in the sight of my God. ³Remember then what you received and heard; obey it, and repent. If you do not wake up, I will come like a thief, and you will not know at what hour I will come to you. ⁴Yet you have still a few persons in Sardis who have not soiled their clothes; they will walk with me, dressed in white, for they are worthy. ⁵If you conquer, you will be clothed like them in white robes, and I will not blot your name out of the book of life; I will confess your name before my Father and before his angels. ⁶Let anyone who has an ear listen to what the Spirit is saying to the churches.

3.1–6: The letter from the spirit possessor to Sardis: Awake. *Sardis* was an inland city, prosperous in John's time but famous for its lost wealth. Its original mountaintop location was thought to be impregnable, but it was twice conquered in surprise nighttime attacks. **3:** The coming *like a thief* is a standard apocalyptic★ warning (Mt 25.42–43; 1 Thess 5.2), but here it is used in an individual and present sense rather than to refer to the end of the age. **5:** The *white robes* may have a sense of purity here, in contrast to the *soiled clothes*, but the basic meaning of white in this story is conquest, and it is in this sense that they are *worthy*. The *book of life* image is used repeatedly in Revelation (13.8; 17.8; 20.12,15). The expression was also used by Paul (Phil 4.3) and occurs in a late first-century Jewish synagogue★ prayer: "May the Nazarenes . . . be blotted out of the book of life" (Twelfth Benediction). The basic metaphor★ of God's keeping track of things in a book occurs in the Exodus story (Ex 32.32).

7 "And to the angel of the church in Philadelphia write:

These are the words of the holy one, the
          true one,
    who has the key of David,
    who opens and no one will shut,
    who shuts and no one opens:

8 "I know your works. Look, I have set before you an open door, which no one is able to shut. I know that you have but little power, and yet you have kept my word and have not denied my name. ⁹I will make those of the synagogue of Satan who say that they

are Jews and are not, but are lying—I will make them come and bow down before your feet, and they will learn that I have loved you. ¹⁰Because you have kept my word of patient endurance, I will keep you from the hour of trial that is coming on the whole world to test the inhabitants of the earth. ¹¹I am coming soon; hold fast to what you have, so that no one may seize your crown. ¹²If you conquer, I will make you a pillar in the temple of my God; you will never go out of it. I will write on you the name of my God, and the name of the city of my God, the new Jerusalem that comes down from my God out of heaven, and my own new name. ¹³Let anyone who has an ear listen to what the Spirit is saying to the churches.

3.7–13: The letter from the door keeper to Philadelphia: Advance. *Philadelphia* was the most remote and least prosperous of the cities. The *key of David* represents the powers of the steward; much of the imagery of this letter is drawn from Isa 22.15–25. **8:** The *word* of Jesus is both his teachings and his testimony (see also 12.11). **9:** The slander that others who claim to be Jews are a *synagogue★ of Satan* shows the strong hostility between the Jews of John's community and others (see also 2.9). **10:** The *hour of trial* indicates an indefinite, but short, period of testing, widely expected in apocalyptic★ writings (see the similar idea at 2.9–10). **11:** The *crown* is the victor's wreath (2.10). **12:** The *temple★* image serves various purposes in Revelation; most often it is the heavenly locus of action (11.19; 14.15; 15.5; 16.1), but here it more likely refers to the people of God among whom God dwells. At 21.22 the image will be reversed: Since God is there, no temple is needed. The *new Jerusalem* is another symbol for the new people of God, here spoken of in the present tense as already coming down from heaven (see 21.2).

14 "And to the angel of the church in Laodicea write: The words of the Amen, the faithful and true witness, the origin*a* of God's creation:

15 "I know your works; you are neither cold nor hot. I wish that you were either cold or hot. ¹⁶So, because you are lukewarm, and neither cold nor hot, I am about to spit you

a Or *beginning*

out of my mouth. ¹⁷For you say, 'I am rich, I have prospered, and I need nothing.' You do not realize that you are wretched, pitiable, poor, blind, and naked. ¹⁸Therefore I counsel you to buy from me gold refined by fire so that you may be rich; and white robes to clothe you and to keep the shame of your nakedness from being seen; and salve to anoint your eyes so that you may see. ¹⁹I reprove and discipline those whom I love. Be earnest, therefore, and repent. ²⁰Listen! I am standing at the door, knocking; if you hear my voice and open the door, I will come in to you and eat with you, and you with me. ²¹To the one who conquers I will give a place with me on my throne, just as I myself conquered and sat down with my Father on his throne. ²²Let anyone who has an ear listen to what the Spirit is saying to the churches."

3.14–22: The letter from the faithful witness to Laodicea: Eat with me. *Laodicea* was a prosperous trading city, originally built as a military colony to protect inland trade routes. It lacked a water supply and had to pipe in its water. The expression *origin of God's creation* is ambiguous and could mean that the speaker was the first to be created, the source of the creation, or the ruler of creation. A similar expression at Col 1.15 links the resurrection with the beginning of the new creation. **15–18:** *I am rich* begins a series of mercantile allusions drawn from the local economy, which included a famous black wool and an eye salve. **16:** The *lukewarm* spiritual state of the Laodiceans is a taunt on their tepid water: neither hot (like Hieropolis to the north) nor cold (like Colossae to the south). **20:**

Map **The seven churches**

The imagery is close to the Jesus story in Luke 12.35–37. **21:** The *throne* image opens the door to the next scene, where God's throne is central.

THE LITURGY* IN HEAVEN

4.1–11.18: The action of this whole section derives from what happens in heaven. It is thus in the most obvious way a revelation: a glimpse into the hidden inner workings of the divine court.

4 After this I looked, and there in heaven a door stood open! And the first voice, which I had heard speaking to me like a trumpet, said, "Come up here, and I will show you what must take place after this." ²At once I was in the spirit,ᵃ and there in heaven stood a throne, with one seated on the throne! ³And the one seated there looks like jasper and carnelian, and around the throne is a rainbow that looks like an emerald. ⁴Around the throne are twenty-four thrones, and seated on the thrones are twenty-four elders, dressed in white robes, with golden crowns on their heads. ⁵Coming from the throne are flashes of lightning, and rumblings and peals of thunder, and in front of the throne burn seven flaming torches, which are the seven spirits of God; ⁶and in front of the throne there is something like a sea of glass, like crystal.

Around the throne, and on each side of the throne, are four living creatures, full of eyes in front and behind: ⁷the first living creature like a lion, the second living creature like an ox, the third living creature with a face like a human face, and the fourth living creature like a flying eagle. ⁸And the four living creatures, each of them with six wings, are full of eyes all around and inside. Day and night without ceasing they sing,

"Holy, holy, holy,
  the Lord God the Almighty,
    who was and is and is to come."

⁹And whenever the living creatures give glory and honor and thanks to the one who is seated on the throne, who lives forever and ever, ¹⁰the twenty-four elders fall before the one who is seated on the throne and worship the one who lives forever and ever; they cast their crowns before the throne, singing,

¹¹ "You are worthy, our Lord and God,
    to receive glory and honor and power,
  for you created all things,
    and by your will they existed and were
      created."

4.1–11: The order of creation. This scene presents the cosmos as it was meant to be, with all creation gathered around the throne of God. The notion of access to heaven through an open *door* is also found in *Testament of Levi* 5.1 and 1 Enoch* 14.8–15. The *first voice* is a reference to the opening vision, 1.10. *Come up here* expresses John's view of the universe as three-leveled with the earth in the center; see also 5.3. The phrase *after this* both opens and closes this sentence. The basic idea is one of correspondence between heaven and earth so that what John sees in heaven must take place on earth. **2:** The phrase *in the spirit* opened the first vision (1.10) also and probably indicates that this was at one time a separate vision. Notice that John ascends by going inward. The *throne* image is central to Revelation, contrasting God's throne with that of Satan (2.13). It is a political image. Such throne visions were a common feature of Jewish mysticism, deriving ultimately from Ezek 1. **3:** We cannot be sure what gems John intended by *jasper* and *carnelian;* it is surprising that God is described as a stone. The *rainbow* is a sign of divine protection (Gen 9.12–13; Ezek 1.28; Rev 10.1). **4:** *Twenty-four* is a doubling of the number of God's people; several explanations have been offered (the 12 tribes plus the 12 apostles;* the 24 orders of priests; the 24 figures associated with the zodiac). The only clear point is that these *elders* represent the heavenly counterpart to the earthly community. The *white robes* signal their victorious lives (3.5) as do the *golden crowns,* for they are the kind given to victors in athletic contests (1 Cor 9.25). **5:** The *lightning, thunder,* and fire signal the manifestation of the divine presence (or theophany;* see Ex 20.18). The *seven spirits* represent the Holy Spirit; see 1.4–5 and Zech 4.2, 10. **6–8:** *Four* marks the *living creatures* as of the earth, probably the four orders of creation; the same four appear in Ezek 1; see also Isa 6. They are *full of eyes* because they have full understanding, deriving from fullness of the spirit (5.6). *Holy, Holy, Holy* derives from Isa 6.3 and had become a traditional part of Jewish and Christian worship in John's time. **9–11:** Notice how the various participants work in concert,

a Or in the Spirit

creating harmony. Such worship is proper, because the object is *worthy,* and this worthiness is based on the act of creation.

~~~~~~~~~~~~~~~~~~~~~~~~~~~~~~~~~~~~~~~

5 Then I saw in the right hand of the one seated on the throne a scroll written on the inside and on the back, sealed[a] with seven seals; 2and I saw a mighty angel proclaiming with a loud voice, "Who is worthy to open the scroll and break its seals?" 3And no one in heaven or on earth or under the earth was able to open the scroll or to look into it. 4And I began to weep bitterly because no one was found worthy to open the scroll or to look into it. 5Then one of the elders said to me, "Do not weep. See, the Lion of the tribe of Judah, the Root of David, has conquered, so that he can open the scroll and its seven seals."

6 Then I saw between the throne and the four living creatures and among the elders a Lamb standing as if it had been slaughtered, having seven horns and seven eyes, which are the seven spirits of God sent out into all the earth. 7He went and took the scroll from the right hand of the one who was seated on the throne. 8When he had taken the scroll, the four living creatures and the twenty-four elders fell before the Lamb, each holding a harp and golden bowls full of incense, which are the prayers of the saints. 9They sing a new song:

"You are worthy to take the scroll
    and to open its seals,
for you were slaughtered and by your
        blood you ransomed for God
    saints from[b] every tribe and language
        and people and nation;
10 you have made them to be a kingdom
    and priests serving[c] our God,
    and they will reign on earth."

11 Then I looked, and I heard the voice of many angels surrounding the throne and the living creatures and the elders; they numbered myriads of myriads and thousands of thousands, 12singing with full voice,

"Worthy is the Lamb that was
        slaughtered
to receive power and wealth and
        wisdom and might
and honor and glory and blessing!"

13Then I heard every creature in heaven and on earth and under the earth and in the sea, and all that is in them, singing,

"To the one seated on the throne and to
        the Lamb
    be blessing and honor and glory and
        might
    forever and ever!"

14And the four living creatures said, "Amen!" And the elders fell down and worshiped.

———————————————————————

5.1–14. The dilemma of the sealed scroll. Whereas the first scene centers on creation and presents an ideal picture (ch. 4), this second scene presents a story of human failure, judgment, and restoration. The first task is to introduce the one with the power to judge and restore. **1–5: The power to open the scroll.** The *right hand* is the hand of power and favor (Ps 20.6; 44.3; 98.1). The *scroll* represents secret knowledge, and access to it is a revelation (see Ps 139.16). Scrolls were ordinarily written only on the *inside* and rarely *on the back;* either there is too much for the scroll to hold or there is a summary on the outside (standard for contracts and wills, which were opened only when they were put to use). The imagery derives from Ezek 2.10 and will be used again in Rev 10. The *seven seals* signify the perfection of the scroll's contents and may also allude to a practice of Roman will-making. The notion that the book contains God's will is intriguing. **2:** *Worthy* signifies having power or position to do the deed; see 5.9 for the basis of this worth. **5:** Both the *Lion* and the *Root of David* are messianic* images (Gen 49.9; Isa 11.10; Jer 23.5). Both are images of power (Prov 30.30) and righteous violence. **6–14: The adoration of the Lamb.** The *Lamb* image is the antithesis* of the lion; it is the recipient of violence, not the author of it. Overwhelmingly, it is an image of sacrifice (Ex 29; Lev 14), but also an image of gentleness (Jer 11.19) and of undeserved suffering (Isa 53.7). *Seven* means perfect here. **8:** The *four creatures* were mentioned at 4.6 and the *twenty-four elders* at 4.4. John makes the meaning of the *incense* symbol explicit: It is the prayers of the saints. That such prayers actually cause divine judgment is portrayed at 8.2. **9:** They sing a *new song* because the Lamb's work has brought a new age. The process by which that new age is brought to reality is detailed in the song. **10:** That the Lamb makes both a *kingdom* and *priests* re-

a Or *written on the inside, and sealed on the back*
b Gk *ransomed for God from*   c Gk *priests to*

veals the dual★ political and religious nature of John's vision; see also 1.9. **13–14:** The scene climaxes★ with *every creature* giving proper praise to God and to the Lamb. It is worth noting that this grand scene of universal redemption precedes all reference to punishment or destruction.

THE UNSEALING OF THE SCROLL

6.1–8.1: With the removal of each seal, we glimpse an aspect of the cosmic drama of human destructiveness, divine justice, and eventual peace. The whole series enacts a unified action.

6 Then I saw the Lamb open one of the seven seals, and I heard one of the four living creatures call out, as with a voice of thunder, "Come!"*a* ²I looked, and there was a white horse! Its rider had a bow; a crown was given to him, and he came out conquering and to conquer.

3 When he opened the second seal, I heard the second living creature call out, "Come!"*a* ⁴And out came*b* another horse, bright red; its rider was permitted to take peace from the earth, so that people would slaughter one another; and he was given a great sword.

5 When he opened the third seal, I heard the third living creature call out, "Come!"*a* I looked, and there was a black horse! Its rider held a pair of scales in his hand, ⁶and I heard what seemed to be a voice in the midst of the four living creatures saying, "A quart of wheat for a day's pay,*c* and three quarts of barley for a day's pay,*c* but do not damage the olive oil and the wine!"

7 When he opened the fourth seal, I heard the voice of the fourth living creature call out, "Come!"*a* ⁸I looked and there was a pale green horse! Its rider's name was Death, and Hades followed with him; they were given authority over a fourth of the earth, to kill with sword, famine, and pestilence, and by the wild animals of the earth.

6.1–8: The four seals of human destructiveness. The *four living creatures* represent all of creation; see 4.6. The colors of the horses have their common meaning: *white* stands for victory or conquest; *red* is the color of blood shed in war; *black* is the color of dead vege-

tation; and *pale green* is the yellowish-gray color of rotting flesh. In addition, each rider is given an instrument appropriate to his task. The *bow* occurs only here in Revelation; it is never an image of Jesus, and thus the first rider is best seen as a military conqueror (in spite of the fact that Jesus will later appear on a white horse; 19.11). The appearance of such a conqueror leads inevitably to war, the second rider; and war leads inevitably to famine, the third rider. **6:** The charge, *do not damage the olive oil and the wine,* is uncertain but may stem from the fact that these are long-term crops not needing yearly planting and thus not as susceptible to the war-induced famine. **8:** *Hades*★ was Zeus's brother and the ruler of the underworld and thus by metaphor★ holder of the dead; see 20.13. There is an escalating destruction in the Apocalypse,★ beginning here with *a fourth;* the next series will destroy one-third (8.7); the last will destroy all (16.1–12).

9 When he opened the fifth seal, I saw under the altar the souls of those who had been slaughtered for the word of God and for the testimony they had given; ¹⁰they cried out with a loud voice, "Sovereign Lord, holy and true, how long will it be before you judge and avenge our blood on the inhabitants of the earth?" ¹¹They were each given a white robe and told to rest a little longer, until the number would be complete both of their fellow servants*d* and of their brothers and sisters,*e* who were soon to be killed as they themselves had been killed.

12 When he opened the sixth seal, I looked, and there came a great earthquake; the sun became black as sackcloth, the full moon became like blood, ¹³and the stars of the sky fell to the earth as the fig tree drops its winter fruit when shaken by a gale. ¹⁴The sky vanished like a scroll rolling itself up, and every mountain and island was removed from its place. ¹⁵Then the kings of the earth and the magnates and the generals and the rich and the powerful, and everyone, slave and free, hid in the caves and among the rocks of the mountains, ¹⁶calling to the mountains and rocks, "Fall on us and hide us from the face of the one seated on the throne and from the wrath of the Lamb;

a Or "Go!" *b* Or *went* *c* Gk *a denarius*
d Gk *slaves* *e* Gk *brothers*

The Meaning of Apocalypse

While in popular usage "apocalypse*" suggests disasters and destruction, this is not the basic meaning of the biblical word. The Greek word "apokalypsis" has the root meaning "to uncover," and thus to cause something to be fully known. It is translated by the Latin word "revelatio," which means a disclosure, a revelation. An apocalypse is grounded in the idea that the meaning of events, of human life in general, is hidden from people and that a vision from beyond our world can "remove the veil" of ordinary perception and show the true, underlying meaning of history. The Apocalypse of John (also called the Book of Revelation) contains many visions of disasters, but its purpose is not to show destruction. Its purpose is to enable us to see behind the scenes where the real struggle is whether or not one follows Jesus (through temptations, suffering, and even death) or whether one follows the way of the world. In this view history is a contest between good and evil, and everyone must eventually choose sides.

17 for the great day of their wrath has come, and who is able to stand?"

6.9–8.1: The three seals of judgment and salvation. 6.9–11: The fifth seal. The *altar* is for sacrifice and these have been *slaughtered*, implying that these lost lives have some significance (see 5.6; 12.11). *Souls* is simply "lives"; thus, the battered lives of the oppressed call for justice. **10:** The call to *avenge* their blood is hardly in the spirit of the Jesus of the gospels (Lk 23.34). However, the retribution John imagines is based on justice (Rev 16.5–6). There is a similar scene in 2 Esd 4.35–37. **11:** The judgment is deferred *until the number would be complete,* implying both the patience of God and the correlation between the extent of evil and its judgment. **12–17: The sixth seal.** All the elements of the final judgment appear here, but no act of judgment is portrayed. We are shown only the anxiety of the judged. For these images see Isa 34.4. This anticipation of universal judgment seems to raise the issue of what will happen to the righteous.

7 After this I saw four angels standing at the four corners of the earth, holding back the four winds of the earth so that no wind could blow on earth or sea or against any tree. 2 I saw another angel ascending from the rising of the sun, having the seal of the living God, and he called with a loud voice to the four angels who had been given power to damage earth and sea, 3 saying, "Do not damage the earth or the sea or the trees, until we have marked the servants[a] of our God with a seal on their foreheads."

4 And I heard the number of those who were sealed, one hundred forty-four thousand, sealed out of every tribe of the people of Israel:

5 From the tribe of Judah twelve thousand sealed,
from the tribe of Reuben twelve thousand,
from the tribe of Gad twelve thousand,
6 from the tribe of Asher twelve thousand,
from the tribe of Naphtali twelve thousand,
from the tribe of Manasseh twelve thousand,
7 from the tribe of Simeon twelve thousand,
from the tribe of Levi twelve thousand,
from the tribe of Issachar twelve thousand,
8 from the tribe of Zebulun twelve thousand,
from the tribe of Joseph twelve thousand,
from the tribe of Benjamin twelve thousand sealed.

a Gk *slaves*

9 After this I looked, and there was a great multitude that no one could count, from every nation, from all tribes and peoples and languages, standing before the throne and before the Lamb, robed in white, with palm branches in their hands. 10They cried out in a loud voice, saying,

> "Salvation belongs to our God who is
>   seated on the throne, and to the
>   Lamb!"

11And all the angels stood around the throne and around the elders and the four living creatures, and they fell on their faces before the throne and worshiped God, 12singing,

> "Amen! Blessing and glory and wisdom
>   and thanksgiving and honor
>   and power and might
>   be to our God forever and ever! Amen."

13 Then one of the elders addressed me, saying, "Who are these, robed in white, and where have they come from?" 14I said to him, "Sir, you are the one that knows." Then he said to me, "These are they who have come out of the great ordeal; they have washed their robes and made them white in the blood of the Lamb.
15 For this reason they are before the throne of God,

>   and worship him day and night within
>   his temple,
>   and the one who is seated on the
>   throne will shelter them.

16 They will hunger no more, and thirst no more;
>   the sun will not strike them,
>   nor any scorching heat;

17 for the Lamb at the center of the throne
>   will be their shepherd,
>   and he will guide them to springs of
>   the water of life,
>   and God will wipe away every tear from
>   their eyes."

7.1–17: The sealing of the servants of God. *Four* is the number of the earth. *Seal* is the same word as the seven seals. The *forehead* was symbolic of human will and worship; see 13.16; Ezek 9.4. **4:** *One hundred forty-four thousand* is a symbolic number built on 12 (God's people) and 10 (all). **5–8:** The regathering of the twelve *tribes* was expected in the end time (Isa 43), but this list is unique in substituting Joseph and Levi

for Dan and Ephraim. **9:** The *great multitude* is either a second group of gentiles* or another image for the same group. **9–12:** The scene of Rev 4–5 is repeated and a central theme of this story, worshipping God, is emphasized. **14:** The *great ordeal* was the time of suffering that would inaugurate the messianic* age; note that in John's story it is already underway. Although sealed from God's wrath, they still suffer. **15–17:** This remarkable vision of divine protection is the antithesis* of the scene in seal five.

~~~~~~~~~~~~~~~~~~~~~~~~~~~~~~~~~~~~~

8 When the Lamb opened the seventh seal, there was silence in heaven for about half an hour. 2And I saw the seven angels who stand before God, and seven trumpets were given to them.

8.1: The seventh seal. The *silence* is both an image of primeval renewal (see 2 Esd 7.26–34) and of the pause before a new action, the sounding of trumpets.

~~~~~~~~~~~~~~~~~~~~~~~~~~~~~~~~~~~~~

3 Another angel with a golden censer came and stood at the altar; he was given a great quantity of incense to offer with the prayers of all the saints on the golden altar that is before the throne. 4And the smoke of the incense, with the prayers of the saints, rose before God from the hand of the angel. 5Then the angel took the censer and filled it with fire from the altar and threw it on the earth; and there were peals of thunder, rumblings, flashes of lightning, and an earthquake.
6 Now the seven angels who had the seven trumpets made ready to blow them.
7 The first angel blew his trumpet, and there came hail and fire, mixed with blood, and they were hurled to the earth; and a third of the earth was burned up, and a third of the trees were burned up, and all green grass was burned up.
8 The second angel blew his trumpet, and something like a great mountain, burning with fire, was thrown into the sea. 9A third of the sea became blood, a third of the living creatures in the sea died, and a third of the ships were destroyed.
10 The third angel blew his trumpet, and a great star fell from heaven, blazing like a torch, and it fell on a third of the rivers and on the springs of water. 11The name of the

star is Wormwood. A third of the waters became wormwood, and many died from the water, because it was made bitter.

12 The fourth angel blew his trumpet, and a third of the sun was struck, and a third of the moon, and a third of the stars, so that a third of their light was darkened; a third of the day was kept from shining, and likewise the night.

8.2–11.19: The sounding of the trumpets. 8.2: The *seven angels* indicate the inner circle of angelic beings; the *trumpets* are more like bugles and were used for signaling in battles. 3–5: The censer of prayer. The small scene is a graphic description of how the prayers of the saints bring judgment to the earth, preparing the repeated scenes of judgment that follow. 6–12: The four blasts of destruction. The destruction of *a third* is an increase over the earlier portrayal that affected one-quarter (6.8). The whole human sphere is contaminated: earth, sea, fresh water, and heavenly bodies. 11: *Wormwood* is a bitter herb; see Amos 5.6–7. 12: The notion that both the *day* and the *night* could be diminished by one-third makes sense only poetically.

THE THREE BLASTS OF WOE

8.13–11.18: As the first four trumpets were introduced by a short dramatic scene (8.3–5), so also are the last three (8.13). Only two of these *woes* are later marked (9.12; 11.14). The last trumpet is hardly a woe, for it contains nothing unpleasant.

13 Then I looked, and I heard an eagle crying with a loud voice as it flew in midheaven, "Woe, woe, woe to the inhabitants of the earth, at the blasts of the other trumpets that the three angels are about to blow!"

9 And the fifth angel blew his trumpet, and I saw a star that had fallen from heaven to earth, and he was given the key to the shaft of the bottomless pit; 2he opened the shaft of the bottomless pit, and from the shaft rose smoke like the smoke of a great furnace, and the sun and the air were darkened with the smoke from the shaft. 3Then from the smoke came locusts on the earth, and they were given authority like the authority of scorpions of the earth. 4They were told not to damage the grass of the earth or any green growth or any tree, but only those people who do not have the seal of God on their foreheads. 5They were allowed to torture them for five months, but not to kill them, and their torture was like the torture of a scorpion when it stings someone. 6And in those days people will seek death but will not find it; they will long to die, but death will flee from them.

7 In appearance the locusts were like horses equipped for battle. On their heads were what looked like crowns of gold; their faces were like human faces, 8their hair like women's hair, and their teeth like lions' teeth; 9they had scales like iron breastplates, and the noise of their wings was like the noise of many chariots with horses rushing into battle. 10They have tails like scorpions, with stingers, and in their tails is their power to harm people for five months. 11They have as king over them the angel of the bottomless pit; his name in Hebrew is Abaddon,*a* and in Greek he is called Apollyon.*b*

12 The first woe has passed. There are still two woes to come.

9.1–11: The fifth trumpet. The *star* that has *fallen* is an apparent reference to the myth of Lucifer (see Isa 14; Luke 10.18). The opening of the *pit* unleashes demonic forces for the first time in the story (it will be closed again at 20.3). 3: The *locusts* echo the plague on Egypt (Ex 10.12–20) and are modeled on Joel 2. 4: The *seal of God* refers to 7.1–3. 10: *Five months* is more than a third of a year; the only other use of five is at 17.10. 11: *Abaddon*⋆ is the Hebrew term for the grave or the pit; *Apollyon* seems to be a pun for its usual Greek translation ("apoleia," destruction), changed to suggest the sun god Apollo.

13 Then the sixth angel blew his trumpet, and I heard a voice from the four*c* horns of the golden altar before God, 14saying to the sixth angel who had the trumpet, "Release the four angels who are bound at the great river Euphrates." 15So the four angels were released, who had been held ready for the hour, the day, the month, and the year, to kill a third of humankind. 16The number of

a That is, *Destruction*   *b* That is, *Destroyer*
c Other ancient authorities lack *four*

the troops of cavalry was two hundred million; I heard their number. 17And this was how I saw the horses in my vision: the riders wore breastplates the color of fire and of sapphire*a* and of sulfur; the heads of the horses were like lions' heads, and fire and smoke and sulfur came out of their mouths. 18By these three plagues a third of humankind was killed, by the fire and smoke and sulfur coming out of their mouths. 19For the power of the horses is in their mouths and in their tails; their tails are like serpents, having heads; and with them they inflict harm.

20 The rest of humankind, who were not killed by these plagues, did not repent of the works of their hands or give up worshiping demons and idols of gold and silver and bronze and stone and wood, which cannot see or hear or walk. 21And they did not repent of their murders or their sorceries or their fornication or their thefts.

9.13–11.14: The sixth trumpet. Like the sixth seal, this is a complicated scene with several actions. 9.13–21: The angels from the Euphrates. The demonic attack continues. The *golden altar* is the incense altar (8.3). 18: *Plagues* that do not cause the recipients to *repent* are both themes from the Exodus story (Ex 8.32; 10.20). 20: The charge that others are *worshiping demons and idols* shows John's utter rejection of Greco-Roman culture.

10 And I saw another mighty angel coming down from heaven, wrapped in a cloud, with a rainbow over his head; his face was like the sun, and his legs like pillars of fire. 2He held a little scroll open in his hand. Setting his right foot on the sea and his left foot on the land, 3he gave a great shout, like a lion roaring. And when he shouted, the seven thunders sounded. 4And when the seven thunders had sounded, I was about to write, but I heard a voice from heaven saying, "Seal up what the seven thunders have said, and do not write it down." 5Then the angel whom I saw standing on the sea and the land

> raised his right hand to heaven
6 and swore by him who lives forever and ever,

who created heaven and what is in it, the earth and what is in it, and the sea and what is in it: "There will be no more delay, 7but in the days when the seventh angel is to blow his trumpet, the mystery of God will be fulfilled, as he announced to his servants*b* the prophets."

8 Then the voice that I had heard from heaven spoke to me again, saying, "Go, take the scroll that is open in the hand of the angel who is standing on the sea and on the land." 9So I went to the angel and told him to give me the little scroll; and he said to me, "Take it, and eat; it will be bitter to your stomach, but sweet as honey in your mouth." 10So I took the little scroll from the hand of the angel and ate it; it was sweet as honey in my mouth, but when I had eaten it, my stomach was made bitter.

11 Then they said to me, "You must prophesy again about many peoples and nations and languages and kings."

11 Then I was given a measuring rod like a staff, and I was told, "Come and measure the temple of God and the altar and those who worship there, 2but do not measure the court outside the temple; leave that out, for it is given over to the nations, and they will trample over the holy city for forty-two months. 3And I will grant my two witnesses authority to prophesy for one thousand two hundred sixty days, wearing sackcloth."

4 These are the two olive trees and the two lampstands that stand before the Lord of the earth. 5And if anyone wants to harm them, fire pours from their mouth and consumes their foes; anyone who wants to harm them must be killed in this manner. 6They have authority to shut the sky, so that no rain may fall during the days of their prophesying, and they have authority over the waters to turn them into blood, and to strike the earth with every kind of plague, as often as they desire.

7 When they have finished their testimony, the beast that comes up from the bottomless pit will make war on them and con-

a Gk *hyacinth*   *b* Gk *slaves*

quer them and kill them, [8]and their dead bodies will lie in the street of the great city that is prophetically[a] called Sodom and Egypt, where also their Lord was crucified. [9]For three and a half days members of the peoples and tribes and languages and nations will gaze at their dead bodies and refuse to let them be placed in a tomb; [10]and the inhabitants of the earth will gloat over them and celebrate and exchange presents, because these two prophets had been a torment to the inhabitants of the earth.

[11] But after the three and a half days, the breath[b] of life from God entered them, and they stood on their feet, and those who saw them were terrified. [12]Then they[c] heard a loud voice from heaven saying to them, "Come up here!" And they went up to heaven in a cloud while their enemies watched them. [13]At that moment there was a great earthquake, and a tenth of the city fell; seven thousand people were killed in the earthquake, and the rest were terrified and gave glory to the God of heaven.

10.1–11.13: John's angelic commission. Encompassed within the sixth trumpet (which ends at 11.14) are two seemingly unrelated scenes of John's encounter with angels; both enact divine protection and thus correlate with the sealing of the saints that was part of seal six (7.1–17). The cloud, rainbow, and pillars of fire all suggest divine presence (Ex 19.16; 13.21; Gen 9.13). 4: The mysterious seven thunders represent additional hidden revelation, known only to John, and also evoke the promise that the seventh trumpet will bring the promised fulfillment. 10: The little scroll is explicitly said to represent another prophetic* announcement (10.11). 11: To prophesy is to announce the revelation of God's judgment and salvation. 11.1–13: The temple* and altar represent the inner reality of the community, which will be protected, even while the outer reality (political, social, and economic well-being) is at the mercy of enemies. 2: Forty-two months is the period of evil; the same as 1,260 days or three and a half years. As a half of seven, the period of evil is always incomplete, broken. 3–4: The two witnesses dramatize what the temple scene symbolized: They are both conquered and victorious. They represent the people of God, characterized both as king and priest (the two olive trees; see Zech 4.12; Rev 1.6) and as the two final prophets,* Moses (plagues;

Ex 7) and Elijah (shutting the sky; 2 Kings 17). Their quality as two emphasizes their function as witnesses (Deut 19.15). 5: The fire from their mouth is their testimony (see Sir 48.1). 7: The beast is prematurely shown here but will be introduced in ch. 13. The war will become the theme of John's new prophecy (chs. 12–22; see 12.17). 8: The great city is a complex symbol; here it stands for Jerusalem; later it symbolizes Rome (17.18). It is prophetically called Sodom and Egypt, places of opposition to God. This is a spiritual or symbolic geography (as is all of John's geography). 9: The three and a half days is yet another symbol for the period of evil. 11: The inward possession of breath of life (the spirit) is the final testimony.

---

14 The second woe has passed. The third woe is coming very soon.

15 Then the seventh angel blew his trumpet, and there were loud voices in heaven, saying,

"The kingdom of the world has become
   the kingdom of our Lord
   and of his Messiah,[d]
and he will reign forever and ever."

16 Then the twenty-four elders who sit on their thrones before God fell on their faces and worshiped God, [17]singing,

"We give you thanks, Lord
      God Almighty,
   who are and who were,
   for you have taken your great power
      and begun to reign.
[18] The nations raged,
   but your wrath has come,
      and the time for judging the dead,
   for rewarding your servants,[e]
      the prophets
   and saints and all who fear
      your name,
   both small and great,
   and for destroying those who destroy
      the earth."

19 Then God's temple in heaven was opened, and the ark of his covenant was seen within his temple; and there were flashes of lightning, rumblings, peals of thunder, an earthquake, and heavy hail.

a Or allegorically; Gk spiritually   b Or the spirit
c Other ancient authorities read I   d Gk Christ
e Gk slaves

11.14–19. 14–18: The seventh trumpet. This announcement that God's kingdom has come symbolizes the final end (see 10.7). The *twenty-four elders* represent God's people (see 4.4), and their *worship* of God enacts God's rule. **16:** *We give you thanks* is the Greek word "eucharistoumen." **18:** This poem represents the desire for justice, *rewarding your servants* and *destroying those who destroy the earth.* **19:** This is pivotal, both closing the action of the throne scene and opening a new action. Seeing the *ark* means John is looking into the inmost sanctuary, thus the traditional elements marking God's manifestation (see comment on 4.5). Note the similar motif* of the splitting of the Temple* curtain at Jesus' crucifixion (Mk 15.38 and parallel references).

THE WAR OF THE COSMOS

12.1–22.5: The focus shifts from what God is doing to the counter-view: what Satan is doing, waging war on the saints.

12 A great portent appeared in heaven: a woman clothed with the sun, with the moon under her feet, and on her head a crown of twelve stars. ²She was pregnant and was crying out in birth pangs, in the agony of giving birth. ³Then another portent appeared in heaven: a great red dragon, with seven heads and ten horns, and seven diadems on his heads. ⁴His tail swept down a third of the stars of heaven and threw them to the earth. Then the dragon stood before the woman who was about to bear a child, so that he might devour her child as soon as it was born. ⁵And she gave birth to a son, a male child, who is to rule*a* all the nations with a rod of iron. But her child was snatched away and taken to God and to his throne; ⁶and the woman fled into the wilderness, where she has a place prepared by God, so that there she can be nourished for one thousand two hundred sixty days.

7 And war broke out in heaven; Michael and his angels fought against the dragon. The dragon and his angels fought back, ⁸but they were defeated, and there was no longer any place for them in heaven. ⁹The great dragon was thrown down, that ancient serpent, who is called the Devil and Satan, the deceiver of the whole world—he was thrown down to the earth, and his angels were thrown down with him.

10 Then I heard a loud voice in heaven, proclaiming,

"Now have come the salvation and the
                    power
    and the kingdom of our God
    and the authority of his Messiah,*b*
for the accuser of our comrades*c* has
                    been thrown down,
    who accuses them day and night
        before our God.
¹¹ But they have conquered him by the
        blood of the Lamb
    and by the word of their testimony,
    for they did not cling to life even in the
        face of death.
¹² Rejoice then, you heavens
    and those who dwell in them!
But woe to the earth and the sea,
    for the devil has come down to you
        with great wrath,
    because he knows that his time
        is short!"

13 So when the dragon saw that he had been thrown down to the earth, he pursued*d* the woman who had given birth to the male child. ¹⁴But the woman was given the two wings of the great eagle, so that she could fly from the serpent into the wilderness, to her place where she is nourished for a time, and times, and half a time. ¹⁵Then from his mouth the serpent poured water like a river after the woman, to sweep her away with the flood. ¹⁶But the earth came to the help of the woman; it opened its mouth and swallowed the river that the dragon had poured from his mouth. ¹⁷Then the dragon was angry with the woman, and went off to make war on the rest of her children, those who keep the commandments of God and hold the testimony of Jesus.

12.1–17: The attack of the dragon on the woman. Three actions are shown: the birth of the son, the war in heaven, and the war on earth. **1–6: The birth of the son.** A *portent* is a token or omen or astrological

a Or *to shepherd*   *b* Gk *Christ*   *c* Gk *brothers*
d Or *persecuted*

sign (here perhaps Virgo). Here *heaven* is the sky. *Twelve stars* recall both the zodiac and the number of God's people; Gen 37.9. The *woman* here is clearly the mother of the messiah,* but this could be understood three ways: Mary, Israel, Eve (see Gen 3.15), or perhaps all three at once. The story of the endangered birth also echoes myths associated with Isis, Leto, and Roma. **2:** The *birth pangs* recall both the story of Eve (Gen 3.16) and the promise of the new age (Mt 24.8). **3:** The *dragon* is God's primal enemy in ancient Near Eastern mythology, leviathan* in Jewish tradition (Isa 27.1; Ps 74.14; see also Dan 7.7); as an astrological sign, perhaps Scorpio, which follows Virgo. **4:** The *stars* probably refer to fallen angels, again echoing the Lucifer myth (see 9.1); this may also be the same event described at 8.12. **5:** The messiah was the one who would *rule* (literally, shepherd) *the nations* (Ps 2). **6:** The *wilderness* is both the place of safety after the Exodus and the place where salvation was to begin; see Isa 40.3 and Mk 1. *One thousand two hundred sixty days* is the time of evil; see 11.2–3. **7–12: The war in heaven.** *Michael* is the prince of Israel (Dan 12.1), hence the heavenly counterpart to Israel—or, in our idiom, the inner reality of Israel. Paradoxically, this war both establishes God's kingdom (v. 10) and unleashes Satan's power on earth (v. 12). **11:** This rests on the greater paradox: Satan's defeat is *by the blood of the Lamb and by the word of their testimony. Testimony* here is "martus" (witness), and it is close to its cognate meaning: martyr.* **13–17: The war on earth.** The escape on *the wings of the great eagle* is an Exodus motif* (Ex 19.4). **15:** The *flood* is appropriate to the ancient sea monster. **16:** The *earth* is feminine, thus, contrary to the expectation that the hero will come to the rescue, we see the rather remarkable picture of one woman being rescued by another. **17:** *The rest of her children* now come under attack, defined more precisely as law-observant followers of Jesus. Most of the rest of the story details this attack.

TWO BEASTS ARISE

12.18–13.18: We first see the dragon preparing for battle.

18 Then the dragon*a* took his stand on the sand of the seashore. ¹And I saw a beast rising out of the sea, having ten horns and seven heads; and on its horns were ten diadems, and on its heads were blasphemous names. ²And the beast that I saw was like a leopard, its feet were like a bear's, and its mouth was like a lion's mouth. And the dragon gave it his power and his throne and great authority. ³One of its heads seemed to have received a death-blow, but its mortal wound*b* had been healed. In amazement the whole earth followed the beast. ⁴They worshiped the dragon, for he had given his authority to the beast, and they worshiped the beast, saying, "Who is like the beast, and who can fight against it?"

5 The beast was given a mouth uttering haughty and blasphemous words, and it was allowed to exercise authority for forty-two months. ⁶It opened its mouth to utter blasphemies against God, blaspheming his name and his dwelling, that is, those who dwell in heaven. ⁷Also it was allowed to make war on the saints and to conquer them.*c* It was given authority over every tribe and people and language and nation, ⁸and all the inhabitants of the earth will worship it, everyone whose name has not been written from the foundation of the world in the book of life of the Lamb that was slaughtered.*d*

9 Let anyone who has an ear listen:

10 If you are to be taken captive,
    into captivity you go;
  if you kill with the sword,
    with the sword you must be killed.

Here is a call for the endurance and faith of the saints.

13.1–10: The *beast* from the *sea* is the ancient sea monster leviathan,* already used as a model for the dragon (12.3). The first description echoes that of the dragon, but this is modified by details from Daniel's beasts (Dan 7.1–7). **3:** *One of its heads* refers to an individual ruler who is cut off, probably referring to the killing of Julius Caesar, whose death did not kill the beast of the empire. *Its mortal wound* refers to the wound of the beast, not to the head. **5:** *Forty-two months* is the period of evil (see 11.2). **6:** The *blasphemies* are the claims to divinity inherent in the cult of the emperors: Julius was divine and all later emperors are sons of the divine Julius. **7:** That the beast is *to*

a Gk *Then he;* other ancient authorities read *Then I stood   b* Gk *the plague of its death   c* Other ancient authorities lack this sentence   *d* Or *written in the book of life of the Lamb that was slaughtered from the foundation of the world* make war on the saints is expected, but it is surprising that it will conquer them (but see 11.7). 9: Let anyone who has an ear, listen repeats the chorus of all seven messages to the churches (chs. 2–3). 10: Both escape and armed rebellion are futile; persistence is called for.

11 Then I saw another beast that rose out of the earth; it had two horns like a lamb and it spoke like a dragon. 12It exercises all the authority of the first beast on its behalf, and it makes the earth and its inhabitants worship the first beast, whose mortal wound[a] had been healed. 13It performs great signs, even making fire come down from heaven to earth in the sight of all; 14and by the signs that it is allowed to perform on behalf of the beast, it deceives the inhabitants of earth, telling them to make an image for the beast that had been wounded by the sword[b] and yet lived; 15and it was allowed to give breath[c] to the image of the beast so that the image of the beast could even speak and cause those who would not worship the image of the beast to be killed. 16Also it causes all, both small and great, both rich and poor, both free and slave, to be marked on the right hand or the forehead, 17so that no one can buy or sell who does not have the mark, that is, the name of the beast or the number of its name. 18This calls for wisdom: let anyone with understanding calculate the number of the beast, for it is the number of a person. Its number is six hundred sixty-six.[d]

13.11–18: The second beast has the external appearance of the Lamb but the internal character of the dragon; this land beast is modeled on the ancient figure of behemoth* (Job 40.15) and represents the civic side of Roman power. 13: The great signs of this beast seem to be connected to the rites honoring the emperor. 15: The image of the beast appeared both on countless statues and on all Roman coins. 16: The right hand represents human work and activity; the forehead represents human spirit and worship (see 14.9). 17: The mark here is spiritual, not visible. No one can buy or sell without using the images on the coins, thus defiling their hands. 18: The number six hundred sixty-six is calculated by adding up the numeric values of each letter of the person's name—in this case probably that of Nero—but its real significance is that of

six. Six is incomplete and imperfect; it is the day humans were created but refuses to move on to day seven, God's day. It is the human (six) claiming to be perfect (seven) that represents the act of the beast.

14 Then I looked, and there was the Lamb, standing on Mount Zion! And with him were one hundred forty-four thousand who had his name and his Father's name written on their foreheads. 2And I heard a voice from heaven like the sound of many waters and like the sound of loud thunder; the voice I heard was like the sound of harpists playing on their harps, 3and they sing a new song before the throne and before the four living creatures and before the elders. No one could learn that song except the one hundred forty-four thousand who have been redeemed from the earth. 4It is these who have not defiled themselves with women, for they are virgins; these follow the Lamb wherever he goes. They have been redeemed from humankind as first fruits for God and the Lamb, 5and in their mouth no lie was found; they are blameless.

14.1–5: The Lamb and the 144,000. Now we see the Lamb's battle preparations. Mount Zion* is the place from which deliverance comes (Ps 14.7; Isa 59.20). For the one hundred forty-four thousand, see 7.4; on the meaning of forehead, see 13.16. 2–3: The voice evokes the opening vision (1.15); the throne scene recalls the second vision (4.2). It is a new song because it belongs to the new age. 4: The characterization of these warriors as those who have not defiled themselves with women, for they are virgins is primarily a spiritual description (contrast 2.20; 14.8). Holy war* demanded ceremonial purity (Lev 15.16–32). Still, the idea shares in the ancient notion that women are corrupt and corrupting. First fruits was an offering (Lev 2.14). 5: Blameless is literally without blemish—the requirement for a sacrificial animal (Lev 1.3).

6 Then I saw another angel flying in midheaven, with an eternal gospel to proclaim to those who live[e] on the earth—to every nation and tribe and language and people. 7He said in a loud voice, "Fear God and give

a Gk whose plague of its death   b Or that had received the plague of the sword   c Or spirit   d Other ancient authorities read six hundred sixteen   e Gk sit him glory, for the hour of his judgment has come; and worship him who made heaven and earth, the sea and the springs of water."

8 Then another angel, a second, followed, saying, "Fallen, fallen is Babylon the great! She has made all nations drink of the wine of the wrath of her fornication."

9 Then another angel, a third, followed them, crying with a loud voice, "Those who worship the beast and its image, and receive a mark on their foreheads or on their hands, 10they will also drink the wine of God's wrath, poured unmixed into the cup of his anger, and they will be tormented with fire and sulfur in the presence of the holy angels and in the presence of the Lamb. 11And the smoke of their torment goes up forever and ever. There is no rest day or night for those who worship the beast and its image and for anyone who receives the mark of its name."

12 Here is a call for the endurance of the saints, those who keep the commandments of God and hold fast to the faith of*a* Jesus.

13 And I heard a voice from heaven saying, "Write this: Blessed are the dead who from now on die in the Lord." "Yes," says the Spirit, "they will rest from their labors, for their deeds follow them."

14 Then I looked, and there was a white cloud, and seated on the cloud was one like the Son of Man, with a golden crown on his head, and a sharp sickle in his hand! 15Another angel came out of the temple, calling with a loud voice to the one who sat on the cloud, "Use your sickle and reap, for the hour to reap has come, because the harvest of the earth is fully ripe." 16So the one who sat on the cloud swung his sickle over the earth, and the earth was reaped.

17 Then another angel came out of the temple in heaven, and he too had a sharp sickle. 18Then another angel came out from the altar, the angel who has authority over fire, and he called with a loud voice to him who had the sharp sickle, "Use your sharp sickle and gather the clusters of the vine of the earth, for its grapes are ripe." 19So the angel swung his sickle over the earth and gathered the vintage of the earth, and he threw it into the great wine press of the wrath of God. 20And the wine press was trodden outside the city, and blood flowed from the wine press, as high as a horse's bridle, for a distance of about two hundred miles.*b*

14.6–20: The announcements of the end. For *angel,* see comment on 2.1. The *eternal gospel* is the central message of Revelation, the proper worship of God. **8:** *Babylon* was the first destroyer of Jerusalem, even as Rome was the second (2 Kings 24; Isa 21.9). **9:** For the *mark on their foreheads,* see 13.16. **10:** The *wine of God's wrath* here launches a series of bitter, violent images of questionable morality if viewed as something separate from the choice to worship the beast. **11:** *There is no rest* implies that this is the present experience; contrast v. 13, those who *die in the Lord will rest.* **12:** The *call for endurance* shows that the real purpose of this section is to admonish the faithful to resistance. **14:** The *white cloud* is the traditional apocalyptic* symbol of the final judgment; Dan 7.13; Mk 13.26. For the *Son of Man,* see 1.13. **15–18:** The *harvest* is both a traditional symbol for judgment and a metaphor* of consequences: *the grapes are ripe* (see Joel 3.13; Rev 16.6). The angel with *authority over fire* recalls 8.3–5, also a judgment scene. **19–20:** The *wine press* is a traditional image of God's wrath (Isa 63.1–4), but here it is *trodden outside the city*—a place of rejection (1 Kings 21.13) but also connected with the place of Jesus' death (Heb 13.11–12). *Two hundred miles* is literally 1,600 stadia, the 1,600 being symbolic of earth (4 X 4) and wholeness (10 X 10): thus the whole earth. Connected as it is with grain and grape—bread and wine—the allusion here is to the blood of Christ that covers the whole earth in the Eucharist.*

THE ACTS OF JUDGMENT

15.1–16.21: The brief symbolic announcements of judgment now open out into a detailed, sequential portrayal.

---

15 Then I saw another portent in heaven, great and amazing: seven angels with seven plagues, which are the last, for with them the wrath of God is ended.

2 And I saw what appeared to be a sea of glass mixed with fire, and those who had conquered the beast and its image and the

---

a Or *to their faith in*   *b* Gk *one thousand six hundred stadia*

Numbers in Revelation

Numbers in Revelation are always symbolic, not meant to communicate a certain quantity but rather a certain quality. The basic meaning of the numbers is standard.

Three	The spiritual order
Four	The created order
Seven (the sum of three and four)	Perfection (contrast six)
Ten	Totality
Twelve (the product of three and four)	Israel (God's people)
Three and one-half	The number of evil
Multiples and repetitions	Intensification

Thus in Revelation there is no important difference between 12, 144, 12,000, or 144,000; they all represent the people of God, with varying emphases on the totality and appropriate to the item counted or measured.

Another facet of numerology stems from the fact that letters of the alphabet* were used for numbers, giving each word also a numerical value. When numerical values corresponded, one could suspect a deeper correspondence as well. This was also true in the general culture. Suetonius reports a wall graffiti from Nero's time: "Count the numerical values of the letters in Nero's name, and in 'murdered his own mother': You will find their sum is the same" (*Nero* 39.2).

John employs a similar technique in identifying the beast from the sea, claiming in Rev. 13.17–18 that: "No one can buy or sell who does not have the mark, that is, the name of the beast or the number of its name. This calls for wisdom: Let anyone with understanding calculate the number of the beast, for it is the number of a person. Its number is six hundred sixty-six."

How one would calculate such a number can be seen by analogy:

A = 1	F = 6	K = 20	O = 60	S = 100	W = 500
B = 2	G = 7	L = 30	P = 70	T = 200	X = 600
C = 3	H = 8	M = 40	Q = 80	U = 300	Y = 700
D = 4	I = 9	N = 50	R = 90	V = 400	Z = 800
E = 5	J = 10				

Caesar Nero = 409

in Greek Χαισαρ Νερον = 1,005

Greek KAISAR NERON transposed into Hebrew קסר נרון = 666

number of its name, standing beside the sea of glass with harps of God in their hands. [3] And they sing the song of Moses, the servant[a] of God, and the song of the Lamb:

"Great and amazing are your deeds,
  Lord God the Almighty!
Just and true are your ways,
  King of the nations![b]

[4] Lord, who will not fear
  and glorify your name?
For you alone are holy.
  All nations will come
  and worship before you,
for your judgments have been revealed."

a Gk *slave*   *b* Other ancient authorities read *the ages*

5 After this I looked, and the temple of the tent[a] of witness in heaven was opened, 6and out of the temple came the seven angels with the seven plagues, robed in pure bright linen,[b] with golden sashes across their chests. 7Then one of the four living creatures gave the seven angels seven golden bowls full of the wrath of God, who lives forever and ever; 8and the temple was filled with smoke from the glory of God and from his power, and no one could enter the temple until the seven plagues of the seven angels were ended.

15.1–8: The preparation. This is the third *portent;* see 12.1, 3. These are the *last* plagues not because they end the story but because they represent the final outcome of the story. The *sea* is the same as in the worship scene, 4.6. **2:** *Those who had conquered* are the 144,000 of 14.1 and those under the altar of 6.9, who conquer by the death of Christ and by their own deaths (12.11). **3:** The *song of Moses* and the *song of the Lamb* is a composite of the Exodus song (Ex 15; Deut 32) with Ps 111.2; 86.8–9; and Jer 10.6–7, 16.19. The community is committed to both Moses and Jesus (see 12.17; 14.2). **6:** The *plagues* are another reference to the Exodus tradition. The scene in the *temple** recalls Isa 6.

16 Then I heard a loud voice from the temple telling the seven angels, "Go and pour out on the earth the seven bowls of the wrath of God."

2 So the first angel went and poured his bowl on the earth, and a foul and painful sore came on those who had the mark of the beast and who worshiped its image.

3 The second angel poured his bowl into the sea, and it became like the blood of a corpse, and every living thing in the sea died.

4 The third angel poured his bowl into the rivers and the springs of water, and they became blood. 5And I heard the angel of the waters say,

"You are just, O Holy One, who are and were,
for you have judged these things;
6 because they shed the blood of saints and prophets,
you have given them blood to drink.
It is what they deserve!"

7And I heard the altar respond,
"Yes, O Lord God, the Almighty,
your judgments are true and just!"

8 The fourth angel poured his bowl on the sun, and it was allowed to scorch people with fire; 9they were scorched by the fierce heat, but they cursed the name of God, who had authority over these plagues, and they did not repent and give him glory.

10 The fifth angel poured his bowl on the throne of the beast, and its kingdom was plunged into darkness; people gnawed their tongues in agony, 11and cursed the God of heaven because of their pains and sores, and they did not repent of their deeds.

12 The sixth angel poured his bowl on the great river Euphrates, and its water was dried up in order to prepare the way for the kings from the east. 13And I saw three foul spirits like frogs coming from the mouth of the dragon, from the mouth of the beast, and from the mouth of the false prophet. 14These are demonic spirits, performing signs, who go abroad to the kings of the whole world, to assemble them for battle on the great day of God the Almighty. 15("See, I am coming like a thief! Blessed is the one who stays awake and is clothed,[c] not going about naked and exposed to shame.") 16And they assembled them at the place that in Hebrew is called Harmagedon.

17 The seventh angel poured his bowl into the air, and a loud voice came out of the temple, from the throne, saying, "It is done!" 18And there came flashes of lightning, rumblings, peals of thunder, and a violent earthquake, such as had not occurred since people were upon the earth, so violent was that earthquake. 19The great city was split into three parts, and the cities of the nations fell. God remembered great Babylon and gave her the wine-cup of the fury of his wrath. 20And every island fled away, and no mountains were to be found; 21and huge hailstones, each weighing about a hundred pounds,[d] dropped from heaven on people, until they cursed God for the plague of the hail, so fearful was that plague.

---

a Or *tabernacle*   *b* Other ancient authorities read *stone*
c Gk *and keeps his robes*   *d* Gk *weighing about a talent*

16.1–21: The pouring out. The effects of the seven bowls mirror those of the seven trumpets—earth, sea, rivers, sun, abyss/throne of the beast, Euphrates River—only now destruction seems to be complete (compare 15.3 with 8.9). **6:** *It is what they deserved* indicates a kind of intrinsic divine justice; evil suffers the inevitable consequences of its actions. **12:** The *Euphrates* marked the eastern border of the Roman Empire, beyond which lay Rome's powerful enemy, the Parthians. **15–16:** *Harmagedon* (Hebrew for Mount Magedon) by contrast is not a place on any map; efforts to identify it with Megiddo in Palestine fail because Megiddo is a plain, not a mountain. This is a spiritual war, as the reference to *coming like a thief* indicates. **17:** *It is done;* the forces of evil are defeated but no battle is ever shown. The saying is reminiscent of Jesus' cry from the cross in John's Gospel: It is finished (Jn 19.30). Both rest on the conviction that the death of Jesus is the victory over evil. Traditional signs of divine presence follow (see 4.5). **19:** *The great city* is primarily Rome (17.18) but can also be Jerusalem (11.8). **21:** The hundred-pound *hailstones* are meant to seem impossibly large, even as the other disasters here are of unimaginable proportions.

17 Then one of the seven angels who had the seven bowls came and said to me, "Come, I will show you the judgment of the great whore who is seated on many waters, ²with whom the kings of the earth have committed fornication, and with the wine of whose fornication the inhabitants of the earth have become drunk." ³So he carried me away in the spirit*a* into a wilderness, and I saw a woman sitting on a scarlet beast that was full of blasphemous names, and it had seven heads and ten horns. ⁴The woman was clothed in purple and scarlet, and adorned with gold and jewels and pearls, holding in her hand a golden cup full of abominations and the impurities of her fornication; ⁵and on her forehead was written a name, a mystery: "Babylon the great, mother of whores and of earth's abominations." ⁶And I saw that the woman was drunk with the blood of the saints and the blood of the witnesses to Jesus.

When I saw her, I was greatly amazed. ⁷But the angel said to me, "Why are you so amazed? I will tell you the mystery of the woman, and of the beast with seven heads and ten horns that carries her. ⁸The beast that you saw was, and is not, and is about to ascend from the bottomless pit and go to destruction. And the inhabitants of the earth, whose names have not been written in the book of life from the foundation of the world, will be amazed when they see the beast, because it was and is not and is to come.

9 "This calls for a mind that has wisdom: the seven heads are seven mountains on which the woman is seated; also, they are seven kings, ¹⁰of whom five have fallen, one is living, and the other has not yet come; and when he comes, he must remain only a little while. ¹¹As for the beast that was and is not, it is an eighth but it belongs to the seven, and it goes to destruction. ¹²And the ten horns that you saw are ten kings who have not yet received a kingdom, but they are to receive authority as kings for one hour, together with the beast. ¹³These are united in yielding their power and authority to the beast; ¹⁴they will make war on the Lamb, and the Lamb will conquer them, for he is Lord of lords and King of kings, and those with him are called and chosen and faithful."

15 And he said to me, "The waters that you saw, where the whore is seated, are peoples and multitudes and nations and languages. ¹⁶And the ten horns that you saw, they and the beast will hate the whore; they will make her desolate and naked; they will devour her flesh and burn her up with fire. ¹⁷For God has put it into their hearts to carry out his purpose by agreeing to give their kingdom to the beast, until the words of God will be fulfilled. ¹⁸The woman you saw is the great city that rules over the kings of the earth."

17.1–18: The vision of the woman in purple. Once again the story moves from summary to detailed narrative,* as the destruction of Babylon is acted out. The mention of the *seven angels* consciously connects this scene with the previous one (chs. 15–16). The *great whore* is a new character, but strongly reminiscent of the prophetic* charge against God's people: Isa 1.21;

a Or *in the Spirit*

Jer 3.1–9; Ezek 16; and throughout Hosea. At the end of the scene John will explicitly identify her with *the great city* (Jerusalem at 11.8) that *rules over the kings of the earth*, which can only mean Rome. This is also the power of the name *Babylon*—the city that, like Rome, destroyed Jerusalem. Nevertheless, the violence of the beast against the whore (v. 16) is strongly suggestive of the destruction of Jerusalem in the Jewish-Roman war (with imagery drawn from Ezek 16.36–42). All who sleep with the beast will be devoured. **3:** *In the spirit* is John's way of signaling the spiritual nature of the vision; see 1.10, 4.2, and 20.10. The *beast* was introduced in ch. 13. **4:** The *purple, scarlet,* and *gold* mark the woman as senatorial class, for only they could wear these colors. **5:** Jeremiah saw *Babylon* as a *golden cup* in God's hand, making the nations *drunk* (51.7–8). *Forehead* (see 13.16). **6:** Being *drunk with blood* echoes the third bowl, 16.6. **8:** The beast who *was, and is not and is to come* is often understood with reference to the ancient myth of the return of Nero, but that myth did not involve Nero's death. Another possibility is that while the present Roman government might not seem so bad, both its past (the death of Jesus) and its future (the final battle) show its beastly or demonic underpinnings. The description satirizes the description of Jesus at 1.17–18. **9:** The *seven kings* are symbolic: There are to be seven emperors (a complete series), but the present emperor is always a sixth (see 666 at 13.11–18). None of the many attempts to count actual rulers has proven convincing.

18 After this I saw another angel coming down from heaven, having great authority; and the earth was made bright with his splendor. 2He called out with a mighty voice,

"Fallen, fallen is Babylon the great!
It has become a dwelling place
        of demons,
a haunt of every foul spirit,
a haunt of every foul bird,
a haunt of every foul and
        hateful beast.*a*
3 For all the nations have drunk*b*
of the wine of the wrath of her
        fornication,
and the kings of the earth have
        committed fornication with her,
and the merchants of the earth have
        grown rich from the power*c* of
        her luxury."

4 Then I heard another voice from heaven saying,
"Come out of her, my people,
        so that you do not take part in her
                sins,
        and so that you do not share in her
                plagues;
5 for her sins are heaped high as heaven,
        and God has remembered
                her iniquities.
6 Render to her as she herself
                has rendered,
        and repay her double for her deeds;
        mix a double draught for her in the
                cup she mixed.
7 As she glorified herself and lived
                luxuriously,
        so give her a like measure of torment
                and grief.
Since in her heart she says,
        'I rule as a queen;
I am no widow,
        and I will never see grief,'
8 therefore her plagues will come in a
                single day—
        pestilence and mourning and famine—
and she will be burned with fire;
        for mighty is the Lord God who
                judges her."

9 And the kings of the earth, who committed fornication and lived in luxury with her, will weep and wail over her when they see the smoke of her burning; 10they will stand far off, in fear of her torment, and say,
"Alas, alas, the great city,
        Babylon, the mighty city!
For in one hour your judgment
        has come."

11 And the merchants of the earth weep and mourn for her, since no one buys their cargo anymore, 12cargo of gold, silver, jewels and pearls, fine linen, purple, silk and scarlet, all kinds of scented wood, all articles of ivory, all articles of costly wood, bronze, iron, and marble, 13cinnamon, spice, incense, myrrh, frankincense, wine, olive oil, choice

a Other ancient authorities lack the words *a haunt of every foul beast* and attach the words *and hateful* to the previous line so as to read *a haunt of every foul and hateful bird*   *b* Other ancient authorities read *She has made all nations drink*   *c* Or *resources* flour and wheat, cattle and sheep, horses and chariots, slaves—and human lives.[a]

14 "The fruit for which your soul longed
 has gone from you,
and all your dainties and your splendor
 are lost to you,
 never to be found again!"

15 The merchants of these wares, who gained wealth from her, will stand far off, in fear of her torment, weeping and mourning aloud,

16 "Alas, alas, the great city,
 clothed in fine linen,
  in purple and scarlet,
 adorned with gold,
  with jewels, and with pearls!

17 For in one hour all this wealth has been
 laid waste!"

And all shipmasters and seafarers, sailors and all whose trade is on the sea, stood far off 18 and cried out as they saw the smoke of her burning,

 "What city was like the great city?"

19 And they threw dust on their heads, as they wept and mourned, crying out,

 "Alas, alas, the great city,
  where all who had ships at sea
  grew rich by her wealth!
For in one hour she has been laid
  waste."

18.1–19.10: The songs over Babylon: lament* and rejoicing. 18.2: *Fallen, fallen* is repeated from 14.8. *Babylon* (Rome; see 14.6; 17.5) is now portrayed as deserted and desolate. **4:** *Another voice* because it now addresses the faithful. *Come out* is a call for separation; the seven messages give some sense of what such separation entailed (see 2.13–16; 3.20–25). **6:** *Render . . . as she . . . rendered* is a call to appropriate justice (see 16.6). **7:** *As . . . . so* is a similar call, but adding the notion that the accumulation of wealth and privilege is itself worthy of retribution. **9–19:** A dirge in three parts. *The kings of the earth* mourn the destruction of *the great city* (see comments on 11.8; 17.18). **11–13:** *The merchants* mourn her lost wealth; notice how the list ends: *slaves—and human lives.* There is an implicit indictment of wealth and oppression in these poems. **17–18:** *The shipmasters* mourn the loss of commerce. The image of *the great city* here is appropriate only to a city like Rome (not Jerusalem, an inland city).

20 Rejoice over her, O heaven, you saints and apostles and prophets! For God has given judgment for you against her.

21 Then a mighty angel took up a stone like a great millstone and threw it into the sea, saying,

 "With such violence Babylon the great
  city
 will be thrown down,
 and will be found no more;

22 and the sound of harpists and minstrels
  and of flutists and trumpeters
 will be heard in you no more;
and an artisan of any trade
 will be found in you no more;
and the sound of the millstone
 will be heard in you no more;

23 and the light of a lamp
 will shine in you no more;
and the voice of bridegroom and bride
 will be heard in you no more;
for your merchants were the magnates
 of the earth,
and all nations were deceived by your
 sorcery.

24 And in you[b] was found the blood of
 prophets and of saints,
 and of all who have been slaughtered
 on earth."

19 After this I heard what seemed to be the loud voice of a great multitude in heaven, saying,

 "Hallelujah!
Salvation and glory and power
 to our God,

2 for his judgments are true and just;
he has judged the great whore
 who corrupted the earth with her
  fornication,
and he has avenged on her the blood of
 his servants."[c]

3 Once more they said,
 "Hallelujah!
The smoke goes up from her forever
 and ever."

4 And the twenty-four elders and the four living creatures fell down and worshiped God who is seated on the throne, saying,

---

a Or *chariots, and human bodies and souls* b Gk *her*
c Gk *slaves*

"Amen. Hallelujah!"

5 And from the throne came a voice
saying,

"Praise our God,
all you his servants,[a]
and all who fear him,
small and great."

[6]Then I heard what seemed to be the voice
of a great multitude, like the sound of many
waters and like the sound of mighty thun-
derpeals, crying out,

"Hallelujah!
For the Lord our God
the Almighty reigns.

[7] Let us rejoice and exult
and give him the glory,
for the marriage of the Lamb has come,
and his bride has made herself ready;

[8] to her it has been granted to be clothed
with fine linen, bright and pure"—

for the fine linen is the righteous deeds of
the saints.

9 And the angel said[b] to me, "Write this:
Blessed are those who are invited to the marriage supper of the Lamb." And he said to
me, "These are true words of God." [10]Then
I fell down at his feet to worship him, but he
said to me, "You must not do that! I am a
fellow servant[c] with you and your comrades[d] who hold the testimony of Jesus.[e]
Worship God! For the testimony of Jesus[e] is
the spirit of prophecy."

18.20–19.10: This passage is a disturbing call to rejoice
at the destruction of Babylon, indicating a deep hostility. **18.20:** They rejoice like someone who has won
a lawsuit: *God has given judgment for you against her.*
21–24: The *millstone* was a common image of judgment (see Mk 9.42); such prophetic-symbolic actions
were common. This is now the third image of Babylon's destruction: 17.16; 18.2; there will be a fourth at
19.3. *The blood of all the prophets* * is found in no one
city, but it is found in the *great city.* **19.1:** In response
to the command of 18.20, the heavenly *multitude*
shout hallelujah, joined by the 24 elders (see 4.4;
11.14). The scene echoes the throne scene in chs. 4–
5; see also 11.15–18. **6:** *The Lord . . . reigns* echoes
11.15. **9:** *The angel said to me* introduces a short exchange between John and the angel, in which John
tries to worship the angel and is rebuked (see the similar scene at 22.8–9). **10:** *The spirit of prophecy* or the

spirit that inspires prophecy; John must not worship
the messenger because the source of the message is
the *testimony of Jesus* (Jesus' life and word).

THE FINAL BATTLE

19.11–20.10: This is the climax* of the third story,
where the war launched by the dragon at 12.17 comes
to its devastating conclusion. Still, the sequence is
complex and unexpected: After the introduction of the
heavenly warrior, the final battle is reported, followed
by a thousand-year reign of peace, then a new battle.

---

11 Then I saw heaven opened, and there
was a white horse! Its rider is called Faithful
and True, and in righteousness he judges
and makes war. [12]His eyes are like a flame
of fire, and on his head are many diadems;
and he has a name inscribed that no one
knows but himself. [13]He is clothed in a robe
dipped in[f] blood, and his name is called The
Word of God. [14]And the armies of heaven,
wearing fine linen, white and pure, were following him on white horses. [15]From his
mouth comes a sharp sword with which to
strike down the nations, and he will rule[g]
them with a rod of iron; he will tread the
wine press of the fury of the wrath of God
the Almighty. [16]On his robe and on his thigh
he has a name inscribed, "King of kings and
Lord of lords."

19.11–16: The heavenly warrior. The *heaven opened*
or the sky opened. The *white horse* symbolizes victory,
but with nearly the opposite meaning as the white
horse at 6.2. There the meaning was the one who
starts wars; here the victory ends war. Elements of the
description were used earlier: *Faithful and True* are
names connected with the death of Jesus at 3.14. **12:**
Eyes like a flame and the sword remind us of the exalted human of the opening vision (1.14). **13–16:** The
robe dipped in blood and the *wine press* echo the
judgment scene at 14.20. The *rod of iron* was the mark
of the woman's son (see 12.5). The *name no one
knows* signals the person is beyond ordinary understanding (see 2.17). *The Word of God* is the third
name given this figure, and the most revealing; it is
connected with the image of the *sword* that comes

a Gk slaves   b Gk he said   c Gk slave
d Gk brothers   e Or to Jesus   f Other ancient
authorities read sprinkled with   g Or will shepherd

from his *mouth*, for this is how the victory over evil will be won: by the word (19.21).

17 Then I saw an angel standing in the sun, and with a loud voice he called to all the birds that fly in midheaven, "Come, gather for the great supper of God, ¹⁸to eat the flesh of kings, the flesh of captains, the flesh of the mighty, the flesh of horses and their riders—flesh of all, both free and slave, both small and great." ¹⁹Then I saw the beast and the kings of the earth with their armies gathered to make war against the rider on the horse and against his army. ²⁰And the beast was captured, and with it the false prophet who had performed in its presence the signs by which he deceived those who had received the mark of the beast and those who worshiped its image. These two were thrown alive into the lake of fire that burns with sulfur. ²¹And the rest were killed by the sword of the rider on the horse, the sword that came from his mouth; and all the birds were gorged with their flesh.

19.17–21: The battle against the beast. The scene opens and closes with the gory spectacle of vultures feasting on the corpses after the battle, but no battle is ever portrayed. The *false prophet** is the same as the beast from the earth (13.11–18). The *lake of fire* combines the image of Dan 7.11 with the Greek idea of hell as a place of torment after death. **20–21:** Here only the beasts are consigned to the fire; *the rest were killed by the sword;* but see 20.15. While the image is violent, the nonviolent meaning is emphasized: The wicked are slain by the word of Jesus (also his testimony; see 12.11; 20.4).

20 Then I saw an angel coming down from heaven, holding in his hand the key to the bottomless pit and a great chain. ²He seized the dragon, that ancient serpent, who is the Devil and Satan, and bound him for a thousand years, ³and threw him into the pit, and locked and sealed it over him, so that he would deceive the nations no more, until the thousand years were ended. After that he must be let out for a little while.

4 Then I saw thrones, and those seated on them were given authority to judge. I also saw the souls of those who had been be-

headed for their testimony to Jesus*a* and for the word of God. They had not worshiped the beast or its image and had not received its mark on their foreheads or their hands. They came to life and reigned with Christ a thousand years. ⁵(The rest of the dead did not come to life until the thousand years were ended.) This is the first resurrection. ⁶Blessed and holy are those who share in the first resurrection. Over these the second death has no power, but they will be priests of God and of Christ, and they will reign with him a thousand years.

20.1–6: The thousand-year peace. This short scene has been of enormous influence; it is the only reference to a thousand-year reign of peace in early Christian literature,* but the idea of a millennium has dominated much later thought. *Angel,* see 2.1; 12.7–12. **2:** *Dragon,* see 12.3. *Bound,* see Mk 3.27. **3:** The *bottomless pit* is the locus of chaos, the antithesis* of the throne of God (see 9.1–11; 11.7; 17.8). **4:** A *thousand years* is a complete time. *Thrones,* see 4.2. *Souls,* see 6.9–11. *Mark,* see 13.11–18. **5:** *The rest of the dead* could mean the righteous who were not martyrs* or, more likely, the unrighteous. **6:** The *second death* implies that those raised later will face only the prospect of a second death.

7 When the thousand years are ended, Satan will be released from his prison ⁸and will come out to deceive the nations at the four corners of the earth, Gog and Magog, in order to gather them for battle; they are as numerous as the sands of the sea. ⁹They marched up over the breadth of the earth and surrounded the camp of the saints and the beloved city. And fire came down from heaven*b* and consumed them. ¹⁰And the devil who had deceived them was thrown into the lake of fire and sulfur, where the beast and the false prophet were, and they will be tormented day and night forever and ever.

20.7–10: The battle against Satan. The persistence of evil is symbolized by the release of *Satan,* who is still able to gather an army and march against the *camp*

a Or *for the testimony of Jesus*   *b* Other ancient authorities read *from God, out of heaven,* or *out of heaven from God* of the saints. **8**: *Gog and Magog*, as well as the general scenario, are drawn from Ezek 37–48. **9**: The *fire . . . from heaven* recalls both the sign of the false prophet/beast (13.13) and the deliverance of the true prophet★ Elijah (2 Kings 1.10); another image for God's word (2 Esd 13.10,38). Again there is no portrayal of a battle (see 16.17). **10**: The *lake of fire*, see 19.20.

THE ACTS OF SALVATION

20.11–22.5: Three visions close out John's story: The dead are raised and judged; the world is renewed; and the city of God is established.

11 Then I saw a great white throne and the one who sat on it; the earth and the heaven fled from his presence, and no place was found for them. 12 And I saw the dead, great and small, standing before the throne, and books were opened. Also another book was opened, the book of life. And the dead were judged according to their works, as recorded in the books. 13 And the sea gave up the dead that were in it, Death and Hades gave up the dead that were in them, and all were judged according to what they had done. 14 Then Death and Hades were thrown into the lake of fire. This is the second death, the lake of fire; 15 and anyone whose name was not found written in the book of life was thrown into the lake of fire.

20.11–15: **The judgment of the dead.** *The great white throne* recalls 4.2, but white now because it represents the victory won in the battles. **12**: The image of the *books* of deeds plays on the metaphor★ of the finality of the written word and the lived life. The *book of life* is the book that gives life (as *tree of life*, 2.7; 22.2). **14**: The *sea, death,* and *Hades*★ (the grave) are the three repositories of the dead, here clearly meaning their bodies. The *second death* is now identified with the *lake of fire* but not described as an eternal torment. This would seem to be the end of evil, but see 22.11,15.

21 Then I saw a new heaven and a new earth; for the first heaven and the first earth had passed away, and the sea was no more. 2 And I saw the holy city, the new Jerusalem, coming down out of heaven from God, prepared as a bride adorned for her husband. 3 And I heard a loud voice from the throne saying,

"See, the home*a* of God is among
  mortals.
He will dwell*b* with them;
  they will be his peoples,*c*
  and God himself will be with them;*d*
4 he will wipe every tear from their eyes.
Death will be no more;
mourning and crying and pain will be
  no more,
for the first things have passed away."

5 And the one who was seated on the throne said, "See, I am making all things new." Also he said, "Write this, for these words are trustworthy and true." 6 Then he said to me, "It is done! I am the Alpha and the Omega, the beginning and the end. To the thirsty I will give water as a gift from the spring of the water of life. 7 Those who conquer will inherit these things, and I will be their God and they will be my children. 8 But as for the cowardly, the faithless,*e* the polluted, the murderers, the fornicators, the sorcerers, the idolaters, and all liars, their place will be in the lake that burns with fire and sulfur, which is the second death."

21.1–8: The new creation. One could not imagine a more stark portrayal of a completely new beginning. The *sea* is an image of chaos, now banished. **2–3:** The descent of the *new Jerusalem* from heaven symbolizes the merging of the two realms: Thus God now lives *among mortals.* **5–6:** *It is done,* see 16.17. This is the first direct word from the one on the *throne* (see 4.2). **8:** It is surprising that the *faithless* are still addressed (see 22.11).

9 Then one of the seven angels who had the seven bowls full of the seven last plagues came and said to me, "Come, I will show you the bride, the wife of the Lamb." 10 And in the spirit*f* he carried me away to a great, high mountain and showed me the holy city Jerusalem coming down out of heaven from God. 11 It has the glory of God and a radiance like a very rare jewel, like jasper, clear as

a Gk *the tabernacle* *b* Gk *will tabernacle* *c* Other ancient authorities read *people* *d* Other ancient authorities add *and be their God* *e* Or *the unbelieving* *f* Or *in the Spirit* crystal. 12It has a great, high wall with twelve gates, and at the gates twelve angels, and on the gates are inscribed the names of the twelve tribes of the Israelites; 13on the east three gates, on the north three gates, on the south three gates, and on the west three gates. 14And the wall of the city has twelve foundations, and on them are the twelve names of the twelve apostles of the Lamb.

15 The angel*a* who talked to me had a measuring rod of gold to measure the city and its gates and walls. 16The city lies four-square, its length the same as its width; and he measured the city with his rod, fifteen hundred miles;*b* its length and width and height are equal. 17He also measured its wall, one hundred forty-four cubits*c* by human measurement, which the angel was using. 18The wall is built of jasper, while the city is pure gold, clear as glass. 19The foundations of the wall of the city are adorned with every jewel; the first was jasper, the second sapphire, the third agate, the fourth emerald, 20the fifth onyx, the sixth carnelian, the seventh chrysolite, the eighth beryl, the ninth topaz, the tenth chrysoprase, the eleventh jacinth, the twelfth amethyst. 21And the twelve gates are twelve pearls, each of the gates is a single pearl, and the street of the city is pure gold, transparent as glass.

22 I saw no temple in the city, for its temple is the Lord God the Almighty and the Lamb. 23And the city has no need of sun or moon to shine on it, for the glory of God is its light, and its lamp is the Lamb. 24The nations will walk by its light, and the kings of the earth will bring their glory into it. 25Its gates will never be shut by day—and there will be no night there. 26People will bring into it the glory and the honor of the nations. 27But nothing unclean will enter it, nor anyone who practices abomination or falsehood, but only those who are written in the Lamb's book of life.

22 Then the angel*d* showed me the river of the water of life, bright as crystal, flowing from the throne of God and of the Lamb 2through the middle of the street of the city. On either side of the river is the tree of life*e* with its twelve kinds of fruit, producing its fruit each month; and the leaves

of the tree are for the healing of the nations. 3Nothing accursed will be found there any more. But the throne of God and of the Lamb will be in it, and his servants*f* will worship him; 4they will see his face, and his name will be on their foreheads. 5And there will be no more night; they need no light of lamp or sun, for the Lord God will be their light, and they will reign forever and ever.

21.9–22.5: The vision of the woman of the Lamb. After the general picture of the new creation we have a detailed portrayal of the new Jerusalem, presented as a paired vision to that of "the great city" (see 17.1). The *bride* motif★ points to the wedding that culminated the holy war★ myth. **10:** *In the spirit,* see 17.3. The *mountain* is traditionally the place of revelation (Ex 19.20–25); John's vision is built on that of Ezekiel (ch. 40). **11:** The *glory of God* was traditional language for God's presence in the Temple★ (see Ezek 10.18; 43.4). God was described as *jasper* at 4.3. **12–21:** All the city's attributes are symbolic of the people of God (whose number is *twelve*). The city has *twelve gates* because the people of God enter here; the *twelve angels* are the heavenly counterparts to the earthly messengers; reference to *twelve tribes* reminds us that those who enter "keep the commandments of God" (12.17; see 7.4–8); the *twelve apostles*★ are now understood as the foundation of God's new work (suggesting that John lived in the post-apostolic generation). The angel with a *measuring rod* provides the symbolic figures that interpret the meaning of the city. It is *foursquare* because it is of the earth. The English measure of *fifteen hundred miles* hides the significance of the Greek's 12,000 stadia. This city would be a hundred times larger than ancient Babylon. The wall is 144 cubits high (twelve squared), about 300 feet. *Every jewel* points to the richness of the city; those named correspond to the jewels associated with the twelve signs of the zodiac, in reverse order (see also Ex 28.17–21; 39.10–14). **22:** There is *no temple* because there is no longer a need to mediate God's presence; this is in some tension with 3.12 on the literal level. **24:** The continued existence of *the nations* shows that with all this change John imagines the world organized in its usual fashion. **22.1–2:** The *river* is perhaps an

---

a Gk He   *b* Gk *twelve thousand stadia*   *c* That is, almost seventy-five yards   *d* Gk *he*   *e* Or *the Lamb.* 2In the middle of the street of the city, and on either side of the river, is the tree of life   *f* Gk *slaves*

Eden motif (Gen 2.10), certainly the *tree of life* is (Gen 2.9, but also see Rev 2.7). **4:** *Foreheads,* see 7.3; 14.9.

~~~~~~

6 And he said to me, "These words are trustworthy and true, for the Lord, the God of the spirits of the prophets, has sent his angel to show his servants*ᵃ* what must soon take place."

7 "See, I am coming soon! Blessed is the one who keeps the words of the prophecy of this book."

8 I, John, am the one who heard and saw these things. And when I heard and saw them, I fell down to worship at the feet of the angel who showed them to me; *⁹*but he said to me, "You must not do that! I am a fellow servant*ᵇ* with you and your comrades*ᶜ* the prophets, and with those who keep the words of this book. Worship God!"

10 And he said to me, "Do not seal up the words of the prophecy of this book, for the time is near. *¹¹*Let the evildoer still do evil, and the filthy still be filthy, and the righteous still do right, and the holy still be holy."

12 "See, I am coming soon; my reward is with me, to repay according to everyone's work. *¹³*I am the Alpha and the Omega, the first and the last, the beginning and the end."

14 Blessed are those who wash their robes,*ᵈ* so that they will have the right to the tree of life and may enter the city by the gates. *¹⁵*Outside are the dogs and sorcerers and fornicators and murderers and idolaters, and everyone who loves and practices falsehood.

16 "It is I, Jesus, who sent my angel to you with this testimony for the churches. I am the root and the descendant of David, the bright morning star."

17 The Spirit and the bride say, "Come."
And let everyone who hears say, "Come."
And let everyone who is thirsty come.
Let anyone who wishes take the water
of life as a gift.

18 I warn everyone who hears the words of the prophecy of this book: if anyone adds to them, God will add to that person the plagues described in this book; *¹⁹*if anyone takes away from the words of the book of this prophecy, God will take away that person's share in the tree of life and in the holy city, which are described in this book.

20 The one who testifies to these things says, "Surely I am coming soon."
Amen. Come, Lord Jesus!

21 The grace of the Lord Jesus be with all the saints. Amen.*ᵉ*

22.6–21: The closing: the voices of the Apocalypse.⋆ The voices of the opening are matched and expanded in the closing (see 1.1–11). They often overlap. **6–11: The voice of the angel.** *These words;* see the same chain of transmission at 1.1. **8: The voice of John.** *I, John,* see 1.9. *Fell down,* see 1.17; 19.10. **9:** *Worship God* is the dominant note of the whole work: 4.10; 7.11; 11.16; 19.4,10; and esp. 14.7. **10:** John is *not to seal* the book (see Dan 12.9) because the words are needed now (see 1.3). **12–16: The voice of Jesus.** *I am coming soon* (see also v. 7) is an odd declaration at this point in the story but underlines the sense of urgency about the whole work (see 1.3; 2.5, 16; 3.11; 16.15). **13:** *Alpha and Omega* was attributed to God at the beginning of the story (1.8). **14:** *Blessed,* see 1.3. To *wash their robes* is to maintain faithful testimony even in the face of death (6.11; 7.14; 19.13; 12.11). The *tree of life* is available now (see 22.2). **15:** *Outside are the dogs* shows that there remains an outside, even at the end of the story. **16:** *I, Jesus* shows that the story makes Jesus present to the audience; see 1.1 for the same chain of transmission. The *root of David* and the *morning star* are messianic⋆ images (see Isa 11; Num 24.17). **7, 17–20: The voice of the reader.** The invitation from the *spirit and the bride* has both heavenly and earthly origins. The warning protects the spoken word. **21: The voice of the letter writer.** This is a standard letter closing, corresponding to the opening at 1.4; see 1 Cor 1.1–2; 16.23–24.

~~~~~~

a Gk *slaves*   *b* Gk *slave*   *c* Gk *brothers*   *d* Other ancient authorities read *do his commandments*
e Other ancient authorities lack *all*; others lack *the saints*; others lack *Amen*

GLOSSARY,
WEIGHTS AND MEASURES,
CONCORDANCE

GLOSSARY

About This Glossary   Like all subjects, biblical studies has developed a specialized vocabulary for various aspects of its discipline. And, like many subjects, biblical studies borrows terms from other disciplines when these can be of assistance in explaining the text or meaning of the Bible. In the study materials, various words are marked with a star symbol ✶, and all these terms are defined here. This glossary includes additional terms, however, in order to give a more complete list of some of the specialized vocabulary. The entries for **ancient translations, calendar, early Christian writings, interpretation, pseudepigrapha,** and **rhetoric** list or discuss a number of terms relating to their particular fields. Finally, many entries refer to the biblical text, where there is an example of the term or where the term itself appears.

How to Use This Glossary   The glossary provides further information and background for the study materials. It lists related entries that help in understanding different areas in biblical studies. It also aids in exploring the text of the Bible by providing examples that can be guides for finding other occurrences.

Abaddon (uh-bad'-dun) "place of destruction," a Hebrew word for the realm of the dead (Job 26.6; Prov 15.11; Ps 88.10–12; also mentioned in Rev 9.11)

Abba the Aramaic word for "father," which Jesus (Mk 14.36) and, following his example, the early church (Rom 8.15), used to address God

accession the act of taking one's place as a ruler

acrostic (ah-cross'-tick) an arrangement of words, or lines in a poem, in which the first letters of each word or line create a pattern. In Hebrew poetry all of the acrostics are alphabetical: the consecutive lines, or groups or lines, each begin with successive letters of the Hebrew alphabet. *See* Figure 1.

The following poems in the Bible are acrostics: Ps 9–10, 25, 34, 37, 111, 112, 119, 145; Prov 31.20–31; Lam 1, 2, 3, 4 (ch 5, while not an acrostic, preserves part of the form by having twenty-two lines, the number of letters in the Hebrew alphabet); Nah 1.2–8 (or 9), which is incomplete; Sir 51.13–30. See sidebar on p. 1107 [OLD TESTAMENT].

Ahikar (uh-hee'-kar) an ancient Near Eastern story of Ahikar, the prime minister to the king of Assyria, who is betrayed by an ungrateful nephew, Nadab, but ultimately vindicated. It is alluded to in Tob 1.21–22. *See* pseudepigrapha.

allegory an extended comparison in which an author, while speaking directly of one reality, intends to mean, and is understood by the reader to be speaking indirectly about, something entirely different. An allegory as a story uses action, setting, and characters to point to a symbolic level.

Examples of biblical allegory include the "Song of the Vineyard" in Isa 5, in which the story of the vineyard is also the story of Judah, and the parable of the sower in Mt 13.1–8, 18–23 (*see* parable). Allegory is infrequent in present-day literature, but allegorical treatments are sometimes present in other areas. The statue of Justice found in many courthouses is an example of an allegorical

Figure 1. Verses 57–72 of Psalm 119 in Hebrew illustrates the acrostic pattern of this psalm. All eight verses in each stanza begin with the same Hebrew letter, and the twenty-two sets of eight verses use the twenty-two Hebrew letters in successive order. The Hebrew letters *heth* and *teth* appear at the right hand side of the text, since Hebrew reads from right to left.

use of art to speak about a different level of reality: a beautiful woman (justice attracts us), blindfolded (justice is not influenced by external appearance), with balancing scales (justice weighs the merits of a case in a publicly observable way), and a sword (justice can punish). This allegorical statue makes clear our ideals of justice. Normally, all important elements in an allegory correspond to elements in another realm of reality.

allegorical a method of reading a work as an allegory; explaining or interpreting elements of a story as if they stood for something else. Paul uses an allegorical method of interpretation in Gal 4.22–26.

alphabet the letters of a given language in a standard order. The Hebrew and Greek alphabets are shown in Figure 4 on the next page. Samples of text are shown in Figures 2 and 3.

anachronism (ah-nah′-krow-nizm) an element in a story that is out of place because it did not exist at the time of the story. Anachronisms can be valuable clues to the time when a story was written.

anadiplosis (a-na-di-plo′-sis) the "doubling," or repetition, of a word or phrase. The author of Isa 40–55 often used this figure; for instance, "Awake, awake, put on strength" (51.9) and "I, I am he who comforts you" (51.12). *See* rhetoric.

anaphora (ah-nah′-for-ah) the repetition of a word or phrase in successive lines or sentences. "As the eyes of servants look to the hand of their master,/ as the eyes of a maid to the hand of her mistress,/ so our eyes look to the LORD our God" (Ps 123.2). *See* rhetoric.

anastrophe (ah-nah′-stro-fee) the repetition at the beginning of one line of the word or words that concluded the previous line. "The voice of the LORD breaks the cedars;/ the LORD breaks the cedars of Lebanon" (Ps 29.5). *See* rhetoric.

ancient translations In the translators' notes to the NRSV and in some of the study materials, there are references to various ancient translations of the Bible. These translations—into Greek, Syriac, Aramaic, and Latin—are called "versions" and are used by biblical scholars to help to translate the Hebrew portion of the Bible. They are useful because they provide a method of checking the Hebrew text, which cannot be done directly in most cases. The oldest complete copies of the Hebrew text are about 1000 years old and are based on the text established by Jewish schol-

1 יְבְּרֵאשִׁ֖ת בָּרָ֣א אֱלֹהִ֑ים אֵ֥ת הַשָּׁמַ֖יִם וְאֵ֥ת הָאָֽרֶץ׃ יְהָאָ֖רֶץ

Figure 2. The first line of the Hebrew Bible: *Bereshith bara elohim eth ha-shamayim w-eth ha-arets.*

1 Ἐν ἀρχῇ ἦν ὁ λόγος, καὶ ὁ λόγος ἦν πρὸς τὸν θεόν, καὶ θεὸς ἦν ὁ λόγος. 2 οὗτος ἦν ἐν ἀρχῇ πρὸς τὸν θεόν.

Figure 3. The beginning of the Gospel of John in Greek: 1. *En archë ën ho logos, kai ho logos ën pros ton theon, kai theos ën ho logos.* 2. *houtos ën en archë pros ton theon.*

ars (the Masoretic text). (Parts of the Hebrew Bible were found among the Dead Sea Scrolls, and these texts date to the second and first centuries BCE.) The ancient versions, however, translated a Hebrew text that was older, and hence provide a window into early forms of the Hebrew text.

When translators cannot make sense of the Hebrew text as it now stands, they can consult these ancient translations to see if any of them offer a clue to a better rendering. Whenever the NRSV translators have done this, they have marked their work with a footnote. In the list of abbreviations you will find the names of the ancient versions. The names and terms associated with the ancient versions of the Bible include: Aramaic, Masoretic text, Old Latin, Peshitta, Septuagint, Syriac, Syriac Hexapla, Targums, Vulgate.

anoint to touch or rub with oil. Both things and people can be anointed. Anointing was a sign that the person or object was dedicated to God: kings (1 Kings 1.39) and priests (Lev 8.30) were anointed, as were the bodies of those who had died (Lk 23.56). *See* Christ, messiah.

antithesis (an-ti′-thuh-sis) the contrast of ideas through closely contrasted words. "A soft answer turns away wrath,/ but a harsh word stirs up anger" (Prov 15.1). *See* rhetoric.

apocalypse (from the Greek word *apokalypsis,* which means "revelation") a narrative in which a revelation is communicated by an angel or otherworldly being to a human being, usually a biblical hero, concerning the divine plan of history and the supernatural world. An apocalypse often consists of a series of visions of heaven and earth that are explained by an angelic being. See sidebar on p. 2071 [NEW TESTAMENT].

apocalyptic having the character of an apocalypse, but more generally referring to a worldview that assumes the existence of a supernatural realm closely related to the natural world. Apocalyptic writings present a reality behind historical

Figure 4: Hebrew and Greek alphabets. At left, the consonantal letters of the Hebrew alphabet. Hebrew vowels are, for the most part, represented by small marks called "points" that appear above and below consonants. At right are the letters of the Greek alphabet.

Hebrew letter and name		Approximate equivalents in English alphabet	Greek letter and name			Approximate equivalents in English alphabet
א	aleph	the unvoiced open sound before a vowel	A	α	alpha	a as in pal
ב	beth	b, v	B	β	beta	b
ג	gimel	g, gh	Γ	γ	gamma	g as in game; γγ, ng as in angry
ד	daleth	d, th as in they	Δ	δ	delta	d
ה	he	h	E	ε	epsilon	e as in bet
ו	waw	w (v in some pronunciations)	Z	ζ	zeta	dz as in adze
ז	zayin	z	H	η	eta	a as in late
ח	heth	ch as in loch	Θ	θ	theta	th as in thin
ט	teth	t	I	ι	iota	i as in bit
י	yod	y, i as in machine	K	κ	kappa	k
כ	kaph	k, kh (approximately ch as in German *Achtung*)	Λ	λ	lambda	l
			M	μ	mu	m
			N	ν	nu	n
ל	lamed	l	Ξ	ξ	xi	x as in axe
מ	mem	m	O	o	omicron	o as in hot
נ	nun	n	Π	π	pi	p
ס	samekh	s	P	ρ	rho	r
ע	ayin	the voiced open sound before a vowel (no English equivalent)	Σ	σ	sigma	s
			T	τ	tau	t
			U	υ	upsilon	u
פ	pe	p, ph	Φ	φ	phi	ph
צ	tsadhe	ts as in itsy	X	χ	chi	ch as in loch
ק	qoph	q, k (spoken at the back of the throat)	Ψ	ψ	psi	ps as in lapse
			Ω	ω	omega	o as in hope
ר	resh	r				
ש	sin, shin	s, sh				
ת	taw	t, th as in thin				

Combinations of vowels, called "diphthongs," include ai (pronounced like eye) and ou (pronounced like oo in hoot). Thus, for instance, "kai," Greek for "and," is pronounced to rhyme with "high."

or natural events; often this reality is presented to the human author as a sign that a final judgment is at hand. See sidebar on p. 1737 [NEW TESTAMENT].

Apocrypha a term, from the Greek *apokryphos*, "hidden," for a group of about 20 mostly Jewish works, many of which were included in the Septuagint (*see*), but which were not ultimately accepted into the Jewish canon. All of these works are considered "apocryphal" or non-canonical in Protestant Bibles and, if included, are grouped together in an appendix to the Old Testament. In Roman Catholic, Greek, and Slavonic Bibles, various groupings of them are considered "deutero-canonical" (*see*) and are included among the canonical Hebrew Scriptures, while others are viewed as non-canonical.

apologetic an account of events or an argument offered as a defense of a particular position or point of view. An apologetic can be a very passionate vindication of the author's position.

aporia (ah-po-ree′-a) pretending doubt about what to say or do next. "Then the manager said to himself, 'What will I do? . . . I have decided . . .'" (Lk 16.3–4). *See* rhetoric.

apostle "one who is sent" (Greek), a delegate or representative. In the New Testament, an apostle was one who had known Jesus and could witness to his resurrection (Acts 1.21–22) or a preacher of the gospel who had been called by God (1 Cor 12.28; Rom 16.7).

Aramaic a semitic language used widely in Syria-Palestine during the Persian period. After the exile of the Jewish people from the land of Israel, those who lived under Persian rule began to speak Aramaic, and it eventually supplanted Hebrew as the language of the ordinary Jewish people. Jesus spoke Aramaic. Aramaic translations of the Hebrew Bible are called Targums (*see*). *See also* ancient translations.

Armageddon (ar-muh-ged'-dun) traditionally, the site of the final battle between good and evil (based on Rev 16.16). The name may be derived from Megiddo, the place of several important battles in Israel's history (Judg 5.19; 2 Kings 9.27).

Asherah pl. **Asherim** a Canaanite goddess, consort of El and often called "mother of the gods," associated in the Bible with a sacred tree (1 Kings 14.15)

Assumption of Moses a legend, the account of which is no longer in existence, that may be the origin of the allusion in Jude 9 to a fight between the archangel Michael and the devil over the body of Moses. ("Assumption" means that one is raised bodily into heaven without dying.)

Astarte (as-star'-tee) (also Ishtar) the spouse of Baal (*see*); a symbol of fertility. The biblical writers denounced worship of "Astartes" (Judg 2.13), which translates the Hebrew word *Ashtoreth*, a plural form of the goddess' name.

atonement the means by which guilt or impurity from the violation of certain rules or commands may be forgiven, compensated, or transferred to another agent (such as the scapegoat—Lev 16.20–23). Such procedures of atonement enable reconciliation between God and the human community so that life and worship may resume without penalty or punishment.

autograph the original author's version of a written work

Baal a Hebrew word, meaning "lord" or "master" (sometimes "husband") but also the name of the chief god of Canaanite religion; the storm god

Baalzebub, Baalzebul *See* Beelzebul.

ban devoting to the LORD the population and sometimes the booty of a captured city by destroying them

baptism ritual purification by immersion in water. Baptism was a practice common to many religions of the ancient Mediterranean world. Christian baptism in the New Testament, based on the reported practice of John the Baptist (Mk 1.4) may have been derived from Jewish purifi-

cation ritual (Lev 15.18) but Paul's connection of Christian baptism with the death and resurrection of Christ (Rom 6.1–14) changed the meaning of the ritual from purification into initiation into a new faith community and a new identity.

Beelzebul (bee-el'-zuh-bull) [also Baalzebul, Baalzebub, Beelzebub] the name for the ruler of the demons (Mt 12.24–27). It is based on the Hebrew form Baalzebul, "lord of heaven," for the Phoenician god at Ekron (2 Kings 1.2–18), transformed (probably as a derogatory name) into Baalzebub, "lord of the flies."

behemoth a mythical beast, sometimes identified with the hippopotamus (Job 40.15–24) who represents violent forces in the created world

calendar any method of enumerating years, differentiating one year from previous and following years, and dividing a year up into groups of days. The **Jewish calendar** consists of the following months:

Nissan	March/ April
Iyyar	April/ May
Siwan/ Sivan	May/ June
Tammuz	June/ July
Ab/ Av	July/ August
Elul	August/ September
Tishri	September/ October
Heshvan/ Marheshvan	October/ November
Chislev	November/ December
Tebeth	December/ January
Shebet	January/ February
Adar	February/ March

The calendar reckons years from the supposed date of creation, 3760/61 BCE. Each month begins on the day of the new moon. Because each month is only 29 or 30 days, a year is only 354 days, so every third (or occasionally second) year is a leap year in which the month of Adar is repeated.

Jewish holy days occur according to this calendar as follows:

The New Year (Rosh Hashanah)	1 Tishri
The Day of Atonement (Yom Kippur)	10 Tishri
Passover: a full week (8 days inclusive) beginning	15 Nisan
Weeks (Shavuot, or Pentecost)	Seven full weeks (50 days inclusive) from Passover
Booths (Sukkot), the harvest festival	15 Tishri
Purim, the festival of deliverance from persecution	14 Adar
Tisha be-Av, the destruction of the Temple	9 Ab
Hanukkuh, the festival of lights, commemorating the rededication of the Temple	25 Chislev

The five festival scrolls (megilloth) are read on five festivals as follows:

Esther is read on Purim
Lamentations is read on Tisha be-Av
Song of Solomon is read on the Sabbath of Passover
Ecclesiastes is read on the Sabbath of Sukkot
Ruth is read on Shavuot

The **Christian calendar** differs slightly between the Orthodox Churches and those derived from Western Christianity. In the Western Christian (Gregorian) calendar, years are reckoned from the supposed dates of the Annunciation (March 25) and the birth of Jesus (December 25) in 1 CE or AD.

The liturgical calendar of Western Christianity follows this scheme:

Advent, the four Sundays preceding Christmas
Christmas, the twelve days from December 25 through January 5
Lent, the 40 Days (excluding Sundays) preceding Easter
Easter, the seven weeks (50 days inclusive) from Easter Sunday through Pentecost Sunday

The pattern is of two major seasons of celebration, devoted to the central beliefs of the Incarnation and Resurrection of Jesus respectively, preceded by seasons of preparation. The Sundays after Epiphany (January 6) until the beginning of Lent, and the Sundays after Pentecost until the beginning of Advent, are not seasons in this sense. Christmas, occurring always on the 25th of December, is a fixed day, but Easter, which depends on the phases of the moon, is a moveable one. Jesus' death took place at the time of Passover, which always begins on a day of the full moon. In the western calendar, Easter Day is the first Sunday after the full moon that falls on or after March 21. It may therefore occur as early as March 22 or as late as April 25. Lent, comprising 40 days (not including the six Sundays that would fall within this time) begins 46 days before: as early as February 4 or as late as March 10.

canon a Greek word meaning "fixed measure," used to describe the official list of books of the Bible. For Judaism the canon consists of the books that Christians refer to as the Hebrew Scriptures; however, for Christianity the canon always includes the New Testament, but differs about the contents of the Old Testament. See "The Nature and Formation of the Biblical Canon" essay on p. 26. *See also* deuterocanonical books.

canonical criticism the interpretation of the meaning of the final form of a biblical text. Canonical criticism assumes that many biblical books were formed from smaller, already-existing units, but it argues that the intentions and mean-

ings of those responsible for putting a book into final form must also be taken into account. Canonical criticism further assumes that the complete canonical text of the Bible is the context from which interpretation draws its essential key. See the essay on "The Nature and Formation of the Biblical Canon" on p. 26. *See also* interpretation.

chaff the husks of grain. *See* thresh, winnow.

cherubim mythical griffin-like creatures with body parts from different creatures, often including human heads, and wings. They were commonly depicted as the guardians of kings, palaces, and temples in the ancient Near East. They also sat atop the ark of the covenant.

chiasmus (ky-az'-muss) inverting the second pair of terms in a parallel structure, so that the corresponding terms, if laid out in a square, would form an X (Greek *chi*). "Righteous lips are the delight of a king,/ and he loves those who speak what is right" (Prov 16.13). The structure is:

Righteous lips — are the — delight of a king

he loves those — who — speak what is right

See rhetoric.

Christ the Greek word for "anointed," translating the Hebrew word *messiah*. In the New Testament and in general usage, "Christ" always refers to Jesus. Although in contemporary Christianity "Christ" functions as a synonym or alternative name for Jesus, that was not the case in the New Testament. Even when used alone, "Christ" is not a name, but a reminder of who the person Jesus is, that is, "the anointed one." "Lord" (Greek *kyrios*) is used in the same way in the New Testament.

chronicle an account of events that is arranged in the order in which they occurred

circumcision the removal of the foreskin of the penis. In the Bible, this is a sign of entry into the covenant community, whether the circumcision is meant literally (Josh 5.5–7) or metaphorically ("uncircumcised heart," Lev 26.41). In the writings of Paul, "the circumcised" and "the uncircumcised" sometimes refer to Jews and Gentiles, respectively (Gal 2.7).

clan a relatively small social unit considered to be descended from a common ancestor; several clans constitute a tribe

Clement, Letter of (or 1 Clement) an early Christian letter, claiming to be written from the church at Rome to the church at Corinth, dealing with a division within the Corinthian church that had caused the established Corinthian leadership to be overthrown. The writer, who is not named in the text but is traditionally given as Clement, third bishop of Rome, presents an early form of a view of authority that later became important: that Jesus chose the apostles, the apostles chose their successors, and so the leaders of all the local churches can trace their authority back to the apostles and ultimately to Jesus. To oppose the leaders of one's church, therefore, is ultimately to oppose Jesus Christ. The letter of Clement was probably written sometime in the 90s of the Common Era. See early Christian writings.

climax a series of clauses in which each succeeding clause repeats the important term from the previous clause, each clause in turn making a more important point (climax means "ladder"). "Suffering produces endurance, and endurance produces character, and character produces hope . . . " (Rom 5.3–4). See rhetoric.

colophon a notice, usually printed at the end of a book, giving information about authorship. There is a colophon at the end of Sirach (50.27).

concubine female slaves used for sexual purposes, having lesser status than wives

covenant a sworn agreement between two parties; in the Old Testament often between God and people

cult prostitute someone available for sexual intercourse with worshippers at the temple of a god. The Bible (Deut 23.17–18; 1 Kings 14.24) accuses non-Israelite religions of having cult prostitutes, but this may be an exaggeration for the sake of polemic.

Cynics popular Greek philosophers, famous for their rude, blunt ways. Some Cynics traveled from place to place, living off of gifts from supporters or what they could beg.

deuterocanonical books ("deuterocanonical" means "second part of the canon") those books, or parts of books, that are not included in the Hebrew Scriptures, but that various Christian churches include as part of the Old Testament because they were included in the Septuagint (see). The NRSV places notices in the Apocryphal/Deuterocanonical books explaining which ones are accepted as canonical by which Christian churches. See canon; see also "The Nature and Formation of the Biblical Canon" on p. 26.

deuteronomistic (dyoo-ter-o-no-mis'-tic) pertaining to editor(s) of the Deuteronomistic His-

tory (the books of Deuteronomy, Joshua, Judges, 1 and 2 Samuel, and 1 and 2 Kings) or to the style of such editorial work. Such style is simple Hebrew and reflects a concern for such matters as obedience to the law of Deuteronomy, centralized worship in Jerusalem, and the choice of the Davidic dynasty.

Diaspora (dee-ah'-spo-rah) the scattering of Jews outside the land of Israel

diatribe an argument against a position or critical of a person or group. Diatribe often includes an imagined dialogue between opposing viewpoints. See rhetoric.

Didache (did'-uh-kay) an early Christian writing, dating from around 150 CE but including earlier materials. Its name means "teaching," and it consists of moral exhortation, a manual of church order, and guidance for community life. It is valuable for providing insight into the concerns of early Christian communities. It contains material similar to that in the Pastoral Letters, 1 and 2 Timothy and Titus. See early Christian writings.

divine warrior God in the role of warrior, leading heavenly armies into battle and fighting for Israel

documentary hypothesis a theory about the formation of the text of the first five books of the Bible. The documentary hypothesis holds that four traditions underlie these books, naming them after a chief characteristic of each: "J" or "The Yahwist" (the letter "J" is derived from the German spelling, "Jahveh") uses the divine name "Yahweh" (the LORD) consistently, and contains much of the oldest material; "E" or "The Elohist" uses the divine name "Elohim" (God) fairly consistently and contains traditions from the northern kingdom of Israel; "P" or "The Priestly Writer" is concerned largely with legal codes and matters of religious practice; and "D" or "The Deuteronomist" represents the traditions gathered mostly in Deuteronomy and continued through the deuteronomistic history in the books of Joshua, Judges, Samuel, and Kings. There have been many modifications in the documentary hypothesis, and most scholars now agree that these "documents" are much more like streams of tradition than they are like fully conceived, written texts that were combined in a cut-and-paste process. See interpretation.

dualism the view that reality consists of two basic elements, often good and evil. Some dualistic thought is primarily ethical, arguing that human actions are ultimately good or evil; other dualistic philosophies see good and evil in the basic nature of the universe.

dynasty a ruling family; when a leader dies, the next leader is always chosen from among the family members

early Christian writings Besides the books contained in the New Testament, many other writings from the first century or so of the Christian church are known to have survived, or are quoted or referred to by later writers. These writings include gospels, letters, narrative books like the Acts of the Apostles, apocalypses, and collections of teachings. In some cases these works provide direct evidence of teachings that were later rejected by the main body of Christians. In other cases they contain similar material, or parallel arguments, to those in parts of the New Testament, such as the instructions to local churches in the Pastoral Letters. In still other cases they provide further examples of kinds of literature found in the New Testament, such as gospels, acts, and apocalypses. Early Christian writings discussed in this glossary are: the Letter of Clement, the Didache, the Letters of Ignatius, the Letter of Polycarp, the Gospel of Thomas, the Shepherd of Hermas.

encomium a formal speech praising someone, as in a funeral oration. Some examples of encomium occur in 4 Macc 7.1–15, 14.2–10, 15.1–32.

Enoch, books of 1 and 2 Enoch are late Jewish or early Christian writings attributed to the ancient patriarch who was the father of Methuselah (Gen 5.22–24). First Enoch is a collection of apocalyptic visions; it is quoted in Jude 14–15. Second Enoch is a vision narrative (a series of linked visions) of ascent through seven heavens, a vision of the LORD, and a return to earth bearing the secrets of creation. *See* pseudepigrapha.

ephod The linen ephod was a kind of apron worn by priests. An ephod could also be an object, carried by priests, that was used to divine the will of God. It was carried in priestly garments, which may explain why the same word was used for both (1 Sam 2.18). "Ephod" in Judg 8.27 seems to be an idol rather than a priestly garment.

Epicureans Greek philosophical school, founded by Epicurus, who taught that human beings naturally seek pleasure, and that the best way to achieve this pursuit was in moderation, since moderation permits the longest possible life of pleasure-seeking

Epiphanes (uh-pi'-fuh-neez) a title, "[God] made manifest," adopted by Antiochus IV, the ruler of the part of the Greek empire that included Israel during the second century BCE. He was the king who forced pagan worship to occur in the Jerusalem Temple, thus provoking the revolt of Maccabees.

epiphany a manifestation, an appearance; in particular, the appearance of God or a divine being

epithet a word or phrase that characterizes a person or thing, and that often can be used by itself to refer to the person. The name "Maccabeus," or "Hammer," is an epithet of Judas, the son of Mattathias and leader of the Jewish revolt against Antiochus IV in 167 BCE.

eschatological (ess-kat-o-lodg'-i-kull) pertaining to the end (Greek *eschaton*) of the present age or world

eschatology (ess-kuh-tol'-uh-gee) writings or teachings about the "last things" (Greek *eschata*), the events at the close of the age

Essenes a communal society in Judaism around the first century BCE to the first century CE which kept the law with utmost rigor and lived apart in communities that were similar in some respects to later monastic groups. It is generally agreed that the Dead Sea Scrolls of Qumran were collected and preserved by an Essene community.

etiology (ee-tee-ol'-uh-gee) a story that explains the origin of something such as a custom, name, place, saying, or the like (Gen 32.28–32)

Eucharist a service of thanksgiving, centering on the sharing of bread and wine, based on the final meal Jesus shared with his followers before his trial and crucifixion; also called Communion or The LORD's Supper. See sidebar on p. 1925 [NEW TESTAMENT].

euphemism (yew'-fuh-mizm) the substitution of an inoffensive word for one that is too explicit. The word "feet" in Isa 6.2, 7.20, and possibly Ruth 3.4, 7, 8, 14 is a euphemism for "genitals." *See* rhetoric.

exhortation urging a particular course of action or behavior by argument or advice

Exile the removal of the Israelite people from the land, first by the Assyrians and then by the Babylonians

fable an illustrative story in which animals or plants have speaking parts. Judges 9.8–15 is a fable.

festival scrolls the five short books that are read on five holy days in the Jewish calendar (*see* calendar): Song of Solomon on Passover, Ruth on Pentecost (Weeks or Shavuot), Lamentations on 9 Ab (the date of the Temple's destruction), Ecclesiastes on Booths (Sukkot), and Esther on Purim

form criticism the interpretation of a text—a parable, a psalm, a proverb—with particular attention to the structure of the text and to the original setting of that form out of which it arose. Form criticism attempts to recover the original context, audience, or situation of a particular kind of literature, before the unit was made a part of a larger narrative such as a gospel or a historical book with its own context, audience, and situation. *See* interpretation.

Gehenna (guh-hen′-nuh) the place of punishment after death (see, for instance, Mt 5.22: the NRSV translates "hell" but gives the Greek word in a note). The name means "valley of Hinnom," a place south of Jerusalem that had been thought to be the area where children were burnt as sacrificial offerings; Josiah (2 Kings 23.10) destroyed the site, but its associations with burning and evil remained, and developed into the image of burning punishment that is found in the New Testament.

genealogy a list or history of the ancestors of an individual or group

genre a form of literature with particular characteristics. The detective story is a genre, for instance. Once a genre is established, the audience for it knows what to expect and can respond more easily to any given work.

gentile a non-Jew

Gilgamesh, epic of a Mesopotamian story narrating the adventures of Gilgamesh, king of Uruk. This epic explores the tension between nature and culture and addresses the nature of humans as mortal. The epic of Gilgamesh contains a parallel to the biblical flood story.

glean to gather or collect, usually by hand, grain that is left behind by reapers. People too poor to own their own fields were permitted to glean in the fields of those better off (Lev 19.9–10; Deut 24.19–24).

gnosticism (nos′-ti-sizm) (from the Greek word *gnosis,* "knowledge") a philosophy that regards spirit and matter as opposites. According to gnostic teaching, human beings are spirits trapped or imprisoned in matter; the material world is an il-

lusion or the work of an inferior or even demonic divine being; and the purpose of life is to learn how to free oneself from material things (including the body) and attain eternal life in the spiritual realm. This is accomplished by learning specialized or secret knowledge about the nature of reality; it is from this emphasis on knowledge that gnosticism gets its name. Gnostic teachings were often in the form of secret doctrines or mysteries (*see*), and many mystery religions were gnostic. Gnosticism, although influential in the first few centuries of the Christian church, was ultimately rejected by the main body of Christians, and most of the gnostic writings were lost or suppressed.

Gospel of Thomas *See* Thomas, Gospel of.

Hades the abode of the dead in Greek religion, used in the New Testament as the general name for the place where souls go after death (for instance, Mt 11.23; Acts 2.27)

Hasidim (hah-suh-deem′) Jewish group in the Maccabean period, concerned with re-establishing Jewish practices in ritual and purity laws, who supported the Maccabees for a time. They may have been the precursors of the Sadducees (*see*).

Hasmoneans The dynasty founded by the Maccabees (164–63 BCE)

Hebrew Scriptures the works, written in the Hebrew language (with a few short Aramaic sections), that are accepted as Scripture in Judaism. Thus, although Sirach, for instance, exists for the most part in Hebrew as well as Greek, it is included in the Apocryphal/Deuterocanonical Books, not in the Hebrew Scriptures, because Judaism does not regard it as canonical. The traditional Jewish order of the Hebrew Scriptures divides the books into three sections: Torah, Nevi'im, Kethubim—the "law" or teachings, the prophets, and the writings (see Prologue to Sirach). Torah (*see*) is the first five books. The prophets are divided into Former Prophets: Joshua, Judges, Samuel, and Kings; and the Latter Prophets: Isaiah, Jeremiah, Ezekiel, and the Twelve (Hosea, Joel, Amos, Obadiah, Jonah, Micah, Nahum, Habakkuk, Zephaniah, Haggai, Zechariah, Malachi). The writings contain all the rest: Psalms, Proverbs, Job, Song of Solomon, Ruth, Lamentations, Ecclesiastes, Esther, Daniel, Ezra, Nehemiah, and Chronicles. See "The Nature and Formation of the Biblical Canon" on p. 26.

Hellenism Greek culture as it spread in the period after the conquests of Alexander the Great (died 323 BCE)

Hellenistic Greek-speaking or influenced by Greek culture after the time of Alexander

Hellenize to bring under the influence of Greek language and culture

Hermas, Shepherd of See Shepherd of Hermas.

hermeneutics the theory and practice of interpretation

high places shrines, usually on a hill or a raised platform, where worship, especially sacrifices, took place. Because they were outside of Jerusalem and sometimes, though not always, used for other gods, they are regularly condemned in the Deuteronomistic History.

holy war battles conducted under divine guidance in which the LORD fought for Israel in the role of divine warrior (Judg 6)

homiletical having the character or function of a sermon

hortatory urging the audience to a certain kind of action or a moral course

hosanna a Hebrew word meaning "Save!" that was used as a cry of acclamation (Ps 118.26; Mt 21.9)

household code a list of rules or prescribed behaviors for the members of an extended family and their servants living under one roof. There are household codes in some of the New Testament letters, for instance Eph 5.22–6.9.

hyperbole (hie-per'-bow-lee) a statement exaggerated in order to make a point or underline its importance. See rhetoric.

hypophora (hie-po-for'-uh) an argument in which the speaker or writer states and answers objections. Sometimes the writer puts the objections in the form of questions and then answers them, often by posing another question. Romans 9.19–24 is an argument using hypophora. See rhetoric.

hyssop a shrub related to mint. It was used as a medicine and, because of its leafy branches, for ritual sprinkling of water or blood (Ex 12.22).

idolatry the worship of anything or any person other than the true God

Ignatius, Letters of early Christian writings of instruction. The author, Ignatius, bishop of Antioch, wrote them (seven are known to have survived) on his way to martyrdom in Rome. They are largely concerned with overcoming divisions in the local churches, combatting false teaching,

and proper conduct of life. They therefore are very similar to some of the canonical New Testament letters, particularly 1 and 2 Timothy and Titus. The letters of Ignatius are addressed to the Ephesians, the Magnesians, the Trallians, the Romans, the Philadelphians, and the Smyrneans, as well as one to Polycarp, bishop of Smyrna. See early Christian writings.

inclusio (in-cloo'-see-oh) the use of the same word or phrase at the end of a passage as appeared at the beginning, thus rounding off or completing it. Sirach 32.14 uses the word *musar,* ("discipline"); the use of the same word in Sir 33.18 (translated "instruction") forms an inclusio. See rhetoric.

interpolation an insertion into a text of materials written by someone other than the original author

interpretation There are a number of different methods of interpreting the Bible, each meant to answer different questions. In general, the purpose of interpretation is to help make the meaning of the text clear, but this sometimes means not only understanding the sentences and paragraphs that we read today, but also understanding the possible ways by which they came to be written, trying to determine the original context of the story or saying, and looking at the different stages through which a biblical text goes on its way to its final form. So interpreters are interested in examining the meanings of words used in the Bible, the historical, religious, or social background of a particular story or saying, the process by which a story was written down, how groups of stories were combined into a longer narrative, how different biblical writers treated the same materials, what the original audience would have gotten out of a story, how a saying was adapted to address the concerns of later readers, and many similar paths of investigation. Terms used by biblical interpreters include: canonical criticism, documentary hypothesis, form criticism, redaction criticism, synoptic problem, tradition criticism, textual criticism. See the essay "What is Bible Study?" on p. 4.

interregnum an interruption or gap between the end of one reign and the beginning of the next

intertextuality the interrelationship between one part of scripture and other parts. Intertextuality can take the form of recurrent images (the vineyard in Isa 5.1–10 and 27.2–4); quotation (1 Cor 3.20 quotes Ps 94.11); or allusion (Isa 48.13 alludes to the creation story in Genesis ch. 1).

irony, ironic a characteristic of literature in which the reader or listener knows more than the characters about the situation in the story. A character in an ironic situation is missing a vital piece of information that is known to the audience. By extension, an ironic aspect of a story, situation, or fact is one that from the outside looks very different than it does from the inside. Irony thus becomes a rhetorical technique in which the author's plain or literal meaning (what the words mean in the dictionary sense) is different from, even in conflict with, the author's intended meaning (what the words mean in their context, with particular emphasis, etc.). Saying "My! Don't you look lovely!" to someone dressed in old work clothes who has just finished a strenuous and messy task is an example of irony in this sense.

Jewish calendar *See* calendar.

Joseph and Aseneth an ancient Greek novel about Joseph's life in Egypt, his marriage to the haughty daughter of an Egyptian priest and her conversion to faith in Joseph's God, and their triumph over a plot to kill them. See sidebar on p. 1322 [APOCRYPHA]. See also pseudepigrapha.

Josephus a Hellenistic Jewish historian who lived from about 37 CE to about 100 CE. Four of his writings have survived: *The Jewish War,* an account of the rebellion against Rome in 66–70 CE, with background information starting at about 200 BCE; *The Antiquities of the Jews,* a complete history from the creation up to the point where *The Jewish War* begins; *Against Apion,* a defense of Judaism; and an autobiography, the *Life.* Josephus provides invaluable historical information about Judaism and its background from 200 BCE to 100 CE; his account of the rebellion, in which he took part, is in part that of an eyewitness. He also provides first-hand information about the Essenes and the Pharisees, since at one time or another he was associated with both groups, as well as giving information about the Sadducees. Josephus is important to scholars in trying to understand the religious context in which Jesus lived and from which early Christianity and rabbinic Judaism developed.

Kethubim (kuh-thoo-veem′) The Writings, the third division of the Hebrew Scriptures (*see*)

kosher the regulations defining which foods and combinations of food observant Jews may eat and how those foods may be prepared

lament a poem of grief or mourning

lectionary a list of readings of Scripture passages for Sabbaths and holy days (in Judaism) or Sundays and holy days (in Christianity). Christian lectionaries also sometimes include readings for weekdays. Lectionaries are partly designed to read certain portions of the Bible—for instance, the Torah, in Jewish lectionaries, or the first three Gospels, in Christian lectionaries—completely through, in order, over a lectionary cycle of a year or several years. In addition, in Christian lectionaries important seasons (for instance, Christmas or Easter) have their own specific readings outside the continuous readings. In the synagogue, the Torah reading is followed by what is called a Haftarah reading ("haphtarah" means "conclusion") from one of the prophets; in addition, the five festival scrolls (*see*) are read on five holy days (*see* calendar). In many Christian churches, the Gospel reading is preceded by a reading from the Hebrew Scriptures, a psalm, and a reading from elsewhere in the New Testament, usually a letter. The Gospel of John is read during Easter season.

legate an official representative

legend, legendary A legend is a popular story, sometimes exaggerated or romanticized, about a holy or righteous person or a special place. The characters in legends can themselves be legends, like Paul Bunyan, or they can be real historical personages about whom stories are told, like George Washington and the cherry tree. Characters that are legendary are those who are famous enough to have legends told about their exploits. Many of the stories told about Elijah and especially Elisha are legends.

Letter of Aristeas the supposed account, by an eyewitness, of the translation of the Torah into Greek. It is the origin of the story that the translators numbered 72 (rounded off to 70 and therefore the reason the ancient Greek translation is called the Septuagint and abbreviated LXX). *See* pseudepigrapha.

leviathan a mythical sea monster, sometimes identified with the crocodile (Job 41.1), that represents the forces of watery chaos which must be overcome at creation (Ps 74.1–17) and that will be finally defeated at the end of time (Isa 27.1). In the Book of Revelation, the dragon, the enemy of God, is identified with the sea (17.1,3), and in the new creation there is no more sea (21.1).

levirate marriage an ancient Hebrew practice requiring the brother of any man who died before fathering a child to marry the widow and father a child to carry on the dead man's name

Liturgical calendar *See* calendar.

liturgy the service of worship, including prayers, hymns, blessings, curses, acclamations, professions of belief, and ritual movements

LXX the roman numeral seventy, the standard abbreviation for the Septuagint (*see*)

martyr (from the Greek word for "witness") a person who demonstrates loyalty by remaining faithful even when threatened with death or killed

Martyrdom of Isaiah a Greco-Roman, Jewish work that is the origin of the legend that Isaiah died by being sawn in two. It is alluded to in Heb 11.37. *See* pseudepigrapha.

Masoretic text the text of the Hebrew Bible, established by Jewish scholars (called Masoretes), which was made up of the Hebrew consonants, vowel signs, accent markings, and other notes (*Masorah* means "tradition"). Texts reflecting this tradition date from circa 900 to 1000 CE. The Masoretic text is the only complete form of the Hebrew Bible that has come down to us. *See* ancient translations.

measures *See* "Weights and Measures," pp. 2109–2110.

megillah pl. **megilloth** scroll, scrolls (Hebrew). See sidebar on p. 1113 [OLD TESTAMENT]. *See also* festival scrolls.

messiah the Hebrew word for "anointed." A king could be referred to as "the LORD's anointed" (1 Sam 24.6); even a foreign king could be called this (Isa 45.1). Later the term came to be used of the expected savior of the Jewish people, and was taken over by Christians to refer to Jesus, whom they believed to be the messiah (Greek *christos*, "Christ").

metaphor a direct comparison between two things. "[God] is a shield" (Ps 18.30). *See* rhetoric.

metonymy (met-on'-uh-mee) a figure of speech in which a word is used in place of another word to which it is closely related. "The coastlands have seen and are afraid" (Isa. 41.5) means "the inhabitants of the coasts," that is, foreigners. *See* rhetoric.

midrash learned biblical interpretation that appears in a highly refined form in rabbinic literature, characterized by very detailed and segmented commentary and the use of one biblical verse to interpret another

motif an image or character type that occurs again and again throughout a literary text. The

Servant motif occurs in Isaiah at 42.1–4, 49.1–6, 50.4–11, 52.13–53.12.

mystery in the New Testament, a divine truth that is kept hidden or secret by God until the right moment for it to be revealed (see Rom 16.25–26). A mystery in this sense is a revelation about God's plan (Eph 1.9–10). The later meaning of mystery, a religious teaching that is based on a revelation from God or other divine messenger, rather than on conclusions from reasoning, and that therefore can never be completely understood by reason alone, is not present in the New Testament.

mystery religion any one of various religious groups in the Greek and Roman empires which practiced secret rites of initiation. These rites often involved rituals enacting the myth of creation or other underlying teaching about the meaning of the universe according to the particular group. Mystery religions taught that the real meaning of life could not be learned without divine guidance and that such guidance was available in their secret teachings and practices. These secret rites were known as "mysteries," and had the sense of a revelation from the divine realm that is similar to some of the New Testament uses of "mystery."

narrative a recounting of an incident, event, or story in an orderly manner. See "A Reader's Guide to the Books of the Bible," p. 17.

Neoplatonism a development of Platonism (*see*). It taught that there were three states of being: the One, the unknowable source of all; Mind, the realm of knowledge; and Soul, the realm of thought and activity. All of existence is a balance between emanation, or movement outward, and contemplation or return, movement back toward the One. There may be early Neoplatonic influence in The Wisdom of Solomon (7.25).

Nevi'im (nuh-vee-eem') The Prophets, the second division of the Hebrew Scriptures (*see*)

new moon the beginning of any month in the Jewish calendar. See calendar.

novel a fictional work in prose. Ancient novels were often romances (*see*).

Old Latin the Latin translation of the Bible based on the Greek text, the Septuagint. The Old Latin version was replaced by Jerome's Latin translation, the Vulgate (*see*). *See* ancient translations.

oracle a statement uttered by a prophet or other sacred person, purporting to be the words of a deity

oracular having the qualities of an oracle or sacred speech

ordination a formal ceremony and process by which certain members of the community are set apart for religious service as priests. See Lev 8.1–46.

oxymoron (ox-ee-more'-on) combining two terms that appear contradictory. "God's foolishness is wiser than human wisdom, and God's weakness is stronger than human strength" (1 Cor 1.25). *See* rhetoric.

parable a statement or story that uses figurative or imaginative language to evoke a reality that lies beyond the literal level of the story or statement. A parable makes its point by analogy, or the comparison of a known fact, situation, or experience with one that is less familiar. The analogy is usually not made explicit; for instance, in the parable of the Prodigal Son (Lk 15.11–32) the father is meant to represent, by analogy, the merciful action of God's forgiveness, but this is not stated. Sometimes an interpretation is added, however, as with the parable of the Sower (Mk 4.1–8, interpreted in vv. 14–20). See sidebar on p. 1687 [NEW TESTAMENT].

parallelism a characteristic of Hebrew poetry in which a thought in one line, or the first part of a line, is echoed, developed, or enlarged in the second part or line. Psalms and Proverbs are largely composed in parallelistic form and demonstrate the great degree of variation that the form permits.

paronomasia (parr-uh-no-may'-zhuh) a play on words, a pun. " 'Jeremiah, what do you see?' . . . 'I see a branch of an almond tree [*shaqed*].' 'You have seen well, for I am watching [*shoqed*] over my word to perform it' " (Jer 1.11–12). *See* rhetoric.

parousia (par-oo'-zhuh) "coming" (Greek). The parousia refers to the second coming of Christ, that is, the expected return of the Messiah at the end of the age or the end of the world.

Passover the festival that commemorates the Exodus of the Israelites from Egypt. The Hebrew name for Passover is *Pesach*. *See* calendar.

Penitential Psalms the seven psalms 6, 32, 38, 51, 102, 130, and 143, used in Christian services of repentance from the earliest times, and by the Middle Ages in regular use during Lent, the penitential season before Easter. *See* calendar.

Pentateuch a Greek word meaning "five books" that refers to the first five books of the Bible, Genesis through Deuteronomy; the Torah (*see*)

Pentecost *See* calendar.

periphrasis (per-ih-fray'-sis) the use of more words than are necessary to express a thought. "No one came to my support, but all deserted me" (2 Tim 4.16). "I am telling the truth, I am not lying" (1 Tim 2.7). *See* rhetoric.

Persian era the period of domination of the Persian Empire over the Near East, beginning at around 550 BCE when Cyrus the Great, King of Persia, defeated the Medes, and lasting until about 330 BCE when Alexander the Great of Macedon conquered the lands surrounding the Mediterranean and brought them under Greek rule. It was during the Persian era that the Israelites were allowed to return to their land from exile (537 BCE) and rebuild the Temple (515 BCE).

personification representing an idea, a value, or other abstract thought as a person. Wisdom is personified as a woman in Prov 8. *See* rhetoric.

Pesach *See* Passover.

Peshitta the Syriac word for "simple." It is the name of the Syriac translation of the Bible (called "simple" because it was a plain translation from Hebrew, not a translation with textual apparatus like the Syrohexapla [*see*]). The Peshitta contains books translated by Jews for Jewish worshippers who spoke Syriac, but it was taken over and completed (including a New Testament) by Syriac speaking Christians. *See* ancient translations.

Pharisees the followers of a movement in Judaism in the second and first centuries BCE through the second century CE, when rabbinic Judaism established itself and took over the Pharisees' major teachings. The Pharisees taught the importance of the Law, which involved keeping the Temple regulations for purity and ritual observance and extending them into the life of the home and table. The Pharisees also taught the importance of both written law and oral law; in effect, they recognized the importance of tradition and interpretation, as well as the importance of written laws. In this belief they were opposed by the Sadducees (*see*).

Philo a Hellenistic Jewish philosopher and interpreter of Scripture, who lived in Alexandria, Egypt, from about 20 BCE to 50 CE. He wrote works in philosophy, scriptural interpretation, and history. In Philo's view, the best insights of Greek philosophy were compatible with the religion of the Hebrew Scriptures and could be found in the Bible by means of allegorical interpretation, which he used in his own interpretive works. He influenced Jewish writers like the author of The Wisdom of Solomon and Christian theologians such as Clement, Origen, and Ambrose.

philology the study of words or language

Platonism a particular philosophy derived from the teaching of Plato, saying that there is a profound difference, even an opposition, between the realm of matter and the realm of spirit, and that the world of sense experience is essentially an illusion, deriving what reality it has from a correspondence with a true, ultimately real world of Forms. The influence of Platonism on religious thought can be seen in The Wisdom of Solomon; it is also apparent in the thought of Philo (*see*) and Christian thinkers like Clement, Origen, and Augustine.

pleonasm (plee'-oh-naz-um) unnecessary words, deliberate repetitiveness. "May you be made strong with all strength" (Col. 1.11). *See* rhetoric.

pogrom (poh-grum') an officially encouraged, organized massacre of a minority group

polemic, polemical an argument or debate in the form of an attack on one's opponent or on the opposing position. Polemical speech is characterized by verbal attacks, exaggerated language, and sometimes violent imagery.

Polycarp, Letter of an early Christian letter of instruction. It was written by Polycarp, bishop of Smyrna, and addressed to the church of Philippi. It gives advice about dealing with problems in the congregation, exhorts readers to behave in a moral fashion, and combats false teachings. It is therefore similar to many canonical New Testament writings, some of which (like the Gospels and Paul's letters) Polycarp seems to know. *See* early Christian writings.

prophet one who speaks in the name of, or at the behest of, God, to exhort, warn, or occasionally to provide hope in time of trouble. Besides the authors of the prophetic books, Moses, Samuel, and others are called prophets. Prophets do not so much predict the future, as the current use would imply, but instead speak about the present situation.

Prophets, The the second division of the Hebrew Scriptures (*see*)

pseudepigrapha (sood-uh-pig'-ruh-fuh) (Greek), "writings with false attributions of authorship," a label for a diverse group of Jewish or Christian religious writings that are not included in the books of the Hebrew Bible, the New Testament, or the Apocrypha. These writings, which date from about 250 BCE to 200 CE, are important for several reasons. Some of them are quoted from or alluded to in the Bible. They are helpful in providing further examples of particular kinds of literature found in the Bible, such as apocalypses and wisdom literature. They help in understanding the concepts, concerns, and development of thought in the Jewish and Christian communities in the centuries just before and just after the beginnings of the Christian movement and the rise of rabbinic Judaism. Among the works included among the pseudepigrapha are: Ahikar, the Assumption of Moses, 1 and 2 Enoch, Joseph and Aseneth, the Letter of Aristeas, the Martyrdom of Isaiah, the Testaments of the Twelve Patriarchs.

pseudonymous written or published under a false name (for example, Testaments of the Twelve Patriarchs). Most pseudonymous writing is attributed to someone much better known than the actual writer, in order to give the text the benefit of the presumed authority of the famous person.

Ptolemies (toll'-uh-meez) the rulers of Egypt and its surrounding areas after the breakup of the Greek empire of Alexander the Great, following his death

Q *See* synoptic problem.

redaction criticism the interpretation of the work of "redactors," or editors who combined already existing units into longer works. Redaction criticism builds on the work of form criticism (*see*) but tries to discover the intentions that shaped the final editing of the text. *See* interpretation.

resident alien a foreigner with legal rights living in Israel or an Israelite residing in the territory of another tribe

rhetoric the art (or study) of persuasive speech or writing. It is a common observation that some writing is more interesting, some less; that some writing is straightforward and direct, some complicated and roundabout; some full of fancy language, some very plain. The study of these aspects of writing (or speaking) is called rhetoric, from the Greek word for "speaker" or "orator," and many of its terms are Greek. They include: anadiplosis, anaphora, anastrophe, antithesis, aporia, chiasmus, climax, diatribe, euphemism, hyperbole, hypophora, inclusio, metaphor, metonymy, oxymoron, paronomasia, periphrasis, personification, pleonasm, simile, sorites, synecdoche.

romance a popular storytelling technique in the ancient Mediterranean world that recounted the situation of young lovers and how they overcome obstacles to their marriage. Tobit is the purest form of romance in biblical literature. In early Christianity the form was modified to tell the stories of early converts and martyrs and the obstacles to their faith.

sackcloth rough cloth, often made from animal hair. A garment made of sackcloth is uncomfortable and is worn to indicate penitence or grief.

Sadducees the followers of a movement in Judaism, probably originating in the second century BCE and ending with the destruction of the Temple in 70 CE. Sadducees were traditionalists who strove to maintain the Temple worship according to the requirements of the law. They were also politically conservative and accommodated themselves to Roman rule as long as they could retain control of the Temple. In keeping with their central belief in the absolute authority of the Torah (*see*), they denied the resurrection of the dead. They were opposed by the early Christians and by the Pharisees (*see*).

Sanhedrin a council, whose membership was drawn from the Jewish ruling classes, responsible for administering the territory of Palestine under the Roman empire. The Sanhedrin was responsible for census-taking and taxation as well as for acting as a court that would decide cases on its own and also, after preliminary determination, send cases on to the Roman governors.

scribe in general, one who could write, especially official documents, and take down dictation for letters, legal proceedings, etc. In the New Testament a scribe was a lawyer, one who was expert in the requirements and meaning of Jewish law.

sect a religious grouping that emphasizes strict adherence to particular teachings and excludes those who do not conform

Seleucids (suh-loo′-sids) the rulers of Syria and its surrounding areas after the breakup of the Greek empire of Alexander the Great, following his death

Septuagint (sep-too′-uh-jint) the ancient Greek translation of the Hebrew Scriptures. The Septuagint was translated over a lengthy period beginning probably in the third century BCE. Traditionally there were 72 translators, a number that is rounded off to 70 and, in roman numerals, used as the abbreviation for this translation (LXX). The Septuagint was prepared for the use of Jews who lived outside the land of Israel and whose main language was Greek. It is important

for several reasons: it translated a version of the Hebrew text that is older than the currently available Hebrew (Masoretic) text (*see*); it contains additional works, grouped in NRSV as the Apocryphal/Deuterocanonical Books, most of which were originally written in Greek; and it was the Bible of early Christians, and therefore represents what they thought of as Scripture. See ancient translations.

Shavuot *See* calendar.

shekel a measure of weight of less than half an ounce

Sheol the abode of the dead according to ancient Israelite belief

Shepherd of Hermas, The an early Christian apocalypse. Hermas was the brother of Pius, bishop of Rome in the first part of the second century CE. The shepherd, a character in the work, is in reality an angel, one of several angels who reveal divine messages and interpret visions. The book consists of visions, commandments, and parables; the main concern is to deal with the issue of Christians who have sinned after they have been baptized. The Shepherd of Hermas presents the view that repentance is possible (but only once) after baptism, countering the even more rigorous view that no repentance is possible for sins committed after one has been baptized. The form of the work, with visions, angelic interpreters, and the view that the day of judgment was coming soon, helps scholars to understand the literary form of apocalypse in early Christianity. *See* early Christian writings.

simile (sim′-uh-lee) a comparison, using "like" or "as." "He made my feet like the feet of a deer" (Ps 18.33). *See* rhetoric.

sorites (so-ry′-tees) a philosophical argument in the form of linked propositions. The second part of each proposition forms the first part of the next, and the series therefore becomes an extended chain of reasoning. Wisdom of Solomon 6.17–20 is a sorites. *See* rhetoric.

Stoics Greek philosophers in the Hellenistic and Roman periods, who taught that emotions should be strictly controlled by reason

synagogue an assembly; a congregation. For Jews who were too distant from the Temple to worship at it, and for all Jews after the final destruction of the Temple by Romans in 70 CE, the synagogue became the only form of worship. Services consisted of prayer, song, and study of the sacred text.

synecdoche (sin-ek'-doe-kee) the use of a part of something to stand for the whole of it. "Do not cheat the poor of their living,/ and do not keep needy eyes waiting" (Sir 4.1). "Needy eyes" represent the whole needy person. *See* rhetoric.

Synoptic Gospels Matthew, Mark, and Luke. "Synoptic" means "view together," and is applied to these writings because they, unlike John, can be readily compared.

synoptic problem the observation that in many passages Matthew and Luke repeat with only minor changes what Mark says, yet in other passages they do not follow Mark, or include stories or sayings that Mark does not have, yet match each other very closely. Many commentators, from the earliest years of Christianity, have tried to understand the relationship among the Synoptic Gospels. According to the most widely-held theory, Matthew and Luke relied on Mark and on another document (now lost) that contained mostly sayings of Jesus; this second document is referred to as "Q" from the German word "Quelle" (source). In addition, Matthew and Luke each had their own sources. *See* interpretation.

Syriac an eastern form of Aramaic (*see*) that was the language of some Jews and of some eastern Christian communities in the early centuries of the Common Era. It is the language of the Peshitta (*see*).

Syrohexapla (see-row-hex-ah'-pluh) or **Syriac hexapla** a Syriac translation of the Septuagint text that provides textual evidence about the nature of the Septuagint. Although the hexapla was translated in the seventh century CE, it is based upon a Septuagint text dating from as early as the third century. *See* ancient translations.

tabernacle the portable sanctuary used by the Israelites during the wandering in the wilderness. It was eventually replaced by the Temple.

Tanakh (tuh-nak') an acronym, a word made up from the beginning letters of the three divisions of the Hebrew Scriptures (*see*): Torah, Nevi'im (prophets), Kethubim (writings)

Targums Aramaic translations or paraphrases of the Hebrew Bible, for use by Aramaic-speaking Jews. The Targums are important for textual criticism of the Hebrew text, since they provide evidence about it at a stage earlier than that of the currently available Hebrew (Masoretic) text. *See* ancient translations.

Temple the central place of worship for Israelite religion in Jerusalem, referring either to the first Temple built by Solomon or the Second Temple of Zerubbabel that was enlarged and rebuilt by Herod

Testaments of the Twelve Patriarchs a text giving the purported last words of the twelve sons of Jacob, each delivered to his sons from his deathbed. Although it may contain material from the second century BCE, and is modeled on speeches in the Bible such as Josh 23–24, as a whole it dates from the second century CE. *See* pseudepigrapha.

textual criticism the study of the significance of the differences among ancient biblical manuscripts. *See* interpretation.

theodicy a defense of the justice of God in the face of the world's evil

theophany a scene that portrays a manifestation of a divine being in the natural order, such as the revelation of God to Moses at Mount Sinai

Thomas, Gospel of an early collection of sayings attributed to Jesus. It contains no miracle stories and no account of Jesus' deeds, his birth, his death, or the resurrection. Some of the sayings resemble those in the canonical Gospels, but others reflect a philosophy that regards spirit and matter as radically different and opposed to each other; in this view, life on earth is one of spirits trapped in matter, and the purpose of life is to free oneself from matter and attain eternal life in the spiritual realm. This philosophy, called gnosticism (*see*), was rejected by the main body of early Christians, and this may explain why the Gospel of Thomas was never accepted as canonical. *See* early Christian writings.

thresh to beat gathered stalks of grain in order to separate the grain from the stems and husks. *See* winnow. A threshing floor, a flat area used for threshing grain, was often built on a hilltop to catch the breeze necessary for winnowing. This made it an ideal location for holding sacrifices (1 Chr 21.18–27).

Torah a Hebrew word meaning "teaching" or "instruction." It is sometimes translated "law" but this can be misleading, since "torah" includes much more than law codes and regulations. Torah is the title of the first five books of the Hebrew Scriptures (*see*), Genesis through Deuteronomy. It is also a general name for the rules for daily living in Jewish tradition.

tradition criticism the interpretation of the history of a tradition, including stages such as oral transmission, the alteration of a tradition to address a changed situation, and the examination of particular kinds of traditions, such as the explanation of place names, the development of religious practices, or the growth or disuse of social practices. *See* interpretation.

uncircumcised, the Gentiles (Rom 4.9; Gal 2.7). *See* circumcision.

Vulgate (from the Latin word for "common," because at the time Latin was the language of ordinary people) the Latin translation of the Bible begun by Jerome in the fourth century CE, who translated directly from the Hebrew and Greek texts and also separated the Old Testament text not part of the Hebrew Bible, but included in the Septuagint, into a separate section of "deuterocanonical" books. In the Middle Ages the Vulgate became the standard translation of the Bible for Western Christians. With the Protestant Reformation, its authority was questioned, but was reaffirmed by the Roman Catholic Church at the Council of Trent (1546). *See* ancient translations.

wadi (Arabic) a stream bed or valley that was dry for much of the year

Weeks, Feast of *See* calendar.

weights See "Weights and Measures," pp. 2109–2110.

winnow to separate grain from its husks (called chaff) after it has been threshed. The method was to place the grain in a wide, flat basket and toss it repeatedly in a breeze, usually in the evening when a breeze is more likely to spring up. Tossing the grain loosens the husks, which are much lighter, and therefore blow away, while the heavier grain drops back down into the basket.

wisdom literature a style of literature in the Hebrew Scriptures that includes Job, Proverbs, and Ecclesiastes; in the Apocrypha it includes Sirach and the Wisdom of Solomon; some Psalms, for instance Ps 37, may also be included. Wisdom literature is concerned with insight, instruction, meditation on the meaning of life, and moral exhortation. It does not generally concern itself with key events in Israel's history, such as the Exodus; the central teachings, such as the covenant; or the focal institutions, such as the Davidic monarchy, prophecy, or the Temple.

Writings, The the third division of the Hebrew Scriptures (*see*)

xenophobia fear of, or contempt for, foreigners; racial exclusiveness

Zealot a member of the Jewish revolutionary movement during the Roman occupation of Palestine; an advocate of armed resistance to Roman rule

Zion the name of the fortified hill within Jerusalem and thus, by extension, an alternative name for Jerusalem itself

WEIGHTS AND MEASURES

I. Hebrew Weights

Hebrew	NRSV	Equivalence	U.S. Avoirdupois
kikkār	talent	60 minas	75.558 pounds
māneh	mina	50 shekels	20.148 ounces
shéqel	shekel	2 bekas	176.29 grains
pîm (or payim)	pim	.667 shekel	117.52 grains
béqa'	beka, half a shekel	10 gerahs	88.14 grains
gērāh	gerah		8.81 grains

The practice of weighing unmarked ingots of metal used in commercial transactions prior to the invention of money explains that the names of the units of weight were used later as indications of value, and as names for monetary standards. There is, however, no direct relation between the shekel-weight and the weight of a shekel piece.

II. Weights in the New Testament

Greek	NRSV	Equivalence	U.S. Avoirdupois
talenton	talent	(Hebrew) talent	see Table I
mna	pound	(Hebrew) mina	see Table I
litra	pound	(Latin) libra	0.719 pound

III. Hebrew Measures of Length

Hebrew	NRSV	Equivalence	U.S. Measures
'ammāh	cubit	2 spans	17.49 inches
zéreth	span	3 handbreadths	8.745 inches
tôphah, téphah	handbreadth	4 fingers	2.915 inches
'esba'	finger		0.728 inch

The cubit described in Ezekiel (40.5; 43.13) is equal to seven (not six) handbreadths, namely 20.405 inches.

IV. Measures of Length in the New Testament

Greek	NRSV	U.S. Measures
pēchus	cubit	about 1.5 feet
orguia	fathom	about 72.44 inches
stadion	stadia, or the equivalent in miles	about 606 feet
milion	mile	about 4,854 feet

V. Hebrew Measures of Capacity

LIQUID MEASURES

Hebrew	NRSV	Equivalence	U.S. Measures
kōr	measure, cor	10 baths	60.738 gallons
bath	bath	6 hins	6.073 gallons
hîn	hin	3 kabs	1.012 gallons
qabh	kab	4 logs	1.349 quarts
lōgh	log		0.674 pint

DRY MEASURES

Hebrew	NRSV	Equivalence	U.S. Measures
hōmer	homer	} 2 lethechs	6.524 bushels
kōr	measure, cor		
léthekh	lethech	5 ephahs	3.262 bushels
'êphāh	ephah, measure	3 seahs	20.878 quarts
se'āh	measure	3.33 omers	6.959 quarts
'ōmer	ōmer	1.8 kabs	2.087 quarts
'issārôn	tenth part (of ephah)		
qabh	kab		1.159 quarts

VI. Measures of Capacity in the New Testament

Greek	NRSV	Equivalence	U.S. Measures
batos	measure	(Hebrew) bath	see Table V
koros	measure	(Hebrew) kōr	see Table V
saton	measure	(Hebrew) se'āh	
metrētēs	measure		10.3 gallons
choinix	quart		0.98 dry quart
modios	bushel	(Latin) modius	7.68 dry quarts
xestēs	pot	(Latin) sextarius	0.96 dry pint, or 1.12 fluid pints

CONCORDANCE

The following abbreviations are used for the Canonical Books:

Ac	Acts	Jas	James	Ne	Nehemiah		
Am	Amos	Jdg	Judges	Nu	Numbers		
1Ch	1 Chronicles	Jer	Jeremiah	Ob	Obadiah		
2Ch	2 Chronicles	Jn	John	1Pe	1 Peter		
1Co	1 Corinthians	1Jn	1 John	2Pe	2 Peter		
2Co	2 Corinthians	2Jn	2 John	Phm	Philemon		
Col	Colossians	3Jn	3 John	Php	Philippians		
Da	Daniel	Jnh	Jonah	Pr	Proverbs		
Dt	Deuteronomy	Job	Job	Ps	Psalms		
Ecc	Ecclesiastes	Joel	Joel	Rev	Revelation		
Eph	Ephesians	Jos	Joshua	Ro	Romans		
Est	Esther	Jude	Jude	Ru	Ruth		
Ex	Exodus	1Ki	1 Kings	1Sa	1 Samuel		
Eze	Ezekiel	2Ki	2 Kings	2Sa	2 Samuel		
Ezr	Ezra	La	Lamentations	SS	Song of Songs		
Gal	Galatians	Lev	Leviticus	1Th	1 Thessalonians		
Ge	Genesis	Lk	Luke	2Th	2 Thessalonians		
Hab	Habakkuk	Mal	Malachi	1Ti	1 Timothy		
Hag	Haggai	Mic	Micah	2Ti	2 Timothy		
Heb	Hebrews	Mk	Mark	Tit	Titus		
Hos	Hosea	Mt	Matthew	Zec	Zechariah		
Isa	Isaiah	Na	Nahum	Zep	Zephaniah		

The following abbreviations are used for the Deuterocanonical Books:

AdE	Additions to Esther	Jdt	Judith	4Mc	4 Maccabees
Aza	Prayer of Azariah	LtJ	Letter of Jeremiah	Pm	Psalm 151
Bar	Baruch	Man	Prayer of Manasseh	Sir	Sirach
Bel	Bel and the Dragon	1Mc	1 Maccabees	Sus	Susanna
1Es	1 Esdras	2Mc	2 Maccabees	Tob	Tobit
2Es	2 Esdras	3Mc	3 Maccabees	Wis	Wisdom

Other abbreviations and special symbols used:

S	Shorter Ending of Mark
T	Psalm Titles
Pr:	Sirach Prologue
*	Entries marked with an asterisk (e.g., ABBA*) contain every reference in the NRSV
→	An arrow following an entry heading points to related words for additional study
=	An equals sign marks an alternate proper name for additional study (e.g., ISRAEL =JACOB)
[[ ]]	Contexts in double brackets are from passages that are similarly bracketed in the NRSV (e.g., John 7:53-8:11)

For further study consult *The Concise Concordance to the New Revised Standard Version* (Oxford University Press, 1993) and *The NRSV Concordance Unabridged* (Zondervan, 1991).

AARON
Genealogy (Ex 6:16-20; Jos 21:4, 10; 1Ch 6:3-15). Priesthood of (Ex 28:1; Nu 17; Heb 5:1-4; 7), vestments of (Ex 28; 39), consecration of (Ex 29), ordination of (Lev 8).

Spokesman for Moses (Ex 4:14-16, 27-31; 7:1-2). Supported Moses' hands in battle (Ex 17:8-13). Built golden calf (Ex 32; Dt 9:20). Spoke against Moses (Nu 12). Priesthood opposed (Nu 16); staff budded (Nu 17). Forbidden to enter the promised land (Nu 20:1-12). Death of (Nu 20:22-29; 33:38-39). Praise of (Sir 45:6-22).

ABANDON → ABANDONED
Nu   32:15 will again a them in the wilderness;
Dt   4:31 will neither a you nor destroy you;
2Ch 15: 2 but if you a him, he will a you.
Mk   7: 8 You a the commandment of God
Ac   2:27 For you will not a my soul to Hades
Heb 10:35 Do not, therefore, a that confidence

ABANDONED → ABANDON
Dt 29:25 they a the covenant of the LORD,
Jdg   2:13 a the LORD, and worshiped Baal
2Ch 12: 5 You a me, so I have a you
Isa 54: 7 For a brief moment I a you,
Sir 49: 4 for they a the law of the Most High;

ABBA*
Mk 14:36 "A, Father, for you all things are possible;

Ro   8:15 When we cry, "A! Father!"
Gal   4: 6 into our hearts, crying, "A! Father!"

ABEDNEGO* → =AZARIAH
Deported to Babylon with Daniel (Da 1:1-6). Name changed from Azariah (Da 1:7). Refused defilement by food (Da 1:8-20). Refused idol worship (Da 3:1-12); saved from furnace (Da 3:13-30).

ABEL
Second son of Adam (Ge 4:2). Offered acceptable sacrifice (Ge 4:4; Heb 11:4; 12:24). Murdered by Cain (Ge 4:8; Mt 23:35; Lk 11:51; 1Jn 3:12).

ABHOR → ABHORRENT
Lev   26:11 and I shall not a you.

ABHORRENT → ABHOR
Dt   14: 3 You shall not eat any a thing.
      18: 9 not learn to imitate the a practices

ABIATHAR
High priest in days of Saul and David (1Sa 22; 2Sa 15; 1Ki 1-2; Mk 2:26). Escaped Saul's slaughter of priests (1Sa 22:18-23). Supported David in Absalom's revolt (2Sa 15:24-29). Supported Adonijah (1Ki 1:7-42); deposed by Solomon (1Ki 2:22-35; cf. 1Sa 2:31-35).

ABIDE → ABIDES, ABODE
Ge   6: 3 My spirit shall not a in mortals forever,
Ps   15: 1 O LORD, who may a in your tent?
      91: 1 a in the shadow of the Almighty,
Jn   15: 4 A in me as I a in you.
1Co   13:13 faith, hope, and love, these three;
1Jn   2:28 And now, little children, a in him,
Wis   3: 9 the faithful will a with him in love,

ABIDES → ABIDE
Hag   2: 5 My spirit a among you; do not fear.
1Jn   3:14 Whoever does not love a in death.

ABIGAIL
1. Sister of David (1Ch 2:16-17).
2. Wife of Nabal (1Sa 25:30); pled for his life with David (1Sa 25:14-35). Became David's wife after Nabal's death (1Sa 25:36-42).

ABIHU
Son of Aaron (Ex 6:23; 24:1, 9); killed for offering illicit fire (Lev 10; Nu 3:2-4; 1Ch 24:1-2).

ABIJAH
1. Second son of Samuel (1Ch 6:28); a corrupt judge (1Sa 8:1-5).
2. An Aaronic priest (1Ch 24:10; Lk 1:5).
3. Son of Jeroboam I; died as prophesied by Ahijah (1Ki 14:1-18).
4. Son of Rehoboam, also called Abijam; king of Judah who fought Jeroboam I attempting to reunite Israel (1Ki 14:31-15:8; 2Ch 12:16-14:1).

ABILITY → ABLE
Ex   31: 3 filled him with divine spirit, with a,
Mt   25:15 to each according to his a.
Ac   2: 4 as the Spirit gave them a.

ABIMELECH
1. King of Gerar who took Abraham's wife Sarah, believing her to be his sister (Ge 20). Covenanted with Abraham (Ge 21:22-33).
2. King of Gerar who took Isaac's wife Rebekah, believing her to be his sister (Ge 26:1-11). Covenanted with Isaac (Ge 26:12-31).
3. Son of Gideon (Jdg 8:31). Attempted to become king (Jdg 9).

ABIRAM
Sided with Dathan in rebellion against Moses and Aaron (Nu 16; 26:9; Dt 11:6; Sir 45:18).

ABISHAI
Son of Zeruiah, David's sister (1Sa 26:6; 1Ch 2:16). One of David's chief warriors (1Ch 11:15-21): against Edom (1Ch 18:12-13), Ammon (2Sa 10), Absalom (2Sa 18), Sheba (2Sa 20). Wanted

---

to kill Saul (1Sa 26), killed Abner (2Sa 2:18-27; 3:22-39).

ABLE → ABILITY
Ex   18:25 Moses chose a men from all Israel
Jos   1: 5 No one shall be a to stand against
      23: 9 no one has been a to withstand you
Da   3:17 God whom we serve is a to deliver
Mt   9:28 "Do you believe that I am a to do
Mk   10:38 you a to drink the cup that I drink,
Ro   14: 4 the Lord is a to make them stand.
2Co   9: 8 God is a to provide you with every
Eph   6:11 a to stand against the wiles of the devil.
2Ti   1:12 he is a to guard until that day
Heb   2:18 a to help those who are being tested.
      5: 2 is a to deal gently with the ignorant
      7:25 he is a for all time to save
Rev   5: 3 a to open the scroll or to look into it.
Jdt   11:18 of them will be a to withstand you.

ABNER
Cousin of Saul and commander of his army (1Sa 14:50; 17:55-57; 26). Made Ish-Bosheth king after Saul (2Sa 2:8-10), but later defected to David (2Sa 3:6-21). Killed Asahel (2Sa 2:18-32), for which he was killed by Joab and Abishai (2Sa 3:22-39).

ABODE → ABIDE
Ps   68:16 mount that God desired for his a,
Pr   3:33 but he blesses the a of the righteous.

ABOLISH → ABOLISHED
Da   11:31 shall a the regular burnt offering
Mt   5:17 I have come not to a but to fulfill.

ABOLISHED → ABOLISH
Eph   2:15 a the law with its commandments
2Ti   1:10 who a death and brought life

ABOMINABLE → ABOMINATION
2Ch   28: 3 the a practices of the nations
Eze   7:20 they made their a images,
1Mc   1:48 to make themselves a by everything

ABOMINATION → ABOMINABLE, ABOMINATIONS
Pr   6:16 seven that are an a to him:
Da   9:27 shall be an a that desolates,
Rev   21:27 anyone who practices a or falsehood
Sir   1:25 but godliness is an a to a sinner.
1Mc   6: 7 that they had torn down the a that

ABOMINATIONS → ABOMINATION
Lev   18:27 committed all of these a,
1Ki   14:24 all the a of the nations that the LORD
Eze   44: 7 broken my covenant with all your a.
Rev   17: 5 mother of whores and of earth's a."

ABOUND → ABOUNDED, ABOUNDING
Dt   28:11 LORD will make you a in prosperity,
Ro   6: 1 in sin in order that grace may a?

ABOUNDED → ABOUND
Ro   5:20 sin increased, grace a all the more,

ABOUNDING → ABOUND
Ex   34: 6 a in steadfast love and faithfulness,
Ps   86: 5 a in steadfast love to all who call on
Joel 2:13 to anger, and a in steadfast love,
Jnh   4: 2 to anger, and a in steadfast love,

ABOVE
Dt   4:39 the LORD is God in heaven a
Jn   3: 7 'You must be born from a.'
Php   2: 9 the name that is a every name,
Col   3: 2 Set your minds on things that are a,

ABRAHAM
Abram, son of Terah (Ge 11:26-27), husband of Sarah (Ge 11:29).
Covenant relation with the LORD (Ge 12:1-3; 13:14-17; 15; 17; 22:15-18; Ex 2:24; Ne 9:8; Ps 105; Mic 7:20; Lk 1:68-75; Ro 4; Heb 6:13-15).
Called from Ur, via Haran, to Canaan (Ge 12:1;

Ac 7:2-4; Heb 11:8-10). Moved to Egypt, nearly lost Sarah to Pharoah (Ge 12:10-20). Divided the land with Lot; settled in Hebron (Ge 13). Saved Lot from four kings (Ge 14:1-16); blessed by Melchizedek (Ge 14:17-20; Heb 7:1-20). Declared righteous by faith (Ge 15:6; Ro 4:3; Gal 3:6-9; 1Mc 2:52). Fathered Ishmael by Hagar (Ge 16).
Name changed from Abram (Ge 17:5; Ne 9:7). Circumcised (Ge 17; Ro 4:9-12). Entertained three visitors (Ge 18); promised a son by Sarah (Ge 18:9-15; 17:16). Questioned destruction of Sodom and Gomorrah (Ge 18:16-33). Moved to Gerar; nearly lost Sarah to Abimelech (Ge 20). Fathered Isaac by Sarah (Ge 21:1-7; Ac 7:8; Heb 11:11-12); sent away Hagar and Ishmael (Ge 21:8-21; Gal 4:22-30). Covenant with Abimelech (Ge 21:22-32). Tested by offering Isaac (Ge 22; Heb 11:17-19; Jas 2:21-24). Sarah died; bought field of Ephron for burial (Ge 23). Secured wife for Isaac (Ge 24). Fathered children by Keturah (Ge 25:1-6; 1Ch 1:32-33). Death (Ge 25:7-11).
Called servant of God (Ge 26:24), friend of God (2Ch 20:7; Isa 41:8; Jas 2:23), prophet (Ge 20:7), father of Israel (Ex 3:15; Isa 51:2; Mt 3:9; Jn 8:39-58). Praised (Sir 44:19-45:1).

ABSALOM
Son of David by Maacah (2Sa 3:3; 1Ch 3:2). Killed Amnon for rape of his sister Tamar; banished by David (2Sa 13). Returned to Jerusalem; received by David (2Sa 14). Rebelled against David (2Sa 15-17). Killed (2Sa 18).

ABSENT
1Co   5: 3 a in body, I am present in spirit;
Col   2: 5 For though I am a in body,

ABUNDANCE → ABUNDANTLY
Lk   6:45 a of the heart that the mouth speaks.
      12:15 one's life does not consist in the a
2Co   9: 8 provide you with every blessing in a

ABUNDANTLY → ABUNDANCE
Jn   10:10 that they may have life, and have it a.
Eph   3:20 to accomplish a far more than all

ABYSS
Lk   8:31 to order them to go back into the a.
Ro   10: 7 'Who will descend into the a?'"

ACCEPT → ACCEPTABLE, ACCEPTED
Pr   19:20 Listen to advice and a instruction,
Jer   32:33 would not listen and a instruction;
Mt   19:11 "Not everyone can a this teaching,
Jn   1:11 his own people did not a him.

ACCEPTABLE → ACCEPT
Ps   19:14 meditation of my heart be a to you,
      51:17 sacrifice a to God is a broken spirit;
Ro   12: 1 a living sacrifice, holy and a to God,

ACCEPTED → ACCEPT
Ge   4: 7 If you do well, will you not be a?
Lk   4:24 no prophet is a in the prophet's hometown.

ACCESS
Ro   5: 2 we have obtained a to this grace
Eph   2:18 have a in one Spirit to the Father.

ACCOMPLISH → ACCOMPLISHED
Isa   55:11 but it shall a that which I purpose,
Eze   17:24 I the LORD have spoken; I will a it.

ACCOMPLISHED → ACCOMPLISH
Mt   5:18 will pass from the law until all is a.

ACCORDING
Ps   28: 4 Repay them a to their work,
      119: 9 By guarding it a to your word.
Mt   9:29 "A to your faith let it be done to you
Ro   8: 4 not a to the flesh but a to the Spirit.
Heb   2: 4 Holy Spirit, distributed a to his will.
1Jn   5:14 that if we ask anything a to his will,

Rev   20:12 dead were judged a to their works,
Sir   16:12 he judges a person a to one's deeds.

ACCOUNT → ACCOUNTABLE
Mt   12:36 judgment you will have to give an a
Heb   4:13 to whom we must render an a.

ACCOUNTABLE → ACCOUNT
Ro   14:12 each of us will be a to God.

ACCURSED → CURSE
Ro   9: 3 I could wish that I myself were a
Rev   22: 3 Nothing a will be found there any

ACCUSATION → ACCUSE
Lk   23: 4 no basis for an a against this man."

ACCUSE → ACCUSATION, ACCUSER
Ps   103: 9 He will not always a,
Zec   3: 1 Satan standing at his right hand to a
Mt   12:10 so that they might a him.

ACCUSER → ACCUSE
Jn   5:45 your a is Moses,
Rev   12:10 the a of our comrades has been
               thrown

ACHAN
    Sinned at Jericho; stoned (Jos 7; 22:20; 1Ch
2:7).

ACHISH
    King of Gath before whom David feigned insan-
ity (1Sa 21:10-15). Later "ally" of David (2Sa 27-
29).

ACKNOWLEDGE
Dt   4:35 you would a that the LORD is God;
Pr   3: 6 In all your ways a him,
Mt   10:32 I also will a before my Father in
Ro   1:28 since they did not see fit to a God,

ACT → ACTED, ACTIVE, ACTS
Ps   37: 5 trust in him, and he will a.
Ro   14:23 because they do not a from faith;
Jas   1:25 hearers who forget but doers who a

ACTED → ACT
Eze   20: 9 But I a for the sake of my name,
Ac   3:17 I know that you a in ignorance,
1Ti   1:13 mercy because I had a ignorantly

ACTIVE → ACT
Heb   4:12 the word of God is living and a,
Jas   2:22 faith was a along with his works,

ACTS → ACT
Ex   6: 6 outstretched arm and with mighty a
Ps   71:15 mouth will tell of your righteous a,
Mt   7:24 hears these words of mine and a

ADAM
    First man (Ge 1:26-2:25; Ro 5:14; 1Ti 2:13; Tob
8:6). Sin of (Ge 3; Hos 6:7 [note]). Children of
(Ge 4:1-5:5). Death of (Ge 5:5; Ro 5:12-21; 1Co 15:22).

ADD → ADDED
Dt   4: 2 You must neither a anything
Pr   30: 6 Do not a to his words, or else
Lk   12:25 by worrying a a single hour to your

ADDED → ADD
Ecc   3:14 nothing can be a to it, nor anything
Sir   42:21 Nothing can be a or taken away,

ADDICTED*
Tit   1: 7 or quick-tempered or a to wine

ADMONISH → ADMONITION
Col   3:16 and a one another in all wisdom;

ADMONITION → ADMONISH
Pr   15: 5 one who heeds a is prudent.

ADONIJAH
    1. Son of David by Haggith (2Sa 3:4; 1Ch 3:2).
Attempted to be king after David; killed at Solomon's order (1Ki 1-2).
    2. Levite; teacher of the Law (2Ch 17:8).

ADOPTION
Ro   8:23 groan inwardly while we wait for a,
Gal   4: 5 that we might receive a as children.

ADORNED → ADORNMENT
Lk   21: 5 how it was a with beautiful stones
Rev   17: 4 a with gold and jewels and pearls,
      21: 2 as a bride a for her husband.

ADORNMENT → ADORNED, ADORNS
Pr   3:22 for your soul and a for your neck;
1Pe   3: 4 let your a be the inner self with the

ADORNS → ADORNMENT
Isa   61:10 as a bride a herself with her jewels.

ADULT* → ADULTS
1Co   13:11 an a, I put an end to childish ways.

ADULTERERS → ADULTERY
Jer   23:10 For the land is full of a;
1Co   6: 9 idolaters, a, male prostitutes,

ADULTERESS → ADULTERY
Lev   20:10 the a shall be put to death.
Pr   2:16 from the a with her smooth words,

ADULTERY → ADULTERERS, ADULTERESS
Ex   20:14 You shall not commit a.
Jer   3: 9 committing a with stone and tree.
Mt   5:28 committed a with her in his heart.
Lk   16:18 and marries another commits a,
Jn   8: 3 [[a woman who had been caught in
               a;]]

ADULTS* → ADULT
1Co   14:20 infants in evil, but in thinking be a.

ADVANTAGE
Ecc   7:12 a of knowledge is that wisdom gives
Ro   3: 1 Then what a has the Jew?
1Co   10:24 Do not seek your own a, but that of

ADVERSARIES → ADVERSARY
Dt   32:41 I will take vengeance on my a,
2Sa   22:49 you exalted me above my a,

ADVERSARY → ADVERSARIES
1Ti   5:14 give the a no occasion to revile us.
1Pe   5: 8 roaring lion your a the devil prowls

ADVERSITY → ADVERSARY
Dt   30:15 life and prosperity, death and a.
Isa   48:10 I have tested you in the furnace of a.

ADVICE → ADVISERS
2Ch   10:13 rejected the a of the older men;
Ps   1: 1 do not follow the a of the wicked,
Pr   8:14 I have good a and sound wisdom;
Tob   4:18 Seek a from every wise person
Sir   37:11 pay no attention to any a they give.

ADVISERS → ADVICE
Pr   15:22 but with many a they succeed.

ADVOCATE
Jn   14:26 But the A, the Holy Spirit,
      15:26 the A comes, whom I will send
1Jn   2: 1 we have an a with the Father,

**AFFLICT → AFFLICTED, AFFLICTION,
              AFFLICTIONS, AFFLICTS**
2Sa   7:10 evildoers shall a them no more,
La   3:33 for he does not willingly a
2Th   1: 6 repay with affliction those who a

AFFLICTED → AFFLICT
Dt   26: 6 Egyptians treated us harshly and a
Na   1:12 Though I have a you, I will afflict
2Co   4: 8 are a in every way, but not crushed;

AFFLICTION → AFFLICT
Dt   16: 3 bread with it—the bread of a—
Ps   25:18 Consider my a and my trouble,
Isa   30:20 of adversity and the water of a,
La   1: 9 "O LORD, look at my a,
2Co   4:17 this slight momentary a is preparing

AFFLICTIONS → AFFLICT
Ps   34:19 Many are the a of the righteous,

AFFLICTS* → AFFLICT
Tob   13: 2 For he a, and he shows mercy;

AFRAID → FEAR
Ge   3:10 and I was a, because I was naked;
      15: 1 not be a, Abram, I am your shield;
Ex   3: 6 his face, for he was a to look at God.
Lev   26: 6 and no one shall make you a;
Dt   20: 3 Do not lose heart, or be a,
Ps   3: 6 I am not a of ten thousands
      27: 1 of whom shall I be a?
      56:11 in God I trust; I am not a.
Isa   12: 2 I will trust, and will not be a,
Eze   2: 6 do not be a of their words,
Mt   10:31 So do not be a; you are of more
      28:10 Jesus said to them, "Do not be a;
Lk   12:32 "Do not be a, little flock,
Heb   13: 6 Lord is my helper; I will not be a.

AGABUS*
    A Christian prophet (Ac 11:28; 21:10).

AGAG
    King of Amalekites; not killed by Saul (1Sa 15).

AGAIN
Job   14:14 If mortals die, will they live a?
Ecc   3:20 and all turn to dust a.
Mk   8:31 and after three days rise a.
Jn   14: 3 I will come a and will take you to
Heb   6: 6 they are crucifying the Son of God
       9:25 Nor was it to offer himself a and a,

AGE → AGES
Ge   21: 2 bore Abraham a son in his old a,
Mt   28:20 with you always, to the end of the
               a."
Gal   1: 4 to set us free from the present evil a,

AGES → AGE
Dt   4:32 For ask now about former a,
1Co   2: 7 decreed before the a for our glory.
Col   1:26 has been hidden throughout the a
1Ti   1:17 To the King of the a, immortal,

AGREE
Mt   18:19 if two of you a on earth about
Mk   14:56 and their testimony did not a.
1Jn   5: 8 and the blood, and these three a.

AGRIPPA
    Descendant of Herod; king before whom Paul
argued his case in Caesarea (Ac 25:13-26:32).

AHAB
    1. Son of Omri; king of Israel (1Ki 16:28-22:40),
husband of Jezebel (1Ki 16:31). Promoted Baal
worship (1Ki 16:31-33); opposed by Elijah (1Ki
17:1; 18; 21), a prophet (1Ki 20:35-43), Micaiah
(1Ki 22:1-28). Defeated Ben-Hadad (1Ki 20).
Killed for failing to kill Ben-Hadad and for murder
of Naboth (1Ki 20:35-21:40).
    2. A false prophet (Jer 29:21-22).

AHASUERUS → ARTAXERXES
    King of Persia (Ezr 4:6), husband of Esther. De-
posed Vashti; replaced her with Esther (Est 1-2).
Sealed Haman's edict to annihilate the Jews (Est
3). Received Esther without having called her (Est
5:1-8). Honored Mordecai (Est 6). Hanged Haman
(Est 7). Issued edict allowing Jews to defend themselves (Est 8). Promoted Mordecai (Est 8:1-2, 15;
9:4, 10). Called Artaxerxes in the Additions to
Esther.

AHAZ
    Son of Jotham; king of Judah, (2Ki 16; 2Ch 28;
Mt 1:9). Idolatry of (2Ki 16:3-4, 10-18; 2Ch
28:1-4, 22-25). Defeated by Aram and Israel (2Ki
16:5-6; 2Ch 28:5-15). Sought help from Assyria
rather than the LORD (2Ki 16:7-9; 2Ch 28:16-21;
Isa 7).

AHAZIAH → =JEHOAHAZ

1. Son of Ahab; king of Israel (1Ki 22:51-2Ki 1:18; 2Ch 20:35-37). Made an unsuccessful alliance with Jehoshaphat (2Ch 20:35-37). Died for seeking Baal rather than the LORD (2Ki 1).

2. Son of Jehoram; king of Judah (2Ki 8:25-29; 9:14-29), also called Jehoahaz (2Ch 21:17-22:9; 25:23). Killed by Jehu while visiting Joram (2Ki 9:14-29; 2Ch 22:1-9).

AHEAD

Mt 11:10 sending my messenger a of you,
Php 3:13 straining forward to what lies a,
Heb 11:26 for he was looking a to the reward.

AHIJAH

1. Priest during Saul's reign (1Sa 14:3,18).
2. Prophet of Shiloh (1Ki 11:29-39; 14:1-18).

AHIKAM

Father of Gedaliah (2Ki 25:22), protector of Jeremiah (Jer 26:24).

AHIMAAZ

1. Father-in-law of Saul (1Sa 14:50).
2. Son of Zadok, the high priest, loyal to David (2Sa 15:27,36; 17:17-20; 18:19-33).

AHIMELECH

1. Priest who helped David in his flight from Saul (1Sa 21-22).
2. One of David's warriors (1Sa 26:6).

AHITHOPHEL

One of David's counselors who sided with Absalom (2Sa 15:12, 31-37; 1Ch 27:33-34); committed suicide when his advice was ignored (2Sa 16:15-17:23).

AI

Jos 7: 4 and they fled before the men of A.

AIR

Eph 2: 2 the ruler of the power of the a,
1Th 4:17 to meet the Lord in the a;
Rev 16:17 angel poured his bowl into the a,

ALARMED

Mk 13: 7 and rumors of wars, do not be a;
2Th 2: 2 to be quickly shaken in mind or a,

ALERT

Lk 12:37 slaves whom the master finds a
1Co 16:13 Keep a, stand firm in your faith,
Eph 6:18 keep a and always persevere
1Pe 5: 8 Discipline yourselves, keep a.

ALEXANDER

1Mc 1: 1 A son of Philip, the Macedonian,

ALIEN → ALIENS

Ex 2:22 an a residing in a foreign land."
Lev 19:34 you shall love the a as yourself,
Dt 24:17 You shall not deprive a resident a

ALIENS → ALIEN

Ge 15:13 your offspring shall be a in a land
Eph 2:19 you are no longer strangers and a,
1Pe 2:11 I urge you as a and exiles to abstain
1Mc 2: 7 the sanctuary given over to a?

ALIVE → LIVE

Ge 6:19 to keep them a with you;
Dt 32:39 I kill and I make a; I wound and I heal;
Ac 1: 3 suffering he presented himself a
Ro 6:11 dead to sin and a to God
Eph 2: 5 made us a together with Christ—
1Th 4:17 Then we who are a, who are left,
Rev 1:18 I am a forever and ever;
19:20 were thrown a into the lake of fire

ALL

Ge 6:13 to make an end of a flesh,
Dt 6: 5 You shall love the LORD your God with a your heart, and with a your soul, and with a your might.
Ps 1: 3 In a that they do, they prosper.

Jer 29:13 if you seek me with a your heart,
Lk 10:27 love the Lord your God with a your
Ro 3:23 a have sinned and fall short of the
6:10 he died to sin, once for a;
1Co 6:12 "A things are lawful for me,"
15:51 not a die, but we will a be changed,
Eph 1:23 the fullness of him who fills a in a.
Php 4:13 I can do a things through him
2Ti 3:16 A scripture is inspired by God
2Pe 3: 9 but a to come to repentance.
Rev 21: 5 "See, I am making a things new."
Sir 7:29 With a your soul fear the Lord,

ALMIGHTY → MIGHT

Ge 17: 1 "I am God A; walk before me,
Ex 6: 3 Isaac, and Jacob as God A,
Ps 91: 1 who abide in the shadow of the A,
Rev 1: 8 who was and who is to come, the A.
21:22 its temple is the Lord God the A
Bar 3: 1 O Lord A, God of Israel,
Man 1: 1 O Lord A, God of our ancestors,

ALMS

Mt 6: 2 "So whenever you give a,
Tob 12: 8 better to give a than to lay up gold.
Sir 7:10 do not neglect to give a.

ALONE → LONELY

Ge 2:18 not good that the man should be a;
Dt 6: 4 The LORD is our God, the LORD a.
Isa 2:11 LORD a will be exalted in that day.
Mk 2: 7 Who can forgive sins but God a?"
10:18 No one is good but God a.
Jas 2:24 justified by works and not by faith a

ALPHA

Rev 1: 8 "I am the A and the Omega,"
22:13 I am the A and the Omega,

ALTAR → ALTARS

Ge 22: 9 Isaac, and laid him on the a,
Ex 27: 1 shall make a of acacia wood,
30: 1 an a on which to offer incense;
Ezr 3: 2 to build the a of the God of Israel,
Mt 5:24 leave your gift there before the a
Heb 13:10 We have an a from which those
Jas 2:21 he offered his son Isaac on the a?
Rev 6: 9 I saw under the a the souls of those
Jdt 4: 1 even draped the a with sackcloth
1Mc 1:54 a desolating sacrilege on the a of
4:47 built a new a like the former one.

ALTARS → ALTAR

Ex 34:13 You shall tear down their a,
Nu 3:31 the table, the lampstand, the a,
1Mc 2:45 went around and tore down the a;

ALWAYS

Mt 28:20 And remember, I am with you a,
Lk 18: 1 to pray a and not to lose heart.
Php 4: 4 Rejoice in the Lord a; again I will

AMALEK

Ex 17: 8 Then A came and fought with Israel
1Sa 15: 3 attack A, and utterly destroy all

AMASA

Nephew of David (1Ch 2:17). Commander of Absalom's forces (2Sa 17:24-27). Returned to David (2Sa 19:13). Killed by Joab (2Sa 20:4-13).

AMAZED → AMAZING

Mt 8:27 a, saying, "What sort of man is this,
Mk 6: 6 And he was a at their unbelief.
Ac 2: 7 A and astonished, they asked,

AMAZIAH

1. Son of Joash; king of Judah (2Ki 14; 2Ch 25). Defeated Edom (2Ki 14:7; 2Ch 25:5-13); defeated by Israel for worshiping Edom's gods (2Ki 14:8-14; 2Ch 25:14-24).

2. Idolatrous priest; opposed Amos (Am 7:10-17).

AMAZING → AMAZED

Mk 12:11 and it is a in our eyes'?"
Rev 15: 3 "Great and a are your deeds,

AMBASSADOR* → AMBASSADORS

Eph 6:20 for which I am an a in chains.

AMBASSADORS → AMBASSADOR

2Co 5:20 So we are a for Christ,

AMBITION

Php 2: 3 Do nothing from selfish a or conceit
Jas 3:14 envy and selfish a in your hearts,

AMEN

Dt 27:15 people shall respond, saying, "A!"
2Co 1:20 through him that we say the "A,"
Rev 3:14 The words of the A, the faithful and

AMMONITE → AMMONITES

Dt 23: 3 No A or Moabite shall be admitted

AMMONITES → AMMONITE

Ge 19:38 the ancestor of the A to this day.
Jer 49: 6 I will restore the fortunes of the A,

AMNON

Firstborn of David (2Sa 3:2; 1Ch 3:1). Killed by Absalom for raping his sister Tamar (2Sa 13).

AMON

1. Son of Manasseh; king of Judah (2Ki 21:18-26; 1Ch 3:14; 2Ch 33:21-25).
2. Ruler of Samaria (1Ki 22:26; 2Ch 18:25).

AMORITES

Ge 15:16 iniquity of the A is not yet complete
Nu 21:31 Israel settled in the land of the A.

AMOS

Prophet from Tekoa (Am 1:1; 7:10-17; Tob 2:6).

ANANIAS

1. Early disciple; died for lying to God (Ac 5:1-11).
2. Disciple who baptized Saul (Ac 9:10-19).
3. High priest at Paul's arrest (Ac 22:30-24:1).

ANCESTOR → ANCESTORS

Dt 26: 5 "A wandering Aramean was my a;
Mt 3: 9 'We have Abraham as our a';

ANCESTORS → ANCESTOR

Ex 3:13 'The God of your a has sent me to
Dt 4:31 not forget the covenant with your a
La 5: 7 Our a sinned; they are no more,
Ac 5:30 The God of our a raised up Jesus,
Heb 1: 1 Long ago God spoke to our a in

ANCHOR

Heb 6:19 a sure and steadfast a of the soul,

ANCIENT

Ps 24: 7 and be lifted up, O a doors!
Jer 6:16 ask for the a paths, where the good
Da 7: 9 and an A One took his throne,
Mic 5: 2 origin is from of old, from a days.
Rev 20: 2 He seized the dragon, that a serpent,

ANDREW*

Apostle; brother of Simon Peter (Mt 4:18; 10:2; Mk 1:16-18, 29; 3:18; 13:3; Lk 6:14; Jn 1:35-44; 6:8-9; 12:22; Ac 1:13).

ANGEL → ANGELS, ARCHANGEL, ARCHANGEL'S

Ge 22:11 the a of the LORD called to him
Ex 3: 2 the a of the LORD appeared to him
23:20 going to send an a in front of you,
Nu 22:22 the a of the LORD took his stand in
1Ch 21:15 sent an a to Jerusalem to destroy it;
Ps 34: 7 The a of the LORD encamps
Isa 37:36 the a of the LORD set out and struck
Da 3:28 who has sent his a and delivered
6:22 God sent his a and shut the lions'
Mt 1:20 an a of the Lord appeared to him in
Lk 1:26 In the sixth month the a Gabriel
Ac 5:19 during the night an a of the Lord
23: 8 say that there is no resurrection, or a,
2Co 11:14 Satan disguises himself as an a of light.

Gal   1: 8 if we or an a from heaven should
Tob   5: 4 the a Raphael standing in front of
Sir 48:21 and his a wiped them out.
LtJ   6: 7 For my a is with you,
Aza   1:26 But the a of the Lord came down
Sus   1:59 a of God is waiting with his sword
Bel   1:34 the a of the Lord said to Habakkuk,
1Mc 7:41 your a went out and struck
2Es 2:44 Then I asked an a, "Who are these,

ANGELS → ANGEL
Ge 19: 1 The two a came to Sodom in the
    28:12 a of God were ascending and
Ps 103:20 Bless the Lord, O you his a,
Mk 12:25 but are like a in heaven.
Lk   4:10 command his a concerning you,
Jn   1:51 and the a of God ascending and
Ro 8:38 that neither death, nor life, nor a,
1Co 6: 3 not know that we are to judge a—
Col 2:18 on self-abasement and worship of a,
Heb 2: 7 for a little while lower than the a;
1Pe 1:12 things into which a long to look!
2Pe 2: 4 not spare the a when they sinned,
Rev 1:20 stars are the a of the seven
           churches,
    7: 1 After this I saw four a standing at
   21:12 and at the gates twelve a,
Tob 11:14 and blessed be all his holy a.

ANGER → ANGRY
Ex 32:19 the dancing, Moses' a burned hot,
    34: 6 merciful and gracious, slow to a,
Dt 32:22 For a fire is kindled by my a,
Jdg 2:12 and they provoked the Lord to a.
1Ki 16:13 God of Israel to a with their idols.
Ps 30: 5 For his a is but for a moment;
Pr 12:16 Fools show their a at once,
Ecc 7: 9 Do not be quick to a,
Isa 48: 9 For my name's sake I defer my a,
Joel 2:13 slow to a, and abounding in
Jnh 4: 2 slow to a, and abounding in
Mk 3: 5 He looked around at them with a;
Eph 4:26 not let the sun go down on your a,
Jas 1:19 slow to speak, slow to a;
Rev 14:10 unmixed into the cup of his a,
Sir 5: 4 for the Lord is slow to a.

ANGRY → ANGER
Ge 4: 5 So Cain was very a, and his
Jer 3:12 I will not be a forever.
Mt 5:22 that if you are a with a brother or

ANGUISH
Isa 53:11 Out of his a he shall see light;
Da 12: 1 There shall be a time of a,
Zep 1:15 a day of distress and a,
Lk 22:44 [[In his a he prayed more
          earnestly,]]

ANIMAL → ANIMALS
Ge 2:19 God formed every a of the field
    9: 2 dread of you shall rest on every a of
Ps 50:10 every wild a of the forest is mine,

ANIMALS → ANIMAL
Ge 3:14 cursed are you among all a
Lev 26: 6 remove dangerous a from the land,
Ps 36: 6 save humans and a alike, O Lord.

ANNA
  1. Prophetess; spoke of the child Jesus (Lk 2:36-38).
  2. Wife of Tobit (Tob 1:20; 2:1, 11).

ANNAS*
  High priest C.E. 6-15 (Lk 3:2; Jn 18:13, 24; Ac 4:6).

ANNOUNCED → ANNOUNCING
Isa 48: 5 before they came to pass I them
1Pe 1:25 the good news that was a to you.

ANNOUNCES → ANNOUNCING
Isa 52: 7 feet of the messenger who a peace,

ANNOUNCING* → ANNOUNCED, ANNOUNCES
Isa 63: 1 I, a vindication, mighty to save."
Ro 1: 9 serve with my spirit by a the gospel

ANNULLED
Jn 10:35 and the scripture cannot be a—

ANOINT → ANOINTED, ANOINTING
Ex 30:30 You shall a Aaron and his sons,
1Sa 15: 1 "The Lord sent me to a you king
Ps 23: 5 you a my head with oil; my cup
Da 9:24 and to a a most holy place.

ANOINTED → ANOINT
1Sa 2:10 and exalt the power of his a."
    26: 9 raise his hand against the Lord's a,
1Ch 16:22 "Do not touch my a ones;
Ps 2: 2 against the Lord and his a, saying,
Isa 61: 1 because the Lord has a me;
Eze 28:14 With a cherub as guardian
Da 9:26 an a one shall be cut off and
Zec 4:14 These are the two a ones who stand
Lk 4:18 he has a me to bring good news to
Jn 1:41 Messiah" (which is translated A).

ANOINTING → ANOINT
Ex 30:25 it shall be a holy a oil.
Jas 5:14 a them with oil in the name of the Lord
1Jn 2:27 as his a teaches you about all things,

ANOTHER
Pr 27: 2 Let a praise you, and not your own
Isa 48:11 My glory I will not give to a.
Jn 14:16 and he will give you a Advocate,
Gal 1: 7 not that there is a gospel,

ANSWER → ANSWERED
1Ki 18:37 A me, O Lord, a me,
Job 30:20 I cry to you and you do not a me;
Ps 65: 2 O you who a prayer!
Pr 15: 1 A soft a turns away wrath,
Isa 65:24 Before they call I will a,
Lk 23: 9 but Jesus gave him no a.

ANSWERED → ANSWER
1Ch 21:26 and he a him with fire from heaven
Ps 118:21 I thank you that you have a me

ANT*
Pr 6: 6 Go to the a, you lazybones;

ANTICHRIST*
1Jn 2:18 As you have heard that a is coming,
    2:22 the a, the one who denies the Father
    4: 3 And this is the spirit of the a,
2Jn 1: 7 person is the deceiver and the a!

ANTIOCH
Ac 11:26 in A that the disciples were first called "Christians."
    13: 1 the church at A there were prophets
Gal 2:11 But when Cephas came to A,

ANTIOCHUS
  Antiochus IV Epiphanes, king of the Syrian Greeks B.C.E. 175-164 (1Mc 1:10-19). Plundered the temple in Jerusalem (1Mc 1:20-28). Attempted to force the Hellenization of the Jewish people (1Mc 1:41-53), including defiling the altar and holy place (1Mc 1:54-64). His policies sparked the Maccabean revolt.

ANXIETIES → ANXIETY
1Co 7:32 I want you to be free from a.

ANXIETY → ANXIETIES
Ecc 11:10 Banish a from your mind,
1Pe 5: 7 Cast all your a on him, because he

ANYTHING
Ge 18:14 Is a too wonderful for the Lord?
Jer 32:27 is a too hard for me?
Mt 18:19 if two of you agree on earth about a
Jn 16:23 if you ask a of the Father in my name,

APART → PART
Jn 15: 5 a from me you can do nothing.
Ro 3:21 a from law, the righteousness of
Jas 2:20 that faith a from works is barren?

APOLLOS
  Christian from Alexandria, learned in the Scriptures; instructed by Aquila and Priscilla (Ac 18:24-28). At Corinth (Ac 19:1; 1Co 1:12; 3; Tit 3:13).

APOSTASIES → APOSTASY
Jer 2:19 and your a will convict you.
Eze 37:23 I will save them from all the a

APOSTASY* → APOSTASIES
1Mc 2:15 officers who were enforcing the a

APOSTLE → APOSTLES
Ro 11:13 as I am an a to the Gentiles,
1Co 9: 1 Am I not an a?
2Co 12:12 signs of a true a were performed
Heb 3: 1 a and high priest of our confession,

APOSTLES → APOSTLE
  See also Andrew, Bartholomew, Barnabas, James, John, Judas, Matthew, Matthias, Nathanael, Paul, Peter, Philip, Simon, Thaddaeus, Thomas.
Mt 10: 2 the names of the twelve a:
Ac 2:43 and signs were being done by the a.
1Co 12:28 has appointed in the church first a,
Eph 2:20 foundation of the a and prophets,
    4:11 he gave were that some would be a,
Rev 21:14 are the twelve names of the twelve a

APPEAL
Mt 26:53 think that I cannot a to my Father,
Ac 25:11 I a to the emperor."
2Co 5:20 God is making his a through us;
Phm 1: 9 rather a to you on the basis of love
1Pe 3:21 an a to God for a good conscience,

APPEAR → APPEARANCE, APPEARANCES, APPEARED, APPEARING
Mt 24:30 the sign of the Son of Man will a in
Mk 13:22 messiahs and false prophets will a
2Co 5:10 a before the judgment seat of Christ,
Heb 9:28 a second time, not to deal with sin,

APPEARANCE → APPEAR
Ex 24:17 Now the a of the glory of the Lord
1Sa 16: 7 not look on his a or on the height
2Co 5:12 those who boast in outward a
Jdt 11:23 You are not only beautiful in a,
AdE 2: 7 The girl was beautiful in a.
Sir 19:29 A person is known by his a,

APPEARANCES → APPEAR
Jn 7:24 not judge by a, but judge with right

APPEARED → APPEAR
Jn 21:14 that Jesus a to the disciples after he
1Co 15: 5 he a to Cephas, then to the twelve.
Heb 9:26 a once for all at the end of the age

APPEARING → APPEAR
Ac 1: 3 a to them during forty days and
2Ti 4: 8 to all who have longed for his a.

APPETITES
Ro 16:18 our Lord Christ, but their own a,
Sir 18:30 base desires, but restrain your a.

APPLE
Dt 32:10 guarded him as the a of his eye.
Zec 2: 8 touches you touches the a of my eye

APPOINT → APPOINTED
1Sa 8: 5 a for us, then, a king to govern us,
Isa 60:17 I will a Peace as your overseer

APPOINTED → APPOINT
Lev 23: 2 the a festivals of the Lord
Ecc 3:17 for he has a a time for every matter,
Hab 2: 3 there is still a vision for the a time;

Mk   3:16 So he a the twelve: Simon (to whom
Ac   3:20 that he may send the Messiah a for
Heb 1: 2 whom he a heir of all things,
     9:27 just as it is a for mortals to die once,

APPORTIONED → PORTION
Dt   32: 8 When the Most High a the nations,
Jos 18:10 Joshua a the land to the Israelites,

APPROACH
Heb 4:16 a the throne of grace with boldness,
     11: 6 whoever would a him must believe
Sir 1:28 do not a him with a divided mind.

APPROVAL → APPROVED
Gal 1:10 I now seeking human a, or God's a?
Heb 11: 2 by faith our ancestors received a.
1Pe 2:20 and suffer for it, you have God's a.

APPROVED → APPROVAL
1Th 2: 4 but just as we have been a by God
2Ti 2:15 to present yourself to God as one a

AQUILA*
   Husband of Priscilla; co-worker with Paul, instructor of Apollos (Ac 18; Ro 16:3; 1Co 16:19;
2Ti 4:19).

ARABS
Ne   4: 7 and the A and the Ammonites
1Mc 5:39 also have hired A to help them,

ARAM → ARAMAIC, ARAMEAN
Jdg 10: 6 the gods of A, the gods of Sidon,
2Ch 16: 7 you relied on the king of A,

ARAMAIC → ARAM
2Ki 18:26 to your servants in the A language,
Ezr 4: 7 the letter was written in A and
Da   2: 4 Chaldeans said to the king (in A),

ARAMEAN → ARAM
Dt   26: 5 "A wandering A was my ancestor;

ARARAT
Ge   8: 4 ark came to rest on the mountains
               of A.

ARAUNAH → =ORNAN
2Sa 24:16 the threshing floor of A the Jebusite.

ARCHANGEL* → ANGEL
Jude 1: 9 a Michael contended with the devil
2Es   4:36 the a Jeremiel answered and said,

ARCHANGEL'S* → ANGEL
1Th 4:16 a call and with the sound of God's

ARCHITECT*
Heb 11:10 whose a and builder is God.

AREOPAGUS
Ac   17:22 Then Paul stood in front of the A

**ARGUE → ARGUES, ARGUMENT,
     ARGUMENTS**
Job 13: 3 and I desire to a my case with God.
Isa 1:18 now, let us a it out, says the LORD;
Ac   18: 4 Every sabbath he would a in the
Ro   9:20 a human being, to a with God?

ARGUES* → ARGUE
Job 40: 2 who a with God must respond."

ARGUMENT → ARGUE
Lk   9:46 An a arose among them as to which
1Ti 2: 8 up holy hands without anger or a;

ARGUMENTS → ARGUE
2Co 10: 4 destroy strongholds. We destroy a
Col 2: 4 may deceive you with plausible a.

ARIMATHEA
Jn   19:38 After these things, Joseph of A,

ARISE → RISE
SS   2:10 "A, my love, my fair one, and
Isa 60: 1 A, shine; for your light has come,
Mt   24:11 false prophets will a and lead many
1Mc 14:41 until a trustworthy prophet should a,

ARK
Ge   6:14 Make yourself an a of cypress wood
Ex   25:10 shall make an a of acacia wood;
1Sa 4:11 The a of God was captured;
1Ki 8: 9 There was nothing in the a except
1Pe 3:20 during the building of the a,
Rev 11:19 the a of his covenant was seen
2Mc 2: 1 that the tent and the a should follow
2Es 10:22 the a of our covenant has been

ARM → ARMIES, ARMOR, ARMS, ARMY
Ex   6: 6 redeem you with an outstretched a
Dt   7:19 mighty hand and the outstretched a
2Ch 32: 8 With him is an a of flesh;
Job 40: 9 Have you an a like God,
Ps   98: 1 his holy a have gotten him victory.
Isa 53: 1 the a of the LORD been revealed?
Jn   12:38 the a of the LORD been revealed?"

ARMIES → ARM
1Sa 17:36 defied the a of the living God."
Lk   21:20 you see Jerusalem surrounded by a,
Rev 19:14 the a of heaven, wearing fine linen,

ARMOR → ARM
1Sa 17:38 Saul clothed David with his a;
Ro   13:12 and put on the a of light;
Eph 6:11 Put on the whole a of God,
Wis 5:17 will take his zeal as his whole a,

ARMS → ARM
Pr   31:17 and makes her a strong.
Hos 11: 3 I took them up in my a;
Mk   10:16 And he took them up in his a,

ARMY → ARM
Ex   15: 4 and his a he cast into the sea;
Jos 5:14 as commander of the a of the LORD
Ps   27: 3 Though an a encamp against me,
     33:16 A king is not saved by his great a;
Rev 19:19 rider on the horse and against his a.

AROMA
2Co 2:15 For we are the a of Christ to God

ARRESTED
Jer 37:14 and a Jeremiah and brought him to
Mt   14: 3 For Herod had a John, bound him,
     26:50 and laid hands on Jesus and a him.
Ac   5:18 the apostles and put them in the
     28:17 yet I was a in Jerusalem and handed

ARROGANCE → ARROGANT
Pr   8:13 Pride and a and the way of evil
Eze 7:24 put an end to the a of the strong,
Jdt 9:10 their a by the hand of a woman.
Sir 10: 7 A is hateful to the Lord and to
1Mc 1:24 much blood, and spoke with great a.

ARROGANT → ARROGANCE
Ps   73: 3 For I was envious of the a;
Da   7:11 a words that the horn was speaking.
1Co 13: 4 love is not envious or boastful or a

ARROW → ARROWS
Ps   64: 7 But God will shoot his a at them;
Isa 49: 2 he made me a polished a,

ARROWS → ARROW
1Sa 20:20 I will shoot three a to the side of it,
Eph 6:16 quench all the flaming a of the evil

ARTAXERXES → =AHASUERUS
   1. King of Persia; allowed rebuilding of temple
under Ezra (Ezr 4; 7), and of walls of Jerusalem
under his cupbearer Nehemiah (Ne 2; 5:14; 13:6).
   2. See Ahasuerus.

ARTEMIS
Ac   19:27 the temple of the great goddess A

ASA
   King of Judah (1Ki 15:8-24; 1Ch 3:10; 2Ch
14-16). Godly reformer (2Ch 15); in later years defeated Israel with help of Aram, not the LORD (1Ki
15:16-22; 2Ch 16).

ASAHEL
   Nephew of David, one of his warriors (2Sa
23:24; 1Ch 2:16; 11:26; 27:7). Killed by Abner
(2Sa 2); avenged by Joab (2Sa 3:22-39).

ASAPH
   1. Recorder to Hezekiah (2Ki 18:18, 37; Isa
36:3, 22).
   2. Levitical musician (1Ch 6:39; 15:17-19; 16:4-
7, 37), seer (2Ch 29:30). Sons of (1Ch 25; 2Ch
5:12; 20:14; 29:13; 35:15; Ezr 2:41; 3:10; Ne 7:44;
11:17; 12:27-47). Psalms of (2Ch 29:30; Ps 50;
73-83).

**ASCEND → ASCENDED, ASCENDING,
     ASCENTS**
Ps   139: 8 If I a to heaven, you are there;
Isa 14:13 in your heart, "I will a to heaven;
Ac   2:34 David did not a into the heavens,
Ro   10: 6 'Who will a into heaven?' "
2Es 4: 8 neither did I ever a into heaven.'

ASCENDED → ASCEND
2Ki 2:11 Elijah a in a whirlwind into heaven.
Jn   3:13 No one has a into heaven except

ASCENDING → ASCEND
Ge   28:12 the angels of God were a and
Jn   1:51 the angels of God a and descending

ASCENTS → ASCEND
   Songs of ascents (Ps 120-134).

ASCRIBE
Dt   32: 3 a greatness to our God!
1Ch 16:29 A to the LORD the glory due his
Ps   68:34 A power to God,
Sir 39:15 A majesty to his name
Bar 2:17 not a glory or justice to the Lord;

ASHAMED → SHAME
Ge   2:25 were both naked, and were not a.
Ps   6:10 All my enemies shall be a and
Isa 29:22 No longer shall Jacob be a,
Mk   8:38 who are a of me and of my words
Ro   1:16 For I am not a of the gospel;
2Ti 2:15 a worker who has no need to be a,
Heb 2:11 Jesus is not a to call them brothers
     11:16 God is not a to be called their God;

ASHER
   Son of Jacob by Zilpah (Ge 30:13; 35:26; 46:17;
Ex 1:4; 1Ch 2:2). Tribe of blessed (Ge 49:20; Dt
33:24-25), numbered (Nu 1:40-41; 26:44-47), al-
lotted land (Jos 10:24-31; Eze 48:2), failed to fully
possess (Jdg 1:31-32), failed to support Deborah
(Jdg 5:17), supported Gideon (Jdg 6:35; 7:23) and
David (1Ch 12:36), 12,000 from (Rev 7:6).

ASHERAH → ASHERAHS, ASTARTE
1Ki 18:19 and four hundred prophets of A,
2Ch 15:16 made an abominable image for A.

ASHERAHS* → ASHERAH
Jdg 3: 7 and worshiping the Baals and the A.

ASHES
Ge   18:27 I who am but dust and a.
Est 4: 1 and put on sackcloth and a,
Job 42: 6 and repent in dust and a."
Jnh 3: 6 himself with sackcloth, and sat in a.
Mt   11:21 long ago in sackcloth and a.
Jdt 4:11 the temple and put a on their heads
Sir 17:32 but all human beings are dust and a.

ASIA
Ac   16: 6 Holy Spirit to speak the word in A.
Rev 1: 4 to the seven churches that are in A:

ASIDE → SIDE
Ex   32: 8 quick to turn a from the way that I
Dt   28:14 if you do not turn a from any of the
Jer 5:23 they have turned a and gone away.
Da   9: 5 turning a from your commandments
Ro   3:12 All have turned a, together they
Heb 12: 1 also lay a every weight and the sin

ASK
Ps   2: 8 A of me, and I will make the nations
Isa 65: 1 sought out by those who did not a,
Mt   6: 8 knows what you need before you a
     7: 7 "A, and it will be given you;
Jn 16:24 A and you will receive,
Jas 4: 3 You a and do not receive, because
             you a wrongly,
1Jn 5:14 we a anything according to his will,

ASLEEP → SLEEP
Jnh 1: 5 had lain down, and was fast a.
Mt   8:24 by the waves; but he was a.
1Th 5: 6 So then let us not fall a as others
             do,

ASSEMBLE → ASSEMBLY
1Ki 18:19 all Israel a for me at Mount Carmel,
Zep 3: 8 to gather nations, to a kingdoms,
Rev 16:14 to a them for battle on the great day

ASSEMBLY → ASSEMBLE
Ne   8: 2 Ezra brought the law before the a,
Ps 149: 1 his praise in the a of the faithful.
Heb 12:23 the a of the firstborn who are

ASSIGNED
Ro 12: 3 the measure of faith that God has a.
1Co 3: 5 as the Lord a to each.
     7:17 lead the life that the Lord has a,

ASSURANCE
Dt 28:66 in dread, with no a of your life.
Heb 6:11 so as to realize the full a of hope
    11: 1 faith is the a of things hoped for,

ASSYRIA
Ge 10:11 From that land he went into A,
2Ki 18:11 of A carried the Israelites away to A,
Jer 50:18 as I punished the king of A.

ASTARTE → ASHERAH, ASTARTES
1Ki 11: 5 Solomon followed A the goddess

ASTARTES → ASTARTE
Jdg 2:13 and worshiped Baal and the A.

ASTONISHED
Isa 52:14 there were many who were a at him
Lk   2:48 his parents saw him they were a;
Gal 1: 6 a that you are so quickly deserting

ASTRAY → STRAY
Dt 30:17 are led a to bow down to other gods
Isa 53: 6 All we like sheep have gone a;
Jer 50: 6 their shepherds have led them a,
Mt 18:12 go in search of the one that went a?
1Pe 2:25 For you were going a like sheep,

ATE → EAT
Ge   3: 6 she took of its fruit and a;
Ex 16:35 The Israelites a manna forty years,
Ps 78:25 Mortals a of the bread of angels;
Eze 3: 3 I a it; and in my mouth it was as
Mt 14:20 And all a and were filled;
    15:37 And all of them a and were filled;
Rev 10:10 from the hand of the angel and a it;

ATHALIAH
   Granddaughter of Omri; wife of Jehoram and
mother of Ahaziah; encouraged their evil ways (2Ki
8:18, 27; 2Ch 22:2). At death of Ahaziah she made
herself queen, killing all his sons but Joash (2Ki
11:1-3; 2Ch 22:10-12); killed six years later when
Joash revealed (2Ki 11:4-16; 2Ch 23:1-15).

ATHLETE → ATHLETES
2Ti 2: 5 And in the case of an a,

ATHLETES → ATHLETE
1Co 9:25 A exercise self-control in all things;

ATONE → ATONEMENT
Da   9:24 an end to sin, and to a for iniquity,
Sir 3: 3 who honor their father a for sins,

ATONED* → ATONEMENT
Pr 16: 6 and faithfulness iniquity is a for,

ATONEMENT → ATONE, ATONED, ATONING
Ex 29:36 a bull as a sin offering for a.
    30:10 Aaron shall perform the rite of a
    32:30 perhaps I can make a for your sin."
Lev 23:28 for it is a day of a,
Ro   3:25 God put forward as a sacrifice of a
Heb 2:17 to make a sacrifice of a for the sins

ATONING → ATONEMENT
1Jn 2: 2 and he is the a sacrifice for our sins,
     4:10 sent his Son to be the a sacrifice for
Sir 28: 5 will make an a sacrifice for his sins?

ATTAIN → ATTAINED
Ps 139: 6 it is so high that I cannot a it.
Pr   8:12 and I a knowledge and discretion.
Da 12:12 those who persevere and a
Php 3:11 a the resurrection from the dead.

ATTAINED → ATTAIN
Ro   9:30 not strive for righteousness, have a
Php 3:16 let us hold fast to what we have a.

ATTENTION
Nu 16:15 "Pay no a to their offering.
Job 24:12 yet God pays no a to their prayer.
Heb 2: 1 greater a to what we have heard,

ATTESTED
Ac   2:22 a man a to you by God with deeds
Ro   3:21 and is a by the law and the
             prophets,

AUTHOR*→
Ac   3:15 and you killed the A of life,
Wis 13: 3 for the a of beauty created them.

AUTHORITIES → AUTHORITY
Ro 13: 1 be subject to the governing a;
Col 2:15 He disarmed the rulers and a and

AUTHORITY → AUTHORITIES
Ge 41:45 Thus Joseph gained a over the land
Pr 29: 2 When the righteous are in a,
Mk   1:27 A new teaching—with a!
Lk   5:24 Son of Man has a on earth to forgive
Ac   5:29 obey God rather than any human a.
Ro 13: 1 for there is no a except from God,
1Co 11:10 woman ought to have a symbol of a
Col 2:10 who is the head of every ruler and a.
1Ti 2:12 no woman to teach or to have a over
Rev 12:10 and the a of his Messiah,
    20: 4 on them were given a to judge.

AVENGE → VENGEANCE
Dt 32:43 he will a the blood of his children,
Joel 3:21 I will a their blood, and I will not
Ro 12:19 Beloved, never a yourselves,
Rev 6:10 and a our blood on the inhabitants
1Mc 2:67 a the wrong done to your people.

AVENGER → VENGEANCE
Nu 35:12 shall be for you a refuge from the a,
Ps   8: 2 to silence the enemy and the a.
1Th 4: 6 the Lord is an a in all these things,

AVENGING → VENGEANCE
Na   1: 2 A jealous and a God is the LORD,

AVOID → AVOIDS
2Ti 2:16 A profane chatter, for it will lead
Tit 3: 9 But a stupid controversies,

AVOIDS → AVOID
Pr 16: 6 by the fear of the LORD one a evil.

AWAKE
Ps 44:23 A, do not cast us off forever!
    57: 8 A, my soul! A, O harp and lyre!
Isa 51: 9 A, a, put on strength, O arm of the
             LORD!
Da 12: 2 in the dust of the earth shall a,
Mk 14:37 Could you not keep a one hour?
Eph 5:14 "Sleeper, a! Rise from the dead,
1Th 5: 6 but let us keep a and be sober;
Rev 16:15 Blessed is the one who stays a and

AWE → AWESOME
Ps 119:161 my heart stands in a of your words.
Isa 29:23 will stand in a of the God of Israel.
Mt   9: 8 saw it, they were filled with a,
Ac   2:43 A came upon everyone, because
Ro 11:20 do not become proud, but stand
             in a.

AWESOME → AWE
Ex 15:11 majestic in holiness, a in splendor,
Dt   6:22 before our eyes great and a signs
    10:17 the great God, mighty and a,
Ne   1: 5 and a God who keeps covenant
Ps 47: 2 For the LORD, the Most High, is a,
    65: 5 By a deeds you answer us with
    68:35 A is God in his sanctuary,
Da   9: 4 saying, "Ah, Lord, great and a God,
Sir 43:29 A is the Lord and very great,

AX
2Ki 6: 5 his a head fell into the water;
Mt   3:10 Even now the a is lying at the root

AZARIAH → =ABEDNEGO, =UZZIAH
   1. King of Judah; see Uzziah (2Ki 15:1-7).
   2. Prophet (2Ch 15:1-8).
   3. Opponent of Jeremiah (Jer 43:2).
   4. Jewish exile; see Abednego (Da 1:6-19).

AZAZEL
Lev 16: 8 for the LORD and the other lot for A.

B

BAAL → BAALS
Nu 25: 3 Israel yoked itself to the B of Peor,
Jdg 2:13 and worshiped B and the Astartes.
1Ki 18:25 Elijah said to the prophets of B,
    19:18 the knees that have not bowed to B,
Jer 2: 8 the prophets prophesied by B,
Hos 2: 8 no longer will you call me, "My B."
Ro 11: 4 not bowed the knee to B."

BAALS → BAAL
Jdg 3: 7 worshiping the B and the Asherahs.
1Sa 7: 4 So Israel put away the B and the

BAASHA
   King of Israel (1Ki 15:16-16:7; 2Ch 16:1-6).

BABEL → BABYLON
Ge 11: 9 Therefore it was called B,

BABES → BABIES
Ps   8: 2 Out of the mouths of b and infants
Isa 3: 4 and b shall rule over them.

BABIES → BABES
Mt 21:16 the mouths of infants and nursing b

BABYLON → BABEL
2Ki 24:15 into captivity from Jerusalem to B.
Ps 137: 1 By the rivers of B—there we sat
Isa 14: 4 this taunt against the king of B:
    21: 9 he responded, "Fallen, fallen is B;
Jer 25:11 serve the king of B seventy years.
1Pe 5:13 Your sister church in B, chosen
Rev 14: 8 "Fallen, fallen is B the great!
Bel 1:36 he set him down in B,

BACK → BACKSLIDING
Ge 19:26 Lot's wife, behind him, looked b,
2Ki 20:11 he brought the shadow b the ten
Lk   9:62 puts a hand to the plow and looks b

BACKSLIDING* → BACK
Jer 8: 5 people turned away in perpetual b?

BAD
Pr 20:14 "B, b," says the buyer, then goes
Mt   7:17 but the b tree bears b fruit.
1Co 15:33 "B company ruins good morals."

BALAAM
   Prophet who attempted to curse Israel (Nu 22-
24; Dt 23:4-5; 2Pe 2:15; Jude 11; Rev 2:14). Killed
in Israel's vengeance on Midianites (Nu 31:8; Jos
13:22).

BALAK
Moabite king who hired Balaam to curse Israel (Nu 22-24; Jos 24:9; Mic 6:5).

BALANCE → BALANCES
Job   31: 6   let me be weighed in a just **b**,
Isa   40:12   in scales and the hills in a **b**?

BALANCES → BALANCE
Lev   19:36   shall have honest **b**, honest weights,
Pr   16:11   Honest **b** and scales are the LORD's,
Sir   28:25   make **b** and scales for your words.

BALM
Jer   8:22   Is there no **b** in Gilead?

BANDIT
Mt   26:55   to arrest me as though I were a **b**?
Jn   10: 1   in by another way is a thief and a **b**.

BANISH
Ecc   11:10   B anxiety from your mind,
Ro   11:26   he will **b** ungodliness from Jacob."

BANNER
Ex   17:15   and called it, The LORD is my **b**.

BAPTISM → BAPTIZE
Mk   1: 4   proclaiming a **b** of repentance for
      10:38   be baptized with the **b** that I am
Lk   20: 4   the **b** of John come from heaven,
Ac   18:25   though he knew only the **b** of John.
      19: 3   They answered, "Into John's **b**."
Ro   6: 4   buried with him by into death,
1Co   15:29   receive **b** on behalf of the dead?
Eph   4: 5   one Lord, one faith, one **b**,
Col   2:12   when you were buried with him in **b**,
1Pe   3:21   **b**, which this prefigured, now saves

BAPTISMS* → BAPTIZE
Heb   6: 2   about **b**, laying on of hands,
      9:10   with food and drink and various **b**,

BAPTIST → BAPTIZE
Mt   3: 1   In those days John the **B** appeared
      11:11   has arisen greater than John the **B**;
      14: 8   the head of John the **B** here on a
      16:14   they said, "Some say John the **B**,

BAPTIZE → BAPTISM, BAPTISMS, BAPTIST, BAPTIZED, BAPTIZING
Mt   3:11   "I **b** you with water for repentance,
Lk   3:16   He will **b** you with the Holy Spirit
1Co   1:17   For Christ did not send me to **b** but

BAPTIZED → BAPTIZE
Mt   3:13   to John at the Jordan, to be **b**
Ac   1: 5   John **b** with water, but you will be **b** with the Holy
      2:38   "Repent, and be **b** every one of you
Ro   6: 3   **b** into Christ Jesus were **b** into his
1Co   10: 2   all were **b** into Moses in the cloud
      12:13   one Spirit we were all **b** into one

BAPTIZING* → BAPTIZE
Mt   28:19   **b** them in the name of the Father
Jn   4: 1   "Jesus is making and **b** more

BARABBAS*
Prisoner released by Pilate instead of Jesus (Mt 27:16-26; Mk 15:7-15; Lk 23:18-19; Jn 18:40).

BARAK*
Judge who fought with Deborah against Canaanites (Jdg 4-5; 1Sa 12:11; Heb 11:32).

BARBARIAN → BARBARIANS
Col   3:11   circumcised and uncircumcised, **b**,

BARBARIANS* → BARBARIAN
Ro   1:14   am a debtor both to Greeks and to **b**,

BARBS*
Nu   33:55   let remain shall be as **b** in your eyes

BARE → BARED
Ps   18:15   were laid **b** at your rebuke,
Heb   4:13   all are naked and laid **b** to the eyes

BARED* → BARE
Isa   52:10   The LORD has **b** his holy arm

BARN → BARNS
Lk   12:24   they have neither storehouse nor **b**,

BARNABAS* → =JOSEPH
Disciple, originally Joseph (Ac 4:36), prophet (Ac 13:1), apostle (Ac 14:14). Brought Paul to apostles (Ac 9:27), Antioch (Ac 11:22-29; Gal 2:1-13), on the first missionary journey (Ac 13-14). Together at Jerusalem Council, they separated over John Mark (Ac 15). Later co-workers (1Co 9:6; Col 4:10).

BARNS* → BARN
Dt   28: 8   the blessing upon you in your **b**,
Ps   144:13   May our **b** be filled, with produce
Lk   12:18   pull down my **b** and build larger

BARREN → BARRENNESS
Ge   11:30   Now Sarai was **b**; she had no child.
Ex   23:26   No one shall miscarry or be **b** in
1Sa   2: 5   The **b** has borne seven, but she who
Ps   113: 9   He gives the **b** woman a home,
Isa   54: 1   Sing, O **b** one who did not bear;
Lk   1: 7   because Elizabeth was **b**,
Heb   11:11   too old—and Sarah herself was **b**—

BARRENNESS* → BARREN
Dt   7:14   neither sterility nor **b** among you
Ro   4:19   considered the **b** of Sarah's womb.

BARTHOLOMEW* → =NATHANAEL*
Apostle (Mt 10:3; Mk 3:18; Lk 6:14; Ac 1:13). Possibly also called Nathanael (Jn 1:45-49; 21:2).

BARUCH*
Jeremiah's secretary (Jer 32:12-16; 36; 43:1-6; 45:1-2). Deuterocanonical book ascribed to (Bar 1:1, 3, 8).

BARZILLAI*
1. Gileadite who aided David during Absalom's revolt (2Sa 17:27; 19:31-39).
2. Son-in-law of 1. (Ezr 2:61; Ne 7:63).

BASED*
Ro   9:31   righteousness that is **b** on the law,
      9:32   but as if it were **b** on works.
Php   3: 9   righteousness from God **b** on faith.

BASHAN
Nu   21:33   King Og of B came out against
Ps   22:12   strong bulls of **B** surround me;
Mic   7:14   let them feed in B and Gilead as in

BASIN
Ex   30:18   You shall make a bronze **b** with a
1Ki   7:30   four corners were supports for a **b**.
Jn   13: 5   **b** and began to wash the disciples'

BASIS
Lk   23: 4   "I find no **b** for an accusation
Phm   1: 9   rather appeal to you on the **b** of love

BASKET
Ex   2: 3   she got a papyrus **b** for him,
Mt   5:15   a lamp puts it under the bushel **b**,
Ac   9:25   in the wall, lowering him in a **b**.

BATHING
2Sa   11: 2   he saw from the roof a woman **b**;

BATHSHEBA*
Wife of Uriah; committed adultery with and married David (2Sa 11; Ps 51), mother of Solomon (2Sa 12:24; 1Ki 1-2; 1Ch 3:5).

BATTLE
1Sa   17:47   the **b** is the LORD's and he will give
2Ch   20:15   for the **b** is not yours but God's.
Ps   24: 8   and mighty, the LORD, mighty in **b**.
Ecc   9:11   nor the **b** to the strong, nor bread to
Rev   16:14   them for **b** on the great day of God

Rev   20: 8   Magog, in order to gather them for **b**;
1Mc   3:19   the army that victory in **b** depends,

BEAR → BEARS, BIRTH, BIRTHRIGHT, BORE, BORN, CHILDBEARING, FIRSTBORN
Ge   4:13   punishment is greater than I can **b**!
      17:19   your wife Sarah shall **b** you a son,
Isa   7:14   is with child and shall **b** a son,
Mt   1:23   virgin shall conceive and **b** a son,
      7:18   A good tree cannot **b** bad fruit,
Lk   11:46   load people with burdens hard to **b**,
Jn   15: 2   he prunes to make it **b** more fruit.
Gal   6: 2   B one another's burdens,
Col   3:13   B with one another and,
Heb   9:28   offered once to **b** the sins of many,
Rev   12: 4   woman who was about to **b** a child,

BEARS → BEAR
Ps   68:19   Blessed be the LORD, who daily **b** us
1Co   13: 7   It **b** all things, believes all things,

BEAST → BEASTS
Rev   11: 7   **b** that comes up from the bottomless pit
      13:18   calculate the number of the **b**,
      16: 2   who had the mark of the **b**
      19:20   who had received the mark of the **b**

BEASTS → BEAST
Da   7: 3   four great **b** came up out of the sea,
Mk   1:13   and he was with the wild **b**;

BEAT → BEATEN, BEATING
Isa   2: 4   shall **b** their swords into plowshares,
Joel   3:10   B your plowshares into swords,
Lk   22:63   began to mock him and **b** him;

BEATEN → BEAT
2Co   11:25   Three times I was **b** with rods.
1Pe   2:20   If you endure when you are **b** for

BEATING → BEAT
Ex   2:11   He saw an Egyptian **b** a Hebrew,
1Co   9:26   nor do I box as though **b** the air;

BEAUTIFUL → BEAUTY
Ge   12:11   you are a woman **b** in appearance;
1Sa   25: 3   The woman was clever and **b**,
Est   2: 7   the girl was fair and **b**,
Job   42:15   no women so **b** as Job's daughters;
Ps   48: 2   **b** in elevation, is the joy of all
SS   1: 5   I am black and **b**, O daughters of
Isa   4: 2   the branch of the LORD shall be **b**
      52: 7   How **b** upon the mountains are the
Ac   3: 2   the temple called the **B** Gate so that
Ro   10:15   **b** are the feet of those who bring
Tob   6:12   girl is sensible, brave, and very **b**,
Jdt   8: 7   She was **b** in appearance,
Wis   7:29   She is more **b** than the sun,
Sir   9: 8   not gaze at **b** belonging to another;
Sus   1: 2   very **b** woman and one who feared

BEAUTY → BEAUTIFUL
2Sa   14:25   so much for his **b** as Absalom;
Ps   27: 4   to behold the **b** of the LORD,
Pr   6:25   Do not desire her **b** in your heart,
      31:30   Charm is deceitful, and **b** is vain,
1Pe   3: 4   with the lasting **b** of a gentle
Jdt   16: 9   her **b** captivated his mind,
Wis   13: 3   for the author of **b** created them.
Sir   9: 8   not gaze at **b** belonging to another;
Sus   1:56   **b** has beguiled you and lust has
1Mc   2:12   And see, our holy place, our **b**,

BED → BEDS
Ge   47:31   bowed himself on the head of his **b**.
Ps   139: 8   if I make my **b** in Sheol, you are
Lk   5:19   let him down with his **b** through the
Heb   13: 4   let the marriage **b** be kept undefiled;

BEDS → BED
Ps   36: 4   They plot mischief while on their **b**;
Mic   2: 1   and evil deeds on their **b**!

BEE* → BEES
Isa   7:18 the **b** that is in the land of Assyria.
Sir 11: 3 The **b** is small among flying

BEER-SHEBA
Ge 21:31 Therefore that place was called **B**;
1Sa   3:20 And all Israel from Dan to **B** knew

BEES → BEE
Jdg 14: 8 a swarm of **b** in the body of the lion,

BEFORE
Ex 20: 3 you shall have no other gods **b** me.
     33: 2 I will send an angel **b** you,
Isa 43:10 **B** me no god was formed,
     65:24 **B** they call I will answer,
Mal   3: 1 my messenger to prepare the way **b**
Mt   6: 8 Father knows what you need **b** you
Lk 22:61 "**B** the cock crows today,
Heb 12: 2 sake of the joy that was set **b** him

BEGGAR → BEGS
Mk 10:46 son of Timaeus, a blind **b**,
Jn   9: 8 who had seen him before as a **b**

BEGINNING
Ge   1: 1 In the **b** when God created the
Ps 111:10 fear of the LORD is the **b** of wisdom;
Pr   1: 7 The fear of the LORD is the **b** of
     8:22 The LORD created me at the **b** of his
Ecc   7: 8 Better is the end of a thing than
             its **b**
Isa 40:21 Has it not been told you from the **b**?
Mt 24: 8 this is but the **b** of the birth pangs.
Jn   1: 1 In the **b** was the Word,
1Jn   1: 1 declare to you what was from the **b**,
2Jn   1: 6 as you have heard it from the **b**—
Rev 21: 6 and the Omega, the **b** and the end.
Wis   6:17 The **b** of wisdom is the most sincere
Sir   1:14 To fear the Lord is the **b** of wisdom;

BEGOTTEN
Ps   2: 7 You are my son; today I have **b** you.
Ac 13:33 are my Son; today I have **b** you.'
Heb   1: 5 are my Son; today I have **b** you"?
2Es   6:58 have called your firstborn, only **b**,

BEGS → BEG
Lk   6:30 Give to everyone who **b** from you;

BEHEADED → HEAD
Lk   9: 9 Herod said, "John I **b**;
Rev 20: 4 the souls of those who had been **b**

BEHEMOTH
Job 40:15 "Look at **B**, which I made just as I
2Es   6:49 the one you called **B** and the name

BEHIND
Isa 38:17 have cast all my sins **b** your back.
Mt 16:23 said to Peter, "Get **b** me, Satan!
Php   3:13 forgetting what lies **b** and straining

BEING
Ge   2: 7 and the man became a living **b**.
Nu 23:19 God is not a human **b**,
Da   7:13 one like a human **b** coming with the
Jn   1: 3 All things came into **b** through him,
1Co 15:45 Adam, became a living **b**,"
Heb   1: 3 the exact imprint of God's very **b**,

BEL*
    Babylonian deity (Isa 46:1; Jer 50:2; 51:44; LtJ
    6:40; Bel 1:3-28).

BELIEF → BELIEVE
2Th   2:13 the Spirit and through **b** in the
          truth.

BELIEVE → BELIEF, BELIEVED, BELIEVER,
        BELIEVERS, BELIEVES, BELIEVING
Ex   4: 5 that they may **b** that the LORD,
Nu 14:11 long will they refuse to **b** in me?
2Ki 17:14 did not **b** in the LORD their God.
Ps 119:66 for I **b** in your commandments.
Pr 14:15 The simple **b** everything,

Jer 12: 6 do not **b** them, though they speak
Hab   1: 5 you would not **b** if you were told.
Mt 18: 6 one of these little ones who **b** in me,
  24:23 or 'There he is!'—do not **b** it.
Mk   1:15 repent, and **b** in the good news."
     9:24 "I **b**; help my unbelief!"
Lk 24:25 how slow of heart to **b** all that the
Jn   1: 7 so that all might **b** through him.
     3:18 who **b** in him are not condemned;
     5:46 believed Moses, you would **b** me,
     6:29 you **b** in him whom he has sent."
  10:38 you do not **b** me, the works,
  14: 1 **B** in God, **b** also in me.
  17:20 will **b** in me through their word,
  20:29 not seen and yet have come to **b**."
Ac 16:31 answered, "**B** on the Lord Jesus,
  28:24 while others refused to **b**.
Ro   3:22 faith in Jesus Christ for all who **b**.
  10: 9 in your heart that God raised him
1Co 15: 2 unless you have come to **b** in vain.
Gal   3: 9 this reason, those who **b** are blessed
1Th   4:14 For since we **b** that Jesus died and
Heb 11: 6 would approach him must **b**
Jas   2:19 Even the demons **b**—and shudder.
1Pe   1: 8 you do not see him now, you **b**
1Jn   4: 1 Beloved, do not **b** every spirit,
Jude   1: 5 destroyed those who did not **b**.
Sir 19:15 so do not **b** everything you hear.

BELIEVED → BELIEVE
Ge 15: 6 And he **b** the LORD;
Ex 14:31 **b** in the LORD and in his servant
Isa 53: 1 Who has **b** what we have heard?
Jn   1:12 received him, who **b** in his name,
  12:38 "Lord, who has **b** our message,
  20: 8 also went in, and he saw and **b**;
Ac   2:44 All who **b** were together and had all
Ro   4: 3 "Abraham **b** God, and it was
  10:16 "Lord, who has **b** our message?"
2Co   4:13 "I **b**, and so I spoke"—
Gal   3: 6 Just as Abraham "**b** God,
1Ti   3:16 **b** in throughout the world, taken up
Heb   4: 3 For we who have **b** enter that rest,
Jas   2:23 that says, "Abraham **b** God,
Jdt 14:10 had done, he **b** firmly in God.
1Mc   2:59 **b** and were saved from the flame.

BELIEVER → BELIEVE
1Co   6: 6 but a **b** goes to court against a **b**—
     7:12 **b** has a wife who is an unbeliever,
2Co   6:15 Or what does a **b** share with an

BELIEVERS → BELIEVE
1Co 14:22 a sign not for **b** but for unbelievers,
Gal   2: 4 because of false **b** secretly brought
2Th   3: 6 keep away from **b** who are living in
1Pe   2:17 Love the family of **b**.

BELIEVES → BELIEVE
Jn   3:15 whoever **b** in him may have eternal
  11:26 everyone who lives and **b** in me
Ro   9:33 whoever **b** in him will not be put to
  10:10 **b** with the heart and so is justified,
1Co 13: 7 It bears all things, **b** all things,

BELIEVING → BELIEVE
Jn 20:31 through **b** you may have life in his
Gal   3: 5 or by your **b** what you heard?

BELLY
Ge   3:14 upon your **b** you shall go,
Lev 11:42 Whatever moves on its **b**,
Jnh   1:17 and Jonah was in the **b** of the fish
Mt 12:40 three days and three nights in the **b**
Php   3:19 is destruction; their god is the **b**;

BELONG → BELONGS
Dt 29:29 The secret things **b** to the LORD our
          God, but the revealed things **b** to us
Ps 82: 8 for all the nations **b** to you!
Da   9: 9 To the LORD our God **b** mercy and
Jn 10:16 sheep that do not **b** to this fold.
  15:19 Because you do not **b** to the world,

Ro   9: 6 not all Israelites truly **b** to Israel,
1Co   3:23 you **b** to Christ, and Christ belongs
  12:15 I do not **b** to the body,"
1Jn   2:19 out from us, but they did not **b** to
          us;

BELONGS → BELONG
Ps 22:28 For dominion **b** to the LORD,
  62:11 I heard this: that power **b** to God,
Jnh   2: 9 Deliverance **b** to the LORD!"
Rev   7:10 "Salvation **b** to our God who is

BELOVED → LOVE
SS   2:16 My **b** is mine and I am his;
Mt   3:17 heaven said, "This is my Son, the **B**,
  12:18 my **b**, with whom my soul is well
  17: 5 "This is my Son, the **B**;
Col   3:12 As God's chosen ones, holy and **b**,
Rev 20: 9 camp of the saints and the **b** city.

BELSHAZZAR*
    King of Babylon (Da 5; Bar 1:11-12).

BELT
1Sa 18: 4 his sword and his bow and his **b**.
Isa 11: 5 Righteousness shall be the **b** around
Mk   1: 6 with a leather **b** around his waist,
Eph   6:14 the **b** of truth around your waist,

BELTESHAZZAR → See DANIEL

BEN-HADAD*
    1. King of Syria in time of Asa (1Ki 15:18-20;
    2Ch 16:2-4).
    2. King of Syria in time of Ahab (1Ki 20; 2Ki
    6:24; 8:7-15).
    3. King of Syria in time of Jehoahaz (2Ki 13:3,
    24-25; Jer 49:27; Am 1:4).

BENAIAH
    A commander of David's army (2Sa 8:18; 20:23;
    23:20-30); loyal to Solomon (1Ki 1:8-2:46; 4:4).

BEND → BENT
Php   2:10 name of Jesus every knee should **b**,
Man   1:11 And now I **b** the knee of my heart,

BENEFICIAL → BENEFIT
1Co   6:12 but not all things are **b**.
  10:23 lawful," but not all things are **b**.

BENEFIT → BENEFICIAL, BENEFITS
Gal   5: 2 Christ will be of no **b** to you.
Phm   1:20 have this **b** from you in the Lord!
Heb   4: 2 message they heard did not **b** them,

BENEFITS → BENEFIT
Ps 103: 2 and do not forget all his **b**—
1Co   9:11 if we reap your material **b**?

BENJAMIN → BENJAMINITE
    Twelfth son of Jacob by Rachel (Ge 35:16-24;
    46:19-21; 1Ch 2:2). Jacob refused to send him to
    Egypt, but relented (Ge 42-45). Tribe of blessed
    (Ge 49:27; Dt 33:12), numbered (Nu 1:37; 26:41),
    allotted land (Jos 18:11-28; Eze 48:23), failed to
    fully possess (Jdg 1:21), nearly obliterated (Jdg
    20-21), sided with Ish-Bosheth (2Sa 2), but turned
    to David (1Ch 12:2, 29). 12,000 from (Rev 7:8).

BENJAMINITE → BENJAMIN
Jdg   3:15 the **B**, a left-handed man.
1Sa   9:21 Saul answered, "I am only a **B**,

BENT → BEND
Hos 11: 4 I **b** down to them and fed them.
Jn   8: 6 [[Jesus **b** down and wrote with his]]
  20: 5 He **b** down to look in and saw

BEREAVE → BEREAVES
Lev 26:22 they shall **b** you of your children
Eze 36:12 No longer shall you **b** them of

BEREAVES* → BEREAVE
La   1:20 In the street the sword **b**;

BESIDES
Dt 32:39 there is no god **b** me.
Ps 18:31 And who is a rock **b** our God?—

Isa 45:21 There is no other god **b** me,
Wis 12:13 For neither is there any god **b** you,
Bel 1:41 there is no other **b** you!"

BEST → GOOD
Dt 33:21 He chose the **b** for himself,
Mk 12:39 the **b** seats in the synagogues and
2Ti 2:15 your **b** to present yourself to God

BETHANY
Mt 26: 6 Jesus was at **B** in the house of
Jn 11: 1 a certain man was ill, Lazarus of **B**,

BETHEL
Ge 12: 8 the east of **B**, and pitched his tent,
28:19 He called that place **B**;
1Sa 7:16 a circuit year by year to **B**, Gilgal,

BETHLEHEM
Ru 4:11 and bestow a name in **B**;
1Sa 17:12 David was the son of an Ephrathite of **B**
Mic 5: 2 But you, O **B** of Ephrathah,
Mt 2: 1 after Jesus was born in **B** of Judea,
Lk 2:15 "Let us go now to **B** and see this

BETRAY → BETRAYED
Mt 10:21 Brother will **b** brother to death,
Mk 14:11 to look for an opportunity to **b** him.
Jn 13:11 For he knew who was to **b** him;

BETRAYED → BETRAY
Lk 21:16 You will be **b** even by parents and
1Co 11:23 Jesus on the night when he was **b**

BETTER → GOOD
1Sa 15:22 Surely, to obey is **b** than sacrifice,
Ps 63: 3 your steadfast love is **b** than life,
Pr 15:16 **B** is a little with the fear of
27: 5 **B** is open rebuke than hidden love.
Ecc 2:24 There is nothing **b** for mortals than
9: 4 a living dog is **b** than a dead lion.
SS 1: 2 For your love is **b** than wine,
Da 1:20 he found them ten times **b** than all
Mt 5:29 it is **b** for you to lose one of your
Mk 14:21 It would have been **b** for that one
Jn 11:50 for you to have one man die for
Ro 14: 5 Some judge one day to be **b** than
Php 1:23 and be with Christ, for that is far **b**;
2: 3 in humility regard others as **b** than
Heb 7:22 the guarantee of a **b** covenant.
9:23 need **b** sacrifices than these.
1Pe 3:17 For it is **b** to suffer for doing good,
Tob 12: 8 A little with righteousness is **b** than
Sir 40:26 the fear of the Lord is **b** than either.

BETWEEN
Ge 3:15 put enmity **b** you and the woman,
9:13 a sign of the covenant **b** me and
16: 5 the Lord judge **b** you and me!"
Isa 2: 4 He shall judge **b** the nations,
Eze 34:17 I shall judge **b** sheep and sheep, **b**
rams and goats:
Jn 19:18 on either side, with Jesus **b** them.
Ro 10:12 no distinction **b** Jew and Greek;
Eph 2:14 dividing wall, that is, the hostility **b**
1Ti 2: 5 one mediator **b** God and humankind

BEWARE
Ecc 12:12 anything beyond these, my child, **b**.
Mt 6: 1 "**B** of practicing your piety before
Php 3: 2 **B** of the dogs, **b** of the evil workers,

BEYOND
Ps 147: 5 his understanding is **b** measure.
2Co 4:17 an eternal weight of glory **b** all
2Jn 1: 9 but goes **b** it, does not have God;
Sir 3:23 not meddle in matters that are **b** you

BEZALEL
Judahite craftsman in charge of building the tabernacle (Ex 31:1-11; 35:30-39:31).

BILDAD*
One of Job's friends (Job 2:11; 8; 18; 25; 42:9).

BILHAH
Servant of Rachel, mother of Jacob's sons Dan and Naphtali (Ge 30:1-7; 35:25; 46:23-25).

BIND → BINDS
Dt 6: 8 **B** them as a sign on your hand,
Pr 6:21 **B** them upon your heart always;
Isa 61: 1 to **b** up the brokenhearted,
Mt 16:19 whatever you **b** on earth will be

BINDS → BIND
Job 5:18 For he wounds, but he **b** up;
Col 3:14 **b** everything together in perfect

BIRD → BIRDS
Ge 1:21 and every winged **b** of every kind.
Lev 20:25 the unclean **b** and the clean;

BIRDS → BIRD
Ge 1:22 and let **b** multiply on the earth."
7: 3 and seven pairs of the **b** of the air
Ps 50:11 I know all the **b** of the air,
Jer 7:33 be food for the **b** of the air, and for
Mt 6:26 Look at the **b** of the air;
Rev 19:21 the **b** were gorged with their flesh.

BIRTH → BEAR
Dt 32:18 you forgot the God who gave you **b**.
Ps 22:10 On you I was cast from my **b**,
Mt 24: 8 is but the beginning of the **b** pangs.
Jas 1:18 he gave us **b** by the word of truth,
1Pe 1: 3 given us a new **b** into a living hope

BIRTHRIGHT → BEAR, RIGHT
Ge 25:34 Thus Esau despised his **b**.
Heb 12:16 who sold his **b** for a single meal.

BISHOP
1Ti 3: 1 whoever aspires to the office of **b**
Tit 1: 7 For a **b**, as God's steward, must be

BIT → BITE, BITS
Nu 21: 9 and whenever a serpent **b** someone,
Ps 32: 9 temper must be curbed with **b** and

BITE* → BIT
Gal 5:15 If, however, you **b** and devour one
Sir 21: 2 if you approach sin, it will **b** you.

BITS → BIT
Jas 3: 3 we put **b** into the mouths of horses

BITTER → BITTERNESS
Ex 1:14 made their lives **b** with hard service
12: 8 with unleavened bread and **b** herbs.
15:23 water of Marah because it was **b**.
Ru 1:13 it has been far more **b** for me than
Rev 8:11 the water, because it was made **b**.

BITTERNESS → BITTER
Nu 5:18 the water of **b** that brings the curse.
Pr 14:10 The heart knows its own **b**,
Ro 3:14 mouths are full of cursing and **b**."
Eph 4:31 Put away from you all **b** and wrath

BLACK
SS 1: 5 I am **b** and beautiful, O daughters
Zec 6: 2 the second chariot **b** horses,
Mt 5:36 cannot make one hair white or **b**.
Rev 6: 5 I looked, and there was a **b** horse!

BLAMELESS
Ge 17: 1 walk before me, and be **b**.
2Sa 22:26 with the **b** you show yourself **b**;
Job 1: 1 That man was **b** and upright,
Ps 37:18 The Lord knows the days of the **b**,
Pr 11:20 but those of **b** ways are his delight.
Eph 1: 4 holy and **b** before him in love.
Php 2:15 so that you may be **b** and innocent,
1Th 5:23 and at the coming of our Lord
Tit 1: 7 bishop, as God's steward, must be **b**
Heb 7:26 **b**, undefiled, separated from sinners,
Rev 14: 5 mouth no lie was found; they are **b**.
1Mc 4:42 chose **b** priests devoted to the law,

BLASPHEME → BLASPHEMED, BLASPHEMER, BLASPHEMES, BLASPHEMIES, BLASPHEMOUS
Ac 26:11 I tried to force them to **b**;
1Ti 1:20 so that they may learn not to **b**.

BLASPHEMED → BLASPHEME
Eze 20:27 In this again your ancestors **b** me,
Mt 26:65 tore his clothes and said, "He has **b**!

BLASPHEMER → BLASPHEME
1Ti 1:13 even though I was formerly a **b**,
Sir 3:16 forsakes a father is like a **b**,

BLASPHEMES → BLASPHEME
Lev 24:16 One who **b** the name of the Lord
Lk 12:10 whoever **b** against the Holy Spirit

BLASPHEMIES → BLASPHEME
Mk 3:28 their sins and whatever **b** they utter;
Rev 13: 6 its mouth to utter **b** against God,
1Mc 2: 6 He saw the **b** being committed in

BLASPHEMOUS → BLASPHEME
Ac 6:11 "We have heard him speak **b** words
Rev 13: 1 and on its heads were **b** names.

BLAZING
Ex 3: 2 he looked, and the bush was **b**,
Dt 4:11 the mountain was **b** up to the very
Heb 12:18 a **b** fire, and darkness, and gloom,

BLEMISH → BLEMISHED
Ex 12: 5 Your lamb shall be without a **b**,
Lev 22:20 not offer anything that has a **b**,
Eph 5:27 that she may be holy and without **b**.
Heb 9:14 offered himself without **b** to God,
1Pe 1:19 that of a lamb without defect or **b**.
Jude 1:24 to make you stand without **b** in the

BLEMISHED* → BLEMISH
Mal 1:14 yet sacrifices to the Lord what is **b**;
Sir 34:21 ill-gotten goods, the offering is **b**;

BLESS → BLESSED, BLESSING, BLESSINGS
Ge 12: 2 I will **b** you, and make your name
17:16 I will **b** her, and moreover I will
22:17 I will indeed **b** you, and I will make
26: 3 I will be with you, and will **b** you;
32:26 not let you go, unless you **b** me."
Ex 20:24 I will come to you and **b** you.
Nu 6:24 The Lord **b** you and keep you;
23:20 See, I received a command to **b**;
Dt 7:13 he will love you, **b** you,
30:16 the Lord your God will **b** you in
1Ch 29:20 "**B** the Lord your God."
Ps 5:12 For you **b** the righteous, O Lord;
29:11 the Lord **b** his people with peace!
34: 1 I will **b** the Lord at all times;
103: 1 **B** the Lord, O my soul,
109:28 Let them curse, but you will **b**.
Hag 2:19 From this day on I will **b** you.
Lk 6:28 curse you, pray
Ro 12:14 **B** those who persecute you;
1Co 4:12 When reviled, we **b**;
Jas 3: 9 With it we **b** the Lord and Father,
Tob 4:19 At all times **b** the Lord God,
Sir 32:13 But above all **b** your Maker,

BLESSED → BLESS
Ge 1:22 God **b** them, saying, "Be fruitful
2: 3 So God **b** the seventh day and
14:19 He **b** him and said, "**B** be Abram
Nu 24: 9 **B** is everyone who blesses you,
Job 1:21 be the name of the Lord."
42:12 The Lord **b** the latter days
Ps 118:26 **B** is the one who comes in the name
Isa 30:18 **b** are all those who wait for him.
Jer 17: 7 **B** are those who trust in the Lord,
Mt 5: 3 "**B** are the poor in spirit,
Mk 10:16 laid his hands on them, and **b** them.
Lk 1:42 "**B** are you among women,
6:20 "**B** are you who are poor,
Jn 12:13 **B** is the one who comes in the name
20:29 **B** are those who have not seen and

Ac 20:35 It is more b to give than to receive.
Gal 3: 8 "All the Gentiles shall be b in you."
Eph 1: 3 who has b us in Christ
1Pe 3:14 for doing what is right, you are b.
Rev 1: 3 B is the one who reads aloud the
22: 7 B is the one who keeps the words of
Tob 3:11 she prayed and said, "B are you,
Jdt 13:17 one accord, "B are you our God,
Aza 1: 3 "B are you, O Lord, God of our
Sus 1:60 raised a great shout and b God,

BLESSING → BLESS
Ge 12: 2 so that you will be a b.
22:18 the nations of the earth gain b for
27:36 now he has taken away my b."
Dt 11:26 before you today a b and a curse:
23: 5 your God turned the curse into a b
Ne 13: 2 our God turned the curse into a b.
Eze 34:26 they shall be showers of b.
Mal 3:10 for you an overflowing b.
Mk 14:22 of bread, and after b it he broke it,
Lk 24:51 While he was b them, he withdrew
1Co 10:16 The cup of b that we bless,
Gal 3:14 in Christ Jesus the b of Abraham
Eph 1: 3 every spiritual b in the heavenly
Rev 5:12 might and honor and glory and b!"
7:12 B and glory and wisdom and
Tob 8:15 you, O God, with every pure b,
Sir 34:20 he gives health and life and b.

BLESSINGS → BLESS
Dt 28: 2 all these b shall come upon you
Jos 8:34 the words of the law, b and curses,
Ps 21: 6 You bestow on him b forever;
144:15 Happy are the people to whom such b
Pr 10: 6 B are on the head of the righteous,
Mal 2: 2 and I will curse your b;
Ro 15:27 come to share in their spiritual b,

BLIND → BLINDED, BLINDNESS
Ex 4:11 mute or deaf, seeing or b?
Dt 27:18 misleads a b person on the road."
Ps 146: 8 the LORD opens the eyes of the b.
Isa 35: 5 the eyes of the b shall be opened,
42:19 Who is b but my servant,
Mt 11: 5 b receive their sight, the lame walk,
Lk 6:39 "Can a b person guide a b person?
Jn 9:25 though I was b, now I see."
Ro 2:19 sure that you are a guide to the b,
2Pe 1: 9 b, and is forgetful of the cleansing
Tob 2:10 until I became completely b.
LtJ 6:37 They cannot restore sight to the b;

BLINDED → BLIND
Zec 11:17 withered, his right eye utterly b!
Jn 12:40 "He has b their eyes and hardened
2Co 4: 4 has b the minds of the unbelievers,

BLINDNESS → BLIND
Ge 19:11 And they struck with b the men
Dt 28:28 will afflict you with madness, b,
1Jn 2:11 the darkness has brought on b.

BLOCK → BLOCKS
Isa 44:19 I fall down before a b of wood?"
Eze 14: 7 their iniquity as a stumbling b
Mt 16:23 You are a stumbling b to me;
Ro 11: 9 a stumbling b and a retribution for
1Co 1:23 stumbling b to Jews and foolishness
Sir 31: 7 It is a stumbling b to those who are

BLOCKS → BLOCK
Jer 6:21 before this people stumbling b
Mt 18: 7 the world because of stumbling b!

BLOOD → BLOODSHED
Ge 4:10 your brother's b is crying out to me
9: 6 sheds the b of a human, by a human shall that person's b be shed;
Ex 7:17 and it shall be turned to b.
12:13 when I see the b, I will pass over
24: 8 the b of the covenant that the LORD
Lev 1: 5 the priests shall offer the b,

Lev 3:17 you must not eat any fat or any b.
17:11 it is the b that makes atonement.
Nu 35:33 for b pollutes the land,
Ps 72:14 and precious is their b in his sight.
Isa 1:11 I do not delight in the b of bulls,
Eze 33: 4 b shall be upon their own heads.
Joel 2:30 b and fire and columns of smoke.
Mt 27: 8 field has been called the Field of B
Mk 14:24 "This is my b of the covenant,
Lk 22:44 [[sweat became like great drops of b]]
Jn 1:13 who were born, not of b
6:53 of the Son of Man and drink his b,
19:34 and at once b and water came out.
Ac 2:20 to darkness and the moon to b,
Ro 5: 9 that we have been justified by his b,
1Co 11:25 cup is the new covenant in my b.
Eph 1: 7 we have redemption through his b,
6:12 not against enemies of b and flesh,
Heb 9:12 the b of goats and calves, but with his own b,
9:22 without the shedding of b there is no
1Jn 5: 6 the one who came by water and b,
Rev 1: 5 and freed us from our sins by his b,
5: 9 by your b you ransomed for God
6:12 the full moon became like b,
8: 9 A third of the sea became b,
12:11 conquered him by the b of the Lamb

BLOODSHED → BLOOD, SHED
Isa 5: 7 he expected justice, but saw b;
Eze 35: 6 you did not hate b, b shall pursue
Hab 2: 8 because of human b, and violence

BLOSSOMS
Ex 25:33 three cups shaped like almond b,
Nu 17: 8 It put forth buds, produced b,

BLOT
Ge 6: 7 "I will b out from the earth
Ex 32:32 b me out of the book that you have
Ps 51: 1 mercy b out my transgressions.
Rev 3: 5 not b your name out of the book of

BLOW → BLOWING
Joel 2: 1 B the trumpet in Zion; sound the
Rev 8: 6 the seven trumpets made ready to b

BOAST → BOASTERS, BOASTFUL, BOASTING
Ps 34: 2 My soul makes its b in the LORD;
Pr 27: 1 Do not b about tomorrow,
Jer 9:24 but let those who b b in this,
Ro 2:23 You that b in the law,
1Co 1:31 the one who boasts, b in the Lord."
2Co 11:30 If I must b, I will b of the things that
Gal 6:14 never b of anything except the cross
Eph 2: 9 of works, so that no one may b.
Sir 25: 6 and their b is the fear of the Lord.

BOASTERS* → BOAST
2Co 11:13 For such b are false apostles,
2Ti 3: 2 b, arrogant, abusive, disobedient to

BOASTFUL → BOAST
Ps 5: 5 The b will not stand before your
1Co 13: 4 love is not envious or b or arrogant

BOASTING → BOAST
1Co 5: 6 Your b is not a good thing.
1Th 2:19 or crown of b before our Lord Jesus

BOAZ
Bethlehemite who showed favor to Ruth (Ru 2), married her (Ru 4). Ancestor of David (Ru 4:18-22; 1Ch 2:12-15), Jesus (Mt 1:5-16; Lk 3:23-32).

BODIES → BODY
Ro 12: 1 present your b as a living sacrifice,
1Co 6:15 that your b are members of Christ?
Heb 10:22 and our b washed with pure water.

BODILY → BODY
Lk 3:22 upon him in b form like a dove.
Col 2: 9 the whole fullness of deity dwells b,

BODY → BODIES, BODILY
2Sa 7:12 who shall come forth from your b,
Mic 6: 7 fruit of my b for the sin of my soul?
Mt 6:22 "The eye is the lamp of the b.
Mk 14:22 and said, "Take; this is my b."
Lk 12: 4 do not fear those who kill the b,
Jn 2:21 speaking of the temple of his b.
Ro 7:24 will rescue me from this b of death?
1Co 6:13 b is meant not for fornication but
15:44 It is sown a physical b, it is raised a spiritual b.
2Co 5: 8 from the b and at home with the Lord.
Eph 4: 4 There is one b and one Spirit,

BOLD → BOLDNESS
Dt 31: 6 Be strong and b; have no fear
Pr 28: 1 but the righteous are as b as a lion.

BOLDNESS → BOLD
Eph 3:12 whom we have access to God in b
Heb 4:16 approach the throne of grace with b,
1Jn 4:17 may have b on the day of judgment,

BONE → BONES
Ge 2:23 "This at last is b of my bones and
Eze 37: 7 the bones came together, b to its b.

BONES → BONE
Ex 12:46 and you shall not break any of its b.
Ps 34:20 He keeps all their b; not one of
Jn 19:36 "None of his b shall be broken."

BOOK → BOOKS
Ex 17:14 "Write this as a reminder in a b and
Dt 31:24 writing down in a b the words of
Jos 1: 8 This b of the law shall not depart
Ps 69:28 be blotted out of the b of the living;
Rev 1:11 "Write in a b what you see and
21:27 who are written in the Lamb's b
1Mc 1:57 possessing the b of the covenant,

BOOKS → BOOK
Ecc 12:12 Of making many b there is no end,
Da 1: 8 in judgment, and the b were opened.
Jn 21:25 world itself could not contain the b
Rev 20:12 the throne, and b were opened.
1Mc 1:56 The b of the law that they found
2Es 14:44 ninety-four b were written.

BOOTHS
Lev 23:34 the festival of b to the LORD.
Ezr 3: 4 kept the festival of b, as prescribed,
Zec 14:16 and to keep the festival of b.

BORE → BEAR
Isa 53:12 yet he b the sin of many,
Mt 8:17 our infirmities and b our diseases."
1Pe 2:24 He himself b our sins in his body

BORN → BEAR
Ecc 3: 2 a time to be b, and a time to die;
Isa 9: 6 For a child has been b for us,
66: 8 Shall a land be b in one day?
Lk 2:11 is b this day in the city of David
Jn 3: 7 'You must be b from above.'
1Co 15: 8 Last of all, as to one untimely b,
1Pe 1:23 You have been b anew,
1Jn 4: 7 everyone who loves is b of God

BORROW → BORROWER
Dt 28:12 to many nations, but you will not b,
Ps 37:21 The wicked b, and do not pay back,
Mt 5:42 anyone who wants to b from you.

BORROWER → BORROW
Pr 22: 7 and the b is the slave of the lender.

BOUGHT → BUY
1Co 6:20 For you were b with a price;
2Pe 2: 1 even deny the Master who b them—

BOW → BOWED, RAINBOW
Ge   9:13 I have set my **b** in the clouds,
Ex   20: 5 You shall not **b** down to them or
Ps   95: 6 O come, let us worship and **b** down,
Isa 45:23 "To me every knee shall **b**,
Ro   14:11 every knee shall **b** to me,

BOWED → BOW
Ps 146: 8 The LORD lifts up those who are **b**
Jn   19:30 he **b** his head and gave up his spirit.

BOWLS
Rev 16: 1 the seven **b** of the wrath of God."

BOY → BOYS
Jer   1: 7 to me, "Do not say, 'I am only a **b**';
Lk   2:43 **b** Jesus stayed behind in Jerusalem,

BOYS → BOY
Ex   1:18 and allowed the **b** to live?"
2Ki   2:24 and mauled forty-two of the **b**.

BRANCH → BRANCHES
Isa   4: 2 On that day the **b** of the LORD shall
     11: 1 and a **b** shall grow out of his roots.
Jer 23: 5 raise up for David a righteous **B**,
Zec   3: 8 going to bring my servant the **B**.
Jn   15: 2 every **b** in me that bears no fruit.

BRANCHES → BRANCH
Ro   11:21 if God did not spare the natural **b**,

BREAD
Ge   3:19 sweat of your face you shall eat **b**
Ex   12: 8 with unleavened **b** and bitter herbs.
     25:30 set the **b** of the Presence on the
            table
Dt   8: 3 that one does not live by **b** alone,
Ecc 11: 1 Send out your **b** upon the waters,
Mt   6:11 Give us this day our daily **b**.
Lk   4: 4 'One does not live by **b** alone.' "
Jn   6:35 Jesus said to them, "I am the **b** of
            life.
Ac   2:42 to the breaking of **b** and the prayers,
1Co 11:26 For as often as you eat this **b** and
Wis 16:20 from heaven with **b** ready to eat,
Sir 15: 3 will feed him with the **b** of learning,

BREAK → BREAKING, BROKEN,
            BROKENHEARTED
Ps   2: 9 You shall **b** them with a rod of iron,
Mt   6:19 where thieves **b** in and steal;
Jn   19:33 they did not **b** his legs.

BREASTPIECE → BREASTPLATE
Ex   28:15 You shall make a **b** of judgment,

BREASTPLATE → BREASTPIECE
Isa 59:17 He put on righteousness like a **b**,
Eph   6:14 and put on the **b** of righteousness.
Wis   5:18 he will put on righteousness as a **b**,

BREATH
Ge   2: 7 into his nostrils the **b** of life;
      6:17 all flesh in which is the **b** of life.
Job   7: 7 "Remember that my life is a **b**;
Ecc 12: 7 the **b** returns to God who gave it.
2Th   2: 8 will destroy with the **b** of his mouth,

BRIBE
Dt   16:19 for a **b** blinds the eyes of the wise
Pr   6:35 and refuses a **b** no matter how great.

BRIDE → BRIDEGROOM
Isa 62: 5 the bridegroom rejoices over the **b**,
Rev 21: 9 the **b**, the wife of the Lamb."

BRIDEGROOM → BRIDE
Mt   9:15 as long as the **b** is with them,
Jn   3:29 He who has the bride is the **b**.

BRIDLE
Ps   32: 9 must be curbed with bit and **b**,
Jas   3: 2 the whole body in check with a **b**,

BRIGHT → BRIGHTNESS
Mt   17: 5 suddenly a **b** cloud overshadowed
Rev 15: 6 robed in pure **b** linen,
     22:16 of David, the **b** morning star."

BRIGHTNESS → BRIGHT
Da   12: 3 wise shall shine like the **b** of the sky
Am   5:20 not light, and gloom with no **b** in it?

BRING → BRINGS, BROUGHT
Ge   6:19 **b** two of every kind into the ark,
Ecc 12:14 will **b** every deed into judgment,
Jer 24: 6 and I will **b** them back to this land.
Mt   10:34 not come to **b** peace, but a sword.
Ro   10:15 the feet of those who **b** good news!"

BRINGS → BRING
1Sa   2: 6 The LORD kills and **b** to life;
Jas   5:20 that whoever **b** back a sinner

BROKE → BREAK
Ex   32:19 tablets from his hands and **b** them
2Ch 36:19 **b** down the wall of Jerusalem,
Jer 31:32 a covenant that they **b**,
Mt   14:19 and blessed and **b** the loaves,
1Co 11:24 he **b** it and said, "This is my body
1Mc   3: 5 and pursued those who **b** the law;

BROKEN → BREAK
Ne   1: 3 the wall of Jerusalem is **b** down,
Ps   51:17 acceptable to God is a **b** spirit;
Mt   15:37 they took up the **b** pieces left over,
Lk   20:18 who falls on that stone will be **b**
Ro   11:20 were **b** off because of their unbelief.

BROKENHEARTED → BREAK, HEART
Ps 147: 3 He heals the **b**, and binds up their
Isa 61: 1 the oppressed, to bind up the **b**,

BRONZE
Nu   21: 9 look at the serpent of **b** and live.
Dt   28:23 The sky over your head shall be **b**,
Da   10: 6 legs like the gleam of burnished **b**,
Rev   1:15 his feet were like burnished **b**,

BROOD
Mt   3: 7 he said to them, "You **b** of vipers!
Lk   13:34 a hen gathers her **b** under her
            wings,

BROTHER → BROTHER'S, BROTHER-IN-
            LAW, BROTHERS
Ge   4: 8 Cain rose up against his **b** Abel,
Mt   5:24 first be reconciled to your **b** or
     10:21 **B** will betray **b** to death,

BROTHER'S → BROTHER
Dt   25: 7 has no desire to marry his **b** widow,
Mk   6:18 lawful for you to have your **b** wife."

BROTHER-IN-LAW* → BROTHER
Ge   38: 8 and perform the duty of a **b** to her;

BROTHERS → BROTHER
Ge   9:25 lowest of slaves shall he be to his **b**.
     37:11 So his **b** were jealous of him,
Mk   3:33 "Who are my mother and my **b**?"
Lk   22:32 turned back, strengthen your **b**."
Heb   2:11 not ashamed to call them **b** and

BROUGHT → BRING
Ge   15: 7 you from Ur of the Chaldeans,
Jdg   2: 1 "I **b** you up from Egypt, and **b** you
            into
2Ch 36:18 all these he **b** to Babylon.
Ezr   6: 5 **b** back to the temple in Jerusalem,
Ro   6:13 who have been **b** from death to life,
1Ti   6: 7 for we **b** nothing into the world,

BUILD → BUILDER, BUILDERS, BUILDING,
            BUILDS, BUILT, REBUILD
Ge   11: 4 "Come, let us **b** ourselves a city,
Dt   6:10 fine, large cities that you did not **b**,
Ps 127: 1 those who **b** it labor in vain.
Isa 57:14 said, "**B** up, **b** up, prepare the way,
Mt   16:18 and on this rock I will **b** my church,
     27:40 destroy the temple and **b** it in three
1Co   3:10 must choose with care how to **b**
     10:23 are lawful," but not all things **b** up.

BUILDER → BUILD
Heb   3: 4 but the **b** of all things is God.)
     11:10 whose architect and **b** is God.

BUILDERS → BUILD
Ps 118:22 The stone that the **b** rejected has
Mk   12:10 'The stone that the **b** rejected has
1Pe   2: 7 "The stone that the **b** rejected has

BUILDING → BUILD
1Co   3: 9 you are God's field, God's **b**.
2Co   5: 1 we have a **b** from God,
Eph   4:12 for **b** up the body of Christ,

BUILDS → BUILD
Ps 127: 1 Unless the LORD **b** the house,
Pr   14: 1 The wise woman **b** her house,
1Co   8: 1 Knowledge puffs up, but love **b** up.

BUILT → BUILD
1Ki   6:14 Solomon **b** the house, and finished
Ne   7: 1 the wall had been **b** and I had set up
Pr   9: 1 Wisdom has **b** her house,
Da   9:25 sixty-two weeks it shall be **b** again
Eph   2:20 **b** upon the foundation of the
Tob 13:16 Jerusalem will be **b** as his house for
1Mc   4:47 **b** a new altar like the former one.

BULL → BULLS
Ps   50: 9 will not accept a **b** from your house,

BULLS → BULL
1Ch 29:21 a thousand **b**, a thousand rams,
Ps   22:12 **b** encircle me, strong **b** of Bashan
Isa   1:11 I do not delight in the blood of **b**,
Heb 10: 4 it is impossible for the blood of **b**

BURDEN → BURDENS, BURDENSOME
Ps   55:22 Cast your **b** on the LORD,
Mt   11:30 my yoke is easy, and my **b** is light."
2Co   5: 4 in this tent, we groan under our **b**,

BURDENS → BURDEN
Ex   6: 6 free you from the **b** of the Egyptians
Lk   11:46 you load people with **b** hard to bear,
Gal   6: 2 Bear one another's **b**, and

BURDENSOME → BURDEN
1Jn   5: 3 And his commandments are not **b**,

BURIED → BURY
Ro   6: 4 have been **b** with him by baptism
1Co 15: 4 he was **b**, and that he was raised on

BURN → BURNED, BURNING, BURNT
Ex   21:25 **b** for **b**, wound for wound,
Ps   79: 5 Will your jealous wrath **b** like fire?
Jer   7:31 to **b** their sons and their daughters
Mal   4: 1 the day that comes shall **b** them up,
Lk   3:17 but the chaff he will **b** with

BURNED → BURN
Ex   3: 3 and see why the bush is not **b** up."
Jn   15: 6 thrown into the fire, and **b**.
1Co   3:15 If the work is **b** up, the builder will

BURNING → BURN
Lk   24:32 "Were not our hearts **b** within us

BURNT → BURN
Ex   40: 6 You shall set the altar of **b** offering
Lev   1: 3 If the offering is a **b** offering from
1Sa 15:22 LORD as great delight in **b** offerings
Ps   51:16 if I were to give a **b** offering,
Da   8:11 it took the regular **b** offering away
Hos   6: 6 the knowledge of God rather than **b**
Mic   6: 6 Shall I come before him with **b**
Mk   12:33 more important than all whole **b**
1Mc   1:45 to forbid **b** offerings and sacrifices
      4:56 and joyfully offered **b** offerings;

BURY → BURIED
Lk   9:60 "Let the dead **b** their own dead;

BUSH
Ex   3: 2 he looked, and the **b** was blazing,
Jnh   4: 6 The LORD God appointed a **b**,

BUY → BOUGHT, BUYS
Pr   23:23 **B** truth, and do not sell it;
Isa   55: 1 b wine and milk without money
Rev   3:18 to **b** from me gold refined by fire so

BUYS → BUY
Pr   31:16 She considers a field and **b** it;
Mt   13:44 sells all that he has and **b** that field.

BYWORD → WORD
Dt   28:37 and a **b** among all the peoples where
Job   17: 6 He has made me a **b** of the peoples,
Ps   44:14 made us a **b** among the nations,

C

CAESAREA
Mt   16:13 came into the district of C Philippi,
Ac   10: 1 C there was a man named Cornelius
   25: 4 that Paul was being kept at C,

CAIAPHAS*
High priest at trial of Jesus (Mt 26:3, 57; Lk 3:2;
Jn 11:49; 18:13-28); at trial of disciples (Ac 4:6).

CAIN*
Firstborn of Adam (Ge 4:1), murdered brother
Abel (Ge 4:1-25; Heb 11:4; 1Jn 3:12; Jude 11; 4Mc
18:11).

CALAMITIES → CALAMITY
1Sa   10:19 who saves you from all your **c** and
2Co   6: 4 in afflictions, hardships, c,
   12:10 and **c** for the sake of Christ;

CALAMITY → CALAMITIES
Pr   1:26 I also will laugh at your c;
Da   9:13 all this **c** has come upon us.
Hab   3:16 wait quietly for the day of **c** to come

CALEB
Judahite who spied out Canaan (Nu 13:6); allowed to enter land (Nu 13:30-14:38; Dt 1:36; Sir
46:7-9; 1Mc 2:56). Given Hebron (Jos 14:6-
15:19).

CALF → CALVES
Ex   32: 4 and cast an image of a c;
Lk   15:23 And get the fatted **c** and kill it,

CALL → CALLED, CALLING
Dt   4:26 I **c** heaven and earth to witness
1Sa   3: 5 But he said, "I did not c; lie down
1Ki   18:24 you **c** on the name of your god and I
   will **c** on the name of the LORD;
1Ch   16: 8 thanks to the LORD, **c** on his name,
Ps   61: 2 From the end of the earth I **c** to
   you,
Pr   8: 1 Does not wisdom c, and does
Isa   65:24 Before they **c** I will answer,
Mt   9:13 to **c** not the righteous but sinners."
Lk   6:46 "Why do you **c** me 'Lord, Lord,'
Jn   15:15 I do not **c** you servants any longer,
Ro   10:12 and is generous to all who **c** on him.
Php   3:14 goal for the prize of the heavenly **c**

CALLED → CALL
2Sa   22: 7 In my distress I **c** upon the LORD;
Isa   43: 1 I have **c** you by name, you are mine.
Mt   23: 8 But you are not to be **c** rabbi,
1Co   7:15 It is to peace that God has **c** you.
Eph   1:18 the hope to which he has **c** you,
1Jn   3: 1 that we should be **c** children of God;

CALLING → CALL
Ro   11:29 and the **c** of God are irrevocable.
Eph   4: 1 lead a life worthy of the **c** to which

CALVES → CALF
1Ki   12:28 and made two **c** of gold.
Mal   4: 2 go out leaping like **c** from the stall.

CAMEL
Mt   23:24 strain out a gnat but swallow a c!
Mk   10:25 **c** to go through the eye of a needle

CANA
Jn   2: 1 there was a wedding in C

CANAAN → CANAANITE, CANAANITES
Ge   9:25 "Cursed be C; lowest of slaves
Nu   13: 2 "Send men to spy out the land of C,
1Ch   16:18 "To you I will give the land of C

CANAANITE → CANAAN
Ge   28: 1 not marry one of the C women.
Mt   15:22 a C woman from that region came

CANAANITES → CANAAN
Ex   33: 2 I will drive out the C, the Amorites,
Jdg   3: 5 So the Israelites lived among the C,

CAPERNAUM
Mt   4:13 and made his home in C by the sea,
Jn   6:59 was teaching in the synagogue at C.

CAPTIVE → CAPTIVITY
2Ki   15:29 he carried the people **c** to Assyria.
   24:16 king of Babylon brought **c** to
Ro   7:23 making me **c** to the law of sin
Eph   4: 8 he made captivity itself a c;

CAPTIVITY → CAPTIVE
Dt   28:41 for they shall go into c.
Ezr   8:35 those who had come from c,

CARE → CAREFUL, CARELESS, CARES, CARING
Ps   8: 4 mortals that you **c** for them?
Heb   2: 6 or mortals, that you **c** for them?
Jas   1:27 to **c** for orphans and widows in

CAREFUL → CARE
Dt   4:23 So be **c** not to forget the covenant
Jos   1: 8 you may be **c** to act in accordance
Eph   5:15 Be **c** then how you live,

CARELESS* → CARE
Pr   14:16 the fool throws off restraint and is **c**.
Mt   12:36 to give an account for every **c** word

CARES → CARE
Lk   8:14 they are choked by the **c** and riches
1Pe   5: 7 on him, because he **c** for you.

CARMEL
1Ki   18:20 assembled the prophets at Mount C.

CARPENTER'S*
Mt   13:55 Is not this the **c** son?

CARRY
Ps   28: 9 their shepherd, and **c** them forever.
Isa   40:11 and **c** them in his bosom,
Lk   14:27 does not **c** the cross and follow me

CASE
Job   13: 3 and I desire to argue my **c** with God.
Isa   41:21 Set forth your c, says the LORD;
Lk   12:58 make an effort to settle the c,
Jn   18:38 "I find no **c** against him.

CAST
Ex   34:17 You shall not make **c** idols.
Est   9:24 Jews to destroy them, and had **c** Pur
Ps   22:18 and for my clothing they **c** lots.
   55:22 C your burden on the LORD,
Pr   16:33 The lot is **c** into the lap,
Mk   3:23 "How can Satan **c** out Satan?
Jn   19:24 and for my clothing they **c** lots."
1Pe   5: 7 C all your anxiety on him,

CATTLE
Ge   1:25 and the **c** of every kind,
Ps   50:10 the **c** on a thousand hills.

CAUGHT
2Co   12: 2 was **c** up to the third heaven—
1Th   4:17 be **c** up in the clouds together with

CAUSE
Job   5: 8 and to God I would commit my c.
Ps   9: 4 For you have maintained my just c;
   140:12 LORD maintains the **c** of the needy,
Jn   15:25 'They hated me without a c.'

CAVE
Ge   23: 9 he may give me the **c** of Machpelah,
1Sa   22: 1 and escaped to the **c** of Adullam;
   24: 3 in the innermost parts of the c.
1Ki   18: 4 hid them fifty to a c,

CEASE
Ge   8:22 winter, day and night, shall not c."
Jer   31:36 If this fixed order were ever to **c**
1Co   13: 8 as for tongues, they will c;

CEDAR
2Sa   7: 2 See now, I am living in a house of c,
Ps   92:12 and grow like a **c** in Lebanon.

CELEBRATE
Lev   23:37 shall **c** as times of holy convocation,
1Co   5: 8 Therefore, let us **c** the festival,

CENSER
Lev   10: 1 Nadab and Abihu, each took his c,
Eze   8:11 Each had his **c** in his hand,
Rev   8: 3 Another angel with a golden **c** came

CENSUS
Nu   1: 2 Take a **c** of the whole congregation
2Sa   24: 2 and take a **c** of the people,

CENTURION
Mt   8: 5 he entered Capernaum, a **c** came to
Lk   23:47 the **c** saw what had taken place,
Ac   10: 1 a man named Cornelius, a **c**

CEPHAS* → =PETER
Name given to the apostle Peter (Jn 1:42; 1Co
1:12; 3:22; 9:5; 15:5; Gal 1:18; 2:9, 11, 14).

CERTIFICATE
Dt   24: 1 and so he writes her a **c** of divorce,
Mt   5:31 let him give her a **c** of divorce.'
Mk   10: 4 a man to write a **c** of dismissal

CHAFF
Ps   1: 4 are like **c** that the wind drives away.
Lk   3:17 **c** he will burn with unquenchable

CHAINED* → CHAINS
2Ti   2: 9 the point of being **c** like a criminal.
   But the word of God is not c.

CHAINS → CHAINED
Eph   6:20 for which I am an ambassador in c.
Heb   11:36 and even **c** and imprisonment.
2Pe   2: 4 them to **c** of deepest darkness

CHALDEANS
Ge   15: 7 who brought you from Ur of the C,
Da   1: 4 the literature and language of the C.

CHANGE → CHANGED, CHANGERS
Ex   32:12 **c** your mind and do not bring
Nu   23:19 a mortal, that he should **c** his mind.
1Sa   15:29 will not recant or **c** his mind;
Ps   46: 2 not fear, though the earth should c,
Jer   18: 8 I will **c** my mind about the disaster
Jas   1:17 is no variation or shadow due to c.

CHANGED → CHANGE
1Co   15:51 will not all die, but we will all be c,
Heb   1:12 and like clothing they will be c.

CHANGERS → CHANGE
Mk   11:15 overturned the tables of the money **c**
Jn   2:15 poured out the coins of the money **c**

CHARACTER
Ro   5: 4 endurance produces c, and **c**
   produces

CHARGE
Mt   25:21 I will put you in **c** of many things;
Mk   15:26 The inscription of the **c** against him
Ro   8:33 will bring any **c** against God's elect?
1Co   9:18 I may make the gospel free of c;

CHARIOT → CHARIOTS
2Ki   2:11 a **c** of fire and horses of fire
Ps   104: 3 you make the clouds your c,

CHARIOTS → CHARIOT
Ex 14:28 waters returned and covered the c
Zec 6: 1 and saw four c coming out from

CHARM
Pr 31:30 C is deceitful, and beauty is vain,
Sir 7:19 for her c is worth more than gold.
26:15 A modest wife adds c to c,

CHASTISEMENT → CHASTISES
La 4: 6 the c of my people has been greater
Sir 16:12 Great as his mercy, so also is his c;

CHASTISES* → CHASTISEMENT
Heb 12: 6 and c every child whom he accepts.

CHEEK
Ps 3: 7 you strike all my enemies on the c;
Mt 5:39 if anyone strikes you on the right c,

CHEERFUL
Pr 15:13 A glad heart makes a c countenance,
17:22 A c heart is a good medicine,
2Co 9: 7 for God loves a c giver.
Jas 5:13 Are any c? They should sing songs

CHEMOSH
1Ki 11: 7 Solomon built a high place for C
Jer 48: 7 C shall go out into exile,

CHERUB → CHERUBIM
2Ch 3:11 touched the wing of the other c;
Ps 18:10 He rode on a c, and flew;
Eze 10:14 the first face was that of the c,
28:14 an anointed c as guardian I placed

CHERUBIM → CHERUB
Ge 3:24 the garden of Eden he placed the c,
Ex 25:18 You shall make two c of gold;
Ps 80: 1 You who are enthroned upon the c,
Heb 9: 5 the c of glory overshadowing the

CHIEF
Ps 118:22 has become the c cornerstone.
Mk 15: 3 the c priests accused him of many
1Pe 5: 4 And when the c shepherd appears,

CHILD → CHILDBEARING, CHILDISH, CHILDREN
Ge 17:17 c be born to a man who is a hundred
1Ki 3: 7 although I am only a little c;
Isa 11: 6 and a little c shall lead them.
49:15 Can a woman forget her nursing c,
Hos 11: 1 When Israel was a c, I loved him,
Mt 1:18 from the Holy Spirit.
Mk 10:15 the kingdom of God as a little c
Lk 2:12 you will find a c wrapped in bands
1Co 13:11 When I was a c, I spoke like a c,
Gal 4: 7 So you are no longer a slave but a c,
Rev 12: 4 that he might devour her c as soon

CHILDBEARING* → CHILD, BEAR
Ge 3:16 greatly increase your pangs in c;
1Ti 2:15 Yet she will be saved through c,

CHILDISH* → CHILD
1Co 13:11 an adult, I put an end to c ways.

CHILDREN → CHILD
Ex 12:26 And when your c ask you,
Dt 6: 7 Recite them to your c and talk about
11:19 Teach them to your c, talking about
Pr 22: 6 Train c in the right way, and when
Mt 3: 9 stones to raise up c to Abraham.
Lk 18:16 "Let the little c come to me,
Jn 1:12 he gave power to become c of God,
Ro 8:14 by the Spirit of God are c of God.
1Co 14:20 do not be c in your thinking,
Eph 6: 4 do not provoke your c to anger,
Heb 12: 7 God is treating you as c;
1Jn 3:10 The c of God and the c of the devil
Sir 30: 1 concerning c He who loves his son

CHOOSE → CHOOSES, CHOSE, CHOSEN
Dt 12:14 at the place that the LORD will c
30:19 C life so that you and your

CHOOSES → CHOOSE
Ro 9:18 he has mercy on whomever he c,

CHOSE → CHOOSE
Dt 4:37 he c their descendants after them.
Ne 9: 7 God who c Abram and brought him
Mk 13:20 for the sake of the elect, whom he c,
1Co 1:27 God c what is foolish in the world

CHOSEN → CHOOSE
Isa 42: 1 my servant, whom I uphold, my c,
Mt 22:14 For many are called, but few are c."
Ro 11: 5 there is a remnant, c by grace.
1Pe 2: 6 a cornerstone c and precious;
2: 9 you are a c race, a royal priesthood,

CHRIST → CHRIST'S, CHRISTIAN, CHRISTIANS, MESSIAH
Jn 4:25 Messiah is coming" (who is called C).
Ro 5: 6 right time C died for the ungodly.
8:35 will separate us from the love of C?
10: 4 For C is the end of the law so that
1Co 1:23 but we proclaim C crucified,
3:11 that foundation is Jesus C.
11: 1 Be imitators of me, as I am of C.
15: 3 C died for our sins in accordance
Gal 5: 1 For freedom C has set us free.
Eph 4:15 into him who is the head, into C,
Php 1:21 to me, living is C and dying is gain.
2:11 should confess that Jesus C is Lord,
Col 1:27 C in you, the hope of glory.
Rev 20: 4 reigned with C a thousand years.

CHRIST'S → CHRIST
Col 1:24 what is lacking in C afflictions
1Pe 4:13 as you are sharing C sufferings,

CHRISTIAN* → CHRIST
Ac 26:28 persuading me to become a C?"
1Pe 4:16 Yet if any of you suffers as a C,

CHRISTIANS* → CHRIST
Ac 11:26 the disciples were first called "C."

CHURCH
Mt 16:18 and on this rock I will build my c,
Ac 8: 1 persecution began against the c
1Co 12:28 has appointed in the c first apostles,
14: 4 those who prophesy build up the c.
Col 1:18 He is the head of the body, the c;

CIRCUMCISE → CIRCUMCISED, CIRCUMCISION
Ge 17:11 shall c the flesh of your foreskins,
Dt 10:16 C, then, the foreskin of your heart,
Lk 1:59 the eighth day they came to c the
Jn 7:22 and you c a man on the sabbath.

CIRCUMCISED → CIRCUMCISE
Ge 17:10 Every male among you shall be c.
Ac 15: 1 c according to the custom of Moses,
Gal 6:13 c do not themselves obey the law,
Col 2:11 also you were c with a spiritual
1Mc 1:60 the women who had their children c,

CIRCUMCISION → CIRCUMCISE
Ro 2:29 and real c is a matter of the heart—
Gal 5: 6 For in Christ Jesus neither c

CISTERN
Pr 5:15 Drink water from your own c,
Jer 38: 6 Jeremiah and threw him into the c

CITIES → CITY
Ge 19:25 and he overthrew those c,
Jos 20: 2 'Appoint the c of refuge,
Rev 16:19 and the c of the nations fell.

CITIZENSHIP
Php 3:20 But our c is in heaven,

CITY → CITIES
1Ch 11: 7 it was called the c of David.
Ps 127: 1 Unless the LORD guards the c,
Pr 31:31 her works praise her in the c gates.
La 1: 1 lonely sits the c that once was full
Da 9:24 for your people and your holy c;
Mt 5:14 A c built on a hill cannot be hid.
Heb 12:22 Zion and to the c of the living God,
Rev 21: 2 I saw the holy c, the new Jerusalem,

CLAP
Ps 47: 1 C your hands, all you peoples;
Isa 55:12 all the trees of the field shall c their

CLAY
Isa 45: 9 Does the c say to the one who
Jer 18: 6 Just like the c in the potter's hand,
Da 2:33 its feet partly of iron and partly of c.
Ro 9:21 Has the potter no right over the c,
2Co 4: 7 But we have this treasure in c jars,
2Ti 2:20 and silver but also of wood and c,

CLEAN → CLEANSE, CLEANSING
Ge 7: 2 seven pairs of all c animals,
Lev 10:10 and between the unclean and the c;
Ps 51: 7 with hyssop, and I shall be c;
Mk 7:19 (Thus he declared all foods c.)
Jn 13:10 you are c, though not all of you."
Ac 10:15 "What God has made c,
Heb 10:22 with our hearts sprinkled c from

CLEANSE → CLEAN
Ps 51: 2 and c me from my sin.
1Jn 1: 9 c us from all unrighteousness.
Sir 38:10 and c your heart from all sin.

CLEANSING → CLEAN
Eph 5:26 by c her with the washing of water
2Pe 1: 9 and is forgetful of the c of past sins.

CLEAR → CLEARING
Ps 19: 8 the commandment of the LORD is c,
Na 1: 3 LORD will by no means c the guilty.
1Ti 3: 9 of the faith with a c conscience.
Rev 21:18 the city is pure gold, c as glass.

CLEARING* → CLEAR
Ex 34: 7 yet by no means c the guilty,

CLEFT
Ex 33:22 I will put you in a c of the rock,
Dt 14: 6 the hoof and has the hoof c in two,

CLINGS
Ge 2:24 and his mother and c to his wife,
Ps 119:25 My soul c to the dust;
Heb 12: 1 weight and the sin that c so closely,

CLOAK
Ex 4: 6 "Put your hand inside your c."
22:26 you take your neighbor's c in pawn,
1Sa 24: 4 cut off a corner of Saul's c.
Mk 15:17 And they clothed him in a purple c,
Heb 1:12 like a c you will roll them up,

CLOTH → SACKCLOTH
Isa 64: 6 righteous deeds are like a filthy c.
Lk 2: 7 and wrapped him in bands of c,

CLOTHE → CLOTHED, CLOTHES, CLOTHING
Col 3:14 Above all, c yourselves with love,
1Pe 5: 5 you must c yourselves with humility

CLOTHED → CLOTHE
2Co 5: 2 longing to be c with our heavenly
Gal 3:27 have c yourselves with Christ.
Rev 12: 1 a woman c with the sun,

CLOTHES → CLOTHE
Zec 3: 3 Joshua was dressed with filthy c as
Lk 8:44 and touched the fringe of his c,

CLOTHING → CLOTHE
Ps 22:18 and for my c they cast lots.
Mt 25:36 I was naked and you gave me c,
Jn 19:24 and for my c they cast lots."

CLOUD → CLOUDS
Ex   13:21 went in front of them in a pillar of c
1Ki   8:10 a c filled the house of the LORD,
         18:44 a little c no bigger than a person's
Eze   10: 4 the house was filled with the c,
Mk   9: 7 Then a c overshadowed them,
Lk   21:27 'the Son of Man coming in a c'
Heb   12: 1 by so great a c of witnesses,
Rev   14:14 on the c was one like the Son of
               Man,

CLOUDS → CLOUD
Ge   9:13 I have set my bow in the c,
Da   7:13 being coming with the c of heaven.
Mt   24:30 'the Son of Man coming on the c of
1Th   4:17 be caught up in the c together with
Rev   1: 7 He is coming with the c;
2Es   13: 3 this man flew with the c of heaven;

CLUSTER
Nu   13:23 from there a branch with a single c

COALS
Ps   11: 6 On the wicked he will rain c of fire
Pr   25:22 will heap c of fire on their heads,
Ro   12:20 will heap burning c on their heads."

CODE*
Ro   2:27 condemn you that have the written c
       7: 6 slaves not under the old written c

COIN*
Mt   17:27 open its mouth, you will find a c;
       22:19 Show me the c used for the tax."
Lk   15: 9 I have found the c that I had lost.'

COLD
Zec   14: 6 that day there shall not be either c
Mt   24:12 the love of many will grow c.
Rev   3:16 lukewarm, and neither c nor hot,

COLLECTOR → COLLECTORS
Mt   10: 3 Thomas and Matthew the tax c;
Lk   18:10 one a Pharisee and the other a tax c.
       19: 2 he was a chief tax c and was rich.

COLLECTORS → COLLECTOR
Mt   5:46 Do not even the tax c do the same?
       11:19 a friend of tax c and sinners!'

COLT
Ge   49:11 his donkey's c to the choice vine,
Zec   9: 9 and riding on a donkey, on a c,
Jn   12:15 coming, sitting on a donkey's c!"

COME → COMES, COMING
Ps   144: 5 your heavens, O LORD, and c down;
Isa   59:20 And he will c to Zion as Redeemer,
Zec   14: 5 Then the LORD my God will c,
Mt   6:10 Your kingdom c. Your will be done,
Lk   7:20 'Are you the one who is to c,
Jn   6:37 the Father gives me will c to me,
1Co   16:22 Our Lord, c!
Rev   1: 4 who is and who was and who is to c,
       22:20 Amen. C, Lord Jesus!

COMES → COME
Ps   118:26 one who c in the name of the LORD.
Lk   19:38 "Blessed is the king who c in the
Jn   14: 6 No one c to the Father except
               through

COMFORT → COMFORTED, COMFORTER,
               COMFORTERS, COMFORTS
Ps   23: 4 your rod and your staff—they c me.
Isa   40: 1 C, O c my people, says your God.

COMFORTED → COMFORT
Ps   86:17 LORD, have helped me and c me.
Isa   49:13 For the LORD has c his people,
Jer   31:15 she refuses to be c for her children,
Mt   5: 4 those who mourn, for they will be c.

COMFORTER* → COMFORT
La   1:16 for a c is far from me,

COMFORTERS → COMFORT
Job   16: 2 miserable c are you all.
Ps   69:20 and for c, but I found none.

COMFORTS → COMFORT
Isa   66:13 As a mother c her child, so I will

COMING → COME
Mal   3: 2 But who can endure the day of his
               c,
Heb   10:37 is c will come and will not delay;
2Pe   3: 4 "Where is the promise of his c?
Rev   22:20 "Surely I am c soon."

COMMAND → COMMANDED,
               COMMANDING, COMMANDMENT,
               COMMANDMENTS
Ex   34:11 Observe what I c you today.
Dt   1:26 rebelled against the c of the LORD
Jdg   2: 2 But you have not obeyed my c.

COMMANDED → COMMAND
Ge   7: 5 Noah did all that the LORD had c
Ex   40:32 as the LORD had c Moses.
Jos   1:16 "All that you have c us we will do,
Mt   28:20 to obey everything that I have c you.
Jn   14:31 but I do as the Father has c me,

COMMANDING → COMMAND
Dt   4:40 c you today for your own well-being
       30:11 c you today is not too hard for you,

COMMANDMENT → COMMAND
Dt   6: 1 Now this is the c—the statutes
Ps   19: 8 c of the LORD is clear,
Mt   22:38 This is the greatest and first c.
Ro   7:12 and the c is holy and just and good.
Gal   5:14 law is summed up in a single c,
1Jn   3:23 this is his c, that we should believe

COMMANDMENTS → COMMAND
Ex   20: 6 those who love me and keep my c.
Dt   4:13 to observe, that is, the ten c;
Ps   119:66 for I believe in your c.
Pr   10: 8 The wise of heart will heed c,
Ecc   12:13 Fear God, and keep his c;
Mt   22:40 On these two c hang all the law and
Jn   14:15 If you love me, you will keep my c.
1Co   7:19 obeying the c of God is everything.
1Jn   5: 3 And his c are not burdensome,
Rev   14:12 those who keep the c of God and
Sir   1:26 If you desire wisdom, keep the c,
1Mc   2:19 and have chosen to obey his c,

COMMENDABLE* → COMMENDATION
Php   4: 8 whatever is pleasing, whatever is c,

COMMENDATION* → COMMENDABLE,
               COMMENDED
1Co   4: 5 each one will receive c from God.

COMMENDED → COMMENDATION
2Co   6: 4 but as servants of God we have c
Heb   11:39 though they were c for their faith,

COMMIT → COMMITS
Dt   5:18 Neither shall you c adultery.
2Ki   17:21 and made them c great sin.
Ps   31: 5 Into your hand I c my spirit;
Pr   16: 3 C your work to the LORD,
Mt   5:27 'You shall not c adultery.'

COMMITS → COMMIT
Jn   8:34 who c sin is a slave to sin.
Jas   4:17 to do and fails to do it, c sin.

COMMON
Lev   10:10 between the holy and the c,
Eze   22:26 between the holy and the c,
Ac   2:44 and had all things in c;
1Co   10:13 has overtaken you that is not c
       12: 7 of the Spirit for the c good.

COMMUNION*
2Co   13:13 the c of the Holy Spirit be with all

COMPANY
1Co   15:33 "Bad c ruins good morals."

COMPARE → COMPARING
Pr   8:11 all that you may desire cannot c
Isa   40:18 or what likeness c with him?
Lk   7:31 I c the people of this generation,

COMPARING* → COMPARE
Ro   8:18 of this present time are not worth c

COMPASSION → COMPASSIONATE
Dt   32:36 will vindicate his people, have c
Ps   103:13 As a father has c for his children,
Isa   54: 8 with everlasting love I will have c
Jer   12:15 I will again have c on them,
Hos   11: 8 my c grows warm and tender.
Mt   14:14 had c for them and cured their sick.
Ro   9:15 I will have c on whom I have c."
Col   3:12 clothe yourselves with c, kindness,
Sir   18:13 the c of the Lord is for every living

COMPASSIONATE → COMPASSION
Ex   22:27 I will listen, for I am c.
Jas   5:11 how the Lord is c and merciful.
Sir   2:11 For the Lord is c and merciful;

COMPETE → COMPETING, COMPETITION
Jer   12: 5 how will you c with horses?
1Co   9:24 that in a race the runners all c,

COMPETING* → COMPETE
Gal   5:26 c against one another, envying one
2Ti   2: 5 is crowned without c according to

COMPLAIN → COMPLAINING,
               COMPLAINT
Nu   14:27 shall this wicked congregation c
Jer   2:29 Why do you c against me?
1Co   10:10 And do not c as some of them did,

COMPLAINING → COMPLAIN
Ex   16: 7 has heard your c against the LORD.
1Pe   4: 9 hospitable to one another without c.

COMPLAINT → COMPLAIN
Job   10: 1 I will give free utterance to my c;
Ps   142: 2 I pour out my c before him;
Hab   2: 1 he will answer concerning my c.
Col   3:13 if anyone has a c against another,

COMPLETE → COMPLETED,
               COMPLETION
Ge   15:16 iniquity of the Amorites is not yet c
Lev   23: 3 seventh day is a sabbath of c rest,
Jn   4:34 him who sent me and to c his work.
Rev   6:11 until the number would be c

COMPLETED → COMPLETE
Jer   25:12 Then after seventy years are c,
Da   11:36 until the period of wrath is c,

COMPLETION → COMPLETE
Php   1: 6 work among you will bring it to c
Jas   2:22 faith was brought to c by the works.

CONCEALED
Lk   9:45 its meaning was c from them,
Sir   11: 4 his works are c from humankind.

CONCEIT → CONCEITED
Php   2: 3 nothing from selfish ambition or c,
1Ti   3: 6 he may be puffed up with c and fall
Sir   3:24 For their c has led many astray,

CONCEITED* → CONCEIT
Gal   5:26 Let us not become c, competing
1Ti   6: 4 is c, understanding nothing,

CONCEIVE → CONCEIVED
Mt   1:23 the virgin shall c and bear a son,
Lk   1:31 you will c in your womb and bear

CONCEIVED → CONCEIVE
1Co   2: 9 ear heard, nor the human heart c,
Jas   1:15 desire has c, it gives birth to sin,

CONDEMN → CONDEMNATION, CONDEMNED
Job 10: 2 I will say to God, Do not c me;
Ps 109:31 save them from those who would c
Lk 11:31 of this generation and c them,
Jn 3:17 not send the Son into the world to c
Ro 8:34 Who is to c?
1Jn 3:21 Beloved, if our hearts do not c us,

CONDEMNATION → CONDEMN
Mk 12:40 They will receive the greater c."
Ro 5:18 one man's trespass led to c for all,
1Ti 3: 6 fall into the c of the devil.
Jas 5:12 so that you may not fall under c.

CONDEMNED → CONDEMN
Mt 12:37 and by your words you will be c."
Lk 24:20 handed him over to be c to death
Jn 3:18 Those who believe in him are not c;
16:11 the ruler of this world has been c.
1Co 11:32 disciplined so that we may not be c

CONDUCT
Eze 22:31 returned their c upon their heads,
Ro 13: 3 For rulers are not a terror to good c,
1Pe 1:15 be holy yourselves in all your c;
Tob 4:14 and discipline yourself in all your c.
Sir 37:17 The mind is the root of all c;

CONFESS → CONFESSES, CONFESSION
Lev 5: 5 you shall c the sin that you have
16:21 c over it all the iniquities of the
Ps 38:18 c my iniquity; I am sorry for my sin.
Php 2:11 should c that Jesus Christ is Lord,
1Jn 1: 9 If we c our sins, he who is faithful
Rev 3: 5 will c your name before my Father
Sir 4:26 Do not be ashamed to c your sins,

CONFESSES → CONFESS
Ro 10:10 c with the mouth and so is saved.
1Jn 2:23 who c the Son has the Father also.

CONFESSION → CONFESS
Da 9: 4 to the LORD my God and made c,
1Ti 6:12 for which you made the good c in
Heb 4:14 let us hold fast to our c.

CONFIDENCE
Ps 118: 8 in the LORD than to put c in mortals.
Php 3: 3 and have no c in the flesh—
Heb 10:19 we have c to enter the sanctuary

CONFIRM → CONFIRMED
2Sa 7:25 c it forever; do as you have
Ps 119:38 C to your servant your promise,
Ro 15: 8 that he might c the promises given

CONFIRMED → CONFIRM
Ps 105:10 which he c to Jacob as a statute,
2Pe 1:19 the prophetic message more fully c.

CONFORMED*
Ro 8:29 predestined to be c to the image of
12: 2 Do not be c to this world,
Php 3:21 may be c to the body of his glory,
1Pe 1:14 do not be c to the desires that you

CONFUSE → CONFUSION
Ge 11: 7 go down, and c their language there,

CONFUSION → CONFUSE
Ex 23:27 and will throw into c all the people
Dt 28:28 blindness, and c of mind;
Ps 44: 7 and have put to c those who hate us.

CONGREGATION
Lev 4:13 c of Israel errs unintentionally
Nu 1: 2 a census of the whole c of Israelites,
Ps 1: 5 nor sinners in the c of the righteous;
Heb 2:12 the midst of the c I will praise you."

CONQUER → CONQUERED, CONQUERORS, CONQUERS
Rev 17:14 and the Lamb will c them,
21: 7 who c will inherit these things,

CONQUERED → CONQUER
Jn 16:33 take courage; I have c the world!"
Heb 11:33 who through faith c kingdoms,
1Jn 2:13 because you have c the evil one.
Rev 15: 2 who had c the beast and its image

CONQUERORS → CONQUER
Ro 8:37 all these things we are more than c

CONQUERS → CONQUER
1Jn 5: 4 victory that c the world, our faith.
Rev 2: 7 To everyone who c, I will give

CONSCIENCE
Ro 2:15 their own c also bears witness;
1Co 8: 7 and their c, being weak, is defiled.
1Ti 1: 5 a good c, and sincere faith.
Heb 9:14 purify our c from dead works to
1Pe 3:21 as an appeal to God for a good c,

CONSECRATE → CONSECRATED
Ex 13: 2 C to me all the firstborn;
40: 9 and c it and all its furniture,

CONSECRATED → CONSECRATE
Lev 8:30 Thus he c Aaron and his vestments,
2Ch 7:16 now I have chosen and c this house
Ne 3: 1 They c it and set up its doors;
1Mc 4:48 of the temple, and c the courts.

CONSIDER → CONSIDERED
Ex 33:13 C too that this nation is your people.
1Sa 12:24 for c what great things he has done
Ps 107:43 and c the steadfast love of the LORD.
Lk 12:27 C the lilies, how they grow:
Ro 6:11 must c yourselves dead to sin
Jas 1: 2 of any kind, c it nothing but joy,

CONSIDERED → CONSIDER
Pr 17:28 fools who keep silent are c wise;
Heb 11:11 he c him faithful who had promised.

CONSOLATION
Lk 2:25 looking forward to the c of Israel,
2Co 1: 3 of mercies and the God of all c,

CONSPIRACY → CONSPIRE
Isa 8:12 not call c all that this people calls c,

CONSPIRE → CONSPIRACY, CONSPIRED
Ps 2: 1 Why do the nations c,
83: 5 They c with one accord;

CONSPIRED → CONSPIRE
Da 6: 6 So the presidents and satraps c
Mt 26: 4 and they c to arrest Jesus by stealth

CONSULT → CONSULTED
1Sa 28: 8 And he said, "C a spirit for me,
Isa 31: 1 Holy One of Israel or c the LORD!
40:14 did he c for his enlightenment,
Sir 8:17 Do not c with fools, for they cannot

CONSULTED → CONSULT
1Ch 10:13 had c a medium, seeking guidance,
Eze 20: 3 Lord God, I will not be c by you.

CONSUME → CONSUMED, CONSUMING
Ex 32:12 c them from the face of the earth'?
Nu 16:21 so that I may c them in a moment.
Mt 6:19 where moth and rust c and where
Jn 2:17 "Zeal for your house will c me."

CONSUMED → CONSUME
Ex 3: 2 bush was blazing, yet it was not c.
Ps 69: 9 zeal for your house that has c me;
90: 7 For we are c by your anger;
Zep 3: 8 all the earth shall be c.
Gal 5:15 that you are not c by one another.

CONSUMING → CONSUME
Heb 12:29 for indeed our God is a c fire.

CONTAIN
2Ch 2: 6 even highest heaven, cannot c him?
Jn 21:25 world itself could not c the books

CONTEMPT
Da 12: 2 some to shame and everlasting c.
Mk 9:12 sufferings and be treated with c?
Heb 6: 6 and are holding him up to c.

CONTEND
Isa 49:25 I will c with those who c with you,
Jude 1: 3 to c for the faith that was once for

CONTENT → CONTENTMENT
2Co 12:10 Therefore I am c with weaknesses,
Php 4:11 learned to be c with whatever I have
Heb 13: 5 and be c with what you have;
Sir 29:23 Be c with little or much,

CONTENTMENT* → CONTENT
1Ti 6: 6 gain in godliness combined with c;

CONTINUE
1Ch 17:27 that it may c forever before you.
Jn 8:31 "If you c in my word,
Ac 13:43 urged them to c in the grace of God.
1Th 3: 8 if you c to stand firm in the Lord.
Heb 8: 9 for they did not c in my covenant,

CONTRARY
Gal 1: 8 a gospel c to what we proclaimed to
1Ti 1:10 else is c to the sound teaching

CONTRIBUTE* → CONTRIBUTING
Ro 12:13 C to the needs of the saints;

CONTRIBUTING* → CONTRIBUTE
Dt 16:10 c a freewill offering in proportion to
Mk 12:43 all those who are c to the treasury.

CONTRITE
Ps 51:17 broken and c heart, O God, you will
Isa 57:15 who are c and humble in spirit,

CONVERT
Mt 23:15 sea and land to make a single c,
1Ti 3: 6 He must not be a recent c,

CONVICT → CONVICTION
Dt 19:15 to c a person of any crime
Jude 1:15 to c everyone of all the deeds of

CONVICTION → CONVICT
Heb 11: 1 the c of things not seen.

CONVINCE → CONVINCED, CONVINCING
Ac 28:23 and trying to c them about Jesus
2Ti 4: 2 c, rebuke, and encourage,

CONVINCED → CONVINCE
Lk 16:31 neither will they be c even if
Ro 8:38 For I am c that neither death, nor
2Co 5:14 we are c that one has died for all;

CONVINCING* → CONVINCE
Ac 1: 3 to them by many c proofs,

CONVOCATIONS
Lev 23: 2 that you shall proclaim as holy c,

COPPER
Lev 26:19 like iron and your earth like c.
Mk 12:42 and put in two small c coins,

COPY
Dt 17:18 he shall have a c of this law written
Heb 9:24 a mere c of the true one,

CORDS
2Sa 22: 6 the c of Sheol entangled me,
Hos 11: 4 led them with c of human kindness,

CORNELIUS*
First Gentile Christian (Ac 10).

CORNER → CORNERSTONE
Pr 1:21 At the busiest c she cries out;
1Pe 2: 7 has become the very head of the c,"

CORNERSTONE → CORNER, STONE
Ps 118:22 rejected has become the chief c.
Isa 28:16 a tested stone, a precious c, a sure
Zec 10: 4 Out of them shall come the c,
Lk 20:17 builders rejected has become the c'?

Eph 2:20 with Christ Jesus himself as the c.
1Pe 2: 6 laying in Zion a stone, a c chosen

CORRECT → CORRECTING, CORRECTION
Ps 141: 5 let the faithful c me.
Jer 10:24 C me, O LORD, but in just measure;
Sir 42: 8 Do not be ashamed to c the stupid

CORRECTING* → CORRECT
2Ti 2:25 c opponents with gentleness.

CORRECTION → CORRECT
Jer 5: 3 but they refused to take c.
2Ti 3:16 c, and for training in righteousness,

CORRUPT → CORRUPTION
Ge 6:11 Now the earth was c in God's sight,
Ac 2:40 yourselves from this c generation."
Eph 4:22 your old self, c and deluded

CORRUPTION → CORRUPT
Ac 2:31 nor did his flesh experience c.'
2Pe 1: 4 you may escape from the c

COST
1Ch 21:24 burnt offerings that c me nothing."
Lk 14:28 not first sit down and estimate the c,

COUNCIL → COUNCILS
Jer 23:18 who has stood in the c of the LORD
Mt 26:59 the whole c were looking for false

COUNCILS* → COUNCIL
Mk 13: 9 for they will hand you over to c;

COUNSEL → COUNSELOR, COUNSELORS
Job 38: 2 that darkens c by words without
Ps 2: 2 and the rulers take c together,
33:11 The c of the LORD stands forever,
Isa 28:29 he is wonderful in c, and excellent

COUNSELOR → COUNSEL
Isa 9: 6 and he is named Wonderful C,
Ro 11:34 Or who has been his c?"
Sir 42:21 and he needs no one to be his c.

COUNSELORS → COUNSEL
Pr 11:14 in an abundance of c there is safety.
24: 6 in abundance of c there is victory.

COUNT → COUNTED, COUNTS
Ge 13:16 if one can c the dust of the earth,
1Ch 21: 1 incited David to c the people of
Ps 90:12 So teach us to c our days

COUNTED → COUNT
Ecc 1:15 and what is lacking cannot be c.
Mt 10:30 even the hairs of your head are all c.

COUNTENANCE
Nu 6:26 the LORD lift up his c upon you,
Ps 89:15 O LORD, in the light of your c;
Pr 15:13 A glad heart makes a cheerful c,

COUNTRY
Ge 12: 1 "Go from your c and your kindred
Jer 31:17 shall come back to their own c.
Jn 4:44 has no honor in the prophet's own
c).
Heb 11:16 they desire a better c, that is,

COURAGE → COURAGEOUS
1Ch 22:13 Be strong and of good c.
Jn 16:33 But take c; I have conquered

COURAGEOUS → COURAGE
Jos 1: 6 Be strong and c; for you shall put
Da 10:19 Be strong and c!"
1Co 16:13 stand firm in your faith, be c,
1Mc 2:64 be c and grow strong in the law,

COURT → COURTS
Ex 27: 9 shall make the c of the tabernacle.
Pr 25: 8 do not hastily bring into c;
Da 7:10 c sat in judgment, and the books
Mt 5:25 while you are on the way to c
1Co 6: 6 believer goes to c against a believer

COURTS → COURT
Ps 84:10 in your c is better than a thousand
96: 8 an offering, and come into his c.

COVENANT → COVENANTS
Ge 6:18 But I will establish my c with you;
9: 9 I am establishing my c with you
15:18 the LORD made a c with Abram,
Ex 2:24 remembered his c with Abraham,
19: 5 you obey my voice and keep my c,
24: 7 Then he took the book of the c,
40: 3 put in it the ark of the c,
Lev 26:42 will I remember my c with Jacob;
Jdg 2: 1 'I will never break my c with you.
1Ki 8:23 keeping c and steadfast love
Ezr 10: 3 now let us make a c with our God
Job 31: 1 "I have made a c with my eyes;
Ps 105: 8 He is mindful of his c forever,
Isa 61: 8 I will make an everlasting c with
Jer 31:31 when I will make a new c with
Eze 16:60 establish with you an everlasting c.
Da 9:27 a strong c with many for one week,
Mal 3: 1 The messenger of the c in whom
Lk 22:20 is the new c in my blood.
1Co 11:25 "This cup is the new c in my blood.
2Co 3: 6 be ministers of a new c, not of letter
Heb 7:22 become the guarantee of a better c.
12:24 the mediator of a new c,
Rev 11:19 the ark of his c was seen within his
Jdt 9:13 planned cruel things against your c,
Sir 28: 7 remember the c of the Most High,
1Mc 1:15 and abandoned the holy c.
2Es 3:15 You made an everlasting c with

COVENANTS → COVENANT
Ro 9: 4 the adoption, the glory, the c,
Gal 4:24 an allegory: these women are two c.

COVER
Ex 33:22 I will c you with my hand
Ps 139:11 "Surely the darkness shall c me,
Isa 11: 9 as the waters c the sea.
Jas 5:20 and will c a multitude of sins.

COVET
Ex 20:17 shall not c your neighbor's house;
Ro 7: 7 had not said, "You shall not c."
Jas 4: 2 you c something and cannot obtain

CRAFTINESS → CRAFTY
Ro 1:29 of envy, murder, strife, deceit, c,
1Co 3:19 "He catches the wise in their c,"

CRAFTY → CRAFTINESS
Ge 3: 1 serpent was more c than any other
2Co 12:16 (you say) since I was c, I took you

CRAVING*
Nu 11: 4 rabble among them had a strong c;
Ps 78:30 But before they had satisfied their c,

CREATE → CREATED, CREATION, CREATOR
Ps 51:10 C in me a clean heart, O God,
Isa 65:17 to c new heavens and a new earth;
Eph 2:15 c in himself one new humanity

CREATED → CREATE
Ge 1: 1 In the beginning when God c the
1:27 So God c humankind in his image,
Dt 4:32 Is not he your Father, who c you,
Pr 8:22 The LORD c me at the beginning of
Mal 2:10 Has not one God c us?
1Co 11: 9 Neither was man c for the sake of
Eph 2:10 c in Christ Jesus for good works,
Col 1:16 all things have been c through him
1Ti 4: 4 For everything c by God is good,
Rev 4:11 for you c all things, and by your will
Jdt 13:18 who c the heavens and the earth,
Wis 2:23 for God c us for incorruption,
Sir 1: 4 Wisdom was c before all other

CREATION → CREATE
Ge 2: 3 all the work that he had done in c.
Mk 10: 6 But from the beginning of c,

Ro 8:19 the c waits with eager longing for
2Co 5:17 anyone is in Christ, there is a new c:
Col 1:15 invisible God, the firstborn of all c;
2Pe 3: 4 they were from the beginning of c!"

CREATOR → CREATE
Ecc 12: 1 Remember your c in the days of
Ro 1:25 served the creature rather than
the C
Col 3:10 according to the image of its c.
1Pe 4:19 to a faithful C,

CREATURE → CREATURES
Ge 2:19 the man called every living c,
Ro 1:25 worshiped and served the c rather

CREATURES → CREATURE
Lev 11: 2 these are the c that you may eat.
Ps 104:24 the earth is full of your c.
Eze 1: 5 was something like four living c.
Rev 4: 6 are four living c, full of eyes
19: 4 elders and the four living c fell

CREDIT → CREDITED
Lk 6:33 what c is that to you?
1Pe 2:20 for doing wrong, what c is that?

CREDITED → CREDIT
Lev 7:18 nor shall it be c to the one who

CREEPING
Ge 1:24 cattle and c things and wild animals
Ps 148:10 c things and flying birds!

CRIED → CRY
Ex 2:23 under their slavery, and c out.
Nu 20:16 when we c to the LORD, he heard
Jdg 3: 9 the Israelites c out to the LORD,
Ps 22: 5 To you they c, and were saved;
Mt 27:46 Jesus c with a loud voice,

CRIMINAL → CRIMINALS
Jn 18:30 "If this man were not a c,
2Ti 2: 9 the point of being chained like a c.
1Pe 4:15 suffer as a murderer, a thief, a c,

CRIMINALS → CRIMINAL
Lk 23:32 Two others also, who were c,

CRIMSON
Ex 25: 4 purple, and c yarns and fine linen,
Lev 14: 4 cedarwood and c yarn and hyssop
Jos 2:21 she tied the c cord in the window.

CROOKED
Dt 32: 5 a perverse and c generation.
Ps 18:26 the c you show yourself perverse.
Ecc 1:15 What is c cannot be made straight,
Lk 3: 5 and the c shall be made straight,
Php 2:15 in the midst of a c and perverse

CROSS → CROSSROADS
Dt 31: 3 your God himself will c over before
Mk 15:30 and come down from the c!"
Lk 14:27 the c and follow me cannot be my
1Co 1:18 the c is foolishness to those who are
Gal 6:14 never boast of anything except the c
Php 2: 8 of death—even death on a c.
Col 1:20 peace through the blood of his c.
Heb 12: 2 was set before him endured the c,

CROSSROADS* → CROSS, ROAD
Pr 8: 2 at the c she takes her stand;
Jer 6:16 Stand at the c, and look, and ask for

CROW*
Lk 22:34 the cock will not c this day,

CROWD → CROWDS
Mk 8: 2 "I have compassion for the c,
14:43 a c with swords and clubs,

CROWDS → CROWD
Mt 7:28 c were astounded at his teaching,

CROWN → CROWNED, CROWNS
Lev 8: 9 the golden ornament, the holy c,
Pr 4: 9 will bestow on you a beautiful c."

La   5:16 The c has fallen from our head;
Jn   19: 2 soldiers wove a c of thorns and put
Php   4: 1 my joy and c, stand firm in the Lord
2Ti   4: 8 there is reserved for me the c
1Pe   5: 4 the c of glory that never fades away.
Rev   6: 2 Its rider had a bow; a c was given
     14:14 with a golden c on his head,
Sir   1:18 fear of the Lord is the c of wisdom,

CROWNED → CROWN
Ps   8: 5 and c them with glory and honor.
2Ti   2: 5 no one is c without competing
Heb   2: 9 now c with glory and honor

CROWNS → CROWN
Rev   4:10 they cast their c before the throne,

CRUCIFIED → CRUCIFY
Mt   27:22 All of them said, "Let him be c!"
Lk   24: 7 c, and on the third day rise again."
Ac   4:10 whom you c, whom God raised
Ro   6: 6 We know that our old self was c
1Co   1:23 but we proclaim Christ c,
Gal   2:19 I have been c with Christ;

CRUCIFY → CRUCIFIED, CRUCIFYING
Lk   23:21 they kept shouting, "C, c him!"
Jn   19:15 asked them, "Shall I c your King?"

CRUCIFYING* → CRUCIFY
Heb   6: 6 they are c again the Son of God

CRUSH → CRUSHED
Job   6: 9 that it would please God to c me,
Isa 53:10 it was the will of the LORD to c him
Da   2:40 it shall c and shatter all these.
Mt   21:44 it will c anyone on whom it falls."
Ro   16:20 will shortly c Satan under your feet.

CRUSHED → CRUSH
Ps   34:18 and saves the c in spirit.
2Co   4: 8 afflicted in every way, but not c;

CRY → CRIED, CRYING
Ex   2:23 Out of the slavery their c for help
Ps   5: 2 Listen to the sound of my c,
    130: 1 Out of the depths I c to you,
Hab   1: 2 how long shall I c for help,
Mk   15:37 Then Jesus gave a loud c

CRYING → CRY
Ge   4:10 your brother's blood is c out to me
Mk   1: 3 the voice of one c out in the
Rev 21: 4 c and pain will be no more,

CRYSTAL
Eze   1:22 shining like c, spread out above
Rev 22: 1 river of the water of life, bright as c,

CUP
Ps   23: 5 my head with oil; my c overflows.
Jer 25:15 my hand this c of the wine of wrath,
Mt   10:42 gives even a c of cold water to one
     26:39 if it is possible, let this c pass from
Mk   10:38 you able to drink the c that I drink,
Lk   22:17 he took a c, and after giving thanks
1Co 11:25 c is the new covenant in my blood.
Rev 14:10 unmixed into the c of his anger,

CURE → CURED
Hos   5:13 But he is not able to c you or heal

CURED → CURE
Mt   8:16 and c all who were sick.
Ac   5:16 and they were all c.

CURSE → ACCURSED, CURSED, CURSES
Ge   8:21 "I will never again c the ground
     12: 3 and the one who curses you I will c;
Nu   22:12 not c the people, for they are blessed
Dt   21:23 hung on a tree is under God's c.
     23: 5 God turned the c into a blessing
Job   2: 9 C God, and die."
Ps 109:28 Let them c, but you will bless.
Mal   4: 6 come and strike the land with a c.

Mk   14:71 he began to c, and he swore an
          oath,
Lk   6:28 bless those who c you, pray
Ro   12:14 bless and do not c them.
Gal   3:13 Christ redeemed us from the c of
Sir   4: 5 and give no one reason to c you;

CURSED → CURSE
Ge   3:17 c is the ground because of you;
      9:25 "C be Canaan; lowest of slaves
     27:29 C be everyone who curses you,
Nu   23: 8 can I curse whom God has not c?
Job   3: 1 Job opened his mouth and c the day
Mk   11:21 fig tree that you c has withered."
Gal   3:10 "C is everyone who does not
Heb   6: 8 and on the verge of being c;
Rev 16: 9 but they c the name of God,

CURSES → CURSE
Lev 24:15 who c God shall bear the sin.
2Ch 34:24 all the c that are written in the book

CURTAIN
Ex   26:31 You shall make a c of blue, purple,
2Ch   3:14 And Solomon made the c of blue
Lk   23:45 the c of the temple was torn in two.
Heb 10:20 that he opened for us through the c

CUSTOM → CUSTOMS
Est   9:23 Jews adopted as a c
Jn   18:39 But you have a c that I release

CUSTOMS → CUSTOM
2Ki 17: 8 the c of the nations whom the LORD
Ac   16:21 advocating c that are not lawful for
1Mc   1:42 all should give up their particular c.

CUT
Ge   9:11 never again shall all flesh be c off
Ps   37: 9 For the wicked shall be c off,
Isa 53: 8 c off from the land of the living,
Da   2:45 a stone was c from the mountain
Mt   3:10 does not bear good fruit is c down
Mk   9:43 hand causes you to stumble, c it off;
Ro   11:22 otherwise you also will be c off.

CYMBAL* → CYMBALS
1Co 13: 1 I am a noisy gong or a clanging c.

CYMBALS → CYMBAL
2Sa   6: 5 tambourines and castanets and c.
Ne   12:27 and with singing, with c,
Ps 150: 5 Praise him with clanging c;

CYRUS
Persian king who allowed exiles to return (2Ch 36:22-Ezr 1:8), to rebuild temple (Ezr 5:13-6:14), as appointed by the LORD (Isa 44:28-45:13).

D

DAGON
Jdg 16:23 a great sacrifice to their god D,
1Sa   5: 2 and brought it into the house of D

DAILY → DAY
Mt   6:11 Give us this day our d bread.
Lk   9:23 take up their cross d and follow me.

DAMASCUS
Ac   9: 3 was going along and approaching D,

DAN
    1. Son of Jacob by Bilhah (Ge 30:4-6; 35:25; 46:23). Tribe of blessed (Ge 49:16-17; Dt 33:22), numbered (Nu 1:39; 26:43), allotted land (Jos 19:40-48; Eze 48:1), failed to fully possess (Jdg 1:34-35), failed to support Deborah (Jdg 5:17), possessed Dan (Jdg 18).
    2. Northernmost city in Israel (Ge 14:14; Jdg 18; 20:1).

DANCE → DANCED
Ps 150: 4 Praise him with tambourine and d;
Ecc   3: 4 a time to mourn, and a time to d;

Lk   7:32 the flute for you, and you did not d;

DANCED → DANCE
2Sa   6:14 David d before the LORD with all
Mt   14: 6 the daughter of Herodias d before

DANIEL → =BELTESHAZZAR
    1. Hebrew exile to Babylon, name changed to Belteshazzar (Da 1:6-7). Refused to eat unclean food (Da 1:8-21). Interpreted Nebuchadnezzar's dreams (Da 2; 4), writing on the wall (Da 5). Thrown into lion's den (Da 6). Visions of (Da 7-12). In deuterocanonical books of Bel and the Dragon, Susanna.
    2. Son of David (1Ch 3:1).

DARE
Mt   22:46 d to ask him any more questions.
Ro   5: 7 someone might actually d to die.

DARIUS
    1. King of Persia (Ezr 4:5), allowed rebuilding of temple (Ezr 5-6).
    2. Mede who conquered Babylon (Da 5:31).

DARK → DARKEST, DARKNESS
Ps 139:12 even the darkness is not d to you;
Lk   12: 3 whatever you have said in the d will
2Pe   1:19 as to a lamp shining in a d place,

DARKEST* → DARK
Ps   23: 4 though I walk through the d valley,

DARKNESS → DARK
Ge   1: 2 the earth was a formless void and d
Ex   10:22 was dense d in all the land of Egypt
Dt   5:23 you heard the voice out of the d,
Isa   9: 2 walked in d have seen a great light;
Joel 2:31 The sun shall be turned to d,
Zep   1:15 a day of d and gloom,
Mt   4:16 who sat in d have seen a great light,
      6:23 light in you is d, how great is the d!
Jn   1: 5 light shines in the d, and the d did
          not
Eph   5: 8 For once you were d, but now in
Col   1:13 from the power of d and transferred
1Jn   1: 5 God is light and in him there is no d

DATHAN*
Involved in Korah's rebellion against Moses and Aaron (Nu 16:1-27; 26:9; Dt 11:6; Ps 106:17; Sir 45:18; 4Mc 2:17).

DAUGHTER → DAUGHTERS
Ex   2: 5 d of Pharaoh came down to bathe at
Est   2: 7 Mordecai adopted her as his own d.
Ps   9:14 and, in the gates of d Zion,
La   2: 1 in his anger has humiliated d Zion!
Mic   7: 6 the d rises up against her mother,
Zec   9: 9 Rejoice greatly, O d Zion!
Mt   14: 6 the d of Herodias danced before the
Lk   12:53 against d and d against mother,
Jdt 10:12 replied, "I am a d of the Hebrews,

DAUGHTERS → DAUGHTER
Ge   6: 4 of God went in to the d of humans,
     19:36 the d of Lot became pregnant by
          their
Nu   27: 1 the d of Zelophehad came forward.
Dt   12:31 even burn their sons and their d in
Job 42:15 no women so beautiful as Job's d;
Joel 2:28 sons and your d shall prophesy,
Ac   2:17 sons and your d shall prophesy,
2Co   6:18 and you shall be my sons and d,
1Pe   3: 6 You have become her d as long

DAVID
Son of Jesse (Ru 4:17-22; 1Ch 2:13-15), ancestor of Jesus (Mt 1:1-17; Lk 3:31). Wives and children (1Sa 18; 25:39-44; 2Sa 3:2-5; 5:13-16; 11:27; 1Ch 3:1-9).
Anointed king by Samuel (1Sa 16:1-13). Musician to Saul (1Sa 16:14-23; 18:10). Killed Goliath (1Sa 17). Relation with Jonathan (1Sa 18:1-4; 19-20; 23:16-18; 2Sa 1). Disfavor of Saul (1Sa

18:6-23:29). Spared Saul's life (1Sa 24; 26).
Among Philistines (1Sa 21:10-14; 27-30). Lament
for Saul and Jonathan (2Sa 1).

Anointed king of Judah (2Sa 2:1-11). Conflict
with house of Saul (2Sa 2-4). Anointed king of Israel (2Sa 5:1-4; 1Ch 11:1-3). Conquered Jerusalem (2Sa 5:6-10; 1Ch 11;4-9). Brought ark to Jerusalem (2Sa 6; 1Ch 13; 15-16). The LORD
promised eternal dynasty (2Sa 7; 1Ch 17; Ps 132).
Showed kindness to Mephibosheth (2Sa 9). Adultery with Bathsheba, murder of Uriah (2Sa 11-12).
Son Amnon raped daughter Tamar; killed by Absalom (2Sa 13). Absalom's revolt (2Sa 14-17);
death (2Sa 18). Sheba's revolt (2Sa 20). Victories:
Philistines (2Sa 5:17-25; 21:15-22; 1Ch 14:8-17;
20:4-8), Ammonites (2Sa 10; 1Ch 19), various
(2Sa 8; 1Ch 18). Mighty men (2Sa 23:8-39; 1Ch
11-12). Punished for numbering army (2Sa 24;
1Ch 21). Appointed Solomon king (1Ki 1:28-2:9).
Prepared for building of temple (1Ch 22-29). Last
words (2Sa 23:1-7). Death (1Ki 2:10-12; 1Ch
29:28).

Psalmist (Mt 22:43-45), musician (Am 6:5),
prophet (2Sa 23:2-7; Ac 1:16; 2:30).

Psalms of: 2 (Ac 4:25), 3-32, 34-41, 51-65, 68-
70, 86, 95 (Heb 4:7), 101, 103, 108-110, 122,
124, 131, 133, 138-145. Deuterocanonical Ps 151
ascribed to.

DAWN → DAWNS
Isa 14:12 from heaven, O Day Star, son of D!
Hos 6: 3 his appearing is as sure as the d;

DAWNS → DAWN
Ps 97:11 Light d for the righteous,
2Pe 1:19 until the day d and the morning star

DAY → DAILY, DAYS
Ge 1: 5 God called the light D, and
8:22 d and night, shall not cease."
Ex 13:21 of them in a pillar of cloud by d,
20: 8 Remember the sabbath d, and keep
Jos 1: 8 you shall meditate on it d and night,
Ps 1: 2 his law they meditate d and night.
118:24 is the d that the LORD has made;
Isa 66: 8 Shall a land be born in one d?
Joel 1:15 For the d of the LORD is near,
Zec 14: 1 See, a d is coming for the LORD,
Mal 3: 2 who can endure the d of his coming,
Mt 25:13 you know neither the d nor the
hour.
Lk 11: 3 Give us each d our daily bread.
24:46 to rise from the dead on the third d,
Jn 6:40 I will raise them up on the last d."
Ro 14: 5 Some judge one d to be better than
2Co 6: 2 see, now is the d of salvation!
1Th 5: 2 very well that the d of the LORD
2Pe 3: 8 the Lord one d is like a thousand
years,
3:10 d of the LORD will come like a thief,
1Jn 4:17 have boldness on the d of judgment,
Rev 1:10 I was in the spirit on the Lord's d,
16:14 for battle on the great d of God

DAYS → DAY
Ge 1:14 and for seasons and for d and years,
7: 4 rain on the earth for forty d and
forty
Ex 24:18 on the mountain for forty d and
1Ki 19: 8 that food forty d and forty nights
Ps 90:10 The d of our life are seventy years,
Mk 1:13 He was in the wilderness forty d,
Eph 5:16 of the time, because the d are evil.
2Ti 3: 1 in the last d distressing times will
Heb 1: 2 last d he has spoken to us by a Son,
1Mc 4:56 dedication of the altar for eight d,
2Es 14:42 They sat forty d; they wrote

DEACON* → DEACONS
Ro 16: 1 a d of the church at Cenchreae,

DEACONS → DEACON
1Ti 3: 8 D likewise must be serious, not

DEAD → DEATH, DIE, DIED, DYING
Nu 16:48 stood between the d and the living;
Dt 18:11 or who seeks oracles from the d.
Ps 115:17 The d do not praise the LORD,
Ecc 9: 4 a living dog is better than a d lion.
Mt 8:22 and let the d bury their own d."
Mk 12:27 God not of the d, but of the living;
Lk 24: 5 look for the living among the d?
Ro 6:11 must consider yourselves d to sin
Eph 2: 1 You were d through the trespasses
Col 1:18 the firstborn from the d,
1Pe 4: 5 ready to judge the living and the d.
Rev 1: 5 witness, the firstborn of the d,
20:12 And the d were judged according to

DEAF
Ex 4:11 Who makes them mute or d,
Isa 29:18 On that day the d shall hear the
Lk 7:22 the lepers are cleansed, the d hear,

DEATH → DEAD
Dt 30:19 that I have set before you life and d,
Ru 1:17 if even d parts me from you!"
Ps 22:15 you lay me in the dust of d.
Pr 18:21 D and life are in the power of the
SS 8: 6 for love is strong as d,
Isa 25: 7 he will swallow up d forever.
Hos 13:14 O D, where are your plagues?
Mt 16:28 standing here who will not taste d
Lk 1:79 in darkness and in the shadow of d,
Jn 5:24 but has passed from d to life.
Ro 6:23 handed over to d for our trespasses
6:23 For the wages of sin is d,
1Co 15:55 "Where, O d, is your victory?
2Co 2:16 to the one a fragrance from d to d,
Heb 2:14 through d he might destroy the one
who has the power of d,
1Jn 3:14 that we have passed from d to life
Rev 1:18 I have the keys of D and of Hades.
20:14 D and Hades were thrown into the
lake
21: 4 D will be no more;
Sir 15:17 Before each person are life and d,

DEBAUCHERY
Ro 13:13 not in d and licentiousness,
Eph 5:18 drunk with wine, for that is d;

DEBORAH
Prophetess; led victory over Canaanites (Jdg 4-
5).

DEBT → DEBTS, INDEBTED
Mt 18:27 released him and forgave him the d.

DEBTS → DEBT
Dt 15: 1 you shall grant a remission of d.
Mt 6:12 And forgive us our d, as we

DECEIT → DECEITFUL, DECEIVE,
DECEIVED, DECEIVERS
Dt 32: 4 A faithful God, without d,
Isa 53: 9 and there was no d in his mouth.
Ro 1:29 Full of envy, murder, strife, d,
1Pe 2:22 and no d was found in his mouth."

DECEITFUL → DECEIT
Ps 35:20 but they conceive d words
Zep 3:13 nor shall a d tongue be found
1Ti 4: 1 by paying attention to d spirits

DECEIVE → DECEIT
Eph 5: 6 Let no one d you with empty words,
1Jn 1: 8 that we have no sin, we d ourselves,
Rev 20: 8 to d the nations at the four corners

DECEIVED → DECEIT
Gal 6: 7 Do not be d; God is not mocked,
1Ti 2:14 was not d, but the woman was d

DECEIVERS* → DECEIT
Tit 1:10 rebellious people, idle talkers and d,
2Jn 1: 7 Many d have gone out into the

DECISION
Pr 16:33 but the d is the LORD's alone.
Joel 3:14 multitudes, in the valley of d!

DECLARE → DECLARED
Ps 50: 6 The heavens d his righteousness,
Col 4: 3 that we may d the mystery of Christ,

DECLARED → DECLARE
Isa 41:26 Who d it from the beginning,
Mk 7:19 (Thus he d all foods clean.)
Ro 1: 4 and was d to be Son of God

DECREASE
Jn 3:30 He must increase, but I must d."

DECREE → DECREED, DECREES
Ps 2: 7 I will tell of the d of the LORD:
Lk 2: 1 d went out from Emperor Augustus

DECREED → DECREE
Da 9:24 "Seventy weeks are d for your

DECREES → DECREE
Dt 6: 2 and keep all his d and his
Ps 19: 7 the d of the LORD are sure,
119: 2 Happy are those who keep his d,

DEDICATED → DEDICATION
1Ki 8:63 all the people of Israel d the house
Lk 21: 5 beautiful stones and gifts d to God,

DEDICATION → DEDICATED
2Ch 7: 9 the d of the altar seven days and
Ezr 6:16 the d of this house of God with joy.
1Mc 4:56 the d of the altar for eight days,

DEED → DEEDS
Ecc 12:14 will bring every d into judgment,
Jer 32:10 I signed the d, sealed it,
Mt 19:16 good d must I do to have eternal life
Col 3:17 And whatever you do, in word or d,

DEEDS → DEED
Dt 3:24 in heaven or on earth can perform d
Ps 9: 1 I will tell of all your wonderful d.
Jer 50:29 Repay her according to her d,
Ob 1:15 your d shall return on your own
Lk 23:41 getting what we deserve for our d,
Ro 2: 6 repay according to each one's d:
Rev 15: 3 "Great and amazing are your d,
19: 8 the righteous d of the saints.

DEEP → DEPTH, DEPTHS
Ge 1: 2 darkness covered the face of the d,
7:11 the fountains of the great d burst
Ro 8:26 with sighs too d for words.

DEFECT
1Pe 1:19 like that of a lamb without d or

DEFEND
Ps 72: 4 May he d the cause of the poor of
Pr 31: 9 d the rights of the poor and needy.
Jdt 5:21 for their Lord and God will d them,

DEFILE → DEFILED
Lev 11:43 you shall not d yourselves
Nu 35:34 You shall not d the land
Mk 7:15 things that come out are what d."

DEFILED → DEFILE
Ps 79: 1 they have d your holy temple;
1Mc 1:37 they even d the sanctuary.

DEFRAUD*
Lev 19:13 You shall not d your neighbor;
Mk 10:19 You shall not d;
1Co 6: 8 you yourselves wrong and d—

DEITY
Col 2: 9 whole fullness of d dwells bodily,

DELAY
Dt 7:10 He does not d but repays
Ps 70: 5 my deliverer; O LORD, do not d!
Heb 10:37 will come and will not d;

DELIGHT → DELIGHTS
1Sa 15:22 "Has the LORD as great d in burnt
Ps 1: 2 but their d is in the law of the
LORD,

Ps   40: 8 I **d** to do your will, O my God;
Pr   8:30 I was daily his **d**, rejoicing before
Ro   7:22 For I **d** in the law of God in my
Sir   1:27 fidelity and humility are his **d**.

DELIGHTS → DELIGHT
Ps   5: 4 not a God who **d** in wickedness;
Isa   42: 1 I chosen, in whom my soul **d**;

DELILAH*
   Philistine who betrayed Samson (Jdg 16:4-22).

DELIVER → DELIVERANCE, DELIVERED,
   DELIVERER, DELIVERS
Ex   3: 8 to **d** them from the Egyptians,
Dt   32:39 and no one can **d** from my hand.
Da   3:17 able to **d** us from the furnace
       6:20 able to **d** you from the lions?"
Mt   27:43 let God **d** him now,

DELIVERANCE → DELIVER
Ex   14:13 and see the **d** that the LORD will
Est   4:14 **d** will rise for the Jews from another
Ps   3: 8 **D** belongs to the LORD;
Php   1:19 this will turn out for my **d**,
Jdt   8:17 while we wait for his **d**,

DELIVERED → DELIVER
Isa   66: 8 Shall a nation be **d** in one moment?
Da   1: 2 at that time your people shall be **d**,

DELIVERER → DELIVER
Ps   140: 7 O LORD, my Lord, my strong **d**,
Ro   11:26 "Out of Zion will come the **D**;

DEMON → DEMONIACS, DEMONIC,
   DEMONS
Mt   11:18 and they say, 'He has a **d**';
      17:18 Jesus rebuked the **d**, and it came out
Jn   8:48 you are a Samaritan and have a **d**?"
      10:21 not the words of one who has a **d**.
Tob   3: 8 the wicked Asmodeus had killed
       6: 8 of a man or woman afflicted by a **d**

DEMONIACS → DEMON
Mt   4:24 **d**, epileptics, and paralytics, and he
       8:28 two **d** coming out of the tombs met

DEMONIC* → DEMON
Rev   16:14 These are **d** spirits, performing signs

DEMONS → DEMON
Dt   32:17 They sacrificed to **d**, not God,
Ps   106:37 and their daughters to the **d**;
Lk   11:18 that I cast out the **d** by Beelzebul.
1Co   10:20 not want you to be partners with **d**.
1Ti   4: 1 deceitful spirits and teachings of **d**,
Jas   2:19 Even the **d** believe—and shudder.
Rev   9:20 their hands or give up worshiping **d**
Bar   4: 7 by sacrificing to **d** and not

DEN
Jer   7:11 a **d** of robbers in your sight?
Da   6: 7 shall be thrown into a **d** of lions.
Mk   11:17 you have made it a **d** of robbers."

DENARIUS
Mk   12:15 Bring me a **d** and let me see it."

DENIED → DENY
Mt   26:70 But he **d** it before all of them,
1Ti   5: 8 has **d** the faith and is worse than an
Rev   3: 8 my word and have not **d** my name.

DENIES → DENY
Lk   12: 9 but whoever **d** me before others
1Jn   2:22 the liar but the one who **d** that Jesus

DENY → DENIED, DENIES
Lev   16:29 you shall **d** yourselves,
      23:27 you shall **d** yourselves
Mt   16:24 let them **d** themselves and take up
2Ti   2:12 if we **d** him, he will also **d** us;
2Pe   2: 1 **d** the Master who bought them—

DEPART → DEPARTED
Ge   49:10 The scepter shall not **d** from Judah,
Jos   1: 8 law shall not **d** out of your mouth;

Ps   34:14 **D** from evil, and do good;
Php   1:23 my desire is to **d** and be with Christ,

DEPARTED → DEPART
1Sa   4:21 "The glory has **d** from Israel,"

DEPRAVED → DEPRAVITY
1Ti   6: 5 among those who are **d** in mind
2Pe   2:10 who indulge their flesh in **d** lust,

DEPRAVITY → DEPRAVED
Lev   20:14 that there may be no **d** among you.

DEPRIVE
Dt   24:17 not **d** a resident alien or an orphan
1Co   7: 5 not **d** one another except perhaps

DEPTH → DEEP
Mt   13: 5 since they had no **d** of soil.
Ro   11:33 O the **d** of the riches and wisdom
Eph   3:18 and length and height and **d**,

DEPTHS → DEEP
Ps   130: 1 Out of the **d** I cry to you, O LORD.
1Co   2:10 even the **d** of God.

DESCENDANTS
Ge   15:18 saying, "To your **d** I give this land,
Dt   4:37 he chose their **d** after them.
Isa   44: 3 I will pour my spirit upon your **d**,
Ro   9: 7 Abraham's children are his true **d**;
Gal   3: 7 who believe are the **d** of Abraham.

DESCENDED → DESCENDING
Ex   34: 5 LORD **d** in the cloud and stood
Jn   3:13 except the one who **d** from heaven,
Eph   4: 9 does it mean but that he had also **d**

DESCENDING → DESCENDED
Ge   28:12 angels of God were ascending and **d**
Mk   1:10 and the Spirit like a dove
Jn   1:51 the angels of God ascending and **d**

DESERT → DESERTED
Ps   106:14 and put God to the test in the **d**;
Isa   40: 3 make straight in the **d** a highway
Mk   8: 4 with bread here in the **d**?"

DESERTED → DESERT
Mt   26:56 all the disciples **d** him and fled.

DESERVE
Pr   14:14 and the good, what their deeds **d**.
Lk   23:15 he has done nothing to **d** death.
Ac   26:31 man is doing nothing to **d** death
Rev   2:23 give to each of you as your works **d**.

DESIRE → DESIRED, DESIRES
Ge   3:16 your **d** shall be for your husband,
Ps   20: 4 May he grant you your heart's **d**,
Pr   3:15 nothing you **d** can compare with her
Hos   6: 6 I **d** steadfast love and not sacrifice,
Mt   9:13 learn what this means, 'I **d** mercy,
Jas   1:14 But one is tempted by one's own **d**,
1Jn   2:16 the **d** of the flesh, the **d** of the eyes,

DESIRED → DESIRE
Ps   19:10 More to be **d** are they than gold,
Lk   22:15 I have eagerly **d** to eat this Passover

DESIRES → DESIRE
Ps   37: 4 he will give you the **d** of your heart.
Gal   5:16 do not gratify the **d** of the flesh.
1Ti   2: 4 who **d** everyone to be saved
2Ti   4: 3 teachers to suit their own **d**,
Sir   18:30 Do not follow your base **d**,

DESOLATE → DESOLATES, DESOLATING
Ex   23:29 or the land would become **d** and
Da   11:31 the abomination that makes **d**.
Mt   23:38 See, your house is left to you, **d**.
1Mc   1:39 sanctuary became **d** like a desert;

DESOLATES → DESOLATE
Da   9:27 shall be an abomination that **d**,

DESOLATING → DESOLATE
Mk   13:14 the **d** sacrilege set up where it ought
1Mc   1:54 erected a **d** sacrilege on the altar

DESPAIR → DESPAIRED
2Co   4: 8 perplexed, but not driven to **d**;

DESPAIRED* → DESPAIR
2Co   1: 8 crushed that we **d** of life itself.

DESPISE → DESPISED
Job   5:17 not **d** the discipline of the Almighty.
Ps   51:17 contrite heart, O God, you will not **d**
Pr   1: 7 fools **d** wisdom and instruction.
Lk   16:13 devoted to the one and **d** the other.

DESPISED → DESPISE
Isa   53: 3 He was **d** and rejected by others;
1Co   1:28 God chose what is low and **d** in the

DESTINED
Eph   1: 5 He **d** us for adoption as his children
1Th   5: 9 For God has **d** us not for wrath but
1Pe   1:11 to the sufferings **d** for Christ

DESTROY → DESTROYED, DESTROYER,
   DESTRUCTION
Ge   6:13 to **d** them along with the earth.
Est   3: 9 Haman plotted to **d** all the Jews,
Mt   10:28 rather fear him who can **d** both soul
Jn   10:10 comes only to steal and kill and **d**.
Jas   4:12 who is able to save and to **d**.
1Jn   3: 8 to **d** the works of the devil.

DESTROYED → DESTROY
Da   6:26 His kingdom shall never be **d**,
1Co   15:26 The last enemy to be **d** is death.
2Co   5: 1 if the earthly tent we live in is **d**,

DESTROYER → DESTROY
Ex   12:23 not allow the **d** to enter your houses
1Co   10:10 and were destroyed by the **d**.

DESTRUCTION → DESTROY
Pr   16:18 Pride goes before **d**, and a haughty
Mt   7:13 and the road is easy that leads to **d**,
Ro   9:22 objects of wrath that are made for **d**;
2Pe   3:16 and unstable twist to their own **d**,

DEVIL
Mt   4: 1 wilderness to be tempted by the **d**.
Lk   8:12 **d** comes and takes away the word
Jn   8:44 You are from your father the **d**,
Eph   4:27 and do not make room for the **d**.
       6:11 to stand against the wiles of the **d**.
1Ti   3: 6 fall into the condemnation of the **d**.
Heb   2:14 the power of death, that is, the **d**,
Jas   4: 7 Resist the **d**, and he will flee from
1Pe   5: 8 lion your adversary the **d** prowls
1Jn   3: 8 to destroy the works of the **d**.
Jude   1: 9 Michael contended with the **d**
Rev   12: 9 who is called the **D** and Satan,
      20: 2 that ancient serpent, who is the **D**

DEVOTED
Ps   86: 2 Preserve my life, for I am **d** to you;
Mt   6:24 **d** to the one and despise the other.

DEVOUR → DEVOURING
Gal   5:15 you bite and **d** one another,
1Pe   5: 8 looking for someone to **d**.
Rev   12: 4 that he might **d** her child

DEVOURING → DEVOUR
Ex   24:17 glory of the LORD was like a **d** fire
Dt   9: 3 crosses over before you as a **d** fire;

DEW
Jdg   6:37 if there is **d** on the fleece alone,

DICTATED*
Jer   36:18 "He **d** all these words to me,
2Es   14:42 and by turns they wrote what was **d**,

DIE → DEAD
Ge   2:17 eat of it you shall **d**."
       3: 4 to the woman, "You will not **d**;
Ex   11: 5 firstborn in the land of Egypt shall **d**
Ru   1:17 Where you **d**, I will—
Job   2: 9 Curse God, and **d**."

Pr   10:21 but fools **d** for lack of sense.
Ecc   3: 2 a time to be born, and a time to **d**;
Isa   22:13 eat and drink, for tomorrow we **d.**"
Jer   31:30 But all shall **d** for their own sins;
Mt   26:35 "Even though I must **d** with you,
Jn   11:26 and believes in me will never **d.**
Ro   14: 8 if we **d**, we **d** to the Lord;
1Co   15:32 eat and drink, for tomorrow we **d.**"
Heb   9:27 it is appointed for mortals to **d** once,

DIED → DEAD
Ro   5: 6 right time Christ **d** for the ungodly.
1Co   15: 3 Christ **d** for our sins in accordance
Gal   2:19 the law I **d** to the law,

DIFFERENT
2Co   11: 4 or a **d** gospel from the one you
Gal   1: 6 and are turning to a **d** gospel—

DIFFICULT
Da   4: 9 and that no mystery is too **d**
Jn   6:60 teaching is **d**; who can accept it?"

DILIGENCE → DILIGENTLY
Ro   12: 8 the leader, in **d**;
Heb   6:11 each one of you to show the same **d**

DILIGENTLY → DILIGENCE
Dt   4: 6 You must observe them **d**,
Pr   8:17 and those who seek me **d** find me.

DINAH*
    Only daughter of Jacob, by Leah (Ge 30:21;
46:15). Raped by Shechem; avenged by Simeon
and Levi (Ge 34).

DIRECT → DIRECTS
Ps 119:128 I **d** my steps by all your precepts;
2Th   3: 5 the Lord **d** your hearts to the love

DIRECTS → DIRECT
Pr   16: 9 but the LORD **d** the steps.
Jas   3: 4 wherever the will of the pilot **d**.

DISAPPOINT*
Ro   5: 5 and hope does not **d** us,

DISASTER
Ex   32:12 your mind and do not bring **d**
Dt   28:20 The LORD will send upon you **d**,
Jer   18: 8 I will change my mind about the **d**
Eze   7: 5 Thus says the Lord God: **D** after **d!**

DISCERNED → DISCERNMENT
1Co   2:14 because they are spiritually **d.**

DISCERNING → DISCERNMENT
Dt   4: 6 nation is a wise and **d** people!"
Pr   1: 5 in learning, and the **d** acquire skill,
1Co   1:19 discernment of the **d** I will thwart."
Sir   1:19 knowledge and **d** comprehension.

DISCERNMENT → DISCERNED,
        DISCERNING
1Ki   4:29 Solomon very great wisdom, **d**,
1Co   12:10 prophecy, to another the **d** of spirits,

DISCIPLE → DISCIPLES
Mt   10:24 "A **d** is not above the teacher,
Lk   14:26 even life itself, cannot be my **d.**

DISCIPLES → DISCIPLE
Isa   8:16 seal the teaching among my **d.**
Mt   26:56 all the **d** deserted him and fled.
      28:19 therefore and make **d** of all nations,
Lk   6:13 he called his **d** and chose twelve of
Jn   8:31 in my word, you are truly my **d**;
Ac   11:26 the **d** were first called "Christians."

DISCIPLINE → DISCIPLINED
Job   5:17 not despise the **d** of the Almighty.
Ps   94:12 Happy are those whom you **d**,
Pr   5:23 They die for lack of **d**,
Jer   7:28 their God, and did not accept **d**;
Eph   6: 4 in the **d** and instruction of the Lord.
Heb   12: 5 not regard lightly the **d** of the Lord,

1Pe   5: 8 **D** yourselves, keep alert.
Sir   1:27 fear of the Lord is wisdom and **d**,

DISCIPLINED → DISCIPLINE
1Co   11:32 **d** so that we may not be condemned
Wis   3: 5 Having been **d** a little, they will

DISEASE → DISEASES
Mt   4:23 of the kingdom and curing every **d**
       9:35 curing every **d** and every sickness.

DISEASES → DISEASE
Ex   15:26 **d** that I brought upon the Egyptians;
Ps   103: 3 your iniquity, who heals all your **d**,
Isa   53: 4 our infirmities and carried our **d**;
Mt   8:17 took our infirmities and bore our **d.**"

DISGRACE
Jos   5: 9 I have rolled away from you the **d**
Pr   11: 2 When pride comes, then comes **d**;
Mt   1:19 unwilling to expose her to public **d**,
1Pe   4:16 do not consider it a **d**,
1Mc   4:58 the **d** brought by the Gentiles was

DISGUISES
2Co   11:14 Satan **d** himself as an angel of light.

DISHONEST
Jer   22:17 and heart are only on your **d** gain,
Lk   16:10 is **d** in a very little is **d** also in much.
Sir   5: 8 Do not depend on **d** wealth,

DISHONOR
Jn   8:49 I honor my Father, and you **d** me.
Ac   5:41 considered worthy to suffer **d** for
1Co   15:43 It is sown in **d**, it is raised in glory.

DISMAYED
Dt   1:21 do not fear or be **d.**"
Jos   1: 9 do not be frightened or **d**,
Jer   17:18 them be **d**, but do not let me be **d**;

DISOBEDIENT → DISOBEY
Ne   9:26 they were **d** and rebelled
Ro   10:21 I have held out my hands to a **d**
      11:30 as you were once **d** to God but have
Tit   3: 3 ourselves were once foolish, **d**, led

DISOBEY → DISOBEDIENT
Lev   26:27 But if, despite this, you **d** me,
1Pe   2: 8 stumble because they **d** the word,
Sir   1:28 Do not **d** the fear of the Lord;

DISPERSION
Jn   7:35 Does he intend to go to the **D**

DISQUALIFIED* → DISQUALIFY
1Co   9:27 to others I myself should not be **d.**

DISQUALIFY* → DISQUALIFIED
Col   2:18 Do not let anyone **d** you,

DISSENSION → DISSENSIONS
1Co   12:25 there may be no **d** within the body,
1Ti   6: 4 From these come envy, **d**, slander,

DISSENSIONS → DISSENSION
Gal   5:20 strife, jealousy, anger, quarrels, **d**,
Tit   3: 9 stupid controversies, genealogies, **d**,

DISTINCTION → DISTINCTIONS
Ex   8:23 I will make a **d** between my people
Lev   11:47 make a **d** between the unclean and
Eze   22:26 have made no **d** between the holy
Ro   3:22 For there is no **d**,

DISTINCTIONS* → DISTINCTION
Jas   2: 4 you not made **d** among yourselves,

DISTRESS → DISTRESSED
Dt   4:30 In your **d**, when all these things
Jdg   2:15 and they were in great **d**.
2Sa   22: 7 In my **d** I called upon the LORD;
Ps   81: 7 In **d** you called, and I rescued you;
Jer   30: 7 it is a time of **d** for Jacob;
Lk   21:23 For there will be great **d** on the
              earth
Ro   8:35 Will hardship, or **d**, or persecution,
Sir   2:11 and saves in time of **d**.

DISTRESSED → DISTRESS
La   1:20 See, O LORD, how **d** I am;

DISTRIBUTED
Jos   13:32 the inheritances that Moses **d**
Ps   112: 9 They have **d** freely,
Ac   4:35 it was **d** to each as any had need.
Heb   2: 4 gifts of the Holy Spirit, **d** according

DIVIDE → DIVIDED
Ex   14:16 your hand over the sea and **d** it,
Ps   22:18 **d** my clothes among themselves,
Lk   23:34 And they cast lots to **d** his clothing.

DIVIDED → DIVIDE
Lev   11: 3 Any animal that has **d** hoofs
Ps   136:13 who **d** the Red Sea in two,
Lk   11:18 If Satan also is **d** against himself,

DIVINATION → DIVINE
Dt   18:10 who practices **d**, or is a soothsayer,
1Sa   15:23 For rebellion is no less a sin than **d**,
2Ki   17:17 they used **d** and augury;

DIVINE → DIVINATION
Ro   1:20 his eternal power and **d** nature,
2Pe   1: 4 become participants of the **d** nature.

DIVORCE → DIVORCED
Dt   24: 1 so he writes her a certificate of **d**,
Isa   50: 1 Where is your mother's bill of **d**
Jer   3: 8 sent her away with a decree of **d**;
Mal   2:16 For I hate **d**, says the LORD,
Mt   5:31 let him give her a certificate of **d**,'
      19: 3 a man to **d** his wife for any cause?"
1Co   7:11 the husband should not **d** his wife.
Sir   7:26 Do not **d** her;

DIVORCED → DIVORCE
Lev   21: 7 neither shall they marry a woman **d**
Mt   5:32 whoever marries a **d** woman

DOCTOR*
Lk   4:23 this proverb, '**D**, cure yourself!'

DOCTRINE → DOCTRINES
Eph   4:14 blown about by every wind of **d**,
1Ti   1: 3 not to teach any different **d**,
2Ti   4: 3 people will not put up with sound **d**,
Tit   1: 9 able but to preach with sound **d**

DOCTRINES → DOCTRINE
Mk   7: 7 teaching human precepts as **d**.'

DOEG*
    Edomite; Saul's chief shepherd; murdered 85
priests at Nob (1Sa 21:7; 22:6-23; Ps 52).

DOERS → DOES, DONE
Jas   1:22 But be **d** of the word,

DOES → DOERS
Ps   135: 6 Whatever the LORD pleases he **d**,
Ecc   3:14 whatever God **d** endures forever;
Mk   3:35 **d** the will of God is my brother

DOG → DOGS
Jdg   7: 5 as a **d** laps, you shall put to one side
Pr   26:11 Like a **d** that returns to its vomit,
2Pe   2:22 "The **d** turns back to its own vomit,"

DOGS → DOG
Mt   7: 6 "Do not give what is holy to **d**;
      15:26 children's food and throw it to the **d**
Php   3: 2 Beware of the **d**, beware of the evil
Rev   22:15 Outside are the **d** and sorcerers

DOMINION
Ge   1:26 and let them have **d** over
Ps   22:28 For **d** belongs to the LORD,
Da   7:14 His **d** is an everlasting
Ro   6:14 For sin will have no **d** over you,
Rev   1: 6 to him be glory and **d** forever

DONE → DOERS
Mt   6:10 Your will be **d**, on earth as it is in
      26:42 unless I drink it, your will be **d.**"

Rev 16:17 from the throne, saying, "It is **d**!"
     21: 6 Then he said to me, "It is **d**!

DONKEY
Nu 22:30 But the **d** said to Balaam,
Jdg 15:15 he found a fresh jawbone of a **d**,
Zec 9: 9 humble and riding on a **d**,
Mt 21: 5 humble, and mounted on a **d**,

DOOM → DOOMED
Dt 32:35 their **d** comes swiftly.
Ps 81:15 and their **d** would last forever.

DOOMED → DOOM
Ps 102:20 to set free those who were **d** to die;
1Co 2: 6 of this age, who are **d** to perish.

DOOR → DOORPOSTS
Mt 7: 7 knock, and the **d** will be opened for
Lk 13:24 Strive to enter through the narrow **d**
Rev 3:20 I am standing at the **d**, knocking;

DOORPOSTS → DOOR
Ex 12: 7 the blood and put it on the two **d**

DORCAS*
  Disciple; raised from the dead (Ac 9:36-43).

DOUBLE → DOUBLE-TONGUED
Ex 22: 7 then the thief, if caught, shall pay **d**.
Dt 21:17 giving him a **d** portion of all that he
1Sa 1: 5 but to Hannah he gave a **d** portion,
2Ki 2: 9 me inherit a **d** share of your spirit."
Rev 18: 6 and repay her **d** for her deeds;

DOUBLE-TONGUED → DOUBLE, TONGUE
1Ti 3: 8 likewise must be serious, not **d**,
Sir 5:14 Do not be called **d** and do not

DOUBT → DOUBTED, DOUBTING
Mt 14:31 of little faith, why did you **d**?"
Jn 20:27 Do not **d** but believe."

DOUBTED* → DOUBT
Mt 28:17 they worshiped him; but some **d**.

DOUBTING* → DOUBT
Jas 1: 6 But ask in faith, never **d**,

DOUGH
Ex 12:39 **d** that they had brought out of Egypt
Gal 5: 9 yeast leavens the whole batch of **d**.

DOVE
Ge 8: 8 Then he sent out the **d** from him,
Mk 1:10 Spirit descending like a **d** on him.

DRAGON
Isa 27: 1 and he will kill the **d** that
Rev 12: 3 a great red **d**, with seven heads and
     20: 2 seized the **d**, that ancient serpent,
Bel 1:23 in that place there was a great **d**,

DRANK → DRINK
Ex 24:11 beheld God, and they ate and **d**.
Mk 14:23 and all of them **d** from it.
1Co 10: 4 and all **d** the same spiritual drink.

DRAW
Jn 12:32 will **d** all people to myself."
Jas 4: 8 **D** near to God, and he will near

DREAM → DREAMED, DREAMER, DREAMS
1Ki 3: 5 LORD appeared to Solomon in a **d**
Da 1:17 Daniel had a **d** and visions of his
Joel 2:28 your old men shall **d** dreams,
Mt 1:20 of the Lord appeared to him in a **d**
Ac 2:17 and your old men shall **d** dreams.

DREAMED → DREAM
Ge 28:12 he **d** that there was a ladder set up
     41: 1 Pharaoh that he was standing by
Da 2: 1 Nebuchadnezzar **d** such dreams
2Es 13: 1 After seven days I **d** a dream in the

DREAMER* → DREAM
Ge 37:19 to one another, "Here comes this **d**.

DREAMS → DREAM
Nu 12: 6 I speak to them in **d**.

1Sa 28: 6 LORD did not answer him, not by **d**,
Sir 34: 7 For **d** have deceived many,

DRIED → DRY
Ge 8:13 the waters were **d** up from the earth;
Jos 5: 1 had **d** up the waters of the Jordan
Isa 51:10 Was it not you who **d** up the sea,

DRINK → DRANK, DRUNK, DRUNKARD, DRUNKENNESS
Ge 19:33 So they made their father **d** wine
Ex 32: 6 the people sat down to eat and **d**,
Ecc 9: 7 and **d** your wine with a merry heart;
Isa 22:13 eat and **d**, for tomorrow we die."
Mt 20:22 to **d** the cup that I am about to **d**?"
Jn 18:11 not to **d** the cup that the Father has
Ro 14:17 kingdom of God is not food and **d**
1Co 12:13 we were all made to **d** of one Spirit.
Rev 14:10 also **d** the wine of God's wrath,

DRIVE → DROVE
Ex 23:30 Little by little I will **d** them out
Nu 33:52 you shall **d** out all the inhabitants of
Jos 13:13 Yet the Israelites did not **d** out the
Mk 11:15 to **d** out those who were selling
Jn 6:37 comes to me I will never **d** away;

DROSS
Ps 119:119 wicked of the earth you count as **d**;
Isa 1:25 I will smelt away your **d** as with lye
Eze 22:18 house of Israel has become **d** to me;

DROVE → DRIVE
Jos 24:18 the LORD **d** out before us all the
Mk 1:12 Spirit immediately **d** him out into

DRUNK → DRINK
Ge 9:21 some of the wine and became **d**,
1Sa 1:13 therefore Eli thought she was **d**.
SS 5: 1 drink, and be **d** with love.
Jn 2:10 after the guests have become **d**.
Ac 2:15 these are not **d**, as you suppose,
Eph 5:18 Do not get **d** with wine,
Jdt 13: 2 on his bed, for he was dead **d**.

DRUNKARD → DRINK
Pr 23:21 for the **d** and the glutton will come
Mt 11:19 they say, 'Look, a glutton and a **d**,
1Co 5:11 is an idolater, reviler, **d**, or robber.
1Ti 3: 3 not a **d**, not violent but gentle,

DRUNKENNESS → DRINK
Ecc 10:17 for strength, and not for **d**!
Gal 5:21 **d**, carousing, and things like these.
Tob 4:15 to excess or let **d** go with you

DRY → DRIED
Ge 1: 9 and let the **d** land appear."
Ex 14:16 may go into the sea on **d** ground.
Jos 3:17 were crossing over on **d** ground,
Jdg 6:37 and it is **d** on all the ground,
Eze 37: 4 **d** bones, hear the word of the LORD.

DUE
1Ch 16:29 Ascribe to the LORD the glory **d** his
Ps 28: 4 render them their **d** reward.
Mal 1: 6 a father, where is the honor **d** me?
Ro 13: 7 Pay to all what is **d** them—

DULL
Isa 6:10 Make the mind of this people **d**,
     59: 1 nor his ear too **d** to hear.
Mt 13:15 For this people's heart has grown **d**,

DUST
Ge 2: 7 LORD God formed man from the **d**
     3:14 and **d** you shall eat all the days of
     3:16 offspring like the **d** of the earth;
1Sa 2: 8 He raises up the poor from the **d**;
Ps 103:14 he remembers that we are **d**.
Ecc 3:20 from the **d**, and all turn to **d** again.
Na 1: 3 and the clouds are the **d** of his feet.
Mt 10:14 shake off the **d** from your feet
1Co 15:47 man was from the earth, a man of **d**;

DWELL → DWELLING, DWELLS
Ex 25: 8 so that I may **d** among them.
1Ki 8:27 But will God indeed **d** on the earth?
Ps 23: 6 and I shall **d** in the house of
Eph 3:17 that Christ may **d** in your hearts
Col 1:19 fullness of God was pleased to **d**,
Rev 21: 3 He will **d** with them as their God;

DWELLING → DWELL
Lev 26:11 I will place my **d** in your midst,
Dt 12:11 will choose as a **d** for his name:
Ps 90: 1 our **d** place in all generations.
Jn 14: 2 my Father's house there are many **d**
2Co 5: 2 to be clothed with our heavenly **d**—
Eph 2:22 spiritually into a **d** place for God.

DWELLS → DWELL
Jn 14:10 but the Father who **d** in me
Ro 7:17 but sin that **d** within me.
1Co 3:16 and that God's Spirit **d** in you?
Col 2: 9 the whole fullness of deity **d** bodily,

DYING → DEAD
2Co 6: 9 as **d**, and see—we are alive;
Php 1:21 living is Christ and **d** is gain.

E

EAGLE → EAGLES, EAGLES'
Eze 1:10 the left side, and the face of an **e**;
     17: 3 A great **e**, with great wings and long
Rev 4: 7 fourth living creature like a flying **e**.
2Es 11: 1 an **e** that had twelve feathered wings

EAGLES → EAGLE
Isa 40:31 shall mount up with wings like **e**,

EAGLES' → EAGLE
Ex 19: 4 and how I bore you on **e** wings
Da 7: 4 like a lion and had **e** wings.

EAR → EARS
Isa 64: 4 has heard, no **e** has perceived,
Lk 22:51 he touched his **e** and healed him.
1Co 2: 9 "What no eye has seen, nor **e** heard,
Rev 2: 7 Let anyone who has an **e** listen

EARLY
Dt 11:14 the **e** rain and the later rain,
Lk 24:22 were at the tomb **e** this morning,
Jas 5: 7 receives the **e** and the late rains.

EARS → EAR
Dt 29: 4 or eyes to see, or **e** to hear.
Isa 35: 5 and the **e** of the deaf unstopped;
Mt 11:15 Let anyone who has **e** listen!
2Ti 4: 3 sound doctrine, but having itching
     e,

EARTH → EARTHLY, EARTHQUAKE, EARTHQUAKES
Ge 1: 1 God created the heavens and the **e**,
     6:11 the **e** was corrupt in God's sight,
Ex 19: 5 Indeed, the whole **e** is mine,
Ps 47: 2 a great king over all the **e**.
Isa 6: 3 the whole **e** is full of his glory."
     65:17 to create new heavens and a new **e**;
Jer 23:24 Do I not fill heaven and **e**?
Mt 5: 5 the meek, for they will inherit the **e**.
     24:35 Heaven and **e** will pass away,
Lk 5:24 has authority on **e** to forgive sins"—
2Pe 3:13 wait for new heavens and a new **e**,
Rev 21: 1 I saw a new heaven and a new **e**;
Sir 40:11 All that is of **e** returns to **e**,

EARTHLY → EARTH
Jn 3:12 If I have told you about **e** things
2Co 5: 1 if the **e** tent we live in is destroyed,

EARTHQUAKE → EARTH, QUAKE
1Ki 19:11 but the LORD was not in the **e**;
Mt 28: 2 And suddenly there was a great **e**;
Ac 16:26 Suddenly there was an **e**,
Rev 6:12 I looked, and there came a great **e**;
2Es 3:19 four gates of fire and **e** and wind

EARTHQUAKES → EARTH, QUAKE
Mt 24: 7 be famines and e in various places:
2Es 9: 3 there shall appear in the world e,

EASIER → EASY
Mt 9: 5 is e, to say, 'Your sins are forgiven,'
Lk 16:17 it is e for heaven and earth to pass
18:25 e for a camel to go through the eye

EAST
Ge 2: 8 planted a garden in Eden, in the e;
Ps 103:12 as far as is the e is from the west,
Mt 2: 1 wise men from the E came to

EASY → EASIER
Mt 7:13 road is e that leads to destruction,
11:30 For my yoke is e, and my burden is

EAT → ATE, EATING, EATS
Ge 2:16 freely e of every tree of the garden;
Ex 12:11 This is how you shall e it:
Lev 3:17 not e any fat or any blood.
11: 4 you shall not e the following:
Ecc 2:24 nothing better for mortals than to e
Mt 26:26 to the disciples, and said, "Take, e;
Ac 10:13 "Get up, Peter; kill and e."
1Co 10:31 whether you e or drink, or whatever
Rev 3:20 I will come in to you and e with you

EATING → EAT
Lk 7:34 the Son of Man has come e and
Ro 14: 2 Some believe in e anything,
1Co 8: 4 as to the e of food offered to idols,

EATS → EAT
Jn 6:51 e of this bread will live forever;
1Co 11:27 e the bread or drinks the cup of the

EDEN
Ge 2: 8 a garden in E, in the east;
Isa 51: 3 and will make her wilderness like E,
Eze 28:13 You were in E, the garden of God;

EDOM → =ESAU
Ge 25:30 (Therefore he was called E.)
Nu 20:18 But E said to him, "You shall not
Ob 1: 1 says the Lord God concerning E:
Mal 1: 4 If E says, "We are shattered but we

EFFORT
Gal 2:17 in our e to be justified in Christ,
Eph 4: 3 every e to maintain the unity of the
Heb 4:11 make every e to enter that rest,
2Pe 1: 5 make every e to support your faith

EGYPT
Ge 12:10 So Abram went down to E to reside
37:28 And they took Joseph to E.
47:27 Thus Israel settled in the land of E,
Ex 1: 8 Now a new king arose over E,
12:40 in E was four hundred thirty years.
Jos 15:47 to the Wadi of E, and the Great Sea
Ne 9:18 God who brought you up out of E,'
Ps 78:51 He struck all the firstborn in E,
Hos 11: 1 and out of E I called my son.
Mt 2:15 "Out of E I have called my son."
Rev 11: 8 prophetically called Sodom and E,

EHUD
Judge of Israel (Jdg 3:12-30).

ELAH
1. Son of Baasha; king of Israel (1Ki 16:6-14).
2. Valley in which David fought Goliath (1Sa 17:2, 19; 21:9).

ELDER → ELDERS
Ge 25:23 the e shall serve the younger."
Ro 9:12 "The e shall serve the younger."
1Ti 5:19 any accusation against an e except
1Pe 5: 1 as an e myself and a witness of the

ELDERS → ELDER
Ex 24: 1 and seventy of the e of Israel,
Jdg 2: 7 days of the e who outlived Joshua,
Isa 3:14 enters into judgment with the e
Mt 27:12 accused by the chief priests and e,

Mk 7: 3 thus observing the tradition of the e;
1Ti 5:17 the e who rule well be considered
Jas 5:14 e of the church and have them pray
1Pe 5: 5 must accept the authority of the e.
Rev 4: 4 on the thrones are twenty-four e,
Sus 1:61 they took action against the two e,

ELEAZAR
1. Third son of Aaron (Ex 6:23-25). Succeeded Aaron as high priest (Nu 20:26; Dt 10:6). Allotted land to tribes (Jos 14:1). Death (Jos 24:33).
2. Brother of Judas Maccabeus (1Mc 2:5; 6:43-46).

ELECT → ELECTION
Mt 24:22 sake of the e those days will be cut
Mk 13:22 to lead astray, if possible, the e.
Wis 4:15 grace and mercy are with his e,
2Es 16:73 Then the tested quality of my e

ELECTION* → ELECT
Ro 9:11 God's purpose of e might continue,
11:28 but as regards e they are beloved,
2Pe 1:10 eager to confirm your call and e,

ELEMENTS
Heb 5:12 the basic e of the oracles of God.
2Pe 3:10 and the e will be dissolved with fire,

ELEVEN
Mt 28:16 Now the e disciples went to Galilee,
Ac 1:26 and he was added to the e apostles.

ELI
1. High priest in youth of Samuel (1Sa 1-4). Blessed Hannah (1Sa 1:12-18); raised Samuel (1Sa 2:11-26). Prophesied against because of wicked sons (1Sa 2:27-36). Death of Eli and sons (1Sa 4:11-22).
2. "Eli, Eli, lema sabachthani?" (Mt 27:46).

ELIAKIM → =JEHOIAKIM
1. Original name of Jehoiakim (2Ki 23:34; 2Ch 36:4).
2. Hezekiah's palace administrator (2Ki 18:17-37; 19:2; Isa 36:1-22; 37:2).

ELIEZER
1. Servant of Abraham (Ge 15:2).
2. Son of Moses (Ex 18:4; 1Ch 23:15-17).

ELIHU
A friend of Job (Job 32-37).

ELIJAH
Prophet; predicted famine in Israel (1Ki 17:1; Jas 5:17). Fed by ravens (1Ki 17:2-6). Raised Sidonian widow's son (1Ki 17:7-24). Defeated prophets of Baal at Carmel (1Ki 18:16-46). Ran from Jezebel (1Ki 19:1-9). Prophesied death of Azariah (1Ki 19:19-21; 2Ki 2:1-18). Succeeded by Elisha (1Ki 19:19-21; 2Ki 2:1-18). Taken to heaven in whirlwind (2Ki 2:11-12; Sir 48:1-12; 1Mc 2:58).
Return prophesied (Mal 4:5-6); equated with John the Baptist (Mt 17:9-13; Mk 9:9-13; Lk 1:17). Appeared with Moses in transfiguration of Jesus (Mt 17:1-8; Mk 9:1-8).

ELIMELECH
Ru 1: 3 But E, the husband of Naomi, died,

ELIPHAZ
A friend of Job (Job 4-5; 15; 22; 42:7, 9).

ELISHA
Prophet; successor of Elijah (1Ki 19:16-21; Sir 48:12-14); inherited his mantle (2Ki 2:1-18). Purified bad water (2Ki 2:19-22). Cursed young men (2Ki 2:23-25). Aided Israel's defeat of Moab (2Ki 3). Provided widow with oil (2Ki 4:1-7). Raised Shunammite woman's son (2Ki 4:8-37). Purified food (2Ki 4:38-41). Fed 100 men (2Ki 4:42-44). Healed Naaman's leprosy (2Ki 5). Made axhead float (2Ki 6:1-7). Captured Arameans (2Ki 6:8-23). Political adviser to Israel (2Ki 6:24-8:6; 9:1-3; 13:14-19), Aram (2Ki 8:7-15). Death (2Ki 13:20).

ELIZABETH*
Mother of John the Baptist (Lk 1:5-58).

ELKANAH
Husband of Hannah, father of Samuel (1Sa 1-2).

EMMANUEL* → =IMMANUEL
Mt 1:23 and they shall name him E,"

EMMAUS
Lk 24:13 were going to a village called E,

EMPEROR
Mt 22:17 Is it lawful to pay taxes to the e, or
Jn 19:12 you are no friend of the e.

EMPTIED → EMPTY
1Co 1:17 cross of Christ might not be e of its
Php 2: 7 but e himself, taking the form of

EMPTY → EMPTIED, EMPTY-HANDED
Ru 1:21 the LORD has brought me back e;
Isa 55:11 it shall not return to me e,
Mt 6: 7 do not heap up e phrases
Eph 5: 6 no one deceive you with e words,

EMPTY-HANDED → EMPTY, HAND
Ex 23:15 No one shall appear before me e.
Ru 3:17 not go back to your mother-in-law e

EN-GEDI
1Sa 23:29 and lived in the strongholds of E.

ENCOURAGE → ENCOURAGEMENT
1Th 4:18 e one another with these words.
1Pe 5:12 written this short letter to e you

ENCOURAGEMENT → ENCOURAGE
Ac 4:36 Barnabas (which means "son of e").
Ro 15: 5 God of steadfastness and e grant
Php 2: 1 If then there is any e in Christ,

END → ENDS
Ge 6:13 determined to make an e of all flesh,
Pr 14:12 but its e is the way to death.
Ecc 12:12 making many books there is no e,
Mt 24:13 but the one who endures to the e
28:20 always, to the e of the age."
Jn 13: 1 he loved them to the e.
Ro 10: 4 For Christ is the e of the law so that
Rev 22:13 the beginning and the e."

ENDOR*
1Sa 28: 7 "There is a medium at E."

ENDS → END
Ps 2: 8 the e of the earth your possession.
Isa 40:28 the Creator of the e of the earth.
Ro 10:18 their words to the e of the world."
1Co 13: 8 Love never e. But as for prophecies,

ENDURANCE → ENDURE
Lk 8:15 and bear fruit with patient e.
Ro 5: 3 knowing that suffering produces e,
1Ti 6:11 godliness, faith, love, e,
Heb 10:36 For you need e, so that when you
Jas 1: 3 the testing of your faith produces e;
2Pe 1: 6 and self-control with e, and e with
Rev 1: 9 and the kingdom and the patient e,

ENDURE → ENDURANCE, ENDURED, ENDURES
Ps 89:29 his throne as long as the heavens e.
Mal 3: 2 who can e the day of his coming,
1Co 10:13 out so that you may be able to e it.
2Ti 2:12 if we e, we will also reign with him;

ENDURED → ENDURE
Heb 12: 2 that was set before him e the cross,

ENDURES → ENDURE
1Ch 16:41 for his steadfast love e forever.
Mt 13:21 but e only for a while,
Jn 6:27 for the food that e for eternal life,
1Co 13: 7 hopes all things, e all things.
1Pe 1:25 but the word of the Lord e forever."
Sir 40:17 and almsgiving e forever.
Bar 4: 1 the law that e forever.

ENEMIES → ENEMY

Ex	23:22	be an enemy to your e and a foe to
Est	9: 5	the Jews struck down all their e
Ps	110: 1	until I make your e your footstool."
Mt	5:44	But I say to you, Love your e and
Lk	20:43	until I make your e your footstool."
Ro	5:10	For if while we were e,
	12:20	"if your e are hungry, feed them;
Jdt	8:35	to take vengeance on our e."
1Mc	4:36	said, "See, our e are crushed;

ENEMY → ENEMIES, ENMITY

Mt	13:39	the e who sowed them is the devil;
1Co	15:26	The last e to be destroyed is death.
Jas	4: 4	of the world becomes an e of God.

ENGAGED

Mt	1:18	mother Mary had been e to Joseph,

ENJOY → ENJOYMENT

Ecc	3:22	that all should e their work,
	9: 9	E life with the wife whom you love,

ENJOYMENT → ENJOY

Ecc	8:15	So I commend e, for there is nothing
1Ti	6:17	with everything for our e.

ENLIGHTENED → LIGHT

Ro	10: 2	have a zeal for God, but it is not e.
Eph	1:18	with the eyes of your heart e,
Heb	6: 4	those who have once been e,

ENLIGHTENS* → LIGHT

Jn	1: 9	The true light, which e everyone,

ENMITY → ENEMY

Ge	3:15	put e between you and the woman,
Jas	4: 4	with the world is e with God?

ENOCH

Walked with God and taken by him (Ge 5:18-24; Heb 11:5; Sir 44:16). Prophet (Jude 14).

ENSLAVE → SLAVE

1Co	9:27	but I punish my body and e it,
Gal	4: 3	so that they might e us—

ENSLAVED → SLAVE

Ro	6: 6	and we might no longer be e to sin.
Gal	4: 9	want to be e to them again?

ENTER → ENTRY

Ex	40:35	Moses was not able to e the tent
Nu	20:24	not e the land that I have given to
Ps	95:11	I swore, "They shall not e my rest."
Mt	5:20	will never e the kingdom of heaven.
	7:13	"E through the narrow gate;
Mk	10:15	as a little child will never e it."
Jn	3: 5	no one can e the kingdom of God
Heb	3:11	'They will not e my rest.' "
	10:19	have confidence to e the sanctuary
Rev	21:27	But nothing unclean will e it,

ENTHRONED → THRONE

1Ch	13: 6	the LORD, who is e on the cherubim,
Ps	9: 7	But the LORD sits e forever,

ENTRUST → TRUST

Jn	2:24	Jesus on his part would not e
1Pe	4:19	e themselves to a faithful Creator,

ENTRUSTED → TRUST

Lk	12:48	the one to whom much has been e,
2Ti	1:12	guard until that day what I have e to
Jude	1: 3	the faith that was once for all e to

ENVY

Pr	23:17	Do not let your heart e sinners,
Mk	7:22	deceit, licentiousness, e, slander,
Ro	1:29	Full of e, murder, strife, deceit,
Jas	3:16	For where there is e and selfish

EPHOD

Ex	28: 6	They shall make the e of gold,
Jdg	8:27	Gideon made an e of it and put it in

EPHRAIM

1. Second son of Joseph (Ge 41:52; 46:20). Blessed as firstborn by Jacob (Ge 48). Tribe of numbered (Nu 1:33; 26:37), blessed (Dt 33:17), allotted land (Jos 16:4-9; Eze 48:5), failed to fully possess (Jos 16:10; Jdg 1:29).

2. Term for the Northern Kingdom (Isa 7:17; Hos 5).

EQUAL → EQUALITY

Isa	40:25	you compare me, or who is my e?
	46: 5	will you liken me and make me e,
Jn	5:18	thereby making himself e to God.

EQUALITY* → EQUAL

Php	2: 6	not regard e with God as something

ERROR

Lev	5:18	for the e that you committed
Ro	1:27	the due penalty for their e.
1Jn	4: 6	the spirit of truth and the spirit of e.
Wis	1:12	Do not invite death by the e of your

ESAU → =EDOM

Firstborn of Isaac, twin of Jacob (Ge 25:21-26). Also called Edom (Ge 25:30). Sold Jacob his birthright (Ge 25:29-34); lost blessing (Gen 27). Married Hittites (Ge 26:34), Ishmaelites (Ge 28:6-9), Reconciled to Jacob (Gen 33). Genealogy (Ge 36), The LORD chose Jacob over Esau (Mal 1:2-3), but gave Esau land (Dt 2:2-12). Descendants eventually obliterated (Ob 1-21; Jer 49:7-22).

ESCAPE

Ge	7: 7	went into the ark to e the waters of
Ps	68:20	the LORD, belongs e from death.
Ro	2: 3	you will e the judgment of God?
1Th	5: 3	and there will be no e!
Heb	12:25	how much less will we e if we reject
2Pe	1: 4	you may e from the corruption

ESTABLISH → ESTABLISHED

Ge	6:18	But I will e my covenant with you;
Dt	28: 9	LORD will e you as his holy people,
Ps	89: 4	'I will e your descendants forever,
Eze	16:60	e with you an everlasting covenant.
Ro	10: 3	and seeking to e their own,
Heb	8: 8	when I will e a new covenant with

ESTABLISHED → ESTABLISH

2Sa	7:16	your throne shall be e forever.
Ps	89: 2	your steadfast love is e forever;
	103:19	The LORD has e his throne in the
Jer	10:12	who e the world by his wisdom,
2Pe	1:12	you know them already and are e in

ESTHER

Jewess, originally named Hadassah, who lived in Persia; cousin of Mordecai (Est 2:7). Chosen queen of Xerxes (Est 2:8-18). Persuaded by Mordecai to foil Haman's plan to exterminate the Jews (Est 3-4). Revealed Haman's plans to Xerxes, resulting in Haman's death (Est 7), the Jews' preservation (Est 8-9), Mordecai's exaltation (Est 8:15; 9:4; 10). Decreed celebration of Purim (Est 9:18-32). See Additions to Esther.

ETERNAL → ETERNITY

Mt	25:46	but the righteous into e life."
Mk	10:17	what must I do to inherit e life?"
Jn	3:16	may not perish but may have e life.
	10:28	I give them e life, and they will
Ro	5:21	e life through Jesus Christ our Lord.
2Co	4:17	an e weight of glory beyond all
Heb	5: 9	the source of e salvation for all who
1Jn	5:13	may know that you have e life.

ETERNITY → ETERNAL

Isa	57:15	high and lofty one who inhabits e,
2Pe	3:18	glory both now and to the day of e.
Wis	2:23	made us in the image of his own e,
Sir	42:21	he is from all e one and the same.

ETHIOPIANS

Jer	13:23	Can E change their skin

EUNUCH → EUNUCHS

Jer	38: 7	Ebed-melech the Ethiopian, a e
Ac	8:27	Now there was an Ethiopian e,

EUNUCHS → EUNUCH

Isa	56: 4	To the e who keep my sabbaths,
Mt	19:12	made themselves e for the sake of the

EUPHRATES

Ge	2:14	And the fourth river is the E.
	15:18	Egypt to the great river, the river E,
Rev	16:12	poured his bowl on the great river E

EUTYCHUS*

Ac	20: 9	A young man named E,

EVANGELIST* → EVANGELISTS

Ac	21: 8	went into the house of Philip the e,
2Ti	4: 5	do the work of an e, carry out your

EVANGELISTS* → EVANGELIST

Eph	4:11	some e, some pastors and teachers,

EVE*

Ge	3:20	The man named his wife E,
	4: 1	Now the man knew his wife E,
2Co	11: 3	afraid that as the serpent deceived E
1Ti	2:13	For Adam was formed first, then E;
Tob	8: 6	his wife E as a helper and support.

EVENING

Ge	1: 5	there was e and there was morning,
Ecc	11: 6	at e do not let your hands be idle;
Zec	14: 7	for at e time there shall be light.

EVERLASTING → LAST

Ge	9:16	remember the e covenant between
Ps	90: 2	from e to e you are God.
Isa	9: 6	God, E Father, Prince of Peace.
	40:28	The LORD is the e God,
Jer	31: 3	I have loved you with an e love;
Da	4: 3	His kingdom is an e kingdom,

EVERY → EVERYTHING

Ge	7:23	He blotted out e living thing that
Ex	11: 5	E firstborn in the land of Egypt
Dt	8: 3	e word that comes from the mouth
Ecc	12:14	God will bring e deed into judgment
Isa	45:23	"To me e knee shall bow,
Mt	12:25	"E kingdom divided against itself
Ro	14:11	e knee shall bow to me, and e tongue
Php	2:10	at the name of Jesus e knee should
2Ti	3:17	equipped for e good work.
1Jn	4: 1	Beloved, do not believe e spirit,
Rev	21: 4	he will wipe e tear from their eyes.

EVERYTHING → EVERY

Ge	1:31	God saw e that he had made,
Ex	19: 8	"E the LORD has spoken we will
Ecc	3: 1	For e there is a season,
1Co	10:31	do e for the glory of God.
1Ti	4: 4	For e created by God is good,
2Pe	1: 3	divine power has given us e needed

EVIDENCE

Dt	17: 6	On the e of two or three witnesses
Mt	18:16	by the e of two or three witnesses.
Sus	1:43	men have given false e against me.

EVIL → EVILDOER, EVILDOERS

Ge	2: 9	tree of the knowledge of good and e.
	3: 5	be like God, knowing good and e."
	6: 5	their hearts was only e continually.
Ex	32:22	the people, that they are bent on e.
Dt	13: 5	So you shall purge the e from your
Jdg	2:11	Then the Israelites did what was e
Ps	23: 4	the darkest valley, I fear no e;
Pr	8:13	The fear of the LORD is hatred of e.
Ecc	12:14	secret thing, whether good or e.
Isa	5:20	you who call e good and good e,
Mt	6:13	but rescue us from the e one.

Mt	12:35	e person brings e things out of an e
Lk	11:13	who are e, know how to give good
Jn	17:15	to protect them from the e one.
Ro	12:17	Do not repay anyone e for e,
Eph	5:16	of the time, because the days are e.
1Ti	6:10	of money is a root of all kinds of e,
1Pe	2:16	use your freedom as a pretext for e.
1Jn	5:18	and the e one does not touch them.
2Jn	1:11	to welcome is to participate in the e
3Jn	1:11	do not imitate what is e but imitate
Tob	12: 7	Do good and e will not overtake
Sir	7: 1	Do no e, and e will never overtake

EVILDOER → EVIL

Ps	52: 6	and will laugh at the e, saying,
Mt	5:39	But I say to you, Do not resist an e.

EVILDOERS → EVIL

2Sa	7:10	and e shall afflict them no more,
Ps	34:16	The face of the LORD is against e,
Lk	13:27	go away from me, all you e!'
1Pe	2:12	though they malign you as e,

EXALT → EXALTED, EXALTS

Ex	15: 2	my father's God, and I will e him.
Pr	4: 8	Prize her highly, and she will e you,
Isa	25: 1	I will e you, I will praise your name;
Lk	14:11	who e themselves will be humbled,
Jas	4:10	before the Lord, and he will e you.

EXALTED → EXALT

Ps	57: 5	Be e, O God, above the heavens.
	97: 9	you are e far above all gods.
Isa	2:11	the LORD alone will be e in that day.
Php	2: 9	highly e him and gave him the name

EXALTS → EXALT

Pr	14:34	Righteousness e a nation,
Sir	7:11	for there is One who humbles and e.

EXAMINE

1Co	11:28	E yourselves, and only then eat of
2Co	13: 5	E yourselves to see whether you
Sir	18:20	Before judgment comes, e yourself;

EXAMPLE → EXAMPLES

Jn	13:15	For I have set you an e,
Php	3:17	according to the e you have in us.

EXAMPLES → EXAMPLE

1Co	10: 6	these things occurred as e for us,
1Pe	5: 3	but be e to the flock.

EXCEL → EXCELLENCE, EXCELLENT

1Co	14:12	strive to e in them for building up
Sir	33:23	E in all that you do;

EXCELLENCE → EXCEL

Php	4: 8	if there is any e and if there is

EXCELLENT → EXCEL

Isa	28:29	in counsel, and e in wisdom.
1Co	12:31	I will show you a still more e way.
Heb	1: 4	the name he has inherited is more e

EXCEPT

2Sa	22:32	And who is a rock, e our God?
Mt	11:27	no one knows the Son e the Father,
Lk	11:29	be given to it e the sign of Jonah.
Jn	14: 6	No one comes to the Father e

EXCHANGED

Ps	106:20	They e the glory of God for the
Ro	1:23	e the glory of the immortal God

EXCUSE

Jn	15:22	but now they have no e for their sin.
Ro	1:20	So they are without e;

EXHORT

Tit	2:15	e and reprove with all authority.
Heb	3:13	But e one another every day,

EXILE → EXILES

2Ki	25:11	carried into e the rest of the people
Ezr	6:21	of Israel who had returned from e,

EXILES → EXILE

1Pe	2:11	I urge you as aliens and e

EXIST → EXISTED, EXISTS

1Co	8: 6	are all things and for whom we e,
Heb	2:10	and through whom all things e,

EXISTED → EXIST

2Pe	3: 5	the word of God heavens e long ago
Rev	4:11	by your will they e and were created

EXISTS → EXIST

Ps	119:89	The LORD e forever;
Heb	11: 6	that he e and that he rewards those

EXPECTING

Lk	6:35	and lend, e nothing in return.
Php	3:20	that we are e a Savior,

EXPLAIN → EXPLAINED, EXPLAINING

2Ch	9: 2	Solomon that he could not e to her.
Da	5:12	to interpret dreams, e riddles,

EXPLAINED → EXPLAIN

Mk	4:34	but he e everything in private to his

EXPLAINING → EXPLAIN

2Ti	2:15	rightly e the word of truth.

EXPOSE → EXPOSED

Mt	1:19	unwilling to e her to public disgrace
Eph	5:11	of darkness, but instead e them.

EXPOSED → EXPOSE

Jn	3:20	so that their deeds may not be e.
Eph	5:13	everything e by the light becomes
Heb	10:33	sometimes being publicly e to abuse

EYE → EYES, EYEWITNESSES

Ex	21:24	e for e, tooth for tooth,
Ps	17: 8	Guard me as the apple of the e;
Mt	5:29	If your right e causes you to sin,
	5:38	An e for an e and a tooth for a tooth.
	7: 3	see the speck in your neighbor's e,
Mk	10:25	to go through the e of a needle
1Co	15:52	in the twinkling of an e, at the last
Rev	1: 7	the clouds; every e will see him,

EYES → EYE

Ge	3: 7	Then the e of both were opened,
Dt	29: 4	or e to see, or ears to hear.
2Ch	16: 9	e of the LORD range throughout the
Ps	121: 1	I lift up my e to the hills—
Pr	3: 7	Do not be wise in your own e;
	22:12	The e of the LORD keep watch over
Isa	11: 3	He shall not judge by what his e see,
Jer	9: 1	and my e a fountain of tears,
Eze	1:18	rims of all four were full of e all
Da	10: 6	lightning, his e like flaming torches,
Zec	4:10	"These seven are the e of the LORD,
Mt	9:30	And their e were opened.
	13:15	that they might not look with their e,
Lk	24:31	their e were opened, and they
Eph	1:18	with the e of your heart enlightened,
1Pe	3:12	e of the LORD are on the righteous,
1Jn	2:16	of the flesh, the desire of the e,
Rev	1:14	his e were like a flame of fire,
	4: 6	full of e in front and behind;
	21: 4	he will wipe every tear from their e.

EYEWITNESSES* → EYE, WITNESS

Lk	1: 2	who from the beginning were e
2Pe	1:16	but we had been e of his majesty.

EZEKIEL

Priest called to be prophet to the exiles (Eze 1-3; Sir 49:8). Symbolically acted out destruction of Jerusalem (Eze 4-5; 12; 24).

EZRA

Priest and teacher of the Law who led a return of exiles to Israel to reestablish temple and worship (Ezr 7-8). Corrected intermarriage of priests (Ezr 9-10; 1Es 8-9). Read Law at celebration of Feast

of Tabernacles (Ne 8; 1Es 9:37-55). Participated in dedication of Jerusalem's walls (Ne 12).

F

FACE → FACES

Ge	1: 2	darkness covered the f of the deep,
	32:30	saying, "For I have seen God f to f,
Ex	3: 6	Moses hid his f, for he was afraid to
	34:30	the skin of his f was shining,
Nu	6:25	LORD make his f to shine upon you,
	12: 8	With him I speak f to f—
Ps	4: 6	Let the light of your f shine on us,
Isa	54: 8	wrath for a moment I hid my f
Eze	39:29	I will never again hide my f from
Lk	9:29	the appearance of his f changed,
2Co	3: 7	not gaze at Moses' f because of the glory
Rev	1:16	his f was like the sun shining with

FACES → FACE

Eze	1: 6	Each had four f, and each
2Co	3:18	And all of us, with unveiled f,
Rev	9: 7	their f were like human f,

FACTIONS

1Co	11:19	there have to be f among you,
Gal	5:20	anger, quarrels, dissensions, f,

FADE → FADES

Ps	37: 2	for they will soon f like the grass,
Isa	64: 6	We all f like a leaf,

FADES → FADE

Isa	40: 7	The grass withers, the flower f,
1Pe	5: 4	crown of glory that never f away.

FAIL → FAILED

Dt	31: 6	he will not f you or forsake you."
Jos	1: 5	I will not f you or forsake you.
Eze	47:12	will not wither nor their fruit f,
Mk	8:18	Do you have eyes, and f to see?

FAILED → FAIL

Jos	23:14	pass for you, not one of them has f.
1Ki	8:56	not one word has f of all his good
Ro	9: 6	not as though the word of God had f

FAINT

Ps	142: 3	When my spirit is f, you know my
Isa	40:31	they shall walk and not f.

FAITH → FAITHFUL, FAITHFULNESS, FAITHLESS

Ps	146: 6	in them; who keeps f forever;
Isa	7: 9	If you do not stand firm in f,
Hab	2: 4	but the righteous live by their f.
Mt	17:20	have f the size of a mustard seed,
Mk	2: 5	When Jesus saw their f, he said to
Lk	7:50	the woman, "Your f has saved you;
	18: 8	comes, will he find f on earth?"
Ac	3:16	and the f that is through Jesus
Ro	1:17	one who is righteous will live by f."
	3:28	that a person is justified by f apart
1Co	13:13	And now f, hope, and love abide,
Gal	3:11	one who is righteous will live by f."
Eph	4: 5	one Lord, one f, one baptism,
Php	3: 9	righteousness from God based on f.
1Ti	6:11	pursue righteousness, godliness, f,
2Ti	4: 7	finished the race, I have kept the f.
Heb	11: 1	f is the assurance of things hoped
	12: 2	the pioneer and perfecter of our f,
Jas	2:17	f by itself, if it has no works, is dead
2Pe	1: 1	a f as precious as ours through the
1Jn	5: 4	that conquers the world, our f.
Jude	1: 3	the f that was once for all entrusted
Rev	2:13	and you did not deny your f in me
Sir	40:12	but good f will last forever.

FAITHFUL → FAITH

Dt	32: 4	A f God, without deceit, just and
Ps	4: 3	LORD has set apart the f for himself;
	116:15	is the death of his f ones.
Mic	7: 2	The f have disappeared from the

Zec 8: 3 Jerusalem shall be called the f city,
Mt 24:45 "Who then is the f and wise slave,
1Co 10:13 God is f, and he will not let you be
1Th 5:24 The one who calls you is f,
Heb 10:23 for he who has promised is f.
1Pe 4:19 to a f Creator,
1Jn 1: 9 is f and just will forgive us our sins
Rev 1: 5 f witness, the firstborn of the dead,
       19:11 Its rider is called F and True,
Wis 3: 9 the f will abide with him in love,
Sir 4:16 If they remain f, they will inherit

FAITHFULNESS → FAITH
Ex 34: 6 abounding in steadfast love and f,
Jos 24:14 and serve him in sincerity and in f;
Ps 26: 3 and I walk in f to you.
       36: 5 to the heavens, your f to the clouds.
Pr 16: 6 By loyalty and f iniquity is atoned
Isa 11: 5 and the f the belt around his loins.
Jer 31: 3 I have continued my f to you.
La 3:23 new every morning; great is your f.
Hos 4: 1 There is no f or loyalty, and no
Ro 3: 3 faithlessness nullify the f of God?
Gal 5:22 patience, kindness, generosity, f,

FAITHLESS → FAITH
Jer 3:14 Return, O f children, says the LORD,
Mt 17:17 "You f and perverse generation,
2Ti 2:13 if we are f, he remains faithful—
Rev 21: 8 But as for the cowardly, the f,

FALL → FALLEN, FALLING, FELL
Ps 91: 7 A thousand may f at your side,
Pr 16:18 and a haughty spirit before a f.
Lk 10:18 "I watched Satan f from heaven like
Ro 9:33 a rock that will make them f,
1Co 10:12 watch out that you do not f.
Heb 10:31 a fearful thing to f into the hands of
Sir 28:23 Those who forsake the Lord will f

FALLEN → FALL
2Sa 1:19 How the mighty have f!
Isa 14:12 f from heaven, O Day Star,
       21: 9 he responded, "F, f is Babylon;
Rev 9: 1 I saw a star that had f from heaven
       18: 2 "F, f is Babylon the great!

FALLING → FALL
Lk 22:44 [[like great drops of blood f down]]
Jude 1:24 him who is able to keep you from f,

FALSE
Dt 5:20 Neither shall you bear f witness
2Ki 17:15 went after f idols and became f;
Mt 7:15 "Beware of f prophets, who come to
Mk 13:22 F messiahs and f prophets will
Heb 6:18 impossible that God would prove f,
2Pe 2: 1 there will be f teachers among you,
Rev 16:13 and from the mouth of the f
              prophet.
       20:10 where the beast and the f prophet
LtJ 6: 8 but they are f and cannot speak.
Sus 1:61 convicted them of bearing f witness;

FAMILIES → FAMILY
Ac 3:25 all the f of the earth shall be
              blessed.
Tit 1:11 are upsetting whole f by teaching

FAMILY → FAMILIES
Pr 6:19 and one who sows discord in a f.
Gal 6:10 especially for those of the f of faith.
Eph 3:15 from whom every f in heaven and
1Pe 2:17 Love the f of believers.

FAMINE
Ge 12:10 Now there was a f in the land.
       41:27 They are seven years of f.
Ru 1: 1 there was a f in the land,
Ps 37:19 in the days of f they have abundance
Am 8:11 not a f of bread, or a thirst for water,
Ac 11:28 there would be a severe f over all
Ro 8:35 or distress, or persecution, or f,

FAR
Nu 16: 3 "You have gone too f!
1Sa 7:12 "Thus f the LORD has helped us."
Isa 57:19 Peace, peace, to the f and the near,
Jer 23:23 and not a God f off?
Mk 7: 6 but their hearts f from me;
       12:34 are not f from the kingdom of God."

FAST → FASTED, FASTING
Isa 58: 5 Is such the f that I choose,
Mt 6:16 "And whenever you f,
Lk 18:12 I f twice a week; I give

FASTED → FAST
Mt 4: 2 He f forty days and forty nights,

FASTING → FAST
Mt 6:16 so as to show others that they are f.

FATHER → FATHER'S
Ge 2:24 a man leaves his f and his mother
Ex 20:12 Honor your f and your mother,
       21:15 Whoever strikes f or mother shall
2Sa 7:14 I will be a f to him, and he shall be
Ps 89:26 cry to me, 'You are my F, my God,
Pr 28:24 Anyone who robs f or mother and
Isa 8: 4 child knows how to call "My f" or
       9: 6 Mighty God, Everlasting F, Prince
Jer 3:19 I thought you would call me, My F,
Mal 1: 6 If then I am a f, where is the honor
Mt 6: 9 Our F in heaven, hallowed be your
       28:19 the name of the F and of the Son
Lk 18:20 Honor your f and mother.' "
Jn 5:18 but was also calling God his own F,
       8:44 You are from your f the devil,
       14: 6 comes to the F except through me.
Ro 8:15 When we cry, "Abba! F!"
Gal 4: 6 into our hearts, crying, "Abba! F!"
Eph 6: 2 "Honor your f and mother"—
Heb 1: 5 be his F, and he will be my Son"?
       12: 9 to be subject to the F of spirits
Jas 1:17 coming down from the F of lights,
Rev 3: 5 confess your name before my F
Wis 2:16 and boasts that God is his f.
Sir 3: 3 who honor their f atone for sins,

FATHER'S → FATHER
Lk 2:49 that I must be in my F house?"
Jn 1:14 the glory as of a f only son,
       2:16 making my F house a marketplace!"
       10:29 can snatch it out of the F hand.
       14: 2 F house there are many dwelling

FAULT
Ro 9:19 "Why then does he still find f?
Sir 11: 7 Do not find f before you investigate;

FAVOR → FAVORITISM
Ge 6: 8 Noah found f in the sight of the
Ex 33:12 you have also found f in my sight.'
Ps 30: 5 his f is for a lifetime.
Isa 49: 8 In a time of f I have answered you,
Zec 11: 7 I named F, the other I named Unity,
Lk 4:19 proclaim the year of the Lord's f."

FAVORITISM* → FAVOR
Jas 2: 1 with your acts of f really believe

FEAR → AFRAID, FEARED, FEARFULLY, FEARS
Ge 22:12 for now I know that you f God,
Dt 6:13 The LORD your God you shall f;
Ps 19: 9 the f of the LORD is pure, enduring
       23: 4 the darkest valley, I f no evil;
       27: 1 and my salvation; whom shall I f?
Pr 1: 7 f of the LORD is the beginning of
Ecc 12:13 F God, and keep his commandments
Mt 10:28 rather f him who can destroy both
Mk 5:36 "Do not f, only believe."
Php 2:12 work out your own salvation with f
1Pe 3:14 Do not f what they f,
1Jn 4:18 but perfect love casts out f;
Rev 14: 7 "F God and give him glory,
Sir 1:11 The f of the Lord is glory

FEARED → FEAR
Ex 14:31 the people f the LORD and believed
Job 1: 1 f God and turned away from evil.
Hag 1:12 and the people f the LORD.

FEARFULLY* → FEAR
Ps 139:14 I am f and wonderfully made.

FEARS → FEAR
Ps 34: 4 and delivered me from all my f.
Pr 31:30 a woman who f the LORD is to be
Jdt 16:16 whoever f the Lord is great forever.
Sir 15: 1 Whoever f the Lord will do this,

FED → FEED
Dt 8:16 f you in the wilderness with manna
Ps 80: 5 have f them with the bread of tears,
Eze 34: 8 but the shepherds have f themselves,

FEED → FED
Isa 40:11 He will f his flock like a shepherd;
       65:25 wolf and the lamb shall f together,
Jn 21:15 Jesus said to him, "F my lambs."
Ro 12:20 "if your enemies are hungry, f them;

FEET → FOOT
Ps 8: 6 you have put all things under their f,
       119:105 Your word is a lamp to my f
Da 2:33 its f partly of iron and partly of clay.
Mt 22:44 I put your enemies under your f' "?
Lk 24:39 Look at my hands and my f;
Jn 13: 5 and began to wash the disciples' f
Ro 16:20 shortly crush Satan under your f.
1Co 15:25 put all his enemies under his f.
Heb 1:13 enemies a footstool for your f"?
Rev 1:15 his f were like burnished bronze,

FELLOWSHIP
Ac 2:42 to the apostles' teaching and f,
2Co 6:14 Or what f is there between light and
1Jn 1: 3 and truly our f is with the Father
              and

FEMALE
Ge 1:27 male and f he created them.
Mk 10: 6 'God made them male and f.'
Gal 3:28 there is no longer male and f;

FESTIVAL → FESTIVALS
Ex 23:14 in the year you shall hold a f for me.
1Co 5: 8 Therefore, let us celebrate the f,

FESTIVALS → FESTIVAL
Lev 23: 2 are the appointed f of the LORD
Ne 10:33 the new moons, the appointed f,
Col 2:16 of food and drink or of observing f,

FEVER
Dt 28:22 will afflict you with consumption, f,
Mk 1:30 mother-in-law was in bed with a f,

FEW
Ps 105:12 When they were f in number,
Ecc 5: 2 therefore let your words be f.
Mt 22:14 many are called, but f are chosen."
Lk 13:23 "Lord, will only a f be saved?"

FIELD → FIELDS
Pr 31:16 She considers a f and buys it;
Mt 6:28 Consider the lilies of the f, how
       13:44 is like treasure hidden in a f,
       24:40 Then two will be in the f;
1Co 3: 9 you are God's f, God's building.

FIELDS → FIELD
Lk 2: 8 there were shepherds living in the f,
Jn 4:35 see how the f are ripe for harvesting.

FIG → FIGS
Ge 3: 7 and they sewed f leaves together
Hab 3:17 Though the f tree does not blossom,
Mt 24:32 "From the f tree learn its lesson:
Lk 13: 6 "A man had a f tree planted in his

FIGHT → FOUGHT
Ex 14:14 The LORD will f for you,

Ps   35: 1 f against those who f against me!
1Ti   1: 18 you may f the good f,
2Ti   4: 7 I have fought the good f,

FIGS → FIG
Jer   24: 1 LORD showed me two baskets of f
Lk   6: 44 F are not gathered from thorns,

FILL → FILLED, FULL, FULLNESS
Ge   1: 28 and f the earth and subdue it;
          9: 1 fruitful and multiply, and f the
                 earth.
Ps   72: 19 may his glory f the whole earth.
Jer   23: 24 Do I not f heaven and earth?
Eph   4: 10 so that he might f all things.)

FILLED → FILL
Ex   1: 7 so that the land was f with them.
         40: 34 glory of the LORD f the tabernacle.
1Ki   8: 11 glory of the LORD f the house of the
Eze   43: 5 the glory of the LORD f the temple.
Lk   1: 15 he will be f with the Holy Spirit.
Ac   2: 4 were f with the Holy Spirit and
Eph   5: 18 but be f with the Spirit,

FILTHY
Isa   64: 6 righteous deeds are like a f cloth.
Zec   3: 3 Joshua was dressed with f clothes
Rev   22: 11 and the f still be f,

FIND → FINDS, FOUND
Nu   32: 23 and be sure your sin will f you out.
Dt   4: 29 you will f him if you search after
Jer   29: 13 you search for me, you will f me;
Mt   11: 29 and you will f rest for your souls.
         16: 25 lose their life for my sake will f it.
Lk   11: 9 search, and you will f;

FINDS → FIND
Pr   8: 35 For whoever f me f life and obtains
         18: 22 He who f a wife f a good thing,

FINGER
Ex   8: 19 "This is the f of God!"
Dt   9: 10 tablets written with the f of God;
Mt   23: 4 themselves are unwilling to lift a f
Lk   11: 20 if it is by the f of God that I cast out

FINISHED
Ge   2: 2 on the seventh day God f the work
Ex   40: 33 So Moses f the work.
Jn   19: 30 received the wine, he said, "It is f."
Sir   38: 8 God's works will never be f;

FIRE → FIERY
Ex   3: 2 appeared to him in a flame of f out
         13: 21 and in a pillar of f by night, to give
Lev   9: 24 F came out from the LORD and
Nu   11: 1 the f of the LORD burned against
Dt   4: 24 the LORD your God is a devouring f,
1Ki   19: 12 but the LORD was not in the f;
2Ki   2: 11 a chariot of f and horses of f
                 separated
2Ch   7: 1 f came down from heaven and
Isa   66: 24 their f shall not be quenched,
Da   3: 25 walking in the middle of the f,
Zec   2: 5 For I will be a wall of f all around it,
Mal   3: 2 For he is like a refiner's f and
Mt   3: 11 baptize you with the Holy Spirit and
                 f.
Mk   9: 43 to go to hell, to the unquenchable f.
Ac   2: 3 Divided tongues, as of f, appeared
1Co   3: 13 the f will test what sort of work each
Heb   12: 29 indeed our God is a consuming f.
Jas   3: 6 And the tongue is a f.
2Pe   3: 10 elements will be dissolved with f,
Rev   20: 14 the second death, the lake of f;
Sir   7: 17 punishment of the ungodly is f and

FIRM → FIRMLY
Ex   14: 13 "Do not be afraid, stand f,
Isa   7: 9 If you do not stand f in faith,
2Co   1: 24 because you stand f in the faith.
Eph   6: 13 having done everything, to stand f.
Heb   3: 6 if we hold f the confidence

FIRMAMENT
Ps   19: 1 and the f proclaims his handiwork.
        150: 1 praise him in his mighty f!

FIRMLY → FIRM
Ps   119: 89 your word is f fixed in heaven.
Ecc   12: 11 like nails f fixed are the collected

FIRST → FIRSTBORN
Ge   1: 5 and there was morning, the f day.
Nu   18: 15 The f issue of the womb of all
Pr   8: 22 the f of his acts of long ago.
Isa   41: 4 I, the LORD, am f,
Mt   6: 33 But strive f for the kingdom of God
Mk   10: 31 But many who are f will be last, and
                 the last will be f."
         16: 2 very early on the f day of the week,
Jn   2: 11 Jesus did this, the f of his signs,
Ac   11: 26 disciples were f called "Christians."
Ro   1: 16 to the Jew f and also to the Greek.
1Co   15: 45 it is written, "The f man, Adam,
1Th   4: 16 and the dead in Christ will rise f.
1Jn   4: 19 We love because he f loved us.
Rev   1: 17 I am the f and the last,
         20: 5 This is the f resurrection.
         21: 1 the f heaven and the f earth

FIRSTBORN → BEAR, FIRST
Ex   4: 22 'Thus says the LORD: Israel is my f
         12: 29 the LORD struck down all the f
         13: 2 Consecrate to me all the f;
Ps   78: 51 He struck all the f in Egypt,
Zec   12: 10 as one weeps over a f,
Lk   2: 7 And she gave birth to her f son and
Col   1: 15 invisible God, the f of all creation;
Heb   1: 6 when he brings the f into the world,
Rev   1: 5 faithful witness, the f of the dead,
Sir   36: 17 whom you have named your f,
2Es   6: 58 whom you have called your f,

FISH
Ge   1: 26 have dominion over the f of the sea,
Jnh   2: 1 his God from the belly of the f,
Mt   7: 10 Or if the child asks for a f, will give
Jn   6: 9 has five barley loaves and two f.

FIVE
1Sa   17: 40 chose f smooth stones from the wadi
Mt   14: 19 Taking the f loaves and the two fish,
1Co   14: 19 church I would rather speak f words

FLAME
Ex   3: 2 in a f of fire out of a bush;
Isa   10: 17 and his Holy One a f;
Rev   19: 12 His eyes are like a f of fire,
Aza   1: 26 drove the fiery f out of the furnace,

FLED → FLEE
Ex   2: 15 But Moses f from Pharaoh.
1Sa   19: 18 Now David f and escaped;
Mk   14: 50 All of them deserted him and f.
Rev   12: 6 the woman f into the wilderness,
         20: 11 and the heaven f from his presence,

FLEE → FLED
Ps   11: 1 "F like a bird to the mountains;
        139: 7 where can I f from your presence?
Isa   30: 17 A thousand shall f at the threat of
1Co   10: 14 f from the worship of idols.
Jas   4: 7 Resist the devil, and he will f from

FLESH
Ge   2: 23 is bone of my bones and f of my f;
          2: 24 and they become one f.
Job   19: 26 then in my f I shall see God,
Eze   36: 26 of stone and give you a heart of f.
Mt   16: 17 For f and blood has not revealed this
         26: 41 but the f is weak."
Jn   1: 14 the Word became f and lived among
          3: 6 What is born of the f is f,
Ro   8: 4 to the f but according to the Spirit.
2Co   12: 7 a thorn was given me in the f,
Gal   5: 19 Now the works of the f are obvious:
Eph   6: 12 not against enemies of blood and f,

1Pe   1: 24 "All f is like grass and all its glory
1Jn   4: 2 that Jesus Christ has come in the f

FLOCK
Isa   40: 11 He will feed his f like a shepherd;
Eze   34: 22 I will save my f, and they shall no
Mt   26: 31 the sheep of the f will be scattered.'
Lk   12: 32 "Do not be afraid, little f,
Jn   10: 16 So there will be one f, one shepherd.
1Pe   5: 3 but be examples to the f.

FLOGGED
Jn   19: 1 Pilate took Jesus and had him f.
Ac   5: 40 the apostles, they had them f.

FLOOD
Ge   7: 7 the ark to escape the waters of the f,
          9: 15 waters shall never again become a f
Ps   29: 10 The LORD sits enthroned over the f;
2Pe   2: 5 a f on a world of the ungodly,
Sir   40: 10 and on their account the f came.

FLOW → FLOWING, FLOWS
Zec   14: 8 waters shall f out from Jerusalem,
Jn   7: 38 'Out of the believer's heart shall f

FLOWER
Isa   40: 7 The grass withers, the f fades,
1Pe   1: 24 The grass withers, and the f falls,

FLOWING → FLOW
Ex   3: 8 a land f with milk and honey,
Jos   5: 6 a land f with milk and honey.
Eze   47: 1 water was f from below the
Rev   22: 1 f from the throne of God and

FOE
Ex   23: 22 and a f to your foes.
Ps   60: 11 O grant us help against the f,

FOLLOW → FOLLOWED
Ex   16: 4 whether they will f my instruction
Dt   6: 14 Do not f other gods, any of the gods
1Ki   18: 21 If the LORD is God, f him;
Ps   23: 6 mercy shall f me all the days of my
Lk   9: 23 take up their cross daily and f me.
Jn   10: 27 I know them, and they f me.
Rev   14: 4 these f the Lamb wherever he goes.

FOLLOWED → FOLLOW
Jdg   2: 12 they f other gods, from among the
Jer   9: 14 have stubbornly f their own hearts
Mk   1: 18 they left their nets and f him.
Rev   13: 3 the whole earth f the beast.

FOLLY → FOOL
Pr   13: 16 but the fool displays f.
         26: 4 not answer fools according to their f
Ecc   2: 13 that wisdom excels f as light excels
Mk   7: 22 envy, slander, pride, f.

FOOD → FOODS
Ge   1: 30 I have given every green plant for f.
          9: 3 thing that lives shall be f for you;
Ps   136: 25 who gives f to all flesh,
Mt   6: 25 Is not life more than f,
Jn   6: 55 for my flesh is true f and my blood
1Co   8: 8 "F will not bring us close to God."
1Mc   1: 63 to die rather than to be defiled by f

FOODS → FOOD
Mk   7: 19 (Thus he declared all f clean.)
1Ti   4: 3 and demand abstinence from f,

FOOL → FOLLY, FOOLISH, FOOLISHNESS, FOOLS
Pr   15: 5 A f despises a parent's instruction,
         20: 3 but every f is quick to quarrel.
Mt   5: 22 'You f,' you will be liable to the
2Co   11: 21 I am speaking as a f—I also dare to

FOOLISH → FOOL
Pr   17: 25 f children are a grief to their father
Jer   5: 21 O f and senseless people,
Mt   7: 26 like a man who built his house
         25: 2 Five of them were f, and five were
1Co   1: 20 Has not God made f the wisdom of

Gal   3: 1   f Galatians! Who has bewitched
Tit   3: 3   For we ourselves were once f,

FOOLISHNESS → FOOL

1Co   1:18   cross is f to those who are perishing,
    3:19   wisdom of this world is f with God.

FOOLS → FOOL

Ps   14: 1   **F** say in their hearts, "There is no
        God."
Pr   1: 7   f despise wisdom and instruction.
    10:21   but f die for lack of sense.
Ecc   5: 4   for he has no pleasure in f.
Ro   1:22   Claiming to be wise, they became f;
1Co   4:10   We are f for the sake of Christ,

FOOT → FEET, FOOTSTOOL

Ps   91:12   will not dash your f against a stone.
Mt   18: 8   or your f causes you to stumble,
Lk   4:11   not dash your f against a stone.' "

FOOTSTOOL → FOOT

Ps   110: 1   until I make your enemies your f."
Isa   66: 1   is my throne and the earth is my f;
Heb   10:13   until his enemies would be made a f

FORCES

Mt   5:41   and if anyone f you to go one mile,
Eph   6:12   spiritual f of evil in the heavenly

FOREHEAD → FOREHEADS

Ex   13: 9   and as a reminder on your f,
1Sa   17:49   and struck the Philistine on his f;
Rev   13:16   marked on the right hand or the f,

FOREHEADS → FOREHEAD

Eze   9: 4   and put a mark on the f of those
Rev   7: 3   of our God with a seal on their f."
    20: 4   not received its mark on their f

FOREIGN → FOREIGNER, FOREIGNERS

Jos   24:23   "Then put away the f gods that are
Ps   81: 9   you shall not bow down to a f god.

FOREIGNER → FOREIGN

Ex   12:43   no f shall eat of it,
1Co   14:11   and the speaker a f to me.

FOREIGNERS → FOREIGN

1Co   14:21   by the lips of f I will speak to this
Heb   11:13   were strangers and f on the earth,

FOREKNEW* → KNOW

Ro   8:29   whom he f he also predestined to
    11: 2   not rejected his people whom he f.

FORERUNNER* → RUN

Heb   6:20   a f on our behalf, has entered,

FORESEEING* → SEE

Ac   2:31   **F** this, David spoke of the
Gal   3: 8   f that God would justify the Gentiles

FORESKIN

Ge   17:14   circumcised in the flesh of his f
Dt   10:16   Circumcise, then, the f of your heart

FORETOLD → TELL

Isa   43: 9   and f to us the former things?
Ac   3:18   this way God fulfilled what he had f

FOREVER

Ge   3:22   the tree of life, and eat, and live f"
    6: 3   spirit shall not abide in mortals f,
Ex   3:15   This is my name f, and this my title
2Sa   7:13   the throne of his kingdom f.
1Ch   16:15   Remember his covenant f,
Ps   19: 9   fear of the LORD is pure, enduring f;
    110: 4   "You are a priest f according to the
    117: 2   faithfulness of the LORD endures f.
Ecc   3:14   that whatever God does endures f;
Isa   40: 8   the word of our God will stand f.
    51: 6   but my salvation will be f,
Jn   6:51   eats of this bread will live f;
    14:16   another Advocate, to be with you f,
Heb   5: 6   "You are a priest f, according to the
    13: 8   the same yesterday and today and f.

1Pe   1:25   but the word of the Lord endures f."
Rev   1:18   I am alive f and ever;
    11:15   and he will reign f and ever."
    22: 5   and they will reign f and ever.
Wis   5:15   But the righteous live f,

FORFEIT

Mk   8:36   the whole world and f their life?

FORGAVE → FORGIVE

Ps   32: 5   and you f the guilt of my sin.
    85: 2   You f the iniquity of your people;
Col   2:13   when he f us all our trespasses,

FORGET → FORGOT, FORGOTTEN

Dt   4:23   So be careful not to f the covenant
    6:12   take care that you do not f the
        LORD,
Ps   137: 5   If I f you, O Jerusalem, let my right
Pr   4: 5   Get wisdom; get insight: do not f,
Isa   49:15   these may f, yet I will not f you.

**FORGIVE → FORGAVE, FORGIVEN,
        FORGIVENESS, FORGIVING**

Ge   18:26   f the whole place for their sake."
Ex   32:32   But now, if you will only f their sin
Nu   14:20   the LORD said, "I do f,
1Ki   8:30   your dwelling place; heed and f.
Ne   9:17   But you are a God ready to f,
Ps   79: 9   and f our sins, for your name's sake.
Eze   16:63   when I f you all that you have done,
Da   9:19   O Lord, hear; O Lord, f;
Mt   6:12   And f us our debts, as we
Lk   5:24   has authority on earth to f sins"—
1Jn   1: 9   is faithful and just will f us our sins
Sir   5: 6   he will f the multitude of my sins,"
Man   1:13   f me, O Lord, f me!

FORGIVEN → FORGIVE

Lev   4:20   for them, and they shall be f.
Ps   32: 1   are those whose transgression is f,
Mt   6:12   as we also have f our debtors.
    12:31   against the Spirit will not be f.
Mk   2: 9   to the paralytic, 'Your sins are f,'
Ac   2:38   so that your sins may be f;
Ro   4: 7   are those whose iniquities are f,
Eph   4:32   as God in Christ has f you.

FORGIVENESS → FORGIVE

Mk   1: 4   a baptism of repentance for the f
    3:29   against the Holy Spirit can never
        have f,
Col   1:14   we have redemption, the f of sins.
Heb   9:22   the shedding of blood there is no f

FORGIVING → FORGIVE

Ex   34: 7   f iniquity and transgression and sin,
Ps   86: 5   For you, O Lord, are good and f,
Eph   4:32   f one another, as God in Christ has

FORGOT → FORGET

Dt   32:18   you f the God who gave you birth.
Jer   23:27   just as their ancestors f my name
Hos   2:13   and went after her lovers, and f me,
Bar   4: 8   You f the everlasting God,

FORGOTTEN → FORGET

Ps   77: 9   Has God f to be gracious?
Isa   49:14   forsaken me, my Lord has f me."
Heb   12: 5   And you have f the exhortation

FORM → FORMED, FORMLESS

Ex   20: 4   in the f of anything that is in heaven
Lk   3:22   descended upon him in bodily f

FORMED → FORM

Ge   2: 7   the LORD God f man from the dust
Ps   139:13   you who f my inward parts;
Gal   4:19   until Christ is f in you,

FORMLESS* → FORM

Ge   1: 2   the earth was a f void and darkness
Wis   11:17   created the world out of f matter,

**FORNICATION → FORNICATOR,
        FORNICATORS**

Mk   7:21   that evil intentions come: f,
1Co   6:13   meant not for f but for the Lord,
Gal   5:19   works of the flesh are obvious: f,
Rev   19: 2   who corrupted the earth with her f,

FORNICATOR* → FORNICATION

1Co   6:18   but the f sins against the body itself.
Eph   5: 5   that no f or impure person,
Sir   23:17   To a f all bread is sweet;

FORNICATORS → FORNICATION

1Ti   1:10   f, sodomites, slave traders, liars,
Rev   22:15   and sorcerers and f and murderers

FORSAKE → FORSAKEN

Dt   31: 6   he will not fail you or f you."
Jos   1: 5   I will not fail you or f you.
Jer   17:13   All who f you shall be put to shame;
Heb   13: 5   "I will never leave you or f you."

FORSAKEN → FORSAKE

Ps   9:10   O LORD, have not f those who seek
    22: 1   my God, why have you f me?
Mt   27:46   my God, why have you f me?"
2Co   4: 9   persecuted, but not f;

FORTRESS

2Sa   22: 2   The LORD is my rock, my f, and my
Ps   71: 3   for you are my rock and my f.

FORTUNES

Dt   30: 3   LORD your God will restore your f
Jer   32:44   I will restore their f, says the LORD.

FORTY

Ge   7: 4   rain on the earth for f days and f
Nu   14:34   f days, for every day a year,
1Ki   19: 8   f days and f nights to Horeb
Jnh   3: 4   And he cried out, "F days more,
Mt   4: 2   He fasted f days and f nights,
Heb   3:17   with whom was he angry f years?
2Es   14:42   They sat f days; they wrote

FOUGHT → FIGHT

Jos   10:42   the LORD God of Israel f for Israel.
2Ti   4: 7   I have f the good fight,
Rev   12: 7   and his angels f against the dragon.

FOUND → FIND

Isa   55: 6   Seek the LORD while he may be f,
    65: 1   be f by those who did not seek me.
Lk   15:24   he was lost and is f!'
Ro   10:20   f by those who did not seek me;
Rev   20:15   not f written in the book of life was

FOUNDATION → FOUNDATIONS

1Ki   6:37   f of the house of the LORD was laid,
Ezr   3: 6   f of the temple of the LORD was not
Isa   28:16   See, I am laying in Zion a f stone,
1Co   3:11   that f is Jesus Christ.
Eph   2:20   built upon the f of the apostles and
2Ti   2:19   But God's firm f stands,

FOUNDATIONS → FOUNDATION

Heb   11:10   looked forward to the city that has f,
Rev   21:14   the wall of the city has twelve f,

FOUNTAIN

Ps   36: 9   For with you is the f of life;
Pr   16:22   Wisdom is a f of life to one who
Jer   9: 1   and my eyes a f of tears,
Joel   3:18   a f shall come forth from the house
Zec   13: 1   a f shall be opened for the house of

FOUR

Eze   1: 5   something like f living creatures.
    10:14   Each one had f faces:
Rev   4: 6   are f living creatures,

FOXES

Jdg   15: 4   went and caught three hundred f,
Lk   9:58   Jesus said to him, "F have holes,

FRAGRANCE → FRAGRANT

2Co   2:14   spreads in every place the f

FRAGRANT → FRAGRANCE
Ex   25: 6 anointing oil and for the f incense,
Eph   5: 2 a f offering and sacrifice to God.

FRANKINCENSE → INCENSE
Isa   60: 6 They shall bring gold and f,
Mt   2:11 gifts of gold, f, and myrrh.

FREE → FREED, FREEDOM, FREEWILL
Ex   21: 2 in the seventh he shall go out a f
Ps   146: 7 The LORD sets the prisoners f;
Jn   8:32 and the truth will make you f."
Ro   6:23 but the f gift of God is eternal life
1Co   9:21 not f from God's law but am under
Gal   3:28 there is no longer slave or f,
Eph   6: 8 whether we are slaves or f.

FREED → FREE
Ac   2:24 having f him from death,
Rev   1: 5 f us from our sins by his blood,

FREEDOM → FREE
2Co   3:17 the Spirit of the Lord is, there is f.
Gal   5: 1 For f Christ has set us free.
1Pe   2:16 not use your f as a pretext for evil.

FREEWILL → FREE, WILL
Ex   35:29 as a f offering to the LORD.
Ps   54: 6 With a f offering I will sacrifice to

FRIEND → FRIENDS, FRIENDSHIP
Ex   33:11 as one speaks to a f.
Pr   17:17 A f loves at all times,
      18:24 but a true f sticks closer than one's
Mt   11:19 a f of tax collectors and sinners!'
Jas   2:23 and he was called the f of God.
       4: 4 a f of the world becomes an enemy
Sir   7:18 Do not exchange a f for money,

FRIENDS → FRIEND
Job   2:11 when Job's three f heard of all
Jn   15:13 to lay down one's life for one's f.
Sir   6:15 Faithful f are beyond price;

FRIENDSHIP → FRIEND
Ps   25:14 The f of the LORD is for those who
Jas   4: 4 know that f with the world is enmity

FRINGES*
Nu   15:38 to make f on the corners of their
Mt   23: 5 phylacteries broad and their f long.

FRUIT → FRUITFUL, FRUITLESS, FRUITS
Ge   3: 6 she took of its f and ate;
Dt   28: 4 Blessed shall be the f of your womb,
Ps   1: 3 which yield their f in its season,
Pr   8:19 My f is better than gold,
Eze   47:12 will not wither nor their f fail,
Hos   14: 2 and we will offer the f of our lips.
Mt   3: 8 Bear f worthy of repentance.
Lk   6:44 for each tree is known by its own f.
Jn   15: 2 branch that bears f he prunes to
              make it bear more f.
Col   1:10 as you bear f in every good work
Heb   13:15 the f of lips that confess his name.
Rev   22: 2 tree of life with its twelve kinds of f,

FRUITFUL → FRUIT
Ge   1:22 Be f and multiply and fill the waters
       9: 1 said to them, "Be f and multiply,
Ex   1: 7 the Israelites were f and prolific;

FRUITS → FRUIT
Ex   23:16 of the first f of your labor,
Pr   3: 9 with the first of all your produce;
Mt   7:16 You will know them by their f.
Ro   8:23 who have the first f of the Spirit,
1Co   15:23 in his own order: Christ the first f,
Rev   14: 4 as first f for God and the Lamb,

FULFILL → FULFILLED, FULFILLING
Ps   20: 5 May the LORD f all your petitions.
Ecc   5: 4 F what you vow.
Mt   5:17 I have come not to abolish but to f.
Gal   6: 2 way you will f the law of Christ.
Jas   2: 8 really f the royal law according to

FULFILLED → FULFILL
Mk   1:15 "The time is f, and the kingdom
Lk   24:44 prophets, and the psalms must be f."
Ro   8: 4 requirement of the law might be f

FULFILLING → FULFILL
Ro   9:31 did not succeed in f that law.
      13:10 love is the f of the law.

FULL → FILL
Isa   6: 3 the whole earth is f of his glory."
Eze   10:12 were f of eyes all around.
      37: 1 it was f of bones.
Mt   6:22 your whole body will be f of light;
Jn   1:14 f of grace and truth.
Rev   4: 6 f of eyes in front and behind:
Sir   42:16 work of the Lord is f of his glory.

FULLNESS → FILL
Jn   1:16 From his f we have all received,
1Co   10:26 "the earth and its f are the Lord's."
Gal   4: 4 But when the f of time had come,
Eph   3:19 may be filled with all the f of God.
Col   1:19 in him all the f of God was pleased

FURNACE
Isa   48:10 have tested you in the f of adversity.
Da   3: 6 be thrown into a f of blazing fire."
Mt   13:42 will throw them into the f of fire,
Aza   1:26 of the Lord came down into the f

FURNITURE
Ex   25: 9 the tabernacle and of all its f,

FURY
Ps   2: 5 and terrify them in his f,
La   2: 4 he has poured out his f like fire.
Ro   2: 8 there will be wrath and f.
Rev   16:19 the wine-cup of the f of his wrath.

FUTILE
Ro   1:21 but they became f in their thinking,
1Co   3:20 thoughts of the wise, that they are f.

FUTURE
Pr   24:20 for the evil have no f;
Jer   31:17 hope for your f, says the LORD:
1Co   3:22 life or death or the present or the
              f—
1Ti   6:19 of a good foundation for the f,

G

GABRIEL*
    Angel who interpreted Daniel's visions (Da 8:16-
26; 9:20-27); announced births of John (Lk 1:11-
20), Jesus (Lk 1:26-38).

GAD
    1. Son of Jacob by Zilpah (Ge 30:9-11; 35:26;
1Ch 2:2). Tribe of blessed (Ge 49:19; Dt 33:20-
21), numbered (Nu 1:25; 26:18), allotted land east
of the Jordan (Nu 32; 34:14; Jos 18:7; 22), west
(Eze 48:27-28), 12,000 from (Rev 7:5).
    2. Prophet; seer of David (1Sa 22:5; 2Sa
24:11-19; 1Ch 29:29).

GAIN
Ecc   1: 3 What do people g from all the toil
Lk   9:25 if they g the whole world,
Php   1:21 living is Christ and dying is g.
       3: 8 in order that I may g Christ
1Ti   6: 5 that godliness is a means of g.

GALILEAN → GALILEE
Mt   26:69 "You also were with Jesus the G."

GALILEANS → GALILEE
Ac   2: 7 not all these who are speaking G?

GALILEE → GALILEAN, GALILEANS
Isa   9: 1 beyond the Jordan, G of the nations.
Mt   4:15 across the Jordan, G of the Gentiles
Jn   7:41 the Messiah does not come from G,

GAMALIEL
    Pharisee (Ac 5:34-39), teacher of Paul (Ac
22:5).

GARDEN
Ge   2: 8 the LORD God planted a g in Eden,
Eze   28:13 You were in Eden, the g of God;
Jn   19:41 and in the g there was a new tomb

GARMENT → GARMENTS
Ge   39:12 she caught hold of his g,
Dt   22: 5 nor shall a man put on a woman's g;
Ps   102:26 they will all wear out like a g.
Lk   5:36 a new g and sews it on an old g;

GARMENTS → GARMENT
Ge   3:21 the LORD God made g of skins for
Isa   61:10 clothed me with the g of salvation,

GATE → GATES
Mt   7:13 "Enter through the narrow g;
Jn   10: 7 I am the g for the sheep.
Heb   13:12 Jesus also suffered outside the city g

GATES → GATE
Ge   24:60 offspring gain possession of the g
Dt   6: 9 of your house and on your g.
Ps   100: 4 Enter his g with thanksgiving,
Mt   16:18 and the g of Hades will not prevail
Rev   21:21 And the twelve g are twelve pearls,

GATH
1Sa   17: 4 Goliath, of G, whose height was six
2Sa   1:20 Tell it not in G, proclaim it not in

GATHER → GATHERED, INGATHERING
Ex   16: 4 and g enough for that day.
Ru   2: 7 and g among the sheaves behind
Isa   11:12 and g the dispersed of Judah from
Mt   12:30 does not g with me scatters.
Lk   13:34 to g your children together as

GATHERED → GATHER
Mt   18:20 two or three are g in my name,
2Th   2: 1 Christ and our being g together
Rev   14:19 and g the vintage of the earth,

GAVE → GIVE
Ge   28: 4 land that God g to Abraham."
Ex   31:18 he g him the two tablets of the
1Ki   4:29 God g Solomon very great wisdom,
Ne   9:15 you g them bread from heaven,
Ecc   12: 7 the breath returns to God who g it.
Mt   25:35 for I was hungry and you g me food,
Jn   1:12 g power to become children of God,
       3:16 loved the world that he g his only
              Son,
Ro   8:32 but g him up for all of us,
Eph   4:11 The gifts he g were that some would
1Ti   2: 6 who g himself a ransom

GEDALIAH
    Governor of Judah (2Ki 25:22-26; Jer 39-41).

GEHAZI*
    Servant of Elisha (2Ki 4:12-5:27; 8:4-5).

GENEALOGIES → GENEALOGY
1Ch   9: 1 So all Israel was enrolled by g;
Ne   7:64 among those enrolled in the g,

GENEALOGY → GENEALOGIES
Mt   1: 1 of the g of Jesus the Messiah,

GENERATION → GENERATIONS
Ge   15:16 come back here in the fourth g;
Ex   20: 6 steadfast love to the thousandth g
      34: 7 to the third and the fourth g."
Da   4:34 his kingdom endures from g to g.
Mt   12:39 evil and adulterous g asks for a sign,
Lk   21:32 this g will not pass away

GENERATIONS → GENERATION
Isa   51: 8 and my salvation to all g.
Lk   1:48 now on all g will call me blessed;

GENEROSITY → GENEROUS
Ro   12: 8 the giver, in g;
Gal   5:22 joy, peace, patience, kindness, g,

GENEROUS → GENEROSITY
Ro   10:12 and is g to all who call on him.
Jas   1:17 Every g act of giving,

GENTILE → GENTILES
Mt   18:17 as a G and a tax collector.
Gal   2:14 live like a G and not like a Jew,
1Mc   1:14 according to G custom,

GENTILES → GENTILE
Lk   21:24 until the times of the G are fulfilled.
Ac   15:19 those G who are turning to God,
Ro   3:29 Is he not the God of G also?
Gal   3: 8 God would justify the G by faith,
Eph   4:17 must no longer live as the G live,
Tob   1:11 from eating the food of the G.
1Mc   1:11 and make a covenant with the G
2Es   4:23 Israel has been given over to the G

GENTLE → GENTLENESS
Pr   15: 4 A g tongue is a tree of life,
Mt   11:29 for I am g and humble in heart,
1Pe   3: 4 with the lasting beauty of a g

GENTLENESS → GENTLE
Gal   5:23 g, and self-control. There is no law
Php   4: 5 Let your g be known to everyone.
1Ti   6:11 godliness, faith, love, endurance, g.

GETHSEMANE
Mk   14:32 They went to a place called G;

GHOST
Mt   14:26 were terrified, saying, "It is a g!"
Lk   24:39 for a g does not have flesh and

GIANT → GIANTS
Sir   47: 4 In his youth did he not kill a g,

GIANTS → GIANT
1Ch 20: 4 was one of the descendants of the g;
Sir   16: 7 He did not forgive the ancient g

GIBEON
Jos   10:12 "Sun, stand still at G, and Moon, in
1Ki   3: 5 G the LORD appeared to Solomon

GIDEON → =JERUBBAAL
    Judge, also called Jerubbaal; freed Israel from
Midianites (Jdg 6-8; Heb 11:32). The fleece (Jdg
8:36-40).

GIFT → GIFTS
Nu   18: 7 I give your priesthood as a g;
Ecc   5:19 this is the g of God.
Mt   5:23 So when you are offering your g at
Jn   4:10 "If you knew the g of God,
Ac   2:38 will receive the g of the Holy Spirit.
Ro   6:23 but the free g of God is eternal life
1Co   7: 7 each has a particular g from God,
Jas   1:17 with every perfect g, is from above,
Rev   21: 6 the thirsty I will give water as a g

GIFTS → GIFT
Dt   12: 6 and your donations, your votive g,
Mt   2:11 offered him g of gold, frankincense,
Lk   11:13 how to give good g to your children,
Ro   11:29 for the g and the calling of God are
1Co   12: 1 Now concerning spiritual g,
Eph   4: 8 he gave g to his people."
Sir   32:13 who fills you with his good g.

GILGAL
Jos   5: 9 so that place is called G to this day.
1Sa   7:16 a circuit year by year to Bethel, G,

GIRL
Ex   1:16 but if it is a g, she shall live."
Mk   5:41 which means, "Little g, get up!"

GIVE → GAVE, GIVEN, GIVER, GIVES
Ge   9: 3 the green plants, I g you everything.
     12: 7 your offspring I will g this land."
1Ki   3: 5 said, "Ask what I should g you."
Pr   25:21 If your enemies are hungry, g them
     30:15 leech has two daughters; "G, g,"
Eze   36:26 A new heart I will g you,

Mt   6:11 G us this day our daily bread.
      7: 6 "Do not g what is holy to dogs;
Mk   10:45 to g his life a ransom for many."
Jn   10:28 I g them eternal life, and they will
Ac   20:35 more blessed to g than to receive.' "
Tob   12: 9 who g alms will enjoy a full life,
Sir   7:10 do not neglect to g alms.

GIVEN → GIVE
Mt   7: 7 "Ask, and it will be g you;
Mk   4:25 to those who have, more will be g;
Lk   22:19 "This is my body, which is g for
Ro   5: 5 the Holy Spirit that has been g to
                us.
Sir   35:12 Give to the Most High as he has g

GIVER → GIVE
Ro   12: 8 the g, in generosity;
2Co   9: 7 for God loves a cheerful g.

GIVES → GIVE
2Co   3: 6 the letter kills, but the Spirit g life.
Jas   4: 6 But he g all the more grace;

GLAD → GLADNESS
Ps   16: 9 Therefore my heart is g, and my
     90:15 Make us g as many days as you
Pr   10: 1 A wise child makes a g father,
Mt   5:12 and be g, for your reward is great in
Ac   2:26 heart was g, and my tongue rejoiced

GLADNESS → GLAD
Ps   100: 2 Worship the LORD with g;
Pr   10:28 The hope of the righteous ends in g,
Isa   16:10 Joy and g are taken away from the
Jer   31:13 and give them g for sorrow.
Zep   3:17 he will rejoice over you with g,
Heb   1: 9 has anointed you with the oil of g

GLASS
Rev   4: 6 there is something like a sea of g,
     21:18 the city is pure gold, clear as g.

GLEAN
Dt   24:21 do not g what is left;
Ru   2: 2 Let me go to the field and g among

GLOOM
Isa   9: 1 there will be no g for those who
Joel   2: 2 a day of darkness and g,
Heb 12:18 and darkness, and g, and a tempest,

GLORIFIED → GLORY
Lev   10: 3 before all the people I will be g.' "
Jn   13:31 "Now the Son of Man has been g,
     17: 4 g you on earth by finishing the work
Ac   3:13 has g his servant Jesus,
Ro   8:30 those whom he justified he also g.

GLORIFY → GLORY
Ps   86:12 and I will g your name forever.
Jn   17: 1 g your Son so that the Son may
                you,
1Co   6:20 therefore g God in your body.
2Co   9:13 you g God by your obedience to
Rev   15: 4 who will not fear and g your name?
Sir   43:30 G the Lord and exalt him as much

GLORIOUS → GLORY
Jas   2: 1 in our g Lord Jesus Christ?
Jdt   16:13 O Lord, you are great and g,
Aza   1: 3 and g is your name forever!

GLORY → GLORIFIED, GLORIFY,
        GLORIOUS
Ex   24:16 The g of the LORD settled on Mount
     33:18 Moses said, "Show me your g,
     40:34 g of the LORD filled the tabernacle.
1Sa   4:21 "The g has departed from Israel,"
1Ki   8:11 g of the LORD filled the house of the
Ps   8: 5 crowned them with g and honor.
     19: 1 heavens are telling the g of God;
     24: 7 that the King of g may come in.
Isa   6: 3 the whole earth is full of his g."
     40: 5 the g of the LORD shall be revealed,

Eze   11:23 g of the LORD ascended from the
     44: 4 g of the LORD filled the temple of
Hos   4: 7 they changed their g into shame.
Mt   25:31 the Son of Man comes in his g,
Lk   2:14 "G to God in the highest heaven,
Jn   1:14 and we have seen his g,
     12:41 Isaiah said this because he saw his g
Ro   3:23 sinned and fall short of the g of
                God;
      8:18 not worth comparing with the g
      9: 4 the g, the covenants, the giving of
1Co   10:31 do everything for the g of God.
2Co   4:17 for an eternal weight of g beyond
Heb   1: 3 reflection of God's g and the exact
2Pe   1:17 conveyed to him by the Majestic G,
Rev   4:11 to receive g and honor and power,
     21:23 for the g of God is its light,
Sir   1:11 The fear of the Lord is g and
Bar   5: 4 "Righteous Peace, Godly G."
1Mc   1:40 dishonor now grew as great as her g

GLUTTON
Pr   23:21 and the g will come to poverty,
Mt   11:19 they say, 'Look, a g and a drunkard,

GNASHING
Mt   8:12 will be weeping and g of teeth.
     25:30 will be weeping and g of teeth.'

GNAT*
Mt   23:24 strain out a g but swallow a camel!

GO
Ex   5: 1 the God of Israel, 'Let my people g,
Jos   1: 9 God is with you wherever you g."
Ru   1:16 Where you g, I will g;
Mt   28:19 G therefore and make disciples of
Jn   14: 3 if I g and prepare a place for you,

GOAT → GOATS
Lev   16: 9 Aaron shall present the g on which
Da   8:21 The male g is the king of Greece,

GOATS → GOAT
Ps   50:13 or drink the blood of g?
Mt   25:32 separates the sheep from the g,
Heb 10: 4 for the blood of bulls and g

*GOD → GOD'S, GODDESS, GODLESS,
        GODLINESS, GODLY, GODS
Ge   1: 1 In the beginning when G created
      1:27 So G created humankind in his
                image,
      3: 5 be like G, knowing good and evil."
      6: 2 sons of G saw that they were fair;
     17: 1 and said to him, "I am G Almighty,"
Ex   3: 4 G called to him out of the bush,
     15: 2 this is my G, and I will praise him,
     20: 5 I the LORD your G am a jealous G,
     34: 6 a G merciful and gracious, slow to
Nu   23:19 G is not a human being,
Dt   4: 7 a g so near to it as the LORD our G
      6: 5 love the LORD your G with all your
Jos   22:34 between us that the LORD is G."
1Sa   2: 2 there is no Rock like our G.
1Ki   8:27 will G indeed dwell on the earth?
     18:24 the g who answers by fire is indeed
                G.
2Ki   17: 7 sinned against the LORD their G,
2Ch   2: 5 for our G is greater than other gods.
Ezr   6:16 the dedication of this house of G
Ne   8:18 read from the book of the law of G.
Ps   19: 1 heavens are telling the glory of G;
     22: 1 My G, my G, why have you forsaken
     46: 1 G is our refuge and strength,
     46:10 "Be still, and know that I am G!
     47: 7 For G is the king of all the earth;
     53: 1 Fools say in their hearts, "There is
                no G."
     68:20 Our G is a G of salvation,
     90: 2 everlasting to everlasting you are G.
    136: 2 O give thanks to the G of gods,
    145: 1 I will extol you, my G and King,

Ecc	12:13	Fear G, and keep his
Isa	9: 6	Wonderful Counselor, Mighty G,
	12: 2	Surely G is my salvation;
	40:28	The LORD is the everlasting G,
	44: 6	besides me there is no g.
Jer	10:10	But the LORD is the true G;
Eze	28: 2	proud and you have said, "I am a g;
Hos	12: 6	But as for you, return to your G,
Am	4:12	prepare to meet your G,
Mic	6: 8	and to walk humbly with your G?
Mal	2:10	Has not one G created us?
Mt	1:23	which means, "G is with us."
	4: 4	that comes from the mouth of G.' "
	4: 7	not put the Lord your G to the test."
	4:10	written, 'Worship the Lord your G,
	6:24	You cannot serve G and wealth.
	27:40	If you are the Son of G,
Mk	1: 1	news of Jesus Christ, the Son of G.
	2: 7	Who can forgive sins but G alone?"
	10: 9	what G has joined together, let no
	12:30	the Lord your G with all your heart,
Lk	2:14	"Glory to G in the highest heaven,
	18:19	No one is good but G alone.
	22:70	"Are you, then, the Son of G?"
Jn	1: 1	was with G, and the Word was G.
	1:18	It is G the only Son,
	3:16	G so loved the world that he gave his only Son,
	5:18	calling G his own Father, thereby making himself equal to G.
	20:28	"My Lord and my G!"
Ac	5:29	"We must obey G rather than any
Ro	4: 3	"Abraham believed G, and it was
	6:23	gift of G is eternal life in Christ
	8:31	If G is for us, who is against us?
1Co	10:31	do everything for the glory of G.
2Co	4: 4	Christ, who is the image of G.
	6:16	we are the temple of the living G;
Eph	4: 6	one G and Father of all,
Php	2: 6	though he was in the form of G,
Col	1:19	fullness of G was pleased to dwell,
Tit	2:13	of our great G and Savior, Jesus
Heb	4:12	the word of G is living and active,
	10:31	to fall into the hands of the living G.
	12:29	indeed our G is a consuming fire.
Jas	2:23	"Abraham believed G,
	4: 8	Draw near to G, and he will draw
1Jn	1: 5	G is light and in him there is no
	4:16	G is love, and those who abide
	5: 2	love G and obey his commandments
Jude	1:21	keep yourselves in the love of G;
Rev	4: 8	"Holy, holy, holy, the Lord G
	19:13	his name is called The Word of G.
	22: 5	for the Lord G will be their light,
Tob	4:19	At all times bless the Lord G,
Sir	32:14	seeks G will accept his discipline,
Bar	8	You forgot the everlasting G,
Bel	1: 4	But Daniel worshiped his own G.
Man	1: 1	Lord Almighty, G of our ancestors,
2Es	16:67	Indeed, G is the judge; fear him!

†GOD → †LORD

Ge	15: 2	But Abram said, "O Lord G,
2Sa	7:18	"Who am I, O Lord G,
Isa	25: 8	Lord G will wipe away the tears
	61: 1	The spirit of the Lord G is upon me,

GOD'S → *GOD

Mt	27:43	for he said, 'I am G Son.' "
	27:54	"Truly this man was G Son!"
Ro	2: 4	that G kindness is meant to lead you
1Co	3: 9	you are G field, G building.
	3:16	you are G temple and that G Spirit
Heb	1: 3	reflection of G glory and the exact imprint of G
1Jn	3: 2	Beloved, we are G children now;

GODDESS → *GOD

1Ki	11: 5	Astarte the g of the Sidonians,
Ac	19:27	the temple of the great g Artemis

GODLESS → *GOD

Job	8:13	the hope of the g shall perish.
Ps	119:122	do not let the g oppress me.
1Ti	1: 9	for the g and sinful,
2Pe	3: 7	judgment and destruction of the g.

GODLINESS → *GOD

1Ti	4: 7	Train yourself in g,
	6: 5	imagining that g is a means of gain.
2Ti	3: 5	outward form of g but denying its
Tit	1: 1	truth that is in accordance with g,
2Pe	1: 3	everything needed for life and g,
Wis	10:12	g is more powerful than anything

GODLY → *GOD

Mal	2:15	the one God desire? G offspring.
2Co	7:10	For g grief produces a repentance
2Ti	3:12	to live a g life in Christ Jesus will
Tit	2:12	are self-controlled, upright, and g,
2Pe	2: 9	how to rescue the g from trial,
Sir	37:12	But associate with a g person
Bar	5	"Righteous Peace, G Glory."

GODS → *GOD

Ge	31:19	stole her father's household g.
Ex	12:12	g of Egypt I will execute judgments;
	20: 3	you shall have no other g before me.
Jdg	2:17	they lusted after other g and bowed
2Ki	7: 7	They had worshiped other g
Jn	10:34	in your law, 'I said, you are g'?
1Co	8: 5	so-called g in heaven or on earth—

GOG

Eze	38:18	G comes against the land of Israel,
Rev	20: 8	G and Magog, in order to gather

GOLD

Ex	20:23	make for yourselves gods of g.
	25:17	shall make a mercy seat of pure g;
	25:31	shall make a lampstand of pure g.
	28: 6	They shall make the ephod of g, a
	32:31	have made for themselves gods of g.
1Ki	6:21	the inside of the house with pure g,
Job	28:15	It cannot be gotten for g,
Ps	119:127	love your commandments more than g,
Isa	60:17	Instead of bronze I will bring g,
Ac	3: 6	Peter said, "I have no silver or g,
1Pe	1: 7	being more precious than g that,
Rev	21:21	and the street of the city is pure g,
Tob	12: 8	better to give alms than to lay up g.
Sir	31: 5	who loves g will not be justified;

GOLGOTHA

Mt	27:33	G (which means Place of a Skull),

GOLIATH

Giant killed by David (1Sa 17; 21:9; Sir 47:4).

GOMORRAH

Ge	19:24	LORD rained on Sodom and G sulfur
Isa	1: 9	like Sodom, and become like G.
Jude	1: 7	Sodom and G and the surrounding

GOOD → BEST, BETTER, GOODNESS

Ge	1:31	and indeed, it was very g.
	2: 9	tree of the knowledge of g and evil.
	3:22	become like one of us, knowing g
	50:20	to me, God intended it for g,
Dt	6:18	Do what is right and g in the sight
2Ch	7: 3	"For he is g, for his steadfast love
Ps	14: 1	there is no one who does g.
	34: 8	O taste and see that the LORD is g;
	84:11	No g thing does the LORD withhold
Pr	18:22	He who finds a wife finds a g thing,
Ecc	12:14	every secret thing, whether g or evil.
Isa	52: 7	who brings g news, who announces
Mt	5:45	his sun rise on the evil and on the g,
	13: 8	Other seeds fell on g soil and
	25:21	'Well done, g and trustworthy slave';
Mk	10:18	No one is g but God alone.

Lk	2:10	I am bringing you g news of great
	6:43	"No g tree bears bad fruit,
Jn	10:11	"I am the g shepherd.
Ro	7:16	I agree that the law is g.
	12: 2	is g and acceptable and perfect.
	12:21	but overcome evil with g.
Eph	2:10	created in Christ Jesus for g works,
1Ti	4: 4	For everything created by God is g,
Heb	10: 1	the law has only a shadow of the g
1Pe	3:17	For it is better to suffer for doing g,
Tob	4: 9	laying up a g treasure for yourself
Aza	1:67	to the Lord, for he is g,

GOODNESS → GOOD

Ex	33:19	will make all my g pass before you,
Ps	23: 6	Surely g and mercy shall follow me
Heb	6: 5	tasted the g of the word of God and
2Pe	1: 5	support your faith with g, and g

GOSHEN

Ge	45:10	You shall settle in the land of G,
Ex	8:22	day I will set apart the land of G,

GOSPEL

Mk	8:35	and for the sake of the g,
Ro	1:16	For I am not ashamed of the g;
1Co	9:16	woe to me if I do not proclaim the g
2Co	4: 3	And even if our g is veiled,
Gal	1: 6	and are turning to a different g—
Php	1:27	life in a manner worthy of the g
Rev	14: 6	an eternal g to proclaim to those

GOSSIP

Pr	11:13	A g goes about telling secrets,
2Co	12:20	selfishness, slander, g, conceit,

GRACE → GRACIOUS

Jn	1:14	father's only son, full of g and truth.
	1:16	we have all received, g upon g.
Ac	15:11	that we will be saved through the g
Ro	3:24	are now justified by his g as a gift,
	6: 1	in sin in order that g may abound?
	6:14	you are not under law but under g.
	11: 6	otherwise g would no longer be g.
2Co	12: 9	"My g is sufficient for you,
Gal	5: 4	you have fallen away from g.
Eph	2: 5	by g you have been saved—
2Th	2:16	through g gave us eternal comfort
Tit	2:11	For the g of God has appeared,
Heb	4:16	approach the throne of g with
Jas	4: 6	But he gives all the more g;
1Pe	5:10	the God of all g,
Jude	1: 4	who pervert the g of our God into
Rev	22:21	The g of the Lord Jesus be with all
Wis	3: 9	g and mercy are upon his holy ones,
2Es	2:32	and my g will not fail."

GRACIOUS → GRACE

Ex	34: 6	the LORD, a God merciful and g,
Nu	6:25	to shine upon you, and be g to you;
Ezr	8:22	of our God is g to all who seek him,
Ne	9:31	for you are a g and merciful God.
Ps	77: 9	Has God forgotten to be g?
	116: 5	G is the LORD, and righteous;
Col	4: 6	Let your speech always be g,

GRAFTED

Ro	11:17	were g in their place to share the

GRAIN

Lev	2: 1	presents a g offering to the LORD,
Dt	25: 4	an ox while it is treading out the g.
Mk	2:23	disciples began to pluck heads of g,
1Ti	5:18	an ox while it is treading out the g,"

GRAPES

Nu	13:23	a branch with a single cluster of g,
Isa	5: 2	to yield g, but it yielded wild g.
Jer	31:29	"The parents have eaten sour g,
Mt	7:16	Are g gathered from thorns, or figs
Rev	14:18	vine of the earth, for its g are ripe."

GRASS

Isa	40: 6	All people are g, their constancy is
Mt	6:30	if God so clothes the g of the field,
1Pe	1:24	"All flesh is like g and all its glory

GRATIFY*
Ro   13:14 for the flesh, to **g** its desires.
Gal   5:16 do not **g** the desires of the flesh.

GRAVE → **GRAVES**
Ps   49:14 straight to the **g** they descend,
Isa   53: 9 They made his **g** with the wicked

GRAVES → **GRAVE**
Eze 37:12 and bring you up from your **g**,
Lk   11:44 For you are like unmarked **g**,

GRAY
Pr   16:31 **G** hair is a crown of glory;
Sir   6:18 **g** hair you will still find wisdom.

GREAT → **GREATER, GREATEST**
Ge   1:16 God made the two **g** lights—
     12: 2 I will make of you a **g** nation,
Ex   32:11 **g** power and with a mighty hand?
Dt   10:17 the **g** God, mighty and awesome,
Ne   8: 6 Ezra blessed the LORD, the **g** God,
Ps   95: 3 the LORD is a **g** God, and a King
Jer   10: 6 you are **g**, and your name is **g**
La   3:23 **g** is your faithfulness.
Da   9: 4 "Ah, LORD, **g** and awesome God,
Joel 2:11 Truly the day of the LORD is **g**;
Mt   4:16 sat in darkness have seen a **g** light,
     13:46 on finding one pearl of **g** value,
     20:26 whoever wishes to be **g** among you
Eph   2: 4 the **g** love with which he loved us
Tit   2:13 of the glory of our **g** God and Savior
Heb   2: 3 if we neglect so **g** a salvation?
     12: 1 by so **g** a cloud of witnesses,
     13:20 the **g** shepherd of the sheep,
Rev 12: 9 The **g** dragon was thrown down,
     14: 8 "Fallen, fallen is Babylon the **g**!
     20:11 I saw a **g** white throne and the one
Jdt 16:13 O Lord, you are **g** and glorious,
Sir 17:29 How **g** is the mercy of the Lord,

GREATER → **GREAT**
Ex   18:11 that the LORD is **g** than all gods,
Mt   12: 6 something **g** than the temple is here.
Mk   12:31 no other commandment **g** than
                these
Jn   14:12 in fact, will do **g** works than these,
     15:13 No one has **g** love than this,
1Jn   4: 4 for the one who is in you is **g** than

GREATEST → **GREAT**
Mt   22:38 the **g** and first commandment.
Lk   9:48 the least among all of you is the **g**."
1Co 13:13 and the **g** of these is love.

GREECE → **GREEK, GREEKS**
Da   8:21 The male goat is the king of **G**,
1Mc   1: 1 had previously become king of **G**.)

GREED → **GREEDY**
Mt   23:25 but inside they are full of **g**
Lk   12:15 on your guard against all kinds of **g**;
Col   3: 5 evil desire, and **g** (which is idolatry)

GREEDY → **GREED**
Pr   28:25 The **g** person stirs up strife,
1Co   6:10 the **g**, drunkards, revilers, robbers—
Tit   1: 7 to wine or violent or **g** for gain;

GREEK → **GREECE**
Jn   19:20 in Hebrew, in Latin, and in **G**.
Ro   1:16 to the Jew first and also to the **G**.
Gal   3:28 There is no longer Jew or **G**,

GREEKS → **GREECE**
1Co   1:22 demand signs and **G** desire wisdom,

GREEN
Ge   1:30 I have given every **g** plant for food."
Ps   23: 2 makes me lie down in **g** pastures;

GREW → **GROW**
1Sa   2:21 boy Samuel **g** up in the presence of
Isa   53: 2 he **g** up before him like a young
Lk   1:80 child **g** and became strong in spirit,
      2:40 child **g** and became strong, filled

GRIEF → **GRIEVE, GRIEVED**
La   3:32 causes **g**, he will have compassion
2Co   7: 9 your **g** led to repentance;

GRIEVE → **GRIEF**
Eph   4:30 do not **g** the Holy Spirit of God,
1Th   4:13 not **g** as others do who have no hope

GRIEVED → **GRIEF**
Isa 63:10 they rebelled and **g** his holy spirit;
Mt   26:38 "I am deeply **g**, even to death;

GRINDING
Lk   17:35 will be two women **g** meal together;

GROAN → **GROANING**
Ro   8:23 **g** inwardly while we wait for
2Co   5: 2 For in this tent we **g**, longing to be
2Es 16:39 and the world will **g**,

GROANING → **GROAN**
Ex   2:24 heard their **g**, and God remembered
Jdg   2:18 would be moved to pity by their **g**
Ps   22: 1 from the words of my **g**?

GROUND
Ge   2: 7 formed man from the dust of the **g**,
      3:17 cursed is the **g** because of you;
Ex   3: 5 which you are standing is holy **g**."
Isa 53: 2 and like a root out of dry **g**;
Mt   13: 5 Other seeds fell on rocky **g**,
Sir 33:10 All human beings come from the **g**,

GROW → **GREW, GROWTH**
Isa 11: 1 and a branch shall **g** out of his roots.
Eze 47:12 will **g** all kinds of trees for food.
Col   1:10 as you **g** in the knowledge of God.
2Pe   3:18 But **g** in the grace and knowledge of

GROWTH → **GROW**
1Co   3: 7 but only God who gives the **g**.
Col   2:19 grows with a **g** that is from God.

GUARANTEE → **GUARANTEED**
2Co   5: 5 who has given us the Spirit as a **g**.
Heb   7:22 Jesus has also become the **g** of a

GUARANTEED* → **GUARANTEE**
Ro   4:16 promise may rest on grace and be **g**
Heb   6:17 he **g** it by an oath,

GUARD → **GUARDIAN, GUARDS**
Pr   2:11 and understanding will **g** you.
2Th   3: 3 and **g** you from the evil one.
2Ti   1:12 to **g** until that day what I have

GUARDIAN → **GUARD**
1Pe   2:25 to the shepherd and **g** of your souls.
Sir 51:12 *Give thanks to the **g** of Israel,*

GUARDS → **GUARD**
Ps 127: 1 Unless the LORD **g** the city,
Mt   28: 4 the **g** shook and became like dead

GUIDANCE → **GUIDE**
Pr   11:14 Where there is no **g**, a nation falls,

GUIDE → **GUIDANCE**
Ps   48:14 He will be our **g** forever.
Isa 58:11 The LORD will **g** you continually,
Lk   6:39 Can a blind person **g** a blind
                person?
Jn   16:13 he will **g** you into all the truth;

GUILT → **GUILTY**
Lev   5:15 as your **g** offering to the LORD,
Ps   32: 5 and you forgave the **g** of my sin.
Hos 14: 2 say to him, "Take away all **g**;
Zec   3: 9 I will remove the **g** of this land

GUILTY → **GUILT**
Ex   23: 7 for I will not acquit the **g**.
Nu   14:18 but by no means clearing the **g**,
Mk   3:29 but is **g** of an eternal sin"—
Sus   1:53 the innocent and acquitting the **g**,

H

HABAKKUK
   Prophet to Judah (Hab 1:1; 3:1; Bel 1:33-39).

HADASSAH → See **ESTHER**

HADES
Mt   16:18 and the gates of **H** will not prevail
Ac   2:27 not abandon my soul to **H**,
Rev   1:18 I have the keys of Death and of **H**.
     20:14 **H** were thrown into the lake of fire.
Sir 21:10 but at its end is the pit of **H**.

HAGAR
   Servant of Sarah, wife of Abraham, mother of
Ishmael (Ge 16:1-6; 25:12). Driven away by Sarah
while pregnant (Ge 16:5-16); after birth of Isaac
(Ge 21:9-21; Gal 4:21-31).

HAGGAI*
   Post-exilic prophet who encouraged rebuilding
of the temple (Ezr 5:1; 6:14; Hag 1-2; 1Es 6:1; 7:3;
2Es 1:40).

HAIL → **HAILSTONES**
Ex   9:19 will die when the **h** comes down
Rev   8: 7 came **h** and fire, mixed with blood,

HAILSTONES → **HAIL**
Jos 10:11 of the **h** than the Israelites killed
Rev 16:21 and huge **h**, each weighing about

HAIR → **HAIRS**
Jdg 16:22 **h** of his head began to grow again
Lk   7:44 her tears and dried them with her **h**
1Co 11: 6 for a woman to have her **h** cut off
1Ti   2: 9 not with their **h** braided, or with

HAIRS → **HAIR**
Ps   40:12 more than the **h** of my head,
Mt   10:30 the **h** of your head are all counted.

HALF
Est   5: 3 even to the **h** of my kingdom."
Mk   6:23 give you, even **h** of my kingdom."
Lk   19: 8 **h** of my possessions, Lord, I will

HALLELUJAH
Rev 19: 1 multitude in heaven, saying, "**H**!
Tob 13:17 and all her houses will cry, '**H**!

HALLOWED
Ge   2: 3 blessed the seventh day and **h** it,
Mt   6: 9 Father in heaven, **h** be your name.

HAM
   Son of Noah (Ge 5:32; 1Ch 1:4), father of Canaan (Ge 9:18; 10:6-20; 1Ch 1:8-16). Saw Noah's
nakedness (Ge 9:20-27).

HAMAN
   Agagite nobleman honored by Xerxes (Est 3:1-
2). Plotted to exterminate the Jews because of Mordecai (Est 3:3-15). Forced to honor Mordecai (Est
5-6). Plot exposed by Esther (Est 5:1-8; 7:1-8).
Hanged (Est 7:9-10). See also Additions to Esther.

HANANIAH → =**SHADRACH**
   1. False prophet; adversary of Jeremiah (Jer 28).
   2. Original name of Shadrach (Da 1:6-19; 2:17).

HAND → **EMPTY-HANDED, HANDED,**
          HANDS
Ex   3:19 unless compelled by a mighty **h**.
     15: 6 Your right **h**, O LORD, glorious in
Dt   19:21 tooth for tooth, **h** for **h**, foot for foot
1Ki 18:44 cloud no bigger than a person's **h** is
Ps   16: 8 he is at my right **h**, I shall not be
     98: 1 right **h** and his holy arm have gotten
    110: 1 says to my lord, "Sit at my right **h**
Pr   3:16 Long life is in her right **h**;
Isa   5:25 and his **h** is stretched out still.
Da   5: 5 the fingers of a human **h** appeared
Hab   2:16 The cup in the LORD's right **h** will
Mt   3:12 His winnowing fork is in his **h**,
Mk   9:43 If your **h** causes you to stumble, cut
Lk   20:42 said to my Lord, "Sit at my right **h**,

Jn	10:28	will snatch them out of my **h**.
Ro	8:34	raised, who is at the right **h** of God,
1Co	12:15	would say, "Because I am not a **h**,
Heb	10:12	"he sat down at the right **h** of God,"
Rev	1:16	In his right **h** he held seven stars,
	5: 1	saw in the right **h** of the one seated
Jdt	9:10	by the **h** of a woman.

HANDED → HAND

Mt	27:26	he **h** him over to be crucified.
Ro	4:25	**h** over to death for our trespasses

HANDS → HAND

Ps	24: 4	who have clean **h** and pure hearts,
	115: 7	They have **h**, but do not feel;
Ecc	11: 6	at evening do not let your **h** be idle;
Isa	49:16	inscribed you on the palms of my **h**;
Da	2:45	was cut from the mountain not by **h**,
Lk	23:46	into your **h** I commend my spirit."
	24:40	he showed them his **h** and his feet.
Jn	3:35	has placed all things in his **h**.
Ac	8:18	the laying on of the apostles' **h**,
Ro	10:21	"All day long I have held out my **h**
Heb	6: 2	laying on of **h**, resurrection of the
	10:31	to fall into the **h** of the living God.

HANNAH*

Wife of Elkanah, mother of Samuel (1Sa 1).
Prayer at dedication of Samuel (1Sa 2:1-10).
Blessed (1Sa 2:18-21).

HAPPY

Ps	1: 1	**H** are those who do not follow the
	33:12	**H** is the nation whose God is the LORD,
	84:12	**h** is everyone who trusts in you.
Pr	3:13	**H** are those who find wisdom,
Ecc	3:12	nothing better for them than to be **h**
Tob	13:14	**H** are those who love you,
Sir	1:13	who fear the Lord will have a **h** end;

HARD → HARD-HEARTED, HARDEN, HARDENED, HARDENING, HARDSHIP, HARDSHIPS

Ex	1:14	made their lives bitter with **h** service
Jer	32:17	Nothing is too **h** for you.
Mt	7:14	the road is **h** that leads to life,
	19:23	**h** for a rich person to enter the

HARD-HEARTED* → HARD, HEART

Dt	15: 7	do not be **h** or tight-fisted toward
Pr	28:14	one who is **h** will fall into calamity.
Mt	19: 8	you were so **h** that Moses allowed

HARDEN → HARD

Ex	4:21	but I will **h** his heart,
Ps	95: 8	Do not **h** your hearts, as at Meribah,
Heb	3: 8	not **h** your hearts as in the rebellion,

HARDENED → HARD

Ex	10:20	But the LORD **h** Pharaoh's heart,
Mk	8:17	Are your hearts **h**?
Ro	11: 7	elect obtained it, but the rest were **h**,
2Co	3:14	But their minds were **h**.

HARDENING* → HARD

Ro	11:25	a **h** has come upon part of Israel,

HARDSHIP → HARD

Ro	8:35	Will **h**, or distress, or persecution,

HARDSHIPS → HARD

2Co	12:10	content with weaknesses, insults, **h**,

HARM

Ge	50:20	though you intended to do **h** to me,
Ne	6: 2	But they intended to do me **h**.
Pr	12:21	No **h** happens to the righteous,
Jer	29:11	plans for your welfare and not for **h**,
1Pe	3:13	who will **h** you if you are eager

HARP → HARPS

Ps	150: 3	praise him with lute and **h**!
Rev	5: 8	each holding a **h** and golden bowls

HARPS → HARP

1Ch	15:16	on **h** and lyres and cymbals,
Ne	12:27	with cymbals, **h**, and lyres.
Ps	137: 2	the willows there we hung up our **h**.

HARSHLY

Dt	26: 6	When the Egyptians treated us **h**
Col	3:19	your wives and never treat them **h**.
1Ti	5: 1	Do not speak **h** to an older man,

HARVEST → HARVESTING

Ge	8:22	the earth endures, seedtime and **h**,
Ex	23:16	You shall observe the festival of **h**,
Mt	13:39	**h** is the end of the age, and the
Lk	10: 2	He said to them, "The **h** is plentiful,
Rev	14:15	the **h** of the earth is fully ripe."

HARVESTING* → HARVEST

Jn	4:35	and see how the fields are ripe for **h**.

HASTENING*

Zep	1:14	day of the LORD is near, near and **h**
2Pe	3:12	and **h** the coming of the day of God,

HATE → HATED, HATING

Ps	45: 7	righteousness and **h** wickedness.
	97:10	The LORD loves those who **h** evil;
Pr	13: 5	The righteous **h** falsehood,
Ecc	3: 8	a time to love, and a time to **h**;
Am	5:15	**H** evil and love good, and establish
Mal	2:16	For I **h** divorce, says the LORD,
Mt	5:43	your neighbor and **h** your enemy.'
Lk	6:27	do good to those who **h** you,
Jn	7: 7	The world cannot **h** you, but it hates
Ro	7:15	but I do the very thing I **h**.

HATED → HATE

Jn	15:18	aware that it **h** me before it **h** you.
Ro	9:13	loved Jacob, but I have **h** Esau."

HATES → HATE

Dt	16:22	things that the LORD your God **h**.
Pr	6:16	six things that the LORD **h**,
Jn	15:23	Whoever **h** me **h** my Father also.
Sir	15:13	The Lord **h** all abominations;

HAUGHTY

Pr	6:17	**h** eyes, a lying tongue, and hands
	16:18	and a **h** spirit before a fall.
1Ti	6:17	command them not to be **h**,

HAY*

1Co	3:12	precious stones, wood, **h**, straw—

HEAD → BEHEADED, HEADS

Isa	59:17	and a helmet of salvation on his **h**;
Mt	8:20	of Man has nowhere to lay his **h**."
Mk	6:28	brought his **h** on a platter,
1Co	11: 3	Christ is the **h** of every man; and the husband is the **h** of his wife,
Eph	1:22	has made him the **h** over all things

HEADS → HEAD

Eze	11:21	bring their deeds upon their own **h**,
Rev	12: 3	a great red dragon, with seven **h**

HEAL → HEALED, HEALING, HEALS, HEALTH, HEALTHY

Dt	32:39	and I make alive; I wound and I **h**;
Ecc	3: 3	a time to kill, and a time to **h**;
Isa	57:19	says the LORD; and I will **h** them.
Jer	3:22	I will **h** your faithlessness.
Hos	14: 4	I will **h** their disloyalty; I will love
Jn	12:40	and turn—and I would **h** them."

HEALED → HEAL

Isa	6:10	their minds, and turn and be **h**."
	53: 5	and by his bruises we are **h**.
Hos	11: 3	but they did not know that I **h** them.
Jas	5:16	one another, so that you may be **h**.
1Pe	2:24	by his wounds you have been **h**.

HEALING → HEAL

Pr	12:18	but the tongue of the wise brings **h**.
Eze	47:12	for food, and their leaves for **h**."
Mal	4: 2	shall rise, with **h** in its wings.
1Co	12: 9	another gifts of **h** by the one Spirit,

Rev	22: 2	leaves of the tree are for the **h** of
Sir	38: 2	gift of **h** comes from the Most High,

HEALS → HEAL

Ex	15:26	for I am the LORD who **h** you."
Ps	103: 3	iniquity, who **h** all your diseases,
Wis	16:12	your word, O Lord, that **h** all people

HEALTH → HEAL

3Jn	1: 2	and that you may be in good **h**,
Sir	30:15	**H** and fitness are better than any

HEALTHY → HEAL

Lk	11:34	If your eye is **h**, your whole body

HEAR → HEARD, HEARERS, HEARING, HEARS

Dt	6: 4	**H**, O Israel: The LORD is our God,
	31:13	may **h** and learn to fear the LORD
1Ki	8:30	O **h** in heaven your dwelling place;
Isa	59: 1	nor his ear too dull to **h**.
Jer	5:21	who have ears, but do not **h**.
Eze	37: 4	dry bones, **h** the word of the LORD.
Mt	13:17	to **h** what you **h**, but did not **h** it.
Mk	12:29	answered, "The first is, '**H**, O Israel:
Lk	7:22	the lepers are cleansed, the deaf **h**,
Heb	3: 7	says, "Today, if you **h** his voice,
Sir	5:11	Be quick to **h**, but deliberate in

HEARD → HEAR

Isa	40:21	not known? Have you not **h**?
1Co	2: 9	"What no eye has seen, nor ear **h**,
1Jn	1: 3	to you what we have seen and **h** so
Rev	22: 8	I, John, am the one who **h** and saw

HEARERS → HEAR

Ro	2:13	For it is not the **h** of the law who
Jas	1:22	merely **h** who deceive themselves.

HEARING → HEAR

Pr	18:13	one gives answer before **h**,
Am	8:11	but of **h** the words of the LORD.
1Co	12:17	If the whole body were **h**,

HEARS → HEAR

Ps	69:33	For the LORD **h** the needy,
Pr	15:29	but he **h** the prayer of the righteous.
Mt	7:24	then who **h** these words of mine
Jn	5:24	I tell you, anyone who **h** my word
1Jn	5:14	according to his will, he **h** us.
Rev	22:18	I warn everyone who **h** the words

HEART → BROKENHEARTED, HARD-HEARTED, HEART'S, HEARTLESS, HEARTS, TENDERHEARTED

Ge	6: 6	and it grieved him to his **h**.
Ex	4:21	but I will harden his **h**,
	14: 4	I will harden Pharaoh's **h**,
Dt	6: 5	the LORD your God with all your **h**,
	30:14	in your mouth and in your **h** for you
Jos	22: 5	all your **h** and with all your soul."
1Sa	16: 7	but the LORD looks on the **h**."
Ps	19:14	meditation of my **h** be acceptable to
	51:10	Create in me a clean **h**, O God,
Pr	3: 5	Trust in the LORD with all your **h**,
	7: 3	write them on the tablet of your **h**.
Jer	9:26	of Israel is uncircumcised in **h**.
Eze	36:26	A new **h** I will give you,
Mt	5: 8	"Blessed are the pure in **h**, for they
	5:28	adultery with her in his **h**.
Mk	12:30	the Lord your God with all your **h**,
Lk	12:34	treasure is, there your **h** will be also.—
Ro	2:29	circumcision is a matter of the **h**—
	10: 9	believe in your **h** that God raised
Heb	10:22	let us approach with a true **h** in full
Sir	1:12	The fear of the Lord delights the **h**,
Aza	1:16	Yet with a contrite **h** and
Man	1:11	And now I bend the knee of my **h**,

HEART'S → HEART

Ps	20: 4	May he grant you your **h** desire,
Ro	10: 1	my **h** desire and prayer to God for

HEARTLESS* → HEART
Ro   1:31 foolish, faithless, **h**, ruthless.

HEARTS → HEART
Ps   95: 8 not harden your **h**, as at Meribah,
Jer 31:33 and I will write it on their **h**;
Mk   7: 6 but their **h** are far from me;
Jn   14: 1 "Do not let your **h** be troubled.
Ro   2:15 law requires is written on their **h**,
Eph   3:17 Christ may dwell in your **h** through
Col   3: 8 the peace of Christ rule in your **h**,
Heb   3: 8 do not harden your **h** as in the
      10:16 I will put my laws in their **h**,
2Pe   1:19 and the morning star rises in your **h**.
1Jn   3:20 for God is greater than our **h**,
Rev   2:23 the one who searches minds and **h**,

HEAVEN → HEAVENLY, HEAVENS
Ge 14:19 by God Most High, maker of **h** and
      28:12 the top of it reaching to **h**;
Ex   16: 4 "I am going to rain bread from **h**
Dt   30:12 "Who will go up to **h** for us,
      31:28 and call **h** and earth to witness
1Ki   8:27 **h** and the highest **h** cannot contain
Job 16:19 now, in fact, my witness is in **h**,
Ecc   3: 1 and a time for every matter under **h**:
Isa 14:12 you are fallen from **h**, O Day Star,
Jer 23:24 Do I not fill **h** and earth?
Mt   3: 2 "Repent, for the kingdom of **h** has
      6: 9 Father in **h**, hallowed be your name.
      24:35 **H** and earth will pass away,
      26:64 and coming on the clouds of **h**."
Mk 10:21 and you will have treasure in **h**;
Lk 10:18 "I watched Satan fall from **h** like a
      19:38 Peace in **h**, and glory in the highest
          h!"
      24:51 and was carried up into **h**.
Jn   3:13 No one has ascended into **h** except
          the one who descended from **h**,
Ac   1:11 same way as you saw him go into **h**.
Ro 10: 6 'Who will ascend into **h**?' "
2Co 12: 2 was caught up to the third **h**—
Php   3:20 But our citizenship is in **h**,
1Th   1:10 to wait for his Son from **h**,
Heb   9:24 but he entered into **h** itself,
2Pe   1:18 heard this voice come from **h**,
Rev   4: 1 and there in **h** a door stood open!
      21: 1 I saw a new **h** and a new earth;

HEAVENLY → HEAVEN
Mt   5:48 as your **h** Father is perfect.
2Co   5: 2 longing to be clothed with our **h**
Eph   1: 3 spiritual blessing in the **h** places,
Heb   3: 1 holy partners in a **h** calling,

HEAVENS → HEAVEN
Ge   1: 1 when God created the **h** and
      11: 4 and a tower with its top in the **h**,
Dt 10:14 the heaven of **h** belong to the LORD
Ps   57: 5 Be exalted, O God, above the **h**.
  115:16 The **h** are the LORD's,
Isa 65:17 to create new **h** and a new earth;
Jer 10:11 The gods who did not make the **h**
Eph   4:10 who ascended far above all the **h**,
Heb   4:14 priest who has passed through the **h**,
2Pe   3:10 the **h** will pass away with a loud

HEAVY
Mt 23: 4 They tie up **h** burdens, hard to bear,
Mk 14:40 for their eyes were very **h**;

HEBREW → HEBREWS
Jnh   1: 9 "I am a **H**," he replied.
Jn 19:20 and it was written in **H**, in Latin,
Php   3: 5 of Benjamin, a **H** born of Hebrews;

HEBREWS → HEBREW
Ex   3:18 The LORD, the God of the **H**, has
2Co 11:22 Are they **H**? So am I.
Jdt 10:12 "I am a daughter of the **H**,

HEBRON
Ge 13:18 the oaks of Mamre, which are at **H**;
2Sa   2:11 The time that David was king in **H**

HEEL
Ge   3:15 your head, and you will strike his **h**;
      25:26 with his hand gripping Esau's **h**;
Ps   41: 9 has lifted the **h** against me.
Jn 13:18 has lifted his **h** against me.'

HEIGHT → HIGH
Ro   8:39 nor **h**, nor depth, nor anything else
Eph   3:18 and length and **h** and depth,

HEIGHTS → HIGH
Ps 148: 1 the heavens; praise him in the **h**!
Hab   3:19 and makes me tread upon the **h**.

HEIR → HEIRS
Ge 15: 4 "This man shall not be your **h**;
Gal   4: 7 then also an **h**, through God.
Heb   1: 2 whom he appointed **h** of all things,

HEIRS → HEIR
Ro   8:17 **h**, **h** of God and joint **h** with
          Christ—
Eph   3: 6 the Gentiles have become fellow **h**,
1Pe   3: 7 also **h** of the gracious gift of life—

HELL
Mt 10:28 both soul and body in **h**.
Mk   9:43 to have two hands and to go to **h**,
2Pe   2: 4 cast them into **h** and committed
2Es   2:29 so that your children may not see **h**.

HELMET
Isa 59:17 and a **h** of salvation on his head;
Eph   6:17 Take the **h** of salvation, and the

HELP → HELPED, HELPER, HELPS
Ex 18: 4 "The God of my father was my **h**,
Ps 33:20 he is our **h** and shield.
      46: 1 a very present **h** in trouble.
Mk   9:24 "I believe; help my unbelief!"
Heb   2:18 able to **h** those who are being tested.
      4:16 receive mercy and find grace to **h**
Jdt   6:21 called on the God of Israel for **h**.
Sir   2: 6 Trust in him, and he will **h** you;

HELPED → HELP
1Sa   7:12 "Thus far the LORD has **h** us."
Ps 118:13 I was falling, but the LORD **h** me.
Isa 49: 8 on a day of salvation I have **h** you;

HELPER → HELP
Ge   2:18 I will make him a **h** as his partner."
Ps 30:10 O LORD, be my **h**!"
Heb 13: 6 Lord is my **h**; I will not be afraid.
Tob   8: 6 Eve as a **h** and support.

HELPS → HELP
Ps 37:40 The LORD **h** them and rescues them;
Ro   8:26 the Spirit **h** us in our weakness;

HERBS
Ex 12: 8 with unleavened bread and bitter **h**.

HERMON
Dt   3: 8 from the Wadi Arnon to Mount **H**
Ps 133: 3 It is like the dew of **H**,

HEROD → HERODIANS
   1. King of Judea; tried to kill Jesus (Mt 2; Lk 1:5).
   2. Son of 1. Tetrarch of Galilee who arrested and beheaded John the Baptist (Mt 14:1-12; Mk 6:14-29; Lk 3:1, 19-20; 9:7-9); tried Jesus (Lk 23:6-15).
   3. Grandson of 1. King of Judea who killed James (Ac 12:2); arrested Peter (Ac 12:3-19). Death (Ac 12:19-23).

HERODIANS → HEROD
Mk   3: 6 immediately conspired with the **H**
      12:13 some **H** to trap him in what he said.

HERODIAS*
   Wife of Herod the Tetrarch who persuaded her daughter to ask for John the Baptist's head (Mt 14:1-12; Mk 6:14-29; Lk 3:19).

HEWN
Ex 20:25 do not build it of **h** stones;
Mk 15:46 laid it in a tomb that had been **h**

HEZEKIAH
   King of Judah (Sir 48:17-25). Restored the temple and worship (2Ch 29-31). Sought the LORD for help against Assyria (2Ki 18-19; 2Ch 32:1-23; Isa 36-37). Illness healed (2Ki 20:1-11; 2Ch 32:24-26; Isa 38). Judged for showing Babylonians his treasures (2Ki 20:12-21; 2Ch 32:31; Isa 39).

HID → HIDE
Ge   3: 8 and his wife **h** themselves from the
Ex   2: 2 a fine baby, she **h** him three months.
      3: 6 Moses **h** his face, for he was afraid
Jos   6:17 live because she **h** the messengers
1Ki 18:13 **h** a hundred of the LORD's prophets
Isa 49: 2 in the shadow of his hand he **h** me;
      54: 8 wrath for a moment I **h** my face
Mt 25:25 and **h** your talent in the ground.

HIDDEN → HIDE
Ps 19:12 Clear me from **h** faults.
Pr   2: 4 and search for it as for **h** treasures—
Isa 40:27 "My way is **h** from the LORD,
Mt 13:44 is like treasure **h** in a field,
Mk   4:22 nothing **h**, except to be disclosed;
Col   3: 3 your life is **h** with Christ in God.
Rev   2:17 the **h** manna, and I will give a white
Sir 42:20 and nothing is **h** from him.

HIDE → HID, HIDDEN
Dt 31:17 I will forsake them and **h** my face
Ps 13: 1 How long will you **h** your face
      17: 8 **h** me in the shadow of your wings,

HIGH → HEIGHT, HEIGHTS, HIGHER, HIGHEST, HIGHLY
Ge 14:18 he was priest of God Most **H**.
1Ki   3: 2 were sacrificing at the **h** places,
Ps 91: 1 live in the shelter of the Most **H**,
Mt   4: 8 a very **h** mountain and showed him
      17: 1 and led them up a **h** mountain,
Mk   5: 7 Jesus, Son of the Most **H** God?
Eph   4: 8 "When he ascended on **h** he made
Heb   2:17 a merciful and faithful **h** priest
      7:26 that we should have such a **h** priest,

HIGHER → HIGH
Ps 61: 2 Lead me to the rock that is **h** than I;
Isa 55: 9 so are my ways **h** than your ways

HIGHEST → HIGH
1Ki   8:27 the **h** heaven cannot contain you,
Mt 21: 9 Hosanna in the **h** heaven!"
Lk   2:14 "Glory to God in the **h** heaven,

HIGHLY → HIGH
Ps 47: 9 to God; he is **h** exalted.
Ro 12: 3 not to think of yourself more **h** than

HILL → HILLS
Ps 15: 1 Who may dwell on your holy **h**?
Isa 40: 4 every mountain and **h** be made low;
Mt   5:14 A city built on a **h** cannot be hid.
Lk   3: 5 mountain and **h** shall be made low,

HILLS → HILL
1Ki 20:23 "Their gods are gods of the **h**,
Ps 50:10 the cattle on a thousand **h**.

HINDER
1Sa 14: 6 nothing can **h** the LORD from saving
Isa 43:13 I work and who can **h** it?
1Pe   3: 7 so that nothing may **h** your prayers.

HIP
Ge 32:25 Jacob's **h** was put out of joint

HIRAM
   King of Tyre; helped David build his palace (2Sa 5:11-12; 1Ch 14:1); helped Solomon build the temple (1Ki 5; 2Ch 2) and his navy (1Ki 9:10-27; 2Ch 8).

HITTITE → HITTITES
Ge   23:10 Ephron the **H** answered Abraham
2Sa 11: 3 the wife of Uriah the **H.**"

HITTITES → HITTITE
Dt   20:17 **H** and the Amorites, the Canaanites
Ezr   9: 1 Canaanites, the **H**, the Perizzites,

HOLD → HOLDS
Ps   73:23 you **h** my right hand.
Isa 41:13 I, the LORD your God, **h** your right
Jn   20:17 Jesus said to her, "Do not **h** on to
Col   1:17 and in him all things **h** together.

HOLDS → HOLD
Ps 37:24 for the LORD **h** us by the hand.
Rev   2: 1 who **h** the seven stars in his right
Wis   1: 7 which **h** all things together

HOLES
Hag 1: 6 to put them into a bag with **h.**
Mt   8:20 Jesus said to him, "Foxes have **h,**

HOLINESS → HOLY
Ex 15:11 Who is like you, majestic in **h,**
Dt 32:51 by failing to maintain my **h** among
Ps 89:35 and for all I have sworn by my **h;**
Ro   1: 4 according to the spirit of **h** by
2Co   6: 6 kindness, **h** of spirit, genuine love,
1Ti   2:15 continue in faith and love and **h,**
Heb 12:14 **h** without which no one will see the

HOLOFERNES
Assyrian general (Jdt 2:4). Beguiled and beheaded by Judith (Jdt 10-13).

HOLY → HOLINESS
Ex   3: 5 which you are standing is **h** ground.
     20: 8 the sabbath day, and keep it **h.**
    26:33 the **h** place from the most **h.**
    29:37 the altar shall be most **h;**
Lev 11:44 and be **h**, for I am **h.**
Jos   5:15 for the place where you stand is **h.**"
1Sa   2: 2 "There is no **H** One like the LORD,
Ps   2: 6 set my king on Zion, my **h** hill."
    11: 4 The LORD is in his **h** temple;
Isa   6: 3 "**H, h, h** is the LORD of hosts;
    40:25 who is my equal? says the **H** One.
Da   9:24 and to anoint a most **h** place.
Mt   1:18 to be with child through the **H** Spirit.
     3:11 baptize you with the **H** Spirit and
    24:15 sacrilege standing in the **h** place,
Mk   1:24 who you are, the **H** One of God."
     3:29 against the **H** Spirit can never have
Lk   3:22 the **H** Spirit descended upon him in
    11:13 heavenly Father give the **H** Spirit
Jn 14:26 But the Advocate, the **H** Spirit,
Ac   2: 4 were filled with the **H** Spirit and
     2:27 your **H** One experience corruption.
     5: 3 your heart to lie to the **H** Spirit
Ro   12: 1 living sacrifice, **h** and acceptable to
Eph   1: 4 to be **h** and blameless
     4:30 do not grieve the **H** Spirit of God,
Heb   6: 4 and have shared in the **H** Spirit,
1Pe   1:16 "You shall be **h**, for I am **h.**"
1Jn   2:20 have been anointed by the **H** One,
Jude 1:14 with ten thousands of his **h** ones,
Rev   4: 8 **H, h, h**, the Lord God the Almighty
    21: 2 I saw the **h** city, the new Jerusalem,
Wis   4:15 he watches over his **h** ones.
1Mc 1:15 and abandoned the **h** covenant.
2Es 14:22 send the **h** spirit into me,

HOME → HOMELESS, HOMETOWN
Dt   6: 7 when you are at **h** and when you
Ps   68: 6 God gives the desolate a **h**
Jn 14:23 to them and make our **h** with them.
2Co   5: 8 the body and at **h** with the Lord.

HOMELESS* → HOME
Isa 58: 7 the **h** poor into your house;
1Co   4:11 poorly clothed and beaten and **h,**

HOMETOWN → HOME, TOWN
Mk   6: 4 not without honor, except in their **h,**

HONEST
Lev 19:36 have **h** balances, **h** weights,
Pr 16:11 **H** balances and scales are the

HONEY
Ex   3: 8 a land flowing with milk and **h,**
Jdg 14: 8 bees in the body of the lion, and **h.**
1Sa 14:26 honeycomb, the **h** was dripping out;
Ps 19:10 sweeter also than **h**, and drippings
Mt   3: 4 and his food was locusts and wild **h.**

HONOR → HONORABLE, HONORED, HONORS
Dt   5:16 **H** your father and your mother,
1Ch 29:12 Riches and **h** come from you,
Ps   8: 5 and crowned them with glory and **h.**
Ecc 10: 1 little folly outweighs wisdom and **h.**
Isa 29:13 and **h** me with their lips,
Mal 1: 6 a father, where is the **h** due me?
Mt 13:57 not without **h** except in their own
    15: 4 For God said, '**H** your father and
Jn 12:26 serves me, the Father will **h.**
Ro 13: 7 **h** to whom **h** is due.
Eph 6: 2 "**H** your father and mother"—
1Ti   5:17 considered worthy of double **h,**
Heb 2: 7 crowned them with glory and **h,**
Rev 4:11 to receive glory and **h** and power,
Tob 4: 3 **H** your mother and do not

HONORABLE → HONOR
Php 4: 8 whatever is true, whatever is **h,**

HONORED → HONOR
Hag 1: 8 I may take pleasure in it and be **h,**
1Co 12:26 if one member is **h**, all rejoice

HONORS → HONOR
Mal 1: 6 A son **h** his father, and servants
Mt 15: 8 'This people **h** me with their lips,

HOOFS
Lev 11: 3 Any animal that has divided **h**

HOOK → HOOKS
Mt 17:27 go to the sea and cast a **h;**

HOOKS → HOOK
Isa 2: 4 and their spears into pruning **h;**
Joel 3:10 and your pruning **h** into spears;

HOPE → HOPED, HOPES
Job 17:15 where then is my **h?**
Ps 62: 5 for my **h** is from him.
  146: 5 whose **h** is in the LORD their God,
Pr 23:18 and your **h** will not be cut off.
Isa 8:17 and I will **h** in him.
Jer 14: 8 O **h** of Israel, its savior in time of
La   3:21 and therefore I have **h:**
Mt 12:21 in his name the Gentiles will **h.**"
Ro   5: 5 and **h** does not disappoint us,
    12:12 Rejoice in **h**, be patient in suffering,
1Co 13:13 And now faith, **h**, and love abide,
Col 1:27 Christ in you, the **h** of glory.
1Th 5: 8 and for a helmet the **h** of salvation.
Heb 6:19 this **h**, a sure and steadfast anchor
     7:19 the introduction of a better **h,**
1Pe 1: 3 a living **h** through the resurrection
1Jn 3: 3 all who have this **h** in him purify
Sir 34:15 their **h** is in him who saves them.
Sus 1:60 who saves those who **h** in him.

HOPED → HOPE
Heb 11: 1 faith is the assurance of things **h** for,
1Pe   3: 5 the holy women who **h** in God

HOPES → HOPE
1Co 13: 7 believes all things, **h** all things,

HOREB → =SINAI
Ex   3: 1 came to **H**, the mountain of God.
Dt   5: 2 God made a covenant with us at **H.**
1Ki 19: 8 forty days and forty nights to **H**

HORN → HORNS
Ps 18: 2 and the **h** of my salvation,
Da   7: 8 when another **h** appeared,
     8: 5 The goat had a **h** between its eyes.

HORNS → HORN
Ge 22:13 caught in a thicket by its **h.**
Ex 27: 2 make **h** for it on its four corners,
Da   7: 7 that preceded it, and it had ten **h.**
     8: 3 Both **h** were long, but one
Zec 1:18 And I looked up and saw four **h.**
Rev 5: 6 having seven **h** and seven eyes,
     9:13 from the four **h** of the golden altar
    17: 3 and it had seven heads and ten **h.**

HORSE → HORSES
Ex 15: 1 **h** and rider he has thrown into the
Ps 33:17 The war **h** is a vain hope for victory,
Zec 1: 8 I saw a man riding on a red **h!**
Rev 6: 2 I looked, and there was a white **h!**
    19:11 and there was a white **h!**

HORSES → HORSE
2Ki 2:11 a chariot of fire and **h** of fire
Ps 20: 7 pride in chariots, and some in **h,**
Joel 2: 4 They have the appearance of **h,**
Rev 9: 7 appearance the locusts were like **h**
    19:14 following him on white **h.**

HOSANNA
Mk 11:10 **H** in the highest heaven!"
Jn 12:13 went out to meet him, shouting, "**H!**

HOSEA
Prophet whose wife and family pictured the unfaithfulness of Israel (Hos 1-3).

HOSHEA → =JOSHUA
1. Original name of Joshua (Nu 13:8, 16).
2. Last king of Israel (2Ki 15:30; 17:1-6).

HOSPITABLE* → HOSPITALITY
1Ti 3: 2 temperate, sensible, respectable, **h,**
Tit   1: 8 but he must be **h**, a lover
1Pe 4: 9 Be **h** to one another without

HOSPITALITY → HOSPITABLE
Ro 12:13 of the saints; extend **h** to strangers.
1Ti   5:10 has brought up children, shown **h,**
Heb 13: 2 not neglect to show **h** to strangers,

HOST → HOSTS
Dt   4:19 all the **h** of heaven,
2Ki 17:16 worshiped all the **h** of heaven
Lk   2:13 angel a multitude of the heavenly **h,**

HOSTILE → HOSTILITY
Ro   8: 7 that is set on the flesh is **h** to God;
Col 1:21 once estranged and **h** in mind,

HOSTILITY → HOSTILE
Eph 2:14 the dividing wall, that is, the **h**
Heb 12: 3 Consider him who endured such **h**

HOSTS → HOST
1Sa 1: 3 and to sacrifice to the LORD of **h**
Ps 46: 7 The LORD of **h** is with us;
Isa 48: 2 the LORD of **h** is his name.

HOT
Rev 3:15 you are neither cold nor **h.**

HOUR
Mt   6:27 by worrying add a single **h** to your
    24:36 about that day and **h** no one knows,
Jn   2: 4 My **h** has not yet come."
    17: 1 "Father, the **h** has come;
Rev 3:10 I will keep you from the **h** of trial
    14: 7 for the **h** of his judgment has come;

HOUSE → HOUSEHOLD, HOUSES, HOUSETOP, HOUSETOPS, STOREHOUSE
Ex 20:17 shall not covet your neighbor's **h;**
2Sa 7:11 that the LORD will make you a **h.**
1Ch 22: 1 "Here shall be the **h** of the LORD
Ezr 1: 5 rebuild the **h** of the LORD in
Ps 69: 9 zeal for your **h** that has consumed
  127: 1 Unless the LORD builds the **h,**
Pr   9: 1 Wisdom has built her **h**, she has
Isa 56: 7 my **h** shall be called a **h** of prayer

Mt 7:24 like a wise man who built his **h**
21:13 'My **h** shall be called a **h** of prayer';
Mk 3:25 And if a **h** is divided against itself,
Jn 2:17 "Zeal for your **h** will consume me."
14: 2 In my Father's **h** there are many
1Pe 2: 5 be built into a spiritual **h**,

HOUSEHOLD → HOUSE
Jos 24:15 and my **h**, we will serve the LORD."
Mic 7: 6 enemies are members of your own **h**
Mt 10:36 will be members of one's own **h**.
1Ti 3: 4 He must manage his own **h** well,
Tit 2: 5 good managers of the **h**, kind,
1Pe 4:17 judgment to begin with the **h** of God

HOUSES → HOUSE
Ex 12:27 passed over the **h** of the Israelites in
Mt 19:29 everyone who has left **h** or brothers

HOUSETOP → HOUSE
Mt 24:17 the one on the **h** must not go down

HOUSETOPS → HOUSE
Mt 10:27 whispered, proclaim from the **h**.

HULDAH*
Prophetess inquired by Hilkiah for Josiah (2Ki 22; 2Ch 34:14-28).

HUMAN → HUMANKIND
Ge 6: 7 blot out from the earth the **h** beings
Ps 8: 4 are **h** beings that you are mindful
Da 2:34 a stone was cut out, not by **h** hands,
5: 5 the fingers of a **h** hand appeared
Hos 11: 4 I led them with cords of **h** kindness,
Mt 15: 9 teaching **h** precepts as doctrines.' "
Ac 5:29 obey God rather than any **h**
1Co 2:13 in words not taught by **h** wisdom
Php 2: 7 being born in **h** likeness.
Rev 4: 7 with a face like a **h** face,
Jdt 8:16 for God is not like a **h** being,

HUMANKIND → HUMAN
Ge 1:26 "Let us make **h** in our image,
Mk 2:27 "The sabbath was made for **h**,
1Ti 2: 5 one mediator between God and **h**,

HUMBLE → HUMBLED, HUMBLY, HUMILITY
Nu 12: 3 Now the man Moses was very **h**,
Dt 8:16 to **h** you and to test you,
Ps 25: 9 He leads the **h** in what is right,
149: 4 he adorns the **h** with victory.
Isa 57:15 to revive the spirit of the **h**,
Zep 2: 3 Seek the LORD, all you **h** of the land
Mt 11:29 for I am gentle and **h** in heart,
21: 5 **h**, and mounted on a donkey,
Jas 4:10 **H** yourselves before the LORD,
1Pe 5: 5 but gives grace to the **h**."
Sir 3:20 but by the **h** he is glorified.

HUMBLED → HUMBLE
Ps 119:71 It is good for me that I was **h**,
Lk 14:11 all who exalt themselves will be **h**,
Php 2: 8 he **h** himself and became obedient

HUMBLY* → HUMBLE
Mic 6: 8 and to walk **h** with your God?

HUMILITY → HUMBLE
Pr 15:33 and **h** goes before honor.
Zep 2: 3 seek righteousness, seek **h**;
Php 2: 3 but in **h** regard others as better than
Col 3:12 with compassion, kindness, **h**,
1Pe 5: 5 must clothe yourselves with **h**
Sir 1:27 fidelity and **h** are his delight.

HUNDRED
Ge 17:17 born to a man who is a **h** years old?
Isa 65:20 one who dies at a **h** years will be
Ro 4:19 (for he was about a **h** years old),

HUNG
Dt 21:23 **h** on a tree is under God's curse.
Ps 137: 2 the willows there we **h** up our harps.
Mk 9:42 if a great millstone were **h** around

HUNGER → HUNGRY
Dt 8: 3 He humbled you by letting you **h**,
Mt 5: 6 "Blessed are those who **h** and thirst
Rev 7:16 will **h** no more, and thirst no more;

HUNGRY → HUNGER
Ps 50:12 "If I were **h**, I would not tell you,
146: 7 who gives food to the **h**.
Pr 25:21 If your enemies are **h**, give them
Mt 12: 1 his disciples were **h**, and they began
Jn 6:35 comes to me will never be **h**,
Ro 12:20 "if your enemies are **h**, feed them;

HUSBAND → HUSBANDS
Ge 3: 6 and she also gave some to her **h**,
3:16 yet your desire shall be for your **h**,
Pr 31:28 her **h** too, and he praises her:
Isa 54: 5 For your Maker is your **h**,
Jer 31:32 they broke, though I was their **h**,
Hos 2:16 the LORD, you will call me, "My **h**,"
1Co 7:10 wife should not separate from her **h**
Eph 5:23 **h** is the head of the wife just as
Rev 21: 2 as a bride adorned for her **h**.
Sir 26: 1 Happy is the **h** of a good wife;

HUSBANDS → HUSBAND
Jn 4:18 for you have had five **h**,
Eph 5:25 **H**, love your wives, just as Christ
Col 3:18 Wives, be subject to your **h**,
Tit 2: 4 the young women to love their **h**,
1Pe 3: 7 **H**, in the same way, show

HUSHAI
Wise man of David; foiled Absalom's revolt (2Sa 15:32-37; 16:15-17:16).

HYMN → HYMNS
Mt 26:30 When they had sung the **h**,
Sir 44: 1 **h** IN HONOR OF OUR ANCESTORS

HYMNS → HYMN
Eph 5:19 psalms and **h** and spiritual songs
Col 3:16 in your hearts sing psalms, **h**,
Aza 1: 1 singing to God and blessing the

HYPOCRISY → HYPOCRITE, HYPOCRITES
Mt 23:28 but inside you are full of **h** and
Mk 12:15 knowing their **h**, he said to them,
Lk 12: 1 of the Pharisees, that is, their **h**.
Jas 3:17 without a trace of partiality or **h**.

HYPOCRITE → HYPOCRISY
Lk 6:42 You **h**, first take the log out of your
Sir 1:29 Do not be a **h** before others,

HYPOCRITES → HYPOCRISY
Mt 6: 5 you pray, do not be like the **h**;
23:13 to you, scribes and Pharisees, **h**!
Mk 7: 6 prophesied rightly about you **h**,

HYSSOP
Ex 12:22 a bunch of **h**, dip it in the blood that
Nu 19: 6 The priest shall take cedarwood, **h**,
Ps 51: 7 Purge me with **h**, and I shall be
Jn 19:29 full of the wine on a branch of **h**

I

I AM
Ex 3:14 God said to Moses, "**I am** WHO I am."
Isa 44: 6 **I am** the first and **I am** the last;
Mt 28:20 **I am** with you always, to the end of
Mk 8:29 "But who do you say that **I am**?"
Jn 6:35 to them, "**I am** the bread of life.
8:12 "**I am** the light of the world.
8:58 before Abraham was, **I am**."
9: 5 **I am** the light of the world."
10: 7 **I am** the gate for the sheep.
10:11 "**I am** the good shepherd.
11:25 "**I am** the resurrection and the life.
14: 6 "**I am** the way, and the truth, and
15: 1 "**I am** the true vine, and my Father

Rev 1: 8 "**I am** the Alpha and the Omega,"
22:20 "Surely **I am** coming soon."

IDLE
Ecc 11: 6 evening do not let your hands be **i**;
2Th 3: 7 were not **i** when we were with you,

IDOL → IDOLS
Ex 20: 4 shall not make for yourself an **i**,
Isa 40:19 An **i**?—A workman casts it,
1Co 10:19 or that an **i** is anything?

IDOLS → IDOL
Ex 34:17 You shall not make cast **i**.
2Ki 17:15 went after false **i** and became false;
Ps 115: 4 Their **i** are silver and gold,
1Co 8: 1 concerning food sacrificed to **i**:
1Mc 1:43 they sacrificed to **i** and profaned the

IGNORANCE → IGNORANT
Ac 17:30 overlooked the times of human **i**,
1Pe 2:15 silence the **i** of the foolish.

IGNORANT → IGNORANCE
Heb 5: 2 He is able to deal gently with the **i**
2Pe 3:16 the **i** and unstable twist to their own

ILL → ILLNESS
1Co 11:30 many of you are weak and **i**,

ILLEGITIMATE
Jn 8:41 said to him, "We are not **i** children;
Heb 12: 8 then you are **i** and not his children.

ILLNESS → ILL
Dt 7:15 will turn away from you every **i**;
Ps 41: 3 their **i** you heal all their infirmities.

IMAGE → IMAGES
Ge 1:26 "Let us make humankind in our **i**,
Dt 27:15 who makes an idol or casts an **i**,
1Co 15:49 the **i** of the man of heaven.
Col 1:15 He is the **i** of the invisible God,
Rev 20: 4 not worshiped the beast or its **i** and
Sir 17: 3 and made them in his own **i**.

IMAGES → IMAGE
Nu 33:52 destroy all their cast **i**,
Ps 97: 7 All worshipers of **i** are put to shame,

IMITATE → IMITATORS
Heb 13: 7 their way of life, and **i** their faith.
3Jn 1:11 not **i** what is evil but **i** what is good.

IMITATORS → IMITATE
1Co 11: 1 Be **i** of me, as I am of Christ.
Eph 5: 1 be **i** of God, as beloved children,

IMMANUEL* → =EMMANUEL
Isa 7:14 bear a son, and shall name him **I**.
8: 8 fill the breadth of your land, O **I**.

IMMORAL → IMMORALITY
1Co 5: 9 not to associate with sexually **i**
Heb 12:16 an **i** and godless person,

IMMORALITY → IMMORAL
2Co 12:21 sexual **i**, and licentiousness
Jude 1: 7 indulged in sexual **i** and pursued
Sir 41:17 Be ashamed of sexual **i**,

IMMORTAL → IMMORTALITY
Ro 1:23 the glory of the **i** God for images
1Ti 1:17 To the King of the ages, **i**, invisible,

IMMORTALITY → IMMORTAL
1Co 15:53 and this mortal body must put on **i**.
1Ti 6:16 It is he alone who has **i** and dwells

IMPERISHABLE
1Co 9:25 a perishable wreath, but we an **i** one.
15:52 and the dead will be raised **i**,
1Pe 1: 4 and into an inheritance that is **i**,

IMPORTANCE* → IMPORTANT
1Co 15: 3 of first **i** what I in turn had received:

IMPORTANT → IMPORTANCE
Mk 12:33 much more **i** than all whole burnt

IMPOSSIBLE
Zec   8: 6 should it also seem i to me,
Mt   17:20 and nothing will be i for you."
Mk   10:27 "For mortals it is i, but not for God;
Heb   11: 6 without faith it is i to please God,

IMPURE* → IMPURITY
Eph   5: 5 that no fornicator or i person,
1Th   2: 3 not spring from deceit or i motives

IMPURITY → IMPURE
Zec   13: 1 to cleanse them from sin and i.
Gal   5:19 fornication, i, licentiousness,
1Th   4: 7 did not call us to i but in holiness.

INCENSE → FRANKINCENSE
Ex   25: 6 anointing oil and for the fragrant i,

INCLINATION
Ge   6: 5 and that every i of the thoughts
Ecc   11: 9 Follow the i of your heart and

INCREASE → INCREASED
Ge   3:16 greatly i your pangs in childbearing;
Lk   17: 5 said to the Lord, "I our faith!"
Jn   3:30 He must i, but I must decrease."

INCREASED → INCREASE
Ro   5:20 but where sin i, grace abounded all

INDEBTED* → DEBT
Lk   11: 4 forgive everyone i to us.

INDEPENDENT*
1Co   11:11 not i of man or man i of woman.

INFANTS
Ps   8: 2 Out of the mouths of babes and i
Mt   21:16 'Out of the mouths of i and nursing
1Co   14:20 i in evil, but in thinking as adults.

INFIRMITIES
Isa   53: 4 borne our i and carried our diseases;
Mt   8:17 took our i and bore our diseases."

INGATHERING → GATHER
Ex   23:16 You shall observe the festival of i

INHERIT → INHERITANCE
Lev   20:24 You shall i their land,
Ps   37:11 But the meek shall i the land,
Zec   2:12 The Lord will i Judah as his portion
Lk   10:25 "what must I do to i eternal life?"
1Co   6: 9 wrongdoers will not i the kingdom
Heb   1:14 sake of those who are to i salvation?

INHERITANCE → INHERIT
Ex   34: 9 and take us for your i."
Eph   1:11 In Christ we have also obtained an i,
Heb   9:15 the promised eternal i,

INIQUITIES → INIQUITY
Lev   16:22 goat shall bear on itself all their i
Ps   103:10 nor repay us according to our i.
Isa   53:11 and he shall bear their i.
Ro   4: 7 are those whose i are forgiven,
Rev   18: 5 and God has remembered her i.

INIQUITY → INIQUITIES
Ex   34: 7 forgiving i and transgression and sin
Ps   103: 3 who forgives all your i,
Isa   53: 6 Lord has laid on him the i of us all.
Tit   2:14 that he might redeem us from all i

INJURY
Lev   24:20 the i inflicted is the i to be suffered.

INJUSTICE
Hos   10:13 wickedness, you have reaped i,
Ro   9:14 Is there i on God's part?

INN*
Lk   2: 7 there was no place for them in the i.
      10:34 brought him to an i, and took care

INNER → INWARDLY
Mt   24:26 He is in the i rooms,' do not believe
2Co   4:16 our i nature is being renewed day
1Pe   3: 4 let your adornment be the i self

INNOCENCE → INNOCENT
Ps   26: 6 I wash my hands in i,
Hos   8: 5 long will they be incapable of i?

INNOCENT → INNOCENCE
Pr   6:17 tongue, and hands that shed i blood,
Mt   10:16 be wise as serpents and i as doves.
      27:24 "I am i of this man's blood;

INQUIRE → INQUIRED
Dt   12:30 do not i concerning their gods,

INQUIRED → INQUIRE
Zep   1: 6 not sought the Lord or i of him.

INSCRIBED → INSCRIPTION
Da   10:21 what is i in the book of truth.
Rev   19:12 he has a name i that no one

INSCRIPTION → INSCRIBED
Mk   15:26 The i of the charge against him read,
2Ti   2:19 foundation stands, bearing this i:

INSIGHT
Pr   3: 5 and do not rely on your own i.
Eph   1: 8 With all wisdom and i
Sir   6:37 It is he who will give i to your mind,

INSPIRED
Ex   35:34 And he has i him to teach,
2Ti   3:16 All scripture is i by God and is

INSTITUTED → INSTITUTION
Ro   13: 1 that exist have been i by God.

INSTITUTION* → INSTITUTED
Nu   10: 8 this shall be a perpetual i for you
1Pe   2:13 the authority of every human i,

INSTRUCT → INSTRUCTED,
**   INSTRUCTION, INSTRUCTOR**
Dt   17:10 observing everything they i you.
Ne   9:20 You gave your good spirit to i them,
Ro   15:14 and able to i one another.
1Co   14:19 in order to i others also,

INSTRUCTED → INSTRUCT
Isa   40:13 or as his counselor has i him?
Jn   8:28 these things as the Father i me.

INSTRUCTION → INSTRUCT
Pr   8:10 Take my i instead of silver,
Mic   4: 2 For out of Zion shall go forth i,
Ro   15: 4 in former days was written for our i,
1Ti   1: 5 But the aim of such i is love
Sir   51:26 and let your souls receive i;

INSTRUCTOR → INSTRUCT
Mt   23:10 for you have one i, the Messiah.

INSULTS
Ps   69: 9 the i of those who insult you have
Lk   22:65 heaping many other i on him.
2Co   12:10 I am content with weaknesses, i,

INTEGRITY
Job   27: 5 until I die I will not put away my i
Pr   14:32 the righteous find a refuge in their i.
Tit   2: 7 and in your teaching show i, gravity,

INTELLIGENCE → INTELLIGENT
Pr   8: 5 acquire i, you who lack it.
Sir   22:11 fool, for he has left i behind.

INTELLIGENT → INTELLIGENCE
Pr   11:12 but an i person remains silent.
Ecc   9:11 nor riches to the i,

INTENDED → INTENTIONS
Ge   50:20 i to do harm to me, God i it for
         good,
Jer   18:10 the good that I had i to do to it.

INTENTIONS → INTENDED
Mk   7:21 the human heart, that evil i come:
Heb   4:12 judge the thoughts and i of the
         heart.

INTERCEDES → INTERCESSION
Ro   8:26 Spirit i with sighs too deep for

INTERCESSION* → INTERCEDES
1Sa   2:25 against the Lord, who can make i?"
Isa   53:12 and made i for the transgressors.
Heb   7:25 he always lives to make i for them.

INTERMARRY → MARRIAGE
Dt   7: 3 Do not i with them, giving your

INTERPRET → INTERPRETATION,
**   INTERPRETATIONS**
Ge   41:15 no one who can i it.
Mt   16: 3 cannot i the signs of the times.
1Co   12:30 Do all speak in tongues? Do all i?

INTERPRETATION → INTERPRET
Da   2: 4 and we will reveal the i."
1Co   12:10 to another the i of tongues.
2Pe   1:20 scripture is a matter of one's own i,
2Es   12:10 "This is the i of this vision

INTERPRETATIONS → INTERPRET
Ge   40: 8 to them, "Do not i belong to God?

INVADE → INVADED
La   1:10 the nations i her sanctuary,
Na   1:15 never again shall the wicked i you;

INVADED → INVADE
2Ki   17: 5 the king of Assyria i all the land

INVISIBLE
Col   1:15 He is the image of the i God,
1Ti   1:17 To the King of the ages, immortal, i,

INVITE → INVITED, INVITES
Lk   14:13 when you give a banquet, i the poor,

INVITED → INVITE
Rev   19: 9 Blessed are those who are i to

INVITES → INVITE
1Co   10:27 If an unbeliever i you to a meal
Sir   13: 9 When an influential person i you,

INVOKE
Ex   23:13 Do not i the names of other gods;
1Pe   1:17 If you i as Father the one who

INWARDLY → INNER
Ro   2:29 a person is a Jew who is one i,
      8:23 groan i while we wait for adoption,

IRON
Ps   2: 9 shall break them with a rod of i,
Pr   27:17 I sharpens i, and one person
Da   2:33 its legs of i, its feet partly of i
Rev   19:15 he will rule them with a rod of i;

IRREVOCABLE
Ro   11:29 gifts and the calling of God are i.

ISAAC
   Son of Abraham by Sarah (Ge 17:19; 21:1-7;
1Ch 1:28). Abrahamic covenant perpetuated with
(Ge 17:21; 26:2-5). Offered up by Abraham (Ge
22; Heb 11:17-19). Rebekah taken as wife (Ge 24).
Inherited Abraham's estate (Ge 25:5). Father of
Esau and Jacob (Ge 25:19-26; 1Ch 1:34). Nearly
lost Rebekah to Abimelech (Ge 26:1-11). Covenant with Abimelech (Ge 26:12-31). Tricked into
blessing Jacob (Ge 27). Death (Ge 35:27-29). Father of Israel (Ex 3:6; Dt 29:13; Ro 9:10).

ISAIAH
   Prophet to Judah (Isa 1:1). Called by the Lord
(Isa 6). Announced judgment to Ahaz (Isa 7), deliverance from Assyria to Hezekiah (2Ki 19; Isa 36-
37), deliverance from death to Hezekiah (2Ki 20:1-
11; Isa 38). Chronicler of Judah's history (2Ch
26:22; 32:32).

ISCARIOT
Mt   10: 4 Judas I, the one who betrayed him.
Lk   22: 1 Satan entered into Judas called I,

ISHBAAL*
   Son of Saul; would-be king (2Sa 2:8-4:12).

ISHMAEL

Son of Abraham by Hagar (Ge 16; 1Ch 1:28). Blessed, but not son of covenant (Ge 17:18-21; Gal 4:21-31). Sent away by Sarah (Ge 21:8-21). Children (Ge 25:12-18; 1Ch 1:29-31). Death (Ge 25:17).

ISRAEL → ISRAELITE, ISRAELITES, =JACOB

1. Name given to Jacob (Ge 32:28; 35:10).
2. Corporate name of Jacob's descendants; often specifically Northern Kingdom.

Ge	49:28	All these are the twelve tribes of I,
Ex	28:11	with the names of the sons of I;
Nu	24:17	and a scepter shall rise out of I;
Dt	6: 4	Hear, O I: The LORD is our God,
Ps	125: 5	Peace be upon I!
Jer	31:31	a new covenant with the house of I
Hos	11: 1	When I was a child, I loved him,
Mt	2: 6	who is to shepherd my people I.' "
Mk	12:29	answered, "The first is, 'Hear, O I:
Lk	22:30	judging the twelve tribes of I.
Ac	1: 6	you will restore the kingdom to I?"
Ro	9: 6	not all Israelites truly belong to I,
Heb	8: 8	a new covenant with the house of I.
Rev	7: 4	out of every tribe of the people of I:
Sir	17:17	but I is the Lord's own portion.

ISRAELITE → ISRAEL

Jn	1:47	an I in whom there is no deceit!"
Ro	11: 1	I myself am an I, a descendant of

ISRAELITES → ISRAEL

Ex	2:23	The I groaned under their slavery,
	29:45	I will dwell among the I, and I will

ISSACHAR

Son of Jacob by Leah (Ge 30:18; 35:23; 1Ch 2:1). Tribe of blessed (Ge 49:14-15; Dt 33:18-19), numbered (Nu 1:29; 26:25), allotted land (Jos 19:17-23; Eze 48:25), assisted Deborah (Jdg 5:15), 12,000 from (Rev 7:7).

ITCHING

2Ti	4: 3	sound doctrine, but having i ears,

J

JACOB → =ISRAEL

1. Son of Isaac, younger twin of Esau (Ge 26:21-26; 1Ch 1:34). Bought Esau's birthright (Ge 26:29-34); tricked Isaac into blessing him (Ge 27:1-37). Fled to Haran (Ge 28:1-5). Abrahamic covenant perpetuated through (Ge 28:13-15; Mal 1:2). Vision at Bethel (Ge 28:10-22). Served Laban for Rachel and Leah (Ge 29:1-30). Children (Ge 29:31-30:24; 35:16-26; 1Ch 2-9). Flocks increased (Ge 30:25-43). Returned to Canaan (Ge 31). Wrestled with God; name changed to Israel (Ge 32:22-32). Reconciled to Esau (Ge 33). Returned to Bethel (Ge 35:1-15). Favored Joseph (Ge 37:3). Sent sons to Egypt during famine (Ge 42-43). Settled in Egypt (Ge 46). Blessed Ephraim and Manasseh (Ge 48). Blessed sons (Ge 49:1-28; Heb 11:21). Death (Ge 49:29-33). Burial (Ge 50:1-14).
2. Corporate name of Jacob's descendants; often specifically Northern Kingdom.

Ps	135: 4	the LORD has chosen J for himself,
Mic	7:20	You will show faithfulness to J
Ro	9:13	"I have loved J,
1Mc	1:28	house of J was clothed with shame.

JAEL*

Woman who killed the Canaanite general, Sisera (Jdg 4:17-22; 5:6, 24-27).

JAIRUS

Synagogue ruler whose daughter Jesus raised (Mk 5:22-43; Lk 8:41-56).

JAMES

1. Apostle; brother of John (Mt 4:21-22; 10:2; Mk 3:17; Lk 5:1-10). At transfiguration (Mt 17:1-13; Mk 9:1-13; Lk 9:28-36). Killed by Herod (Ac 12:2).
2. Apostle (Mt 10:3; Mk 3:18; Lk 6:15).
3. Brother of Jesus (Mt 13:55; Mk 6:3; Lk 24:10; Gal 1:19) and Judas (Jude 1). With believers before Pentecost (Ac 1:13). Leader of church at Jerusalem (Ac 12:17; 15; 21:18; Gal 2:9, 12). Author of epistle (Jas 1:1).

JAPHETH

Son of Noah (Ge 5:32; 1Ch 1:4-5). Blessed (Ge 9:18-28). Sons of (Ge 10:2-5).

JAR → JARS

1Ki	17:14	The j of meal will not be emptied
Mk	14: 3	alabaster j of very costly ointment
Lk	22:10	man carrying a j of water will meet

JARS → JAR

Jn	2: 6	there were six stone water j for
2Co	4: 7	But we have this treasure in clay j,

JEALOUS

Ex	34:14	whose name is J, is a j God).
Dt	4:24	God is a devouring fire, a j God.
	32:16	They made him j with strange gods,
Eze	39:25	and I will be j for my holy name.
Ro	10:19	"I will make you j of those

JEBUSITES

Ex	3: 8	the Perizzites, the Hivites, and the J.
Jos	15:63	Judah could not drive out the J,

JECONIAH → See JEHOIACHIN

JEHOAHAZ

1. Son of Jehu; king of Israel (2Ki 13:1-9).
2. Son of Josiah; king of Judah (2Ki 23:31-34; 2Ch 36:1-4).

JEHOASH → =JOASH

1. Son of Ahaziah, king of Judah (2Ki 12). See Joash, 1.
2. Son of Jehoahaz; king of Israel. Defeat of Aram prophesied by Elisha (2Ki 13:10-25). Defeated Amaziah in Jerusalem (2Ki 14:1-16). See Joash, 2.

JEHOIACHIN → =CONIAH, =JECONIAH

Son of Jehoiakim; king of Judah exiled by Nebuchadnezzar (2Ki 24:8-17; 2Ch 36:8-10; Eze 1:2). Status improved (2Ki 25:27-30; Jer 52:31-34).

JEHOIADA

Priest who sheltered Joash from Athaliah (2Ki 11-12; 2Ch 22:11-24:16).

JEHOIAKIM → =ELIAKIM

Son of Josiah; made king of Judah by Nebuchadnezzar (2Ki 23:34-24:6; 2Ch 36:4-8; Jer 22:18-23). Burned scroll of Jeremiah's prophecies (Jer 36).

JEHORAM → =JORAM

1. Son of Jehoshaphat; king of Judah. Prophesied against by Elijah; killed by the LORD (2Ch 21). See Joram, 1.
2. Son of Ahab; king of Israel (2Ch 22:5). Joined Jehoshaphat against Moab (2Ki 3). See Joram, 2.

JEHOSHAPHAT

1. Son of Asa; king of Judah. Strengthened his kingdom (2Ch 17). Joined Ahab against Aram (2Ki 22; 2Ch 18). Established judges (2Ch 19). Joined Joram against Moab (2Ki 3; 2Ch 20).
2. Valley of judgment (Joel 3:2, 12).

JEHU

1. Prophet against Baasha (2Ki 16:1-7).
2. King of Israel. Anointed by Elijah to obliterate house of Ahab (1Ki 19:16-17); anointed by servant of Elisha (2Ki 9:1-13). Killed Joram and Ahaziah (2Ki 9:14-29; 2Ch 22:7-9), Jezebel (2Ki 9:30-37), relatives of Ahab (2Ki 10:1-17; Hos 1:4), ministers of Baal (2Ki 10:18-29). Death (2Ki 10:30-36).

JEPHTHAH

Judge from Gilead who delivered Israel from Ammon (Jdg 10:6-12:7). Made rash vow concerning his daughter (Jdg 11:30-40).

JEREMIAH

Prophet to Judah (Jer 1:1-3). Called by the LORD (Jer 1). Put in stocks (Jer 20:1-3). Threatened for prophesying (Jer 11:18-23; 26). Opposed by Hananiah (Jer 28). Scroll burned (Jer 36). Imprisoned (Jer 37). Thrown into cistern (Jer 38). Forced to Egypt with those fleeing Babylonians (Jer 43).

JERICHO

Jos	6: 2	"See, I have handed J over to you,
1Ki	16:34	In his days Hiel of Bethel built J;
Lk	18:35	As he approached J, a blind man

JEROBOAM

1. Official of Solomon; rebelled to become first king of Israel (1Ki 11:26-40; 12:1-20; 2Ch 10). Idolatry (1Ki 12:25-33; Tob 1:5; Sir 47:23); judgment for (1Ki 13-14; 2Ch 13).
2. Son of Jehoash; king of Israel (1Ki 14:23-29).

JERUSALEM

2Sa	5: 5	and at J he reigned over all Israel
	15:29	carried the ark of God back to J,
2Ki	25:10	broke down the walls around J.
Ezr	2: 1	they returned to J and Judah,
Ne	2:17	Come, let us rebuild the wall of J,
Isa	40: 2	Speak tenderly to J,
La	1: 8	J sinned grievously, so she has
Da	9:25	went out to restore and rebuild J
Joel	3: 1	I restore the fortunes of Judah and
Mic	4: 2	and the word of the LORD from J.
Zec	1:14	I am very jealous for J and for Zion.
	14: 8	living waters shall flow out from J,
Mt	23:37	"J, J, the city that kills the prophets
Lk	4: 9	Then the devil took him to J,
Gal	4:25	corresponds to the present J,
Heb	12:22	of the living God, the heavenly J,
Rev	21: 2	And I saw the holy city, the new J,
1Mc	1:29	and he came to J with a large force.

JESSE

Father of David (Ru 4:17-22; 1Sa 16; 1Ch 2:12-17).

JESUS

1. Jesus the Messiah.

LIFE: Genealogy (Mt 1:1-17; Lk 3:21-37). Birth announced (Mt 1:18-25; Lk 1:26-45). Birth (Mt 2:1-12; Lk 2:1-40). Escape to Egypt (Mt 2:13-23). As a boy in the temple (Lk 2:41-52). Baptism (Mt 3:13-17; Mk 1:9-11; Lk 3:21-22; Jn 1:32-34). Temptation (Mt 4:1-11; Mk 1:12-13; Lk 4:1-13). Ministry in Galilee (Mt 4:12-18:35; Mk 1:14-9:50; Lk 4:14-13:9; Jn 1:35-2:11; 4; 6). Transfiguration (Mt 17:1-8; Mk 9:2-8; Lk 9:28-36), on the way to Jerusalem (Mt 19:20; Mk 10; Lk 13:10-19:27), in Jerusalem (Mt 21-25; Mk 11-13; Lk 19:28-21:38; Jn 2:12-3:36; 5; 7-12). Last supper (Mt 26:17-35; Mk 14:12-31; Lk 22:1-38; Jn 13-17). Arrest and trial (Mt 26:36-27:31; Mk 14:43-15:20; Lk 22:39-23:25; Jn 18:1-19:16). Crucifixion (Mt 27:32-66; Mk 15:21-47; Lk 23:26-55; Jn 19:28-42). Resurrection and appearances (Mt 28; Mk 16; Lk 24; Jn 20-21; Ac 1:1-11; 7:56; 9:3-6; 1Co 15:1-8; Rev 1:1-20).

MIRACLES. *Healings:* official's son (Jn 4:43-54), demoniac in Capernaum (Mk 1:23-26; Lk 4:33-35), Peter's mother-in-law (Mt 8:14-15; Mk 1:29-31; Lk 4:38-39), leper (Mt 8:2-4; Mk 1:40-45; Lk 5:12-16), paralytic (Mt 9:1-8; Mk 2:1-12; Lk 5:17-26), cripple (Jn 5:1-9), shriveled hand (Mt 12:10-13; Mk 3:1-5; Lk 6:6-11), centurion's servant (Mt 8:5-13; Lk 7:1-10), widow's son raised (Lk 7:11-17), demoniac (Mt 12:22-23; Lk 11:14), Gadarene demoniacs (Mt 8:28-34; Mk 5:1-20; Lk 8:26-39), woman's bleeding and Jairus' daughter (Mt 9:18-26; Mk 5:21-43; Lk 8:40-56), blind man (Mt 9:27-31), mute man (Mt 9:32-33), Canaanite woman's daughter (Mt 15:21-28; Mk 7:24-30), deaf man (Mk 7:31-37), blind man (Mk 8:22-26), demoniac boy (Mt 17:14-18; Mk 9:14-29; Lk 9:37-43), ten lepers (Lk 17:11-19), man born blind (Jn 9:1-7), Lazarus raised (Jn 11), crippled woman (Lk 13:11-17), man with dropsy (Lk 14:1-6), two blind men (Mt 20:29-34; Mk 10:46-52; Lk 18:35-43), Malchus' ear (Lk 22:50-51). *Other Miracles:* water to wine (Jn 2:1-11), catch of fish (Lk 5:1-11), storm stilled (Mt 8:23-27; Mk 4:37-41; Lk 8:22-25), 5,000 fed (Mt 14:15-21; Mk 6:35-44; Lk 9:10-17; Jn 6:1-14), walking on water (Mt 14:25-33; Mk 6:48-52; Jn 6:15-21), 4,000 fed (Mt 15:32-39; Mk 8:1-9), money from fish (Mt 17:24-27), fig tree cursed (Mt 21:18-22; Mk 11:12-14), catch of fish (Jn 21:1-14).

MAJOR TEACHING: Sermon on the Mount (Mt 5-7; Lk 6:17-49), to Nicodemus (Jn 3), to Samaritan woman (Jn 4), Bread of Life (Jn 6:22-59), at Feast of Tabernacles (Jn 7-8), woes to Pharisees (Mt 23; Lk 11:37-54), Good Shepherd (Jn 10:1-18), Olivet Discourse (Mt 24-25; Mk 13; Lk 21:5-36), Upper Room Discourse (Jn 13-16).

PARABLES: Sower (Mt 13:3-23; Mk 4:3-25; Lk 8:5-18), seed's growth (Mk 4:26-29), wheat and weeds (Mt 13:24-30, 36-43), mustard seed (Mt 13:31-32; Mk 4:30-32), yeast (Mt 13:33; Lk 13:20-21), hidden treasure (Mt 13:44), valuable pearl (Mt 13:45-46), net (Mt 13:47-51), house owner (Mt 13:52), good Samaritan (Lk 10:25-37), unmerciful servant (Mt 18:15-35), lost sheep (Mt 18:10-14; Lk 15:4-7), lost coin (Lk 15:8-10), prodigal son (Lk 15:11-32), dishonest manager (Lk 16:1-13), rich man and Lazarus (Lk 16:19-31), persistent widow (Lk 18:1-8), Pharisee and tax collector (Lk 18:9-14), payment of workers (Mt 20:1-16), tenants and the vineyard (Mt 21:28-46; Mt 12:1-12; Lk 20:9-19), wedding banquet (Mt 22:1-14), faithful servant (Mt 24:45-51), ten virgins (Mt 25:1-13), talents (Mt 25:1-30; Lk 19:12-27).

DISCIPLES see APOSTLES. Call (Jn 1:35-51; Mt 4:18-22; 9:9; Mk 1:16-20; 2:13-14; Lk 5:1-11, 27-28). Named Apostles (Mk 3:13-19; Lk 6:12-16). Twelve sent out (Mt 10; Mk 6:7-11; Lk 9:1-5). Seventy sent out (Lk 10:1-24). Defection of (Jn 6:60-71; Mt 26:56; Mk 14:50-52). Final commission (Mt 28:16-20; Jn 21:15-23; Ac 1:3-8).

Ac 9: 5 "I am J, whom you are persecuting,
1Co 8: 6 and one Lord, J Christ,
Php 2:10 name of J every knee should bend,
2Th 2: 1 the coming of our Lord J Christ
1Ti 1:15 J came into the world to save
Heb 12: 2 to J the pioneer and perfecter of our
      13: 8 J Christ is the same yesterday and
1Jn 1: 7 the blood of J his Son cleanses us
Rev 1: 1 The revelation of J Christ,
      22:20 Amen. Come, Lord J!

2. Disciple, also called Justus (Col 4:11).
3. Writer of Sirach (Sir Pr:1; 50:27; 51:1).

JETHRO
Father-in-law and adviser of Moses (Ex 3:1; 4:18; 18). Also known as Reuel (Ex 2:18).

JEW → JEWS, JUDAISM
Est 10: 3 Mordecai the J was next in rank to
Zec 8:23 shall take hold of a J,
Ro 1:16 to the J first and also to the Greek.
      2:29 a person is a J who is one inwardly,
1Co 9:20 To the Jews I became as a J,
Col 3:11 there is no longer Greek and J,

JEWEL → JEWELS
Pr 20:15 by knowledge are a precious j.
Rev 21:19 of the city are adorned with every j;

JEWELS → JEWEL
Pr 3:15 She is more precious than j,
Isa 54:12 your gates of j, and all your wall
Rev 17: 4 adorned with gold and j and pearls,

JEWS → JEW
Ne 4: 1 enraged, and he mocked the J.
Est 3:13 to kill, and to annihilate all J,
Mt 2: 2 who has been born king of the J?
      27:11 "Are you the King of the J?"
Jn 4:22 for salvation is from the J.
Ro 3:29 Or is God the God of J only?

JEZEBEL*
Sidonian wife of Ahab (1Ki 16:31). Promoted Baal worship (1Ki 16:32-33). Killed prophets of the LORD (1Ki 18:4, 13). Opposed Elijah (1Ki 19:1-2). Had Naboth killed (1Ki 21). Death (1Ki 21:17-24; 2Ki 9:30-37). Metaphor of immorality (Rev 2:20).

JEZREEL
2Ki 10: 7 in baskets and sent them to him at J.
Hos 1: 4 the LORD said to him, "Name him J;

JOAB
Nephew of David (1Ch 2:16). Commander of his army (2Sa 8:16). Victorious over Ammon (2Sa 10; 1Ch 19), Rabbah (2Sa 11; 1Ch 20), Jerusalem (1Ch 11:6), Absalom (2Sa 18), Sheba (2Sa 20). Killed Abner (2Sa 3:22-39), Amasa (2Sa 20:1-13). Numbered David's army (2Sa 24; 1Ch 21). Sided with Adonijah (1Ki 1:17, 19). Killed by Benaiah (1Ki 2:5-6, 28-35).

JOASH → =JEHOASH
1. Son of Ahaziah; king of Judah. Sheltered from Athaliah by Jehoiada (2Ki 11; 2Ch 22:10-23:21). Repaired temple (2Ch 24). See Jehoash, 1.
2. Son of Jehoahaz, king of Israel (2Ki 13; 2Ch 25:17-25). See Jehoash, 2.

JOB
Wealthy man from Uz; feared God (Job 1:1-5). Integrity tested by disaster (Job 1:6-22), personal affliction (Job 2). Maintained innocence in debate with three friends (Job 3-31), Elihu (Job 32-37). Rebuked by the LORD (Job 38-41). Vindicated and restored to greater stature by the LORD (Job 42). Example of righteousness (Eze 14:14, 20; Sir 49:9).

JOEL
1. Son of Samuel (1Sa 8:2; 1Ch 6:28).
2. Prophet (Joel 1:1; Ac 2:16).

JOHANAN
1. First high priest in the temple (1Ch 6:9-10).
2. Jewish leader who tried to save Gedaliah from assassination (Jer 40:13-14); took Jews, including Jeremiah, to Egypt (Jer 40-43).

JOHN
1. Son of Zechariah and Elizabeth (Lk 1). Called the Baptist (Mt 3:1-12; Mk 1:2-8). Witness to Jesus (Mt 3:11-12; Mk 1:7-8; Lk 3:15-18; Jn 1:6-35; 3:27-30; 5:33-36). Doubts about Jesus (Mt 11:2-6; Lk 7:18-23). Arrest (Mt 4:12; Mk 1:14). Execution (Mt 14:1-12; Mk 6:14-29; Lk 9:7-9). Ministry compared to Elijah (Mt 11:7-19; Mk 9:11-13; Lk 7:24-35).
2. Apostle; brother of James (Mt 4:21-22; 10:2; Mk 3:17; Lk 5:1-10). At transfiguration (Mt 17:1-13; Mk 9:2-13; Lk 9:28-36). Desire to be greatest (Mk 10:35-45). Leader of church at Jerusalem (Ac 4:1-3; Gal 2:9). Elder who wrote epistles (2Jn 1; 3Jn 1). Prophet who wrote Revelation (Rev 1:1; 22:8).
3. Cousin of Barnabas, co-worker with Paul, (Ac 12:12-13:13; 15:37; see Mark).
4. Son of Simon Maccabeus (1Mc 13:53; 16).

JOIN → JOINED
Eze 37:17 and them together into one stick,
2Ti 1: 8 j with me in suffering for the gospel

JOINED → JOIN
Mt 19: 6 what God has j together, let no one
Eph 2:21 the whole structure is j together and

JOINT → JOINTS
Ge 32:25 and Jacob's hip was put out of j
Ps 22:14 and all my bones are out of j;
Ro 8:17 heirs of God and j heirs with Christ

JOINTS → JOINT
Heb 4:12 soul from spirit, j from marrow;

JONAH
Prophet in days of Jeroboam II (2Ki 14:25). Called to Nineveh; fled to Tarshish (Jnh 1:1-3). Cause of storm; thrown into sea (Jnh 1:4-16). Swallowed by fish (Jnh 1:17). Prayer (Jnh 2). Preached to Nineveh (Jnh 3). Attitude reproved by the LORD (Jnh 4). Sign of (Mt 12:39-41; Lk 11:29-32).

JONATHAN
1. Son of Saul (1Sa 13:16; 1Ch 8:33). Valiant warrior (1Sa 13-14). Relation to David (1Sa 18:1-4; 19-20; 23:16-18). Killed at Gilboa (1Sa 31). Mourned by David (2Sa 1).
2. Brother and successor of Judas Maccabeus (1Mc 2:5; 9:28-31).

JOPPA
Jnh 1: 3 down to J and found a ship going
Ac 9:43 he stayed in J for some time with

JORAM → =JEHORAM
1. Son of Jehoshaphat; king of Judah (2Ki 8:16-24). See Jehoram, 1.
2. Son of Ahab; king of Israel. Killed with Ahaziah by Jehu (2Ki 8:25-29; 9:14-26; 2Ch 22:5-9). See Jehoram, 2.

JORDAN
Ge 13:10 the plain of the J was well watered
Nu 34:12 the boundary shall go down to the J,
Jos 3:17 dry ground in the middle of the J,
Mt 3: 6 were baptized by him in the river J,

JOSEPH → =BARNABAS, =BARSABBAS
1. Son of Jacob by Rachel (Ge 30:24; 1Ch 2:2). Favored by Jacob, hated by brothers (Ge 37:3-4). Dreams (Ge 37:5-11). Sold by brothers (Ge 37:12-36). Served Potiphar; imprisoned by false accusation (Ge 39). Interpreted dreams of Pharaoh's servants (Ge 40), of Pharaoh (Ge 41:41-57). Made greatest in Egypt (Ge 41:41-57). Sold grain to brothers (Ge 42-45). Brought Jacob and sons to Egypt (Ge 46-47). Sons Ephraim and Manasseh blessed (Ge 48). Blessed (Ge 49:22-26; Dt 33:13-17). Death (Ge 50:22-26; Ex 13:19; Heb 11:22). 12,000 from (Rev 7:8).
2. Husband of Mary mother of Jesus (Mt 1:16-24; 2:13-19; Lk 1:27; 2; Jn 1:45).
3. Disciple from Arimathea; buried Jesus in his tomb (Mt 27:57-61; Mk 15:43-47; Lk 24:50-52).
4. Original name of Barnabas (Ac 4:36).

JOSHUA → =HOSHEA, =JESHUA
1. Son of Nun; name changed from Hoshea (Nu 13:8, 16; 1Ch 7:27). Fought Amalekites under Moses (Ex 17:9-14). Servant of Moses on Sinai (Ex 24:13; 32:17). Spied Canaan (Nu 13). With Caleb, allowed to enter land (Nu 14:6, 30). Succeeded Moses (Dt 1:38; 31:1-8; 34:9).

Charged Israel to conquer Canaan (Jos 1). Crossed Jordan (Jos 3-4). Circumcised sons of wilderness wanderings (Jos 5). Conquered Jericho (Jos 6), Ai (Jos 7-8), five kings at Gibeon (Jos 10:1-28), southern Canaan (Jos 10:29-43), northern Canaan (Jos 11-12). Defeated at Ai (Jos 7). Deceived by Gibeonites (Jos 9). Renewed covenant (Jos 8:30-35; 24:1-27). Divided land among tribes (Jos 13-22). Last words (Jos 23). Death (Jos 24:28-31).
2. High priest during rebuilding of temple (Hag 1-2; Zec 3:1-9; 6:11). See Jeshua.

JOSIAH
Son of Amon; king of Judah (2Ki 21:26; 1Ch 3:14). Prophesied (1Ki 13:2). Book of the Law dis-

covered during his reign (2Ki 22; 2Ch 34:14-31). Reforms (2Ki 23:1-25; 2Ch 34:1-13; 35:1-19; Sir 49:1-4). Killed in battle (2Ki 23:29-30; 2Ch 35:20-27).

JOTHAM
1. Son of Gideon (Jdg 9).
2. Son of Azariah (Uzziah); king of Judah (2Ki 15:32-38; 2Ch 26:21-27:9).

JOY → JOYFUL
Ne 8:10 the j of the LORD is your strength."
Job 20: 5 j of the godless is but for a moment?
Ps 51:12 Restore to me the j of your salvation
Pr 21:15 When justice is done, it is a j to the
Isa 12: 3 With j you will draw water from
35:10 everlasting j shall be upon their
La 2:15 of beauty, the j of all the earth?"
Mt 28: 8 tomb quickly with fear and great j,
Mk 4:16 they immediately receive it with j.
Lk 1:44 the child in my womb leaped for j.
2:10 bringing you good news of great j
Jn 16:22 no one will take your j from you.
Ro 14:17 but righteousness and peace and j in
Gal 5:22 the fruit of the Spirit is love, j,
Php 4: 1 I love and long for, my j and crown,
Heb 12: 2 j that was set before him endured
Jas 1: 2 consider it nothing but j,
Tob 13:17 Jerusalem will sing hymns of j,
Bar 5: 9 For God will lead Israel with j,

JOYFUL → JOY
Ps 98: 4 Make a j noise to the LORD,
Jdt 14: 9 and made a j noise in their town.

JUBILEE
Lev 25:10 It shall be a j for you:
Nu 36: 4 when the j of the Israelites comes,

JUDAH → JUDEA
1. Son of Jacob by Leah (Ge 29:35; 35:23; 1Ch 2:1). Did not want to kill Joseph (Ge 37:26-27). Among Canaanites, fathered Perez by Tamar (Ge 38). Tribe of blessed as ruling tribe (Ge 49:8-12; Dt 33:7), numbered (Nu 1:27; 26:22), allotted land (Jos 15; Eze 48:7), failed to fully possess (Jos 15:63; Jdg 1:1-20).
2. Name used for Southern Kingdom.
2Sa 2: 4 David king over the house of J.
La 1: 3 J has gone into exile with suffering
Joel 3: 1 when I restore the fortunes of J and
Mic 5: 2 who are one of the little clans of J,
Mt 2: 6 least among the rulers of J;
Heb 7:14 our Lord was descended from J,
Rev 5: 5 See, the Lion of the tribe of J,

JUDAISM → JEW
Ac 13:43 devout converts to J followed Paul
Gal 1:13 no doubt, of my earlier life in J.

JUDAS → =BARSABBAS, =JUDE, =THADDAEUS, MACCABEUS
1. Apostle; son of James (Lk 6:16; Jn 14:22; Ac 1:13). Probably also called Thaddaeus (Mt 10:3; Mk 3:18).
2. Brother of James and Jesus (Mt 13:55; Mk 6:3), also called Jude (Jude 1).
3. Christian prophet (Ac 15:22-32).
4. Apostle, also called Iscariot, who betrayed Jesus (Mt 10:4; 26:14-56; Mk 3:19; 14:10-50; Lk 6:16; 22:3-53; Jn 6:71; 12:4; 13:2-30; 18:2-11). Suicide of (Mt 27:3-5; Ac 1:16-25).
5. Leader of the Maccabean revolt (1Mc 2:4, 66). Recaptured Jerusalem and rededicated the temple and altar (1Mc 4:36-61). Death of (1Mc 9).

JUDE → See JUDAS, 2

JUDEA → JUDAH
Mt 2: 1 Jesus was born in Bethlehem of J,
Lk 3: 1 Pontius Pilate was governor of J,
Ac 1: 8 my witnesses in Jerusalem, in all J

JUDGE → JUDGED, JUDGES, JUDGMENT, JUDGMENTS
Ge 16: 5 the LORD j between you and me!"
Ex 2:14 made you a ruler and j over us?
1Sa 2:10 LORD will j the ends of the earth;
Ps 96:13 for he is coming to j the earth.
Isa 11: 3 He shall not j by what his eyes see,
Jer 11:20 O LORD of hosts, who j righteously,
Eze 34:17 I shall j between sheep and sheep,
Lk 6:37 not j, and you will not be judged;
Jn 7:24 Do not j by appearances,
18:31 "Take him yourselves and j him
Ac 4:19 rather than to God, you must j;
Ro 3: 6 then how could God j the world?
1Co 6: 2 that the saints will j the world?
2Ti 4: 1 to j the living and the dead,
Heb 12:23 and to God the j of all,
Jas 5: 9 See, the J is standing at the doors!
Rev 20: 4 on them were given authority to j.
Sir 35:15 for the Lord is the j,

JUDGED → JUDGE
Mt 7: 1 not judge, so that you may not be j.
1Co 11:31 if we j ourselves, we would not be j.
Jas 3: 1 know that we who teach will be j
Rev 20:12 dead were j according to their works

JUDGES → JUDGE
Jdg 2:16 Then the LORD raised up j
Lk 11:19 Therefore they will be your j.
Jas 4:11 evil against the law and j the law;
Rev 19:11 righteousness he j and makes war.
Sir 16:12 j a person according to one's deeds.

JUDGMENT → JUDGE
Ex 6: 6 arm and mighty acts of j.
Ps 1: 5 wicked will not stand in the j,
119:66 Teach me good j and knowledge,
Ecc 12:14 God will bring every deed into j,
Jer 25:31 he is entering into j with all flesh,
Da 7:22 j was given for the holy ones of the
Mal 3: 1 Then I will draw near to you for j;
Mt 11:24 day of j it will be more tolerable for
Jn 16:11 about j, because the ruler
Ro 14:10 we will all stand before the j seat of
2Co 5:10 all of us must appear before the j
Heb 9:27 to die once, and after that the j,
10:27 but a fearful prospect of j,
Jas 2:13 mercy triumphs over j.
1Pe 4:17 for j to begin with the household of
1Jn 4:17 may have boldness on the day of j,
Rev 18:10 For in one hour your j has come."
Wis 12:12 Or will resist your j?
Sir 18:20 Before j comes, examine yourself;
2Es 7:70 the things that pertain to the j.

JUDGMENTS → JUDGE
Ps 119:75 that your j are right,
Ro 11:33 How unsearchable are his j and
Rev 19: 2 for his j are true and just;

JUDITH
Virtuous widow and heroine of the deuterocanonical book of Judith (Jdt 8-16).

JUST → JUSTICE, JUSTIFICATION, JUSTIFIED, JUSTIFY
Ge 18:25 Judge of all the earth do what is j?"
Dt 32: 4 without deceit, j and upright is he;
Ps 111: 7 works of his hands are faithful and j
Eze 33:17 "The way of the Lord is not j,"
Ro 7:12 the commandment is holy and j and
1Jn 1: 9 he who is faithful and j will forgive
Rev 15: 3 J and true are your ways, King of
Tob 3: 2 O Lord, and all your deeds are j;
Sir 18: 2 the Lord alone is j.

JUSTICE → JUST
Ex 23: 6 not pervert the j due to your poor
1Ki 7: 7 pronounce judgment, the Hall of J,
Job 19: 7 I call aloud, but there is no j.
37:23 he is great in power and j,

Ps 33: 5 He loves righteousness and j;
106: 3 Happy are those who observe j,
Pr 21:15 j is done, it is a joy to the righteous,
Isa 30:18 For the LORD is a God of j;
42: 4 until he has established j in the earth
Jer 9:24 I act with steadfast love, j,
Hos 12: 6 to your God, hold fast to love and j.
Am 5:24 But let j roll down like waters,
Mal 2:17 by asking, "Where is the God of j?"
Lk 11:42 and neglect j and the love of God;

JUSTIFICATION → JUST
Ro 4:25 trespasses and was raised for our j.
2Co 3: 9 more does the ministry of j abound
Gal 2:21 for if j comes through the law,

JUSTIFIED → JUST
Job 32: 2 he j himself rather than God;
Mt 12:37 for by your words you will be j,
Ro 3:24 they are now j by his grace as a gift,
5: 1 Therefore, since we are j by faith,
10:10 believes with the heart and so is j,
Gal 2:16 that we might be j by faith in Christ,
Jas 2:24 is j by works and not by faith alone.

JUSTIFY → JUST
Ro 3:30 and he will j the circumcised on the
Gal 3: 8 that God would j the Gentiles

K

KADESH → KADESH-BARNEA
Nu 20: 1 and the people stayed in K.
Dt 1:46 you had stayed at K as many days

KADESH-BARNEA → KADESH
Nu 32: 8 sent them from K to see the land.

KEEP → KEEPER, KEEPS, KEPT
Ge 17: 9 for you, you shall k my covenant,
Ex 19: 5 obey my voice and k my covenant,
Nu 6:24 The LORD bless you and k you;
Dt 5:10 love me and k my commandments.
Ne 1: 5 love him and k his commandments;
Pr 7: 2 k my commandments and live,
Ecc 3: 6 time to k, and a time to throw away;
12:13 Fear God, and k his commandments
Lk 17:33 those who lose their life will k it.
Jude 1:24 Now to him who is able to k you
Rev 22: 9 those who k the words of this book.
Sir 1:26 wisdom, k the commandments,

KEEPER → KEEP
Ge 4: 9 am I my brother's k?"
Ps 121: 5 The LORD is your k;

KEEPS → KEEP
Ps 121: 3 he who k you will not slumber.
Jas 2:10 whoever k the whole law but fails

KEPT → KEEP
Mt 19:20 said to him, "I have k all these;
Jn 17: 6 and they have k your word.
2Ti 4: 7 finished the race, I have k the faith.

KEY → KEYS
Isa 22:22 on his shoulder the k of the house
Lk 11:52 taken away the k of knowledge;
Rev 3: 7 true one, who has the k of David,

KEYS* → KEY
Mt 16:19 you the k of the kingdom of heaven,
Rev 1:18 I have the k of Death and of Hades.

KIDNAPS*
Ex 21:16 Whoever k a person, whether

KIDRON
2Sa 15:23 the king crossed the Wadi K,
Jn 18: 1 his disciples across the K valley

KILL → KILLED, KILLS
Ex 4:23 now I will k your firstborn son.' "
Ecc 3: 3 a time to k, and a time to heal;

Mt 10:28 not fear those who **k** the body but cannot **k** the soul;
Mk 14: 1 to arrest Jesus by stealth and **k** him;

KILLED → KILL
Mk 9:31 after being **k**, he will rise again."
Ac 3:15 and you **k** the Author of life,
Ro 7:11 deceived me and through it **k** me.
2Co 6: 9 as punished, and yet not **k**;

KILLS → KILL
1Sa 2: 6 The LORD **k** and brings to life;
2Co 3: 6 the letter **k**, but the Spirit gives life.

KIND → KINDNESS, KINDS
Ge 6:20 two of every **k** shall come in to you,
Ps 145:17 and **k** in all his doings.
1Co 13: 4 Love is patient; love is **k**;
Eph 4:32 and be **k** to one another,

KINDNESS → KIND
Pr 31:26 teaching of **k** is on her tongue.
Hos 11: 4 I led them with cords of human **k**,
Ro 2: 4 **k** is meant to lead you to repentance
Gal 5:22 joy, peace, patience, **k**, generosity,

KINDS → KIND
Lev 19:19 not sow your field with two **k** of
1Co 12:10 to another various **k** of tongues,
1Ti 6:10 of money is a root of all **k** of evil,

KING → KINGDOM, KINGS
Ex 1: 8 Now a new **k** arose over Egypt,
Dt 17:14 and you say, "I will set a **k** over me,
1Sa 8: 7 rejected me from being **k** over them.
2Sa 2: 4 there they anointed David **k** over
Ps 2: 6 set my **k** on Zion, my holy hill."
10:16 The LORD is **k** forever and ever;
Isa 6: 5 have seen the **K**, the LORD of hosts!
Jer 10:10 living God and the everlasting **K**.
Mt 2: 2 who has been born **k** of the Jews?
27:37 "This is Jesus, the **K** of the Jews."
Lk 19:38 "Blessed is the **k** who comes in the
Jn 1:49 You are the **K** of Israel!"
1Ti 1:17 To the **K** of the ages, immortal,
Rev 19:16 "**K** of kings and Lord of lords."
Tob 10:13 Lord of heaven and earth, **K** over all
Jdt 9:12 **K** of all your creation,

KINGDOM → KING
Ex 19: 6 you shall be for me a priestly **k** and
2Sa 7:12 and I will establish his **k**.
1Ki 11:31 "See, I am about to tear the **k**
Ps 145:13 Your **k** is an everlasting **k**,
Da 4: 3 His **k** is an everlasting **k**,
Mt 4:17 "Repent, for the **k** of heaven has
5: 3 for theirs is the **k** of heaven.
6:10 Your **k** come. Your will be done,
13:24 "The **k** of heaven may be compared
Mk 6:23 I will give you, even half of my **k**."
10:24 how hard it is to enter the **k** of God!
12:34 You are not far from the **k** of God."
13: 8 and **k** against **k**;
Lk 17:21 in fact, the **k** of God is among us."
22:16 not eat it until it is fulfilled in the **k**
Jn 18:36 "My **k** is not from this world.
Ac 1: 6 you will restore the **k** to Israel?"
Ro 14:17 the **k** of God is not food and drink
1Co 6: 9 wrongdoers will not inherit the **k**
Eph 5: 5 any inheritance in the **k** of Christ
Col 1:13 transferred us into the **k** of his
1Th 2:12 calls you into his own **k** and glory.
Heb 12:28 receiving a **k** that cannot be shaken,
2Pe 1:11 entry into the eternal **k** of our Lord
Rev 11:15 world has become the **k** of our Lord
Wis 10:10 she showed him the **k** of God,

KINGS → KING
Ge 17: 6 and **k** shall come from you.
Ps 2: 2 The **k** of the earth set themselves,
138: 4 All the **k** of the earth shall praise
Pr 8:15 By me **k** reign, and rulers decree

Isa 52:15 **k** shall shut their mouths because of
Da 7:24 of this kingdom ten **k** shall arise,
Ac 4:26 The **k** of the earth took their stand,
1Ti 6:15 the King of **k** and Lord of lords.
Rev 19:16 "King of **k** and Lord of lords."
Sir 51:12 *Give thanks to the King of the **k** of,*

KISS
Ps 2:12 **k** his feet, or he will be angry,
SS 1: 2 Let him **k** me with the kisses of his
Mt 26:48 "The one I will **k** is the man; arrest
2Co 13:12 Greet one another with a holy **k**.

KNEE → KNEES
Isa 45:23 "To me every **k** shall bow,
Ro 14:11 says the Lord, every **k** shall bow to
Php 2:10 at the name of Jesus every **k** should

KNEEL → KNELT
Ps 95: 6 let us **k** before the LORD, our Maker

KNEES → KNEE
1Ki 19:18 the **k** that have not bowed to Baal,
Eph 3:14 I bow my **k** before the Father,

KNELT → KNEEL
2Ch 6:13 he **k** on his knees in the presence of
Lk 22:41 about a stone's throw, **k** down,

KNEW → KNOW
Dt 34:10 whom the LORD **k** face to face.
Jer 1: 5 I formed you in the womb I **k** you,
Mt 7:23 will declare to them, 'I never **k** you;
Ro 1:21 they **k** God, they did not honor him

KNOCK → KNOCKING
Lk 11: 9 **k**, and the door will be opened for

KNOCKING → KNOCK
Rev 3:20 I am standing at the door, **k**;

KNOW → FOREKNEW, KNEW, KNOWING, KNOWLEDGE, KNOWN, KNOWS
Ge 22:12 for now I **k** that you fear God,
Ex 6: 7 **k** that I am the LORD your God,
1Ki 8:39 only you **k** what is in every human
Job 19:25 For I **k** that my Redeemer lives,
Ps 46:10 "Be still, and **k** that I am God!
Ecc 8:16 I applied my mind to **k** wisdom,
Isa 1: 3 Israel does not **k**, my people do not
Jer 31:34 "**K** the LORD," for they shall all **k**
Mt 6: 3 left hand **k** what your right hand is
24:42 do not **k** on what day your LORD is
Lk 11:13 how to give good gifts to your
22:34 denied three times that you **k** me."
Jn 10:14 I **k** my own and my own **k** me,
13:35 will **k** that you are my disciples,
21:24 and we **k** that his testimony is true.
Ac 1: 7 **k** the times or periods that the
Ro 8:28 We **k** that all things work together
1Co 8: 2 Anyone who claims to **k** something
13:12 I **k** only in part; then I will **k** fully,
Eph 3:19 the love of Christ that surpasses
Php 3:10 to **k** Christ and the power of his
Tit 1:16 profess to **k** God, but they deny him
Heb 8:11 '**K** the Lord,' for they shall all **k** me,
1Jn 2: 4 Whoever says, "I have come to **k**
3:16 **k** love by this, that he laid down his
Rev 3: 3 not **k** at what hour I will come to

KNOWING → KNOW
Ge 3:22 like one of us, **k** good and evil;
Jn 18: 4 Jesus, **k** all that was to happen to
Php 3: 8 surpassing value of **k** Christ Jesus
Heb 13: 2 have entertained angels without **k** it.

KNOWLEDGE → KNOW
Ge 2: 9 the tree of the **k** of good and evil.
Job 21:22 Will any teach God **k**,
Pr 1: 7 of the LORD is the beginning of **k**;
8:10 and **k** rather than choice gold;
Ecc 1:18 who increase **k** increase sorrow.
Isa 11: 2 spirit of **k** and the fear of the LORD.
Hos 4: 6 people are destroyed for lack of **k**;

Lk 11:52 you have taken away the key of **k**;
Ro 11:33 riches and wisdom and **k** of God!
1Co 8: 1 **K** puffs up, but love builds up.
Eph 3:19 the love of Christ that surpasses **k**,
Col 2: 3 the treasures of wisdom and **k**.
1Ti 6:20 of what is falsely called **k**;
2Pe 1: 5 goodness, and goodness with **k**,
1Jn 2:20 and all of you have **k**.
Sir 3:25 without **k** there is no wisdom.

KNOWN → KNOW
Ps 139: 1 you have searched me and **k** me.
Lk 6:44 for each tree is **k** by its own fruit.
Jn 1:18 Father's heart, who has made him **k**.
Ro 7: 7 I would not have **k** sin.
1Co 2:16 For who has **k** the mind of the Lord
Eph 1: 9 made **k** to us the mystery of his will,

KNOWS → KNOW
Ps 94:11 The LORD **k** our thoughts,
103:14 For he **k** how we were made;
Mt 6: 8 your Father **k** what you need before
24:36 about that day and hour no one **k**,
Ro 8:27 **k** what is the mind of the Spirit,
2Ti 2:19 "The Lord **k** those who are his,"
1Jn 4: 7 loves is born of God and **k** God.
Sir 42:18 Most High **k** all that may be known;

KORAH → KORAHITES
Levite; led rebels against Moses (Nu 16; Jude 11).

KORAHITES → KORAH
Psalms of: Pss 42; 44-49; 84; 85; 87; 88.

L

LABAN
Brother of Rebekah (Ge 24:29), father of Rachel and Leah (Ge 29:16). Received Abraham's servant (Ge 24:29-51). Provided daughters as wives for Jacob in exchange for Jacob's service (Ge 29:1-30). Provided flocks for Jacob's service (Ge 30:25-43). Pursued and covenanted with Jacob (Ge 31).

LABOR → LABORER
Ex 1:11 to oppress them with forced **l**.
20: 9 Six days you shall **l** and do all your
Jn 4:38 reap that for which you did not **l**.

LABORER → LABOR
Lev 19:13 the wages of a **l** until morning.
Lk 10: 7 for the **l** deserves to be paid.
1Ti 5:18 and, "The **l** deserves to be paid."

LACKED → LACKING
Dt 2: 7 with you; you, you have **l** nothing."

LACKING → LACKED
Ecc 1:15 and what is **l** cannot be counted.
Lk 18:22 "There is still one thing **l**.
Col 1:24 completing what is **l** in Christ's

LADDER
Ge 28:12 that there was a **l** set up on the earth,

LAID → LAY
Isa 53: 6 the LORD has **l** on him the iniquity
Mk 16: 6 Look, there is the place they **l** him.
1Jn 3:16 that he **l** down his life for us—

LAKE
Rev 19:20 were thrown alive into the **l** of fire
20:14 This is the second death, the **l** of fire

LAMB → LAMBS
Ge 22: 8 "God himself will provide the **l** for
Ex 12:21 and slaughter the passover **l**.
Isa 53: 7 like a **l** that is led to the slaughter,
Mk 14:12 when the Passover **l** is sacrificed,
Jn 1:29 **L** of God who takes away the sin of
1Co 5: 7 For our paschal **l**, Christ, has been
1Pe 1:19 like that of a **l** without defect or
Rev 5:12 the **L** that was slaughtered to
21:23 and its lamp is the **L**.

LAMBS → LAMB
Isa 40:11 he will gather the l in his arms,
Jn   21:15 Jesus said to him, "Feed my l."

LAME
Isa 35: 6 then the l shall leap like a deer,
Zep 3:19 And I will save the l and gather the
Mt 11: 5 the l walk, the lepers are cleansed,

LAMENTATION
La   2: 5 in daughter Judah mourning and l.

LAMP → LAMPS, LAMPSTAND, LAMPSTANDS
1Ki 11:36 servant David may always have a l
Ps   18:28 It is you who light my l;
   119:105 Your word is a l to my feet and a
Mt   5:15 lighting a l puts it under the bushel
   6:22 "The eye is the l of the body.
Rev 22: 5 they need no light of l or sun,

LAMPS → LAMP
Ex 25:37 You shall make the seven l for it;
Mt 25: 1 Ten bridesmaids took their l and

LAMPSTAND → LAMP
Ex 25:31 You shall make a l of pure gold.
Zec 4: 2 And I said, "I see a l all of gold,
1Mc 4:50 and lit the lamps on the l,

LAMPSTANDS → LAMP
Rev 1:20 the seven l are the seven churches.
   11: 4 the two l that stand before the Lord

LAND
Ge   1:10 God called the dry l Earth,
   12: 7 your offspring I will give this l."
Ex   3: 8 a l flowing with milk and honey,
   20: 2 brought you out of the l of Egypt,
Nu 13: 2 to spy out the l of Canaan,
Jos 11:23 So Joshua took the whole l,
Jdg   1:27 Canaanites continued to live in that l
2Ki 17: 5 the king of Assyria invaded all the l
   25:21 So Judah went into exile out of its l.
2Ch 7:14 will forgive their sin and heal their l.
Ps   37:11 But the meek shall inherit the l,
Jer 22:29 O l, l, l, hear the word of the Lord!
Da   11:41 He shall come into the beautiful l,
Mal 4: 6 come and strike the l with a curse.

LANGUAGE
Ge 11: 9 Lord confused the l of all the earth;
Ac   2: 6 speaking in the native l of each.

LAP
Jdg 7: 5 who l the water with their tongues,
Pr 16:33 The lot is cast into the l,

LASHES
Dt   25: 3 Forty l may be given but not more;
2Co 11:24 from the Jews the forty l minus one.

LAST → EVERLASTING
2Sa 23: 1 Now these are the l words of David:
Isa 44: 6 I am the first and I am the l;
Mt 19:30 first will be l, and the l will be first.
Mk 9:35 first must be l of all and servant of
1Co 15:26 l enemy to be destroyed is death.
   15:52 twinkling of an eye, at the l trumpet.
2Ti   3: 1 that in the l days distressing times
Heb 1: 2 l days he has spoken to us by a Son,
1Jn 2:18 Children, it is the l hour!
Rev 1:17 I am the first and the l,

LAUGH → LAUGHINGSTOCK, LAUGHTER
Ge 18:13 said to Abraham, "Why did Sarah l,
Ecc 3: 4 a time to weep, and a time to l;
Lk   6:21 you who weep now, for you will l.

LAUGHINGSTOCK → LAUGH
Ps 44:14 the nations, a l among the peoples.
La   3:14 have become the l of all my people,

LAUGHTER → LAUGH
Ps 126: 2 Then our mouth was filled with l,
Jas   4: 9 Let your l be turned into mourning

LAW → LAWFUL, LAWLESSNESS
Dt   1: 5 Moses undertook to expound this l
   31: 9 Then Moses wrote down this l,
Jos   1: 8 book of the l shall not depart out of
Ps   1: 2 their delight is in the l of the Lord,
   119:97 Oh, how I love your l!
Jer 31:33 I will put my l within them,
Mt   5:17 come to abolish the l or the prophets
   23:23 the weightier matters of the l:
Lk   24:44 written about me in the l of Moses,
Jn   1:17 l indeed was given through Moses;
Ro   6:14 you are not under l but under grace.
   10: 4 For Christ is the end of the l so that
Gal   2:19 through the l I died to the l,
Heb 10: 1 Since the l has only a shadow of the
Jas   2:10 For whoever keeps the whole l but
1Mc 2:48 They rescued the l out of the hands

LAWFUL → LAW
Mt 12:12 So it is l to do good on the sabbath."
1Co 6:12 "All things are l for me,"
   10:23 "All things are l," but

LAWLESSNESS → LAW
2Th 2: 7 the mystery of l is already at work,
1Jn 3: 4 commits sin is guilty of l; sin is l.
Sir 21: 3 All l is like a two-edged sword;

LAY → LAID
Mt   8:20 of Man has nowhere to l his head."
   28: 6 Come, see the place where he l.
Jn 10:15 And I l down my life for the sheep.
1Co 3:11 no one can l any foundation other

LAZARUS*
   1. Poor man in Jesus' parable (Lk 16:19-31).
   2. Brother of Mary and Martha whom Jesus raised from the dead (Jn 11:1-12:19).

LAZY
Ex   5:17 He said, "You are l, l;
Pr 13: 4 The appetite of the l craves,

LEAD → LEADER, LEADERS, LEADS, LED
Ex 32:34 l the people to the place
Ps   61: 2 L me to the rock that is higher than
Isa 11: 6 and a little child shall l them.
Mk 13:22 to l astray, if possible, the elect.
Ro   2: 4 meant to l you to repentance?

LEADER → LEAD
1Ch 28: 4 for he chose Judah as l,
Ro 12: 8 the l, in diligence;

LEADERS → LEAD
Isa 3:12 O my people, your l mislead you,
Lk 19:47 the l of the people kept looking for
Heb 13: 7 Remember your l, those who spoke

LEADS → LEAD
Ps 23: 2 he l me beside still waters;
Mk 13: 5 "Beware that no one l you astray.
Ro   6:16 obedience, which l to righteousness

LEAH
   Wife of Jacob (Ge 29:16-30); bore six sons and one daughter (Ge 29:31-30:21; 34:1; 35:23; Ru 4:11).

LEAPING
1Ch 15:29 and saw King David l and dancing;
Ac   3: 8 walking and l and praising God.

LEARN → LEARNED, LEARNING
Dt   4:10 that they may l to fear me as long as
Isa 1:17 l to do good; seek justice,
1Ti 2:11 Let a woman l in silence with full

LEARNED → LEARN
Jn   6:45 l from the Father comes to me.
Php 4:11 I have l to be content with whatever

LEARNING → LEARN
Jn   7:15 "How does this man have such l,
Ac 26:24 Too much l is driving you insane!"

LEAST → LESS
Mt   2: 6 are by no means l among the rulers
   5:19 called l in the kingdom of heaven;
Lk   9:48 l among all of you is the greatest."

LEAVE → LEFT
Nu 11:20 'Why did we ever l Egypt?' "
Mk 10: 7 this reason a man shall l his father
Jn 14:18 not l you orphaned; I am coming to
Heb 13: 5 said, "I will never l you or forsake

LEAVEN → LEAVENS
Ex 12:15 on the first day you shall remove l

LEAVENS → LEAVEN
Gal   5: 9 A little yeast l the whole batch of

LEAVES
Ge   3: 7 and they sewed fig l together
Eze 47:12 and their l for healing."
Rev 22: 2 l of the tree are for the healing of

LEBANON
Dt 11:24 from the wilderness to the L and
Isa 40:16 L would not provide fuel enough,

LED → LEAD
Isa 53: 7 like a lamb that is l to the slaughter,
Jer 50: 6 their shepherds have l them astray,
Hos 11: 4 I l them with cords of human
Mt   4: 1 Then Jesus was l up by the Spirit
   27:31 they l him away to crucify him.
Lk 21: 8 "Beware that you are not l astray;
Ro   8:14 For all who are l by the Spirit

LEFT → LEAVE
Dt 28:14 either to the right or to the l,
Mt   6: 3 your l hand know what your right
   25:33 his right hand and the goats at the l.
Lk 17:34 one will be taken and the other l.

LEGION
Lk   8:30 He said, "L"; for many demons

LEGS
Da 10: 6 l like the gleam of burnished bronze
Jn 19:33 they did not break his l.
Rev 10: 1 and his l like pillars of fire.

LENDER
Pr 22: 7 the borrower is the slave of the l.

LEPER → LEPROUS
Mt   8: 2 and there was a l who came to him
   26: 6 in the house of Simon the l,

LEPERS → LEPROUS
Lk   7:22 the lame walk, the l are cleansed,

LEPROUS → LEPER, LEPERS
Ex   4: 6 he took it out, his hand was l,
Nu 12:10 Miriam had become l,

LESS → LEAST
Ex 30:15 and the poor shall not give l,
Ezr 9:13 punished us l than our iniquities

LETTER
Mt   5:18 not one l, not one stroke of a l,
2Co 3: 6 the l kills, but the Spirit gives life.

LEVI → LEVITES, LEVITICAL, =MATTHEW
   1. Son of Jacob by Leah (Ge 29:34; 46:11; 1Ch 2:1). With Simeon avenged rape of Dinah (Ge 34). Tribe of blessed (Ge 49:5-7; Dt 33:8-11), chosen as priests (Nu 3-4), numbered (Nu 3:39; 26:62), given cities, but not land (Nu 18; 35; Dt 10:9; Jos 13:14; 21), land (Eze 48:8-22), 12,000 from (Rev 7:7).
   2. See Matthew.

LEVIATHAN
Job 41: 1 you draw out L with a fishhook,
Ps   74:14 You crushed the heads of L;
2Es 6:49 and the name of the other L.

LEVITES → LEVI
Nu   1:53 L shall camp around the tabernacle
Jos 14: 4 no portion was given to the L in the
Ne   8: 9 L who taught the people said to all

LEVITICAL → LEVI
Heb 7:11 attainable through the l priesthood

LIAR → LIE
Pr   19:22 and it is better to be poor than a l.
Jn   8:44 for he is a l and the father of lies.
Ro   3: 4 Although everyone is a l,
1Jn 2:22 l but the one who denies that Jesus

LIARS → LIE
1Ti 1:10 sodomites, slave traders, l, perjurers,
Rev 21: 8 the sorcerers, the idolaters, and all l,

LIBERTY
Lev 25:10 shall proclaim l throughout the land
Isa 61: 1 to proclaim l to the captives,
1Co 8: 9 this l of yours does not somehow

LICENTIOUSNESS
Mk   7:22 avarice, wickedness, deceit, l, envy,
Gal 5:19 fornication, impurity, l,
Jude 1: 4 pervert the grace of our God into l

LIE → LIAR, LIARS, LIES, LYING
Nu   23:19 that he should l, or a mortal,
Ps   23: 2 makes me l down in green pastures;
Isa 11: 6 leopard shall l down with the kid,
Ac   5: 3 your heart to l to the Holy Spirit
1Jn 2:21 know that no l comes from the
          truth.

LIES → LIE
Ps   5: 6 You destroy those who speak l;
Php 3:13 forgetting what l behind and
          straining forward to what l ahead,

LIFE → LIVE
Ge   2: 7 into his nostrils the breath of l;
     2: 9 the tree of l also in the midst of the
     9: 5 require a reckoning for human l.
Ex   21:23 then you shall give l for l,
Dt   12:23 for the blood is the l,
     30:19 Choose l so that you and your
Ps   34:12 Which of you desires l, and covets
Pr   18:21 Death and l are in the power of the
          tongue,
Ecc 7:12 that wisdom gives l to the one who
Isa 53:10 you make his l an offering for sin,
Da   12: 2 shall awake, some to everlasting l,
Mt   7:14 and the road is hard that leads to l,
     10:39 Those who find their l will lose it,
     20:28 to give his l a ransom for many."
Mk   10:30 and in the age to come eternal l.
Lk   12:25 a single hour to your span of l?
Jn   1: 4 in him was l, and the l was the light
     3:15 believes in him may have eternal l.
     6:35 said to them, "I am the bread of l.
     11:25 "I am the resurrection and the l.
     14: 6 "I am the way, and the truth, and
          the l.
Ac   3:15 and you killed the Author of l,
Ro   5:21 eternal l through Jesus Christ our
     8:38 convinced that neither death, nor l,
2Co 3: 6 the letter kills, but the Spirit gives l.
Eph 4: 1 to lead a l worthy of the calling
Php 4: 3 whose names are in the book of l.
1Jn 3:14 that we have passed from death to l
     5:20 He is the true God and eternal l.
Rev 2: 8 who was dead and came to l:
     20: 4 came to l and reigned with Christ
     20:12 book was opened, the book of l.
     22: 2 the tree of l with its twelve kinds
Sir 4:12 Whoever loves her loves l,
2Es 8:52 the tree of l is planted,

LIFTED
Isa 52:13 he shall be exalted and l up,
Jn   3:14 so must the Son of Man be l up,

LIGHT → ENLIGHTENED, ENLIGHTENS, LIGHTS
Ge   1: 3 "Let there be l"; and there was l.
Ex   13:21 pillar of fire by night, to give them l,
Ps   27: 1 The LORD is my l and my salvation;
Pr   4:18 the path of the righteous is like the l
Ecc 2:13 that wisdom excels folly as l excels
Isa 9: 2 in darkness have seen a great l;
     42: 6 as a covenant to the people, a l
     60: 1 Arise, shine; for your l has come,
Mt   4:16 in darkness have seen a great l,
     5:14 "You are the l of the world.
     11:30 my yoke is easy, and my burden is l.
Jn   1: 9 true l, which enlightens everyone,
     8:12 saying, "I am the l of the world.
Ro   13:12 and put on the armor of l,
2Co 11:14 Satan disguises himself as an angel
          of l.
1Pe 2: 9 of darkness into his marvelous l.
1Jn 1: 7 walk in the l as he himself is in the l
Rev 22: 5 for the Lord God will be their l,

LIGHTNING
Ex   19:16 third day there was thunder and l,
Da   10: 6 body was like beryl, his face like l,
Lk   10:18 from heaven like a flash of l.
Rev 4: 5 from the throne are flashes of l,

LIGHTS → LIGHT
Ge   1:16 God made the two great l—
Jas 1:17 coming down from the Father of l,

LIKE → LIKENESS
Ge   3: 5 be l God, knowing good and evil."
Ex   15:11 "Who is l you, O LORD, among the
2Sa 7:22 for there is no one l you,
Ps   113: 5 Who is l the LORD our God,
Isa 46: 9 I am God, and there is no one l me,
Jer 10: 6 There is none l you, O LORD;
Lk   13:18 "What is the kingdom of God l?
1Co 13:11 When I was a child, I spoke l a child
Rev 1:13 I saw one l the Son of Man,
     10: 1 his face was l the sun,
     16:15 ("See, I am coming l a thief!

LIKENESS → LIKE
Ge   1:26 in our image, according to our l;
Ro   8: 3 his own Son in the l of sinful flesh,
Php 2: 7 of a slave, being born in human l.

LILIES
Lk   12:27 Consider the l, how they grow:

LINE
Isa 28:10 l upon l, l upon l, here a little,
Am   7: 7 with a plumb l in his hand.

LINEN
Ex   26: 1 with ten curtains of fine twisted l,
Da   10: 5 and saw a man clothed in l,
Rev 19: 8 for the fine l is the righteous deeds

LION → LION'S, LIONS
1Sa 17:34 and whenever a l or a bear came,
Ecc 9: 4 a living dog is better than a dead l.
Isa 11: 7 and the l shall eat straw like the ox.
Da   7: 4 first was like a l and had eagles'
Rev 4: 7 the first living creature like a l,
     5: 5 See, the L of the tribe of Judah,

LION'S → LION
2Ti 4:17 So I was rescued from the l mouth.

LIONS → LION
Da   6:20 able to deliver you from the l?"

LIPS
Dt   23:23 Whatever your l utter you must
Job 2:10 Job did not sin with his l.
Isa 6: 5 am lost, for I am a man of unclean l,
Mt   15: 8 with their l, but their hearts are far
Heb 13:15 the fruit of l that confess his name.

LISTEN → LISTENS
Ex   23:22 But if you l attentively to his voice
2Ki 17:40 They would not l, however,

Ps   5: 2 L to the sound of my cry, my King
Pr   4: 1 L, children, to a father's instruction,
Ecc 5: 1 l is better than the sacrifice offered
Mk   9: 7 my Son, the Beloved; l to him!"
Lk   16:31 'If they do not l to Moses and the
Ac   3:22 You must l to whatever he tells you.
Jas 1:19 be quick to l, slow to speak,
Sir 11: 8 Do not answer before you l,

LISTENS → LISTEN
Jn   18:37 Everyone who belongs to the truth l
1Jn 4: 6 Whoever knows God l to us,

LITTLE
Ex   16:18 who gathered l had no shortage;
Ps   8: 5 have made them a l lower than God,
Pr   15:16 Better is a l with the fear of
Mt   8:26 "Why are you afraid, you of l faith?
     19:14 "Let the l children come to me,
2Co 8:15 one who had l did not have too l."
Gal 5: 9 A l yeast leavens the whole batch of
Rev 10: 2 He held a l scroll open in his hand.
Sir 29:23 Be content with l or much,

LIVE → ALIVE, LIFE, LIVED, LIVES, LIVING
Ge   3:22 and eat, and l forever"—
Ex   1:16 but if it is a girl, she shall l."
     33:20 for no one shall see me and l."
Lev 18: 5 by doing so one shall l:
Dt   8: 3 one does not l by bread alone,
Ps   91: 1 l in the shelter of the Most High,
Hab 2: 4 but the righteous l by their faith.
Mt   4: 4 'One does not l by bread alone,
Jn   11:25 even though they die, will l,
Ro   1:17 one who is righteous will l by faith."
     14: 8 If we l, we l to the Lord,
2Co 5:15 those who l might l no longer for
Gal 3:12 does works of the law will l
Wis 5:15 But the righteous l forever,
Sir 34:14 those who fear the Lord will l,

LIVED → LIVE
Ro   14: 9 to this end Christ died and l again,

LIVES → LIVE
Job 19:25 For I know that my Redeemer l,
Ps   18:46 The LORD l! Blessed be my rock,
Jn   11:26 and everyone who l and believes
Ro   6:10 the life he l, he l to God.
1Jn 3:16 to lay down our l for one another.
Rev 15: 7 of God, who l forever and ever;
Tob 13: 1 "Blessed be God who l forever,

LIVING → LIVE
Ge   2: 7 and the man became a l being.
     3:20 because she was the mother of all l.
     6:19 And of every l thing, of all flesh,
Dt   5:26 the voice of the l God speaking out
Jer 2:13 forsaken me, the fountain of l water,
Zec 14: 8 that day l waters shall flow out from
Mt   16:16 the Messiah, the Son of the l God."
Jn   4:10 he would have given you l water."
     6:51 I am the l bread that came down
Ro   12: 1 present your bodies as a l sacrifice,
2Co 6:16 For we are the temple of the l God;
Heb 4:12 the word of God is l and active,
1Pe 2: 4 l stone, though rejected by mortals

LOAVES
Mk   6:41 Taking the five l and the two fish,
     8: 6 and he took the seven l,

LOCK
Mt   23:13 you l people out of the kingdom of

LOCUST → LOCUSTS
2Ch 6:28 if there is plague, blight, mildew, l,
Joel 2:25 years that the swarming l has eaten,

LOCUSTS → LOCUST
Ex   10: 4 I will bring l into your country.
Mt   3: 4 and his food was l and wild honey.
Rev 9: 3 from the smoke came l on the earth,

LOG
Mt   7: 3 do not notice the l in your own eye?

LONELY → ALONE
Ps 25:16 for I am l and afflicted.
La   1: 1 How l sits the city that once was full

LONG → LONGING
Ex 20:12 that your days may be l in the land
Ps 13: 1 How l, O LORD?
Pr   3:16 L life is in her right hand;
1Co 11:14 that if a man wears l hair,
1Pe   1:12 things into which angels l to look!
      2: 2 Like newborn infants, l for the pure,
Rev   6:10 how l will it be before you judge

LONGING → LONG
Ro   8:19 the creation waits with eager l for
2Co   5: 2 l to be clothed with our heavenly

LOOK → LOOKED, LOOKS
Ex   3: 6 for he was afraid to l at God.
Ps   8: 3 When I l at your heavens,
   80:14 I l down from heaven, and see;
Lk 24:39 L at my hands and my feet;

LOOKED → LOOK
Ge 19:26 But Lot's wife, behind him, l back,
Ex   2:25 God l upon the Israelites,
Sir 16:29 Then the Lord l upon the earth,

LOOKS → LOOK
1Sa 16: 7 but the LORD l on the heart."
Ps 14: 2 The LORD l down from heaven
Mt   5:28 who l at a woman with lust

*LORD → *LORD'S, LORDS
Ge 18:27 take it upon myself to speak to the L
Ex   4:10 Moses said to the LORD, "O my L,
Dt 10:17 God is God of gods and L of lords,
Ps 16: 2 I say to the LORD, "You are my L;
  110: 1 The LORD says to my l,
Isa   6: 1 I saw the L sitting on a throne, high
Da   2:47 God is God of gods and L of kings
Mic   1: 2 The L from his holy temple.
Mt   7:22 many will say to me, 'L, L,
    9:38 the L of the harvest to send out
  12: 8 the Son of Man is L of the sabbath."
Mk   1: 3 'Prepare the way of the L,
  12:29 The L our God, the L is one;
Lk   2:11 who is the Messiah, the L.
  10:27 "You shall love the L your God
  19:38 who comes in the name of the L!
Jn 13:13 You call me Teacher and L—
  20:28 "My L and my God!"
Ac   2:34 'The L said to my L, "Sit at my
Ro   4:24 in him who raised Jesus our L
  10:12 the same L is L of all and
1Co   2:16 who has known the mind of the L
   8: 6 and one L, Jesus Christ,
2Co   3:17 Now the L is the Spirit,
Eph   4: 5 one L, one faith, one baptism,
Php   2:11 that Jesus Christ is L, to the glory
   4: 5 The L is near.
Col   3:13 just as the L has forgiven you,
1Th   4:15 are left until the coming of the L,
1Ti   6:15 the King of kings and L of lords
Heb 12:14 without which no one will see the L.
Jas   4:10 Humble yourselves before the L,
1Pe   3:15 in your hearts sanctify Christ as L.
2Pe   3: 9 The L is not slow about his promise,
Jude   1: 4 and deny our only Master and L,
Rev   4: 8 "Holy, holy, holy, the L God
  19:16 "King of kings and L of lords."
  22:20 Amen. Come, L Jesus!
Jdt   6:19 L God of heaven, see their
Wis   8: 3 and the L of all loves her.
Sir   1: 1 All wisdom is from the L,
Aza 1:35 Bless the L, all you works of the L;
Sus   1: 2 and one who feared the L.

†LORD → †GOD, †LORD'S
Ge   2: 7 L God formed man from the dust of
   6: 6 the L was sorry that he had made

  13: 4 Abram called on the name of the L.
  18:14 Is anything too wonderful for the L?
  22:14 that place "The L will provide";
Ex   3:15 shall say to the Israelites, 'The L,
   5: 2 But Pharaoh said, "Who is the L,
   6: 7 know that I am the L your God,
  15: 3 The L is a warrior; the L is his name.
  34: 6 and proclaimed, "The L, the L,
Lev 19: 2 for I the L your God am holy.
Nu   6:24 The L bless you and keep you;
  14:18 'The L is slow to anger,
Dt   6: 4 The L is our God, the L alone.
Jos 24:15 my household, we will serve the L."
1Sa   2: 2 "There is no Holy One like the L,
1Ki   8:11 of the L filled the house of the L.
  18:21 If the L is God, follow him;
1Ch 16:11 Seek the L and his strength,
Ezr   7:10 his heart to study the law of the L,
Ne   8:10 the joy of the L is your strength."
Job   1:21 the L gave, and the L has taken
  42:12 The L blessed the latter days
Ps   1: 2 their delight is in the law of the L,
  10:16 The L is king forever and ever;
  18: 1 I love you, O L, my strength.
  23: 1 The L is my shepherd, I shall not
  33:12 Happy is the nation whose God is the L
  84:11 For the L God is a sun and shield;
  110: 1 The L says to my lord,
  113: 5 Who is like the L our God,
  125: 2 so the L surrounds his people,
  128: 1 Happy is everyone who fears the L,
  145:18 The L is near to all who call on him,
  150: 6 that breathes praise the L!
Pr   1: 7 fear of the L is the beginning of
   3: 5 Trust in the L with all your heart,
  19:23 The fear of the L is life indeed;
  21: 2 but the L weighs the heart.
Isa   2:11 L alone will be exalted in that day.
   6: 3 "Holy, holy, holy is the L of hosts;
  33:22 the L is our judge, the L is our ruler;
  53: 6 the L has laid on him the iniquity
  64: 8 Yet, O L, you are our Father;
Jer   4: 4 Circumcise yourselves to the L,
  31:34 "Know the L," for they shall all
  32:27 I am the L, the God of all flesh;
La   3:25 The L is good to those who wait for
Eze   3:23 and the glory of the L stood there,
  10:18 the glory of the L went out from
  37: 4 O dry bones, hear the word of the L.
  44: 4 glory of the L filled the temple
  48:35 time on shall be, The L is There.
Hos 14: 1 Return, O Israel, to the L your God,
Joel   1:15 For the day of the L is near,
Am   5: 6 Seek the L and live,
Ob   1:15 the day of the L is near against all
Na   1: 3 The L is slow to anger but great in
Zep   1:14 The great day of the L is near,
Zec 14: 9 the L will be one and his name one.
Mal   3: 6 For I the L do not change;
   4: 5 and terrible day of the L comes.

*LORD'S → *LORD
Mk 12:11 was the L doing, and it is amazing
Lk   4:19 to proclaim the year of the L favor."
Ro 14: 8 or whether we die, we are the L.
1Co 10:26 the earth and its fullness are the L."
Sir 17:17 but Israel is the L own portion.

†LORD'S → †LORD
Nu 11:23 "Is the L power limited?
Dt 32: 9 the L own portion was his people,
Ps 24: 1 The earth is the L and all that is in it
Isa 59: 1 the L hand is not too short to save,
Ob   1:21 and the kingdom shall be the L.

LORDS → *LORD
Dt 10:17 God is God of gods and Lord of l,
Ps 136: 3 O give thanks to the Lord of l,

1Co   8: 5 there are many gods and many l—
Rev 19:16 "King of kings and Lord of l."

LOSE → LOSS, LOST
Mk   8:35 who l their life for my sake,
Jn 12:25 Those who love their life l it,
2Co   4: 1 in this ministry, we do not l heart.
Heb 12: 3 you may not grow weary or l heart.
2Jn   1: 8 do not l what we have worked for,

LOSS → LOSE
1Co   3:15 burned up, the builder will suffer l;
Php   3: 8 I regard everything as l because of
Sir 32:24 who trusts the Lord will not suffer l.

LOST → LOSE
Ps 119:176 I have gone astray like a l sheep;
Jer 50: 6 My people have been l sheep;
Eze 34:16 I will seek the l, and I will bring
Mt 10: 6 to the l sheep of the house of Israel.
Lk 15: 6 I have found my sheep that was l.'
  19:10 came to seek out and to save the l."

LOT → LOT'S, LOTS
  1. Nephew of Abraham (Ge 11:27; 12:5). Chose to live in Sodom (Ge 13). Rescued from four kings (Ge 14). Rescued from Sodom (Ge 19:1-29; 2Pe 2:7). Fathered Moab and Ammon (Ge 19:30-38).
  2. Object cast to make decisions.
Nu 33:54 You shall apportion the land by l
Est   3: 7 they cast Pur—which means "the l"
Pr 16:33 The l is cast into the lap,
Jnh   1: 7 cast lots, and the l fell on Jonah.
Ac   1:26 and the l fell on Matthias;

LOT'S → LOT, 1
Ge 19:26 L wife, behind him, looked back,
Lk 17:32 Remember L wife.

LOTS → LOT, 2
Ps 22:18 and for my clothing they cast l.
Mt 27:35 among themselves by casting l;

LOVE → BELOVED, LOVED, LOVER,
        LOVERS, LOVES
Ex 20: 6 but showing steadfast l to the
  34: 6 and abounding in steadfast l and
Lev 19:18 shall l your neighbor as yourself:
Nu 14:18 and abounding in steadfast l,
Dt   6: 5 You shall l the LORD your God
2Sa   7:15 not take my steadfast l from him,
1Ki 11: 2 Solomon clung to these in l.
2Ch   6:42 Remember your steadfast l
Ezr   3:11 his steadfast l endures forever
Ne   1: 5 steadfast l with those who l him
Ps 18: 1 I l you, O LORD, my strength.
  86: 5 abounding in steadfast l to all who
  116: 1 I l the LORD, because he has heard
  119:97 Oh, how I l your law!
  136: 1 for his steadfast l endures forever.
Pr   5:19 be intoxicated always by her l.
   8:17 I l those who l me,
  19: 8 To get wisdom is to l oneself;
Ecc   3: 8 a time to l, and a time to hate;
SS   1: 2 For your l is better than wine,
   8: 6 for l is strong as death,
Isa 54: 8 but with everlasting l I will have
La   3:22 steadfast l of the LORD never ceases,
Da   9: 4 steadfast l with those who l you
Hos   6: 4 Your l is like a morning cloud,
  11: 4 of human kindness, with bands of l.
  14: 4 heal their disloyalty; I will l them
Joel   2:13 and abounding in steadfast l,
Jnh   4: 2 and abounding in steadfast l,
Mt   5:44 L your enemies and pray
   6:24 either hate the one and l the other,
Mk 12:31 shall l your neighbor as yourself.'
Lk   6:27 For even sinners l those who l them.
  10:27 "You shall l the Lord your God
Jn 12:25 Those who l their life lose it,
  13:34 new commandment, that you l one

Jn 14:15 "If you l me, you will keep my
15:13 No one has greater l than this,
21:16 "Simon son of John, do you m me?"
Ro 5: 8 But God proves his l for us in that
12: 9 Let l be genuine; hate what is evil,
13: 8 anything, except to l one another;
1Co 8: 1 Knowledge puffs up, but l builds up.
13: 4 L is patient; l is kind;
13:13 and the greatest of these is l.
Gal 5: 6 is faith working through l.
5:22 the fruit of the Spirit is l, joy,
Eph 3:19 l of Christ that surpasses knowledge
5:25 Husbands, l your wives,
Col 3:14 Above all, clothe yourselves with l,
1Th 5: 8 put on the breastplate of faith and l,
1Ti 6:10 For the l of money is a root of all
Tit 2: 2 in faith, in l, and in endurance.
Heb 10:24 provoke one another to l and good
13: 5 your lives free from the l of money,
Jas 2: 8 shall l your neighbor as yourself."
1Pe 1: 8 you have not seen him, you l him;
2Pe 1: 7 and mutual affection with l.
1Jn 2:15 not l the world or the things in the
3: 1 See what l the Father has given us,
3:16 We know l by this, that he laid
5: 3 For the l of God is this,
2Jn 1: 6 And this is l, that we walk according
Jude 1:21 keep yourselves in the l of God;
Rev 2: 4 abandoned the l you had at first.
Sir 2:15 and those who l him keep his ways.
7:30 With all your might l your Maker,
Bel 1:38 have not forsaken those who l you,"
1Mc 4:33 with the sword of those who l you,

LOVED → LOVE
Dt 4:37 And because he l your ancestors,
Jer 31: 3 have l you with an everlasting love;
Hos 11: 1 When Israel was a child, I l him,
Mal 1: 2 I have l you, says the LORD.
Jn 3:16 God so l the world that he gave his
13: 1 he l them to the end.
15: 9 the Father has l me, so I have l you;
15:12 love one another as I have l you.
Gal 2:20 who l me and gave himself for me.
Eph 5: 2 Christ l us and gave himself up for
1Jn 4:19 We love because he first l us.

LOVER → LOVE
Ps 99: 4 Mighty King, l of justice,
Ecc 5:10 l of money will not be satisfied with
1Ti 3: 3 quarrelsome, and not a l of money.

LOVERS → LOVE
Jer 3: 1 have played the whore with many l;
La 1: 2 all her l she has no one to comfort
Hos 2: 5 For she said, "I will go after my l;
Lk 16:14 Pharisees, who were l of money,
2Ti 3: 2 For people will be l of themselves,

LOVES → LOVE
Ps 33: 5 He l righteousness and justice;
Pr 3:12 For the LORD reproves the one he l,
17:17 A friend l at all times,
Mt 10:37 Whoever l father or mother more
Lk 7:47 to whom little is forgiven, l little."
Ro 13: 8 who l another has fulfilled the law.
Eph 5:28 He who l his wife l himself.
Heb 12: 6 Lord disciplines those whom he l,
1Jn 4: 7 who l is born of God and knows
Rev 1: 5 who l us and freed us from our sins
Wis 8: 3 and the Lord of all l her.
Sir 4:12 Whoever l her l life,

LOW → LOWER, LOWLY
Ps 136:23 who remembered us in our l estate,
Isa 40: 4 every mountain and hill be made l;
Lk 3: 5 mountain and hill shall be made l,

LOWER → LOW
Ps 8: 5 have made them a little l than God,
Heb 2: 7 made them for a little while l than

LOWLY → LOW
Pr 16:19 It is better to be of a l spirit
Lk 1:52 their thrones, and lifted up the l;
Ro 12:16 but associate with the l;
Jdt 9:11 But you are the God of the l,

LOYAL → LOYALTY
2Sa 22:26 With the l you show yourself l;
Da 11:32 who are l to their God

LOYALTY → LOYAL
Dt 7: 9 God who maintains covenant l
Ru 3:10 this last instance of your l
Ps 101: 1 I will sing of l and of justice;
Hos 4: 1 There is no faithfulness or l,

LUKE*
Associate of Paul (Col 4:14; 2Ti 4:11; Phm 24).

LUKEWARM*
Rev 3:16 because you are l, and neither cold

LUST → LUSTS
Mt 5:28 looks at a woman with l has already
2Pe 1: 4 that in the world because of l,

LUSTS → LUST
Ro 1:24 gave them up in the l of their hearts
Eph 4:22 old self, corrupt and deluded by its l
2Pe 3: 3 scoffing and indulging their own l

LYDIA
Ac 16:14 named L, a worshiper of God,

LYING → LIE
1Ki 22:23 a l spirit in the mouth of all these
Pr 6:17 a l tongue, and hands that shed
Hos 4: 2 Swearing, l, and murder,
Wis 1:11 and a l mouth destroys the soul.

LYRE
1Sa 18:10 while David was playing the l,
Ps 33: 2 Praise the LORD with the l;
Da 3: 5 pipe, l, trigon, harp, drum,

M

MACCABEUS → JUDAS
1Mc 2:66 Judas M has been a mighty warrior

MACEDONIA
Ac 16: 9 a man of M pleading with him and

MADE → MAKE
Ge 1:31 God saw everything that he had m,
2:22 he m into a woman and brought her
3:21 the LORD God m garments of skins
6: 6 was sorry that he had m humankind
15:18 the LORD m a covenant with Abram,
Ex 20:11 For in six days the LORD m heaven
36: 8 the workers m the tabernacle with
Ps 8: 5 have m them a little lower than God
118:24 This is the day that the LORD has m;
139:14 I am fearfully and wonderfully m.
Jer 27: 5 outstretched arm have m the earth,
Mk 2:27 "The sabbath was m for humankind,
Ac 2:36 that God has m him both Lord and
Eph 2: 5 m us alive together with Christ—
Rev 14: 7 and worship him who m heaven
Sir 43:33 For the Lord has m all things,

MADNESS
Dt 28:28 The LORD will afflict you with m,
Ecc 9: 3 m is in their hearts while they live,

MAGDALENE
Mt 27:56 Among them were Mary M,

MAGICIANS
Ex 7:11 and they also, the m of Egypt,
Da 2: 2 So the king commanded that the m,

MAGNIFIES* → MAGNIFY
Lk 1:46 Mary said, "My soul m the Lord,

MAGNIFY → MAGNIFIES
Ps 34: 3 O m the Lord with me,

MAJESTIC → MAJESTY
Ex 15:11 Who is like you, m in holiness,
Ps 8: 1 how m is your name in all the earth!
2Pe 1:17 conveyed to him by the M Glory,

MAJESTY → MAJESTIC
1Ch 29:11 the glory, the victory, and the m;
Ps 93: 1 The LORD is king, he is robed in m;
Isa 53: 2 or m that we should look at him,
Heb 1: 3 sat down at the right hand of the M
2Pe 1:16 we had been eyewitnesses of his m.

MAKE → MADE, MAKER
Ge 1:26 "Let us m humankind in our image,
2:18 will m him a helper as his partner."
12: 2 I will m of you a great nation,
Ex 20: 4 You shall not m for yourself an idol,
32: 1 "Come, m gods for us, who shall go
Nu 6:25 LORD m his face to shine upon you,
Isa 61: 8 I will m an everlasting covenant
66:22 and the new earth, which I will m,
Jer 31:31 when I will m a new covenant with
Mt 28:19 and m disciples of all nations,
Mk 1:17 and I will m you fish for people."

MAKER → MAKE
Ge 14:19 God Most High, m of heaven and
Job 4:17 beings be pure before their M?
Ps 95: 6 kneel before the LORD, our M!
Isa 54: 5 For your M is your husband,
Sir 7:30 With all your might love your M,

MALACHI*
Post-exilic prophet (Mal 1:1; 2Es 1:40).

MALE
Ge 1:27 m and female he created them.
17:10 m among you shall be circumcised.
Lev 20:13 If a man lies with a m as with a
Mt 19: 4 'made them m and female,'
Rev 12: 5 she gave birth to a son, a m child,

MALICE
Ro 1:29 wickedness, evil, covetousness, m.
1Co 5: 8 the old yeast, the yeast of m and

MAN → MEN
Ge 2: 7 LORD God formed m from the dust
2:18 not good that the m should be
alone;
32:24 m wrestled with him until daybreak.
1Sa 13:14 sought out a m after his own heart;
Mt 9: 6 Son of M has authority on earth to
Lk 6: 5 The Son of M is lord of the sabbath.
Jn 9:35 "Do you believe in the Son of M?"
1Co 11: 3 that Christ is the head of every m,
Rev 1:13 I saw one like the Son of M,
14:14 cloud was one like the Son of M,

MANAGE → MANAGERS
1Ti 3: 4 He must m his own household well,
5:14 children, and m their households,

MANAGERS* → MANAGE
Tit 2: 5 chaste, good m of the household,

MANASSEH
1. Firstborn of Joseph (Ge 41:51; 46:20).
Blessed by Jacob but not as firstborn (Ge 48). Tribe
of blessed (Dt 33:17), numbered (Nu 1:35; 26:34),
half allotted land east of Jordan (Nu 32; Jos 13:8-
33), half west (Jos 16; Eze 48:4), failed to fully
possess (Jos 17:12-13; Jdg 1:27), 12,000 from (Rev
7:6).
2. Son of Hezekiah; king of Judah (2Ki 21:1-18;
2Ch 33:1-20). Judah exiled for his detestable sins
(2Ki 21:10-15). Repented (2Ch 33:12-19; Man
1-15).

MANGER
Lk 2:12 in bands of cloth and lying in a m."

MANNA
Ex 16:31 The house of Israel called it m;
Jos 5:12 The m ceased on the day they ate

Jn 6:49 ate the **m** in the wilderness,
Rev 2:17 I will give some of the hidden **m**,

MANNER
1Co 11:27 cup of the Lord in an unworthy **m**
Php 1:27 life in a **m** worthy of the gospel

MANTLE
1Ki 19:19 and threw his **m** over him.
2Ki 2: 8 Elijah took his **m** and rolled it up,

MANY
Isa 53:12 yet he bore the sin of **m**,
Mt 22:14 **m** are called, but few are chosen."
Mk 10:45 and to give his life a ransom for **m**."
Jn 20:30 Now Jesus did **m** other signs in the
Ro 12: 5 who are **m**, are one body in Christ,

MARAH
Ex 15:23 That is why it was called **M**.

MARK → MARKED, MARKS
  1. Cousin of Barnabas (Ac 12:12; 15:37-39; Col 4:10; 2Ti 4:11; Phm 24; 1Pe 5:13), see John.
  2. Brand or symbol:
Ge 4:15 And the LORD put a **m** on Cain,
Eze 9: 6 but touch no one who has the **m**.
Rev 14: 9 receive a **m** on their foreheads or
  19:20 who had received the **m** of the beast

MARKED → MARK
Hab 1:12 you have **m** them for judgment;
Eph 1:13 **m** with the seal of the promised

MARKET → MARKETPLACE
Mk 7: 4 not eat anything from the **m** unless
1Co 10:25 Eat whatever is sold in the meat **m**

MARKETPLACE → MARKET
Jn 2:16 Stop making my Father's house a **m**

MARKS → MARK
1Co 7:18 to remove the **m** of circumcision.
Gal 6:17 I carry the **m** of Jesus branded on
1Mc 1:15 and removed the **m** of circumcision.

MARRIAGE → INTERMARRY, MARRIED, MARRIES
Mt 22:30 are given in **m**, but are like angels
Heb 13: 4 Let **m** be held in honor by all,
Rev 19: 7 for the **m** of the Lamb has come,

MARRIED → MARRIAGE
Mal 2:11 has **m** the daughter of a foreign god.
Mk 12:23 For the seven had her **m**."
1Ti 3: 2 be above reproach, **m** only once,
Tit 1: 6 **m** only once, whose children are

MARRIES → MARRIAGE
Mk 10:11 and **m** another commits adultery
Ro 7: 3 if she **m** another man, she is not an
1Co 7:28 and if a virgin **m**, she does not sin.

MARTHA*
  Sister of Mary and Lazarus (Lk 10:38-42; Jn 11; 12:2).

MARVELOUS
Ps 98: 1 for he has done **m** things.
  131: 1 things too great and too **m** for me.
Sir 39:20 and nothing is too **m** for him.

MARY
  1. Mother of Jesus (Mt 1:16-25; Lk 1:27-56; 2:1-40). With Jesus at temple (Lk 2:41-52), at the wedding in Cana (Jn 2:1-5), questioning his sanity (Mk 3:21), at the cross (Jn 19:25-27). Among disciples (Ac 1:14).
  2. Magdalene; former demoniac (Lk 8:2). Helped support Jesus' ministry (Lk 8:1-3). At the cross (Mt 27:56; Mk 15:40; Jn 19:25), burial (Mt 27:61; Mk 15:47). Saw angel after resurrection (Mt 28:1-10; Mk 16:1-9; Lk 24:1-12); also Jesus (Jn 20:1-18).
  3. Sister of Martha and Lazarus (Jn 11). Washed Jesus' feet (Jn 12:1-8).
  4. Mother of James and Joses; witnessed cruci-

fixion (Mt 27:56; Mk 15:40) and empty tomb (Mk 16:1; Lk 24:10).

MASTER → MASTERS, TASKMASTERS
Ge 4: 7 desire is for you, but you must **m** it.
Mal 1: 6 if I am a **m**, where is the respect due
Mt 25:21 enter into the joy of your **m**.'
Jn 15:20 Servants are not greater than their **m**
2Pe 2: 1 deny the **M** who bought them—

MASTERS → MASTER
Mt 6:24 "No one can serve two **m**;

MATTANIAH → See ZEDEKIAH

MATTATHIAS
  Priest who started the Maccabean revolt (1Mc 2).

MATTER
Ecc 3: 1 a time for every **m** under heaven:
  12:13 end of the **m**; all has been heard.

MATTHEW* → =LEVI
  Apostle; former tax collector (Mt 9:9-13; 10:3; Mk 3:18; Lk 6:15; Ac 1:13). Also called Levi (Mk 2:14-17; Lk 5:27-32).

MATTHIAS
  Disciple chosen to replace Judas (Ac 1:23-26).

MATURE → MATURITY
1Co 2: 6 among the **m** we do speak wisdom,
Php 3:15 who are **m** be of the same mind;
Col 4:12 you may stand **m** and fully assured
Heb 5:14 But solid food is for the **m**,

MATURITY → MATURE
Eph 4:13 to **m**, to the measure of the full

MEAN → MEANING, MEANS
Ex 12:26 What do you **m** by this observance?
Jos 4: 6 'What do those stones **m** to you?'

MEANING → MEAN
Ge 40: 5 and each dream with its own **m**.
Dt 6:20 "What is the **m** of the decrees

MEANS → MEAN
Mt 9:13 learn what this **m**, 'I desire mercy,
1Co 9:22 that I might by all **m** save some.

MEASURE
Dt 25:15 have only a full and honest **m**,
Mk 4:24 **m** you give will be the **m** you get,
Lk 6:38 A good **m**, pressed down, shaken
Jn 3:34 for he gives the Spirit without **m**.

MEAT
Ex 16:12 'At twilight you shall eat **m**,
Ro 14:21 not to eat **m** or drink wine or do

MEDIA
Da 8:20 these are the kings of **M** and Persia.

MEDIATOR
Gal 3:19 ordained through angels by a **m**.
1Ti 2: 5 between God and humankind,
Heb 8: 6 he is the **m** of a better covenant,

MEDICINE
Pr 17:22 A cheerful heart is a good **m**,
Sir 6:16 Faithful friends are life-saving **m**;

MEDITATE → MEDITATION
Jos 1: 8 you shall **m** on it day and night,
Ps 1: 2 on his law they **m** day and night.
  119:15 I will **m** on your precepts,
Wis 12:22 we may **m** upon your goodness,
Sir 6:37 and **m** at all times on his

MEDITATION → MEDITATE
Ps 19:14 of my mouth and the **m** of my heart
  119:97 It is my **m** all day long.

MEDIUM
Lev 20:27 A man or a woman who is a **m**
1Ch 10:13 moreover, he had consulted a **m**,

MEEK → MEEKNESS
Ps 37:11 But the **m** shall inherit the land,
Mt 5: 5 "Blessed are the **m**, for they will

MEEKNESS → MEEK
Col 3:12 kindness, humility, **m**, and patience.
Jas 1:21 with **m** the implanted word

MEET → MEETING
Ex 30:36 tent of meeting where I shall **m** with
Am 4:12 prepare to **m** your God,
1Th 4:17 together with them to **m** the Lord

MEETING → MEET
Ex 27:21 In the tent of **m**, outside the curtain
  40:34 the cloud covered the tent of **m**,

MELCHIZEDEK
Ge 14:18 King **M** of Salem brought out bread
Ps 110: 4 forever according to the order of **M**."
Heb 7: 1 This "King **M** of Salem, priest of

MELT
Dt 1:28 made our hearts **m** by reporting,
Ps 97: 5 The mountains **m** like wax before
2Pe 3:12 and the elements will **m** with fire?

MEMBERS
Ro 7:23 I see in my **m** another law at war
1Co 6:15 that your bodies are **m** of Christ?
  12:18 God arranged the **m** in the body,

MEMORIAL
Lev 5:12 a handful of it as its **m** portion.
Jos 4: 7 stones shall be to the Israelites a **m**

MEN → MAN
Ge 18: 2 and saw three **m** standing near him.
Da 3:25 "But I see four **m** unbound,
Mt 2: 1 wise **m** from the East came to
Lk 9:30 they saw two **m**, Moses and Elijah,
Sir 44: 1 now sing the praises of famous **m**,

MENAHEM*
  King of Israel (2Ki 15:14-23).

MENE
Da 5:25 inscribed: **m**, **m**, TEKEL, and PARSIN.

MEPHIBOSHETH
  Son of Jonathan shown kindness by David (2Sa 4:4; 9; 21:7). Accused of siding with Absalom (2Sa 16:1-4; 19:24-30).

MERCIES → MERCY
La 3:22 his **m** never come to an end;
2Co 1: 3 the Father of **m** and the God of all

MERCIFUL → MERCY
Dt 4:31 the LORD your God is a **m** God,
Ps 111: 4 the LORD is gracious and **m**.
Jer 3:12 not look on you in anger, for I am **m**
Mt 5: 7 "Blessed are the **m**, for they will
Lk 6:36 Be **m**, just as your Father is **m**.
Heb 2:17 be a **m** and faithful high priest
Sir 2:11 the Lord is compassionate and **m**;

MERCY → MERCIES, MERCIFUL
Ex 25:17 make a **m** seat of pure gold;
1Ch 21:13 of the LORD, for his **m** is very great;
Ps 40:11 Do not, O LORD, withhold your **m**
Da 9: 9 To the Lord our God belong **m**
Hab 3: 2 in wrath may you remember **m**.
Zec 1:12 will you withhold **m** from Jerusalem
Mt 9:13 learn what this means, 'I desire **m**,
  23:23 of the law: justice and **m** and faith.
Ro 9:15 "I will have on whom I have **m**,
Eph 2: 4 But God, who is rich in **m**,
1Ti 1:13 **m** because I had acted ignorantly
Tit 3: 5 had done, but according to his **m**,
Heb 4:16 so that we may receive **m** and find
Jas 2:13 **m** triumphs over judgment.
Sir 2:17 for equal to his majesty is his **m**,

MERIBAH
Ex 17: 7 He called the place Massah and **M**,
Ps 95: 8 Do not harden your hearts, as at **M**,

MESHACH → =MISHAEL
Hebrew exiled to Babylon; name changed from Mishael (Da 1:6-7). Refused defilement by food (Da 1:8-20). Refused to worship idol (Da 3:1-18); saved from furnace (Da 3:19-30).

MESSAGE → MESSENGER
Jn 12:38 "LORD, who has believed our **m**,
1Co 1:18 the **m** about the cross is foolishness
2Co 5:19 entrusting the **m** of reconciliation to

MESSENGER → MESSAGE
Isa 42:19 or deaf like my **m** whom I send?
Mt 11:10 I am sending my **m** ahead of you,
2Co 12: 7 a **m** of Satan to torment me,

MESSIAH → CHRIST, MESSIAHS
Mt 16:16 Peter answered, "You are the **M**,
Lk 2:11 a Savior, who is the **M**, the Lord.
Ac 2:36 God has made him both Lord and **M**
Ro 9: 5 according to the flesh, comes the **M**,
Rev 11:15 kingdom of our Lord and of his **M**,
2Es 7:28 For my son the **M** shall be revealed

MESSIAHS → MESSIAH
Mk 13:22 False **m** and false prophets will

MICAH
1. Idolater from Ephraim (Jdg 17-18).
2. Prophet from Moresheth (Jer 26:18-19; Mic 1:1).

MICAIAH
Prophet of the LORD who spoke against Ahab (1Ki 22:1-28; 2Ch 18:1-27).

MICHAEL
Archangel (Jude 9); warrior in angelic realm, protector of Israel (Da 10:13, 21; 12:1; Rev 12:7).

MICHAL*
Daughter of Saul, wife of David (1Sa 14:49; 18:20-28). Warned David of Saul's plot (1Sa 19). Saul gave her to Paltiel (1Sa 25:44); David retrieved her (2Sa 3:13-16). Criticized David for dancing before the ark (2Sa 6:16-23; 1Ch 15:29).

MIDDLE
Ge 3: 3 tree that is in the **m** of the garden,
Rev 22: 2 the **m** of the street of the city.

MIDIAN → MIDIANITES
Ex 18: 1 Jethro, the priest of **M**, Moses'

MIDIANITES → MIDIAN
Ge 37:36 the **M** had sold him in Egypt to
Nu 31: 2 "Avenge the Israelites on the **M**;

MIDWIVES
Ex 1:17 But the **m** feared God; they did not

MIGHT → ALMIGHTY, MIGHTY
2Ch 6:41 you and the ark of your **m**.
  20: 6 In your hand are power and **m**,
Ps 54: 1 and vindicate me by your **m**.
Ecc 9:10 hand finds to do, do with your **m**;
Zec 4: 6 **m**, nor by power, but by my spirit,
Sir 7:30 With all your **m** love your Maker,

MIGHTY → MIGHT
Ge 49:24 by the hands of the **M** One of Jacob,
Ex 6: 1 by a **m** hand he will let them go;
Dt 5:15 a **m** hand and an outstretched arm;
2Sa 1:19 How the **m** have fallen!
Ps 99: 4 **M** King, lover of justice, you have
Isa 9: 6 Wonderful Counselor, **M** God,
Lk 1:49 the **M** One has done great things
Rev 18: 8 for **m** is the Lord God who judges

MILE
Mt 5:41 one **m**, go also the second **m**.

MILK
Ex 3: 8 a land flowing with **m** and honey,
Heb 5:12 You need **m**, not solid food;
1Pe 2: 2 long for the pure, spiritual **m**,

MILLSTONE → STONE
Lk 17: 2 better for you if a **m** were hung

MIND → MINDFUL, MINDS
Nu 23:19 mortal, that he should change his **m**.
1Ch 28: 9 for the LORD searches every **m**,
Ps 110: 4 sworn and will not change his **m**,
Jnh 3: 9 God may relent and change his **m**;
Mt 22:37 all your soul, and with all your **m**.'
Ro 1:28 God gave them up to a debased **m**
  8: 6 but to set the **m** on the Spirit is life
1Co 2:16 who has known the **m** of the Lord
Php 2: 5 same **m** be in you that was in Christ
Heb 7:21 sworn and will not change his **m**,
Sir 37:17 The **m** is the root of all conduct;

MINDFUL → MIND
Ps 8: 4 beings that you are **m** of them,
  111: 5 he is ever **m** of his covenant.
Heb 2: 6 beings that you are **m** of them,

MINDS → MIND
2Co 4: 4 blinded the **m** of the unbelievers,
Eph 4:23 be renewed in the spirit of your **m**,
Php 4: 7 guard your hearts and your **m**

MINISTER → MINISTERS, MINISTRY
Ex 28:43 to **m** in the holy place;
Ps 101: 6 that is blameless shall **m** to me.

MINISTERS → MINISTER
2Co 3: 6 to be **m** of a new covenant,
  11:15 if his **m** also disguise themselves as **m**

MINISTRY → MINISTER
2Co 5:18 has given us the **m** of reconciliation;
Eph 4:12 equip the saints for the work of **m**,
Heb 8: 6 now obtained a more excellent **m**,

MIRACLES → See also JESUS: MIRACLES
Ps 78:11 and the **m** that he had shown them.
Ac 19:11 did extraordinary **m** through Paul,
1Co 12:29 Are all teachers? Do all work **m**?
Heb 2: 4 signs and wonders and various **m**,

MIRIAM
Sister of Moses and Aaron (Nu 26:59). Led dancing at Red Sea (Ex 15:20-21). Struck with leprosy for criticizing Moses (Nu 12). Death (Nu 20:1).

MIRROR
1Co 13:12 For now we see in a **m**, dimly,
2Co 3:18 as though reflected in a **m**,
Jas 1:23 who look at themselves in a **m**;

MISHAEL → See MESHACH

MISUSES
Ex 20: 7 not acquit anyone who **m** his name.

MOAB → MOABITE
Ge 19:37 bore a son, and named him **M**;
Ru 1: 1 went to live in the country of **M**,
Isa 15: 1 An oracle concerning **M**.

MOABITE → MOAB
Dt 23: 3 **M** shall be admitted to the assembly

MOCK → MOCKED
Ps 22: 7 All who see me **m** at me;
Mk 10:34 they will **m** him, and spit upon him,

MOCKED → MOCK
1Ki 18:27 At noon Elijah **m** them, saying,
Gal 6: 7 God is not **m**, for you reap

MOLECH
Lev 18:21 to sacrifice them to **M**,

MOMENT → MOMENTARY
Ex 33: 5 single **m** I should go up among you,
Ps 30: 5 For his anger is but for a **m**;
Isa 54: 7 For a brief **m** I abandoned you,
  66: 8 a nation be delivered in one **m**?
1Co 15:52 in a **m**, in the twinkling of an eye,

MOMENTARY* → MOMENT
2Co 4:17 this slight **m** affliction is preparing

MONEY
Ecc 10:19 and **m** meets every need.
Mk 11:15 the tables of the **m** changers
1Ti 3: 3 quarrelsome, and not a lover of **m**.
  6:10 love of **m** is a root of all kinds
Heb 13: 5 your lives free from the love of **m**,

MONTH
Ex 12: 2 be the first **m** of the year for you.
Eze 47:12 they will bear fresh fruit every **m**,
Rev 22: 2 producing its fruit each **m**;

MOON → MOONS
Ge 37: 9 the sun, the **m**, and eleven stars
Dt 17: 3 the sun or the **m** or any of the host
Jos 10:13 sun stood still, and the **m** stopped,
Joel 2:31 to darkness, and the **m** to blood,
Ac 2:20 to darkness, and the **m** to blood,
Rev 6:12 the full **m** became like blood,
  21:23 no need of sun or **m** to shine on it,

MOONS → MOON
2Ch 8:13 the new **m**, and the three annual
Col 2:16 or of observing festivals, new **m**,

MORALS*
1Co 15:33 "Bad company ruins good **m**."

MORDECAI
Benjamite exile who raised Esther (Est 2:5-15). Exposed plot to kill Xerxes (Est 2:19-23). Refused to honor Haman (Est 3:1-6; 5:9-14). Charged Esther to foil Haman's plot against the Jews (Est 4). Xerxes forced Haman to honor Mordecai (Est 6). Mordecai exalted (Est 8-10). Established Purim (Est 9:18-32). See also Additions to Esther.

MORE → MOST
Ps 19:10 **M** to be desired are they than gold,
  69:31 will please the LORD **m** than an ox
Ecc 6:11 The **m** words, the **m** vanity,
Mk 4:25 to those who have, **m** will be given;
Lk 12:23 For life is **m** than food,
Ro 8:37 things we are **m** than conquerors
1Co 12:31 a still **m** excellent way.
Jas 4: 6 But he gives all the **m** grace;
Rev 7:16 will hunger no **m**, and thirst no **m**;
  21: 4 Death will be no **m**;

MORIAH*
Ge 22: 2 you love, and go to the land of **M**,
2Ch 3: 1 the LORD in Jerusalem on Mount **M**,

MORNING
Ge 1: 5 and there was **m**, the first day.
Ps 30: 5 but joy comes with the **m**.
La 3:23 every **m**; great is your faithfulness.
Lk 24:22 They were at the tomb early this **m**,
2Pe 1:19 the day dawns and the **m** star rises
Rev 22:19 of David, the bright **m** star."

MORTAL
Nu 23:19 **m**, that he should change his mind.
1Sa 15:29 **m**, that he should change his mind."
1Co 15:53 **m** body must put on immortality.
2Co 5: 4 is **m** may be swallowed up by life.

MOSES
Levite; brother of Aaron (Ex 6:20; 1Ch 6:3). Put in basket into Nile; discovered and raised by Pharaoh's daughter (Ex 2:1-10). Fled to Midian after killing Egyptian (Ex 2:11-15). Married to Zipporah, fathered Gershom (Ex 2:16-22).
Called by the LORD to deliver Israel (Ex 3-4). Pharaoh's resistance (Ex 5). Ten plagues (Ex 7-11). Passover and Exodus (Ex 12-13). Led Israel through Red Sea (Ex 14). Song of deliverance (Ex 15:1-21). Brought water from rock (Ex 17:1-7). Raised hands to defeat Amalekites (Ex 17:8-16). Delegated judges (Ex 18; Dt 1:9-18).
Received Law at Sinai (Ex 19-23; 25-31; Jn

1:17). Announced Law to Israel (Ex 19:7-8; 24; 35). Broke tablets because of golden calf (Ex 32; Dt 9). Saw glory of the LORD (Ex 33-34). Supervised building of tabernacle (Ex 36-40). Set apart Aaron and priests (Lev 8-9). Numbered tribes (Nu 1-4; 26). Opposed by Aaron and Miriam (Nu 12). Sent spies into Canaan (Nu 13). Announced forty years of wandering for failure to enter land (Nu 14). Opposed by Korah (Nu 16). Forbidden to enter land for striking rock (Nu 20:1-13; Dt 1:37). Lifted bronze snake for healing (Nu 21:4-9; Jn 3:14). Final address to Israel (Dt 1-33). Succeeded by Joshua (Nu 27:12-23; Dt 34). Death and burial by God (Dt 34:5-12). Praise of (Sir 45).
Law of (1Ki 2:3; Mk 12:26; Lk 24:44). Book of (2Ch 25:12; Ne 13:1). Song of (Ex 15:1-21; Rev 15:3). Prayer of (Ps 90).

MOST → MORE
Ge	14:18	he was priest of God M High.
Ex	26:33	the holy place from the m holy.
Ps	91: 1	live in the shelter of the m High,
Mk	5: 7	Jesus, Son of the M High God?
Col	4: 5	making the m of the time.
Jude	1:20	yourselves up on your m holy faith;

MOTH
Ps	39:11	consuming like a m what is dear to
Mt	6:19	where m and rust consume and

MOTHER → MOTHER'S, MOTHERS
Ge	2:24	a man leaves his father and his m
	3:20	because she was the m of all living.
Ex	20:12	Honor your father and your m,
Jdg	5: 7	Deborah, arose as a m in Israel.
Pr	31: 1	An oracle that his m taught him:
Isa	66:13	As a m comforts her child, so I will
Mt	10:37	loves father or m more than me is
Lk	14:26	and does not hate father and m,
Jn	19:27	to the disciple, "Here is your m."
Eph	5:31	a man will leave his father and m
Rev	17: 5	m of whores and of earth's
Tob	4: 3	Honor your m and do not abandon
Sir	3: 6	who honor their m obey the Lord;

MOTHER'S → MOTHER
Job	1:21	"Naked I came from my m womb,
Pr	1: 8	and do not reject your m teaching;
Jn	3: 4	a second time into the m womb and

MOTHERS → MOTHER
Pr	15:20	but the foolish despise their m.
Mk	10:30	brothers and sisters, m and children,

MOUNT → MOUNTAIN, MOUNTAINS
Ge	22:14	"On the m of the LORD it shall be
Ex	19:20	the LORD descended upon M Sinai,
Dt	11:29	blessing on M Gerizim and the curse
Ps	78:68	M Zion, which he loves.
Mic	4: 7	will reign over them in M Zion
Zec	14: 4	the M of Olives shall be split in two
Mk	13: 3	he was sitting on the M of Olives
Heb	12:22	But you have come to M Zion and
Rev	14: 1	the Lamb, standing on M Zion!

MOUNTAIN → MOUNT
Ex	3: 1	and came to Horeb, the m of God.
	24:18	on the m for forty days and
Isa	2: 2	the m of the LORD's house shall be
Da	2:45	saw that a stone was cut from the m
Mt	4: 8	a very high m and showed him all
	17:20	you will say to this m, 'Move from
2Pe	1:18	we were with him on the holy m.

MOUNTAINS → MOUNT
Ge	7:20	the waters swelled above the m,
Ps	125: 2	As the m surround Jerusalem,
Isa	52: 7	beautiful upon the m are the feet of
1Co	13: 2	have all faith, so as to remove m,
Rev	16:20	and no m were to be found;

MOURN → MOURNFUL, MOURNING
Ecc	3: 4	a time to m, and a time to dance;
Zec	12:10	they shall m for him,

Mt	5: 4	"Blessed are those who m,
Sir	7:34	but m with those who m.

MOURNING → MOURN
Ps	30:11	You have turned my m into dancing
Isa	61: 3	the oil of gladness instead of m,
Rev	21: 4	m and crying and pain will be no

MOUTH → MOUTHS
Ex	4:12	Now go, and I will be with your m
Dt	8: 3	that comes from the m of the LORD.
Ps	19:14	Let the words of my m and
Ecc	5: 2	Never be rash with your m,
Isa	49: 2	He made my m like a sharp sword,
Mt	4: 4	every word that comes from the m
	15:11	it is not what goes into the m
Jas	3:10	From the same m come blessing and
Rev	19:15	From his m comes a sharp sword
Sir	28:25	and a bolt for your m.

MOUTHS → MOUTH
Ps	115: 5	They have m, but do not speak;
Da	6:22	sent his angel and shut the lions' m

MUCH
Ps	19:10	they than gold, even m fine gold;
Ecc	12:12	m study is a weariness of the flesh.
Lk	12:48	to whom m has been given, m will be required;
Jn	12:24	but if it dies, it bears m fruit.
1Jn	4:11	since God loved us so m,

MUD
Jn	9: 6	and spread the m on the man's eyes,
2Pe	2:22	washed only to wallow in the m."

MULTIPLY
Ge	1:28	to them, "Be fruitful and m,
	9: 7	And you, be fruitful and m,
Dt	6: 3	that you may m greatly in a land

MULTITUDE → MULTITUDES
Jas	5:20	and will cover a m of sins.
1Pe	4: 8	for love covers a m of sins.

MULTITUDES → MULTITUDE
Joel	3:14	M, m, in the valley of decision!
Rev	17:15	are peoples and m and nations

MURDER → MURDERER, MURDERERS
Ex	20:13	You shall not m.
Hos	4: 2	lying, and m, and stealing and
Mt	5:21	of ancient times, 'You shall not m';

MURDERER → MURDER
Nu	35:16	the m shall be put to death.
Jn	8:44	He was a m from the beginning

MURDERERS → MURDER
1Jn	3:15	who hate a brother or sister are m,
Rev	21: 8	the faithless, the polluted, the m,

MUSIC
1Sa	19: 9	while David was playing m.
Ps	92: 3	to the m of the lute and the harp,

MUSTARD
Mt	17:20	have faith the size of a m seed,
Mk	4:31	It is like a m seed, which,

MUTUAL
Ro	12:10	love one another with m affection;
Heb	13: 1	Let m love continue.

MYRRH
Mt	2:11	gifts of gold, frankincense, and m.
Mk	15:23	offered him wine mixed with m;

MYSTERY
Da	2:19	m was revealed to Daniel in a vision
Ro	11:25	I want you to understand this m:
1Co	15:51	Listen, I will tell you a m!
Eph	3: 4	my understanding of the m of Christ
1Ti	3: 9	must hold fast to the m of the faith
Rev	17: 5	a name, a m: "Babylon the great,

MYTHS
2Pe	1:16	did not follow cleverly devised m

N

NAAMAN
Aramean general whose leprosy was cleansed by Elisha (2Ki 5; Lk 4:27).

NABAL
Wealthy Carmelite the LORD killed for refusing to help David (1Sa 25). David married Abigail, his widow (1Sa 25:39-42).

NABOTH
Jezreelite killed for his vineyard (1Ki 21). Ahab's family punished (1Ki 21:17-24; 2Ki 9:21-37).

NADAB
1. Firstborn of Aaron (Ex 6:23); killed with Abihu for offering unauthorized fire (Lev 10; Nu 3:4).
2. Son of Jeroboam I; king of Israel (1Ki 15:25-32).

NAHUM
Prophet against Nineveh (Na 1:1; Tob 14:4).

NAILING* → NAILS
Col	2:14	He set this aside, n it to the cross.

NAILS → NAILING
Ecc	12:11	like n firmly fixed are the collected
Jn	20:25	put my finger in the mark of the n

NAKED → NAKEDNESS
Ge	2:25	the man and his wife were both n,
Job	1:21	"N I came from my mother's womb, and n shall
2Co	5: 3	taken it off we will not be found n.

NAKEDNESS → NAKED
Ro	8:35	or persecution, or famine, or n,

NAME → NAME'S, NAMES
Ge	2:19	every living creature, that was its n.
	4:26	people began to invoke the n of
	12: 2	bless you, and make your n great,
Ex	3:15	my n forever, and this my title
	20: 7	wrongful use of the n of the LORD
	34: 5	and proclaimed the n, "The LORD."
Nu	17: 2	Write each man's n on his staff,
Dt	12:11	as a dwelling for his n:
Ps	9:10	know your n put their trust in you,
Pr	18:10	The n of the LORD is a strong tower;
Isa	42: 8	I am the LORD, that is my n;
Eze	20: 9	But I acted for the sake of my n,
Joel	2:32	on the n of the LORD shall be saved;
Zec	14: 9	the LORD will be one and his n one.
Mt	1:21	a son, and you are to him Jesus,
	6: 9	Father in heaven, hallowed be your n.
	28:19	baptizing them in the n of the Father
Jn	1:12	received him, who believed in his n,
	20:31	believing you may have life in his n.
Ac	4:12	for there is no other n under heaven
Php	2: 9	gave him the n that is above every n.
Rev	13:17	n of the beast or the number of its n.
	19:13	his n is called The Word of God.
	22: 4	and his n will be on their foreheads.
Sir	2:17	and equal to his n are his works.

NAME'S → NAME
Ps	23: 3	in right paths for his n sake.

NAMES → NAME
Ge	2:20	The man gave n to all cattle,
Ex	28: 9	engrave on them the n of the
Mt	10: 2	are the n of the twelve apostles:
Rev	21:14	the twelve n of the twelve apostles

NAOMI*
Wife of Elimelech, mother-in-law of Ruth (Ru 1:2, 4). Left Bethlehem for Moab during famine (Ru 1:1). Returned a widow, with Ruth (Ru 1:6-22). Advised Ruth to seek marriage with Boaz (Ru

2:17-3:4). Cared for Ruth's son Obed (Ru 4:13-17).

NAPHTALI
Son of Jacob by Bilhah (Ge 30:8; 35:25; 1Ch 2:2). Tribe of blessed (Ge 49:21; Dt 33:23), numbered (Nu 1:43; 26:50), allotted land (Jos 19:32-39; Eze 48:3), failed to fully possess (Jdg 1:33), supported Deborah (Jdg 4:10; 5:18), David (1Ch 12:34), 12,000 from (Rev 7:6).

NARROW
Lk 13:24 "Strive to enter through the n door;

NATHAN
Prophet and chronicler of Israel's history (1Ch 29:29; 2Ch 9:29). Announced the Davidic covenant (2Sa 7; 1Ch 17). Denounced David's sin with Bathsheba (2Sa 12). Supported Solomon (1Ki 1).

NATHANAEL → =BARTHOLOMEW?
Apostle (Jn 1:45-49; 21:2). Probably also called Bartholomew (Mt 10:3).

NATION → NATIONS
Ge 12: 2 I will make of you a great n, and
Ex 32:10 and of you I will make a great n."
Ps 33:12 Happy is the n whose God is the LORD
Pr 14:34 Righteousness exalts a n,
Isa 2: 4 n shall not lift up sword against n,
66: 8 a n be delivered in one moment?
Mt 24: 7 For n will rise against n,
1Pe 2: 9 a holy n, God's own people,

NATIONS → NATION
Ge 18:18 the n of the earth shall be blessed in
2Ki 17:15 followed the n that were around
Ps 47: 8 God is king over the n;
Isa 2: 2 all the n shall stream to it.
42: 1 he will bring forth justice to the n.
Am 9:12 and all the n who are called
Mt 28:19 and make disciples of all n,
Mk 11:17 a house of prayer for all the n'?
Ro 4:18 become "the father of many n,"
Rev 22: 2 the tree are for the healing of the n.

NATURAL → NATURE
Nu 16:29 If these people die a n death,
Ro 11:21 if God did not spare the n branches,

NATURE → NATURAL
Ro 1:20 his eternal power and divine n,
2Pe 1: 4 become participants of the divine n.

NAZARETH
Mt 2:23 made his home in a town called N,
Jn 1:46 Can anything good come out of N?
19:19 "Jesus of N, the King of the Jews."

NAZIRITE
Nu 6: 2 make a special vow, the vow of a n,
Jdg 13: 5 boy shall be a n to God from birth.

NEAR → NEARSIGHTED
Dt 4: 7 has a god so n to it as the LORD
30:14 No, the word is very n to you;
Isa 55: 6 call upon him while he is n;
Zep 1:14 The great day of the LORD is n,
Lk 10: 9 'The kingdom of God has come n
to
Jas 4: 8 Draw n to God, and he will draw n to
Rev 22:10 of this book, for the time is n.

NEARSIGHTED* → NEAR, SEE
2Pe 1: 9 lacks these things is n and blind,

NEBUCHADNEZZAR
Babylonian king, also spelled Nebuchadrezzar. Subdued and exiled Judah (2Ki 24-25; 2Ch 36; Jer 39). Dreams interpreted by Daniel (Da 2; 4). Worshiped God (Da 3:28-29; 4:34-37).

NECK → STIFF-NECKED
Pr 3:22 your soul and adornment for your n.
Mt 18: 6 were fastened around your n

NECO
Pharaoh who killed Josiah (2Ki 23:29-30; 2Ch 35:20-22), deposed Jehoahaz (2Ki 23:33-35; 2Ch 36:3-4).

NEED → NEEDY
Mt 6: 8 for your Father knows what you n
1Co 12:21 to the hand, "I have no n of you,"
Heb 4:16 and find grace to help in time of n.
1Jn 2:27 you do not n anyone to teach you.

NEEDLE
Lk 18:25 a camel to go through the eye of a n

NEEDY → NEED
1Sa 2: 8 he lifts the n from the ash heap,
Job 29:16 I was a father to the n,
Ps 113: 7 and lifts the n from the ash heap,

NEGLECT
Lk 11:42 and n justice and the love of God;
1Ti 4:14 Do not n the gift that is in you,
Heb 2: 3 escape if we n so great a salvation?

NEHEMIAH
Cupbearer of Artaxerxes (Ne 2:1); governor of Israel (Ne 8:9). Returned to Jerusalem to rebuild walls (Ne 2-6). With Ezra, reestablished worship (Ne 8). Prayer confessing nation's sin (Ne 9). Dedicated wall (Ne 12). Story of the miraculous fire (2Mc 1).

NEIGHBOR
Lev 19:18 shall love your n as yourself:
Dt 5:20 bear false witness against your n.
Mt 19:19 You shall love your n as yourself."
Jas 2: 8 "You shall love your n as yourself."

NESTS
Mt 8:20 and birds of the air have n;
Lk 13:19 made n in its branches."

NEVER
Ps 15: 5 do these things shall n be moved.
La 3:22 steadfast love of the LORD n ceases,
Da 2:44 will set up a kingdom that shall n
Mt 7:23 will declare to them, 'I n knew you;
Jn 10:28 eternal life, and they will n perish.
1Co 13: 8 Love n ends. But as for prophecies,
Heb 13: 5 he has said, "I will n leave you or

NEW
Ex 1: 8 Now a n king arose over Egypt,
Ps 33: 3 Sing to him a n song;
Ecc 1: 9 there is nothing n under the sun.
Isa 43:19 I am about to do a n thing;
65:17 create n heavens and a n earth;
Jer 31:31 I will make a n covenant with the
La 3:23 they are n every morning;
Eze 36:26 A n heart I will give you,
Mt 9:17 is n wine put into old wineskins;
Mk 1:27 A n teaching—with authority!
Lk 22:20 is the n covenant in my blood.
Jn 13:34 I give you a n commandment,
2Co 3: 6 to be ministers of a n covenant,
Col 3:10 clothed yourselves with the n self,
Heb 8: 8 when I will establish a n covenant
1Pe 1: 3 mercy he has given us a n birth
2Pe 3:13 we wait for n heavens and a n earth,
1Jn 2: 7 writing you no n commandment,
Rev 21: 1 I saw a n heaven and a n earth;
21: 2 I saw the holy city, the n Jerusalem,
21: 5 "See, I am making all things n."

NEWS
Isa 52: 7 who brings good n, who announces
Mt 11: 5 the poor have good n brought to
Mk 1:15 repent, and believe in the good n."

NICODEMUS
Pharisee who visted Jesus at night (Jn 3). Argued for fair treatment of Jesus (Jn 7:50-52). With Joseph, prepared Jesus for burial (Jn 19:38-42).

NIGHT → NIGHTS
Ge 1: 5 and the darkness he called N.

Ex 13:21 a pillar of fire by n, to give them
Jos 1: 8 you shall meditate on it day and n,
Mt 24:43 part of the n the thief was coming,
1Th 5: 2 Lord will come like a thief in the n.
Rev 22: 5 And there will be no more n;

NIGHTS → NIGHT
Ge 7:12 on the earth forty days and forty n.
Ex 24:18 mountain for forty days and forty n.
1Ki 19: 8 of that food forty days and forty n
Jnh 1:17 of the fish three days and three n.
Mt 4: 2 He fasted forty days and forty n,
12:40 for three days and three n the Son

NILE
Ex 7:17 will strike the water that is in the N,

NINEVEH
Jnh 1: 2 "Go at once to N, that great city,
Na 1: 1 An oracle concerning N.
Mt 12:41 The people of N will rise up at the

NOAH
Righteous man (Eze 14:14, 20) called to build ark (Ge 6-8; Heb 11:7; 1Pe 3:20; 2Pe 2:5). God's covenant with (Ge 9:1-17). Drunkenness of (Ge 9:18-23). Blessed sons, cursed Canaan (Ge 9:24-27). Praised (Sir 44:17-18).

NOISE
Ex 32:17 "There is a n of war in the camp."
Ps 66: 1 Make a joyful n to God, all the earth
2Pe 3:10 will pass away with a loud n,

NOON
Am 8: 9 I will make the sun go down at n,
Mk 15:33 When it was n, darkness came over

NORTH
Jer 4: 6 I am bringing evil from the n,
Da 11: 6 come to the king of the n to ratify

NOTHING
Ecc 1: 9 there is n new under the sun.
Jer 32:17 N is too hard for you.
Mt 17:20 and n will be impossible for you."
Jn 15: 5 apart from me you can do n.
1Co 13: 2 but do not have love, I am n.
Sir 39:20 and n is too marvelous for him.

NULLIFY
Ro 3: 3 n the faithfulness of God?
Gal 2:21 I do not n the grace of God;

NUMBER → NUMBERED, NUMEROUS
Nu 1:45 So the whole n of the Israelites,
26:51 the n of the Israelites enrolled;
Ro 11:25 until the full n of the Gentiles has
Rev 13:18 Its n is six hundred sixty-six.

NUMBERED → NUMBER
2Sa 24:10 because he had n the people.

NUMEROUS → NUMBER
Ge 17: 2 and will make you exceedingly n."
Ex 1: 9 the Israelite people are more n
Zec 10: 8 shall be as n as they were before.

NURSING
Isa 49:15 Can a woman forget her n child,

O

OATH
Dt 7: 8 and kept the o that he swore to your
Ne 13:25 them take an o in the name of God,
Ps 132:11 a sure o from which he will not turn
Heb 7:20 This was confirmed with an o;

OBADIAH
1. Believer who sheltered 100 prophets from Jezebel (1Ki 18:1-16).
2. Prophet against Edom (Ob 1; 2Es 1:39).

OBEDIENCE → OBEY
Ro 5:19 so by the one man's o the many will
Heb 5: 8 learned o through what he suffered;

OBEDIENT → OBEY
Ex   24: 7 spoken we will do, and we will be o.
Php   2: 8 and became o to the point of death

OBEY → OBEDIENCE, OBEDIENT, OBEYED
Ex   19: 5 if you o my voice and keep my
Dt   12:28 Be careful to o all these words that
Jos 24:24 we will serve, and him we will o."
Mt   28:20 o everything that I have commanded
Ac   5:29 "We must o God rather than any
Eph   6: 1 Children, o your parents in the
           Lord,
1Jn   5: 3 love of God is this, that we o his

OBEYED → OBEY
Jer   3:13 have not o my voice, says the LORD.
Heb 11: 8 By faith Abraham o when he was

OBSERVE
Lev 20: 8 Keep my statutes, and o them;
Ps 119: 8 I will o your statutes;

OBSTACLE
1Co   9:12 o in the way of the gospel of Christ.
2Co   6: 3 are putting no o in anyone's way,

OBTAIN → OBTAINED
Ro   11: 7 Israel failed to o what it was seeking
2Ti   2:10 that they may also o the salvation

OBTAINED → OBTAIN
Php   3:12 Not that I have already o this
Heb   8: 6 Jesus has now o a more excellent

ODOR
Ge   8:21 the LORD smelled the pleasing o,
Ex   29:18 it is a pleasing o, an offering

OFFENSE
Mk   6: 3 And they took o at him.
Gal   5:11 o of the cross has been removed.

OFFER → OFFERING, OFFERINGS
Ps   4: 5 O right sacrifices, and put your trust
Hos 14: 2 and we will o the fruit of our lips.
Heb   9:25 Nor was it to o himself again and

OFFERING → OFFER
Ge   4: 4 LORD had regard for Abel and his o,
     22: 8 will provide the lamb for a burnt o,
2Ch   7: 1 heaven and consumed the burnt o
Ps   40: 6 Sacrifice and o you do not desire,
Da   11:31 shall abolish the regular burnt o
Eph   5: 2 a fragrant o and sacrifice to God.
Heb 10:14 For by a single o he has perfected
1Mc   4:44 what to do about the altar of burnt
           o,

OFFERINGS → OFFER
1Sa 15:22 the LORD as great delight in burnt o
Hos   6: 6 of God rather than burnt o.
Mk   12:33 important than all whole burnt o
1Mc   1:45 to forbid burnt o and sacrifices

OFFSPRING
Ge   3:15 and between your o and hers;
     12: 7 "To your o I will give this land."
2Sa   7:12 I will raise-up your o after you,

OHOLIAB
Craftsman who worked on the tabernacle (Ex
31:6; 35:34; 36:1-2; 38:23).

OIL
Ex   25: 6 o for the lamps, spices for the
           anointing o
Dt   14:23 your wine, and your o, as well
Ps   23: 5 you anoint my head with o;
Heb   1: 9 with the o of gladness beyond your
Jas   5:14 anointing them with o in the name

OLD
Ge   21: 7 I have borne him a son in his o age."
Ps   74:12 Yet God my King is from of o,
Mk   2:22 puts new wine into o wineskins;
Ro   4:19 he was about a hundred years o),
Eph   4:22 your o self, corrupt and deluded by

OLIVE → OLIVES
Zec   4: 3 And by it there are two o trees,
Ro   11:17 and you, a wild o shoot,
Rev 11: 4 two o trees and the two lampstands

OLIVES → OLIVE
Zec 14: 4 Mount of O shall be split in two
Mt   24: 3 he was sitting on the Mount of O,

OMEGA
Rev   1: 8 "I am the Alpha and the O,"

OMRI
King of Israel (1Ki 16:21-26).

ONCE → ONE
Ex   30:10 O a year Aaron shall perform the
Ro   6:10 he died, he died to sin, o for all;
Heb   7:27 this he did o for all when he offered
      9:27 it is appointed for mortals to die o,

ONE → FIRST, ONCE
Ge   2:24 and they become o flesh.
Zec 14: 9 the LORD will be o and his name o.
Mk   12:29 the Lord our God, the Lord is o;
Jn   10:30 The Father and I are o."
1Co 12:13 For in the o Spirit we were all
           baptized
Eph   4: 5 o Lord, o faith, o baptism,

ONLY
Ge   22: 2 "Take your son, your o son Isaac,
1Ki 18:22 "I, even I o, am left a prophet
Jn   1:14 the glory as of a father's o son,
      3:16 that he gave his o Son,
1Ti   1:17 the o God, be honor and glory
1Jn   4: 9 God sent his o Son into the world so

OPEN → OPENED, OPENS
Isa 53: 7 so he did not o his mouth.
Rev   5: 2 "Who is worthy to o the scroll

OPENED → OPEN
Ge   3: 7 Then the eyes of both were o,
Da   7:10 in judgment, and the books were o.
Zec 13: 1 a fountain shall be o for the house
Lk   11: 9 knock, and the door will be o for
Heb 10:20 new and living way that he o for us
Rev 20:12 book was o, the book of life.

OPENS → OPEN
Rev   3: 7 who o and no one will shut,

OPPORTUNITY
Mt   26:16 began to look for an o to betray him.
Gal   5:13 not use your freedom as an o for

OPPRESSED → OPPRESSION
Ge   15:13 shall be o for four hundred years;
Ex   1:12 But the more they were o,
Ps 146: 7 who executes justice for the o;
Isa 53: 7 He was o, and he was afflicted,
Jdt   9:11 God of the lowly, helper of the o,

OPPRESSION → OPPRESSED
Jer   9: 6 O upon o, deceit upon deceit!
Eze 45: 9 Put away violence and o,

ORACLES
Ro   3: 2 entrusted with the o of God.

ORDAIN → ORDINANCE, ORDINANCES
Ex   29: 9 shall then o Aaron and his sons.
1Ti   5:22 Do not o anyone hastily,

ORDER
Ps 110: 4 according to the o of Melchizedek."
Heb   5:10 according to the o of Melchizedek.

ORDINANCE → ORDAIN
Ex   12:17 your generations as a perpetual o.
     29: 9 shall be theirs by a perpetual o.

ORDINANCES → ORDAIN
Ps   19: 9 o of the LORD are true and righteous

ORIGIN
Mt   21:26 But if we say, 'Of human o,'
Ac   5:38 or this undertaking is of human o,

ORNAMENTS
Ex   33: 6 stripped themselves of their o,
1Pe   3: 3 by wearing gold o or fine clothing;

ORPHAN → ORPHANED, ORPHANS
Ex   22:22 You shall not abuse any widow or o.
Hos 14: 3 In you the o finds mercy."

ORPHANED → ORPHAN
Jn   14:18 will not leave you o; I am coming

ORPHANS → ORPHAN
Jas   1:27 to care for o and widows in their
Sir   4:10 Be a father to o, and be like a

OTHER → OTHERS
Ex   20: 3 you shall have no o gods before me.
Jdg   2:19 following o gods,
2Ki 17: 7 They had worshiped o gods
Isa 45: 5 I am the LORD, and there is no o;
Mt   6:24 to the one and despise the o.

OTHERS → OTHER
Lk   6:31 Do to o as you would have them do
Php   2: 3 but in humility regard o as better

OTHNIEL
Nephew of Caleb (Jos 15:15-19; Jdg 1:12-15).
Judge who freed Israel from Aram (Jdg 3:7-11).

OUTSIDE
Lk   11:39 Pharisees clean the o of the cup and
Heb 13:12 Jesus also suffered o the city gate in
Rev 22:15 O are the dogs and sorcerers and

OUTSTRETCHED → STRETCH
Ex   6: 6 I will redeem you with an o arm
Ps 136:12 an o arm, for his steadfast love
Jer 27: 5 by my great power and my o arm

OUTWARD
1Sa 16: 7 they look on the o appearance,
2Co   5:12 those who boast in o appearance
2Ti   3: 5 the o form of godliness but denying

OVERCOME
Jn   1: 5 and the darkness did not o it.
Ro   12:21 Do not be o by evil, but o with
1Jn   2:14 and you have o the evil one.

OVERSHADOW* → OVERSHADOWED
Lk   1:35 power of the Most High will o you;

OVERSHADOWED → OVERSHADOW
Lk   9:34 a cloud came and o them;

OWE → OWES
Mt   18:28 he said, 'Pay what you o.'
Ro   13: 8 O no one anything, except to love

OWN
Isa 53: 6 we have all turned to our o way,
Jer 31:30 But all shall die for their o sins;
Jn   1:11 He came to what was his o, and his
           o people did not accept him.
     10:18 but I lay it down of my o accord.
1Co   6:19 and that you are not your o?

OX → OXEN
Dt   25: 4 not muzzle an o while it is treading
Isa 65:25 the lion shall eat straw like the o;
Eze   1:10 the face of an o on the left side,
1Ti   5:18 not muzzle an o while it is treading
Rev   4: 7 the second living creature like an o,

P

PAGANS
1Co   5: 1 that is not found even among p;
      12: 2 You know that when you were p,

PAIN → PAINS
Ge   3:16 in p you shall bring forth children,
1Pe   2:19 endure p while suffering unjustly.
Rev 21: 4 and crying and p will be no more,

PAINS → PAIN
Ro   8:22 creation has been groaning in labor
          p
1Th   5: 3 as labor **p** come upon a pregnant

PALM → PALMS
Jn   12:13 So they took branches of **p** trees
Rev   7: 9 robed in white, with **p** branches in

PALMS → PALM
Isa   49:16 I have inscribed you on the **p** of my

PANGS
Ge   3:16 increase your **p** in childbearing;
Mk   13: 8 but the beginning of the birth **p.**
Rev   12: 2 and was crying out in birth **p,**

PARABLE → PARABLES
Ps   78: 2 I will open my mouth in a **p;**
Mt   13:18 "Hear then the **p** of the sower.

PARABLES → PARABLE; See also JESUS:
          PARABLES
Mt   13:35 I will open my mouth to speak in **p;**
Sir   39: 2 penetrates the subtleties of **p;**

PARADISE
Lk   23:43 today you will be with me in **P.**"
2Co   12: 4 was caught up into **P** and heard
Rev   2: 7 tree of life that is in the **p** of God.
2Es   8:52 for you that **p** is opened,

PARALYTIC → PARALYZED
Mt   9: 2 saw their faith, he said to the **p,**

PARALYZED → PARALYTIC
Jn   5: 3 many invalids—blind, lame, and **p.**
Ac   8: 7 who were **p** or lame were cured.

PARCHMENTS*
2Ti   4:13 also the books, and above all the **p.**

PARDON
Ex   34: 9 **p** our iniquity and our sin,
Isa   55: 7 our God, for he will abundantly **p.**

PARENT → PARENTS
Dt   8: 5 that as a **p** disciplines a child
Eze   18:20 nor a **p** suffer for the iniquity of a

PARENTS → PARENT
Mal   4: 6 turn the hearts of **p** to their children
Lk   1:17 turn the hearts of **p** to their
          children,
Eph   6: 1 Children, obey your **p** in the Lord,
Sir   48:10 turn the hearts of **p** to their
          children,

PART → APART
1Co   13: 9 For we know only in **p,** and we
          prophesy only in **p;**

PARTAKE
1Co   10:17 for we all **p** of the one bread.

PARTIALITY
Dt   16:19 distort justice; you must not show **p;**
Pr   24:23 **P** in judging is not good.
Ro   2:11 For God shows no **p.**
Jas   3:17 without a trace of **p** or hypocrisy.
Sir   35:15 and with him there is no **p.**

PARTICIPANTS → PARTICIPATE
2Pe   1: 4 may become **p** of the divine nature.

PARTICIPATE* → PARTICIPANTS
1Ti   5:22 and do not **p** in the sins of others;
2Jn   1:11 for to welcome is to **p** in the evil

PARTNER → PARTNERS, PARTNERSHIP
Pr   2:17 who forsakes the **p** of her youth
1Co   7:15 But if the unbelieving **p** separates,

PARTNERS → PARTNER
1Co   10:20 not want you to be **p** with demons.
Heb   3: 1 holy **p** in a heavenly calling,

PARTNERSHIP* → PARTNER
2Co   6:14 **p** is there between righteousness

PASHHUR
  Priest; opponent of Jeremiah (Jer 20:1-6).

PASS → PASSED, PASSING
Ex   12:13 when I see the blood, I will **p** over
          33:19 make all my goodness **p** before you,
Am   5:17 I will **p** through the midst of you,
Mt   24:35 Heaven and earth will **p** away, but
          my words will not **p**
2Pe   3:10 then the heavens will **p** away

PASSED → PASS
Ge   15:17 torch **p** between these pieces.
Ex   12:27 he **p** over the houses of the Israelites
          33:22 with my hand until I have **p** by;
2Co   5:17 everything old has **p** away;
1Jn   3:14 that we have **p** from death to life
Rev   21: 4 for the first things have **p** away."

PASSING → PASS
1Co   7:31 present form of this world is **p** away
1Jn   2:17 the world and its desire are **p** away,

PASSIONS
Gal   5:24 have crucified the flesh with its **p**
2Ti   2:22 Shun youthful **p** and pursue

PASSOVER
Ex   12:11 It is the **p** of the LORD.
Dt   16: 1 the month of Abib by keeping the **p**
Mk   14:12 when the **P** lamb is sacrificed,

PASTORS*
Eph   4:11 evangelists, some **p** and teachers,

PASTURE → PASTURES
Ps   100: 3 his people, and the sheep of his **p.**
Jer   50: 7 the LORD, the true **p,** the LORD,

PASTURES → PASTURE
Ps   23: 2 He makes me lie down in green **p;**

PATH → PATHS
Ps   16:11 You show me the **p** of life.
          119:105 lamp to my feet and a light to my **p.**
Mt   13: 4 he sowed, some seeds fell on the **p,**

PATHS → PATH
Ps   23: 3 in right **p** for his name's sake.
Pr   3: 6 and he will make straight your **p.**
Mt   3: 3 of the Lord, make his **p** straight.'"
Heb   12:13 and make straight **p** for your feet,

PATIENCE → PATIENT
Mic   2: 7 Is the LORD's **p** exhausted?
Ro   2: 4 his kindness and forbearance and **p?**
Gal   5:22 fruit of the Spirit is love, joy, peace,
          p,
2Pe   3:15 regard the **p** of our Lord as salvation

PATIENT → PATIENCE
Lk   8:15 and bear fruit with **p** endurance.
Ro   12:12 Rejoice in hope, be **p** in suffering,
1Co   13: 4 Love is **p;** love is kind;
2Pe   3: 9 as some think of slowness, but is **p**

PATTERN
Ex   25:40 make them according to the **p** for
Heb   8: 5 make everything according to the **p**

PAUL → =SAUL
  Also called Saul (Ac 13:9). Pharisee from Tarsus
  (Ac 9:11; Php 3:5). Apostle (Gal 1). At stoning of
  Stephen (Ac 8:1). Persecuted Church (Ac 9:1-2;
  Gal 1:13). Vision of Jesus on road to Damascus (Ac
  9:4-9; 26:12-18). In Arabia (Gal 1:17). Preached
  in Damascus; escaped death through the wall in a
  basket (Ac 9:19-25). In Jerusalem; back to Tarsus
  (Ac 9:26-30).
  Brought to Antioch by Barnabas (Ac 11:22-26).
  First missionary journey to Cyprus and Galatia (Ac
  13-14). Stoned at Lystra (Ac 14:19-20). At Jeru-
  salem council (Ac 15). Split with Barnabas over
  Mark (Ac 15:36-41).
  Second missionary journey with Silas (Ac 16-
  20). Called to Macedonia (Ac 16:6-10). Freed from

prison in Philippi (Ac 16:16-40). In Thessalonica
(Ac 17:1-9). Speech in Athens (Ac 17:16-33). In
Corinth (Ac 18). In Ephesus (Ac 19). Return to
Jerusalem (Ac 20). Farewell to Ephesian elders (Ac
20:13-38). Arrival in Jerusalem (Ac 21:1-26). Arrested (Ac 21:27-36). Addressed crowds (Ac 22),
Sanhedrin (Ac 23:1-11). Sent to Caesarea (Ac
23:12-35). Trial before Felix (Ac 24), Festus (Ac
25:1-12). Before Agrippa (Ac 25:13-26:32). Voyage to Rome; shipwreck (Ac 27). Arrival in Rome
(Ac 28).

PAVEMENT
Ex   24:10 his feet there was something like a **p**
Jn   19:13 bench at a place called The Stone **P,**

PAY → REPAY
Ex   22: 4 the thief shall **p** double.
Dt   24:15 You shall **p** them their wages daily
Mt   22:17 lawful to **p** taxes to the emperor, or
Ro   13: 7 **P** to all what is due them—

PEACE → PEACEMAKERS
Lev   26: 6 And I will grant **p** in the land,
Ps   122: 6 Pray for the **p** of Jerusalem:
Isa   26: 3 in **p** because they trust in you.
          57:19 **P, p,** to the far and the near,
          57:21 no **p,** says my God, for the wicked.
Jer   6:14 saying, "**P, p,**" when there is no **p.**
Mic   5: 5 and he shall be the one of **p.**
Lk   2:14 on earth **p** among those whom he
Jn   14:27 **P** I leave with you; my **p** I give
Ro   16:20 God of **p** will shortly crush Satan
1Co   14:33 is a God not of disorder but of **p.**
Gal   5:22 the fruit of the Spirit is love, joy,
Eph   4: 3 unity of the Spirit in the bond of **p.**
Php   4: 7 the **p** of God, which surpasses all
2Ti   2:22 righteousness, faith, love, and **p,**

PEACEMAKERS* → PEACE
Mt   5: 9 "Blessed are the **p,** for they will be

PEARL* → PEARLS
Mt   13:46 on finding one **p** of great value,
Rev   21:21 each of the gates is a single **p,**

PEARLS → PEARL
Mt   7: 6 do not throw your **p** before swine,

PEKAH*
  King of Israel (2Ki 15:25-31; 2Ch 28:6; Isa 7:1).

PEKAHIAH*
  Son of Menahem; king of Israel (2Ki 15:22-26).

PENALTY
Ro   1:27 in their own persons the due **p**
2Pe   2:13 suffering the **p** for doing wrong.

PENTECOST
Ac   2: 1 When the day of **P** had come,

PEOPLE → PEOPLES
Ex   5: 1 the God of Israel, 'Let my **p** go,
          33:13 that this nation is your **p.**"
Dt   4:20 a **p** of his very own possession,
          32: 9 the LORD's own portion was his **p,**
Ru   1:16 your **p** shall be my **p,**
2Sa   5: 2 shall be shepherd of my **p** Israel,
Ps   29:11 the LORD bless his **p** with peace!
          125: 2 so the LORD surrounds his **p,**
Isa   40: 1 Comfort, O comfort my **p,** says
          42: 6 give you as a covenant to the **p,**
          53: 8 for the transgression of my **p.**
Jer   50: 6 My **p** have been lost sheep;
La   1: 1 sits the city that once was full of **p!**
Da   9:24 "Seventy weeks are decreed for your
          p
Zec   13: 9 I will say, "They are my **p**";
Mt   1:21 he will save his **p** from their sins."
Jn   11:50 the **p** than to have the whole nation
          18:14 to have one person die for the **p.**
Ro   9:25 not my **p** I will call 'my **p,**'
Heb   8:10 their God, and they shall be my **p.**
1Pe   2: 9 a holy nation, God's own **p,**

PEOPLES → PEOPLE
Ge 17:16 kings of p shall come from her."
Dt 7: 7 for you were the fewest of all p.
Ps 117: 1 Extol him, all you p!
Rev 21: 3 they will be his p, and God himself

PERFECT → PERFECTED, PERFECTER,
PERFECTION
Lev 22:21 to be acceptable it must be p;
2Sa 22:31 This God—his way is p;
Ps 19: 7 The law of the LORD is p, reviving
Mt 5:48 Be p, therefore, as your heavenly
Father is p.
Ro 12: 2 what is good and acceptable and p.
2Co 12: 9 for power is made p in weakness."
Heb 7:19 (for the law made nothing p);
1Jn 4:18 in love, but p love casts out fear;

PERFECTED → PERFECT
Heb 10:14 For by a single offering he has p
1Jn 4:12 God lives in us, and his love is p in

PERFECTER* → PERFECT
Heb 12: 2 Jesus the pioneer and p of our faith,

PERFECTION → PERFECT
Heb 6: 1 Therefore let us go on toward p,
1Jn 2: 5 the love of God has reached p.

PERISH → PERISHABLE
Lev 26:38 You shall p among the nations,
Jos 23:13 until you p from this good land that
Est 4:16 and if I p, I p."
Ps 1: 6 but the way of the wicked will p.
Lk 21:18 But not a hair of your head will p.
Jn 3:16 who believes in him may not p
2Pe 3: 9 with you, not wanting any to p,

PERISHABLE → PERISH
1Co 9:25 they do it to receive a p wreath,
15:42 What is sown is p, what is raised is
1Pe 1:23 not of p but of imperishable seed,

PERMANENT → PERMANENTLY
2Co 3:11 much more has the p come in glory!

PERMANENTLY* → PERMANENT
Heb 7:24 but he holds his priesthood p,

PERSECUTE → PERSECUTED,
PERSECUTION
Mt 5:44 and pray for those who p you,
Ac 9: 4 "Saul, Saul, why do you p me?"
Ro 12:14 Bless those who p you; bless

PERSECUTED → PERSECUTE
Ps 119:86 I am p without cause; help me!
Jn 15:20 they p me, they will persecute you;
2Co 4: 9 p, but not forsaken; struck down,
2Ti 3:12 godly life in Christ Jesus will be p.

PERSECUTION → PERSECUTE
Mt 13:21 or p arises on account of the word,
Ro 8:35 Will hardship, or distress, or p, or
Heb 10:33 publicly exposed to abuse and p,

PERSEVERANCE* → PERSEVERE
Heb 12: 1 let us run with p the race that is set

PERSEVERE → PERSEVERANCE
Da 12:12 Happy are those who p
Ro 12:12 be patient in suffering, p in prayer.

PERSIA → PERSIANS
Ezr 1: 1 the spirit of King Cyrus of P
Da 8:20 these are the kings of Media and P.

PERSIANS → PERSIA
Da 6:15 a law of the Medes and P that

PESTILENCE
Dt 32:24 burning consumption, bitter p.
Ps 91: 6 or the p that stalks in darkness,

PETER → =CEPHAS, =SIMON
Apostle, brother of Andrew, also called Simon
(Mt 10:2; Mk 3:16; Lk 6:14; Ac 1:13), and Cephas
(Jn 1:42). Confession of Christ (Mt 16:13-20; Mk
8:27-30; Lk 9:18-27). At transfiguration (Mt

17:1-8; Mk 9:2-8; Lk 9:28-36; 2Pe 1:16-18).
Caught fish with coin (Mt 17:24-27). Denial of Jesus predicted (Mt 26:31-35; Mk 14:27-31; Lk
22:31-34; Jn 13:31-38). Denied Jesus (Mt 26:69-
75; Mk 14:66-72; Lk 22:54-62; Jn 18:15-27).
Commissioned by Jesus to shepherd his flock (Jn
21:15-23).
   Speech at Pentecost (Ac 2). Healed beggar (Ac
3:1-10). Speech at temple (Ac 3:11-26), before
Sanhedrin (Ac 4:1-22). In Samaria (Ac 8:14-25).
Sent by vision to Cornelius (Ac 10). Announced
salvation of Gentiles in Jerusalem (Ac 11; 15).
Freed from prison (Ac 12). Inconsistency at Antioch (Gal 2:11-21). At Jerusalem Council (Ac 15).

PHARAOH → PHARAOH'S
Ge 41:14 Then P sent for Joseph,
Ex 3:11 "Who am I that I should go to P,
14:17 I will gain glory for myself over P
Ro 9:17 For the scripture says to P,

PHARAOH'S → PHARAOH
Ex 7: 3 But I will harden P heart,
Heb 11:24 refused to be called a son of P

PHARISEE → PHARISEES
Lk 11:37 a P invited him to dine with him;
Jn 3: 1 a P named Nicodemus,
Ac 5:34 a P in the council named Gamaliel,
Php 3: 5 as to the law, a P;

PHARISEES → PHARISEE
Mt 5:20 that of the scribes and P,
16: 6 beware of the yeast of the P and
23:13 "But woe to you, scribes and P,

PHILEMON*
Phm 1: 1 To P our dear friend and co-worker,

PHILIP
1. Apostle (Mt 10:3; Mk 3:18; Lk 6:14; Jn
1:43-48; 14:8; Ac 1:13).
2. Deacon (Ac 6:1-7); evangelist in Samaria (Ac
8:4-25), to Ethiopian (Ac 8:26-40).

PHILISTINE → PHILISTINES
1Sa 17:37 save me from the hand of this P."
Pm 151: 6 I went out to meet the P,

PHILISTINES → PHILISTINE
Ge 26: 1 Gerar, to King Abimelech of the P.
1Sa 5: 1 the P captured the ark of God,
17: 1 the P gathered their armies for
battle
2Sa 8: 1 David attacked the P and subdued
Am 1: 8 the remnant of the P shall perish,

PHILOSOPHERS* → PHILOSOPHY
Ac 17:18 Epicurean and Stoic p debated with

PHILOSOPHY → PHILOSOPHERS
Col 2: 8 no one takes you captive through p

PHINEHAS
1. Grandson of Aaron (Ex 6:25; Jos 22:30-32).
Zeal for the LORD (Nu 25:7-13; Ps 106:30).
2. A wicked priest (1Sa 1:3; 2:12-17; 4:1-19).

PHOEBE*
Ro 16: 1 I commend to you our sister P,

PHYSICAL
1Co 15:44 It is sown a p body, it is raised a
1Ti 4: 8 while p training is of some value,

PHYSICIAN → PHYSICIANS
Mt 9:12 who are well have no need of a p,
Col 4:14 Luke, the beloved p, and Demas

PHYSICIANS → PHYSICIAN
Job 13: 4 all of you are worthless p.
Mk 5:26 had endured much under many p,

PIECES
Ge 15:17 torch passed between these p.
Mt 14:20 what was left over of the broken p,
15:37 they took up the broken p left over,
Lk 20:18 on that stone will be broken to p;

PIERCED
Zec 12:10 look on the one whom they have p,
Jn 19:37 look on the one whom they have p."
Rev 1: 7 even those who p him;

PIG
Dt 14: 8 the p, because it divides the hoof

PILATE
Governor of Judea. Questioned Jesus (Mt 27:1-
26; Mk 15:15; Lk 22:66-23:25; Jn 18:28-19:16);
sent him to Herod (Lk 23:6-12); consented to his
crucifixion when crowds chose Barabbas (Mt
27:15-26; Mk 15:6-15; Lk 23:13-25; Jn 19:1-10).

PILLAR → PILLARS
Ge 19:26 back, and she became a p of salt.
Ex 13:21 and in a p of fire by night,

PILLARS → PILLAR
Jdg 16:29 Samson grasped the two middle p
1Ki 7:15 He cast two p of bronze.
Pr 9: 1 she has hewn her seven p.

PIONEER*
Heb 2:10 make the p of their salvation perfect
12: 2 Jesus the p and perfecter of our
faith

PIT
Rev 20: 3 into the p, and locked and sealed it
Sir 21:10 but at its end is the p of Hades.

PITY
Dt 7:16 showing them no p;
Hos 1: 6 for I will no longer have p
2:23 And I will have p on Lo-ruhamah,

PLACE → PLACES
Ge 28:16 "Surely the LORD is in this p—
Ex 26:33 shall separate for you the holy p
Ps 24: 3 And who shall stand in his holy p?
32: 7 You are a hiding p for me;
Jn 14: 3 And if I go and prepare a p for you,

PLACES → PLACE
Lev 26:30 I will destroy your high p
Ps 78:58 him to anger with their high p;

PLAGUE → PLAGUES
Ex 32:35 the LORD sent a p on the people,
Nu 25: 8 So the p was stopped among the
Zec 14:12 the p with which the LORD will
Rev 11: 6 strike the earth with every kind of p,

PLAGUES → PLAGUE
Hos 13:14 O Death, where are your p?
Rev 15: 1 seven angels with seven p, which
22:18 God will add to that person the p

PLAIN
Ge 13:12 among the cities of the P and
Isa 40: 4 and the rough places a p.

PLANNED
Ex 32:14 his mind about the disaster that
he p
Isa 46:11 I have p, and I will do it.

PLANT → PLANTED
Ge 1:29 I have given you every p yielding
Ecc 3: 2 time to p, and a time to pluck up

PLANTED → PLANT
Ge 2: 8 the LORD God p a garden in Eden,
Ps 1: 3 like trees p by streams of water,
1Co 3: 6 I p, Apollos watered, but God gave

PLEA
1Ki 8:28 your servant's prayer and his p,
La 3:56 heard my p, "Do not close your ear

PLEASE → PLEASED, PLEASES, PLEASING,
PLEASURE
Ps 69:31 will p the LORD more than an ox
Ro 8: 8 who are in the flesh cannot p God.
15: 3 For Christ did not p himself;

1Co 10:33 as I try to p everyone in everything
1Th 4: 1 how you ought to live and to p God
Heb 11: 6 without faith it is impossible to p God,
Sir 2:16 Those who fear the Lord seek to p

PLEASED → PLEASE
Ps 40:13 Be p, O LORD, to deliver me;
Mic 6: 7 Will the LORD be p with thousands
Mt 3:17 Beloved, with whom I am well p."
Col 1:19 the fullness of God was p to dwell,
2Pe 1:17 Beloved, with whom I am well p."

PLEASES → PLEASE
Ps 115: 3 the heavens; he does whatever he p.
1Jn 3:22 commandments and do what p him.

PLEASING → PLEASE
Ps 104:34 May my meditation be p to him,
Eph 5:10 to find out what is p to the Lord.
Php 4:18 a sacrifice acceptable and p to God.

PLEASURE → PLEASE
Pr 21:17 Whoever loves p will suffer want;
Eze 18:32 I have no p in the death of anyone,
Eph 1: 5 according to the good p of his will,
2Ti 3: 4 lovers of p rather than lovers of God

PLENTIFUL → PLENTY
Lk 10: 2 He said to them, "The harvest is p,

PLENTY → PLENTIFUL
Php 4:12 and I know what it is to have p.

PLOT → PLOTTED
Ps 2: 1 and the peoples p in vain?
Na 1: 9 Why do you p against the LORD?

PLOTTED → PLOT
Est 9:24 p against the Jews to destroy them,

PLOWSHARES
Isa 2: 4 they shall beat their swords into p,
Joel 3:10 Beat your p into swords, and your

PLUNDER
Ex 3:22 and so you shall p the Egyptians."
Est 9:10 but they did not touch the p.
Eze 39:10 and p those who plundered them,

POISON
Ps 69:21 They gave me p for food,
Jas 3: 8 a restless evil, full of deadly p.

POLE → POLES
Nu 21: 8 poisonous serpent, and set it on a p;
Dt 16:21 not plant any tree as a sacred p

POLES → POLE
2Ki 17:10 for themselves pillars and sacred p

POLLUTED → POLLUTES
Ac 15:20 from things p by idols and from
Rev 21: 8 the cowardly, the faithless, the p,

POLLUTES* → POLLUTED
Nu 35:33 blood p the land, and no expiation

POOR → POVERTY
Ex 23: 6 not pervert the justice due to your p
1Sa 2: 8 He raises up the p from the dust,
Ps 113: 7 He raises the p from the dust,
Pr 19:22 and it is better to be p than a liar.
Mt 5: 3 "Blessed are the p in spirit,
Mk 10:21 own, and give the money to the p,
12:42 p widow came and put in two small
Jn 12: 8 You always have the p with you,
2Co 6:10 as p, yet making many rich;
8: 9 yet for your sakes he became p,
Jas 2: 5 Has not God chosen the p in the

PORTION → APPORTIONED
Dt 32: 9 the LORD's own p was his people,
Jos 18: 7 The Levites have no p among you,
Ps 142: 5 my p in the land of the living."
La 3:24 "The LORD is my p," says my soul,
Sir 17:17 Israel is the Lord's own p.

POSSESS → POSSESSED, POSSESSION, POSSESSIONS
Dt 28:21 the land that you are entering to p.
Ezr 9:11 that you are entering to p is a land
Isa 60:21 they shall p the land forever.

POSSESSED → POSSESS
Mt 8:16 many who were p with demons;
Heb 10:34 you yourselves p something better

POSSESSION → POSSESS
Ex 19: 5 treasured p out of all the peoples.
Jos 1:11 to go in to take p of the land that
Ps 2: 8 and the ends of the earth your p.

POSSESSIONS → POSSESS
Lk 12:15 not consist in the abundance of p."
1Co 13: 3 If I give away all my p,

POSSIBLE
Mt 19:26 but for God all things are p."
26:39 if it is p, let this cup pass from me;

POTIPHAR*
Egyptian who bought Joseph (Ge 37:36; 39:1-6), sent him to prison (Ge 39:7-30).

POTTER → POTTER'S
Isa 64: 8 we are the clay, and you are our p;
Ro 9:21 Has the p no right over the clay,
Sir 33:13 Like clay in the hand of the p,

POTTER'S → POTTER
Jer 18: 2 go down to the p house,
Mt 27: 7 to buy the p field as a place to bury

POUR → POURED
Dt 12:16 p it out on the ground like water.
Isa 44: 3 I will p my spirit upon your
Eze 39:29 I p out my spirit upon the house of
Joel 2:28 I will p out my spirit on all flesh;
Ac 2:17 I will p out my Spirit upon all flesh,
Rev 16: 1 p out on the earth the seven bowls

POURED → POUR
Mt 26:28 is p out for many for the forgiveness
Ac 2:33 he has p out this that you both see
Tit 3: 6 This Spirit he p out on us richly

POVERTY → POOR
Pr 30: 8 give me neither p nor riches;
Mk 12:44 out of her p has put in everything
2Co 8: 9 by his p you might become rich.
Sir 11:14 p and wealth, come from the Lord.

POWER → POWERFUL, POWERS
Ex 9:16 show you my p, and to make
15: 6 right hand, O LORD, glorious in p—
1Ch 29:11 O LORD, are the greatness, the p,
Ps 68:34 Ascribe to God, whose majesty is
Pr 18:21 and life are in the p of the tongue,
Isa 40:29 He gives p to the faint,
Zec 4: 6 by might, nor by p, but by my spirit,
Mt 22:29 the scriptures nor the p of God.
Mk 13:26 coming in clouds' with great p and
Ro 1:20 creation of the world his eternal p
1Co 1:17 might not be emptied of its p.
15:24 and every authority and p.
Eph 1:19 the immeasurable greatness of his p
Php 3:10 Christ and the p of his resurrection
2Ti 3: 5 form of godliness but denying its p.
2Pe 1: 3 divine p has given us everything
Rev 19: 1 and glory and p to our God,
20: 6 these the second death has no p,
Jdt 9:14 the God of all p and might,
Sir 39:18 and none can limit his saving p.

POWERFUL → POWER
Mk 1: 7 one who is more p than I is coming
1Co 1:26 not many were p,
Heb 1: 3 he sustains all things by his p word.

POWERS → POWER
Ro 8:38 present, nor things to come, nor p,
Eph 6:12 against the cosmic p of this present

PRACTICE → PRACTICES
Mt 23: 3 for they do not p what they teach.
Sir 50:29 For if they put them into p,

PRACTICES → PRACTICE
Ex 23:24 or worship them, or follow their p,
Col 3: 9 stripped off the old self with its p

PRAISE → PRAISED, PRAISES
Ex 15: 2 this is my God, and I will p him,
Dt 10:21 He is your p; he is your God,
Ps 56: 4 whose word I p, in God I trust;
150: 6 that breathes the LORD!
Pr 27: 2 Let another p you, and not your own
31:31 let her works p her in the city gates.
Mt 21:16 nursing babies you have prepared p
1Co 14:15 but I will sing p with the mind also.
Rev 19: 5 "P our God, all you his servants,
Tob 12: 6 Bless and sing p to his name.
Sir 24: 1 THE p OF WISDOM Wisdom praises

PRAISED → PRAISE
Ps 48: 1 is the LORD and greatly to be p
Lk 23:47 what had taken place, he p God and

PRAISES → PRAISE
Ps 47: 6 Sing p to God, sing p;

PRAY → PRAYED, PRAYER, PRAYERS
1Sa 12:23 against the LORD by ceasing to p
2Ch 7:14 humble themselves, p, seek my face
Ps 5: 2 King and my God, for to you I p.
122: 6 P for the peace of Jerusalem:
Jer 7:16 As for you, do not p for this people,
Mt 5:44 and p for those who persecute you,
6: 5 you p, do not be like the hypocrites;
Lk 11: 1 teach us to p, as John taught his
Ro 8:26 do not know how to p as we ought,
1Co 14:15 but I will p with the mind also;
1Th 5:17 p without ceasing,
Jas 5:16 and p for one another, so that you
Sir 37:15 But above all p to the Most High

PRAYED → PRAY
Mk 1:35 to a deserted place, and there he p,
14:35 threw himself on the ground and p

PRAYER → PRAY
Ps 6: 9 the LORD accepts my p.
Pr 15:29 but he hears the p of the righteous.
Isa 56: 7 house shall be called a house of p
Mt 21:13 house shall be called a house of p';
Mk 11:24 I tell you, whatever you ask for in p,
Ro 12:12 patient in suffering, persevere in p.
Jas 5:16 The p of the righteous is powerful

PRAYERS → PRAY
Mk 12:40 the sake of appearance say long p.
Heb 5: 7 Jesus offered up p and supplications
Rev 5: 8 which are the p of the saints.

PREACH → PREACHING
Tit 1: 9 able both to p with sound doctrine

PREACHING → PREACH
1Ti 5:17 those who labor in p and teaching;

PRECEPT → PRECEPTS
Isa 28:10 For it is p upon p, p upon p,

PRECEPTS → PRECEPT
Ps 19: 8 the p of the LORD are right,
119:15 I will meditate on your p,
Mt 15: 9 teaching human p as doctrines.'"

PRECIOUS
Ps 72:14 and p is their blood in his sight.
Pr 3:15 She is more p than jewels,
Isa 28:16 a tested stone, a p cornerstone,
1Pe 1:19 but with the p blood of Christ,
2: 6 a cornerstone chosen and p;
2Pe 1: 1 received a faith as p as ours

PREDESTINED
Ro 8:30 those whom he p he also called;

PREDICTION* → PREDICTIONS
Isa 44:26 and fulfills the p of his messengers;

PREDICTIONS* → PREDICT
Jude 1:17 the p of the apostles of our Lord

PREPARE → PREPARED
Ps 23: 5 You p a table before me in the
Mal 3: 1 sending my messenger to p the way
Mt 3: 3 'P the way of the Lord, make his
Jn 14: 2 I have told you that I go to p a place

PREPARED → PREPARE
Lk 1:17 make ready a people p for the Lord.
1Co 2: 9 God has p for those who love him"

PRESENCE → PRESENT
Ex 25:30 the bread of the P on the table
  33:14 He said, "My p will go with you,
Ps 51:11 Do not cast me away from your p,
  139: 7 Or where can I flee from your p?
Jn 17: 5 with the glory that I had in your p
Heb 9:24 now to appear in the p of God

PRESENT → PRESENCE
Ro 6:13 but p yourselves to God as
1Co 3:22 or death or the p or the future—
Eph 5:27 the church to himself in splendor,
2Ti 2:15 p yourself to God as one approved

PRESS → PRESSED
Php 3:14 I p on toward the goal for the prize

PRESSED → PRESS
Lk 6:38 A good measure, p down, shaken
Php 1:23 I am hard p between the two:

PREVAIL → PREVAILED
1Sa 2: 9 for not by might does one p.

PREVAILED → PREVAIL
Ge 32:28 God and with humans, and have p."
Hos 12: 4 He strove with the angel and p,

PRICE
Mt 27: 9 the one on whom a p had been set,
1Co 6:20 For you were bought with a p;

PRIDE → PROUD
Ps 20: 7 our p is in the name of the LORD
Pr 16:18 P goes before destruction,
Mk 7:22 licentiousness, envy, slander, p,
1Jn 2:16 the desire of the eyes, the p in riches
Sir 10:13 For the beginning of p is sin,

PRIEST → PRIESTHOOD, PRIESTS
Ge 14:18 he was p of God Most High.
Ex 2:16 p of Midian had seven daughters.
Ne 8: 9 and Ezra the p and scribe,
Ps 110: 4 "You are a p forever according to
Mk 14:63 Then the high p tore his clothes and
Heb 3: 1 apostle and high p of our confession
  7: 3 the Son of God, he remains a p
  10:21 since we have a great p over the

PRIESTHOOD → PRIEST
Ex 29: 9 the p shall be theirs by a perpetual
Heb 7:24 but he holds his p permanently,
1Pe 2: 5 a holy p, to offer spiritual sacrifices

PRIESTS → PRIEST
Ex 28: 1 the Israelites, to serve me as p—
Dt 31: 9 this law, and gave it to the p,
Mic 3:11 its p teach for a price, its prophets
Mk 15: 3 the chief p accused him of many
Heb 7:27 Unlike the other high p, he has no
Rev 20: 6 they will be p of God and of Christ,

PRINCE → PRINCES
Isa 9: 6 Everlasting Father, P of Peace.
Eze 37:25 David shall be their p forever.
Da 10:21 princes except Michael, your p.

PRINCES → PRINCE
1Sa 2: 8 to make them sit with p and inherit
Da 8:25 even rise up against the Prince of p.

PRISCILLA*
  Wife of Aquila, also called Prisca; co-worker
with Paul (Ac 18; Ro 16:3; 1Co 16:19; 2Ti 4:19);
instructor of Apollos (Ac 18:24-28).

PRISON → PRISONER, PRISONERS
Ge 39:20 he remained there in p.
Mt 14:10 and had John beheaded in the p.
Ac 12: 5 While Peter was kept in p,
  16:26 foundations of the p were shaken;

PRISONER → PRISON
Mk 15: 6 at the festival he used to release a p
Eph 3: 1 that I Paul am a p for Christ Jesus

PRISONERS → PRISON
Ps 146: 7 The LORD sets the p free;
Isa 61: 1 to the captives, and release to the p;

PRIZE
1Co 9:24 but only one receives the p?
Php 3:14 the p of the heavenly call of God in

PROCLAIM → PROCLAIMED
Ex 33:19 p before you the name, 'The LORD';
Ps 97: 6 The heavens p his righteousness;
Mt 10:27 whispered, p from the housetops.
Lk 4:19 to p the year of the Lord's favor."
Ro 10: 8 the word of faith that we p);

PROCLAIMED → PROCLAIM
Mk 13:10 the good news must first be p to all
Col 1:23 which has been p to every creature

PRODUCE → PRODUCES
Nu 18:12 choice p that they give to the LORD,
Jos 5:11 they ate the p of the land,
Pr 3: 9 with the first fruits of all your p;

PRODUCES → PRODUCE
2Co 7:10 For godly grief p a repentance that
Jas 1: 3 testing of your faith p endurance;

PROFANE
Lev 22:32 You shall not p my holy name,
1Mc 1:45 to p sabbaths and festivals,

PROFIT
Mt 16:26 For what will it p them if they gain
Sir 29:11 and it will p you more than gold.

PROMISE → PROMISED, PROMISES
Ps 105:42 For he remembered his holy p,
Ac 2:39 the p is for you, for your children,
Eph 2:12 and strangers to the covenants of p,
1Ti 4: 8 holding p for both the present life
2Pe 3: 9 The Lord is not slow about his p,

PROMISED → PROMISE
Dt 1:11 and bless you, as he has p you!
2Sa 7:28 p this good thing to your servant;
Lk 24:49 sending upon you what my Father p
Ac 13:23 to Israel a Savior, Jesus, as he p;
Eph 1:13 with the seal of the p Holy Spirit;
Heb 10:23 for he who has p is faithful.

PROMISES → PROMISE
Jos 21:45 the good p that the LORD had made
Ps 12: 6 p of the LORD are p that are pure,
2Co 1:20 every one of God's p is a "Yes."
Heb 8: 6 has been enacted through better p.

PROOFS* → PROVE
Isa 41:21 bring your p, says the King of Jacob
Ac 1: 3 to them by many convincing p,

PROPHECIES → PROPHESY
1Co 13: 8 as for p, they will come to an end;

PROPHECY → PROPHESY
Ac 21: 9 daughters who had the gift of p.
1Co 12:10 to another p, to another
2Pe 1:20 that no p of scripture is a matter
Rev 22:18 who hears the words of the p

PROPHESY → PROPHECIES, PROPHECY,
  PROPHET, PROPHETS
Joel 2:28 sons and your daughters shall p,

Mt 7:22 Lord, did we not p in your name,
1Co 13: 9 only in part, and we p only in part;
Rev 11: 3 my two witnesses authority to p

PROPHET → PROPHESY
Ex 7: 1 your brother Aaron shall be your p.
Dt 18:18 a p like you from among their own
Mal 4: 5 the p Elijah before the great and
Lk 4:24 no p is accepted in the prophet's
  20: 6 are convinced that John was a p."
Rev 16:13 and from the mouth of the false p.
  20:10 where the beast and the false p were
1Mc 4:46 until a p should come to tell what

PROPHETS → PROPHESY
Nu 11:29 that all the LORD's people were p,
1Ki 18:40 said to them, "Seize the p of Baal;
Ps 105:15 anointed ones; do my p no harm."
Mt 5:17 come to abolish the law or the p;
  22:40 hang all the law and the p."
Lk 24:44 p, and the psalms must be fulfilled."
1Co 12:28 the church first apostles, second p,
Eph 2:20 the foundation of the apostles and
  p,
  4:11 some p, some evangelists,
Rev 11:10 these two p had been a torment to
  18:20 you saints and apostles and p!
1Mc 9:27 that p ceased to appear among
  them.

PROSPER → PROSPERING, PROSPERITY,
  PROSPEROUS
Ge 39: 3 LORD caused all that he did to p
Ps 1: 3 In all that they do, they p.
Isa 53:10 the will of the LORD shall p.

PROSPERING → PROSPER
Dt 30: 9 will again take delight in p you,

PROSPERITY → PROSPER
Dt 30:15 have set before you today life and p,
Ps 73: 3 I saw the p of the wicked.
Isa 48:18 your p would have been like a river,

PROSPEROUS → PROSPER
Jos 1: 8 For then you shall make your way p

PROSTITUTE → PROSTITUTES
Ex 34:15 they p themselves to their gods
Jos 2: 1 a p whose name was Rahab.
1Co 6:15 make them members of a p?
Heb 11:31 By faith Rahab the p did not perish

PROSTITUTES → PROSTITUTE
Mt 21:31 the p are going into the kingdom of
1Co 6: 9 idolaters, adulterers, male p,
Sir 9: 6 Do not give yourself to p,

PROTECT → PROTECTS
Ps 91:14 I will p those who know my name.
Jn 17:11 p them in your name that you have

PROTECTS → PROTECT
Ps 116: 6 The LORD p the simple;
Jdt 9:14 no other who p the people of Israel

PROUD → PRIDE
Ps 94: 2 give to the p what they deserve!
Pr 21: 4 Haughty eyes and a p heart—
Jas 4: 6 God opposes the p, but gives grace
Sir 10: 9 How can dust and ashes be p?

PROVE → PROOFS, PROVED
Heb 6:18 impossible that God would p false,

PROVED → PROVE
Ro 3: 4 let God be p true,

PROVERBS
1Ki 4:32 He composed three thousand p,
Pr 1: 1 The p of Solomon son of David,
Ecc 12: 9 and studying and arranging many p.
Sir 39: 3 seeks out the hidden meanings of p

PROVIDE → PROVIDES
Ge 22: 8 "God himself will p the lamb for
1Co 10:13 testing he will also p the way out

PROVIDES → PROVIDE
Ps 111: 5 He **p** food for those who fear him;
1Ti 6:17 who richly **p** us with everything

PROVOKE → PROVOKED
Dt 32:21 **p** them with a foolish nation.
Jer 25: 6 not **p** me to anger with the work of
Heb 10:24 how to **p** one another to love

PROVOKED → PROVOKE
Ps 78:41 and **p** the Holy One of Israel.

PROWLS*
1Pe 5: 8 your adversary the devil **p** around,

PRUNES
Jn 15: 2 he **p** to make it bear more fruit.

PSALM → PSALMS
Ps 47: 7 sing praises with a **p**.
Jdt 16: 1 Raise to him a new **p**;

PSALMS → PSALM
Lk 24:44 and the **p** must be fulfilled."
Eph 5:19 you sing **p** and hymns and spiritual

PUBLIC
Mt 1:19 to expose her to **p** disgrace,
Col 2:15 and made a **p** example of them,
1Ti 4:13 to the **p** reading of scripture,

PUFFED → PUFFS
Col 2:18 **p** up without cause by a human way
1Ti 3: 6 or he may be **p** up with conceit

PUFFS* → PUFFED
1Co 8: 1 Knowledge **p** up, but love builds up.

PUNISH → PUNISHING, PUNISHMENT
Ex 32:34 I will **p** them for their sin."
2Sa 7:14 I will **p** him with a rod such as
Jer 21:14 I will **p** you according to the fruit of
1Pe 2:14 by him to **p** those who do wrong

PUNISHING → PUNISH
Dt 5: 9 **p** children for the iniquity of parents
Joel 2:13 in steadfast love, and relents from **p**.

PUNISHMENT → PUNISH
Ge 4:13 "My **p** is greater than I can bear!
Isa 53: 5 was the **p** that made us whole,
Mt 25:46 these will go away into eternal **p**,
1Jn 4:18 for fear has to do with **p**,

PURE → PURIFICATION, PURIFIED, PURIFY, PURITY
2Sa 22:27 with the **p** you show yourself **p**,
Ps 19: 9 the fear of the LORD is **p**, enduring
  119: 9 can young people keep their way **p**?
Hab 1:13 Your eyes are too **p** to behold evil,
Mt 5: 8 "Blessed are the **p** in heart, for they
Php 4: 8 whatever is **p**, whatever is pleasing,
Tit 1:15 To the **p** all things are **p**,
1Jn 3: 3 purify themselves, just as he is **p**.

PURIFICATION → PURE
Jn 2: 6 water jars for the Jewish rites of **p**,
Heb 1: 3 When he had made **p** for sins,

PURIFIED → PURE
Da 12:10 Many shall be **p**, cleansed, and
1Pe 1:22 **p** your souls by your obedience to

PURIFY → PURE
Tit 2:14 **p** for himself a people of his own
Heb 9:14 **p** our conscience from dead works

PURIM
Est 9:26 are called **P**, from the word Pur.

PURITY → PURE
2Co 6: 6 by **p**, knowledge, patience, kindness
1Pe 3: 2 the **p** and reverence of your lives.

PURPLE
Ex 25: 4 **p**, and crimson yarns and fine linen,
Mk 15:17 And they clothed him in a **p** cloak;

PURPOSE
Ps 57: 2 to God who fulfills his **p** for me.
Isa 46:10 saying, "My **p** shall stand,

Ro 8:28 who are called according to his **p**.
Eph 3:11 was in accordance with the eternal **p**
2Ti 1: 9 works but according to his own **p**

PURSUE → PURSUED, PURSUES
Ps 34:14 and do good; seek peace, and **p** it.
Ro 14:19 Let us then **p** what makes for
  peace
1Ti 6:11 **p** righteousness, godliness, faith,
Sir 27: 8 If you **p** justice, you will attain it

PURSUED → PURSUE
Ex 14:23 Egyptians **p**, and went into the sea
Ps 18:37 I **p** my enemies and overtook them;

PURSUES → PURSUE
Pr 21:21 Whoever **p** righteousness
Sir 31: 5 **p** money will be led astray by it.

PUT
Isa 42: 1 I have **p** my spirit upon him;
Eze 36:27 I will **p** my spirit within you,
Mt 12:18 I will **p** my Spirit upon him,
Eph 6:11 **P** on the whole armor of God,

Q

QUAILS
Ex 16:13 In the evening **q** came up
Nu 11:31 and it brought **q** from the sea and

QUARRELED → QUARRELSOME
Ex 17: 7 the Israelites **q** and tested the LORD,
Nu 20: 3 The people **q** with Moses and said,

QUARRELSOME → QUARRELED
1Ti 3: 3 not **q**, and not a lover of money.
2Ti 2:24 the Lord's servant must not be **q**

QUEEN
1Ki 10: 1 the **q** of Sheba heard of the fame of
Est 2:17 and made her **q** instead of Vashti.
Mt 12:42 The **q** of the South will rise up at
Rev 18: 7 in her heart she says, 'I rule as a **q**;

QUESTIONS
2Ch 9: 1 to Jerusalem to test him with hard **q**,
Mt 22:46 anyone dare to ask him any more **q**.

QUICK → QUICKLY
Jas 1:19 be **q** to listen, slow to speak,
Sir 5:11 Be **q** to hear, but deliberate

QUICKLY → QUICK
Jn 13:27 "Do **q** what you are going to do."
Ro 9:28 execute his sentence on the earth **q**
Gal 1: 6 so **q** deserting the one who called

QUIET
1Ti 2: 2 **q** and peaceable life in all godliness
1Pe 3: 4 beauty of a gentle and **q** spirit,

QUIVER
Ps 127: 5 Happy is the man who has his **q** full
  of
Isa 49: 2 in his **q** he hid me away.

R

RABBI
Mt 23: 8 But you are not to be called **r**,
Jn 1:38 "**R**" (which translated means
  Teacher),

RACE
Ecc 9:11 the sun the **r** is not to the swift,
1Co 9:24 that in a **r** the runners all compete,
Heb 12: 1 let us run with perseverance the **r**
1Pe 2: 9 But you are a chosen **r**, a royal

RACHEL
Daughter of Laban (Ge 29:16); wife of Jacob (Ge 29:28); bore two sons (Ge 30:22-24; 35:16-24; 46:19). Stole Laban's gods (Ge 31:19, 32-35). Death (Ge 35:19-20).

RAHAB
Prostitute who hid Israelite spies (Jos 2; 6:22-25; Heb 11:31; Jas 2:25). Mother of Boaz (Mt 1:5).

RAIN → RAINBOW, RAINED, RAINS
Ge 7: 4 For in seven days I will send **r** on
1Ki 17: 1 neither dew nor **r** these years,
Isa 45: 8 let the skies **r** down righteousness;
Mt 5:45 sends **r** on the righteous and on the
Rev 11: 6 so that no **r** may fall during the days

RAINBOW → BOW
Rev 4: 3 the throne is a **r** that looks like an

RAINED → RAIN
Ge 19:24 **r** on Sodom and Gomorrah sulfur
Ex 9:23 LORD **r** hail on the land of Egypt;

RAINS → RAIN
Lev 26: 4 I will give you your **r** in their season
Jas 5: 7 receives the early and the late **r**.

RAISE → RISE
Dt 18:15 God will **r** up for you a prophet
Jn 2:19 and in three days I will **r** it up."
2Co 4:14 who raised the Lord Jesus will **r** us

RAISED → RISE
Mt 17:23 and on the third day he will be **r**."
Ac 2:24 God **r** him up, having freed him
Ro 4:25 and was **r** for our justification.
1Co 15: 4 **r** on the third day in accordance

RAM → RAMS
Ge 22:13 and took the **r** and offered it up as
Ex 29:22 (for it is a **r** of ordination),
Da 8: 3 saw a **r** standing beside the river.

RAMS → RAM
1Sa 15:22 and to heed than the fat of **r**.

RANSOM → RANSOMED
Ps 49: 8 For the **r** of life is costly, and can
Mt 20:28 and to give his life a **r** for many."
1Ti 2: 6 who gave himself a **r** for all

RANSOMED → RANSOM
Isa 35:10 And the **r** of the LORD shall return,
Rev 5: 9 by your blood you **r** for God saints

RAVENS
1Ki 17: 6 **r** brought him bread and meat in
Lk 12:24 Consider the **r**: they neither sow

READ → READING
Ex 24: 7 and **r** it in the hearing of the people;
Jos 8:34 he **r** all the words of the law,
Ne 8: 8 they **r** from the book, from the law
Lk 4:16 as was his custom. He stood up to **r**,
2Co 3:15 this very day whenever Moses is **r**,

READING → READ
Ac 8:30 you understand what you are **r**?"

READY
Lk 1:17 a people prepared for the Lord."
Rev 19: 7 and his bride has made herself **r**;

REAP
Gal 6: 7 for you **r** whatever you sow.
Rev 14:15 for the hour to **r** has come,

REBEKAH
Sister of Laban, secured as bride for Isaac (Ge 24). Mother of Esau and Jacob (Ge 25:19-26). Taken by Abimelech as sister of Isaac; returned (Ge 26:1-11). Encouraged Jacob to trick Isaac out of blessing (Ge 27:1-17).

REBEL → REBELLED, REBELLION
Ex 23:21 do not **r** against him, for he will
1Sa 12:14 not **r** against the commandment

REBELLED → REBEL
Nu 20:24 because you **r** against my command
Ne 9:26 they were disobedient and **r**

REBELLION → REBEL
1Sa 15:23 For **r** is no less a sin than divination,
2Th 2: 3 the **r** comes first and the lawless one

REBUILD → BUILD
Ezr 1: 3 and **r** the house of the LORD,
Ne 2:17 let us **r** the wall of Jerusalem,
Da 9:25 went out to restore and **r** Jerusalem
Ac 15:16 and I will **r** the dwelling of David,

REBUKE
Ps 6: 1 O LORD, do not **r** me in your anger,
Pr 27: 5 Better is open **r** than hidden love.
Zec 3: 2 said to Satan, "The LORD **r** you,
Mk 8:32 Peter took him aside and began to **r**
2Ti 4: 2 convince, **r**, and encourage,

RECEIVE → RECEIVED
Jn 16:24 Ask and you will **r**, so that your joy
Ac 2:38 you will **r** the gift of the Holy Spirit.
20:35 'It is more blessed to give than to **r.**'
Rev 4:11 to **r** glory and honor and power,

RECEIVED → RECEIVE
Mt 6: 2 I tell you, they have **r** their reward.
Jn 1:12 But to all who **r** him, who believed
1Co 11:23 I **r** from the Lord what I also handed

RECKONED → RECKONING
Ge 15: 6 LORD **r** it to him as righteousness.
Ro 4: 3 it was **r** to him as righteousness."

RECKONING → RECKONED
Ge 9: 5 I will require a **r** for human life.
Sir 2:14 you do when the Lord's **r** comes?

RECONCILE → RECONCILED, RECONCILIATION
Ac 7:26 were quarreling and tried to **r** them,
Col 1:20 God was pleased to **r** to himself all

RECONCILED → RECONCILE
Mt 5:24 first be **r** to your brother or sister,
1Co 7:11 let her remain unmarried or else be **r**

RECONCILIATION → RECONCILE
Ro 5:11 whom we have now received **r.**
2Co 5:18 and has given us the ministry of **r**;

RED
Ex 15: 4 officers were sunk in the **R** Sea.
Mt 16: 3 for the sky is **r** and threatening.'
Rev 12: 3 a great **r** dragon, with seven heads

REDEEM → REDEEMED, REDEEMER, REDEMPTION
Ex 6: 6 I will **r** you with an outstretched
2Sa 7:23 whose God went to **r** it as a people,
Gal 4: 5 to **r** those who were under the law,

REDEEMED → REDEEM
Dt 15:15 and the LORD your God **r** you;
Ps 107: 2 Let the **r** of the LORD say so,

REDEEMER → REDEEM
Job 19:25 For I know that my **R** lives,
Ps 19:14 O LORD, my rock and my **r.**
Isa 48:17 Thus says the LORD, your **R,**

REDEMPTION → REDEEM
Lk 21:28 because your **r** is drawing near."
Eph 1: 7 In him we have **r** through his blood,
Heb 9:12 own blood, thus obtaining eternal **r.**

REFINE → REFINED
Jer 9: 7 I will now **r** and test them,
Zec 13: 9 **r** them as one refines silver,

REFINED → REFINE
Da 12:10 shall be purified, cleansed, and **r,**

REFLECTED → REFLECTION
2Co 3:18 though **r** in a mirror,

REFLECTION → REFLECTED
1Co 11: 7 since he is the image and **r** of God;
Heb 1: 3 He is the **r** of God's glory

REFUGE
Nu 35:11 select cities to be cities of **r** for you,
Ps 2:12 Happy are all who take **r** in him.

Pr 30: 5 a shield to those who take **r** in him.
Jer 16:19 my **r** in the day of trouble,

REFUSE
Ex 8: 2 If you **r** to let them go,
Eze 3:27 and let those who **r** to hear, **r**;
Heb 12:25 do not **r** the one who is speaking;

REGARD
Isa 8:13 of hosts, him you shall **r** as holy;
Php 2: 6 did not **r** equality with God as
3: 7 these I have come to **r** as loss
Heb 12: 5 not **r** lightly the discipline of the

REGULATIONS
Col 2:20 Why do you submit to **r,**
Heb 9:10 **r** for the body imposed until the

REHOBOAM
Son of Solomon (1Ki 11:43; 1Ch 3:10). Harsh treatment of subjects caused divided kingdom (1Ki 12:1-24; 14:21-31; 2Ch 10-12).

REIGN → REIGNS
Ex 15:18 The LORD will **r** forever and ever."
Ps 146:10 The LORD will **r** forever,
1Co 15:25 **r** until he has put all his enemies
2Ti 2:12 we will also **r** with him;
Rev 11:15 and he will **r** forever and ever."
22: 5 and they will **r** forever and ever.

REIGNS → REIGN
Isa 52: 7 who says to Zion, "Your God **r.**"
Rev 19: 6 the Lord our God the Almighty **r.**

REJECT → REJECTED
Ex 20: 5 generation of those who **r** me,
Isa 30:12 Because you **r** this word,

REJECTED → REJECT
1Sa 8: 7 but they have **r** me from being king
Ps 60: 1 O God, you have **r** us, broken our
118:22 The stone that the builders **r**
Isa 53: 3 He was despised and **r** by others;
Mt 21:42 'The stone that the builders **r**
1Pe 2: 4 though **r** by mortals yet chosen and

REJOICE → REJOICING
Ps 5:11 But let all who take refuge in you **r**;
118:24 let us **r** and be glad in it.
Isa 62: 5 so shall your God **r** over you.
Zep 3:17 he will **r** over you with gladness,
Lk 6:23 **R** in that day and leap for joy,
Php 4: 4 **R** in the Lord always; again I will say, **R.**

REJOICING → REJOICE
2Sa 6:12 to the city of David with **r**;
Ne 8:17 And there was very great **r.**
2Co 6:10 as sorrowful, yet always **r**;

RELEASE
Isa 61: 1 liberty to the captives, and **r** to
Mt 27:15 the governor was accustomed to **r**

RELENT → RELENTED
Eze 24:14 I will not spare, I will not **r.**
Joel 2:14 whether he will not turn and **r,**
Jnh 3: 9 God may **r** and change his mind;

RELENTED → RELENT
1Ch 21:15 LORD took note and **r** concerning
Jer 4:28 I have not **r** nor will I turn back.

RELIGION
Jas 1:27 **R** that is pure and undefiled before

RELY
2Ch 14:11 O LORD our God, for we **r** on you,
Pr 3: 5 and do not **r** on your own insight.
Gal 3:10 all who **r** on the works of the law
Sir 5: 1 Do not **r** on your wealth,

REMAIN → REMAINS
1Co 7:20 Let each of you **r** in the condition
Heb 1:11 they will perish, but you **r**;

REMAINS → REMAIN
Jos 13: 2 This is the land that still **r**:
Heb 7: 3 Son of God, he **r** a priest forever.
10:26 there no longer **r** a sacrifice for sins,

REMEMBER → REMEMBERED, REMEMBRANCE
Ge 9:15 I will **r** my covenant that is between
Ex 20: 8 **R** the sabbath day, and keep it holy.
Dt 8:18 But **r** the LORD your God,
Job 10: 9 **R** that you fashioned me like clay;
Ecc 12: 1 **R** your creator in the days of your
Jer 31:34 and **r** their sin no more.
2Ti 2: 8 **R** Jesus Christ, raised from the dead
Heb 8:12 and I will **r** their sins no more."
Sir 23:18 The Most High will not **r** sins."

REMEMBERED → REMEMBER
Ex 2:24 God **r** his covenant with Abraham,
Ps 78:35 They **r** that God was their rock,
106:45 For their sake he **r** his covenant,
Rev 16:19 God **r** great Babylon and gave her

REMEMBRANCE → REMEMBER
Lk 22:19 Do this in **r** of me."

REMNANT
Ge 45: 7 before you to preserve for you a **r**
Isa 10:21 A **r** will return, the **r** of Jacob,
Jer 50:20 will pardon the **r** that I have spared.
Ro 9:27 only a **r** of them will be saved;

REMOVE
Eze 36:26 **r** from your body the heart of stone
Lk 22:42 if you are willing, **r** this cup from

RENEW → RENEWAL, RENEWED, RENEWING
Isa 40:31 for the LORD shall **r** their strength,
La 5:21 **r** our days as of old—

RENEWAL → RENEW
Mt 19:28 I tell you, at the **r** of all things,
Col 3:11 In that **r** there is no longer Greek

RENEWED → RENEW
2Co 4:16 inner nature is being **r** day by day.
Eph 4:23 to be **r** in the spirit of your minds,

RENEWING* → RENEW
Ro 12: 2 transformed by the **r** of your minds,

REPAY → PAY
Ps 28: 4 **R** them according to their work,
Isa 59:18 to their deeds, so will he **r**;
Ro 12:17 Do not **r** anyone evil for evil,
Rev 18: 6 and **r** her double for her deeds;

REPENT → REPENTANCE
1Ki 8:47 **r**, and plead with you in the land
Job 42: 6 and **r** in dust and ashes."
Mt 3: 2 "**R,** for the kingdom of heaven has
Ac 2:38 "**R,** and be baptized every one of
Rev 16: 9 they did not **r** and give him glory.
Sir 18:21 and when you have sinned, **r.**

REPENTANCE → REPENT
Mk 1: 4 a baptism of **r** for the forgiveness
Lk 3: 8 Bear fruits worthy of **r.**
Ro 2: 4 kindness is meant to lead you to **r**?
2Co 7:10 **r** that leads to salvation and brings
2Pe 3: 9 any to perish, but all to come to **r.**

REPROVE
Pr 19:25 **r** the intelligent, and they will gain
Tit 2:15 exhort and **r** with all authority.
Rev 3:19 **r** and discipline those whom I love.

REQUIRE
Dt 10:12 does the LORD your God **r** of you?
Mic 6: 8 the LORD **r** of you but to do justice,

RESCUE → RESCUED, RESCUES
Ps 22: 8 him **r** the one in whom he delights!"
Mt 6:13 but **r** us from the evil one.
2Pe 2: 9 the Lord knows how to **r** the godly

RESCUED → RESCUE
Col   1:13 has r us from the power of darkness
Sir   51:12 and r me in time of trouble.

RESCUES → RESCUE
Ps   37:40 The LORD helps them and r them;
Da   6:27 and r, he works signs and wonders
1Th   1:10 Jesus, who r us from the wrath that

RESIST
Mt   5:39 I say to you, Do not r an evildoer.
Ro   9:19 For who can r his will?"
Jas   4: 7 R the devil, and he will flee from

RESPECT
Mal   1: 6 if I am a master, where is the r due
Ro   13: 7 r to whom r is due,

REST → RESTED, RESTS
Ex   31:15 seventh day is a sabbath of solemn r
2Sa   7:11 give you r from all your enemies.
Ps   95:11 swore, "They shall not enter my r."
Mt   11:28 and I will give you r.
Heb   4:10 those who enter God's r also cease

RESTED → REST
Ge   2: 2 he r on the seventh day from all the
Ex   20:11 all that is in them, but r the seventh

RESTORE → RESTORES
Dt   30: 3 LORD your God will r your fortunes
Ps   51:12 R to me the joy of your salvation,
Da   9:25 the word went out to r and rebuild
Mt   17:11 "Elijah is indeed coming and will r

RESTORES → RESTORE
Ps   23: 3 he r my soul. He leads me in right

RESTS → REST
Ps   16: 9 my body also r secure.
Pr   19:23 one r secure and suffers no harm.

RESURRECTION
Mt   22:30 For in the r they neither marry nor
Mk   12:18 Sadducees, who say there is no r,
Jn   11:25 said to her, "I am the r and the life.
1Co   15:12 you say there is no r of the dead?
Php   3:10 know Christ and the power of his r
Rev   20: 5 This is the first r.
2Es   2:23 will give you the first place in my r.

RETURN
Ge   3:19 you are dust, and to dust you shall r.
Dt   30: 2 and r to the LORD your God,
Ps   116:12 What shall I r to the LORD
Hos   14: 1 R, O Israel, to the LORD your God,
Mal   3: 7 R to me, and I will r to you,

REUBEN
Firstborn of Jacob by Leah (Ge 29:32; 46:8; 1Ch 2:1). Attempted to rescue Joseph (Ge 37:21-30). Lost birthright for sleeping with Bilhah (Ge 35:22; 49:4). Tribe of blessed (Ge 49:3-4; Dt 33:6), numbered (Nu 1:21; 26:7), allotted land east of Jordan (Nu 32; 34:14; Jos 13:15), west (Eze 48:6), failed to help Deborah (Jdg 5:15-16), supported David (1Ch 12:37), 12,000 from (Rev 7:5).

REVEAL → REVEALED, REVELATION, REVELATIONS
Mt   11:27 to whom the Son chooses to r him.

REVEALED → REVEAL
Isa   40: 5 the glory of the LORD shall be r,
Mt   16:17 flesh and blood has not r this to you
Lk   17:30 on the day that the Son of Man is r.
Ro   1:17 in it the righteousness of God is r
2Th   1: 7 the Lord Jesus is r from heaven
1Jn   3: 2 we do know is this: when he is r,

REVELATION → REVEAL
1Co   14: 6 some r or knowledge or prophecy
Eph   3: 3 was made known to me by r,
Rev   1: 1 The r of Jesus Christ, which God

REVELATIONS → REVEAL
2Co   12: 1 but I will go on to visions and r of

REVERE → REVERENCE
Jos   24:14 "Now therefore r the LORD,
Mal   4: 2 But for you who r my name the sun
Tob   4: 5 "R the Lord all your days,

REVERENCE → REVERE
Eph   5:21 subject to one another out of r for
1Pe   3: 2 see the purity and r of your lives.

REVILE → REVILED
Ex   22:28 You shall not r God, or curse
Mt   5:11 people r you and persecute you

REVILED → REVILE
1Co   4:12 When r, we bless;
1Pe   4:14 If you are r for the name of Christ,

REWARD → REWARDED
Ps   19:11 in keeping them there is great r.
Isa   40:10 r is with him, and his recompense
Mt   6: 5 I tell you, they have received their r.
Lk   6:23 for surely your r is great in heaven;
Heb   11:26 for he was looking ahead to the r.
Rev   22:12 I am coming soon; my r is with me,

REWARDED → REWARD
2Sa   22:21 The LORD r me according to my

RIB
Ge   2:22 r that the LORD God had taken from

RICH → RICHES
Pr   23: 4 Do not wear yourself out to get r;
Mt   19:23 hard for a r person to enter the
Lk   12:21 but are not r toward God."
2Co   8: 9 by his poverty you might become r.
Eph   2: 4 But God, who is r in mercy,
1Ti   6:18 to do good, to be r in good works,
Jas   1:10 and the r in being brought low,

RICHES → RICH
Ps   62:10 if r increase, do not set your heart
Pr   30: 8 give me neither poverty nor r;
Lk   8:14 they are choked by the cares and r
Ro   11:33 O the depth of the r and wisdom
1Jn   2:16 the desire of the eyes, the pride in r
Sir   13:24 R are good if they are free from sin;

RID
Col   3: 8 But now you must get r of all such
1Pe   2: 1 R yourselves, therefore, of all

RIDER → RIDES, RIDING
Rev   19:11 Its r is called Faithful and True,

RIDES → RIDER
Dt   33:26 r through the heavens to your help,
Ps   68: 4 a song to him who r upon the clouds

RIDING → RIDER
Zec   9: 9 humble and r on a donkey,

RIGHT → BIRTHRIGHT
Ex   15: 6 Your r hand, O LORD, glorious in
Dt   6:18 Do what is r and good in the sight
Job   42: 7 have not spoken of me what is r,
Ps   110: 1 says to my lord, "Sit at my r hand
Pr   14:12 a person,
Mt   25:33 sheep at his r hand and the goats at
Ac   2:34 said to my Lord, "Sit at my r hand,
Heb   1:13 "Sit at my r hand until I make your
1Pe   3:14 if you do suffer for doing what is r,

RIGHTEOUS → RIGHTEOUSNESS
Ge   18:23 "Will you indeed sweep away the r
Job   4:17 'Can mortals be r before God?
Ps   11: 7 For the LORD is r; he loves r deeds;
Pr   10: 6 Blessings are on the head of the r,
   11:23 desire of the r ends only in good;
   15:29 but he hears the prayer of the r.
Jer   23: 5 I will raise up for David a r Branch,
Eze   3:20 if the r turn from their righteousness
Hab   2: 4 but the r live by their faith.
Mt   5:45 rain on the r and on the unrighteous.
Mk   2:17 come to call not the r but sinners."
Ro   1:17 one who is r will live by faith."

RIGHTEOUSNESS → RIGHTEOUS
Ro   5:19 the many will be made r.
Heb   10:38 but my r one will live by faith.
1Jn   2: 1 with the Father, Jesus Christ the r;
Rev   19: 8 the fine linen is the r deeds of the
Wis   5:15 r live forever, and their reward
Sir   35:22 and does justice for the r,

RIGHTEOUSNESS → RIGHTEOUS
Ge   15: 6 the LORD reckoned it to him as r.
Ps   9: 8 He judges the world with r;
Pr   12:28 In the path of r there is life,
Ecc   7:15 people who perish in their r,
Isa   11: 5 R shall be the belt around his waist,
Jer   23: 6 be called: "The LORD is our r."
Da   9:24 to bring in everlasting r,
   12: 3 and those who lead many to r,
Hos   10:12 Sow for yourselves r; reap steadfast
Mt   5: 6 those who hunger and thirst for r,
Jn   16: 8 about sin and r and judgment:
Ro   5:18 act of r leads to justification
   10: 4 be r for everyone who believes.
Gal   3: 6 and it was reckoned to him as r,"
Eph   6:14 and put on the breastplate of r.
1Pe   2:24 free from sins, we might live for r;
2Pe   3:13 heavens and a new earth, where r is
Rev   19:11 and in r he judges and makes war.

RIPE
Joel   3:13 Put in the sickle, for the harvest is r.
Jn   4:35 how the fields are r for harvesting.
Rev   14:15 the harvest of the earth is fully r."

RISE → ARISE, RAISE, RAISED, ROSE
Nu   24:17 and a scepter shall r out of Israel;
Ps   94: 2 R up, O judge of the earth;
Da   12:13 shall r for your reward at the end of
Mal   4: 2 the sun of righteousness shall r,
Mt   27:63 'After three days I will r again.'
Eph   5:14 R from the dead, and Christ will
1Th   4:16 and the dead in Christ will r first.

RIVER → RIVERS
Ps   46: 4 a r whose streams make glad the
Isa   48:18 prosperity would have been like a r,
Eze   47:12 On the banks, on both sides of the r,
Mt   3: 6 baptized by him in the r Jordan,
Rev   22: 1 showed me the r of the water of life,

RIVERS → RIVER
Ps   137: 1 By the r of Babylon—there we sat
Rev   8:10 it fell on a third of the r and on the

ROAD → CROSSROADS
Mt   7:13 and the r is easy that leads to

ROAR → ROARING, ROARS
Ps   46: 3 though its waters r and foam,
Jer   25:30 The LORD will r from on high,

ROARING → ROAR
1Pe   5: 8 a r lion your adversary the devil

ROARS → ROAR
Hos   11:10 the LORD, who r like a lion;
Joel   3:16 The LORD r from Zion,

ROB → ROBBER, ROBBERS
Mal   3: 8 anyone r God? Yet you are robbing

ROBBER → ROB
1Co   5:11 an idolater, reviler, drunkard, or r.

ROBBERS → ROB
Jer   7:11 become a den of r in your sight?
Mt   21:13 but you are making it a den of r."

ROBE → ROBED, ROBES
Ge   37: 3 had made him a long r with sleeves.
Ex   28: 4 a breastpiece, an ephod, a r,
Jn   19: 5 crown of thorns and the purple r.
Rev   6:11 They were each given a white r and
   19:13 He is clothed in a r dipped in blood,

ROBED → ROBE
Ps   93: 1 LORD is king, he is r in majesty;
Rev   15: 6 r in pure bright linen,

ROBES → ROBE
Mk   12:38 who like to walk around in long r,
Rev   22:14 Blessed are those who wash their r,

ROCK
Ex   17: 6 Strike the r, and water will come
Nu   20: 8 you shall bring water out of the r
1Sa   2: 2 there is no R like our God.
Ps   19:14 O LORD, my r and my redeemer.
Isa   44: 8 There is no other r; I know not one.
Mt   16:18 and on this r I will build my church,
Mk   15:46 that had been hewn out of the r.
1Pe   2: 8 and a r that makes them fall."

ROD
2Sa   7:14 I will punish him with a r such as
Ps   2: 9 shall break them with a r of iron,
       23: 4 your r and your staff—they comfort
Pr   13:24 who spare the r hate their children,
Heb   9: 4 and Aaron's r that budded,
Rev   2:27 to rule them with an iron r,

ROLL
Am   5:24 But let justice r down like waters,
Mk   16: 3 "Who will r away the stone for us

ROOF
Jos   2: 6 to the r and hidden them
2Sa   11: 2 he saw from the r a woman bathing;
Mk   2: 4 they removed the r above him;

ROOM
Mk   14:15 He will show you a large r upstairs,
Ro   12:19 but leave r for the wrath of God;
Eph   4:27 and do not make r for the devil.

ROOT → ROOTED
Isa   11:10 On that day the r of Jesse
       53: 2 and like a r out of dry ground;
Ro   15:12 "The r of Jesse shall come,
1Ti   6:10 For the love of money is a r of all
Rev   5: 5 the tribe of Judah, the R of David,

ROOTED → ROOT
Eph   3:17 are being r and grounded in love.

ROSE → RISE
SS   2: 1 I am a r of Sharon, a lily
1Th   4:14 believe that Jesus died and r again,

ROUGH
Isa   40: 4 and the r places a plain.
Lk   3: 5 and the r ways made smooth;

ROYAL
Jas   2: 8 if you really fulfill the r law
1Pe   2: 9 are a chosen race, a r priesthood,

RUBBISH
1Co   4:13 have become like the r of the world,
Php   3: 8 and I regard them as r,

RUIN → RUINS
Eze   21:27 A r, a r, a r—I will make it!
Zep   1:15 a day of r and devastation,

RUINS → RUIN
Ezr   9: 9 the house of our God, to repair its r,
Ne   2:17 Jerusalem lies in r with its gates
Ac   15:16 from its r I will rebuild it,
1Co   15:33 "Bad company r good morals."
1Mc   3:43 "Let us restore the r of our people,

RULE → RULER, RULER'S, RULERS, RULES
Ge   3:16 husband, and he shall r over you."
Ps   110: 2 R in the midst of your foes.
Eph   1:21 far above all r and authority and
Col   3:15 the peace of Christ r in your hearts,
Rev   19:15 he will r them with a rod of iron;

RULER → RULE
Ex   2:14 made you a r and judge over us?
Mt   2: 6 a r who is to shepherd my people
1Co   15:24 after he has destroyed every r
Rev   1: 5 and the r of the kings of the earth.

RULER'S → RULE
Ge   49:10 the r staff from between his feet,

RULERS → RULE
Ps   2: 2 and the r take counsel together,
Isa   40:23 makes the r of the earth as nothing.
Eph   6:12 against the r, against the authorities,

RULES → RULE
Ps   66: 7 who r by his might forever,
Isa   40:10 and his arm r for him;
2Ti   2: 5 competing according to the r.

RUMORS
Mt   24: 6 you will hear of wars and r of wars;

RUN → FORERUNNER, RUNNERS
Isa   40:31 they shall r and not be weary,
Gal   2: 2 or had not r, in vain.
Heb   12: 1 let us r with perseverance the race

RUNNERS* → RUN
1Co   9:24 that in a race the r all compete,

RUST
Mt   6:19 where moth and r consume
LtJ   6:12 cannot save themselves from r

RUTH
       Moabitess; widow who went to Bethlehem with
   mother-in-law Naomi (Ru 1). Gleaned in field of
   Boaz (Ru 2). Proposed marriage to
   Boaz (Ru 3). Married (Ru 4:1-12); bore Obed, ancestor of David (Ru 4:13-22), Jesus (Mt 1:5).

S

SABBATH
Ex   20: 8 Remember the s day, and keep it
                holy.
2Ch   36:21 the days that it lay desolate it kept s,
Mt   12: 1 through the grainfields on the s;
Mk   2:28 Son of Man is lord even of the s."
1Mc   1:43 to idols and profaned the s.

SACKCLOTH → CLOTH
Da   9: 3 supplication with fasting and s and
Mt   11:21 would have repented long ago in s

SACRED
Ex   28: 2 You shall make s vestments for
       34:13 and cut down their s poles

SACRIFICE → SACRIFICED, SACRIFICES
Ex   12:27 'It is the passover s to the LORD,
Lev   3: 1 If the offering is a s of well-being,
1Sa   15:22 Surely, to obey is better than s,
Ps   40: 6 S and offering you do not desire,
Pr   15: 8 s of the wicked is an abomination
Da   9:27 he shall make s and offering cease;
Hos   6: 6 For I desire steadfast love and not s,
Mt   9:13 this means, 'I desire mercy, not s.'
Ro   3:25 put forward as a s of atonement
Php   4:18 as acceptable and pleasing to God.
Heb   13:15 let us continually offer a s of praise
1Jn   2: 2 and he is the atoning s for our sins,

SACRIFICED → SACRIFICE
1Co   5: 7 our paschal lamb, Christ, has been
                s.
        8: 1 Now concerning food s to idols:

SACRIFICES → SACRIFICE
Mk   12:33 all whole burnt offerings and s."
Heb   7:27 has no need to offer s day after day,

SADDUCEES
Mt   16: 6 the yeast of the Pharisees and S."
Mk   12:18 S, who say there is no resurrection,

SAFE → SAFETY
Ps   37:28 righteous shall be kept s forever,
Pr   18:10 the righteous run into it and are s.

SAFETY → SAFE
Dt   12:10 around so that you live in s,
Eze   34:28 they shall live in s,

SAINTS
Ps   31:23 Love the LORD, all you his s.
Ro   8:27 the Spirit intercedes for the s

1Co   6: 2 that the s will judge the world?
Eph   4:12 equip the s for the work of ministry,
Rev   5: 9 by your blood you ransomed for
                God s

SALT
Ge   19:26 back, and she became a pillar of s.
Mt   5:13 "You are the s of the earth;

SALVATION → SAVE
Ex   15: 2 and he has become my s;
Ps   27: 1 The LORD is my light and my s;
       51:12 Restore to me the joy of your s,
Isa   12: 3 draw water from the wells of s.
       52: 7 brings good news, who announces s,
La   3:26 one should wait quietly for the s
Hab   3:18 I will exult in the God of my s.
Lk   3: 6 all flesh shall see the s of God.'"
Ac   4:12 There is s in no one else,
2Co   6: 2 see, now is the day of s!
Php   2:12 work out your own s with fear
Heb   2: 3 escape if we neglect so great a s?
2Pe   3:15 regard the patience of our Lord as s.
Rev   19: 1 S and glory and power to our God,
Bar   4:29 everlasting joy with your s.

SAMARIA → SAMARITAN
1Ki   16:24 and called the city that he built, S,
2Ki   17: 6 the king of Assyria captured S;
Jn   4: 4 But he had to go through S.
Ac   1: 8 in all Judea and S, and to the ends

SAMARITAN → SAMARIA
Lk   10:33 But a S while traveling came near
Jn   4: 7 A S woman came to draw water,

SAME
Ro   10:12 the s Lord is Lord of all
1Co   12: 4 varieties of gifts, but the s Spirit;
Heb   13: 8 Jesus Christ is the s yesterday and

SAMSON*
       Danite judge. Birth promised (Jdg 13). Married
   a Philistine, but his wife given away (Jdg 14). Vengeance on the Philistines (Jdg 15). Betrayed by Delilah (Jdg 16:1-22). Death (Jdg 16:23-31). Feats of
   strength: killed lion (Jdg 14:6), 30 Philistines (Jdg
   14:19), 1,000 Philistines with jawbone (Jdg 15:13-
   17), carried off gates of Gaza (Jdg 16:3), pushed
   down temple of Dagon (Jdg 16:25-30; Heb 11:32).

SAMUEL
       Ephraimite judge and prophet (Heb 11:32).
   Birth prayed for (1Sa 1:10-18). Dedicated to temple by Hannah (1Sa 1:21-28). Raised by Eli (1Sa
   2:11, 18-26). Called as prophet (1Sa 3). Led Israel
   to victory over Philistines (1Sa 7). Asked by Israel
   for a king (1Sa 8). Anointed Saul as king (1Sa 9-
   10). Farewell speech (1Sa 12). Rebuked Saul for
   sacrifice (1Sa 15). Anointed David as king (1Sa 16). Protected David from Saul (1Sa 19:18-24). Death
   (1Sa 25:1). Returned from dead to condemn Saul
   (1Sa 28).

SANCTIFICATION → SANCTIFY
Ro   6:19 as slaves to righteousness for s.
1Th   4: 3 For this is the will of God, your s:

SANCTIFIED → SANCTIFY
Ex   29:43 and it shall be s by my glory;
Jn   17:19 so that they also may be s in truth.
1Co   6:11 But you were washed, you were s,

**SANCTIFY → SANCTIFICATION,
                SANCTIFIED**
Lev   11:44 s yourselves therefore, and be holy,
Heb   13:12 to s the people by his own blood.

SANCTUARY
Ex   25: 8 And have them make me a s,
1Ch   22:19 build the s of the LORD God
Eze   37:26 and will set my s among them

Da 9:26 shall destroy the city and the **s**.
Heb 9:24 Christ did not enter a **s** made by
1Mc 1:21 He arrogantly entered the **s**
4:36 cleanse the **s** and dedicate it."

SAND
Ge 22:17 as the stars of heaven and as the **s**
Hos 1:10 Israel shall be like the **s** of the sea,
Mt 7:26 foolish man who built his house
on **s**,

SANDALS
Ex 3: 5 Remove the **s** from your feet,
Mt 3:11 I am not worthy to carry his **s**.

SARAH
Wife of Abraham, originally named Sarai; barren
(Ge 11:29-31; 1Pe 3:6). Taken by Pharaoh as
Abraham's sister; returned (Ge 12:10-20). Gave
Hagar to Abraham; sent her away in pregnancy (Ge
16). Name changed; Isaac promised (Ge 17:15-21;
18:10-15; Heb 11:11). Taken by Abimelech as
Abraham's sister; returned (Ge 20). Isaac born;
Hagar and Ishmael sent away (Ge 21:1-21; Gal
4:21-31). Death (Ge 23).

SAT → SIT
Heb 10:12 "he **s** down at the right hand of God,
Rev 3:21 and **s** down with my Father

SATAN
1Ch 21: 1 **S** stood up against Israel,
Job 1: 6 and **S** also came among them.
Zec 3: 2 "The LORD rebuke you, O **S**!
Mt 4:10 Jesus said to him, "Away with you,
S!
12:26 If **S** casts out **S**, he is divided
16:23 said to Peter, "Get behind me, **S**!
2Co 11:14 **S** disguises himself as an angel of
light.
Rev 12: 9 who is called the Devil and **S**,
20: 7 **S** will be released from his prison

SATISFIED → SATISFY
Ps 17:15 I shall be **s**, beholding your likeness.
Joel 2:26 You shall eat in plenty and be **s**,

SATISFY → SATISFIED
Isa 55: 2 labor for that which does not **s**?
Jer 31:25 I will **s** the weary, and all who are

SAUL → =PAUL
1. Benjamite; anointed by Samuel as first king
of Israel (1Sa 9-10). Defeated Ammonites (1Sa
11). Rebuked for offering sacrifice (1Sa 13:1-15).
Defeated Philistines (1Sa 14). Rejected as king for
failing to annihilate Amalekites (1Sa 15). Soothed
from evil spirit by David (1Sa 16:14-23). Sent David against Goliath (1Sa 17). Jealousy and attempted murder of David (1Sa 18:1-11). Gave David Michal as wife (1Sa 18:12-30). Second attempt
to kill David (1Sa 19). Anger at Jonathan (1Sa
20:26-34). Pursued David: killed priests at Nob
(1Sa 22), went to Keilah and Ziph (1Sa 23), life
spared by David at En Gedi (1Sa 24) and in his
tent (1Sa 26). Rebuked by Samuel's spirit for consulting witch at Endor (1Sa 28). Wounded by Philistines; took his own life (1Sa 31; 1Ch 10). Lamented by David (2Sa 1:17-27). Children (1Sa
14:49-51; 1Ch 8).
2. See Paul.

SAVE → SALVATION, SAVED, SAVIOR
Ps 54: 1 **S** me, O God, by your name,
Isa 59: 1 LORD's hand is not too short to **s**,
Jer 15:20 for I am with you to **s** you
Mt 1:21 he will **s** his people from their sins."
16:25 who want to **s** their life will lose it,
Lk 19:10 came to seek out and to **s** the lost."
Heb 7:25 to **s** those who approach God

SAVED → SAVE
Isa 45:22 Turn to me and be **s**,
Joel 2:32 on the name of the LORD shall be **s**;
Mt 10:22 who endures to the end will be **s**.

Mk 15:31 He **s** others; he cannot save himself.
Lk 13:23 "Lord, will only a few be **s**?"
Ac 2:21 on the name of the Lord shall be **s**.'
16:30 "Sirs, what must I do to be **s**?"
Ro 10:13 on the name of the Lord shall be **s**."
Eph 2: 8 For by grace you have been **s**

SAVIOR → SAVE
Ps 106:21 They forgot God, their **S**,
Isa 49:26 know that I am the LORD your **S**,
Hos 13: 4 and besides me there is no **s**.
Lk 2:11 this day in the city of David a **S**,
Ac 13:23 to Israel a **S**, Jesus, as he promised;
1Ti 4:10 who is the **S** of all people,
Tit 2:13 of the glory of our great God and **S**,
2Pe 3:18 knowledge of our Lord and **S** Jesus

SCARLET
Isa 1:18 your sins are like **s**, they shall be
Mt 27:28 stripped him and put a **s** robe on
him

SCATTER → SCATTERED
Dt 4:27 LORD will **s** you among the peoples;
Jer 9:16 I will **s** them among nations that

SCATTERED → SCATTER
Dt 30: 3 the LORD your God has **s** you.
Jer 31:10 "He who **s** Israel will gather him,
Mk 14:27 "the shepherd, and the sheep will
be **s**.'

SCEPTER
Ge 49:10 The **s** shall not depart from Judah,
Nu 24:17 and a **s** shall rise out of Israel;
Heb 1: 8 righteous **s** is the **s** of your kingdom.

SCOFFED → SCOFFERS
Lk 23:35 but the leaders **s** at him, saying,

SCOFFERS → SCOFFED
Ps 1: 1 or sit in the seat of **s**;
Pr 19:29 Condemnation is ready for **s**,
2Pe 3: 3 that in the last days **s** will come,

SCRIBES
Mt 7:29 having authority, and not as their **s**.
23:13 "But woe to you, **s** and Pharisees,

SCRIPTURE → SCRIPTURES
Lk 4:21 "Today this **s** has been fulfilled in
Jn 10:35 and the **s** cannot be annulled—
1Ti 4:13 attention to the public reading of **s**,
2Ti 3:16 All **s** is inspired by God and is useful

SCRIPTURES → SCRIPTURE
Mt 22:29 know neither the **s** nor the power
Lk 24:45 their minds to understand the **s**,
Jn 5:39 "You search the **s** because you think
1Co 15: 3 our sins in accordance with the **s**,

SCROLL
Lk 4:17 the **s** of the prophet Isaiah was given
Rev 5: 2 to open the **s** and break its seals?"

SEA
Ge 1:26 have dominion over the fish of the **s**,
Ex 15: 1 and rider he has thrown into the **s**.
Dt 30:13 Neither is it beyond the **s**, that you
Ps 95: 5 The **s** is his, for he made it,
Da 7: 3 great beasts came up out of the **s**,
Mic 7:19 all our sins into the depths of the **s**.
Rev 4: 6 there is something like a **s** of glass,
13: 1 a beast rising out of the **s** having
21: 1 and the **s** was no more.

SEAL → SEALS
Da 8:26 As for you, **s** up the vision,
2Co 1:22 by putting his **s** on us and giving us
Eph 1:13 the **s** of the promised Holy Spirit;
Rev 7: 3 our God with a **s** on their foreheads.
22:10 not **s** up the words of the prophecy

SEALS → SEAL
Rev 5: 2 to open the scroll and break its **s**?"

SEARCH → SEARCHES
Dt 4:29 if you **s** after him with all your heart
Ps 139:23 **S** me, O God, and know my heart;
Eze 34:11 I myself will **s** for my sheep,

SEARCHES → SEARCH
Ro 8:27 And God, who **s** the heart,
1Co 2:10 the Spirit **s** everything,

SEASON → SEASONS
Ps 1: 3 which yield their fruit in its **s**,
Ecc 3: 1 For everything there is a **s**,

SEASONS → SEASON
Ge 1:14 let them be for signs and for **s** and
Gal 4:10 and months, and **s**, and years.
1Th 5: 1 Now concerning the times and the **s**,

SEAT → SEATED
Ex 25:17 make a mercy **s** of pure gold;
Ps 1: 1 or sit in the **s** of scoffers;
Ro 14:10 stand before the judgment **s** of God.
2Co 5:10 must appear before the judgment **s**

SEATED → SEAT
Lk 22:69 the Son of Man will be **s** at the right
Eph 1:20 and **s** him at his right hand
Rev 4: 4 **s** on the thrones are twenty-four
elders,
19: 4 and worshiped God who is **s** on

SECOND → TWO
Mt 22:39 And a **s** is like it:
Rev 20:14 This is the **s** death, the lake of fire;

SECRET
Dt 29:29 The **s** things belong to the LORD
Ro 2:16 will judge the **s** thoughts of all.

SECURITY → SECURE
Pr 12: 3 No one finds **s** by wickedness,
1Th 5: 3 they say, "There is peace and **s**,"

**SEE → FORESEEING, NEAR-SIGHTED,
SEEN, SEES, SIGHT**
Ex 12:13 when I **s** the blood, I will pass over
33:20 for no one shall **s** me and live."
Ps 115: 5 eyes, but do not **s**.
Jn 9:25 that though I was blind, now I **s**."
1Co 13:12 we **s** in a mirror, dimly,
1Jn 3: 2 for we will **s** him as he is.
Rev 1: 7 the clouds; every eye will **s** him,

SEED → SEEDS, SEEDTIME
Isa 6:13 The holy **s** is its stump.
Mt 17:20 have faith the size of a mustard **s**,
1Pe 1:23 of perishable but of imperishable **s**,

SEEDS → SEED
Mt 13: 8 Other **s** fell on good soil
Mk 4:31 the smallest of all the **s** on earth;

SEEK
1Ch 28:9 If you **s** him, he will be found by
Ps 34:10 those who **s** the LORD lack no good
119:10 With my whole heart I **s** you;
Isa 55: 6 **S** the LORD while he may be found,
65: 1 found by those who did not **s** me.
Lk 19:10 came to **s** out and to save
Heb 11: 6 that he rewards those who **s** him
Sir 2:16 who fear the Lord **s** to please him,

SEEMS
Pr 16:25 there is a way that **s** to be right,
Heb 12:11 discipline always **s** painful rather

SEEN → SEE
Jn 1:18 No one has ever **s** God.
14: 9 Whoever has **s** me has **s** the Father.
20:29 Blessed are those who have not **s**
1Pe 1: 8 you have not **s** him, you love him;

SELF-CONTROL → SELF-CONTROLLED
1Co 7: 5 tempt you because of your lack of **s**.
2Pe 1: 6 with **s**, and **s** with endurance,

SELF-CONTROLLED → SELF-CONTROL
Tit 1: 8 prudent, upright, devout, and **s**.
2: 5 to be **s**, chaste, good managers

SELFISH → SELFISHNESS
Ps 119:36 to your decrees, and not to s gain.
Php 1:17 proclaim Christ out of s ambition,
Jas 3:14 if you have bitter envy and s

SELFISHNESS* → SELFISH
2Co 12:20 anger, s, slander, gossip, conceit,

SELL
Pr 23:23 Buy truth, and do not s it;
Mk 10:21 s what you own, and give the money

SEND → SENT
Ex 33: 2 I will s an angel before you,
Isa 6: 8 And I said, "Here am I; s me!"
Jn 3:17 God did not s the Son into the world to
  14:26 whom the Father will s in my name,

SENNACHERIB
  Assyrian king; siege of Jerusalem was overthrown by the LORD following prayer of Hezekiah and Isaiah (2Ki 18:13-19:37; 2Ch 32:1-21; Isa 36-37).

SENT → SEND
Ex 3:14 'I am has s me to you.' "
Lk 10:16 rejects me rejects the one who s me.
Jn 17:18 As you have s me into the world,
  20:21 the Father has s me, so I send you."
1Jn 4:10 and s his Son to be the atoning

SEPARATE → SEPARATED
Mt 19: 6 joined together, let no one s."
Ro 8:35 will us from the love of Christ?
1Co 7:10 wife should not s from her husband

SEPARATED → SEPARATE
Lev 20:24 I have s you from the peoples.
Heb 7:26 s from sinners, and exalted above

SERPENT → SERPENTS
Ge 3: 1 the s was more crafty than any other
Nu 21: 9 Moses made a s of bronze,
2Co 11: 3 the s deceived Eve by its cunning,
Rev 20: 2 He seized the dragon, that ancient s,

SERPENTS → SERPENT
Mt 10:16 wise as s and innocent as doves.

SERVANT → SERVANTS
Ps 19:11 Moreover by them is your s warned;
Isa 42: 1 Here is my s, whom I uphold,
  43:10 and my s whom I have chosen,
  53:11 my s, shall make many righteous,
Zec 3: 8 going to bring my s the Branch.
Lk 1:38 "Here am I, the s of the Lord;
Ac 3:13 has glorified his s Jesus,
2Ti 2:24 Lord's s must not be quarrelsome
Heb 3: 5 faithful in all God's house as a s,

SERVANTS → SERVANT
2Ki 17:23 as he had foretold through all his s
Jn 15:15 I do not call you s any longer,
1Pe 2:16 As s of God, live as free people,
Rev 7: 3 marked the s of our God with a seal

SERVE
Jos 24:15 my household, we will s the LORD."
1Sa 12:20 but s the LORD with all your heart;
Mt 6:24 You cannot s God and wealth.
Mk 10:45 Son of Man came not to be served but to s,
1Pe 4:10 s one another with whatever gift

SETH
Ge 4:25 she bore a son and named him S,

SETTLE
Ge 26: 2 s in the land that I shall show you.
Nu 33:53 possession of the land and s in it,

SEVEN → SEVENTH
Ge 7: 2 with you s pairs of all clean animals,
Ex 25:37 You shall make the s lamps for it;
Jos 6: 4 march around the city s times,
Da 9:25 prince, there shall be s weeks;

Mt 18:22 "Not s times, but, I tell you, seventy-seven
Rev 1:12 turning I saw s golden lampstands,
  5: 1 and on the back, sealed with s seals;
  8: 2 I saw the s angels who stand before
  12: 3 a great red dragon, with s heads and
  15: 1 s angels with s plagues,

SEVENTH → SEVEN
Ge 2: 2 on the s day God finished the work
Ex 20:10 the s day is a sabbath to the LORD
  23:11 but the s year you shall let it rest
Heb 4: 4 God rested on the s day from all his

SEVENTY → SEVENTY-SEVEN
Ge 46:27 who came into Egypt were s.
2Ch 36:21 it kept sabbath, to fulfill s years.
Jer 25:12 Then after s years are completed,
Da 9:24 S weeks are decreed for your people

SEVENTY-SEVEN → SEVENTY
Mt 18:22 "Not seven times, but, I tell you, s

SEXUAL
1Co 10: 8 not indulge in s immorality as some

SHADOW
2Ki 20:11 brought the s back the ten intervals,
Ps 17: 8 hide me in the s of your wings,
  91: 1 who abide in the s of the Almighty,
Mt 4:16 and s of death light has dawned."
Col 2:17 are only a s of what is to come,

SHADRACH → =HANANIAH
  Hebrew exiled to Babylon; name changed from Hananiah (Da 1:6-7). Refused defilement by food (Da 1:8-20). Refused to worship idol (Da 3:1-18); saved from furnace (Da 3:19-30).

SHALLUM
  King of Israel (2Ki 15:10-16).

SHALMANESER
  King of Assyria; conquered and deported Israel (2Ki 17:3-4; 18:9; Tob 1:2).

SHAME → ASHAMED, SHAMEFUL
Ps 69: 6 who hope in you be put to s because
Eze 39:26 They shall forget their s, and all
Da 12: 2 some to s and everlasting contempt;
1Co 1:27 foolish in the world to s the wise;
Heb 12: 2 endured the cross, disregarding its s,
1Jn 2:28 be put to s before him at his coming.

SHAMEFUL → SHAME
2Co 4: 2 We have renounced the s things
Eph 5:12 For it is s even to mention

SHAMGAR*
  Judge; killed 600 Philistines (Jdg 3:31; 5:6).

SHARE
Nu 18:20 I am your s and your possession
Lk 3:11 "Whoever has two coats must s
Ro 15:27 for if the Gentiles have come to s
Col 1:12 to s in the inheritance of the saints
Heb 12:10 in order that we may s his holiness.
Jude 1: 3 to you about the salvation we s,

SHARP → SHARPENS, SHARPER
Pr 5: 4 s as a two-edged sword.
Rev 19:15 a s sword with which to strike down

SHARPENS → SHARP
Pr 27:17 Iron is iron, and one person s

SHARPER* → SHARP
Heb 4:12 s than any two-edged sword,

SHEBA
  1. Benjamite; rebelled against David (2Sa 20).
  2. Queen of Sheba (1Ki 10; 2Ch 9; Mt 12:42; Lk 11:31).

SHECHEM
  1. Raped Jacob's daughter Dinah; killed (Ge 34).
  2. City where Joshua renewed the covenant (Jos 24). Abimelech as king (Jdg 9).

SHED → BLOODSHED, SHEDDING
Ge 9: 6 shall that person's blood be s;
Pr 6:17 and hands that s innocent blood,
Mt 23:35 may come all the righteous blood s
Rev 16: 6 s the blood of saints and prophets,

SHEDDING → SHED
Heb 9:22 without the s of blood there is no
  12: 4 resisted to the point of s your blood.

SHEEP
1Ki 22:17 like s that have no shepherd;
Ps 100: 3 people, and the s of his pasture.
Isa 53: 6 All we like s have gone astray;
Eze 34:15 myself will be the shepherd of my s,
Zec 13: 7 shepherd, that the s may be scattered;
Mt 9:36 like s without a shepherd.
Lk 15: 4 a hundred s and losing one of them,
Jn 10: 7 I am the gate for the s.
  10:15 And I lay down my life for the s.
Heb 13:20 the great shepherd of the s,
1Pe 2:25 For you were going astray like s,

SHELTER
Ps 91: 1 who live in the s of the Most High,
Rev 7:15 is seated on the throne will s them.

SHEM
  Son of Noah (Ge 5:32; 6:10). Blessed (Ge 9:26). Descendants (Ge 10:21-31; 11:10-32; Lk 3:36).

SHEOL
Nu 16:30 and they go down alive into S,
Job 26: 6 S is naked before God,
Ps 139: 8 if I make my bed in S, you are there.
Isa 28:15 and with S we have an agreement;
Hos 13:14 O S, where is your destruction?

SHEPHERD → SHEPHERDS
2Sa 7: 7 whom I commanded to s my people
Ps 23: 1 The LORD is my s, I shall not want.
Ecc 12:11 sayings that are given by one s.
Isa 40:11 He will feed his flock like a s;
Mt 2: 6 ruler who is to s my people Israel.' "
  26:31 strike the s, and the sheep of the flock
Jn 10:11 "I am the good s.
Heb 13:20 the great s of the sheep,
1Pe 5: 4 And when the chief s appears,

SHEPHERDS → SHEPHERD
Eze 34: 2 prophesy against the s of Israel:
Lk 2: 8 there were s living in the fields,

SHIELD
Ge 15: 1 I am your s; your reward shall be
Ps 7:10 God is my s, who saves the upright
Eph 6:16 With all of these, take the s of faith,

SHILOH
1Sa 1:24 to the house of the LORD at S;

SHIMEI
  Cursed David (2Sa 16:5-14); spared (2Sa 19:16-23). Killed by Solomon (1Ki 2:8-9, 36-46).

SHINE → SHINES, SHINING
Nu 6:25 LORD make his face to s upon you,
Ps 4: 6 light of your face s on us, O LORD!"
Isa 60: 1 s; for your light has come,
Da 12: 3 Those who are wise shall s like the
Mt 5:16 let your light s before others,
Eph 5:14 the dead, and Christ will s on you."

SHINES → SHINE
Jn 1: 5 The light s in the darkness,

SHINING → SHINE
2Pe 1:19 to this as to a lamp s in a dark place,
1Jn 2: 8 and the true light is already s.

SHORT

Isa 59: 1 the LORD's hand is not too s to save,
Mt 24:22 if those days had not been cut s,
Ro 3:23 sinned and fall s of the glory of God;

SHOUT

Ps 47: 1 s to God with loud songs of joy.
Zec 9: 9 S aloud, O daughter Jerusalem!
Lk 19:40 were silent, the stones would s out."

SHOW → SHOWED

Ge 12: 1 to the land that I will s you.
Ex 33:18 Moses said, "S me your glory,
Ps 85: 7 S us your steadfast love, O LORD,
Jn 14: 8 said to him, "Lord, s us the Father,
1Co 12:31 will s you a still more excellent way
Rev 4: 1 I will s you what must take place

SHOWED → SHOW

Dt 34: 1 the LORD s him the whole land:
Jn 20:20 he s them his hands and his side.

SHOWERS

Dt 32: 2 rain on grass, like s on new growth.
Eze 34:26 they shall be s of blessing.

SHUT

Isa 22:22 he shall open, and no one shall s;
Da 6:22 God sent his angel and s the lions'
Rev 3: 7 who opens and no one will s,

SICK → SICKNESS

Mt 8:16 and cured all who were s.
9:12 of a physician, but those who are s.
Jas 5:14 Are any among you s?

SICKLE

Joel 3:13 Put in the s, for the harvest is ripe.
Rev 14:14 and a sharp s in his hand!

SICKNESS → SICK

Ex 23:25 I will take s away from among you.
Mt 4:23 and curing every disease and every s

SIDE → ASIDE

Ps 91: 7 A thousand may fall at your s,
124: 1 the LORD who was on our s
Jn 19:34 soldiers pierced his s with a spear,

SIFT

Isa 30:28 to s the nations with the sieve of
Lk 22:31 Satan has demanded to s all of you

SIGHT → SEE

Ge 6:11 the earth was corrupt in God's s,
Ps 72:14 and precious is their blood in his s.
Mt 11: 5 blind receive their s, the lame walk,
2Co 5: 7 for we walk by faith, not by s.
1Pe 3: 4 which is very precious in God's s.

SIGN → SIGNS

Ge 9:12 the s of the covenant that I make
17:11 a s of the covenant between me
Isa 7:14 the Lord himself will give you a s.
Mt 24: 3 the s of your coming and of the end
Mk 8:12 does this generation ask for a s?

SIGNS → SIGN

Ge 1:14 be for s and for seasons and for days
Ex 7: 3 I will multiply my s and wonders in
Da 6:27 he works s and wonders in heaven
Mt 16: 3 cannot interpret the s of the times.
Jn 20:30 Jesus did many other s in the
1Co 1:22 Jews demand s and Greeks desire
Rev 16:14 demonic spirits, performing s,

SILAS

Prophet (Ac 15:22-32); co-worker with Paul on second missionary journey (Ac 16-18; 2Co 1:19). Co-writer with Paul (1Th 1:1; 2Th 1:1); Peter (1Pe 5:12).

SILENT

Isa 53: 7 sheep that before its shearers is s,
Zep 1: 7 Be s before the Lord God!
Mk 14:61 But he was s and did not answer.
1Co 14:34 women should be s in the churches.

SILVER

Ps 66:10 you have tried us as s is tried.
Pr 8:10 Take my instruction instead of s,
Isa 48:10 I have refined you, but not like s;
Zec 13: 9 refine them as one refines s,
Mt 26:15 They paid him thirty pieces of s.
Ac 3: 6 But Peter said, "I have no s or gold,
1Co 3:12 on the foundation with gold, s,

SIMEON → =SIMON

1. Son of Jacob by Leah (Ge 29:33; 35:23; 1Ch 2:1). With Levi killed Shechem for rape of Dinah (Ge 34:25-29). Held hostage by Joseph in Egypt (Ge 42:24-43:23). Tribe of blessed (Ge 49:5-7), numbered (Nu 1:23; 26:14), allotted land (Jos 19:1-9; Eze 48:24), 12,000 from (Rev 7:7).
2. Godly Jew who blessed the infant Jesus (2:25-35).
3. See Peter (Ac 15:14; 2Pe 1:1).

SIMON → =PETER, =SIMEON

1. See Peter.
2. Apostle; the Zealot (Mt 10:4; Mk 3:18; Lk 6:15; Ac 1:13).
3. Samaritan sorcerer (Ac 8:9-24).

SIMPLE

Ps 19: 7 are sure, making wise the s;
Pr 1:22 O s ones, will you love being s?
14:15 The s believe everything,

SIN → SINFUL, SINNED, SINNER, SINNERS, SINS

Ge 4: 7 not do well, s is lurking at the door;
Ex 32:32 if you will only forgive their s—
Nu 32:23 and be sure your s will find you out.
1Ki 8:46 "If they s against you—
2Ch 7:14 forgive their s and heal their land.
Ps 119:11 so that I may not s against you.
Isa 53:12 yet he bore the s of many,
Mt 5:29 If your right eye causes you to s,
Jn 1:29 who takes away the s of the world!
Ro 6:23 For the wages of s is death,
2Co 5:21 made him to be s who knew no s,
Heb 4:15 tested as we are, yet without s.
1Jn 1: 7 Jesus his Son cleanses us from all s.
Tob 12:10 but those who commit s
Wis 10:13 but delivered him from s.
Sir 3:30 so almsgiving atones for s.

SINAI → =HOREB

Ex 19:20 the LORD descended upon Mount S,
Ps 68:17 the Lord came from S into the holy
Gal 4:25 Now Hagar is Mount S in Arabia

SINFUL → SIN

Lk 5: 8 from me, Lord, for I am a s man!"
Ro 8: 3 Son in the likeness of s flesh,
1Mc 1:10 From them came forth a s root,

SING → SINGERS, SONG, SONGS, SUNG

Ex 15: 1 "I will s to the LORD,
Ps 47: 6 S praises to God, s praises;
Isa 5: 1 s for my beloved my love-song
1Co 14:15 I will s praise with the spirit,
Col 3:16 gratitude in your hearts s psalms,
Rev 5: 9 They s a new song:
Jdt 16:13 I will s to my God a new song:
Aza 1:35 s praise to him and highly exalt him

SINGERS → SING

1Ch 15:16 to appoint their kindred as the s
Ezr 2:70 and the s, the gatekeepers,

SINGLE

Mt 6:27 worrying add a s hour to your span
Rev 21:21 each of the gates is a s pearl,

SINNED → SIN

Nu 14:40 LORD has promised, for we have s."
Ps 51: 4 Against you, you alone, have I s,
La 5: 7 Our ancestors s; they are no more,
Ro 3:23 all have s and fall short of the glory of God;

1Jn 1:10 If we say that we have not s,
Sir 18:21 and when you have s, repent.

SINNER → SIN

Lk 15: 7 over one s who repents than
Jas 5:20 that whoever brings back a s

SINNERS → SIN

Ps 1: 1 or take the path that s tread,
Pr 23:17 Do not let your heart envy s,
Lk 6:33 For even s do the same.
Ro 5: 8 we still were s Christ died for us.
1Ti 1:15 Jesus came into the world to save s

SINS → SIN

1Sa 2:25 but if someone s against the LORD,
Ps 103:10 not deal with us according to our s,
Isa 1:18 your s are like scarlet, they shall be
Eze 18: 4 only the person who s that shall die.
Mic 7:19 cast all our s into the depths of the
Mt 9: 6 has authority on earth to forgive s"—
Mk 1: 5 the river Jordan, confessing their s.
Lk 11: 4 forgive us our s, for we ourselves
Ac 3:19 to God so that your s may be wiped
1Co 15: 3 Christ died for our s in accordance
Heb 9:28 offered once to bear the s of many,
1Jn 1: 9 If we confess our s, he who is faithful
Rev 1: 5 loves us and freed us from our s
Sir 2:11 he forgives s and saves

SISTER

Ge 12:13 Say you are my s, so that it may go
20: 2 of his wife Sarah, "She is my s."
Pr 7: 4 Say to wisdom, "You are my s,"
Mk 3:35 the will of God is my brother and s

SIT → SAT, SITS

Ps 1: 1 or s in the seat of scoffers;
110: 1 says to my lord, "S at my right hand
Jer 33:17 never lack a man to s on the throne
Mt 20:23 to s at my right hand and at my left,
Heb 1:13 "S at my right hand until I make

SITS → SIT

Ps 2: 4 He who s in the heavens laughs;
Isa 28: 6 to the one who s in judgment,

SIX

Ex 20: 9 S days you shall labor and do all
Pr 6:16 are s things that the LORD hates,
Isa 6: 2 above him; each had s wings:
Rev 4: 8 each of them with s wings,

SKILL

Ex 28: 3 whom I have endowed with s,
1Ki 7:14 he was full of s, intelligence,

SKIN

Job 2: 4 Satan answered the LORD, "S for s!
19:26 after my s has been thus destroyed,
Jer 13:23 Can Ethiopians change their s

SKULL

2Ki 9:35 they found no more of her than the s
Mt 27:33 Golgotha (which means Place of a S)

SKY

Dt 28:23 s over your head shall be bronze,
Mt 16: 3 to interpret the appearance of the s,
Rev 6:14 The s vanished like a scroll rolling

SLANDER → SLANDERED

Ps 15: 3 who do not s with their tongue,
Pr 10:18 and whoever utters s is a fool.
Mt 15:19 fornication, theft, false witness, s,
1Pe 2: 1 all guile, insincerity, envy, and all s.

SLANDERED → SLANDER

1Co 4:13 when s, we speak kindly.

SLAUGHTER → SLAUGHTERED

Pr 7:22 and goes like an ox to the s,
Isa 53: 7 like a lamb that is led to the s,

Zec 11: 4 a shepherd of the flock doomed to s.
Ac   8:32 "Like a sheep he was led to the s,

SLAUGHTERED → SLAUGHTER
Rev   5: 6 a Lamb standing as if it had been s,
      6: 9 who had been s for the word of God

SLAVE → ENSLAVE, ENSLAVED, SLAVERY, SLAVES
Ge   21:10 Cast out this s woman with her son;
Mk   10:44 first among you must be s of all.
Jn   8:34 who commits sin is a s to sin.
Gal   3:28 there is no longer s or free,

SLAVERY → SLAVE
Ex   20: 2 out of the house of s;
Ro   7:14 of the flesh, sold into s under sin.
Gal   5: 1 do not submit again to a yoke of s.

SLAVES → SLAVE
Ro   6:16 are s of the one whom you obey,
2Pe   2:19 people are s to whatever masters

SLEEP → ASLEEP, SLEEPER, SLEEPING
Ge   2:21 God caused a deep s to fall upon
     15:12 a deep s fell upon Abram,
Ps   121: 4 keeps Israel will neither slumber
            nor s.
Da   12: 2 Many of those who s in the dust of

SLEEPER → SLEEP
Eph   5:14 "S, awake! Rise from the dead,

SLEEPING → SLEEP
Mt   9:24 for the girl is not dead but s."
     26:40 to the disciples and found them s;

SLING
1Sa 17:50 over the Philistine with a s and a
            stone,

SLIP
Dt   32:35 for the time when their foot shall s;
Ps   37:31 their steps do not s.

SLOW → SLOWNESS
Ex   34: 6 merciful and gracious, s to anger,
Nu   14:18 'The LORD is s to anger,
Ps 145: 8 s to anger and abounding in
Na   1: 3 The LORD is s to anger but great in
Lk   24:25 and how s of heart to believe all that
2Pe   3: 9 The Lord is not s about his promise,
Tob 12: 6 Do not be s to acknowledge him.
Sir   5: 4 for the Lord is s to anger.

SLOWNESS → SLOW
2Pe   3: 9 think of s, but is patient with you,

SMALL → SMALLEST
Jas   3: 5 So also the tongue is a s member,

SMALLEST → SMALL
Mk   4:31 is the s of all the seeds on earth;

SMOKE → SMOKING
Ex   19:18 Now Mount Sinai was wrapped in s,
Isa   6: 4 and the house filled with s.
Joel 2:30 blood and fire and columns of s.
Rev 15: 8 with s from the glory of God and

SMOKING → SMOKE
Ge   15:17 s fire pot and a flaming torch passed
Ex   20:18 of the trumpet, and the mountain s,

SNAKE
Ex   4: 3 and it became a s; and Moses drew
Lk   11:11 will give a s instead of a fish?

SNARE
Ex   23:33 it will surely be a s to you.
Jdg   2: 3 their gods shall be a s to you."

SNOW
Ps   51: 7 and I shall be whiter than s.
Isa   1:18 sins are like scarlet, they shall be
            like s;
Da   7: 9 his clothing was white as s,
Rev   1:14 as white wool, white as s;

SOBER
1Th   5: 6 but let us keep awake and be s;
2Ti   4: 5 always be s, endure suffering,

SODOM
Ge   19:24 rained on S and Gomorrah sulfur
Isa   1: 9 we would have been like S,
Lk   10:12 it will be more tolerable for S than
Rev 11: 8 city that is prophetically called S

SOLDIERS
Mt   28:12 give a large sum of money to the s,
Jn   19:23 When the s had crucified Jesus,

SOLID
1Co   3: 2 I fed you with milk, not s food,
Heb   5:14 But s food is for the mature,

SOLOMON
     Son of David by Bathsheba; king of Judah (2Sa
12:24; 1Ch 3:5, 10). Appointed king by David (1Ki
1); adversaries Adonijah, Joab, Shimei killed by Benaiah (1Ki 2). Asked for wisdom (1Ki 3; 2Ch 1).
Judged between two prostitutes (1Ki 3:16-28).
Built temple (1Ki 5-7; 2Ch 2-5); prayer of dedication (1Ki 8; 2Ch 6). Visited by Queen of Sheba
(1Ki 10; 2Ch 9). Wives turned his heart from God
(1Ki 11:1-13). Jeroboam rebelled against (1Ki
11:26-40). Death (1Ki 11:41-43; 2Ch 9:29-31).
     Proverbs of (1Ki 4:32; Pr 1:1; 10:1; 25:1);
psalms of (Ps 72; 127); song of (SS 1:1).

SON → SONS
Ge   21: 2 conceived and bore Abraham a s
Ex   4:23 now I will kill your firstborn s.' "
2Sa   7:14 and he shall be a s to me.
Ps   2: 7 He said to me, "You are my s;
Isa   7:14 is with child and shall bear a s,
Mt   1:23 virgin shall conceive and bear a s,
      2:15 "Out of Egypt I have called my s."
      3:17 from heaven said, "This is my S,
     12: 8 the S of Man is lord of the sabbath."
     16:16 the Messiah, the S of the living
            God."
Mk   10:45 S of Man came not to be served but
            to
Lk   1:35 he will be called S of God.
     20:44 so how can he be his s?"
Jn   1:34 testified that this is the S of God."
      3:16 loved the world that he gave his only
            S,
Ro   8:29 be conformed to the image of his S,
1Th   1:10 to wait for his S from heaven,
Heb   1: 2 last days he has spoken to us by a S,
      1: 5 my S; today I have begotten you"?
2Pe   1:17 saying, "This is my S, my Beloved,
1Jn   4: 9 God sent his only S into the world
Rev 12: 5 she gave birth to a s, a male child,
     14:14 the cloud was one like the S of
            Man,
Sir   4:10 be like a s of the Most High,
2Es 13:32 then my S will be revealed,

SONG → SING
Ex   15: 1 sang this s to the LORD:
Dt   31:21 s will confront them as a witness,
Ps   40: 3 He put a new s in my mouth,
Rev   5: 9 They sing a new s: "You are worthy
     15: 3 and the s of the Lamb;

SONGS → SING
1Ki   4:32 his s numbered a thousand and five.
Ps 137: 3 "Sing us one of the s of Zion!"
Col   3:16 hymns, and spiritual s to God.

SONS → SON
Ge   6: 2 the s of God saw that they were fair;
     35:22 Now the s of Jacob were twelve.
Dt   7: 3 giving your daughters to their s
Ac   2:17 s and your daughters shall prophesy,
2Co   6:18 you shall be my s and daughters,

SOON
Isa 56: 1 for s my salvation will come,
Rev 22:20 says, "Surely I am coming s."

SORCERERS → SORCERY
Rev 22:15 Outside are the dogs and s and

SORCERY → SORCERERS
Gal   5:20 s, enmities, strife, jealousy, anger,
Rev 18:23 all nations were deceived by your s.

SORROW → SORROWFUL
Est   9:22 turned for them from s into gladness
Ecc   1:18 who increase knowledge increase s.
Isa 35:10 and s and sighing shall flee away.

SORROWFUL → SORROW
2Co   6:10 as s, yet always rejoicing;

SOUL → SOULS
Dt   6: 5 all your s, and with all your might.
Jos 22: 5 all your heart and with all your s."
Ps   16: 9 heart is glad, and my s rejoices;
     25: 1 To you, O LORD, I lift up my s.
     42: 1 so my s longs for you, O God.
Mic   6: 7 fruit of my body for the sin of my
            s?"
Mt   10:28 fear him who can destroy both s and
Heb   4:12 piercing until it divides s from spirit
Jas   5:20 will save the sinner's s from death
3Jn   1: 2 just as it is well with your s.
Sir   7:29 With all your s fear the Lord,

SOULS → SOUL
Jer   6:16 walk in it, and find rest for your s.
Mt   11:29 and you will find rest for your s.
1Pe   2:25 the shepherd and guardian of your s.

SOUND
Eze   1:24 like the s of mighty waters,
1Co 15:52 For the trumpet will s, and the dead
2Ti   4: 3 will not put up with s doctrine,
Tit   1: 9 able both to preach with s doctrine
Rev   1:15 voice was like the s of many waters.

SOUR
Jer 31:29 "The parents have eaten s grapes,
Mk   15:36 filled a sponge with s wine,

SOVEREIGN → SOVEREIGNTY
1Ki   4:21 Solomon was s over all the
Rev   6:10 "S Lord, holy and true, how long

SOVEREIGNTY → SOVEREIGN
Da   4:34 For his s is an everlasting s,

SOW → SOWED, SOWS
Ex   23:10 For six years you shall s your land
Ecc 11: 6 In the morning s your seed,
Hos 10:12 S for yourselves righteousness;
Mt   13: 3 A sower went out to s.
1Co 15:36 s does not come to life unless it dies.

SOWED → SOW
Mt   13:24 to someone who s good seed
Lk   13:19 took and s in the garden;

SOWS → SOW
Jn   4:37 'One s and another reaps.'
2Co   9: 6 who s sparingly will also reap

SPAN
Isa 40:12 marked off the heavens with a s,
Mt   6:27 add a single hour to your s of life?

SPARE
Ro   11:21 perhaps he will not s you.
2Pe   2: 4 if God did not s the angels when

SPARROWS
Lk   12: 7 you are of more value than many s.

SPEAK → SPEAKING, SPEECH, SPOKE
Ge   18:27 take it upon myself to s to the Lord,
Nu   12: 8 With him I s face to face—
Dt   18:20 presumes to s in my name a word
Job 13: 3 But I would s to the Almighty,
Ecc   3: 7 time to keep silence, and a time to s;
Mt   13:13 The reason I s to them in parables is
Ac   2: 4 began to s in other languages,

1Co 12:30 Do all s in tongues?
Jas   1:19 be quick to listen, slow to s,
Sir   4:25 Never s against the truth,

SPEAKING → SPEAK
1Co 14:39 and do not forbid s in tongues;
Eph   4:15 But s the truth in love,

SPEAR → SPEARS
1Sa 19:10 to pin David to the wall with the s;
Jn   19:34 the soldiers pierced his side with a s,

SPEARS → SPEAR
Joel   3:10 and your pruning hooks into s;
Mic   4: 3 and their s into pruning hooks;

SPECK
Mt   7: 4 'Let me take the s out of your eye, '

SPECTACLE
1Co   4: 9 we have become a s to the world,

SPEECH → SPEAK
Ex   4:10 I am slow of s and slow of tongue."
Ps   19: 3 There is no s, nor are there words;
1Ti   4:12 set the believers an example in s
1Jn   3:18 let us love, not in word or s,
Sir   4:29 Do not be reckless in your s,

SPICES
Ex   25: 6 s for the anointing oil and for
Jn   19:40 wrapped it with the s in linen cloths,

SPIES → SPY
Nu   13:32 we have gone through as s
Jos   2: 1 two men secretly from Shittim as s,

SPIRIT → SPIRITS, SPIRITUAL
Ge   6: 3 My s shall not abide in mortals
            forever,
Nu   11:25 s rested upon them, they
            prophesied.
2Ki   2: 9 inherit a double share of your s."
Ne   9:20 You gave your good s to instruct
Job 33: 4 The s of God has made me,
Ps   31: 5 Into your hand I commit my s;
     51:17 acceptable to God is a broken s;
Pr   16:18 and a haughty s before a fall.
Isa 42: 1 I have put my s upon him;
Eze 36:26 and a new s I will put within you;
Joel 2:28 I will pour out my s on all flesh;
Mt   1:18 to be with child from the Holy S.
     5: 3 "Blessed are the poor in s,
     12:31 against the S will not be forgiven.
     26:41 the s indeed is willing, but the flesh
Mk   1: 8 will baptize you with the Holy S."
Jn   3: 5 without being born of water and S.
     4:24 God is s, and those who worship
            him must worship in s and truth."
     6:63 It is the s that gives life;
     14:26 But the Advocate, the Holy S,
Ac   2: 4 of them were filled with the Holy S
Ro   8: 9 not in the flesh; you are in the S,
     8:26 the S helps us in our weakness;
1Co   6:19 your body is a temple of the Holy S
     12: 4 are varieties of gifts, but the same S;
2Co   3: 6 the letter kills, but the S gives life.
Gal   5:22 the fruit of the S is love, joy, peace,
Eph   1:13 the seal of the promised Holy S;
     4:30 do not grieve the Holy S of God,
     5:18 but be filled with the S,
1Th   5:19 Do not quench the S.
Heb   4:12 piercing until it divides soul from s,
1Pe   3: 4 lasting beauty of a gentle and quiet s
1Jn   4: 1 Beloved, do not believe every s,
Rev   1:10 I was in the s on the Lord's day,

SPIRITS → SPIRIT
Nu   16:22 the God of the s of all flesh,
Dt   18:11 or who consults ghosts or s,
Lk   4:36 power he commands the unclean s,
1Co 12:10 to another the discernment of s,
Gal   4: 3 we were enslaved to the elemental s
Rev   1: 4 seven s who are before his throne,

SPIRITUAL → SPIRIT
Ro   7:14 For we know that the law is s;
1Co   2:13 interpreting s things to those who
            are s.
     12: 1 Now concerning s gifts,
     14: 1 Pursue love and strive for the s gifts,
     15:46 the s that is first, but the physical,
Eph   1: 3 every s blessing in the heavenly
Col   1: 9 of God's will in all s wisdom
1Pe   2: 2 infants, long for the pure, s milk,
     2: 5 yourselves be built into a s house,

SPIT
Mk   14:65 began to s on him, to blindfold him,
Rev   3:16 am about to s you out of my mouth.

SPLENDOR
1Ch 16:29 Worship the LORD in holy s;
Eph   5:27 to present the church to himself
            in s,

SPOKE → SPEAK
Mk   4:33 many such parables he s the word
1Co 13:11 When I was a child, I s like a child,
Heb   1: 1 Long ago God s to our ancestors in
2Pe   1:21 moved by the Holy Spirit s from

SPOT
Eph   5:27 without a s or wrinkle or anything
2Pe   3:14 at peace, without s or blemish;

SPRING
Isa 45: 8 earth open, that salvation may s up,
Jn   4:14 a s of water gushing up to eternal
            life."
Rev 21: 6 from the s of the water of life.

SPRINKLE → SPRINKLED
Nu   8: 7 s the water of purification on them,
Eze 36:25 I will s clean water upon you,

SPRINKLED → SPRINKLE
Lev   8:11 He s some of it on the altar seven
Heb 10:22 with our hearts s clean from an evil
1Pe   1: 2 and to be s with his blood:

SPY → SPIES
Nu   13: 2 men to s out the land of Canaan,
Jos   6:25 whom Joshua sent to s out Jericho.

STAFF
Ge   49:10 the ruler's s from between his feet,
Ex   4: 4 and it became a s in his hand—
Nu   17: 6 the s of Aaron was among theirs.
Ps   23: 4 your rod and your s—they comfort
            me.
Zec 11:10 I took my s Favor and broke it,

STAND → STANDING
Ex   14:13 "Do not be afraid, s firm,
Job 19:25 at the last he will s upon the earth;
Ps   1: 5 wicked will not s in the judgment,
Isa 7: 9 If you do not s firm in faith,
Mt   12:25 house divided against itself will s.
Ro   14: 4 for the Lord is able to make them s.
     14:10 all s before the judgment seat of
            God.
Eph   6:11 may be able to s against the wiles of

STANDARDS
Jn   8:15 You judge by human s; I judge no
1Co   1:26 of you were wise by human s,

STANDING → STAND
1Co 10:12 So if you think you are s,
Jas   5: 9 See, the Judge is s at the doors!
Rev   3:20 I am s at the door, knocking;

STAR → STARS
Nu   24:17 a s shall come out of Jacob,
Isa 14:12 are fallen from heaven, O Day S,
Mt   2: 2 For we observed his s at its rising,
2Pe   1:19 day dawns and the morning s rises
Rev   9: 1 saw a s that had fallen from heaven
     22:16 of David, the bright morning s."

STARS → STAR
Ge   1:16 to rule the night—and the s.
Job 38: 7 when the morning s sang together
Ps   148: 3 praise him, all you shining s!
Da   12: 3 like the s forever and ever.
Php   2:15 you shine like s in the world.
Rev   1:16 In his right hand he held seven s,
     12: 4 a third of the s of heaven and threw

STATUE
Da   2:31 there was a great s.

STATUTE → STATUTES
Lev 16:29 This shall be a s to you forever:
Nu   19:21 It shall be a perpetual s for them.

STATUTES → STATUTE
Ge   26: 5 commandments, my s, and my laws.
Dt   4: 1 give heed to the s and ordinances
Ne   9:13 good s and commandments,
Ps   119: 8 I will observe your s;

STEADFAST
Ex   34: 6 abounding in s love and faithfulness
Nu   14:18 and abounding in s love,
2Sa   7:15 I will not take my s love from him,
Ps   57: 7 My heart is s, O God, my heart is s.
     136: 1 for his s love endures forever.
Heb   6:19 a sure and s anchor of the soul,
1Pe   5: 9 Resist him, s in your faith,

STEAL
Ex   20:15 You shall not s.
Mt   6:19 and where thieves break in and s;
Jn   10:10 The thief comes only to s and kill

STEPHEN*
    Early church leader (Ac 6:5). Arrested (Ac 6:8-
15). Speech to Sanhedrin (Ac 7). Stoned (Ac 7:54-
60; 8:2; 11:19; 22:20).

STEPS
Pr   16: 9 but the LORD directs the s.
1Pe   2:21 so that you should follow in his s.

STIFF-NECKED → NECK
Ex   32: 9 "I have seen this people, how s
Ac   7:51 "You s people, uncircumcised in

STILL
Ex   14:14 and you have only to keep s."
Jos 10:13 sun stood s, and the moon stopped,
Ps   46:10 "Be s, and know that I am God!
Mk   4:39 said to the sea, "Peace! Be s!"
Ro   5: 8 we s were sinners Christ died for us.
Heb 11: 4 but through his faith he s speaks.

STING
1Co 15:55 Where, O death, is your s?"

**STONE → CORNERSTONE, MILLSTONE,
          STONED, STONES**
Ge   28:18 the s that he had put under his head
Ex   28:10 six of their names on the one s,
     31:18 tablets of s, written with the finger
            of
1Sa 17:50 the Philistine with a sling and a s,
Ps   118:22 The s that the builders rejected has
Isa 28:16 in Zion a foundation s, a tested s,
Eze 36:26 from your body the heart of s
Mt   4: 6 will not dash your foot against a s.' "
Mk   12:10 'The s that the builders rejected has
     16: 3 "Who will roll away the s for us
Ro   9:32 have stumbled over the stumbling s,
2Co   3: 3 not on tablets of s but on tablets
1Pe   2: 4 living s, though rejected by mortals
Rev   2:17 and I will give a white s,

STONED → STONE
2Ch 24:21 by command of the king they s him
Ac   14:19 Then they s Paul and dragged him
Heb 11:37 s to death, they were sawn in two,

STONES → STONE
Ex   28:21 twelve s with names corresponding
Jos   4: 3 'Take twelve s from here out of the

1Sa 17:40 chose five smooth s from the wadi,
Mt 3: 9 God is able from these s to raise
Lk 19:40 were silent, the s would shout out."
1Co 3:12 precious s, wood, hay, straw—
1Pe 2: 5 like living s, let yourselves be built

STORE → SHOREHOUSE, STORING
Pr 7: 1 and s up my commandments
Mt 6:19 Do not s up for yourselves treasures

STOREHOUSE → HOUSE, STORE
Dt 28:12 LORD will open for you his rich s,
Mal 3:10 Bring the full tithe into the s,

STORING* → STORE
Ro 2: 5 you are s up wrath for yourself
1Ti 6:19 s up for themselves the treasure of

STRAIGHT
Pr 3: 6 and he will make s your paths.
Isa 40: 3 s in the desert a highway for our
God.
Mt 3: 3 way of the Lord, make his paths s.' "
Ac 9:11 Get up and go to the street called S,
Sir 2: 6 make your ways s, and hope in him.

STRANGE → STRANGER, STRANGERS
Dt 32:16 They made him jealous with s gods,
1Co 14:21 "By people of s tongues and by the

STRANGER → STRANGE
Dt 10:19 You shall also love the s,
Mt 25:35 I was a s and you welcomed me,

STRANGERS → STRANGE
Dt 10:19 for you were s in the land of Egypt.
Ro 12:13 extend hospitality to s.
Eph 2:12 and s to the covenants of promise,
Heb 11:13 They confessed that they were s

STRAW
Ex 5:10 says Pharaoh, 'I will not give you s.
1Co 3:12 precious stones, wood, hay, s—

STRAY → ASTRAY
Ps 119:10 not let me s from your
commandments.
Pr 22: 6 and when old, they will not s.

STREAM → STREAMS
Isa 2: 2 all the nations shall s to it.
Am 5:24 righteousness like an ever-flowing s

STREAMS → STREAM
Ps 1: 3 like trees planted by s of water,
42: 1 As a deer longs for flowing s,

STREET
Pr 1:20 Wisdom cries out in the s;
Mt 6: 5 the synagogues and at the s corners,
Rev 21:21 and the s of the city is pure gold,

STRENGTH → STRONG
Ex 15: 2 The LORD is my s and my might,
1Ch 16:11 Seek the LORD and his s,
Ne 8:10 for the joy of the LORD is your s."
Ps 46: 1 God is our refuge and s,
Pr 31:25 S and dignity are her clothing,
Isa 40:31 for the LORD shall renew their s,
Mk 12:30 all your mind, and with all your s.'
1Co 1:25 God's weakness is stronger than
human s.
Jdt 9:11 your s does not depend on numbers,
1Mc 3:19 but s comes from Heaven.

STRENGTHEN → STRONG
Jdg 16:28 and s me only this once, O God,
Ps 119:28 s me according to your word.
Lk 22:32 have turned back, s your brothers."
Heb 12:12 hands and s your weak knees,

STRENGTHENS → STRONG
Isa 40:29 to the faint, and s the powerless.
Php 4:13 do all things through him who s me.

**STRETCH → OUTSTRETCHED,
STRETCHED**
Ex 14:16 and s out your hand over the sea
Mk 3: 5 to the man, "S out your hand."

STRETCHED → STRETCH
2Sa 24:16 angel s out his hand toward
Jerusalem
Isa 5:25 and his hand is s out still.

STRIFE → STRIVE
Pr 23:29 Who has sorrow? Who has s?
Ro 1:29 Full of envy, murder, s, deceit,
Gal 5:20 enmities, s, jealousy, anger,

STRIKE
Ge 3:15 he will s your head, and you will s
Ex 17: 6 S the rock, and water will come out
Zec 13: 7 S the shepherd, that the sheep may
Mal 4: 6 come and s the land with a curse.
Mk 14:27 'I will s the shepherd, and the sheep
Rev 19:15 to s down the nations,

STRIVE → STRIFE
Mt 6:33 But s first for the kingdom of God
1Co 12:31 But s for the greater gifts.
2Pe 3:14 s to be found by him at peace,

**STRONG → STRENGTH, STRENGTHEN,
STRENGTHENS, STRONGHOLD**
Dt 31: 6 Be s and bold; have no fear
Jos 1: 6 Be s and courageous; for you shall
Ps 140: 7 O LORD, my Lord, my s deliverer,
Pr 18:10 The name of the LORD is a s tower;
Ecc 9:11 nor the battle to the s, nor bread to
SS 8: 6 for love is as death, passion fierce
Ro 15: 1 We who are s ought to put up with
1Co 1:27 in the world to shame the s;
2Co 12:10 whenever I am weak, then I am s.
Eph 6:10 be s in the Lord and in the strength

STRONGHOLD → STRONG
Ps 9: 9 The LORD is a s for the oppressed,
Na 1: 7 a s in a day of trouble;

STRUGGLE
Eph 6:12 our s is not against enemies of
Heb 12: 4 In your s against sin you have not
yet

STUBBORN
Dt 9: 6 for you are a s people.
Hos 4:16 Like a s heifer, Israel is s;

STUDY
Ezr 7:10 Ezra had set his heart to s the law
Ecc 12:12 much s is a weariness of the flesh.

STUMBLE → STUMBLING
Ps 37:24 we s, we shall not fall headlong,
Pr 4:12 and if you run, you will not s.
Mt 18: 9 And if your eye causes you to s,
Ro 9:33 a stone that will make people s,
1Pe 2: 8 s because they disobey the word,

STUMBLING → STUMBLE
Eze 14: 3 placed their iniquity as a s block
Mt 16:23 You are a s block to me;
Ro 11: 9 a s block and a retribution for them;
1Co 8: 9 not somehow become a s block to

STUMP
Isa 6:13 The holy seed is its s.
11: 1 shall come out from the s of Jesse,

SUBDUE
Ge 1:28 and fill the earth and s it;
1Ch 17:10 and I will s all your enemies.

SUBJECT → SUBJECTED
Ro 13: 1 be s to the governing authorities,
Gal 4:21 who desire to be s to the law,
Eph 5:21 s to one another out of reverence

SUBJECTED → SUBJECT
Ro 8:20 for the creation was s to futility,
1Co 15:28 When all things are s to him,

SUBMISSION* → SUBMIT
1Ti 2:11 a woman learn in silence with full s.
Heb 5: 7 was heard because of his reverent s.

SUBMISSIVE → SUBMIT
1Ti 3: 4 keeping his children s and respectful
Tit 2: 5 kind, being s to their husbands,

SUBMIT → SUBMISSION, SUBMISSIVE
Ps 81:11 Israel would not s to me.
Gal 5: 1 do not s again to a yoke of slavery.
Heb 13:17 Obey your leaders and s to them,

SUCCEED → SUCCESS, SUCCESSFUL
Pr 15:22 but with many advisers they s.
Ecc 10:10 but wisdom helps one to s.

SUCCESS → SUCCEED
Ps 118:25 O LORD, we beseech you, give us s!
Sir 10: 5 Human s is in the hand of the Lord,

SUCCESSFUL → SUCCEED
Jos 1: 7 that you may be s wherever you go.

SUDDENLY
Mal 3: 1 LORD whom you seek will s come to
Mk 13:36 find you asleep when he comes s.

**SUFFER → SUFFERED, SUFFERING,
SUFFERINGS, SUFFERS**
Lk 22:15 this Passover with you before I s;
24:46 the Messiah is to s and to rise from
Heb 9:26 then he would have had to s again
1Pe 3:17 For it is better to s for doing good,

SUFFERED → SUFFER
Php 3: 8 For his sake I have s the loss of all
1Pe 2:21 because Christ also s for you,

SUFFERING → SUFFER
Job 2:13 they saw that his s was very great.
Isa 53: 3 a man of s and acquainted with
Mk 8:31 Son of Man must undergo great s,
Ro 12:12 Rejoice in hope, be patient in s,

SUFFERINGS → SUFFER
Ro 8:18 the s of this present time are not
1Pe 4:13 insofar as you are sharing Christ's s,

SUFFERS → SUFFER
1Co 12:26 If one member s, all suffer together

SUFFICIENT
2Co 12: 9 "My grace is s for you,

SULFUR
Ge 19:24 rained on Sodom and Gomorrah s
Ps 11: 6 he will rain coals of fire and s;
Rev 21: 8 in the lake that burns with fire
and s,

SUMMED*
Ro 13: 9 commandment, are s up in this word
Gal 5:14 the whole law is s up in a single

SUN
Jos 10:13 And the s stood still,
Ps 84:11 For the LORD God is a s and shield;
Ecc 1: 9 there is nothing new under the s.
Joel 2:31 The s shall be turned to darkness,
Mal 4: 2 the s of righteousness shall rise,
Mt 5:45 he makes his s rise on the evil and
Ac 2:20 The s shall be turned to darkness
Rev 1:16 his face was like the s shining with
19:17 I saw an angel standing in the s,
22: 5 they need no light of lamp or s,

SUPERIOR
Heb 1: 4 having become as much s to angels
7: 7 that the inferior is blessed by the s.

SUPPER
Lk 22:20 he did the same with the cup after s,
Rev 19: 9 to the marriage s of the Lamb."

SUPPLICATION → SUPPLICATIONS
Ps 6: 9 The LORD has heard my s;
Zec 12:10 a spirit of compassion and s
Eph 6:18 at all times in every prayer and s.

SUPPLICATIONS → SUPPLICATION
1Ti 2: 1 then, I urge that s, prayers,
Heb 5: 7 Jesus offered up prayers and s,

SUPPORT
Ps 18:18 but the LORD was my s.
Ro 11:18 that it is not you that s the root,

SURE
Nu 32:23 and be your sin will find you out.
Ps 19: 7 the decrees of the LORD are s,
Isa 28:16 a s foundation: "One who trusts
Heb 6:19 a s and steadfast anchor of the soul,

SURPASSES → SURPASSING
Eph 3:19 the love of Christ that s knowledge,
Php 4: 7 the peace of God, which s all
Sir 25:11 Fear of the Lord s everything;

SURPASSING → SURPASSES
Ps 150: 2 according to his s greatness!
2Co 9:14 pray for you because of the s grace

SURPRISE → SURPRISED
1Th 5: 4 for that day to s you like a thief;

SURPRISED → SURPRISE
1Pe 4:12 do not be s at the fiery ordeal that is

SURROUNDED → SURROUNDS
Lk 21:20 you see Jerusalem s by armies,
Heb 12: 1 s by so great a cloud of witnesses,
Rev 20: 9 of the earth and s the camp of

SURROUNDS → SURROUNDED
Ps 89: 8 Your faithfulness s you.
125: 2 so the LORD s his people,

SURVIVORS
Isa 1: 9 of hosts had not left us a few s,
Eze 14:22 Yet, s shall be left in it,

SUSA
Ne 1: 1 while I was in S the capital,
Est 1: 2 his royal throne in the citadel of S,

SUSANNA
Righteous woman wrongly accused of immorality (Sus 1:1-44); vindicated by Daniel (Sus 1:45-64).

SUSTAINS
Ps 3: 5 for the LORD s me.
Heb 1: 3 he s all things by his powerful word.

SWALLOW → SWALLOWED
Jnh 1:17 provided a large fish to s up Jonah;
Mt 23:24 You strain out a gnat but s a camel!

SWALLOWED → SWALLOW
Ge 41: 7 The thin ears s up the seven plump
Nu 16:32 earth opened its mouth and s them
1Co 15:54 "Death has been s up in victory."

SWEAR → SWORE, SWORN
Dt 10:20 and by his name you shall s.
Ps 24: 4 and do not s deceitfully.
Mt 5:34 Do not s at all, either by heaven,

SWEAT
Ge 3:19 By the s of your face you shall eat
Lk 22:44 [[s became like great drops of blood]]

SWEET → SWEETER
Ex 15:25 the water, and the water became s.
Ps 119:103 How s are your words to my taste,
Eze 3: 3 in my mouth it was as s as honey.
Rev 10:10 it was s as honey in my mouth,

SWEETER → SWEET
Jdg 14:18 "What is s than honey?
Ps 19:10 s also than honey, and drippings of

SWIFT
Ecc 9:11 the race is not to the s, nor the battle
2Pe 2: 1 bringing s destruction on themselves

SWINE
Mt 7: 6 do not throw your pearls before s,
Mk 5:12 "Send us into the s;
1Mc 1:47 sacrifice s and other unclean animals,

SWORD → SWORDS
Ge 3:24 and a s flaming and turning to guard
1Sa 17:47 LORD does not save by s and spear;
1Ch 21:30 he was afraid of the s of the angel
Isa 2: 4 shall not lift up s against nation,
49: 2 He made my mouth like a sharp s,
Hos 2:18 and I will abolish the bow, the s,
Mt 10:34 not come to bring peace, but a s.
Eph 6:17 the s of the Spirit, which is the word
Heb 4:12 sharper than any two-edged s,
Rev 1:16 mouth came a sharp, two-edged s,
19:15 a sharp s with which to strike down
Sir 21: 3 All lawlessness is like a two-edged s

SWORDS → SWORD
Isa 2: 4 shall beat their s into plowshares,
Joel 3:10 Beat your plowshares into s,

SWORE → SWEAR
Ex 6: 8 the land that I s to give to Abraham,
32:13 how you s to them by your own self,
Ps 132:11 The LORD s to David a sure oath
Heb 6:13 by whom to swear, he s by himself,

SWORN → SWEAR
Ge 22:16 "By myself I have s, says the LORD:
Ps 110: 4 The LORD has s and will not change
Heb 7:21 "The Lord has s and will not change

SYMPATHIZE* → SYMPATHIZE
Heb 4:15 unable to s with our weaknesses,

SYMPATHY → SYMPATHIZE
Php 2: 1 any compassion and s,
1Pe 3: 8 all of you, have unity of spirit, s,

SYNAGOGUE → SYNAGOGUES
Lk 4:16 he went to the s on the sabbath day,
8:41 man named Jairus, a leader of the s.
Ac 18:26 He began to speak boldly in the s;

SYNAGOGUES → SYNAGOGUE
Mt 4:23 teaching in their s and proclaiming
Jn 18:20 always taught in s and in the temple,

T

TABERNACLE
Ex 25: 9 concerning the pattern of the t
40:34 the glory of the LORD filled the t.
1Ch 6:48 for all the service of the t of the house

TABITHA* → See DORCAS

TABLE → TABLES
Ex 25:23 You shall make a t of acacia wood,
Ps 23: 5 a t before me in the presence of my

TABLES → TABLE
Mk 11:15 overturned the t of the money changers

TABLET → TABLETS
Pr 3: 3 write them on the t of your heart.

TABLETS → TABLET
Ex 31:18 gave him the two t of the covenant,
2Co 3: 3 not on t of stone but on t of human hearts.

TAKE → TAKEN, TAKES
Dt 12:32 do not add to it or t anything from
Mt 11:29 T my yoke upon you, and learn
Mk 8:34 deny themselves and t up their cross

TAKEN → TAKE
Ecc 3:14 added to it, nor anything t from it;
Heb 11: 5 By faith Enoch was t so that he did
Sir 44:16 Enoch pleased the Lord and was t

TAKES → TAKE
Jn 1:29 t away the sin of the world!
10:18 No one t it from me,
Rev 22:19 if anyone t away from the words of

TALENT
Mt 25:25 and hid your t in the ground.

TAMAR
1. Wife of Judah's sons Er and Onan (Ge 38:1-10). Children by Judah (Ge 38:11-30; Mt 1:3).
2. Daughter of David, raped by Amnon (2Sa 13).

TASTE → TASTED
Ps 34: 8 O t and see that the LORD is good;
Mt 16:28 not t death before they see the Son
Col 2:21 not handle, Do not t, Do not touch"?

TASTED → TASTE
Heb 6: 4 and have t the heavenly gift,
1Pe 2: 3 you have t that the Lord is good.

TAUGHT → TEACH
Isa 40:14 Who t him knowledge,
Jn 6:45 'And they shall all be t by God.'

TAX → TAXES
Mt 11:19 a friend of t collectors and sinners!'
Lk 18:10 Pharisee and the other a t collector.

TAXES → TAX
Mt 22:17 Is it lawful to pay t to the emperor,
Ro 13: 7 t to whom t are due,

TEACH → TAUGHT, TEACHER, TEACHERS, TEACHING
Dt 6: 1 to t you to observe in the land that
Ps 90:12 So t us to count our days that we
Jer 31:34 No longer shall they t one another,
Jn 14:26 will t you everything,
Col 3:16 t and admonish one another in all
1Ti 2:12 I permit no woman to t or
1Jn 2:27 so you do not need anyone to t you.

TEACHER → TEACH
Ecc 1: 1 words of the T, the son of David,
Mt 10:24 "A disciple is not above the t,
Jn 1:38 "Rabbi" (which translated means T)
1Ti 3: 2 respectable, hospitable, an apt t,

TEACHERS → TEACH
Ps 119:99 more understanding than all my t,
1Co 12:28 second prophets, third t;
Eph 4:11 evangelists, some pastors and t,
Jas 3: 1 Not many of you should become t,

TEACHING → TEACH
Mk 1:27 A new t—with authority!
Tit 1:11 by t for sordid gain what it is not right
2Jn 1: 9 who does not abide in the t of Christ,

TEAR → TORN
Mk 2:21 from the old, and a worse t is made.
Rev 7:17 God will wipe away every t from

TEETH → TOOTH
Mt 8:12 will be weeping and gnashing of t."

TEKEL
Da 5:27 t, you have been weighed on the scales

TELL → FORETOLD
Ps 50:12 "If I were hungry, I would not t you,
105: 2 t of all his wonderful works.
1Co 15:51 Listen, I will t you a mystery!

TEMPERATE
1Ti 3: 2 married only once, t, sensible,
Tit 2: 2 Tell the older men to be t, serious,

TEMPLE
1Sa 3: 3 Samuel was lying down in the t of the
2Ch 2:12 who will build a t for the LORD,

Ps   11: 4 The LORD is in his holy t;
Mt   4: 5 placed him on the pinnacle of the t,
      12: 6 something greater than the t is here.
Jn   2:21 was speaking of the t of his body.
1Co 3:16 you are God's t and that God's Spirit
Eph 2:21 and grows into a holy t in the Lord;
Rev 21:22 its t is the Lord God the Almighty
          and
1Mc 4:48 sanctuary and the interior of the t,

TEMPTATION* → TEMPTED, TEMPTER
1Ti   6: 9 who want to be rich into t and
Jas   1:12 Blessed is anyone who endures t.

TEMPTED → TEMPTATION
Mk 1:13 wilderness forty days, t by Satan;
Gal 6: 1 care that you yourselves are not t.

TEMPTER* → TEMPTATION
Mt   4: 3 The t came and said to him,
1Th 3: 5 that somehow the t had tempted
          you

TEN → TENTH
Ex 34:28 the covenant, the t commandments.
Da   7:24 out of this kingdom t kings shall
          arise,
Mt 25: 1 T bridesmaids took their lamps and
Rev 17:12 the t horns that you saw are t kings

TENDER → TENDERHEARTED
Hos 11: 8 my compassion grows warm and t.
Lk   1:78 By the t mercy of our God,

TENDERHEARTED* → HEART, TENDER
Eph 4:32 t, forgiving one another,

TENT
Ex 27:21 the t of meeting, outside the curtain
2Sa 7: 2 but the ark of God stays in a t."
2Co 5: 1 the earthly t we live in is destroyed,

TENTH → TEN
Ge 14:20 Abram gave him one t of everything
Isa   6:13 Even if a t part remain in it,

TERROR
Ex 23:27 I will send my t in front of you,
Ps   91: 5 You will not fear the t of the night,
Ro 13: 3 rulers are not a t to good conduct,

TEST → TESTED, TESTING
Dt   6:16 not put the LORD your God to
          the t,
Lk   4:12 not put the Lord your God to
          the t.'
   10:25 then a lawyer stood up to t Jesus.
2Co 13: 5 indeed, you fail to meet the t!
1Jn 4: 1 t the spirits to see whether they are
Sir 37:27 My child, t yourself while you live;

TESTED → TEST
Ge 22: 1 After these things God t Abraham.
Ps 78:41 They t God again and again,
Heb 4:15 been t as we are, yet without sin.

TESTIFIED → TESTIFY
Jn   1:15 (John t to him and cried out,
1Pe 1:11 it t in advance to the sufferings

TESTIFIES → TESTIFY
1Jn 5: 6 Spirit is the one that t,

TESTIFY → TESTIFIED, TESTIFIES, TESTIMONY
Jn 15:26 he will t on my behalf.
1Jn 5: 7 There are three that t:

TESTIMONY → TESTIFY
Nu 35:30 put to death on the t of a single
Mk 14:59 on this point their t did not agree.
Rev 1: 9 the word of God and the t of Jesus.

TESTING → TEST
1Co 10:13 No t has overtaken you that is not
Jas 1: 3 t of your faith produces endurance;

THADDAEUS* → =JUDAS
    Apostle (Mt 10:3; Mk 3:18); probably also
known as Judas son of James (Lk 6:16; Ac 1:13).

THANK → THANKS, THANKSGIVING
2Ch 29:31 bring sacrifices and t offerings to
Ps 52: 9 I will t you forever,
Sir 35: 4 gives alms sacrifices a t offering.

THANKS → THANK
1Ch 16: 8 give t to the LORD, call on his name,
Ps 107: 1 O give t to the LORD, for he is
          good;
Ro   1:21 not honor him as God or give t to
1Co 11:24 and when he had given t,
2Co 9:15 T be to God for his indescribable
Rev 4: 9 give glory and honor and t to

THANKSGIVING → THANK
Lev 7:12 If you offer it for t,
Ps 50:14 Offer to God a sacrifice of t,
Php 4: 6 with t let your requests be made
          known
Rev 7:12 glory and wisdom and t and honor

THEFT → THIEF
Mt 15:19 fornication, t, false witness, slander.

THEFTS* → THIEF
Rev 9:21 or their fornication or their t.

THIEF → THEFT, THEFTS, THIEVES
Ex 22: 1 The t shall make restitution,
Jn 10:10 The t comes only to steal and kill
1Th 5: 2 day of the Lord will come like a t in
Rev 16:15 ("See, I am coming like a t!

THIEVES → THIEF
Mt   6:19 and where t break in and steal;
Eph 4:28 T must give up stealing;

THINK → THINKING, THOUGHT, THOUGHTS
Ro 12: 3 not to t of yourself more highly than
1Co 10:12 So if you t you are standing,

THINKING → THINK
Ro   1:21 but they became futile in their t,
1Co 14:20 infants in evil, but in t be adults.

THIRD → THREE
Hos 6: 2 on the t day he will raise us up,
Mt 26:44 and prayed for the t time,
Lk 18:33 and on the t day he will rise again."
2Co 12: 2 was caught up to the t heaven—

THIRST → THIRSTY
Mt   5: 6 who hunger and t for righteousness,
Rev 7:16 will hunger no more, and t no more;

THIRSTY → THIRST
Mt 25:35 I was t and you gave me something
Jn   6:35 believes in me will never be t.
Rev 22:17 And let everyone who is t come.

THOMAS*
    Apostle (Mt 10:3; Mk 3:18; Lk 6:15; Jn 11:16;
14:5; 21:2; Ac 1:13). Doubted resurrection (Jn
20:24-28).

THORN → THORNS
2Co 12: 7 a t was given me in the flesh,

THORNS → THORN
Ge   3:18 t and thistles it shall bring forth for
Mt 13: 7 Other seeds fell among t,
Jn 19: 2 the soldiers wove a crown of t and

THOUGHT → THINK
1Co 13:11 I spoke like a child, I t like a child,
2Co 10: 5 take every t captive to obey Christ.

THOUGHTS → THINK
Isa 55: 8 For my t are not your t,
1Co 3:20 "The Lord knows the t of the wise,
Heb 4:12 judge the t and intentions of the
          heart.

THOUSAND → THOUSANDS
Ps 50:10 the cattle on a t hills.
    90: 4 t years in your sight are like
         yesterday
2Pe 3: 8 one day is like a t years, and a t
         years
Rev 20: 4 and reigned with Christ a t years.

THOUSANDS → THOUSAND
1Sa 18: 7 has killed his t, and David his ten t."
Da   7:10 A thousand t served him,
Rev 5:11 myriads of myriads and t of t,

THREE → THIRD
Ge 18: 2 and saw t men standing near him.
Ex 23:14 T times in the year you shall hold a
Mt 18:20 two or t are gathered in my name,
   26:34 you will deny me t times."
Mk 8:31 be killed, and after t days rise again.
2Co 12: 8 T times I appealed to the Lord
1Jn 5: 7 There are t that testify:

THRONE → THRONES
2Sa 7:13 the t of his kingdom forever.
Ps 45: 6 Your t, O God, endures forever
Isa   6: 1 I saw the LORD sitting on a t, high
Jer 33:21 not have a son to reign on his t,
Mt 19:28 the Son of Man is seated on the t
Heb 4:16 approach the t of grace with
         boldness,
    12: 2 his seat at the right hand of the t
Rev 4:10 they cast their crowns before the t,
   20:11 I saw a great white t and the one

THRONES → THRONE
Da   7: 9 t were set in place,
Rev 4: 4 Around the throne are twenty-four t,

THROW → THROWN
Ex   1:22 Hebrews you shall t into the Nile,
Mt   7: 6 do not t your pearls before swine,

THROWN → THROW
Ex 15: 1 horse and rider he has t into the
         sea.
Da   3:21 t into the furnace of blazing fire.
    6:12 shall be t into a den of lions?"
Rev 20:10 t into the lake of fire and sulfur,

THUMMIM
Ex 28:30 you shall put the Urim and the T,

THUNDER → THUNDERS
Ex   9:23 the LORD sent t and hail,
Rev 4: 5 and rumblings and peals of t,

THUNDERS → THUNDER
Rev 10: 3 he shouted, the seven t sounded.

TIBNI*
    King of Israel (1Ki 16:21-22).

TIE
Pr   6:21 t them around your neck.
Mt 23: 4 t up heavy burdens, hard to bear,

TIME → TIMES
Est   4:14 dignity for just such a t as this."
Ecc 3: 1 a t for every matter under heaven:
Da   7:25 for a t, two times, and half a t.
Ro   5: 6 the right t Christ died for the
         ungodly.
2Co 6: 2 See, now is the acceptable t;
Gal 4: 4 when the fullness of t had come,
Col 4: 5 making the most of the t.
Rev 12:14 for a t, and times, and half a t.
   22:10 of this book, for the t is near.

TIMES → TIME
Jos 6: 4 march around the city seven t,
Mt 16: 3 cannot interpret the signs of the t.
   18:22 seven t, but, I tell you, seventy-seven
         t.
Mk 14:30 you will deny me three t."
Sir 20:12 but pay for it seven t over.

TIMOTHY

Believer from Lystra (Ac 16:1). Joined Paul on second missionary journey (Ac 16-20). Sent to settle problems at Corinth (1Co 4:17; 16:10). Led church at Ephesus (1Ti 1:3). Co-writer with Paul (1Th 1:1; 2Th 1:1; Phm 1).

TITHE

Dt 12:17 the t of your grain, your wine, and
Mal 3:10 Bring the full t into the storehouse,

TITUS

Gentile co-worker of Paul (Gal 2:1-3; 2Ti 4:10); sent to Corinth (2Co 2:13; 7-8; 12:18), Crete (Tit 1:4-5).

TOBIAH

Enemy of Nehemiah (Ne 2:10-19; 4; 6; 13:4-9).

TOBIT

Tob 1: 1 This book tells the story of T

TODAY

Dt 30:15 set before you t life and prosperity,
Ps 2: 7 my son; t I have begotten you.
Lk 23:43 t you will be with me in Paradise."
Heb 1: 5 my Son; t I have begotten you"?
13: 8 Christ is the same yesterday and t and

TOGETHER

Mt 19: 6 God has joined t, let no one separate."
Eph 2: 5 made us alive t with Christ—

TOLA

A judge of Israel (Jdg 10:1-2).

TOMB

Mk 15:46 laid it in a t that had been hewn out
Lk 24: 2 the stone rolled away from the t,

TOMORROW

Isa 22:13 "Let us eat and drink, for t we die."
Mt 6:34 "So do not worry about t,
Jas 4:14 do not even know what t will bring.

TONGUE → DOUBLE-TONGUED, TONGUES

Ex 4:10 I am slow of speech and slow of t."
Ps 139: 4 before a word is on my t, O LORD,
Pr 18:21 Death and life are in the power of the t,
Isa 45:23 shall bow, every t shall swear."
1Co 14:19 than ten thousand words in a t.
Php 2:11 every t should confess that Jesus Christ
Jas 3: 8 but no one can tame the t—
Sir 20:18 is better than a slip of the t;
23: 7 DISCIPLINE OF THE t

TONGUES → TONGUE

Ac 2: 3 Divided t, as of fire, appeared
1Co 12:10 of t, to another the interpretation of t.
14: 5 in t, unless someone interprets,

TOOTH → TEETH

Ex 21:24 t for t, hand for hand, foot for foot,
Mt 5:38 'An eye for an eye and a t for a t.'

TORCHES

Da 10: 6 lightning, his eyes like flaming t,
Rev 4: 5 of the throne burn seven flaming t,

TORMENTED

Rev 20:10 they will be t day and night forever

TORN → TEAR

1Sa 28:17 has t the kingdom out of your hand,
Lk 23:45 curtain of the temple was t in two.

TORTURED

Mt 18:34 handed him over to be t until
Heb 11:35 were t, refusing to accept release,

TOUCH

Ge 3: 3 nor shall you t it, or you shall die.' "
Mt 9:21 only t his cloak, I will be made well.

Lk 24:39 T me and see;
Col 2:21 not handle, Do not taste, Do not t"?

TOWER

Ge 11: 4 and a t with its top in the heavens,
Pr 18:10 The name of the LORD is a strong t;

TRADITION

Mt 15: 2 disciples break the t of the elders?
Col 2: 8 empty deceit, according to human t,

TRAIN → TRAINING

Pr 22: 6 T children in the right way, and
1Ti 4: 7 T yourself in godliness,

TRAINING → TRAIN

1Ti 4: 8 while physical t is of some value,
2Ti 3:16 and for t in righteousness,

TRAITOR

Lk 6:16 and Judas Iscariot, who became a t.

TRANSFIGURED

Mt 17: 2 And he was t before them,

TRANSFORM* → TRANSFORMED

Php 3:21 will t the body of our humiliation

TRANSFORMED → TRANSFORM

Ro 12: 2 be t by the renewing of your minds,
2Co 3:18 are being t into the same image

TRANSGRESSION → TRANSGRESSIONS, TRANSGRESSORS

Ex 23:21 for he will not pardon your t;
Da 9:24 to finish the t, to put an end to sin,
Gal 6: 1 if anyone is detected in a t,

TRANSGRESSIONS → TRANSGRESSION

Ps 103:12 so far he removes our t from us.
Isa 53: 5 But he was wounded for our t,

TRANSGRESSORS → TRANSGRESSION

Ps 51:13 Then I will teach t your ways,
Isa 53:12 and was numbered with the t;

TRAP

Lk 20:20 in order to t him by what he said,
Ro 11: 9 their table become a snare and a t,

TREAD → TREADING

Mic 7:19 he will t our iniquities under foot.
Rev 19:15 he will t the wine press of the fury

TREADING → TREAD

Dt 25: 4 not muzzle an ox while it is t out
1Co 9: 9 not muzzle an ox while it is t out

TREASURE → TREASURED, TREASURES

Ps 119:11 I treasure your word in my heart,
Mt 6:21 where your t is, there your heart
2Co 4: 7 But we have this t in clay jars,
2Ti 1:14 Guard the good t entrusted to you,

TREASURED → TREASURE

Ex 19: 5 be my t possession out of all the

TREASURES → TREASURE

Col 2: 3 are hidden all the t of wisdom

TREE → TREES

Ge 3:24 to guard the way to the t of life.
Dt 21:23 hung on a t is under God's curse.
Mt 12:33 for the t is known by its fruit.
Ac 5:30 had killed by hanging him on a t.
Ro 11:24 grafted back into their own olive t.
Rev 22: 2 the t of life with its twelve kinds

TREES → TREE

Ps 96:12 all the t of the forest sing for joy
Zec 4:11 "What are these two olive t on the
Rev 11: 4 two olive t and the two lampstands

TREMBLE → TREMBLED, TREMBLING

Ps 114: 7 T, O earth, at the presence of the LORD
Hab 3: 6 he looked and made the nations t.

TREMBLED → TREMBLE

Ex 20:18 they were afraid and t and stood at

TREMBLING → TREMBLE

Ps 2:11 Serve the LORD with fear, with t
Php 2:12 your own salvation with fear and t;

TRESPASS → TRESPASSES

Ro 5:15 But the free gift is not like the t.

TRESPASSES → TRESPASS

Mt 6:14 For if you forgive others their t,
2Co 5:19 not counting their t against them,

TRIAL → TRIALS

Lk 11: 4 do not bring us to the time of t."
2Pe 2: 9 knows how to rescue the godly from t,
Rev 3:10 I will keep you from the hour of t

TRIALS → TRIAL

Jas 1: 2 whenever you face t of any kind,
1Pe 1: 6 you have had to suffer various t,

TRIBE → TRIBES

Nu 1: 4 A man from each t shall be with you
Ps 78:68 but he chose the t of Judah,
Rev 5: 5 See, the Lion of the t of Judah,

TRIBES → TRIBE

Ge 49:28 All these are the twelve t of Israel,
Ex 24: 4 to the twelve t of Israel.
Mt 19:28 judging the twelve t of Israel.
Rev 21:12 inscribed the names of the twelve t

TRIUMPH → TRIUMPHAL, TRIUMPHS

Ps 112: 8 they will look in t on their foes.
Pr 28:12 the righteous t, there is great glory,

TRIUMPHAL* → TRIUMPH

2Co 2:14 Christ always leads us in t procession,

TRIUMPHS → TRIUMPH

Jas 2:13 mercy t over judgment.

TROUBLE → TROUBLED

Job 14: 1 few of days and full of t,
Ps 9: 9 a stronghold in times of t.
Pr 11: 8 The righteous are delivered from t,
Isa 33: 2 our salvation in the time of t.
Mt 6:34 Today's t is enough for today.
Sir 51:10 do not forsake me in the days of t,

TROUBLED → TROUBLE

Jn 14: 1 "Do not let your hearts be t.

TRUE → TRUTH

Ps 119:151 and all your commandments are t.
Jn 1: 9 The t light, which enlightens
21:24 and we know that his testimony is t.
Ro 3: 4 everyone is a liar, let God be proved t,
1Jn 5:20 He is the t God and eternal life.
Rev 3:14 the Amen, the faithful and t witness,
19:11 its rider is called Faithful and T,
22: 6 "These words are trustworthy and t,

TRUMPET → TRUMPETS

Ex 19:16 a blast of a t so loud that all the
Joel 2:15 Blow the t in Zion; sanctify a fast;
1Co 15:52 twinkling of an eye, at the last t.
1Th 4:16 and with the sound of God's t,

TRUMPETS → TRUMPET

Nu 10: 2 Make two silver t; you shall make
Rev 8: 2 and seven t were given to them.

TRUST → ENTRUST, ENTRUSTED, TRUSTED, TRUSTEES, TRUSTS, TRUSTWORTHY

Ps 9:10 know your name put their t in you,
37: 3 T in the LORD, and do good;
119:42 for I t in your word.
Pr 3: 5 T in the LORD with all your heart,
Isa 12: 2 Surely God is my salvation; I will t,
Jer 17: 7 Blessed are those who t in the LORD,
Heb 2:13 And again, "I will put my t in him."
Sir 2: 6 T in him, and he will help you;

TRUSTED → TRUST
Ps 22: 4 they **t**, and you delivered them.
Da 3:28 delivered his servants who **t** in him.
 6:23 because he had **t** in his God.
Sus 1:35 for her heart **t** in the Lord.

TRUSTS → TRUST
Ps 86: 2 save your servant who **t** in you.
Mt 27:43 He **t** in God; let God deliver him

TRUSTWORTHY → TRUST
Ps 111: 7 and just; all his precepts are **t**.
Rev 22: 6 "These words are **t** and true,
1Mc 14:41 until a **t** prophet should arise,

TRUTH → TRUE
Ps 25: 5 Lead me in your **t**, and teach me,
 119:142 and your law is the **t**.
Pr 23:23 Buy **t**, and do not sell it;
Jn 1:17 grace and **t** came through Jesus
 Christ.
 4:23 worship the Father in spirit and **t**,
 8:32 and the **t** will make you free."
 14: 6 "I am the way, and the **t**, and the
 life.
 14:17 This is the Spirit of **t**,
Eph 4:15 But speaking the **t** in love,
2Ti 2:15 rightly explaining the word of **t**,
Tob 3: 2 all your ways are mercy and **t**;

TUNIC
Lk 9: 3 nor money—not even an extra **t**.
Jn 19:23 **t** was seamless, woven in one piece

TURN → TURNED
Ex 32:12 **T** from your fierce wrath;
Jos 1: 7 do not **t** from it to the right hand or
Isa 6:10 and **t** and be healed."
 45:22 **T** to me and be saved,
Mal 4: 6 He will **t** the hearts of parents to
 their
Lk 1:17 **t** the hearts of parents to their
 children

TURNED → TURN
Dt 23: 5 your God **t** the curse into a blessing
Isa 53: 6 we have all **t** to our own way,
Ro 3:12 All have **t** aside, together they have

TWELVE
Ge 49:28 All these are the **t** tribes of Israel,
Ex 24: 4 the mountain, and set up **t** pillars,
Jos 4: 3 'Take **t** stones from here out of the
Mt 10: 1 Jesus summoned his **t** disciples
Lk 9:17 **t** baskets of broken pieces.
Rev 21:12 inscribed the names of the **t** tribes
 22: 2 tree of life with its **t** kinds of fruit,

TWINKLING*
1Co 15:52 in the **t** of an eye, at the last
 trumpet

TWO → TWICE, TWO-EDGED
Ge 1:16 God made the **t** great lights—
 6:19 bring **t** of every kind into the ark,
Ex 31:18 the **t** tablets of the covenant,
Dt 17: 6 or three witnesses the death
Mt 6:24 "No one can serve **t** masters;
 19: 5 and the **t** shall become one flesh'?

TWO-EDGED → TWO
Heb 4:12 sharper than any **t** sword,
Rev 1:16 his mouth came a sharp, **t** sword,

TYRE
1Ki 5: 1 King Hiram of **T** sent his servants to
Eze 28:12 a lamentation over the king of **T**,
Mt 11:22 be more tolerable for **T** and Sidon

U

UNBELIEF → UNBELIEVER, UNBELIEVERS
Mk 6: 6 And he was amazed at their **u**.
 9:24 cried out, "I believe; help my **u**!"
Ro 11:20 were broken off because of their **u**,
1Ti 1:13 because I had acted ignorantly in **u**,

UNBELIEVER → UNBELIEF
1Co 10:27 If an **u** invites you to a meal and
2Co 6:15 does a believer share with an **u**?

UNBELIEVERS → UNBELIEF
2Co 6:14 Do not be mismatched with **u**.
2Es 15: 4 For all **u** shall die in their unbelief.

UNCHASTITY*
Mt 5:32 except on the ground of **u**,
 19: 9 divorces his wife, except for **u**,

UNCIRCUMCISED → UNCIRCUMCISION
Ex 12:48 But no **u** person shall eat of it;
Ac 7:51 people, **u** in heart and ears,
Ro 4:11 he had by faith while he was still **u**.
Col 3:11 circumcised and **u**, barbarian,
1Mc 1:48 and to leave their sons **u**.

UNCIRCUMCISION → UNCIRCUMCISED
1Co 7:19 Circumcision is nothing, and **u** is
Gal 5: 6 neither circumcision nor **u** counts

UNCLEAN → UNCLEANNESS
Lev 5: 2 when any of you touch any **u** thing
Isa 52:11 Touch no **u** thing;
Mk 3:11 Whenever the **u** spirits saw him,
Rev 21:27 But nothing **u** will enter it,

UNDER
Ps 8: 6 you have put all things **u** their feet,
Ac 4:12 for there is no other name **u** heaven
Ro 6:14 since you are not **u** law but **u** grace.
Eph 1:22 And he has put all things **u** his feet

UNDERSTAND → UNDERSTANDING
Job 42: 3 I have uttered what I did not **u**,
Pr 2: 5 then you will **u** the fear of the LORD
Hos 14: 9 Those who are wise **u** these things;
Mt 13:15 and **u** with their heart and turn—
Lk 24:45 opened their minds to **u** the
 scriptures,
Ac 8:30 "Do you **u** what you are reading?"
Eph 5:17 but **u** what the will of the Lord is.

UNDERSTANDING → UNDERSTAND
Ex 36: 1 has given skill and **u** to know how
Pr 2: 6 from his mouth come knowledge
 and **u**
Isa 40:14 and showed him the way of **u**?
Lk 2:47 heard him were amazed at his **u**
Php 4: 7 peace of God, which surpasses all **u**,
2Ti 2: 7 Lord will give you **u** in all things.

UNEXPECTED
Mt 24:44 Son of Man is coming at an **u** hour.

UNFAITHFUL → UNFAITHFULNESS
Ro 3: 3 What if some were **u**?

UNFAITHFULNESS → UNFAITHFUL
1Ch 9: 1 exile in Babylon because of their **u**.

UNGODLY
Ro 5: 6 the right time Christ died for the **u**.
2Pe 2: 6 example of what is coming to the **u**;
Sir 12: 5 but do not give to the **u**;

UNINTENTIONALLY
Lev 4: 2 When anyone sins **u** in any of
Nu 15:22 if you **u** fail to observe all these

UNITY
Ps 133: 1 when kindred live together in **u**!
Eph 4: 3 to maintain the **u** of the Spirit in the

UNJUST
Ro 3: 5 That God is **u** to inflict wrath on us?
Heb 6:10 For God is not **u**; he will

UNLEAVENED
Ex 12:17 shall observe the festival of **u** bread,
Mt 26:17 first day of **U** Bread the disciples

UNPRODUCTIVE*
1Co 14:14 my spirit prays but my mind is **u**.
Tit 3:14 so that they may not be **u**.

UNRIGHTEOUS → UNRIGHTEOUSNESS
Mt 5:45 rain on the righteous and on the **u**.
2Pe 2: 9 **u** under punishment until the day

UNRIGHTEOUSNESS → UNRIGHTEOUS
Ps 92:15 and there is no **u** in him.
1Jn 1: 9 and cleanse us from all **u**.

UPHOLD
Isa 42: 1 my servant, whom I **u**, my chosen,
Ro 3:31 On the contrary, we **u** the law.

UPRIGHT
Job 1: 1 That man was blameless and **u**,
Ps 7:10 God is my shield, who saves the **u**
Tit 1: 8 a lover of goodness, prudent, **u**,

UR
Ge 15: 7 LORD who brought you from **U** of

URIAH
Hittite husband of Bathsheba, killed (2Sa 11).

URIM
Ex 28:30 of judgment you shall put the **U**

USE → USEFUL
Ex 20: 7 not make wrongful **u** of the name of
Gal 5:13 only do not use your freedom as an
2Ti 2:20 for special **u**, some for ordinary.

USEFUL → USE
Eph 4:29 but only what is **u** for building up,
2Ti 3:16 scripture is inspired by God and is **u**

UZZIAH → =AZARIAH
 Son of Amaziah; king of Judah also known as
Azariah (2Ki 15:1-7; 1Ch 6:24; 2Ch 26). Struck
with leprosy because of pride (2Ch 26:16-23).

V

VAIN → VANITY
Lev 26:16 You shall sow your seed in **v**,
Ps 2: 1 and the peoples plot in **v**?
Mt 15: 9 in **v** do they worship me,
Php 2:16 that I did not run in **v** or labor in **v**.

VALLEY
Ps 23: 4 through the darkest **v**, I fear no evil;
Isa 40: 4 Every **v** shall be lifted up,
Joel 3:14 multitudes, in the **v** of decision!
Lk 3: 5 Every **v** shall be filled, and every

VALUE
Mt 13:46 on finding one pearl of great **v**,
Ro 3: 1 Or what is the **v** of circumcision?
1Ti 4: 8 while physical training is of some **v**,

VANITY → VAIN
Ecc 1: 2 **v** of vanities! All is **v**.
 12: 8 **V** of vanities, says the Teacher; all
 is **v**.

VASHTI
 Persian queen replaced by Esther (Est 1-2; AdE
1-2).

VEIL
Ex 34:33 he put a **v** on his face;
2Co 3:15 a **v** lies over their minds.

VENGEANCE → AVENGE, AVENGER, AVENGING
Ps 94: 1 O LORD, you God of **v**,
Isa 34: 8 For the LORD has a day of **v**,
Na 1: 2 the LORD takes **v** on his adversaries

VICTORY
Pr 21:31 but the **v** belongs to the LORD.
1Co 15:54 Death has been swallowed up in **v**."
1Jn 5: 4 the **v** that conquers the world, our
 faith.

VINDICATE → VINDICATED
Ps 26: 1 **V** me, O LORD, for I have walked
 135:14 For the LORD will **v** his people,

VINDICATED → VINDICATE
Job 13:18 I know that I shall be v.
Mt 11:19 Yet wisdom is v by her deeds."
1Ti 3:16 He was revealed in flesh, v in spirit,

VINE → VINEYARD
Ps 80: 8 You brought a v out of Egypt;
Jer 2:21 Yet I planted you as a choice v,
Jn 15: 1 "I am the true v, and my Father is
Rev 14:18 gather the clusters of the v of the

VINEYARD → VINE
1Ki 21: 1 Naboth the Jezreelite had a v in
Isa 5: 1 I had a v on a very fertile hill.
Mt 21:33 a landowner who planted a v,

VIOLENCE → VIOLENT
Ge 6:11 and the earth was filled with v.
Isa 53: 9 although he had done no v,
Hab 2:17 because of human bloodshed and v

VIOLENT → VIOLENCE
1Ti 3: 3 not v but gentle, not quarrelsome,
Tit 1: 7 or addicted to wine or v or greedy

VIPERS
Mt 23:33 You snakes, you brood of v!
Ro 3:13 venom of v is under their lips."

VIRGIN
Jer 31:21 Return, O v Israel, return to these
Mt 1:23 the v shall conceive and bear a son,
Lk 1:34 "How can this be, since I am a v?"
2Co 11: 2 present you as a chaste v to Christ.

VISION → VISIONS
Isa 22: 1 oracle concerning the valley of v.
Da 8:26 As for you, seal up the v,
Ac 26:19 not disobedient to the heavenly v,

VISIONS → VISION
Nu 12: 6 make myself known to them in v;
Eze 1: 1 were opened, and I saw v of God.
Da 1:17 Daniel also had insight into all v
Joel 2:28 and your young men shall see v.
Ac 2:17 and your young men shall see v,

VOICE
Isa 40: 3 A v cries out: "In the wilderness
Jn 1:23 v of one crying out in the wilderness
10: 3 and the sheep hear his v.
Heb 3: 7 says, "Today, if you hear his v,
Rev 3:20 if you hear my v and open the door,

VOID
Ge 1: 2 the earth was a formless v
Mt 15: 6 you make v the word of God.

VOW → VOWS
Ecc 5: 4 Fulfill what you v.
Sir 18:23 Before making a v, prepare yourself

VOWS → VOW
Ps 22:25 my v I will pay before those who fear

W

WAGES
Ro 6:23 For the w of sin is death,

WAIT → WAITS
Ps 27:14 W for the LORD; be strong,
La 3:26 should w quietly for the salvation of
Hab 2: 3 If it seems to tarry, w for it;
Ro 8:23 while we w for adoption,
1Th 1:10 to w for his Son from heaven,
Sir 2: 7 fear the Lord, w for his mercy;

WAITS → WAIT
Ps 130: 6 my soul w for the Lord more than
Ro 8:19 the creation w with eager longing

WALK → WALKED
Ge 17: 1 w before me, and be blameless.
Dt 10:12 to w in all his ways, to love him,

Ps 23: 4 I w through the darkest valley, I fear no
Isa 2: 5 let us w in the light of the LORD!
40:31 they shall w and not faint.
Jer 6:16 w in it, and find rest for your souls.
Jn 8:12 follows me will never w in darkness
2Co 5: 7 for we w by faith, not by sight.
Rev 21:24 The nations will w by its light,

WALKED → WALK
Ge 5:24 Enoch w with God; then he was no

WALL
Jos 6:20 shout, and the w fell down flat;
Ne 2:17 let us rebuild the w of Jerusalem,
Zec 2: 5 I will be a w of fire all around it,
Eph 2:14 has broken down the dividing w,

WANT → WANTING
Ps 23: 1 LORD is my shepherd, I shall not w.
Php 3:10 I w to know Christ and the power

WANTING → WANT
2Pe 3: 9 not w any to perish, but all to come to

WAR → WARRIOR, WARS
Ecc 3: 8 a time for w, and a time for peace.
Da 9:26 and to the end there shall be w.
Ro 7:23 in my members another law at w
Rev 19:11 righteousness he judges and makes w.

WARRIOR → WAR
Ex 15: 3 LORD is a w; the LORD is his name.

WARS → WAR
Mt 24: 6 you will hear of w and rumors of w;

WASH → WASHED
Ps 51: 7 w me, and I shall be whiter than snow.
Jn 13: 5 and began to w the disciples' feet
Rev 22:14 Blessed are those who w their robes,

WASHED → WASH
1Co 6:11 you were w, you were sanctified,
2Pe 2:22 sow is w only to wallow in the mud.

WATCH → WATCHES
Lk 2: 8 keeping w over their flock by night.
Heb 13:17 they are keeping w over your souls

WATCHES → WATCH
Ps 1: 6 LORD w over the way of the righteous,
Wis 3: 9 and he w over his elect.

WATER → WATERS
Ex 17: 1 no w for the people to drink.
Nu 20: 2 there was no w for the congregation;
Jer 2:13 the fountain of living w,
Eze 36:25 I will sprinkle clean w upon you,
Mk 1: 8 I have baptized you with w;
Jn 2: 9 tasted the w that had become wine,
3: 5 without being born of w and Spirit.
4:10 he would have given you living w."
1Jn 5: 6 the one who came by w and blood,
Rev 22: 1 showed me the river of the w of life,

WATERS → WATER
Ge 7: 7 the ark to escape the w of the flood.
Ex 14:21 dry land; and the w were divided.
Ecc 11: 1 Send out your bread upon the w,
Isa 55: 1 who thirsts, come to the w;

WAVERING
Heb 10:23 confession of our hope without w,
Jude 1:22 have mercy on some who are w;

WAY → WAYS
Ps 1: 6 watches over the w of the righteous,
86:11 Teach me your w, O LORD,
Pr 12:15 Fools think their own w is right,
22: 6 Train children in the right w,
Isa 40: 3 wilderness prepare the w of the LORD,

Mal 3: 1 sending my messenger to prepare the w
Mt 3: 3 'Prepare the w of the Lord,
Jn 14: 6 "I am the w, and the truth, and the life.
Ac 9: 2 found any who belonged to the W,
1Co 12:31 show you a still more excellent w.
Heb 10:20 the new and living w that he opened

WAYS → WAY
Dt 10:12 to walk in all his w, to love him,
Hos 14: 9 For the w of the LORD are right,
Rev 15: 3 Just and true are your w, King of
Sir 2:15 who love him keep his w.

WEAK → WEAKNESS, WEAKNESSES
Mt 26:41 indeed is willing, but the flesh is w."
Ro 14: 1 Welcome those who are w in faith,
1Co 1:27 God chose what is w in the world
2Co 12:10 whenever I am w, then I am strong.

WEAKNESS → WEAK
Ro 8:26 the Spirit helps us in our w;
1Co 15:43 It is sown in w, it is raised in power.

WEAKNESSES → WEAK
2Co 12:10 I am content with w, insults,
Heb 4:15 to sympathize with our w,

WEALTH
Ps 49: 6 those who trust in their w and boast
Pr 19: 4 W brings many friends,
Mt 13:22 and the lure of w choke
Rev 5:12 receive power and w and wisdom
Sir 5: 1 Do not rely on your w,

WEAPONS
Ecc 9:18 Wisdom is better than w of war,
2Co 6: 7 the w of righteousness for the right

WEAR
Isa 51: 6 the earth will w out like a garment,
Mt 6:31 or 'What will we w?'

WEARY
Isa 40:31 they shall run and not be w,
Heb 12: 3 you may not grow w or lose heart.

WEDDING
Jn 2: 1 there was a w in Cana of Galilee,

WEEKS
Ex 34:22 You shall observe the festival of w,
Lev 23:15 you shall count off seven w;
Da 9:24 "Seventy w are decreed for your

WEEP → WEEPING
Ecc 3: 4 a time to w, and a time to laugh;
Ro 12:15 w with those who w.

WEEPING → WEEP
Ps 30: 5 W may linger for the night,
Mt 2:18 Rachel w for her children;
8:12 will be w and gnashing of teeth."

WEIGHED
1Sa 2: 3 and by him actions are w.
Da 5:27 you have been w on the scales

WELL
Dt 6: 3 so that it may go w with you,
Mt 3:17 with whom I am w pleased."
17: 5 I am w pleased; listen to him!"
2Pe 1:17 with whom I am w pleased."

WEST
Ps 103:12 as far as the east is from the w,
Isa 43: 5 and from the w I will gather you;

WHEAT
Mt 13:25 and sowed weeds among the w,
Lk 22:31 demanded to sift all of you like w,
Jn 12:24 grain of w falls into the earth and dies,

WHIRLWIND → WIND
2Ki 2:11 Elijah ascended in a w into heaven.
Na 1: 3 His way is in w and storm,

WHITE → WHITER

Da	7: 9	his clothing was w as snow,
Mt	5:36	cannot make one hair w or black.
Rev	1:14	his hair were w as w wool, w as snow;
	20:11	a great w throne and the one who sat

WHITER → WHITE

Ps	51: 7	wash me, and I shall be w than snow.

WICKED → WICKEDNESS

Ge	13:13	Now the people of Sodom were w,
	18:23	the righteous with the w?
Ps	1: 5	the w will not stand in the judgment,
	73: 3	I saw the prosperity of the w.
Isa	48:22	no peace," says the LORD, "for the w."
Eze	18:23	any pleasure in the death of the w,
Da	12:10	None of the w shall understand,

WICKEDNESS → WICKED

Ge	6: 5	The LORD saw that the w of
Ps	45: 7	you love righteousness and hate w.
Lk	11:39	inside you are full of greed and w.

WIDE

Mt	7:13	the gate is w and the road is easy

WIDOW → WIDOWS

Ex	22:22	shall not abuse any w or orphan.
Ps	146: 9	he upholds the orphan and the w,
1Ti	5: 4	If a w has children or grandchildren,
Rev	18: 7	I am no w, and I will never see grief

WIDOWS → WIDOW

1Ti	5: 3	Honor w who are really w.
Jas	1:27	to care for orphans and w in their

WIFE → WIVES

Ge	2:24	and his mother and clings to his w,
Ex	20:17	shall not covet your neighbor's w,
Pr	18:22	who finds a w finds a good thing,
Mt	5:32	that anyone who divorces his w,
	19: 3	to divorce his w for any cause?"
Eph	5:28	He who loves his w loves himself.
Rev	21: 9	the bride, the w of the Lamb."
Tob	8: 6	his w Eve as a helper and support.
Sir	26: 3	A good w is a great blessing;

WILD

Ex	32:25	saw that the people were running w
Mk	1:13	and he was with the w beasts;
Ro	11:17	a w olive shoot,

WILDERNESS

Isa	40: 3	the w prepare the way of the LORD,
Mt	3: 3	voice of one crying out in the w:

WILL → FREEWILL, WILLING

Ps	40: 8	I delight to do your w, O my God;
	143:10	Teach me to do your w,
Isa	53:10	it was the w of the LORD to crush him
Mt	6:10	Your w be done, on earth as it is in
Lk	22:42	yet, not my w but your w be done."
Jn	4:34	"My food is to do the w of him who
Ro	9:19	For who can resist his w?"
Eph	6: 6	doing the w of God from the heart.
1Jo	5:14	if we ask anything according to his w,

WILLING → WILL

Mt	26:41	spirit indeed is w, but the flesh is weak.
Lk	22:42	if you are w, remove this cup from

WIND → WHIRLWIND

1Ki	19:11	but the LORD was not in the w;
Ps	1: 4	like chaff that the w drives away.
Ecc	1:14	all is vanity and a chasing after w.
Jn	3: 8	The w blows where it chooses,
Ac	2: 2	a sound like the rush of a violent w,

WINE

Dt	7:13	your grain and your w and your oil,
Ps	104:15	and w to gladden the human heart,
Pr	20: 1	W is a mocker, strong drink a
SS	1: 2	For your love is better than w,
Mt	9:17	is new w put into old wineskins;
Jn	2: 9	tasted the water that had become w,
Eph	5:18	Do not get drunk with w, for that is
Rev	18: 3	have drunk of the w of the wrath
Sir	40:20	W and music gladden the heart,

WINGS

Ex	19: 4	and how I bore you on eagles' w
Ps	17: 8	hide me in the shadow of your w,
Mal	4: 2	shall rise, with healing in its w.
Lk	13:34	hen gathers her brood under her w,

WIPE → WIPED

Isa	25: 8	God will w away the tears from all faces,
Rev	21: 4	he will w every tear from their eyes.

WIPED → WIPE

Ac	3:19	so that your sins may be w out,

WISDOM → WISE

Dt	4: 6	will show your w and discernment
1Ki	4:29	God gave Solomon very great w,
Job	11: 6	the secrets of w! For w is many-sided.
Pr	1:20	W cries out in the street;
	9:10	fear of the LORD is the beginning of w,
Ecc	1:13	to search out by w all that is done
Jer	9:23	Do not let the wise boast in their w,
Mt	13:54	this man get this w and these deeds
Lk	2:52	Jesus increased in w and in years,
Ro	11:33	the depth of the riches and w and
1Co	1:19	"I will destroy the w of the wise,
Col	2: 3	whom are hidden all the treasures of w
Jas	3:17	But the w from above is first pure,
Rev	5:12	wealth and w and might and honor
Wis	6:12	W is radiant and unfading,
Sir	1: 1	All w is from the Lord,
	24: 1	THE PRAISE OF w

WISE → WISDOM

Dt	4: 6	great nation is a w and discerning
Ps	19: 7	are sure, making w the simple;
Pr	3: 7	Do not be w in your own eyes;
	13:20	walks with the w becomes w,
Ecc	12:11	The sayings of the w are like goads,
Da	12: 3	are w shall shine like the brightness
Mt	25: 2	were foolish, and five were w.
1Co	1:26	not many of you were w by human
Eph	5:15	not as unwise people but as w,

WITHER → WITHERED, WITHERS

Ps	1: 3	and their leaves do not w.
Eze	47:12	Their leaves will not w nor their

WITHERED → WITHER

Mt	13: 6	since they had no root, they w away.
	21:19	And the fig tree w at once.

WITHERS → WITHER

Jn	15: 6	is thrown away like a branch and w;
1Pe	1:24	The grass w, and the flower falls,

WITHHOLD

Ps	84:11	No good thing does the LORD w from
Ro	8:32	He who did not w his own Son,

WITHOUT

2Ch	18:16	like sheep w a shepherd;
Pr	19: 2	Desire w knowledge is not good,
Mt	9:36	helpless, like sheep w a shepherd.
Jn	3:34	for he gives the Spirit w measure.
Eph	2:12	no hope and w God in the world.
Heb	4:15	tested as we are, yet w sin.

WITNESS → EYEWITNESSES, WITNESSES

Dt	19:15	single w shall not suffice to convict
Job	16:19	in fact, my w is in heaven,
Ro	2:15	their own conscience also bears w;
Rev	1: 5	faithful w, the firstborn of the dead,

WITNESSES → WITNESS

Mt	26:60	though many false w came forward.
Heb	12: 1	surrounded by so great a cloud of w,
Rev	11: 3	my two w authority to prophesy

WIVES → WIFE

1Ki	11: 3	and his w turned away his heart.
Eph	5:22	W, be subject to your husbands as
1Pe	3: 1	W, in the same way, accept the

WOE

Mt	23:13	"But w to you, scribes and Pharisees
Rev	8:13	"W, w, w to the inhabitants of the

WOLF → WOLVES

Isa	11: 6	The w shall live with the lamb,
Jn	10:12	sees the w coming and leaves the sheep

WOLVES → WOLF

Mt	7:15	but inwardly are ravenous w.

WOMAN → WOMEN

Ge	2:22	he made into a w and brought her to
	3:15	enmity between you and the w,
Ps	113: 9	He gives the barren w a home,
Pr	11:16	A gracious w gets honor,
	31:30	w who fears the LORD is to be praised.
Isa	54: 1	of the desolate w will be more than
Rev	12: 1	a w clothed with the sun,
Jdt	16: 5	foiled them by the hand of a w.
Sus	1: 2	a very beautiful w and one who feared

WOMB

Job	1:21	Naked I came from my mother's w,
Ps	139:13	knit me together in my mother's w.
Lk	1:44	the child in my w leaped for joy.

WOMEN → WOMAN

Ezr	10: 2	married foreign w from the peoples
Mt	24:41	Two w will be grinding meal
Lk	1:42	"Blessed are you among w,
	23:55	w who had come with him from
1Pe	3: 5	that the holy w who hoped in God

WONDERFUL → WONDERS

Ge	18:14	Is anything too w for the LORD?
Jdg	13:18	do you ask my name? It is too w."
Ps	107: 8	for his w works to humankind.
Isa	9: 6	named W Counselor, Mighty God,

WONDERS → WONDERFUL

Ex	3:20	and strike Egypt with all my w that
Ps	136: 4	who alone does great w,
Jn	4:48	signs and w you will not believe."
2Th	2: 9	who uses all power, signs, lying w,

WOOD

Dt	28:64	serve other gods, of w and stone,
1Co	3:12	silver, precious stones, w, hay,

WORD → BYWORD, WORDS

Dt	30:14	No, the w is very near to you;
1Ki	8:56	not one w has failed of all his good
Ps	56: 4	In God, whose w I praise,
	119:105	Your w is a lamp to my feet and
Pr	30: 5	Every w of God proves true;
Isa	40: 8	the w of our God will stand forever.
	55:11	my w be that goes out from my mouth;
Mk	4:14	The sower sows the w.
Jn	1: 1	In the beginning was the W, and the W was with God, and the W was God.

Jn 1:14 the W became flesh and lived among
17:17 in the truth; your w is truth.
Ro 9: 6 as though the w of God had failed.
2Ti 2:15 rightly explaining the w of truth.
Jas 1:22 But be doers of the w,
1Jn 2: 5 but whoever obeys his w,
Rev 19:13 his name is called The W of God.

WORDS → WORD
Ex 20: 1 Then God spoke all these w:
Dt 11:18 put these w of mine in your heart
Ps 5: 1 Give ear to my w, O LORD;
Pr 30: 6 not add to his w, or else he will rebuke
Hos 6: 5 killed them by the w of my mouth,
Mt 24:35 but my w will not pass away.
Lk 6:47 hears my w, and acts on them.
1Co 2:13 in w not taught by human wisdom
Rev 22:19 takes away from the w of the book

WORK → WORKS
Ge 2: 2 the seventh day God finished the w
Ex 20:10 you shall not do any w—
Ps 8: 3 heavens, the w of your fingers,
Jn 6:27 Do not w for the food that perishes,
Php 1: 6 who began a good w among you will
2:12 w out your own salvation with fear
2Ti 3:17 equipped for every good w.

WORKS → WORK
Ps 8: 6 given them dominion over the w
92: 5 How great are your w, O LORD!
Gal 2:16 and not by doing the w of the law,
5:19 the w of the flesh are obvious:
Eph 2: 9 not the result of w, so that no one may
1Ti 6:18 to do good, to be rich in good w,

WORLD
Ps 9: 8 He judges the w with righteousness;
Mt 5:14 "You are the light of the w.
16:26 gain the whole w but forfeit their life?
Jn 1:10 yet the w did not know him.
3:16 loved the w that he gave his only Son,
8:12 saying, "I am the light of the w.
16:33 courage; I have conquered the w!"
1Ti 6: 7 we brought nothing into the w,
Jas 4: 4 friend of the w becomes an enemy of
1Jn 2: 2 but also for the sins of the whole w.
2:15 not love the w or the things in the w.
Rev 11:15 kingdom of the w has become the

WORM
Ps 22: 6 But I am a w, and not human;
Mk 9:48 where their w never dies,

WORRY
Mt 6:25 do not w about your life,
10:19 not w about how you are to speak

WORSHIP → WORSHIPED
Ex 20: 5 not bow down to them or w them;
Ps 100: 2 W the LORD with gladness;
Mt 4: 9 if you will fall down and w me."
Jn 4:24 who w him must w in spirit and truth."
Ro 12: 1 which is your spiritual w.
Rev 22: 3 and his servants will w him;
Sir 35:10 Be generous when you w the Lord,

WORSHIPED → WORSHIP
Mt 28: 9 took hold of his feet, and w him.
Rev 5:14 And the elders fell down and w.

WORTHY
2Sa 22: 4 LORD, who is w to be praised,
Mt 10:38 and follow me is not w of me.

Eph 4: 1 to lead a life w of the calling
Heb 3: 3 Jesus is w of more glory than Moses
Rev 4:11 "You are w, our Lord and God,
5:12 W is the Lamb that was slaughtered

WOUND → WOUNDS
Ex 21:25 burn for burn, w for w, stripe for
Rev 13: 3 but its mortal w had been healed.

WOUNDS → WOUND
Ps 147: 3 brokenhearted, and binds up their w.
1Pe 2:24 by his w you have been healed.

WRAPPED
Mk 15:46 the body, w it in the linen cloth,
Lk 2: 7 w him in bands of cloth,

WRATH
Nu 16:46 For w has gone out from the LORD;
Ps 2: 5 Then he will speak to them in his w,
6: 1 or discipline me in your w.
Pr 15: 1 A soft answer turns away w,
Jer 25:15 my hand this cup of the wine of w,
La 4:11 The LORD gave full vent to his w;
Zep 1:15 That day will be a day of w,
Mt 3: 7 you to flee from the w to come?
Ro 1:18 w of God is revealed from heaven
1Th 1:10 rescues us from the w that is coming
Rev 6:17 the great day of their w has come,
Sir 16:11 For mercy and w are with the Lord;

WRESTLED
Ge 32:24 a man w with him until daybreak.

WRITE → WRITING, WRITTEN, WROTE
Ex 34:27 LORD said to Moses: W these words;
Nu 17: 2 W each man's name on his staff,
Dt 6: 9 w them on the doorposts of your house
Pr 7: 3 w them on the tablet of your heart.
Jer 31:33 and I will w it on their hearts,
Heb 8:10 and w them on their hearts,
Rev 21: 5 "W this, for these words are trustworthy

WRITING → WRITE
Ex 32:16 and the w was the w of God,
Da 5: 1 "Whoever can read this w
2Es 14:24 prepare for yourself many w tablets,

WRITTEN → WRITE
Jos 23: 6 to observe and do all that is w in
Da 12: 1 who is found w in the book.
Lk 24:44 everything w about me in the law
Jn 21:25 if every one of them were w down,
Rev 21:27 are w in the Lamb's book of life.
2Es 14:44 forty days, ninety-four books were w.

WRONG → WRONGDOING, WRONGED
Nu 5: 7 shall make full restitution for the w,
Lk 23:41 but this man has done nothing w."
Ac 23: 9 "We find nothing w with this man.
Ro 13:10 Love does no w to a neighbor;

WRONGDOING → DO, WRONG
Ex 23: 2 You shall not follow a majority in w
1Jn 5:17 All w is sin, but there is sin that is not

WRONGED → WRONG
1Co 6: 7 Why not rather be w?

WROTE → WRITE
Ex 24: 4 And Moses w down all the words
34:28 he w on the tablets the words of the
Jn 5:46 believe me, for he w about me.

Y

YEAR → YEARS
Ex 23:14 Three times in the y you shall hold a
Heb 10: 1 continually offered y after y,

YEARS → YEAR
Ge 1:14 and for seasons and for days and y,
Ex 12:40 in Egypt was four hundred thirty y.
Nu 14:34 forty y, and you shall know my
2Ch 36:21 it kept sabbath, to fulfill seventy y.
Ps 90: 4 For a thousand y in your sight are like
Jer 25:12 Then after seventy y are completed,
Da 9: 2 of Jerusalem, namely, seventy y.
Gal 4:10 and months, and seasons, and y.
2Pe 3: 8 the LORD one day is like a thousand y,
Rev 20: 2 and bound him for a thousand y,

YEAST
Mt 16: 6 beware of the y of the Pharisees and
Gal 5: 9 A little y leavens the whole batch of

YESTERDAY
Heb 13: 8 Jesus Christ is the same y and today

YOKE
Mt 11:30 my y is easy, and my burden is light."
Gal 5: 1 not submit again to a y of slavery.

YOUNG → YOUTH
Ps 119: 9 can y people keep their way pure?
Joel 2:28 and your y men shall see visions.
Ac 2:17 and your y men shall see visions,

YOUTH → YOUNG
Ps 71: 5 my trust, O LORD, from my y.
Ecc 12: 1 Remember your creator in the days of your y,

Z

ZACCHAEUS
Lk 19: 2 A man was there named Z;

ZEAL → ZEALOUS
Ps 69: 9 z for your house that has consumed me
Isa 37:32 The z of the LORD of hosts will do this.
Jn 2:17 Z for your house will consume me.
Ro 10: 2 testify that they have a z for God,
Php 3: 6 as to z, a persecutor of the church;
1Mc 2:26 Thus he burned with z for the law,

ZEALOUS → ZEAL
Nu 25:13 because he was z for his God,
1Ki 19:10 "I have been very z for the LORD,

ZEBULUN
Son of Jacob by Leah (Ge 30:20; 35:23; 1Ch 2:1). Tribe of blessed (Ge 49:13; Dt 33:18-19), numbered (Nu 1:31; 26:27), allotted land (Jos 19:10-16; Eze 48:26), failed to fully possess (Jdg 1:30), supported Deborah (Jdg 4:6-10; 5:14, 18), David (1Ch 12:33), 12,000 from (Rev 7:8).

ZECHARIAH
1. Son of Jeroboam II; king of Israel (2Ki 15:8-12).
2. Post-exilic prophet who encouraged rebuilding of temple (Ezr 5:1; 6:14; Zec 1:1).

ZEDEKIAH → =MATTANIAH
1. False prophet (1Ki 22:11-24; 2Ch 18:10-23).
2. Mattaniah, son of Josiah (1Ch 3:15), made king of Judah by Nebuchadnezzar (2Ki 24:17-25:7; 2Ch 36:10-14; Jer 37-39; 52:1-11).

ZEPHANIAH
Prophet; descendant of Hezekiah (Zep 1:1).

ZERUBBABEL
Descendant of David (1Ch 3:19; Mt 1:3). Led return from exile (Ezr 2:2; Ne 7:7). Governor of Israel; helped rebuild temple (Ezr 3; Hag 1-2; Zec 4).

ZIMRI

    King of Israel (1Ki 16:9-20).

ZION

2Sa   5: 7 David took the stronghold of Z,
Ps   2: 6 I have set my king on Z, my holy
            hill.
    48: 2 is the joy of all the earth, Mount Z,

Ps 78:68 Mount Z, which he loves.
Isa 28:16 I am laying in Z a foundation
            stone,
Mic   4: 2 For out of Z shall go forth
            instruction,
Zec   9: 9 Rejoice greatly, O daughter Z!
Mt 21: 5 "Tell the daughter of Z,
Ro 11:26 "Out of Z will come the Deliverer;

1Pe   2: 6 "See, I am laying in Z a stone,
Rev 14: 1 the Lamb, standing on Mount Z!

ZIPPORAH*

    Daughter of Reuel; wife of Moses (Ex 2:21-22; 4:20-26; 18:1-6).

ZOPHAR*

    One of Job's friends (Job 2:11; 11; 20; 42:9).

MAP 1

Jerusalem in the Late Second Temple Period

Approximate lines of City Walls:
- Medieval and Ottoman Jerusalem
- under Herod the Great
- added by Agrippa I
- Modern roads
- Original Rock Contours are shown.

B = Bridge
C. of I. = Court of Israel
C. of P. = Court of Priests
C. of W. = Court of Women
G = Gate
G* = Gate of Coponius = Barclay's Gate
G** = ? Double (Huldah) Gate

Mount of Olives
Bethany
Gethsemane

Kidron Valley
Jehoshaphat Valley
Tyropoeon Valley
Hinnom Valley

? Psalms Tower
Pool
Shalem Gate
Solomon's
Beautiful Gate
Portico
TEMPLE
Court of Gentiles
Royal Portico
Pinnacle of Temple
Ophel
Kidron Spring
Conduit
Solomon's Pool
Pool of Siloam
Bethesda
Pool of Bethesda
Antonia Tower
Aqaba
Caverns
BEZETHA
Warren's Gate
Western Gate
Western Wall
Gate (by Wilson's Arch)
Gate (by Robinson's Arch)
ROYAL WALL
Damascus Gate
? Peristinum
Jewish Tombs
Golgotha
? Mariamne
Phasael
? Hippicus
? Peristinum
Pool
Tomb of Helena Princess of Adiabene
Emmaus
ROYAL PALACE
PRAETORIUM
Tomb Gate
Gate (Kaaba)
Pool
Ottoman Wall
Aqueduct
Essene Gate
Family Tomb of Herod
Pool
Bethlehem

OUTWORK OF UNCERTAIN ORIGIN

300 Metres
300 Yards

© Oxford University Press

Jerusalem in the 1st Millennium BCE

Approximate lines of City Walls:
- Medieval and Ottoman Jerusalem
- of original Zion (2 Sam 5:7)
- extended during the Monarchy extended after the Exile (by Maccabees, 2nd Cent. BCE)
- Eastern wall of Nehemiah's city
- Modern roads
- Original Rock Contours are shown.

Mount of Olives
Kidron Valley
Hinnom Valley (? Topheth)

Post-exilic Jewish tombs
Monument of Bene Hezir
Pre-exilic tombs

TEMPLE
Solomon's
ALTAR
? PALACE
Barris
? Tower of Hananel
Manasseh's Wall
Solomon's
Wall
LOWER CITY
CITY OF DAVID
SILOAM
Old Conduit
Conduit
Gihon Spring
En-rogel Spring
Central (Cheesemakers') Valley
Tombs
Wall of Zion
Lower Pool
Old Pool
? MISHNA (SECOND QUARTER)
UPPER CITY
Wall of Hezekiah (Maccabees?)
Wall

This lines of the southern walls of the city after the Exile are uncertain

OTTOMAN WALL

300 Metres
300 Yards

© Oxford University Press

OUTER BORDER SHOWS 200 YARD SUBDIVISIONS

MAP 2

The Land of Canaan

GAD, etc. Tribes of Israel said to have settled in Transjordan

EDOM, etc. Kingdoms said to have been encountered by the Israelites at the time of the settlement

Cities mentioned in Numbers and Deuteronomy, but not in Genesis

20 Miles

20 Kilometres

A R A M
(S Y R I A)

Damascus

Mt. Hermon (Sirion, Senir)

Mt. Lebanon

ARGOB

B A S H A N

MANASSEH

Edrei

Ramoth-gilead

Karnaim
Ashtaroth
Golan

GESHUR

MAACAH

Laish (Dan)

Ijon

Aduru

Abel

Beth-anath?

Kedesh

Hazor

R. Jordan

Sea of Chinnereth

Chinnereth

HAVVOTH-JAIR

Yanoam

Beth-yerah (Philoteria)

Madon

Hannathon

Shimron
Japhia

Anaharath?

G i l e a d

Ham

Pehel (Pella)

Jordan

A r a b a h

Beth-shean
Rehob

Beth-haggan (En-gannim)
Ibleam
Dothan

Tirzah

Mt. Ebal

Sidon

Tyre

Uzu

Acco

Achzib

Achshaph?

Mt. Carmel

Jokneam

Dor

Janoah

Merom

Kanah

Shunem

Megiddo

Taanach

Aruna

Migdal
Gath of Sharon
Arubboth
Yehem
Socoh

Vale of Sharon

h i l l   c o u n t r y

T H E

G R E A T

S E A

MAP 2

OUTER BORDER SHOWS 10 MILE SUBDIVISIONS

(The Western Sea)

AMMON

GAD

REUBEN

AMORITES

MOAB

EDOM

Salt Sea (Sea of the Arabah)

Hill Country of Israel

Hill Country of Judah

The Shephelah

The Negeb

Possible location of the cities of Sodom, Gomorrah, Admah, Zeboiim, and Zoar in the Valley of Siddim

Joppa, Beth-dagon, Ashdod, Ashkelon, Gaza, Beth-eglaim (Eglaim), Yurza, Sharuhen, Rehoboth, Beer-sheba, Moladah, Hormah, Aroer, Arad?, ARAD?, Debir, Ziph, Hazazon-tamar, Ascent of Akrabbim, Khanazir, Feifa, Zoar, es-Safi, Numeira, Bab ed-Dra, Ar, Aroer, Dibon, Kedemoth?, Mattanah, Bezer?, Elealeh, Heshbon, Medeba, Baal-meon (Beon), Kiriathaim, Ataroth, Mt. Nebo, Mts. of Abarim, Pisgah, Beth-jeshimoth, Gilgal, Jericho, Abel-shittim (Shittim), Beth-nimrah, Jazer, Jogbehah, Rabbah, Penuel, Mahanaim, Succoth, Shechem, Mt. Gerizim, Bethel (Luz), Ai, Gibeon, Jerusalem (Salem), Bethlehem (Ephrath), Mamre, Hebron (Kiriath-arba), Beth-tappuah, Adullam, Keilah, Lachish, Socoh, Chezib, Gath?, Timnah, Beth-shemesh, Aijalon, Beth-horon, Gezer, Lod, Ono, Aphek, Ekron, Eglon?, Gerar, Ziklag?, River Jabbok, Plains of Moab, R. Nahaliel, R. Arnon, Brook Zered

MAP 3

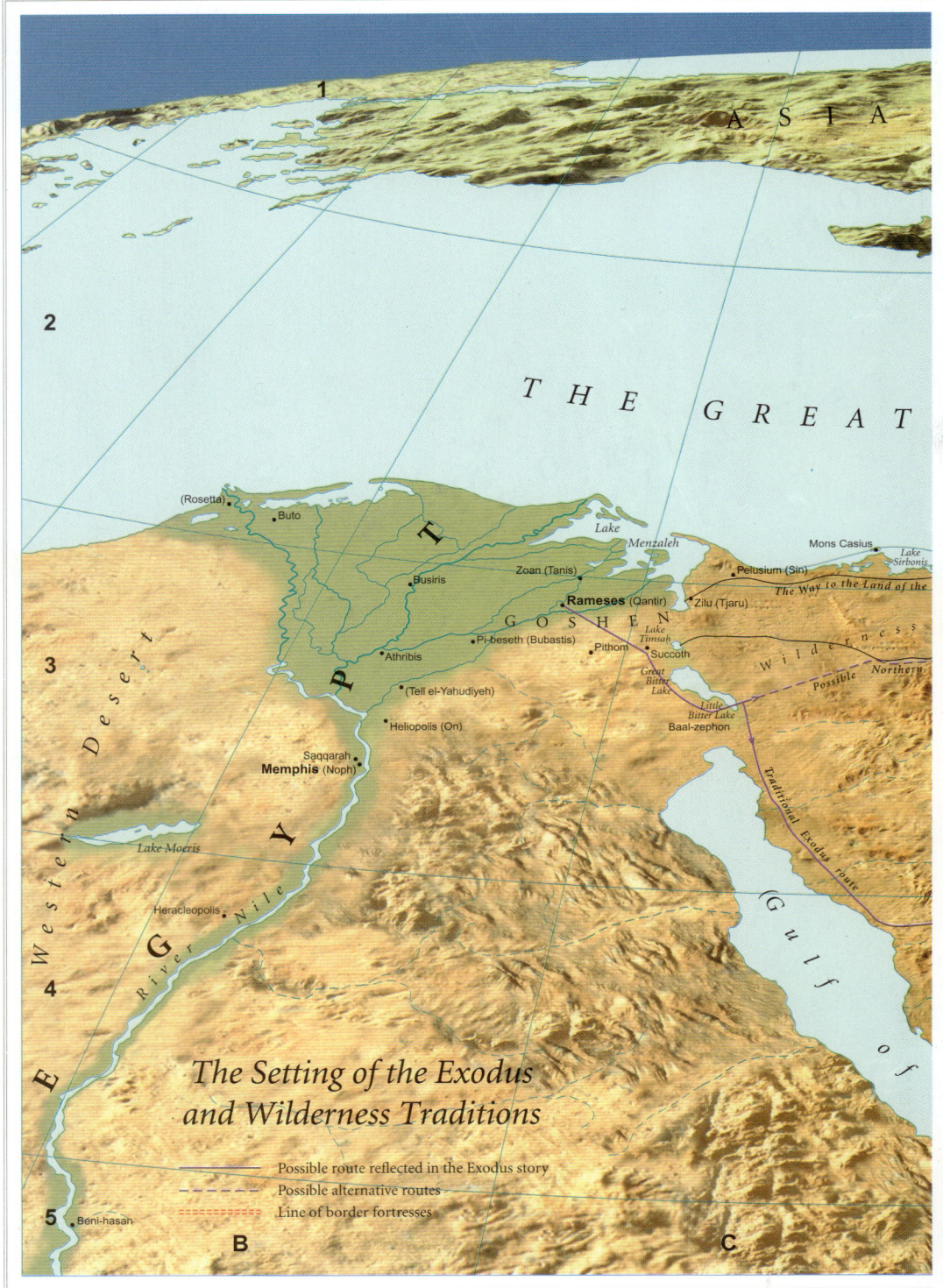

1

ASIA

2

THE GREAT

(Rosetta)

Buto

Busiris

Zoan (Tanis)

Lake Menzaleh

Mons Casius

Lake Sirbonis

Pelusium (Sin)

Rameses (Qantir)

Zilu (Tjaru)

The Way to the Land of the

GOSHEN

Pi-beseth (Bubastis)

Pithom

Lake Timsah

Succoth

3

Western Desert

Athribis

E   G   Y   P   T

(Tell el-Yahudiyeh)

Great Bitter Lake

Little Bitter Lake

Wilderness

Possible   Northern

Heliopolis (On)

Baal-zephon

Saqqarah

Memphis (Noph)

Traditional Exodus route

Lake Moeris

(Gulf of

Heracleopolis

River Nile

4

The Setting of the Exodus and Wilderness Traditions

——————— Possible route reflected in the Exodus story

– – – – – Possible alternative routes

┅┅┅┅┅┅ Line of border fortresses

5

Beni-hasan

B

C

MAP 3

M I N O R

Cyprus

River Euphrates

1

2

S E A

Sea of Chinnereth

Bethel
Ai
Jerusalem • Jericho
Ashdod • *Philistia*
Azekah
Gezer
Libnah?
Lachish
Gaza
Hebron
Debir
Juttah
ARAD?
Beer-sheba
Gerar
Arad?
Hormah
The Negeb
Wilderness of Zin
Bene-jaakan (Beeroth)
Hazar-addar
Azmon
Hazazon-tamar
Mt. Sinai? (Horeb)
(Jebel Helal)
Kadesh-barnea
(Meribah)
Oboth
Philistines
Brook of Egypt
The Way to Shur
of Shur
Exodus routes

C A N A A N
Plain of

Shittim
Rabbah
Heshbon
Mt. Nebo
Medeba
Dibon
Salt Sea
R. Arnon
M O A B
Kir-hareseth
Sela
Punon
Bozrah
The Arabah
E D O M
The King's Highway
Alternative Exodus route

A r a b i a n

3

Ezion-geber

D e s e r t

S I N A I

Wilderness of Sin?

M I D I A N

(Gulf of 'Aqaba)

Mt. Sinai (Horeb)?
(Jebel Musa)

4

S u e z)

© Oxford University Press

5

D   R e d   S e a   E

MAP 4

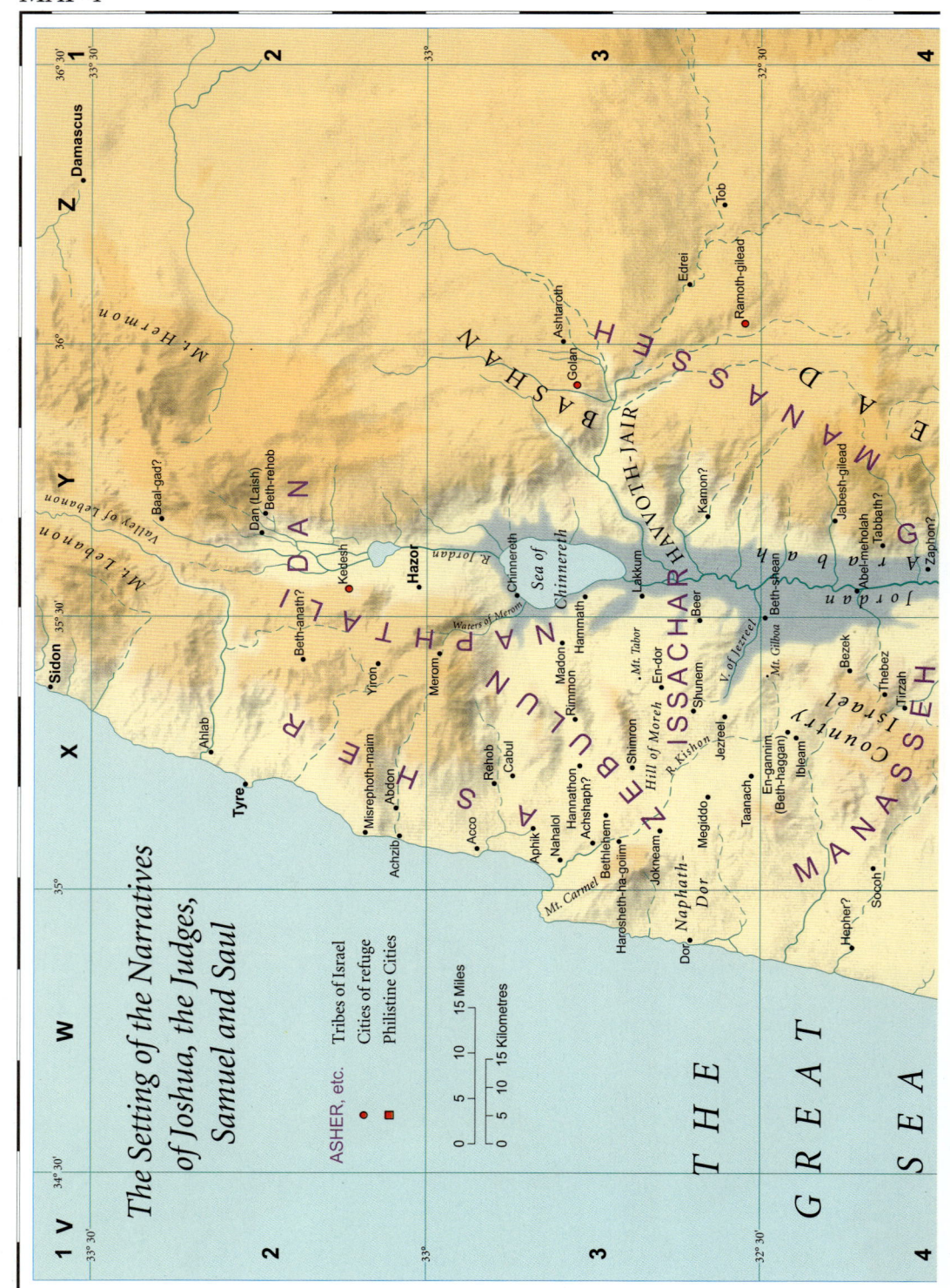

The Setting of the Narratives of Joshua, the Judges, Samuel and Saul

ASHER, etc. Tribes of Israel
● Cities of refuge
■ Philistine Cities

0   5   10   15 Miles
0 5 10 15 Kilometres

Damascus

Mt. Hermon

Mt. Lebanon
Valley of Lebanon
Baal-gad?

Sidon

Tyre
Ahlab
Achzib
Abdon
Misrephoth-maim
Acco
Aphik
Nahalol
Rehob
Cabul

ASHER

Dan (Laish)
Beth-rehob
Kedesh
Beth-anath?
Yiron
Merom
Waters of Merom

NAPHTALI

Hazor
Chinnereth
Sea of Chinnereth
R. Jordan

DAN

Madon
Rimmon
Hammath
Hannathon
Achshaph?
Bethlehem
Harosheth-ha-goiim
Joknеam
Shimron
Hill of Moreh
Mt. Tabor

ZEBULUN

ISSACHAR

Beer
Lakkum
Hammath

HAVVOTH-JAIR

BASHAN

Golan
Ashtaroth
Edrei
Tob
Ramoth-gilead
Kamon?

MANASSEH

GAD

Jabesh-gilead
Tabbath?
Abel-meholah
Zaphon?

Jordan

Beth-shean
Mt. Gilboa
Beth-haggan
En-gannim
Jezreel
Taanach
Megiddo
Dor
Naphath-Dor
Mt. Carmel

Shunem
En-dor
V. of Jezreel
R. Kishon
Ibleam

MANASSEH

Country of Israel

Bezek
Thebez
Tirzah
Socoh
Hepher?

THE GREAT SEA

MAP 4

OUTER BORDER SHOWS 10 MILE SUBDIVISIONS

AMMON

MOAB

EDOM

Karkor
[33° 36'E]

Jogbehah

Rabbah

Bezer?

Succoth Penuel

R. Jabbok

Zarethan?

Adam

River Jabbok

Betonim

Beth-nimrah

Atarotth

Kedemoth?

Medeba

Dibon   Aroer

Heshbon

Mt. Pisgah

Shittim

Beth-peor

Beth-jeshimoth

Kiriathaim

Mt. Nebo?

Beth-baal-meon

Zereth-shahar

R. Arnon

REUBEN

GILEAD

Arumah

Shechem

Mt. Ebal

Mt. Gerizim

Pirathon

Tappuah

Lebonah

Shiloh

Hill   *of*   **EPHRAIM**

Timnath-serah

Ephron (Ophrah)

Rimmon

Michmash

Bethel   Ai

Naarah   Gilgal

Jericho

Middin?

Secacah?

Nibshan?

V. of Achor

Mizpah

Upper Beth-horon

Gibeon

Ramah

Anathoth

Jerusalem
(Jebus)

BENJAMIN

Beeroth?

Gibeah?

Zela

Bethlehem

Etam

Beth-zur

Hebron

Ziph

Maon

Eshtemoa

En-gedi

Sea of the Arabah
(The Salt Sea)

Hill   *Country*   *of*   *Judah*

Shaalbim

Ajalon

Lower Beth-horon

Chephirah

Baalah

Kiriath-jearim

Lehi?

Zorah

Jarmuth

Timnah

Giloh

Adullam

Keilah

Socoh

Mareshah

Jezreel?

Debir

Goshen?

Jattir

Anab

Betkul (Bethuel)

Kabzeel?

Beer-sheba

Hazar-shual

Hormah

Madmannah?

Ashan

Adadah (Aroer)

Arad?

ARAD?

Ascent of
Akrabbim

SIMEON

The Negeb

Ziph?

Gath-rimmon?

Joppa

Beth-dagon

Asor

Ramathaim-zophim

Aphek

Baal-shalishah

EPHRAIM

Gibbethon

Gezer

Shikkeron

DAN

Ekron

Timnah*

Beth-shemesh

Makkedah?

Gath?

Azekah?

V. of Elah

Libnah

Lachish

Jabneel

Mount Baalah

Baalath?

Ashdod

Ashkelon

Gaza

Eglon?

Gerar

Ziklag?

The   *Shephelah*

Brook Besor

PHILISTINES

Brook Zered

MAP 5

The Setting of the Narratives
of David and Solomon

SYRIA, etc.   Non-Israelite peoples
■   Places fortified by Solomon
I–XII   Solomon's administrative
          districts (1 Kgs. 4. 7–19)

20 Miles

20 Kilometres

MAP 5

© Oxford University Press

OUTER BORDER SHOWS 10 MILE SUBDIVISIONS

AMMON

Rabbah (Rabbath-ammon)

GAD

Lo-debar?
Succoth
Zarethan?
Mahanaim
Jazer

R. Jabbok

Shechem
Pirathon
Mt. Gerizim
Shiloh

Baal-hazor
Ephraim
Bethel
Upper Beth-horon
Gibeon
Geba
Beeroth?
Anathoth
Jerusalem
Gilgal
Jericho

Heshbon
Medeba

MOAB

Dibon
Aroer

R. Nahaliel
R. Arnon

Kir-hareseth

EDOM

Brook Zered

Salt Sea
(Sea of the Arabah)

Wilderness of Judah

ISRAEL

Zeredah
Gath-rimmon
Joppa

Beth-hanan
Lower Beth-horon
Shaalbim
Gezer
Makaz
Baalath?
Ashdod
Ekron

Kiriath-jearim
Sorek
Elon
Beth-shemesh
Gath?
Libnah?
Adullam
Giloh

Bethlehem
Netophah
Tekoa

Hebron
Carmel

Arad

JUDAH

Debir
Kabzeel?

Valley of Salt

The Negeb

Beer-sheba

The Shephelah (Lowland)

Ashkelon

Gaza

Gerar
Ziklag?

Brook Besor

AMALEKITES

Tamar
(30° 48'N)

PHILISTINES

MAP 6

The Kingdoms of
Israel and Judah

ISRAEL, JUDAH   Hebrew kingdoms
ASHER, etc.   Tribal areas
SYRIA, etc.   Non-Israelite peoples
- - - -   Approximate boundary
                 between Israel, Judah
                 and Philistia

20 Miles
20 Kilometres
0   10   20
0   10

SYRIA (ARAM)

ZOBAH
Damascus
R. Pharpar
R. Abana

BASHAN

HAURAN

Karnaim
Ashtaroth
Edrei
Ramoth-gilead

MANASSEH
HAVVOTH-JAIR
Aphek
Beth-arbel

Mt. Hermon
Entrance to Hamath
Mt. Lebanon

Dan
Ijon
Kedesh
Hazor
Chinnereth
Sea of Chinnereth
R. Jordan

Tishbe
Brook Cherith
Abel-meholah

ISRAEL

GILEAD

Abel-beth-maacah
(Abel-maim)

NAPHTALI

Yiron
Merom
Chinnereth

Sidon
Zarephath

SIDONIANS

ASHER

GALILEE
Janoah
Rumah
Hannathon

ZEBULUN
Gath-hepher
Mt. Tabor

ISSACHAR
V. of Jezreel
Shunem
Jezreel

MANASSEH
Beth-haggan
Ibleam
Dothan

Tirzah
Mt. Ebal

Tyre
Acco
R. Kishon
Mt. Carmel
Jokmeam
Megiddo
Taanach
Borim

Socoh
Yazith
Samaria
Siphtan

Dor

of Sharon

THE GREAT SEA

Sidon

MAP 6

© Oxford University Press

OUTER BORDER SHOWS 10 MILE SUBDIVISIONS

AMMON

Rabbah

Penuel
Lo-debar?
Mahanaim

GILEAD

River Jabbok

Er-Jabbok

The Jordan River

EPHRAIM

Shechem
Mt. Gerizim

Pirathon
Baal-shalishah
Tappuah
Zeredah

Shiloh
Jeshanah
Ephron
Baal-hazor
Ai
Bethel
Zemaraim
Mizpah
Geba
Ramah
Gibeah?
Ajjalon
Beth-horon

BENJAMIN

Gilgal
Jericho
Baal-peor

Heshbon
Bezer? (Bozrah?)
Nebo
Kiriathaim
Medeba
Beth-meon (Baal-meon)
Beth-diblathaim
Jahaz?

R. Nahaliel
Ataroth
Dibon
Aroer

R. Arnon

MOAB

Kir-hareseth

Brook Zered

EDOM

Waters of Nimrim

Zoar

X ▸ Hazazon-tamar
(30° 48')

Sea of the Arabah (Salt Sea)

City of Salt?
Secacah?
Middin
Nibshan?
Anathoth
Jerusalem

V. of Achor
Br. Kidron
Ascent of Ziz
V. of Berachah

En-gedi

Wilderness of Judah

Etam
Tekoa
Bethlehem
Beth-zur
Zair
Hebron
Adoraim
Ziph
Carmel

JUDAH

Gimzo
Gath
Gibbethon
Shikkeron
Ekron
Timnah
Zorah
Azekah
Socoh
Adullam
Libnah
Mareshah
Lachish
Beth-shemesh
Gath?

V. of Zephathah?

The Shephelah (Lowland)

Great Arad
Gurbaal
Arad of Beth-yeroham?

Valley of Salt

Beer-sheba

SIMEON

The Negeb

Joppa

Jabneel (Jabneh)
Mount Baalah
Baalath?
Ashdod

PHILISTIA

Ashkelon

Gaza

Gerar
Brook Besor
Yurza
Sharuhen
Raphia

32°
31° 30'
31°
36° 30'
36°
35° 30'
35°
34° 30'
31° 30'

5
6
7
V
W
Y
Z

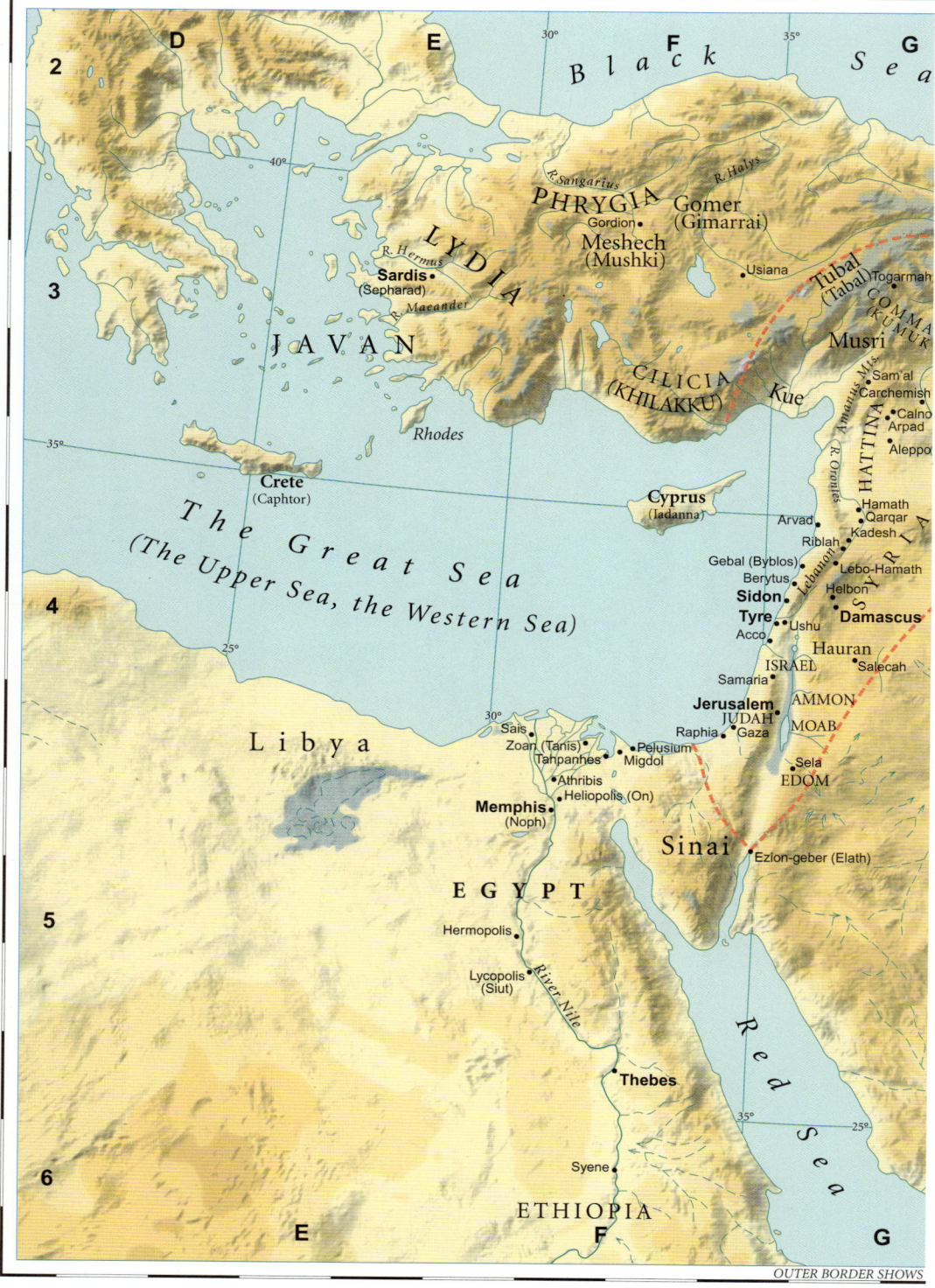

MAP 7

D E F G

2

Black Sea

30° 35°

40°

R. Sangarius *R. Halys*

PHRYGIA Gomer
(Gimarrai)

Gordion

Meshech
(Mushki)

Usiana

Tubal
(Tabal) Togarmah

3

R. Hermus LYDIA

Sardis
(Sepharad)

R. Maeander

COMMA-
GUMUK

Musri

JAVAN

CILICIA
(KHILAKKU)

Kue

Sam'al
Carchemish

Calno
Arpad
Aleppo

Rhodes

HATTINA

35°

The Great Sea

Crete
(Caphtor)

Cyprus
(Iadanna)

Arvad

Riblah

Gebal (Byblos)

Berytus

R. Orontes

SYRIA

Hamath
Qarqar
Kadesh

Lebo-Hamath

Helbon

(The Upper Sea, the Western Sea)

4

25°

Sidon

Tyre

Ushu

Acco

Lebanon

Damascus

Hauran

Salecah

Samaria

ISRAEL

AMMON

L i b y a

30°

Sais

Zoan (Tanis)

Tahpanhes

Pelusium
Migdol

Jerusalem

JUDAH

Raphia Gaza

MOAB

Athribis

Heliopolis (On)

Memphis
(Noph)

Sela

EDOM

Sinai

Ezion-geber (Elath)

E G Y P T

5

Hermopolis

Lycopolis
(Siut)

River Nile

Red Sea

35° 25°

Thebes

6

Syene

ETHIOPIA

E F G

MAP 7

ARARAT
(URARTU)

(Til-garimmu)

Milid (Melitene)   Nairi   Lake Van   Turushpa
(Tuspar)

GENE
HU
R. Balikh   Haran   Gozan   Lake   Minni
Urmia   (Mannai)

Beth-eden   A S S Y R I A   Dur-sharrukin   MADAI
(Bit-adini)   Nineveh   Calah   Arbela   (MEDES)

Tiphsah   R. Habor   Upper Zab
Rezeph   Asshur   Lower Zab   Arrapkha   Ecbatana

River   River Tigris   R.Adhaim   R.Diyala

Euphrates

Tadmor (Tadmar)

Kedar   E L A M
(Qidri)   Sippar   Cuthah   Pekod
Babylon   (Puqudu)
Borsippa   Nippur   Susa (Shushan)

A   BABYLONIA
R   Erech (Uruk)   Larsa
Dumah   A   Ur

B
I   ancient coastline
Tema   A

Dedan   *The Assyrian Empire*

The Lower (Eastern) Sea

- - - - Approximate extent of Assyrian domination
in the latter part of the 8th. century.
(Later, under Esarhaddon (680-669), Assyria conquered Egypt.)

0   100   200 Miles

0   100   200 Kilometres

SHEBA   © Oxford University Press
(SABA) OPHIR

Caspian Sea

100 MILE SUBDIVISIONS

MAP 8

The Persian Empire

– – – Approximate boundary
of the Persian Empire

OUTER BORDER SHOWS

MAP 8

200 MILE SUBDIVISIONS

MAP 9

Judah/Yehud/Judea and
Neighboring Regions
in the Persian and
Hellenistic Periods

MAP 9

5

B

Samaga

Heshbon

Medeba

Dabaloth?

Libba

Machaerus

31° 30'

M O A B

N A B A T A E A N S

6

R. Arnon

(Khirbet Qumran)

Ain Feshkha

Lake
Asphaltitis
(Dead Sea)

En-gedi

Masada

35° 30'

X

31°

7

© Oxford University Press

Y

Anathoth

Jerusalem

Ananiah

Beth-haccherem

Beth-basi

Kiriath-jearim

Beeroth (Berea)?

Netophah

J U D A H

(YEHUD, JUDEA)

Zorah

Zanoah

Bethlehem

Tekoa

Beth-zaith

Nebo

Beth-zur

Beth-zechariah

Adullam

Elam

Hebron (Kiriath-arba)

Ekron

Jarmuth

Azekah

Harim

Keilah

Adoraim

I D U M E A

Jeshua?

Hormah

Marisa

En-rimmon

Lachish

Eglon?

Jekabzeel?

Moladah

Beer-sheba

Hazar-shual

LAND OF THE PHILISTINES

Ziklag?

Ashdod
(Azotus)

Ashkelon
(Ascalon)

Gerar

34° 30'

W

Anthedon

Gaza

31°

Raphia

V

5

6

7

MAP 10

The Empire of Alexander and His Successors

- - - Approximate boundary of Alexander's Empire

2

MACEDONIA
EPIRUS
Pella
Thessalonica
Thasos
THRACE
Philippi
Doriscus
Byzantium
Lysimachia
Calchedon
Nicaea
Heraclea
Dascylium
Black Sea
Sinope
PAPHLAGONIA
PONTUS
Trapezus
R. Sangarius

THESSALY
AETOLIA
Delphi
ACHAEA
Olympia
Thebes
Athens
Corinth
Sparta
Mytilene
Pergamum
Magnesia
IONIA
Sardis
Ephesus
Samos
Miletus
Didyma
CARIA
Halicarnassus
Illium (Troy)
R. Maeander
PHRYGIA
Gordium (Gordion)
Ipsus
Apamea (Calaenae)
S
PISIDIA
PAMPHYLIA
Perga
LYCIA
Xanthus
Phaselis
CILICIA
GALATIA
Ancyra
Pteria?
CAPPADOCIA
Tyana
Cilician Gates
Soli
Tarsus
Issus
E
Melitene
R. Halys
COMMAGENE
Carchemish
Alexandria
Aleppo
Antioch
L
ARMENIA
L. Van
L. Urmia
Nisibis
Gaugamela
Arbela
U

Rhodes
Cydonia
Knossos
Gortyna
Crete

Cyprus
Salamis
Citium
Paphos
Laodicea
Marathus
Tripolis
Byblos
Berytus
Sidon
Tyre
Ptolemais
Dora
Samaria
Emesa
SYRIA
Coele Syria
Damascus
Paneas
Palmyra
Thapsacus
R. Euphrates
Dura-Europus
R. Tigris
Ctesiphon
Seleucia
BABYLO
Babylon
Nippur
Uruk
E

Mediterranean Sea

Cyrene
CYRENAICA
4
PTOLEMAIC
Paraetonium
Alexandria
Sais
Bubastis
Heliopolis
Memphis
Arsinoe
Pelusium
Azotus
Gaza
Raphia
Antioch (Gerasa)
Philadelphia
Jerusalem
Petra
NABATAEANS
ARABI

5
Oasis of Ammon (Siwa)
Crocodilopolis
EGYPT
Hermopolis
Lycopolis
R. Nile
Ptolemais
Nag Hammadi
Thebes
EMPIRE
Syene
Red Sea

| 0 | 100 | 200 | 300 Miles |
| 0 | 100 | 200 | 300 Kilometres |

MAP 10

J

K

L

M

N   SAKA (SCYTHIANS)   2

50°

Hyrcanian   Cyropolis

CHORASMIA

SOGDIANA   3

40°

R. Oxus

R. Cyrus

R. Araxes

Sea

Alexandria (Antiochia-Margiana)

B A C T R I A

Astrabad (Gorgan)   Zadrakarta (Turang Tepe)

Alexandria Kapisa

HYRCANIA

Hecatompylus (?)

Ortospana (Kabul)

M

Rages (Rhagae)

P A R T H I A

Alexandria Arion   R. Areius

A R I A

Alexandria Arachosion   4

E

Ecbatana

D

C

I

DRANGIANA

Gabae

A

ARACHOSIA

Alexandropolis (Kandahar)

SUSIANA

Susa

D

P

Parsagarda

I

Persepolis

R

C A R M A N I A

E

GEDROSIA   5

PERSIS

Alexandria (Gulashkird)

Pura

HINDUSH

R. Indus

NIA

Pattala

Persian   Harmozeia

50°

Gulf

55°

25°   25°

A

Erythraean Sea

© Oxford University Press   6

J

K

L

M

N

60°   65°

MAP 11

The Kingdom of Herod
and His Successors

Boundary of Herod's kingdom
at its greatest extent

Divisions, CE 6–37

Fortresses

MAP 11

© Oxford University Press

OUTER BORDER SHOWS 10 MILE SUBDIVISIONS

NABATAEAN KINGDOM

Philadelphia (Rabbah)

OLIS

Medeba

Betharamphtha

PEREA

Gadara

R. Jabbok

River

Machaerus

Callirrhoe

R. Arnon

(Kh. Qumran:
settlement of
Dead Sea sect)

Lake

Asphaltitis

Engaddi (En-gedi)

(Dead
Sea)

Alexandrium

Phasaelis

Archelais

Jericho

Cyprus

Jerusalem

Bethany

Hyrcania

Herodium

Wilderness of Judah

Masada

Mt. Gerizim

Neapolis

SAMARIA

Thamna

Gophna

Emmaus (Nicopolis)

JUDEA

Bethlehem

Hebron

Malatha

IDUMEA

Mampsis

Antipatris

Plat...

Apollonia
Sozusa

Joppa

Lydda

Gazara

Jamnia

Azotus

Betogabri

Marisa

Adora

Bersabe
(Beersheba)

Ascalon
(Free City)

Agrippias
(Anthedon)

Gaza

Raphia

KINGDOM

Medite

MA

PEREA

Z

Y

X

W

V

5

6

7

32°

5

31° 30'

6

31°

7

36°

35° 30'

35°

34° 30'

31° 30'

32°

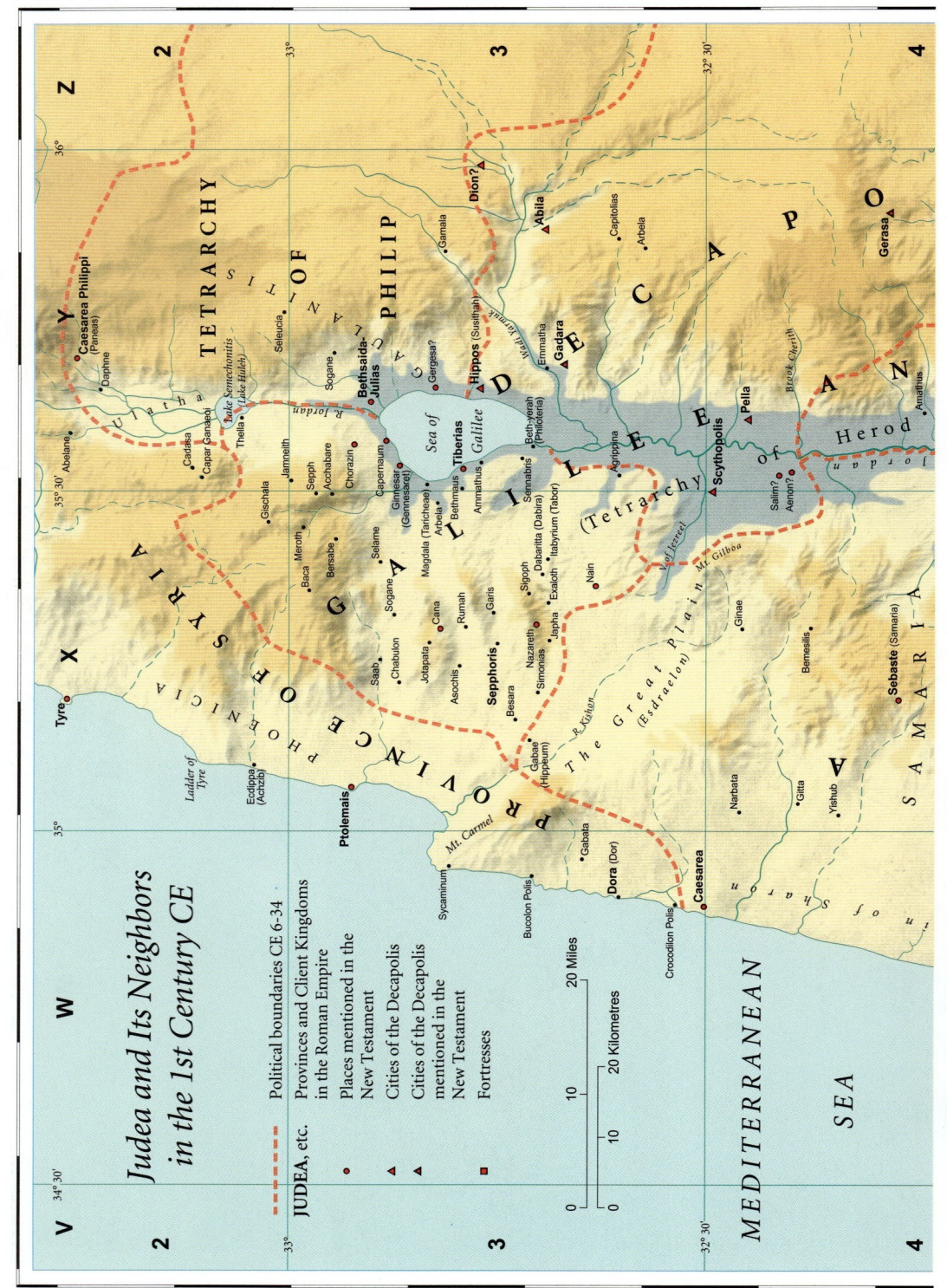

MAP 12

Judea and Its Neighbors in the 1st Century CE

Political boundaries CE 6–34
Provinces and Client Kingdoms in the Roman Empire
Places mentioned in the New Testament
Cities of the Decapolis
Cities of the Decapolis mentioned in the New Testament
Fortresses

JUDEA, etc.

20 Miles
20 Kilometres

MEDITERRANEAN SEA

TETRARCHY OF PHILIP

PROVINCE OF SYRIA

PHOENICIA

GALILEE

DECAPOLIS

SAMARIA

(Tetrarchy of Herod

Tyre
Caesarea Philippi (Paneas)
Daphne
Abelene
Cadisa
Capar Canaboi
Thella
Seleucia
Sogane
Bethsaida-Julias
Gamala
Dion?
Abila
Gadara
Hippos (Susithah)
Emmatha
Capernaum
Gergesa?
Sea of Galilee
Tiberias
Bethmaus
Ammathus
Beth-yerah (Philoteria)
Gamaia
Capitolias
Arbela
Gerasa
Sepph
Acchabare
Chorazin
Ginnesar (Gennesaret)
Magdala (Taricheae)
Arbela
Pella
Scythopolis
Agrippina
Salim?
Aenon?
Amathus
Jamneith
Gischala
Meroth
Baca
Bersabe
Sogane
Selame
Cana
Rumah
Garis
Sigoph
Dabaritta (Dabira)
Exaloth
Itabyrium (Tabor)
Mt. Gilboa
Nain
Ssab
Chabulon
Jotapata
Asochis
Nazareth
Simonias
Japha
Sepphoris
Besara
Gabae (Hippeum)
Ginae
Bernesilis
Sebaste (Samaria)
Narbata
Gitta
Yishub
Ecdippa (Achzib)
Ptolemais
Sycaminum
Mt. Carmel
Gabata
Dora (Dor)
Caesarea
Bucolon Polis
Crocodilon Polis

Ladder of Tyre

R. Jordan
R. Kishon
The Great Plain (Esdraelon)
Plain of Jezreel
Plain of Sharon
Wadi Yarmuk
Brook Cherith

MAP 12

OUTER BORDER SHOWS 10 MILE SUBDIVISIONS

Philadelphia (Rabbah)

LIS

D P E R E A

Antipas)

Zia

Gadara

Betharamphtha (Livias=Julias)

Esbus

Medeba (Madaba)

Callirrhoe

R. Nebo(?)

Machaerus

Lake Asphaltitis (Dead Sea)

NABATAEAN KINGDOM

Areopolis (Rabbathmoab)

R. Arnon

Coreae (Wadi Farah)

Alexandrium

Phasaelis

Archelais

Jericho

Cyprus

Taurus

(Kh. Qumran; settlement of Dead Sea sect)

Hyrcania

Wadi Jiphlie

Wilderness of Judah

Engedi (En-gedi)

Masada

Acrabbein

Anathu Borcaeus

Selo (Shiloh)

Tephon

Ilon

Thanna (Timnath)

Neapolis

Sychar

Tirathana

Mt. Gerizim;

Mt. Ebal

Mahnaym

Pharalon

Arus

Berzetho

Gophna

Bethel

Lower Beth-horon,

Upper Beth-horon,

Berea?

Gabaon

Adasa

Capharsalama?

Gabath Saul

Anathoth

Ephraim (Aphairema)

Aialon?

Michmash

Colonia Amasa,

Emmaus?

Jerusalem

Bethphage

Bethany

Mt. Scopus

E D U

Cappareetaea

Antipatris (Pegai)

Tower of Aphek

Rathamin (Arimathea?)

Adida

Modein

Sappho

Emmaus (Nicopolis)

Cariathiarim

I U D E A

Bethlehem

Etam

Herodium

Beth-basi

W. Marhabia

Thecoa (Thekoa)

Bethzachariah

Beth-zaith

Beth-zur)

Beth-zur,

Terebinthus (Mamre)

Hebron

Aristoboulias

?Caparorsa

(under Roman administration)

Caparnsaba

Gazara

Bethletepha

Betogabri

Capharabis

Gemmaruris

Capharobas

Adora

I D U M E A

Mampsis (37°)

Malatha

Apollonia Sozusa

Joppa

Lydda

Jamnia

Kedron

Accaron (Ekron)

Azotus

(Wadi Qubeiba)

Bersabe (Beersheba)

Iamnitarum Portus (Jamnia Harbour)

Azotus Paralius (Azotus-on-Sea)

Ascalon (Free city)

Maiumas Ascalon (Baths of Ascalon)

Agrippias (Anthedon)

Gaza

?To Province of Syria

Brook Besor

R. Pelus (Kedron)

Brook of Kanah

Pla

V W X Y Z

MAP 13

R. Po
Genua
Portus Veneris
Luca
Florentia
Bononia
Ravenna
Pola
Ariminum
Arretium
Perusia
Ancona
CORSICA
Apennine Mts
R. Tiber
Sea of
ROME ITALY
Ostia
Three Taverns
Antium
Forum of Appius
(Appii Forum)
Tarracina
Capua
Beneventum
Puteoli
Neapolis
Canusium
Pompeii
Appian Way
Capreae
(Capri)
Paestum
Tarentum
SARDINIA
Tyrrhenian Sea
Sybaris
Croton
Corcyra
R O M A N
Lesser Syrtis
Panormus
Messana
Rhegium
SICILY
Catana
Agrigentum
Utica
Carthage
Thapsus
St. Paul's Bay
Malta (Melita)
Syracuse

2
3

PANNONIA
Siscia
Sirmium
ILLYRICUM (DALMATIA)
Salonae
Scodra
Dyrrhachium
Apollonia
Brundisium
Adria
Corcyra
Nicopolis
Actium
Olympia

C
Sirmium
Singidunum
Viminacium
R. Danube
Oescus
Niassus
Novae
DACIA
MOESIA
Scupi
Sardica
Philippopolis
THRACE
Mesembria
Odessus
MACEDONIA
Philippi
Neapolis
Beroea
Thessalonica
Egnatian Way
THESSALY
Larissa
Cyzicus
Troas (Alexandria)
Assos
Adramyttium
Lesbos
Pergamum
Thyatira
A
Chios
Smyrna
Sardis
Philadelphia
Ephesus
Miletus

D
DACIA
Oescus
Novae
Odessus

E

40°

Aegean Sea
Corinth
Cenchreae
Athens
Sparta (Lacedaemon)
Cnidus
Rhodes
Rhodes

A C H A I A

N

E

M

P

CRETE
Phoenix
Fair Havens
Cauda
Salmone
Lasea

Mediterranean Sea
(Mare Internum, Mare Nostrum)

Sabratha
Oea
Lepcis Magna
TRIPOLITANIA
15°
Greater Syrtis
20°
Cyrene
CYRENAICA
25°

A F R I C A
LIBYA
Alexandria
EGY

Sahara Desert

4
5

45°
40°
35°

B
C
D
E

MAP 13

The Roman Empire

MAP 14

Scupi

Dyrrhachium

Philippopolis

Mesembria

D **E**

2 Egnation Way

R. Strymon

R. Axius

T H R A C E

M A C E D O N I A

Doberus?

Philippi

Beroea

Thessalonica

Neapolis

Amphipolis

25°

Apollonia

Doriscus

Egnation Way

E P I R U S

T H E S S A L Y

Larissa

Samothrace

Imbros

Hellespont

Abydos

Propontis

Cyzicus

Nicopolis

Actium

Pharsalus

40°

Lemnos

M Y S I A

(Alexandria) Troas

Assos

Adramyttium

Delphi

Euboea

Lesbos

Mytilene

Pergamum

L Y D I A

Thyatira

Patrae

Thebes

Chios

R. Hermus

Sardis

3

Olympia

A C H A I A

Corinth

Cenchreae

Eleusis

Athens

Piraeus

Smyrna

Philadelphia

Ephesus

R. Maeander

Sparta

(Lacedaemon)

Samos

Magnesia

Laodicea

Trogyllium

C A R I

Delos

Patmos

Didyma

Miletus

35°

Halicarnassus

Cos

Cos

Cnidus

Rhodes

Rhodes

A e g e a n   S e a

Heracleon

Phoenix

C R E T E

Salmone

(Sammanion)

Fair Havens

Lasea

Cauda

(Gaudos)

M e d i t e r r a n e

(Ma

r e

I n t e

4

25°

D   © Oxford University Press   **E**

MAP 14

*The Setting of
Early Christian Missions*

50 MILE SUBDIVISIONS

INDEX TO MAPS